INTERNATIONAL SHOWBUSINESS
REFERENCE

Garland Reference Library
of the Humanities
(Volume 292)

INTERNATIONAL SHOWBUSINESS REFERENCE

Mike Kaplan
Editor

Garland Publishing, Inc.
New York & London
1981

© 1981 Daily Variety, Ltd.
All rights reserved

Library of Congress Cataloging in Publication Data

Main entry under title:

Variety international showbusiness reference.

(Garland reference library of the humanities ; v. 292)
 1. Performing arts—Dictionaries.   I. Kaplan, Mike,
1918–   . II. Daily variety. III. Series.
PN1579.V3   790.2′03′21   81-2329
ISBN 0-8240-9341-0   AACR2

Printed on acid-free, 250-year-life paper
Manufactured in the United States of America

CONTENTS

Abbreviations	1
Biographies	3
Distributor Code	309
Film Credits 1976–1980	317
Oscars	573
All-Time Film Rental Champs	659
Festivals, Markets and Conventions 1981	661
TV Credits 1976–1980	663
Emmys	773
Top 50 Nielsen-Rated TV Shows	915
Broadway Play Credits 1976–1980	917
Plays Abroad Credits 1976–1980	947
Tonys	987
Pulitzer Prize Plays	1015
Long-Running Broadway Plays	1017
Grammys	1019
Platinum Records 1976–1980	1111
Necrology 1976–1980	1115

FOREWORD

In its 75 years of existence, VARIETY has been the largest single source of information about the entertainment industry worldwide. At first, it covered only the field of live showbusiness, specializing in U.S. activities but gradually broadening its base. As the entertainment business grew and became global, VARIETY's coverage grew with it. As a result, no showbusiness event of any significance anywhere in the world escapes its attention. It pioneered in film reviews when "films" were generally less than a minute long, and currently reviews more films each year than any other publication in the world.

This first VARIETY international showbusiness reference volume is a distillation of key information from VARIETY files. The material was selected on the basis of possible reference need, judged by the queries which the publication receives daily for specific showbusiness information.

Thus, the Awards section comprises the first complete tabulation of nominees as well as winners of Oscar, Tony, Emmy and Grammy Awards from their inceptions through the 1980 presentations. It should be noted that the year associated with an award is the year of performance; the Oscars presented in April of 1980 were for films released in 1979.

Probably the most frequently requested type of information is credits—the listing of personnel involved in films, plays and television programs. These credits have been assembled here by category and alphabetically within each category for ready reference, and dated so that researchers can, if necessary, find the entire printed review by consulting the microfilmed back copies of VARIETY which can be found in all leading libraries. Since VARIETY reviews in these categories cover the entire world, translations of foreign titles are provided as a cross-index.

The almost 6,000 current biographies in this volume represent the largest single such compilation for actors, actresses, choreographers, cinematographers, composers, dancers, designers, directors, executives, film editors, journalists, musicians, producers, singers, songwriters and writers ever achieved. Included also are career profiles for personalities who died between Jan. 1, 1979, and Dec. 31, 1980. The credits reflect work reviewed by VARIETY through Dec. 31, 1980, and are thus as up to date as printing schedules permit; the career listings include Oscar, Tony, Emmy and Grammy Awards won, including the year in which they were won.

The necrology section lists showbusiness deaths for the last five years.

Future VARIETY volumes will maintain a continuing current record of activity in all of these categories to provide a single source of information on all facets of show business.

Mike Kaplan
Editor

NOTE TO USERS

The VARIETY INTERNATIONAL SHOWBUSINESS REFERENCE is designed for quick, uncomplicated use.

Biographies and the necrology are listed in alphabetical order.

Film, play and television credits are also listed in alphabetical order, the date below the credits indicating when the review was printed in VARIETY.

In film credits, the abbreviation at the beginning of the first paragraph indicates the distributor of the film. The Distributor Code lists the names of the companies indicated by the abbreviations. Where an "X" appears, the distributor is unknown. All production credits are listed in the first paragraph. The number at the end of this paragraph is the running time of the film. The second paragraph contains acting credits. Special information, such as DOCUMENTARY, is listed at the bottom.

In play credits, the first paragraph lists production personnel and opening date, the second lists actors. In the case of musicals, the third paragraph lists the musical numbers.

In television credits, the letter after some of the dates serves to identify the type of review—F for Foreign; S for Syndication; C for Cable Television; PI for Prix Italia contestants.

All awards are listed by year. In the cases of Oscar, Tony, Emmy and Grammy Awards, categories within each year follow the form set down by the individual Academies involved. In all cases, winners are indicated by boldface type.

Platinum Records are listed by year, and alphabetically by artist's name within each year.

Abbreviations found throughout the text are detailed in the section which follows.

ABBREVIATIONS

AADA American Academy of Dramatic Art

AAMDA American Academy of Music and Dramatic Art

ABT American Ballet Theatre

Act actor, actress

ACT American Conservatory Theatre

ADMN administration, administrator

ADV advertising

ADVR advisor

AFF affairs

AK Alaska

AL Alabama

ANI Animation, animator

AR Arkansas

ARR arrangements

AS American Samoa

ASSO associate

ASST assistant

AZ Arizona

b. born

B of brother of

BCST broadcast

BCSTNG broadcasting

BD CHMN board chairman

BR branch

CA California

CAM camera

CEO Chief Executive Officer

CHF chief

CHG charge

CHMN chairman

CIN cinematographer, cinematography

CLASS classical

CM Northern Mariana Islands

CNSL counsel

CNSLTS consultants

CO Colorado

COLLAB collaborator, collaborating

COMP Composer

COMPS Compositions

CONT controller

COO chief operating officer

CORP corporation

CORR Correspondent

COS costume

CREA creative, creator

CT Connecticut

CZ Canal Zone

D of daughter of

DC District of Columbia

DE Delaware

DEL delegate

DIR director

DIST district

DIV division

DOM domestic

DSGN design, designer

DVLP Development

e. education

E East, Eastern

EDTR editor

ENG engineer, engineering

ENT entertainment, entertainer

ENTS Enterprises

EQPT Equipment

EXEC executive

EXP export

F of father of

FIN Finance, financing, financial

FL Florida

GA Georgia

GEN General

GU Guam

H of Husband of

HD head

HI Hawaii

IA Iowa

ID Idaho

IDHEC Institute des Hautes Etude Cinematographiques

IL Illinois

IMP import

IN Indiana

INC include, including

IND industry

INST Instrumental

INTL international

KS Kansas

KY Kentucky

LA Louisiana

LAMDA London Academy of Musical and Dramatic Art

LCL local

LIC licensing

M of mother of

M-DIR managing director

MA Massachusetts

MAN ED managing editor

MAT Material

MD Maryland

MDSNG Merchandising

ME Maine

MGR manager

MI Michigan

MIN miniatures

MINS minutes

MKTG Marketing

MN Minnesota

MO Missouri

MS Mississippi

MT Montana

MUS music, musical, musician

MUSICOMEDY musical comedy

N North, Northern

NC North Carolina

ND North Dakota

NE Nebraska

NET network

NH New Hampshire

NJ New Jersey

NM New Mexico

NRE Northeast

NV Nevada

2 ABBREVIATIONS

NW Northwest
NY New York
O&O owned and operated
OFC office
OH Ohio
OK Oklahoma
OPS operations
OR Oregon
OWN owner
P Pres
PA Pennsylvania
PERF performer
PERS personality
PGM program
PGMG programming
PHO photographer, photography
PLYWRI playwright
PR Puerto Rico
PRCTS practices
PROD producer
PRODN production
PROJ projects
PROJST projectionist
PUB Publicity
PUBL publisher, publishing
RADA Royal Academy of Dramatic Art
REG regulatory
REGL regional
REL releasing
RES research
RESD resigned
RET retired
RETD returned
RI Rhode Island
S South, Southern
S of son of
Sis of sister of
SC South Carolina
SCH scheduling
SD South Dakota
SE Southeast

SEC secretary
SLS sales
SNGWRI songwriter
SP Screenplay
SPEC Special
STA station
STNDS standards
STV Subscription television
SUPV supervisor, supervising, supervisory
SVS service
SW Southwest
SYN syndication
TECH technical
TN Tennessee
TREAS treasurer
TT Trust Territories
TV television
TX Texas
UT Utah
VA Virginia
VAUDE vaudeville
VI Virgin Islands
VOC vocal, vocalist
VP vice president
VT Vermont
W West, Western
w of wife of
WA Washington
WI Wisconsin
WLD world
WLDWDE worldwide
WRI writer
WV West Virginia
WY Wyoming

BIOGRAPHIES

These career profiles reflect credits through Dec. 31, 1980. Personalities who died between Jan. 1, 1979, and Dec. 31, 1980, are included.

AALBERG, John O: Sound Eng. b. Chicago, Apr 3, 1897. e. IL Institute of Technology, EE. Head of sound department RKO Studios, 1932-57. During this period RKO sound dept. won 3 Oscars; Academy "Medal of Commendation" awarded 1980.

AAMES, Willie: Act. b. CA, Jul 15, 1960. TV inc: We'll Get By; Swiss Family Robinson; Wait Til Your Father Gets Home; Eight Is Enough.
Films inc: Hog Wild; Scavenger Hunt.

AARON, Paul: Dir. Bway inc: Salvation; Paris is Out; '70 Girls '70; That's Entertainment; Love Me, Love My Children; The Burnt Flowerbed.
Films inc: A Different Story; A Force of One.
TV inc: The Miracle Worker.

AARON, Roy H: Exec. b. LA, Apr 8, 1929. e. UCLA, BA; USC, LLB. Specialist in exhibition law, handled acquisition and disposition of major theatres and circuits while with LA firm of Pacht, Ross, Warne, Bernhard & Sears; joined Plitt Companies 1978 as sr vp, genl counsel; 1980 P & CEO Plitt Theatres and related companies.

ABBA: Swedish Rock Group. Members inc: Bjorn Ulvaeus, Agnetha Faltskog, Anni-Frid Lyngstad, Benny Andersson.
Albums inc: Waterloo; ABBA; Greatest Hits; Arrival; The Album.
Films inc: ABBA, the Movie.

ABBOTT, George: Wri-Prod-Dir. b. Forestville, NY, Jun 25, 1887. e. Rochester U, BA; Harvard. Began on Bway (1913) as act in Misleading Lady; Queen's Enemies; Daddies; The Broken Wing; Hell-Bent Fer Heaven; Lazybones; Processional; 1926 co-wrote The Fall Guy with James Gleason and thereafter appeared only in A Holy Terror (& co-wri); Cowboy Crazy; Those We Love (& co-wri); John Brown (& prod-dir); revival of The Skin of Our Teeth.
As co-wri-dir: Broadway; Four Walls; Coquette; Ringside; Lilly Turner (& co-prod); Heat Lightning; Page Miss Glory; Three Men on a Horse; On Your Toes; The Boys from Syracuse (solo wri); Best Foot Forward; Where's Charley?; A Tree Grows in Brooklyn; The Pajama Game *(Tony*-author-1955); Damn Yankees *(Tony*-author-1956); New Girl In Town; Fiorello *(Tonys*-author & dir-1960); also Pulitzer Prize); Tenderloin, Flora, The Red Menace; Anya.
As dir: Chicago, Jarnegan; The Great Magoo; Twentieth Century (& co-prod); Small Miracle; Jumbo; Boy Meets Girl (& prod); Brother Rat (& prod); Room Service (& prod); Brown Sugar (& prod); Too Many Girls (& prod); Barefoot Boy with Cheek (& wri); High Button Shoes (& prod); Call Me Madam; Wonderful Town; Me and Juliet; Once Upon a Mattress; Take Her, She's Mine; A Funny Thing Happened on the Way to the Forum *(Tony*-dir-1963); Fade Out-Fade In; How Now, Dow Jones; The Education of H*Y*M*A*N* K*A*P*L*A*N; Norman, Is That You?;
Lawrence Langner Award-1976.
Films inc: (As wri-dir) Half-Way To Heaven; Why Bring That Up; All Quiet on the Western Front (sp only); Manslaughter; Secrets of a Secretary; My Sin; The Cheat; (As dir): Too Many Girls; The Pajama Game; Damn Yankees.

ABBOTT, John: Act. b. London, 1905. Films inc: Mademoiselle Docteur; The Return of the Scarlet Pimpernel; The Saint in London; Mrs Miniver; They Got Me Covered; Jane Eyre; Secret Motive; The Woman in White; The Merry Widow; Gigi; Who's Minding the Store; Greatest Story Ever Told; Gambit; Two Thousand Years Later.
TV inc: The Harmfulness of Tobacco; Tender is the Night; Child of Virtue; The Glorious Gift of Mollie Malone; The Song of David; The Suicide Club; The Waltz of the Toreadors; The Cat Creature.

ABBOTT, L B (Lenwood Ballard Abbott): Cin. b. Pasadena, CA, Jun 13, 1908. Specializing in visual effects. Films inc: Three Faces of Eve; Peyton Place; Some Like It Hot; South Pacific; Journey to the Center of the Earth; The Longest Day; Cleopatra; The Agony and the Ecstacy; The Sound of Music; Von Ryans Express; Sand Pebbles; Fantastic Voyage; Dr Doolittle *(Oscar*-1967); Planet of the Apes; The Prime of Miss Jean Brodie; Hello Dolly; Butch Cassidy and the Sundance Kid; Mash; The Great White Hope; Patton; Tora, Tora, Tora *(Oscar*-1970); The Poseidon Adventure *(Oscar*-1972); Logan's Run *(Oscar*-1976).
TV inc: Voyage to the Bottom of the Sea *(Emmys*-(2)-1965 & 1966); Time Tunnel *(Emmy*-1967); City Beneath the Sea *(Emmy*-1971).

ABBOTT, Philip (nee Alexander): Act. b. Lincoln, NE, Mar 21, 1923. e. Fordham U. Bway inc: Harvest of Years; Detective Story; Springtime Folly; Square Root of Wonderful; Two for the Seesaw; Robert Frost (adapt & dir): Promises to Keep; O Socrates.
Films inc: The Bachelor Party; The Invisible Boy; The Miracle of the White Stallions; Those Calloways; Sweet Bird of Youth; The Spiral Road; Hangar 18.
TV inc: The House on High Street; The FBI; Tailgunner Joe; Rich Man, Poor Man.

ABDUL-JABBAR, Kareem (Lew Alcindor): Act. b. NYC, Apr 16, 1947. e. UCLA. Pro basketball player with Milwaukee Bucks, LA Lakers. Films inc: Game of Death; The Fish That Saved Pittsburgh.

ABEL, Walter: Act. b. St Paul, Jun 6, 1898. e. AADA. In vaudeville, summer stock, Bway stage. Screen debut, 1936, The Three Musketeers. Films inc: The Witness Chair; Fury; Portia on Trial; Racket Busters; King of the Turf; Miracle on Main Street; Arise My Love; Hold Back the Dawn; Beyond the Blue Horizon; Star Spangled Rhythm; Holiday Inn; Wake Island; So Proudly We Hail; Mr Skeffington; The Affairs of Susan; Kiss and Tell; 13 Rue Madelaine; Dream Girl; Bernardine; Raintree County; Mirage; Quick Let's Get Married.
TV inc: The Man Without a Country.
Bway inc: Saturday, Sunday, Monday; Trelawney of the Wells.

ABELES, Arthur: Exec. b. 1914. e. Duke, U; Columbia. Began with WB 1941 as gm West Indies; 1942 asst gm U, Brazil; 1945 supv WB various South American countries; 1968 m-dir WB, vp Warner Intl; 1970 M-dir U, vp U Int'l in chg U.K., Europe, Middle East; when U and Par formed Cinema International Corp in 1970 he became co-chmn with Henri Michaud; 1977 formed, with Michaud, A-M Film Consultants Ltd.

ABRAHAMS, Doris Cole: Prod. b. NYC, Jan 29, 1925. e. Ohio U, Leland Powers School of Theatre. Briefly an actress and agent, turned to prodn 1945 with Blue Holiday.
Bway inc: Equus *(Tony*-1975); Travesties; Once a Catholic. (London) Enter A Free Man; Out of the Question; Enemy; Child's Play.

ABRAHAMS, Mort: Prod. b. NYC, Mar 26, 1916. e. NYU, BA, Columbia U, MA. TV inc: Tales of Tomorrow; GE Theatre; Producer's Showcase; Suspicion; Target: The Corrupters; Route 66; Kraft Suspense Theatre; Man from U.N.C.L.E; The House on Garibaldi Street.
Films inc: Dr Doolittle; Planet of the Apes; Goodbye Mr Chips; The Chairman; Beneath the Planet of the Apes (& sp); Luther (exec prod); Man in the Glass Booth; Homecoming; Lost in the Stars; Rhinocerous; The Greek Tycoon (exec prod).

ABRAMS, Gerald W: Exec prod. b. West Chester, PA, Sep 26, 1939. e. Penn State U. TV inc: Red Alert; Ski Lift to Death; James Dean--Portrait of a Friend; The Defection of Simas Kudirka; Flesh and Blood; Steeltown; Letters From Frank; The Gift; Act of Love.

ABULADZE, Tengiz: Dir-Wri. b. Russia, Jan 31, 1924. e. Moscow Film Institute. Films inc: (doc) Dmitry Arakishvili; Our Palace; The Georgian State Dancing Company; An Open Air Museum. (Features) Magdan's Donkey; Someone Else's Children; Me, Grandma, Iliko and Hillarion; The Entreaty; A Necklace for My Beloved; A Tree of Wishes.

ACKER, Sharon: Act. b. Apr 2, 1935.
Films inc: Lucky Jim, Point Blank.
TV inc: A Cry for Justice; Dallas; Stone; Battles--The Murder That Wouldn't Die.

ACKERMAN, Bettye: Act. b. Cottageville, SC, Feb 28, 1928. e. Columbia U. W of Sam Jaffe. Bway inc: No Count Boy; Tartuffe; Sophocles; Antigone; Oedipus at Colonus.
Films inc: Face of Fire; Companions in Nightmare; Rascal.
TV inc: Heat of Anger; Ben Casey; Medical Center; Trouble In High Timber Country.

ACKERMAN, Forrest J: Act-Wri-Prod. b. LA, Nov 24, 1916. Films inc: The Time Travelers (cameo); Queen (aka Planet) of Blood; Dracula vs. Frankenstein; Schlock; Hollywood Boulevard; Kentucky Fried Movie; Aftermath.

ACKERMAN, Harry S: Prod. b. Albany, NY, Nov 17, 1912. e. Dartmouth Coll. Began as writer, actor. Joined Young & Rubicam adv. agency, 1936; exec prod. CBS, 1948; VP chge network programs CBS-TV. 1950; formed ind co, 1957; VP and exec prod. Screen Gems Inc., 1958-77; pres. Harry Ackerman Prods. TV inc: Gunsmoke (also radio); Dennis the Menace; The Farmer's Daughter; Bewitched; The Flying Nun; Hazel.

ACKLAND, Joss: Act. b. London, England, Feb 29, 1928. Appeared in rep; member of Old Vic with whom he toured Russia, US; spent some time in Central Africa as tea planter; in thea and deejay, South Africa. Thea inc: (London) The Hasty Heart; The Rising Sun; Arms and the Man; Lock Up Your Daughters; The Life of Galileo; The Possessed; The Baccchae; The Professor; Hotel in Amsterdam; Come As You Are; A Streetcar Named Desire; A Little Night Music.
Films inc: Seven Days to Noon; Royal Flash; Crescendo; The House That Dripped Blood; Villain; England Made Me; Penny Gold; The Black Windmill; Great Expectations; The Little Prince; Seven Men At Daybreak; Silver Bears; Who Is Killing the Great Chefs of Europe?; Watership Down (voice); Saint Jack; The Apple; Rough Cut.

ACKROYD, David: Act. b. Orange, NJ, May 30, 1940. e. Bucknell, BA; Yale, MFA. TV inc: Secret Storm; The Great American Dream Machine; Another World; Harvest Home; Joanne and Tom; The Word; And I Alone Survived; Women in White; Mind Over Murder; The Yeagers.
Films inc: The Mountain Men.
Bway inc: Hamlet; Unlikely Heroes; Full Circle; Hide and Seek.

ACUFF, Roy: Mus. b. Maynardsville, TN, Sep 15, 1903. Joined Grand Ole Opry, 1940; shortly after organized his band, the Smokey Mountain Boys; entered mus publishing business in the 50s; elected to Country Mus Hall of Fame, 1962. TV inc: Merry Christmas From the Grand Ole Opry House; The Concrete Cowboys.

ADAM, Ken: Art dir. b. Berlin, Feb 5, 1921. Films inc: Around the World in 80 Days; Trials of Oscar Wilde; Dr. No; Sodom and Gomorrah; Dr. Strangelove; Ipcress File; Goldfinger; You Only Live Twice; Funeral in Berlin; Chitty Chitty Bang Bang; Goodbye Mr. Chips; The Owl and the Pussycat; Thunderball; Diamonds are Forever; The Spy Who Loved Me; Moonraker.

ADAM, Ronald, OBE: Act-Prod-Plywri. b. Herefordshire, England, Dec 31, 1896. Originally an accountant, became mgr at various London Theatres after WW1; began prod 1932, later act. Thea inc: (Prod) Ten Minute Alibi; Close Quarters; The Dominant Sex; Judgement Day. (Act) The Ascent of F6; Judgment Day; Virtuoso; Antony and Cleopatra; The Manor of Northstead; Billy Bunter; Wolf's Clothing; Policy for Murder; Windfall; Barn Dance; Hostile Witness; The Deadly Game; Gone With the Wind; Born Yesterday.
Plays inc: An English Summer; A Wind on the Heath; Marriage Settlement; Black on Magenta; Open Verdict; The Little Doctor.
Films inc: (Act) The Drum; Escape to Danger; Green For Danger; Bonnie Prince Charlie; Angels One Five; Private's Progress; Reach for the Sky; Cleopatra; The Tomb of Ligeia; Who Killed the Cat; The Song of Norway; Zeppelin; The Ruling Class; The Zoo Robbery; Brothers; The Man in Black; The Greek Tycoon.
(Died March 27, 1979).

ADAMS, Berle: Exec. b. Chicago, Jan 11, 1917. e. Northwestern U, BA. Started with GAC, Chicago, 1940; formed Mutual Entertainment Agency, 1942; formed (with Irving Green) Mercury Records, 1945; served as p; sold Mercury Records in 1948, joined MCA 1950; became vp of MCA TV, 1952; created MCA mus publ co; elected vp of MCA Inc in Jan 1965; named exec vp, 1968; left MCA to head WM Sports; p, BAC, Inc. Films inc: (prod) Brass Target.

ADAMS, Brooke: Act. b. NYC, Feb 8, 1949. e. NY High School for Performing Arts.
Films inc: Days of Heaven; Invasion of the Body Snatchers; Shock Waves; A Man, A Woman, and a Bank; Cuba; Shock Waves; Tell Me A Riddle.
TV inc: Rex Stout's Nero Wolfe; Family.

ADAMS, Catlin (nee Barab): Act. b. LA, Oct 11, 1950. Thea inc: Safe House; Scandalous Memories; Dream of a Blacklisted Actor; The Candy Store.
Films inc: Katherine; Panic in Needle Park; The Jerk; The Jazz Singer.
TV inc: How to Survive the 70's and Maybe Even Bump Into A Little Happiness; She Loves Me, She Loves Me Not.

ADAMS, Don (nee Yarmy): Act. b. NYC, Apr 13, 1926. Nitery impressionist, won Arthur Godfrey talent contest, began guesting on tv shows.
TV inc: The Bill Dana Show; Get Smart (Emmy-1967, 1968,1969); The Partners; Hooray for Hollywood; Don Adams Screen Test; Three Times Daley; Billy.
Films inc: The Nude Bomb.

ADAMS, Edie (nee Enke): Act-Singer. b. Kingston, PA, Apr 16, 1931. e. Juilliard, Columbia U. Thea inc: Wonderful Town; Li'l Abner; Anything Goes.
Films inc: The Apartment; It's A Mad, Mad, Mad, Mad World; Call Me Bwana; Under the Yum Yum Tree; Love With The Proper Stranger; Lover Come Back; The Best Man; Maid in Paris; The Honey Pot; The Happy Hooker Goes to Washington; Cheech & Chong's Up in Smoke; The Happy Hooker Goes To Hollywood.
TV inc: The Ernie Kovacs Show; Cinderella; Here's Edie; The Edie Adams Show; Fast Friends; The Seekers; Make Me An Offer; Portrait of an Escort; Bosom Buddies.

ADAMS, Joey: Wri-Comedian. b. NYC, Jan 6, 1911. e. CCNY. Syndicated humor columnist; host daily radio show WEVD, NY. Toastmaster, emcee niteries, concerts.
Bway inc: Guys and Dolls; The Gazebo.
Films inc: (prod-act) Ringside; Singing in the Dark.

ADAMS, Julie (Betty May Adams): Act. b. Waterloo, IA, Oct 17, 1928. Films inc: Bright Victory; Bend of the River; Mississippi Gambler; The Creature from the Black Lagoon; One Desire; Away all Boats; Slaughter on Tenth Avenue; Valley of Mystery; The Private War of Major Benson; The Last Movie; McQ; The Wild McCulloughs; Killer Force; The Killer Inside Me; The Fifth Floor.
TV inc: The Jimmy Stewart Show; Greatest Heroes of the Bible.

ADAMS, Mason: Act. b. NYC, Feb 26. e. U of WI. Started on radio 1946; spent nearly two decades in Pepper Young's Family. Bway inc: Get Away Old Man; Inquest; The Sign in Sidney Brustein's Window; Tall Story; You Know I Can't Hear You When the Water's Running; The Trial of the Catonsville Nine; The Shortchanged Review; Checking Out.
TV inc: Another World; The Deadliest Season; Lou Grant; And Baby Makes Six; A Shining Season; Flamingo Road; Murder Can Hurt You!; Revenge of the Stepford Wives.

ADAMS, Neile: Act. b. Jul 10, 1936. Films inc: This Could Be the Night.
Bway inc: Kismet; Me and Juliet; Best Foot Forward; Pajama Game.
TV inc: Women in Chains; Fuzz.

ADAMS, Peter: Act. b. LA, Sep 22, 1917. e. Williams Coll., BA. Films inc: Turnabout; Fountainhead; Battle Zone; Flat Top; Dragonfly; Ruby Gentry; Courtmartial of Billy Mitchell; Brigadoon; Bullwhip; The Big Fisherman; Midnight Lace; How to Murder Your Wife; Funny Girl.

ADAMS, Phillip: Prod-Columnist-Broadcaster. b. Victoria, Australia, Jul 12, 1939. Films inc: Jack and Jill: A Postscript; The Naked Bunyip; The Adventures of Barry McKenzie; Don's Party; The Getting of Wisdom; Grendel, Grendel, Grendel.

ADAMS, Stanley: Lyr. b. NYC, Aug 14, 1907. e. NYU, NYU Law School. Began with songs for Connie's Inn Revue. Bway inc: The Show Is On; The Lady Says Yes; Shoestring Revue.
Films inc: Everyday's a Holiday; Duel in the Sun; My Reputation; The Great Lie; Road Show; Viva Villa!; Strategic Air Command.
Songs inc: Little Old Lady; My Shawl; What A Diff'rence A Day Made; La Cucaracha; My Silent Mood; Rollin' Down the River; You Stole My Heart.

ADAMS, Tony: Prod. b. Dublin, Ireland, Feb 15, 1953. Films inc: (assoc prod) Return of the Pink Panther; The Pink Panther Strikes Again. (exec prod) Revenge of the Pink Panther; 10.
TV inc: Julie Andrews in Japan.

ADAMSON, Harold: Lyr. b. Greenville, NJ, Dec 10, 1906. e. U of KS, Harvard U. Film scores inc: Dancing Lady; The Great Ziegfeld; Banjo on My Knee; Top of the Town; You're a Sweetheart; That Certain Age; Four Jills and a Jeep; Gentlemen Prefer Blondes; An Affair to Remember.
Bway inc: Smiles; Earl Carroll's Vanities; Banjo Eyes; As the Girls Go; Around the World in Eighty Days.
Songs inc: Time on My Hands; Did I Remember; Change of Heart; Everything I Have Is Yours; With a Banjo on My Knee; My Own; I Couldn't Sleep a Wink Last Night; An Affair to Remember; Ferryboat Serenade.
(Died Aug 17, 1980).

ADATO, Perry Miller: Prod-Dir. TV inc: Dylan Thomas--The World I Breathe (Emmy-prod-1968); Gertrude Stein--When You See This, Remember Me; An Eames Celebration; Frankenthaler--Toward a New Climate; Mary Cassatt--Impressionist from Philadelphia; Georgia O'-Keefe.

ADDAMS, Dawn: Act. b. Felixstowe, Suffolk, Eng, Sep 21, 1930. e. RADA. In repertory in Europe, on British stage. Moved to Hollywood, 1950. Films inc: Night into Morning; Singin' in the Rain; The Robe; The Silent Enemy; The Two Faces of Dr. Jekyll; Come Fly With Me; The Vault of Horror.
Thea inc: Peter Pan; The Coming Out Party; The Wild Duck. TV inc: Romans and Friends; Star Maidens.

ADDISON, John: Comp. b. Chobham, Surrey, Eng, Mar 16, 1920. e. Wellington Coll, Royal College of Music. Film scores inc: The Guinea Pig; Seven Days to Noon; Private's Progress; I Reach for the Sky; I Was Monty's Double; Look Back in Anger; The Entertainer; A Taste of Honey; The Loneliness of the Long Distance Runner; Tom Jones (Oscar-1963); Guns at Batasi; Torn Curtain; The Honey Pot; Mr Forbush and the Penguin; Sleuth; Dead Cert; A Bridge Too Far; The Charge of the Light Brigade; The 7% Solution; Joseph Andrews.
TV inc: Centennial; Pearl.
Thea inc: The Entertainer; The Chairs; Luther; Bloomsbury.
(Grammy-Soundtrack-1963).

ADDISON, Nancy: Act. b. NYC, Mar 21. e. Fisher Coll, NYU. TV inc: The Guiding Light; Ryan's Hope; The Dain Curse.
Thea inc: The Impossible Years.

ADDY, Wesley: Act. b. Omaha, NE, Aug 4, 1913. Films inc: The First Legion; The Big Knife; Whatever Happened to Baby Jane?; Hush, Hush, Sweet Charlotte; Seconds; Tora! Tora! Tora!; The Grissom Gang; Network; The Europeans.
Bway inc: Hamlet; Twelfth Night; Romeo and Juliet; Antigone; Candida; Invitation to a March; A Month in the Country.
TV inc: The Edge of Night; Days of Our Lives.

ADELMAN, Joseph A: Exec. b. Winnipeg, Man, Can, Dec 27, 1933. e. NYU, BA; Harvard Law School, JD; 1957, Attorney, UA, NY; 1958, West Coast Counsel; 1964, exec asst to VP in chg prodn; 1968, VP West Coast business, legal affairs; 1972, exec VP AMPTP; 1977, admitted to NY, CA, Supreme Court bars; 1979 VP in chg of bus aff, PAR.

ADELSON, Merv: Prod. b. LA, Oct 23, 1929. e. UCLA. Chmn Board Lorimar Prodns, Inc. Films inc: Twilight's Last Gleaming; The Choirboys; Who's Killing the Great Chefs of Europe; Avalanche Express; The Big Red One.
TV inc: The Waltons; Eight is Enough; Dallas; Kaz; The Waverly Wonders; Knots Landing; Sybil; A Man Called Intrepid; The Blue Knight; Helter-Skelter.

ADJANI, Isabelle: Act. b. Germany, Jun 27, 1955. Films inc: The Slap; The Story of Adele H; The Tenant; Faustine; Barocco; The Driver; NOSFERATU--The Vampire; The Bronte Sisters.

ADLER, Gerald L: Exec. b. Pittsburgh, PA, Jan 30, 1931. e. Carnegie Mellon U, BFA; Syracuse U, MS. VP U-TV 1956-68; VP Cinema Center 100, 1968-71; Exec VP WB-TV 1971; Prod Sandy Howard Prodns 1975-76; Prod-Dir Teens World Intl 1977-1979; VP in chg tv prodn Melvin Simon Prodns Jan 1980.

ADLER, Jerry: Mus. b. Baltimore, MD, Oct 30, 1918. e. Baltimore City Coll. Command perf before King George V & Queen Mary and King George VI & Queen Elizabeth. Toured as solo perf. Recorded over 150 Film and TV sound tracks.

ADLER, Jerry: Dir. b. NYC, Feb 4, 1929. e. Syracuse U. Bway inc: Fun City; We Interrupt This Program; Words And Music; Good Evening; Checking Out; My Fair Lady (revival).

ADLER, Larry: Mus. b. NYC, Feb 10, 1914. Virtuoso who raised what the Musicians Union considered a toy to the level of a musical instrument. Started in showbusiness in 1928 when Rudy Vallee gave him a brief job at the Heigh-Ho Club; Bway inc: Smiles, Clowns in Clover, Flying Colors; and the English revues Streamline and Time Inn; during World War II teamed with dancer Paul Draper for USO tours that led to post-war concert engagements around the world.
Films inc: Many Happy Returns; The Singing Marine; St. Martin's Lane; Sidewalks of London; The Big Broadcast of 1937; Music for Millions.
TV inc: The Monte Carlo Show.

ADLER, Lou: Prod. b. LA. Began wri, prod records 1958 with Herb Alpert. In 1963 formed Dunhill Records, sold to ABC; started Ode Records, joined Alpert in A&M Records.
(Grammys-Record of the Year-Album of the Year-1971).
Films inc: Monterey Pop (doc); Brewster McCloud; The Rocky Horror Picture Show; Cheech and Chong's Up In Smoke.

ADLER, Luther: Act. b. NYC, May 4, 1903. Studied under his father, Jacob P Adler and appeared with Adler Yiddish Theatre Company from 1908 through 1921. Bway inc: Humoresque; The Monkey Talks; Money Business; We Americans; Is Zat So?; Street Scene; Night Over Taos; Success Story; Alien Corn; Men In White; Golden Boy; Rocket to the Moon; Thunder Rock; Two On An Island; Dunnigan's Daughter; A Flag Is Born (& prod); The Passion of Joseph D.; Three Sisters; toured in Fiddler on the Roof.
Films inc: Lancer Spy; Cornered; Saigon; Loves of Carmen; Wake of the Red Witch; House of Strangers; D.O.A.; South Sea Sinner; Under My Skin; Kiss Tomorrow Goodbye; The Desert Fox; The Hoodlum Empire; The Last Angry Man; Crazy Joe; Murph The Surf.
TV inc: Hedda Gabler; Billy Budd; The Plot to Kill Stalin; The Lincoln Murder Case; The Brotherhood.

ADLER, Richard: Comp-Lyr-Prod. b. NYC, Aug 3, 1921. Bway inc: (mus-lyr) John Murray Anderson's Almanac; Pajama Game (Tony-comp-1955); Damn Yankees (Tony-comp-1956); Kwamina; A Mother's Kisses; Rex (prod only); Music Is (prod only).
TV inc: (scores) The Gift of the Magi (& co-prod); Little Women (& co-prod).

ADLER, Stella: Act-Dir-Teacher. b. NYC, Feb 10, 1902. Sis of Luther Adler. Studied with her father, Jacob Adler; Maria Ouspenskaya; Constantin Stanislavsky. Thea inc: debut at age 4 with father's company in Yiddish Theatre and appeared with him for many years; in vaude for year; starred in repertory of plays all over the world; joined Group Theatre 1931; directs and teaches at Stella Adler Conservatory, NY.
Bway inc: The House of Connelly; 1931; Night Over Taos; Success Story; Big Night; Hilda Cassidy; Gentlewoman; Gold-Eagle Guy; Awake and Sing!; Paradise Lost; Sons and Soldiers; Manhattan Nocturne (dir); Pretty Little Parlor; Polonaise (dir); He Who Gets Slapped; Sunday Breakfast (dir); Johnny Johnson (dir).
Films inc: Love On Toast; The Thin Man; My Girl Tisa.

ADRIAN, Iris (nee Hostetter): Act. b. LA, May 29, 1913. In Ziegfeld Follies, 1931. Films inc: Paramount on Parade; Rumba; Our Relations; Professional Bride; The G-String Murders; I'm From Arkansas; The Paleface; G.I. Jane; The Buccaneer; That Darn Cat; The Odd Couple; Scandalous John.
TV inc: Murder Can Hurt You!

AGAR, John: Act. b. Chicago, Jan 31, 1921. Films inc: Fort Apache; Sands of Iwo Jima; The Magic Carpet; Joe Butterfly; Journey to the Seventh Planet; Of Love and Desire; Waco; The St. Valentine's Day Massacre; The Curse of the Swamp Creature; The Undefeated; Big Jake; King Kong.

AGER, Milton: Comp. b. Chicago, IL, 1893. H of Celia, Ager, former Variety columnist. F of Shana Alexander, news commentator. Songs inc: Everything is Peaches Down in Georgia; Ain't She Sweet; Happy Days Are Here Again; Hardhearted Hannah; If I Didn't Care; Rain or Shine.
(Died May 6, 1979).

AGHAYAN, Ray: Cos dsgn. b. Jul 29, 1934. e. LA City Coll, BA, UCLA. Films inc: The Art of Love; Do Not Disturb; Our Man Flint; The Glass Bottom Boat; In Like Flint; Caprice; Dr Doolittle; Gaily, Gaily; Hannie Caulder; Lady Sings the Blues; The Four Musketeers; Funny Lady.
TV inc: The Judy Garland Show; The Dick Van Dyke Show; Robin Hood; Alice Through the Looking Glass (Emmy-1966); Carol Channing & 101 Men; Carol Channing & Pearl Bailey on Broadway; Leslie Uggams Show; Jim Nabors Show; Diahann Carroll Variety Show (prod); The Tenth Month.
Bway inc: Catch My Soul; Applause; On the Town; Lorelei.

AGUTTER, Jenny: Act. b. London, Dec 20, 1952. Film debut age 11, East of Sudan. Films inc: Gates To Paradise; Star!; Walkabout; The Railway Children; Logan's Run; The Eagle Has Landed; Equus; China 9, Liberty 37; Riddle of the Sands; Sweet William.
TV inc: Ballerina; The Wild Duck; The Snow Goose (Emmy-supp-1972). Shelley; War of Children; School Play; Mayflower: The Pilgrim's Adventure; Beulah Land. Thea: School For Scandal; Rooted; Arms and the Man; The Ride Across Lake Constance; The Tempest; Spring Awakening.

AHERNE, Brian: Act. b. Worcestershire, Eng, May 2, 1902. In films since 1924. On stage in London. On Bway in Barretts of Wimpole Street; Romeo and Juliet; St. Joan; She Stoops To Conquer.
Films inc: Song of Songs; Juarez; Constant Nymph; Beloved Enemy; The Great Garrick; Captain Fury; The Appointment; The Mandarins.

AIDMAN, Charles: Act-Dir-Wri. b. Frankfort, IN, Jan 31, 1929. e. IN U. Films inc: Pork Chop Hill; War Hunt; Count Down; Hour of the Gun; Dirty Little Billy; Kotch; Twilight's Last Gleaming.
TV inc: Spoon River Anthology (dir); The Picture of Dorian Gray; The Red Badge of Courage; Amelia Earhart; The Last Song; Alcatraz-The Whole Shocking Story.
Bway inc: Spoon River Anthology (conceived-dir-lyr); Julius Caesar; The Cretan Woman; Macbeth; Career; After the Fall; Zoot Suit.

AIELLO, Danny: Act. b. Jun 20, 1933. Films inc: Blood Brothers; Fingers; Defiance; Hide in Plain Sight.
Bway inc: Lampost Reunion; Wheelbarrow Closers; Knockout.
TV inc: Family of Strangers.

AILES, Roger: Prod-Dir. b. Warren, OH, May 15, 1940. e. OH U, BFA. TV inc: The Last Frontier (& dir); Fellini--Wizards, Clowns and Honest Liars (& dir).
Bway inc: Mother Earth; Hot L Baltimore.

AILEY, Alvin: Chor-Dir. b. Rogers, TX, Jan 5, 1931. Began as a member of Lester Horton Dance Troupe in LA; chor Mourning Morning; According to St Francis; Darius Milhaud's Creation of the World; formed Alvin Ailey Dancers; chor Revelations; Knoxville Summer of 1915; Been Here and Gone; Feast of Ashes; Labrynth; Ariadne.
Films inc: Carmen Jones (dancer).
Bway inc: The Carefree Tree; The House of Flowers; Sing, Man, Sing; Jamaica; Tiger, Tiger Burning Bright (act).

AIMEE, Anouk (Francoise Sorya): Act. b. Paris, Apr 27, 1934. Films inc: Les Amants de Verone; The Golden Salamander; Pot Bouille; La Dolce Vita; Eight and a Half; The Journey; A Man and a Woman; Un Soir Un Train; The Appointment; The Model Shop; Justine; If It Were to do Over Again; My First Love; Leap Into The Void.

AJAYE, Franklyn: Act. b. Brooklyn, May 13, 1949. Nightclubs, TV, records. Films inc: The All-American Girl; Car Wash; Convoy; Sweet Revenge; The Jazz Singer.
TV inc: The Cheap Detective.

AKINS, Claude: Act. b. Nelson, GA, May 25, 1918. e. Northwestern U. Films inc: From Here to Eternity; The Caine Mutiny; The Sea Chase; Johnny Concho; Porgy and Bess; Inherit The Wind; How the West Was Won; The Killers; Return of the Seven; Skyjacked; Waterhole Three; The Devil's Brigade; Flap; Battle for the Planet of the Apes; The Great Train Robbery; Timber Tramps; Tentacles.
TV inc: Movin' On; Nashville 99; Murder In Music City; Ebony, Ivory and Jade; The Misadventures of Sheriff Lobo; The Concrete Cowboys.

ALBECK, Andy: Exec. b. Russia, Sep 25, 1921. Entered film industry 1939 with Columbia Pictures Int'l, worked for Central Motion Picture Exchange and Eagle Lion Classics before joining UA Int'l dept 1951; named VP UA & UA Broadcasting 1972; became P UA Broadcasting following year; became UA sr vp ops 1976; P, CEO 1978; Dec 1980, ChmnB.

ALBEE, Denny: Act. b. Oklahoma City, OK, Mar 19, 1949. e. TN State U, BA; FL State U, MFA. Thea inc: An American Dream; Halloween. TV inc: The Edge of Night.

ALBEE, Edward: Wri-Dir-Prod. b. Washington, DC, May 12, 1928. e. Trinity Coll. Plays inc: The Zoo Story; The Death of Bessie Smith; The American Dream; Who's Afraid of Virginia Woolf?; The Ballad of the Sad Cafe; Tiny Alice; A Delicate Balance; All Over; Seascape (& dir) (Pulitzer Prize-1975); Lady From Dubuque. Dir: The Sandbox; The Palace at 4 a.m. (Prod) Corruption in the Palace of Justice; Two Executioners; The Dutchman; The Butter and Egg Man; Night of the Dunce; The Front Page.
(Grammy-Drama Recording-1963).

ALBERG, Mildred Freed: Prod. b. Montreal. TV inc: Playhouse 90; Our American Heritage series; The Story of Jacob and Joseph; The Story of David; The Royal Archives of Elba; Archeological Dig in Syria.

ALBERGHETTI, Anna Marie: Act. b. Pesaro, Italy, May 15, 1936. US debut Carnegie Hall, 1950. Films inc: Here Comes the Groom; The Stars Are Singing; The Medium; The Last Command; Ten Thousand Bedrooms; Cinderfella.
TV inc: Forever and a Day; Smart Woman; The Locket; Titanic; The Swan; Lancelot and Guinevere; The Waltz King; Rosie.
Bway inc: Carnival (Tony-1962).

ALBERT, Chris: Mus. b. Gottingen, W Germany, Jun 17, 1963. See Blood, Sweat & Tears.

ALBERT, Eddie (nee Heimberger): Act. b. Rock Island, IL, Apr 22, 1908. Started career as a singer; Bway debut in Brother Rat. Films inc: Brother Rat;
Bway inc: Say Darling; The Music Man. Room Service; Roman Holiday; Captain Newman, MD; The Longest Day; The Young Doctors; Teahouse of the August Moon; Roots of Heaven; Carrie; You're in the Navy Now; The Heartbreak Kid; The Longest Yard; The Concorde - Airport '79; Yesterday; Foolin' Around; How To Beat The High Cost of Living.
TV inc: Miracle of the White Stallion; Seven Women; Green Acres; Switch; Trouble In High Timber Country; Beulah Land.

ALBERT, Edward: Act. b. LA, Feb 20, 1951. S of Margo and Eddie Albert. Films inc: Midway; Butterflies are Free; Forty Carats; The Purple Taxi; The Domino Principle; The Greek Tycoon; When Time Ran Out; The Squeeze.
TV inc: The Word; Silent Victory - The Kitty O'Neil Story; The Last Convertible.

ALBERTSON, Jack: Act. b. Malden, MA, Jun 16, 1907. Films inc: Top Banana; The Harder They Fall; Man of a Thousand Faces; The Shaggy Dog; Period of Adjustment; A Tiger Walks; How to Murder Your Wife; The Subject Was Roses *(Oscar-*supp-1968); Justine; Rabbit Run; Willy Wonka and the Chocolate Factory; The Poseidon Adventure; Pick Up on 101.

TV inc: Ensign O'Toole; The Thin Man; The Defenders; Cher *(Emmy-*supp-1975); Chico and the Man *(Emmy-*1976); Grandpa Goes to Washington; Uptown - A Tribute to the Apollo Theatre; Valentine; Marriage Is Alive and Well.

Bway inc: Make Mine Manhattan; High Time; Strip for Action; The Lady Says Yes; Showboat; The Red Mill; The Subject Was Roses *(Tony-*1964).

ALBERTSON, Mabel: Act. b. 1901. Films inc: Mutiny on the Blackhawk; She's Back on Broadway; Ransom; Forever Darling; The Long Hot Summer; Home Before Dark; The Gazebo; Period of Adjustment; Barefoot in the Park.

TV inc: The Tom Ewell Show.

ALBRIGHT, Lola: Act. b. Akron, OH, Jul 20, 1925. Screen debut, 1948, The Pirate. Films inc: Champion; The Good Humor Man; Arctic Flight; The Tender Trap; Seven Guns to Mesa; A Cold Wind in August; Kid Galahad; The Love Cage; Lord Love a Duck; The Way West; Where Were You When the Lights Went Out?; The Impossible Years; The Money Jungle.

TV inc: Peter Gunn.

ALCOTT, John: Cin. b. England. Films inc: A Clockwork Orange; Barry Lyndon *(Oscar-*1975); March or Die; Who is Killing the Great Chefs of Europe; Terror Train.

ALDA, Alan: Act. b. NYC, Jan 28, 1936. e. Fordham U. S of Robert Alda. Studied at Cleveland Playhouse; performed with Second City. Bway inc: The Owl and the Pussycat; Purlie Victorious; Fair Game for Lovers; The Apple Tree. Films inc: Gone Are the Days; The Moonshine War; Jenny; The Mephisto Waltz; Paper Lion; To Kill a Clown; California Suite; Same Time, Next Year; The Seduction of Joe Tynan (& sp).

TV inc: That Was the Week That Was; M*A*S*H *(Emmy-*actor, 1974; dir, 1977; wri, 1979 also actor of the year 1974); The Glass House; Kill Me If You Can; 6 Rms Riv Vu (& dir); Greatest Heroes of the Bible.

ALDA, Robert (Alphonso D'Abruzzo): Act. b. NYC, Feb 26, 1914. e. NYU. Radio; dramatic stock; signed by WB 1943. Films inc: Cinderella Jones; Rhapsody in Blue; Cloak and Dagger; The Man I Love; Nora Prentiss; The Beast with Five Fingers; Beautiful but Dangerous; Musketeers of the Sea; Revenge of the Barbarians; Cleopatra's Daughter; A Soldier and One Half; Imitation of Life; I Will, I Will . . . For Now; Bittersweet Love; The Squeeze.

Bway inc: Guys and Dolls *(Tony-*1951); Harbor Lights; What Makes Sammy Run; My Daughter, Your Son; Front Page.

TV inc: Police Story; The Invisible Man; Rhoda; Fame; Supertrain; Lucy Moves to NBC; Perfect Gentlemen.

ALDEN, Norman: Act. b. Fort Worth, TX, Sep 13, 1924. e. TCU. Films inc: The Walking Target; Portrait of a Mobster; Operation Bottleneck; Bedtime Story; The Wild Angels; Tora Tora Tora; The Great Bank Robbery; I Never Promised You a Rose Garden; Hindenburg; Where Does It Hurt; Semi-Tough; Cloud Dancer; Borderline.

TV inc: No Other Love; Flamingo Road.

ALDERTON, John: Act. b. Gainsborough, Lincs, England, Nov 27, 1940. Thea inc: Spring and Port Wine; Dutch Uncle; The Night I Chased the Women With an Eel; Punch and Judy Stories; Birthday Party; Confusions; Rattle of a Simple Man.

Films inc: The System; Duffy; Hannibal Brooks; Please Sir; Zardoz; It Shouldn't Happen to a Vet; All Things Bright and Beautiful.

TV inc: Emergency Ward 10; Please Sir; My Wife Next Door.

ALDREDGE, Theoni V (nee Vachlioti): Costume Des. b. Salonika, Greece. Bway inc: The Distaff Side; Subject to Fits; Underground; The Basic Training of Pavlo Hummel; Timon of Athens; Two Gentlemen of Verona; Sticks and Stones; Voices; The Hunter; The Wedding Band; The Three Sisters; The Dance of Death; Music! Music!; An American Millionaire; In Praise of Love; Little Black Sheep; A Chorus Line; The Au Pair Man; Annie *(Tony-*1977); Clothes For A Summer Hotel; Break A Leg; I Remember Mama; Barnum *(Tony-*1980); 42d Street.

Films inc: Girl of the Night; You're a Big Boy Now; No Way to Treat a Lady; Uptight; Last Summer; I Never Sang for My Father; Promise at Dawn; The Great Gatsby *(Oscar-*1974); The Fury; The Cheap Detective; Eyes of Laura Mars; The Champ; Semi-Tough; The Rose.

ALDREDGE, Tom: Act. b. Dayton, OH, Feb 28, 1928. e. U of Dayton. Bway inc: Electra; The Nervous Set; The Tempest; Between Two Thieves; Love's Labour's Lost; Troilus and Cressida; The Mutilated; The Butter and Egg Man; Romeo and Juliet; Twelfth Night; The Boys in the Band; The Happiness Cage (dir only); How the Other Half Loves; Sticks and Bones; The Leaf People; Rex; Vieux Carre; Stages; Saint Joan; On Golden Pond.

Films inc: The Mouse on the Moon; The Troublemaker; The Rain People.

TV inc: Nurse; Henry Winkler Meets William Shakespeare *(Emmy-*1978).

ALDRICH, Adell: Dir. b. LA, Jun 11, 1943. e. USC. D of Robert B. Aldrich. Films inc: Daddy, I Don't Like It Like This.

TV inc: The Kid from Left Field.

ALDRICH, Robert: Dir. b. Cranston, RI, Aug 9, 1918. e. U of VA. Films inc: The Big Leaguer; World for Ransom (& prod); Apache; Vera Cruz; Kiss Me Deadly (& prod); The Big Knife (& prod); Attack (& prod); Autumn Leaves; The Ride Back (& exec prod); Ten Seconds to Hell; The Angry Hills; The Last Sunset; Sodom and Gomorrah; Whatever Happened to Baby Jane? (& prod); Four For Texas (& prod); Hush, Hush Sweet Charlotte (& prod); Flight of the Phoenix (& prod); The Dirty Dozen; The Legend of Lylah Claire (& prod); The Killing of Sister George (& prod); Whatever Happened to Aunt Alice (prod only); Too Late the Hero (& prod); The Grissom Gang (& prod); Ulzana's Raid; Emperor of the North; The Longest Yard; Hustle (& prod); Twilight's Last Gleaming; Choirboys; No Knife; The Frisco Kid.

TV inc: China Smith; The Doctor; Adventures in Paradise; Sundance Kid.

ALDRICH, William McLaughry: Prod. b. LA, Oct 17, 1944. e. USC. S of Robert B. Aldrich. P Aldrich Co, Inc. Films inc: Who's Killing the Great Chefs of Europe; The Choirboys.

ALDRIDGE, Michael: Act. b. Glastonbury, Somerset, England, Sep 9, 1920. Thea inc: With Old Vic in various Shakespearean roles; Escapade; Salad Days; Free As Air; A Moon for the Misbegotten; State of Emergency; Vanity Fair; The Fighting Cock; The Farmer's Wife; Heartbreak House; The Unknown Soldier and His Wife; The Tempest; The Cocktail Party; Caucasian Chalk Circle; The Magistrate; A Bequest to the Nation; Reunion in Vienna; Absurd Person Singular; Jeeves; Lies!; The Last of Mrs. Cheyney.

ALEXANDER, Denise: Act. b. Long Island, NY, Nov 11, 1939. Performed in 5,000 radio programs inc A Tree Grows in Brooklyn; I Remember Mama; Perry Mason; Martin Kane, Private Eye.

Bway inc: Children's Hour; A Member of the Wedding.

TV inc: Days of Our Lives; General Hospital.

ALEXANDER, Jane (nee Quigley): Act. b. Boston, Oct 28, 1939. e. Sarah Lawrence Coll, U of Edinburgh. Films inc: The Great White Hope; A Gun Fight; The New Centurions; All the President's Men; The Betsy; Kramer vs Kramer; Brubaker.

TV inc: Eleanor and Franklin; Death Be Not Proud; A Question of Love. Mourning Becomes Electra; The Time of Your Life; Find Your Way Home; Hamlet; Playing For Time.

Bway inc: The Great White Hope *(Tony-*1969); The Merry Wives of Windsor; First Monday in October; Goodbye Fidel.

ALEXANDER, Jeff: Comp-Cond. b. Seattle, WA, Jul 2, 1910. e. Becker Cons. Film scores inc: The Tender Trap; Escape From Fort Bravo; The Mating Game; The Gazebo; It Started with a Kiss; Kid Galahad; The George Raft Story; The Rounders; The Sea Gypsies.

TV inc: Sam Benedict; The Lieutenant; The Greatest Show on Earth; Valentine's Day; More Wild Wild West.

ALEXANDER, Shana: Wri-TV pers. b. NYC, Oct 6, 1925. D Cecelia Ager and the late Milton Ager. With PM (NYC newspaper) 1944-46; Harper's Bazaar, 1946-47; reporter Life Mag 1951-1961; staff wri 1961-64; edtr McCall's Mag 1969-71.

TV inc: 60 Minutes.

ALEXANDER, Van: Cond-Arr-Comp. b. NYC, May 2, 1915. e. Columbia U. Formed own orch, played in theatres, radio; arr for Benny Goodman, Paul Whiteman. Film scores inc: Baby-Face Nelson; Straight-Jacket; Big Operation; Andy Hardy Comes Home.

TV inc: Hazel; Dean Martin's Xmas In California.

Songs: A Tisket a Tasket (collab. w. Ella Fitzgerald); I'll Close My Eyes; Where, O Where Has My Little Dog Gone?.

ALGAR, James Nelson: Prod-Wri-Dir. b. Modesto, CA, Jun 11, 1912. e. Stanford U, BA, MA Journalism. With Walt Disney Prods. since 1934. Animator: Snow White. Directed: Fantasia; Bambi; Ichabod & Mr. Toad. Films inc: Ten Who Dared; The Incredible Journey; The Jungle Cat; Run, Cougar, Run.

TV inc: Run Light Buck, Run; The Not So Lonely Lighthouse Keeper; Two Against The Arctic; Wild Geese Calling.

ALI, Muhammad (Cassius Clay): Act. b. Louisville, KY, Jan 18, 1942. Former champion fighter. Films inc: Requiem for a Heavyweight; The Greatest.

TV inc: Freedom Road.

ALJIAN, James D: Exec. b. Oakland, CA, Nov 5, 1932. Senior v.p.-finance, MGM.

ALLAN, Ted: Wri. Films inc: Lies My Father Told Me; Falling In Love Again.

ALLAN, Ted: Cin. b. Clifton, AZ. Portrait pho for MGM, FOX; Selznick. Featurettes for the following films: Von Ryan's Express; Fantastic Voyage; Sand Pebbles; Dr Doolittle; Lady in Cement; Tora! Tora! Tora!; The Hindenburg; The 7% Solution; Rollercoaster; Two Minute Warning; House Calls; Dracula; Same Time Next Year.

ALLAND, William: Prod. b. Delmar, DE, Mar 4, 1916. Originally with Orson Welles' Mercury Theatre; acted in Citizen Kane; later staff producer for U-I. Films inc: It Came from Outer Space; This Island Earth; The Lady Takes a Flyer; The Rare Breed; Look in Any Window (& dir).

ALLBRITTON, Louise: Act. b. Oklahoma City, OK, Jul 3, 1920. On screen from 1942, Not a Ladies Man. Films inc: Who Done It?; A Date with an Angel; Son of Dracula; Her Primitive Man; Men in Her Diary; San Diego I Love You; Tangier; The Egg and I; Walk a Crooked Mile; Sitting Pretty; The Great Manhunt.

(Died Feb 16, 1979).

ALLEGRET, Yves: Dir. b. Asnieres, France, Oct 13, 1907. Films inc: Les Deux Timides; Dedee; Une St Jolie Petite Plage; Maneges; Les Orgueilleux; Oasis; Germinal; Mam'zelle Nitouche; La Meilleure Part.

ALLEN, Corey: Wri-Dir. b. Cleveland, OH, Jun 29, 1934. e. UCLA, BA. On stage dir. Death of a Salesman; Who's Afraid of Virginia Woolf?; The Time of Your Life.

TV inc: Dr. Kildare; Stone; The Return of Frank Cannon.

Films inc: Thunder and Lightning; Avalanche (& wri).

ALLEN, Dede: Flm Ed. b. Cleveland, OH, 1924. Films inc: Odds Against Tomorrow; Bonnie and Clyde; Rachel, Rachel; Serpico; Dog Day Afternoon; Slap Shot; The Wiz.

ALLEN, Duane: Singer-Sngwri. b. Taylortown, TX, Apr 29, 1943. e. U of TX, BS. Deejay KPLT (Paris, TX) before joining Oak Ridge Boys (see group listing for Grammys). Songs inc: Here's A Song for The Man; How Much Further Can We Go; I Will Follow The Sun; He Did It All For Me.

ALLEN, Elizabeth (nee Gillease): Act. b. Jersey City, NJ, Jan 25 1934. Films inc: From the Terrace; Diamond Head; Donovan's Reef; The Carey Treatment; Star Spangled Girl.

Thea inc: Romanoff & Juliet; Lend An Ear; The Gay Life; Do I Hear a Waltz?; Sherry; Cactus Flower; California Suite.

TV inc: Jackie Gleason Show; The Jimmy Walker Story; Bracken's World; The Paul Lynde Show; No Other Love.

ALLEN, Irving: Dir-Prod. b. Poland, Nov 24, 1905. e. Georgetown, PhD. Film editor U, PAR, REP, 1929-40. Shorts director RKO, WB. 1941-42. WW II, 1942-45. Debut as director Strange Voyage, 1945. Films inc: Avalanche; Fire Down Below; No Time To Die; Trials of Oscar Wilde; Hammerhead; The Wrecking Crew; The Desperados; Run Wild, Run Free; Cromwell.

ALLEN, Irwin: Prod. b. NYC, 1916. e. Columbia U, CCNY. Films inc: The Sea Around Us; The Animal World; The Story of Mankind (& dir); The Big Circus; The Lost World; A Voyage to the Bottom of the Sea (& dir); Five Weeks in a Balloon (& dir); The Poseidon Adventure; The Towering Inferno (& co dir); The Swarm (& dir); Beyond The Poseidon Adventure (& dir); When Time Ran Out.

TV inc: Voyage to the Bottom of the Sea; Lost in Space; Time Tunnel; Land of the Giants; The Swiss Family Robinson; The Time Travelers; The Memory of Eva Ryker.

ALLEN, Jay Presson: Wri. b. Fort Worth, TX, Mar 3, 1922. Films inc: Marnie; Prime of Miss Jean Brodie; Travels with My Aunt; Cabaret; Funny Lady; Just Tell Me What You Want; It's My Turn (exec prod).

Plays inc: Prime of Miss Jean Brodie; Forty Carats.

TV inc: Prime of Miss Jean Brodie.

ALLEN, Karen: Act. b. MD, Oct 5, 1951. Films inc: A Small Circle of Enemies; Cruising; The Wanderers; National Lampoon's Animal House.

ALLEN, Lewis M: Prod. b. Berryville, VA, 1922. e. U. of VA, BA. Bway inc: Ballad of the Sad Cafe; Big Fish, Little Fish; The Physicists; Half a Sixpence; Annie *(Tony-*1977); Billy Bishop Goes To Washington.

Films inc: Lord of the Flies; Fahrenheit 451; The Balcony; The Connection.

ALLEN, Marty: Comedian. b. Pittsburgh, PA, Mar 23, 1922. Began working niteries while USC student after WW2 service; appeared as opening act with Nat "King" Cole; Eydie Gorme; teamed with Steve Rossi for several years in niteries; solo since 1968, niteries, tv guestings. Other TV inc: Mr. Jericho; The Ballad of Billie Blue; Comedy Is Not Pretty; Murder Will Kill You.

ALLEN, Mel: Sportscaster. b. Birmingham, AL, Feb 14, 1913. e. U of AL, AB, AL Law School, LLB. Staff announcer CBS, early 30s. Commentator NY Yankees three decades. Also sports commentator Fox Movietone Newsreel (1946-64).

ALLEN, Nancy: Act. b. NYC, Jun 24. Films inc: The Last Victim; The Last Detail; Carrie; I Wanna Hold Your Hand; Home Movies; 1941; Dressed To Kill.

ALLEN, Patrick: Act. b. Malawi, Mar 17, 1927. Thea inc: The Desperate Hours; The Rough and Ready Lot; Ondine; The Devils; Troilus and Cressida; The Flip Side; The Sandboy; The Island of the Mighty; Present Laughter.

Films inc: 1984; High Tide At Noon; The Long Haul; Dunkirk; I Was Monty's Double; The Traitors; Captain Clegg; Night of the Big Heat; When Dinosaurs Ruled the Earth; Persecution.

ALLEN, Philip: Act. b. Pittsburgh, PA, Mar 26, 1939. e. Neighborhood Playhouse. Bway inc: Sticks and Bones. Films inc: The Onion Field; Special Delivery; Midway.

TV inc: Helter Skelter; Washington--Behind Closed Doors; Trapped Beneath the Sea; Mary Jane Harper Cried Last Night; Bad News Bears; A Family Upside Down; Friendly Fire.

ALLEN, Rex: Act. b. Wilcox, AZ, Dec 31, 1922. Started in radio, vaudeville, rodeo perf, rec artist. Films inc: Arizona Cowboy; Hills of Oklahoma; I Dream of Jeanie; Phantom Stallion; For the Love of Mike; Tomboy and the Champ.

TV inc: Frontier Doctor; Town Hall Party.

ALLEN, Sian Barbara: Act. b. Reading, PA, Jul 12, 1946. e. Pasadena Playhouse. Films inc: You'll Like My Mother; Billy Two Hats.

TV inc: The Waltons; The Lindbergh Kidnapping Case; Captains and the Kings; Scream, Pretty Peggy; The Family Rico; Eric.

ALLEN, Steve: Act-Comp. b. NYC, Dec 26, 1921. Started career as announcer-writer-pianist at KOY, Phoenix. On TV in N.Y. in '50. TV inc: What's My Line; Tonight; Steve Allen Show. Stone; The Big Show; The Gossip Columnist; 32d Annual Emmy Awards (host); Steve Allen Comedy Hour; A Funny Thing Happened On The Way to the White House (cable TV).

Films inc: Down Memory Lane; I'll Get By; The Benny Goodman Story; Warning Shot; College Confidential.

Songs inc: This Could Be the Start of Something Big; South Rampart Street Parade; Picnic; Houseboat; On The Beach.

(Grammy-original Jazz comp-1963).

ALLEN, Woody (Allen Stewart Konigesberg): Act-Dir-Wri. b. NYC, Dec 1, 1935. Began writing comedy at age 17, contributing to various magazines and top comics. Started career as stand-up comic 1961, in niteries. On screen from 1963. Films inc: What's New Pussycat? (wri-act); Casino Royale (act); What's Up Tiger Lily? (dubbed scr, act); Take the Money and Run (dir-wri-act); Bananas (dir-wri-act); Play It Again, Sam (wri-act); Everything You Always Wanted to Know About Sex But Were Afraid To Ask (dir-wri-act); Sleeper (dir-wri-act); Love and Death (wri-act) The Front (act); Annie Hall (wri-dir-act) *(Oscars*-1977 for dir-wri); Interiors (wri-dir); Manhattan (wri-dir-act); Stardust Memories (wri-dir-act).

Bway inc: Play It Again, Sam (auth); Don't Drink the Water.

ALLIO, Rene: Dir. b. Marseilles, France, 1924. Films inc: Les Ames Mortes; La Meule; The Shameless Old Lady; Skin Deep; Pierre et Paul; Les Camisards; Rude Journee pour la Reine; Return to Marseilles (& wri).

ALLISON, Charles Gary: Wri-Prod. b. Newport, RI, Jul 12, 1940. e. USC. TV inc: Fraternity Row (& prod): C.C. Julian; In Country (& co-prod); The Hanoi Hilton (co-prod); The 33rd of August (& co-prod). VP, Troystar Prodns.

ALLISON, Fran: Act. b. LaPorte City, IA, circa 1920. e. Coe Coll. Started as radio singer, 1934; moved to Chicago 1937 where for many years portrayed Aunt Fanny on Don McNeill's Breakfast Club; best known as the live member of the puppet TV series, Kukla, Fran & Ollie (1947-57 and since revived). TV inc: Happy Birthday, Beulah Witch.

ALLMAN, Sheldon: Act. b. Chicago, Jun 8, 1924. Films inc: Hud; Good Neighbor Sam; Pattern for Murder; The Sons of Katie Elder; Nevada Smith; In Cold Blood.

ALLYSON, June (Ella Geisman): Act. b. Westchester, NY, Oct 7, 1917. Started as chorus girl. Screen debut Best Foot Forward, 1943. Films inc: Girl Crazy; Thousands Cheer; The Stratton Story; Executive Suite; My Man Godfrey; They Only Kill Their Masters; That's Entertainment; Blackout.

ALMEIDA, Laurindo: Comp-Mus. b. Sao Paulo, Brazil, Sep 2, 1917. To US 1947. Guitarist in Stan Kenton orch; left Kenton 1950 to record, compose, tour US.

Film scores inc: Maracaibo; Cry Tough; The Naked Sea.

Comps inc: Naked Sea; Johnny Peddler; Sighs; Gold Brazilian Sun; The Gypsy with Fire in His Shoes; Sunset in Copacabana; Pancho's Guitar; Guitar Tristesse.

(Grammys-(5)-Class Perf Vocal/Inst-1960; Class Perf Inst 1960, 1961; Class Comp 1961; Inst Jazz 1964).

ALMENDROS, Nestor: Cin. b. Barcelona, Spain, 1930. Films inc: La Collectionneuse; My Night At Maud; Clare's Knee; Wild Child; The Gentleman Tramp; The Marquise of O; Bed and Board; Story of Adele H; The Man Who Loved Women; Days of Heaven *(Oscar*-1978); Goin' South; Madame Rosa; Perceval; Kramer vs Kramer; The Green Room; Love On The Run; The Valley; The Blue Lagoon; The Last Metro.

ALMOND, Paul: Prod-Dir-Wri. b. Montreal, Apr 26, 1931. e. McGill U., Balliol College, Oxford. Toured British Isles with Shakespearean company. Joined CBS as a prod-dir, 1954. Prod, dir over 100 TV dramas in Canada, England, U.S. Films inc: Isabel; Act of the Heart; Journey.

ALONSO, Alicia: Dancer. b. Havana, Cuba, Dec 21, 1921. Debut 1938, Musicomedy, Great Lady; also appeared in Stars In Your Eyes; joined American Ballet Caravan 1939 as soloist; moved to American Ballet Theatre following year; career interrupted 1942 when she suffered detached retina; replaced ailing Alicia Markova in Giselle 1943, thereafter a star member of American Ballet Theatre with Markova, Anton Dolin, Andre Eglevsky, Igor Youskevitch; promoted to principal dancer 1964 danced Fall River Legend; Undertow; Romeo and Juliet; Billy The Kid; founded Ballet Alicia Alonso, Havana, 1948, company disbanded mid-fifties after Batista government cut its susbsidies; joined Ballet Russe de Monte Carlo 1955; 1957 first Western dancer invited to dance in USSR; 1959, with help from Castro goverment, founded Ballet Nacional de Cuba of which she, despite growing blindness, continues as prima ballerina.

Films inc: Alicia (doc).

ALONZO, John A: Cin-Dir. b. Dallas, TX, 1934. Films inc: (as cin) Bloody Mama; Vanishing Point; Chinatown; Harold and Maude; Lady Sings the Blues; The Bad News Bears; Black Sunday; Sounder; Pete 'n' Tillie; Conrack; Casey's Shadow; The Cheap Detective; Norma Rae; Tom Horn; FM (dir).

TV inc: Champions, A Love Story; Belle Starr (dir-cin); Blinded By The Light (dir-cin).

ALPERT, Herb: Mus. b. LA, Mar 31, 1935. Leader, trumpeter of Tijuana Brass. Formed A&M Records 1962.

Recordings inc: The Lonely Bull, Tijuana Taxi; Spanish Flea; A Taste of Honey *(Grammys*-(3)-record of year, non-jazz inst, inst arr-1965); Zorba the Greek; What Now, My Love *(Grammys*-non-jazz inst, inst arr-1966); This Guy's In Love With You; Solid Brass; Summertime; Rise *(Grammy*-pop inst-1979); You Smile-the Song Begins; Main Event; Beyond.

ALSTON, Howard P: Exec. b. Glendale, CA, Jan 26, 1921. Joined CBS TV as prodn asst 1951; dir of ops Television City, 1956; later prodn mgr. Filmaster Prodns, CBS Films, Goodson-Todman, QM Prodns; joined U 1977 as prod.

TV inc: Centennial.

ALSWANG, Ralph: Dsgn-Dir-Prod. b. Chicago, Apr 12, 1916. Debut as set designer on Revelation, 1942. Bway inc: Fair Game for Lovers; The Committee; Comedy in Music: devised Living Screen process (live action and film) for Is There Intelligent Life on Earth? The Bernard Shaw Story; Hostile Witness; The Effect of Gamma Rays on Man-in-the-Moon Marigolds; At the Drop of Another Hat; The Hemingway Hero; Halfway Up the Tree; Fun City, 1972. Designed the Uris Theatre, NY; the New Orleans Civic Center Theatre and Pine Knob Pavillion, MI, 1972.

(Died Feb 15, 1979).

ALTER, Louis: Comp. b. Haverhill, MA, Jun 18, 1902. Piano accomp to Nora Bayes, Irene Bordoni, Helen Morgan, Beatrice Lillie. Film scores inc: Hollywood Revue; Rainbow on the River; The Trail of the Lonesome Pine; Sing, Baby, Sing; Make a Wish; Las Vegas Nights; New Orleans.
    Bway inc: Ballyhoo.
    (Died Nov 5, 1980).

ALTMAN, Robert: Dir-Wri-Prod. b. Kansas City, MO, Feb 20, 1922. e. U of MO. Films inc: The Delinquents; The James Dean Story (co-dir & prod); Countdown; That Cold Day in the Park; M*A*S*H; Brewster McCloud; McCabe and Mrs. Miller; Images; The Long Goodbye; Thieves Like Us; California Split; Nashville; Buffalo Bill and the Indians; The Late Show (& prod); 3 Women (wri-prod); Welcome to LA (prod); Remember My Name (prod); A Wedding (& wri-prod); A Perfect Couple (& wri-prod); Quintet (& wri-prod); Rich Kids (prod); Health; Popeye (dir).
    TV inc: Bonanza; The Roaring Twenties; Bus Stop; Combat.

ALVES, Joe: Dsgn-Prod. b. San Leandro, CA, May 21, 1938. e. San Jose State, USC. Films inc: Sugarland Express; Jaws; Close Encounters; Jaws II (assoc prod & 2nd unit dir).
    TV inc: Night Gallery.

ALVIN, John (nee Hoffstadt): Act. b. Chicago, Oct 24, 1917. Screen debut, 1944, Destination Tokyo. Films inc: Missing Women; Two Guys from Texas; Train to Alcatraz; Shanghai Chest; Carrie; April in Paris; Torpedo Alley; Somewhere In Time.
    TV inc: Police Woman; MASH; Mannix; All in the Family; Visions.

ALWYN, William: Comp. b. Northampton, Eng, 1905. e. Royal Academy of Music. Films inc: Odd Man Out; Fallen Idol; Svengali; Cure for Love; The Ship that Died of Shame; Manuela; I Accuse; Silent Enemy; Swiss Family Robinson; The Running Man.

AMATEAU, Rod: Dir-Wri. b. NYC, Dec 20, 1927. Films inc: Pussy Cat, I Love You; The Statue; Where Does It Hurt?; The Wild Conspiracy; Drive-In; Seniors; Hitler's Son.
    TV inc: Private Secretary; Dobie Gillis; Lassie; Dennis Day Show; Dukes of Hazzard; Enos (& supv prod).

AMATI, Giovanni: Exhib. b. Rome, Italy, 1906. Leading Italian exhibitor. Started as a prize-fight promoter, entered exhibition in the 20's. At one time operated a chain of 50 theatres in Rome. Active in the exhibitors' association, he tried unsuccessfully to enter politics.
    (Died June 30, 1980).

AMBLER, Eric: Wri. b. England, 1909. Films inc: The Way Ahead; The October Man; The Magic Box; The Card; The Cruel Sea; A Night to Remember; The Wreck of the Mary Deare.

AMECHE, Don: Act. b. Kenosha, WI, May 31, 1908. In stock, on radio before screen debut 1936. Films inc: Sins of Man; Ramona; You Can't Have Everything; Alexander's Ragtime Band; Kiss The Boys Goodbye; Alexander Graham Bell; Suppose They Gave A War And Nobody Came; The Boatniks.

AMES, Ed: Singer-Act. b. Jul 9. Originally a member of the Ames Brothers singing act, went solo and studied acting under Herbert Berghof. Bway inc: One Flew Over the Cuckoo's Nest. TV inc: Daniel Boone.
    Recordings inc: Try to Remember; My Cup Runneth Over; Who Will Answer.

AMES, Leon (nee Wycoff): Act. b. Portland, IN, Jan 20, 1903. Screen debut, 1932, Murders in the Rue Morgue. Films inc: The Count of Monte Cristo; Charlie Chan on Broadway; Ellery Queen and the Murder Ring; Meet Me in St. Louis; Thirty Seconds Over Tokyo; Little Women; On Moonlight Bay; Peyton Place; From the Terrace; The Absent-Minded Professor; On a Clear Day You Can See Forever; Hammersmith Is Out; Just You And Me Kid.
    TV inc: Life with Father; Father of the Bride; Mister Ed; The Best Place To Be.

AMES, Rachel: Act. b. Portland, OR, Nov 2. Films inc: When Worlds Collide.
    TV inc: General Hospital.

AMFITHEATROF, Daniele: Comp-Cond. b. St. Petersburg, Russia, Oct 29, 1901. e. Royal Conservatory of Music, Rome. Guest cond symphony orchs Paris, Rome, Budapest, Vienna, Boston. Film scores inc: Lassie Come Home; Song of the South; O.S.S.; I'll Be Seeing You; The Senator Was Indiscreet; Letter From an Unknown Woman; Desert Fox; Human Desire; The Mountain; Unholy Wife; Heller in Pink Tights; Edge of Eternity; Major Dundee.

AMOS, John: Act-Wri-Prod. b. Dec 27, 1941. Films inc: The World's Greatest Athlete; Vanishing Point; Let's Do It Again; Touched By Love.
    TV inc: Tim Conway Hour; Mary Tyler Moore; Good Times; Roots; Willa; Alcatraz--The Whole Shocking Story.

AMRAN, Robert: Prod-Dir-Wri. b. Budapest, Hungary, Jun 12, 1938. e. London School of Economics, BS. Films inc: The Mini Affair; Sentinels of Silence (Oscar-1972); Sky High!; Pacific Challenge; The Late Great Planet Earth.

AMSTERDAM, Morey: Act-Wri-Comp. b. Chicago, Dec 14, 1914. Radio, 1922. Nightclub performer. Films inc: Don't Worry. . . We'll Think Of A Title; Machine Gun Kelly; Murder, Inc.
    TV inc: Stop Me If You've Heard This One; Morey Amsterdam Silver Swan Show; Dick Van Dyke Show; Can You Top This; Sooner or Later.
    Songs inc: Rum and Coca Cola; Why Oh Why Did I Ever Leave Wyoming, Yak A Puk.

ANDERS, Luana: Act. b. 1940. Films inc: Life Begins at Seventeen; The Pit and the Pendulum; The Young Racers; Dementia; B.J. Presents; When the Legends Die; Shampoo; Goin' South; Harper Valley PTA.

ANDERS, Merry: Act. b. 1932. Films inc: Les Miserables; Phfft; The Dalton Girls; Violent Road; The Hypnotic Eye; 20,000 Eyes; Tickle Me; Legacy of Blood.
    TV inc: How to Marry a Millionaire.

ANDERSEN, Carl: Act. b. Lynchburg, VA, Feb 27, 1945. Started career with rock group in Washington, D.C. Joined road tour as Judas in Jesus Christ Superstar. Repeated role in film version.

ANDERSON, Daphne (nee Scrutton): Act. b. London, Apr 27, 1922. London stage debut, 1938. Thea inc: Three Penny Opera; Blithe Spirit; Cat on a Hot Tin Roof; Spring and Port Wine; A Woman Named Anne; Sadler's Wells; Lord Arthur Savile's Crime; Alice Through the Looking Glass; Jane Eyre; The Sleeping Beauty; Lloyd George Knew My Father.
    Films inc: Trottie True; The Beggar's Opera; Hobson's Choice; A Kid for Two Farthings; The Prince and the Showgirl; Snowball; Captain Clegg; The Launching; I Want What I Want.
    TV inc: Silas Marner; Gideon's Way; The Imposter; The Whitehall Worrier; The Suede Jacket; Casanova; Justice Is A Woman.

ANDERSON, Daryl: Act. b. Seattle, WA, Jul 11, 1951. e. U of WA, BFA. Films inc: Sweet Revenge; Butch and Sundance - The Early Days.
    TV inc: Lou Grant.

ANDERSON, Don: Prod. b. Hobart, Tasmania, Australia, Jul 29, 1929. Dir or prod over 200 doc inc Challenge; For Better - For Worse; Hard to Windward; I Hate Holidays; Noise Annoys; Olives Don't Float; Tasmanian Wild Life; The Big Catch; Winter.

ANDERSON, Howard A: Cin. b. LA, Mar 31, 1920. e. UCLA. specialist in special effects. Films inc: Jack the Giant Killer; Tobruk; Superman.
    TV inc: Star Trek; My World and Welcome to It.

ANDERSON, Jack: Syndicated columnist-TV reporter. b. Long Beach, CA, Oct 19, 1922. Pulitzer Prize 1972, nat'l reporting. TV inc: Good Morning America.

ANDERSON, John: Act. b. Clayton, IL, Oct 20, 1922. e. U of IA, MA. Films inc: Psycho; Ride the High Country; Cotton Comes to Harlem; Soldier Blue; Executive Action; The Lincoln Conspiracy; In Search of Historic Jesus.

TV inc: The Deerslayer; Shadow of Fear; Backstairs At The White House; Mark Twain's America--Young Will Rogers.

ANDERSON, Judith, Dame: Act. b. Adelaide, Australia, Feb 10, 1898. Stage debut (Sydney) in Royal Divorce, 1915. Bway, stock, 1918. Screen debut Blood Money, 1933. Films inc: King's Row; Rebecca; Laura; Specter of the Rose; Tycoon; Salome; Cat on a Hot Tin Roof; A Man Called Horse.

TV inc: Macbeth *(Emmy-*1954), Macbeth *(Emmy-*1961).

Bway inc: Dear Brutus; Cobra; Strange Interlude; Mourning Becomes Electra; Macbeth; Medea *(Tony-*1948); Toured in Dame Judith Anderson as Hamlet.

ANDERSON, Lindsay: Dir. b. Bangalore, India, Apr 17, 1923. e. Cheltenham Coll, Wadham Coll, Oxford. Started as film critic, doc dir. Films inc: O Dreamland; Thursday's Children; Every Day Except Christmas; This Sporting Life; If. . . ; O Lucky Man!; In Celebration.

Thea inc: The Long and the Short and the Tall; Billy Liar; The Fire Raisers; Diary of a Madman; The Cherry Orchard; Inadmissible Evidence; In Celebration; The Changing Room; What the Butler Saw; The Sea Gull; The Bed Before Yesterday; Kingfisher; Alice's Boys; Early Days.

TV inc: Robin Hood.

ANDERSON, Loni: Act. b. St Paul, MN, Aug 5. e. U of MN. Taught school briefly.

TV inc: WKRP in Cincinnati; Three on A Date; The Fantastic Funnies; 4th Annual Circus of the Stars; Christmas in Opryland; Shaun Cassidy Special; Bob Hope's All-Star Comedy Birthday Party; The Jayne Mansfield Story; Bob Hope's All-Star Comedy Christmas Special.

ANDERSON, Marian: Singer. b. South Phila, PA, Feb 27, 1902. Appeared on concert stages throughout the world. Received Presidential Medal of Freedom, 1963.

ANDERSON, Melissa Sue: Act. b. Berkeley, CA, Sep 26, 1962. TV inc: The Brady Bunch; Shaft; Very Good Friends; James at 15; The Loneliest Runner; Little House on the Prairie; The Survival of Dana; Which Mother Is Mine? *(Emmy-*1980).

ANDERSON, Melody: Act. b. Edmonton, Canada. Worked as radio reporter for Canadian Broadcasting Corp; later in Australia; to Hollywood as model before act. TV inc: Pleasure Cove; Elvis; Battlestar Galactica.

Films inc: Flash Gordon.

ANDERSON, Michael: Dir. b. London, Jan 3, 1920. Debuted in films as actor, 1936, asst. dir. on In Which We Serve, Pygmalion, French Without Tears. Dir. The Dam Busters; Hell Is Sold Out; Around the World in 80 Days; The Wreck of the Mary Deare; All The Fine Young Cannibals; The Naked Edge; Operation Cross Bow; The Quiller Memorandum; Shoes of the Fisherman; Pope Joan; Conduct Unbecoming; Logan's Run; Orca; Dominique.

TV inc: The Martian Chronicles.

ANDERSON, Michael Jr: Act. b. London, 1943. Started as child actor. Films inc: Tiger Bay; The Sundowners; Greatest Story Ever Told; Major Dundee; The Sons of Katie Elder; Logan's Run.

TV inc: Queen's Champion; Ivanhoe; The Monroes; The Martian Chronicles.

ANDERSON, Richard: Act. b. Long Branch, NJ, Aug 8, 1926. Films inc: 12 O'Clock High; The People Against O'Hara; Escape from Fort Bravo; The Long Hot Summer; Compulsion; Paths of Glory; Tora! Tora! Tora!; Play It As It Lays.

TV inc: Perry Mason; Dan August; Six Million Dollar Man; Bionic Woman; Pearl; The Immigrants; The French Atlantic Affair.

ANDERSON, Robert: Wri. b. NYC, Apr 28, 1917. e. Harvard U, AB, MA. Films inc: Tea and Sympathy; Until They Sail; The Nun's Story; The Sand Pebbles; I Never Sang for My Father.

Plays inc: All Summer Long; Tea and Sympathy; Silent Night, Lonely Night; The Days Between; You Know I Can't Hear You When the Water's Running; I Never Sang for My Father; Solitaire, Double Solitaire.

TV inc: Biography; The Old Lady Shows Her Medals.

ANDERSON, William H: Prod. b. Smithfield, UT, Oct 12, 1911. e. Compton Coll. Films inc: Old Yeller; Third Man on the Mountain; Swiss Family Robinson; Moon Pilot; Savage Sam; A Tiger Walks; The Happiest Millionaire; The One and Only, Genuine, Original Family Band; The Barefoot Executive; The Biscuit Eater; Superdad; The Strongest Man in the World; The Apple Dumpling Gang; The Treasure of Matecumbe; The Shaggy D.A.

TV inc: Zorro; The Wonderful World of Disney; Daniel Boone; The Swamp Fox; Pop Warner Football; The Scarecrow of Romney Marsh; The Legend of Young Dick Turpin; Willie and the Yank; A Boy Called Nuthin'; The Young Loner; The Mystery of Dracula's Castle; The Bull from the Sky; Adventure in Satan's Canyon; Three on the Run.

ANDERSSON, Bibi (Berit Elisabet Andersson): Act. b. Stockholm, Nov 11, 1939. e. Royal Dramatic Theatre School. Films inc: Smiles of a Summer Night; The Seventh Seal; Wild Strawberries; Brink of Life; The Face; So Close to Life; The Mistress; The Devil's Eye; My Sister My Love; Duel at Diablo; A Question of Rape; The Story of a Woman; The Kremlin Letter; The Passion of Anna; The Touch; I Never Promised You a Rose Garden; Quintette; The Concorde - Airport '79; Tree Vrouwen; Not For Children; Enemy of the People; The Marmalade Revolution.

Thea inc: Who's Afraid of Virginia Woolf?; Dollhouse; After the Fall; The Night of the Tribades.

ANDERSSON, Harriet: Act. b. Stockholm, 1932. Films inc: Medan Staden Sover; Anderssonskans Kalle; Biffen Och Bananen; Sabotage; Summer With Monika; Ubat 39; Trots; Sawdust and Tinsel; A Lesson in Love; Journey Into Autumn; Smiles of a Summer Night; Kvinna i leopard; Britt i paradiset; Through a Glass Darkly; Siska; Now About These Women; To Love; Loving Couples; The Deadly Affair; The Girls; Anna; Cries and Whispers; Linus; Monismanien; La Sabina.

ANDES, Keith: Act. b. Ocean City, NJ, Jul 12, 1920. e. Temple U, Oxford. Films inc: The Farmer's Daughter; Clash by Night; Blackbeard the Pirate; Split Second; Back from Eternity; Damn Citizen; Surrender Hell!; Tora! Tora! Tora!; And Justice For All.

TV inc: Glynis; This Man Dawson; The Ultimate Impostor; Blinded By The Light.

Thea inc: Wildcat; Winged Victory; Kiss Me Kate; Maggie.

ANDRESS, Ursula: Act. b. Berne, Switzerland, Mar 19, 1938. Films inc: The Loves of Casanova; Dr. No; Four For Texas; Fun in Acapulco; She; Nightmare in the Sun; What's New Pussycat?; Once Before I Die; The Blue Max; Casino Royale; The Southern Star; Perfect Friday; Red Sun; Five Against Capricorn; The Fifth Musketeer.

ANDREWS, Dana: Act. b. Collins, MS, Jan 1, 1909. With Pasadena Playhouse. Screen debut 1939, The Westerner. Films inc: Best Years of Our Lives; Foolish Heart; The Crowded Sky; Devil's Brigade; Innocent Bystander; The Last Tycoon; Airport, 1975; Born Again; Good Guys Wear Black.

TV inc: The Right Hand Man; One Small Step Forward; A Wind of Hurricane Force; The Town That Died; Last of the Big Spenders; Ike.

ANDREWS, Eamonn: TV pers-Wri. b. Dublin, Dec 19, 1922. Radio Eireann bcaster 1941-1950; BBC 1950, switched to BBC-TV 1951. Host of British versions of What's My Line; This Is Your Life; host Eamonn Andrews Show; World of Sport; Today; Time for Business. Served 1960-66 as chmn Radio Telefis Eireann, statutory authority charged with establishment of TV in Ireland. Author play The Moon is Black.

ANDREWS, Edward: Act. b. Griffin, GA, Oct 9, 1915. e. U of VA. Bway debut 1935, How Beautiful with Shoes. Films inc: The Phenix City Story; The Tattered Dress; Tea and Sympathy; The Fiend Who Walked the West; Elmer Gantry; Advise and Consent; Kisses for My President; Youngblood Hawke; Send Me No Flowers; The Glass Bottom Boat; Birds Do It; Tora! Tora! Tora!; Avanti; Charley and the Angel; Seniors.

TV inc: Supertrain; Undercover With The KKK.

Bway inc: So Proudly We Hail; Of Mice and Men; The Time of Your Life; The Knew What They Wanted; I Am a Camera; A Visit to a Small Planet; The Gazebo.

ANDREWS, Harry: Act. b. Tonbridge, Kent, Eng, Nov 10, 1911. e. Wrekin Coll. Thea inc: Worse Things Happen at Sea; Snow in Summer; Hamlet; He Was Born Gay; The School for Scandal; Three Sisters; Hundreds and Thousands; The Critic; An Inspector Calls; The Cherry Orchard; Caesar and Cleopatra; Antony and Cleopatra; Camino Real; Coriolanus; The Lizard on the Rock; Baal; You Never Can Tell.

Films inc: The Red Beret; A Hill in Korea; Moby Dick; Ice Cold in Alex; The Devil's Disciple; Solomon and Sheba; The Best of Enemies; Lisa; 55 Days at Peking; The Informers; The Hill; The Deadly Affair; The Charge of the Light Brigade; The Night They Raided Minsky's; The Seagull; A Nice Girl Like Me; Wuthering Heights; Nicholas and Alexandra; Man of La Mancha; The Mackintosh Man; Man at the Top; The Bluebird; The Big Sleep; Crossed Swords; Equus; Death on the Nile; The Medusa; Superman; Watership Down.

TV inc: S O S Titanic; The Four Feathers; The Curse of King Tut's Tomb; Hawk, The Slayer.

ANDREWS, Julie (Julia Wells): Act. b. Walton-on-Thames, Eng, Oct 1, 1935. Films inc: Mary Poppins (Oscar-1964); The Americanization of Emily; The Sound of Music; Torn Curtain; Hawaii; Thoroughly Modern Millie; Star!; Darling Lili; The Tamarind Seed; 10; Little Miss Marker.

Bway inc: The Boy Friend; My Fair Lady; Camelot.

TV inc: High Tor; Julie and Carol at Carnegie Hall; The Julie Andrews Hour (Emmy-1973); An Evening with Julie Andrews and Harry Belafonte; Julie Andrews and Jackie Gleason Together; Julie Andrew's Invitation to the Dance With Rudolf Nureyev.

(Grammy-childrens recording-1964).

ANDREWS, Peter: Dir. TV inc: How to Survive a Marriage; The Guiding Light; Search for Tomorrow; The Doctors; One Life to Live; All My Children; Gold Coast; Take Five.

ANDREWS, Ralph: Prod. b. Chicago, 1928. e. Tulane U, U of Michigan, LA City Coll. TV inc: Wedding Party; Mickie Finn; Mickie Finn's Happy Time Hour; Liars Club; Celebrity Sweepstakes; Divorce Hearing; You Don't Say.

ANDREWS, Tige: Act. b. Brooklyn, Mar 19. e. U of Beirut, AADA. Films inc: Mr. Roberts; Imitation General; China Doll; Until They Sail; Onion Head; The Last Tycoon.

TV inc: Sgt. Bilko; Detectives; Mod Squad; Werewolf of Woodstock; Skyway to Death; Raid on Entebbe; Return of the Mod Squad.

Thea inc: Threepenny Opera; Mr. Roberts; Hidden Horizons; Guys and Dolls; Hasty Heart; My Sister Eileen.

ANDREWS, Tina: Act. b. Chicago, Apr 23. Films inc: Hit; Conrack; Shoot It; Crawly; Carny.

TV inc: McNaughton's Daughter; Born Innocent; The Weekend Nun; The Girls of Huntington House; Billy; Days of Our Lives; Roots, Part II; The Contender.

ANDREWS SISTERS: Singing Trio. Patty (1918), Maxine (1916), Laverne (1913-67). Popular singing trio of the forties. Films inc: Argentine Nights; In the Navy; Buck Privates; Hold that Ghost; Give Out Sisters; Private Buckaroo; What's Cookin'?; Always a Bridesmaid; Follow the Boys; Hollywood Canteen; Moonlight and Cactus; Her Lucky Night; Make Mine Music (voices); Road to Rio; Melody Time (voices).

Bway inc: Over Here.

ANDRIOT, Lucien: Cin. b. France, 1897. Films inc: Two Lives; Why Trust Your Husband; Gigolo; White Gold; Hallelujah I'm a Bum; Anne of Green Gables; The Hairy Ape; And Then There Were None; Dishonoured Lady.

(Died Mar 19, 1979).

ANGEL, Heather: Act. b. Oxford, Eng, Feb 9, 1909. On stage 1926-30. US screen debut, 1932, Pilgrimage. Films inc: Berkeley Square; The Informer; The Mystery of Edwin Drood; Last of the Mohicans; Army Girl; Pride and Prejudice; Time to Kill; Lifeboat; In the Meantime, Darling; The Saxon Charm; Alice In Wonderland; Peter Pan; The Premature Burial.

TV inc: Peyton Place; Family Affair; Backstairs at the White House.

ANGELOU, Maya (Marguerite Johnson): Wri-Dir-Act. b. St. Louis, MO, Apr 4, 1928. Studied dance with Pearl Primus; worked as singer-dancer in niteries; toured Europe and Africa for two years in State Department sponsored production Porgy and Bess; wrote, produced (with Godfrey Cambridge) performed in Cabaret for Freedom; act in The Blacks, off-Broadway. Thea inc: Look Away (act); Ajax (wri).

Films inc: Georgia, Georgia, (wri).

TV inc: The Slave Coast (narr); Circles (dir); Tapestry (dir); I Know Why The Caged Bird Sings (wri).

ANHALT, Edna: Wri. b. NYC, Apr 10, 1914. Films inc: Panic in the Streets (Oscar-1950); The Sniper; Not As A Stranger; Pride and the Passion; Girls, Girls, Girls; Decision at Delphi; Becket (Oscar-1964).

ANHALT, Edward: Wri. b. NYC, 1914. Films inc: Bulldog Drummond Strikes Back; Panic in the Streets (Oscar-1950); The Sniper; Not as a Stranger; The Pride and the Passion; The Young Lions; A Girl Named Tamiko; Becket (Oscar-1964); Hour of the Gun; The Boston Strangler; The Mad Woman of Chaillot; Jeremiah Johnson; Luther; Escape to Athena.

TV inc: Q.B. VII; The Day Christ Died.

Plays inc: Thomas and the King.

ANKA, Paul: Singer-Sngwri. b. Ottawa, Canada, Jul 30, 1941. At age 16, launched career with recording of Diana, which he wrote. Since then has written more than 400 songs, inc My Way; You Are My Destiny; Puppy Love; Lonely Boy. Appears in niteries, TV specials.

Films inc: Girls' Town; Look in Any Window; The Longest Day; Atlantic City, USA (song).

TV inc: Sinatra--The First 40 Years.

ANNABELLA (Suzanne Charpentier): Act. b. France, 1909. Films inc: Napoleon; Le Million; Under the Red Robe; Dinner at the Ritz; Wings of the Morning; Suez; Hotel du Nord; Bridal Suite; Bomber's Moon; Tonight We Raid Calais; 13 Rue Madeleine; Don Juan (sp).

ANNAKIN, Ken: Dir. b. Yorkshire, Eng, 1914. Film inc: Holiday Camp; Miranda; Quartet (part); Trio (part); Hotel Sahara; Robin Hood; The Sword and the Rose; Three Men in a Boat; Loser Take All; Across the Bridge; The Swiss Family Robinson; Third Man on the Mountain; Very Important Person; The Longest Day; The Fast Lady; Those Magnificent Men in Their Flying Machines; Battle of the Bulge; Monte Carlo or Bust; Call of the Wild; White Fang; Paper Tiger; Behind the Iron Mask; The Fifth Musketeer; Cheaper To Keep Her.

TV inc: The Pirate; Institute for Revenge; Hunter's Moon.

ANNIS, Francesca: Act. b. England, 1944. Films inc: The Cat Gang; Cleopatra; Flipper and the Pirates; The Pleasure Girls; The Walking Stick; Macbeth; Stronger than the Sun.

TV inc: Lillie/Emilie; Why Didn't They Ask Evans?

ANN-MARGRET (Ann-Margret Olsson): Act. b. Stockholm, Sweden, Apr 28, 1941. Toured with bands. Worked with George Burns in Las Vegas. Made TV debut with Jack Benny. Films inc: Pocketful of Miracles; State Fair; Bye, Bye Birdie; Carnal Knowledge; The Pleasure Seekers; Once A Thief; Joseph Andrews; The Twist (Folies Bourgeoises); The Last Remake of Beau Geste; The Cheap Detective; Magic; The Villain; Middle Age Crazy.

TV inc: Ann-Margret Olsson; Ann-Margret Smith; Ann-Margret-Rhinestone Cowgirl; A Holiday Tribute to the Radio City Music Hall; Hollywood Movie Girls.

ANOUILH, Jean: Plywri. b. Bordeaux, France, Jun 23, 1907. e. College Chaptal, U of Paris. Plays inc: The Ermine; Thieves' Carnival; Mandarin; Y Avait un Prisonnier; Traveller Without Luggage; La Sauvage; Cavalcade D'Amour; Time Remembered; Point of Departure; Antigone; Oreste; Jezabel; Ring Around the Moon; The Rehearsal; Colombe; Waltz of the Toreadors; The Lark; The Fighting Cock; Becket (Tony-1961); Catch As Catch Can; The Cavern; Dear Antoine; Ne Reveillez pas Madame; Le Directeur de L'Opera; The Arrest; The Scenario.

Films inc: Monsieur Vincent; Pattes Blanches.

ANSARA, Michael: Act. b. Lowell, MA, Apr 15, 1922. Early training Pasadena Playhouse. Films inc: The Robe; Julius Caesar; Soldiers Three; Only the Valiant; New Orleans, Uncensored; Guns of the Magnificent Seven; The Greatest Story Ever Told; Mohammad-Messenger of God; Day of the Animals; The Manitou; Target - Harry.

TV inc: Ordeal; Broken Arrow; Law of the Plainsman; Deadly Target; Shootout in a One-Dog Town; Centennial.

ANSPACH, Susan: Act. b. NYC, 1939. e. Catholic U of America. Films inc: The Landlord; Five Easy Pieces; Play It Again, Sam; Blume in Love; Nashville; The Big Fix; Running.

TV inc: The Last Giraffe; Portrait of an Escort.

Bway inc: A View From the Bridge; Journey to the Fifth House.

ANSTEY, Edgar: Prod. b. Watford, Eng, 1907. Films inc: (doc) Housing Problems; Enough to Eat?; Journey Into Spring; The England of Elizabeth; Terminus; Snow; Wild Wings.

ANTHONY, Joseph (nee Deuster): Dir-Act. b. Milwaukee, WI, May 24, 1912. e. U of WI. Bway inc: (act) Mary of Scotland; Professor Mamlock; On the Rocks; Liberty Jones; The Country Girl; Flight Into Egypt; Anastasia. (Dir) Celebration; Bullfight; The Rainmaker; Once Upon a Tailor; The Lark; The Most Happy Fella; Rhinocerous; Mary, Mary; Happily Never After; Finishing Touches.

Films inc: (act) Hat, Coat and Glove; She; Joe Smith, American; Shadow of the Thin Man. (Dir): The Rainmaker; The Matchmaker; Career; All in a Night's Work; Captive City; Tomorrow.

TV inc: (dir) Brenner; Profiles in Courage; Return at Night.

ANTHONY, Ray: Orch Ldr. b. Bentleville, PA, Jan 20, 1922. Recorded for Capitol Records 19 years; Ranwood Records, 9 years. Films inc: Daddy Long Legs; Five Pennies; High School Confidential; This Could Be the Night.

TV inc: Variety shows; summer replacement for Perry Como on CBS, ABC.

ANTON, Susan: Act-Singer. b. Oak Glen, CA, Oct 12. Recording artist; niteries. Films inc: Golden Girl.

TV inc: The Cliffhangers; Presenting Susan Anton.

ANTONELLI, Laura: Act. Films inc: Lovers and Other Relatives; The Divine Nymph; Wifemistress; Till Marriage Do Us Part; The Innocent; The Hypochondriac.

ANTONIO, Lou: Act-Wri-Dir. b. Oklahoma City, OK, Jan 23, 1934. e. U of OK, BA. Films inc: The Strange One; Splendor in the Grass; America, America; Hawaii; Cool Hand Luke; The Phynx, Mission Batangas (wri).

Bway inc: The Girls of Summer; The Good Soup; The Garden of Sweets; Andorra; The Lady of the Camellias; The Ballad of the Sad Cafe; Ready When You Are, C.B.

TV inc: (act) Piece of Blue Sky; The Power and the Glory; Danny Thomas Hour; Partners in Crime; Sole Survivor; Where The Ladies Go; Snoop Sisters; Dog and Cat; Making It. (Dir) Gentle Ben (& wri); Flying Nun; McCloud; Rockford Files; Delvecchio; Three for the Road; Rich Man, Poor Man; Lannigan's Rabbi; The Young Rebels (& wri); Someone I Touched; The Girl in the Empty Grave; Something for Joey; The Critical List; Silent Victory--The Kitty O'Neil Story; Breaking Up Is Hard To Do; The Contender.

ANTONIONI, Michelangelo: Dir. b. Ferrara, Italy, Sep 29, 1912. e. Bologna U. Films inc: Le Amiche; Il Grido; L'Avventura; La Notte; L'Eclisse; The Red Desert; Blow-Up; Zabriskie Point; Chung Kuo; The Passenger; Story of a Love Affair; The Mystery of Oberwald.

ANTONOWSKY, Marvin: Exec. b. NYC, Jan 31, 1929. e. CCNY, BA, MBA. With adv agencies Kenyon & Eckhardt; Norman Craig & Kummel; J. Walter Thompson before joining ABC 1969 as vp research svs; 1972 VP-asso dir planning, Mktg Dvlpmt, Research; July 1973, NBC VP pgm dvlpmnt; Sept 1973, VP Pgms East Coast; 1975, VP Pgms NBC-TV net; 1977 sr vp U-TV; 1979, Sr vp, asst to pres Col; 1980 exec vp mktg.

ANTOON, A J: Dir. b. Lawrence, MA, Dec 7, 1944. e. Boston Coll. Bway inc: Subject to Fits; The Tale of Cumbeline; That Championship Season (Tony-1973); Much Ado About Nothing; The Good Doctor; The Dance of Death; Trelawney of the Wells; The Effect of Gamma Rays on Man-In-the-Moon Marigolds.

TV inc: Much Ado About Nothing.

ANZARUT, Raymond: Exec Prod. b. Lebanon, 1912. Films inc: (prod mgr) Flight From Folly; Caesar and Cleopatra; Meet Me at Dawn; Scott of the Antartic. (Prod): Sea Devils; Man Between; An Inspector Calls; The Man Who Loved Redheads; Summer Madness; Storm Over the Nile. (Asso prod): The Silent Enemy; Room at the Top; Our Man in Havana; The Hill; The Dirty Dozen.

APTED, Michael: Dir. b. Aylesbury, Eng, Feb 10, 1941. e. Cambridge. Began in tv in England. Films inc: Triple Echo; Stardust; The Squeeze; Agatha; Coal Miner's Daughter.

ARBUS, Allan: Act. b. NYC, Feb 15, 1918. Films inc: Putney Swope; The Christian Licorice Store; Cisco Pike; Coffy; The Young Nurses; Cinderella Liberty; Law and Disorder; W C Fields and Me; Damien-Omen II; Americathon; The Electric Horseman; The Last Married Couple in America.

TV inc: The Trial of Ethel and Julius Rosenberg.

Bway inc: Dreyfus in Rehearsal.

ARCHARD, Bernard: Act. b. England, 1922. Films inc: Village of the Damned; The List of Adrian Messenger; Face of a Stranger; The Song of Norway; The Horror of Frankenstein; The Sea Wolves.

Thea inc: (London) The Case of the Oily Levantine.

TV inc: A Tale of Two Cities.

ARCHER, Anne: Act. b. Aug 25, 1947. Films inc: Cancel My Reservations; Paradise Alley; Good Guys Wear Black; Hero at Large; Raise The Titanic.

TV inc: The Pirate.

ARCHER, Ronald Graham: Exec. b. Brisbane, Australia, Oct 25, 1933. GM Channel O, commercial TV.

ARCHERD, Army (Armand Archerd): Columnist. b. NYC, Jan 13. e. UCLA, BA. Joined AP Hollywood Bureau 1945; Herald-Express; Daily Variety columnist since 1953. MC Hollywood premieres; Pre-show MC Academy Awards. P, founder Hollywood Press Club. Films inc: California Suite.

TV inc: Movie Game; People's Choice Awards TV Show.

ARCHINAL, Harry: Exec. b. NYC, Jun 3, 1928. e. Wagner College, BA; Georgetown U, MH. Began working for Buena Vista 1954 as part-time clerk in foreign dept while at Georgetown; became Latin American sales supv, later gen sls mgr BV's foreign division; vp Buena Vista Int'l; named P BVI 1972.

ARDEN, Eve (Eunice Quedens): Act. b. Mill Valley, CA, Apr 12, 1912. Appeared with Alcazar stock co., Bandbox Repertory Co. B'way debut, Ziegfeld Follies of 1936. On Screen from 1937. Films inc: Oh, Doctor; Stage Door; A Letter of Introduction; Eternally Yours; Comrade X; That Uncertain Feeling; Ziegfeld Girl; She Knew all the Answers; Manpower; Cover Girl; The Doughgirls; Mildred Pierce; Night and Day; Voice of the Turtle; Tea for Two; Goodbye My Fancy; Our Miss Brooks; Anatomy of a Murder; The Dark at the Top of the Stairs; Sgt. Deadhead, the Astronaut; The Strongest Man in the World; Grease.

Bway inc: Mame; Hello Dolly; Butterflies Are Free.

TV inc: Our Miss Brooks; The Eve Arden Show; The Mothers-in-Law (Emmy-female personality-1953); The Dream Merchants.

ARDOLINO, Emile: Prod-Dir. TV inc: Dance in America--Live From Lincoln Center; Balanchine IV--Dance in America; Great Performances (Emmy-series coord prod-1979).

ARDREY, Robert: Wri. b. Chicago, 1909. Films inc: They Knew What They Wanted; The Green Years; The Three Musketeers; Madame Bovary; The Wonderful Country; Four Horsemen of the Apocalypse; Khartoum.
Plays inc: Thunder Rock; Sing Me No Lullaby; Shadow of Heroes; Casey Jones; Jeb.
(Died Jan 14, 1980).

ARGO, Allison: Act. b. Richmond, VA, Dec 23. Bway inc: Grease; Night of the Iguana; Lady From the Sea.
TV inc: Search for Tomorrow; The Gift; High Ice; Casino; The Return of Frank Cannon; Ladies' Man.

ARKIN, Adam: Act. b. NYC, Aug 19, 1956. S of Alan Arkin. Debuted, 1969, in Short People Soup, prod by his father. Films inc: Made for Each Other; Baby Blue Marine.
TV inc: We'll Get By; All Together Now; It Couldn't Happen to a Nicer Guy; Busting Loose; Pearl; Mark Twains's America-Tom Edison.

ARKIN, Alan: Act-Dir. b. NYC, Mar 26, 1934. e. LA City Coll, LA State Coll, Bennington Coll. Professional debut, 1959, St Louis in improvisations; later joined Second City Group, Chicago. NY debut, 1961, revue, From the Second City; Bway inc: Man Out Loud; Girl Quiet; Enter Laughing (Tony-supp-1963); Luv; The Opening; (dir): Hail Scrawdyke!; Little Murders; The White House Murder Case; The Sunshine Boys; Molly; Joan of Lorraine.
Films inc: The Russians Are Coming, The Russians Are Coming; Woman Times Seven; Wait Until Dark; Inspector Clouseau; The Heart Is a Lonely Hunter; Popi; the Monitors; Catch 22; Little Murders (& dir); Last of the Red Hot Lovers; Freebie and the Bean; Rafferty and the Gold Dust Twins; Hearts of the West; The Seven Per Cent Solution; Fire Sale (& dir); The In-Laws; The Magician of Lublin; Simon.
TV inc: (dir) Twigs; Fay.

ARKOFF, Louis S: Exec. b. LA, Jan 4, 1950. e. USC, BA. S of Samuel Z Arkoff. Prodn Asst 1967, Wild in the Streets; Asst to VP Prodn (part time), 1967-69; Legal Admin & Asst to VP bus aff AIP, 1973-74; Prodn super 1975, Return to Macon County; Exec Prod 1976, Small Town in Texas; VP Prodn AIP, 1977; Exec in charge Prodn 1978, Our Winning Season; California Dreaming; Gorp.

ARKOFF, Samuel Z: Exec. b. Fort Dodge, IA, Jun 12, 1918. e. U of CO, U of IA, Loyola U School of Law, JD. Prod; ChmnB & P, AIP until Dec 1979. Prod more than 150 films inc: The House of Usher; The Pit and the Pendulum; The Raven; Comedy of Terrors; Wild in the Streets; Scream and Scream Again; Cry of the Banshee; Bloody Mama; Wuthering Heights; Frogs; Blacula; Dillinger; The Great Scout and Cathouse Thursday; A Matter of Time; The Island of Dr Moreau; Our Winning Season; The Amityville Horror; California Dreaming; C.H.O.M.P.S.; How To Beat The High Cost Of Living; Dressed To Kill.

ARLEDGE, Roone: Exec. b. NYC, Jul 8, 1931. e. Columbia U. Leading figure in TV sports since 1960 when as vp ABC-Sports he developed programs such as Wide World of Sports and The American Sportsman. Named p ABC Sports, 1968; developed Monday Night Football; acquired Olympics for ABC 1968, 1972, 1976. In Spring of 1977, also named p ABC-News.
(14 Emmys-8 as prod Wide World of Sports-1966, 1968, 1970, 1971, 1972, 1973, 1974, 1976; 19th Summer Olympics, 1969; 20th Summer Olympics 1973; Munich Olympic Tragedy, 1973; NFL Monday Night Football, 1976; XII Winter Olympics 1976; NCAA Football, 1980).

ARLEN, Harold (Hyman Arluck): Comp. b. Buffalo, NY, Feb 15, 1905. Films inc: Strike Me Pink; Let's Fall in Love; The Wizard of Oz; A Day at the Circus; The Sky's the Limit; Cabin in the Sky; The Farmer Takes a Wife; A Star is Born; Country Girl; Gay Purr-ee; I Could Go On Singin'.
Bway inc: You Said It; Earl Carroll's Vanities; Americana; Life Begins at 8:40; Bloomer Girl.
Songs inc: Over the Rainbow (Oscar-1939); Stormy Weather; I've Got the World on a String; Let's Fall in Love; Blues in the Night; Happiness is a Thing Called Joe; My Shining Hour; Black Magic; Accentuate the Positive; The Man That Got Away.

ARLETTY (Arlette-Leonie Bathiat): Act. b. Courbevoie, France, 1898. Films inc: Un Chien Qui Rapporte; La Guerre des Valses; Aloha; Hotel du Nord; Le Jour Se Leve; Les Enfants du Paradis; L'Air de Paris; Les Petits Matins; La Gamberge.

ARLING, Arthur: Cin. b. Missouri, Sep 2, 1906. e. NY Institute of Photography. Joined Fox Studio 1927 as asst cameraman; op cameraman on Gone With the Wind, 1939. Films inc: The Yearling (Oscar-1946); Homestretch; Mother Was A Freshman; My Blue Heaven; I'll Cry Tomorrow; Story of Ruth; Pillow Talk; Notorious Landlady; Boys Night Out; My Six Loves.

ARLISS, Dimitra: Act. b. Oct 23, 1932. Films inc: The Sting; A Perfect Couple; Xanadu.
TV inc: The Pirate; Guyana Tragedy--The Story of Jim Jones.

ARLT, Lewis: Act. b. Kingston, NY, Dec 5, 1949. e. Carnegie Tech, BFA. Started in repertory. Thea inc: Murder Among Friends. TV inc: As the World Turns.

ARMATRADING, Joan: Singer-Comp. b. St Kitts, West Indies, Dec 9, 1950. Singer; recording artist. Films inc: Wild Geese (Title Song).

ARMER, Alan A: Prod. b. LA, Jul 7, 1922. e. Stanford, BA. TV inc: My Friend Flicka; Broken Arrow; Man Without a Gun; The Untouchables; The Dick Powell Theatre; The Fugitive (Emmy-1966); The Invaders; Lancer; Name of the Game; Cannon; Westside Medical; Along Came a Spider; Birds of Prey; The Stranger.

ARMSTRONG, R G: Act. b. Apr 7, 1917. Films inc: Garden of Eden; From Hell to Texas; Never Love a Stranger; The Fugitive Kind; Ride the High Country; Major Dundee; El Dorado; The Great White Hope; The Car; Mr. Billion; Going South; Fast Charlie, the Moonbeam Rider; Good Luck, Miss Wyckoff; Where the Buffalo Roam; Steel.
TV inc: Last Ride of the Dalton Gang.

ARNALL, Ellis G: Exec. b. Newman, GA, Mar 20, 1907. Former gov of GA. P Society Independent Motion Picture Producers (SIMPP) 1948-1960, P Independent Producers Export Corp 1953-60.

ARNAUD, Leo: Comp. b. Lyons, France, Jul 24, 1904. Music dir & arr in France and England, 1927-30; to U.S. 1931; music dir MGM, 1936-44. Film scores inc: One Touch of Venus; Easter Parade; Date with Judy; Three Little Words; Lovely to Look At; Stars & Stripes Forever; Rose Marie; Seven Brides for Seven Brothers; The Unsinkable Molly Brown.

ARNAZ, Desi: Act-Mus. b. Santiago, Cuba, Mar 2, 1917. Began as vocalist with a band at age 17. Later with own rhumba band. N.Y. nightclubs, on Bway in Too Many Girls. Screen debut in Too Many Girls, 1940. Films inc: Father Takes A Wife; Four Jacks and a Jill; Bataan; Holiday in Havana; Forever Darling.
TV inc: Bob Hope Show (mus dir); I Love Lucy (act-exec prod); The Lucille Ball-Desi Arnaz Show (act-exec prod).

ARNAZ, Desi Jr: Act-Singer. b. Los Angeles, Jan 19, 1953. S of Lucille Ball and Desi Arnaz. Began appearing on I Love Lucy show on TV in infancy. Gained own status as rock singer and musician with the Dino, Desi and Billy group. Film debut in Red Sky at Morning, 1972. Films inc: Marco; She Lives; Joyride; A Wedding.
TV inc: The Great American Traffic Jam.

ARNAZ, Lucie: Act. b. LA, Jul 17, 1951. D of Lucille Ball and Desi Arnaz. Bway inc: Cabaret; Once Upon A Mattress; Bye, Bye Birdie; Mack and Mabel; Goodbye Charlie; Lil Abner; They're Playing Our Song.
TV inc: Here's Lucy; The Black Dahlia; The Mating Season. Films inc: Billy Jack Goes To Washington; The Jazz Singer.

ARNE, Peter: Act. b. British Malaya, 1922. Films inc: Time Slip; The Purple Plain; The Moonraker; Danger Within; The Hellfire Club; Khartoum; Battle Beneath the Earth; Murders in the Rue Morgue; Straw Dogs; Antony and Cleopatra; Return of the Pink Panther; Providence; Agatha; The Passage.
TV inc: The Mask of Janus; The Third Man; The Champions; The Shattered Eye; The Stallion; Rivals of Sherlock Holmes; Task Force; The Fox; The Venturers; Quiller; The Expert.

ARNESS, James: Act. b. Minneapolis, MN, May 26, 1923. Films inc: Farmer's Daughter; Battleground; Hell Gate; Man from Texas; Island in the Sky; Hondo; Flame of the Islands; Sea Chase.
TV inc: Gunsmoke; How the West Was Won.

ARNOLD, Danny (Arnold Rothman): Wri-Act. b. NYC, Jan 23, 1925. Appeared in summer stock, nightclubs, vaudeville. Started in films as sound effects ed., Columbia, 1944-46. Films inc: (act) Breakthrough; Inside the Walls of Folsom Prison; Sailor Beware; Scared Stiff; Stars Are Singing. (Wri): The Caddy; Desert Sands; Fort Yuma; Rebel in Town; Outside the Law.
TV inc: My World and Welcome To It *(Emmy-prod-1970)*.

ARNOLD, Eddy: Singer. b. Henderson, TN, May 15, 1918. Country singer, recording artist since 1946. Nicknamed The Tennessee Plowboy. TV inc: The Eddy Arnold Show; Eddy Arnold Time. Elected to Country Mus Hall of Fame, 1966.

ARNOLD, Jack: Prod-Dir. b. New Haven, CT, Oct 14, 1916. e. OH State U, AADA. US Air Force, 1942-45; Prod documentary films for State Dept., Army, private industry. Films inc: The Mouse That Roared; Bachelor in Paradise; Global Affair; The Incredible Shrinking Man; It Came From Outer Space; The Creature from the Black Lagoon; Revenge of the Creature; The Glass Web; Man in the Shadow; The Tattered Dress; The Lady Takes a Flyer; Tarantula; Outside the Law; Man From Bitter Ridge; High School Confidential; Blackeye; The Swiss Conspiracy; Red Sundown; No Name on the Bullet; The Lively Set.
TV inc: The Sid Caesar, Imogene Coca, Carl Reiner, Howard Morris Special *(Emmy-prod-1967)*; It Takes a Thief (exec prod); Marilyn--The Untold Story (dir).

ARNOLD, Malcolm: Comp. b. England, 1921. Films inc: The Sound Barrier; Island in the Sun; The Bridge on the River Kwai *(Oscar-1957)*; Inn of the Sixth Happiness; Tunes of Glory; The Chalk Garden; The Heroes of Telemark; The Reckoning.

ARNOUL, Francoise (nee Gautsch): Act. b. Constantine, Algeria, 1931. Films inc: Forbidden Fruit; Companions of the Night; The Sheep Has Five Legs; French Can-Can; The Face of the Cat; The Devil and the Ten Commandments; Le Dimanche de la Vie.

ARNSTEIN, Eugene: Exec. b. Milwaukee, WI, Aug 13, 1907. e. Marquette U. Exhibitor, 1926-44; Sec-Treas, Film Classics; controller, Eagle Lion Classics; exec Pathe Lab; left NY for LA, 1951, to be Studio M, Monogram; 1962-64, Exec VP Society of Independent Producers; 1964-74, VP AMPTV. Since 1974 motion picture industrial labor relations consultant.

ARONSON, Boris: Dsgn. b. Kiev, Russia, Oct 15, 1900. e. State Art School, Kiev: School of Modern Painting, Moscow. Bway inc: Tenth Commandment (Yiddish Art Theatre): Tragedy of Nothing: 2x25, Jew Suss; Roaming Stars; Walk A Little Faster; Small Miracle; Three Men on a Horse; Awake and Sing; Paradise Lost; The Body Beautiful; Radio City Music Hall prodns; Merchant of Yonkers; Ladies and Gentlemen; The Unconquered; Heavenly Express; Cabin In the Sky; Clash by Night; RUR; Cafe Crown; Snow Maiden (ballet); South Pacific; The Red Poppy (ballet); Sadie Thompson; Pictures at an Exhibition (ballet); The Desert Song; Truckline Cafe; Sweet Bye and Bye; Skipper Next to God; The Survivors: Detective Story; The Bird Cage; The Rose Tattoo; Season in the Sun; The Country Girl *(Tony-1951-for last 3 shows named)*; Barefoot in Athens; I Am A Camera; The Rose Tattoo; I've Got Sixpence; Ballade (ballet): The Crucible; My Three Angels; Mlle Colombe; Bus Stop; A View From The Bridge; The Master Builder; Diary of Anne Frank; A Hole in the Head; Orpheus Descending; Rope Dancers; Small War on Murray Hill; The Cold Wind and the Warm; J B; Flowering Cherry; Do-Re-Mi; A Gift of Time; Fiddler on the Roof; Incident at Vichy; Cabaret *(Tony-1966)*; The Price (& costumes); Zorba *(Tony-1969)*; Fidelio (Metropolitan Opera); Company *(Tony-1971)*; Follies *(Tony-1972)*; The Creation of the World and Other Business; The Great God Brown; A Little Night Music; Dreyfus in Rehearsal; Pacific Overtures *(Tony-1976)*.
(Died Nov 16, 1980).

ARRANTS, Rod: Act. b. LA. e. U of Pacific. TV inc: The Young and the Restless; McCoy; Helter Skelter; The Lives of Jenny Dolan; Cross Current; Lisa Bright and Dark; Lovers and Friends; Search for Tomorrow.

ARTHUR, Beatrice: Act. b. NYC, May 13, 1926. Films inc: That Kind of Woman; Lovers and Other Strangers; Mame.
TV inc: Maude *(Emmy-1977)*; The Beatrice Arthur Special; Hope, Women & Song; 30 Years of TV Comedy's Greatest Hits (co-host).
Bway inc: Dog Beneath The Skin; Gas; Yerma; No Exit; Six Characters in Search of an Author; The Owl and the Pussycat; Ulysses in Nighttown; Chic; Mame *(Tony-supp-1966)*; Fiddler on the Roof.

ARTHUR, Jean (Gladys Greene): Act. b. NYC, Oct 17, 1905. Film debut 1928 Warming Up. Films inc: Cameo Kirby; The Canary Murder Case; Diamond Jim; The Whole Town's Talking; Mr. Deeds Goes To Town; The Plainsman; History Is Made at Night; You Can't Take It With You; Only Angels Have Wings; Mr Smith Goes to Washington; Too Many Husbands; The Devil and Miss Jones; The Talk of the Town; The Lady Takes a Chance; The More the Merrier; A Foreign Affair; Shane.
TV inc: The Jean Arthur Show.

ARTHUR, Karen (nee Jensen): Dir. b. Omaha, NE, Aug 24, 1941. Started as perf, chor; then dir. Films inc: Legacy; The Mafu Cage (& prod). TV inc: Charleston.

ARTHUR, Robert: Prod. b. NYC, Nov 1, 1909. Joined MGM as writer, 1937. Films inc: Buck Private Come Home; For The Love of Mary; Mexican Hayride; Abbott And Costello in the Foreign Legion; Abbott And Costello Meet Frankenstein; Bedtime Story; Father Goose; Shenandoah; A Man Could Get Killed; Sweet Charity.

ARZNER, Dorothy: Dir. b. San Francisco, Jan 3, 1900. e. USC. Best known woman dir of the 30s. Started as script girl, then film edtr on Blood and Sand & The Covered Wagon; Worked on sp Old Ironsides before first directorial chore, Fashions for Women, 1927.
Films inc: The Wild Party; Manhattan Cocktail; Anybody's Woman; Honour Among Lovers; Working Girls; Merrily We Go to Hell; Christopher Strong; Nana; Craig's Wife; The Bride Wore Red; Dance, Girls, Dance; First Comes Courage; during WW II, prod training films for WAC.
(Died Oct 1, 1979).

ASHBY, Hal: Dir. b. Ogden, UT, 1936. e. UT State U. Started as flm ed. Films inc: In the Heat of the Night *(Oscar-1967)*; The Cincinnati Kid; The Russians Are Coming, The Russians Are Coming; The Thomas Crown Affair. (Dir) The Landlord; Harold and Maude; The Last Detail; Shampoo; Bound for Glory; Coming Home; Being There; Second-Hand Hearts.

ASHCROFT, Dame Peggy: Act. b. Croydon, England, Dec 22, 1907. London debut 1927, One Day More. Thea inc: When Adam Delved; The Way of the World; The Land of Heart's Desire; A Hundred Years Old; Requital; Jew Suss; Othello; The Breadwinner; various Shakespearean roles for Old Vic and Sadlers Wells Companies; She Stoops to Conquer; School for Scandal; The Importance of Being Earnest; Rebecca; Edward My Son; The Deep Blue Sea; Hedda Gabler; The Good Woman of Setzuan; Ghosts; The Hollow Crown; A Delicate Balance; Lloyd George Knew My Father; Happy Days; Hullabaloo Over George and Bonnie's Pictures; Watch On The Rhine (rev).

Films inc: The Wandering Jew; The 39 Steps; Rhodes of Africa; The Nun's Story; Secret Ceremony; Sunday, Bloody Sunday; Joseph Andrews.

TV inc: Shadow of Heroes; The Cherry Orchard; The Wars of the Roses; Days in the Trees; Edward and Mrs Simpson; Cream In My Coffee.

ASHER, Jane: Act. b. London, England, Apr 5, 1946. Thea inc: (London) Will You Walk A Little Faster?; Peter Pan; Level Crossing; Summer; Look Back In Anger; The Philanthropist; Treats; Whose Life Is It Anyway? (Bway) Measure for Measure; The Philanthropist.

Films inc: The Greengage Summer; The Girl in the Headlines; The Masque of Red Death; Alfie; Deep End; The Buttercup Chain; Henry VIII and his 6 Wives.

ASHERSON, Renee: Act. b. London, England, 1921. Thea inc: Within Seven Hours; Wuthering Heights; with repertory groups and Old Vic in London and on tour; Lottie Dundass; The Cure for Love; Much Ado About Nothing; The Animal Kingdom; The Taming of the Shrew; The Government Inspector; A Streetcar Named Desire; Spring at Marino; Three Sisters; The Big Knife; The Dazzling Hour; Kill Two Birds; Portrait of Murder; The Magistrate; Dear Antoine; All Over.

Films inc: Henry V; The Way Ahead; The Way to the Stars; The Small Back Room; The Cure for Love; The Day The Earth Caught Fire; Rasputin The Mad Monk; The Smashing Bird I Used to Know.

ASHLEY, Elizabeth (nee Cole): Act. b. Ocala, FL, Aug 20, 1939. Bway inc: The Highest Tree; Take Her, She's Mine (Tony-supp-1962); Barefoot in the Park; Cat on a Hot Tin Roof; The Skin of Our Teeth; Caesar and Cleopatra.

Films inc: The Carpetbaggers; Ship of Fools; The Third Day; Marriage of a Young Stockbroker; The Paperback Hero; 92 in the Shade; Great Scout and Cathouse Thursday; Coma; Windows.

TV inc: When Michael Calls; The Face of Fear; Second Chance; Sad Figure Laughing; One of My Wives Is Missing; A Fire in the Sky.

ASHLEY, Ted: Exec. b. NYC, Aug 3, 1922. e. CCNY. With William Morris Agency, 1939-46; formed Ted Ashley Assoc, 1946; pres Ashley Famous Agency, 1954; dir & chmn of exec committee of Warner Communications 1967-74; bd chmn-CEO WB, 1969 to Nov 1980 when became consultant.

ASKIN, Leon: Act. b. Vienna, Sep 18, 1907. e. Max Reinhardt School of Acting. Performed in Europe, stage, cabarets. To US, 1940. In stock as actor, dir. Films inc: Road to Bali; South Sea Woman; The Robe; Secret of the Incas; Valley of the Kings; One Two Three; What Did You Do in the War Daddy?; Guns for San Sebastian.

TV inc: Hogans Heroes.

ASLAN, Gregoire (G Krikor Arslanian): Act. b. Constantinople, Mar 28, 1908. Films inc: Sleeping Car to Trieste; Innocents in Paris; Last Holiday; Cairo Road; Cage of Gold; He Who Must Die; Act of Love; Oasis; Joe Macbeth; The Criminals; King of Kings; The Rebel; The Devil at 4 O'Clock; Cleopatra; Marco Polo; Paris When It Sizzles; The Yellow Rolls Royce; Moment to Moment; The Centurions; A Man Could Get Killed; A Flea in Her Ear; Tiffany Memorandum; Dubious Patriots; Sinbad's Golden Voyage; The Girl from Petrovka; Return of the Pink Panther; Gloria; Meetings With Remarkable Men.

TV inc: Q.B. VII; The Killer Who Wouldn't Die.

ASLEEP AT THE WHEEL: Band. Members are Ray Benson, lead guitar-voc; Chris O'Connell, voc; Mary Ann Price, voc; Pat "Taco" Ryan, horns; Dean Merritt, bass; Billy Estes, drums; Paul Anastasio, fiddle; Dan Tyack, steel guitar. Albums inc: Comin' Right At Ya; Texas Gold; Wheelin' and Dealin'; The Wheel; Collision Course; Served Live; Framed.

(Grammy-country instr-1979).

ASNER, Edward: Act. b. Kansas City, MO, Nov 15, 1929. Films inc: Peter Gunn; The Slender Thread; The Satan Bug; Kid Galahad; The Wrestler.

TV inc: Mary Tyler Moore Show (Emmys-supp-1971, 1972, 1975); Hey, I'm Alive; Rich Man, Poor Man (Emmy-1976); Roots Part I (Emmy-supp-1977); Lou Grant (Emmys-1978, 1980); Insight--This Side of Eden; The Family Man; Combat In The Classroom (host); Narco (narr).

ASPINALL, David Roy: Exec. b. New South Wales, Australia, May 19, 1947. Sr exec m, TV Channel 9, Perth.

ASSANTE, Armand: Act. b. NYC, Oct 4, 1949. e. AADA. Appeared off-Bway, with regional theatre groups. Bway inc: Why I Went Crazy; Boccaccio; Comedians; Romeo and Juliet.

TV inc: Human Feelings; Lady of the House; The Pirate; Sophia Loren--Her Own Story.

Films inc: Lords of Flatbush; Paradise Alley; Prophecy; Little Darlings; Love and Money; Private Benjamin.

ASSAYEV, Tamara: Prod. b. 1942. Started in films as asst to Roger Corman on Targets; Pit Stop; Saint Valentine's Day Massacre; Devil's Angels; The Trip; The Pit and the Pendulum. Became ind prod 1967: The Wild Racers, Paddy; The Arousers; teamed with Alex Rose on Drive In; I Wanna Hold Your Hand; Big Wednesday; Norma Rae.

ASSELIN, Diane (nee Dailey): Prod. b. Detroit, MI, Mar 11, 1941. e. Miami U of OH, BA. before indie. Reporter-researcher Time Inc; asso prod David Wolper Prodns; asso prod PBS TV inc: Journey Together; I Can; Dinky Hocker; Once Upon a Midnight Dreary (Emmy-1980); Animal Talk (Emmy-1980); The Treasure of Alpheus T Winterborn.

ASSELIN, Paul: Prod. b. Lynn, MA, Dec 23, 1935. e. Yale, BA. H of Diane Asselin. With ABC News; CBS News; Wolper Prodns before forming Asselin Prodns. TV inc: An American Portrait; The National Disaster Survival Test; CBS Mystery Theatre; CBS Television Library; Dinky Hocker; Once Upon a Midnight Dreary (Emmy-1980); Animal Talk (Emmy-1980); The Treasure of Alpheus T Winterborn.

ASTAIRE, Fred (nee Austerlitz): Perf. b. Omaha, NE, May 10, 1900. Formed dance team with sister, Adele. Vaudeville debut 1908. On screen from 1933 in Dancing Lady. (Oscar-Special-1949, "for his unique artistry and his contribution to the technique of musical pictures.") Films inc: The Gay Divorcee; Roberta; Top Hat; Swing Time; The Story of Vernon and Irene Castle; Holiday Inn; The Sky's the Limit; Ziegfeld Follies; Blue Skies; Easter Parade; The Barkleys of Broadway; Let's Dance; Three Little Words; Royal Wedding; The Band Wagon; Daddy Long Legs; Funny Face; Silk Stockings; On the Beach; The Pleasure of His Company; The Notorious Landlady; Finian's Rainbow; Midas Run; The Towering Inferno; That's Entertainment, Part Two; The Purple Taxi.

Bway inc: Over the Top; Passing Show of 1918; Apple Blossoms; Lady Be Good; Smiles; Funny Face; Gay Divorcee; The Bandwagon.

TV inc: An Evening with Fred Astaire (Emmy-1959); Astaire Time (Emmy-1961); Alcoa Premiere; The Fred Astaire Show; It Takes a Thief; A Family Upside Down (Emmy-1978); The Man in the Santa Claus Suit.

ASTIN, John: Act. b. Baltimore, Mar 30, 1930. e. John Hopkins U, BA. First prof. job off-Broadway in Threepenny Opera. Broadway debut, Major Barbara. Did voices in cartoon. Films inc: West Side Story; That Touch of Mink; Candy; Viva Max!; Freaky Friday.

TV inc: (dir) Getting There; Ethel Is An Elephant.

ASTIN, Patty Duke (See DUKE, Patty):

ASTOR, Mary (Lucile V Langhanke): Act. b. Quincy, IL, May 3, 1906. Beauty contest winner, 1920. Screen debut in Beggar's Maid, 1920. On stage in Among the Married; Tonight at 8:30; Male Animal. Films inc: (silent) Don Juan; Bright Shawl; Beau Brummel; (sound) Lost Squadron; The Great Lie (Oscar-supp-1941); Maltese Falcon; Meet Me in St. Louis; Cass Timberlane; Act of Violence; Any Number Can Play; Youngblood Hawke; Hush, Hush Sweet Charlotte.

ASTRUC, Alexandre: Dir. b. Paris, 1923. Originally a critic and novelist, started in films as asst to Marc Allegret on Blanche Fury.
Films inc: Aller-Retour; Ulysses et les Amauvaise Recontres; The Crimson Curtain (short); Une Vie; La Proie pour l'ombre; Education Sentimentale; Le Puits et Le Pendule (short); La Longue Marche; Flammes sur l'Adriatique.

ATHERTON, William: (nee Knight): Act. b. New Haven, CT, 1947. Films inc: Class of '44; The New Centurions; The Sugarland Express; The Day of the Locust; The Hindenberg; Looking for Mr. Goodbar.
Bway inc: The House of Blue Leaves; The Basic Training of Pavlo Hummel; The Sign in Sidney Brustein's Window; The American Clock.
TV inc: Centennial.

ATKINS, Chet: Guitarist-Comp. b. Luttrell, TN, Jun 20, 1924. Started as mus on WRBL, Columbus GA; worked several other stations before joining Grand Ole Opry 1950; later worked with Carter Sisters; recorded with Hank Williams; Elvis Presley; Dolly Parton, others; finally solo. Albums inc: Chet Atkins Plays Guitar; Chet Atkins in Three Dimensions; Chet Atkins Picks the Best (Grammy-inst-1967); Chet Atkins Picks on the Beatles; Me and Jerry (Grammy-country inst-1970); Snowbird (Grammy-country inst-1971); The Atkins-Travis Traveling Show (Grammy-country inst-1974); The Entertainer (Grammy-country inst-1975); Chester and Lester (Grammy-country inst-1976).
Songs inc: Country Gentleman; Midnight; How's The World Treating You?; Heartbreak Avenue.

ATKINS, Eileen: Act. b. London, Jun 16, 1934. First professional appearance in Love's Labours Lost. Thea inc: Semi-Detached; Exit the King; The Promise; She Fell Among Thieves.
Films inc: Inadmissable Evidence; Equus.
TV inc: The Lady's Not for Burning; Party Games; Major Barbara.

ATTENBOROUGH, Sir Richard: Prod-Dir-Act. b. Cambridge, Eng, Aug 29, 1923. e. RADA. Made London stage debut Awake and Sing, 1942. Film debut In Which We Serve, 1942.
Thea inc: The Little Foxes; Brighton Rock; The Way Back Home (Home of the Brave); To Dorothy, A Son; Sweet Madness; The Mousetrap; Double Image; Rape of the Belt.
Films inc: (as act) School for Secrets; The Man Within; Brighton Rock; London Belongs To Me; The Magic Box; Gift Horse; Eight O'-Clock Walk; The Ship That Died of Shame; Private's Progress; Dunkirk; The Man Upstairs; I'm All Right Jack; SOS Pacific; The Angry Silence (& co-prod); Leaque of Gentlemen; Whistle Down the Wind (prod); Only Two Can Play; The L-Shaped Room (prod only); The Great Escape; Seance on a Wet Afternoon (& prod); The Third Secret; Guns at Batasi; Flight of the Phoenix; The Sand Pebbles; The Bliss Of Miss Blossom; Only When I Larf; Dr. Dolittle; David Copperfield; 10 Rillington Place; Ten Little Indians; Rosebud; Brannigan; Conduct Unbecoming; The Chess Players; The Human Factor. (Dir) Oh! What A Lovely War; Young Winston; A Bridge Too Far; Magic.

ATTERBURY, Malcolm: Act. b. Philadelphia, PA, Feb 20, 1907. In vaude. Bway inc various Shubert musicals; One Flew Over the Cuckoo's Nest.
Films inc: Dragnet; Storm Center; Crime in the Streets; Toward The Unknown; No Time for Sergeants; Rio Bravo; North By Northwest; From the Terrace; Summer and Smoke; Advise and Consent; The Birds; The Chase; Hawaii.

AUBERJONOIS, Rene: Act. b. NYC, Jun 1, 1940. Bway inc: Dark of the Moon; The Hostage; Beyond the Fringe; Tartuffe; Charley's Aunt; King Lear; A Cry of Players; Chemin de Fer; Coco (Tony-supp-1970); Tricks; The Ruling Class; Break A Leg; Every Good Boy Deserves Favor.
Films inc: M*A*S*H; Brewster McCloud; McCabe and Mrs Miller; Pete 'n Tillie; Hindenberg; King Kong; Eyes of Laura Mars; Where the Buffalo Roam.
TV inc: The Wild Wild West Revisited; More Wild Wild West.

AUBREY, James T: Exec Prod. b. LaSalle, IL, Dec 14, 1918. e. Princeton. Started as account exec KNX (radio) LA; M KNXT (TV) 1952; vp creative svcs CBS 1955-56. VP pgms & talent ABC-TV 1957; exec vp CBS-TV 1958-59. P CEO MGM 1969-1973; ind prodn. Films inc: Futureworld (prod).
TV inc: Dallas Cowboys Cheerleaders I & II; When Hell Was in Session; Fugitive Family; Mark, I Love You.

AUDLEY, Maxine: Act. b. London, Apr 29, 1923. Thea inc: Old Vic Co; Carissima; Celestina; Thieves Carnival; The Constant Couple; A Letter from Paris; Angels in Love; Love Affair; Speaking of Murder; Present Laughter; Conduct Unbecoming; All My Sons; A Touch of Purple; Private Lives; A Streetcar Named Desire; Saratoga.
Films inc: Anna Karenina; The Sleeping Tiger; The Barretts of Wimpole Street; The Vikings; Our Man in Havana; The Trials of Oscar Wilde; A Jolly Bad Fellow; Here We Go Round The Mulberry Bush; Frankenstein Must Be Destroyed.

AUDRAN, Stephane: Act. b. Versailles, France, 1936. Films inc: The Champagne Murders; Les Biches; La Femme Infidele; The Beast Must Die; Le Boucher; Dead Pigeon on Beethoven Street; And Then There Were None; The Black Bird; The Twist (Folies Bourgeoises); Silver Bears; Violette; The Eagle's Wing; Face to the Sun; The Big Red One; Le Coeur L'envers (My Heart is Upside Down).

AUERBACH, Norbert: Exec. b. Vienna, Nov 4, 1922. e. UCLA. Entered film industry in 1946. Held numerous managerial posts in foreign depts of COL, Seven Arts, WB, Cinema Center Films & UA. In 1977, named UA sales m for Europe and the Middle East; named senior vp Int'l Dept UA in 1978; Dec. 1980, P & COO, UA.

AUGER, Claudine: Act. b. France, 1942. Films inc: Testament of Orpheus; Terrain Vague; A Certain Desire; Thunderball; Our Man From Marrakesh; Operation San Genero; The Killing Game; Triple Cross; The Devil in Love; Love Birds; Equinoxe; A Bay of Blood; The Eiger Sanction; Flic Story; Paris Mon amour; A Butterfly On The Shoulder; Travels With Anita; L'Associe; Fantastica.

AUMONT, Jean-Pierre: Act. b. Paris, Jan 5, 1909. e. Conservatoire of Drama. Films inc: The Cross of Lorraine; Scheherazade; Blindman's Buff; Castle Keep; Lili; The Horse Without a Head; Day for Night; Two Solitudes; Blackout; Cat and Mouse; Something Short of Paradise.
TV inc: The French Atlantic Affair; Beggarman, Thief; The Memory of Eva Ryker; A Time For Miracles.

AUSSIE-STONE, Marc: Exec. b. Australia, Oct 8, 1937. National dir of Australian National Motion Picture Assn.

AUSTIN, Bud (Harold M Austin): Exec. b. NYC. e. U of NC, NYU. Initially with Official Films and NTA in the early 50s; then Goodson-Todman, 1956-65; Filmways, 1965-71, as exec VP; joined PAR 1973; head PAR TV, 1974-76; P, Bud Austin Prodns.

AUSTIN, Ronald: Prod-Wri-Dir. b. LA, Apr 9, 1934. e. UCLA, BA. TV inc: Death Squad; Jigsaw John; Charlie's Angels; The Return of Frank Cannon (wri).
Films inc: (sp) Harry in Your Pocket; Beach Patrol.

AUTANT-LARA, Claude: Dir. b. Luzarches, France, 1903. Film inc: Ciboulette; Fric Frac; Lettres de l'Amour; Le Diable au Corps; The Red Inn; Ripening Seed; Le Rouge et le Nolr; En Cas de Malheur; The Green Mare's Nest; The Count of Monte Cristo; The Seven Deadly Sins; Oh Amelia; Game of Love.

AUTRY, Gene: Act-Exec. b. Tioga, TX, Sep 29, 1908. Started as unpaid radio singer (KVOO, Tulsa) while working as railroad telegrapher. Co-wrote "That Silver-Haired Daddy Of Mine," which became one of all-time top-selling records. Began working on WLS, Chicago, 1930, appearing on such programs as National Barn Dance; became network performer when station was sold; signed by Republic as film's first singing cowboy after appearing in serial The Phantom Empire. Between films and radio he was the top western personality through early 1942, when he enlisted in the Army. Returning after the war, he made three more films for Republic and then formed own company which produced films and several tv series. Owner of radio and tv stations and the California Angels Baseball Team.

TV inc: Gene Autry--An American Hero.

Songs inc: You're the Only Star in My Blue Heaven; Be Honest With Me; Back in the Saddle Again.

AVAKIAN, Aram: Dir. b. NYC. Still photog and editor before dir The End of the Road. Films inc: Cops and Robbers; 11 Harrowhouse.

AVALON, Frankie (nee Avallone): Act. b. Philadelphia, Sep 18, 1940. Trumpet prodigy at age 9. TV variety shows; niteries; recording artist. Films inc: Jamboree; Guns of the Timberland; The Alamo; Voyage to the Bottom of the Sea; Sail a Crooked Ship; Panic in the Year Zero; Bikini Beach; Beach Blanket Bingo; Jet Set; I'll Take Sweden; Fireball 500; How to Stuff a Wild Bikini; The Take; Grease.

TV inc: Ed Sullivan; Perry Como; Pat Boone; Dick Clark Shows; Milton Berle; Golden Circle Spectacular; Dinah Shore Show; Frankie and Annette--The Second Time Around; Beach Girls.

AVALON, Phillip: Prod-Wri-Act. b. Australia, Feb 24, 1945. Films inc: Backstreet General (sp-dir-prod); Double Dealer (sp-prod-act); Summer City (sp-prod-act); Little Boy Lost (prod).

AVERBACK, Hy: Dir. b. 1925. Films inc: Chamber of Horrors; Where Were You When The Lights Went Out; I Love You Alice B. Toklas; The Great Bank Robbery; Suppose They Gave a War and Nobody Came.

TV inc: The Brothers; The Real McCoys; Donna Reed Show; Richie Brockelman; Quark; M*A*S*H; Friends; The New Maverick; Anna and the King; Needles and Pins; Movin' On; Look Out World; Friends; Pearl; The Night Rider.

AVERY, Margaret: Act. b. Mangum, OK. Films inc: Magnum Force; Which Way Is Up?; The Fish that Saved Pittsburgh.

TV inc: Hudson Street; Louis Armstrong, Chicago Style; Scott Joplin.

Thea inc: Sistuhs; Revolution; Does a Tiger Wear a Necktie; Baby, I'm Back.

AVIDAN, David: Dir-Wri-Prod. b. Tel Aviv, Feb 21, 1934. Films inc: You Name It; Split; Sex; Telepathic Codes (anim); Stress.

TV inc: Multivista (series of talkshows in Israel).

AVILDSEN, John G: Dir. b. Oak Park, IL. e. NYU. Films inc: Turn on to Love; Out of It (& cin); Sweet Dreams (& cin); Guess What We Learned in School Today? (& cin); Joe (& cin); Cry Uncle (& cin); Save the Tiger; W W and the Dixie Dancekings; The President's Women; Rocky (Oscar-1976); Slow Dancing in the Big City (& prod-edtr); The Formula (& edtr).

AVNET, Jon: Prod-Dir. b. Brooklyn, NY. e. U of PA; Sarah Lawrence; dir fellowship at AFI. Films inc: Confusion's Circle; Thursday Night Woman. (Asso prod) It's Showtime; Checkered Flag or Crash; Trial By Combat; Outlaw Blues. (Prod) Coast to Coast.

TV inc: No Other Love; Homeward Bound.

AXELROD, George: Wri. b. NYC, Jun 9, 1922. Films inc: Phffft; The Seven Year Itch; Bus Stop; Will Success Spoil Rock Hunter; Breakfast at Tiffany's; The Manchurian Candidate; How to Murder Your Wife (& prod); Goodbye Charlie; Lord Love a Duck (& prod-dir); The Secret Life of an American Wife (& prod); The Lady Vanishes.

Plays inc: The Seven Year Itch; Will Success Spoil Rock Hunter; Visit to a Small Planet; Once More with Feeling; Goodbye Charlie.

AXELROD, Jonathan: Wri. b. NYC, Jul 9, 1948. Stepson of George Axelrod. Films inc: The Dirty Movie; Every Little Crook and Nanny.

AXTON, Hoyt: Singer-Comp. b. Oklahoma, Mar 25, 1938. Films inc: Smoky; The Black Stallion; Cloud Dancer. TV inc: Skinflint.

AYCKBOURN, Alan: Wri-Dir. b. London, Apr 12, 1939. e. Haileybury Coll. Plays inc: Mr Whatnot; Relatively Speaking; How The Other Half Loves; Ernie's Incredible Illucinations; Family Circles; Time and Again; Absurd Person Singular; The Norman Conquests; Absent Friends; Confusions; Jeeves; Bedroom Farce (& co-dir) (Tony-dir-1979); Just Between Ourselves; Ten Times Table (& dir); Joking Apart (& dir); Sisterly Feelings; Taking Steps; Men on Women on Men.

TV inc: Relatively Speaking; Service Not Included.

AYKROYD, Dan: Wri-Act. b. Ottawa, Can, Jul 1. TV inc: Coming Up Rosie (Canadian TV series); Beach Boys Special; All You need is Cash; Saturday Night Live (Emmy-wri-1977). Also performs and records with John Belushi as Blues Brothers. Albums inc: Briefcase Full of Blues.

Films inc: Mr Mike's Mondo Video; Love At First Sight; 1941; The Blues Brothers.

AYLMER, Felix: Act. b. Corsham, Wilts, Eng, Feb 21, 1889. e. Oxford. Thea inc: Bird in Hand; The Nelson Touch; The Flashing Stream; Daphne Laureola; The Chalk Garden; The Prescott Proposals.

Films inc: Victoria The Great; Quo Vadis; St. Joan; Separate Tables; Exodus; The Chalk Garden.

(Died Sept 2, 1979).

AYRES, Lew: Act. b. Minneapolis, MN, Dec 28, 1908. Originally musician, toured Mexico with own band, sideman with Henry Halstead Orch before films; during WW2 served as medic, asst chaplin. Screen debut 1929 The Sophomore.

Films inc: The Kiss; All Quiet on the Western Front; Common Clay; Doorway to Hell; State Fair; Servants Entrance; Dr. Kildare Series; Hearts In Bondage (dir); Dark Mirror; Unfaithful; Johnny Belinda; The Capture; Donovan's Brain; The Carpetbaggers; Altars to The East (& prod-dir-narr); Advise and Consent; The Last Generation; The Biscuit Eater; The Man; Planet of the Apes; Damien--Omen II; Battlestar Galactica.

TV inc: Greatest Heroes of the Bible; Suddenly Love; Salem's Lot; Letters From Frank; Reunion.

AZENBERG, Emanuel: Prod. b. Bronx, NY, Jan 22, 1934. e. NYU, BA. Bway inc: The Lion in Winter; Mark Twain Tonight; The Investigation; Something Different; Ain't Supposed to Die a Natural Death; The Sunshine Boys; The Poison Tree; The Good Doctor; Scapino; God's Favorite; California Suite; Something Afoot; Chapter Two; They're Playing Our Song; Ain't Misbehavin' (Tony-1978); Whose Life is it Anyway?; Devour the Snow; Last Licks; Children of a Lesser God; (Tony-1980) I Ought to Be in Pictures; Division Street.

AZNAVOUR, Charles: Act. b. Paris, May 22, 1924. Films inc: Shoot The Pianist; Passage du Rhin; Candy; The Adventurers; The Games; Un Beau Monstre; And Then There Were None; The Twist (Folies Bourgeoises); Ciao, Les Mecs; The Tin Drum.

BABBIN, Jacqueline: Prod. Started as prodn sec to agent Audrey Wood; worked with Irene Selznick on A Streetcar Named Desire; worked for David Susskind as story edtr, later asso prod, prod.

TV inc: DuPont Theatre; Armstrong Circle Theatre; Beacon Hill; Sybil (Emmy-1977); Friendships, Secrets and Lies; Once Upon a Family; Brave New World.

BACALL, Lauren (Betty Perske): Act. b. NYC, Sep 16, 1924. e. AADA. Screen debut in: To Have and Have Not, 1944. Films inc: The Big Sleep; Key Largo; Young Man with a Horn; How To Marry a Millionaire; Written on the Wind; Designing Woman; Sex and the Single Girl; Murder on the Orient Express; The Shootist; Health.

Bway inc: Cactus Flower; Goodbye Charlie; Applause (Tony-1970).

TV inc: Applause; Perfect Gentlemen.

BACH, Barbara: Act. b. NYC, Aug 27, 1950. Films inc: The Odyssey; Il Mio Monsignore; Masculi Ruspanti; Paolo Il Caldo; The Sea Wolf; Last Chance; The Spy Who Loved Me; Force 10 From Navarone; The Sensual Man; Jaguar Lives!; Up The Academy.

BACH, Catherine: Act. b. Warren, OH, Mar 1, 1954. Films inc: The Widow; The Midnight Man; Thunderbolt and Lightfoot; Hustle.
TV inc: Strange New World; Enos.

BACH, Steven: Prod-Exec. b. Pocatello, ID, Apr 29, 1940. Former teacher, became asst to Gordon Davidson at Mark Taper Theatre, LA, 1967; story ed for Gabriel Katzka; 1970 prodn exec with Palomar; 1974 formed Palladium Productions with Katzka; May 1978 named sr. vp prodn East Coast for UA; Jan 1980 named Sr vp worldwide prodn UA.
Films inc: The Taking of Pelham 1-2-3; The Parallax View; Mr. Billion; Butch and Sundance--The Early Days.

BACHARACH, Burt: Comp-Cond-Arr. b. Kansas City, MO, May 12, 1928. e. McGraw U, Mannes School of Music, Music Academy of the West. Cond. for Vic Damone, Ames Bros., Marlene Dietrich. Films inc: What's Up Pussycat; Butch Cassidy and the Sundance Kid *(Oscars-*(2)-1969-score & best song, Raindrops Keep Fallin' on My Head); Lost Horizon.
Songs inc: It's Great to be Young; Any Day Now; Baby, It's You; Only Love Can Break a Heart; I Wake Up Crying; A Lifetime of Loneliness; What the World Needs Now. Film title songs inc: Wives and Lovers; A House Is Not a Home; Send Me No Flowers; What's New Pussycat; Promise Her Anything.
TV inc: Burt Bacharach Special *(Emmy-*1971).
(Grammys-(3)-Arr-1967; Film Score & Orig cast album-1969).

BACKES, Alice: Act. b. Salt Lake City, UT, May 17. e. U of UT. Films inc: I Want to Live; It Started with a Kiss; Touch of Mink; Glory Guys; The Boatniks; Snowball Express; Gable and Lombard; The Cat from Outer Space.
TV inc: Young and the Restless; Vicky; Bachelor Father; Mayberry RFD; Hazel; Rich Man, Poor Man; Fear on Trial; Maude; Man from Independence.

BACKUS, Jim: Act. b. Cleveland, OH, Feb 25, 1913. e. AADA. Began in stock & vaudeville; voice of Oscar winning cartoon Mr Magoo. Films inc: The Great Lover; Hollywood Story; His Kind of Woman; Pat and Mike; Rebel Without a Cause; The Great Man; Ice Palace; Boys' Night Out; It's Mad, Mad, Mad, Mad World; Advance to the Rear; Where Were You When the Lights Went Out?; Now You See Him, Now You Don't; Good Guys Wear Black; C.H.O.M.P.S.; There Goes The Bride.
TV inc: I Married Joan; Hot Off the Wire; Gilligan's Island; Blondie; The Jim Backus Show. The Gift of the Magi; The Castaways on Gilligan's Island; The Rebels; The Gossip Columnist.
Bway inc: Our Town.

BADDELEY, Hermione: Act. b. Shropshire, Eng, Nov 13, 1908. Films inc: Passport to Pimlico; Quartet; Christmas Carol; The Pickwick Papers; Mr Prohack; Room at the Top; Let's Get Married; Midnight Lace; Rag Doll; Mary Poppins; The Unsinkable Molly Brown; C.H.O.M.P.S.; There Goes The Bride.
TV inc: Richard of Bordeaux; Drink Doggie Drink; The Gambler; Airmail from Cypress; The Castaway; Maude.
Thea inc: The Milk Train Doesn't Stop Here Anymore; Canterbury Tales.

BADEL, Alan: Act. b. Manchester, Eng, Sep 11, 1923. e. RADA Performed in Oxford Repertory Theatre. Following WW II, on London stage. Films inc: The Stranger Who Left No Card; Arabesque; This Sporting Life; Otley; Day of the Jackal; Luther; Telefon; Force 10 from Navarone; The Medusa Touch; Agatha; Riddle of the Sands; Nijinsky.
TV inc: Shogun.

BADHAM, John: Dir. b. England, 1939. e. Yale. Started Universal mail room clerk. TV credits inc: The Impatient Heart; Isn't It Shocking; Diabolique; The Gun; The Law.
Films inc: The Bingo Long Traveling All-Stars and Motor Kings; Dracula; Saturday Night Fever.

BADHAM, Mary: Act. b. 1952. Films inc: To Kill a Mockingbird; This Propery is Condemned; Let's Kill Uncle.

BADIYI, Reza: Dir. b. Iran, Apr 17, 1936. e. U of Tehran. Cin for 15 years in Iran, Europe, US; then dir. TV inc: Hawaii Five-O; The Doris Day Show; Cades County; The Eyes of Charles Sand; Switch; Incredible Hulk; Quincy; Rockford Files; Baretta; Starsky & Hutch; W.E.B.; Million Dollar Man; Bionic Woman; The Hardy Boys.

BAER, Art: Wri-Prod. b. NYC, Sep 17, 1925. e. Washington Square Coll, BA. TV inc: Dick Van Dyke; Good Times; The Jeffersons; Hogan's Heros; Gomer Pyle; Get Smart; Victor Borge Show; Perry Como Show; Jim Nabors Hour; Jonathan Winters Show; Carol Burnett Show *(Emmy-*wri-1972); The Cop & the Kid (prod); The Love Boat (& prod).

BAER, Max: Prod-Dir. b. Oakland, CA, 1937. e. U of Santa Clara. TV inc: (act) The Beverly Hillbillies. Films inc: (prod) The McCullochs; Ode to Billie Joe; Hometown, USA (dir); The Asphalt Cowboy (act).

BAEZ, Joan: Singer. b. NYC, Jan 9, 1941. e. Boston U. Films inc: Sacco and Vanzetti (sang and wrote lyrics for theme ballad); Don't Look Back (doc); Carry It On (doc); Woodstock; Celebration at Big Sur; Banjo Man; Renaldo & Clara.

BAGGETTA, Vincent: Act. b. Paterson, NJ, Dec 7. e. LA City Coll. Films inc: Embryo; Two Minute Warning.
TV inc: The Rhinemann Exchange; In the Matter of Karen Ann Quinlan; Murder on Flight 502; The Eddie Capra Mysteries; Eischeid-Only the Pretty Girls Die.

BAGNOLD, Enid: Wri. b. Eng, Oct 27, 1889. Plays inc: Lottie Dundass; National Velvet; Poor Judas; Gertie; The Chalk Garden; The Last Joke; The Chinese Prime Minister; Call Me Jacky; A Matter of Gravity.

BAIL, Chuck: Dir. Started as 2d unit dir. Films inc: Cleopatra Jones and the Casino of Gold; Gumball Rally (& prod); Black Sampson; The Stunt Man (act).

BAILEY, Jack: Bcast personality. b. Hampton, IA, Sep 15, 1907. e. Drake U. An itinerant actor, worked with Ralph Bellamy Stock Co, became radio announcer San Diego 1938; became net announcer handling such shows as Ozzie and Harriet, Duffy's Tavern; 1945 became host of radio's Queen for Day; show went to tv in 1955, continued through 1960, ranking as number one afternoon show for many years; also hosted Truth or Consequences; was voice of Goofy character in Walt Disney cartoons.
(Died Feb 1, 1980).

BAILEY, Pearl: Singer-Act. b. Newport News, VA, Mar 29, 1918. Started show business age 15 as singer and dancer in vaudeville, NY clubs. Stage debut, St. Louis Woman, 1946. Other Bway appearances inc: Arms and the Girl; Bless You All; House of Flowers; Hello, Dolly. *(Special Tony-*1968).
Films inc: Carmen Jones; Isn't it Romantic; That Certain Feeling; Porgy and Bess; All the Fine Young Cannibals; Norman Is That You?.
TV inc: The Pearl Bailey Show.

BAILEY, Robin: Act. b. Hucknall, Nottingham, Eng, Oct 5, 1919. Films inc: School for Secrets; Private Angelo; For Better for Worse; The Spy with a Cold Nose; The Whisperers; You Only Live Twice; The Eliminator; Blind Terror; Nightmare Rally; The Four Feathers.
TV inc: Seven Deadly Sins; The Power Game; Person to Person; The Newcomers; Murder Must Advertise; Upstairs, Downstairs; I Didn't Know You Cared; The Velvet Glove; Crown Court.
Thea inc: Barretts of Wimpole Street; You'll Never be Michael Angelo.

BAIN, Barbara: Act. b. Sep 13, 1931. e. U IL, BA. W of Martin Landau. Former fashion model. TV inc: Mission Impossible *(Emmys-*1967, 1968, 1969); Goodnight My Love; Murder Once Removed; Savage; A Summer Without Boys; Space 1999.

BAIN, Conrad: Act. b. Alberta, Canada, Feb 4, 1923. e. AADA. Thea inc: The Iceman Cometh; Sixth Finger in a Five Finger Glove; Candide; Dark of the Moon; Lost in the Stars; The Family Reunion.
Films inc: Who Killed Mary What's Her Name?; Up the Sandbox; A Fan's Notes; I Never Sang for My Father; A Pleasure Doing Business; C.H.O.M.P.S.
TV inc: The Defenders; Look Up and Live; Grandpa Goes to Washington; The Waverly Wonders; Diff'rent Strokes.

BAIO, Jimmy: Act. b. Brooklyn, NY, Mar 15. Bway inc: All God's Chillun Got Wings. TV inc: Joe and Sons; Soap.

BAIO, Scott Vincent: Act. b. NYC, Sep 22, 1961. Films inc: Bugsy Malone; Skatetown USA; Foxes.
TV inc: Luke Was There; Muggsy; Happy Days; Blansky's Beauties; Who's Watching the Kids; The Boy Who Drank Too Much; Stoned.

BAIRD, Roy: Prod. b. London. Films inc: Our Mother's House; Women in Love; The Devils; If. . .; Spring and Port Wine; The Music Lovers; That'll Be the Day; Stardust; The Final Program; Henry VIII and His Six Wives; Mahler; Quadrophenia; McVicar.

BAKER, Benny (nee Zifkin): Act. b. St Joseph, MO, May 5, 1907. Started in George Cukor's stock co in Rochester, NY; later in vaude with Lou Holtz; began in films in shorts; made 57 features inc: The Hell Cat; Belle of the Nineties; Big Broadcast of 1936; Thanks A Million; Rose Bowl; Champagne Waltz; Up In Arms; My Girl Tisa; The Inspector General; Public Pigeon No. 1; Thunder Birds; Boy Did I Get a Wrong Number; Papa's Delicate Condition; Paint Your Wagon; Car Wash.
Bway inc: The Tempest; Front Page; DuBarry Was a Lady; Let's Face It; Jackpot; No, No Nanette (rev).

BAKER, Blanche: Act. b. Dec 20, 1956. Films inc: French Postcards; The Seduction of Joe Tynan.
TV inc: Holocaust (Emmy-supp-1978); Mary and Joseph-A Story of Faith.

BAKER, Buddy (Norman Dale Baker): Comp-Cond. b. Springfield, MO, Jan 4, 1918. Prior to 1954 did arranging for Stan Kenton; Harry James; Bob Crosby; Glen Gray; for radio: Bob Hope; Jack Benny; Kay Kyser Shows. TV inc: Pearl Bailey Show. 1954, composer for Walt Disney Productions.
Films inc: Napoleon and Samantha; The Apple Dumpling Gang; The Shaggy D.A.; The Treasure of Matacumbe; Hot Lead and Cold Feet; The Apple Dumpling Gang Rides Again.

BAKER, Carroll: Act. b. Johnstown, PA, May 28, 1931. Films inc: Easy to Love; Giant; Baby Doll; The Miracle; Something Wild; Bridge to the Sun; How the West Was Won; The Carpetbaggers; Station Six Sahara; The Greatest Story Ever Told; Sylvia; Harlow; Jack of Diamonds; The Sweet Body of Deborah; Paranoia; Captain Apache; Andy Warhol's Bad; The World is Full of Married Men; The Watcher in the Woods.

BAKER, Diane: Act. b. Hollywood, 1938. Films inc: The Diary of Anne Frank; Journey to the Centre of the Earth; Hemingway's Adventures of a Young Man; Strait Jacket; The Prize; Marnie; Mirage; The Horse in the Grey Flannel Suit; East of Java; Baker's Hawk.
TV inc: The Badge or the Cross; Do You Take This Stranger; Congratulations, It's a Boy; Here We Go Again; Fugitive Family.

BAKER, Herbert (nee Abrahams): Wri. b. Dec 25, 1920. e. Yale U, BA. S of late Belle Baker, and late Maurice Abrahams. Films inc: So This Is New York; Jumping Jacks; Scared Stiff; Loving You; The Silencers; King Creole; Murderers Row; Sextette; The Jazz Singer.
TV inc: An Evening With Fred Astaire (Emmy-1959); John Denver and the Muppets; Danny Kaye Show; Perry Como Show; Danny Kaye's Lock-in At the Met; Ted Knight Special; Gladys Knight and the Pips; Mac Davis Show; Flip Wilson Show (Emmy-1971); Norman Rockwell's America; Some of Manie's Friends; Specials for Perry Como; Frank Sinatra; Danny Kaye; Dean Martin; John Denver and the Muppets--A Christmas Get Together.
Bway: lyr for Helen Goes to Troy. Special material for Belle Baker; Danny Kaye; Lena Horne.

BAKER, Jim B: Act. b. Great Falls, MT, Jul 12. e. U of MT. Worked with ACT, various repertory groups. Films inc: Manny's Orphans. TV inc: In Memory Of; Flo.

BAKER, Joe Don: Act. b. Groesbeck, TX, Feb 12, 1936. Films inc: Adam at 6 A.M.; Wishbone Cutter; Charley Varrick; Walking Tall; Golden Needles; Cool Hand Luke; Mitchell; Wild Rovers; The Pack; Checkered Flag or Crash; Speedtrap.
TV inc: Mongo's Back in Town; That Certain Summer; To Kill a Cop; Power.

BAKER, Roy: Dir. b. England, 1916. With Gainsborough studios prior to WW2. Films inc: The October Man; The Weaker Sex; Morning Departure; I'll Never Forget You; Inferno; Don't Bother To Knock; Passage Home; Tiger in the Smoke; That One That Got Away; A Night to Remember; The Singer not the Song; Flame in the Streets; Quatermass and the Pit; The Anniversary; Moon Zero Two; The Vampire Lovers; Dr. Jekyll and Sister Hyde; Asylum; Vault of Horror; Legend of the Seven Golden Vampires; The Seven Brothers Meet Dracula.

BAKER, Suzanne: Prod. b. London, 1942. Freelance interviewer/researcher, wri Australian TV & radio, 1962-64; prod-dir-wri Australia network, 1964-68; dir BBC-TV, 1968; Women's Edtr, Sydney Morning Herald, 1971-73; prod, Film Australia, 1974-78. Films inc: Leisure (Oscar-ss-1976).

BAKEWELL, William: Act. b. LA, May 2, 1908. Films inc: The Iron Mask; All Quiet on the Western Front; Dance, Fools, Dance; The Spirit of Notre Dame; Back Street; Quality Street; Three Cornered Moon; Seven Sinners; Come, Fill the Cup; Davy Crockett; The Strongest Man in the World.

BAKSHI, Ralph: Ani. b. NYC. Films inc: Fritz the Cat; Heavy Traffic; Coonskin; Wizards; The Lord of the Rings.

BALABAN, A J: Thea Exec. b. Chicago, Aug 18, 1889. Began as operator of nickelodeon in Chicago, 1907. Co-founder Balaban & Katz Corp, 1917. Affiliated with Paramount, named director of entertainment, then VP. Abroad 9 years, returned to U.S. as circuit exhibitor, 1935. General manager Roxy Theatre, NY, 1942-52.

BALANCHINE, George (Georges Malitonovitch Balanchivadze): Chor. b. St Petersburg, Russia, Jan 22, 1904. e. Imperial School of Ballet in St Petersburg. Began as a dancer, 1923-24; appointed ballet master and chor to Les Ballets Russes de Diaghilev; ballet master to the Royal Danish Ballet, 1931; formed the School of American Ballet, NY, which later became the American Ballet Co, 1934; chor to Metropolitan Opera, NY, 1935-38; founded Ballet Society, 1946, renamed the NY City Ballet, 1948, toured US & abroad.
Bway inc: (chor) Wake Up and Dream; Cochran's 1931 Revue; The Ziegfeld Follies; On Your Toes; Babes in Arms; The Boys from Syracuse; Louisiana Purchase; Cabin in the Sky; The Song of Norway; Where's Charley?.
Films inc: Goldwyn Follies; On Your Toes; I Was an Adventuress.
TV inc: (chor) Stravinsky's The Flood; Ringling Bros Barnum & Bailey Circus.

BALDWIN, Bill: Act. Films inc: New York, New York; The One and Only; The Champ; Rocky II; Voices.
TV inc: Evita Peron; Goldie and the Boxer Go to Hollywood.

BALIN, Ina: Act. b. NYC, 1937. Films inc: The Black Orchid; From the Terrace; The Young Doctors; The Greatest Story Ever Told; The Patsy; Act of Reprisal; Run Like a Thief; Charro; The Projectionist; The Comeback Trail; The Don Is Dead.
TV inc: The Lonely Profession; Desperate Mission; The Immigrants; The Children of An Lac.

BALL, Lucille: Act-Prod. b. Celoron, NY, Aug 11, 1911. Worked as model in NY. To Hollywood as a Goldwyn Girl in Roman Scandals. Under contract to Columbia, later to RKO in number of un-billed parts, including two-reelers with Leon Errol and The Three Stooges. First credit in Carnival.

Films inc: Roberta; The Three Musketeers; I Dream Too Much; That Girl From Paris; Stage Door; Affairs of Annabel; Annabel Takes a Tour; Five Came Back; Dance, Girl, Dance; Too Many Girls; The Big Street; Best Foot Forward; Thousands Cheer; DuBarry Was A Lady; Meet the People; Lured; Her Husband's Affairs; Sorrowful Jones; Fancy Pants; Easy Living; Miss Grant Takes Richmond: Fuller Brush Girls; Facts of Life; Critic's Choice; Yours, Mine And Ours; Mame.

Radio inc: Phil Baker Show; Jack Haley's Wonder Bread Show; Screen Guild Playhouse; My Favorite Husband.

TV inc: I Love Lucy (with former husband Desi Arnaz) (Emmys-1952, 1955); The Lucy Show (Emmys-1967, 1968); Here's Lucy; Happy Anniversary and Goodbye; What Now, Catherine Curtis; The Lucille Ball Specials; Lucy Moves to NBC; The Steve Allen Comedy Hour.

Bway: Wildcat.

BALLARD, Carroll: Dir. b. LA, Oct 14, 1937. e. UCLA. Film: The Black Stallion.

BALLARD, Kaye (Catherine Gloria Balota): Act-Singer. b. Cleveland, OH, Nov 20, 1926. Began show business 1946 at The Bowery, Detroit, as impressionist. Toured vaudeville houses with Spike Jones, Vaughn Monroe, Stan Kenton. Films inc: The Girl Most Likely; A House is Not a Home; The Ritz; Freaky Friday; Falling In Love Again. TV inc: Red Skelton Show; Ed Sullivan; Perry Como Show; Laugh-In; The Mothers-in-Law; The Dream Merchants.

Bway inc: Three To Make Ready; Carnival!; Molly; The Beast in Me; Reuben, Reuben.

BALLARD, Lucien: Cin. b. Miami, OK, May 6, 1908. e. U of OK, U of PA. Films inc: Crime and Punishment; Craig's Wife; Blind Alley; Wild Geese Calling; The Lodger; Laura; Inferno; The Killing; Al Capone; Pay or Die; The Caretakers; Nevada Smith; Hour of the Guns; Will Penny; The Wild Bunch; True Grit; The Ballad of Cable Hogue; What's the Matter with Helen; Junior Bonner; The Getaway; Breakout; Rabbit Test.

BALLARD, Lucinda: Dsgn. b. Apr 13, 1908. W of Howard Dietz. Bway inc: Happy Birthday; Another Part of the Forest (Tony-1947); John Loves Mary; Chocolate Soldier (& sets); I Remember Mama; Annie Get Your Gun; Show Boat; Fourposter; A Streetcar Named Desire; The Gay Life (Tony-1962). Silk Stockings.

Opera inc: Peter and the Wolfe; Giselle.

BALNAVES, Neil Richard: Prod. b. Adelaide, S Australia, May 5, 1944. M dir Hanna-Barbera Pty, Ltd. Films inc: (exec prod) Last of the Mohicans; Five Weeks in a Balloon; Black Beauty. TV inc: Clue Club; The Robonic Stooges; Undercover Elephant; The Popeye Show.

BALSAM, Martin: Act. b. NYC, Nov 4, 1919. TV inc: Playhouse 90; Studio One; Philco Playhouse; Doctor Kildare; Naked City; The Defenders; The Millionaire; Rainbow; The Seeding of Sarah Burns; The House on Garibaldi Street; Archie Bunkers Place; Aunt Mary; The Love Tapes.

Bway inc: You Know I Can't Hear You When the Water's Running (Tony-1968); Cold Storage.

Films inc: On the Waterfront; Twelve Angry Men; Psycho; Breakfast at Tiffanys; The Carpetbaggers; Seven Days in May; Harlow; A Thousand Clowns (Oscar-supp-1965); 2001-A Space Odyssey; Tora! Tora! Tora!; Little Big Man; Summer Wishes-Winter Dreams; Catch 22; The Taking of Pelham 1-2-3; Murder On the Orient Express; All the President's Men; Two Minute Warning; The Sentinel; Silver Bears; Cuba; There Goes The Bride.

BALTER, Allan: Wri-Prod. b. Detroit, MI, Aug 28, 1925. e. U of MI, BA. TV inc: Adventures in Paradise; Outer Limits; Voyage to the Bottom of the Sea (& assoc prod); Mission: Impossible (& prod); San Francisco International Airport (& prod); Earth II (& prod); Shaft (& prod); The Man with the Power (& prod); Just a Little Inconvenience (& prod); Six Million Dollar Man (exec prod); Captain America (exec prod); Samurai (prod); Where the Ladies Go.

BANAS, Robert Joseph: Dir-Chor. b. NYC, Sep 20, 1933. TV inc: Judy Garland Show; Tony Martin Special; Tennessee Ernie Ford Special; Jonathan Winters Show; Frank Sinatra Special II; Eleanor and Franklin; Lindsey Wagner Special; Bud and Lou; Kaz; Quincy.

BANCROFT, Anne (nee Italiano): Act. b. NYC, Sep 17, 1931. e. AADA. W of Mel Brooks. On screen from 1952 in Don't Bother to Knock. Films inc: Tonight We Sing; The Kid From Left Field; Demitrius and the Gladiators; Gorilla at Large; The Raid; New York Confidential; The Brass Ring; Naked Street; The Miracle Worker (Oscar-1962); The Pumpkin Eater; The Slender Thread; The Graduate; Young Winston; The Prisoner of Second Avenue; The Hindenburg; The Turning Point; Fatso (& dir-sp); The Elephant Man.

Bway inc: Two for the Seasaw (Tony-1958); The Miracle Worker (Tony-1960); The Devils; A Cry of Players; Golda.

TV inc: Torrents of Spring; Annie, the Woman in the Life of Men (Emmy-1970); Annie and the Seven Hoods.

BAND, Albert: Prod-Wri-Dir. b. Paris, May 7, 1924. e. Lyceum Louis le Grand. Started as film cutter Pathe Lab; Prodn Asst MGM. Films inc: The Young Guns (dir); I Bury the Living (prod-dir); Face of Fire (prod-dir); The Avenger (dir); The Tramplers (prod-dir); The Hellbenders (prod); A Minute to Pray, A Second to Die (prod-dir); Little Cigars (prod); Dracula's Dog (prod); She Came to the Valley (prod-dir).

BANGERT, Charles A: Prod-Dir. b. Kansas City, MO, Oct 14, 1943. e. Hofstra. TV inc: Lifeline; The Body Human--The Sexes; The Body Human--The Magic Sense (Emmy-co-prod-1980); The Body Human--The Body Beautiful; The Body Human--The Sexes II.

BANKY, Vilma (nee Lonchit): Act. b. Budapest, Hungary, Jan 9, 1903. Silent screen star. Films inc: The Dark Angel; The Eagle; Son of the Sheik; The Winning of Barbara Worth; A Lady to Love; The Rebel.

BANNEN, Ian: Act. b. Airdrie, Scotland, Jun 29, 1928. e. Ratcliffe Coll. Films inc: Private's Progress; The Birthday Present; Macbeth; A French Mistress; Suspect; Station Six Sahara; Rotten to the Core; The Hill; The Flight of he Phoenix; Penelope; Lock Up Your Daughters; Too Late the Hero; Fright; Doomwatch; The Offence; The Mackintosh Man; Bite the Bullet; Sweeney; Inglorious Bastards; The Watcher in the Woods.

Bway inc: A View From the Bridge; The Iceman Cometh; Long Day's Journey Into Night; Hedda Gabler; Toys in the Attic; Sergeant Musgrave's Dance.

TV inc: Johnny Belinda; Tinker, Tailor, Soldier, Spy.

BANNER, Bob: Prod-Dir. b. Ennis, TX, Aug 15, 1921. e. SMU, BA, Northwestern U, MA. Staff dir, NBC-TV Chicago-1949-50; TV inc: The Dinah Shore Chevy Show (Emmy-dir-1957); The Garry Moore Show; Garroway at Large; Candid Camera. His co, Bob Banner Assoc, prod specials inc Carnegie Hall Salutes Jack Benny; Julie and Carol at Carnegie Hall; Here's Peggy Fleming; The John Davidson Shows; Love! Love! Love!; To Europe with Love; Perry Como's Early American Christmas; The Darker Side of Terror; If Things Were Different; Perry Como's Bahama Holiday.

BANNON, Jack: Act. b. LA, Jun 14, 1940. e. UCSB, BA. TV inc: Petticoat Junction; Quincy; Tail Gunner Joe; Amelia Earhart; Lou Grant.

BARASH, Olivia: Act. b. Miami, FL, Jan 11, 1965. Films inc: Who Is Harry Kellerman. . . ?; American Hot Wax.

TV inc: A World Apart; Big Blue Marble; Code R; The Secret Storm; Michel's Bird; The Ghost Belongs to Me; In the Beginning.

Bway inc: Gypsy; Panama Hattie.

BARBEAU, Adrienne: Act. b. Sacramento, CA, Jun 11. Bway inc: Fiddler on the Roof; Grease; The Owl and the Pussycat.

TV inc: Maude; Houdini; Having Babies; Red Alert; Someone is Watching Me; The Darker Side of Terror; The Top of the Hill; Valentine Magic On Love Island; Tourist.

Films inc: The Fog.

BARBER, Red (Walter L Barber): Sportscaster. b. Columbus, MS, 1908. Chiefly assoc with baseball. Play-by-play Cincinnati Reds, 1934-39; Brooklyn Dodgers, 1939-54; NY Yankees, 1954-66. Ret.

BARBERA, Joseph R: Exec. b. NYC, Mar 24. e. NYU, American Institute of Banking. Started submitting cartoons to leading magazines; joined Van Buren Associates as a sketch artist; later worked in the animation department of MGM where he met William Hanna in 1937; they were teamed to produce a single animated short and developed Tom & Jerry, the first of seven Academy Award winning cartoons. Left MGM in 1957 to form Hanna-Barbera Prods to make cartoons for TV. Cartoon series inc: Yogi Bear; Huckleberry Hound; The Flintstones. Company entered theatrical prod with Charlotte's Web in 1973.

TV inc: The Curlews (*Emmy*-1973); The Runaways (*Emmy*-1974); The Gathering (*Emmy*-exec prod-1978); The Popeye Valentine Special - Sweethearts At Sea; Beach Girls; The Gathering, Part II; Scooby Goes Hollywood; Belle Starr; The Flintstone's New Neighbors.

Films inc: C.H.O.M.P.S.

BARBOUR, John: Comedian-TV pers. b. Toronto, Canada, Apr 24. Started as nitery comic. Hosted 4 LA area tv shows. TV inc: The Tonight Show; The Dean Martin Show; The Marty Feldman Show; Gomer Pyle USMC (wri); My Mother, The Car (wri); Real People (Cohost).

BARDEM, Juan-Antonio: Dir-Wri. b. Madrid, Jun 2, 1922. Films inc: Welcome, Mr Marshall; Death of a Cyclist; Calle/Mayor; La Venganza; Los Innocentes; The Uninhibited; El Puente; 7 dias de Enero.

Thea inc: (Dir) The House of Bernarda Alba.

BARDOT, Brigitte: Act. b. Paris, Sept 28, 1934. Began as model. Films inc: Le Trou Normand; Helen of Troy; Doctor at Sea; The Bride Is Much Too Beautiful; Will You Dance With Me; And God Created Woman; Love Is My Profession; Babette Goes To War; A Very Private Affair; Two Weeks in September; Spirits of the Dead; Les Femmes.

BARE, Richard L: Prod-Dir. b. Turlock, CA, 1909. e. USC. Films inc: This Rebel Breed; Girl on the Run; Return of the Frontiersman; Shootout at Medicine Bend; This Side of the Law; Smart Girls Don't Talk; Flaxy Martin; House Across the Street; Wicked, Wicked.

TV inc: Green Acres; 77 Sunset Strip; Cheyenne; The Islanders; Man Against Crime; Gangbusters; So This Is Hollywood; Walt Disney Presents; You're Only Young Once; Run for Your Life; Bus Stop; Gallant Men; Casablanca; Nanny and the Professor; Petticoat Junction; Donna Reed Show; Topper; Behind the Eightball; Alias Smith and Jones; The Virginian; Maverick; Lawman; Sugarfoot.

BARGERON, Dave: Trombonist. b. Athol, MA, Sep 6, 1942. See Blood, Sweat & Tears.

BARI, Lynn (Marjorie Bitzer): Act. b. Roanoke, VA, 1917. First appeared on screen as dancing girl in Dancing Lady. Films inc: Shock; Home Sweet Homicide; Sunny Side of the Street; I Dream of Jeanie; Damn Citizen; Trauma.

BARKER, Bob: TV Host. b. Darrington, WA, Dec 12. e. Drury Coll. Started as news wri, announcer, disc jockey. MC Truth or Consequences, 1956. Formed Bob Barker Prods, Inc. Since 1967, MC for both the Miss Universe Beauty Pageant and the Miss USA Beauty Pageant; also created Lucky Pair; prod the Pillsbury Bake-Off Special; host of the Indianapolis 500 Parade; The Price is Right.

BARKLEY, Deanne: Prod. b. New Orleans, LA, 1930. e. Northwestern U. Began in public affairs at WDSU-TV, New Orleans; to NYC as headwriter for Dick Cavett A.M. Shows; prod Virginia Graham Show; Helen Gurley Brown Show; network staff writer; joined Robert Stigwood Organization as vp crea aff, exec prod Virginia Hill Story; All Together Now; Death Scream; 1975 to NBC as vp pgm dev West Coast; 1976 vp Dramatic Problems; 1977, vp motion pictures for tv and miniseries; joined Paul Klein in indie prodn as part of Osmond Group Productions, Oct 1979.

TV inc: Valentine Magic on Love Island; The Day The Women Got Even (exec prod).

BARNES, Binnie: Act. b. London, May 25, 1905. W of Mike Frankovich. On screen from 1931. Films inc: Love Lies; Murder at Covent Gardens; The Private Life of Henry VIII; The Private Life of Don Juan; Diamond Jim; Three Smart Girls; The Adventures of Marco Polo; The Three Musketeers; Tight Shoes; Three Girls About Town; Up in Mabel's Room; It's in the Bag; The Trouble with Angels; Forty Carats.

BARNES, Joanna: Act. b. Nov 15, 1934. e. Smith Coll. Films inc: Auntie Mame; Spartacus; The Parent Trap; Goodbye Charlie; The War Wagon; I Wonder Who's Killing Her Now.

TV inc: Beacon Street; Trial of O'Brien; Dateline, Hollywood.

BARON, Allen: Dir-Wri. b. NYC, 1935. Films inc: Blast of Silence (wri-dir-act); Pie in the Sky (prod-dir).

BARR, Anthony (Morris Yaffe): Prod-Dir. b. St Louis, MO, Mar 14, 1921. e. WA U, BS. TV inc: (dir) Art Linkletter's Houseparty; About Faces; Climax; Shower of Stars; Playhouse 90; The Law and Mr. Jones.

Films inc: Dime with A Halo (co-prod).

BARR, Julia: Act. b. Fort Wayne, IN, Feb 8, 1949. e. Purdue. TV inc: Gathering of One; The Adams Chronicles; Ryan's Hope; All My Children.

BARR, Richard (nee Baer): Dir-Prod. b. Washington, DC, Sep 6, 1917. e. Princeton U. Began as an actor with Orson Welles' Mercury Theatre Co, 1938. Later moved to dir & prod. Bway inc: Who's Afraid of Virginia Woolf? (*Tony*-prod-1963); Tiny Alice; A Delicate Balance; Everything in the Garden; Johnny-No-Trump; The Front Page; All Over; Seascape; The Grass Harp; The Last of Mrs Lincoln; Noel Coward in Two Keys; PS Your Cat is Dead; Sweeney Todd (*Tony*-prod-1979); The Lady From Dubuque.

BARRAULT, Marie-Christine: Act. Films inc: My Night at Maud's; The Daydreamer; Lancelot of the Lake; The Aspern Papers; Les Intrus; La Famille Grossfelder; John Gluckstadt; Cousin Cousine; By The Tennis Courts; L'Etat Sauvage; Perceval; The Medusa Touch; Tout est a nous; Femme Entre Chien et Loup; Ma Cherie; Stardust Memories.

BARRETT, James Lee: Wri-Prod. b. Charlotte, NC, Nov 19, 1929. e. Furman U, Penn State U. Films inc: The D.I.; The Greatest Story Ever Told; The Truth About Spring; Shenandoah; Bandolero; The Green Berets; The Cheyenne Social Club (& prod); Fools' Parade; Smokey and the Bandit.

Plays inc: The Wiz (*Tony*-book-1975).

TV inc: Mayflower - The Pilgrims' Adventure; The Day Christ Died; Belle Starr; Angel City.

BARRETT, Rona: Journalist. b. NYC, Oct 8, 1936. e. NYU. Syndicated Hollywood gossip columnist. Created first daily syndicated TV news segment for Metromedia; Hollywood corr ABC's Good Morning, America; 1980, Tomorrow Show. Films inc: Sextette.

BARRIE, Barbara: Act. b. Chicago, IL, May 23, 1931. e. U TX Austin. Bway inc: The Wooden Dish; The Selling of the President; Company; Killdeer; The Prisoner of Second Avenue; California Suite.

Films inc: One Potato, Two Potato; The Caretakers; Giant; Breaking Away; Private Benjamin.

TV inc: Barney Miller; Diana; Tell Me My Name; 79 Park Avenue; The Summer of My German Soldier; Breaking Away.

BARRIE, George: Exec-Sngwri. b. NYC, Feb 9, 1918. Chmn & CEO, Faberge, Inc; p Brut Prods. Films inc: A Touch of Class; Night Watch; Welcome to Arrow Beach; Book of Numbers; Hang-Up; Miracles Still Happen; I Will, I Will. . . for Now; Hugo the Hippo (ani); Whiffs; Thieves; Nasty Habits; Hedda; Fingers; The Class of Miss MacMichael.

Songs inc: All That Love Went to Waste, Now That We're in Love.

BARRIS, Chuck: Prod-TV Host. b. Philadelphia, Jun 3. e. U of Miami, Drexel Institute of Technology. TV shows inc: Dream Girl; Operation: Entertainment; The Newlywed Game; The Dating Game; How's Your Mother-In-Law?; The Family Game; The Etiquette Game; The Game Game; The Cass Elliott Special; The New Treasure Hunt; Your Hit Parade; The Bobby Vinton Show; The Gong Show.

Films inc: The Gong Show Movie.

BARRON, William A Jr: Dir-Prod. b. St. Louis, MO, Sep 8, 1927. e. Hobart Coll, BA. Staff dir WABC-TV, 1962-63. Freelance next 12 years; many Gemini (space probe) missions; first live Gemini telecast from ship at sea; many Apollo Missions; now Mellow Prods, children's programming.

BARROW, Bernard: Act. b. NYC, Dec 30. Films inc: Serpico; Rachel, Rachel; Glass Houses; Claudine.
TV inc: The Edge of Night; The Secret Storm; Where the Heart Is; Ryan's Hope.

BARRY, Dave: Comedian. b. NYC, Aug 26, 1918. Started on radio, vaudeville. Later in big band shows, niteries; with Wayne Newton Show, Las Vegas.

BARRY, Donald (Red) (Donald Barry de Acosta): Act. b. Houston, TX, 1912. On stage prior to Hollywood.
Films inc: Night Waitress; The Woman I Love; Sinners in Paradise; star of Red Ryder series; Untamed Heiress; The Purple Heart; I'll Cry Tomorrow; Bandolero; Shalako; Fastest Gun in the West; Orca.
(Died July 18, 1980).

BARRY, Gene (Eugene Klass): Act. b. NYC, Jun 14, 1921. Films inc: Atomic City; War of the Worlds; Those Redheads from Seattle; Soldier of Fortune; Back from Eternity; Maroc 7; Red Garters; Naked Alibi; China Gate; Thunder Road; Subterfuge; Guyana, Cult of the Damned.
TV inc: Bat Masterson; Burke's Law *(Emmy*-1965); The Name of the Game; The Adventurer; Istanbul Express; Prescription Murder; The Devil and Miss Sarah; Aspen. Thea inc: Rosalinda; Catherine Was Great; The Would Be Gentleman; Glad to See You; Happy Is Larry; Bless You All; The Merry Widow.

BARRY, Jack: TV Prod-Act. b. Lindenhurst, NY, Mar 20, 1918. e. U of PA. TV shows inc: The Jokers Wild; Blank Check; Break the Bank; Juvenile Jury; Life Begins at 80; Tic Tac Dough; 21.

BARRY, John (J B Prendergast): Comp-Arr-Cond. b. York, Eng, 1933. Films inc: Beat Girl; Amorous Prawn; From Russia with Love; Zulu; Goldfinger; The Ipcress File; Thunderball; King Rat; The Chase; Born Free *(Oscars*-(2)-Best Score, Title Song-1966); The Wrong Box; The Quiller Memorandum; Petulia; Boom; Deadfall; The Lion in Winter *(Oscar*-1968); Midnight Cowboy; Murphy's War; The Might Be Giants; Diamonds Are Forever; Robin and Marian; King Kong; The Deep; The Betsy; The White Buffalo; Hanover Street; Moonraker; Starcrash; The Black Hole; Night Games; Touched by Love; Raise The Titanic; Somewhere In Time; Inside Moves.
TV inc: Elizabeth Taylor in London; Sophia Loren in Rome; Eleanor and Franklin; Eleanor and Franklin-The White House Years; Love Among The Ruins.
(Grammy-inst theme-1969).

BARRY, John: Art dir. b. London, England, 1936. Films inc: A Clockwork Orange; Star Wars *(Oscar*-1977); Superman; Saturn 3 (orig story).
(Died May 31, 1979).

BARRY, Philip: Prod. b. NYC. e. Yale U. S of late Philip Barry. Films inc: The Mating Game; Sail a Crooked Ship.
TV inc: The Elgin Hour; The Motorola Playhouse; The Alcoa Hour; The Goodyear Playhouse; Just an Old Sweet Song; Kinfolks; The Animals; First You Cry. Friendly Fire *(Emmy*-1979); Father Brown, Detective; Bogie.

BARRY, W Russell: Exec. b. Brooklyn, Mar 7, 1936. e. Dartmouth, Harvard Grad School of Business. Joined WBBM TV, Chicago, as acct exec 1960; vp CBS radio div 1969; vp TV stations div & gen mgr KNXT 1973; named network sales vp 20th Fox 1976; vp sals & syndication 1977; named prexy 20th Fox TV 1979; P Playboy Productions, July 1980.

BARSTOW, Richard: Dir-Chor. b. Ashtabula, OH. In stock companies, vaude, played Palace as dancer.
Films inc: (chor) Buck Benny Rides Again; Love Thy Neighbor; Swing Fever; Girl Next Door; New Faces; Greatest Show on Earth; A Star Is Born.
TV inc: Colgate Hour.
Bway inc: Olsen and Johnson's Carnival Night Club (prod). Also chor Ringling Bros & Barnum and Bailey Circus 1949-1951.

BART, Lionel: Comp-Lyr-Plywri. b. Aug 1, 1930. Thea inc: Fings Ain't Wot They Used T' Be (mus-lyr); Lock Up Your Daughters (lyr); Oliver! (book-lyr-mus) *(Tony*-1963); Blitz (co-book-lyr-mus-dir); Merry Roosters panto (contributed mus-lyr); Maggie May (mus-lyr); Twang! (book-mus-lyr); Lock Up Your Daughters; La Strada (mus-lyr); The Londoners (songs); Costa Packet (songs); So You Want To Be In Pictures (mus supv).
Films inc: The Tommy Steele Story; The Duke Wore Jeans; Tommy The Toreador; Oliver!.
Title songs inc: From Russia With Love; Man in the Middle.

BART, Peter: Exec. b. Jul 24, 1932. e. Swarthmore College, London School of Economics. Joined Paramount Pictures 1965; exec asst to Robert Evans, exec in charge world wide prod; VP prod; resigned 1973; pres Lorimar Films April '78-June '79; co-prod: Islands in the Stream; Fun with Dick and Jane.

BARTEL, Paul: Dir. b. NYC, Aug 6, 1938. e. UCLA, BA. Films inc: The Secret Cinema; Naughty Nurse; Private Parts; Death Race 2000; Cannonball; Piranha (act); Rock 'n' Roll High School (act).

BARTHOLOMEW, Freddie: Act. b. London, Mar 28, 1924. Stage debut, 1927. Screen debut, David Copperfield, 1935. Films inc: Anna Karenina; Lloyds of London; Little Lord Fauntleroy; Kidnapped; Swiss Family Robinson; Yank at Eton; The Town Went Wild; St. Benny the Dip.

BARTLETT, Hall: Prod-Dir-Wri. b. Kansas City, MO, Nov 27, 1925. e. Yale U, BA. Films inc: Navajo; Crazy-Legs; Unchained; Drango; Zero Hour; All the Young Men; The Caretakers; A Global Affair; Changes; The Sandpit Generals; Jonathan Livingston Seagull; The Children of Sanchez.
TV inc: Cleo Laine Special; The Search of Zubin Mehta.

BARTOK, Eva (nee Szoke): Act-Wri-Prod. b. Hungary, Jun 18, 1926. In films since 1933 in Crimson Pirate; Tale of Five Cities; The Venetian Bird; Spaceways; Park Plaza; Front Page Story; The Gamma People; Carnival Story; Operation Amsterdam; S.O.S. Pacific; Beyond the Curtain; 10,000 Bedrooms; Blood and Back Lace.

BARTON, Charles T: Dir. b. CA, May 25, 1902. In vaude and stock before becoming film prop man. Began directing at Par.
Films inc: Wagon Wheels; Rocky Mountain Mystery; Last Outpost; And Sudden Death; Nevada; Rose Bowl; Murder with Pictures; Crime Nobody Saw; Thunder Train; Five Little Peppers and How they Grew; Island of Doomed Men; Out West with the Peppers; Five Little Peppers in Trouble; Phantom Submarine; Harmon of Michigan; Two Latins from Manhattan; Sing for Your Supper; Hello Annapolis; Parachute Nurse; Sweetheart of the Fleet; A Man's World; Spirit of Stanford; Reveille with Beverly; She Has What it Takes; Jam Session; Louisiana Hayride; Beautiful Cheat; Men in Her Diary; White Tie and Tails; The Time of Their Lives; Wistful Widow of Wagon Gap; Buck Privates Come Home; Mexican Hayride; Abbott and Costello Meet Frankenstein; The Noose Hangs High; Abbott and Costello Meet the Killer; Double Crossbones; The Milkman; Ma and Pa Kettle at the Fair; Dance With Me Henry; Shaggy Dog; Swinging Along.
TV inc: Amos 'n' Andy; Oh, Susannah!; Zorro; McHale's Navy; Dennis The Menace; Hazel; Petticoat Junction; A Family Affair.

BARTY, Billy: Act. b. Millsboro, PA, Oct 25 (circa 1919). Films inc: Footlight Parade; Golddiggers of 1933; A Midsummer Night's Dream; The Day of the Locust; The Happy Hooker Goes to Washington; W C Fields and Me; Rabbit Test; Foul Play; Firepower; Skatetown USA.

BARUCH, Andre: Radio-TV pers. b. Paris. e. Pratt Institute of Fine Arts; Columbia U; Ecole de Beaux Arts . H of Bea Wain. Started as radio announcer, became voice of some of top-rated radio programs of era inc: Your Hit Parade; The United States Steel Hour; The Kate Smith Show; The Shadow; Exploring the Unknown. Did play-by-play broadcasts for Brooklyn Dodgers Baseball team; was voice of Pathe News (newsreel); news commentator on CBS and ABC networks. With wife conducted Mr and Mrs Music Show, later did the Bea and Andre show on WPBR, Palm Beach. TV and radio commercials for top sponsors. Inducted into National Broadcasters Hall of Fame 1979.

BARWOOD, Hal: Wri. b. Hanover, NH, Apr 16. e. Brown U; USC. Made prize-winning A Child's Introduction to the Cosmos while at USC; teamed with Matthew Robbins. Films inc: Sugarland Express; The Bingo Long Traveling All-Stars and Motor Kings; MacArthur; Corvette Summer (& prod).

BARYSHNIKOV, Mikhail: Dancer-Act. b. Riga, Latvia, Jun 1947. Joined Korov ballet, Leningrad; then American Ballet Theatre in US; New York City Ballet Company. Films inc: The Turning Point.
   TV inc: Baryshnikov at the White House (*Emmy*-1979); Bob Hope on the Road to China; Baryshnikov on Broadway.

BASEHART, Richard: Act. b. Zanesville, OH, Aug 31, 1914. Debuted with local stock company age 13. Joined Hedgerow Theatre, Moylan, PA, played in repertory there, 1938-42. Broadway debut in Counterattack, 1943. Film debut, Cry Wolf, 1945. Films inc: Roseanna McCoy; Tension; Outside the Wall; Fourteen Hours; The House on Telegraph Hill; Titanic; Rage; Time Limit; Four Days in November; The Satan Bug; Island of Dr. Moreau; Shenanigans; Being There.
   TV inc: Voyage to the Bottom of the Sea; Let My People Go (*Emmy*-narr-1965); The Andersonville Trial; The Critical List; The Girl Who Saved Our America; The Rebels; Eric Hoffer--The Crowded Life; Marilyn--The Untold Story; The Ten Thousand Day War.
   Bway inc: Land of Fame; Othello; Hickory Stick; The Hasty Heart.

BASIE, Count (William Basie): Comp-Pianist. b. Red Bank, NJ, Aug 21, 1906. Accompanist to vaude acts; later organized own orch; appeared in hotels, theatres, niteries. Songs inc: One O'Clock Jump; Good Morning Blues; Basie Boogie; Gone with the Wind; I Left My Baby.
   (*Grammys*-(6)-Dance Band-1958, 1960, 1963; Jazz Large Group-1958; Jazz solo-1976; Jazz Big Band-1977).

BASS, Alfie (Alfred Bass): Act. b. London, Apr 8, 1921. Thea inc: Those Were The Days; He Who Gets Slapped; Headlights; Finian's Rainbow; The Golden Door; The Gentle People; Trelawney of the Wells; Starched Aprons; The Bespoke Overcoat; The World of Sholem Aleichem; The Punch Revue; The Silver Whistle; Fiddler on the Roof.
   Films inc: Holiday Camp; It Always Rains on Sunday; Lavender Hill Mob; The Hasty Heart; The Bespoke Overcoat; A Kid for Two Farthings; A Tale of Two Cities; I Only Asked; The Millionairess; Alfie; The Fearless Vampire Killers; The Magnificent Seven Deadly Sins; Up the Junction; Moonraker.
   TV inc: Robin Hood; The Army Game; Bootsie and Snudge; Till Death Do Us Part.

BASS, Saul: Title Dsgn-Prod-Dir. b. NYC, May 8, 1920. e. Arts Students League. Films inc: (shorts) The Searching Eye; From Here to There; Why Man Creates; (titles): Carmen Jones; The Man With the Golden Arm; Around the World in Eighty Days; Vertigo; Bonjour Tristesse; North by Northwest; Psycho; A Walk on the Wild Side; It's a Mad, Mad, Mad, Mad World; Bunny Lake is Missing. Directorial debut, 1974, Phase IV.

BASSEY, Shirley: Singer. b. England, 1937. Nitery and concert performer, recording artist.

BATES, Alan: Act. b. Derbyshire, Eng, Feb 17, 1934. e. RADA. London Stage debut 1956 in The Mulberry Bush; Bway 1958 in Look Back in Anger. Thea inc: Hamlet; The Taming of the Shrew; The Seagull; Life Class; Butley (*Tony*-1973); Otherwise Engaged; Stage Struck.
   Films inc: The Entertainer; The Caretaker; Zorba the Greek; Georgy Girl; Three Sisters; Far From the Madding Crowd; The Fixer; Royal Flash; An Unmarried Woman; The Shout; The Rose; Nijinsky.
   TV inc: The Thug; A Memory of Two Mondays; The Square Ring; Look Back in Anger; A Hero for Our Time; The Mayor of Casterbridge.

BATES, Michael: Act. b. Jhansi, India, Dec 4, 1920. e. Cambridge. Films inc: I'm All Right Jack; Bedazzled; Here We Go Round the Mulberry Bush; Salt and Pepper; Don't Raise the Bridge, Lower the River; Hammerhead; Patton; The Rise and Rise of Michael Rimmer; A Clockwork Orange; No Sex Please, We're British.
   Thea inc: HMS Pinafore; The Birdwatcher; Forget-Me-Not Lane; Made in Heaven.
   TV inc: The Navy Lark; Last of the Summer Wine; It Ain't Half Hot, Mum.

BAUER, Jaime Lyn: Act. b. Phoenix, AZ, Mar 9, 1949. Former fashion model. TV inc: The Young and the Restless.

BAUGHN, David: Exec. b. LA, May 3, 1939. e. Santa Monica City College. P Scope III, Inc.; exec VP Intercontinental Releasing Corp; Films inc: Beyond Evil.

BAUM, Martin: Exec. b. NYC, Mar 2, 1924. Formed Baum & Newborn Thea Agency; sold agency to GAC; head of West Coast office, GAC; sr exec vp Creative Management Corp; left 1968 to become p ABC Pictures; returned to agency work and in 1973 became sr exec vp, Creative Management Corp.

BAUR, John F (Jack): Exec. b. 1915. Extra cast dir; 1937 asst cast dir MGM; after WW2 worked as cast dir for Enterprise Pictures, Samuel Goldwyn, U, Disney; 1968 cast dir Fox.
   (Died Aug 13, 1980).

BAVA, Mario: Dir. b. San Remo, Italy, 1914. Cin for almost 20 years.
   Films inc: (cin) Il Tacchino Prepotente; Uomini e Cieli; Cose da Pazzi; Terza Liceo; Mio Figlio Nerone; Il Diavolo Bianco; Esther and the King; The Giant of Marathon (& asst dir). (Dir): Black Sunday (& sp-cin); Hercules in the Center of the Earth (& sp-cin); Erik the Conqueror (& sp); La Ragazza che Sapeva Troppo; Black Sabbath (& sp); The Evil Eye (& sp-cin); Blood and Black Lace (& sp-cin); Planet of Blood; Dr Goldfoot and the Girl Bombs; Curse of the Dead (& sp); Five Dolls for An August Moon; The Antecedent; Quella Notte; Il Diavolo et il Morto.

BAXTER, Anne: Act. b. Michigan City, IN, May 7, 1923. e. Theodora Ervine School of Drama. Summer stock Cape Cod. Bway in Madam Carpet, 1938. Screen debut, Twenty Mule Team, 1940. Films inc: The Great Profile; Charley's Aunt; Magnificent Ambersons; The Razor's Edge (*Oscar*-supp-1946); All About Eve; The Spoilers; Cimarron; The Ten Commandments; The Late Liz; Jane Austen In Manhattan.
   Bway inc: Applause; Noel Coward in Two Keys.
   TV inc: The Moneychangers; Rex Stout's Nero Wolfe.

BAXTER, Les: Comp-Cond-Arr. b. Mexia, TX, Mar 14, 1922. Films inc: Hot Blood; The Black Sheep; Macabre; Goliath and the Barbarians; House of Usher; The Pit and the Pendulum; The Raven; The Comedy of Terrors; Muscle Beach Party; Dr. G and the Bikini Machine; Wild in the Streets; The Dunwich Horror; Cry of the Banshee; Frogs; Escape from Devil's Island; Born Again; Target - Harry.
   TV inc: Cond., choral dir., Bob Hope Show; Halls of Ivy. Arr. for Nat King Cole; Margaret Whiting.

BAXTER-BIRNEY, Meredith: Act. b. LA, Jun 21, 1947 Films inc: Ben; Bittersweet Love; All the President's Men.
   TV inc: The Interns; Bridget Loves Bernie; The Imposter; The Night That Panicked America; Target Risk; The Stranger Who Looks Like Me; Family; Little Women; The Family Man; Beulah Land.
   Bway inc: Guys and Dolls.

THE BAY CITY ROLLERS: Group. Originally formed in Scotland in 1967 as The Saxons; name changed 1969. Members are Stuart (Woody) Wood; Leslie McKeown, Alan Longmuir; Derek Longmuir; Eric Faulkner. Concerts, several world tours. TV inc: The Krofft Superstar Hour (hosts).

Albums inc: Bay City Rollers; Rock and Roll Love Letter; Dedication.

BAYNES, Andrea L: Exec. b. Sep 27, 1946. e. USC, BA. Started with NBC-TV; 1974 west coast mgr pgm dvlpt; 1977, vp Columbia Pictures-TV; 1979, sr vp; Sept. 1980, exec vp chg prodn Fox-TV.

THE BEACH BOYS: Group. Organized 1960. Members are Brian Wilson, Carl Wilson, Dennis Wilson, Al Jardine, Mike Love. Albums inc: Surfin' Safari; Surfin' USA; Surfer Girl; Little Deuce Coupe; Pet Sounds; All Summer Long; Beach Boys in Concert; Wild Honey; Sunflower; Surfs Up; Endless Summer; Good Vibrations; Spirit of America; Love You; Light Album.

BEAL, John (Alexander Bliedung): Act. b. Joplin, MO, Aug 13, 1909. e. U of PA. Bway inc: Another Language; She Loves Me Not; Petrified Forest. Screen debut, 1933, Another Language. Films inc: The Little Minister; Les Miserables; Laddie; The Man Who Found Himself; I Am the Law; The Cat and the Canary; The Great Commandment; Edge of Darkness; Alimony; My Six Convicts; Remains to be Seen; That Night; The Vampire; Ten Who Dared.

TV inc: The Legend of Lizzie Borden; Jennifer--A Woman's Story.

BEAN, Orson (Dallas Frederick Burroughs): Act. b. Burlington, VT, Jul 22, 1928. Performed in niteries. Bway inc: Men of Distinction; The School for Scandal; Almanac; Will Success Spoil Rock Hunter; Mr Roberts (rev); Nature's Way; Subways Are for Sleeping; Never Too Late; Warm Heart, Cold Feet; The Roar of the Grease Paint-The Smell of the Crowd; Ilya Darling.

Films inc: Lola; Skateboard.

TV inc: Return of the King (voice).

BEASLEY, Irene: Singer-Prod. b. 1903. In vaude, playing Keith Orpheum circuit, the Palace, entered radio 1927 WMC, Memphis; wrote, prod, dir many shows; singer on early network shows; created and prod game shows inc Raising a Husband, Grand Slam.

(Died Jan 7, 1980).

THE BEATLES: Group. British pop group whose unprecedented popularity in the early sixties sparked a musical revolution before they split up to go their separate ways. (See HARRISON, George; LENNON, John; McCARTNEY, Paul; STARR, Ringo).

Films inc: A Hard Day's Night; Help!; Yellow Submarine; Let It Be (*Oscar*-Song Score-1970).

(*Grammys*-(4)-vocal Group and new artist-1964; Album of Year and Contemporary Album-1967).

BEATON, Alex: Prod-Dir. TV inc: Centennial; The Duke; The Night Rider (Exec prod); Stone (supv prod); 10 Speed and Brownshoe (prod); Nightside (prod).

BEATON, Cecil: Dsgn-Photographer. b. London, Jan 14, 1904. e. Cambridge U. Debut as stage designer 1935 Follow The Sun. Bway inc: Quadrille (*Tony*-1955); My Fair Lady (*Tony*-1957); Saratoga (*Tony*-1960); Coco (*Tony*-1970).

Films inc: Gigi (*Oscar*-cost-1958); My Fair Lady (*Oscar*-cost-1964); The Doctor's Dilemma.

(Died Jan 17, 1980).

BEATTS, Anne: Wri. TV inc: Saturday Night Live (*Emmys*-wri-1976, 1980).

BEATTY, Ned: Act. b. Lexington, KY, Jul 6, 1937. Films inc: Deliverance; The Thief Who Came to Dinner; White Lightning; W W and the Dixie Dancekings; Nashville; All the President's Men; Silver Streak; Mickey and Nicky; Network; Exorcist II-The Heretic; Shenanigans; Gray Lady Down; Superman; Promises in the Dark; The America Success Company; Wise Blood; 1941; Hopscotch; Superman II.

TV inc: The Execution of Private Slovik; Attack on Terror; The Marcus-Nelson Murders; A Question of Love; Friendly Fire; Guyana Tragedy-The Story of Jim Jones; All God's Children.

BEATTY, Roger: Wri-Dir. b. LA, Jan 24, 1933. TV inc: The Carol Burnett Show (*Emmy*-wri-1972, 1973, 1974, 1975, 1978); I Do, I Don't; Tim Conway Show; Dolly and Carol in Nashville; The Grass is Always Greener Over the Septic Tank; Carol Burnett and Co.

Films inc: Billion Dollar Hobo (wri).

BEATTY, Warren: Act. b. Richmond, VA, Mar 30, 1938. e. Northwestern U. B of Shirley Mac Laine. Films inc: Splendor in the Grass; Roman Spring of Mrs. Stone; Lilith; Promise Her Anything; Bonnie and Clyde (& prod); The Only Game in Town; Shampoo (& prod-wri); The Fortune; Heaven Can Wait (& prod-dir-wri).

Bway inc: A Loss of Roses.

BEAUDINE, William Jr: Prod-Dir. b. Hollywood, Apr 28, 1921. e. USC, BS. TV inc: Prod Lassie, 1968-72; Prod-Dir two shows for Disney's Wonderful World of Color, 1973; (Assoc Prod), Sandburg's Lincoln; Roots. Prod TV pilot Lasie, the New Beginning; Escape.

Film inc: The Magic of Lassie (prod).

BECK, John: Act. b. Chicago, Jan 28. Films inc: Three in the Attic; The Unexpected Mrs Pollifax; The Lawman; Deadly Honeymoon; The Paper Back Hero; Pat Garrett and Billy the Kid; Sleepers; Only God Knows; Rollerball; Sky Riders; The Big Bus; Call of the Wild; Audrey Rose; Nightmare Honeymoon; The Other Side of Midnight.

TV inc: Nichols; Nourish the Beast; Greatest Heroes of the Bible; The Buffalo Soldiers; Flamingo Road; The Great American Traffic Jam.

BECK, Michael: Act. b. Memphis, TN, Feb 4, 1949. Films inc: The Warrior; Xanadu.

TV inc: Holocaust; Mayflower--the Pilgrims' Adventure; Alcatraz--The Whole Shocking Story.

BECKER, Ivan Lawrence: Wri-Prod. b. Harrison Co, NE, Aug 13, 1911. e. Columbia U. Plays inc: Etched in Granite; The King's Darling; Ruby; The Vapor Trail; This Kiss for this Kingdom; After the Rocks, the Martini.

BECKETT, Samuel: Plywri. b. Dublin, Apr 13, 1906. e. Trinity College. Plays inc: Waiting for Godot; Endgame; Krapp's Last Tape; Happy Days; and one-acters The Old Tune; That Time; Footfalls. (Awarded Nobel Prize Literature 1969).

BEDELIA, Bonnie: Act. b. 1946. Films inc: The Gypsy Moths; They Shoot Horses Don't They?; Lovers and Other Strangers; The Strange Vengeance of Rosalie; The Big Fix.

TV inc: Hawkins on Murder; A Question of Love; Salem's Lot; Fighting Back.

BEE GEES: Group. Group consisting of the Gibb Brothers, Andy, Barry, Robin and Maurice. Albums inc: Children of the World; Here At Last--Bee Gees Live; Main Course; Saturday Night Fever; Spirits Having Flown; Too Much Heaven; Tragedy; Bee Gees Greatest.

(*Grammys*-(6)-group vocal-1977; Album of the year (2 awards, one as artists one as prods), group vocal, arr for voices, prod of year-1978).

BEE, Molly: Act-Singer. b. Oklahoma City, OK, Aug 18, 1939. TV inc: Hometown Jamboree; Swingin' Country. Appearances in niteries, fairs, club circuit. Records inc: I Saw Mommy Kissing Santa Claus.

BEERY, Noah Jr: Act. b. NYC, Aug 10, 1916. Travelled with parents in stock company. Appeared as child in Mark of Zorro, 1920. Films inc: Father and Son; Only Angels Have Wings; Two Flags West; Cimarron Kid; Wagons West; Story of Will Rogers; Jubal; Fastest Gun Alive; Walking Tall; The Spikes Gang; The Asphalt Cowboy.

TV inc: Rockford Files; Revenge of the Red Chief; The Bastard; The Great American Traffic Jam.

BEGELMAN, David: Exec. b. NYC, 1922. Started as agent with MCA 1949; resigned as vp - special projects 1960 to form agency with Freddie Fields; firm acquired General Artists Agency 1968, merger resulting in formation of Creative Management Associates, of which he was vice-chmn; resigned 1973 to become pres Columbia Pictures; in 1977 took added duties as pres tv divison; forced to leave Columbia 1978 following charges of fiscal irregularities; re-united with Fields in Begelman-Fields prodn co, releasing through Columbia; named P-CEO MGM Film Div Jan 1980; prod doc short Angel Dust as part of legal arrangement leading to probation on charges growing out of Columbia resignation. Films inc: (exec prod) Wholly Moses.

BEICH, Albert: Wri. b. Bloomington, IL, Jun 25, 1919. e. McGill U. Wrote for radio. Films inc: Girls in Chains; The Perils of Pauline; The Bride Goes Wild; Key to the City; The Lieutenant Wore Skirts; Dead Ringer.

BELAFONTE, Harry: Act-Singer. b. NYC, Mar 1, 1927. Started professionally as singer in NY clubs. Films inc: Bright Road; Carmen Jones; Uptown Saturday Night; Island in the Sun; Odds Against Tomorrow; The World, The Flesh & The Devil; The Angel Levine; Buck and the Preacher; Uptown Saturday Night (& prod).

TV: Tonight With Belafonte (*Emmy*-1960); The Strollin' Twenties; A Time For Laughter.

Bway inc: Three For Tonight; John Murray Anderson's Almanac (*Tony*-supp-1954); A Night with Belafonte.

(*Grammys*-(3)-Folk perf-1960; Folk recording-1961, 1965).

BELASCO, Leon (Leonid Simeonovich Berladsky): Act. b. Odessa, Russia, Oct 11, 1902. e. St. Josephs Coll, Yokohama, Japan. Began as violinist, orch. leader. Performed in niteries, hotels; in 1936, added the Andrews Sisters to orchestra in Kansas City. On screen from 1939 in Topper Takes a Trip. Films inc: Broadway Serenade; Comrade X; Design for Scandal; Road to Morocco; Over My Dead Body; Holiday Inn; Yankee Doodle Dandy; Earl Carroll Vanities; Suspense; Bagdad; Ma and Pa Kettle Go to Town; Abbott & Costello in the Foreign Legion; Son of Ali Baba; Call Me Madam; Geraldine; Jalopy; Art of Love; The Woman of the Year.

BELFER, Hal B: Chor-Dir. b. LA, Feb 16. Head of dance department U, 20th Century Fox, 1949-54. Dir of entertainment Riviera Hotel, Flamingo Hotel, Las Vegas, 1955-mid-60s. Exec prod Premore Prodns since 1970.

BELFORD, Christine: Act. b. Amityville, NY, Jan 14, 1949. TV inc: Vanished; Ironside; World Premier; Banacek; Cool Million; High Midnight; Kenny Rogers as the Gambler; Desperate Voyage.

Films inc: Pocket Money; The Groundstar Conspiracy.

BEL GEDDES, Barbara: Act. b. NYC, Oct 31, 1922. NY stage debut 1941, Out of the Frying Pan. Films inc: The Gangster; The Long Night; I Remember Mama; Blood on the Moon; Caught; Panic in the Streets; Fourteen Hours; Vertigo; The Five Pennies; Five Branded Women; By Love Possessed; The Todd Killings; Summertree.

Bway inc: The Moon Is Blue; The Living Room; Cat on a Hot Tin Roof; Silent Night, Lonely Night; Mary, Mary; LUV; Finishing Touches; Ah, Wilderness.

TV inc: Dallas (*Emmy*-1980).

BELL, Steve: TV newsman. b. Oskaloosa, IA, Dec 9, 1935. e. Central College, Pella IA, BA; Northwestern U, MSJ. Started 1955 as anncr KBOE, Oskaloosa; 1959, reporter WOI-TV, Ames, IA; 1960, wri WGN-TV Chicago; 1962, anchor WOW-TV, Omaha; 1965, anchor WNEW (radio), NYC; 1967 corr ABC; 1970, combat corr Vietnam; 1972 ABC Bureau chief Hong Kong; 1974 White House Corr; 1975, anchor news segs Good Morning America. TV doc inc: The People of People's China.

BELLAMY, Earl: Prod-Dir. b. Minneapolis, MI, Mar 13, 1917. e. LA City Coll. Films inc: Fluffy; Gunpoint; Incident at Phantom Hill; Seven Alone; Part Two Walking Tall; Sidewinder; Speedtrap (dir).

TV inc: Bachelor Father; Wells Fargo; Lone Ranger; Rawhide; The Donna Reed Show; Andy Griffith Show; Wagon Train; Laramie; Laredo; I Spy; Mod Squad; Medical Center; Fantasy Island; Castaways on Gilligan's Island; Valentine Magic on Love Island (dir).

BELLAMY, Madge (Margaret Derden Philpott): Act. b. Hillsboro, TX, Jun 30, 1902. Silent screen star. Films inc: The Riddle Woman; Hail the Woman; Lorna Doone; The Hottentot; Love's Whirlpool; Love and Glory; The Iron Horse; The Parasite; Lightnin'; Summer Bachelors; Bertha, the Sewing Machine Girl; The Telephone Girl; Silk Legs; The Play Girl; White Zombie; Charlie Chan in London; the Daring Young Man; Northwest Mounted.

Bway inc: The Love Mill; Dear Brutus; Pollyanna; Peg O'My Heart; Intermission; Holiday Lady; See My Lawyer.

BELLAMY, Ralph: Act. b. Chicago, Jun 17, 1905. In stock, repertory, 1922-30. Films inc: Secret Six; The Awful Truth; Forbidden Company; Flying Devils; Spitfire; Hands Across the Table; The Man Who Lived Twice; The Court-Martial of Billy Mitchell; Sunrise at Campobello; Rosemary's Baby; Cancel My Reservation; Oh, God!

Bway inc: Town Boy; Roadside; Tomorrow the World; State of the Union; Detective Story; Sunrise at Campobello (*Tony*-supp-1958).

TV inc: The Eleventh Hour; The Survivors; The Immortal; The Most Deadly Game; The Clone Master; The Millionaire; The Billion Dollar Threat; Power; The Memory of Eva Ryker.

BELLAVER, Harry: Act. b. Feb 12, 1905. Films inc: Another Thin Man; The House on 92d St; No Way Out; The Lemon Drop Kid; From Here to Eternity; Miss Sadie Thompson; Love Me or Leave Me; Slaughter on Tenth Avenue; The Birds and the Bees; The Old Man and The Sea; One Potato, Two Potato; Madigan; Blue Collar; Hero at Large.

TV inc: Naked City; Murder in Music City.

BELLE, Barbara (nee Einhorn): Sngwri. b. NYC, Nov 22, 1922. e. NYU. Wrote special material for Louis Armstrong; Louis Prima; pers mgr for Jose Ferrer; Penny Singleton; Keely Smith. Songs inc: A Sunday Kind of Love; You Broke the Only Heart That Ever Loved You; Early Autumn.

BELLER, Kathleen: Act. b. Westchester, NY, 1955. TV inc: Search for Tomorrow; Something for Joey; Mary White; Are You in the House Alone?; Mother and Daughter--The Loving War.

Films inc: The Godfather, Part II; The Betsy; Promises in the Dark.

BELLOCCHIO, Marco: Dir. b. Italy, 1940. Films inc: Fists in the Pocket; China Is Near; Leap Into the Void (& wri); Vacations in Val Trebbia (& wri).

BELLSON, Louis: Drummer. b. Rock Falls, IL, Jul 6, 1924. e. Augustana College. H of Pearl Bailey. With Ted Fio Rito orch 1942; Benny Goodman, 1943-44; Tommy Dorsey 1947-1950; Duke Ellington, 1951-54; Jazz At Philharmonic; formed own orch; backs Pearl Bailey in nitery, concert dates.

BELLWOOD, Pamela: Act. b. NYC, Jun 26. Films inc: Two Minute Warning; Airport '77; Serial; Hangar 18.

TV inc: The War Widow; Emily, Emily; W.E.B.; The Girl Who Saved Our America.

Bway inc: Butterflies are Free; Finishing Touches; Philadelphia, Here I Come; The Tenth Man; The Effect of Gamma Rays on Man-in-the-Moon Marigolds.

BELMONDO, Jean-Paul: Act. b. Neuilly-sur-Seine, France, Apr 9, 1933. e. Conservatoire d'Art Dramatique. Films inc: A Double Tour; A Bout de Souffle; Moderato Cantabile; La Viaccia; Two Women; Cartouche; Un Singe en Hiver; That Man from Rio; Weekend in Dunkirk; Is Paris Burning?; The Brain; Ho!; The Mississippi Mermaid; A Man I Like; Borsalino; Scoundrel; Le Magnifique; Stavisky; L'Incorrigible; Le Corps de Mon Ennemi; Flic ou Voyou; Le Guignolo.

Thea inc: Caesar and Cleopatra; Treasure Party.

BELUSHI, John: Wri-Act. b. Chicago, Jan 24, 1949. Performs and records with Dan Aykroyd as the Blues Brothers. Albums inc: Briefcase Full of Blues. Films inc: Goin' South; National Lampoon's Animal House; Old Boyfriends; 1941; The Blues Brothers.

TV inc: Saturday Night Live (*Emmy*-wri-1977); The Beach Boys; All You Need Is Cash.

BENCHLEY, Peter: Wri. b. NYC, May 8, 1940. e. Harvard, BA. S of Nathaniel Benchley, Grandson Robert Benchley. Films inc: Jaws; The Deep; The Island.

TV inc: Sharks (narr).

BENEDEK, Laslo: Dir. b. Budapest, Mar 5, 1907. e. U of Vienna. Films inc: The Kissing Bandit; Port of New York; Storm Over the Tiber; Death of a Salesman; The Wild One; Affair in Havana; Moment of Danger; Namu the Killer Whale (& prod.); The Daring Game; The Night Visitor.

TV inc: Dupont Theatre; Loretta Young Show; Perry Mason; Naked City; Untouchables; Outer Limits; etc.

Thea inc: Belial; Twelfth Night.

BENEDICT, Dirk (nee Niewoehner): Act. b. Helena, MT, Mar 1. e. Whitman Coll, BFA. Started in repertory. Films inc: Georgia, Georgia; Sssssss; Battlestar Galactica; Scavenger Hunt.

Thea inc: Abelard and Heloise; Butterflies Are Free.

TV inc: Chopper One; Battlestar Galactica; Georgia Peaches.

BENEDICT, Nick: Act. b. LA, Jul 14. TV inc: Medical Center; Emergency; All My Children.

Thea inc: Of Mice and Men; Hello Out There; The Glass Menagerie; Lovers and Other Strangers.

BENEDICT, Paul: Act. b. Silver City, NM, Sep 17, 1938. Started with Boston's Image Theatre; Theatre Company of Boston. Bway inc: Little Murders; The White House Murder Case; Bad Habits.

Films inc: Taking Off; Up the Sandbox; Jeremiah Johnson; The Front Page; The Goodbye Girl.

TV inc: Sesame Street; The Jeffersons.

BENENSON, Bill: Prod. e. Hobart Coll; Ecole Nationale de Beaux Arts, Paris; Columbia. Films inc: (doc) Easter Island Raises; The Marginal Way; Diamond Rivers. (Fea) Boulevard Nights.

BENJAMIN, Richard: Act. b. NYC, May 22, 1939. e. Northwestern U. Thea: toured in Tchin Tchin; A Thousand Clowns; Barefoot in the Park; The Odd Couple. Bway debut, The Star Spangled Girl. Directed London prodn Barefoot in the Park.

Films inc: Thunder Over the Plains; Crime Wave; Diary of a Mad Housewife; Catch 22; Goodbye, Columbus; Westworld; Sunshine Boys; House Calls; Love at First Bite; Scavenger Hunt; The Last Married Couple in America; How To Beat The High Cost Of Living; First Family.

TV inc: He and She; Fame; Quark.

BENJAMIN, Robert S: Exec. b. NYC, May 14, 1909. e. CCNY, BA, Fordham U, JD Sr member of NY law firm of Phillips, Nizer, Benjamin & Krim. Pres J Arthur Rank, Inc, 1946-67; chmn UA, 1951-69; formed Orion Pictures with other former UA execs Feb 6, 1978. Posthumous Jean Hersholt Award 1980.

(Died Oct 22, 1979).

BENNENT, Heinz: Act. b. Aachen, Germany, Jul 23, 1921. Films inc: Katharina Blum; Wild Ducks; The Net; NEA; Ich Will Leben; Special Section; Femme Fatale; Rendezvous; Serpent's Egg; Hitler's Son; The Tin Drum; Lulu; From the Life of the Marionettes; Clair de Femme; The Last Metro.

BENNET, Spencer G: Dir. b. NYC, Jan 5, 1893. Started as stunt man, then dir from 1925-64. Films inc: numerous serials; Submarines Seahawk; Atomic Submarine; Bounty Killer; Requiem for a Gunfighter.

BENNETT, Alan: Act-Wri. b. Leeds, England, May 9, 1934. e. Oxford. Thea inc: (London) Beyond the Fringe (& co-wri); Blood of the Bambergs; A Cuckoo in the Nest; Forty Years On (& wri); Getting On (wri); Habeas Corpus (& wri); The Old Country (wri).

(Bway): Beyond the Fringe. (Special Tony 1963); Enjoy (wri).

TV inc: A Day Out; Sunset Across the Bay; On the Margin (& wri).

BENNETT, Bruce (Herman Brix): Act. b. Tacoma, WA, 1909. e. U of WA. Films inc: Student Tour; The New Adventures of Tarzan; Before I Hang; Atlantic Convoy; The More the Merrier; Sahara; Mildred Pierce; The Treasure of Sierra Madre; Task Force; Without Honor; Sudden Fear; Dream Wife; Strategic Air Commmand; Three Violent People; The Outsider.

BENNETT, Charles: Wri. b. Shoreham, Eng, 1899. Films inc: Blackmail; The Man Who Knew Too Much; The Thirty-nine Steps; Secret Agent; Sabotage; King Solomon's Mines; Balalaika; Foreign Correspondent; Reap the Wild Wind; The Story of Dr. Wassell; Ivy; Madness of the Heart (& dir); Black Magic; Where Danger Lives; No Escape (& dir.); The Story of Mankind; The Lost World; Five Weeks in a Balloon; War Gods of the Deep.

Plays inc: Blackmail; The Last Hour; Sensation; The Danger Line; Page from a Diary; After Midnight.

TV inc: Cavalcade of America; The Christophers.

BENNETT, Harve (nee Fischman): Prod. b. Chicago, IL, Aug 17, 1930. e. UCLA. Member Quiz Kids radio show as child; special events prod CBS-TV; vp pgms ABC-TV; 1977-1980 partnered with Harris Katleman.

TV inc: Mod Squad (& wri); Six Million Dollar Man; Bionic Woman; Rich Man, Poor Man; The Gemini Man; American Girls; Salvage; From Here To Eternity; Legend of the Golden Gun; From Here to Eternity--The War Years; Alex and the Doberman Gang; Nick and the Dobermans.

BENNETT, Hywel: Act. b. South Wales, Apr 8, 1944. e. RADA. Thea inc: In repertory, appeared with Young Vic; Dear Wormwood; A Smashing Day; Henry IV; Bakke's Night of Fame; The Birthday Party; Night Must Fall; Look Back in Anger; Toad of Toad Hall; I Must Have Been Here Before; Rosencrantz and Guildenstern are Dead; A Man For All Seasons; The Case of the Oily Levantine.

TV inc: Romeo and Juliet; The Idiot; Three's One; Tinker, Tailor, Soldier, Spy.

Films inc: The Virgin Soldiers; Loot; Alice in Wonderland.

BENNETT, Jill: Act. b. Penang, Federated Malay States, Dec 24, 1931. Thea inc: Captain Cavallo; Antony and Cleopatra; Caesar and Cleopatra; The Seagull; The Seagull; The Bald Prima Donna; Dinner with the Family; Castle in Sweden; Time Present; Hedda Gabler; The End of Me Old Cigar; Loot; Watch It Come Down.

Films inc: Moulin Rouge; Hell Below Zero; The Criminal; Lust for Life; The Skull; The Nanny; The Charge of the Light Brigade; Inadmissible Evidence; I Want What I Want; Quilp; Full Circle.

TV inc: The Heiress; Trilby; Jealousy; The Three Sisters; Intent Is Murder; Almost a Vision; Hello Lola.

BENNETT, Joan: Act. b. Palisades, NJ, Feb 27, 1910. On stage with father, Richard Bennett. Screen debut in Bulldog Drummond, 1929. Films inc: Three Live Ghosts; Disraeli; Moby Dick; Reckless Moment; Little Women; Woman in the Window; Father of the Bride; Father's Little Dividend; There's Always Tomorrow; Navy Wife; Desire in the Dust; Suspiria.

TV inc: Dark Shadows; Suddenly Love.

BENNETT, Julie: Act. b. Beverly Hills, CA, Jan 24, 1943. Films inc: Hey There, It's Yogi Bear; What's Up, Tiger Lily; On a Clear Day You Can See Forever; Westworld.

BENNETT, Meg: Act. b. LA, Oct 4. e. Northwestern U, BA. Bway inc: Grease. TV inc: Search for Tomorrow; After Hours; Camera Three; The Young and the Restless.

BENNETT, Michael: (nee diFiglia): Dir-Chor. b. Buffalo, NY, 1943. Bway: (Chor) A Joyful Noise; Henry, Sweet Henry; Promises, Promises (& dir); Coco (& dir); (Company (& co-dir); Follies (& co-dir) *(2 Tonys-*dir, chor-1972); Twigs (dir); God's Favorite (dir); Seesaw (& dir) *(Tony*-chor-1974); A Chorus Line (& conceived-dir) (Pulitzer Prize; 2 Tonys-dir-chor-1976); Ballroom *(Tony*-chor-1979).

BENNETT, Richard Charles: Dir. b. Milwaukee, WI, Apr 24, 1923. e. UCLA. TV inc: Girl from UNCLE; The Bold Ones; Alias Smith & Jones; Insight; Toma; Barnaby Jones; Emergency; Lucas Tanner; Apples Way; Waltons; Gibbsville; This Is the Life.
Films inc: Harper Valley PTA.

BENNETT, Richard Rodney: Comp. b. Eng, 1936. Films inc: Interpol; Indiscreet; Only Two Can Play; One Way Pendulum; The Nanny; Far from the Madding Crowd; Nicholas and Alexandra; Murder on the Orient Express; The Brinks Job; Equus; Permission To Kill; Yanks.

BENNETT, Robert Russell: Comp-Cond. b. Kansas City, MO, Jun 15, 1894. e. Studied with Carl Busch, Nadia Boulanger. Started as thea violinist, became arr for Bway shows inc: Rose Marie; Sunny; The Band Wagon; Of Thee I Sing; The Cat and the Fiddle; Face the Music; Showboat; Oklahoma!; Carousel; Kiss Me Kate; South Pacific; The King and I; The Sound of Music; My Fair Lady; Bells Are Ringing; On a Clear Day You Can See Forever.
(Special Tony-1957).
Films inc: Oklahoma! *(Oscar*-1955).
TV inc: Victory at Sea; Project 20; He is Risen *(Emmy*-score-1963).

BENNETT, Tony: (nee Benedetto): Singer. b. NYC, Aug 3, 1926. Recording artist, niteries. *(Grammys*-(2)-solo vocal & record of year-1962). TV inc: King.

BENNINGTON, William A (Bill): TV inc: Hawaii Calls; 19th Summer Olympics *(Emmy*-1969); Wide World of Sports; Macy Thanksgiving Day Parade; NCAA Football; Tournament of Roses Parade; The Pet Set.

BENSON, George: Singer-Guitarist. b. Pittsburgh, PA, Mar 22, 1943. Recordings inc: This Masquerade; Body Talk; White Rabbit. Albums inc: Breezin'; In Flight; Weekend In LA; Give Me the Night.
(Grammys-(5)-Record of Year-1976; Pop inst-1976; R&B inst-1976; R&B vocal-1978; inst arr-1979).

BENSON, Hugh: Prod. b. NYC, Sep 7, 1917. During WW II was master sergeant in charge of Special Service units under Joshua Logan. Asst to prods of Ed Sullivan Show 1947. Joined WB 1955 as head of radio-TV promotion. In 1956 exec. asst. to William T. Orr, Warner Production VP; Exec. prod. Screen Gems; prod. MGM.
TV inc: Contract on Cherry Street; A Fire in the Sky; The Child Stealer; Goldie and the Boxer; Confessions of a Lady Cop; The Dream Merchants.
Films inc: Nightmare Honeymoon.

BENSON, Lucille: Act. b. AL, Jul 17, 1922. Films inc: Little Fauss and Big Halsey; Slaughterhouse Five; Mame; Tom Sawyer; Huck Finn; The Greatest; Silver Streak.
TV inc: Women in Chains; Duel; Petrocelli; Murder in Music City.

BENSON, Ray (nee Seifert): Mus-Act. b. Philadelphia, PA, Mar 16, 1951. Founder of group Asleep at the Wheel, 1970. Leader, lead singer of band. *(Grammy*-country instrumental-1978).

BENSON, Robby (nee Segal): Act. b. Dallas, Jan 21, 1955. Appeared Bway at age of 5, The King and I. Films inc: Ode to Billy Joe; Jeremy; Joey; The Godfather Part II; Lucky Lady; One On One (& wri); The End; Ice Castles; Walk Proud (& comp); Die Laughing (& prod-wri-comp); Tribute.
TV inc: Death Be Not Proud; Search For Tomorrow; All the Kind Strangers; Virginia Hill; Remember When; The Death of Richie.

BENTON, Barbi: Act-Sing. b. Sacramento, CA, Jan 28, 1950. e. UCLA. TV inc: Laugh-In; Playboy After Dark (host); Hee Haw; Love on the Run; The Great American Beauty Pageant; Murder at the Mardi Gras; Sugartime; A Barbi Doll for Christmas; A Country Christmas; For the Love of It.

BENTON, Doug: Prod. b. Hollis, OK, Sep 24, 1925. e. Northwestern U. TV inc: Thriller; Wide Country; Dr Kildare; The Girl from UNCLE; Cimmaron Strip; Name of the Game; Columbo *(Emmy*-1974); Ironside; Hec Ramsey; The Rookies; Police Woman; A Last Cry for Help; Transplant; Undercover with the KKK; Skag; Gauguin the Savage.

BENTON, Robert: Wri-Dir. b. Waxahachie, TX, 1933. e. U of TX, BA. Films inc: Bonnie and Clyde; There Was A Crooked Man; What's Up Doc?; Bad Company (& dir); The Late Show (& dir); Superman; Money's Tight; Kramer vs Kramer (& dir) *(Oscars*-dir-wri-1979).
Bway inc: It's a Bird. . . It's a Plane. . . It's Superman (libretto); Oh, Calcutta (one sketch).

BERADINO, John: Act. b. LA, May 1, 1917. Former pro baseball player. TV inc: The New Breed; I Led Three Lives; Do Not Fold, Spindle or Mutilate; Moon of the Wolf; General Hospital.

BERCOVICI, Eric: Wri-Prod. b. NYC, Feb 27, 1933. e. St John's Coll, Yale Drama School. Films inc: The Culpepper Cattle Company; Hell in the Pacific.
TV inc: Police Story; Strange Homecoming; Washington Behind Closed Doors; Flesh and Blood; The Top of the Hill; Shogun.

BERCOVICI, Leonardo: Wri. b. NYC, Jan 4. Films inc: Puccini; Under Ten Flags; The Bishop's Wife; The Lost Moment; The Unafraid; Kiss the Blood Off My Hands; Portrait of Jennie; Dark City; Monsoon; Square of Violence (& prod-dir); Story of a Woman (& prod-dir).

BERCOVITCH, Reuben: Wri-Prod. Films inc: Hell in the Pacific; What's Up, Tiger Lilly? (prod only); Out of Season.
TV inc: (wri) Bonanza; Virginian; Bold Ones; Richard Boone Theatre.

BERENGER, Tom: Act. b. May 31, 1950. Films inc: Looking for Mr. Goodbar; The Sentinel; Butch and Sundance--The Early Days; In Praise of Older Women; The Dogs of War.
TV inc: Flesh and Blood.

BERENSON, Marisa: Act. b. Feb 15, 1947. Fashion model. Films inc: Death in Venice; Cabaret; Barry Lyndon; Killer Fish.
TV inc: Tourist; Playing For Time.

BERESFORD, Bruce: Dir. b. Australia, 1940. Films inc: The Adventures of Barry McKenzie; The Getting of Wisdom; Don's Party; Breaker Morant; The Club.

BERG, Dick: Exec Prod. TV inc: Are You in the House Alone; The Word; The Martian Chronicles; A Rumor of War; Rape and Marriage--The Rideout Case.

BERGEN, Candice: Act. b. Beverly Hills, May 9, 1946. e. U of PA. D the late Edgar Bergen. Model, freelance photographer. Films inc: The Group; The Sand Pebbles; The Day The Fish Came Out; Carnal Knowledge; T.R. Baskin; 11 Harrowhouse; The Wind And The Lion; The Domino Principle; The End of the World in Our Usual Bed in a Night Full of Rain; Oliver's Story; Starting Over.

BERGEN, Polly: Singer-Act. b. Knoxville, TN, Jul 4, 1930. Started on radio at age 14; in light opera, summer stock, niteries. Films inc: At War with the Army; That's My Boy; Warpath; The Stooge; Escape from Fort Bravo; Cape Fear; Move Over Darling; Kisses for My President; A Guide for the Married Man.
TV inc: Belle Sommers; The Life of Helen Morgan *(Emmy*-1957); Death Cruise.

BERGER, Helmut: Act. b. Salzburg, Aus, circa 1942. e. Feldkirk Coll & U of Perugia. Films inc: The Damned; Un Beau Monstre; The Garden of the Finzi, Continis; Dorian Gray; Ash Wednesday; Ludwig; Conversation Piece; The Romantic Englishwoman; Madam Kitty; The Roses of Danzig; Heroin.

BERGER, Richard L: Exec. b. Oct 25, 1939. e. UCLA, BA. Joined 20th Century-Fox in 1966; vp in charge of programs, 1972; asst vp, Feature Films Prodn, 1975-76; vp dramatic development, CBS, 1976-78; Retd to Fox 1978 vp, World Wide Prodn.

BERGER, Robert: Prod. TV inc: Holocaust *(Emmy-*1978); Hollow Image; Doctor Franken; Death Penalty; FDR-The Last Year; The Henderson Monster; King Crab.

BERGER, Senta: Act. b. Austria, May 13, 1941. Films inc: The Secret Ways; The Good Soldier Schweik; The Victors; Major Dundee; The Glory Guys; Cast a Giant Shadow; The Quiller Memorandum; Our Man in Marrakesh; The Ambushers; Treasure of San Gennaro; De Sade; Percy; The Swiss Conspiracy; Cross of Iron; Killing Me Softly; The Chinese Miracle; Goodnight Ladies and Gentlemen; Nest of Vipers; La Giacla Berger.

BERGERAC, Jacques: Act. b. Biarritz, France, 1927. Films inc: Les Girls; Gigi; Thunder in the Sun; The Hypnotic Eye; Taffy and the Jungle Hunter; The Emergency Operation; Lady Chaplin; The Last Party; One Plus One.

BERGHOF, Herbert: Act-Dir. b. Vienna, Sep 13, 1909. Stage debut Vienna, 1927. Appeared in more than 120 plays during the next 12 years. In 1939 to Bway to dir From Vienna; appeared in Reunion in New York; The Innocent Voyage; Jacobowski and the Colonel; The Man Who Had All the Luck; The Key and Rip Van Winkle (dir); Waiting for Godot (dir); The Infernal Machine (dir); The Queen and the Rebels (dir); The Andersonville Trial; Do You Know the Milky Way (dir); In the Matter of J Robert Openheimer; The Unknown Soldier; Marius; The Doctor's Dilemma; The Sponsor (dir); Poor Murderer (dir); Charlotte (dir).

Films inc: Five Fingers; Red Planet Mars; Cleopatra; Voices; Those Lips, Those Eyes; Times Square.

BERGMAN, Alan: Lyr. b. NYC, Sep 11, 1925. e. U of NC, BA, UCLA. Films inc: In the Heat of the Night; The Thomas Crown Affair *(Oscar*-song, The Windmills of Your Mind-1968); Happy Ending; Gaily, Gaily; Pieces of Dreams; Sometimes A Great Notion; The Way We Were *(Oscar*-title song-1974); A Star Is Born; John and Mary; Life and Times of Judge Roy Bean; The One and Only; Same Time Next Year; And Justice For All; The Promise; A Change of Seasons.

TV inc: Queen of the Stardust Ballroom *(Emmy*-1975); Sybil *(Emmy*-1977); themes for: Maude; Good Times; Alice; Nancy Walker Show; Sandy Duncan Show.

Bway inc: Something More.

Chief Collaborators: Marilyn Bergman (wife); Lew Spence; Norman Luboff; Paul Weston; Sammy Fain; Alex North. Songs inc: Yellow Bird; Nice 'n' Easy; Cheatin' Billy; Outta My Mind; Sentimental Baby; Pieces of Dreams; All His Children; The Last Time I Felt Like This; Sleep Warm.

(Grammys-(2)-film score & song of the year-1974).

BERGMAN, Ingmar: Wri-Dir. b. Uppsala, Sweden, Jul 14, 1918. e. Stockholm U. Directed University plays. First theatrical success as director, Macbeth, 1940. Wri-Dir Svensk Film-Industri, 1942. First screenplay, Frenzy, 1943. First directorial assignment, Crisis, 1946.

Films inc: Night Is My Future; Port of Call; The Devil's Wanton; Three Strange Loves; Wild Strawberries; Brink of Life; The Magician; The Virgin Spring; Through a Glass Darkly; Shame; Face to Face; The Serpent's Egg; Autumn Sonata; Summer Paradise (Prod); From The Life of the Marionettes (dir-wri); Faro Document.

Irving Thalberg Award 1969.

TV inc: The Magic Flute.

BERGMAN, Ingrid: Act. b. Stockholm, Sweden, Aug 24, 1915. e. Royal Dramatic Theatre School. Screen debut, Intermezzo, 1939. Films inc: Adam Had Four Sons; Rage in Heaven; Dr. Jekyll and Mr. Hyde; For Whom The Bells Toll; Notorious; Saratoga Trunk; Spellbound; Gaslight *(Oscar*-1944); Joan of Arc; Anastasia *(Oscar*-1956); Indiscreet; The Inn of the Sixth Happiness; Cactus Flower; Murder on the Orient Express *(Oscar*-supp-1974); A Matter of Time; Autumn Sonata.

Bway inc: Joan of Lorraine *(Tony*-1947); Captain Brassbound's Conversion; More Stately Mansions; Constant Wife. London Thea inc: Waters of the Moon.

TV inc: The Turn of the Screw *(Emmy*-1960); 24 Hours in the Life of A Woman.

BERGMAN, Jules: TV News. b. NYC, Mar 21, 1929. e. CCNY, Columbia. Started 1947 on news desk, CBS; 1948 to Time Mag; 1950 asst news dir WFDR; 1951 prod-wri ABC news; 1955 science wri; 1959 science edtr; covered space program for ABC.

TV inc: Closeup on Fire *(Emmy*-narr-1973); Closeup on Oil--The Policy Crisis; Closeup on the Danger in Sports--Paying the Price; Closeup on Crashes--The Illusion of Safety; Union in Space; Closeup on Automobiles; Closeup--the Weekend Athlete; Asbestos--the Way to a Dusty Death.

BERGMAN, Marilyn: Lyr. b. NYC, Nov 10, 1929. e. NYU, BA. W of Alan Bergman. Films inc: In the Heat of the Night; The Thomas Crown Affair *(Oscar*-song, The Windmills of Your Mind, 1968); Happy Ending; Gaily, Gaily; Pieces of Dreams; Sometimes A Great Notion; The Way We Were *(Oscar*-title song-1974); A Star Is Born; John and Mary; Life and Times of Judge Roy Bean; The One and Only; Same Time Next Year; And Justice For All; The Promise; A Change of Seasons.

TV inc: Queen of the Stardust Ballroom *(Emmy*-1975); Sybil *(Emmy*-1977); themes for: Maude; Good Times; Alice; Nancy Walker Show; Sandy Duncan Show.

Bway inc: Something More.

Chief Collaborators: Alan Bergman (husband); Lew Spence; Norman Luboff; Sammy Fain; Alex North. Songs inc: Yellow Bird; Nice 'n' Easy; Outta My Mind; Sentimental Baby; Sleep Warm; Pieces of Dreams; All His Children; The Last Time I Felt Like This. *(Grammys*-(2)-film score & song of the year-1974).

BERGMANN, Alan: Act-Dir. b. Brooklyn, NY. e. Syracuse U, BS. Bway inc: Danton's Death; Gideon; Night Life; Lorenzo; Luther.

TV inc: (Dir) Operation Petticoat; Flying High.

BERGNER, Elisabeth: Act. b. Vienna, Aug 22, 1900. e. Vienna Conservatory. On stage since 1919. Recent plays inc: The Gay Invalid; Long Day's Journey Into Night; First Love; The Madwoman of Chaillot; Catsplay.

Films inc: Der Evangelimann; Der Traumende Mund; Ariane; Catherine the Great; Escape Me Never; As You Like It; Dreaming Lips; Stolen Life; Paris Calling; Cry of the Banshee; Courier to the Tsar; Der Fussganger; Michael Strogoff; Der Pfingstausflug.

BERKOWSKY, Paul B: Thea prod-Gen mgr. b. Cornwall, NY, Sep 8, 1932. e. Hobart Coll, BA, Yale U, MFA. GM for NY's Phoenix Theatre; VP League of Off-Bway Theatres and Producers. Bway inc: (GM) Yentl; Molly; Les Blancs; The Enemy Is Dead; Dear Oscar; You Know I Can't Hear You When the Water's Running; The Club; What the Wine-Sellers Buy; Showdown; The Fabulous Miss Marie; The Prodigal Sister. (Prod) Medal of Honor Rag.

BERLE, Milton (nee Berlinger): Perf. b. NYC, Jul 12, 1908. Film debut at age 5 in Tillie's Punctured Romance. Stage debut 1920 revival of Floradora, Atlantic City. Played Palace, starred in Ziegfeld Follies, headlined top night clubs.

TV inc: Star of own NBC show; *(Emmy*-Kinescoped Personality-1950); Texaco Star Theatre; Kraft Music Hall; The Milton Berle Show *(Specail Emmy*-to "Mr. Television").

Films inc: Tall, Dark and Handsome; Sun Valley Serenade; Margin for Error; It's A Mad Mad Mad World; The Happening; Who's Minding The Mint; Lepke; The Muppet Movie.

BERLIN, Irving (Israel Baline): Comp-Sngwri. b. Russia, May 11, 1888. Began as singing waiter. Started writing songs in 1907 (Marie From Sunny Italy).

Bway scores inc: Watch Your Step; Stop! Look! Listen!; The Century Girl; Cohan Revue of 1918; Yip Yap Yaphank (all soldier show); Music Box Revue; The Cocoanuts; Ziegfeld Follies of 1927; Face the Music; As Thousands Cheer; Louisiana Purchase; This Is the Army (all-soldier show); Annie Get Your Gun; Miss Liberty; Call Me Madam; Mr President.

Film scores inc: Top Hat; Follow The Fleet; On the Avenue; Alexander's Ragtime Band; Carefree; Second Fiddle; Holiday Inn; Blue Skies; Easter Parade; White Christmas; There's No Business Like Show Business.

Also wrote songs for films: Puttin' on the Ritz; Hallelujah; Reaching for the Moon; Sayonara.

Songs inc: My Wife's Gone to the Country, Hurrah, Hurrah; Alexander's Ragtime Band; Everybody's Doin' It; Call Me Up Some Rainy Afternoon; When the Midnight Choochoo Leaves for Alabam; Play A Simple Melody; Oh, How I Hate to Get Up in the Morning; Mandy; A Pretty Girl Is Like a Melody; All By Myself; Say It With Music; Crinoline Days; All Alone; What'll I Do; Always; How Many Times; Remember; Blue Skies; Russian Lullaby; The Song Is Ended; Coquette; Marie; Puttin' On The Ritz; Reachin' for the Moon; Soft Lights and Sweet Music; How Deep Is the Ocean?; Let's Have Another Cup o' Coffee; Easter Parade; Heat Wave; I Never Had A Chance; Cheek to Cheek; Isn't This a Lovely Day; The Piccolino; Top Hat, White Tie and Tails; I'm Putting All My Eggs in One Basket; Let's Face the Music and Dance; I've Got My Love To Keep Me Warm; This Year's Kisses; Change Partners; God Bless America (received Congressional Medal of Honor--all proceeds from song to God Bless America Fund); It's A Lovely Day Tomorrow; Happy Holiday; White Christmas (Oscar-1942); This is the Army, Mr Jones; You Keep Coming Back Like a Song; Doin' What Comes Natur'lly; The Girl That I Marry; There's No Business Like Showbusiness; You Can't Get a Guy With a Gun'; A Couple of Swells; It's A Lovely Day Today; You're Just In Love; Count Your Blessings.

(Special Tony-Award 1963). (Special Grammy-Award 1968).

BERLIN, Jeannie: Act. b. 1949. D of Elaine May. Films inc: On a Clear Day You Can See Forever; Getting Straight; Move; The Strawberry Statement; The Baby Maker; Bone; Why; Portnoy's Complaint; The Heartbreak Kid; Sheila Levine.

BERLIND, Roger S: Prod. b. NYC, Jun 27, 1930. e. Princeton, AB. Former stockbroker. Bway inc: Rex; Music Is; Diversions and Delights; The Merchant; The 1940's Radio Hour; The Lady from Dubuque; Passione; Amadeus.

BERLINGER, Warren: Act. b. Brooklyn, Aug 31, 1937. e. Columbia U. Films inc: Teenage Rebel; Three Brave Men; Blue Denim; The Wackiest Ship in the Army; All Hands on Deck; Thunder Alley; Lepke; I Will. . . I Will. . . For Now; Harry and Walter Go to New York; The Shaggy D.A; The Magician of Lublin.

TV inc: The Funny Side; Touch of Grace; The Most Wanted Woman; Sex and the Single Parent; Holy Moses.

Bway inc: Annie Get Your Gun; The Happy Time; Bernardine; Come Blow Your Horn; Take a Giant Step; Anniversary Waltz; Who's Happy Now; California Suite (tour).

BERMAN, Henry: Prod-Flm ed. b. Newcastle, PA, Jan 1, 1914. B of Pandro S Berman. Films inc: Just This Once; Torch Song; Men of the Fighting Lady; Bedevilled; It's a Dog's Life; The Great American Pastime; Grand Prix (Oscar-edit-1966); Pacific Challenge.

TV inc: Babe (edit).

(Died June 12, 1979).

BERMAN, Monty: Prod. b. London, 1913. Films inc: Jack the Ripper (& dir); The Flesh and the Fiends; Sea of Sand; Blood of the Vampire; The Hellfire Club; What a Carve Up.

TV inc: The Saint; Gideon's Way; The Adventurer.

BERMAN, Monty M: Cost. b. London, 1912. Films inc: Doctor Zhivago; Tom Jones; Chitty Chitty Bang Bang; The Longest Day; My Fair Lady; Oliver; Battle of Britain; Where Eagles Dare; Cromwell; Patton; The Devils; Fiddler on the Roof; A Bridge Too Far; The Other Side of Midnight; Julia; The Seven Per Cent Solution; The Slipper and the Rose.

BERMAN, Pandro S: Prod. b. Pittsburgh, Mar 28, 1905. Started as Asst Film Ed FBO (later RKO) 1923; asst to prod heads William Le Baron & David Selznick; became prod 1931; head of prodn RKO 1937-1940. Joined MGM 1940. Films inc: What Price Hollywood; Symphony of Six Million; Bachelor Mother; The Gay Divorcee; Of Human Bondage; Morning Glory; Roberta; Alice Adams; Top Hat; Winterset; Stage Door; Vivacious Lady; Gunga Din; Hunchback of Notre Dame; Ziegfeld Girl; Honky Tonk; Seventh Cross; National Velvet; Dragon Seed; Portrait of Dorian Grey; Love Affair; Undercurrent; Sea of Grass; The Three Musketeers; Madame Bovary; Father of the Bride; Father's Little Dividend; The Prisoner of Zenda; Ivanhoe; All the Brothers Were Valiant; Knights of the Round Table; Long, Long Trailer; Blackboard Jungle; Bhowani Junction; Something of Value; Tea and Sympathy; Brothers Karamazov; Reluctant Debutante; Butterfield 8; Sweet Bird of Youth; The Prize; A Patch of Blue; Justine; Move.

(Irving Thalberg Award 1976).

BERMAN, Shelley: Act. b. Chicago, Feb 3, 1926. Appears mostly in niteries. Films inc: The Best Man; The Wheeler Dealer; Divorce American Style; Every Home Should Have One.

TV inc: Brenda Starr.

(Grammy-Comedy Performance-1959).

BERNARD, Ed: Act. b. Philadelphia, Jul 4. e. Temple U. Films inc: Across 110th Street; The Hot Rock; Shaft; Julia.

TV inc: The Doctors; As the World Turns; Somerset; One Life to Live; Police Woman; The Last Song.

Bway inc: Ceremonies in Dark Old Men; A Man's Man; Oedipus Rex; The Blacks.

BERNARD, Judd (Sherman Bernard Goldberg): Wri-Prod. b. Chicago, Jun 20, 1927. Films inc: Double Trouble; Point Blank; Blue; Fade In; Negatives; The Man Who Had Power Over Women; Deep End; And Now for Something Completely Different; Glad All Over; The Marseilles Contract; Inside Out; The Class of Miss MacMichael.

BERNARDI, Herschel: Act. b. NYC, Oct 20, 1923. Films inc: Green Fields; Miss Susie Slagle's; Stakeout on Dope Street; Irma La Douce; Murder by Contract; A Cold Wind in August; The George Raft Story; Love with the Proper Stranger; The Honey Pot.

TV inc: A Hatful of Rain; Arnie; But I Don't Want to Get Married; No Place To Run; Sandcastles; The Miracle of Hannukah.

Bway inc: The Goodbye People.

BERNEAU, Christopher: Act. b. Santa Barbara, CA, Jun 2, 1940. e. UCSB. Bway inc: Lloyd George Knew My Father; The Jockey Club Stakes; The Boys in the Band; The Real Inspector Hound; Sweet Bird of Youth; The Passion of Dracula (off-Bway).

TV inc: Dark Shadows; Guiding Light.

BERNHARD, Harvey: Prod. b. Seattle, WA, Mar 5, 1924. e. Stanford U. Films inc: Thomasine & Bushrod; The Mack; The Omen; Damien-Omen II.

BERNHARDT, Curtis: Dir. b. Worms, Germany, Apr 15, 1899. In US since 1940. Films inc: My Love Came Back; Lady with Red Hair; Million Dollar Baby; Juke Girl; Devotion; A Stolen Life; Possessed; Payment on Demand (& sp); Sirocco; The Blue Veil; Miss Sadie Thompson; Beau Brummell; Interrupted Melody; Gaby; Kisses for My President (& prod).

BERNHARDT, Melvin: Dir. b. Buffalo, NY, Feb 26. e. U of Buffalo, Yale U. Thea inc: Conerico Was Here To Stay; 110 in the Shade; Father Uxbridge Wants to Marry; A View From the Bridge; Who's Happy Now?; Honour & Offer; Homecoming; Cop-Out; The Effects of Gamma Rays On Man-In-The-Moon Marigolds; Early Morning; And Miss Reardon Drinks A Little; Other Voices, Other Rooms; The Killdeer; DA (Tony-1978).

TV inc: Another World.

BERNHEIM, Alain: Exec prod. b. Paris, Oct 5, 1922. Films inc: The Good Leviathan; Fun & Games.

BERNS, Seymour: Dir. Started as Radio Dir. Shows inc: Art Linkletter's House Party; Double or Nothing; Hollywood Barn Dance; Free for All.
    TV inc: Art Linkletter's House Party; Meet Millie; The Red Skelton Show; Shower of Stars; My Friend Irma; Jack Benny Show; Gunsmoke; Lineup.

BERNSEN, Randy: Mus. b. Needham, MA, Jul 15, 1954. See Blood, Sweat & Tears.

BERNSTEIN, Charles: Comp. b. NYC. e. Juilliard School of Music, UCLA, BA. Films inc: The Honey Factor; Grasslands; White Lightning; Mr. Majestik; A Small Town in Texas; Viva Knievel!; Outlaw Blues; Love at First Bite; Foolin' Around.
    TV inc: Kate McShane; Look What's Happened To Rosemary's Baby; Leonard; Cops and Robin; Wild & Wooly; Thaddeus Rose and Eddy; Scruples; Bogie; Foolin' Around; Coast to Coast.
    Documentaries: The New Indians; Last Jews from Poland; Helen Keller Story; Soutine; Czechoslovakia.

BERNSTEIN, Elmer: Comp-Cond. b. NYC, Apr 4, 1922. e. NYU, Juilliard. Concert career 1939 to 1950, except for WW 2 service in Air Force; wrote scores for Army radio shows; two United Nations shows; debut as film composer 1950, Saturday's Hero.
    Films inc: Sudden Fear; Man With the Golden Arm; To Kill a Mockingbird; Summer and Smoke; The Magnificent Seven; Walk on the Wild Side; Hud; Love with a Proper Stranger; Return of the Seven; Hawaii; Thoroughly Modern Millie *(Oscar-*1967); The Great Escape; The Carpetbaggers; True Grit; The Shootist; Bloodbrothers; Casey's Shadow; National Lampoon's Animal House; Saturn 3; Airplane.
    TV inc: Hollywood-The Golden Years; The Race for Space; D-Day; The Making of the President *(Emmy-*1963); Four Days in November; Julia; Owen Marshall; The Rookies; Little Women; Guyana Tragedy--The Story of Jim Jones; Moviola.
    Songs inc: Wherever Love Takes Me; Baby the Rain Must Fall; Walk on the Wild Side; My Wishing Doll; True Grit.

BERNSTEIN, Jay: Prod. b. Oklahoma City, OK, Jun 7, 1937. Films inc: Sunburn; Nothing Personal. TV inc: Wild Wild West Revisited; More Wild Wild West.

BERNSTEIN, Leonard: Cond-Comp. b. Lawrence, MA, Aug 25, 1918. e. Harvard, BA. Asst cond NY Philharmonic 1943-44; cond NY Symphony 1945-48; prof of music Brandeis U, 1951-56. Film scores inc: On the Waterfront.
    Bway inc: On the Town; Fancy Free (ballet); Facsimile (ballet); Wonderful Town *(Tony-*1953); The Age of Anxiety (Ballet); Candide; West Side Story; Peter Pan; The Lark; The Firstborn; By Bernstein; 1600 Pennsylvania Avenue; *(Special Tony-*1969).
    TV inc: Omnibus *(Emmys-*1956, 1957); Leonard Bernstein and the New York Philharmonic *(Emmys-*1960, 1961, 1976); New York Philharmonic Young People's Concerts *(Emmy-*1965); Beethoven's Birthday-A Celebration in Vienna *(Emmy-*1972); A Time There Was; The Kennedy Center Honors 1980.
    Songs inc: New York, New York; Lonely Town; It's Love; Maria; Tonight; America.
    (Grammys-(9)-Spoken Word-1961; Children's Recording, 1961-1962-1963); Classical Album of the year, 1964, 1967, 1977; Classical choral performance 1967; opera recording 1973).

BERNSTEIN, Sidney, Lord: Exec. b. Jan 30, 1899. Founder member of British Film Society 1924; founder of the Granada entertainment group, entertainment industry complex which started with theatres and now includes television, publishing; originator (1927) of Saturday Morning film matinees for children; served as film adviser to British Ministry of Information during WW2; Chief of Film Section, Allied Forces in North Africa 1942-43, Allied Forces in Europe 1943-45.
    Films inc: (as prod) Under Capricorn; I Confess.
    Life peerage created 1969.

BERNSTEIN, Walter: Wri. b. NYC. Films inc: Kiss the Blood Off My Hands; Heller in Pink Tights; Fail-Safe; The Money Trap; Paris Blues; The Molly Maguires; Semi-Tough; The Front (drawn from experience as blacklisted writer); The Betsy; An Almost Perfect Affair; Yanks; Little Miss Marker (& dir).
    TV inc: Rich Boy.

BERRI, Claude (nee Langmann): Act-Dir-Prod. b. Paris, Jul 1, 1934. Began in films in 1966 prod & dir Le Poulet which won an Oscar for short subjects.
    Films inc: The Two Of Us (dir); Marry Me, Marry Me (dir-act); Le Pistonne (dir); Le Cinema de Papa (prod-dir); Sex Shop (dir-sp); Male of the Century (dir-sp-act); The First Time (dir-sp); Tess (prod); Inspecteur la Bavure (Inspector Blunder) (prod).

BERRY, Chuck: Mus-Singer-Sngwri. b. San Jose, CA, Jan 15, 1926. Creator of rock 'n' roll classics Roll Over Beethoven; Rock 'n' Roll Music; Johnny B. Goode. Credited with being the most influential figure in the development of rock music in the '50s and 60s.
    Films inc: Rock, Rock, Rock; American Hot Wax.

BERRY, John: Dir. b. NYC, 1917. Films inc: Cross My Heart; From This Day Forward; Miss Susie Slagle's; Casbah; Tension; He Ran All The Way; The Great Lover; Je Suis un Sentimental; Tamango; Maya; Claudine; The Bad News Bears Go to Japan; Thieves.
    TV inc: One Drink at a Time; Farewell Party; Mr. Broadway; Angel on my Shoulder.

BERRY, Ken: Act. b. Moline, IL, Nov 3. Films inc: Two for the Seesaw; Hello Down There; Herbie Rides Again; The Cat from Outer Space.
    TV inc: Soldier Parade; Every Man Needs One; The Reluctant Heroes; Wake Me When the War is Over; The Ken Berry WOW Show; Mayberry RFD; F Troop.

BERTINELLI, Valerie: Act. b. Wilmington, DE, Apr 23, 1960. TV inc: The Secret of Charles Dickens; One Day at a Time; Young Love, First Love; The Promise of Love.
    Films inc: C.H.O.M.P.S.

BERTOLUCCI, Bernardo: Dir. b. Parma, Italy, Mar 16, 1941. Films inc: The Grime Reaper; Before the Revolution; Once Upon A Time in the West (sp only); The Spider's Stratagem; The Conformist; Last Tango in Paris; 1900; Luna.

BERTOLUCCI, Giovanni: Prod. b. Parma, Italy, Jun 24, 1940. e. U of Parma. Films inc: Partner; The Spider's Stratagem; The Conformist; Conversation Piece; The Intruder; One Evening at Dinner; The Bishop's Room; Nene; Just As You Are; Theresa The Thief; The Innocent; Cose Come Sei; Luna.

BERTOLUCCI, Giuseppe: Wri-Dir. b. Parma, Italy, Feb 27, 1947. B of Bernardo Bertolucci. Films inc: 1900; Luna; Berlinguer, I Love You; Lost and Found.
    TV inc: Going, Coming.

BERUH, Joseph: Prod. b. Pittsburgh, PA, Sep 27, 1924. e. Carnegie Institute, Mellon U. Bway inc: Kittiwake Island; Promenade; Long Day's Journey Into Night; Godspell; Nourish the Beast; American Buffalo; Gypsy (London); Blasts and Bravos; An Evening with H L Mencken; Night that Made America Famous.
    Films inc: The Wild Party; Blue Sunshine; He Knows You're Alone.

BESCH, Bibi: Act. b. Vienna, Feb 1. e. Studied with Herbert Berghof. D of Gusti Huber. Bway inc: Fame; The Chinese Prime Minister; Here Lies Jeremy Troy; Once For the Asking.
    Films inc: The Pack; Hardcore; Meteor; The Promise.
    TV inc: Love Is A Many Splendored Thing; Victory at Entebbe; Transplant; Peter Lundy and the Medicine Hat Stallion; Backstairs at the White House; Secret of Midland Heights.

BESSELL, Ted: Act. b. Flushing, NY, Mar 20, 1935. Studied with Sanford Meisner at Neighborhood Playhouse, NY. Films inc: The Outsider; Lover, Come Back; Captain Newman, M.D.; Don't Drink the Water.
    TV inc: Your Money or Your Wife; That Girl; It's A Man's World; The Ted Bessell Show; Breaking Up Is Hard to Do; Good Time Harry.

BESSIE, Alvah: Wri. Films inc: Northern Pursuit; The Very Thought of You; Hotel Berlin, Objective, Burma!; Smart Woman. Career halted when he was imprisoned for contempt of Congress after refusing to testify before the House Un-American Activities Committee.

BEST, James: Act. b. Corydon, IN, Jul 26, 1926. Films inc: Winchester 73; Commanche Territory; The Cimarron Kid; Apache Drums; The Caine Mutiny; Come Next Spring; The Naked and the Dead; Shenandoah; First to Fight; Gaby; The Rack; Sounder; Ode to Billy Joe; The End (& prod); Hooper; Rolling Thunder.

TV inc: The Runaway Barge; Savages.

BETHUNE, Zina: Act. b. NYC, Feb 17, 1950. Films inc: Sunrise at Campobello; Who's That Knocking At My Door?; Tuesday's Child; August, September.

TV inc: The Nurses; The Guiding Light; Young Dr Malone; Love of Life.

Thea inc: Most Happy Fella; Nutcracker Suite.

BETTGER, Lyle: Act. b. Philadelphia, Feb 13, 1915. e. AADA. Films inc: No Man of Her Own; Union Station; All I Desire; The Greatest Show on Earth; Gunfight at OK Corral; Nevada Smith; The Fastest Guitar Alive; The Seven Minutes.

TV inc: Grand Jury; Court of Last Resort.

Bway inc: John Loves Mary; Love Life; Eve of St. Mark; M Station-Hawaii.

BETTIS, Valerie: Act-Dir-Chor. b. Houston, TX. First appeared on NY stage 1937, with the Hanya Holm Dance Co; danced and toured in her own and others' ballets, 1942-44. Bway (chor): Beggar's Holiday; Two On the Aisle; Pousse Cafe. (Act): Inside U S A; Great to be Alive; Bless You All; Ulysses in Nighttown.

Films inc: Affair in Trinidad; Salome; Athena.

BEY, Turhan: Act. b. Vienna, Mar 30, 1920. US screen debut, 1941. Films inc: Footsteps in the Dark; Drums of the Congo; The Mummy's Tomb; Arabian Nights; Ali Baba and the Forty Thieves; Dragon Seed; The Climax; A Night in Paradise; Out of the Blue; Adventures of Casanova; Song of India; Prisoners of the Casbah; Stolen Identity (prod).

BEYMER, Richard: Act. b. Avoca, IA, Feb 21, 1939. Films inc: Indiscretions of an American Wife; So Big; Diary of Anne Frank; High Time; West Side Story; Bachelor Flat; Five Finger Exercise; Hemingway's Adventures of a Young Man; The Longest Day; The Stripper.

TV inc: God in the Dock.

BICK, Jerry: Prod. b. NYC, Apr 26, 1923. e. U of GA, OH State U, Columbia U, Sorbonne. Films inc: Michael Kohlhaas (1969 in Czechoslovakia); The Long Goodbye; Thieves Like Us; Russian Roulette; Farewell My Lovely; The Big Sleep.

BIGARD, Barney (nee Leon Albany Bigard): Comp-Mus. b. 1906. Began as teenager playing clarinet with top bands of era including King Oliver, later joining Duke Ellington with whom he stayed 15 years. Later with Freddie Slack, formed his own band until joining Louis Armstrong All-Stars 1947.

Composer Mood Indigo; Clarinet Lament; C-Jam Blues.

(Died June 27, 1980).

BIKEL, Theodore: Act-Singer. b. Vienna, May 2, 1924. e. RADA. Stage debut 1943, Habimah Theatre, Israel. On London stage 1948, You Can't Take It With You. Films inc: The African Queen; Never Let Me Go; The Little Kidnappers; A Day to Remember; The Pride and the Passion; The Enemy Below; The Defiant Ones; I Want to Live; A Dog of Flanders; My Fair Lady; Sands of Kalahari; The Russians Are Coming, The Russians Are Coming; My Side of the Mountain; Nobody Loves a Drunken Indian; The Little Ark; Two Hundred Motels.

Bway: Tonight In Samarkand; The Lark; The Rope Dancers; The Sound of Music; Cafe Crown; Pousse-Cafe; Fiddler on the Roof.

TV inc: The Eternal Light; Look Up and Live; Who Has Seen the Wind?; Diary of Anne Frank; Hallmark Hall of Fame; Killer by Night; The Return of the King (voice).

BILL, Tony: Prod-Act. b. San Diego, CA, Aug 23, 1940. e. Notre Dame, BA, MA. Films inc: (act) Come Blow Your Horn; None But the Brave; You're a Big Boy Now; Never a Dull Moment; Ice Station Zebra; Castle Keep; Shampoo; Las Vegas Lady; Heart Beat. (Prod): Deadhead Miles; Steelyard Blues; The Sting (Oscar-1973); Hearts of the West; Harry & Walter Go to New York (exec prod); Boulevard Nights (exec prod); Little Dragons (exec prod); Going in Style; My Bodyguard (dir only).

TV inc: (act) Are You in the House Alone?; Portrait of an Escort.

BILSON, Bruce: Dir. b. NYC, May 19, 1928. e. UCLA, BA. TV inc: Hawaii 5-0; Barney Miller; Get Smart (Emmy-1968); BJ and the Bear; Pleasure Cove; The Dallas Cowboys Cheerleaders; The Halloween That Almost Wasn't; The Ghosts of Buxley Hall.

Films inc: The North Avenue Irregulars.

BINDER, Steve: Prod-Dir-Wri. b. LA. e. USC. TV inc: Soupy Sales; A Funny Thing Happened on the Way to the White House; Hulabaloo; America; Liza Minelli Special; Elvis Presley Special; Mac Davis Show; Shields & Yarnell; Barry Manilow Special (Emmy-1977); Olivia Newton-John; Star Wars Holiday Special; Dorothy Hamill Special.

Films inc: Give 'em Hell Harry!

BING, Sir Rudolph: Opera Mgr. b. Vienna, Austria, Jan 9, 1902. Opera and concert agent in Germany, 1921-1933; became GM Glyndebourne Festival, England, 1934 to 1939; artistic dir Edinburgh Int'l Festival 1947-1949; GM Metropolitan Opera NY, 1950-1972.

TV inc: A Time There Was.

BINNS, Edward: Act. b. PA. Films inc: Fail-Safe; Twelve Angry Men; Compulsion; Patton; The Americanization of Emily; Judgement at Nuremberg; Lovin' Molly; Night Moves; Oliver's Story; The Man You Love To Hate (narr).

Bway inc: Command Decision; Detective Story; Caligula; The Caine Mutiny Court Martial; A Touch of the Poet.

TV inc: The Power Within; Battles - The Murder That Wouldn't Die; FDR - The Last Year.

BIRCH, Patricia: Chor. Originally dancer with Martha Graham Dance Company, later with NYC Light Opera Company. Thea inc: Up Eden; Fireworks; The Me Nobody Knows; F. Jasmine Addams; The Real Inspector Hound; After Magritte; A Little Night Music; Candide; Diamond Studs; Grease; Over Here!; Pacific Overtures; Music Is.

BIRKIN, Jane: Act. b. England, 1949. Films inc: The Knack; Blow-Up; Don Juan; Slogan; Swimming Pool; Je t'aime moi non plus; Le Diable au Coeur; The Wild Goose Chase; Projection Privee; Love at the Top; Death on the Nile; Melancholy Baby; A Bout du Bout de Banc; La Miel (Honey).

BIRNEY, David: Act. b. Washington, DC, Apr 23, 1944. e. Dartmouth, AB, UCLA, MA. On stage Lincoln Center Repertory Theatre; NY Shakespeare Festival; The American Shakespeare Festival. Films inc: Caravan to Vaccares; Trial by Combat; Au Revoir. . .A Lundi; Oh, God! Book II.

TV inc: Bridget Loves Bernie; Serpico; The Adams' Chronicles; Greatest Heroes of the Bible; High Midnight; Ohms; Mom, the Wolfman and Me.

BIROC, Joseph: Cin. b. NYC, Feb 12, 1903. Films inc: Bwana Devil; The Tall Texan; The Ride Back; Home Before Dark; Hitler; The Devil at Four O'Clock; Bullet for a Badman; Hush, Hush Sweet Charlotte; The Flight of the Phoenix; The Russians Are Coming, The Russians Are Coming; The Killing of Sister George; Whatever Happened to Aunt Alice?; Too Late the Hero; The Grissom Gang; The Organization; Blazing Saddles; The Longest Yard; The Towering Inferno (Oscar-1974); Hustle; The Duchess and the Dirtwater Fox; The Choirboys; Beyond The Poseidon Adventure; Airplane.

TV inc: Wonder Woman; Honky Tonk; The Moneychangers; Washington D C; Scruples; Kenny Rogers as the Gambler.

BISHOP, Joey (Joseph Abraham Gottlieb): Act. b. NYC, 1918. Films inc: The Naked and the Dead; Ocean's Eleven; Sergeants Three; Texas Across the River; A Guide for the Married Man; Who's Minding the Mint?.

TV inc: The Joey Bishop Show.

BISHOP, Julie: Act. b. Denver, CO, Aug 30, 1914. On screen as Jacqueline Wells from 1923 in Maytime; Tarzan the Fearless; Happy Landing; Paid to Dance; Coronado; Torture Ship; The Girl in 313. Since 1941 billed as Julie Bishop. Films inc: Northern Passage; Rhapsody in Blue; Sands of Iwo Jima; Westward the Women; The High and the Mighty; The Big Land.

BISHOP, Stephen: Singer-Comp. b. San Diego, CA, Nov 14, 1951. Films inc: Phantom of the Paradise; Kentucky Fried Movie; Sgt Pepper's Lonely Hearts Club Band; National Lampoon's Animal House; The China Syndrome (comp).

BISOGLIO, Val: Act. b. NYC, May 7, 1926. Films inc: Saturday Night Fever; The Frisco Kid.
TV inc: The Mary Tyler Moore Show; All in the Family; The Marcus-Nelson Murders; Quincy.
Bway inc: Wait Until Dark.

BISSELL, Whit: Act. b. NYC, Oct 25, 1909. e. U of NC, BA. Films inc: (more than 85) Destination Tokyo; Another Part of the Forest; It Should Happen to You; The Young Stranger; I Was A Teenage Frankenstein; The Time Machine; Hud; Seven Days in May; Covenant with Death; Airport; Pete and Tillie; Soylent Green; Psychic Killer; Casey's Shadow; Conspiracy to Kill Lincoln.
More than 350 TV roles inc: Andersonville Trial; A Tattered Web; Cry Rape; Mark Twain's America - Abe Lincoln: Freedom Fighter.

BISSET, Jacqueline: Act. b. Weybridge, Eng, Sep 13, 1946. Model. Film debut in The Knack. Pictures inc: Cul de Sac; Casino Royale; Two for the Road; The Sweet Ride; The Detective; Airport; Day for Night; End of the Game; Bullitt; Murder on the Orient Express; The Deep; The Greek Tycoon; Sunday Woman; Secrets; Who's Killing The Great Chefs of Europe; When Time Ran Out; Amo Non Amo.

BIXBY, Bill: Act. b. San Francisco, Jan 29, 1934. Stage debut Detroit Civic Theatre production The Boy Friend. TV inc: Dobbie Gillis; Joey Bishop Show; My Favorite Martian; The Courtship of Eddie's Father; The Magician; The Incredible Hulk; How To Survive The 70's and Maybe Bump Into A Little Happiness.
Films inc: Lonely Are The Brave; Irma La Douce; Yum Yum Tree; The Apple Dumpling Gang; Kentucky Fried Movie.
Bway inc: The Paisley Convertible; Sunday in New York.

BLACK, David: Prod-Dir. b. NYC, Nov 20, 1931. e. Harvard U, BA. Performed in operetta, opera, musical comedy, 1951-61. Dir: As You Like It; The Killing of Sister George; The Typists; The Children's Hour; Girl in My Soup; Two for the Seasaw; The Advertisement; Eros in Exile; Augusta; Rosewood; The Last Minstrel Show; Spotlight; Cabaret. Prod: Look We've Come Through; The Aspen Papers; Semi-Detached; Cambridge Circus; Ready When You Are C.B.; The Knack; The Ides of March; The Impossible Years; Those That Play the Clowns; The Natural Look; To Clothe the Naked; George M!; Fire!; Paris Is Out; Salvation; W.C.; A Funny Thing Happened On The Way to the Forum; Lysistrata; Fearless Frank.

BLACK, Karen: Act. b. Park Ridge, IL, Jul 1, 1946. Bway: We're Civilized; The Uncommon Denominator; Happily Never After; On a Clear Day You Can See Forever; After the Fall.
Films inc: Five Easy Pieces; Easy Rider; A Gunfight; Born to Win; Portnoy's Complaint; You're A Big Boy Now; Law and Disorder; Airport 1975; Family Plot; Capricorn One; In Praise of Older Women; Killer Fish; The Last Word; The Squeeze.
TV inc: Power; Where The Lady's Go; Confessions of a Lady Cop.

BLACK, Noel: Dir. b. Jun 30, 1940. Films inc: Skaterdater (The American Boy) (short); Pretty Poison; A Man, A Woman and A Bank (A Very Big Withdrawal); The Golden Honeymoon.

BLACKMAN, Honor: Act. b. London, 1926. Films inc: Fame Is the Spur; Diamond City; The Rainbow Jacket; Breakaway; A Night to Remember; The Square Peg; Goldfinger; The Secret of My Success; Life at the Top; Moment to Moment; A Twist of Sand; Shalako; The Last Grenade; The Virgin and the Gypsy; Fright; To the Devil a Daughter; The Cat and the Canary.
Thea inc: The Exorcism.

BLACKSTONE, Milton Wri-Prod. b. NYC, May 5, 1924. e. U of Miami, NYU. Thea Agent & personal mgr 1948-66. Prod-wri Guy Lombardo New Years Eve Specials 1960-65; Arthur Murray Show 1955-64; prod Comedians' Golf Classic since 1961; Andy Williams Golf Special 1977.

BLACKTON, Jay S: (Jacob Schwartzdorf): Comp-Arr. b. NYC, Mar 25, 1909. e. Juilliard. Musical dir for Bway prodns inc: Oklahoma!; Annie Get Your Gun; Miss Liberty; Call Me Madam; New Faces of 1956; Redhead; Mr President; Sherry; George M; Two By Two; Rex; Revivals of Oklahoma!; Finian's Rainbow; Showboat.
Films inc: Oklahoma (*Oscar*-1955); Guys and Dolls. Named to recording Academy Hall of Fame for dir orig cast album of Oklahoma!.

BLAIN, Gerard: Act-Dir. b. Paris, Oct 23, 1930. Films inc: (act) Avant le deluge; Escalier de service; Le Temps des Assassins; Crime et Chatiment; Desire Takes the Men; Les Mistons; Le Beau Serge; Charlotte et son Jules; Les Cousins; Les Dauphins; Hatari!; La Frenesie; Les Vierges; La Bonne Soupe; Via Veneto; Il Generale; Joe Caligula; Un Homme de Trop; Ripley S'Amuse; La Guepe. (Dir): Les Amis (& co-sp); Le Pelican (& sp-act); un enfant dans la foule (& co-sp); A Second Wind (& sp); The Rebel (& sp).

BLAINE, Vivian (nee Stapleton): Act. b. Newark, NJ, Nov 21, 1924. Singer with various bands, 1937-39, then nightclubs; 20th-Fox contract, 1942. Appeared in Guys and Dolls, Broadway, London stage. Films inc: He Married His Boss; Guys and Dolls; Greenwich Village; Nob Hill; State Fair; Skirts Ahoy; Public Pigeon No. 1; The Dark.
TV inc: The Cracker Factory; Fast Friends; Sooner or Later.

BLAIR, Betsy (nee Boger): Act. b. NYC, Dec 11, 1923. Films inc: The Guilt of Janet Ames; A Double Life; Another Part of the Forest; The Snake Pit; Kind Lady; Marty; The Halliday Brand; All Night Long; A Delicate Balance.
TV inc: Steel Hour; Ford Theatre; Kraft; Philco.
Bway inc: Beautiful People; Richard II.

BLAIR, Janet (Martha Lafferty): Act. b. Blair, PA, Apr 23, 1921. Films inc: Three Girls About Town; Two Yanks in Trinidad; Broadway; My Sister Eileen; Something to Shout About; Tonight and Every Night; Gallant Journey; The Fabulous Dorseys; The Fuller Brush Man; Public Pigeon Number One; Boys' Night Out; Night of the Eagle; The One and Only Genuine Original Family Band.
TV inc: The Smith Family.

BLAIR, Linda: Act. b. Westport, CT, 1959. Model for children's apparel and TV commercials. Films inc: The Exorcist; Airport 1975; The Heretic; Wild Horse Hank; Roller Boogie.
TV inc: Born Innocent.

BLAKE, Amanda (Beverly Neill): Act. b. Buffalo, NY, Feb 20, 1929. Films inc: Duchess of Idaho; Stars in My Crown; Lili; Sabre Jet; A Star Is Born; About Mrs. Leslie; High Society.
TV inc: Exposure; Cavalcade of America; Gunsmoke.

BLAKE, Eubie (James Hubert Blake): Comp. b. Baltimore, MD, Feb 7, 1883. Began career at 15 playing pianos in Baltimore bordellos; joined traveling medicine show at 17; following year made NY debut in cast of musical In Old Kentucky; teamed with Noble Sissle, first as songwriting team with Sissle handling lyrics, later as vaudeville act touring U.S., Europe; later teamed with Andy Razaf as songwriting team; in 1946 began studying Schillinger system of Composition at NYU, completing four year course in 30 months; career was basis of Broadway musical Eubie, 1979.
Bway inc: Shuffle Along; Blackbirds of 1929; Singing the Blues (cond only); Swing It; C.B. Cochran's Revue; Will Morrisey's Folies Bergere; Brown Skin Models of 1954; Eubie.
Songs inc: Love Will Find a Way; Memories of You; You Were Meant For Me; Strange What Love Will Do; Baby Mine; I'm Just Wild About Harry; You're Lucky To Me; Lindy Hop; Green Pastures; Lovin You the Way I Do.

BLAKE, Robert (Michael Gubitosi): Act. b. Nutley, NJ, Sep 18, 1934. Child actor in Our Gang comedies, also Little Beaver in Red Ryder series. Later films inc: Andy Hardy's Double Life; The Horn Blows at Midnight; Treasure of Sierra Madre; Revolt in the Big House; The Purple Gang; The Greatest Story Ever Told; In Cold Blood; Tell Them Willie Boy Is Here; Corky; Electra Glide in Blue; Second Hand Hearts; Coast to Coast.

TV inc: Baretta (*Emmy*-1975).

BLAKE, Yvonne: Cost desgn. Films inc: Nicholas and Alexandra (*Oscar*-1971); The Four Musketeers; The Eagle Has Landed; Superman; Escape to Athena.

BLAKELY, Colin: Act. b. Bangor, County Down, Northern Ireland, Sep 23, 1930. Stage debut Ulster Group, Belfast. London debut 1959. Joined Royal Shakespeare Co. Stratford-on-Avon, 1961. Thea inc: Enjoy.

Films inc: Murder on the Orient Express; The Pink Panther Strikes Again; Saturday Night and Sunday Morning; The Informers; Young Winston; Equus; All Things Bright and Beautiful; The Big Sleep; Nijinsky; Meetings With Remarkable Men; The Dogs of War.

TV inc: The Day Christ Died; Vikings.

BLAKELY, Susan: Act. b. Germany, 1949. e. U of TX. Started as commercial model. Screen debut 1972, Savages. Films inc: The Lords of Flatbush; The Towering Inferno; Report to the Commissioner; Shampoo; Capone; Dreamer; The Concorde - Airport '79.

TV inc: Rich Man, Poor Man; Secrets; Make Me An Offer.

BLAKLEY, Ronee: Act. b. Caldwell, ID, 1946. e. Stanford U, Juilliard. Recording artist, niteries. Films inc: Nashville; Renaldo & Clara; The Driver; Good Luck Miss Wyckoff; The Baltimore Bullet; Lightning Over Water (Nick's movie) (& mus).

BLANC, Mel: Voice specialist. b. San Francisco, May 30, 1908. Voice of Warner Bros cartoon characters, Bugs Bunny, Porky Pig, Daffy Duck, since 1937. TV inc: (voice) The Bugs Bunny Show; The Porky Pig Show; The Munsters; Flintstones; The Bugs Bunny Mothers Day Special; Daffy Duck's Easter Show; Murder Can Hurt You! (act); Bugs Bunny's Bustin' Out All Over; Daffy Duck's Thanks-For-Giving Special.

Occasional cameo appearance in films inc: Neptune's Daughter; Kiss Me Stupid; Buck Rogers in the 25th Century.

BLANCO, Ray: Dist-Prod. b. Havana, Cuba, Oct 31, 1955. e. CCNY, NYU. Exec dir, Independent Film Critics Assn, 1973-75; Chmn/Admin. Bauer Int'l, Art Film Distributors USA, 1975; 1977, co-prod, The Red Dress; 1978, prod, The Lonely Road.

BLANE, Sally (Elizabeth Jung): Act. b. Salt Lake City, UT, 1910. Sis of Loretta Young. Films inc: Sirens of the Sea; Rolled Stockings; The Vagabond Lover; Once a Sinner; Ten Cents a Dance; I Am a Fugitive from a Chain Gang; Advice to the Lovelorn; The Silver Streak; One Mile from Heaven; Charlie Chan at Treasure Island; A Bullet for Joey.

BLANK, Tom: Dir. b. Minneapolis, MN, Dec 29, 1938. e. Northwestern U. TV inc: Bionic Woman; American Girls; Spiderman; Dinky Hockey; Harris & Company-Choices.

BLANKE, Henry: Prod-Exec. b. Berlin-Steglitz, Germany, Dec 30, 1901. To US 1922; with UA, then Warner Bros. Films inc: The Story of Louis Pasteur; Satan Met a Lady; The Petrified Forest; Green Pastures; The Life of Emile Zola; Jezebel; The Adventures of Robin Hood; Juarez; The Sea Hawk; The Maltese Falcon; The Mask of Dimitrios; The Treasure of Sierra Madre; The Fountainhead; Come Fill the Cup; King Richard and the Crusaders; Too Much Too Soon; The Nun's Story; Ice Palace; Hell Is for Heroes.

BLANKFORT, Michael: Wri. b. NYC, Dec 10, 1907. e. U of PA, BA, Princeton U, MA. Films inc: Blind Alley; Texas; Adam Had Four Sons; An Act of Murder; Broken Arrow; Halls of Montezuma; Untamed; The Vintage; The Plainsman; See How They Run; The Other Man; Lydia Bailey; The Juggler; My Six Convicts; Tribute to a Bad Man; The Caine Mutiny.

TV inc: A Fire In The Sky.

BLATTY, William Peter: Wri-Prod. b. NYC, Jan 7, 1928. Films inc: The Man from the Diners' Club; A Shot in the Dark; John Goldfarb, Please Come Home; What Did You Do in the War, Daddy?; Gunn; The Great Bank Robbery; Darling Lili; The Exorcist (& prod) (*Oscar*-1973-wri); The Ninth Configuration (prod-dir-wri).

BLAUSTEIN, Julian: Prod. b. NYC, May 30, 1913. e. Harvard. Reader, Universal, 1935; story ed. 1936-38; headed story dept. MCA, 1938-39; story ed. Paramount, 1939-41; U.S. Signal Corps, 1941-46; edit. supv Selznick, 1946-48; 20th-Fox as prod., 1949; exec. prod. 1951-52. Films inc: Broken Arrow; Mister 880; Day the Earth Stood Still; Don't Bother to Knock; Desiree; The Racers; The Wreck of the Mary Deare; The Four Horsemen of the Apocalypse, Khartoum.

BLECKNER, Jeffrey: Dir. b. Brooklyn, NY. e. Amherst, BA; Yale, MFA. Dir at the Long Wharf; Yale. Bway inc: The Basic Training of Pavlo Hummel; Sticks and Bones. Other thea inc: Secret Affairs of Mildred West; Death and Life of Jesse James.

Films inc: A Sunday Dinner. TV inc: Sticks and Bones; Another World; Doc; Guilding Light; The Stockard Channing Show; Willow B--Women in Prison.

BLEES, Robert: Wri-Prod. b. Lathrop, MO, Jun 9, 1922. e. Dartmouth. Films inc: Paid in Full; The Glass Web; Slightly Scarlet; Magnificent Obsession; Autumn Leaves; Night Games.

TV inc: Climax; Westinghouse Playhouse; Alfred Hitchcock Presents; Zane Grey Theater; Bonanza; Bus Stop; Combat!; Harry O; The Class of '65; Quincy; Columbo.

BLEIFER, John: Act. b. Zawiercie, Poland, Jul 26, 1901. Films inc: We Americans; Captured; Black Fury; Les Miserables; Charlie Chan at Monte Carlo; Mr. Moto Takes A Vacation; The Mark of Zorro; In Our Town; The Juggler; The Hook; F.I.S.T.; The Frisco Kid.

BLESSED, Brian: Act. b. Yorkshire, England. e. Bristol Old Vic. Thea inc: Incident at Vichy; Oedipus. TV inc: Z Cars; The Three Musketeers; Son of a Man; I Claudius.

Films inc: Barry Lyndon; Man of La Mancha; The Trojan Women; A Last Valley; Henry VIII; Flash Gordon.

BLIER, Bernard: Act. b. France, 1916. Films inc: Hotel du Nord; Quai des Orfevres; Dedee d'Anvers; L'Ecole Buissoniere; The Wanton; Souvenirs Perdus; Les Miserables; Les Grandes Familles; A Question of Honor; Breakdown; Catch Me a Spy; Cher Victor; Daydreamer; Serie Noire; Cold Cuts. The Hypochondriac.

BLIER, Bertrand: Prod-Dir. b. Paris, Mar 14, 1939. S of Bernard Blier. Researched contemporary cinema verite film project for prod Andre Michelin and launched directorial career with the film, Hitler, Connais Pas which featured on-camera interviews with 11 French teenagers.

Films inc: La Grimace (short); Breakdown; Going Places; Femmes Fatales; Calmos; The Body of My Enemy; Get Out Your Handkerchiefs; Buffet Froid (& sp).

BLOCH, Charles B: Exec Prod. b. NYC, Mar 31, 1915. e. Columbia U, CCNY. Pres Globe Photos until 1972 when formed Charles Publishing Co, Inc; West Coast editorial rep Bantam books. Films inc: (exec prod) The Fog. TV inc: (exec prod) The House on Garibaldi Street.

BLOCH, Richard L: Exec. b. Pontiac, MI, Jun 12, 1929. e. U of Chicago, BS. On boards of Center Theatre Group; American Ballet Theatre; American Film Institute; became director Filmways 1969, elected chmn, CEO 1971.

BLOCH, Robert: Wri. b. Chicago, Apr 5, 1917. Films inc: Psycho; The Cabinet of Caligari; Strait Jacket; The Night Walker; The Psychopath; The Deadly Bees; The Torture Garden; The House That Dripped Blood.

TV inc: The Cat Creature; The Dead Don't Die; A Man Called Satan.

BLOCK, David Greenberg: Exec. b. Johannesburg, S Africa, Mar 21, 1936. To Australia, 1964. Investment banker; part time commissioner, Australian Film Commission.

BLONDELL, Joan: Act. b. NYC, Aug 30, 1906. On stage from childhood. In stock, Dallas. Bway inc: Tarnish; Trial of Mary Dugan; Ziegfeld Follies. On screen from 1929. Films inc: Three on a Match; Gold Diggers (various years); East Side of Heaven; Lady For A Night; Nightmare Alley; Blue Veil; The Cincinnati Kid; Support Your Local Sheriff; Grease; The Champ.
    TV inc: Here Come The Brides; Banyon; Battered; The Rebels.
    (Died Dec 25, 1979).

BLONDIE: Group. Members are Deborah Harry, Christ Stein, Clem Burke, Jimmy Destri, Nigel Harrison, Frank Infante.
    Albums inc: Parallel Lines; Eat to the Beat. Films inc: Roadie. TV inc: Pink Lady.

BLOOD, SWEAT & TEARS: Rock Band. Members of group inc: David Clayton-Thomas; Dave Bargeron; Larry Willis; Tony Klatka; Gregory Herbert; Randy Bernsen; Bobby Colomby; Neil Stubenhaus; Chris Albert. Films inc: The Owl and the Pussycat (score).
    (*Grammys*-(2)-Album of Year; Best Inst-1969)

BLOOM, Arthur: Dir-Prod. b. NYC, Apr 19, 1940. e. NYU, BS. TV inc: 60 Minutes; Democratic & Republican National Conventions; Carter-Ford Presidential Debate from San Francisco; Tricia Nixon tour of White House; CBS Election Night, 1974-76-78; CBS Reports; The American Assassins (series).

BLOOM, Claire: Act. b. London, Feb 15, 1931. Stage debut at Playhouse, Oxford, 1947. Screen debut in Limelight, 1951. Films inc: Innocents in Paris; Richard III; Alexander The Great; The Brothers Karamazov; Look Back in Anger; The Chapman Report; The Spy Who Came In From The Cold; The Illustrated Man; A Doll's House; Islands in the Stream.
    TV inc: Anna Karenina; Wuthering Heights; An Imaginative Woman; In Praise of Love; Backstairs At The White House; Hamlet.
    Thea inc: A Streetcar Named Desire; The Innocents.

BLOOM, Verna: Act. b. Lynn, MA, Aug 7, 1939. e. Boston U. Films inc: Medium Cool; The Hired Hand; High Plains Drifter; Badge 373. National Lampoon's Animal House.
    Bway inc: Marat/Sade.
    TV inc: Playing For Time.

BLOOMFIELD, George: Dir. b. Montreal, Canada. e. McGill U. Started as act; later dir for Nat'l Film Board, Canada and CBC. TV inc: Riel; Hedda Gabler; Love on the Nose; Saturday, Sunday, Monday; Paradise Lost; Second City.
    Films inc: Jenny (& co-sp); To Kill A Clown; Child Under A Leaf (& sp); Nothing Personal; Double Negative.

BLOSSOM, Roberts: Act. Bway inc: The Physicists. Films inc: Deranged; Slaughterhouse Five; Handle With Care; Hospital; The Great Gatsby; Close Encounters of the Third Kind; Escape From Alcatraz; Resurrection.
    TV inc: Mourning Becomes Electra.

BLUE SKY BOYS: Country Music Group. The Bolick brothers, both born in Hickory, NC, Earl (Dec 16, 1919); Bill (Oct 28, 1917). Began performing during the late 20s. Retired 1961, reappeared in 1964, performing on college campuses and recording for Capitol.

THE BLUES BROTHERS: (See BELUSHI, John and AYKROYD, Dan).

BLUHDORN, Charles G: Exec. b. Sep 20, 1926. e. CCNY, Columbia. After Air Force Service, entered export import business, launched his own firm in 1949; 1956 acquired Michigan Plating and Stamping Co.; 1958 merged it with a Houston automotive parts distribution company to form Gulf & Western Industries; merged with Paramount Oct 19, 1966, With G&W as the surviving corporation and Bluhdorn as Chmn and CEO.

BLUM, Harry N: Prod. b. Cleveland, OH, Oct 3, 1932. e. U of MI; BA, LLB. Films inc: The Bluebird; Diamonds; At The Earth's Core; Obsession; Skateboard; The Magician of Lublin.

BLUM, Stanford: Prod-Dir. b. Baltimore, MD, Jul 8, 1940. e. U of MD. Film inc: (shorts) The Thrill of Victory, the Agony of the Feet; Kathy Rigby; Joan Baez; Burton Cummings; Foreigner; Circle of Sound.

BLUMENTHAL, Ann (nee Jacobs): Prod. b. St Louis, MO, Apr 24, 1942. TV inc: (Asso prod) The Patriots; Uncommon Women and Others; mus specials for PBS. Series prod for WNET int'l co-prodns inc the plays of Shakespeare. Also prod Tartuffe; Mourning Becomes Electra; The Sorrows of Gin; O Youth and Beauty!; Big Blonde.

BLUMOFE, Robert F: Prod. b. NYC. e. Columbia Coll, AB, Columbia U, JD. Director, The American Film Institute, West. Films inc: Yours, Mine & Ours; Pieces of Dreams; Bound for Glory.

BLYE, Allan: Wri-Prod. b. Winnipeg, Canada, Jul 19, 1937. Worked in Canadian TV as singer, wri, act; to Hollywood 1967 as wri for Smothers Brothers Comedy Hour (*Emmy*-1969); also wri for Glen Campbell Summer Series, Elvis Presley's 1st TV special, two Andy Williams specials, Petula Clark's 1st TV special. From 1967-70, joined with Chris Beard to prod: The Sonny and Cher Show; The Sonny Comedy Review; Lil' Abner; Wow; The American Bag; Ray Stevens (summer series); That's My Mama. In 1975, partnered with Bob Einstein and produced Van Dyke and Company (*Emmy*-1977); Lola Falana specials; Redd Foxx Show.

BLYTH, Ann: Act. b. Mt. Kisco, NY, Aug 16, 1928. Films inc: Chip off the Old Block; The Merry Monahans; Mildred Pierce; Brute Force; Killer McCoy; Another Part of the Forest; Mr. Peabody and the Mermaid; Once More My Darling; The Great Caruso; I'll Never Forget You; The World in His Arms; One Minute to Zero; Rose Marie; The Student Prince; Kismet; Slander; The Buster Keaton Story; The Helen Morgan Story.

BOARDMAN, True: Wri-Act-Dir. b. Seattle, WA, Oct 25, 1909. e. UCLA, AB, Occidental Coll, MA. Started as child actor; later wrote for radio, screen. Films inc: (as wri) Son of the Navy; Ride 'em Cowboy; Keep 'em Flying; Pardon My Sarong; Between Us Girls; Arabian Nights; The Painted Hills.
    TV inc: Colgate Theatre; Revlon Playhouse; Donna Reed Show; Perry Mason; My Three Sons; Ironside; The Virginian; Bonanza.

BOASBERG, Charles: Exec. b. Buffalo, NY, Aug 20, 1906. e. Cornell U. Started with MGM in 1927; then salesman for RKO, 1930; named gen sales mgr, dir, RKO, 1952; joined Par, 1955, in charge of worldwide sales of The Ten Commandments; gen sales mgr, p WB Dist Corp, 1958; domestic gen sales mgr & vp Par Dist Corp, 1962; p, Par Film Dist Corp, 1963; vp Par Pictures, Inc, 1967; vp National General Corp, 1968; P, 1969. In 1974 formed Boasberg-Goldstein, consultants to film producers, now Charles Boasberg, Inc.

BOBKER, Lee R: Dir. b. NYC, Jul 19, 1925. e. NYU, BA. Over 600 docus.

BOCHCO, Steven: Prod-Wri. b. NYC, 1945. e. Carnegie Tech, MFA. Won MCA fellowship while in college, joined U-TV as apprentice. TV inc: (wri & story ed) Name of the Game; Columbo; McMillan and Wife; Delvecchio (wri-prod); Paris (Exec prod); Richie Brockelman (co-crea); Turnabout (wri); Invisible Man (wri); Vampire (wri).
    Films inc: Silent Running (co-wri).

BOCHNER, Lloyd: Act. b. Canada, Jul 29, 1924. Films inc: Drums of Africa; The Night Walker; Sylvia; Tony Rome; Point Blank; The Detective; The Horse in the Gray Flannel Suit; Tiger By the Tail; Ulzana's Raid; The Man in the Glass Booth.
    TV inc: A Fire in the Sky; Greatest Heroes of the Bible; The Immigrants; The Best Place To Be; The Golden Gate Murders; Mary and Joseph--A Story of Faith.

BOCK, Jerry: Comp. b. New Haven, CT, Nov 23, 1928. e. U of WI. Bway inc: Catch A Star (songs); Mr. Wonderful; The Ziegfeld Follies; The Body Beautiful; Fiorello!; She Loves Me; Fiddler on the Roof; The Apple Tree; The Rothschilds.
    TV inc: The Admiral Broadway Revue; The Show of Shows; The Mel Torme Show; The Kate Smith Hour.
    (*Grammy*-cast album-1963).

BOCK, Jerry: Comp. b. New Haven, CT, Nov 23, 1928. e. U of WI. Bway inc: Catch A Star (songs); Mr Wonderful; The Ziegfeld Follies; The Body Beautiful; Fiorello!; She Loves Me; Fiddler on the Roof (Tony-1965); The Apple Tree; The Rothschilds.
TV inc: The Admiral Broadway Revue; The Show of Show; The Mel Torme Show; The Kate Smith Hour.
(Grammy-cast album-1963).

BODARD, Mag: Prod. b. Sweden, 1927. Films inc: The Umbrellas of Cherbourg; The Young Girls of Rochefors; Le Bonheur; Mouchette; Benjamin; Le Viol; La Chinoise; Peau d'Ane; The Best Way.

BOEHM, Karl: Act. b. Germany, 1928. Films inc: Peeping Tom; Too Hot to Handle; The Magnificent Rebel; The Four Horsemen of the Apocalypse; The Wonderful World of the Brothers Grimm; Come Fly with Me; The Venetian Affair.

BOEHM, Sydney: Wri. b. Philadelphia, Apr 4, 1908. e. Lehigh U. Films inc: High Wall; The Undercover Man; Side Street; Mystery Street; Union Station; When Worlds Collide; The Savage; The Big Heat; The Atomic City; The Secret of the Incas; Rogue Cop; Black Tuesday; Violent Saturday; The Tall Men; Hell on Frisco Bay; The Revolt of Mamie Stover; Harry Black; A Woman Obsessed (& prod.); Seven Thieves (& prod.); Shock Treatment; Sylvia; Rough Night in Jericho.

BOETTICHER, Budd (Oscar Boetticher): Prod-Dir-Wri. b. Chicago, Jul 29, 1916. e. OH State U. Former Bullfighter, served as tech dir, Blood and Sand, 1941; became feature dir, 1944. Films inc: The Missing Juror; Assigned to Danger; Sword of D'Artagnan; The Bullfighter and the Lady (& sp-prod); Red Ball Express; Horizons West; City Beneath The Sea; East of Sumatra; The Magnificent Matador (& sp); Decision at Sundown; Buchanan Rides Alone; Ride Lonesome; The Rise and Fall of Legs Diamond; Arruza; A Time for Dying.

BOFFETY, Jean: Cin. b. France. Films inc: Act of the Heart; Journey; Cesar and Rosalie; Thieves Like Us; A Simple Story; Un Mauvais Fils (A Bad Son).

BOGARDE, Dirk (Derek van den Bogaerde): Act. b. London, Mar 28, 1921. Films inc: Quartet (Alien Corn episode); So Long at the Fair; Penny Princess; Doctor in the House; The Sea Shall Not Have Them; The Spanish Gardener; A Tale of Two Cities; The Doctor's Dilemma; Libel; Song Without End; Victim; I Could Go On Singing; The Servant; Doctor in Distress; The High Bright Sun; King and Country; Darling; Accident; Our Mother's House; Sebastion; The Fixer; Justine; Oh What a Lovely War; The Damned; Death in Venice; Le Serpent; The Night Porter; Permission to Kill; Providence; A Bridge Too Far; Despair.
TV inc: The Little Moon of Alban; Blythe Spirit; Upon This Rock.

BOGART, Neil: Exec. b. NYC. Began as pop singer; moved into record prodn and promo. First assoc with Cameo/Parkway Records Co; then p of Buddah Records; formed Casablanca Records in 1974. Expanded into films in 1978. Sold Casablanca to Polygram, formed The Boardwalk with Jon Peters, Peter Guber, 1980. Exec prod of Thank God It's Friday.

BOGART, Paul: Dir. b. NYC, Nov 21, 1919. Films inc: Marlowe, Halls of Anger; Skin Game; Class of '44; Mr Ricco.
TV inc: Ages of Man; The Defenders (Emmy-1965); Mark Twain Tonight; The Final War of Ollie Winter; Dear Friends (Emmy-1968); The House Without a Christmas Tree; Look Homeward Angel; The Country Girl; Double Solitaire; Tell Me Where It Hurts; Shadow Game (Emmy-1970); All in the Family (Emmy-1978); The Adams Chronicles.

BOGDANOVICH, Peter: Prod-Dir. b. Kingston, NY, Jul 30, 1939. Actor summer stock 1955-58. Prod off-Bway plays, The Big Knife; Once in a Lifetime.
Films inc: Targets (dir-act-sp); The Last Picture Show (dir-sp); What's Up Doc? (dir-prod-sp); Paper Moon (dir-prod); Daisy Miller (dir-prod); At Long Last Love (dir-prod-sp); Nickelodeon (dir-prod-wri); Saint Jack (dir-act-sp). Books inc: Orson Welles; Howard Hawks; Alfred Hitchcock; John Ford; Fritz Lang in America; Allan Dwan--The Last Pioneer; Pieces of Time--Peter Bogdanovich on the Movies.

BOHEM, Endre: Wri. b. Hungary. e. U of Vienna. Films inc: Night Has a Thousand Eyes; The Redhead and the Cowboy; Alias Nick Beal; Streets of Laredo; Thirst; House with a Thousand Candles; Two Wise Maids; Little Orphan Annie; Lord Jeff; Crime of the Century; Twin Stars; Bengazi.
TV inc: Revlon Mirror; Ford Theatre; Rawhide.

BOISSETT, Yves: Dir. b. Paris, Mar 14, 1939. Worked as an assistant to Jean-Pierre Melville, Vittorio De Sica and Rene Clement; location scout for James Bond films; made directorial debut with Coplan Saves His Skin.
Films inc: Cran D'Arret (& co-sp); Angel's Leap (& co-sp); The French Conspiracy; R.A.S.; Rape of Innocence; The Purple Taxi; La Cle Sur La Porte; La Femme Flic (& co-sp).

BOLGER, Ray: Act. b. Dorchester, MA, Jan 10, 1906. Stage debut with a musicomedy repertory company touring New England. Screen debut in The Great Ziegfeld, 1936; own TV show, ABC, 1954-55. Films inc: Rosalie; Wizard of Oz; Where's Charley?; April in Paris; Babes in Toyland; Four Jacks and a Jill; Look For The Silver Lining; The Entertainer; Just You And Me Kid; The Runner Stumbles.
Bway inc: Scandals of 1931; Life Begins at 8:40; On Your Toes; By Jupiter; All American; Come Summer; Where's Charley? (Tony-1949); Three to Make Ready.

BOLKAN, Florinda: Act. b. 1945. Films inc: Candy; The Damned; Investigation of a Citizen; The Last Valley; Romance; The Island; A Man to Respect; Hearts and Minds; Royal Flash; Assassination in Sarajevo; Manaos.
TV inc: The Word.

BOLOGNA, Joseph: Act-Plywri. b. Dec 30, 1936. H of Renee Taylor. (Writes in collaboration with wife).
Bway inc: Lovers and Other Strangers (& wri).
Films inc: Honor Thy Father; Cops and Robbers; Lovers and Other Strangers (& wri); Made for Each Other (& wri); Mixed Company; The Big Bus; Torn Between Two Lovers; Chapter Two.
TV inc: (wri): Acts of Love and Other Comedies (Emmy-1973); Paradise; Calucci's Department (created); The American Dream Machine; Drink, Drank, Drunk.

BOLOGNINI, Mauro: Dir. b. Italy, 1923. Worked as asst to Yves Allegret, Mario Zampi, Luigi Zampi; directed films for tv.
Feature films inc: I Cavalieri della Regina; Gli Inamorati; Marisa la Civetta; Giovanni Mariti; La Viaccia; La Corruzione; Madamigella di Maupin; Un Bellissimo Novembre; Metello; Down the Ancient Staircase; Libera, Amore mio; The Inheritance; Dove Va In Vacanza (When Are You Going on Vacation?).

BOLT, Robert: Wri. b. Manchester, Eng, Aug 15, 1924. e. Manchester U. Films inc: Lawrence of Arabia; Doctor Zhivago (Oscar-1965); A Man For All Seasons (Oscar-1966); Ryan's Daughter; Lady Caroline Lamb (& dir).
Plays inc: The Critic and the Heart; Flowering Cherry; The Tiger and the Horse; A Man for All Seasons (Tony-1962); Brother and Sister; State of Revolution.

BOLTON, Guy: Wri. b. Broxburne, Herts, Eng, Nov 23, 1884. Plays inc: The Drone; The Rule of Three; The Fallen Idol; Ninety in the Shade; The Sea Wolf; Nobody Home; Have a Heart; Leave it to Jane; Adam and Eve; The Rose of China; Sally; Sitting Pretty; Grounds for Divorce; Lady Be Good; Oh, Kay!; Top Speed; Simple Simon; Girl Crazy; The Song of the Drums; Anything Goes; Going Places; Hold On to Your Hats; Guardian Angel; Come On, Jeeves; A Man and His Wife.
(Died Sep 5, 1979).

BOMBECK, Erma: Wri-TV pers. b. Dayton, OH, Feb 21, 1927. e. U Dayton, BA. Syndicated columnist. TV inc: Good Morning, America.

BOND, Sudie: Act. b. Louisville, KY, Jul 13, 1923. e. Intermont College; NYU. Studied dance with Jose Limon, Martha Graham, Merce Cunningham. Bway inc: Waltz of the Toreadors; Grease; A Piece of Blue Sky; The Sandbox; The American Dream.
Films inc: Cold Turkey; Where Lilies Bloom; A Thousand Clowns; They Might Be Giants.
TV inc: Philco Playhouse; Mary Hartman, Mary Hartman; The Greatest Man in the World; Jolly Corner; Flo.

BONDARCHUK, Sergei: Act-Dir. b. Russia, Sep 25, 1920. Films inc: (act) The Young Guard; Taras Shevchenko; A Night of The Gold Star; The Grasshopper; An Unfinished Story; Othello; The Soldiers Marched On; It Was Night in Rome; The Battle of the Neretva; Uncle Vanya; Dr. Evans' Silence; Such High Mountains; The Choice of a Goal; The Fate of a Man (& dir); War and Peace; Waterloo (& dir); They Fought for Their Motherland (& dir; co-sp); The Steppe (& dir-sp).

BONDELLI, Phil: Dir. b. Chicago, Dec 10, 1927. e. Crane Coll. TV inc: The Mikado; First Nixon-Kennedy Debates; Something Special; Jack Carter Special; Mod Squad; The Rookies; Six Million Dollar Man; The Bionic Boy; The Bionic Woman; SWAT; Charlie's Angels; Switch; CHiPs.

BONDI, Beulah: Act. b. Chicago, May 3, 1892. Stage debut in Little Lord Fauntleroy in stock and repertory. Bway debut, Wild Birds, 1925. Screen debut in 1932. Films inc: Trail of the Lonesome Pine; Maid of Salem; Of Human Bondage; Mr. Smith Goes to Washington; Our Town; One Foot in Heaven; The Big Fisherman; Tammy, Tell Me True.
TV inc: The Jimmy Stewart Show; Dirty Sally; Crossing Fox River; The Waltons *(Emmy-1977)*.

BONERZ, Peter: Act-Dir. b. Portsmouth, NH, Aug 6, 1918. e. Marquette U. Films inc: Funnyman; Medium Cool; Catch-22; Jennifer on My Mind; Fuzz; The Committee.
TV inc: (act): Bob Newhart Show; The Bastard. (Dir) Szysznyk (all episodes); Love, Natalie; G.I.'s.
Thea inc: The White Murder Case.

BONNER, Frank: Act. b. Little Rock, AR, Feb 28, 1942. Films inc: Hearts of the West; Las Vegas Lady; The Equinox; The Hoax; Stop Me.
TV inc: The Lives of Jenny Dolan; Fer-de-Lance; The Amazing Howard Hughes; WKRP in Cincinnati.

BONO, Sonny (Salvatore Bono): Singer-Act. b. Detroit, Feb 16, 1935. Started writing songs at age 16. Entered record business with Specialty Records as apprentice prod Became asst to Phil Spector, rock music prod and did background singing. Recorded albums with then wife Cher and formed nightclub act with her.
Films inc: Good Times; Chastity; Escape To Athena.
TV: Sonny & Cher Comedy Hour; Sonny Comedy Revue; Murder in Music City; The Top of the Hill.

BONSALL, Joe See Oakridge Boys

BOOKE, Sorrell: Act. b. Buffalo, NY, Jan 4, 1930. e. Columbia U, Yale U. Bway inc: The White Devil; Moby Dick; A Month in the Country; The Sleeping Prince; Nature's Way; Heartbreak House; Finian's Rainbow; Fiorello!; The White House; Come Live With Me; Night.
Films inc: Gone Are the Days; Fail Safe; Black Like Me; Lady in a Cage; Up the Down Staircase; Slaughterhouse Five; The Take; The Iceman Cometh; Bank Shot; The Other Side of Midnight; Special Delivery; Devil Times Five.
TV inc: Greatest Heroes of the Bible.

BOOKMAN, Robert: Exec. b. LA, Jan 29, 1947. e. UC Berkeley, Yale Law School. VP in charge of worldwide prodns, ABC Motion Pictures.

BOONE, Ashley: Exec. b. Springfield, MA, Dec 8, 1938. e. Brandeis U, BA. Dir of Foreign Adv & pub, UA, 1963-68; dir Foreign Adv & Pub, Cinema Center Films, 1968-69; asst to ChmnB, Motown Records, 1970; moved to 20th Century-Fox Film Corp in 1972; named sr vp domestic mktg & dist, 1979; resigned Jan. 1980 to form own marketing firm, ABJ Enterprises; also vp mktg The Ladd Co.

BOONE, Debby: Singer. b. Hackensack, NJ, Sep 22, 1956. D of Pat Boone. TV inc: The Gift of the Magi; Pat Boone and Family Christmas Special; Hope, Women and Song; Debby Boone--The Same Old Brand New Me; The Magic of David Copperfield; A Country Christmas.
(Grammy-new artist-1977).

BOONE, Pat: Singer-Act. b. Jacksonville, FL, Jun 1, 1934. e. Columbia U, Magna Cum Laude with a BS. Winner of Ted Mack's TV Amateur Show, joined Arthur Godfrey TV Show, 1955. Recordings inc: Ain't That A Shame; I Almost Lost My Mind; Friendly Persuasion; Love Letters in the Sand; April Love; Tutti Frutti; Speedy Gonzalez; Days of Wine & Roses; Moody River. Films inc: Bernadine; April Love; Mardi Gras; Journey to the Center of the Earth; All Hands on Deck; State Fair; The Main Attraction; The Yellow Canary; The Horror of it All; The Perils of Pauline; The Cross and the Switchblade. Author: Twixt Twelve and Twenty; Between You & Me and the Gatepost.
TV inc: The Miracle of America; Pat Boone and Family Christmas Special.

BOONE, Richard: Act. b. LA, 1917. e. Stanford U, Actors Studio. NYC. Summer stock, TV shows. Screen debut in Halls of Montezuma. Films inc: Call Me Mister; Man on a Tightrope; The Robe; Battle Stations; The Alamo; The War Lord; Hombre; The Arrangement; The Kremlin Letter; The Shootist; The Last Dinosaur; The Big Sleep; Winter Kills.
TV inc: Medic; Have Gun Will Travel; The Richard Boone Show; Hec Ramsey.

BOORMAN, John: Dir. b. London, 1933. Films inc: Catch Us If You Can; Point Blank; Hell In the Pacific; Leo the Last; Deliverance; Zardoz (& sp); Exorcist II - The Heretic; The Long Shot (act).
The Hard Way (exec prod).

BOOTH, James (nee Geeves-Booth): Act. b. London, Dec 19, 1933. e. RADA. Member of Old Vic Company 1956-57. Thea inc: King Lear; Comedy of Errors; A Thousand Clowns; The Entertainer; The Tempest.
Films inc: The Trials of Oscar Wilde; The Hellions; Sparrows Can't Sing; Zulu; Robbery; The Bliss of Mrs. Blossom; Macho Callahan; Revenge; Brannigan; Airport '77; It's Not The Size That Counts; The Jazz Singer.
TV inc: The Ruffians; The Great Gold Bullion Robbery; Stray Cats and Empty Bottles.

BOOTH, Margaret: Film ed. b. LA, 1898. Films inc: Why Men Leave Home; Husbands and Lovers; The Gay Deceiver; Bringing Up Father; Mysterious Lady; Bridge of San Luis Rey; Redemption; The Lady of Scandal; A Lady's Morals; New Moon; The Southerner; Susan Lenox; Strange Interlude; Smilin' Through; Peg O' My Heart; Riptide; The Barretts of Wimpole Street; Mutiny on the Bounty; Romeo and Juliet; Camille; A Yank at Oxford; supv film ed: The Owl and the Pussycat; To Find a Man; Fat City; The Way We Were; Funny Lady; The Sunshine Boys; Murder by Death; The Goodbye Girl; California Suite; The Cheap Detective (assoc prod); Chapter Two. *(Honorary Oscar*-1977).

BOOTH, Shirley: Act. b. NYC, Aug 20, 1907. Stage debut 1919 with Poli Stock Co., Hartford, CT.; starred on radio in Duffy's Tavern for several years.
Bway inc: Hell's Bells; Laff That Off; The Mask and the Face; After Such Pleasures; Three Men on a Horse; Philadelphia Story; My Sister Eileen; Tomorrow The World; Goodbye, My Fancy *(Tony*-supp-1949); Come Back Little Sheba *(Tony*-1950); A Tree Grows in Brooklyn; Time of the Cuckoo *(Tony*-1953); Desk Set; Loot to The Lilies; Hay Fever (rev); toured in Harvey; Mourning in a Funny Hat.
Films inc: Come Back Little Sheba *(Oscar*-1952); About Mrs. Leslie; Hot Spell; The Matchmaker. Starred on radio in Duffy's Tavern for several years.
TV inc: Perle Mesta Story; Hazel (from 1961-68) *(Emmys*-1962 & 1963).

BOOTHE, Powers: Act. b. Snyder, TX, 1949. Bway inc: Love Star. TV inc: Skag; Guyana Tragedy--The Story of Jim Jones *(Emmy*-1980).

BORCHERS, Cornell (Cornelia Bruch): Act. b. Heydekrug, Germany, Mar 16, 1925. Films inc: The Big Lift; The Divided Heart; Never Say Goodbye; Istanbul; Oasis; Alone Together.

BORETZ, Alvin: Wri. Films inc: My Pleasure Is My Business; Brass Target. TV inc: Follow the North Star; Young Dr. Kildare; Medical Center; Murder By Proxy; The Rookies; Swiss Family Robinson; Kojak; ADA; Spider Man; Stedman; Crisis At Sun Valley.

BORGE, Victor: Perf. b. Copenhagen, Denmark, Jan 3, 1909. Child piano prodigy at age 10. Later became humorous concert artist. Wrote and starred in musical plays and films in Denmark. Fled Nazis in 1941, came to U.S. Concert and nightclub tours. One-man Broadway show. TV variety shows.

BORGNINE, Ernest: Act. b. Hamden, CT, Jan 24, 1918. In stock companies: on Bway in Harvey; Mrs. McThing. Film debut in Whistle at Eaton Falls. Films inc: Vera Cruz; Bad Day at Black Rock; Marty (Oscar-1955); Run For Cover; Catered Affair; Dirty Dozen; Bunny O'Hare; The Revengers; Convoy; Crossed Swords; Ravagers; The Greatest; The Double McGuffin; The Black Hole; When Time Ran Out.

TV inc: Wagon Train; Laramie; Zane Grey Theater; McHale's Navy; All Quiet on the Western Front.

BOROWCZYK, Walerian: Wri-Dir. b. Poland, 1923. Films inc: (Shorts) Photographies Vivantes; Striptease; Dom; Szkola; Terra Incognita; Le Magicien; Solitude; Le Concert de Monsieur et Madame Kabal; Les Jeux des Anges; Rosalie; Gavotte; Le Theatre de Monsieur et Madame Kabal; Le Phonographe. (Features): Goto, the Island of Love; Blanche; Interior of a Convent; Private Collections; Lulu.

BOSLEY, Tom: Act. b. Chicago, Oct 1, 1927. e. De Paul U. Films inc: The Street with No Name; Call Northside 777; The World of Henry Orient; Love with the Proper Stranger; Divorce American Style; The Secret War of Harry Frigg; Yours, Mine and Ours; To Find a Man.

Bway inc: Golden Boy; Fiorello! (Tony-1960); Nowhere to Go But Up; Natural Affection; The Education of H*Y*M*A*N K*A*P*L*A*N.

TV inc: Arsenic and Old Lace; Debbie Reynolds Show; Happy Days; Return of the Mod Squad; Stingiest Man In Town; Doug Hennings World of Magic; Triangle Factory Fire Scandal; The Bastard; With This Ring; Death Trap; Castaways of Gilligan's Island; The Rebels; Pat Boone and Family Christmas Special; The California Earthquake Test; For The Love Of It.

BOSTWICK, Barry: Act. Bway inc: The Robber Bridegroom (Tony-1977).

TV inc: Once Upon a Family; Scruples; Moviola-The Silent Lovers. Films inc: Movie Movie.

BOSUSTOW, Nick: Prod. b. LA, Mar 28, 1940. e. Menlo Coll, BS. S of Stephen R Bosustow. P. Bosustow Entertainment Inc. Prod more than 100 short ani films inc Is It Always Right To Be Right? (Oscar-1970); The Legend of John Henry.

TV inc: The Running Condition; Segs of Sesame Street, The Electric Company; The Incredible Book Escape.

BOSUSTOW, Stephen: Exec Prod. b. Victoria, BC, Canada, Nov 6, 1911. Started in animated cartoon bus. as artist for Disney, others. Founded UPA Pictures, Inc, 1943; founder and Chmn. Stephen Bosustow Prodns, 1961. Ani shorts inc: Magic Fluke; Gerald McBoing Boing (Oscar-1950); Trouble Indemnity; Tooty Tooty Toot; Christopher Crumpet; The Tell Tale Heart; Madeline; Romance of Transportation; When Magoo Flew (Oscar-1954); Gerald McBoing Boing on Planet Moo; Magic Jaywalker; The Jaywalker and His Bird; Magoo's Puddle Jumper (Oscar-1956); Trees and Jamaica Daddy; The Legend of John Henry.

BOTKIN, Perry Jr: Comp-Arr-Mus. b. NYC, Apr 16, 1933. Films scores inc: R.P.M.; Bless the Beasts and the Children; Sky Terror; They Only Kill Their Masters; Lady Ice; Your Three Minutes Are Up.

Provided mus arrs for Andy Williams; Barbra Streisand; Herb Alpert; George Burns; Sammy Davis.

TV inc: Co-author of Nadia's Theme (Grammy-1977); When She Was Bad; The Golden Moment--An Olympic Love Story; Landon, Landon and Landon.

BOTTOMS, Joseph: Act. b. Santa Barbara, CA, Apr 22, 1954. Films inc: The Dove; Crime and Passion; The Black Hole; Cloud Dancer. TV inc: Winesburg, Ohio; Adventures of Major Effects.

BOTTOMS, Sam: Act. b. Santa Barbara, CA, Oct 17, 1955. B of Timothy, Joseph Bottoms. Films inc: The Last Picture Show; Class of '44; Zandy's Bride; The Outlaw Josey Wales; Apocalypse Now; Up From the Depths; Bronco Billy.

TV inc: Savages; Greatest Heroes of the Bible.

BOTTOMS, Timothy: Act. b. Santa Barbara, CA, Aug 30, 1951. Film debut in Johnny Got His Gun. Films inc: Rollercoaster; The Last Picture Show; Love and Pain and the Whole Damn Thing; The Paper Chase; The Moneychangers; Operation Daybreak; A Small Town in Texas; The Other Side of the Mountain, Part II; Hurricane.

TV inc: The Gift of Love; A Shining Season; Escape.

BOULEZ, Pierre: Comp-Cond. b. Montbrison, France, Mar 26, 1925. e. Paris Conservatory of Music. Named mus dir Jean-Louis Barrault's Theatre co 1948, toured world with Barrault; principal guest cond Cleveland Symphony 1970-71; mus dir NY Philharmonic 1971-77; guest cond major orchs, Bayreuth Festival, Edinburgh Festival.

(Grammys-(8)-class alb of year-1967, 1973; opera rec-1967; class perf-1968, 1969, 1970, 1973, 1975).

BOULTING, John: Prod-Dir-Wri. b. Bray, Buchinghamshire, Eng, Nov 21, 1913. With twin brother Roy, formed Charter Film Productions, 1937. Films listed are joint efforts unless otherwise noted: Consider Your Verdict; Inquest; True Crime; Pastor Hall; Thunder Rock; Journey Together (John); Fame Is the Spur; Brighton Rock; The Guinea Pig; Seven Days to Noon; The Magic Box; Seagulls Over Sorrento; Josephine and Men; Private's Progress; Brothers in Law; Lucky Jim; Happy Is the Bride; I'm All Right Jack; Suspect; A French Mistress; Heavens Above; Rotten to the Core; Twisted Nerve; There's a Girl in My Soup (John); Endless Night.

BOULTING, Roy: Prod-Dir. b. Bray, Buckinghamshire, Eng, Nov 21, 1913. See films listed under twin brother John Boulting. Solo film credits inc: Desert Victory; Sailor of the King; Run for the Sun; Soft Beds and Hard Battles; The Last Word.

BOUQUET, Michel: Act. b. Paris, Nov 1926. Films inc: Monsieur Vincent; Brigade Criminelle; Manon; Trois Femmes; La Tour de Nesle; Le Piege; Katia; Lamiel; La Femme Infidele; La Sirene du Mississippi; Borsalino; Un Conde; La Raison d'Etat; The Order and Security of the World; The Toy.

BOURGIGNON, Serge: Wri-Dir. b. France, 1928. Films inc: Sundays and Cybele (Oscar-wri-1963); The Reward; Two Weeks in September; The Picasso Summer.

BOURKE, Terry: Wri-Prod-Dir. b. Bairnsdale, Australia, Apr 19, 1940. Films inc: Sampan; Noon Sunday; Night of Fear; Inn of the Damned; Plugg; Little Boy Lost.

TV inc: Spyforce; Catch Kandy; Murcheson Creek.

BOWDEN, Charles: Prod-Dir. b. Somerville, MA, Aug 7, 1913. e. Harvard U. Began career as actor, Wharf Players, Provincetown, MA, 1929. Thea inc: (act) Ah, Wilderness; Meet the Prince; Hedda Gabler; Dr. Knock; The Three Sisters; Ten Million Ghosts; Antony and Cleopatra; Hamlet; The Taming of the Shrew. US Army, 1941-45. On return to civilian life was tech dir for the Lunts' prod of O Mistress Mine; tech dir, 1949, I Know My Love, also starring the Lunts; M Dir Westport, CT, Country Playhouse, 1948-53; owned, operated New Parsons Theatre, Hartford, CT, Bahama Playhouse, Nassau, 1950-54.

Bway inc: (prod or co-prod) Seagulls Over Sorrento (& dir); At Home with Ethel Waters; Ruth Draper; Ruth Draper and Paul Draper; All in One; Twenty-Seven Wagons Full of Cotton; Fallen Angels (& dir); Hotel Paradiso; Auntie Mame (road shows, & dir); Romanoff and Juliet (& dir); Caligula; The Night of the Iguana (& dir); Slapstick Tragedy; A Streetcar Named Desire (road show); The Changing Room. In 1974 joined NY Telephone Co. as creative consultant.

BOWEN, Bill: Exec. b. Amsterdam, Aug 19, 1936. Chmn, Council for Childrens Film and TV; member of West Australian Film Council.

BOWER, Dallas: Prod-Dir. b. London, 1907. Originally snd recorder, edtr, wri; then dir of BBC-TV, 1939; supv of Ministry of Information film prodn, 1940-42. Asso prod: As You Like It; Henry V; prod: Sir Lancelot, TV series; dir: Alice in Wonderland; The Second Mrs. Tanqueray; Doorway to Suspicion.

BOWERS, William: Wri-Prod. b. Las Cruces, NM, Jan 17, 1916. e. U of MO. Plays inc: Where Do We Go from Here; Back to Eden. Films inc: My Favorite Spy; Night and Day; The Web; Black Bart; Larceny; The Gunfighter; Cry Danger; The Mob; Split Second; Five Against the House; The Best Things in Life Are Free; The Sheepman; Alias Jesse James; The Last Time I Saw Archie; Advance to the Rear; Support Your Local Sheriff.
TV inc: The Wild Wild West Revisited; More Wild Wild West.

BOWIE, David: Singer-Act. b. London, Jan 8, 1947. Films inc: The Man who Fell to Earth; Just a Gigolo.
TV inc: Start Chart.

BOWMAN, Lee: Act. b. Cincinnati, OH, Dec 26, 1914. e. Cincinnati U; AADA; Grenoble U. Started as radio singer.
Films inc: Having a Wonderful Time; The Great Victor Herbert; Buck Privates; Model Wife; Smash-up; Impatient Years; Tonight and Every Night; Cover Girl; Love Affair.
TV inc: Robert Montgomery Presents; Studio One; Miami Undercover; Ellery Queen.
(Died Dec 25, 1979).

BOX, Betty E: Prod. b. Beckenham, Kent, Eng, 1920. Films inc: Miranda; Here Come the Huggetts; Doctor in the House; The Iron Petticoat; A Tale of Two Cities; The Thirty-nine Steps; No Love for Johnnie; A Pair of Briefs; No My Darling Daughters; Deadlier Than the Male; The High Commissioner; The Love Ban; Percy's Progress; It's Not the Size that Counts!.

BOX, Muriel: Wri-Prod-Dir. b. Surrey, Eng, 1905. W of Sydney Box. Films inc: The Seventh Veil (*Oscar*-sp-1946); The Man Within (sp); The Brothers (sp); A Girl in a Million (sp & prod); The Happy Family (& dir); The Beachcomber (& dir); Cash On Delivery (dir); Simon and Laura (dir); Eyewitness (dir); To Dorothy A Son (dir); The Truth About Women (prod-dir); Subway in the Sky (dir); This Other Eden (dir); Rattle of a Simple Man (dir).

BOX, Sydney: Prod-Dir-Wri. b. Kent, England, Apr 29, 1907. Films inc: The Seventh Veil; The Years Between; Holiday Camp; Jassy; The Brothers; Dear Murderer; Quartet; Don't Take It To Heart; Broken Journey; Daybreak; A Girl in a Million; So Long at the Fair; The Prisoner.

BOXLEITNER, Bruce: Act. b. Elgin, IL, May 12. TV inc: How the West Was Won; Jack and the Princess; The Last Convertible; Wild Times; Kenny Rogers As The Gambler.
Films inc: The Baltimore Bullet.

BOYAR, Sully: Act. b. NYC, Dec 14, 1923. Films inc: Car Wash; King of Marvin Gardens; The Gambler; Panic in Needle Park; Made for Each Other; Last of the Red Hot Lovers; Dog Day Afternoon; Oliver's Story; The Jazz Singer.

BOYETT, Bob: Prod. TV inc: Happy Days (crea cons); Laverne & Shirley (crea cons); Angie (supv prod); Out of the Blue (supv prod); Goodtime Girls (exec prod); Bosom Buddies (exec prod-crea).

BOYLE, Peter: Act. b. Philadelphia, Oct 18, 1935. e. La Salle U, BA. Stage debut road company The Odd Couple. Performed in Chicago's Second City Improvisational Repertory Co. Bway inc: The Roast.
Films inc: Joe; T.R. Baskin; Steelyard Blues; Kid Blue; Slither; The Candidate; Taxi Driver; Swashbuckler; The Brink's Job; F.I.S.T.; Hardcore; Beyond The Poseidon Adventure; Where The Buffalo Roam; In God We Trust.
TV inc: From Here To Eternity.

BOZZETTO, Bruno: Prod-Dir. b. Milan, 1939. Prod, Tampu! A History of Weapons, 1958 (short). Started own studio 1960. Films inc: (shorts) An Oscar for Mr Rossi; Mr Rossi Buys a Car; Alpha Omega; The Two Castles; Pickles; Opera; Self-Service. (Features) West and Soda; VIP - My Brother Superman; Allegro Non Troppo.

BRABOURNE, John, Lord: Prod. b. London, Nov 9, 1924. Films inc: Harry Black; Sink the Bismarck; HMS Defiant; The Mikado; Romeo and Juliet; Tales of Beatrix Potter; Murder on the Orient Express; Death on the Nile; Stories From A Flying Trunk; The Mirror Crack'd.

BRACHMAN, Leon S: Exec. b. NYC, Nov 28, 1929. e. U of OK; Brooklyn Law School LLB. With UA as an atty; 1965 legal dept Col; 1978, bus aff vp UA; 1980 sr vp wldwde bus aff Fox thea films.

BRACKEN, Eddie: Act. b. NYC, Feb 7, 1920. Stage debut, Lottery, 1930. Screen debut in, Life With Henry, 1940. Films inc: Fleet's In; Sweater Girl; Miracle of Morgan's Creek; About Face; We're Not Married; Slight Case of Larceny.
Bway inc: The Lady Refuses; So Proudly We Hail; Brother Rat; Seven Year Itch; You Know I Can't Hear You When the Water's Running; The Odd Couple; Sunshine Boys; Hello, Dolly! (London): Hello, Dolly!.
TV inc: Masquerade Party.

BRADBURY, Ray: Wri. b. Waukegan, IL, Aug 22, 1920. Films inc: It Came from Outer Space; The Beast from 20,000 Fathoms; Moby Dick; Fahrenheit 451; The Illustrated Man.
TV inc: Infinite Horizons-Space Beyond Apollo.

BRADLEY, Ed: Newscaster. b. PA. e. Cheyney State Coll, BS. Joined CBS as stringer in the Paris Bureau, 1971; transferred to the Saigon Bureau; named CBS News Corr, 1973; named CBS News White House Corr and anchorman of CBS Sunday Night News, 1976.
TV inc: Return of the CIA; Miami. . .The Trial That Sparked the Riot; The Saudis.

BRADY, Scott (Jerry Tierney): Act. b. NYC, Sep 13, 1924. e. Bliss-Hayden Drama School, Beverly Hills. Films inc: Born to Fight; He Walked by Night; Perilous Journey; Johnny Guitar; Vanishing American; Fort Utah; The Loners; Wicked, Wicked; The China Syndrome.
TV inc: The Last Ride of the Dalton Gang; Power.

BRAEDEN, Eric (Hans Gudegast): Act. b. Kiel, Germany. Films inc: Colossus: The Forbin Project; The Law and Jake Wade; The Ultimate Thrill; Morituri; Escape from the Planet of the Apes; Lady Ice; A Hundred Rifles; Herbie Goes to Monte Carlo.
TV inc: Jack and the Princess; The Power Within; The Aliens Are Coming.

BRAHM, John: Dir. b. Hamburg, Germany, Aug 17, 1893. Films inc: Counsel for Crime; Penitentiary; Escape to Glory; The Undying Monster; Tonight We Raid Calais; The Lodger; Wintertime; Hangover Square; Thief of Venice; Face to Face; The Miracle of Fatima; The Diamond Queen; The Mad Magician; Special Delivery; Bengazi; Hot Rods to Hell.

BRAMBELL, Wilfrid: Act. b. Dublin, Ireland, 1912. Thea inc: Blind Man's Bluff; Stop It, Whoever You Are; The Ghost Train.
Films inc: Dry Rot; Serious Charge; What a Whopper; In Search of the Castaways; Thomasina; A Hard Day's Night; Crooks in Cloisters; Where the Bullets Fly; Witchfinder General; The Adventures of Picasso.
Radio & TV: Steptoe and Son.

BRAND, Neville: Act. b. Kewanee, IL, Aug 13, 1921. Studied acting in NY. Screen debut in D.O.A. Films inc: Halls of Montezuma; Stalag 17; Riot in Cell Block 11; Prince Valiant; The Prodigal; The Adventures of Huckleberry Finn; Birdman of Alcatraz; Psychic Killer; Eaten Alive; The Mouse and His Child; Five Days From Home; The Ninth Configuration; Without Warning.
TV inc: Laredo; The Captain and the Kings; The Seekers.

BRANDO, Jocelyn: Act. b. San Francisco, 1919. e. Lake Forest Coll. Sis of Marlon Brando. Films inc: The Big Heat; China Venture; Nightfall; The Explosive Generation; The Ugly American; Bus Riley's Back in Town; The Chase; The Appaloosa; Movie Movie; Good Luck, Miss Wyckoff; Why Would I Lie?

Bway inc: Mr. Roberts; Desire Under the Elms; Golden State.

TV inc: A Question of Love.

BRANDO, Marlon: Act. b. Omaha, NE, Apr 3, 1924. e. Dramatic Workshop, NY. Played stock. Bway in I Remember Mama; Truckline Cafe; Candida; A Flag Is Born; Streetcar Named Desire. Films inc: The Men; Streetcar Named Desire; Viva Zapata; Julius Caesar; On The Waterfront (Oscar-1954); Sayonara; Teahouse of the August Moon; The Young Lions; Mutiny on the Bounty; Reflections in a Golden Eye; Last Tango In Paris; The Missouri Breaks; The Godfather (Oscar-1972); Superman; Apocalypse Now; The Formula.

TV inc: Roots-The Next Generation (Emmy-supp-1979).

BRANDON, Clark: Act. b. NYC, Dec 30. Films inc: Chicken Chronicles. TV inc: When, Jenny, When; Like Mother, Like Me; Teenage Millionaire; The Fitzpatricks; Out of the Blue.

BRANDON, Michael: Act. b. Brooklyn, NY. e. AADA. Bway inc: Does a Tiger Wear a Necktie? Films inc: Lovers and Other Strangers; Jennifer on My Mind; FM; Promises in the Dark; A Change of Seasons.

TV inc: Third Girl From the Left; The Red Badge of Courage; The Queen of the Stardust Ballroom; James Dean, Portrait of a Friend; Red Alert; Scot Free; Hitchhike; Vacation in Hell; Comedy Company; A Perfect Match; A Change of Seasons.

BRANDT, Victor: Act. b. LA, Sep 19. e. UCLA; AADA. Films inc: Battle of the Bulge; Point Blank; Three the Hard Way. TV inc: Assignment Vienna; Cry Rape; Strange Homecoming; Nobody's Perfect.

BRASSEUR, Claude: Act. b. Paris, 1936. Youngest of an acting family famous in France since 1820. Films inc: Rue Des Prairies; Green Harvest; The Soft-Hearted Guy; Dr. Faustus' Horror Chamber; Les Menteurs; Les Distractions; The Elusive Corporal; Les Ennemis; The Seven Deadly Sins; Banana Peel; Lucky Jo; Du Rififi a Paname; Such A Gorgeous Kid Like Me; Act of Aggression; An Elephant Can Be Extremely Deceptive; Barocco; The Big Operator; Pardon Mon Affaire; Pardon Mon Affaire, Too; Other People's Money; Au Revoir. . .a Lundi; A Simple Story; La Guerre des Policiers; These Kids are Grown Ups; La Banquiere (The Woman Banker).

BRAUDY, Susan: Exec. b. Jul 8, 1941. e. Bryn Mawr, BA; U PA; Yale. Wri-edtr Newsweek; wri-edtr, MS Magazine; dvlpmt exec for Alberto Grimaldi; Dec 1980 named East Coast prodn vp, WB.

BRAUN, Zev: Prod. b. Chicago, Oct 19, 1928. e. U of Chicago. Films inc: Goldstein; The Pedestrian; Angela (exec prod); The Little Girl Who Lives Down the Lane; The Fiendish Plot of Dr. Fu Manchu.

TV inc: Freedom Road.

BRAUS, Mort: Wri. b. NYC, Nov 21, 1908. e. Cornell U, AB, DL. Films inc: Women in Prison; The Other One Am I; Three Loves Has Nancy; The Postman Didn't Ring; Wing and a Prayer; Strange Triangle; Let's Make it Legal; Hannibal.

TV inc: Loretta Young Show; Lassie; Lux Theatre; G E Theatre; Kraft Theatre.

BRAVERMAN, Bart: Act. b. LA, Feb 1. e. Carnegie Tech, MFA. B of Charles Braverman. TV inc: Started as child actor on Bob Hope Show; Red Skelton Show; I Love Lucy; Magic Mongo; Vega$; Fast Lane Blues. Films inc: Alligator.

Thea inc: Godspell; The Rocky Horror Show.

BRAVERMAN, Charles: Prod-Dir. b. LA, Mar 3, 1944. e. USC, BA. Films inc: Dillinger; Soylent Green (titles and montages).

TV inc: An American Time Capsule; The World of '68; Moon Journey; The Smothers Brothers; How to Stay Alive; David Hartman. . . Birth and Babies; Breathe a Sigh of Relief; Getting Married; The Making of a Live TV Show; Televisionland.

BRAXTON, Anthony: Mus-Comp. b. Chicago, Jun 4, 1945. e. Roosevelt U, Chicago Musical College. Multi-instrumentalist of int'l stature; recording artist.

BRAZZI, Rossano: Act. b. Bologna, Italy, 1916. e. U of Florence. Started career on Italian stage. Films inc: (U.S.) Three Coins in the Fountain; Barefoot Contessa; Summertime; South Pacific; Light in the Piazza; Rome Adventure; Woman Times Seven; The Adventurers; The Great Waltz; A Time For Miracles.

BREALEY, Gil: Prod. b. Australia, Apr 9, 1932. Chmn, Tasmanian Film Corp. TV inc: After the Miracle; Two Trumpets for St Andrew; The Lad that Waited; Legend of Damien Parer.

Films inc: My Brother Jack; The Stranger; Three to Go; The Gallery; Sunday Too Far Away.

BREAM, Julian: Classical guitarist. b. London, Jul 15, 1933. e. Royal Coll of Music. London debut 1950. Formed Julian Bream Consort 1960; expert in Elizabethan lute music; Malcolm Arnold Guitar Concerto written for him.

Albums inc: The Art of Julian Bream; An Evening of Elizabethan Music (Grammy-Chamber Music-1963); Popular Classics for Spanish Guitar; Julian Bream in Concert; Baroque Guitar (Grammy-class inst-1966); 20th Century Guitar; Julian Bream and His Friends; Dances of Dowland; Bach and Vivaldi Sonatas for Lute and Harpsichord; Villa Lobos Concerto for Guitar (Grammy-class inst with orch-1971); Julian and John (Grammy-chamber music-1972); Concerto for Guitar and Chamber Ensemble; Julian and John Vol. 2; Berkeley Guitar Concerto/Rodrigo concierto de Aranjuez for Guitar.

TV inc: A Time There Was.

BRECHER, Irving: Wri. b. NYC, Jan 17, 1914. Radio writer for Milton Berle; Willie Howard; Al Jolson. Films inc: New Faces of 1937; At the Circus; Go West; Shadow of the Thin Man; Dubarry Was a Lady; Meet Me in St. Louis; Yolanda and the Thief; Summer Holiday; The Life of Riley (& dir-prod); Somebody Loves Me (& dir); Cry for Happy; Sail a Crooked Ship ((& dir); Bye Bye Birdie.

TV inc: People's Choice; The Life of Riley.

BREGMAN, Buddy: Dir-Prod. b. Chicago, Jul 9, 1940. e. UCLA. Started as an arranger, composer, conductor for such artists as: Judy Garland; Ella Fitzgerald; Sammy Davis Jr, Joel Grey; Debbie Reynolds; Jerry Lewis. Films scores inc: The Delicate Delinquent; Secret of the Purple Reef; The Wild Party; Five Guns West; Born Reckless; Pajama Game.

TV inc: (prod-dir) Richard Rodgers Special; Chicago in the Roaring Twenties; Saga of the Wild West; The American Civil War; Miriam Makeba; George Gershwin Special; Cole Porter Special; An Evening with Ethel Merman; Juliet Prowse Special; Diahann Carroll Special; Bing Crosby in Dublin; Superkid; Great American Music Celebration; Circus of the Stars; Pure Gold; The Danny Thomas Special; Sunpower; The Force Is With Us.

BREGMAN, Martin: Prod. b. NYC. e. IN U, NYU. Business rep 1960 for Barbra Streisand; Elliott Gould; Joel Gray; Candice Bergen; Alan Alda; formed Artists Entertainment Complex in 1971, functioning as career counselor, prod. Films inc: Serpico; Dog Day Afternoon; The Next Man; The Seduction of Joe Tynan; Simon. TV inc: S*H*E.

BREN, Milton: Prod. b. 1905. H of Claire Trevor. Producer and later studio exec with Hal Roach and MGM. Films inc: (as prod) Topper; Merrily We Live; Wyoming; Remember?; There Goes My Heart; Tars and Spars; Borderline. Retired from film industry in 1954.

(Died Dec 15,1979)

BRENNAN, Eileen: Act. b. LA, Sep 3, 1937. e. Georgetown U, AADA. Summer stock. Off-Broadway: Little Mary Sunshine. Films inc: Divorce, American Style; The Last Picture Show; The Sting; At Long Last Love; Hustle; Murder By Death; The Cheap Detective; FM; The Great Smokey Roadblock; Private Benjamin.

Bway inc: The Miracle Worker; Hello, Dolly!; revivals of The King And I; Guys and Dolls; Camelot.

TV inc: A New Kind of Family; When She Was Bad; My Old Man.

BRENNAN, Richard: Prod. b. Sydney, Australia, Jun 24, 1945. e. U of Sydney. Films inc: Lend Me Your Stable; Or Forever Hold Your Peace; The Adventures of Barry McKenzie; The Great McCarthy; The Trespassers; Death Cheaters; News Front.

BRENT, George: (nee Nolan): Act. b. Dublin, Mar 15, 1904. e. Dublin U. Started in silents. Films inc: Lily Turner; Jezebel; Dark Victory; Painted Veil; Stranded; Special Agent; Tomorrow Is Forever; The Spiral Staircase; Luxury Liner; Bride For Sale; Man Bait; Tangier Incident; The Rains Came; The Gay Sisters; Affairs of Susan; Mexican Manhunt; Born Again.
(Died May 25, 1979).

BRENTON, Howard: Plywri. b. Portsmouth, England, Dec 13, 1942. e. St Catherine's Coll, Cambridge. Plays inc: Ladder of Fools; It's My Criminal (one-act); Christie in Love; Fruit; Winter; Daddykins; Revenge; Wesley; Scott of the Antarctic; A Sky-Blue Life; Hitler Dances; Brass Neck; The Churchill Play; Weapons of Happiness; The Romans in Britain.
Films inc: Skinflicker.
TV inc: Lushly; The Saliva Milkshake; The Paradise Run.

BRESLER, Jerry: Prod. b. CO, 1912. Films inc: (Shorts): Heavenly Music *(Oscar-1943)*; Main Street Today; Luckiest Guy In The World; Stairway To Light *(Oscar-1944)*. (Fea): Main Street after Dark; Dr Kildare series; Bewitched; The Web; Another Part of the Forest; Shop Around The Corner; Ziegfeld Girl; The Flying Missile; The Mob; Assignment Paris; Lizzie; The Vikings; Gidget Goes Hawaiian; Diamond Head; Major Dundee; Pussycat Pussycat I Love You.
TV inc: Ray Bolger Show.

BRESSLAW, Bernard: Act. b. England, 1933. Films inc: I Only Arsked; Too Many Crooks; The Ugly Duckling; Morgan; Carry on Screaming; Up Pompeii; Vampire; One of our Dinosaurs Is Missing; The Fifth Musketeer; Jabberwocky; Hawk, the Slayer.
TV inc: The Army Game. Thea inc: (London) Lancelot and Guinevere.

BRESSON, Robert: Wri-Dir. b. France, Sep 25, 1907. Films inc: Les Anges du Peche; Les Dames du Bois de Boulogne; Le Journal d'un Cure de Campagne; Pickpocket; The Trial of Joan of Arc; Au Hazard Balthasar; Mouchette; Une Femme Douce; Lancelot du Lac; Le Diable Probablement.

BREST, Martin: Dir-Wri. b. NYC, 1951. e. NYU, AFI. Films inc: Hot Dogs for Gauguin (short made at NYU); Hot Tomorrows; Going In Style.

BRETT, Jeremy (nee Huggins): Act. b. Berkswell, Eng, Nov 3, 1935. e. Eton Coll. Thea inc: Richard II; Troilus and Cressida; Meet Me by Moonlight; Variations on a Theme; Mr. Fox of Venice; Hamlet; Saint Joan; A Measure of Cruelty; Hedda Gabler; A Voyage Round My Father; The Way of the World.
Films inc: War and Peace; The Wild and the Willing; The Very Edge; My Fair Lady; The Medusa Touch.
TV inc: The Picture of Dorian Gray; Dinner with the Family; The Merry Widow; School for Scandal.

BREWER, Teresa: Singer. b. Toledo, OH, May 7, 1931. Recording artist; on radio, TV and in niteries. Films inc: Three Red Heads from Seattle.

BRIALY, Jean-Claude: Act-Dir. b. Algeria, Mar 30, 1933. Films inc: Elena et les Hommes; Lift to the Scaffold; Le Beau Serge; The Four Hundred Blows; Tire au Flane; La Chambre Ardente; The Devil and Ten Commandments; La Ronde; Un Homme de Trop; King of Hearts; Le Rouge et le Noir; Claire's Knee; Le Fantome de la Liberte; Catherine et Cie; The Accuser; L'Annee Sainte; La Banquiere (The Woman Banker). (Dir-sp) Eglantine; Les Volets Clos; L'oiseau Rare; Un Amour De Pluie; Bobo Jacco; L'oeil Du Maitre; Robert and Robert.

BRIAN, David: Act. b. NYC, Aug 5, 1914. Films inc: Flamingo Road; Beyond the Forest; Intruder in the Dust; The Damned Don't Cry; This Woman Is Dangerous; The High and the Mighty; The First Travelling Saleslady; The Rabbit Trap; A Pocketful of Miracles; How the West Was Won; The Rare Breed; The Destructors; The Seven Minutes.
Bway inc: New Moon; Bittersweet; Let 'Em Eat Cake; Beat the Band; Candle in the Wind.
TV inc: Mr. District Attorney.

BRICKMAN, Marshall: Wri-Dir. b. Rio de Janeiro. e. U WI. With folk groups The Tarriers, The Journeymen, began writing for tv.
TV inc: Candid Camera; The Tonight Show.
Films inc: Sleeper; Annie Hall *(Oscar-1977)*; Manhattan; Simon (& dir).

BRICUSSE, Leslie: Wri-Comp-Lyr-Prod. b. London, Jan 29, 1931. e. Cambridge, MA. Thea inc: book mus & lyr (with Anthony Newley) for: Stop the World--I Want to Get Off. The Roar of the Grease Paint--the Smell of the Crowd; The Good Old Bad Old Days; Kings and Clowns; The Traveling Music Show.
Films inc: Sp, mus & lyrics: Pickwick; Goodbye Mr Chips; Scrooge; Doctor Doolittle; Sammy Stops The World. Film scores inc: Willy Wonka and the Chocolate Factory; Revenge of the Pink Panther; Superman (lyr only); Sunday Lovers (sp only).
Songs inc: Goldfinger; You Only Live Twice; If I Ruled The World; What Kind of Fool Am I *(Grammy-1962)*; We Were Lovers; Talk to the Animals *(Oscar-1967)*. TV inc: I'm a Big Girl Now (lyr).

BRIDGES, Beau: Act. b. Hollywood, 1941. S of Lloyd Bridges. Began film career age 4, The Red Pony. On stage 1947, in All My Sons. Films inc: The Incident; For Love of Ivy; Gaily, Gaily; The Landlord; Hammersmith Is Out; The Other Side of the Mountain; Two-Minute Warning; The Fifth Musketeer; Greased Lightning; Norma Rae; The Runner Stumbles; Silver Dream Racer.
TV inc: Sea Hunt; Ensign O'Toole; Man Without A Country; The Stranger Who Looks Like Me; The Four Feathers; The Child Stealer; United States.

BRIDGES, James: Wri-Dir. b. Paris, AR, Feb 3, 1936. Originally actor in Johnny Trouble; Faces; numerous tv segs. Films inc: (wri) Appaloosa; Colossus: The Forbin Project; Limbo. (Wri-dir): The Baby Maker; The Paper Chase; The China Syndrome; Urban Cowboy.
TV inc: (wri) 18 Alfred Hitchcock Presents; The Paper Chase.

BRIDGES, Jeff: Act. b. Los Angeles, Dec 4, 1949. S of Lloyd Bridges. Appeared in TV series Sea Hunt at age 8. On stage, NY, Hollywood. Films inc: Halls of Anger; The Last Picture Show; The Iceman Cometh; Thunderbolt and Lightfoot; Rancho Deluxe; Hearts of the West; Somebody Killed Her Husband; Winter Kills; The American Success Company; Heaven's Gate.
TV inc: Heroes of Rock N Roll.

BRIDGES, Lloyd: Act. b. San Leandro, CA, Jan 15, 1913. e. UCLA. Films inc: High Noon; The Master Race; A Walk in the Sun; Home of the Brave; White Tower; The Rainmaker; The Goddess; Around the World Under the Sea; The Fifth Musketeer; Bear Island; Airplane.
Thea inc: Oh, Men! Oh, Women!; The Dead Pigeon.
TV inc: Sea Hunt; The Loner; The Critical List; Disaster On The Coastline; Moviola-This Year's Blonde.

BRIGHT, Richard S: Prod. b. New Rochelle, NY, Feb 28, 1936. e. Hotchkiss School; Wharton School of Finance; U PA. Partner in Persky-Bright Org arr film financing before turning prod. Films inc: Tribute.
TV inc: The President's Mistress.
Bway inc: A History of the American Film.

BRINCKERHOFF, Burt: Dir. b. Oct 25, 1936. Films inc: Dogs.
TV inc: The Cracker Factory; The Funny Side of Love; Can You Hear The Laughter?-The Story of Freddie Prinze; Mother and Daughter-The Loving War; Rollergirls; Brave New World; The Day The Women Got Even.

BRINKLEY, David: News Commentator. b. Wilmington, NC, Jul 20, 1920. Started writing for hometown newspaper. Joined United Press before serving in Army, WW II. After discharge in 1943, joined NBC News in Washington as White House corr. Co-anchored NBC Nightly News with late Chet Huntley. TV inc: David Brinkley's Journal; The American Presidency; NBC Reports--Gambling (wri-corr).

BRISEBOIS, Danielle: Act. b. NYC, Jun 28, 1969. Films inc: The Premonition; If Ever I See You Again; King of the Gypsies; Slow Dancing In The Big City.
   TV inc: All My Children; As the World Turns; All in the Family; Archie Bunker's Place; Mom, the Wolfman and Me.
   Bway inc: The Saint of Bleecker Street; Annie.

BRISKIN, Irving: Prod. b. NYC, Feb 28, 1903. e. NYU. Joined Banner Prods, 1923; then Sterling Pictures; founded Meteor Pictures, which prod Tim McCoy Westerns for Columbia; when Meteor purchased by Columbia, became vp Col.
   Films inc: Jam Session; Calling All Stars.

BRISKIN, Mort: Prod-Wri. b. Oak Park, IL, 1919. e. USC, Harvard and Northwestern Law Schools. Films inc: The River; The Magic Face; No Time for Flowers; The Second Woman; Quicksand, The Big Wheel; The Jackie Robinson Story; Ben; Willard; You'll Like My Mother; Walking Tall; Framed.
   TV inc: Sheriff of Cochise; U S Marshall; The Texan; Grand Jury; The Walter Winchell File; Official Detective; Whirlybirds.

BRISSON, Frederick: Prod. b. Copenhagen, Denmark, Mar 17, 1913. e. Rossall College, England. H of the late Rosalind Russell. Formerly actor's agent. First stage production at the Hippodrome, London, Sep, 1933. Came to U.S. in 1939. Bway inc: The Pajama Game *(Tony*-1955); Damn Yankees *(Tony*-1956); The Pleasure of His Company; The Gazebo; Five Finger Exercise; Under the Yum-Yum Tree; Jumpers; So Long 174th St; Mixed Couples.
   Founded Independent Artists Pictures 1948; Films inc: The Velvet Touch; Never Wave at a WAC; The Pajama Game; Damn Yankees; Five Finger Exercise; Under the Yum-Yum Tree; Generation; Mrs. Pollifax-Spy.

BRITT, Elton: Singer. b. Marshall, AR, Jul 7, 1917. Country and western perf during the 40s and 50s. Films inc: Laramie; The Prodigal Son.

BRITT, Mai (Maybritt Wilkens): Act. b. Sweden, 1933. Films inc: Affairs of a Model; La Lupa; The Young Lions; The Hunters; The Blue Angel; Murder Inc.; Secrets of a Woman; The Ship of Condemned Women; Haunts.

BRITTANY, Morgan (Suzanne Cupito): Act. b. Hollywood, Dec 5, 1951. Films inc: Marnie; The Birds; Gypsy; Gable and Lombard. TV inc: Amazing Howard Hughes; Delta County; Initiation of Sarah; Samurai; Fantastic Seven; Going Home Again; The Dream Merchants; Moviola.

BRITTEN, Benjamin: Comp. b. Lowestoft, England, Nov 22, 1913. Operas inc: Peter Grimes; The Rape of Lucretia; Albert Herring; The Beggar's Opera (new version); Billy Budd; The Turn of the Screw; A Midsummer Night's Dream; Death in Venice. Numerous choral works inc War Requiem (*Grammys*-class album of year, class perf choral, class comp-1963).
   TV inc: A Time There Was.

BRITTON, Barbara (nee Brantingham): Act. b. Long Beach, CA, 1923. Films inc: Wake Island; Till We Meet Again; The Virginian; Return of Monte Cristo; Great John L.; Ain't Misbehavin'; The Spoilers.
   Thea inc: Born Yesterday; The Rainmaker; Berkeley Square; Once More With Feeling; Plaza Suite; Relatively Speaking.
   TV inc: Mr. & Mrs. North.
   (Died Jan 17, 1980).

BRITTON, Tony: Act. b. Birmingham, Eng, Jun 9, 1924. Performed in repertory; first London stage appearance 1952, The Firstborn. Films inc: Salute the Toff; Loser Take All; The Rough and the Smooth; Suspect; Stork Talk; The Break; There's a Girl in My Soup; Sunday, Bloody Sunday; The Day of the Jackal; The People That Time Forgot; Night Watch; Agatha.
   TV inc: Melissa; Romeo and Juliet; The Nearly Man.
   Thea inc: Move Over Mrs. Markham; No, No, Nanette; The Dame of Sark; The Chairman; The Bells of Hell; My Fair Lady (rev); Murder Among Friends.

BROCCOLI, Albert R: Prod. b. NYC, Apr 5, 1909. Began as asst dir, Fox, 1938; exec. prod., Warwick Films. Films inc: Cockleshell Heroes; No Time To Die; The Black Knight; Red Beret; Hell Below Zero; Fire Down Below; The Trials of Oscar Wilde; Dr. No; From Russia With Love; Goldfinger; Thunderball; You Only Live Twice; On Her Majesty's Secret Service; Chitty Chitty Bang Bang; Diamonds Are Forever; Live and Let Die; Man With The Golden Gun; The Spy Who Loved Me; Moonraker.

BROCKMAN, Michael: Exec. e. Ithaca Coll. With ABC 1974 as vp, daytime programming, ABC Entertainment, later vp, tape prod ops and admin. Joined NBC Nov 1977 as vp, daytime programs, NBC Entertainment.

BRODERICK, James: Act. b. Charlestown, NH, Mar 7, 1930. Films inc: Girl of the Night; The Group; Alice's Restaurant; The Tree; The Todd Killings; Dog Day Afternoon.
   TV inc: Brenner; The Iceman Cometh; Children of Innocence; John Brown; Family; The Shadow Box.
   Bway inc: Maggie, A Touch of the Poet; A View From The Bridge; Let Me Hear You Smile.

BRODKIN, Herbert: Prod. b. NYC, Nov 9, 1912. e. MI U, Yale Drama School. TV inc: The Defenders; The Nurses; Shane; Coronet Blue; Holocaust (*Emmy*-exec prod-1978); Hollow Image; Doctor Franken; Death Penalty; FDR - The Last Year; The Henderson Monster; Pueblo; The Missiles of October; F Scott Fitzgerald; Last of the Belles; King Crab.

BRODNEY, Oscar: Wri-Prod. b. Boston, 1905. e. Boston U, LLB, Harvard, LLM. Films inc: When Johnny Comes Marching Home; Are You With It?; Yes Sir, That's My Baby; Francis; Little Egypt; The Glenn Miller Story; Lady Godiva; Tammy and the Bachelor; The Bobbikins; Tammy and the Doctor; The Brass Bottle; I'd Rather be Rich.

BRODZIAK, Kenn: Prod. b. Sydney, Australia, May 31, 1913. Joint Man Dir Playbox Theatres Pty, Ltd; Chmn, Man Dir, J C Williamson Prods Ltd.

BROIDY, Steve: Exec. b. Malden, MA, Jun 14, 1905. b. Boston U. Started in sls, Franklin Film Co, then U & WB, before joining Monogram as sls m, 1933; in 1940, elected to bd of dir; in 1945, vp-oper; then p until 1964. P Associated Films Ents.
   Jean Hersholt Humanitarian Award, 1962.

BROKAW, Norman R: Exec. b. NYC, Apr 21, 1927. e. UCLA. Joined William Morris Agency as trainee, 1943. Sr agent, exec. in m.p., TV, 1951; 1974, VP William Morris Agency, World Wide, all areas.

BROKAW, Tom: TV Host. b. Yankton, SD, Feb 6, 1940. e. U of SD. Former NBC anchor, LA; NBC White House corr, 1973-76. Host of Today pgm since Aug, 1976. TV inc: To Be A Doctor.

BROLIN, James: Act. b. LA, Jul 18, 1942. TV inc: The Monroes; Marcus Welby, M.D. (*Emmy*-supp-1970); A Short Walk To Daylight; Trapped.
   Films inc: Take Her, She's Mine; Von Ryan's Express; Morituri; Fantastic Voyage; Our Man Flint; The Car; Gable and Lombard; Capricorn One; The Amityville Horror; Night of the Juggler.

BROMFIELD, John: Act. b. South Bend, IN, Jun 11, 1922. e. St Mary's Coll. Films inc: Harpoon; Rope of Sand; Paid in Full; The Furies; Flat Top; Easy to Love; Ring of Fear; Crime Against Joe; Manfish; Hot Cars.
   TV inc: Sheriff of Cochise; U.S. Marshall.

BRON, Eleanor: Act. b. Stanmore, Middlesex, Eng, 1934. Films inc: Help; Alfie; Two for the Road; Bedazzled; Women in Love; The Millstone.
TV inc: Not So Much a Programme, More a Way of Life.
Thea inc: The Doctor's Dilemma; Howard's End; The Prime of Miss Jean Brodie; Two for the Seesaw; The Prince of Darkness.

BRONSON, Charles (nee Buchinsky): Act. b. Ehrenfeld, PA, 1921. Stock companies, off-Broadway. Films inc: You're in the Navy Now; Red Skies of Montana; Pat and Mike; House of Wax; The Magnificent Seven; The Dirty Dozen; The Great Escape; The Sandpiper; Rider In The Rain; You Can't Win 'em All; The Valachi Papers; The Stone Killer; Mr Majestyk; Death Wish; Breakout; Hard Times; Break Heart Pass; From Noon Till Three; St. Ives; The White Buffalo; Telefon; Love and Bullets; Borderline.
TV inc: The Lineup; The Legend of Jesse James.

BRONSON, Lillian: Act. b. Lockport, NY, Oct 21, 1902. e. U of MI. Films inc: Happy Land; What a Man; A Tree Grows in Brooklyn; Junior Miss; Sentimental Journey; The Hucksters; Sleep My Love; No Room for the Groom; Walk on the Wild Side; Spencer's Mountain; Fail Safe; The Americanization of Emily.
TV inc: Playhouse 90; Studio One; Playhouse of Stars.
Bway inc: Five Star Final; Camille; The Druid Circle.

BRONSTON, Samuel: Prod. b. Bessarabia, Russia, Mar 26, 1908. e. Sorbonne. Films inc: Martin Eden; City Without Men; Jack London; Ten Little Indians; A Walk in the Sun; The Count of Monte Cristo; John Paul Jones; King of Kings; El Cid; 55 Days at Peking; Fall of the Roman Empire; Circus World.

BROOK, Peter: Dir. b. London, Mar 21, 1925. e. Magdalen Coll, Oxford. Films inc: The Beggar's Opera; Moderato Cantabile; Lord of the Flies; Marat/Sade; Tell Me Lies; King Lear; Meetings With Remarkable Men.
Thea inc: Pygmalion; Man and Superman; King John; The Lady from the Sea; The Brothers Karamazov; The Little Hut; Faust; The Dark is Light Enough; Both Ends Meet; The House of Flowers; Irma La Douce; The Visit; The Fighting Cock; Marat/Sade (Tony-1966); The Physician; The Investigation; A Midsummer Night's Dream (Tony-1971).
TV inc: (wri) The Birthday Present; Box for One.

BROOKS, Albert (nee Einstein): Dir-Wri-Act. b. LA, Jul 22, 1947. e. Carnegie Tech. S of late comedian Harry Einstein (Parkyakarkus). TV inc: (Act) Steve Allen Show; Gold-Diggers of 1969; Tonight Show; Saturday Night Live (& wri). Films inc: Taxi Driver (Act); Real Life (Dir-wri-act); Private Benjamin. Recordings inc: Comedy Minus One; A Star is Bought.

BROOKS, Donald: Cos dsgn. b. NYC, Jan 10, 1928. e. Fine Arts School, Syracuse; Parsons School of Design. Films inc: The Cardinal; Star!; Darling Lili; The Bell Jar.
Bway inc: No Strings; Barefoot in the Park; Fade Out, Fade In; The Third Day; Flora, The Red Menace; On A Clear Day You Can See Forever; Promises, Promises.

BROOKS, Foster: Act-Singer. b. Louisville, KY, May 11, 1912. In baseball's Hall of Fame for writing Riley on the Mound. Films inc: Tammy; The Great Race; Yours, Mine and Ours; The Villain.
TV inc: Love on a Rooftop; Dean Martin Roasts; Bobby Vinton Show.

BROOKS, James L: Prod-Wri. b. Brooklyn, NY, May 9, 1940. With CBS News as wri, 1964-1966; to David Wolper Prodns 1966 as wri-prod of docs.
TV inc: Room 222 (crea-exec story ed); Mary Tyler Moore (Emmys-wri-1971,1977; exec prod 1975, 1976, 1977); Thursday's Game (wri-prod); The End (prod); Paul Sand in Friends and Lovers (Exec Prod); Rhoda (co-crea-exec prod); Lou Grant; Cindy (wri); Taxi (co-crea-exec prod) (Emmys-1979,1980); The Associates.
Films inc: Starting Over (prod-wri).

BROOKS, Joseph: Sngwri-Prod-Dir. With ad agency. Wrote jingles inc the Pepsi Generation. Films inc: You Light Up My Life (sp-prod-dir-mus score); (Oscar-song-1977) If Ever I See You Again (sp-act-comp); Heading For Broadway (prod-dir-sp-comp).
(Grammy-song-1977).

BROOKS, Louise: Act. b. Cherryvale, KS, 1906. Originally a dancer with Ruth St. Denis, later on Bway.
Films inc: (silent) The Street of Forgotten Men; The American Venus; A Social Celebrity; It's the Old Army Game; The Show-Off; Just Another Blonde; Love 'em and Leave 'em; Rolled Stockings; The City Gone Wild; A Girl in Every Port; Beggars of Life; went to Europe to make Pandora's Box (snd); Diary of a Lost Girl; Prix de Beaute; returned to Hollywood and made It Pays To Advertise; God's Gift to Women; Empty Saddles; When You're In Love; King of the Gamblers; Overland Stage Riders before retiring in 1938.

BROOKS, Mel (nee Kaminsky): Act-Wri-Dir. b. NYC, 1926. H of Anne Bancroft. First appeared as actor in Golden Boy, Red Bank, NJ; also dir and social dir, Catskills. Became wri for Sid Caesar on TV's Broadway Revue & Your Show of Shows; teamed with Carl Reiner for comedy record album, 2000 Year Old Man & The 2000 and 13 Year Old Man. Films inc: The Critic (short-sp-narr); The Producers (Oscar-sp-1968); The Twelve Chairs (sp); Blazing Saddles (sp-prod-co-dir); Young Frankenstein (prod-sp-dir-act); High Anxiety (prod-sp-dir-act); The Muppet Movie.
TV inc: Sid Caesar, Imogene Coca, Carl Reiner, Howard Morris Special (Emmy-wri-1967); Get Smart (wri); When Things Were Rotten (creator).
Thea inc: (wri) Shinbone Alley; All American.

BROOKS, Richard: Wri-Dir. b. Philadelphia, May 18, 1912. e. Temple U. Films inc: White Savage; The Killers; Brute Force; Crossfire; Key Largo; Any Number Can Play; Crisis; Storm Warning; Deadline; The Last Time I Saw Paris (dir only); Take the High Ground (dir only); The Blackboard Jungle; The Last Hunt; The Catered Affair (dir only); Something of Value; The Brothers Karamazov; Cat on a Hot Tin Roof (dir only); Elmer Gantry (Oscar-sp-1960); Lord Jim (& prod); The Professionals (& prod); In Cold Blood (& prod); The Happy Ending (& prod.); Dollars (& prod); Bite the Bullet (& prod); Looking for Mr. Goodbar.

BROOKSHIER, Tom: Sportscaster. b. Roswell, NM, 1931. e. U of CO. Former pro football player. Host of CBS Sports Spectacular.

BROOME, Peter J: Sls Exec. b. Sydney, Australia, Feb 22, 1930. VP 20th Century Fox Int'l, Inc.

BROSTEN, Harve: Wri-Dir-Prod. b. May 15, 1943. e. Goodman Memorial Theatre-Art Institute, BA. TV inc: All in the Family (Emmy-wri-1978); The Jeffersons; The Guiding Light (dir). Prod various industrial shows and Bway revues at St. Regis Hotel, NY.

BROTHERS JOHNSON: Group. Band featuring Louis Johnson, bass; George Johnson, guitar and voc. Albums inc: Look Out For #1; Right On Time; Blam!; Light Up the Night.
(Grammy-R&B inst-1977).

BROTHERS, Dr Joyce: (nee Bauer): Bcst personality. b. NYC, Sep 20, 1928. e. Cornell U, BS, Columbia U, PHD. TV inc: Dr Joyce Brothers; Consult Dr Brothers; Ask Dr Brothers; An Appointment with Dr Joyce Brothers; Beggarman, Thief; Daytime Star; More Wild Wild West. Films inc: Oh God! Book II.

BROUGH, Walter: Prod-Wri. b. Phila, Dec 19, 1935. e. La Salle Coll, USC. Films inc: (as wri) The Desperados; Run Wild, Run Free; A New Life; No Place to Hide; Jed & Sonny (& prod); Funeral for An Assassin (& prod); On a Dead Man's Chest (& prod).
TV inc: (as wri) Doctor Kildare; The Fugitive; Branded; Name of the Game; Mannix; Mission: Impossible; The Magician; Man from Atlantis; Police Story; Lucan.

BROUMAS, John G: Exec. b. Youngstown, OH, Oct 12, 1917. GM, Pitts & Roth Theatres 1946-54; P, Broumas Theatres; P, Showcase Theatres; secy & treas Tenley Circle Twin Theatre Corp; P, Cinema Mgt Corp.

BROWN, Charlotte: Wri-Dir. b. Cleveland, OH, Oct 20, 1943. e. UCLA, BA. TV inc: (wri) Mary Tyler Moore Show; Bob Newhart Show; Doris Day Show; Mitzi Gaynor Tribute To American Housewife: Rhoda (& dir, exec prod); The Associates (dir).

BROWN, Clarence: Dir. b. Clinton, MA, May 10, 1890. e. U of TN. Dir debut 1920, The Great Redeemer. Joined MGM 1924. Launched Greta Garbo as star U.S. 1926, Flesh and the Devil. Films inc: The Last of the Mohicans; The Eagles; The Goose Woman; A Woman of Affairs; Anna Christie; Romance; Inspiration; A Free Soul; Possessed; Chained; Anna Karenina; Ah Wilderness; Conquest; Idiot's Delight; The Rains Came; Edison, the Man; Come Live with Me (& prod); The Human Comedy (& prod); The White Cliffs of Dover; National Velvet; The Yearling; Song of Love (& prod); Intruder in the Dust (& prod); To Please a Lady (& prod); Angels in the Outfield (& prod); When in Rome (& prod); Plymouth Adventure; Never Let Me Go (prod. only).

BROWN, David: Prod. b. NYC, Jul 28, 1916. e. Stanford U, AB, Columbia, MS. Reporter, edtr, drama critic. Story ed, head of scenario dept. 20th-Fox; apptd member of exec staff, Darryl F Zanuck; exec VP Warner Bros. Partnered with Richard D. Zanuck in Zanuck-Brown Prods. Films inc: Sssssss; Willie Dynamite; The Sugarland Express; Black Windmill; The Eiger Sanction; The Girl from Petrovka; The Sting (*Oscar*-1973); Jaws; MacArthur; Jaws 2; The Island.

BROWN, Denys E: Prod. b. Eng, Aug 8, 1915. e. Oxford U, BA, MA. From 1948 to 1966, prod more than 100 docs, travelogues, educ films before becoming prod-in-chief at Film Australia.

BROWN, Georg Sanford: Act. b. Havana, Jun 24. Films inc: The Comedians; Dayton's Devils; Bullitt; Colossus; The Forbin Project; The Man; God Bless You, Uncle Sam.
TV inc: The Rookies; Barefoot in Athens; The Young Lawyers; Next Time; My Love; Dawn; Portrait of a Teenage Runaway; Roots; The Night the City Screamed.
Thea inc: All's Well That Ends Well; Measure for Measure; Macbeth; Murderous Angels; Hamlet; Detective Story.

BROWN, George H: Prod. b. London, 1913. Films inc: Sleeping Car to Trieste; The Chiltern Hundreds; The Seekers; Jacqueline; Dangerous Exile; Tommy the Toreador; Murder at the Gallop; Guns at Batasi; The Trap; Finders Keepers; Assault; Revenge; Innocent Bystander; Open Season.

BROWN, Georgia (nee Klot): Act. b. London, Oct 21, 1933. Stage debut, 1956, The Threepenny Opera, London. Films inc: Running Scared; The Fixer; The Raging Moon; Lock Up Your Daughters; Nothing But the Night; The Seven-Per-Cent Solution.
TV inc: Upstairs, Downstairs; Shoulder to Shoulder; The Roads to Freedom.
Thea inc: Oliver!; Maggie May.

BROWN, Harry: Wri. b. Portland, ME, Apr 30, 1917. e. Harvard. Films inc: The True Glory; A Walk in the Sun; Arch of Triumph; Sands of Iwo Jima; A Place in the Sun (*Oscar*-sp-1951); Bugles in the Afternoon; The Sniper; Eight Iron Men; All the Brothers Were Valiant; D-Day the Sixth of June; Between Heaven and Hell; Ocean's II; El Dorado.

BROWN, James H: Prod-Dir. b. Berkeley, CA, Jul 26. e. Stanford U, UCLA. TV inc: (dir) Wagon Train; Honey West. (Prod) Gibbsville; The First 36 Hours of Dr Durant; Joe Forrester; Magnificent Magical Magnet of Santa Mesa; The Quest; Alcatraz--The Whole Shocking Story.

BROWN, Jim: Act. b. St Simons Island, GA, Feb 17, 1936. e. Syracuse U. Played pro football, Cleveland Browns. Won Hickock Belt as Professional Athlete of year, 1964. Films inc: Rio Conchos; The Dirty Dozen; 100 Rifles; Slaughter; The Slams; Three the Hard Way; Take A Hard Ride; Superbug; The Wild Ones; Fingers.

BROWN, Johnny: Perf. b. St Petersburg, FL, Jun 11, 1937. TV inc: The Leslie Uggams Show; Laugh-In; Sammy & Company. Thea inc: Golden Boy.

BROWN, Les: Comp-Cond. b. Reinerton, PA, Mar 14, 1912. e. Duke U. Started own band while in college; worked as arr, freelance mus. formed Band of Reknown for recs, tours; cond for Steve Allen; Bob Hope. Songs inc: Trylon Stomp; Duckfoot Waddle; Bill's Well; Bill's III; We Wish You the Merriest; Sentimental Journey.

BROWN, Peter: Act. Films inc: Darby's Rangers; Merrill's Marauders; Ride The Wind; Surf; Kitten With a Whip; Three Guns from Texas; Backtrack; Chrome and Hot Leather.
TV inc: Lawman; Laredo; Salvage; The Top of the Hill; Days of Our Lives; The Girl, The Gold Watch and Everything.

BROWN, Ruth: Singer-Act. b. Portsmouth, VA, Jan 12. Worked top niteries as singer, appeared at Tokyo Jazz Festival; Montery Jazz Festival. Thea inc: Living Fat; Selma; Guys and Dolls.
TV inc: Hello, Larry.

BROWN, Tom: Act. b. NYC, Jan 6, 1913. On radio, then stage. Screen debut in A Lady Lies, 1929. Films inc: Buck Privates Come Home; Duke of Chicago; Operation Haylift; Fireman Save My Child.
TV inc: General Hospital.

BROWN, Vanessa (Smylla Brind): Act. b. Vienna, 1928. e. UCLA. W of Mark Sandrich, Jr. Films inc: Margie; The Late George Apley; Mother Wore Tights; The Foxes of Harrow; The Heiress; Tarzan and the Slave Girl; The Bad and the Beautiful; Rosie; Bless the Beasts and the Children.

BROWNE, Coral: Act. b. Melbourne, Australia, Jul 23, 1913. W of Vincent Price. Thea inc: Lover's Leap; Mated; Basalik; This Desirable Residence; The Golden Gander; Heroes Don't Care; Death Asks a Verdict; The Great Romancer; The Man Who Came to Dinner; Bonne Soupe; The Rehearsal; Lady Windermere's Fan; What the Butler Saw; My Darling Daisy; The Waltz of the Toreadors.
Films inc: The Amateur Gentlemen; Pygmalion; The Prime Minister; Quartet; Madeleine; All at Sea; Rooney; The Ruling Class; Theatre of Blood; The Drowning Pool.
TV inc: Time Express.

BROWNE, Jackson: Songwri-Act. b. Heidelberg, Germany, Oct 9, 1948. Songs inc: Fountain of Sorrow; Before the Deluge; Doctor My Eyes; Here Comes Those Tears; The Pretender.
Albums inc: The Pretender; Running On Empty; Hold Out. Films inc: No Nukes.

BROWNE, Leslie Act. b. NYC, 1958. e. School of American Ballet, NY. Debut in the corps de ballet of Balanchine's Symphony in C, Lincoln Center, 1974; Union Jack, 1976. Hired by Dir Herbert Ross for minor parts in film The Turning Point. When girl originally chosen for key role became ill, Browne replaced her and received Oscar nomination; Nijinsky.

BROWNE, Roscoe Lee: Act-Dir-Wri. b. Woodbury, NJ, 1940. e. Lincoln U, Middlebury Coll, Columbia U. International track star, 1946-56; published poet, short story writer. Films inc: The Comedians; Uptight; The Liberation of L.B. Jones; The Cowboys; World's Greatest Athlete; Superfly T.N.T.; Logan's Run; Twilight's Last Gleaming; Nothing Personal.
Bway inc: The Ballad of the Sad Cafe; The Cool World; Tiger, Tiger Burning Bright!; The Old Glory; A Hand Is On the Gate (& dir).
TV inc: King.

BROWNING, Kirk: Dir. b. NYC, Mar 28, 1921. e. Cornell. Worked as reporter; with American Field Services; as ad writer before joining NBC-TV 1949 as floor mgr. TV inc: Trial of Mary Lincoln; Jascha Heifetz Special; Harry and Lena; NBC Opera Theatre (40 programs); Producers Showcase; Evening with Toscanini; Bell Telephone; The Flood; Beauty and the Beast; Lizzie Borden; World of Carl Sandburg; La Gioconda (*Emmy*-1980); Big Blonde.

BRUBECK, Dave: Comp-Mus. b. Concord, CA, Dec 6, 1920. e. U Pacific, BA. Studied under Darius Milhaud. One of the pioneers of modern jazz, formed own trio 1950, quartet following year; played niteries; several Carnegie Hall appearances; disbanded quartet 1967.
Compositions inc: The Light in the Wilderness; Beloved Son; Gates of Justice.

BRUCE, Brenda: Act. b. Manchester, Eng, 1918. Stage debut, 1934, Babes in the Wood. Films inc: Night Boat to Dublin; Millions Like Us; Piccadilly Incident; My Brother's Keeper; Marry Me; The Final Test; Law and Disorder; Nightmare; The Uncle.

Thea inc: Gently Does It; Woman in a Dressing Gown; Merry Wives of Windsor; Little Murders; Winters Tale; Pericles; Hamlet.

TV inc: Nearer to Heaven; Wrong Side of the Park; The Lodger; Love Story; Give the Clown His Supper; Knock on Any Door; Death of a Teddy Bear; Family at War; Henry IV.

BRUCE, Carol (Shirley Levy): Act-Singer. b. NYC, Nov 15, 1919. Professional debut as bandsinger. As single, headlined top U.S. niteries. Bway inc: George White's Scandals of 1939; Nice Goin'; Louisiana Purchase; New Priorities of 1943; Show Boat; Along Fifth Avenue; Pal Joey; A Family Affair; Do I Hear a Waltz; Henry, Sweet Henry.

Films inc: This Woman Is Mine; Keep 'Em Flying; Behind the Eight Ball; The Messenger; American Gigolo.

TV inc: Ed Sullivan show; Studio One; Armstrong Circle Theatre; Love Of Life; WKRP in Cincinnati.

BRUNDIN, Bo: Act. b. Stockholm, Apr 25, 1937. Arrived U.S. in 1958. Worked in summer stock and off-Broadway. Since 1964 has alternated time between U.S. and Sweden. Films inc: The Great Waldo Pepper; Russian Roulette; The Day The Clown Cried; Meteor; Raise The Titanic.

TV inc: The Word; Centennial; Swan Song.

BRUNING, Robert: Prod. b. Western Australia. TV inc: The Godfathers; The Spoilers; Crisis; The People Next Door; The True Blue Show; Paradise; Is There Anybody There; Mama's Gone A-Hunting; The Alternative; Gone to Ground; The Night Nurse; Plunge Into Darkness; Image of Death; The Death Train; Roses Bloom Twice; Demolition.

BRUNNER, Robert F: Comp-Cond-Arr. b. Pasadena, CA, Jan 9, 1938. Comp., arr., Walt Disney Studios. Scores inc: That Darn Cat; The Computer Wore Tennis Shoes; The Barefoot Executive; Snowball Express; The Castaway Cowboy; The Strongest Man in the World; The North Avenue Irregulars.

TV inc: Gallegher Goes West; Salute to Alaska; The Owl That Didn't Give a Hoot; Hamad and the Pirates; Cavalcade of Songs; Mustang; Adventure in Satan's Canyon; Coomba, Dingo of the Outback; The Young Runaways; The Wonderful World of Disney Special.

BRYAN, Dora (nee Broadbent): Act. b. Southport, Eng, Feb 7, 1924. Stage debut, 1935; screen debut, 1948, Fallen Idol. Films inc: The Cure for Love; The Blue Lamp; High Treason; Lady Godiva Rides Again; Fast and Loose; See How They Run; Cockleshell Heroes; The Green Man; The Night We Got the Bird; A Taste of Honey; The Great St. Trinian's Train Robbery; The Sandwich Man; Two a Penny; Hands of the Ripper; Up the Front.

BRYANT, Anita: Act. b. Barnsdall, OK, Mar 25, 1940. Former Miss Oklahoma. Recording artist. Does promo work for Florida Citrus Commission.

BRYNNER, Yul: Act. b. Sakhalin Island, Japan, Jul 11, 1920. Started singing in night clubs in Paris at age 12. Later joined circus as trapeze artist. Performed with repertory co. in Paris, made American stage debut in Twelfth Night. Bway inc: Lute Song; Dark Eyes; The King and I *(Tony*-supp-1952); Home, Sweet Homer; The King and I (Rev). (London) The King and I.

Films inc: Port of New York; The King and I *(Oscar*-1956); Ten Commandments; Anastasia; Solomon and Sheba; The Magnificent Seven; Taras Bulba; Invitation to a Gunfighter; Return of the Seven; Madwoman of Chaillot; Romance of a Horsethief; Fuzz; Futureworld.

TV inc: Anna and the King of Siam.

BUCHANAN, Edgar: Act. b. Humansville, MO. e. U of OR. Films inc: My Son is Guilty; Arizona; The Desperados; Buffalo Bill; Framed; The Best Man Wins; Red Canyon; Devil's Doorway; The Great Missouri Raid; Shane; The Sheepman; Edge of Eternity; Cimarron; Ride the High Country; McLintock; The Rounders; Welcome to Hard Times.

TV inc: Hopalong Cassidy; Judge Roy Bean; Petticoat Junction; Cade's County.

(Died Apr 4, 1979).

BUCHANAN, James D: Wri-Prod. b. Detroit, MI, Dec 17, 1929. e. MI State. TV inc: Death Squad (wri); Paperman (wri); Jigsaw John (wri-prod); Charlie's Angels (prod); Beach Patrol (wri); The Return of Frank Cannon (wri).

Films inc: Harry in Your Pocket (wri).

BUCHHOLZ, Horst: Act. b. Berlin, Dec 4, 1933. In radio, stage plays. Screen debut in Marianne (French), 1955. Films inc: Robinson Must Not Die; The Confessions of Felix Krull; Tiger Bay; Fanny; One, Two, Three; Nine Hours to Rama; The Empty Canvas; The Great Waltz; Cervantes; From Hell to Victory; Avalanche Express.

TV inc: Raid on Entebbe; The French Atlantic Affair.

BUCK, Jules: Prod. b. St Louis, MO, Jul 30, 1917. Films inc: Love Nest; Fixed Bayonets; Treasure of the Golden Condor; The Day They Robbed the Bank of England; Great Catherine. Under Milkwood; The Ruling Class; Man Friday; The Great Scout and Cathouse Thursday.

TV inc: O.S.S.

BUCKLEY, Anthony: Prod. b. Sydney, Australia, Jul 27, 1937. Films inc: Caddie; The Irishman; The Night of the Prowler.

BUCKLEY, Betty: Act. b. Big Springs, TX, Jul 3, 1947. Films inc: Carrie. TV inc: Eight is Enough.

Bway inc: 1776; Promises, Promises; Pippin.

BUFFUM, Ray: Wri-Prod. b. 1904. Began as radio wri for Al Jolson; later wri-prod Big Town; Lux Theatre; The Whistler; Sam Spade; Rogue's Gallery; Joe Penner Show; Eddie Cantor Show. TV inc: Broadway Open House; Colgate Comedy Hour.

Films inc: (wri) Girls in the Night; Playgirl; The Black Dakotas; Teenage Crime Wave; The Brain from Planet Arous; Teenage Monster; Island of Lost Women.

(Died Dec 13, 1980).

BUFMAN, Zev: Act-Prod. b. Tel Aviv, Israel, Oct 11, 1931. e. LA City College, MA. Films inc: Bengal Rifles; Flight to Tangiers; The Prodigal; The Ten Commandments; Buccaneer.

Thea inc: (act) See How They Run; Lady in the Dark; Brigadoon; Caesar and Cleopatra; Merton of the Movies. (Prod): A Hole in the Head; Laffcapades; Fair Game; Murder in the Red Barn; The Barber of Seville; Our Town; Pajama Tops. (Bway) The Egg; Fair Game for Lovers; Minor Miracle; Marat/Sade; Spofford; Your Own Thing; Jimmy Shine; Big Time Buck White; Oklahoma! (rev); West Side Story (rev); Peter Pan (rev); Brigadoon (rev).

BUJOLD, Genevieve: Act. b. Montreal, Jul 1, 1942. e. Montreal Conservatory of Drama. On screen from 1967. Films inc: La Guerre est Finie; La Fleur de L'age; King of Hearts; The Thief; Isabel; Anne of The Thousand Days; The Act of the Heart; The Journey; Earthquake; Swashbuckler; Obsession; Alex and the Gypsy; Another Man, Another Chance; Coma; Murder By Decree; The Last Flight of Noah's Ark; Final Assignment.

TV inc: St. Joan; Anthony and Cleopatra.

Thea inc: The Barber of Seville; A Midsummer Night's Dream; A House. . .A Day.

BUKTENICA, Raymond: Act. b. NYC, Aug 6. e. UCLA. TV inc: Rhoda; The Amazing Mr. Hughes; Circle of Children; Mary Jane Harper Cried Last Night; The Amazing Nellie Bly; House Calls; The Jayne Mansfield Story.

Films inc: King Kong; Annie Hall.

BULIFANT, Joyce: Act. b. Newport News, VA, Dec 16. e. AADA. Bway inc: Tall Story; Whisper to Me; The Paisley Convertible. TV inc: 90 Bristol Court; Love Thy Neighbor; Big John, Little John; Darn You, Harry Landers; Hanging By A Thread; Flo. Films inc: The Happiest Millionaire; Airplane.

BULOFF, Joseph: Act-Dir. b. Wilno, Lithuania, Dec 6, 1907. To US in 1928. Joined Yiddish Art Theatre, NY, in 1930; Bway inc: Don't Look Now; Morning Star; Oklahoma!; Mrs McThing (dir); The Fifth Season; Once More with Feeling; Moonbirds; Slow Dance on a Killing Ground; The Price.

Films inc: Let's Make Music; Somebody Up There Likes Me; Silk Stockings.

BUMSTEAD, Henry: Art dir. Films inc: To Kill a Mockingbird (Oscar-1962); The Sting (Oscar-1973); Rollercoaster; Slap Shot; House Calls; Same Time Next Year; A Little Romance; The Concorde--Airport 79; Smokey and The Bandit II.

BUNIM, Mary-Ellis: Prod. b. Northampton, MA, Jul 9, 1946. e. Fordham U. TV inc: Search for Tomorrow, exec prod, since 1975.

BUNUEL, Luis (Jean-Louis Bunuel): Wri-Dir. b. Calanda, Spain, 1900. Films inc: Un Chien Andalou; L'Age d'Or; Land Without Bread; Los Olvidados; The Brute; Wuthering Heights; Robinson Crusoe; La Ilusion Viaja en Tranvia; La Mort en ce Jardin; The Young One; Viridiana; The Exterminating Angel; Diary of a Chambermaid; Belle de Jour; The Milky Way; Tristana; The Discreet Charm of the Bourgeoisie; The Phantom of Liberty; That Obscure Object of Desire.

BUONO, Victor: Act. b. San Diego, CA, 1939. Films inc: What Ever Happened to Baby Jane?; Four for Texas; Hush, Hush Sweet Charlotte; The Greatest Story Ever Told; Who's Minding the Mint?; The Wrath of God; Arnold; The Evil; Target-Harry; The Man With Bogart's Face.
   TV inc: Return of the Mod Squad; Better Late Than Never; Murder Can Hurt You; More Wild Wild West.

BURGE, Stuart, CBE: Dir. b. Essex, England, Jan 15, 1918. Originally act with Old Vic. Thea inc: (Dir) Let's Make an Opera; Hook, Line and Sinker; Henry V (& overseas tour); Public and Confidential (Bway); Serjeant Musgrave's Dance (Bway); The Judge; Two Gentlemen of Verona; The Ruling Class; The Demonstration; The Daughter-in-law; The Rivals; A Close Shave; See How They Run; The White Raven; The Devil Is An Ass; The London Cuckolds.
   Films inc: There Was a Crooked Man; Othello; The Mikado; Julius Caesar.
   TV inc: The Power and the Glory; The Devil and John Brown; Luther; School for Scandal.

BURGESS, Wilma: Act. b. Orlando, FL, Jun 11, 1939. e. Stetson Coll. Country mus perf, recording artist.

BURGHOFF, Gary: Act. b. Bristol, CT, May 24. Films inc: M*A*S*H; B S I Love You.
   TV inc: An Evening's Journey to Conway, Mass; M*A*S*H (Emmy-1977); The Man In The Santa Claus Suit; Casino.
   Thea inc: You're a Good Man, Charlie Brown; Finian's Rainbow; Look Homeward, Angel; Bells Are Ringing; Sound of Music; The Boy Friend; Romanoff and Juliet.

BURKE, Alfred: Act. b. London, Feb 28, 1918. e. RADA. Films inc: The Angry Silence; Moment of Danger; The Man Inside; The Man Upstairs; No Time to Die; Law and Disorder; Yangtse Incident; Interpol; Bitter Victory.
   TV inc: The Crucible; Mock Auction; Parole; The Big Knife; Parnell; The Strong are Lonely; Home of the Brave; The Birthday Party; The Watching Eye; The House on Garabaldi Street.
   Thea inc: The Universal Legacy; Henry VI; The MacRoary Whirl; The Father; Pictures in a Bath of Acid; Murder in the Cathedral; Dr. Knock.

BURKE, David: Act. b. Liverpool, England, May 25, 1934. e. RADA. Thea inc: (London) War and Peace; Hotel in Amsterdam; several seasons with Royal Lyceum Company Edinburgh; A Pagan Place; Absurd Person Singular; Watch on the Rhine.

BURKE, Delta: Act. b. Orlando, FL, Jul 30, 1956. e. LAMDA. TV inc: The Seekers; Charleston; A Last Cry for Help; The Chisholms.

BURKE, Graham William: Exec. b. Australia, Jun 10, 1942. Member, Australian Film Commission.

BURKE, Joseph Francis (Sonny): Comp-Cond-Recording exec. b. Scranton, PA, 1914. With Jimmy Dorsey band, later led his own group. A&R exec for Decca, Capitol, other labels, produced scores of albums inc Sinatra-A Man And His Music (Grammy-album of the year-1965); September of My years (Grammy-album of the Year-1966); Trilogy. Composed score for Disney's Lady and the Tramp. Songs inc: You're A Lucky Fellow Mr Smith; Star Dreams; Black Coffee; How It Lies, How It Lies; You Was.
   (Died May 31, 1980).

BURKE, Patricia: Act. b. Milan, Italy, Mar 23, 1917. London stage debut 1933, I Hate Men. Films inc: The Lisbon Story; The Trojan Brothers; Love Story; While I Live; Forbidden; The Happiness of Three Women; Spider's Web; The Day the Fish Came Out.
   TV inc: Robin Hood; For Dear Life; Sword of Freedom.

BURKE, Paul: Act. b. New Orleans, Jan 21, 1929. Films inc: South Sea Woman; Screaming Eagles; Valley of the Dolls; The Thomas Crown Affair; Once You Kiss A Stranger; Daddy's Gone A-Hunting.
   TV inc: Noah's Ark; Five Fingers; Harbor Master; Naked City.

BURMESTER, Leo: Act. b. Louisville, KY, Feb 1. e. Western KY Coll, BA; U Denver, MA. Films inc: Cruising. Bway inc: Lone Star.
   TV inc: All My Children; The Caretaker; Flo.

BURNETT, Carol: Act. b. San Antonio, TX, Apr 26, 1934. e. UCLA. W of Joe Hamilton. Summer stock and nitery experience prior to appearance on Jack Paar show and subsequent Garry Moore daytime tv show. Bway debut in Once Upon a Mattress.
   TV inc: Garry Moore Show (Emmy-1962); Julie and Carol at Carnegie Hall (Emmy-1963); Carol & Company; Calamity Jane; Once Upon a Mattress; Carol Burnett Show (Emmys-1972, 1974, 1975); Julie and Carol at Lincoln Center; 6 Rms Riv Vu; Twigs; Sills and Burnett at the Met; Dolly and Carol in Nashville; The Grass is Always Greener Over the Septic Tank; Friendly Fire; The Tenth Month; This Side Of Eden.
   Films inc: Who's Been Sleeping in My Bed; Pete'n Tillie; The Front Page; A Wedding; Health.
   (Special Tony-1969).

BURNETT, W R: Wri. b. Springfield, OH, Nov 25, 1899. e. OH State U. Films inc: Little Caesar (from own novel); Scarface; Dr Socrates; High Sierra; Crash Dive; Wake Island; This Gun for Hire; The Asphalt Jungle; I Died a Thousand Times; Captain Lightfoot; Sergeants Three.

BURNS, Allan: Wri-Prod. b. Baltimore. Films inc: A Little Romance; Butch and Sundance, The Early Years.
   TV inc: He and She (Emmy-1968); Mary Tyler Moore Show (Emmys-(5)-wri-1971 & 1977; exec prod-1975, 1976, 1977); Rhoda; Lou Grant.

BURNS, Bonnie: Prod. b. Seattle, May 28, 1949. e. U of WA, BA. TV inc: (prod): Don Kirshners Rock Concert; The Jacksons; Rock Music Awards; The World's Most Spectacular Stuntman.

BURNS, Catherine: Act. b. NYC, Sep 25, 1945. e. AADA. Thea inc: The Crucible; The Prime of Miss Jean Brodie.
   Films inc: Last Summer; Red Sky At Morning.

BURNS, George (Nathan Birnbaum): Act. b. NYC, 1896. In show business from age of seven. Vaudeville song and dance man. Teamed with Gracie Allen, 1925 for long career on radio, TV.
   Films inc: The Big Broadcast; We're Not Dressing; Many Happy Returns; International House; Love in Bloom; College Swing; Honolulu; Two Girls and A Sailor; The Sunshine Boys (Oscar-supp-1975); Oh, God!; Sgt. Pepper's Lonely Hearts Club Band; Just You and Me Kid; Going in Style; Oh, God! Book II.
   TV inc: Wendy and Me; Ann-Margret - Hollywood Movie Girls; George Burns In Nashville???

BURNS, Ralph J: Comp-Cond. Films inc: Cabaret (Oscar-adapt-1972); Movie Movie; All That Jazz (Oscar-adapt-1979); Urban Cowboy; First Family (adapt-cond). TV inc: IBM Presents Baryshnikov on Broadway (Emmy-arr-1980).

BURR, Raymond: Act. b. New Westminister, BC, Canada, May 21, 1917. e. Stanford U; U CA; Columbia U; U Chungking. Appeared on stage in many countries in Night Must Fall; Mandarin; Crazy With The Heat; Duke in Darkness. Dir, Pasadena Community Playhouse, 1943.

Films inc: Pitfall; Raw Deal; Place in the Sun; Rear Window; A Man Alone; Count Three and Pray; Great Day in the Morning; Cry in the Night; P.J.; Out of the Blue.

TV inc: Perry Mason (Emmys-1959, 1961); Ironside; Love's Savage Fury; The Bastard (narr); The Jordan Chance; Centennial; Only The Pretty Girls Die; Disaster on the Coastline; The 13th Day - The Story of Esther; The Curse of King Tut's Tomb (narr); The Night the City Screamed.

BURROWS, Abe: Comp-Wri-Dir. b. NYC, Dec 18, 1910. e. CCNY, NYU. Began as radio script writer: Duffy's Tavern; Rudy Vallee; Joan Davis Show; Dinah Shore Show; Texaco Star Theatre; Abe Burrows Show. Performed in nighteries, TV. Bway librettist, Guys and Dolls (Tony-1951). (Dir): Happy Hunting; Silk Stockings; Can-Can; Say, Darling; How to Succeed in Business Without Really Trying (dir-co-wri) (Tony & Pulitzer Prize-1962); Two on the Aisle; The Golden Fleecing; What Makes Sammy Run?; Cactus Flower (& wri); Three Wishes For Jamie (& co-wri); Can Can (& wri).

Films inc: Reclining Figure; Say Darling; Forty Carats; The Solid Gold Cadillac.

Songs inc: The Girl With the Three Blue Eyes; Leave Us Face It, We're in Love.

BURROWS, James: Dir. b. LA, Dec 30, 1940. e. Oberlin, BA; Yale, MFA. S of Abe Burrows. Dir for off-Bway dinner theatres.

TV inc: Mary Tyler Moore; Bob Newhart; Laverne & Shirley; Phyllis; Rhoda; Fay; Bustin Loose; More Than Friends; Like Father Like Daughter; Taxi (Emmy-dir-1980) Lou Grant; The Associates.

BURRUD, Bill: Prod. b. Hollywood, Jan 12, 1925. e. USC, Harvard, Notre Dame. Started as child actor; formed Bill Burrud Prods, 1952. TV inc: Vagabond; Holiday; Wanderlust; Islands in the Sun; True Adventure; Challenging Sea; Animal World; Safari to Adventure; World of the Sea; Wildlife Adventure; Wonderful World of Travel.

Open Heart Surgery; This Nation Israel; Is There an Ark?; Centerfold Pets; Where Did All the Animals Go?; Baja; Secret World of Reptiles; Vanishing Africa; The Great American Wilderness; Predators of the Sea; The Amazing Apes; Curse of the Mayan Temple; Montezuma's Lost Gold.

BURSTYN, Ellen (Edna Rae Gilhooley): Act. b. Detroit, Dec 7, 1932. Worked as fashion model, dancer, bit player under names of Keri Flynn, Erica Dean, Edna Rae, Ellen McRae. Films inc: Goodbye Charlie; For Those Who Think Young; Tropic of Cancer; Alex in Wonderland; King of Marvin Gardens; The Last Picture Show; Exorcist; Alice Doesn't Live Here any More (Oscar-1974); Harry and Tonto; Providence; A Dream of Passion; Same Time Next Year; Resurrection.

Bway inc: Fair Game; Same Time Next Year (Tony-1975).

TV inc: The Doctors; Thursday's Game.

BURTON, Al: Prod-Wri-Dir-Exec. b. Chicago, IL, Apr 4, 1928. e. Northwestern U, BS. TV consultant to Edgar Bergen, 1948; prod-dir-act Al Burton Productions, 1948-1972; wri Oscar Levant Show 1958-59; dev dir TAT Communications 1974, sr vp-exec vp Tandem/TAT. TV inc: All in the Family (Emmy-exec prod-1979).

BURTON, Gary: Mus. b. Anderson, IN, Jan 23, 1943. e. Boston Conservatory of Music.

(Grammys-(2)-jazz solo-1972; jazz duet-1979).

BURTON, LeVar: Act. b. Landsthul, Germany, Feb 16, 1957. e. USC. Films inc: Looking for Mr. Goodbar.

TV inc: Roots; Almos' a Man; Billy: Portrait of a Street Kid; Battered; One in a Million--The Ron Leflore Story; Dummy; Guyana Tragedy - The Story of Jim Jones; The Hunter.

BURTON, Richard (Richard Jenkins): Act. b. Pontrhydyfen, So Wales, Nov 10, 1925. Thea inc: (London) The Lady's Not For Burning; Montserrat; Dark Summer; A Phoenix Too Frequent. Bway inc: The Lady's Not For Burning; Camelot (Tony-1961); Hamlet; Legend of Lovers; Time Remembered; Camelot (rev).

TV inc: Anna Christie; Wuthering Heights; The Fifth Column; The Broadway of Lerner and Loewe.

Films inc: The Last Days of Dolwyn; Now Barabbas; Waterfront; The Woman With No Name; My Cousin Rachel; The Robe; Alexander The Great; Look Back in Anger; The Spy Who Came In From The Cold; Becket; Night of The Iguana; The Sandpiper; Who's Afraid of Virginia Woolf?; Anne of the Thousand Days; Doctor Faustus; Where Eagles Dare; The Voyage; Exorcist II - The Heretic; Equus; The Medusa Touch; The Wild Geese; Breathrough; Circle of Two.

(Grammy-children's recording-1975).

BURTON, Val: Wri-Prod. b. Kent, England, Feb 22, 1900. Films inc: The Ghost Steps Out; Everything But The Truth; Two Years Before the Mast; Henry Aldrich (series); The Time of Their Lives; Bedtime for Bonzo; So This is Harris (short); The Preferred List (short); Passport to Destiny; Lord Jeff; Girl Without A Room; Melody Cruise; Carnival.

BURY, John: Set dsgn. b. Wales, Jan 27, 1925. e. University Coll, London. Thea inc: The Cruel Daughters; The Chimes; Richard III; Volpone; The Quare Fellow; Love and Lectures/Man of Destiny (& dir); A Taste of Honey; A Christmas Carol; Fings aint Wot They Used To Be; Ned Kelly; Sparrers Can't Sing; Oh, What A Lovely War!; numerous plays as head of design for Royal Shakespeare Company; Indians; A Delicate Balance; Dutch Uncle; The Homecoming; The Government Inspector; Old Times; The Silver Tassie; The Blood Knot; The Lionel Touch; several plays as head of design The National Theatre. (Bway) The Homecoming; The Rothschilds; Hedda Gabler; A Doll's House; Via Galactica; Old Times.

BUSCH, Lou (aka Joe (Fingers) Carr): Act-Arr. b. Louisville, KY, 1910. Recording artist; arr for The Young Americans; exec at Columbia Records.

(Died Sep 19, 1979.)

BUSCH, Niven: Wri. b. NYC, Apr 26, 1903. e. Princeton U. Films inc: Babbitt; In Old Chicago; The Westerner; Duel in the Sun; Pursued; The Furies; The Moonlighter; Treasure of Pancho Villa.

BUSEY, Gary: Act-Mus. b. Goose Creek, TX, Jun 29, 1944. Films inc: Last American Hero; Lolly Madonna; Gumball Rally; Alex and the Gypsy; A Star is Born; The Buddy Holly Story; Straight Time; Big Wednesday; Foolin' Around; Carny.

TV inc: Bloodsport; The Execution of Private Slovik.

BUTLER, Bill: Cin. b. Colorado, Apr 7, 1921. e. IA Wesleyan, State U of IA. Films inc: The Rain People; The Conversation; Jaws; One Flew Over the Cuckoo's Nest; Bingo Long; Lipstick; Demon Seed; Capricorn One; Grease; Omen II; Ice Castles; Uncle Joe Shannon; Rockey II; Discoland; It's My Turn.

TV inc: Sunshine; The Execution of Pvt Slovak; Hustling; Fear on Trial; Raid on Entebbe (Emmy-1977).

BUTLER, David: Prod-Dir. b. San Francisco, 1894. e. Stanford U. Silent screen actor before becoming a director, in: The Greatest Thing in Life; Upstairs and Down; The Sky Pilot; The Village Blacksmith; The Temple of Venus; Private Affairs; His Majesty Bunker Bean; Seventh Heaven; Salute. (Dir): The Princess and the Pirate; San Antonio; The Time, the Place and the Girl; My Wild Irish Rose; Two Guys from Milwaukee; It's a Great Feeling; John Loves Mary; Look for the Silver Lining; The Story of Seabiscuit; Tea for Two; Lullaby of Broadway; Painting the Clouds with Sunshine; Where's Charlie?; April in Paris; By the Light of the Silvery Moon; Calamity Jane; The Command; King Richard and the Crusaders; Jump into Hell; Glory; Girl He Left Behind.

TV inc: Wagon Train; Leave it to Beaver; 3 Bob Hope Specials; Seven Little Foys.

(Died June 15, 1979).

BUTLER, Daws (Charles Dawson Butler): Act. b. Toledo, OH, Nov 16, 1916. Voice of many cartoon characters inc Yogi Bear; Huckleberry Hound; Peter Potamus; etc.

BUTLER, Michael: Cin. b. 1944. Films inc: Charley Varrick; Harry and Tonto; The Car (wri); Telefon; Jaws 2; Smokey and The Bandit II.

BUTLER, Robert: Dir. b. LA, Nov 16, 1927. TV inc: Gunsmoke; Cimarron Strip; Hennessey; Star Trek (pilot); Hogan's Heroes (pilot); Batman (pilot); Death Takes A Holiday; Strange New World; The Blue Knight (Emmy-1974 & dir of year 1974); Dark Victory; Mayday at 40,000 Feet; The Andros Targets (pilot); In the Glitter Palace; James Dean, Portrait of a Friend; A Question of Guilt; Lacy and the Mississippi Queen.

Films inc: The Secret of Boyne Castle; The Computer Wore Tennis Shoes; The Barefoot Executive; Scandalous John; Now You See Him, Now You Don't; Hot Lead and Cold Feet; Night of the Juggler.

BUTTOLPH, David: Comp-Cond. b. NYC, Aug 3, 1902. e. Juilliard. Films inc: Show Them No Mercy; Nancy Steele is Missing; Four Sons; The Mark of Zorro; Tobacco Road; This Gun for Hire; Wake Island; Moontide; My Favorite Blonde; Crash Dive; The Hitler Gang; The House on 92nd Street; Somewhere in the Night; Kiss of Death; Rope; Roseanna McCoy; Three Secrets; The Enforcer; My Man and I; House of Wax; Secret of the Incas; The Lone Ranger; The Big Land; The Horse Soldiers; Guns of the Timberland; Steel Jungle; Santiago; The Burning Hills; Cry in the Night.

TV inc: Maverick.

BUTTONS, Red (Aaron Chwatt): Act. b. Bronx, NY, Feb 5, 1919. Began singing for pennies on street corners as a teenager. Comic, Minsky's Burlesque Shows. After WW 2 appeared on Broadway in Barefoot Boy With Cheek. TV inc: The Red Buttons Show; The Secret Life of Henry Phyfe; Rudolph and Frosty's Christmas in July (voice); Power; The Dream Merchants.

Films inc: Sayonara (Oscar-supp-1957); Imitation General; The Big Circus; Five Weeks in a Balloon; Stagecoach; Harlow; They Shoot Horses Don't They?; Who Killed Mary What's Her Name?; Pete's Dragon; The Poseidon Adventure; Gable and Lombard; Viva Knievel; Movie Movie; C.H.O.M.P.S.; When Time Ran Out.

BUTTS, R Dale: Comp-Arr-Cond. b. Lamasco, KY, Mar 12, 1910. e. Louisville Conservatory of Music. Pianist, arr with dance orchs; also in radio. Film scores inc: My Buddy; The Catman of Paris; My Pal Trigger; Gay Blades; One Exciting Week; Flame of Barbary Coast; Night Train to Memphis.

TV inc: Laramie; Wagon Train; The Virginian; Whispering Smith.

Songs inc: I'm in Love with a Guy Who Flies in the Sky; Please Take Me Home This Moment; I Get to Feeling Like This: Lilacs in the Spring; Will You Marry Me, Mr. Larramie; Welcome to My Heart.

BUXTON, Frank: Wri-Dir. b. Wellesley, MA, Feb 13. e. Northwestern U, BS; Syracuse U, MS. TV inc: (wri) Discovery; The Wonder of it all; The Second Bill Cosby Special; Me and the Chimp; Children's Letters to God (dir); Hot Dog (& prod-dir).

BUYSE, Emile: Exec. b. Brussels, Belgium, Apr 16, 1927. e. College Ecole Normale Charles Buls, Brussels. Pub-ad Mgr, 1952, Col; transferred to Paris, 1957 pub-ad Mgr for France, Belgium, Col; 1962, pub-ad-pro dir for Continental Europe, UA; 1966, Fox, Paris, pub-ad-pro Dir for continental Europe; 1969, VP of Fox Int'l Corp, Paris; 1973, VP, mktg mgr, Paris; 1975, VP, GM for Europe & Middle East, Paris; 1976, appointed VP Fox Int'l Dist in LA and P, Fox Int'l Corp; Dec 1980 resd to form ind prods rep-mktg firm.

BUZZELL, Edward: Dir. b. NYC, Nov 13, 1905. 60 films inc: Best Foot Forward; Youngest Profession; Keep Your Powder Dry; Three Wise Fools; Song of Thin Man; Neptune's Daughter; At the Circus; Women of Distinction; Emergency Wedding; Easy to Wed; Confidentially Connie; Ain't Misbehavin'; My Favorite Husband.

BUZZI, Ruth: Act. b. Westerly, RI, Jul 24, 1936. Studied at Pasadena Playhouse. Stage debut San Francisco with Rudy Vallee in Jenny Kissed Me. Played summer stock, off-Bway. Bway inc: Sweet Charity. Films inc: Freaky Friday; The North Avenue Irregulars; The Apple Dumpling Gang Rides Again; The Villain; Skatetown, USA.

TV inc: Laugh-In; Almost Anything Goes; Medical Center; The Lost Saucer; Linus the Lionhearted; That Girl; The Incredible Book Escape (voice).

BYERS, Bill: Mus-Comp-Arr. b. May 1, 1927. Bway inc: (orchs) A Chorus Line; Perfectly Frank.

TV inc: (Arr) America Salutes Richard Rodgers--The Sound of His Music; Ben Vereen--His Roots; IBM Presents Baryshnikov on Broadway (Emmy-1980).

BYGRAVES, Max: Act. b. London, Oct 16, 1922. Films inc: Skimpy in the Navy; Tom Brown's Schooldays; Charley Moon; A Cry from the Streets; Bobbikins; Spare the Rod. TV inc: Roamin Holiday.

BYRNE, Anne: Act. Films inc: Papillon; The End of the World in Our Usual Bed in a Night Full of Rain; Manhattan; Why Would I Lie?.

BYRNE, Eddie: Act. b. Dublin, 1911. Films inc: Odd Man Out; The Gentle Gunman; Time, Gentlemen Please; A Kid for Two Farthings; The Mummy; The Bulldog Breed; Devils of Darkness; Island of Terror; Never Mind the Quality, Feel the Width; The MacIntosh Man; Stardust.

BYRNE, Patsy: Act. b. Ashford, England, Jul 13, 1933. Thea inc: Chicken Soup With Barley; Roots; Serjeant Musgrave's Dance; One Way Pendulum; joined Royal Shakespeare Company for numerous Shakespearean roles 1960-62; again in 1964; Caucasian Chalk Circle; Virtue In Danger; Endgame; Eh?; The Government Inspector; Equus; The Streets of London.

BYRNES, Edd (nee Breitenberger): Act. b. NYC, Jul 30, 1933. Films inc: Girl On The Run; Darby's Rangers; Up Periscope; Marjorie Morningstar; Yellowstone Kelly; Secret Invasion; Wicked, Wicked; Payment in Blood; Tunisia; Any Gun Can Play; Star Wars; Grease.

TV inc: 77 Sunset Strip; Crossroads; Wire Service; Where The Action Is.

BYRON, Kathleen: Act. b. London, Jan 11, 1922. e. London U. Screen debut 1943, Young Mr. Pitt. Films inc: The Silver Fleet; A Matter of Life and Death; Black Narcissus; The Small Back Room; Madness of the Heart; The Reluctant Widow; Four Days; The Gambler and the Lady; Hand in Hand; Night of the Eagle; Private Road; Twins of Evil; One of Our Dinosaurs Is Missing.

TV inc: Emergency Ward 10; Design for Murder; Breaking Point; Young Bess; Secret Venture; Heidi.

BYRUM, John: Wri-Dir. b. Evanston, IL, Mar 14, 1947. Films inc: (wri) Mahogany; Harry and Walter Go to New York. (Wri-dir) Inserts; Heart Beat.

CAAN, James: Act. b. NYC, Mar 26, 1939. Appeared off-Broadway in La Ronde, 1961. Films inc: Lady in a Cage; Games; Journey to Shiloh; Rain People; Rabbit; The Godfather; Slither; Godfather II; Funny Lady; Silent Movie; Another Man, Another Chance; A Bridge Too Far; Comes A Horseman; Chapter Two; Hide In Plain Sight (& dir).

TV inc: Ben Casey; Wagon Train; Combat; Naked City; Brian's Song; Playboy's 25th Anniversary Celebration.

CACAVAS, John: Comp-Cond-Arr. b. Aberdeen, SD, Aug 13, 1930. e. Northwestern U, BM. Films inc: Blade; Horror Express; Satanic Rites of Dracula; Redneck; Airport 75; Airport 77; Once Upon A Spy.

TV inc: She Cried Murder; Linda; Elevator; Hazard's People; Kate McShane; Murder at the World Series; SST Death Flight; Human Feelings; Kojak; Hawaii Five-O; segments of Quincy; Bionic Woman; The Contest Kid Strikes Again.

CACOYANNIS, Michael: Prod-Dir-Wri. b. Cyprus, Jun 11, 1922. e. Admitted to bar, London. Producer of BBC's wartime Greek programs. Films inc: Windfall; Stella; A Girl in Black; A Matter of Dignity; One Last Spring; The Wastrel; Electra; Zorba the Greek; The Day the Fish Came Out; The Trojan Women; Iphigenia; Attila, '74. Bway inc: The Bacchae (dir-translator).

CAESAR, Irving: Lyr-Comp-Act. b. NYC, Jul 4, 1895. Toured in vaudeville. First lyric for the theater was Swanee, with George Gershwin as composer, for Al Jolson in Sinbad. Songs inc: Tea for Two; Sometimes I'm Happy; I Want to be Happy; Lady Play Your Mandolin; Songs of Safety; Songs of Friendship; Songs of Health; Pledge of Allegiance to the Flag.

Films scores inc: George White's Scandals. Bway scores inc: Greenwich Village Follies; Betty Lee; Sweetheart Time; No, No, Nanette; Ziegfeld Revue; Yes, Yes, Yvette; Here's How; Americana; The Wonder Bar; George White's Scandals of 1928; Hit the Deck; White Horse Inn; My Dear Public.

CAESAR, Sid: Act. b. Yonkers, NY, Sep 8, 1922. Band musician. Film debut Tars and Spars. Worked nightclubs, Bway. Films inc: The Guilt of Janet Ames; It's A Mad, Mad, Mad World; Guide For The Married Man; The Busy Body; Airport '75; Silent Movie; Fire Sale; The Cheap Detective; Grease; The Fiendish Plot of Dr. Fu Manchu.

TV inc: Your Show of Shows (Emmy-1952); Caesar's Hour (Emmy-1956); Thanksgiving In The Land of Oz (narr).

CAGNEY, James: Act. b. NYC, Jul 17, 1899. e. Columbia U. In vaudeville, 1924. Later Bway as dancer. On screen from 1930. Films inc: Doorway to Hell; A Midsummer Night's Dream; The Strawberry Blonde; Angels With Dirty Faces; Yankee Doodle Dandy (Oscar-1942); Each Dawn I Die; Johnny Come Lately; 13 Rue Madeleine; Time of Your Life; White Heat; The West Point Story; Come Fill The Cup; What Price Glory?; A Lion Is in the Streets; Run For Cover; Love Me or Leave Me; Mister Roberts; Seven Little Foys; Tribute To A Bad Man; Man With A Thousand Faces; Shake Hands With the Devil; The Gallant Hours; One, Two, Three.

TV inc: The Kennedy Center Honors, 1980.

CAGNEY, Jeanne: Act. b. NYC, Mar 25, 1919. e. Hunter. Sis of James Cagney. Films inc: All Women Have Secrets; Golden Gloves; Queen of the Mob; Yankee Doodle Dandy; Time of Your Life; Don't Bother to Knock; A Lion Is in the Streets; Man of a Thousand Faces; Town Tamer.

TV inc: Big Hello; Legal Tender; Mr. and Mrs. North; Big Town; Wild Bill Hickok.

CAGNEY, William: Prod. b. NYC, 1902. B of James Cagney. Films inc: (asso prod): Strawberry Blonde; Bride Came C.O.D.; Captains of the Clouds; Yankee Doodle Dandy. (Prod): Johnny Come Lately; Blood on the Sun; The Time of Your Life; Kiss Tomorrow Goodbye; A Lion is in the Streets.

CAHN, Sammy: Lyr. b. NYC, Jun 18, 1913. Organized band with Saul Chaplin, duo also wrote songs for niteries; Vitaphone shorts before Hollywood.

Films inc: Anchors Aweigh; Three Coins in a Fountain; Romance on the High Seas; The Kid from Brooklyn; Two Guys from Texas; West Point Story, April in Paris; Three Sailors and a Girl; Love Me or Leave Me; The Court Jester; Meet Me in Las Vegas; Road to Hong Kong; Robin and the Seven Hoods; The Tender Trap; Pocketful of Miracles; Thoroughly Modern Millie.

Bway inc: High Button Shoes; Two's Company; Skyscraper; Walking Happy; Words and Music (& act); Falling In Love Again.

Songs (chief collaborators Chaplin, Jule Styne, James Van Heusen-)inc: Rhythm Is Our Business; Shoe Shine Boy; Until the Real Thing Comes Along; Bei Mir Bist du Schon; Joseph Joseph; Please Be Kind; Saturday Night is the Loneliest Night in the Week; Let It Snow; Let It Snow; I Should Care; It's Been A Long, Long Time; It Seems to Me I've Heard That Song Before; I'll Walk Alone; It's Magic; Be My Love; Teach Me Tonight; Three Coins in a Fountain (Oscar-1954); Love and Marriage (Emmy-1955); The Tender Trap; All the Way (Oscar-1957); High Hopes (Oscar-1959); Second Time Around; Pocketful of Miracles; Call Me Irresponsible (Oscar-1962) My Kind of Town; Thoroughly Modern Millie; Star; All That Love Went to Waste.

CAIN, Christopher (Bruce Doggett): Prod-Dir-Wri. b. Sioux Falls, SD, Oct 29, 1943. e. Dakota Wesleyan U, BA. Films inc: Brother, My Son; Elmer; Buzzard; Grand Jury; Sixth & Main; Key West Crossing (dir only).

CAINE, Howard (nee Cohen): Act. b. Nashville, TN, Jan 2, 1928. e. Columbia U, BS. Films inc: Pay or Die; From the Terrace; Judgment at Nuremberg; Pressure Point; The Man from the Diners' Club; Alvarez Kelly; Watermelon Man; 1776; Helter Skelter.

Thea inc: Wonderful Town; Inherit the Wind; Lunatics and Lovers; Tiger at the Gates; Damn Yankees. TV inc: Marilyn--The Untold Story.

CAINE, Michael (Maurice Joseph Micklewhite): Act. b. London, 1933. Asst. stage mgr. Acted with repertory group. Films inc: Zulu; The Ipcress File; Alfie; The Wrong Box; Gambit; Funeral in Berlin; Hurry Sundown; Deadfall; The Magus; The Battle of Britain; Play Dirty; Too Late The Hero; Get Carter; Kidnapped; X, Y and Zee; A Bridge Too Far; The Eagle Has Landed; The Man Who Would Be King; California Suite; Silver Bears; The Swarm; Beyond The Poseidon Adventure; Ashanti; The Island; Dressed to Kill.

TV inc: The Compartment; The Playmates; Hobson's Choice; Hamlet; Luck of the Draw.

CAIROLI, Charlie: Clown. b. Italy, 1910. One of the last of the British circus clowns, has starred in Blackpool circus since 1939.

(Died Feb 17, 1980).

CALDER-MARSHALL, Anna: Act. b. Kensington, Eng, Jan 11, 1947. Thea inc: Uncle Vanya; The Lady's Not for Burning; The Country Wife; Absurd Person Singular; Objections to Sex and Violence; Dear Janet Rosenberg; Too True to be Good.

Films inc: Pussycat, Pussycat I Love You; Wuthering Heights; Zulu Dawn.

TV inc: The Male of the Species (Emmy-supp-1969).

CALDICOT, Richard: Act. b. London, Oct 7, 1908. e. RADA. Thea inc: Major Barbara; The Critic; Journey's End; She Stoops to Conquer; Caravan; Within the Gates; Floodlight; Edward My Son; Six Months Grace; The Kidder; A Shred of Evidence; No Sex Please, We're British; My Fair Lady (rev).

Films inc: The Card; The VIPs; The Spy Who Came in from the Cold.

CALDWELL, Zoe, OBE: Act. b. Australia, 1934. Bway inc: The Mad Woman of Chaillot; The Way of the World; The Caucasian Chalk Circle; Slapstick Tragedy (Tony-supp-1966); The Prime of Miss Jean Brodie (Tony-1968); A Bequest to the Nation; The Creation of the World and Other Business; Love and Master Will; An Almost Perfect Person.

TV inc: The Apple Cart; Macbeth; The Lady's Not for Burning.

CALHOUN, Rory (Francis Timothy Durgin): Act. b. LA, Aug 8, 1923. Screen debut, 1944, Something for the Boys. Films inc: The Red House; Miraculous Journey; I'd Climb the Highest Mountain; With a Song in My Heart; Powder River; How to Marry a Millionaire; Dawn at Socorro; Treasure of Pancho Villa; The Spoilers; Domino Kid (& prod-dir-sp); Hired Gun (& prod-dir); The Colossus of Rhodes; Marco Polo; A Face in the Rain; Apache Uprising; Night of the Lepus; Koo Lau (doc: prod-dir); Operation Crosseagles; Mule Feathers; Bitter Heritage; Just Not the Same Without You; Midnight Auto Supply; The Main Event; Motel Hell.

TV inc: The Road Ahead; Bet the Wild Queen; Suspicion; The Texan (prod-dir-sp many segments). Flatbed Annie & Sweetiepie, Lady Truckers; The Rebels; Harris & Co, Pottsville. Thea inc: (London) Belle Star.

CALLAN, Michael: Act. b. Philadelphia, 1935. Bway inc: The Boy Friend. Films inc: They Came to Cordura; Pepe; Mysterious Island; The Victors; The Magnificent Seven Ride Again; Lepke; The Cat and the Canary.

TV inc: Blind Ambition; Mark Twain's America - Tom Edison; Scruples.

CALLAS, Charlie: Act. b. NYC, Dec 20. Started as a drummer with various bands; later became night club comedian. Films inc: The Big Mouth; High Anxiety; Pete's Dragon. TV inc: The Andy Williams Show; The Flip Wilson Show; Switch.

CALLEY, John: Exec. b. NJ, 1930. Dir nighttime prog NBC, 1951-57; prod exec Henry Jaffee Enterprises, 1957; joined Filmways, Inc, 1960; exec vp and prod to 1969; exec vp - world-wide prod Warner Bros; p WB; Nov 1980 became cnsltnt. Films inc: (Prod): Wheeler Dealer; The Americanization of Emily; Topkapi; The Cincinnati Kid; Loved One; Don't Make Waves; Ice Station Zebra; Catch-22.

CALLOWAY, Cab: Orch leader-Singer-Act. b. Dec 24, 1907. In vaudeville, playing top theatres inc The Palace; band was one of the top attractions during the big band era. Bway inc: Porgy and Bess; Cotton Club Revue of 1957; Hello Dolly!; Pajama Game. Films inc: The Big Broadcast; International House; The Singing Kid; Manhattan Merry-Go-Round; Stormy Weather; Sensations of 1945; St. Louis Blues; The Cincinnati Kid; A Man Called Adam; The Blues Brothers.

CALVERT, Phyllis (nee Bickle): Act. b. London, Feb 18, 1915. On stage at age 10. Most recent thea inc: A Woman of no Importance; Blithe Spirit; The Cherry Orchard; Hay Fever; The Reluctant Debutante; Dear Daddy; Before The Party.

Films inc: Two Days to Live; They Came by Night; Kipp; The Young Mr. Pitt; The Man in Grey; Fanny by Gaslight; Madonna of the Seven Moons; My Own True Love; Appointment with Danger; Mandy; It's Never Too Late; Indiscreet; Oscar Wilde; Twisted Nerve; Oh! What a Lovely War; The Walking Stick.

TV inc: Kate.

CALVET, Corinne (nee D'ibos): Act. b. Paris, Apr 30, 1925. e. U of Paris School of Fine Arts. Screen debut 1945, La Part de l'Ombre. Hollywood debut 1949, Rope of Sand. Films inc: When Willie Comes Marching Home; My Friend Irma Goes West; On the Riviera; What Price Glory?; Powder River; The Far Country; So This is Paris; The Plunderers; Painted Flats; Bluebeard's Ten Honeymoons; Hemingway's Adventures of a Young Man; Apache Uprising; Quebec; On the Riviera; Too Hot To Handle; Dr. Heckyl and Mr. Hype.

TV inc: She's Dressed To Kill.

CAMERON, John: Comp. b. England. Films inc: Every Home Should Have One; Kes; Night Watch; A Touch of Class; Scalawag; Nasty Habits; Made; The Bermuda Triangle; Lost and Found; Sunburn; The Mirror Crack'd.

TV inc: She Fell Among Thieves.

CAMERON, Rod (nee Cox): Act. b. Calgary, Alberta, Canada, Dec 7, 1912. Films inc: Christmas in July; North West Mounted Police; Henry Aldrich for President; Panhandle; Plunderers; Wagons West; Santa Fe Passage; The Bounty Killer; Evel Knievel; Psychic Killer; Midnight Auto Supply.

CAMP, Joe: Prod-Dir-Wri. b. St Louis, Apr 20, 1939. e. U of MS, BA. Films inc: Benji; Hawmps; For the Love of Benji; The Double McGuffin; Oh, Heavenly Dog.

TV inc: The Phenomenon of Benji; Benji's Very Own Christmas Story; Benji at Cannes; Benji at Work.

CAMPANELLA, Joseph: Act. b. 1927. Films inc: Murder Inc; The Young Lovers; The St. Valentine's Day Massacre; Ben; Meteor; Hangar 18.

TV inc: Mannix; The Bold Ones; Greatest Heroes of the Bible; Rex Stout's Nero Wolfe; The Plutonium Incident.

CAMPBELL, Glen: Singer-Act. b. Billstown, AR, Apr 22, 1935. Films inc: Baby, the Rain Must Fall; The Cool Ones; True Grit; Norwood.

TV Inc: Solid Gold '79; A Country Christmas. (Grammys-(5)-vocal-contemp vocal-c & w, rec-c & w, vocal-1967; album of year-1968).

CAMPBELL, Judy (nee Gamble): Act. b. Grantham, Lincs, Eng, May 31, 1916. On stage since 1935. Screen debut 1940, Saloon Bar. Films inc: Breach of Promise; The World Owes Me a Living; Green for Danger; Bonnie Prince Charlie; There's a Girl in My Soup; Forbush and the Penguins.

Thea inc: You Never Can Tell; Mourning Becomes Electra; Relatively Speaking; Hay Fever; Death on Demand.

TV inc: The Chinese Prime Minister.

CAMPBELL, William: Act. b. Newark, NJ, 1926. Films inc: The Breaking Point; The People Against O'Hara; Escape from Port Bravo; The High and the Mighty; Man Without a Star; Cell 2455 Death Row; Backlash; The Naked and the Dead; Hush, Hush Sweet Charlotte; Dementia; Blood Bath; Black Gunn; Dirty Mary, Crazy Larry.

CAMPOS, Rafael: Act. b. Santiago, Dominican Republic, May 13, 1936. Films inc: Blackboard Jungle; Trial; This Could Be the Night; Tonka; The Light in the Forest; Mister Buddwing; Lady in a Cage; The Appaloosa; The Doll Squad; Oklahoma Crude; Let the Good Times Roll; Slumber Party '57; Where The Buffalo Roam.

TV inc: Centennial; Return of the Mod Squad; The Return of Frank Cannon.

Thea inc: Infidel Caesar; The Oxcart; Ten Years of Love; Ceremony for an Assassinated Black Man.

CANALE, Gianna Maria: Act. b. Reggio Calabria, Italy, Sep 12, 1927. Films inc: Rigoletto; Go for Broke; The Man from Cairo; The Silent Enemy; The Whole Truth; Queen of the Pirates; Scaramouche.

CANDOLI, Pete: Trumpeter-Act. b. Mishawaka, IN. e. Purdue U. H of Edie Adams. Films inc: Bell, Book and Candle (& score); Meet Me After the Show; Presenting Lily Mars; Dubarry was a Lady.

TV inc: Al Hirt Special; One Step Beyond; Peter Gunn; Johnny Staccato.

CANNELL, Stephen J Wri-Prod. TV inc: The Rockford Files (Emmy-supv prod-1978); The Jordan Chance; The Duke; The Night Rider; Stone (Exec prod-co-crea); 10 Speed and Brownshoe; Nightside.

CANNON, Dyan (Samille Diane Friesen): Act. b. Tacoma, WA, Jan 4, 1937. Acting debut TV's Playhouse 90 in Ding-A-Ling Girl. Bway debut The Fun Couple. Films inc: The Last of Sheila; The Love Machine; Bob and Carol and Ted and Alice; Number One (doc: prod-dir-ed); Such Good Friends; The Burglars; Shamus; Doctors' Wives; Heaven Can Wait; Revenge of the Pink Panther; Honeysuckle Rose; Coast To Coast.

TV inc: Matinee Theatre; 77 Sunset Strip; Full Circle; Lady of the House.

CANNON, J D: Act. b. Apr 24, 1922. e. AADA. Started with Joe Papp's NY Shakespeare Festival. Other thea inc: Peer Gynt; Great God Brown; Great Day in the Morning.

Films inc: An American Dream; Cool Hand Luke; Cotton Comes to Harlem; The Lawman; Scorpio; Raise The Titanic.

TV inc: The Defenders; Profiles in Courage; Wedding Band; McCloud; Testimony of Two Men; Ike; The Top of the Hill; Pleasure Palace; My Kidnapper, My Love.

CANOVA, Diana: Act. b. West Palm Beach, FL, Jun 1, 1953. D of Judy Canova. Films inc: The First Nudie Musical. TV inc: Happy Days; Mel & Susan Together; Love Boat; Fantasy Island; Soap; With This Ring; Perry Como's Early American Christmas; The Death of Ocean View Park; I'm A Big Girl Now.

CANOVA, Judy: Act-Singer. b. Jacksonville, FL, Nov 20, 1916. On radio with Paul Whiteman for 10 Years; Woodbury Soap Hour; Judy Canova Show; Colgate Show. TV inc: Colgate Comedy Hour; Love American Style; numerous guest star shots.

Films inc: In Caliente; Broadway Gondolier; Going High Brow; Artists and Models; Thrill of a Lifetime; Scatter Brain; Sis Hopkins; Puddinhead; Sleepy Time Gal; True to the Army; Joan of the Ozarks; Chatter Box; Sleepy Lagoon; Louisiana Hayride; Hit the Hay; Singin' in the Corn; Honey Chile; Oklahoma Annie; The WAC from Walla Walla; Untamed Heiress; Carolina Cannonball; Lay That Rifle Down; Adventures of Huckleberry Finn; Cannonball.

Bway inc: Calling All Stars; Ziegfeld Follies, Yokel Boy.

CANTAMESSA, Gene S: Sound. b. NYC, Feb 17, 1931. Films inc: The Candidate; Blazing Saddles; Nickel Ride; Young Frankenstein; Leadbelly; Smile; Bad News Bears; Black Sunday; Close Encounters of the Third Kind; Citizen Band; Sextette; High Anxiety; Bad New Bears Go to Japan; Same Time Next Year; Prophecy; 1941.

CANTINFLAS (Mario Moreno): Act. b. Mexico, Aug 12, 1911. Clown, acrobat, bullfighter in Mexican comedies for years. Films inc: Neither Blood Nor Sand; Romeo and Juliet; Around the World in Eighty Days; Pepe; The Minister and Me.

CANTON, Mark C: Exec. b. NYC, Jun 19, 1949. e. UCLA. 1978, VP Motion Picture Development, MGM; 1979, exec vp JP Organization; 1980 vp prodn WB. Films inc: Die Laughing (prod).

CANTOR, Arthur: Prod. b. Boston, Mar 12, 1920. e. Harvard, BA. Started as press rep in 1945; entered prod Nov 1959, The Tenth Man. Bway inc: All the Way Home; Gideon; A Thousand Clowns; Man in the Moon; Put it in Writing; The Golden Age; The Passion of Josef D; The Committee; The Trigon (& dir); The World of Gunter Grass; The Concept; The Wizard of Oz; Tango; Winnie the Pooh; Golden Bat. In London, 1970-71, (co-prod): Vivat! Vivat!; A Bequest to the Nation; The Winslow Boy; Butterflies Are Free; The Patrick Pearse Motel. Bway: Old Times; Promenade, All!; Captain Brassbound's Conversion; The Little Black Book; 42 Seconds from Broadway; In Praise of Love; Private Lives; The Constant Wife; Emlyn Williams as Charles Dickens; A Party With Betty Comden and Adolph Green.

CANTRELL, Lana: Singer-Act. b. Sydney, Australia, Aug 7, 1943. Nitery singer Australia 1958. To US 1962, debut on Tonight Show. Nitery, recording star. U.S. rep Int'l Song Festival Poland 1966.

CANUTT, Yakima: Dir. b. Colfax, WA, Nov 29, 1895. World's champion All-around Rodeo, 1917-24. In 1924 became stunt man, double for such stars as Clark Gable, Errol Flynn, John Wayne. Received special Oscar 1966. Films inc: (dir) The Angel and the Badmen; Oklahoma Badlands; Carson City Raiders; Sons of Adventure; G-Men Never Forget; Dangers of the Canadian Mounted; Adventures of Frank and Jesse James; Lawless Rider.

CAPERS, Virginia: Act. b. Sumter, SC, Sep 22. Films inc: House of Women; Ride the Hangman Tree; The World's Greatest Athlete; Five on the Black Hand Side; Trouble Man; Lady Sings the Blues; The Lost Man; The North Avenue Irregulars.
TV inc: Mannix; Breaking Point; Ben Casey; Class of '65; White Mama; Willow B-Women in Prison.
Bway inc: Saratoga; Jamaica; Raisin (Tony-1974).

CAPICE, Philip: Prod. b. Bernardsville, NJ, Jun 24, 1931. e. Dickinson, BA; Columbia, MFA. 1965 vp pgm dvlp Benton & Bowles; 1969 dir special pgms CBS-TV; 1974, Sr VP Crea aff Lorimar Prodns; 1978 P Lorimar; 1979 resd to enter indie prodn.
TV inc: Sybil (Emmy-exec prod-1977); Long Journey Back; Some Kind of Miracle; Studs Lonigan; A Man Called Intrepid.

CAPLAN, Harry: Exec. b. New Haven, CT, Jun 2, 1908. e. UCLA, Southwestern U. With Paramount 1940-60 as asst dir and unit prod m; assoc prod UA, 1960; prod m Filmways, 1962; unit prod m and 2d unit dir, 20th Century Fox, 1963-66; exec prod m National General Productions Inc, 1966-69. Prod: Charro.

CAPOTE, Truman: Wri. b. New Orleans, LA, Sep 30, 1924. Films inc: Breakfast at Tiffany's; In Cold Blood; Other Voices, Other Rooms. Murder by Death (act); CS Blues (act).
TV inc: A Christmas Memory (Emmy-adapt-1967).

CAPRA, Frank: Dir. b. Palermo, Sicily, May 18, 1897. e. CalTech. Wrote 26 Mack Sennett comedies, Two Harry Langdon features. Films inc: (as dir) Platinum Blonde; American Madness; Bitter Tea of General Yen; Lady for a Day; Broadway Bill; It Happened One Night (Oscar-1934); Mr. Deeds Goes to Town (Oscar-1936); Lost Horizon; You Can't Take it With You (Oscar-1938); Mr. Smith Goes to Washington; Meet John Doe; Prelude to War (Doc); Why We Fight (war doc series 1942-44); Arsenic and Old Lace; It's a Wonderful Life; State of the Union; Riding High; Here Comes the Groom; A Hole in the Head; A Pocketful of Miracles.
TV inc: Four one-hour science films for AT&T.

CAPTAIN AND TENNILLE: Husband and wife singing duo. See DRAGON, Daryl and TENNILLE, Toni.

CAPUCINE (Germaine Lefebvre): Act. b. Toulon, France, Jan 6, 1933. Model. Films inc: Song Without End; A Walk on the Wild Side; The Pink Panther; The Seventh Dawn; What's New Pussycat?; The Honey Pot; The Queens; Fellini's Satyricon; Red Sun; Jaguar Lives!; Arabian Adventure; From Hell To Victory.

CARDIFF, Jack: Dir-Cin. b. Yarmouth, Eng, Sep 18, 1914. Films inc: (cin) Wings of the Morning; The Four Feathers; Caesar and Cleopatra; A Matter of Life and Death; Black Narcissus (Oscar-1947); The Red Shoes; Pandora and the Flying Dutchman; The Barefoot Contessa; War and Peace; The Vikings; Crossed Swords; Death on the Nile; The Fifth Musketeer; The Prince and the Pauper; A Man, A Woman and a Bank; Avalanche Express; The Awakening; The Dogs of War. (Dir): Intent to Kill; Beyond this Place; Scent of Mystery; Sons and Lovers; My Geisha; The Lion; The Long Ships; Young Cassidy; The Liquidator; Dark of the Sun; Girl on a Motorcycle (& prod-cin); The Mutations; Penny Gold.

CARDINALE, Claudia: Act. b. Italy, Apr 15, 1939. Films inc: Persons Unknown; Upstairs and Downstairs; Il Bell'Antonio; Rocco and his Brothers; Cartouche; The Leopard; The Pink Panther; Blindfold; Lost Command; The Professionals; Don't Make Waves; Day of the Owl; The Hell with Heroes; A Fine Pair; Adventures of Brigadier Gerard; Popsy Pop; The Red Tent; Papal Audience; Days of Fury; The Gun; The Little Girl In Blue Velvet; Escape To Athena; Corleone.

CARELLI, Joann: Prod. b. NYC. Films inc: The Deer Hunter (asso prod); Heaven's Gate.

CAREY, Harry Jr: Act. b. Saugus, CA, May 16, 1921. Performed in summer stock with father, silent screen western star. Screen debut in Pursued. Films inc: Three Godfathers; She Wore A Yellow Ribbon; Rio Grande; Warpath; Wild Blue Yonder; Monkey Busines; Beneath the 12-Mile Reef; The Long Gray Line; Mister Roberts; House of Bamboo; The Undefeated; One More Train To Rob; The Long Riders.
TV inc: Wild Times.

CAREY, MacDonald: Act. b. Sioux City, IA, Mar 15, 1913. e. U of IA. Performed in summer stock, radio. On Bway in Anniversary Waltz. Screen debut in 1942. Films inc: Dr. Broadway; Take a Letter Darling; Wake Island; Suddenly It's Spring; Hazzard; Excuse My Dust; Let's Make It Legal; My Wife's Best Friend; Fire Over Africa; Stranger at My Door; American Gigolo; End of the World.
TV inc: Days of Our Lives (Emmys-1974, 1975); Roots; The Rebels; The Top of the Hill; The Girl, The Gold Watch and Everything.

CAREY, Phil: Act. b. Hackensack, NJ, Jul 15, 1925. Films inc: Operation Pacific; Pushover; Mister Roberts; Afrique; Wicked as they Come; Screaming Mimi; Tonka; The Great Sioux Massacre; The Seven Minutes.
TV inc: 77th Bengal Lancers; Philip Marlowe; Laredo.

CAREY, Ron: Act. b. Newark, NJ, Dec 11, 1935. Films inc: The Out-of-Towners; Silent Movie; High Anxiety; Fatso.
TV inc: The Corner Bar; The Montefuscos; Barney Miller.

CARIOU, Len: Act-Dir. b. St Boniface, Manitoba, Canada, Sep 30, 1939. e. St Paul's Coll. NY debut, 1968, The House of Atreus. Thea inc: Much Ado about Nothing; The Three Sisters; Henry V; Applause; Cyrano de Bergerac; The Taming of the Shrew; became assoc dir of The Tyrone Guthrie in 1972; Of Mice and Men (dir); Sondheim: A Musical Tribute; The Petrified Forest (dir); King Lear; The Crucible; Don't Call Back (dir); One Man; A Little Night Music; Cold Storage; Sweeney Todd (Tony-1979).
TV inc: The Master Builder; Juno and the Paycock; Don't Forget; Drying up The Streets.
Films inc: A Little Night Music.

CARLIN, George: Act. b. NYC, May 12, 1937. Deejay, nightclub comedian. TV debut 1965 on Merv Griffin Show. Films inc: Car Wash; Americathon. (Grammy-comedy-1972).

CARLIN, Lynn: Act. b. LA, Jan 31, 1930. Films inc: Faces; Tick. . .Tick. . .Tick; Taking Off; Wild Rovers; Baxter. TV inc: Silent Night, Lonely Night; The Morning After; The Honorable Sam Houston; The Tenth Level; The Waltons; James at 16; French Postcards; Battle Beyond The Stars.

CARLINO, Lewis John: Wri. b. NYC, Jan 1, 1932. e. El Camino College BA, USC MA. Films inc: Seconds; The Fox; The Brotherhood; The Mechanic; A Reflection of Fear; Crazy Joe; The Sailor Who Fell From Grace With the Sea (& dir); I Never Promised You a Rose Garden; The Great Santini (& dir); Resurrection.

TV inc: The Brick and The Rose; Where Have All the People Gone?; Doc Elliot; In Search of America; Honor Thy Father.

Plays inc: The Brick and the Rose; Cages (2 plays); Telemachus Clay; Double Talk (2 plays); The Exercise.

CARLISLE, Kitty (Catherine Conn): TV Pers. b. New Orleans, Sep 3, 1914. Widow of Moss Hart. Former opera singer. Films inc: Murder at the Vanities; She Loves Me Not; Here Is My Heart; A Night at the Opera; Hollywood Canteen.

TV inc: What's My Line?; To Tell the Truth.

CARLSEN, Henning: Dir-Wri. b. Aalborg, Denmark, Jun 4, 1927. Made more than 30 shorts before turning to features. Films inc: Dilemma; Epilogue (dir); The Cats (dir); Hunger; Two People Meet and Sweet Music Fills The Heart; We Are All Demons; Are You Afraid?; Oh, to Be On the Bandwagon; A Happy Divorce (dir); Da Svante Forsvandt; Did Somebody Laugh?

CARLSON, Linda: Act. b. Knoxville, TN, May 12. e. IA U, NYU. TV inc: Westside Medical; Kaz. Thea inc: Full Circle.

CARMEN, Julie: Act. b. Millburn, NJ, 1955. e. State U NY, BFA; studied with Sanford Meisner at Neighborhood Playhouse and with Uta Hagen. Bway inc: Zoot Suit. TV inc: The Guiding Light; Love of Life; As The World Turns; Can You Hear the Laughter--The Story of Freddie Prinze.

Films inc: Night of the Juggler; Gloria.

CARMET, Jean: Act. b. France. Films inc: The Tall Blond Man With One Black Shoe; La Raison du plus Fou; Don't Cry With Your Mouth Full; Le Concierge; Les Gaspards; Bons Baisers a Lundi; Return of the Tall Blond Man; Rape of Innocence; Black and White in Color; Alice ou la Derniere Fugue; Plus Ca Va, Moins Ca Va, The Sugar; Violette; Such a Lovely Town.

CARMICHAEL, Hoagy (Hoagland Howard Carmichael): Sngwri-Act. b. Bloomington, IN, Nov 22, 1899. e. IN U, LLB. Wrote a few songs during college years; started law practice but abandoned it when offered job with Jean Goldkette's band; later formed own group.

Bway inc: The Show is On; Walk With Music.

Films inc: (Songs) Anything Goes; Topper; Every Day's A Holiday; Sing You Sinners; Thanks for the Memory; True to Life; Stork Club; Johnny Angel; College Swing; St. Louis Blues; Canyon Passage; Here Comes the Groom. (Act) To Have and Have Not; Canyon Passage; The Best Years of Our Lives; Night Song; Young Man With a Horn; Las Vegas Story.

Songs inc: Stardust; Lazybones; Little Old Lady; Riverboat Shuffle; Georgia on My Mind; Lazy River; In the Still of the Night; Small Fry; Two Sleepy People; Heart and Soul; Skylark; The Nearness of You; In the Cool, Cool, Cool of the Evening (Oscar-1951); Ole Buttermilk Sky; Doctor, Lawyer, Indian Chief; I Get Along With You Very Well; The Old Music Master; The Lamplighter's Serenade; My Resistance is Low.

CARMICHAEL, Ian: Act. b. Hull, Eng, Jun 18, 1920. Films inc: Meet Mr. Lucifer; The Colditz Story; Storm Over the Nile; Simon and Laura; Private's Progress; Brothers in Law; Lucky Jim; Left, Right and Centre; School for Scoundrels; I'm All Right Jack; Light Up the Sky; The Amorous Prawn; Heavens Above; Smashing Time; The Magnificent Seven Deadly Sins.

TV inc: Twice Upon a Time; Lady Luck; The Importance of Being Earnest; Simon and Laura; The Last of the Big Spenders; The Coward Revue.

CARMICHAEL, Ralph R: Comp-Arr-Cond. b. Quincy, IL, May 27, 1927. TV inc: (Arr) Campus Christian Hour; I Love Lucy (& comp); Nat King Cole (& cond).

Films inc: (Comp): Series of films for Billy Graham inc Mr Texas; Joni.

Songs inc: He's Everything To Me; Tell It Like It Is; The Saviour Is Waiting.

CARNE, Judy: Act. b. Southampton, Eng, 1939. Films inc: A Pair of Briefs; The Americanization of Emily; All the Right Noises.

TV inc: Love on a Rooftop; Laugh-In.

CARNE, Marcel: Dir. b. Paris, 1909. Films inc: Jenny; Drole de Drame; Quai des Brumes; Le Jour Se Leve; Les Visiteurs du Soir; Les Enfants du Paradis; L'Air de Paris; Terrain Vague; Three Rooms in Manhattan; The Young Wolves; Les Assassins de L'Ordre; La Merveilleuse Visit.

CARNEY, Art: Act. b. Mt Vernon, NY, Nov 4, 1918. In vaudeville and on broadway prior to radio and tv. TV inc: Cavalcade of Stars; The Jackie Gleason Show (Emmy-supp-1953 & 1954); Harvey; The Honeymooners (Emmy-1955); Art Carney Meets Peter and the Wolf; Our Town; Very Important People; You Can't Take It With You; Letters From Frank; Alcatraz--The Whole Shocking Story; Fighting Back. (Special Emmys-1967 & 1968).

Films inc: A Guide for the Married Man; The Yellow Rolls Royce; Harry and Tonto (Oscar-1974); Scott Joplin; The Late Show; House Calls; Movie Movie; Sunburn; Ravagers; Going In Style; Defiance; Roadie; Steel.

Bway inc: The Rope Dancers; The Odd Couple; Lovers; The Prisoner of Second Avenue.

CARNOVSKY, Morris: Act-Dir. b. St Louis, MO, Sep 5, 1897. First NY stage appearance 1922 in The God of Vengeance. Joined the Group Theatre, 1931. Has appeared regularly with the American Shakespeare Festival Company of Stratford, CT. Thea inc: Saint Joan; Doctors Dilemma; View From The Bridge.

Films inc: The Life of Emile Zola; Rhapsody in Blue; Address Unknown; Our Vines Have Tender Grapes; Cornered; Miss Susie Slagle's; Cyrano de Bergerac; Tovarich.

TV inc: Medea; The World of Sholom Aleichem.

CARON, Leslie: Act. b. Paris, Jul 1, 1931. e. Nat'l Conservatory of Dance. Joined Ballet des Champs Elysees. Screen debut 1951 as star An American in Paris. Films inc: The Story of Three Loves; Lili; Daddy Longlegs; Gaby; Gigi; The Doctor's Dilemma; The Subterraneans; Fanny; The L-Shaped Room; Father Goose; A Very Special Favour; Promise Her Anything; Is Paris Burning?; Head of the Family; Madron; Chandler; The Man Who Loved Women; Serail; Valentino; Goldengirl; Tous Vedettes; Kontrakt.

TV inc: QB VII.

CAROTHERS, A J: Wri. b. Houston, TX, Oct 22, 1931. e. UCLA. Films inc; Miracle of the White Stallions; Emil and the Detectives; The Happiest Millionaire; Never a Dull Moment; Hero at Large.

TV inc: Goldilocks and the Crosby Family; Nanny and the Professor; Topper Returns; Shakespeare Loves Rembrandt; Forever.

CARPENTER, Carleton: Act. b. Bennington, VT, Jul 10, 1926. Thea inc: Bright Boy; Career Angel; Three to Make Ready; The Magic Touch; The Big People; Art of Dust; Almanac.

Films inc: Summer Stock; Father of the Bride; Two Weeks with Love; Whistle at Eaton Falls; Fearless Fagan; Sky Full of Moon; Take the High Ground; Some of My Best Friends Are. . .

CARPENTER, Freddie: Dir. b. Melbourne, Australia, Feb 15, 1908. Appeared on stage as dancer in Australia, New York, London. Thea (dance dir) inc: Tulip Time; Life Begins at Oxford Circus; The Town Talks; Mother Goose; And On We Go; Maritza; The Dancing Years; Lady Behave; Irene. (Dir): The Sleeping Beauty; Dear Miss Phoebe; One Fair Daughter; Never Too Late; The World of Jamie; Let's Get Swinging; Cinderella; Hans Andersen.

Films inc: (arr dances) Carnival; London Town; The Winslow Boy.

TV (dance numbers) inc: Tribute to Sir Winston Churchill; Noel Coward Revue; Tarbuck's Luck.

CARPENTER, John: Dir-Wri. b. Carthage, NY, Jan 16, 1948. e. USC. H of Adrienne Barbeau. Films inc: Dark Star; Assault on Precinct 13; Halloween (& mus); Eyes of Laura Mars (wri); The Fog (& mus).

TV inc: Someone Is Watching Me; Better Late Than Never (wri); Elvis.

CARPENTER, Robert L: Exec. b. Memphis, TN, Mar 20, 1927. Joined U Memphis exchange 1949 as booker; named branch mgr 1958; moved to LA as branch mgr 1963; to NY 1971 as asst gen sls mgr; became gen sls mgr 1973 when H.H. Martin moved up to president of company.

CARPENTERS: Singers. b. New Haven, CT, Richard, 1945, Karen 1950. Brother and sister recording duo. TV inc: Christmas Portrait (1978); Music, Music, Music. *(Grammys*-(3)-New Artist & Group Vocal-1970; Group Vocal-1971).

CARR, Allan: Prod. b. Highland Park, IL, 1939. e. Lake Forest College, Northwestern U. Entered showbusiness on production staff of Playboy Penthouse TV series. Produced plays at Chicago Civic Theatre; Asst to Nicholas Ray on film King of Kings; became personal mgr; Prod West Coast version of Sunday in New York, introducing Marlo Thomas; Creative consultant on Tommy for Robert Stigwood Organization; presented Survive! in assoc with Stigwood; Films inc: The First Time; C.C. and Company; Grease (co-prod & wri); Can't Stop the Music (& wri). TV inc: Ann-Margret Olsson (exec prod).

CARR, Darleen (nee Farnon): Act. b. Chicago, 1950. Films inc: The Sound of Music (voice only); Monkeys Go Home; Death of a Gunfighter; The Impossible Years; The Beguiled.

TV inc: The Smith Family; Streets of San Francisco; Once an Eagle; Young Joe Kennedy; Miss Winslow and Son.

CARR, Martin: Prod-Dir-Wri. b. NYC, Jan 20, 1932. e. Williams Coll. TV inc: Dublin Through Different Eyes; The Search for Ulysses; CBS Reports - Gauguin in Tahiti *(Emmy-*1968); Hunger in America *(Emmy-*1969); The Search For Ulysses; Five Faces of Tokyo; NBC White Paper-Migrant; This Child is Rated X; Leaving Home Blues; ABC Closeup - The Culture Thieves.

CARR, Richard: Wri. b. Cambridge, OH, Feb 24, 1929. e. Pasadena City Coll. Films inc: The Man from Del Rio; Hell Is for Heroes; Too Late Blues; Heaven with a Gun.

TV inc: Four Star Playhouse; Richard Diamond (pilot); Maverick; Zane Grey Theatre; G.E. Theatre; Guns of Will Sonnett (created); The Waltons; Charlie's Angels; Vegas.

CARR, Vikki (Florencia Bisenta de Casillas Martinez Cardona): Singer. b. El Paso, TX, 1942. Sang with bands and in night clubs. Appeared on TV as guest star with Dean Martin, Ed Sullivan, Jack Gleason, Bob Hope, Red Skelton, Carol Burnett. Hosted the Tonight Show.

CARRADINE, David: Act. b. Hollywood, Oct 8, 1940. S of John Carradine. TV inc: Shane; Kung Fu; Mr Horn; Gauguin The Savage; High Noon Part II--The Return of Will Kane. Thea inc: The Deputy; Royal Hunt of the Sun.

Films inc: Taggart; The Violent Ones; Heaven With A Gun; McCabe and Mrs. Miller; Boxcar Bertha; Bound for Glory; The Serpent's Egg; Thunder and Lightning; Deathsport; Gray Lady Down; Circle of Iron; Fast Charlie The Moonbeam Rider; The Long Riders; Cloud Dancer.

CARRADINE, John: Act. b. NYC, Feb 5, 1908. On Bway in Shakespearean roles. On screen from 1936. Films inc: Fallen Angel; House of Dracula; House of Frankenstein; Johnny Guitar; The Egyptian; Stranger on Horseback; Desert Sands; The Kentuckian; Dark Venture; Black Sheep; Everything You Always Wanted to Know About Sex; Boxcar Bertha; The Shootist; The Killer Inside Me; The Last Tycoon; The Sentinel; Crash; Journey Into Beyond (narr); Satan's Cheerleaders; Shock Waves; The White Buffalo; The Bees; The Mouse and His Child; The Boogey Man.

TV inc: The Seekers.

CARRADINE, Keith: Act. b. San Mateo, CA, Aug 8, 1950. S of John Carradine. Bway inc: Hair. Films inc: A Gunfight; McCabe and Mrs. Miller; Idaho Transfer; Emperor of the North; Thieves Like Us; Nashville *(Oscar*-best song-1975); Lumiere; Welcome to L.A.; The Duellists; Pretty Baby; An Almost Perfect Affair; Old Boyfriends; The Long Riders. TV inc: A Rumor of War.

CARRADINE, Robert: Act. b. Mar 24, 1954. S of John Carradine. Films inc: Joyride; Orca; Blackout; Coming Home; The Long Riders; The Big Red One.

CARRERA, Barbara: Act. b. Nicaragua. Was top model. Films inc: The Master Gun Fighter; Embryo; The Island of Dr. Moreau; When Time Ran Out. TV inc: Centennial.

CARRERAS, Sir James: Exec. b. England, 1910. British prod. exec; former exhibitor; chmn. Hammer Films.

CARRERAS, Michael: Prod. b. England, 1927. S of James Carreras. M-dir. Hammer Films since 1971. Films inc: Blackout; The Snorkel; Ten Seconds to Hell; Passport to China; What a Crazy World; She; One Million Years BC; The Lost Continent; The 7 Brothers Meet Dracula; The Lady Vanishes.

CARRIERE, Jean-Claude: Wri-Prod. b. France, 1931. Films inc: Viva Maria; Heureux Anniversaire (Happy Anniversary) *(Oscar*-short coprod-1962); Borsalino; Taking Off; The Discreet Charm of the Bourgeoisie; That Obscure Object of Desire; Leonor; L'Associe; The Tin Drum (wri).

CARROLL, Carroll: Wri. b. NYC, Apr 11, 1902. Started as newspaperman; film critic NY Sunday World; joined J Walter Thompson Agency 1932 as head wri, edit supv radio shows inc Bing Crosby; Rudy Vallee; Al Jolson; Eddie Cantor; Burns & Allen; Joe Penner; Kraft Music Hall; Frank Sinatra; ghosted bios of Henny Youngman; Ed McMahon; Liberace; Mike Douglas; Bob Hope; columnist (And Now A Word From. . .) Variety.

TV inc: Bob Crosby Show; Fred Allen; General Electric Hour.

CARROLL, Diahann: Act-Singer. b. NYC, Jul 17, 1935. Films inc: Carmen Jones; Porgy and Bess; Goodbye Again; Paris Blues; Hurry Sundown; The Split; Claudine.

TV inc: Julia; A Holiday Tribute To Radio City Music Hall; I Know Why The Caged Bird Sings; Hope Women & Song.

Bway inc: No Strings *(Tony*-1962).

CARROLL, John (Julien LaFaye): Act. b. New Orleans, 1908. Studied opera in Europe. Films inc: Rose of the Rio Grande; Susan and God; Marx Brothers Go West; Rio Rita; Flying Tigers; A Letter for Evie; Bedside Manner; Fiesta; The Flame; Hit Parade of 1951; The Farmer Takes a Wife; Decision at Sundown; The Plunderers of Painted Flats; Teenage Graffiti.

(Died Apr 24, 1979).

CARROLL, Madeleine: Act. b. West Bromwich, Eng, Feb 26, 1906. e. Birmingham U, BA. Films inc: The Guns of Loos; The American Prisoner; Atlantic; Young Woodley; French Leave; School for Scandal; Madame Guillotine; I Was a Spy; Thirty-Nine Steps; Case Against Mrs. Ames; Secret Agent; The General Died at Dawn; Lloyds of London; On The Avenue; Prisoner of Zenda; It's All Yours; Blockade; Honeymoon in Bali; Cafe Society; Safari; Northwest Mounted Police; One Night in Lisbon; Bahama Passage; Lady in Distress; My Favorite Blonde; Don't Trust Your Husband; The Fan.

CARROLL, Matt: Prod. b. Sydney, Australia, Jun 6, 1944. e. Sydney U. Films inc: Shirley Thompson Versus the Aliens; Sunday Too Far Away; Fourth Wish; Storm Boy; Money Movers; Weekend of Shadows; Blue Fin; The Plumber; Breaker Morant; The Club.

CARROLL, Pat: Act. b. Shreveport, LA, May 5, 1927. e. Immaculate Heart Coll, Catholic U. Films inc: With Six You Get Egg Roll. TV inc: Cinderella; Caesar's Hour *(Emmy*-supp-1956); The Danny Thomas Show; Busting Loose; Getting Together.

Bway inc: Catch A Star!; On the Town (rev).

CARROLL, Vinnette: Act-Dir. b. NYC, Mar 11, 1922. e. Long Island U, BA; NYU, MA. In stock, repertory, toured in one-woman variety show; artistic dir Urban Arts Corps; teacher at NYC High School for Performing Arts. Bway inc: (act) A Streetcar Named Desire; Small War on Murray Hill; The Crucible; Jolly's Progress; Moon On A Rainbow Shawl (off-Bway); The Octoroon; Your Arms Too Short To Box With God (& co-wri & dir). (Dir) Don't Bother Me I Can't Cope (& conceived); Bury The Dead; Croesus and the Witch; Step Lively Boy; But Never Jam Today; I'm Laughin' But I Ain't Tickled (& conceived). London inc: Moon On A Rainbow Shawl (act); Black Nativity (dir).

Films inc: A Morning for Jimmy; One Potato, Two Potato; Up The Down Staircase; Alice's Restaurant.

THE CARS: Group. Members inc: Ric Ocasek, Elliot Easton, David Robinson, Benjamin Orr, Greg Hawkes. Began as regional group in New England.

Albums inc: The Cars; Candy-O; Panorama.

CARSEY, Marcia: Exec. b. South Weymouth, MA, Nov 21, 1944. e. U of NH. Joined ABC July 1974 as general program exec in comedy programming; May 1976 named VP Prime Time Comedy Development; Oct. 1976 VP Prime Time Comedy Programs-VP Comedy and Variety Programs; June 1978 Sr VP Comedy & Variety Programs; June 1979 SR VP all Prime Time Series; Dec 1980, resd to go into indie prodn.

CARSON, Dick: Dir. TV inc: Merv Griffin Show (Emmy-1974); The Don Rickles Show; Tonight Show.

CARSON, Jeannie (Jean Shufflebottom): Act. b. Yorkshire, Eng, 1928. Films inc: Love in Pawn; As Long as They're Happy; An Alligator Named Daisy; Rockets Galore; Seven Keys.

TV inc: Hey Jeannie!; Best Foot Forward; Jeannie Carson Show.
Thea inc: (tour) Sound of Music; Camelot; 110 in the Shade.

CARSON, Johnny: TV Pers. b. Corning, IA, Oct 23, 1925. e. U of NE. Started on radio station KFAB, Lincoln, NE. Then to WOW, WOW-TV, Omaha, 1948; announcer, KNXT, LA, 1950; then Carson's Cellar; quizmaster, Earn Your Vacation, 1954; writer for Red Skelton; Johnny Carson Show, CBS-TV; Who Do You Trust, ABC-TV; The Tonight Show, NBC-TV (Emmys-1976, 1977, 1978, 1979); Lucy Moves To NBC (ATAS Governors Award-1980).

CARSON, Robert: Wri. b. Clayton, WA, Oct 6, 1909. Wri-prod CBS 1954-55. Films inc: Men With Wings; The Light That Failed; Bundle of Joy; Action of the Tiger; Beau Geste; Western Union; The Desperadoes; A Star Is Born (Oscar-1937).

CARSON, Sunset (Kit) (Michael Harrison): Act. b. Plainview, TX, Nov 12, 1927. Films inc: Stage Door Canteen; Janie; Call of the Rockies; Code of the Prairie; The Oregon Trail; Days of Buffalo Bill; Alias Billy the Kid; The El Paso Kid Deadline; Rio Grande; Outlaw Grizzly; Buckstone County Prison; Marshall of Windy Hollow.

TV inc: Six Gun Heroes; Dukes of Hazard.

CARTER, Bennett Lester (Benny): Comp-Saxophonist-Arr-Act. b. NYC, Aug 7, 1907. e. Wilberforce U. To Paris 1935, joined Willie Lewis orch; staff arr, BBC, Eng. Formed own band in NY, Hollywood. Films inc: A Man Called Adam (score); The View From Pompey's Head (act); Snows of Kilimanjaro (act). TV background score: M Squad.

Songs inc: Because of You; When Lights Are Low; Manhattan Mood; Cow Cow Boogie.

CARTER, Dixie: Act. b. McLemoresville, TN, May 25. Thea inc: (Bway) Pal Joey; Sextet. (Off-Bway) Jesse and the Bandit Queen; Fathers and Sons; Taken In Marriage.

TV inc: On Our Own; The Andros Targets; The Edge of Night; Out of the Blue.

CARTER, Jack (nee Chakrin): Act. b. NYC, Jun 24, 1923. e. Brooklyn College. Stage debut, 1947, Call Me Mister. Films inc: The Horizontal Lieutenant; Viva Las Vegas; The Extraordinary Seaman; The Resurrection of Zachary Wheeler; The Happy Hooker Goes To Washington; The Octagon; Alligator.

TV inc: Kraft 75th Anniversary Show; Rainbow; The Gossip Columnist; The Hustler of Muscle Beach; For The Love Of It.

Bway inc: Top Banana; Mr. Wonderful.

CARTER, June: Singer. b. Maces Spring, VA, Jun 23, 1929. W of Johnny Cash. Member of Carter Family Singing Group; member Grand Ole Opry; co-wri song Ring of Fire. TV inc: A Johnny Cash Christmas (1979); A Johnny Cash Christmas (1980). (Grammys-(2)-Group country voc/inst-1967; Country Group-1970).

CARTER, Lynda: Act. b. Phoenix, AZ, Jul 24. Named Miss World--USA 1973. TV inc: The New Adventures of Wonder Woman; Lynda Carter's Special; Lynda Carter Encore!; The Last Song.

CARTER, Peter: Dir. b. England, Aug 12, 1933. Films inc: The Powderman; Rituals; High-ballin'; Klondike Fever. TV inc: A Man Called Intrepid.

CARTER, Ralph: Act. b. NYC, May 30, 1961. TV inc: Sesame Street; I'm a Fan; Good Times. Thea inc: Tough to Get Help; Dude; Via Galactica; Raisin.

CARTER, Terry: Act. b. NYC, Dec 18. Films inc: Abby; Foxy Brown; Benji. TV inc: Dr Kildare; Mannix; Six Million Dollar Man; Sgt Bilko; Julia; Battlestar Galactica.

Thea inc: The Hostage; Mrs Patterson; Kwamina.

CARTWRIGHT, Angela: Act. b. Cheshire, England, Sep 9, 1952. Films inc: The Sound of Music; Lad: A Dog; Somebody Up There Likes Me; Something of Value; Beyond The Poseidon Adventure.

TV inc: The Danny Thomas Show; Lost in Space; Make Room for Granddaddy; Room 222; My Three Sons; Adam 12; Logan's Run; Scout's Honor.

Thea inc: Forty Carats.

CARVER, Randall: Act. b. Fort Worth, TX, May 25. Films inc: Midnight Cowboy; Time to Run. TV inc: Forever Fernwood; The Waltons; The Daughters of Joshua Cabe; Taxi.

CARVER, Steve: Dir. b. Brooklyn, NY, Apr 5, 1945. e. U of Buffalo; WA U. Films inc: Big Bad Mama; Capone; Drum; Moonbeam Rider; Steel.

CASARES, Maria (nee Quiroga): Act. b. France, 1922. Films inc: Les Enfants du Paradis; Les Dames du Bois de Boulogne; Orphee; Le Testament d'Orphee; The Rebel Nun.

CASEY, Bernie: Act. b. WV. e. Bowling Green U, MFA. Pro football player with San Francisco 49ers, LA Rams. Studied with Jeff Corey. Films inc: Guns of the Magnificent Seven; Box Car Bertha; Tick, Tick, Tick; Black Gun; Hit Man; Cleopatra Jones; Maurie; Cornbread Earl and Me; Brothers; The Watts Monster.

TV inc: Mary Jane Harper Cried Last Night; Brian's Song; Gargoyles; Ring of Passion; Love Is Not Enough; Harris and Company; The Martian Chronicles.

CASH, Johnny: Act-Folk singer. b. Kingsland, AR, Feb 26, 1932. Films inc: Hootenanny Hoot; Five Minutes to Live; Festival; A Gunfight; The Gospel Road.

TV inc: The Johnny Cash Show; The Unbroken Circle - A Tribute to Mother Maybelle Carter; A Johnny Cash Christmas 1979; Johnny Cash - The First 25 Years; A Johnny Cash Christmas 1980.

(Grammys-(6)-country vocal group-1967, 1970; country vocal-1968, 1969; Album Notes-1968, 1969.)

CASH, June Carter: (See CARTER, June).

CASH, Rosalind: Act. b. Atlantic City, NJ, Dec 31, 1938. e. CCNY. Films inc: Klute; The Omega Man; The New Centurians; Hickey and Boggs; Melinda; Uptown Saturday Night; Amazing Grace; Hit the Open Man; The Class of Miss McMichael; The Watts Monster.

Thea inc: The Wayward Stork; Junebug Graduates Tonight!; Fiorello!; God Is a (Guess What?); Ceremonies in Dark Old Men;

TV inc: Ceremonies in Dark Old Men; Angel Dust - The Wack Attack; Guyana Tragedy - The Story of Jim Jones.

CASON, Barbara: Act. b. Memphis, TN, Nov 15. e. U of MS, BA, MA. Bway inc: Oh, Coward; Marat/Sade.

TV inc: Carter Country.

CASS, Peggy: Act. b. Boston, May 21, 1924. Bway inc: Burlesque; The Live Wire; Bernardine; Othello; Oh Men! Oh Women!; Auntie Mame (*Tony*-supp-1957); A Thurber Carnival; Don't Drink the Water; The Front Page; Plaza Suite; Last of the Red Hot Lovers; Once A Catholic.

Films inc: The Marrying Kind; Auntie Mame; Gidget Goes Hawaiian; The Age of Consent; If It's Tuesday, This Must be Belgium; Paddy.

TV inc: The Hathaways; The Garry Moore Show; To Tell the Truth; The Jack Paar Show.

CASSAVETES, John: Act-Dir. b. NYC, 1929. H of Gena Rowlands. Film debut in The Night Holds Terror, 1953. Films inc: (act) Crime in The Streets; Rosemary's Baby; Edge of the City; Affair in Havana; Saddle The Wind; The Dirty Dozen; Two Minute Warning; Brass Target; The Fury. (Dir): Shadows; Too Late Blues; A Child Is Waiting; Faces; Husbands; Minnie and Moskowitz (& sp); A Woman Under The Influence (& sp); Killing of a Chinese Bookie (& sp); Mikey and Nicky; Opening Night (& sp-act); Gloria (& sp).

TV inc: Flesh and Blood.

CASSEL, Jean-Pierre: Act. b. France, Oct 27, 1932. Films inc: Les Jeux de l'Amour; L'Amant de Cinq Jours; The Vanishing Corporal; La Ronde; Those Magnificent Men in Their Flying Machines; Is Paris Burning?; Baxter; The Discreet Charm of the Bourgeoisie; The Three Musketeers; Murder on the Orient Express; That Lucky Touch; No Time For Breakfast; Who's Killing The Great Chefs of Europe?; From Hell To Victory; Le Soleil en Face; 5% Risk; Je Me Tiens, Tu Me Tiens par La Barbichette.

CASSEL, Seymour: Act. b. Jan 22, 1935. Films inc: Murder Inc; Too Late Blues; Juke Box Racket; Coogan's Bluff; The Revolutionary; Faces; Minnie and Moskowitz; Black Oak Conspiracy; Valentino; Killing of a Chinese Bookie; Convoy; Sunburn; Ravagers; California Dreaming; The Mountain Men.

TV inc: Angel on My Shoulder.

CASSIDY, David: Act. b. Apr 12, 1950. S of Shirley Jones and the late Jack Cassidy. TV inc: The Partridge Family; Man Undercover; The Night the City Screamed.

CASSIDY, Joanna: Act. b. 1944. Films inc: The Laughing Policeman; The Outfit; Bank Shot; Stay Hungry; Prime Time; The Late Show; Night Child; Stunts; Our Winning Season; Night Games.

TV inc: 240-Robert; Reunion.

CASSIDY, Shaun: Singer-Act. b. LA, Sep 27, 1958. S of Shirley Jones and the late Jack Cassidy. Films inc: Born of Water. TV inc: Hardy Boys Mysteries; Like Normal People; Breaking Away.

Thea inc: On a Clear Day; The Sound of Music; High Button Shoes. Recordings inc: Da Doo Ron Ron; That's Rock n' Roll; Hey Deanie. Albums inc: Shaun Cassidy; Born Late; Under Wraps; Wasp.

CASTELLANO, Richard S: Act. b. NYC, Sep 4, 1933. e. Columbia U. Films inc: A Fine Madness; Lovers and Other Strangers; The Godfather; Night of the Juggler.

Thea inc: A View from the Bridge; The Investigation; That Summer, That Fall; Sheep on the Runway; Lovers and other Strangers; Night of the Juggler.

CATES, Gilbert: Prod-Dir. b. NYC, Jun 6, 1934. e. Syracuse U, BS, MA. Films inc: The Painting (short); Rings Around the World; I Never Sang for My Father; Summer Wishes, Winter Dreams; Dragonfly; The Promise; The Last Married Couple in America (& exec prod); Oh, God! Book II.

TV inc: International Showtime (exec prod-dir); To All My Friends on Shore (dir-prod); The Affair (dir); After the Fall (dir- prod); Johnny We Hardly Knew Ye (dir-prod); Have I Got a Christmas for You (dir-prod); Fame; The Berenstain Bears - Xmas Tree (exec prod); Skinflint (exec prod); Elvis Remembered - Nashville to Hollywood (exec prod).

Bway inc: (Dir): Voices; The Price. (Prod) You Know I Can't Hear You When the Water's Running; I Never Sang for My Father; The Chinese and Dr. Fish; Tricks of the Trade (& dir).

CATES, Joseph: Prod-Dir. b. 1924. e. NYU. B of Gilbert Cates. One of the first producers of live tv with Bess Myerson's Wish Upon a Star, 1947; asso prod Jackie Gleason Show.

(Prod) Stop the Music; $64,000 Question; Johnny Carson All Star Comedy Hour; Ethel Merman Chevy Special; Annie The Women in The Life of A Man (*Emmy*-exec prod-1970). 'S Wonderful, 'S Marvelous, 'S Gershwin (*Emmy*-exec prod-1972); George M; Monte Carlo International Circus Special; Circus Lions, Tigers and Melissas Too; Fame; Spoon River; Dames at Sea; Berenstain Bears' Christmas Tree; Johnny Cash Christmas (1979); Skinflint; Fame; Elvis Remembered--Nashville to Hollywood; Comedy is Not Pretty; All Commercials; The Berenstain Bears Meet Bigpaw (exec prod); Daredevils (exec prod); A Johnny Cash Christmas (1980).

Bway inc: Spoon River Anthology; Joe Egg.

Films inc: The Last Married Couple in America.

CATTRALL, Kim: Act. b. Aug 21, 1956. TV inc: The Bastard; The Night Rider; The Rebels; Scruples; The Gossip Columnist.

Films inc: Tribute.

CAULFIELD, Joan: Act. b. Orange, NJ, Jun 1, 1922. e. Columbia U. Screen debut 1945, Miss Susie Slagle's. Films inc: Dear Ruth; Variety Girl; Unsuspected; Sainted Sisters; Larceny; Dear Wife; The Petty Girl; The Rains of Ranchipur; Cattle King; Red Tomahawk; Buckskin.

TV inc: My Favorite Husband.

CAVALCANTI, Alberto: Dir. b. Rio de Janeiro, Feb 6, 1897. e. Geneva Fine Arts School. Films inc: North Sea; Squadron 992; Men of the Lightship; The Foreman Went to France; Halfway House; Dead of Night; They Made Me a Fugitive; For Them that Trespass.

TV inc: Thus Spake Theodore Herzl; Les Empailles; La Vista de la Vieille Dame.

Thea inc: Blood Wedding; Fuente-Ovejuna.

CAVETT, Dick: Act-Wri. b. Kearny, NE, Nov 19, 1936. e. Yale U. Writer for Jack Parr and his successors on the Tonight Show and had comedy writing assignments with Merv Griffin, Jerry Lewis, Johnny Carson. In 1967 wrote for and appeared in night clubs. Performed in TV specials for ABC-TV. TV inc: The Dick Cavett Show, PBS. (*Emmys*-1972, 1974).

Films inc: Annie Hall; CS Blues; Power Play; Health.

CAVILL, Joy: Prod-Wri. b. Sydney, Australia, Feb 2. Films inc: King of the Coral Sea; Walk into Paradise; Dust in the Sun; The Stowaway; The Dispossessed; Nickel Queen.

TV inc: Adventure Unlimited; Seaway; Skippy; Barrier Reef; Boney; Shannon's Mob.

CAYATTE, Andre: Wri-Dir. b. Carcassonne, France, 1909. Films inc: Justice est Faite; Nous Sommes Tous les Assassins; An Eye for an Eye; The Mirror Has Two Faces; The Crossing of the Rhine; La Vie Conjugale; A Trap for Cinderella; Die of Loving.

CECIL, Jonathan: Act. b. England, 1939. Films inc: The Yellow Rolls Royce; Otley; The Private Life of Sherlock Holmes; Barry Lyndon; Joseph Andrews.

CELI, Adolfo: Act. b. Italy, 1922. Films inc: Escape into Dreams; The Man from Rio; Von Ryan's Express; Thunderball; El Greco; Grand Prix; The Honey Pot; Grand Slam; Fragment of Fear; Murders in the Rue Morgue; Hitler-The Last Ten Days; And Then There Were None; The Big Operator; Goodnight Ladies and Gentlemen; Cafe Express.

CHABROL, Claude: Dir. b. Sardent, France, 1930. Films inc: Le Beau Serge (& sp); Les Cousins (& sp); A Double Tour; Ophelia (& sp); The Third Lover; The Seven Deadly Sins; Landru; Marie Chantal; Line of Demarcation; The Champagne Murders; The Road to Corinth; Les Biches (& sp); La Femme Infidele (& sp); The Beast Must Die; The Butcher (& sp); Just Before Night (& sp); Blood Wedding; Ten Days Wonder; The Wolf Trap; Scoundrel in White; Une Partie de Plaisie; Les Magiciens; Folies Bourgeoises; Alice Ou La Derniere Fugue (& sp); Violette Noziere; Dirty Hands (& sp); Rascals (act only); Le Cheval D'orgeuil (& sp).

CHAFFEY, Don: Dir. b. England, 1917. Films inc: Time is My Enemy; The Girl in the Picture; The Flesh is Weak; A Question of Adultery; The Man Upstairs; Dentist in the Chair; Nearly a Nasty Accident; A Matter of Who; The Prince and the Pauper; Jason and the Argonauts; A Jolly Bad Fellow; One Million Years B.C.; The Viking Queen; A Twist of Sand; Creatures the World Forgot; Persecution; Pete's Dragon; The Magic of Lassie; C.H.O.M.P.S.
  TV inc: The Gift of Love; Casino; Riding For the Pony Express.

CHAIKIN, William E: Exec. b. Cleveland, OH, Apr 7, 1919. e. OH State U, BS, MS. Newspaper reporter, columnist before joining Fox publicity dept, 1945. Also in pub. depts of Republic, Eagle Lion. Later p of Chaikin-Perrett, p.r. firm. Became vp-treas of Standard Capital, investment banking firm which financed over 60 films. In 1963 named p, board chairman of Charter Title Ins. Co, LA. From 1968-74 was vp in charge of West Coast operation of Avco Embassy Pictures Corp. In July, 1974, p Avco Embassy. Ret 1980.

CHAKIRIS, George: Act-Dancer. b. Norwood, OH, Sep 16, 1934. Films inc: Brigadoon; Two and Two Make Six; West Side Story (Oscar-supp-1961); Diamond Head; King of the Sun; Flight from Ashiya; Squadron; The High Bright Sun; Is Paris Burning?; The Young Girls of Rochefort; The Big Cube.

CHALLIS, Christopher: Cin. b. England, 1919. Films inc: Theirs is the Glory; The Small Back Room; Tales of Hoffman; The Elusive Pimpernel; Genevieve; The Story of Gilbert and Sullivan; Malaga; The Flame and the Flesh; Footsteps in the Fog; Miracle in Soho; Sink the Bismark; The Grass is Greener; The Captain's Table; The Long Ships; Those Magnificent Men in Their Flying Machines; The Victors; The Americanization of Emily; Arabesque; Chitty Chitty Bang Bang; Villain; Catch Me a Spy; Mary Queen of Scots; The Boy who Turned Yellow; The Little Prince; Quilp; The Incredible Sarah; The Deep; Force 10 From Navarone; Riddle of the Sands; The Mirror Crack'd.

CHAMBERLAIN, Richard: Act. b. LA, Mar 31, 1935. Films inc: A Thunder of Drums; Twilight of Honor; Joy in the Morning; Petulia; The Madwoman of Chaillot; Julius Caesar; The Music Lovers; The Three Musketeers; The Towering Inferno; The Slipper and the Rose; The Swarm; The Last Wave.
  TV inc: Dr. Kildare series (1961-65); Hamlet; F. Scott Fitzgerald and the Last of the Belles; The Lady's Not For Burning; The Man in the Iron Mask; The Count of Monte Cristo; The Woman I Love; Centennial; Shogun.
  Thea inc: Hamlet (London & Bway); The Lady's Not For Burning.

CHAMBERLIN, Lee: Act. b. NYC, Feb 14. e. NYU, Sorbonne. Originally dancer with Pearl Primus and Alvin Ailey companies, then studied with Herbert Berghof and Uta Hagen. Thea inc: Your Own Thing; Slave Ship; King Lear.
  TV inc: The Electric Company (Grammy-childrens rec-1972); All's Fair; Roots--The Next Generation; Paris.
  Films inc: Uptown Saturday Night; Let's Do It Again.

CHAMBERS, Everett: Prod-Dir-Wri. b. Montrose, CA, Aug 19, 1926. e. New School for Social Research; Dramatic Workshop, NY. TV inc: Target - The Corruptors; The Lollipop Cover; Peyton Place; Nightslaves; Monty Nash; Moon of the Wolf; Trouble Comes to Town; Can Ellen be Saved?; The Girl Must Live; They Only Come Out at Night; Variety '77-The Year In Entertainment; Rex Stout's Nero Wolfe; B.A.D. Cats; Turnover Smith.
  Films inc: Tess of the Storm Country.

CHAMCHOUM, Georges Farouk N: Prod-Dir. b. Niamey, Niger, Jul 16, 1946. Founder Cam 9 - Group 4 Prodns. Films inc: Inside Out; Salam, After Death; Lebanon. . .Why? (doc).

CHAMIE, Alfred P: Atty. b. NYC, Jun 1, 1910. e. UCLA, AB, Harvard, LLB. Legal counsel Assn. Motion Picture Prods Inc.; sec. Central Casting Corp; VP, sec, gen counsel Assn Motion Pictures and TV; bd dirs Motion Picture and TV Relief Fund; pres. LA Film Development Committee; chmn. Motion Picture & TV Fund Investment Committee.

CHAMPION, Gower: Dir-Act-Chor. b. Geneva, IL, Jun 22, 1921. Started as dancer. Teamed with then wife, Marge, in nightclubs, featured, Radio City Music Hall. Screen debut Till The Clouds Roll By, 1946. Films inc: Show Boat; Lovely to Look At; Everything I Have Is Yours; Three For the Show; Jupiter's Darling. (Dir): My Six Loves; Bank Shot.
  Bway inc: (perf) Streets of Paris; Count Me In. (Dir. chor): Lend An Ear (Tony-chor-1949); Bye Bye Birdie (Tonys-dir & chor-1961); Carnival; Hello Dolly (Tonys-dir & chor-1964); I Do I Do; Happy Time (Tonys-dir & chor-1968), Mack and Mabel; Rockabye Hamlet; 42d Street.
  TV inc: NBC color specials 1958-59-60 (dir-chor); Mary Martin Special; Oscar Show 1969; Julie Andrews Special; Irene.
  (Died Aug 25, 1980).

CHAMPION, John: Prod-Dir. b. Denver, CO, Oct 13, 1923. Films inc: Panhandle; Stampede; Hellgate; Dragonfly Squadron; Zero Hour; The Last Escape; Mustang Country.

CHAMPION, Marge: Dancer-Chor. b. LA, Sep 2, 1923. W of Boris Sagal. Appeared in Blossom Time, Student Prince for LA Civic Opera. Made debut with then husband Gower Champion as nightclub dance team, Bway, films. TV inc: Queen of the Stardust Ballroom (Emmy-chor-1975).

CHANCELLOR, John: TV Anchorman. b. Chicago, 1927. e. U. of Il. Joined Chicago Sun Times, 1948. To NBC News as Midwest corr. 1950. Subsequently Vienna Bureau, Chief of Moscow Bureau before returning to US. Host Today program for one year, 1961. Served as dir. of Voice of America, 1965-67. Then anchorman, principal reporter on NBC TV News, commentator on NBC Radio.

CHANDLER, George: Act. b. Waukegan, IL, Jun 30, 1898. In vaudeville as The Musical Nut. On screen from 1927. Films inc: Tenderfoot Thrillers; Pretty Baby; This Woman Is Dangerous; Meet Me at the Fair; Hans Christian Anderson; Island in the Sky; Only Saps Work; In Gay Madrid; Too Many Cooks; The Country Doctor; Libeled Lady; Second Fiddle; The Return of Frank James; The Great Man's Lady; Since You Went Away; Lover Come Back; Perfect Strangers; Across the Wide Missouri; Apache Uprising; The Ghost and Mr. Chicken; One More Train to Rob; Every Which Way But Loose; The Apple Dumpling Gang Rides Again.
  TV inc: Waterfront; Lassie.

CHANDLER, John Davis: Act. b. 1937. Films inc: The Young Savages; Mad Dog Coll; Major Dundee; Once a Thief; The Good Guys and the Bad Guys; Barquero; Shootout; Capone; The Jaws of Death; Scorchy.

CHANNING, Carol: Act. b. Seattle, WA, Jan 30, 1923. Starred in West Coast revue, Lend an Ear. On Broadway 1950, Gentlemen Prefer Blondes; Hello, Dolly! (Tony-1964); Lorelei; Hello, Dolly! (rev). (London) Hello, Dolly!. (Special Tony-1968).
  Films inc: Thoroughly Modern Millie.
  TV inc: An Evening With Carol Channing.

CHANNING, Stockard (Susan Stockard): Act. b. NYC, Feb 13, 1944. Films inc: The Fortune; The Big Bus; Sweet Revenge; The Cheap Detective; Grease; The Fish That Saved Pittsburgh.
  TV inc: The Girl Most Likely To . . .; The Stockard Channing Show.
  Thea inc: Absurd Person Singular; No Hard Feelings.

CHAPIN, Harry: Act-Sngwri. b. NYC, Dec 7, 1942. Recording artist; tours with own band. Thea inc: The Night That Made America Famous (score). TV inc: Mother and Daughter - The Loving War (score).

CHAPLIN, Geraldine: Act. b. Santa Monica, CA, Jul 31, 1944. D of late Charles Chaplin. Films inc: Doctor Zhivago; Stranger in the House; I Killed Rasputin; The Hawaiians; Zero Population Growth; Innocent Bystanders; The Three Musketeers; Nashville; Buffalo Bill and the Indians; Cria!; Roseland; Welcome to L.A.; Northwest Wind; Remember My Name; Elisa My Love; A Wedding; Blindfolded Eyes; Mama Cumple 100 Anos; L'Adoption; Travels on the Sly; La Viuda De Monteil; The Mirror Crack'd.

CHAPLIN, Saul: Prod-Sng wri. b. NYC, Feb 19, 1912. e. NYU. Sgwri at Vitaphone Corp. NY, 1937-39; to Hollywood 1940.
Films inc: (Mus dir) Cover Girl; The Jolson Story; Down To Earth; Jolson Sings Again; On The Town; An American in Paris *(Oscar-*scoring-1951); Lovely To Look At; Kiss Me Kate; Seven Brides for Seven Brothers *(Oscar-*scoring-1954); High Society. (Asso prod) Les Girls; Merry Andrew; Can Can; West Side Story *(Oscar-*scoring-1961) also *(Grammy-*for soundtrack album); I Could Go On Singing; The Sound of Music; Man of La Mancha. (Prod) Star!; That's Entertainment II.
Songs inc: Bei Mir Bist Du Schoen; Shoe Shine Boy; Please Be Kind; Until The Real Thing Comes Along; Anniversary Song.

CHAPLIN, Sydney: Act. b. Beverly Hills, CA, 1926. S of Charles Chaplin. Films inc: Limelight; Confession; Land of the Pharaohs; Four Girls in Town; Quantez; Follow that Man; A Countess from Hong Kong; The Sicilian Clan; Satan's Cheerleaders.
Bway inc: Bells Are Ringing *(Tony-*supp-1957).

CHAPMAN, Marguerite: Act. b. Chatham, NY, 1916. Films inc: Charlie Chan at the Wax Museum; The Body Disappears; Parachute Nurse; Destroyer; Pardon My Past; The Walls Came Tumbling Down; Mr. District Attorney; Kansas Raiders; Man Bait; Flight to Mars; The Seven Year Itch; The Amazing Transparent Man.

CHAPMAN, Michael: Cin. b. MA, Nov 21, 1935. Films inc: The Last Detail; White Dawn; Taxi Driver; The Front; The Next Man; The Last Waltz; Invasion of the Body Snatchers; Hardcore; The Wanderers; Raging Bull.
TV inc: Death Be Not Proud; King.

CHARISSE, Cyd (Tula Ellice Finklea): Act. b. Amarillo, TX, Mar 8, 1923. W of Tony Martin. Toured U.S. & Europe with Ballet Russe. Screen debut in Something to Shout About, 1943. Films inc: Mission to Moscow; Till The Clouds Roll By; Words and Music; Kissing Bandit; East Side, West Side; Bandwagon; Brigadoon; Silk Stockings; Two Weeks in Another Town; The Silencers; Maroc 7; Warlords of Atlantis. TV inc: Portrait of an Escort.

CHARLES, Lewis (nee Cholost): Act. b. NYC, Nov 2, 1920. e. St. Johns U. Films inc: Panic in the Streets; To Catch a Thief; Jodie; Sweet Smell of Success; A House is Not a Home; Barney Ross Story; Soldier in the Rain; Al Capone; Island in the Sun; Penelope; Who's Got the Action; Topaz; The Midnight Oil; The Rose Tattoo; Our Man Flint; Now You See Her, Now You Don't; Maurie; I Love A Mystery.

CHARLES, Ray (nee Robinson): Singer-Mus-Wri. b. Sep 23, 1930. Blind since birth, became musician in teens, played with bands in the South; developed own style of "soul music"; formed singing group; has toured around the world.
TV inc: Hit Parade; The First Nine Months Are the Hardest *(Emmy-*spec material-1971); The Funny Side of Marriage *(Emmy-*spec material-1972); Perry Como Show; The Unbroken Circle--a Tribute to Mother Maybelle Carter; John Denver and the Muppets--A Christmas Get Together (choral dir & spec material); Perry Como's Christmas in New Mexico (spec material); Perry Como's Bahama Holiday (choral dir & spec material); John Schneider--Back Home.
(Grammys-(10)-R&B Rec-1960, 1961, 1962, 1963, 1966, 1975; Voc (single) 1960; voc (album) 1960; pop single artist (1960); R&B solo voc 1966).

CHARLESON, Leslie: Act. b. Feb 22, 1945. Films inc: Day of the Dolphin.
Bway inc: One Night Stand.
TV inc: A Flame in the Wind (later called a Time for Us); Love Is a Many Splendored Thing; General Hospital.

CHARMOLI, Tony: Chor-Dir-Prod. b. MN. e. College of St Thomas. TV inc: Hit Parade *(Emmy-*chor-1955); Dinah Shore Show; Mitzi--A Tribute To The American Housewife *(Emmy-*chor-1974); Gypsy in My Soul *(Emmy-*chor-1976); The Nutcracker; John Denver and the Muppets; John Davidson Christmas Show; Third Annual Circus of the Stars; John Denver and The Muppets - A Christmas Get Together; From Raquel With Love; Julie Andrews' Invitation to the Dance with Rudolf Nureyev.

CHARNIN, Martin: Dir-Lyr. b. NYC, Nov 24, 1934. e. Cooper Union, BFA. Bway inc: Hot Spot (lyr); Mata Hari (lyr); Two by Two (lyr); Nash at Nine (dir); Music! Music! (dir); Annie *(Tony-*lyr-1977); I Remember Mama; The Bar Mitzvah Boy.
TV inc: Anne Bancroft Special; Jackie Gleason Show; Annie, The Women in the Life of a Man *(Emmy-*prod-1970); 'S Wonderful, 'S Marvelous, 'S Gershwin *(Emmys-*prod & dir-1972).
*(Grammy-*Cast Album-1977.)

CHARO (Maria Rosario Pilar Martinez): Singer-Act. b. Murcia, Spain, Jan 15, 1951. Recording artist. Numerous TV and nitery appearances. Films inc: Don Juan Teniorio (in Spain); The Concorde - Airport '79.

CHARTERIS, Leslie: Wri-Prod. b. Singapore, 1907. e. Cambridge, Eng. Novelist. Creator The Saint, series of mystery novels on which several films, TV series based.

CHARTOFF, Robert: Prod. b. NYC, Aug 26, 1933. e. Columbia U, LLB. Films inc: Double Trouble; Point Blank; The Split; They Shoot Horses, Don't They?; The Strawberry Statement; Believe in Me; The Gang that Couldn't Shoot Straight; The Mechanic; The New Centurions; Up the Sandbox; Busting; S.P.Y.S.; Fat Chance; Breakout; Nickelodeon; Rocky *(Oscar-*1976); New York, New York; Valentino; Comes a Horseman; Uncle Joe Shannon; Rocky II; Raging Bull.

CHASE, Chevy (Cornelius Crane Chase): Act-Wri. b. NYC, Oct 8, 1943. e. Bard College, BA, Columbia MA; MIT, MA. TV inc: Great American Dream Machine; Saturday Night Live *(Emmys-*supp act & wri-1976); Chevy Chase Special; Paul Simon Special *(Emmy-*wri-1978).
Films inc: Foul Play; Oh Heavenly Dog; Caddyshack; Seems Like Old Times.

CHASE, David: Wri-Prod. b. Aug 22, 1945. e. Stanford, MFA. TV inc: The Magician (wri); The Nightstalker (story ed); The Rockford Files (prod-wri) *(Emmy-*prod-1978); Off The Minnesota Strip *(Emmy-*wri-1980).

CHASE, Mary (nee Coyle): Wri. b. West Denver, CO, Feb 25, 1907. e. U of Denver, U of CO. Former reporter. Plays inc: Me Third; Now You've Done It; A Slip of a Girl; Harvey *(Pulitzer Prize-*1944); The Next Half Hour; Mrs. McThing; Bernardine; Lolita; Midge Purvis; Cocktails for Mimi.

CHASE, Sylvia: TV news. b. St Paul, MN, Feb 23, 1938. e. UCLA, BA. Action reporter KNX, LA, 1969; 1971 CBS News corr; 1977, ABC Weekend News co-anchor, corr.
TV inc: Magazine; Caution--Drinking Water May Be Hazardous to your Health; The American Woman; 20/20; (ATAS broadcast journalism award-1978).

CHASMAN, David: Prod-Exec. b. NYC, Sep 28, 1925. With various film cos inc UA; Fox; Col; Samuel Goldwyn; City Film. In 1974, p Convivium Prod, Inc; 1979 exec vp chg prodn Col; June 1980 exec vp film prodn MGM; Dec 1980 exec vp in chg wldwde theatrical prodn.
TV inc: Murder on Flight 502.

CHAYEFSKY, Paddy: Wri. b. NYC, Jan 29, 1923. e. CCNY. Wrote musical comedy, No T.O. For Love, produced by Army Special Service and entertained GIs throughout Europe. Films inc: Marty (Oscar-1955); The Hospital (Oscar-1971); Middle of the Night; Network (Oscar-1976); The Goddess.
    TV inc: Marty; Danger; Manhunt; Holiday Song; The Catered Affair; Bachelor Party.
    Plays inc: Middle of the Night; The Tenth Man; Gideon; The Passion of Josef D (& dir).

CHEAP TRICK: Rock group. Members are Rick Nielsen, Pete Comita, Bun E. Carlos, Robin Zander.
    Albums inc: In Color; Live At Budokan; Dream Police.

CHECCO, Al: Act. b. Pittsburgh, Jul 21, 1925. e. Carnegie Mellon U, BA. Films inc: Skipping; Super Dad; Pete's Dragon; Move Over Darling; Hotel; The Ghost and Mr. Chicken; Bullitt; Movie Maker; Daddy's Gone A Hunting; There Was a Crooked Man; I Love My Wife; How to Frame a Fig; Get to Know Your Rabbit; Skin Game; Repo; How To Beat The High Cost of Living.
    TV inc: The Blue Knight; Helter Skelter; 79 Park Ave; Some Kind of Miracle.
    Thea inc: An Inspector Calls; Lend an Ear; Two on the Aisle; The Gazebo; Damn Yankees; Leave It To Jane; Reuben-Reuben.

CHECKER, Chubby (Ernest Evans): Singer. b. Philadelphia, 1941. Films inc: Twist Around the Clock; Don't Knock the Twist. (Grammy-Rock & Roll-1961).

CHEECH AND CHONG: (See MARIN, Richard and CHONG, Tommy).

CHENAULT, Robert: Prod-Dir. TV inc: The Big Hex of Little Lulu; The Contest Kid Strikes Again; The Girl with ESP; The Ghost of Thomas Kempe; Where Do Teen Agers Come From?

CHER (Cherilyn Sarkisian): Singer-Act. b. El Centro, CA., May 20, 1946. Began singing 1965 with Sonny Bono to whom she was then married. First hit record, I Got You Babe, sold 3 million; nitery performer. Films inc: Good Times; Chastity. TV inc: Sonny & Cher Hour; Cher.

CHERMAK, Cy: Wri-Prod. b. Bayonne, NJ, Sep 20, 1929. e. Brooklyn Coll, Ithaca Coll. TV inc: (wri) Rocky King; Detective; Philco Playhouse. (Prod): The Virginian; Convoy; Ironside; The New Doctors; Amy Prentiss; The Night Stalker; CHiPS; Murder at the World Series.

CHERRY, Helen: Act. b. England, 1915. W of Trevor Howard. Films inc: The Courtneys of Curzon Street; Adam and Evelyn; Morning Departure; Young Wives' Tale; Castle in the Air; Three Cases of Murder; High Flight; The Naked Edge; Flipper's New Adventure; Hard Contract; Harrowhouse. Thea inc: The Streets of London.

CHERTOK, Jack: Prod. b. Atlanta, GA, Jul 13, 1906. Worked as script clerk, asst dir, head of music dept, shorts prod at MGM; features prod inc The Penalty; Joe Smith, American; Kid Glove Killer; The Omaha Trail; Eyes in the Night; The Corn is Green; Northern Pursuit.
    TV inc: Private Secretary; The Lawless Years; Johnny Midnight; My Favorite Martian.

CHESTER, Hal E: Prod. b. Brooklyn, NY, Mar 6, 1921. Child actor (Little Tough Guys, etc).
    Films inc: (prod) Joe Palooka series; Underworld Story; The Highwayman; Triple Cross; Models, Inc; Beast from 20,000 Fathoms; Crashout; The Bold and the Brave; The Weapon; The Haunted; School for Scoundrels; Two-Headed Spy; Hide and Seek; The Secret War of Harry Frigg; The Double Man; The Comedy Man.

CHETWYND, Lionel: Wri. b. London, 1940. e. Sir George Williams U, McGill U, Trinity Coll, Oxford. Joined Col Pictures Int'l, NY, 1968; transferred to Col, London, 1968; asst man dir, 1969; asst man dir Columbia-Warner UK, 1971; freelance wri. Films inc: The Apprenticeship of Duddy Kravitz; It Happened One Christmas; Hanoi Hilton; Two Solitudes (& dir); Johnny We Hardly Knew Ye; Goldenrod; Quintet.
    TV inc: The Adams Chronicles; The Guest Room; Please, Remember Me; Quintet.
    Plays inc: Bleeding Great Orchids.

CHEW, Richard: Flm Ed. b. LA, Jun 28, 1940. e. UCLA, AB. Films inc: The Conversation; One Flew Over the Cuckoo's Nest; Star Wars (Oscar-1977); Goin' South; When You Comin' Back, Red Ryder; Saint Jack.

CHIARI, Walter (nee Annichiarico): Act. b. Italy, 1924. Films inc: Bellissima; OK Nero; The Moment of Truth; Nana; The Little Hut; Bonjour Tristesse; Pepote; Chimes at Midnight; They're a Weird Mob; Squeeze a Flower; The Valachi Papers.

CHIC: Group. Members are Bernard Edwards, bass & voc; Nile Rodgers, guitar; Tony Thompson, drums; Alfa Anderson, voc; Luci Martin, voc. Group formed by Edwards and Rodgers in 1977.
    Albums inc: Chic; C'est Chic; Risque; Les Plus Grands Succes De Chic. Singles inc: Dance, Dance, Dance; Le Freak; I Want Your Love.

CHICAGO: Group. Members are Peter Cetera, voc-bass; Laudir De Oliveira, percussion; Robert Lamm, voc-keyboard; Lee Loughnane, trumpet-flugelhorn-voc; Danny Seraphine, drums. All write group's songs.
    Albums inc: Chicago Transit Authority; Chicago at Carnegie Hall; Hot Streets; Chicago II through XIII.
    (Grammy-group pop vocal-1976).

CHILD, Julia: TV pers. b. Pasadena, CA, Aug 15, 1912. e. Smith College, BA. With adv dept W & J Sloane; served with OSS in Washington and Ceylon during WW2.
    TV inc: The French Chef (Emmy-1966); Julia Child and Co; Julia Child and More Company.

CHILES, Lois: Act. b. Alice, TX. Former model. Films inc: The Way We Were; The Great Gatsby; Coma; Death on the Nile; Moonraker.

CHISHOLM, Samuel Hewlings: TV Exec. b. Auckland, New Zealand, Oct 8, 1939. GM TCN Channel Nine Pty Ltd Willoughby NSW.

CHODOROV, Edward: Wri-Prod. b. NYC, Apr 17, 1904. Films inc: The World Changes; Kind Lady; The Story of Louis Pasteur; Yellow Jack; Undercurrent; The Hucksters; Roadhouse; Craig's Wife.
    Plays inc: Wonder Boy; Kind Lady; Cue for Passion; Those Endearing Young Charms; Decision; Common Ground; Signor Chicago; Oh Men, Oh Women, Listen to the Mocking Bird.

CHODOROV, Jerome: Wri-Dir. b. NYC, Aug 10, 1911. Films inc: Louisiana Purchase; My Sister Eileen; Junior Miss; Happy Anniversary.
    Plays inc: My Sister Eileen; Pretty Penny; Wonderful Town (Tony-1953); The Girl in Pink Tights; The Tunnel of Love; Three Bags Full; The Student Prince; Make a Million (& dir); The Gazebo (& dir); Blood Sweat and Stanley Poole (dir only).

CHOMSKY, Marvin J: Dir. b. NYC, May 23, 1929. e. Syracuse U, BS, Stanford U, MA. Films inc: Maya; Evel Knievel; Murph the Surf; Mackintosh and TJ; Good Luck Miss Wyckoff.
    TV inc: The Wild, Wild West; Gunsmoke; Star Trek; Then Came Bronson; Victory at Entebbe; Roots; Holocaust (Emmy-1978); Hollow Image; Doctor Franken; Attica (Emmy-1980); King Crab.

CHONG, Tommy: Singer-Act-Wri. b. Edmonton, Alta, Canada. Guitar player with various Canadian R&B combos, teamed wth Richard Marin (Cheech) in improvisational group; spotted by Lou Adler at Hollywood's Troubadour club began comedy recordings (Grammy-1973).
    Films inc: Cheech and Chong's Up in Smoke, Cheech and Chong's Next Movie.

CHOOLUCK, Leon: Prod-Dir. b. NYC, Mar 19, 1920. Worked as Asst Dir, apprentice cutter, projectionist, film examiner, cin. Films inc: (prod): Hell on Devil's Island; Plunder Road; Murder by Contract; City of Fear; Take A Hard Ride. (Assoc prod): The Fearmakers; Day of the Outlaw; The Bramble Bush; The Rise and Fall of Legs Diamond; Studs Lonigan; Three the Hard Way. Dir: Three Blondes in His Life. (Prodn supv): God's Little Acre; Anna Lucasta; El Cid; Battle of the Bulge; The Midas Run; The Grissom Gang; The Phynx; Kotch; Slaughter; Apocalypse Now.

TV inc: The Pinky Lee Show; The Outer Limits; I Spy; Highway Patrol; Lockup; Stoney Burke; Dynasty; Judge Horton and the Scottsboro Boys.

Thea inc: Boy Meets Girl.

CHOW, Raymond: Prod-Exec. b. Hong Kong, May 17, 1927. e. St John's U, Shanghai, BAJ. Journalist with US Information Service; pub dir Shaw Brothers. Formed Golden Harvest group of companies in 1970; has produced more than 100 films inc: Fists of Fury; Chinese Connection; Enter The Dragon; The Contract; Return Of the Dragon; Game of Death; Night Games; The Big Brawl.

CHRISTENBERRY, Chris: Prod-Dir. b. 1923. Originally a musician with Jimmy Dorsey, Johnny "Scat" Davis, others; made theatre debut as asst to Orson Welles at Mercury Players; pioneered in live tv.

TV inc: Night Must Fall; You Are There; Robert Montgomery Presents; Studio One. (Dir) Marcus Welby; Bancek; Ironsides.

Bway inc: Salvation on a String; Hit the Trail; Idiot's Delight (rev); touring companies of Harvey; Our Town; I Shall Return.

Films inc: Bandolier; Two Mules for Sister Sarah; The Big Bus. (Died Feb 15, 1980).

CHRISTIAN-JAQUE (Christian Maudet): Dir. b. Paris, Sep 4, 1904. Les Disparus de Saint-Agil; La Symphonie Fantastique; Sortileges; Un Revenant; D'Homme a Hommes; Bluebeard; Fanfan la Tulipe; Lucrezia Borgia; Nana; Race for Life; Babette Goes to War; The Black Tulip; The Secret Agents; Two Tickets to Mexico; Doctor Justice; La Vie Parisienne; The Making of a Lady (& sp).

CHRISTIAN, Linda (Blanca Rosa Welter): Act. b. Tampico, Mexico, Nov 13, 1924. Screen debut 1946, Holiday in Mexico. Films inc: Green Dolphin Street; Tarzan and the Mermaid; The Happy Time; Athena; Thunderstorm; The House of Seven Hawks; The VIPs; How to Seduce a Playboy.

CHRISTIANSEN, Robert: Prod. b. Porterville, CA. Prod asst Monte Walsh; Hail Hero.

Films inc: (prod) Adam at Six A.M.; Hide in Plain Sight.

TV inc: Suddenly Single; The Glass House; A Brand New Life; The Autobiography of Miss Jane Pittman (Emmy-1974); I Love You. . .Goodbye; Queen of the Stardust Ballroom; Born Innocent; A Death in Canaan; Strangers.

CHRISTIE, Audrey: Act. b. Chicago, Jun 27, 1912. NY stage debut 1928, Palace Theatre, in a dancing act. Bway inc: Good News; Follow Thru; Sweet and Low; Of Thee I Sing; Shady Lady; Sailor Beware; No, No, Nanette; A Connecticut Yankee; The Red Mill; I Married an Angel; My Sister Eileen; The Voice of the Turtle; Light Up the Sky; Holiday for Lovers; Mame.

Films inc: Deadline; Carousel; Splendour in the Grass; The Unsinkable Molly Brown; The Ballad of Josie; Harlow; Mame; Harper Valley PTA.

TV inc: Fair Exchange; The Streets of L.A.

CHRISTIE, Howard J: Prod. b. San Francisco, Sep 16, 1912. e. UC Berkeley, BA. Began career as actor, 1934; Asst dir 1936-40; Assoc prod 1942-44, Deanna Durbin pictures. Films inc: Lady on a Train; Because of Him; Abbott and Costello Meet the Invisible Man (7 other A&C pictures); Comin' Round the Mountain; Lost in Alaska; Against All Flags; Yankee Buccaneer; Seminole; Back to God's Country; Yankee Pasha; Smoke Signal; The Looters; Price of Fear; Congo Crossing; Showdown at Abilene; Toy Tiger; Away All Boats; I've Lived Before; Wagon Train; The Raiders; Sword of Ali Baba; Laredo; Ride to Hangman's Tree; Journey to Shiloh; Nobody's Perfect; A Man Called Gannon.

TV inc: Wagon Train; Laredo; The Virginian.

CHRISTIE, Julie: Act. b. Assam, India, Apr 14, 1941. Joined a repertory company at Sussex, England. Performed in TV. Films inc: Billy Liar; Young Cassidy; Darling (Oscar-1965); Doctor Zhivago; Fahrenheit 451; Far From the Madding Crowd; Petulia; In Search of Gregory; The Go-Between; McCabe and Mrs Miller; Don't Look Now; Shampoo; Demon Seed; Heaven Can Wait.

CHRISTINE, Virginia (nee Kraft): Act. b. Stanton, IA, Mar 5, 1920. e. UCLA. W of Fritz Feld. In addition to appearing for 15 years as Mrs. Olson in Folger's coffee commercials, film and TV credits number more than 400. Films inc: Edge of Darkness; Mission to Moscow; Counter Attack; The Killers; Cover Up; The Men; Cyrano De Bergerac; Cobweb; High Noon; Not as a Stranger; The Spirit of St. Louis; Three Brave Men; Judgment at Nuremberg; The Prize; Four For Texas; A Rage to Live; Guess Who's Coming to Dinner; Hail Hero; Daughter of the Mind.

Thea inc: Hedda Gabler; Mary, Queen of Scots; Miss Julie; Desdemona.

CHRISTOPHER, Jordan: Mus-Act. b. Youngstown, OH, Oct 23, 1942. Formed band, The Wild Ones which played Peppermint Lounge; became mus dir Arthur, NYC discotheque.

Films inc: Return of the Seven; The Fat Spy; The Tree; Pigeons; Angel, Angel Down We Go.

Bway inc: Black Comedy; Sleuth.

TV inc: Heart in Hiding; The Secret of Midland Heights.

CHRISTOPHER, William: Act. b. Evanston, IL, Oct 20, 1932. e. Wesleyan U. Films inc: The Fortune Cookie; With Six You Get Eggroll; The Shakiest Gun in the West; The Private Navy of Sgt. O'Farrell; Hearts of the West.

TV inc: Gomer Pyle, USMC; Hogan's Heroes; The Andy Griffith Show; M*A*S*H; For The Love Of It.

CHUA, Robert (Robert Chua Wah Peng): Prod. b. Singapore, May 20, 1946. M-dir, Robert Chua Productions; Robert Chua TV Academy. Created & prod Hong Kong's longest running variety show, 90 min. strip, Enjoy Yourself Tonight. TV inc: Miss Hong Kong Contest; Popular Song Contest; Amateur Song Contest.

CHURCHILL, Sarah: Act. b. London, Oct 7, 1916. D of Winston Churchill. Made first appearance in chorus of Follow the Sun, London. Films inc: When In Rome; Daniele Cortis; The Royal Wedding; All Over The Town.

Bway inc: Gramercy Ghost.

TV inc: Hallmark Hall of Fame, (act & host).

CILENTO, Diane: Act. b. Rabaul, New Guinea, Apr 2, 1934. e. Studied ballet. Attended AADA, RADA. Films inc: Moulin Rouge; Angel Who Pawned Her Harp; Passing Stranger; Passage Home; Admirable Crichton; Hombre; Tom Jones; The Wicker Man.

London Thea inc: The Big Knife; Arms and The Man; Tiger at the Gates; I Thank a Fool; The Third Secret; Tom Jones; The Streets of London (dir).

TV inc: La Belle France; Court Martial; Blackmail; Dial M for Murder; Big Toys.

CIMINO, Michael: Wri-Dir. b. 1943. e. Yale, BFA, MFA. Films inc: Silent Running (sp only); Magnum Force (sp only); Thunderbolt and Lightfoot; Deer Hunter (& co-prod), (Oscars-picture, dir-1978); Heaven's Gate.

CINADER, Robert A: Prod. b. NYC, Nov 10, 1924. e. NYU. TV inc: Adam-12; Emergency; Chase; Sierra; Pine Canyon Is Burning; The Two-Five; the Immigrants; The Rebels; The Seekers; Condominium.

CIOFFI, Lou: TV newsman. b. NYC, Apr 30, 1926. e. CCNY; Muhlenberg. Joined CBS 1947 as copyboy; 1948 wri; 1950 Washington News Bureau edtr; 1952 Korean War corr; 1954 NY Bureau CBS; 1956, Paris corr; 1961, CBS Washington corr; 1961 joined ABC News; corr Viet Nam; 1968, headed Tokyo Bureau; 1970, Bonn Bureau; 1973, Paris Bureau; 1977 named UN corr ABC.

CLAIR, Rene (nee Chomette): Prod-Dir-Wri. b. France, 1898. Films inc: Paris Qui Dort; An Italian Straw Hat; Le Million; Le Quatorze Juliet; The Ghost Goes West; Break The News; The Flame of New Orleans; I Married a Witch; Forever and a Day (part); It Happened Tomorrow; And Then There Were None; Le Silence est d'Or; Porte des Lilas; Les Fetes Galantes.

CLAIRE, Ina (nee Fagan): Act. b. Washington, DC, Oct 15, 1892. In vaude as child, noted for imitation of Sir Harry Lauder. Legit debut at age 16, Jumping Jupiter.
Bway inc: Quaker Girl; Lady Luxury; Ziegfeld Follies of 1915; Polly With A Past (first straight comedy role); The Gold Diggers; Bluebeard's Eighth Wife; The Awful Truth; Grounds for Divorce; The Last of Mrs. Cheyney; Biography; Ode to Liberty; End of Summer; Once is Enough; Ninotchka; The Talley Method; The Fatal Weakness; The Confidential Clerk (1954, last Bway appearance).
Films inc: Polly With Past (1915); The Awful Truth; The Royal Family of Broadway; Rebound; The Greeks Had a Word for Them; Ninotchka; Claudia (1943, last film).

CLAMPETT, Bob: Ani-Wri-Prod-Dir. b. San Diego, CA, May 8. e. Otis Art School. Creator of cartoon characters. Ani cartoons inc: Bugs Bunny; Porky Pig; Daffy Duck; Tweety; Beany and Cecil; Thunderbolt the Wonder Colt; Time for Beany; Lone Stranger and Porky; Bugs Bunny Superstar (host).

CLAPTON, Eric: Singer-Sngwri. b. Ripley, Surrey, England, Mar 30, 1945. With various groups inc Casey Jones and the Engineers; Yardbirds; Joe Mayall's Bluesbreakers; Cream; Blind Faith; Delaney and Bonnie and Friends; Derek and the Dominoes before going solo.
Recordings inc: Concert for Bangladesh (*Grammy*-Album of Year-1972); 461 Ocean Boulevard; There's One In Every Crowd; E.C. Was Here; No Reason to Cry; Slowhand; Backless.
Films inc: Concert for Bangladesh; Tommy; The Last Waltz.
Songs inc: Let It Rain; Layla.

CLARK, Bob: Dir. b. New Orleans, LA, 1941. e. Hillsdale College, MI. Films inc: The Emperor's New Clothes; Children Shouldn't Play With Dead Things; Dead of Night; Black Christmas; Breaking Point; Murder By Decree; Tribute.

CLARK, Brian: Wri. b. Bristol, England. Plays inc: Whose Life Is It, Anyway?; Can You Hear Me At The Back?
TV inc: Achilles Heel; Magic Carpet; Parole; Easy Go; The Saturday Party; The Country Party; All Creatures Great and Small; Telford's Change.

CLARK, Candy: Act. b. Oklahoma, Jun 20, 1947. Model. Films inc: Fat City; American Graffiti; The Man Who Fell to Earth; Citizens Band; The Big Sleep; When You Comin' Back, Red Ryder; More American Graffiti.
TV inc: Amateur Night at the Dixie Bar and Grill; Where The Ladies Go; Rodeo Girl.

CLARK, Dane: Act. b. NYC, Feb 18, 1915. e. Cornell U, John Hopkins U. Started in radio. Bway inc: Of Mice and Men; Dead End. Films inc: The Glass Key; Pride of the Yankees; Destination Tokyo; God Is My Co-Pilot; Whiplash; Go Man Go; Blackout; Thunder Pass; Toughest Man Alive.
TV inc: No Exit; The Closing Door; Bold Venture; The French Atlantic Affair.

CLARK, Dick: TV Pers. b. Mt Vernon, NY, Nov 30, 1929. e. Syracuse U. Started as radio announcer. Host of American Bandstand; Dick Clark Beechnut Show; Dick Clark's World of Talent; The Object Is; Missing Links. Formed Dick Clark Productions, 1956 to produce films, TV.
Films inc: Because They're Young; The Young Doctor; Psychout; The Savage Seven; Killers Three; The Dark.
TV inc: Dick Clark's Live Wednesday; Dick Clark's Rockin' New Year's Eve; Elvis; Birth of the Beatles; The Man in the Santa Claus Suit; The Sensational Shocking Wonderful Wacky 70's; $20,000 Pyramid (*Emmy*-host-1979); Valentine Magic on Love Island; 32d Annual Emmy Awards (host).

CLARK, John Richard: Dir. b. Hobart, Tasmania, Oct 30, 1932. e. U of Tasmania, BA, UCLA, MA. Thea inc: The Merchant of Venice; The Country Wife; A Midsummer Night's Dream; Major Barbara; The Alchemist.
Films inc: Lagged, The Story of a Convict.

CLARK, Marilyn: Act. b. Spokane, WA, Sep 28, 1929. e. UCLA, BA. W of Philip Langner. Films inc: Shadows; Husbands; Too Late Blues; A Child Is Waiting; Slaves.
Thea inc: Seven Year Itch; Middle of the Night; Dinner at Eight.

CLARK, Oliver: Act. b. Buffalo, NY, Jan 4. e. U of Buffalo. Films inc: The Landlord; End of the Road; They Might Be Giants; A Star is Born; Another Man, Another Chance; Fire Sale. TV inc: We've Got Each Other; Fame.

CLARK, Petula: Singer-Act. b. Ewell, Surrey, Eng, Nov 15, 1932. Films inc: The Huggets; Dance Hall; Made in Heaven; Runaway Bus; Finian's Rainbow; Goodbye Mr. Chips.
(*Grammys*-(2)-Rock & Roll-1964; Contemporary R & R-1965).

CLARK, Roy Linwood: Singer. b. Meherrin, VA, Apr 15, 1933. C&W recording artist. TV inc: The Sensational, Shocking, Wonderful, Wacky 70's.

CLARK, Susan: Act. b. Sarnia, Ont, Canada, Mar 8, 1940. e. RADA. Films inc: Ganning; Madigan; Coogan's Bluff; The Forbin Project; Tell Them Willie Boy is Here; Skullduggery; Valdez is Coming; The Skin Game; Showdown; Airport 75; The Midnight Man; The Apple Dumpling Gang; Murder By Decree; The North Avenue Irregulars; Real Life; City on Fire; Promises in the Dark; Double Negative.
TV inc: Trapped; Amelia Earhart; Babe (*Emmy*-1976); Jimmy B and Andre (& prod).

CLARKE, T.E.B: Wri. b. England, 1907. Films inc: Johnny Frenchman; Hue and Cry; Passport to Pimlico; The Blue Lamp; The Lavender Hill Mob (*Oscar*-1952-story & sp); The Titfield Thunderbolt; Barnacle Bill; Law and Disorder; Sons and Lovers; The Horse Without a Head; A Man Could Get Killed.

CLARY, Robert (nee Widerman): Act-Singer. b. Paris, Mar 1, 1926. Films inc: Ten Tall Men; Thief of Damascus; New Faces; A New Kind of Love; The Hindenburg.
Thea inc: New Faces of 1952; Seventh Heaven; La Plume de ma Tante; Around the World in 80 Days; Sugar.
TV inc: Hogan's Heroes; The Young and the Restless; Days of Our Lives.

CLAVELL, James: Dir-Wri. b. Australia, 1922. Film inc: (sp only) The Fly; Watusi; The Great Escape; 633 Squadron; The Satan Bug. (Prod-dir-sp) Five Gates to Hell; Walk Like a Dragon; To Sir with Love; Where's Jack?; Last Valley.
Plays inc: Countdown to Armageddon. TV inc: Shogun (author & exec prod).

CLAXTON, William: Dir-Prod. b. CA, Oct 22, 1914. Films inc: God Is My Partner; Young and Dangerous; Desire in the Dust.
TV inc: Twilight Zone; Bonanza; High Chaparral; Little House on the Prairie.

CLAYTON, Jack: Prod-Dir. b. England, 1921. Films inc: The Bespoke Overcoat; Three Men in a Boat (prod); Room at the Top (dir); The Innocents (dir); The Pumpkin Eater (dir); Our Mother's House (dir); The Great Gatsby (dir).

CLAYTON, Jan: Act. b. Tularosa, NM, Aug 26, 1917. Films inc: Flight Angels; several Hopalong Cassidy westerns; This Man's Navy; The Snake Pit.
TV inc: Lassie; Scruples.
Bway inc: Show Boat; Carousel.

CLAYTON-THOMAS, David: Singer. b. Canada, Sep 13, 1941. See Blood, Sweat & Tears.

CLAYBURGH, Jill: Act. b. NYC, Apr 30, 1944. Films inc: The Wedding Party; Portnoy's Complaint; the Thief Who Came to Dinner; The Terminal Man; Gable and Lombard; Griffin and Phoenix; Silver Streak; Semi-Tough; An Unmarried Woman; Luna; Starting Over; It's My Turn.
   TV inc: Search for Tomorrow; The Choice; Hustling.
   Bway inc: The Rothschilds; Pippin; Jumpers.

CLEESE, John: Act. b. England, 1939. Films inc: Interlude; The Best House in London; The Rise and Rise of Michael Rimmer; The Love Ban; And Now For Something Completely Different; Monty Python and the Holy Grail; Life of Brian (& sp).

CLEMENS, Brian: Wri-Prod-Dir. b. Croydon, England, 1931. Films inc: Station Six Sahara; The Corrupt Ones; And Soon the Darkness; See No Evil; Dr. Jekyll and Sister Hyde; Captain Kronos - Vampire Hunter; The Golden Voyage of Sinbad; The Watcher in the Woods (sp).
   TV inc: Danger Man; Scene of the Crime; The Avengers.

CLEMENT, Dick: Wri-Dir. b. Eng, 1937. Films inc: The Jokers; Otley; A Severed Head (dir); Villain; Catch Me a Spy; The Likely Lads; The Prisoner of Zenda.
   Plays inc: Billy.
   TV inc: My Wife Next Door.

CLEMENT, Rene: Dir. b. France, 1913. Films inc: Bataille du Rail; Les Maudits; Knave of Hearts; Gervaise; The Sea Wall; The Day and the Hour; The Love Cage; Is Paris Burning?; Rider on the Rain; The House under the Trees; And Hope to Die.

CLIBURN, Van (Harvey Lavan Cliburn Jr): Concert pianist. b. Shreveport, LA, Jul 12, 1934. e. Juilliard. Debut 1947 with Houston Symphony; guest soloist NY Philharmonic 1954; winner Moscow International Tschaikowsky Piano Competition 1958; guest with major world orchestras.
   (*Grammys*-(2)-class inst solo-1958, 1959).

CLIFTON, Peter: Prod-Dir. b. Sydney, Australia, Apr 1, 1943. e. Sydney U. Films inc: Popcorn; The London Rock & Roll Show; The Song Remains the Same.

CLOONEY, Rosemary: Singer. b. Maysville, KY, 1928. Niteries; recording artist. Films inc: The Stars Are Singing; Here Come the Girls; Red Garters; White Christmas; Deep in My Heart.
   TV inc: Pat Boone and Family Christmas Special.

CLOTHIER, William H: Cin. b. 1903. Films inc: Sofia; Track of the Cat; Blood Alley; The Horse Soldiers; The Alamo; The Deadly Companions; The Man Who Shot Liberty Valance; A Distant Trumpet; Cheyenne Autumn; Shenandoah; The War Wagon; Firecreek; The Devil's Brigade; The Cheyenne Social Club; Big Jake.

CLOUSE, Robert: Dir. Started making shorts inc: The Cadillac; The Legend of Jimmy Blue Eyes.
   Films inc: Happy Mothers Day; Love George (wri); Darker Than Amber; Enter the Dragon; Golden Needles; The Ultimate Warrior; The Amsterdam Kill; The Pack; Game of Death; The Big Brawl (& wri).
   TV inc: The Omega Connections; The Kids Who Knew Too Much.

CLURMAN, Harold: Prod-Dir-Wri. b. NYC, Sep 18, 1901. e. Columbia U; Sorbonne. Joined Theatre Guild 1925 as asst stage mgr; appeared in small parts in The Goat Song; The Chief Thing; Juarez and Maximilian. Critic for The Nation; New Republic; London Observer.
   Founded Group Theatre 1931; Plays prod under his management inc: Night Over Taos; House of Connelly; Success Story; Men In White; Awake and Sing; Johnny Johnson; Golden Boy; Waiting for Lefty; Rocket to the Moon; Truckline Cafe; All My Sons.
   (Dir) Beggars Are Coming to Town; the Whole World Over; The Young and Fair; The Member of the Wedding; The Bird Cage; The Autumn Garden; Desire Under The Elms; Time of the Cuckoo; The Emperor's Clothes; The Ladies of the Corridor; Mademoiselle Colombe; Bus Stop; Pipe Dream; Waltz of the Toreadors; Orpheus Descending; The Day the Money Stopped; Heartbreak House; A Shot in the Dark; Incident at Vichy; Where's Daddy.
   (Died Sep 9, 1980).

COBE, Sandy: Exec. b. NYC, Nov 30, 1928. e. Columbia U, Tulane U. P Intercontinental Releasing Corp, P Sandy Cobe Productions, P Sandon Companies, Inc.

COBLENZ, Walter: Prod. Films inc: The Candidate; All the President's Men; The Onion Field.
   TV inc: The Blue Knight.

COBURN, D L (Donald Lee Coburn): Plywri. b. Baltimore, MD, Aug 4, 1938. Ad salesman, later ad agcy exec. Plays inc: The Gin Game *(Pulitzer Prize*-1978); Bluewater Cottage.

COBURN, James: Act. b. Laurel, MD, Aug 31, 1928. e. LA City Coll. Films inc: Ride Lonesome; The Magnificent Seven; Hell is for Heroes; The Great Escape; Charade; The Americanization of Emily; Major Dundee; A High Wind in Jamaica; Our Man Flint; What Did You Do in the War Daddy?; Dead Heat on a Merry-Go-Round; In Like Flint; The President's Analyst; Duffy; Candy; A Fistful of Dynamite; The Honkers; A Reason to Live, A Reason to Die; Pat Garrett and Billy the Kid; The Intercine Project; Hard Times; Sky Riders; Cross of Iron; The Last Hard Man; Firepower; Circle of Iron (wri); The Muppet Movie; Goldengirl; The Baltimore Bullet; Mr Patman; Loving Couples.
   TV inc: Klondike; Acapulco; The Dain Curse.

COCA, Imogene: Act. b. Philadelphia, Nov 18, 1908. Debut as tap dancer in vaudeville at age 11. Solo dancer in Broadway musicals then comedienne on Broadway in New Faces, 1934. Night clubs.
   TV inc: Your Show of Shows *(Emmy*-1952); Imogene Coca Show; Sid Caesar Invites You.
   Films inc: Under the Yum Yum Tree; Rabbit Test.
   Bway inc: On The 20th Century.

COCHRAN, Hank: Singer-Comp. b. Greenville, MS, Aug 2, 1935. Comp C & W songs for such artists as Patsy Cline; Eddy Arnold; Burl Ives; Ray Price. Also appeared on radio, TV; recorded for RCA Victor.

COCKER, Joe (John Robert Cocker): Singer-Mus. b. Sheffield, England, May 21, 1944. With groups the Cavaliers; Vance Arnold and the Avengers before starting The Grease Band; hit single With A Little Help from My Friends.
   Albums inc: Mad Dogs and Englishmen; Cocker Happy; Something to Say; I Can Stand a Little Rain; Jamaica Say You Will; Stingray.

COCO, James: Act. b. NYC, Mar 21, 1930. Films inc: A New Leaf; The Strawberry Statement; Tell Me That You Love Me, Junie Moon; Such Good Friends; Man of La Mancha; The Wild Party; Murder by Death; Bye Bye Monkey; Charleson; The Cheap Detective; Scavenger Hunt; Wholly Moses!
   Bway inc: Hotel Paradiso; Last of the Red Hot Lovers; The Devils; Passage to India; Man of La Mancha; Everybody Loves Opal; Next.
   TV inc: The Flip Wilson Show; The Trouble with People; Calucci's Dept; The Dumplings; The French Atlantic Affair; The Diary of Anne Frank; From Raquel With Love.

CODRON, Michael: Prod. b. London, Jun 8, 1930. e. Oxford. Thea inc: (London) Ring for Catty; A Month of Sundays; Share My Lettuce; The Birthday Party; Fool's Paradise; Pieces of Eight; Stop It, Whoever You Are; Everything in the Garden; A Cheap Bunch of Nice Flowers; The Cloud; Hedda Gabler; A Scent of Flowers; The Killing of Sister George; Ride a Cock Horse; Entertaining Mr Sloane; There's a Girl in My Soup; The Flip Side; Not Now, Darling; The Philanthropist; Butley; Absurd Person Singular; Crown Matrimonial; My Fat Friend; The Golden Pathway Annual; John, Paul, George, Ringo. . . and Bert; A Family and a Fortune; Otherwise Engaged; The Old Country; The Homecoming; Alice's Boys; Night and Day; The Unvarnished Truth; Ten Times Table; The Rear Column; Joking Apart; Stage Struck; Taking Steps; Enjoy; Make and Break; Hinge & Brackett; The Dresser.

CODUN, Sergio (Bruno Blumer): Dir. b. St Galen, Swi, Dec 29, 1949. Dir of Swiss docs, industrial, adv films.

COE, Fred: Prod-Dir. b. Alligator, MS, Dec 23, 1914. e. Peabody Coll, Yale U. Films inc: The Left-Handed Gun; The Miracle Worker; A Thousand Clowns; Me, Natalie.
    Bway inc: A Trip to Bountiful; Two for the Seesaw; The Miracle Worker (Tony-1960); All the Way Home; Gideon; A Thousand Clowns; Fiddler on the Roof; Wait Until Dark; In Praise of Love (dir).
    TV inc: Theatre Guild; TV Playhouse; Mr. Peepers; Bonino; Producers Showcase (Emmy-1955); The Miracle Worker (Emmy-1980).
    (Died Apr 29, 1979).

COE, Peter: Dir. b. London, Apr 18, 1929. e. London Academy of Music and Dramatic Art. Thea inc: (London) Lock Up Your Daughters; The World of Suzie Wong; Treasure Island; Oliver!; The Miracle Worker; Caligula; In White America; In the Matter of J Robert Oppenheimer; The Silence of Lee Harvey Oswald; World War 2 1/2; Kiss Me Kate; Fish Out of Water; Black Macbeth; Games; Poets to the People; The Exorcism; Ride, Ride, Lucy Crown; Cages (& wri). (Bway) Oliver!; On a Clear Day You Can See Forever; Next Time I'll Sing To You; Golden Boy; Pickwick; Six; Woman of the Dunes (& wri); A Life. Films inc: Lock Up Your Daughters.

COEN, Franklin: Wri. b. NYC, Apr 25, 1912. e. U of VA. Films inc: Till We Meet Again; We're On the Jury; Exposed; Glory Brigade; Four Guns to the Border; Johnny Dark; Chief Crazy Horse; The Island Earth; Kiss of Fire; Interlude; Night of the Quarter Moon; The Train; Alvarez Kelly; Black Gunn; The Take.

COHEN, Alexander H: Prod. b. NYC, Jul 24, 1920. e. NYU. Bway inc: Angel Street; The Duke in Darkness; King Lear; The First Gentleman; At the Drop of a Hat; An Evening with Mike Nichols and Elaine May; Beyond the Fringe; Maurice Chevalier at 77; The School for Scandal; Ages of Man; Man and Boy; Victor Borge's Comedy in Music; A Time for Singing; At the Drop of Another Hat; The Homecoming (Tony-1967); Little Murders; The Unknown Soldier and His Wife; Marlene Dietrich; Halfway Up the Tree; Dear World; Home; Good Evening; Ulysses in Nighttown; Words and Music; Who's Who in Hell; Comedians; Anna Christie; I Remember Mama; A Day in Hollywood and a Night in the Ukraine. London inc: The Doctor's Dilemma; Man and Boy; Ivanov; You Never Can Tell; Season of Goodwill; The Merchant of Venice; The Rivals; Plaza Suite; The Price; Come As You Are; 1776; The Happy Apple; Who Killed Santa Claus?; Applause; Harvey.
    TV inc: Since 1967 has produced the annual TV coverage of the Tony Awards (Emmy-1980); On the Air (50th anniversary celebration of seven special programs, 1978).

COHEN, Herman: Prod-Wri. b. Detroit, MI, Aug 27, 1928. Films inc: Two Dollar Bettor; The Basketball Fix; Bela Lugosi Meets the Brooklyn Gorilla; River Beat; Crime of Passion; I Was a Teenage Werewolf; How to Make a Monster; The Traitors; Berserk; Crooks and Coronets; Trog; Today We Kill--Tomorrow We Die; Craze; The Dragon Lives.

COHEN, Larry: Wri. b. Chicago, Apr 20, 1947. e. U of WI, BA. Films inc: Alice Doesn't Live Here Anymore (prodn exec); Carrie; God Told Me To; No Mean Feat (co-sp); The American Success Company (sp).
    Plays inc: Trick (& dir).

COHEN, Rob: Prod. b. Cornwall-on-the-Hudson, NY, Mar 12, 1949. e. Harvard, BA. Films inc: Mahogany; Bingo Long; Scott Joplin; The Wiz; Almost Summer; Thank God It's Friday; A Small Circle of Friends (dir).

COHN, Bruce: Prod. b. San Francisco, Apr 8, 1931. e. UC Berkeley, BA, MJ. News dir KNBC-TV 1962; West Coast prod ABC News 1966; exec prod National Public Affairs Center for TV 1972.
    Films inc: Dogs; Acapulco Gold; Good Guys Wear Black (wri only).
    TV inc: 1968-A Crack In Time (& wri).

COHN, Robert: Prod. b. Avon, NJ, Sep 6, 1920. e. U of MI, BA. Joined Columbia as asst dir; later headed Robert Cohn prodn unit at Columbia; formed Robert Cohn Productions. Film inc: Black Eagle; Rusty Leads the Way; Palomino; Kazan; Killer that Stalked New York; The Barefoot Mailman; Mission Over Korea; The Interns; The New Interns; The Young Americans.

COLASANTO, Nicholas: Dir-Act. b. Providence, RI, Jan 19, 1924. Films inc: (act) Fat City; Family Plot; Raging Bull.
    TV inc: (dir) Name of the Game; Felony Squad; Hawaii 5-0; Police Story; Streets of San Francisco; SWAT.
    Bway inc: (act) A Hatful of Rain.

COLBERT, Claudette (Lily Chauchoin): Act. b. Paris, Sep 13, 1905. Films inc: For the Love of Mike; The Sign of the Cross; I Cover the Waterfront; Three Cornered Moon; It Happened One Night (Oscar-1934); Cleopatra; Private Worlds; Imitation of Life; Under Two Flags; Maid of Salem; I Met Him in Paris; Bluebeard's Eighth Wife; Midnight; Drums Along the Mohawk; Boom Town; Arise My Love; The Palm Beach Story; Since You Went Away; Tomorrow is Forever; The Egg and I; Three Came Home; Let's Make It Legal; The Planter's Wife; Si Versailles M'Etait Conte; Texas Lady; Parrish.
    Bway inc: See Naples and Die; Marriage-Go-Round; Jake, Julia and Uncle Joe; The Irregular Verb to Love; Diplomatic Relations; A Community of Two; Kingfisher.
    TV inc: The Royal Family; The Guardsman; Blithe Spirit.

COLE, George: Act. b. London, Apr 22, 1925. Films inc: Cottage to Let; Quartet; Lady Godiva Rides Again; Top Secret; The Belles of St. Trinian's; The Green Man; Too Many Crooks; The Bridal Path; Cleopatra; The Legend of Young Dick Turpin; The Great St. Trinian's Train Robbery; Fright; Take Me High; The Bluebird.
    TV inc: Life of Bliss; A Man of Our Times; Don't Forget to Write.

COLE, Lester: Wri. b. NYC, Jun 19, 1904. Began writing career 1930 with co-sp credit If I had A Million. Films inc: Charlie Chan's Greatest Case; Pursued; Follow Your Heart; The President's Mystery; Affairs of Cappy Ricks; Some Blondes Are Dangerous; Crime of Dr. Hallet; Midnight Intruder; Winter Carnival; I Stole a Million; Invisible Man Returns; House of Seven Gables; Hostages; None Shall Escape; Objective Burma; Blood On the Sun; Fiesta; Romance of Rosy Ridge; High Wall; one of "Hollywood Ten" who declined (Oct. 1947) to testify before House of Un-American Activities Committee, imprisoned for contempt of Congress. While blacklisted wrote (under pseudonyms) Operation Eichman; Born Free.
    TV inc: (under pseudonyms) Time-Life TV plays; Pied Piper.
    Plays inc: Love Technique; Still Life; Honorable Johnson; Potiphar's House; My Uncle's Dream (adapt from Dostoievski); Say Uncle.

COLE, Maria: Singer. b. Boston, MA, Aug 1, (circa 1920). Widow of Nat King Cole. Singer with Duke Ellington Band, 1945-46. TV inc: Tempo (hosted 1968-69).

COLE, Natalie: Singer. b. LA, Feb 6, 1950. e. U MA. D of Maria and the late Nat "King" Cole. TV inc: Uptown--A Tribute to the Apollo Theatre.
    Albums inc: Unpredictable; Thankful.
    (Grammys-(3)-new artist-1975; R&B vocal-1975, 1976).

COLE, Olivia: Act. b. Memphis, TN, Nov 26, 1942. e. RADA. Bway inc: NY Shakespeare Festival; Skin of Our Teeth; Three-Penny Opera; Black Comedy; The National Health.
    TV inc: Guiding Light; Roots (Emmy-Supp-1977); Szysznk; Backstairs at the White House; Children of Divorce.
    Films inc: Heroes; Coming Home.

COLEMAN, Cy: Comp. b. NYC, Jun 14, 1929. e. NY Coll of Music. Piano debut at age 7, Town Hall & Steinway Hall. Played bars, niteries; then formed trio, performed in hotels. Songs inc: Witchcraft; The Best Is Yet to Come; Hey, Look Me Over; I'm Gonna Laugh You Out of My Life; Real Live Girl; Big Spender.
    Film scores inc: Father Goose; The Art of Love.
    Bway inc: Wildcat; Little Me; Sweet Charity; Compulsion (background music); On the 20th Century (Tony-1978); Barnum (& prod).
    TV inc: Shirley MacLaine-If They Could See Me Now (Emmy-wri-1975); Gypsy In My Soul (Emmy-prod-1976).

COLEMAN, Dabney: Act. b. Austin, TX, Jan 3, 1932. Films inc: This Property is Condemned; The Slender Thread; The Scalp Hunters; The Other Side of the Mountain; The Black Streetfighter; Rolling Thunder; Viva Knievel!; North Dallas Forty; Nothing Personal; How To Beat The High Cost of Living; Melvin and Howard; Nine To Five.

TV inc: Mary Hartman; Forever Fernwood; Apple Pie; When She Was Bad.

COLEMAN, Gary: Act. b. Zion, IL, Feb 8, 1968. TV inc: The Little Rascals; America 2-Night; Good Times; The Jeffersons; Diff'rent Strokes; The Kid From Left Field; Lucy Moves to NBC; The Big Show (host); Scout's Honor.

COLEMAN, Nancy: Act. b. Everett, WA, 1917. e. U of WA. In radio serials; NY stage; repertory. Films inc: Kings' Row; Dangerously They Live; The Gay Sisters; Desperate Journey; Edge of Darkness; In Our Time; Devotion; Her Sister's Secret; Mourning Becomes Electra; That Man from Tangier; Slaves.

COLEMAN, Ornette: Mus. b. Fort Worth, TX, Mar 19, 1930. Rec artist; band ldr.

COLICOS, John: Act. b. Toronto, Can, Dec 10, 1928. NY stage debut 1956, City Center in King Lear. Joined American Shakespeare Festival Theatre 1957, Stratford, CT. Films inc: Anne of the Thousand Days; Raid on Rommel; Red Sky at Morning; Doctor's Wives; The Wrath of God; Scorpio; Drum; Breaking Point; Battlestar Galactica; The Changeling; Phobia.

TV inc: Beaverbrook--The Life and Times of Max Aitken; The Bastard; The Girl Who Saved Our America.

COLLA, Richard: Dir. b. Milwaukee, WI, Apr 18, 1918. e. Marquette U, BA, MA. Films inc: Zig Zag; Sometimes A Great Notion; Fuzz; Battlestar Galactica. TV inc: Live Again, Die Again; Jake's Way.

COLLINS, Gary: Act. b. Boston, MA, 1938. Films inc: Cleopatra; The Pigeon That Took Rome; The Longest Day; Airport; Angel in My Pocket; Killer Fish; Hangar 18.

TV inc: The Secret of Lost Valley; Hour Magazine (host); Daredevils.

COLLINS, Hal: Wri. b. NYC, 1920. Began writing material for Milton Berle at age 15, wrote for him for almost 40 years; also wri for Red Buttons. Invented off-line video tape editing technique. TV inc: (edit) All in the Family; Maude; Sanford and Son; The Jeffersons; Good Times; Carter Country; Lucille Ball Specials; Bob Hope Specials.

(Died Nov 7, 1980).

COLLINS, Joan: Act. b. London, May 23, 1933. Films inc: I Believe in You; Judgement Deferred; Decameron Nights; The Square Ring; The Good Die Young; Land of the Pharaohs; Virgin Queen; Island in the Sun; Wayward Bus; The Bravados; The Bawdy Adventures of Tom Jones; Empire of the Ants; The Big Sleep; Sunburn; The Bitch. Thea inc: The Last of Mrs. Cheyney.

COLLINS, Judy: Folksinger-Sngwri. b. Denver, CO, May 1, 1939. Albums inc: A Maid of Constant Sorrow; Who Knows Where the Time Goes; Whalers and Nightingales; Living; Judith; Colors of the Day; The Best of Judy Collins.

(Grammy-folk rec-1968).

COLLINS, Pat (nee Allan): Hypnotist. b. Detroit, May 7, 1935. Works niteries, tv guestints.

COLLINS, Richard: Wri-Prod. b. NYC, Jul 20, 1914. e. Stanford U. Films inc: Rulers of the Sea; One Crowded Night; Lady Scarface; Thousands Cheer; Little Giant; China Venture; Riot in Cell Block 11; The Adventures of Hajji Baba; The Bob Mathias Story; Kiss of Fire; My Gun Is Quick; Spanish Affair; The Badlanders; Edge of Eternity; Pay or Die.

TV inc: Clown; Shadow On the Heart; That's the Man; The Great Alberti; The Breaking Point; Sarah; Chrysler Theatre; The Family Holvak; The Godchild; Breaking Point; The Immigrants.

COLLINS, Stephen: Act. b. Hastings-on-Hudson, NY, Oct 1, 1947. e. Amherst. Bway inc: Macbeth; More Than You Deserve; Last Days of British Honduras; Moonchildren; Censored Scenes From King Kong.

Films inc: All The President's Men; Between The Lines; Fedora; The Promise; Star Trek--The Motion Picture; Loving Couples.

TV inc: The Best of Families; The Rhineman Exchange; Brinks--The Great Robbery; The Henderson Monster.

COLLINSON, Peter: Dir. b. Lincs, England, 1936. Films inc: The Penthouse; Up the Junction; The Italian Job; You Can't Win 'em All; Fright; Straight on till Morning; Innocent Bystanders; The Man Called Noon; Open Season; The Spiral Staircase; The Sell Out; The Earthling.

TV inc: The House on Garibaldi Street.

(Died Dec 16, 1980).

COLOMBY, Bobby: Drummer. b. Miami, FL, Jan 12, 1954. See Blood, Sweat & Tears.

COLONNA, Jerry: Act. b. Boston, 1903. Films inc: College Swing; Little Miss Broadway; Sis Hopkins; True to the Army; Star Spangled Rhythm; Ice Capades; Atlantic City; It's in the Bag; Road to Rio; Kentucky Jubilee; Meet Me in Las Vegas; Andy Hardy Comes Home.

COMDEN, Betty (Elizabeth Cohen): Wri. b. NYC, May 3, 1918. e. NYU. Films inc: Good News; The Barkleys of Broadway; On the Town; Singin' in the Rain; Band Wagon; It's Always Fair Weather; Auntie Mame; What a Way to Go.

Bway inc: Wonderful Town (Tony-1953); Peter Pan; Do Re Mi; On the Town; Billion Dollar Baby; Two on the Aisle; Bells Are Ringing; Subways Are for Sleeping; Hallelujah Baby (Tonys-best musical & lyr-1968); Fade Out - Fade In; Applause (Tony-best musical-1970); On the 20th Century (Tonys-book & lyr-1978); A Party With Betty Comden and Adolph Green; Peter Pan.

Songs: New York, New York; Lonely Town; Ohio; Give a Little, Get A Little; The Party's Over; Just in Time; Make Someone Happy.

TV inc: The Kennedy Center Honors, 1980.

COMER, Anjanette: Act. b. 1942. Films inc: Quick Before it Melts; The Loved One; The Appaloosa; Banning; Rabbit, Run; The Baby; Lepke; Fire Sale.

TV inc: The Firechasers.

THE COMMODORES: Group. Members are Lionel Richie, lead singer-sngwri; Thomas McClary, guitar-sngwri; Walter Orange, lead singer-drummer; William King, trumpet-sngwri; Ronald LaPread, bass-sngwri; Milan Williams, keyboard-sngwri. Formed 1969, made world tours before signing with Motown.

Albums inc: Machine Gun; The Commodores; Commodores Live; Natural High; Midnight Magic.

COMO, Perry (Nick Perido): Act. b. Canonsburg, PA, May 18, 1912. Barber at age 15; joined Carlone Band, then Ted Weems, 1936; performed in niteries. Screen debut, Something for the Boys, 1944. Films inc: Doll Face; If I'm Lucky; Words and Music.

TV inc: The Chesterfield Supper Club; The Perry Como Show; The Kraft Music Hall. (Emmy-male singer-1954 & 55); (Emmy-host-1955); (Emmy-male personality-1957); (Emmy-act-mus-1959); Perry Como's Early American Christmas; Perry Como's Christmas in New Mexico; Perry Como's Bahama Holiday.

(Grammy-vocal-1958).

COMPTON, Forrest: Act. b. Reading, PA, Sep 15. Films inc: Inherit the Wind; The Children's Hour; The Outsider; Kings Go Forth.

TV inc: Gomer Pyle, USMC; Hogan's Heroes; That Girl; Mayberry RFD; Bright Promise; The Brighter Day; The Edge of Night.

Thea inc: Look Homeward, Angel; An Evening with Oscar Wilde; Under The Yum Yum Tree; Detective Story; The Happy Time; Othello.

COMPTON, Richard B: Dir. Films inc: Angels Die Hard; Welcome Home Soldier Boys; Macon County Line; Return to Macon County; Maniac; Ravagers; Wild Times.

TV inc: The California Kid.

CONAWAY, Jeff: Act. b. NYC, Oct 5. Films inc: Jennifer On My Mind; The Eagle Has Landed; Pete's Dragon; I Never Promised You a Rose Garden; Grease.
TV inc: The Mary Tyler Moore Show; Happy Days; Movin' On; Having Babies; Delta County, U S A; Taxi; Breaking Up Is Hard to Do; For The Love Of It.
Bway inc: All The Way Home; Grease.

CONLEY, Renie: Cost Dsgn. b. Republic, WA, Jul 31, 1919. e. UCLA, Chouinard School of Art. Under contract RKO 10 years, Fox 6 years using first name only on credits.
Films inc: The Model and the Marriage Broker; The President's Lady; The Big Fisherman; Cleopatra (Oscar-1953); The Legend of Lylah Clare; The Killing of Sister George; Whatever Happened to Aunt Alice; Great Scout and Cathouse Thursday; Caravans.
TV inc: Haywire; Woman's Room.
Desgnd all costumes for Disneyland when park opened; dsgnr for Shipstad and Johnson's Ice Follies 7 years.

CONNELLY, Marc: Wri-Act. b. McKeesport, PA, Dec 13, 1890. Films inc: (act) Cradle Song; Captains Courageous; I Married a Witch; The Spirit of St Louis
Plays inc: Dulcy; To The Ladies; The 49-ers; Merton of the Movies; Helen of Troy, New York; The Deep-Tangled Wildwood; Beggars on Horseback; Be Yourself; Green Pastures; Having a Wonderful Time (dir); Hunter's Moon (dir); Tall Story (act).
(Died Dec 21, 1980).

CONNERY, Sean: Act. b. Edinburgh, Scotland, Aug 25, 1930. Stage debut chorus of London company South Pacific. On screen from 1955. Films inc: No Road Back; Another Time, Another Place; Tarzan's Greatest Adventure; Dr. No; From Russia With Love; Goldfinger; Thunderball; A Fine Madness; You Only Live Twice; The Anderson Tapes; Diamonds Are Forever; The Offence; Ransom; Murder on the Orient Express; The Wind and the Lion; The Man Who Would Be King; Robin and Marian; The Last Man; A Bridge Too Far; The Great Train Robbery; Meteor; Cuba.
TV inc: Requiem for a Heavyweight; Anna Karenina; Age of Kings;
Thea inc: (London) I've Seen You Cut Lemons (dir).

CONNIFF, Ray: Comp-Cond. b. Attleboro, MA, Nov 6, 1916. Played trombone and arranged for Bunny Berigan; Bob Crosby; Artie Shaw; Glen Gray; Mitch Miller; arr for Col Records; formed own orch and chorus; recorded 63 albums. (Grammy-Chorus-1966).

CONNORS, Carol: Songwri. Films inc: (Lyr) Rocky; Orca; The Other Side of Midnight; Looking for Mr. Goodbar; Heroes; Matilda (mus); Fast Break; Golden Girl; Mountain Family Robinson; The Onion Field; Scavenger Hunt; Cheaper To Keep Her; Resurrection; Falling in Love Again; Dressed to Kill; Fade to Black.
TV inc: American Gothic; Dallas Cowboy Cheerleaders I & II; Next Step Beyond (& mus); Archie's Prime Time (& mus); San Pedro Beach Bums (& mus); A Sensitive Passionate Man (& mus); Zuma Beach.
Songs inc: Gonna Fly Now; Someone's Waiting for You.

CONNORS, Chuck (Kevin Joseph Connors): Act. b. NYC, Apr 10, 1924. e. Seton Hall Coll. Former professional baseball player. Films inc: Pat and Mike; Dragonfly Squadron; Target Zero; Hold Back The Night; Geronimo; Kill Them All And Come Back Alive; The Deserter; Support Your Local Gunfighter; 99 and 44/100ths % Dead; Tourist Trap; Virus.
TV inc: Dennis Day Show; Gunsmoke; West Point; Rifleman; Roots.

CONNORS, Mike (Kregor Ohanian): (early billing as Touch Connors). Act. b. Fresno, CA, Apr 15, 1925. e. UCLA. Films inc: Sudden Fear; The Ten Commandments; Where Love Has Gone; Good Neighbor Sam; Situation Hopeless But Not Serious; Harlow; Stagecoach; Kiss the Girls and Make Them Die; Avalanche Express.
TV inc: The Killer Who Wouldn't Die; Tightrope; Mannix; Long Journey Back; Death of Ocean View Park; High Midnight; Casino; Nightkill.

CONRAD, Robert (nee Falk): Act. b. Chicago, Mar 1, 1935. e. Northwestern U. Films inc: Thundering Jets; Palm Springs Weekend; Young Dillinger; Murph the Surf; Sudden Death; Hotel Madrid; You Can't Steal Love; The Lady in Red.
TV inc: Hawaiian Eye; Wild, Wild West; The D A; Baa, Baa, Black Sheep; Weekend of Terror; Five Desperate Men; The Adventures of Nick Carter; Centennial; The Duke; Wild Wild West Revisited; Breaking Up is Hard to Do; A Man Called Sloane; More Wild Wild West; Daredevils (host); Coach of the Year.

CONRAD, Scott: Film ed. Films inc: Rocky (Oscar-1976); Outlaw Blues; Cheech and Chong's Up in Smoke; Wanda Nevada.

CONRAD, William: Act. b. Louisville, KY, Sep 27, 1920. e. Fullerton Coll. Radio station KMPC, LA, wri, anncr, dir. WW 2 fighter pilot. Returned to radio drama as original Matt Dillon of Gunsmoke series. Films inc: The Killers; Body and Soul; Sorry, Wrong Number; The Naked Jungle; Moonshine County Express.
TV inc: This Man Dawson; The Brotherhood of the Bell; The D A; Conspiracy to Kill; O'Hara, U.S. Treasury; Cannon; The Rebels; The Lost Treasure of the Conception (narr); The Murder That Wouldn't Die; Return of the King (voice); Turnover Smith (& prod); The Return of Frank Cannon.

CONRIED, Hans: Act. b. Baltimore, Apr 15, 1917. Films inc: Dramatic School; Crazy House; Mrs. Parkington; The Senator Was Indiscreet; My Friend Irma; The Twonky; The 5,000 Fingers of Doctor T; Bus Stop; Rockabye Baby; The Patsy; The Brothers O'Toole; The Cat From Outer Space; Oh, God! Book II.
Bway inc: Can-Can; 70 Girls 70; Irene. Other thea inc: Tall Story; The Absence of a Cello; Don't Drink the Water; Norman, Is That You?; Something Old, Something New.
TV inc: The Danny Thomas Show; Quark; The Adventures of Major Effects; The Incredible Book Escape (voice); Scruffy (voice).

CONSTANTINE, Eddie: Act. b. Oct 29, 1915. Films inc: SOS Pacific; Treasure of San Teresa; Riff Raff Girls; Alphaville; The Lemmy Caution series; The Third Generation; It Lives Again; Portrait of a Female Drunkard; The Long Good Friday; Panische Zeiten (Panic Times); Exit. . .But No Panic; Tango Through Germany.

CONSTANTINE, Michael (Constantine Joanides): Act. b. Reading, PA, May 22, 1927. Films inc: Hustler; Quick Before It Melts; Hawaii; Fat Chance; Skidoo; Justine; Don't Drink the Water; If It's Tuesday, This Must be Belgium; Voyage of the Damned; The North Avenue Irregulars.
TV inc: Hey Landlord; Room 222 (Emmy-1970); Sirota's Court; The Pirate; The Love Tapes.
Bway inc: Inherit the Wind; Compulsion; The Miracle Worker; The Egg; Arturo UI.

CONTE, John: Act. b. MA. Former actor now P KMIR-TV, Channel 36, Desert Empire TV Corp, Palm Springs. TV inc: John Conte's Little Show; Matinee Theatre (host); Mantovani Welcomes You.
Thea inc: Windy City; Allegro; Carousel; Arms and the Girl.

CONTI, Bill: Comp. b. Providence, RI, Apr 13, 1942. e. LSU, BM, Juilliard School of Music. Film scores inc: Blume in Love; Harry & Tonto; Next Stop Greenwich Village; Rocky; Citizen Band; Pacific Challenge; Slow Dancing in the Big City; An Unmarried Woman; F.I.S.T.; The Big Fix; Paradise Alley; Uncle Joe Shannon; Dreamer; Five Days From Home; Rocky II; Goldengirl; A Man, A Woman and a Bank; The Seduction of Joe Tynan; Gloria; Private Benjamin; The Formula.
TV inc: Executive Suite; The Andros Targets; Pappa and Me; Smashup On Interstate 5; A Sensitive, Passionate Man; Kill Me If You Can; In the Matter of Karen Ann Quinlan; Ring of Passion; The Pirate.

CONTI, Tom: Act. b. Scotland, Nov 22, 1941. Films inc: Full Circle; The Duelists. Bway inc: Whose Life Is It Anyway? (Tony-1979); Last Licks (dir); Before the Party (dir). (London) They're Playing Our Song; Whose Life Is It Anyway?
TV inc: Blade on the Feather.

CONVERSE, Frank: Act. b. St Louis, MO, May 22, 1938. e. Carnegie Tech. Films inc: Hurry Sundown; Hour of the Gun; The Rowdyman. TV inc: Movin' On; Marilyn--The Untold Story.
Thea inc: The Seagull; Death of a Salesman; Night of the Iguana; A Man for All Seasons; The House of Blue Leaves; First One Asleep Whistle; Arturo Ui; The Philadelphia Story.

CONVERSE, Tony: Prod-Exec. b. 1936. e. Yale, BA. Worked as asst dir CBS-TV prior to Army service as pgm dir AFRN Europe; 1971 joined CBS as pgm exec; 1974 vp special pgms; 1977 vp-exec prod EMI Televison Programs Inc.
TV inc: (Prod) Secret Storm; Love of Life. (Exec Prod) Forever; Deadman's Curve; Special Olympics; Just Me and You; Steel Cowboy; One In a Million; Betrayal; The Cracker Factory; Survival of Dana; Can You Hear The Laughter--The Story of Freddie Prinze; Orphan Train; My Kidnapper, My Love.

CONVY, Bert: Act. b. St Louis, Jul 23, 1934. e. UCLA, BA. Former professional baseball player. Bway inc: The Matchmaker; Billy Barnes Revue. Films inc: Gunman's Walk; Susan Slade; Act One; Semi-Tough; Jennifer; Hero at Large.
TV inc: Dallas Cowboys Cheerleaders; Ebony, Ivory and Jade; Man in the Santa Claus Suit.

CONWAY, Gary (Gareth Monello Carmody): Act. b. Boston, Feb 4, 1936. e. UCLA. Films inc: Young Guns of Texas; Once Is Not Enough; The Farmer (& prod.). TV inc: Burke's Law; Land of the Giants.

CONWAY, James L: Wri-Prod-Dir. b. NYC, Oct 27, 1950. e. U of Denver, BA. TV inc: (Dir) Grizzly Adams; Last of the Mohicans; The Incredible Rocky Mountain Race; Greatest Heroes of the Bible; House of Usher (& prod); The Legend of Sleepy Hollow (prod).
Films inc: Beyond and Back; In Search of Historic Jesus (prod); Hangar 18.

CONWAY, Kevin: Act. b. NYC, May 29, 1942. Bway inc: When You Comin Back, Red Ryder; One Flew Over the Cuckoo's Nest; Moonchildern; The Plough and the Stars; Indians; Saved; Muzeeka; Long Day's Journey Into Night; The Elephant Man.
Films inc: Slaughterhouse Five; Shamus; Portnoy's Complaint; F.I.S.T.; Paradise Alley.
TV inc: Johnny We Hardly Know You; The Deadliest Season; Lathe of Heaven.

CONWAY, Russ (nee Zink): Act. b. Brandon, Manitoba, Can, Apr 25, 1913. e. UCLA. Films inc: The Heiress; War of the Worlds; Fort Dobbs; Bramble Bush; Tomahawk; The Lively Set; Our Man Flint.
TV inc: Wagon Train; Mission Impossible; Bonanza; Sea Hunt; The Hardy Boys.
Thea inc: Prologue To Glory; The American Way; Johnny 2 by 4; The Land Is Bright.

CONWAY, Tim: Act. b. Willoughby, OH, Dec 15, 1933. e. Bowling Green State U. Joined KWY-TV, Cleveland as wri, dir and occasional performer. Films inc: McHale's Navy; The World's Greatest Athlete; The Apple Dumpling Gang; Gus; The Shaggy D.A.; Billion Dollar Hobo (& wri); They Went Thataway and Thataway (& wri); The Apple Dumpling Gang Rides Again; The Prizefighter (& wri); Private Eyes (& wri).
TV inc: Carol Burnett Show (4 Emmys-supp-1973, 1977, 1978; wri-1978); Steve Allen Show; McHale's Navy; Red Skelton; Danny Kaye; Dean Martin; Cher; Doris Day Shows; The Tim Conway Show.

COOGAN, Jackie: Act. b. LA, Oct 26, 1914. e. Villanova Coll. Film debut in The Kid at age 4. Films inc: Peck's Bad Boy; My Boy Trouble; Daddy; Oliver Twist; Circus Days; Long Live the King; Boy of Flanders; Rag Man; Johnny Get Your Gun; Buttons; Tom Sawyer; Huckleberry Finn; Million Dollar Legs; Kilroy Was Here; Lost Women; Marlowe; Human Experiments; Dr. Heckyl and Mr. Hype.
TV inc: The Kids Who Knew Too Much.

COOK, Elisha Jr: Act. b. San Franciso, Dec 26, 1902. Films inc: Sergeant York; The Maltese Falcon; I Wake Up Screaming; Casanova Brown; Up in Arms; Dillinger; The Big Sleep; The Fall Guy; The Gangster; Shane; The Killing; Welcome to Hard Times; El Condor; The Outfit; The Black Bird; Messiah of Evil; Winterhawk; St. Ives; The Champ; Carny; 1941.
TV inc: Salem's Lot.

COOK, Fielder: Prod-Dir. b. Atlanta, GA, Mar 9, 1923. Films inc: Patterns of Power; Home Is the Hero; Big Hand for a Little Lady; How to Save a Marriage; Prudence and the Pill; Eagle in a Cage; From the Mixed Up Files of Mrs. Basil E. Frankenweiler.
TV inc: Studio One; Theatre Guild of the Air; Playhouse 90; Brigadoon (Emmys-prod & dir-1967); The Price (Emmy-dir-1971); The Fifty-Minute Hour; Ben Casey; The Eleventh Hour; The Waltons; Beacon Hill; Too Far To Go; Gauguin the Savage.
Bway inc: A Cook for Mr General.

COOK, Peter: Act-Wri. b. Torquay, Eng, Nov 17, 1937. e. Cambridge. Beyond the Fringe; Behind the Fringe; Good Evening. (Special Tonys-1963 & 1974).
Films inc: (act) A Dandy in Aspic; The Wrong Box; Bedazzled; The Bed Sitting Room; The Rise and Rise of Michael Rimmer; Hound of the Baskervilles.
(Grammy-spoken word-1974).

COOK, Dr Robin: Wri. b. NYC, 1940. e. Columbia U, College of Physicians and Surgeons. MD, Ophthalmic surgeon, clinical instructor at Harvard Medical School.
Films inc: Coma.

COOK, T S (Thomas S Cook): Wri. b. Cleveland, OH, Aug 25, 1947. e. Denison U, BA; U of TX, MFA. Films inc: China Syndrome.
TV inc: Baretta; Paper Chase; Project UFO; Scared Straight!--Another Story.

COOK, Tommy: Act-Wri-Prod. b. Duluth, MN, Jul 5, 1930. e. UCLA. On screen from 1942. Films inc: The Tuttles of Tahiti; Hi, Buddy; Wanderer of the Wasteland; Gallant Journey; Panic in the Streets; Mohawk; Alaska Passage; Rollercoaster (asso prod); Players (prod).
TV inc: (co-creator) The Challenge of the Sexes; Celebrity challenge of the Sexes.

COOKE, Alan: Prod-Wri-Dir. b. England, Mar 29, 1935. e. Merton College Oxford. TV inc: (England) Armchair Theatre; BBC Play of the Month; Play for Today; A Picture of Katherine Mansfield; Shades of Green; Devil's Crown; Cover; Brack Report. (US) NBC Matinee Theatre; Dear Detective; Lou Grant; Quincy; Hart to Hart.
Films inc: Mind of Mr. Soames.

COOKE, Alistair: Journalist-TV Commentator. b. England, Nov 20, 1908. e. Jesus Coll, Cambridge, Yale, Harvard. Film critic, BBC, 1934-37. London corr NBC, 1936-37. BBC commentator in U.S. since 1933. Chief Amer corr Manchester Guardian since 1948. TV inc: (emcee) Omnibus; America (2 Emmys-narr & wri-1973); Masterpiece Theatre (Emmy-1974); Pride and Prejudice; Testament of Youth.

COOLIDGE, Rita: Singer. b. Nashville, TN, 1944. Singer with Delaney and Bonnie Bramlett; Joe Cocker; Leon Russell; Kris Kristofferson before going solo.
Records inc: Rita Coolidge; Nice Feelin' The Lady's Not for Sale; Love Me Again; Satisfied; Anytime, Anywhere.
(Grammys-(2)-country vocal duo-1973, 1975).
Films inc: Pat Garrett and Billy the Kid.
TV inc: The Christmas Raccoons.

COONEY, Dennis: Act. b. NYC. e. Fordham. Thea inc: (Off-Bway) Whisper To Me; Every Other Evil; Young Jefferson; In The Summer House. (Bway) Ross; Love and Kisses; The Last of Mrs Lincoln; Sherlock Holmes.
TV inc: Love of Life; The Magnificent Yankee; The Secret Storm; As The World Turns.

COONEY, Ray: Prod-Act-Dir-Wri. b. London, May 30, 1932. Thea inc: (act) Simple Spymen; One for the Pot (& wri); The Mousetrap; Doctor at Sea; Uproar in the House. (Dir): Thark; In at the Death; Press Cuttings; Not Now, Darling; Move Over, Mrs. Markham; The Mating Game; Why Not Stay for Breakfast; Birds of Paradise (& prod). (Prod): Lloyd George Knew My Father; Two and Two Make Sex; Say Goodnight to Grandma; At the End of the Day; The Dame of Sark; The Bedwinner; Jack the Ripper; A Ghost on Tiptoe; The Sack Race; Murder at the Vicarage; A Ghost on Tiptoe; Hello Dolly; Beatlemania; They're Playing Our Song; Duet For One.
Films inc: There Goes The Bride (prod).

COOPER, Alice (Vincent Damon Furnier): Singer-Songwri. b. Detroit, MI, 1948. Pioneer of Shockrock; concert tours featuring bizarre and elaborate equipment.
Films inc: Welcome to My Nightmare (doc); Sgt. Pepper's Lonely Hearts Club Band; Sextette; Roadie.

COOPER, Ben: Act. b. Hartford, CT, Sep 30, 1930. e. Columbia U. Films inc: The Woman They Almost Lynched; Perilous Journey; Johnny Guitar; Jubilee Trail; The Eternal Sea; The Rose Tattoo; Red Tomahawk; The Fastest Gun Alive; One More Train to Rob; Support Your Local Gunfighter.
Thea inc: Life With Father.

COOPER, Hal: Dir. b. NYC, Feb 23, 1923. e. U MI, BA. TV inc: TV Babysitter; Magic Cottage; Search for Tomorrow; Valiant Lady; Portia Faces Life; Kitty Foyle; Death Valley Days; Dick Van Dyke Show; I Spy; Courtship of Eddie's Father; Mary Tyler Moore Show; Odd Couple; All in the Family; Maude (exec prod); Insight/Holy Moses; Pottsville; Mr. & Mrs. . .and Mr.; Did You Hear About Josh and Kelly (& prod-song); The Long Road Home.

COOPER, Jackie: Act-Dir-Prod. b. LA, Sep 15, 1922. e. Notre Dame, BA. On screen at age 3, Our Gang Comedies. First starring role 1930, Skippy. Films inc: (act) Sunny Side Up; Sooky; The Champ; When a Fellow Needs a Friend; Lumpy; Lost; The Bowery; Treasure Island; The Devil Is a Sissy; Gangster's Boy; Seventeen; Her First Beau; Stork Bites Man; Kilroy Was Here; Everything's Ducky; The Love Machine; Chosen Survivors; Superman; Superman II. (Dir): Stand Up and Be Counted.
TV inc: People's Choice (act & dir 71 segments); Hennessy (act & dir 91 segments); Mobile Two (act). VP in chg. of TV Prodn, Screen Gems, 1964-69; resd to return to acting, dir, prod. TV inc: (dir) M*A*S*H (*Emmy*-dir-1974); White Shadow (*Emmy*-dir-1979); Sex and the Single Parent; Trapper John; Paris; White Mama; Rodeo Girl.

COOPER, Lester: Prod. b. NYC, Jan 20, 1919. e. NYU. Freelance screenwriter, joined CBS News 1953 as wri; 1956 wri Today Show, NBC; 1961, head-wri, supv prod PM; 1967 exec prod ABC News doc unit; 1969 exec prod ABC Summer Focus Series.
TV inc: (exec prod-wri) Heart Attack; This Land is Mine; Can You Hear Me; The Right to Live; Hemingway's Spain--A Love Affair; Make A Wish (*Emmy*-prod-children's series-1974); Animals, Animals, Animals (& crea) (*Emmy*-1978).

COOPER, Robert: Prod-Bdcstr. b. Montreal, Dec 3, 1944. TV inc: Ombudsman (host). Films inc: Power Play (exec prod); Running (prod); Middle Age Crazy (prod).

COOPERMAN, Alvin: Prod. b. NYC, Jul 24, 1923. e. NYU. Served with NBC-TV on three separate occasions as program exec. Also exec dir of the Shubert Theaters; P of Madison Square Garden Prodns; chmn, Athena Communications Corp (a cable TV co).
TV inc: The Bolshoi Ballet; Romeo and Juliet; Producers Showcase; Wide Wide World; 1972 Republican National Convention in Miami Beach (conceived format & prod); Live from Studio 8H--A Tribute to Toscanini (*Emmy*-1980).

COOTE, Robert: Act. b. London, Feb 4, 1909. e. Hurstpierpoint Coll. Stage debut 1925, The Private Secretary. Thea inc: The Windmill Man; Sweet Lavender; The Love of Four Colonels; Dear Charles; My Fair Lady; Camelot; Birds of Paradise.
Films inc: Sally in Our Alley; A Yank at Oxford; Prudence and the Pill; Up the Front; Theatre of Blood.
TV inc: The Rogues; Best of Enemies; Institute for Revenge; A Room With a View.

COPELAND, Joan (nee Miller): Act. b. NYC, Jun 1, 1922. e. AADA, Actors Studio. Sis of Arthur Miller. Bway inc: Othello; Sundown Beach; Detective Story; Not For Children; The Grass Is Always Greener; The Miser; Handful of Fire; Tovarich; My Fair Lady (tour); Something More!; The Price; Two By Two; The American Clock.
Films inc: The Goddess; Middle of the Night; It's My Turn.
TV inc: Search For Tomorrow; The Iceman Cometh; How To Survive A Marriage.

COPLAND, Aaron: Comp-Cond. b. NYC, Nov 14, 1900. Film scores inc: The City; Of Mice and Men; Our Town; North Star; The Red Pony; The Heiress (*Oscar*-1949); Something Wild. TV inc: Kennedy Center Honors-A Celebration of the Performing Arts.
Works: Dance Symphony; Piano Variations; El Salon Mexico; Outdoor Adventure.
(*Grammy*-classical comp-1960); Presidential Medal of Freedom 1964.

COPPERFIELD, David: Illusionist-Act. b. 1957. Admitted to American Society Magicians at age 12, youngest member ever admitted. In musicomedy Magic Man, Chicago. Films inc: Terror Train.
TV inc: The Magic of ABC; The Magic of David Copperfield; The Magic of David Copperfield II.

COPPOLA, Carmine: Comp-Cond. b. NYC, Jun 11, 1910. e. Manhattan School of Music, BA, MA, Juilliard, MM. F of Francis Ford Coppola. Chief arr Radio City Music Hall; 1st flutist, Detroit Symphony & Toscanini Symphony; cond David Merrick Productions. Films inc: Wide Open Places; Once Upon a Mattress; Kismet; La Plume de Ma Tante; Godfather Part II (*Oscar*-1974); Apocalypse Now; The Black Stallion.
TV inc: The People.
Works: Flute Fling; Phantom Cavalry; Woodwind Quintet; Oboe Fantasie.

COPPOLA, Francis Ford: Dir-Wri-Prod. b. Detroit, MI, Apr 7, 1939. e. Hofstra, BA; UCLA, MFA. Owns Omni Zoetrope Prodn facility San Francisco; 1980 purchased Hollywood General Studios.
Films inc: (dir) Dementia 13; You're A Big Boy Now; Finian's Rainbow; The Rain People (& wri); The Godfather (& wri) (*Oscar*-sp-1972); The Conversation (& wri-prod); The Godfather, Part 2 (& wri-prod) (*Oscars*-picture-dir-sp-1974); Apocalypse Now (& wri-prod-mus). (Wri) Is Paris Burning?; This Property is Condemned; Reflections In a Golden Eye; Patton (*Oscar*-sp-1970). (Prod): American Graffiti; THX 1138; The Black Stallion (exec prod).

CORBETT, Gretchen: Act. b. Camp Sherman, OR, Aug 13, 1947. Films inc: The Other Side of the Mountain, Part II. TV inc: The Rockford Files; Mandrake; She's Dressed to Kill; High Ice. Thea inc: Forty Carats.

CORBETT, Harry H: Act. b. Rangoon, 1925. Films inc: Floods of Fear; Nowhere to Go; Cover Girl Killer; What a Crazy World; Ladies Who Do; Rattle of a Simple Man; Joey Boy; The Sandwich Man; Carry on Screaming; Crooks and Coronets; The Magnificent Seven Deadly Sins; Jabberwocky; It's Not the Size That Counts; Silver Dream Racer.
TV inc: Song in a Strange Land; Thunder on the Snow; Steptoe and Son; Mr. Aitch.

CORBY, Ellen (nee Hansen): Act. b. Racine, WI, 1913. Films inc: The Dark Corner; The Spiral Staircase; I Remember Mama; Fighting Father Dunne; Madame Bovary; On Moonlight Bay; About Mrs. Leslie; The Seventh Sin; Macabre; Visit to a Small Planet; The Strangler; The Gnome Mobile.
TV inc: The Waltons (*Emmys*-supp-1973-1975-1976).

CORD, Alex (nee Viespi): Act. b. Floral Park, NY, Aug 3, 1935. Films inc: Synanon; Stagecoach; The Brotherhood; Stiletto; Dead or Alive. The Last Grenade; The Dead Are Alive; Chosen Survivors; Sidewinder 1; Grayeagle.

TV inc: Genesis II; The Girl Who Saved Our America; Beggarman, Thief; Hunter's Moon.

CORDAY, Mara (Marilyn Watts): Act. b. Santa Monica, CA, Jan 3, 1932. Films inc: Drums Across the River; Playgirl; Dawn at Socorro; Francis Joins the WACS; So This Is Paris; Man Without a Star; Man from Bitter Ridge; Tarantula; A Day of Fury; Girl on Death Row; The Gauntlet.

COREA, Chick (Armando Corea): Pianist-Comp. b. Chelsea, MA, Jun 12, 1941. e. Juilliard. With Blue Mitchell, Stan Getz, Miles Davis, Sarah Vaughan before starting own group Return to Forever.

Recordings inc: No Mystery; Leprechaun; My Special Heart; Mad Hatter; Light as a Feather.

(Grammys-(5)-group jazz-1975, 1976, 1978, 1979; inst arr-1976).

COREA, Nicholas: Wri. b. St Louis, MO, Apr 7, 1943. TV inc: Police Woman, The Blue Knight; Kingston Confidential (story ed); Oregon Trail (exec story ed); Starsky & Hutch; Black Sheep Squadron; The Incredible Hulk (prod-dir).

COREY, Irwin: Act. b. NYC, Jan 29, 1912. Stage debut in musical, Pins and Needles. Developed into double-talking comedian. Bway inc: Mrs. McThing; Happy as Heaven.

Films inc: Thieves; Car Wash; How to Commit Marriage.

COREY, Jeff: Act-Dir. b. NYC, Aug 10, 1914. e. UCLA, BA. On stage 1936, Hamlet. Screen debut 1940, All That Money Can Buy. Films inc: The Killers; Ramrod; Joan of Arc; In Cold Blood; The Boston Strangler; True Grit; Butch Cassidy and the Sundance Kid; Beneath the Planet of the Apes; They Call Me Mr. Tibbs; A Clear and Present Danger; Catlow; Something Evil; Premonition; Moonshine County Express; The Last Tycoon; Oh, God!; Jennifer; Butch and Sundance-The Early Years; Battle Beyond The Stars.

TV inc: Sixth Sense; Sons and Daughters; Greatest Heroes of the Bible; The Pirate; Homeward Bound.

CORMAN, Gene: Prod. b. Detroit, Sep 24, 1927. e. Stanford U. Partner with brother Roger in Corman Co. and New World Distrib. Films inc: Secret of the Purple Reef; Beast from Haunted Cave; The Intruder; Secret Invasion; Ski Party; Blood and Steel; Girls on the Beach; Tobruk; What's in it for Harry?; You Can't Win 'Em All; Cool Breeze; Hit Man; Private Parts; I Escaped From Devil's Island; Vigilante Force; F.I.S.T.; Target Harry; The Big Red One.

TV inc: Mary and Joseph-A Story of Faith.

CORMAN, Roger William: Exec-Prod-Dir. b. Detroit, Apr 5, 1926. e. Stanford U, Oxford U. Joined Fox prod dept 1948; then story analyst, literary agent; formed Roger Corman Prod. and Filmgroup, prod over 200 feature films & dir over 60 of them; 1970, formed New World Pictures, Inc, production-releasing co.

Films inc: Five Guns West; Apache Woman; The Day the World Ended; Swamp Woman; The Gunslinger; Naked Paradise; Not of this Earth; War of the Satellites; Machine Gun Kelly; A Bucket of Blood; House of Usher; The Last Woman on Earth; The Pit and the Pendulum; The Intruder; The Raven; The Man with X-ray Eyes; The Masque of the Red Death; The St. Valentine's Day Massacre. (Prod): Boxcar Bertha; I Escaped from Devil's Island (co-prod); Big Bad Mama; Cockfighter; Grand Theft Auto; I Never Promised You A Rose Garden; Thunder and Lightning; Avalanche; Deathsport; Piranha; Rock 'n' Roll High School; Saint Jack; Fast Charlie the Moonbeam Rider; Humanoids From the Deep; Battle Beyond The Stars; Georgia Peaches.

CORNEAU, Alain: Wri-Dir. b. Meung-sur-Loire, France, 1943. e. ID-HEC. Films inc: France Societe Anonyme; Police Python 357; La Menace; Serie Noire.

CORNFIELD, Hubert: Dir-Wri. b. Istanbul, Turkey, 1929. e. U of PA. Films inc: Sudden Danger; Lure of the Swamp; Plunder Road; The Third Voice; Angel Baby; Pressure Point; Night of the Following Day; Les Grand Moyens; Short and Sweet.

CORSARO, Frank: Act-Dir. b. NYC, Dec 22, 1924. e. Yale Drama School; Actors Studio. Thea inc: dir numerous off-Bway prodns inc No Exit; Family Reunion; Heartbreak House; The Scarecrows; A Hatful of Rain; Fitz and Biscuit; Baby Want a Kiss; The Sweet Enemy. (Bway) The Night of the Iguana; Treemonisha; Knockout; It's So Nice To Be Civilized. (Opera) La Traviata; Mme Butterfly; Prince Igor; Rigoletto; Don Giovanni; Manon Lescaut.

Bway (act); The Taming of the Shrew; Mrs. McThing; The Merchant of Venice.

TV inc: A Piece of Blue Sky (dir-wri).

CORSAUT, Aneta: Act. b. Hutchinson, KS, Nov 3. e. Northwestern U; studied with Lee Strasberg. TV inc: Philco Playhouse; Studio One; Kraft Theatre; Andy Griffith Show; Mrs G Goes to College; Bad Ronald; The Runaways; House Calls.

CORT, Bud (Walter Edward Cox): Act. b. New Rochelle, NY, Mar 29, 1950. Started as standup comic in NY niteries. Films inc: M*A*S*H; Brewster McCloud; Harold and Maude; Why Shoot The Teacher; Die Laughing. TV inc: Brave New World.

CORTESE, Valentina: Act. b. Milan, Italy, Jan 1, 1925. Started career at 15 in Rome. Screen debut in La Cens Delle Beffe, 1941. Films inc: A Yank in Rome; Cagliostro; Glass Mountain; House on Telegraph Hill; The Dinner of Jests; No One Turns Back; Barefoot Contessa; Legend of Lylah Clare; Day for Night; Widow's Nest; The Big Operator; When Time Ran Out.

CORTEZ, Stanley (nee Kranz): Cin. b. NYC, 1908. Films inc: Four Days Wonder; The Black Doll; Lady in the Morgue; The Last Express; Risky Business; Alias the Deacon; The Leatherpushers; San Antonio Rose; The Magnificent Ambersons; The Secret Beyond the Door; The Man on the Eiffel Tower; Abbott and Costello Meet Captain Kidd; The Night of the Hunter; The Three Faces of Eve; Back Street; The Candidate; The Naked Kiss; The Bridge at Remagen; The Date; Another Man, Another Chance.

TV inc: Do Not Fold, Spindle or Mutilate.

CORWIN, Bruce C: Exec. b. LA, Jun 11, 1940. e. Wesleyan U. S of late Sherrill Corwin. P Metropolitan Theatres Corp.

CORWIN, Norman: Wri-Dir-Prod. b. Boston, May 3, 1910. Films inc: Once Upon a Time; Blue Veil; The Grand Design; Scandal in Scourie; Lust for Life; The Story of Ruth.

TV inc: Inside the Movie Kingdom; The FDR series; The Plot to Overthrow Christmas; Norman Corwin Presents; The Court Martial of General Yamashita.

Plays inc: The Rivalry; The World of Carl Sandburg; The Hyphen; Together Tonight- Jefferson, Hamilton and Burr.

Radio inc: Words Without Music series; Ballad for Americans; Pursuit of Happiness; 26 by Corwin; We Hold These Truths; Bill of Rights Show; On a Note of Triumph; The Lonesome Train; One World Flight; Word from the People.

CORWIN, Sherrill: Exh. b. Sioux City, IA, Sep 21, 1908. e. USC, U of IA. Entered film industry, 1928; partner Principal Theatres and Fox West Coast Theatres 1933-1949; partner Principal Theatres and Fox West Coast Theatres 1933-1949, operating 40 theatres in Southern Calif; ChmnB Metropolitan Theatres Corp, a So. Calif. theatre circuit headquartered in LA; dir KAKE Radio and Television, Inc, Wichita, KS; founding trustee (1967) American Film Institute; first full-time pres. (1966) NATO, also its chmn. of bd. (1967); exec prod. Viva Knievel.

(Died May 8, 1980).

COSBY, Bill: Act. b. Philadelphia, Jul 12, 1938. e. Temple U. Night club, TV comedian. Recorded comedy and musical albums. Films inc: Uptown Saturday Night; Man and Boy; Hickey and Boggs; Let's Do It Again; A Piece of the Action; California Suite.

TV inc: I Spy (Emmy-1966-1967-1968); Bill Cosby Special (Emmy-1969); Bill Cosby Show; Fat Albert.

(Grammys-(8)-comedy 1964-65-66-67-68-69; rec for children (2) 1971).

COSCARELLI, Don: Wri-Dir. b. Tripoli, Libya, Feb 17, 1954. Films inc: Jim the World's Greatest; Kenny and Company; Phantasm.

COSELL, Howard: TV Pers. b. Winston-Salem, NC, Mar 21, 1920. Hosted own TV show; commentator on ABC's Monday Night Football & Monday Night Baseball. TV inc: Fighting Back. Films inc: Bananas; Sleeper; The World's Greatest Athlete.

COSLOW, Sam: Comp-Wri-Prod. b. NYC, Dec 27, 1902. Film scores inc: College Humor; Two Much Harmony; Hello Everybody; Belle of the Nineties; Murder at the Vanities; True Confession. In 1940, co-prod 2 reel short, Heavenly Music (Oscar-1943). Apptd Paramount prod, 1944; joined Mary Pickford Prodns as prod, 1945. Films inc: (prod) Out of This World; Copacabana; Dreaming Out Loud.

Songs inc: Cocktails for Two; Just One More Chance; Sing You Sinners.

COSMATOS, George Pan: Dir-Wri-Prod. b. Jan 4, 1941. e. London Film School, London U. Prod-dir of TV commercials in Europe. Asst dir Zorba the Greek; Exodus.

Films inc: Massacre in Rome; The Cassandra Crossing; Escape to Athena.

COSSETTE, Pierre: Prod. b. LA, Dec 15, 1928. e. USC. Personal manager, Ann-Margret. Founder Dunhill Records. TV inc: Andy Williams Show; Sammy Davis Jr. Show; Sammy & Co; Sha Na Na; Hollywood Diamond Jubilee; Grammy Awards; Super Night at Super Bowl; New Adventures of Heidi; Alcatraz--The Whole Shocking Story; The Promise of Love.

COSTA-GAVRAS, Henri: Dir. b. Athens, 1933. Studied at the Sorbonne. Worked as asst to Rene Clair, Rene Clement, Jacques Demy. Directorial debut, The Sleeping Car Murders. Films inc: The Thieves; Un Homme De Trop; The Vow; Z; State of Siege; Special Section; Clair de Femme; Madame Rosa (act).

COSTELLO, Dolores: Act. b. Pittsburgh, Sep 17, 1905. Films inc: Lawful Larceny; The Sea Beast; Old San Francisco; The Redeeming Sin; Noah's Ark; Show of Shows; Expensive Women; Little Lord Fauntleroy; King of the Turf; The Magnificent Ambersons; This is the Army.

(Died Mar 1, 1979).

COSTELLO, Elvis (Declan Patrick McManus): Singer. b. London, 1954. Recordings inc: My Aim Is True; This Year's Model; Armed Forces.

Films inc: Americathon.

COSTELLO, Mariclare: Act. b. Peoria, IL, Feb 3. Films inc: Tiger Makes Out; Let's Scare Jessica to Death; Ordinary People. TV inc: The Waltons; The Execution of Pvt Slovak; Raid on Entebbe; A Sensitive, Passionate Man; The Fitzpatricks; A Family of Winners; All God's Children.

Thea inc: The Hostage; Lovers and Other Strangers.

COSTELLO, Robert E: Prod. b. Chicago, IL, Apr 26, 1921. e. Dartmouth, BA; Yale Drama School, MFA. Began 1952 as NBC unit mgr. TV inc: Mr. Peepers; Family Classics; Armstrong Circle Theatre; Patty Duke Show; Dark Shadows; Strange Paradise; Secret Strom; Adams Chronicles; Ryan's Hope (Emmys-1977, 1979); Another World.

COSTER, Nicholas: Act. b. London, England. e. RADA; Neighborhood Playhouse, NY; studied with Lee Strasberg. Films inc: My Blood Runs Cold; The Sporting Club; MacArthur; Slow Dancing in the Big City; The Big Fix; Concorde--Airport '79; Just You and Me Kid; The Electric Horseman; Goldengirl; Little Darlings; Why Would I Lie?; Stir Crazy.

TV inc: Elizabeth the First; Another World; The Word; A Fire in the Sky; Bender; The Women's Room.

COSTIGAN, James: Wri. TV inc: The Turn of the Screw; The Little Moon of Alban (Emmy-1959); War of Children; Last of the Belles; In This House of Brede; Love Among the Ruins (Emmy-1975); Eleanor and Franklin (Emmy-1976); F Scott Fitzgerald in Hollywood; Eleanor and Franklin--The White House Years; Titanic.

COTLER, Kami: Act. b. Long Beach, CA, Jun 17, 1965. TV inc: The Waltons.

COTTEN, Joseph: Act. b. Petersburg, VA, May 15, 1905. H of Patricia Medina. Bway inc: Absent Father; Jezebel; Accent on Youth; The Postman Always Rings Twice. 1936 joined Orson Welles Federal Theatre project, remained with him through Mercury Players productions; Horse Eats Hat; Dr. Faustus; Julius Caesar; Shoemaker's Holiday; Danton's Death; Philadelphia Story; Sabrina Fair; Once More With Feeling; Calculated Risk.

Films inc: Citizen Kane; The Magnificent Ambersons; Journey Into Fear; Shadow of a Doubt; Gaslight; Since You Went Away; Love Letters; I'll Be Seeing You; Duel in the Sun; Farmer's Daughter; Portrait of Jennie; Under Capricorn; The Third Man; September Affair; Man With a Cloak; Peking Express; Steel Trap; Niagara; Blue Print for Murder; The Angel Wore Red; The Last Sunset; Hush, Hush Sweet Charlotte; Petulia; Days of Fire; Doomsday Voyage; Tora, Tora, Tora; Soylent Green; A Delicate Balance; Twilight's Last Gleaming; Airport 77; F For Fake; The Order and Security of the World; Caravans; Guyana - Cult of the Damned; The Hearse; Heaven's Gate.

Numerous radio shows inc: War of the Worlds.

TV inc: Hollywood and the Stars (Narr); Casino.

COULOURIS, George: Act. b. Manchester, Eng, Oct 1, 1903. Stage debut Manchester 1926, Outward Bound. On screen from 1933. Films inc: Christopher Bean; All This and Heaven Too; Citizen Kane; Watch on the Rhine; Hotel Berlin; Sleep My Love; A Southern Yankee; An Outcast of the Islands; Doctor in the House; The Runaway Bus; I Accuse; King of Kings; The Skull; Arabesque; Papillon; Mahler; Murder on the Orient Express; The Antichrist; The Tempter; It's Not the Size That Counts.

Thea inc: The Alchemist; The Moon of the Caribbees; The Insect Comedy; The Admirable Crichton; The Provok'd Wife.

COURTENAY, Tom: Act. b. Hull, Eng, Feb 25, 1937. e. University Coll, London; RADA. Films inc: Billy Liar; The Loneliness of the Long Distance Runner; King and Country; Operation Crossbow; King Rat; Doctor Zhivago; The Day the Fish Came Out; A Dandy in Aspic; Otley; One Day in the Life of Ivan Denisovitch.

Thea inc: The Seagull; Peer Gynt; Charley's Aunt; Time and Time Again; Arms and the Man; The Prince of Homburg; The Rivals; The Norman Conquest; The Fool; Otherwise Engaged; The Dresser.

TV inc: Private Potter; The Lads.

COURTLAND, Jerome (Courtland Jourolmon): Act-Prod-Dir. b. Knoxville, TN, Dec 27, 1926. Film debut in Together Again, 1944. Films inc: (act) Tonka; Bamboo Prison; Take The High Ground; Tokyo Joe; Battleground. (Prod): Pete's Dragon; Ride A Wild Pony; Escape to Witch Mountain; Return From Witch Mountain. TV inc: (dir) Flying Nun; Nancy; The Wonderful World of Disney; The Partridge Family; The Sky Trap; The Sultan and the Rock Star; The Ghosts of Buxley Hall (prod).

Bway inc: Flahooley.

COURTNEIDGE, Dame Cicely: Act. b. Sydney, Australia, Apr 1, 1893. Stage debut, 1901, Manchester, A Midsummer Night's Dream. On screen from 1929. Films inc: The Ghost Train; Jack's the Boy; Aunt Sally; Me and Marlborough; The Imperfect Lady; Take My Tip; Under Your Hat; The L-Shaped Room; Those Magnificent Men in Their Flying Machines; The Wrong Box; Not Now Darling.

Thea inc: The Reluctant Peer; Dear Octopus; Oh, Clarence; The Hollow; Breath of Spring; Once More with Music.

(Died April 26, 1980).

COURTNEY, Jacqueline: Act. b. East Orange, NJ, Sep 24, 1946. Former child act. TV inc: The Edge of Night; Our Five Daughters; Secret Storm; Another World (11 years); One Life To LIve.

COUSTEAU, Jacques-Yves: Prod. b. France, 1910. Films inc: The Silent World; The Golden Fish (Oscar-ss-1959); World Without Sun; Voyage To The Edge of the World.

TV inc: Blind Prophets of Easter Island; Time Bomb at 50 Fathoms; The Nile (narr); The Undersea World of Jacques Cousteau.

COUTARD, Raoul: Cin. b. France, 1924. Films inc: Ranuntcho; A Bout de Souffle; Shoot the Pianist; Lola; Jules et Jim; Bay of Angels; Les Carabiniers; Silken Skin; Sailor from Gibraltar; The Bride Wore Black; Z; L'Aveu; L'Explosion.

COVER, Franklin: Act. b. Cleveland, OH, Nov 20, 1928. e. Denison U, BA; Western Reserve U, MA, MFA. Bway inc: Applause; Forty Carats; A Warm Body; The Investigation; Any Wednesday; Calculated Risk. Films inc: The Stepford Wives; The Great Gatsby; Such Good Friends; Mirage; What's So Bad About Feeling Good?

TV inc: The Day The Bubble Burst; The Connection; The Investigation; What Makes Sammy Run?; The Jeffersons.

COWITT, Ben L: Exec. b. LA, Nov 23, 1934. e. Claremont Men's Coll; U of So CA. Studio mgr MGM 1958; studio mgr Hollywood Zoetrope, 1980.

COX, Ronny: Act. b. Aug 23, 1938. Films inc: The Happiness Cage; Deliverance; Hugo the Hippo (voice only); Gray Lady Down; Harper Valley PTA; The Onion Field.

TV inc: Apple's Way; Transplant; When Hell Was in Session; Kavik the Wolf Dog; One Last Ride; Fugitive Family; The Last Song; First Time, Second Time--For Better or Worse; Alcatraz--The Whole Shocking Story.

CRABBE, Larry (Buster): Act. b. Oakland, CA, Feb 7, 1907. e. USC. A 1932 Olympic swimming champ, on screen since 1933. Films inc: Tarzan series; Sweetheart of Sigma Chi; The Thundering Herd; Million Dollar Legs; Flash Gordon (serial); Pirates of the High Seas (serial); Billy the Kid; Badman's Country; Comeback Trail.

TV inc: The Foreign Legion.

CRAIG, Helen: Act. b. San Antonio, TX, May 13, 1912. W of John Beal. With Hedgerow Repertory Theatre 1929-1934; various stock cos. Bway inc: Russet Mantle; New Faces; Julius Caesar; Soliloquoy; Family Portrait; The Unconquered; Johnny Belinda; As You Like It; Lute Song; Land's End; The House of Bernarda Alba; Medea; More Stately Mansions.

Films inc: They Live By Night; The Keys of the Kingdom; The Snake Pit; The Sporting Club; Heroes.

CRAIG, Michael (nee Gregson): Act. b. Poona, India, Jan 27, 1928. e. Upper Canada Coll, Toronto. London stage debut, 1949, The Merchant of Venice. Bway inc: Homecoming. Films inc: Malta Story; The Love Lottery; High Tide at Noon; The Silent Enemy; Sea of Sand; Sapphire; Upstairs and Downstairs; The Angry Silence (& sp); Cone of Silence; Mysterious Island; Payroll; Stolen Hours; Life at the Top; Sandra; Star!; The Royal Hunt of the Sun; Twinky; Brotherly Love; A Town Called Bastard; Vault of Horror; The Irishman.

TV inc: Saint Joan; Spoiled; The Hotel in Amsterdam; The Timeless Land.

CRAIG, Tony (nee Kulasa). Act. b. Pittsburgh, PA, Dec 23, 1946. e. Mansfield, OH, State College; OH U. High school English and drama teacher before turning pro. TV inc: Love Is A Many Splendored Thing; Search for Tomorrow; The Edge of Night.

CRAIG, Wendy: Act. b. England, Jun 20, 1934. e. Central School Dramatic Art. Thea inc: (London) Soho So What; Mr Kettle and Mrs Moon; Man Alive!; A Resounding Tinkle; Epitaph for George Dillon; The Ginger Man; Three (triple bill); Something from Collette; Ride a Cock Horse; Happy Family; Finishing Touches; Hobson's Choice.

Films inc: The Mind Benders; The Servant; The Nanny; Just Like A Woman; I'll Never Forget Whatshisname; Joseph Andrews.

TV inc: Not in Front of the Children; And Mother Makes Five.

CRAIN, Jeanne: Act. b. Barstow, CA, May 25, 1925. Model; Miss Long Beach of 1941. Films inc: Home in Indiana; Winged Victory; State Fair; Leave Her to Heaven; Margie; Centennial Summer; Apartment for Peggy; Letter To Three Wives; Vicki; Gentlemen Marry Brunettes; Fastest Gun Alive; The Joker; Skyjacked.

CRAIN, William: Dir. b. Jun 20, 1943. Films inc: Blacula; The Watts Monster. TV inc: Mod Squad; Rookies; S.W.A.T.; Starsky & Hutch; Roots-The Next Generation.

CRAMER, Douglas Schoolfield: Prod. b. Louisville, KY, Aug 22, 1931. e. Columbia U, Sorbonne, Paris. Exec VP Development ABC-TV & Fox; Exec VP Paramount TV; P Douglas S. Cramer Co; 1978, exec VP Aaron Spelling Productions. TV inc: Bridget Loves Bernie; QB VII; The Cat Creature; The Dead Don't Die; The Black Dahlia; Nightmare in Badham County; Dawn-Portrait of a Teenage Runaway; Snowbeast; Love Boat; Wonder Woman; Love's Savage Fury; Friends-Going Out; The Power Within; The French Atlantic Affair; B.A.D. Cats; Waikiki; Murder Can Hurt You; Casino.

CRAMER, Floyd: Mus. b. Shreveport, LA, Oct 27, 1933. Recording artist; between 1952-55, toured country with such performers as Hank Williams and Elvis Presley; became regular perf on the Grand Ole Opry in mid-50s.

CRAMPHORN, Rex: Dir. b. Brisbane, Australia, Jan 10, 1945. Thea inc: Jesus Christ Superstar; The Tempest; Measure for Measure; Interplay.

CRAVEN, Gemma: Act. b. Dublin, Jun 1, 1950. e. Loretto Coll. Thea inc: Fiddler on the Roof; Audrey; Saturnalia; Sabrina Fair; Trelawny; The Confederacy; A Month in the Country; Underground; The Threepenny Opera; Black Comedy; Songbook; They're Playing Our Song.

Films inc: The Slipper and the Rose. TV inc: Pennies From Heaven.

CRAWFORD, Broderick: Act. b. Philadelphia, Dec 9, 1911. Films inc: Submarine D-1; Ambush; Undercover Doctor; Slightly Honorable; Butch Minds The Baby; Anna Lucasta; All The King's Men (Oscar-1949); Born Yesterday; New York Confidential; Not as a Stranger; The Oscar; The Private Files of J. Edgar Hoover; A Little Romance; Harlequin; There Goes The Bride.

TV inc: Highway Patrol; The Interns; True Position.

Thea inc: That Championship Season.

CRAWFORD, Cheryl: Prod. b. Akron, OH, Sep 24, 1902. e. Buchtel Coll, Smith Coll. Thea inc: All the Living; Porgy and Bess (revival 1941); The Flowers of Virtue; A Kiss for Cinderella; One Touch of Venus; The Perfect Marriage; The Tempest; founded the American Repertory Theatre, as m-dir co-prod Henry VIII; What Every Woman Knows; John Gabriel Borkman; Androcles and the Lion; A Pound on Demand; Alice in Wonderland; Through the Looking Glass; appointed joint-gen dir of the ANTA play series 1950.

Plays at ANTA Playhouse inc: The Tower Beyond Tragedy; Peer Gynt; The Rose Tattoo (Tony-1951); Paint Your Wagon; Camino Real; Oh, Men! Oh, Women!; The Honeys; Girls of Summer; The Shadow of a Gunman; Sweet Bird of Youth; Period of Adjustment; Brecht on Brecht; Jennie; Doubletalk; Celebration; Colette; The Love Suicide at Schofield Barracks; The Web and the Rock; Yentl; Do You Turn Somersaults?

CRAWFORD, Henry James: Prod. b. Woodend, Victoria, Australia, Feb 8, 1947. TV inc: Homicide; Mattlock Police; Young Ramsay; Solo One; (& creator); The Sullivans; Against the Wind; A Town Like Alice.

Films inc: No Nukes.

CRAWFORD, Joanna Jane: Wri. b. Jan 14, 1943. Films inc: My Side of the Mountain; The Little Ark; Birch Interval.

TV inc: Betrayal; Friendships, Secrets and Lies; Sophia Loren--Her Own Story.

CRAWFORD, Johnny: Act. b. LA, Mar 26, 1946. On stage at age 5 in Mr. Belvedere. At 9 title role in film Little Boy Lost. Films inc: Village of the Giants; Indian Paint; Outlaw Blues; Dreamer; The Apple Dumpling Gang Rides Again.

TV inc: The Rifleman.

CRAWFORD, Michael: Act. b. Salisbury, England, Jan 19, 1942. Thea inc: (London) Striplings; Travelling Light; The Anniversary; Come Blow Your Horn; No Sex Please, We're British; Billy; Same Time, Next Year; Flowers for Algernon. (Bway) White Lies & Black Comedy (double bill).

Films inc: Two Left Feet; The War Lover; Two Living, One Dead; The Knack; A Funny Thing Happened on the Way to the Forum; How I Won the War; The Jokers; Hello, Dolly!; The Games; Hello and Goodbye; Alice in Wonderland.

TV inc: Not Such Much a Programme, More a Way of Life; Some Mothers Do 'Ave 'Em; Private View; Audience; Chalk and Cheese.

CREMER, Bruno: Act. b. Paris, 1929. Appeared in plays on French stage. Films inc: Marco Polo; Is Paris Burning?; One Man Too Many; Breakdown; Special Section; The Good and the Bad; Sorcerer; The Order and Security of the World; On Efface Tout (We Forget Everything); A Simple Story; Cet Age Sans Pitie.

CRENNA, Richard: Act. b. Los Angeles, Nov 30, 1927. e. USC. On radio in Boyscout Jamboree; A Date With Judy; The Great Gildersleeve; Our Miss Brooks. Films inc: Pride of St. Louis; It Grows On Trees; John Goldfarb, Please Come Home; The Sand Pebbles; Star!; The Deserter; Catlow; Dirty Money; The Evil; Stone Cold Dead; Death Ship.

TV inc: Our Miss Brooks; The Real McCoys; Slattery's People; All's Fair; First You Cry; A Fire in the Sky; Better Late Than Never; Turnabout (dir); Joshua's World; Fugitive Family.

CRICHTON, Dr Michael: Wri-Dir. b. Chicago, Oct 23, 1942. e. Harvard Medical School. While there completed 1st novel, Easy God. Has written 15 books under four different names, inc A Case of Need (filmed as The Carey Treatment); The Andromeda Strain; Dealing; The Terminal Man, all filmed. Films inc: Westworld; Coma; The Great Train Robbery.

TV inc: Pursuit (dir).

CRISTALDI, Franco: Prod. b. Turin, Italy, Oct 3, 1924. Films inc: White Nights; The Strawman; The Challenge; Big Deal On Madonna Street; Kapo; The Dauphins; The Assassin; Divorce Italian Style; The Organizer; Seduced and Abandoned; Time of Indifference; Sandra; A Rose for Every-One; China Is Near; A Quiet Couple; The Red Tent; Christ Stopped at Eboli; Wife-Mistress; Ogro; Ratataplan; The Persian Lamb Coat; Cafe Express.

CRISTOFER, Michael (nee Procaccino): Plywri-Act. b. Jan 22, 1945. Plays inc: The Shadow Box *(Pulitzer Prize & Tony-1977)*; Ice; Black Angel; The Lady and the Clarinet.

Bway inc: (act) Cherry Orchard.

Films inc: (act) Enemy of the People.

TV inc: (act) Family; Sad Figure Laughing; Crime Club; The Shadow Box (wri).

CROFTS, Dash: Mus-Singer. b. Cisco, TX. With The Champs, The Dawnbreakers before teaming with James Seals. Albums inc: Seals and Crofts I and II; Year of Sunday; Summer Breeze; Diamond Girl; Unborn Child; I'll Play For You; Greatest Hits; Get Closer; Sudan Village; Takin It Easy.

CROMWELL, John: Dir-Act-Prod. b. Toledo, OH, Dec 23, 1887. Started on stage as actor, then dir & prod; became film dir for Par, 1929. Films inc: (dir) Close Harmony; The Mighty; Street of Chance; The Texan; For the Defense; Tom Sawyer; Rich Man's Folly; The Silver Cord; Of Human Bondage; Little Lord Fauntleroy; To Mary-With Love; The Prisoner of Zenda; Algiers; In Name Only; Abe Lincoln in Illinois; Son of Fury; Since You Went Away; The Enchanted Cottage; Anna and the King of Siam; Dead Reckoning; Caged; The Company She Keeps; The Racket; The Goddess; The Scavengers; A Matter of Morals; 3 Women (act); A Wedding (act).

(Died Sep 26, 1979).

CRONKITE, Walter: TV Newsman. b. St Joseph, MO, Nov 4, 1916. e. U of TX. Joined CBS as Washington news correspondent 1950; mng ed-anchorman CBS Evening News 1963.

TV inc: You Are There; Twentieth Century; Eyewitness to History; CBS Reports; Universe (narr); Man on the Moon--The Epic Journey of Apollo XI *(Emmy-1970)*; Space Coverage *(Emmy-1971)*; U S Soviet Wheat Deal--Is There a Scandal? *(Emmy-exec prod-1973)*; The Watergate Affair *(Emmy-1973)*; The Shooting of Gov Wallace *(Emmy-1973)*; The Agnew Resignation *(Emmy-1974)*; Watergate--The White House Transcripts *(Emmy-1974)*; The Key Biscayne Bank Charter Struggle; The Rockefellers *(Emmy-1974)*; Solzhenitsyn *(Emmy-1974)*; Sadat's Eternal Egypt; A Private Battle (act).

(ATAS second annual Governors Award).

CRONYN, Hume: Act-Dir. b. London, Ontario, Canada, Jul 18, 1911. e. AADA; Mozarteum. Worked at Barter Theatre. Bway inc: (Act) Hipper's Holiday; Boy Meet Girl; Room Service; High Tor; Escape This Night; There's Always a Breeze; Off to Buffalo; The Weak Link; The Survivors; Now I Lay Me Down To Sleep (dir only); Hilda Crane (Dir only); The Fourposter; Madame Will You Walk (& dir); The Egghead (dir only); Triple Play (& dir); Hamlet *(Tony-supp-1964)*; The Physicists; Slow Dance on a Killing Ground (prod only); Promenade All; Act Without Words; Krapp's Last Tape; Noel Coward in Two Keys; The Many Faces of Love; The Gin Game.

Films inc: Cross of Lorraine; Lifeboat; The Seventh Cross; Main Street After Dark; The Sailor Takes a Wife; A Letter for Evie; The Green Years; Brute Force; The Bride Goes Wild; The Postman Always Rings Twice; Top O' The Morning; People Will Talk; Crowded Paradise; Sunrise at Campobello; Cleopatra; Gaily, Gaily; The Arrangement; There Was a Crooked Man; Conrack; The Parallax View.

TV inc: The Bridge of San Luis Rey; The Fourposter; The Moon and Sixpence; The Marriage (also on radio).

CROSBY, Bob: Orch Ldr. b. Spokane, WA, Aug 23, 1913. e. Gonzaga U. B of late Bing Crosby. Began as singer; featured vocalist with Jimmie & Tommy Dorsey band. Org own band, the Bobcats. Films inc: Sis Hopkins; Reveille With Beverly; As Thousands Cheer; Kansas City Kitty; Pardon My Rhythm; Singing Sheriff; Two Tickets to Broadway.

TV inc: The Bob Crosby Show.

CROSBY, Cathy Lee: Act. b. LA. e. USC. Films inc: Call Me by my Rightful Name; The Laughing Policeman; Trackdown; The Coach; The Dark.

TV inc: Third Annual Circus of the Stars; The Funny Side of Love; That's Incredible! (host); Roughnecks; The World's Most Spectacular Stuntmen (host).

CROSBY, David: Sngwri-Singer-Mus. b. LA, Aug, 1941. Member of Les Baxter's Balladeers before going solo; With Roger McGuinn and Gene Clark formed The Byrds; 1967 teamed with Graham Nash and Stephen Sills to form Crosby, Stills & Nash *(Grammy-new artist-1969)*.

Songs inc: Everybody's Been Burned; Renaissance Fair; What's Happening.

CROSBY, Floyd Delafield: Cine (ret). b. NYC, Dec 12, 1899. Lensed 80 films inc: Tabu *(Oscar-1930-31)*; High Noon; Wonderful Country; Cold Wind in August; The Explosive Generation; Tales of Terror; The Firebrand; The Raven; The Comedy of Terrors; Pajama Party; Beach Blanket Bingo; Sallah; Fireball 500; The Cool Ones.

Docs inc: The River; Power and the Land; The Fight for Life.

CROSBY, Kathryn: Act. b. Houston, TX, Nov 25, 1933. e. U of TX, UCLA. W of late Bing Crosby. Films inc: Forever Female; Rear Window; Cassanova's Big Night; Unchained; Five Against the House; Phoenix City Story; The Night the World Exploded; The Big Circus; Operation Mad Ball.

TV inc: The Bing Crosby Christmas Specials; Suspense Theatre; Ben Casey; The Kathryn Crosby Show.

CROSBY, Mary: Act. b. LA, Sep 14, 1959. e. U TX, Austin. D of Kathryn Grant and the late Bing Crosby. TV inc: various specials with parents; With This Ring; Guide for the Married Women; Brothers and Sisters; Pearl; Dallas.

CROSBY, Norm: Comedian. b. Boston, MA, Sep 15, 1927. Nitery and concert perf; opening act for Robert Goulet for three years.
TV inc: Norm Crosby's Comedy Shop; A Funny Thing Happened on the Way to the White House (cable TV).

CROSS, Beverley: Wri. b. London, Apr 13, 1931. e. Nautical Coll, Oxford. H of Maggie Smith. Former actor. Plays inc: The Singing Dolphin; The Three Cavaliers; Boeing-Boeing (adapted from the French of Marc Camoletti); Half-a-Sixpence (book of musical); The Mines of Sulphur (libretto); The Rising of the Moon (libretto); Victory (libretto); Spook; The Great Society; Hans Andersen (book).
Films inc: Jason and the Argonauts; The Long Ships; Ghenghis Khan; Half-a-Sixpence; Sinbad and The Eye of the Tiger.
TV inc: The Dark Pits of War; Catherine Howard.

CROSS, Irv: Sportscaster. b. Hammond, IN, Jul 27, 1939. e. Northwestern U. Former pro football player. Joined CBS sports 1971. Commentator for The NFL Today.

CROTHERS, Joel: Act. b. Cincinnati, OH, Jan 28, 1941. e. Harvard, BA. Bway debut age 12, The Remarkable Mr. Pennypacker. TV inc: Studio One; Playhouse 90; Goodyear Playhouse; Dark Shadows; The Secret Storm; Somerset Five; The Edge of Night.

CROTHERS, Scatman (Sherman Crothers): Act. b. Terre Haute, IN, May 23, 1910. Started own band; made recordings; on TV with Dixie Showboat, 1949. Films inc: Bloody Mama; Black Belt Jones; Truck Turner; Coonskin; One Flew Over the Cuckoo's Nest; Friday Foster; The Cheap Detective; Scavenger Hunt; The Shining.
TV inc: The Puppy's Great Adventure (voice).

CROUCH, Andrae: Singer-Mus-Comp. b. LA, Jul 1, 1942. Organizer and leader of The Disciples.
Recordings inc: Live at Carnegie Hall; Just Andrae; Take Me Back. (Grammy-soul gospel-1975); This is Another Day; Crouch in London (Grammy-soul gospel-1978); Crouch Alone (Grammy-soul Gospel-1979).

CROUSE, Lindsay: Act. b. NYC. e. Radcliffe. D of Russell Crouse. Films inc: All the President's Men; Between the Lines; Slap Shot.
TV inc: Eleanor and Franklin; The Tenth Level.

CROWLEY, Mart: Plywri. Plays inc: The Boys in the Band; Remote Asylum; A Breeze from the Gulf.

CROWLEY, Pat: Act. b. Olyphant, PA, Sep 17, 1933. Films inc: Forever Female; Money From Home; Red Garters; There's Always Tomorrow; Hollywood or Bust; Key Witness; To Trap a Spy.
TV inc: Please Don't Eat the Daisies; The Millionaire; The Sky Trap; Confessions of a Lady Cop.

CRYSTAL, Billy: Act. b. Long Beach, NY, Mar 14. Films inc: Rabbit Test. TV inc: That Was The Year That Was; Death Flight; The Love Boat; Soap; Breaking Up Is Hard to Do; Enola Gay--The Men, The Mission, The Atomic Bomb.

CRYSTAL, Lester M: Exec. b. Duluth, MI, Sep 13, 1934. e. Northwestern U. P, NBC News since Oct 5, 1977. Prior to that served as exec prod, NBC Nightly News; vp, special programming, NBC News: exec vp, NBC TV News. TV inc: An Investigation of Teenage Drug Addiction (Emmy-prod-1970); Reports on World Hunger (Emmy-exec prod-1974).

CUGAT, Xavier: Orch Ldr. b. Barcelona, Spain, Jan 1, 1900. Films inc: You Were Never Lovelier; Two Girls and a Sailor; Holiday in Mexico; This Time for Keeps; A Date with Judy; Neptune's Daughter; Chicago Syndicate.

CUKOR, George: Dir. b. NYC, Jul 7, 1899. Started as asst Stage M, Chicago, NY. In 1926 dir first Bway play, The Great Gatsby. Bway inc: The Dark; The Furies; A Free Soul; Young Love; Gypsy. To Hollywood in 1929 as dialogue dir for River of Romance; All Quiet on the Western Front; then co-dir Grumpy; The Virtuous Sin; The Royal Family of Broadway.
Solo dir debut 1931, Tarnished Lady. Films inc: One Hour With You; What Price Hollywood?; A Bill of Divorcement; Dinner at Eight; Little Women; Susan and God; The Philadelphia Story; Two-faced Woman; Her Cardboard Lover; A Double Life; Keeper of the Flame; Gaslight; Winged Victory; Adam's Rib; Edward My Son; A Life of Her Own; Born Yesterday; The Marrying Kind; Pat and Mike; The Actress; A Star Is Born; Les Girls; Wild Is the Wind; Song Without End; The Chapman Report; My Fair Lady (Oscar-1964); Justine; Travels With My Aunt; The Bluebird.
TV inc: Love Among the Ruins (Emmy-1975); The Corn Is Green.

CULLEN, Bill: Act. b. Pittsburgh, PA, Feb 18, 1920. e. U of Pittsburgh, BA. Started as radio announcer, Pittsburgh, then staff announcer for CBS, 1944. Game show host since the 50's. Shows inc: Where Was 1?; Place the Face; Hit the Jackpot; Give and Take; The Price is Right; I've Got a Secret; To Tell the Truth; $25,000 Pyramid; Blockbusters.

CULLEN, William Kirby: Act. b. Santa Ana, CA, Mar 9, 1952. TV inc: General Hospital; Portrait of a Teen-Age Alcoholic; The Force of Evil; How the West Was Won; Fugitive Family.

CULLUM, John: Act-Singer. b. Knoxville, TN, Mar 2, 1930. e. U of TN. Bway inc: NY Shakespeare Festival Theatre in various roles; Camelot; Infidel Caesar; Hamlet; On a Clear Day You Can See Forever; The Man of La Mancha (matinees); 1776; Vivat! Vivat Regina!; Shenandoah (Tony-1975); The Elizabethans; On the 20th Century (Tony-1978).
Films inc: 1776.

CULP, Robert: Act. b. Berkeley, CA, Aug 16, 1930. Films inc: P.T. 109; The Raiders; Sunday in New York; Rhino; The Hanged Man; Bob & Carol & Ted & Alice; Hickey and Boggs; Sky Riders; The Great Scout & Cathouse Thursday; Goldengirl.
TV inc: Trackdown; I Spy; Greatest Heroes of the Bible; Women in White; A Cry for Justice; The Dream Merchants; The Night the City Screamed.
Thea inc: The Prescott Proposals; A Clearing in the Woods.

CULVER, Roland: Act. b. London, Aug 31, 1900. e. RADA. London stage debut 1925 with the Greater London Players. Thea inc: Gentlemen Prefer Blondes; The Stranger Within; Dance With No Music; An Ideal Husband; Who Is Sylvia?; The Deep Blue Sea; The Little Hut; Five Finger Exercise; Sergeant Dower Must Die; His, Hers, and Theirs; The Bedwinner; Hamlet.
Films inc: French Without Tears; To Each His Own; The Greek Tycoon.
TV inc: The Pallisers; The Word.

CUMBUKA, Ji-Tu: Act. b. Montgomery County, AL, Mar 4. e. Columbia Coll, MA. Films inc: Uptight; Bound for Glory; Mandingo; Fun With Dick and Jane; Walk Proud.
TV inc: Roots; Young Dan'l Boone; A Man Called Sloane; Night of the Wizard; Flesh and Blood.

CUMMINGS, Constance (nee Halverstadt): Act. b. Seattle, WA, May 15, 1910. NY stage debut, 1928, in chorus of Treasure Girl. On screen from 1931. Films inc: The Criminal Code; The Guilty Generation; Movie Crazy; Channel Crossing; Glamour; Looking for Trouble; Remember Last Night?; Blithe Spirit; John and Julie; In the Cool of the Day; Battle of the Sexes; A Boy 10 Feet Tall.
TV inc: Touch of the Sun; The Last Tycoon; Ruth; Late Summer.
Bway inc: This Man's Town; June Moon; Accent on Youth; Young Madame Conti; Madame Bovary; If I Were You; Goodbye Mr. Chips; The Jealous God; Saint Joan; The Petrified Forest; The Shrike; Trial and Error; Lysistrata; Fallen Angels, Hamlet; The Milk Train Doesn't Stop Here Any More; The Visit; Children; Stripwell; The Cherry Orchard; Wings (Tony-1979).

CUMMINGS, Jack: Prod. b. New Bedford, Canada, Feb 16, 1905. Films inc: The Winning; Born to Dance; Go West; Ship Ahoy; Bathing Beauty; Neptune's Daughter; Three Little Words; The Last Time I Saw Paris; Romance of Rosy Ridge; The Stratton Story; Lovely to Look At; Kiss Me Kate; Seven Brides for Seven Brothers; Interrupted Melody; Many Rivers to Cross; The Teahouse of the August Moon; The Blue Angel; Can Can; Bachelor Flat; Viva Las Vegas.

CUMMINGS, Quinn: Act. b. LA, Aug 13, 1967. Discovered by cin. James Wong Howe, first work in TV commercials. TV inc: Big Eddie; Intimate Stranger; Night Terror; The Dancing Bear; Family; The Incredible Book Escape; The Baby Sitter.
Films inc: The Goodbye Girl.

CUMMINGS, Robert: Act. b. Joplin, MO, Jun 9, 1910. e. Drury Coll; Carnegie Tech; AADA. Films inc: The Virginia Judge; Last Train from Madrid; Three Smart Girls Grow Up; The Devil and Mrs. Jones; It Started with Eve; King's Row; Saboteur; The Bride Wore Boots; Heaven Only Knows; The Accused; Paid in Full; Dial M for Murder; My Geisha; What a Way to Go; The Carpetbaggers; Promise Her Anything; Stagecoach; Five Golden Dragons.
TV inc: The Bob Cummings Show; My Hero; Twelve Angry Men (*Emmy*-1954).

CURB, Mike: Exec. b. Savannah, GA, Dec 24, 1944. Began as jingle wri; formed Sidewalk Prodns, handling mus dir, prodn for records and films inc Mondo Hollywood; 1968 sold Sidewalk Prodns to Transcontinental Investing for $2,000,000, became P MGM Records; created Mike Curb Congregation; 1974 formed Mike Curb Prodns, organized Warner-Curb Records; 1979 elected Lt-Gov CA; formed Elektra/Curb Records and Mike Curb Records.

CURBISHLEY, Bill (William George Curbishley): Prod. b. London, Mar 13, 1942. Trinifold Ltd., William Tell Music Publishing Ltd.; Manager of The Who' for seven years; became film prod 1979.
Films inc: Quadrophenia; The Kids Are Alright (doc); McVicar.

CURRLIN, Lee: Exec. b. NY. e. CCNY, Hofstra U. Started with Benton & Bowles advertising agency; joined CBS-TV in 1968 as dir of mktg; subsequently vp, sales admn; joined NBC in July, 1978 as vp, broadcast planning; appointed vp, program planning, NBC Entertainment, March 1979.

CURTIN, Jane: Act. b. Cambridge, MA, Sep 6, 1947. e. Northeastern U. Thea inc: Proposition (improvisational group); Last of the Red Hot Lovers (tour); Pretzels (off-Bway).
TV inc: Saturday Night Live; 30 Years of TV Comedy's Greatest Hits.
Films inc: Mr. Mike's Mondo Video; How To Beat the High Cost of Living.

CURTIN, Valerie: Act. Films inc: Alice Doesn't Live Here Anymore; All The President's Men; Silver Streak; Silent Movie; And Justice For All (wri); Why Would I Lie?; Inside Moves (wri).
TV inc: A Christmas Without Snow (wri).

CURTIS, Dan: Dir. b. Bridgeport, CT, Aug 12. e. Syracuse U, BA. Head of Dan Curtis Prodns. Films inc: House of Dark Shadows; Night of Dark Shadows.
TV inc: Dark Shadows; The Night Strangler; The Norliss Tapes; Dracula; Kolchak- The Night Stalker; Mrs R's Daughter; Last Ride of the Dalton Gang; The Long Days of Summer (& prod).

CURTIS, Jamie Lee: Act. b. LA, Nov 22, 1958. D of Janet Leigh and Tony Curtis. Films inc: Halloween; The Fog; Terror Train.
TV inc: Operation Petticoat.

CURTIS, Tony (Bernard Schwartz): Act. b. NYC, Jun 3, 1925. Films inc: Criss Cross; Winchester 73; Son of Ali Baba; Houdini; Six Bridges to Cross; The Square Jungle; Trapeze; Sweet Smell of Success; The Defiant Ones; Some Like It Hot; Spartacus; Taras Bulba; Captain Newman, M.D.; The Boston Strangler; Lepke; The Last Tycoon; The Bad News Bears Go to Japan; The Manitou; Sextette; Title Shot; Little Miss Marker; The Mirror Crack'd.
TV inc: The Persuaders; Second Girl on the Right; Vega$; Centerfold-Playboy's 25th Anniversary Celebration; Moviola-The Scarlett O'Hara War.

CUSACK, Cyril: Act. b. Durban, S Africa, Nov 26, 1910. e. University College Dublin. Joined Abbey Theatre, Dublin 1932, appearing in approximately 75 prodns; London debut Ah, Wilderness.
Thea inc: Playboy of the Western World; The Plough and the Stars; Les Parents Terribles; The Doctors Dilemma; Pommy; formed own company presenting several classics and premiere of O'Casey's The Bishop's Bonfire. Bway inc: A Moon for the Misbegotten.
Films inc: Odd Man Out; The Blue Lagoon; The Blue Veil; Soldiers Three; The Man Who Never Was; Jacqueline; Shake Hands With the Devil; Waltz of the Toreadors; The Spy Who Came in From the Cold; Fahrenheit 451; Oedipus the King; Galileo; David Copperfield; The Day of the Jackal; The Homecoming. TV inc: The Big Toe; Moon in the Yellow River; Deirdre; The Golden Bowl; Cry of the Innocent.

CUSHING, Peter: Act. b. Kenley, Surrey, England, May 26, 1913. Films inc: Vigil in the Night; Moulin Rouge; The Black Knight; Hamlet; Alexander the Great; The Curse of Frankenstein; The Abominable Snowman; Dracula; John Paul Jones; The Hound of the Baskervilles; The Revenge of Frankenstein; Cone of Silence; The Naked Edge; Cash on Demand; The Man Who Finally Died; The Frightened Island; Torture Garden; Some May Live; Scream and Scream Again; The House That Dripped Blood; Tales From the Crypt; Fear in the Night; Horror Express; Frankenstein and the Monster from Hell; The Revenge of Dr. Death; Golden Vampires; The Ghoul; Legend of the Werewolf; The Devil's People; Trial by Combat; At the Earth's Core; Land of the Minotaur; Shock Waves; Star Wars; Battleflag; The Uncanny; Count Dracula and His Vampire Bride; The 7 Brothers Meet Dracula; Arabian Adventure; Shock Waves.
TV inc: Asmodee; Anastasia; 1984; Gaslight; Home at Seven; Tovarich; Beau Brummell; Epitaph for a Spy; Pride and Prejudice; The Moment of Truth; The Browning Version; The Winslow Boy; Julius Caesar; Monica; Sherlock Holmes; Orson Welles Great Mysteries; Space 1999; The New Avengers; The Great Houdini; A Tale of Two Cities.

Da COSTA, Morton (nee Tecosky): Dir-Act. b. Philadelphia, Mar 7, 1914. e. Temple U, BS. Bway inc: (act) The Skin of Our Teeth; War President; It's a Gift; Hamlet; Man and Superman (dir): Captain Brassbound's Conversion; Dream Girl; The Wild Duck; Dark Legend; The Grey-Eyed People; Plain and Fancy; No Time for Sergeants; Auntie Mame; The Music Man; Saratoga; The Wall; Hot Spot; To Broadway with Love; The Coffee Lover; Maggie Flynn; Show Me where the Good Times Are; The Women; Musical Jubilee.
Films inc: (dir) Auntie Mame; The Music Man; Island of Love.

DAGOVER, Lil (Marta Maria Liletts): Act. b. Java, 1897. Films inc: The Cabinet of Dr. Caligari; The Spiders; Dr. Mabuse; Between Worlds; Tartuffe; Love Makes Us Blind; Discord; Hungarian Rhapsody; The White Devil; The Woman From Monte Carlo (only U. S. film); Congress Dances; Madame Blaubart; The Kreutzer Sonata; Strife Over The Boy; Fredericus; Murder on the Bridge; Tales From the Vienna Woods; The Pedestrian.
(Died Jan 23, 1980).

DAHL, Arlene: Act. b. Minneapolis, MN, Aug 11, 1928. On radio at age 8. Broadway debut in Mr. Strauss Goes to Boston, 1946. On Screen from 1947. Films inc: My Wild Irish Rose; Reign of Terror; Three Little Words; Journey to the Center of the Earth; Kisses for My President; Land Raiders.
Bway inc: Applause; The King and I; Pal Joey; One Touch of Venus; Liliom; Blithe Spirit.

DAHL, Roald: Wri. b. Norway, 1916. H of Patricia Neal. Films inc: Chitty Chitty Bang Bang; You Only Live Twice; Willy Wonka and the Chocolate Factory; Hair.

DAILEY, Irene: Act-teacher. b. NYC, Sep 12, 1920. e. Actors Studio. Sis of late Dan Dailey. Founder, artistic dir School of the Actors Company. Bway inc: Nine Cards; Truckline Cafe; Idiot's Delight; Good Woman of Setzuan; Miss Lonely hearts; Andorra; The Subject Was Roses; Rooms; The Effect Gamma Rays on Man-In-the Moon Marigolds; You Know I Can't Hear You When the Water's Running. Other thea inc: Tomorrow--With Pictures (London); Laughing Water (tour); Skylark (tour); various stock appearances. Films inc: Five Easy Pieces; The Grissom Gang; No Way To Treat A Lady; Daring Game; The Amityville Horror. TV inc: Robert Montgomery Presents; Another World (Emmy-1979).

DAKIN, A Douglas: Exec. b. Gloucester, England, Apr 20, 1913. 1932 extra casting dir Fox; 1943-1960 chief casting dir Central Casting; 1960-1975 gm Central Casting. Ret. 1975.

DALE, Jim (nee Smith): Act. b. Rothwell, Northants, Eng, Aug 15, 1935. Made debut as solo comedian, 1951, at the Savoy. Joined National Theatre Company at the Old Vic. Appeared in numerous plays, touring Europe and appearing in NY in The Taming of the Shrew; Scapino (& co-dir & mus); Barnum (Tony-1980).
Films inc: Raising the Wind; Carry On Spying; Carry On Cleo; The Big Job; Carry On Cowboy; Carry on Screaming; Lock Up Your Daughter; The National Health; Digby; Joseph Andrews; Pete's Dragon; Unidentified Flying Oddball.

DALEY, Robert H: Prod. Films inc: Dirty Harry; Play Misty For Me; Joe Kidd; High Plains Drifter; Breezy; Magnum Force; Thunderbolt and Lightfoot; The Eiger Sanction; The Outlaw Josey Wales; The Enforcer; The Gauntlet; Every Which Way But Loose; Escape from Alcatraz; Bronco Billy; Any Which Way You Can.

DALIO, Marcel: Act. b. Paris, 1900. Films inc: La Grande Illusion; Pepe le Moko; La Regle du Jeu; Unholy Partners; Casablanca; The Song of Bernadette; Wilson; A Bell for Adano; To Have and Have Not; On the Riviera; The Happy Time; The Snows of Kilimanjaro; Sabrina Fair; Miracle in the Rain; Pillow Talk; Can Can; Jessica; Wild and Wonderful; Lady L; The 25th Hour; How Sweet It is; Catch 22; The Great White Hope; The Mad Adventures of Rabbi Jacob.

DALRYMPLE, Ian Murray: Wri-Prod. b. England, Aug 26, 1903. e. Cambridge. Films inc: The Citadel; Pygmalion (Oscar-1938); The Lion Had Wings; Once a Jolly Swagman; The Woman in the Hall; The Wooden Horse; The Heart of the Matter; Three Cases of Murder; The Admirable Crichton; A Cry from the Streets.

DALRYMPLE, Jean: Prod. b. Morristown, NJ, Sep 2, 1910. Former act. Started play prodn 1945, Hope for the Best. Subsequently prod: Harvey; The Voice of the Turtle; The Second Man. In 1953 became Gen Dir, NY City Center Drama Company and the City Center Light Opera Company;
Thea inc: Cyrano de Bergerac; The Shrike; King Lear; The Teahouse of the August Moon; The Glass Menagerie; The Beggar's Opera; Brigadoon; The Pajama Game; South Pacific; Porgy and Bess; Oklahoma; Pal Joey; The King and I; My Fair Lady; West Side Story; Kiss Me Kate.
Films inc: The Children of Theatre Street (doc).

DALTON, Timothy: Act. b. Colwyn Bay, Wales, Mar 21, 1946. Films inc: The Lion in Winter; Cromwell; The Voyeur; Wuthering Heights; Mary, Queen of Scots; Permission to Kill; Sextette; Agatha; Flash Gordon.
TV inc: Five Finger Exercise; Candida; Centennial; The Flame is Love.

DALTREY, Roger: Singer-Act. b. London, Mar 1, 1944. Lead Voc with The Who.
Films inc: Woodstock; Tommy; Lisztomania; The Legacy; The Kids Are Alright; McVicar (& prod).

DALY, John C: Newscaster-TV pers. b. Johannesburg, S Africa, 1914. Newsman and panel-show personality during the 50's and 60's; What's My Line? (moderator); VP in charge of news, special events and public affairs for ABC (1953-60). (Emmy-Commentator-1954). TV inc: We Take Your Word; News of the World; Critique.

DALY, Robert A: Exec. b. NYC, Dec 8, 1936. e. Brooklyn Coll. Joined CBS TV in 1955; served successively as dir of program accounting; dir of research and cost planning; dir of business affairs, NY; vp, business affairs, NY; exec vp of the network on Apr 1976; named p, CBS Entertainment in Oct 1977; Nov 1980, co-chmn, co-CEO, WB.

DALY, Tyne: Act. b. Madison, WI, Feb 21. W of Georg Stanford Brown. D of late James Daly. Films inc: John and Mary; Play It as It Lays; The Entertainer; The Enforcer; Telefon; Speedtrap.
Thea inc: Butter & Egg Man; The Summer, The Fall; Ashes; Three Sisters.
TV inc: Larry; Greatest Heroes of the Bible; Better Late Than Never; The Women's Room.

DAMITA, Lili: Act. b. Paris, Jul 20, 1907. Films inc: The Rescue; The Bridge of San Luis Rey; The Cock-Eyed World; This is the Night; Goldie Gets Along; The Frisco Kid; L'Escadrille de la Chance.

DAMON, Cathryn: Act. b. Seattle, WA, Sep 11. TV inc: The Love Boat; Soap (Emmy-1980); The Hal Linden Special; Friendship Secrets and Lies.
Thea inc: The Secret Life of Walter Mitty; LA Under Siege; Siame; The Prodigal; L'Histoire Du Soldat; Criss-Crossing; Show Me Where the Good Times Are; Your Own Thing; The Effect of Gamma Rays on Man-in-the Moon Marigolds.
Films inc: How To Beat the High Cost of Living.

DAMON, Stuart: (nee Zonis): Act. b. NYC, Feb 5, 1937. e. Brandeis U. Thea inc: Irma La Douce; Entertain a Ghost; The Boys from Syracuse; Do I Hear a Waltz?; Houdini-Man of Magic; Macbeth; Cadenza; The Sunshine Boys.
TV inc: The Champions.

DAMONE, Vic (Vito Farinola): Act. b. NYC, Jun 12, 1928. Winner Arthur Godfrey talent show, 1945. Nightclubs, radio, theatres, hotels. Screen debut in Rich, Young and Pretty. Films inc: The Strip; Athena; Deep in My Heart; Hit the Deck; Kismet; From Hell to Eternity.
TV inc: The Vic Damone Show; The Lively Ones.

DANA, Bill: Act-Wri. b. Quincy, MA, 1924. Niteries, TV. Films inc: The Barefoot Executive; The Nude Bomb (& wri).

DANA, Leora: Act. b. NYC, Apr 1, 1923. e. RADA. Stage debut London, 1947, Chiltern Hundreds. Returned to U.S. 1948. Bway inc: The Madwoman of Chaillot; Point of No Return; Sabrina Fair; The Milktrain Doesn't Stop Here Anymore; The Trojan Woman; A Place Without Mornings; The Last of Mrs Lincoln (Tony-supp-1973); Mourning Pictures.
Films inc: The 3:10 to Yuma; Kings Go Forth; Some Came Running; A Gathering of Eagles; The Norman Vincent Peale Story.
TV inc: The Barretts of Wimpole Street; Rip Van Winkle; Nurse; Another World.

DANA, Viola: Act. b. Brooklyn, Jun 26, 1897. Sis of Shirley Mason. On Bway in The Poor Little Rich Girl. Film debut in A Christmas Carol.
Films inc: The Flower of No Man's Land; Blue Jeans; The Winding Trail; A Weaver of Dreams; The Willow Tree; Merton of the Movies.
Briefly in vaudeville in a skit, The Ink Well, written by Anita Loos, after retiring from films with advent of sound.

DANDREA, Ron: Exec. b. Montreal, Feb 27, 1930. e. Loyola U. Chief financial officer Golden Harvest Group; former Bank of America vp.

DANELIA, Georgy: Dir. b. Russia, Aug 25, 1930. e. Moscow Architectural Institute. Films inc: Seryozha; The Way to the Harbour; Walking the Streets of Moscow; 33; Don't Grieve; Hopelessly Lost; Afonya; Mimino; Autumn Marathon.

DANGERFIELD, Rodney: Act. b. Babylon, NY, 1921. Films inc: The Projectionist; Caddyshack.

DANIEL, Eliot: Comp-Lyr-Cond. b. Jan 7, 1910. Radio during 30s and 40s for Rudy Vallee Fleischmann Hour; Frank Morgan Show; Danny Thomas Show; Fibber McGee. TV inc: I Love Lucy (theme and all original music); September Bride; The Whiting Girls; Willy; Angel; various Bob Hope specials.

Films: with Disney in the 40s; then to 20th Century-Fox in 50s; later freelanced at Paramount, Columbia, RKO.

Songs for films inc: Lavender Blue; So Dear to My Heart; Never.

DANIELS, Billy: Act. b. Jacksonville, FL, Sep 12, 1915. Started as singing waiter; then band singer; niteries. Films inc: Cruising Down the River; Sunny Side of the Street; Rainbow Round My Shoulder. TV inc: The Big Operator; Night of the Quarter Moon; Beat Generation; All God's Children Got Rhythm.

Thea inc: Memphis Bound; Golden Boy; Norman, Is That You?; Hello, Dolly!; Bubbling Brown Sugar.

DANIELS, Charlie: Mus-Sngwri. b. NC, Oct 28, 1936. Began professional career in teens as guitarist in smalltown bars; organized the Jaquars; went to Nashville, began working as recording session musician for Bob Dylan, Flatt & Scruggs, Marty Robbins, Claude King, Pete Seeger, Ringo Starr before forming Charlie Daniels Band, 1971.

TV inc: Crystal.

Recordings inc: Grease and Wolfman; Honey in Rock; Orange Blossom Special; Long Haired Country Boy; Night Rider; Saddle Tramp; High Lonesome; The South's Gonna Do It; Midnight Wind; Million Mile Reflection; Full Moon.

(Grammy-country vocal-1979).

DANIELS, William: Act. b. Brooklyn, NY, Mar 31, 1927. e. Northwestern U, BS. Bway inc: The Zoo Story; Dear Me The Sky Is Falling; One Flew Over the Cuckoo's Nest; A Thousand Clowns; On A Clear Day You Can See Forever; Daphne in Cottage D.

Films inc: The Graduate; Two For the Road; The President's Analyst; 1776; A Thousand Clowns; Black Sunday; Oh, God!; The One and Only; Sunburn; The Blue Lagoon.

TV inc: A Case of Rape; One of Our Own; Sarah T--Portrait of a Teenage Alcoholic; The Adams Chronicles; Francis Gary Powers; The Bastard; Blind Ambition; The Rebels; City in Fear; Damien. . .The Leper Priest; Freebie and the Bean.

DANKWORTH, John: Mus-Comp. b. England. H of Cleo Laine. Organized Johnny Dankworth Seven, debut London Palladium 1950; John Dankworth Band 1953; mus dir Nat "King" Cole; Buddy Greco; Mel Torme; Ella Fitzgerald; guest cond London Symphony, London Philharmonia; London Philharmonic; Los Angeles Philharmonic.

Films inc: (comp) We Are The Lambeth Boys; Saturday Night and Sunday Morning; The Servant; Darling; Morgan; The Idol; Perfect Friday; The Engagement; 10 Rillington Place; Modesty Blaise.

Thea inc: Midsummer Night's Dream; Twelfth Night; Colette.

DANN, Michael H (Mike): Exec. Began as comedy wri late 40's; moved to pub dept, later pgm dept CBS; 1958, vp NY pgms CBS; 1963, head of pgms; 1966, sr vp pgms; 1970, vp & asst to P of Childrens Television Workshop; 1979 consltnt to Disney on planned experimental prototype community; 1980 sr pgm advsr ABC Video Enterprises.

DANNER, Blythe: Act. b. Phila, Feb 3. e. Bard College. Films inc: 1776; To Kill a Clown; Lovin' Molly; Hearts of the West; Futureworld; The Great Santini.

TV inc: Dr Cook's Garden; To Confuse the Angel; George M; To Be Young Gifted and Black; The Scarecrow; Adam's Rib; F Scott Fitzgerald and the Last of the Belles; Eccentricities of a Nightingale; Too Far to Go; You Can't Take It With You; Are You in the House Alone?

Bway inc: Cyrano de Bergerac; Up Eden; The Miser; Butterflies Are Free (Tony-supp-1970); Major Barbara; The Seagull; Ring Around the Moon; Betrayal; The Philadelphia Story.

DANO, Royal: Act. b. NYC, Nov 16, 1922. Films inc: Undercover Girl; Red Badge of Courage; Bend of the River; The Far Country; Moby Dick; Never Steal Anything Small; The Adventures of Huckleberry Finn; Welcome to Hard Times; Death of a Gunfighter; The Undefeated; The Wild Party; The Outlaw Josey Wales; The Killer Inside Me; In Search of Historic Jesus.

TV inc: Lights Out; Lost in Space; Death Valley Days; Planet of the Apes; How the West Was Won; Heroes of the Bible; The Raid on Coffeyville; Murder In Peyton Place; Greatest Heroes of the Bible; The Last Ride of the Dalton Gang; From Here to Eternity-The War Years.

Thea inc: Finian's Rainbow; Three Wishes for Jaimey; Stalag 17; White Cargo.

DANOVA, Cesare: Act. b. Rome, Mar 1. Films inc: The Captain's Son; King of Kings; Tender Is the Night; Cleopatra; Gidget Goes to Rome; Boy, Did I Get a Wrong Number!; Che!; Mean Streets; Scorchy; Tentacles; National Lampoon's Animal House.

TV inc: The Magician; Police Story; The Manhunters; A Matter of Wife. . .and Death.

DANTE, Nicholas: Plywri. b. NYC, Nov 22, 1941. Originally a dancer, worked summer stock. Bway inc: I'm Solomon; Applause.

Plays inc: A Chorus Line (Pulitzer Prize & Tony-1976).

DANTINE, Helmut: Act. b. Vienna, 1918. Films inc: Mrs. Miniver; Passage to Marseilles; Hotel Berlin; Escape in the Desert; Northern Pursuit; Shadow of a Woman; Call Me Madam; War and Peace; Fraulein; Operation Crossbow; Bring Me the Head of Alfredo Garcia (& exec prod); The Wilby Conspiracy (& exec prod); The Killer Elite (& exec prod); The 5th Musketeer.

DANTON, Ray: Act. b. NYC, Sep 19, 1931. Began as radio actor; in summer stock. Films inc: Chief Crazy Horse; The Looters; The Spoilers; The Night Runner; Onionhead; Legs Diamond; Majority of One; The George Raft Story; The Chapman Report; The Longest Day.

TV inc: (dir) Psychic Killer; Bender.

D'ANTONI, Philip: Prod-Dir. b. NYC, Feb 19, 1929. e. Fordham U. Films inc: Bullitt; The French Connection (Oscar-1971); The Seven Ups.

TV inc: Elizabeth Taylor in London; Sophia Loren in Rome; Melina Mercouri in Greece; This Proud Land; Movin' On; Mr Inside/Mr Outside; Strike Force; The Connection.

DANZA, Tony: Act. b. Brooklyn, NY, Apr 21, 1951. e. U Dubuque. TV inc: Fast Lane Blues; Taxi. Films inc: The Hollywood Knights.

DARBY, Ken: Comp-Lyr-Cond-Arr. b. Hebron, NE, May 13, 1909. e. Chapman Coll. Originated the King's Men, male quartet, 1929, appearing on radio, TV, films, records; leader arr. Ken Darby Singers; asso mus supv, cond. for films inc: The Wizard of Oz; Elmer Gantry; The King and I (Oscar-1956); South Pacific; Porgy and Bess (Oscar-1959); Camelot (Oscar-1967); Finian's Rainbow; The Great Bank Robbery; Airport.

Songs inc: Barbie; This Friendly World; Forever Hold Me; The Story of Christmas; Whispering Wind; How the West Was Won; No Goodbye; Come Share My Life; Daniel Boone Theme for TV.

(Grammy-soundtrack-1959).

DARBY, Kim (Deborah Zerby): Act. b. LA, Jul 8, 1948. Films inc: Bus Riley's Back in Town; True Grit; Generation; Norwood; The Strawberry Statement; The Grissom Gang; The One and Only.

TV inc: Eleventh Hour; Gunsmoke; Flesh and Blood; Flatbed Annie & Sweetiepie-Lady Truckers; The Last Convertible; Enola Gay--The Men, The Mission, The Atomic Bomb.

DARC, Mireille: Act. b. Toulon, France, May 15, 1940. Films inc: Galia; Du Rififi a Paname; Weekend; Jeff; The Blonde from Peking; There Was Once a Cop; Return of the Big Blonde; Le Telephone Rose; Man In A Hurry; Les Passagers; Mort d'un Pourri.

DARCEL, Denise (nee Billecard): Act. b. Paris, 1925. Films inc: To the Victor; Battleground; Tarzan and the Slave Girl; Westward the Women; Dangerous When Wet; Flame of Calcutta; Vera Cruz; Seven Women from Hell.

DARDEN, Severn: Act. b. Nov 9, 1929. Films inc: Dead Heat on a Merry-Go-Round; The President's Analyst; Luv; Pussycat, Pussycat I Love You; Vanishing Point; The Hired Hand; Cisco Pike; The War Between Men and Women; Who Fears the Devil; Wanda Nevada; Why Would I Lie?; In God We Trust.
TV inc: Love for Rent; Orphan Train.

DARLING, Joan (nee Kugell): Dir-Act. b. Apr 14, 1935. TV inc: (dir) Mary Hartman, Mary Hartman; Chuckles Bites the Dust; Phyllis; Doc; Rhoda; Rich Man, Poor Man; M*A*S*H; The Nurses. (Perf): Frieda; Owen Marshal; Margret; Viola; The Two Worlds of Jenny Logan.
Films inc: (perf) The Troublemaker; The President's Analyst; Fearless Frank; Kansas City Bomber; Sunnyside; First Love (dir).

DARREN, James: Act. b. Philadelphia, Jun 8, 1936. Films inc: Rumble on the Docks; The Brothers Rico; The Guns of Navarone; Gidget Goes Hawaiian; The Lively Set; Venus in Furs. TV inc: Turnover Smith.

DARRIEUX, Danielle: Act. b. Bordeaux, France, May 1, 1917. On screen from the early 30s. Films inc: Mayerling; Rage of Paris; Rich, Young and Pretty; Alexander the Great; Loss of Innocence; Friend of the Family; 24 Hours in a Woman's Life; Le Cavaleur; Divine.
Bway inc: Coco.

DA SILVA, Howard (nee Silverblatt): Act. b. Cleveland, OH, May 4, 1909. e. Carnegie Tech. Steel worker prior to joining Civic Repertory Theatre, NY 1929. Remained with CRT five years appearing in The Would Be Gentleman; The Green Cockatoo; The Three Sisters; The Cherry Orchard.
Bway inc: Ten Million Ghosts; Golden Boy; The Cradle Will Rock; Casey Jones; Abe Lincoln in Illinois; Two on an Island; Oklahoma!; Burning Bright; The World of Sholem Aleichem (& dir-coprod); The Adding Machine; Volpone; Fiorello!; Compulsion; Purlie Victorious (dir); Dear Me, The Sky is Falling; The Zulu and the Zayda (co-auth); My Sweet Charlie (dir); 1776.
Films inc: I'm Still Alive; Abe Lincoln in Illinois; Sea Wolf; Big Shot; Omaha Trail; Tonight We Raid Calais; Lost Weekend; Two Years Before the Mast; Duffy's Tavern; Unconquered; Blaze of Noon; They Live By Night; Tripoli; Underworld Story; Three Husbands; 14 Hours; M; David and Lisa; 1776; The Great Gatsby.
TV inc: Walter Fortune; For the People; Missiles of October; Stop, Thief; Smile Jenny, You're Dead; Hollywood on Trial; Verna--USO Girl (Emmy-supp-1978); When the Boat Comes In (host); Power.

DASSIN, Jules: Dir-Wri. b. Middletown, CT, Dec 18, 1911. H of Melina Mercouri. Started as actor on stage. Joined MGM 1941 as dir. Films inc: Nazi Agent; The Affairs of Martha; The Canterville Ghost; A Letter for Evie; Brute Force; Naked City; Thieves Highway; Rififi (& sp-act); He Who Must Die (& sp); Where the Hot Wind Blows (& sp); Never on Sunday (& sp-act); Phaedra (& sp); Topkapi; 10:30 P M Summer (& sp); Survival; Uptight (& sp); Promise at Dawn (& sp-act); A Dream of Passion (& prod-sp); Circle of Two.
Bway: Magdalena (dir); Ilya, Darling (wri-dir).

DAVENPORT, Nigel: Act. b. Cambridge, England, May 23, 1928. e. Trinity Coll, Oxford. Thea inc: Relative Values; The Country Wife; The Mulberry Bush; The Crucible; The Death of Satan; Cards of Identity; Good Woman of Setzuan; Epitaph for George Dillon; A Resounding Tinkle; A Taste of Honey; Bonne Soupe; Incident at Vichy; Notes on a Love Affair; Three Sisters.
Films inc: Peeping Tom; A High Wind in Jamaica; Where the Spies Are; A Man For All Seasons; Royal Hunt of the Sun; The Virgin Soldiers; A Last Valley; No Blade of Grass; Villain; Living Free; Mary, Queen of Scots; The Island of Dr. Moreau; Zulu Dawn.
TV inc: South Riding; Dracula; Oil Strike North; Phase IV; The Ordeal of Dr. Mudd; Cry of the Innocent.

DAVID, Hal: Lyr. b. May 25, 1921. e. NYU. B of Mack David. Songs inc: American Beauty Rose; My Heart is an Open Book; Magic Moments; Blue on Blue; Walk On By; Any Old Time of Day; The First Night of the Full Moon; There's Always Something To Remind Me; Trains and Boats and Planes; What The World Needs Now Is Love; The Look of Love; Raindrops Keep Fallin on My Head (Oscar-1969). Send Me No Flowers; Alfie; What's New Pussycat; Promise Her Anything; Moonraker. Film title songs inc: Wives and Lovers; A House is Not a Home; (Grammy-cast album-1969).

DAVID, Mack: Comp. b. NYC, Jul 5, 1912. e. Cornell U, St Johns U Law School. Film scores inc: Cinderella; At War with the Army; Sailor Beware; Jumping Jacks.
Songs inc: Falling Leaves; A Sinner Kissed an Angel; Lili Marlene; Spellbound; Chi-Baba Chi-Baba; La Vie en Rose; Bibbidi Bobbidi Boo; I Don't Care if the Sun Don't Shine; It Only Hurts for a Little While; My Wishing Doll.
Film title songs inc: The Hanging Tree; Walk on the Wild Side; To Kill a Mockingbird; It's a Mad Mad Mad Mad World; Cat Ballou.

DAVID, Saul: Prod. b. NYC, Jun 27, 1921. Radio, newspaper work, editorial dir Bantam Books. With Col, 1960-62; WB, 1962-62; Fox, 1963-67; U, 1968-69; Exec story edtr MGM, 1972. Films inc: Von Ryan's Express; Our Man Flint; Fantastic Voyage; In Like Flint; Skullduggery; Logan's Run; Ravagers.

DAVIDSON, Gordon: Dir-Prod. b. NYC, May 7, 1933. e. Cornell U, BA, Case Western Reserve U, MA. Artistic dir Mark Taper Forum. Thea inc: Savages; In the Matter of J Robert Oppenheimer; Leonard Bernstein's Mass; Who's Happy Now?; Murderous Angels; Rosebloom; The Trial of the Catonsville Nine; The Shadow Box (Tony-1977); And Where She Stops Nobody Knows; Black Angel; Children of a Lesser God; Zoot Suit.
Films inc: The Trial of the Catonsville Nine. TV inc: Who's Happy Now?

DAVIDSON, John: Act. b. Pittsburgh, Dec 13, 1941. Films inc: The Happiest Millionaire; The Concorde-Airport '79. TV inc: The Entertainer; The Fantasticks; The Interns; The Girl With Something Extra; The John Davidson Christmas Show; Dallas Cowboys Cheerleaders; That's Incredible! (host); The Carpenters-Music, Music, Music. Bway inc: Foxy.

DAVIDSON, Martin: Dir. b. NYC, Nov 7, 1939. Films inc: The Lords of Flatbush (co-dir); Almost Summer (& sp); If Ever I See You Again (sp); Hero at Large.

DAVIS, Allan: Prod-Dir. b. London, Aug 30, 1913. e. Sydney U, Australia. Started as act; after WW2 service became asst-dir, later dir Bristol Old Vic. Thea inc: (London) Arabian Nightmare; The Shadow of Doubt; Breath of Spring; Joshua Tree; Fool's Paradise (& co-prod); A Shred of Evidence; The Bird of Time (& co-prod); The Big Killing; The Apricot Season; Honey, I'm Home; Did You Feel It Move?; The Sacred Flame (co-prod); The Night I Chased the Women With an Eel; Come As You Are (& co-prod); No Sex Please--We're British; Friends, Romans, and Lovers; Signs of the Times (& co-prod); A Touch of Spring (& co-prod); In The Red (& prod).

DAVIS, Ann B: Act. b. Schenectady, NY, May 5, 1926. e. U MI, BA. With stock and repertory companies. Bway inc: Once Upon a Mattress.
TV inc: The Bob Cummings Show (Emmy-supp-1957, 1958, 1959); Keefe Brasselle Show; John Forsythe Show; The Brady Bunch.

DAVIS, Benny: Sngwri-Vaudevillian. b. NYC, Aug 21, 1895. In vaude at age 14 as accomp for Benny Fields and Blossom Seeley. Later soloed on vaude's bigtime, headlined at the Palace.
Bway inc: (scores) Future Broadway Stars; Cotton Club Revue; Artists and Models of 1927, Sons O'Guns, three editions of Cotton Club Revue (also prod vaude revues with which he toured country).
Songs inc: Goodbye Broadway, Hello France; Margie; Baby Face; There Goes My Heart; Carolina Moon; Sleepyhead; I Still Get a Thrill; I'm Nobody's Baby.
(Died Dec 20, 1979).

DAVIS, Bette (Ruth Elizabeth Davis): Act. b. Lowell, MA, Apr 5, 1908. Performed in stock and repertory company. Bway debut 1929, Broken Dishes. Film debut Bad Sister, 1931. Films inc: Dangerous (*Oscar*-1935); Jezebel (*Oscar*-1938); Dark Victory; The Letter; The Little Foxes; Now Voyager; Pocketful of Miracles; Mr Skeffington; All About Eve; The Star; Whatever Happened to Baby Jane?; Hush, Hush Sweet Charlotte; The Anniversary; Burnt Offerings; Death on the Nile; Return From Witch Mountain; The Watcher in the Woods.

TV inc: The Dark Secret of Harvest Home; Strangers-The Story of a Mother and Daughter (*Emmy*-1979); White Mama; Skyward.

Toured US, Australia, New Zealand with "Bette Davis in Person and on Film."

DAVIS, Bill: Dir. b. Belleville, Ontario, Canada, Aug 13, 1931. e. Ryerson Inst of Tech. TV inc: Hullabaloo; Smothers Brothers; Hee Haw; Jonathan Winters; Lennon Sisters; Julie Andrews Special (*Emmy*-1973); Herb Alpert; Lily Tomlin; Frank Sinatra; John Denver (*Emmy*-1975); Gabe Kaplan; Marlo Thomas.

DAVIS, Brad: Act. b. Nov 6, 1949. Films inc: Midnight Express; A Small Circle of Friends.

TV inc: Sybil; A Rumor of War.

DAVIS, Clifton: Act. b. Chicago, Oct 4, 1945. Films inc: Scott Joplin. TV inc: Little Ladies of the Night; The Clifton Davis Show; That's My Mama; The Night The City Screamed.

DAVIS, Jim: Act. b. Edgerton, MO, Aug 26, 1915. Films inc: White Cargo; Swing Shift Maisie; Gallant Bess; Winter Meeting; Brimstone; The Last Command; Timberjack; The Maverick Queen; Alias Jesse James; Rio Lobo; Big Jake; The Honkers; Bad Company; Monte Walsh; The Choirboys; Comes A Horseman; The Day Time Ended.

TV inc: Satan's Triangle; Stone; Just a Little Inconvenience; Dallas.

DAVIS, Jimmie: Act. b. Quitman, LA, Sep 11, 1902. e. LA Coll, BA. Co-author western song standard You Are My Sunshine. Toured country as singer and guitarist. Twice elected governor of Louisiana.

DAVIS, Luther: Prod-Wri. b. NYC, Aug 29, 1921. e. Yale U. Films inc: (sp); The Hucksters; B.F.'s Daughter; Black Hand; A Lion Is in the Streets; The Gift of Love; Holiday for Lovers; The Wonders of Alladin; Across 110th St. (prod) Lady in the Cage.

Plays inc: Kismet (*Tony*-prod & co-author-1954); Timbuktu (prod & author).

TV inc: Arsenic and Old Lace; Bus Stop series; Daughters of the Mind; The Old Man Who Cried Wolf.

DAVIS, Mac: Act-Lyr. b. Lubbock, TX, Jan 21, 1942. Began as country-western sngwri; has written for Elvis Presley, Kenny Rogers, Andy Williams, Sammy Davis Jr, Dolly Parton.

Songs inc: In the Ghetto; Baby Don't Get Hooked On Me; One Hell of a Woman; I Believe in Music; Stop and Smell the Roses; Watching Scotty Grow; You're Good For Me; Friend, Lover, Woman, Wife; Daddy's Little Man; Something's Burning; I'll Paint You A Song; Everything a Man Could Ever Need; A Little Less Conversation; Memories; Don't Cry Daddy.

TV inc: Mac Davis Special--Christmas Odyssey; Kenny Rogers--The American Cowboy; Mac Davis--A Christmas Special With Love; The Mac Davis Show; The Monte Carlo Show; A Johnny Cash Christmas (1980); I'll Be Home For Christmas.

Films inc: North Dallas Forty; Cheaper to Keep Her.

DAVIS, Madelyn Pugh: Wri. b. Indianapolis, IN. e. IN U. TV inc: I Love Lucy; Lucy; Here's Lucy; Mothers-in-Law; Lucille Ball Special; Alice (prod).

DAVIS, Miles: Mus-Comp. b. Alton, IL, May 25, 1926. e. Juilliard. With Charlie Parker and Benny Carter bands before solo.

Films inc: (scores) Elevator to the Gallows; Jack Johnson. (*Grammys*-(2)-original comp-1960; jazz group-1970).

DAVIS, Nancy: Act. b. NYC, Jul 6, 1921. W of Ronald Reagan. Films inc: Shadow on the Wall; The Doctor and the Girl; Night and Morning; It's a Big Country; Donovan's Brain; Crash Landing; Hellcats of the Navy.

DAVIS, Ossie: Act-Wri-Dir. b. Cogdell, GA, 1917. e. Howard U. H of Ruby Dee. Stage debut with Rose McClendon Players in Harlem, 1941; Bway debut 1946, Jeb. Thea inc: (act) Anna Lucasta; The Washington Years; The Leading Lady; The Smile of the World; The Royal Family; Touchstone; Green Pastures; A Raisin in the Sun; Purlie Victorious (& wri).

Films inc: (act) The Scalphunters; The Slaves; The Hill; The Cardinal; Purlie Victorious. (Dir): Cotton Comes to Harlem; Kongi's Harvest; Black Girl; Gordon's War; Countdown at Kusini; Hot Stuff.

TV inc: Teacher, Teacher; The Defenders; The Sheriff; The Tenth Level; King; Roots-The Next Generation; Freedom Road (narr); All God's Children.

DAVIS, Phyllis: Act. b. Nederland, TX, Jul 17, 1940. Films inc: Day of the Dolphin; The Choirboys.

TV inc: Love American Style; Vega$.

DAVIS, Sammy Jr: Act. b. NYC, Dec 8, 1925. On stage at age 2 in act with father, uncle, Will Mastin. Bdwy inc: Mr. Wonderful; Golden Boy. Niteries.

Films inc: Anna Lucasta; Porgy & Bess; Ocean's 11; Robin and the Seven Hoods; Salt and Pepper; A Man Called Adam; Sweet Charity; One More Time; Sammy Stops The World.

TV inc: The Sammy Davis Jr. Show; Sammy and Company; Mod Squad; Name of the Game; The Trackers.

DAVIS, Skeeter (Mary Frances Penick): Act. b. Dry Ridge, KY, Dec 30, 1931. C & W rec artist. Started as teenager; formed duo, The Davis Sisters; went solo in 1955; regular on Nashville's Grand Ole Opry; performed at Carnegie Hall, 1950.

DAWBER, Pam: Act. b. Detroit, MI, Oct 18, 1951. Films inc: A Wedding. TV inc: Sister Terri; Mork & Mindy; The Girl, The Gold Watch and Everything.

DAWSON, Richard: Act. b. Gosport, Hampshire, Eng, Nov 20. Films inc: The Devil's Brigade; King Rat; Munsters Go Home; Promises, Promises.

TV inc: The New Dick Van Dyke Show; Hogan's Heroes; I've Got a Secret; Match Game; Masquerade Party; Laugh-In; Family Feud. (*Emmy*-host-1978).

DAY, Dennis (Eugene Denis McNulty): Act. b. NYC, May 21, 1917. e. Manhattan Coll. Debut on Jack Benny radio show. Films inc: Buck Benny Rides Again; Music in Manhattan; One Sunday Afternoon; I'll Get By; Golden Girl; The Girl Next Door.

DAY, Doris (nee Kappelhoff): Act. b. Cincinnati, Apr 3, 1924. Toured as dancer, radio, band singer. Screen debut, Romance on the High Seas, 1948. Films inc: Young Man With a Horn; Tea for Two; On Moonlight Bay; I'll See You in My Dreams; By the Light of the Silvery Moon; Calamity Jane; With Six You Get Eggroll; Where Were You When the Lights Went Out?; Glass Bottom Boat; Young at Heart; Love Me or Leave Me; Man Who Knew Too Much; Pajama Game; That Touch of Mink; Teacher's Pet; Pillow Talk;

TV inc: The Doris Day Show. Please Don't Eat the Daisies; Midnight Lace; Lover Come Back; Jumbo; The Thrill of It All.

DAY, Laraine (nee Johnson): Act. b. Roosevelt, UT, Oct 13, 1920. Screen debut Border G-Men, 1938. Films inc: Story of Dr. Wassell; Those Endearing Young Charms; Tycoon; My Son, My Son; The High and the Mighty; Mr. Lucky; Bride By Mistake; My Dear Secretary.

TV inc: Playhouse 90; Let Freedom Ring; The Name of the Game; Medical Center; Murder on Flight #504; Love Boat.

DEAN, Isabel (nee Hodgkinson): Act. b. Eng, May 29, 1918. London stage debut 1940, Peril at End House. Thea inc: All's Well that Ends Well; Witch Errant; Night of the Fourth; The Centaur; What the Butler Saw; Claw; The Fool; Half-Life; Dear Daddy.

Films inc: The Light in the Piazza; A High Wind in Jamaica; Inadmissible Evidence; Catch Me a Spy; Rough Cut.

TV inc: The Quatermass Experiment; The Parachute; Sense and Sensibility.

DEAN, Morton: TV news. b. Fall River, MA, Aug 22, 1935. e. Emerson Coll, BA. News dir NY Herald Tribune radio net 1957; corr WBZ 1960; 1964 corr WCBS-TV; 1967 anchor WCBS-TV News; joined CBS News 1967 as corr; 1975 anchor CBS Sunday Night News; 1976 anchor Sunday edition CBS Evening News; also anchors Newsbreak.

TV inc: The Case of Plastic Peril; Vietnam--A War That is Finished; Energy--The Facts, The Fears, The Future; Pope John Paul II--The American Journey; Iran--A Week of Tumult.

De BONT, Jan: Cin. b. Netherlands, Oct 22, 1943. e. Amsterdam Film Academy. Films inc: Turkish Delight; Keetje Tippel; Last Train; Joao; Paranoia; White Slave; The Family; Max Havelaar; Expresse; Dakota; What Do I See.

De BROCA, Philippe: Dir. b. France, 1933. Films inc: Playing at Love; Infidelity; That Man From Rio (sp); Un Monsieur de Compagnie; Tribulations Chinoise en Chine; King of Hearts; Devil by the Tail; Give Her the Moon; Chere Louise; Le Magnifique; Dear Inspector (& sp); Le Cavaleur; Premier Voyage.

DECAE, Henri: Cin. b. France, 1915. Films inc: Le Silence de la Mer; Les Enfants Terribles; Lift to the Scaffold; Le Beau Serge; A Double Tour; Les Quatre Cents Coup; Les Cousins; Les Bonnes Femmes; Sundays and Cybele; Viva Maria; Weekend at Dunkirk; Night of the Generals; La Voleur; The Comedians; Castle Keep; The Sicilian Clan; The Light at the Edge of the World; Bobby Deerfield; The Wild Goose Chase; The Boys From Brazil; An Almost Perfect Affair; The Island; Le Guignol; Le Coup du Parapluie (The Umbrella Coup); Inspector la Bavure (Inspector Blunder).

De CAMP, Rosemary: Act. b. Prescott, AZ, Nov 14, 1910. Films inc: Hold Back the Dawn; Cheers for Miss Bishop; The Jungle Book; Yankee Doodle Dandy; Practically Yours; Weekend at the Waldorf; Many Rivers to Cross; Tora! Tora! Tora!

TV inc: Robert Cummings Show; That Girl; Life of Riley; Death Valley Days; Partridge Family; Blind Ambition; Mark Twain's America-Thomas Edison.

DE CARLO, Yvonne (Peggy Middleton): Act. b. Vancouver, BC, Sep 1, 1924. Began as dancer. Screen debut This Gun For Hire, 1942. Films inc: The Story of Dr. Wassell; Salome; Frontier Gal; Brute Force; Casbah; Criss Cross; Calamity Jane; The Ten Commandments; McClintock; A Global Affair; Blazing Stewardesses; Satan's Cheerleader; It Seemed Like a Good Idea At the Time; Guyana-Cult of The Damned; Silent Scream; The Man With Bogart's Face.

De CORDOVA, Frederick: Dir. b. NYC, Oct 27, 1910. e. Northwestern U, BS. Gen stage dir, Shubert enterprises, 1938-41; prod Louisville (KY) Amphitheatre, 1942-43. Films inc: Too Young to Know; Her Kind of Man; Wallflower; For the Love of Mary; Peggy; Desert Hawk; Yankee Buccaneer; Columns South.

TV inc: (prod-dir) Burns and Allen; Jack Benny Program; Smothers Bros Show; My Three Sons (dir). Tonight Show (prod) *(Emmys-1976-1977-1978-1979).*

De CUIR, John: Art dir. b. San Francisco, 1918. Films inc: The Naked City; Snows of Kilimanjaro; My Cousin Rachel; Call Me Madam; Three Coins in the Fountain; Daddy Long Legs; The King and I *(Oscar-*1956); Island in the Sun; South Pacific; The Big Fisherman; Cleopatra *(Oscar-*1963); The Agony and the Ecstacy; The Honey Pot; Hello, Dolly! *(Oscar-*1969); The Great White Hope; Once Is Not Enough; That's Entertainment!; Ziegfeld-The Man and His Women; Love and Bullets; Raise The Titanic.

DEE, Frances: Act. b. LA, Nov 26, 1907. e. Chicago U. W of Joel McCrea.

Films inc: Follow Through; Playboy of Paris; American Tragedy; Rich Man's Folly; King of the Jungle; This Reckless Age; If I Had a Million; Silver Cord; Little Women; Of Human Bondage; Becky Sharp; Meet The Stewarts; If I Were King; So Ends Our Night; Happy Land; Patrick the Great; Private Affairs of Bel Ami; Four Faces West; Payment on Demand; Reunion in Reno; Because of You; Mr. Scoutmaster; Gypsy Colt. Ret 1955.

DEE, Ruby (nee Wallace): Act. b. Cleveland, OH, Oct 27, 1923. e. Hunter Coll. W of Ossie Davis. Bway debut 1943, South Pacific. Thea inc: Walk Hard; Jeb; Anna Lucasta; Purlie Victorious; King Lear; The Imaginary Invalid; Wedding Band; Hamlet.

Films inc: No Way Out; The Jackie Gleason Story; St Louis Blues; Take a Giant Step; A Raisin in the Sun; The Balcony; Buck and the Preacher; Black Girl; Countdown at Kusini.

TV inc: Actor's Choice; Seven Times Monday; Go Down Moses; Twin-Bit Gardens; I Know Why the Caged Bird Sings; All God's Children.

DEE, Sandra: Act. b. Bayonne, NJ, Apr 23, 1942. Began as model. Films inc: Until They Sail; The Restless Years; The Reluctant Debutante; Gidget; Imitation of Life; Romanoff and Juliet; Tammy Tell Me True; Tammy and the Doctor; The Dunwich Horror.

DEELEY, Michael: Prod. b. London, Aug 6, 1932. Started as film editor. Ind. prod 1961-63; Gen M Woodfall Films, 1964-67; Ind Prod 1967-72; M-dir EMI Films, 1976-77; Chief Exec EMI Films, 1978. Films inc: Robbery; Italian Job; The Knack; Murphy's War; Conduct Unbecoming; The Man Who Fell to Earth; The Deer Hunter *(Oscar-*1978); Convoy.

De FARIA, Walt: Prod-Dir-Wri. b. Sep 3, 1929. e. St Mary's Coll. Film inc: The Mouse and His Child; Winds of Change; Nutcracker Fantasy.

TV inc: The Wonderful World of Pizzazz; Children's Letters to God; The Unexplained; Travels With Charley (& dir); Snoopy at the Ice Follies; Snoopy Directs the Ice Follies; The Borrowers; Wild Science; The Wild Places; The Rivalry; The Yellow Bus; Beach Girls; Hanna-Barbera Happy Hour.

De FELITTA, Frank: Wri. b. NYC, Aug 3, 1921. Films inc: The First of January; The Savage Is Loose; Trapped; Audrey Rose (& prod).

TV inc: Chosen Child (doc); Odyssey; The Two Worlds of Jenny Logan (& dir).

De FORE, Don: Act. b. Cedar Rapids, IA, Aug 25, 1917. e. Pasadena Community Theatre. Bway inc: Where Do We Go From Here; Steel; The Male Animal.

Films inc: We Go Fast; The Male Animal; City Without Men; The Human Comedy; A Guy Named Joe; Thirty Seconds Over Tokyo; Affairs of Susan; You Came Along; Stork Club; It Happened On Fifth Avenue; Romance on the High Seas; One Sunday Afternoon; My Friend Irma; Southside 1-1000; Girl In Every Port; She's Working Her Way Through College; No Room for the Groom; Jumping Jacks; Battle Hymn.

TV inc: Lux Theatre; Philco Playhouse; Mr and Mrs Detective; Ozzie and Harriet; Hazel; A Punt, A Pass and a Prayer.

De FUNES, Louis: Act. b. Paris, Jul 31, 1914. Films inc: The Seven Deadly Sins; No Exit; The Sheep Has Five Legs; Lock Up the Spoons; Femmes de Paris; Taxi; A Pied a Chevel et en Spoutnik; The Sucker; Fantomas; Fantomas vs Scotland Yard; Don't Look Now; Jo; The Mad Adventures of Rabbi Jacob; L'aile ou la Cuisse; La Zizanie; The Miser; The Gendarme and the Creatures from Outer Space.

DEGERMARK, Pia: Act. b. Sweden. Films inc: Elvira Madigan; The Looking Glass War.

DE HARTOG, Jan: Plywri. b. Haarlem, Netherlands, Apr 22, 1914. Plays inc: Skipper Next To God; This Time Tomorrow; The Fourposter *(Tony-*1952); William and Mary; I Do, I Do (mus version of Fourposter).

De HAVEN, Carter III: Prod. b. LA, Feb 16, 1932. e. UCLA, BS. Films inc: Dead Heat On a Merry-Go-Round; The Kremlin Letter; A Walk With Love and Death; The Last Run; Ulzana's Raid; The Outfit; Seven Men At Daybreak; The Seniors.

TV inc: Make Me An Offer.

De HAVEN, Gloria: Act. b. LA, Jul 23, 1925. Films inc: Susan and God; Thousands Cheer; Two Girls and a Sailor; The Thin Man Goes Home; Summer Holiday; Three Little Words; Two Tickets to Broadway; So This Is Paris; The Girl Rush.

TV inc: Call Her Mom; Who Is the Black Dahlia?; Lucy Moves to NBC.

de HAVILLAND, Olivia: Act. b. Tokyo, Jul 1, 1916. Sis of Joan Fontaine. Film debut, A Midsummer's Night Dream. Films inc: Captain Blood; The Charge of The Light Brigade; The Adventures of Robin Hood; To Each His Own (*Oscar*-1946); The Snake Pit; The Heiress (*Oscar*-1949); Airport '77; The Swarm; The Fifth Musketeer.

DEHNER, John (nee Forkum): Act. b. NYC, Nov 23, 1915. e. UC Berkeley. Films inc: Thirty Seconds Over Tokyo; The Corn is Green; Ten Tall Men; Scaramouche; Man on a Tightrope; The Prodigal; Carousel; Fastest Gun Alive; Left Handed Gun; The Chapman Report; Critics Choice; Youngblood Hawke; Cheyenne Social Club; Dirty Dingus McGee; Day of the Dolphin; The Killer Inside Me; Fun with Dick and Jane; The Lincoln Conspiracy; The Boys from Brazil.

TV inc: The Roaring Twenties; The Baileys of Balboa; The Westerner; Doris Day Show; The Virginian; Missiles of October; Big Hawaii; Greatest Heroes of the Bible; Young Maverick; Enos.

DELAIR, Suzy: Act. b. Paris, Dec 31, 1931. Films inc: Le Dernier des Six; Defense D'Aimer; Quai des Orfevres; Lady Paname; Robinson Crusoe Land; Gervaise; Rocco and his Brother; Is Paris Burning?; The Mad Adventures of Rabbi Jacob.

DE LAURENTIIS, Dino: Prod. b. Torre Annunziata, Italy, Aug 8, 1919. Films inc: The Bandit Mussolino; Bitter Rice; War and Peace; Ulysses; Mambo; La Strada; The Bible; Anzio; Barbarella; Waterloo; The Vilachi Papers; Serpico; The Stone Killer; Three Days of the Condor; Death Wish; The Shootist; King Kong. Orca; The Serpent's Egg; Hurricane; Mean Frank, Crazy Tony; Flash Gordon.

DELERUE, Georges: Cond-Comp. b. Roubaix, France, 1924. Film scores inc: Hiroshima Mon Amour; King of Hearts; Shoot the Pianist; The Pumpkin Eater; Viva Maria; Interlude; Anne of the Thousand Days; The Day of the Dolphin; Julia; An Almost Perfect Affair; The Inspector; The Little Girl In Blue Velvet; Get Out Your Handkerchiefs; A Little Romance (*Oscar*-1979); Your Turn, My Turn; Richard's Things; The Last Metro.

TV inc: Our World (*Emmy*-1968).

DELFONT, Bernard, Lord: Exec. b. Tomak, Russia, Sep 5, 1909. B of Lord Lew Grade. Entered thea mgt in Great Britain, 1941; first London prodn, 1942; presenter with Louis Benjamin annual Royal Variety Performance; chmn and chief exec EMI film & Theatre Corp, 1969; chmn EMI Cinemas Ltd; EMI Leisure Enterprises; EMI Films; EMI-Elstree Studios; dir Bernard Delfont Organisation, Blackpool Tower Co; vice chmn Associated Film Distrib Corp, USA.

Thea inc: Henry IV; Ulysses in Nighttown; The Good Companions; Harvey; Dad's Army; It's Alright If I Do It; An Evening with Tommy Steele; Mardi Gras.

De LIAGRE, Alfred Jr: Prod-Dir. b. NYC, Oct 6, 1904. e. Yale U. Bway inc: Three Cornered Moon; By Your Leave; Pure in Heart (co-prod); Petticoat Fever; Fresh Fields; Yes, My Darling Daughter; I am My Youth; No Code to Guide Her; Mr and Mrs North; The Walrus and the Carpenter; Ask My Friend Sandy; The Voice of the Turtle (prod); The Madwoman of Chaillot; The Golden Apple; The Caine Mutiny Court Martial (tour); Photo Finish; The Irregular Verb to Love; J B (*Tony*-1959); Deathtrap; as exec prod for ANTA presented The American Conservatory Theatre in The Three Sisters; Tiny Alice; A Flea in Her Ear.

DELL, Gabriel (nee del Vecchio): Act. b. Barbados, BWI, Oct 7, 1919. Studied with Lee Strasberg. Bway debut age 9 in The Good Earth; in orig co Dead End; went to Hwd for film version.

Bway inc: Tickets Please; Ankles Aweigh; Can-Can; Wonderful Town; Marathon; Anyone Can Whistle; The Sign in Sidney Brustein's Window; Luv; Something Diff'rent; Fun City; The Prisoner of Second Avenue; Lamppost Reunion.

Films inc: Dead End; Angels With Dirty Faces; Crime School; Little Tough Guy; They Made Me A Criminal; Angels Wash Their Faces; Tough as They Come; Bowery Champs; Million Dollar Kid; Hard-Boiled Ma honey; Jinx Money; Fighting Fools; Blonde Dynamite; Triple Trouble; Who is Harry Kellerman; Framed; Earthquake.

TV inc: Broadway Open House; The Corner Bar; Risko.

DELL, Wanda: Prod. b. Miami, FL, 1941. Partner, co-founder TriStar Pictures Inc. Films inc: The Billion Dollar Hobo (asso prod); They Went That-A-Way and That-A-Way (asso prod); Prize Fighter (co-prod); The Private Eyes (co-prod).

DELON, Alain: Act. b. Paris, Nov 8, 1935. Films inc: Plein Soleil; The Eclipse; The Big Snatch; The Yellow Rolls Royce; The Love Cage; Once a Thief; Lost Command; Is Paris Burning; Texas Across the River; Histoires Extraordinaires; Diabolically Yours; Girl on a Motorcycle; Borsalino; The Sicilian Clan; Red Sun; The Assassination of Trotsky; Scorpio; Borsalino and Co; Shock; Mr Klein; Like A Boomerang; Le Gang; L'Homme Presse; Mort d'un Pourri; The Concorde-Airport '79; Le Toubib; Trois Hommes a Abattre (Three Men To Destroy).

DEL RIO, Dolores (nee Ansunsolo): Act. b. Durango, Mexico, Aug 3, 1905. Studied voice in Madrid, Paris. Screen debut in Joanna, 1925. Films inc: What Price Glory?; Resurrection; Ramona; Flying Down to Rio; Wonderbar; Madame DuBarry; Journey Into Fear; Portrait of Maria; The Fugitive; Cheyenne Autumn; The Children of Sanchez.

De LUISE, Dom: Act. b. NYC, Aug 1, 1933. Launched TV career as bumbling magician on Gary Moore Show. Films inc: Fail Safe; The Busybody; The Glass Bottom Boat; Who Is Harry Kellerman?; Every Little Crook and Nanny; The Adventures of Sherlock Holmes' Smarter Brother; The World's Greatest Lover; Silent Movie; The Cheap Detective; The End; Sextette; Hot Stuff (& dir); The Muppet Movie; The Last Married Couple in America; Fatso; Wholly Moses!; Smokey and the Bandit II.

TV inc: The Entertainers; The Dean Martin Summer Show; The Dom DeLuise Variety Show; Lotsa Luck; Ann-Margret-Hollywood Movie Girls.

DELVAUX, Andre: Dir. b. Belgium, 1926. Originally a teacher. Made docs before turning to features.

Film inc: The Man Who Had His Hair Cut Short; Un soir--Un Train; Rendezvous at Bray; Belle; Femme Entre Chien et Loup; To Woody Allen, From Europe With Love (& wri).

DEMAREST, William: Act. b. St Paul, MN, Feb 27, 1894. Films inc: When the Wife's Away; The Jazz Singer; The Gracie Allen Murder Case; Mr Smith Goes to Washington; The Farmer's Daughter; The Miracle of Morgan's Creek; Duffy's Tavern; Along Came Jones; The Jolson Story; When Willie Comes Marching Home; What Price Glory?; The Private War of Major Benson; Lucy Gallant; Pepe; Son of Flubber; It's a Mad, Mad, Mad, Mad World; That Darn Cat; The Wild McCullochs; Won Ton Ton, the Dog Who Saved Hollywood.

TV inc: Wells Fargo; Love and Marriage; My Three Sons; The Millionaire.

De MILLE, Agnes: Chor-Act. b. NYC, 1905. D of late William C DeMille. First appeared as a dancer in NY, 1927, in La Finta Giardiniera; danced in US, England, France, Denmark, 1928-41. Thea inc: The American Legend: Oklahoma!; One Touch of Venus; Bloomer Girl; Carousel; Brigadoon (*Tony*-1947); Allegro; Gentlemen Prefer Blondes (& dir); Paint Your Wagon; The Girl in Pink Tights; Goldilocks; Juno; Bitter Weird; Kwamina (*Tony*-1962); 110 in the Shade; The Wind in the Mountains; Carousel.

TV inc: Narrator for the TV programs of the Bolshoi Ballet; The Kennedy Center Honors, 1980.

DEMME, Jonathan: Wri-Dir. Films inc: Caged Heat; Crazy Mama (dir only); Fighting Mad; Citizens Band; Murder in Aspic; The Incredible Melting Man (act); Last Embrace; Melvin and Howard.

DEMY, Jacques: Dir. b. Pont-Chateau, France, 1931. Films inc: Lola; la Baie des Anges; The Umbrellas of Cherbourg (& sp); The Young Girls of Rochefort (& mus); The Model Shop; Donkey-Skin; The Pied Piper of Hamelin; The Most Important Event Since Man Walked on the Moon; Lady Oscar.

Songs inc: I Will Wait for You.

DENCH, Judi: Act. b. York, Eng, Dec 9, 1934. Thea inc: Hamlet; Twelfth Night; Henry V; Midsummer Night's Dream; Importance of Being Earnest; Romeo and Juliet; A Shot in the Dark; The Promise; Cabaret; The Merchant of Venice; Macbeth; King Lear; Juno and the Paycock.
Films inc: He Who Rides a Tiger; Study in Terror; The Third Secret; Dead Cert.
TV inc: Major Barbara; Pink String and Sealing Wax; Age of Kings; Neighbours; Emilie; A Village Wooing; On Giant's Shoulders.

DENEUVE, Catherine (nee Dorleac): Act. b. France, Oct 22, 1943. Films inc: The Doors Slam; Vice and Virtue; Satan Leads the Dance; Umbrellas of Cherbourg; Repulsion; Le Chant du Monde; La Vie de Chateau; Les Creatures; The Young Girls of Rochefort; Belle de Jour; Benjamin; Manon; Mayerling; The April Fools; The Mississippi Mermaid; Tristana; Hustle; La Grande Bourgeoise; Le Sauvage; March or Die; If It Were To Do Over Again; The Forbidden Room; L'argent des Autres (Other People's Money); Ils Sont Grand Ces Petits; Courage Fuyons; A Nous Deux; The Last Metro.

DENHAM, Reginald: Dir. b. London, Jan 10, 1894. Thea inc: Rope; Jew Suss; An Object of Virtue; Cold Blood; Jupiter Laughs; Ladies in Retirement; Play with Fire; The Devil Also Dreams; Dial M for Murder; Be Your Age; A Date with April; Sherlock Holmes; The Bad Seed; Hostile Witness; Minor Murder; Grass Widows; The Last Straw; Wallflower; The Man They Acquitted; Sweet Peril; A Dash of Bitters; Stars in My Hair.

De NIRO, Robert: Act. b. NYC, Aug 17, 1943. Films inc: The Wedding Party; Greetings; Hi, Mom; Bloody Mama; The Gang That Couldn't Shoot Straight; Bang the Drum Slowly; Mean Streets; The Last Tycoon; 1900; The Godfather, Part II (*Oscar*-supp-1974); Taxi Driver; New York, New York; The Deer Hunter; Raging Bull.

DENISON, Michael: Act. b. Eng, Nov 1, 1915. e. Oxford. Stage debut 1938, Charlie's Aunt. Thea inc: Ever Since Paradise: Let Them Eat Cake; Candida; Where Angels Fear to Tread; Hostile Witness; At The End of the Day; The Sack Race; The Black Mikado; The First Mrs Fraser; Robert and Elizabeth; The Cabinet Minister.
Films inc: Hungry Hill; The Blind Goddess; The Glass Mountain; Angels One Five; Tall Headlines; Importance of Being Earnest; The Truth About Women; Faces in the Dark.
TV inc: Funeral Games; Tale of Piccadilly; The Provincial Lady.

DENKER, Henry: Wri. b. NYC, Nov 25, 1912. e. NY Law School, LLB. Lawyer and tax consultant before turning to writing. Wrote, prod-dir radio series The Greatest Story Ever Told.
Plays inc: Time Limit; Venus at Large; A Case of Libel; What Did We Do Wrong?; Something Old, Something New; Horowitz and Mrs. Washington; The Name of the Game; A Sound of Distant Thunder; A Far Country.
Films inc: The Heartfarm; The Hook; Twilight of Honor; Time Limit.
TV inc: Give Us Barabbas; The Court Martial of Lt. Calley; Neither Are We Enemies; The Choice; A Time For Miracles.

DENNEHY, Brian: Act. b. Bridgeport, CT, Jul 9. e. Columbia U, BA. Thea inc: Shadow of a Gunman; Julius Caesar; Sez I, Sez He; Streamers (Bway).
Films inc: Looking for Mr Goodbar; Semi-Tough; Foul Play; F.I.S.T.; Butch and Sundance--The Early Days; 10; Little Miss Marker.
TV inc: A Real American Hero; Dummy; Silent Victory--The Kitty O'Neil Story; Pearl; Big Shamus, Little Shamus; The Seduction of Miss Leona.

DENNING, Richard: Act. b. Poughkeepsie, NY, 1914. Films inc: Hold 'Em Navy; Buccaneer; Illegal Traffic; Adam Had Four Sons; Glass Key; Black Beauty; The Fabulous Suzanne; Caged Fury; No Man of Her Own; Hangman's Knot; The Glass Web; Creature of the Black Lagoon; The Gun That Won the West; An Affair to Remember; Twice Told Tales.
TV inc: Mr and Mrs North; Flying Doctor; Hawaii Five-O; The Asphalt Cowboy.

DENNIS, Sandy: Act. b. Hastings, NE, Sep 27, 1937. Films inc: Splendor in the Grass; Who's Afraid of Virginia Woolf? (*Oscar*-supp-1966); Up the Down Staircase; The Fox; Sweet November; That Cold Day in the Park; A Touch of Love; The Out-of-Towners; The Only Way Out is Dead; Nasty Habits; God Told Me To.
Bway inc: A Thousand Clowns (*Tony*-supp-1963); Any Wednesday (*Tony*-1964); Absurd Person Singular.
TV inc: Perfect Gentlemen.

DENOFF, Sam: Wri-Prod. Partnered with Bill Persky for 21 years, originally writing nitery acts.
TV inc: Steve Allen Show; Andy Williams Show; Dick Van Dyke Show (& prod) (*Emmy*-wri-1964, 1966); Sid Caesar-Imogene Coca-Carl Reiner-Howard Morris Special (*Emmy*-1967); McHale's Navy; Dick Van Dyke and the Other Woman (& prod); The First Nine Months are the Hardest (crea-prod); Pure Goldie (& prod); Confessions of Dick Van Dyke (prod); The Funny Side (crea-exec prod); Don Rickles Show (crea-exec prod); Lotsa Luck (crea-exec prod); That Girl (crea-exec prod); Bill Cosby Special; The Man Who Came to Dinner.
Since splitting with Persky: Turnabout (exec prod); On Our Own (prod); Harper Valley PTA (exec prod).

DENVER, Bob: Act. b. New Rochelle, NY, 1935. Films inc: Take Her She's Mine; For Those Who Think Young; Who's Minding the Mint?; The Sweet Ride; Do You Know the One About the Travelling Saleslady?
TV inc: Dobie Gillis; Gilligan's Island; Dusty's Trail; The Castaways on Gilligan's Island.

DENVER, John (Henry John Deutchendorf): Singer-Act. b. Roswell, NM, Dec 31, 1943. Recording artist; concerts; niteries. Films inc: Oh, God! TV inc: An Evening with John Denver (*Emmy*-1975); Rocky Mountain Christmas; John Denver and the Muppets, A Christmas Get Together; The Higher We Fly (host).
Albums inc: Spirit; I Want to Live; A Christmas Together.

De PALMA, Brian: Dir. b. Newark, NJ, Sep 11, 1940. e. Columbia Coll, BA, Sarah Lawrence Coll, MA. Films inc: Murder a la Mod; Greetings; Hi Mom; Get to Know Your Rabbitt; Sisters; Phantom of the Paradise; Obsession; Carrie; The Fury; The Wedding Party; Home Movies (& prod); Dressed To Kill.

DEPARDIEU, Gerard: Act. b. Chateauroux, France, Dec 27, 1948. Films inc: Le Cormoran le soir au-dessus des Jonques; Le Tueur; L'Affaire Dominici; Un peu de Soleil dans l'eau froide; Au rendez-vous de la mort Joyeuse; La Scoumoune; Deux Hommes dans la Ville; 1900; The Wonderful Crook; Bye Bye Monkey; Sugar; The Last Woman; Get Out Your Handkerchiefs; L'Ingorgo; Cold Cuts; Mistress; My American Uncle; Les Chiens; The Last Metro; Inspector la Bavure (Inspector Blunder).

De PATIE, David H: Prod. b. LA, Dec 24, 1930. e. UC Berkeley, AB. Partner DePatie-Freleng Ent, 1963-80. Films inc: Pink Panther; Return to the Planet of the Apes. Shorts inc: The Pink Phink (*Oscar*-1964); Super President; Super Six; The Inspector; Roland & Rattfink; The Ant and the Aardvark; The Tijuana Toads; Here Comes the Grump; The Adventures of Dr. Dolittle; My World and Welcome To It; The Blue Racer; The Houndcats; The Barkleys; Bailey's Comets; Sheriff Hoot Kloot; The Oddball Couple; Baggy Pants & The Nitwits; What's New Mr. Magoo?
TV inc: My Mom's Having a Baby (*Emmy*-1974); Halloween Is Grinch Night (*Emmy*-1978); The Bear Who Slept Through Christmas; Pink Panther in Olympinks; Where Do Teen Agers Come From?; Dr Seuss' Pontoffel Pock Where Are You?

De PAUL, Gene: Comp-Arr-Pianist. b. NYC, Jun 17, 1919. Songs inc: Pig Foot Pete; I'll Remember April; Mister Five by Five; He's My Guy; Cow Cow Boogie; Irresistible You; Sobbin' Women; Namely You; Cornpone; Your Red Wagon; A Song Was Born; Teach Me Tonight; You Can't Run Away From It;
Film Scores inc: Seven Brides for Seven Brothers; You Can't Run Away From It.

DEREK, Bo (Mary Cathleen Collins): Act. b. Long Beach, CA, Nov 20, 1956. W of John Derek. Films inc: Once Upon A Time; Orca; 10; A Change of Seasons.

DEREK, John (Derek Harris): Act. b. Aug 12, 1926. Films inc: I'll Be Seeing You; Knock on Any Door; All the King's Men; Rogues of Sherwood Forest; Mask of the Avenger; Scandal Sheet; Mission Over Korea; Prince of Players; Run for Cover; The Ten Commandments; Omar Khayyam; Exodus; Nightmare in the Sun; Once Before I Die (& dir); Childish Things (& dir).

DERN, Bruce: Act. b. Chicago, Jun 4, 1936. e. U of PA. On screen from 1960, Wild River. Films inc: Marnie; Hush, Hush Sweet Charlotte; The Wild Angels; The St. Valentine's Day Massacre; Waterhole #3; Psyche-Out; The War Wagon; Will Penny; Castle Keep; They Shoot Horses, Don't They?; Bloody Mama; The Incredible Two-Headed Transplant; Drive, He Said; Suport Your Local Sheriff; The Cowboys; Silent Running; King of Marvin Gardens; The Laughing Policeman; The Great Gatsby; Posse; Smile; Family Plot; Won Ton Ton, the Dog Who Saved Hollywood; The Twist (Folies Bourgeoises); Black Sunday; Coming Home; Driver; Middle Age Crazy.

Bway inc: Strangers.

DESCHANEL, Caleb: Cin. b. Philadelphia, PA, Sep 21, 1944. e. Johns Hopkins U; USC. Films inc: The Black Stallion; More American Graffiti; Being There.

DESNY, Ivan: Act. b. 1922. Films inc: Madeleine; The Respectful Prostitute; Lola Montes; The Mirror Has Two Faces; The Magnificent Rebel; I Killed Rasputin; Mayerling; Adventures of Gerard; Paper Tiger; The Conquest of the Citadel; Fifty-Fifty; Sidney Sheldon's Bloodline; The Marriage of Maria Braun; Berlin Alexanderplatz; Fabian.

De TOTH, Andre (Andreas Toth): Dir. b. Mako, Hungary, 1913. Worked for Alexander Korda as edtr, asst dir, in Eng. In 1943, dir in Hollywood. Films inc: Passport to Suez; None Shall Escape; Since You Went Away; Pitfall; Springfield Rifle; The Gunfighter (co-sp); House of Wax; Bounty Hunter; Monkey on My Back; Two-Headed Spy; Man on a String; The Mongols; Gold for the Caesars; Billion Dollar Brain; Play Dirty; El Condor; The Dangerous Game; Omar Mukhtar-Lion of the Desert.

DEUBEL, Robert E: Dir-Prod. b. Cleveland, Oct 12, 1933. e. Cleveland Inst of Art, Western Reserve U. TV inc: Norman Rockwell's World-. . . An American Dream; The American Woman; Portraits of Courage.

DEUTSCH, Adolph: Comp-Cond-Arr. b. London, Oct 20, 1897. e. Royal Academy of Music. Film scores inc: The Maltese Falcon; High Sierra; The Mask of Dimitrios; Father of the Bride; Some Like It Hot; The Apartment; Annie Get Your Gun (*Oscar*-1950); Show Boat; The Band Wagon; Seven Brides for Seven Brothers (*Oscar*-1954); Oklahoma (*Oscar*-1955).

(Died Jan 1, 1980).

DEUTSCH, Armand: Prod. b. Chicago, IL, Jan 25, 1913. e. U Chicago, BA. Films inc: Ambush; Right Cross; Magnificent Yankee; Three Guys Named Mike; Kind Lady; Girl in White; Carbine Williams; The Girl Who Had Everything; Slander.

DEUTSCH, Helen: Wri. b. NYC, Mar 21, 1912. e. Barnard Coll, BA. Films inc: Seventh Cross; Golden Earrings; National Velvet; King Solomon's Mines; Kim; Plymouth Adventure; Lili; I'll Cry Tomorrow; The Unsinkable Molly Brown; Valley of the Dolls.

TV inc: Jack & the Beanstalk; GM's 50th Anniversary Show; Hallmark Christmas Show.

Plays inc; Love on an Island; Carnival.

DEUTSCH, Stephen: Prod. b. LA, Jun 30, 1946. e. UCLA, BA; Loyola Law School. S of the late S Sylvan Simon. Stepson of Armand Deutsch. Was adm asst John Tunney's senatorial campaign 1968-70; in private law practice until joined Rastar 1976 as asst to Ray Stark; 1977, sr vp Rastar Films; resd 1978 to enter indie prodn. Films inc: Somewhere In Time.

DEVANE, William: Act. b. Albany, NY, Sep 5, 1939. e. AADA. Appeared in Othello, Coriolanus, Hamlet during NY Shakespeare Festival. b. Aug 30, 1917. Bway inc: G. R. Point (dir).

Films inc: Lady Liberty; Report to the Commissioner; McCabe and Mrs. Miller; Family Plot; Marathon Man; Bad News Bears in Breaking Training; Rolling Thunder; The Dark; Yanks.

TV inc: Missiles of October; Fear on Trial; From Here to Eternity; From Here to Eternity-The War Years.

DEVILLE, Michel: Dir. b. Boulogne-sur-Seine, France, Apr 13, 1931. Films inc: Une Balle Dans le Canon; Ce Soir ou Jamais; L'Apartment de Filles; Tricky Jo; Benjamin; Bye Bye Barbara; The Bear and the Doll; La Femme en Bleu; Love at the Top; L'Apprenti Salaud; Dossier 51; Travels on the Sly.

De VITO, Danny: Act. b. Neptune, NJ, Nov 17, 1944. Films inc: One Flew Over the Cuckoo's Nest; The Van; The World's Greatest Lover; Goin' South.

TV inc: Taxi; Like Father, Like Daughter; Valentine; Ann-Margret-Hollywood Movie Girls.

De VOL, Frank: Comp-Cond-Arr. b. Moundsville, WV, Sep 20, 1911. e. Miami U. Film scores inc: The Big Knife; Good Neighbor Sam; Send Me No Flowers; Pillow Talk; Cat Ballou; Hush, Hush, Sweet Charlotte; The Flight of the Phoenix; Guess Who's Coming to Dinner; The Glass Bottom Boat; The Choirboys; Herbie Goes to Monte Carlo; The Frisco Kid (& act); Herbie Goes Bananas. (Act): Boys Night Out; Parent Trap; WC Fields and Me.

TV inc: Family Affair; GE Theatre; The Colgate Hour; The George Gobel Show; My Three Sons; The Brady Bunch; The Ghosts of Buxley Hall.

DEVON, Richard: Act. b. Glendale, CA, Dec 11, 1931. Films inc: The Prodigal; The Undead; Viking Women; Gunfighters of Abilene; Machine Gun Kelly; 3:10 to Yuma; The Bandlanders; The Comancheros; Kid Galahad; Cattle King; The Silencers; Magnum Force.

Thea inc: It Pays to Advertise; A Light From Saint Agnes; Maisie; The Same Old Thing.

De VORZON, Barry: Comp. b. NYC, Jul 31, 1934. e. Pasadena City College. Films inc: Dillinger; Bless the Beasts and Children; The Warriors; The Ninth Configuration; Xanadu.

TV inc: The Young and the Restless; S.W.A.T.; Stunts Unlimited; The Comeback Kid; Reward.

Songs inc: Nadia's Theme (*Grammy*-inst arr-1977); Treasure of Your Love; Dreamin'; Hey Little One; I Wonder What She's Doin' Tonight; Bless the Beasts and Children; Theme from S.W.A.T.; In the City.

DEWAERE, Patrick: Act. b. Saint-Brieuc, France, 1947. Member of a theatrical family, worked with the experimental French Group, Cafe de la Gare.

Films inc: Going Places; The Best Way; F as in Fairbanks; Victory March; Catherine and Co; Le Sheriff; Bishop's Bedroom; La Cle sur la Porte; Coupe de tete; Get Out Your Hankerchiefs; Serie Noire; L'Ingorgo; Paco the Infallible; Un Mauvais Fils (A Bad Son).

DEWELL, Michael: Prod. b. Woodbridge, CT, 1931. e. Yale, BA, RADA. Thea inc: Elizabeth the Queen; Mary Stuart; Hedda Gabler; Liliom; The Crucible; The Seagull; Ring Round the Moon; Madwoman of Chaillot; The Trojan Women; The Imaginary Invalid; As You Like It; Macbeth; The Comedy of Errors.

TV inc: Mary Stuart; Inaugural Night at Ford's.

DEWHURST, Colleen: Act. b. Montreal, Jun 3, 1926. Bway inc: Desire Under the Elms (rev); The Ballad of the Sad Cafe; Hello and Goodbye; The Good Woman of Setzuan; All the Way Home *(Tony-supp-1961)*; The Big Coca Cola Swamp in the Sky; Mourning Becomes Electra; A Moon for the Misbegotten *(Tony-1973)*; Who's Afraid of Virginia Woolf?

Films inc: The Nun's Story; McQ; Annie Hall; Ice Castles; When a Stranger Calls; Arthur Miller on Home Ground; Final Assignment; Tribute.

TV inc: No Exit; Antony and Cleopatra; Medea; Focus; Silent Victory-The Kitty O'Neil Story; Studs Lonigan; And Baby Makes Six; Mary and Joseph-A Story of Faith; Death Penalty; Escape; Guyana Tragedy-The Jim Jones Story; The Women's Room; A Perfect Match; Baby Comes Home.

De WITT, Joyce: Act. b. Wheeling WV, Apr 23, 1949. e. Ball State U, BA. TV inc: The Osmond Family Hour; Susan Anton Show; With This Ring; Three's Company; John Ritter, Being of Sound Mind and Body.

DEXTER, Alan (nee Dreeben): Act. b. Seychelles Island, Africa, Oct 21, 1925. e. Hammadryad U, Zanzibar. Films inc: It Came from Outer Space; Time Limit; The Enemy Below; Paint Your Wagon; Kiss Me Stupid; Gable and Lombard.

TV inc: Helter Skelter.

Thea inc: Call Me Mister; The G.I. Hamlet; The Music Man.

DEXTER, John: Dir. b. Eng, 1935. Thea inc: Each in His Own Wilderness; Chicken Soup with Barley; Toys in the Attic; The Sponge Room; Saint Joan; Hobson's Choice; Othello; A Woman Killed with Kindness; The Misanthrope; Equus *(Tony-1975)*; The Party; Phaedra Britannica; Black Comedy and White Lies; The Unknown Soldier and His Wife; In Praise of Love; The Merchant. Films inc: The Virgin Soldiers; Sidelong Glances of a Pigeon Kicker; I Want What I Want.

De YOUNG, Cliff: Act. b. Inglewood, CA, Feb 12. e. CA State Coll, BA, IL State U. Films inc: Sunshine; A Perfect Couple. TV inc: Sticks and Bones; Centennial; The Seeding of Sarah Burns; Hunter's Moon; King; Fun and Games; Scared Straight.

Thea inc: Hair.

DIAMOND, David: Prod. b. NYC, Feb 2, 1900. Films inc: Damaged Lives; Mussolini Speaks; The Modern Marriage; I Was an American Spy; A Bullet for Joey; The Phoenix City Story; Operation Eichmann; King of the Roaring Twenties; The Strangler.

(Died Nov 9, 1979).

DIAMOND, I A L: Wri. b. Unghani, Rumania, Jun 27, 1920. e. Columbia U, BA. Films inc: Murder in the Blue Room; Never Say Goodbye; Love and Learn; Always Together; The Girl from Jones Beach; Monkey Business; Something for the Birds; That Certain Feeling; Love in the Afternoon; Merry Andrew; Some Like It Hot; The Apartment *(Oscar-1960)*; One, Two, Three; Irma la Douce; Kiss Me, Stupid; The Fortune Cookie; Cactus Flower; The Private Life of Sherlock Holmes; The Front Page; Avanti; Fedora (& prod).

DIAMOND, Neil: Singer-Sngwri. b. Brooklyn, NY, Jan 24, 1941. Recording artist; concerts.

Films inc; Jonathan Livingston Seagull (mus) *(Grammy-score-1973)*; Every Which Way But Loose (mus); The Last Waltz (act); The Jazz Singer (act & mus).

Bway inc: Dancin'.

Songs inc: Kentucky Woman; Sweet Caroline; I'm A Believer; Cherry, Cherry, Cherry: Solitary Man; You'll Be a Woman Now; Song Sung Blue; Play Me; Walk on Water.

Albums inc: Beautiful Noise; Love At the Greek; I'm Glad You're Here Tonight; You Don't Bring Me Flowers; September Morn.

DICKINSON, Angie: Act. b. Kulm, ND, Sep 30, 1936. Films inc: Sins of Rachel Cade; Rio Bravo; Oceans 11; The Killers; Point Blank; The Outside Man; Klondike Fever; Dressed To Kill.

TV inc: Police Woman; Overboard; Pearl; The Suicide's Wife; Alan King's Thanksgiving Special--What Do We Have To Be Thankful For.

DICKINSON, Thorold: Dir. b. Bristol, England, 1903. Films inc: The High Command; Spanish ABC; The Arsenal Stadium Mystery; Gaslight; The Prime Minister; Next of Kin; Men of Two Worlds; The Queen of Spades; Secret People; Hill 24 Doesn't Answer.

Ret. 1956 to teach film at Slade School, London.

DIDION, Joan: Wri. b. Sacramento, CA, Dec 5, 1934. e. UC Berkeley. Winner of Vogue mag contest for young writers, began with mag writing promotional copy; later asso feature ed; film reviewer. Films inc: (in collab with husband John Gregory Dunne) Panic in Needle Park; Play It As It Lays (from her novel); A Star Is born (Remake).

DIEHL, Walter: Union Exec. b. Revere, MA, Apr 13, 1907. e. Northeastern U. Started as proj 1927; 1946; bus agt Local 182 1953 Int'l Rep IATSE; 1957 Int'l asst p; 1974, IATSE p; *(Tony-special-1979)*.

DIENER, Joan: Act. b. Cleveland, OH, Feb 24. e. Sarah Lawrence Coll. NY stage debut, 1948, Small Wonder. Bway inc: Season in the Sun; Kiss Me Kate; Kismet; Ziegfeld Follies; At the Grand; Destry Rides Again; La Belle; Man of La Mancha; Cry for us All; Odyssey; Home Sweet Homer.

TV inc: Androcles and the Lion.

DIERKOP, Charles: Act. b. LaCrosse, WI, Sep 11, 1936. Films inc: Butch Cassidy and the Sundance Kid; Pound; The Pawnbroker; The Sting. TV inc: Police Woman; The Deerslayer.

DIETRICH, Dena: Act. Bway inc: The Prisoner of Second Avenue; Here's Where I Belong; The Freaking out of Stephanie Blake; Cindy; The Rimers of Eldritch.

TV inc: Adam's Rib; Karen; Friends and Lovers; The Practice; Trouble With People; Turnabout; Baby Comes Home.

Films inc: The Wild Party; Crazy World of Julius Vrooder; North Avenue Irregulars; Captain Midnight.

DIETRICH, Marlene (Maria Magdalene von Losch): Act. b. Berlin, Dec 27, 1904. Attended Max Reinhardt's School of Drama. Debut in Viennese version of play, Broadway. Films inc: (in Germany) Blue Angel. (In Hollywood): Morocco; Blonde Venus; Desire; Destry Rides Again; Manpower; Pittsburgh; The Spoilers; Golden Earrings; Witness for the Prosecution; Judgment at Nuremberg; Just A Gigolo.

(Special Tony 1968).

DIETZ, Howard M: Lyr-Wri. b. NYC, Sep 8, 1896. H of Lucinda Ballard. Publicist, became Dir Pub MGM 1924, remained that position until 1957. Named VP Loew's Inc, 1957. Began writing for Broadway 1924, Dear Sir, in collab with Jerome Kern.

Shows inc: Poppy; Ziegfeld Follies; Merry-Go-Round; Keep Off the Grass; Inside USA; The Gay Life; Jennie; Three's A Crowd; The Band Wagon; Flying Colors; Revenge With Music; At Home Abroad.

Films inc: The Band Wagon, That's Entertainment; That's Entertainment II.

Opera inc: English versions of Die Fledermaus; La Boheme.

Songs inc: Moanin' Low; I Guess I'll Have To Change My Plans; I Love Louisa; Dancing in the Dark; A Shine On Your Shoes; You and The Night and the Music; That's Entertainment.

DIFFRING, Anton: Act. b. Koblenz, Germany, Oct 20, 1918. e. Berlin Acad of Drama. Films inc: State Secret; Albert RN; The Sea Shall Not Have Them; The Colditz Story; I Am a Camera; The Man Who Could Cheat Death; Circus of Horrors; The Heroes of Telemark; Fahrenheit 451; Counterpoint; Where Eagles Dare; Zeppelin; Operation Daybreak; Valentino; The Accuser; The Swiss Conspiracy; Tusk.

TV inc: The Last Hours; A Small Revolution; The Fourposter; The Million Pound Note; A Place in the Sun.

DIGHTON, John: Wri. b. London, Dec 8, 1909. e. Cambridge. Films inc: Champagne Charlie; Nicholas Nickleby; Saraband for Dead Lovers; Kind Hearts & Coronets; The Happiest Days of Your Life; The Man in the White Suit; Who Goes There!; Roman Holiday; The Swan; The Devil's Disiciple.

DILLER, Barry: Exec. b. Feb 2, 1942. Joined ABC 1966. In 1968, made exec asst to vp in chg pgmng and dir of feature films; 1971, made vp feature films and Circle Entertainment, responsible for, The Tuesday Movie of the Week, The Wednesday Movie of the Week and Circle Film original features for airing on ABC-TV; also acquired and scheduled theatrical features for TV on ABC Sunday Night Movie and ABC Monday Night Movie. In 1974 joined Par Pictures, ChmnB and CEO.

DILLER, Phyllis: Act. b. Lima, OH, Jul 17, 1917. On stage for 1st time at age 37, stand-up comedienne, San Francisco's Purple Onion. Bway inc: Hello, Dolly. Films inc: Boy, Did I Get a Wrong Number!; Eight on the Lam; Did You Hear the One About the Traveling Saleslady?; The Private Navy of Sgt. O'Farrell; The Adding Machine.
    TV inc: The Phyliss Diller Show; The Beautiful Phyllis Diller Show; The Monte Carlo Show.

DILLMAN, Bradford: Act. b. San Francisco, Apr 14, 1930. e. Yale. Films inc: A Certain Smile; In Love and War; Compulsion; Francis of Assisi; A Rage to Live; Jigsaw; Escape from the Planet of the Apes; The Iceman Cometh; The Enforcer; The Lincoln Conspiracy; The Amsterdan Kill; Piranha; The Swarm; Love & Bullets; Guyana-Cult of the Damned.
    TV inc: Last Bride of Salem (Emmy-1975); Jennifer-A Woman's Story; Before and After; The Memory of Eva Ryker; Tourist.

DILLON, Matt: Act. b. Westchester, NY, Feb 18, 1964. Films inc: Over The Edge; Little Darlings; My Bodyguard.

DILLON, Melinda: Act. b. Hope, AR. Films inc: Bound for Glory; Slap Shot; Close Encounters of the Third Kind; F.I.S.T. Thea inc: Who's Afraid of Virginia Woolf?; You Know I Can't Hear You When the Water's Running; A Way of Life.
    TV inc: The Critical List; Transplant; Marriage Is Alive and Well; The Shadow Box.

DIMMOCK, Peter: Exec. b. England, Dec 6, 1920. e. Dulwich Coll. Prod and Commentator BBC-TV. Head of BBC Outside Broadcasts, 1954-72; Head of BBC Enterprises, 1973; joined ABC Sports as an exec, 1977.

DIRE STRAITS: Group. Members are Mark Knopfler, guitar; David Knopfler, guitar; John Illsley, bass; Pick Withers, drums.
    Albums inc: Dire Straits; Communique.

DISHY, Bob: Act. Bway inc: Chic; From A to Z; Second City; Flora, The Red Menace; By Jupiter; Something Different; The Goodbye People; A Way of Life; The Creation of the World and Other Business; An American Millionaire; The Good Doctor; Murder at Howard Johnsons; Sly Fox.
    Films inc: Lovers and Other Strangers; The Big Bus; The Last Married Couple in America; First Family.

DIXON, Ivan: Act-Dir. b. NYC, Apr 6, 1931. e. Western Reserve U. Began as extra in Edge of the City. Films inc: Car Wash (act); Trouble Man (dir); The Spook Who Sat By The Door (dir).
    TV inc: Studio One.

DIZON, Jesse: Act. b. Oceanside, CA, Jun 16, 1950. e. UC Santa Barbara. Films inc: Cambodian; Prisoners; Midway; MacArthur.
    TV inc: Lady of the House; Critical List; Operation Petticoat; Gold Watch; Dinky Hocker; Court Martial of General Yamashita.

DMYTRYK, Edward: Dir. b. Grand Forks, B C, Can, Sep 4, 1908. Films inc: The Hawk; The Devil Commands; Seven Miles from Alcatraz; Hitler's Children; Murder My Sweet; Till the End of Time; Crossfire; Obsession; (career interrupted when, as one of so-called Unfriendly 10, went to prison for contempt of Congress for refusal to testify before House Un-American Activities Committee; after serving term he testified and resumed career). The Sniper; Eight Iron Men; The Juggler; The Caine Mutiny; Broken Lance; The Young Lions; Warlock; The Blue Angel; A Walk on the Wild Side; The Carpetbaggers; Where Love Has Gone; Mirage; Alvarez Kelly; Anzio; Shalako; Bluebeard; Hollywood on Trial (act) (Doc).

DOBSON, Kevin: Act. b. NYC, Mar 18, 1944. Films inc: Love Story; Bananas; Klute; The Anderson Tapes; The French Connection; Carnal Knowledge; Midway.
    TV inc: The Nurses; The Doctors; Kojack; Stranded; Greatest Heroes of the Bible; The Immigrants; Transplant; Orphan Train; Hardhat and Legs; Reunion; Mark, I Love You.

DOBSON, Tamara: Act. b. Baltimore, MD, May 14. e. MD Inst of Art, BA. Films inc: Fuzz; Cleopatra Jones; Cleopatra Jones and the Casino of Gold; Norman, Is That You?
    TV inc: Murder at the World Series; Jason of Star Command.

DOCKRY, Nancy: Exec. b. Niagara Falls, NY, Mar 24. e. Syracuse U, BS chem eng; Columbia, PhD, Math. Started as wri on soaps; joined ABC 1960 in corporate training program; 1962 dir pgm dept Dancer-Fitzgerald-Sample; 1964 media dir Procter and Gamble; 1967, account exec Procter & Gamble; 1969 account supv Procter & Gamble; 1970 vp-adv American Home Products; 1975 vp, sr agent William Morris NY office; 1976 moved to Coast office; 1978 vp for pgm devlpt & prodn Nephi Productions; 1979, vp Universal TV; 1980 vp of network tv for Time-Life TV.

DR HOOK: Group. Members are Ray Sawyer, lead voc-guitar-percussions; Dennis Locorriere, lead voc-guitar; Bill Francis, keyboards-voc; Rik Elswit, guitar-voc; Jance Garfat, bass-voc; John Wolters, drums-voc; Bob "Willard" Henke, guitar-voc.
    Albums inc: Bankrupt; A Little Bit More; Makin' Love and Music; Pleasure and Pain.

DR SEUSS: (See GEISEL, Ted).

DODERER, Joop: Act. b. Velsen, Holland, Aug 28, 1921. Early career with Amsterdam City Theatre interrupted by WW2; resumed stage career; in 1958 began children's TV series Swiebertga which ran 17 years becoming most popular tv show in Holland before he decided to end it; continued local theatre career while on TV.
    TV inc: Mother Makes Five (Britain); Wuthering Heights; Professor Stranger.
    Films inc: The Human Factor.

DOLIN, Anton: (Sydney Patrick Healey-Kay): Dancer-Chor. b. Sussex, England, 1904. First English dancer in 20th century to achieve world recognition. Joined Diaghilev's Ballet Russe as soloist, 1924-25, again in 1928-29, Train Bleu created for him; 1934, Principal dancer with Old Vic Sadlers Wells ballet, dancing Giselle with Markova; 1935 formed Markova-Dolin Company; 1939 joined American Ballet Theatre; during WW2 toured extensively again with Markova; 1949 formed group which became London Festival Ballet; 1962-64, dir Rome Opera Ballet; art advisor Les Grands Ballets Canadiens.

DOMERGUE, Faith: Act. b. New Orleans, Jun 16, 1925. Films inc: Vendetta; Where Danger Lives; This Island Earth; California; One on Top of the Other; Legacy of Blood; The House of the Seven Corpses.

DOMINO, Fats (Antoine Domino): Pianist-Singer-Sngwri. b. New Orleans, Feb 26, 1928. Albums inc: Here Comes Fats Domino; Fats On Fire; Getaway With Fats Domino; Stompin' Fats Domino; Trouble in Mind; Fats Is Back.

DONAHUE, Phil: TV pers. b. Cleveland, OH, Dec 21, 1935. e. Notre Dame, BBA. H of Marlo Thomas. Began working as anncr at KYW-TV & AM, Cleveland, news dir WABJ, Adrian, MI, moved to WHIO-TV & AM, Dayton, to do morning newscasts; interviews with Teamster Boss Jimmy Hoffa and Billy Sol Estes were picked up nationally by CBS; became host of Conversation Piece, phone-in talk show; debuted the Phil Donahue Show Nov 6, 1967 on WLWD-TV, Dayton; show syndicated two years later; moved to Chicago 1974 where program, now called Donahue, rated as reaching more households than any other syndicated talk show (Emmy-1978, 1979, 1980); does tri-weekly segments for Today Show.

DONAHUE, Troy (Merle Johnson, Jr): Act. b. NYC, Jan 17, 1937. Summer stock, Bucks County Playhouse, Sayville Playhouse. Films inc: A Summer Place; The Crowded Sky; Rome Adventure; A Distant Trumpet; Sweet Savior; Godfather, Part II.
TV inc: Surfside 6; Hawaiian Eye; CHiPS.

DONALDSON, Roger: Dir-Prod. b. Ballarat, Australia, Nov 15, 1945. Films inc: The Adventure World of Sir Edmund Hillary; Winners & Losers; Sleeping Dogs.

DONAT, Peter: Act. b. Kentville, Nova Scotia, Jan 20. Films inc: Russian Roulette; The Godfather II; The Hindenburg; A Different Story; F I S T; The China Syndrome; City on Fire.
TV inc: Cyrano de Bergerac; The Missiles of October; The Suicide's Wife; Fun and Games.
Thea inc: The Chinese Prime Minister; A Touch of Spring.

DONATI, Danilo: Cos dsgn. b. Luzzara, Italy. dsgn for Luchino Visconti stage prodns, Italy; supervising art dir RAI, Italian tv net. Films inc: La Mandragola; The Gospel According to St. Matthew; The Taming of the Shrew; Romeo and Juliet (Oscar-1968); Oedipus Rex; Medea; The Clowns; Decameron; Fellini's Satyricon; Brother Sun, Sister Moon; Fellini's Amarcord; Fellini's Casanova (Oscar-1976); Hurricane; Flash Gordon.

DONEN, Stanley: Prod-Dir. b. Columbia, SC, Apr 13, 1924. On Broadway as dancer in Pal Joey; Best Foot Forward; Beat The Band. (Dance dir) Cover Girl; Anchors Aweigh. Films inc: (dir) Kiss Them For Me; Seven Brides For Seven Brothers; Funny Face; On The Town; Damn Yankees; Indiscreet (& co-prod). (Prod-dir) Once More, With Feeling; Surprise Package; Arabesque; Staircase; Two for the Road; Bedazzled; The Little Prince; Lucky Lady; Movie, Movie; Saturn 3.

DONFELD (Donald Lee Feld): Cos dsgn. b. LA, Jul 3, 1934. e. Chouinard Art Institute; LA Trade Tech Jr Coll. Films inc: Hemingway's Adventures of a Young Man; The Second Time Around; Under the Yum Yum Tree; Hombre; The Chase; The Outrage; The Cincinnati Kid; Days of Wine and Roses; The Great Race; The April Fools; They Shoot Horses, Don't They?; Fun With Dick and Jane; Who'll Stop The Rain (Tuesday Weld cos only); Le Magnifique; Diamonds Are Forever; One on One; Who Is Killing the Great Chefs of Europe?; The China Syndrome.
TV inc: The Pirate; Wonder Woman; Herb Alpert and the Tijuana Brass Specials; Dinah Shore in Las Vegas.

DONIGER, Walter: Dir-Wri-Prod. b. NYC, 1917. e. Duke U, Harvard Grad School of Business. Films inc: Rope of Sand (sp); Duffy of San Quentin (prod-dir-sp); Along the Great Divide (sp); The Steel Cage (prod-dir-sp); Safe at Home Cease Fire (sp); The Steel Jungle (dir-sp); Unwed Mother (dir); Tokyo Joe (adapt); Alaska Seas (sp); Hold Back the Night (sp); Guns of Fort Petticoat (sp).
TV inc: Peyton Place; The Survivors (exec prod); Jigsaw; The Bold Ones; Bracken's World; Maverick; The Man Who Never Was; Checkmate; Bat Masterson; Men Into Space; MacKenzie's Raiders; 77 Sunset Strip; Bourbon Street; Cheyenne; Movin' On; Switch; McCloud; Delvecchio; Roots (sp).

DONLAN, Yolande: Act. b. Jersey City, NJ, Jun 2, 1920. Thea inc: School for Brides; Kiss and Tell; Three's a Family; Born Yesterday.
Films inc: Turnabout; Miss Pilgrim's Progress; Mr Drake's Duck; Penny Princess; They Can't Hang Me; Expresso Bongo; Jigsaw; Eighty Thousand Suspects; Seven Nights in Japan.

DONLEAVY, J P (James Patrick Donleavy): Wri. b. NYC, Apr 23, 1926. e. Trinity Coll. Plays inc: Fairy Tales of New York; What They Did in Dublin with the Ginger Man; A Singular Man; The Onion Eaters; The Plays of J P Donleavy. Novels inc: The Ginger Man.

DONNELL, Jeff: Act. b. S Windham, ME, Jul 10, 1921. Films inc: A Night to Remember; He's My Guy; In a Lonely Place; Sweet Smell of Success; Gidget Goes Hawaiian; The Iron Maiden; Stand Up and Be Counted.
TV inc: Portrait of a Stripper.

DONNELLY, Donal: Act. b. Bradford, Yorks, Eng, Jul 6, 1931. Thea inc: Serjeant Musgrave's Dance; The Playboy of the Western World; The Scatterin'; Red Roses for Me; Philadelphia, Here I Come; The Mundy Scheme (dir); Sleuth; My Astonishing Self; Faith Healer (Bway).
Films inc: Shake Hands With The Devil; The Knack; The Mind of Mr Soames; Waterloo.
TV inc: Juno and the Paycock; The Plough and the Stars; Yes Honestly; The Statesman-Benjamin Franklin.

DONNELLY, Ralph E: Exec. b. Lynbrook, NY, Jan 20, 1932. Started at Variety 1949; 1951 to Long Island Press; gm, Associated Independent Theatres, 1953-65; film buyer, AIT, 1965-73; Independent film buyer, 1973-76; head film buyer, RKO Stanley Warner, 1976-79; dir of ops & film buying, Cinema Five, 1979.

DONNELLY, Ruth: Act. b. Trenton, NJ, May 17, 1896. Films inc: Rubber Heels; The Spider; Make Me A Star; Hard to Handle; 42d Street; Goodbye Again; Hands Across the Table; Mr Deeds Goes to Town; Cain and Mabel; Portia on Trial; Holiday; Affairs of Annabel; A Slight Case of Murder; Mr Smith Goes to Washington; Model Wife; Bells of St Mary's; Little Miss Broadway; Fighting Father Dunne; The Snake Pit; Where the Sidewalk Ends; The Secret of Convict Lake; Autumn Leaves.

DONNENFELD, Bernard: Exec. b. NYC, Oct 28, 1926. e. NYU, NYU School of Law, LLB. Supv corp affairs, Legal Dept Par Pictures, 1957-61; exec asst, asst secy Par Hollywood studio, 1961-64; asst to p 1964-65; vp, World Wide prod & admin 1965-69; p, The Filmmakers group, 1970.

DONNER, Clive: Dir. b. London, 1926. Films inc: The Secret Place; Heart of a Child; A Marriage of Convenience; Here We Go Round the Mulberry Bush; Alfred the Great; Vampire; The Nude Bomb.
TV inc: Danger Man; Sir Francis Drake; Mighty and Mystical; British Institutions; Tempo; Rogue Male; The Thief of Baghdad; She Fell Among Thieves. Thea inc: Kennedy's Children.

DONNER, Jorn: Wri-Dir. b. Helsinki, Feb 5, 1933. e. Helsinki U. Dir at Swedish Film Institute, 1972-75; then prod of feature films; dir, prod Jorn Donner Prodns. Films inc: (in Sweden & Finland) A Sunday in September; To Love; Rooftree; Black and White (& prod); Portraits of Women (& prod); Three Scenes with Ingmar Bergman (& prod); The Bergman File (& prod); Home and Refuge; Black Sun (A Necessary Action).

DONNER, Richard: Dir. Films inc: X-15; Salt and Pepper; Twink; The Omen; Superman; Inside Moves.

DONSKOY, Mark: Dir. b. Odessa, Russia, Mar 6, 1901. A published poet at age 14, studied medicine, then law; turned to film at age 25; worked as extra, editing asst, directed Life (short) then feature In the Big City (& sp); spent six years at Leningrad Studios learning all phases of film.
Films inc: The Song of Happiness; The Gorky Trilogy (Gorky's Childhood; My Apprenticeship; My Universities); Romantiki; The Rainbow; The High Cost; How the Steel Was Tempered; Mother (& co-sp); Hello, Children; A Mother's Heart; A Mother's Loyalty; Nadezhda.

DOOBIE BROTHERS: Seven-member band. Members are: Patrick Simmons, vocals and guitar; Michael McDonald, keyboards; Tiran Porter, bass; Keith Knudsen, drums; Cornelius Bumpus, keyboards, sax; John McFee, guitars and strings; Chet McCracken, drums and vibes. All except McCracken double on vocals.
Films inc: No Nukes.
Albums inc: Best of the Doobies; Takin' It To the Streets; Minute By Minute; One Step Closer. (Grammys-(2) record of year & pop vocal-1979).

DOOHAN, James Montgomery: Act. b. Vancouver, BC, Mar 3, 1920. Films inc: The Wheeler Dealers; The Satan Bug; Bus Riley's Back in Town; Pretty Maids All in a Row; Star Trek-the Movie.
TV inc: Star Trek.

DORAN, Ann: Act. b. Amarillo, TX, Jul 28, 1911. On screen from 1934 in numerous two-reelers with Three Stooges, Harry Langdon, Andy Clyde; Films inc: Zoo in Budapest; Way Down East; Penny Serenade; Air Force; I Love a Soldier; Pride of the Marines; Roughly Speaking; The Strange Love of Martha Ivers; Magic Town; No Sad Songs for Me; The High and the Mighty; Rebel Without a Cause; The Female Animal; Where Love Has Gone; Topaz; There Was a Crooked Man; The Hired Hand.

TV inc: National Velvet; Jesse James; Hey, Landlord; Longstreet; How the West Was Won; Peter Lundy and the Medicine Hat Stallion; Little Mo; Greatest Heroes of the Bible; Backstairs at the White House; Shirley.

DORATI, Antal: Comp-Cond. b. Budapest, 1906. e. Budapest Academy of Music, becoming at 18 youngest person ever to receive degree. On graduation appointed coach, later cond of Budapest Royal Opera House; 1928-33 permanent First Cond Munster Opera House; 1934-41 mus dir Ballet Russe de Monte Carlo; US debut as cond with National Symphony Orch, Washington, 1937; 1941-42 dir NY Opera Co; 1942-45 Mus Dir American Ballet Theatre; org Dallas Symphony Orch 1945. Remained as mus dir until 1949 when he was named mus dir Minneapolis Symphony; 1963-1967 Chief Cond BBC Symphony; 1967-74 Chief Cond Stockholm Symphony; since Sep 1977 Mus Dir Detroit Symphony; made more than 500 recordings.

DORS, Diana (nee Fluck): Act. b. Swindon, Eng, Oct 23, 1931. e. London Academy of Music and Dramatic Art. Films inc: Lady Godiva Rides Again; The Weak and the Wicked; Is Your Honeymoon Really Necessary?; Miss Tulip Stays the Night; Yield to the Night; I Married a Woman; The Unholy Wife; The Long Haul; On the Double; The Sandwich Man; Berserk; There's a Girl in My Soup; The Amazing Mr Blunden; The Amorous Milkman; Confessions of a Driving Instructor.

TV inc: The Innocent.

DORTORT, David: Wri-Prod. b. NYC, Oct 23, 1920. e. CCNY BA. Films inc: The Lusty Men; Cry in The Night; The Big Land; Reprisal; Clash By Night; TV inc: (wri) Cavalcade of America; Panic; Waterfront; Public Defender; An Error in Chemistry; The Ox Bow Incident. (Prod) The Cowboys; The Restless Gun; Hunter's Moon (& wri). (Crea-exec prod) Bonanza; High Chaparral.

DOTY, Dennis E: Exec. b. Newhall, CA, Jul 20, 1941. e. USC, BA. VP primetime variety programs, ABC-TV; vp TV crea aff, Marble Arch Prodns; 1980 sr vp crea aff.

DOUGLAS, Gordon: Dir. b. NYC, Dec 15, 1907. Small roles in Eastern studios. To Hollywood 1932. Hal Roach Co. Writer; collab. Topper series; The Housekeeper's Daughter. Dir 30 Our Gang Shorts. Films inc: Saps at Sea; Broadway Limited; The Devil with Hitler; First Yank into Tokyo; Walk a Crooked Mile; Mr. Soft Touch; Between Midnight and Dawn; Kiss Tomorrow Goodbye; The Great Missouri Raid; Only the Valiant; I Was a Communist for the FBI; Come Fill the Cup; Mara Maru; Them; So This Is Love; The Charge at Feather River; The McConnell Story; Sincerely Yours; Santiago; The Big Land; Bombers B-52; Fort Dobbs; Yellowstone Kelly; Follow That Dream; Rio Conchos; Robin and the Seven Hoods; Sylvia; Harlow; Stagecoach (remake); In Like Flint; Chuka; Tony Rome; The Detective; The Lady in Cement; Barquero; They Call Me Mr. Tibbs; Slaughter's Big Rip Off; Viva Knievel.

TV inc: Nevada Smith.

DOUGLAS, Helen Gahagan: Act. b. Boontown, NJ, 1900. An opera star as well an actress, last screen appearance She, 1935. Also in stage version. Turned to politics in the '40s and was twice elected (in '44 and '46) a congresswoman from Cal. In 1950 ran for the US Senate, defeated by Richard Nixon.

(Died June 28, 1980).

DOUGLAS, Kirk (Issur Danielovich): Act. b. Amsterdam, NY, Dec 9, 1916. e. St Lawrence U, BA. Bway inc: Spring Again; The Sisters; Kiss and Tell; The Wind Is Ninety. On screen from 1946. Films inc: Out of the Past; I Walk Alone; Mourning Becomes Electra; The Walls of Jericho; A Letter to Three Wives; Champion; Young Man With a Horn; The Glass Menagerie; Along the Great Divide; Detective Story; The Big Sky; The Juggler; Ulysses; 20,000 Leagues Under the Sea; Lust for Life; Gunfight at the OK Corral; Paths of Glory; The Vikings (& prod); Spartacus (& prod); Town Without Pity; Lonely Are the Brave (& prod); Two Weeks in Another Town; The List of Adrian Messenger (& prod); Seven Days in May (& prod); Cast a Giant Shadow; The War Wagon; There Was a Crooked Man; Catch Me a Spy; A Man to Respect; The Fury; Indian Fighter; The Brotherhood (& prod); Summertree (& prod); Scalawag (& dir); Once Is Not The Villain; Saturn 3; The Final Countdown.

TV inc: Mousey; The Money Changers. Enough (& prod-dir); Posse (& prod-dir); Holocaust 2000 (& prod-dir); The Chosen; Home Movies;

DOUGLAS, Melvyn (nee Hesselberg): Act. b. Macon, GA, Apr 5, 1901. Bway inc: Tonight or Never; On the Loose; Inherit the Wind; Jealousy; The Best Man (Tony-1960). Screen debut in Tonight or Never, 1931. Films inc: As You Desire Me; Counsellor-at-Large; The Gorgeous Hussy; Arsene Lupin Returns; Ninotchka; He Stayed for Breakfast; Hud (Oscar-Supp-1963); One Is a Lonely Number; The Candidate; The Tenant; I Never Sang for My Father; Twilight's Last Gleaming; The Seduction of Joe Tynan; Being There (Oscar-supp-1979); The Changeling; Tell Me A Riddle.

TV inc: Do Not Go Gentle Into That Good Night (Emmy-1968); The Statesman-Benjamin Franklin.

DOUGLAS, Michael Kirk: Act-Prod. b. New Brunswick, NJ, Sep 25, 1944. e. U of CA at Santa Barbara, BA. S of Kirk Douglas. Films inc: (act) Hail Hero!; Adam at 6 A.M.; Summertree; Napoleon & Samantha; Coma; The China Syndrome (& prod); Running (& prod); It's My Turn. (Prod): One Flew Over the Cuckoo's Nest (Oscar-best film-1975).

TV inc: (act) When Michael Calls; The Streets of San Francisco.

DOUGLAS, Mike: TV Pers. b. Chicago, 1925. Syndicated host of daily talk-variety program, The Mike Douglas Show. Originally a singer; hosted a celebrity talk-show on radio in Chicago before moving to TV in the Early 60s. TV show started in Cleveland, then Philadephia; moved to Hollywood in 1978; (Emmy-1967)

DOUGLAS, Robert (nee Finlayson): Act-Dir. b. Bletchley, Eng, Nov 9, 1909. e. Bickley Hall Coll, RADA. Films inc: (act) The Decision of Christopher Blake; The Adventures of Don Juan; The Fountainhead; The Buccaneer's Girl; The Flame and the Arrow; Kim; Thunder on the Hill; At Sword's Point; The Prisoner of Zenda; The Desert Rats; Saskatchewan; The Virgin Queen; Good Morning, Miss Dove; Helen of Troy.

TV inc: (dir) 12 O'Clock High; Fugitive; Cannon; Streets of San Francisco; Barnaby Jones; Medical Center; Baretta; Columbo; Big Hawaii; Hunter; Man from Atlantis; Quincy; Centennial; Hart to Hart.

DOUGLAS, Wallace: Dir. b. Winnipeg, Canada, Aug 15, 1911. Former actor. Thea inc: Zoo in Silesia; Love Goes to Press; Twice Upon a Time; Collector's Item; A Month of Sundays; Let Them Eat Cake; Let Sleeping Wives Lie; She's Done It Again; Don't Just Lie There, Say Something; A Bit Between the Teeth; Fringe Benefits.

DOURIF, Brad: Act. b. Huntington, WV. Thea inc: The Ghost Sonata; The Doctor In Spite of Himself; Three Sisters; Future is the Eggs; Time Shadows; When You Comin Back, Red Ryder?.

Films inc: Split; W W and the Dixie Dancekings; One Flew Over the Cuckoos's Nest; Group Portrait With Lady; Eyes of Laura Mars; Wise Blood; Heaven's Gate.

TV inc: The Mound Builders; The Gardener's Son; Studs Lonigan; Guyana Tragedy--The Story of Jim Jones.

DOVE, Billie (Lilian Bohny): Act. b. May 14, 1900. Originally a model. Joined Ziegfeld Follies 1917. Films inc: Beyond the Rainbow; Polly of the Follies; Wanderer of the Wasteland; The Black Pirate; All the Brothers Were Valiant; The Marriage Clause; The Yellow Lily; The Night Watch; One Night at Susie's; Painted Angel; Blondie of the Follies; Diamond Head; The Age of Love.

DOWD, Nancy: Wri. b. Framingham, MA. e. Smith Coll. Films inc: Slap Shot; Coming Home *(Oscar-*story-1978).

DOWELL, Anthony J: Dancer. b. London, Feb 16, 1943. e. Royal Ballet School. Principal dancer the Royal Ballet since 1963; principal dancer American Ballet Theatre since 1978.

DOWLING, Doris: Act. b. 1921. Films inc: The Lost Weekend; The Blue Dahlia; Bitter Rice; Othello; Running Target; The Car.
TV inc: Scruples.

DOWN, Lesley-Anne: Act. b. London, Mar 17, 1957. Child model for TV and film commercials. Film debut at age 14 in All the Right Noises. Films inc: Pope Joan; Scalawag; Brannigan; The Pink Panther Strikes Again; A Little Night Music; The Betsy; Hanover Street; The Great Train Robbery; Rough Cut.
TV inc: Upstairs, Downstairs; Heartbreak House; The One and Only Phyllis Dixie.
Thea inc: Great Expectations; Hamlet.

DOWNS, Hugh: Bcaster-Act. b. Akron, OH, Feb 14, 1921. e. Columbia U. Supv of Science Programming, NBC's Science Dept. TV inc: Hawkins Falls; Kukla, Fran & Ollie; American Inventory; Home; Sid Caesar Show; Tonight (Jack Paar Show); Concentration; Today. Radio inc: NBC's Monitor. Films inc: Oh, God! Book II.

DOYLE, David: Act. b. Omaha, NE, Dec 1. Films inc: A New Leaf; April Fools; Loving; Six Gates to Hell; Capricorn One.
TV inc: 200 Years of American Humor;The New Dick Van Dyke Show; The Confessions of Dick Van Dyke; Bridget Loves Bernie; A Very Special Love. Charlie's Angels; John Ritter-Being of Sound Mind and Body.
Bway inc: Will Success Spoil Rock Hunter?; Promises, Promises; The Beauty Part; I Was Dancing.

DOZIER, William: Exec (ret). b. Omaha, NE, Feb 13, 1908. e. Creighton U, AB. Head of story & writing dept Paramount, 1941-45; exec asst to vp in chg. prod RKO, 1945-48; asso head of prod, Universal, 1948-51; CBS-TV, vp chg. programs, 1951-59; vp chg. production & member bd of dir, Screen Gems (Col) 1959-64; p of own co. Greenway Prods, 1964-72. Films inc: Harriet Craig; Two of a Kind; Batman.
TV inc: Batman; The Green Hornet; The Donna Reed Show; Bewitched; The Farmer's Daughter. Literary agent for: Sinclair Lewis; Kathleen Norris; Erle Stanley Gardner; F. Scott Fitgerald.

DRABINSKY, Garth H: Prod. b. Toronto, Canada, 1950. e. U Toronto, LLD. Co-founder Pan-Canadian Film Distributors; P Cineplex Corp., Canadian multi-screen circuit; dir CFMT-TV, Toronto; former publ Canadian Film Digest. Films inc: The Disappearance; The Silent Partner; The Changeling; Tribute.
Bway inc: A Broadway Musical.

DRAGON, Carmen: Comp-Cond. b. Antioch, CA, Jul 28, 1914. e. San Jose State College, MA. F of Daryl Dragon. Cond Hollywood Bowl Symphony; Capitol Symph; Royal Philharmonic, BBC Symphony. Films inc: Cover Girl *(Oscar-*1944).

DRAGON, Daryl: Mus. b. Pasadena, CA, Aug 27, 1942. S of Carmen Dragon. With The Beach Boys before teaming with wife Toni Tennille as The Captain and Tennille.
*(Grammy-*Record of the Year-1975). TV inc: The Toni Tennille Show.

DRAKE, Alfred (nee Capurro): Act-Dir. b. NYC, Oct 7, 1914. e. Brooklyn Coll, BA. Bway inc: (act) Oklahoma!; Sing Out, Sweet Land; Beggar's Holiday; Kiss Me Kate; succeeded Yul Brunner in The King and I; Kismet *(Tony-*1954); Much Ado About Nothing. (Dir): The Liar; Courtin' Time; Salt of the Earth; Millicent's Castle; Love Me Little; Lock Up Your Daughter; The Skin of Our Teeth.
Films inc: (act) Tars and Spars.

DRAKE, Betsy: Act. b. Paris, 1923. Films inc: Every Girl Should be Married; Room for One More; Pretty Baby; The Second Woman; Clarence the Cross-Eyed Lion.

DRAKE, Jim: Dir. e. Columbia U. TV inc: Mary Hartman, Mary Hartman (150 episodes); Fernwood 2Night; Alice; Ball Four; The Supreme Court and Civil Liberties; Young and Restless; Love of Life; Where the Heart Is; Sanford.

DRAKE, Tom (Alfred Alderdice): Act. b. NYC, 1919. Films inc: Two Girls and a Sailor; Meet Me in St. Louis; The Green Years; I'll Be Yours; Master of Lassie; Never Trust a Gambler; Sudden Danger; The Sandpiper; Red Tomahawk; The Spectre of Edgar Allan Poe; The Return of Joe Forrester.

DREIFUSS, Arthur: Dir-Wri-Prod. b. Frankfurt, Ger, Mar 25, 1908. e. U of Frankfurt, NYU, Columbia. Former child cond and chor. Films inc: (dir) Mystery in Swing; Baby Face Morgan; The Payoff; Campus Rhythm; Ever Since Venus; Eadie Was a Lady; Boston Blackie's Rendezvous; Two Blondes and a Redhead; Manhattan Angel; The Quare Fellow; The Love-Ins; For Singles Only; The Young Runaways.
TV inc: Wildlife in Crisis.
Thea inc: Allure; Baby Pompadour.

DREYFUSS, Richard: Act. b. NYC, 1949. Films inc: Dillinger; American Graffiti; The Apprenticeship of Duddy Kravitz; Jaws; Inserts; Close Encounters of the Third Kind; The Goodbye Girl *(Oscar-*1977); The Big Fix (& prod); The Competition.
Thea inc: Journey to the Day; Incident at Vichy; People Need People; Major Barbara; Line; But Seriously; Whose Little Boy Are You?; The Time of Your Life.

DRIVAS, Robert (nee Choromokos): Act-Dir. b. Chicago, Nov 21, 1938. e. U of Chicago, U of Miami. Bway inc: (act) The Firstborn; One More River; The Wall; Diff'rent; Mrs Daly Has a Lover; The Irregular Verb to Love; And Things That Go Bump in the Night. (Dir): Bad Habits; The Ritz; Legend; Cheaters.
Films inc: (act) Where It's At; Janice; God Told Me To; Road Movie.
TV inc: (dir) The Ugily Family.

DROMGOOLE, Patrick: Dir. b. Chile, Aug 30, 1930. e. Dulwich Coll; University Coll, Oxford. Thea inc: Periphery (& act); Cockade; Entertaining Mr. Sloane; The Love Game; Little Malcolm and His Struggle Against the Eunuchs; The Anniversary; Say Goodnight to Grandma; The Case of the Oily Levantine.
TV inc: (Prod) Armchair Theatre; Sunday Night Theatre; The Curse of King Tut's Tomb.

DRU, Joanne (nee La Cock): Act. b. Logan, WV, Jan 31, 1923. On screen from 1946, Abie's Irish Rose. Films inc: Red River; She Wore a Yellow Ribbon; All the King's Men; Wagonmaster; 711 Ocean Drive; Vengeance Valley; Mr Belvedere Rings the Bell; Return of the Texan; The Pride of St Louis; Hell on Frisco Bay; Sincerely Yours; The Light in the Forest; September Storm; The Wild and the Innocent; Sylvia.
TV inc: Guestward Ho.

DRURY, James: Act. b. NYC, 1934. Films inc: Forbidden Planet; Love Me Tender; Bernardine; Pollyanna; Ride the High Country; The Young Warriors.
TV inc: The Virginian; Firehouse.

DRYSDALE, Don: Sports Commentator. b. Van Nuys, CA, Jul 23, 1936. Former pitcher LA Dodgers. TV inc: ABC's Monday Night Baseball; World Championship Tennis.

DUART, Louise: Act. b. Quincy, MA, Oct 30, 1950. TV inc: Kapt Kool and the Kongs; Ace's Diner; Krofft Superstars. Various voices for cartoons.

DUBIN, Charles S: Dir. b. NYC, Feb 1, 1919. e. Brooklyn Coll. TV inc: Kojak; Baretta; Movin' On; Toma; Kung Fu; Sanford and Son; The New Dr Kildare; Room 222; Hawaii Five-0; Bracken's World; Omnibus; M*A*S*H; Roots; Rodgers and Hammerstein's Cinderella; Bolshoi Ballet; Never Say Never; Topper; The Gathering, Part II; Landon, Landon and Landon; Nightengales; Man's Greatest Sports--Dribble.

DU BOIS, Ja'net: Act. b. Philadelphia, Aug 5. Films inc: Diary of a Mad Housewife; Five on the Black Hand Side; A Piece of the Action; The Pawnbroker; Love With the Proper Stranger.

TV inc: Love of Life; Sammy Davis Special; On Being Black; Another World; As the World Turns; J.T.; Good Times.

Thea inc: Golden Boy; A Raisin in the Sun; Nobody Loves an Albatross.

DUBOIS, Marie: Act. b. Paris, Jan 12, 1937. e. Conservatoire of Dramatic Arts. Films inc: Le Signe de Lion; Une Femme est une Femme; Jules et Jim; La Ronde; Les Fetes Galantes; Le Voleur; Gonfles a Bloc; La Maison des Bories; The Innocent; My American Uncle.

DU BOIS, Raoul Pene: Dsgn. b. NYC, Nov 29, 1914. First des in NY were costumes for Life Begins at 8:40, 1934. Bway inc: Jumbo; The Ziegfeld Follies; Du Barry Was a Lady; Panama Hattie; Carmen Jones; Heaven on Earth; Lend an Ear; Call Me Madam; Wonderful Town (Tony-sets-1953); Plain and Fancy; Bells Are Ringing; The Student Gypsy; Maurice Chevalier; P.S. I Love You; Rain; Irene; No, No, Nanette (Tony-costumes-1971); Gypsy; Dr. Jazz; Sugar Babies. Also des for The Ballet Russe de Monte Carlo.

Films inc: Louisiana Purchase; Lady in the Dark; Dixie.

DUBOV, Paul: Wri-Prod. b. Chicago, 1924. TV inc: Backstairs at the White House; Shirley (co-prod).

Films inc: With Six You Get Eggroll.

(Died Sep 20, 1979).

DU BREY, Claire: Act. b. Bonner's Ferry, ID, Aug 31, 1892. Silent screen star. Films inc: Reward of the Faithless; Heart of a Child; Two Sisters; Broadway to Hollywood; The Sin of Nora Moran; The Devil Doll; Ramona; Wife, Doctor and Nurse; Nothing Sacred; The Baroness and the Butler; Everybody's Baby; Alexander Graham Bell; The Blue Bird; Charlie Chan's Murder Cruise; Brigham Young; Black Diamonds; Juke Box Jenny. Ret May 1962.

DUFF, Howard: Act. b. Bremerton, WA, Nov 24, 1917. Repertory Playhouse, Seattle. With KOMO radio. In Army, 1941-45. Radio's original Sam Spade. Films inc: Brute Force; All My Sons; Private Hell 36; Broken Star; Naked City; While the City Sleeps; Boy's Night Out; Panic in the City; The Late Show; A Wedding; Kramer vs Kramer; Double Negative; Oh God! Book II.

TV inc: Mr Adams and Eve; Dante; Felony Squad; The D.A.; Battered; The Heist; Valentine Magic on Love Island; Flamingo Road; The Dream Merchants.

DUFFY, James E: Exec. b. Decatur, IL. Joined ABC in Chicago, 1949. Moved to ABC TV, 1955. Returned to radio as dir of sls, ABC Central Div; named exec vp, national dir of sls for ABC Radio, 1962. In 1963, named vp in charge of sls for ABC TV; 1970 P ABC-TV Network.

DUFFY, Patrick: Act. b. Townsend, MT, Mar 17. e. U of WA. TV inc: The Stranger Who Looks Like Me; Hurricane; The Last of Mrs Lincoln; Man From Atlantis; Dallas; Knot's Landing; Enola Gay--The Men, The Mission, The Atomic Bomb.

DUFOUR, Val: Act. b. New Orleans, Feb 5, 1927. e. LA State U, BA, Catholic U of America, MA. Films inc: The Lonely Night; Ben Hur; LA Confidential; King of Kings; Land of Plenty.

TV inc: The Edge of Night; Another World; Search for Tomorrow.

Thea inc: High Button Shoes; South Pacific; Picnic; Mister Roberts; Stalag 17.

DUGGAN, Andrew: Act. b. Dec 28, 1923. Films inc: Patterns; The Bravados, The Chapman Report; FBI Code; Westbound; Merrill's Marauders; Seven Days in May; Secret War of Harry Frigg; The Glory Guys; The Skin Game; It's Alive; The Bears and I.

TV inc: Jigsaw; Bourbon Street Beat; Room for One More; Lancer; Overboard; A Fire in the Sky; The Incredible Journey of Dr. Meg Laurel; Backstairs at the White House; One Last Ride; The Long Days of Summer; M-Station-Hawaii; Jake's Way.

DUKE, Daryl: Dir. TV inc: The Senator (Emmy-The Day the Lion Died-1971). I Heard the Owl Call My Name (& prod).

Films inc: Payday; Griffin & Phoenix; The Silent Partner.

DUKE, Patty: Act. b. NYC, Dec 14, 1947. W of John Astin (since marriage billed as Patty Duke Astin). Bway inc: The Miracle Worker; Isle of Children. Films inc: The Miracle Worker (Oscar-supp-1962); Billie; The Valley of the Dolls; My Sweet Charlie; Me, Natalie; You'll Like My Mother; The Swarm.

TV inc: Armstrong Circle Theatre; The Prince and the Pauper; Wuthering Heights; US Steel Hour; Meet Me in St. Louis; Swiss Family Robinson; My Sweet Charlie (Emmy-1970); The Power and the Glory; The Patty Duke Show; Captains and Kings (Emmy-1977); Before and After; Women in White; The Miracle Worker (Emmy-1980); The Women's Room; The Baby Sitter; Mom, The Wolfman and Me.

DUKES, David: Act. b. San Francisco. Bway inc: School for Wives; The Great God Brown; Don Juan; The Visit; Holiday; Love for Love; Rules of the Game; Travesties; Rebel Women; Dracula; Bent.

Films inc: The Wild Party; A Little Romance; The First Deadly Sin.

TV inc: Glory Hallelujah; Beacon Hill; 79 Park Avenue; Family; A Fire In the Sky; Go West, Young Girl; Some Kind of Miracle; The Triangle Factory Fire Scandal; Mayflower--The Pilgrim Adventure; Portrait of a Rebel--Margaret Sanger.

DULLEA, Keir: Act. b. Cleveland, OH, May 30, 1936. Films inc: The Hoodlum Priest; David and Lisa; Mail Order Bride; The Thin Red Line; Bunny Lake is Missing; Madame X; The Fox; 2001, A Space Odyssey; Last of the Big Guns; Paperback Hero; Paul and Michelle; Black Christmas; Because He's My Friend.

TV inc: Brave New World; The Legend of John Hammer; Starlost; Legend of the Golden Gun; Brave New World; The Hostage Tower.

Bway inc: Cat on a Hot Tin Roof; Bus Stop.

DUNAWAY, Faye: Act. b. Bascom, FL, Jan 14, 1941. e. Boston U. Films inc: Doc; Puzzle of A Downfall Child; The Arrangement; The Happening; Hurry Sundown; Bonnie and Clyde; The Thomas Crown Affair; Oklahoma Crude; Little Big Man; The Three Musketeers; Chinatown; The Towering Inferno; Network (Oscar-1976); The Champ; Arthur Miller on Home Ground; The First Deadly Sin.

TV inc: Trials of O'Brien; On the Seaway; After the Fall; Hogan's Goat; The Woman I Love.

Bway inc: A Man for All Seasons; After the Fall; But for Whom Charlie?; Hogan's Goat; Candida; Old Times; Streetcar Named Desire.

DUNCAN, Sandy: Act. b. Henderson, TX, Feb 20, 1946. Bway inc: Music Man; Carousel; The Sound of Music; Finian's Rainbow; Life with Father; Canterbury Tales; The Boy Friend; Peter Pan.

Films inc: Million Dollar Duck; Star Spangled Girl; The Cat From Outer Space.

TV inc: Funny Face; Sandy in Disneyland; The Sandy Duncan Special; Christmas at Disneyland; Pinocchio; Roots.

DUNHAM, Katherine: Dancer-Chor. b. Joliet, IL, 1910. e. U Chicago. Formed own dance school, created idea of Negro Ballet; formed Katherine Dunham Dancers, debut with Chicago Opera Co at Chicago World's Fair; chor Aida for Metropolian Opera 1963.

Bway inc: Cabin In the Sky; Windy City; Bal Negre; Bamboche.

Films inc: Cabin In the Sky; Carnival of Rhythm (short); Star Spangled Rhythm; Stormy Weather; Pardon My Sarong (chor only); Casbah.

DUNING, George: Comp-Arr-Cond. b. Richmond, IN, Feb 25, 1908. e. Cincinnati Conservatory of Music. Arr. for Kay Kyser orch; dir. radio program Kollege of Musical Knowledge. Film scores inc: From Here to Eternity; Salome; The Jolson Story; All Ashore; My Sister Eileen; Pal Joey; Picnic; The Eddie Duchin Story; Cowboy; Houseboat; Bell, Book and Candle; The World of Suzy Wong; That Touch of Mink; Toys in the Attic; The Man With Bogart's Face.

TV inc: The Naked City; Tightrope; The Big Valley; The Farmer's Daughter; Glynis; No Time for Sergeants; The Silent Force; The Partridge Family; The Top of the Hill; The Dream Merchants.

Songs inc: Cry for Happy; My Kind of Guy; Picnic; Song Without End; Strangers When We Met; You Are My Dream.

DUNLAP, Richard D: Dir-Prod. b. Pomona, CA, Jan 30, 1923. e. Yale, BA, MFA. TV inc: Kraft Theatre; Omnibus; Bell Telephone Hour; Frank Sinatra & Mitzi Gaynor Specials; The Young and the Restless (Emmys-dir-1975-1978).

DUNLOP, Frank: Dir. b. Leeds, Eng, Feb 15, 1927. e. University Coll. Thea inc: The Bishop's Bonfire; Schweik in the Second World War; Son of Oblomov; The Taming of the Shrew; Any Wednesday; Too True to be Good; Saturday Night and Sunday Morning; The Trojan Women; Edward H; Home and Beauty; The White Devil; The Captain of Kopenick; The Maids; Deathwatch; The Alchemist; Bible One; French Without Tears; Scapino; Macbeth; Habeas Corpus; Antony and Cleopatra; Camelot.

DUNNE, Irene: Act. b. Louisville, KY, Dec 20, 1904. e. Chicago College of Music. Screen debut 1931. Films inc: Cimarron; Back Street; The Age of Innocence; Sweet Adeline; Roberta; The Magnificent Obsession; Showboat; The Awful Truth; Love Affair; Anna and the King of Siam; Life With Father; I Remember Mama; The Mudlark; Theodora Goes Wild.

DUNNE, Philip: Wri-Dir-Prod. b. NYC, Feb 11, 1908. e. Harvard U. Films inc: The Count of Monte Cristo; The Rains Came; Stanley and Livingston; Johnny Apollo; How Green Was My Valley; The Late George Apley; The Ghost and Mrs. Muir; Pinky; David and Bathsheba; Prince of Players (prod-dir); The View from Pompey's Head (& Prod-dir); Three Brave Men (& dir); Ten North Frederick (& dir); Blue Denim (& dir); Blindfold (& dir). Plays inc: Mr. Dooley's America.

DUNNING, John: Prod. b. Montreal, Canada, May 27, 1927. Films inc: The House By the Lake; Rabid; Blackout (& wri); Meatballs; Happy Birthday to Me; My Bloody Valentine.

DUNNOCK, Mildred: Act. b. Baltimore, MD, Jan 25, 1904. Films inc: The Corn Is Green; Kiss of Death; Death of a Salesman; Viva Zapata; The Jazz Singer; The Trouble with Harry; Love Me Tender; Peyton Place; Baby Doll; The Nun's Story; Sweet Bird of Youth; Behold a Pale Horse; Seven Women; Whatever Happened to Aunt Alice; The Spiral Staircase; Arthur Miller on Home Ground.
TV inc: Death of a Salesman; The Best Place to Be; And Baby Makes Six; Baby Comes Home.
Bway inc: The Corn is Green; Foolish Notion; Lute Song; Another Part of the Forest; Death of a Salesman; Cat on a Hot Tin Roof; The Milk Train Doesn't Stop Here Anymore; The Chinese; Colette; Days in the Trees; Tartuffe.

DURANTE, Jimmy: Act. b. NYC, Feb 10, 1893. Nitery, Broadway, radio. Films inc: Roadhouse Nights; Get Rich Quick Wallingford; The Cuban Love Song; Her Cardboard Lover; Two Girls and a Sailor; Ziegfeld Follies; Music For Millions; This Time For Keeps; On An Island With You; The Great Rupert; Yellow Cab Man; The Milkman; Jumbo; It's a Mad, Mad, Mad, Mad, World.
TV inc: Colgate Comedy Hour *(Emmy-*1952); Jimmy Durante Show; Jimmy Durante Presents The Lennon Sisters.
(Died Jan 29, 1980).

DURAS, Marguerite: Wri. b. Indo-China, 1914. e. Sorbonne, Paris. Plays inc: The Square; La Musica; The Viaduct; Days in the Trees; The Truck; A Place Without Doors; The Lovers of Viorne.
Films inc: Hiroshima Mon Amour; Nathalie Granger; India Song (dir).

DURBIN, Deanna: Act. b. Winnipeg, Can, Dec 4, 1922. Films inc: Three Smart Girls; One Hundred Men and a Girl; Mad About Music; That Certain Age; Three Smart Girls Grow Up; First Love; It Started with Eve; The Amazing Mrs Holliday; Christmas Holiday; Can't Help Singing; Because of Him; I'll Be Yours; Something in the Wind; Up in Central Park; For the Love of Mary (last film 1948).
*(Honorary Oscar-*1938).

DURNING, Charles: Act. b. Highland Falls, NY. Bway inc: The Andersonvillle Trial; The Championship Season; The Au Pair Man.
Films inc: Hi, Mom!; The Fury; Sisters; The Sting; Twilight's Last Gleaming; Dog Day Afternoon; The Hindenburg; Harry and Walter Go To New York; The Choir Boys; Tilt; When a Stranger Calls; The Greek Tycoon; The Muppet Movie; Starting Over; Enemy of the People; North Dallas 40; Die Laughing; The Final Countdown.
TV inc: The Connection; Queen of the Stardust Ballroom; Studs Lonigan; Attica; A Perfect Match.

DURRELL, Michael: Act. b. Brooklyn, Oct 6, 1943. Bway inc: Phedre; Hamlet; Murder Among Friends: Death of a Salesman (rev.); Emperor Henry IV; Cock-A-Doodle Dandy; The Sunshine Boys.
TV inc: The Guiding Light; Search for Tomorrow; The Class of '65; When Every Day Was the 4th of July; A Killing Affair; Harvest Home; The Immigrants; The Sunshine Boys.
Films inc: Thank God It's Friday.

DURRENMATT, Friedrich: Wri. b. Berne, Switzerlnd, Jan 5, 1921. e. U of Zurich, U of Berne. Plays inc: Es Steht Geschrieben; Der Blinde; Romulus Der Grosse; The Marriage of Mr Mississippi; An Angel Comes to Babylon; The Visit; The Physicists; Portrait of a Planet; Der Mitmacher.
Films inc: Es Gesachah am Hellichten Tage; The Marriage of Mr Mississippi; The Visit.
TV inc: Breakdown; The Physicists.

DUSAY, Marj (nee Mahoney): Act. b. Russell, KS, Feb 20, 1936. Films inc: Sweet November; Pendulum; Breezy; Clam Bake; 30 Dangerous Seconds; MacArthur.
TV inc: Peace in the Family; Climb An Angry Mountain; Most Wanted; Murder in Peyton Place; A Fire in the Sky; Paradise Connection; Battles - The Murder That Wouldn't Die.

DUSSAULT, Nancy: Act. b. Pensacola, FL, Jun 30, 1936. e. Northwestern U. Bway inc: Street Scene; Dr Willy Nilly; The Mikado; The Cradle Will Rock; Do Re Mi; The Sound of Music; Bajour; Carousel; Half a Sixpence; Fiorello!; Detective Story; The Gershwin Years.
TV inc: The Beggar's Opera; Love Is; Good Morning America (co-host); Too Close For Comfort.
Films Inc: The In-Laws.

d'USSEAU, Loring: Prod-Dir. b. LA, Dec 19, 1930. In prodn dept KTLA, LA, 1959; pgm dir 1964; exec prod NBC/KNBC 1971; sr pgm exec KCET 1975; entered indie prodn 1979.
TV inc: (Prod) Steve Allen Show; Korean Legacy; Harkness Ballet; Up Through the Ranks; And the Children Die; Meeting of the Minds; Nancy Wilson Show; James Wong Howe--The Man and His Movies; Handle With Care and Dignity; Number Our Days; The Good Old Days of Radio; Agnes DeMille and the Joffrey Ballet.

DUVALL, Robert: Act. b. San Diego, CA, 1931. e. Principia College. Neighborhood Playhouse, NY. Broadway, off-Broadway prodns. Films inc: To Kill A Mockingbird; Captain Newman, M.D.; The Chase; The Detective; M*A*S*H; Bullitt; The Godfather; The Godfather Part II; The Conversation; The 7 1/2% Solution; Network; The Eagle Has Landed; The Greatest; The Betsy; Apocalypse Now; The Great Santini.
TV inc: Ike.

DUVALL, Shelley: Act. b. Houston, TX, 1949. Films inc: Brewster McCloud; McCabe and Mrs Miller; Thieves Like Us; Nashville; Three Women; Annie Hall; The Shining; Popeye.

DVORAK, Ann (nee McKim): Act. b. NYC, Aug 2, 1912. Films inc: Hollywood Revue; The Guardsman; The Crowd Roars; Scarface; Three on a Match; Heat Lightning; Housewife; G Men; Follies Bergere; Dr Socrates; We Who Are About to Die; Merrily We Live; Blind Alley; Escape to Danger; The Long Night; The Walls of Jericho; A Life of Her Own; I Was an American Spy; The Secret of Convict Lake (last film, 1951).
(Died Dec 10, 1979).

DWAN, Allan: Dir. b. Toronto, Canada, Apr 3, 1885. e. Notre Dame. Pioneer dir. During 1911-14, made one & two reelers at The American Film Co; moved to Famous Players, 1914, and then to Griffith's Triangle Co in 1915. Films inc: Wildflower; The Good Bad Man; Luck of the Irish; Robin Hood; Zaza; Manhandled; Stage Struck; The Iron Mask; Human Cargo; Heidi; Suez; The Three Musketeers (Ritz Bros version); Rise and Shine; Abroad with Two Yanks; Up in Mable's Room; Brewster's Millions; Getting Gertie's Garter; Sands of Iwo Jima; The Wild Blue Yonder; The Woman They Almost Lynched; Silver Lode; Hold Back the Night; Slightly Scarlet; The River's Edge; The Most Dangerous Man Alive.

DYER-BENNET, Richard: Singer-Comp. b. Leicester, Eng, Oct 6, 1913. e. UC Berkeley. Recognized as a major innovator in folk mus.

DYKSTRA, John: Cin. b. Long Beach, CA, Jun 3, 1947. Films inc: Silent Running; Star Wars (*Oscar*-visual effects-1977; also Class II Academy Technical Award 1977); Battlestar Galactica; Star Trek - The Movie.
    TV inc: Battlestar Galactica (*Emmy*-1979) (prod first five hours and theatrical).

DYLAN, Bob (nee Zimmerman): Act-Comp. b. Duluth, MN, May 24, 1941. Recording artist; concert tours in US, Europe. Films inc: Don't Look Back; The Last Waltz; Renaldo and Clara (prod-dir-wri-act-edtr). Albums inc: Desire; Slow Train Coming.
    (*Grammys*-album of the year-1972; rock vocal-1979).

DYSART, Richard A: Act. Bway inc: The Quare Fellow; Six Characters in Search of an Author; A Man for All Seasons; All In Good Time; The Little Foxes; The Ruffian on the Stair; A Place Without Doors; That Championship Season.
    Films inc: The Crazy World of Julius Vrooder; The Terminal Man; Meteor; Enemy of the People; Prophecy; Being There.
    TV inc: First You Cry; Bogie; The Ordeal of Dr. Mudd.

EAGLES: Group. Members are Glenn Frey, guitar-voc-keyboard; Don Henley, drum-voc; Don Felder, guitar-pedal steel-banjo-voc; Joe Walsh, guitar-voc; Timothy B Schmit, bass-voc.
    Albums inc: Eagles; Desperado; On the Border; One of These Nights; Eagles--Their Greatest Hits; Hotel California; The Long Run.
    Singles inc: Take It Easy; Witchy Woman; Tequila Sunrise; Outlaw Man; Lyin' Eyes (*Grammy*-pop voc group-1975); Take It To the Limit; New Kid in Town (*Grammy*-arr for voices-1977); Hotel California (*Grammy*-record of year-1977); Life in the Fast Lane; Heartache Tonight (*Grammy*-rock voc-1979); The Long Run.

EARLEY, Candice: Act. b Ft Hood, TX, Aug 18, 1950. e. Trinity U. Bway inc: Hair; Jesus Christ, Superstar; Grease. TV inc: All My Children.

EARTH, WIND AND FIRE. Band. Organized by Maurice White. Members are: Maurice White, lead voc-drums-kalimba; Verdine White, bass; Fred White, drums; Philip Bailey, lead voc-percussion-congas; Larry Dunn, piano-moog; Al McKay, guitar; Ralph Johnson, percussion; Johnny Graham, guitar; Andrew Woolfolk, tenor sax; Don Myrick, alto-tenor-baritone sax; Louis Satterfield, trombone; Rahmlee Michael Davis, trumpet.
    Films inc: Sgt. Pepper's Lonely Hearts Club Band.
    TV inc: Star Chart.
    Albums inc: Gratitude; Spirit; All n' All; I Am; Best of Volume I.
    (*Grammy*-(5)-R&B voc group-1975, 1978, 1979; R&B inst-1978, 1979).

EASDALE, Brian: Comp. b. England, 1909. Film scores inc: Ferry Pilot; Black Narcissus; The Red Shoes (*Oscar*-1948); An Outcast of the Islands; The Battle of the River Plate.

EASTHAM, Richard (Dickinson Swift Eastham): Act-Singer. b. Opelousas, LA, Jun 22, 1918. Films inc: There's No Business Like Show Business; Man on Fire; Toby Tyler; That Darned Cat; Not With My Wife You Don't; Murderers Row; Tom Sawyer; Battle for the Planet of the Apes; McQ.
    Bway inc: A Flag is Born; Medea; South Pacific; Call Me Madam.
    TV inc: Tombstone Teritory; Wonder Woman; Silent Night, Lonely Night; The President's Plane Is Missing; Missiles of October; Attack on Terror; Rich Man, Poor Man; Salvage.

EASTON, Robert (nee Burke): Act. b. Milwaukee, WI, Nov 23, 1930. Quiz Kid on radio 1945. Films inc: The Red Badge of Courage; Belles on Their Toes; Comin' Round the Mountain; The Warlover; The Loved One; Paint Your Wagon; Pete's Dragon; When You Comin' Back, Red Ryder.
    TV inc: Burns and Allen; Playhouse 90; Climax; Hallmark Hall of Fame; Profiles in Courage; Centennial. Dialect Coach for many top stars.

EASTWOOD, Clint: Act. b. San Francisco, May 31, 1930. In TV series Rawhide for seven and one-half years. Formed Malpaso Productions, 1969. Films inc: A Fistful of Dollars; The Good, The Bad and The Ugly; The Beguiled; Paint Your Wagon; Where Eagles Dare; Two Mules for Sister Sara; Dirty Harry; Magnum Force; Play Misty For Me (& dir); High Plains Drifter (& dir); Joe Kidd; The Outlaw Josey Wales (& dir); The Eiger Sanction (& dir); The Gauntlet (& dir); Thunderbolt & Lightfoot; The Enforcer; Every Which Way But Loose; Escape From Alcatraz; Bronco Billy (& dir); Any Which Way You Can.

EBB, Fred: Lyr. b. NYC, Apr 8, 1933. Bway inc: Cabaret (*Tony*-1967); The Happy Time; Zorba; 70, Girls, 70; Liza; Chicago.
    Films inc: Funny Lady; Lucky Lady; Cabaret (*Tony*-lyr-1967); A Matter of Time; New York, New York; French Postcards.
    TV inc: Liza; Liza with a Z (*Emmys*-prod & special material-1973); Ole Blue Eyes Is Back; Gypsy in My Soul; (*Emmy*-prod-1976) Goldie and Liza Together (wri-prod).
    (*Grammy*-cast album-1973).

EBERLE, Ray: Singer. b. 1919. Recording artist and big band singer. Films inc: Sun Valley Serenade; Orchestra Wives.
    (Died Aug 25, 1979).

EBSEN, Buddy: Act. b. Belleville, IL, Apr 2, 1908. Bway debut dancer in Ziegfeld's Whoopee, 1928. Dance team with sister, Vilma; played nightclubs. Films inc: Broadway Melody of 1936; Captain January; Banjo On My Knee; Red Garters; Davy Crockett; Attack; Breakfast at Tiffany's; Mail Order Bride; The Family Band.
    TV inc: The Beverly Hillbillies; Davy Crockett; Barnaby Jones; The Bastard; The Critical List; Paradise Connection (& prod).
    Thea inc: Take Her, She's Mine; Our Town.

ECKSTINE, Billy: (William Clarence Eckstine): Singer. b. Pittsburgh, PA, Jul 8, 1914. Band singer with Earl 'Fatha' Hines then solo as headliner niteries, vaude.
    Films inc: Skirts Ahoy!; Let's Do It Again.
    Recording inc: Prime of My Life; For the Love of Ivy; My Way; Senior Soul; Feel the Warm; Stormy; If She Walked Into My life; Soul Session.

EDELMAN, Herb: Act. b. NYC, 1930. Films inc: In Like Flint; Barefoot in the Park; The Odd Couple; The Front Page; The Yakuza; California Suite; Goin' Coconuts.
    TV inc: Marathon.

EDEN, Barbara (nee Huffman): Act. b. Tucson, AZ, Aug 23, 1934. Films inc: Back from Eternity; Twelve Hours to Kill; Flaming Star; Voyage to the Bottom of the Sea; Five Weeks in a Balloon; The Wonderful World of the Brothers Grimm; The Brass Bottle; Seven Faces of Dr Lao; Harper Valley PTA. TV inc: The Feminist and the Fuzz; A Howling in the Woods; How to Marry a Millionaire; I Dream of Jeannie.

EDGLEY, Michael Christopher: Impresario. b. Melbourne, Australia, Dec 17, 1940. e. Christian Brothers Coll. Chmn of Directors of Michael Edgley International Pty, Ltd.

EDLUND, Richard: Cin. b. Fargo, ND, Dec 6, 1940. e. USC, US Naval Photographic School. Films inc: Star Wars (*Oscar*-visual effects-1977).
    TV inc: Battlestar Galactica (*Emmy*-1979).

EDOUART, Alexander Farciot: Cin. b. LA, Nov 5, 1894. Films inc: Alice in Wonderland; Lives of a Bengal Lancer; Spawn of the North (*Oscar*-honorary-1938); I Wanted Wings (*Oscar*-sfx-1941); Reap the Wild Wind (*Oscar*-sfx-1942); Unconquered; Ace in the Hole; The Mountain.
    (Died Mar 17, 1980).

EDWARDS, Blake: Prod-Dir-Wri. b. Tulsa, OK, Jul 26, 1922. H of Julie Andrews. Films inc: Panhandle; Stampede; Rainbow Round My Shoulder; Drive A Crooked Road; Notorious Landlady; Breakfast at Tiffany's; Experiment in Terror; Days of Wine and Roses; Soldier in the Rain; The Pink Panther; A Shot in the Dark; The Great Race; The Tamarind Seed; The Return of the Pink Panther; The Pink Panther Strikes Again; Revenge of the Pink Panther; 10.

TV inc: (crea) Dante's Inferno; Peter Gunn; Mr. Lucky.

EDWARDS, Douglas: Newscaster. b. Ada, OK. e. U of AL, Emory U, U of GA Evening Coll. Joined CBS Radio News, 1942; served as chief of CBS News' Paris Bureau; has anchored a daily CBS tv news broadcast since 1949.

EDWARDS, Geoff: Act. b. Westfield, NJ, Feb 15. e. Duke U, BA. Daily morning radio show KMPC, LA. TV host of Jackpot, The New Treasure Hunt; Shoot for the Stars. Films inc: W.U.S.A.; The Comic.

EDWARDS, Ralph: Prod-TV Pers. b. Merino, CO, Jun 13, 1913. e. U of CA, Berkeley, AB. Started in radio, 1929, as wri-act-prod-anncr station KROW, Oakland. Later joined CBS & NBC Radio, New York, as announcer. 1940, orig, prod, emceed Truth or Consequences for both radio & TV (Emmy-1950). Other shows inc: This Is Your Life (crea-prod-MC) (Emmys-1953,-1954); The Ralph Edwards Show (crea-prod-MC); Place the Face; Funnyboners; It Could Be You; End of the Rainbow; About Faces; Wide Country; Who in the World; The Woody Woodbury Show; Name That Tune; The Cross Wits; Knockout.

EDWARDS, Sherman: Comp-Lyr. b. NYC, Apr 3, 1919. e. NYU, Cornell. Bway inc: 1776 (& conceived) (Tony-1969).

Films inc: Kid Galahad; GI Blues; 1776.

EDWARDS, Vince: Act. b. NYC, Jul 9, 1928. e. OH State U; U of HI, AADA. Films inc: Sailor Beware; Rogue Cop; The Night Holds Terror; The Killing; The Three Faces of Eve; Devil's Brigade; The Desparados; Las Vegas.

TV inc: Studio One; Ben Casey; The Untouchables; The Deputy; The Rhinemann Exchange.

EGAN, Eddie: Act. b. NYC, Jan 3, 1930. Former NYC Detective. Films inc: The French Connection; Prime Cut; Badge 272.

TV inc: Joe Forrester; Eischied; Police Story.

EGAN, Richard: Act. b. San Francisco, Jul 29, 1923. e. U of SF, BA, Stanford U, MA. Films inc: The Damned Don't Cry; Split Second; Demetrius and the Gladiators; Wicked Woman; Gog; Untamed; Violent Saturday; The View from Pompey's Head; Love Me Tender; Tension at Table Rock; These Thousand Hills; A Summer Place; Pollyanna; Esther and the King; The 300 Spartans; The Destructors; Chubasco; The Big Cube; The Amsterdam Kill.

TV inc: The Day of the Wolves; Empire; Redigo.

EGGAR, Samantha: Act. b. London, Mar 5, 1939. Films inc: The Wild and the Willing; Dr. Crippen; Doctor in Distress; Psyche; The Collector; Walk Don't Run; Doctor Doolittle; The Walking Stick; The Lady in the Car; The Light at the End of the World; The Sellout; The Seven Per Cent Solution; Why Shoot The Teacher?; The Brood; The Exterminator.

TV inc: Anna and the King.

EGGLESTON, Colin Richard Francis: Prod-Dir-Wri. b. Melbourne, Australia, Sep 23, 1941. Films inc: Long Weekend. TV inc: Matlock Police; Rush; The Sullivans; Cop Shop; Lap Dog; Lion's Share.

EICHHORN, Lisa: Act. b. NY, Feb 4, 1952. e. Oxford; RADA. Films inc: Yanks; The Europeans; Why Would I Lie?

EIKENBERRY, Jill: Act. b. New Haven, CT, Jan 21, 1947. e. Yale Drama School. Bway inc: All Over Town; The Primary English Class; Just Spokes; Watch on the Rhine (rev); Onward Victoria.

Films inc: Between The Lines; The End of the World In Our Usual Bed in a Night Full of Rain; An Unmarried Woman; Butch and Sundance--The Early Days; Orphan Train; Rich Kids; Hide in Plain Sight.

TV inc: Swan Song.

EILBACHER, Cynthia (Cindy): Act. b. Saudi Arabia, Jul 7. TV inc: My Mother, the Car; Crowhaven Farm; The Senator; The Great Man's Whiskers; A Fire in the Sky; Donner Pass; The Road to Survival; Shirley; City In Fear.

Films inc: The Big Bounce; Golden Girl.

EINHORN, Lawrence C: Prod-Dir. b. Chicago, IL, Jan 18, 1936. e. U MI. TV inc: Warner Brothers--a 50 Year Salute; Paramount Presents; Mrs America Pageant; Victor Awards; Rona Barrett Specials; That's Hollywood; Kids are People Too (Emmy-exec prod-1979).

EINSTEIN, Bob: Wri-Prod. b. LA, Nov 20, 1940. e. Chapman Coll. S of late Harry (Parkyakarkus) Einstein. TV inc: (wri) Smothers Brothers Show (Emmy-1969); Andy Williams Show; Love Concert; Just Friends; Pat Paulsen Show; Three for Tahiti; Sonny and Cher Show; Sonny Comedy Revue. (Prod) Van Dyke and Company (Emmy-1977); Lola Falana Specials; Redd Foxx Show.

Films inc: Another Nice Mess (wri-dir).

EISNER, Michael: Exec. b. NYC, 1942. e. Denison U, BA. Started with programming dept, CBS-TV; joined ABC, 1966, as asst to vp & nat'l pgm dir; 1968, became dir of pgm dev, east coast; 1971, named vp daytime pgmng, ABC-TV; May, 1976, named sr vp, prime time prod and dev; Nov, 1976, left ABC to join Par as p & CEO.

EKBERG, Anita: Act. b. Malmo, Sweden, Sep 29, 1931. Model. Films inc: Man in the Vault; Blood Alley; Artists and Models; War and Peace; Sheba and the Gladiator; La Dolce Vita; Boccaccio '70; The Cobra; Fellini's Clowns.

TV inc: Gold of the Amazon Women; S*H*E*.

EKLAND, Britt: Act. b. Stockholm, Sep 29, 1931. Films inc: After the Fox; The Bobo; The Double Man; The Night They Raided Minsky's; Stiletto; Percy; A Time for Loving; Baxter; Endless Night; Asylum; The Man with the Golden Gun; Royal Flash; Slaves; The Wicker Man.

TV inc: A Cold Peace; Trials of O'Brien; The Hostage Tower.

ELAM, Jack: Act. b. Miami, AZ, Nov 13, 1916. Films inc: The Sundowners; Rawhide; Ride Vaquero; Kansas City Confidential; Jubilee Trail; Kiss Me Deadly; The Man from Laramie; Kismet; Jubal; Night Passage; Gunfight at the O.K. Corral; Baby Face Nelson; Day of the Gun; The Rare Breed; Firecreek; Support Your Local Sheriff; Cockeyed Cowboys of Calico County; Support Your Local Gunfighter; Dirty Dingus Magee; Rio Lobo; Daughters of Joshua Cabe; Sidekicks; Huckleberry Finn; The Winds of Autumn; Grayeagle; The Norseman; Hot Lead and Cold Feet; The Apple Dumpling Gang Rides Again; The Villain.

TV inc: The Dakotas; Temple Houston; The Texas Wheelers; Daughters of Joshua Cabe; How the West Was Won; Black Beauty; Lacy & the Mississippi Queen; Struck By Lightning; Revenge of the Red Chief; Mark Twain's America--Young Will Rogers.

ELCAR, Dana: Act. b. Ferndale, MI, Oct 10. Films inc: Report to the Commissioner; The Sting; The Northfield; Minnesota Raid; A Gunfight; Soldier Blue; The Amazing Mrs Pollifax; W.C. Fields and Me; The Champ; Good Luck Miss Wyckoff; The Nude Bomb; The Last Flight of Noah's Ark.

TV inc: St Joan; Elizabeth the Queen; Centennial; Samurai; Death Penalty; Mark, I Love You.

Bway inc: The Pinter Plays; Summer of the 17th Doll; As Good As Gold.

ELDER, Ann: Wri. TV inc: Mitzi Gaynor Special; Perry Como Special; Flip Wilson Show; Lily Tomlin (Emmy-1974); Paul Lynde Comedy Hour; 3 Girls 3; Lily Tomlin Show (Emmy-1976); Osmond Specials; Marilyn Monroe; Collegiate Cheerleaders Championships; Carol Burnett & Co; Playboy Pajama Party; The Big Hex of Little Lulu; The Girl With ESP; Zack and the Magic Factory.

ELDER, Lonne III: Wri. b. Dec 26, 1931. e. Yale School of Drama. Films inc: Melinda; Sounder; Sounder Part 2.

TV inc: The Terrible Veil; N.Y.P.D.; Toma; Ceremonies in Dark Old Men; A Woman Called Moses.

Plays inc: Kissin' Rattle Snakes Can Be Fun; Seven Comes Up & Seven Comes Down (Two one act plays prod off Bdway); Charades On East Fourth Street; Ceremonies in Dark Old Men.

ELDRIDGE, Florence: Act. b. NYC, 1901. Widow of Fredric March. Films inc: The Greene Murder Case; The Divorcee; The Matrimonial Bed; The Great Jasper; The Story of Temple Drake; Les Miserables; Mary of Scotland; Another Part of the Forest; An Act of Murder; Christopher Columbus; Inherit the Wind.

TV inc: First You Cry.

ELFAND, Martin: Prod. b. 1937. Started as agent, with William Morris; Chasin-Park-Citron; CMA; joined Artists Entertainment Complex as prod; 1976 exec vp chg wldwde prodn WB; resd 1977.

Films inc: Kansas City Bomber; Dog Day Afternoon; It's My Turn.

ELG, Taina: Act. b. Helsinki, Finland, Mar 9, 1931. With Sadler Wells Ballet. Films inc: The Prodigal; Diane; Gaby; Les Girls; Imitation General; The 39 Steps; The Bacchantes; The Great Experiment

Bway inc: Where's Charley; The Utter Glory of Morrissey Hall.

ELIAS, Hal: Exec. b. NYC, Dec 23. Western exploitation m MGM, 1926-34; exec asst to Fred Quimby, MGM Studios, 1935-55; head MGM cartoon studio, 1955-58; VP & studio m UPA, 1959-62. Honorary Oscar 1979.

ELIKANN, Larry: Dir. b. NYC, Jul 4, 1923. e. Brooklyn Coll, Walter Hervey Coll. TV inc: James at 16; Westside Medical; Weekend Specials; After School Specials; The Great Wallendas; Charlie and the Great Balloon Chase; Supertrain; Grandpa Goes to Washington; Paper Chase; The Seven Wishes of a Rich Kid; The Revenge of the Red Chief; Where Do Teenagers Come From?; Here's Boomer.

ELINSON, Jack: Prod-Wri. Began as radio wri on Jimmy Durante Show; Ed Wynn Show; Garry Moore Show. TV inc: The Danny Thomas Show; Gomer Pyle, USMC; Andy Griffith (wri); The Real McCoys (wri); That Girl; The Doris Day Show; One Day at a Time; Good Times; Joe's World; Facts of Life.

ELIZONDO, Hector: Act. b. NYC, Dec 22, 1936. Films inc: Valdez is Coming; Pocket Money; Stand Up and Be Counted; Born To Win. The Taking of Pelham One Two Three; Report to the Commissioner; Thieves; Cuba; The Eves; American Gigolo. The Prisoner of Second Avenue; The Dance of Death.

Bway inc: Mr. Roberts; Great White Hope; So Proudly We Hail;
TV inc: Popi; The Impatient Heart; Freebie and the Bean.

ELKINS, Hillard: Prod. b. NYC, Oct 18, 1929. e. Brooklyn Coll, NYU. Bway inc: Come on Strong; Golden Boy; Oh, Calcutta!; The Rothschilds; A Doll's House; An Evening with Richard Nixon and. . .; Sizwe Banzi is Dead.

Films inc: Alice's Restaurant; A New Leaf; A Doll's House.
TV inc: The Importance of Being Earnest.

ELKINS, Saul: Prod-Dir-Wri. b. NYC, Jun 22, 1907. e. CCNY. Started in radio as wri-dir-prod. To Hollywood 1934 as dialogue dir-wri Fox; contract wri Fox, Col, RKO, Rep; 1947 became prod WB. Films inc: Younger Brothers; One Last Fling; Homicide; House Across the Street; Flaxy Martin; Barricade; Return of the Frontiersman; This Side of the Law; Colt .45; Sugarfoot; Raton Pass; The Big Punch; Smart Girls Don't Talk; Embraceable You.

ELLIMAN, Yvonne: Singer. b. HI, 1953. Singer with Eric Clapton before solo. Recordings inc: I Don't Know How to Love Him; Food of Love; Rising Sun; Night Flight; If I Can't Have You.

Bway inc: Jesus Christ Superstar.
Films inc: Jesus Christ Superstar; Saturday Night Fever.
(*Grammy*-album of year-1978).

ELLIOTT, Denholm: Act. b. London, May 31, 1922. e. RADA. Stage debut 1945, The Drunkard. Films inc: The Sound Barrier; The Cruel Sea; The Heart of the Matter; They Who Dare; The Night My Number Came Up; Station Six Sahara; Nothing But the Best; King Rat; Alfie; The Spy with a Cold Nose; Here We Go Round the Mulberry Bush; The Night They Raided Minsky's; The Rise and Rise of Michael Rimmer; A Doll's House; Madame Sin; Robin and Marian; The Little Girl In Blue Velvet; Russian Roulette; Hound of the Baskervilles; The Boys From Brazil; Partners; Watership Down; It's Not The Size That Counts; Saint Jack; Zulu Dawn; Cuba; Bad Timing; Rising Damp; Sunday Lovers.

TV inc: Sextet; Clayhanger. Thea inc: King of Hearts; Traveller without Luggage; Write Me a Murder; The Crucible; The Imaginary Invalid; Chez Nous; The Return of A J Raffles; Blade on the Feather.

ELLIOTT, James S (Dimitri Eliopoulos): Prod-Dir. b. NYC, Jan 15, 1926. Prod on Bway at age 17. Bway inc: The First Million; 27 Wagons Full of Cotton; Lord Byrons' Love Letters; Rats of Norway; Accidentally Yours; Too Hot for Maneuvers; Arlene; The Sun Looks Down; Sodom and Gomorrah (dir); Farewell Apollo (dir).

Films inc: It Happened in Athens; Death Awaits Below; Time and Touch; A Dream of Kings; Once Upon a Scoundrel.

ELLIOTT, Lang: Prod. b. LA, 1950. Co-founder The International Picture Show; co-founder, P, TriStar Pictures Inc. Films inc: They Went That-A-Way and That-A-Way; The Billion Dollar Hobo; Prize Fighter; The Private Eyes.

TV inc: Experiment in Love (doc).

ELLIOTT, Paul: Prod. b. Bournemouth, Eng, Dec 9, 1941. Former actor. Has presented over 100 touring shows. Thea inc: (London) When We Are Married; The Chalk Garden; Big Bad Mouse; Grease; The King and I. Bway inc: Brief Lives; I Do, I Do; 13 Rue de l'Amour; Bus Stop; Hello, Dolly!; Beatlemania.

ELLIOTT, Sam: Act. b. Aug 9, 1944. Films inc: The Games; Frogs; Molly and Lawless John; The Legacy.

TV inc: Wild Times.

ELLIOTT, Stephen: Act. b. NYC, Nov 27. Bway inc: Command Decision; Livin' the Life; Roman Candle; Traveller Without Luggage; Marat/Sade; A Cry of Players; In the Matter of J Robert Oppenheimer; The Miser; A Whistle in the Dark; Georgy; The Good Woman of Setzuan; The Playboy of the Western World; An Enemy of the People; A Ride Across Lake Constance; The Crucible; The Creation of the World and Other Business.

Films inc: The Hospital; Death Wish; Report to the Commissioner; The Hindenburg.

TV inc: Beacon Hill; Son Rise: A Miracle of Love; The Golden Honeymoon.

ELLIS, Brian James: Prod. b. Cheyenne, WY, Apr 3, 1953. e. USC. Films inc: Whitewater Sam; Time for the Arrow; Avalanche.

ELSOM, Isobel (nee Reed): Act. b. England, 1893. Films inc: A Debt of Honor; Dick Turpin's Ride to York; The Sign of Four; The Wandering Jew; Illegal; Ladies in Retirement; You Were Never Lovelier; Forever and a Day; First Comes Courage; Casanova Brown; The Unseen; Of Human Bondage; Ivy; Love from a Stranger; The Ghost and Mrs. Muir; Monsieur Verdoux; Desiree; The Paradine Case; 23 Paces to Baker Street; Love is a Many Splendored Thing; Lust for Life; The Bellboy; Who's Minding The Store?; My Fair Lady. Ret 1965.

EMERSON, Faye: Act. b. Elizabeth, LA, Jul 7, 1917. Films inc: Between Two Worlds; The Mask of Dimitrios; Hotel Berlin; Danger Signal; Nobody Lives Forever; Guilty Bystander; A Face in the Crowd.

EMERY, Katherine: Act. b. 1907. Bway inc: Carry Nation; The Children's Hour; Strangers at Home; As You Like It; Everywhere I Roam; The Three Sisters; Proof Through the Night; The Cherry Orchard.

Films inc: The Locket; The Private Affairs of Bel Ami; Chicken Every Sunday; Isle of the Dead.

(Died Feb 6, 1980).

EMHARDT, Robert: Act. b. Jul 24, 1914. Films inc; The Iron Mistress; 3.10 to Yuma; Underworld USA; The Stranger; Kid Galahad; The Group; Where Were You When the Lights Went Out; Seniors.
TV inc: Greatest Heroes of the Bible; Institute for Revenge; Aunt Mary; One Last Ride.

ENBERG, Dick: Sportscaster. e. Central MI U; IN U, PhD. Asso prof & asst baseball coach CA State Northridge before becoming voice of CA Angels baseball team; became NBC sportscaster 1975. TV inc: Sports Challenge; Three For The Money; Sportsworld; The Way It Was.

ENDELSON, Robert Allen: Prod-Dir. b. NYC, Dec 9, 1947. e. Adelphi U, BS. Films inc: The Filthiest Show in Town; Fight for Your Life.

ENDERS, Howard: Wri-Prod-Dir. b. Philadelphia, Jul 31, 1926. e. Johns Hopkins U. TV inc: How Life Begins; The Other Walls; Black Fiddler; Rape: The Unspeakable Crime; Americans All (21 episodes); The Religions of Asia; Gerim Means Strangers; Television in America.

ENDERS, Robert J: Prod-Wri. Films inc: A Thunder of Drums (prod); The Maltese Bippy (prod); How Do I Love Thee (prod); Voices; The Maids (sp); Winter Rules (exec prod); Conduct Unbecoming (sp); Hedda (prod); Nasty Habits; Stevie (prod & dir).
TV inc: The Best of the Post; Ben Franklin; Acad Awards Show, 1968 (co-prod).

ENFIELD, Cy: Prod-Dir-Wri. b. Nov 1914. Films inc: Gentleman Joe Palooka; Stork Bites Man; The Argyle Secrets; Underworld Story; The Sound of Fury; The Search; Child in the House; Hell Drivers; Sea Fury; Jet Storm; Mysterious Island; Zulu; Sands of Kalahari; De Sade; Universal Soldier; Zulu Dawn.

ENGEL, Charles F: Exec. b. LA, Aug 30, 1937. e. MI State U, BA; UCLA. S of Samuel G Engel. In pgm development dept ABC-TV 1964-1968; 1969 exec prod Run a Crooked Mile; The Aquarians; 1972 named vp U TV; 1977 sr vp; 1980, exec vp.

ENGEL, Georgia: Act. b. Washington, DC, Jul 28, 1948. e. HI U, BA. Bway inc: Hello, Dolly!. Films inc: Taking Off.
TV inc: Mary Tyler Moore Show; Betty White Show; Good Time Girls; The Day The Women Got Even.

ENGEL, Samuel G: Prod. b. Woodbridge, NY, Dec 29, 1904. e. Union U. Films inc: Wrote and produced several of the Charlie Chan & Cisco Kid films for Fox; My Darling Clementine (& sp); Sitting Pretty; Daddy Long Legs; The Jackpot; Come to the Stable; The Frogmen; A Man Called Peter; The Story of Ruth; Boy on a Dolphin; The Lion; Belles on Their Toes.

ENGELBERG, Mort: Prod. b. Memphis, TN, Aug 20, 1937. e. U of IL, U of MO. Films inc: Smokey and the Bandit; Hot Stuff; The Villain; The Hunter.

ENGLANDER, Roger: Prod-Dir. b. Cleveland, OH, Nov 23, 1926. e. U of Chicago, PhB. TV inc: (dir) Omnibus; Odyssey; Let's Take a Trip; Twentieth Century; Great American Dream Machine; 60 Minutes; The Performing Arts. (Prod) Young People's Concerts; What Is Sonata Form? *(Emmy*-1965); Vladimir Horowitz at Carnegie Hall; S Hurok Presents; The Bell Telephone Hour; Candid Camera.

ENGLUND, George H: Prod-Dir. b. Washington, DC, Jun 22, 1926. Films inc: The World, The Flesh and the Devil (prod); The Ugly American; Signpost to Murder (dir); Dark of the Sun (prod); Zachariah (dir); Snowjob (dir); A Christmas To Remember; The Streets of L.A. (prod).

ENGLUND, Ken: Wri. b. Chicago, May 6, 1914. Films inc: Big Broadcast of 1928; Artists and Models; No, No Nanette; Sweet Rosie O'-Grady; Secret Life of Walter Mitty; A Millionaire for Christy; The Wicked Dream of Paula Schultz; Surviving the Savage Sea.
TV inc: Jackie Gleason Show; Ray Milland Show; Loretta Young Show; My Three Sons; Bewitched; Dr. Joyce Brothers.

ENRIGHT, Dan (nee Ehrenreich): Prod. e. CCNY, RCA Institute. TV inc: Juvenile Jury; Life Begins at 80; The Joe DiMaggio Show; You're On Your Own; Tic Tac Dough; Twenty One; Concentration; Dough Re Mi; Magistrate's Court; Family Court; Line 'Em Up; Hi-Do; Oh Baby!; Break the Bank; The Hollywood Connection; Crossfire; Meet the McGees; It's the Barrys; Marriage Confidential; The James Beard Show; Junior Celebrities; The Fred Davis Show; Winky Dink; Make a Face.

ENTWISTLE, John: Comp-Mus. b. London, Oct 9, 1944. Member of The Who rock group for 15 years.
Films inc: (as mus dir) Quadrophenia; The Kids Are Alright (doc).

EPHRON, Amy: Exec. b. Beverly Hills, CA, Oct 21, 1952. D of Phoebe and Henry Ephron. With Sidney Beckerman Prodns; Marty Ehrlichman Prodns; joined Martin Bregman Prodns as vp Acquisition & Dvlpment; 1980 VP prodn, Col.

EPHRON, Henry: Wri. b. 1912. Collaborated with wife, Phoebe, until her death in 1971. Films inc: Bride by Mistake; Always Together; John Loves Mary; The Jackpot; On the Riviera; Belles on Their Toes; There's No Business Like Show Business; Daddy Long Legs; Carousel (& prod); The Best Things in Life are Free (prod only); Desk Set; Take Her She's Mine; Captain Newman, MD.

EPHRON, Nora: Wri. b. NYC, May 19, 1941. e. Wellesley. D of Phoebe and Henry Ephron. Sis of Amy Ephron. TV inc: Perfect Gentlemen.

EPSTEIN, Alvin: Act-Dir. b. NYC, May 14, 1925. e. Queens Coll. Bway inc: Clerambard; No Strings; Waiting for Godot; King Lear; Passion of Josef D.; The Tempest; The Government Inspector; The Bacchae; The Merchant of Venice; Enrico IV; Ivanov; Don Juan.
TV inc: Waiting for Godot; Prayers from the Ark; Terezin Requiem; Histoire Du Soldat; Grimm's Fairy Tales.

EPSTEIN, Julius: Wri. b. NYC, Aug 22, 1909. e. Penn State Coll. Collab. with twin brother Philip until latter's death, 1952. Films inc: Four Daughters; Four Wives; No Time for Comedy; Strawberry Blonde; The Man Who Came to Dinner; Casablanca (*Oscar*-1942); Mr Skeffington (& prod); Romance on the High Seas; My Foolish Heart; Forever Female; The Last Time I Saw Paris; (solo): The Tender Trap; Tall Story; Take a Giant Step (& prod); Fanny; Send Me No Flowers; Any Wednesday (& prod); Pete 'n Tillie (& prod); House Calls.
TV inc: The Pirate.

ERDMAN, Richard: Act-Dir. b. Enid, OK, Jun 1, 1925. Films inc: Janie; The Very Thought of You; Danger Signal; Too Young to Know; Nobody Lives Forever; The Time of His Life; Easy Living; Jumping Jacks; The Stooge; Stalag 17; The Brass Bottle; A Delicate Balance. (Dir): Bleep; The Brothers O'Toole.
TV inc: The Great Mans Whiskers; The Dick Van Dyke Show; The Tab Hunter Show.

ERICKSON, Leif: Act. b. Alameda, CA, Oct 27, 1911. On stage in A Midsummer Night's Dream. Joined Olsen & Johnson comedy team. Screen debut, Wanderer of the Wasteland, 1935. On Broadway in Tea and Sympathy, 1953-55. Films inc: Sorry, Wrong Number; Joan of Arc; Snake Pit; Perilous Journey; On the Waterfront; Fastest Gun Alive; Twilight's Last Gleaming.
TV inc: High Chapparal; Hunter's Moon; Wild Times.

ERICSON, Devon: Act. b. Salt Lake City, UT, Dec 21. e. USIU. Films inc: Return to Macon County. TV inc: The Waltons; Eleanor and Franklin; The Dream Makers; The Skating Rink; Testimony of Two Men; The Bluegrass Special; Young Dan'l Boone; Baby Comes Home.

ERICSON, John: Act. b. Dusseldorf, Ger, Sep 25, 1926. e. AADA. On stage Stalag 17. Films inc: Teresa; Rhapsody; Green Fire; Bad Day at Black Rock; The Return of Jack Slade; Forty Guns; Pretty Boy Floyd; Under Ten Flags; The Seven Faces of Dr Lao; The Destructors; Operation Bluebook; Bedknobs and Broomsticks; Hustler Squad.
TV inc: Honey West.

ERMAN, John: Dir. b. Chicago. e. UCLA, BA. Films inc: (as act) Blackboard Jungle; Anything Goes; The Benny Goodman Story; (as dir): Making It; Ace Eli and Rodger of the Skies.

TV inc: (dir) Stoney Burke; My Favorite Martian; Please Don't Eat the Daisies; That Girl; The Fugitive; Ben Casey; Peyton Place; Gomer Pyle; Star Trek; The Flying Nun; Letters From Three Lovers; Green Eyes; Child of Glass; Just Me and You; Moviola.

ERSKINE, Howard: Prod-Dir. b. Bronxville, NY, Jun 29, 1926. e. Williams Coll. Act in stock before prodn. Bway inc: (Prod) Late Love; The Desperate Hours *(Tony*-prod-1955); The Happiest Millionaire (& dir); The Midnight Sun; Calculated Risk; Any Wednesday (& dir); Minor Miracle.

ESMOND, Carl (Willy Eichberger): Act. b. Vienna, Jun 14, 1908. e. Academy of Dramatic Arts. On stage in many European cities. On screen in Germany, then USA. Films inc: Evensong; Invitation to the Waltz; Dawn Patrol; Thunder Afloat; The Story of Dr. Wassell; Ministry of Fear; Address Unknown; Catman of Paris; Smash-Up; Walk a Crooked Mile; From the Earth to the Moon; Thunder in the Sun; Agent for HARM; Morituri; Kiss of Evil.

TV inc: Climax; Playhouse 90; Four Star Playhouse.

ESSERT, Gary: Film Fest Exec. b. Oakland, CA, Oct 15, 1938. e. UCLA, BA. Between 1964-67 coordinated and supervised the design and planning of UCLA Motion Pictures Center; designed the m.p. exhibition facilities at the U of CA, Berkeley; 1965-67 San Francisco Int'l Film Festival; 1968-1970 Tech coordinator for the American Film Institute's Center for Advanced Film Studies; Co-founded (1971) Los Angeles Film Exposition (Filmex).

ESSEX, Harry: Wri-Dir. b. NYC, Nov 29, 1915. e. St Johns U, BA. Films inc: He Walked By Night; Man and Boy; The Amigos; The Sons of Katie Elder; It Came From Outer Space; The Creature From the Black Lagoon.

TV inc: The Untouchables; The Racers; The Corrupters; Bewitched.

Thea inc: Something for Nothing; One for the Dame.

ESTRADA, Erik: Act. b. NYC, Mar 16, 1949. Films inc: The Cross and the Switchblade; The New Centurions; Airport '75; Midway; Trackdown.

TV inc: CHiPs; Donnie and Marie Christmas Special; Dean Martin Christmas Special 1980.

ETAIX, Pierre: Act. b. Roanne, France, 1928. Films inc: Rupture (short); Heureux Anniversaire (Happy Anniversary) *(Oscar*-short, co-prod-1962); The Suitor; Yo Yo; As Long As You Have Your Health; Le Grand Amour; Pays de Cocagne.

ETKES, Raphael: Exec. b. Paris, May 6, 1930. e. USC. 1961 joined MCA as exec in int'l sales dept; In London as prodn exec; retd to studio, sr vp U and vp MCA; Feb 1980, named p, CEO Filmways Pictures.

EUARD, Opal: Act. Started as understudy for Laurette Taylor in 1910, toured with many of the latter's productions throughout the US. Became a teacher with drama department U of Miami; co-founder of Equity Library Theatre, Hollywood; numerous film and tv appearances.

(Died May 13, 1980).

EUBANKS, Bob: TV host. b. Flint, MI. e. CA State Northridge. Worked as deejay, KRLA, LA; launched string of young adult niteries called The Cinnamon Cinder; promoter first West Coast concert of Beatles at Hollywood Bowl; formed Concert Express which books acts around the country.

TV inc: Rhyme and Reason; The Diamond Head Game; The Newlywed Game; All Star Secrets; The Toni Tennille Show (exec prod); You Bet Your Life (exec prod).

EVANS, Bill (nee William John Evans): Jazz pianist. b. Plainfield, NJ, Aug 16, 1929. e. Southwestern LA Coll. Played Chicago niteries, worked with Tony Scott, Miles Davis before forming own trio 1959.

Albums inc: Conversation With Myself *(Grammy*-inst jazz-1963); Alone *(Grammy*-small group jazz-1970); The Bill Evans Album *(Grammy*-solo jazz-1971); Tony Bennett/Bill Evans.

(Died Sep 15, 1980).

EVANS, Clifford: Act. b. Cardiff, Wales, Feb 17, 1912. e. RADA. London stage debut 1930 in The Witch; Bway debut in The Distaff Side, 1934. Films inc: The Mutiny of the Elsinore; Love on the Dole; Stryker of the Yard; Passport to Treason; The Curse of the Werewolf; Kiss of the Vampire; Twist of Sand; One Brief Summer.

TV inc: The Accused; Treason; The Quiet Man; War and Peace; Who's for Tennis.

EVANS, Dale (Frances O Smith): Act. b. Uvalde, TX, Oct 31, 1912. W of Roy Rogers. Started as band singer. Films inc: Orchestra Wives; Swing Your Partner; Casanova in Burlesque; The Yellow Rose of Texas; Utah; My Pal Trigger; Apache Rose; Susanna Pass; Twilight in the Sierras; Trigger Jr; Pals of the Golden West.

EVANS, Gene: Act. b. Holbrooke, AZ, Jul 11, 1924. Films inc: Under Colorado Skies; Berlin Express; Park Row; Donovan's Brain; Hell and High Water; The Sad Sack; Operation Petticoat; Apache Uprising; Support Your Local Sheriff; The Ballad of Cable Hogue; Walking Tall; The Magic of Lassie; Devil Times Five.

TV inc: My Friend Flicka; Matt Helm; Spencer's Pilots; The Concrete Cowboys; Wild Times; Casino; Mark Twain's America--The Young Will Rogers.

EVANS, Jerry: Dir. e. UC Berkeley, Yale U School of Drama. TV inc: Secret Storm; Love of Life; Ryan's Hope *(Emmys*-1979, 1980).

EVANS, Linda: Act. b. Hartford, CT, Nov 18, 1942. Films inc: Those Callaways; The Klansman; Mitchell; Twilight of Honor; Avalanche Express; Tom Horn.

TV inc: The Big Valley; Hunter.

EVANS, Maurice: Act. b. Dorchester, Eng, Jun 3, 1901. On stage since 1926. London theatrical career inc: Justice; Loyalties; Diversion; Journey's End. To U.S. in 1935, appeared in Romeo and Juliet; Hamlet; Richard II; Macbeth; Man and Superman; The Devil's Disciple; Dial M for Murder; Tenderloin; The Aspern Papers; Program for Two Players; Teahouse of the August Moon (co-prod) *(Tony*-1954). Honorary Tony, 1950.

Films inc: Kind Lady; Androcles and the Lion; Gilbert and Sullivan; Macbeth; Planet of the Apes; Rosemary's Baby; The Body Stealers; The Jerk.

TV inc: Hamlet; Richard II; Macbeth *(Emmy*-1961); Devil's Disciple; Taming of the Shrew; St. John (series of 7 plays for Hallmark, NBC); Caesar & Cleopatra; The Girl, The Gold Watch and Everything.

EVANS, Mike: Act-Wri. b. Salisbury, NC, Nov 3. e. LACC. TV inc: All in the Family; Call Her Mom; Now You See Him, Now You Don't; The Voyage of the Yes; Rich Man, Poor Man, Book I; The Jeffersons; Good Times (crea).

EVANS, Ray: Comp. b. Salamanca, NY, Feb 4, 1915. e. Wharton School, U of PA. Wrote special material for Olsen & Johnson; Betty Hutton; Joel Gray; Mitzi Gaynor; Cyd Charisse; Polly Bergen. Film scores inc: My Friend Irma; Red Garter; All Hands on Deck; Monsieur Beaucaire; The Paleface; Sorrowful Jones; The Lemon Drop Kid; Fancy Pants.

Songs: Buttons and Bows *(Oscar*-1948); A Thousand Violins; Mona Lisa *(Oscar*-1950); Silver Bells; Misto Cristofo Columbo; My Beloved; Never Let Me Go; Que Sera Sera *(Oscar*-1956); Almost in Your Arms; Dear Heart.

Film title songs: To Each His Own; Golden Earrings; Another Time, Another Place; Tammy; Saddle the Wind. TV title songs: Bonanza; Mr. Lucky; Mr. Ed; To Rome with Love.

Thea inc: Oh Captain; Let It Ride.

EVANS, Robert: Prod. b. NYC, Jun 29, 1930. Former actor, later business exec, became Paramount head of prod, 1966. After 10 years resigned to become indie prod. Films inc: (act) Lydia Bailey; The Man of a Thousand Faces; The Sun Also Rises; The Fiend Who Walked the West; The Best of Everything. (Prod): Chinatown; Marathon Man; Black Sunday; Players; Urban Cowboy; Popeye.

EVERETT, Chad (Ray Canton): Act. b. South Bend, IN, Jun 11, 1936. Films inc: Claudelle Inglish; The Chapman Report; The Singing Nun; The Last Challenge; Made in Paris; Return of the Gunfighter; The Impossible Years.
TV inc: Hawaiian Eye; 77 Sunset Strip; Lawman; The Dakotas; Redigo; Route 66; Ironside; Medical Center; Centennial; The French Atlantic Affair; Hagen.

EVERLY BROTHERS: Mus. b. Brownie, KY, Don, Feb 1, 1937, Phil, Jan 19, 1939. Country mus recording artists.

EVIGAN, Greg: Act. b. South Amboy, NJ, Oct 14. Thea inc: Jesus Christ, Superstar; Grease.
TV inc: A Year at the Top; Operation Runaway; BJ and the Bear; Debby Boone--The Same Old Brand New Me; The Osmond Family Christmas Show.

EWELL, Tom (Yewell Tompkins): Act. b. Owensboro, KY, Apr 29, 1909. e. U of WI. Bway debut, They Shall Not Die, 1934. In Navy, 1942-46. Returned to Bway in John Loves Mary; The Seven-Year Itch (Tony-1953); Tunnel of Love.
Films inc: Adam's Rib; A Life of Her Own; Up Front; Finders Keepers; The Seven-Year Itch; Tender Is the Night; State Fair; They Only Kill Their Masters; The Great Gatsby.
TV inc: Only the Pretty Girls Die.

FABARES, Shelley: Act. b. Jan 19, 1944. Films inc: Never Say Goodbye; Rock Pretty Baby; Summer Love; Ride the Wild Surf; Girl Happy; Hold On; Spin Out; Clambake; A Time to Sing; UMC.
TV inc: Pleasure Cove; Donovan's Kid; Friendships, Secrets and Lies; The Great American Traffic Jam.

FABER, Robert: Prod-Dir-Wri. b. NYC, Jun 6, 1908. e. CCNY. Started with Paramount in adv dept 1928; National Screen Service, 1933; Universal 1938 until retirement in 1979, when formed own firm. Prod features, featurettes, trailers.
Features inc: Easy To Look At; The Crimson Canary; (short) The World's Most Beautiful Girls. Doc featurettes: The Far Country; 1954 Hollywood Spotlight Series; Focus on Airport; Gambit; The Changing Image of the Western Hero; The Andromeda Strain; From Then Till Now; Swashbuckler; Thoroughly Modern Millie; The Hindenburg; Midway; Same Time Next Year; The Island.

FABIAN (Fabian Forte Bonaparte): Act. b. Philadelphia, 1943. Teenage singer, guitarist. Films inc: The Hound Dog Man; North to Alaska; Mr Hobbs Takes a Vacation; Dear Brigitte; Ten Little Indians; Fireball 500; The Devil's Eight; A Bullet for Pretty Boy; Lovin' Man.

FABIAN, Francoise (Michele Cortes de Leon): Act. b. Algiers, May 10, 1935. Films inc: Le Feu Aux Poudres; Les Fanatiques; Les Violents; La Brune Que Voila; Maigret Voit Rouge; Le Voleur; Ma Nuit Chez Maud.

FABRAY, Nanette (nee Fabares): Act. b. San Diego, CA, Oct 27, 1920. e. Juillard. First appeared as Baby Nanette in vaudeville. On screen in Our Gang Comedies. Films inc: Elizabeth and Essex; A Child is Born; The Happy Ending; Cockeyed Cowboys; Wonderful Town; Last of the Red Hot Lovers; Never Too Late.
Bway inc: Meet the People; By Jupiter; Jackpot; Bloomer Girl; High Button Shoes; Love Life (Tony-1949); Mr President; No Hard Feelings; Wonderful Town.
TV inc: Yes, Yes Nanette; Caesar's Hour (Emmys-(3)-supp & comedienne of year-1955; comedienne of year-1956); Man in the Santa Claus Suit.

FABRIZI, Aldo: Act. b. Italy, 1905. Films inc: Go Ahead Passengers; Square of Rome; Open City; My Son, the Professor; To Live in Peace; Christmas at Camp; Emigrants; Father's Dilemma; Mishappy Family; Cops and Robbers; Times Gone By; Lucky Five; The Angel Wore Red; Three Bites of the Apple; Those Were The Days; We All Loved Each Other So Much.

FACTOR, Alan Jay: Prod-Dir. b. Chicago, Dec. 25, 1925. e. Northwestern U. Former actor under name Alan Frost. P Factor-Newland Production Corp. Thea inc: Richard II; Pick Up Girl; Battle for Heaven.
Films inc: Portrait of Jennie; All Hands on Deck; Double Lift; The Right Approach; Female Jungle.
TV inc: (prod) Something Evil; Terror on the Beach; A Sensitive, Passionate Man; Overboard; The Suicide's Wife; The Next Step Beyond; Angel City.

FADIMAN, Clifton: Ed-TV pers. b. NYC, May 15, 1904. e. Columbia U. Contributor to magazines since 1924. Asst. editor Simon & Schuster, 1927-29, ed. 1929-35; Book Editor The New Yorker, 1933-43; MC on Information Please radio program, 1938-48, TV '52; MC This Is Show Business, TV; MC Conversation, 1954; MC Quiz Kids, 1956; Board of Editors, Encyclopaedia Britannica; Edit. consultant Encyclopaedia Britannica Educational Corp; Senior Editor, Cricket: The Magazine for Children;

FAIN, Sammy: Comp. b. NYC, Jun 17, 1902. Self-taught pianist; worked as staff comp-pianist for various mus pubs; in vaude.
Bway inc: Everybody's Welcome; Hellzapoppin'; Sons o' Fun; George White's Scandals of 1939; Toplitzky of Notre Dame; Flahooley; Ankles Aweigh; Christine; Around the World in 80 Days.
Films inc: Young Man of Manhattan; Footlight Parade; Sweet Music; New Faces of 1937; No Leave, No Love; Alice in Wonderland; George White's Scandals; Call Me Mister; Peter Pan; Weekend at the Waldorf; Anchors Aweigh; Calamity Jane; Marjorie Morningstar; Love Is a Many-Splendored Thing; Tender is the Night.
Songs inc: I Left My Sugar Standing in the Rain; Let A Smile Be Your Umbrella; Wedding Bells Are Breaking Up That Old Gang of Mine; You Brought a New Kind of Love to Me; When I Take My Sugar To Tea; Was That the Human Thing To Do; By A Waterfall; That Old Feeling; I Can Dream, Can't I; I'll Be Seeing You; Secret Love (Oscar-1953); Dear Heats and Gentle People; April Love; A Certain Smile; Love Is A Many-Splendored Thing (Oscar-1955); Tender Is the Night; Strange Are The Ways of Love; A World That Never Was.

FAIRBANKS, Douglas Jr (nee Ullman): Act. b. NYC, Dec. 9, 1909. Son of silent screen star. Began screen career 1923 in Stephen Steps Out. On stage in NY, England. In US Navy during WW II. Films inc: Dawn Patrol; Little Caesar; Union Depot; Catherine the Great; Accused; The Prisoner of Zenda; Gunga Din; The Corsican Brothers; Sinbad the Sailor; State Secret. Prod: Another Man's Poison; Chase a Crooked Shadow.
TV inc: (prod) Douglas Fairbanks Presents; The Hostage Tower (act); From Raquel With Love.
Thea inc: The Pleasure of His Company.

FAIRBANKS, Jerry: Exec prod. b. San Francisco, Nov 1, 1904. Started as projectionist, cameraman; indep shorts prod. Formed Jerry Fairbanks Productions, 1944. Prod shorts for Par; films for TV; developed Zoomar Lens. Films inc: Who's Who In Animal Land (Oscar-short subj-1944); Moon Rockets; Lost Wilderness; Down Liberty Road; With This Ring; Counterattack; Collision Course; Land of the Sea; Brink of Disaster; The Legend of Amaluk; North of the Yukon; Damage Report.
TV inc: Front Page Detective; Crusader Rabbit.

FAIRCHILD, Morgan: Act. b. Dallas, TX, Feb 3, 1950. e. SMU. Films inc: Bullet for Pretty Boy.
TV inc: Search for Tomorrow; Murder in Music City; The Memory of Eva Ryker; Flamingo Road; The Dream Merchants.

FAIRCHILD, William: Wri. b. Cornwall, Eng, 1918. Films inc: Morning Departure; An Outcast of the Islands; The Gift Horse; The Net; The Malta Story; Front Page Story; John and Julie (& dir); Value for Money; The Silent Enemy (& dir); Star!; Embassy.

TV inc: The Man with the Gun; No Man's Land; Four Just Men; Some Other Love; The Zoo Gang.

Plays inc: Sound of Murder; The Pay-Off; The Flight of the Bumble B.

FAIRE, Virginia Browne (nee LaBuna): Act. b. NYC, 1905. An extra in silent films in NY, came to Hollywood with U contract after winning Motion Picture Classic Fame and Fortune contest in 1919.

Films inc: Monte Cristo; Peter Pan; The Temptress, Trapped by the Police; A Race for Life; The Donovan Affair; numerous westerns with Buck Jones, Hoot Gibson, Ken Maynard, John Wayne before settling in Chicago to do radio.

Ret. 1940. (Died June 30, 1980).

FAISON, George: Dir-Chor. Bway inc: 1600 Pennsylvania Ave; The Wiz *(Tony*-chor-1975).

FALANA, Lola: Singer-Act. b. Camden, NJ, 1945. Started as dancer-singer in niteries. Films inc: The Liberation of Lord Byron Jones; The Klansman; Lady Coco.

TV inc: Ben Vereen NBC Summer Variety Show.

Thea inc: Golden Boy; Dr Jazz.

FALK, Peter: Act. b. NYC, Sep 16, 1927. Off-Bway, The Iceman Cometh; The Lady's Not For Burning; St. Joan; Diary of a Scoundrel; The Prisoner of Second Avenue. Films inc: Murder; Pocketful of Miracles; Robin and the Seven Hoods; It's A Mad, Mad, Mad, Mad World; Griffin and Phoenix; Mikey and Nicky; Murder by Death; The In-Laws; The Brink's Job.

TV inc: The Price of Tomatoes *(Emmy*-1962); Brenner; The Untouchables; Sacco-Vanzetti Story; Columbo *(Emmys*-1972-1975-1976).

FAPP, Daniel: Cin. b. Kansas City, KS, Apr 4, 1921. Films inc: Five Card Stud; Double Trouble; The Pleasure Seekers; Send Me No Flowers; The Unsinkable Molly Brown; Move Over Darling; The Great Escape; One, Two, Three; Kings Go Forth; Desire Under the Elms; Joker is Wild; West Side Story *(Oscar*-1961); Let's Make Love; I'll Take Sweden; Our Man Flint; Lord Love a Duck; Sweet November; Ice Station Zebra; Marooned.

FARBER, Sandy: Thea prod. b. NYC, May 16, 1941. Thea inc: Student Gypsy; Riverside Drive; Babes in the Wood; Family Way; Summer Tree; Frank Merriwell; Tough to Get Help.

FARENTINO, James: Act. b. NYC, Feb 24, 1938. Films inc: Psychomania; Ensign Pulver; The War Lord; The Pad; Banning; Rosie; Me Natalie; The Story of a Woman; The Final Countdown.

TV inc: Death of a Salesman; The Bold Ones; Cool Million; Silent Victory - The Kitty O'Neil Story; Son Rise - A Miracle of Love.

Thea inc: The Night of the Iguana; One Flew over the Cucko's Nest; Desire (rev); Death of a Salesman (rev).

FARGAS, Antonio: Act. b. NYC, Aug 14. Films inc: Putney Swope; Shaft; Pound; Across 110th Street; Cleopatra Jones; Bustin'; Car Wash; Pretty Baby; Up the Academy.

TV inc: Starsky & Hutch; Hereafter; Huckleberry Finn; Escape; Nurse; All Commercials. Huckleberry Finn; The Roast.

Thea inc: The Great White Hope; The Slave; The Toilet; The Amen Corner;

FARGO, Donna: Singer-Sngwri. b. Mt Airy, NC, 1945. C & W Recording artist. *(Grammy*-1972).

FARGO, James: Dir. b. Republic, WA, Aug 14, 1938. e. U of WA, BA. Films inc: The Enforcer; Caravans; Every Which Way But Loose; Game for Vultures.

FARINA (See HOSKINS, Alan).

FARLEIGH, Lynn: Act. b. Bristol, Eng, May 3, 1942. Joined Royal Shakespeare Co, 1966. Thea inc: The Homecoming; All's Well that Ends Well; The Relapse; Julius Caesar; Exiles; Suzanne Andler; Ashes; The Doctor's Dilemma; Sex and Kinship in a Savage Society; Twelfth Night; Close Of Play.

Films inc: Three Into Two Won't Go; A Phoenix Too Frequent; Watership Down (voice only).

TV inc: The Rivals; Force of Circumstance; Eyeless in Gaza; The Word.

FARMER, Mimsy: Act. b. 1945. Films inc: Spencer's Mountain; Bus Riley's Back in Town; Hot Rods to Hell; The Devil's Angels; Move; The Road to Salina; Four Flies on Gray Velvet; Autopsy; L'amant de Poche (The Pocket Lover).

FARNSWORTH, Richard: Act. b. LA. Spent 40 years as stuntman. Films inc: (act) Comes a Horseman; Tom Horn; Resurrection.

FARR, Derek: Act. b. London, Feb 7, 1912. On screen From 1940. Films inc: The Outsider; Spellbound; Quiet Wedding; Wanted for Murder; Teheran; Noose; Silent Dust; Man on the Run; Reluctant Heroes; The Dam Busters; Town on Trial; Doctor at Large; The Truth About Women; The Projected Man; Thirty Is a Dangerous Age; Cynthia; Pope Joan.

TV inc: The Saint; The Human Jungle.

FARR, Felicia: Act. b. Westchester, NY, Oct 4, 1932. e. Penn State Coll. W of Jack Lemmon. Films inc: Timetable; Jubal; 3:10 to Yuma; The Last Wagon; Hell Bent for Leather; Kiss Me Stupid; The Venetian Affair; Charley Varrick.

FARR, Jaimee (Jameel Joseph Farah): Act. b. Toledo, OH, Jul 1, 1934. Films inc: The Blackboard Jungle; No Time for Sergeants; The Greatest Story Ever Told; Who's Minding the Mint?; With Six You Get Egg Roll.

TV inc: The Red Skelton Show; The Danny Kaye Show; The Chicago Teddy Bears; M*A*S*H; Amateur Night at the Dixie Bar & Grill; Murder Can Hurt You.

FARRAR, David: Act. b. Forest Gate, Eng, 1908. Films inc: Return of the Stranger; Danny Boy; The Night Invader; The Dark Tower; The World Owes Me a Living; Meet Sexton Blake; The Lisbon Story; Black Narcissus; Mr Perrin and Mr Traill; The Small Back Room; Night Without Stars; The Golden Horde; Duel in the Jungle; Lilacs in the Spring; The Sea Chase; I Accuse; Solomon and Sheba; John Paul Jones; Best Girl; The 300 Spartans.

FARRELL, Charles: Act. b. Onset Bay, MA, Aug 9, 1901. e. Boston U. Started in silent films. Films inc: Seventh Heaven; Sandy; Street Angel; Lucky Star; Sunny Side Up; Tess of the Storm Country; The First Year; Change of Heart; Moonlight Sonata; Just Around the Corner; Tailspin.

TV inc: My Little Margie; The Charles Farrell Show.

FARRELL, Mike: Act. b. St Paul, MN, Feb 6, 1939. Films inc: Capt Newman, MD; The Graduate; The Americanization of Emily; Targets. TV inc: The Interns; The Man and the City; M*A*S*H; The Longest Night; The Questor Tapes; Battered; Ladies of the Corridor; Sex and the Single Parent; Letters From Rank; Damien. . .The Leper Priest.

FARRELL, Sharon: Act. b. Dec 24, 1946. Films inc: The Spy With My Face, A Lovely Way to Die; The Reivers; The Love Machine; The Premonition; The Fifth Floor; Out of the Blue; The Stunt Man.

TV inc: The Last Ride of the Dalton Gang.

FARROW, Mia: Act. b. LA, Feb 9, 1947. D of Maureen O'Sullivan and John Farrow. Summer stock, off-Bway. NY debut 1963, The Importance of Being Earnest. Screen debut, 1964, Guns at Batasi. Films inc: A Dandy in Aspic; Rosemary's Baby; Secret Ceremony; John and Mary; See No Evil; The Public Eye; The Great Gatsby; Full Circle; A Wedding; Death on the Nile; Avalanche; Hurricane.

TV inc: Peyton Place; Johnny Belinda.

Thea inc: Mary Rose; The House of Bernarda Alba; The Three Sisters; The Marrying of Anne Leete; Zykovs; Ivanov; Romantic Comedy.

FARROW, Tisa: Act. b. Jul 22, 1951. D of Maureen O'Sullivan, Sis of Mia Farrow. Films inc: Homer; Strange Shadows in an Empty Room; Fingers; Manhattan; Winter Kills; Zombie.

FASSBINDER, Rainer Werner: Dir. b. Bad Worrishofen, Germany, May 31, 1946. Films inc: Love Is Colder Than Death; Katzelmacher; Rio das Mortes; The Agitator Niklashauser; The American Soldier; Whitey; Beware of A Holy Whore; Martha; Effi Briest; The Merchant of Four Seasons; The Bitter Tears of Petra von Kant; All Fear Eats the Soul; Fox and His Friends (& wri-perf); Despair; Chinese Roulette; The Third Generation (& sp-cin); Game Pass; Eight Hours Are Not a Day; A Little Godard. Berlin Alexanderplatz. The Marriage of Maria Braun; In a Year of 13 Months; Mother Kusters Goes To Heaven;

FAST, Howard: Wri. b. NYC, Nov 11, 1914. Foreign corr, mag wri; author several historical novels which have been filmed.
  Plays inc: The Crossing; The Hill.
  TV inc: The Ambassador (Ben Franklin) (*Emmy*-1975); The Immigrants.

FATHER GUIDO SARDUCCI: (See NOVELLO, Don).

FAWCETT, Farrah: Act. b. Corpus Christi, TX, Feb 2, 1942. Made TV commercials. (Billed as Fawcett-Majors while married to Lee Majors). Films inc: Love Is a Funny Thing; Myra Breckenridge; Logan's Run; Somebody Killed Her Husband; Sunburn (dropped Majors from name); Saturn 3.
  TV inc: Owen Marshall, Counselor at Law; The Six Million Dollar Man; The Feminist and the Fuzz; Harry O.; Charley's Angels.

FAYE, Alice: Act-Singer. b. May 5, 1915. W of Phil Harris. On screen From 1934. Films inc: George White's Scandals; The King of Burlesque; Poor Little Rich Girl; Wake Up and Live; In Old Chicago; Alexander's Ragtime Band; Sally, Irene and Mary; Rose of Washington Square; Lillian Russell; Tin Pan Alley; The Great American Broadcast; State Fair.
  Bway inc: Good News (rev).
  TV inc: The Magic of Lassie.

FAYE, Herbie: Act. b. 1900. In vaudeville and on Bway for almost 50 years.
  Films inc: Thoroughly Modern Millie; The Night They Raided Minsky's; The Family Jewels; The Fortune Cookie; Maurie.
  TV inc: The Phil Silvers Show.
  (Died June 28, 1980).

FAYE, Joey (Joseph Antony Palladino): Act-comedian. b. NYC, Jul 12, 1909. In vaudeville, burlesque in the early 30's. Bway inc: Room Service; The Milky Way; Boy Meets Girl; High Button Shoes; Top Banana; Strip for Action; DuBarry Was a Lady; Waiting for Godot; Guys and Dolls; Anatomy of Burlesque (& wri-dri); Man of La Mancha.
  Began in films in 30's in WB shorts. Features inc: Top Banana; The Tender Trap; Ten North Frederick; North to Alaska; The Grissom Gang; The War Between Men and Women.

FAYLEN, Frank: Act. b. 1907. Films inc: Bullets or Ballets; The Grapes of Wrath; Top Sergeant Mulligan; The Lost Weekend; Blue Skies; Road to Rio; Detective Story; Riot in Cell Block Eleven; Killer Dino; The Monkey's Uncle; Funny Girl.
  TV inc: The Doby Gillis Show; That Girl.

FEDDERSON, Don: Prod. b. Beresford, SD, Apr 16. Created and prod: Liberace Show, 1950; Life with Elizabeth; Betty White Show; The Millionaire; consultant Lawrence Welk Show, 1954-70; 1971, began syndication Welk Show. Other TV Shows inc: Date with Angels; Do You Trust Your Wife?; Who Do You Trust?; Charley Weaver Show; My Three Sons; Family Affair; To Rome with Love; Smith Family.

FEHMIU, Bekim: Act. b. Yugoslavia, Jun 1, 1936. Films inc: Cagliostro; Black Sunday; Madam Kitty; Special Education; Permission to Kill.

FEIFFER, Jules: Wri. b. NYC, Jan 26, 1929. Syndicated cartoonist. Films inc: Little Murders; Carnal Knowledge.
  Plays inc: Little Murders; The White House Murder Case; Knock Knock; Popeye.

FEINSTEIN, Alan: Act. b. NYC, Sep 8. Films inc: Looking For Mr Goodbar. TV inc: Edge of Night; Love of Life; Search for Tomorrow; Jigsaw John; Alexander; The Other Side of Dawn; The Users; Visions; The Runaways; The Two Worlds of Jenny Logan. Thea inc: Malcolm; Zelda.

FELD, Donald Lee (See: DONFELD)

FELD, Fritz: Act. b. Berlin, Oct 15, 1900. e. Berlin U, Max Reinhardt School of Drama. H of Virginia Christine. On screen From 1918, The Golem. In more than 400 films inc: Wives and Lovers; Promises, Promises; Who's Minding the Store?; Four for Texas; The Patsy; Harlow; The Comic; Barefoot in the Park; Hello, Dolly!; The Phynx; Which Way to the Front?; The Strongest Man in the World; Only with Married Men; The Sunshine Boys; Won Ton Ton, the Dog Who Saved Hollywood; Broadway Rose; Silent Movie; Pennsylvania Lynch; Freaky Friday; The World's Greatest Lover; Herbie Goes Bananas.
  TV inc: Please Don't Eat the Daises; The Smothers Bros.; Bewitched; The Beverly Hillbillies; Land of the Giants; Arnie; Love, American Style; The New Bill Cosby Show; The Julie Andrews Hour; The Odd Couple; The Night Stalker; The Mike Douglas Show.
  Thea inc: Once More with Feeling; Would Be Gentleman; Midsummer Night's Dream; Arsenic and Old Lace.

FELD, Irvin: Prod. b. Hagerstown, MD, May 9, 1918. Pres, prod and CEO Ringling Bros-Barnum & Bailey Combined Shows. TV inc: (exec prod): Klowns; Highlights of Ringling Bros and Barnum and Bailey Circus; Gunther Gebel Williams-Lord of the Rings; International Circus Festival of Monte Carlo; Circus Super Heroes; Siegfried and Roy--Superstars of Magic.
  Bway inc: Barnum.

FELDKAMP, Fred: Prod-Reporter-Wri-Ed. b. Newark, NJ, Mar 2, 1914. Films inc: Silken Affair; Triple Cross.
  TV inc: Crusade in Europe; Crusade in the Pacific.

FELDMAN, Edward S: Prod. b. NYC, Sep 5, 1929. e. MI State U. Publicist Fox; Paramount; Embassy; Seven Arts. Vp-Exec Asst to head of Prod WB-Seven Arts, 1967; P mp dept, Filmways, 1970.
  Films inc: (exec prod) What's the Matter with Helen?; Fuzz; Save The Tiger; The Other Side of the Mountain; Two-Minute Warning; The Other Side of The Mountain, Part II; The Last Married Couple in America.
  TV inc: King (Exec Prod); Valentine; Pioneer Woman; The Stranger Who Looks Like Me; My Father's House; Smashup on Interstate 5.

FELDMAN, Marty: Act-Wri. b. London, England, Jul 8, 1934. TV inc: Every Home Should Have One; Marty. Films inc: (Act) The Bed Sitting Room; Young Frankenstein; The Adventure of Sherlock Holmes Smarter Brother; Silent Movie; The Last Remake of Beau Geste (& dir-wri).

FELDMAN, Philip: Exec. b. Boston, MA, Jan 22, 1922. e. Harvard; Georgetown; Harvard Law School; Harvard Business School. Entered ind as legal counsel for Famous Artists; 1953 asso dir bus aff CBS; 1954, dir bus aff; 1957, vp talent CBS; 1960 exec vp Broadcast Management Inc; 1962 prodn vp Seven Arts Corp; formed Phil Feldman Prodns; 1972 vp Rastar Prodns; 1975, P First Artists Prodns; 1980 exec vp Rastar Films.
  Films inc: The Wild Bunch; The Ballad of Cable Hogue; You're A Big Boy Now; Posse.

FELDON, Barbara: Act. b. Pittsburgh, Mar 12, 1941. Fashion model. TV commercials. TV inc: East Side, West Side; Get Smart; Man From U.N.C.L.E.; Profiles in Courage; Children of Divorce.
  Films inc: Fitzwilly; Smile; No Deposit, No Return; Sooner or Later; A Vacation in Hell; Before and After; The Bear Who Slept Through Christmas (voice).
  Bway inc: Past Tense.

FELDSHUH, Tovah: Act. b. NYC, Dec 27, 1953. e. Sarah Lawrence Coll, BA; U of MN, MA. TV inc: The Amazing Howard Hughes; Holocaust; Connecticut Yankee in King Arthur's Court; Terror in the Sky; The Great Triangle Factory Fire; Beggarman, Thief; The Women's Room.

Bway inc: Cyrano; Brainchild; Straws in the Wind; Three Sisters; Dreyfus in Rehearsal; Rodgers and Hart; Yentl; Sarava.

Films inc: Cheaper to Keep Her; The Idolmaker.

FELICIANO, Jose: Singer-Comp. b. Lares, Puerto Rico, Sep 10, 1945. Recording artist. Film scores inc: Aaron Loves Angels; TV theme songs Chico and the Man; Love at First Sight. (Grammys-(2)-new artist, contemporary pop voc-1968).

FELL, Norman: Act. b. Philadelphia, Mar 24, 1924. e. Temple U, BA. Films inc: The Graduate; Oceans 11; Pork Chop Hill; Bullitt; If It's Tuesday This Must Be Belgium; The Stone Killer; The End; Rabbit Test.

TV inc: 87th Precinct; Dan August; Needles and Pins; Rich Man, Poor Man (Part 1); Three's Company; The Ropers; Pat Boone and Family Christmas Special; Moviola (This Year's Blonde); For The Love Of It.

FELLINI, Federico: Dir. b. Rimini, Italy, Jan 8, 1920. Cartoonist, caricaturist, writer. Wrote scripts for films Open City; Paisan. Dir debut, Variety Lights 1950. Films inc: La Dolce Vita; The Clowns; Juliet of the Spirits; Fellini's Rome; The Wastrels; La Strada; Vitelloni; Fellini's 8-1/2; Fellini's Satyricon; Amarcord; Fellini's Casanova; Orchestra Rehearsal; City of Woman.

FELTON, Norman: Prod. b. London, Eng, Apr 29. e. U of IA; BFA, MA. TV inc: (Wri-dir) Dave Garroway Show; Robert Montgomery Presents; US Steel Hour; Studs Place; Alcoa Playhouse; Studio One. (Prod) Studio One; Playhouse 90; Dr. Kildare; The 11th Hour; The Man From UNCLE; The Psychiatrist; Mr. Novak; Babe.

FENADY, Andrew J: Prod-Wri. b. Toledo, OH, Oct 4, 1928. e. U of Toledo, BA. Films inc: Stakeout on Dope Street; The Young Captives; Ride Beyond Vengeance; Chisum; Terror in the Wax Museum; Arnold; The Man With Bogart's Face.

TV inc: Black Noon; The Woman Hunter; The Stranger; The Mask of Alexander; The Hostage Heart.

FENADY, George J: Dir. b. Toledo, OH, Jul 2, 1930. e. U of Toledo. Films inc: Arnold; Terror In the Wax Museum.

TV inc: Mission Impossible; Sarge; Emergency; Chase; Code R; Hanging by a Thread; Cave In; The Night the Bridge Fell Down; Firehouse; CHiPS; Sierra.

FENDER, Freddy (Baldemar Huerta): Mus. b. San Benito, TX, Jun 4, 1937. Country mus recording artist.

FENNELL, Albert: Prod. b. Eng, 1920. Films inc: The Green Scarf; Next to No Time; Tunes of Glory; The Innocents; Night of the Eagle; And Soon the Darkness; Dr. Jekyll and Sister Hyde; The Legend of Hell House.

TV inc: The Avengers.

FERBER, Mel: Prod-Dir. b. NYC, Oct 2, 1922. TV inc: Adventure; Seven Lively Arts; That Was the Week That Was; Alias Smith and Jones; Mary Tyler Moore; The Odd Couple; CPO Sharkey; From Here to the Seventies; Polynesian Adventure; A Bell for Adano; Comedy in Music; Wonderful Town; (prod pilot) Sixty Minutes; Calendar; exec prod: Democratic National Committee Convention 1972; Good Morning America; Clonemaster.

FERDIN, Pamelyn: Act. b. Feb 4, 1959. Films inc: What a Way To Go!; Never Too Late; Beguiled; The Mephisto Waltz; Happy Birthday, Wanda June; The Tool Box Murders.

TV inc: A Tree Grow In Brooklyn; Miles to Go Before I Sleep.

FERGUSON, Allyn M Jr: Comp-Cond-Arr. b. San Jose, CA, Oct 18, 1924. e. San Jose State U, AB, MA; Stanford U, PhD; studied with Nadia Boulanger, Ernest Toch, Aaron Copland. Films inc: Avalanche Express.

TV inc: Johnny Mathis Show; Andy Williams Show; Fast Freight; The Count of Monte Cristo; Captains Courageous; Man in The Iron Mask; All Quiet on the Western Front; Big Island; The Gossip Columnist; Cry of the Innocent; A Country Christmas--1979; Beulah Land; Love Boat; Pleasure Palace; House Calls; Little Lord Fauntleroy; A Tale of Two Cities.

FERGUSON, Graeme: Dir. b. Toronto, Can, Oct 7, 1929. e. U of Toronto, BA. P IMAX Systems Corp since 1967. Films inc: The Love Goddesses; The Virgin President. TV inc: The Legend of Rudolph Valentino.

FERGUSON, Jay: Mus. b. LA, May 10, 1943. Pianist with two groups, Spirit and Jo Jo Gunne, before launching solo career in 1975.

FERGUSON, Maynard: Mus. b. Montreal, Canada, May 4, 1928. Briefly with Boyd Rayburn orch, then Jimmy Dorsey. To the US permanently 1949 with Charlie Barnet; worked with Stan Kenton 1950-1953 then freelance as studio musician before becoming charter member all-star Birdland Dream Band; formed sextet 1965.

Albums inc: Maynard Ferguson; Maynard Ferguson Horn 1-2-3-4-5; Live at Jimmy's; Primal Scream; Montreaux Summit 1 & 2; New Vintage; Carnival; Hot; It's My Time.

FERRELL, Conchata: Act. b. WV. Bway inc: Hot L Baltimore. TV inc: Hot L Baltimore; Network; A Death in Canaan; Hatter Fox; The Seduction of Miss Leona; Reunion; Rape and Marriage--The Rideout Case.

FERRER, Jose: Act-Prod-Dir. b. Santurce, Puerto Rico, Jan 8, 1912. e. Princeton U. Dir, act Bway prior to film career. Films inc: Joan of Arc; Whirlpool; Cyrano de Bergerac (Oscar-1950); Moulin Rouge; Lawrence of Arabia; Enter Laughing; Forever Young, Forever Free; The Sentinel; The Swarm; Fedora; Dracula's Dog; Natural Enemies; The Big Brawl.

TV inc: Fame; The French Atlantic Affair; Battles-The Murder That Wouldn't Die; Gideon's Trumpet; The Dream Merchants; Debbie Boone--The Same Old Brand New Me; Pleasure Palace.

Bway inc: Cyrano de Bergerac (Tony-1947); The Shrike (prod-dir-act) (Tonys-dir-act-1952); The Chase (prod-dir); Stalag 17.

FERRER, Mel: Prod-Dir-Act. b. Elberon, NJ, Aug 25, 1917. e. Princeton U. Spent early career in summer stock, Cape Cod Playhouse. Bway as dancer, You'll Never Know; Everywhere I Roam. Later prod-dir NBC. Started in films, 1945, as dial dir. Films inc: The Secret Fury; The Brave Bulls; Scaramouche; Lili; War and Peace; The Flesh and the Devil; Blood and Roses; The Net; The Black Pirate. (Prod) Wait Until Dark; "W"; The Norseman; The Tempter; The Fifth Floor; The Visitor.

Bway inc: Lost Boundaries; Born To Be Bad; Ondine.

TV inc: (act) The Top of the Hill; The Memory of Eva Ryker; Fugitive Family.

FERRERI, Marco: Dir. b. Italy, 1928. Films inc: El Pisito; The Wheelchair; Queen Bee; The Bearded Lady; Wedding March; Dillinger is Dead; Blowout.

FERRIGNO, Lou: Act. b. NYC, Nov 9, 1952. Won Mr America contest, 1973; won Mr Universe contest, 1974 & 1975. TV inc: The Incredible Hulk. Films inc: Pumping Iron.

FERTIK, Bill: Dir. b. NYC, Nov 28, 1942. e. Syracuse U, BA, NYU, MA. Films inc: Ga Guerre; Forty-One North, Sixty-One West; The Bolero (Oscar-ss-1973); Relations; The 1812 Overture; Ernest Bloch, A Portrait; Ned Williams Dance Theatre.

FERZETTI, Gabrielle: Act. b. Italy, 1925. Films inc: William Tell; Puccini; L'Avventura; Torpedo Bay; Once Upon a Time in the West; On Her Majesty's Secret Service; Hitler-The Last 10 Days; Night Porter; The Order and Security of the World; The Psychic; Gli anni Struggenti (The Burning Years).

FETCHIT, Stepin (Lincoln Theodore Perry): Act-Comedian. b. Key West, FL, 1892. On screen From 1927. Films inc: In Old Kentucky; Showboat; The Galloping Ghost; Stand Up and Cheer; David Harum; Miracle in Harlem; Bend of the River; Won Ton Ton, The Dog Who Saved Hollywood; Amazing Grace.
TV inc: Cutter.

FEUER, Cy: Prod-Dir. b. NYC, Jan 15, 1911. e. Juilliard. Bway (Prodns) (in assoc with Ernest N Martin): Where's Charley?; Guys and Dolls (Tony-1951); Can-Can; The Boy Friend; Silk Stockings; How to Succeed in Business Without Really Trying (Tony-1962); Little Me; Skyscraper; Walking Happy; The Goodbye People; The Act. Also prod-co-wri Whoop-up; On the 20th Century; I Remember Mama (rev).
Films inc: (with Martin); Cabaret; Piaf.

FEUILLERE, Edwige: Act. b. France, 1907. Topaze; I Was An Adventuress; Lucrezia Borgia; The Idiot; Blind Desire; The Eagle With Two Heads; Woman Hater; Olivia; Adorable Creatures; The Fruits of Summer; Love is My Profession; Crime Doesn't Pay.

FICKETT, Mary: Act. b. Bronxville, NY, May 23. Films inc: Man in Fire; Kathy O.
TV inc: Edge of Night; The Nurses; Pueblo; All My Children (Emmy-1973).
Bway inc: Sunrise at Campobello; I Know My Love; Tea and Sympathy; Love and Kisses.

FIEDEL, Brad: Comp-Wri-Singer. b. NYC, Mar 10, 1951. Films inc: Deadly Hero. TV inc: Mayflower--The Pilgrim Adventure; Hardhat and Legs; Seven Wishes of a Rich Kid; A Movie Star's Daughter; Playing for Time; The Day The Women Got Even.
Songs inc: I Don't Want To Be Your Fool Anymore; The Love That I Give You.

FIEDLER, Arthur: Cond. b. Boston, Dec 17, 1894. e. Royal Academy of Music, Berlin. Cond since 1923. Founder Boston Esplanade Concerts; also cond Boston Symphony Pop Concerts.
(Died July 9, 1979).

FIEDLER, John: Act. b. 1925. Films inc: Twelve Angry Men; Stage Struck; That Touch of Mink; The World of Henry Orient; Kiss Me Stupid; Fitzwilly; The Odd Couple; True Grit; Making It; Boulevard Nights.

FIELD, Leonard S: Prod. b. St Paul, MN, Jul 10, 1908. e. U of MN. Bway inc: Good Hunting; Pretty Penny; Bell, Book and Candle (Gen M); Porgy and Bess (Gen M); The Hostage; The Birthday Party; The Au Pair Man; Susanna Andler; Passion of Dracula.

FIELD, Sally: Act. b. Pasadena, CA, Nov 6, 1946. Films inc: The Way West; Stay Hungry; Smokey and the Bandit; Heroes; The End; Norma Rae (Oscar-1979); Beyond the Poseidon Adventure; Smokey and The Bandit II.
TV inc: Gidget; The Flying Nun; The Girl With Something Extra; Home for the Holidays; Maybe I'll Come Home in the Spring; Marriage Year One; Sybil (Emmy-1977).

FIELD, Shirley Ann: Act. b. London, 1938. Films inc: Dry Rot; Once More With Feeling; The Entertainer; Saturday Night and Sunday Morning; The Man in the Moon; The Damned; The War Lover; Lunch Hour; Kings of the Sun; Doctor in Clover; Hell is Empty; Risking It.

FIELDING, Harold: Prod. b. England. Originally concert violinist, later concert impresario. Thea inc: (London) Cinderella; Aladdin; The Gazebo; The Billy Barnes Revue; The Music Man; Progress to the Park; The Bird of Time; Critic's Choice; A Thurber Carnival; How Are You Johnny?; Half A Sixpence; Looking For the Action; Fielding's Music Hall; Charlie Girl; Man of Magic; Sweet Charity; You're a Good Man Charlie Brown; Mame; Phil the Fluter; The Great Waltz; Show Boat; Gone With the Wind; Finishing Touches; Let My People Come; The Charles Pierce Show; The Biograph Girl.

FIELDING, Jerry: Comp. b. Pittsburgh, Jun 17, 1922. Film scores inc: Advise and Consent; The Wild Bunch; Straw Dogs; Josey Wales; The Big Sleep; Gray Lady Down; Beyond the Poseidon Adventure; Escape From Alcatraz; Below The Belt.
TV inc: Betty Hutton series; Hogan's Heroes; Bionic Woman; McMillan and Wife; High Midnight (Emmy-1980).
(Died Feb 17, 1980).

FIELDS, Freddie: Prod. b. Ferndale, NY, Jul 12, 1923. VP, member of bd of dir, MCA Corp; p Freddie Fields Assoc Ltd, 1961; p, chief exec ofcr Creative Management Assoc Ltd Agency; resigned CMC (now int'l Creative Mgt), 1975; became indy prod. Films inc: Handle With Care; Looking for Mr Goodbar; American Gigolo; Wholly Moses!

FIELDS, Gracie: Act-Singer. b. Rochdale, Eng, 1898. Appeared in vaudeville, music halls. On screen in England From 1931. Films inc: Sally in Our Alley; Sing As We Go; The Show Goes On; Smiling Along; Shipyard Sally; (In U.S.) Stage Door Canteen; Holy Matrimony; Molly and Me; Paris Underground.
(Died Sep 27, 1979).

FIELDS, Verna: Exec-Film ed. b. St Louis, MO, Mar 21, 1918. Films inc: Studs Lonigan; Savage Eye; Track of Thunder; Affair of the Skin; Medium Cool; American Graffiti (co-ed); What's Up Doc; Paper Moon; Daisy Miller; The Sugarland Express (co-ed); Jaws (Oscar-1975). 1976 named VP, Universal.

FIGUEROA, Gabriel: Cin. b. Mexico, 1907. Films inc: The Fugitive; Maclovia; Night of the Iguana; Kelly's Heroes; The Children of Sanchez.

FINCH, Jon: Act. b. England, 1941. Films inc: The Vampire Lovers; Horror of Frankenstein; Macbeth; Sunday Bloody Sunday; Frenzy; Lady Caroline Lamb; The Final Program; A Faithful Woman; The Second Power; Battleflag; Death on the Nile; La Sabina; Breaking Glass.
TV inc: Henry IV.

FINE, Sylvia: Wri. b. NYC, Aug 29. e. Brooklyn Coll. Wrote special material for husband, Danny Kaye. Stage scores inc: Straw Hat Review; Films inc: The Court Jester (score); Up in Arms (songs).
TV inc: Danny Kaye's Look-In At The Metropolitan Opera (Emmy-exec prod-1976); Musical Comedy Tonight.
Songs inc: The Moon Is Blue; The Five Pennies.

FINKEL, Robert S (Bob): Prod-Dir-Wri. b. Pittsburgh, PA, Mar 25, 1918. TV inc: (prod) Andy Williams Show (Emmys-1966, 1967); Elvis Presley Special; Bing Crosby Christmas Special; Julie Andrews Hour; Circus of the Stars. (Dir): Bob Newhart; Barney Miller; McMillan & Wife; The John Davidson Christmas Show; Third Annual Circus of the Stars; John Denver and the Muppets, A Christmas Get Together.

FINLAY, Frank: Act. b. Farnworth, Lancs, Eng, Aug 6, 1926. e. RADA. Appeared with Guildford Repertory Theatre Co, 1957. Thea inc: The Telescope; The Queen and the Welshman; Chicken Soup with Barley; The Happy Haven; The Workhouse Donkey; Hamlet; The Crucible; Othello; Filumena.
Films inc: The Informer; Othello; Inspector Clouseau; Twisted Nerve; Cromwell; Gumshoe; Danny Jones; Sitting Target; Shaft in Africa; The Three Musketeers; The Four Musketeers; Murder by Decree.
TV inc: Casanova; The Adventures of Don Quixote; The Death of Adolph Hitler; The Thief of Baghdad.

FINNERMAN, Gerald Perry: Cin. b. LA, Dec 17, 1931. e. Loyola U of LA. TV inc: Night Gallery (& dir); Star Trek; Kojak; Planet of the Apes; Police Woman; Joe Forrester; Salvage I (& dir); The Last Hurrah; Ziegfeld--The Man and His Woman (Emmy-1978); The Dream Merchants; From Here To Eternity; To Find My Son.

FINNEY, Albert: Act. b. Salford, Eng, May 9, 1936. e. RADA. Stage debut, 1956, Birmingham Repertory Theatre. Screen debut, 1960, The Entertainer. Films inc: Saturday Night and Sunday Morning; Tom Jones; Night Must Fall; Two for the Road; Charlie Bubbles; Scrooge; Gumshoe; Alpha Beta; Murder on the Orient Express; The Duelists.

Thea inc: The Party; Coriolanus; The Lily White Boys; Billy Liar; Luther; Much Ado About Nothing; Love for Love; Miss Julie; A Flea in Her Ear; Joe Egg; Alpha Beta; Krapp's Last Tape; Cromwell; Chez Nous; Hamlet; Loot; Tamburlaine; The Country Wife; Uncle Vanya; The Cherry Orchard; Present Laughter.

TV inc: View Friendship and Marriage; The Claverdon Road Job; The Miser.

FINNEY, Edward F: Exec. b. NYC, Apr 18, 1913. e. CCNY. In 1941 org Edward Finney Productions. Discovered the late Tex Ritter and made his first 40 features. TV inc: Things that Make America Great; Baron Munchhausen; Seven Wonders of Arkansas; Journey to Freedom; Call of the Forest.

FINSTON, Nathaniel: Cond-Mus dir. b. 1890. Conducted orchestras accompanying silent film presentations various theatres, NYC and Chicago; concert master under Walter Damrosch; to Hollywood with advent of sound to set up industry's first sound music dept at Par; remained at Par through 1935; shifted to MGM as general mus dir until 1944; collaborated on indie prodns and travelogs until his retirement.

(Died Dec 19, 1979).

FIRESTONE, Eddie: Act. b. San Francisco, Dec 11, 1920. Films inc: Jackpot; With a Song in My Heart; One Minute to Zero; The Revolt of Mamie Stover; Bail Out at 40,000; Two for the Seesaw; A Man Called Cannon; Suppose They Gave a War and Nobody Came?; Play It As It Lays.

TV inc: The Big Slide; Revenge of the Red Chief.

FIRKUSNY, Rudolf: Pianist. b. Czechoslovakia, Feb 11, 1912. Debut 1922, Prague; fled Czechoslovakia after German occupation; has performed all over the world.

FIRSTENBERG, Jean (nee Picker): Exec. b. NYC, Mar 13, 1936. e. Boston U, BS. D of Eugene Picker. With WRC-TV, Washington as asst prod pub aff tv shows; J. Walter Thompson Agcy; 1972 Princeton U, dir publications; in chg of grants for Markle Foundation; Jan 1980 dir AFI.

FIRTH, Peter: Act. b. Bradford, Yorkshire, England, 1955. First appeared in TV series, The Flaxton Boys, at age 15. Films inc: Here Come the Double Deckers; Brother Sun and Sister Moon; Equus; When You Comin' Back, Red Ryder; Tess.

Thea inc: Spring Awakening; Equus; Romeo and Juliet.

FISHER, Art: Dir-Prod-Wri. b. NYC, Feb 2, 1934. TV inc: Andy Williams Special; Sunny & Cher Comedy Hour *(Emmy-*dir-1972); Chevy Chase Show; Neil Diamond; Ann-Margret; Bing Crosby; Elton John; Tom and Dick Smothers Brothers Special I; Siegfried and Roy-Superstars of Magic (dir).

FISHER, Carrie: Act. b. Beverly Hills, CA, Oct 21, 1956. e. London Central School of Speech and Drama. D of Debbie Reynolds and Eddie Fisher. Films inc: Shampoo; Star Wars; Mr. Mike's Mondo Video; The Empire Strikes Back; The Blues Brothers.

Bway inc: Irene (rev); Censored Scenes from King Kong.
TV inc: Come Back, Little Sheba; Saturday Night Live (guest host).

FISHER, Eddie: Act. b. Philadelphia, Aug 10, 1928. Niteries, Radio, TV performer. Discovered by Eddie Cantor, 1949. Films inc: All About Eve; Bundle of Joy; Butterfield 8.

FISHER, Lucy: Exec. b. Oct 2, 1949. e. Harvard U, BA. Story ed, Samuel Goldwyn Jr Prodns; exec story ed, MGM; exec in charge of creative affairs, MGM; vp creative affairs, Fox; vp prodn, Fox. Resigned Feb 1980.

FISHER, Steve: Wri. b. 1913. Films inc: Destination Tokyo; The Lady in the Lake; Dead Reckoning; Song of the Thin Man; To the Shores of Tripoli; Tokyo Joe: Vicki; Johnny Angel; Battle Zone; Susan Slept Here; The Restless Breed; I, Monster.

TV inc: McMillan and Wife; Barnaby Jones; Starsky and Hutch; Fantasy Island.

(Died Mar 27, 1980).

FISHER, Terence: Dir. b. London, 1904. Started as ed. Films inc: Colonel Bogey; To the Public Danger; Marry Me; The Astonished Heart (co-dir); So Long at the Fair (co-dir); Home to Danger; The Last Page; Stolen Face; Wings of Danger; Four-Sided Triangle; Murdered By Proxy; The Curse of Frankenstein; Kill Me Tomorrow; Dracula; The Mummy; The Hound of the Baskervilles; The Man Who Could Cheat Death; The Two Faces of Dr Jekyll; Phantom of the Opera; Sherlock Holmes; The Gorgon; Dracula-Prince of Darkness; Night of the Big Heat; The Devil Rides Out; Frankenstein and the Monster from Hell.

FITZGERALD, Ella: Singer. b. Newport News, VA, 1918. Films inc: Ride Em Cowboy; Pete Kelly's Blues; St Louis Blues; Let No Man Write My Epitaph.

TV inc: The Kennedy Center Honors - A Celebration of the Performing Arts; The Carpenters - Music, Music, Music. *(Grammys-*(9)-vocal-1958, 1959, 1960, 1962; jazz-vocal-1958, 1959, 1976, 1979; vocal album 1960).

FITZGERALD, Geraldine: Act. b. Dublin, Ireland, Nov 24, 1914. e. Dublin Art School. On stage Gate Theatre, Dublin. British films inc: Turn of the Tide; Mill on the Floss. To Hollywood 1939. Films inc: Wuthering Heights; Dark Victory; Till We Meet Again; Flight From Destiny; Watch on the Rhine; Wilson; Obsessed; Ten North Frederick; The Pawnbroker; Rachel, Rachel; The Last American Hero; Harry and Tonto; Echoes of a Summer; Bye Bye Monkey.

Bway inc: A Long Day's Journey Into Night; Ah, Wilderness!; A Touch of the Poet; The Shadow Box.

TV inc: The Best of Everything.

FITZPATRICK, James A: Prod. b. Shelton, CT, Feb 26, 1902. e. Yale, AADA. Prod and narr many travel shorts (Fitzpatrick Traveltalks). Wrote, prod, dir one fea, Song of Mexico, 1945.

(Died June 12, 1980).

FITZSIMMONS, Tom: Act. b. San Francisco, Oct 28, 1947. e. Yale, BA, Yale School of Drama, MFA. Films inc: Swashbuckler. TV inc: June Moon; The Last of the Belles; The Paper Chase.

FIX, Paul: Act. b. Dobbs Ferry, NY, Mar 13, 1902. Films inc: The First Kiss; The Last Mile; Back Street; The Prisoner of Shark Island; The Ex-Mrs Bradford; The Buccaneer; Dr. Cyclops; Back to Bataan; Wake of the Red Witch; The Plunderers; Red River; Island in the Sky; The High and the Mighty; The Bad Seed; Giant; Santiago; To Kill a Mockingbird; The Sons of Katie Elder; Shenandoah; Welcome to Hard Times; The Ballad of Josie; Day of the Evil Gun; Dirty Dingus Magee; Zabriskie Point; Shoot Out; Night of the Lepus; Pat Garrett & Billy the Kid; Cahill, United States Marshal; Grayeagle; Wanda Nevada.

TV inc: The Rifleman; The Rebels.

FLACK, Roberta: Singer-Comp. b. Black Mountain, NC, Feb 10, 1940. e. Howard U. Recording artist *(Grammys-*(4)-record of year-1972, 1973; pop vocal-1972, 1973).

TV inc: The Bill Cosby Show; The First Time Ever.
Films inc: Renaldo and Clara.

FLAGG, Fannie (Patricia Neal): Act. b. Birmingham, AL, Sep 21. e. U of AL. Films inc: Five Easy Pieces; Stay Hungry; Rabbit Test; Grease.

TV inc: Fernwood 2Night; Match Game; Sex and the Married Woman; Candid Camera; The New Dick Van Dyke Show; The New Wonder Woman.

Thea inc: Here Today; Gingerbread Lady; Little Mary Sunshine; Come Back to the Five and Dime, Jimmy Dean, Jimmy Dean.

FLAMM, Donald J: Exec. b. Pittsburgh, PA, Dec 11, 1899. Started as publicist for the Shuberts, 1918; a pioneer in radio, he owned and operated WMCA, NYC, 1925-1941; WPCH NYC 1927-1932 and co-owned WPAT, Paterson, NJ, 1942-1948. Founded Intercity Network, one of first regional networks in US, 1927; with OWI during World War II conceived and executed plan for American Broadcasting Station in England which became basis for Voice of America; co-prod of plays in London and NY through directorship in Oscar Lewenstein Plays Ltd.

FLANAGAN, Fionnuala: Act. b. Dec 10, 1941. Films inc: Ulysses; Sinful Davey; Mr. Patman.
TV inc: The Legend of Lizzie Borden; Rich Man, Poor Man (*Emmy*-supp-1976); Young Love, First Love.
Bway inc: Ulysses in Nighttown.

FLANDERS, Ed: Act. b. Minneapolis, MN. Bway inc: The Birthday Party; The Trial of the Catonsville Nine; A Moon for the Misbegotten (*Tony*-supp-1974).
TV inc: The Legend of Lizzie Borden; A Moon for the Misbegotten (*Emmy*-supp-1976); Harry S Truman - Plain Speaking (*Emmy*-1977); Backstairs at the White House; Blind Ambition; Eleanor and Franklin; Meeting at Potsdam; Howard, The Amazing Mr. Hughes; Salem's Lot; Last Licks.
Films inc: MacArthur; The Ninth Configuration.

FLANNERY, Susan: Act. b. NYC, Jul 31, 1943. Films inc: The Towering Inferno; The Gumball Rally.
TV inc: Voyage to the Bottom of the Sea; The Time Tunnel; Days of Our Lives (*Emmy*-1975); The Moneychangers; Women in White; Anatomy of a Seduction.

FLATT, Ernest O: Chor. b. Oct 30, 1928. Bway inc: Fade Out, Fade In; It's A Bird, It's A Plane, It's Superman; Sugar Babies (& dir). Films inc: Anything Goes.
TV inc: Your Hit Parade (1955-1958); Garry Moore Show (1958-1963); Julie and Carol at Carnegie Hall; Julie and Carol at Lincoln Center; Carol Burnett Show (*Emmy*-1971); Bubbles and Burnett at the Met; Annie Get Your Gun; Damn Yankees; Kiss Me Kate; Calamity Jane.

FLATT, Lester Raymond: Act. b. Overton County, TN, Jun 28, 1914. With Earl Scruggs, formed the Foggy Mountain Boys, playing Bluegrass mus, the oldest form of rural mus in America. Team of Flatt & Scruggs were fixtures of the Grand Ole Opry. After 25 years team split up in March 1969. (*Grammy*-country-1968). (See also SCRUGGS, Earl).
(Died May 11, 1979).

FLAUM, Marshall: Prod-Wri-Dir. b. NYC, Sep 13, 1930. e. U of IA, BA, U of S IL, DFA. TV inc: The Twentieth Century (series CBS-TV); Let My People Go; The Yanks Are Coming; Day of Infamy; Battle of Britain; Berlin: Kaiser to Khruschev; Hollywood--The Great Stars; Bogart; Hollywood: The Selznick Years; The Time of Man; Jane Goodall and the World of Animal Behaviour (*Emmy*-1973); Killy Le Champion; Bing Crosby - His Life and Legend. Exec prod & co-wri 25 Jacques Cousteau Specials; Playboy's 25th Anniversary Celebration (& dir).

FLEETWOOD MAC: Recording artists. Group members inc: Mick Fleetwood, (b. 1947) drummer; John McVie, (b. 1947) bassist; Lindsey Buckingham, (b. 1950) guitarist; singers Christine McVie, (b. 1944) and Stevie Nicks. (b. 1948).
(*Grammy*-album of year-1978; also prod award to Fleetwood).

FLEISCHER, Dave: Animator. b. NYC, Jul 14, 1894. e. Cooper Union. Created and prod animated cartoons with brother, Max. Their cartoons inc: Out of the Inkwell; Betty Boop; Bouncing Ball; Bimbo; Popeye; Imagination (*Oscar*-short-1943). Features inc: Gulliver's Travels; Mr Bug Goes to Town. In 1942 appointed head of Screen Gems for Columbia Studios.
(Died Jun 25, 1979).

FLEISCHER, Richard: Dir. b. NYC, Dec. 8, 1916. e. Brown U, BA; Yale, MFA. Films inc: Design for Death (*Oscar*-short-co-prod-1947); Child of Divorce; Banjo; So This Is New York; Bodyguard; Follow Me Quietly; The Clay Pigeon; Trapped; The Narrow Margin; The Happy Time; Arena; 20,000 Leagues Under the Sea; Violent Saturday; The Girl in the Red Velvet Swing; Bandido; Between Heaven and Hell; The Vikings; These Thousand Hills; Compulsion; Crack in the Mirror; The Big Gamble; Barabbas; Fantastic Voyage; Doctor Dolittle; The Boston Strangler; Che; Tora, Tora, Tora; 10 Rillington Place; See No Evil; The Last Run; The New Centurians; Soylent Green; The Don Is Dead; The Spikes Gang; Mr. Majestyk; Mandingo; The Incredible Sarah; The Prince and the Pauper; Ashanti; Crossed Swords; The Jazz Singer.

FLEISCHMAN, Stephen: Prod-Wri. b. NYC, Feb 19, 1919. e. Haverford Coll, BA. H of Dede Allen. TV inc: The Search series; Let's Take a Trip (prod); The Twentieth Century; CBS Reports; joined ABC News 1964 as prod doc unit; Close Up series; Life, Liberty and the Pursuit of Oil; Assault on Privacy; The Long Childhood of Timmy; Anatomy of Pop--The Music Explosion; Oil; Nobody's Children; Death In A Southwest Prison.

FLEMING, Art: Act-TV Personality. b. NYC. TV inc: The Californians; International Detective; Jeopardy (host). Films inc: The Moneychanger; Conspiracy to Assassinate President Lincoln; MacArthur.

FLEMING, Rhonda (Marilyn Lewis): Act. b. LA, Aug. 10, 1923. Films inc: Spellbound; Spiral Staircase; A Connecticut Yankee in King Arthur's Court; The Redhead and the Cowboy; Crosswinds; Inferno; While the City Sleeps; Gunfight at the OK Corral; The Buster Keaton Story; The Crowded Sky; Won Ton Ton, The Dog Who Saved Hollywood; The Nude Bomb.
Bway: The Women (rev).
TV inc: Love For Rent.

FLETCHER, Bramwell: Act. b. Bradford, Eng, Feb 20, 1904. London stage debut, 1927, Paul I. Films inc: Chick; To What Red Hell; Raffles; Svengali; The Mummy; The Scarlet Pimpernel; Random Harvest; White Cargo; The Immortal Sergeant.
Thea inc: Tonight at 8:30; Margin for Error; The Doctor's Dilemma; The Bernard Shaw Story; Pygmalion.

FLETCHER, Louise: Act. b. Birmingham, AL, 1938. Appeared in Playhouse 90, other TV shows. Retired for 10 years to raise family. Returned in Thieves Like Us; One Flew Over The Cuckoo's Nest, (*Oscar*-1975); Russian Roulette; Exorcist II: The Heretic; The Cheap Detective; The Lady In Red; Natural Enemies; Magician of Lublin; The Lucky Star.

FLICKER, Theodore J: Wri-Dir-Prod-Act. b. Freehold, NJ, Jun 6, 1930. e. Bard Coll, RADA. Plays inc: The Nervous Set (& dir); The Premise (& prod-dir-act).
Films inc: The Trouble Maker (dir); The President's Analyst (sp-dir); Jacob Two-Two Meets The Hooded Fang (sp-dir).
TV inc: (dir) Andy Griffith; Dick Van Dyke; Man From UNCLE; Barney Miller (co-creator & dir, pilot); Just a Little Inconvenience (wri-dir); Last of the Good Guys (wri-dir); Where The Ladies Go.

FLINN, John C Jr: Publicist. b. Yonkers, NY, May 4, 1917. e. UCLA. Publicist, Warner Bros 1936-46; joined Monogram 1946; Allied Artists 1951; dir of adv & pub Columbia 1959; joined MGM 1973; rejoined Columbia Pictures 1974, studio pub dir; 1979 named dir Industry Relations.

FLOOD, Ann: Act. b. Jamaica, NY, Nov 12. Bway inc: Kismet; Holiday for Lovers.
TV inc: West Point; Annapolis; Matinee Theatre; From These Roots; The Edge of Night (since 1962).

FLOREA, John: Dir-Wri-Prod. b. Alliance, OH, May 28, 1920. Films inc: A Time to Every Purpose; The Astral Strangler.
TV inc: The Island of the Lost; The Americans; Wide Country; Daniel Boone; Sea Hunt; Everglades; Primus; Convoy; Firehouse; Bonanza; The Virginian; High Chapparral; Destry Rides Again; Mission Impossible; Not for Hire; Highway Patrol; Target; CHiPs; Daktari; Gentle Ben; Flipper; The Runaways.

FLOREN, Myron: Comp-Mus-Singer. b. Webster, SD, Nov 5, 1919. With USO during WW 2, touring front lines. On radio, St Louis, postwar while head accordion dept St Louis Coll of Music. Soloist with various orchs; featured perf with Lawrence Welk orch.

Comps inc: Skating Waltz in Swing; Swingin' in Vienna; Kavallo's Kapers; Windy River; Dakota Polka; Long Long Ago in Swing; Minute Waltz in Swing.

FLOREY, Robert: Dir. b. Paris, 1900. In Hollywood since 1921. Films inc: The Romantic Age; The Coconuts; The Murders in the Rue Morgue; The Woman in Red; Hollywood Boulevard; The Face Behind The Mask; God Is My Co-Pilot; The Beast with Five Fingers; Rogues' Regiment; Johnny One Eye; The Gangster We Made.

TV inc: The Loretta Young Show; Alfred Hitchcock Presents.

(Died May 16, 1979).

FLUELLEN, Joel: Act. b. Dec 1, 1910. Films inc: The Burning Cross; The Jackie Robinson Story; Miss Lucy Gallant; The Decks Ran Red; Friendly Persuasion; Porgy and Bess; A Raisin in the Sun; Sitting Bull; Imitation of Life; Run Silent, Run Deep; He Rides Tall; Good Neighbor Sam; The Chase; The Learning Tree; The Great White Hope; The Skin Game; Man Friday; Casey's Shadow; Butch and Sundance Kid-The Early Days.

TV inc: Roots 2; Freedom Road.

FLYNN, John: Dir. Films inc: The Sergeant; The Jerusalem File; The Outfit (& sp); Rolling Thunder; Defiance.

TV inc: Marilyn--The Untold Story.

FOCH, Nina: Act. b. Leyden, Holland, Apr 20, 1924. On screen since 1943. Films inc: Return of the Vampire; Strange Affair; My Name Is Julia Ross; Ten Commandments; The Guilt of Janet Ames; An American in Paris; Spartacus; Prescription: Murder; Executive Suite; Such Good Friends; Jennifer.

TV inc: Ebony, Ivory and Jade; Pottsville.

FOGEL, Ira: Dir. TV inc (flr mgr): One Life to Live; All My Children; Sammy & Co. (Asso dir) Inside Pro Football; Stiller and Meara Take Five; AM America; Good Night America; Good Morning America. (Dir) Rona Barrett segs of Good Morning America.

FOGELBERG, Dan (Daniel Grayling Fogelberg): Sngwi-Mus. b. Peoria, IL, Aug 13, 1951. e. U IL. Albums inc: Home Free; Souvenirs; Captured Angel; Nether Lands; Twin Sons of Different Mothers; Phoenix.

FOGELMAN, Ted: Exec. b. Minneapolis, Feb 5, 1913. Bd member, Sec-Treas, then chmn local section SMPTE. Bd member, local chmn, SMPTE International. Assoc member ASC, ACE.

FOGELSON, Andrew M: Exec. b. New Rochelle, NY, Aug 5, 1942. e. Union Coll. 1968, ad coypwriter WB; 1971 vp mktg svs; 1973 vp wldwde pub-ad Col; 1975, vp & exec asst to P; 1977, exec vp wldwde pub-ad WB; 1979 P Rastar Pictures.

FOGERTY, John C; Sngwri-Singer b. Berkeley, CA, May 28, 1945. With Creedence Clearwater Revival 1968-1972 as writer-performer; later with Blue Ridge Rangers before solo.

Songs inc: Proud Mary; Have You Ever Seen the Rain; Who'll Stop the Rain; Bad Moon Rising; Fortunate Son; Travelin' Band; Look Out My Back Door; Down on the Corner; Green River; Run Through The Jungle; Hey Tonight; Up Around the Bend; It Came Out of The Sky; Commotion; Born on the Bayou; Rockin' All Over the World.

FOLSEY, George: Cin. b. 1898. Films inc: The Fear Market; Born Rich; Applause; Reunion in Vienna; The Smiling Lieutenant; Reckless; The Gorgeous Hussy; The Great Ziegfeld; Meet Me in St. Louis; White Cliffs of Dover; A Guy Named Joe; Under The Clock; The Green Years; Green Dolphin Street; State of the Union; Take Me Out to the Ballgame; The Great Sinner; Adam's Rib; Million Dollar Mermaid; Executive Suite; Seven Brides for Seven Brothers; All the Brothers Were Valiant; The Fastest Gun Alive; Imitation General; The Balcony.

TV inc: Here's Peggy Fleming (Emmy-1969).

FONDA, Henry: Act. b. Grand Island, NE, May 16, 1905. e. U of MN. F of Jane and Peter. Screen debut 1935, The Farmer Takes A Wife. Bway debut 1929, The Game of Life and Death (walkon).

Films inc: Way Down East; I Dream Too Much; Trail of the Lonesome Pine; The Moon's Our Home; You Only Live Once; Wings of the Morning; That Certain Woman; I Met My Love Again; Jezebel; Blockade; The Mad Miss Manton; Jesse James; Let Us Live; The Story of Alexander Graham Bell; Young Mr Lincoln; Drums Along the Mohawk; The Grapes of Wrath; Lillian Russell; Chad Hanna; The Lady Eve; The Male Animal; The Magnificent Dope; Tales of Manhattan; The Immortal Sergeant; The Ox-Bow Incident; My Darling Clementine; The Long Night; The Fugitive; Daisy Kenyon; Mister Roberts; War and Peace; 12 Angry Men; The Tin Star; Stage Struck; Warlock; Advise and Consent; The Longest Day; How the West Was Won; The Best Man; Fail Safe; In Harm's Way; Battle of the Bulge; Welcome to Hard Times; Yours, Mine and Ours; The Boston Strangler; Once Upon a Time in the West; The Cheyenne Social Club; Sometimes a Great Notion; Ash Wednesday; My Name is Nobody; Midway; Roller Coaster; Tentacles; The Great Smokey Roadblock; The Swarm; Meteor; City on Fire; Wanda Nevada.

Bway inc: I Loved You Wednesday; The Farmer Takes A Wife; Blow Ye Winds; Mister Roberts (Tony-1948); Point of No Return; Caine Mutiny Court Martial; Two for the Seesaw; Silent Night, Lonely Night; Critic's Choice; A Gift of Time; Generation; Our Town; Fathers Against Sons Against Fathers; The Time of Your Life; Clarence Darrow; First Monday in October. (Special Tony-1979).

TV inc: The Decision of Arrowsmith; Clown (& prod); The Petrified Forest; The Deputy; The Fabulous Fifties (host); Henry Fonda and Family; Hollywood--the Fabulous Era (host); Stranger on the Run; John Steinbeck's America and Americans (Host-narr); The Smith Family; The Red Pony; The Alpha Caper; Clarence Darrow; FDR--The man Who Changed America; Collision Course; The Henry Fonda Special; Travels With Charley; Home to Stay; The Man Who Loved Bears (narr); The Golden Honeymoon (Host); The Oldest Living Graduate; Gideon's Trumpet.

FONDA, Jane: Act. b. NYC, Dec 21, 1938. D of Henry Fonda. Screen debut 1960 Tall Story. Films inc: Walk on the Wild Side; The Chapman Report; Period of Adjustment; In the Cool of the Day; Sunday in New York; La Ronde; Cat Ballou; Hurry Sundown; Barefoot in the Park; Barbarella; They Shoot Horses Don't They?; Klute (Oscar-1971); Steelyard Blues; A Doll's House; Fun with Dick and Jane; Julia; Coming Home (Oscar-1978); California Suite; Comes A Horseman; The China Syndrome; The Electric Horseman; Nine To Five.

FONDA, Peter: Act. b. NYC, 1939. e. NE U. S of Henry Fonda. Acting debut at Lincoln (NE) Playhouse, where his father had made pro bow 35 years earlier. Bway: Blood, Sweat and Stanley Poole. On screen from 1963, Tammy and the Doctor. Films inc: The Victors; Lilith; The Wild Angels; The Trip; Easy Rider (& prod); The Last Movie; The Hired Hand (& dir); Two People; Dirty Mary, Crazy Larry; Open Season; Race with the Devil; Fighting Mad; Outlaw Blues; High Ballin'; Wanda Nevada (& dir).

TV inc: The Hostage Tower.

FONG, Kam: Act. b. Honolulu, May 27. Films inc: Gidget Goes Hawaiian; Ghost of the China Sea; Seven Women From Hell; Diamond Head.

TV inc: Hawaii Five-O.

FONTAINE, Joan: Act. b. Tokyo, Oct 22, 1917. Sis of Olivia de Havilland. On Broadway in Tea and Sympathy. Screen debut, Quality Street, 1937. Films inc: Rebecca; Suspicion (Oscar-1941); Women; The Constant Nymph; Gunga Din; This Above All; Jane Eyre; Frenchman's Creek; Affairs of Susan; Emperor Waltz; September Affair; Ivanhoe; Casanova's Big Night; Island in the Sun; Until They Sail; A Certain Smile; Tender is the Night; The Devil's Own.

FONTANNE, Lynn: Act. b. Woodford, Eng, Dec 6, 1897. Widow of Alfred Lunt. London stage debut 1905, in pantomine, Cinderella. Bway debut 1910, Mr Preedy and the Countess. Films inc: Second Youth; The Guardsman; Stage Door Canteen.

TV inc: The Great Sebastians; The Magnificent Yankee (Emmy-1965).

Bway inc: Pygmalion; Strange Interlude; Reunion in Vienna; Point Valaine; The Seagull; The Taming of the Shrew; There Shall Be No Night; O Mistress Mine; Quadrille; The Visit; The Kennedy Center Honors, 1980.

(Special Tony-1974). Received the Peace Medal From Pres Johnson, 1964.

FONTEYN, Dame Margot (Margaret Hookham): Ballerina. b. Surrey, Eng, May 18, 1919. Prima Ballerina of Britain's Royal Ballet, Dame Margot made her professional debut, 1934. Starred with Royal Ballet until 1970, then guest starring appearances with the Stuttgart Ballet, The National Ballet in Washington, DC, and other companies.

FOOTE, Horton: Wri. b. Wharton, TX, Mar 14. Former act. Plays inc: Out of My House; Only the Heart; Celebration; The Chase; The Trip to Bountiful; The Traveling Lady; book for the musical Gone With the Wind.

Films inc: To Kill a Mockingbird (Oscar-1962).

TV inc: The Trip to Bountiful; Young Lady of Property; Death of the Old Man; The Dancers; Flight; Tomorrow; the Night of the Storm.

FORAN, Dick: Act. b. Flemington, NJ, Jun 18, 1910. e. Princeton. Screen debut, Stand Up and Cheer, 1934. Films inc: Change of Heart; Accent on Youth; The Perfect Specimen; Boy Meets Girl; The Fighting 69th; The House of Seven Gables; Unfinished Business; Fort Apache; Please Murder Me; Donovan's Reef; Brighty of the Grand Canyon.

(Died Aug 10, 1979).

FORAY, June: Act. b. Springfield, MA. Voice specialist; on radio for several years; to Hollywood to do voice characterizations for Capital Records (PO)TV inc: The Bugs Bunny Mother's Day Special; Rikki Tikki Tavi; Raggedy Childrens Albums; voice of many cartoon characters. Ann and Andy in the Pumpkin Who Couldn't Smile; Yankee Doodle Cricket; The White Seal; Mowgli's Brothers; The Incredible Book Escape; Scruffy.

FORBES, Bryan (John Theobald Clarke): Act-Wri-Prod-Dir. b. London, Jul 22, 1926. e. RADA. Head of Prodn EMI Films, 1969-1971. London Stage debut, 1942, The Corn Is Green. Screen debut, 1948, The Small Back Room. Films inc: The Wooden Horse; The Million Pound Note; The Colditz Story; The World in His Arms; The Black Night; The Cockleshell Heroes (& sp); The Black Tent; The Body and the Battleship (& sp); The Key; I Was Monty's Double (& sp); Only Two Can Play; Of Human Bondage; Station Six Sahara; The League of Gentlemen. (Wri-co-prod), The Angry Silence. (Dir): Whistle Down the Wind; Seance on a Wet Afternoon; The L-Shaped Room; King Rat (& sp). The Wrong Box (& prod); The Whisperers (& sp-prod); Deadfall (& sp); Madwoman of Chaillot; The Stepford Wives. (Dir): The Slipper and the Rose (dir, co-sp): International Velvet (sp-prod-dir): Hopscotch (wri); Sunday Lovers (dir).

TV inc: (prod-dir): I Caught Acting Like the Measles; Goodbye, Norma Jean (dir); Elton John.

Thea inc: Macbeth (dir).

FORBES, David: Exec. b. Omaha, NE, Nov 9, 1945. e. U NE. Started with MGM, 1968 as field man in Detroit; later asst natl field coordinator at studio; 1973, dir Metrovision; 1974, dir special projects Fox; 1976 natl dir mktg svs Fox; 1977, mktg dir Rastar Prodns; 1980, vp & asst to pres, Columbia Pictures.

FORBES, Lou: Comp-Cond. b. St Louis, MO, Aug 12, 1902. Film scores inc: Intermezzo; Up in Arms; Wonder Man; This is Cinerama. Mus dir Intermezzo; Gone With the Wind.

FORD, Cecil: Prod. b. Dublin, 1911. e. Trinity Coll. Began career as an actor. Films inc: (Asst dir): Odd Man Out. (Prodn Mgr): Moby Dick; Around the World in 80 Days; The Bridge on the River Kwai; The Inn of the Sixth Happiness; Young Winston. (Prod): The Guns of Navarone; Squadron 64; All Things Bright and Beautiful.

FORD, Glenn: Act. b. Quebec, May 1, 1916. Bway inc: Groom for a Bride; Soliloquy. Screen debut, 1940, Heaven With a Barbed Wire Fence. U.S. Marine Corps, 1942-45. Films inc: So Ends Our Night; Desperadoes; Gilda; Framed; The Mating of Millie; Loves of Carmen; The Redhead and the Cowboy; Follow the Sun; The Secret of Convict Lake; Affair in Trinidad; Man From the Alamo; Appointment in Honduras; The Americano; Violent Men; Blackboard Jungle; Ransom; Fastest Gun Alive; Jubal; Teahouse of the August Moon; Don't Go Near the Water; The Sheepman; Imitation General; Torpedo Run; It Started With a Kiss; The Gazebo; Cimarron; The Four Horsemen of the Apocalypse; Experiment in Terror; The Courtship of Eddie's Father; The Rounders; The Money Trap; Fate Is the Hunter; Dear Heart; Time for Killing; Heaven With a Gun; Santee; Midway; Superman; The Visitor; Virus.

TV inc: The Brotherhood of The Bell; Cade's Country; Jarret; The Holvak Family; When The West Was Fun; Once An Eagle; Beggarman, Thief; The Gift.

FORD, Harrison: Act. b. Chicago, Jul 13, 1942. e. Ripon Coll. Films inc: Dead Heat on a Merry-Go-Round; Luv; Getting Straight; The Long Ride Home; Journey To Shiloh; Zabriskie Point; The Conversation; American Graffiti; Star Wars; Heroes; Force 10 From Navarone; Hanover Street; Apocalypse Now; The Frisco Kid; The Empire Strikes Back.

TV inc: Dynasty; The Trial of Lt. Calley; The Possessed.

FORD, Tennessee Ernie: Singer. b. Bristol, TN, Feb 13, 1919. e. Cincinnati Conserv. of Music. Radio announcer, 1939-41; U.S. Air Force, 1942-45; hillbilly disc jockey, Pasadena; Capital Recording artist. TV inc: Tennessee Ernie Show; I Love Lucy; Red Skelton Show; Perry Como Show; George Gobel Show.

(Grammy-Gospel-1964).

FORD, Tony: Exec. b. NYC, Aug 6, 1925. e. St Johns U. Agent with MCA, 1949-53; Indy prod tv specials for Ringling Bros Circus, Victor Borge; reentered agency business, General Artists Corp, vp, tv dept. Headed own agency, Tony Ford Mgt, Inc, which was acquired by William Morris Agency; headed creative services division WMA; left Morris Agency 1977; to re-open own agency; Oct 1979 named sr vp crea aff Metromedia Producers Corp.

FOREIGNER: Group. Members are Mick Jones, lead guitar-voc; Lou Gramm, lead voc; Ian McDonald, guitars-keyboard-horns-voc; Al Greenwood, keyboard-synthesizer; Dennis Elliott, drums; Rick Wills, bass guitar-voc.

Albums inc: Foreigner; Double Vision; Head Games; Little River Band.

FOREMAN, Carl: Wri-Prod-Dir. b. Chicago, Jul 23, 1914. e. U of IL, Northwestern U. Films inc: So This Is New York (sp); The Clay Pigeon (sp); Home of the Brave (sp); Champion (sp); The Men (sp); Cyrano de Bergerac (sp); High Noon (sp); The Key (sp & prod); The Mouse That Roared (exec prod); The Guns of Navarone (sp & prod); The Victors (sp, dir & prod); Born Free (prod); MacKenna's Gold (prod); Otley (prod); The Virgin Soldiers (prod); Living Free (prod); Young Winston (sp & prod); Force 10 From Navarone (sp); When Time Ran Out (sp).

TV inc: The Golden Gate Murders.

FOREMAN, John: Prod. b. Idaho Falls, ID. Co-founder of CMA Agency. Resigned 1968 to found Newman-Foreman Co. Films inc: Winning; Butch Cassidy and the Sundance Kid; WUSA; Puzzle of a Downfall Child; They May Be Giants; Pocket Money; The Effect of Gamma Rays on Man-in-the-Moon Marigolds; The Macintosh Man; The Man Who Would Be King; The Great Train Robbery.

FORMAN, Milos: Dir. b. Caslaz, Czechoslovakia, Feb 18, 1932. e. Academy of Music and Dramatic Arts, Prague. Wrote scripts, radio commentator. First directorial job, Magic Lantern. Films inc: Black Peter; Loves of A Blonde; Talent Competition; Fireman's Ball; One Flew Over the Cuckoo's Nest (Oscar-1975); Hair.

FORMAN, William R: Exh. P Cinerama; Pacific Theatres; Nationwide Theatres; Consolidated Amusements; Cinema 5; RKO- Stanley Warner.

FORREST, George (Chet): Lyr-Comp. b. NYC, Jul 31, 1915. At 13 became partner of Robert Wright; as team, under contract to MGM Studios; wrote songs for films inc: Maytime: Sweethearts; Firefly; Balalaika; The New Moon; I Married an Angel.

Bway scores inc: Song of Norway; Kismet *(Tony*-1954); Magdalena.

Songs inc: Always and Always; It's a Blue World; Elena; Donkey Serenade; Stranger in Paradise; Baubles, Bangles and Beads; And This is My Beloved.

FORREST, Steve (William Forrest Andrews): Act. b. Huntsville, TX, Sep 29, 1924. B of Dana Andrews. Films inc: The Bad and the Beautiful; Phantom of the Rue Morgue; Prisoner of War; Bedevilled; The Living Idol; Heller in Pink Tights; The Yellow Canary; Rascal; The Wild Country; The Late Liz; North Dallas Forty.

TV inc: The Baron; S.W.A.T.; Wanted, the Sundance Woman; The Deerslayer; Roughnecks; A Rumor of War.

FORSTER, Robert: Act. b. Rochester, NY, Jul 13, 1941. e. Heidelberg Coll; Alfred U; Rochester U, BS. Thea inc: Mrs. Dally; A Streetcar Named Desire (tour).

Films inc: Reflections in a Golden Eye; Medium Cool; Justine; Journey Through Rosebud; The Don Is Dead; Avalanche; The Black Hole; Alligator.

TV inc: Judd for the Defense; Banyon; The Darker Side of Terror.

FORSYTH, Bruce: Act. b. London, Feb 22, 1928. Started in vaudeville, worked as comic at Windmill Theatre, London, 1949-1951. Thea inc: Little Me; Birds on the Wing; Bruce Forsyth (one-man show); The Travelling Music Show.

Films inc: Star!; Hieronymus Merkin; Bedknobs and Broomsticks; The Magnificent Seven Deadly Sins.

TV inc: Sunday Night at the London Palladium (host for three years); The Generation Game.

FORSYTHE, John (John Lincoln Freund): Act. b. Carney's Point, NJ, Jan 29, 1918. Early career as sports announcer, radio. Bway debut, 1942, Vickie. On screen From 1944, Destination Tokyo. Films inc: The Captive City; It Happens Every Thursday; The Glass Web; Escape From Fort Bravo; The Trouble With Harry; The Ambassador's Daughter; See How They Run; Madame X; In Cold Blood; The Happy Ending; Topaz; And Justice For All.

TV inc: Studio One; Kraft Theatre; Robert Montgomery Presents; Bachelor Father; To Rome with Love; Charlie's Angels (voice); A Time For Miracles.

Thea inc: Mr. Roberts; All My Sons; Yellow Jack; Teahouse of the August Moon; Detective Story; Weekend.

FORTE, Chet: Prod-Dir. b. Hackensack, NJ, Aug 7, 1935. e. Columbia Coll. TV inc: (Dir) Monday Night Football; Monday Night Baseball; World Series; Wide World of Sports; Kentucky Derby; Indianapolis 500; Preakness; Prime Time Fights. (Prod) Wide World of Sports *(Emmy*-1976); Olympic Games 1968 through 1980 *(Emmy*-1976).

FOSSE, Bob: Dir-Chor-Act. b. Chicago, 1927. On stage as dancer at age 13. Toured in Call Me Mister. Signed by MGM, 1953. Films inc: (act): Give a Girl A Break; The Affairs of Dobie Gillis; Kiss Me Kate; The Little Prince. (Chor): My Sister Eileen. (Dir-chor): Sweet Charity; Cabaret *(Oscar*-dir-1972); All That Jazz. (Dir): Lenny.

Bway inc: (chor): Pajama Game *(Tony*-chor-1955); How to Succeed in Business Without Even Trying. (Dir-chor): Redhead *(Tony*-chor-1959); Damn Yankees *(Tony*-chor-1956); New Girl In Town; Little Me *(Tony*-chor-1963); Sweet Charity *(Tony*-chor-1966); Pippin *(Tonys*-dir-chor-1973); Chicago; Dancin' *(Tony*-chor-1978).

TV inc: Liza With A Z *(Emmys*-(3)-Prod-Dir-Chor-1973).

FOSSEY, Brigitte: Act. b. France, 1945. Films inc: Jeux Inderdits; Le Grand Meaulnes; Adieu l'ami; M Comme Matthieu; The Man Who Loved Women; The Good and the Bad; The Swiss Affair; Blue Country; Quintet; Mais ou et donc Orincar; The Triple Death of the Third Character; A Bad Son.

FOSTER, David: Prod. b. NYC, Nov 25, 1929. Entered ind prod, 1968. Films inc: McCabe and Mrs. Miller; The Getaway; The Nickel Ride (exec prod); The Drowning Pool; First Love; Heroes; The Legacy; Tribute (exec prod).

FOSTER, Desmond Lionel: Exec. b. Wellington, Australia, Jan 14, 1924. Broadcast industry association dir.

FOSTER, Jodie: Act. b. LA, Nov 19, 1962. Made TV commercials starting at age 3. Screen debut in Disney's Napoleon and Samantha, 1972. Films inc: Tom Sawyer; One Little Indian; Alice Doesn't Live Here Anymore; Echoes of Summer; Bugsy Malone; Taxi Driver; Freaky Friday; The Little Girl Who Lives Down The Lane; Candleshoe; Foxes; Carny; Cassotto.

TV inc: The Courtship of Eddie's Father; My Three Sons; Paper Moon; Smile Jenny, You're Dead; Rookie of the Year.

FOSTER, Julia: Act. b. Lewes, Sussex, Eng, 1942. Films inc: The Small World of Sammy Lee; Two Left Feet; The System; The Bargee; One-Way Pendulum; Alfie; Half a Sixpence; All Coppers Are.

TV inc: Crime and Punishment; Good Girl; Moll Flanders.

Thea inc: Travelling Light; What the Butler Saw; Notes on a Love Affair; Saint Joan.

FOSTER, Meg: Act. e. NY Neighborhood Playhouse. Films inc: Adam at 6 A.M.; Promise Her Anything; A Different Story; Once In Paris; Carny.

TV inc: Sunshine Christmas; Things In Their Season; James Dean, Portrait of a Friend; Washington Behind Closed Doors; Scarlet Letter; Guyana Tragedy--the Story of Jim Jones; The Legend of Sleepy Hollow.

FOSTER, Paul: Wri. b. Penn's Grove, NJ, 1931. e. Rutgers U, St John's U. Plays inc: Hurrah for the Bridge; The Recluse; The Madonna in the Orchard; The Hessian Corporal; Tom Paine Satyricon; Silver Queen Saloon.

FOSTER, Phil: Act. b. NYC, Mar 29, 1914. Nitery Comic. Films inc: Conquest of Space. TV inc: Laverne & Shirley; The Great American Traffic Jam.

FOWLEY, Douglas: Act. b. NYC, May 30, 1911. Films inc: Let's Talk it Over; Crash Donovan; Charlie Chan on Broadway; Mr Moto's Gamble; Dodge City; Tanks a Million; The Kansan; The Hucksters; Battleground; Edge of Doom; Singin' in the Rain; The High and the Mighty; Desire in the Dust; Barabbas; The Good Guys and the Bad Guys; Homebodies; Black Oak Conspiracy; The White Buffalo; The North Avenue Irregulars.

TV inc: Pistols and Petticoats.

FOX, Charles: Comp-Cond. b. NYC, Oct 30, 1940. e. Fontainbleu Conservatory of Music and with Nadia Boulanger. Films inc: Barbarella; Goodbye, Columbus; A Separate Peace; Pufnstuf; The Laughing Policeman; The Last American Hero; The Other Side of The Mountain; The Duchess and the Dirtwater Fox; Two Minute Warning; Victory at Entebbe; Foul Play; Our Winning Season; One on One; Little Darlings; Why Would I Lie?; Oh, God! Book II; Nine To Five.

TV inc: Love American Style *(Emmys*-1970, 1973); Shirley.

FOX, Edward: Act. b. Eng, 1937. Films inc: The Naked Runner; The Long Duel; Oh! What a Lovely War; Skullduggery; The Go-Between; The Day of the Jackal; Doll's House; The Squeeze; A Bridge Too Far; The Cat and the Canary; The Big Sleep; The Duellists; Force 10 From Navarone; Soldier of Orange; The Miror Crack'd.

TV inc: Edward and Mrs Simpson.

FOX, James: Act. b. Eng, 1939. Film debut as child actor 1950, The Magnet. Films inc: The Loneliness of the Long-Distance Runner; The Servant; Tamahine; Those Magnificent Men in Their Flying Machines; King Rat; The Chase; Thoroughly Modern Millie; Duffy; Isadora; Arabella; Performance.

TV inc: The Door; Espionage.

FOX, Maxine: Prod. b. Baltimore, MD, Dec 26, 1946. e. Boston U. Plays inc: Grease; Over Here!; And Miss Reardon Drinks a Little; Fortune and Men's Eyes.

FOX, Ray Errol: Lyr. b. Jul 13, 1941. Films inc: La Guerre Est Finie; The Clowns. Plays inc: The Sign in Sidney Brustein's Window.

FOXWORTH, Robert: Act. b. Houston, TX, Nov 1. e. Mellon U. Films inc: Treasure of Matecumbe; The Astral Factor; Airport '77; Damien-Omen II; Prophecy; The Black Marble.

TV inc: The Storefront Lawyers; Mrs Sundance; Hogan's Goat; The Memory of Eva Ryker; Act of Love.

FOXX, Redd: Act. b. St Louis, MO, Dec 9, 1922. Nightclub performer; recording artist. TV inc: Soul; Green Acres; Sanford and Son. Films inc: Norman. . .Is That You?

FOY, Eddie Jr: Act. b. New Rochelle, NY, Feb 4, 1905. Films inc: Fugitive From Justice; The Farmer Takes a Wife; Lucky Me; The Pajama Game; Bells are Ringing; Thirty is a Dangerous Age; Cynthia.

TV inc: Fair Exchange.

FRAKER, William A: Cin. b. LA, 1923. e. USC. Films inc: Games; The President's Analyst; Rosemary's Baby; Bullitt; Paint Your Wagon; Dusty and Sweets McGee; Day of the Dolphin; The Killer Inside Me; Bobby and Rose; Gator; Close Encounters of the Third Kind; The Exorcist; Looking for Mr. Goodbar; American Hot Wax; Heaven Can Wait; Old Boyfriends; 1941; The Hollywood Knights; Divine Madness. (Dir): Monte Walsh; Reflection of Fear.

FRAMPTON, Peter: Singer-Mus. b. Beckenham, Kent, England, Apr 22, 1950. With groups The Herd, Humble Pie, Frampton's Camel before solo.

Albums inc: Winds of Change; Something's Happening; Frampton; Frampton Comes Alive; I'm in You; Where I Should Be.

Films inc: Sgt Pepper's Lonely Hearts Club Band.

FRANCIOSA, Anthony: Act. b. NYC, Oct 25, 1928. Films inc: A Face in the Crowd; This Could Be the Night; A Hatful of Rain; Wild Is the Wind; The Long Hot Summer; The Naked Maja; The Story on Page One; Period of Adjustment; Rio Conchos; The Pleasure Seekers; A Man Could Get Killed; Assault on a Queen; The Swinger; In Enemy Country; A Man Called Gannon; Across 110th Street; The Drowning Pool; Firepower.

TV inc: Valentine's Day; Name of the Game; Search; Matt Helm; Earth II; Hide and Go Seek; The Deadly Hunt; Ryan's the Name; The Black Widow; Side Show; The World is Full of Married Men.

Bway inc: End as a Man; Wedding Breakfast; A Hatful of Rain.

FRANCIS, Anne: Act. b. Ossining, NY, Sep 16, 1932. Radio, TV shows as child. Films inc: Summer Holiday; So Young So Bad; Elopement; Lydia Bailey; Susan Slept Here; Bad Day at Black Rock; The Blackboard Jungle; Forbidden Planet; Don't Go Near the Water; Girl of the Night; The Satan Bug; Funny Girl; The Love God; More Dead than Alive; Pancho Villa; Born Again.

TV inc: Haunts of the Very Rich; Honey West; Greatest Heroes of the Bible; The Rebels; Beggarman, Thief; Detour to Terror.

FRANCIS, Arlene (nee Kazanjian): Act. b. Boston, MA, 1908. W of Martin Gabel. Films inc: All My Sons; One, Two, Three; The Thrill of it All.

Thea inc: All That Glitters; Once More With Feeling; Dinner at Eight; Pal Joey; Who Killed Santa Claus?; Gigi.

TV inc: Regular panelist What's My Line; Arlene Francis Show; Talent Patrol.

FRANCIS, Connie (Constance Franconero): Act. b. Newark, NJ, Dec 12, 1938. Won Arthur Godfrey's Talent Scout Show at age 12. Films inc: Where The Boys Are; Follow The Boys; Looking For Love.

FRANCIS, Freddie: Cin-Dir. b. London, 1917. Films inc: (Cin) Mine Own Executioner; Time Without Pity; Room at the Top; Sons and Lovers (Oscar-cin-1960); The Innocents; The Elephant Man. (Dir): Two and Two Make Six; Vengeance; Paranoiac; Nightmare; The Evil of Frankenstein; The Skull; They Came From Beyond Space; The Torture Garden; Dracula Has Risen From the Grave; Tales From the Crypt; Asylum; Tales that Witness Madness; Legend of the Werewolf.

FRANCIS, Genie: Act. b. LA, May 26, 1962. TV inc: Family; General Hospital.

FRANCISCUS, James: Act. b. Clayton, MO, Jan 31, 1934. e. Yale U. Films inc: Four Boys and a Gun; I Passed for White; The Outsider; The Miracle of the White Stallions; Youngblood Hawke; The Valley of Gwangi; Marooned; Beneath the Planet of the Apes; Cat O'Nine Tails; City on Fire; Killer Fish; When Time Ran Out.

TV inc: Mr Novak; Longstreet; Hunter; The Dream Makers; The 500 Pound Jerk; The Pirate; Nightkill.

FRANJU, Georges: Dir. b. Fougeres, France, 1912. Films inc: (doc) Le Sange des Betes; Hotel des Invalides; Le Grand Melies; (features): La Tete Contre les Murs; Eyes Without a Face; Spotlight on a Murderer; Jude; Thomas the Impostor; Les Rideaux Blancs; The Last Melodrama.

FRANK, Gary: Act. b. Spokane, WA, Oct 9. TV inc: General Hospital; Senior Year; Family (Emmy-supp-1977); The Gift; Enola Gay--The Men, The Mission, The Atomic Bomb; The Night the City Screamed.

FRANK, Harriet: Wri. W of Irving Ravetch. Films inc: Silver River; Whiplash; The Long Hot Summer; The Sound and the Fury; Home from the Hill; The Dark at the Top of the Stairs; Hud; Hombre; The Reivers; Conrack; Norma Rae.

FRANK, Melvin: Wri. b. 1917. Films inc: (collab) My Favorite Blonde; Thank Your Lucky Stars; Road to Utopia; Monsieur Beaucaire; Mr Blanding Builds His Dream House; The Reformer and the Redhead; Above and Beyond; White Christmas; That Certain Feeling; Lil Abner; The Facts of Life; The Road to Hong Kong; Strange Bedfellows; (solo): A Funny Thing Happened on the Way to the Forum (& prod); Buona Sera Mrs. Campbell (& prod-dir); A Touch of Class (& prod-dir); The Dutchess and the Dirtwater Fox (& prod-dir); Lost and Found (& prod-dir).

FRANK, Reuven: Prod-Exec. b. Montreal, Can, Dec 7, 1920. e. CCYN, BS; Columbia, MSJ. On staff ABC News, 1950-1967; named exec vp 1967; P 1968-1972; sr exec prod 1972; prod political convention news coverage.

TV inc: (prod) Huntley-Brinkley Reports; Berlin - Window on Fear (& wri); The Road To Spandau; Outlook; Time Present; The S-Bahn Stops at Freedom; The Big Ear; Our Man in the Mediterranean; Our Man in Hong Kong; Our Man in Vienna; The Problem With Water Is People; Weekend.

FRANK, Sandy: Exec. b. Mt Kisco, NY, Jul 11, 1929. e. Columbia U; NYU. P Sandy Frank tv prodn & dist company.

FRANKEL, Gene: Dir. b. NYC, Dec 23, 1923. e. NYU. Thea inc: Salem Story; They Shall Not Die; All My Sons; Stalag 17; Country Girl; Volpone; An Enemy of the People; Brecht on Brecht; Split Lip; The Night That Made America Famous.

FRANKEN, Al: Wri. TV inc: Saturday Night Live (Emmys-1976, 1977); Paul Simon Special (Emmy-1978).

FRANKEN, Steve: Act. b. Brooklyn. Bway inc: Inherit the Wind. TV inc: Dobie Gillis; The Ghosts of Buxley Hall. Films inc: Follow Me Boys; Westworld; The Party; Which Way To The Front?; The Americanization of Emily; Avalanche; Hardly Working; 10; The Fiendish Plot of Dr. Fu Manchu; There Goes The Bride.

FRANKENHEIMER, John: Dir. b. Malba, NY, Feb 19, 1930. e. Williams Coll. Act-dir summer stock. Joined CBS. TV inc: Mama; You Are There; Danger; Climax; Studio One; Ford Startime; Sunday Showcase.

Films inc: The Young Stranger; The Young Savages; Birdman of Alcatraz; The Manchurian Candidate; Seven Days in May; The Iceman Cometh; 99 and 44/100% Dead; The French Connection II; Black Sunday; Prophecy.

FRANKLIN, Aretha: Singer. b. Memphis, TN, Mar 25, 1942. Recording artist. (Grammys-(10)-R&B-1967; R&B vocal-1967, 1968, 1969, 1970, 1971, 1972, 1973, 1974; Gospel-1972).

Films inc: The Blues Brothers.

FRANKLIN, Bonnie: Act. b. Santa Monica, CA, Jan 6, 1944. e. UCLA, BA. TV inc: Broadway; The Law; One Day at a Time; Breaking Up Is Hard To Do; Portrait Of A Rebel-Margaret Sanger.
Bway inc: Dames at Sea; Your Own Thing; Applause.

FRANKLIN, Michael H: Exec. b. LA, Dec 25, 1923. e. UCLA, AB, USC, LLB. Pvt. practice 1951-52; CBS, 1952-54, atty; 1954-58, Paramount, atty; 1958-78, Exec Dir, Writers Guild of America; 1978, National Exec Sec, Directors Guild of America.

FRANKLIN, Pamela: Act. b. Tokyo, Feb 4, 1950. Films inc: The Innocents; The Lion; Flipper's New Adventure; The Prime of Miss Jean Brodie; The Night of the Following Day; And Soon the Darkness; The Legend of Hell House; Food of the Gods.

FRANKLIN, Richard: Dir. b. Melbourne, Australia, Jul 15, 1948. Films inc: The True Story of Eskimo Nell; Fantasm; Patrick. TV inc: Homicide.

FRANKOVICH, M J: Exec. b. Bisbee, AZ, Sep 29,1910. e. UCLA, BA. Started in radio, 1934, as prod, commentator. Wrote screen plays for Universal, Republic. In Army during WW II. In Europe, 1949, to make Fugitive Lady; Lucky Nick Kane; Thief of Venice; 1955 appointed man. dir. Columbia in U.K., Eire; 1958, VP Columbia Pics Int.; 1959, VP Col. Pics. Corp.; first VP chg wldwde prodn Columbia; resd 1967 to return to ind prodn.
Films inc: Bob & Carol & Ted & Alice; Cactus Flower; There's A Girl in My Soup; The Love Machine; Butterflies Are Free; Stand Up And Be Counted; From Noon Till Three; The Shootist.

FRANZ, Arthur: Act. b. Perth Amboy, NJ, Feb 29, 1920. Films inc: Jungle Patrol; Sands of Iwo Jima; Abbott and Costello Meet the Invisible Man; The Sniper; Eight Iron Men; The Caine Mutiny; The Unholy Wife; Running Target; Hellcats of the Navy; Alvarez Kelly; Anzio; The Human Factor.
Thea inc: Streetcar Named Desire; Second Threshold.
TV inc: Bogie.

FRANZ, Eduard: Act. b. Milwaukee, WI, Oct 31, 1902. Thea inc: Miss Swan Expects; The Brown Danube; Farm of Three Echoes; First Stop to Heaven; Cafe Crown; The Russian People; Outrageous Fortune; The Cherry Orchard; Embezzled Heaven; The Stranger; Home of the Brave; The Egghead; Conversation at Midnight; In the Matter of J Robert Oppenheimer.
Films inc: The Iron Curtain; The Magnificent Yankee; The Ten Commandments; Johnny Got His Gun.
TV inc: The Breaking Point.

FRASER, Fil: Prod-Broadcaster. b. Montreal, Can, Aug 19, 1932. Films inc: Why Shoot the Teacher?; Marie Anne; Back to Beulah; The Hounds of Notre Dame.

FRASER, Ian: Comp-Con-Arr. b. Hove, England, Aug 23, 1933. Arr-Cond for: Liza Minnelli; Sammy Davis Jr.; Anthony Newley; Petula Clark; Paul Anka. Films inc: Doctor Doolittle; Goodbye Mr. Chips; Scrooge; Hopscotch.
TV inc: Julie Andrews Specials; Bing Crosby Christmas Shows, 1975/77; America Salutes Richard Rodgers (Emmy-1977). Sentry collection presents Ben Vereen--His Roots (Emmy-1978); IBM presents Baryshnikov on Broadway (Emmy-1980); Linda In Wonderland.

FRASER, Ronald: Act. b. Ashton-under-Lynn, Eng, 1930. Films inc: The Sundowners; The Pot Carriers; The Punch and Judy Man; Crooks in Cloisters; The Beauty Jungle; The Flight of the Phoenix; The Killing of Sister George; Sinful Davey; Too Late the Hero; The Rise and Rise of Michael Rimmer; The Magnificent Seven Deadly Sins; Swallows and Amazons; Paper Tiger.
TV inc: Sealed with a Loving Kiss; Stray Cats and Empty Bottles; All the Walls Came Tumbling Down; The Corn Is Green; The Brahmin Widow.

FRAYN, Michael: Wri. b. London, Sep 8, 1933. e. Cambridge. Plays inc: The Sandboy; Alphabetical Order; Donkey's Years; Clouds; Make and Break.
TV inc: Jamie; Birthday.

FRAZER, Dan: Act. b. NYC, Nov 20. Films inc: Lilies of the Field; Requiem for a Heavyweight; Counterpoint; Bananas; Take the Money and Run; Fuzz; Cleopatra Jones; Super Cops.
TV inc: Kojak; Greatest Heroes of the Bible.
Thea inc: Once More With Feeling; Who Was That Lady I Saw You With?; Golden Boy; Goodbye Charlie; Christopher Blake; Play It Again, Sam; Conflict of Interest.

FRAZIER, Dallas: Singer. b. Spiro, OK, 1939. C & W recording artist.

FRAZIER, Sheila E: Act. b. NYC, Nov 13, 1948. Former fashion model. Studied drama with NY Negro Ensemble Co; NY Federal Theatre. Films inc: Super Fly; Super Fly T.N.T.; The Super Cops; California Suite.

FREBERG, Stan: Act. b. LA, Aug 7, 1926. Developed TV puppet series: Time for Beany, 1949-54; did voice for UPA cartoon characters, Walt Disney films; had own radio show; wrote commercials. Films inc: Calloway Went Thataway. P, Freberg, Ltd, adv firm.
(Grammy-Spoken Word-1958).

FREDERICKSON, H Gray Jr: Prod. b. Oklahoma City, OK, Jul 21, 1937. e. U of Lausanne, Switzerland, U of OK, BA. Films inc: Candy; Inspector Sterling; An Italian in America; The Man Who Wouldn't Die; The Good, Bad & Ugly; Intrigue in Suez; Wedding March; An American Wife; Echoes in the Village; Little Fauss & Big Halsey; Making It; The Godfather; The Godfather Part II (Oscar-1974); Hit (exec prod); Big Wednesday; Apocalypse Now.
TV inc: Thunder Guys.

FREED, Bert: Act. b. NYC, Nov 3, 1919. Films inc: Where the Sidewalk Ends; No Way Out; Detective Story; Desperate Hours; Paths of Glory; The Swinger; Wild in the Streets; There Was a Crooked Man; Evel Knievel; Billy Jack; La Devoradora des Hombres (Venezuela); Barracuda; Norma Rae.
TV inc: Shane; Skag.
Thea inc: One Touch of Venus; Joy to the World; Annie Get Your Gun; Stone for Danny Fisher; Romanoff and Juliet; Rope Dancers; Time of Your Life.

FREEDMAN, Gerald: Dir-Prod-Wri. b. Lorain, OH, Jun 25, 1927. e. Northwestern U. London directorial debut 1957, Bells Are Ringing; NY debut 1959, On the Town (revival). Thea inc: The Taming of the Shrew; Rosemary; The Alligators; The Gay Life; The Tempest; West Side Story; Electra; The Day the Whores Came Out to Play Tennis; A Time For Singing; artistic dir of the New York Shakespeare Festival prodn of All's Well That Ends Well; The Comedy of Errors; Hair; Hamlet; Titus Adronicus; Sambo; No Place to be Somebody; Colette; The Incomparable Max; The Au Pair Man; The Robber Bridegroom; Mrs Warren's Profession; The Grand Tour.
TV inc: Antigone; Ford Theatre; Du Pont Show of the Week.

FREEMAN, Al Jr: Act. b. San Antonio, TX, Mar 21, 1934. e. LA City Coll. Bway inc: The Long Dream; Kicks and Co; Tiger Tiger Burnin Bright; Trumpets of the Lord; Blues for Mister Charlie; Conversation at Midnight; Look to the Lilies; Are You Now or Have You Ever Been?; The Poison Tree.
Films inc: Torpedo Run; Dutchman; Finian's Rainbow; Sweet Charlie; A Fable (& dir).
TV inc: My Sweet Charlie; Roots; King; One Life To Live (Emmy-1979).

FREEMAN, Devery: Wri. b. NYC, Feb 13, 1913. e. Brooklyn Coll, BA. Films inc: Main Street Lawyer; Guilt of Janet Ames; Dear Brat; The Fuller Brush Man; Tell It To the Judge; Miss Grant Takes Richmond; Three Sailors and a Girl; Francis in the WACS; Francis Joins the Navy; Dance With Me, Henry; Three Bad Sisters; The Girl Most Likely.
TV inc: Ford Theatre; Climax; Loretta Young Show; Sugarfoot; Belevedere; Dear Midge; The Thin Man; Pete and Gladys; Happily Ever After; Harris Against the World.

FREEMAN, Everett: Wri. b. NYC, 1912. Films inc: George Washington Slept Here; Larceny Inc; Thank Your Lucky Stars; The Princess and the Pirate; It Happened on Fifth Avenue; The Secret Life of Walter Mitty; Jim Thorpe--All American; Million Dollar Mermaid; Destination Gobi; My Man Godfrey; Marjorie Morningstar; Sunday in New York; The Glass Bottomed Boat; Where Were You When the Lights Went Out? The Maltese Bippy; Zig Zag.

FREEMAN, Joel: Prod. b. Newark, NJ, Jun 12, 1922. e. Upsala Coll. Films inc: The Farmer's Daughter; The Setup; Battleground; Bad Day at Black Rock; Blackboard Jungle; Music Man; Finian's Rainbow; Camelot; The Heart Is a Lonely Hunter; Trouble Man; Shaft; Love At First Bite; The Octagon.

FREEMAN, Kathleen: Act. b. Circa 1919. Films inc: Naked City; Lonely Heart Bandits; Athena; The Fly; The Ladies' Man; The Disorderly Orderly; Three on Couch; Support Your Local Gunfighter; Stand Up and Be Counted; The Norsemman; The Blues Brothers.

Bway inc: 13 Rue de l'amour.

FREEMAN, Seth: Wri. TV inc: The Waltons; Fish; The Blue Knight; Doc; Rhoda; Phyllis; The New Zoo Revue; Lou Grant (& prod) *(Emmy-prod-1979, 1980; wri 1980).*

FREES, Paul: Act. b. Chicago, Jun 22, 1920. In vaude as child. Later host of radio shows, Suspense; Escape. Films inc: Red Light; A Place in the Sun; The Big Sky; War of the Worlds; Riot in Cellblock II; Suddenly; The Raven; Wild in the Streets.

TV inc: Jack Benny Show; My Friend Irma; voice for TV cartoons inc Rudolph and Frosty's Christmas in July.

FREGONESE, Hugo: Dir. b. Argentina, 1908. Films inc: Pampa Barbara; Donde Mueren las Palabras; Saddle Tramp; One Way Street; Apache Drums; Mark of the Renegade; My Six Convicts; Untamed Frontier; Decameron Nights; Blowing Wild; The Man in Attic; Black Tuesday; Live in Fear; Marco Polo; Apaches Last Battle; Savage Pampas; Beyond the Sun.

FREIBERGER, Fred: Wri-Prod. b. NYC, Feb 19, 1915. e. Pace Inst. Films inc: (wri) Garden of Evil; Beast From 40,000 Fathoms; Crash Landing; The Weapon.

TV inc: (wri) Climax; Fireside Theatre; Zane Grey Theatre; Ben Casey; Slattery's People; The Senator; Trackdown; Rawhide; Starsky and Hutch. (Wri-prod) Ben Casey; Star Trek; Wild Wild West; Space 1999; Iron Horse; Big Shamus, Little Shamus.

FRELENG, Friz: Prod-Dir. b. Kansas City, MO, Aug 21, 1906. Animator, Walt Disney Studio, 1928-29; animator, Charles Mintz Studio, NY, 1929-30; prod-dir., Warner Bros., 1930-63; partner DePatie-Freleng Ent., 1963-1980. Cartoons inc: Tweetie Pie; Speedy Gonzales; Birds Anonymous; Knighty Knight Bugs; Halloween is Grinch Night *(Emmy-1978);* The Bear Who Slept Through Christmas; Pink Panther In Olympinks; Where Do Teenagers Come From?; Dr Seuss' Pontoffel Pock, Where Are You?

FRENCH, Valerie (nee Harrison): Act. b. London, Mar 11, 1932. London stage debut 1954, Cockles and Champagne. NY stage debut 1965, Inadmissible Evidence. Films inc: Jubal; Garment Center; Decision at Sundown; The Four Skulls of Jonathan Drake; Shalako.

TV inc: The Nurses.

FRENCH, Victor: Act. b. Santa Barbara, CA, Dec 4. e. LA (CA) State Coll. Studied With Herbert Berghoff. TV inc: Gunsmoke; It's A Great Life; TV Readers Digest; Carter Country; Amateur Night at the Dixie Bar and Grill; Riding for the Pony Express; The Ghosts of Buxley Hall.

FRENKE, Eugene: Prod. b. Russia, Jan 1, 1907. e. Moscow U. H of Anna Sten. Films inc: Life Returns (& dir); Two Who Dared (& dir); Three Russian Girls (& dir); Let's Live a Little; Lady in the Iron Mask; Miss Robinson Crusoe (& dir); Heaven Knows, Mr. Allison; Barbarian and the Geisha; The Last Sunset.

FREY, Leonard: Act. Bway inc: The Boys in the Band; Fiddler On the Roof; Beggar on Horseback; The National Health; Knock Knock.

Films inc: The Boys in the Band; Fiddler on the Roof; Where The Buffalo Roam.

TV inc: Leonard; Testimony of Two Men.

FRIDELL, Squire: Act. b. Oakland, CA, Feb 9, 1943. e. U of Pacific, BA, Occidental Coll, MA. TV inc: Adam 12; Ironside; Police Story; Bold Ones; Love Story; The Heist; Rossetti and Ryan.

FRIED, Gerald: Comp. b. NYC, Feb 13, 1928. e. Juilliard. Film scores inc: Killer's Kiss; Terror in a Texas Town; A Cold Wind in August; The Cabinet of Caligari; One Potato, Two Potato; The Killing of Sister George; Too Late the Hero; The Grissom Gang; Soylent Green; Birds Do It, Bees Do It; Vigilante Force; Survive; The Bell Jar.

TV inc: Francis Gary Powers; Roots *(Emmy-1977);* Sex and the Married Woman; Testimony of Two Men; Son Rise; The Ordeal of Dr. Mudd; Gauguin The Savage; Flamingo Road; Moviola (The Silent Lovers); The Wild and The Free; Number 96.

FRIEDBERG, A Alan: Exec. b. NYC, Apr 13, 1932. e. Columbia Coll, BA; Harvard Law School. Pres. Sack Theatres; P, Theatre Owners of New England; Board of Dir, NATO.

FRIEDHOFER, Hugo: Comp. b. 1903. Films inc: The Adventures of Marco Polo; China Girl; The Lodger; The Woman in the Window; Joan of Arc; The Best Years of Our Lives *(Oscar-1946);* Ace in the Hole; Above and Beyond; Hondo; Vera Cruz; Between Heaven and Hell; The Rains of Ranchipur; Soldier of Fortune; The Harder They Fall; One Eyed Jacks; An Affair to Remember; The Secret Invasion; The Revolt of Mamie Stover; Boy on a Dolphin; The Young Lions.

FRIEDKIN, Johnny: Exec. b. NYC, Dec 9, 1926. e. Columbia U. Publicist Col, NY, 1946-48; Young & Rubicam, 1948-57; Partner, Sumner & Friedkin, 1957-60; VP, Rogers & Cowan, 1960-67; to Fox, 1967; 1978, VP, World Wide Publicity & Promotion; 1979, vp Intl ad-pub WB.

FRIEDKIN, William: Dir. b. Chicago, 1939. Joined NBC-TV, 1957. Worked for National Educational TV. Films inc: Good Times; The Night They Raided Minsky's; The French Connection *(Oscar-1971);* The Birthday Party; The Exorcist; Sorcerer (& prod); The Brink's Job; Cruising (& sp).

FRIEDLAND, Louis N: Exec. b. NYC, Apr 18, 1913. e. NYU, BS, MA. ChmnB, MCA-TV & vp MCA Inc.

FRIEDMAN, Seymour Mark: Dir. b. Detroit, Aug 17, 1917. e. Cambridge, BS. Films inc: To the Ends of the Earth; Rusty's Birthday; Prison Warden; Her First Romance; Son of Dr Jekyll; Loan Shark; Flame of Calcutta; I'll Get You; Saint's Girl Friday; African Manhunt; Secret of Treasure Mountain.

FRIEDMAN, Stephen: Prod-Wri. b. NYC. e. U of PA, Harvard Law School. Film inc: The Last Picture Show; Lovin' Molly (& sp); Slap Shot; Fast Break; Bloodbrothers; Little Darlings; Hero At Large.

FRIENDLY, Ed: Exec-Prod. b. NYC. Indy tv prod since 1967. Previously with BBD&O and vp - special pgms at NBC-TV. Teamed with George Schlatter to produce Laugh-In. Formed own prod co.

TV inc: Little House on the Prairie; Peter Lund and the Medicine Hat Stallion; Backstairs at the White House; The Flame Is Love.

FRIES, Charles: Exec. b. Cincinnati, OH, Sep 30, 1928. e. OH State U, BS. Exec Prod Ziv TV; VP, Prodn Screen Gems; VP, Prodn Columbia; Exec VP, Prodn & Exec Prod Metromedia Producers Corp, 1970-74; formed own co.

TV inc: Are You In The House Alone?; The Word; Winds of Kitty Hawk; The Martian Chronicles; Bogie; A Rumor of War; For the Love Of It; The Home Front; The Children of An Lac; High Noon, Part II--The Return of Will Kane.

FRINGS, Ketti (nee Hartley): Wri. b. Columbus, OH. Plays inc: Mr. Sycamore; Look Homeward Angel *(Pulitzer Prize-*1958); The Long Dream; Angel (mus version of Look Homeward Angel).
    Films inc: Come Back, Little Sheba; About Mr. Leslie; Fox Fire; The Shrike.

FRISBY, Terence: Act-Dir-Wri. b. London, Nov 28, 1932. Perf & dir 1957-66 under the name of Terence Holland. London stage debut 1958, Gentlemen's Pastime. Plays inc: The Subtopians; There's a Girl in My Soup; The Bandwagon; It's All Right If I Do It.
    TV (wri) inc: Take Care of Madam; Don't Forget the Basics.

FRIZZELL, Lou: Act. b. Jun 10, 1925. e. UCLA. Films inc: Summer of '42; The Stalking Moon; Tell Them Willie Boy Was Here; The Reivers; The Other; Lawman; Our Time; Capricorn One.
    TV inc: Bonanza; The Streets of San Francisco; Rockford File; Police Story; The Anderson Trial; Steel Cowboy; Centennial.
    Thea inc: Oklahoma!; Red Roses for Me; Once Upon a Tailor; The Andersonville Trial; Great Day in the Morning; Desire Under the Elms; The Balcony; The Quare Fellow.
    (Died June 17, 1979).

FROEBE, Gert: Act. b. Germany, 1912. Films inc: The Heroes Are Tired; He Who Must Die; Goldfinger; Those Magnificent Men in Their Flying Machines; Is Paris Burning?; Rocket to the Moon; Monte Carlo or Bust; Dollars; And Then There Were None; The Serpent's Egg; Sidney Sheldon's Bloodline; The Umbrella Coup.

FROESCHEL, George: Wri. b. Vienna, 1891. Novelist and mag writer in Europe before emigrating to US in late 30's; under contract to MGM where he co-wrote The Mortal Storm; Waterloo Bridge; Mrs Miniver *(Oscar-*1942) Random Harvest; The White Cliffs of Dover; Command Decision; The Miniver Story; Scaramouche; Story of Three Loves; Never Let Go; Rose Marie; Betrayed; Me and the Colonel; I Aim at the Stars.
    (Died Nov 22, 1979).

FROMAN, Jane: Singer. b. St Louis, MO, Nov 10, 1907. e. Christian Coll U of MO. Started as singer for radio commercials; joined Paul Whiteman Band; later solo, headlining niteries. Bway inc: Ziegfeld Follies of 1933; Artists and Models; Laugh Town Laugh; Keep off the Grass. Badly injured in plane crash in Lisbon in 1943 while on USO tour; required many operations over several years before she was able to resume career.
    TV inc: Jane Froman's USA Canteen; The Jane Froman Show
    Films inc: vocals for With a Song in My Heart, based on her career.
    (Died April 22, 1980).

FRONTIERE, Dominic: Comp. b. New Haven, CT, Jun 17, 1931. e. Yale School of Mus. Films inc: Giant; The Marriage Go Round; Hero's Island; Billie; Hang 'Em High; Popi; Chisum; Cancel My Reservation; Hammersmith is Out; Defiance; The Stunt Man.
    TV inc: The New Breed; Stoney Burke; Outer Limits; Branded; Iron Horse; Rat Patrol; Twelve O'Clock High; Zig Zag; The Love War; Swing Out Sweet Land *(Emmy-*1971).

FROST, David: TV Pers. b. Tenterdon, England, Apr 7, 1939. e. Cambridge U. TV inc: That Was the Week That Was; The David Frost Show *(Emmys-*1970, 1971); The Nixon Interviews.

FRYE, Dwight: Prod. b. Spokane, WA, Dec 26, 1930. e. U of ME; BS, MS. Thea inc: Man of La Mancha (prod-dir London & Paris companies); Chu Chem; Halloween; Cry For Us All; Odyssey (Home Sweet Homer); So Long 174th Street.

FRYE, William: Prod. Started as talent agent; entered prodn 1953 as assoc prod of the Four Star Playhouse TV series. Films inc: The Trouble With Angels; Where Angels Go, Trouble Follows; Airport 1975; Airport 1977; Raise The Titanic.
    TV inc: General Electric Theatre; The Alfred Hitchcock Hour; The Deputy; Thriller; The Elevator; Linda; The Other Man; the Longest Night; The Screaming Woman.

FRYER, Robert: Prod. b. Washington, DC, Dec 18, 1920. e. Western Reserve U, BA. Films inc: The Boston Strangler; The Prime of Miss Jean Brodie; Myra Breckenridge; The Salzburg Connection; Travels with My Aunt; Mame; The Abdication; Great Expectations; Voyage of the Damned; The Boys From Brazil.
    Bway inc: A Tree Grows in Brooklyn; Wonderful Town *(Tony-*1953); By the Beautiful Sea; The Desk Set; Shangri-La; Auntie Mame; Redhead *(Tony-*1959); Saratoga; Hot Spot; There Was A Little Girl; Advise and Consent; A Passage to India; Roar Like a Dove; A Dream of Swallows; Sweet Charity; Mame; Chicago; California Suite; On The 20th Century; Sweeney Todd *(Tony-*1979).
    TV inc: Wonderful Town.

FUCHS, Daniel: Wri. b. NYC, Jun 1909. e. CCNY, BA. Films inc: The Day the Bookies Wept; The Hard Way; Love Me or Leave Me *(Oscar-*1955); Jeanne Eagels.

FUCHS, Leo: Prod. b. Vienna, Jun 14, 1929. Films inc: Gambit; Secret War of Harry Frigg; A Fine Pair; Jo; La Mandarine; La Femme en Bleu; Le Moutun Enrage; Les Passagers; Sunday Lovers.

FUCHS, Michael: Pay TV Exec. b. NYC, Mar 9, 1946. e. Union Coll, NYU. VP & exec. prod. Home Box Office.

FUDGE, Alan: Act. b. Wichita, KS, Feb 27, 1944. e. U of AZ. Films inc: Two People; Family Plot; Airport '75; Capricorn One.
    TV inc: Sunshine; The Marcus-Nelson Murders; Man From Atlantis; Eischeid; Golden Gate Murders; The Children of An Lac.

FUEST, Robert: Dir. Joined ABC-TV as designer, 1958. Dir docs, commercials, 1962. TV (as dir) inc: Just Like A Woman; The Avengers; And Soon the Darkness; Wuthering Heights; Doctor Phibes; Doctor Phibes Rises Again; The Final Programme; The Devils Rain; A Movie Star's Daughter; The Gold Bug; Family of Strangers; Revenge of the Stepford Wives.

FUGARD, Athol: Wri-Dir-act. b. South Africa, 1932. e. U of Cape Town. Plays inc: No-Good Friday; Blood-Knot (& act-dir); People Are Living There; Hello and Goodbye; Boesman and Lena; Sizwe Bansi is Dead (& dir); The Island; Statements After an Arrest under the Immorality Act (& dir); Dimetos; A Lesson From Aloes (& dir).
    Films inc: Marigolds In August (Sp & act).

FUISZ, Dr. Robert E Wri-Prod. b. Pennsylvania, Oct 15, 1934. e. Georgetown School of Medicine. TV inc: The Body Human--The Sexes; Lifeline *(Emmy-*1979); The Body Human--The Magic Sense *(Emmy-*1980); The Body Human--The Body Beautiful; The Body Human--The Sexes II; The Body Human--The Facts for Boys (& wri).

FULLER, Robert: Act. b. Troy, NY, Jul 29, 1934. Films inc: Teenage Thunder; Return of the Seven; Whatever Happened to Aunt Alice?; King Gun; The Hard Ride; The Gatling Gun.
    TV inc: Laramie; Wagon Train; Emergency; Disaster on the Coastliner; Jake's Way.

FULLER, Samuel: Wri-Dir-Prod. b. NYC, 1911. Films inc: I Shot Jesse James; The Baron of Arizona; Fixed Bayonets; The Steel Helmet; Park Row; Pickup On South Street; Hell and High Water; House of Bamboo; Forty Guns; The Crimson Kimona; Underworld USA; Merrill's Marauders; The Naked Kiss; Shark; Dead Pigeon on Beethoven Street; The American Friend (act); The Big Red One.

FUNICELLO, Annette: Act. b. LA, Oct 22, 1942. Films inc; Johnny Tremaine; The Shaggy Dog; Babes in Toyland; Misadventures of Merlin Jones; Bikini Beach; Beach Party; Pajama Party; How to Stuff A Wild Bikini; The Monkey's Uncle; Fireball 500.
    TV inc: Easy Does It; Frankie and Annette--The Second Time Around; The Mouseketeer Reunion.

FUNT, Allen: Act. b. NYC, 1914. Host of Candid Camera TV show. Films inc: What Do You Say to a Naked Lady? (act & prod); Candid Camera Special.

FURIA, John: Wri. TV inc: The FBI; The Name of the Game; Hawaii Five-O; Kung Fu; The Waltons; The Healers; Death of Ocean View Park; 240-Robert; The Hustler of Muscle Beach.
Films inc: The Singing Nun.

FURIE, Sidney J: Dir-Wri-Prod. b. Toronto, Can, Feb 28, 1933. Films inc: Dangerous Age; A Cool Sound From Hell; The Ipcress File; The Appaloosa; The Naked Runner; Hit!; Gable and Lombard; The Boys In Company C.

FURNEAUX, Yvonne: Act. b. France, 1928. Films inc: Meet Me Tonight; The Dark Avenger; Lisbon; The Mummy; La Dolce Vita; Repulsion; The Scandal; The Man Who Never Was.
TV inc: Tigress on the Hearth; Danger Man; The Baron; The Survivors.

FURNESS, Betty: Act. b. NYC, Jan 3, 1916. On screen From 1933. Films inc: Professional Sweetheart; Emergency Call; Lucky Devils; Beggars in Ermine; Keeper of the Bees; Magnificent Obsession; Swing Time; The President's Mystery; Mama Steps Out; North of Shanghai. Consumer Advocate for NBC-TV.

FURTH, George: Wri-Act. b. Dec 14, 1932. e. Northwestern U, BS. Stage debut 1961, A Cook for Mr. General. Films inc: Butch Cassidy and the Sundance Kid; Myra Breckenridge; Blazing Saddles; Hooper. Plays inc: Company *(Tony*-1971); Twigs; The Act.

GABEL, Martin: Act-Prod-Dir. b. Philadelphia, Jun 19, 1912. e. AADA. H of Arlene Francis. Bway debut 1933, Man Bites Dog. Films inc: The Lost Moment (dir only); Fourteen Hours; The Thief; Tip on a Dead Jockey; Marnie; Lord Love a Duck; Divorce American Style; Lady in Cement; There Was a Crooked Man; The Front Page; The First Deadly Sin.
Bway inc: Will Success Spoil Rock Hunter?; The Hidden River (co-prod); Once More with Feeling (co-prod); Big Fish, Little Fish *(Tony*-Supp-1961); Children From Their Games; Baker Street; Sheep on the Runway; In Praise of Love.
TV inc: The Making of the President, 1964 (narr).

GABOR, Eva: Act. b. Budapest, Feb 11, 1921. Films inc: The Wife of Monte Cristo; The Last Time I Saw Paris; Artists and Models; My Man Godfrey; Don't Go Near the Water; Gigi; The Trouble with Woman; New Kind of Love; It Started with a Kiss; The Rescuers; Nutcracker Fantasy.
TV inc: Green Acres; The Eva Gabor Show; Almost Heaven.
Thea inc: The Happy Time; Present Laughter; Blithe Spirit; Strike a Match; Oh Men, Oh Women; Her Cardboard Lover; Uncle Vanya; A Shot in the Dark; Private Lives.

GABOR, Zsa Zsa: Act. b. Hungary, Feb 6, 1919. Stage debut in Europe. Films inc: Lovely to Look At; We're Not Married; Lili; Moulin Rouge; Boys' Night Out; Picture Mommy Dead; Jack of Diamonds.

GABRIEL, John: Act. b. Niagara Falls, NY, May 25, 1931. e. UCLA, BA. Bway inc: the Happy Time; Applause.
Films inc: Redline 7000; El Dorado; Network.
TV inc: Mary Tyler Moore Show; Ryan's Hope.

GAFFNEY, Robert: Prod-Dir. b. NYC, Oct 8, 1931. e. Iona Coll. Films inc: Rooftops of New York (Short); Man on a String; Light Fantastic; Troublemaker; Frankenstein Meets the Space Monster.

GAIDAI, Leonid: Wri-Dir. b. Russia, Jan 30, 1923. e. Moscow Film Institute. Films inc: Lyana (act); The Long Path (co-dir); A Fiancee from the Other world (dir); Barbos, the Dog and a Cross-Country Run; Bootleggers; Business People; Operation "Y" and Shurik's Other Adventures; Prisoner of the Caucasus: The Diamond Hand; The Twelve Chairs; Ivan Vasillievich Changes His Profession; It Can't Be!.

GAIL, Maxwell: Act. b. Detroit, MI, Apr 5. e. U of MI. Films inc: The Organization; Dirty Harry.
TV inc: Like Mom, Like Me; Pearl; Desperate Women; Barney Miller; The 11th Victim; The Aliens Are Coming; Fun & Games.

GALABRU, Michel: Act. Films inc: The Groper; Group Portrait With Lady; The Gendarme and the Creature from Outer Space; Surprise Sock; The Pawn; Confidences for Confidences; Cop or Hood; The Bit Between the Teeth;La Cage Aux Folles; A Week's Vacation; Le Guignolo; It All Depends on Girls; Les Sous-Doues (The Under Gifted); La Cage Aux Folles II.

GALLAGHER, Helen: Act. b. NYC, Jul 19, 1926. Bway debut 1945, The Seven Lively Arts. Bway inc: Mr. Strauss Goes to Boston; Billion Dollar Baby; Brigadoon; High Button Shoes; Make a Wish; Pal Joey *(Tony*-Supp-1952); Hazel Flagg; Guys and Dolls; Finian's Rainbow; Sweet Charity; No, No, Nanette *(Tony*-1971).
TV inc: Ryan's Hope *(Emmys*-1976 & 1977). Films inc: Roseland.

GALLERY, Michele: Wri. TV inc: Lou Grant *(Emmy*-1979).

GALLO, Lew: Prod. b. Mt Kisco, NY, Jun 12, 1928. e. Ithaca Coll, Columbia U. TV inc: The Ghost and Mrs. Muir; That Girl; Love American Style; Lucan; Having Babies; Don Rickles Show.

GALLO, Lillian B: Prod. b. Springfield, MA, Apr 12. e. U of MI, BA. TV inc: The Natural Look; Hustling; The Stranger Who Looks Like Me; What Are Best Friends For?; Playmates; The Haunts of the Very Rich; Fun & Games.

GALLOWAY, Don: Act. b. Brooksville, KY, Jul 27, 1937. e. KY U AB. Films inc: The Rare Breed; Gunfight in Abilene; The Ride To Hangman's Tree; Rough Night in Jericho.
TV inc: Tom, Dick And Mary; Arrest And Trial; The Virginian; Boot Hill; Ironside; The Life and Times of Grizzly Adams.

GAM, Rita: Act. b. Pittsburgh, Apr 2, 1928. Films inc: The Thief; Sign of the Pagan; Night People; Magic Fire; Mohawk; King of Kings; Klute; Such Good Friends. TV inc: Greatest Heroes of the Bible.

GANCE, Abel: Prod-Dir. b. Paris, 1889. Pioneer of wide-screen techniques. Films inc: Baberousse; J'Accuse; La Roue; Napoleon; La Fin du Monde; Lucrezia Borgia; Une Grande Amour de Beethoven; Paradis Perdu; La Tour de Nesie; The Battle of Austerlitz; Bonaparte et la Revolution.

GANG, Martin: Atty. b. Passaic, NJ, Mar 12, 1901. e. Harvard U, BA; Heidelberg, PhD; U CA, JurD. Film Business Atty.

GANS, Sharon: Act. b. NY, Jul 29, 1942. Films inc: Zabriskie Point; Tell Me Lies; Slaughterhouse Five.

GARAGIOLA, Joe: TV Pers. b. St Louis, MO, 1926. Former Pro baseball player. TV inc: NBC's Today Show; Baseball Game of the Week; The Baseball World of Joe Garagiola; He Said, She Said (host).

GARAS, Kaz: Act-Wri. b. Kaunas, Lithuania, Mar 4, 1940. e. U CT, BA. Films inc: The Last Safari; Ben; Love Is a Funny Thing.
TV inc: Separate Lives; Strange Report.

GARBO, Greta (nee Gustafson): Act (ret). b. Stockholm, Sep 18, 1906. On screen in Sweden in Peter The Tramp; Atonement of Gosta Berlibg; Joyless Street; brought to Hollywood 1926 by Swedish dir Mauritz Stiller and made Hollywood debut in Torrent.
Films inc: The Temptress; Flesh and the Devil; Love; Mysterious Lady; The Divine Woman; The Kiss; A Woman of Affairs; Wild Orchids; The Single Standard; Anna Christie; Romance; Inspiration; Susan Lennox; Mata Hari; Grand Hotel; As You Desire Me; Queen Christina; The Painted Veil; Anna Karenina; Camille; Conquest; Ninotchka; Two-Faced Woman.
(Honorary Oscar 1954 "for her unforgettable film performances.")

GARCIA, Jerry: Mus. b. Aug 1, 1942. Founder-member Grateful Dead; occasionally records with other musicians. Albums inc: Garcia; Cats Under the Stars; Garcia/Reflections.
(See The Grateful Dead for group credits).

GARDENIA, Vincent: Act. b. Naples, Jan 7, 1922. Bway inc: The Visit; The Prisoner of Second Ave (Tony-Supp-1971); God's Favorite.
Films inc: Cop Haters; Little Murders; Murder, Inc.; Jenny; Cold Turkey; Hickey and Boggs; Death Wish; Bang The Drum Slowly; The Front Page; Heaven Can Wait; Firepower; Home Movies; The Last Flight of Noah's Ark.
TV inc: All in the Family; The Untouchables; The Rookies; Marciano; Goldie and the Boxer; Insight/Holy Moses; The Dream Merchants; Breaking Away.

GARDINER, Frank Reid: Atty. b. Australia, Nov 26, 1938. Member Australian Film Commission. Films inc: Final Cut (exec prod).

GARDINER, Reginald: Act. b. Wimbledon, Surrey, Eng, Feb 27, 1903. e. RADA. London stage debut 1923, Prisoner of Zenda. Thea inc: Naughty Cinderella; The Lady Known as Lou; Chance Acquaintance; Pleasure Cruise; Mother of Pearl; Indoor Fireworks; Hi-Diddle-Diddle.
In Hollywood From 1936. Films inc: Born to Dance; Everybody Sing; Marie Antoinette; Sweethearts; The Great Dictator; The Man Who Came to Dinner; Captains of the Clouds; The Immortal Sergeant; Molly and Me; Cluny Brown; Fury at Furnace Creek; Halls of Montezuma; The Black Widow; Ain't Misbehaving; The Birds and the Bees; Mr Hobbs Takes a Vacation; Do Not Disturb.
TV inc: The Pruitts of Southampton.
(Died July 7, 1980).

GARDNER, Arthur (nee Goldberg): Prod. b. Marinette, WI. Started as screen actor, 1929; asst dir 1941; then asst prod; formed Allart Pictures Corp; then VP Levy-Gardner-Laven Productions. Films inc: Without Warning; Vice Squad; Geronimo; The Glory Guys; Scalphunters; The Honkers; Hunting Party; Kansas City Bomber; White Lightning; McQ; Brannigan; Gator.
TV inc: Rifleman; Law of the Plainsman; The Big Valley.

GARDNER, Ava: Act. b. Smithfield, NC, Dec 24, 1922. Films inc: We Were Dancing; Joe Smith; American; Whistle Stop; The Killers; The Hucksters; One Touch of Venus; Show Boat; Pandora and the Flying Dutchman; Snows of Kilimanjaro; Mogambo; Barefoot Contessa; The Naked Maja; Bhowani Junction; On the Beach; Night of the Iguana; 55 Days at Peking; Mayerling; Life and Times of Judge Roy Bean; Earthquake; Permission to Kill; The Bluebird; The Cassandra Crossing; The Sentinel; City on Fire; The Kidnapping of the President.

GARDNER, Herb: Wri. Originally a commercial artist, drew comic strip, The Nebbishes, for eight years before devoting time to writing. Plays inc: A Thousand Clowns; Thieves.
Films inc: A Thousand Clowns; Who is Harry Kellerman? (& prod); Thieves.
TV inc: Happy Endings; Word of Mouth.

GARFIELD, Allen See: GOORWITZ, Allen.

GARFINKLE, Louis: Wri. b. Seattle, WA, Feb 11, 1928. e. UC Berkeley; U of WA, USC. Films inc: The Young Guns; I Bury the Living; Face of Fire; The Hellbenders; A Minute to Pray, A Second to Die; The Love Doctors; Beautiful People; The Doberman Gang; Little Cigars; The Deer Hunter.
Plays inc: Molly; I Shall Return.

GARFUNKEL, Art: Act. b. NYC, Oct 13, 1942. e. COL U. Formed vocal and instrumental duo with Paul Simon, dissolved in 1970 to go their separate ways. Garfunkel continued as a recording artist; also turned actor. Films inc: Catch-22; Carnal Knowledge; Bad Timing. (Grammys-(4)-Record of year-1968; Record of year-album of year-best arr-1970.)

GARGAN, William: Act. b. NYC, Jul 17, 1905. On Bway in Aloma of the South Seas. Screen debut 1932, Misleading Lady. Films inc: Rain; Animal Kingdom; They Knew What They Wanted; I Wake Up Screaming; Destination Unknown; The Bells of St. Mary's; Behind Green Lights; Miracle in the Rain; Rawhide Years.
TV inc: Martin Kane; Private Eye.
(Died Feb 16, 1979).

GARGIULO, Mike: Prod-Dir. b. Sep 23, 1926. e. U of MO, BA. TV inc: Jackpot (Emmy-dir-1974); $20,000 Pyramid (Emmys-dir-1976, 1978); Thanksgiving Day Parade; Cotton Bowl Parade; Leningrad Ice Show; Rose Parade; Happy New Year America.

GARLAND, Beverly (nee Fessenden): Act. b. Santa Cruz, CA, Oct 17, 1930. Films inc: The Mad Room; Where the Red Fern Grows; Airport, 1975; Roller Boogie; It's My Turn.
TV inc: Decoy.

GARLAND, Patrick: Dir-Wri. b. Eng. e. Oxford. Thea (dir) inc: Brief Lives; Forty Years On; The Stiffkey Scandals of 1932; A Doll's House; Hedda Gabler; Getting On; Kilvert and His Diary; Mad Dog; Billy; Enemy of the People; Signed and Sealed; Chichester; Beecham.
TV inc: On the Margin; The Snow Goose.

GARNER, Erroll: Comp-pianist. b. Pittsburgh, PA, Jun 15, 1923. In niteries; concerts; European tours. Film scores inc: A New Kind of Love.

GARNER, James: Act. b. Norman, OK, Apr 7, 1928. Films inc: Toward the Unknown; The Jolly Pink Jungle; Hour of the Guns; Sayonara; Cash McCall; Children's Hour; Duel at Diablo; Grand Prix; The Great Escape; The Americanization of Emily; A Man Could Get Killed; Mister Buddwing; Support Your Local Sheriff; Marlowe; Skin Game; They Only Kill Their Masters; One Little Indian; Hawaiian Cowboy; Health.
TV inc: Cheyenne; Maverick; Rockford Files (Emmy-1977); Young Maverick.

GARNER, Peggy Ann: Act. b. Canton, OH, Feb 8, 1933. Screen debut 1938, Little Miss Thoroughbred. Honorary oscar 1945, as "outstanding child actress." Films inc: Blondie Brings Up Baby; Abe Lincoln in Illinois; The Pied Piper; Jane Eyre; A Tree Grows in Brooklyn; The Keys of the Kingdom; Nob Hill; Home Sweet Homicide; Daisy Kenyon; The Sign of the Ram; Bomba the Jungle Boy; The Big Cat; Teresa; The Black Widow; Eight Witnesses; The Black Forest; The Cat; A Wedding.
TV inc: Studio One; Lux Playhouse; Betrayal.

GARNETT, Gale: Singer-Songwri-Act. b. Auckland, NZ. Thea inc: Stratford Shakespeare Festival; Factory Theatre Lab. (Bway) Ulysses in Nighttown; Ladyhouse Blues; Crack; Jesse and the Bandit Queen.
Films inc: The Children; Tribute.
Songs inc: We'll Sing in the Sunshine (Grammy-Folk Recording-1964); Down Here on the Ground; Street Tattoo.

GARRETT, Betty: Act. b. St Joseph, MO, May 23, 1919. Bway debut 1938, Danton's Death. Films inc: Big City; Words and Music; Take Me Out to the Ball Game; Neptune's Daughter; On the Town; My Sister Eileen; The Shadow on the Window.
TV inc: All in the Family; Laverne and Shirley.
Bway inc: Beg, Borrow, or Steal; A Girl Could Get Lucky; Who's Happy Now?; Plaza Suite; And Miss Reardon Drinks a Little.

GARRETT, Lila: Prod-Wri-Dir. b. NYC. TV inc: Mother of the Bride (2 Emmys-Writing & Daytime Wri of Year-1974); The Girl Who Couldn't Lose (prod) (Emmy-1975); Another April (wri); Dick Van Dyke pilot; MacLeish (wri & prod); Newman's Drugstore pilot (wri); This Better Be It (prod-wri); Instant Family (exec prod); Terraces (prod-wri & dir); Baby I'm Back (prod-wri); Getting There (exec prod-wri).

GARROWAY, Dave: TV Pers. b. Schenectady, NY, Jul 13, 1913. U.S. Navy, 1942-45. TV inc: Garroway at Large, NBC, 1948-51; Today Show, 1952-61; Dave Garroway Show, NBC radio; Wide Wide World; Exploring the Universe; NET, 1962-63; Dave Garroway Show (syndication), 1969-71; Jack Frost (voice).

GARSON, Greer: Act. b. County Down, Northern Ireland, Sep 29, 1908. e. London U, BA cum laude; Grenoble U. Stage debut Birmingham Rep. theatre 1932; London debut 1935, Golden Arrow. Screen debut 1939, Goodbye, Mr. Chips. Films inc: Pride and Prejudice; When Ladies Meet; Mrs. Miniver (Oscar-1942); Random Harvest; Mme. Curie; Mrs. Parkington; Valley of Decision; Adventure; Desire Me; That Forsythe Woman; The Miniver Story; Scandal at Scourie; Julius Caesar; Strange Lady in Town; Sunrise at Campobello; The Singing Nun; The Happiest Millionaire.

TV inc: Crown Matrimonial; My Father Gave Me America; Little Women; Holiday Tribute to Radio City; Perry Como's Christmas in New Mexico.

Bway inc: The Madwoman of Chaillot; On Golden Pond (prod).

GARY, Lorraine: Act. b. NYC, Aug 16, 1937. e. Columbia U. W of Sidney J Sheinberg. Films inc: Jaws; Car Wash; Jaws 2; Just You and Me Kid; 1941.

GASSMAN, Vittorio: Act. b. Genoa, Italy, Sep 1, 1922. e. Academy Dramatic Art, Rome. Screen deubt, 1946. Films inc: Daniele Cortis; Mysterious Rider; Bitter Rice; The Outlaws; Cry of the Hunted; Sombrero; The Glass Wall; Mambo; War and Peace; The Tiger; Woman Time Seven; Ghosts-Italian Style; Scent of a Woman; Desert of the Tartars; Goodnight Ladies and Gentlemen; The Forbidden Room; Due Pezzi Di Pane; Viva Italia; A Wedding; Quintet; Caro Papa; La Terrazza (The Terrace); The Nude Bomb.

GASTONI, Lisa: Act. b. Italy, 1935. Films inc: The Runaway Bus; Man of the Moment; The Baby and the Battleship; Intent to Kill; Hello London; Passport to China; Maddalena; The Last Days of Mussolini.

GATELY, Frederick: Cin. b. Oct 5, 1909. Films inc: Harpoon; Four Seasons.

TV inc: Operation Petticoat; Nancy Drew; Executive Suite; Medical Center; Nanny and the Professor; Lancer; Hazel; My Sister Eileen; Father Knows Best; Ozzie and Harriet; Dragnet.

GATES, Larry: Act. b. St Paul, MN, Sep 24, 1915. Films inc: Has Anybody Seen My Gal?; The Girl Rush; Invasion of the Body Snatchers; Jeanne Eagels; Cat on a Hot Tin Roof; One Foot in Hell; The Hoodlum Priest; Some Came Running; Toys in the Attic; The Sand Pebbles; Airport.

Bway inc: Shakespeare repertory; Teahouse of the August Moon; Bell, Book and Candle; Love of Four Colonels; Hamlet; Poor Murderer; First Monday in October.

TV inc: Backstairs at the White House; FDR-The Last Year; The Henderson Monster.

GAUTIER, Dick: Act. b. 1939. Films inc: Wild in the Sky; The Manchu Eagle Murder Caper Mystery; Fun with Dick and Jane.

TV inc: Here We Go Again; Marathon.

GAVIN, Bill: Exec. b. Wellington, New Zealand, Oct 8, 1936. Man-dir GTO Films, London, 1973-78; GM (Films and Mktg) Hoyts Theatres Ltd, Sydney, 1978.

GAVIN, John: Act. b. LA, Apr 8, 1928. e. Stanford. Brief job as a press agent. On screen From 1956. Films inc: Behind the High Wall; Four Girls in Town; Quantez; A Time to Love and a Time to Die; Imitation of Life; Spartacus; A Breath of Scandal; Psycho; Midnight Lace; Romanoff and Juliet; Tammy and the Professor; Back Street; Thoroughly Modern Millie; The Madwoman of Chaillot; Jennifer.

TV inc: Convoy; Destry; Cutter's Trail; Doris Day Show; New Adventures of Heidi.

Bway inc: Seesaw; Equus; Heaven Can Wait.

GAY, John: Wri. b. Whittier, CA, Apr 1, 1924. e. LA City Coll. Films inc: Run Silent, Run Deep; Separate Tables; The Happy Thieves; Four Horsemen; The Courtship of Eddie's Father; The Hallelujah Trail; The Last Safari; The Power; No Way to Treat a Lady; Soldier Blue; Sometimes a Great Notion; Hennessey; Matter of Time.

TV inc: Amazing Howard Hughes; Kill Me If You Can; Captains Courageous; Red Badge of Courage; All My Darling Daughters; Les Miserables; Transplant; A Private Battle; A Tale of Two Cities.

GAYE, Marvin: Singer-Sngwri. b. Washington, DC, Apr 2, 1939. With the Rainbows; co-founder The Marquees (later the Moonglows) before going solo 1962.

Recordings inc: What's Going On?; Trouble, Man; Let's Get It On; Marvin Gaye Live; Live at the London Palladium; I Want You.

Songs inc: What's Going On?; Mercy, Mercy Me; Inner City Blues.

GAYLE, Crystal: Singer. b. Paintsville, KY. Sis of Loretta Lynn. Albums inc: Crystal Gayle; Somebody Loves You; We Must Believe in Magic; When I Dream. Singles inc: Somebody Loves You; Don't It Make My Brown Eyes Blue (Grammy-c&w vocal-1977); Ready for the Times to Get Better.

TV inc: Midnight Special; Dean Martin Christmas Special; Wayne Newton Special; Merry Christmas from Grand Ole Opry; Crystal Gayle Special; Crystal.

GAYNOR, Janet (Laura Gainer): Act. b. Philadelphia, 1906. Films inc: The Johnstown Flood; Seventh Heaven, Sunrise, Street Angel (Oscar-1927-28); Sunny Side Up; High Society Blues; Daddy Longlegs; Merely Mary Ann; Tess of the Storm Country; State Fair; Carolina; The Farmer Takes a Wife; Ladies in Love; A Star is Born; Three Loves Has Nancy; The Young in Heart; Bernardine.

Bway inc: Harold and Maude.

GAYNOR, Mitzi (nee von Gerber): Act. b. Chicago, 1931. Studied ballet From age 4. Appeared in light opera. Screen debut, 1950, My Blue Heaven. Films inc: The I Don't Care Girl; We're Not Married; There's No Business Like Show Business; Anything Goes; Les Girls; South Pacific; Happy Anniversary; For Love or Money. Opera: The Fortune Teller; Song of Norway; Louisiana Purchase; Naughty Marietta; The Great Waltz.

TV: Mitzi Gaynor Specials.

GAZZARA, Ben: Act. b. NYC, 1930. Won scholarship to study with Erwin Piscator. Joined Actor's Studio, performing in improvised play, End As A Man. Screen debut 1957 in film version of that play retitled The Strange One. Films inc: Anatomy of a Murder; The Passionate Thief; The Young Doctors; Convicts Four; A Rage to Live; The Bridge at Remagen; Husbands; Capone; Killing of a Chinese Bookie; Voyage of the Damned; Saint Jack; Sidney Sheldon's Bloodline.

Thea inc: Cat on a Hot Tin Roof; A Hatful of Rain; Who's Afraid of Virginia Woolf?

TV inc: Arrest and Trial; Run For Your Life.

GAZZO, Michael V: Act-Wri. b. 1923. Bway (act) inc: Arsenic and Old Lace; The Petrified Forest; Shadow of a Gunman; The Little Foxes; The Aristocrats; Juno and the Paycock; A Hatful of Rain (wri).

Films inc: On the Waterfront; (act) The Godfather, Part II; Fingers; King of the Gypsies; Love and Bullets; The Fish that Saved Pittsburgh (sp); King Creole; Cuba Crossing; Alligator.

GEESON, Judy: Act. b. Arundel, Sussex, Eng, Sep 10, 1948. Films inc: To Sir With Love; Here We Go Round The Mulberry Bush; Three Into Two Won't Go; The Executioner; Brannigan; The Eagle Has Landed; Carry On England; It's Not the Size That Counts.

TV inc: Dance of Death; Lady Windermere's Fan; The Skin Game; She; A Room With a View.

Thea inc: Othello; Two Gentlemen of Verona; An Ideal Husband.

GEFFEN, David: Exec. b. 1944. Started as agent with William Morris; opened own agcy with Elliott Roberts; founded Asylum Records, 1970. 1973, sold to Warners, merged with Elektra with Geffen as P; 1975 vice chmn Warner Brothers Pictures; 1977 exec asst to Warner Communications chmn Steven J Ross; resd 1978 to teach music at Yale; 1980 P new diskery bankrolled by WCI.

GEISEL, Ted (Dr Seuss): Prod-Wri-Ani. b. Springfield, MA, Mar 2, 1904. e. Dartmouth; Oxford. Started as adv artist; cartoons inc: "Quick Henry the Flit" campaign, wri of children's books. Films inc: Oscar-winning shorts If Hitler Lives; Design for Death; Gerald McBoing-Boing.
   TV inc: (prod-wri) How the Grinch Stole Christmas; Horton Hears A Who; The Cat in the Hat; The Lorax; Dr. Seuss on the Loose; The Hoober Blood Highway; Hallowe'en is Grinch Night *(Emmy-*1978); Dr. Seuss' Pontoffel Pock, Where Are You?

GEISINGER, Elliot: Wri-Dir-Prod. b. NYC, Feb 8, 1930. e. Columbia U, BS. Films inc: The Prince and the Pauper (sp-prod-dir); The Great Adventure (sp-prod); The Amityville Horror (prod).
   TV inc: Meteor-Messenger From Space.

GELBART, Larry: Wri. b. Chicago, Feb 25, 1928. Films inc: The Notorious Landlady; The Wrong Box; Oh, God!; Movie, Movie.
   TV inc: M*A*S*H *(Emmy-*prod-1974); United States (exec prod-wri).
   Plays inc: A Funny Thing Happened on the Way to the Forum *(Tony-*1963); Sly Fox.

GELIN, Daniel: Act. b. Angers, France, 1921. Films inc: Rendezvous de Juillet; Edouard et Caroline; La Ronde; Les Mains Sales; Rue de l'Estrapade; The Lovers of Lisbon; The Man Who Knew Too Much; Charmants Garcons; There's Always a Price Tag; Carthage in Flames; The Season for Love; Black Sun; Le Souffle au Coeur; Pardon Mon Affaire, Too; L'Oeil du Maitre (His Master's Eye).
   Thea inc: Le Scenario.

GENET, Jean: Wri. b. France, Dec 19, 1910. Plays inc: Haute Surveillance (Deathwatch); Le Balcon (The Balcony); Les Negres (The Blacks); Les Paravents (The Screens). Films inc: Un Chant d'Amour (Love Song).

GENTRY, Bobbie: Comp-Singer. b. Chickasaw Co, MS, 1944. Recording artist. *(Grammys-*(3)-new artist-vocal-contemporary solo-1967).

GEORGE, Chief Dan: Act. b. Canada, Jul 24, 1899. Films inc: Smith; Little Big Man; Alien Thunder; Harry and Tonto; The Outlaw Josey Wales; Shadow of the Hawk; Americathon; Spirit of the Wind.

GEORGE, Christopher: Act. b. Royal Oak, MN, Feb 25, 1929. e. U of Miami. Thea inc: Mr Roberts; Petrified Forest; Streetcar Named Desire.
   TV inc: Rat Patrol; The Immortal; Last Survivors; Voyage into Evil.
   Films inc: El Dorado; In Harms Way; The Delta Factor; Chisum; Day of the Animals; Grizzly; Tiger by the Tail; The Exterminator.

GEORGE, Linda Day: Act. b. San Marcos, TX, Dec 11. W of Christopher George. Films inc: Chisum; Day of the Animals; Gentle Rain; Racquet; Beyond Evil.
   TV inc: Mission Impossible; Once an Eagle; Roots; Rich Man, Poor Man; Murder at the World Series; Trial of Capt Jensen; Casino.
   Thea inc: The Devils; The Crucible.

GEORGE, Phyllis: TV Pers. b. Denton, TX. Former Miss America (1971). Joined CBS, 1975. Co-Host of The NFL Today. Co-host, with Bert Parks, The Miss America Pageant TV Broadcast. Macy's Thanksgiving Day Parade telecast; People.

GEORGE, Susan: Act. b. Eng, 1950. Former child actress. Films inc: Billion Dollar Brain; The Strange Affair; Twinky; Spring and Port Wine; The Looking Glass War; Die Screaming, Marianne; Eye Witness; Fright; The Straw Dogs; Dirty Mary, Crazy Larry; Sonny and Jed; Mandingo; Out of Season; Tintorera.

GERAGHTY, Maurice: Wri-Dir-Prod. b. Rushville, IN, Sep 29, 1908. e. Princeton U. Films inc: Red Canyon; Dakota Lil; Calamity Jane and Sam Bass; Tomahawk; Sword of Monte Cristo; Rose of Cimarron; Mohawk; Love Me Tender.
   TV inc: Virginian; Bonanza; Daniel Boone; 87th Precinct; Beacon St; Cavalcade of America; No Warning; Flight; Laramie; Lassie.

GERARD, Gil: Act. b. Little Rock, AR, Jan 23, 1943. TV inc: The Doctors; Killing Stone; Buck Rogers in the 25th Century.
   Films inc: Airport '77; Buck Rogers in the 25th Century.
   Thea inc: I Do! I Do!

GERASIMOV, Sergei: Dir-Wri. b. May 21, 1906. Started as actor, films inc: The Bears Versus Yudenich; The Devil's Wheel; The Overcoat; Buddy; S.V.D.; The New Babylon; Alone; Three Soldiers; The Deserter; The Boarder; The Vyborg Side. (Dir-wri): Twenty-Two Mishaps; (co-dir) Solomon's Heart; If I Love You; The Brave Seven; Komsomolsk; The Teacher; Masquerade (& act); The Mainland; The Young Guard; Nadezhda; Men and Beasts; The Journalist; At the Lake; For The Love of Man. (Dir only): The Old Guard; The Village Doctor. (Sp only) The The Road of Truth; And Quiet Flows the Don; Memory of the Heart.

GERBER, David: Exec. b. NYC. e. U of Pacific. Before joining 20th Century-Fox as vp-TV sales, 1965, was packaging agent with GAC and Famous Artists Corp; became ind prod 1972. TV inc: Exec prod, Nanny and the Professor; The Ghost and Mrs. Muir; Cade's County; Police Story *(Emmy-*1976); Police Woman; Needles and Pins; Born Free; Joe Forrester; The Quest; Bibbsville; Man Undercover; Doctor's Private Lives; The Billion Dollar Threat; Only the Pretty Girls Die; Power; Once Upon A Spy; Beulah Land; The Night the City Screamed.

GERE, Richard: Act. b. Philadelphia, PA, Aug 31, 1949. Films inc: Report to the Commissioner; Baby Blue Marine; Days of Heaven; Looking for Mr Goodbar; Bloodbrothers; Days of Heaven; Yanks; American Gigolo. Bway inc: Grease; Bent. (London): Grease; Habeus Corpus; The Taming of the Shrew.

GERSHENSON, Joseph: Comp-Cond. b. Russia, Jan 12, 1904. Cond orch B F Keith Theatres 1920-28; music dir RKO Theatres, 1928-33; joined Universal 1933; 1941 apptd exec prod, head of music dept UI. Film scores inc: Glenn Miller Story; Magnificent Obsession; There's Always Tomorrow; Written in the Wind; My Man Godfrey; Imitation of Life; Pillow Talk; Operation Petticoat; Father Goose; Shenandoah; Blindfold; Thoroughly Modern Millie; Sweet Charity.

GERSHWIN, Ira: Lyr. b. NYC, Dec 6, 1896. e. CCNY. B of late George Gershwin. Bway inc: Two Little Girls in Blue (under name of Arthur Francis); Lady Be Good; Tell Me More; Tip-Toes; Oh, Kay; Funny Face; Rosalie; Treasure Girl; Show Girl; Strike Up The Band; Girl Crazy; of Thee I Sing *(Pulitzer Prize-*1932); Let 'Em Eat Cake; Life Begins at 8:40; Ziegfeld Follies of 1936; Porgy and Bess; Lady in the Dark; Park Avenue.
   Films inc: Delicious; Shall We Dance; A Damsel in Distress; The Goldwyn Follies; Cover Girl; The Shocking Miss Pilgrim; The Barkleys of Broadway; An American In Paris; A Star is Born; Country Girl; Kiss Me Stupid.
   Songs inc: Fascinatin' Rhythm; Oh, Lady Be Good; The Man I Love; Do Do Do; Someone to Watch Over Me; Strike Up the Band; Funny Face; 'S Wonderful; Liza; Bidin' My Time; Embraceable You; I Got Rhythm; But Not For Me; Cheerful Little Earful; Wintergreen for President; Of Thee I Sing; Who Cares; I Got Plenty of Nuttin; It Aint Necessarily So; Let's Call The Whole Thing Off; Shall We Dance; They Can't Take That Away From Me; A Foggy Day; Nice Work If You Can Get It; Love Walked In; Saga of Jenny; My Ship; Long Ago; The Man That Got Away.

GERTZ, Irving: Comp-Mus dir. b. Providence, RI, May 19, 1915. e. Providence Coll of Music. US Army, 1941-46; then comp, arranger, Mus Dir for Col, 1946-49; NBC, 1949-51; U Pictures, 1951-60; Fox, 1960-70. Films inc: Bandits of Corsica; Gun Belt; Long Wait; The Fiercest Heart; First Travelling Saleslady.
   TV inc: America; The Golden Voyage; Across the Seven Seas; The Legend of Jesse James; Daniel Boone; Voyage to the Bottom of the Sea; Peyton Place; Land of the Giants; Lancer; Medical Center.

GETHERS, Steven: Wri-Dir-Prod. b. Jun 8, 1922. e. AADA. Plays inc: A Cook for Mr. General.
   TV inc: (Wri) It's Good To Be Alive; A Circle of Children (& prod); Billy--Portrait of a Street Kid (& dir); Silent Victory; Damien. . .The Leper Priest (& dir).

GETZ, Stan: Mus. b. Philadelphia, Feb 2, 1927. Sideman with Jack Teagarden; Stan Kenton; Jimmy Dorsey; Benny Goodman; Woody Herman bands before forming own group in 1949. Films inc: The Benny Goodman Story; Get Yourself a College Girl; The Hanged Man; Mickey One.
(Grammy-(4)-jazz solo-1962; record of year-1964; album of year-1964; small group jazz-1964).

GEWALD, Robert M: Prod. b. NYC, Mar 8, 1934. Prod first appearance at Lincoln Center of an American Symphony Orchestra, 1963; prod First Children's Folk Festival at Lincoln Center, 1965; prod An Evening of Rodgers and Hammerstein; mgr: Jose Iturbi; Eleanor Steber; Pittsburgh Ballet Theatre; Rochester Philharmonic.

GHIA, Fernando: Prod. b. Rome, Jul 22, 1935. e. U of Rome. Thea (Rome). inc: Miracle Worker; Requiem for a Man; Becket.
Films inc: China Is Near; The Red Tent; The Audience; A Fine Pair; The Mattei Affair; Lady Caroline Lamb.

GHOSTLEY, Alice: Act. b. Eve, MO, Aug 16, 1926. e. U of OK. Films inc: New Faces; To Kill a Mockingbird; My Six Loves; Ace Eli and Rodger of the Skies; Rabbit Test; Grease.
Bway inc: New Faces of 1952; Sandhog; Trouble in Tahiti; Maybe Tuesday; A Thurber Carnival; Gentlemen Be Seated; The Sign in Sidney Brustein's Window (Tony-supp-1965); Stop, Thief, Stop.

GIANNINI, Giancarlo: Act. b. Spezia, Italy, Aug 1, 1942. Films inc: Love and Anarchy; The Seduction of Mimi; How Funny Can Sex Be?; Seven Beauties; The End of the World In Our Usual Bed In A Night Full of Rain; The Innocent; Buone Notizie (& prod); Revenge; Travels with Anita.
Thea inc: Two Plus Two No Longer Make Four.

GIBB, Andy: Mus-Prod. TV inc: Dean Martin Christmas Special 1980. Albums inc: Shadow Dancing; Shadow Gibb; Flowing Rivers.
See also BEEGEES.

GIBB, Barry: Mus-Prod. b. Sep 1, 1946. Films inc: Saturday Night Fever; Sgt. Pepper's Lonely Hearts Club Band.
See also BEEGEES.

GIBB, Maurice: Mus-Prod. b. Dec 22, 1949. Films inc: Saturday Night Fever; Sgt. Pepper's Lonely Hearts Club Band.
See also BEEGEES.

GIBB, Robin: Mus-Prod. b. Dec 22, 1949. Films inc: Saturday Night Fever; Sgt. Pepper's Lonely Hearts Club Band.
See also BEEGEES.

GIBBONS, Peter (Walter Peter Gibbons-Fly): Cin. b. Philadelphia, Jan 15, 1913. e. NYU, BS, USC, MFA. Tech advisor on: Seven Wonders of the World; Search for Paradise; South Seas Adventure; Wonderful World of the Brothers Grimm; How the West Was Won. Personal tech advisor to George Stevens on The Greatest Story Ever Told; (Cin) Fraternity Row.

GIBBS, Marla: Act. b. Chicago, IL, Jun 14, 1946. Films inc: Black Belt Jones; Sweet Jesus, Preacher Man.
TV inc: The Moneychanger; Tell Me Where It Hurts; You Can't Take It With You; The Jeffersons.

GIBNEY, Sheridan: Wri. b. NYC, Jun 11, 1903. e. Exeter, Amherst, AB, MA. Films inc: I Am A Fugitive From a Chain Gang; The Story of Louis Pasteur (Oscar-1936); Anthony Adverse; Letter of Introduction; Cheers For Miss Bishop; Once Upon a Honeymoon; The Locket; Our Hearts Were Young and Gay.
Plays inc: The Wiser They Are; Encore; Merry Madness.

GIBSON, Henry: Act. b. Germantown, PA, 1935. e. Catholic U. Broadway, My Mother, My Father and Me. Film debut in The Long Goodbye. Films inc: Kiss Me Stupid; The Nutty Professor; The Gunslingers; Evil Roy Slade; The Last Remake of Beau Geste; A Perfect Couple; The Blues Brothers; Health.
TV inc: Mister Roberts; F-Troop; Laugh-In; The Halloween That Almost Wasn't; For the Love of It.

GIBSON, William: Wri. b. NYC, Nov 13, 1914. e. CCNY. Plays inc: I Lay in Zion; A Cry of Players; The Miracle Worker (Tony-1960); Dinny and the Witches; John and Abigail; The Butterfingers Angel; A Season in Heaven; Golda.
Films Inc: Two for the Seesaw; The Miracle Worker; The Cobweb.
TV inc: The Miracle Worker.

GIDDING, Nelson: Wri. b. 1915. Films inc: I Want to Live; Odds Against Tomorrow; Nine Hours to Rama; The Inspector; The Haunting; Lost Command; Skullduggery; The Andromeda Strain; Beyond the Poseidon Adventure.

GIELGUD, Sir John: Act. b. London, Apr 14, 1904. e. RADA. Knighted, 1953. Began stage career in Shakespearean roles London stage; also in The Constant Nymph; The Good Companions; The Importance of Being Earnest; Half-Life. (Bway): various Shakespearean roles; Bingo; No Man's Land; also dir Big Fish, Little Fish (Tony-1961); Private Lives; The Constant Wife; No Man's Land; The Gay Lord Quex (Special Tony-1959).
Films inc: Secret Agent; Julius Caesar; Richard III; Around the World in 80 Days; The Barretts of Wimpole Street; Becket; The Loved One; St. Joan; The Charge of the Light Brigade; The Shoes of the Fisherman; Oh What a Lovely War; Lost Horizon; Murder on the Orient Express; Portrait of the Artist As A Young Man; Joseph Andrews; Providence; Murder By Decree; Caligula; The Human Factor; Drygent (The Orchestra Conductor); The Elephant Man; The Formula.
TV inc: A Day by the Sea; The Browning Version; Mayfly and the Frog; The Cherry Orchard; From Chekov With Love; St. Joan; Deliver Us From Evil; Heartbreak House; To Be An Actor; Les Miserables; Why Didn't They Ask Evans?
(Grammy-spoken word-1979).

GIFFORD, Alan: Act. b. Boston, Mar 11, 1911. Films inc: The Iron Petticoat; The Flying Scot; Screaming Mimi; Onionhead; Mouse That Roared; The Royal Game; The Road to Hong Kong; Town Without Pity; One Spy Too Many; 2001: A Space Odyssey; Isadora.
TV inc: High Tension; Philadelphia Story; A Quiet Game of Cards; Portrait of a Lady; The Male Animal; As The World Turns.

GIFFORD, Frank: Sports Commentator. b. Santa Monica, CA, Aug 16, 1930. e. USC. Former football great (Hall of Fame 1977). ABC sportscaster. TV inc: Monday Night Football; Olympic Games 1972 and 1976; Superstar series (host); (Emmy-outstanding sports personality-1977).

GIL, David: Prod. b. Tel Aviv, Israel, Jan 24, 1930. e. U of Jerusalem. Headed Gilart Productions, 1962-68; Foreign sls dir, Commonwealth United, 1968. Films inc: Guess What We Learned in School Today; Joe; A Journey Through Rosebud; A Change in the Wind; Gas Pump Girls.
TV inc: Nightkill.

GILARDI, Jack Leo: Agent. b. Chicago, Oct 5, 1930. e. Loras Coll. H of Annette Funicello. Started as agent at GAC; then sr vp ICM.

GILBERT, Bruce: Prod. b. LA, 1948. e. UC Berkeley. Partnered with Jane Fonda in IPC Films; story ed CineArtists. Films inc: Coming Home (asso prod); The China Syndrome (exec prod); Nine To Five.

GILBERT, Lewis: Dir. b. London, Mar 6, 1920. Films inc: Little Ballerina; Bismarck; The Sea Shall Not Have Them; The Admirable Crichton; Carve Her Name With Pride; Alfie; You Only Live Twice; H.M.S. Defiant; Loss of Innocence; The Spy Who Loved Me; Moonraker.

GILBERT, Melissa: Act. b. LA, May 8, 1964. TV inc: Gunsmoke; Tenafly; The Hanna-Barbera Happy Hour; Christmas Miracle; Little House on the Prairie; The Miracle Worker; The Diary of Anne Frank. Films inc: Nutcracker Fantasy.

GILBERT, Ray: Lyr-Comp. b. Hartford, CT, Sep 15, 1912. Wrote special material for Sophie Tucker; Harry Richman; Buddy Rogers. To Hollywood 1939. Films scores inc: The Three Caballeros; Make Mine Music; Song of the South; A Date with Judy.
Songs inc: You Belong to My Heart; Two Silhouettes; Zip-a-Dee-Doo-Dah (Oscar-1947); My Fickle Eye; Bahia; Muskrat Ramble; Casey at the Bat; Bonita; If You Went Away.

GILBRIDE, Andrew D: Mus. b. Seattle, WA, Jul 5, 1953. Performs on 5-string banjo. On tour with the Bunk Hokum travelling Bluegrass Show.

GILFORD, Jack (nee Gellman): Act. b. NYC, Jul 25, 1907. Started in vaudeville, niteries. Films inc: Hey Rookie; A Funny Thing Happened on the Way to the Forum; Mister Buddwing; Enter Laughing; The Happening; Who's Minding the Mint? They Might be Giants; Catch 22; Save the Tiger; Wholly Moses!; Cheaper to Keep Her.

TV inc: Once Upon a Mattress; Of Thee I Sing; Friends and Lovers; The World of Sholem Aleichem; The Diary of Anne Frank; The Tenth Man; Apple Pie.

Bway inc: The Sunshine Boys; No, No Nanette; Cabaret; Sly Fox.

GILKYSON, Terry: Act-Comp. b. Phoenixville, PA, circa 1919. One of the pioneers of the pop folk movement of the 50s and 60s.

GILLESPIE, Dizzy (John Birks Gillespie): Mus-Comp. b. Cheraw, SC, Oct 21, 1917. e. Laurinburg Inst. Trumpet player with Teddy Hill; Cab Calloway; Earl "Fatha" Hines before forming own group 1944; world tours for State Dept; concerts; later rec artist with Charlie Parker; Miles Davis; Stan Getz; Oscar Peterson.

Songs inc: A Night in Tunisia; Groovin' High; Tour de Force; Con Alma; This Is The Way; Manteca; Lorraine; Cool World; Something Old, Something New; Swing Low Sweet Cadillac.

(*Grammy*-jazz solo-1975).

GILLIATT, Penelope: Wri. b. England, 1933. Films inc: Sunday, Bloody Sunday.

GILLING, John: Wri-Dir-Prod. b. England, 1912. Films inc: Interpol; The Man Inside; Odongo; High Flight; The Flesh and the Fields; The Challenge; The Pirates of Blood River; The Shadow of the Cat; Scarlet Blade; Plague of the Zombies; The Reptile; The Night Caller.

GILMAN, Sam: Act. b. Lynn, MA. Films inc: Shadow of the Window; Somebody Up There Likes Me; Away All Boats; Desiree; PT 109; One-Eyed Jacks; Burn; Gator Bait; Fluffy; Wild Rovers; Macon County Line; Missouri Breaks; Sometimes a Great Notion; Every Which Way But Loose; Gatorbait.

GILMORE, William S: Prod. b. LA, Mar 10, 1934. e. UC Berkeley. Films inc: The Last Remake of Beau Geste; Defiance.

TV inc: S O S Titanic.

GILROY, Frank D: Wri. b. NYC, Oct 13, 1925. e. Dartmouth. Films inc: The Fastest Gun Alive; The Subject Was Roses; The Gallant Hours; The Only Game in Town; Desperate Characters (& dir); From Noon Till Three (& dir); Once in Paris (& dir).

TV inc: Studio One; Playhouse 90; Kraft Theatre; Rex Stout's Nero Wolfe.

Plays inc: Who'll Save the Plowboy (& prod); The Subject Was Roses (& prod); (*Pulitzer Prize & Tony*-1965) That Summer--That Fall; The Only Game in Town; Present Tense; Last Licks.

GIMBEL, Norman: Lyr. b. Brooklyn, Nov 16, 1927. e. Baruch Coll, BBA. Bway inc: Whoop Up; The Conquering Hero.

Songs inc: Ready To Take A Chance Again; Canadian Sunset; Girl From Ipanema; Watch What Happens; Live for Life; I Got a Name; I Will Wait For You; Richard's Window; Killing Me Softly With His Song (*Grammy*-song of year-1973); Love Is; Sail On; Love Theme from Five Days From Home; Are You Ready for the Summer; Meatballs; Good Friend; Moondust; It Goes Like It Goes (*Oscar*-1979); Here Is Where The Love Is.

GIMBEL, Peter: Wri-Dir-Prod. b. NYC, Feb 14, 1928. e. Yale. Films inc: Blue Water, White Death; Mystery of the Andrea Doria.

GIMBEL, Roger: Exec prod. b. Philadelphia, Mar 11, 1925. e. Yale. Copy and creative chief of RCA Victor TV; Became assoc prod, Tonight Show; made head of pgm dvlpt of NBC daytime programming; later named prod of Tonight specials, including the Jack Paar, Ernie Kovacs shows; also responsible for the Bing Crosby/Mary Martin Special; the Dean Martin Special; in 1969 prod, co-packager The Glen Campbell Goodtime Hour; 1971, named prodn vp, Tomorrow Entertainment, Inc.

TV inc: The Autobiography of Miss Jane Pittman; Born Innocent; Glass House; A War of Children (*Emmy*-1973); Gargoyles; I Heard the Owl Call My Name; I Love You, Goodbye; Tell Me Where It Hurts; Things in Their Season; Minstrel Man; Miles to Go Before I Sleep; Queen of the Stardust Ballroom. June 1976, merged with EMI, became the first P, of EMI TV, Inc., prod. The Amazing Howard Hughes; TVTV; Hatter Fox; Lawman Without a Gun; Forever; Deadman's Curve; Deathmoon; Just Me and You; Peterbilt; The Ron Le Flore Story-One in a Million; Betrayal; Steel Cowboy; The Cracker Factory; This Man Stands Alone; The Survival of Dana; Can You Hear the Laughter-The Story of Freddie Prinze; S.O.S. Titanic; Orphan Train; Sophia Loren--Her Own Story; My Kidnapper, My Love.

GINGOLD, Dan: Prod-Dir. b. LA, Jan 1, 1928. Started 1951 as staff dir KNXT (CBS); 1959, staff prod-dir; 1972, exec news prod; 1976, exec prod pgms; 1979 field prod Real People. TV inc: Combat in the Classroom; Hard Time; Whatever Happened to Lori Jean Lloyd? (& wri).

GINGOLD, Hermione: Act. b. London, Dec 9, 1897. Thea inc: (London) Pinkie and the Fairies; The Merry Wives of Windsor; The Merchant of Venice; Little Lord Fauntleroy.

Films inc: Around the World in 80 Days; Bell, Book and Candle; Gigi; The Naked Edge; The Music Man; Promise Her Anything; Those Fantastic Flying Fools.

(*Grammy*-childrens record-1976).

GINN, Robert: Prod. b. Melbourne, Australia, Jun 6, 1943. Exec Dir J C Williamson Productions Ltd. Plays prod inc: (Australia) A Chorus Line; Funny Peculiar; Boeing-Boeing; Dracula; Annie.

GINSBERG, Henry: Prod. b. NYC, Apr 29, 1897. GM-Sls Educational Pictures; then joined Preferred Pictures; entered indy prod as head of Sterling Pictures; exh in PA, 1931; joined Hal Roach Studios; resigned to join Selznick Int'l Pictures as gm; later vp; in 1940 vp and gm in charge of studio oper, Par; resig Par 1950; partnered with George Stevens to prod Giant, 1953.

(Died May 10, 1979).

GINSBERG, Sidney: Exec. b. NYC, Oct 26, 1920. e. CCNY. Started as asst mgr Loew's Theatres; joined Trans-Lux, 1943, as thea mgr; film booker; helped form Trans-Lux Dist. Corp, 1956; vp in charge of world wide sls, 1969; Haven Int'l Pictures, Inc, 1970; vp-sls, Scotia Int'l. Films Inc, 1971; exec vp, Scotia American Prods; 1977, p, Rob-Rich Films Inc.

GINTY, Robert: Act. b. NYC, Nov 14, 1948. Films inc: Bound for Glory; Two Minute Warning; Incident of October 20th; Coming Home.

TV inc: Police Story; The Rockford Files; Baa Baa Black Sheep.

Thea inc: My Three Angels; Once in a Lifetime; The Lion in Winter; The Indian Wants the Bronx.

GIRARDOT, Annie: Act. b. France, Oct 25, 1931. Films inc: Rocco and His Brothers; Maigret Sets a Trap; Vice and Virtue; Dillinger Is Dead; A Man I Like; The Novices; Story of a Woman; Love Is a Funny Thing; The Slap; Love and Cool Water; To Each His Hell; Dear Inspector; No Time for Breakfast; Go On, Mama; The Last Kiss; The Key Is in the Door; L'ingorgo; Bobo, Jacco; Le Coeur a L'envers (My Heart Is Upside Down).

GISH, Lillian: Act. b. Springfield, OH, Oct 14, 1899. Sis of Dorothy Gish. On stage age 5. In 1913 on Bway with Mary Pickford in A Good Little Devil. Film debut 1912 under direction of D.W. Griffith, for whom she made The Birth of a Nation; Intolerance; Hearts of the World; Broken Blossoms; Way Down East; Orphans of the Storm. Other films inc: Duel in the Sun; A Wedding. 1969-71, one woman int'l tour in Lillian Gish and the Movies. Received honorary Oscar, 1971.
1974, Int'l tour with illustrated lecture on the art of film and TV; 1975 Bway; A Musical Jubilee.
TV inc: Sparrow.

GLASER, Paul Michael: Act. b. Cambridge, MA, Apr 25. Films inc: Fiddler on the Roof; Butterflies Are Free; Phobia.
TV inc: Trapped Beneath the Sea; The Great Houdini; Starsky & Hutch.

GLASS, George: Prod. b. LA, Aug 19, 1910. Former publicist. Founder member Publicists Guild, founder member Producers Guild of America. Films inc: (asso prod) The Men; Cyrano de Bergerac; Death of a Salesman; Guess Who's Coming to Dinner; The Secret of Santa Victoria; Bless the Beasts and the Children. (Co-prod) Shake Hands with the Devil; The Naked Edge; Paris Blues. (Exec prod): One Eyed Jacks.

GLASS, Ned: Act. b. Poland, Apr 1, 1906. e. CCNY. Films inc: The Bad and Beautiful; Julius Caesar; West Side Story; Experiment in Terror; Lady Sings the Blues; Charade; Save the Tiger.
TV inc: The Phil Silvers Shows; Julia *(Emmy*-supp-1969); Bridget Loves Bernie; Goldie and the Boxer.

GLASS, Ron: Act. b. Evansville, IN, Jul 10, 1945. e. U of Evansville, BA. TV inc: Beg, Borrow or Steal; Shirts and Skins; Change at 125th Street; Crash; Barney Miller.

GLAZER, Tom: Act-Comp. b. Philadelphia, Sep 3, 1914. e. CCNY. Folk singer; NY debut, 1948, Town Hall. Film scores inc: A Face in the Crowd.

GLAZIER, Sidney: Prod. b. Philadelphia, May 29, 1918. Films inc: The Eleanor Roosevelt Story *(Oscar*-doc-1965); Take the Money and Run; The Gamblers; Quackser Fortune Has a Cousin in the Bronx; The 12 Chairs; Glen and Panda; The Night Visitor; The Only Way.

GLEASON, Jackie: Act. b. NYC, Feb 26, 1916. Started as nitery entertainer. Films inc: The Hustler; Requiem For A Heavyweight; Gigot; Soldier in the Rain; Smokey and the Bandit; Smokey and the Bandit II.
TV inc: The Life of Riley; Cavalcade of Stars; The Jackie Gleason Show; The Honeymooners.
Bway inc: Take Me Along *(Tony*-1960); Hellzapoppin'; Artists and Models.

GLEASON, Joanna: Act. b. Toronto, Can, Jun 2. e. Occidental Coll. D of Monty Hall. Thea inc: I Love My Wife; As You Like It; A Midsummer Night's Dream; Hamlet.
TV inc: Hello, Larry.

GLENVILLE, Peter: Act-Dir. b. London, Eng, Oct 28, 1913. e. Oxford U. Professional debut with Manchester Repertory Co, 1934; act in various prodns before dir the following plays; Point Valaine; Major Barbara; The Giaconda Smile; Crime Passionnel; The Browning Version; Summer and Smoke; Under the Sycamore Tree; The Innocents; Letter From Paris; The Living Room; Separate Tables; Rashomon; Take Me Along; Silent Night, Lonely Night; Becket; Tovarich; Dylan; A Patriot for Me; A Bequest to the Nation; Outcry.
Films inc: (dir) The Prisoner; Term of Trial; Becket; Summer and Smoke; The Comedians; Hotel Paradiso.

GLESS, Sharon: Act. b. LA, May 31, 1943. TV inc: The Longest Night; All My Darling Daughters; My Darling Daughters' Anniversary; Switch; The Immigrants; The Scream of Eagles; The Last Convertible; Hardhat and Legs; The Kids Who Knew Too Much; Turnabout; Moviola (The Scarlett O'Hara War); Revenge of the Stepford Wives.

GLICKMAN, Fred: Comp. b. Chicago, Sep 22, 1903. Violinist in dance bands, symph orchs; also cond own orch; has own recording, publ cos.
Songs inc: Mule Train; Little Old Band of Gold; Angel of Mine.

GLICKMAN, Joel: Prod. b. LA, Jul 29, 1930. e. UCLA, BA. Early TV work on series, documentaries, commercials. Prodn assoc, Wedding and Babies, 1958.
Films inc: Terror in the City; The Balcony; All the Way Home; Last Summer; Hamlet; Brother John; Buck and the Preacher; Trial of the Catonsville Nine.
TV inc: East Side, West Side; Mr. Broadway; N.Y.P.D.; Among the Paths to Eden; Night Terror; Angel on Horseback; The Kennedy-Hoffa War.

GLOBUS, Yoram: Prod. Films inc: Marriage Tel Aviv Style; The Godsend; The Apple; The Happy Hooker Goes to Washington; The Magician of Lublin; Operation Thunderbolt; It's A Funny, Funny World; Dr. Heckyl and Mr. Hype; Schizoid; The Apple.

GLOUNER, Richard C: Cin. b. LA, Aug 12, 1931. e. LA City Coll, Glendale Coll. Films inc: Payday; Gumball Rally.
TV inc: Cry for Help; Louis Armstrong; Bloodsport; Savage Swarm; Sweet Hostage; Columbo *(Emmy*-1974, 75). Bud and Lou.

GLUCKSMAN, Ernest D: Prod-Dir-Wri. b. Vienna, Mar 21. Films inc: The Nutty Professor; The Errand Boy; The Patsy; Rock-A-Bye-Baby; The Bell Boy; Cinderfella; Geisha Boy.
TV inc: Here Come the Stars; Can You Top This; (specials): Sonny & Cher; Bobby Darin; Fifth Dimension; Lou Rawls; George Kirby; Dr Jekyll and Mr Hyde; Charles Aznavour & Liza Minnelli.
Bway inc: The Odd Couple.
(Died July 7, 1979).

GOBEL, George: Act. b. Chicago, 1919. Played with country western group on radio. Appeared in niteries.
TV inc: The George Gobel Show *(Emmy*-1954); Better Late Than Never; A Country Christmas; The Incredible Book Escape (voice).
Bway, Three Men on a Horse (musical).
Films inc: Rabbit Test.

GODARD, Jean-Luc: Wri-Dir. b. Paris, Dec 3, 1930. Films inc: A Bout de Souffle; Une Femme Est Une Femme; Vivre Sa Vie; Le Petit Soldat; Les Carabiniera; Bande a Part; Une Femme Mariee; A Little Godard; Pierrot Le Fou; Made in USA; Weekend; Tout va Bien.

GODDARD, Paulette: Act. b. Great Neck, NY, Jun 3, 1911. Bway inc: Rio Rita. On screen from 1931.
Films inc: City Lights; Roman Scandals; Modern Times; The Cat and the Canary; Northwest Mounted Police; The Great Dictator; So Proudly We Hail; Hold Back the Dawn; Reap the Wild Wind; I Love a Soldier; Standing Room Only; Kitty; Unconquered; Anna Lucasta; Sins of Jezebel; Time of Indifference.

GODFREY, Arthur: Act. b. NYC, Aug 31, 1903. News commentator; act-wri-narr-on radio, TV.
Films inc: The Glass Bottom Boat; Where Angels Go. . .Trouble Follows; Four for Texas; Shenanigans.
TV inc: The Arthur Godfrey Show (also radio); The Arthur Godfrey Talent Show; Flatbed Annie and Sweetie Pie-Lady Truckers.

GODFREY, Bob: Prod. b. Eng, 1921. Animated shorts inc: The Do It Yourself Cartoon Kit; The Plain Man's Guide to Advertising; Kama Sutra Rides Again; Great *(Oscar*-1975).

GOETZ, Ben: Exec. b. NYC, Jan 2, 1891. Joined MGM in 1934; sent to London to run the studio's English prodn arm. Headed London prod office until 1955. (Died Aug 22, 1979).

GOETZ, Ruth Goodman: Wri. b. Philadelphia, Jan 11, 1918. Formerly a story edtr. Plays (with late husband Augustus Goetz) inc: Franklin Street; One Man Show; The Heiress The Immoralist; The Hidden River; also Here Today (with George Oppenheimer); adapted Madly in Love from the French of Andre Broussin.
Films inc: (with husband) The Heiress; Sister Carrie; Rhapsody; Trapeze; Stage Struck.

GOFF, Ivan: Wri. b. Australia, 1910. Usually in collab with Ben Roberts. Films inc: My Love Came Back; White Heat; Captain Horatio Hornblower; Come Fill the Cup; King of the Khyber Rifles; Green Fire; Serenade; Man of a Thousand Faces; Shake Hands with the Devil; Portrait in Black.
TV inc: The Rogues; Charlie's Angels; Time Express.

GOLAN, Menahem: Dir. b. Israel, 1931. Films inc: Sallah; Tevye and His Seven Daughters; What's Good for the Goose?; Lepke; Diamonds; The Magician of Lublin; Marriage Tel Aviv Style; The Godsend; The Apple (& prod-wri); The Happy Hooker Goes to Hollywood; It's A Funny Funny World (prod); The Uranium Conspiracy (& prod); Dr. Heckyl and Mr. Hype; Schizoid.

GOLD, Ernest: Comp-Cond. b. Vienna, Jul 13, 1921. Film scores inc: Too Much, Too Soon; On the Beach; Inherit the Wind; Exodus (Oscar-1960); Judgment at Nuremberg; A Child Is Waiting; It's a Mad, Mad, Mad, Mad World; Ship of Fools; The Secret of Santa Vittoria; Fun With Dick and Jane; Cross of Iron; Good Luck, Miss Wyckoff; Tom Horn.
Songs inc: On the Beach; It's a Mad, Mad, Mad, Mad World. (Grammys-(2)-song of year & soundtrack-1960).

GOLD, Missy: Act. b. Great Falls, MT, Jul 14, 1970.
TV inc: How The West Was Won, Captains and Kings; Nancy Drew; Benson.

GOLD, Tracey: Act. b. May 16, 1969. TV inc: Jennifer-A Woman's Story; The Dark Secrets of Harvest Home; The Child Stealers; Shirley.

GOLDBECK, Willis: Wri-Dir-Prod. b. NYC, Oct 24, 1898. Films inc: Where the Pavement Ends; Wild Orchids; Peter Pan; Lilac Time; Mare Nostrum; Dr Gillespie's New Assistant; Rationing; Between Two Women; Three Men in White; She Went to the Races; Love Laughs at Andy Hardy; Ten Tall Men.
(Died Sep 17, 1979.)

GOLDBERG, Fred: Exec. b. NYC, Aug 26, 1921. e. Pace Coll. Exec asst to dir pub, adv, UA, 1958; exec dir pub, adv, exp 1961; named vp, 1962; sr vp, 1972; sr vp, dir of mktg, 1977; 1978, sr vp ad-pub-prom, Col.

GOLDBERG, Gary David: Prod. b. Brooklyn, NY, Jun 25, 1944. TV inc: Bob Newhart Show (wri); Tony Randall Show (1976 story ed; 1978 co-prod); Lou Grant (co-prod) (Emmy-1979); The Last Resort (prod-crea-wri).

GOLDBERG, Leonard: Prod. b. NYC, Jan 24, 1934. e. U PA, BS. Joined research dept CBS 1956; to NBC research 1957 as supv special proj; 1961 BBD&O agcy in chg daytime tv; 1963 mgr pgm dvlpt ABC; 1964 vp daytime pgm & dir pgm dvlpt; 1965 vp network pgms; 1966 vp chg prodn Screen Gems; 1969 teamed with Aaron Spelling in Spelling- Goldberg Prodns; 1972 Leonard Goldberg Prodns; 1978 Goldberg-Weintraub Prodns.
TV inc: The Rookies; People's Choice; Charley's Angels; Starsky and Hutch; Beach Patrol; Hart to Hart; When the Whistle Blows; Blue Jeans.

GOLDENBERG, Billy: Comp. b. NYC, Feb 10, 1936. e. Columbia Coll, BA. Films inc: Red Sky At Morning; Play It Again, Sam; Up The Sandbox; The Grasshopper; The Domino Principle; Scavenger Hunt; The Last of Sheila.
TV inc: Queen of the Stardust Ballroom; The Rebel--Benjamin Franklin (Emmy-1975); Duel; The Neon Ceiling; The Miracle Worker; The Glass House; The Incredible Machine; Helter Skelter; An Evening with Diana Ross (Emmy-spec mat-1977); King (Emmy-1978); All God's Children; The Love Tapes; Haywire; The Women's Room; Act of Love; A Perfect Match; Father Figure; The Diary of Anne Frank.
TV themes inc: Kojak; Rhoda; Alias Smith and Jones; Banacek; Columbo; Harry-O; The Sixth Sense; Delvecchio.

GOLDENSON, Leonard: Exec. b. Scottsdale, PA, Dec 7, 1905. e. Harvard Coll, BA, Harvard Law School, LLB. Counsel in reorg. Paramount theatres in New England, 1933-37. Appointed asst to vp Paramount in charge theatre operations, 1937. Became head of theatre operations, 1938; elected pres. Paramount Theatre Service Corp., vp Paramount Theatres Inc., 1938. Then pres, CEO, director United Paramount Theatres, Inc. and American Broadcasting Companies which merged into American Broadcasting Companies, Inc. Chairman of the Board and CEO of ABC since 1972.

GOLDMAN, Bo: Wri. Films inc: One Flew Over the Cuckoo's Nest (Oscar-1975); The Rose; Melvin and Howard.

GOLDMAN, James: Wri. Plays inc: Blood, Sweat and Stanley Poole; They Might Be Giants; The Lion in Winter; Family Affair; Follies; Waldorf; Myself as Witness.
Films inc: The Lion in Winter (Oscar-1968); They Might Be Giants; Nicholas and Alexandra; Robin and Marian.
TV inc: Evening Primrose.

GOLDMAN, William: Wri. b. Chicago, 1931. e. Oberlin Coll, BA, Columbia U, MA. Films inc: Soldier in the Rain; Masquerade; Harper; No Way to Treat a Lady; Butch Cassidy and the Sundance Kid (Oscar-story-sp-1969); The Hot Rock; The Great Waldo Pepper; All the President's Men (Oscar-sp-1976); A Bridge Too Far; Magic; Butch and Sundance-The Early Days.
TV inc: Mr Horn.

GOLDONI, Lelia: Act. b. NYC. Films inc: Shadows; Day of the Locust; Alice Doesn't Live Here Anymore; Baby Blue Marine; Bloodbrothers; Invasion of the Body Snatchers.
TV inc: Espionage; Secret Agent; Attorneys At Law; The Spider's Web; Blackmail; The Dream Divided; Scott and Zelda Fitzgerald; A Kiss is Just a Kiss; Sister Aimee; Scruples.

GOLDSBORO, Bobby: Mus. b. Marianne, FL, 1941. Recording artist. TV inc: The Bobby Goldsboro Show.

GOLDSMITH, David: Prod. b. LA, Jul 22, 1948. e. USC, BS; Southwestern U School of Law. Member The Thomas Group (rock band) while in college; 1970 prodn asst T&L Prodns, Paramount TV; 1972, mgr pgm dvlpmt Screen Gems; 1974, dir films for tv & pgm dvlpmt MGM TV; 1977 vp pgm devlpmt Bennett-Katleman Prodns; 1978, vp dramatic pgms, Paramount TV; 1980 joined Charles Fries Prodns to develop projects under David Goldsmith Prodns banner in ass'n with Fries.
TV inc: (Exec prod) Mind Over Murder; Comedy Company; Deadly Tower.

GOLDSMITH, Jerry: Comp. b. LA, 1930. e. LA City Coll. Film scores inc: Lonely Are The Brave; Freud; Lilies of the Field; The Blue Max; Seven Days in May; Von Ryan's Express; A Patch of Blue; The Sand Pebbles; Planet of the Apes; Patton; Papillon; Mephisto Waltz; The Wild Rovers; Chinatown; The Wind and the Lion; Logan's Run; Islands in the Stream; MacArthur; The Omen (Oscar-1976); The Cassandra Crossing; The Boys From Brazil; Coma; Damien-Omen II; Capricorn One; Magic; The Swarm; The Great Train Robbery; Alien; Players; Star Trek-The Motion Picture.
TV inc: Climax; Playhouse 90; The Man From UNCLE; Dr. Kildare; Gunsmoke; The Red Pony (Emmy-1973); QB-VII (Emmy-1975); The Waltons; Babe (Emmy-1976).

GOLDSMITH, Lester: Prod. b. Chicago, IL, Mar 2, 1934. e. U of IL, BSJ. Northwestern U; MA. VP Radio-TV Edward Weiss Adv Agency; VP Paramount; Prod UPA Pictures.
TV inc: Watch Mr Wizard.
Films inc: Happy Birthday, Wanda June; The Passage.
Bway inc: Happy Birthday, Wanda June.

GOLDSMITH, Martin M: Wri. b. NYC, Nov 6, 1913. Films inc: Detour; Blind Spot; The Narrow Margin; Mission Over Korea; Overland Pacific; Hell's Island.

GOLDSTEIN, Milton: Exec. b. NYC, Aug 1, 1926. e. NYU. Exec vp worldwide dist Cinerama, 1967-68,; Cinema Center Films, 1969-73, exec vp, then P; 1973-74 vp theatrical dist worldwide, Metromedia; 1974-75 p Boasberg-Goldstein; 1975-77, exec vp Avco Embassy Pictures; 1977, exec vp Mel Simon Productions.

GOLDSTONE, James: Dir. b. LA, Jun 8, 1931. e. Dartmouth, B.A. TV inc: Star Trek; Ironside; Studs Lonigan.
Films inc: Jigsaw; Man Called Gannon; The Gang That Couldn't Shoot Straight; Swashbuckler; Rollercoaster; When Time Ran Out.

GOLDSTONE, Richard: Prod. b. NYC, Jul 14, 1912. e. UCLA, BA. Films inc: The Outsider; Inside Straight; The Tall Target; The Devil Makes Three; Cinerama's South Seas Adventure; No Man Is an Island (& sp-dir); Rage; The Sergeant; The Babymaker.
TV inc: Adventures in Paradise; Combat; Peyton Place.

GOLDWURM, Jean: Exec. b. Bucharest, Romania, Feb 21, 1893. e. U of Vienna. Founder-pres of Times Film Corp., which has been importing European films to the U.S. since 1945. Ownr-opr of the Little Carnegie and World Theatres. Began import business with To Live In Peace; has since imported Two Cents Worth of Hope; Forbidden Games; One Summmer of Happiness and some 200 other films. Founder of the International Film Importers and Distributors Association of America.

GOLDWYN, Samuel Jr: Prod-Dir. b. LA, Sep 7, 1926. e. U of VA. U.S. Army, 1944. After war, writer, assoc. prod. J. Arthur Rank Org. Prod. Gathering Storm London stage. Returned to US, 1948; prod. Adventure TV series for CBS; The Unexpected. Formed Formosa Prod. Inc., 1955.
Films inc: Man With the Gun; The Sharkfighters; The Proud Rebel; The Adventures of Huckleberry Finn; The Young Lovers; Cotton Comes to Harlem; Come Back Charleston Blue.

GOLITZEN, Alexander: Art Dir (ret). b. Moscow, USSR, Feb 28, 1907. Films inc: Phantom of the Opera; Spartacus (*Oscar*-1960); To Kill a Mockingbird (*Oscar*-1962).

GOLOD, Jerry: Exec. b. NY. e. CCNY. Joined CBS in 1975 as an exec in the children's programming area; moved to NBC; named vp, National Program Dir, NBC Entertainment, in Apr, 1979.

GOMBERG, Sy: Wri-Prod. b. NYC, Aug 19, 1918. e. USC, BA. Films inc: When Willie Comes Marching Home; Summer Stock; Toast of New Orleans; Because You're Mine; Bloodhounds of Broadway; Joe Butterfly; The Wild and the Innocent; Three Warriors.
TV inc: The Law and Mr. Jones; Accidental Family; Good Heavens; Margaret Jean; Bender; High Ice; The Ghosts of Buxley Hall. World Premiere Theatre; The Wonderful World of Disney; The Snatching of Little Freddie and

GONZALEZ-GONZALEZ, Pedro: Act. b. Aguilares, TX, Dec 21, 1926. Films inc: Wings of the Hawk; Ring of Fear; The High and the Mighty; Strange Lady in Town; The Sheepman; Rio Bravo; The Adventures of Bullwhip Griffin; The Love Bug; Support Your Local Gunfighter; Dreamer; There Goes The Bride.
TV inc: O'Henry Stories; Hostile Guns.

GOODEVE, Grant: Act. b. Middlebury, CT, Jul 6, 1952.
Films inc: All the King's Horses.
TV inc: Eight Is Enough; Hot Rod; A Last Cry for Help.

GOODFRIED, Bob: Pub. b. NYC, Apr 8, 1913. Started with Skouras Theatres. To west coast 1945 as PA mgr Columbia Pictures; vp in charge of studio and West Coast publicity, Paramount pictures, 1971; became PR Consultant for Paramount 1980.

GOODMAN, Benny: Act. b. Chicago, May 30, 1909. Played in Broadway theater orchestras. Organized own band 1933. Appeared in hotels, ballrooms, night clubs.
Films inc: Hollywood Hotel; The Big Broadcast of 1937; Stage Door Canteen; The Powers Girl; Sweet and Low Down; A Song Is Born.

GOODMAN, David Zelag: Wri. Films inc: Monte Walsh; Lovers and Other Strangers; The Straw Dogs; Man on the Swing; Farewell My Lovely; Logan's Run; March Or Die; The Eyes of Laura Mars.
TV inc: Freedom Road.

GOODMAN, Dody: Act. b. Columbus, OH, 1929. Joined ballet companies of the Radio City Music Hall, the Metropolitan Opera. Danced on Broadway in High Button Shoes, Call Me Madam, Wonderful Town. Started career as comic on TV, nightclubs, off-Broadway revues.
Films inc: Bedtime Story; Women, Women, Women!; Grease.
TV inc: Jack Paar Show; Mary Hartman, Mary Hartman; Search for Tomorrow; Fernwood Tonight; The Treasure of Alpheus T. Winterborn.
Bway inc: Period of Adjustment; My Daughter, Your Son; Rainy Day in Newark; Valentine Magic on Love Island.

GOODMAN, Julian: Exec. b. Glasgow, KY, May 2, 1922. e. Western KY U, BA. Joined NBC as a news wri for WRC, Washington 1945. Appointed M, News, Special Events, NBC TV, 1951; in 1959, assigned to NBC News, NY, as dir News Public Affairs; appointed vp, NBC News, Jan 1961, and exec vp, Oct 1965. Became chief admin officer NBC with title sr exec vp, Dec 1965. Elected to NBC Board of Dir, Jan 1966; P, NBC March 1, 1966. ChmnB, April 1974.
Retired May 31, 1979.

GOODRICH, Frances: Wri. b. 1901. Usually in collab with husband, Albert Hackett.
Films inc: The Thin Man; After the Thin Man; Naughty Marietta; Another Thin Man; The Hitler Gang; It's A Wonderful Life; Summer Holiday; Father of the Bride; Seven Brides for Seven Brothers; The Diary of Anne Frank.
Bway: The Diary of Anne Frank (*Tony*-1956).
TV inc: The Diary of Anne Frank.

GOODSON, Mark: TV Prod. b. Sacramento, CA, Jan 24, 1915. e. U of CA, AB. Anncer, newscaster, dir. radio, KFRC, San Francisco, 1938-41. Anncer dir. NY, 1941-43. Dir. for ABC, 1943. Formed Goodson-Todman Prodns., 1946.
Originated radio shows: Winner Take All; Stop the Music; Hit the Jackpot. Creator of TV game shows: What's My Line (*Emmy*-1952); News to Me; The Name's the Same; I've Got a Secret; To Tell the Truth; The Price Is Right; Password; Match Game.
TV films: The Web; The Rebel; Branded.

GOODWIN, Ron: Comp-Arr-Cond. b. Plymouth, Eng, 1930. Films inc: I'm All Right, Jack; The Trials of Oscar Wilde; Murder She Said; 633 Squadron; Operation Crossbow; Those Magnificent Men in Their Flying Machines; The Alphabet Murders; Where Eagles Dare; Battle of Britain; Frenzy; The Happy Prince; One of Our Dinosaurs is Missing; Escape From the Dark; Force 10 From Navarone.

GOORWITZ, Allen (formerly billed as Allen Garfield): Act. b. Newark, NJ, Nov 22, 1939. Films inc: (as Garfield) Orgy Girls; Greetings; Putney Swope; The Owl and the Pussycat; Roommates; The Commitment; Bananas; Cry Uncle; The Organization; The Candidate; Slither; Busting; The Conversation; The Front Page; Nashville; Paco; Gable and Lombard; Skateboard. (As Goorwitz) The Brink's Job; The Stunt Man; One Trick Pony.

GORDON, Alex: Prod. b. London, Sep 8, 1922. Films inc: Lawless Rider; Bride of the Monster; Apache Woman; The Day the World Ended; Oklahoma Woman; Shake, Rattle and Rock; Flesh and the Spur; Voodoo Woman; Dragstrip Girl; Submarine Seahawk; Atomic Submarine; The Underwater City; The Bounty Killer; Requiem for a Gunfighter.
TV inc: Movie of the Year; Golden Century; Great Moments in Motion Pictures.

GORDON, Bert: Prod-Dir-Wri. b. Kenosha, WI, 1922. e. U of WI. Films inc: The Beginning of the End; The Amazing Colossal Man; Cyclops; The Boy and the Pirates; The Magic Sword; Picture Mommy Dead; Necromancy; The Mad Bomber; The Police Connection; The Food of the Gods; Empire of the Ants.

GORDON, Don: Act. b. LA, Nov 23, 1926. Films inc: Bullitt; WUSA; Cannon for Cordoba; The Gamblers; The Last Movie; Fuzz; Slaughter; ZPG; The Mack; Papillon; The Education of Sonny Carson.
TV inc: Street Killing; The Sparrow; The Contender; Out of The Blue.

GORDON, Gale (Charles T Aldrich Jr): Act. b. NYC, Feb 2, 1906. Films inc: The Pilgrimage Play; Rally 'Round The Flag, Boys; All in a Night's Work; Don't Give up the Ship; Visit To a Small Planet; All Hands on Deck.
TV inc: Dennis the Menace; Our Miss Brooks; Here's Lucy; The Lucy Show; Lucy Moves to NBC.

GORDON, Hayes: Act-Dir-Prod. b. Boston, MA, Feb 25, 1920. Studied for stage under Lee Strasberg, Sandy Meisner.
Bway (act) inc: Oklahoma!; Winged Victory; Show Boat; Brigadoon; Sleepy Hollow; Small Wonder; Along Fifth Avenue; went to Australia 1952 to star in Kiss Me Kate; Annie Get Your Gun; Kismet; founded Ensemble Theatre, Sydney, 1958, has since prod more than 30 plays.
TV (US) inc: Hayes Gordon Presents; Potted Musicals; The Fashion Story. (Australia) Medico; The Late Show; The Dawn Lake Show.
Films inc: Winged Victory; Stage Door Canteen.

GORDON, Lawrence: Prod. b. Belzoni, MS. e. Tulane. TV inc: Burke's Law (asso prod-wri); joined ABC TV as head West Coast Talent Dvlpmnt; vp Screen Gems; vp chg wldwde prodn AIP; left to form own company.
TV inc: Nightengales; Stunts Unlimited.
Films inc: Dillinger (exec prod); Heavy Traffic; Hard Times; Rolling Thunder; The Driver; The End; Hooper.

GORDON, Leo: Act-Wri. b. Dec 2, 1922. Films inc: China Venture; Riot in Cell Block 11; Seven Angry Men; The Man Who Knew Too Much; Cry Baby Killer (& sp); The Big Operator; The Stranger; The Terror (& sp); The Haunted Palace; Beau Geste; Tobruk (& sp); The St. Valentine's Day Massacre; You Can't Win 'Em All.
TV inc: (Act) Directors Playhouse; Playhouse 90; The Untouchables. (Wri) Adam 12, Bonanza; Maverick; Black Sheep Squadron; Little House on the Prairie.

GORDON, Michael: Dir. b. Baltimore, Sep, 1909. e. Johns Hopkins U, BA; Yale, MFA. Films inc: Boston Blackie Goes Hollywood; Underground Agent; One Dangerous Night; Texas Across The River; Pillow Talk; Move Over Darling.
Bway inc: The Tender Trap; Deadfall; The Lovers.

GORDON, Ruth (nee Jones): Act-Wri. b. Wollaston, MA, Oct 30, 1896. e. AADA. W of Garson Kanin. Stage debut, 1915, Peter Pan. Films inc: (act) Abe Lincoln in Illinois; Two Faced Woman; Edge of Darkness; Inside Daisy Clover; Whatever Happened to Aunt Alice?; Rosemary's Baby (Oscar-supp-1968); Where's Poppa?; Harold and Maude; The Big Bus; Every Which Way But Loose; Boardwalk; My Bodyguard; Any Which Way You Can. (Wri): A Double Life; Adam's Rib; Pat and Mike; The Marrying Kind.
Bway: A Doll's House; Ethan Frome; Three Cornered Moon; Saturday's Children; The Matchmaker; (also London, Berlin); My Mother, My Father and Me; Mrs Warren's Profession; Over 21 (& wri); Years Ago (& wri); Leading Lady (& wri).
TV inc: Taxi (Emmy-1979); Hardhat and Legs (wri); Perfect Gentlemen.

GORDY, Berry: Exec. Founded Motown record co in 1961; expanded into mus publishing, personal mgt, recording studios, film, TV; now bd chmn Motown Industries. Films inc: Lady Sings the Blues (prod); Mahogany (dir); Almost Summer.
TV inc: Scott Joplin, King of Ragtime.

GORETTA, Claude: Dir. b. Geneva, Italy, Jun 23, 1929. e. U of Geneva, British Film Inst. Films inc: The Madman; The Wedding Day; The Invitation; The Wonderful Crook; The Lace Maker; The Provincial (& sp).

GORING, Marius: Act. b. Newport, Isle of Wight, May 23, 1912. e. Cambridge. Films inc: Consider Your Verdict; Rembrandt; The Case of the Frightened Lady; A Matter of Life and Death; The Red Shoes; Mr Perrin and Mr Traill; So Little Time; Ill Met by Moonlight; Exodus; Up From the Beach; Girl on a Motorcycle; Subterfuge; First Love; Zeppelin; The Little Girl in Blue Velvet.
TV inc: Man in a Suitcase; The Scarlet Pimpernel; The Expert; Edward and Mrs Simpson.

GORMAN, Cliff: Act. b. NYC, Oct 13. e. UCLA; U of NM; NYU. Stage debut 1965, Hogan's Goat. Films inc: Justine; Boys in the Band; Cops and Robbers; Rosebud; An Unmarried Woman; Night of the Juggler.
TV inc: Paradise Lost; Class of '63.
Bway inc: Ergo; Lenny (Tony-1971).

GORME, Eydie: Act. b. NYC, Aug 16, 1931. In niteries, TV. Usually performs with husband, Steve Lawrence. TV inc: Steve and Eydie Celebrate Irving Berlin (Emmy-1979).
(Grammys-vocal group-1960; Vocal, female-1966).

GOROG, Laszlo: Wri. b. Hungary, Sep 30, 1903. Films inc: Tales of Manhattan; The Affairs of Susan; She Wouldn't Say Yes; The Land Unknown.
TV inc: The Roaring Twenties; 77 Sunset Strip; Maverick.

GORSHIN, Frank: Act. b. Pittsburgh, PA, 1935. Films inc: The True Story of Jesse James; Warlock; Studs Lonigan; Ring of Fire; The George Raft Story; Batman.
TV inc: Batman; Greatest Heroes of the Bible; Death Car on the Freeway.

GORTNER, Marjoe: Act. b. Long Beach, CA, Jan 14, 1944. Former child evangelist. Screen debut, 1972, Marjoe, full-length autobiographical documentary.
Films inc: Earthquake; Bobbie Jo and the Outlaws; The Food of the Gods; Viva Knievel!; Starcrash; When You Comin Back, Red Ryder (& prod).
TV inc: The Marcus Nelson Murders; The Gun and the Pulpit; Pray for the Wildcats; Speak Up America.

GOSSETT, Louis Jr: Act. b. May 27. e. NYU, BS. Films inc: The Landlord; River Niger; Choirboys; The Deep; It Rained All Night the Day I Left.
TV inc: Roots-Part I (Emmy-1977); To Kill a Cop; Backstairs at the White House; Critical List; Africans; This Man Stands Alone; The Lazarus Syndrome.
Thea inc: Take a Giant Step; The Desk Set; Lost in the Stars; A Raisin in the Sun; Golden Boy; The Zula and the Zayda; The Blacks; My Sweet Charley; Blood Knot; Murderous Angels.

GOTTLIEB, Alex: Wri-Prod. b. Russia, Dec 21, 1906. e. U of WI, BA. Plays inc: Wake Up Darling; Separate Rooms; Susan Slept Here; Stud; Your Place or Mine?; Divorce Me, Darling; September Song.
Films inc: I'll Take Sweden; Frankie and Johnny; Arizona Ranger; The Pigeon; Blue Gardenia; Macao; Susan Slept Here.
TV (wri-prod) inc: Dear Phoebe; The Gale Storm Show; The Tab Hunter Show; Bob Hope Chrysler Theatre Show; Donna Reed Show; The Smothers Brothers.

GOTTLIEB, Carl: Wri. b. Mar 18, 1938. Films inc: Jaws; Which Way Is Up?; The Committee (act); Jaws 2; The Jerk (& act).
TV inc: Smothers Brothers Show (Emmy-1969); The Odd Couple; Flip Wilson; Bob Newhart Show; The Super; Crisis at Sun Valley.

GOTTLIEB, Linda (nee Salzman): Prod. b. NJ, 1939. e. Wellesley, BA; Columbia U, Russian Institute, MA. Films inc: Limbo.
TV inc: Big Henry and The Polka Dot Kid (Emmy-1977); Snowbound; Summer of My German Soldier; The Tap Dance Kid (Emmy-exec prod-1979); Seven Wishes of a Rich Kid; A Movie Star's Daughter; Make-Believe Marriage; The Gold Bug; A Family of Strangers; Stoned; The Mating Season.

GOTTLIEB, Morton: Prod-Mgr. b. NYC, May 2, 1921. e. Yale U, BA. Made pro stage debut 1941, Liberty Jones. Turned to press rep then business Mgr 1946 for Dream Girl; Joan of Lorraine; prod first show 1953, tour of Arms and the Man.

Bway inc: His and Hers; Waiting for Gillian; The Stronger Sex; The Last Tycoon; The Facts of Life; A Palm Tree in a Rose Garden; The Better Mousetrap; The Amazing Adele; An Adventure; Enter Laughing; The Killing of Sister George; The Promise; Lovers; We Bombed in New Haven; The White House; The Mundy Scheme; Sleuth *(Tony*-1970); Veronica's Room; Same Time Next Year; Romantic Comedy.

Films inc: Same Time, Next Year.

GOTTSCHALK, Robert: Exec. b. Chicago, IL, Mar 12, 1918. e. Carleton Coll, BA. Entered film ind as prod shorts; 1949 formed Robert E. Gottschalk Inc, camera equip firm; 1953 Panavision, Inc; Academy Award of Merit 1978 to Panavision for concept, dvlpmnt Panaflex System.

GOUDAL, Jetta: Act. b. France, 1898. Silent star in The Bright Shawl; The Green Goddess; Open All Night; Salome of the Tenements; Road To Yesterday; Three Faces East; White Gold; Forbidden Woman; Her Cardboard Lover; Lady of the Pavements; Plutocrat (sound); Business and Pleasure; (sound) Tarnished Youth. (sound) Ret. 1935.

GOUGH, Michael: Act. b. Malaya, Nov 23, 1917. e. Old Vic School. Films inc: Blanche Fury; The Small Back Room; The Man in the White Suit; Dracula; The Horse's Mouth; Konga; Circus of Blood; The Corpse; The Go-Between; Henry VIII and His Six Wives; The Boys From Brazil; Horror Hospital.

Bway inc: Love of Women; The Hollow Crown; Maigret and the Lady; The Prime of Miss Jean Brodie; Free for All; King Lear; Events in an Upper Room; Phaedra Brittanica; Counting the Ways; Bedroom Farce *(Tony*-supp-1979); Before the Party.

GOULD, Elliott: Act. b. NYC, Aug 29, 1938. Films inc: The Night They Raided Minsky's; Bob & Carol & Ted & Alice; M*A*S*H; I Will. . .I Will. . .For Now; Harry and Walter Go To New York; A Bridge Too Far; Capricorn One; Escape to Athena; The Muppet Movie; The Lady Vanishes; The Silent Partner; The Last Flight of Noah's Ark; Falling In Love Again.

TV inc: Once Upon A Mattress; Saturday Night Live.

Thea inc: Rumple; Say Darling; Irma La Douce; I Can Get It For You Wholesale.

GOULD, Harold: Act. b. Schenectady, NY, Dec 10, 1923. e. Cornell U, MA, PhD. Films inc: Two for the Seesaw; Harper; Inside Daisy Clover; Marnie; The Arrangement; The Lawyer; Where Does It Hurt?; The Sting; Love and Death; The Front Page; The Silent Movie; The One and Only; Seems Like Old Times.

TV inc: Washington--Behind Closed Doors; Soap; Love Boat; Feather and Father; Rhoda; Gunsmoke; Petrocelli; Double Solitaire; Streets of San Francisco; Mary Tyler Moore Show; The 11th Victim; Aunt Mary; Man in the Santa Claus Suit; Insight/Holy Moses; Kenny Rogers as the Gambler; Moviola (The Scarlett O'Hara Wars & The Silent Lovers); King Crab; The Long Road Home.

Thea inc: Once in a Lifetime; The Miser; The Devils; The Birthday Party; The House of Blue Leaves; The Price; The World of Ray Bradbury; Rhinocerous; Seidman and Son.

GOULET, Robert: Singer-Act. b. Lawrence, MA, Nov 26, 1933. Made concert debut in Edmonton, Canada, 1951, Handel's Messiah. Other stage appearances in Canada inc: The Beggar's Opera; South Pacific; Finian's Rainbow; Gentlemen Prefer Blondes.

Bway inc: Camelot; The Happy Time *(Tony*-1968); prod the US tour of Gene Kelly's Salute to Broadway, 1975.

Films inc: Honeymoon Hotel; I'd Rather Be Right; I Deal in Danger; Underground; Atlantic City, USA.

TV inc: The Broadway of Lerner and Loewe; The Robert Goulet Show; Brigadoon; Carousel; Kiss Me Kate; The Dream Merchants. (*Grammy*-new artist-1962).

GOWDY, Curt: Sportscaster. b. Green River, WY, 1919. Basketball star, U. of Wyoming. In Air Force, WW II, then became sportscaster. Voted Sportscaster of the Year, 1967.

TV inc: American Sportsman; The Way It Was (host).

GRADE, Lew, Lord: Exec. b. Russia, 1907. B of Lord Delfont. Chmn & Man dir, Incorporated TeleVision Co, Ltd; Chmn Assoc Television Corp Ltd; Chmn, Marble Arch Productions. Life Peerage created 1976. Thea inc: Sly Fox. Films inc: From the Life of the Marionettes.

GRAF, William N: Prod. b. NYC, Oct 11, 1912. Films inc: A Man for All Seasons (exec prod); Sinful Davey; The African Elephant. VP Columbia Pictures Intl Corp; head of prodn for Europe, 1952-65; asst to head wldwde prodn, 1962-65.

GRAHAM, Martha: Dancer-Cho. b. Pittsburgh, PA, May 11, 1894. Studied with Ruth St. Denis. Soloist 1920 with Denishawn Dancers; Greenwich Village Follies 1923. debut as chor-dancer 1926; founded Martha Graham Dancers, Martha Graham School of Contemporary Dance; guest soloist with leading orchs in Judith; Triumph of St. Joan. Has made eight world tours, some under sponsorship of US State Dept.

Chor more than 150 ballets inc: Appalachian Spring; Clytemestra; Tragic Pattern; A Time of Snow; Holy Jungle; Dream; Scarlet Letter; Point of Crossing. TV inc: The Kennedy Center Honors--A Celebration of the Performing Arts.

GRAHAM, Ronny: Act-Dir-Comp-Wri. b. Philadelphia, PA, Aug 26, 1919. Started as comedian in niteries. Wrote songs for Bway revues.

Bway inc: (dir) Free Fall; Grin and Bare It!; Postcards; A Place for Polly.

Films inc: New Faces (& sp); Dirty Little Billy.

TV inc: Omnibus; Toast of the Town.

GRAHAM, Sheilah: Wri. b. England, 1912. Hollywood columnist since 1936. Had own radio & TV shows. Books inc: Beloved Infidel; The Rest of the Story; The Garden of Allah; Confessions of a Hollywood Columnist; How to Marry Super Rich; The Real Scott Fitzgerald.

GRAHAM, Virginia: Act. b. Chicago, IL, Jul 4, 1913. e. U of Chicago, BA, Northwestern MJ. Originally on radio, At Home With Virginia Graham; Week Day.

TV inc: Week Day; Girl Talk; Virginia Graham Show. Films inc: The Carpetbaggers; Face in the Crowd.

Thea inc: Any Wednesday; Butterflies Are Free; Barefoot in the Park.

GRAHAME, Gloria (nee Hallward): Act. b. LA, Nov 28, 1929. Screen debut, 1944, Blond Fever. Films inc: The Bad and the Beautiful (*Oscar*-supp-1952); Star of Tomorrow; It Happened in Brooklyn; Crossfire; Merton of the Movies; The Greatest Show on Earth; Man on a Tight Rope; The Good Die Young; Not as a Stranger; The Man Who Never Was; Ride Out For Revenge; The Todd Killing; Head Over Heels; Melvin and Howard.

Thea inc: (London) The Glass Menagerie.

GRAINGER, James Edmund: Prod. b. NYC, 1906. e. Fordham U. Films inc: Diamond Jim; Sutter's Gold; International Squadron; Wake of the Red Witch; Sands of Iwo Jima; Flying Leathernecks; One Minute to Zero; Treasure of Pancho Villa; Green Mansions; Home From the Hill; Cimarron.

GRANDY, Fred: Act. b. Sioux City, IA, Jun 29. e. Harvard U. Films inc: Death Race 2000; The Lincoln Conspiracy.

TV inc: Love Boat; Blind Ambition.

GRANET, Bert: Wri-Prod. b. NYC, Jul 10, 1910. e. Yale U, School of Fine Arts. Films inc: Quick Money; The Affairs of Annabel; Mr. Doodle Kicks Off; Laddie; My Favorite Wife; Bride by Mistake; Those Endearing Young Charms; Do You Love Me?; The Marrying Kind; Berlin Express; The Torch; Scarface.

TV inc: Desilu; Twilight Zone; The Mob; The Untouchables; Loretta Young Show; Walter Winchell File; Lucille Ball-Desi Arnaz Show; The Great Adventure.

GRANGER, Farley: Act. b. San Jose, CA, Jul 1, 1925. Screen debut, 1943, North Star. In Army, 1944-46. Films inc: They Live By Night; Side Street; Edge of Doom; Strangers on a Train; Three Loves; Arrowsmith; The Heiress; The Prisoner of Zenda; Call Me Trinity; Arnold; A Crime for a Crime.

TV inc: One Life to Live; Wagon Train; Masquerade Party.

GRANGER, Stewart (James Stewart): Act. b. London, May 6, 1913. On stage From 1935 with Hull Repertory, Birmingham Repertory. Screen debut in So This Is London, 1940.

Films inc: Convoy; Secret Mission; Thursday's Child; Madonna of the Seven Moons; Caesar and Cleopatra; King Solomon's Mines; Scaramouche; The Prisoner of Zenda; Salome; Beau Brummel; Green Fire; Flaming Frontier; The Trygon Factor; The Last Safari; The Wild Geese.

GRANT, B Donald (Bud): Exec. b. Baltimore, MD, 1934. e. John Hopkins U, BS. Joined NBC 1958 on Today show; subsequently mgr nightime pgms, later daytime pgms; 1967, nat'l dir daytime pgms; 1972 to CBS as vp daytime pgms; 1976 vp-pgms; 1977 vp-pgms for CBS Entertainment; Nov 1980, P CBS Entertainment.

GRANT, Cary (Archibald Alexander Leach): Act. b. Bristol, Eng, Jan 18, 1904. On stage in England, then to US, appearing for a season with St. Louis Municipal Opera Co. Screen debut, 1932, This Is The Night.

Films inc: Gambling Ship; Alice in Wonderland; Sylvia Scarlett; Suzy; Gunga Din; The Philadelphia Story; Penny Serenade; Suspicion; Mr Lucky; Destination Tokyo; None But The Lonely Heart; Arsenic and Old Lace; The Bachelor and the Bobby Soxer; The Bishop's Wife; Mr Blandings Builds His Dream House; I Was a Male War Bride; Room for One More; Dream Wife; To Catch a Thief; The Pride and the Passion; An Affair to Remember; Charade; Father Goose; Walk Don't Run.

Special Academy Award, 1969. Houseboat; North by Northwest; Operation Petticoat; The Grass Is Greener; The Touch of Mink;

GRANT, Lee: Act. b. NYC, Oct 31, 1927. e. Julliard School of Music. Debut age 4 on stage of Metropolitan Opera; member American Ballet at age 11. Bway inc: Joy to the World; Detective Story; Arms and the Man; A Hole in the Head; Wedding Breakfast; Plaza Suite; Prisoner of Second Avenue.

Films inc: Detective Story; Terror in the Streets; Portnoy's Complaint; The Landlord; In the Heat of the Night; Buona Sera, Mrs. Campbell; Plaza Suite; Marooned; Shampoo (Oscar-supp-1975); Voyage of the Damned; Airport 77; The Swarm; The Mafu Cage; Damien--Omen 2; When You Comin' Back, Red Ryder; Little Miss Marker.

TV inc: Peyton Place (Emmy-1966); The Neon Ceiling (Emmy-1971); Why Me (doc); Fay; Rape-The Hidden Crime (doc); The Spell; Princess Grace, Once Upon a Time is Now; For the Use of the Hall (dir); The Shape of Things (dir); You Can't Go Home Again; Tell Me A Riddle (dir).

GRANT, Merrill: Prod. b. NYC, Jul 9, 1932. Joined Benton & Bowles ad agency 1957, becoming vp & dir pgmg; 1970 sr vp & dir radio-tv, Grey Ad agency; 1972 vp Viacom; 1974 P Don Kirshner Prodns; left to go into indie prodn.

TV inc: The Triangle Factory Fire Scandal; She's Dressed to Kill; OHMS; That's Incredible!; Those Amazing Animals; The World's Most Spectacular Stuntman; 30 Years of TV Comedy's Greatest Hits.

GRANVILLE, Bonita: Act. b. NYC, Feb 2, 1923. W of Jack Wrather. On screen as child.

Films inc: Westward Passage; Cradle Song; Ah Wilderness; These Three; Merrily We Live; Maid of Salem; Call it a Day; Nancy Drew Detective (and subsequent series); Angels With Dirty Faces; H M Pulham, Esq; The Glass Key; Hitler's Children; Love Laughs at Andy Hardy; The Guilty; Treason; The Lone Ranger. (Prod): Lassie's Greatest Adventure; The Magic of Lassie.

TV inc: Lassie (prod).

GRAPPELLI, Stephane: Violinist. b. Paris, Jan 27, 1908. Founder with Django Reinhardt of Hot Club of Paris. Recording artist, concerts.

GRASSHOFF, Alex: Prod-Dir. b. Boston, MA, Dec 10, 1930. e. USC, BA. Films inc: Young Americans; The Jailbreakers.

TV inc: Future Shock; Frank Sinatra-Family and Friends; Journey to the Outer Limits (Emmy-1974); Rockford Files; Night Stalker; Toma; Barbary Coast; Movin' On; CHiPs.

GRASSLE, Karen: Act. b. Berkeley, CA, Feb 25, 1944. e. UC Berkeley, LAMDA. TV inc: Little House on the Prairie; Battered (& wri).

Thea inc: The Gingham Dog; Butterflies Are Free; Cymbeline.

THE GRATEFUL DEAD: Rock group. Originally formed 1964 by Jerry Garcia, Bob Weir, Ron McKernan as Mother McCree's Uptown Jug Champions; following year switched from jug band to electric rock, adopting name The Warlocks; in 1966 changed name to The Grateful Dead; world tours inc concerts at Great Pyramid in Egypt. Members inc Garcia, Weir, Bill Kreutzman, Phil Lesh, Mickey Hart, Brent Mydland.

Albums inc: The Grateful Dead; Anthem of the Sun; Aoxomoxoa; Live Dead; Workingman's Dead; American Beauty; Europe 72; Wake of the Flood; Mars Hotel; Blues for Allah; Terrapin Station; Shakedown Street; Go to Heaven.

Films inc: The Grateful Dead Concert Film.

GRAUMAN, Walter: Dir. b. Milwaukee, WI, Mar 17, 1922. Films inc: Lady in a Cage; 633 Squadron; A Rage to Live; I Deal in Danger; The Last Escape.

TV inc: The Untouchables; Naked City; Route 66; The Felony Squad; Are You in the House Alone?; The Golden Gate Murders; The Top of the Hill; To Race the Wind (& prod); Crisis In Mid-Air; The Memory of Eva Ryker; Pleasure Palace.

GRAVES, Peter: Act. b. Minneapolis, MN, Mar 18, 1936. e. U of MN. B of James Arness. Appeared in summer stock. Screen debut Rogue River.

Films inc: Fort Defiance; Stalag 17; Beneath The 12-Mile Reef; Black Tuesday; The Long Gray Line; Night of the Hunter; Court Martial of Billy Mitchell; The Five Man Army; Sidecar Racers. Clonus Horror; Survival Run; Airplane.

TV inc: Fury; Mission Impossible; The Gift of the Magi; The Rebels; Death Car on the Freeway; Comedy Is Not Pretty; The Memory of Eva Ryker.

GRAY, Coleen (Doris Jensen): Act. b. Staplehurst, NE, Oct 23, 1922. e. Hamline U, BA, summa cum laude. Screen debut, 1945, State Fair. Films inc: Kiss of Death; Nightmare Alley; Fury at Furnace Creek; Father Is A Bachelor; The Killing; Copper Sky; The Phantom Planet; The Late Liz.

TV inc: Days of Our Lives; Family Affair; Name of the Game; The Best Place to Be.

GRAY, Dolores: Act. b. Chicago, Jun 7, 1924. Started as singer in niteries. NY stage debut 1944, Seven Lively Arts.

Bway inc: Are You With It; Sweet Bye and Bye; Annie Get Your Gun; Two on the Aisle; Carnival in Flanders (Tony-1954).

Films inc: It's Always Fair Weather; Kismet; The Opposite Sex; Designing Woman.

GRAY, Dulcie: Act-Wri. b. Kuala Lumpur, Federated Malay States, Nov 20, 1919. London stage debut 1939 in Hay Fever. Thea inc: The Little Foxes; Rain on the Just; Candida; An Ideal Husband; Where Angels Fear to Tread; Out of the Question; At the End of the Day; A Murder has been Announced; The Sack Race; The Pay Off.

Films inc: Two Thousand Women; Mine Own Executioner; The Glass Mountain; Wanted for Murder; Angels One Five; A Man Could Get Killed.

TV inc: Milestones; The Will; Lesson in Love; Winter Cruise; Unexpectedly Vacant; The Importance of Being Earnest; Crown Court; Making Faces.

GRAY, Erin: Act. b. Honolulu, HI. Former model. TV inc: Police Story; Gibbsville; Evening in Byzantium; Buck Rogers in the 25th Century; Coach of the Year.

Films inc: Winter Kills.

GRAY, Linda: Act. b. Santa Monica, CA, Sep 12, 1940. Films inc: Fun With Dick and Jane; The World Between; Under the Yum Yum Tree; Palm Springs Weekend; Dogs.

TV inc: Murder in Peyton Place; All That Glitters; The Grass Is Greener Over the Septic Tank; The Two Worlds of Jenny Logan; The Starmakers; Haywire; Dallas; The Wild and the Free; I'll Be Home For Christmas.

GRAY, Simon: Wri. b. Hayling Island, Hants, Eng, Oct 21, 1936. e. Cambridge. Plays inc: Wise Child; Dutch Uncle; The Idiot (adapt); Spoiled; Butley; Otherwise Engaged; Stage Struck; Close Of Play.

TV inc: Death of a Teddy Bear; Defendants; Two Sundays.

GRAY, Tom (Thomas Robert Gray Jr V): Exec. b. Jasper, AL, Mar 19, 1939. e. U MO; Southern IL U. After service as Army Public Information Officer, joined Atlanta Constitution 1965 as ent edtr; 1966 MGM fieldman, Chicago & Washington; 1967 asst to pub dir Par; 1969 pub for new talent program U; dir corp pub Lion Country Safari; 1976 LA press contact, U; 1978 unit pub Hurricane; The Villain; Health; 1979 natl pub dir U; 1980 VP & studio pub dir UA.

GRAYSON, Kathryn (Zelma Hedrick): Act. b. Winston-Salem, NC, Feb 9, 1923. Films inc: The Vanishing Virginian; Rio Rita; Seven Sweethearts; Thousands Cheer; Ziegfeld Follies; Anchors Aweigh; Two Sisters From Boston; Till the Clouds Roll By; The Kissing Bandit; Showboat; The Grace Moore Story (So This Is Love); Kiss Me Kate; The Vagabond King; That's Entertainment; That's Entertainment, Part 2; The Amazing World of Psychic Phenomena; Now I Lay Me Down to Sleep.

TV inc: GE Theatre; Die Fledermaus.

Thea inc: Rosalinda; Merry Widow; Kiss Me Kate; Showboat.

GREAVES, William: Prod-Dir. b. NYC, Oct 8, 1926. e. CCNY, McGill U. Docs inc: Black Journal (Emmy-1970); From These Roots; In the Company of Men; Voice of La Raza.

GRECO, Jose: Dancer. b. Abruzzi, Italy, 1918. Flamenco dancer. Final U.S. performance 1975, retired to Marbella, Spain, to operate dance school. On screen From the '50s.

Films inc: Sombrero; Around the World in 80 Days; Holiday for Lovers; Ship of Fools.

GREEN, Adolph: Wri-Act. b. NYC, Dec 2, 1915. e. CCNY. Usually collab with Betty Comden on books, lyr for shows, musical films. Bway scores inc: Wonderful Town (Tony-1952); Peter Pan; Do Re Mi; On the Town; Two on the Aisle; Bells Are Ringing; Subways Are For Sleeping; Fade Out-Fade In; Hallelujah, Baby (Tony-1968); Applause (Tony-1970); On the 20th Century (Tony-1978); A Party With Betty Comden and Adolph Green (& act); Peter Pan.

Film score, sp inc: The Band Wagon; It's Always Fair Weather; On the Town; Good News; The Barkleys of Broadway; Auntie Mame; Bells Are Ringing; What a Way to Go; Simon (act).

Songs inc: New York, New York; Lonely Town; Ohio; Give a Little, Get a Little; The Party's Over; Just in Time; Make Someone Happy; Get Acquainted.

TV inc: The Kennedy Center Honors, 1980.

GREEN, Bud: Sngwri. b. Austria, Nov 19, 1897. Wrote special vaude material, Bway scores for various musicals; staff wri for music publishers, before founding own firm 1928. Songs inc: Alabamy Bound; That's My Weakness Now; I'll Always Be In Love With You; Moon On The River; Once In A While; The Man Who Comes Around; Flat Foot Floogie; Sentimental Journey.

GREEN, Gerald: Wri. b. Brookyn, NY, 1922. e. Columbia. Novelist, writer of tv docs.

TV inc: Today Show With Dave Garroway; Wide Wide World; Chet Huntley Reporting; Holocaust (Emmy-1978).

GREEN, Guy: Dir. b. Frome, Somerset, Eng, 1913. Started as cin. Films inc: (cin) In Which We Serve; The Way Ahead; Great Expectations (Oscar-1947); Take My Life; Oliver Twist; Captain Horatio Hornblower; The Beggar's Opera; Rob Roy. (Dir): River Beat; Portrait of Alison; Postmark for Danger; House of Secrets; Sea of Sand; SOS Pacific; The Mark; The Angry Silence; Diamond Head; A Patch of Blue; The Magus; A Walk in the Spring Rain; Luther; Once Is Not Enough; The Devil's Advocate.

TV inc: (dir) The Incredible Journey of Dr Meg Laurel; Jennifer: A Woman's Story; Jimmy B and Andre.

GREEN, John: Mus Dir-Cond-Comp. b. NYC, Oct 10, 1908. e. Harvard U, AB. Started as rehearsal pianist. Comp-cond 1930-32, Paramount Astoria, NY; accompanist to: Ethel Merman; Gertrude Lawrence; James Melton; led own orch., Bway shows, niteries. Radio inc: Jack Benny; Philip Morris Shows. Comp, cond, arr 1942-46, MGM; WB and U, 1947-48; Gen Mus Dir & Exec-in-charge-of-Mus, MGM 1949-58; Prod, TV Desilu, 1959-60. Guest cond major symphony orchestras since 1959.

Songs inc: Coquette; I'm Yours; Out of Nowhere; The Waterfront; I Wanna Be Loved; Body and Soul.

Films inc: Easter Parade (Oscar-1951); Fiesta; Bathing Beauty; The Toast of New Orleans; An American in Paris (Oscar-1953); Merry Wives of Windsor Overture (Oscar-short-1953); Royal Wedding; High Society; Meet Me in Las Vegas; Raintree County; Pepe; West Side Story (Oscar-1961); Bye Bye Birdie; Oliver! (Oscar-1968); They Shoot Horses, Don't They?;

(Grammy-soundtrack-1961).

GREEN, Paul Eliot: Wri. b. Lillington, NC, Mar 17, 1894. e. U of NC. Plays inc: No 'Count Boy; In Abraham's Bosom (Pulitzer Prize-1927); Roll, Sweet Chariot; The Enchanted Maze; The Confederacy; The Wilderness Road; Cross and Sword.

Films inc: Cabin in the Cotton; State Fair; Dr. Bull; Voltaire; David Harum; Black Like Me.

GREEN, Walon: Prod-Dir-Wri. b. Baltimore, Dec 15, 1936. e. U of Barcelona, U of Gottingin. Films inc: The Wild Bunch (sp); Hellstrom Chronicles (Oscar-doc-1971) (prod); Sorcerer (sp); Brink's Job (sp); Secret Life of Plants (doc) (dir-sp).

TV inc: Mysteries of the Sea (wri).

GREENBAUM, Everett: Wri. b. Buffalo, NY, Dec 20, 1919. e. MIT; Sorbonne. TV inc: Mr Peepers; The George Gobel Show; The Real McCoys; The Andy Griffith Show; M*A*S*H; Lou Grant; Semi-Tough.

Films inc: Good Neighbor Sam; The Ghost and Mr. Chicken; The Shakiest Gun in the West; The Reluctant Astronaut; Angel in My Pocket.

GREENBERG, Stanley R: Wri. b. Chicago, IL, Sep 3. e. Brown U. TV inc: The Defenders; East Side, West Side; Route 66; Nurses; A Day Like Today; Welcome Home Johnny; Pueblo; The Missiles of October; The Silence; Blind Ambition; FDR--The Last Year.

Films inc: Skyjacked; Soylent Green.

Play: Pueblo.

GREENE, Clarence: Wri. b. 1918. Films inc: The Town Went Wild; D O A; The Well; New York Confidential; Pillow Talk (Oscar-story & sp-1959); A House Is Not a Home; The Oscar; Caper of the Golden Bulls.

TV inc: Tightrope.

GREENE, David: Dir. b. Manchester, England, Feb 22, 1921. Films inc: The Shuttered Room; Sebastian; The Strange Affair; I Start Counting; Madame Sin; Godspell; Gray Lady Down.

TV inc: The Defenders; The Count of Monte Cristo; The People Next Door (Emmy-1969); Rich Man, Poor Man (Emmy-1976); Roots Part 1 (Emmy-1977); The Trial of Lee Harvey Oswald; Friendly Fire (Emmy-1979); A Vacation in Hell (& exec prod).

GREENE, Graham: Wri. b. England, 1904. Author of books that provided material for the screen. Novels which became films inc: This Gun for Hire; The Ministry of Fear; Confidential Agent; The Fugitive; The Fallen Idol; The Third Man; The Stranger's Hand; The End of the Affair; The Quiet American; Our Man in Havana; The Comedians; Travels with My Aunt.

Plays inc: The Return of A J Raffles.

GREENE, Lorne: Act. b. Ottawa, Can, 1915. e. Queen's U, New York's Neighborhood Playhouse. Films inc: The Silver Chalice; Tight Spot; The Hard Man; The Buccaneer; Peyton Place; Battlestar Galactica; Klondike Fever.

TV inc: Bonanza; Big Brother; The Bastard; Battlestar Galactica; A Time For Miracles.

Bway: Speaking of Murder; Edwin Booth.

GREENE, Mort: Lyr. b. Cleveland, OH, Oct 3, 1912. e. U of PA. Wri-dir night club acts; then wrote songs for films inc; The Big Street; Call Out the Marines; Beyond the Blue Horizon; Tulsa.

TV theme songs inc: Leave It to Beaver; Restless Gun; Tales of Wells Fargo; Lawrence Welk Champagne Time.

Songs inc: High Society; Stars in Your Eyes; A Full Moon and an Empty Heart; Sioux City Sue; My Grandfather's Clock.

GREENE, Shecky (Sheldon Greenfield): Act. b. Chicago, 1925. Films inc: Tony Rome; The Love Machine.

TV inc: The Colgate Comedy Hour; Combat; Hal Linden's Big Apple.

GREENFELD, Josh: Wri. b. Malden, MA, Feb 27, 1934. e. U of MI, Columbia U. Films inc: Harry and Tonto.

TV inc: Lovey; A Circle of Children Part II.

GREENFIELD, Leo: Exec. b. NYC, Apr 25, 1916. e. St John's U. Joined Buena Vista 1956, mgr east sls div; 1961 west div mgr; 1966 domestic sls mgr; 1966 vp, gm-sls Cinerama Release Corp; 1969 vp, gm-sls Warners; 1975 sr vp, worldwide dist, MGM.

GREENLAW, Charles F: Exec. b. CA, Jan 18, 1914. Prodn dept, WB, 1933-42; asst prodn m, 1942-56; studio prodn m, 1956-65; vp, prod exec U, 1965-69; vp prod & studio ops, WB, 1969-73; exec vp worldwide prod mgt. WB, 1973; Ret. Dec 31, 1980.

Films inc: Superman, The Movie (asso prod).

GREENSPAN, Lou: Exec. b. Chicago, May 14. Started as reporter; ed, Heard & Seen magazine; Variety staffer; PA, wri, prod asst Universal Studios, 1931-35; wri Republic studio, 1936; wri, assoc prod, Grand National Pictures, 1937-38; spec West Coast rep ASCAP, 1938-39; ed Hollywood Reporter, 1939-43; exec to prod Joseph Breen, RKO; PR dir, studio liaison Office of Coord of Inter-American Affairs, 1942-45; ind prod, wri 1945-50; coord of Council of Motion Picture Organizations Round Table Conf, 1950; dir of industry-wide PR pgm under auspices of United Par Theatres, 1950-51; exec secy Motion Picture Industry Council, 1951-59; exec dir Producers Guild of America and ed of PGA Journal, 1959-78.

GREENWALD, Robert: Prod-Dir. b. NYC, Aug 28, 1943. e. NYC High School of Performing Arts; Antioch Coll. Dir off-Bway; teacher NYU; New School for Social Research; ran experimental theatre program Mark Taper Forum, LA. Thea inc: Soon; The Amazing Flight of the Goonie Bird; Me and Bessie. Bway inc: I Have A Dream.

TV inc: (prod) The Desperate Miles; 21 Hours at Munich; Delta County, USA; Escape From Bogen County; Getting Married; Portrait of a Stripper. (Dir) Sharon--Portrait of a Mistress; Katie--Portrait of a Centerfold; Flatbed Annie and Sweetipie--Lady Truckers.

Films inc: Xanadu (dir).

GREENWOOD, Joan: Act. b. London, Mar 4, 1921. e. RADA. Thea inc: (London) The Robust Invalid; Little Ladyship; The Women; Rise Above It; Peter Pan; Striplings; Damaged Goods; It Happened in New York; Frenzy; Young Wives Tale; Bell, Book and Candle; Cards of Identity; Lysistrata; The Grass is Greener; Hedda Gabler; Fallen Angels; The Au Pair Man; The Chalk Garden. (Bway) The Confidential Clerk; Those That Play the Clowns. Films inc: My Wife's Family; He Found a Star; The Gentle Sex; The Man Within; The October Man; The White Unicorn; Saraband for Dead Lovers; Whiskey Galore; Kind Hearts and Coronets; The Man in the White Suit; The Importance of Being Earnest; Father Brown; Moonfleet; Mysterious Island; The Amorous Prawn; Tom Jones; Moon Spinners; Girl Stroke Boy; Hound of The Baskervilles; The Water Babies.

GREER, Dabbs: Act. b. Fairview, MO, Apr 2, 1917. e. Drury Coll, AB. On screen From 1948. Films inc: The Black Book; House of Wax; Affair with a Stranger; Riot in Cell Block 11; Bitter Creek; Invasion of the Body Snatchers; The Vampire; Baby Face Nelson; I Want to Live; The Lone Texan; Roustabout; Shenandoah; Cheyenne Social Club; Rage; White Lightning.

TV inc: Big Town; Gunsmoke; Hank; The Ghost and Mrs. Muir; Little House on the Prairie; The Winds of Kitty Hawk.

GREER, Jane: Act. b. Washington, DC, Sep 9, 1924. Films inc: Pan Americana; Two O'Clock Courage; George White's Scandals; Dick Tracy; Bamboo Blonde; Sunset Pass; Sinbad the Sailor; They Won't Believe Me; Out of the Past; Station West; The Big Steal; The Prisoner of Zenda; Desperate Search; The Clown; Down Among the Sheltering Palms; Run for the Sun; Man of a Thousand Faces; Where Love Has Gone; Billie; The Outfit.

TV inc: A Christmas for Boomer.

GREFE, William: Dir-Prod. b. Miami, May 17. e. U of Miami. Films inc: The Checkered Flag; Racing Fever; Devil Sisters; Sting of Death; Tartu; Wild Rebels; Hooked Generation; The Grove; Electric Shades of Grey; Stanley; Impulse; Jaws of Death; Godmothers; Whiskey Mountain; Live and Let Die. P Ivan Tors Studios, Miami.

GREGG, Virginia: Act. On screen From 1947. Films inc: Body and Soul; Dragnet; I'll Cry Tomorrow; The D.I.; Twilight for the Gods; Operation Petticoat; Spencer's Mountain; A Big Hand for a Little Lady; Madigan; A Walk in the Spring Rain.

TV inc: Little Women.

GREGORY, James: Act. b. NYC, Dec 23, 1911. Films inc: The Naked City; The Young Stranger; Onionhead; Al Capone; The Manchurian Candidate; Twilight of Horror; The Great Escape; PT-109; Captain Newman, M.D.; Quick, Before It Melts; The Sons of Katie Elder; The Ambushers; The Secret War of Harry Frigg; Beneath the Planet of the Apes; The Late Liz; The Strongest Man in the World; The Main Event; The In-Laws.

TV inc: Studio One; Climax!; Suspense; The Lawless Years; Big Valley; The Bastard; Detective School; The Comeback Kid; The Great American Traffic Jam.

Bway inc: Death of a Salesman; The Desperate Hours; Fragile Fox; All My Sons; Dream Girl; Key Largo; Dead Pigeon.

GREGORY, Paul (nee Lenhart): Prod. b. Waukee, IA, Aug 27, 1920. H of Janet Gaynor. Began as agent; 1947 headed MCA Concert Div, launched Charles Laughton reading tours; became prod 1951.

Thea inc: Don Juan in Hell; John Brown's Body; Caine Mutiny Court Martial; Elsa Lanchester's Private Music Hall; Three for Tonight; Rivalry; The Pink Jungle; Captains and Kings; Prescription for Murder; Lord Pengo; Dame Judith Anderson as Hamlet.

Films inc: Night of the Hunter; The Naked and the Dead.

TV inc: Caine Mutiny Court Martial (*Emmy*-adapt-1955).

GRENFELL, Joyce (nee Phipps): Act-Wri. b. London, Feb 10, 1910. Originally journalist; stage debut 1939 playing her own monologues. Thea inc: Diversion; Light and Shade; Sigh No More; Tuppence Coloured; Joyce Grenfell Requests the Pleasure; Joyce Grenfell.

Films inc: Happiest Days of Your Life; The Belles of St Trinian's; A Run for Your Money; Stage Fright; Laughter in Paradise; Genevieve; The Million Pound Note; Happy is the Bride; Blue Murder at St Trinian's; Pure Hell of St Trinian's; The Americanization of Emily; The Yellow Rolls Royce.

(Died Nov 30, 1979).

GREY, Joel (nee Katz): Act. b. Cleveland, OH, Apr 11, 1932. S of Mickey Katz. Worked in father's stage revues, niteries. Bway inc: Cabaret *(Tony-*supp-1967); George M!; Goodtime Charley; Marco Polo Sings a Solo; The Grand Tour.

Films inc: Cabaret *(Oscar*-supp-1972); The Seven-Per-Cent Solution; Man on a Swing; Buffalo Bill and the Indians.

TV inc: Colgate Comedy Hour; Jack and the Beanstalk; Live From Wolf Trap (host); Evening at Pops '79.

GREY, Nan (Eschal Miller): Act. b. 1918. W of Frankie Laine. Films inc: Dracula's Daughter; Three Smart Girls; Three Smart Girls Grow Up; Tower of London; The Invisible Man Returns; Sandy Is a Lady; Under Age.

TV inc: Rawhide.

GREY, Virginia: Act. b. LA, Mar 22, 1917. On screen From 1927, Uncle Tom's Cabin.

Films inc: Secrets; Dames; The Firebird; The Great Ziegfeld; Rosalie; Test Pilot; The Hardys Ride High; Hullaballoo; Idaho; Strangers in the Night; Unconquered; Who Killed Doc Robbin?; Jungle Jim; The Last Command; Crime of Passion; The Restless Years; Back Street; Love Has Many Faces; Madame X; Rosie; Airport.

TV inc: General Hospital.

GRIER, Pam: Act. b. Winston-Salem, NC. Films inc: Beyond the Valley of the Dolls; Twilight People; Blacula; Hit Man; Coffy; Black Mama, White Mama; The Arena; The Big Doll House; Greased Lightning.

GRIFFETH, Simone: Act. b. Savannah, GA, Apr 14. e. U of SC. Films inc: Death Race; Slap Shot. TV inc: Mandrake; Ladies Man; Fighting Back.

GRIFFIN, Merv: TV Pers. b. San Mateo, CA, Jul 6, 1925. Sang on local radio station, San Francisco. Joined Freddy Martin band.

Films inc: This Is Love; The Boy From Oklahoma; By The Light of the Silvery Moon; The Phantom of the Rue Morgue; The Seduction of Joe Tynan.

TV inc: The Merv Griffin Show *(Emmy*-wri-1974); Keep Talking; The Jack Paar Show; The Robert Q Lewis Show.

GRIFFITH, Andy: Act. b. Mount Airy, NC, Jun 1, 1926. e. NC U. Performed on TV, Niteries. Starred in outdoor pageant, The Lost Colony. Screen debut, 1957, A Face in the Crowd.

Films inc: No Time for Sergeants; Onionhead; The Second Time Around; Angel in My Pocket; Hearts of the West.

TV inc: The Andy Griffith Show; Andy of Mayberry; No Time for Sergeants; The Headmaster; Go Ask Alice. Salvage; Centennial; From Here to Eternity; The Yeagers.

Thea inc: No Time for Sergeants; Destry Rides Again.

GRIFFITH, Corinne: Act. b. TX, Jun 1899. Films inc: The Yellow Girl; Six Days; Lilies of the Field; The Marriage Whirl; Infatuation; The Garden of Eden; Saturday's Children; Back Pay; Lily Christine.

(Died Jul 13, 1979).

GRIFFITH, Hugh: Act. b. Marian Glas, Anglesey, N Wales, May 30, 1912. Stage debut 1939, Playboy of the Western World.

Films inc: Neutral Port; The Three Weird Sisters; London Belongs to Me; Laughter in Paradise; The Beggar's Opera; The Titfield Thunderbolt; Lucky Jim; Ben Hur *(Oscar*-supp-1959); The Day They Robbed the Bank of England; Exodus; The Counterfeit Traitor; Tom Jones; Oh Dad, Poor Dad; How to Steal a Million; The Chastity Belt; Oliver; The Fixer; Start The Revolution Without Me; City of the Banshee; Wuthering Heights; Who Slew Auntie Roo?; What; Craze; Take Me High; The Last Remake of Beau Geste; Joseph Andrews; The Hound of the Baskervilles.

TV inc: Walrus and the Carpenter.

(Died May 14, 1980).

GRILLO, Basil: Exec (ret). b. Antel's Camp, CA, Oct 8, 1910. e. U of CA, Berkeley. Dir Seven League Ent, Inc; dir Electrovision Prodns; CEO, Bing Crosby Enterprises.

GRIMALDI, Alberto: Prod. b. Naples, 1927. Pres of PEA (Produzioni Europee Assoc, S.A.S.). Films inc: For a Few Dollars More; The Good, The Bad, and The Ugly; Three Steps in Delirium; Satyricon; Burn!; The Decameron; The Canterbury Tales; 1001 Nights; Salo, or the 100 Days of Sodom; Bawdy Tales; Man of La Mancha; Last Tango in Paris; Avanti; Fellini's Casanova; 1900; The True Story of General Custer.

GRIMES, Gary: Act. b. San Francisco, 1955. Films inc: Summer of 42; The Culpepper Cattle Co; Class of 44; Cahill; The Spikes Gang; Gus.

GRIMES, Tammy: Act. b. Lynn, MA, Jan 30, 1934. e. Stephens Coll. Bway inc: Bus Stop (replaced Kim Stanley). The Amazing Adele; The Lark; Look After Lulu; The Unsinkable Molly Brown *(Tony-*supp-1961); Rattle of a Simple Man; High Spirits; Finian's Rainbow; The Decline and Fall of the Whole World as Seen Through the Eyes of Cole Porter; The Only Game in Town; Private Lives *(Tony*-1970); In Praise of Love; Trick; A Musical Jubilee; California Suite; Tartuffe; Father's Day; 42d Street.

Films inc: Three Bites of an Apple; Play It As It Lays; Somebody Killed Her Husband; The Runner Stumbles; Can't Stop the Music; Just Crazy About Horses (narr).

TV inc: Holiday; You Can't Go Home Again; The Incredible Book Escape (voice).

GRINDE, Harry A (Nickey): Dir. b. Madison, WI, Jan 12, 1894. Films inc: The Bishop Murder Case; Good News; White Bondage; Million Dollar Legs; Hitler, Dead or Alive; Gangbusters.

(Died June 19, 1979).

GRIZZARD, George: Act. b. Roanoke Rapids, NC, Apr 1, 1928.

Films inc: From The Terrace; Advise and Consent; Warning Shot; Happy Birthday, Wanda June; Comes a Horseman; Fire Power; Seems Like Old Times.

Bway inc: The Desperate Hours; The Happiest Millionaire; The Country Girl; The Royal Family; Who's Afraid of Virginia Woolf?; You Know I Can't Hear You When the Water's Running; The Gingham Dog; Inquest; California Suite.

TV inc: My Three Angels; Notorious; A Case of Libel; The Front Page; Travis Logan, D.A.; The Night Rider; Attica; The Oldest Living Graduate *(Emmy*-supp-1980).

GRODIN, Charles: Act-Dir-Wri. b. Pittsburgh, Apr 21, 1935. e. U of Miami. NY stage debut 1962 in Tchin-Tchin. Plays inc: Absence of a Cello; wrote the book and lyr for Hooray! It's a Beautiful Day. . .And All That (also dir); Lovers and Other Strangers (dir); Steambath; Thieves (prod); Same Time, Next Year; Unexpected Guests (prod-dir).

Films inc: (act) Rosemary's Baby; Catch 22; The Heartbreak Kid; 11 Harrowhouse; King Kong; Heaven Can Wait; Real Life; Sunburn; It's My Turn; Seems Like Old Times.

TV inc: Simon and Garfunkel Special (wri-dir); Paradise (prod-dir); The Paul Simon Special *(Emmy*-wri-1978).

GROH, David: Act. b. Brooklyn, May 21. e. Brown U; London Academy of Music and Fine Arts on Fulbright Scholarship. Films inc: Change in the Wind; Two-Minute Warning.

TV inc: Love Is A Many-Splendored Thing; Edge of Night; Rhoda; The Child Stealer; Power; The Dream Merchants; Tourist.

Bway inc: Antony and Cleopatra; Elizabeth The Queen; Hot L Baltimore.

GROSBARD, Ulu: Dir. b. Antwerp, Belgium, Jan 9, 1929. e. U of Chicago, BA; Yale Drama School. Bway inc: The Days and Nights of Beebee Fenstermaker; The Subject Was Roses; A View from the Bridge; The Investigation; That Summer-That Fall; American Bufalo.

Films inc: Splendor in the Grass (asst dir); West Side Story (asst dir): The Subject Was Roses (dir); Who Is Harry Kellerman and Why Is He Saying Those Terrible Things About Me? (dir); Straight Time (dir).

GROSS, Shelly: Thea Prod. b. Philadelphia, May 20, 1921. e. U of PA, AB, Northwestern U, MSJ. Bway inc: Catch Me If You Can; Sherry; Inquest; Grand Music Hall of Israel; Lorelei; The King and I.

GROSS, Yoram Jerzy: Prod-Dir. b. Poland. Film inc: Joseph the Dreamer; Chansons sans Paroles; One Pound Only; Dot and the Kangaroo (animated); The Little Convict (animated); Magician of Lublin (prod).

GROSSBERG, Jack: Prod. b. NYC, Jun 5, 1927. Films inc: Requiem for a Heavyweight; Pretty Poison; The Producers; Take the Money and Run; Don't Drink the Water; They Might Be Giants; Bananas; Everything You Always Wanted to Know About Sex; The Betsy; Fast Break.

GROSSMAN, Kenneth Lewis: Exec (ret 1976). b. Minneapolis, MN, Apr 11, 1905. e. USC. Prod TV sports programs; business mgr, MGM Radio; asso to Louis K Sidney, exec vp MGM Studios, 1948-55; asso to Edward J. Mannix, vp, gm, MGM, 1955-57; Universal City Studios prodn mgr, 1960-76.

GROTTA, Kare J: Exec. b. Andalsnes, Norway, Jan 21, 1943. Dir PR Norwegian Cinema and Film Foundation; M-dir, founder Royal Film AS; Grotta Invest AS; founder Norwegian Film Festival.

GROVENOR, Linda: Act. b. Baltimore, MD, Feb 6, 1956. e. Villa Julie Coll, BS. TV inc: The Tenth Month; The Terrible Secret; Valentine; Secret of Midland Heights.

Films inc: Die Laughing.

GRUENBERG, Leonard: Exec. b. Minneapolis, MN, Sep 10, 1913. e. U of MN. Began as salesman Republic Pictures, 1935; with RKO in same capacity, 1936; then branch thea mgr, 1941; later that year apptd dist mgr; vp NTA; vp Cinemiracle Prodn; p, ChmnB, Sigma III Corp, 1962; ChmnB Filmways, 1967; ChmnB Gamma III Dist Co & ChmnB and p Gamma III Group Ltd, 1976.

GRUNDY, Reg: Prod. b. Sydney, Australia, Aug 4, 1923. TV inc: Pass Word; Junior Money Makers; Price is Right; Penthouse Club; Gambit; Emergency Line.

Films inc: Barry McKenzie Holds His Own; Abba--The Movie.

GRUSIN, Dave: Comp-Cond. Films inc: Divorce American Style; The Graduate; Candy; Winning; Tell Them Willie Boy Is Here; The Pursuit of Happiness; The Great Northfield Minnesota Raid; The Front; Murder By Death; The Yakuza; Three Days of the Condor; Bobby Deerfield; Fire Sale; The Goodbye Girl; Mr. Billion; Heaven Can Wait; And Justice For All; The Champ; The Electric Horseman; My Bodyguard.

GUARDINO, Harry: Act. b. NYC, Dec 22, 1925. Films inc: Houseboat; The Five Pennies; Five Branded Women; The Pigeon That Took Rome; Madigan; The Hell With Heroes; The Enforcer; Goldengirl; Any Which Way You Can.

Bway inc: End As A Man; A Hatful of Rain; Anyone Can Whistle; One More River; Natural Affection; Seven Descents of Myrtle. Seven Descents of Myrtle.

TV inc: Studio One; Playhouse 90; The Reporter; Pleasure Cove; Bender.

GUBER, Lee: Thea Prod. b. Philadelphia, Nov 20, 1920. e. Temple U, MA. With partners, Shelly Gross & Frank Ford, owns, operates and produces musicals at six summer theatres.

Bway inc: The Happiest Girl in the World; Catch Me If You Can; Inquest; Grand Music Hall of Israel; Lorelei; The King and I.

GUBER, Peter: Prod-Exec. b. 1939. e. Syracuse U, BA; NYU Law School, JD, LLM. Recruited by Col as mgt trainee while working to MBA degree at NYU; 1973 exec vp chg wldwide prodn; 1975 formed Peter Guber Filmworks; 1976 merged with Neil Bogart's Casablanca Records to form Casablanca Record & Filmworks Inc; March 1980, firm bought by Polygram, Guber remaining as bd chmn; May 1980 formed Boardwalk with Bogart, Jon Peters but retained connection with Polygram Pictures of which he is 50% owner.

Films inc: The Deep; Midnight Express.

TV inc: Mysteries of the Sea (doc).

GUENETTE, Robert: Prod-Dir-Wri. b. Holyoke, MA, Jan 12, 1935. TV inc: William Faulkner's Mississippi; Our War In Vietnam; The Hungry Americans; The Defector; They've Killed President Lincoln (Emmy-wri-1971); The Tree; The Plot to Murder Hitler; The Crucifixion of Jesus; Peary's Race to the North Pole; Monsters! Mysteries or Myths?; The World Turned Upside Down; Bigfoot; The Amazing World of Psychic Phenomena; The National Disaster Survival Test; I Can; Journey Together; Dinky Hocker Shoots Smack; The Making of Star Wars; SPFX--The Empire Strikes Back; Roots--One Year Later; Do You Know How to Talk To Your Kids About Sex?

GUEST, Val: Wri-Prod-Dir. b. London, 1911. Films inc: Miss Pilgrim's Progress; The Body Said No; Happy Go Lovely; Another Man's Poison; Men of Sherwood Forest; Lyons in Paris; It's a Great Life; They Can't Hang Me; The Abominable Snowman; Carry on Admiral; Up the Creek; Further Up the Creek; Hell is a City; The Day the Earth Caught Fire; Jigsaw; Where the Spies Are; Casino Royale; When Dinosaurs Ruled the Earth; The Adventurers; Confessions of a Window Cleaner; Killer Force; Diamond Mercenaries; The Shillingbury Blowers.

TV inc: Space 1999; Return of the Saint.

GUETTEL, Henry: Prod-Exec. b. Kansas City, MO, Jan 8, 1928. e. U of PA; U of Kansas City. Act and stg mgr in stock and Bway; Mgr Royal Winnipeg Ballet; Gen Mgr Sacramento Music Circus; Sombrero Theatre; gen mgr Music Theatre of Lincoln Center.

Bway inc: Romulus (asso prod); The Merry Widow; The King and I; Kismet; Carousel; Show Boat; Annie Get Your Gun.

Thea prodns inc: The Best Man; The Sound of Music; Camelot; Oliver. Originated Music Theatre Concerts at Philharmonic Hall. VP Cinema 5 Ltd.; VP crea aff Col; 1980, Sr. VP Prodn Fox (NY).

GUFFEY, Burnett: Cin. b. Del Rio, TN, May 26, 1905. Films inc: The Informer; Foreign Correspondent; All the King's Men; The Sniper; From Here to Eternity (Oscar-1953); The Harder They Fall; Birdman of Alcatraz; King Rat; Bonnie and Clyde (Oscar-1967); The Split; The Madwoman of Chaillot; The Great White Hope.

GUILLAUME, Robert: Act. b. St Louis, MO, Nov 30. e. WA U. Bway inc: Carousel; Guys and Dolls; Purlie; Golden Boy; Othello; Porgy and Bess; Jacques Brel.

TV inc: Mel and Susan Together; Rich Little's Washington Follies; S'Wonderful, S'Marvelous, S'Gershwin; Soap (Emmy-1979); Benson; The Kid From Left Field; The Starmakers; Hal Linden's Big Apple.

Films inc: Seems Like Old Times.

GUILLERMIN, John: Dir. b. London, 1925. Films inc: Torment; Smart Alec; Miss Robin Hood; Adventures in the Hopfields; The Crowded Day; Town on Trial; I Was Monty's Double; Tarzan's Greatest Adventure; The Day They Robbed the Bank of England; Waltz of the Toreadors; Tarzan Goes to India; Guns at Batasi; Rapture; The Blue Max; P.J.; House of Cards; The Bridge at Remagen; El Condor; Skyjacked; Shaft in Africa; The Towering Inferno; King Kong; Death on the Nile; Mr. Patman.

GUINNESS, Alec Sir: Act. b. London, Apr 2, 1914. Knighted, 1959. Stage debut London, 1934. Also on stage in NY, Europe. On screen From 1934, Evensong.

Films inc: Great Expectations; Oliver Twist; Kind Hearts and Coronets; The Lavender Hill Mob; The Man in the White Suit; The Promoter; The Malta Story; Captain's Paradise; The Detective; To Paris With Love; The Prisoner; The Lady Killers; The Swan; The Bridge on the River Kwai *(Oscar-*1957); The Horse's Mouth; The Scapegoat; Our Man in Havana; Tunes of Glory; A Majority of One; H.M.S. Defiant; Lawrence of Arabia; Dr. Zhivago; The Comedian; Cromwell; Scrooge; Brother Sun and Sister Moon; Hitler; The Last Ten Days; Murder by Death; Star Wars; The Empire Strikes Back; Raise The Titanic.

Honorary Oscar (April 1980) for advancing the art of screen acting through a host of memorable performances.

TV inc: The Wicked Scheme of Jebel Deeks; Twelfth Night; Conversation at Night; Solo; E.E. Cummings; Little Gidding; The Gift of Friendship; Caesar & Cleopatra; Tinker, Tailor, Soldier, Spy; Little Lord Fauntleroy.

Bway inc: Dylan *(Tony-*1964); The Cocktail Party (prod-act); Time Out of Mind; A Voyage Round My Father; Macbeth; Yahoo; The Old Country.

GULAGER, Clu: Act. b. Holdenville, OK, Nov 16, 1928. e. Baylor U. Studied with Jean Louis Barrault and Etienne Decroix in Paris.

Films inc: The Killers; Winning; The Last Picture Show; Company of Killers; McQ; The Other Side of Midnight; A Force of One; Touched by Love.

TV inc: A Different Drummer; The Virginian; SFX; A Question of Love; Willa; Once An Eagle; This Man Stands Alone; Sticking Together; King; MacKenzies of Paradise Cove; Kenny Rogers as the Gambler; Skyward.

GULKIN, Harry: Prod. b. Montreal, Nov 14, 1927. Films inc: Two Solitudes; Jacob Two-Two Meets the Hooded Fang; Lies My Father Told Me.

GUMBEL, Bryant: Sportscaster. b. Chicago, IL. e. Bates College. Sports dir KNBC, LA since 1976. Network tv inc: (host) NCAA Basketball Championships; Super Bowl XI; Super Bowl XII; Games People Play; Different as Night and Day.

GUNN, Moses: Act. b. St Louis, MO, Oct 2, 1929. e. TN State U. Films inc: The Great White Hope; The Wild Rovers; Shaft; The Hot Rock; Rollerball; Aaron Loves Angela; Remember My Name; The Ninth Configuration.

TV inc: Mr Carter's Army; Of Mice and Men; Haunts of the Very Rich; If You Give a Dance, You Gotta Pay the Band; The Cowboys; Roots; The Contender.

Thea inc: In White America; Song of the Lusitanian Bogey; Measure for Measure; Romeo and Juliet; As You Like It; Macbeth; Othello; A Hand Is on the Gate.

GURLEY, Randy: Mus. b. Salem, MA, Nov 29, 1952. Recording artist. TV inc: Hee Haw; Good Old Nashville Music.

GUTHRIE, Arlo: Act. b. NYC, Jul 10, 1947. S of Woody Guthrie. Films inc: Alice's Restaurant; Renaldo and Clara.

GWYNNE, Anne (Marguerite Gwynne Trice): Act. b. Waco, TX, Dec 10, 1918. e. Stephens Coll. Films inc: Framed; Unexpected Father; Honeymoon Deferred; House of Frankenstein; Fear; The Ghost Goes West; Dick Tracy Meets Gruesome; Call of the Klondike; Breakdown; Teenage Monster.

Thea inc: Stage Door; Inside Story; The Colonel's Lady.

GWYNNE, Fred: Act. b. NYC, Jul 10, 1926. e. Harvard U. Thea inc: Mrs McThing; Love's Labour's Lost; Irma la Douce; The Lincoln Mask; More Than You Deserve; Cat On a Hot Tin Roof; The Winter's Tale; Angel.

Films inc: Luna; Simon.

TV inc: The Munsters.

HAACK, Morton R: Cos Dsgn. b. LA, Jun 26, 1924. Films inc: Games; Walk Don't Run; The Unsinkable Molly Brown; Jumbo; Come September; Please Don't Eat the Daisies; Planet of the Apes.

Bway inc: Make Mine Manhattan. Has also des prima donna costumes for LaScala.

HACK, Shelley: Act. b. CT, Jul 6. e. Smith Coll. Former model. TV inc: Death Car; Charlie's Angels.

Films inc: Annie Hall; If I Ever See You Again.

HACKETT, Albert: Wri. b. 1900. Usually in collab with wife, Frances Goodrich. Films inc: The Thin Man; After the Thin Man; Naughty Marietta; Another Thin Man; The Hitler Gang; It's A Wonderful Life; Summer Holiday; Father of the Bride; Seven Brides for Seven Brothers; The Diary of Anne Frank.

Bway inc: The Diary of Anne Frank *(Tony-*1956).

TV inc: The Diary of Anne Frank.

HACKETT, Buddy: Comedian-Act. b. NYC, Aug 31, 1924. Began professional career in the Catskills.

Bway inc: Lunatics and Lovers; I Had a Ball.

Films inc: Walking My Baby Back Home; Fireman, Save My Child; God's Little Acre; All Hands on Deck; The Music Man; The Wonderful World of the Brothers Grimm; It's A Mad, Mad, Mad, Mad World; The Love Bug; The Good Guys and the Bad Guys.

TV inc: Jack Frost (voice); You Bet Your Life.

HACKETT, Joan: Act. b. NYC, 1942. Films inc: The Group; Will Penny; Support Your Local Sheriff; Assignment to Kill; The Rivals; The Last of Sheila; Mr Mike's Mondo Video; One-Trick Pony.

TV inc: The Young Country; Class of '63; Reflections of Murder; Pleasure Cove; Long Days of Summer.

Thea inc: Laurette; She Didn't Say Yes.

HACKFORD, Taylor: Dir. b. 1945. Started with KCET (LA) as prod-dir. Films inc: Teenage Father *(Oscar-*short-1978). TV inc: The Idolmaker (dir).

HACKMAN, Gene: Act. b. San Bernardino, CA, Jan 30, 1931. Films inc: Lilith; Bonnie And Clyde; I Never Sang for My Father; The French Connection *(Oscar-*1971); The Poseidon Adventure; Bite The Bullet; The Domino Principle; A Bridge Too Far; March Or Die; Superman; Superman II.

HADJIDAKIS, Manos: Comp. b. Greece, 1925. Films inc: Stella; A Matter of Dignity; Never On Sunday *(Oscar-*song-1959); America, America; Blue; Topkapi.

Bway inc: Ilya, Darling.

HAEBERLE, Horatius: Wri-Prod. b. Berlin, Feb 24, 1940. Films inc: Fort Travis; Anaconda Run.

HAENSCHEN, Gus (Walter Gustave Haenschen): Comp-Cond. b. East St Louis, MO, 1890. e. WA U. Exec with Brunswick Records in early years of diskery; cond top radio programs inc American Album of Familiar Music; Maxwell House Show Boat; Bayer Musical Review; Coca Cola Song Shop; Chevrolet Hour; Palmolive Show; Chase and Sanborn Hour; Pet Milk Saturday Serenade; after retiring as cond was associated with NY Philharmonic and Metropolitan Opera radio broadcasts.

Songs inc: Rosita; Manhattan Merry-Go-Round; Silver Star; Lullaby of Love; Easy Melody; Under the Japanese Moon.

(Died March 27, 1980).

HAGEN, Jean (nee Verhagen): Act. b. Chicago, 1924. Films inc: Side Street; Adam's Rib; The Asphalt Jungle; Singin' in the Rain; Carbine Williams; Latin Lovers; Half a Hero; Spring Reunion; The Shaggy Dog; Sunrise at Campobello; Panic in Year Zero; Dead Ringer.

TV inc: Make Room for Daddy.

HAGEN, Uta: Act. b. Gottingen, Ger, Jun 12, 1919. e. RADA. Stage debut 1937, with Eva Le Gallienne's Civic Repertory Co.
Bway inc: The Seagull; Happiest Days; Key Largo; Othello; Faust; A Streetcar Named Desire; The Country Girl *(Tony*-1950); The Affairs of Anatol; Island of Goats; Who's Afraid of Virginia Woolf? *(Tony*-1962); The Cherry Orchard; Charlotte (& translator).
TV inc: Macbeth; Out of the Dust; A Month in the Country. Films inc: The Other; The Boys From Brazil.

HAGGARD, Merle: Singer. b. Bakersfield, CA, Apr 6, 1937. C & W recording artist. TV inc: Huck Finn; Movin' On (score); Centennial.

HAGGARD, Piers: Dir. b. Scotland, 1939. e. U of Edinburgh. Worked in various Scottish theatrical prodns before joining Britain's National Theatre where he spent two years as asst to Franco Zeffirelli and Laurence Olivier. Asst to Michaelangelo Antonioni on Blow Up.
Films inc: Wedding Night; Satan's Skin; Quatermass Conclusion; The Fiendish Plot of Dr. Fu Manchu.
TV inc: A Divorce; The Chester Mystery Plays; Poor Cherry; Pennies from Heaven.

HAGGERTY, Dan: Act. b. Hollywood, CA, Nov 19. Films inc: Where the North Wind Blows; Wild Country; Grasslands; Easy Rider.
TV inc: The Life and Times of Grizzly Adams; Terror Out of the Sky.

HAGMAN, Larry: Act. b. Ft Worth, TX, Sep 21, 1931. S of Mary Martin. Films inc: Fail Safe; Ensign Pulver and the Captain; The Cavern; Stardust; 3 in the Cellar; Mother, Jugs and Speed; Harry and Tonto; The Eagle Has Landed; Checkered Flag or Crash; Superman.
TV inc: The President's Mistress; Last of the Good Guys; Battered; I Dream of Jeannie; The Good Life; Here We Go Again; Dallas; A Cry for Justice.
Thea inc: Once Around the Block; Career; Comes a Day; A Priest in the House.

HAGMANN, Stuart: Dir. b. Sturgeon Bay, WI, Sep 2, 1942. Films inc: The Strawberry Statement; Believe In Me; Good Night, Socrates (short).
TV inc: Mission Impossible; Mannix; Code Three; Sparrow; She Lives; Tarantula.

HAILEY, Arthur: Wri. b. Luton, Eng, Apr 4, 1920. Wrote for TV before turning to novels. Authored Airport. Other novels made into films inc: Hotel; The Young Doctors; Zero Hour.

HAILEY, Oliver: Wri. b. Pampa, TX, Jul 7, 1932. e. U of TX, Yale School of Drama, MFA. Plays inc: Hey You, Light Man!; First One Asleep; Father's Day; Continental Divide; And Where She Stops Nobody Knows; Tryptich.
TV inc: McMillan & Wife (ed); Mary Hartman, Mary Hartman (cnsltnt); Another Day (co-prod).
Films inc: Just You and Me Kid.

HAINES, Larry: Act. Bway inc: Twigs; Last of the Red Hot Lovers; Promises, Promises; A Thousand Clowns; Generation; Paris Is Out.
TV inc: Search for Tomorrow *(Emmy*-1976); Doc; Maude; Sunshine Boys; Phil & Mikky.
Films inc: The Odd Couple.

HAKIM, Raymond: Prod. b. Aug 16, 1909. Partnered with brother Robert in Paris Films Co.
Films inc: Pepe Le Moko; La Bete Humaine; Le Jour Se Leve; The Southerner; Her Husband's Affairs; The Long Night; The Blue Veil; Belle De Jour; Isadora; La Marge.
(Died Aug 14, 1980).

HAKIM, Robert: Prod. b. Egypt, 1907. Partnered with brother Raymond in Paris Film Prodns. For credits see HAKIM, Raymond.

HALAS, John: Prod-Dir. b. Budapest, Hungary, Apr 16, 1912. Prod over 500 docs, educational shorts & cartoons.
Films inc: Animal Farm; Ruddigore; The Kid From Outer Space; Parkinson's Law.

HALE, Alan Jr: Act. b. LA, 1918. Films inc: I Wanted Wings; Spirit of West Point; It Happens Every Spring; Lady in the Iron Mask; Springfield Rifle; Destry; Many Rivers to Cross; The Sea Chase; The True Story of Jesse James; Bullet for a Bad Man; Hang 'Em High; Dead Heat; There Was a Crooked Man; The Fifth Musketeer; The North Avenue Irregulars.
TV inc: Wagon Train; Cheyenne; Maverick; Biff Baker, USA; Casey Jones; Gilligan's Island; The Castaways on Gilligan's Island; Revenge of the Red Chief.

HALE, Barbara: Act. b. DeKalb, IL, Apr 18, 1922. Films inc: Higher and Higher; The Falcon in Hollywood; First Yank into Tokyo; Lady Luck; The Boy with Green Hair; The Window; Jolson Sings Again; The Jackpot; Lorna Doone; A Lion is in the Streets; Unchained; The Far Horizons; The Oklahoman; Airport; Big Wednesday.
TV inc: Perry Mason *(Emmy*-supp-1959).

HALEY, Alex: Wri-Prod. b. Ithaca, NY, Aug 11, 1921. Books inc: Autobiography of Malcolm X; Roots (Special Pulitzer Prize citation, 1977). TV inc: Palmerstown USA (exec prod).

HALEY, Jack: Act. b. Boston, Aug 10, 1897. Vaudeville, stage. On screen From 1930.
Films inc: Follow Through; Redheads on Parade; Pigskin Parade; Poor Little Rich Girl; Wake Up and Live; Alexander's Ragtime Band; The Wizard of Oz; Navy Blue; Scared Stiff; People Are Funny; Make Mine Laughs; Norwood. (Died June 6, 1979).

HALEY, Jack Jr: Prod-Dir-Wri. b. LA, Oct 25, 1933. e. Loyola U, BS. Joined David L Wolper Prodns 1959; named sr vp 1967; in 1973 moved to MGM as dir of creative arts; in 1975 became p, Fox TV; indie prod in 1976.
TV inc: The Incredible World of James Bond; The General; The Legend of Marilyn Monroe; The Supremes; The Hidden World; Movin' with Nancy *(Emmy*-dir-1968); With Love, Sophia; Monte Carlo, C'est La Rose; The Best of the Brass; Academy Award Show dir, 1970, prod, 1974; Life Goes to War: Hollywood and the Homefront; Heroes of Rock n' Roll (exec prod); 51st Annual Academy Awards *(Emmy*-1979).
Films inc: Norwood; The Love Machine; That's Entertainment.

HALEY, Jackie Earle: Act. b. Northridge, CA, Jul 14, 1961. Films inc: The Outside Man; The Day of the Locust; Damnation Alley; Bad News Bears; The Bad News Bears Break Training; The Bad News Bears in Japan; Breaking Away.
TV inc: Breaking Away.

HALL, Conrad: Cin. b. Tahiti, 1927. Films inc: Morituri; Harper; The Professionals; Cool Hand Luke; In Cold Blood; Hell in the Pacific; Butch Cassidy and the Sundance Kid *(Oscar*-1969); Tell Them Willie Boy is Here; The Happy Ending; Fat City; The Day of the Locust; Smile; Marathon Man.

HALL, Huntz: Act. b. NYC, 1920. Films inc: Dead End; Crime School; Angels with Dirty Faces; The Return of Dr X; Give Us Wings; Wonder Man; Bowery Bombshell; Angels in Disguise; Lucky Losers; Loose in London; Paris Playboys; High Society; Spook Chasers; The Gentle Giant; The Love Bug Rides Again; Gas Pump Girls.
TV inc: Chicago Teddy Bears.

HALL, Jon (Charles Locher): Act. b. near San Francisco, Feb 23, 1913. Films inc: Charlie Chan in Shanghai; The Girl From Scotland Yard; The Hurricane; Kit Carson; South of Pago Pago; Arabian Nights; White Savage; Ali Baba and the Forty Thieves; The Invisible Man's Revenge; Prince of Thieves; Hurricane Island; Last Train From Bombay; The Beachgirls and the Monster (& dir); Five the Hard Way (co-prod & cin only).
TV inc: Ramar of the Jungle.
(Died Dec 13, 1979).

HALL, Ken G: Prod-Dir. b. Sydney, Australia, Feb 22, 1901. Films inc: On Our Selections; Squatter's Daughter; Tall Timbers; Lovers and Luggers; Mr Chedworth Steps Out; Vengeance of the Deep; Pacific Adventure (ret).

HALL, Monty: Act. b. Winnipeg, Canada, 1923. e. U of Manitoba, BS. Teenage radio actor, 1940. TV since 1952.
TV inc: (host) Let's Make a Deal; Strike It Rich; Video Village; Your First Impression.
Films inc: Courage and the Passion.

HALL, Sir Peter: Prod-Dir. b. Suffolk, Eng, Nov 22, 1930. e. Cambridge. Dir Oxford Playhouse 1954-55; Arts Theatre 1955-57; M-Dir Royal Shakespeare Company 1960-68, creating RSC as permanent ensemble; succeeded Lord Olivier as dir National Theatre Company of Great Britain 1973.
Thea inc; The Lesson; Waiting for Godot; Waltz of the Toreadors; Becket; The Collection; The Homecoming *(Tony-*1967); A Delicate Balance; Old Times; Tristan und Isolde; Via Galactica; Happy Days; John Gabriel Borkman; No Man's Land; Judgement; Tamburlaine the Great; Bedroom Farce; Betrayal; Amadeus (London & Bway); numerous Shakespearean prodns for RSC.
Films inc: A Midsummer Night's Dream; Three Into Two Won't Go; Perfect Friday; Landscape; The Homecoming; Akenfield.
TV inc: The Wars of the Roses (adaptation of four Shakespeare plays).

HALL, Tom T: Singer-Sngwri. b. Olive Hill, KY, May 25, 1936. Worked as deejay, WMOR; with groups Tom Hall and the Kentucky Travelers; The Technicians; The Story Tellers. Albums inc: In Search of Song; We All Got Together and--; The Story Teller; Songs of Fox Hollow; Magnificent Music Machine; Tom T Hall's Greatest Hits.

HALLER, Daniel: Dir. b. Glendale, CA, 1928. Films inc: Die Monster Die; The Devil's Angels; The Wild Racers; Paddy; The Dunwich Horror; Pieces of Dreams; Buck Rogers in the 25th Century.
TV inc: Sword of Justice; Kojack; Owen Marshall; Black Beauty; Little Mo; High Midnight; Georgia Peaches.

HALSEY, Richard: Film edtr. Films inc: Payday; Harry and Tonto; W.W. and the Dixie Dancekings; Next Stop Greenwich Village; Rocky *(Oscar-*1976); Thank God It's Friday; Boulevard Nights; American Gigolo; Tribute.
TV inc: Peyton Place (more than 500 episodes).

HAMBLEN, Stuart: Act-Comp. b. Kellyville, TX, Oct 20, 1908. One of the major C&W recording artists; also performed on radio. Ran for P of the U S in 1952 on the Prohibition Party ticket.

HAMBLETON, Thomas Edward: Prod. b. Towson, MD, Feb 12, 1911. e. Yale U, BA. Founder (1953) and M-dir Phoenix Theatre, NY. Prodns inc: Robin Landing; I Know What I Like; The First Crocus; The Great Campaign; Galileo; Temporary Island; Ballet Ballads; Pride's Crossing; The American Bell; Once Upon a Mattress; Saint Joan; Diary of a Scoundrel; The Power and the Glory; The Matchmaker; Man and Superman; War and Peace; Judith; You Can't Take It With You; Cock-A-Doodle-Dandy; Harvey; The Criminals; The Persians; The School for Wives; The Trial of the Cantonsville 9; Murderous Angels.

HAMILL, Mark: Act. b. San Francisco, Sep 25, 1951. TV inc: General Hospital; Texas Wheelers; Sarah: Portrait of a Teenage Alcoholic; Erick; Mallory; SPFX--The Empire Strikes Back (host).
Films inc: Star Wars; Corvette Summer; The Empire Strikes Back; The Big Red One.

HAMILL, Pete (William Hamill): Wri. b. Brooklyn, NY, Jun 24, 1935. Columnist, NY newspapers.
Films inc: Doc; Badge 373.

HAMILTON, Arthur: Comp-Lyr. b. Seattle. TV inc: I Love Lucy.
Thea inc: What A Day.
Songs inc: He Needs Me; Sing a Rainbow; Cry Me a River; You'll Remember Me; Till Love Touches Your Life.

HAMILTON, Bernie: Act. b. LA, Jun 12. Films inc: The Jackie Robinson Story; Let No Man Write My Epitaph; The Devil at 4 O' Clock; One Potato, Two Potato; Synanon; The Swimmer; The Losers; The Organization.
TV inc: That's My Mama; Hec Ramsey; The Bold Ones; Starsky & Hutch.
Thea inc: Take a Giant Step; The Petrified Forest; Othello; Waiting for Lefty; No Time for Sergeants.

HAMILTON, Dirk: Sngwri-Singer. b. Indiana, Aug 31, 1949. Recording artist.

HAMILTON, George: Act. b. Memphis, TN, Aug 12, 1939. Films inc: Crime and Punishment U.S.A; Home From The Hill; Where the Boys Are; All the Fine Young Cannibals; Light in the Piazza; Two Weeks in Another Town; Act One; Your Cheatin' Heart; Viva Maria!; The Power; Evel Knievel; Once Is Not Enough; Sextette; Love at First Bite (& prod); From Hell to Victory.
TV inc: Institute for Revenge; Death Car on the Freeway; The Seekers; The Great Cash Giveaway.

HAMILTON, Guy: Dir. b. Paris, Sep 1922. Former asst to Carol Reed. Films inc: The Ringer; The Intruder; An Inspector Calls; The Colditz Story; Charley Moon; The Devil's Disciple; A Touch of Larceny; The Best of Enemies; Live and Let Die; The Man with the Golden Gun; The Man in the Middle; Goldfinger; The Battle of Britain; Diamonds are Forever; Force 10 From Navarone; The Mirror Crack'd.

HAMILTON, Joe: Prod. b. LA, Jan 6. H of Carol Burnett. Orig singer with the Skylarks.
TV inc: The Gary Moore Show; exec prod Carol Burnett Show *(3 Emmys-*1972, 1974, 1975); Julie and Carol at Carnegie Hall; Calamity Jane; Once Upon A Mattress; 6 Rms Riv Vu; Twigs; Sills and Burnett at the Met; The Grass Is Always Greener Over the Septic Tank; The Tenth Month.

HAMILTON, Linda: Act. b. Salisbury, MD, Sep 26. Studied with Lee Strasberg. TV inc: Rape and Marriage--The Rideout Case; Reunion; Secrets of Midland Heights.

HAMILTON, Margaret: Act. b. Cleveland, OH, Dec 9, 1902. Films inc: Another Language; These Three; Nothing Sacred; The Wizard of Oz; Invisible Woman; Guest in the House; Mad Wednesday; State of the Union; The Great Plane Robbery; Thirteen Ghosts; The Daydreamer; Rosie; The Anderson Tapes; Brewster McCloud.
TV inc: Letters From Frank.

HAMILTON, Murray: Act. b. 1923. Films inc: Bright Victory; No Time for Sergeants; The FBI Story; Seconds; The Graduate; No Way to Treat a Lady; The Boston Strangler; If It's Tuesday This Must Be Belgium; The Way We Were; Jaws; Jaws II; Casey's Shadow; The Amityville Horror; 1941; Brubaker.
TV inc: Donovan's Kid; Swan Song.

HAMILTON, Neil: Act. b. Lynn, MA, Sep 9, 1899. Films inc: White Rose; America; Isn't Life Wonderful; Beau Geste; The Great Gatsby; Keeper of the Bees; The Dawn Patrol; The Animal Kingdom; Tarzan the Ape Man; One Sunday Afternoon; Tarzan and His Mate; The Little Shepherd of Kingdom Come; Madame X.
TV inc: Batman.

HAMLISCH, Marvin: Comp-Cond. b. NYC, Jun 2, 1944. e. Juilliard. Films inc: Flap; The Sting *(Oscar-*adapt-score-1973); The Way We Were *(Oscar-*score-1973), *(Oscar-*best song-1973); The Spy Who Loved Me; Same Time, Next Year; Ice Castles; Starting Over; Ordinary People; Seems Like Old Times.
Bway inc: A Chorus Line *(Tony-*1975); They're Playing Our Song.
TV inc: The Entertainer (prod); Omnibus (theme).
(Grammys-(4)-New Artist, Song of Year, Film Score, Pop Instrumental-1974).

HAMMOND, Peter: Act-Wri-Dir. b. London, Nov 15, 1923. Films inc: They Knew Mr Knight; Holiday Camp; Fly Away Peter; Morning Departure; Vote for Huggett; The Adventurers; Spring and Port Wine (dir only).

TV inc: William Tell; Robin Hood; The Buccaneers; Three Musketeers; Treasure Island; Our Mutual Friend; The House that Jack Built; The Black Knight.

HAMNER, Earl: Prod-Wri. b. Schuyler, VA, Jul 10, 1923. With WLW, Cincinnati as radio-wri-prod; joined NBC 1949 as wri; 1960 freelance.

TV inc: The Waltons (crea-co-prod); Joshua's World.

Films inc: Spencers Mountain; You Can't Get There From Here; The Homecoming.

HAMPSHIRE, Susan: Act. b. London, May 12, 1942. Films inc: Upstairs and Downstairs; During One Night; The Long Shadow; The Three Lives of Thomasina; Night Must Fall; Wonderful Life; The Fighting Prince of Donegal; The Trygon Factor; Monte Carlo or Bust; A Time for Loving; Living Free.

TV inc: David Copperfield; Baffled; (series): The Forsyte Saga (*Emmy*-1970); The First Churchills (*Emmy*-1971); The Pallisers; Vanity Fair (*Emmy*-1973).

Thea inc: Expresso Bongo; Follow That Girl; Fairy Tales of New York; Ginger Man; Past Imperfect; She Stoops to Conquer; Peter Pan; Romeo & Jeanette; The Circle; Arms and the Man; Man and Superman; The Crucifer of Blood.

HAMPTON, James: Act. b. Oklahoma City, OK, Jul 9, 1936. e. North TX State U. Films inc: Fade In; Soldier Blue; The Man Who Loved Cat Dancing; The Longest Yard; W.W. and the Dixie Dance Kings; Hustle; The Cat From Outer Space; The China Syndrome; Champs; McIntosh and TJ; Eyewitness; Hangar 18.

TV inc: F Troop.

HAMPTON, Lionel: Mus. b. Birmingham, AL, Apr 12, 1913. Virtually self-taught on drums, vibraharp; worked with Les Hite and Eddie Elkins Bands while attending USC; guest drummer with Louis Armstrong on recording dates; with Benny Goodman Quartet 1936 to 1940; organized own band; a top attraction during big band era, band toured the world.

Films inc: No Maps On My Taps (doc).

HANCOCK, John: Dir. b. Kansas City, MO, Feb 12, 1939. e. Harvard U. Films inc: Let's Scare Jessica to Death; Bang the Drum Slowly; Baby Blue Marine; Foul Play; California Dreaming; The In-Laws.

HANCOCK, Sheila, OBE: Act. b. Isle of Wight. e. RADA. Thea inc: (London) Breath of Spring; One to Another; Make Me an Offer; One Over the Eight; Rattle of a Simple Man; The Anniversary; The Soldier's Fortune; Fill The Stage With Happy Hours; A Delicate Balance; So What About Love; All Over; Absurd Person Singular; Deja Revue; Annie.

Films inc: Light Up the Sky; A Girl in a Boat; Night Must Fall; The Anniversary; Take A Girl Like You.

TV inc: Mr. Digby Darling; Now Take My Wife; But Seriously, It's Sheila Hancock.

HANDEL, Leo A: Dir-Prod-Wri. b. Vienna. P Handel Film Corp.

TV inc: Everyday Adventures; Magic of the Atom; The American Indian; Police Dog. Films inc: The Case of Patty Smith (prod-dir-wri); Phantom Planet (prod).

HANDELMAN, Stanley Myron: Comedian. Worked top niteries as single, opening act for Frank Sinatra, Bobbie Gentry. TV inc: Dean Martin Show; Golddiggers; Merv Griffin Show; Hollywood Squares; Make Room for Granddaddy; numerous guestar spots.

HANNA, William: Exec. b. Melrose, NM, Jul 14, 1911. e. Compton Coll. Worked briefly as a structural engineer; turned to cartooning with Leon Schlessinger's company In Hollywood; in 1937 hired by MGM as dir and story man in cartoon dept; met Joseph R Barbera and created Tom & Jerry, the first of seven Academy Award winning cartoons; left MGM in 1957 to form Hanna-Barbera Prodns (of which Hanna is VP) to make cartoons for TV.

TV inc: Jack and the Beanstalk; The Last of the Curlews (*Emmy*-1973); The Runaways (*Emmy*-1974); The Popeye Valentine Special; Sweethearts at Sea; Scooby Goes to Hollywood; The Flintstone's New Neighbors.

Films inc: Charlotte's Web.

HANNAY, David: Wri-Prod. b. Wellington, New Zealand, Jun 23, 1939. e. Scots Coll, Auckland U. Films inc: The Set; Stone; The Man From Hong Kong; Solo; Alison's Birthday.

TV inc: Crisis; Spoiler; Polly My Love; Paradise; Is There Anybody There; Mama's Gone A-Hunting; The Alternative; The Godfathers; The Spoiler; The People Next Door; The Unisexers; Kung Fu Killers.

HANNEMANN, Walter: Film edtr. b. Atlanta, GA, May 2, 1914. e. USC, Pomona Coll. Films inc: Hell's Five Hours; Getting Gertie's Garter; Guest in the House; Fabulous Dorseys; Blood on the Sun; Johnny Come Lately; A Lion Is In The Streets; Only the Valiant; Kiss Tomorrow Goodbye; Search for Paradise; Wagons Westward; Jet Pilot; Fort Vengeance; The Rose Bowl Story; The Bob Mathias Story; Pay or Die; Al Capone; A Cannon for Cordova; Guns of the Magnificent Seven; El Condor; A Dream of Kings; Lost in the Stars; Maurie; Two Minute Warning; Smokey and the Bandit; The Other Side of the Mountain Part II; The Villain; The Nude Bomb.

TV inc: Gene Autry; Annie Oakley; Range Riders; Death Valley Days; Dr Christian; June Allyson Show; Wagons West; The Rifleman; The Fugitive; 12 O'Clock High; The Invaders; Streets of San Francisco; Barnaby Jones; Storefront Lawyers; Hawaii Five-O.

HANSON, Barry Anthony: Prod. b. England, Aug 10, 1943. TV inc: Gangsters; The Naked Civil Servant; Plays for Britain; ITV Playhouse.

Films inc: The Long Good Friday.

HARBACH, William O: Prod. b. NYC, Oct 12, 1919. e. Brown U. S of late Otto Harbach. TV inc: Tonight Show (Steve Allen); Steve Allen Show; Bing Crosby Specials (& dir); Hollywood Palace; Julie Andrews Show (*Emmy*-1973); Gypsy in My Soul (*Emmy*-Exec prod-1976); Steve Allen Comedy Hour; The Kennedy Center Honors, 1980 (cnsltnt).

HARBURG, E Y (Yip): Lyr. b. NYC, Apr 8, 1896. e. CCNY, BA. Bway scores inc: Earl Carroll's Sketch Book; The Garrick Gaieties; Earl Carroll's Vanities of 1930; Ziegfeld Follies of 1934; Hold on to Your Hat; Bloomer Girl; Finian's Rainbow.

Film scores inc: Gold Diggers of 1937; The Wizard of Oz; Cabin in the Sky; Ship Ahoy; Meet the People; Gay Purr-ee.

TV inc: They Write The Songs--Yip Harburg.

Songs inc: Brother, Can You Spare a Dime; Thrill Me; Speaking of Love; That's Life; April in Paris; Suddenly; It's Only a Paper Moon; Over the Rainbow (*Oscar*-1939); Happiness Is a Thing Called Joe; More and More; If This Isn't Love; Adrift on a Star; I Could Go on Singing.

HARDIN, Tim: Sngwri-Folksinger. b. Eugene, OR, 1940. Worked Eastern clubs as folksinger. Songs inc: If I Were A Carpenter; Reason to Believe.

(Died Dec 29, 1980).

HARDING, Ann (Dorothy Walton Gatley): Act. b. Fort Sam Houston, TX, Aug 17, 1904. Performed in summer stock. Bway in Trial of Mary Dugan. Screen debut, Paris Bound, 1929.

Films inc: Westward Passage; Animal Kingdom; Holiday; The Fountain; Peter Ibbetson; Love From a Stranger; Stella Dallas; The Male Animal; The Man in the Gray Flannel Suit; Strange Intruder (Last film, 1956). Last on Bway in Abraham Cochrane, 1964.

HARDY, Joseph: Dir-Prod. b. Carlsbad, NM, Mar 8, 1929. e. NM Highland U, BA, MA, DFA, Yale U School of Drama, MFA. Bway inc: (as dir) You're a Good Man, Charlie Brown; Play It Again, Sam; Child's Play *(Tony*1970); What the Butler Saw; Bob and Ray; The Two and Only; Children! Children!; The Crucible.

TV inc: (as prod) Love of Life; The Secret Storm; Time for Us; Love Is a Many Splendored Thing; James at 15 (& dir); The Paper Chase; Love's Savage Fury; The Seduction of Miss Leona.

HARGROVE, Dean: Wri-Prod-Dir. b. Iola, KS, Jul 27, 1938. TV inc: wrote Bob Newhart Show, 1961-62; Man From Uncle series; Ransom for a Dead Man (wri-prod); Columbo (wri-prod) *(Emmy*-exec prod-1974); McCloud; Name of the Game; McCoy; The Family Holvak; Madigan (exec prod); Alias Sherlock Holmes (dir); Manchu Eagle Murder Caper Mystery (co-wrote & dir).

HARMAN, Barry: Wri. TV inc: Carol Burnett Show *(Emmy*-1974); Joe and Sons; All in the Family *(Emmy*-1978); The Jeffersons.

HARMON, Mark: Act. b. Burbank, CA, Nov 2, 1951. e. UCLA. S of Tom Harmon. Films inc: Comes A Horseman; Beyond the Poseidon Adventure.

TV inc: Eleanor and Franklin; The White House Years; Sam; Centennial; Little Moe; Getting Married; 240-Robert; Flamingo Road; The Dream Merchants.

HARMON, Tom: Sportscaster. b. Rensselaer, IN, Sep 28, 1919. e. U of MI, BS. All-American Football player, 1939-40. U.S. Air Force, 1941-46. After service became sportscaster, joined Columbia Pacific Radio Network as sports dir, 1948-61; Tom Harmon Sports Show, ABC, 19621-70; Golden West Broadcasters, 1970-74; Hughes TV Network sports dir, 1974. Editor-Publisher Tom Harmon's Football Today.

HARNICK, Sheldon M: Lyr. b. Chicago, Apr 30, 1924. e. Northwestern U. Bway inc: New Faces of 1932; Two's Company; John Murray Anderson's Almanac; Shoestring Revue; The Littlest Revue; Body Beautiful; Fiorello *(Pulitzer Prize & Tony*-1960); Tenderloin; She Loves Me; Fiddler on the Roof *(Tony*-1965); Apple Tree; The Rothschilds; Smiling the Boy Fell Dead; Rex; Capt. Jinks of the Horse Marines; Dr Heidegger's Fountain of Youth.

(Grammy-cast album-1963).

HARPER, Gregory W: Prod. b. Bethesda, MD, May 4, 1952. e. Amherst Coll, BA. TV inc: 1971-74 CBS News Paris freelance; 1975-76 WGBY TV/WGBH Educational Foundation; 1976-78 $128,000 Question; World Chess Championship.

HARPER, Ron: Act. b. Turtle Creek, PA, Jan 12. e. Princeton U. TV inc: 87th Precinct; Wendy and Me; Garrison's Gorillas; Planet of the Apes; Land of the Lost; Love of Life; Where the Heart Is.

Thea inc: A Palm Tree in a Rose Garden; Night Circus; Sweet Bird of Youth; 6 Rms Riv Vu.

Films inc: Splendor in the Grass; The Savage Season.

HARPER, Valerie: Act. b. Suffern, NY, Aug 22, 1940. TV inc: The Mary Tyler Moore Show *(3 Emmys*-supp-1971, 1972, 1973); Rhoda *(Emmy*-1975); The Shadow Box.

Bway inc: Story Theater; Second City; Take Me Along; Wildcat; Subways Are for Sleeping.

Films inc: Chapter Two; The Last Married Couple in America; Fun and Games.

HARPER, William A: Prod. b. Port Jervis, NY, Sep 3, 1915. e. USC, BS. Prod/dir commercial & industrial films, 1945-51. Films inc: The Silken Affair; S O S Ecuador; The Last Blitzkreig. 1964, organized American-European Film Service, Paris, as prod rep.

HARRINGTON, Curtis: Dir. b. LA, Sep 17, 1928. Films inc: Night Tide; Queen of Blood; Games; What's the Matter with Helen?; Who Slew Auntie Roo?

TV inc: The Dead Don't Die; The Deadly Bees.

HARRINGTON, Pat: Act. b. NYC, 1929. Launched career on Jack Paar Show. Later joined Steve Allen's show, then became a regular on the Danny Thomas Show. Also worked niteries.

Films inc: The President's Analyst.

TV inc: One Day At A Time; Mr. Deeds Goes To Town; Counsellor-at-Law.

HARRIS, Barbara: Act. b. Evanston, IL, Jul 25, 1935. Bway inc: Oh Dad, Poor Dad, Mamma's Hung You in the Closet and I'm Feelin' So Sad; On a Clear Day You Can See Forever; The Apple Tree *(Tony*-1967).

Films inc: A Thousand Clowns; Who Is Harry Kellerman?; The War Between Men and Women; Nashville; Family Plot; Movie Movie; The North Avenue Irregulars; The Seduction of Joe Tynan; Second Hand Hearts.

HARRIS, Emmylou: Singer. b. NC, 1947. Recording artist. *(Grammys*-(2)-country vocal-1976, 1979).

Films inc: The Last Waltz; Honeysuckle Rose.

TV inc: The Unbroken Circle-A Tribute to Mother Maybelle Carter.

HARRIS, Harry: Dir. b. Kansas City, MO, Sep 8, 1922. Started as flm edtr. TV inc: (dir) The Texan; Death Valley Days; Wanted Dead or Alive; The Islanders; Gunsmoke; Voyage to the Bottom of the Sea; Lost in Space; Time Tunnel; High Chaparral; Bonanza; Shenandoah; The Waltons; Blue Knight; Spencer's Pilots; Naked City; Swiss Family Robinson; Love American Style; Kung Fu; The Runaways; The Home Front.

HARRIS, James B: Prod-Dir. b. NYC, Aug 3, 1928. e. Juilliard School of Music. Films inc: The Killing; Paths of Glory; Lolita; The Bedford Incident (& dir); Some Call It Loving (& sp, dir); Telefon.

Thea inc: Make A Million; Tovarich; Sweet Charity; Mame.

HARRIS, Jed (nee Horowitz) Prod-Dir. b. Vienna, Feb 25, 1900. Dropped out of Yale while an undergraduate to work on Bway. Prodns inc: Broadway; Coquette; The Front Page; The Royal Family (these four shows were all hits during the 1927-28 Bway season, quickly establishing Harris as a major--and temperamental--force in the theatre); Uncle Vanya; The Green Bay Tree; The Lake; Our Town; A Doll's House; The Crucible; Child of Fortune (dir).

Films inc: Night People (wri).

(Died Nov 15, 1979).

HARRIS, Julie: Act. b. Grosse Pointe, MI, Dec 2, 1925. e. Yale Drama School. Films inc: Member of the Wedding; East of Eden; I Am a Camera; The Truth About Women; Requiem for a Heavyweight; The Haunting; Reflections in a Golden Eye; The Hiding Place; The Voyage of the Damned; The Bell Jar.

Bway inc: Sundown Beach; The Young and The Fair; Magnolia Alley; The Member of the Wedding; I Am a Camera *(Tony*-1952); Mlle Colombe; The Lark *(Tony*-1956); The Country Wife; Little Moon of Alban; Skyscraper; A Streetcar Named Desire; Forty Carats *(Tony*-1969); And Miss Reardon Drinks a Little; The Last of Mrs Lincoln *(Tony*-1973); The Au Pair Man; In Praise of Love; The Belle of Amherst *(Tony*-1976); Break A Leg; Mixed Couples.

TV inc: Little Moon of Alban *(Emmy*-1959); Victoria Regina *(Emmy*-1962); Backstairs at the White House; The Gift. *(Grammys*-spoken word-1977).

HARRIS, Louis: Prod-Dir. b. NYC, Jan 18, 1906 (ret). Assoc prod C B Demille, 1941-42; assoc prod & prod Par short subjects, 1943-46. Prod trailers for Par and National Screen Service to 1970.

Film shorts inc: Mardi Gras; Bombalera; Caribbean Romance; Lucky Cowboy; Bonnie Lassie.

HARRIS, Phil: Orch Ldr. b. Linton, IN, Jun 24, 1904. H of Alice Faye. Appeared on TV, radio. On screen From 1933.

Films inc: Turn Off the Moon; Buck Benny Rides Again; Dreaming Out Loud; I Love a Bandleader; Wabash Avenue; The High and the Mighty; The Patsy; King Gun.

HARRIS, Richard: Act. b. Limerick, Ireland, Oct 1, 1930. On screen since 1958.

Films inc: Alive and Kicking; Shake Hands with the Devil; The Long, The Short and The Tall; The Guns of Navarone; Mutiny on the Bounty; This Sporting Life; The Heroes of Telemark; The Bible; Hawaii; A Man Called Horse; Robin and Marian; The Cassandra Crossing; Orca; Return of a Man Called Horse; Echoes of a Summer; Golden Rendezvous; The Ravagers; The Last Word.

(Grammy-spoken word-1973).

HARRIS, Rosemary: Act. b. Ashby, Suffolk, Eng, Sep 19, 1930. Films inc: Beau Brummel; The Shiralee; A Flea in Her Ear; The Boys From Brazil.

TV inc: Othello; The Prince and the Pauper; Wuthering Heights; Dial M for Murder; Notorious Woman (Emmy-1976); Blithe Spirit; The Chisholms.

Bway inc: Climate of Eden; Seven Year Itch; The Crucible; Much Ado About Nothing; The Lion in Winter (Tony-1966).

HARRIS, Stan: TV Prod-Dir. b. Toronto, Feb 3, 1932. e. Ryerson Institute of Technology. TV inc: Nat King Cole Special; Perry Como Presents; Bing Crosby Special; Jim Nabors Special; Milton Berle Show; The Smothers Brothers Comedy Hour; Bob Hope Specials (1968 & 69); The Dick Van Dyke Show; Jack Benny Special; John Wayne Special; The Mancini Generation; Duke Ellington Special; George Burns' One Man Show; The Phenomenon of Benji; George Burns 100th Birthday; Rich Littles' Washington Follies; Pat Boone's Thanksgiving; The Muppets Go Hollywood; The Magic of David Copperfield; Kenny Rogers and The American Cowboy; Lynda Carter's Special; Lynda Carter Encore; Country Gold--The First Fifty Years; The Nashville Palace.

HARRISON, George: Singer-Mus-Comp. b. Liverpool, England, Feb 25, 1943. Member of The Beatles (see group listing).

Individual film credits inc: Let It Be (score); Life of Brian (exec prod).

(Grammys-(2)-(in addition to group awards): Film Soundtrack-1970; album of year-1972).

HARRISON, Gregory: Act. b. Avalon, Catalina Island, CA, May 31, 1950. Films inc: Jim, the World's Greatest; Fraternity Row.

TV inc: Logan's Run; The Gathering; Centennial; Trapper John; The Women's Room; Enola Gay--The Men, The Mission, The Atomic Bomb.

HARRISON, Joan: Wri-Prod. b. Guildford, Eng, 1911. Films inc: (wri) Jamaica Inn; Rebecca; Foreign Correspondent; Saboteur; Dark Waters. (Prod) Phantom Lady; Uncle Harry; Ride the Pink Horse; Circle of Danger.

TV inc: Alfred Hitchcock Presents.

HARRISON, Rex: Act. b. Derry House, Huyton, Lancashire, Eng, Mar 5, 1908. Stage debut, Thirty Minutes in a Street, Liverpool Repertory theatre, 1924. London debut, Getting George Married, 1930. To NY in Sweet Aloes, 1936. Screen debut 1929.

Films inc: Cleopatra; The School for Scandal; Storm in a Teacup; The Citadel; Night Train; Blithe Spirit; Anna and the King of Siam; Notorious Gentleman; The Ghost and Mrs. Muir; The Foxes of Harrow; The Four Poster; The Reluctant Debutante; Midnight Lace; My Fair Lady (Oscar-1964); The Yellow Rolls-Royce; The Agony and the Ecstasy; Doctor Doolittle; A Flea in Her Ear; Staircase; The Prince and the Pauper; Ashanti.

Bway inc: Anne of 1000 Days (Tony-1949); Cocktail Party; Bell, Book and Candle; Venus Observed; My Fair Lady (Tony-1957); Henry IV; In Praise of Love (Special Tony-1969).

HARRISON, Robert A: Exec. b. Aurelia, IA, Sep 10, 1926. e. USC, BS. Joined MGM as asst. Studio Controller 1959. Named Controller of MGM, 1973.

HART, Bruce: Prod-Wri-Sngwri. TV inc: Sesame Street (wri & title song); Free To Be. . .You and Me; Sooner Or Later (dir-lyr); Hot Hero Sandwich (Emmy-exec prod-1980).

Songs inc: You Take My Breath Away; Bang the Drum Slowly; Who Are You Now?; One Way Ticket.

HART, Carole: Prod-Wri. TV inc: Sesame Street (wri); Free to Be. .You and Me (Emmy-prod-1974); It Happened One Christmas; Sooner or Later; Hot Hero Sandwich (Emmy-exec prod-1980).

HART, Dolores (nee Hicks): Act. b. 1938. Gave up film career after 1963 to enter convent of Regina Laudis in Bethlehem, CT. She remains there as Mother Dolores. On screen From 1957.

Films inc: Loving You; Wild in the Wind; Lonely Hearts; Where the Boys Are; Francis of Assisi; Sail a Crooked Ship; Come with Me; Lisa.

In 1971 subject of David Wolper TV doc.

HART, Harvey: Dir. b. Canada, 1928. Films inc: Dark Intruder; Bus Riley's Back in Town; Sullivan's Empire; The Sweet Ride; Fortune and Men's Eyes; The Pyx; The Aliens Are Coming.

HART, Mickey: Mus. Member of The Grateful Dead since 1967. Also records with own band. Albums inc: Rolling Thunder; Diga.

(See The Grateful Dead for group credits).

HARTFORD-DAVIS, Robert: Prod-Dir. b. Eng, 1923. Films inc: That Kind of Girl; The Yellow Teddybears; Saturday Night Out; Black Torment; The Sandwich Man; Corruption; The Smashing Bird I Used to Know; The Field; Black Gunn; The Take.

HARTLEY, Mariette: Act. b. NYC, Jun 21, 1941. Films inc: Ride the High Country; Marooned; Skyjacked; Marnie.

TV inc: Peyton Place; Stone; The Incredible Hulk (Emmy-1979); The Second Time Around; The Halloween That Almost Wasn't; The Love Tapes; The Secret War of Jackie's Girls.

HARTMAN, David: Act-TV Personality. b. Pawtucket, RI, May 19, 1937. e. Duke U, AADA. Off-Broadway, summer stock; toured with Belafonte Singers. Bway debut, Hello, Dolly.

Films inc: The Ballad of Josie; Nobody's Perfect; Ice Station Zebra; The Island at the Top of the World.

TV inc: The Virginian; The Bold Ones; Lucas Tanner; host of Good Morning, America; The Shooters (wri-exec prod-narr).

HARTMAN, Elizabeth: Act. b. Youngstown, OH, Dec 23, 1943. Cleveland Playhouse. Thea inc: The Madwoman of Chaillot; Becket; Everyone Out the Castle is Sinking.

Films inc: A Patch of Blue; The Group; The Fixer; Beguiled; You're a Big Boy Now; Walking Tall.

TV inc: Willow B-Women in Prison.

HARTMANN, Edmund: Wri-Prod. b. St Louis, MO, Sep 24, 1911. Films inc: The Feminine Touch; Ali Baba and the 40 Thieves; The Naughty Nineties; The Paleface; Sorrowful Jones; Lemon Drop Kid; Fancy Pants; Mr. Casanova; Sherlock Holmes and the Scarlet Claw.

TV inc: My Three Sons; Family Affair; To Rome With Love; The Smith Family.

HARVEY, Anthony: Dir. b. London, Jun 5, 1931. e. RADA. Films inc: Dutchman; The Lion in Winter; They Might Be Giants; The Abdication; Players; The Eagle's Wing; Richard's Things.

TV inc: The Glass Menagerie; The Disappearance of Aimee.

HARVEY, Kenneth: Act-Wri. b. 1919. Started on radio, various road shows.

Bway inc: Pipe Dream; Calculated Risk; The Sound of Music; The Old Glory.

TV inc: Search for Tomorrow.

(Died June 6, 1979).

HASKELL, Jimmie: Comp-Cond-Arr. b. Brooklyn, NY. e. LA City Coll. Started as prod-arr for Rick Nelson. Owner Horn Records. TV inc: (Comp) See How She Runs (Emmy-1978); The Jericho Mile; Silent Victory--The Kitty O'Neill Story; One Last Ride; The Jayne Mansfield Story; Mark, I Love You.

(Grammys-(3)-arr accomp voc-1967, 1970, 1976).

HASKELL, Peter: Act. b. Oct 15, 1934. Films inc: Passages from Joyce's Finnegan's Wake; Christina.

TV inc: The Jordan Chance; Mandrake; Shadow of Fear; The Cracker Factory; Stunt Seven; God In The Dock.

HASSANEIN, Salah M: Exec. b. Egypt, May 31, 1921. e. British School, Alexandria. Exec vp United Artists Theatre Circuit, Inc; P, United Artists Eastern Theatres, Inc; P, Todd AO Corp; Bd of dir, NATO.

HASSETT, Marilyn: Act. b. LA, Dec 17, 1947. Films inc: They Shoot Horses, Don't They?; Shadow of the Hawk; The Other Side of the Mountain; Two-Minute Warning; The Other Side of the Mountain--Part 2; The Bell Jar.

HASSO, Signe: Act. b. Stockholm, Aug 15, 1915. Films inc: Assignment in Brittany; The Seventh Cross; The House on 92nd Street; Johnny Angel; A Scandal in Paris; Where There's Life; To the Ends of the Earth; A Double Life; Outside the Wall; Crisis; Picture Mommy Dead; Reflection of Fear; The Black Bird.

HASTINGS, Don: Act-Wri. b. Brooklyn, NY. On radio at age six; toured in Life With Father three years. Bway inc: I Remember Mama; On Whitman Avenue; A Young Man's Fancy; Summer and Smoke.
    TV inc: (Act) Captain Video; Studio One; Crunch and Des; The Edge of Night; As The World Turns (since 1960). (Wri) As The World Turns; Guiding Light.

HATCH, Richard: Act. b. Santa Monica, CA, May 21. TV inc: All My Children; Addy and the King of Hearts; The Last of the Belles; Streets of San Francisco; Battlestar Galactica; The Hustler of Muscle Beach.

HATFIELD, Hurd: Act. b. NYC, 1918. Films inc: Dragon Seed; The Picture of Dorian Gray; The Diary of a Chambermaid; The Beginning or the End; The Unsuspected; The Checkered Coat; Joan of Arc; Tarzan and the Slave Girl; The Left Handed Gun; King of Kings; El Cid; Mickey One; The Boston Strangler; Von Richthofen and Brown.
    TV inc: You Can't Go Home Again.

HATHAWAY, Henry (Henri Leopold de Fiennes): Dir. b. Sacramento, CA, Mar 13, 1898. More than 60 films inc: Wild Horse Mesa; Sunset Pass; Now and Forever; Lives of a Bengal Lancer; Peter Ibbetson; Trail of the Lonesome Pine; Spawn of the North; Shepherd of the Hills; The Real Glory; Brigham Young; Johnny Apollo; China Girl; Wing and a Prayer; Nob Hill; House on 92nd Street; 13 Rue Madeleine; Kiss of Death; Call Northside 777; Down to the Sea in Ships; The Black Rose; The Desert Fox; 14 Hours; Rawhide; Prince Valiant; Garden of Evil; 23 Paces to Baker Street; Legend of the Lost; How the West Was Won; Circus World; Nevada Smith; The Sons of Katie Elder; The Last Safari; 5 Card Stud; True Grit; Raid on Rommel; Shoot Out.

HATLEY, Marvin T: Comp-Cond. b. Reed, OK, Apr 3, 1905. e. UCLA. Head of mus dept Hal Roach Studios; comp-cond-arr for Our Gang; Charlie Chase; Laurel & Hardy films. Films inc: Way Out West; Captain Fury; Merrily We Live; Broadway Limited; Topper Takes a Trip; There Goes My Heart; Blockheads.

HAUBEN, Lawrence: Wri. b. Mar 3, 1931. e. UC Santa Barbara, BFA. Films inc: One Flew Over the Cuckoo's Nest (Oscar-1975).

HAUER, Rutger: Act. b. Breukelen, Netherlands, Jan 23, 1944. On stage in Amsterdam for six years. Films inc: Turkish Delight; Repelstweltje; Pusten Blume; Konter Bande; The Wilby Conspiracy; Keetje Tipple; Max Havelaar; Soldier of Orange; Pastorale 1943; Femme Entre Chien et Loup; Mysteries.

HAUFF, Reinhard: Dir. b. Marburg/Lahn, Germany, May 23, 1939. Films inc: Mathias Kneissl; The Brutalization of Franz Blum; Fuses; Paule Paulander; The Main Actor (& sp).

HAUSER, Robert B: Cin. b. Spokane WA, Mar 25, 1919. Films inc: The Odd Couple; The Riot; Willard; A Man Called Horse; Soldier Blue; Le Mans; Twilight's Last Gleaming; The Frisco Kid; Walking Tall--Final Chapter.
    TV inc: Peyton Place (3 Yrs); The Legend of Lizzie Borden; Combat; When Hell Was In Session; Roll of Thunder Hear My Cry; Fugitive Family; Alcatraz--The Whole Shocking Story.

HAVELOCK-ALLEN, Sir Anthony: Prod. b. Durham County, Eng, 1905. Films inc: This Man is News; In Which We Serve; Blithe Spirit; Brief Encounter (co-sp); Great Expectations (co-sp); Oliver Twist; The Small Voice; Never Take No for an Answer; The Young Lovers; Orders to Kill; The Quare Fellow; An Evening with the Royal Ballet; Othello; The Mikado.

HAVER, June (nee Stovenour): Act. b. Rock Island, IL, Jun 10, 1926. W of Fred McMurray. Films inc: The Gang's All Here; Home in Indiana; The Dolly Sisters; Three Little Girls in Blue; I Wonder Who's Kissing Her Now; Scudda Hoo, Scudda Hay; Oh You Beautiful Doll; Look for the Silver Lining; The Daughter of Rosie O'Grady; Love Nest; The Girl Next Door.

HAVOC, June (nee Hovick): Act. b. Seattle, WA, Oct 8, 1916. Sis of the late Gypsy Rose Lee. Film debut at age 2 in Hal Roach comedy. Danced with Anna Pavlova troupe, then entered vaudeville in own act. To Hollywood in 1942.
    Films inc: Hello Frisco, Hello; No Time for Love; Sweet and Low Down; Intrigue; Gentleman's Agreement; Once a Thief; Follow the Sun; Lady Possessed; Can't Stop The Music.
    Thea inc: Pal Joey; Sadie Thompson; Mexican Hayride; The Infernal Machine; The Beaux Strategem; Habeas Corpus.
    TV inc: Anna Christie; The Bear; Cakes and Ale; The Untouchables.

HAWES, Bess Lomax: Act-Comp. b. Austin, TX, Jan 21, 1921. Folklore authority. An accomplished guitarist; performs at concerts, festivals.

HAWES, Stanley Gilbert: Prod. b. London, Jan 19, 1905. Prod or dir 10 documentary films for Strand Films, London; 100 for National Film Board of Canada; 400 for the Australian Commonwealth Film Unit (now Film Australia).

HAWKINS, Rick: Wri. TV inc: Dorothy; Welcome Back, Kotter; Carol Burnett Show (Emmy-1978); Love Boat.

HAWKINS, Robert F: Journalist. b. Genoa, Italy, Jun 18, 1924. e. Princeton. Became Variety stringer, Rome, 1948; freelance photographer, regular contributor NY Times 1948-1960; became Rome bureau chief Variety 1954; London bureau chief & European mgr 1966; exec vp & int'l editor 1977, based in NY.

HAWN, Goldie: Act. b. Washington, DC, Nov 21, 1945. Began professionally as dancer in Can-Can, NY Worlds Fair, 1964.
    Films inc: The One and Only Genuine Original Family Band; Cactus Flower (Oscar-supp-1969); There's a Girl in My Soup; Dollars; Butterflies Are Free; The Sugarland Express; The Girl From Petrovka; Shampoo; The Dutchess and the Dirtwater Fox; Travels With Anita; Foul Play; Private Benjamin (& exec prod); Seems Like Old Times.
    TV inc: Good Morning World; Laugh-In; Goldie & Liza Together.

HAWORTH, Ted: Art Dir. b. Willoughby, OH, 1917. Films inc: Strangers on a Train; The Body Snatcher; Sayonara (Oscar-1957); Some Like It Hot; The Getaway; Jeremiah Johnson; The Professionals; The Longest Day; Claudine; Harry and Tonto; Bloodline; I Want to Live; Marty; Half a Sixpence; The Bachelor Party; Beguiled; What a Way to Go; Somebody Killed Her Husband; When You Comin' Back, Red Ryder; Sidney Sheldon's Bloodline.

HAYDEN, Jeffrey: Dir. b. NYC, Oct 15, 1926. e. U of NC. H of Eva Marie Saint. TV inc: Omnibus; The Big Payoff; The Bert Parks Show; Lassie; Leave it to Beaver; Dennis the Menace; 77 Sunset Strip; Peyton Place; The Bold Ones; Batman; Mannix; Ironsides; The Incredible Hulk; Cliff Hangers.

HAYDEN, Sterling: Act. b. Montclair, NJ, Mar 26, 1916. Films inc: Virginia; Bahama Passage; The Asphalt Jungle; Hellgate; Flat Top; So Big; Johnny Guitar; Shotgun; The Killing; The Godfather; The Long Goodbye; King of the Gypsies; Winter Kills; The Outsider; Nine to Five.

HAYDN, Richard: Act. b. Eng, 1905. Films inc: Ball of Fire; Charley's Aunt; Forever and a Day; And Then There Were None; Cluny Brown; Sitting Pretty; Jupiter's Darling; Please Don't Eat the Daisies; The Lost World; Mutiny on the Bounty; Five Weeks in a Balloon; The Sound of Music; Clarence the Cross-Eyed Lion; Bullwhip Griffin; Young Frankenstein.

HAYES, Helen (nee Brown): Act. b. Washington, DC, Oct 10, 1901. On screen From the teens in a few silents.
Films inc: Arrowsmith; The White Sister; Another Language; A Farewell to Arms; The Sin of Madelon Claudet (Oscar-1931-32); My Son, John; Anastasia; Airport (Oscar-supp-1970); Herbie Rides Again; One of Our Dinosaurs Is Missing; Candleshoe.
TV inc: Twelve Pound Look (Emmy-1952); Mary of Scotland; Dear Brutus; The Skin of Our Teeth; Christmas Tie; Drugstore on a Sunday Afternoon; Omnibus.
Thea inc: What Every Woman Knows; Coquette; The Good Fairy; Mary of Scotland; Victoria Regina; Wisteria Trees; Happy Birthday (Tony-1947); Mrs McThing; Glass Menagerie; The Show Off; Time Remembered (Tony-1958); Front Page. Lawrence Langner Award (1980).
(Grammy-spoken word-1976).

HAYES, Isaac: Comp-Singer. b. Covington, KY, Aug 20, 1942. Recordings inc: Hot Buttered Soul; B-A-B-Y; Soul Man; Chocolate Chip; Juicy Fruit; A Man and a Woman; Tough Guys; Shaft (Grammy-inst arr-1971); Black Moses (Grammy-pop inst-1972).
Films inc: Shaft (Oscar-song-1971) (Grammy-film score-1972).

HAYES, John Michael: Wri. b. Worcester, MA, May 11, 1919. e. U of MA. Films inc: Rear Window; To Catch a Thief; The Trouble with Harry; Peyton Place; The Carpetbaggers; Where Love Has Gone; Harlow; Judith; Nevada Smith.

HAYES, Peter Lind: Act. b. San Francisco, Jun 25, 1915. On radio as singer. Also performed in vaudeville, niteries.
Films inc: Million Dollar Legs; Seventeen; Dancing on a Dime; Playmates; Seven Days Leave.

HAYES, Raphael: Wri. b. Mar 2, 1915. Films inc: One Potato, Two Potato.
TV inc: The Defenders; Lamp Unto My Feet.
Thea inc: Man Most Likely.

HAYMES, Dick: Singer. b. Argentina, Sep 13, 1918. e. Loyola U. Radio anncer, then singer with various bands. Screen debut, Irish Eyes Are Smiling, 1944.
Films inc: Diamond Horseshoe; State Fair; Up in Central Park; All Ashore; Cruisin' Down the River.
(Died Mar 28, 1980).

HAYS, Robert: Act. b. Bethesda, MD, Jul 24, 1947. Films inc: Airplane.
TV inc: Will Rogers-Champion of the People; California Gold Rush; The Girl, The Gold Watch and Everything; Angie; Mark Twain's America--The Young Will Rogers.

HAYWARD, Louis: Act. b. Johannesburg, So Africa, Mar 19, 1909. On London stage in Dracula; Vinegar Tree; Conversation Piece. To Bway in 1935. In Point Valaine. Screen debut in Self-Made Lady.
Films inc: Anthony Adverse; Man in the Iron Mask; My Son, My Son; And Then There Were None; Walk A Crooked Mile; Camelot; Search for Bridey Murphy; Chuka.
TV inc: The Lone Wolf; Climax; Pursuers; The Survivors.

HAYWORTH, Rita (Margarita Carmen Cansino): Act. b. NYC, Oct 17, 1918. On stage as dancer From age 6.
Films inc: Dante's Inferno; Charlie Chan in Egypt; Human Cargo; A Message to Garcia; Only Angels Have Wings; The Lady in Question; The Strawberry Blonde; Blood and Sand; You'll Never Get Rich; Tales of Manhattan; Cover Girl; Gilda; Affair in Trinidad; Tonight and Every Night; The Lady From Shanghai; Salome; Miss Sadie Thompson; Fire Down Below; Pal Joey; Separate Tables; They Came to Cordura; Circus World; The Money Trap; The Poppy is also a Flower; The Rover; Sons of Satan; The Road to Salina; The Wrath of God.

HEAD, Edith: Dsgn. b. LA, Oct 28, 1907. e. Stanford U, MA; Otis Art School; Chouinard Art School. Films inc: She Done Him Wrong; The Emperor Waltz; The Heiress (Oscar-B&W-1949); All About Eve (Oscar-B&W-1950); Samson and Delilah (Oscar-Color-1950); A Place in the Sun (Oscar-B&W-1951); Carrie; The Greatest Show on Earth; Roman Holiday (Oscar-B&W-1953); Sabrina (Oscar-B&W-1954); The Rose Tattoo; To Catch a Thief; The Proud and the Profane; The Ten Commandments; Funny Face; THe Buccaneer; Career; The Five Pennies; Pepe; Pocketful of Miracles; The Man Who Shot Liberty Vallance; My Geisha; Love With the Proper Stranger; What a Way to Go; Inside Daisy Clover; The Facts of Life (Oscar-B&W-1969); Airport; Butch Cassidy and the Sundance Kid; The Sting (Oscar-1973); The Man Who Would Be King; The Big Fix; Sextette.

HEARNE, Richard: Act. b. Eng, 1909. Best known for his Mr Pastry characterization.
Films inc: Dance Band; The Butler's Dilemma; Capt Horatio Hornblower; Madame Louise; Something in the City; Tons of Trouble.
(Died Aug 25, 1979).

HEATHERTON, Joey: Act. b. Rockville Centre, NY, Sep 14, 1944. Films inc: Twilight of Honor; Where Love has Gone; My Blood Runs Cold; Bluebeard; The Happy Hooker Goes to Washington.

HECHT, Harold: Prod. b. NYC, Jun 1, 1907. Former dance dir, literary agent. From 1947 prod jointly with Burt Lancaster and later James Hill.
Films inc: Vera Cruz; Marty (Oscar-1955); Trapeze; Separate Tables; Taras Bulba; Cat Ballou; The Way West.

HECKART, Eileen: Act. b. Columbia, OH, Mar 29, 1919. e. OH State U. Films inc: Miracle in the Rain; The Bad Seed; Somebody Up There Likes Me; Hot Spell; Heller in Pink Tights; No Way to Treat a Lady; Butterflies Are Free (Oscar-supp-1972); Zandy's Bride; The Hiding Place; Burnt Offerings.
Bway inc: The Time of the Cuckoo; And Things That Go Bump in the Night; A View From the Bridge; The Dark at the Top of the Stairs; Barefoot in the Park; Butterflies Are Free; Picnic; Ladies at the Alamo.
TV inc: Save Me a Place at Forest Lawn; Mary Tyler Moore Show; Suddenly Love; Backstairs at the WHite House; White Mama; FDR-The Last Year.

HEDISON, David (nee Heditsian): Act. b. Providence, RI, May 20, 1929. Films inc: The Enemy Below; The Fly; Son of Robin Hood; The Lost World; Marines Let's Go; The Greatest Story Ever Told; Live and Let Die; Ffolkes.
TV inc: Five Fingers; Voyage to the Bottom of the Sea; The Power Within.

HEDREN, Tippi: Act. b. 1935. Films inc: The Birds; Marnie; A Countess From Hong Kong; The Man with the Albatross; Tiger by the Tail; Satan's Harvest; Mr Kingstreet's War; The Harrad Experiment.

HEELEY, David E: Dir-Prod. b. England, Dec 26, 1940. e. Oxford, BA. With BBC London, 1961-69 as dir Late Night Line Up; How It Is; Music Now; then to WNET, NY 1969.
TV inc: (dir) Free Time; How Do Your Children Grow; Behind the Lines; The Arc of Civilization; We Interrupt This Week; (prod & dir): Skyline (series); Fred Astaire-Puttin' On His Top Hat (Emmy-Prod-1980).

HEFFLEY, Wayne: Act. b. Bakersfield, CA, Jul 15, 1927. TV inc: Highway Patrol; Voyage to the Bottom of the Sea; Nichols; Little House on the Prairie; Roots.
Films inc: Tora, Tora, Tora; Lonely Are the Brave; The Outsider; Johnny Got His Gun.

HEFFRON, Richard: Dir. b. Chicago, Oct 6, 1930. e. Harvard. Started as dir documentaries, political films.
TV inc: The Bold Ones; Banacek; Toma; A Rumor of War.
Films inc: Newman's Law; Foolin' Around.

HEFNER, Hugh M: Exec. b. Chicago, IL, Apr 9, 1926. e. U KS. In promotion dept Esquire Magazine; Childrens Activities Magazine; started Playboy Magazine 1953; P Playboy Enterprises which inc film activities, tv.
    Films inc: (prod) Saint Jack; The Fiendish Plot of Dr. Fu Manchu.

HEFTI, Neal: Comp-Cond. b. Hastings, NE, Oct 29, 1922. Trumpeter with Woody Herman and Harry James Orchs before starting own orch 1950. Cond on TV for Arthur Godfrey Show; Kate Smith Show; American Bandstand.
    Films inc: Sex and the Single Girl; How To Murder Your Wife; Synanon; Harlow; Boeing-Boeing; Lord Love a Duck; Duel at Diablo; Oh Dad, Poor Dad; Barefoot in the Park; PJ; Odd Couple.
    TV inc: Fred Astaire Show; Odd Couple; Batman (*Grammy*-inst theme-1966).
    Songs inc: Lil Darlin'; Don't Dream of Anyone But Me; Girl Talk; Batman Theme.

HEIDT, Horace: Band Ldr (ret). b. Oakland, CA, 1901. e. U CA Berkeley. Formed own orch, Horace Heidt and his Musical Knights. On radio, TV. Radio inc: Pot O'Gold. TV inc: Youth Opportunity Program.

HEIFETZ, Jascha: Violinist. b. Vilna, Russia, Feb 2, 1901. Child prodigy; became int'l concert artist. (*Grammys*-(3)-classical-1961, 1962, 1964).

HEIFITS, Iossif: Wri-Dir. b. Russia, Dec 17, 1905. Began as a writer, collaborating with Alexander Zarkhi while both students at the Leningrad Film Factory; after two films, The Moon On Your Left and The Fiery Transport, they began directing in tandem and turned out a dozen films inc: Wind in The Face; Midday; My Homeland; Those Were the Days!; The Baltic Deputy; Member of the Government; His Name is Sukhe-Bator; Precious Grains; The Lights of Baku. Solo dir inc: The Big Family; The Rumyantsev Case (& co-sp); My Dear Man (& co-sp); The Lady With a Dog (& sp); The Horizon; A Day of Happiness (& co-sp); Salute, Maria (& co-sp); A Bad Goody (& sp); The Only One (& co-sp); Asya (& sp); Married for the First Time.

HEINDORF, Ray: Comp-Arr-Cond. b. Haverstraw, NY, Aug 25, 1908. Film scores inc: Yankee Doodle Dandy (*Oscar*-1942); This is the Army (*Oscar*-1943); Up in Arms; Rhapsody in Blue; Young Man with a Horn; The Jazz Singer; Night and Day; Look for the Silver Lining; Calamity Jane; A Star is Born; Damn Yankees; Finian's Rainbow; The Music Man (*Oscar*-score adapt-1962);
    (Died Feb 3, 1980).

HEINEMAN, Laurie: Act. TV inc: Almost Heaven; Terror on the 40th Floor; Mad Bull; Another World (*Emmy*-1978); An Apple and An Orange; Loose Change; Holier Than Thou; Studs Lonigan.
    Films inc: Inaugural Ball; Save The Tiger; The Lady in Red.

HEISLER, Stuart R: Dir. b. LA, 1897. Films inc: Wedding Night; Dark Angel; Peter Ibbetson; Big Broadcast of 1937; Glass Key; Along Came Jones; Blue Skies; Smashup; Storm Warning; Dallas; Tokyo Joe; Chain Lightning; Island of Desire; The Star; Beachhead; I Died a Thousand Times; Lone Ranger; Burning Hills.
    (Died Aug 21, 1979).

HELDFOND, Susan: Act. b. LA. TV inc: Kingston Confidential; C O P; The Trial of Lee Harvey Oswald; Fast Friends. Films inc: Why Would I Lie?

HELLER, Paul M: Prod. b. NYC, Sep 25, 1927. Films inc: David & Lisa; The Eavesdropper; Once Upon a Tractor; Red Over Red; Secret Ceremony; Enter the Dragon; Black Belt Jones; Golden Needles; Hot Potato; Dirty Knight's Work; Crash; Those Cuckoo Crazy Animals; Outlaw Blues; Checkered Flag or Crash; The Pack; The Promise (& sp).

HELLMAN, Jerome: Prod. b. NYC, Sep 4, 1928. e. NYU. With William Morris and Jaffee Agencies before forming own agency, Ziegler, Hellman, and Ross. Switched to feature prod with The World of Henry Orient, 1964.
    Films inc: A Fine Madness; Midnight Cowboy (*Oscar*-1969); The Day of the Locust; Coming Home; Promises in the Dark (& dir).

HELLMAN, Lillian: Plywri. b. New Orleans, LA, Jun 20, 1905. e. NYU, Columbia U. Plays inc: The Children's Hour; Days to Come; The Little Foxes; Watch on the Rhine; The Searching Wind; Another Part of the Forest (& dir); Montserrat (& dir); Autumn Garden; Toys in the Attic; My Mother, My Father and Me.
    Films inc: These Three; Dead End; The Little Foxes; The North Star; The Searching Wind; The Chase.

HELLMAN, Monte: Dir-Wri-Prod. b. NYC, Jul 12, 1932. e. Stanford U, BA. Films inc: Beast From Haunted Cave; Back to Hell; Flight to Fury; The Shooting (& prod); Ride in the Whirlwind (& prod); Two-Lane Blacktop; Cockfighter; China 9-Liberty 37 (& prod).

HELLMAN, Richard: Prod. b. Bucharest, Oct 8, 1936. e. Oxford U, London Polytechnic. P, Dasar Film Inc, Montreal, exec vp Canafox Films Inc & Prospec Films Inc.
    Films inc: Secret War (asso prod); Surcouf; Killer Likes Candy; Montreal; Tiens Toi Bien; Le Petit Vient Vite; Les Corps Celestes; Il Etait Une Fois Dans L'est; Sweet Movie; Les Beaux Dimanches.
    TV inc: Nightkill.

HELLWIG, Klaus: Dist-Prod. b. Frankfurt, Germany, Jul 20, 1941. P Janus Film, 1965; P Action Films, Paris.
    Films inc: Your Turn, My Turn.

HELMOND, Katherine: Act. b. Galveston, TX, Jul 5. Films inc: Baby Blue Marine; The Hindenberg; Family Plot.
    TV inc: Wanted-The Sundance Woman; The Legend of Lizzie Borden; Little Ladies of the Night; Getting Married; Soap; Scout's Honor.
    Thea inc: Great God Brown; House of Blue Leaves. Pearl; Diary of a Teenage Hitchhiker.

HELPMAN, Sir Robert: Act-Dancer. b. Mount Gambler, Australia, Apr 9, 1909. e. Prince Alfred's Coll. Films inc: One of Our Aircraft is Missing; Henry V; The Red Shoes; Tales of Hoffman; 55 Days in Peking; The Quiller Memorandum; Chitty Chitty Bang Bang; Alice's Adventures in Wonderland; Don Quixote; Patrick.
    Thea inc: Hamlet; The Fairy Queen; He Who Gets Slapped; Camelot (dir); Duel of Angels; La Contessa; Conduct Unbecoming (dir); Peter Pan (dir).
    Chor numerous ballets; dir Dame Margot Fonteyn's World Tour.

HEMINGWAY, Margaux: Act. b. Portland, OR, Feb 1955. Grand D of the late Ernest Hemingway. Model. Films inc: Lipstick; Killer Fish.

HEMINGWAY, Mariel: Act. Sis of Margaux Hemingway. Films inc: Lipstick; Manhattan. TV inc: I Want To Keep My Baby.

HEMION, Dwight A: Dir-Prod. b. New Haven, CT, Mar 14, 1926. Asso dir ABC-TV. 1946-49; dir Tonight Show, NBC-TV, 1950-60; Perry Como Show, 1960-67; prod-dir Yorkshire Prods, 1967-70; prod-dir TV specials with ATV, London 1971-75; prod-dir Smith-Hemion Prods, 1975-present.
    TV inc: My Name Is Barbra (dir); Frank Sinatra: A Man and His Music (*Emmy*-prod-1966); The Sound of Burt Bacharach (*Emmy*-dir-1970); Singer presents Burt Bacharach (*Emmy*-prod-1971); Barbra Streisand and Other Musical Instruments (*Emmy*-dir-1974 & dir of year); Steve and Eydie-Our Love Is Here to Stay (*Emmy*-dir-1976); American Salutes Richard Rodgers-The Sound of His Music (*Emmy*-Dir-1977); Bette Midler-Ol Red Hair is Back (*Emmy*-prod-1978); Ben Vereen-His Roots (*Emmy*-dir-1978); Merry Christmas From the Grand Ole Opry House (1978); A Holiday Tribute to Radio City Music Hall (dir); Cheryl Ladd Special; Steve and Eydie Celebrate Irving Berlin (*Emmy*-exec prod-1979); Merry Christmas From the Grand Ole Opry House (1979); Kraft Salutes Disneyland's 25th Anniversary; Baryshnikov on Broadway (dir) (*Emmy*-1980); Ann Margret-Hollywood Movie Girls; Shirley MacLaine-Every Little Movement; Uptown-A Tribute to the Apollo Theatre; Linda In Wonderland.

HEMMINGS, David: Act. b. Guildford, Eng, 1941. Films inc: No Trees in the Street; The Wind of Change; Live It Up; Dateline Diamonds; Eye of the Devil; Blow Up; Camelot; The Charge of the Light Brigade; A Long Day's Dying; Only When I Larf; Barbarella; Alfred the Great; The Walking Stick; Fragment of Fear; The Love Machine; Running Scared; The Squeeze; Dripping Deep Red; Islands in the Stream; Disappearance (& prod); Crossed Swords; Power Play (& co-prod); Murder by Decree; Just a Gigolo (dir); Thirst; Harlequin; Beyond Reasonable Doubt.

Thea inc: Dylan Thomas in Adventures in the Skin Trade.
TV inc: Auto Stop; The Big Toe; Out of the Unknown.

HEMMINGS, Peter Williams: Exec. b. London, Apr 10, 1934. e. Cambridge U. 1959-65, Repertory & Planning Mgr Sadlers Wells Opera; gen administrator Scottish Opera, 1962-77; gm The Australian Opera since 1977.

HEMPHILL, Shirley: Act. b. Asheville, NC, Jul 1. TV inc: Rich Man, Poor Man, Book II; Richard Pryor Special; What's Happening; One in a Million.

HEMSLEY, Sherman: Act. b. Philadelphia, Feb 1, 1938. Films inc: Love at First Bite.
TV inc: All in the Family; The Jeffersons;
Thea inc: Purlie.

HENDERSON, Florence: Singer-Act. b. Dale, IN, Feb 14, 1934. e. AADA. Bway inc: Wish You Were Here; Oklahoma!; The Great Waltz; Fanny; The Sound of Music; The Girl Who Came to Supper; South Pacific (rev); Annie Get Your Gun (tour).
TV inc: Rodgers and Hammerstein Anniversary Show; The Gershwin Years; Huckleberry Finn; Little Women; The Brady Bunch.
Films inc: Song of Norway.

HENDERSON, Skitch (Lyle Henderson): Orch Ldr. b. Halstad, MN, 1918. e. U of CA. TV inc: Steve Allen Show; Tonight Show.

HENDLER, Lauri: Act. b. Ft Belvoir, VA, Apr 22, 1965. Appeared on juvenile news program KRON-TV, San Francisco. TV inc: It Isn't Easy Being a Teenage Millionaire; The Grass is Always Greener Over the Septic Tank; Little Lulu Goes to Camp; The Big Hex of Little Lulu; Three's Company; The Child Stealer; You Can't Keep A Horse In The Garage (host); A New Kind of Family; The Promise of Love.

HENDRIX, Wanda: Act. b. Jacksonville, FL, Nov 3, 1928. Films inc: Ride the Pink Horse; Miss Tatlock's Millions; Prince of Foxes; Captain Carey, USA; The Highwayman; The Last Posse; The Black Dakotas; Johnny Cool; Stage to Thunder Rock.

HENEKER, David: Comp-Lyr. b. Southsea, England, Mar 31, 1906. e. Wellington Coll & Royal Military College. Thea inc: Expresso Bongo; Make Me An Offer; Irma La Douce (adapt); The Art of Living; Half a Sixpence; Charlie Girl; Jorrock; Phil the Fluter; Popkiss.
Films inc: Half a Sixpence; The Two Faces of Dr Jekyll; I've Got a Horse.

HENNER, Marilu: Act. b. Chicago, Apr 6. e. U of Chicago. Films inc: Between the Lines; Blood Brothers.
TV inc: The Paper Chase; Off-Campus; Seventh Avenue; Leonard; Like Father, Like Daughter; Taxi.
Thea inc: Grease; Over Here; Pal Joey (rev).

HENNING, Doug: Act. b. Winnipeg, Canada, May 3, 1947. Toured colleges with lectures, demos entitled Illusion and Reality; also toured major US cities with magic show. Bway in The Magic Show; created stage illusions for rock band Earth, Wind and Fire's 1978 touring show.
TV inc: Doug Henning's World of Magic (Emmy-1976); The Crystal Gayle Special; The Osmond Family Christmas Show.

HENNING, Paul: Prod-Wri. b. Independence, MO, Sep 16, 1911. e. Kansas City School of Law. Started as radio wri for Rudy Vallee, Fibber McGee and Molly, Joe E Brown, Burns and Allen.
TV inc: (created, wrote & prod) The Beverly Hillbillies; Petticoat Junction; Bob Cummings Show; exec prod Green Acres.
Films inc: Lover Come Back; Bedtime Story.

HENREID, Paul: Act-Dir. b. Trieste, Italy, 1908. On stage, in films Vienna, London, before U.S.
Films inc: Joan of Paris; Now Voyager; Casablanca; Of Human Bondage; Devotion; Deception; Between Two Worlds; Song of Love; Stolen Face; Man in Hiding; Pirates of Tripoli; Holiday for Lovers; Madwoman of Chaillot; Colors of Love; Exorcist II;
TV inc: (dir) Bracken's World; The Man And The City.

HENRY, Buck (nee Zuckerman): Wri. b. 1930. Films inc: Troublemaker; The Graduate; Candy; Catch 22; The Owl and the Pussycat; What's Up Doc?; The Day of the Dolphin; The Man Who Fell To Earth; Heaven Can Wait (Act, Co-Sp, Co-Dir) Old Boyfriends (act); Gloria (act); First Family (wri-dir-act).
TV inc: Get Smart (Emmy-wri-1967).

HENSHAW, Jere C: Exec. b. Kansas City, MO, Sep 7, 1932. e. UCLA, BA. Started with Col 1954 in mail room; successively wardrobe dept stock clerk, casting clerk, asst casting dir; in 1956 exec in chg casting, 1959 vp-exec in chg talent & casting, Revue Prodns; 1962 vp-exec in chg talent & casting U-TV; 1964, vp-exec in chg talent & casting U; 1966, vp-exec in chg crea aff for World Premiere films for tv U-TV; 1967, vp chg crea aff Cinema Center Films; 1968, vp in chg wldwide prodn theatrical and tv film; 1972 vp crea aff Fox; 1973, vp chg wldwde prodn Fox; 1975, vp for prodn, U; 1977 sr vp chg wldwde theatrical prodn; 1980, exec vp in chg wldwde prodn Polygram Group.

HENSLEY, Pamela: Act. b. LA, Oct 3, 1950. e. RADA. TV inc: Owen Marshall, Counselor at Law; Toma; Marcus Welby, M.D.; Ironsides; The Rebels; Buck Rogers In the 25th Century.
Films inc: Doc Savage; Rollerball; The Nude Bomb.

HENSON, Jim: Puppeteer-Prod. b. Greenville, MS, Sep 24, 1936. e. U MD, BA. Created the Muppetts, 1954.
TV inc: Sesame Street (Emmys-childrens pgm-1974, 1976); The Muppet Show (Emmys-prod & perf-1978); Emmet Otter's Jug Band Christmas.
Films inc: The Time Piece (short); The Muppet Movie.

HEPBURN, Audrey: Act. b. Brussels, May 4, 1929. On London stage. Screen debut, Laughter in Paradise.
Bway inc: Ondine (Tony-1954); Gigi. Special Tony 1968.
Films inc: Laughter in Paradise; Roman Holiday (Oscar-1958); One Wild Oat; Lavender Hill Mob; Sabrina; War and Peace; Funny Face; Love in the Afternoon; The Nun's Story; Breakfast at Tiffany's; Charade; My Fair Lady; Wait Until Dark; Robin and Marian; Sidney Sheldon's Bloodline.
TV inc: Producers Showcase; Mayerling.

HEPBURN, Katharine: Act. b. Hartford, CT, Nov 9, 1909. e. Bryn Mawr Coll. Films inc: A Bill of Divorcement; Morning Glory (Oscar-1932-33); Little Women; Spitfire; The Little Minister; Mary of Scotland; Stage Door; Bringing Up Baby; Holiday; The Philadelphia Story; Woman of the Year; Keeper of the Flame; Dragon Seed; Sea of Grass; State of the Union; Adam's Rib; The African Queen; Pat and Mike; Summertime; The Rainmaker; Desk Set; Suddenly Last Summer; Long Day's Journey Into Night; Guess Who's Coming to Dinner (Oscar-1967); The Lion in Winter (Oscar-1968); The Madwoman of Chaillot; A Delicate Balance; Rooster Cogburn; Olly, Olly, Oxen Free.
Bway inc: Night Hostess; The Lake; Jane Eyre; The Philadelphia Story; Without Love; The Millionairess; Antony and Cleopatra; Coco; A Matter of Gravity.
TV inc: Love Among the Ruins (Emmy-1975); The Corn Is Green.

HERBERT, Gregory: Saxaphonist. b. Philadelphia, May 19, 1947. See Blood, Sweat & Tears.

HEREFORD, Kathryn: Act-Prod. b. Campbell, VA. W of Pandro Berman. Films inc: (prod or asso prod) Something of Value; Jailhouse Rock; Brothers Karamzov; The Reluctant Debutante; All the Fine Young Cannibals; Key Witness; Butterfield 8; Sweet Bird of Youth; The Prize; Honeymoon Hotel; Patch of Blue; Justine.

HERLIE, Eileen (nee Herlihy): Act. b. Glasgow, Scotland, Mar 8, 1920. Films inc: Hungry Hill; Hamlet; The Angel with the Trumpet; The Story of Gilbert and Sullivan; Isn't Life Wonderful; For Better, For Worse; She Didn't Say No; Freud; The Seagull.

Thea inc: Take Me Along; All American; Hamlet; Halfway Up the Tree; Who's Afraid of Virginia Woolf?; Crown Matrimonial; The Great Sebastians.

HERMAN, Jerry: Comp-Lyr. b. NYC, Jul 10, 1933. e. Parsons School of Design, U of Miami, AB. Bway inc: I Feel Wonderful; Nightcap; Parade; Milk and Honey; Madame Aphrodite; Hello, Dolly! (*Tony*-comp-1964); Mame; Dear World; Mack and Mabel; Grand Tour.

(*Grammys*-(2)-song of the year-1964; cast album-1966).

HERMAN, Kenn R: Dir. b. Detroit, Jul 2, 1930. e. MI State U. TV inc: General Hospital (1961-1978); Days of Our Lives.

HERMAN, Norman T: Prod-Dir. b. Newark, NJ, Feb 10, 1924. e. Rutgers U BA. (Prod), Sierra Stranger; Crime Beneath the Seas; Hot Rod Rumble; Hot Rod Girl; Rolling Thunder; Dirty Mary, Crazy Larry; Legend of Hill House. (Prod-dir), Tokyo After Dark; Mondo Teeno (Co-prod), Killers Three; Bunny O'Hare; Angel Unchained; Bloody Mama; Dillinger (Wri only); In God We Trust (exec prod).

TV inc: (wri) Lancer; Adam 12; Invaders; You Are the Judge; Hannibal Cobb; Iron Horse.

HERMAN, Pinky: Sngwri. b. NYC, Dec 23, 1905. Songs inc: Boom Ta Ra Ra; It Must Be LUV; Manhattan Merry Go Round; If I Had A Million Dollars.

HERMAN, Woody: Band Ldr. b. Milwaukee, WI, May 16, 1913. e. Marquette U. Played clarinet, sax with dance bands; formed own orch appearing in hotels, theatres, ballrooms, toured Europe. Films inc: What's Cookin'?; Winter Time; Sensations of 1945; Earl Carroll's Vanities.

(*Grammys*-(3)-jazz perf large group-1963; jazz perf-big band-1973, 1974).

HEROUX, Claude: Prod. b. Montreal, Jan 26, 1942. e. U of Montreal. Films inc: Valerie; L'Initiation; L'Amour Humain; Un enfant comme les autres; J'ai mon voyage; Je t'aime; Echoes of a Summer; Jacques Brel Is Alive and Well and Living in Paris; Breaking Point; Born for Hell; Angela; The Uncanny; In Praise of Older Women; The Brood; City on Fire; Hog Wild. Named Prod VP Film Plan International, Montreal, 1979.

HERRMANN, Edward: Act. b. Washington, DC, Jul 31, 1943. e. Bucknell U. Films inc: The Paper Chase; The Day of the Dolphin; The Great Gatsby; The Great Waldo Pepper; The Betsy; The North Avenue Irregulars; Brass Target; Take Down.

TV inc: Beacon Hill; Eleanor and Franklin; Eleanor and Franklin-The White House Years; The Lou Gehrig Story; Portrait of a Stripper; The Sorrows of Gin; Freedom Road.

Bway inc: Mrs. Warren's Profession (*Tony*-1976); The Philadelphia Story.

HERSHEY, Barbara (nee Hertzstein; also known as Barbara Seagull): Act. b. LA, Feb 5, 1948. Films inc: With Six You Get Eggroll; Last Summer; The Liberation of L B Jones; The Pursuit of Happiness; The Baby Maker; Boxcar Bertha; Diamonds; The Last Hard Men; The Stunt Man.

TV inc: The Monroes; From Here To Eternity-The War Years; A Man Called Intrepid; Angel on My Shoulder.

HERSKOVITZ, Arthur M: Exec. b. Mukden, China, Nov 28, 1920. e. CCNY. Joined RKO scenario dept, 1939; m RKO Radio Pictures of Peru, 1955; Warner Bros. Peru, 1958-64; MGM, Panama, 1965-67; MGM rep in Japan, 1968; Far East Supv, 1970; joined National General Pictures, 1973, as foreign sls m; in 1974 appt dir of sls, JAD Films International.

HERTZ, William F: Exec. b. Wishek, ND, Dec 5, 1923. e. U of MN. Thea Mgr, Fox West Coast Theatres, 1946; LA 1st-run district Mgr, National General Corp, 1965; Pacific Coast Div Mgr NGC, 1967; vp & So Pac Div M, NGC, 1971; now dir thea ops, Mann Theatres.

HERZOG, Werner: Dir. b. Germany, 1942. Films inc: Signs of Life; Even Dwarfs Started Small; Fata Morgana; The Land of Silence Darkness; Aguirre-Wrath of God; Soufriere; Heart of Glass; Stroszek; Kaspar Hauser; Nosferatu; Woyzeck (& sp).

HESSEMAN, Howard: Act. b. Salem, OR, Feb 27, 1940. With the San Francisco group The Committee. Films inc: Petulia; Billy Jack; Steelyard Blues; Shampoo; The Sunshine Boys; Jackson County Jail; The Big Bus; The Other Side of Midnight; Silent Movie.

TV inc: Mary Hartman, Mary Hartman; Fernwood 2night; Hustling; The Life and Times of Sen. Joseph McCarthy; The Amazing Howard Hughes; The TV TV Show; Tarantulas--The Deadly Cargo; The Ghost on Flight 401; WKRP in Cincinnati; John Ritter, Being of Sound Mind and Body; The Great American Traffic Jam; Skyward; 30 Years of TV Comedy's Greatest Hits.

HESSLER, Gordon: Prod-Dir. b. Berlin, 1930. Films inc: The Last Shot You Hear; The Oblong Box (& prod); Scream and Scream Again; Cry of the Banshee (& prod); Murders in the Rue Morgue (& prod); Embassy; Sinbad's Golden Voyage; Medusa; Next Week Rio; Puzzle.

TV inc: Alfred Hitchcock Presents; Alfred Hitchcock Hour; Run For Your Life; Bob Hope Chrysler Show; Lucas Tanner; Night Stalker; Switch; Kung Fu; Hawaii Five-O; The Secret War of Jackie's Girls.

HESTON, Charlton: Act. b. Evanston, IL, Oct 4, 1924. e. Northwestern U Films inc: Dark City; The Greatest Show on Earth; The Savage; Ruby Gentry; The President's Lady; Arrowhead; The Naked Jungle; Far Horizons; Private War of Major Benson; Lucy Gallant; The Ten Commandments; Three Violent People; Touch of Evil; The Big Country; Ben Hur (*Oscar*-1959); The Wreck of the Mary Deare; El Cid; The Pigeon That Took Rome; 55 Days at Peking; The Greatest Story Ever Told; The Agony and the Ecstasy; The War Lord; Khartoum; Will Penny; Planet of the Apes; Beneath the Planet of the Apes; Julius Caesar; The Omega Man; Antony and Cleopatra; Skyjacked; Call of the Wild; Soylent Green; Airport 1975; Earthquake; The Four Musketeers; The Last Hard Men; Midway; Two Minute Warning; Crossed Swords; Gray Lady Down; The Mountain Men; The Awakening.

Bway inc: Antony and Cleopatra; Leaf and Bough; Cockadoodle Doo; Design for a Stained Glass Window.

TV inc: Macbeth; The Taming of the Shrew; Of Human Bondage; Julius Caesar; A Man For All Seasons.

Jean Hersholt Humanitarian Award, 1977.

HEYES, Doug: Act. b. LA, May 22, 1956. TV inc: The Barbary Coast; City of Angels; Captains and the Kings; Aspen; The Hardy Boys; The French Atlantic Affair (dir-wri).

HEYMAN, John: Prod. b. Leipzig, Germany, 1933. Publicist, later pers mgr for stars. Films inc: Boom; Privilege; Jesus.

HEYWARD, Louis M: Exec. b. NYC, Jun 29, 1920. e. NYU, Brooklyn Law School. Radio writer, CBS: Garry Moore Show; Ernie Kovacs Show; co-owner Heyward-Wilkes Industrial Film Co.; vp prodn AIP; m-dir AIP, London; Hanna-Barbera Prods. 1973, vp live prodn, asst to pres.

Films inc: Chomps; Dr. Phibes; Dr. Phibes Rises Again; Wuthering Heights (remake); Scream and Scream Again.

TV inc: (prod over 5000 shows): Bell Telephone Hour; Dick Clark Show; The Gathering; Beasts Are in the Street; Kiss Meets Phantom of the Park.

HEYWOOD, Anne (Violet Pretty): Act. b. Eng, 1931. W of Raymond Stross. Films inc: Find the Lady; Checkpoint; Dangerous Exile; The Depraved; Violent Playground; Floods of Fear; Upstairs and Downstairs; A Terrible Beauty; Petticoat Pirates; Stork Talk; Vengeance; Ninety Degrees in the Shade; The Fox; The Chairman; The Midas Run; I Want What I Want; Trader Horn; The Nun and the Devil; The Most Dangerous Man in the World; And Presumed Dead. Good Luck Miss Wyckoff.

HIBBLER, Al: Act. b. Little Rock, AR, Aug 16, 1915. Born blind. Vocalist with Duke Ellington, 1943-51. Left Ellington for career as solo recording artist.

HICKMAN, Darryl: Act-TV Prod. b. Hollywood, Jul 28, 1931. On screen since 1939. Films inc: The Star Maker; The Grapes of Wrath; Joe Smith, American; Keeper of the Flame; Captain Eddie; Leave Her to Heaven; Destination Gobi; Tea and Sympathy; Network.
TV inc: Love of Life (Exec prod).

HICKS, Catherine: Act. b. Scottsdale, AZ, Aug 6, 1951. e. Notre Dame, BA Bway inc: Tribute. TV inc: Ryan's Hope; Sparrow; The Bad News Bears; Marilyn--the Untold Story.

HICKSON, Joan: Act. b. Northampton, England, Aug 5, 1906. e. RADA. Thea inc: (London) A Damsel in Distress; Baa Baa Black Sheep; The Middle Watch; Leave it to Psmith; Crime at the Blossoms; Crime on the Hill; Distinguished Gathering; Murder Gang; Festival Time; The Gusher; It's A Wise Child; The Proposal; See How They Run; Appointment With Death; The Guinea Pig; Foxhole in the Parlor; Rain Before Seven; The Gay Dog; Man Alive!; A Day in the Death of Joe Egg; The Card; The Freeway; Blithe Spirit. (Bway) A Day in the Death of Joe Egg; Bedroom Farce *(Tony*-supp-1979).
Films inc: Widow's Might; Love From a Stranger; I See a Dark Stranger; The Guinea Pig; Seven Days to Noon; The Card; The Man Who Never Was; Happy Is The Bride; The 39 Steps; A Day in the Death of Joe Egg; Theatre of Blood; Yanks.
TV inc: Sinister Street; Bachelor Father.

HIELSCHER, Leo Arthur: Exec. b. Eumundi, Queensland, Australia, Oct 1, 1926. Commissioner, Queensland Film Corp.

HIGGINS, Colin: Wri-Dir. Former actor. Films inc: Harold and Maude (wri); Silver Streak (wri); Foul Play; Nine to Five.

HIKEN, Gerald: Act-Dir. b. Milwaukee, WI, May 23, 1927. e. U of WI. Bway inc: The Lovers; Good Woman of Szetzuan; The Cave Dwellers; The Nervous Set; The Fighting Cock; The 49th Cousin; Gideon; Brecht on Brecht; Strider.
Films inc: Uncle Vanya; The Goddess; Invitation to a Gunfighter; Funnyman.

HILL, Arthur: Act. b. Melfort, Saskatchewan, Can, Aug 1, 1922. Bway: The Matchmaker; The Gang's All Here; A Death in the Family; All The Way Home; Who's Afraid of Virginia Woolf? *(Tony*-1963).
Films inc: The Deep Blue Sea; Harper; The Ugly American; Petulia; Don't Let The Angels Fall; The Chairman; Killer Elite; Futureworld; The Andromeda Strain; A Bridge Too Far; The Champ; The Glacier Fox; A Little Romance; Butch and Sundance-The Early Years.
TV inc: Owen Marshall; Death Be Not Proud; Hagen; The Ordeal of Dr. Mudd; Revenge of the Stepford Wives; The Return of Frank Cannon.

HILL, Benny (Alfred Hawthorn Hill): Act. b. Southampton, Eng, 1925. TV inc: The Service Show; Showcase; The Benny Hill Show; Midsummer Night's Dream.
Films inc: Who Done It?; Light Up the Sky; Those Magnificent Men in Their Flying Machines; Chitty Chitty Bang Bang.

HILL, Debra: Prod. Films inc: Halloween (& co-wri); The Fog (& co-wri).

HILL, George Roy: Prod-Dir. b. Minneapolis, MS, Dec 20, 1922. e. Yale U, BA, Trinity Coll, Dublin. Films inc: Period of Adjustment; Toys in the Attic; The World of Henry Orient; Hawaii; Thoroughly Modern Millie; Butch Cassidy and the Sundance Kid; Slaughterhouse Five; The Sting *(Oscar*-1973); The Great Waldo Pepper; Slap Shot; A Little Romance.
Bway inc: Look Homeward Angel; The Gang's All Here; Greenwillow; Period of Adjustment; Moon on a Rainbow Shawl; Henry, Sweet, Henry.
TV inc: A Night to Remember; Helen Morgan; Child of Our Time; Judgment at Nuremberg.

HILL, Pamela: (nee Abel): Exec. b. Winchester, IN, Aug 18, 1938. e. Bennington Coll. Researcher, asso prod, dir NBC News, 1965-1973; dir White Paper Series, 1969-1972; prod, Edwin Newman's Comment, 1972; prod ABC News Closeup doc series, 1973-1978; vp ABC News, 1979. TV inc: Fire! *(Emmys*-prod & dir-1974); Nobody's Children; Escape From Justice-Nazi War Criminals in the U.S.; This Shattered Land; To Die For Ireland; Lights, Camera; Can't It Be Anyone Else; Death In A Southwest Prison; The Apocalypse Game; The Shattered Badge; A Matter of Survival.

HILL, Sandy: Newscaster. b. Centralia, WA. e. U of WA. One of first women to co-anchor early evening news in the country (Channel 7, LA). In April 1977, joined ABC TV's Good Morning America.

HILL, Steven (Solomon Berg): Act. b. Seattle, WA. Studied with Lee Strasberg; Elia Kazan; Joshua Logan. Bway inc: Mister Roberts; The Lady from the Sea; The Country Girl.
Films inc: Lady Without a Passport; The Goddess; A Child Is Waiting; The Slender Thread; It's My Turn.
TV inc: Mission Impossible; King.

HILL, Terrence (Mario Girotti): Act. b. Venice, Italy, Mar 1941. Screen debut age 12, Holiday for Gangsters.
Films inc: My Name is Nobody; They Call Me Trinity; Trinity Is Still My Name; Boot Hill; Ace High; Mr Billion; March or Die.

HILL, Walter: Wri-Dir. b. Long Beach, CA, Jan 10, 1942. e. MI State U. Films inc: Hickey & Boggs; The Getaway; The Thief Who Came to Dinner; The Mackintosh Man; The Drowning Pool; Hard Times (& dir); The Driver (& dir); The Warriors (& dir); Alien (prod); The Long Riders (dir).

HILLAIRE, Marcel: Act. b. Cologne, Germany, Apr 23, 1908. Films inc: Sabrina; Seven Thieves; The Honeymoon Machine; The Wheeler Dealers; A Very Special Favor; Made in Paris.
TV inc: Adventures in Paradise; Beggerman, Thief.

HILLER, Arthur: Dir. b. Edmonton, Canada, Nov 22, 1923. Films inc: The Careless Years; The Americanization of Emily; Tobruk; The Tiger Makes Out; Poppi; The Out of Towners; Love Story; Plaza Suite; Hospital; Man of La Mancha; WC Fields and Me; Man in the Glass Booth; Silver Streak; Nightwing; The In-Laws.
TV inc: Matinee Theatre; Climax; Playhouse 90; Alfred Hitchcock Presents; Naked City; Massacre at Sand Creek.

HILLER, Wendy: Act. b. Bramhall, Cheshire, Eng, Aug 15, 1912. Performed with Manchester Repertory Theatre. London debut, Love on the Dole, 1935. Screen debut, Lancashire Luck, 1937.
Films inc: Pygmalion; Major Barbara; Something of Value; Separate Tables *(Oscar*-supp-1958); Sons and Lovers; Toys in the Attic; A Man for All Seasons; Murder on the Orient Express; Voyage of the Damned; The Cat and The Canary; The Elephant Man.
Thea inc: Wings of the Dove; Sacred Flame; Crown Matrimonial; John Gabriel Borkman; Lies; Waters of the Moon.
TV inc: The Curse of King Tut's Tomb.

HILLERMAN, John: Act. b. Denison, TX, Dec 30, 1932. e. U of TX. Films inc: Paper Moon; The Day of the Locust; Chinatown; Audrey Rose; Sunburn.
TV inc: Ellery Queen; The Law; The Betty White Show; Beane's of Boston; Marathon; Battles-The Murder That Wouldn't Die; Don't Eat the Snow In Hawaii (Magnum P.I. pilot).

HILO HATTIE (Clara Haili): Act. b. Honolulu, HI, 1901. Hula dancer and teacher; performed at Royal Hawaiian Hotel. Films inc: Song of the Islands. TV inc: Harry Owens Show; Arthur Godfrey Show; retired 1969.
Died Dec 12, 1979)

HINCK, Jon W: Dist. b. CA, Jan 1954. e. U of PA, BA. Northwest Diversified Entertainment, 1977; Cinemaworld Releasing, 1978.

HINES, Earl Kenneth (Fatha): Comp-Cond. b. Duquesne, PA, Dec 28, 1905. Formed own band, 1928; recorded with Louis Armstrong; toured Europe; performed at White House 1969, 1976,1977.

HINGLE, Pat: Act. b. Denver, CO, Jul 19, 1923. e. U of TX. Stage debut, 1950, Johnny Belinda.
Films inc: On the Waterfront; The Strange One; No Down Payment; Splendor in the Grass; The Ugly American; Invitation to a Gunfighter; Nevada Smith; Hang 'Em High; Bloody Mama; Norwood; The Carey Treatment; One Little Indian; Run Wild; Norma Rae; When You Comin' Back Red Ryder;
Bway inc: Man for all Seasons; A Girl Could Get Lucky; The Odd Couple; Johnny No-Trump; A Grave Undertaking; A Life.
TV Inc: Elvis; Stone; Disaster on the Coastliner; Wild Times.

HINKLE, Robert: Act-Dir-Prod. b. Brownfield, TX, Jul 25, 1930. Rodeo performer. Films inc: The First Texan; Dakota Incident; Gun The Man Down; Ole Rex; Stuntman; Texas Long Horns; Country Music (prod-dir); Guns of a Stranger (prod-dir).
TV inc: Test Pilot; Dial 111; Juvenile Squad; Giant; Opposite Sex.

HIRSCH, Judd: Act. b. NYC, Mar 15. e. CCNY, Cooper Union Coll. Films inc: Serpico; King of the Gypsies; Ordinary People.
TV inc: The Law; Delvecchio; Valentino; Fear on Trial; Like Father, Like Daughter; Taxi; Sooner or Later; The Halloween That Almost Wasn't; Marriage is Alive and Well.
Bway inc: The Hot L Baltimore; Knock Knock; Chapter Two; Talley's Folly.

HIRSCHFELD, Gerald: Cin. b. NYC, Apr 25, 1921. e. Columbia U. Films inc: Fail Safe; The Incident; Goodbye Columbus; Last Summer; Cotton Comes to Harlem; Diary of a Mad Housewife; Child's Play; Summer Wishes, Winter Dreams; Young Frankenstein; Two-Minute Warning; The Car; The World's Greatest Lover; The Bell Jar; Americathon; Why Would I Lie?

HIRSCHFIELD, Alan J: Exec. b. Oklahoma City, OK, Oct 10, 1935. e. U of OK; Harvard Business School, MA. 1959 joined Allen & Co., investment bankers, later becoming vp; 1966 financial vp WB-Seven Arts; 1970, vp American Diversified Enterprises, investment firm; 1973 p, CEO Columbia Pictures Industries; July 1978, fired in furore over his handling of David Begelman situation; 1979 consultant to Warner Communications; Oct 1979 vice chmn, COO Fox.

HIRSCHHORN, Joel: Sngwri. Writes in collaboration with Al Kasha.
Songs inc: My Empty Arms; I'm Comin' On Back To You; Let's Start All Over Again; Wake Up; Your Time Hasn't Come Yet Baby; Will You Be Staying After Sunday?; One More Mountain To Climb; The Subject Was Roses; Living Is Dying Without You; The Morning After (Oscar-1972); We May Never Love Like This Again (Oscar-1974); Candle on the Water; I'd Like To Be You For a Day; May the Best Man Win; Mississippi Magic; Pass A Little Love Around.

HIRSCHMAN, Herbert: Prod-Dir. b. NYC, Apr 13. e. U of MI, BA, Yale U, MFA. Films inc: (prod.): Halls of Anger; They Call Me Mr. Tibbs.
Thea inc: (London) (dir) A Thousand Clowns.
TV inc: (dir) Omnibus; Starlight Theatre; Mr. I-Magination; Steve Allen Show; Celebrity Time; What's My Line; The Defenders; For the People; Iron Horse; Felony Squad. (Prod. & dir.): The Web; Alcoa Hour; Goodyear Playhouse; Studio One; Playhouse 90; Perry Mason; Dr. Kildare; Twilight Zone; Wackiest Ship in the Army; Men From Shiloh; Young Lawyers; The Bold Ones; Tell Me Where It Hurts; Returning Home; Eric; The Zoo Gang; The Amazing Howard Hughes; Morris Bird III; Flesh and Blood; And Baby Makes Six; The Scarlet Letter. (Exec prod): Iron Horse; Planet of the Apes.

HIRT, Al: Act. b. New Orleans, LA, Nov 7, 1922. e. Cincinnati Conservatory of Music. Played with Tommy and Jimmy Dorsey bands, Ray McKinley, Horace Heidt; worked niteries, TV.
Films inc: World By Night; Rome Adventure.
(Grammy-orch perf-1963).

HITCHCOCK, Sir Alfred: Dir. b. Leytonstone, Essex, Eng, Aug 13, 1899. Directorial debut 1925, The Pleasure Garden. Films inc: The Lodger; Easy Virtue; The Ring; The Farmer's Wife; Blackmail; Juno and the Paycock; Murder; Number Seventeen; The Man Who Knew Too Much; The Thirty-Nine Steps; Sabotage; The Lady Vanishes; Rebecca; Foreign Correspondent; Suspicion; Saboteur; Shadow of a Doubt; Lifeboat; Spellbound; Notorious; The Paradine Case; Stage Fright; Strangers on a Train; Dial M for Murder; Rear Window; To Catch a Thief; The Trouble with Harry; Vertigo; North by Northwest; Psycho; The Birds; Marnie; Torn Curtain; Topaz; Frenzy; Family Plot.
Irving Thalberg Award, 1967.
TV inc: Alfred Hitchcock Presents.
Knighted Jan. 1, 1980.
(Died April 29, 1980).

HO, Don: Singer-Act. b. Oahu, HI, Aug 13, 1930. Nightclubs. TV inc: The Don Ho Show.

HOBERMAN, Ben: Exec. b. 1923. Started as anncr-slsm WMFG, Hibbing, MN. Enlisted as private in WW2, won field commission as lieutenant, in chg American Forces Network stations France, England. 1946, asst gm WELI, New Haven, CT; 1948, gm WDET (FM), Detroit, MI; 1950 joined WXYZ-TV Detroit (ABC O&O) as first fulltime slsmn; 1958 gm WABC (AM) (ABC flagship NY); 1960 gm KABC-AM (ABC O&O); 1961, vp ABC; 1980, P ABC Radio net.

HOBIN, Bill: Prod-Dir. b. Evanston, IL, Nov 12, 1923. e. USC. TV inc: Garroway at Large; Assignment Manhattan; Fred Waring Show; Andy Williams Show; Pat Boone; The Bell Telephone Hour; Sing Along with Mitch; Meredith Wilson Special; Red Skelton Hour; The Bill Cosby Special; The Tim Conway Comedy Hour; The CBS Newcomers series; An Evening with My Three Sons; Fred Astaire Special; A Touch of Grace; Bobby Goldsboro Show; Welcome Back Kotter; Bert Convy Show; George Burns Special; Three's Company.

HOCH, Winton C: Cin. b. IA, 1907. Originally a research physicist, joined Technicolor 1934 to work on development of three-color process; with US Naval Photographic Science Lab During WW 2, became cin after retiring from Navy.
Films inc: So Dear to My Heart; Tulsa; Joan of Arc (Oscar-1948); She Wore a Yellow Ribbon (Oscar-1949); Halls of Montezuma; Jet Pilot; The Quiet Man (Oscar-1952); Darby O'Gill and the Little People; The Lost World; The Searchers; Five Weeks in a Balloon; Mr. Roberts; Robinson Crusoe on Mars; The Green Berets. TV inc: Voyage to the Bottom of the Sea (Emmy-1966); Time Tunnel.
(Died March 20, 1979).

HODGES, Mike: Dir. TV inc: Sunday Break; World in Action; Tempo; Suspect; Rumour.
Films inc: Get Carter; The Terminal Man; Flash Gordon.

HOFFMAN, Dustin: Act. b. LA, Aug 8, 1934. e. Santa Monica City Coll, Pasadena Playhouse. Films inc: The Graduate; Midnight Cowboy; John and Mary; Little Big Man; Who is Harry Kellerman and Why Is He Saying those Terrible Things about Me?; Straw Dogs; Alfredo, Alfredo; Papillon; Lenny; All the President's Men; Marathon Man; Straight Time; Agatha; Kramer vs Kramer (Oscar-1979).
Bway inc: A Cook for Mr General; Harry, Noon and Night; Journey of the Fifth Horse; Eh?; Jimmie Shine; All Over Town (dir).
TV inc: To Be An Actor.

HOFFMAN, Joseph: Wri-Prod. b. NYC, Feb 20, 1909. e. UCLA. Started as newspaperman, radio wri. TV prod. for Screen Gems, Warner Bros., Four Star; later TV and screen freelance wri.
Films inc: China Sky; Don't Trust Your Husband; Gung Ho; And Baby Makes Three; At Sword's Point; Against All Flags; No Room for the Groom; Yankee Pasha; Tall Man Riding; Live a Little; How to Make Love and Like It; Sex and the Single Girl.
TV (prod) inc: Ford Theatre; Celebrity Theatre; Damon Runyon Theatre; Colt 45.

HOFFMAN, Ross A: Cin (ret). b. Mar 30, 1905. Specialized in special photography. Films inc: Island Earth; Incredible Shrinking Man; The Brass Bottle; Pillow Talk; Earthquake. With U 50 years.

HOFSISS, Jack: Dir. b. Brooklyn, NY, Sep 28, 1950. e. Georgetown. Dir for NY Shakespeare Festival 1976; ANTA.
Bway inc: The Elephant Man (Tony-1979).
TV inc: For Richer for Poorer; The Sorrows of Gin; The Oldest Living Graduate.

HOLBROOK, Hal: Act. b. Cleveland, OH, Feb 17, 1925. Bway debut 1959, one-man show, Mark Twain Tonight!; then toured US, Europe, Saudi Arabia. Screen debut, 1966, The Group.
Films inc: Wild in the Streets; The People Next Door; The Great White Hope; They Only Kill Their Masters; Magnum Force; The Girl from Petrovka; All the President's Men; Midway; Julia; Capricorn One; Natural Enemies; The Fog.
TV inc: Mark Twain Tonight!; A Clear and Present Danger; The Glass Menagerie; The Senator (Emmy-1970); Pueblo (Emmy-1974); Legend of the Golden Gun; Sandburg's Lincoln (Emmy-1976); When Hell Was In Session; Off The Minnesota Strip; Omnibus (host); The Kidnapping of the President.
Bway inc: The Apple Tree; I Never Sang For My Father; Man of La Mancha; Mark Twain Tonight (Tony-1966); Does a Tiger Wear a Necktie?.

HOLDEN, Gloria: Act. b. London, Sep 5, 1911. e. AADA. Films inc: Dracula's Daughter; The Life of Emile Zola; Test Pilot; A Child Is Born; The Corsican Brothers; Behind the Rising Sun; The Hucksters; Dream Wife; The Eddie Duchin Story; This Happy Feeling.

HOLDEN, William: Act. b. O'Fallon, IL, Apr 17, 1918. Films inc: Golden Boy; Those Were the Days; Our Town; Arizona; I Wanted Wings; The Remarkable Andrew; The Fleet's In; Deear Ruth; Rachel and the Stranger; Apartment for Peggy; Dear Wife; Miss Grant Takes Richmond; Blaze of Noon; Union Station; Sunset Boulevard; Born Yesterday; Force of Arms; Boots Malone; Stalag 17 (Oscar-1953); The Moon is Blue; Escape From Fort Bravo; Executive Suite; Sabrina; Bridges at Toko-Ri; Country Girl; Love is a Many-Splendored Thing; Picnic; Proud and Profane; Bridge on the River Kwai; The Horse Soldiers; The World of Suzie Wong; The Counterfeit Traitor; The Longest Day; Paris When it Sizzles; Alvarez Kelley; Casino Royale; Devil's Brigade; The Wild Bunch; The Revengers; Breezy; The Towering Inferno; Network; Damien--Omen 2; Fedora; When Time Ran Out; The Earthling.
TV inc: The Blue Knight (Emmy-1974); Mysteries of the Sea.

HOLDER, Geoffrey: Chor-Act-Dir. b. Trinidad, West Indies, Aug 1, 1930. e. Queens Royal Coll. Made US debut with own dance co in 1953; perf as solo dancer Metropolitan Opera in Aida & La Perichole, 1956-57 season; dramatic debut 1957, Waiting for Godot; toured with own dance co. Bway inc: I Got a Song (chor); The Wiz (chor & cos dsgn) (2 Tonys-1975); Timbuktu, (chor & cos dsgn) 1977.
Films inc: All Night Long; Everything You've Ever Wanted to Know About Sex but Were Afraid to Ask; Live and Let Die; The Gold Bug.

HOLLAND, Anthony: Dsgn. b. England, Jun 3, 1912. e. Manchester School of Art. Thea inc: The King and Mistress Shore; The Eagle Has Two Heads; Edward My Son; The Sleeping Clergyman; Life With Father; The Indifferent Shepherd; Traveller's Joy; People Like Us; The Philadelphia Story; The Cocktail Party; The Four Poster; The Seventh Veil; The Three Sisters; The Amorous Prawn; A Visit to a Small Planet; Miss Pell is Missing; Menage a Trois; Reluctant Peer; Hostile Witness; Wait Until Dark; Let's All Go Down to the Strand; The Jockey Club Stakes; Birds of Paradise; The Dame of Sark; The Last of Mrs Cheyney.
Ice shows inc: Robinson Crusoe; The Sleeping Beauty; Aladdin; The Babes in the Wood; Cinderella; Snow White; Around the World in 80 Days; Ali Baba and the 40 Thieves.

HOLLIDAY, Kene: Act. b. NYC, Jun 25. e. U of MD. TV inc: Burglar-Proofing; Carter Country. Thea inc: Streamers.

HOLLIDAY, Polly: Act. b. Jasper, AL, Jul 2. Films inc: All the President's Men; W W and the Dixie Dance Kings; Distance; The One and Only.
TV inc: The Silence; The 34th Star; Bernice Bobs Her Hair; Alice; You Can't Take It With You; Flo.

HOLLIMAN, Earl: Act. b. Delhi, LA, 1928. On stage in Camino Real; Streetcar Named Desire.
Films inc: Bridges of Toko-Ri; Giant; Gunfight at the OK Corral; Summer and Smoke; Good Luck Miss Wyckoff.
TV inc: The Dark Side of the Earth; Alexander; The Other Side of Dawn; Police Woman; The Solitary Man; Where The Ladies Go; The Real Rookies (narr).

HOLLOWAY, Stanley: Act. b. London, Oct 1, 1890. London stage debut in Kissing Time, 1919. Screen debut, 1921, in The Rotter. On Bway, London Stage in My Fair Lady, 1956-59.
Films inc: Hamlet; Snowbound; Passport to Pimlico; Lavender Hill Mob; The Beggar's Opera; An Alligator Named Daisy; Ten Little Indians; My Fair Lady; The Private Life of Sherlock Holmes; Run A Crooked Mile; Flight of the Doves; Journey into Fear; Target-Harry.

HOLLOWAY, Sterling: Act. b. Cedartown, GA, Jan 4, 1905. Films inc: Casey at the Bat; Alice in Wonderland; Life Begins at Forty; The Bluebird; A Walk in the Sun; The Beautiful Blonde from Bashful Bend; Shake, Rattle and Roll; Live a Little, Love a Little; The Aristocrats; Won Ton Ton, The Dog Who Saved Hollywood; Super Seal; Thunder and Lightning.
TV inc: The Life of Riley; Willy; The Baileys of Balboa.
(Grammy-childrens recording-1974).

HOLLY, Edwin E: Exec. b. Elizabethtown, TN, Oct 3, 1926. e. U of TN. P First Artists Production Co.

HOLM, Celeste: Act. b. NYC, Apr 29, 1919. On screen from 1946. Films inc: Three Little Girls in Blue; Gentlemen's Agreement (Oscar-supp-1947); Snake Pit; Chicken Every Sunday; All About Eve; Come to the Stable; Tom Sawyer; Bittersweet Love.
Bway inc: Time of Your Life; Return of the Vagabond; Oklahoma; Bloomer Girl; Candida; Habeas Corpus; Utter Glory of Morrissey Hall.
TV inc: Clearing House in the Wood; Play of the Week; Cinderella; Backstairs at the White House.

HOLM, Hanya: Chor-Dancer. b. Wurms-am-Rhein, Germany, circa 1900. e. Hoch Conservatory, Frankfurt; Dalcroze Institute; Wigman School of Dance, Dresden. Appeared in Max Reinhardt's The Miracle before joining Wigman company where she was a member of the original company and later chief instructor; formed own dance company, toured Europe; to U.S. 1931, founded the NY Wigman School which later became the Hanya Holm School; prodns include Trend; Metropolitan Daily; Tragic Exodus.
Bway inc: Ballet Ballads; Kiss Me, Kate (received first copyright for choreographic composition); The Insect Comedy; Blood Wedding; Out of This World; My Darlin' Aida; The Golden Apple; My Fair Lady; Anya.
Films inc: The Vagabond King.
TV inc: Pinocchio; Dinner With the President.

HOLM, Ian (Ian Holm Cuthbert): Act. b. Ilford, Essex, England, Sep 12, 1931. e. RADA. Thea inc: (London) Love Affair; Titus Andronicus; various roles with Royal Shakespeare Company; Ondine; Becket; The Cherry Orchard; The Homecoming; The Friends; A Bequest to the Nation; The Sea. (Bway) The Homecoming (Tony-supp-1967).
Films inc: A Midsummer Night's Dream; The Fixer; The Homecoming; Juggernaut; Shout at the Devil; Alien.
TV inc: Les Miserables; S.O.S. Titanic; All Quiet on the Western Front.

HOLT, Charlene: Act. TV inc: Faith For Today; The Hero. Films inc: Zig Zag; Eldorado; Man's Favorite Sport; Redline 7000; Melvin and Howard.

HOLTZ, Lou: Act. b. San Francisco, Apr 11, 1898. In vaude prior to WW1, played the Palace. On radio.
Bway inc: Scandals of 1919; Scandals of 1920; George White's Scandals; Tell Me More; Manhattan Mary; You Said It.
Films inc: Follow the Leader; Manhattan Mary.
(Died Sep 22, 1980).

HOLZER, Adela: Prod. Bway inc: (Voices) Dude; Bad Habits; Sherlock Holmes; All Over Town; Hair; The Ritz; Treemonisha (opera); Something Old, Something New.

HOME, William Douglas: Wri. b. Edinburgh, Scotland, Jun 3, 1912. e. Oxford. Plays inc: Great Possessions; Passing By; Now Barabbas; The Chiltern Hundreds; Up a Gum Tree; The Cigarette Girl; The Reluctant Peer; The Secretary Bird; A Friend In Need; The Grouse Moor Image; The Jockey Club Stakes; Lloyd George Knew My Father; The Dame of Sark; The Lord's Lieutenant; In The Red; Rolls Hyphen Royce; The Kingfisher; The Perch; The Eleventh Hour.

Films inc: Now Barrabas; The Chiltern Hundreds; The Colditz Story; The Reluctant Debutante.

HOMEIER, Skip: Act. b. Chicago, IL, Oct 5, 1930. e. UCLA. On radio as child actor; Bway in Tomorrow the World.

Films inc: Tomorrow The World; Boy's Ranch; Mickey; Arthur Takes Over; The Big Cat; The Gunfighter; Halls of Montezuma; The Black Widow; Cry Vengeance; The Captives; No Road Back; Decision at Durango; The Greatest.

TV inc: Playhouse 90; Kraft Theatre; Studio One; Overboard; Helter Skelter; The Wild Wild West Revisited.

HONEY, John: Prod-Dir-Wri. b. Tasmania, Australia, Jul 10, 1944. TV reporter, 1968-72; prod-wri-dir short films, 1972; exec prod TV series; 1978, prod-wri-dir Tasmanian Film Corp.

HOOKS, Kevin: Act. b. Philadephia, PA, Sep 19, 1958. S of Robert Hooks. TV inc: Just an Old Sweet Song; The Greatest Thing That Almost Happened; Friendly Fire; Backstairs at the White House; White Shadow; Can You Hear The Laughter?--The Story of Freddie Prinze.

Films inc: Sounder; Aaron and the Angels; A Hero Ain't Nothin' But A Sandwich; Take Down.

HOOKS, Robert: Act. b. Washington, DC, Apr 18, 1937. Films inc: Sweet Love, Bitter; Hurry Sundown.

TV inc: N Y P D; Crosscurrent; Trapped; Ceremonies In Dark Old Men; Backstairs at the White House; Hollow Image.

HOOL, Lance: Prod. b. Mexico City, May 11, 1948. Exec dir, Mexico Film International, 1977-78; ChmnB, Azteca Films, 1978-79.

Films inc: Survival Run; Wolf Lake.

HOPE, Bob: Perf. b. Eltham, Eng, May 29, 1903. Started in vaudeville.

Bway inc: Ballyhoo; Roberta; Ziegfeld Follies; Red Hot and Blue.

On screen from 1938 (after shorts made in 1934). Films inc: The Big Broadcast of 1938; College Swing; Thanks for the Memory; The Road to Singapore (and 6 other "Road" pictures); My Favorite Blonde; Lets Face It; Nothing But The Truth; Monsieur Beaucaire; The Paleface; Sorrowful Jones; Fancy Pants; The Lemon Drop Kid; Seven Little Foys; That Certain Feeling; Beau James; Critic's Choice; Alias Jesse James; Boy Did I Get a Wrong Number; The Private Navy of Sergeant O'Farrell; A Global Affair; I'll Take Sweden; Eight on the Lam; How to Commit Marriage; Cancel My Reservation. The Muppet Movie.

Many times MC of Oscar presentations, (4 Special Oscar citations).

TV inc: Bob Hope Shows; Chrysler Presents The Bob Hope Christmas Specials (*Emmys*-1966-exec prod & star); On the Road to China; Kenny Rogers and the American Cowboy; Hope, Women and Song; Lucy Moves to NBC; The Starmakers; Bob Hope's Birthday Party; Debbie Boone--The Same Old Brand New Me; Hope For President.

HOPE, Harry: Prod-Wri. b. May 26, 1926. e. UCLA. Films inc: Arch of Virtue; #13 Sin Alley; The Mad Butcher; The War of the Tongs; The Wild Girl; Doomsday Machine; Thunderfist; Sunset Cove; Save Our Beach; Death Dimension.

HOPKINS, Anthony: Act. b. Port Talbot, S Wales, Eng, Dec 31, 1941. e. RADA. Films inc: The Lion in Winter; A Bridge Too Far; A Doll's House; Young Winston; Dark Victory; Audrey Rose; International Velvet; Magic; The Elephant Man; A Change of Seasons.

TV inc: All Creatures Great and Small; The Lindbergh Kidnapping Case (*Emmy*-1976); Kean; Mayflower-The Pilgrims' Adventure.

Bway inc: Equus.

HOPKINS, Bo: Act. b. Greenville, SC, Feb 2, 1942. Films inc: White Lightning; The Moonshine War; Macho Callahan; Culpepper Cattle Co; Killer Elite; A Small Town in Texas; The Wild Bunch; The Bridge at Remagen; The Getaway; American Graffiti; The Day of the Locust; Posse; Tentacles; Midnight Express; More American Graffiti; The Fifth Floor.

TV inc: Kansas City Massacre; The Courtmartial of Lt William Calley; Aspen; Dawn: Portrait of a Teen-Age Runaway; The Last Ride of the Dalton Gang; Beggarman, Thief; The Plutonium Incident; Casino; Rodeo Girl.

HOPKINS, Linda: Singer-Act. Bway inc: Purlie; Inner City (*Tony*-supp-1972); Me and Bessie; An Evening with Linda Hopkins.

TV inc: Mitzi--Roarin' Into the 20's.

HOPPER, Dennis: Act. b. Dodge City, KS, May 17, 1936. Films inc: Johnny Guitar; Rebel Without a Cause; From Hell to Texas; The Young Land; Giant; Cool Hand Luke; Panic in the City; Hang 'Em High; Easy Rider (& sp-dir); True Grit; The Last Movie; The American Friend; The Order and Security of the World; The Apprentice Soldiers; Apocalypse Now; Out of the Blue (& dir).

TV inc: Medic; Loretta Young Show; Wild Times.

HOPPER, Jerry: Dir. b. Guthrie, OK, Jul 29, 1907. Films inc: The Atomic City; Hurricane Smith; The Secret of the Incas; Naked Alibi; The Private War of Major Benson; One Desire; The Square Jungle; Toy Tiger; The Sharkfighters; Everything But the Truth; The Missouri Traveller; Blueprint for Robbery; Madron.

TV inc: Kung Fu.

HORDERN, Michael: Act. b. Berkhampstead, Eng, 1911. e. Brighton Coll. On Screen from 1939, The Girl in the News. Films inc: Mine Own Executioner; Passport to Pimlico; The Heart of the Matter; Sink the Bismark; El Cid; Genghis Khan; The Spy Who Came in From the Cold; Khartoum; A Funny Thing Happened on the Way to the Forum; Where Eagles Dare; The Bed-Sitting Room; Anne of the Thousand Days; Alice's Adventures in Wonderland; The Mackintosh Man; Mister Quilp; Royal Flash; Lucky Lady; The Slipper and the Rose; The Medusa Touch; Watership Down.

TV inc: Tartuffe; Don Juan in Hell; The Magistrate; King Lear; Cakes and Ale; Gauguin The Savage; The Tempest; Shogun.

HORN, Alan: Exec. b. NYC, Feb 28, 1943. e. Union Coll, Harvard Business School. Joined Tandem Productions, 1972; became vp of business affairs, 1973, of Tandem and its sister company T A T Communications Co; named exec vp and COO in 1977; 1978, named p with complete creat control.

HORNBECK, William: Exec-Film ed. b. LA, Aug 23, 1901. Began in motion pictures in 1916 in film lab., Keystone Comedies. Then editor. 1964 named VP Universal Pictures; retired 1976.

Films inc: The Scarlet Pimpernel; Ghost Goes West; Things To Come; (Supv Ed) It's A Wonderful Life; State of the Union; Heiress; Shane; A Place in the Sun (*Oscar*-1951); Act of Love; Barefoot Contessa; Giant; The Quiet American; I Want To Live.

HORNE, Lena: Act. b. NYC, Jun 30, 1917. Performed in supper clubs. Screen debut, Panama Hattie. Films inc: Death of a Gunfighter; Meet Me in Las Vegas; Words and Music; Ziegfeld Follies; Till The Clouds Roll By; Patch; The Wiz.

Bway inc: Blackbirds; Dance With Your Gods.

HORNE, Marilyn: Mezzo-soprano. b. Bradford, PA, Jan 16, 1934. e. USC. As child teamed with sis Gloria as Horne Sisters, playing dates around LA. Operatic debut with LA Guild Opera; soloist with LA Philharmonic; member Roger Wagner Chorale; concerts and opera in Europe; first major US opera appearance with San Francisco Opera 1960; soloist with NY Philharmonic; with Metropolitan Opera; La Scala; Covent Garden.

Recordings inc: The Age of Bel Canto; Presenting Marilyn Horne; Souvenir of a Golden Era.

(*Grammy*-most promising new artist-1964).

HORNER, Harry: Art Dir-Dir. b. Holitsch, Czechoslovakia, Jul 24, 1910. Films inc: (art dir) Our Town; The Little Foxes; A Double Life; The Heiress *(Oscar-1949)*; Born Yesterday; The Hustler *(Oscar-1961)*; They Shoot Horses Don't They?; Who is Harry Kellerman?; Sandbox; The Black Bird; Harry and Walter Go to New York; Audrey Rose; The Driver; Moment By Moment; The Jazz Singer. (Dir): The Wild Party; Beware My Lovely.

TV inc: (dir) Omnibus; Four Star Theatre; Gunsmoke; Dupont Theatre.

HOROVITZ, Israel: Wri. b. Wakefield, MA, Mar 31, 1939. e. RADA. Plays inc: The Comeback; The Hanging of Emanuel; The Indian Wants the Bronx; Line; Rats; Chiaroscuro; The Honest-to-God Schnozzola; The World's Greatest Play; Acrobats; Shooting Gallery; Hero; The Reason We Eat; Sunday Runners in the Rain; The Widow's Blind Date.

Films inc: Speed is of the Essence; Camerian Climbing; The Sad-Eyed Girls in the Park; The Strawberry Statement.

TV inc: Play for Trees; Funny Books; Happy.

HOROWITZ, Norman: Exec. Started with Col in shipping dept, 1956; with Col in various sls & exec positions for 24 years except for two year period, 1968-70 as dir int'l sls CBS Enterprises; became sr vp worldwide dist Col TV syndication 1976; became P 1978; 1980, P & CEO Polygram Television.

HOROWITZ, Vladimir: Pianist. b. Kiev, Russia, Oct 1, 1904. Launched career in Berlin, 1926. *(Grammys*-(17)-album of year-1962, 1965, 1971 1977; classical perf-1962, 1963, 1964, 1965, 1967, 1968, 1971, 1972, 1973, 1976, 1978 (2), 1979).

HORTON, Dutch (Howard William Horton): Loc Mgr. b. England, Feb 24, 1906. Started with MGM 1929, misc. duties. Asst. location mgr., 1936; head location dept. 1942; mandatory retirement 1971; joined Disney Studios 1971, location mgr.

HORTON, Robert: Act. b. LA, Jul 29, 1924. e. Miami U; UCLA. Films inc: The Tanks are Coming; Bright Road; Prisoner of War; This Man is Armed; The Dangerous Days of Kiowa Jones; The Green Slime.

TV inc: Wagon Train; A Man Called Shenandoah.

HOSKINS, Allen (Farina): Act. b. LA, 1921. On screen in Our Gang and Little Rascals series.

(Died July 26, 1980).

HOSSEIN, Robert: Act-Dir. b. France, 1927. Films inc: Rififi; Crime and Punishment; The Wicked Go To Hell (& dir); Nude in a White Car; Paris Pickup; Love on a Pillow; Enough Rope; Marco the Magnificent; I Killed Rasputin (& dir); The Burglars (& dir).

Thea inc: (Dir) Notre Dame de Paris; Les Miserables.

HOUGH, John: Dir. b. London, Nov 21, 1941. Films inc: Wolfshead; Eye Witness; Twins of Evil; Treasure Island; The Legend of Hell House; Dirty Mary, Crazy Larry; Escape to Witch Mountain; Return to Witch Mountain; Brass Target; The Watcher In The Woods.

TV inc: The Avengers; The Zoo Gang.

HOUSEMAN, John (Jean Haussmann): Prod-Dir-Wri-Act. b. Rumania, Sep 22, 1902. Came to U.S. 1925. In 1932 prod Four Saints in Three Acts on Broadway; later dir Valley Forge; Panic. Helped Orson Welles launch Mercury Theatre, 1927. Wrote radio scripts for Helen Hayes. Exec, Selznick Prods, 1941-42. Chief of overseas radio div OWI, 1942-43.

Films inc: Jane Eyre (sp); (prod) The Blue Dahlia; Julius Caesar; Letters from An Unknown Woman; The Bad and the Beautiful; Executive Suite; The Cobweb; Lust for Life. Acting debut 1964, Seven Days In May. Films inc: The Paper Chase *(Oscar-supp-1973)*; Rollerball; Three Days of the Condor; St. Ives; The Cheap Detective; Old Boyfriends; The Fog; My Bodyguard; Wholly Moses.

TV inc: The Paper Chase; The Last Convertible; The French Atlantic Affair; Gideon's Trumpet (& exec prod); Justice--A Matter of Balance; The Baby Sitter; A Christmas Without Snow.

Bway inc: (Dir) Lute Song; King Lear; Coriolanus; Measure For Measure; Clarence Darrow.

HOUSER, John: Act. b. LA, Jul 14, 1952. Films inc: Summer of '42; Bad Company; Class of '44; Slap Shot.

TV inc: Maude; Phyllis; Barnaby Jones; Three Times Daley.

HOUSTON, David: Act. b. Shreveport, LA, Dec 9, 1938. Country mus recording artist. Films inc: Cottonpickin' Chickenpickers. *(Grammys*-C&W rec, C&W vocal-1966).

HOUWER, Rob: Prod. b. Holland. e. German Institute for Film. Films inc: A Degree of Murder; Business is Business; Turkish Delight; Keetje Tippel; Soldier of Orange.

HOWAR, Barbara: TV pers. b. Nashville, TN, Sep 27, 1934. Wri for Washington Post; New Yorker mag; TV inc: Panorama (host); CBS-TV corr; Who's Who (host).

HOWARD, Cy: Prod-Dir. b. Milwaukee, WI, Sep 27, 1915. Radio Wri for Jack Benny; Milton Berle; Danny Thomas; Bert Lahr; Jerry Lewis; created My Friend Irma; Life with Luigi (radio & TV); exec prod Desilu Studios, created and prod Harrigan & Son; Westward Ho; Fair Exchange; My Friend Irma Goes West.

Films inc: Lovers and Other Strangers; Won Ton Ton, The Dog Who Saved Hollywood; Every Little Crook and Nanny.

HOWARD, John C: Film Edtr. b. LA, Jul 1, 1930. Films inc: Butch Cassidy and the Sundance Kid; Blazing Saddles; Young Frankenstein; W C Fields and Me; Silent Movie; High Anxiety; Sgt Pepper's Lonely Hearts Club Band; Nightwing; Why Would I Lie.

HOWARD, Ken: Act. b. El Centro, CA, Mar 28, 1944. Films inc: Tell Me That You Love Me Junie Moon; Such Good Friends; The Strange Vengeance of Rosalie; 1776.

TV inc: Adam's Rib; Manhunter; The White Shadow; A Real American Hero; Damien...The Leper Priest; The Body Human--The Facts for Boys (host).

Bway inc: Child's Play *(Tony-supp-1970)*; The Norman Conquests; 1600 Pennsylvania Ave.

HOWARD, Ron: Act. b. Duncan, OK, Mar 1, 1954. Films inc: The Journey; Mother's Day; Five Minutes to Live; Music Man; Eat My Dust; The Courtship of Eddie's Father; Village of the Giants; Wild Country; American Graffiti; Run, Stranger, Run; The Shootist; Grand Theft Auto (& co-wri, dir); More American Graffiti; Leo and Loree.

TV inc: Migrants; Locust; Smith Family; Huck Finn; Happy Days; Cotton Candy (co-wrote, dir, exec-prod); Act of Love; Skyward (dir).

HOWARD, Sandy: Prod. b. NYC, Aug 1, 1927. Films inc: A Man Called Horse; Man in the Wilderness; The Neptune Factor; Together Brothers; Embryo; Return of a Man Called Horse; Sky Riders; The Island of Dr. Moreau; The Silent Flute; Circle of Iron; Jaguar Lives; Meteor; City on Fire; Death Ship.

HOWARD, Trevor: Act. b. Clifton, Eng, Sep 29, 1916. e. RADA. Stage debut, 1933, Revolt in a Reformatory. Screen debut, The Way Ahead.

Films inc: Brief Encounter; So Well Remembered; The Third Man; Sons and Lovers; Heart of the Matter; Cockleshell Heroes; Around the World in 80 Days; Mutiny On The Bounty; Father Goose; Von Ryan's Express; Morituri; The Lion; The Battle of Britain; Ryan's Daughter; Pope Joan; 11 Harrowhouse; Hennessy; Conduct Unbecoming; The Bawdy Adventures of Tom Jones; The Last Remake of Beau Geste; Slaves; Stevie; Superman; Hurricane; Meteor; The Shillingbury Blowers; The Sea Wolves; Sir Henry At Rawlinson End; Windwalker.

TV inc: The Invincible Mr. Disraeli *(Emmy-1963)*; Catholics; The Count of Monte Cristo; Night Flight.

HOWELLS, Ursula: Act. b. London, Sep 17, 1922. Films inc: Flesh and Blood; The Constant Husband; They Can't Hang Me; The Long Arm; Dr Terror's House of Horrors; Mumsy, Nanny, Sonny and Girly; Crossplot.

TV inc: The Small Back Room; A Woman Comes Home; For Services Rendered; Mine Own Executioner; The Cocktail Party.

Thea inc: The Gimmick; Doctors of Philosophy; Return Ticket; Dear Octopus; The Lion in Winter; Two and Two Make Sex.

HOWERD, Frankie: Act. b. York, Eng, Mar 6, 1921. Films inc: The Runaway Bus; Jumping for Joy; The Ladykillers; A Touch of the Sun; Further Up the Creek; The Cool Mikado; The Great St Trinian's Train Robbery; Carry on Doctor; Up Pompeii; Up the Chastity Belt; Up the Front; The House in Nightmare Park.

TV inc: Frankie Howerd Show; Comedy Playhouse.

Thea inc: A Funny Thing Happened on the Way to the Forum; Way Out in Picadilly; Wind in the Sassafras Trees.

HOWES, Sally Ann: Act. b. London, 1934. Films inc: Thursday's Child; Halfway House; Dead of Night; Pink String and Sealing Wax; My Sister and I; Anna Karenina; The History of Mr Polly; Fool Rush In; Honeymoon Deferred; The Admirable Crichton; Chitty Chitty Bang Bang; Death Ship.

TV inc: The Hounds of the Baskervilles.

HOWLAND, Beth: Act. b. Boston, May 28, 1947. Films inc: Bye Bye Birdie.

TV inc: The Ted Bessel Show; Bronk; Cannon; Little House on the Prairie; Alice.

Bway inc: George M; Company; A Tribute to Stephen Sondheim.

HOYT, John (nee Hoysradt): Act. b. 1905. Films inc: OSS; The Unfaithful; Brute Force; Winter Meeting; The Great Dan Patch; The Desert Fox; When Worlds Collide; Androcles and the Lion; Julius Caesar; The Girl in the Red Velvet Swing; Baby Face Nelson; The Blackboard Jungle; Never So Few; Spartacus; Cleopatra; Duel at Diablo.

TV inc: Greatest Heroes of the Bible; The Winds of Kitty Hawk; Rex Stout's Nero Wolfe.

HU, King (Chin-Ch'uan Hu): Dir. b. Peking, 1931. e. Peking National Art Coll. Began as journalist, artist, act. Films inc: The Love Eterne; Sons of the Good Earth; Come Drink With Me; Dragon Inn; A Touch of Zen; Four Moods; The Fate of Lee Khan; The Valiant Ones; Legend of the Mountain.

HUBLEY, Faith: Prod-Dir. b. NYC, Sep 16, 1924. W of John Hubley. Worked as mus edtr Spectre of the Rose; script supv 12 Angry Men; became prod ani films after marrying Hubley.

Films inc: Women of the World; Second Chance; The Hole (Oscar-cartoon-1962); Herb Alpert and the Tijuana Brass Double Feature (Oscar-cartoon-1966); Windy Day; Of Men and Demons; Everybody Rides the Carousel; Voyage to Next; The Doonesbury Special.

HUBLEY, John: Ani-Prod-Dir. b. Marinette, WI, 1914. With Disney; art dir Pinocchio; Bambi; Rite of Spring; Fantasia (section).

Films inc: (Dir) Robin Hoodlum; Magic Fluke; Ragtime Bear. (Prod) Moonbird (Oscar-cartoon-1959); The Hole (Oscar-cartoon-1962); Herb Alpert and the Tijuana Brass Double Feature (Oscar-cartoon-1966); Windy Day; Of Men and Demons; Everybody Rides the Carousel (& Dir); Voyage to Next; The Doonesbury Special.

HUDDLESTON, David: Act-Prod. b. Vinton, VA, Sep 17, 1930. e. AADA. Films inc: All the Way Home; A Lovely Way to Die; Slaves; Norwood; Rio Lobo; Fools Parade; Country Blue; Bad Company; Billy Two-Hats; Blazing Saddles; McQ; The Klansman; Capricorn I; I Superpiedi Quasipiatti; The World's Greatest Lover; Gorp; Smokey and the Bandit II.

TV inc: Gunsmoke; Brian's Song; Suddenly Last Summer; The Homecoming; The Waltons; Heat Wave; Dirty Sally; Hizzonner (prod & act); The Kallikaks.

Thea inc: Woman Is My Idea; A Man for all Seasons; My Three Angels; Front Page; Everybody Loves Opal; Ten Little Indians; Silk Stockings; Can-Can; Fanny; Guys and Dolls; The Music Man; Desert Song; Mame; The Roast.

HUDSON, Rock (Roy Fitzgerald): Act. b. Winnetka, IL, Nov 17, 1925. Films inc: Fighter Squadron; Pillow Talk; A Gathering of Eagles; Blindfold; Tobruk; The Undefeated; Showdown; Embryo; Seconds; Avalanche; The Mirror Crack'd.

TV inc: McMillan & Wife; Wheels; The Martian Chronicles.

Thea inc: I Do! I Do!; John Brown's Body; Camelot; On the 20th Century.

HUEBING, Craig: Act. b. Reedsburg, WI, Mar 4. TV inc: From These Roots; The Doctors; General Hospital.

Thea inc: The Thurber Carnival; Time of the Cuckoo.

HUGGINS, Roy: Wri-Dir. b. Litelle, WA, Jul 18, 1914. Films inc: I Love Trouble; Too Late for Tears; Lady Gambler; Fuller Brush Man; Good Humor Man; Woman in Hiding; Sealed Cargo; Hangman's Knot; Three Hours to Kill; Pushover; A Fever in the Blood.

TV inc: Cheyenne; Conflict; Colt 45; 77 Sunset Strip; Maverick; The Fugitive; Run for Your Life (exec prod); The Outsiders; The Bold Ones; Alias Smith and Jones; Toma; The Rockford Files; Captains and the Kings (exec prod); Aspen; Wheels (exec prod); The Jordan Chance (exec prod); The Last Convertible.

HUGHES, Barnard: Act. b. Bedford Hills, NY, Jul 16, 1915. Thea inc: Please, Mrs. Garibaldi; A Majority of One; All Over Town; Hamlet; Advise and Consent; How Now, Dow Jones; Sheep on the Runway; Abelard and Heloise; The Good Doctor; Da (Tony-1978).

Films inc: Midnight Cowboy; Oh, God!; Where's Poppa; The Hospital; Rage; Sisters; Cold Turkey; Pursuit of Happiness; Deadhead Miles.

TV inc: Doc; See How She Runs; The Caryl Chessman Story; Tell Me My Name; Look Homeward, Angel; Judge (Lou Grant Series) (Emmy-1978); Father Brown, Detective; Nova--The Wizard Who Spat on the Floor (host); Homeward Bound.

HUGHES, Del: Dir-Act. b. Detroit, Sep 4, 1909. Thea inc: Vickie; Open House; Rip Van Winkle; Command Decision; Death of a Salesman; Legend of Sarah; The Autumn Garden; The Crucible.

TV inc: (act) The Brighter Day; (dir) One Life to Live; All My Children.

Films inc: (act) A Face in the Crowd.

HUGHES, Kathleen (Betty von Gerkan): Act. b. LA, Nov 14, 1928. Films inc: Mother is a Freshman; For Men Only; The Golden Blade; It Came From Outer Space; The Glass Web; Dawn at Socorro; Cult of the Cobra; Promise Her Anything; The President's Analyst; The Take.

TV inc: The Ghost and Mrs Muir; Bracken's World; Babe (movie).

HUGHES, Ken: Dir. b. Liverpool, Eng, 1922. Films inc: Wide Boy; Black Thirteen; Joe Macbeth; Wicked as They Come (& sp); The Long Haul; In the Nick; The Trials of Oscar Wilde (& sp); Of Human Bondage; Drop Dead Darling (& sp); Casino Royale; Chitty Chitty Bang Bang (& sp); Cromwell (& sp); The Internecine Project; Alfie Darling; Sextette.

TV inc: Solo for Canary; Eddie (Emmy-wri-1959); An Enemy of the State; Sammy; The Haunting; The Voice.

HUMBERSTONE, Bruce: Dir. b. Buffalo, NY, Nov 18, 1903. e. OH State U. Films inc: If I Had a Million; Crooked Circle; Pack Up Your Troubles; Tall, Dark and Handsome; I Wake Up Screaming; Sun Valley Serenade; To the Shores of Tripoli; Iceland; Hello, Frisco, Hello; Pin-Up Girl; Wonder Man; Three Little Girls in Blue; The Homestretch; Fury at Furnace Creek; Happy Go Lovely; Desert Song; Ten Wanted Men; Purple Mask.

HUMPERDINCK, Engelbert (Arnold George Dorsey): Singer. b. India, May 3, 1936. TV inc: The Engelbert Humperdinck Show.

Albums inc: Release Me; A Man Without Love; Last Waltz; We Made It Happen; Miracles; Last of the Romantics; After the Lovin'.

HUNNICUT, Gayle: Act. b. Ft Worth, TX, Feb 6, 1943. Films inc: The Wild Angels; P.J.; Marlowe; Eye of the Cat; Fragment of Fear; Running Scared; The Legend of Hell House; The Sellout; The Ambassadors; Return of the Saint; Once In Paris.

TV inc: Man and Boy; The Golden Bowl; The Ripening Seed; Fall of Eagles; The Switch; Humboldt Girl; Strange Shadows In An Empty Room; A Man Called Intrepid; The Martian Chronicles.

Thea inc: The Ride Across Lake Constance; Twelfth Night; The Tempest; Dog Days; The Admirable Crichton.

HUNNICUTT, Arthur: Act. b. Gravelly, AR, Feb 17, 1911. Films inc: Wildcat; Lust for Gold; Broken Arrow; The Red Badge of Courage; The Big Sky; The Last Command; The Kettles in the Ozarks; Apache Uprising; Cat Ballou; Million Dollar Duck; The Revengers; Harry and Tonto; The Spikes Gang; Moonrunners.

Thea inc: Love's Old Sweet Song; The Time of Your Life; Apple of His Eye; Tobacco Road.

(Died Sep 26, 1979).

HUNT, Marsha: Act. b. Chicago, Oct 17, 1917. Films inc: The Virginia Judge; Gentle Julia; Pride and Prejudice; Cheers for Miss Bishop; Joe Smith, American; Cry Havoc; Blue Denim; The Plunderers; Johnny Got His Gun.

TV inc: Twelfth Night; The Breaking Point; Profiles in Courage; Accidental Family; The Young Lawyers.

Thea inc: Joy to the World; The Devil's Disciple; Banned in Texas; Legend of Sarah; The Tunnel of Love; The Paisley Convertible.

HUNT, Peter: Dir. b. Pasadena, CA, Dec 16, 1938. Films inc: 1776; Gold; On Her Majesty's Secret Service; Bully.

TV inc: Adams Rib; Hello Mother Goodbye; Karen Valentine Show; Ivan the Terrible; When Things Were Rotten; Mixed Nuts; Rendezvous Hotel; When She Was Bad. . .; Life On the Mississippi (& prod).

Bway inc: 1776 *(Tony*-1969); Georgy; Scratch; Goodtime Charley; Give 'Em Hell, Harry; Magnificent Yankee; Bully.

HUNT, Walter (Pee Wee): Mus-Singer. b. 1908. Trombonist, also handled novelty singing chores, with big bands inc: Paul Whiteman; Glen Gray; after service in World War II formed own band for recordings and ballroom dates.

(Died June 22, 1979).

HUNTER, Evan: Wri. b. 1926. Films inc: The Blackboard Jungle; Strangers When We Meet; The Young Savages; The Birds; Mister Buddwing; Walk Proud.

TV inc: 87th Precinct.

HUNTER, Kim (Janet Cole): Act. b. Detroit, Nov 12, 1922. Started in summer stock. Films inc: The Seventh Victim; Stairway to Heaven; A Streetcar Named Desire *(Oscar*-supp-1951); Anything Can Happen; Deadline: U.S.A.; Lilith; Planet of the Apes; The Swimmer; Escape From the Planet of the Apes. Blacklisted during the 50s she later testified for radio personality John Henry Faulk who sued after he was similarly blacklisted. Her testimony paved the way for clearance of many performers unjustly accused of Communist connections.

Bway inc: A Streetcar Named Desire; Darkness at Noon; The Children's Hour; The Tender Trap; Write Me a Murder; The Women; And Miss Reardon Drinks a Little.

TV inc: Requiem for a Heavyweight; The Comedian; Give Us Barabbas; Lamp at Midnight; The Prodigal; Bad Ronald; This Side of Innocence; Backstairs at the Whitehouse; Golden Gate Murders; FDR-The Last Year; Edge of Night.

HUNTER, Ronald: Act. b. Boston, Jun 14, e. U of PA, AB; NYU, MFA. Bway inc: The Basic Training of Pavlo Hummel; Hamlet; Richard III.

Films inc: The Sentinel; The Seduction of Joe Tynan.

TV inc: The Edelin Conviction; One Life to Live ; The Lazarus Syndrome.

HUNTER, Ross (Martin Fuss): Prod. b. Cleveland, May 6, 1916. e. Western Reserve U, MA. School teacher, 1938-43; actor, under contract at Columbia 1944-46; returned to teaching; Dial Director-Assoc Prod U, 1950-51; Prod U, 1951; to Col, 1971; to Par 1974.

Films inc: Louisiana Hayride; Ever Since Venus; The Bandit of Sherwood Forest; The Groom Wore Spurs; Son of Cochise; Magnificent Obsession; Naked Alibi; Yellow Mountain; Captain Lightfoot; One Desire; The Spoilers; All That Heaven Allows; There's Always Tomorrow; Battle Hymn; Tammy and the Bachelor; Interlude; My Man Godfrey; The Wonderful Years; Stranger in My Arms; Imitation of Life; Pillow Talk; Portrait in Black; Midnight Lace; Back Street; Flower Drum Song; Tammy and the Doctor; The Thrill of It All; The Chalk Garden; I'd Rather Be Rich; The Art of Love; Madame X; The Pad; Thoroughly Modern Millie; Rosie; Airport; Lost Horizon.

TV inc: Suddenly Love; The Best Place To Be.

HUNTER, Tab: Act. b. NYC, Jul 11, 1931. Screen debut, 1950, The Lawless.

Films inc: Island of Desire; Track of the Cat; Battle Cry; Lafayette Escadrille; Damn Yankees; That Kind of Woman; Pleasure of his Company; They Came to Cordura; Ride the Wild Surf; The Life and Times of Judge Roy Bean.

TV inc: The Kid From Left Field.

HUPPERT, Isabelle: Act. b. Paris, Mar 16, 1955. Films inc: Faustine et le Bel Ete; Cesar and Rosalie; Going Places; Rosebud; Aloise; Serieux Comme le Plaisir; The Rape of Innocence; No Time for Breakfast; Silence. . .on Tourne; The Lacemaker; The Indians Are Still Far Away; Violette; The Bronte Sisters; Loulou; Sauve Qui Peut la Vie; Orokseg; Heaven's Gate.

HURKOS, Peter (Pieter Van der Hurk): Act-Psychic. b. Dordrecht, Holland, May 21, 1911. Films inc: The Peter Hurkos Story; Sixth Sense; New World; Boston Strangler; The Mysterious Monsters; The Amazing World of Psychic Phenomena; Now I Lay Me Down to Sleep.

HURST, Rick: Act. b. Houston, TX, Jan 1. e. Tulane. Worked niteries. Films inc: W W and the Dixie Dance Kings; The Cat From Outer Space.

TV inc: On the Rocks; Amateur Night at the Dixie Bar and Grill; The Dukes of Hazzard; Enos.

HURT, John: Act. b. Lincolnshire, Eng, Jan 22, 1940. e. RADA. Films inc: The Wild and the Willing; A Man for All Seasons; Before Winter Comes; Spectre; Sinful Davey; In Search of Gregory; 10 Rillington Place; Little Malcolm; East of Elephant Rock; The Shout; The Disappearance; Midnight Express; The Lord of the Rings; Watership Down; Alien; The Elephant Man; Heaven's Gate.

TV inc: The Stone Dance; The Playboy of the Western World; The Naked Civil Servant; Nijinksy; I, Claudius; Crime and Punishment.

Thea inc: The Dwarfs; Man and Superman; Ride a Cock-Horse; The Caretaker; The Only Secret; The Dumb Waiter; Travesties; Chips with Everything; Inadmissible Evidence.

HURT, Mary Beth: Act. b. IA. Thea inc: More Than You Deserve; Boy Meets Girl; Love for Love; Trelawney of the Wells.

Films inc: Interiors; Change of Seasons.

TV inc: Head Over Heels; The 5:48.

HUSKY, Ferlin: Act. b. Flat River, MO, Dec 3, 1927. Also sang under the name of Simon Crum. Country & Pop Mus recording artist. On radio, TV. Film inc: Country Music Holiday.

HUSSEIN, Waris: Dir. b. India, 1938. Films inc: A Touch of Love; Quackser Fortune; Melody; The Possession of Joel Delaney; The Six Wives of Henry VIII.

TV inc: Shoulder to Shoulder; Notorious Woman; Sleeping Dogs; St. Joan; A Casual Affair; A Passage To India; Chips With Everything; And Baby Makes Six; Edward and Mrs. Simpson; Death Penalty; The Henderson Monster.

Thea inc: Half-Life.

HUSSEY, Olivia: Act. b. Buenos Aires, Apr 17, 1951. Films inc: The Battle of the Villa Florita; Cup Fever; Romeo and Juliet; All the Right Noises; Summertime Killer; Lost Horizon; Black Christmas; Death On The Nile; The Cat and the Canary; Virus; The Man With Bogart's Face.

TV inc: Jesus of Nazareth; The Pirate; The Bastard; The Thirteenth Day-The Story of Esther.

HUSSEY, Ruth: Act. b. Providence, RI, Oct 30, 1917. Films inc: Madame X; Judge Hardy's Children; Marie Antoinette; Time Out for Murder; Spring Madness; Maisie; The Women; Another Thin Man; Fast and Furious; Northwest Passage; Susan and God; The Philadelphia Story; Married Bachelor; H M Pulham Esq.; The Uninvited; Marine Raiders; Jane Doe; The Great Gatsby; Louisa; Stars and Stripes Forever; The Lady Wants Mink; The Facts of Life.

HUSTON, Anjelica: Act. b. 1952. D of John Huston. Films inc: Sinful Davey; A Walk with Love and Death; The Last Tycoon.

HUSTON, John: Dir-Wri-Act. b. Nevada, MO, Aug 5, 1906. S of late Walter Huston. Films inc: (Wri) Dr. Ehrich's Magic Bullet; Sergeant York; Maltese Falcon (& dir); Three Strangers; The Treasure of the Sierra Madre *(Oscars-*dir & sp-1948); Key Largo; Beat the Devil; The Red Badge of Courage; The Asphalt Jungle; The African Queen; Heaven Knows Mr. Allison; Moulin Rouge; The Misfits; Reflections in a Golden Eye; The Man Who Would Be King; Tentacles (act); Jaguar Lives (act); Winter Kills (act); Wise Blood (dir-act); The Visitor (act); Phobia; Agee (act).

TV inc: The Word; Return of the King (voice).

HUTCHINS, Will (Marshall Lowell Hutchason): Act. b. LA, May 5, 1932. e. Pomona Coll, BA. TV inc: Sugarfoot; Hey Landlord!; Blondie; then toured for two years with circus (clown & ringmaster): Films inc: Teenage Slumber Party; No Time for Sergeants; Claudelle Inglish; Merrill's Marauders; The Shooting; Spin-Out; Clambake; Roar!

HUTTON, Betty: Act. b. Battle Creek, MI, Feb 26, 1921. Screen debut, 1942, The Fleet's In. Last seen on screen in Spring Reunion, 1957.

Films inc: Star-Spangled Rhythm; The Miracle of Morgan's Creek; Incendiary Blonde; The Perils of Pauline; Annie Get Your Gun; Let's Dance; The Greatest Show on Earth; Somebody Loves Me.

HUTTON, Brian: Dir. b. NYC, 1935. Films inc: The Wild Seed; The Pad; Sol Madrid; Where Eagles Dare; Kelly's Heroes; X Y and Z; Night Watch; The First Deadly Sin.

HUTTON, Jim: Act. b. Binghamton, NY, May 31, 1938. Performed in summer stock. Screen debut 1950. Films inc: Where the Boys Are; Honeymoon Machine; Period of Adjustment; The Horizontal Lieutenant; Walk Don't Run; The Trouble with Angels; Who's Minding the Mint?; The Green Berets; Psychic Killer.

TV inc: Ellery Queen; The Sky Trap.

(Died June 2, 1979).

HUTTON, Lauren (Mary Hutton): Act. b. Charleston, SC, 1944. Films inc: Little Fauss and Big Halsy; The Gambler; Welcome to LA; A Wedding; American Gigolo.

TV inc: Someone Is Watching Me; Institute For Revenge.

HUTTON, Robert (nee Winne): Act. b. Kingston, NY, Jun 11, 1920. Films inc: Destination Tokyo; Janie; Too Young To Know; Always Together; The Steel Helmet; Cassanova's Big Night; Cinderfella; The Slime People; The Secret Man; Finders Keepers; Torture Garden; Tales from the Crypt.

HUTTON, Tim: Act. b. LA, Aug 16, 1960. S of the late Jim Hutton. TV inc: Zuma Beach; The Best Place To Be; Friendly Fire; And Baby Makes Six; Young Love, First Love; The Sultan and the Rock Star; Father Figure.

Films inc: Ordinary People.

HYAMS, Nessa: Dir. b. NYC, Nov 21, 1941. e. Syracuse U. W of David Picker. TV inc: Mary Hartman, Mary Hartman.

HYAMS, Peter: Wri-Dir. b. NYC, Jul 26, 1943. e. Hunter College; Syracuse U. With CBS News, NY before going to Par as writer. Films inc: T.R. Baskin (wri-prod); Busting; Our Time (dir); Peeper (dir); Telefon (wri); Capricorn One; Hanover Street; The Hunter (wri).

TV inc: The Rolling Man; Goodnight My Love.

HYDE-WHITE, Wilfrid: Act. b. Bourton-on-the-Water, Eng, May 12, 1903. Films inc: Murder by Rope; Rembrandt; The Third Man; The Story of Gilbert and Sullivan; See How They Run; North-West Frontier; Carry on Nurse; Two-Way Stretch; My Fair Lady; John Goldfarb Please Come Home; Ten Little Indians; The Liquidator; Our Man in Marrakesh; Chamber of Horrors; Skullduggery; Gaily Gaily; Fragment of Fear; The Cat and the Canary; Battlestar Galactica; In God We Trust; Oh, God! Book II.

Thea inc: The Philadelphia Story; Caesar and Cleopatra; Antony and Cleopatra; The Reluctant Debutante; The Happiest Millionaire; Not in the Book; The Pleasure of His Company; Rolls Hyphen Royce.

TV inc: The Rebels; The Associates; The Cat and the Canary; Scout's Honor; Damien. . .The Leper Priest.

HYER, Martha: Act. b. Fort Worth, TX, Aug 10, 1930. e. Northwestern U, Pasadena Playhouse. W of Hal Wallis. Screen debut 1946. Films inc: The Locket; The Judge Steps Out; Sabrina; Cry Vengeance; Battle Hymn; The Big Fisherman; Some Came Running; The Carpetbaggers; The Sons of Katie Elder; House of a Thousand Dolls; Once You Kiss A Stranger.

HYLTON, Jane: Act. b. London, Jul 16, 1927. Films inc: The Upturned Glass (as Gwen Clark); My Brother's Keeper; Passport to Pimlico; Here Comes the Huggetts; Secret Venture; Circus of Horrors; One Man's Navy.

TV inc: Sir Lancelot; The Four Seasons of Rosie Carr; Nightmare on Installments.

HYMAN, Eliot: Exec. b. CT, 1905. Entered film industry after World War II following careers in tire and microfilm businesses. Formed Associate Artists Prodns in 1948 to buy Monogram Pictures library for sale to tv; partnered in Motion Pictures for Television and Moulin Prodns, latter financing John Huston's Moulin Rouge and Moby Dick; in 1956 acquired entire pre-1948 WB films for $21,0000,000, considered a phenomenal price at the time, but within less than five years the Looney Tunes and Merrie Melodie cartoons alone had been sold to tv stations for more than $10,000,000; Associated Artists Productions purchased by UA in 1958 with Hyman becoming P of United Artists Associated which acquired screen rights to several key Bway and literary properties.

In 1960 formed Seven Arts which became top films-to-tv distrib, financed or produced Lolita; Whatever Happened to Baby Jane? Seven Days in May; Night of the Iguana; Sunday in New York and Bway prodns of Iguana; Suzie Wong; Funny Girl; The Owl and the Pussycat; Seven Arts acquired WB in 1967, with Hyman remaining as head of new WB-Seven Arts until 1969 when firm was acquired by Kinney; formed Feature House, 1971.

(Died July 23, 1980).

HYMAN, Kenneth: Prod. b. NYC, 1928. e. Columbia U. S of Eliot Hyman. Entered films as packager; exec vp Associated Artists; exec VP Seven Arts Prodns; Exec vp world-wide prodn WB-Seven Arts 1967-69; Films inc: (exec prod) Hound of the Baskervilles; Small Sad World of Sammy Lee; Whatever Happened to Baby Jane?; Emperor of the North Pole. (Prod) The Hill; The Dirty Dozen.

IAN, Janis: Singer. b. NJ, Apr 7, 1951. Films inc: Virus (theme song). TV inc: Star Chart. *(Grammy-*pop vocal-1975).

IBBETSON, Arthur: Cin. b. England, 1922. Films inc: The Horse's Mouth; The Angry Silence; The League of Gentlemen; Tunes of Glory; Whistle Down the Wind; The Inspector; Nine Hours to Rama; The Chalk Garden; The Countess from Hong Kong; Inspector Clouseau; Where Eagles Dare; Anne of the Thousand Days; The Railway Children; Willie Wonka and the Chocolate Factory; A Doll's House; Harrowhouse 11; All Things Bright and Beautiful; The Medusa Touch; The Prisoner of Zenda; Hopscotch. TV inc: Frankenstein--The True Story; Little Lord Fauntleroy.

IHNEN, Wiard (Bill): Art Dir. b. Jersey City, NJ, 1898. H of Edith Head. Retired 1963. Worked in many different studios starting in 1919. Films inc: Wilson *(Oscar-*1944); Blood on the Sun *(Oscar-*1945).

(Died Jun 22, 1979).

ILLES, Robert: Wri. Works with James R Stein. TV inc: Lily *(Emmy-*1974); Van Dyke and Co; What's Happening; One Day at a Time; Love Boat (Pilot); Fernwood 2Night; Carol Burnett Show *(Emmy-*1978); Lou Rawls Special; America 2night; Mary Tyler Moore Show; Helen Reddy Special; New Kind of Family; Dick Clark Specials; Flo; Steve Allen Comedy Hour.

ILSON, Saul: Wri-Prod. Writer for Canadian TV, to Hollywood in late 50's; from 1967 to 1978 partnered with Ernie Chambers in indie firm producing variety shows; April 1980 named vp pgms & talent NBC Entertainment; Oct 1980, vp comedy and variety.

TV inc: Dinah Shore; Smothers Brothers; Tony Orlando and Dawn; Lynda Carter Special; Beatrice Arthur Special.

IMMEL, Jerrold: Comp-Cond. b. LA. TV inc: Gunsmoke; Hawaii Five-O; The Macahans; How The West Was Won; The Fitzpatricks; Harry-O; Dallas; The American Girls; Married, The First Year; Alcatraz--The Whole Shocking Story; Secret of Midland Heights.

IMMERMAN, William J: Exec. b. NYC, Dec 29, 1937. e. U of WI, BS, Stanford U, JD. VP, AIP, 1965-72; sr vp Twentieth Fox, 1972-77; pres Scoric Prodns, Inc, 1977.

INGELS, Marty: Act. b. NYC, Mar 9, 1936. H of Shirley Jones. Arranges star commercials for various firms. Films inc: Armored Command; The Horizontal Lieutenant; The Ladies Man; Irving's Root Canal; For Singles Only; Monsieur Bouquet; If It's Tuesday This Must Be Belgium.
    TV inc: Dickens and Fenster; Burke's Law; Pat Boone and Family Christmas Special.

IONESCU, Eugene: Plywri. b. Romania, Nov 13, 1912. Plays inc: The Lesson; The Chairs; The Bald Prima Donna; Amedee; Victims of Duty; The New Tenant; Rhinocerous; The Killer; The Man With the Suitcases; Pedestrian in the Air; Ce Formidable Bordel.

IRELAND, Jill: Act. b. London, Apr 24, 1936. Began career in music halls age 12, played Palladium, toured continent. Film contract with J. Arthur Rank. Screen debut as a ballet dancer in Oh, Rosalinda.
    Films inc: Three Men in a Boat; Carry On, Nurse; The Mechanic; The Valachi Papers; Hard Times; From Noon Till Three; Love and Bullets.
    TV inc: Shane; Night Gallery; Ben Casey; Daniel Boone; Mannix; Star Trek; The Girl, The Gold Watch and Everything.

IRELAND, John: Act. b. Vancouver, BC, Jan 30, 1915. Films inc: A Walk in the Sun; All the King's Men; My Darling Clementine; Red River; I Shot Jesse James; Little Big Horn; Gunfight at the O.K. Corral; Spartacus; 55 Days at Peking; The Fall of the Roman Empire; Farewell, My Lovely; The Adventurers; Madam Kitty; Maniac; Midnight Auto Supply; The Swiss Conspiracy; Guyana, Cult of the Damned.
    TV inc: The Millionaire; Kavik The Wolf Dog; Crossbar; Tourist; Marilyn--The Untold Story.

IRVING, Amy: Act. b. Palo Alto, CA, Sep 10, 1953. e. American Conservatory Theatre; London Academy of Dramatic Art. D of the late Jules Irving. Films inc: Carrie; The Fury; Honeysuckle Rose; The Competition. TV inc: I'm A Fool; Dynasty; Voices; Once an Eagle.

IRVING, George S (nee Shelasky): Act-Singer. b. Springfield, MA, Nov 1, 1922. In stock and touring companies before Bway debut in chorus of Oklahoma!
    Bway inc: Lady in the Dark; Call Me Mister; Along Fifth Avenue; Gentlemen Prefer Blondes; Two's Company; Me and Juliet; Can-Can; Bells Are Ringing; The Beggar's Opera; Oh Kay; Irma La Douce; Seidman and Son; Tovarich; A Murderer Among Us; An Evening With Richard Nixon and. . .; Irene (Tony-supp-1972); Who's Who in Hell.
    Opera inc: The Telephone and The Medium (London); Boris Godunov (Montreal).
    TV inc: Omnibus; Barry Wood's Variety Show; I Remember Mama; Getting There; Pinocchio's Christmas (voice).

IRVING, Jules (Israel): Dir-Prod. b. NYC, Apr 13, 1925. e. NYU, Stanford U. Taught drama at San Francisco State College, 1949-62. Co-founded the San Francisco Actor's Workshop in 1952. Appointed co-dir of The Repertory Theatre of Lincoln Center, 1965; became dir 1967-73.
    Bway inc: The Condemned of Altona; The Little Foxes; Tiger at the Gates; Cyrano de Bergerac; King Lear; In the Matter of J Robert Oppenheimer; The Year Boston Won the Pennant; Beggar on Horseback; The Playboy of the Western World; An Enemy of the People; Delicate Champions; The Crucible; Act Without Words.
    TV inc: Loose Change; Rich Man, Poor Man.
    (Died July 28, 1979).

IRVING, Richard: Prod-Dir. b. NYC, Feb 13, 1917. e. NYU. TV inc: Biff Baker, USA; State Trooper; The Virginian; Court Martial; Laredo; Columbo; Name of the Game; Six Million Dollar Man; Seventh Avenue; Class of '65; Quincy.

ISAACS, Phil: Exec. b. NYC, May 22, 1922. e. CCNY. Joined Par 1946 as booker's asst; worked up to asst eastern sls mgr; 1966 natl sls mgr Ten Commandments; 1967 vp dom dist Cinema Center Films; 1972 mktg vp Tomorrow Entertainment; 1975, vp gen sls mgr Avco Embassy; 1978 vp General Cinema Corp; 1980 vp gen sls mgr Orion Pictures.

ISCOVE, Rob Dir-Chor. b. Toronto, CA, Jul 4, 1947. e. Juilliard School of Music. TV inc: (Chor); Dorothy Hamill Special; Rock Awards 1976; Super Night at the Super Bowl; three Burt Bacharach specials; Steve and Eydie Celebrate Irving Berlin; 50th Academy Awards. (dir) Mary; Pontiac Special with Raquel Welch; Welcome to My Nightmare; Rock Awards; Roller Revolution; Jack; Clowns.
    Films inc: (chor) Jesus Christ Superstar; Duchess and the Dirtwater Fox; Silent Movie.
    Thea inc: Peter Pan (dir-chor).

ISENBERG, Gerald I: Prod. b. Cambridge, MA, May 13, 1940. e. Bowdoin Coll, BA, Harvard Business School, MBA. TV inc: The People; Go Ask Alice; Great American Tragedy; Sandcastles; It's Good to be Alive; Where Have All the People Gone; The Last Angry Man; Betrayal; It Couldn't Happen to a Nicer Guy; Winner Take All; Katherine. (Exec prod); James Dean; Portrait of a Friend; The Bureau; Having Babies; Secrets; The Secret Life of John Chapman; Red Alert; The Defection of Simas Kudirka; Having Babies II; Having Babies III; Seizure-The Story of Kathy Morris (& dir).
    Thea inc: Let the Good Times Roll.

ISHERWOOD, Christopher: Wri. b. Aug 26, 1904. Plays inc: Dog Beneath the Skin, or Where is Francis; Ascent of F 1; On the Frontier. His short stories, Goodbye to Berlin, formed the basis of the play I Am a Camera, subsequently musicalized as Cabaret; both versions subsequently filmed.
    Films inc: The Loved One.
    Bway inc: A Meeting by the River.

ISRAEL, Neil: Wri-Dir. TV inc: (wri) Lola Falana Special; Mac Davis Show; Ringo; Marie (prod).
    Films inc: Tunnelvision (exec prod-wri); Americathon.

ITO, Robert: Act. b. Vancouver, BC, Jul 2. Films inc: Midway; Rollerball; Special Delivery.
    TV inc: Men of the Dragon; Helter Skelter; Kung Fu; Quincy.
    Thea inc: Flower Drum Song; What Makes Sammy Run.

ITURBI, Jose: Pianist. b. Valencia, Spain, Nov 28, 1895. Screen debut, 1943, Thousands Cheer.
    Films inc: Two Girls and a Sailor; Anchors Aweigh; Holiday in Mexico; Three Daring Daughters. Last Film, 1949, That Midnight Kiss.
    (Died June 28, 1980).

IVES, Burl: Act-Singer. b. Hunt Township, IL, Jun 14, 1909. On screen from 1946. Films inc: The Big Country (Oscar-supp-1958); Smoky; East of Eden; Cat on a Hot Tin Roof; Desire Under the Elms; Let No Man Write My Epitaph; Ensign Pulver; Those Fantastic Flying Fools; The Only Way Out Is Dead; Baker's Hawk; Hugo The Hippo (voice); Just You and Me, Kid.
    TV inc: The New Adventures of Heidi.

IVORY, James: Dir. b. Jun 7, 1928. e. U of OR, BA, USC, MA. Films inc: The Householder; Shakespeare Wallah; The Guru; Bombay Talkie; Savages; The Wild Party; Autobiography of a Princess; Roseland; The Europeans (& prod); Jane Austen In Manhattan.
    TV inc: The Five Forty Eight.

JACKS, Robert L: Prod. b. Oxnard, CA, Jun 14, 1927. e. USC. Films inc: Man on a Tightrope; Prince Valiant; Gambler from Natchez; White Feather; Black Tuesday; Stranger on Horseback; A Kiss Before Dying; Man in the Middle; Guns at Batasi; Zorba The Greek; Bandolero; The Undefeated.
    TV inc: Honeymoon with a Stranger; Victor Borge Show; Three Coins in the Fountain; Arnie; The Homecoming; Pomeroy's People; The Waltons (Emmy-1973); Crunch; State Fair; Eight Is Enough; Mr. Horn; The Wild, Wild West Revisited; Young Love, First Love; The Young Pioneers; Murder Can Hurt You.

JACKSON, Anne: Act. b. Allegheny, PA, Sep 3, 1926. W of Eli Wallach. Films inc: So Young So Bad; The Journey; Tall Story; The Tiger Makes Out; How to Save a Marriage; The Secret Life of an American Wife; Lovers and Other Strangers; Zigzag; Dirty Dingus Magee; Nasty Habits; The Bell Jar; The Shining.

TV inc: The Family Man; A Private Battle.

JACKSON, Calvin: Pianist-Comp. b. Philadelphia, PA, May 26, 1919. Films inc: Blood and Steel; The Unsinkable Molly Brown. TV inc: Asphalt Jungle; Rehearsal With Calvin.

JACKSON, Eddie: Act. b. 1896. Partnered with the late Jimmy Durante and the late Lou Clayton since 1916; song and dance man best known for strutting version of Bill Bailey. With partners worked NY niteries during and after the prohibition era, headlined the Ziegfeld musical Show Girl; Trio went to Hollywood for series of films; Clayton died in 1950 but Jackson continued to team with Durante in club dates and on tv until Durante retired. (Died July 16, 1980).

JACKSON, Freda: Act. b. Nottingham, Eng, Dec 29, 1909. Films inc: Henry V; Great Expectations; No Room at the Inn; Bhowani Junction; The Flesh Is Weak; A Tale of Two Cities; The Shadow of the Cat; Tom Jones; House at the End of the World.

TV inc: Macadam and Eve; Sorry Wrong Number; Release; Maigret in Montmartre; Knock on Any Door; Midland Profile.

Thea inc: Tell Tale Murder; Starched Aprons; The Lady of the Camellias; Camino Real; The Man on the Stairs; Error of Judgement; The Devil's Disciple; The White Devil.

JACKSON, Glenda: Act. b. Cheshire, Eng, May 9, 1936. Films inc: Marat-Sade; Negatives; Women in Love *(Oscar-*1970); The Music Lovers; Sunday Bloody Sunday; Mary Queen of Scots; A Touch of Class *(Oscar-*1973); The Triple Echo; A Bequest to the Nation; Hedda; The Incredible Sarah; Nasty Habits; House Calls; Stevie; Lost & Found; Class of Miss MacMichael; Hopscotch; Health.

TV inc: Elizabeth R *(Emmy-*1972); Shadow In The Sun *(Emmy-*1972).

Thea inc: Hedda Gabler; The White Devil; Stevie; Rose.

JACKSON, Gordon: Act. b. Glasgow, Dec 19, 1923. Films inc: The Foreman Went to France; Millions Like Us; Pink String and Sealing Wax; Tight Little Island; Tunes of Glory; The Great Escape; The Ipcress File; Cast a Giant Shadow; The Prime of Miss Jean Brodie; Kidnapped; Russian Roulette; Medusa Touch.

TV inc: Upstairs, Downstairs *(Emmy-*supp-1976).

Thea inc: What Every Woman Knows; Macbeth; Noah.

JACKSON, Kate: Act. b. Birmingham, AL, Oct 29, 1948. e. AADA. Thea inc: Night Must Fall; Constant Wife; Little Moon of Alban. Films inc: Limbo; Night of Dark Shadows; Thunder and Lightning.

TV inc: Dark Shadows; The Rookies; Charlie's Angels; Homicide; Killer Bees; Topper (& exec prod).

JACKSON, Keith: Sportscaster. b. GA. TV inc: Monday Night Baseball; NCAA Football; Wide World of Sports; The Superstars; The Woman Superstars; Superteams.

JACKSON, Sherry: Act. Films inc: The Breaking Point; The Miracle of Our Lady of Fatima; The Lion and the Horse; Trouble Along the Way; Come Next Spring; Wild on the Beach; Gunn; The Silent Treatment; The Mini-Skirt Mob; Bare Knuckes; Stingray.

TV inc: Brenda Starr.

JACKSONS, THE: Musical group. Members of the group (all brothers) are: Sigmund (Jackie) b. May 4, 1951; Toriano Aldryll (Tito) b. Oct 15, 1953; Marlon David b. Mar 12, 1957; Michael Joe, b. Aug 29, 1958; Steven Randall (Randy) b. Oct 29, 1961. Recording artists, concert tours.

Films inc: The Wiz.

Albums inc: Destiny; Shake Your Body; Triumph.

JACOBI, Derek: Act. b. London, Oct 22, 1938. e. Cambridge. Films inc: The Day of the Jackal; Blue Blood; The Odessa File; The Medusa Touch; The Human Factor.

TV inc: She Stoops to Conquer; Man of Straw; The Pallisers; I Claudius.

Thea inc: Pericles; A Month in the Country; The Hollow Crown; Pleasure and Repentance; Hobson's Choice; The Suicide.

TV inc: Philby, Burgess and MacLean; Hamlet.

JACOBI, Lou: Act. b. Toronto, Ont, Canada, Dec 28, 1913. Stage experience in Canada before debuting London. Thea inc: (London) Remains to Be Seen; Pal Joey; Bontche Schweig; Embassy. (Bway) The Diary of Anne Frank; The Tenth Man; Come Blow Your Horn; Fade Out-Fade In; Don't Drink The Water; A Way of Life; Norman, Is That You?; Cheaters.

Films inc: The Diary of Anne Frank; Song Without End; Irma La-Douce; Everything You've Ever Wanted To Know About Sex But Were Afraid To Ask; Penelope; Roseland; Magician of Lublin; The Lucky Star.

TV inc: Rheingold Theatre; Better Late Than Never.

JACOBS, Lawrence-Hilton: Act. b. NYC, Sep 4. Films inc: Claudine; Cooley High; Young Blood.

TV inc: Roots; Welcome Back, Kotter; For the Love of It.

JACOBS, Newton P (Red): Exec. b. Pittsburgh, PA, Mar 10, 1900. Joined Selznick Film Exchange as a clerk in 1918; then to Associated Films National and later to Film Booking Office where he became booker, salesman and asst to m. In 1924 appointed LA branch m for RKO Radio Pictures; in 1928 formed Favorite Films of California, distributing product in 13 Western states. In 1959 became p of Crown International Pictures; ChmnB of Crown in 1973.

Films inc: (exec prod) Malibu Beach; Coach; Van Nuys Boulevard; The Hearse.

(Died Nov 6, 1980).

JACOBS, Seaman: Wri. b. Kingston, NY. Films inc: It Happened at the World's Fair; Oh, God! Book II.

TV inc: Ed Wynn; Bing Crosby; Johnny Carson; Edgar Bergen; My Favorite Martian; Petticoat Junction; My Three Sons; F Troop; Adams Family; Bachelor Father; Family Affair; The Lucy Show; Tony Orlando & Dawn; The Jeffersons; Maude; Alice; Love Boat; George Burns In Nashville?

JACOBY, Coleman: Wri. TV inc: Phil Silvers Show *(Emmys-*1955, 1956, 1957); Dick Cavett Show; Alan King Specials; The Hallowe'en That Almost Wasn't.

JACOBY, Scott: Act. Films inc: The Little Girl Who Lives Down the Lane; Midnight Auto Supply; Our Winning Season.

TV inc: That Certain Summer *(Emmy-*supp-1973); No Other Love; The Diary of Anne Frank.

JACQUES, Hattie (Josephine Edwina Jacques): Act. b. Kent, England, Feb 7, 1924. Toured with Young Vic Co. Thea inc: Beauty and the Beast; Ali Baba (& adapt); The Bells of St. Martin's; The Sleeping Beauty in the Wood; Albertine by Moonlight; Large as Life.

Films inc: Nicholas Nickleby; The Magic Christian; The Carry On Series; Make Mine Mink; Crooks and Coronets.

(Died Oct 6, 1980).

JADE, Claude: Act. b. Dijon, France. Films inc: Stolen Kisses; Topaz; Le Temoin; Domicile Conjugal; Le Miroir Ecarlate; Home Sweet Home; Number One; Le Malin Plaisir; Trop, C'est Trop; The Pawn; Le Choix; Cap Du Nord.

TV inc: Les Oiseaux Rares.

JAE, Jana: Singer. b. Great Falls, MT, Aug 30, 1946. e. CO Women's Coll. C&W recording artist.

JAECKEL, Richard: Act. b. Long Beach, NY, Oct 10, 1926. Films inc: Guadalcanal Diary; A Wing and a Prayer; Battleground; Sands of Iwo Jima; Come Back, Little Sheba; The Naked and the Dead; The Gallant Hours; The Dirty Dozen; Sometimes a Great Notion; The Devil's Brigade; Chisum; Ulzana's Raid; The Drowning Pool; Walking Tall, Part II; Twilight's Last Gleaming; Speedtrap; The Dark; Herbie Goes Bananas.

TV inc: U.S. Steel Hour; Elgin Hour; Goodyear Playhouse; Firehouse; Champions-A Love Story; Salvage; The $5.20 An Hour Dream; Princess; Reward.

JAECKIN, Just: Dir. b. 1940. Originally a Fashion photographer. Films inc: Emmanuelle; Story of O; Madame Claude; Le Dernier Amant Romantique; Private Collections.

JAFFE, Herb: Prod. b. NYC. e. Brooklyn Coll, Columbia U. Started as press agent, then talent agent. Joined UA in 1965 as vp in charge of worldwide prod; left in 1973 and for short time served as p of Rastar Pictures; then entered indy prod.

Films inc: The Wind and the Lion; Demon Seed; Who'll Stop the Rain; Time after Time; Those Lips, Those Eyes; Motel Hell.

JAFFE, Leo: Exec. b. NYC, Apr 23, 1909. e. NYU. Joined accounting dept of Columbia 1930. Became vp, Columbia, 1954; 1st vp, treas, member of the board; 1958; exec vp, 1962; pres, 1968; pres Columbia Pictures Industries, Inc, 1970; pres & CEO, 1973; chm, 1973.

Jean Hersholt Humanitarian Award 1978.

JAFFE, Michael: Prod. b. NYC, Jan 9, 1945. e. Yankton Coll, BA; U of Chicago; Cornell. S of Jean Muir and Henry Jaffe. TV inc: Alexander; Death of Richie; Emily, Emily; A Woman Called Moses; Battered; When She Was Bad; Aunt Mary; Escape.

JAFFE, Sam: Act. b. NYC, Mar 10, 1891. e. CCNY, BS. Bway inc: The Clod; Samson and Delilah; The Jazz Singer; The Eternal Road; A Doll's House; The Merchant of Venice; Cafe Crown; Mademoiselle Columbo; The Seagull; The Lark; A Meeting By the River.

Films inc: The Scarlet Empress; Lost Horizon; Gunga Din; Gentleman's Agreement; The Asphalt Jungle; The Barbarian and the Geisha; Ben Hur; Guns for San Sebastian; The Kremlin Letter; Bedknobs and Broomsticks; Battle Beyond The Stars.

TV inc: Ben Casey; Gideon's Trumpet.

JAFFE, Stanley R: Prod. b. New Rochelle, NY, Jul 31, 1940. e. U of PA. S of Leo Jaffe. Joined Seven Arts Associated Corp 1962; named exec asst to P 1964; dir pgmg 1965; 1969 exec vp Par; 1970 P Par Pictures Corp and Par TV; 1971 P Jafilms, Inc; 1975 exec vp Col; 1976 P Stanley Jaffe Prodns.

Films inc: Goodbye, Columbus; A New Leaf (exec prod); Bad Company; The Bad News Bears; Kramer Vs. Kramer (Oscar-1979).

JAGGER, Dean: Act. b. Lima, OH, Nov 7, 1903. Vaudeville, Bway prior to screen debut, 1929, Woman from Hell.

Films inc: Star for a Night; Western Union; Valley of the Sun; Sister Kenny; 12 O'Clock High (Oscar-supp-1949); Driftwood; Executive Suite; White Christmas; Elmer Gantry; Jumbo; The Kremlin Letter; Vanishing Point; Game of Death; Alligator.

TV inc: Gideon's Trumpet; Haywire; Independence and 76 (Emmy-1980).

JAGGER, Mick: Singer-Sngwri-Act. b. Dartford, Kent, England, Jul 26, 1943. Lead Singer with Rolling Stones. Films inc: Performance; Ned Kelly; Gimme Shelter; Sympathy for the Devil; Ladies and Gentlemen, The Rolling Stones.

Songs inc: Satisfaction; Get Off My Cloud; Paint It Black; Let's Spend the Night Together; Ruby Tuesday; Stray Cat Blues.

JAGLOM, Henry: Wri-Dir. b. London, Jan 26, 1941. e. U of PA. Films inc: A Safe Place; Tracks; Hearts and Minds (presenter only); Sitting Ducks (& act).

JAMAL, Ahmad: Pianist-Comp. b. Pittsburgh, PA, Jul 2, 1930. Albums inc: One For Miles; Minor Moods; Extension; Jamal Plays Jamal; Jamalca; The Awakening; Poinciana Revisited; Tranquility; Cry Young; Heatwave.

JAMES, Dennis: Act-TV host. b. Jersey City, NJ, Aug 24, 1917. TV Shows inc: Price Is Right; Name That Tune.

Films inc: The One and Only.

JAMES, Emrys: Act. b. England, Sep 1, 1930. With Old Vic; Royal Shakespeare Co. Thea inc: The Long and the Short and the Tall; Macbeth; Indians; Relapse; The Plebeians Rehearse the Uprising; Othello; The Merchant of Venice; The Island of Mighty; Dr Faustus; King John; Merry Wives of Windsor.

Films inc: Darling.

TV inc: Pygmalion; Twelfth Night; Testament of Youth.

JAMES, Harry: Orch Ldr. b. Albany, GA, May 15, 1916. As a child performed as contortionist with circus. Played trumpet with Benny Goodman band. Formed own orchestra 1939. On screen from 1942.

Films inc: Private Buckaroo; Springtime in the Rockis; Two Girls and a Sailor; Young Man with a Horn; To Catch a Thief; Anything Goes.

JAMES, Monique: Exec. b. Paris, France, Apr 2, 1926. e. Vassar, BA. Started 1949 in cast dept CBS NY; 1950 in partnership with Eleanor Kilgallen in Casting Consultants; 1952, MCA, NY; 1958, MCA West Coast; 1962 vp talent dept U; 1980 formed K-S Productions with Eleanor Kilgallen.

JAMES, Sonny (Jimmie Loden): Act. b. Hackleburg, AL, May 1, 1929. Recording artist; Grand Ole Opry perf.

Films inc: Second Fiddle to a Steel Guitar; Las Vegas Hillbillies; Nashville Rebel; Hillbilly in a Haunted House.

JAMESON, Jerry: Dir. b. Hollywood. Began as editorial asst, later edtr, supv edtr Danny Thomas prodns, before dir. TV inc: Mod Squad; Dan August; Ironside; Hawaii Five-O; Cannon; Streets of San Francisco; The Elevator; Heat Wave; Hurricane; Terror on the Fortieth Floor; The Secret Night Caller; The Lives of Jenny Dolan; The Deadly Tower; Call of the Wild; Brahman; A Fire in the Sky; High Noon Part II--The Return of Will Kane.

Films inc: Dirt Gang; The Bat People; Brute Core; Airport 77; Raise the Titanic.

JANIS, Conrad: Act. b. NYC, Feb 11, 1928. Films inc: Snafu; Margie; That Hagen Girl; Airport 75; The Duchess and the Dirtwater Fox; Roseland; The Buddy Holly Story; Oh, God! Book II.

TV inc: Mork and Mindy; Quark.

Bway inc: Junior Miss; Dark of the Moon; The Next Half Hour; The Brass Ring; Time Out for Ginger; Visit to a Small Planet; Make a Million; Sunday in New York; Marathon 33; The Front Page; Same Time Next Year.

JANKOWSKI, Gene F: Exec. b. Buffalo, NY, May 21, 1934. e. Canisius, BS, MI State U, MA. Joined CBS Radio Network Sales 1961 as account exec; eastern sls mgr 1966; moved to CBS TV network as account exec 1969; gen sls mgr WCBS-TV 1970; dir sales 1970; vp sales, CBS TV 1973; vp finance & planning 1974; vp, controller 1976; vp adm/Jan 1977; exec vp CBS Broadcast Group July 1977; named pres Oct 1977.

JANNEY, Leon: Act. b. 1917. In vaude as child; in silent films Old Dutch; The Wind; member original Our Gang; on radio in Charlie Chan series. Films inc: Father's Son; Handful of Clouds; Old English; Doorway to Hell; Penrod and Sam; Police Court; Should Ladies Behave?; Son of Mine; The Last Mile; Charly.

Bway inc: The Simpleton of Unexpected Isles; Parade; The Bough Breaks; The Flowering Peach.

(Died Oct 28, 1980).

JANNI, Joseph: Prod. b. Milan, Italy, May 21, 1916. e. Milan U, Rome Film School. Films inc: The Glass Mountain; White Corridors; Something Money Can't Buy; Romeo and Juliet; A Town Like Alice; Savage Innocents; Billy Liar; Darling; Modesty Blaise; Far From the Madding Crowd; Poor Cow; Sunday, Bloody Sunday; Made; Yanks.

JANSSEN, David: Act. b. Naponee, NE, Mar 27, 1931. Screen debut age 9, Swamp Fire. Films inc: Hell to Eternity; Marooned; Where It's At; Once Is Not Enough; Two-Minute Warning; Covert Action; The Swiss Conspiracy.

TV inc: Richard Diamond; Detective; The Fugitive; O'Hara, U.S. Treasury; Harry O; The Longest Night; Hijack; Pioneer Woman; Centennial; The Word; SOS Titanic; High Ice; City In Fear.

(Died Feb 13, 1980).

JANSSEN, Werner: Comp-Cond. b. NYC, Jun 1, 1900. e. Dartmouth Coll. Cond symph orchs throughout world.

Film scores inc: The General Died at Dawn; Blockade; Eternally Yours, Captain Kidd; Guest in the House; The Southerner.

Bway inc: Ziegfeld Follies of 1925-26.

TV inc: Ghost of Canterville.

JARMAN, Claude Jr: Act. b. Nashville, TN, Sep 27, 1934. e. Vanderbilt U. Started as child actor. Dir San Francisco Int'l Film Festival, 1967-1979.

Films inc: The Yearling (Honorary Oscar-1946); High Barbaree; Intruder in the Dust; Rio Grande; Hangman's Knot; Fair Wind to Java; The Great Locomotive Chase.

TV inc: Centennial.

JARRE, Maurice: Comp. b. Lyon, France, 1924. Films inc: Hotel des Invalides; La Tetre Contre les Murs; Eyes Without a Face; Crack in the Mirror; The Longest Day; Lawrence of Arabia (Oscar-1962); Sundays and Cybele; Weekend at Dunkirk; Dr Zhivago (Oscar-1965); Is Paris Burning?; The Professionals; Five Card Stud; Isadora; The Damned; Ryan's Daughter; Mohammad, Messenger of God; Two Solitudes; Crossed Swords; Winter Kills; The Black Marble; The Last Flight of Noah's Ark; Resurrection.

TV inc: Shogun; Enola Gay--The Men, The Mission, The Atomic Bomb.

JARREAU, Al: Singer. b. Mar 12, 1940. Recording artist. (Grammys-(2)-jazz vocalist-1977 & 1979.)

JARRICO, Paul: Wri. b. LA, Jan 12, 1915. Films inc: Salt of the Earth; Tom, Dick and Harry; Thousands Cheer; The White Tower; Not Wanted; The Girl Most Likely; Assassination in Sarajevo.

JARROTT, Charles: Dir. b. London, Jun 16, 1927. Films inc: Anne of the Thousand Days; Mary, Queen of Scots; Lost Horizon; The Dove; The Littlest Horse Thieves; The Other Side of Midnight; The Last Flight of Noah's Ark.

TV inc: The Hot Potato Boys; Roll On; Girls in a Birdcage; The Picture of Dorian Gray; Rain; The Young Elizabeth; A Case of Libel; Dr. Jekyll and Mr. Hyde.

Thea inc: The Duel; Galileo; The Basement; Tea Party; The Dutchman.

JARVIS, Graham: Act. b. Toronto, Canada, Aug 25, 1930. e. Williams Coll. Bway inc: The Best Man; The Investigation; Halfway Up a Tree; The Rocky Horror Show.

Films inc: The Out of Towners; Cold Turkey; The Organization; What's Up, Doc?; Prophecy; Middle Age Crazy.

TV inc: Mary Hartman, Mary Hartman; Forever Fernwood.

JASON, Rick: Act. b. NYC, May 21, 1926. e. AADA. Bway debut, 1949, Now I Lay Me Down to Sleep.

Films inc: Sombrero; Saracen Blade; This Is My Love; The Lieutenant Wore Skirts; The Wayward Bus.

TV inc: The Case of the Dangerous Robin; Combat; The Best Place To Be.

JAYSTON, Michael: Act. b. Nottingham, Eng, Oct 28, 1935. With Old Vic Theatre Co., Bristol Old Vic.

Films inc: Cromwell; The Nelson Affair; Nicholas and Alexandra; A Midsummer Night's Dream; The Public Eye.

TV inc: She Fell Among Thieves; Tinker, Tailor, Soldier, Spy.

JEAKINS, Dorothy: Dsgn. b. San Diego, CA, Jan 11, 1914. Films inc: Joan of Arc (Oscar-1948); Samson and Delilah (Oscar-1950); My Cousin Rachel; The Greatest Show on Earth; The Ten Commandments; The Childrens Hour; The Music Man; The Night of the Iguana (Oscar-1964); The Sound of Music; Hawaii; The Way We Were; The Betsy; North Dallas Forty.

Bway inc: Major Barbara; Too Late The Phalarope; The World of Suzie Wong.

JEAN, Gloria (nee Schoonover): Act. b. Buffalo, NY, Apr 14, 1928. Films inc: The Underpup; Pardon My Rhythm; If I Had My Way; Moonlight in Vermont; She's My Lovely; I'll Remember April; Fairy Tale Murder; Copacabana; I Surrender, Dear; There's a Girl in My Heart; The Ladies' Man.

JEAN, Norma: Singer. b. Wellston, OK, Jan 30, 1938. C&W recording artist. Joined Porter Wagner Show on national TV in the Mid 60's; later joined the Grand Ole Opry.

JEANMAIRE, Renee (Zizi): Act-Ballet star. b. Paris, 1924. Films inc: Hans Christian Andersen; Anything Goes; Folies Bergere; Charmante Garcons; Black Tights.

JEFFERSON Herb Jr: Act. b. Jersey City, NJ, Sep 28. TV inc: The Silent Force; Battlestar Galactica.

Thea inc: The Great White Hope; Murderous Angels; The Blacks; Dream on Monkey Mountain.

JEFFREY, Tom M: Prod-Dir. b. Sydney, Australia, Sep 26, 1938. Films inc: The Removalists; Weekend of Shadows; The Odd Angry Shot.

TV inc: Pastures of the Blue Crane; Devlin.

JEFFREYS, Anne: Act. b. Goldsboro, NC, Jan 26, 1923. Powers model. On screen from 1943.

Films inc: X Marks the Spot; I Married an Angel; Step Lively; Sing Your Way Home; Riffraff; Return of the Bad Men.

Bway inc: Street Scene; Kiss Me Kate; Three Wishers for Jamie; Kismet.

TV inc: Topper; Love That Jill; Delphi Bureau; Beggarman, Thief.

JEFFRIES, Lionel: Act. b. London, England. Films inc: High Terrace; Bhowani Junction; Lust for Life; The Nun's Story; Two-Way Stretch; The Trials of Oscar Wilde; Fanny; The Notorious Landlady; Wrong Arm of the Law; The First Men in the Moon; Call Me Bwana; You Must Be Joking; The Crimson Blade; Arriverderci Baby; Spy With the Cold Nose; Camelot; Chitty Chitty Bang Bang; Who Slew Auntie Roo?; Eye Witness; Railway Children (& dir-sp); Gingerbread House; Baxter (& dir); The Amazing Mr. Blundern; Water Babies (dir).

TV inc: Cream in My Coffee.

JENNER, Bruce: TV Pers. b. Mt Kisco, NY, Oct 28, 1949. Former Olympic decathlon champ. TV inc: America Alive! (co-host).

JENNINGS, Talbot: Wri. b. Shoshone, ID. e. Harvard, MA. Films inc: Mutiny on the Bounty; The Good Earth; Romeo and Juliet; Northwest Passage; Frenchman's Creek; Anna and the King of Siam; Across the Wide Missouri; Escape to Burma; Pearl of the South Pacific; Untamed; The Naked Maja; The Sons of Katy Elder.

JENNINGS, Waylon: Singer. b. Littlefield, TX, Jun 15, 1937. C&W recording artist. Featured on Grand Ole Opry TV shows. Films inc: Nashville Rebel. TV Inc: Anatomy of Pop; American Swing-Around; Carl Smith's Country Music Hall; The Unbroken Circle-A Tribute To Mother Maybelle Carter; Waylon--Starring Waylon Jennings.

Albums inc: The Outlaws; Ol' Waylon; Waylon & Willie; Greatest Hits.

(Grammy-country vocal duo-1969).

JENS, Salome: Act. b. Milwaukee, WI, May 8, 1935. e. Northwestern U. Thea inc: Sixth Finger in a Five Finger Glove; The Bald Soprano; The Disenchanted; Deirdre of the Sorrows; USA; Freud in A Far Country; Night Life; The Winter's Tale; First One Asleep; I'm Solomon; A Patriot for Me; Mary Stuart; The Ride Across Lake Constance; Antony and Cleopatra; A Break in the Skin.

Films inc: Angel Baby; The Fool Killer; Seconds; Me, Natalie; Cloud Dancer.

TV inc: From Here To Eternity; From Here To Eternity-The War Years; The Golden Moment-An Olympic Love Story.

JENSEN, Maren: Act. b. Arcadia, CA, Sep 23. TV inc: Hardy Boys/Nancy Drew Mysteries; Battlestar Galactica.

JENSON, Roy Cameron: Act. b. Calgary, Canada, Feb 1935. e. UCLA, BA. Films inc: Harper; Will Penny; Water Hole 3; Paint Your Wagon; Fools; Big Jake; Sometimes a Great Notion; Judge Roy Bean; The Glass House; The Getaway; Deadly Honeymoon; Dillinger; Chinatown; Breakout; The Wind and the Lion; Breakout Pass; The Dutchess and the Dirt Water Fox; The Car.

TV inc: The Wish; Bonanza.

JERGENS, Adele: Act. b. NYC, Nov 28, 1922. Films inc: Edge of Doom; Side Street; Sugarfoot; Show Boat; Somebody Loves Me; Overland Pacific; Miami Story; Fireman Save My Child; Strange Lady in Town; The Cobweb.

JESSEL, George: Perf. b. NYC, Apr 3, 1898. On stage as child singer. Appeared in NY, London; toured US vaudeville circuit. Film debut 1911, Widow at the Races (with Eddie Cantor).

Films inc: Private Izzy Murphy; Lucky Boy; Happy Days; Four Jills and a Jeep; Valley of the Dolls; The Busy Body; The Phynx. (Prod) The Dolly Sisters; Nightmare Alley; Dancing in the Dark; When My Baby Smiles at Me; Tonight We Sing.

Bway inc: The Jazz Singer; Sweet and Low; Box of Tricks; Casino de Paree; Show Time.

Radio: Jessel's Jamboree; Jessel's Celebrity Program; The George Jessel Show.

TV inc: George Jessel's Show Business; Here Come the Stars.
Jean Hersholt Humanitarian Award 1969.

JEWISON, Norman: Prod-Dir. b. Toronto, Can, Jul 21, 1926. e. U of Toronto, BA. Act, wri for BBC. Prod, dir TV for CBC.

Films inc: Forty Pounds of Trouble; The Thrill of it All; Send Me No Flowers; The Cincinnati Kid; In The Heat of the Night; The Russians Are Coming, The Russians Are Coming; Fiddler On The Roof; Jesus Christ, Superstar; Rollerball; F.I.S.T.; And Justice For All; The Dogs of War (exec prod).

TV inc: Judy Garland; Harry Belafonte; Danny Kaye; Andy Williams specials; Wayne and Shuster; Showtime; Barris Beat.

JOBERT, Marlene: Act. b. Algiers, 1943. Films inc: Masculin Feminin; Le Voleur; L'Astragale; Rider on the Rain; Last Known Address; Catch Me a Spy; Ten Days' Wonder; The Good and the Bad; The Wonderful Crook; The Accuser; Your Turn, My Turn; La Guerre Des Policiers.

TV inc: Mademoiselle Pygmalion; Les Quatre Chemins.

JOBIM, Antonio Carlos: Comp-Mus. b. Rio de Janeiro, 1927. Mus dir with Odeon Records, credited with introducing bossa nova with Joao Gilberto recording. Comps inc: Desafinado; One Note Samba; The Girl From Ipanema; Quiet Nights; Meditation.

Films inc: Black Orpheus; The Adventurers.

JOEL, Billy: Singer. b. NYC, May 9, 1949. Singer, songwriter, musician. Recording artist. (Grammys-(4)-record of year, song of year-1978; album of year, pop vocal-1979).

Albums inc: The Stranger; 52d Street; Glass Houses.

JOFFE, Charles H: Exec Prod. b. NYC. Films inc: Don't Drink the Water; Take the Money and Run; Everything You Always Wanted to Know About Sex But Were Afraid to Ask; Love and Death; Annie Hall (Oscar-1977); Play It Again, Sam; Bananas; Sleeper; Interiors; Manhattan; Stardust Memories.

TV inc: Woody Allen Specials; Good Time Harry.

JOFFREY, Robert: Dancer-Chor. b. Seattle, WA, Dec 24, 1930. On faculty of High School for the Performing Arts, NYC, 1950-55; faculty American Ballet Theatre school; resident chor NY City Center Opera 1955-1961; founded City Center Joffrey Ballet 1956; chor NBC-TV operas 1955, 1957, 1958.

Ballets inc: Persephone; Scaramouche; Bal Masque, Pierot Lunaire; Harpsichord; Astarte; Remembrances.

JOHAR, I S: Act. b. India. Films inc: Harry Black and the Tiger; North West Frontier; Lawrence of Arabia; Death on the Nile.

JOHN, Elton (Reginald Kenneth Dwight): Act-Sngwri. b. Pinner, Mx, Eng, Mar 25, 1947. Played (as Reg Dwight) with nondescript rock groups around London; In 1967 met Berni Taupin, changed his name, they began collaborating, in 1969 first hit album Elton John led to p.a.'s which established him as a leading rock star, retired in 1975 having split with Taupin; resumed career 1979.

Songs inc: (with Taupin) The Bitch Is Back; Someone Saved My Life Tonight; Country Comfort.

Albums include Honky Chateau; Don't Shoot Me I'm Only the Piano Player; Yellow Brick Road; Blue Moves; Elton John's Greatest; A Single Man.

Films inc: Friends (score); Tommy (act); Oh Heavenly Dog (songs).

JOHNS, Glynis: Act. b. Pretoria, South Africa, Oct 5, 1923. In ballet, London stage, films as child. Thea debut 1935, Buckie's Bears; film debut 1936 South Riding.

Thea inc: (London) St Helena; The Children's Hour; The Melody That Got Lost; Quiet Weekend; The Way Things Go; The King's Mare; Come As You Are; 13 rue de l'Amour. (Bway) Gertie; Major Barbara; Too True to be Good; A Little Night Music (Tony-1973).

Films inc: Prison Without Bars; 49th Parallel; Perfect Strangers; Frieda; Miranda; An Ideal Husband; State Secret; The Card; Rob Roy; The Beachcomber; The Court Jester; The Day They Gave Babies Away; The Sundowners; The Spider's Web; The Chapman Report; Mary Poppins; Dear Brigitte; Don't Just Stand There; Lock Up Your Daughters; Under Milkwood; Vault of Horror.

TV inc: Glynis; Noel Coward's Star Quality; Mrs Amworth; All You Need is Love; Across a Crowded Room.

JOHNSON, Arte: Act. b. Chicago, Jan 20. Films inc: Miracle in the Rain; The Subterraneans; The Third Day; The President's Analyst; Love At First Bite.

TV inc: Laugh-In (Emmy-1969); Knockout; Baggy Pants and the Nitwits (voice); The Bear Who Slept Through Christmas (voice); Detour To Terror; The Love Tapes; The Incredible Book Escape (voice).

JOHNSON, Ben: Act. b. Foreacre, OK, Jun 13, 1918. Began film career as a wrangler, stuntman. Competed in rodeos. Acting debut, Mighty Joe Young.

Films inc: The Sugarland Express; Dillinger; The Getaway; The Train Robbers; The Last Picture Show (Oscar-supp-1971); The Wild Bunch; Grayeagle; The Swarm; The Hunter; Terror Train.

TV inc: Wild Times.

JOHNSON, Bruce: Prod-Wri. b. Oakland, CA, Jul 7, 1939. e. USC, BA. TV inc: Gomer Pyle; Jim Nabors Hour; Arnie; The Little People; The New Temperatures Rising Show; Sierra; Excuse My Friend; Alice; Blansky's Beauties; Quark; Mork and Mindy; Angie.

JOHNSON, Celia (CBE): Act. b. Richmond, Surrey, Eng, Dec 18, 1908. e. RADA. Thea inc: A Hundred Years Old; The Artist and the Shadow; Three Sisters; It's Never too Late; The Grass Is Greener; The Tulip Tree; The Cherry Orchard; Hay Fever; Lloyd George Knew My Father; The Dame of Sark; The Kingfisher.

Films inc: In Which We Serve; Dear Octopus; This Happy Breed; Brief Encounter; A Kid for Two Farthings; The Good Companions; The Prime of Miss Jean Brodie.

TV inc: Les Miserables; The Hostage Tower.

JOHNSON, Don: Act. b. Flatt Creek, MO, Dec 15. Worked with ACT, San Francisco. Films inc: The Magic Garden of Stanley Sweetheart; The Harrad Experiment; A Boy and His Dog.

TV inc: Amateur Night; The Rebels; From Here To Eternity--The War Years; Beulah Land; Revenge of the Stepford Wives.

JOHNSON, Kenneth A: Dir-Wri-Prod. b. Pine Bluff, AR, Oct 26, 1942. e. Carnegie Tech. TV inc: The Mike Douglas Show (prod); An Evening of Edgar Allan Poe (prod-wri); The Last Bride of Salem (wri-prod); The Bionic Woman (exec prod); The Incredible Hulk (wri-prod); A Death in the Family (wri-prod).

JOHNSON, Lamont: Dir-Prod. b. Stockton, CA, Sep 30, 1922. Films inc: Covenant with Death; The Mackenzie Break; A Gunfight; The Groundstar Conspiracy; You'll Like My Mother; The Last American Hero; Lipstick; One on One; Somebody Killed Her Husband.

TV inc: The Defenders; Profiles in Courage; Twilight Zone; My Sweet Charlie; The Execution of Private Slovik; Fear on Trial; Sunnyside; Off The Minnesota Strip.

Thea inc: The Egg; Yes is for a Very Young Man.

JOHNSON, Mary Lea: Prod. W of Martin Richards. Bway inc: Sweeney Todd (Tony-1979); Goodbye, Fidel.

JOHNSON, Richard: Act. b. Upminster, Eng, Jul 30, 1927. e. RADA. Films inc: Captain Horatio Hornblower; Never So Few; Cairo; The Haunting; The Pumpkin Eater; Operation Crossbow; Khartoum; Deadlier Than the Male; Oedipus the King; A Twist of Sand; Lady Hamilton; Some Girls Do; Julius Caesar; Hennessy; Aces High; The Making of a Lady; Zombie.

Thea inc: The Complaisant Lover; The Devils; Thomas and the King; Blithe Spirit; The Guardsman.

TV inc: A Marriage; Murder on Your Mind; Portrait of a Rebel-Margaret Sanger; Haywire.

JOHNSON, Van: Act. b. Newport, RI, Aug 28, 1916. In vaudeville, on Bway, New Faces of 1937. On screen in 1941 in Murder in the Big House.

Films inc: The War Against Mrs. Hadley; Thirty Seconds Over Tokyo; Romance of Rosy Ridge; State of the Union; Command Decision; Remains to be Seen; The Caine Mutiny; Brigadoon; Miracle in the Rain; Battle Squadron; Spider on the Wall; Eagles Over London; The Kidnapping of the President.

TV inc: The Girl on the Late Late Show; McMillan & Wife.

Thea inc: The Bells Are Ringing; I Do! I Do!; The Music Man.

JOLLEY, Stan: Art Dir. b. NYC, May 17, 1926. e. USC, BA. Films inc: The Good Guys and The Bad Guys; The Phynx; City Beneath the Sea; The War Between Men and Women; Walking Tall; Framed; Drum; Swarm; Superman; Americathon.

TV inc: The Strangers; Punch and Jody; Eagle One; Swiss Family Robinson; Flood; Howard; The Amazing Mr Hughes; Rescue from Gilligan's Island; Happily Ever After; A Very Special Love.

JONES, Allan: Singer-Act. b. Scranton, PA, 1907. Films inc: A Night at the Opera; Rose Marie; Showboat; A Day at the Races; The Firefly; Honeymoon in Bali; The Great Victor Herbert; The Boys from Syracuse; One Night in the Tropics; Moonlight in Havana; Crazy House; The Singing Sheriff; The Senorita From the West; Stage to Thunder Rock; A Swingin' Summer.

JONES, Carolyn: Act. b. Amarillo, TX, Apr 28, 1932. On screen from 1952 in The Turning Point.

Films inc: Road to Bali; Desiree; Baby Face Nelson; House of Wax; Seven Year Itch; The Tender Trap; The Bachelor Party; A Hole in the Head; Ice Palace; Sail a Crooked Ship; A Ticklish Affair; Good Luck, Miss Wyckoff.

TV inc: Roots; The French Atlantic Affair; The Dream Merchants.

Thea inc: Summer and Smoke; Live

JONES, Chuck: Prod-Dir. b. Spokane, WA, Sep 21, 1912. e. Chouinard Art Institute. Dir, Warner Bros Animation until 1962 where he created and dir Roadrunner & Coyote; Pepe le Pew; dir and helped create Bugs Bunny; Porky Pig; Daffy Duck.

Cartoons inc: Nelly's Folly; Ersatz; (Oscar-1961); Beep Prepared; The Dot and the Line (Oscar-1965).

Films inc: Gay Purree; The Phantom Tollbooth.

TV inc: Raggedy Ann and Andy in the Pumpkin Who Couldn't Smile; Bugs Bunny's Bustin' Out All Over; Daffy Duck's Thanks-For-Giving Special.

JONES, Clark: Dir. TV inc: Your Hit Parade; Ford 50th Anniversary Show; Sleeping Beauty; Cinderella; Romeo and Juliet; The Fourposter; Peter Pan; Sid Caesar Show; Patrice Munsel Series; Bell Telephone Hour; Perry Como Specials; Carol Burnett Show; Dinah Shore Special; Carol Channing Specials; Twigs; 6 Rms Rv Vu; Tony Awards (Emmy-1978).

JONES, Dean: Act. b. Decatur, AL, Jan 25, 1931. e. Asbury Coll, UCLA. Films inc: The Great American Pastime; Jailhouse Rock; Under the Yum Yum Tree; That Darn Cat; Any Wednesday; The Horse in the Gray Flannel Suit; The Love Bug; Snowball Express; The Shaggy D.A.; Herbie Goes to Monte Carlo.

TV inc: Ensign O'Toole; The Teddy Bears; The Long Days of Summer.

Thea inc: There Was a Little Girl; Company.

JONES, Gemma: Act. b. London, Dec 4, 1942. e. RADA. Thea inc: Baal; Alfie; The Cavern; The Pastime of M Robert; Portrait of a Queen; Next of Kin; The Marriage of Figaro; And A Nightingale.

TV inc: The Lie; The Way of the World; The Duchess of Duke Street.

Films inc: The Devils.

JONES, Henry: Act. b. Philadelphia, Aug 1, 1912. e. St Joseph's Coll, AB. Films inc: Never Too Late; Stay Away Joe; Support Your Local Sheriff; Rascal; Angel in My Pocket; Butch Cassidy & the Sundance Kid; Rabbit Run; Cock-eyed Cowboys of Calico County; Dirty Dingus Magee; Support Your Local Gunman; Skin Game; Napoleon & Samantha; Tom Sawyer; Pete n Tillie; The Outfit; Nine to Five. Bway inc: Hamlet; The Time of your Life; Village Green; My Sister Eileen; This Is the Army; The Solid Gold Cadillac; The Bad Seed; Sunrise at Campobello (Tony-supp-1958) Advise and Consent; Comedians.

JONES, Jack: Singer-Act. b. LA, Jan 14, 1942. S of Irene Hervey and Allan Jones. Professional debut with parents act, Las Vegas; works nitieries, concerts. Films inc: (Act) Juke Box Rhythm; The Comeback. (Title Song) Love With the Proper Stranger; Where Love Has Gone; A Ticklish Affair; A Battle For Anzio Kotch.

TV inc: (act) The Palace; Holiday Tribute to Radio City. (Title song) Funny Face; Love Boat.

Recs inc: Lollipops and Roses (Grammy-voc-1961); Wive and Lovers (Grammy-voc-1963).

JONES, James Cellan: Dir. b. Swansea, Wales, Jul 13, 1935. Films inc: The Nelson Affair.

TV inc: The Ambassadors, The Scarlet and the Black; The Forsyte Saga; The Day Christ Died.

JONES, James Earl: Act. b. Arkabutla, MS, Jan 17, 1931. e. U of MI, BA. S of Robert Earl Jones. Films inc: Dr. Strangelove; The Comedians; The End of the Road; The Great White Hope; The Man; Malcolm X (doc); Claudine; The Swashbuckler; The Bingo Long Traveling All-Stars and Motor Kings; The River Niger; The Heretic; The Greatest; The Last Remake of Beau Geste; A Piece of the Action; The Bushido Blade.

TV inc: Trumpets of the Lord; Black Omnibus (host-narrator); King Lear; The Cay; Interrupted Journey; A Day Without Sunshine; Jesus of Nazareth; The Greatest Thing that Almost Happened; Roots; Paris; Paul Robeson; Guyana Tragedy--The Story of Jim Jones; Golden Moment-An Olympic Love Story; Philby, Burgess and MacLean; The Knowledge.

Bway inc: Sunrise at Campobello; The Cool World; Infidel Caesar; A Hand is on the Gate; The Great White Hope (Tony-1969); Les Blancs; The Iceman Cometh; Of Mice and Men; Paul Robeson; A Lesson From Aloes.

(Grammy-spoken word-1976).

JONES, Jennifer (Phyllis Isley): Act. b. Tulsa, OK, 1919. e. AADA. Toured with parents' stock company as a child. On screen in 1939 under real name in New Frontier; Dick Tracy's G-Men. On screen from 1942 as Jennifer Jones.

Films inc: The Song of Bernadette (Oscar-1944); Since You Went Away; Love Letters; Duel in the Sun; Love is a Many Splendored Thing; Portrait of Jennie; Ruby Gentry; The Barretts of Wimpole Street; A Farewell to Arms; Tender is the Night; The Towering Inferno; Eagles Over London.

JONES, Preston: Wri-Act. b. 1936. Plays inc: Texas Trilogy (The Knights of the White Magnolia; Lu Ann Hampton Laverty Oberlander; The Oldest Living Graduate); A Place On Magdalena Flats; Remember.
(Died Sep 19, 1979.)

JONES, Quincy: Comp-Arr-Cond-Prod. b. Chicago, Mar 14, 1933. e. Seattle U, Berklee School of Mus, Boston Cons. Trumpeter, arr for Lionel Hampton orch, 1950-53; arr for orchs, singers, inc: Ray Anthony; Count Basie; Sarah Vaughn; Peggy Lee; prod 10 gold records for pop songstress Lesley Gore in the 60s; also introduced and prod The Brothers Johnson.

Films inc: Pawnbroker; Mirage; The Slender Thread; For The Love Of Ivy; In Cold Blood; In the Heat of the Night; The Wiz.

TV inc: Roots (Emmy-1977).

Songs inc: Evening in Paris; The Boy in the Tree Theme; Je ne sais pas; Jasmin. (Grammys-(5)-inst arr-1963, 1973, 1978; group jazz-1969; pop inst-1971).

JONES, Robert C: Wri-Flm Ed. b. LA, Mar 30, 1930. S of Harmon Jones. Films inc: (ed) I Love You Alice B Toklas; Tobruk; Mad, Mad, Mad, Mad, World; A Child is Waiting; Ship of Fools; Guess Who's Coming to Dinner; Love Story; Man of La Mancha; The Last Detail; Shampoo; Bound for Glory; Heaven Can Wait (& mus); Coming Home (sp) (Oscar-1978).

JONES, Sam J: Act. b. Chicago, IL, Aug 24, 1954. TV inc: Stunts Unlimited. Films inc: 10; Flash Gordon.

JONES, Shirley: Act. b. Smithton, PA, Mar 31, 1934. Thea inc: Lady in the Dark; Call Me Madam; South Pacific.

Films inc: Elmer Gantry (Oscar-supp-1960); Oklahoma; Carousel; A Ticklish Affair; The Music Man; Bedtime Story; The Cheyenne Social Club; Beyond The Poseidon Adventure.

TV inc: Silent Night, Lonely Night; The Partridge Family; Shirley; Hope, Women & Song; The Children of An Lac.

JONES, Tom (nee Woodward): Singer. b. Pontypridd, Wales, Jun 7, 1940. Began singing in village stores at age 3. Organized group the Playboys 1964 for recordings, London nitery dates. U.S. tours in 1965 and 1968.

Recordings inc: It's Not Unusual (Grammy-new artist-1965).

TV inc: This is Tom Jones; Pleasure Cove; Lynda Carter Encore!

JORDAN, Glenn: Dir-Prod. e. Harvard Coll, BA, Yale Drama School. TV inc: Hogan's Goat; Paradise Lost; Eccentricities of a Nightingale; Benjamin Franklin (Emmy-prod-1975); The Oath; Shell Game; In the Matter of Karen Ann Quinlan; Sunshine Christmas; The Court Martial of Gen Armstrong Custer; Les Miserables; Son-Rise; The Family Man; The Women's Room.

JORDAN, Richard: Act. b. 1938. Films inc: The Yakuza; Kamouraska; Rooster Cogburn; Old Boyfriends; Interiors; Raise The Titanic.

TV inc: Captains and the Kings; Les Miserables; The French Atlantic Affair.

JORDAN, Will: Act. b. Jul 27. e. AADA. Comedian and impressionist; over 400 major TV credits including 22 appearances on the Ed Sullivan Show where he created imitation of Sullivan.

Bway inc: Bye Bye Birdie.

Films inc: The Buddy Holly Story; I Wanna Hold Your Hand.

JORY, Victor: Act. b. Dawson City, Canada, Nov 28, 1902. Screen debut, 1932, Sailor's Luck.

Films inc: Leather Burners; Unknown Guest; Cariboo Trail; The Highwayman; Cave of Outlaws; Son of Ali Baba; Toughest Man in Arizona; Valley of the Kings; Desperado; The Miracle Worker; A Time for Dying; Papillon; The Mountain Men.

Thea inc: Berkeley Square; Tonight or Never; What Every Woman Knows; The Truth Game.

TV inc: Kings Row; Manhunt; Banacek; Mannix; Name of the Game; High Chaparral; Ironside; Virginian; Voyage to the Bottom of the Sea; Greatest Heroes of the Bible; Power.

JOSEFSBERG, Milt: Wri-Prod. b. NYC, Jun 29, 1911. Wri for Bob Hope; Jack Benny; Joey Bishop; Lucille Ball; Here's Lucy (created format); All in the Family (prod-wri-script supv) (Emmy-prod-1978).

JOSEPHSON, Marvin A: Agt. b. NYC, Jun 5, 1935. e. Long Island U, BA. Liebling-Wood Agency; Music Corp of America; General Artists Corp; Agency for the Performing Arts; ChmnB Marvin Josephson Associates, Parent Company of International Creative Mgt.

JOURDAN, Louis: Act. b. Marseilles, France, Jun 19, 1921. On stage prior to screen debut 1939.

Films inc: Her First Affair; The Paradine Case; Letter from an Unknown Woman; Madame Bovary; Three Coins in the Fountain; Gigi; Can-Can; A Flea in Her Ear; To Commit a Murder; The More It Goes, The Less It Goes; Silver Bears.

TV inc: The French Atlantic Affair.

Bway inc: 13 Rue de l'Amour.

JOUVE, Nicole: Dist exec. b. Paris, 1928. M-dir, Interama.

JULIA, Raul: Act. b. San Juan, Puerto Rico, Mar 9, 1940. e. U of Puerto Rico. Bway inc: The Marriage Proposal; Mobile; Macbeth; Titus Andronicus; No Exit; Your Own Thing; The Cuban Thing; Indians; Two Gentlemen of Verona; Via Galactica; As You Like It; King Lear; Where's Charley; Three Penny Opera.

Films inc: The Eyes of Laura Mars.

JULIEN, Jay: Prod. b. NYC, Aug 11, 1924. e. CCNY, BSS, Georgetown, LLB. Bway inc: A Hatful of Rain; The Night Circus; The Fun Couple; Hostile Witness; Hughie/Duet; It's So Nice to Be Civilized.

JUMP, Gordon: Act. b. Dayton, OH, Apr 1, 1932. e. KS State U. Started as prodn dir WIBW-TV, Topeka, KS, wri-prod WLWD, Dayton.

Films inc: Conquest of the Planet of the Apes; Trouble Man; Adam at 6 A.M.

TV inc: Goldie; WKRP in Cincinnati.

JURADO, Katy (Maria Christina Jurado): Act. b. Guadalajara, Mexico, 1927. In Mexican films, Hollywood debut 1951. Films inc: The Bullfighter and the Lady; High Noon; Broken Lance; Trapeze; One-Eyed Jacks; Barabbas; A Covenant with Death; The Bridge in the Jungle; The Children of Sanchez; La Viuda De Montiel; El Recurso Del Metedo.

JURGENS, Curt: Act. b. Munich, Dec 12, 1915. On German stage then screen in 1939.

Films inc: The Enemy Below; And God Created Woman; The Longest Day; Of Love and Desire; Lord Jim; The Assassination Bureau; Legion of the Damned; Nicholas and Alexandra; Kill Kill Kill; Undercover Hero; Die Patriotin; Goldengirl; La Gueble de l'Autre; Breakthrough.

JUROW, Martin: Prod. b. NYC, Dec 14, 1911. e. Harvard Law, BA, JD. Agent with MCA, William Morris, Famous Artists before becoming prod.

Films inc: The Hanging Tree; The Fugitive Kind; Breakfast at Tiffanys; Soldier in the Rain; The Pink Panther; The Great Race.

JUSTIN, John: Act. b. London, Nov 23, 1917. Films inc: Thief of Bagdad; The Sound Barrier; The Village; Melba; Crest of the Wave; King of the Khyber Rifles; Untamed; Safari; Island in the Sun; The Savage Messiah; Barcelona Kill; Lisztomania; Valentino; The Big Sleep.

KACZENDER, George: Dir. b. Apr 19, 1933, Budapest. e. Film Academy. Films inc: Don't Let the Angels Fall; U-Turn; In Praise of Older Women; Agency.

KADAR, Jan: Dir. b. Budapest, Hungary, Apr 1, 1918. Films inc: Life Is Rising From The Ruins (doc); Katya; Kidnapped; Music from Mars; The Terminal; Three Wishes; A Shop on Main Street *(Oscar-*foreign film-1965); The Angel Levine; Adrift; Lies My Father Told Me.

TV inc: Blue Hotel; Case Against Milligan; Mandelstam's Witness; Hope Against Hope; Freedom Road.

(Died June 1, 1979).

KAEMPFERT, Bert: Comp. b. Germany, 1924. Songs inc: Spanish Eyes; Strangers in the Night; Danke Schoen.

(Died June 22, 1980).

KAGAN, Jeremy Paul: Dir-Wri. b. Mt Vernon, NY, Dec 14, 1945. e. Harvard, NYU, MFA. TV inc: Columbo; The Bold Ones; Unwed Father; Judge Dee; My Dad Lives in a Downtown Hotel; Katherine (& wri); Scott Joplin; Heroes; The Big Fix.

KAHN, Madeline: Act. b. Boston, 1942. Films inc: What's Up Doc?; Paper Moon; Blazing Saddles; Young Frankenstein; The Adventures of Sherlock Holmes' Smarter Brother; At Long Last Love; Won Ton Ton, The Dog Who Saved Hollywood; The Cheap Detective; The Muppet Movie; Simon; Happy Birthday, Gemini; Wholly Moses; First Family.

Bway inc: La Boheme; Showboat; Two by Two; Candide; In the Boom Boom Room; On the 20th Century.

KAHN, Michael: Dir. b. NYC. e. Columbia U, BA. Prod-dir McCarter Theatre, Princeton; dir NY Shakespeare Festival. Thea inc: The Love Nest; Funnyhouse of a Negro; Victims of Duty; America Hurrah; Here's Where I Belong; As You Like It; The Crucible; Winter's Tale; Our Town; Cat on a Hot Tin Roof; Romeo and Juliet; Macbeth; Julius Caesar; Mourning Becomes Electra; All's Well That Ends Well.

KAHN, Richard: Exec. b. New Rochelle, NY, Aug 19, 1929. e. U of PA, BS. Joined MGM 1974 from Columbia Pictures, where he was vp in charge of Worldwide special marketing projects; 1975, MGM's vp worldwide advertising, publicity and exploitation; 1978, Sr VP Worldwide Mktg; 1979, P MGM Int'l.

KAHN, Sheldon: Film Edtr. b. Mar 21, 1940. e. USC, BA. Films inc: One Flew Over The Cuckoo's Nest; Great Scout and Cathouse Thursday; Mikey and Nicky; Enemy of the People; Blood Brothers; Same Time Next Year; The Electric Horseman; Private Benjamin.

KALBER, Floyd: TV Newsman. b. Omaha, NE, Dec 23, 1924. e. Creighton U. Joined NBC News in 1960 after 11 years as news dir KMTV, Omaha; anchorman for NBC Sunday News; newscaster on Today.

KALSER, Konstantin: Prod. Act. b. Munich, Germany, Sep 4, 1920. Founded Marathon International Prodns, Inc, p, exec prod; p, Kleinerman-Kalser Asso, Ltd.

Films inc: Crashing the Water Barrier *(Oscar-*1956-ss); Give and Take; Right Hand of Plenty; The Carmakers; I'm Takin' the Time; Each Day at Dawn; In Spite of Walls; The One for the Road (dir).

KAMINSKA, Ida: Act-Prod-Dir. b. Odessa, Russia, Sep 4, 1899. Stage debut age 5 with parents who were celebrated Yiddish stage actors in Poland; perf in Jewish and classical repertory in Poland and Russia; founded Warsaw Jewish Art Theatre; Ida Kaminska Theatre; to Russia in 1939, remaining until 1945, touring key cities in repertory; 1945 founded Jewish State Theatre Poland, remained there as artistic dir; 1967 brought troupe to US to present Mirele Efrom; Mother Courage; 1968 emigrated to US; worked to re-establish Yiddish Theatre in US.

Films inc: The Shop on Main Street.

TV inc: Mandelstam's Witness.

(Died May 21, 1980).

KAMM, Larry: Dir-Prod. b. Long Branch, NJ, Oct 10, 1939. e. Northwestern U, BS. TV inc: 1972 Winter Olympics; 1976 Winter Olympics *(Emmy-*dir); Indianapolis 500; Grand Prix of Monaco; NCAA Football; Frankie Valli On Stage; Friday Night at the Kentucky Derby.

KANALY, Steve: Act. b. Burbank, CA, Mar 14. Films inc: The Life and Times of Judge Roy Bean; Dillinger; The Sugarland Express; Terminal Man; The Wind and the Lion; Midway. TV inc: The Lost; Young Joe--The Forgotten Kennedy; Amelia Earhart; Melvin Purvis; To Find My Son; Dallas.

KANDER, John: Comp. b. Kansas City, MO, Mar 18, 1927. e. Columbia, MA. Bway inc: A Family Affair; Flora, The Red Menace; Cabaret *(Tony-*1967); The Happy Time; Zorba; 70 Girls 70; The Act.

Films inc: Cabaret; Chicago; Funny Lady; Lucky Lady; New York, New York.

TV inc: Liza with a Z *(Emmy-*1973).

*(Grammy-*cast album-1967).

KANE, Carol: Act. b. OH, Jun 18, 1952. Bway inc: The Prime of Miss Jean Brodie; The Effect of Gamma Rays on Man-in-the-Moon Marigolds.

Films inc: Carnal Knowledge; Wedding in White; Desperate Characters; The Last Detail; Hester Street; Dog Day Afternoon; Harry and Walter Go To New York; Valentino; The Mafu Cage; When A Stranger Calls; The Muppet Movie; La Sabina.

KANE, Josh: Exec. b. NYC. e. Brooklyn Coll, BA. Joined NBC in 1965 as a page; In pub dept 1969-1976; to program dept 1976; named vp, programs, East Coast, Nov 1977.

KANE, Thomas J: Story Ed. b. Chicago, Mar 24, 1920. e. Northwestern U, BA. With Batjac Prods; worked on all John Wayne films since 1952. Sec, asst treas Batjac Prods.

KANIN, Fay (nee Mitchell): Wri. b. NYC. e. Elmira Coll, USC. W of Michael Kanin. Films inc: Blondie for Victory; Sunday Punch; My Pal Gus; Rhapsody; The Opposite Sex; Teacher's Pet; Swordsman of Siena; The Right Approach; The Outrage.

Plays inc: Goodbye My Fancy; His and Hers; Rashomon; The Gay Life.

TV inc: Heat of Anger; Tell Me Where It Hurts *(Emmy-*1974-also wri of the year); Hustling; Friendly Fire *(Emmy-*co-prod-1979); Fun & Games (co-prod).

KANIN, Garson: Prod-Dir-Wri. b. Rochester, NY, Nov 24, 1912. e. AADA. H of Ruth Gordon. Briefly Bway actor then prod asst to George Abbott. Dir, Hitch Your Wagon; Too Many Heroes. Joined Samuel Goldwyn's prod staff, 1937. To RKO, 1938 as prod-dir. Films inc: Adam's Rib; Born Yesterday; Pat and Mike; Tom, Dick and Harry; The Rat Race; Woman of the Year; The More the Merrier.

Plays inc: Born Yesterday; The Diary of Anne Frank; Hole in the Head; Sunday in New York; Funny Girl; Idiot's Delight. Bway (dir) Dreyfus In Rehearsal.

TV inc: Hardhat & Legs.

KANIN, Michael: Wri-Prod. b. Rochester, NY, Feb 1, 1910. Worked as commercial and scenic artist, musician and entertainer before turning to writing.

Films inc: They Made Her a Spy; Panama Lady; Anne of Windy Poplars; Woman of the Year *(Co-Oscar-*1942); The Cross of Lorraine; Centennial Summer; Honeymoon; Sunday Punch; My Pal Gus; Rhapsody; The Swordsman of Siena; The Opposite Sex; Teacher's Pet; The Outrage; How to Commit Marriage. When I Grow Up (& dir); prod A Double Life.

Bway inc: (prod) Goodbye My Fancy; Seidman and Son. Wrote (with wife Fay Kanin) His and Hers; Rashomon; The Gay Life.

KANTER, Hal: Wri-Dir-Prod. b. Savannah, GA, Dec 18, 1918. Wri: Danny Kaye Show; Amos 'n Andy; Bing Crosby Show; Ed Wynn TV Show, 1949. Paramount, 1951-54; dir RKO Radio, 1956; prod, dir, wri, Kraft Music Hall, 1958-59.

TV inc: Chrysler Theatre; George Gobel Show *(Emmy-*1954); Julia; Jimmy Stewart; All in the Family; Chico & The Man; Lucy Moves To NBC (prod-wri); For the Love of It (dir).

Films inc: My Favorite Spy; Road to Bali; Artists and Models; Rose Tattoo; Pocketful of Miracles; Move Over, Darling; Brigitte.

KANTER, Jay: Exec. b. 1927. Started as agent with MCA, when agency dissolved became European prodn head for U, which MCA had acquired; resd to enter indie prodn with Elliott Kastner; 1972, P First Artists Prodns; 1975 to Fox as prodn vp; 1976 sr vp; 1978 sr vp wldwde prodn; resd 1979 with Alan Ladd Jr, Gareth Wigan, joining them in new indie The Ladd Co.

KAPER, Bronislau: Comp. b. Warsaw, Poland, Feb 5, 1902. Film scores inc: Gaslight; Without Love; Green Dolphin Street; The Forsyte Saga; The Red Badge of Courage; Lili (*Oscar*-1953); Them; The Swan; The Brothers Karamazov; Butterfield 8; Mutiny on the Bounty; Kisses for My President; Lord Jim; Tobruk; A Flea in Her Ear.

KAPLAN, Gabe: Act. b. NYC, Mar 31, 1946. Nitery comic.
TV inc: Welcome Back Kotter. Films inc: Fast Break.

KAPLAN, Jonathan: Dir-Wri. b. Paris, Nov 25, 1947. e. U of Chicago, BA; NYU, MFA. Films inc: The Slams; Truck Turner; White Line Fever; Mr Billion; Over the Edge.
TV inc: The 11th Victim; The Hustler of Muscle Beach.

KAPLAN, Mike: Newspaperman. b. Salem, MA, May 7, 1918. Reporter Playhouse (thea tradepaper) 1933, asso edtr 1934; 1936 city edtr Boston Bureau Transradio Press; 1939 man edtr Boston City News Bureau; 1942 night newscast edtr NY Daily News; 1947 West Coast edtr Variety (weekly) and legit, nitery critic for Daily Variety; 1958-1961 freelance film publicist, Europe; 1961-1964 with Stanley Kramer Prodns; 1964 pub dir Robert Wise Prodns; 1966 exec asst to Wise; 1973 organized National News Service for U; 1978 returned to Variety to create, edit International Reference.

KAPROFF, Dana: Comp-Cond. b. LA, Apr 24, 1954. e. UCLA. TV inc: Once An Eagle; Ellery Queen; The Bionic Woman; Hawaii 5-0; Belle Starr; Scared Straight.
Films inc: The Late Great Planet Earth; When A Stranger Calls; The Big Red One.

KARGER, Fred: Comp-Orch Ldr. b. 1916. Under contract to Columbia's mus dept for many years. Wrote theme song for From Here to Eternity.
(Died Aug 5, 1979.)

KARINA, Anna (Hanne Karin Beyer): Act. b. Copenhagen, 1940. Films inc: She'll Have To Go; Une Femme Est Une Femme; Vivre Sa Vie; Le Petit Soldat; Bande a Part; Alphaville; The Magus; Before Winter Comes; Laughter in the Dark; Justine; Rendezvous At Bray; The Salzburg Connection; Surprise Sock; Bread and Chocolate; Vivre Ensemble (& dir); Story of a Mother.

KARLAN, Richard: Act. b. NYC, Apr 24, 1919. e. Brooklyn Coll. Films inc: Union Station; The Lemon Drop Kid; Sailor Beware; The Racket; Wait Till The Sun Shines Nellie; Blowing Wild; All the Brothers Were Valiant; I Died a Thousand Times; While the City Sleeps; Inside the Mafia; Star!
TV inc: Betrayal; Missiles of October; The Blue Knight; The Partners.

KARLIN, Fred: Comp-Cond. b. Chicago, Jun 16, 1936. e. Amherst Coll, BA. Comp, arr for orchs inc: Benny Goodman; Harry James.
Films inc: Up the Down Staircase; Yours, Mine and Ours; The Sterile Cuckoo; Lovers and Other Strangers (*Co-Oscar*-song, For All We Know-1970); Westworld; Gravy Train; Mixed Company; Leadbelly; Minstrel Man; California Dreaming; Ravagers; Cloud Dancer; Loving Couples.
TV inc: Autobiography of Miss Jane Pittman (*Emmy*-1974); Once Upon A Family; Marriage Is Alive and Well; The Plutonium Incident; Baby Comes Home; Sophia Loren--Her Own Story; Homeward Bound; The Secret War of Jackie's Girls; Fighting Back; My Kidnaper, My Love; Mom, The Wolfman and Me; A Time For Marriage.
Songs: Come Saturday Morning; Come Follow, Follow Me; Early in the Morning.

KARLSON, Phil (nee Karlstein): Dir. b. Chicago, 1980. Films inc: A WAVE, a WAC and a Marine; Swing Parade; Dark Alibi; The Missing Lady; Black Gold; Kilroy was Here; Thunderhoof; The Big Cat; Down Memory Lane; Lorna Doone; The Texas Rangers; Scandal Sheet; Kansas City Confidential; Hell's Island; Five Against the House; The Phenix City Story; The Brothers Rico; Key Witness; The Young Doctors; Kid Galahad; Rampage; The Silencers; A Time for Killing; Hornet's Nest; Ben; Walking Tall; Framed.

KARP, David: Wri. Films inc: Sol Madrid; Cervantes; Che!.
TV inc: The Defenders (*Emmy*-1965); Garrison's Gorillas; The Storefront Lawyers (& crea); The Family Rico; Hawkins (& crea); Archer (developed); W.E.B. (crea).

KARP, Jacob H (Jack): Exec. b. NYC, Jan 2, 1903. e. NYU, Columbia Law School. Entered ind 1929, legal dept Par, NY; transferred to studio 1932; became resident atty in chg legal dept 1935; made exec asst to studio head 1941; named vp chg studio 1959; resd 1964 to enter indie prodn; later returned as legal consultant.
(Died Oct 12, 1980).

KARRAS, Alex: Act. b. Gary, IN, Jul 15, 1935. e. IA U. Former pro football player.
Films inc: Blazing Saddles; Another Day at the Races; Jacob Two-Two Meets The Hooded Fang; Mad Bull; When Time Ran Out.
TV inc: The Paper Lion; Hardcase; The 500 Lb Jerk; Babe; For As Long As the Water Flows; The Longhorns; The Big Event; The Storm; The Crime; The Winds of Change; The Winds of Death; Jimmy B & Andre; Alcatraz--The Whole Shocking Story.

KASHA, Al: Sngwri. b. NYC, Jan 22, 1937. e. NYU, BS; Juilliard. Writes in collaboration with Joel Hirschhorn.
Songs inc: My Empty Arms; I'm Comin' On Back To You; Let's Start All Over Again; Wake Up; Your Time Hasn't Come Yet, Baby; Will You Be Staying After Sunday?; One More Mountan to Climb; The Subject Was Roses; Living is Dying Without You; The Morning After (*Oscar*-1972); We May Never Love Like This Again (*Oscar*-1974); Candle on the Water; I'd Like To Be You for a Day; May the Best Man Win; Mississippi Magic; Pass A Little Love Around.

KASHA, Lawrence N: Prod-Dir-Plywri. b. NYC, Dec 3, 1932. e. NYU, BA, MA. Dir nat'l companies L'il Abner; Camelot; Funny Girl; Cactus Flower; Star Spangled Girl; Bway prodn Bajour; Lovely Ladies, Kind Gentlemen before becoming prod. Bway inc: She Loves Me; Hadrian VII; Applause (*Tony*-1970); Father's Day; Inner City; Seesaw; No Hard Feelings; Seven Brides for Seven Brothers.
TV inc: Applause; Another April; Rosenthal and Jones; Busting Loose; Komedy Tonite; Willow B--Women in Prison.
Plays inc: The Pirate; Where Have You Been, Billy Boy?; Heaven Sent; Seven Brides for Seven Brothers.

KASTNER, Elliott: Prod. b. NYC, Jan 7, 1933. e. U of Miami, Columbia U. Started as agent with MCA, named vp 1960; became prod when MCA took over Universal; became ind prod with Harper.
Films inc: Kaleidoscope; The Bobo; Sweet November; Sol Madrid; Laughter In the Dark; The Night of the Following Day; Where Eagles Dare; A Severed Head; When Eight Bells Toll; Tam Lin; X Y and Zee; The Nightcomers; Big Truck and Poor Clare; Fear is the Key; The Long Goodbye; Cops and Robbers; 11 Harrowhouse; Rancho Deluxe; 92 in the Shade; Farewell, My Lovely; Russian Roulette; Breakheart Pass; The Missouri Breaks; Swashbuckler; Black Joy; A Little Night Music; Equus; The Stick Up; The Medusa Touch; The Big Sleep; Goldengirl; Yesterday's Hero; Ffolkes; The First Deadly Sin.

KASZNAR, Kurt: Act. b. Vienna, Aug 12, 1913. Films inc: The Light Touch; The Last Time I Saw Paris; Lili; Kiss Me Kate; A Farewell to Arms; Legend of the Lost; Lovely to Look At; My Sister Eileen; 55 Days at Peking; Casino Royale; The Ambushers; Torn Curtain.
Thea inc: The Sound of Music; Barefoot in the Park; Waiting for Godot; Henry V; Montserrat; The Happy Time; Mack the Knife.
TV inc: Land of the Giants; Suddenly Love.
(Died Aug 6, 1979.)

KATLEMAN, Harris L: Exec. b. Omaha, NE, Aug 19, 1928. e. UCLA, BA. Joined MCA in 1949; joined Goodson-Todman Prodns in 1955; named vp in 1956; exec vp in 1958; sr exec vp in 1968; joined MGM in 1972 as vp MGM-TV; 1973, P MGM-TV, sr vp MGM Inc; resd 1977 to enter indie prod with Harve Bennett; partnership dissolved, became chmn Fox-TV May 1, 1980.

TV inc: Salvage; From Here to Eternity; The Golden Gun; From Here To Eternity-The War Years; Alex and the Doberman Gang; Nick and the Dobermans.

KATSELAS, Milton: Dir. b. Pittsburgh, PA, Feb 22, 1933. e. Carnegie Institute of Technology. Thea inc: The Zoo Story; Call Me By My Rightful Name; The Garden of Sweets; On an Open Roof (& co-prod); The Rose Tattoo (rev); Butterflies Are Free; Camino Real.

Films inc: Butterflies Are Free; 40 Carats; Report to the Commissioner; When You Coming Back, Red Ryder.

KATZ, Norman B: Exec. b. Scranton, PA, Aug 23, 1919. Exec asst to head of prodn, Discina-Speva Films (Paris), 1948-49; 1950-53, vp, exec vp, Discina International Films; 1954-57, foreign Mgr, Asso Artists Prodns; 1958-59, dir of foreign operations, UA Prodns; 1959-61, dir of foreign operations, UA; 1961-64, vp in charge, foreign operations, Seven Arts Associates Corp; 1964-67, exec vp, Seven Arts Prodns Intl; 1967-69, exec vp, WB-Seven Arts Intl; 1969-72, exec vp, chief exec ofcr, WB Intl, board member WB, Inc; 1975, P, Cinema Arts Assoc Corp; 1979 exec vp American Communications Industries; 1980 p American Communications Intl.

KATZENBERG, Jeff: Exec. Joined Par NY 1975 as asst to chmn of board; 1976, exec dir mktg & adm; 1977 to Hollywood as vp film div; 1978, prodn vp in chg acquisitions, pickups; 1980 sr vp prodn.

KATZIN, Lee H: Dir. b. Detroit, Apr 12, 1935. e. Harvard Coll, AB. Films inc: Heaven with a Gun; Whatever Happened to Aunt Alice?; The Phynx; Le Mans; The Salzburg Connection.

TV inc; The Rat Patrol; Wild, Wild West; Hondo; Felony Squad; Mission Impossible; It Takes a Thief; The Mod Squad; Mannix; Along Came a Spider; Visions; Strange Homecoming; Savages; Space 1999; McMillan & Wife; Sky Heist; The Last Survivor; Firebird; Police Story; Relentless; McLaren's Riders; Man from Atlantis; The Quest; The Bastard; Broken Badge; River of Promises; Terror Out Of The Sky; Samurai; Zuma Beach; T. R. Sloane.

KATZKA, Gabriel: Prod. b. NYC, Jan 25, 1931. e. Kenyon Coll. Films inc: Marlowe; Kelly's Heroes; Soldier Blue; The Parallax View; The Taking of Pelham 1-2-3; The Heartbreak Kid; Sleuth; A Bridge Too Far; Who'll Stop the Rain; Meteor; Butch and Sundance--The Early Days. Bway inc: Pal Joey; Hamlet; The Little Foxes; Anna Christie; Same Time Next Year; The Comedians; Hughie; A View From the Bridge. TV inc: Kavik-the Wolf Dog.

KAUFER, Jonathan: Wri. b. LA, Mar 14, 1955. TV inc: The Practice; Alice; Destination: Uranus; Quark (story ed).

KAUFMAN, Andy: Act. b. NYC, Jan 17, 1949. TV inc: Saturday Night Live; The New Dick Van Dyke Show; Taxi; Johnny Cash Christmas. Films inc: In God We Trust.

KAUFMAN, Boris: Cin. b. Poland, 1897. Began as cin in France, Worked for Canadian Film Board and U.S. Office of War Information during WW2 making documentaries; emigrated to US where he established himself as leading East Coast lenser.

Films inc: (Europe) 24 Hours in 30 Minutes; Seine; A Propos de Nice; Zero de Conduite; L'Atalanta. (U.S.): On the Waterfront (Oscar-1954); Patterns; Baby Doll; Twelve Angry Men; That Kind of Woman; The Fugitive Kind; Splendor in the Grass; Long Day's Journey Into Night; Gone Are the Days; All the Way Home; The World of Henry Orient; The Pawnbroker; The Group; Uptight; The Brotherhood; Tell Me That You Love Me, Junie Moon.

Ret 1972. (Died June 24, 1980).

KAUFMAN, Leonard: Prod-Wri. b. Newark, NJ, Aug 31, 1927. e. NYU. Films inc: Clarence, the Cross-eyed Lion (prod); Birds Do It (sp only). TV inc: (prod) Daktari; Jambo; O'Hara, US Treasury; Escape; Archer; Grizzly Adams; Sam; Hawaii Five-O; (wri): Hawaii Five-O; Baretta; Grizzly Adams; Policewoman; Harry-O; Chase; Adam 12; Maude; Daktari; Barbary Coast; The Danger Game; Archer; Flipper; King Family; (dir-wri-crea): Jambo; (wri-prod): Keeper of the Wild (pilot); African Queen (pilot); Mr. & Mrs. Cop (pilot); Time Express (prod); Scruples (prod).

KAUFMAN, Millard: Wri. b. NYC, Mar 12, 1917. e. Johns Hopkins U, BA. Films inc: To the Center of the Earth; Take the High Ground; Bad Day at Black Rock; Raintree County; Never So Few; Reprieve (& dir); War Lord; John Collier; Living Free; The Klansman.

TV inc: The Nativity; Enola Gay--The Men, The Mission, The Atomic Bomb.

KAUFMAN, Philip: Dir. b. Chicago, Oct 23, 1936. e. Chicago U. Films inc: Goldstein; Fearless Frank; The Great Northfield; Minnesota Raid; Invasion Of The Body Snatchers; The Wanderers (& sp).

KAUFMAN, Robert: Wri-Prod. b. NYC. e. Columbia U. Films inc: (wri) Ski Party; Dr. Goldfoot and the Bikini Machine; Divorce American Style; I Love My Wife; Freebie and the Bean; Harry and Walter Go To New York; Love at First Bite (& co-exec prod); How to Beat the High Cost of Living.

TV inc: Ben Casey; Get Smart; McHale's Navy; Alfred Hitchcock Presents; The Bob Newhart Show.

KAUTNER, Helmut: Dir. b. Dusseldorf, Germany, 1908. Originally an actor, he specialized in satirical comedy in cabarets. Worked as an act and dir in theatres in Leipzig, Munich and Berlin. Went to Hollywood in the 50's where he made a few films before returning to Europe. Films inc: Kitty and the World Conference; The Last Bridge; The Devil's General; The Captain From Kopenick; Der Rest ist Schweigen; Anuschka; Romanze im Moll; Unter den Bruecken; Der Apfel is Ab; Himmel Ohne Sterne; The Wonderful Years (Hollywood); Stranger In My Arms (Hollywood).

(Died Apr 20, 1980).

KAVNER, Julie: Act. b. LA, Sep 7. e. CSU San Diego. TV inc: Rhoda (Emmy-supp-1978); No Other Love; Revenge of the Stepford Wives.

KAYDEN, William: Prod. b. NYC. TV inc: I Heard the Owl Call My Name; The Family Nobody Wanted; Yesterday's Child; Final Eye; Cops and Robin; Lady of the House; To Race The Wind.

KAYE, Buddy: Sngwri-Mus. b. NYC, Jan 3, 1918. Began career as saxophonist; wrote special material for Mills Bros; Ted Lewis; McGuire Sisters; wrote songs for Walt Disney Films; also for Popeye the Sailor cartoons; Bouncing Ball series.

Films inc: The Trouble with Girls; Change of Habit; Not as a Stranger; Treasure of Sierra Madre; Twist Around the Clock.

TV inc: I Dream of Jeannie; Cross Wits.

Songs: Till the End of Time; Full Moon and Empty Arms; A-You're Adorable; Quiet Nights; What You See Is Who I Am.

KAYE, Caren: Act. b. NYC, Mar 12. e. Carnegie Tech. TV inc: The Betty White Show; Blansky's Beauties; Who's Watching the Kids.

Thea inc: USA; Barefoot in the Park (road co).

KAYE, Danny: Act. b. NYC, Jan 18, 1913. Performed on stage, night clubs. Screen debut, 1944, Up In Arms. Films inc: The Secret Life of Walter Mitty; A Song Is Born; Hans Christian Andersen; White Christmas; The Court Jester; The Madwoman of Chaillot (retired from screen after this film, 1969).

TV inc: The Danny Kaye Show (Emmy-1964); Kraft Salutes Disneyland's 25th Anniversary (host).

(Tony-special-1953); (Oscar-special-1954).

KAYE, Nora: Dancer-Prod. b. NYC, 1920. e. NY Metropolitan Opera Ballet School. W of Herbert Ross. As a child performed with Met Opera Ballet and at Radio City. Joined American Ballet Theatre at its inception; hailed as leading drama dancer of her time after appearance in Hagar; also danced classic roles; 1951-54 with NYC Ballet where Jerome Robbins created Cage for her; 1954-1960 returned to ABT where Kenneth MacMillan created ballets Winters Eve and Journey for her; married Herbert Ross and with him formed Ballet of Two worlds with which she toured extensively as prima ballerina. Retired from dancing 1961 to work with Ross.

Films inc: (prod) Turning Point; Nijinsky.

KAYE, Sammy: Orch ldr-Comp. b. Rocky River, OH, Mar 13, 1910. e. OH U. Organized own band while in college; played niteries, radio. Started radio pgm So You Want To Lead a Band.

Films inc: Iceland; Song of the Open Road.

Songs inc: Until Tomorrow; Hawaiian Sunset; Tell Me That You Love Me; Wanderin'.

KAYE, Stubby: Act. b. NYC, Nov 11, 1918. Toured as a comedian in vaudeville, 1939-42.

Thea inc: Guys and Dolls; Li'l Abner; Everybody Loves Opal; Good News; The Ritz.

Films inc: Guys and Dolls; Li'l Abner; The Dirtiest Girl I Ever Met; 40 Pounds of Trouble; Cat Ballou; Sweet Charity.

KAZAN, Elia: Dir. b. Constantinople, Sep 7, 1909. e. Williams Coll, Yale Drama School. Stage, films as actor before becoming dir.

Films inc: Gentleman's Agreement (Oscar-1947); Boomerang; A Streetcar Named Desire; On the Waterfront (Oscar-1954); Man on a Tightrope; East of Eden; Splendor in the Grass; The Arrangement; The Last Tycoon.

Thea inc: (as act) Waiting for Lefty; Golden Boy; Gentle People; Liliom. (Dir) The Skin of Our Teeth; A Streetcar Named Desire; All My Sons (Tony-1947); Death of a Salesman (Tony-1949); Cat On a Hot Tin Roof; One Touch Of Venus; Jacobowsky and the Colonel; Tea and Sympathy; JB (Tony-1959); Sweet Bird of Youth.

Author of The Arrangement; The Assassins; The Understudy.

KAZAN, Lainie (nee Levine): Singer. b. NY, May 15, 1943. e. Hofstra U. On stage, niteries, TV.

Films inc: Romance of a Horse Thief; Lady in Cement; Dayton's Devils.

KEACH, Stacy: Act. b. Savannah, GA, Jun 2, 1941. Films inc: The Heart is a Lonely Hunter; End of the Road; The Travelling Executioner; Brewster McCloud; Judge Roy Bean; The New Centurions; Fat City; The Gravy Train; The Killer Inside Me; Conduct Unbecoming; The Squeeze; Cheech & Chong's Up In Smoke; Gray Lady Down; Big Wednesday; Street People; The Search For Solutions (narr); The Ninth Configuration.

TV inc: Caribe; Odyssey-Seeking The First Americans; A Rumor of War.

KEANE, James: Act. b. Buffalo, NY, Sep 26, 1952. Films inc: Three Days of the Condor; Close Encounters of the Third Kind; The Ninth Configuration; Uncle Joe Shannon; Apocalypse Now.

TV inc: Intimate Strangers; Night Cries; The Paper Chase; Life On The Mississippi.

KEATON, Diane: Act. b. Santa Ana, CA, Jan 5, 1949. Performed in summer stock. Bway debut 1968, Hair.

Bway inc: Play It Again, Sam; The Primary English Class. Screen debut 1970, Lovers and Other Strangers.

Films inc: The Godfather; Play It Again, Sam; Sleeper; The Godfather, Part II; Love and Death; I Will, I Will. . .For Now. . .; Harry and Walter Go to New York; Annie Hall (Oscar-1977); Looking for Mr. Goodbar; Interiors; Manhattan.

TV inc: Love American Style; The FBI; Mannix.

KEDROVA, Lila: Act. b. USSR, 1918. Films inc: Zorba the Greek (Oscar-supp-1964); A High Wind in Jamaica; Torn Curtain; Penelope; The Kremlin Letter; Soft Beds, Hard Battles; The Tenant; Widow's Nest; March or Die; Le Cavaleur; Claire De Femme; The Sewers of Paradise; Tell Me A Riddle.

KEEFER, Don: Act. b. High Spire, PA. e. AADA. Films inc: Death of a Salesman; Riot in Cell Block II; Away All Boats; Six Bridges to Cross; Caine Mutiny; The Russians Are Coming! The Russians Are Coming!; Butch Cassidy and the Sundance Kid; The Way We Were; Sleeper; The Car; Firesale; Not So Big; Marathon.

Thea inc: Junior Miss; Harriet; Othello; Death of a Salesman; Flight Into Egypt.

TV inc: Moviola (The Scarlett O'Hara War).

KEEL, Howard: Act. b. Gillespie, IL, Apr 13, 1919. Stage debut, 1945, Carousel. Screen debut, 1948, The Small Voice.

Films inc: Three Guys Named Mike; Ride Vaquero; Desperate Search.

Bway inc: Oklahoma; South Pacific; The Rainmaker; Mr. Roberts; Sunrise at Campobello; I Do, I Do.

KEELER, Ruby: Act. b. Halifax, NS, Aug 25, 1909. Films inc: 42nd Street; Gold Diggers of 1933; Footlight Parade; Dames; Flirtation Walk; Go Into Your Dance; Shipmates Forever; Colleen; Ready Willing and Able; Mother Carey's Chickens; Sweetheart of the Campus; The Phynx.

Bway inc: The Rise Of Rosie O'Reilly; Bye, Bye Bonnie; Sidewalks of New York; Whoopee; Show Girl. Retired 1941. Retd to Bway 1971 revival No, No Nanette.

KEEP, Stephen: Act. b. Camden, SC, Aug 24. e. Columbia U; Yale School of Drama. Bway inc: Metamorphosis; Story Theatre; The Shadow Box.

Films inc: The Front; Love and Money.

TV inc: A Rumor of War; Bogie; Moviola; When Hell Was In Session; Panic On Page One; Billion Dollar Threat.

KEESHAN, Bob: Act. b. Lynbrook, NY, Jun 27, 1927. Hosted from its inception (1955) the children's program, Captain Kangaroo, on CBS-TV. Prior to that he was Clarabelle the Clown on Howdy Doody. Also created Tinker the Toymaker and prod and performed in the program Tinker's Workshop.

KEHOE, Jack: Act. b. NYC, Nov 21, 1938. Films inc: Panic in Needle Park; The Gang That Couldn't Shoot Straight; Law and Disorder; Serpico; The Sting; The Fish That Saved Pittsburgh; On The Nickel; Melvin and Howard.

TV inc: Shell Game; Most Wanted.

KEIGHLEY, William: Dir. b. Philadelphia, PA, 1893. Asst dir and dir Bway before turning to Hollywood in 1932.

Films inc: The Match King (co-dir); Ladies They Talk About (co-dir); Easy to Love; Big Hearted Herbert; Kansas City Priness; Babbitt; G-Men; Mary Jane's Pa; Special Agent; Stars Over Broadway; Green Pastures (co-dir); Bullets or Ballots; Prince and the Pauper; Adventures of Robin Hood (co-dir); Brother Rat; Yes, My Darling Daughter; Each Dawn I Die; The Fighting 69th; Torrid Zone; No Time for Comedy; The Bride Came C.O.D.; The Man Who Came to Dinner; George Washington Slept Here; The Street With No Name; Close to My Heart; The Master of Ballantrae.

KEIR, Andrew: Act. b. Scotland, 1926. Films inc: Scotch on the Rocks; High and Dry; Cleopatra; Lord Jim; The Long Duel; Five Million Years to Earth; Attack on the Iron Coast; Zeppelin; Blood from the Mummy's Tomb.

KEITEL, Harvey: Act. b. NYC, May 13, 1939. Films inc: Who's that Knocking at My Door?; Alice Doesn't Live Here Anymore; Taxi Driver; Mother, Jugs and Speed; Welcome to LA; Blue Collar; The Duellists; Fingers; The Eagle's Wing; Deathwatch; Bad Timing.

KEITH, Brian: Act. b. Bayonne, NJ, Nov 14, 1921. Bway inc: Mister Roberts; Darkness at Noon. Screen debut 1953, Arrowhead.
Films inc: Jivaro; Tight Spot; Storm Center; Chicago Confidential; The Parent Trap; The Pleasure Seekers; Moon Pilot; The Russians Are Coming, The Russians Are Coming; Reflections in a Golden Eye; Gaily, Gaily; Suppose They Gave a War And Nobody Came; With Six You Get Eggroll; The Wind and the Lion; Nickelodeon; Hooper; Meteor; Moonraker; The Mountain Men.
TV inc: Studio One; Suspense; Philco Playhouse; The Crusader; The Westerner; Family Affair; Little People; Centennial; The Seekers; Power; Moviola (The Silent Lovers).

KELLER, Harry: Dir. b. LA, Feb 22, 1913. Former film editor. Dir debut 1949, The Blonde Bandit.
Films inc: The Unguarded Moment; The Brass Bottle; Send Me No Flowers; That Funny Feeling; Voice in the Mirror; Tammy Tell Me True; Mirage; Texas Across the River; In Enemy Country; The Skin Game (& prod); Stir Crazy.
TV inc: The Loretta Young Show; Schlitz Playhouse; Four Star Theatre; The Swamp Fox (pilot); Texas John Slaughter.

KELLER, Marthe: Act. b. Switzerland. e. Stanislavsky School, Munich, Brecht Theatre, East Berlin. Films inc: The Devil By the Tail; Les Caprices de Marie; And Now My Love; Down the Ancient Stairs; The Hornet's Nest; Marathon Man; Black Sunday; Bobby Deerfield; Fedora; The Formula.
TV inc: (France) Arsene Lupin; Le Demoiselle d'Avignon.
Thea inc: (Paris) A Day In the Death of Joe Egg.

KELLERMAN, Sally: Act. b. Long Beach, CA, Jun 2, 1936. Films inc: The Boston Strangler; The April Fools; M*A*S*H; Brewster McCloud; Last of the Red Hot Lovers; Lost Horizon; Slither; Rafferty and the Gold Dust Twins; The Big Bus; Welcome to LA; The Mouse and his Child (voice); A Little Romance; Foxes; Serial; Loving Couples; Head On.
TV inc: Centennial; Verna--USO Girl; Big Blonde.

KELLEY, DeForest: Act. b. Atlanta, GA, Jan 20, 1920. Films inc: Fear in the Night; Canon City; The Men; House of Bamboo; Man in the Gray Flannel Suit; Tension at Tablerock; Gunfight at the OK Corral; Raintree County; The Law and Jake Wade; Warlock; Where Love Has Gone; Marriage on the Rocks; Star Trek-The Motion Picture.
TV inc: Star Trek.

KELLEY, William: Wri. b. NYC, May 27, 1929. e. Brown U, AB; Harvard U, AM. TV inc: Route 66; Gunsmoke; Kung Fu; Serpico; Petrocelli; How the West Was Won; The Winds of Kitty Hawk.

KELLIN, Mike: Act. Films inc: So Young, So Bad; At War With the Army; Lonely Hearts; The Great Imposter; The Wackiest Ship In the Army; Invitation To A Gunfighter; Banning; The Boston Strangler; The Maltese Bippie; Fool's Parade; Freebie and the Bean; Girl Friends; Midnight Express; On the Yard; The Jazz Singer.
TV inc: Battles--The Murder That Wouldn't Die; FDR--The Last Year.
Bway inc: The Ritz.

KELLY, Emmett: Clown. b. Sedan, KS, Dec 9, 1898 Member of the Ringling Brothers and Barnum & Bailey Circus, 1942-56.
Films inc: The Greatest Show on Earth; Wind Across the Everglades.
(Died Mar 28, 1979).

KELLY, Gene: Act-Dir. b. Pittsburgh, Aug 23, 1912. e. U of Pittsburgh, BA. Bway debut, 1938, Leave It To Me. Film debut, 1942, For Me and My Gal.
Films inc: Du Barry Was A Lady; Thousands Cheer; Cross of Lorraine; Cover Girl; Christmas Holiday; Anchors Aweigh (chor); Ziegfeld Follies; The Three Musketeers; The Pirate; Words and Music; Take Me Out to the Ball Game (chor); On The Town; An American in Paris (chor); Singin' in the Rain (chor & co-dir); Brigadoon (chor); Invitation to the Dance (dir & chor); Marjorie Morningstar; Les Girls; Inherit the Wind; Gigot (dir); What a Way to Go!; A Guide for the Married Man; Hello, Dolly (dir); The Cheyenne Social Club (dir); 40 Carats.
(Oscar-special-1951).
Bway inc: Pal Joey; The Time of Your Life; One for the Money.
TV inc: Jack and the Beanstalk (Emmy-prod-1967); Julie Andrews Show; New York, New York (host, chor); Gene Kelly and 50, Count 'Em Girls; The Funny Side; Lucy Moves To NBC; Debby Boone--The Same Old Brand New Me (prod).
Sep 1980 signed with Francis Ford Coppola to create musical prodn unit at Zoetrope Studio.

KELLY, Grace: Act. b. Philadelphia, PA, Nov 12, 1929. e. AADA. Appeared on stage, TV. Screen debut in Fourteen Hours, 1951.
Films inc: High Noon; The Country Girl (Oscar-1954); Dial M for Murder; Rear Window; The Bridges of Toko-Ri; To Catch A Thief; The Swan; High Society. Married Prince Rainier of Monaco, Apr 19, 1956.

KELLY, Jack: Act. b. NYC, 1927. Films inc: Where Danger Lives; Drive a Crooked Road; To Hell and Back; Hong Kong Affair; Love and Kisses; Young Billy Young.
TV inc: King's Row; Maverick.

KELLY, Nancy: Act. b. Lowell, MA, Mar 25, 1921. On Bway as child in Give Me Yesterday.
Bway inc: Susan and God; The Big Knife; Bad Seed (Tony-1955); Season In The Sun; The Gingerbread Lady.
Films inc: (silent) Untamed Lady; Great Gatsby. (Sound) Stanley and Livingston; Tailspin; To The Shores of Tripoli; Murder in the Music Hall; Jesse James; Friendly Enemies.

KELLY, Patsy: Act. b. NYC, Jan 12, 1910. Bway inc: Sketch Book; Vanities; Wonder Bar; Flying Colors. No, No, Nanette (rev) (Tony-1971); Irene.
Films inc: Going Hollywood; The Girl From Missouri; Ever Since Eve; The Cowboy And The Lady; Please Don't Eat The Daisies; The Crowded Sky; The Naked Kiss; C'mon Let's Live A Little; Freaky Friday; The North Avenue Irregulars.
TV inc: The Cop and the Kid.

KELMAN, Alfred R: Prod. b. NYC, May 17, 1936. e. Boston U, MJ. TV inc: Agassiz the Man; Martin Luther King in Boston; The Face of Genius; This Week; The Government; Scopitone; The Transplanter; Drug of Choice; The Body Human (Emmy-1978); Lifeline (Emmy-1979); The Body Human--The Sexes; The Body Human--The Magic Sense (Emmy-1980); The Body Human--The Body Beautiful; The Body Human--The Sexes II; The Body Human--Facts for Boys (& dir).

KELSEY, Linda: Act. b. Minneapolis, MN, Jul 28, 1946. e. U of MI, BA.
TV inc: Picture of Dorian Gray; Something for Joey; Eleanor and Franklin; Lou Grant; A Perfect Match. Thea inc: The Tempest; Summer and Smoke; The Crucible; A Pagan Place.

KEMENY, John: Prod. b. Budapest, Hungary, Apr 17, 1925. Films inc: Don't Let the Angels Fall; Sept Fois Par Jour; Un Enfant Comme Les Autres; The Apprenticeship of Duddy Kravitz; White Line Fever; Shadow of the Hawk; Ice Castles.

KEMP, Jeremy: Act. b. Chesterfield, Eng, Feb 3, 1935. Films inc: Cast a Giant Shadow; Operation Crossbow; The Blue Max; Twist of Sand; Strange Affair; Darling Lili; The Games; The Salzburg Connection; The Seven-Per-Cent Solution; Caravans; Prisoner of Zenda.
TV inc: Z Cars; Colditz; The Rainmaker; The Lovers of Florence; School Play; The Last Roundup; Vikings.

KEMPSON, Rachel: Act. b. Darmouth, Devon, Eng, May 28, 1910. e. RADA. W of Sir Michael Redgrave. M of Lynn & Vanessa Redgrave. London stage debut 1933 in the Lady from Alfaqueque.
Thea inc: Twelfth Night; Love's Labour's Lost; Venus Observed; Hedda Gabler; Not for Children; Romeo and Juliet; Teresa of Avila; Saint Joan of the Stockyards; The Freeway; A Family and a Fortune; The Old Country.
Films inc: The Captive Heart; Georgy Girl; The Jokers; Charge of the Light Brigade; The Virgin Soldiers; Jane Eyre.
TV inc: Little Lord Fauntleroy.

KEMP-WELCH, Joan: Act-Dir. b. Wimbledon, England, 1906. Thea inc: (Act) John Gabriel Borkman; Silent Witness; Glory Be; Nina; The Melody That Got Lost; Nora; Lady Fanny; Ladies in Retirement; It Happened In September. (Dir) Desire Under The Elms; Dead On Nine; dir various repertory and festival prodns.
Films inc: (Act) Once A Thief; The Girl in the Taxi; Busman's Honeymoon; Pimpernel Smith; They Flew Alone; Goodbye Mr. Chips; The Citadel; Jeanie.
TV inc: (Dir) A Birthday Party; A View From the Bridge; A Midsummer Night's Dream; Elektra.

KENDAL, Felicity: Act. b. Birmingham, Eng, 1946. Stage debut age 9 months in parents' Shakespearean productions. Toured with them in India, Far East through childhood. London debut 1967 in Minor Murder.
Thea inc: Various Shakespearean roles, The Norman Conquest; Clouds; Amadeus; Othello. Films inc: Shakespeare Wallah; Valentino.
TV inc: The Good Life; Edward the Seventh; The Mayfly And The Frog.

KENDALL, Suzy (Frieda Harrison): Act. b. Belper, Eng, 1943. Film inc: Circus of Fear; To Sir with Love; Penthouse; Up the Junction; Thirty is a Dangerous Age; Cynthia; Fraulein Doktor; The Betrayal; Darker than Amber; The Bird with the Crystal Plumage; Assault; Craze; Fear is the Key.

KENDALL, William: Act. b. London, Aug 26, 1903. Thea inc: The Royal Visitor; Old Heidelberg; March Hares; The Command Performance; This'll Make You Whistle; Between the Devil; The Lady Asks for Help; Primrose and the Peanuts; Castle in the Air; Night Call; The Nest Egg; It's Different for Men; Star Maker; Towards Zero; The Brides of March; August for the People; The Circle; Highly Confidential.

KENNEDY, Arthur: Act. b. Worcester, MA, Feb 17, 1914. On screen from 1940 in City for Conquest.
Films inc: Champion; Bright Victory; Trial; Peyton Place; Some Came Running; High Sierra; They Died With Their Boots On; The Glass Menagerie; The Desperate Hours; Elmer Gantry; Lawrence of Arabia; The Sentinel; The Tempter; Covert Action.
Bway inc: Merrily We Roll Along; Life and Death of an American; All My Sons; Death of a Salesman (Tony-supp-1949); See The Jaguar; The Crucible; Time Limit.

KENNEDY, Betty: Act. b. Roswell, NM, Oct 2. Films inc: Cheech and Chong's Next Movie. TV inc: Rockford Files; Ladies Man.

KENNEDY, Burt: Wri-Dir. b. Muskegon, MI, Sep 3, 1922. Films inc: Rounders (sp-dir); War Wagon (dir); Support Your Local Sheriff (dir); Mail Order Bride (sp-dir); Welcome to Hard Times (sp-dir); Return of the Seven (dir); Good Guys Bad Guys (dir); Dirty Dingus Magee (sp-prod-dir); Train Robbers (sp-dir); Wolf Lake (sp-dir). TV inc: (dir) The Wild, Wild West Revisited; The Concrete Cowboys; More Wild Wild West.

KENNEDY, Byron Eric: Prod. b. Melbourne, Aug 18, 1949. Films inc: Mad Max.

KENNEDY, George: Act. b. NYC, Feb 18, 1927. Started career at age 2 in touring company of Bringing Up Father.
Films inc: Lonely Are The Brave; Strait Jacket; Charade; Shenandoah; The Dirty Dozen; Cool Hand Luke (Oscar-supp-1967); Airport; Airport '75; The Eiger Sanction; Airport '77; Brass Target; Death on the Nile; Concorde-Airport '79; The Double McGuffin; Death Ship; Virus; Steel.
TV inc: Sarge; The Blue Knight; Backstairs At The White House; Never Say Never; Hard Times (host); Steve Allen Comedy Hour.

KENNEDY, Jayne: Act-TV pers. b. Washington, DC, Oct 27, 1951. TV inc: The NFL Today; Speak Up America (Co-host).
Films inc: Big Time; Death Force; The Muthers; Group Marriage; Lady Sings The Blues; Let's Do It Again.

KENNEDY, Madge: Act. b. Chicago, IL, 1892. Bway inc: Little Miss Brown; Twin Beds; Fair and Warmer; Cornered; Poppy; Paris Bound; Bridal Wise.
Films inc: Baby Mine; The Danger Game; The Fair Pretender; Friendly Husband; A Perfect Lady; A Kingdom of Youth; Leave It to Susan; Three Miles Out; Bad Company; Lying Wives; Oh, Baby!; The Marrying Kind; The Rains of Ranchipur; Catered Affair; Lust For Life; A Nice Little Bank That Should Be Robbed; Let's Make Love; They Shoot Horses, Don't They?; The Baby Maker; Day of the Locust.

KENNEY, Douglas: Wri-Prod. b. West Palm Beach, FL, 1947. e. Harvard. Edited Harvard Lampoon while in college, launched National Lampoon mag 1970. Films inc: National Lampoon's Animal House (wri); Caddyshack.
TV inc: Delta House (wri).
(Died Aug 1980).

KENNEY, H Wesley: Dir. TV inc: All in the Family; Days of Our Lives (& exec prod); (Emmys (4) dir drama, dir special pgm, dir of year-1974; exec prod-1978).

KENTON, Stan: Orch Ldr. b. Wichita, KS, Feb 19, 1912. Known for his experimentation and innovations in jazz arrangements. (Grammys-jazz group-1961 & 1962).
(Died Aug 25, 1979).

KENWITH, Herbert: Prod-Dir. TV inc: Daktari; Star Trek; Temperatures Rising; The Partridge Family; Love American Style; Mary Tyler Moore; Marcus Welby; All That Glitters; Good Times; One Day at a Time; Different Strokes; Me and Maxx.

KENYON, Curtis: Wri. Films inc: Woman Who Dared; Lloyds of London; Wake Up and Live; Love and Hisses; She Knew All the Answers; Seven Days Leave; Thanks for Everything; Princess and the Pirate; Bathing Beauty; Fabulous Dorseys; Tulsa; Two Flags West.
TV inc: Cavalcade of America; Fireside Theatre; U.S. Steel Hour; Waikiki.

KENYON, Doris: Act. b. 1897. On screen from 1916. Films inc: The Pawn of Fate; Loose Ankles; Voltaire; Girls' School; Counsellor-at-Law; The Man in the Iron Mask.
(Died Sept 1, 1979).

KERCHEVAL, Ken: Act. b. Wolcottville, IN, Jul 15. e. U of IN; Pacific U. Bway inc: Who's Afraid of Virginia Woolf?; Fiddler on the Roof; Cabaret; The Apple Tree; Who's Happy Now?; Father's Day.
Films inc: Pretty Poison; The Seven-Ups; Network; F.I.S.T.
TV inc: The Coming Asunder of Jimmy Bright; The Scottsboro Boys; Separating; Something in the Air; Dallas.

KERKORIAN, Kirk: Exec. b. Fresno, CA, Jun 6, 1917. A captain in the RAF Transport Command during WW2, he opened flight training school after war, branched into non-sked airline field, later charter; subsequently sold 58% interest in Trans International Airlines to Transamerica Corp for $104 million; bought Flamingo Hotel, Las Vegas, began acquiring land Las Vegas, built International Hotel; began acquiring MGM stock, became majority owner 1974, served as vice chmn, CEO until Nov 1978 when, having acquired large interest in Columbia Pictures, he stepped down from executive positions while retaining financial interest; with split of MGM into two companies (films and hotels) is biggest stockholder in each.

KERR, Anita (nee Grilli): Comp-Arr-Vocalist. b. Memphis, TN, Oct 13. Founder of the Anita Kerr Singers; co-founder of the San Sebastian Strings. Films scores inc: Limbo. *(Grammys*-(3)-vocal group-1965, 1966; Gospel-1965).

KERR, Deborah (nee Kerr-Trimmer): Act. b. Helensburgh, Scotland, Sep 30, 1921. London stage debut, 1938, Sadler's Wells ballet. Screen debut, 1940, Major Barbara. Bway debut 1953, Tea and Sympathy.
 Films inc: Love on the Dole; The Life and Death of Colonel Blimp; Perfect Strangers; I See a Dark Stranger; Black Narcissus; The Hucksters; Edward, My Son; Quo Vadis; Julius Caesar; From Here to Eternity; The King and I; Tea and Sympathy; Heaven Knows, Mr. Allison; An Affair to Remember; Separate Tables; Bonjour Tristesse; The Sundowners; The Journey; The Grass Is Greener; The Innocents; The Chalk Garden; The Night of the Iguana; Casino Royale; Prudence and the Pill; The Gypsy Moths; The Arrangement.
 Bway inc: The Day After the Fair; Seascape; Souvenir; Long Day's Journey Into Night; Last of Mrs. Cheyney; Candida; Seascape.

KERR, Elizabeth: Act. b. Kansas City, MO, Aug 12. e. Northwestern U. Became actress 1944 after her sons were grown. Bway inc: Angel in the Pawnshop; The Righteous Are Bold; Conquering Hero ; Redhead. (Tours) Music Man; The Front Page; Joe Egg; Anything Goes; Harvey.
 Films inc: Coma; Matilda; Spree; Dogs.
 TV inc: Hitch Hike; Mork and Mindy.

KERR, Jean (nee Collins): Plywri. b. Scranton, PA, Jul 10, 1923. e. Marywood Coll, Catholic U. W of Walter Kerr. Plays inc: Song of Bernardette (with husband); Jenny Kissed Me; Touch and Go (with husband); sketches for John Murray's Almanac; King of Hearts (with Eleanor Brooke); Goldilocks (with husband); Mary, Mary; Poor Richard; Finishing Touches; Penny Candy; Lunch Hour.
 TV inc: The Good Fairy. (Book: Please Don't Eat the Daisies was adapted as a tv series).

KERR, John: Act. b. NYC, Nov 15, 1931. Films inc: The Cobweb; Gaby; Tea and Sympathy; South Pacific; The Pit and the Pendulum; Seven Women From Hell.
 TV inc: Peyton Place.
 Thea inc: Tea and Sympathy *(Tony*-supp-1954).

KERR, Walter: Wri-Dir. b. Evanston, IL, Jul 8, 1913. e. Northwestern U. H of Jean Kerr. Drama Critic For Commonweal; NY Herald Tribune; NY Times.
 Plays inc: Song of Bernardette (with wife); Count Me In (co-author); Swing Out Sweet Land (& dir); Touch and Go (with wife); King of Hearts (dir); Goldilocks (with wife).
 TV inc: Esso Repertory Theatre (host).
 (Pulitzer Prize-for criticism-1978).

KERSHNER, Irvin: Dir. b. Philadelphia, Apr 29, 1923. e. Temple U, USC. Films inc: Stakeout on Dope Street; The Young Captives; The Hoodlum Priest; Face in the Rain; The Luck of Ginger Coffey; A Fine Madness; The Flim Flam Man; Loving; Up the Sandbox; S P Y S; The Return of a Man Called Horse; Eyes of Laura Mars; The Empire Strikes Back.
 TV inc: Raid on Entebbe.

KERWIN, Brian: Act. b. Chicago, Oct 25, 1949. e. USC. TV inc: The Young and Restless; American Girls; The Chisholms; A Real American Hero; Power; The Misadventures of Sheriff Lobo.
 Films inc: Hometown U.S.A.; Soft Explosion.

KERWIN, Lance: Act. b. Newport Beach, CA, Nov 6, 1960. Films inc: Escape to Witch Mountain.
 TV inc: Reflections of Terror; Pssst, Hammerman's After You; The Healers; The Cloning of Richard Swimmer; James at 16; Salem's Lot; The Boy Who Drank Too Much; Animal Talk; Children of Divorce.

KESSLER, Bruce: Dir. b. CA, Mar 23, 1936. Films inc: Angels From Hell; Killers Three; Gay Deceivers; Simon.

KESSLER, Ralph: Comp-Cond. b. NYC, Aug 1, 1919. e. Juilliard School of Music, BS, MS. Trumpeter with dance bands, Bway pit orchs inc: This Is The Army; created original music treatments and sketches for Man of La Mancha. P Ralph Kessler Prodns, specializing in music for commercials.
 TV inc: arr-comp for Arthur Godfrey Show, 1951-1959; scores inc Barnaby Jones; Police Story.

KEYES, Evelyn: Act. b. Port Arthur, TX, 1919. Began career as a dancer in niteries.
 Films inc: Gone With The Wind; Union Pacific; The Jolson Story; The Prowler; The Killer That Stalked New York; The Iron Man; 99 River Street; Seven-Year Itch; Around the World in 80 Days.
 Thea inc: No, No, Nanette.

KIBBEE, Roland: Wri. b. Monongahela, PA, Feb 15, 1914. Writer for Fred Allen Show; Fanny Brice; Groucho Marx.
 Films inc: A Night in Casablanca; Angel on my Shoulder; The Crimson Pirate.
 TV inc: (wri-prod) The Ford Show; The Deputy; The Bob Cummings Show; The Bob Newhart Show; Columbo *(Emmy*-exec prod-1974).

KIBLER, William Stephan (Steve): Prod. b. St Louis, MO, Sep 8, 1941. e. Eastern KY U, BA. Started as agent with William Morris; exec dir development Aaron Spelling Prodns & Spelling-Goldberg Prodns; became m-dir Seven Keys TV, Sydney, Australia; exec prod Gemini Prodns, Sydney; exec prod Reg Grundy Prodns, Sydney.

KIDD, Michael (Milton Greenwald): Dir-Chor-Act. b. NYC, Aug 12, 1919. e. CCNY, School of the American Ballet. On stage as dancer from 1938.
 Films inc: (chor) Where's Charley?; The Band Wagon; Seven Brides for Seven Brothers; Guys and Dolls; Merry Andrew (dir only); Star!; Hello, Dolly!; Smile (perf); Movie Movie (chor & perf). Bway inc: (chor) Finian's Rainbow *(Tony*-1947); Hold It; Love Life; Arms and the Girl; Guys and Dolls *(Tony*-1951); Can-Can *(Tony*-1954); Skyscraper; Li'l Abner *(Tony*-1957); Wildcat (& prod); Destry Rides Again *(Tony*-1960); Subways Are for Sleeping; Ben Franklin in Paris; The Rothschilds; Cyrano; Good News; The Music Man (rev).
 Ballets inc: Pillar of Fire; Dim Lustre; Fancy Free; Romeo & Juliet; Giselle; Copellia.

KIDD, Robert: Dir. b. Scotland, Feb 23, 1943. Thea inc: (London) When Did You Last See My Mother?; The Man of Destiny; The Restoration of Arnold Middleton; The Philanthropist; Siege; Butley; Savages; Treats; joint artistic director Royal Court Theatre.
 (Died July 18, 1980). Bway: The Philanthropist.

KIDDER, Margot: Act. b. Yellowknife, Can, Oct 17, 1948. Films inc: Gaily, Gaily; Quackser Fortune Has A Cousin in the Bronx, Sisters; The Great Waldo Pepper; Superman; Mr. Mike's Mondo Video; The Amityville Horror; Willy & Phil; Superman II.

KIEL, Richard: Act. b. Detroit, Sep 13, 1939. Films inc: Eegah; The Human Duplicators; Skidoo; The Longest Yard; The Spy Who Loved Me; Force 10 From Navarone; They Went Thataway & Thataway; Flash and the Firecat; Moonraker.
 TV inc: Klondike; The Riflemen; I Spy; The Barbary Coast.

KIERNAN, Laurence James: Exec. b. Perth, Western Australia, Jun 1, 1927. Exec dir Swan Television Ltd, 1969; m-dir, 1971.

KILEY, Richard: Act. b. Chicago, Mar 31, 1922. e. Loyola U. Began in radio. Films inc: The Mob; The Sniper; Pick-up on South Street; The Blackboard Jungle; Pendulum; The Little Prince; Looking for Mr. Goodbar.
 Bway inc: A Streetcar Named Desire; A Month of Sundays; Kismet; Redhead *(Tony*-1959); Advise and Consent; Man of LaMancha *(Tony*-1966); The Heiress (rev); Knickerbocker Holiday (rev); The Incomparable Max; Absurd Person Singular.
 TV inc: Patterns; Arrowsmith; POW; Close Quarters; Angel On My Shoulder.

KILIAN, Victor: Act. b. Jersey City, NJ, Mar 6, 1891. Bway debut, 1923, Desire Under the Elms. Films inc: Gentlemen's Agreement; The Tall Target; Spellbound; Dr. Cyclops.
TV inc: Gunsmoke; Planet of the Apes; McCloud; Kojak.
(Died Mar 11, 1979).

KING, Alan: Act. b. NYC, 1927. Performs on stage, TV. Films inc: Hit the Deck; Miracle in the Rain; The Helen Morgan Story; Operation Snafu; Bye Bye Braverman; The Anderson Tapes; Just Tell Me What You Want; Happy Birthday, Gemini (exec prod).
TV inc: Alan King's Energy Crisis; Alan King's Third Annual Final Warning; Seventh Avenue; Alan King's Thanksgiving Special--What Do We Have To Be Thankful For; Pinocchio's Christmas (voice).
Bway inc: The Impossible Years; Dinner at Eight; The Lion in Winter.

KING, Andrea: Act. b. Paris, Feb 7, 1915. Films inc: Mr. Skeffington; The Very Thought of You; My Wild Irish Rose; Ride the Pink Horse; Hollywood Canteen; God Is My Co-Pilot; Hotel Berlin; Roughly Speaking; The Man I Love; Shadow of a Woman; Mr. Peabody and the Mermaid; Dial 1119; The World In His Arms; The Lemon Drop Kid; Red Planet Mars; Band of Angels; Darby's Rangers; Daddy's Gone A Hunting; Prescription Murder.
TV inc: The Days of Our Lives.

KING, Bob: Wri-Exec. b. Cincinnati, OH, Aug 1, 1928. Dir Mktg Svs, Disney; 1980, VP Mktg. Films inc: Now You See Him, Now You Don't (orig story). TV inc: 50 Happy Years; Disney's Greatest Villains.

KING, Carole: Singer-Sngwri. b. Brooklyn, NY, Feb 9, 1942. Songs inc: Will You Love Me Tomorrow; He's A Rebel; Go Away, Little Girl; Up on the Roof; Natural Woman; Take Good Care of My Baby; You've Got a Friend *(Grammy*-song of year-1971); It's Too Late.
(Grammys-(3)-album of year-record of year-pop vocal-1971).

KING, Frank (PeeWee): Comp-Mus. b. Milwaukee, WI, Feb 18, 1914. Country mus recording artist; TV inc Grand Ole Opry. Films inc: Gold Mine in the Sky; Riding the Outlaw Trail.
Songs inc: Tennessee Waltz.

KING, Henry: Dir. b. Christianburg, VA, Jan 24, 1896. Toured in stock, circuses, vaudeville, burlesque. Wri, dir, prod with Inspiration Co. Joined Fox Film Co, remaining with them after merger with 20th Century.
Films inc: Tol'able David; Stella Dallas; The Winning of Barbara Worth; State Fair; Lloyds of London; In Old Chicago; Ramona; Alexander's Ragtime Band; Stanley and Livingston; A Yank In The R.A.F.; Song of Bernadette; A Bell for Adano; Captain From Castile; Twelve O'Clock High; The Gunfighter; David and Bathsheba; Wait Till The Sun Shines, Nelly; Snows of Kilimanjaro; Love Is A Many Splendored Thing; The Sun Also Rises; Tender Is The Night.

KING, Larry L: Wri-Act. b. Putnam, TX, Jan 1, 1929. e. TX Tech; Nieman Fellow at Harvard. Bway inc: Co-author Best Little Whorehouse in Texas (& act); The Kingfish.

KING, Mabel: Act. b. Charlestown, SC, Dec 25. Films inc: Blood Couple; The Bingo Long Traveling All-Stars and Motor Kings; The Wiz.
Bway inc: Hello Dolly; Don't Play Us Cheap; The Wiz.
TV inc: What's Happening!.

KING, Paul: Exec. b. LA. e. Loyola U, USC. Started as a wri. Films inc: Operation Petticoat; Wild Heritage; Canyons of Jade; The Iron Horse.
With CBS from 1966 to 1976, rising to vp of development, then vp, program prodns. Moved to WB; then Quinn Martin Prodns; joined NBC; appointed vp, Prime Time Series, NBC Entertainment, Oct 1978.

KINGI, Henry: Act. b. LA, Dec 2, 1943. Films inc: R.P.M.; Buck and the Preacher; Cleopatra Jones; Uptown Saturday Night; Smoke in the Wind; Swashbuckler; Car Wash.
TV inc: Search for the Gods.

KINGSLEY, Dorothy: Wri. b. NYC, Oct 14, 1909. Radio wri for Bob Hope; Edgar Bergen.
Films inc: Date With Judy; Neptune's Daughter; When in Rome; It's A Big Country; Kiss Me Kate; Seven Brides for Seven Brothers; Pal Joey; Can Can; Pepe; Half a Sixpence; Valley of the Dolls.
TV inc: created series Bracken's World.

KINGSLEY, Sidney (nee Kirchner): Wri-Prod-Dir. b. NYC, Oct 22, 1906. e. Cornell U. H of Madge Evans. Plays inc: Men in White *(Pulitzer Prize*-1934); Dead End; Ten Million Ghosts (& dir); The World We Make (& dir); The Patriots; Detective Story; Lunatics and Lovers; Darkness At Noon; Night Life (prod); Detective Story.
TV inc: The Patriots (prod).

KINSKI, Klaus: Act. b. Berlin, 1926. Films inc: For A Few Dollars More; Dr. Zhivago; Circus of Fear; Aguirre-Wrath of God; The Bloody Hands of the Law; Nuit D'or; Mort D'un Pourri; L'importance C'est D'aimer; The Net; Madame Claude; Woyzeck; Nosferatu The Vampire; Haine; La Femme Enfant; Schizoid.

KINSKI, Nastassia: Act. b. Berlin, Jan 24, 1960. D of Klaus Kinski. Films inc: To The Devil A Daughter; Passion Flower Hotel; Cosi Come Sei (Stay As You Are); Tess.

KINTNER, Robert E: Exec. b. Stroudsburg, PA, Sep 12, 1909. e. Swarthmore, BA. With NY Herald-Tribune, later columnist; teamed with Joseph Alsop on Washington column, 1937-1941; following war service joined ABC radio 1944 as vp pub-relations, later shifting to news; 1950 became pres ABC net; resd 1956, following year became NBC vp in chg coordinating color tv; 1958 pres NBC-TV, later corporate pres; 1965 became chmn, CEO NBC; 1966, resd to become spec asst Pres Lyndon B Johnson; 1967 resd due to illness, retired.
(Died Dec 22, 1980).

KIPNESS, Joseph: Prod. Bway inc: Bright Lights of 1944; The Duke in Darkness; Star Spangled Family; High Button Shoes; All You Need Is One Good Break; Women of Twilight; Conscience; Be Your Age; La Plume de Ma Tante; Have I Got a Girl For You!; I Had a Ball; But, Seriously. . .; Applause *(Tony*-1970); Father's Day; Inner City; Seesaw; No Hard Feelings; Teibele And Her Demon.

KIRGO, George: Wri-Prod. b. Hartford, CT, Mar 26, 1926. e. Wesleyan U Films inc: Red Line 7000; Spinout; Don't Make Waves; Voices; No Room to Run; Shimmering Light.
TV inc: Norby; Home; Young Dr. Kildare; Adam's Rib; Get Christie Love (created); Another Day (prod); Topper; The Man In The Santa Claus Suit; Angel On My Shoulder.

KIRK, Lisa: Singer-Act. b. Brownsville, PA, Sep 18, 1925. Bway inc: Good Night, Ladies; Allegro; Kiss Me Kate; Here's Love; Applause; Mack and Mabel; An Evening with Jerry Herman; Me Jack, You Jill.
TV inc: A Toast to Jerome Kern; The Man in the Moon; Shubert Alley; The Taming of the Shrew.

KIRK, Phyllis (nee Kirkegaard): Act. b. Syracuse, NY, Sep 18, 1926. Films inc: Our Very Own; The Iron Mistress; House of Wax; Canyon Crossroads; The Sad Sack; The Woman Opposite; City After Midnight.
Bway inc: My Name is Aquilon; Point of No Return.
TV inc: The Thin Man.

KIRKLAND, Sally: Act. b. NYC, Oct 31, 1944. e. Actors Studio. Thea inc: The Love Nest; Fitz; Tom Paine; Futz!; Sweet Eros; Witness; The Noisy Passenger; The Justice Box; Delicate Champion; Felix; Chicken Coop Chinaman; Has Tommy Flowers Gone?; Canadian Gothic.
Films inc: Blue; Futz!; Comin' Apart; The Way We Were; Cinderella Liberty; Big Bad Mama; Bite The Bullet; Pipe Dreams.
TV inc: Willow B--Women in Prison; Georgia Peaches.

KIRKWOOD, Gene: Prod. Films inc: New York, New York (asso prod); Comes A Horseman; Uncle Joe Shannon; The Idolmaker.

KIRSTEN, Dorothy: Soprano. b. 1917. Diva with the Metropolitan Opera for more than 30 years until her retirement in 1975.
Films inc: Mr. Music; The Great Caruso.

KIRTLAND, Louise: Act. b. Lynn, MA, Aug 4, 1905. Has appeared in more than 300 plays, inc Night Hostess; Light Wines and Beer; Murder at the Vanities; The Only Girl; Few Are Chosen; No, No Nanette; Little Women; Alive and Kicking; Gigi; Tea and Sympathy; Waltz of the Toreadors; Church Mouse; The Tunnel of Love; Tovarich; Music Man; Take Me Along; Forty Carats; The Torch Bearers; Mame.

TV inc: Search for Tomorrow; Love of Life.

KISS: Hard rock band consisting of Gene Simmons, bass; Paul Stanley, Ace Frehley, guitars; Peter Criss, drums.

Albums inc: Destroyer; Kiss Alive; Rock and Roll Over; Love Gun; Kiss Alive II; Double Platinum; Dynasty.

KITT, Eartha: Singer. b. Columbia, SC, 1928. Began career as a dancer, touring US, Mexico, Europe with Katherine Dunham group. Opened nitery in Paris. Returned to US, appearing in niteries, stage. Screen debut, 1954, New Faces.

Films inc: St. Louis Blues; Anna Lucasta; Synanon; Friday Foster. Bway inc: Timbuktu.

KIVLER, Steve: Exec prod. b. St Louis, MO, Sep 8, 1941. e. Eastern KY U, BA. Agent with William Morris Agency; then exec dir of dev for Aaron Spelling Prodns & Spelling-Goldberg Prodns; M-dir Seven Keys Television, Sydney, Australia; exec prod, Gemini Prodns, Sydney; exec prod, Reg Grundy Prodns, Sydney.

KJELLIN, Alf: Act-Dir. b. Sweden, 1920. Films inc: (act) Frenzy; My Six Convicts; The Iron Mistress; The Juggler; Ship of Fools; Assault on a Queen. (Dir) The Midas Run; The McMasters.

KLEIN, Allen: Prod. b. Dec 18, 1931. Pres ABKCO Industries Inc. Films inc: Force of Impulse; Pity Me Not; Strangers in Town; The Stranger Returns; Samurai on a Horse; El Topo; The Silent Stranger; Pete, Pearl & the Pole; The Grand Boufe; The Greek Tycoon; Concert For Bangladesh.

KLEIN, Eugene V: Exec. b. NYC, Jan 29, 1921. Automobile dealer, later chmn bd Columbia Savings & Loan, entered ind with National Theatres; P National Theatres 1955; P & chmn bd National General Theatres 1961; owner San Diego Chargers football team.

KLEIN, Robert: Act-Wri-Comedian. b. NYC, Feb 8, 1942. e. Alfred U, BA, Yale Drama School. Worked with Chicago's Second City group, on Bway with Second City Revue; The Apple Tree; They're Playing Our Song.

Films inc: The Landlord; The Owl and the Pussycat; The Pursuit of Happiness; Rivals; The Bell Jar; Hooper.

TV inc: Tonight Show (guest host); Saturday Night Live; A Secret Space; All Commercials.

Recordings inc: Child of the Fifties; Mind Over Matter.

KLEINER, Harry: Wri. b. Philadelphia, 1916. e. Temple U, BS, Yale U, MFA. Films inc: Fallen Angel; The Street With No Name; Red Skies of Montana; Salome; Miss Sadie Thompson; Carmen Jones; The Garment Jungle (& prod); Ice Palace; Fantastic Voyage; Bullitt; Le Mans.

TV inc: The Virginian; Bus Stop; The Rosenberg Trial.

KLEINERMAN, Isaac (Ike): Prod. Has prod more than 400 network docs. Began at NBC 1951 as film edtr Victory at Sea series; became prod in NBC's Project 20 unit; between 1952-57 prod The Great War; The Twisted Cross; The Jazz Age; Nightmare in Red; Wisdom; 1957 to CBS to organize Twentieth Century unit; also prod CBS Reports; The 21st Century (Emmy-1968); The Trail of the Feathered Serpent; Hitler and His Henchmen; Lure of the Tall Ships; Mr. Justice Dogulas; The Great Depression; Gandhi; Revolt in Hungary; The Violent World of Sam Huff; The Age of Anxiety; Who Killed Anne Frank?; The Dissenter--Norman Thomas; The Majestic Polluted Hudson; resd 1976 to enter indie prodn.

KLEINSCHMITT, Carl: Wri-Prod. b. LA, Aug 28. TV inc: (as wri) Gomer Pyle; That Girl; The Dick Van Dyke Show; My World and Welcome To It; Odd Couple; M*A*S*H; Funny Face (created & prod); Karen (prod); Pete N'Tillie (wri & prod).

KLEISER, Randal: Dir. b. Jul 20, 1946. e. USC. Films inc: Grease; Street People; The Blue Lagoon.

TV inc: Marcus Welby, M D; The Rookies; Starsky & Hutch; Family; All Together Now; Dawn; Portrait of a Teenage Runaway; Boy in the Plastic Bubble; Portait of Grandpa Doc; The Gathering.

KLEMPERER, Werner: Act. b. Cologne, Germany, 1920. S of late Otto Klemperer. Films inc: Death of a Scoundrel; Five Steps to Danger; The Goddess; Operation Eichmann; Judgment at Nuremberg; Escape from East Berlin; Youngblood Hawke; Ship of Fools; The Wicked Dreams of Paula Schultz.

TV inc: Hogan's Heroes (Emmys-1968 & 1969).

KLINE, Richard: Cin. b. 1926. Films inc: Camelot; The Boston Strangler; A Dream of Kings; The Andromeda Strain; Kotch; Black Gunn; The Harrad Experiment; Mandingo; King Kong; The Fury; Who'll Stop the Rain; Star Trek-The Motion Picture; Touched By Love; The Competition.

KLING, Woody: Wri-Prod. b. NYC. e. Wesleyan Coll. TV inc: Milton Berle Show; Jackie Gleason Show; Carol Burnett Show (Emmys-wri-1972, 1973); A Year at the Top (crea-wri); All in the Family (co-exec prod); Sanford Arms (prod); Hot L Baltimore (prod); Hello, Larry (prod).

KLINGER, Michael: Prod. b. Eng, Nov 2, 1920. Managing dir Avton Films; Tonav Films; Three Michaels Films.

Films inc: That Kind of Girl; Saturday Night Out; Repulsion; Cul de Sac; The Yellow Teddy Bears; Penthouse; A Study in Terror; Baby Love; Something To Hide; Get Carter; Pulp; Gold; Shout at the Devil; Blood Relatives.

KLOTZ, Florence: Cos Dsgn. b. NYC. Bway inc: A Call on Kuprin; Take Her, She's Mine; Never Too Late; On an Open Roof; Nobody Loves an Albatross; Everybody Out, The Castle Is Sinking; The Owl and the Pussycat; The Mating Dance; Best Laid Plans; This Winter's Hobby; It's A Bird. . .It's A Plane. . .It's Superman; Norman, Is That You?; Paris Is Out; Follies (Tony-1972); A Little Night Music (Tony-1973); Sondheim--A Musical Tribute; Dreyfus In Rehearsal; Pacific Overtures (Tony-1976); Legend.

Films inc: Something for Everyone; A Little Night Music.

KLUGMAN, Jack: Act. b. Philadelphia, PA, Apr 27, 1922. Bway inc: Saint John; Stevedore; Gypsy. Films inc: Timetable; Twelve Angry Men; The Days of Wine and Roses; Act One; The Detective; Goodbye Columbus; Two-Minute Warning.

TV inc: The Defenders (Blacklist) (Emmy-1964); The Odd Couple (Emmys-1971, 1973); Quincy; Packy; Lucy Moves To NBC; The Magic of David copperfield.

KNEF, Hildegarde (aka NEFF): Act. b. Ulm, Germany, Dec 18, 1925. e. Art Academy, Berlin. Film cartoonist for UFA, Berlin. Films inc: Between Yesterday and Tomorrow; The Sinner; Decision Before Dawn; Diplomatic Courier; The Snows of Kilimanjaro; Sunderlin; Svengali; Catherine of Russia; Valley of the Doomed; The Threepenny Opera; Escape From Sahara; Subway in the Sky; Mozambique; Everyone Dies In His Own Time; Fedora.

KNIEVEL, Evel: Stuntman. b. Butte, MT, Oct 17, 1939. Films inc: Viva Knievel.

TV inc: The Sensational Shocking Wonderful Wacky 70's.

KNIGHT, David (nee Mintz): Act. b. Niagara Falls, NY, Jan 16, 1927. e. Syracuse U, RADA. Films inc: The Young Lovers; Lost; Across the Bridge; Nightmare.

London thea inc: The Caine Mutiny Court Martial; The Iceman Cometh; The Tenth Man; A Present for the Past; Out of the Question.

TV inc: Abe Lincoln in Illinois; Strange Interlude; Berkeley Square; Kate.

KNIGHT, Gladys: Singer-Lyr. b. Atlanta, GA, May 28, 1944. Winner Ted Mack Amateur Hour 1952; toured with Morris Brown Choir; with Terry Lloyd Jazz Ltd, before organizing Gladys Knight and the Pips.

Songs inc: I Don't Want to do Wrong; Do You Love Me Just A Little Honey; Me and My Family; Way Back Home.

(Grammys-(2)-pop vocal group & R&B vocal group-1973).

TV inc: Uptown--A Tribute to the Apollo Theatre.

KNIGHT, Shirley: Act. b. Gossell, KS, Jul 5, 1936. e. Lake Forrest Coll. Films inc: Five Gates to Hell; Ice Palace; The Dark at the Top of the Stairs; The Couch; Sweet Bird of Youth; House of Women; Flight from Ashiya; The Group; The Counterfeit Killer; The Rain People; Juggernaut; Beyond The Poseidon Adventure.

TV inc: The Lie; The Country Girl; Champion-A Love Story; Playing For Time.

Bway inc: Journey to the Day; The Three Sisters; We Have Always Lived in the Castle; The Watering Place; Kennedy's Children *(Tony-supp-1976).*

KNIGHT, Ted: (Tadeus Wladyslaw Konopka): Act. b. Terryville, CT, Dec 7. TV inc: Mary Tyler Moore Show *(2 Emmys-supp-1973 & 1976);* Mac Davis Special; The Sensational, Shocking, Wonderful Wacky 70's; Too Close For Comfort.

Films inc: Caddyshack.

KNOPF, Edwin H: Prod-Dir-Wri. b. NYC, Nov 11, 1899. e. Amherst Coll. Films inc: The Cross of Lorraine; Cry Havoc; Valley of Decision; The Sailor Takes a Wife; Secret Heart; B F's Daughter; Edward My Son; Malaya; Fearless Fagan; Scandal at Scourie; Lili; The Vintage; Tip on a Dead Jockey; Fast Company; Slightly Scarlet; Santa Fe Trail; Light

Films inc: Caddyshack. of the Western Stars; Nice Women; Law and the Lady.

KNOTTS, Don: Act. b. Morgantown, WV, Jul 21, 1924. e. WV U, BA. In Army Special Services during WW2. On radio after war; on Bway in No Time for Sergeants.

Films inc: No Time for Sergeants; Wake Me When It's Over; It's A Mad, Mad, Mad, Mad World; Move Over Darling; The Incredible Mr Limpet; The Ghost and Mr Chicken; The Reluctant Astronaut; The Shakiest Gun in The West; How to Frame a Figg; The Apple Dumpling Gang; No Deposit, No Return; Gus; Herbie Goes to Monte Carlo; Hot Lead and Cold Feet; The Apple Dumpling Gang Rides Again; The Prize Fighter; The Private Eyes.

TV inc: The Garry Moore Show; The Steve Allen Show; The Mouse Factory; The Andy Griffith Show *(Emmys-supp-1961, 1962, 1963, 1966, 1967);* The Don Knotts Show.

KNOWLES, Patric: Act. b. Leeds, England, Nov 11, 1911. Films inc: Irish Hearts; Charge of the Light Brigade; Honour's Easy; Mister Hobo; Give Me Your Heart; It's Love I'm After; Adventures of Robin Hood; How Green Was My Valley; Forever and a Day; Of Human Bondage; The Bride Wore Boots; Kitty; Monsieur Beaucaire; Three Came Home; Mutiny; Jamaica Run; Flame of Calcutta; Khyber Patrol; No Man's Woman; Auntie Mame; The Devil's Brigade; In Enemy Country; Chisum: Terror in The Wax Museum.

KNOX, Alexander: Act. b. Strathroy, Ont, Jan 16, 1907. On screen in England from 1938 in Four Feathers; in U.S. from 1941 in The Sea Wolf.

Films inc: Khartoum; Puppet on a Chain; Nicholas and Alexandra; You Only Live Twice; Oscar Wilde; Wilson; Sister Kenny; The Longest Day; Wreck of the Mary Deere; Mr Moses; Villa Rides; Shalako; Skullduggery; Khartoum; Nicholas and Alexander; Potsdam; The Chosen.

TV inc: Cry of the Innocent; Tinker, Tailor, Soldier, Spy.

KNUDSEN, Peggy: Act. b. Duluth, MN, Apr 27, 1923. Started as actress on radio inc Lux Radio Theatre; Junior Miss; Women in White. Films inc: Humoresque; The Big Sleep; A Stolen Life; Stallion Road; Trouble Preferred; Unchained; Good Morning Miss Dove; Copper Canyon.

Bway inc: My Sister Eileen.

(Died July 11, 1980).

KOBAYASHI, Masaki: Dir. b. Otaru, Japan, Jan 14, 1916. e. Waseda U. Served as apprentice (asst dir) to Keisuke Kinoshita, 1946-52. Films inc: My Son's Youth; Room with Thick Walls; Three Loves; Beneath the Wide Sky; Beautiful Days; Fountain Head; I'll Buy You; Black River; The Human Condition; The Inheritance; Harakiri; The Black Hair; In A Cup of Tea; Hymn to a Tired Man; Inn of Evil; Kaseki.

KOCH, Howard: Wri. b. NYC, Dec 12, 1902. e. Bard Coll, Columbia U. Films inc: The Sea Hawk; The Letter; Sergeant York; Casablanca *(Oscar-1943);* Three Strangers; No Sad Songs For Me; Letter From An Unknown Woman; The Thirteenth Letter; The War Lover; The Fox.

Plays inc: In Time To Come; Straitjacket.

Radio plays inc: War of the Worlds.

KOCH, Howard W: Prod-Dir. b. NYC, Apr 11, 1916. Asst dir, 20th-Fox; Eagle Lion; MGM. Exec prod Frank Sinatra Enterprises; vp chg prod Paramount, 1965.

Films inc: Beachhead; The Manchurian Candidate; Four For Texas; None But The Brave; The Odd Couple; Plaza Suite; Once Is Not Enough.

TV inc: The Untouchables; Maverick; Cheyenne; Hawaiian Eye; The Pirate; Who Loves Ya Baby; 50th Annual Academy Awards *(Emmy-prod-1978);* Oscar's Best Movies.

KOCH, Howard W Jr: Prod. b. LA, Dec 14, 1945. e. UCLA. Worked various positions in industry inc asst dir before becoming prod. Films inc: Heaven Can Wait; The Other Side of Midnight; The Frisco Kid; The Idolmaker.

KOENEKAMP, Fred J: Cin. b. LA, Nov 11, 1922. Films inc: Heaven with a Gun; The Great Bank Robbery; Patton; Billy Jack; Skin Game; Rage; Kansas City Bomber; Papillon; Doc Savage; Towering Inferno *(Oscar-1974);* Posse; Embryo; Islands in the Stream; Fun with Dick and Jane; Domino Principle; The Other Side of Midnight; Swarm; The Champ; Amityville Horror; The Day the World Ended; Love and Bullets; When Time Ran Out; The Hunter; First Family.

TV inc: Disaster on the Coastline.

KOHAN, Buz (Alan W Kohan): Wri-Comp-Prod. b. NYC, Aug 9, 1933. e. Eastman School of Music, BM, MM. TV inc: Perry Como Specials, 1963-1967 (wri); Carol Burnett Show, 1967-1973 (wri-prod) *(Emmy-wri-1973);* Ann-Marget Smith (wri); Ann-Margret--Rhinestone Cowgirl (wri); America Salutes Richard Rodgers--The Sound of His Music *(Emmy-wri-1977);* 50th Annual Academy Awards *(Emmy-mus-1978);* Kraft 75th ANniversary Special (wri); A Country Christmas--1979 (prod-wri); Merry Christmas From Grand Ole Opry House (wri); Kraft Salutes Disneyland's 25th Anniversary (prod); Debby Boone--The Same Old Brand New Me; Shirley MacLaine...Every Little Movement *(Emmy-wri-1980);* 30 Years of TV Comedy's Greatest Hits (wri); A Country Christmas--1980 (prod-wri); Julie Andrews' Invitation to the Dance with Rudolf Nureyev (wri).

KOHNER, Pancho: Prod. b. LA, Jan 7, 1939. e. USC, U of Mexico, Sorbonne. Films inc: The Bridge in the Jungle (& dir-wri); The Lie; Mr Sycamore; St Ives; The White Buffalo; Love and Bullets; Why Would I Lie?

KOHNER, Susan: Act. b. LA, Nov 11, 1936. Films inc: To Hell and Back; The Last Wagon; Dino; Imitation of Life; The Big Fisherman; The Gene Krupa Story; All the Fine Young Cannibals; By Love Possessed; Freud.

Bway inc: Love Me Little; He Who Gets Slapped; Rose Tattoo; Bus Stop; St Joan; Sunday in New York; Take Her, She's Mine; Hiawatha.

KOKUBO, Christina: Act. b. Detroit, Jul 27, 1950. In ballet, on stage, US, Europe.

Films inc: The Yakuza, Midway.

KOMACK, James: Wri-Prod-Dir-Act. b. NYC, Aug 3, 1930. Films inc: (act) Damn Yankees; Hole in the Head; Senior Prom; Bell Boy; Contessa Azura.

TV inc: Hennessey (& wri); My Favorite Martian (wri); Mr. Roberts (prod & dir); Courtship of Eddie's Father (crea, wri, act & dir); Chico and the Man (dir & crea); Welcome Back Kotter (dir & crea); Sugar Time (dir & crea); Another Day (dir & crea); Rollergirls (dir & crea); Me and Maxx (wri-crea-exec prod). Bway inc: (act) Damn Yankees.

KONIGSBERG, Frank: Prod. Started ind prodn co with Stirling Silliphant in 1975; 1979 exec prod Fox TV. TV inc: Pearl; Bing Crosby Christmas Shows; Bing Crosby: Life and Legend; Before and After; Dummy; Dorothy; Guyana Tragedy-The Story of Jim Jones (exec prod); A Christmas Without Snow (exec prod).

KONVITZ, Jeffrey Steven: Wri-Prod. b. NYC, Jul 22, 1944. e. Cornell U, BA, Columbia U School of Law, JD. Films inc: Silent Night, Bloody Night; The Sentinel; Gorp.

KOPELL, Bernie: Act. b. NYC, Jun 21, 1933. Films inc: The Loved One. TV inc: Jack Benny Show; Steve Allen; Danny Kaye; My Favorite Martian; The Farmer's Daughter; Get Smart; That Girl; Doris Day Show; Mr. Deeds Goes to Washington; Bewitched; Needles and Pins; When Things Were Rotten; Love Boat; Greatest Heroes of the Bible.

KOPELSON, Arnold: Prod. b. NYC, Feb 14, 1935. e. NY Law School, LLB. Films inc: Lost and Found; The Legacy; Night of the Juggler; Foolin' Around; Final Assignment.

KOPIT, Arthur: Wri. b. NYC, May 10, 1937. e. Harvard U, BA. Plays inc: Gemini; On the Runway of Life; You Never Know What's Coming Off Next; Across the River and into the Jungle; Sing to Me Through Open Windows; To Dwell in a Palace of Strangers; Oh Dad, Poor Dad, Mama's Hung You in the Closet and I'm Feelin' So Sad; Indians; The Day the Whores Came Out to Play Tennis; What the Gentlemen Are Up To, and As for the Ladies; Wings.

TV inc: The Conquest of Everest; Starstruck.

KORDA, David: Prod. b. England. Films inc: (asso prod) A Day in the Death of Joe Egg; The Ruling Class; Cattle Annie and Little Britches. (Prod) Great Scout and Cathouse Thursday; Man Friday.

KORJUS, Miliza: Coloratura soprano. b. Poland, 1906. Concert star in Europe and the U.S., retired in the 50's. Films inc: The Great Waltz; Caballeria del Imperio.

(Died Aug 26, 1980).

KORMAN, Harvey: Act. b. Chicago, IL, Feb 15, 1927. TV inc: Danny Kaye Show; Carol Burnett Show (*Emmys*-1969, 1971, 1972, 1974); How To Survive The 70's and Maybe Even Bump Into A Little Happiness; The John Davidson Christmas Show.

Films inc: Three Bites of an Apple; Lord Love a Duck; The April Fools; Blazing Saddles; Huckleberry Finn; Americathon; Herbie Goes Bananas; First Family.

KORTY, John: Dir-Wri-Ani. b. Lafayette, IN, Jun 22, 1936. e. Antioch Coll. Animator of Breaking the Habit; A Scrap of Paper and a Piece of String; The Owl and the Pussycat.

Films inc: The Crazy Quilt; Funnyman; Riverrun; Silence; Alex & the Gypsy; Who Are the DeBolts? And Where Did They Get Nineteen Kids? (*Oscar*-doc fea-1977); Oliver's Story (dir & sp). TV inc: The Autobiography of Miss Jane Pittman (*Emmy*-dir-1974); Farewell to Manzanar; The Music School; Who Are The DeBolts? And Where Did They Get 19 Kids? (*Emmy*-dir-1978); Can't It Be Anyone Else? (exec prod); A Christmas Without Snow (wri-dir-prod).

KOSCINA, Sylva: Act. b. Yugoslavia, Aug 22, 1933. Films inc: Hercules Unchained; Jessica; Hot Enough for June; Juliet of the Spirits; Three Bites of the Apple; Deadlier Than the Male; A Lovely Way to Die; The Battle for Neretva; The Secret War of Harry Frigg; Hornet's Nest; Sunday Lovers.

KOSLECK, Martin: Act. b. Barketzen, Germany, Mar 24, 1907. Films inc: Confessions of a Nazi Spy; Foreign Correspondent; The Mad Doctor; Nazi Agent; Manila Calling; The Hitler Gang; Crime of the Century; House of Horrors; Assigned to Danger; Smuggler's Cove; Hitler; 36 Hours; The Flesh Eaters; Which Way to the Front; A Day at the White House.

KOSSOFF, David: Act. b. London, Nov 24, 1919. Stage debut with Unity Theatre, later joined BBC repertory group.

Thea inc: The Love of Four Colonels; The Shrike; The Bespoke Overcoat; The World of Sholem Aleichem; Stars in Your Eyes; The Tenth Man; Come Blow Your Horn; Seidman and Son; Enter Solly Gold. On Such a Night (& wri).

TV inc: The Larkins; Little Big Business; Storytime.

Films inc: The Good Beginning; The Young Lovers; A Kid for Two Farthings; The Bespoke Overcoat; The Journey; Freud; Ring of Spies.

KOSTAL, Irwin: Mus Dir. b. Chicago, Oct 1, 1911. Films inc: West Side Story (*Oscar*-1961); Mary Poppins; The Sound of Music (*Oscar*-scoring adapt-1965); Bedknobs and Broomsticks; Chitty Chitty Bang Bang; Pete's Dragon; The Magic of Lassie.

TV inc: Your Show of Shows; Julie Andrews Specials; Brigadoon.

Bway inc: West Side Story; Fiorello; A Funny Thing Happened on the Way to the Forum; Sail Away (*Grammy*-soundtrack-1961).

KOSTELANETZ, Andre: Cond. b. St Petersburg, Russia, 1901. e. St Petersburg Conservatory of Music. Made his concert debut as pianist at age eight. Came to US 1923, Worked as accompanist for the Metropolitan and Chicago Opera Companies. Made radio debut 1928, became regular cond on CBS radio 1931; has made more radio, tv appearances then any other cond; known for popularizing both jazz and classical music, he commissioned many symphonic compositions from such composers as Aaron Copland, Jerome Kern, Virgil Thompson, Ferde Grofe; has made more than 200 different recordings; guest cond with NY Philharmonic, many other top orchestras.

Films inc: I Dream Too Much; Artists and Models; Hitting a New High.

(Died Jan 13, 1980).

KOSTER, Henry: Dir. b. Berlin, May 1, 1905. Films inc: 100 Men and a Girl; Rage of Paris; It Started With Eve; Music for Millions; Two Sisters from Boston; The Bishop's Wife; Come to the Stable; My Blue Heaven; Harvey; Mr Belvedere Rings the Bell; Stars and Stripes Forever; The Robe; Desiree; A Man Called Peter; D-Day, the Sixth of June; My Man Godfrey; The Naked Maja; The Story of Ruth; Flower Drum Song; Mr Hobbs Takes a Vacation; Take Her She's Mine; Dear Brigitte; The Singing Nun.

KOTCHEFF, Ted: Dir. b. Toronto, Canada, 1931. Films inc: Life at the Top; Two Gentlemen Sharing; Outback; Billy Two Hats; The Apprenticeship of Duddy Kravitz; Fun with Dick and Jane;

Thea inc: Play with a Tiger; Luv; Have You Any Dirty Washing, Mother Dear? Who Is Killing The Great Chefs of Europe?; North Dallas 40 (& sp).

KOTTO, Yaphet: Act. b. 1937. Films inc: The Thomas Crown Affair; Across 110th Street; Live and Let Die; Truck Turner; Friday Foster; Report to the Commissioner; Drums; The Shootist; Blue Collar Alien; Brubaker.

Thea inc: The Great White Hope; The Zulu and the Zayda; Black Monday; In White America.

KOVACS, Laszlo: Cin. Films inc: Targets; Easy Rider; Five Easy Pieces; Alex in Wonderland; The Last Movie; What's Up Doc?; Freebie and the Bean; Shampoo; At Long Last Love; Nickelodeon; Harry and Walter Go to New York; New York, New York; F.I.S.T.; The Last Waltz; Paradise Alley; Butch and Sundance-The Early Days; The Runner Stumbles; Inside Moves.

KOWAL, Stefanie: Exec. b. Chicago, Dec 18, 1941. e. U of IL, Webster Coll. Wri-prod Ann Landers Radio Show, 1970-72; asso prod Kennedy & Co, 1972-74; prod A M Chicago, 1975-77; Development exec, Universal TV, 1977-79; VP movies & mini series, Universal TV, 1979.

TV inc: Story of Esther; The Thirteenth Day-The Story of Ruth.

KOWALSKI, Bernard L: Dir. b. Brownsville, TX, Aug 2, 1929. Act as a child before becoming dir. TV inc: The Nativity; Marciano; B.A.D. Cats; Nick and the Dobermans; Baretta (& exec prod); Turnover Smith; Nightside.

Films inc: Hot Car Girl; Attack of the Giant Leeches; Night of the Blood Beast; Blood and Steel; Krakatoa--East of Eden; Stiletto; Macho Callahan.

KOZLENKO, William: Wri. b. Philadelphia, PA. Plays inc: Jacob Comes Home; This Earth is Ours; A Fearful Madness.

Films inc: Stranger In Town: Holiday in Mexico; The Man Who Loved Children; Stone Wall; The Raw Edge.

TV inc: Pulitzer Prize Playhouse; Lux Video Theatre; Climax; G.E. Theatre; Playhouse of the Stars; also served as story consltnt G.E. Theatre; Alfred Hitchcock; Hubbell Robinson Prodns.

KRAMER, Lee: Prod. b. England, Nov 3, 1951. Personal mgr of Olivia Newton-John. TV inc: The Silver Surfer. Films inc: Xanadu.

KRAMER, Stanley: Prod-Dir. b. NYC, Sep 29, 1913. e. NYU. Films inc: The Moon and Sixpence; Home of the Brave; The Men; Death of a Saleman; High Noon; My Six Convicts; The Member of the Wedding; The Fourposter; The Juggler; The Wild One; The Caine Mutiny; Not as a Stranger (& dir); The Pride and Passion (& dir); The Defiant Ones (& dir); On the Beach (& dir); Inherit the Wind (& dir); Judgment at Nurenberg (& dir); Pressure Point; A Child Is Waiting; It's a Mad, Mad, Mad, Mad, Mad World (& dir); Invitation to a Gunfighter; Ship of Fools (& dir); Guess Who's Coming to Dinner (& dir); The Secret of Santa Vittoria (& dir); R P M (& dir); Bless the Beasts and Children (& dir); Oklahoma Crude (& dir); The Domino Principle (& dir); The Runner Stumbles (& dir).

Irving Thalberg Award 1961.

TV inc: The Trial of Julius and Ethel Rosenberg; The Court Martial of the Tiger of Malaya - Gen Tomobumi Yamashita; The Court Martial of Lt. William Calley.

KRAMM, Joseph: Wri-Dir-Act. b. Philadelphia, Sep 30, 1907. e. U of PA, BA. Bway debut as act 1928, Lilac Time.

Bway inc: L'Aiglon; Bury the Dead; Golden Boy; Liliom; Journey to Jerusalem; Uncle Harry; Hope Is The Thing with Feathers (dir).

Plays inc: The Shrike (*Pulitzer Prize*-1952); Build With One Hand; Giants, Sons of Giants; The Gypsies Wore High Hats; All Honourable Men.

KRANTZ, Steve: Prod. b. NYC, May 20, 1923. e. Columbia, BA. TV dir with NBC 1953; dir pgm dvlpt Screen Gems; formed Steve Krantz Films 1964.

TV inc: (wri) Steve Allen Show; Kate Smith Show; Winston Churchill-The Valiant Years.

Films inc: (Prod) Fritz the Cat; Heavy Traffic; Ruby (& wri); Which Way Is Up?; Jennifer (& wri); Swap Meet (& wri).

KRASNA, Norman: Wri-Prod. b. NYC, Nov 7, 1909. e. NYU, Columbia U, Brooklyn Law School. N.Y. drama edtr before joining Warner publicity dept, began writing for films 1932.

Films inc: Fury; It Started With Eve; Princess O'Rourke (*Oscar*-sp-1943); White Christmas; Indiscreet; My Geisha; I'd Rather Be Rich.

Plays inc: Louder, Please; John Loves Mary; Sunday In New York; Lady Harry.

KRASNY, Paul: Dir. b. Cleveland, OH, Aug 8, 1935. TV inc: Mission Impossible (*Emmy*-ed-1967); Mannix; Police Story; Born Free; Blue Knight; Quincy; Chips; Islander; Centennial; Christina; Joe Panther; 240 Robert; When Hell Was In Session; Fugitive Family; Alcatraz--The Whole Shocking Story.

KRESKIN (legal single name; nee Kresge): Mentalist. b. Montclair, NJ, Jan 12, 1935. e. Seton Hall U. TV inc: Amazing World of Kreskin; Misadventures of Ichabod Crane.

KRESS, Carl: Film Edtr. b. LA, Feb 3, 1937. S of Harold Kress. Films inc: The Liberation of L Q Jones; Doctor's Wives; Watermelon Man; Towering Inferno (*Oscar*-1974); Audrey Rose; Meteor; Hopscotch.

KRESS, Harold F: Flm Ed. b. Pittsburgh, PA, Jun 26, 1913. e. UCLA. Films inc: Command Decision; Madame Curie; Mrs Miniver; The Yearling; How the West was Won (*Oscar*-1963); Poseidon Adventure; The Iceman Cometh; 99-44/100ths % Dead; The Towering Inferno (*Oscar*-1974); The Other Side of Midnight; Viva Knievel; Swarm.

KREUGER, Kurt: Act. b. Switzerland, Jul 23, 1919. e. U of Lausanne. Films inc: Mademoiselle Fifi; Hotel Berlin; Paris Underground; Dark Corner; Unfaithfully Yours; Fear; The St. Valentine's Day Massacre; What Did You Do in the War Daddy?

KREUTZMAN, Bill: Mus. b. Jun 7, 1946. Founder--member of The Grateful Dead.

(See The Grateful Dead for group credits).

KRIM, Arthur B: Atty. b. NYC, 1910. e. Columbia U. Became member of law firm, Philips, Nizer, Benjamin & Krim, NY. P, Eagle Lion Films 1946-49; elected P, United Artists, 1951; ChmnB, 1969. Co-founder Orion Pictures Corp, 1978.

Jean Hersholt Humanitarian Award 1974.

KRIMS, Milton: Wri. b. NYC, Feb 7, 1904. e. OR Inst Tech, OR U, U of Rome. Films inc: Strangers All; Dude Ranch; West of the Pecos; Harmony Lane; The Great O'Malley; Confessions of a Nazi Spy; We Are Not Alone; Prince of Foxes; Iron Curtain; Crossed Swords; One Minute To Zero.

TV inc: Perry Mason; Wagon Train; Hotel deParis.

KRISTEL, Sylvia: Act. b. Sep 28, 1952. Films inc: Because of the Cats; Living Apart Together; Naakt over de Schutting; Emmanuelle; Un Lincoln n'a pas de poches; Le Jeu avec le Feu; Julia; Eswar die nachtigall und Night die Lerche; Emmanuelle 2; La Marge; Alice ou la Derniere Fugue; Une Femme Fidele; Fene La Canne; Behind the Iron Mask; Good-bye Emmanuelle; Mysteries; The Fifth Musketeer; Concorde--Airport 79.

KRISTOFFERSON, Kris: Act. b. Brownsville, TX, Jun 22, 1936. Rock mus comp, singer. Songs inc: Me and Bobby McGee; Why Me, Lord; Sunday Mornin' Comin' Down; Help Me Make It Through The Night (*Grammy*-1971).

Films inc: Cisco Pike; Pat Garrett And Billy The Kid; Bring Me The Head of Alfredo Garcia; Blume In Love; Alice Doesn't Live Here Anymore; Vigilante Force; The Sailor Who Fell From Grace with the Sea; A Star Is Born; Semi-Tough; Convoy; Heaven's Gate.

TV inc: Freedom Road; The Unbroken Circle-A Tribute to Mother Maybelle Carter.

(*Other Grammys*-(2)-C&W perf-1973, 1975).

KROFFT, Marty: Puppeteer-Prod. b. Montreal, Canada. Member of family that has operated puppet theatre in Athens since 18th century. TV inc: H R Pufnstuf; Land of the Lost; Sigmund and the Sea Monsters; Lost Saucer; Far Out Space Nuts; Donny and Marie Series; Brady Bunch Variety Hour; Really Raquel; Kaptain Kool and the Kongs Present ABC All-Star Saturday; Jimmy Osmond Special; Krofft Comedy Hour; Krofft Superstars Hour; Pink Lady; Barbara Mandrell and the Mandrell Sisters. 0

Films inc: Middle Age Crazy.

KROFFT, Sid: Puppeteer-Prod. b. Athens, Greece. B of Marty Krofft. Created Les Poupees de Paris. For other credits see KROFFT, Marty.

KROLL, Nathan: Prod-Dir. b. NYC, Nov 5, 1911. e. Juilliard. TV inc: A Dancer's World; Appalachian Spring; Night Journey; The World of Carl Sandburg; Who's Afraid of Opera?; Portrait of an American Actress; Prado Museum - Masterpieces and Music; Casals at Marlboro; Impact.

Films inc: The Guns of August (doc).

KRONENBERGER, Louis: Wri. b. Cincinnati, Dec 9, 1904. e. U Cincinnati. Drama critic Time Mag 1938-1940; PM 1940-1948; Time 1948-1961, prof theatre arts Brandeis U, 1953-1970; author of idiomatic stage adapt Mademoilselle Colombe.

(Died April 30, 1980).

KRUGER, Hardy: Act. b. Berlin, Apr 12, 1928. On screen since 1943.
Films inc: As Long As You're Near Me; Taxi For Tobruk; Sundays and Cybele; The Flight of the Phoenix; The Defector; The Battle on the Neretva; The Secret of Santa Vittoria; The Red Tent; Paper Tiger; Barry Lyndon; A Bridge Too Far; The Wild Geese; Blue Fin.

KRUGER, Jeffrey S: Prod. b. London, England, Apr 19, 1931. Prod numerous concerts with top US, British stars. Pres Ember Enterprises which includes mus pub, concert promotion, film dist & prodn.
Films inc: Sweetbeat; Rock You Sinners; The Amorous Sex.

KRUGMAN, Lou: Act. b. Chicago, Jul 19, 1914. Started as radio actor, 1929.
Films inc: To the Ends of the Earth; The Lady of Fatima; Kim; Caper of the Golden Bulls; I Want to Live; Irma La Douce.
Thea inc: Yoshe Kalb; Midsummer Night's Dream; Cafe Crown; Cotton Candy; Diary of Anne Frank.

KRUMGOLD, Joseph: Wri. b. Jersey City, NJ, 1908. e. NYU. Films inc: And Now Miguel; Dream No More; Magic Town; Seven Miles From Alcatraz; The Crooked Road; The Phantom Submarine; Main Street Lawyer; Speed to Burn; Blackmailer; Adventure in Manhattan; Lady from Nowhere; Join the Marines.

KRUSCHEN, Jack: Act. b. Winnipeg, Canada, Mar 20, 1922. Films inc: Red Hot and Blue; The Last Voyage; The Apartment; Lover Come Back; The Unsinkable Molly Brown; Harlow; Caprice; McClintock; Cry Terror; Freebie and the Bean; Satan's Cheerleader; Sunburn.
TV inc: Deadly Harvest; Busting Loose; The Life and Times of Grizzly Adams.

KUBRICK, Stanley: Dir-Prod-Wri. b. NYC, Jul 26, 1928. Films inc: (doc) Day of the Fight; Flying Padre. (Features) Fear and Desire; Killer's Kiss; The Killing; Paths of Glory; Spartacus; Lolita; Dr Strangelove; 2001: A Space Odyssey; A Clockwork Orange; Barry Lyndon; The Shining.

KULIK, Seymour (Buzz): Prod-Dir. b. NYC, 1923. Films inc: The Explosive Generation; The Yellow Canary; Warning Shot (& prod); Villa Rides; Riot; To Find a Man; The Hunter.
TV inc: Brian's Song; Vanished; The Lindbergh Kidnapping Case; From Here To Eternity.

KULUKUNDIS, Eddie: Prod. b. London, Apr 20, 1932. e. Yale. Thea inc: (London) Enemy; Happy Apple; Poor Alice; How the Other Half Loves; The Disorderly Woman; Skyvers; The Plotters of Cabbage Patch Corner; Straight Up; Small Craft Warnings; A Private Matter; Cromwell; The Waltz of the Toreadors; A Little Night Music; The Gay Lord Quex; What the Butler Saw; A Room With a View; Dimetos; Outside Edge; Once A Catholic; Born In the Gardens; Beecham; Censored Scenes from King Kong. (Bway): How the Other Half Loves; Sherlock Holmes; London Assurance; Travesties.

KUPCINET, Irv: Columnist-TV host. b. Jul 31. e. U of ND, BA.

KURALT, Charles: TV newsman. b. Wilmington, NC, Sep 10, 1934. e. U NC, BA. Reporter Charlotte News 1955; reporter CBS 1957-1959, then spec assignments.
TV inc: On the Road with Charles Kuralt (Emmy-1969; ATAS Broadcast Journalism Award 1978.)

KUROSAWA, Akiro: Dir. b. Japan, Mar 23, 1910. Films inc: Rashomon; Scandal; The Idiot; Red Beard; I Live in Fear; Doomed; The Hidden Fortress; The Cobweb Castle; Stray Dog; Seven Samurai; High and Low; The Man Who Tread on A Tiger's Tail; Sanjuro; The Bad Sleep Well; Drunken Angels; Lower Depths; No Regret for Our Youth; A Quiet Duel; Dodes'ka-den; Yojimbo; The Double.

KURTZ, Gary: Prod. b. 1941. e. USC. Worked with Roger Corman, Monte Hellman, other dirs as cin, soundman, edtr. Became asst prod on Two Lane Blacktop. Films inc: Chandler (asst prod); American Graffiti (co-prod); Star Wars (prod); The Empire Strikes Back (prod).

KURTZ, Swoozie: Act. b. Omaha, NE, Sep 6. Bway inc: Enter A Free Man; Tartuffe; A History of The American Film; Fifth of July.
TV inc: Uncommon Women; Ah, Wilderness; Marriage Is Alive and Well; The Mating Season.
Films inc: Slap Shot; First Love; Oliver's Story.

KURTZMAN, Katy: Act. b. Washington, DC, Sep 16, 1965. TV inc: Child of Class; When Every Day Was the 4th of July; Little House on the Prairie; The New Adventures of Heidi; Long Journey Back; Donovan's Kid.

KWAN, Nancy: Act. b. Hong Kong, 1939. Films inc: The World of Suzie Wong; Flower Drum Song; The Main Attraction; Honeymoon Hotel; Fate Is the Hunter; The House of Seven Joys; The Wrecking Crew; Fortress in the Sun; Night Creature.

KYSER, Kay: Orch Ldr. b. Rocky Mt, NC, 1905. Retired in 1947. Now lives in Boston where he is manager of the film and broadcasting departments of the Christian Science church.

LA BONTE, C Joseph: Exec. b. Salem, MA, Sep 23, 1939. e. Northeastern U, BS; Harvard, MBA. Exec with H. P. Hood & Sons, 1958-1963; mktg coord Market Forge Co., 1963; vp food svs ARA 1969; exec vp 1971; Aug. 1979 P 20th-Fox Enterprises & sr vp 20th Century-Fox; Sept 1979 named P 20th Century-Fox.

LABORTEAUX, Matthew: Act. b. LA, Dec 1965. Films inc: Woman Under the Influence.
TV inc: Poppa and Me; Little House on the Prairie.

LACHMAN, Mort: Wri-Dir-Prod. b. Seattle, WA, Mar 20, 1918. e. U WA, BA. TV inc: Bob Hope TV Specials; Flip Wilson Specials; Oscar Shows; Emmy Shows; The Girl Who Couldn't Lose (Emmy-dir-1975); All in the Family (Emmy-exec prod-1978); One Day at a Time (exec prod).
Films inc: Yours, Mine and Ours (wri); Mixed Company (wri).

LADD, Alan Walbridge Jr: Exec. b. LA, Oct 22, 1937. e. USC. S of late Alan Ladd. Agent, CMA, 1962-68; prod, 1969-73. Films inc: Walking Stick; A Severed Head; Tam Lin; Nightcomers; Fear Is the Key; with 20th Century-Fox Film Corp 1973; Sr vp Worldwide Prod, 1974-76; appointed pres 20th Century-Fox, Aug 30, 1976; resigned June 1979; formed The Ladd Company, Oct 1979.

LADD, Cheryl (nee Stoppelmoor): Act. b. Huron, SD, Jul 2. TV inc: Charlie's Angels; Ben Vereen. . . His Roots; General Electric's All-Star Anniversary; John Denver and the Ladies; The Cheryl Ladd Special; When She Was Bad; Cheryl Ladd Special-Souvenirs.

LADD, David Alan: Act. b. LA, Feb 5, 1947. e. USC, BA. S of late Alan Ladd. Films inc: The Lone Ranger (at age 9); The Big Land; Raymie; Misty; R.P.M.; Catlow; Deathline; Jamaica Reef; Jonathan Livingston Seagull; Day of the Locusts; Kansan; Wild Geese.
TV inc: Zane Gray Theatre; Wagon Train; Playhouse 90; Pursuit; Ben Casey; Gunsmoke; Love American Style; Kojak; When She Was Bad (prod).
Thea inc: The Glass Menagerie; Alpha Beta.

LADD, Diane (nee Ladnier): Act. b. Nov 29, 1939. Films inc: White Lightning; Chinatown; Alice Doesn't Live Here Any More.
TV inc: Willa; Guyana Tragedy-The Story of Jim Jones.
Bway inc: Lu Ann Hampton Laverty Oberlander.

LAEMMLE, Carl Jr: Exec. b. Chicago, Apr 28, 1908. At age 21 became gm in charge of prodn at Universal, which his father had founded.
Films inc: Frankenstein; The Invisible Man; Bride of Frankenstein; Waterloo Bridge; King of Jazz; The Spirit of Notre Dame; Strictly Dishonorable; Imitation of Life; The Good Fairy; Remember Last Night?
(Died Sep 24, 1979).

LAFFERTY, Perry: Exec. b. Oct 3, 1920. Former vp, pgms, Hollywood, for the CBS TV Network from 1965-1976. In 1976 with Filmways as an exec prod; June 1979 named sr vp pgms and talent, West Coast, NBC Entertainment.

TV inc: The Danny Kaye Show; Robert Montgomery Presents; U S Steel Hour; Studio One; Twilight Zone; Mary Tyler Moore Show; The Funny Side of Love.

LAFONT, Bernadette: Act. b. Nimes, France, Oct 28. Films inc: Le Beau Serge; Bal De Nuit; A Double Tour; Les Bonnes Femmes; Les Mordus; Tire Au Flanc; Un Clair De Lune A Maubeuge; La Chasse A L'Homme; Le Bons Vivante; Le Voleur; Le Trouble-Fesses; Noroit; La Tortue sur le dos; Violette Noziere; Chaussette Surprise; Nous Maigrirons Ensemble; La Guele de l'autre; Retour En Force; Il Ladrone.

LAI, Francis: Comp. b. France, 1933. Film scores inc: A Man and a Woman; Mayerling; House of Cards; Rider on the Rain; Love Story (Oscar-1970); Le Petit Matin; Another Man, Another Chance; Bilitis; The Good and the Bad; Widow's Nest; Cat and Mouse; International Velvet; Oliver's Story (Oscar-1970).

LAINE, Cleo (Clementina Dinah Campbell): Singer-Act. b. Southall, Middlesex, England, 1934. W of John Dankworth. Singing debut 1952 with Dankworth Seven, later John Dankworth Orch. U S debut Lincoln Center 1972; appeared Carnegie Hall; world tours. Albums inc: I Am A Song; Cleo Laine Live at Carnegie Hall; A Beautiful Thing; Born on a Friday; Porgy and Bess; Best Friends.

Thea inc: (London) The Seven Deadly Sins; Show Boat; Valmouth; Flesh to a Tiger; Hedda Gabler; A Time to Laugh; A Midsummer Night's Dream; Colette.

TV inc: The Monte Carlo Show.

LAINE, Frankie: Act. b. Chicago, Mar 30, 1913. Recording, nitery star. Films inc: When You're Smiling; Make Believe Ballroom; The Sunny Side of the Street; Rainbow Round My Shoulder; Bring Your Smile Along; He Laughed Last; Viva Las Vegas.

LAIRD, Jack: Prod-Wri-Dir. b. Bombay, India, May 8, 1923. Prod with Bing Crosby Prodns 1961; U, 1963. Films inc: Dark Intruder; Destiny of a Spy; Intrigue at Monte Carlo; Perilous Voyage.

TV inc: Ben Casey; Kraft Suspense Theatre; The Bold Ones; Night Gallery; Kojak; Doctors Hospital; Whatever Happened to the Class of '65?; Testimony of Two Men; Beggarman, Thief; The Dark Secret of Harvest Home.

LAKE, Arthur (nee Silverlake): Act. b. Corbin, KY, 1905. On screen since 1924.

Films inc: Skinner's Dress Suit; The Irresistible Lover; Harold Teen; On with the Show; Indiscreet; Midshipman Jack; Orchids to You; Topper; Blondie series; Three is a Family; Sixteen Fathoms Deep.

LAKIN, Rita: Wri. b. NYC. e. Hunter Coll, BA. TV inc: The Doctors; Peyton Place; Mod Squad; Death Takes a Holiday; Women in Chains; A Summer Without Boys; Message to My Daughter; Last Bride of Salem; Medical Center; Hey, I'm Alive; A Sensitive; Passionate Man; Executive Suite; Flamingo Road; The Home Front (& supv prod).

LAMARR, Hedy: Act. b. Vienna, Nov 9, 1915. On screen in Europe from 1929.

Films inc: One Doesn't Need Money; Storm in a Water Glass; Ecstasy. In US from 1938 in: Algiers; I Take This Woman; Boom Town; Comrade X; H.M. Pulham, Esq.; Tortilla Flat; Crossroads; White Cargo; Samson and Delilah; Lady Without A Passport; Dishonored Lady; Experiment Perilous; My Favorite Spy; The Female Animal.

LAMAS, Fernando: Act-Dir. b. Buenos Aires, Jan 9, 1923. After 24 European and Latin-American films came to Hollywood in 1951. Films inc: Rich, Young and Pretty; The Merry Widow; Rose Marie; Duel of Fire; Kill a Dragon; 100 Rifles; Backtrack; The Cheap Detective.

TV inc: (dir) Run For Your Life; The Bold Ones; Mannix; The Rookies; SWAT; Carl Reiner Show; Starsky and Hutch; Samurai; The Dream Merchants.

LAMAS, Lorenzo: Act. b. LA, Jan 20, 1958. S of Arlene Dahl and Fernando Lamas. Films inc: Grease; Tilt; Take Down.

TV inc: California Fever; Detour to Terror; Secret of Midland Heights.

LAMB, Gil: Dancer-Act. b. Minneapolis, MN, Jun 14, 1906. In Vaude, on Bway. Films inc: The Fleet's In; Ridin' High; Rainbow Island; Practically Yours; Hit Parade of 1947; Make Mine Laughs; Humphrey Takes a Chance; Bye, Bye Birdie; The Gnomemobile; Blackbeard's Ghost; The Love Bug.

TV inc: For The Love of It.

LAMBERT, Gavin: Wri. b. Eng, 1924. Films inc: Bitter Victory; Sons and Lovers; The Roman Spring of Mrs Stone; Inside Daisy Clover; I Never Promised You a Rose Garden.

LAMOUR, Dorothy (Dorothy Raumeyer): Act. b. New Orleans, LA, Dec 10, 1914. Screen debut, 1938, Jungle Princess.

Films inc: Hurricane; Johnny Apollo; Typhoon; The Road to Singapore (and 4 other "Road" pix); Star Spangled Rhythm; The Fleet's In; Beyond the Blue Horizon; A Medal for Benny; Duffy's Tavern; My Favorite Brunette; Lulu Belle; The Greatest Show on Earth; Donovan's Reef; The Phynx.

LAMPELL, Millard: Wri. b. Paterson, NJ, Jan 10, 1919. e. WV U. Films inc: The Hero; Chance Meeting; Escape from East Berlin; The Idol.

TV inc: No Hiding Place; Eagle In a Cage (Emmy-1966); The Deadly Visitor; Grand Ole Opry at 50; Rich Man, Poor Man; Wheels; Orphan Train.

LAMPERT, Zohra: Act. b. May 13, 1937. Films inc: Odds Against Tomorrow; Posse from Hell; Splendor in the Grass; A Fine Madness; Bye, Bye Braverman; Let's Scare Jessica To Death; Opening Night.

TV inc: The Nurses; Lady of the House; The Suicide's Wife; The Girl, The Gold Watch and Everything; Children of Divorce.

Bway inc: Look, We've Come Throught; Mother Courage and Her Children; Unexpected Guests.

LANCASTER, Burt: Act. b. NYC, Nov 2, 1913. Screen debut, 1946, The Killers.

Films inc: Desert Fury; Brute Force; All My Sons; The Flame and the Arrow; Jim Thorpe-All American; Crimson Pirate; Come Back, Little Sheba; From Here To Eternity; His Majesty O'Keefe; Apache; Vera Cruz; The Rose Tattoo; Trapeze; The Rainmaker; Gunfight At The OK Corral; Sweet Smell of Success; Separate Tables; Elmer Gantry (Oscar-1960); Judgment at Nuremberg; Bird Man of Alcatraz; Seven Days in May; The Swimmer; The Gypsy Moths; Airport; Scorpio; Executive Action; Conversation Piece; Buffalo Bill and the Indians; The Cassandra Crossing; Twilight's Last Gleaming; The Island of Dr. Moreau; Go Tell The Spartans; Zulu Dawn; Arthur Miller On Home Ground; Atlantic City, USA.

LANCHESTER, Elsa: Act. b. London, Oct 28, 1902. W of late Charles Laughton. Performed on stage with husband in London, NY. On screen in England from 1938. On screen in US from 1935.

Films inc: David Copperfield; Naughty Marietta; The Razor's Edge; Bell, Book and Candle; Come To The Stable; Witness for the Prosecution; Mary Poppins; Murder by Death; Die Laughing.

TV inc: Where's Poppa?

LANDAU, Ely: Prod. b. NYC, Jan 20, 1920. Films inc: Long Day's Journey Into Night; The Pawnbroker; The Madwoman of Chaillot; A Filmed Record. . .Montgomery to Memphis (doc); A Face of War (doc); The Iceman Cometh; Rhinoceros; Lost in the Stars; The Homecoming; A Delicate Balance; Luther; In Celebration; Butley; Galileo; The Man in the Glass Booth (all under the banner of the American Film Theatre Subscription series); The Greek Tycoon; Hopscotch.

In the 50's he founded and headed NTA (National Telefilm Associates). During this period he created and developed Play of the Week series, inc such plays as Medea; The World of Sholem Aleichem, No Exit; Tiger at the Gates.

LANDAU, Martin: Act. b. NYC, Jun 20, 1930. H of Barbara Bain. Films inc: Pork Chop Hill; North by Northwest; The Gazebo; Cleopatra; The Hallelujah Trail; Nevada Smith; They Call Me Mr Tibbs; Strange Shadows in an Empty Room; Meteor; The Last Word; Without Warning.

TV inc: Mission Impossible; Space 1999; The Death of Ocean View Park.

Bway inc: Middle of the Night; Uncle Vanya; Stalag 17; First Love; The Goat Song.

LANDAU, Richard: Wri. b. NYC, Feb 21, 1914. e. U of AZ; Yale. Started as agent; became wri with MGM Shorts Dept. Films inc: Gun In His Hand; Strange Confession; Back To Bataan; Christmas Eve; Crooked Way; Johnny One Eye; The Lost Continent; FBI Girl; Stolen Face; Bad Blonde; The Sins of Jezebel; Blackout; Pearl of the Pacific; Creeping Unknown; Fort Courageous; The Black Hole.

TV inc: The FBI; Manhunter; Run, Joe, Run; Cannon; Switch; The $6 Million Man; The Incredible Hulk; American Girls; Misadventures of Sheriff Lobo; One Last Ride.

LANDER, David L: Act. b. Brooklyn, NY, Jun 22. e. NYC High School for Performing Arts; Carnegie Tech. Teamed with Michael McKean in comedy group The Credibility Gap, toured US for four years. TV inc: Viva Valdez; The Bob Newhart Show; The Hollywood Squares; Kids Are People Too; Laverne & Shirley.

LANDERS, Hal (nee Waxlander): Prod. b. Chicago, Jun 26, 1928. Films inc: Joy Ride; Damnation Alley; Gypsy Moths; Monte Walsh; The Hot Rock; Back Shot; Death Wish.

LANDESBERG, Steve: Act. b. NYC, Nov 23. TV inc: Johnny Carson Show; Paul Sand Show; Barney Miller; The Steve Allen Comedy Hour.

LANDIS, John: Dir. b. Chicago, IL, 1951. Films inc: Schlock; Kentucky Fried Movie; National Lampoon's Animal House; The Blues Brothers (& wri).

LANDON, Michael (nee Orowitz): Act-Wri-Dir. b. Forest Hills, NY, Oct 31, 1937. e. USC. Films inc: I Was a Teenage Werewolf; God's Little Acre; The Legend of Tom Dooley.

TV inc: (as actor) Restless Gun; Bonanza; Little House on the Prairie (& co-prod). Love Came Laughing (wri-dir); The Loneliest Runner; Killing Stone (wri-dir-prod); The Roy Campanella Story (dir); Highlights of Ringling Bros and Barnum & Bailey Circus (host).

LANDRES, Paul: Dir. b. NYC, Aug 21, 1912. Films inc: Miracle of the Hills: Johnny Rocco; Vampire; Flame Barrier; Oregon Passage; Last of the Badmen; Son of a Gunfighter.

TV approximately 400 segments of various shows inc: The Outcasts; Bonanza; Daktari; The Rifleman; 77 Sunset Strip; Maverick; Hawaiian Eye.

LANDSBURG, Alan W: Exec prod. b. NYC, May 10, 1933. e. NYU. Prod NBC News, 1951-59; prod-wri CBS, 1959-60; exec prod, Wolper Prodns/Metromedia Prods Corp, 1961-70; p Alan Landsburg Prodn 1970.

TV inc: A Storm In Summer (Emmy-prod-1970); Terror Out Of The Sky; The Triangle Factory Fire Scandal; And Baby Makes Six; Mysterious Island of Beautiful Women; Marathon; The Chisholms; That's Incredible; Those Amazing Animals; No Holds Barred; Baby Comes Home; The World's Most Spectacular Stuntman; 30 Years of TV Comedy's Greatest Hits.

LANE, Abbe: Singer. b. NYC, 1932. Appeared with bands, in niteries. Films inc: Wings of the Hawk; Ride Clear of Diablo; The Americano.

LANE, Burton (nee Levy): Comp. b. NYC. b. Feb 2, 1912. Bway scores inc: Hold On to Your Hats; Laffing Room Only; Finian's Rainbow; On a Clear Day You Can See Forever.

Songs inc: Everything I Have Is Yours; The Lady's in Love with You; I Hear Music; How Are Things in Glocca Morra; That Old Devil Moon; When I'm Not Near The Girl I Love; On a Clear Day You Can See Forever.

Film scores inc: Dancing Lady; College Swing; St. Louis Blues; Babes on Broadway; Ship Ahoy; Royal Wedding.

(Grammy-cast album-1965).

LANE, Diane: Act. b. NYC, 1965. Films inc: A Little Romance; Touched By Love.

Thea inc: The Cherry Orchard; Agamemnon; Runaways.

LANE, Lola: Act. b. Macy, IN, 1906. Screen debut, 1929, Speakeasy.

Films inc: The Girl from Havana; Burn 'em Up Barnes; Murder on a Honeymoon; Torchy Blane in Panama; Four Daughters; Deadline at Dawn.

LANG, Charles B Jr: Cin. b. Bluff, UT, Mar 27, 1902. Began in film laboratory, then asst cameraman; dir of photography, Paramount, 1929-52, then freelance.

Films inc: The Right To Love; A Farewell to Arms (Oscar-1933); The Ghost and Mrs. Muir; Ace In The Hole; Sundown; Sabrina; Sudden Fear; The Uninvited; The Rainmaker; So Proudly We Hail; Some Like It Hot; Separate Tables; How The West Was Won; The Magnificent Seven; Charade; The Love Machine; Doctor's Wives; Bob and Carol & Ted & Alice; Butterflies Are Free.

LANG, Jennings: Exec. b. NYC, May 28, 1915. e. St Johns U, BS, JD. H of Monica Lewis. Law practice, 1937. Opened own office as actor's agent, Hollywood. In 1940 joined Jaffee Agency; made partner and vp in 1942; pres from 1948-50; resigned to join MCA; in 1952 made vp of MCA-TV Ltd and bd member; exec prod, MCA (Universal). Creator and developer of the Sensurround System which won (Oscar-1974).

Films inc: Winning; Puzzle of a Downfall Child; Coogan's Bluff; Joe Kidd; High Plains Drifter; Play Misty For Me; Charley Varrick; Pete 'N Tillie; Slaughterhouse Five; Breezy; The Great Waldo Pepper; Airport 75; The Eiger Sanction; Airport 77; The Front Page; The Hindenburg; Rollercoaster; House Calls; Nunzio; The Concorde-Airport '79; Real Life (act); Little Miss Marker; The Nude Bomb.

TV inc: Wagon Train; The Robert Cummings Show; Bachelor Father; Wells Fargo; Mike Hammer.

LANG, Otto: Prod-Dir. b. Austria, Jan 21, 1908. Films inc: (docs) New Guinea; New Zealand; Australia; Philippines; Thailand; Singapore; Turkey. (Features) Five Fingers; Call Northside 777; White Witch Doctor; Lowell Thomas' Search for Paradise; Tora! Tora! Tora! (asso prod).

TV inc: Beethoven - Ordeal and Triumph; Man from UNCLE; Daktari; Iron Horse; Cheyenne; Bat Masterson; Rifleman; Sea Hunt.

LANG, Richard (W Richard Lang Jr): Dir. Films inc: Wind River; Rough Mix; The Mountain Men; A Change of Seasons.

TV inc: Fantasy Island; Vega$ (pilot); The Word.

LANGDON, Sue Ane: Act. b. Mar 8, 1936. Films inc: The Outsider; The Rounders; A Fine Madness; A Guide For The Married Man; Cheyenne Social Club; The Evictors; Without Warning.

TV inc: Arnie.

LANGE, Hope: Act. b. Redding Ridge, CT, Nov 28, 1933. Bway debut age 12, The Patriots. Screen debut, 1956, Bus Stop.

Films inc: Peyton Place; The Young Lions; In Love and War; A Pocketful of Miracles; How the West Was Won; Jigsaw; Death Wish.

TV inc: The Ghost and Mrs. Muir (Emmys-1969, 1970); That Certain Summer; The Day Christ Died; Beulah Land; Pleasure Palace.

LANGE, Jessica: Act. b. Apr 20, 1949. Films inc: King Kong; All That Jazz; How to Beat the High Cost of Living.

LANGE, Ted: Perf. b. Oakland, CA, Jan 5. Films inc: Love Gift; Trick Baby; Wattstax; Black Belt Jones; Friday Foster; Record City.
TV inc: The Last Detail; A.F.I. Salute to James Cagney; That's My Mama; Mr. T. and Tina; The Love Boat.
Thea inc: Hair; Ain't Supposed to Die a Natural Death.

LANGELLA, Frank: Act. b. Bayonne, NJ, Jan 1, 1940. e. Syracuse U. Bway inc: The Immoralist; Benito Cereno; A Cry of Players; The Relapse; Seascape (Tony-1975); Ring Around the Moon; Dracula; Passione (dir).
Films inc: The Twelve Chairs; Diary of a Mad Housewife; The House Under the Trees; The Deadly Trap; The Wrath of God; Dracula; Those Lips, Those Eyes.

LANGFORD, Francis: Act. b. Lakeland, FL, Apr 4, 1913. Stage, vaudeville, niteries prior to screen debut Broadway Melody of 1936.
Films inc: Born to Dance; The Hit Parade; This Is the Army; Follow the Band; Radio Stars on Parade; The Purple Heart Diary; The Glenn Miller Story.

LANGNER, Philip: Prod. b. NYC, Aug 24, 1926. e. Yale U, BS. S of Armina Marshall and late Lawrence Langner. Films inc: Judgment at Nuremburg; A Child is Waiting; The Pawnbroker; Slaves; Born to Win.
Bway inc: Seagulls Over Sorrento; The Tunnel of Love; The Summer of the Seventeenth Doll; Sunrise at Campobello (Tony-1957); Third Best Sport; The 49th Cousin; Help Stamp Out Marriage; The Homecoming; Absurd Person Singular. Ownr Westport Country Playhouse, Westport CT.

LANKFORD, Kim: Act. b. Montebello, CA. Films inc: Harry and Walter Go To New York; Malibu Beach; Convoy; The Octagon.
TV inc: Terror Among Us; Three Eyes; Knots Landing.

LANSBURY, Angela: Act. b. London, Oct 16, 1925. Screen debut, 1943, Gaslight.
Films inc: National Velvet; The Picture of Dorian Gray; The Hoodlum Saint; Till the Clouds Roll By; If Winter Comes; State of the Union; The Three Musketeers; Samson and Delilah; Kind Lady; Mutiny; Remains to be Seen; A Life at Stake; Please Murder Me; The Court Jester; The Long Hot Summer; The Dark at the Top of the Stairs; A Breath of Scandal; All Fall Down; The Manchurian Candidate; Dear Heart; The Greatest Story Ever Told; Harlow; Mister Buddwing; Something for Everyone; Bedknobs and Broomsticks; Death on the Nile; The Lady Vanishes; The Mirror Crack'd.
Bway inc: Mame (Tony-1966); Dear World (Tony-1979); Hamlet; Gypsy (Tony-1975); Sweeney Todd (Tony-1979).

LANSBURY, Bruce: Prod. b. London, Jan 12, 1930. e. UCLA, BA. Wri, prod KABC-TV, LA, 1957-59; joined CBS-TV 1959, supervised daytime and nighttime programming; promoted to vp 1964; joined Paramount TV 1969 as prod; appointed vp 1972; joined Columbia TV as indie prod, 1975.
TV inc: Wild, Wild West; Mission Impossible; Silent Gun; Assault on the Wayne; Escape; Banjo Hackett; Bell, Book and Candle; The Fantastic Journey (exec prod); Mobile Medics (exec prod); The Aeromeds (exec prod; New Adventures of Wonder Woman (supv prod); Buck Rogers (supv prod).

LANSBURY, Edgar: Prod-Desgn. b. London, Jan 12, 1930. e. UCLA. Began career as scenic dsgn and art dir. First designs in NY were for The Wise Have Not Spoken, 1954, Cherry Lane Theatre. Art dir CBS, 1955-60; exec art dir, prod for WNDT educational TV, NY, 1962-63; art dir for award winning TV series The Defenders.
Films inc: (prod) The Subject Was Roses; Godspell; The Wild Party; Squirm; Blue Sunshine; He Knows You're Alone.
Bway inc: (prod) The Subject Was Roses (Tony-1964); The Only Game in Town; That Summer-That Fall; Promenade; Waiting for Godot; Long Day's Journey Into Night; Nourish the Beast; The Enclave; Gypsy; The Night That Made America Famous; The Magic Show; Godspell; American Buffalo.

LANSING, Robert (nee Broom): Act. b. San Diego, 1929. Films inc: The 4-D Man; A Gathering of Eagles; Under the Yum, Yum Tree; The Grissom Gang; Wild in the Sky; Bittersweet Love; Scalpel.
TV inc: 87th Precinct; 12 O'Clock High; S*H*E*; Life On The Mississippi.
Bway inc: Stalag 17; Suddenly Last Summer; Great God Brown.

LANSING, Sherry Lee: Exec. b. Chicago, Jul 31, 1944. e. Northwestern, BS. Films (as act) Loving; Rio Lobo; Then Story Ed Talent Associates; exec story ed, MGM 1975-77; vp, Creative Affairs, MGM; vp, prod, Col; sr vp prodn, Col, 1978; Resigned to become P 20th Fox Jan 1980.

LANTEAU, William (nee Lanctot): Act. b. St Johnsbury, VT, Nov 17, 1922. e. Yale School of Drama. Films inc: Li'l Abner; The Honeymoon Machine; The Facts of Life; Hotel; That Touch of Mink; From Noon Till Three.
TV inc: Our Town; All in the Family; Bronk; Sanford and Son; First You Cry.
Bway inc: At War With the Army; Mrs. McThing; The Remarkable Mr. Pennypacker; What Every Woman Knows; The Matchmaker; Li'l Abner.

LANTOS, Robert: Prod. b. Budapest, Hungary, Apr 3, 1949. e. McGill U, BA, MA. Pres R.S.L. Films, Ltd, pres Viva Film. Films inc: L'Ange et la Femme; In Praise of Older Women; Suzanne.

LANTZ, Walter: Prod. b. New Rochelle, NY, Apr 27, 1900. Cartoonist for Hearst, 1916-20; prod cartoons for J. R. Bray Studios, 1922-27; then for Universal; became independent prod, 1937; pres Walter Lantz Prods. Created Woody Woodpecker; Chilly Willy; Oswald Rabbit; Katzenjammer Kids; Happy Hooligan; Krazy Kat. Also prod educational & commercial pictures for non-theatrical release & TV; prod, the Woody Woodpecker Show (TV). (Honorary Oscar-1978).

LA PLANTE, Laura: Act. b. St Louis, MO, Nov 1, 1904. On screen from 1921. Films inc: The Old Swimming Hole; Perils of the Yukon; Sporting Youth; The Cat and the Canary; Show Boat; Spring Reunion.

LARDNER, Ring W Jr: Wri. b. Chicago, IL, Aug 19, 1915. e. Princeton. Originally a reporter then pub for Selznick Int'l before writing. Films inc: Woman of the Year (Oscar-1942); The Cross of Lorraine; Forever Amber; Forbidden Street; Four Days Leave; Cloak and Dagger; (career interrupted when, as member of so-called Unfriendly 10, he served year in prison for refusing to testify before House Committee on UnAmerican Activities); The Cincinnati Kid; M*A*S*H (Oscar-1970); The Greatest; Hollywood on Trial (act).

LARNER, Jeremy: Wri. Films inc: Drive, He Said; The Candidate (Oscar-1972).

LA ROSA, Julius: Singer. b. NYC, 1930. Pop singer of the 50's. TV inc: Arthur Godfrey and His Friends; Another World.

LARSON, Glen: Prod-Wri. Member of the Four Preps singing group in the 1950's, moved to tv 1960.
TV inc: It Takes a Thief; McCloud; The Virginian; Get Christie Love; Six Million Dollar Man; Sword of Justice; Battlestar Galactica; BJ and the Bear; Evening in Byzantium; Quincy; The Misadventures of Sheriff Lobo; Buck Rogers in the 25th Century; Battles--The Murder That Wouldn't Die; Nightside; Magnum P.I.

LARSON, Jack: Act. b. Feb 8, 1933. Films inc: (perf) Fighter Squadron; Star Lift; Three Sailors and a Girl; Kid Monk Baroni; Battle Zone; Man Crazy; Johnny Trouble.
Thea inc: The Great Man; Androcles and the Lion.
TV inc: Superman.

LA RUE, Jack: Act. b. NYC, 1900. Screen debut, 1932, When Paris Sleeps. On stage in Diamond Lil.
Films inc: Three on a Match; A Farewell to Arms; Valley of the Giants; Charlie Chan in Panama; Murder in the Music Hall; Robin and the Seven Hoods; A Voice in the Night.

LASKY, Jesse Jr: Wri. b. NYC, Sep 19, 1910. Worked in foreign dept, Paramount, Spain. Asst to Sol Wurtzel, Fox.
Films inc: Secret Agent; The Redhead; Union Pacific; Northwest Mounted Police; Reap The Wild Wind; Samson and Delilah; Ten Commandments; John Paul Jones.
TV inc: Naked City; Avengers; The Saint; The Baron; The Protectors; Danger Man; The World of Lowell Thomas.

LASSER, Louise: Act. b. NYC, Apr 11, 1939. Films inc: Everything You Always Wanted to Know About Sex and Were Afraid to Ask; Slither; In God We Trust.
TV inc: Mary Hartman, Mary Hartman.

LASTFOGEL, Abe: Agt. b. May 20, 1898. Ret p of William Morris Agency.

LASZLO, Andrew: Cin. b. Hungary, 1926. Films inc: You're a Big Boy Now; The Night They Raided Minsky's; Popi; Teacher, Teacher; The Out of Towners; Lovers and Other Strangers; The Owl and the Pussycat; Class of 44; The Warriors.
TV inc: The Man Without a Country; Shogun.

LASZLO, Ernest: Cin. b. Yugoslavia, Apr 23, 1905. Films inc: The Hitler Gang; Two Years Before the Mast; The Steel Trap; Stalag 17; Vera Cruz; Inherit the Wind; Judgment at Nuremberg; It's a Mad, Mad, Mad, Mad World; Ship of Fools (Oscar-1965); Fantastic Voyage; Star!; Airport; Logan's Run; The Domino Principle.

LATHAM, Louise: Act. Films inc: Marnie; Firecreek; Adam at 6 A.M.; 92 in the Shade.
TV inc: Amateur Night at the Dixie Bar and Grill; Backstairs at the White House; Scruples; The Contender; The Ghost of Buxley Hall.

LATHROP, Philip: Cin. b. 1916. Films inc: The Monster of Piedras Blancas; Experiment in Terror; Lonely are the Brave; Days of Wine and Roses; The Pink Panther; The Americanization of Emily; The Cincinnati Kid; What Did You Do in the War, Daddy?; The Russians Are Coming; The Happening; Point Blank; Finian's Rainbow; The Gypsy Moths; The Illustrated Man; They Shoot Horses Don't They?; Von Richthofen and Brown; Airport '77; Earthquake; A Different Story; The Driver; The Concorde-Airport '79; Little Miss Marker; Foolin' Around; Loving Couples; A Change of Seasons.

LAUCK, Chester H (Lum): Act-Wri. b. 1900. With Norris Goff created Lum & Abner characters for radio series that spanned quarter of a century, inc six films.
(Died Feb 21, 1980).

LAUGHLIN, Tom: Dir-Prod-Act. b. Minneapolis, MN, 1938. P Billy Jack Enterprises.
Films inc: The Young Sinner; Born Losers; Billy Jack; The Trial of Billy Jack; The Master Gunfighter; Billy Jack Goes to Washington.

LAUREN, Tammy: Act. b. San Diego, CA, Nov 16, 1969. TV inc: Who's Watching the Kids; Angie; Out of the Blue.

LAURENCE, Douglas: Prod. b. Totowa, NJ, Dec 16, 1922. Films inc: Quick Before It Melts; Mister Buddwing; Dr. You've Got to be Kidding; Speedway; Stay Away Joe; Live a Little, Love a Little.
TV inc: Strange Wills; Some of the Pioneers; All Star Hit Parade; John Gunther's High Road.
Industrial, Trade Shows inc: LA Auto Show; LA Home Show; California State Fair; Wisconsin State Fair; Texas State Fair; Miami Auto Show.

LAURENTS, Arthur: Wri-Dir. b. NYC, Jul 14, 1918. e. Cornell U. Plays inc: Home of the Brave; The Bird Cage; The Time of the Cuckoo; A Clearing in the Woods; West Side Story; Gypsy; Invitation to March (& dir); Anyone Can Whistle (& dir); Do I Hear a Waltz; Hallelujah, Baby (Tony-1968); dir musical I Can Get It for You Wholesale; The Enclave (& dir); The Madwoman of Central Park West (& dir).
Films inc: The Snake Pit; Rope; Anna Lucasta; Caught; Anastasia; Bonjour Tristesse; The Way We Were; The Turning Point.

LAURIE, John: Act. b. Scotland, Mar 25, 1897. Thea inc: What Every Woman Knows; most major Shakespearean roles; Love's Labour's Lost; The Improper Duchess; Crime on the Hill; The Duchess of Malfi; Hedda Gabler; MacAdam and Eve; The Cherry Orchard; Dad's Army.
Films inc: Juno and the Paycock; The 39 Steps; Tudor Rose; As You Like It; Farewell Again; Edge of the World; Henry V; Caesar and Cleopatra; Hamlet; Laughter in Paradise; The Fake; Hobson's Choice; The Black Knight; Campbell's Kingdom; Kidnapped; Siege of the Saxons; Mr. Ten Percent.
TV inc: Dad's Army.
(Died June 23, 1980).

LAURIE, Piper (Rosetta Jacobs): Act. b. Detroit, Jan 22, 1932. Screen debut 1950, Louisa.
Films inc: The Milkman; The Prince Who Was a Thief; Mississippi Gambler; Smoke Signal; Kelly and Me; Until They Sail; The Hustler; Carrie; Tim.
TV inc: Quality Town; The Road that Led Afar; The Days of Wine and Roses; The Lee Wiley Story; The Woman Rebel; In The Matter Of Kathleen Ann Quinlan; Rainbow; Skag.
Bway inc: The Glass Menagerie.

LAUTER, Ed: Act. b. Long Beach, NY, Oct 30, 1940. Films inc: The Last American Hero; Executive Action; Lolly Madonna; The Longest Yard; The French Connection II; Breakheart Pass; Family Plot; King Kong; Magic.
TV inc: Last Hours Before Morning; Love's Savage Fury; The Clone Master; The Greatest Heroes of the Bible; The Jericho Mile; Undercover With The KKK; The Boy Who Drank Too Much; Guyana Tragedy-The Story of Jim Jones; Alcatraz--The Whole Shocking Story.

LAVEN, Arnold: Dir. b. Chicago, Feb 23, 1922. Films inc: Without Warning; Vice Squad; Down Three Dark Streets; The Rack; Slaughter on 10th Avenue; Anna Lucasta; The Glory Guys; Rough Night In Jericho; Sam Whiskey.
TV inc: The Rifleman; The Detective; The Plainsman; Friends; Time Express.

LAVERY, Emmet: Wri. b. Poughkeepsie, NY, Nov 2, 1902. e. Fordham U, LLB. Research dir of Hallie Flanagan's History of Federal Theatre. Plays inc: The First Legion; Monsignor's Hour; Second Spring; The Magnificent Yankee; Tarquin; Fenelon; Hail to the Chief; Dawn's Early Light; Ladies of Soissons.
Films inc: Hitler's Children; Behind the Rising Sun; The First Legion; Guilty of Treason; The Magnificent Yankee; Bright Road; The Court Martial of Billy Mitchell.
TV inc: The Magnificent Yankee; Gideon's Trumpet.

LAVERY, Emmet Jr: Prod. b. Poughkeepsie, NY, Aug 10, 1927. e. UCLA, AB, LLB. In law practice; 1965, dir bus aff Fox; 1967 vp buss aff Par-TV; 1967 exec vp Par-TV; became prod 1974.
TV inc: Serpico; Rex Stout's Nero Wolfe; Ghost of Flight 401.

LAVIN, Linda: Act. b. Portland, ME, Oct 15, 1937. e. William and Mary Coll. Bway inc: A Family Affair; Cop Out; On a Clear Day; Last of the Red Hot Lovers; Superman; Something Different.
TV inc: Phyllis; Rhoda; Barney Miller; Like Mother, Like Me; Sad Bird; Alice; The John Davidson Christmas Show; The $5.20 An Hour Dream; Linda in Wonderland.

LAW, John Philip: Act. b. LA, 1937. e. U of HI. Films inc: The Russians Are Coming, The Russians Are Coming; Hurry Sundown; Barbarella; Skidoo; The Sergeant; Danger: Diabolik; The Hawaiians; Von Richthofen and Brown; The Love Machine; The Last Movie; The Golden Voyage of Sinbad; The Cassandra Crossing; The Pioneers.

LAWFORD, Peter: Act. b. London, Sep 7, 1923. On screen at 7 in Britain. U.S. screen debut 1938, Lord Jeff.
Films inc: Mrs. Miniver; Good News; Mrs. Parkinton; Little Women; Easter Parade; A Yank at Eton; White Cliffs of Dover; Canterville Ghost; Never So Few; Royal Wedding; The Picture of Dorian Gray; Advise and Consent; Harlow; Exodus; The Longest Day; Sergeants Three; Salt and Pepper; They Only Kill Their Masters; Seven From Heaven; That's Entertainment; Rosebud.
TV inc: Phoebe; The Thin Man; A Step Out of Line; The Doris Day Show; How I Spent My Summer Vacation; Island Of Beautiful Women.

LAWRENCE, Barbara: Act. b. Carnegie, OK, Feb 24, 1930. e. UCLA. Films inc: Billy Rose's Diamond Horse Shoe; Margie; Captain from Castile; Give My Regards to Broadway; Street With No Name; Unfaithfully Yours; Letter to Three Wives; Mother is a Freshman; Thieves' Highway; Two Tickets to Broadway; Jessie James Versus the Daltons; Oklahoma; Joe Dakota.

LAWRENCE, Carol: Act. b. Melrose Park, IL, 1934. Bway inc: Me and Juliet; Guys and Dolls; Finian's Rainbow; Plain and Fancy; South Pacific; West Side Story; Funny Girl.
TV inc: Indiscriminate Woman; Rashomon; The Dybbuk; Run For Your Life; Kraft Theatre; Medical Center; Greatest Heroes of the Bible; Mr. and Mrs. Dracula.

LAWRENCE, Elliot (nee Broza): Comp-Cond. b. Philadelphia, PA, Feb 14, 1925. Had own orch. Bway inc: (mus dir) How To Succeed in Business Without Really Trying *(Tony-*1962); Golden Boy. TV inc: The Berenstain Bear's Christmas Tree.
Songs inc: Heart to Heart; Sugartown Road; Once Upon a Moon.

LAWRENCE, Jerome: Wri. b. Cleveland, OH, Jul 14, 1915. e. OH State U. Plays inc: (with Robert E Lee) Look, Ma. I'm Dancin'!; Inherit the Wind; Auntie Mame; Shangri La (based on Lost Horizon); Only in America; A Call on Kuprin; Turn on the Night; Sparks Fly Upward; The Incomparable Max; The Night Thoreau Spent in Jail; Jabberwock; First Monday In October.

LAWRENCE, Marc (Max Goldsmith): Act-Dir-Prod. b. NYC, Feb 17, 1914. Films inc: White Woman; Shepherd of the Hills; Ox Bow Incident; Key Largo; Cloak and Dagger; Asphalt Jungle; Nightmare in the Sun (prod only); The Marathon Man; Man with the Golden Gun; Foul Play; Goin' Coconuts; Hot Stuff.

LAWRENCE, Steve; (Sidney Liebowitz) Act. b. NYC, Jul 8, 1935. In niteries, TV.
Films inc: Stand Up and Be Counted; The Blues Brothers.
TV inc: Steve and Eydie Celebrate Irving Berlin *(Emmys-*exec prod & star-1979).
*(Grammy-*vocal group-1960).

LAWRENCE, Vicki: Act. b. LA, Mar 26. Recording artist. Appeared with Young Americans singing group for three years. TV inc: The Carol Burnett Show *(Emmy-*supp-1976).

LAYE, Dilys: Act. b. London, Mar 11, 1934. Thea inc: (London) And So To Bed; High Spirits; Intimacy at 8:30; For Amusement Only; The Boy Friend; The Purging and The Singer. (Bway): Tunnel of Love; Make Me An Offer; Say Who You Are; Children's Day The Bewitched; The Purging and the Singer.
Films inc: Doctor at Large; The Carry On series.

LAYE, Evelyn, CBE: Act-Singer. b. London, Jul 10, 1900. Thea inc: (London) The Beauty Spot; Going Up; The Kiss Call; The Shop Girl; Nighty Night; The Merry Widow; Madame Pompadour; The Dollar Princess; Cleopatra; Mayfair; Princess Charming; Lilac Time; The New Moon; Bitter Sweet; Paganini; The Sleeping Beauty; Lights Up; Sunny River; School for Scandal; Two Dozen Red Roses; The Amorous Prawn; Never Too Late; The Circle; Let's All Go Down to the Strand; Charlie Girl; No Sex Please-We're British; Ladies in Retirement. (Bway) The New Moon; Sweet Aloes; Between the Devil. Films inc: Luck of the Navy; One Heavenly Night; Waltz Time; Princess Charming; Evensong; The Night is Young; Make Mine a Million; Theatre of Death; Say Hello to Yesterday.

LAYTON, Joe: Chor. b. NYC, May 3, 1931. Bway inc: (dancer) Oklahoma!; High Button Shoes; Gentlemen Prefer Blondes; Wonderful Town. (Chor) Once Upon a Mattress; The Sound of Music; Sail Away; No Strings *(Tony-*1962); The Girl Who Came to Supper (& dir); Peter Pan (& dir); Drat the Cat (& dir); Sherry!; George M! *(Tony-*1969); Carol Channing and Her Ten Stout-Hearted Men (London); Two by Two; The Grand Tour (ballet); Gone With the Wind (& dir); Clams on the Half Shell Revue (& dir); Barnum.
TV inc: The Gershwin Years; Once Upon a Mattress; My Name is Barbra *(Emmy-*1965); Color Me Barbra (& dir).
Films inc: Thoroughly Modern Millie.

LAZARUS, John T: Exec. b. NYC, Dec 27, 1940. e. U of VT, BA. NBC-TV Sales; Foote Cone & Belding; ABC Sports, acct exec; dir radio/TV, Major League Baseball; vp Sports sales, ABC-TV.

LAZARUS, Paul N: Exec (ret). b. NYC, Mar 31, 1913. e. Cornell U, BA. Joined Warner Bros, 1933, ad-pub dept; became ad mgr; 1942, ad-pub dir, UA; then exec asst to pres Gradwell Sears; 1950-62, vp Columbia Pictures; 1962-64, exec vp Samuel Bronson Prods, Madrid; 1964, vp Subscription TV, LA; 1964-65, exec vp Landau Releasing Org; 1965-75, exec vp and dir, National Screen Service Corp, NY.

LAZARUS, Paul N III: Prod. b. NYC, May 25, 1938. e. Williams Coll, BA, Yale Law School, LLB. Exec vp Palomar Pictures, 1967-69; joined ABC Pictures, 1969-71; then P, CRM Prods., 1970-74; Film VP Marble Arch 1979-1980; Resd to become ind prod with ties to Marble Arch.
Films inc: Extreme Close-up; Westworld; Futureworld; Capricorn One; Hanover Street.

LAZARUS, Thomas: Wri. b. NYC, Nov 5, 1942. TV inc: The President's Mistress; Uncle Bill and the Queen of Hollywood; Revenge or Justice; Columbo.
Film inc: Just You and Me Kid.

LAZENBY, George: Act. b. Goulburn, Australia, Sep 5, 1939. Films inc: On Her Majesty's Secret Service; Universal Soldier; Stoner; The Man From Hong Kong; Operation Regina; Saint Jack.
TV inc: Jack of Hearts.

LEACHMAN, Cloris: Act. b. Des Moines, IA, Apr 30, 1930. Films inc: Kiss Me Deadly; The Rack; The Chapman Report; Butch Cassidy and the Sundance Kid; The Last Picture Show *(Oscar-*supp-1971); Dillinger; Charley and the Angel; Daisy Miller; Crazy Mama; The North Avenue Irregulars; High Anxiety; The Mouse and His Child (voice); The North Avenue Irregulars; The Muppet Movie; Scavenger Hunt; Foolin' Around; Herbie Goes Bananas.
TV inc: The Migrants; A Brand New Life *(Emmy-*1973); Phyllis; Mary Tyler Moore Show *(Emmy-*supp-1974 & 1975); Cher *(Emmy-*supp-1975); A Girl Named Sooner; Death Sentence; Long Journey Back; Backstairs At The White House; Willa; Mrs R's Daughter; SOS Titanic; The Oldest Living Graduate.
Bway inc: Come Back Little Sheba; As You Like It; South Pacific.

LEACOCK, Philip: Dir-Prod. b. London, Oct 8, 1917. Films inc: The Brave Don't Cry; Appointment in London; The Kidnappers; Escapade; The Spanish Gardener; High Tide at Noon; Innocent Sinners; The Rabbit Trap; Let No Man Write My Epitaph; Hand in Hand; Take a Giant Step; The War Lover; Tamahine; Adam's Woman.
TV inc: The Birdmen; The Great Man's Whiskers; When Michael Calls; Key West; The Daughters of Joshua Cabe; Baffled; Killer Aboard; Wild and Wooly; (series prod): Gunsmoke; Cimarron Strip; Hawaii 5-0; The Curse of King Tut's Tomb; Angel City.

LEADER, Anton M: Dir-Prod. b. Boston, Dec 23, 1913. Films inc: It Happened Every Thursday; Sally and St Anne; Go Man Go!; Children of the Damned; The Cockeyed Cowboys of Calico County.
TV inc: The Virginian; Rawhide; Tarzan; Daniel Boone; Father of the Bride; It Takes a Thief; Ironside; Star Trek; Lost in Space; I Spy; Get Smart; Hawaii Five-O; Movin' On; This Is the Life.

LEAF, Paul: Wri-Dir-Prod. b. NYC, May 2, 1929. e. CCNY, BA. TV inc: Top Secret (dir); Sergeant Matlovich vs. The Air Force (prod-dir); Every Man a King; Sister Aimee (prod); Judge Horton and the Scottsboro Boys (prod).

LEAN, David: Dir. b. Croydon, Eng, Mar 25, 1908. Films inc: Escape Me Never; Pygmalion; The Invaders; In Which We Serve; This Happy Breed; Blithe Spirit; Brief Encounter; Great Expectations; Oliver Twist; The Passionate Friends; Madeleine; The Sound Barrier; Hobson's Choice; Summertime; The Bridge on the River Kwai *(Oscar-*1957); Lawrence of Arabia *(Oscar-*1962); Dr Zhivago; Ryan's Daughter.

LEAR, Norman: Prod-Dir-Wri. b. New Haven, CT, Jul 27, 1922. Began in TV as co-wri of weekly variety show, The Ford Star Revue in 1950; then wrote for Dean Martin & Jerry Lewis, Martha Raya, George Gobel, Carol Channing, Don Rickles.

Films inc: (prod-wri) Come Blow Your Horn; Never Too Late; Divorce-American Style; The Night They Raided Minsky's; Start the Revolution Without Me; Cold Turkey.

TV inc: All in the Family *(Emmys-*(4)-comedy series-1971; 1972; 1973; New Series-1971); Maude; Good Times; Sanford and Son; The Jeffersons; Mary Hartman, Mary Hartman; The Dumplings; One Day at a Time; All's Fair; A Year At The Top; All That Glitters; Fernwood 2Night; America 2Night; The Baxters; Palmerstown, USA.

LEARNED, Michael: Act. b. Washington, DC, Apr 9, 1939. TV inc: Gunsmoke; Hurricane Hunters; Widow; Little Mo; The Waltons *(Emmy-*(3)-1973, 1974 & 1976); Politics of Poison; Nurse; Off The Minnesota Strip; A Christmas Without Snow.

Films inc: Touched By Love.

LEAUD, Jean-Pierre: Act. b. Paris, 1944. Films inc: Les Quatre Cent Coups; Le Testament d'Orphee; L'Amour a Vingt Ans.

LEAVITT, Sam: Cin. b. 1917. Films inc: The Thief; A Star is Born; Carmen Jones; The Man with the Golden Arm; The Defiant Ones *(Oscar-*1958); Anatomy of a Murder; Exodus; Advise and Consent; Two on a Guillotine; Major Dundee; Brainstorm; An American Dream; Guess Who's Coming to Dinner; The Desperados; The Grasshopper; Star Spangled Girl; The Man in the Glass Booth.

LEBER, Steven E: Agt-Prod. b. NYC, Dec 12, 1941. e. Northeastern U. Former head of music dept, William Morris Agency. Partner with David Krebs in agency. Bway inc: Beatlemania.

LEBER, Dr Titus: Dir-Prod-Wri. b. Zellam See, Austria, Mar 2, 1951. e. Lycee Francais de Vienna, U of Vienna. Films inc: On Plato's Banquet; Sisyphus; Ophelia; Melancolie D'Un Fou; Hyperhidrosis; Neue Coelome; Kindertotenlieder; A Stranger I Came.

LE BORG, Reginald (nee Grobel): Dir. b. Vienna, Dec 11, 1902. Films inc: She's for Me; The Mummy's Ghost; Jungle Woman; Destiny; Honeymoon Ahead; Philo Vance's Secret Mission; The Squared Circle; G I Jane; Great Jesse James Raid; Sins of Jezebel; Joe Palooka; Port Said; Fall Guy; Black Sheep; Voodoo Island; War Drums; The Dalton Girls.

TV inc: Wire Service; Navy Log; Maverick; Court of Last Resort; The Flight That Disappeared; Deadly Duo; The Diary of a Madman; The Eyes of Annie Jones; So Evil My Sister.

LEDERER, Francis: Act. b. Prague, Nov 6, 1902. On screen in Europe from 1929. Hollywood debut 1934, Man of Two Worlds. Films inc: The Pursuit of Happiness; The Gay Deception; Confessions of a Nazi Spy; The Man I Married; One Rainy Afternoon; The Lone Wolf in Paris; A Voice in the Wind; Diary of a Chambermaid; Million Dollar Weekend; Captain Carey USA; Stolen Identity; Lisbon; Terror Is A Man; The Bridge of San Luis Rey; The Curse of Dracula; A Breath of Scandal.

LEDERER, Richard: Exec. b. NYC, Sep 22, 1916. e. U of VA, BS. Adv copywriter, Columbia, 1946-50; to Warners, adv copywriter, 1950-53; copy chief, 1953-57; asst Nat'l Adv Mgr, 1957-59; prod, theatrical TV Warner Bros. Studios, 1959-60; adv-pub dir, Warner, 1960; vp Warner, 1963; vp prod, Warner, 1969-70; ind prod, to May, 1971; returned Warners as ad-pub vp; resumed ind prodn. Films inc: The Hollywood Knights.

LEDERER, Suzanne: Act. b. Great Neck, NY, Sep 29. e. Hofstra U. Thea inc: The National Health; Days in the Trees; Ah, Wilderness.

TV inc: The Best of Families; Judge Horton and the Scottsboro Boys; Power; Eischied; Power.

LEDNER, Caryl: Wri. TV inc: The Waltons; Apple's Way; Gibbsville; Winner Take All; The Great American Tragedy; Mary White *(Emmy-*1978); A Gift of Love.

LED ZEPPELIN: Group. Members are John Paul Jones, bass-keyboards; Robert Plant, voc; Jimmy Paige, guitar; John Bonham, drums; disbanded Dec 1980 after Bonham's death.

Films inc: The Song Remains The Same.

Recordings inc: Stairway to Love; Whole Lotta Love; Immigrant Song; Presence; The Song Remains the Same; In Through the Out Door.

LEE, Anna (Joanna Winnifrith): Act. b. Eng, 1914. Films inc: Ebb Tide; The Camels Are Coming; King Solomon's Mines; The Four Just Men; My Life with Caroline; Summer Storm; Fort Apache; Whatever Happened to Baby Jane?; The Sound of Music; Seven Women; In Like Flint.

TV inc: Scruples.

LEE, Bernard: Act. b. London, Jan 10, 1908. e. RADA. Films inc: The Fallen Idol; Quartet; The Third Man; The Ship that Died of Shame; Dunkirk; The Man Upstairs; The Key; The Angry Silence; Dr No; Two Left Feet; From Russia with Love; Goldfinger; Thunderball; The Spy Who Came in from the Cold; You Only Live Twice; Dulcima; Frankenstein and the Monster from Hell; The Man with the Golden Gun; The Spy Who Loved Me; It's Not The Size That Counts; Moonraker.

TV inc: The Interrogator; Human Jungle; King of the River; Man in the Suitcase; General Hospital; The Skin Game; The Foundation; School for Scandal. Thea inc: If I Were You; Blind Man's Buff; The Long Mirror; Peace in Our Time; Seagulls Over Sorrento; The Desperate Hours.

LEE, Brenda: Singer-Act. Began singing professionally at age six. Films inc: Two Little Bears; Smokey and The Bandit II.

LEE, Christopher: Act. b. London, May 27, 1922. On screen since 1947 in more than 50 films inc: Corridor of Mirrors; Hamlet; Moulin Rouge; The Crimson Pirate; Moby Dick; Curse of Frankenstein; Tale of Two Cities; Dracula; The Hound of the Baskervilles; The Man Who Could Cheat Death; The Mummy; Hands of Orlac; Sherlock Holmes and the Deadly Necklace; The Face of Fu Manchu; Rasputin the Mad Monk; Julius Caesar; The Three Musketeers; The Man With The Golden Gun; To The Devil A Daughter; Killer Force; Dracula, Father and Son; Airport 77; Alien Encounter; Return from Witch Mountain; Caravans; Count Dracula and His Vampire Bride; Starship Invasions; Circle of Iron; The Passage; The Wicker Man; The Nutcracker Fantasy; Jaguar Lives; Count Dracula and His Vampire Bride; Arabian Adventure; 1941; Bear Island; Serial.

TV inc: Once Upon A Spy.

LEE, Jack: Dir. b. Eng, 1913. Films inc: Close Quarters; Children on Trial; The Woman in the Hall; Once a Jolly Swagman; The Wooden Horse; Turn the Key Softly; A Town Like Alice; Robbery Under Arms; The Captain's Table; Circle of Deception.

LEE, Joanna: Wri-Prod-Dir. TV inc: Babe; Cage Without a Key; I Want to Keep My Baby; Mary Jane Harper Died Last Night; Tell Me My Name; The Thanksgiving Story *(Emmy-*wri-1974); Mulligan's Stew; Mirror, Mirror; Like Normal People; The Love Tapes; Children of Divorce.

LEE, Michele (nee Dusiak): Act. b. Jun 24, 1942. Films inc: How to Succeed in Business Without Really Trying; The Love Bug; The Comic.

TV inc: Knots Landing; The Tim Conway Show.

Bway inc: Seesaw.

LEE, Peggy (Norma Egstrom): Singer-Act. b. Jamestown, ND, May 26, 1920. In niteries, on radio, with Will Osborne, Benny Goodman Bands. Screen debut, 1950, Mr. Music.

Films inc: The Jazz Singer; Pete Kelly's Blues. Comp (with Sonny Burke) music for Lady and the Tramp. *(Grammy-*pop vocalist-1969).

LEE, Robert E: Wri. b. Elyria, OH, Oct 15, 1918. e. Northwestern U, OH Wesleyan, Drake U. Plays inc: (with Jerome Lawrence) Look Ma, I'm Dancin'!; Inherit the Wind; Auntie Mame; Shangri La (based on Lost Horizon); The Gang's All Here; Only in America; A Call on Kuprin; Turn on the Night; Sparks Fly Upward; The Night Thoreau Spent in Jail; The Incomparable Max; Jabberwock; First Monday in October.
    TV inc: Lincoln.

LEE, Ruta: Act. b. May 30, 1936. Films inc: Twinkle in God's Eye; Funny Face; Marjorie Morningstar; Operation Eichman; Sergeants 3; Bullet for a Badman.
    TV inc: Lucy Moves to NBC; The Ghosts of Buxley Hall.

LEE, William: Singer. b. 1914. Founder of Mellomen singing group; regarded as one of top studio singers in Hollywood; soloist Hollywood Bowl; one of original members Norman Luboff Choir. Films inc: South Pacific; Lady and the Tramp; The Sound of Music (voc for Christopher Plummer). Chor dir Disney on Parade; several Academy Awards Shows.
    (Died Nov 15, 1980).

LEEDS, Andrea: Act. b. 1914. Films inc: Come and Get It; Stage Door; It Could Happen To You; The Goldwyn Follies; Letter of Introduction; Swanee River; Earthbound. Ret 1941.

LEEWOOD, Jack: Prod. b. NYC, May 20, 1913. e. Upsala Coll. Films inc: Holiday Rhythm; Gunfire; Hijacked; Roaring City; Lost Continent; F B I Girl; Train to Tombstone; I Shot Billy the Kid; Motor Patrol; Three Desperate Men; Thundering Jets; Little Savage; Alligator People; 13 Fighting Men; Young Jesse James; We'll Bury You; 20,000 Eyes; Thunder Island; The Plainsman; Longest 100 Miles; Escape to Mindanao.

LEFKOWITZ, Nat: Exec. b. NYC, Jul 24, 1905. e. CCNY; Brooklyn Law School. Co-Chmn, William Morris Agency, Inc.

LE GALLIENNE, Eva: Act. b. London, Jan 11, 1899. Stage debut London as page in Monna Vanna; appeared briefly on London stage before going to U.S.
    Bway inc: Mrs. Boltay's Daughters; Melody of Youth; Saturday to Monday; The Off-Chance; Elsie Janis and Her Gang; Not So Long Ago; Liliom; The Rivals (& dir); Hannele; The Master Builder; John Gabriel Borkman; Founded Civic Repertory Theatre which she operated between 1926 and 1933; Alison's House; Camille; The Rivals; Uncle Harry; The Cherry Orchard (& dir); All's Well That Ends Well; Exit the King; founder (with Cheryl Crawford and Margaret Webster), the American Repertory Theatre 1946. *(Tony*-special-1964).
    Films inc: Prince of Players; The Devil's Disciple; Resurrection.
    TV inc: Alice In Wonderland; The Corn Is Green; The Bridge of San Luis Rey; Mary Stuart; The Royal Family *(Emmy*-supp-1978).

LEGRAND, Michel Jean: Comp-Cond. b. Paris, 1932. e. Paris Conservatory. Film scores inc: Lola; Eva; The Umbrellas of Cherbourg; Un Femme Mariee; Les Demoiselles de Rochefort; Ice Station Zebra; The Thomas Crown Affair, *(Oscar*-song-The Windmills of Your Mind-1968); Summer of '42 *(Oscar*-1971); A Time for Loving; One Is a Lonely Number; Portnoy's Complaint; Cops and Robbers; The Three Musketeers; The Hunter; Atlantic City, USA; Falling In Love Again.
    TV inc: Brian's Song.
    (Grammys-(5)-inst comp-1971, 1972, 1975; arr accomp voc-1972; Jazz Big Band-1975).

LEHMAN, Ernest: Wri-Prod-Dir. b. NYC, 1920. Films inc: The King and I; Somebody Up There Likes Me; Inside Story; Executive Suite; Sabrina; The Sweet Smell of Success; North by Northwest; From The Terrace; West Side Story; The Prize; The Sound of Music; Who's Afraid of Virginia Woolf? (& prod); Hello Dolly (& prod); Portnoy's Complaint (& prod-dir); Family Plot; Black Sunday.

LEHMANN, Beatrix: Act. b. Bourne End, Bucks, Eng, Jul 1, 1903. e. RADA. Thea inc: The Way of the World; The Green Hat; Hoopla; The Race With the Shadow; Late Night Final; Success Story; Up the Garden Path; Suddenly Last Summer; A Cuckoo in the Nest; Peer Gynt; The Island of the Mighty; Richard II.
    Films inc: The Passing of the Third Floor Back; Black Limelight; The Rat; The Key; Psyche 59; The Spy Who Came in from the Cold; Staircase.
    TV inc: Coriolanus; Crime and Punishment.
    (Died July 31, 1979.)

LEHRER, Jim: TV newsman. b. 1935. e. U of MO. Reporter Dallas Morning News, Dallas Times Herald 1959-1966; became city ed 1968; moved to public tv 1969, exec dir pub aff KERA-TV; edtr Newsroom; joined Nat'l Public Affairs Center for TV 1973.
    TV inc: Senate Watergate Hearings *(Emmy*-1974); MacNeil-Lehrer Report; House Impeachment Inquiry; Washington Straight Talk; Washington Connection.

LEHRER, Tom: Act. b. NYC, Apr 9, 1928. e. Harvard U, BA, MA. Comp-perf. Wrote special material for films, TV; recording artist, singer-pianist niteries, concerts. Wrote songs for A Gathering of Eagles (film); The Electric Company (TV).

LEIBMAN, Ron: Act. b. NYC, Oct 11, 1938. Films inc: Where's Poppa?; Hot Rock; Slaughterhouse Five; Super Cops; Won-Ton-Won, The Dog Who Saved Hollywood; Your Three Minutes Are Up; Norma Rae; Up The Academy.
    TV inc: A Question of Guilt; Kaz *(Emmy*-1979); Linda In Wonderland.
    Bway inc: Dear Me, the Sky is Falling; Bicycle Ride to Nevada; The Deputy; We Bombed in New Haven; I Ought To Be In Pictures.

LEIDER, Jerry (Gerald J Leider): Prod. b. Camden, NJ, May 28, 1931. e. Syracuse U, BA. Fulbright Fellow U of Bristol, Eng, 1954. Thea prod NYC & London 1956-1959; prod John Gielgud's Ages of Man; dir spec pgms CB TV 1960-61; dir pgm sls 1961-62; vp tv operations Ashley Famous Agency 1962-69; pres WB TV 1969-74; exec vp foreign prodn WB 1975-76; launched indie GJL prods 1977.
    TV inc: And I Alone Survived; Willa; The Hostage Tower.
    Films inc: The Jazz Singer.

LEIGH, Janet (nee Jeanette Helen Morrison): Act. b. Merced, CA, Jul 6, 1927. e. Coll of the Pacific. Films inc: Romance of Rosy Ridge; If Winter Comes; Hills of Home; Words and Music; Act of Violence; Little Women; That Forsythe Woman; Jet Pilot; It's A Big Country; Two Tickets to Broadway; Strictly Dishonorable; Angels in the Outfield; Night of the Lepus; Harper; The Naked Spur; Houdini; Walking My Baby Back Home; Prince Valiant; The Black Shield of Falworth; Rogue Cop; My Sister Eileen; Pete Kelly's Blues; Touch of Evil; The Vikings; Psycho; The Manchurian Candidate; Bye Bye Birdie; Wives and Lovers; Grand Slam; The Deadly Dream; One is a Lonely Number.
    TV inc: Death's Head; The Monk; Honeymoon With a Stranger; House on Green Apple Road; The Chairman; World Series Murders.

LEIGH, Mitch: Comp. b. Brooklyn, NY, Jan 30, 1928. e. Yale, BA, MA. Studied with Hindemith.
    Bway inc: Too True to Be Good; Never Live Over a Pretzel Factory; Man of La Mancha *(Tony*-score-1966); Home Sweet Homer; Sarava.

LEIGH-HUNT, Barbara: Act. b. Bath, Somerset, Eng, Dec 14, 1935. Films inc: Frenzy; Henry VIII and his Six Wives; The Nelson Affair; A Bequest to the Nation; Oh Heavenly Dog.
    Thea inc: Measure for Measure; Hamlet.

LEINSDORF, Erich: Cond. b. Vienna, Feb 4, 1912. Asst cond Salzburg Festival 1934; to US 1937 cond Metropolitan Opera; 1943 Cleveland Orchestra; 1947 Rochester Philharmonic; 1956 dir NY Center Opera; 1957-1962 Metropolitan Opera; guest cond major orchs inc Philadelphia, Los Angeles; St. Louis; Minneapolis; Concertgebouw, Amsterdam; Israel Philharmonic.
    (Grammys-(8)-class perf-1959, 1960, 1963, 1964, 1966; opera-1963, 1968, 1971).

LELOUCH, Claude: Dir. b. Paris, Oct 30, 1937. Formed Films 13, prod, dir shorts. Films inc: A Man and A Woman (Oscar-foreign film-1966); Live for Life; To Be A Crook; Love, Life, Death; A Man I Like; Smic Smac Smoc; Adventure Is Adventure; La Bonne Annee; Marriage; Another Man, Another Chance; The Good and the Bad; Robert et Robert; And Now My Love; A Nous Deux (& sp).

LE MAIRE, George: Prod. b. LA, Aug 6, 1935. exec MGM-TV, 1958-68; left to form Chamberlain-LeMaire Prods, 1972-76, pgm exec Par-TV; formed George LeMaire Prods, 1977; Aug 1980, Sr vp feature prodn COL.
    TV inc: Hamlet; The Family Rico; The Legend of Lizzie Borden; Some Kind of Miracle.

Le MAT, Paul: Act. b. NJ. Studied with Milton Katselas; Herbert Berghof; ACT. Films inc: American Graffiti; Aloha, Bobby and Rose; Citizen's Band; More American Graffiti; Melvin and Howard.
    TV inc: Firehouse.

LE MESURIER, John: Act. b. Eng, 1912. Films inc: Death in the Hand; Beautiful Stranger; Private's Progress; Happy Is the Bride; I Was Monty's Double; School for Scoundrels; Only Two Can Play; The Pink Panther; Masquerade; Where the Spies Are; The Midas Run; The Magic Christian; The Garnett Saga; Confessions of a Window Cleaner; Stand Up Virgin Soldiers; Who Is Killing The Great Chefs of Europe?; Unidentified Flying Oddballs; The Shillingbury Blowers; The Fiendish Plot of Dr. Fu Manchu.
    TV inc: Dad's Army.
    Thea inc: Dad's Army.

LEMMON, Jack: Act. b. Boston, Feb 8, 1925. e. Harvard U. Started in stock, then radio. Bway inc: Room Service; Face of a Hero; Tribute.
    Films inc: It Should Happen to You; Three For The Show; My Sister Eileen; Mister Roberts (Oscar-supp-1955); Operation Mad Ball; Bell, Book and Candle; Some Like It Hot; The Apartment; The Notorious Landlady; Days of Wine and Roses; Irma La Douce; How To Murder Your Wife; The Great Race; The Fortune Cookie; The Out-of-Towners; The Odd Couple; The April Fools; Kotch (dir only); The War Between Men and Women; Avanti; Save the Tiger (Oscar-1973); The Front Page; The Prisoner of Second Avenue; Alex and the Gypsy; Airport '77; The Gentleman Tramp (& narr); The China Syndrome; Portrait of a 60% Perfect Man (doc); Tribute.
    TV inc: The Entertainer; 'S Wonderful, 'S Marvelous, 'S Gershwin (Emmy-1972); An All-Star Party for Jack Lemmon.

LEMON, Meadowlark: Act. b. Wilmington, NC, Apr 25. Former trick shot basketball player with the Harlem Globetrotters.
    Films inc: Sweepstakes; The Fish That Saved Pittsburgh.
    TV inc: Hello, Larry.

LENNON, John: Singer-Mus-Comp. b. Liverpool, England, Oct 9, 1940. Member of The Beatles (see group listing).
    Individual film credits inc: Let It Be (score); How I Won The War (act).
    (Grammys-(2)-(in addition to group awards); song of the year-1966; Film soundtrack-1970).
    (Died Dec 8, 1980).

LENYA, Lotte: Act. b. Vienna, Oct 18, 1900. German musical stage after World War I. Screen debut in The Threepenny Opera, 1931, following stage production.
    Films inc: The Roman Spring of Mrs. Stone; From Russia With Love; The Appointment; Semi-Tough.
    Thea inc: Threepenny Opera (Tony-1956); Rise and Fall of Mahagonny; The Seven Deadly Sins; The Eternal Road; Brecht on Brecht; Mother Courage and Her Children.

LENZ, Kay: Act. b. LA, Mar 4, 1953. W of David Cassidy. Films inc: American Graffiti; Breezy; White Line Fever; The Great Scout and Cathouse Thursday; The Passage.
    TV inc: Playmates; Weekend Nun; Lisa Bright and Dark; Heart in Hiding (Emmy-1975); The Seeding of Sarah Burns; Escape; The Hustler of Muscle Beach.

LENZ, Rick: Act. b. 1939. Films inc: Cactus Flower; Where Does It Hurt?; The Little Dragons; Melvin and Howard. TV inc: Reunion.

LEO, Malcolm: Prod-Dir-Wri. b. LA, Oct 9, 1944. e. UC at Santa Barbara. Films inc: (doc) Up Here Looking Down; Search for the Vampire Bat; Flight; The Sky's the Limit; Banapple Gas; Majacat, Cat Stevens in Concert; Birds Do It, Bees Do It.
    TV inc: (doc) Life Goes to the Movies; Life Goes to War; Hollywood and the Homefront; Heroes of Rock 'N Roll.

LEONARD, Bill (William Augustus Leonard): Exec. b. NYC, Apr 9, 1916. Started in radio in 1946, with CBS station in NY; shifted to WCBS-TV; moved to the CBS News division in 1959 as prod-correspondent of CBS Reports; in 1965 became an exec responsible for editorial policies, prodn planning and special events coverage; in 1975, named Washington, DC vp and chief liaison between CBS Inc and Capital Hill; named CBS p of News, Mar 30, 1979.

LEONARD, Herbert B: Prod. b. NYC, Oct 8, 1922. e. NYU. Began as ind prod 1945; vp Allied Artists TV 1974-1977; 1980 signed with Playboy to develop films and TV.
    TV inc: Rin Tin Tin; Circus Boy; Naked City; Route 66; Starstruck; Breaking Away.

LEONARD, Hugh (John Keyes Byrne): Playwri. b. Dublin, Eire, Nov 9, 1926. Plays inc: The Big Birthday; A Leap in the Dark; Madigan's Lock; A Walk on the Water; The Passion of Peter Ginty; Stephen D; Dublin One; The Poker Session; The Family Way; When the Saints Go Cycling In; Mick and Mick; The Quick and the Dead; The Au Pair Man; The Barracks; The Patrick Pearse Motel; Da (Tony-1977); Summer; A Suburb of Babylon; A Life.
    TV inc: Me Mammy; Tales from the Lazy Acre; Country Matters; Father Brown.

LEONARD, Sheldon: Act-Dir-Prod. b. NYC, Feb 22, 1907. e. Syracuse U, BA. Films inc: Another Thin Man; Tall, Dark and Handsome; Tortilla Flat; Somewhere in the Night; Her Kind of Man; If You Knew Susie; Sinbad the Sailor; Here Come the Nelsons; Stop You're Killing Me; Money From Home; Guys and Dolls. (Dir): The Real McCoys; Pocketful of Miracles; The Brink's Job.
    TV inc: (dir) Make Room for Daddy; Damon Runyon; Jimmy Durante Show; prod & dir Danny Thomas Show (Emmys-dir-1956 & 1961); exec prod Gomer Pyle, USMC; I Spy; My World and Welcome to It (Emmy-exec prod-1970); Big Eddie (act).

LEONETTI, Tommy: Comp-Act. b. Bergen, NJ, Sep 10, 1929. Vocalist with Charlie Spivak, other bands; featured singer on TV's Hit Parade; comp scores for several episodes of Fantasy Island.
    (Died Sep 15, 1979).

LEONTOVICH, Eugenie: Act. b. Moscow, Mar 21, 1900. e. Imperial School of Dramatic Art. Member of Moscow Art Theatre, left Moscow after Revolution, worked in Europe before arriving U.S., 1922; appeared as showgirl in Topics of 1923; Artists and Models while learning English, in later years operated own theatre, LA; on faculty Goodman School of Drama, Chicago.
    Bway inc: Revue Russe; Candlelight; Grand Hotel; Twentieth Century; Blood Wedding; Antony and Cleopatra; Dark Eyes; Obsession; Anastasia; The Cave Dwellers (& dir); A Call on Kuprin.
    Films inc: Anything Can Happen; Four Sons; The Man In Her Arms.

LERNER, Alan Jay: Wri. b. NYC, Aug 31, 1918. e. Harvard, BS. Bway inc: What's Up; The Day Before Spring; Brigadoon; My Fair Lady; (Tony-1956); Camelot; Coco; On A Clear Day You Can See Forever; Gigi (Tony-1974); 1600 Pennsylvania Ave.
    Films inc: Royal Wedding; An American in Paris (Oscar-story & sp-1951); Gigi (Oscars-sp & best song-1958); Camelot; Paint Your Wagon; On A Clear Day You Can See Forever; The Little Prince; Tribute.
    (Grammy-best score-1965).

LEROY, Mervyn: Prod-Dir. b. San Francisco, Oct 15, 1900. In vaudeville prior to films. Dir debut, 1928, No Place To Go. Films inc: Little Caesar; I Am A Fugitive From A Chain Gang; Five Star Final; Three On A Match; Two Seconds; Golddiggers of 1938; Tugboat Annie; Oil For The Lamps of China; Sweet Adeline; Anthony Adverse; The Wizard of OZ; Waterloo Bridge; Blossoms in the Dust; Johnny Eager; Random Harvest; Madame Curie; Thirty Seconds Over Tokyo; Homecoming; Any Number Can Play; Little Women; Quo Vadis; Mister Roberts; Strange Lady in Town; No Time For Sergeants; The FBI Story; Gypsy; Devil At Four O'Clock; Majority of One; Moment to Moment.
(Oscar-special-1945). Irving Thalberg Award, 1975.

LESH, Phil: Mus. b. Mar 15, 1940. Founder-member of The Grateful Dead. Solo albums inc: Seastones.
(See The Grateful Dead for group credits).

LESLIE, Bethel: Act. Films inc: The Rabbit Trap; Captain Newman, M.D.; A Rage To Live; The Molly Maguires; Old Boyfriends.
TV inc: The Richard Boone Show; White Shadow; The Gift of Love; A Christmas for Boomer.

LESLIE, Joan (nee Brodell): Act. b. Detroit, Jan 26, 1925. Films inc: Camille; Men with Wings; Foreign Correspondent; High Sierra; Sergeant York; The Male Animal; Yankee Doodle Dandy; This is the Army; Thank Your Lucky Stars; Hollywood Canteen; Rhapsody in Blue; Too Young to Know; Cinderella Jones; Royal Flush; Repeat Performance; Born to be Bad; The Woman They Almost Lynched; The Revolt of Mami Stover;
TV inc: The Keegans.

LESSER, Sol: Prod. b. Spokane, WA, Feb 17, 1890. Founded Fox West Coast Theatres (now Mann Theatres) and Principal Theaters which was sold to Pacific Drive-In Theatres.
Prod 117 films inc: Oliver Twist (with Lon Chaney); Our Town; The Red House; Stage Door Canteen; 6 Jackie Coogan features; 10 Tarzan films; Kon-Tiki (Oscar-doc-1951).
Jean Hersholt Humanitarian Award 1960.
(Died Sept 19, 1980).

LESTER, Mark: Act. b. Oxford, Eng, 1958. Films inc: Our Mother's House; Oliver; Run Wild, Run Free; The Boy Who Stole the Elephant; Eye Witness; Black Beauty; Whoever Slew Antie Roo?; Redneck; Crossed Swords; Roller Boogie.
TV inc: Scalawag; Graduation Trip; Seen Dimly Before Dawn; Gold of the Amazon Women (dir).
Thea inc: The Murder Game; The Prince and the Pauper.

LESTER, Richard: Dir-Comp. b. Philadelphia, 1932. Films inc: It's Trad Dad; The Mouse on the Moon; A Hard Day's Night; The Knack; A Funny Thing Happened on the Way to the Forum; How I Won the War; Petulia; The Three Musketeers; Juggernaut; The Four Musketeers; Royal Flash; Robin and Marian; The Ritz; Butch and Sundance-The Early Days; Cuba; Superman II.

LETTERMAN, David: Wri-Act. b. Indianapolis, IN, Apr 12, 1947. e. Ball State U, IN. Started as weatherman, talk show host on Indianapolis tv before going to Hollywood.
TV inc: (wri) Good Times; Paul Lynde Comedy Hour; John Denver Special; Bob Hope Special. (Act) Mary; Good Friends; guesthost Tonight Show; David Letterman Show.

THE LETTERMEN: Recording artists. Trio members: Tony Butala and Gary and Donny Pike.

LEVATHES, Peter G: Exec. b. Pittsburgh, PA, Jul 28, 1911. e. George Washington U, Georgetown U, AB, MA, Law. Exec VP charge of prodn, 20th Century-Fox Films; VP TV Young & Rubicam Adv; Currently dir pgm development, Corp for Public Broadcasting.

LEVEN, Boris: Art Dir. b. Moscow. Films inc: Alexander's Ragtime Band; Second Chorus; The Shanghai Gesture; Tales of Manhattan; Hello, Frisco, Hello; Mr Peabody and the Mermaid; I Wonder Who's Kissing Her Now; Criss Cross; The Prowler; Sudden Fear; Giant; Anatomy of a Murder; West Side Story (Oscar-1961); Two For The Seesaw; The Sound of Music; The Sand Pebbles; Star!; A Dream of Kings; The Andromeda Strain; Jonathan Livingston Seagull; Mandingo; New York, New York; The Last Waltz; Matilda.

LEVENE, Sam: Act. b. Russia, 1905. Bway inc: Three Men on a Horse; Guys and Dolls; Seidman and Sons; Paris Is Out; The Sunshine Boys; Dreyfus In Rehearsal; Horowitz and Mrs. Washington.
Films inc: Three Men on a Horse; Shopworn Angel; Golden Boy; Shadow of the Thin Man; Destination Unknown; Gung Ho; Boomerang; Crossfire; Brute Force; Killer McCoy; Dial 1119; A Dream of Kings; God Told Me To; And Justice For All; Last Embrace.
(Died Dec 26, 1980).

LEVENSON, Sam: Act. b. NYC, Dec 28, 1911. e. Brooklyn Coll, Columbia U. TV inc: The Sam Levinson Show; This Is Show Business; Two for the Money; To Tell the Truth; Password.
(Died Aug 28, 1980).

LEVEY, William A: Prod-Dir. Films inc: To Be A Rose (& wri); A Make Believe Mind (dir); Blackenstein (dir); Wham, Bam, Thank You Spaceman; Slumber Party '57; The Happy Hooker Goes to Washington; Skatetown, USA.

LEVI, Alan J: Dir. TV inc: ABC Wide World of Sports; Gemini Man; The Invisible Man; Oregon Trail; Class of '65; $6 Million Man; The Bionic Woman; The Incredible Hulk; Battlestar Galactica; The Immigrants; Legend of the Golden Gun; A Man Called Sloan; Scruples; The Last Song.

LEVIN, Alan M: Exec. b. NYC, 1943. e. Brooklyn Coll; Brooklyn Law School. In law practice before joining CBS News Bus Affairs Dept 1969 as asst dir; 1970, talent & pgm negotiator for network bus affairs; 1971, asso dir bus affairs; 1974, dir talent & pgm contracts; 1975, dir talent & pgm negotiations; 1976, vp bus affairs CBS NY; 1977, vp bus affairs CBS Entertainment; April 1978, vp & asst to pres; Sept 1978, vp bus affairs; 1980, bus affairs & administration.

LEVIN, Henry: Dir. b. Trenton, NJ, Jun 5, 1909. e. U of PA, BS. Films inc: Cry of the Werewolf; I Love a Mystery; Jolson Sings Again; The Petty Girl; The President's Lady; Gambler from Natchez; Bernadine; The Remarkable Mr Pennypacker; Holidays for Lovers; Journey to the Center of the Earth; Where the Boys Are; The Wonderful World of the Brothers Grimm; Come Fly with Me; Genghis Khan; Kiss the Girls and Make them Die; Murderers' Row; The Desperados; That Man Bolt; On a Deadman's Chest; The Thoroughbreds.
TV inc: Knots Landing.
(Died May 1, 1980).

LEVIN, Herman: Prod. b. Philadelphia, Dec 1, 1907. e. U of PA, St Johns U Law School. Admitted to NY Bar, 1935, practiced until 1946.
Bway inc: Call Me Mister; No Exit; Bonanza Bound; Richard III; Gentlemen Prefer Blondes; Bless You All; My Fair Lady (Tony-1957); The Girl Who Came to Supper; The Great White Hope; Lovely Ladies, Kind Gentlemen.

LEVIN, Ira: Wri. b. NYC, Aug 27, 1929. e. Drake U, BA. Films inc: A Kiss Before Dying; Rosemary's Baby; This Perfect Day; The Stepford Wives; The Boys From Brazil.
Plays inc: No Time for Sergeants; Interlock; Critic's Choice; General Seeger; Drat! The Cat; Dr. Cook's Garden; Veronica's Room; Deathtrap; Break A Leg.

LEVIN, Irving H: Exec. b. Chicago, Sep 8, 1921. e. U of IL. Entered flm industry as partner of Kranz-Levin Pictures and Realart Pictures, 1948; formed Mutual Prodns, 1952; p, Filmakers Releasing Org, 1953; p AB-PT Picture Corp, 1956; p, exec prod Oakhurst TV Prod Inc; p, exec prod Atlas Enterprises; p Atlantic Pictures, 1959; exec vp, member of bd of dir National General Corp, 1961; p National General, 1966; p & COO NGC; formed Levin-Schulman Prodns, 1975; formed Group L Prodns, 1978; acquired ownership of Royal Theatres, Hawaii, 1979.

LEVIN, Michael: Act. b. Minneapolis, MN, Dec 8. e. U of MN. TV inc: Adams Chronicles; Two Faces West; Ryan's Hope.
Thea inc: The Royal Hunt of the Sun.

LEVIN, Peter: Dir. TV inc: James at 15; James at 16; Family; Kaz; Lou Grant; Starsky and Hutch; Beacon Hill; The Best of Families; Married; Rape and Marriage--The Rideout Case.

LEVINE, Joseph E: Exec. b. Boston, MA, Sep 9, 1905. Former theatre owner. Formed Embassy Pictures in late 50's; financed foreign films Eight and a Half; Divorce Italian Style; Boccaccio.
Films inc: (prod) The Carpetbaggers; Darling; Woman Times Seven; Carnal Knowledge; Where Love Has Gone; Harlow; The Graduate; The Producers; The Lion In Winter; A Bridge Too Far; Magic.

LEVINSON, Barry: Prod. b. NYC, 1932. Films inc: The Only Way; First Love; The Night Visitor; The Amazing Mr. Blunden; Catholics; The Internecine Project (& wri); And Justice for All (wri); Inside Moves (wri).

LEVINSON, Richard L: Wri-Prod. b. Philadelphia, PA, Aug 7, 1934. e. U of PA, BS. Partnered with William Link in TV-film prod. Plays inc: Prescription Murder.
TV inc: Mannix (& crea); Ellery Queen (& crea); Tenafly (& crea); That Certain Summer; My Sweet Charlie *(Emmy*-wri-1970); Columbo (& crea) *(Emmy*-wri-1972); The Execution of Private Slovik; The Gun; Stone.

LEVITT, Alan J: Wri. TV inc: The Courtship of Eddie's Father; Three's Company; Maude; All in the Family; Baretta; Miss Winslow and Son (& prod).
(Died Feb 20, 1980).

LEVITT, Gene: Wri-Dir-Prod. b. NYC, May 28, 1920. e. U of WY, BA. Started writing for radio, then TV (over 100 hour shows).
TV inc: (prod) Adventures In Paradise; Combat; The Outsider; Any Second Now; (as dir): Run a Crooked Mile; Alias Smith and Jones (pilot); Cool Million (pilot); Phantom of Back Lot; Maggie and the Lady; Fantasy Island (crea).

LEVY, Edmond A: Dir-Wri. b. Toronto, Canada, Sep 26, 1929. e. Harvard. Has made more than 100 documentary and entertainment shorts inc A Year Toward Tomorrow *(Oscar*-1967); Beyond Silence; Trouble In the Family; After the Applause.
TV inc: The Farmer's Daughter.

LEVY, Jules V: Prod. b. LA, Feb 12, 1923. e. USC. P, Levy-Gardner-Laven Prodns. Films inc: Without Warning; Vice Squad; Down Three Dark Streets; Geronimo; The Glory Guys; Sam Whiskey; Scalphunters; The McKenzie Break; The Honkers; Kansas City Bomber; White Lightning; McQ; Brannigan; Gator. TV inc: The Rifleman; The Detectives; The Plainsman; The Big Valley.

LEVY, Melvin: Wri. b. 1902. Plays inc: Gold Eagle Guy. Films inc: Robin Hood of El Dorado; Hilter's Hangman; First Comes Courage; Sunday Dinner for a Soldier; She's A Soldier Too; Renegades; Bandit of Sherwood Forest; Calamity Jane and Sam Bass; career interrupted by blacklisting, wrote several years under pseudonyms.
TV inc: Wild Bill Hickok; Daniel Boone; Bonanza.
(Died Dec 1, 1980).

LEVY, Norman: Exec. b. NYC, Jan 3, 1935. e. CCNY, BA. Joined U 1957, various sales positions; moved to Nat'l General Pictures 1967-74; moved to Col 1974, vp & gm-sls; exec vp marketing 1975-77; p, domestic distrib 1978; became P 20th-Fox Entertainment Feb. 19, 1980.

LEWIN, Albert E: Wri-Story Edtr. b. Chicago, Jul 29, 1916. e. Art Institute of Chicago. Wrote for radio: Scattergood Baines; Eddie Cantor Comedy Hour; Edgar Bergen.
Films inc: Alice in Wonderland; Call Me Mister; Down Among the Sheltering Palms; Boy, Did I Get a Wrong Number; Eight on the Lamb; I Will, I Will. . .For Now.
TV inc: My Friend Irma; Life with Luigi; The Dennis Day Show; The West Point Story; Alfred Hitchcock Presents; the Ray Milland Show; The Hathaways; Margie; The Farmer's Daughter; McHales Navy; The Donna Reed Show; Bob Hope Special; My Favorite Martian. Plays inc: A Gift Horse; Trashman.

LEWIS, Arthur: Prod-Dir-Wri. b. NYC, Sep 15, 1916. e. USC, Yale U. Started film career as a writer, 1941. Films inc: Oh, You Beautiful Doll (wri); Golden Girl (wri); Conquest of Cochise (wri); Loot (prod); Brass Target (prod).
Thea inc: Three Wishes for Jamie; dir first London prodn Guys and Dolls, 1953; returned to Bway as asso prod of Can Can; The Boy Friend; Silk Stockings; in 1963 returned to London to take over operation of the Shaftsbury Theatre where he prod or presented How to Succeed in Business Without Really Trying; A Thousand Clowns; The Brig; Little Me (also dir); The Solid Gold Cadillac (also dir); Barefoot in the Park; The Owl and the Pussycat; Funny Girl; The Odd Couple; Golden Boy. Bway 1968, Rockefeller and the Red Indian.
TV inc: Brenner; The Asphalt Jungle; The Nurses; The Diary of Anne Frank.

LEWIS, David: Act-Dir. b. Pittsburgh, Oct 19, 1916. Thea inc: Goodbye Again; Take It As It Comes; The Three Sisters; The King of Hearts; Anastasia.
TV inc: The John Forsythe Show; The Farmer's Daughter.
Films inc: That Certain Feeling; The Apartment; Honeymoon Hotel; John Goldfarb, Please Come Home; Generation.

LEWIS, Geoffrey: Act. b. San Diego, CA, Jan 1, 1935. Films inc: The Wind and the Lion; Dillinger; Return of a Man Called Horse; Lucky Lady; The Great Waldo Pepper; The Culpepper Cattle Company; Macon County Line; Every Which Way But Loose; Human Experiments; Bronco Billy; Any Which Way You Can.
TV inc: The Jericho Mile; Samurai; Salem's Lot; Flo; Belle Starr.

LEWIS, Jerry: Act-Dir. b. Newark, NJ, Mar 16, 1925. Formed comedy team with Dean Martin, Atlantic City, 1946. Appeared in niteries, TV. Made screen debut as team in My Friend Irma, 1949.
Films inc: (as team) At War with the Army; That's My Boy; The Stooge; Sailor Beware; Jumping Jacks; The Caddy; Artists and Models; Hollywood or Bust. Team split, 1956.
Lewis solo films inc: Delicate Delinquent; The Sad Sack; The Geisha Boy; Visit to A Small Planet; The Errand Boy; The Patsy; Big Mouth.

LEWIS, Jerry Lee: Mus-Singer. b. Ferriday, LA, Sep 29, 1935. Films inc: Disc Jockey Jamboree; High School Confidential; American Hot Wax.
Recordings inc: Crazy Arms; Whole Lotta Shakin' Goin' On; Great Balls of Fire; Original Golden Hits; Rare Jerry Lee Lewis; Rockin' Up A Storm; The Greatest Live Show on Earth; Best of Jerry Lee Lewis; The Killer Rocks On.

LEWIS, Joseph H: Dir. b. NYC, Apr 6, 1900. Films inc: Two-Fisted Rangers; The Mad Doctor of Market Street; Bombs Over Burma; Minstrel Man; My Name is Julia Ross; So Dark the Night; The Jolson Story (musical numbers only); The Swordsman; The Return of October; The Undercover Man; Gun Crazy; Retreat Hell; The Big Combo; A Lawless Street; Seventh Cavalry; The Halliday Brand; Terror in a Texas Town.

LEWIS, Monica: Act. b. Chicago, May 5, 1925. e. Hunter Coll. W of Jennings Lang. Radio, band singer. Films inc: Inside Straight; Excuse My Dust; The Strip; Everything I Have is Yours; Affair with a Stranger; D.I.; Charlie Varrick; Earthquake; Roller Coaster; Airport '77; Nunzio; Concorde-Airport '79.
TV inc: The Immigrants.

LEWIS, Morton M: Prod-Dir. b. NYC, Oct 25, 1917. Started at B.I.P. Elstree, 1931; with Warner Bros., Hollywood, 1937-42; currently chmn, Meadway Prodns Ltd, Overseas Prodn Services Ltd, E.P.A. International Programmers Ltd.
TV inc: World Cup Mexico, 1970; The World at Their Feet; Suburban Wives; Secret Rights; Commuter Husbands; Heading for Glory; TV series of World Cup 1974 Munich games; Diary of a Space Virgin; Sexplorer; Secrets of a Super Stud; Golfing with Jacklin; Sex Is No Alibi.

LEWIS, Richard: Prod. b. NYC, Jan 2, 1920. e. Yale, BA. Radio producer Take It or Leave It; Crime Doctor, Philip Morris Playhouse.
TV inc: Blind Date; Mr. & Mrs. North; Quick as a Flash; Mike Hammer; Jake's Way (exec prod).
Films inc: The Borgia Stick; A Lovely Way To Die.

LEWIS, Robert Michael: Dir. TV inc: The Alpha Caper (pilot); The Invisible Man (pilot); Married (pilot); The Astronaut; Money to Burn; Message to My Daughter; The Day The Earth Moved; Guilty or Innocent--The Sam Sheppard Murder Case; The Night They Took Miss Beautiful; Ring of Passion; If Things Were Different; Escape; S*H*E*; A Private Battle; Secret of Midland Heights.

LEWIS, Robert Q: TV Pers. b. NYC, 1924. Hosted or was a panelist on numerous game shows, conducted Robert Q. Lewis Show.
Films inc: An Affair to Remember; Good Neighbor Sam; How to Succeed in Business Without Really Trying; CHOMPS.

LEWIS, Roger H: Exec. b. NYC, Mar 14, 1918. e. Lafayette Coll; UCLA; Columbia. Joined WB 1939 as apprentice pub dept; after WW II service, to Fox as spec asst to dir pub-ad-exploit; vp Monroe Greenthal agcy; 1952, adv mgr UA; 1956 natl dir pub-ad-exploit; 1959, vp; resd 1961 to enter prodn, exec vp Garrick Prodns; prodn exec National General; prodn exec, WB; vp Max Youngstein Enterprises.
Films inc: The Pawnbroker; The Swimmer; Shaft; Shaft's Big Score; Shaft in Africa; Night Games.

LEWIS, Shari (nee Hurwitz): Puppeteer-Ventriloquist. b. NYC, Jan 17, 1934. TV inc: Shari Lewis Show (both U.S. and Britain); A Picture of Us; Magic. Recordings inc: Fun in Shariland; The Kids; Shari in Storyland.

LEYTES, Josef: Wri-Dir-Prod. b. Warsaw, Poland, Nov 22, 1901. Dir 23 features, many docs in Poland where he lectured at State Drama School.
Films inc: The Young Fores; The Day of the Great Adventure; Les Hommes Maudits; during WW 2 made several docs for British Government inc From Homes to Tobruk; made The Great Promise (doc) and features Ein Breira and The Faithful City in Israel before coming to US in 1958.
Films in Hollywood inc: Valley of Mystery; The Movie Maker; The Counterfeit Killers. TV inc: Sugarfoot; Adventures in Paradise; June Allyson Show; Target-The Corruptors; Dick Powell Theatre; The Outlaws; Alfred Hitchcock Presents; 12 O'Clock High; Voyage to the Bottom of the Sea; Bonanza; Marcus Welby MD.

L'HERBIER, Marcel: Dir. b. France, 1888. Founded Institute des Hautes Etudes Cinematographiques, Paris film school, 1943.
Films inc: Rose-France; Eldorado; The Late Mathias Pascal; Mystery of the Yellow Room; Money; L'Epervier; Le Bonheur; Nuits de Feu; The Cheat; La Nuit Fantastique; Last Days of Pompeii.
(Died Nov 26, 1979).

LIBERACE (Wladziu Valentino Liberace): Mus. b. Milwaukee, WI, May 29, 1917. e. WI Coll of Music. Guest soloist with the Chicago Symphony age 16. Performed in niteries, TV.
Films inc: South Sea Sinner; Footlight Varieties; Sincerely Yours; When the Boys Meet the Girls; The Loved One.
TV inc: The Liberace Show (Emmy-male personality-1953).

LIBERACE, George J: Mus. b. Menasha, WI, Jul 31, 1911. e. Chicago Conservatory of Music. B of Liberace. Violinist in orchs inc: Anson Weeks; Orrin Tucker; musical dir for brother; founded Geo Liberace Enterprises, 1957; cond of symph orchs inc Kansas City, Dallas, St Louis, Phila., Denver, LA Philh. Films inc: Girl in the Convertible; Sincerely Yours.

LIEBERSON, Sandy: Exec. b. 1936. Started as agent. Became ind film prod; joined CMA as exec in chg European activities; 1979 named P 20th Century Fox Prodns; resgd 1980 to join The Ladd Co. as Int'l vp.
Films inc: Jabberwocky; Swastika; All This and World War II.

LIEBMAN, Max: Prod-Wri. b. Vienna, Aug 5, 1902. Wrote sketches, songs for Bway musicals; dir summer shows; prod-dir Your Show of Shows starting in 1949; prod Bob Hope's TV debut and NBC spectaculars, 1954.

LIGHT, Judith: Act. b. Trenton, NJ, Feb 9, 1949. e. Carnegie-Mellon U, BFA. Bway inc: A Doll's House; Last of the Red Hot Lovers; Our Town; Measure for Measure; Herzl.
TV inc: One Life to Live (Emmy-1980).

LIGHTFOOT, Gordon: Singer-Sngwri. b. Orillia, Ont, Canada, Nov 17, 1938. Songs inc: Early Morning Rain; Canadian Railroad Trilogy; If You Could Read My Mind; Sundown; Carefree Highway; Wreck of the Edmund Fitzgerald; Race Among the Ruins.

LILLIE, Beatrice: Act. b. Toronto, Canada, May 29, 1898. London stage debut age 16, The Daring of Diane. Screen debut, 1926, Exit Smiling.
Films inc: Around The World In 80 Days; Thoroughly Modern Millie; On Approval; Dr. Rhythm.
Bway inc: A Late Evening With Beatrice Lillie; High Spirits; Ziegfeld Follies; Seven Lively Arts. (Tony-special-1953).

THE LIMELITERS: Folk trio. Members are Alex Hassilev, Lou Gottlieb, Glenn Yarbrough. Formed in the 60's, became top recording and concert attraction before breaking up in 1977. Re-grouped in 1980.

LINDEN, Hal (nee Lipshitz): Act. b. NYC, Mar 20, 1931. e. CCNY, BA. Sax player, perf with Sammy Kaye Band. Bway inc: Bells are Ringing; On a Clear Day; Wildcat; Subways Are for Sleeping; On a Clear Day; Pajama Game; The Love Match; The Rothschilds (Tony-1971); Wildcat; Ilya Darling; The Apple Tree; Education of H*Y*M*A*N K*A*P*L*-A*N; The Sign in Sidney Brustein's Window.
Films inc: When You Comin' Back Red Ryder.
TV inc: Barney Miller; Animals, Animals, Animals (Host); Hal Linden Special; Hal Linden's Big Apple; Father Figure.

LINDFORS, Viveca: Act. b. Uppsala, Sweden, Dec 29, 1920. e. Royal Dramatic School. On screen, Sweden 1941, The Crazy Family; If I Should Marry the Minister. Hollywood debut 1948, Night Unto Night.
Films inc: Adventures of Don Juan; Dark City; Flying Missile; Gypsy Fury; No Sad Songs For Me; Journey Into Light; Four in a Jeep; The Raiders; No Time for Flowers; Run for Cover; Captain Dreyfus; Coming Apart; Puzzle of a Downfall Child; The Way We Were; Welcome to L.A.; Girlfriends; A Wedding; Voices; Linus; Natural Enemies.
TV inc: The Diary of Anne Frank; Medical Center; FBI; Interns; Marilyn--The Untold Story; Playing For Time; Mom, The Wolfman and Me.

LINDGREN, Goran: Exec. b. Stockholm, Oct 5, 1927. Pres Sandrew Films & Theater, AB, since 1969.

LINDLEY, Audra: Act. b. LA, Sep 24. Films inc: Taking Off; The Heartbreak Kid; When You Comin' Back, Red Ryder? TV inc: Bridget Loves Bernie; Fay; Doc; Another World; Three's Company; Getting Married; Pearl; The Ropers; Pat Boone and Family Christmas Special; Moviola (The Silent Lovers); Revenge of the Stepford Wives.
Bway inc: The Young and Fair; Spofford; Take Her, She's Mine; A Case of Libel.

LINDSAY, Margaret: Act. b. Dubuque, IA, 1910. Screen debut, 1932, The All-American.
Films inc: Cavalcade; Voltaire; The House on 56th Street; Jezebel; The Spoilers; Ellery Queen, Master Detective (six others in this series); Seven Keys to Baldpate; Cass Timberlane; Please Don't Eat the Daisies.

LINK, Andrea: Prod. b. Hungary, Jul 25, 1932. Films inc: Shivers; Rabid; The House By the Lake; Meatballs; Happy Birthday to Me; My Bloody Valentine.

LINK, William: Wri-Prod. Partnered with Richard L Levinson in TV-film prod. Plays inc: Prescription Murder.
TV inc: Mannix (& crea); Ellery Queen (& crea); Tenafly (& crea); That Certain Summer; My Sweet Charlie (*Emmy*-wri-1970); Columbo (& crea) (*Emmy*-wri-1972); The Execution of Private Slovik; The Gun; Stone.

LINKLETTER, Art: TV Pers. b. Moose Jaw, Sask, Can, Jul 17, 1912. Radio pgm mgr San Diego Exposition, 1935; radio pgm mgr S.F. World's Fair, 1937-39; freelance radio anncr, 1939-42.
TV inc: MC People Are Funny; Inside Beverly Hills; Art Linkletter's Secret World of Kids; Art Linkletter's House Party; The Linkletter Show. (*Grammy*-spoken word-1969).

LINKLETTER, Jack: TV Pers. b. San Francisco, Nov 20, 1937. e. USC, BA. S of Art Linkletter. TV inc: America Alive! (Co-host).

LINSK, Lester: Prod. b. Philadelphia, Jan 19, 1919. e. U of MI, Columbia U. Films inc: The Games; Run Shadow Run; Mr & Mrs Bo Jo Jones.

LINSON, Art: Prod. b. Chicago. Films inc: Rafferty and the Gold Dust Twins; Car Wash; American Hot Wax; Where The Buffalo Roam; Melvin and Howard.

LINVILLE, Larry: Act. b. Ojai, CA, Sep 29, 1939. e. RADA. Bway inc: More Stately Mansions. Films inc: Kotch.
TV inc: M*A*S*H; Grandpa Goes to Washington; A Christmas for Boomer.

LIPPERT, Robert L Jr: Exec. b. Alameda, CA, Feb 28, 1928. e. St Mary's Coll. S of exhib-prod. Operated d.i. theatre San Francisco; filmed on 65 films his father prod; now P Robert L. Lippert Theatres. Fangs of the Wild; The Big Chase; Black Pirates; Bandit Island; The Charge of the Rurales; Massacre.

LIPSTONE, Howard: Exec Prod. b. Chicago, Sep 28, 1928. e. USC, BA. 1950-55, asst to GM KTLA; 1955-64, Film/pgm dir, KABC-TV; 1964-69, exec asst to p, exec prod, Selmur Prodns, Inc; 1969-70, exec vp, Ivan Tors Films & studios; 1970-present, P Alan Landsburg Prodns, Inc.
Films inc: The Outer Space Connection; The Bermuda Triangle Mysteries.
TV inc: Shindig; In Search of Ancient Astronauts; The American Idea; The Small Miracle; The Savage Bees; Ruby and Oswald; The Triangle Factory Fire Scandal.

LIPTON, David A: Exec. b. Chicago, Nov 6, 1906. Started 1921 as office boy for Balaban and Katz Theatres, in Chicago, later pub dept; 1933 pub for Sally Rand; 1938 NY pub dir U; later studio pub dir; 1941 COL as pub-ad-exp dir; retd to Universal after war as exec/coordinator of advertising and promotion; 1949, nat'l pub-ad dir; 1951, VP; 1974 in charge of pub-ad, MCA Discovision; 1979 Consultant.

LISI, Virna: Act. b. Ancona, Italy, Nov 8, 1937. Films inc: How To Murder Your Wife; Casanova 70, Not With My Wife You Don't; Assault On A Queen; The Lady And The General; Arabella; Better A Widow; Ernesto.

LISTER, Moira: Act. b. Cape Town, S Africa, Aug 6, 1923. On stage as a child. Thea inc: Felicity Jasmine; Juliet; Desdemona; Twelfth Night; Anthony and Cleopatra; Don't Listen, Ladies!; French Without Tears; The Gazebo; Any Wednesday; Move Over Mrs Markham; Bird of Paradise; Great Expectations; Murder Among Friends.
Films inc: The Shipbuilders; The Deep Blue Sea; The Yellow Rolls Royce; The Double Man.
TV inc: Major Barbara; Simon and Laura; The Very Merry Widow.

LITTLE, Cleavon: Act. b. Chickasha, OK, Jun 1, 1939. e. AADA. Bway inc: Macbeth; Scuba Duba; Hamlet; Jimmy Shine; Someone's Comin' Hungry; Purlie (*Tony*-1970); All Over Town; The Poison Tree.
Films inc: Vanishing Point; Blazing Saddles; FM; Scavenger Hunt.

LITTLE, Rich: Act. b. Ottawa, Can, 1938. Impersonator in niteries; TV inc: Rich Little's Christmas Carol; Rich Little's Washington Follies; The Christmas Raccoons (narr).

LITTO, George: Prod. b. Philadelphia, PA, Dec 9, 1930. e. Temple U. Started as agent with William Morris; later had own literary agcy. Films inc: Thieves Like Us; Drive-In; Over The Edge; Dressed to Kill.

LIVINGSTON, Alan W: Exec. b. McDonald, PA. e. Wharton School of Finance and Commerce, BS. Wri-prod, VP-A&R Capitol Records, Inc., 1946-55; VP-TV programming NBC, 1955-60; then P and ChmnB, Capitol Records and P, Capitol Industries, Inc., 1960-68; from 1968-76, P and ChmnB, Mediarts, Inc. and Investment Fund M; 1976 to present, P Entertainment Group, Twentieth Century-Fox Film Corp; 1980 P Atlanta Investment Co.
TV inc: One In A Million (wri).

LIVINGSTON, Bob (nee Randell): Act. b. Quincy, IL, Dec 8, 1904. Studied at Pasadena Playhouse, signed by MGM as a contract player. Later under contract to Republic, became western star in studio's Three Mesquiteer series.
Films inc: Mutiny on the Bounty; The Vigilantes Are Coming; Lone Ranger Rides Again; Bold Caballero; later starred in PRC's Lone Ranger Series.
Ret 1955.

LIVINGSTON, Harold: Wri. b. Haverhill, MA, Sep 4, 1924. e. Brandeis U. Films inc: The Hell With Heroes; The Street is My Beat; Star Trek--The Motion Picture.
TV inc: Mission Impossible; Barbary Coast; Mannix; Banacek; Mannix; Star Trek; Destination Mindanao.

LIVINGSTON, Jay: Comp. b. McDonald, PA, Mar 28, 1915. e. U of PA, BA. Film scores inc: My Friend Irma; Red Garters; All Hands on Deck; The Paleface; Fancy Pants; Captain Carey, USA; The Lemon-Drop Kid; Houseboat; Tammy and the Bachelor; The Man Who Knew Too Much; Dear Heart; This Property is Condemned; The Oscar; Harlow; What Did You Do in the War, Daddy?; Wait Until Dark.
Songs inc: To Each His Own; Golden Earrings; Silver Bells; Button and Bows (*Oscar*-1948); Mona Lisa (*Oscar*-1950); Tammy; Dear Heart; Wish Me a Rainbow; Que Sera Sera (*Oscar*-1956); Almost in Your Arms.
TV title songs inc: Bonanza; Mr. Lucky; Mr. Ed.

LIVINGSTON, Jerry: Comp-Arr. b. Denver, CO, Mar 25, 1909. e. U of AZ. Films scores inc: Cinderella; At War with the Army; Sailor Beware; Jumping Jacks. TV scores inc: Shirley Temple Storybook; Jack and the Beanstalk.
Songs inc: Under a Blanket of Blue; What's the Good Word, Mr Bluebird?; Mairzy Doats; Promises; Chi-Baba Chi-Baba; Wake the Town and Tell the People; The Hanging Tree; The Ballad of Cat Ballou.
TV title songs inc: 77 Sunset Strip; Bourbon Street Beat; Hawaiian Eye; The Roaring Twenties; Lawman.

LIZZANI, Carlo: Dir. b. Italy, 1922. Films inc: Bitter Rice (co-sp only); Achtung Banditi; The Great Wall; Hunchback of Rome; The Hills Run Red; The Violent Four; Crazy Joe; The Last Days of Mussolini; Fontamara (& wri).

LLOYD, Christopher: Act. b. Stamford, CT, Oct 22, 1938. Started with Neighborhood Playhouse, NY. Bway inc: Happy End; Red, White and Maddox.
Films inc: The Onion Field; Butch and Sundance--The Early Days; One Flew Over the Cuckoo's Nest; Another Man, Another Chance; The Black Marble; Three Warriors.
TV inc: The Word; Lacy and the Mississippi Queen; Visions; Stunt Seven; Taxi.

LLOYD, Euan: Prod. b. Rugby, Eng, Dec 6, 1923. Films inc: April in Portugal; Invitation to Monte Carlo; The Secret Ways; Genghis Khan; Murderer's Row; Shalako; Catlow; The Man Called Noon; Paper Tiger; The Wild Geese; The Sea Wolves.

LLOYD, Kathleen: Act. Winner of UCLA Hugh O'Brian Best Actress Award 1969. Films inc: Missouri Breaks; The Car; Take Down; Skateboard.
TV inc: Incident on a Dark Street; Sorority Kill; Lacy and the Mississippi Queen; House Hunting; High Midnight; Make Me an Offer; The Jayne Mansfield Story.

LLOYD, Norman: Prod. b. Jersey City, NJ, Nov 8, 1914. e. NYU. Former act.
Films inc: (act) Spellbound; The Southerner; The Green Years; Limelight; The Nude Bomb. (Prod) Arch of Triumph; The Red Pony.
TV inc: The Alfred Hitchcock Show; Beggarman, Thief (act); The Dark Secret of Harvest Home (act). Bway inc: (act) Noah; Liberty Jones; Everywhere I Roam; The Cocktail Party; The Lady's Not for Burning; The Golden Apple.

LOBELL, Michael: Prod. b. NYC, May 7, 1941. e. MI State U. Films inc: Dreamer; Windows.

LO BIANCO, Tony: Act. b. NYC. Films inc: The Honeymoon Killers; The Merciless Man; The Roots of the Mafia; The Seven-Ups; The French Connection; God Told Me To; F.I.S.T.; Bloodbrothers.
Thea inc: The Office; The Royal Hunt of the Sun; The Rose Tattoo; The 90 Day Mistress; The Goodbye People; The Threepenny Opera; The Nature of the Crime.
TV inc: Mr Inside, Mr Outside; Shadow in the Streets; Jesus of Nazareth; Third Annual Circus of the Stars; The Last Tenant; Champions (A Love Story); The Last Cry For Help; Marciano.

LOCKE, Sondra: Act. b. Shelbyville, TN, May 28, 1947. Films inc: The Heart Is a Lonely Hunter; Willard; A Reflection of Fear; The Second Coming of Suzanne; The Outlaw Josey Wales; The Gauntlet; Every Which Way but Loose; Any Which Way You Can.
TV inc: Friendships, Secrets and Lies.

LOCKHART, June: Act. b. NYC, Jun 25, 1925. D of the late Gene and Kathleen Lockhart. Professional debut at eight in Metropolitan Opera production of Peter Ibbetson. Film debut 1938, A Christmas Carol. Films inc: All This and Heaven Too; Sergeant York; Adam Had Four Sons; The White Cliffs of Dover; Meet Me in St Louis; The Yearling; Son of Lassie; Keep Your Powder Dry; Bury Me Dead; Time Limit.
TV inc: Lassie; Lost in Space; Petticoat Junction; Dinky Hocker; The Gift of Love.
Bway inc: For Love or Money (Special Tony 1948).

LOCKWOOD, Gary (John Gary Yusolfsky): Act. b. 1937. Films inc: Tall Story; Splendor in the Grass; Wild in the Country; The Magic Sword; It Happened at The World's Fair; Firecreek; 2001--A Space Odyssey; They Came to Rob Las Vegas; Model Shop; RPM; Stand Up and Be Counted.
TV inc: Follow the Sun; The Incredible Journey of Dr. Meg Laurel; The Top of the Hill.

LOCKWOOD, Margaret (nee Day): Act. b. Karachi, Pakistan, Sep 15, 1916. e. RADA. Thea inc: Subway in the Sky; Suddenly It's Spring; Signpost to Murder; An Ideal Husband; On a Foggy Day; Lady Frederick; Relative Values; Double Edge; Mother Dear.
Films inc: Lorna Doone; Some Day; Honours Easy; Jury's Evidence; The Amateur Gentleman; The Lady Vanishes; The Stars Look Down; Rulers of the Sea; Night Train to Munich; Alibi; The Man in Grey; Dear Octopus; Love Story; The Wicked Lady; Hungry Hill; Jassy; Cardboard Cavalier; Trent's Last Case; Trouble in the Glen; Cast a Dark Shadow; The Slipper and the Rose.

LODEN, Barbara: Act-Dir-Wri. b. Marion, NC, 1932. W of Elia Kazan. Bway inc: Compulsion; Look After Lulu; The Highest Tree; The Long Dream; Night Circus; Winter Journey; After the Fall (*Tony*-1964); The Changeling.
Films inc: Wild River; Splendor in the Grass; Wanda (& dir).
(Died Sep 5, 1980).

LOEWE, Frederick: Comp. b. Vienna, Jun 10, 1901. Usually collab with Alan Jay Lerner.
Films inc: Brigadoon; Paint Your Wagon; My Fair Lady; Gigi (*Oscar*-song-1958); Camelot; The Little Prince.
Bway inc: Petticoat Fever; Salute to Spring; The Day Before Spring; Brigadoon; Paint Your Wagon; My Fair Lady; Camelot; Gigi (*Tony*-1973).
TV inc: Salute to Lerner and Loewe; The Lerner and Loewe Songbook.

LOGAN, Joshua: Dir-Wri-Prod. b. Texarkana, TX, Oct 5, 1908. e. Princeton U, Moscow Art Theatre. Films inc: I Met My Love Again; Picnic; Bus Stop; Sayonara; South Pacific; Tall Story; Fanny; Ensign Pulver; Camelot; Paint Your Wagon.
Bway inc: To See Ourselves; Stars In Your Eyes; Charley's Aunt; Mister Roberts (*Tony*-co-author-1948); South Pacific (3 *Tonys*-wri, prod, & dir-1950; also Pulitzer Prize); The Wisteria Trees; Picnic (*Tony*-dir-1953); Fanny; Bus Stop; The World of Suzie Wong; All American; Tiger, Tiger Burning Bright; Look at the Lilies; Miss Moffat; Rip Van Winkle; Lysistrata (new adaptation); Joshua Logan (act); Trick (prod); Horowitz and Mrs. Washington.

LOGGIA, Robert: Act. b. NYC, Jan 3, 1930. e. U MO. Films inc: Somebody Up There Likes Me; Cop Hater; The Nine Lives of Elfego Baca; Cattle King; The Greatest Story Ever Told; Che; First Love; Revenge of the Pink Panther; The Sea Gypsies; The Ninth Configuration.
TV inc: T.H.E. Cat; No Other Love; Casino.
Plays inc: Toys in the Attic; Three Sisters; Boom Boom Room; Wedding Band.

LOGGINS, Kenny: Singer-Comp. b. Jan 7, 1947. With groups Second Helping, Loggins and Messina, Electric Prunes before going solo.
Songs inc: Danny's Songs; Love Song; House at Pooh Corner; Your Mama Don't Dance; Celebrate Me Home; Whenever I Call You Friend; This Is It; What A Fool Believes, (*Grammy*-song of year-1979).
Albums inc: Nightwatch; Celebrate Me Home.
Films inc: Caddyshack (songs). TV inc: Fridays.

LOLLOBRIGIDA, Gina: Act. b. Auviaco, Italy, Jul 4, 1928. e. Academy Fine Arts, Rome. Films inc: Love of a Clown; Fanfan The Tulip; Pagliacci; Beat the Devil; Crossed Swords; Trapeze; Woman of Rome; Bread, Love and Dreams; Bread, Love and Jealousy; Solomon and Sheba; Go Naked in the World; Come September; Strange Bedfellows; Assassination Bureau; Hotel Paradiso; Buena Sera Mrs. Campbell; Bambole; Plucked.

LOM, Herbert (Herbert Kuchacevich ze Schluderpacheru): Act. b. Prague, 1917. Films inc: Mein Kampf; The Young Mr Pitt; The Dark Tower; The Seventh Veil; Dual Alibi; State Secret; The Ladykillers; War and Peace; I Aim at the Stars; Mysterious Island; El Cid; Phantom of the Opera; Return from the Ashes; Uncle Tom's Cabin (Ger); Gambit; Assignment to Kill; Murders in the Rue Morgue; Asylum; The Return of the Pink Panther; And Then There Were None; The Pink Panther Strikes Again; Revenge of the Pink Panther; Charleston; The Lady Vanishes; The Man With Bogart's Face; Hopscotch.
TV inc: The Human Jungle.

LOMAX, Alan: Act-Author. b. Austin, TX, Jan 15, 1915. e. Harvard, U of TX. Folk music collector. With father, the late John Avery Lomax, helped make the Archive of American Folk Song of the Library of Congress one of the most comprehensive in the world. Author of many books on folk music.

LONDON, Jerry: Dir. b. LA, Jan 21, 1937. TV inc: Mary Tyler Moore Show; Hogans Heroes; Kojack; Police Story; Swan Song; Women In White; Evening in Byzantium; Wheels; Swan Song; Shogun; Father Figure.

LONDON, Julie: Act. b. Santa Rosa, CA, Sep 26, 1926. Began as singer in niteries. Screen debut, 1944, Jungle Woman.
Films inc: A Night in Paradise; The Red House; Tap Roots; Task Force; Drango; Saddle the Wind; A Question of Adultery; The George Raft Story.
TV inc: Emergency.

LONGET, Claudine: Act. b. France, Jan 29, 1942. Films inc: McHale's Navy; The Party; The Scavengers.

LONGSTREET, Stephen: Wri. b. NYC, Apr 18, 1907. e. Rutgers U. Films inc: The Jolson Story; The Greatest Show on Earth; The First Travelling Saleslady; The Helen Morgan Story; Untamed Youth; Duel in the Sun; The Crime. TV inc: Casey Jones; Clipper Ship; Agent of Scotland Yard. Plays inc: High Button Shoes.

LOO, Richard: Act. b. HI, 1903. Films inc: Thank You, Mr Moto; The Good Earth; Bombs Over Burma; China; Jack London; The Keys to the Kingdom; The Story of Dr Wassell; God is My Co-Pilot; Back to Bataan; Tokyo Rose; The Clay Pigeon; I Was an American Spy; Hell and High Water; Soldier of Fortune; Around the World in 80 Days; The Quiet American; Confessions of a Opium Eater; A Girl Named Tamiko; The Sand Pebbles; One More Train to Rob; Chandler; The Man with the Golden Gun.

LOOS, Anita: Wri. b. Sisson, CA, Apr 26, 1893. Plays inc: The Whole Town's Talking; The Fall of Eve; Gentleman Prefer Blondes (musical version); Gigi; Cheri; Gogo Loves You. Films inc: Gentlemen Prefer Blondes; Red Headed Woman; Riff Raff; San Francisco; Saratoga; The Women; Susan and God; I Married An Angel.

LOPEZ, Priscilla: Act. Bway inc: A Chorus Line; A Day in Hollywood; A Night in the Ukraine *(Tony*-supp-1980).

LOPEZ, Trini: Act. b. Dallas, TX, 1937. Bandleader, recording artist. Films inc: Marriage on the Rocks; The Poppy is Also a Flower; The Dirty Dozen.

LOQUASTO, Santo: Dsgn. e. Yale School of Drama Repertory Theatre. Set and costume dsgn for repertory companies. Bway inc: Sticks and Bones; That Championship Season; The Secret Affairs of Mildred Wild; Siamese Connections; The Orphans; As You Like It; King Lear; The Tempest; The Dance of Death; Mert and Phil; Kennedy's Children; Murder Among Friends; American Buffalo; The Three Penny Opera; The Cherry Orchard *(Tony*-costumes-1977).
Films inc: Sammy Stops The World.

LORD, Jack (John Joseph Ryan): Act-Wri. b. NYC, Dec 30, 1930. e. NYU, BS in Fine Arts. Thea inc: Traveling Lady; Cat on a Hot Tin Roof.
Films inc: Court Martial of Billy Mitchell; Tip on a Dead Jockey; God's Little Acre; Walk Like A Dragon; Dr. No; Doomsday Flight; Ride to Hangman's Tree; Counterfeit Killer.
TV inc: Omnibus; Studio One; Playhouse 90; Stoney Burke; Hawaii Five-0; M Station--Hawaii.

LORD, Stephen: Wri-Dir. b. New Orleans, LA, Dec 14, 1933. e. Notre Dame, Tulane, Loyola. TV inc: Loretta Young Show; Johnny Ringo; Zane Grey Theatre; Death Valley Days; Outer Limits; Virginian; Ironside; Banacek; Madigan; McCloud; Hawaii 5-0; Fantasy Island; CHiPS; Widow's Peak; Last of the Mohicans; Heroes of the Bible; Fall of the House of Usher; California Beat; Earthbound.
Films inc: From Hell to Eternity; Bourbon Street Beat; Blood Hunt; The Devil's Hand; Tarzan and the Jungle Boy; The Fur and Feather Cops; Beyond and Back; The Bermuda Triangle.

LOREN, Sophia (nee Scicoloni): Act. b. Rome, Italy, Sep 20, 1934. W of Carlo Ponti. On screen from 1950 (as extra).
Films inc: The Sign of Venus; Attila; The Gold of Naples; The Miller's Wife; The Pride and the Passion; Boy on a Dolphin; Desire Under the Elms; The Key; Houseboat; Black Orchid; That Kind of Woman; Heller in Pink Tights; A Breath of Scandal; Two Women *(Oscar*-1961); The Millionairess; El Cid; Boccaccio '70; The Condemned of Altona; Five Miles to Midnight; Yesterday, Today and Tomorrow; The Fall of the Roman Empire; Lady L; Marriage Italian Style; Judith; Arabesque; Lady L; A Countess from Hong Kong; More Than a Miracle; Sunflower; Cinderella Italian Style; Ghosts Italian Style; Man of La Mancha; Lady Liberty; The Voyage; The Cassandra Crossing; Revenge; A Special Day; Brass Target; Firepower.
TV inc: Brief Encounter; Sophia Loren--Her Own Story.

LOSEY, Joseph: Dir. b. La Crosse, WI, Jan 14, 1909. e. Dartmouth U, BA. Stage mgr in NY, inc opening of Radio City Music Hall.
Films inc: The Boy With Green Hair; The Prowler; The Lawless; The Big Night; The Servant; King and Country; The Damned; Accident; Boom!; The Go-Between; Assassination of Trotsky; A Doll's House; Mr. Klein; Don Giovanni.

LOTITO, Louis A: Exec. b. 1901. Started on Bway as usher, became theatre treasurer, press agent; named mgr Center Theater, Rockefeller Center 1934; mgr Martin Beck Theatre 1938-1969; became head of City Playhouses 1943, controlling several key Bway legit showcases; backer many Bway shows inc Death of a Salesman; Guys and Dolls; Damn Yankees; ret. 1967.
(Died Feb 12, 1980).

LOUDON, Dorothy: Act. b. Boston, MA, Sep 17, 1933. Worked niteries before Bway debut in Nowhere to Go But Up, 1962.
Other Bway inc: Sweet Potato; The Fig Leaves Are Falling; Three Men on a Horse (rev); The Women (rev); Annie *(Tony*-1977); Ballroom; Sweeney Todd.
TV inc: Kraft Music Hall; Dean Martin Show; Dupont Project 20; Dorothy.

LOUIS, Jean: Des. b. Paris, Oct 5, 1907. Head designer for Hattie Carnegie before accepting post as chief designer Columbia Pictures. Later Universal Studios. Then freelance in motion pictures, TV. President Jean-Louis Inc.
Films inc: Born Yesterday; Affair in Trinidad; From Here To Eternity; It Should Happen To You; A Star Is Born; Queen Bee; The Solid Gold Cadillac *(Oscar*-1956); Pal Joey; Bell, Book and Candle; Judgement at Nuremberg; Back Street; Ship of Fools; Gambit; Thoroughly Modern Millie.

LOUISE, Tina: Act. b. NYC, 1934. e. Miami U. Films inc: God's Little Acre; Day of the Outlaw; Armored Command; For Those Who Think Young; Wrecking Crew; The Good Guys and the Bad Guys; How to Commit Marriage; The Stepford Wives.
TV inc: Gilligan's Island; Friendships, Secrets and Lies; The Day the Women Got Even.

LOURIE, Eugene: Dsgn-Dir. b. France, 1908. Prodn dsgn many films in France inc: Las Bas Fonds; La Grande Illusion; La Regle du Jeu. In Hollywood dsgd This Land Is Mine; The Southerner; The River; Battle of the Bulge; Krakatoa--East of Java. (Dir) The Beast from 20,000 Fathoms; Behemoth (& wri); Gorgo (& wri).

LOVE, Bessie (Juanita Horton): Act. b. Midland, TX, 1898. On screen from childhood. Films inc: Intolerance; The Aryan; A Sister of Six; The Song and Dance Man; Has Anybody Here Seen Kelly?; Broadway Melody; Conspiracy; Touch and Go; The Wild Affair; Isadora; Sunday, Bloody Sunday.
TV inc: Mousey; S.O.S. Titanic; Edward and Mrs. Simpsons.
Thea inc: (London) Gone With the Wind.

LOVE, Cecil D: Cin. b. Roseland, LA, Feb 7, 1898. Special Academy Award for design of Acme-Dunn optical printer.

LOVELL, Dyson: Prod. b. Salisbury, Rhodesia, Aug 8, 1939. Films inc: Brother Sun, Sister Moon; Murder on the Orient Express; Galileo; Death on the Nile; Jesus of Nazareth; The Champ.

LOVELL, Patricia: Prod. b. Sydney, Australia. Films inc: Picnic at Hanging Rock; Break of Day; Summerfield.

LOWTISCH, Klaus: Act. b. Berlin, Germany, Feb 8, 1936. On stage in Germany before films and tv. Films inc: Madchen Mit Gewalt; Pioneers in Ingolstadt; The Merchant of Four Seasons; Disaster; The Odessa File; Rosebud; Schatten der Engel; Cross Of Iron; Despair; The Marriage of Maria Braun.

LOY, Myrna (nee Williams): Act. b. Helena, MT, Aug 2, 1905. Appeared on stage in ballet chorus of Grauman's Chinese Theatre.
Films inc: What Price Beauty; The Thin Man; After the Thin Man; Test Pilot; The Rains Came; The Best Years of Our Lives; Mr Blandings Builds His Dream House; Red Pony; Cheaper By The Dozen; The Prizefighter and the Lady; Lonelyhearts; From the Terrace; Midnight Lace; Airport '75; The End; Just Tell Me What You Want.
Thea inc: Marriage-Go-Round; There Must Be A Pony; Barefoot in the Park; Dear Love.

LOY, Nanni: Dir. b. Italy, 1925. Films inc: Parola di Ladra; The Four Days of Naples; Made in Italy; Cafe Express.

LUBOFF, Norman: Comp-Cond. b. Chicago, IL, May 14, 1917. e. Chicago U. Arr and coach for shows in early days of Chicago radio. After WW2 service, to Hollywood to work on Railroad Hour; under contract WB, formed choral group for concerts, recordings.
Songs inc: Yellow Bird; Warm; It's Some Spring.
(Grammy-chorus-1960).

LUCAS, George: Prod-Dir-Wri. b. Modesto, CA, May 14, 1944. e. USC. Made short film, THX and won National Student Film Festival Grand Prize, 1967. Joined WB; asst to Francis Ford Coppola on the Rain People; made 2-hr documentary on filming of that feature. Debut as dir. with THX 1138.
Films inc: American Graffiti (dir, co-sp); Star Wars (dir-sp); More American Graffiti (prod); The Empire Strikes Back (exec prod).

LUCAS, Marcia (nee Griffin): Film edtr. b. Modesto, CA, Oct 4, 1945. e. LA City College, USC. W of George Lucas Films inc: American Graffiti; Alice Doesn't Live Here Anymore; Taxi Driver; Star Wars *(Oscar*-1977); New York, New York.

LUCAS, Nick: Act. b. NJ, 1897. Known as the Singing Troubadour during the '20s and '30s. His singing has been used on the soundtracks of The Day of the Locust; The Great Gatsby; Hearts of the West. On screen from 1929.
Films inc: The Gold Diggers of Broadway; The Show of Shows; numerous musical shorts.

LUCE, Claire: Act. b. Syracuse, NY, Oct 15, 1901. On stage from 1921 in Little Jessie James; Dear Sir; in 1924 appeared for a time as a dancer with Texas Guinan's troupe; made first appearance in London 1928 in Burlesque;
Bway inc: Atlantic City; Society Girl; The Taming of the Shrew; A Doll's House; Rain; Mary Stuart, Queen of Scots; And So, Farewell; The Wedding and the Funeral; The Cave Dwellers. On screen in 1930 in Up the River.
TV inc: Peer Gynt; Becky Sharp.

LUCE, Clare Boothe: Wri. b. NYC, Apr 10, 1903. Plays inc: Abide With Me; The Women; Kiss The Boys Goodbye; Margin for Error; Child of the Morning; Slam the Door Softly.
Films inc: Come to the Stable.

LUCKINBILL, Laurence George: Act. b. Fort Smith, AR, Nov 21, 1934. e. U of AR, Catholic U of America. Bway inc: Oedipus Rex; There Is a Play Tonight; A Man for All Seasons; Arms and the Man; The Boys in the Band; What the Butler Saw; Alpha Beta; The Shadow Box; Poor Murderer; Past Tense.
Films inc: The Boys in the Band; Such Good Friends; The Money; The Promise.
TV inc: As I Lay Dying; The Secret Storm; The Boston Massacre; The Senator; Ike; Delphi Bureau; The Mating Season; Our Brother's Keeper.

LUDDEN, Allen: Prod-TV Pers. b. Mineral Point, WI, Oct 5, 1929. e. U TX Austin; BA, MA. H of Betty White. On radio in Mind Your Manners; prod Monitor.
TV inc: GE College Bowl; Password *(Emmy*-host-1976); Stumpers; The Gossip Columnist (act).

LUDWIG, Jerry: Wri-Prod. b. NYC, Jan 23, 1934. e. CCNY, BA. Films inc: Fade In (sp); Three the Hard Way (sp); Take A Hard Ride (sp).
TV inc: (wri) I Spy; Run For Your Life; The Virginian; Mission Impossible; Hawaii Five-O; Police Story; (wri-prod) Assignment: Munich; Assignment: Vienna; Wheeler & Murdoch; Strange Homecoming; Bunco; In the Glitter Palace; Samurai.

LUFT, Lorna: Act. b. LA, Nov 21, 1952. D of late Judy Garland. Vaude and concert appearances with mother inc: London Palladium. Also played niteries. Bway debut Promises, Promises.

LUISI, James: Act. Films inc: The Tiger Makes Out; Ben; Moment By Moment; Norma Rae.
TV inc: The Asphalt Cowboy.

LUKE, Keye: Act. b. Canton, China, 1904. Began as artist for Fox West Coast Theatres & RKO Studios. Also technical advisor on Chinese Films Screen debut, 1935, Painted Veil.
Films inc: Oil for the Lamps of China; The Good Earth; First Yank in Tokyo; Tokyo Rose; Love Is A Many Splendored Thing; Ten Charlie Chan Films; The Chairman, Won Ton Ton, The Dog That Saved Hollywood; The Amsterdam Kill; Just You and Me Kid.
TV inc: Anna and the King of Siam; Follow the Sun; Kung Fu.

LULU BELLE (Myrtle Wiseman): Act. b. Boone, NC, Dec 24, 1913. Country music singer-guitarist; teamed with husband, Scotty Wiseman. They performed on radio, TV, Grand Ole Opry, National Barn Dance.

LUMET, Sidney: Dir. b. Philadelphia, PA, Jun 15, 1924. On stage age 9, The Eternal Road. Also appeared on Broadway in Dead End; George Washington Slept Here; My Heart's in the Highlands. In 1947 began directing off-Broadway and summer stock prodns. Became staff dir at CBS-TV in 1950. Screen directorial debut, 1957, Twelve Angry Men.
Films inc: A View From The Bridge; Long Day's Journey into Night; Fail-Safe; The Pawnbroker; The Hill; The Anderson Tapes; Dog Day Afternoon; Network; WIZ; Just Tell Me What You Want.

LUPINO, Ida: Act. b. London, Feb 4, 1918. e. RADA. D of Stanley Lupino. Screen debut, 1932, Her First Affair. To Hollywood, 1934, Money for Speed.
Films inc: Peter Ibbetson; Artists and Models; The Light that Failed; The Adventures of Sherlock Holmes; High Sierra; Ladies in Retirement; In Our Time; Escape Me Never; Road House; Outrage; Beware My Lovely; The Hitch-Hiker; The Bigamist; Private Hell 36; The Big Knife; While the City Sleeps; The Devil's Rain; The Food of the Gods.
TV inc: Mr Adams & Eve; The Trial of Mary Surrat; The Bill Cosby Show. Dir many TV segs.

Lu PONE, Patti: Act. b. Northport, NY. e. Juilliard. Thea inc: The School for Scandal; The Three Sisters; The Beggers Opera; The Robber Bridegroom; Measure for Measure; Edward II; The Water Engine; Working; The Time of Your Life; Evita *(Tony*-1980).

LYLES, A C: Prod. b. Jacksonville, FL, May 17, 1912. Started as mailboy Paramount Studios; 1938 to pub dept; 1940 ad-pub head for Pine-Thomas unit; became asso prod, then prod. Films inc: The Mountain; Short Cut to Hell; Raymie; The Young and the Brave; The Law of the Lawless; Stage to Thunder Rock; Young Fury; Black Spur; Hostile Guns; Arizona Bushwackers; Town Tamer; Apache Uprising; Johnny Reno; Waco; Red Tomahawk; Fort Utah; Buckskin; Rogue's Gallery; Night of the Lepus; The Last Day.
TV inc: A Christmas for Boomer; Here's Boomer.

LYNCH, Richard: Act. b. Apr 29, 1936. Bway inc: The Devils; The Lion in Winter. Films inc: Scarecrow; Steel; Formula.
TV inc: Vampire; Buck Rogers in the 25th Century; Alcatraz--The Whole Shocking Story.

LYNDE, Paul: Act. b. Mt Vernon, OH, Jun 13, 1926. e. Northwestern U. In niteries, on Bway in New Faces of 1952; Bye Bye Birdie.
Films inc: The Glass Bottom Boat; Under the Yum-Yum Tree; Send Me No Flowers; Hugo The Hippo; Rabbit Test; The Villain.
TV inc: Bewitched; The Paul Lynde Show; Hollywood Squares.

LYNLEY, Carol: Act. b. NYC, Feb 13, 1942. Films inc: The Light in the Forest; Holiday for Lovers; Blue Denim; The Hound Dog Man; Return to Peyton Place; The Last Sunset; The Stripper; Under the Yum Yum Tree; The Cardinal; Shock Treatment; The Pleasure Seekers; Bunny Lake is Missing; The Shuttered Room; Danger Route; The Maltese Bippy; Norwood; Once You Kiss a Stranger; The Poseidon Adventure; Cotter; The Cat and the Canary; The Shape of Things to Come.

TV inc: Harlow; Weekend of Terror; Crosscurrent; The Night Stalker; Death Stalk; Willow B-Women in Prison.

LYNN, Ann: Act. b. London, 1934. Films inc: Piccadilly Third Stop; The Wind of Change; Strongroom; Flame in the Streets; Black Torment; Four in the Morning; Baby Love; Hitler - The Last Ten Days.

TV inc: The Cheaters; After the Show; All Summer Long; Trump Card; The Zoo Gang.

LYNN, Jeffrey (Ragnar Lind): Act. b. Auburn, MA, 1909. On screen from 1938. Films inc: Four Daughters; Yes, My Darling Daughter; Espionage Agent; The Roaring Twenties; A Child Is Born; Fighting 69th; All This and Heaven Too; Four Mothers; Million Dollar Baby; The Body Disappears; Whiplash; Black Bart; A Letter to Three Wives; Up Front; Captain China; Come Thursday; Tony Rome.

Bway inc: Dinner at Eight (rev).

LYNN, Judy: Act. b. Boise, ID, Apr 12, 1936. C&W recording artist; appeared with Grand Ole Opry.

TV inc: Judy Lynn Show.

LYNN, Loretta (nee Webb): Act. b. Butchers Hollow, KY, Apr 14, 1935. C&W recording artist. Toured US, Europe; joined Grand Ole Opry.

TV inc: A Country Christmas, 1979; George Burns In Nashville?; A Country Christmas, 1980. (Grammy-country vocal-1971).

LYNTON-WILLIAMS, David Bruce: Exec. b. Sydney, Australia, Nov 23, 1925. e. Sydney U. M dir, Greater Union Organisation, Pty, Ltd.

LYON, Ben: Act. b. Atlanta, GA, Feb 5, 1901. Films inc: Open Your Eyes; Potash and Perlmutter; So Big; Bluebeard's Seven Wives; The Prince of Tempters; The Air Legion; Alias French Gertie; Hell's Angels; Hat Check Girl; I Cover the Waterfront; Crimson Romance; Dancing Feet; I Killed the Count; Hi Gang.

(Died March 22, 1979).

LYON, Francis D: Dir. b. Bowbells, ND, Jul 29, 1905. e. UCLA. Started as edtr. Films inc: Shape of Things to Come; Knight Without Armor; Intermezzo; Adam Had Four Sons; The Great Profile; Daytime Wife; Body and Soul (Oscar-1947); He Ran All the Way. (Dir) Crazylegs; The Bob Mathias Story; Cult of the Cobra; The Great Locomotive Chase; The Oklahoman; Gunsight Ridge; Bail out at 43,000; Escort West; Cinerama South Seas Adventure; The Tomboy and the Champ; Destination Inner Space; The Destructors; The Money Jungle; The Girl Who Knew Too Much; Tiger By the Tail.

TV inc: Laramie; Zane Grey Theatre; Perry Mason; Bus Stop; M Squad; Wells Fargo.

LYON, Ron: Prod-Exec. Asso prod at MGM 1970-1973; formed Ronald Lyon Prodns 1973; joined with Jim Aubrey in Aubrey-Lyon Prodns 1976; joined MGM-TV Feb 1980; Sept 1980 became P Rastar Televison. TV inc: The Other Side of Hell; Love's Savage Fury; City In Fear.

LYON, Sue: Act. b. Davenport, IA, Jul 10, 1946. Films inc: Lolita; Seven Women; Night of the Iguana; The Flim Flam Man; Evel Knievel; Crash!; End of the World; Who Stole My Wheels?.

LYONS, Stuart: Prod. b. Manchester, England, Dec 27, 1928. e. Manchester U, BA. Asst dir TV, 1955-56; casting dir Associated British, 1956-60; joined 20th Century-Fox Prodns as casting dir, 1963; apptd dir 20th Century-Fox Prodns Ltd, 1967; M dir 1968; left Fox 1971 on closure European prodn. Joined Hemdale Group as head of prodn, 1972; left Hemdale 1973 to resume ind prodn.

Films inc: Those Magnificent Men in Their Flying Machines; High Wind in Jamaica; The Blue Max; The Slipper and the Rose; Meetings with Remarkable Men.

MABRY, Moss: Cos Dsgn. b. FL, Jul 5. Desgd more than 75 films inc: Giant; The Manchurian Candidate; What A Way To Go; Morituri; The Cactus Flower; Butterflies Are Free; The Way We Were; King Kong; Casey's Shadow; The One and Only; Sunburn.

MacARTHUR, James: Act. b. LA, CA, Dec 8, 1937. e. Harvard. S of Helen Hayes, Charles MacArthur. Films inc: The Young Stranger; The Light in the Forest; Kidnapped; Swiss Family Robinson; The Interns; Spencer's Mountain; Angry Breed.

TV inc: Strike a Blow; Hawaii Five-0; Alcatraz--The Whole Shocking Story.

MacCORKINDALE, Simon: Act. b. England, 1953. Films inc: Death on the Nile; Riddle of the Sands; Quatermass Conclusion.

TV inc: I Claudius; The Life and Times of Shakespeare; Just Williams; Romeo and Juilet; Within These Walls; Jesus of Nazareth.

Thea inc: The Dark Lady of the Sonnets; Pygmalion; French Without Tears.

MacDONALD, Philip: Wri. b. Scotland, 1900. Films inc: Sahara; The Body Snatchers; Action in Arabia; Strangers in the Night; Dangerous Intruder; The Man Who Cheated Himself; Circle of Danger; Mask of the Avenger; Ring of Fear; Tobor the Great.

MacDONNELL, Norman: Dir. b. Pasadena, CA, Nov 8, 1916. Asst dir network radio, CBS; then full network prod and dir. Radio inc: Gunsmoke; Escape; Fort Laramie.

TV inc: The Virginian; Kraft Suspense Theatre; Gunsmoke.

Films inc: The Ballad of Josie.

(Died Nov 28, 1979).

MacGRAW, Ali: Act. b. Pound Ridge, NY, Apr 1, 1939. Began career as a model. Films inc: Goodbye Columbus; Love Story; The Getaway; Convoy; Players; Just Tell Me What You Want.

MACHT, Stephen: Act. b. Philadelphia, May 1, 1942. e. Dartmouth, Tufts, U of IN, PhD. Films inc: Ring of Passion; The Choirboys; Nightwing; The Mountain Men; Galaxina.

TV inc: The Tenth Level; Raid on Entebbe; Amelia Earhart; Big Hawaii; The Immigrants; Enola Gay--The Men, The Mission, The Atomic Bomb.

Thea inc: When You Comin' Back, Red Ryder; A Man For All Seasons.

MACK, Austin: Pianist. b. 1894. Originally a bandleader, became accompanist for comedian Joe E. Lewis, remained with him until Lewis died in 1971.

(Died Oct 15, 1980).

MACKAILL, Dorothy: Act. b. Hull, England, 1903. Began as chorus girl at London Hippodrome; came to U.S., joined Ziegfeld's Midnight Follies; replaced Marilyn Miller in Sally, spotted by Marshall Neilan and brought to Hollywood.

Films inc: The Lotus Eaters; Twenty One; Dancer of Paris; Convoy; Children of the Ritz; Once a Sinner; Lady Be Good; Kept Husbands; No Man of Her Own; Bulldog Drummond at Bay; The Man Who Came Back.

MacKENZIE, Giselle: Singer. b. Winnipeg, Canada, Jan 10, 1927. With CBC 1946-1950; to U.S. 1951.

TV inc: Bob Crosby Show; Mario Lanza; Your Hit Parade; Giselle MacKenzie Show; Kraft Theatre; General Electric Theatre; Studio One.

MACKIE, Bob: Des. Films inc: Lady Sings the Blues; Funny Lady; Goin' Coconuts; The Villain.

MacLAINE, Shirley: Act. b. Richmond, VA, Apr 24, 1934. On Bway in chorus of Me and Juliet; understudied Carol Haney in Pajama Game; took over starring role on fourth night when Haney fractured ankle. Signed by Hal Wallis; made screen debut in The Trouble With Harry, 1955.

Films inc: Artists and Models; Around the World in 80 Days; The Matchmaker; Some Came Running; Can-Can; The Apartment; My Geisha; The Children's Hour; Two for the Seasaw; Irma La Douce; What A Way To Go; John Goldfarb; Please Come Home; Sweet Charity; Two Mules for Sister Sara; Desperate Characters; The Possession of Joel Delaney; The Turning Point; Being There; Loving Couples; A Change of Seasons.

TV inc: Shirley's World; If They Could See Me Now; Gypsy In My Soul (Emmy-1976); Shirley Mac Laine at the Lido; Shirley Mac Laine-Every Little Movement.

World tour with one-woman show. Prod, co-dir of doc on China, The Other Half of the Sky.

MacLEOD, Gavin: Act. b. Feb 28, 1931. Films inc: I Want To Live; Compulsion; Operation Petticoat; McHale's Navy; The Sand Pebbles; Deathwatch; The Party; Kelly's Heroes.

TV inc: Hogan's Heroes; Mary Tyler Moore Show; The Love Boat; Captains and the Kings; Alan King's Third Annual Final Warning; Murder Can Hurt You; Scruples.

MacMAHON, Aline: Act. b. McKeesport, PA, May 3, 1899. Screen debut 1931 Five Star Final.

Films inc: The Mouthpiece; Life Begins; Once In A Lifetime; Gold Diggers of 1933; Heroes For Sale; Babbitt; Kind Lady; Ah, Wilderness; When You're In Love; Back Door to Heaven; The Lady Is Willing; Dragon Seed; Guest In the House; The Search; The Flame and the Arrow; The Eddie Cantor Story; The Man from Laramie; All the Way Home.

Bway inc: The Dover Road; Artists and Models; Beyond the Horizon; Once in a Lifetime; Eve of St. Mark; Galileo; Cyrano De Bergerac; The Crucible; Trelawny of the Wells.

MacMURRAY, Fred: Act. b. Kankakee, IL, Aug 30, 1908. Sang, played with band. Also performed in vaudeville, niteries. On screen since 1935.

Films inc: The Gilded Lily; The Trail of the Lonesome Pine; Maid of Salem; Cafe Society; Dive Bomber; Above Suspicion; Double Indemnity; Captain Eddie; The Egg and I; The Caine Mutiny; The Apartment; The Absent Minded Professor; The Happiest Millionaire; Charley and the Angel; The Shaggy Dog; Kisses For My President; Son of Flubber; The Swarm.

TV inc: My Three Sons.

MacNEE, Patrick: Act. b. London, 1922. Films inc: The Life and Death of Colonel Blimp; Hamlet; Flesh and Blood; Three Cases of Murder; Les Girls; Incense for the Damned; The Sea Wolves.

TV inc: Mr Jericho; The Avengers; The New Avengers; The Billion Dollar Threat; Stunt Seven.

MacNEIL, Robert: TV newsman. b. Canada, 1932. e. Dalhousie U; Carleton U. Worked for CBS before moving to England for Reuters; 1960 joined NBC News as London corr; 1963, Washington bureau; 1964, co-anchor Scherer-MacNeil Report; 1967 joined BBC Panorama news pgm; 1968 joined Public Broadcasting Laboratory.

TV inc: The Big Ear; The Right to Bear Arms; The Whole World is Watching; America 73; Senate Watergate Hearings (Emmy-1974); The MacNeil-Lehrer Report; Goodbye America; Mountbatten; Edward the King; Artur Rubenstein at 90; A Conversation With Miss Lillian.

MacRAE, Gordon: Act. b. E Orange, NJ, Mar 12, 1921. Performed in stock, radio, TV. On screen from 1948.

Films inc: Look for the Silver Lining; The Daughter of Rosie O'Grady; Tea for Two; West Point Story; On Moonlight Bay; By the Light of the Silvery Moon; The Desert Song; Oklahoma!; Carousel; The Best Things in Life Are Free.

MacRAE, Meredith: Act. b. Houston, TX, 1945. D of Gordon MacRae. Film debut age seven as extra, By The Light Of The Silvery Moon.

Films inc: Beach Party; Bikini Beach; Footsteps in the Snow; Norwood; Chinese Caper; Grand Jury.

TV inc: My Three Sons; The Young Marrieds; Petticoat Junction.

MacRAE, Sheila (nee Stephens): Act. b. London, Sep 24. TV inc: Jackie Gleason Show; Sheila MacRae Show; The Secret War of Jackie's Girls.

MACY, Bill (William Macy Garber): Act. b. Revere, MA, May 18, 1922. e. NYU. Films inc: The Late Show; The Jerk; Serial.

TV inc: Maude; Moviola (The Scarlett O'Hara War).

Bway inc: The Threepenny Opera; The Balcony; America Hurrah; The Cannibals; Oh, Calcutta!; And Miss Reardon Drinks a Little; The Roast.

MADISON, Guy (Robert Moseley): Act. b. Bakersfield, CA, Jan 19, 1922. Films inc: Since You Went Away; Till the End of Time; Honeymoon; Texas; Drums in the Deep South; Hilda Crane; Adventures of Tortuga; Duel at Rio Bravo; Shatterhand.

TV inc: The Rebels.

MAGEE, James E: Wri. b. Chicago, IL. e. Loyola U, Chicago. Creator & Pres International Producers Center, Grand Bahama; Pres Media Finance Corp; vp Cinemerica Satellite Network.

TV inc: Jerry Lester Show; GE Theatre; Schiltz Playhouse; Zane Grey Theatre; Four Star Playhouse; Jackie Gleason Show; Bob Newhart Show; Tonight Show.

MAGEE, Patrick: Act. b. Armagh, Northern Ireland. Thea inc: (London) The Iceman Cometh; The Buskers; Cock-a-Doodle Dandy; A Whistle in the Dark; The Birthday Party; Afore Night Come; Marat/Sade; The Meteor; Staircase; Dutch Uncle; Endgame. (Bway) Marat/Sade (Tony-supp-1966); Keep It In the Family.

Films inc: The Birthday Party; Hard Contract; Barry Lyndon; Telefon; The Bronte Sisters; Rough Cut; Sir Henry at Rawlinson's End.

MAGIDSON, Herb: Comp. b. Braddock, PA, Jan 7, 1906. e. U of Pittsburgh. Film inc: The Great Ziegfeld; Life of the Party; Music in Manhattan; Sing Your Way Home.

Songs inc: The Continental (Oscar-1934); Music, Maestro, Please; Gone With the Wind; Enjoy Yourself (It's Later Than You Think); Say A Prayer For The Boys Over There; The Masquerade Is Over; Roses In December; I'll Buy That Dream; A Pink Cocktail For A Blue Lady.

MAGUIRE, Charles H: Exec. b. NYC. e. Fordham U. Started as asst dir, later unit mgr, prodn mgr. VP Athena Enterprises Corp, 1954-1978; exec prodn consltnt & prod, WB, 1967-1970; exec prod Dogwood Prodns 1978-1979; named vp & exec prodn mgr features div Par 1980. Films inc: (asso prod) America, America; The Sand Pebbles; Bye Bye Braverman; The Arrangement; Fuzz; The Friends of Eddie Coyle; The Parallax View; Shampoo; Audrey Rose. (prod) I Love You Alice B Toklas. (Exec prod) Heaven Can Wait.

MAHARIS, George: Act. b. Sep 1, 1928. Films inc: Exodus; Sylvia; Quick Before It Melts; The Satan Bug; Covenant With Death; The Happening; The Desperadoes.

TV inc: Route 66; The Most Deadly Game; Rich Man, Poor Man.

MAHIN, John Lee: Wri. b. Evanston, IL, 1907. Films inc: Scarface; Captains Courages; Naughty Marietta; Treasure Island; Too Hot to Handle; Dr Jekyll and Mr Hyde; Red Dust; Boom Town; Tortilla Flat; Down to the Sea in Ships; Quo Vadis; Johnny Eager; Elephant Walk; Mogambo; Heaven Knows Mr Allison; Bad Seed; The Horse Soldiers (& prod); The Spiral Road; Moment to Moment.

MAHONEY, Jock (Jacques O'Mahoney): Act. b. Chicago, Feb 7, 1919. e. U of IA. Films inc: The Doolins of Oklahoma; A Day of Fury; Away All Boats; I've Lived Before; A Time to Love and a Time to Die; Tarzan the Magnificent; Tarzan Goes to India; Tarzan's Three Challenges; The Walls of Hell; The End.

TV inc: The Range Rider; Yancey Derringer.

MAIBAUM, Richard: Wri-Prod. b. NYC, May 26, 1909. e. NYU, U of IA, BA, MA. Films inc: They Gave Him a Gun; I Wanted Wings; Ten Gentlemen From West Point; O.S.S. (& prod); The Great Gatsby; The Big Clock; Ransom; Cockleshell Heroes; The Day They Robbed the Bank of England; Battle at Bloody Beach; Dr. No; From Russia With Love; Goldfinger; Thunderball; Chitty, Chitty, Bang, Bang; On Her Majesty's Secret Service; Diamonds Are Forever; The Man with the Golden Gun; The Spy Who Loved Me.

Plays inc: The Tree; Birthright; Sweet Mystery of Life; See My Lawyer.

TV inc: Fearful Decision; S*H*E.

MAIN, David: Prod-Dir-Wri. b. Essex, Eng, 1929. Films inc: Sunday in the Country (sp); It Seemed Like a Good Idea at the Time (sp); Find the Lady (sp & prod); Double Negative (prod).

TV inc: (dir) Moment of Truth; Quentin Durgens M.P.; Famous Jury Trials.

MAJORS, Lee: Act. b. Wyandotte, MI, Aug 23, 1940. Films inc: Strait-Jacket; Will Penny; The Liberation of Lord Byron Jones; The Norsemen; Naked Sun; Killer Fish; Agency; Steel (& exec prod).

TV inc: The Big Valley; The Man from Shiloh; Owen Marshall, Counselor-at-Law; The Six-Million Dollar Man; The Bionic Woman; Weekend of Terry; The Gary Francis Powers Story; High Noon Part II--The Return of Will Kane.

MAKAROVA, Natalia: Dancer. b. Leningrad, Russia, Nov 21, 1940. With Leningrad Kirov Ballet; toured to Britain, U.S.; Defected 1970, joined American Ballet Theatre; danced with Nureyev. Roles inc: Giselle; Swan Lake; Les Sylphides; Sleeping Beauty.

MAKEBA, Miriam: Act. b. Johannesburg, S Africa, Mar 4, 1932. Brought to the US by Harry Belafonte, 1959, to appear with his group. Then made recordings, appeared on radio, TV. (*Grammy*-Folk Recording-1965).

MAKO (Mako Iwamatsu): Act. Films inc: The Ugly Dachshund; The Sand Pebbles; The Private Navy of Sgt O'Farrell; The Hawaiians; Tora! Tora! Tora!; The Killer Elite; Prisoners; The Big Brawl.

TV inc: When Hell Was in Session.

Bway inc: Pacific Overtures.

MALDEN, Karl (Mladen Sekulovich): Act. b. Gary, IN, Mar 22, 1914. Screen debut 1940 They Knew What they Wanted.

Films inc: Boomerang; The Gunfighter; A Streetcar Name Desire (*Oscar*-supp-1951); Ruby Gentry; Desperate Hours; The Hanging Tree; On the Waterfront; Bombers B-52; Fear Strikes Out; Time Limit (dir only); One Eyed Jacks; How the West Was Won; Patton; Meteor; Beyond The Poseiden Adventure.

Bway: Golden Boy; Key Largo; All My Sons; Meteor; A Streetcar Named Desire; Desperate Hours.

TV inc: The Streets of San Francisco; Skag.

MALICK, Terrence: Dir-Wri. b. IL, Nov 30, 1944. e. Harvard U, Oxford U. Films inc: Badlands; Days of Heaven.

MALLE, Louis: Dir. b. Thumeries, France, Oct 30, 1932. Started as cin. Co-dir Oscar-winning doc, The Silent World. Doc inc: Humain, Trop Humain; Vive Le Tour; Phantom India; Calcutta; Place de la Republique.

Films inc: Elevator to the Gallows; The Lovers; Zazie dans le Metro; Vie Privee; Viva Maria; The Fire Within; The Thief; Le Souffle au Coeur; Lacombe, Lucien; Black Moon; Pretty Baby (& prod-sp); Atlantic City, USA.

MALLORY, Victoria: Act. b. Fort Lee, VA, Sep 20, 1948. e. AMDA. Bway inc: West Side Story (rev); Carnival (rev); Follies; A Little Night Music.

TV inc: After Hours--Singin', Swingin' and All That Jazz; The Emperor's New Clothes; Aladdin; The Young and the Restless.

MALONE, Dorothy: Act. b. Chicago, IL, Jan 30, 1930. Screen debut 1946, The Big Sleep.

Films inc: Young at Heart; Battle Cry; Written on the Wind (*Oscar*-supp-1956); Man of a Thousand Faces; The Last Voyage; Warlock; Fate Is the Hunter; Winter Kills; Good Luck Miss Wyckoff; The Day Time Ended.

TV inc: Dr. Kildare; The Untouchables; The Greatest Show on Earth; Peyton Place.

MALTBY, Richard E: Comp-Cond-Mus. b. Chicago, Jun 26, 1914. e. Northwestern U. Cond of own orch, 1945; recording artist. Works inc: Requiem for John F Kennedy.

MALTZ, Albert: Wri. b. NYC, Oct 28, 1908. e. Columbia Coll, AB. Films inc: This Gun for Hire; Destination Tokyo; Pride of the Marines; Cloak and Dagger; Naked City; (career interrupted when he served year in jail for refusing to testify before Un-American Activities Committee 1950, subsequently on blacklist for years); Two Mules for Sister Sara.

Special Oscar for writing The House I Live In, (Doc) 1945. Also wrote Oscar-winning Moscow Strikes Back (Doc).

MAMOULIAN, Rouben: Dir. b. Russia, Oct 8, 1897. e. Lycee Montaigne, Paris, Moscow U (law). Stage dir since 1918. Came to US in 1923. Prod dir, Eastman Theatre, Rochester, NY, 1923-26. After that dir operas, operettas, musicals.

Films inc: Applause; City Streets; Dr. Jekyll and Mr. Hyde; Song of Songs; Queen Christine; Gay Desperado; Becky Sharp; Golden Boy; Mark of Zorro; Blood and Sand; Summer Holiday; Silk Stockings; Never Steal Anything Small (co-author).

Bway inc: Porgy; Marco's Millions; Wings Over Europe; Sadie Thompson; Farewell to Arms; Porgy and Bess; Oklahoma!; Carousel; St. Louis Woman; Lost in the Stars; Arms and the Girl.

MANCHESTER, Melissa: Singer. b. Bronx, NY, Feb 15, 1951. e. Performing Arts High School. Singer with Bette Midler before going solo.

Recordings inc: Home to Myself; Bright Eyes; Melissa; Better Days and Happy Endings; Help is on the Way.

Bway inc: Dancin'. TV inc: I'll Be Home for Christmas.

MANCINI, Henry: Comp-Arr-Cond. b. Cleveland, OH, Apr 16, 1924. Film scores inc: Breakfast at Tiffany's (*Oscars*-score and song-Moon River-1962); Days of Wine and Roses (*Oscar*-song-1963); Hatari; The Pink Panther; Charade; Two for the Road; Darling Lili; Sunflower; Alex and the Gypsy; W.C. Fields and Me; The Pink Panther Strikes Again; Silver Streak; House Calls; Revenge of the Pink Panther; Who Is Killing The Great Chefs of Europe; Nightwing; The Prisoner of Zenda; A Change of Seasons.

TV inc: The Shadow Box.

Guest cond with the leading symphony orchestras in the US and around the world.

(*Grammys*-(20)-record of the year-1961, 1963; song of the year-1961, 1963; album of the year-1958; arrangement-1958, 1960, 1961; inst arr-1962, 1964, 1969, 1970; orch-1960, 1961; Jazz group-1960; soundtrack-1961; background arr-1963; inst composition-1964; inst perf-1964; contemporary inst perf-1970).

MANCUSO, Frank: Exec. b. Buffalo, NY, Jul 25, 1933. Started in exhib; film buyer Basil Circuit; 1962 booker Buffalo branch Par; 1964 branch sales rep; 1967 branch mgr; 1970, vp-gen sls mgr Par Canada; 1972, P Par Canada; 1976 Par Western Div mgr, hq in LA; 1977, gen sls mgr, NY, later vp dom dist Par; 1979, mktg & dist vp.

MANDAN, Robert: Act. b. Clever, MO, Feb 2. e. Pomona Coll, NYU. TV inc: Search for Tomorrow; One Day at a Time; Caribe; Soap; You Can't Take it With You.

Bway inc: There's a Girl in My Soup; Applause.

MANDEL, John Alfred (Johnny): Comp-Arr-Cond. b. NYC, Nov 23, 1935. Trumpeter, trombonist with numerous orchs.

Film scores inc: You're Never Too Young; I Want to Live; The Americanization of Emily; The Sandpiper; Harper; The Russians Are Coming, the Russians Are Coming; An American Dream; Deadly Hero; Agatha; The Baltimore Bullet; Caddyshack.

Songs inc: Emily; The Shadow of your Smile (Oscar-1965); A Time for Love. TV inc: Markham; GE Theatre; Too Close For Comfort. (Grammys-(2)-song & soundtrack album-1965).

MANDELKER, Philip: Exec Prod. b. NYC, May 18, 1938. e. Northwestern U. Dir daytime pgmg CBS, 1971; dir primetime dvlpt ABC, 1972; exec prod Warner Bros TV, 1973-79; exec prod, Time-Life Films, Inc, 1979.

TV inc: The New Land; The Dark Side of Innocence; Sidekicks; The Possessed; The Fitzpatricks; Champions--A Love Story; The Dukes of Hazzard; Sex and the Single Parent; Cruisin'; Amber Waves; The Women's Room; Blinded By the Light.

MANDRELL, Barbara: Act. b. Houston, TX, Dec 25, 1948. Recording artist; niteries.

TV inc: Merry Christmas From the Grand Ole Opry House; The Concrete Cowboys; Elvis Remembered-Nashville to Hollywood; Bob Hope's Birthday Party; John Schneider--Back Home; Barbara Mandrell and the Mandrell Sisters.

MANGANO, Silvana: Act. b. Rome, 1930. Films inc: Bitter Rice; Ulysses; The Sea Wall; Gold of Naples; Tempest; Five Branded Women; Barabbas; Theorem; The Decameron; Death in Venice.

MANGIONE, Chuck: Comp-Mus. b. Rochester, NY, Nov 29, 1940. Formed jazz quartet; toured Europe. Recording artist. Film scores inc: The Children of Sanchez. TV theme music for: The Dorothy Hamill Special; ABC Super Stars; ABC Wide World of Sports; NBC Tomorrow Show; World Championship Tennis.

(Grammys-(2)-inst comp-1976; pop inst perf-1978).

MANILOW, Barry: Act-Sngwri. b. Brooklyn, Jun 17, 1946. e. NY College of Music, Juilliard. Started with CBS TV in mailroom, became night flm ed, arranged new musical theme for The Late Show; left CBS to do nitery tour with Jeanie Lucas; mus dir Callback, WCBS-TV; mus dir Ed Sullivan Prodns; mus dir off-Bway prodn The Drunkard; wrote & sang commercials for radio, tv; mus dir for Bette Midler; went solo as recording artist, perf; two-week stand at Uris Theatre, NY (Special Tony-1977); (Grammy-male vocal-1979).

TV inc: Barry Manilow Specials (Emmy-variety show-1977).

Films inc: Tribute (mus).

Songs inc: Sweet Life; I Am Your Child; Sweetwater Jones; Could It Be Magic?

Albums inc: This One's For You; Barry Manilow Live; Even Now; Greatest Hits; One Voice.

MANKIEWICZ, Don: Wri. b. Berlin, Jan 20, 1922. e. Columbia U, BA. S of late Herman J Mankiewicz. Films inc: Trial; House of Numbers; I Want to Live.

TV inc: On Trial; One Step Beyond; Profiles in Courage; Ironside; Sarge; Lanigans Rabbi; Father Brown, Detective.

MANKIEWICZ, Frank: Wri-Exec. b. NYC, May 16, 1924. e. UCLA, AB; Columbia, MS; Berkeley, LLB. S of late Herman Mankiewicz. Syndicated columnist, TV commentator. P National Public Radio 1977.

MANKIEWICZ, Joseph L: Prod-Wri-Dir. b. Wilkes-Barre, PA, Feb 11, 1909. e. Columbia U. B of late Herman J Mankiewicz. Films inc: (wri) Skippy; Million Dollar Legs; Forsaking All Others; (wri-dir) Dragonwyck; Somewhere in the Night; The Late George Apley; The Ghost and Mrs Muir; A Letter for Three Wives (Oscars-dir & sp-1949); House of Strangers (dir only); No Way Out; All About Eve (Oscars-dir & sp-1950); People Will Talk; Julius Caesar; Five Fingers; The Barefoot Contessa; Guys and Dolls; The Quiet American (& prod); Suddenly Last Summer (dir only); Cleopatra; The Honey Pot; There Was a Crooked Man; Sleuth (dir only). (As prod) Fury; The Bride Wore Red; Three Comrades; Huckleberry Finn; Strange Cargo; The Philadelphia Story; Woman of the Year; The Keys to the Kingdom.

MANKIEWICZ, Tom: Wri-Prod-Dir. b. LA, Jun 1, 1942. e. Exeter Acad, Yale. S of Joseph Mankiewicz. Films inc: (sp) The Sweet Ride; Diamonds Are Forever; Live and Let Die; The Man With The Golden Gun; The Eagle Has Landed; Mother, Jugs & Speed (and co-prod); served as creative consultant Superman, the Movie; Superman II.

TV inc: Hart to Hart (dir-wri).

MANKOWITZ, Wolf: Wri. b. London, 1924. Films inc: A Kid for Two Farthings; Expresso Bongo; Waltz of the Toreadors; The Day the Earth Caught Fire; Where the Spies Are; Casino Royale; Dr Faustus; The 25th Hour; Bloomfield; The Hireling.

TV inc: Make Me an Offer; It Should Happen to a Dog; Conflict; The Killing Stones; The Model Marriage; The Battersea Miracle; Dickens of London.

MANN, Abby: Wri. b. Philadelphia, 1927. e. NYU. Films inc: Judgment at Nuremberg (Oscar-1961); Ship of Fools; A Child Is Waiting; The Detective.

TV inc: The Marcus-Nelson Murders (exec prod & wri) (Emmy-wri-1973); Medical Story (exec. prod & wri); King (co-prod, wri, dir); This Man Stands Alone; Skag (exec prod-wri).

MANN, Daniel: Dir. b. NYC, Aug 8, 1912. Films inc: Come Back Little Sheba; About Mrs Leslie; I'll Cry Tomorrow; The Teahouse of the August Moon; Hot Spell; The Last Angry Man; Butterfield 8; Ada; Who's Got the Action?; Who's Been Sleeping in My Bed?; Our Man Flint; For Love of Ivy; Willard; The Revengers; Maurie; Interval; Lost in the Stars.

Bway inc: Come Back Little Sheba; Rose Tattoo; A Streetcar Named Desire; Paint Your Wagon.

Playing For Time.

MANN, Delbert: Dir. b. Lawrence, KS, Jan 30, 1920. e. Vanderbilt U, Yale U. School of Drama. Films inc: Marty (Oscar-1955); Bachelor Party; Desire Under the Elms; Separate Tables; The Dark at the Top of the Stairs; Lover Come Back; That Touch of Mink; A Gathering of Eagles; Quick Before It Melts; Mister Buddwing; The Pink Jungle; Kidnapped; The Birch Interval.

TV inc: TV Playhouse; Producer's Showcase; Omnibus; Playhouse 90; Lights Out; Masterpiece Theatre; Ford Startime; Heidi; David Copperfield; Jane Eyre; The Man Without A Country; A Girl Named Sooner; Torn Between Two Lovers; All Quiet on the Western Front; To Find My Son.

Bway inc: A Quiet Place; Speaking of Murder; Zelda Wuthering Heights.

MANN, Johnny (John R): Comp-Cond-Prod. b. Baltimore, Aug 30, 1928. e. Baltimore City Coll, Peabody Cons. Choral dir NBC; arr and cond for various artists inc: Danny Kaye, George Gobel, Julie London; cond The Johnny Mann Singers (Grammys-(2)-chorus-1961, 1967).

Film title song: Hang Up Your Stockin'.

MANN, Larry D: Act. b. Toronto, Dec 18, 1922. e. Oxford, BA. Films inc: The Singing Nun; The Russians Are Coming, The Russians Are Coming; The Appaloosa; In the Heat of the Night; The Wicked Dreams of Paula Schultz; Oklahoma Crude; Black Eye; The Sting; Pony Express Rider; The Octagon.

TV inc: Columbo; Quincy; Hogan's Heroes; It Takes a Thief; Donovan's Kid.

MANN, Michael: Wri. TV inc: Police Story; Gibbsville; Bronk; Vega$ (& crea); The Jericho Mile (Emmy-1979); Swan Song.

MANN, Stanley: Wri. b. Aug 8, 1928. e. McGill U. Films inc: The Mouse That Roared; The Mark; High Wind in Jamaica; The Collector; Naked Runner; Circle of Iron; Damien - Omen II; Meteor.

MANN, Ted: Exec. b. Wishek, ND, Apr 15, 1916. e. U of MN. Acquired first theatre 1935, St Paul: expanded into other states, 1968, entered film prodn 1973, took over National General Theatres (266 in 27 states).

Films inc: Extreme Close-Up (exec prod); The Illustrated Man (co-prod); Buster and Billie (exec prod); Lifeguard (exec prod); Brubaker (exec prod).

MANN, Theodore (nee Goldman): Prod-Dir. b. Brooklyn, NY, May 13, 1924. e. Columbia U; NYU; Brooklyn Law School. Co-founder Circle in the Square. Bway inc: Summer and Smoke; The Grass Harp; American Gothic; The Iceman Cometh; The Quare Fellow; And Things That Go Bump in the Night; A Moon for the Misbegotten; The Waltz of the Toreadors; Hot L Baltimore; An American Millionaire; Scapino; The Royal Hunt of the Sun; The Zulu and the Zayda; Past Tense.

MANNE, Shelley: Mus-Comp. b. NYC, Jun 11, 1920. Drummer with various bands inc Bobby Byrne; Bob Astor; Joe Marsala; Raymond Scott; Stan Kenton; Jazz at the Philharmonic; Woody Hermann.
Films inc: (act) I Want To Live; Five Pennies; The Gene Krupa Story. (Scores) Proper Time; The Trial of the Catonsville Nine; Trader Horn.
TV inc: (score) Daktari!

MANNERS, Sam (Savino Maneri): Prod. b. Cleveland, OH, Mar 29, 1921. e. UCLA, BA. TV inc: Before and After; Hot Rod; Dummy; Pearl; Sparrow; Guyana Tragedy-The Story of Jim Jones.
Films inc: Dead Man's Chest.

MANNI, Ettore: Act. b. Rome, 1928. Films inc: White Slavery; Women Alone; She Wolf; Girlfriends; Poveri ma belli; Revolt of the Gladiators; Revolt of the Slaves; Cleopatra's Legions; The Conquest of Atlantide; Yursus; Goliath; Fatti de Gente per bene; The Divine Nymph; In the Name of the Pope-King; Defiance.
(Died July 27, 1979).

MANOFF, Dinah: Act. Films inc: Possessed; Grease; Ordinary People.
TV inc: Like Mother, Like Me; The Great Cherub; Night Drive; Raid on Entebbe; Sweepstakes; Soap.
Bway inc: I Ought To Be In Pictures (Tony-supp-1980).

MANSON, Arthur: Exec. b. NYC, Feb 21, 1928. e. CCNY. Prod pub rep, Stanley Kramer Corp, Samuel Goldwyn Prodns, 1950-52; regional ad-pub dir, Stanley Warner Cinerama Corp, 1953-58; worldwide ad-pub dir, 1958-61; adv Mgr, Col, 1961-62; national ad-pub dir, Dino De Laurentiis, 1962-64; exec asst to vp, adv and pub, Fox, 1964-67; worldwide ad-pub VP, Cinerama, Inc, Cinerama Releasing Corp, 1967-74; exec VP, sls mktg, BCP, Feature Film Div of Cox Broadcasting Corp, 1974-75; worldwide ad-pub VP WB, 1976-77; P, Cinemax Marketing and Distributing Corp, 1977.

MANSON, Eddy Lawrence: Comp-Arr. b. NYC, May 9, 1925. e. Juilliard. Harmonica soloist, Town Hall; Carnegie Hall; also on TV and on Russian tour with Ed Sullivan show.
Film background scores inc: The Little Fugitive; Lovers and Lollipops; Johnny Jupiter; Day of the Painter; The River Nile; Polaris Submarine.
TV inc: American Spectacle; DuPont, Kraft, Armstrong series. Songs and instrumentals: Paisano; Boy on a Carousel; New Gray Mare; Fandango; The Lovers; Cornball Rag; Night Beat; Joey's Theme; Day of the Painter; Theme for Strings.

MANTEE, Paul (nee Marianetti): Act. b. San Francisco, Jan 9, 1936. e. U of CA, BA. Films inc: Robinson Crusoe on Mars; Blood on the Arrow; An American Dream; A Man Called Dagger; They Shoot Horses Don't They?; Day of the Animals; The Greatest; The Manitou; Wolf Lake; The Great Santini; Fugitive Family; Alcatraz--The Whole Shocking Story.

MANTLEY, John: Exec Prod. b. Toronto, Can, Apr 25, 1920. e. U of Toronto. Pasadena Playhouse MTA. Started as actor, became live TV prod-dir in early days of TV. Exec prod Gunsmoke 11 years.
TV inc: Wild Wild West; Dirty Sally; How the West Was Won. Author of more than 50 teleplays and two novels "27th Day" and "Snow Birch," both made into films.

MANTOOTH, Randolph: Act. b. Sacramento, CA, Sep 19, 1945. e. AADA. TV inc: Marcus Welby, MD; Emergency; The Seekers.

MANTOVANI, Annunzio: Cond. b. 1905. Began playing violin professionally at age 15; had own orch at 17; on radio and in concerts; began recording in England, emphasizing waltzes; for first U.S. recordings utilized 40 piece orch, of which 28 were strings, creating new easy-listening style that maintained his position as top orch leader for more than two decades.
(Died March 30, 1980).

MANULIS, Martin: Prod. b. NYC, May 30, 1915. e. Columbia U, BA. M, dir, Westport Country Playhouse, 1945-50; staff prod, dir CBS-TV, 1951-58; prod, 20th Century-Fox-TV. P, Martin Manulis Prodns, Ltd.
Films inc: Days of Wine and Roses; The Out-of-Towners; Luv; Duffy.
TV inc: Suspense; Studio One; Climax; Best of Broadway; Playhouse 90; The Day Christ Died.
Thea inc: Private Lives; Made in Heaven; The Philadelphia Story; Laura; The Men We Marry; The Hasty Heart; The Show Off.

MANZ, Linda: Act. b. NYC, Aug 20, 1961. Films inc: Days of Heaven; King of the Gypsies; Boardwalk; Out of the Blue; The Wanderers.
TV inc: The Orphan Train.

MARA, Adele: Act. b. Dearborn, MI, Apr 28, 1923. Singer, dancer with Xavier Cugat. Films inc: Shut My Big Mouth; Blondie Goes to College; Alias Boston Blackie; Passkey to Danger; Traffic in Crime; Exposed; Blackmail; Sands of Iwo Jima; Count the Hours; Wake of the Red Witch; Back from Eternity.

MARAIS, Jean (Jean Villain): Act. b. Cherbourg, France, 1913. Films inc: Histoires de ma Vie; L'Eternel Retour; La Belle et la Bete; Les Parents Terrible; Orphee; Le Paria; Peau d'Ane.

MARCEAU, Marcel: Act. b. Strasbourg, France, Mar 22, 1923. Gives concerts as mime.
Films inc: Barbarella; Shanks; Silent Movie. TV inc: numerous guest shots. (Emmy-specialty act-1955).

MARCH, Donald: Exec. b. NYC, Jul 26, 1942. e. Fordham U, BA. West Coast story ed RSO Films 1974; dir limited series ABC-TV, 1976; vp in chg telefilm CBS 1977; p feature film div Filmways March 1979; returned to CBS Oct. 1979 as vp theatrical films.

MARCH, Elspeth: Act. b. London, England. Thea inc: The Writing on the Wall; Autumn; Playboy of the Western World; Lady Precious Stream; Duet for Two Hands; The Turn of the Screw; Peace in Our Time; The King of Friday's Men; The Darling Buds of May; Arms and the Man; On the Town; The Wings of the Dove; A Public Mischief; Abelard and Heloise; Parents Day; Snap; Anastasia; The Last of Mrs Cheyney.
Films inc: Mr Emmanuel; The Rise and Rise of Michael Rimmer; Promise at Dawn; Goodbye, Mr. Chips; The Magician of Lublin.

MARCHAND, Nancy: Act. b. Buffalo, NY, Jun 19, 1928. Films inc: The Rise and Rise of Michael Rimmer; Promise at Dawn; Goodbye Mr Chips; Ladybug, Ladybug; Me, Natalie; Tell Me That You Love Me, Junie Moon.
TV inc: Lou Grant (Emmys-supp-1978, 1980); Some Kind of Miracle; Willa; Once Upon a Family; The Golden Moment-An Olympic Love Story.
Bway inc: The Playboy of the Western World; On the Town; The Eccentricities of a Nightingale; The Duel; Parents' Day; Death on Demand; Morning's at Seven (Rev).

MARCOVICCI, Andrea: Act-Singer. b. NYC, Nov 18, 1948. TV inc: The Ascent of Mt. Fuji; Cry Rape ; Some Kind of Miracle; A Vacation in Hell. Films inc: The Front; The Concorde-Airport 79. Bway inc: Hamlet.

MARCUS, Louis: Prod-Dir-Wri. b. Cork, Ireland, 1936. e. National U of Ireland. Prod & dir for Louis Marcus Documentary Film Prod of Dublin and Louis Marcus Films Ltd of London. Has made more than 30 documentaries.
Films inc: Woes of Golf; Children at Work; Conquest of Light.

MARGO (Maria Marguerita Guadalupe Boldao y Castilla): Act. b. Mexico City, May 10, 1918. W of Eddie Albert. Performed as dancer with Xavier Cugat. Films inc: Winterset; Lost Horizon; Crime without Passion; Viva Zapata; I'll Cry Tomorrow; From Hell to Texas; Taffy and the Jungle Hunter.

MARGOLIN, Janet: Act. b. NYC, 1943. Films inc: David and Lisa; Bus Riley's Back in Town; The Greatest Story Ever Told; The Saboteur; Nevada Smith; Enter Laughing; Buona Sera Mrs Campbell; Take the Money and Run; Annie Hall; The Last Embrace.

TV inc: The Triangle Factory Fire Scandal; The Plutonium Incident.

MARGOLIN, Stuart: Act-Dir. b. Davenport, IA, Jan 31. TV inc: Love American Style; My World and Welcome to It; Occasional Wife; The Rockford Files (*Emmys*-supp-1979, 1980); Suddenly, Love (dir); A Shining Season (dir).

Films inc: Texas Wheelers (dir); Kelly's Heroes; The Gamblers; Limbo; Death Wish; Days of Heaven.

MARGULIES, Stan: Prod. b. NYC, Dec 14, 1920. e. NYU, BS. Publicist: RKO; CBS-Radio; 20th Century-Fox; Walt Disney. Bryna Films, 1955; became vp, 1958; prod aide Spartacus, 1968. vp Wolper Pictures.

Films inc: Forty Pounds of Trouble; Those Magnificent Men in their Flying Machines; Don't Just Stand There; The Pink Jungle; If It's Tuesday, This Must Be Belgium; I Love My Wife; Willy Wonka and the Chocolate Factory; One Is A Lonely Number; Visions of Eight.

TV inc: The 500LB Jerk; She Lives; The Morning After; Unwed Father; Men of the Dragon; The Honorable Sam Houston; I Will Fight No More Forever; Collision Course; Roots (*Emmy*-prod-1977); Roots-The Next Generation (*Emmy*-1979); Moviola.

MARIN, Richard (Cheech): Act-Wri. b. LA, Jul 13, 1946. Teamed with Tommy Chong in improvisational group; spotted by Lou Adler at Hollywood's Troubadour club; began comedy recordings (*Grammy*-1973).

Films inc: Cheech and Chong's Up in Smoke; Cheech and Chong's Next Movie.

MARKEY, Gene: Wri-Prod. b. Jackson, MI, 1895. e. Dartmouth. Novelist who became a screenwriter with the advent of sound. Films inc: King of Burlesque; Girls Dormitory; On the Avenue; Wee Willie Winkie (& prod).

(Died May 1, 1980).

MARKHAM, Monte: Act. b. Manatee, FL, Jun 21, 1938. e. U of GA. Films inc: One Is a Lonely Number; Hour of the Gun; Guns of the Magnificent Seven; Airport '77; Midway.

TV inc: The Second Hundred Years; Mr. Deeds Goes to Town; The New Perry Mason; Visions; The Astronaut; Death Takes a Holiday; Hustling; The Littlest Hobo; The Ghosts of Buxley Hall.

Bway inc: Same Time Next Year; Irene.

MARKLE, Fletcher: Wri-Dir-Prod. b. Winnipeg, Can, Mar 21, 1921. With Canadian Broadcasting Co and BBC, London, 1942-46; prod-dir Studio One series, CBS, 1947-48; wri, edtr, narr of prize-winning documentary short, V-1, Story of the Robot Bomb, 1944.

Films inc: Jigsaw; Night Into Morning; The Man With a Cloak. TV inc: Life With Father; Front Row Center; Mystery Theatre; Panic; No Warning; M Squad; Buckskin; Rendezvous; Tales of the Vikings; Hong Kong; Father of the Bride; The Play's the Thing; The Olympics.

MARKOVA, Alicia, Dame (Lillian Alicia Marks): Ballerina. b. London, Dec 1, 1910. Studied under Astafieva. Taken into Russian Ballet 1924 by Serge Diaghilev (Song of the Nightingale created for her); first prima ballerina of the Vic-Sadlers Wells (Now Royal) Ballet, 1933-1935; with Anton Dolin formed Markova-Dolin Ballet 1935, toured United Kingdom until 1938; Ballet Russe de Monte Carlo 1938-1941; Ballet Theatre 1941-1944; reactivated Markova-Dolin ballet 1944-45; formed Festival Ballet 1950 with Dolin; guest artist principal ballets.

MARKS, Alfred OBE: Act. b. London, 1921. Films inc: Desert Mice; There Was a Crooked Man; Weekend with Lulu; Frightened City; She'll Have to Go; Scream and Scream Again; Our Miss Fred; Valentino.

TV inc: Blanding's Castle; Hobson's Choise; Paris 1900; The Memorandum; Alfred Marks Time.

Thea inc: Can Can; Pleasures and Palaces; Dead Silence; Don't Just Lie There, Say Something; The Entertainer; The Sunshine Boys; Bus Stop; Rolls Hyphen Royce.

MARKS, Arthur: Prod-Dir. b. LA, Aug 2, 1927. e. USC. Films inc: Togetherness; Bonnie Kids; Roommates: Detroit 9000; A Woman for all Men; Class of '74; Bucktown; Friday Foster; J D's Revenge; Monkey Hustle.

TV inc: (prod-dir) Perry Mason; (dir) I Spy; Mannix; Starsky and Hutch.

MARKS, Richard: Film Edtr. b. NYC, Nov 10, 1943. Films inc: Little Big Man; Bang The Drum Slowly; Lies My Father Told Me; Serpico; Godfather Part II; The Last Tycoon; Apocalypse Now.

MARLEY, John: Act. On screen from 1952. Films inc: My Six Convicts; Faces; Cat Ballou; Love Story; The Godfather; W C Fields and Me; The Car; The Greatest; Hollywood Stuntmen; Hooper; Tribute.

TV inc: Greatest Heroes of the Bible; Moviola (This Year's Blonde).

MARLOW, Lucy (nee McAleer): Act. b. LA, Nov 20, 1932. Films inc: A Star Is Born; Lucky Me; Tight Spot; My Sister Eileen; Queen Bee; Bring Your Smile Along.

MARLOWE, Hugh (nee Hipple): Act. b. Philadelphia, PA, Jan 20, 1911. On screen from 1937. Films inc: Mrs Parkington; Meet Me in St Louis; Twelve O'Clock High; All About Eve; The Day the Earth Stood Still; Wait Till the Sun Shines Nellie; Monkey Business; Thirteen Frightened Girls; Castle of Evil; The Last Shot You Hear.

Bway inc: Kiss the Boys Goodbye; Margin for Error; Flight to the West; The Land is Bright; Lady in the Dark; Laura; Woman is My Idea; All My Sons.

TV inc: Ellery Queen; Another World.

MARMELSTEIN, Linda: Prod. b. Washington, DC. TV inc: Over Seven; Wide World of Adventure; Little Vic; Henry Winkler Meets William Shakespeare; The Great Wallendas; The Secret Life of Charles Dickens; The Bloodhound Gang; Jennifer's Journey; New York City Too Far From Tampa Blues; The Late Great Me--The Story of a Teeenage Alcoholic (*Emmy*-1980).

MARON, Mel: Dist. b. NYC, Apr 21, 1931. e. CCNY. P Maron Films Ltd; exec vp Trans America Film Corp; p Cinema Shares Int'l Dist Corp; exec vp United Prodns of America; exec vp World Northal Corp.

MARRE, Albert: Dir-Prod. b. NYC, Sep 20, 1925. e. Oberlin Coll, Harvard. Bway inc: The Little Blue Light; Love's Labour's Lost; Misalliance; Kismet; Festival; The Chalk Garden; Shangri-La; Fledermaus; Saint Joan; Good as Gold; South Pacific; Time Remembered; Rape of the Belt; Milk and Honey; Too True to be Good; A Rainy Day in Newark; Never Live Over a Pretzel Factory; Man of La Mancha (*Tony*-1966); Cry for Us All (& wri); Home Sweet Home; A Meeting by the River.

TV inc: Androcles and the Lion; Craig's Wife.

MARSAC, Maurice: Act. b. La Croix, France, Mar 23, 1920. Films inc: (in US) How to Marry a Millionaire; What a Way to Go; The Art of Love; Dien Bien Phu Story; Pleasure Seekers; Clarence; Caprice; How Do I Love Thee?; The Jerk; Big Red One. European films inc: Sa Petite Folie; King of Kings; Armored Command; La Chapelle Noire; Scent of Mystery; Natika; Come Fly With Me; Lycantropus; Stray Dog. Thea inc: Saint Joan; The Happy Time; Sabrina Fair.

TV inc: Studio One; Climax; Our Miss Brooks; Combat; FBI; It Takes a Thief; Mission Impossible; Legendary Curse of the Hope Diamond; Tony Randall Show; Rockford Files; Ike, the War Years.

MARSHALL, Armina: Prod-Act-Wri. b. Alfalfa County, OK, 1899. e. UCLA. M of Philip Langner. NY stage debut, 1928, in The Tidings Brought to Mary. Bway inc: Peer Gynt; The Race with the Shadow; Fata Morgana; The Glass Slipper; Merchants of Glory; Right You Are If You Think You Are; Man's Estate; The Pillars of Society; The Bride the Sun Shines On; If This be Treason. Ret from acting in 1935 to write and produce plays with her husband, the late Lawrence Langner, inc: Pursuit of Happiness; Suzanna and the Elders; co-prod Sunrise at Campobello *(Tony*-prod-1958); Absurd Person Singular; Golda.

MARSHALL, E G: Act. b. Owatonna, MI, Jun 18, 1910. e. Carlton Coll, U of MN. Films inc: The House on 92nd Street; The Caine Mutiny; Pushover; Twelve Angry Men; The Bachelor Party; Town Without Pity; The Chase; The Bridge at Remagen; The Pursuit of Happiness; Billy Jack Goes To Washington; Interiors; Superman II.

TV inc: The Plot to Kill Stalin; Look Homeward Angel; A Quiet Game of Cards; The Defenders *(Emmys*-1962 & 1963); The Bold Ones; The Poppy is Also a Flower; Collision Course; Gold!; The Lazarus Syndrome; Vampire; Disaster on the Coastline; National Geographic Special (host); Mysteries of the Mind (host); Superliners-Twilight of an Era (host).

Bway inc: The Skin of Our Teeth; The Survivors; The Crucible; Red Roses for Me; The Little Foxes; The Imaginary Invalid; Old Movies; John Gabriel Borkman.

MARSHALL, Garry: Prod-Dir-Wri. b. NYC, Nov 13, 1934. e. Northwestern U, BS. Worked as copy boy, later reporter NY Daily News while writing comedy material for Phil Foster, Joey Bishop; partnered with Jerry Belson for almost ten years.

TV inc: (wri) Jack Paar Show; Joey Bishop Show; Danny Thomas Show; Lucy; Dick Van Dyke Show; I Spy; Hey, Landlord (& crea); The Odd Couple (& exec prod). (Crea-exec prod) The Little People; Happy Days; Laverne & Shirley; Mork and Mindy; Angie; Sitcom--The Adventures of Garry Marshall; Beane's of Boston; Who's Watching the Kids; Evil Roy Slade (& wri).

Films inc: (wri-prod) How Sweet It Is; The Grasshopper.

MARSHALL, Penny: Act. b. NYC, Oct 15, 1944. W of Rob Reiner. Sis of Garry Marshall. TV inc: Happy Days; Let's Switch; Paul Sands' Friends and Lovers; More Than Friends; Barry Manilow Special; Laverne & Shirley; Working Stiffs (dir).

Films inc: 1941.

MARSHALL, Peter (Pierre La Cock): Act. b. Huntington, WV, Mar 30. Films inc: The Rookies; Swingin' Along; Ensign Pulver; The Cavern; Americathon.

TV inc: The Hollywood Squares *(Emmys*-host-1974, 1975, 1980; Host of Year-1974).

MARTIN, Allan: Exec. b. Auckland, NZ, May 2, 1926. Dir gen SPTV; p Prods & Dirs Guild of Australia.

MARTIN, Charles E: Wri-Dir-Prod. b. Newark, NJ, 1916. e. NYU, NJ Law School. Films inc: My Dear Secretary; No Leave No Love; Death of a Scoundrel; If He Hollers Let Him Go; Remember Vivian Valentine; Seduction American Style; How to Seduce a Woman; Hotshot; The Cop Who Played God; One Man Jury.

TV inc: Tallulah Bankhead Show; Gertrude Lawrence Show; Philip Morris Playhouse.

MARTIN, David Lloyd: Thea Mgr. b. Sydney, Australia, Apr 30, 1934. Tivoli Circuit Australia 1954; chmn, joint m dir, 1961-66; chmn & m dir Sydney Opera House, 1966-72; deputy GM, 1973.

MARTIN, Dean

(Dino Crocetti): Act. b. Steubenville, OH, Jun 7, 1917. Joined Jerry Lewis, 1946, in Atlantic City. The duo played niteries, theatres before making screen debut in My Friend Irma. They appeared together until 1956. From 1957 Martin appeared in: Ten Thousand Bedrooms; Some Come Running; Rio Bravo; Toys in the Attic; The Sons of Katie Elder; Airport; Showdown; Mr. Ricco.

TV inc: Dean Martin Show; Celebrity Roasts; Dean Martin's Christmas in California; Dean Martin Christmas Special.

MARTIN, Dick: Act. b. Detroit, 1922. Half of the Rowan-Martin comedy team. Films inc: Once Upon a Horse; The Glass Bottom Boat; The Maltese Bippy.

TV inc: Laugh-In *(Emmy*-1969).

MARTIN, Elliot: Thea Prod. b. Denver, CO, Feb 25, 1924. e. U of Denver. Bway inc: A Moon for the Misbegotten ; Henry IV; Of Mice and Men; When You Comin' Back, Red Ryder? (off-Bway); More Stately Mansions; Dinner at Eight (all-star revival); A Touch of the Poet; Clothes For a Summer Hotel.

MARTIN, Ernest H: Prod. b. Pittsburgh, PA, Aug 28, 1919. e. UCLA, AB. Plays inc: Where's Charley; Guys and Dolls; Can-Can; The Boy Friend; Silk Stockings; How to Succeed in Business Without Really Trying *(Tony*-1962); Skyscraper; Walking Happy; The Goodbye People; The Act (all in asso with Cy Feuer).

Films inc: Cabaret; Piaf. M-dir LA and San Francisco Civic Light Opera Assn, 1975.

MARTIN, Freddy: Orch Leader. b. Cleveland, OH, Dec 5, 1906. Formed own orchestra 1931. Performed in St. Regis; Waldorf; Astor; Pennsylvania; Commodore Hotels, NY; St. Francis Hotel, SF; Los Angeles Cocoanut Grove from 1940-70; made coast-to-coast tours, inc Carnegie Hall.

MARTIN, Henry H (Hi): Exec. b. Holcomb, MS, Mar 22, 1912. Joined Universal as accessory mgr in 1935. Moved on to booker, salesman, branch mgr, div mgr. Named gen sls mgr in 1957, became vp 1959. Succeeded Milton R. Rackmil as president Universal Pictures on Jan 1, 1973. Ret 1978.

MARTIN, Mary: Act. b. Wetherford, TX, Dec 1, 1914. On screen from 1939 in The Great Victor Herbert; Rhythm on the River; Kiss the Boys Goodbye; Birth of the Blues; Happy Go Lucky; Night and Day.

Bway: *(Special Tony Award*-1948) Lute Song; Leave It to Me; One Touch of Venus; South Pacific; Annie Get Your Gun; Kind Sir; Peter Pan *(Tony*-1955); Jennie; The Sound of Music *(Tony*-1960); I Do I Do; Do You Turn Somersaults?.

TV inc: Peter Pan *(Emmy*-1955); Valentine.

MARTIN, Millicent: Act. b. Romford, England, Jun 8, 1934. Thea inc: (London) Expresso Bongo; The Crooked Mile; The Dancing Heiress; The Lord Chamberlain Regrets; State of Emergency; Our Man Crichton: Peter Pan; The Beggar's Opera; Absurd Person Singular; Side by Side by Sondheim. (Bway) The Boy Friend; Side by Side by Sondheim; King of Hearts.

TV inc: That Was The Week That Was; Mainly Millicent.

MARTIN, Nan: Act. Films inc: For the Love of Ivy; Goodbye Columbus; Toys in the Attic; Three in the Attic; The Other Side of the Mountain; The Other Side of the Mountain, Part 2. TV inc: A Circle of Children.

Bway inc: A Story for a Sunday Evening; The Constant Wife; J.B.; The Great God Brown; The Merchant of Venice; Hamlet; A Sign of Affection; Come Live With Me; The Taming of the Shrew; Summer Brave.

MARTIN, Pamela Sue: Act. b. Westport, CT, Jan 5, 1959. Model, TV commercials. Films inc: To Find A Man; The Poseidon Adventure; Buster and Billie; Our Time; The Lady In Red.

TV inc: The Hemingway Play; Nancy Drew Mysteries.

MARTIN, Peter G: Exec. b. Sydney, Australia, Sep 12, 1940. Commissioner (full time), Australian Film Commission.

MARTIN, Quinn: Prod. b. LA, May 22, 1927. e. Berkeley. Formed Quinn Martin Prods which subsequently sold to Taft Broadcasting. TV inc: The Untouchables; The Fugitive; The FBI; The New Breed; Cannon; Banyon; Barnaby Jones; Dan August; Manhunter; Most Wanted; Streets of San Francisco; 12 O'Clock High.

MARTIN, Ross (Martin Rosenblatt): Act. b. Poland, Mar 22, 1920. e. CCNY, BA. Films inc: Underwater Warrior; Geronimo; Experiment in Terror; The Ceremony; The Great Race.
    Bway inc: Hazel Flagg; Guys & Dolls.
    TV inc: (act) Dorso D.A.; Mr. Lucky; Stump the Stars; Wild Wild West; Skyway to Death; Yesterday's Child; Donovan's Kid. The Wild, Wild West Revisited; Return of the Mod Squad; The Seekers; More Wild Wild West. (Dir) Here's Lucy; Love American Style; Big George Diamond. Shinbone Alley.

MARTIN, Steve: Act. b. Waco, TX, 1945. e. Long Beach State Coll; UCLA. Writer for various TV shows inc: The Smothers Brothers Comedy Hour; Sonny and Cher. TV inc: (act) Steve Martin--A Wild and Crazy Guy; Comedy Is Not Pretty; All Commercials; Steve Allen Comedy Hour.
    Films inc: The Kids Are Alright; The Muppet Movie; The Jerk (& wri).
    Albums inc: Let's Get Small *(Grammy-*1977); A Wild and Crazy Guy *(Grammy-*1978).

MARTIN, Strother: Act. b. Kokomo, IN, Mar 26, 1919. Began career on a TV kiddie show. Screen debut in The Asphalt Jungle. Films inc: The Wild Bunch; The Ballad of Cable Hogue; The Man Who Shot Liberty Valance; Cool Hand Luke; The Wild Bunch; True Grit; Slap Shot; Cheech and Chong's Up in Smoke; The Champ; Love and Bullets; Nightwing; The Villain; The Secret of Nikola Tesla.
    TV inc: Gunsmoke; Have Gun, Will Travel; Better Late Than Never. (Died Aug 1, 1980).

MARTIN, Tony: Act. b. Oakland, CA, Dec 25, 1913. H of Cyd Charisse. Performed with bands; played niteries. Screen debut 1936, Pigskin Parade. Films inc: Sing, Baby, Sing; Follow the Fleet; You Can't Have Everything; Sally, Irene and Mary; Ziegfeld Girl; Two Tickets to Broadway; Hit the Deck.

MARTINDALE, Wink: Bcast Personality. b. Jackson, TN, Dec 4. e. Memphis State Coll. Game show host; LA disc jockey. TV game shows inc: Words and Music; How's Your Mother-in-Law?; What's the Song?; Everbody's Talking; Can You Top This?; Gambit; The New Tic Tac Dough; Las Vegas Gambit.

MARTINSON, Leslie: Dir. b. Boston. Films inc: Hot-Rod Girl; Hot-Rod Rumble; Lad: A Dog; Black Gold; FBI Code 98; PT-109; For Those Who Think Young; Batman; Fathom; The Challengers; Millions May Die; Mrs Pollifax-Spy; Escape from Angola; Cruise Missile.
    TV inc: Big Shamus, Little Shamus.

MARTON, Andrew: Dir-Prod. b. Budapest, Hungary, Jan 26, 1904. To Hollywood with Ernst Lubitsch, 1923. Directed chariot race in Ben Hur; amphibious landings in The Longest Day; battle scenes in 55 Days at Peking. Films inc: (as dir) The Thin Red Line; Crack in the World; Green Fire; The Devil Makes Three.
    TV inc: Man and the Challenge; Daktari; Cowboy in Africa; The Sea Hunt.

MARVIN, Lee: Act. b. NYC, Feb 19, 1924. Films inc: You're in the Navy Now; Duel at Silver Creek; Eight Iron Men; The Wild One; Gorilla at Large; The Caine Mutiny; Bad Day at Black Rock; Violent Saturday; Not as a Stranger; Pete Kelly's Blues; Attack; Raintree County; The Man Who Shot Liberty Valance; Donovan's Reef; The Killers; Attack!; Cat Ballou *(Oscar-*1965); Ship of Fools; The Professionals; The Dirty Dozen; Point Blank; Paint Your Wagon; The Iceman Cometh; Emperor of the North; Shout at the Devil; The Great Scout and Cathouse Thursday; Avalanche; The Big Red One.
    TV inc: M Squad; Lawbreaker.

MARX, Samuel: Wri-Prod. b. NYC, Jan 26, 1902. e. Columbia U. Started as story ed MGM, later prod at MGM, Goldwyn, Col, U.
    Films inc: Lassie Come Home; This Man's Navy; My Brother Talks to Horses; The Beginning or the End; A Lady Without A Passport; Grounds for Marriage; Kiss of Fire; Ain't Misbehavin'; Waterloo; Rome; The Ravine.
    June 1980, special story assignment for MGM.

MARX, Zeppo (Herman Marx): Act. b. NYC, 1900. Youngest of The Marx Brothers. Films inc: Cocoanuts; Animal Crackers; Monkey Business; Horse Feathers; Duck Soup.
    Ret from act, operated talent agency 1933-1960, then retired (Died Nov 29, 1979).

MASINA, Giulietta: Act. b. Bologna, Italy, Feb 22, 1921. e. U of Rome. W of Federico Fellini. School teacher before becoming act. On radio, Rome stage; met Fellini when he asked her to audition for radio soap opera. Films inc: Without Pity; The White Sheik; Lights of Variety; La Strada; Il Bidone; The Nights of Cabiria; Europa; Fortunella; Juliet of the Spirits.

MASLANSKY, Harris J: Exec. b. NYC, May 25, 1944. e. NYU Law School, LLM. Sr. VP Col, NY; 1980 P Motion Picture Division Time-Life Films.

MASLANSKY, Paul: Prod. b. NYC, Nov 23, 1933. e. Washington & Lee U, NYU Law School. Films inc: Jason and the Argonauts; The Long Ships; The Running Man; Castle of the Living Dead; The Blood Beast; The Red Tent; Deathline; Gun in the Pulpit; Hard Times; Race with the Devil; The Black Bird; Damnation Alley; Circle of Iron; When You Comin' Home, Red Ryder?; Hot Stuff; The Villain; Scavenger Hunt.
    TV inc: King.

MASON, James: Act. b. Huddersfield, Eng, May 15, 1909. e. Marlborough Coll. On screen from 1935. More than 120 films inc: Late Extra; I Met a Murderer; The Night Has Eyes; The Man in Grey; The Seventh Veil; The Wicked Lady; Odd Man Out; Pandora and the Flying Dutchman; The Desert Fox; Five Fingers; The Prisoner of Zenda; Julius Caesar; 20,000 Leagues Under the Sea; A Star is Born; Journey to the Center of the Earth; Lolita; The Pumpkin Eater; The Blue Max; Georgy Girl; The Deadly Affair; Harrowhouse; Inside Out; Cross of Iron; Heaven Can Wait; The Boys from Brazil; Murder by Decree; The Passage; Sidney Sheldon's Bloodline; The Water Babies; Ffolkes.
    TV inc: The Pioneers (narr).

MASON, Marsha: Act. b. St Louis, MO, Apr 3, 1943. W of Neil Simon. Films inc: Blume in Love; Cinderella Liberty; Audrey Rose; The Goodbye Girl; The Cheap Detective; Promises in the Dark; Chapter Two.
    TV inc: The Love of Life.
    Bway inc: Cactus Flower; Whatever Happened to Lori Jean Lloyd?; Faith Healer.

MASON, Pamela: Act-Wri. b. Westgate, Eng, Mar 10, 1918. Stage debut, 1936, The Luck of the Devil. Films inc: I Met a Murderer; They Were Sisters; The Upturned Glass; Pandora and the Flying Dutchman; Lady Possessed.
    TV inc: Pamela Mason Show.

MASON, Paul: Wri-Prod. b. Chicago, IL, Jun 21, 1936. e. Northwestern U. Films inc: Angel Baby; Action in the North Atlantic; To Die In Paris; King Kong Vs Godzilla; California Kid.
    TV inc: Chrysler Theatre; Eleventh Hour; Laredo; Tammy; Ironsides; It Takes a Thief; McMillan and Wife; SFX; Chico and the Man; Welcome Back, Kotter; The Wolper Specials; 1980, joined Danny Thomas and Ronald Jacobs as partner in Danny Thomas Prodns.

MASON, Shirley (Leonie Flugrath): Act. b. NYC, 1900. Sis of Viola Dana. Films inc: Treasure Island; Vanity Fair; So This is Paris. (Died July 27, 1979.)

MASON, Tom: Act. b. Brooklyn, NY, Mar 1. Bway inc: Kid Champion. Films inc: King of the Gypsies; Apocalypse Now.
    TV inc: Feasting With Panthers; Brother to Dragons; Walking Through Fire; Grandpa Goes to Washington; Nero Wolfe; Alien Force; Freebie and the Bean.

MASSARI, Lea: Act. b. France. Films inc: L'avventura; From a Roman Balcony; Colossus of Rhodes; Made In Italy; Murmur of the Heart; Impossible Object; Escape to Nowhere; Christ Stopped at Eboli; Le Divorcement.

MASSEY, Anna: Act. b. Sussex, Eng, Aug 11, 1937. D of Raymond Massey. Films inc: Peeping Tom; Bunny Lake is Missing; The Looking Glass War; David Copperfield; Frenzy; A Little Romance; Sweet William.

Thea inc: (London) The Reluctant Debutante; Slag; Spoiled; Flipside; The Doctor's Dilemma; School for Scandal; Close of Play.

TV inc: A Doll House; Remember the Germans; Wicked Woman; The Corn is Green.

MASSEY, Daniel: Act. b. London, Oct 10, 1933. S of Raymond Massey. Films inc: Girls At Sea; Girls in Arms; Upstairs and Downstairs; Mary, Queen of Scots; Fragment of Fear; Star!; The Jokers; The Incredible Sarah; Bad Timing.

Thea inc: (London) The Happiest Millionaire; Living for Pleasure; School for Scandal; The Rivals; Barefoot in the Park; She Loves Me; The Importance of Being Ernest; Bloomsbury; The Gay Lord Quex; Heloise and Abelard.

TV inc: Venus Observed; On Approval; War and Peace; Vikings.

MASSEY, Raymond: Act. b. Toronto, Aug 30, 1896. On stage from 1922 in England and U.S. On screen from 1931. Films inc: The Scarlet Pimpernel; The Prisoner of Zenda; Reap the Wild Wind; Action in the North Atlantic; Lincoln in Illinois; Arsenic and Old Lace; Stairway to Heaven; Mourning Becomes Electra; The Fountainhead; East of Eden; The Naked and the Dead; The Great Impostor; How the West Was Won; Mackenna's Gold.

Bway inc: Ethan Frome; Abe Lincoln in Illinois; Pygmalion; John Brown's Body.

MASSINE, Leonid: Chor. b. Moscow, 1896. A major force in dance from 1910. Choreographed 15 full-length ballets. Appeared in the film The Red Shoes. (Died Mar 16, 1979).

MASTERSON, Peter: Act. b. Houston, TX, Jun 1, 1934. e. Rice U. Thea inc: Marathon 33; Blues for Mr. Charlie; Trail of Lee Harvey Oswald; Great White Hope; That Championship Season; Poison Tree. Co-wri, co-dir Best Little Whorehouse In Texas.

Films Inc: Ambush Bay; Counterpoint; In the Heat of the Night; Exorcist; Von Richtofen and Brown; Man on a Swing; Stepford Wives.

TV inc: Pueblo; Delta County; A Question of Guilt; City in Fear (exec prod).

MASTROIANNI, Marcello: Act. b. Fontane Liri, Italy, Sep 28, 1924. On screen from 1947. Films inc: Three Girls from Rome; The Miller's Beautiful Wife; Fever to Live; The Ladykillers of Rome; Love a La Carte; La Dolce Vita; Divorce Italian Style; La Notte; A Very Private Affair; Where the Hot Wind Blows; The Organizer; Yesterday, Today and Tomorrow; Marriage Italian Style; Casanova '70; Kiss the Other Sheik; The Poppy Is Also a Flower; A Place for Lovers; Sunflower; Jealousy Italian Style; The Priest's Wife; The Grande Bouffe; Massacre in Rome; Down the Ancient Stairs; The Sunday Woman; The Divine Creature; Goodnight Ladies and Gentlemen; A Special Day; We All Loved Each So Much; Revenge; Wifemistress; Bye Bye Monkey; Cosi Come Sei; L'ingorgo; The Terrace; Todo Modo; City of Women.

MATALON, Vivian: Dir. b. Manchester, Eng, Oct 11, 1929. e. Munro College, Jamaica. Thea inc: (London as act) The Caine Mutiny Court Martial; A Hatful of Rain; The Iceman Cometh. (Dir) The Admiration of Life; Season of Goodwill; The Chinese Prime Minister; The Glass Menagerie; Suite in Three Keys; First Day of a New Season; Two Cities; I Never Sang for My Father; The Gingerbread Lady.

Bway inc: (dir) After the Rain; Noel Coward in Two Keys; PS Your Cat is Dead; Brigadoon (rev); Mornings at Seven (rev) (Tony-1980); The American Clock.

MATHESON, Richard: Wri. Films inc: The Incredible Shrinking Man; Somewhere In Time.

TV inc: Twilight Zone; Night Gallery; The Night Stalker; Duel; The Martian Chronicles.

MATHESON, Tim: Act. b. LA, Dec 31, 1949. Films inc: Divorce American Style; Yours, Mine and Ours; How to Commit Marriage; The Apple Dumpling Gang Rides Again; 1941. Magnum Force; Almost Summer; National Lampoon's Animal House; Dreamer;

TV inc: The Quest; Lock, Stock and Barrel; Hitched; Remember When; The Runaway Barge; The Last Day; What Ever Happened to the Class of '65?.

MATHEWS, Carole: Act. b. Montgomery, IL, Sep 13. Started as nightclub, radio entertainer. To Hollywood 1944. Films inc: Massacre River; The Great Gatsby; Meet Me at the Fair; Shark River; Requirement for a Redhead; Look in Any Window; Thirteen Men; Tender Is the Night; End of the Road.

MATHIS, Johnny: Singer. b. San Francisco, Sep 30, 1935. Recording artist. Performs in niteries; tours U S, abroad. Films inc: Lizzie; Wild in the Wind (sang title song); A Certain Smile.

MATTHAU, Walter: (nee Matuschanskayasky) Act. b. NYC, Oct 1, 1923. On screen from 1955 in The Kentuckian. Other films inc: A Face in the Crowd; Lonely Are the Brave; Charade; Fail Safe; The Odd Couple; The Fortune Cookie (Oscar-supp-1966); Hello, Dolly!; Cactus Flower; Kotch; The Front Page; Earthquake; The Bad News Bears; The Sunshine Boys; House Calls; California Suite; Casey's Shadow; Little Miss Marker (& exec prod); Portrait of a 60% Perfect Man (doc); Hopscotch.

Bway inc: Anne of the Thousand Days; Will Success Spoil Rock Hunter; A Shot in the Dark (Tony-supp-1962); The Odd Couple (Tony-1965).

MATTHEWS, Jessie, OBE: Act. b. London, Mar 11, 1907. Started as child dancer. Thea inc: Charlot's Revue of 1924; Earl Carroll's Vanities; One Dam Thing After Another; Wake Up and Dream; Aladdin; The Lady Comes Across; The Browning Version; Pygmalion; Private Lives; Sauce Tartare; Five Finger Exercise; The Killing of Sister George; toured extensively with one woman show.

Films inc: The Beloved Vagabond (1923); The Good Companions; Evergreen; Out of the Blue; The Man From Toronto; Friday The Thirteenth; Victory Wedding (dir); Making the Grade; Tom Thumb.

TV inc: Edward and Mrs. Simpson.

MATURE, Victor: Act. b. Louisville, KY, Jan 29, 1916. Early training in Pasadena Theatre, Playbox Theatre. On Broadway in Lady in the Dark. On screen from 1939 in The Housekeeper's Daughter; One Million B.C.; Captain Caution; I Wake Up Screaming; My Darling Clementine; Kiss of Death; Samson and Delilah; Androcles and the Lion; The Robe; The Big Circus; The Tartars; Every Little Crook and Nanny; Firepower.

MATZ, Peter: Comp-Cond. b. Pittsburgh, PA, Nov 6, 1928. e. UCLA. TV inc: (mus dir) My Name is Barbra (Emmy-1965); The Sound of Burt Bacharach (Emmy-1970); The Carol Burnett Show 1971-1978 (Emmy-1973); The Big Show; Fun and Games; Omnibus; Good Time Harry; Damien. . .The Leper Priest; From Raquel With Love (mus dir); The Mouseketeer Reunion (cond).

Films inc: Private Eyes (mus).

(Comp) First You Cry; Father Damien; White Mama; Tenta Monta; Doug Henning's Magic Show.

Recordings (arr) for Barbra Streisand (Grammy-1964); Tony Bennett; Chicago.

MAULDIN, Bill: Cartoonist. b. Santa Fe, NM, 1922. Winner of two Pulitzer Awards for his cartoons. Appeared on screen in films: Teresa; The Red Badge of Courage; Up Front.

MAXWELL, Lois: Act. That Hagen Girl; The Big Punch; The Decision of Christopher Blake; The Dark Past; The Crime Doctor's Diary; Scotland Yard Inspector; Satellite in the Sky; Lolita; The Haunting; Dr No; From Russia With Love; Goldfinger; Thunderball; The Man With the Golden Gun; You Only Live Twice; Diamonds Are Forever; The Spy Who Loved Me; Lost and Found; Moonraker.

MAXWELL, Ronald: Dir. b. Tripoli, Libya. e. NYU. TV inc: Theatre In America; Sea Marks; Verna--Uso Girl. Films inc: Little Darlings.

MAY, Billy: Comp-Arr-Cond. b. Pittsburgh, Nov 10, 1916. Arr & cond for many leading vocalists, 1950-60; comp & cond for TV shows inc: Naked City; Batman; Green Hornet; Mod Squad; Emergency; CHiPS.
(*Grammys*-best orch-1958; best arr-1959).

MAY, Elaine: Act-Wri. b. Philadelphia, Apr 21, 1932. Comedy team with Mike Nichols. Films inc: Luv; Enter Laughing; A New Leaf (& dir, sp); Such Good Friends (sp); The Heartbreak Kid; Mikey and Nicky (dir, sp); California Suite; Heaven Can Wait (sp).
(*Grammy*-comedy perf-1961).

MAYBERRY, Russ: Dir. Films inc: The Jesus Trip; Unidentified Flying Oddballs.
TV inc: The Monkees; Love on a Rooftop; Fer De Lance; Who Killed the Centerfold Model; The Million Dollar Dixie Deliverance; The Snatching of Little Freddie; The Young Runaways; Arnie; Probe; Baa Baa Black Sheep; The Rebels; The $5.20 an Hour Dream; Marriage Is Alive and Well; Reunion.

MAYER, Arthur L: Exec. b. Demopolis, AL, May 28, 1886. e. Harvard AB. Early career in exhib with Lubliner & Trinz; Balaban & Katz; Publix Theatres; became mgr Rialto Theatre, NY, 1933; formed Mayer-Burstyn (with Joseph Burstyn) 1937 to distrib foreign films; sold holdings to Burstyn 1950, formed Mayer-Kingsley Inc; ret from firm 1954; professor at Stanford, USC, Dartmouth ù1965-76.
Served as film consultant to Secretary of War during WW2, later rep American Military Government, Germany in charge of films; awarded Medal of Merit by Pres. Truman; author of Merely Colossal: The Movies.

MAYER, Roger L: Exec. b. NYC, Apr 21, 1926. e. Yale U, BA, Yale Law School, LLB, JD. Atty for Columbia Pictures, 1952-57; then corporate exec from 1957-61; joined MGM as both VP-operations & asst sec; currently VP-administration, exec VP-MGM laboratories.

MAYES, Wendell: Wri. b. Hayti, MO, Jul 21, 1919. Films inc: Spirit of St. Louis; The Way to the Gold; The Hanging Tree; The Enemy Below; The Hunters; Anatomy of a Murder; Advise & Consent; In Harm's Way; Von Ryan's Express; Hotel; Poseidon Adventure; The Revengers; The Stalking Moon; The Bank Shot; Death Wish; Love and Bullets, Charlie; Go Tell the Spartans; Love and Bullets.

MAYFIELD, Curtis: Mus-Comp-Singer. b. Chicago, IL, Jun 3, 1942. With group Impression 1958-1970 before going solo. Albums inc: Curtis; Curtis Live; Roots; Back to the World; Sweet Exorcist; America Today; Never Say You Can't Survive; Do It.
Films inc: (scores) Superfly; Short Eyes; A Piece of the Action.

MAYO, Virginia (nee Jones): Act. b. St. Louis, MO, Nov 30, 1920. Performed on stage in stock, niteries. Screen debut in 1944. Films inc: Jack London; Up in Arms; The Princess and the Pirate; The Best Years of Our Lives; The Secret Life of Walter Mitty; White Heat; The Flame and the Arrow; West Point Story; Captain Horatio Hornblower; Painting the Clouds with Sunshine; The Proud Ones; The Big Land; Castle of Evil.
TV inc: Police Story.

MAYRON, Melanie: Act. b. Philadelphia, PA, Oct 20, 1952. e. AADA. Films inc: Car Wash; Gable and Lombard; Harry and Tonto; Girlfriends; The Great Smoky Roadblock.
TV inc: Hustling; Playing For Time.
Thea inc: Godspell (tour); The Goodbye People (Bway).

MAZURKI, Mike: Act. b. Tarnopal, Austria, Dec 25, 1909. e. Manhattan College, NY, BA. Toured US, Canada, as heavyweight wrestler. Screen debut 1941 Shanghai Gesture. Films inc: I Walk Alone; Unconquered; Nightmare Alley; Come to the Stable; Rope of Sand; Samson and Delilah; Ten Tall Men; My Favorite Spy; The Egyptian; New York Confidential; Some Like It Hot; A Pocketful of Miracles; Requiem for a Heavyweight; Challenge to be Free; Agnes; The Magic of Lassie; Gas Pump Girls; The Man with Bogart's Face.

MAZURSKY, Paul: Prod-Dir-Wri. b. NYC, Apr 25, 1930. Films inc: I Love You Alice B Toklas (co-sp); Bob and Carol and Ted and Alice (co-sp, dir); Alex in Wonderland (co-sp, dir); Blume in Love (sp-dir); Harry and Tonto; Next Stop Greenwich Village; An Unmarried Woman (& act); A Man, A Woman, And A Bank (act); Willie & Phil.

Mc ANALLY, Ray: Act. b. Buncrana, Donegal, Ireland, Mar 30, 1926. e. St Eunan's Coll, St Patrick's Coll. Appeared in over 150 plays with the Abbey Theatre Company, 1947-63. On London stage 1964 in Who's Afraid of Virginia Woolf?. Thea inc: Lorna and Ted; The Devil's Disciple; The Devil's Own People; Living Quarters; Translations.
Films inc: She Didn't Say No!; Shake Hands With the Devil; The Naked Edge; Billy Budd; The Outsider.
TV inc: Leap in the Dark; The Little Father; Court Martial.

McARDLE, Andrea: Act. b. Philadelphia, Nov 5, 1963. Thea inc: Annie.
TV inc: Search for Tomorrow; Rainbow; Come On Saturday.

Mc CALLION, James: Act. b. Glasgow, Scotland, Sep 27, 1918. Films inc: Boy Slaves; Code of the Streets; Gantry the Great; Hero for a Day; Tribute to a Bad Man; Vera Cruz; North by Northwest; How Do I Love Thee. TV inc: National Velvet.

Mc CALLISTER, Lon: Act (Ret. b. LA, Apr 17, 1923. Started as an extra, 1935. Films inc: Stage Door Canteen; Home In Indiana; Winged Victory; The Red House; Thunder in the Valley; Scudda Hoo, Scudda Hay; The Big Cat; The Story of Seabiscuit; The Boy from Indiana; A Yank in Korea; Montana Territory; Combat Squad (last film, 1953).

Mc CALLUM, David: Act. b. Scotland, Sep 19, 1933. Films inc: Prelude to Fame; The Secret Place; Violent Playground; The Long, the Short and the Tall; Billy Budd; Freud; The Great Escape; The Greatest Story Ever Told; Around the World Under the Sea; Three Bites of the Apple; Sol Madrid; Mosquito Squadron; Frankenstein, The True Story; Dogs; The Watcher in the Woods.
TV inc: The Man from UNCLE; Colditz; The Invisible Man.

Mc CALLUM, John: Prod-Dir-Act. b. Brisbane, Australia, Mar 14, 1918. In reportory theatres 1937-39; Man dir J C Williamson Theatres, Aus, 1959-66; Chmn, exec dir John McCallum Prods, 1976; prod TV series: Skippy; Barrier Reef; Boney.

Mc CAMBRIDGE, Mercedes: Act. b. Joliet, IL, Mar 17, 1918. e. Mundelein College, BA. Performed on radio, stage. Films inc: All The King's Men (*Oscar*-Supp-1950); Giant; Lightning Strikes Twice; Johnny Guitar; A Farewell to Arms; Suddenly Last Summer; The Exorcist (voice of Satan on soundtrack); Thieves; Concorde-Airport '79.
Bway inc: Hope for the Best; A Place of Our Own; Woman Bites Dog.

Mc CARTHY, Frank: Prod. b. Richmond, VA, Jun 8, 1912. e. VMI, U of VA. In WW II was Asst Secy later Secy of War Dept General Staff, Secy to Chief of Staff Gen. Marshall. Joined MPAA, 1946, serving as asst to vp, later European mgr. Joined Darryl F. Zanuck as a 20th Century-Fox exec prod, 1948.
Films inc: Decision Before Dawn; Sailor of the King; A Guide for the Married Man; Patton (*Oscar*-best pic-1970); MacArthur.

Mc CARTHY, Kevin: Act. b. Seattle, WA, Feb 15, 1915. Bway debut in Abe Lincoln in Illinois. Screen debut 1951 Death of a Salesman. Films inc: Drive a Crooked Road; Stranger on Horseback; The Misfits; A Gathering of Eagles; Mirage; A Time for Heroes; Buffalo Bill and the Indians; Invasion of the Body Snatchers; Piranha; Hero At Large.
TV inc: Flamingo Road; Portrait of An Escort.

Mc CARTHY, Nobu (nee Atsumi): Act. b. Ottawa, Can, Nov 13, 1940. e. LACC. Films inc: The Hunters; Geisha Boy; Five Gates to Hell; Wake Me When It's Over; Two Loves; Walk Like a Dragon.
TV inc: Lost Flight; Farewell to Manzanar; The Man On The Beach.

McCARTNEY, Paul: Singer-Mus. b. Liverpool, England, Feb 25, 1943. Member of The Beatles (see group listing). Individual film credits inc: Live and Let Die (title song); Oh Heavenly Dog (songs); Rock Show.
Formed group Wings for p.a. and recordings.
(*Grammys*-(5)-(in addition to group awards). Song of Year, 1966; Contemporary vocal solo, 1966; Soundtrack, 1970; Arrangement-vocalists, 1971; Pop vocal group, 1974).

Mc CARTY, Mary: Act. b. KS, 1923. Bway inc: Sleepy Hollow; Miss Liberty; A Rainy Day in Newark; Follies; Sondheim; Chicago; Anna Christie.
Films inc: French Line; Babes in Toyland; Pillow Talk; My Six Loves; Somebody Killed Her Husband.
TV inc: Trapper John. (Died April 3, 1980).

McCASHIN, Constance (nee Broman): Act. b. Chicago, Jun 18. e. Manhattanville Coll. Worked with off-Bway group; in tv prodn WPIX, NY. TV inc: Daddy, I Don't Like It Like This; A Special Kind of Love; First Ladies Diaries--Edith Bolling Wilson; The Two Worlds of Jennie Logan; Are You A Missing Heir?; Married--The First Year; Knots Landing.

Mc CAUGHEY, William L: Snd. b. Kansas City, MO, Dec 21, 1929. Films inc: Logans Run; Audrey Rose; Norman Is that You?; Piece of the Action; King Kong; Deer Hunter (*Oscar*-1978); California Suite; Voices; The Runner Stumbles; The Champ; Fast Break; Voices; The Villian.

Mc CLANAHAN, Rue: Act. b. Healdton, OK, Feb 21. e. Tulsa U. TV inc: Maude; Who's Happy Now; Move Over, Mrs Markham; Apple Pie; Rainbow; Mother and Me; Topper; The Great American Traffic Jam.
Bway inc: The Secret Life of Walter Mitty; Jimmy Shine; California Suite.

Mc CLORY, Sean: Act. b. Dublin, Ireland, Mar 8, 1924. e. U of Galway. With Abbey Theatre. Came to U S 1946. Films inc: Dick Tracy vs The Claw; Beyond Glory; Storm Warning; What Price Glory; The Quiet Man; Ring of Fear; The Long Grey Line; Botany Bay; Moonfleet; Day of the Wolves; Follow Me Boys; The Gnomobile; Well of the Saints; Roller Boogie.
Thea inc: Shining Hour; Juno and the Paycock; Anna Christie; The Lady's Not for Burning; Billy Budd; Dial M for Murder; Shadows of a Gunman; Saint Joan.
TV inc: Captains and the Kings; Once an Eagle; Kate McShane; Battlestar Galactica.

Mc CLURE, Doug: Act. b. Glendale, CA, 1935. Films inc: Because They're Young; The Unforgiven; Shenandoah; Beau Geste; The King's Pirate; Nobody's Perfect; The Land that Time Forgot; At the Earth's Core; Warlords of Atlantis; Humanoids From the Deep.
TV inc: Checkmate; Overland Trail; The Virginian; Search; The Judge and Jake Wyler; The Rebels.
Bway inc: The Roast.

Mc CLURE, Marc: Act. b. San Mateo, CA, Mar 31, 1957. Films inc: Freaky Friday; Coming Home; Superman; I Wanna Hold Your Hand. TV inc: The Cop and the Kid; numerous segs.

McCOOK, John: Act-Singer-Cond. b. Ventura, CA, Jun 20, 1945. In stock, touring shows; cond for various headline acts in Las Vegas. Bway inc: West Side Story (rev).
TV inc: The Young and the Restless; From Janice and John and Mary and Michael. . .With Love; Singin', Swingin', and All That Jazz; Mitzi--What's Hot, What's Not.

Mc CORD, Kent: Act. b. LA, Sep 26, 1942. Began acting career on Ozzie and Harriet Show. TV inc: The Virginian; Jigsaw; Dragnet; Adam 12.
Films inc: The Young Warriors.

Mc CORMACK, Patricia: Act. b. Aug 21, 1945. Made Bway debut at age 6 (billed as Patty McCormack). Bway inc: Touchstone; The Bad Seed. Films inc: The Bad Seed; The Day They Gave Babies Away; Huckleberry Finn; Kathy-O; Explosive Generation; The Young Runaways.
TV inc: I Remember Mama; The Miracle Worker; Shower of Stars; Peck's Bad Girl; The New Breed; The Best of Everything; Friends; As The World Turns; The Ropers.

McCORMICK, Pat (Arley D McCormick): Wri-Act. b. Jul 17, 1934. Comedy writer for Phyllis Diller, Jonathan Winters, Henny Youngman. TV inc: (wri) Jack Paar Show; Don Rickles Show; Tonight Show.
Films inc: (act); Buffalo Bill and the Indians; If You Don't Stop It You'll Go Blind; Smokey and the Bandit; A Wedding; Hot Stuff; Scavenger Hunt; Smokey and The Bandit II.

Mc COWEN, Alec: Act. b. Tunbridge Wells, Eng, May 26, 1925. e. RADA. In repertory 1943-45. Thea inc: (London) Ivanhoe; The Mask and the Face; Tishoo. (Bway) Antony and Cleopatra; The Holy Terrors; Escapade; The Matchmaker; The Caine Mutiny Court Martial; No Laughing Matter; The Elder Statesman; After the Rain; Hadrian the Seventh.
Films inc: The Cruel Sea; Time Without Pity; A Midsummer Night's Dream; The Loneliness of the Long Distance Runner; The Agony and the Ecstasy; The Devil's Own; The Hawaiians; Frenzy; Travels With My Aunt; Stevie; Hanover Street.

Mc COY, Van: Mus-Comp-Prod. b. Washington, DC, Jan 6, 1944. (*Grammy*-pop inst-1975). (Died Jul 6, 1979).

Mc CREA, Joel: Act. b. LA, Nov 5, 1905. H of Frances Dee. On screen from 1923. Films inc: Penrod and Sam; The Jazz Age; The Silver Cord; Private Worlds; Barbary Coast; Dead End; Union Pacific; Foreign Correspondent; Sullivan's Travels; The Great Man's Lady; The More The Merrier; Ramrod; Four Faces West; Stars in my Crown; Buffalo Bill; The Oklahoman; Fort Massacre; Mustang Country.

Mc DOUGALL, Gordon: Dir. b. Inverness, Scotland, May 4, 1941. e. Cambridge. Started in repertoire, then artistic dir of the Traverse, Edinburgh, 1966-68. Later dir The Vicar of Soho; The Dark River; Twelfth Night; The Country Wife; in 1974 became artistic dir of the Oxford Playhouse Company; prodns inc: The Government Inspector; As You Like It; Happy End; Uncle Vanya; Fitting for Ladies; For Heaven's Sake Don't Walk Around With Nothing On.

Mc DOWALL, Roddy: Act. b. London, Sep 17, 1928. On screen in England from 1936 in Murder in the Family. Films in U.S. inc: How Green Was My Valley; Confirm or Deny; The Pied Piper; My Friend Flicka; Lassie Comes Home; Keys of the Kingdom; Midnight Lace; Cleopatra; Inside Daisy Clover; Planet of the Apes (and its sequels); The Poseidon Adventure; Funny Lady; The Cat From Outer Space; Laserblast; Rabbit Test; Circle of Iron; Nutcracker Fantasy; Scavenger Hunt.
Bway inc: Misalliance; Escapade; The Doctor's Dilemma; No Time for Sergeants; Compulsion; A Handful of Fire; Look After Lulu; The Fighting Cock (*Tony*-supp-1960); Camelot.
TV inc: Not Without Honor (*Emmy*-1961); The Thief of Baghdad; The Immigrants; The Martian Chronicles; The Memory of Eva Ryker; The Return of the King (voice).

Mc DOWELL, Malcolm: Act. b. Leeds, Eng, Jun 1943. Films inc: If. . .; Figures in a Landscape; The Raging Moon; A Clockwork Orange; O Lucky Man!; Royal Flash; Aces High; Voyage of the Damned; The Passage; Time After Time; Caligula.
TV inc: She Fell Among Thieves.

McEVEETY, Bernard: Dir. B of Vincent McEveety. Films inc: Napoleon and Samantha; One Little Indian; The Bears and I.
TV inc: Bonanza; Gunsmoke; Combat; Cimarron Strip (& prod); Man Undercover; Donovan's Kid; Young Maverick; Roughnecks.

McEVEETY, Vincent: Dir. TV inc: Gunsmoke; High Flying Spy; The Buffalo Soldiers.
    Films inc: The $1,000,000 Duck; The Biscuit Eater; Charley and the Angel; Superdad; The Strongest Man in the World; Treasure of Matecumbe; Herbie Goes to Monte Carlo; The Apple Dumpling Gang Rides Again; Herbie Goes Bananas.

Mc GAVIN, Darren: Act. b. Spokane, WA, May 7, 1922. Bway inc: Death of a Salesman; My Three Angels; The Rainmaker; Dinner at Eight (revival).
    Films inc: A Song to Remember; Counter Attack; Summertime; The Man with the Golden Arm; Beau James; Ride the High Wind; Mrs. Polifax, Spy; Run, Stranger, Run (dir); American Reunion (dir); No Deposit, No Return; Airport '77; Hot Lead and Cold Feet; Hangar 18.
    TV inc: Mike Hammer; The Outsider; Riverboat; The Night Stalker; Tribes; Something Evil; Say Goodbye Maggie Cole; Cyborg; Crime of the Century-The Brink's Robbery; Ike; Love For Rent; The Martian Chronicles; Waikiki.

Mc GOOHAN, Patrick: Act. b. NYC, Mar 19, 1928. Films inc: Passage Home; Zarak; High Tide at Noon; Hell Drivers; The Gypsy and the Gentleman; Two Living One Dead; The Quare Fellow; Life for Ruth; Dr Syn; Ice Station Zebra; Mary Queen of Scots; Catch My Soul (dir only); The Genius; Silver Streak; Brass Target; Escape From Alcatraz.
    TV inc: Danger Man (Secret Agent); The Prisoner; Columbo (*Emmy*-supp-1975).

McGRAW, Charles: Act. b. May 10, 1914. Films inc: The Moon Is Down; The Killers; Armored Car Robbery; The Narrow Margin; The Bridges of Toko-Ri; Away All Boats; Slaughter on Tenth Avenue; The Defiant Ones; Wonderful Country; Spartacus; Cimarron; It's A Mad, Mad, Mad, Mad World; In Cold Blood; Pendulum; Johnny Got His Gun; Twilight's Last Gleaming.
    TV inc: The Falcon; Casablanca.
    (Died Jul 29, 1980).

Mc GREGOR, Angela Punch: Act. b. Sydney, Australia, Jan 21, 1953. e. Natl Institute of Dramatic Arts. Worked with Old Tote Theatre, Tasmanian Theatre Company, Nimrod Theatre in Australia. Thea inc: Playboy of the Western World; Collaborators; Kennedy's Children; Case for the Defense; Mother Courage; Romeo and Juliet; The Bride of Gospel Place.
    TV inc: La Boheme; Alvin Purple; Kiss and Ride a Ferry; The Timeless Land.
    Films inc: The Chant of Jimmie Blacksmith; Newsfront; The Island.

Mc GUIRE, Biff (William J): Act. b. New Haven, CT, Oct 25, 1926. e. MA State, Shrivenham U, Eng. Bway inc: Make Mine Manhattan; South Pacific; The Moon Is Blue; The Time of Your Life; A View From the Bridge; Greatest Man Alive; Happy Town; Beg Borrow or Steal; Beggar on Horseback;Trial of the Catonsville Nine; That Championship Season.
    Films inc: Serpico; The Last Word.
    TV inc: Act of Violence; Rex Stout's Nero Wolfe.

Mc GUIRE, Dorothy: Act. b. Omaha, NE, Jun 14, 1919. Films inc: Claudia; A Tree Grows in Brooklyn; The Spiral Staircase; Claudia and David; Gentlemen's Agreement; Mister 880; Three Coins in a Fountain; Friendly Persuasion; Old Yeller; The Remarkable Mr Pennypacker; The Earth Is Mine; Dark at the Top of the Stairs; Swiss Family Robinson; Flight of the Doves; Summer Magic; The Greatest Story Ever Told; Jonathan Livingston Seagull (voice only).
    TV inc: She Waits; The Runaways; Rich Man, Poor Man; The Outlander; Little Women; The Incredible Journey of Dr Meg Laurel.
    Bway inc: A Kiss for Cinderella; Our Town; Kind Lady; Medicine Show; Claudia; Summer and Smoke; Legend of Lovers; Winesburg, Ohio; The Night of the Iguana.

Mc HUGH, Frank: Act. b. Homestead, PA, May 23, 1899. Bway inc: Fall Guy; Tenth Avenue; Excess Baggage; Conflict.
    Films inc: Bright Lights; Little Caesar; The Front Page; One Way Passage; Bullets or Ballets; Three Men on a Horse; Boy Meets Girl; Going My Way; Back Street; State Fair; The Last Hurrah; Say One for Me.

Mc INTIRE, John: Act. b. Spokane, WA, Jun 27, 1907. H of Jeanette Nolan. Films inc: Asphalt Jungle; Saddle Tramp; Winchester 73; A Lion Is In the Streets; Apache; Phenix City Story; The Lawless Breed; The Tin Star; Psycho; Summer and Smoke; Rough Night in Jericho; Two Rode Together; Challenge To Be Free; Herbie Rides Again; Rooster Cogburn; The Rescuers (voice).
    TV inc: Naked City; Wagon Train; The Virginian; The Jordan Chance; Mrs. R's Daughter; Shirley.

Mc KAY, Bruce: Exec. b. Helena, MT. e. Gettsburg Coll, Syracuse U. Joined NBC TV in 1973. Appointed vp, Variety Programs, NBC Entertainment in April, 1979.

McKAY, Jim (nee McManus): TV Sportscaster. b. Philadelphia, Sep 24, 1921. e. Loyola College, Baltimore. Reporter, Baltimore Sunpapers, joined Sunpapers' WMAR-TV 1974 as wri-prod-dri; 1950 CBS as variety show host, sports commentator; 1961, host ABC Wide World of Sports (*Emmys*-1968, 1971, 1974, 1975, 1976, 1980); also (*Emmy*-1973 for coverage of Munich Olympic Tragedy); commentator all Olympiads since 1960; Indianapolis 500; Kentucky Derby; Masters & PGA Golf Championships.

Mc KAY, Scott: (Carl Gore): Act. b. Pleasantville, IA, May 28, 1922. e. U of CO. Films inc: Duel in the Sun; Kiss and Tell; A Guest in the House; Thirty Seconds Over Tokyo; The Front; The Bell Jar.
    TV inc: Love of Life; Edge of Night; Search for Tomorrow.
    Bway inc: Good Hunting; Three Sisters; Letters to Lucerne; The Eve of St. Mark; Dark Eyes; The Moon is Down; Requiem for a Nun; Pillar to Post; Another Part of the Forest; The Night Before Christmas; The American Way; Sabrina Fair; Dream Girl; Born Yesterday; Bell, Book and Candle; The Little Foxes; The Live Wire; Once for the Asking.

McKEAN, Michael: Act-Mus-Sngwri. b. NYC, Oct 17. e. NYU, Carnegie Tech. Teamed with David L. Lander in comedy group The Credibility Gap, toured US for four years. TV inc: More Than Friends; American Bandstand; Laverne & Shirley.
    Films inc: 1941.

McKECHNIE, Donna: Act-Dancer-Singer. b. Detroit, MI, 1940. Bway inc: How to Succeed in Business Without Really Trying; The Education of H*Y*M*A*N K*A*P*L*A*N; Promises, Promises; Company; On the Town; Sondheim--A Musical Tribute (& chor); Music, Music, Music; A Chorus Line (*Tony*-1976).

McKENNA, Siobhan: Act. b. Belfast, N Ireland, May 24, 1923. e. Natl U of Ireland. Appeared in Galway Theatre, Abbey Theatre Dublin before London stage bow 1947, The White Steed. Thea inc: (London) Berkeley Square; Ghosts; Heloise; Joan of Arc; Playboy of the Western World; Play With A Tiger; The Cavern; On a Foggy Day; Best of Friends; Memoir. (Bway) The Chalk Garden; Saint Joan; The Rope Dancers; A Meeting by the River.
    Films inc: Hungry Hill; Daughter of Darkness; The Lost People; The Adventurers; King of Kings; Of Human Bondage; Dr Zhivago.
    TV inc: The Letter; Cradle Song; What Every Woman Knows.

McKENNA, T P (Thomas Patrick McKenna): Act. b. County Cavan, Eire, Sep 7, 1929. e. Abbey Theatre School. With the Abbey Theatre for eight years before going to London. Thea inc: Stephen D; Julius Caesar; Too True to be Good; Recall the Years (opening prodn of new Abbey); Breakdown; The Contractor; Exiles; The Balcony; Sleuth; The Devil's Disciple; Nightshade.
    Films inc: Ulysses; The Charge of the Light Brigade; Anne of the Thousand Days; Straw Dogs; It's Not The Size That Counts; The Outsider; Portrait of the Artist as a Young Man.
    TV inc: The Rivals; The Duchess of Malfi; The Changeling.

McKENNA, Virginia: Act. b. London, England, Jun 7, 1931. Thea inc: (London) A Penny for a Song; The Winter's Tale; The River Line; The Bad Samaritan; I Capture the Castle; various Shakespearean roles with Old Vic; The Devils; The Beggar's Opera; The Beheading; A Little Night Music; The King and I. Films inc: The Second Mrs. Tanqueray; Father's Doing Fine; The Cruel Sea; Simba; The Ship That Died of Shame; A Town Like Alice; The Smallest Show on Earth; The Barretts of Wimpole Street; Carve Her Name With Pride; The Wreck of the Mary Deare; Born Free; Ring of Bright Water; An Elephant Called Slowly; Waterloo; Swallows and Amazons; The Chosen.

Mc KEON Philip: Act. b. Westbury, NY, Nov 11, 1964. Films inc: Up the Sandbox; Once Is Not Enough; American Moments.
TV inc: Alice.
Bway inc: Medea and Jason.

Mc KERN, Leo (Reginald Mc Kern): Act. b. Sydney, NSW, Mar 16, 1920. Thea inc: Love's Labour's Lost; She Stoops to Conquer; Hamlet; The Merry Wives of Windsor; Timon of Athens; Toad of Toad Hall; The Queen and the Rebels; The Good Sailor; Cat on a Hot Tin Roof; A Man for All Seasons; Peer Gynt; The Alchemist; Coriolanus.
Films inc: A Man for All Seasons; Ryan's Daughter; Candleshoe; The Blue Lagoon.
TV inc: The House on Garibaldi Street.

Mc KINSEY, Beverlee: Act. b. McAlester, OK, Aug 9. Began on children's show The Make-Believe Playhouse on PBS. Bway inc: Man and Boy; Who's Afraid of Virginia Woolf?; Barefoot in the Park.
TV inc: Another World; Texas.

McKUEN, Rod: Comp-Act-Poet. b. Oakland, CA, Apr 29, 1933. Concert, nitery perf; record prod for Frank Sinatra, Kingston Trio, Petula Clark, others. Film scores inc: Joanna; The Prime of Miss Jean Brodie; Me, Natalie; A Boy Named Charlie Brown; Come to Your Senses; Wildflowers; Lisa, Bright and Dark; The Borrowers; Emily; The Unknown War.
Songs inc: Jean; Love's Been Good To Me; Listen to the Warm; Olly Olly Oxen Free; The Lovers; Joanna; I'll Catch the Sun; The Ever Constant Sea; April People; Forever Young Forever Free; The Winds of Change; If You Go Away; Seasons in the Sun; I'm Not Afraid.
(*Grammy*-spoken word-1968).

Mc LAGLEN, Andrew V: Dir. b. London, Jul 28, 1920. Began career as Asst Dir, 1944. Films inc: Man in the Vault; Gun the Man Down; The Abductors; Freckles; The Little Shepherd of Kingdom Come; McLintock!; Shenandoah; The Rare Breed; Seven Men from Now; The Way West; The Ballad of Josie; Monekys, Go Home; The Devil's Brigade; Bandolero; The Undefeated; Fool's Parade; Something Big; One More Train to Rob; Cahill, United States Marshall; Mitchell; Breakthrough; The Last Hard Men; Ffolkes; The Sea Wolves.
TV inc: Gunsmoke; Have Gun-Will Travel; Perry Mason; Rawhide; The Lineup; The Lieutenant.

Mc LAREN, Norman: Dir. b. Eng, 1914. Specializes in animated shorts. Films inc: Allegro; Dots and Loops; Boogie Doodle; Hoppity Pop; Fiddle-de-dee; Begone Dull Care; Around is Around; Neighbours; Blinkety Blank; Rhythmetic; A Chairy Tale; Blackbird; Parallels; Pas de Deux; Mosaic.

Mc LAUGHLIN, Emily: Act. b. White Plains, NY, Dec 1, 1928. e. Middlebury Coll, BA. Theatre inc: The Frogs of Spring; The Lovers.
TV inc: Studio One; Kraft Theatre; Young Dr. Malone; General Hospital (since April 1963).

Mc LENDON, Gordon Barton: Broadcast Exec-Prod. b. Paris, TX, Jun 8, 1921. e. Yale U, Harvard Law School. Established Liberty Broadcasting System with Baseball's Game of the Day and football Game of the Week. Known as The Old Scotchman since days of sports broadcasting. Owned and operated numerous radio and tv stations. Films prod inc: The Giant Gila Monster; The Killer Shrews; My Dog Buddy.

Mc LERIE, Allyn Ann: Act. b. Grand'Mere, Quebec, Canada, Dec 1, 1926. Films inc: Words and Music; Where's Charley; Desert Song; Battle Cry; The Reivers; They Shoot Horses Don't They; Cowboys; The Way We Were; Cinderella Liberty; All the President's Men.
TV inc: Music for a Summer Night; Shadow of a Gunman; A Tree Grows in Brooklyn; Born Innocent; Death Scream; Sister Terri; Return Engagement; And Baby Makes Six; A Shining Season; Beulah Land; To Find My Son.
Bway inc: One Touch of Venus; On the Town; Finian's Rainbow; Time Limit; West Side Story; South Pacific; My Fair Lady; The Beast in Me; The Mind with the Dirty Man; The Night of the Iguana.

Mc LIAM, John (John Joseph Williams): Act. b. Alberta, Can, Jan 24, 1918. e. St Mary's Coll, BA. Films inc: RPM; Halls of Anger; The Reivers; Cool Hand Luke; My Fair Lady; In Cold Blood; Lucky Lady; The Iceman Cometh; The Missouri Breaks.
Bway inc: Barefoot in Athens; Tiger at the Gates; Desire Under the Elms; St Joan; One More River.

Mc MAHON, Ed: Act. b. Detroit, Mar 6, 1923. e. Boston Coll. Films inc: The Incident; Fun with Dick and Jane.
TV inc: Who Do You Trust; The Tonight Show (since 1962); Fortune Phone; The Missing Links; The Kid From Left Field; The Golden Moment-An Olympic Love Story; The Great American Traffic Jam.

McMAHON, Jenna: Wri. TV inc: Carol Burnett Show (*Emmys*-1974, 1975, 1978); Carol Burnett and Co; Facts of Life (& crea); The Grass Is Always Greener Over the Septic Tank; Flo (& crea).

McMAHON, John J: Exec. b. Chicago, IL, 1932. e. Northwestern U, BA. Began on staff WGN-TV, Chicago; 1952 Ziv-UA TV Prodns; 1958, vp-gm WXYZ-TV, Detroit; 1968, vp-gm WABC-TV, LA; joined NBC 1972 as vp pgms, West Coast; 1974, vp pgm ops; 1978 sr vp pgms & talent; 1979, P Rastar TV.

McNAIR, Barbara: Singer-Act. b. Racine, WI, Mar 4, 1934. Bway inc: The Body Beautiful; No Strings.
Films inc: Spencer's Mountain; Stiletto; Change of Habit; Venus in Furs; They Call Me Mr. Tibbs.
TV inc: The Barbara McNair Show.

McNALLY, Stephen (Horace McNally): Act. b. NYC, Jul 29. e. Fordham, U, LLB. Practiced law for two years before becoming act. Films inc: The Man From Down Under; The Harvey Girls; Johnny Belinda; Rogue's Regiment; Winchester 73; Wyoming Mail; No Way Out; Air Cadet; Apache Drums; Raging Tide; The Lady Pays Off; Devil's Canyon; Make Haste to Live; A Bullet is Waiting; The Man from Bitter Ridge; Panic in the Streets; Tribute to a Bad Man; Once You Kiss a Stranger; Requiem for a Gunfighter. TV inc: Target--The Corruptors.

Mc NALLY, Terrence: Wri. b. St Petersburg, FL, Nov 3, 1939. e. Columbia U, BA. Plays inc: And Things That Go Bump in the Night; Sweet Eros; Witness; Where Has Tommy Flowers Gone; Bad Habits; The Ritz; Broadway, Broadway.

McNEILL, Don: Radio-TV Pers. b. Gelena, IL, Dec 23, 1907 e. Marquette U. Started on radio with WISN, Milwaukee 1928, also worked in Louisville and San Francisco before returning to Chicago to start Breakfast Club on ABC 1933; pgm spanned 36 years of radio, later tv; has made numerous guest appearances, specials for PBS.

Mc NICHOL, James Vincent:

(Jimmy) Act. b. LA, Jul 2, 1961. TV inc: Sunshine; The Fitzpatricks; Champions-A Love Story; The Carpenters-A Christmas Portrait; California Fever; Blinded By the Light.

Mc NICHOL, Kristy: Act. b. LA, Sep 9, 1963. Films inc: Black Sunday; The End; Little Darlings.
TV inc: Fawn Story; Me and Dad's New Wife; The Pinballs; Family (*Emmy*-supp-1977, 1979). Summer of My German Soldier; The Carpenters-A Christmas Portrait; My Old Man; Blinded By the Light.

Mc QUAID, John: Exec. b. Brewarrina, NSW, Australia, Oct 16, 1932. Commissioner, Australian Film Commission. Member Australian Film Institute; member National Film Theatre of Australia.

Mc QUEEN, Butterfly: Act. b. Tampa, FL, 1911. Films inc: Gone With the Wind; Cabin in the Sky; Flame of the Barbary Coast; Mildred Pierce; Duel in the Sun; The Phynx.
TV inc: The Seven Wishes of a Rich Kid (*Emmy*-1980); The Seven Wishes of Joanna Peabody.

Mc QUEEN, Steve: Act. b. Indianapolis, IN, Mar 24, 1930. On screen from 1956 in Somebody Up There Likes Me. Films inc: The Magnificent Seven; The Honeymoon Machine; Hell Is For Heroes; The Great Escape; Love With The Proper Stranger; Soldier in the Rain; The Cincinnati Kid; Nevada Smith; The Sand Pebbles; The Thomas Crown Affair; Bullitt; The Reivers; Le Mans; Junior Bonner; The Getaway; Papillon; The Towering Inferno; Enemy Of The People; Tom Horn (& exec prod); The Hunter.

TV inc: Wanted--Dead or Alive.

(Died Nov 7, 1980).

McWILLIAMS, Caroline: Act. b. Seattle, WA, Apr 4, 1945. e. Carnegie Institute of Tech. Bway inc: The Rothschilds; Cat On a Hot Tin Roof.

TV inc: Guiding Light; Barney Miller; Soap; Benson; Alien Force; Amusement Park.

MEADOWS, Audrey: Act. b. Wu Chang, China, 1924. Sis of Jayne Meadows. Films inc: That Touch of Mink; Take Her She's Mine; Rosie. TV inc: The Honeymooners (*Emmy*-supp-1954).

MEADOWS, Jayne: Act. b. Wu Chang, China, 1926. W of Steve Allen. Films inc: Undercurrent; Dark Delusion; Lady in the Lake; Song of the Thin Man; Luck of the Irish; Enchantment; David and Bathsheba; College Confidential.

TV inc: Danger; Robert Montgomery Presents; I've Got A Secret; What's My Line; Laugh-Back; Sex and the Married Woman; Ten Speed and Brownshoe; The Gossip Columnist; A Funny Thing Happened On the Way to the White House (cable TV).

MEARA, Anne: Act. b. NYC, Sep 20, 1929. W of Jerry Stiller. Films inc: Lovers and Other Strangers; The Out-Of-Towners; Nasty Habits; The Boys From Brazil; Fame.

TV inc: Kate McShane; Take Five; Archie Bunker's Place.

Thea inc: A Month in the Country; Maedchen in Uniform; Ulysses in Nighttown; member Joseph Papp's Shakespeare Co; toured in a comedy act with husband Jerry Stiller.

MEDAVOY, Mike: Exec. b. Shanghai, China, Jan 21, 1941. e. UCLA. Came to US in 1957. Started in mail room at U; became a casting dir; joined GAC, CMA where he was a vp in the motion picture dept. In 1971 joined IFA as vp; involved in packaging The Sting; Young Frankenstein; Jaws before joining UA May 1974 as sr vp in charge of West Coast prod. Resigned 1978, joined other former UA execs in forming Orion Pictures Co of which he is exec vp.

MEDFORD, Don: Dir. TV inc: Kraft Theatre; US Steel Hour; Climax; General Electric Theatre; Dr Kildare; Alfred Hitchcock Presents; The Fugitive; The Man From UNCLE; 12 O'Clock High; The FBI; Baretta; Police Story; Kaz; Coach of the Year.

Films inc: The Hunting Party; The Organization.

MEDFORD, Kay: Act. b. NYC, 1920. Films inc: The War Against Mrs Hadley; Swing Shift Maisie; Adventure; A Face in the Crowd; The Rat Race; Butterfield 8; Two Tickets to Paris; Ensign Pulver; A Fine Madness; Funny Girl; Angel in My Pocket; Twinky; Fire Sale; Windows.

(Died April 10, 1980).

MEDINA, Patricia: Act. b. England, Jul 19, 1921. W of Joseph Cotten. Films inc: Double or Quit; Secret Journey; Kiss The Bride Goodbye: They Met in the Dark; Hotel Reserve; Waltz Time; The Secret Heart; The Three Musketeers; The Fighting O'Flynn; Lady in the Iron Mask; Siren of Baghdad; Lady and the Bandit; Moss Rose; Foxes of Harrow The Black Knight; Pirates of Tripoli; Count Your Blessings; The Killing of Sister George; Stranger at My Door.

MEDOFF, Mark: Plywri. b. Mt Carmel, IL, Mar 18, 1940. e. U of Miami (FL), BA; Stanford, MA. Plays inc: When You Comin' Back, Red Ryder?; The Wager; The Kramer; The Halloween Bandit; The Conversion of Aaron Weiss; Firekeeper; The Last Chance Saloon; Children of A Lesser God (*Tony*-1980). Films inc: When You Comin' Back, Red Ryder?

MEEKER, Ralph (nee Rathgeber): Act. b. Minneapolis, MI, Nov 21, 1921. e. Northwestern U. Films inc: Teresa; Four in a Jeep; The Naked Spur; Jeopardy; Code Two; Kiss Me Deadly; Desert Sands; Paths of Glory; Ada; The Dirty Dozen; The St Valentine's Day Massacre; Gentle Giant; The Detective; The Anderson Tapes; The Happiness Cage; The Food of the Gods; The Alpha Incident; Winter Kills; Without Warning.

TV inc: Lost Flight.

Bway inc: Doughgirls; Strange Fruit; Cyrano de Bergerac; Mr Roberts; A Streetcar Named Desire; Picnic.

MEHTA, Zubin: Cond. b. Bombay, India, Apr 29, 1926. e. State Academy of Music, Vienna. Mus dir Montreal Symphony, 1961-67; Los Angeles Philharmonic 1967-1978; New York Philharmonic 1978; guest conductor Salzburg Festival; Berlin Philharmonic; Metropolitan Opera; Vienna Philharmonic; La Scala.

MEKKA, Eddie: Act. b. Worcester, MA, Jun 14, 1952. Bway inc: Jumper; The Magic Show; The Lieutenant.

TV inc: Laverne and Shirley.

MELATO, Mariangela: Act. b. Milan, Italy, 1938. Films inc: Nada; The Seduction of Mimi; Dear Michael; Love and Anarchy; Swept Away; To Forget Venice; Flash Gordon; The Beach House.

MELCHIOR, Ib Jorgen: Wri-Dir-Prod. b. Copenhagen, Denmark, Sep 17, 1917. e. Stenhus Coll, U of Copenhagen. S of the late Lauritz Melchior. Films inc: (wri) Live Fast, Die Young; When Hell Broke Loose; The Angry Red Planet (& dir); Robinson Crusoe on Mars; Reptilicus; Journey to the Seventh Planet; The Time Travelers (& dir); Ambush Bay; Planet of the Vampires; Death Race 200; The Gingerbread Man (& prod).

TV inc: (wri) Men Into Space; The Outer Limits; (dir) The Perry Como Show; The Eddie Arnold Show; The March of Medicine.

MELLE, Gil: Comp-Cond. b. Jersey City, NJ, Dec 31, 1935. Films inc: The Ultimate Warrior; Starship Invasion; Secret Life of Plants; Embryo; You'll Like My Mother; The Savage Is Loose; The Sentinel; The Andromeda Strain; Borderline.

TV inc: Perilous Voyage; Legend In Granite; Killdozer; Hitchhiker; If Tomorrow Comes; The President's Plane Is Missing; A Cry for Help; Frankenstein-The True Story; That Certain Summer; My Sweet Charlie; Starship Invasions; Colombo; Night Gallery; The Night Stalker; Executive Suite; The Curse of King Tut's Tomb; Rape and Marriage--The Rideout Case.

MELNICK, Dan: Exec. b. NYC, Apr 21, 1934. Joined CBS TV 1954 as staff prod, later exec prod; vp chg prgmg ABC-TV; 1964 partner in Talent Associates; 1972 VP chg wldwde prodn MGM; 1974 sr vp; 1976 left to go into indie prodn; 1977 prodn head Col; 1978 P Columbia Pictures Industry film ops; 1979 retd to indie prodn.

TV inc: Ages of Man (*Emmy*-prod-1966).

Films inc: (exec prod) All That Jazz; Altered States; First Family.

MELVILLE, Sam: Act. b. Utah, Aug 20, 1940. e. Brigham Young U, U of UT. Films inc: Hour of the Gun; The Thomas Crown Affair; Big Wednesday.

TV inc: Terror in the Sky; Lust; City by Night; Roughnecks.

MEMMOLI, George: Act. b. NYC, Aug 3, 1938. Former member of Ace Trucking Company (group). Films inc; Means Streets; Rocky; New York, New York; Phantom of the Paradise.

TV inc: Hello, Larry.

MENDELSON, Lee: Prod-Dir-Wri. b. San Francisco, Mar 24, 1933. e. Stanford U. TV inc: A Man Named Mays; Travels With Charley; Hot Dog; It Couldn't Be Done; Wild Places; The Fabulous Funnies (& dir-wri); exec prod all Charlie Brown features and specials inc A Charlie Brown Christmas (*Emmy*-1966); John Steinbeck's America and the Americans (*Emmy*-1968); You're A Good Sport, Charlie Brown (*Emmy*-1976); Happy Anniversary Charlie Brown (*Emmy*-1976); Happy Birthday Charlie Brown; You're The Greatest Charlie Brown; She's A Good Skate Charlie Brown; The Fantastic Funnies; Life Is A Circus Charlie Brown.

Films inc: Bon Voyage Charlie Brown (And Don't Come Back).

MENDES, Sergio: Mus. b. Nitero, Brazil, Feb 11, 1941. Formed Brasil 65; later with Tijuana Brass; Brasil 77. Albums inc: Vintage 74; So Nice; Paris Tropical; Sergio Mendes.

MENGERS, Sue: Agent. b. NYC. Joined MCA NY 1961 as receptionist, later secy. Became agent 1963 with small agency, joined Creative Management Associates 1965; tsfd to Hwd; remained as exec with International Creative Management when CMA merged with Marvin Josephson.

MENON, Vijaya Bhaskar: Exec. b. Trivandrum, India, May 29, 1934. e. St. Stephens Coll, BA, U of Delhi, MA, U of Oxford. Chmn & chief exec Capitol Records, Inc.; dir EMI Ltd, London; P & CEO Capitol Industries-EMI, Inc.

MENOTTI, Gian Carlo: Comp. b. Caddegliano, Italy, Jul 7, 1911. Operas: Amelia Goes to the Ball; The Telephone; The Medium; The Consul *(Pulitzer Prize-*1950); The Saint of Bleecker Street *(Pulitzer Prize-*1955); Vanessa *(Pulitzer Prize-*1958); The Last Savage. Ballets: Sebastian; The Unicorn, the Gorgon and the Manticore; Errand into the Maze.

MENUHIN, Yehudi: Violinist. b. NYC, Apr 22, 1916. Began playing at age 4; soloist with San Francisco Orchestra at 7; recital at Manhattan Opera House at 8; debut Carnegie Hall at 10 with NY Symphony; soloist with Berlin Symphony at 12; toured Europe and U.S. at 15; debut as cond American Symphony 1966. *(Grammys-*chamber mus-1967; class album of year-1977).

MENZIES, Heather: Act. b. Toronto, Dec 3, 1949. Screen debut, 1965 Sound of Music. Films inc: Hawaii; Sssssssss; Piranha.
TV inc: The Farmer's Daughter; Tail Gunner Joe; Logan's Run.

MERCER, David: Plywri. b. Wakefield, Yorks, England, Jun 27, 1928. Plays inc: The Buried Man; The Governor's Lady (one-act); Ride A Cock Horse; Belcher's Luck; After Haggerty; Flint.
TV inc: Where the Difference Begins; A Suitable Case for Treatment; Let's Murder Vivaldi; On the Eve of Publication; Emma's Time.
Films inc: Morgan (based on A Suitable Case for Treatment); Providence.
(Died Aug 8, 1980).

MERCER, Marian: Act-Singer. b. Akron, OH, Nov 26, 1935. e. U MI, BMus. In stock and on tour before Bway debut Greenwillow (understudy) 1960. Bway inc: Fiorello!; Little Mary Sunshine; New Faces of 1962; Your Own Thing; Promises, Promises *(Tony-*supp-1969); A Place for Polly.
TV inc: Dean Martin Show; Bosoms and Neglect; The Cracker Factory; It's A Living.
Films inc: Oh, God! Book II.

MERCHANT, Ismail: Prod. Films inc: The Creation of Woman (short); The Householder; Shakespeare Wallah; The Guru; The Wild Party; Roseland; Hullabaloo Over Georgie and Bonnie's Pictures; The Europeans; Jane Austen In Manhattan.

MERCHANT, Vivien: Act. b. Manchester, Eng, Jul 22, 1929. Toured with repertory company at age 14. Thea inc: (London) Sigh No More; Sweet Bird of Youth; Mary Stuart, Queen of Scots; Tea Party; Mixed Doubles. (Bway) The Homecoming. Films inc: The Way Ahead; Alfie; Accident; Frenzy; Under Milk Wood; The Homecoming; The Maids.
TV inc: The Protest; The Collection; Weather in the Streets; The Lover; A Month in the Country; Don Juan in Hell.

MERCOURI, Melina: Act. b. Athens, Greece, Apr 18, 1915. Appeared on stage in Athens, Paris. Thea inc: Medea. Screen debut in Stella. Films inc: Never On Sunday; He Who Must Die; The Gypsy and the Gentleman; The Victors; Never on Sunday; Where the Hot Wind Blows; Phaedra; Topkapi; 10:30 pm Summer; A Man Could Get Killed; Gaily, Gaily; Once Is Not Enough; Nasty Habits; Promise At Dawn.

MEREDITH, Burgess: Act-Dir. b. Cleveland, OH, Nov 16, 1908. e. Amherst Coll. On stage from 1929. Bway inc: The Barretts of Wimpole Street; Little Old Boy; She Loves Me Not; The Star Wagon; Winterset; High Tor; The Remarkable Mr Pennypacker; Teahouse of the August Moon; Ulysses in Nighttown (dir); God and Kate Murphy (dir); A Thurber Carnival *(Tony-*special-1960); An Evening with Burgess Meredith; Blues for Mr Charlie (dir); The Latent Homosexual (dir); Love Remembered (dir). Films inc: Winterset; Idiot's Delight; Of Mice and Men; That Uncertain Feeling; Tom, Dick and Harry; The Story of G.I. Joe; Miracles Can Happen; The Diary of a Chambermaid; Magnificent Doll; Mine Own Executioner; The Man of the Eiffel Tower; Joe Butterfly; Advise and Consent; The Cardinal; In Harm's Way; A Big Hand for the Little Lady; Madame X; Batman; Hurry Sundown; Mackenna's Gold; There was a Crooked Man; Such Good Friends; Golden Needles; The Day of the Locust; The Hindenberg; Rocky; The Sentinel; Shenanigans; Foul Play; The Manitou; Magic; Rocky 2; When Time Ran Out; Final Assignment.
TV inc: Search; U.F.O.'s; Johnny We Hardly Knew Ye; Tail Gunner Joe *(Emmy-*supp-1977); SST-Earth Flight; The Last Hurrah; How the West Was Won; The Return of Capt Nemo; Kate Bliss; Puff the Magic Dragon in the Land of the Living Lies (voice); Those Amazing Animals (host).

MEREDITH, Don: Sports Commentator-Act. b. Mt Vernon, TX, Apr 10, 1938. Former pro-football star. TV inc: Monday Night Football *(Emmy-*1971); Undercover With the KKK; The Night the City Screamed.

MERIWETHER, Lee: Act. b. LA, May 27. Former Miss America, 1955. Films inc: 4-D Man; Batman; Namu, the Killer Whale; The Legend of Lylah Clare; The Courtship of Eddie's Father; Angel in My Pocket; The Undefeated.
TV inc: The Clear Horizon; The Young Marrieds; Time Tunnel; The New Andy Griffith Show; Barnaby Jones; Dean Martin's Xmas in California; True Grit; Tourist.

MERKEL, Una: Act. b. Covington, KY, Dec 10, 1903. On screen since 1921 in more than 100 films inc: Eyes of the World; Abraham Lincoln; Command Performance; The White Robe; Love's Old Sweet Song; Daddy Long Legs; Private Lives; Reunion in Vienna; Bombshell; The Maltese Falcon; Day of Reckoning; Merry Widow; Born to Dance; Riffraff; Saratoga; Test Pilot; On Borrowed Time; Road to Zanzibar; Twin Beds; This is the Army; It's A Joke Son; The Bride Goes Wild; Emergency Wedding; My Blue Heaven; Rich, Young and Pretty, Golden Girl; Millionaire for Christy; With A Song in My Heart; The Kentuckian; I Love Melvin; Bundle of Joy; The Mating Game; Summer and Smoke; Summer Magic; A Tiger Walks; Spin-out.
Bway inc: Two By Two; Poor Nut; Pigs; Gossipy Sex; Coquette; Salt Water; The Ponder Heart *(Tony-*supp-1956); Take Me Along.

MERLIS, George: Prod. e. U of PA; Columbia. Began as sports editor Rome (Italy) Daily American; with NY World-Telegram-Sun, World-Journal-Tribune, Daily News before joining ABC pub relations dept; 1973 ABC Evening News; ABC Weekend News; 1975 Good Morning America; 1978, sr. prod; 1979 exec prod.

MERMAN, Ethel (nee Zimmerman): Act. b. NYC, Jan 16, 1909. Started in niteries, vaudeville. On stage in: Girl Crazy; George White's Scandals; Stars in Your Eyes; Du Barry Was A Lady; Panama Hattie; Annie Get Your Gun; Call Me Madam *(Tony-*1951); Happy Hunting; Hello Dolly! *(Special Tony-*1972). Screen debut 1930 Follow the Leader.
Films inc: The Big Broadcast of 1932; Kid Millions; Strike Me Pink; Alexander's Ragtime Band; Call Me Madam; There's No Business Like Show Business; It's a Mad, Mad, Mad, Mad World. *(Grammy-*cast album-1959).

MERRICK, David (nee Margulies): Prod. b. Hong Kong, 1911. Plays inc: Fanny; The Matchmaker; Look Back in Anger; Romanoff and Juliet; The Entertainer; The World of Suzie Wong; La Plume de Ma Tante; Destry Rides Again; Gypsy; A Taste of Honey; Becket (*Tony*-1961; also special award); Irma La Douce; Carnival; Sunday in New York; Subways Are for Sleeping; I Can Get it for you Wholesale; Stop the World, I Want to Get Off; Oliver!; Rattle of a Simple Man; One Flew Over the Cuckoo's Nest; Hello, Dolly (*Tony*-1964); The Milk Train Doesn't Stop Here Anymore; Oh, What a Lovely War!; I Was Dancing; The Roar of the Greasepaint-The Smell of the Crowd; Hot September; Inadmissible Evidence; The Cactus Flower; Marat/Sade; Don't Drink the Water; I Do! I Do!; Keep It In the Family; Rosencrantz and Guildenstern Are Dead; The Seven Descents of Myrtle; Rockefeller and the Red Indians; Promises, Promises; Play It Again Sam; Mack and Mabel; The Misanthrope; Dreyfus in Rehearsal; Very Good Eddie; Travesties; (*Special Tony*-1968); 42nd Street.
Films inc: The Great Gatsby; Semi-Tough; Rough Cut.

MERRILL, Bob: Comp. b. Atlantic City, NJ, May 17, 1920. e. Temple U. Started as nightclub singer, comedian. Bway scores inc: New Girl in Town; Take Me Along; Carnival; Funny Girl; Henry, Sweet Henry.
Films scores inc: The Wonderful World of the Brothers Grimm. Songs inc: How Much is that Doggie in the Window; My Truly, Truly Fair; If I Knew You Were Comin' I'd've Baked a Cake; Take Me Along; Love Makes the World Go Round; I Am Woman; Don't Rain on My Parade.
(*Grammy*-show score-1964).

MERRILL, Dina (Nedinia Hutton): Act. b. NYC, Dec 9, 1925. e. George Washington U, AADA. Films inc: Desk Set; Catch Me If You Can; The Sundowners; The Courtship of Eddie's Father; The Pleasure Seekers; I'll Take Sweden; Running Wild; The Greatest; A Wedding; Just Tell Me What You Want.
Bway inc: My Sister Eileen; Major Barbara; Misalliance; Angel Street. TV inc: The Tenth Month.

MERRILL, Gary: Act. b. Hartford, CT, 1914. e. Bowdoin Coll, Trinity Coll. Films inc: Winged Victory; Slattery's Hurricane; Twelve O'Clock High; All About Eve; Decision Before Dawn; Phone Call From a Stranger; Blueprint for Murder; Bermuda Affair; The Pleasure of His Company; The Woman Who Wouldn't Die; Around the World Under the Sea; Destination Inner Space; The Power; Huckleberry Finn; Thieves. TV inc: The Mask; Justice; Dr Kildare; The Seekers.
Bway inc: Born Yesterday; At War With the Army; Morning's at Seven (rev).

MERRILL, Kieth W: Dir-Wri-Prod. b. May 22, 1940. e. Brigham Young U, BA. Films inc: Matter of Winning; The Great American Cowboy (*Oscar*-doc-1973); Indian; Three Warriors; Take Down; Windwalker.
TV inc: Kenny Rogers and the Cowboys; Mr Kreuger's Christmas.

MERRILL, Robert: Baritone. b. Brooklyn, NY, Jun 4, 1919. Winner Metropolitan Opera Audition of the Air 1945; made opera debut 1945; with NBC 1946; opened Met Opera Season 1950; guest artist Covent Garden; with Toscanini for latter's final opera and recording sessions; with 1973 appearance became first American singer to do 500 performances at Metropolitan Opera.
Bway inc: Fiddler on the Roof.

MERZBACH, Susan K: Exec. b. Amherst, MA, Apr 20, 1946. e. Bucknell. 1972, story analyst MGM; 1978 story ed; 1978 exec story ed Col; 1980 vp crea aff Fox.

METCALFE, Burt: Prod-Dir. b. Saskatchewan, Can, Mar 19, 1935. e. UCLA, BA. TV inc: M*A*S*H, asso prod, 1971-75; co-prod, '76; prod, (& dir) '77-'78; Little House on the Prairie.

MEYER, Nicholas: Wri-Dir. b. NYC. Films inc: The Seven-Per-Cent Solution (sp); Time After Time (sp & dir).

MEYER, Russ: Prod-Dir. b. Oakland, CA, Mar 21, 1922. Films inc: The Immoral Mr Teas: Fanny Hill; Finders Keepers, Lovers Weepers; Lorna; Motorpsycho; Faster Pussycat; Kill, Kill; Goodmorning and Goodbye; Vixen; Beyond the Valley of the Dolls; The Seven Minutes; Blacksnake; Supervixens; Up!; Beneath the Valley of the Ultravixens.

MICHAELS, Joel B: Prod. b. Buffalo, NY. Studied acting with Stella Adler. Films inc: The Peace Killers; Your Three Minutes Are Up (prodn supv); Student Teachers (prodn supv); Lepke (asso prod); The Four Deuces (asso prod); Bittersweet Love; The Silent Partner; The Changeling; Tribute.

MICHAELS, Lorne: Wri-Prod. b. Toronto, Canada, Nov 17. TV inc: Lily (*Emmy*-wri-1974); Laugh-In; Lily Tomlin (*Emmy*-1976-wri); Flip Wilson Special (& prod); NBC's Saturday Night Live (*Emmys*-prod-wri-1976; wri-1977; wri-1978); The Paul Simon Special (*Emmy*-wri-1978); NBC's Saturday Night Live (prod).
Films inc: Gilda Live (prod-wri).

MICHAELS, Richard: Dir. TV inc: Ellery Queen; Love American Style; The Odd Couple; Delvecchio; Bewitched; Charlie Cobb; My Husband Is Missing; Having Babies II; Leave Yesterday Behind; Once Upon A Family; And Your Name Is Jonah; Scared Straight! Another Story; Homeward Bound.

MICHAUD, Henri (Ricky): Exec. b. Ismailia, Egypt, Sep 24, 1912. Joined WB Paris 1934; To Par Int'l 1944; when Par and U formed Cinema International Corp 1970, became co-chmn with Arthur Abeles, also P Par Int'l; 1977, formed, with Abeles, A-M Film Consultants Ltd.

MICHEL, Werner: Exec. b. Germany, Mar 5, 1910. e. U of Berlin; U of Paris. Radio wri prior to WW 2; dir Voice of America Bcast Div 1942-1946; with CBS as prod-dir, pgm dir 1946-1950; dir tv dept Kenyon & Eckhart ad agcy 1950; prod Dumont TV net 1952; prod Benton & Bowles agcy, Proctor & Gamble, NW Ayer before joining ABC-TV Hollywood 1975 as pgm exec; 1976 dir dramatic pgms; 1977 sr vp crea aff MGM-TV; 1979 exec vp Wrather Entertainment Intl; 1980 sr vp pgms MGM-TV.

MICHELET, Michel: Comp. b. Kiev, Russia, Jun 27, 1899. e. Graduate of three conservatories: Leipzig (Germany), St. Petersburg (Russia), Lev (Russia). Scored 108 movies in Paris, Italy, Germany, Spain, US. To US, 1941.
Films inc: Diary of a Chambermaid; Anastasia; The Journey; The Man on the Eiffel Tower; Lured; Outpost in Morocco; Music for Millions; Impact; Voice in the Wind; The Challenge-A Tribute to Modern Art (documentary, narrated by Orson Welles).
Compositions inc: Memories; Hommage to Bach; Concert Songs and Arias; Hanelle.

MICHELL, Keith: Act. b. Adelaide, Australia, Dec 1, 1928. e. Adelaide U. Thea inc: (London) And So to Bed; Troilus and Cressida; Romeo and Juliet; The Lady's Not for Burning; Antony and Cleopatra; Irma La Douce; The Art of Seduction; Abelard and Heloise; Man of La Mancha; On The 20th Century. (Bway) Irma La Douce; The Rehearsal; Man of La Mancha. Hamlet; Dear Love; Tonight We Improvise; Cyrano de Bergerac; The Apple Cart; The Crucifer of Blood.
Films inc: Hell Fire Club; All Night Long; Seven Seas to Calais.
TV inc: Pygmalion; The Mayerling Affair; Traveller Without Luggage; Tiger at the Gates; Catherine Howard (*Emmy*-1972); Ring Around the Moon; The Six Wives of Henry VIII; The Tenth Month; The Day Christ Died; The Treasure of Alpheus T. Winterborn.

MICHENER, James A: Wri. b. NYC, Feb 3, 1907. Works filmed inc: South Pacific; Return to Paradise; The Bridges of Toko Ri; Sayonara; Hawaii.
TV inc: Centennial (narr).

MIDDLETON, Ray: Act. b. Chicago, IL, Feb 8, 1907. e. Juilliard School of Music. Bway inc: Roberta; Annie Get Your Gun; South Pacific; Man of La Mancha.
Films inc: Knickerbocker Holiday; American Jubilee; Lady for a Night; I Dream of Jeannie; Sweethearts on Parade; Road to Denver; 1776.

MIDGLEY, Leslie: Exec. b. Salt Lake City, Jan 18, 1915. H of Betty Furness. TV inc: prod Eyewitness, CBS 1959-1963; prod CBS Evening New with Walter Cronkite 1967-1972; has produced hundreds of documentaries and special report broadcasts including four one-hour reports on Robert Kennedy assassination 1967; The Senate and the Watergate Affair; *(Emmy*-exec prod-1974) resigned CBS news after 24 years to join NBC News as vp special pgms Oct 1979.

MIDGLEY, Robin: Dir. b. Torquay, Eng, Nov 10, 1934. e. King's College, Cambridge. Dir debut The Seagull; London dir debut Kill Two Birds (1961); B'way debut Those That Play The Clowns 1967.
Thea inc: Victor; Picnic on the Battlefield; The Pedagogue (all for Royal Shakespeare Co); Oedipus The King; Right You Are If You Think So; The Professor; Let's Get a Divorce; Rafferty's Chant; Young Churchill; How the Other Half Loves; Lloyd George Knew My Father; Six of One; Cause Celebre; Oliver! (rev); My Fair Lady (rev); Sextet.
TV inc: Royal Shakespeare Co prodn of The Wars of the Roses; The Mayfly and the Frog.

MIDLER, Bette: Act. b. Honolulu, 1945. Recording artist; niteries; TV guest shots. Films inc: The Divine Mr J; The Rose; Divine Madness (doc). Bway inc: Fiddler on the Roof; Bette! Divine Madness (& dir). TV inc: Ol' Red Hair is Back *(Emmy*-1978). *(Grammy*-new artist-1973). *(Special Tony*-1974).

MIFUNE, Toshiro: Act. b. Tsing-tao, China, Apr 1, 1920. Film debut in 1946 These Foolish Times. Films inc: Rashomon; Scandal; The Seven Samurai; Throne of Blood; Rickshaw Man; Red Beard; Midway; Love and Faith; Shag (& prod); Winter Kills; Oginsaga; 1941. TV inc: Shogun.

MIGDEN, Chester L: Exec. b. NYC, May 21, 1921. e. CCNY, BA, Columbia U, LLB. National exec secy, Screen Actors Guild; vp, California Labor Federation; p, Film and Television Coordinating Committee; vp, Associated Actors and Artists of America; vp, International Federation of Actors (FIA); vp, Hollywood Film Council.

MIGHTY CLOUDS OF JOY: Gospel Singers. Group inc: Johnny Martin, Joe Ligon, Elmo Franklin, Richard Wallace, Paul Beasley.
(Grammys-Soul Gospel Performance, traditional-1979, 1980).

MIKHALKOV-KONCHALOVSKY, Andrei: Dir. b. Russia, Aug 20, 1937. Films inc: A Boy and a Pigeon (short) (& sp); The First Teacher; Asya's Happiness; A Nest of the Gentry (& co-sp); Uncle Vanya (& sp); A Lover's Romance; Siberiade.

MILES, Bernard, Sir: Act. b. Hillingdon, Eng, Sep 27, 1907. Films inc: Channel Crossing; Quiet Wedding; In Which We Serve; (& sp-co-dir); Great Expectations; Never Let Me Go; The Man Who Know Too Much; Moby Dick; The Smallest Show on Earth; Tom Thumb; Sapphire; Heavens Above; Run Wild Run Free; The Specialist.
TV inc: Treasure Island; Why Didn't They Ask Evans?
Thea inc: Various Shakespearean roles with Old Vic Company; Lock Up Your Daughters; John Gabriel Borkman; All in Good Time; Schweyk in the Second World War; Treasure Island; The Great Society; On the Rocks; Tawny Pipit.

MILES, Christopher: Dir. b. Eng, 1939. Films inc: Up Jumped a Swagman; The Virgin and the Gypsy; Time for Loving; The Maids; That Lucky Touch.

MILES, Sarah: Act. b. Eng, Dec 31, 1941. e. RADA. Films inc: Term of Trial; The Ceremony; Those Magnificent Men in Their Flying Machines; Blow Up; Ryan's Daughter; Lady Caroline Lamb; The Hireling; The Man Who Loved Cat Dancing; The Sailor Who Fell with Grace from the Sea; The Big Sleep.
TV inc: Great Expectations; Dynasty.
Thea inc: Vivat! Vivat Regina!

MILES, Sylvia: Act. b. 1932. Films inc: Midnight Cowboy; Heat; Farewell My Lovely; 92 in the Shade; The Great Scout and Cathouse Thursday; The Sentinel.

MILES, Vera: Act. b. Boise City, OK, Aug 23, 1930. Screen debut 1952, For Men Only. Films inc: The Wild Country; Hellfighters; It Takes All Kinds; Gentle Giant; The Man Who Shot Liberty Valance; Kona Coast; Run for the Roses.
TV inc: Climax; Ford Theatre; Pepsi Cola Playhouse; And I Alone Survived; Rougnecks.

MILESTONE, Lewis: Dir. b. Russia, Sep 30, 1895. Started as cutter. Later signed by Howard Hughes' Caddo Co. Loaned to UA to dir. Garden of Eden. Films inc: Two Arabian Knights *(Oscar*-comedy dir-1927/28); The Racket; Betrayal; All Quiet on the Western Front *(Oscar*-1929/30); Front Page; Rain; The General Died at Dawn; Of Mice and Men; Report from Russia; Edge of Darkness; North Star; Purple Heart; A Walk in the Sun; Red Pony; Arch of Triumph; No Minor Vices; Les Miserables; Pork Chop Hill; Melba; Ocean's 11; Mutiny on the Bounty (remake).
(Died Sep 25, 1980).

MILFORD, John: Act. b. Johnstown, NY, Sep 7, 1929. e. Union Coll. Films inc: Marty.
TV inc: Wyatt Earp; The Lieutenant; The Legend of Jesse James; The Bold Ones; Enos.

MILFORD, Penelope: Act. b. St Louis, MO. Films inc: Maidstone; Man on a Swing; Valentino; Coming Home.
Bway inc: Lenny; Shenandoah; Seizure-The Story of Kathy Morris; The Oldest Living Graduate.

MILIAN, Tomas: Act. b. Italy, Mar 3, 1938. Films inc: The Fine Night; The Dolphins; A Day of Lions; The Casaroli Gang; Time of Indifference; The Money; Bounty Killer; Run, Man, Run; Face to Face; The Cannibals; Conjugal Love; The Chosen Victims; A Man With Tough Skin; The J and S Gang; Criminal Story of the West; The Last Movie; Antimafia Squad; Luna; Winter Kills; Almost Human; Crime at Porta Romana.
TV inc: The Day Christ Died.

MILIUS, John: Wri-Dir. b. St Louis, MO, Apr 11, 1944. e. LA City College; USC. Films inc: (sp) Devil's 8; Evel Knievel; Dirty Harry; Jeremiah Johnson; The Life and Times of Judge Roy Bean; Magnum Force; Dillinger (& dir); The Wind and the Lion (& dir); Big Wednesday (& dir); Apocalypse Now; Used Cars (exec prod).

MILKIS, Edward K: Prod. b. LA, Jul 16, 1931. e. USC. Started as asst edtr ABC-TV 1952; Disney 1954; MGM 1957; edtr MGM 1960-65; asso prod Star Trek 1966-1969; exec in chg post prodn Par 1969-1972; formed Miller-Milkis Prodns 1972; Miller-Milkis-Boyett, 1979.
TV inc: (exec prod) Happy Days; Laverne and Shirley; Petrocelli; Angie; Out of the Blue; Goodtime Girls; Bosom Buddies (& crea).
Films inc: (co-prod); Silver Streak; Foul Play.

MILLAND, Ray (Reginald Truscott-Jones): Act. b. Neath, Wales, Jan 3, 1908. On screen, England, from 1929, in US, from 1931. Films inc: Ambassador Bill; We're Not Dressing; Charlie Chan in London; Jungle Princess; Ebb Tide; Men with Wings; Beau Geste; The Major and the Minor; Lady in the Dark; Kitty; I Wanted Wings; The Lost Weekend *(Oscar*-1945); Reap the Wild Wind; The Major and the Minor; Golden Earrings; Big Clock; Bugles in the Afternoon; The Thief; Dial M for Murder; Hostile Witness; Love Story; The House in Nightmare Park; Escape to Witch Mountain; Swiss Conspiracy; The Last Tycoon; Slaves; Blackout; Oliver's Story; Battlestar Galactica; Survival Run.
TV inc: Rich Man, Poor Man; Seventh Avenue; Testimony of Two Men; The Darker Side of Terror; The Dream Merchants.

MILLAR, Stuart: Dir. b. NYC, 1929. e. Stanford, Sorbonne, Paris. Wrote, directed documentary films for US State Dept; to Hollywood as asso to William Wyler. Films inc: The Young Stranger; Stage Struck; The Birdman of Alcatraz; The Best Man; Paper Lion; Little Big Man; When Legends Die; Rooster Cogburn.

MILLER, Ann (Lucille Ann Collier): Act. b. Houston, TX, Apr 12, 1923. In vaudeville. Screen debut New Faces of 1937. Films inc: Life of the Party; Stage Door; Room Service; You Can't Take it with You; Eadie Was a Lady; Easter Parade; On the Town; Lovely to Look At; Kiss Me Kate; Deep in My Heart; Hit the Deck; The Opposite Sex; The Great American Pastime.

Bway inc: George White's Scandals; Mame; Sugar Babies.

MILLER, Arthur: Wri. b. NYC, Oct 17, 1915. e. U of MI, BA. Plays inc: All My Sons; *(Special Tony*-1947) Death of a Salesman; *(Pulitzer Prize*-1948-9); The Crucible *(Tony*-1953); A View from the Bridge; After the Fall; Incident at Vichy; The Price; Up for Paradise (& dir-act) Situation Normal; The American Clock.

Film: The Misfits.

TV inc: Death of a Salesman *(Emmy*-1976); Fame; Playing For Time.

MILLER, Burton: Cos dsgn. b. Pittsburgh, PA, Jan 17, 1928. e. Carnegie Tech; Parsons School of Design. Films inc: Counterpoint; Sugarland Express; Earthquake; The Front Page; Roller Coaster; Swashbucker; When You Comin' Back, Red Ryder?; The Omen II; Airport '77; House Calls; The Concorde--Airport '79; The Nude Bomb.

TV inc: Chrysler Theatre; Run For Your Life; It Takes A Thief; Switch; The $6 Million Man; The Immigrants, The Gossip Columnist; Condominium.

MILLER, Cheryl: Act. b. Sherman Oaks, CA, Feb 4, 1943. Appeared in over 100 films as child. Recent films inc: The Monkey's Uncle; Clarence the Cross-Eyed Lion; The Initiation; The Man from Clover Grove; Doctor Death.

MILLER, David: Dir. b. Paterson, NJ, Nov 28, 1909. Films inc: Billy the Kid; Sunday Punch; Flying Tigers; Love Happy; Top o' the Morning; Saturday's Hero; Sudden Fear; Twist of Fate; The Opposite Sex; Happy Anniversary; Midnight Lace; Back Street; Lonely are the Brave; Captain Newman, M.D.; Hammerhead; Hail, Hero; Executive Action; Bittersweet Love.

TV inc: The Best Place To Be; Love for Rent; Goldie and the Boxer.

MILLER, Dick: Act-Wri. b. NYC, Dec 25, 1928. e. CCNY, Columbia U. Films inc: Not of This Earth; Thunder over Hawaii; Rock All Night; Sorority Girl; The Terror; War of the Satellites; The Long Ride Home; St Valentine Day Massacre; Capone; Cannonball; New York, New York; Corvette Summer; I Wanna Hold Your Hand; Piranha; Starhops; The Lady in Red; Rock 'n' Roll High School (sp) TNT Jackson; Which Way to the Front; Four Rode Out.

MILLER, Harvey. Wri-Prod. b. NYC, Jun 15, 1935. e. Emerson College, BS. Began as comedy wri for Dick Gregory; Alan King; Shecky Greene. TV inc: The Odd Couple (&-dir). Films inc: Private Benjamin.

MILLER, Jack: Wri. b. 1935. TV inc: Run for Your Life; Name of the Game; The Deadly Game; Dirty Sally (crea); The Quest (exec story cnsltnt); Gunsmoke (exec story ed) 1971-74.

(Died Jan 12, 1980).

MILLER, Jason: Wri-Act. b. NYC, Apr 22, 1939. e. U of Scranton; Catholic U. Made stage debut as actor, 1969, Pequod; as plywri: That Championship Season *(Tony & Pulitzer Prize*-1973).

Films inc: The Exorcist (act); That Championship Season (sp) The Nickel Ride (act); A Home of Our Own (act); Fitzgerald in Hollywood (act); A Love Story (sp); The Ninth Configuration (act).

TV inc: Vampire (act); Reward (wri); The Henderson Monster (act); Marilyn--The Untold Story.

MILLER, JP: Wri. b. San Antonio, TX, Dec 18, 1919. e. Rice U. Films inc: The Rabbit Trap; Days of Wine and Roses; The Young Savages; Behold a Pale Horse; The People Next Door.

TV inc: Hide and Seek; Old Tassletoot; The Pardon-me Boy; The People Next Door *(Emmy*-1969); Days of Wine and Roses; The Lindbergh Kidnapping Case; Helter Skelter; Gauguin the Savage.

MILLER, Marvin (nee Mueller): Act. b. St Louis, MO, Jul 18, 1913. Films inc: Johnny Angel; Intrigue; Off Limits; Peking Express; The Naked Ape; Where Does It Hurt; I Wonder Who's Killing Her Now; Prime Time.

TV inc: The Millionaire; The FBI (narr); Burrud Nature Specials (nar). Radio: Marvin Miller, Storyteller.

MILLER, Mitch: Mus-Cond. b. Rochester, NY, Jul 4, 1911. e. Eastman School of Music, BA. Oboist with Rochester Philharmonic 1931-1933; Metropolitan Museum of Art concerts 1934; oboe soloist CBS Symphony 1935-1947; also with Saidenburg Little Symphony, Budapest String Quartet; A&R dir Mercury Records 1947-1950; head pop records div Columbia Records 1950-1961; guest cond major symphonies.

TV inc: Sing Along With Mitch.

MILLER, Robert Ellis: Dir. b. NYC, Jul 18, 1932. e. Harvard U. Films inc: Any Wednesday; Sweet November; The Heart Is a Lonely Hunter; The Buttercup Chain; Big Truck and Poor Claire; The Girl from Petrovka; The Baltimore Bullet.

TV inc: The Voice of Charlie Pont; And James Was a Very Small Snail; Ishi, The Last of His Tribe.

MILLER, Roger: Singer-Sngwri. b. Fort Worth, TX, Jan 3, 1936. Song inc: Chug-A-Lug; Dang Me *(Grammys*-(4)-C&W single-C&W vocal-C&W song-new C&W artist-1964); King of the Road *(Grammys*-(5)-contemporary (R&R) single-contemporary voc-C&W single-C&W voc-C&W song-1965); In the Summertime; England Swings; You Can't Rollerskate in a Buffalo Herd; Hey Little Star.

Albums inc: Dang Me/Chug-a-Lug *(Grammy*-C&W album-1964); Return of Roger Miller *(Grammy*-C&W album-1965); Roger Miller's Golden Hits; Roger Miller--Off The Wall.

MILLER, Ronald W: Prod. b. LA, Apr 17, 1933. e. USC. Asso prod. TV series Walt Disney Presents; asso or co-prod 37 one-hour episodes Disney TV; exec prod. Walt Disney's Wonderful World of Color.

Films inc: Bon Voyage; Summer Magic; Son of Flubber; Moon Pilot; The Monkey's Uncle; That Darn Cat; Lt. Robin Crusoe, U.S.N.; Monkeys, Go Home!; Never a Dull Moment; The Boatniks; Wild Country; Now You See Him, Now You Don't; Snowball Express; The Castaway Cowboy; No Deposit, No Return; Gus; Freaky Friday; Herbie Goes to Monte Carlo; The Rescuers; Pete's Dragon; Candleshoe; The Littlest Horse Thieves; The Cat From Outer Space; Hot Lead and Cold Feet; Return From Witch Mountain; The North Avenue Irregulars; The Apple Dumpling Gang Rides Again; Unidentified Flying Oddballs; The Black Hole; Midnight Madness; The Kids Who Knew Too Much; The Watcher in the Woods; The Last Flight of Noah's Ark; Herbie Goes Bananas.

TV inc: Donovan's Kid; The Omega Connection; The Sky Trap; The Secret of Lost Valley.

MILLER, Sidney: Act-Mus-Comp-Dir. b. Shenandoah, PA, Oct 22, 1916. In films as child act, later in vaude, on radio; became dir on Saturday Night Show for NBC; wrote spec material and staged acts for Eddie Albert; George Gobel; Totie Fields; Milton Berle; Red Buttons, others; teamed with Donald O'Connor in nitery act for 9 years.

TV inc: (Dir) Get Smart; Bewitched; Please Don't Eat the Daisies; Broadside; McHale's Navy; Disneyland Anniversary; Celebrity Playhouse; Mouseketeers; Honey West; Tightrope; Saturday Night Revue; What's Happening; Toni Tennille Talk Show (wri); Lucy Moves to NBC (act).

Films inc: (Scores) Chip Off the Old Block; Babes on Swingstreet; Patrick the Great; On Stage, Verybody; Are You With It? (Dir) Get Yourself a College Girl; Secret Bride.

MILLER, Steve: Mus. b. Dallas. Started the Ardells with Boz Scaggs; later with Barry Goldberg in Goldberg-Miller Blues Band.

Recordings inc: Children of the Future; Sailor; Brave New World; Your Saving Grace; Number Five; Rock Love; Recall The Beginning; Fly Like an Eagle; Book of Dreams; Steve Miller Band's Greatest Hits 1974-1978.

MILLS BROTHERS: Singing Act. On radio, in niteries for more than a half century. There are only three now. Originals were Harry, Don, Herb and John Jr, who died in 1968. Began as children on small Ohio radio station in 1925.

Films inc: The Big Broadcast of 1932; Broadway Gondolier; He's My Guy; Reveille With Beverly; Chatterbox. They have recorded more than 1,300 songs inc: Tiger Rag (their first); Dinah; Goodbye Blues (their theme); Paper Doll (their greatest success, 6 million copies); I'll Be Around; You Always Hurt the One You Love.

MILLS, Donna: Act. b. Chicago, IL, Dec 11. TV inc: The Secret Storm; Love Is a Many Splendored Thing; The Good Life; Waikiki; Doctor's Private Lives; Superdome; The Hunted Lady; Woman on the Run; Fire; Curse of the Black Widow; Hanging By a Thread; Knots Landing.

Films inc: The Incident; Play Misty for Me.

MILLS, Hayley: Act. b. London, Apr 18, 1946. D of John Mills. Screen debut 1959, Tiger Bay. Films inc: Pollyana *(Special Oscar-1960)*; The Parent Trap; Whistle Down the Wind; In Search of the Castaways; Summer Magic; The Chalk Garden; The Trouble with Angels; The Family Way; A Matter of Innocence; Take a Girl Like You; Silhouettes; What Changed Charley Farthing; The Diamond Hunters.

MILLS, Sir John: Act. b. Suffolk, Eng, Feb 22, 1908. On screen from 1932. Films inc: The Midshipmaid; Born for Glory; Nine Days a Queen; Goodbye, Mr. Chips; The Young Mr. Pitt; In Which We Serve; The Happy Breed; Great Expectations; The Rocking Horse Winner; The Colditz Story; Hobson's Choice; War and Peace; I Was Monty's Double; Tunes of Glory; The Desert Hawk; The Chalk Garden; Operation Crossbow; King Rat; Africa--Texas Style; Chuka; Ryan's Daughter *(Oscar-supp-1970)*; Young Winston; Lady Caroline Lamb; Oklahoma Crude; The Human Factor; The Big Sleep; The Making of a Lady; 39 Steps (remake); Zulu Dawn; Quatermass Conclusion.

Thea inc: Good Companions; Great Expectations; Separate Tables.

MILLS, Juliet: Act. b. London, Nov 21, 1941. D of John Mills. Stage debut age 14, Alice Through the Looking Glass. On screen as an infant, 1942.

Films inc: So Well Remembered; The History of Mr. Polly; No, My Darling Daughter; Twice Around the Daffodils; Nurse on Wheels; Carry On, Jack; The Rare Breed; Wings of Fire; Oh! What a Lovely War; The Challengers; Avanti!; Riata; Beyond the Door; The Second Power; The Last Melodrama.

TV inc: Mrs. Miniver; The Morning After; QB VII *(Emmy-supp-1975)*; Man of the World; The Cracker Factory.

MILLS, Dr Peter B: Prod-Exec. b. Chicago, May 11, 1936. e. Harvard U. Films inc: The Farmer (exec prod); ofcr of numerous record cos. Medical examiner, DeKalb County, GA.

MILNE, Lennox: Act. b. Scotland, 1910. e. Edinburgh College of Drama, RADA. Founder member Edinburgh Gateway Theatre Company; career devoted mostly to Scottish theatre, except for brief period as BBC prod. On Bway in The Prime of Miss Jean Brodie.

(Died July 2, 1980).

MILNER, Martin: Act. b. Detroit, Dec 26, 1927. e. USC. Films inc: Life with Father; Our Very Own; I Want You; Pete Kelly's Blues; The Sweet Smell of Success; Marjorie Morningstar; Thirteen Ghosts; Sullivan's County; Valley of the Dolls.

TV inc: The Trouble with Father; The Life of Riley; Route 66; Adam 12; The Last Convertible; The Seekers.

MIMIEUX, Yvette: Act. b. LA, Jan 8, 1942. Screen debut 1960 Platinum High School. Films inc: The Time Machine; Light in the Piazza; The Wonderful World of the Brothers Grimm; Diamond Head; Toys in the Attic; The Mercenaries; Skyjacked; The Neptune Factor; Journey Into Fear; Jackson County Jail; The Black Hole.

TV inc: Tyger Tyger; Most Deadly Game; Death Takes a Holiday; Black Noon; Diaster on the Coastline.

Bway inc: I Am a Camera; The Owl and the Pussycat.

MINER, Jan: Act. b. Boston, MA, Oct 15, 1917. Studied with Lee Strasberg. In rep, stock. Bway inc: Obbligato; Viva Madison Avenue; The Decameron; Cricket; The Milk Train Doesn't Stop Here Anymore; The Freaking Out of Stephanie Blake; Othello; Butterflies Are Free; The Women; Saturday, Sunday, Monday; The Heiress.

Films inc: Lenny.

TV inc: Pottsville; Willy and Phil.

MINNELLI, Liza: Act. b. LA, Mar 12, 1946. D of Judy Garland and Vincente Minnelli. Films inc: Charlie Bubbles; Tell Me That You Love Me, Junie Moon; The Sterile Cuckoo; Cabaret *(Oscar-1972)*; A Matter of Time; Lucky Lady; New York, New York.

Bway inc: Flora, The Red Menace *(Tony-1965)*; The Act *(Tony-1978)*; *(Special Tony-1974)*.

TV inc: Liza With a Z *(Emmy-1973)*; Goldie and Liza Together; Baryshnikov On Broadway.

MINNELLI, Vincente: Dir. b. Chicago, Feb 28, 1910. As child toured circuses, carnivals with Minnelli Bros. Served as Art Dir for Radio City Music Hall during 30s. Designed sets, costumes for editions of Ziegfeld Follies and Earl Carroll Vanities. Signed by MGM. 1st directorial film 1943, Cabin in the Sky. Films inc: Brigadoon; An American in Paris; The Cobweb; Kismet; Lust for Life; Designing Woman; The Reluctant Debutante; Gigi *(Oscar-1958)*; Some Came Running; Home from the Hill; Bells Are Ringing; The Four Horsemen of the Apocalypse; Two Weeks in Another Town; The Courtship of Eddie's Father; Goodbye Charlie; The Sandpiper; On a Clear Day You Can See Forever; A Matter of Time.

MINOW, Newton: Exec. b. Milwaukee, WI, Jan 17, 1926. e. Northwestern U, BA, JD. Chmn FCC 1961-1963; chmn Board of Govs PBS, 1979.

MINSKY, Howard G: Prod. Agency exec Wm Morris; p Cinema Consultants. Prod Love Story.

MINTER, Mary Miles: Act. b. 1902. One of the top stars of the silent screen, made approximately 50 films between 1912 and 1923 when she retired. Films inc: The Nurse; Emma of Stork's Nest; Barbara Frietchie; Dimples; Lovely Mary; The Gentle Intruder; Melissa of the Hills; Her Country's Call; The Mate of Sally Ann; A Bit of Jade; The Ghost of Rosy Taylor; A Bachelor's Wife; Anne of Green Gables; Nurse Marjorie; Jenny Be Good; The Little Clown; Moonlight and Honeysuckle; Tillie; The Heart Specialist; South of Suva; The Trail of the Lonesome Pine; The Cowboy and the Lady.

MINTZ, Robert: Prod. b. LA, Jul 7, 1929. e. UCLA BA F. TV inc: (wri) Room 222; Outer Limits; Batman, David Cassidy-Man Under Cover. (co-prod) Feather and Father Gang; Tabitha. (Prod) The French Atlantic Affair.

MIOU-MIOU: Act. b. Paris, Feb 22, 1950. Films inc: La Cavale; Themroc; Quelques Messieurs trop Tranquilles; Les Granges Brulees; Elle court, elle court la banlieue; The Mad Adventures of Rabbi Jacob; Going Places; Tendre Dracula; Pas de Probleme; La Marche Triomphante; F Comme Fairbanks; Love and Cool Water; We've Seen Everything; The Bottom Line; Dites-lui que je l'aime; Les Routes du Sud; La Femme Flic; Jonah, Who Will Be 25 in the Year 2000; La Derobade; Au Revoir. . .a Lundi; L'Ingorgo.

MIRANDA, Isa (Ines Sampietro): Act. b. Milan, Italy Jul 5, 1917. Films inc: Darkness; Everybody's Lady; Red Passport; Hotel Imperial; Adventure in Diamonds; La Ronde; Seven Deadly Sins; Rasputin; We Women; Summertime; The Yellow Rolls Royce; The Great Train Robbery; The Shoes of the Fisherman.

MIRISCH, Marvin E: Exec. b. NYC, Mar 19, 1918. e. CCNY, BA. Print dept, contract dept, asst booker, NY Exchange, head booker, Grand National Pictures, Inc, 1936-40; GM vending concession operation 800 theatres, Midwest Theatres Candy Co, Inc, 1941-52; corporate ofcr in chge, ind prod negotiations, Allied Artists Pictures, 1953-57; ChmnB, CEO in chg of all business affairs, admin & financing, distr liaison, The Mirisch Co, Inc, 1957 to present. P, Mirisch Films Inc; Prod Dracula.

MIRISCH, Walter: Exec. b. NYC, Nov 8, 1921. e. U WI, BA, Harvard Grad. School. Partnered with brother, Marvin, in The Mirisch Corp, formed 1957. Serves as pres, exec prod

Films inc: The Magnificent Seven; Two for the Seasaw; Toys in the Attic; Hawaii; In the Heat of the Night; Midway; Gray Lady Down; Same Time Next Year; Dracula; The Prisoner of Zenda.

Irving Thalberg Award 1977.

MIRREN, Helen: Act. b. England, 1946. Thea inc: (London) Various Shakespearean roles; The Silver Tassie; Bartholomew Fair; Enemies; The Man of Mode; Miss Julie; The Balcony; Teeth 'n' Smiles; The Sea Gull; The Bed Before Yesterday.

Films inc: Age of Consent; Savage Messiah; O! Lucky Man; Hamlet; Caligula; The Long Good Friday; The Fiendish Plot of Dr. Fu Manchu.

TV inc: Miss Julie; The Applecart; The Little Minister.

MISCHER, Donald L: Dir. b. San Antonio, TX, Mar 5, 1941. e. U of TX; BA, MA. TV inc: Great American Dream Machine (& prod) (Emmy-1972); Making Television Dance with Twyla Tharp; Goldie Hawn Special; Kennedy Center Honors; John Denver and the Ladies; The Third Barry Manilow Special; Goldie and Liza Together (& prod); The Barbara Walters Specials; The Donna Summer Special; Cheryl Ladd Special--Souvenirs; Omnibus; The Kennedy Center Honors, 1980.

MISSEL, Renee: Prod. b. Montreal, Canada. e. UCLA; McGill U. Freelance photojournalist; prodn asst New World Pictures; post prodn supv Tomorrow Entertainment; story ed Kings Road Prodns. Films inc: Main Event; Resurrection.

TV inc: The Great American Dream Machine.

MITCHELL, Cameron: Act. b. Dallastown, PA, Nov 4, 1918. Films inc: They Were Expendable; Cass Timberlane; High Barbaree; Command Decision; Homecoming; Some Like It Hot; Slaves; Viva Knievel; Haunts; The Swarm; The Toolbox Murders; Supersonic Man; Silent Scream; Without Warning.

TV inc: High Chaparral; Andersonville Trial; Swiss Family Robinson; Ohms; Wild Times; The Bastard.

Bway inc: The Taming of the Shrew; The November People.

MITCHELL, David: Set Dsgn. Bway inc: Medea; Macbeth; Volpone; Hamlet; The Increased Difficulty of Concentration (& cos); Grin and Bare It; Postcards; Steambath; Trelawny of the "Wells"; Colette; How the Other Half Loves; The Basic Training of Pavlo Hummel; The Incomparable Max; The Cherry Orchard; Barbary Shore; In the Boom Boom Room; Enter a Free Man; Annie (Tony-1977); Working; Barnum (Tony-1980).

MITCHELL, George A: Cin-Inventor. b. TN, 1891. With U.S. Signal Corps as cin; to Hollywood 1911; joined U 1916 in camera service dept, becoming cin following year; invented Mitchell Camera 1920 which became standard for industry for serveral decades, founded Mitchell Camera Co; later desgd portable cameras, eqpt for 70 mm and reflex cameras. Special Oscar 1952 for design and development of Mitchell camera.

(Died April 16, 1980).

MITCHELL, Keith: Act. b. Palm Springs, CA, Jan 13, 1970. Grandson of Jackie Coogan. Started in commercials. TV inc: The Waltons; a Question of Love; Battered; Animal Talk.

MITCHELL, Wayne: Cin-Dir. b. Detroit, Apr 5, 1926. e. USC. TV inc: Holiday USA; Confidential File; Viet Nam.

Films inc: Attack of the Jungle Women; Gangster Story; Surf Monster; Philippine Adventure.

MITCHELL, Yvonne: Act-Wri. b. London, 1925. Thea inc: The Cradle Song; The Seagull; Twelfth Night; Jassy; A Month in the Country; The Flies; The Merchant of Venice; The Taming of the Shrew; Less Than Kind (dir); The Wall; The Oresteia; Ivanov; Horizontal Hold; Out of Order; Children of the Wolf; Electra; Bloomsbury; The Same Sky (wri). Films inc: The Queen of Spades; Turn the Key Softly; The Divided Heart; Woman in a Dressing Gown; Tiger Bay; Sapphire; The Trials of Oscar Wilde; Genghis Khan; The Corpse; The Great Waltz; The Incredible Sarah; Widow's Nest.

MITCHUM, Robert: Act. b. Bridgeport, CT, Aug 6, 1917. On screen from 1943. Films inc: Hopalong Cassidy Series; Gung Ho!; The Story of G.I. Joe; Undercurrent; Till the End of Time; Crossfire; Rachel and the Stranger; Red Pony; Blood on the Moon; Macao; Racket; She Couldn't Say No; River of No Return; Track of the Cat; Night of the Hunter; Heaven Knows, Mr. Allison; Not As a Stranger; The Sundowners; Cape Fear; The Longest Day; Two for the Season; Secret Ceremony; Ryan's Daughter; Farewell My Lovely; Friends of Eddie Coyle; Midway; The Last Tycoon; Amsterdam Kill; The Big Sleep; Breakthrough; Nightkill.

MITGANG, Herbert: Wri. b. NYC, Jan 20, 1920. e. St. John's Law School. With NY Times as copy edtr; reviewer; supv ed Sunday drama section.

Plays inc: Mr. Lincoln.

MOBLEY, Mary Ann: Act. b. Biloxi, MS, Feb 17, 1939. Former Miss America, 1959. Films inc: Girl Happy; Get Yourself a College Girl; Young Dillinger; Harum Scarum; Three on a Couch; For Singles Only; Istanbul Express.

Bway inc: Nowhere to Go but Up.

TV inc: The Lie; Third Annual Circus of the Stars; The Secret of Lost Valley.

MOCKRIDGE, Cyril: Comp. b. England, 1896. Film scores inc: The Sullivans; My Darling Clementine; How to Marry a Millionaire; Guys and Dolls; Many Rivers to Cross; Flaming Star.

(Died Jan 18, 1979).

MOFFAT, Donald: Act-Dir. b. Plymouth, England, Dec 26, 1930. e. RADA. London stage debut 1954; Macbeth. Films inc: Pursuit of the Graf Spee; Rachel, Rachel; The Great Northfield Minnesota Raid; Showdown; The Trial of the Catonsville Nine; Earthquake; The Terminal Man; Winter Kills; Promises in the Dark; On The Nickel; Health; Popeye.

Bway inc: Under Milk Wood; A Passage to India; The Affair; Much Ado About Nothing; The Tumbler; The Hostage; The Wild Duck; Right You Are (If You Think You Are); Forget-Me-Not Lane; Cock-A-Doodle Dandy (dir); Father's Day (dir).

TV inc: The Snoop Sisters; The New Land; The Word; The Gift of Love; Logan's Run; Mrs. R's Daughter; The Long Days of Summer.

MOFFIT, John C: Dir. TV inc: Andy Williams Show; Perry Como Show; New Year's Rockin' Eve; Good Vibrations from Central Park; 4 AM Music Awards; 28th annual Emmy Awards (Emmy-1977); Lily Tomlin's 4th Special; Van Dyke and Company; Dick Clark's Live Wednesday; Circus Festival of Monte Carlo (& prod); Ringling Bros. Circus Highlights (& prod); Low Moan Spectacular (& prod); Helen Reddy Special; 31st annual Emmy Awards (& prod).

MOGULL, Artie: Exec. b. NYC, Mar 26, 1927. e. Columbia U, BA. Partner, Tetragrammaton Records, 1966-68; vp Capitol 1970; vp MCA (1972-74); ownr, Signpost Records, 1974; United Artists Records, 1976-77; bought UA Records 1978, co-ownr & co-chmn with Jerry Rubinstein of UA Records.

MOHLA, J G: Prod. b. India, Nov 26, 1909. e. U of Lahore. Films inc: Insaan; Ehsaan; Senapati; Adarsh; Yogeshwar Krishna.

MOHYEDDIN, Zia Act. b. Lyallpur, Pakistan, Jun 20, 1933. e. Punjab U, RADA. Thea inc: A Passage to India; The Alchemist; Volpone; The Guide; The Merchant of Venice; On the Rocks.

Films inc: Lawrence of Arabia; Sammy Going South; The Sailor From Gibraltar; Ashanti.

TV inc: Death of a Princess.

MOISEIWITSCH, Tanya, CBE: Dsgn. b. London, England, Dec 3, 1914. Thea inc: More than 50 prodns at Abbey Theatre Dublin. (London) The Golden Cuckoo; Uncle Vanya; The Critic; Cyrano de Bergerac; The Time of Your Life; The Beggar's Opera (Sadlers Wells); The Cherry Orchard; A Month in the Country; Passing Day; Figure of Fun; Othello (Royal Shakespeare prodn); The Deep Blue Sea; Two Gentlemen of Verona; Wrong Side of the Park; Ondine; The Alchemist; Volpone; Phaedra Brittanica; in US des several prodns for Tyrone Guthrie Theatre, Minneapolis; The Misanthrope (Bway).

MOLINARO, Al: Act. b. Kenosha, WI, Jun 24, 1919. Started as guitarist in four-piece combo; became local tv producer in LA, before act.

TV inc: Get Smart; The Odd Couple; Happy Days; Anson and Lorrie; The Ugily Family; The Great American Traffic Jam.

MOLINARO, Edouard: Dir-Wri. b. Bordeaux, France, May 13, 1928. Started out making short documentaries. Films inc: Back to the Wall; Des Femmes Disparaissent; A Mistress for the Summer; The Passion of Slow Fire; A Touch Of Treason; The Seven Deadly Sins; Arsene Lupin against Arsene Lupin; The Warm Blooded Spy; Male Hunt; Quand Passent Les Faisans; Peau D'Espion; Oscar; Hibernatus; Mon Oncle Benjamin; Les Aveux Les Plus Doux; Le Gang des Otages; The Pain in the Ass; L'Ironie du sort; The Pink Telephone; Dracula, Father & Son; L'Homme Presse; La Cage Aux Folles; Sunday Lovers; La Cage Aux Folles II.

MONASH, Paul: Prod-Wri. b. NYC, Jun 14, 1917. e. U of WI, BA, Columbia U, MA. Started as TV script wri. Authored two-part teleplay which launched The Untouchables.

Films inc: Butch Cassidy and the Sundance Kid (exec prod); Slaughter House Five (prod); The Friends of Eddie Coyle (prod & sp); Front Page (prod); Carrie (prod).

TV inc: The Lonely Wizard (wri) *(Emmy*-1957); Cain's Hundred (prod); Peyton Place (prod); Judd for the Defense (prod); All Quiet on the Western Front (wri); Salem's Lot (wri).

MONICELLI, Mario: Dir. b. Rome, May 15, 1915. Films inc: Big Deal on Madonna Street; The Great War; Tears of Joy; Boccaccio; The Organizer; Casanova; Girl With a Pistol; Amici Mie; Viva Italia!; Travels With Anita.

MONKEES, THE: Novelty quartet popular in the 60's. Members were Peter Tork (nee Torkelson); Mike Nesmith; Micky Dolenz; Davy Jones. Films inc: Head.

TV inc: The Monkees.

MONKHOUSE, Bob: Act. b. Beckenham, Kent, Eng, Jun 1, 1928. e. Dulwich Coll. Started with BBC 1949 on Works Wonders radio show; first tv series 1953 Monkhouse, Fast & Loose.

TV inc: Bob Monkhouse Comedy Hour; The Golden Shot (8 yrs); What's My Line (Brit vers); Celebrity Squares (Brit vers: since 1974); Candid Camera (Brit vers) I'm Bob, He's Dickie; Mad Movies; Family Fortunes.

Films inc: Carry On Sergeant; Dentist in the Chair; Weekend with Lulu; She'll Have to Go; The Bliss of Mrs. Blossom.

Thea inc: Start Time with Bob; Aladdin; Boy from Syracuse; Come Blow Your Horn;

MONTAGNE, Edward J: Prod-Dir. b. NYC. e. Loyola Coll, Notre Dame. Films inc: McHale's Navy Joins the Air Force; The Ghost and Mr Chicken; The Reluctant Astronaut; Shakiest Gun in the West; P J; Travelling Saleslady; Angel in my Pocket; How to Frame a Fig; They Went Thataway & Thataway.

TV inc: Man Against Crime; You'll Never Get Rich; McHale's Navy; Hurricane; Terror on the 40th Floor; Francis Gary Powers; Million Dollar Rip Off; Spider Man; Crash; Quincy; Delta House; High Noon Part II--The Return of Will Kane.

MONTALBAN, Ricardo: Act. b. Mexico City, Nov 25, 1920. Attended school in US before returning to Mexico to make 13 Spanish-language films. US screen debut, 1947, Fiesta. Films inc: The Kissing Bandit; Border Incident; My Man and I; Sombrero; Latin Lovers; A Life in the Balance; Sayonara; The Money Trap; Madame X; Sol Madrid; The Singing Nun; Blue; Sweet Charity; The Train Robbers; Return to the Planet of the Apes; TV inc: Desperate Mission; Captains Courageous; Fantasy Island; How the West Was Won Part 2 *(Emmy*-1978).

Bway inc: Her Cardboard Lover; The King and I; Don Juan In Hell.

MONTANA, Montie (Owen Harlan Mickel): Act. b. Wolf Point, MT, 1910. On screen from 1930 in many Tom Mix and Buck Jones westerns. Films inc: Circle of Death; Riders of the Deadline; Down Dakota Way; Arizona Bushwackers.

MONTAND, Yves (Yvo Livi): Act. b. Monsumano, Italy, Oct 13, 1921. H of Simone Signoret. Singer niteries, music halls. On screen since 1946 in: Star Without Light; Where the Hot Wind Blows; My Geisha; The Sleeping Car Murder; Is Paris Burning?; Grand Prix; Live For Life; Z; On a Clear Day You Can See Forever; The Confession; State of Siege; Gates of the Night; The Wages of Fear; Witches of Salem; Let's Make Love; Vincent, Francois, Paul and the Others; Lovers Like Us; The Menace; Police Phython 357; The Big Operator; Les Routes De Sud; Claire De Femme; I Comme Icarus.

MONTANUS, Edward A: Exec. b. 1931. e. OH State. Started as slsmn NBC Films 1952; mgr central div sls ABC 1962; to MGM 1964; sr vp 1973; exec vp 1976; p MGM-TV 1977; resd 1980 to enter indie prodn.

MONTGOMERY, Belinda: Act. b. Winnipeg, Manitoba, Canada, Jul 23. Films inc: The Other Side of the Mountain; The Other Side of the Mountain, Part II; Blackout; Stone Cold Dead.

TV inc: The Man from Atlantis; Murder in the Music City; Marciano; Turnover Smith; Trouble In High Timber Country.

MONTGOMERY, Elizabeth: Act. b. LA, Apr 15, 1933. D of Robert Montgomery. Films inc: The Court Martial of Billy Mitchell; Johnny Cool; Who's Been Sleeping in My Bed?

TV inc: Bewitched; Jennifer-A Woman's Story; Act of Violence; The Legend of Lizzie Borden. Belle Starr.

MONTGOMERY, Ralph: Act. b. Ohio, Jul 4, 1911. Films inc: Willy Dynamite; How to Frame a Figg; Which Way to the Front; The Day the President's Plane Was Missing; Terminal Man; Watermelon Man; Soylent Green; Hello Dolly; Hustle; Which Way Is Up.

TV inc: Sam Houston; Woman of the Year; Helter Skelter; Ziegfeld, the Man and His Woman.

MONTGOMERY, Robert (Henry Montgomery, Jr): Act-Dir-Prod. b. Beacon, NY, May 21, 1904. Consultant to Pres Dwight Eisenhower on radio-TV 1952-60.

Films inc: Sins of the Children; Big House; When Ladies Meet; Private Lives; Petticoat Fever; Cat and the Canary; Night Must Fall; Here Comes Mr. Jordan; They Were Expendable; The Saxon Charm; Lady in the Lake; Eye Witness; Ride the Pink Horse; Once More, My Darling; The Gallant Hours.

Bway inc: Dawn Mack; One of the Family; The Desperate Hours *(Tony*-dir-1955);

MONTY PYTHON'S FLYING CIRCUS: Group of British comedians who performed for BBC during the 60's and 70's. Now seen in the US. Regular cast inc: Eric Chapman. John Cleese, Terry Gilliam, Eric Idle, Terry Jones and Michael Palin.

MOODY, Ron (nee Moodnick): Act. b. London, Jan 8, 1924. e. London U. Thea inc: (London) Intimacy at Eight; For Amusement Only; For Adults Only; Candide; Oliver! (& wri-comp); Joey; Peter Pan; The Clandestine Marriage; Saturnalia (& dir-wri-comp); Move Along Sideways. (Bway) Candide; Oliver!.

Films inc: Davy; Summer Holiday; Mouse on the Moon; Ladies Who Do; Murder Most Foul; The Sandwich Man; Oliver!; David Copperfield; Twelve Chairs; Flight of the Doves; Dominique; Legend of the Werewolf; Unidentified Flying Oddballs.

TV inc: I Want to Go Home; Who's a Good Boy, Then; The Word; Benji's Very Own Christmas.

MOONJEAN, Hank: Prod. b. Evanston, IL, Jan 19, 1935. e. USC. Films inc: Child's Play; The Great Gatsby; The Fortune; The End; Beauty and the Beast; Hooper; Smokey and The Bandit II.

MOORATOFF, George Walter: Exec. b. Shanghai, China, Sep 14, 1933. M dir Par Pictures (Australia) P/L.

MOORE, Clayton: Act. b. 1908. Best known for TV role: The Lone Ranger. Films inc: Kit Carson; Black Dakotas; The Cowboy and the Indians; Along the Oregon Trail; Night Stage to Galveston; Montana Territory; Down Laredo Way.

MOORE, Colleen: Act. b. Port Huron, MI, Aug, 19 1900. On screen from 1917 to 1934. Films inc: Bad Boy; An Old Fashioned Young Man; A Hoosier Romance; The Busher; The Wall Flower; Flaming Youth; The Perfect Flapper; Irene; Ella Cinders; Twinkletoes; The Power and the Glory; The Scarlet Letter.

MOORE, Constance: Act. b. Sioux City, IA, Jan 18, 1920. On screen since 1938. Films inc: A Letter of Introduction; The Crime of Dr. Hallet; You Can't Cheat an Honest Man; Charlie McCarthy, Detective; Framed; I Wanted Wings; Take a Letter, Darling; Earl Carroll's Sketch Book; Hit Parade of 1947.
 Bway inc: The Boys From Syracuse; By Jupiter.

MOORE, Dickie: Act. b. LA, Sep 12, 1925. First screen appearance 1926 at 11 mos old in The Beloved Rogue. Films inc: Oliver Twist; Peter Ibbetson; Dangerous Years; Out of the Past; Eight Iron Men; Member of the Wedding.

MOORE, Dudley: Act-Comp. b. London, Apr 19, 1935. e. Oxford. H of Tuesday Weld. Thea inc: Beyond the Fringe; Play It Again, Sam; Serjeant Musgrave's Dance (comp music); The Caucasian Chalk Circle (comp music); Good Evening (*Grammy*-spoken word-1974); (*Special Tony Awards*-1969 & 1974).
 Film inc: The Wrong Box; Bedazzled; Thirty Is a Dangerous Age; Cynthia; The Bed-Sitting Room; Alice in Wonderland; Foul Play; The Hound of the Baskervilles; 10; Wholly Moses!

MOORE, Garry (Thomas Garrison Morfit): Act. b. Baltimore, MD, Jan 31, 1915. On radio as announcer, sports commentator, comedian, writer. Teamed with Jimmy Durante on radio to 1947. MC Take It or Leave It; Breakfast in Hollywood.
 TV inc: Garry Moore Show; I've Got a Secret; To Tell the Truth.

MOORE, Juanita: Act. b. 1922. Films inc: Lydia Bailey; Witness to Murder; Ransome; The Girl Can't Help It; Imitation of Life; Walk on the Wild Side; The Singing Nun; Rosie; Fox Style.

MOORE, Kevan: Exec. b. Bradford, Eng, Dec 29, 1937. Pgm controller, South Pacific Television, New Zealand.

MOORE, Mary Tyler: Act. b. NYC, Dec 29, 1936. Films inc: X15; Thoroughly Modern Millie; What's So Bad About Feeling Good?; Don't Just Stand There; Change of Habit; Ordinary People.
 TV inc: Richard Diamond; Steve Canyon; The Dick Van Dyke Show (*Emmys*-1964 & 1966); The Mary Tyler Moore Show (*Emmys*-1973, 1974, 1976 and actress of year-1974). Run a Crooked Mile; How To Survive The 70's and Maybe Even Bump Into Happiness; First You Cry; The Mary Tyler Moore Hour.
 Bway inc: Whose Life Is It Anyway (*Special Tony*-1980).

MOORE, Melba: Singer-Act. b. NYC, Oct 29, 1945. Rec artist; niteries. Bway inc: Hair; Purlie (*Tony*-supp-1970); Timbuktu.
 Films inc: Pigeons; Cotton Comes to Harlem; Hair.
 TV inc: The Melba Moore-Clifton Davis Show; The Beatrice Arthur Special; Flamingo Road.

MOORE, Richard: Cin-Dir. b. Jacksonville, IL, Oct 4, 1925. e. Westminster College; USC. Films inc: (as cin) The Wild Angels; Wild in the Streets; The Scalphunters; Winning; The Rievers; WUSA; Myra Breckinridge; Sometimes a Great Notion; The Life and Times of Judge Roy Bean; The Stonekillers. (As dir) The Circle of Iron.

MOORE, Robert: Act-Dir. b. Detroit, Aug 17, 1927. e. Catholic U of America. First appeared on stage under name of Brennan Moore, 1948, in Jenny Kissed Me. Plays inc: (dir) The Boys in the Band; Promises, Promises; Last of the Red Hot Lovers; The Gingerbread Lady; Lorelei; My Fat Friend; Deathtrap; They're Playing Our Song.
 Films inc: (act) Tell Me That You Love Me, Junie Moon; (dir) Murder by Death; The Cheap Detective; Chapter Two.

MOORE, Roger: Act. b. London, Oct 14, 1927. e. RADA. Films inc: Last Time I Saw Paris; Interrupted Melody; King's Thief; Rachel Cade; Caesar and Cleopatra; Trottie True; Live and Let Die; Gold; The Man With the Golden Gun; The Lucky Touch; Street People; Shout at the Devil; Sherlock Holmes in New York; The Spy Who Loved Me; The Wild Geese; Escape to Athena; Ffolkes; The Sea Wolves; Sunday Lovers.
 TV inc: The Persuaders; The Saint; Maverick; Ivanhoe.

MOORE, Terry (Helen Koford): Act. b. LA, Jan 1, 1929. Photographer's model as a child; on radio; Pasadena Playhouse. On screen under four different names. As child in: The Howards of Virginia (as Helen Koford); My Gal Sal; Gaslight; Son of Lassie; Sweet and Low Down (as Judy Ford); The Devil on Wheels (as Jan Ford); The Return of October (The first as Terry Moore). Other films inc: Mighty Joe Young; The Barefoot Mailman; Man on a Tightrope; Beneath the 12-Mile Reef; King of the Khyber Rifles; Daddy Long Legs; Peyton Place; A Private Affair; Waco; A Man Called Dagger.

MOORE, Thomas W: Prod-Exec. Former adv mgr, entered tv as account exec CBS-TV film sales; 1965 Gen sls mgr CBS-TV film sales; 1958, vp chg pgmg & talent; 1962 P ABC-TV net; 1968, bd chmn Ticketron; 1971 P Tomorrow Entertainment.
 TV inc: (exec prod) The Body Human (*Emmy*-1978); I Know Why The Caged Bird Sings; The Body Human--The Sexes; Lifeline (*Emmy*-1979); Roll of Thunder, Hear My Cry; The Body Human--The Magic Sense (*Emmy*-1980); White Mama; The Body Human--The Body Beautiful; Damien. . .The Leper Priest; The Body Human--The Sexes II; Gnomes; The Body Human--The Facts For Boys.

MORAHAN, Christopher: Dir. b. London, Jul 9, 1929. Thea inc: Little Murders; This Story of Yours; The Caretaker; State of Revolution; Brand.
 Films inc: Diamonds for Breakfast; All Neat in Black Stockings; Fruits of Enlightment; Sisterly Feelings.
 TV inc: Talking to a Stranger; Uncle Vanya; The Gorge.

MORAN, Erin: Act. b. Burbank, CA, Oct 18, 1961. Films inc: How Sweet It Is; 80 Steps to Jonah; Watermelon Man.
 TV inc: Stanley vs. the System; Daktari; Don Rickles Show; Mirror, Mirror; Lisa, Bright and Dark; Happy Days; Greatest Heroes of the Bible; Sweepstakes.

MORAN, Lois: Act. b. Pittsburgh, PA, 1907. Raised and educated in France where she entered films with a French firm while dancing in the ballet of the Paris Grand Opera Company. Returned to the US to star in Stella Dallas. Films inc: Just Suppose; The Road To Mandalay; The Music Master; Sharp Shooters; Prince of Sinners; Behind That Curtain; Love Hungry; The River Pirate; The Dancers; Transatlantic; The Spider; The Men in Her Life; West of Broadway.
 Bway inc: Of Thee I Sing,
 TV inc: Waterfront.

MORE, Kenneth: Act. b. Gerrards Cross, Eng, Sep 20, 1914. Films inc: Look Up and Laugh; Windmill Revels; Carry on London; Man on the Run; The Franchise Affair; Appointment with Venus; Brandy for the Parson; Never Let Me Go; Genevieve; Our Girl Friday; Doctor in the House; Deep Blue Sea; Reach for the Sky; The Sheriff of Fractured Jaw; Sink the Bismarck; The Longest Day; The Mercenaries; Oh What a Lovely War; Battle of Britain; Scrooge; The Slipper and the Rose; Unidentified Flying Oddballs.
 TV inc: Father Brown; An Englishman's Castle; The Forsyte Saga.
 Thea inc: The Deep Blue Sea; And No Birds Sing; The Angry Deep (prod-dir); Our Man Crichton; The Secretary Bird; The Winslow Boy; Signs of the Times; On Approval.

MOREAU, Jeanne: Act. b. Paris, Jan 23, 1928. Films inc: The She Wolves; The Lovers; Les Liaisons Dangereuses; La Notte; Jules et Jim; Eva; The Trial; The Victors; Diary of a Chambermaid; The Yellow Rolls-Royce; The Train; Mata Hari; Viva Maria; Chimes at Midnight; Sailor from Gibraltar; The Bride Wore Black; Great Catherine; Monte Walsh; Alex in Wonderland; Louise; Mr Klein; The Last Tycoon; Lumiere (& dir-sp); L'Adolescente (dir-sp).

MORECAMBE, Eric (John Eric Bartholomew, OBE): Comedian. b. England, May 14, 1926. Teamed with Ernie Wise beginning 1941. On radio, tv with Morecambe and Wise Shows. Films inc: The Intelligence Man; That Riviera Touch; The Magnificent Two.

MORENO, Rita (Rosa Dolores Alvario): Act. b. Humacao, Puerto Rico, Dec 11, 1931. Films inc: Pagan Love Song; Singin' in the Rain; Garden of Evil; The Vagabond King; The King and I; West Side Story *(Oscar-*supp-1961); The Night of the Following Day; Popi; Carnal Knowledge; The Ritz; Happy Birthday, Gemini.

Bway inc: The Sign in Sidney Brustein's Window; Gantry; Last of the Red Hot Lovers; Detective Story; The National Health; The Ritz *(Tony*-supp-1975); She Loves Me.

TV inc: The Muppet Show *(Emmy*-1977); Rockford Files *(Emmy*-1978); Anatomy of a Seduction.

(Grammy-childrens rec-1972).

MORGAN, Dennis (nee Stanley Morner): Act. b. Prentice, WI, Dec 10, 1910. e. Carroll Coll. Films inc: Suzy; The Great Ziegfeld; Kitty Foyle; Captains of the Clouds; Thank Your Lucky Stars; Two Guys from Texas; My Wild Irish Rose; Painting the Clouds with Sunshine; The Gun that Won the West; Uranium Boom; Rogues' Gallery.

TV inc: Beacon Street.

MORGAN, Harry (also billed as Henry Morgan) (nee Bratsburg): Act. b. Detroit, Apr 10, 1915. Screen debut, 1942, The Omaha Trail. Films inc: To the Shores of Tripoli; Crash Dive; Wing and a Prayer; A Bell for Adano; State Fair; Dragonwyck; All My Sons; The Saxon Charm; Madame Bovary; High Noon; What Price Glory?; Not as a Stranger; The Teahouse of the August Moon; Inherit the Wind; How the West Was Won; John Goldfarb, Please Come Home; The Flim Flam Man; Charlie and the Angel; Support Your Local Sheriff; Viva Max; Snowball Express; The Apple Dumpling Gang; The Barefoot Executive; The Shootist; The Cat From Outer Space; The Apple Dumpling Gang Rides Again.

TV inc: December Bride; Pete and Gladys; The Richard Boone Show; Oh, Those Bells; Dragnet; The D.A.; Hec Ramsey; M*A*S*H *(Emmy*-supp-1980); Backstairs at the White House; The Wild Wild West Revisited; The Bastard; Better Late Than Never; Scout's Honor; More Wild Wild West.

MORGAN, Jaye P: Singer. b. Mancos, CO, Dec 3, 1931. With Frank De Vol Orch 1950-53 then solo. Recordings inc: That's All I Want From You; Life Is Just a Bowl of Cherries; The Longest Walk.

Films inc: The Gong Show Movie.

MORGAN, Michele (Simone Roussel): Act. b. Paris, Feb 29, 1920. First Amer film 1942, Joan of Paris. Films inc: Higher and Higher; Passage to Marseilles; The Fallen Idol; The Seven Deadly Sins; The Mirror Has Two Faces; Landru; Lost Command; Benjamin; Cat and Mouse.

MORIARTY, Michael: Act. b. Detroit, 1942. e. Dartmouth, London Academy of Mus and Dramatic Art. Films inc: Glory Boy; Hickey & Boggs; Shoot It; Bang the Drum Slowly; The Last Detail; Report to the Commissioner; The Dog Soldiers; Shoot It: Black Shoot It; Blue!. TV inc: The Glass Menagerie *(Emmys*-supp and supp act of year-1974); Girls of Summer; The Deadliest Season; Holocaust *(Emmy*-1978); The Winds of Kitty Hawk; Too Far To Go.

Bway inc: Find Your Way Home *(Tony*-1974); Richard III; G R Point.

MORIN, Alberto (Salvador R Lopez): Act-Dial Coach. b. Puerto Rico, Nov 26, 1902. Films inc: Wings of the Navy; Gone with the Wind; The Desert Song; House of Strangers; The Gunfighter; Tripoli; Lydia Bailey; Rio Grande; My Sister Eileen; Will Success Spoil Rock Hunter?; Two Mules for Sister Sara; The Cheyenne Social Club; Chisum; The Mephisto Waltz.

TV inc: The Wild, Wild West Revisited.

MORISON, Patricia: Act. b. NYC, 1915. Films inc: Persons in Hiding; I'm from Missouri; Untamed; One Night in Lisbon; A Night in New Orleans; Beyond the Blue Horizon; Are Husbands Necessary; Silver Skates; Hitler's Madman; The Fallen Sparrow; The Song of Bernadette; Lady on a Train; Dressed to Kill; Queen of the Amazons; Tarzan and the Huntress; Son of the Thin Man; Walls of Jericho; The Return of Wildfire; Sofia; Song without End.

MORITZ, Milton I: Exec. b. Pittsburgh, PA, Apr 27, 1933. Owned and operated theatres in in LA from 1953-55; U.S. Navy 1955-1957; joined AIP 1957 as asst gen sls mgr; 1958 nat'l pub-ad dir; 1967, vp & bd member; 1975, sr vp; 1980 resigned to form own mdsng & cnsltng firm.

MORLEY, Karen (Mildred Linton): Act. b. Ottumwa, IA, 1905. Films inc: Inspiration; Scarface; Dinner at Eight; Our Daily Bread; Beloved Enemy; Kentucky; Pride and Prejudice; Jealousy; 13th Hour; The Unknown; 'M'.

MORLEY, Robert: Act-Wri. b. Wiltshire, Eng, May 26, 1908. e. RADA. Films inc: Marie Antoinette; Major Barbara; The Young Mr Pitt; African Queen; Edward My Son; Melba; Gilbert and Sullivan; Beat the Devil; Around the World in 80 Days; The Doctor's Dilemma; The Journey; Oscar Wilde; Nine Hours to Rama; Murder at the Gallop; Those Magnificent Men in their Flying Machines; Topkapi; The Alphabet Murders; Genghis Khan; A Study in Terror; Hotel Paradiso; Way, Way, Out; The Trygon Factor; When Eight Bells Toll, Theatre of Blood; Song of Norway; The Blue Bird; Hugo the Hippo (voice only); Who Is Killing The Great Chefs of Europe; The Human Factor; Scavenger Hunt; Oh Heavenly Dog.

Thea inc: Pygmalion; Edward My Son (co-author & perf).

TV inc: Call My Bluff.

MOROSS, Jerome: Comp. b. NYC, Aug 1, 1913. e. NYU, BS, Juilliard. Film scores inc: Hans Christian Andersen; The Big Country; Seven Wonders of the World; The Cardinal; The War Lord. TV inc: Wagon Train; Lancer; Gunsmoke; Have Gun Will Travel.

Thea inc: Parade; Ballet Ballads; The Golden Apple; Gentlemen, Be Seated.

Songs inc: You Ain't So Hot; I've Got Me; Yellow Flower; Lazy Afternoon; My Rebel Heart; Stay With Me.

MORRICONE, Ennio: Comp-Arr. b. Rome, 1928. Films inc: A Fistful of Dollars; El Greco; Fists in the Pocket; The Good, the Bad, and the Ugly; The Big Gundown; Matchless; Theorem; Once Upon a Time in the West; Investigation of a Citizen; Fraulein Doktor; Cat O'Nine Tails; The Decameron; The Burglars; The Black Belly of the Tarantula; Bluebeard; The Serpent; Down the Ancient Stairs; Divine Creature; Desert of the Tartars; Exorcist II-The Heretic; La Grande Bourgeoise; 1900; Orca; Sunday Woman; Days of Heaven; Leone; The Tempter; La Cage Aux Folles; Sidney Sheldon's Bloodline; La Banguiere (The Woman Banker); Uomini e no (Men or Not Men); La Cage Aux Folles II.

MORRIS, Garrett: Act. b. New Orleans, Feb 1, 1937. Singer, arr with Harry Belafonte Folk Singers.

Bway inc: Hallelujah Baby; I'm Solomon; Porgy and Bess; Showboat; Ain't Supposed To Die A Natural Death; Great White Hope; What The Winesellers Buy.

Films inc: The Angel Levine; Where's Papa?; The Anderson Tapes; Car Wash; Cooley High.

TV inc: NBC Saturday Night Live.

MORRIS, Greg: Act. b. Cleveland, OH, Sep 27, 1934. e. OH State U, U of IA. Films inc: The New Interns; The Lively Set; The Sword of Ali Baba; S.T.A.B.

TV inc: Mission Impossible; Vega$.

MORRIS, Howard: Dir-Act. b. NYC, Sep 4, 1919. e. NYU. Films inc: Boys Night Out; Who's Minding the Mint?; With Six You Get Egg Roll; Don't Drink the Water; High Anxiety; Goin' Coconuts.

TV inc: Your Show of Shows; Caesar's Hour.

Bway inc: Hamlet; Call Me Mister; John Loves Mary; Gentlemen Prefer Blondes.

MORRIS, John Jackson: Wri-Dir-Prod. b. Sydney, Australia, Nov 11, 1933. Head of Prod, South Australian Film Corp; dir, South Australian Film Corp, 1976. Deputy Chmn, Australian Film and TV School.

MORRIS, John: Comp. b. Elizabeth, NJ, Oct 18, 1926. e. Juilliard; U WA. TV inc: The Adams Chronicles; The Scarlet Letter; The Tap Dance Kid; Doctor Franken.

Films inc: The Producers; The 12 Chairs; Blazing Saddles; Young Frankenstein; Silent Movie; High Anxiety; Sherlock Holmes' Smarter Brother; The Last Remake of Beau Geste; The In-Laws; The Bank Shot; The Elephant Man; In God We Trust.

Bway inc: Bye Bye Birdie; Bells are Ringing; Mack and Mabel.

MORRIS, Oswald: Cin. b. London, 1915. Films inc: Green for Danger; Moulin Rouge; Beat the Devil; Beau Brummell; Moby Dick; A Farewell to Arms; Heaven Knows, Mr. Allison; The Key; Look Back in Anger; Our Man in Havana; The Entertainer; Lolita; Of Human Bondage; The Pumpkin Eater; The Hill; The Spy Who Came in From the Cold; Stop the World I Want to Get Off; The Taming of the Shrew; Oliver; Goodbye Mr Chips; Scrooge; Fiddler on the Roof (Oscar-1971); Lady Caroline Lamb; The Mackintosh Man; The Odessa File; The Man Who Would be King; The Seven Per Cent Solution; Equus; The Wiz.

MORRISON, Hobe: Wri-Critic. b. Germantown, PA, Mar 24, 1904. 1943, drama ed Philadelphia Record; joined Variety 1937; drama ed-critic.

(Tony-honorary-1980).

MORROW, Jeff: Act. b. NYC, Jan 13, 1917. e. Pratt Institute. Films inc: The Robe; Tangier; Siege at Red River; Tanganyika; Sign of the Pagan; Captain Lightfoot; The Giant Claw; The Story of Ruth; Harbour Lights. Bway inc: Romeo and Juliet; St Joan; January Thaw; Billy Budd; Three Wishes for Jamie; The Suspects.

TV inc: Iron Horse.

MORROW, Karen: Act-Singer. b. Des Moines, IA, Dec 15. e. Clarke Coll. Thea inc: (Bway) I Had a Ball; A Joyful Noise; I'm Solomon; The Grass Harp; The Selling of the President; Oklahoma!; Most Happy Fella; Brigadoon; Carnival; teamed with Nancy Dussault for Town Hall concert appearances. (Off-Bway) Sing Muse; The Boys From Syracuse.

TV inc: The Jim Nabors Show; The Boy in the Plastic Bubble; Tabitha; Friends; Song by Song; Ladies Man.

MORROW, Richard T: Exec. b. Glendale, CA, 1926. e. UCLA, BA, USC, LLB. Became a vp at Walt Disney Productions in 1964. Elected to the Board of Directors in Dec, 1971; trustee of the Disney Foundation.

MORROW, Vic: Act-Wri-Dir. b. NYC, Feb 14, 1931. Dir off-Broadway, Deathwatch; The Maids; The Firstborn. Appeared in A Streetcar Named Desire. On screen since 1955. Films inc: Blackboard Jungle; Tribute to a Bad Man; God's Little Acre; The Bad News Bears; Last Year at Malibu; Dirty Mary, Crazy Larry; Message From Space; Target-Harry; The Evictors; Humanoids From the Deep.

TV inc: Bonanza; The New Breed; Roots; Captain and the Kings; Stone; The Last Convertible; The Seekers; B.A.D. Cats; The Secret of Lost Valley (Dir).

MORSE, Barry: Act. b. England 1919. Films inc: The Goose Steps Out; When We Are Married; There's A Future In It; Late At Night; No Trace; Kings of the Sun; Justine; Asylum; Love at First Sight; Power Play; The Shape of Things To Come; Klondike Fever; The Changeling; The Hounds. . .of Notre Dame.

TV inc: The Fugitive; The Zoo Gang; The Adventurer; Space 1999; The Martian Chronicles; The Deptford Trilogy.

MORSE, Hollingsworth: Dir. b. LA, 1910. Has directed approximately 2,000 tv shows. Films inc: Pufnstuf; Daughters of Satan.

TV inc: The Lone Ranger; The Mark of Zorro; The Grey Ghost; Riverboat; Laramie; No Time for Sergeants; Adam 12; Man from Shiloh; Emergency; Marcus Welby; Dukes of Hazzard; National Lampoon Delta House; Crash Island; Secret of Isis; Ark II; The Oregon Trail.

MORSE, Robert: Act. b. Newton, MA, May 18, 1931. Films inc: The Matchmaker; Honeymoon Hotel; Quick Before it Melts; The Loved One; Oh Dad, Poor Dad; How to Succeed in Business Without Really Trying; Where Were You When the Lights Went Out?; The Boatniks.

TV inc: That's Life; The Stingiest Man In Town; Jack Frost (voice).

Bway inc: Darling; Take Me Along; How to Succeed in Business Without Really Trying (Tony-1962); Sugar; Damn Yankees; So Long 174th St.

MORTON, Bruce: TV newsman. b. Norwalk, CT. e. Harvard. With various broadcasting organizations before joining CBS as Washington Bureau reporter 1964; 1966 named Washington correspondent; 1974 Washington correspondent CBS Morning News; 1975 Washington anchorman. TV inc: Reports from Lt. Calley Trial (Emmy-1971); Watergate--The White House Transcripts (Emmy-1974).

MOSES, Gilbert III: Dir. b. Cleveland, OH, Aug 20, 1942. e. Oberlin Coll. Thea inc: LeRoi Jones' Slaveship; Bloodknot; Rigoletto; Mother Courage; No Place to be Somebody; Charlie Was Here and Now He's Gone; Aint Supposed to Die a Natural Death; The Duplex; Don't Let It Go to Your Head; The Taking of Miss Janie; 1600 Pennsylvania Avenue.

Films inc: Willie Dynamite (& comp); The Fish That Saved Pittsburgh.

MOSES, Sir Charles: Exec. b. Lancashire, Eng, Jan 21, 1900. e. Royal Military Coll, Sandhurst. GM, Australian Broadcasting Comm, 1935-65; secy-gen Asian Broadcasting Union, 1965-77.

MOSS, Arnold: Act-Dir. b. NYC, Jan 28, 1910. e. CCNY, BA Columbia U, MA, NYU, PHD. Films inc: Temptation; The Black Book; Kim; Viva Zapata; Casanova's Big Night; The Twenty-Seventh Day; The Fool Killer; Gambit; Caper of the Golden Bulls.

MOSS, Irwin: Exec. Started with Dancer-Fitzgerald-Sample ad agcy pgm dept; joined CBS-TV as dir bus aff, later dir bus aff Cinema Center Films; joined ICM agency as sr vp bus aff, creating & packaging pgms; to NBC Entertainment as sr vp entertainment acquisitions; Aug 1980 named P Marble Arch Television.

MOST, Donny: Act. b. NYC, Aug 8, 1953. Films inc: American Dream; Leo and Loree.

TV inc: Huckleberry Finn; Mel and Susan Together; The Donna Fargo Show; With This Ring; The $1,000 Bill; Happy Days.

MOUNT, Thom: Exec. b. May 26, 1948. e. Bard College; CA Institute of the Arts, MFA. Started in industry as asso prod Selznick/Glickman Prod; 1976 asst to U exec vp Ned Tanen; 1977, vp supv feature films; 1978 exec vp in chg prodn.

MOUSSA, Ibrahim: Prod. b. Alexandria, Egypt, Sep 30, 1946. Talent agent before turning prod in 1979. Films inc: La Cicala (The Cricket).

MOXEY, John Llewellyn: Dir. TV inc: Mission Impossible; Mannix; Hawaii 5-0; Judd for the Defense; Charlie's Angels (pilot); San Francisco International (pilot); Intimate Strangers; The President's Mistress; Foster and Laurie; The Night Stalker; Father Brown, Detective; The Power Within; Ebony, Ivory and Jade; The Solitary Man; The Children of An Lac; The Mating Season.

Films inc: Horror Hotel; Circus of Fear; Foxhole in Cairo.

MOYERS, Bill: TV Newsman. b. Hugo, OK, Jun 5, 1934. e. U TX, BJ; Southwestern Baptist Theological Sem. Asst to Sen Lyndon B Johnson 1959-1960, 1961-63; asso dir Peace Corps 1961-63; spec asst to Pres Johnson 1963-1967 also press sec 1965-1967.

TV inc: A Question of Impeachment (Emmy-1964); Henry Steele Commager (Emmy-1974); Essay on Watergate (Emmy-1974) (all aired on PBS show Bill Moyers Journal); edtr & chf corr CBS Reports; winner ATAS Broadcast Journalism Award 1978.

MUDD, Roger: TV News. b. Washington, DC, Feb 9, 1928. e. Washington & Lee U, AB; U NC, MA. Reporter Richmond News-Leader 1953; news dir WRNL 1954; WTOP, Washington 1956; joined CBS News 1961 as Congressional corr; 1977 Nat'l Aff Corr; 1978, corr CBS Reports; 1980 joined ABC as Chief Washington Corr.

TV inc: The Selling of the Pentagon; The Shooting of Gov. Wallace (Emmy-1973); The Agnew Resignation (Emmy-1974); Watergate--The White House Transcripts (Emmy-1974); The Senate and the Watergate Affair (Emmy-1974).

MUHL, Edward E: Exec. b. Richmond, IN, Feb 17, 1907. GM Universal, 1948-53 vp chg prod, 1953-68; consultant, 1969-72. Ret.

MULDAUR, Diana: Act. b. NYC, Aug 19, 1943. e. Sweet Briar Coll, BA. Films inc: The Swimmer; Number One; The Lawyer; The Other; One More Train to Rob; McQ; The Chosen Survivors.

TV inc: McCloud; Ordeal; The Word; A Cry For Justice; The Miracle Worker; The Return of Frank Cannon.

Bway inc: Seidman and Son; Poor Bitos; A Very Rich Woman.

MULGREW, Kate: Act. b. Dubuque, IA, Apr 29, 1955. e. NYU. TV inc: Ryan's Hope; The Word; Jennifer: A Woman's Story; Kate Columbo; A Time For Miracles.

Thea inc: Othello; Three Sisters; The Plow and the Stars; Orpheus Descending.

MULHALL, Jack: Act. b. Wappingers Falls, NY, Oct 7, 1891. Started in vaudeville; in films in the 1910's. Films inc: Sirens of the Sea; Mickey; All of a Sudden Peggy; Molly 'O; The Bad Man; The Goldfish; Friendly Enemies; The Poor Nut; Dark Streets; Hollywood Boulevard.

(Died Jun 1, 1979).

MULHARE, Edward: Act. b. Ireland, Apr 8, 1923. Films inc: Hill Twenty-Four Doesn't Answer; Signpost to Murder; Von Ryan's Express; Our Man Flint; Eyes of the Devil; Caprice.

TV inc: The Ghost and Mrs Muir; Gidget Grows Up.

MULHOLLAND, Robert E: Exec. b. 1934. e. Northwestern U, BA, MA. Joined NBC Chicago 1962 as newswriter, became field prod for Huntley-Brinkley report; 1964 to London as European prod NBC News; 1967, Washington prod Huntley-Brinkley; 1967, news dir West Coast; 1972, exec prod NBC Nightly News; 1973, vp NBC News; 1974, exec vp NBC News; 1977 P NBC TV network.

MULL, Martin: Act-Wri. b. Chicago, IL, Aug 18, 1943. Humorist, hired by Warner Records to develop hit singles, wrote A Girl Named Johnny Cash; recorded for Capricorn, ABC Records, Electra-Asylum Records.

Films inc: FM; Serial; My Bodyguard.

TV inc: Mary Hartman, Mary Hartman; Fernwood 2 Night; America 2 Night; guest host Tonight Show; Johnny Cash Spring Special; Chevy Chase National Humor Test; Big City Comedy; Tom and Dick Smothers Brothers Special.

MULLANEY, Jack: Act. b. Pittsburgh, Sep 18, 1932. Films inc: The Young Stranger; The Vintage; Kiss Them for Me; All the Fine Young Cannibals; The Honeymoon Machine; The Absent Minded Professor; Seven Days in May; South Pacific; Tickle Me; Spinout; Little Big Man; When the Legends Die; George; Where Does It Hurt?

TV inc: Ann Sothern Show; My Living Doll; Ensign O'Toole; It's About Time.

Bway inc: The Amazing Mr. Pennypacker.

MULLAVEY, Greg: Act. b. Buffalo, NY, Sep 10, 1939. e. Hobart. H of Meredith MacRae. Bway inc: Romantic Comedy.

TV inc: Mary Hartman, Mary Hartman; Centennial; Children of Divorce; Number 96.

Films inc: Raid on Rommel; The Hindenburg; The Love Machine.

MULLIGAN, Richard: Act. b. NYC, Nov 13, 1932. Films inc: The Mixed Up Files of Mrs. Basil E. Frankweiler; Irish Whiskey Rebellion; One Potato, Two Potato; The Group; The Big Bus; Little Big Man; Scavenger Hunt.

Thea inc: All the Way Home; Never Too Late; Nobody Loves an Albatross; Thieves.

TV inc: Having Babies; The Hero; The Diana Rigg Show; Soap (Emmy-1980).

MULLIGAN, Robert: Dir. b. NYC, Aug 23, 1925. e. Fordham U. Films inc: Fear Strikes Out; The Rat Race; The Great Impostor; Come September; The Spiral Road; To Kill a Mockingbird; Summer of '42; Love with a Proper Stranger; Inside Daisy Clover; Up the Down Staircase; The Stalking Moon; The Pursuit of Happiness; Baby, The Rain Must Fall; The Nickel Ride; The Other; Bloodbrothers; Same Time Next Year.

TV inc: Philco-Goodyear Playhouse; Alcoa-Goodyear Playhouse; The Moon and Sixpence (Emmy-1960); Billy Budd; Ah, Wilderness; The Human Comedy, What Every Woman Knows; The Member of the Wedding; The Catered Affair; A Tale of Two Cities.

Bway inc: Comes a Day.

MUNSEL, Patrice: Soprano. b. 1925. Made Metropolitan Opera debut at age 17. Opera, concert appearances.

Bway inc: A Musical Jubilee.

Films inc: Melba

MURPHY, Ben: Act. b. Jonesboro, AR, Mar 6, 1942. e. U IL, BA; Pasadena Playhouse. TV inc: The Name of the Game; Alias Smith and Jones; Griff; Gemini Man; The Chisholms; The Secret War of Jackie's Girls.

MURPHY, George: Act. b. New Haven, CT, Jul 4, 1902. e. Yale U. Vaude, nitery dancer, stage debut in 1927 Good News; Of Thee I Sing; Roberta. Screen debut 1934 Kid Millions, 1934. Films inc: Broadway Melody of 1938; A Letter of Introduction; Two Girls on Broadway; A Guy, A Girl and A Gob; Tom, Dick and Harry; For Me and My Gal; This Is the Army; Bataan; Cynthia; Battleground; It's a Big Country; Walk East on Beacon. (Special Oscar-1950.) U S Senator (Cal) 1964-1971.

MURPHY, Michael: Act. Films inc: That Cold Day in the Park; Brewster McCloud; McCabe and Mrs. Miller; What's Up, Doc?; Phase IV; Nashville; The Front; The Class of Miss McMichael; An Unmarried Woman; Manhattan.

TV inc: The Autobiography of Miss Jane Pittman.

MURPHY, Richard: Wri-Dir. b. Boston, 1912. e. Williams Coll. Films inc: Boomerang; Deep Waters; Cry of the City; Panic in the Streets; Les Miserables; The Desert Rats; Broken Lance; The Wackiest Ship in the Army; Compulsion; The Last Angry Man; The Kidnapping of the President (wri).

TV inc: Our Man Higgins; The Felony Squad (creator).

MURRAY, Anne: Singer. b. Springhill, Nova Scotia, Jun 20, 1945. e. U of New Brunswick. Recording artist.

Albums inc: Let's Keep It That Way; Greatest Hits.

(Grammy-country vocal-1974; pop vocal-1979).

TV inc: The Johnny Cash Christmas; Perry Como's Christmas in New Mexico.

MURRAY, Bill: Wri-Act. b. Evanston, IL, Sep 21, 1950. With Second City group; wrote and performed in National Lampoon Show off-Bway and National Lampoon Radio Hour.

TV inc: All You Need is Cash; Saturday Night Live (Emmy-wri-1977).

Films inc: Next Stop, Greenwich Village; Coming Attractions; Meatballs; Mr Mike's Mondo Video; Where the Buffalo Roam; Caddyshack.

MURRAY, Don: Act-Dir-Wri. b. LA, Jul 31, 1929. Films inc: Bus Stop; Bachelor Party; A Hatful of Rain; The Hoodlum Priest; Shake Hands With The Devil; Advise and Consent; The Cross and the Switchblade;; Conquest of the Planet of the Apes; The Plainsman; Escape from East Berlin; The Borgia Stick; Deadly Hero; Damien--Omen II.

Bway inc: Insect Comedy; The Rose Tattoo; The Skin of Our Teeth; The Hot Corner; The Norman Conquest.

TV inc: Rainbow; Knots Landing; If Things Were Different; The Boy Who Drank Too Much; Confessions of a Lady Cop; Fugitive Family.

MURRAY, Jan: Act. b. NYC, 1917. Performed in niteries, vaudeville, Bway, radio. TV inc: (MC) Songs for Sale, Sing It Again; Jan Murray Time; Treasure Hunt. (Act) The Dream Merchants.

Films inc: Who Killed Teddy Bear?; The Busy Body; Thunder Alley; A Man Called Dagger.

MURRAY, Ken (Don Court): Act. b. NYC, 1903. On NY stage as MC; Hollywood stage in Ken Murray's Blackouts, 1942-9. Screen debut 1929 in Half-Marriage. Films inc: Leathernecking; A Night at Earl Carroll's; Juke Box Jenny; The Man Who Shot Liberty Valance; Son of Flubber; The Power; Ken Murray's Shooting Stars. *(Oscar Special-1947).*

TV inc: Ken Murray Show; Hollywood Without Makeup.

MUSANTE, Tony: Act. b. Bridgeport, CT, Jun 30, 1936. e. Oberlin Coll. Films inc: Once A Thief; The Incident; The Detective; A Professional Gun; The Love Circle; The Bird with the Crystal Plummage; The Last Run; Anonymous Venetian.

TV inc: Toma; Breaking Up Is Hard To Do; The Thirteenth Day-The Story of Ruth.

Bway inc: 27 Wagons Full of Cotton; Memory of Two Mondays; Lady From Dubuque.

MUSBURGER, Brent: Sportscaster. b. Portland, OR, May 26, 1940. Joined CBS sports 1975. Hosts The NFL Today and Sports Time.

Films inc: The Main Event; Rocky 2.

MUSE, Clarence: Act-Wri. b. Baltimore, MD, Oct 7, 1889. e. Dickerson School of Law. On concert stage, radio, in circus, vaudeville. Screen debut 1928, Hearts in Dixie. Films inc: If I Had A Million; Sun Shines Bright; Broadway Bill; Night and Day; Huckleberry Finn; The Great Dan Patch; Car Wash.

(Died Oct 13, 1979).

MUSSER, Tharon: Light dsgn. b. Roanoke, VA, Jan 8, 1925. e. Yale School of Drama, MFA. Light dsgn for Provincetown Playhouse; Jose Limon tour; Stratford (CT) Shakespeare. Bway inc: The Rivalry; The Great God Brown; Only in America; Five Finger Exercise; Giants, Sons of Giants; The Crucible; All in Good Time; Flora, The Red Menace; The Lion in Winter; House of Flowers; Applause; The Boy Friend; Follies *(Tony-*1972); The Trial of the Catonsville Nine; The Prisoner of Second Avenue; The Creation of the World and Other Business; The Sunshine Boys; A Little Night Music; Sondheim--a Musical Tribute; The Wiz; Same Time Next Year; A Chorus Line *(Tony-*1976); Pacific Overtures; The Act; Ballroom; They're Playing Our Song; Whose Life Is It Anyway?

MUTI, Ornella (Francesca Romana Rivelli): Act. b. Rome, 1955. Films inc: La Moglie Piu Bella; Breakup; Viva Italia; A Man Alone in Revolt; Primo Amore; Bishop's Bedroom; Nest of Vipers; Flash Gordon.

MYERS, Carmel: Act. b. LA, 1900. In short films as child, became silent screen star specializing in vamp roles. Films inc: Sirens of the Sea; The Haunted Pajamas; The Famous Mrs. Fair; The Slave of Desire; Beau Brummel; Ben Hur; Tell It To The Marines; Sorrell and Son; A Certain Young Man; Dream of Love; Broadway Scandals; Svengali; The Mad Genius; The Countess of Monte Cristo; Lady For a Night; Whistle Stop; Won Ton Ton, The Dog Who Saved Hollywood.

(Died Nov 9, 1980).

MYERS, Harold: Journalist. b. London, Jul 10, 1912. Started as reporter with the Daily Film Renter, London, 1933; resigned in 1946; edtr, Cine-Technician, 1946-48; joined Variety 1948 as London Bureau Chief; named first European mgr in 1957; later named senior international correspondent on world-wide assignments.

MYERS, Peter S: Exec. b. Toronto, May 13, 1920. e. U of Toronto. Salesman Warners, 1946; Toronto br mgr Eagle Lion, 1947; Toronto br mgr 20th Century-Fox, 1948; Canadian div mgr, 1951; Canadian GM, 1955; gen sls mgr in charge of dom. distribution 1968; named vp, 1969; sr vp Fox Entertainment Inc, 1980.

NAAR, Joseph T: Prod. b. San Diego, CA, Apr 25, 1925. e. UCLA, BA. TV inc: GE Theatre; Schlitz Playhouse; Checkmate; Starsky and Hutch.

Films inc: All American Boy; Blacula.

NABORS, Jim: Act. b. Sylacauga, AL, Jun 12, 1932. TV inc: Andy Griffith Show; Gomer Pyle, USMC; The Jim Nabors Show.

NADEL, Arthur H: Wri-Prod-Dir. b. NYC, Apr 25. Films inc: Clambake; Lola; Underground; No Trumpets, No Drum.

TV inc: The Rifleman; The Plainsman; Arrest and Trial; The Virginian; Daniel Boone; Cowboy in Africa; Bonanza; Banyon; Welcome Home; The Chase; Crime Without Passion.

NADER, George: Act. b. LA, Oct 19, 1921. e. Occidental Coll. Films inc: Monsoon; Six Bridges to Cross; Lady Godiva; Away All Boats; Four Girls in Town; Joe Butterfly; The Human Duplicators; The Million Eyes of Sumuru.

NAGY, Ivan: Wri-Dir. b. Budapest, Hungary, Jan 23, 1938. e. UCLA, MFA. Films inc: Deadly Hero; Five Minutes of Freedom. TV inc: Midnight Lace; A Gun in the House; Once Upon a Spy; Captain America II; Mind Over Murder.

NAGY, Ivan: Dancer-Chor. b. Debrecen, Hungary, Apr 28, 1943. e. Budapest State Opera House School. With Budapest Opera House Ballet; 1965 won silver medal at Int'l Ballet Competition, Bulgaria; joined Nat'l Ballet of Washington as guest artist; 1968 joined NYC Ballet, 1969 principal dancer; 1970 became premier dancer; has danced with may leading ballerinas inc Dame Margot Fonteyn; Makarova; Cynthia Gregory.

NAKADAI, Tatsuya: Act. b. Tokyo, 1932. Films inc: Seven Samurai; Black River; The Human Condition; Enjo; Odd Obsession; Sanjuro; Yojimbo; High and Low; Harakiri; Kwaidan; Rebellion; I Am A Cat; Queen Bee; Bird of Fire; Kagemusha.

NAMATH, Joe: Act. b. Beaver Falls, PA, May 31, 1943. e. U of AL. Former pro football star. Films inc: Norwood; C C & Co; The Last Rebel; Avalanche Express.

TV inc: The Waverly Wonders; Marriage Is Alive and Well; All American Pie.

NANKIN, Michael: Wri-Dir. b. LA, Dec 26, 1955. e. UCLA, BFA. Films inc: Gravity (short); Junior High School (short); Midnight Madness.

NAPIER, Alan: Act. b. Birmingham, Eng, Jan 7, 1903. Films inc: The Uninvited; In a Monastery Garden; Loyalties; For Valour; The Four Just Men; The Invisible Man Returns; Ministry of Fear; Lost Angel; Forever Amber; Julius Caesar; The Court Jester; Journey to the Center of the Earth; Marnie.

TV inc: Batman; Centennial; The Contest Kid Strikes Again.

Thea inc: 10 yrs leading roles London inc Old Vic; Lady in Waiting.

NARDINO, Gary: Exec. b. Garfield, NJ, Aug 26, 1935. e. Seton Hall U, BS. Joined ICM agency, became Sr VP; moved to William Morris as VP in chg NY TV Dept; became P Paramount Television Prodns 1977.

NARIZZANO, Silvio: Dir. b. Montreal, Feb 8, 1928. e. U of Bishop's, BA. Films inc: Die, Die, My Darling: Georgy Girl; Blue; Loot; Redneck; The Sky Is Falling; Why Shoot the Teacher?; The Class of Miss MacMichael.

TV inc: Death of a Salesman; War and Peace; The Little Farm.

NASATIR, Marcia: Prod. b. NYC, May 18, 1925. Ed Dell Publishing, Bantam Books; ed, The Ladies Home Journal; East Coast story ed National General Pictures; vp in charge of Motion Picture Dev, UA; vp in charge of Motion Picture Dev, Orion Pictures.

NASH, N Richard (nee Nusbaum): Wri. b. Philadelphia, Jun 8, 1913. e. U of PA. Plays inc: The Young and Fair; See the Jaguar; The Rainmaker; Girls of Summer; Handful of Fire; Echoes.
    Films inc: Nora Prentiss; Welcome Stranger; Porgy and Bess; The Rainmaker.

NAT, Marie-Jose: Act. b. Corsica, 1940. Films inc: Crime et Chatiment; Club de Femmes; Secret Professional; Rue des Prairies; Safari Diamant; Le Paria; Elise ou La Vraie Vie.

NATHANSON, Don Paul: Exec. b. 1914. e. U MN. Started own ad agcy in Minneapolis 1937; later joined Grey Advertising, from 1952 to 1977 was P, later bd chmn Grey-North, agency's Chicago div; credited with originating key ad campaign for Toni, Lanvin; entered bcasting 1953 as exec vp Harriscope Broadcasting Corp; founded Harriscope Cable TV, later merged with Cypress Communications; co-owner Falcon Communications.
    (Died Dec 24, 1980).

NATHANSON, Paul Louis: Exhib. b. Canada, 1913. S of Nathan L Nathanson (founder of Famous Player Circuit in Canada). Founded Odeon Chain; for more than three decades controlled more than 75% of all Canadian film houses.
    (Died Nov 13, 1980).

NATWICK, Mildred: Act. b. Baltimore, MD, Jun 19, 1908. e. Bryn Mawr. Films inc: The Long Voyage Home; The Enchanted Cottage; The Late George Apley; Three Godfathers; The Kissing Bandit; She Wore a Yellow Ribbon; Cheaper by the Dozen; The Quiet Man; The Trouble with Harry; The Court Jester; Tammy and the Bachelor; Barefoot in the Park; If It's Tuesday This Must be Belgium; The Maltese Bippy; Daisy Miller; At Long Last Love.
    TV inc: Do Not Fold, Spindle or Mutilate; The Snoop Sisters (Emmy-1974); The Easter Promise; Little Women; You Can't Take It With You.
    Bway inc: End of Summer; Love from a Stranger; Candida; Missouri Legend; Blithe Spirit; Waltz of the Toreadors; Critic's Choice; Barefoot in the Park; Our Town.

NAUGHTON, Bill: Wri. b. Ballyhaunis, Ireland, Jun 12, 1910. Plays inc: All In Good Time; Alfie; Spring and Port Wine; He Was Gone When They Got There; June Evening; Keep It In the Family; Lighthearted Intercourse.
    Films inc: Alfie.

NAUGHTON, David: Act-Singer. b. Hartford, CT, Feb 13, 1955. e. U PA, BA. Numerous commercials inc all Dr Pepper mus commercials since 1978. TV Inc: Making it.
    Films inc: Midnight Madness
    Bway inc: Hamlet; Da.

NAZARRO, Ray: Dir. b. Boston. e. Boston Coll. Films inc: The Tougher They Come; Counterspy; Palomino; Bullfighter and Lady (co-sp); Cripple Creek; Bandits of Corsica; Top Gun; Apache Territory; The Night Is Fatal; Arrivederci Cowboy.
    TV inc: Mickey Spillane; State Trooper; Fury.

NEAGLE, Anna, Dame (Marjorie Robertson): Act. b. Forest Gate, Eng, Oct 20, 1904. On screen since 1929 in Mary Was Love (as Marjorie Robertson). Films inc: Bitter Sweet; Victoria the Great; Nurse Edith Cavell; Irene; No, No, Nanette; Forever and a Day; The Yellow Canary; Odette; The Man Who Wouldn't Talk; The Lady is a Square.
    Thea inc: (London) This Year of Grace; Wake Up and Dream; As You Like It; Peter Pan; Charlie Girl; No, No, Nanette; Maggie; My Fair Lady.
    TV inc: The Spice of Life; What's My Line; The Elstree Story; A Letter From The General; Shadow of the Sun.

NEAL, Patricia: Act. b. Packard, KY, Jan 20, 1926. W of Roald Dahl. In summer stock. Bway debut in Another Part of the Forest (Tony-supp-1947). Also in Children's Hour. Screen debut 1948, John Loves Mary.
    Films inc: The Fountainhead; The Day the Earth Stood Still; A Face in the Crowd; Breakfast at Tiffany's; Hud (Oscar-1963); In Harm's Way; The Subject Was Roses (first film after recovering from a stroke); Happy Mother's Day. . .Love, George; Baxter; Widow's Nest; The Passage.
    TV inc: All Quiet On The Western Front.

NEAME, Ronald: Dir-Prod. b. London, Apr 23, 1911. Started as asst cam 1929, Blackmail, first British sound film. Films inc: (as cin) Drake of England; The Gaunt Stranger; The Crimes of Stephen Hawke; Major Barbara; In Which We Serve; Blithe Spirit; Brief Encounter; Great Expectations.
    (dir) Take My Life; The Golden Salamander; The Card (& prod); The Million Pound Note; The Man Who Never Was; Windom's Way; The Horse's Mouth; Tunes of Glory; The Chalk Garden; Mister Moses; A Man Could Get Killed; Gambit; The Prime of Miss Jean Brodie; The Poseidon Adventure; The Odessa File; Meteor; Hopscotch.
    TV inc: The Knowledge (prod).

NEDERLANDER, James: Prod-Thea Ownr. b. Detroit, Mar 31, 1922. e. Detroit Inst Tech, U of ND. P Nederlander Theatre Cos. Bway inc: (prod or co-prod) On a Clear Day You Can See Forever; The Ninety-Day Mistress; Applause; Not Now, Darling; Abelard and Heloise; Seesaw; Annie; My Fat Friend; Otherwise Engaged; Night and Day; Oklahoma! (rev); Betrayal; West Side Story (rev); Peter Pan; Whose Life Is It Anyway.

NEEDELMAN, Julius: Dist. b. NYC, Jul 1, 1918. e. USC, BA, U of Denver, MBA. VP Tower Film Corp, 1968-72; p Tower Film Corp. 1972-present.

NEEDHAM, Hal: Dir. b. Memphis, TN, Mar 6, 1931. From 1956-76, stuntman, stunt coordinator, second unit dir. Films inc: (dir) Smokey and the Bandit; Hooper; Foul Play; Hooper; The Villain; Smokey and the Bandit II.
    TV inc: Death Car on the Freeway; Hal Needham's Wild World of Stunts; Stunts.

NEELEY, Ted: Act. b. Ranger, TX, 1943. Formed rock group while in college. Performed in clubs, Las Vegas, LA.
    Films inc: Jesus Christ Superstar; The Last Picture Show; A Perfect Couple (& mus).

NEFF, Hildegarde. (See KNEF, Hildegarde).

NEGRI, Pola: Act. b. Poland, 1897. On screen in US from 1922 in: The Red Reacock; Bella Donna; Passion; Forbidden Paradise; East of Suez; A Woman of the World; Loves of an Actress; The Woman from Moscow; Forbidden Paradise; Madame Bovary; Hi Didle Diddle; The Moonspinners.

NEGULESCO, Jean: Dir. b. Rumania, Feb 29, 1900. Films inc: Kiss and Make Up; The Mask of Dimitrios; The Conspirators; Three Strangers; Humoresque; Roadhouse; Johnny Belinda; Under My Skin; Three Came Home; The Mudlark; Phone Call from a Stranger; Titanic; How to Marry a Millionaire; Three Coins in the Fountain; Woman's World; Daddy Longlegs; The Rains of Ranchipur; Boy on a Dolphin; Count Your Blesings; The Best of Everything; Jessica; The Pleasure Seekers; The Invincible Six; Hello and Goodbye.

NEILSON, James: Dir. b. NYC, 1909. Began as legitimate thea stage manager, into tv in early days directing various programs inc: General Electric Theatre. Recommended by James Stewart to direct film Night Passage. Films inc: Moon Pilot; Bon Voyage; Summer Magic; Dr. Syn; The Moonspinners; The Adventures of Bullwhip Griffin; Return of the Gunfighter; Gentle Giant; Where Angels Go-Trouble Follows; The First Time; Flareup.
    (Died Dec 9, 1979)

NELLIGAN, Kate: Act. b. London, Mar 16, 1951. Thea inc: Barefoot in the Park; Misalliance; A Streetcar Named Desire; The Playboy of the Western World; Private Lives; Knuckle; Heartbreak House; Films inc: The Count of Monte Cristo; The Romantic Englishwoman; Dracula; Mr Patman.
TV inc: The Onedin Line; The Lady of the Camelias.

NELSON, Barry (Robert Neilson): Act. b. Oakland, CA, Apr 16, 1920. Screen debut, 1941, Johnny Eager. Films inc: Shadow of the Thin Man; Dr. Kildare's Victory; Stand By for Action; Eyes in the Night; A Yank on the Burma Road; The Human Comedy; Bataan; A Guy Name Joe; Undercover Maisie; Tenth Avenue Angel; The Man With My Face; Forty Guns; Mary, Mary; The Only Game in Town; Airport; Pete 'n Tillie; The Shining.
Bway inc: Light Up the Sky; Rat Race; The Moon Is Blue; Mary, Mary; Cactus Flower; Every Thing in the Garden; Seascape; The Norman Conquests; The Act.
TV inc: The Hunter; My Favorite Husband; Washington: Behind Closed Doors; Greatest Heroes of the Bible.

NELSON, David: Act. b. NYC, Oct 24, 1936. e. USC. S of Harriet Hilliard and the late Ozzie Nelson. Films inc: Here Come the Nelsons; Peyton Place; The Remarkable Mr. Pennypacker; Day of the Outlaw; The Big Circus; 30; The Sinners; Cheech and Chong's Up in Smoke.
TV inc: Adventures of Ozzie and Harriet; Annual Circus of the Stars.

NELSON, Ed: Act. b. Dec 21, 1928. Films inc: Attack of the Crab Monsters; New Orleans Uncensored; Hell on Devil's Island; Invasion of the Saucer Men; Street of Darkness; The Young Captives; Soldier in the Rain; Judgment at Nuremberg; Elmer Gantry; The Man From Galveston; Time to Run; Airport '75; That's The Way of the World; The Silent Force; Midway; For the Love of Benji.
TV inc: Peyton Place; Doctor's Private Lives (High Rollers); Anatomy of a Seduction; The Girl, The Gold Watch and Everything; The Return of Frank Cannon; Enola Gay--The Men, The Mission, The Atomic Bomb.

NELSON, Gene (Eugene Leander Berg): Act-Dir. b. Seattle, WA, Mar 24, 1920. Began dancing and singing while in high school; joined Sonja Henie and toured in her ice shows, 1940-41; during WW II played in Irving Berlin's GI prodn of This Is The Army.
Films inc: I Wonder Who's Kissing Her Now; Apartment for Peggy; Gentlemen's Agreement; The Daughter of Rosie O'Grady; Tea for Two; Lullaby of Broadway; She's Working Her Way Through College; Three Sailors and a Girl; The West Point Story; Oklahoma!; Atomic Man; So This Is Paris; (dir) Wake Me When the War Is Over; The Cool One; Harum Scarum; Your Cheatin' Heart.
TV inc: (dir) McNaughton's Daughter; The Invisible Man; Starsky and Hutch; Christy Love; New Land; Diana Rigg Show; Barnaby Jones; Cannon; Rookies; The Letters; Salvage.
Bway inc: (act) Lend An Ear; Music, Music; Good News; Hit the Deck; Oklahoma!; Pal Joey.

NELSON, Harriet (nee Hilliard): Act. b. Des Moines, IA, Jul 18, 1914. Singer with late husband Ozzie Nelson's band, later appeared in dramatic and musical roles with him. On radio shows: Believe It Or Not; Seeing Stars; Adventures of Ozzie & Harriet. On Screen in Here Come the Nelsons.
TV inc: Adventures of Ozzie & Harriet; Death Car On The Freeway; A Christmas For Boomer.
Thea inc: Marriage-Go-Round; Impossible Years; State Fair.

NELSON, Haywood: Act. b. NYC, Mar 25, 1960. Films inc: Mixed Company. Thea inc: Thieves. TV inc: As the World Turns; What's Happening!.

NELSON, Ralph: Dir. b. NYC, Aug 12, 1916. Started as act on Bway in Cyrano De Bergerac, 1934; Bway inc: Romeo and Juliet; Taming of the Shrew; Hamlet; There Shall Be No Night. (Dir) Here's Mama; The Trouble Makers; Man In the Dog Suit; (prod) Look to the Lilies; (wri) Mail Call; The Wind Is Ninety.
From 1948 to 1960 dir more than 1,000 tv shows inc: Playhouse 90; Studio One; Philco Playhouse; Dupont Show of the Month; Requiem For a Heavyweight (Emmy-1956); Doyle Against The House; The Old Vic Hamlet; Man In the Funny Suit; Rodgers & Hammerstein's Cinderella; Cole Porter's Aladdin; This Happy Breed; Lady of the House; You Can't Go Home Again; Christmas Lilies of the Field (& exec prod).
Films inc: Requiem For a Heavyweight (& act); Lilies of the Field (& prod-act); Soldier in the Rain (& act); Fate is the Hunter; Father Goose; Duel at Diablo (& prod-act); Charly (& prod); Counterpoint (& act); Soldier Blue (& act); Flight of the Doves (& prod-wri); The Wrath of God (& prod-wri); The Wilby Conspiracy; Embryo (& act); A Hero Ain't Nothin' But a Sandwich.

NELSON, Rick: Act. b. Teaneck, NJ, May 8, 1940. S of Ozzie and Harriet Nelson. Recorded for Decca Records. Films inc: Here Come the Nelsons; Wackiest Ship in the Army; Rio Bravo; A Story of Three Loves; Love and Kisses.
TV inc: Adventures of Ozzie and Harriet.

NELSON, Willie: Comp-Singer. b. Abbott, TX, Apr 30, 1933. Began writing songs in the 60's, started performing in 1970.
Songs inc: Family Bible; Funny How Time Slips Away.
Films inc: Electric Horseman; Honeysuckle Rose.
Albums inc: Stardust; Willie Nelson & Family Live. (Grammys-(3)-country vocal male-1975, 1978; country vocal group-1978).

NERO, Franco: Act. b. Italy, 1942. Films inc: The Tramplers; The Bible; Camelot; The Day of the Owl; A Quiet Place in the Country; Tristana; The Virgin and the Gypsy; The Battle of Neretva; Pope Joan; The Monk; Victory March; Force 10 from Navarone; Roses of Danzig; Mimi; The Man With Bogart's Face.

NESBITT, Cathleen: Act. b. Belfast, 1889. Stage debut with the Irish Players, 1911. First London appearance 1913, The Winter's Tale. Screen debut 1932, The Case of the Frightened Lady. Films inc: Separate Tables; The Parent Trap; Staircase; An Affair to Remember; Villain; Family Plot.
Thea inc: King Lear; The Cocktail Party; Sabrina Fair; My Fair Lady.
TV inc: Mask of Love (Emmy-1974; & daytime actress of year 1974).

NETHERTON, Tom: Act. b. Munich, Germany, Jan 11. Singer with Lawrence Welk Show; recording artist, niteries.

NETTER, Douglas: Exec. b. Seattle, WA, May 23, 1921. e. Holy Cross, BS. After WW2 joined PRC (later merged with Eagle Lion) in sales dept; 1947-55 gen sls mgr Altec; 1955-58, vp & gm Todd-AO; 1958, Samuel Goldwyn Prodns; 1964 formed own firm as prods rep; 1969 vp MGM; 1970-73 exec vp; 1974 into ind prodn.
Films inc: Mr Ricco.
TV inc: The Buffalo Soldiers; Wild Times; Roughnecks.

NETTLETON, Lois: Act. b. Oak Park, IL, circa 1929. Films inc: Period of Adjustment; Come Fly with Me; Mail Order Bride; The Good Guys and the Bad Guys; Dirty Dingus Magee; Sidelong Glances of a Pigeon Kicker; The Honkers; Echoes of a Summer.
Thea inc: The Biggest Thief in Town; Darkness at Noon; God and Kate Murphy; Silent Night, Lonely Night; The Wayward Stork; The Hemingway Hero; The Only Game in Town; Strangers.
TV inc: The Brighter Day; Portrait of Emily Dickinson; Duet for Two Hands; The Hidden River; Centennial; Tourist.

NEUCHATEAU, Corinne: Act. b. Staten Island, NY, Jul 20, 1952. Thea inc: Golda; The Three Sisters; A View from the Bridge; The Story Teller; In the Beginning; Skipping.
TV inc: Love of Life.
Films inc: The Last Tycoon (VO).

NEUFELD, Mace: Prod-Comp-Dir. b. NYC, Jul 13, 1928. e. Yale U, BA, NYU Law School. Films inc: The Omen (exec prod); The Frisco Kid (prod).
TV inc: Angel On My Shoulder (exec prod).

NEUFELD, Sigmund Jr Dir. b. LA, May 12, 1931. TV inc: Lassie; Kojak; Invisible Man; Doctors Hospital; Serpico; Baretta; Switch; Project UFO; Incredible Hulk; Buck Rogers in the 25th Century.

NEUMAN, E Jack: Wri-Prod. b. Toledo, OH, Feb 27, 1921. e. U of MO, BJ, UCLA, LLD. Films inc: Viva Vasquez; Seven Cakes for Christmas; Man From Tomorrow; The Outlanders; Heat Wave; Most Dangerous Game; The Venetian Affair (& prod); Company of Killers (& prod); The Berlin Affair (& prod); The Cable Car Murder (& prod); Snow Job (& prod); Occurrence On A Dark Street (& prod); Police Story (& prod); The Blue Knight (& prod).
TV (prod-wri) Dr Kildare; Sam Benedict; Mr Novak; A Man Called Shenandoah; Night Games; Kate McShane; Law and Order.

NEWAY, Patricia: Act. b. NYC, Sep 30, 1919. e. Notre Dame Coll for Women. Bway inc: The Consul; Sound of Music (Tony-supp-1960); Morning Sun; The King and I; Salome.
TV inc: The Dialogue of the Carmelites; Golden Child; The Consul; Marie Golovin; Macbeth; Wozzeck.

NEWHART, Bob: Act. b. Oak Park, IL, Sep 5, 1929. Performed in niteries before cutting talk album; weekly TV variety show, 1961. Films inc: Hell Is for Heroes; Hot Millions; Catch-22; On a Clear Day You Can See Forever; Cold Turkey; Little Miss Marker; First Family.
TV inc: The Bob Newhart Show; Thursday's Game; Packy; Marathon. (Grammys-(3)-new artist-comedy-artist of year-1960).

NEWLAND, John: Act-Dir-Prod. b. Cincinnati, OH, Nov 23, 1917. Films inc: Bulldog Drummond; That Night; The Violators; The Spy with My Face; Hush-a-Bye Murder.
TV inc: Robert Montgomery Show (& dir); My Lover, My Son; One Step Beyond (host & dir); The Next Step Beyond; The Suicide's Wife; Angel City (prod).

NEWLEY, Anthony: Act. b. Hackney, Eng, Sep 24, 1931. On screen from 1946 in: Adventures of Dusty Bates; Little Ballerina; Oliver Twist; The Weak and the Wicked; Fire Down Below; How to Murder a Rich Uncle; Killers of Kilimanjaro; The Small World of Sammy Lee; Willi Wonka and the Chocolate Factory; Doctor Doolittle; Sweet November; Mr. Quilp.
TV inc: Sammy; Sunday Night at the Palladium; The Strange World of Gurney Slade; Saturday Spectaculars; Hollywood Squares; The Tonight Show; Animal Talk; Linda In Wonderland.
Bway inc: Stop the World--I Want To Get Off; Roar of the Greasepaint; Good Old Bad Old Days. (London) The Traveling Music show (mus & lyr).
(Grammy-song of year-1962).

NEWMAN, Barry: Act. b. Boston, MA, Nov 7, 1938. e. Brandeis U. Films inc: Pretty Boy Floyd; The Lawyer; Vanishing Point; The Salzburg Connection; Fear is the Key; City on Fire.
TV inc: Petrocelli; Sex and the Married Woman; King Crab.

NEWMAN, David: Wri. b. NYC, Feb 4, 1937. e. U MI. Films inc: (all in collab with Robert Benton) Bonnie and Clyde; There was a Crooked Man; Floreana; What's Up Doc; Money's Tight; Bad Company; Superman; Superman II.
Plays inc: It's A Bird, It's A Plane, It's Superman; Oh! Calcutta (one Sketch).

NEWMAN, Edwin: TV Newsman. b. NYC, 1919. Joined NBC News in London, 1952; served as bureau chief London, Rome, Paris. Based in NY since 1961. Serves as newscaster, anchors specials.
TV inc: Reading, Writing and Reefer; The American Family; An Endangered Species; No More Vietnams. . .But.

NEWMAN, Joseph M: Dir. b. Logan, UT, Aug 7, 1909. Dir short subjects 1938. Films inc: Jungle Patrol; 711 Ocean Drive; The Outcasts of Poker Flats; Pony Soldier; The Human Jungle; Dangerous Crossing; Kiss of Fire; This Island Earth; Flight to Hong Kong (prod); Gunfight at Dodge City; The Big Circus; Tarzan the Ape Man; King of the Roaring Twenties; A Thunder of Drums; The George Raft Story.
TV inc: The Twilight Story.

NEWMAN, Laraine: Act. b. LA, Mar 2. Films inc: American Hotwax; Wholly Moses! TV inc: NBC's Saturday Night Live.

NEWMAN, Lionel: Comp-Cond. b. LA. B the late Alfred Newman. Began career age 16 as lead pianist Earl Carroll's Vanities, wrote first song, Dust in your Eyes, which was featured in Vanities; 1943 joined brother who was head of Fox music dept; became head of dept when Alfred died 1970; 1977 named vp Fox.
Films inc: The Cowboy and the Lady; Street With No Name; Cheaper By the Dozen; I'll Get By; There's No Business Like Show Business; The Best Things In Life Are Free; Mardi Gras; Move Over Darling; Do Not Disturb; The Pleasure Seekers; Hello, Dolly! (Oscar-scoring-1969); Salzburg Connection.
TV inc: Daniel Boone; Adventures in Paradise; Hong Kong; Dobie Gillis.
Songs inc: Kiss; Never; Adventures in Paradise; Again.

NEWMAN, Paul: Act-Dir. b. Cleveland, OH, Jan 26, 1925. H of Joanne Woodward. Started in summer stock, Woodstock (IL) Players. Bway in Picnic. Screen debut in The Silver Chalice.
Films inc: (act) Somebody Up There Likes Me; The Long Hot Summer; Cat on a Hot Tin Roof; Rally Round The Flag Boys; The Young Philadelphians; Exodus; The Hustler; Hud; Sweet Bird Of Youth; The Prize; The Outrage; What A Way To Go; Lady L; Harper; Hombre; Cool Hand Luke; Secret War of Harry Frigg; Winning; Butch Cassidy and the Sundance Kid; Sometimes A Great Notion (& dir); Pocket Money; Life and Times of Judge Roy Bean; The Mackintosh Man; The Sting; The Towering Inferno Slap Shot; The Drowning Pool; Buffalo Bill and the Indians; Quintet; Angel Dust (doc-narr); When Time Ran Out. (Dir) The Effect of Gamma Rays on Man-in-the-Moon Marigolds; Rachel, Rachel.
TV inc: The Shadow Box (dir).

NEWMAN, Phyllis: Act-Singer. b. Jersey City, NJ, Mar 19, 1935. e. Columbia U. W of Adolph Green. Bway inc: Wish You Were Here; I Feel Wonderful; Bells Are Ringing; First Impressions; Moonbirds; Subways Are for Sleeping (Tony-supp-1962); The Apple Tree; On the Town; The Madwoman of Central Park West (one woman show).
Films inc: Picnic; Let's Rock; To Find a Man.

NEWMAN, Randy: Songwri. Act. b. LA, Nov 28, 1943. Songs inc: Mama Told Me Not To Come; I Think It's Going to Rain Today; Short People.

NEWMAN, Robert: Exec. b. New Haven, CT, Jul 21, 1905. Started as press agent various Bway producers inc George M Cohan, George White; became producer. Bway inc: Off Key; The Sap From Syracuse; The Poor Nut; Twelve Miles Out; Bad Girl; Trick for Trick.
Entered film ind 1942 as exec asst William Goetz; later exec prod Fox; 1945, vp Republic Pictures; 1951, vp Samuel Goldwyn Prodns; 1958, P Batjac Prodns; 1964, exec prod & dir studio ops Paramount; 1972, gm Summa Prodns; 1975 retd to Paramount as exec.

NEWMAN, Stanley: Exec. b. NYC, Jul 24, 1935. e. Columbia Coll, BA. VP, MCA, Inc; VP U TV; VP U Pictures.

NEWMAN, Susan Kendall: Act. b. NYC, Feb 21, 1953. D of Paul Newman. Bway inc: We Interrupt This Program.
Films inc: The Wedding; I Wanna Hold Your Hand.
TV inc: The Shadow Box (prod).

NEWMAN, Walter: Wri. Films inc: Ace in the Hole; Underwater; The Man With the Golden Arm; The True Story of Jesse James; Crime and Punishment USA; The Interns; Cat Ballou; Bloodbrothers; The Champ.

NEWMAR, Julie: Act. b. Hollywood, Aug 16, 1935. Screen debut, 1954, Seven Brides for Seven Brothers. Films inc: Li'l Abner; The Rookie; Marriage-Go-Round; For Love or Money; MacKenna's Gold.

TV inc: My Living Doll; Monster Squad; Batman; Omnibus; Route 66.

Bway inc: Marriage Go 'Round *(Tony*-supp-1959); Dames at Sea; Ziegfeld Follies.

NEWTON, Connie: Act. b. Anaheim, CA, Dec 5, 1962. TV inc: The New Mickey Mouse Club Show; Jimmy Osmond Special; Eight is Enough.

NEWTON, Wayne: Act. b. Roanoke, VA, Apr 3, 1942. Recording artist. Appears in niteries. Purchased Aladdin Hotel, Las Vegas, 1980. Films inc: 80 Steps to Jonah.

NEWTON-JOHN, Olivia: Singer-Act. b. Cambridge, England, Sep 26, 1948. Singer in Australia before coming to U S in 1965. Films inc: Grease; Xanadu.

Recordings inc: If Not For You; Let Me Be There *(Grammy*-country voc-1973); I Honestly Love You *(Grammys*-record of year & pop voc-1974); You're The One That I Want; Hopelessly Devoted To You; Summer Nights; Totally Hot.

NICHOLL, Don: Wri-Prod. b. England, 1926. Writer for BBC radio and tv, emigrated to US in 1968.

TV inc: story ed, later exec prod All In The Family; creat-prod The Jeffersons; Three's Company; partner in NRW Productions.

(Died July 5, 1980).

NICHOLLS, Allan: Act-Wri-Comp. b. Montreal, Canada. Worked with rock groups. Bway inc: Hair; Jesus Christ Superstar; Sgt Pepper's Lonely Hearts Club Band.

Films inc: (act) Nashville (& songs); Buffalo Bill and the Indians; Welcome to L A; A Wedding; Slap Shot; A Perfect Couple (& songs); Quintet (asso prod); Health; Popeye.

NICHOLS, Charles August: Dir. b. Milford, UT, Sep 15, 1910. Ani and live action dir Walt Disney Prodns, 1935-61; sr ani dir Hanna-Barbera Prodns, 1961; vp, exec - ani feature films, Hanna-Barbera. Dir Oscar winning cartoon Toot, Whistle, Plunk and Boom, 1954. Other films inc: Last of the Curlews; Charlotte's Web. TV inc: Scruffy.

NICHOLS, Mike (Michael Igor Peschkowsky): Dir. b. Berlin, Nov 6, 1931. Stage, nitery performer. Films inc: Who's Afraid of Virginia Woolf?; The Graduate *(Oscar*-1967); Catch 22; Carnal Knowledge; The Day of the Dolphin; The Fortune; Gilda Live.

TV inc: An Evening with Mike Nichols and Elaine May.

Bway inc: Barefoot in the Park *(Tony*-1964); The Knack; LUV *(Tony*-1965); The Odd Couple *(Tony*-1965); The Apple Tree; The Little Foxes; Plaza Suite *(Tony*-1968); Uncle Vanya; Prisoner of Second Ave *(Tony*-1972); Annie *(Tony*-exec prod-1977); Billy Bishop Goes To War (prod); Lunch Hour.

(Grammy-Comedy-1961).

NICHOLS, Peter: Wri. b. England, Jul 31, 1927. The Hooded Terror; A Day in the Death of Joe Egg; The National Health; Forget-Me-Not Lane; Chez Nous; The Freeway; Harding's Luck; Jungle Jamboree. Films inc: Georgy Girl; Joe Egg; National Health.

NICHOLSON, Jack: Act-Prod. b. Neptune, NJ, Apr 22, 1936. Fims inc: (act) Easy Rider; Five Easy Pieces; Ride the Whirlwind (wri-prod); Drive, He Said (wri-dir-prod); Carnal Knowledge; The Last Detail; Chinatown; Tommy; The Shooting (prod); Head (wri-prod); One Flew Over the Cuckoo's Nest *(Oscar*-1975); The Missouri Breaks; The Last Tycoon; Goin' South (& dir); The Shining.

NICKS, Stevie: Singer-Sngwri. b. LA, May 26, 1948. With Lindsay Buckingham; Fleetwood Mac before solo. Songs inc: Rhiannon. Recordings inc: Whenever I Call You Friend.

NICOL, Alex: Act-Dir. b. Ossining, NY, Jan 20, 1916. e. UCLA. Films inc: The Sleeping City; Because of You; Law and Order; The Man from Laramie; Under Ten Flags; Three Came Back (& prod-dir); The Savage Guns; Ride and Kill; Bloody Mama; Point of Terror (dir only); The Night God Screamed; King Kong. TV inc: (dir) The Westerners; The Wackiest Ship in the Army; Jesse James; Daniel Boone; Wild, Wild West; Tarzan; Escape. Thea inc: (dir) The Best Man; Cat on a Hot Tin Roof; River in a High Place; La Ronde.

NIELSEN, Leslie: Act. b. Regina, Sask, Can, Feb 11, 1922. Summer stock, TV. Screen debut, 1956, Vagabond King. Films inc: Forbidden Planet; Ransom!; The Opposite Sex; Hot Summer Night; Tammy and the Bachelor; Night Train to Paris; Harlow; Dark Intruder; Beau Geste; Gunfight in Abilene; The Reluctant Astronaut; Counterpoint; Rosie; Dayton's Devil; How to Commit Marriage; Change of Mind; The Resurrection of Zachary Wheeler; The Poseidon Adventure; Viva Knievel!; The Amsterdam Kill; City On Fire; Airplane; Prom Night.

TV inc: Studio One; Kraft Playhouse; Robert Montgomery Presents; Suspense; Danger; Man Behind the Badge; Death of a Salesman; The New Breed; Swamp Fox; Peyton Place; Ben Casey; The Loner; Institute For Revenge; Backstairs At The White House; OHMS; National Geographic Society Special (narr).

NIMOY, Leonard: Act. b. Boston, Mar 26, 1931. Screen debut 1951 Queen For A Day. Films inc: Deathwatch; The Balcony; Francis Goes To West Point; Kid Monk Baroni; Invasion of the Body Snatchers; Star Trek-The Movie.

TV inc: Bonanza; Dr Kildare; Gunsmoke; Dragnet; Star Trek; Mission Impossible; Seizure-The Story of Kathy Morris. Thea inc: My Fair Lady; Sherlock Holmes; Twelfth Night; Caligula; Fourposter.

NIMS, Ernest J: Exec. b. Des Moines, IA, Nov 15, 1908. e. U of IA. Started in cutting dept Fox Films, 1930; joined Universal Pictures 1946; post prod exec, 1949-58; asso prod CBS-TV, 1958-61; pre prod exec Universal, 1962-64; vp & pre prod exec, 1965-75. Retired.

NITZSCHE, Jack: Comp. b. Chicago, IL, 1937. Films inc: Performance; One Flew Over the Cuckoo's Nest; The Exorcist; Blue Collar; Hardcore; Greaser's Palace; When You Comin' Back Red Ryder; Cruisin.

NIVEN, David: Act. b. Kirriemuir, Scotland, Mar 1, 1910. Films inc: Thank You Jeeves; Dodsworth; The Charge of the Light Brigade; The Prisoner of Zenda; Three Blind Mice; Wuthering Heights; Raffles; Stairway to Heaven; The Bishop's Wife; Around the World in 80 Days; Oh Men! Oh Women!; Bonjour Tristesse; Separate Tables *(Oscar*-1958); The Guns of Navarone; The Pink Panther; The Impossible Years; The Kremlin Letter; The Paper Tiger; No Deposit, No Return; Murder by Death; Death On The Nile; Escape To Athena; Rough Cut; The Sea Wolves.

TV inc: A Man Called Intrepid.

NIVEN, David Jr: Exec. b. London, Dec 15, 1942. Joined William Morris Agency, 1963; next five yrs worked for agency's European offices in Rome, Madrid, London; in 1968 joined Columbia UK office as prodn exec; 1972, named UK m-dir Paramount; 1976, became indep prod, forming partnership with Jack Wiener.

Films inc: The Eagle Has Landed; Escape To Athena.

NIVEN, Kip: Act. b. Kansas City, MO, May 27, 1945. Films inc: In Cold Blood; Magnum Force; Newman's Law; Earthquake; Airport '75; The Hindenburg.

TV inc: A Fire In the Sky; Shadow of Fear; The Sky Trap; Blind Ambition.

NIXON, Graeme Lewis: Sls Exec. b. Gillingham, Kent, Eng, Jan 13, 1936. e. Auckland U Coll. GM, TV Int'l Ent Ltd, UK 1962-67; European controller MCA records & U Pictures, UK 1967; 70: group controller Cinema Int'l Corp, Holland 1970-74; Far East and Australia sls supv CIC TV, Australia 1976.

NIXON, Marni: Act. b. 1929. Singer, who "ghost-sang" for many stars inc: Margaret O'Brien in Big City; Deborah Kerr in The King and I; Natalie Wood in West Side Story; Audrey Hepburn in My Fair Lady. Appeared in The Sound of Music, 1965.

NIZER, Louis: Atty. b. London, Feb 6, 1902. e. Columbia Coll, BA, Columbia U, LLB. Exec secy NY Film Board of Trade since 1928. Atty for many personalities in films; stage; opera; counsel to mp cos, prods, film, stage, radio execs. Author: Analysis of Standard Exhibition Contract; Analysis of Motion Picture Code.

NOBLE, James: Act. b. Dallas, TX, Mar 5, 1922. e. SMU. TV inc: As The World Turns; The Doctors; Circle of Children, Part II; The Split; Equal and Orderly Justice; The Summer of My German Soldier; Benson; Baby Comes Home.
    Films inc: What's So Bad About Feeling Good?; The Sporting Club; 1776; Being There; 10; The Nude Bomb.
    Bway inc: Come of Age; A Far Country; Johnny No Trump; 1776; The Runner Stumbles.

NOIRET, Philippe: Act. b. France, 1931. With Theatre National Populaire, worked as nitery entertainer before film debut in Agnes Varda's short La Pointe Court.
    Films inc: Zazie; Ravissante; The Billionaire; Crime Does Not Pay; Therese Desqueyroux; None But the Lonely Spy; Death, Where Is Thy Victory; Les Copains; Lady L; La Vie de Chateau; Tender Scoundrel; Night of the Generals; Woman Times Seven; The Assassination Bureau; Mr Freedom; Justine; Topaz; Clerambard; Give Her the Moon; A Room in Paris; Murphy's War; The French Conspiracy; The Serpent; La Grande Bouffe; Custer; Let Joy Reign Supreme; The Old Gun; The Judge and the Assassin; A Woman at Her Window; Desert of the Tartars; Dear Inspector; Due Pezzi di Pane; Who Is Killing the Great Chefs of Europe; Death Watch; Rue du Pied-de-grue; Une Semaine de Vacances; Pile Ou Face (Heads or Tails).

NOLAN, Bob: Sngwri-Singer. b. Canada, 1909. Joined Roy Rogers' Rocky Moutaineers 1931, left after year; 1933 joined Rogers, Tim Spencer in the Pioneer Trio on KFWB radio, LA; named changed to Sons of the Pioneers after an anncr mistakenly introed the expanded group under that name; Rogers left in 1937 but group remained together until 1949, selling an estimated 35,000,000 records. Nolan wrote more than 1,000 C&W songs including Cool Water; Tumbling Tumbleweeds which was group's theme song.
    (Died June 16, 1980).

NOLAN, Jeanette: Act. b. LA, Dec 30, 1911. With Dick Powell in radio series, Hollywood Hotel. Also played other roles on radio. On screen from 1948.
    Films inc: Words and Music; Macbeth; No Sad Songs for Me; The Big Heat; Tribute to a Bad Man; April Love; The Great Impostor; Two Rode Together; The Man Who Shot Liberty Valance; My Blood Runs Cold; The Reluctant Astronaut; Did You Hear the One about the Traveling Saleslady; Avalanche; The Manitou.
    TV inc: Hotel de Paree; Better Late Than Never; The Hustler of Muscle Beach.

NOLAN, Kathleen: Act. b. St. Louis, Sep 27, 1933. Career began on a Mississippi show boat which traveled between Cincinnati and New Orleans. Elected 1st woman pres Screen Actors Guild, 1975; reelected 1977. Films inc: The Desperadoes Are in Town; No Time to be Young; Benjie Gault; Limbo. TV inc: The Real McCoys; Playhouse 90; Jamie; Broadside; Name of the Game; The Immigrants.

NOLAN, Lloyd: Act. b. San Francisco, Aug 11, 1902. Joined Pasadena Playhouse 1927. Worked as stage hand, Cape Cod. On screen from 1934. Films inc: Stolen Harmony; Guadalcanal Diary; Bataan; Circumstantial Evidence; Captain Eddie; The House on 92nd Street; Lady in the Lake; Wild Harvest; Two Smart People; Street with No Name; Easy Living; Bad Boy; The Lemon Drop Kid; Island in the Sky; Crazylegs; Santiago; Abandon Ship; A Hatful of Rain; Peyton Place; Susan Slade; Circus World; Sergeant Ryker; Airport; Earthquake.
    Thea inc: The Front Page; Reunion in Vienna; One Sunday Afternoon; Caine Mutiny Court Martial.
    TV inc: The Caine Mutiny Court Martial (Emmy-1955); Martin Kane Private Eye; Julia; Valentine.

NOLAN, Patrick J: Wri. b. Bronx, NY, Jan 2, 1933. e. Villanove, BA; Detroit U, MA; Bryn Mawr, Phd. TV inc: Hourglass Movement; The Jericho Mile (Emmy-1979).

NOLTE, Nick: Act. b. Omaha, NE, 1934. Appeared in repertory. Films inc: The Deep; Dog Soldiers; Who'll Stop the Rain; North Dallas Forty; Heart Beat.
    TV inc: Rich Man, Poor Man.

NOONE, Peter: Singer-Mus. b. Nov 5, 1947. Original Herman of Herman's Hermits; ret for some years, returned with group The Tremblers.

NORGARD, John Davey: Exec. b. Adelaide, Australia, Feb 3, 1914. Chmn, Australian Broadcasting Commission.

NORRIS, Christopher: Act. b. NYC, Oct 7, 1953. Bway inc: The Sound of Music; The Secret Life of Walter Mitty; The Playroom. TV inc: Mr and Mrs Bo Jo Jones; Lady of the House; Great American Beauty Contest; Suddenly Love; Trapper John; The Great American Traffic Jam. Films inc: Summer of '42; Airport 75; Mortadella; Eat My Dust.

NORTH, Alex: Comp. b. Chester, PA, Dec 4, 1910. e. Curtis Institute, Juilliard, Moscow Conservatory. Film scores inc: Death of a Salesman; Viva Zapata!; A Streetcar Named Desire; Member of the Wedding; Desiree; I'll Cry Tomorrow; The Rose Tattoo; The Rainmaker; Unchained; The Bad Seed; The Long Hot Summer; The Sound and The Fury; Spartacus; The Misfits; Cleopatra; The Agony and the Ecstasy; Who's Afraid of Virginia Woolf?; The Devil's Brigade; The Shoes of the Fisherman; Lost in the Stars; Shanks; Bite the Bullet; Passover Plot; Somebody Killed Her Husband; Carny.
    TV inc: Playhouse 90; Nero Wolfe; I'm a Lawyer; F D Roosevelt Series; Silent Night; The Man and the City; Rich Man, Poor Man (Emmy-1976).
    Bway inc: Death of a Saleman; Innocents; Coriolanus; Richard III; 'Tis of Thee; Queen of Sheba; The Great Campaign.

NORTH, Edmund H: Wri. b. NYC, Mar 12, 1911. e. Stanford. Films inc: One Night of Love; I Dream Too Much; Dishonored Lady; Flamingo Road; Young Man With A Horn; Day The Earth Stood Still; Outcasts of Poker Flat; Destry; Cowboy; Sink the Bismarck; H M S Defiant; Patton (Oscar-1970); Meteor.

NORTH, Sheree Act. b. LA, Jan 17, 1933. Films inc: Excuse My Dust; How to be Very Popular; The Best Things in Life are Free; The Way to the Gold; No Down Payment; Mardi Gras; Madigan; The Gypsy Moths; Charley Varick; Breakout; The Shootist; Only Once In A Lifetime; Rabbit Test.
    TV inc: Eddie; Breaking Point; A Real American Hero; Amateur Night At The Dixie Bar & Grill; Women In White; Portrait of a Stripper; A Christmas For Boomer; Marilyn--The Untold Story; I'm A Big Girl Now.
    Bway inc: Hazel Flagg; I Can Get It for You Wholesale.

NORTON, William Lloyd: Wri-Dir. b. CA, Aug 13, 1943. Films inc: Cisco Pike (& dir); Outlaw Blues; Convoy; More American Graffiti (& dir).
    TV inc: Gargoyles.

NORVET, Robert W: Exec. b. Forest City, IA, Aug 17, 1922. e. Grinnell Coll, BA. Bus M, MGM-TV, 1952-60; dir, film prod operations, CBS-TV; GM, CBS Studio Center; VP, CBS Studio Center; VP, Prodn facilities, CTN Hollywood.

NORVO, Red: Mus. b. Beardstown, IL, Mar 31, 1908. First to play jazz on xylophone, vibraharp. Began as sideman with Paul Ash orch; with Victor Young as staff musican NBC; sideman Paul Whiteman Band; married Mildred Bailey, formed own orch which backed her for nitery, recording dates; later with Benny Goodman; Woody Herman.

NOVAK, Kim (Marilyn Novak): Act. b. Chicago, Feb 13, 1933. Began as model. Screen debut, 1953, The French Line. Films inc: Pushover; Phfft; Five Against the House; Picnic; Man with the Golden Arm; The Eddie Duchin Story; Jeanne Eagles; Pal Joey; Middle of the Night; Bell, Book and Candle; Vertigo; Pepe; Strangers When We Meet; The Notorious Landlady; Boys' Night Out; Of Human Bondage; Kiss Me, Stupid; The Amorous Adventures of Moll Flanders; The Legend of Lylah Clare; The Great Bank Robbery; Tales That Witness Madness; The White Buffalo; Just A Gigolo; The Mirror Crack'd.

TV inc: Third Girl from the Left.

NOVELLO, Don (Father Guido Sarducci): Act-Wri. b. Ashtabula, OH. Ad agency copywriter, began writing comedy material, emerged as stand-up comic; created character of Father Guido Sarducci, performs under that name but writes as Novello. TV inc: Smothers Brothers Show; Saturday Night Live.

Bway inc: Gilda Radner--Live from New York.

Films inc: Gilda Live.

NUGENT, Elliott: Plywri-Prod-Act. b. Dover, OH, Sep 20, 1899. Vaude debut age 4 in parents act, in vaude throught teens. On Bway (act) Dulcy, Kempy (& co-wri); Poor Nut (& co-wri); Voice of the Turtle; The Male Animal (co-wri);

Films inc: (act) College Life; Not So Dumb; Richest Man in the World; Unholy Three, Stage Door Canteen. (Dir) The Mouthpiece; And So They Were Married; Professor Beware; Give Me A Sailor; Cat and the Canary; Nothing But the Truth; Up in Arms; My Favorite Brunette; Mr. Belvedere Goes to College; Just for You.

(Died Aug 9, 1980)

NUGENT, Ted: Sngwri-Singer. b. Detroit, MI, Dec 13, 1948. Started group Amboy Dukes, name later changed to Ted Nugent and the Amboy Dukes, finally Ted Nugent. Albums inc: Journey to the Center of the Mind; Migration; Survival of the Fittest; Tooth, Fang and Claw; Ted Nugent; Free for All; Cat Scratch Fever; Double Live Gonzo; Weekend Warriors; Scream Dream.

NUNN, Trevor: Dir. b. Ipswich, Suffolk, England, Jan 14, 1940. e. Downing College Cambridge. Thea inc; (London) The Thwarting of Baron Bolligrew; Henry IV; Tango; The Revenger's Tragedy; The Taming of the Shrew; King Lear; Much Ado About Nothing; The Winter's Tale; Henry VIII; Hamlet; The Romans; Macbeth; Hedda Gabler; Antony and Cleopatra; The Comedy of Errors; Once In a Lifetime; The Life and Adventures of Nicholas Nickleby; Juno and the Paycock.

NUREYEV, Rudolf: Act. b. Russia, Mar 17, 1938. Attended Leningrad Ballet School. Joined Kirov Ballet Company as soloist. While performing in Paris in 1961, asked for and was granted political asylum. Joined Marquis de Cuevan Ballet Company. Films inc: An Evening With the Royal Ballet; Swan Lake; Romeo and Juliet; The Sleeping Beauty; Don Quixote; Valentino. TV inc: Julie Andrew's Invitation to the Dance with Rudolf Nureyev.

NUYEN, France: Act. b. Marseilles, Jul 31, 1939. Began career as an artists' model. Films inc: South Pacific; In Love and War; The Last Time I Saw Archie; Diamond Head; A Girl Named Tamiko; Man in the Middle; Dimension 5; One More Train to Rob.

NYBY, Christian: Dir. b. LA, Sep 1, 1913. Films inc: The Thing; Hell on Devil's Island; Six-Gun Law; Young Fury; Operation CIA; First to Fight.

NYBY, Christian II: Dir-Wri. b. Glendale, CA, Jun 1, 1941. e. USC, BA. TV inc: Emergency; Ironside; Adam 12; Six Million Dollar Man; Rockford Files; Sword of Justice; Swiss Family Robinson; CHiPs; The Hardy Boys; Battlestar Galactica; B J and the Bear.

NYKVIST, Sven: Cin. b. Sweden, 1922. Films inc: Sawdust and Tinsel; Karin Mansdotter; The Virgin Spring; Winter Light; The Silence; Loving Couples; Persona; Hour of the Wolf; The Last Run; One Day in the Life of Ivan Denisovitch; Cries and Whispers (Oscar-1973); Black Moon; The Tenant (& act); Serpent's Egg; Pretty Baby; Autumn Sonata; Starting Over; Hurricane;. Marmalad Upporet (The Marmalade Revolution); From the Life of the Marionettes; Willie & Phil.

NYPE, Russell: Act. b. Zion, IL, Apr 26, 1924. e. Lake Forest College, BA. Bway inc: Regina; Great To Be Alive; Call Me Madam (Tony-supp-1951); Wake Up, Darling; Carousel; Goldilocks (Tony-supp-1959); Brigadoon; My Fair Lady; The Girl in the Freudian Slip; Hello, Dolly!.

TV inc: The Milton Berle Show; Ed Sullivan Show; One Touch of Venus.

Films inc: Can't Stop the Music.

OAKLAND, Ben (nee Oaklander): Comp-Prod. b. NYC, Sep 24, 1907. Vaudeville pianist for Helen Morgan; George Jessel. Wri, dir, prod, personal appearances of Jeanette MacDonald; Tony Martin; Joe E. Lewis; Nelson Eddy; Josephine Baker; Nanette Fabray; Bob Hope; Jimmy Durante; Dorothy Lamour.

Films inc: (songs & background music) The Big Store; The Eddie Duchin Story; Jeanne Eagles Story; Jolson Sings Again; They Shoot Horses Don't They; Funny Lady.

Bway inc: Ziegfeld Follies; Earl Carrolls Vanities; Sketch Book; Casino De Paree; How It Looks From Here.

TV inc: Down Tin Pan Alley (prod); George Jessel Show; Texaco Star Theatre; Here Come the Stars.

Songs inc: If I Love Again; I'll Take Romance; Gone with the Wind; Roses in December; Two Loves Have I; Pink Cocktail for a Blue Lady.

(Died Aug 26, 1979).

OAKLAND, Simon: Act. b. NYC, 1922. Films inc: The Brothers Karamazov; I Want to Live; Psycho; West Side Story; Wall of Noise; The Satan Bug; The Plainsman; The Sand Pebbles; Tony Rome; Chubasco; On a Clear Day You Can See Forever; Chato's Land; Happy Mother's Day. . .Love, George.

TV inc: Man Undercover.

Bway inc: The Shadow Box.

OAK RIDGE BOYS: Country Music Group. Members: William Lee Golden; Richard Sterban; Joe Bonsall; Duane Allen. TV inc: A Country Christmas.

(Grammys-(4)-gospel perf-1970, 1974, 1976, 1977).

OATES, Warren: Act. b. Depoy, KY, 1932. Films inc: Yellowstone Kelly; Private Property; Hero's Island; Mail Order Bride; Major Dundee; Return of the Seven; In the Heat of the Night; Crooks and Coronets; The Wild Bunch; There Was a Crooked Man; Tom Sawyer; Dillinger; The White Dawn; Badlands; 92 in the Shade; Race with the Devil; Drum; China 9 Liberty 37; The Brink's Job; 1941.

TV inc: And Baby Makes Six; True Grit; My Old Man; Baby Comes Home.

OBERON, Merle (Estelle Merle O'Brien Thompson): Act. b. Tasmania, Feb 19, 1911. Screen debut 1930, Wedding Rehearsal. Films inc: The Private Life of Henry VIII; Folies Bergere (her first in Hollywood); The Scarlet Pimpernel; Dark Angel; Beloved Enemy; Wuthering Heights; The Cowboy and the Lady; Till We Meet Again; The Lodger; A Song To Remember; Lydia; Forever And a Day; Berlin Express; Desiree; Deep In My Heart; The Oscar; Hotel; Interval.

(Died Nov 23, 1979).

OBOLER, Arch: Prod-Dir-Wri. Started as wri on radio; created series Lights Out. Films inc: Escape (sp); Bewitched; The Arnelo Affair; Five; The Twonky; Bwana Devil (in 3-D); The Bubble.

O'BRIAN, Hugh (Hugh J Krampe): Act. b. Rochester, NY, Apr 19, 1930. Films inc: Young Lovers; Vengeance Valley; Sally and St. Anne; Meet Me at the Fair; Saskatchewan; Broken Lance; There's No Business Like Show Business; Come Fly With Me; Strategy of Terror; Killer Force; The Shootist; Game of Death.

TV inc: Wyatt Earp; Dial M for Murder; A Punt, A Pass and A Prayer; Murder on Flight 502; Greatest Heroes of the Bible; The Seekers.

Bway credits inc: Destry Rides Again; First Love; Guys and Dolls.

O'BRIEN, Edmond: Act-Dir. b. NYC, Sep 10, 1915. Films inc: The Hunchback of Notre Dame; Parachute Battalion; The Killers; The Web; A Double Life; Another Part of the Forest; An Act of Murder; White Heat; Between Midnight and Dawn; Two of a Kind; Julius Caesar; The Hitch Hiker; Man in the Dark; The Bigamist; The Barefoot Contessa (*Oscar*-supp-1954); Shield for Murder; 1984; The Third Voice; Mantrap (prod-dir); The Great Imposter; The Man Who Shot Liberty Valance; Birdman of Alcatraz; Seven Days in May; Sylvia; Fantastic Voyage; The Viscount; The Wild Bunch; The Love God; Jigsaw; 99 44/100ths% Dead.

TV inc: Johnny Midnight; Wyatt Earp; 333 Montgomery Street; Flesh and Blood; Sam Benedict.

O'BRIEN, Jack: Dir. b. Saginaw, MI, Jun 18, 1939. e. U of MI, AB, MA. APA staff dir, 1964-1969; San Diego Shakespeare Festival, 1969-1977; Houston Grand Opera, 1976-1979. Bway inc: Cock-A-Doodle-Dandy; The Time of Your Life (rev); Porgy and Bess (rev).

O'BRIEN, Margaret: Act. b. LA, Jan 15, 1937. Screen debut age 4, Babes in Arms. (*Honorary Oscar*-1944). Films inc: Journey for Margaret; Lost Angel; Thousands Cheer; Jane Eyre; The Canterville Ghost; Meet Me in St. Louis; Three Wise Fools; Tenth Avenue Angel; Secret Garden; Little Women; Her First Romance; Anabelle Lee; Diabolic Wedding.

O'BRIEN, Pat: Act. b. Milwaukee, WI, Nov 11, 1899. Started career as a chorus boy on Bway, 1919. Screen debut 1931, The Front Page. Films inc: Oil For The Lamps Of China; Knute Rockne; Ceiling Zero; Angels With Dirty Faces; Having A Wonderful Crime; The Fighting 69th; The Iron Major; The Last Hurrah; Fighting Father Dunne; The Boy With Green Hair; Some Like It Hot; The Phynx; The End.

TV inc: The Other Woman (2 *Emmys*-actor in daytime special & daytime actor of year-1974); Scout's Honor.

O'BRIEN, Virginia: Singer-Act. b. LA, 1921. Originated "deadpan" singing technique in stage revue Meet the People.

Films inc: Hullabaloo; The Big Store; Ship Ahoy; Lady Be Good; Ringside Maisie; Thousands Cheer; Meet the People; DuBarry Was A Lady; Two Girls and a Sailor; The Harvey Girls; Ziegfeld Follies; Till The Clouds Roll By; Ziegfeld Follies; Merton of the Movies.

O'BRIEN-MOORE, Erin: Act. b. LA. Films inc: The Life of Emile Zola; Black Legion; Little Men; Destination Moon; The Long Grey Line; Phantom of the Rue Morgue; How to Succeed in Business Without Really Trying.

TV inc: The Ruggles; Peyton Place.

Thea inc: Street Scene; Riddle Me This; Tortilla Flat; Men Must Fight; State of the Union.

(Died May 3, 1979).

O'CONNELL, Arthur: Act. b. NYC, Mar 29, 1908. In vaudeville, stock. Films inc: Murder in Soho; Picnic; Solid Gold Cadillac; Man in the Gray Flannel Suit; Bus Stop; Picnic; Anatomy of a Murder; The Proud Ones; There Was a Crooked Man; The Poseidon Adventure; The Hiding Place; Suppose They Gave a War and Nobody Came. Thea inc: Golden Boy; Picnic; Anna Christie; Lunatics and Lovers.

O'CONNELL, Helen: Singer. b. Lima, OH, 1920. Singer with name bands, recording artist.

TV inc: Co-host Miss USA Beauty Pageant; Miss Universe Beauty Pageant; numerous guest appearances; segs.

O'CONNOR, Carroll: Act. b. NYC, Sep 2, 1925. e. U Coll, Dublin, U of MT. With Dublin Gate Theatre, then NY stage in Ulysses in Nighttown; Playboy of the Western World; The Big Knife. Screen debut, 1960, Fever in the Blood.

Films inc: By Love Possessed; Lonely Are the Brave; Cleopatra; In Harm's Way; What Did You Do in the War Daddy?; Hawaii; Not With My Wife You Don't; Waterhole No. 3; The Devil's Brigade; For Love of Ivy; Kelly's Heroes; Doctors' Wives; Law and Disorder.

TV inc: US Steel Hour; Armstrong Circle Theatre; Kraft Theatre; All In The Family (*Emmys*-1972-1977-1978-1979); The Last Hurrah (& wri); Bender (exec prod); Archie Bunker's Place. Author: (play) Ladies of Hanover Tower; (screenplays) Little Anjie Always; The Great Robinson.

O'CONNOR, Donald: Act. b. Chicago, Aug 28, 1925. In vaudeville before screen debut 1938, Sing You Sinners. Films inc: Men With Wings; Million Dollar Legs; Beau Geste; On Your Toes; What's Cookin'?; The Merry Monahans; Singin' in the Rain; No Business Like Show Business; The Buster Keaton Story; Cry Me Happy; That Funny Feeling; That's Entertainment; The Big Fix.

TV inc: The Donald O'Connor Show (*Emmy*-1953); Lucy Moves To NBC.

O'DAY, Anita: Singer. b. Chicago, IL, Dec 18, 1919. Singer with Gene Krupa, Stan Kenton. Recordings inc: Let Me Off Uptown; And Her Tears Flowed Like Wine. Albums inc: Anita Swings Cole Porter; Anita Sings; The Lady is a Tramp; Anita Sings the Winners.

ODETTA (Odetta Holmes): Act. b. Birmingham, AL, Dec 31, 1930. Folk music recording artist; recitals inc: Town Hall; Carnegie Hall. Films inc: Cinerama Holiday.

TV inc: TV Tonight.

OGIER, Bulle: Act. Films inc: Les idoles; L'amour feu; Pierre et Paul; 48 Hours of Love; Piege; Paulina s'en va; M comme Mathieu; Out One; Les stances a Sophie; Rendezvous at Bray; The Salamander; The Valley; The Discreet Charm of the Bourgeoisie; Meet Some of My Best Friends; Bel Ordure; Projection Privee; Celine and Julie Go Boating; La Paloma; Mariage; Un divorce heureux; Maitresse; Flocons d'or; A Short Memory; Never Again Always; Serail; Les Aventures de Holly and Wood; Navire Night; The Third Generation.

O'HARA, Gerry: Dir. b. Boston-Lincs, Eng, 1924. Film inc: That Kind of Girl; Game for Three Lovers; Pleasure Girls (& sp); Maroc 7; Love in Amsterdam; All the Right Noises (& sp); The Bitch.

TV inc: The Avengers; Man in a Suitcase; Journey into the Unknown.

O'HARA, Maureen (nee FitzSimons): Act. b. Dublin, Aug 17, 1920. e. Abbey School of Acting. On Screen from 1938. Films inc: Kicking the Moon Around; Jamaica Inn; The Hunchback of Notre Dame; A Bill of Divorcement; How Green Was My Valley; To the Shores of Tripoli; Ten Gentlemen from West Point; The Black Swan; The Fallen Sparrow; Buffalo Bill; The Spanish Main; Do You Love Me?; Miracle on 34th Street; The Foxes of Harrow; The Homestretch; Sitting Pretty; Sentimental Journey; Sinbad the Sailor; Father Was a Fullback; Comanche Territory; Tripoli; Bagdad; Rio Grande; At Sword's Point; Flame of Araby; The Quiet Man; Against All Flags; The Redhead from Wyoming; Fire Over Africa; Lady Godiva; The Long Gray Line; Wings of Eagles; The Deadly Companions; Our Man in Havana; Dr. Hobbs Takes a Vacation; McLintock!; Spencer's Mountain; The Parent Trap; The Rare Breed; The Battle of Villa Fiorita; How Do I Love Thee?; Big Jake; The Red Pony.

O'HERLIHY, Dan (Daniel Peter O'Herlihy): Act. b. Wexford, Ireland, May 1, 1919. e. National U of Ireland. With Abbey Theatre, Dublin. Films inc: Odd Man Out; At Swords Point; Actors and Sin; Adventures of Robinson Crusoe; Black Shield of Falworth; Bengal Brigade; Purple Mask; The Virgin Queen; That Woman Opposite; City After Midnight; Failsafe; Home Before Dark; 100 Rifles; The Tamarind Seed; MacArthur.

Thea inc: The Ivy Green; Red Roses For Me.

TV inc: A Man Called Sloan; Hunter's Moon; Mark Twain--Beneath the Laughter.

O'HERLIHY, Michael: Dir. b. Dublin, Ireland, Apr 1, 1928. e. Castleknock Coll, Dublin. TV inc: Maverick; 77 Sunset Strip; Hawaiian Eye; Surfside 6; Mr. Novak; Richard Boone Theatre; Profiles in Courage; Rawhide; Gunsmoke; Fighting Prince of Donegal; The One and Only Family Band; Smith; Willie and the Yank; The Loner; Hawaii Five-0 (42 episodes); Deadly Harvest; Young Pioneers I; Young Pioneers II; Kiss Me, Kill Me; Peter Lundy and the Medicine Hat Stallion; The Magnificent Hustle; The Dublin Incident (& prod); Backstairs at the White House; The Flame Is Love; Dallas Cowboy Cheerleaders II; Detour to Terror; The Great Cash Giveaway; Cry of the Innocent; Desperate Voyage; A Time For Miracles.

OHLMEYER, Don: Prod. e. Notre Dame. Joined ABC Sports 1967 as prod-dir all leading sports events; 1977 to NBC as exec prod sports.
    TV inc: NFL Monday Football *(Emmy-*1976); Monday Night Baseball; Wide World of Sports *(Emmy-*1976); Superstars; 1968, 1972, 1976 Summer Olympics; 1976 Winter Games (Emmy); Battle of The Network Stars; US against the World; Super Bowl Saturday Night; The Golden Moment--An Olympic Love Story; Games People Play.

OHLSSON, Terry: Dir. b. Sydney, Australia, Dec 30, 1938. Films inc: Year of the Cortina; Cortina Conquest; Mountain Men; David's Day; Call for a Bird; Corsair; First Time Around; She's a Lady; The Green Machine; The Overseas Connection.

OISTRAKH, David: Violinist. b. Odessa, Russia, 1908. e. Odessa Conservatory. Made professional debut age 12; toured USSR several times, later made world tours as guest soloist major symphonies. Recs inc: Brahms Double Concerto *(Grammy-*class inst solo-1970); Shostakovich Violin Concerto No. 1 *(Grammy-*class inst solo with orch-1974).

OKUN, Milt: Act. b. NYC, Dec 23, 1923. e. CCNY, Oberlin Conservatory of Mus. Folk Mus recording artist; mus dir for various groups.

OLIANSKY, Joel: Wri-Dir. b. NYC, Oct 11, 1935. e. Yale, MFA. TV inc: The Senator *(Emmy-*1971); Kojak; Quincy; The Law.
    Films inc: The Competition.

OLIM, Dorothy: Prod-Manager. b. Oct 14, 1934. Thea inc: (prod) I Must Be Talking to My Friends; Pimpernel!; The Golden Apple; The Lion in Love; A Worm in Horseradish. (asso prod): The Fantasticks.

OLIVER, Gordon: Prod-Act. b. LA, Apr 27, 1910. On screen from 1936 in Draegerman Courage. Films inc: Fugitive in the Sky; The Go Getter; War Lords; Since You Went Away; The Spiral Staircase; Born to be Bad; Station West; Las Vegas Story.
    TV inc: (prod) Peter Gunn series; Mr. Lucky; Profiles in Courage; It Takes a Thief.

OLIVER, Susan (Charlotte Gercke): Act. b. NYC, Feb 13, 1937. e. Swarthmore Coll. Films inc: Green-Eyed Blonde; The Gene Krupa Story; Looking for Love; The Disorderly Orderly; Your Cheating Heart; A Man Called Gannon; Change of Mind; Widow's Nest. TV inc: Peyton Place.

OLIVIER, Laurence, Lord: Act. b. Dorking, Eng, May 22, 1907. On stage London, NY since 1925. Films inc: As You Like It; Romeo and Juliet; Fire Over England; Wuthering Heights; Rebecca; Henry V (& dir); Hamlet (& prod-dir) *(Oscar-*act-1948); Term of Trial; Prince and the Showgirl; Devil's Disciple; Three Sisters; Sleuth; Nicholas & Alexandra; The Ruling Class; Lady Caroline Lamb; Marathon Man; A Bridge Too Far; The Betsy; The Boys From Brazil; A Little Romance; Dracula; The Jazz Singer. *(Honorary Oscars-*1948, 1978).
    TV inc: The Moon and Sixpence *(Emmy-*1960); The Power and the Glory; Uncle Vanya; Long Day's Journey into Night *(Emmy-*1973); Love Among the Ruins *(Emmy-*1975).
    Thea inc: Antony & Cleopatra; Venus Observed; Sleeping Prince; The Entertainer; Becket; Othello; The Crucible; Long Day's Journey into Night; Amphitryon 38 (dir); Saturday, Sunday, Monday; Eden End (dir); Filumena (dir).

OLIVO, Frank: Dir. b. NYC, Nov 18, 1941. e. Queens College, NY. TV inc: Eyewitness News Conference; A.M. New York. (Docs): NYPD; Paul Robeson - The Man; City in Crisis; Harlem; Black Out; Underground Railroad; Tribute to Paul Robeson; Israel Today; Littlest Junkie; Teenage Alcoholics; Dr Luther King; Sidney Poitier; Harry Belafonte; Count Basie; Lionel Hampton; Jazz Today.

O'LOUGHLIN, Gerald S: Act. b. NYC, Dec 23, 1921. e. U of Rochester. Bway inc: Streetcar Named Desire; Shadow of a Gunman; The Dark at the Top of the Stairs; A Touch of the Poet; A Cook for Mr. General; One Flew Over the Cuckoo's Nest;
    Films inc: Lovers and Lollypops; Cop Hater; Hatful of Rain; Ensign Calculated Risk. Pulver; A Fine Madness; In Cold Blood; The Valachi Papers; Desperate Characters; The Organization; Twilight's Last Gleaming.
    TV inc: For the People; Going My Way; The Rookies; Women in White; Blind Ambition; Detour to Terror; Pleasure Palace.

OLSEN, Merlin: Act. b. Logan, UT, Sep 15, 1940. e. UT State, BS, MS. Former pro football star. Films inc: Mitchell; Something Big; One More Train to Rob; The Undefeated.
    TV inc: Little House on the Prairie; The Golden Moment-An Olympic Love Story.

OLSON, James: Act. b. Evanston, IL, Oct 8, 1930. Bway inc: The Young and the Beautiful; Romulus; The Chinese Prime Minister; Breakfast at Tiffany's.
    Films inc: Moon Zero Two; Rachel, Rachel; The Andromeda Strain; The Groundstar Conspiracy; The Mafu Cage.
    TV inc: Greatest Heroes of the Bible; Moviola.

OLSON, Nancy: Act. b. Milwaukee, WI, 1928. e. U of WI, UCLA. Films inc: Canadian Pacific; Union Station; Sunset Boulevard; Submarine Command; Force of Arms; So Big; Battle Cry; Pollyanna; The Absent Minded Professor; Son of Flubber; Smith!; Snowball Express; Airport 1975.

OLSSON, Nigel: Act-Sngwri. b. Wallasey, Eng, Feb 10, 1949. Recording artist. Played drums behind Elton John, Rod Stewart, Linda Ronstadt before writing and recording own songs.

O'NEAL, Patrick: Act. b. Ocala, FL, Sep 26, 1927. Films inc: The Mad Magician; From the Terrace; The Cardinal; In Harm's Way; King Rat; A Fine Madness; Alvarez Kelly; Assignment to Kill; Castle Keep; The Kremlin Letters; Corky; The Way We Were; The Stepford Wives.
    TV inc: Dick and the Duchess; Kaz; Make Me An Offer; True Position (dir).
    Thea inc: Oh Men, Oh Women; Laurette; A Far Country; Stalag 17; The Night of the Iguana.

O'NEAL, Ron: Act. b. Utica, NY, Sep 1, 1937. Began as member of Karamu Theatre, Cleveland; then off-Bway in American Pastorale; The Mummer's Play; No Place to Be Somebody.
    Films inc: Move; The Organization; Super Fly; Super Fly TNT; The Master Gunfighter; When a Stranger Calls; The Final Countdown.
    TV inc: Freedom Road; Brave New World; Guyana Tragedy--The Story of Jim Jones.

O'NEAL, Ryan (Patrick Ryan O'Neal): Act. b. LA, Apr 20, 1941. Films inc: The Big Bounce; The Games; Love Story; Wild Rovers; What's Up, Doc?; Paper Moon; The Thief Who Came to Dinner; Barry Lyndon; Nickelodeon; A Bridge Too Far; The Driver; Oliver's Story; The Main Event.
    TV inc: Peyton Place; Dobie Gillis; The Untouchables; Bachelor Father; My Three Sons; Under the Yum Yum Tree; Love Hate Love.

O'NEAL, Tatum: Act. b. LA, Nov 5, 1963. D of Ryan O'Neal. Debuted on screen age 9, Paper Moon *(Oscar-*supp-1973). Films inc: The Bad News Bears; Nickelodeon; International Velvet; Little Darlings; Circle Of Two.

O'NEIL, Barbara: Act. b. St Louis, MO, Jul 10, 1911. Films inc: Stella Dallas; The Toy Wife; When Tomorrow Comes; Tower of London; Gone With the Wind; All This and Heaven Too; I Remember Mama; Whirlpool; Flame of the Islands; The Nun's Story.
    (Died Sep 3, 1980).

O'NEILL, Jennifer: Act. b. Rio de Janeiro, Feb 20, 1949. Model. Films inc: Rio Lobo; Summer of '42; Such Good Friends; The Carey Treatment; The Reincarnation of Peter Proud; The Flower in the Mouth; The Intruder; Caravans; The Innocent; The Psychic; A Force Of One; Steel.

ONTKEAN, Michael: Act. b. Jan 24, 1946. Films inc: Slap Shot; Voices; Willie & Phil.
TV inc: The Rookies.

OOSTHOEK, Eric: Dir-Prod. b. Bilthoven, Holland, Sep 13, 1948. From 1970-77, with political and educational theatre, Holland; now TV director, Dutch Television.

OPATOSHU, David: Act. b. NYC, Jan 30, 1918. Films inc: Exodus; Guns of Darkness; Torn Curtain; The Defector; Enter Laughing; Death of a Gunfighter; Romance of a Horse Thief; Who'll Stop The Rain; Americathon; Beyond Evil.
Thea inc: Me and Molly; Once More with Feeling; Silk Stockings; The Wall; Bravo Giovanni.

OPPENHEIMER, Alan: Act. b. NYC, Apr 23. e. Carnegie Institute of Technology. Films inc: Star!; The Hindenburg; Freaky Friday; Little Big Man.
TV inc: Washington - Behind Closed Doors; Helter Skelter; Tail Gunner Joe; To Kill A Cop; Dinky Hocker; Six Million Dollar Man; Bionic Woman; Blind Ambition; Eischied.
Thea inc: The Devils; The Latent Heterosexual.

OPPENHEIMER, Jess: Wri-Prod-Dir. b. San Francisco, Nov 11, 1913. Wri: (Radio) Packard Hour, Fred Astaire, 1936-38; Rudy Vallee, 1940-41; Fanny Brice Baby Snooks Show, 1942-47 (also dir & prod).
TV inc: Head wri, prod, dir Lucille Ball My Favorite Husband, 1948-51; I Love Lucy (prod & wri) 1951-56; exec prod General Motors Fiftieth Anniversary Show, 1956; exec prod, creator, Angel, 1960-61; exec prod, creator, Glynis Johns Show; 1963-64; prod, dir, wri, Bob Hope Chrysler Theatre; prod, wri, dir Get Smart; exec prod, creator, wri, Debbie Reynolds Show; prod Danny Kaye Show with Lucille Ball.

ORBACH, Jerry: Act. b. NYC, Oct 20, 1935. e. U of IL, Northwestern U. Thea inc: Threepenny Opera; The Fantasticks; Carnival; The Cradle Will Rock; Guys and Dolls; Carousel; Annie Get Your Gun; The Natural Look; Scuba Duba; Promises, Promises (Tony-1969); The Rose Tattoo; The Trouble with People. . .and Other Things; Chicago; 42d Street.
Films inc: Please Come Home; The Sentinel.
TV inc: The Nurses.

ORBISON, Roy: Act-Comp. b. Wink, TX, Apr 23, 1936. C&W recording artist. Films inc: Fastest Guitar Alive; Roadie.

OREAR, Richard H: Exec. b. Kansas City, MO, Jun 11, 1911. e. Findlay Engineering College. In exhibition since 1931 in all phases; publicist-purchasing agent for Hughes-Franklin, which carried over to newly formed Commonwealth Theatres; 1947 elected to board of Commonwealth; 1955 exec vp; 1959 bd chmn.

ORGOLINI, Arnold: Prod. b. LA, Oct 16, 1936. e. USC, BS, MBA. Films inc: Cactus; Embryo; Meteor.

ORLANDO, Tony (Michael Orlando Cassivitis): Singer. b. NYC, Apr 3, 1944. Record promoter for April/Blackwood Records; formed group Dawn with Thelma Hopkins and Joyce Vincent Wilson, 1970 before solo.
TV inc: Tony Orlando and Dawn.
Recordings inc: Halfway to Paradise; Knock Three Times; Tie a Yellow Ribbon Round the Old Oak Tree. Albums inc: Greatest Hits; Before Dawn; The World of Tony Orlando and Dawn; Tony Orlando.

ORMANDY, Eugene: Cond. b. Budapest, Hungary, Nov 18, 1899. Child prodigy at 3; at 5 1/2, youngest pupil ever admitted to Royal State Academy of Music, received BA at 14 1/2. Toured Hungary as child prodigy. To US 1921, subbed for Toscanini as cond Philadelphia Orchestra; cond Minneapolis Symphony 1931-1936; Philadelphia Orchestra 1936; guest conductor major world orchestras.
(Grammy-class performance choral-1967).

ORNITZ, Arthur J: Cin-Dir. b. NYC, Nov 28, 1916. e. UCLA. S of Sam Ornitz. Films inc: (Cin) The Goddess; Requiem for a Heavyweight; The World of Henry Orient; A Thousand Clowns; Serpico; Death Wish; Next Stop Greenwich Village; An Unmarried Woman.
TV inc: Make A Wish (dir); Playing for Time.

ORR, Mary: Act-Wri. b. NYC, Dec 21, 1918. e. Briarcliff, Syracuse U. Bway debut 1938, Bachelor Born. Bway inc: Of Mice and Men; Jupiter Laughs; Jeannie; Without Love; Wallflower; Dark Hammock; Sherlock Holmes; The Desperate Hours.
Films inc: Pigeons.
TV inc: Suspect.
Plays inc: Wall Flower; Dark Hammock; Round Trip; The Platinum Set; Be Your Age. Short story Wisdom of Eve was basis of film All About Eve.

ORR, William T: Exec. b. NYC, Sep 27, 1917. Started in niteries, Bway. Joined WB 1947 as exec, talent dept; later named asst to Steve Trilling, exec asst to Jack Warner; VP in charge of prod both features and TV, 1961-62; asst to P, exec prod, TV div, 1963-65; formed Wm T Orr Co, 1966, for prodn of film and TV.
Films inc: My Love Come Back; Thieves Fall Out; Navy Blues; The Mortal Storm; The Big Street; Unholy Partners; Wicked, Wicked.

ORTOLANI, Riziero (Riz): Comp. b. Pesaro, Italy, Mar 25, 1931. e. Giaocchino Rossini Conservatory. Films inc: Mondo Cane; The Yellow Rolls Royce; The Seventh Dawn; Woman Times Seven; Buona Sera Mrs. Campbell; The Mackenzie Break; Say Hello to Yesterday; The Valachi Papers; Madrom; Drama Borghese; The Fifth Musketeer; From Hell to Victory.
Songs inc: More (Grammy-instrumental theme-1963); Forget Domani; Till Love Touches Your Life.

OSBORN, Paul: Wri. b. Evansville, IN, Sep 4, 1901. e. U MI, AB, MA, Yale Dramatic Workshop. Plays inc: The Vinegar Tree; Oliver Oliver; On Borrowed Time; Morning's At Seven; The Innocent Voyage; A Bell for Adano; The World of Suzie Wong; Maiden Voyage; Hot September;
Films inc: The Yearling: Mme. Curie; The Young in Heart; East of Eden; Homecoming; Contessa. Portrait of Jennie; Sayonara; South Pacific; Wild River; John Brown's Body.

OSBORNE, John: Wri-Act. b. London, Dec 12, 1929. e. Belmont Coll. Plays inc; Look Back in Anger; Epitaph for George Dillon; The Entertainer; The World of Paul Stickey; Luther (Tony-1964); Inadmissible Evidence; Watch It Come Down.
Films inc: Look Back in Anger; The Entertainer; Tom Jones (Oscar-1963).
TV inc: The Right Prospectus; Very Like A Whale; A Subject of Scandal and Concern; Almost a Vision.

O'SHEA, John: Prod-Dir. b. New Plymouth, New Zealand, 1920. e. Victoria U, U of New Zealand. Films inc: Broken Barrier; Runaway; Don't Let It Get You.

O'SHEA, Tessie: Act. b. England, Mar 13, 1918. Films inc: The Shiralee; The Russians Are Coming, The Russians Are Coming; The Best House in London; Bedknobs and Broomsticks.
Bway inc: The Girl Who Came to Supper (Tony-supp-1964); Something's Afoot.
TV inc: The Word.

OSMOND, Cliff: Act. b. Feb 26, 1937. Films inc: Irma La Douce; Kiss Me Stupid; The Fortune Cookie; Three Guns for Texas; The Devil's Eight; The Front Page; Shark's Treasure; The Mouse and His Child (voice only); The Apple Dumpling Gang Rides Again; The North Avenue Irregulars; Hangar 18.
TV inc: Beggarman, Thief.

OSMOND, Donny: Act. b. Ogden, UT, Dec 9, 1957. The fifth member of the Osmond Family to become a professional singer. First appeared on The Andy Williams Show at age 4.
TV inc: The Donny & Marie Show; The Gift of Love; Donnie and Marie Christmas Special; The Osmond Family Christmas Show.
Films inc: Goin' Coconuts.

OSMOND, Marie: Act. b. Ogden, UT, Oct 13, 1959. Began career at age 7 while touring with her brothers. When she joined the group the act was changed from the Osmond Brothers to the Osmonds.
TV inc: Donny & Marie Show; The Gift Of Love; The Donnie and Marie Christmas Special; The Osmond Family Christmas Show.

O'STEEN, Sam: Dir-Edtr. b. Nov 6, 1923. Films inc: (edtr) Kisses for My President; Robin and the 7 Hoods; Youngblood Hawke; Marriage on the Rocks; None But the Brave; Who's Afraid of Virginia Woolf; Cool Hand Luke; The Graduate; Rosemary's Baby; The Sterile Cuckoo (supv ed); Catch-22; Carnal Knowledge; Portnoy's Complaint; Day of the Dolphin; Chinatown; Straight Time; Sparkle (dir); Hurricane.
TV inc: (dir) A Brand New Life; I Love You, Goodbye; Queen of the Stardust Ballroom; High Risk; Look What's Happened to Rosemary's Baby.

OSTERMAN, Lester: Thea prod. b. NYC, Dec 31, 1914. e. U of VA. Member of NY Stock exchange 1945-59; began theatrical career as prod Mr. Wonderful, 1956, has prod or co-prod Candide; High Spirits; Fade Out Fade In; Hadrian VII; Butley; The Rothschilds; Sizwe Banzi Is Dead; The Island; A Moon for the Misbegotten; The Shadow Box (*Tony*-1977); Da (*Tony*-1978); Crucifer of Blood; Watch on the Rhine (rev); The Lady From Dubuque; A Life.
TV inc: The Littlest Angel; Raggedy Ann.

OSTERWALD, Bibi: Act. b. New Brunswick, NJ, Feb 3, 1920. e. Catholic U. Films inc: Parris; The World of Henry Orient; Tiger Makes Out; Bank Shot; The Great Smokey Road Block.
TV inc: Captain Billy's Mississippi Music Hall; Our Town; Where the Heart Is; Beulah Land.
Bway inc: Sing Out Sweet Land; Gentlemen Prefer Blondes; Three to Make Ready; Bus Stop; Golden Apple; Hello Dolly.

OSTROW, Stuart: Prod. b. NYC, Feb 8, 1932. Bway inc: We Take the Town; Here's Love; The Apple Tree, 1776; Scratch; Pippin; Stages.

O'SULLIVAN, Maureen: Act. b. Voyle, Ireland, May 17, 1911. M of Mia Farrow. On screen from 1930. Films inc: Song O' My Heart; MGM Tarzan series; The Barretts of Wimpole Street; The Thin Man; Anna Karenina; A Day at the Races; Cardinal Richelieu; David Copperfield; A Yank at Oxford; The Big Clock; As I Desire; The Steel Cage; Never Too Late.
Thea inc: The Front Page; No Sex Please, We're British; Morning's At Seven (rev).

OSWALD, Gerd: Dir. b. Berlin, Jun 9, 1919. Films inc: A Kiss Before Dying; Brass Legend; Crime of Passion; Fury at Showdown; Valerie; Paris Holiday; Screaming Mimi; The Day the Rains Came (sp, prod); The Longest Day (sequence); Scarlet Eye; Agent for Harm; 80 Steps to Jonah (sp, prod); Bunny O'Hare; To the Bitter End.
TV inc: Ford Theatre; GE Hour; Playhouse 90; Perry Mason; Rawhide; Outer Limits; Star Trek; Shane; Gentle Ben; Bonanza; It Takes a Thief; Nichols.

OSWIN, James Henry Martin: Exec. b. Lismore, Australia, Aug 5, 1923. e. Scots College. Station mgr ATN Channel 7 Syd, 1955-57; gm ATN Channel 7 Syd, 1957-72; dir M7 Records 1971-72; m dir 7 Network 1972-73; secy Australian Govt Dept of the Media 1973-75; Australian ambassador, Permanent Delegate to UNESCO, Paris 1975-76; vice chmn Australian Broadcasting Tribunal.

O'TOOLE, Peter: Act. b. Ireland, Aug 2, 1932. e. RADA. Early career with Bristol Old Vic. Thea inc: (London) The Long, The Short and the Tall; Macbeth. Dead Eyed Dicks (Dublin).
Screen debut 1959, Kidnapped. Films inc: The Day They Robbed the Bank of England; Lawrence of Arabia; Becket; The Lion in Winter; Goodby Mr. Chips; The Ruling Class; What's New Pussycat?; Lord Jim; How to Steal a Million; Murphy's War; Man of La Mancha; Rosebud; Man Friday; Power Play; Foxtrot; Zulu Dawn; Caligula; The Stunt Man.
TV inc: Rogue Male.

OURY, Gerard: Act-Dir-Wri. b. Paris, Apr 29, 1919. e. Nat'l Conservatory Dramatic Art. On stage in Paris at Comedie Francaise, also in Geneva.
Films inc: (act) Antoine and Antoinette; Jo la romance; La Belle que voila; Le Passe-Muraille; Le Nuit est mon Royaume; The Rose and the Sword; Sea Devils; The Heart of the Matter; Father Brown; La Fille du Fleuve; La Meiullure Part; The House of Secrets; Le Septieme Ciel; The Mirror has Two Faces; The Journey; The Prize. (Dir): La main chaude (& wri); La Menace; Crime Does Not Pay (& wri); The Sucker (& wri); Don't Look Now (& wri); The Brain (& wri); Delusions of Grandeur (& wri); The Mad Adventures of Rabbi Jacob (& wri); La Carapate; Le Coup du Parapluie (& wri).

OWEN, Alun: Wri. b. Liverpool, Eng, Nov 24, 1925. Plays inc: a Little Winter Love; Maggie May; Progress in the Park; The Rough and Ready Lot; There'll Be Some Changes Made; Fashion of Your Time; The Male of the Species. Films inc: The Criminal; A Hard Day's Night.
TV inc: No Trams to Lime Street; After the Funeral; Lena, Oh My Lena; The Ruffians; The Ways of Love; You Can't Win 'Em All; The Stag; Park People; Giants and Ogres; Just the Job; Forget Me Not.

OWENS, Bonnie: Act-Sngwri. b. Blanchard, OK, Oct 1, 1933. W of Buck Owens. C&W recording artist. Teamed with Merle Haggard.

OWENS, Buck: Act. Sngwri. b. Sherman, TX, Aug 12, 1929. Country mus artist. TV inc: Hee Haw.
Films inc: Murder Can Hurt You.
Songs inc: Crying Time; Together Again.

OWENS, Gary: Act-TV pers. b. Mitchell, SD, May 10, 1936. e. Wesleyan U. Disc jockey, KMPC Hollywood. TV inc: Laugh-In; host of Letters to Laugh-In; The Hudson Brothers; The Green Hornet; Gong Show (orig host).
Cartoons inc: (voice) Roger Ramjet; Space Ghost; The Blue Falcon; Perils of Penelope Pitstop!

OWENSBY, Earl: Prod-Act. b. North Carolina, 1936. Has own studio in Shelbyville, NC. Films inc: Challenge; Dark Sunday; Buckstone County Prison; Frank Challenge--Manhunter; Death Driver; Wolfman; Seabo; Day of Judgment; Living Legend; Lady Grey.

OZAWA, Seiji: Cond. b. Shenyang, China, Sep 1, 1935. e. Toho School of Music. Studied with Herbert Von Karajan, Leonard Bernstein. Asst cond NY Philharmonic 1961-1962; dir Ravinia Festival, 1964-1969; cond Toronto Symphony 1965-1969; mus dir San Francisco Symphony 1970-76; mus dir Berkshire Music Festival Tanglewood 1970-1973; mus dir Boston Symphony. TV inc: Central Park In The Dark/A Hero's Life (*Emmy*-mus dir-1976).

PAAR, Jack: TV Pers. b. Canton, OH, 1918. Host NBC's Tonight show, 1957; in 1958 network changed title to The Jack Paar Show. Switched to weekly variety show in 1962. In 1973, signed with ABC and for a time did a one-month-a-week show.

PACINO, Al: Act. b. NYC, 1940. Thea inc: The Indian Wants the Bronx; Does a Tiger Wear a Necktie? (*Tony*-supp-1969); The Connection; Hello Out There; Tiger at the Gates; The Basic Training of Pablo Hummel (*Tony*-1977); Richard III.
Films inc: Panic in Needle Park; The Godfather; Scarecrow; Serpico; The Godfather Part II; Dog Day Afternoon; Bobby Deerfield; And Justice For All; Cruising.

PACKER, Kerry Francis Bullmore: Exec. b. Sydney, Australia, Dec 17, 1937. Chmn, Australian Consolidated Press Ltd & Publishing and Broadcasting Ltd; dir, General Television Ltd.

PAGE, Anthony: Dir. b. Bangalore, India, Sep 21, 1935. e. Oxford. Films inc: Inadmissible Alpha Beta; The Lady Vanishes.
Thea inc: Inadmissible Evidence; Evidence; A Cuckoo in the Nest; Waiting for Godot; A Patriot for Me; Diary of a Madman; Look Back in Anger; Uncle Vanya; The Rules of the Game.
TV inc: Stephen D; The Parachute; The Hotel in Amsterdam; F.D.R. - The Last Year.

PAGE, Genevieve: Act. b. France, 1931. Films Inc: Fanfan La Tulippe; The Silken Affair; Michael Strogoff; Song Without End; El Cid; Paris Blues; Grand Prix; Youngblood Hawke; Belle De Jour; Decline and Fall; Private Life of Sherlock Holmes; Buffet Froid (Cold Cuts).

PAGE, Geraldine: Act. b. Kirkville, MO, Nov 22, 1924. W of Rip Torn. Bway debut 1945, Seven Mirrors. On screen from 1953. Films inc: Hondo; Summer and Smoke; Sweet Bird of Youth; Toys in the Attic; Dear Heart; The Happiest Millionaire; You're a Big Boy Now; Trilogy; Whatever Happened to Aunt Alice; The Beguiled; J.W. Cooper; Pete 'N' Tillie; The Day of the Locust; Nasty Habits; Interiors.

Thea inc: Mid-Summer; The Immoralist; Summer and Smoke (rev); The Rainmaker; Separate Tables; Sweet Bird of Youth; Strange Interlude; Absurd Person Singular; The Three Sisters; Angela; Black Comedy; Clothes For A Summer Hotel; Mixed Couples.

TV inc: A Christmas Memory *(Emmy-*1967); The Thanksgiving Visitor *(Emmy-*1969); Barefoot in Athens; The Name of the Game.

PAGE, LaWanda: Act. b. Cleveland, OH, Oct 19, 1920. Started as dancer in nieteries. TV inc: The Sanford Arms; B.A.D. Cats.

PAGE, Patti (Clara Ann Fowler): Act. b. Claremore, OK, Nov 8, 1927. Staff performer, radio sta KTUL, Tulsa. Appeared on CBS radio; Patti Page Show; TV film series, The Big Record.

Films inc: Elmer Gantry; Dondi; Boys Night Out.

PAGET, Debra (Debralee Griffin): Act. b. Denver, CO, Aug 19, 1933. Films inc: Cry of the City; House of Strangers; Broken Arrow; Les Miserables; Prince Valiant; Love Me Tender; From the Earth to the Moon; Tales of Terror; The Haunted Palace.

PAGETT, Nicola (Scott): Act. b. Cairo, Egypt, Jun 15, 1945. e. RADA. Thea inc: A Boston Story; Widowers' Houses; The Misanthrope; A Voyage Round My Father; The Ride Across Lake Constance; Ghosts; The Seagull; A Family and a Fortune; Gaslight; Yahoo; Taking Steps.

Films inc: Anne of the Thousand Days; There's a Girl in My Soup; Operation Daybreak; Oliver's Story.

TV inc: Upstairs Downstairs; The Timeless Land.

PAIGE, Janis (Donna Mae Jaden): Act. b. Tacoma, WA, Sep 16, 1923. Sang with Tacoma Opera Co. Screen debut 1944, Hollywood Canteen. Films inc: Of Human Bondage; The Time, the Place and the Girl; Her Kind of Man; Silk Stockings; Please Don't Eat the Daisies; Bachelor in Paradise; The Caretakers; Follow the Boys; Welcome to Hard Times.

TV inc: Columbo; Mannix; Hec Ramsey; Valentine Magic On Love Island; Angel On My Shoulder.

Thea inc: The Pajama Game; Remains to be Seen.

PAKULA, Alan: Prod-Dir. b. NYC, Apr 7, 1928. e. Yale, BA. Joined MGM 1950, prod apprentice; prod asst Para 1951; prod Para 1955; own prod co, Pakula-Mulligan Prod.

Films inc: (prod) Fear Strikes Out; To Kill a Mockingbird; Love With the Proper Stranger; Baby the Rain Must Fall; Inside Daisy Clover; Up the Down Staircase; The Stalking Moon; (dir) The Sterile Cuckoo; Klute; Love and Pain and the Whole Damned Thing; The Parallax View; All the President's Men; Coms A Horseman; Starting Over.

Thea inc: There Must Be a Pony; Blood and Thunder; Comes a Day; Laurette.

PAL, George: Prod. b. Cegled, Hungary, Feb 1, 1908. Devised prodn system for Puppetoons in London. To US, 1940; prod cartoons, Paramount. Special Oscar 1943 "for the development of novel methods and techniques."

Films inc: Destination Moon *(Oscar-*spec effects-1950); When Worlds Collide *(Oscar-*spec effects-1951); The War of the Worlds *(Oscar-*spec effects-1953); The Naked Jungle; Tom Thumb *(Oscar-*spec effects-1958); The Time Machine; Atlantis, the Lost Continent (& co-dir); first Cinerama; The Wonderful World of the Brothers Grimm; Seven Faces of Dr. Lao; The Power; Doc Savage. . .the Man of Bronze; Days of the Comet.

(Died May 2, 1980).

PALANCE, Jack: Act. b. Lattimer, PA, Feb 18, 1920. On screen from 1950. Films inc: Star of Tomorrow; Flight to Tangier; Man in the Attic; Sign of the Pagen; Sudden Fear; Shane; Silver Chalice; Kiss of Fire; The Big Knife; I Died a Thousand Times; Attack!; Lonely Man; House of Numbers; Ten Seconds to Hell; Warriors Five; Barabbas; Contempt; Torture Garden; Kill a Dragon; They Came to Rob Las Vegas; The Desperadoes; Che; The Mercenary; Justine; Legion of the Damned; A Bullet for Rommel; The McMasters; Monte Walsh; Companeros; The Horsemen; The Professionals; Oklahoma Crude; Craze; The Four Deuces; The Diamond Mercenaries; The Shape of Things to Come; Without Warning; Hawk The Slayer.

TV inc: Requiem For A Heavyweight *(Emmy-*1956); Dr. Jekyll and Mr. Hyde; Dracula; Bronk; The Last Ride of the Dalton Gang; The Golden Moment-An Olympic Love Story.

Thea inc: The Big Two; Temporary Island; The Vigil; A Streetcar Named Desire; Darkness at Noon.

PALEY, William S: Exec. b. Chicago, Sep 28, 1901. e. U of PA. Pres. Columbia Broadcasting System 1928; chairman of board since 1946. During WW II, on leave to supervise OWI radio in Mediterranean area. Chief of radio of Psychological Warfare Division, SHAFE, 1944-45. Dep Chief Info Control Div of USGCC 1945. Colonel, AUS Deputy Chief Psychological Warfare Div, SHAFE, 1945.

(First Annual Academy of Television Arts & Sciences Governor's Award 1978.)

PALMER, Betsy (Patricia Hrunek): Act. b. East Chicago, IN, Nov 1, 1929. e. IN U, De Pauw U. Thea inc: The Grand Prize; Affair of Honor; Roar Like a Dove; Cactus Flower; A Doll's House. Films inc: The Long Gray Line; The Tin Star; The Last Angry Man; Mister Roberts; Friday The 13th.

TV inc: Studio One; US Steel Hour; Climax; Kraft Theatre; Number 96.

PALMER, Lilli: Act. b. Austria, 1914. On screen in England from 1934. Films in US from 1946 inc: Cloak and Dagger; My Girl Tisa; Body and Soul; No Minor Vices; The Fourposter; But Not For Me; The Pleasure of His Company; The Counterfeit Traitor; Maedchen in Uniform; Sebastian; Murders in the Rue Morgue; The House That Screamed; The Boys From Brazil.

Thea inc: Bell, Book and Candle; Suite in 3 Keys; Venus Observed; Love of Four Colonels.

TV inc: Lilli Palmer Presents.

PALMER, Maria: Act. b. Vienna, Austria, Sep 5, 1924. e. Vienna Acad Music & Interpretive Arts. Joined Reinhardt's Theatre in Josefstadt, Vienna, 1938 as youngest member of company. Films inc: Mission to Moscow; Days of Glory; Lady on a Train; Surrender; Strictly Dishonorable; By the Light of the Silvery Moon; Flight Nurse; City of Women.

Bway inc: The Moon is Down; The Girl on the Via Flaminia; The Heiress; A Streetcar Named Desire; The Diary of Anne Frank; The Happy Time.

TV inc: Schlitz Playhouse; Robert Montgomery Presents; Playhouse 90; The Diamond Necklace; Sincerely Maria Palmer (& wri).

PALUZZI, Luciana: Act. b. Italy, 1939. Films inc: Three Coins in the Fountain; Sea Fury; Thunderball; The Venetian Affair; Chuka; Women; The Green Slime; Black Gunn; War Goddess; The Greek Tycoon.

TV inc: Five Fingers.

PAN, Hermes: Chor. Films inc: Roberta; Damsel in Distress *(Oscar-*1938); Top Hat; Old Man Rhythm; Follow the Fleet; Swing Time; Shall We Dance; Let's Dance; Three Little Words; Texas Carnival; Lovely to Look At; Kiss Me Kate; Student Prince; Hit the Deck; Jupiter's Darling; Meet Me In Las Vegas; Porgy and Bess; Can-Can; Flower Drum Song; Cleopatra; My Fair Lady; Finian's Rainbow; Darling Lili; Lost Horizon.

TV inc: Frances Langford Show; Sounds of America; Astaire Time; An Evening with Fred Astaire *(Emmy-*chor-1959).

PANAMA, Norman: Wri-Prod-Dir. b. Chicago, Apr 21, 1914. e. U of Chicago. Films inc: My Favorite Blonde; Happy Go Lucky; Star Spangled Rhythm; And the Angels Sing; The Road to Utopia; Duffy's Tavern; Monsieur Beaucaire; The Return of October; Mr Blanding Builds His Dream House; The Reformer and the Redhead; Strictly Dishonorable; Callaway Went Thataway; Knock on Wood; White Christmas; The Court Jester; That Certain Feeling; Li'l Abner; The Facts of Life; The Road to Hong Kong; Strange Bedfellows; Not With My Wife, You Don't!; How to Commit Marriage.

TV inc: Coffee, Tea, or Me; Li'l Abner.

PAPAS, Irene: Act. b. Corinth, Greece, 1926. Films inc: The Man from Cairo; Tribute to a Bad Man; Attila the Hun; The Guns of Navarone; Antigone; Zorba the Greek; The Brotherhood; A Dream of Kings; Anne of the Thousand Days; The Trojan Women; Moses; Mohammed, Messenger of God; Iphigenia; Christ Stopped At Eboli; Sidney Sheldon's Bloodline.

Thea inc: The Idiot; Journey's End; Inherit the Wind; Iphigenia in Aulis.

PAPP, Joseph (nee Papirofsky): Prod-Dir. b. NYC, Jun 22, 1921. Worked wth Actors Lab in Hollywood; 1953 founded Shakespeare Workshop which became basis of NY Shakespeare Festival; prod & dir complete Shakespearean repertory; founded Public Theatre. Prod inc: Hair; Ergo; The Memorandum (& dir); Huui, Huui (& dir); The Expressway; Romania; That's The Old Country; Invitation to a Beheading; No Place to be Somebody; Sambo; The Wonderful Years; Play on the Times; X Has No Value; Subject to Fits; Slag; Here are Ladies; Sticks and Bones (Tony-1972); musical version of Two Gentlemen of Verona (Tony-1972); The Black Terror; The Wedding of Iphigenia; Iphigenia in Concert; That Championship Season (Tony-1973); The Hunter; The Corner; Boom Boom Room; The Au Pair Man; More Than You Deserve; What the Wine Sellers Buy; The Kildeer; Where Do We Go From Here; Mert and Phil (& dir); Last Days of British Honduras; Black Picture Show; Little Black Sheep; A Chorus Line (Tony-1976); Streamers; The Leaf People; For Colored Girls Who Considered Suicide; Sticks and Bones; Jesse and the Bandit Queen; Runaways; The Water Engine.

(Tony-special-1958).

PARAMOR, Norrie: Orch ldr-Comp. b. London, 1914. Producer for Columbia Records; formed own prod co. Film scores inc: The Frightened City.

(Died Sep 9, 1979.)

PARIS, Jerry: Prod-Dir-Act. b. San Francisco, Jul 25, 1925. e. NYU, UCLA. On stage in Medea, revival of Anna Christie; toured in Front Page. Films inc: (act) Marty; The Wild One; The Caine Mutiny; The Naked and the Dead; D Day; The Sixth of June; Good Morning, Miss Dove; Cyrano De Bergerac. (Dir) inc: The Grasshopper; Viva Max; How Sweet It Is; Don't Raise the Bridge; Star-Spangled Girl; Leo and Loree (& act).

TV inc: (dir) That Girl; The Partridge Family; The Dick Van Dyke Show (Emmy-1964); Love, American Style; Odd Couple; The Feminist and the Fuzz; Evil Roy Slade; How to Break Up a Happy Divorce; Happy Days; Beane's of Boston; Make Me An Offer.

PARKER, Alan: Dir. b. London, Feb 14, 1944. Films inc: Bugsy Malone (& sp); Midnight Express; Fame.

TV inc: The Evacuees.

PARKER, Eleanor: Act. b. Cedarville, OH, Jun 26, 1922. In summer stock Martha's Vineyard; at Pasadena Playhouse. On screen from 1941 in They Died With Their Boots On; Mission to Moscow; Of Human Bondage; Caged; Detective Story; Valentino; Scaramouche; Above and Beyond; Interrupted Melody; The Man with the Golden Arm; A Hole in the Head; Return to Peyton Place; The Sound of Music; Warning Shot; The Tiger and the Pussycat; Eye of the Cat; Sunburn.

TV inc: Bracken's World; Vanished; The Bastard; She's Dressed To Kill; Once Upon A Spy.

PARKER, Fess: Act. b. Ft Worth, TX, Aug 16, 1925. e. U of TX. Thea inc: 1951, nat'l co Mr. Roberts. Films inc: Untamed Frontier; No Room for the Groom; Springfield Rifle; Thunder Over the Plains; Island in the Sky; Them; Battle Cry; Davy Crockett, King of the Wild Frontier; The Great Locomotive Chase; Westward Ho the Wagons; Old Yeller; The Light in the Forest; The Hangman; The Jayhawkers; Hell Is for Heroes; Smoky.

TV inc: Mr. Smith Goes to Washington Daniel Boone; Jonathan Winters; Phyllis Diller; Joey Bishop; Dean Martin; Red Skelton; Glen Campbell.

PARKER, Jameson: Act. b. Baltimore, MD. e. Beloit Coll. Worked with stock groups, in commercials. Films inc: The Bell Jar; A Small Circle of Friends.

TV inc: Somerset; One Life to Live; Women at West Point; Anatomy of a Seduction; The Promise of Love.

PARKER, Jean (Lois Stephanie Zelinska): Act. b. Butte, MT, 1915. On screen from 1932. Films inc: Rasputin and the Empress; Little Women; Two Alone; Caravan; Princess O'Hara; Penitentiary; Beyond Tomorrow; Torpedo Boat; Alaska Highway; Minesweeper; The Navy Way; One Body Too Many; The Gunfighter; Toughest Man in Arizona; Those Redheads from Seattle; Black Tuesday; The Parson and the Outlaw; Apache Uprising.

Thea inc: Dream Girl; Born Yesterday; Burlesque.

PARKER, Suzy (Cecelia Parker): Act. b. San Antonio, TX, Oct 28, 1932. Former model. Films inc: Kiss Them for Me; Ten North Frederick; The Best of Everything; Circle of Deception; The Interns; Chamber of Horrors.

PARKER, Tom: Prod-Dist. b. New Haven, CT, Dec 20, 1913. Films inc: Initiation; Somebody Help Me; Amazing Love Secret; Frustrations; Love Clinic; Country Girl; Streets of Paris; Reunion; Antique Shop; Wacky Wagon Train.

PARKINS, Barbara: Act. b. Vancouver, Can, May 22, 1942. Films inc: Valley of the Dolls; Bear Island; The Kremlin Letter; Puppet On A Chain; The Mephisto Waltz; Bear Island.

TV inc: Peyton Place; Captains And The Kings; Young Joe; The Forgotten Kennedy; Ziegfeld--The Man And His Women; The Critical List.

PARKS, Bert: TV MC. b. Atlanta, GA, 1914. Network announcer for Eddie Cantor Show; TV inc: MC for Xavier Cugat's show; Miss America Pageant; Break the Bank; Stop the Music; Fast Lane Blues; Replaced As MC Miss America Jan 1980.

Films inc: That's the Way of the World.

PARKS, Gordon: Wri-Dir. Films inc: The Learning Tree; Shaft; Shaft's Big Score (& mus); Supercops (dir); Leadbelly (dir).

PARKS, Michael: Act. b. 1938. Films inc: Wild Seed; Bus Riley's Back in Town; The Bible; The Idol; The Happening; The Last Hard Men; Sidewinder One; The Evictors; ffolkes.

TV inc: Can Ellen Be Saved; Bronson; Rainbow; Fast Friends; Reward; Turnover Smith.

PARRISH, Robert: Dir-Prod. b. Columbus, GA, Jan 4, 1916. Films inc: Body and Soul (Oscar-ed-1947). (Dir) Cry Danger; The Mob; My Pal Gus; The San Francisco Story; The Purple Plain; Lucy Gallant; Fire Down Below; Saddle the Wind; In the French Style; Up from the Beach; The Bobo; Duffy; Journey to the Far Side of the Sun; A Town Called Bastard; The Marseilles Contract.

PARSONS, Estelle: Act. b. Marblehead, MA, Nov 20, 1927. e. CT Coll for Women, BA. Joined NBC-TV's Today Show as prodn asst, then wri, feature prod, commentator. Films inc: Ladybug, Ladybug; Bonnie and Clyde *(Oscar-*supp-1967); Rachel, Rachel; Don't Drink the Water; I Never Sang for My Father; The Watermelon Man; I Walk the Line; Two People; For Pete's Sake.

Thea inc: Happy Hunting; Next Time I'll Sing to You; Suburban Tragedy; Ready When You Are, C.B.; The Seven Descents of Myrtle; And Miss Reardon Drinks A Little; Mert and Phil; The Norman Conquests; Ladies at the Alamo; Miss Margarida's Way; A Way of Life.

TV inc: The Gambling Heart; The Nurses; The Verdict Is Yours; Faith for Today; A Memory of Two Mondays; The UFO Incident.

PARSONS, Lindsley Sr: Prod-Exec. b. Tacoma, WA, Sep 12, 1915. With Monogram, Allied Artists, Warner Bros. Columbia, 20th Century-Fox since early 40s. Films inc: Big Timber; Call of the Klondike; Sierra Passage; Yukon; Manhunt; Yellow Fin; Northwest Territory; Desert Pursuit; Torpedo Alley; Jack Slade; Cry Vengeance; Finger Man; Return of Jack Slade; The Intruder; Cruel Tower; Dragon Wells Massacre; Portland Expose; Oregon Passage; Wolf Larsen; Crash Boat; The Purple Gang; Good Times; The Big Cube; Bravo Hennessey; Coasts of War.

TV inc: Gray Ghost.

PARTON, Dolly: Singer-Sngwri. b. Sevierville, TN, Jan 19, 1946. Recording artist, has own diskery, White Diamond Records. Records inc: Here You Come Again *(Grammy-*country vocal-1979).

TV inc: A Christmas Special With Love, Mac Davis; Barbara Mandrell and the Mandrell Sisters.

Films inc: Nine To Five (act).

PASETTA, Marty: Prod-Dir. b. Jun 16, 1932. e. U of Santa Clara. TV inc: A Gift of Song; Salute to Israel; Gene Kelly Special; Elvis in Hawaii; Oscar, Emmy and Grammy Award Shows; A Country Christmas, 1979; Debbie Boone--The Same Old Brand New Me; The Monte Carlo Show (exec prod); A Country Christmas, 1980.

PASTERNAK, Joe: Prod. b. Hungary, Sep 19, 1901. 2nd asst dir Paramount, 1923; asst dir Universal, 1926; then prod mgr Berlin; made pictures in Vienna and Budapest; returned to Hollywood, 1937; asso prod then prod. Films inc: Three Smart Girls; 100 Men and a Girl; That Certain Age; Three Smart Girls Grow Up; Mad About Music; Destry Rides Again; It Started With Eve; Presenting Lily Mars; Thousands Cheer; Anchors Aweigh; The Great Caruso; Student Prince; Hit the Deck; Where the Boys Are; Jumbo; A Ticklish Affair; Girl Happy; Penelope.

PATAKI, Michael: Act. b. Jan 16, 1938. e. USC. Films inc: The Return of Count Yorga; Airport '77; Love At First Bite; Dracula's Dog; The Onion Field.

TV inc: Samurai; The Survival of Dana; Marciano; Phyl & Mikhy; High Noon Part II--The Return of Will Kane.

PATERSON, Neil: Wri. b. Scotland, 1916. e. Edinburgh U. Films inc: Man on a Tight Rope; The Little Kidnappers; High Tide at Noon; Room at the Top *(Oscar-*1959); The Spiral Road; Mister Moses.

PATINKIN, Mandy: Act. b. Chicago, Nov 30, 1952. e. U KS; Juilliard. Films inc: Night of the Juggler; The Big Fix; The Last Embrace; French Postcards.

Bway inc: The Shadow Box; Evita *(Tony-*supp-1980).

TV inc: That Thing on ABC; Charleston.

PATRICK, Gail (Margaret Fitzpatrick): Act-Prod. b. Birmingham, AL, 1912. On screen from 1932, The Phantom Broadcast. Films inc: Cradle Song; No More Ladies; Artists and Models; Reno; Quiet, Please, Murder; Calendar Girl; Inside Story. Retired from acting to become exec prod of the Perry Mason TV series.

(Died July 6, 1980).

PATRICK, John: Wri. b. Louisville, KY, May 17, 1907. e. Holy Cross Coll, Columbia U. Films inc: Three Coins in a Fountain; Love is a Many Splendored Thing; The Teahouse of the August Moon; High Society; Les Girls; Some Came Running; The World of Suzie Wong; The Shoes of the Fisherman. Plays inc: Hell Freezes Over; The Hasty Heart; The Teahouse of the August Moon *(Pulitzer Prize & Tony-*1954); Good as Gold; Everybody's Girl; Scandal Point; A Barrelful of Pennies; Love Is a Time of Day; Opal Is a Diamond; Macbeth Did It; A Bad Year for Tomatoes; Noah's Animals; Enigma (& dir).

PATRICK, Lee: Act. b. NYC, Nov 22, 1911. Bway inc: The Green Beetle; The Bunch and Judy; June Moon; Little Women; Blessed Event; Abide With Me; Pearl of Great Price; Stage Door.

Films inc: Strange Cargo; The Sisters; The Maltese Falcon; Now Voyager; George Washington Slept Here; Mrs Parkington; Mildred Pierce; City for Conquest; Footsteps in the Dark; Inner Sanctum; Snake Pit; Caged; Tomorrow Is Another Day; There's No Business Like Show Business; Vertigo; Auntie Mame; Visit to a Small Planet; Pillow Talk; Summer and Smoke; A Girl Named Tamiko; Wives and Lovers; The Seven Faces of Dr Lao; The New Interns; The Black Bird.

TV inc: Chevy Mystery Show; Topper.

PATRICK, Nigel: Act-Dir. b. London, May 2, 1913. Stage debut 1932, The Life Machine. Screen debut 1939, Mrs Pim of Scotland Yard. Films inc: Spring in Park Lane; Noose; Trio; The Browning Version; The Sound Barrier; The Pickwick Papers; Raintree County; How to Murder a Rich Uncle (& dir); Sapphire; The League of Gentlemen; The Trials of Oscar Wilde; Johnny Nobody (& dir); The Informers; The Executioner; The Great Waltz; The Mackintosh Man.

TV inc: Zero One.

Thea inc: The Payoff (& dir); Dear Daddy; Avanti (dir); They Ride On Broomsticks; Night Must Fall; The Last of Mrs. Cheyney (dir).

PAUL, M B (nee Bloomfield): Cin-Dir. b. Montreal, Sep 30, 1909. e. St. Paul U. Newsreel, publicity, picture service, 1925-30; part. Seymour Studious, 1930-33; Film test biz own studio, Hollywood, 1933-35. Oscar 1949, for the first successful large-area seamless translucent backgrounds. Designed, patented, Scenoramic process, 1965. Sceno 360 surround system development. Sidney Sheldon's Bloodline.

PAULEY, Jane: TV Newscaster. b. Indianapolis, IN, Oct 31, 1950. e. IN U, BA. Reporter WISH-TV, Indianapolis, 1972; anchor WMAQ-TV, Chicago, 1975; joined NBC Today show, Oct. 1976 after Barbara Walters left show; 1980 anchor Saturday edition NBC Nightly News.

PAULSEN, Albert: Act. b. Guayaquil, Ecuador, Dec 13, 1929. Bway inc: Night Circus; Three Sisters; Only Game in Town.

Films inc: The Manchurian Candidate; Gunn; Che!; The Amazing Mrs Pollifax; The Laughing Policeman; The Next Man.

TV inc: A Day in the Life of Ivan Denisovich *(Emmy-*1964).

PAULSEN, Pat: Comedian. Featured on Smothers Brothers Comedy Show *(Emmy-*special-1968). TV inc: Pat Paulsen Show; You Had To Be There; The Palace; Tom and Dick Smothers Brothers Special I.

PAVAN, Marisa (nee Pierangeli): Act. b. Cagliari, Sardinia, Jun 19, 1932. Sis of Pier Angeli. In US from 1950. Films inc: What Price Glory?; The Rose Tattoo; The Man in the Grey Flannel Suit; Solomon and Sheba; John Paul Jones.

PAVAROTTI, Luciano: Lyric Tenor. b. Modena, Italy, Oct 12, 1935. Former teacher and insurance salesman; operatic debut 1961 in La Boheme.

Operas inc: Lucia de Lammermoor; Rigoletto; Daughter of the Regiment; guest artist at La Scala; Vienna Staatsopera; Metropolitan Opera; San Francisco Opera; Paris Opera; Chicago Opera.

Recordings inc: Hits From Lincoln Center *(Grammy-*class voc-1978); O Sole Mio *(Grammy-*class voc-1979).

PAVLIK, John Michael: Exec. b. Melrose, IA, Dec 3, 1939. e. U of MN, BA. Joined Assoc of Motion Picture and Television Prod, 1968, as asst dir of PR; then dir of PR, 1972; vp 1978-79; resigned to become exec administrator Academy of Motion Picture Arts and Sciences, 1979.

PAXTON, John: Wri. b. Kansas City, MO, Mar 21, 1911. e. U of MO. Films inc: Murder My Sweet; Cornered; So Well Remembered; Crossfire; Crack-Up; Rope of Sand; Fourteen Hours; The Cobweb; How to Murder a Rich Uncle; On the Beach; Kotch.

PAXTON, Tom: Act-Sngwri. b. Chicago, Oct 31, 1937. Folksinger and recording artist; appeared in clubs throughout US; later concentrated on writing for major folk groups.

PAYCHECK, Johnny: Act-Sngwri. b. OH, May 31, 1941. Country mus recording artist. Started as a sngwri; later sang background for recording artists, then solo.

PAYNE, John: Act. b. Roanoke, VA, 1912. On screen from 1936 in Dodsworth. Films inc: Wings of the Navy; To the Shores of Tripoli; Indianapolis Speedway; Tin Pan Alley; The Great American Broadcast; Moon Over Miami; Footlight Serenade; Iceland; Sentimental Journey; The Vanquished; Hold Back the Night; Hidden Fear.

TV inc: Gunsmoke; Columbo.

Thea inc: Good News.

PEARL, Minnie (Sarah Ophelia Cannon): Singer-Act. b. Centerville, TN, Oct 25, 1912. With Grand Ole Opry since 1940. TV inc: Grand Ole Opry; Jubilee USA; HeeHaw; A Country Christmas, 1979; George Burns In Nashville?; A Country Christmas, 1980.

Albums inc: Minnie Pearl; Minnie Pearl at the Party; Answer to Giddyup and Go.

PECK, Gregory: Act. b. La Jolla, CA, Apr 5, 1916. On screen from 1944 in Days of Glory. Films inc: The Keys of the Kingdom; The Yearling; Gentleman's Agreement; Paradine Case; Twelve O'Clock High; The Valley of Decision; Spellbound; Duel in the Sun; The Macomber Affair; The Paradine Case; The Gunfighter; David and Bathsheba; Captain Horatio Hornblower; The Snows of Kilimanjaro; Roman Holiday; The Man in the Gray Flannel Suit; Moby Dick; Pork Chop Hill; On The Beach; Beloved Infidel; The Guns of Navarone; To Kill A Mockingbird (Oscar-1962); Captain Newman, MD; How the West Was Won; Arabesque; Mackenna's Gold; The Chairman; Marooned; The Stalking Moon; I Walk the Line; Billy Two Hats; The Omen; MacArthur; The Boys From Brazil; The Sea Wolves. (Prod) Trial of the Catonsville Nine; The Dove.

(Jean Hersholt Humanitarian Award-1967).

TV inc: A Holiday Tribute to Radio City Music Hall.

PECKINPAH, Sam: Dir. b. Fresno, CA, Feb 21, 1925. e. USC, MA. Produced, directed shows for the Huntington Park Theatre near LA. Wrote for TV series Gunsmoke. Continued in TV as prod, dir, wri on such series as Broken Arrow; Tales of Wells Fargo; The Westerner; The Rifleman; Route 66; The Dick Powell Theatre.

Films inc: Deadly Companions; The Wild Bunch; The Ballad of Cable Hogue; Straw Dogs; The Getaway; The Killer Elite; Cross of Iron; Convoy; Il Visitatore (The Visitor).

PEERCE, Jan (Jacob Pincus Perelmuth): Tenor. b. NYC, 1904. F of Larry Peerce. Originally a violinist, playing with pickup bands, worked Borscht belt; hired by Roxy Rothafel as singer at Radio City Music Hall; appeared on Roxy Sunday radio shows; starred at NY Paramount; started "tabloid" versions of opera at Music Hall, remaining there 10 seasons and appearing on Music Hall of Air; started concert career 1937; debuted Metropolitan Opera House 1941. Bway inc: Fiddler on the Roof.

PEERCE, Larry: Wri-Dir. b. NYC. S of Jan Peerce. Films inc: One Potato, Two Potato; Goodbye Columbus; A Separate Peace; Ash Wednesday; The Other Side of the Mountain; Two Minute Warning; The Other Side of the Mountain Part II; The Bell Jar; Why Would I Lie?

PELIKAN, Lisa: Act. b. Berkeley, CA. Studied at Juilliard. Thea inc: Dynamo; Spring Awakening; Elephant in the House.

TV inc: The Country Girl; The Blue Hotel; Beacon Hill; Valley Forge; Perfect Gentlemen; True Grit; I Want to Keep My Baby; The Best of Families; James at 15; The Last Convertible; Studs Lonigan; The Women's Room.

Films inc: Julia; Jennifer; Labrynth; The House of God.

PENDERGRASS, Teddy: Mus-Singer. b. Philadelphia, Mar 26, 1950. Drummer with various groups, became lead singer with reorganized Blue Notes 1970; solo 1977. Albums inc: Teddy Pendergrass; Life Is A Song Worth Singing; Teddy; TP.

PENDLETON, Austin: Act. b. Warren, OH, Mar 27, 1940. e. Yale U. Thea inc: Oh Dad, Poor Dad, Mama's Hung You in the Closet and I'm Feelin' So Sad; Fiddler on the Roof; Hail Scrawdyke!; The Little Foxes; The Last Sweet Days of Isaac; American Glands; An American Millionaire; The Runner Stumbles; Say Goodnight Gracie (dir); John Gabriel Borkman (dir).

Films inc: What's Up Doc?; Every Little Crook and Nanny; The Thief Who Came to Dinner; The Front Page; The Great Smokey Roadblock; Starting Over; The Muppet Movie; Simon; First Family.

PENN, Arthur: Dir. b. Philadelphia, Sep 27, 1922. e. Black Mountain College, Ashville, NC; Universities of Perugia and Florence, Italy. Began stage career as actor, Neighborhood Playhouse, Philadelphia, 1940. Dir first Bway prodn, Two for the Seesaw, 1958. Thea inc: The Miracle Worker (Tony-1960); Toys in the Attic; An Evening with Mike Nichols and Elaine May; Golden Boy; Wait Until Dark; The Sly Fox.

Films inc: The Left-Handed Gun; The Miracle Worker; Bonnie and Clyde; Alice's Restaurant; Little Big Man; Visions of Eight; Night Moves.

TV inc: Man on a Mountain; The Miracle Worker.

PENN, Bill: Act-Prod-Dir. b. Reading, PA, Jun 15, 1931. e. Franklin and Marshall Coll, UCLA. Bway debut 1953, The Fifth Season. Toured in Stalag 17. Since 1958, dir, prod. Thea inc: The Potting Shed; Fugue for Three Marys; The Women at the Tomb; Susannah and the Elders; The Bible Salesman; Tobacco Road; Medium Rare; The Miracle; Double Entry; Bartleby; Put It In Writing; Three Cheers for the Tired Businessman; That Thing at the Cherry Lane; By Hex.

PEPPARD, George: Act-Prod-Dir. b. Detroit, Oct 1, 1928. e. Carnegie Mellon Institute, BFA. Early experience on stage. Screen debut 1957, The Strange One. Films inc: Pork Chop Hill; Home from the Hill; Breakfast at Tiffany's; How the West Was Won; The Carpetbaggers; The Blue Max; Tobruk; What's So Bad About Feeling Good?; Pendulum; The Executioner; Cannon for Cordoba; One More Train to Rob; The Groundstar Conspiracy; Newman's Law; Damnation Alley; Five Days from Home; From Hell to Victory (& prod-dir); Battle Beyond the Stars.

TV inc: The Bravos; One of Our Own; Guilty or Innocent; The Sam Sheppard Murder Case; Banacek; Doctors Hospital; Torn Between Two Lovers.

PERELMAN, S J: Wri. b. NYC, Feb 1, 1904. Films inc: Monkey Business; Horse Feathers; Ambush; The Golden Fleecing; Around the World in 80 Days

(Oscar-1956).

(Died Oct 17, 1979).

PERENCHIO, Jerry (Andrew Jerrold Perenchio): Exec. b. Fresno, CA, Dec 20, 1930. e. UCLA. Started as agent; 1958 vp MCA; 1962 vp GAC; 1964 formed Chartwell Artists; 1973 bd chmn Tandem Productions/TAT Communications; also pres ON TV.

PERKINS, Anthony: Act. b. NYC, Apr 14, 1932. e. Columbia U, Rollins Coll. S of late Osgood Perkins. Screen debut, 1953, The Actress. Films inc: Friendly Persuasion; The Lonely Man; Fear Strikes Out; The Tin Star; This Bitter Earth; Desire Under the Elms; The Matchmaker; Green Mansions; On the Beach; Tall Story; Psycho; Goodbye Again; Phaedra; The Trail; The Fool Killer; The Champagne Murders; Pretty Poison; Catch-22; Someone Behind the Door; Ten Days' Wonder; WUSA; Play It As It Lays; Lovin' Molly; Murder on the Orient Express; Mahogany; Remember My Name; Winter Kills; Tree Vrouwen; The Black Hole; ffolkes; Double Negative.

Thea inc: Greenwillow; Look Homeward Angel; Steambath (& dir); Equus; Romantic Comedy.

TV inc: Kraft Theatre; Studio One; US Steel Hour; Armstrong Theatre; First You Cry; Les Miserables.

PERKINS, Millie: Act. b. 1939. Films inc: The Diary of Anne Frank; Wild in the Country; Wild in the Streets; Lady Cocoa.

PERLMAN, Itzhak: Concert violinist. b. Tel Aviv, Aug 31, 1945. e. Juilliard. Guest soloist with Indianapolis Symphony; NY Philharmonic; National Symphony; Philadelphia Orchestra; Baltimore Symphony; Cleveland Orchestra; Buffalo Symphony; major festivals.

(Grammys-(3)-class inst-1977; class album of year & chamber mus perf-1978).

PERLMUTTER, David M: Prod. b. Toronto, Sep 22, 1934. e. U of Toronto. P, Quadrant Films Ltd. Films inc: The Neptune Factor; Dead of Night; Blue Blood; Sunday in the Country; It Seemed Like a Good Idea at the Time; Love at First Sight; Find the Lady; Blood and Guts; Nothing Personal; Double Negative.

PERRINE, Valerie: Act. b. Galveston, TX, Sep 3, 1943. Performed as showgirl in Las Vegas. Screen debut, 1972, Slaughterhouse Five. Films inc: The Last American Hero; Lenny W.C. Fields and Me; Mr. Billion; Superman; The Electric Horseman; Magician of Lublin; Can't Stop The Music; Superman II.

PERRY, Barbara: Act. Films inc: Period of Adjustment; From the Terrace; I was a Male War Bride; The Mirage; Maybe I'll be Home in the Spring; Thief; Opening Night.

TV inc: Family Affair; Andy Griffth Show; Side by Side.

Thea inc: Rumple; Happy as Larry; Swan Song; If the Shoe Fits.

PERRY, Eleanor: Wri. Films inc: David and Lisa; Ladybug, Ladybug; The Swimmer; Last Summer; Trilogy; Diary of a Mad Housewife; The Lady in the Car; The Man Who Loved Cat Dancing.

TV inc: A Christmas Memory (Emmy-adapt-1967); The House Without A Christmas Tree (Emmy-1973).

PERRY, Frank: Dir. b. 1930. Films inc: David and Lisa; Ladybug, Ladybug; The Swimmer; Trilogy; Last Summer; Diary of a Mad Housewife; Doc; Play It as it Lays; Man on a Swing; Rancho de Luxe.

Thea inc: Ladies at the Alamo (dir).

TV inc: Skag; The Dummy.

PERRY, John Bennett: Act. b. Williamstown, MA, Jan 4, 1941. e. St Lawrence U. Lead singer with Serendipity Singers before act. Thea inc: (tours) Irma La Douce; Annie Get Your Gun; Hello, Dolly!; Leonard Bernstein's Mass.

Films inc: Midway; Lipstick.

TV inc: EveryDay (host); 240-Robert.

PERSKY, Bill: Wri-Dir. b. New Haven, CT, 1931. e. Syracuse. Ad writer, teamed with Sam Denoff (1953), writing nitery acts, then tv; partnership lasted 21 years.

TV inc: Steve Allen Show; Andy Williams Show; Dick Van Dyke Show (& prod) (Emmys-wri-1964,1966); Sid Caesar-Imogene Coca-Carl Reiner-Howard Morris Special (Emmy-1967); McHale's Navy; Dick Van Dyke and the Other Woman (& prod); The First Nine Months Are the Hardest (crea-prod); Pure Goldie (& prod); Confessions of Dick Van Dyke (prod); The Funny Side (crea-exec prod); Don Rickles Show (crea-exec prod); Lotsa Luck (crea-exec prod); That Girl (crea-exec prod); Bill Cosby Special; The Man Who Came To Dinner. Since splitting with Denoff, dir Big City Boys; Joe and Valerie; How to Survive the 70's and Maybe Even Bump Into Happiness; The Single Life; My Wife Next Door; Love at First Sight.

PERSKY, Lester: Prod. b. NYC, Jul 6, 1927. e. Brooklyn College. Former ad agcy owner. Formed Persky-Bright organization which financed indie films, company then became Persky-Bright Prodns.

Films inc: Fortune and Men's Eyes; Equus; Hair; Yanks.

TV inc: Almost Heaven.

PERSOFF, Nehemiah: Act. b. Israel, Aug 14, 1920. e. Hebrew Tech Inst. Films inc: On the Waterfront; The Harder They Fall; The Angry Age; Never Steal Anything Small; Al Capone; Some Like It Hot; The Big Show; The Hook; Fate is the Hunter; The Greatest Story Ever Told; Panic in the City; Red Sky at Morning; Psychic Killer; In Search of Historic Jesus.

Thea inc: Only in America; Galileo; Richard III; Peter Pan; Peer Gynt; Tiger at the Gates.

TV inc: The Word; Greatest Heroes of the Bible; A Cry For Justice; The Rebels; The French Atlantic Affair; The Thirteenth Day-The Story of Esther; B.A.D. Cats; F.D.R-The Last Year; The Henderson Monster; Turnover Smith.

PERTWEE, Michael: Wri. b. London, Apr 24, 1916. Thea inc: Death on the Table; The Paragon; It's Different for Men; She's Done It Again; Don't Just Lie There, Say Something!; A Bit Between the Teeth; Birds of Paradise; Six of One; Ace in a Hole.

Films inc: Silent Dust; The Interrupted Journey; Daughter in Paradise; The Naked Truth; The Mouse on the Moon; Ladies Who Do; A Funny Thing Happened on the Way to the Forum; Finders Keepers; The Magnificent Two; Salt and Pepper; One More Time; Digby the Biggest Dog in the World.

TV inc: The Paragon; Chain Male; Strictly Personal; The Frightened Man; Never a Cross Word; Men of Affairs.

PESCOW, Donna: Act. b. NYC, Mar 24, 1954. Films inc: Saturday Night Fever. TV inc: Angie.

PETER, PAUL, AND MARY: Trio. Members are Peter Yarrow, Noel Paul Stookey and Mary Travers. Recs inc: If I Had a Hammer (Grammys-group & folk-1962); Blowin' In The Wind (Grammys-group & folk-1963); Peter Paul and Mommy (Grammy-children-1969); Puff the Magic Dragon; Reunion.

PETERS, Bernadette: Act. b. NYC, Feb 28, 1944. Professional debut at age 5 on TV's Horn and Hardart Children's Hour. Also on Juvenile Jury, Name That Tune. Legit debut NY City Center production The Most Happy Fella. At age 13 toured in Gypsy, playing Baby June. Screen debut, Ace Eli And Rodger of the Skies. Films inc: W.C. Fields & Me; Vigilante Force; The Silent Movie; The Jerk.

TV inc: All's Fair; They Said It With Music; Sha Na Na; The Tim Conway Special; A Mac Davis Special Christmas Odyssey; The Martian Chronicles; The Starmakers.

PETERS, Brock: Act. b. NYC, 1927. Films inc: Carmen Jones; Porgy and Bess; To Kill a Mockingbird; Major Dundee; The Pawnbroker; The Incident; P.J.; Daring Game; Ace High; The McMasters; Black Girl; Soylent Green; Framed; Lost in the Stars; Two-Minute Warning.

Thea inc: King of the Dark Chamber; Othello; The Great White Hope; Lost in the Stars; Framed.

TV inc: It Takes a Thief; Judd for the Defense; Felony Squad; Gunsmoke; Mannix; Mod Squad; Welcome Home, Johnny Bristol; The Incredible Journey of Doctor Meg Laurel; Mark Twain's America-Abe Lincoln, Freedom Fighter.

PETERS, Jean: Act. b. Canton, OH, Oct 15, 1926. Gave up career 1957 to marry Howard Hughes. Div 1971. On screen from 1947. Films inc: The Captain from Castile; Deep Waters; It Happens Every Spring; Anne of the Indies; Wait Till the Sun Shines, Nellie; Take Care of My Little Girl; As Young as You Feel; Viva Zapata; Lure of the Wilderness; O'Henry's Full House; Niagara; Pickup on South Street; Blueprint for Murder; Vicki; Three Coins in the Fountain; Apache; Broken Lance; A Man Called Peter.

TV inc: Winesburg, Ohio.

PETERS, Jon: Prod. b. Van Nuys, CA, 1947. Started local hair-styling business, built it into multi-million dollar corporation before turning prod with Jon Peters Organization; 1980 joined with Peter Guber, Neil Bogart to form new entity, The Boardwalk Co.

Films inc: A Star Is Born; The Eyes of Laura Mars; The Main Event; Die Laughing; Caddyshack.

PETERS, Roberta: Opera singer-Act. b. NYC, May 4, 1930. Soloist with Metropolitan Opera since 1951 with Royal Opera-Covent Garden; Salzburg Festival; Vienna State Opera; Munich Opera; Berlin Opera; Kirov Opera (Leningrad); Bolshoi Opera; frequent guest tv appearances.

PETERSDORF, Rudy: Exec. b. Germany, Jan 24, 1930. e. UC Berkeley, LLB. 1955 with Capitol Records legal dept; 1957, vp bus aff Desilu Prodns; 1963 vp bus aff U; 1978, vp bus aff WB; 1980 P Australian Film Office.

PETERSON, Arthur: Act. b. Mandan, ND, Nov 18, 1912. e. U of MN. Began on radio in hundreds of dramas inc original Guiding Light. Films inc: Call Northside 777.
TV inc: That's O'Toole (& crea); Soap.

PETERSON, Oscar: Mus. b. Montreal, Canada, Aug 15, 1925. With Johnny Holmes Orch in Canada; with Jazz at the Philharmonic; toured U.S. & Europe; established own trio with Ray Brown, Irving Ashby.
(Grammys-(4)-jazz group-1974; jazz soloist 1977, 1978, 1979).

PETIT, Roland: Chor. b. Paris, Jan 13, 1924. e. Paris Opera Ballet School. H of Rene Jeanmaire. Premier Danseur Paris Opera 1940-1944; founder Les Vendredis de la Danse; Les Ballets de Champs Elysees; Les Ballets de Paris; Les Ballets de Marseille; dir Paris Opera Ballet 1970.
Chor works inc: Le Rossignold et la Rose; Le Demoiselles de la nuit; Le Loup; Cyrano de Bergerac; Carmen; Hans Christian Anderson; Folies Bergere; Paradise Lost; Pelleas et Melisande.

PETITCLERC, Denne Bart: Wri. b. Montesano, WA, May 15, 1929. Former newspaper reporter. TV inc: Bonanza; High Chaparral; Shane; Then Came Bronson.
Films inc: Red Sun; Islands in the Stream.

PETRIE, Daniel: Dir. b. Glace Bay, Nova Scotia, Nov 26, 1920. e. St. Francis Xavier U, BA, Columbia U, MA. Films inc: The Bramble Bush; A Raisin in the Sun; Stolen Hours; The Idol; The Spy with a Cold Nose; Buster and Billie; Lifeguard; The Betsy; Resurrection.
TV inc: Eleanor and Franklin (Emmy-1976); Sybil; Eleanor and Franklin-The White House Years (Emmy-1977); Harry Truman-Plain Speaking.

PETTET, Joanna: Act. b. 1944. Films inc: The Group; Night of the Generals; Robbery; Blue; The Evil.
TV inc: The Weekend Nun; Captains and the Kings; The Return of Frank Cannon.

PEVNEY, Joseph: Dir. b. NYC, 1920. Former actor. Films inc: (act) Nocturne; Outside the Wall; Body and Soul. (Dir) Counsellor at Law; Key Largo; Stage Door; Iron Man; Flesh and Fury; It Happens Every Thursday; Six Bridges to Cross; Away All Boats; Tammy; Man of a Thousand Faces; Twilight for the Gods; Cash McCall; Night of the Grizzly.
TV inc: Mysterious Island of Beautiful Women.

PEYSER, John J: Wri-Prod-Dir. b. NYC, Aug 10, 1916. e. Colgate U, BA. Films inc: Spain; The Open Door; Kashmiri Run; Honeymoon with a Stranger; Four Rode Out; Massacre Harbor.
TV inc: Hawaii 5-O; Mannix; Movin' On; Swiss Family Robinson; Bronk; Combat; The Untouchables; Rat Patrol; Stunt Seven.

PFEIFFER, Jane C: Exec. b. Sep 29, 1932. Named Bd chmn NBC and a member of the RCA board since Oct 4, 1978; Relieved of duties Jul 9, 1980 by Fred Silverman.

PFLUG, Jo Ann: Act. Films inc: M*A*S*H; Catlow; Where Does It Hurt?. TV inc: Shakespeare Loves Rembrandt; The Day The Women Got Even.

PHILLIPS, Bernard: Act. b. St. Louis, Oct 20, 1913. e. WA U, AB. Films inc: Ruby Gentry; Eight Iron Men; Blue Print for Murder; The Decks Ran Red; Julie; All American; Drango; Cry Terror; The Sand Pebbles; Matti; The Square Jungle; Hijack. TV inc: Dragnet, 12 O'Clock High; Cade's County.

PHILLIPS, Julia: Prod. b. NYC. e. Mt Holyoke Coll. Films inc: Steelyard Blues; The Sting (Oscar-1973); Taxi Driver; The Big Bus; Close Encounters of the Third Kind.

PHILLIPS, MacKenzie: Act. b. Richmond, VA, Nov 10, 1959. Screen debut, 1973, American Graffiti. Films inc: The Conversation; Rafferty and the Gold Dust Twins; More American Graffiti.
TV inc: Go Ask Alice; One Day At A Time; Fast Friends; Moviola (The Silent Lovers).

PHILLIPS, Michael: Prod. b. NYC, Jun 29, 1943. e. Dartmouth Coll, AB, NYU Law School, JD. Films inc: Steelyard Blues; The Sting (Oscar-1973); Taxi Driver; The Big Bus (exec prod); Close Encounters of the Third Kind.

PHILLIPS, Robert: Act. b. Chicago, Apr 10. e. IN U. Films inc: The Silencers; The Dirty Dozen; Hour of the Gun; MacKenna's Gold; Telefon; Killing of a Chinese Bookie.

PHILLIPS, Wendy: Act. b. NYC, Jan 2, 1952. e. UC at Berkeley. Films inc: Fraternity Row. TV inc: Executive Suite; Capra.

PHILLPOTTS, Ambrosine: Act. b. London, England, Sep 13, 1912. e. RADA. Thea inc: (London) The Ringer; No Sleep for the Wicked; The Morning Star; The Man Who Came to Dinner; Emma; The Anonymous Lover; Point Valaine; Marriage Playground; It's Never Too Late; Spring Awakening; Thark; The Killing of Sister George; Sign Here Please; Half Way Up the Tree; A Ghost on Tiptoe; numerous tours of provinces and Europe.
Films inc: Room At the Top; Ooh, You Are Awful; Expresso Bongo; Doctor in Love; Captain's Paradise; This Man is Mine; Life at the Top.
TV inc: Hadleigh; Follyfoot; Doctor at Large.
(Died Oct 12, 1980).

PHIPPS, Nicholas: Act-Wri. b. London, England, Jun 23, 1913. Thea inc: (London) Love In a Mist; Spring Meeting; First Stop North; The Gate Revue; Blithe Spirit; Bold Lover; The Hungry God; Letter from Paris; Past Imperfect; Fallen Angels.
Plays inc: First Stop North; Bold Lover; The Burning Boat.
Films inc: (wri) Spring In Park Lane; Maytime in Mayfair; The Captain's Paradise; Doctor in the House; Doctor at Sea; Doctor at Large; Doctor in Love; No Love for Johnnie.
(Died Apr 11, 1980).

PICCOLI, Michel: Act. b. Paris, Dec 27, 1925. Films inc: French Cancan; The Witches of Salem; Le Bal des Espiona; Le Mepris; Diary of a Chambermaid; De L'Amour; Lady L; La Curee; The Young Girls of Rochefort; Un Homme de Trop; Belle de Jour; Diabolik; La Chamade; Dillinger Est Mort; Topaz; L'Invasion; The Last Woman; Leonor; Mado; The Accuser; Le Mors Aux Dents (The Bit Between The Teeth); The Little Girl In Blue Velvet; The Price of Survival; Le Sucre; Le Divorcement; Todo Modo; Salto Nel Vuoto (Leap Into The Void); Atlantic City, USA.

PICERNI, Paul: Act. b. NYC, Dec 1, 1922. e. Loyola U. Films inc: Breakthrough; I Was a Communist for the FBI; Mara Maru; Desert Song; House of Wax; Omar Khayyam; Strangers When We Meet; The Scalphunters; The Land Raiders; Airport; Kotch; Capricorn One; Beyond the Poseidon Adventure.
TV inc: The Untouchables; Marciano; Alcatraz--The Whole Shocking Story.

PICKENS, Slim (Louis Bert Lindley, Jr): Act. b. Kingsberg, CA, Jun 29, 1919. Rodeo performer 1931-36. On screen from 1940. Films inc: Rocky Mountain; The Boy From Oklahoma; The Outcast; Santa Fe Passage; Last Command; When Gangland Strikes; Stranger at My Door; The Great Locomotive Chase; One-Eyed Jacks; Dr. Strangelove; The Honkers; Pat Garrett and Billy the Kid; Blazing Saddles; Rancho Deluxe; White Line Fever; Mr. Billion; The White Buffalo; The Swarm; Beyond the Poseidon Adventure; Spirit of the Wind; 1941; Tom Horn; Honeysuckle Rose.
TV inc: Bonanza; Mannix; Ironside; Name of the Game; Gunsmoke; Alias Smith and Jones; The Devil and Miss Sarah; Undercover with the KKK; Swan Song; Jake's Way.

PICKER, David V: Exec. b. NYC, May 14, 1931. e. Dartmouth, BA. S of Eugene Picker. United Artists, 1956-73; P, 1969-73; P, Paramount, 1976-77; ind prod. Films inc: Juggernaut; Lenny; Smile; Royal Flash; Oliver's Story; The One and Only; Sidney Sheldon's Bloodline; The Jerk.

PICKER, Eugene D: Exec. b. NYC, Nov 17, 1903. e. NYU School of Business. F of David V Picker. Entered films bus with father operating theatres Bronx, NY; joined Loew's, NY 1920; vp Loews Theratres 1954; exec vp 1958; p 1959; to UA as vp 1961; Trans-Lux Corp. exec vp Jan 1967; p & CEO Sept 1967; formed EDP Films 1974.

PICKFORD, Mary (Gladys Mary Smith): Act. b. Toronto, Apr 8, 1893. W of Charles (Buddy) Rogers. On stage at age 5 with Valentine Stock Co.; toured in The Little Red School House; Uncle Tom's Cabin; East Lynne. On screen from 1909. Films inc: Pollyanna; Little Lord Fauntleroy; Tess of the Storm Country; My Best Girl; Coquette *(Oscar-1928-29-her 1st talking picture)*; The Taming of the Shrew; Kiki; Secrets (her last film, 1933). Special Oscar 1976, "in recognition of her unique contribution to the film industry and the development of film as an artistic medium." One of the founders United Artists Corp, 1919, VP, 1935-37; formed Mary Pickford Co, 1926; Co-Prod Pickford-Lasky Co, 1936. Formed Pickford Prods Inc (with Sam Coslow), 1945; org (with Edward J Peskay) Comet Prodns; co-org P.R.B., Inc, to prod radio & TV programs; sold interest in UA Corp, 1956.
(Died May 29, 1979).

PICON, Molly: Act. b. NYC, Feb 28, 1898. Appeared in vaudeville, Yiddish repertory. On screen from 1937. Films inc: Yiddle and His Fiddle (Poland); Mamale (Poland); Come Blow Your Horn; Fiddler on the Roof; For Pete's Sake.
Bway inc: A Majority of One; Milk and Honey; Dear Me, the Sky Is Falling; Madame Mousse; How to Be a Jewish Mother; Paris Is Out; The Front Page; How Do You Live with Love?; Something Old, Something New.

PIDGEON, Walter: Act. b. East St. John, NB, Can, Sep 23, 1897. In vaudeville with Elsie Janis prior to appearing on Broadway in You Never Can Tell, 1925. On screen from 1925. Films inc: The Gorilla; Turn Back the Hours; Saratoga; Shopworn Angel; Nick Carter, Master Detective; Man Hunt; How Green Was My Valley; Madame Curie; Mrs. Parkington; If Winter Comes; Command Decision; That Forsythe Woman; Mrs. Miniver; Executive Suite; Men of the Fighting Lady; Hit the Deck; Forbidden Planet; Voyage to the Bottom of the Sea; Advise and Consent; Funny Girl; Skyjacked; The Neptune Factor; Harry in Your Pocket; Two Minute Warning. Thea inc: Take Her She's Mine; Dinner at Eight; The Happiest Millionaire; Take Me Along. TV inc: Swiss Family Robinson; Meet Me in St. Louis; The Vanishing 400.

PIERCE, Frederick S: Exec. b. NYC, Apr 8, 1933. e. CCNY. Joined ABC, 1956 as research analyst. Named dir of Sales Planning and Sales Development, 1962; elected vp, 1964; national dir of sales for ABC-TV, 1964-68; vp in charge of planning and asst to the p of ABC-TV until 1972; named p of ABC-TV, 1974; also exec vp ABC Inc, 1979.

PIERSON, Frank: Dir-Wri. b. NYC, May 12, 1925. Films inc: Cat Ballou (co-sp); Cool Hand Luke (sp); The Anderson Tapes (sp); The Looking Glass War (sp & dir); Dog Day Afternoon *(Oscar-sp-1975)*; A Star is Born (sp & dir); King of the Gypsies (sp & dir).
TV inc: Nichols (prod); Haywire (wri).

PILBROW, Richard: Prod. b. Beckenham, Kent, Eng, Apr 28, 1933. Former lighting des. As prod, plays inc: A Funny Thing Happened on the Way to the Forum; She Loves Me; A Scent of Flowers; Fiddler on the Roof; Cabaret; The Beggar's Opera; She Stoops to Conquer; Edward II; Richard II; Erb; Catch My Soul; Company; I and Albert; The Good Companions; A Little Night Music. Films inc: Swallows and Amazons. TV inc: All You Need Is Love — The Story of Popular Music

PINE, Phillip: Act. b. Hanford, CA, 1925. e. UC Berkeley. Films inc: The Lost Missile; Murder by Contract; Price of Fear; Men in War; Glass Houses.
TV inc: Playhouse 90; Studio One; Stone; The Gift; Enola Gay--The Men, The Mission, The Atomic Bomb.
Thea inc: A Stone for Danny Fisher; The Immoralist; See the Jaguar; One Bright Day.

PINE, Robert: Act. b. Scarsdale, NY, Jul 10, 1941. e. OH Wesleyan U. Films inc: Gunpoint; Young Warriors; Out of Sight; Munster, Go Home; Faceless Man; Journey to Shiloh; Day of the Locust; The Graduate; One Little Indian; The Bears and I; The Apple Dumpling Gang Rides Again. TV inc: Brotherhood of the Bell; Incident on a Dark Street; Young Prosecutors; CHiPs; Enola Gay--The Men, The Mission, The Atomic Bomb.

PINTER, Harold: Dir-Wri-Act. b. London, Oct 10, 1930. Started as actor; then wri, dir. Plays inc: The Birthday Party (& dir); The Caretaker; The Homecoming; Landscape; Silence; Old Times; No Man's Land; The Hot House (& dir).
Thea inc: (dir) The Man in the Glass Booth; Exiles; Butley; Otherwise Engaged; Blithe Spirit; The Rear Column; Close of Play.
Films inc: The Servant; The Pumpkin Eater; The Quiller Memorandum; Accident; The Go-Between; The Last Tycoon.
TV inc: A Night Out; Night School; The Lover; Tea Party; The Basement.

PINTOFF, Ernest: Dir-Wri-Prod. b. Dec 15, 1931. Dir Oscar winning short, The Critic (1963). Films inc: Who Killed Mary Whats'ername; Blade; Harvey Middleman; Fireman; Dynamite Chicken; Jaguar Lives.
TV inc: Hawaii Five-0; Kojak; Bionic Woman; The Six Million Dollar Man; James at Sixteen; Movin' On; Feather and Father; Young Dan'l Boone; The White Shadow; The Wild Wild West; This is Marshall McLuhan; This Is Sholem Aleichem; This is Al Capp; Human Feelings.

PIROSH, Robert: Wri. b. 1910. Films inc: The Winning Ticket; A Day at the Races; I Married a Witch; Rings on Her Fingers; Up in Arms; Battleground *(Oscar-1949)*; Go For Broke (& dir); Washington Story (& dir); Valley of the Kings (& dir); Spring Reunion (& dir); Hell is for Heroes; A Gathering of Eagles; What's so Bad about Feeling Good? TV inc: (wri-prod pilots) Laramie; Combat.

PISIER, Marie-France: Act. b. Dalat, Indo-China, 1944. Films inc: Love at Twenty; Les Saintes Nitouches; Les Amoureux du France; La Mort D'Un Tuer; Les Yeaux Cernes; The Vampire of Dusseldorf; Trans-Europe Express; Stolen Kisses; L'Ecume Des Jours; Nous N'Irons Plus Au Bois; Journal of a Suicide; Feminin, Feminin; Celine and Julie Go Boating; French Provincial; The Phantom of Liberte; Cousin Cousine; Serail; Barocco; Le Corps De Mon Ennemi; Barocco; Serail; The Other Side of Midnight; Les Apprentis Sourciers; The Bronte Sisters; French Postcards; Love on the Run; La Banquiere (The Woman Banker).
TV inc: The French Atlantic Affair; Scruples.

PITLIK, Noam: Dir. b. Philadelphia, PA, Nov 4, 1932. e. Temple U, BA; NYU, MA. Films inc: (act) The Graduate; The Fortune Cookie; The Hallelujah Trail; Front Page.
TV inc: (dir) The Dick Van Dyke Show; The Practice; Barney Miller (& prod) *(Emmy-dir-1979)*; I'm A Big Girl Now.

PLACE, Mary Kay: Act-Sing-Wri. b. Sep 23, 1947. TV inc: (wri) The Mary Tyler Moore Show; Phyllis; M*A*S*H. (act) Mary Hartman, Mary Hartman *(Emmy-supp-1977)*; Fernwood Forever; Act of Love.
Films inc: (act) Bound for Glory; New York, New York; More American Graffiti; Starting Over; Private Benjamin.

PLATO, Dana: Act. b. Maywood, CA, Nov 7, 1964. Films inc: The Heretic; Beyond the Bermuda Triangle; California Suite.
TV inc: Diff'rent Strokes.

PLEASENCE, Angela: Act. b. Chapeltown, Yorkshire, Eng. e. RADA. D of Donald Pleasence. Thea inc: A Midsummer Night's Dream; The Ha-Ha; The Three Sisters; The Tempest; The Plough and the Stars; You Were So Sweet When You Were Little; The Entertainer; Round House; The Journey; The Bitter Tears of Petra von Kant; The Hothouse.

Films inc: Here We Go Round the Mulberry Bush; Hitler - The Last Ten Days; Symptoms; The Godsend.

TV inc: The Six Wives of Henry VIII; Breath; The Wood Demon; Les Miserables.

PLEASENCE, Donald: Act. b. Worksop, England, Oct 5, 1919. Thea inc: (London) Twelfth Night; The Brothers Karamazov; Hobson's Choice; Ebb Tide (& wri); The Impresario from Smyrna; The Rules of the Game; The Lark; Misalliance; The Caretaker; The Man in the Glass Booth; Reflections. (Bway) Caesar and Cleopatra; Antony and Cleopatra; The Caretaker; Poor Bitos; The Man in the Glass Booth; Wise Child.

Films inc: Tale of Two Cities; The Shakedown; Spare The Rod; The Caretaker; The Great Escape; The Greatest Story Ever Told; The Hallelujah Trail; Fantastic Voyage; Cul-de-Sac; You Only Live Twice; Arthur, Arthur; THX 1138; Soldier Blue; Jerusalem File; Innocent Bystanders; Death Line; The Black Windmill; Journey Into Fear; Escape to Witch Mountain; Hearts of the West; The Last Tycoon; The Passover Plot; The Eagle Has Landed; Oh, God!; Fear; The Uncanny; Telefon; Halloween; Sgt. Pepper's Lonely Hearts Club Band; The Order and Security of the World; Power Play; Jaguar Lives; Night Creature; Dracula; Good Luck, Miss Wyckoff.

TV inc; Fate and Mr. Browne; The Silk Purse; A House of His Own; The Traitor; The Millionairess; The Bastard; All Quiet on the Western Front; The French Atlantic Affair; Blade On The Feather.

PLESHETTE, John: Act. b. NYC, Jul 27. e. Brown U; Carnegie-Mellon; studied with Stella Adler and Sanford Meisner. Bway inc: The Zulu and the Zayda; Jimmy Shine; Love's Labour's Lost; Measure for Measure; Richard III. Other thea inc MacBird!; Green Julia; It's Called the Sugar Plum; Says I, Says He.

Films inc: The End of the Road; Won Ton Ton--The Dog That Saved Hollywood; Slap Shot; Rocky II.

TV inc: The Trial of Lee Harvey Oswald; The Users; Seventh Avenue; Once Upon a Marriage; Knots Landing.

PLESHETTE, Suzanne: Act. b. NYC, Jan 31, 1937. e. Syracuse U. Screen debut, 1958, The Geisha Boy. Films inc: Rome Adventure; The Birds; 40 Pounds of Trouble; Wall of Noise; A Rage to Live; Youngblood Hawke; A Distant Trumpet; The Ugly Dachshund; Bullwhip Griffin; Fate Is The Hunter; Mr. Buddwing; Nevada Smith; Bluebeard's Ghost; The Power; If It's Tuesday This Must Be Belgium; Suppose They Gave a War and Nobody Came; Support Your Local Gunfighter; The Shaggy D.A.; Hot Stuff; Target Harry; Oh, God! Book II.

Bway inc: Compulsion; The Cold Wind and the Warm; The Golden Fleecing; The Miracle Worker; Two for the Seesaw.

TV inc: The Bob Newhart Show; Wings of Fire; Along Came a Spider; Hunters Are for Killing; River of Gold; In Broad Daylight; Flesh and Blood; If Things Were Different.

PLESKOW, Eric: Exec. b. Vienna, Apr 24, 1924. Started in 1948 as asst GM, Motion Picture Export Assoc, Germany; 1950-51, continental rep, Sol Lesser Prodns; joined UA in 1951 as Far East sls mgr; 1952, named mgr, S Africa; 1953-58, mgr, Germany; 1958-59, exec asst, to continental mgr; 1959-60, asst continental mgr; 1960-62, continental mgr; 1962, in charge of foreign dist; 1973, exec VP & COO; 1973, P, & CEO; resigned 1978, formed Orion Pictures Co, P, CEO.

PLOWRIGHT, Joan: Act. b. Brigg, Eng, Oct 18, 1929. W of Laurence Olivier. Performed in repertory; member of Old Vic Co during tour of S. Africa, 1952.

Thea inc: (London) Saint Joan; Uncle Vanya; Hobson's Choice; The Master Builder; The Three Sisters; Tartuffe; Love's Labour's Lost. (Co-Dir) An Evasion of Women; The Travails of Sancho Panza. (Dir) Rites; Enjoy. (Bway) The Chairs; The Lesson; A Taste of Honey *(Tony-*1961); Eden End; The Sea Gull; The Bed Before Yesterday; Filumena.

Films inc: Moby Dick; The Entertainer; Three Sisters; Equus.

TV inc: Odd Man In; The Secret Agent; The School for Scandal; The Diary of Anne Frank.

PLUMMER, Christopher: Act. b. Toronto, Dec 13, 1929. Professional debut with Canadian Repertory Theatre, Ottawa. Broadway debut 1954 The Constant Wife. Films inc: Across the Everglades; Stage Struck; The Sound of Music; Triple Cross; Lock Up Your Daughters; The Man Who Would Be King; The Return of the Pink Panther; The Disappearance; Assassination In Sarajevo; The Assignment; International Velvet; Murder by Decree; Starcrash; Hanover Street; The Silent Partner; Arthur Miller on Home Ground; Somewhere In Time.

Bway inc: A Night of the Auk; J.B.; The Lark; Hamlet; Macbeth; Cyrano de Bergerac *(Tony-*1974).

TV inc: The Moneychangers *(Emmy-*1977); The Shadow Box.

PLUNKETT, Walter: Des. b. Oakland, CA, Jun 5, 1902. Films inc: Rio Rita; Cimarron; Little Women; The Gay Divorcee; Of Human Bondage; Gone With the Wind; The Hunchback of Notre Dame; Stagecoach; Duel in the Sun; The Three Musketeers; That Forsythe Woman; The Magnificent Yankee; Kind Lady; An American in Paris *(Oscar-*1951); The Prisoner of Zenda; Kiss Me Kate; Seven Brides for Seven Brothers; Lust For Life; Pollyanna; How the West Was Won; Seven Women.

POCO: Group. Members are Paul Cotton, lead guitar-sngwri; Rusty Young, multi-inst & voc; Steve Chapman, drums; Charlie Harrison, bass; Kim Bullard, keyboard. Originally formed 1968 by Richie Furay, Jim Messina and Young as Pogo but name changed to avoid lawsuit from cartoonist Walt Kelly. Albums inc: Pickin' Up the Pieces; Poco; Deliverin'; From the Inside; Good Feeling to Know; Crazy Eyes; Seven; Cantamos; Head Over Heels; Rose of Cimarron; Indian Summer; Legend; Under the Gun.

PODESTA, Rossana: Act. b. Libya, Jun 20, 1934. Films inc: Luxury Girls; Cops and Robbers; Ulysses; Raw Wind in Eden; The Slave of Rome; Sodom and Gemorrah; Helen of Troy; The Golden Arrow; Seven Golden Men; Man of the Year; Sunday Lovers.

POE, James: Wri. b. Dobbs Ferry, NY, 1923. Films inc: Around the World in 80 Days *(Oscar-*co-sp-1956); Attack; Cat on a Hot Tin Roof; Last Train from Gun Hill; Summer and Smoke; Toys in the Attic; Lilies of the Field; The Bedford Incident; They Shoot Horses Don't They? (Died Jan 24, 1980).

TV inc: Enola Gay--The Men, The Mission, The Atomic Bomb.

POITIER, Sidney: Act-Dir. b. Miami, Feb 20, 1924. Formed First Artists Prod Co Ltd, 1969, with Paul Newman and Barbara Streisand. On screen from 1949. Films inc: No Way Out; Cry the Beloved Country; Red Ball Express; Go Man Go; The Blackboard Jungle; Good-Bye My Lady; Edge of the City; Something of Value; Porgy and Bess; All the Young Men; Devil at Four O'Clock; A Raisin in the Sun; The Long Ships; Lilies of the Field *(Oscar-*1963); Slender Thread; A Patch of Blue; Duel at Diablo; To Sir With Love; In the Heat of the Night; Guess Who's Coming to Dinner; The Lost Man; They Call Me Mr. Tibbs; Brother John; For Love of Ivy; Buck and the Preacher. (Dir-act) A Warm December; Uptown Saturday Night; The Wilby Conspiracy; Let's Do It Again; A Piece of the Action. (Dir) Stir Crazy.

Thea inc: Lysistrata; Anna Lucasta; Freight.

POLAN, Lou: Act. b. Ukrain, Russia, Jun 15, 1904. To US as youth. Early training Neighborhood Playhouse; NY School of the Theatre. Bdwy debut, 1922, in walk-on part. First speaking role 1922. The Bootlegger; toured in vaudeville.

Thea inc: The Gentleman from Athens; Desire Under the Elms; Coriolanus; Saint Joan; Seidman and Son; Hamlet; The Tenth Man; The Creation of the World and Other Business. Films inc: Fourteen Hours; You Never Can Tell; Murder, Inc; The Seven Ups.

POLANSKI, Roman: Dir-Wri-Act. b. Paris, Aug 18, 1933. e. Polish National Film Academy. Originally and actor in several Polish films, entered dirs school of Polish Academy where he made several shorts inc Two Men and a Wardrobe, Le Gros et le Maigre; Mannals. Films inc: Knife in the Water; Repulsion; Cul de Sac; The Fearless Vampire Killers or Pardon Me But Your Teeth Are in My Neck; Rosemary's Baby; The Tenant (& act); Chinatown. Arrested in 1978 in Hollywood on sex charges involving a minor, he jumped bail while awaiting sentence and returned to France. Resumed career in France with Tess (dir-wri).

POLIKOFF, Gerald: Dir. Staff dir NBC News. TV inc: No More Vietnams, but; We're Moving Up--The Hispanic Migration; American Fashion--Rags to Riches; Gambling.

POLITO, Gene: Cin. b. NYC, Sep 13, 1918. e. USC. Films inc: Downhill Racer; Prime Cut; Five on the Black Hand Side; Futureworld; Westworld; Trackdown; That's Entertainment; Bad News Bears Go To Japan; Cheech and Chong's Up in Smoke.

TV inc: A Time for Love; Sam Hill; Judge Dee; Delaney; The Man Who Could Talk to Kids; All Together Now; My Sweet Charlie; Death Scream; Life Goes To War; Profiles in Courage; Lost in Space.

POLL, Martin: Prod. b. NYC, Nov 24, 1924. Films inc: Love Is a Ball; Sylvia; The Lion in Winter; The Appointment; The Magic Garden of Stanley Sweetheart; The Man Who Loved Cat Dancing; Night Watch; Love and Death; The Sailor Who Fell From Grace With the Sea; Somebody Killed Her Husband.

TV inc: Stunt Seven.

POLLACK, Sydney: Dir. b. South Bend, IN, Jul 1, 1934. Films inc: The Slender Thread; This Property is Condemned; The Scalphunters; Castle Keep; They Shoot Horses, Don't They?; Jeremiah Johnson; The Way We Were; The Yakuza; Three Days of the Condor; Bobby Deerfield; The Electric Horseman; Honeysuckle Rose.

TV inc: A Cardinal Act of Mercy; Something About Lee Willey; Two is the Number; The Game (*Emmy*-1966).

POLLARD, Michael J: (nee Pollack): Act. b. 1939. Films inc: Adventures of a Young Man; Summer Magic; The Stripper; Bonnie and Clyde; Hannibal Brooks; Little Fauss and Big Halsy; Dirty Little Billy; Sunday in the Country; Between the Lines; Melvin and Howard.

POLONSKY, Abraham: Dir-Wri. b. NYC, 1910. e. CCNY, BA, Columbia Law School. Golden Earrings; I Can Get It for You Wholesale; Body and Soul; Madigan; Tell Them Willie Boy is Here (& dir); Romance of a Horse Thief (dir); Avalanche Express (wri).

PONTI, Carlo: Prod. b. Milan, Italy, Dec 11, 1913. e. U of Milan. H of Sophia Loren. Films inc: Little Old World; A Dog's Life; The Knight Has Arrived; Musolino; The Outlaw; Romanticism; Sensuality; The White Slave; Toto in Color; The Three Corsairs; Ulysses; The Woman of the River; An American of Rome; Attila; War and Peace; La Strada (*Oscar*-Foreign film-1956); The Last Lover; The Great Spy Mission; Happily Ever After; The Girl and the General; Sunflower; Best House in London; Lady Liberty; White Sister; What?; Andy Warhol's Frankenstein; The Passenger; The Cassandra Crossing; A Special Day.

PORTER, Don: Act. b. Miami, OK, Sep 24, 1912. Films inc: Top Sergeant; Night Monster; The Curse of the Allenbys; Ocean Drive; Because You're Mine; The Racket; Our Miss Brooks; Bachelor In Paradise; Youngblood Hawke; The Candidate; Forty Carats; White Line Fever.

TV inc: Private Secretary; Our Miss Brooks; The Ann Sothern Show; Murder or Mercy; The President's Mistress; Happy Birthday Charlie Brown; The Legend of Lizzie Borden; Battles-The Murder That Wouldn't Die; The Last Song.

PORTER, Eric: Act. b. London, Apr 8, 1928. Films inc: The Heroes of Telemark; Kaleidoscope; The Lost Continent; Hands of the Ripper; Antony and Cleopatra; Nicholas and Alexandra; The Day of the Jackal; The Belstone Fox; Callan; Hennessy.

TV inc: The Forsyte Saga; Hamlet; Little Lord Fauntleroy.

PORTER, Nyree Dawn: Act. b. New Zealand, 1940. Films inc: Two Left Feet; The Cracksman; Jane Eyre; The House That Dripped Blood; From Beyond the Grave.

TV inc: The Forsyte Saga; The Protectors; The Martian Chronicles.

PORTMAN, Richard: Snd. b. LA, Apr 2, 1934. Films inc: Kotch; The Candidate; Paper Moon; Day of the Dolphin; Young Frankenstein; Godfather; Nashville; Funny Lady; The End; The Deer Hunter (*Oscar*-1978); A Perfect Couple; Quintet; Rich Kids.

TV inc: Dynasty; Eleanor and Franklin Part II; The White House Years.

POST, Ted: Prod-Dir. b. NYC. Films inc: Hang 'Em High; Beneath the Planet of the Apes; The Harrad Experiment; Magnum Force; Go Tell The Spartans; Good Guys Wear Black; Whiffs; Nightkill.

TV inc: Studio One; Ford Theatre; Playhouse of Stars; Fred Astaire Show; Gunsmoke; Rawhide; Twilight Zone; Wagon Train; Combat; Peyton Place; Defenders; Route 66; Baretta; Columbo; Diary of a Teenage Hitchhiker; The Girls in the Office; Beyond Westworld.

Thea inc: The Happy Dollar; Claudia; The Eve of St. Mark; Watch on the Rhine; The Male Animal; Counsellor-at-Law; The Philadelphia Story; Yes, My Darling Daughter; Room Service; Home of the Brave; The Front Page; Three Men on a Horse; The Fatal Weakness; Made in Heaven; George Washington Slept Here; Anna Lucasta; The Dark Tower; Burlesque.

POSTON, Tom: Act. b. Columbus, OH, Oct 17, 1927. Films inc: The City that Never Sleeps; Zotz!; Soldier in the Rain; The Old Dark House; Cold Turkey; The Happy Hooker; Rabbit Test; Up The Academy.

TV inc: Macbeth; The Tempest; Steve Allen Show (*Emmy*-supp-1959); On the Rocks; We've Got Each Other; To Tell the Truth; Fame; Beane's of Boston; Mork and Mindy.

POWELL, Anthony: Dsgn. b. Chortlon-Cum-Hardy, England, Jun 2, 1935. e. Central School of Art and Design. Thea inc: Women, Beware Women; The Rivals; School for Scandal; Fish Out of Water; Comedy of Errors; Private Lives; Ring Round the Moon. Films inc: Royal Hunt of the Sun; Joe Egg; A Town Called Bastard; Nicholas and Alexandra (advsr); Travels With My Aunt (*Oscar*-cos-1972); Papillon; That Lucky Touch; Buffalo Bill and the Indians; Sorcerer; Death on the Nile (*Oscar*-cos-1978); Tess.

POWELL, Charles M: Exec. b. NYC, Feb 17, 1934. e. NYU, BS. Col Natl pub-exp mgr 1959. Natl Pub Coord Par, 1963-64; WNBC Radio/TV, adv Promo Mgr, 1965; ad-pub-dir M J Frankovich, 1969-71; joined MGM as ad-pub-expl dir; 1972; named div vp & corp vp, 1974; Columbia Pictures vp, ad-pub-expl; 1975; Universal Pictures vp ad-pub-prom 1976; formed ind pub-marketing firm with Buddy Young, Jan 1980.

POWELL, Eleanor: Act. b. Springfield, MA, Nov 21, 1912. On stage, niteries. Screen debut, George White's Scandals of 1935. Films inc: Broadway Melody of 1936; Born to Dance; Rosalie; Broadway Melody of 1938; Honolulu; Broadway Melody of 1940; Lady Be Good; Ship Ahoy; I Dood It; Sensations of 1945; Thousands Cheer; The Duchess of Idaho.

TV inc: Faith of Our Children; Bob Hope on the Road to China.

POWELL, Jane (Suzanne Burce): Act. b. Portland, OR, Apr 1, 1929. On screen from 1944 in Song of the Open Road. Films inc: Holiday in Mexico; Three Daring Daughters; Luxury Liner; Two Weeks with Love; Royal Wedding; Seven Brides for Seven Brothers; Athena; Hit the Deck; Enchanted Island.

Thea inc: Irene; I Do! I Do!

POWELL, Michael: Wri-Prod-Dir. b. Canterbury, Kent, England, Sep 30, 1905. Teamed for 15 years with Emeric Pressburger in a series of prodns. Films inc: Caste (wri); Park Lane (wri); Hotel Splendide (wri); Night of the Party (wri); Lazy Bones (wri); The Man Behind the Mask (wri); The Edge of the World; The Spy in Black; The Lion Has Wings; The Thief of Baghdad; 49th Parallel; One Of Our Aircraft Is Missing; The Life and Death of Col Blimp; The Silver Fleet; A Canterbury Tale; I Know Where I'm Going; A Matter of Life and Death; Black Narcissus; The Red Shoes; The Small Back Room; The Elusive Pimpernel; The Tales of Hoffman; The Battle of the River Plate; Ill Met By Moonlight; Honeymoon; Age of Consent; The Boy Who Turned Yellow.

POWELL, Michael: Wri-Prod-Dir. b. Canterbury, Eng, Sep 30, 1905. Films inc: The Edge of the World; The Spy in Black; The Lion Has Wings; The Thief of Baghdad; Contraband; One of Our Aircraft is Missing; The Life and Death of Colonel Blimp; A Canterbury Tale; I Know Where I'm Going; A Matter of Life and Death; The Red Shoes; The Tales of Hoffman; The Battle of the River Plate; Peeping Tom; The Queen's Guard; Sebastian; Age of Consent; The Boy Who Turned Yellow.

POWELL, Norman: Prod. b. LA, 1934. e. Cornell U, BA. S of Joan Blondell and Dick Powell. Dir movies-for-tv, CBS Entertainment. TV inc: (Prod) Flatbush; Salvage I; More Than Friends; Rafferty; Washington Behind Closed Doors.

POWELL, Randolph: Act. b. Iowa City, IA, Apr 14, 1950. e. U Denver. TV inc: Babe; Eleanor and Franklin--The White House Years; Logan's Run; Doctors' Private Lives; The Concrete Cowboys; Dallas.

POWELL, William: Act. b. Pittsburgh, PA, Jul 29, 1892. e. AADA. Began in stock; on NY stage, 1920, in Spanish Love. Screen debut, 1922, in Sherlock Holmes. Films inc: Under the Red Robe; Beau Geste; The Great Gatsby; The Canary Murder Case; One Way Passage; Reckless; The Great Ziegfeld; The Thin Man; My Man Godfrey; Life With Father; Mr. Peabody and the Mermaid; How to Marry a Millionaire; Mister Roberts.

POWERS, Dave (David Price Powers): Dir. b. LA, Dec 2, 1932. Began as prodn asst CBS 1953; stage mgr 1957; asso dir 1964; dir since 1968.
    TV inc: Carol Burnett Show (Emmys-1974, 1975, 1977, 1978); John Ritter, Being of Sound Mind and Body.

POWERS, James: Exec. b. Duluth, MN, Jul 12, 1918. Former journalist. Dir, Seminars and Publications, Center for Advanced Film Studies, The American Film Institute, since 1972. Editor, Filmmaking: The Collaborative Art.
    (Died July 4, 1980).

POWERS, Mala: Act. b. San Francisco, Dec 20, 1931. Films inc: Rage at Dawn; Tammy; City Beneath the Sea; Outrage; Edge of Doom; Cyrano De Bergerac; Daddy's Gone A-Hunting; Six Tickets to Hell.
    TV inc: Hazel; The Man and the City; SWAT.
    Thea inc: Absence of a Cello; The Rivalry; Night of the Iguana; Hogan's Goat; Critic's Choice; Sabrina Fair; Roman Candle; King of Hearts.

POWERS, Stefanie: Act. b. Hollywood, Nov 2, 1942. On screen from 1961. Films inc: Among the Thorns; Experiment in Terror; The Interns; If a Man Answers; McLintock!; Tammy Tell Me True; Die! Die! My Darling; Stagecoach; Love Has Many Faces; Warning Shot; The Love Bug Rides Again; Crescendo; Escape to Athena.
    TV inc: The Girl From UNCLE; The Interns; Fanatic; Feather and Father; Washington--Behind Closed Doors; Hart to Hart.

PRECHT, Robert H: Prod. b. Douglas, AZ, May 12, 1930. e. UCLA, UC Berkeley, BA. CBS-TV 1956-60, assoc. prod.; 1960-71, prod. Ed Sullivan Show; since; 1971 ind, prod. network specials inc: Lily Tomlin; Carroll O'Connor; Andy Williams; Grammy Awards; 50th Anniversary of Grand Ole Opry; The Crystal Gayle Special; Crystal.

PREMINGER, Otto: Dir-Prod. b. Vienna, Dec 5, 1906. e. U of Vienna. At 17, actor with Max Reinhardt troupe; 1935-40, stage prod & dir in US; on faculty Yale Drama School. Films inc: Royal Scandal; Forever Amber; Laura; Centennial Summer; Daisy Kenyon; In the Meantime Darling; Fallen Angel; Whirlpool; Where the Sidewalk Ends; The 13th Letter; Angel Face; The Moon Is Blue; River of No Return; Carmen Jones; Court Martial of Billy Mitchell; The Man with the Golden Arm; St. Joan; Bonjour Tristesse; Porgy and Bess; Anatomy of a Murder; Exodus; Advise & Consent; The Cardinal; In Harm's Way; Bunny Lake Is Missing; Hurry Sundown; Skidoo; Tell Me that You Love Me Junie Moon; Such Good Friends; Rosebud; The Human Factor.
    Bway inc: Margin for Error; The Moon Is Blue; Critic's Choice; Full Circle.

PRENTISS, Paula (nee Ragusa): Act. b. San Antonio, TX, Mar 4, 1939. e. Northwestern U, BA. W of Richard Benjamin. On screen from 1961 in Where the Boys Are. Films inc: Bachelor in Paradise; The Horizontal Lieutenant; Follow the Boys; Man's Favorite Sport; What's New Pussycat?; Catch 22; Last of the Red Hot Lovers; The Stepford Wives; The Black Marble.
    TV inc: He & She; Friendships, Secrets and Lies; The Top of the Hill.
    Thea inc: As You Like It; Arf!; The Norman Conquests.

PRESLE, Micheline (nee Chassagne): Act. b. Paris, Aug 22, 1922. Films inc: Jeunes Filles en Detress; La Nuit Fantastique; Boule de Suif; Le Diable au Corps; Under My Skin; The Adventures of Captain Fabian; Villa Borghese; The She Wolves; Blind Date; The Prize; King of Hearts; Peau d'Ane; Nea; We Forget Everything; Je Te Tiens, Tu Me Tiens par la Barbichette; Your Turn, My Turn; Rien Ne Va Plus; Demons du Midi.
    Thea inc: Colinette; Am Stram Gram; La Main Passe; Tout Depend Des Filles (It All Depends on Girls).

PRESSBURGER, Emeric: Wri. b. Hungary, 1902. Films inc: The Invaders (Oscar-1942-orig story); Twice Upon a Time (& prod-dir); Miracle in Soho (& prod); Behold a Pale Horse; Operation Crossbow; They're a Weird Mob; The Boy Who Turned Yellow.

PRESSMAN, David: Dir. b. Tiflis, Russia, Oct 10, 1913. e. Columbia; NY Neighborhood Playhouse. Started as act on Bway in Brooklyn, USA; Eve of St. Mark; Dream Girl; began dir at Toronto Theatre of Action.
    Bway inc: The Disenchanted; Roman Candle; A Cook for Mr. General; Summertree.
    TV inc: Actors Studio Theatre; T-Men in Action; Westinghouse Summer Theatre; The Nurses; Another World; One Life To Live (10 years) (Emmys-1976, 1977).

PRESSMAN, Edward R: Prod. b. NYC. e. Stanford U. Films inc: Girl (short); Out Of It; The Revolutionary; Dealing; Lost Bag Blues; Sisters; Badlands, Phantom of the Paradise; Paradise Alley; Old Boyfriends; Heart Beat; Despair; You Better Watch Out.

PRESSMAN, Lawrence: Act. b. Cynthiana, KY, Jul 10, 1939. e. KY Northwestern U, BA. Bway inc: Man in the Glass Booth; Never Live Over a Pretzel Factory; Play It Again Sam. Also did Man in the Glass Booth, London.
    TV inc: Rich Man, Poor Man; A Bedtime Story; Blind Ambition; The Gathering, Part 2; Ladies Man.
    Films inc: Man in the Glass Booth; The Crazy World of Julius Vrooder; Helstrom Chronicles; Shaft; Making It; Nine To Five.

PRESSMAN, Michael: Dir. b. NYC, Jul 1, 1950. e. CA Inst of the Arts. Films inc: The Great Texas Dynamite Chase; The Bad News Bears in Breaking Training; Boulevard Nights; Those Lips, Those Eyes.
    TV inc: Like Mom, Like Me.

PRESTON, Robert (nee Meservey): Act. b. Newton Highlands, MA, Jun 8, 1918. e. Pasadena Playhouse. Screen debut, 1938, King of Alcatraz. Films inc: Illegal Traffic; Disbarred; Union Pacific; Beau Geste; Typhoon; Moon Over Burma; Northwest Mounted Police; The Macomber Affair; Wild Harvest; Tulsa; Whispering Smith; The Sundowners; When I Grow Up; Cloudburst; Face to Face; The Last Frontier; Dark at the Top of the Stairs; The Music Man; Junior Bonner; Child's Play; Mame; Semi-Tough.
    Thea inc: 20th Century; The Male Animal; His and Hers; The Tender Trap; Janus; The Hidden River; The Music Man (Tony-1958); To True to be Good; Nobody Loves an Albatross; The Lion in Winter; I Do! I Do! (Tony-1967); Mack and Mabel.
    TV inc: Playhouse 90; Omnibus; The Bells of St. Mary's; Dupont Show of the Month; The Chisholms.

PREVIN, Andre: Comp-Cond. b. Berlin, Apr 6, 1929. Conductor, London Symphony Orchestra; guest cond. of major symphony orchestras, US, Europe. Films inc: Three Little Words; Cause for Alarm; It's Always Fair Weather; Bad Day at Black Rock; Invitation to the Dance; Catered Affair; Designing Woman; Silk Stockings; Gigi (Oscar-1958); Porgy and Bess (Oscar-co-score-1959); Subterraneans; The Bells Are Ringing; Pepe; Elmer Gantry; Four Horsemen of the Apocalypse; One Two Three; Two for the Seesaw; Long Day's Journey Into Night; Irma La-Douce (Oscar-1963); My Fair Lady (Oscar-1964); Goodbye Charlie; Inside Daisy Clover; The Fortune Cookie; Thoroughly Modern Millie; Valley of the Dolls; Paint Your Wagon; The Music Lover; Jesus Christ, Superstar; Every Good Boy Deserves Favor. (Grammys-(7)-soundtrack-1958, 1959; orch perf-1959; jazz perf-1960, 1961; choral perf, classical, 1973, 1976).

PREVIN, Dory (nee Langan): Sngwri-Singer. b. Rahway, NJ, Oct 22, 1930. Lyricist for Andre Previn, also collab with Harold Arlen, Johnny Green; Jimmy Van Heusen; John Williams.

Songs inc: You're Gonna Hear From Me; A Faraway Part of Town; Second Chance; Valley of the Dolls; Come Saturday Morning; With My Daddy in the Attic; Esther's First Communion; Third Girl from the Left.

PREVIN, Steve: Exec. b. NYC, Oct 21, 1925. Film edtr 1943-50, UI & MGM; to Europe, 1950-60, dir TV series; Foreign Intrigue; Sherlock Holmes; Captain Gallant; The Vikings (for Disney): Almost Angels; Waltz King; Escapade in Florence; 1966-69, Paramount, London, prodn exec; 1969-72, Commonwealth United, London, prodn exec; 1973, Paramount, prodn exec; 1974 AIP, VP in charge of European prodn.

PRICE, Frank: Exec. b. Decatur, IL, 1930. e. MI State. Joined CBS-TV NY 1951 as story ed; to Hollywood as story ed Screen Gems; story ed NBC; 1959joined U-TV as asso prod-wri; 1961 exec prod; 1971, Sr vp U-TV; 1973, exec vp; 1974 P U-TV & VP MCA; 1978 resd to become P Columbia Pictures Prodns; 1979 P Columbia Pictures.

TV inc: (exec Prod) The Virginian; Ironside; It Takes A Thief; The Doomsday Flight; Kojak; $6 Million Man; Bionic Woman; Rockford Files; Quincy; Rich Man, Poor Man; 79 Park Ave.; Captains and the Kings.

PRICE, Leontyne: Opera singer. b. Laurel, MS, Feb 10, 1927. e. Central State College OH, BA. Played Bess in State Dept European tour of Porgy and Bess; guest soloist with major orchs around world; NBC-TV 1955-1958, other starring appearances 1960, 1962, 1964; guest soloist Vienna Staadtopera; Berlin Opera; Rome Opera; Paris Opera; Covent Garden; Salzburg Festival; Metropolitan Opera where now resident member.

(*Grammys*-(10)-class voc solo-1960, 1963, 1964, 1965, 1966, 1967, 1969, 1971, 1973, 1974).

TV inc: The Kennedy Center Honors, 1980.

PRICE, Lorin E: Prod. b. NYC, Apr 1, 1921. e. Yale, BA. Bway inc: The Moon Besieged; The Natural Look; George M; Seesaw; No Hard Feelings.

PRICE, Paul B: Act. b. Carteret, NJ, Oct 7, 1933. e. U of AL, BS. TV inc: Sesame Street; Naked City; Get Smart; The Hero; Hey, Landlord; Busting Loose.

Thea inc: A Cook for Mr General; Let Me Hear You Smile; Bad Habits; The Ritz.

Films inc: Butch and Sundance-The Early Days.

PRICE, Ray: Act-Sngwri. b. Perryville, TX, Jan 12, 1926. C&W recording artist. Started on radio; became regular on the Grand Ole Opry. (*Grammy*-C&W vocal-1970).

PRICE, Roger: Wri-Act. b. Charleston, VW, Mar 6, 1922. e. U MI, American Academy of Art; studied in Max Reinhardt School, LA. Worked niteries, TV. Bway inc: Tickets Please. TV inc: Whatever Turns You On; For The Love of It.

Films inc: Pete's Dragon; The Cat From Outer Space; Just You and Me, Kid.

PRICE, Stanley: Wri. b. London, Dec 8, 1931. e. Cambridge U, MA. Films inc: Arabesque; Gold; The Devil Within Her; Shout at the Devil; The Last Pentathlon.

Plays inc: Come Live with Me; Horizontal Hold; The Two of Me; The Starving Rich.

PRICE, Vincent: Act. b. St. Louis, MO, May 27, 1911. e. Yale U, U of London, Nuremberg U. On screen from 1938 in Service de Luxe. Films inc: The Tower of London; The Private Lives of Elizabeth and Essex; The Invisible Man Returns; The Song of Bernadette; Laura; The Keys of the Kingdom; Leave Her to Heaven; Dragonwyck; The Three Musketeers; Rogues' Regiment; The Web; Up in Central Park; House of Wax; The Mad Magician; The Ten Commandments; The Raven; The Last Man on Earth; Scream and Scream Again; The Devil's Triangle; Dr. Phibes; Dr. Phibes Rises Again; Madman; It's Not The Size That Counts; Scavenger Hunt.

TV inc: Time Express; John Ritter, Being of Sound Mind and Body.

Bway inc: Diversions and Delights.

PRIDE, Charley: Singer. b. Sledge, MS, Mar 8, 1938. C&W recording artist. (*Grammys*-(3)-sacred perf, gospel perf-1971; C&W-1972).

PRIESTLEY, J B: Wri. b. Bradford, Eng, Sep 13, 1894. e. Cambridge, MA, LLD, DLitt. Plays inc: The Roundabout; People at Sea; When We Are Married; They Came to a City; An Inspector Calls; The Linden Tree; Dragon's Mouth; Mr Kettle and Mrs Moon; The Golden Entry; A Severed Head; Eden End.

Films inc: The Foreman Went to France; Britain at Bay; Priestley's Postscripts; Battle for Music; They Came to a City; Last Holiday; The Inspector Calls.

TV inc: Lost City (& act); You Know What People Are (& act).

PRIMUS, Barry: Act. b. NYC, Feb 16, 1938. Lincoln Center Repertory Company; improvisational theatre, St. Louis; Bway inc: Teibele and Her Demon; off-Bway, Huui, Huui; The Changeling. Films inc: The Brotherhood; Been Down So Long It Looks Like Up to Me; Gravy Train; Avalanche; Night Games; Heartland.

PRINCE, Harold S: Prod-Dir. b. NYC, Jan 30, 1928. e. U of PA, AB. Worked as stage mgr for George Abbott, later coproduced and/or dir the following: The Pajama Game (*Tony*-1954); Damn Yankees (*Tony*-1955); New Girl in Town; West Side Story; Fiorello; (*Tony and Pulitzer Prize*-1959); Tenderloin; A Call on Kuprin; They Might Be Giants (London); Take Her She's Mine; A Funny Thing Happened on the Way to the Forum (*Tony*-1962); She Loves Me (London); Fiddler on the Roof (*Tony*-1964); Poor Bitos; Flora The Red Menace; Superman; Cabaret (*Tony*-1966); Zorba; Company (*Tonys*-musical & dir-1970); Follies (*Tony*-dir-1972); A Little Night Music (*Tony*-1973); Love For Love; Candide (*Tony*-dir-1974); Pacific Overtures; Side by Side by Sondheim; Some of My Best Friends; On the Twentieth Century; Sweeney Todd (*Tony*-dir-1978); Evita (*Tony*-dir-1980).

Films inc: (co-prod) The Pajama Game; Damn Yankees; (dir) Something For Everyone; A Little Night Music.

PRINCE, William: Act. b. Nichols, NY, Jan 26, 1913. On screen from 1943. Films inc: Destination Tokyo; Cinderella Jones; The Very Thought of You; Roughly Speaking; Objective Burma; Pillow to Post; Lust for Gold; Cyrano de Bergerac; Secret of Treasure Mountain; Macabre; Sacco and Vanzetti; The Heartbreak Kid; The Stepford Wives; Rollercoaster; The Cat From Outer Space; The Promise; Bronco Billy.

Thea inc: Guest in the House; Across the Board on Tomorrow Morning; The Eve of St. Mary; John Loves Mary; As You Like It; I Am a Camera; Forward the Heart; Affair of Honor; Third Best Sport; The Highest Tree; Venus at Large; Strange Interlude; The Ballad of the Sad Cafe; Mercy Street.

TV inc: The Jericho Mile; City in Fear; Gideon's Trumpet.

PRINCIPAL, Victoria: Act. b. Fulipla, Japan, Jan 30, 1950. Films inc: The Life and Times of Judge Roy Bean; The Naked Ape; Earthquake; I Will, I Will. . . For Now; Vigilante Force.

TV inc: The Night They Stole Miss Beautiful; Dallas; Pleasure Palace.

PRINE, Andrew: Act. b. Jennings, FL, Feb 14, 1936. e. U of Miami. Films inc: Advance to the Rear; Company of Cowards; Generation; The Devil's Brigade; Chisum; Grizzly; The Evil.

TV inc: Tail Gunner Joe; Last of the Mohicans; Law of the Land; The Road West; Wide Country; W.E.B.; The Girl Who Saved Our America; Mark Twain's America.

Thea inc: Look Homeward, Angel; A Distant Bell. Mark Twain's America-Abe Lincon-Freedom Fighter; Mind Over Murder.

PRINZ, Le Roy: Prod-Dir-Chor. b. St. Joseph, MO, Jul 14, 1895. Ran away from home at 15, joined French Foreign Legion, served with French aerial corps; remained Paris after WW1 as chor, Folies Bergere. To Hwd 1931 as chor for Cecil B DeMille.

Films inc: Sign of the Cross; The Bing Crosby-Bob Hope Road films; Yankee Doodle Dandy; Desert Song; This Is The Army; Night and Day; The Ten Commandments; Helen Morgan Story; Sayonara; South Pacific. Dir Oscar-winning short A Boy and His Dog; prod-dir films for U.S. Navy; commercial films.

Prod-dir stage revue Red, White and Blue for the American Legion.

PROVINE, Dorothy: Act. b. Deadwood, SD, Jan 20, 1937. e. U of WA. On screen from 1958 in The Bonnie Parker Story. Films inc: The Thirty Foot Bride of Candy Rock; It's a Mad, Mad, Mad, Mad World; Good Neighbor Sam; That Darn Cat; The Great Race; One Spy Too Many; Who's Minding the Mint?; Never a Dull Moment.

TV inc: The Alaskan; The Roaring 20's.

PROWSE, Juliet: Act. b. Bombay, 1937. On screen from 1960. Films inc: Can-Can; G.I. Blues; The Second Time Around; The Right Approach; Who Killed Teddy Bear?; Dingaka; Run for Your Wife; Spree.

Thea inc: I Do! I Do!

PRYCE, Jonathan: Act. b. North Wales, 1947. e. RADA. Thea inc: (London) Comedians; joined Royal Shakespeare Co appearing in The Taming of the Shrew; Measure for Measure; Antony and Cleopatra; Hamlet. Bway inc: Comedians (*Tony*-1977).

TV inc: Comedians; Playthings; Daft as a Brush; Partisans; For Tea on Sunday; Glad Day.

Films inc: Voyage of the Damned; Breaking Glass; Loophole.

PRYOR, Nicholas: Act. Bway inc: That Championship Season; Thieves; The Boys in the Band.

Films inc: The Fish That Saved Pittsburgh; The Gumball Rally; Damien--Omen II; Smile; The Formula; Airplane.

TV inc: Element of Risk; Night Terror; Rainbow; Marriage is Alive and Well in the USA; Washington Behind Closed Doors; Gideon's Trumpet; The $5.20 an Hour Dream; The Plutonium Incident; Reunion; The Last Song.

PRYOR, Richard: Act. b. Peoria, IL, 1940. Worked as standup comic in niteries, TV. Wrote scripts for Lily Tomlin, Flip Wilson; co-sp of film, Blazing Saddles; recorded several albums.

Films inc: (perf) Lady Sings the Blues; Bingo Long and the Travelin' All Stars; Silver Streak; Greased Lightning; Blue Collar; California Suite; The Wiz; Richard Pryor Live in Concert; The Muppet Movie; Wholly Moses; In God We Trust; Stir Crazy.

TV inc: Lily (*Emmy*-wri-1974).

(*Grammys*-comedy recording-1974, 1975, 1976).

PRYOR, Thomas M: Newspaperman. b. NYC, May 22, 1912. Joined NY Times, 1929; mp dept 1931 as reporter, edtr, asst film critic; Hollywood bureau chief, NY Times, 1951-59. Editor Daily Variety, 1959.

PUCK, Eva: Act. b. 1892. A Vaude star with brother Harry (Puck & Puck), she married Sammy White and couple became top vaude attraction. Appeared in musicomedies Greenwich Village Follies of 1923; Melody Man; Boy Friend, which Rodgers & Hart had written for her; created role of Ellie in Showboat. Retired in 1935 having made several Vitaphone shorts but no feature films.

(Died Oct 24, 1979).

PURCELL, Lee: Act. b. NC, Jun 15, 1949. Films inc: Adam at 6 A.M.; Stand Up and Be Counted; Dirty Little Billy; Necromancy; Mr. Majestyk; Almost Summer; Big Wednesday; Stir Crazy.

TV inc: Death Works Overtime; The Amazing Mr. Hughes; Summer of Fear; Murder in Music City. Kenny Rogers as the Gambler; My Wife Next Door; The Secret War of Jackie's Girls.

PURCELL, Noel: Act. b. Dublin, Dec 23, 1900. e. Irish Christian Brothers. Started as child actor, appeared with Abbey Players; also worked in vaude as comedian.

Films inc: Odd Man Out; The Blue Lagoon; Captain Boycott; Island Rescue; Crimson Pirate; Shake Hands With the Devil; Pickwick Papers; Doctor in the House; Moby Dick; Doctor at Sea; Lust for Life; Lord Jim; Arriverderci, Baby; Sinful Davy.

PURDOM, Edmund: Act. b. Welwyn Garden City, England, Dec 19, 1924. Thea inc: (London) The Way Things Go; Malade Imaginaire; Caesar and Cleopatra; Antony and Cleopatra.

Films inc: Titanic; The Student Prince; The Egyptian; The Prodigal; The Kings Thief; The Cossacks; Nights of Rasputin; The Comedy Man; The Beauty Jungle; The Yellow Rolls Royce; The Man in the Golden Mask; The Black Corsair; Evil Fingers.

TV inc: Sophia Loren--Her Own Story.

PURL, Linda: Act. b. Greenwich, CT, Sep 2, 1955. Moved to Japan at age 2. Appeared in Japanese theatre, TV. To US in 1971. Films inc: Jory; W C Fields & Me; Crazy Mama; Leo and Loree.

TV inc: The Secret Storm; Happy Days; Eleanor and Franklin; Beacon Hill; Little Ladies of the Night; Testimony of Two Men; A Last Cry for Help; Women at West Point; The Young Pioneers; A Very Special Love; Like Normal People; The Flame Is Love; The Night the City Screamed.

PUTTNAM, David: Prod. b. London, 1941. Films inc: Melody; The Pied Piper; That'll Be the Day; Mahler; Bugsy Malone; The Duellists; Midnight Express; Foxes.

PUZO, Mario: Wri. b. NYC, Oct 15, 1920. Films inc: The Godfather (*Oscar*-1972); The Godfather Part II (*Oscar*-1974); Earthquake; Superman; Superman II.

PYLE, Denver: Act. b. Bethune, CO, May 11, 1920. Films inc: The Man from Colorado; To Hell and Back; Shenandoah; Bonnie and Clyde; Five Card Stud; Something Big; Cahill; Escape to Witch Mountain; The Adventures of Frontier Fremont; Welcome to LA; Return from Witch Mountain.

TV inc: The Doris Day Show; The Life and Times of Grizzly Adams.

QUAID, Dennis: Act. b. Houston, TX, Apr 9, 1953. e. U of Houston. Films inc: Crazy Mama; 9/30/55; Our Winning Season; Seniors; Breaking Away; Gorp; The Long Riders.

QUAID, Randy: Act. b. 1950. Films inc: The Last Picture Show; What's Up Doc?; The Last Detail; Lolly Madonna XXX; Paper Moon; The Apprenticeship of Duddy Kravitz; Breakout; The Missouri Breaks; Bound for Glory; Three Warriors; The Choirboys; Midnight Express; Foxes; The Long Riders.

TV inc: The Last Ride of the Dalton Gang; Guyana Tragedy-The Story of Jim Jones.

QUALEN, John (nee Oleson): Act. b. Vancouver, BC, 1899. Films inc: Arrowsmith; Black Fury; Seventh Heaven; The Grapes of Wrath; All That Money Can Buy; Casablanca; The Fugitive; The Big Steal; Hans Christian Andersen; The High and the Mighty; Two Rode Together; The Man Who Shot Liberty Valance; The Prize; The Seven Faces of Dr Lao; Cheyenne Autumn; The Sons of Katie Elder; A Patch of Blue; A Big Hand for the Little Lady; Firecreek; Criss Cross.

TV inc: Mr Ed; Hazel; Partridge Family.

QUAYLE, Anna: Act. b. Birmingham, Eng, Oct 6, 1937. e. RADA. Thea inc: Do You Mind?; Look Who's Here!; Stop the World - I Want to Get Off; (*Tony*-supp-1963); Homage to T S Eliot; Full Circle; Out of Bounds; Pal Joey; Kings and Clowns; The Case of the Oily Levantine.

Films inc: Drop Dead Darling; Smashing Time; Chitty Chitty Bang Bang; Up the Chastity Belt.

TV inc: S O S Titanic.

QUAYLE, Anthony CBE: Act. B. Ainsdale, Lancashire, Eng, Sep 7, 1913. e. RADA. Stage debut London 1931, Robin Hood. Thea inc: (London) various Shakespearean roles with Old Vic Co; Anna Christie; Pride and Prejudice; The Silent Knight; Trelawney of the Wells; The Rivals; Crime and Punishment (dir); director of Shakespeare Memorial Theatre 1948-1956; A View from the Bridge; Look After Lulu; Incident at Vichy; Sleuth; Harvey (dir). (Bway): The Country Wife; Tamburlaine The Great; The Firstborn (& dir); Galileo; Halfway Up the Tree; Sleuth; Do You Turn Somersaults?

Films inc: Hamlet; Battle of the River Plate; The Wrong Man; No Time for Tears; The Man Who Would Not Talk; Ice Cold in Alex; The Nelson Affair; Guns of Navarone; Lawrence of Arabia; Barefoot in Athens; Fall of the Roman Empire; MacKenna's Gold; Anne of the Thousand Days; The Tamarind Seed; The Eagle Has Landed; The Chosen; Murder By Decree.

TV inc: QB VII *(Emmy*-supp-1975); Henry IV.

QUEEN: Group. Members are Freddie Mercury; John Deacon; Brian May, Roger Taylor. Formed in Britain in 1971. Innovators of effects, costumes for rock tours of US, Japan. Albums inc: Queen; Sheer Heart Attack; A Night at the Opera; A Day At The Races; News of the World; We Are The Champions; Jazz; The Game.

Films inc: Flash Gordon (score).

QUESTED, John: Dir-Prod. Started as asst dir, later prodn mgr for Col, France; WB, Spain; UA, Ireland. Films inc: A Lion in Winter (asso prod); All The Right Noises (prod); Philadelphia, Here I Come; The Brute; Leopard in the Snow (prod); The Stud (prod); The Passage (prod); Sunburn (exec prod); Loophole (dir).

QUIGLEY, Martin Jr: Edit-Wri-Publ. b. Chicago, IL, Nov 24, 1917. e. Georgetown U, AB; Columbia U, Ed.D. S of founder of Motion Picture Herald, Motion Picture Daily.

Special edit rep, later asso edtr, edtr Quigley Publications Author Magic Shadows (on origins of film business); New Screen Techniques; co-author Films in America.

QUILLAN, Eddie: Act. b. Philadelphia, PA, Mar 31, 1907. In vaude as child with family act.

Films inc: Up and At 'Em; Night Work; Big Money; A Little Bit of Everything; The Big Shot; Mutiny on the Bounty; Young Mr. Lincoln; Grapes of Wrath; This is the Life; A Guy Could Change; Flying Blind; Sideshow; Brigadoon; The Ghost and Mr. Chicken; How to Frame a Figg.

TV inc: White Mama; The Great Cash Giveaway Getaway; For The Love Of It.

QUINE, Richard: Dir. b. Detroit, MI, Nov 12, 1920. Former act. on Bway in Very Warm For May; My Sister Eileen. Films inc: (act) The World Changes; Babes on Broadway; My Sister Eileen; For Me and My Gal. (Dir) The Sunny Side of the Street; Drive a Crooked Road; My Sister Eileen; The Solid Gold Cadillac; Operation Mad Ball; Bell, Book and Candle; The World of Suzie Wong; The Notorious Landlady; Paris When It Sizzles; How to Murder Your Wife; Oh Dad, Poor Dad, Mama's Hung You in the Closet and I'm Feelin' So Sad; Hotel; A Talent for Loving; The Moonshine War; W.; Prisoner of Zenda.

QUINLAN, Kathleen: Act. b. Pasadena, CA, Nov 19, 1954. Films inc: American Graffiti; Lifeguard; I Never Promised You a Rose Garden; The Promise; The Runner Stumbles; Sunday Lovers.

QUINN, Anthony: Act. b. Chihuahua, Mexico, Apr 21, 1916. Films inc: Guadalcanal Diary; Buffalo Bill; China Sky; Back to Bataan; Black Gold; Tycoon; The Brave Bulls; Against All Flags; East of Sumatra; Ulysses; Viva Zapata *(Oscar*-supp-1952); La Strada; Attila the Hun; Hunchback of Notre Dame; Lust For Life *(Oscar*-supp-1956); The Guns of Navarone; Barabbas; Requiem for a Heavyweight; Zorba the Greek; The Don Is Dead; Mohammed, Messenger of God; The Shoes of the Fisherman; The Destructors; Caravans; The Children of Sanchez; The Greek Tycoon; The Inheritance; The Passage.

QUINTERO, Jose: Dir. b. Panama City, Panama, Oct 15, 1924. e. USC. Thea inc: Long Day's Journey Into Night *(Tony*-co-prod-1957); Pousse Cafe; More Stately Mansions; The Seven Decents of Myrtle; Ghandi; A Moon for the Misbegotten *(Tony*-1973); The Skin of Our Teeth; Anna Christie; A Touch of the Poet; Clothes For A Summer Hotel.

Opera inc: Pagliacci; Cavalleria Rusticana.

Films inc: The Roman Spring of Mrs Stone.

TV inc: Medea; Our Town.

RABAL, Francisco: Act. b. Aguilas, Spain, 1925. Legitimate theatre, Madrid. Films inc: The Eclipse; Nazaran; Viridiana; Belle du Jour; Desert of the Tartars; Sorcerer; Stay As You Are; Corleone.

RABB, Ellis: Act-Dir-Prod-Wri. b. Memphis, TN, Jun 20, 1930. e. U of AZ, Carnegie Institute of Technology, BFA, Yale U. Made stage debut 1952, King John. NY debut 1956, A Midsummer Night's Dream; founded and became artistic dir of the Association of Producing Artists, 1960; also dir for the Old Globe Theatre; the Kansas City Center of the Performing Arts; Dallas Civic Opera. Bway inc: (dir) The School for Scandal; The Tavern; The Seagull; The Grass Harp; Sleuth; Veronica's Room; Who's Who In Hell; Edward II; Caesar and Cleopatra (rev); The Royal Family *(Tony*-1976); In A Life in the Theatre (act); The Man Who Came To Dinner (rev); The Philadelphia Story (rev).

TV inc: The Royal Family; The Dain Curse (act).

RABBIT, Eddie (Edward Thomas Rabbit): Singer-Sngwri. b. Brooklyn, Nov 27, 1941. Songs inc: Kentucky Rain; Pure Love; Forgive and Forget; Rocky Mountain Music; Drinkin' My Baby Off My Mind; Two Dollars in the Jukebox.

TV inc: The Eddie Rabbit Show; Crystal.

RABE, David William: Plywri. b. Dubuque, IA, Mar 10, 1940. Plays inc: The Basic Training of Pavlo Hummel; Stickes and Bones; The Orphan; In the Boom Boom Room; Streamers.

RACHMIL, Lewis J: Exec. b. NYC, Jul 3, 1908. e. NYU, Yale School of Fine Arts. Started as art dir Par (Long Island Studios) 1930; to Hollywood as art dir, asst prod.

Films inc: Parson of Panamint; Tombstone; Hopalong Cassidy Series; Bunco Squad; Crackdown; Hunt The Man Down; Roadblock; Androcles and the Lion (co-prod); Whiphand; Gun Fury; Human Desire; They Rode West; Violent Men; Tight Spot; The Brothers Rico; Gidget; Reprisal; Kings of the Sun; 633 Squadron; 1977 vp & exec prodn mgr MGM.

RADEMAKERS, Fons (Alphonse M Rademakers): Prod-Dir. b. Roosendaal, Netherlands, Sep 5, 1920. Films inc: Village on the River; That Joyous Eve; The Knife; The Spitting Image; The Dance of the Heron; Because of the Cats; Max Havelaar; Mun Vriend; Mysteries (act).

RADIN, Paul B: Prod. b. NYC, Sep 15, 1913. e. NYU. Assoc prod: The Journey; Once More with Feeling; Surprise Package. Prod: Born Free; Living Free; Phase IV; The Blue Bird.

TV inc: Born Free; Kate; The Incredible Journey of Doctor Meg Laurel; The Two Worlds of Jenny Logan; The Ordeal of Dr. Mudd; The Wild and the Free.

RADNER, Gilda: Act. b. Detroit, MI, Jun 28. TV inc: The Muppet Show; All You Need is Cash; Saturday Night Live *(Emmy*-supp-1978).

Films inc: Mr. Mike's Mondo Video; Gilda Live; First Family.

Bway inc: Lunch Hour.

RADNITZ, Robert B: Prod. b. Great Neck, NY, Aug 9, 1924. e. U of VA. Reader for Bway dir Harold Clurman. Wrote doc scripts for RKO-Pathe; worked as stage mgr; produced (Bway and London) The Young and the Beautiful. First feature film, A Dog of Flanders, 1960.

Films inc: Misty; Island of the Blue Dolphins; My Side of the Mountain; Little Ark; Sounder; Birch Interval; Sounder II; A Hero Ain't Nothin' But A Sandwich.

TV inc: Mary White.

RAE, Charlotte (nee Lubotsky): Act. b. Milwaukee, WI, Apr 22, 1926. e. Northwestern U, BS. Bway inc: Romeo and Juliet; Li'l Abner; Pickwick; Morning, Noon and Night.
Films inc: Rabbit Test; Hair.
TV inc: Sesame Street; Car 54 Where Are You?; Hot L Baltimore; Queen of the Stardust Ballroom; The Triangle Factory Fire Scandal; Beane's of Boston; Diff'rent Strokes; Facts of Life; Emily Dickinson.

RAFELSON, Bob: Prod-Dir-Wri. b. NYC, 1935. Films inc: Head (co-sp); Five Easy Pieces (co-prod-dir); The King of Marvin Gardens (prod-dir); Stay Hungry (co-prod, co-sp, dir).
TV inc: The Monkees (*Emmy*-prod-1967).

RAFFIN, Deborah: Act. b. LA, 1953. Former model. Films inc: 40 Carats; The Dove; God Told Me To; The Sentinel; Once Is Not Enough; Maniac; Touched By Love.
TV inc: Willa; The Last Convertible; Mind Over Murder; Haywire; For The Love Of It.

RAFT, George (nee Rauft): Act. b. NYC, 1895. Started as dancer. Bway inc: The City Chap; Padlocks of 1927.
Films inc: Queen of the Night Clubs; Quick Millions; Hush Money; Palmy Days; Scarface; Night After Night; If I Had A Million; The Bowery; All of Me; Bolero; The Trumpet Blows; Limehouse Blues; Rumba; The Glass Key; Every Night at Eight; Souls at Sea; Each Dawn I Die; I Stole a Million; The House Across the Bay; They Drive By Night; Broadway; Stage Door Canteen; Follow the Boys; Nob Hill; Johnny Angel; Whistle Stop; Mr. Ace; Intrigue; Outpost in Morocco; Johnny Allegro; Rogue Cop; Lucky Nick Cain; A Bullet for Joey; Around the World In 80 Days; Some Like It Hot; Ocean's Eleven; Ladies Man; The Patsy; Casino Royal; Du Rififi a Paname; Five Golden Dragons; Skidoo; Hammersmith Is Out; Sextette; The Man With Bogart's Face.
(Died Nov. 24, 1980).

RAGAWAY, Martin: Wri-Prod. b. Jan 29, 1928. e. NYU. TV inc: Peter Donald; Milton Berle; Abbott & Costello, Phil Baker; Bob Hope; I Love Lucy, Phil Silvers; Red Skelton (*Emmy*-wri-1961); Dick Van Dyke Show; Mary Tyler Moore Show; The Courtship of Eddie's Father. Films inc: Ma and Pa Kettle Go to New York; The Milkman.

RAGIN, John S: Act. b. Newark, NJ, May 5. e. Carnegie Tech. Films inc: Earthquake; The Parallax View; Marooned; I Love You, Alice B Toklas. TV inc: Sons and Daughters; Quincy.

RAGLAND, Robert Oliver: Comp-Arr-Cond. b. Chicago, Jul 3, 1931. e. Northwestern U, BS, Amer Cons, BA, MA. Comp, arr, pianist for orchs inc Tommy & Jimmy Dorsey; Ralph Marterie; Dick Contino; Woody Herman. Film scores inc: Grizzly; Sharks Treasure; Seven Alone; The Saga of Jimmy D; The Kill Machine; Return to Macon County; Where's Willie?; Only Once in a Lifetime; The Babysitter; Weekend with the Babysitter; Jaguar Lives.

RAILSBACK, Steve: Act. b. Dallas, TX. Studied with Lee Strasberg. Thea inc: Bluebird; Orpheus Descending; This Property Condemned; One Sunday Afternoon; The Cherry Orchard; The Skin of Our Teeth.
Films inc: The Visitors; Angela; The Stunt Man.
TV inc: Helter Skelter; From Here To Eternity.

RAINER, Luise: Act. b. Vienna, 1910. On stage in Austria 1930; to Hollywood 1934. Films inc: Escapade; The Great Ziegfeld (*Oscar*-1936); The Good Earth (*Oscar*-1937); The Emperor's Candlesticks; The Big City; The Toy Wife; The Great Waltz; Dramatic School; Hostages.

RAINES, Cristina: Act. b. Manila, Philippines, Feb 28, 1953. Films inc: Hex; The Stone Killer; Nashville; Russian Roulette; The Sentinel; The Duellists; Silver Dream Racer; Touched By Love. TV inc: Sunshine; The Tenth Month; Centennial; The Child Stealer; Flamingo Road.

RAINES, Ella Act. b. Snowquainde Falls, WA, Aug 6, 1921. On screen from 1943 in Corvette K-225; Hail the Conquering Hero; Tall in the Saddle; White Tie and Tails; Time Out Of Mind; The Web; Brute Force; The Senator Was Indiscreet; Impact; Ride the Man Down; Man in the Road.
TV inc: Janet Dean, R.N.

RAINS, Robert H: Exec. b. NYC, Aug 12, 1921. e. NYU. Started as PA with International Pictures, 1946; dir of radio activities; asst casting dir, 1952; radio-TV activities, 1955; exec in chg of TV press dept, Universal City, 1961; Universal vp, 1966; ret Apr 21, 1978.

RAITT, Bonnie: Singer. b. Burbank, CA, Nov 8, 1949. D of John Raitt. Recording artist; concerts.
Films inc: No Nukes.

RAITT, John: Act. b. Santa Ana, Jan 29, 1917. Bway from 1945 in Carousel; Magdalena; Three Wishes For Jamie; Carnival in Flanders; The Pajama Game; A Joyful Noise; A Musical Jubilee.
Films from 1940 inc: Flight Command; Billy The Kid; Ziegfeld Girl; The Pajama Game.
TV inc: Buick Circus Hour; Chevy Show; Annie Get Your Gun; America Sing.

RAKSIN, David: Comp-Cond-Arr. b. Philadelphia, Aug 4, 1912. Films scores inc: Modern Times; Laura; The Bad and the Beautiful; Forever Amber; The Secret Life of Walter Mitty; Suddenly; Separate Tables; Force of Evil; The Magnificent Yankees; Al Capone; Sylvia; A Big Hand for the Little Lady. Songs inc: Laura; Forever Amber; The Bad and the Beautiful; A Song After Sundown. TV themes inc: Ben Casey; The Breaking Point.

RALSTON, Esther: Act. b. Bar Harbor, ME, Sep 27, 1902. Starred on radio series Portia Faces Life for two years. In over 150 films from 1917 to 1942. Vaudeville headliner. Films inc: The Phantom Fortune (serial); Peter Pan; A Kiss for Cinderella; Lucky Devil; Old Ironsides; Figures Don't Lie; The Sawdust Paradise; The Prodigal; Sadie McKee; Hollywood Boulevard; Tin Pan Alley.

RALSTON, Vera (nee Hruba): Act. b. Prague, 1919. Widow of Herbert J Yates. Ice skating champion in Europe. Appeared in ice shows in U.S. Screen debut, 1941, Ice Capades (as Vera Hruba); The Lady and the Monster; Lake Placid; Murder in the Music Hall (billed Vera Hruba Ralston); and, after 1946 billed Vera Ralston, The Plainsman and the Lady; The Flame; Wyoming; I, Jane Doe; The Wild Blue Yonder; Hoodlum Empire; Fair Wind to Java; Timberjack; Accused of Murder; The Man Who Died Twice.

RAMBALDI, Carlos: Dsgn-Sculptor. b. Ferrara, Italy, Sep 16, 1925. e. Academy of Fine Arts, Bologna. Creator of special effects for screen, stage, TV. Films inc: King Kong (*Oscar*-special-1976); The White Buffalo; Barabbas; Frankenstein; Dracula; Last Woman; Alien (*Oscar*-visual effects-1979).

RAMBO, Dack: Act. b. Delano, CA, Nov 13, 1941. TV inc: Never Too Young; The Guns of Will Sonnett; Dirty Sally; River of Gold; Hit Lady; Sword of Justice; Waikiki.

RAMIN, Sid: Comp-Cond. b. Boston, Jan 22, 1924. e. Boston U, Columbia U. Bway inc: West Side Story; Gypsy; A Funny Thing Happened On the Way to the Forum; Wildcat; I Can Get It For You Wholesale; The Girls Against the Boys; Kwamina.
TV Musical dir inc: Patty Duke Show; Milton Berle Show; Candid Camera.
Films inc: West Side Story (*Oscar*-1961).
Songs inc: Simon Says; Where There's a Man; Ecstasy Waltz; Come Alive (Pepsi Cola Commercial).
(*Grammy*-soundtrack-1961).

RAMPLING, Charlotte: Act. b. Stumer, Eng, Feb 5, 1946. Films inc: The Knack; Rotten to the Core; Georgy Girl; Ski Bum; Corky; Tis a Pity She's A Whore; Asylum; The Night Porter; Zardoz; Farewell My Lovely; Foxtrot; Orca; The Purple Taxi; Target-Harry; Stardust Memories.
TV inc: The Six Wives of Henry VIII; The Strangers.

RAND, Sally: Fan Dancer. b. Hickory Country, MO, Jan 2, 1904. Appeared on screen in 1924 in The Dressmaker from Paris. Other films inc: Man Bait; The Night of Love; Getting Gertie's Garter; A Girl in Every Port; The King of Kings; Bolero. Gave up films in 1933 when she debuted fan, bubble dancing act, Chicago World's Fair. Toured this act throughout world.
(Died Aug 13, 1979).

RANDALL, Tony: Act. b. Tulsa, OK, Jul 26, 1920. e. Northwestern U. On screen from 1957 in Oh Men! Oh Women!. Films inc: Will Success Spoil Rock Hunter?; The Mating Game; Pillow Talk; Boy's Night Out; The Seven Faces of Dr. Lao; Send Me No Flowers; The Alphabet Murders; Everything You Always Wanted to Know About Sex. TV inc: One Man's Family; Mr. Peepers; Playhouse 90; The Odd Couple (*Emmy*-1975); The Tony Randall Show; Sleep From A to Zzzz (host).

Bway inc: Circle of Chalk; The Corn is Green; Antony & Cleopatra; Caesar and Cleopatra; Oh, Men! Oh, Women!; The Barretts of Wimpole Street; Inherit the Wind; Oh Captain.

RANDELL, Ron: Act. b. New South Wales, Australia, Oct 8, 1923. e. St Mary's Coll, Sydney. Bway inc: The Browning Version; Harlequinade; The World of Suzie Wong. (London) Candide; Sweet Peril; The Fifth Season; Sabrina Fair; Mary, Mary; The Button; The Passionate Husband; Mrs Warren's Profession; Bent.

Films inc: Pacific Adventure; I Am a Camera; King of Kings.

RANDOLPH, Lillian: Act. On radio, later tv as Madame Queen of Amos 'N' Andy shows.

Films inc: At the Circus; Little Men; It's A Wonderful Life; The Bachelor and the Bobby Soxer; Bend of the River; Hush, Hush, Sweet Charlotte; The Great White Hope; Once Is Not Enough; The Onion Field; Magic.

TV inc: Sanford and Son; Redd Foxx Show; The Jeffersons; The Autobiography of Miss Jane Pittman; Roots.

(Died Sep 12, 1980).

RANSOHOFF, Martin: Exec. b. New Orleans, LA, 1927. e. Colgate U. With Young & Rubicam, 1948-49. Wri, dir, Gravel Films, 1951; formed Filmways, 1952, later formed Filmways TV Prod, Filmways, Inc, Filmways of Calif. Resigned as bd chmn. Filmways 1972 to start new independent co. Films inc: The Loved One; The Cincinnati Kid; Ten Rillington Place; King Lear; Topkapi; Ice Station Zebra; Catch 22; Save the Tiger; The White Dawn; Silver Streak; Nightwing; The Wanderers; A Change of Seasons.

TV inc: Mister Ed; The Beverly Hillbillies; Petticoat Junction; The Addams Family.

RAPF, Matthew: Prod. b. NYC, Oct 22, 1920. Films inc: Adventures of Gallant Bess; Desperate Search; Big Leaguer; Half a Hero. TV inc: Loretta Young Show; Frontier; The Great Gildersleeve; The Web; Two Faces West; Ben Casey; Slattery's People; The Young Lawyers; Terror in the Sky; On the Land; Marcus-Nelson Murders; Kojack; Doctor's Private Lives; Eischeid.

RAPHAEL, Frederic: Wri. b. Chicago, 1931. e. Cambridge. Films inc: Nothing But the Best; Darling (*Oscar*-1965); Two for the Road; Far from the Madding Crowd; A Severed Head; Daisy Miller; The Glittering Prices; Rogue Male; Roses, Roses; Richard's Things.

TV inc: School Play.

RAPHAELSON, Samson: Wri. b. NYC, Mar 30, 1896. e. U IL. Play inc: The Jazz Singer; Young Love; The Wooden Slipper; Accent on Youth; White Man; Skylark; Jason; The Perfect Marriage.

Films inc: The Magnificent Lie; The Smiling Lieutenant; Trouble In Paradise; Broken Lullaby; One Hour With You; Angel; Shop Around the Corner; Suspicion; Heaven Can Wait; Green Dolphin Street; That Lady in Ermine; A Prince In Disguise; Main Street to Broadway.

RAPHEL, David: Exec. b. Boulogne-sur-Seine, France, Jan 9, 1925. 1950 asst sls mgr Fox France; 1951 asst mgr Italy; 1954 mgr Holland; 1957 asst European mgr; 1959 European mgr for TV; 1961 Continental mgr; 1964 vp chg intl sls (NY); 1973 P Fox Int'l; 1975 sr vp wldwde mktg features; 1976 ousted from Fox, joined International Creative Management heading new unit to rep indie prods; 1979 p ICM Film Marketing; 1980 founded Cambridge Film Group Ltd.

RAPPAPORT, Michelle: Prod. b. NY, Mar 15, 1952. e. Simmons Coll. Films inc: Old Boyfriends (co-prod).

RAPPER, Irving: Dir. b. London, England, 1900. e. NYU. Films inc: Shining Victory; One Foot in Heaven; The Gay Sisters; Adventures of Mark Twain; Rhapsody in Blue; The Corn is Green; Deception; Now, Voyager; Voice of the Turtle; Anna Lucasta; Glass Menagerie; Bad for Each Other; The Brave One; Marjorie Morningstar; The Miracle; Joseph and His Brethren; The Christine Jorgensen Story; Born Again.

RASKER, Frans: Prod. b. Amsterdam, Jul 12, 1945. Prod mgr, Scorpio Films; then independent prod, 1976. Films inc: Blind Spot; Pastorale 1943. Shorts: (Dir) Wintertime Love; Hairdressers.

RASKIN, Carolyn: Prod. b. IA, Aug 22. e. U of IA. TV inc: Rowan & Martin's Laugh In (*Emmys*-1968 & 1969); Arte Johnson Pilot; Frank Sinatra Special; Wacky World Special; Hellzapoppin; Up With People; John Ford Tribute; Helen Reddy Summer Series; The Shape of Things; One More Time; Travelin' On; Funny World of Sports; Dinah! (*Emmys*-1975 & 1976); Jim Nabors Show; All Star Salute to Women's Sports; Us Against the World; Beverly and Friends; Big City Comedy.

RASKY, Harry: Prod-Dir-Wri. b. Toronto, May 9, 1928. e. U of Toronto, BA. Films inc: Homage to Chagall; The Colours of Love; Arthur Miller on Home Ground.

TV inc: The 49th State; Perspective on Greatness; Meet the Professor; Cuba and Castro; The African Revolution; A Child is to Love; The Lion and the Cross; This Proud Land; Hall of Kings (*Emmy*-doc-1967); The Legend of Silent Night; Tennessee Williams' South; The Wit and World of George Bernard Shaw; The Song of Leonard Cohen.

RASULALA, Thalmus (Jack Crowder): Act. b. 1939. Films inc: Cool Breeze; Blacula; Willie Dynamite; Mr Ricco; Bucktown; Fun with Dick and Jane; The Last Hard Men; The Bermuda Triangle.

RATHER, Dan: TV Newsman. b. Wharton, TX, 1931. Member of the CBS staff since 1962. Served as White House Correspondent anchorman, CBS Evening News. (*Emmys*-(5)-Coverage of The Watergate Affair, 1973; shooting of Gov Wallace, 1973; Agnew resignation-1974; Watergate, The White House transcripts-1974; The Senate and the Watergate Affair-1974). Named co-edtr 60 Minutes, Oct 1975; Named to succeed Walter Cronkhite on latter's retirement as CBS Anchorman.

RAVETCH, Irving: Wri-Dir-Prod. b. 1915. H of Harriet Frank. Films inc: The Long Hot Summer; The Sound and the Fury; Home from the Hill; The Dark at the Top of the Stairs; Hud; Hombre; The Reivers (& prod); Conrack; Norma Rae.

RAWLINS, Lester (nee Rosenberg): Act. b. Sharon, PA, Sep 24, 1924. e. Carnegie-Mellon, BFA. Charter founder member of Arena Stage, Washington. In repertory, stock and off Bway inc: The Quare Fellow; Camino Real; Nightride; Hedda Gabler; Benito Cereno. Bway inc: Othello; Henry IV; Macbeth; Romeo and Juliet; The Lovers; Hamlet; A Man for All Seasons; The Golden Age; The Child Buyer; The Reckoning; Da (*Tony*-supp-1978).

Films inc: Mr Congressman; Diary of a Mad Housewife; They Might Be Giants.

TV inc: Salome; The Life of Samuel Johnson; Secret Storm; Edge of Night; The Nurses.

RAWLS, Eugenia: Act. b. Macon, GA, Sep 11, 1916. e. U of NC. Bway inc: Member of Clare Tree Major's childrens theatre; The Children's Hour; Pride and Prejudice; Strange Fruit; The Little Foxes; Fanny Kemble (one woman show); Just the Immediate Family; The Daughter of the Regiment (Boston Opera Co).

TV inc: Hedda Gabler; The Great Sebastians; The Doctors; The Nurses.

RAWLS, Lou: Singer. b. Chicago, IL, Dec 1, 1936. Started as member of Pilgrim Travelers, gospel group; solo in 1962; recordings (*Grammys*-R&B vocal-1961, 1971, 1977).

Films inc: Angel, Angel Down We Go; Believe in Me.

TV inc: Soul; Lou Rawls and the Golddiggers; Uptown--A Tribute to the Apollo Theatre.

RAY, Aldo (Aldo DaRe): Act. b. Pen Argyl, PA, Sep 5, 1926. Screen debut, 1951, Saturday's Hero. Films inc: The Marrying Kind; Pat and Mike; Miss Sadie Thompson; Battle Cry; The Naked and the Dead; God's Little Acre; What Did You Do in the War, Daddy?; Welcome to Hard Times; The Violent Ones; The Green Berets; Inside Out; Seven Alone; Psychic Killer; Haunts; Sweet Savage; Human Experiments.
TV inc: Women in White.

RAY, Johnnie: Singer. b. Dallas, OR, 1927. Performs in niteries. Known for his rendition of song, Cry. On screen 1954, There's No Business Like Show Business.

RAY, Nicholas (Raymond N Kienzie): Dir-Wri. b. La Crosse, WI, Aug 7, 1911. Films inc: They Live By Night; A Woman's Secret; A Tree Grows In Brooklyn; Knock On Any Door; Born to be Bad; In a Lonely Place; Flying Leathernecks; On Dangerous Ground; The Lusty Men; Johnny Guitar; Run for Cover; Rebel Without a Cause; Hot Blood; Bigger Than Life; The True Story of Jesse James; Bitter Victory; Wind Across the Everglades; Party Girl; Savage Innocents; King of Kings; 55 Days at Peking; Dreams of Thirteen; Hair.
Bway inc: Lute Song; Beggar's Holiday.
TV inc: Sorry, Wrong Number.
(Died June 16, 1979).

RAY, Satyajit: Dir. b. India, May 2, 1921. Films inc: Pather Panchali; The Unvanquished; The Music Room; The World of Apu; The Goddess; The Adventures of Goopy and Bagha; The Adversary; Distant Thunder; The Middle Man; The Chess Player; The Elephant God (& wri-mus); The Kingdom of Diamonds (& wri-mus).

RAYBOULD, Harry: Act-Prod-Dir. b. Jun 16, 1932. Films inc: The Amazing Colossal Man; Girl in the Woods; The Wizard of Bagdad; The Scorpio Letters; The Young Goodman Brown; Genesis II.
TV inc: Playhouse 90; Twilight Zone; Ozzie and Harriet; Lost in Space; Meeting of the Minds.

RAYBURN, Gene: TV Pers. b. Christopher, IL, Dec 22, 1917. Started as radio announcer. Rayburn and Finch Show, WNEW, NY, 1945-52; Gene Rayburn Show, NBC radio; TV variety shows; game shows. TV inc: Tonight; Helluva Town; Amateur's Guide to Love; The Match Game.
Bway inc: Bye Bye Birdie; Come Blow Your Horn.

RAYE, Martha (Margaret Theresa Yvonne Reed): Act. b. Butte, MT, Aug 27, 1916. In vaudeville, 1919-29, with parents. Bway debut 1934, Calling All Stars. Bway inc: Earl Carroll's Sketchbook; Hold on to Your Hats; Annie Get Your Gun; The Solid Gold Cadillac; Personal Appearance; Separate Rooms; Call Me Madam; Everybody Loves Opal; Hello Dolly!.
First appeared on screen 1934 in short subjects. Films inc: Rhythm on the Range; The Big Broadcast of 1937; Waikiki Wedding; Mountain Music; Double or Nothing; Artists and Models; College Swing; Give Me a Sailor; $1,000 a Touchdown; The Boys from Syracuse; Navy Blues; Keep 'Em Flying; Hellzapoppin; Pin-Up Girl; Four Jills in a Jeep; Monsieur Verdoux; Jumbo; The Phynx; Puf n Stuf; Concorde-Airport '79.
TV inc: All Star Revue; The Martha Raye Show; Carol Burnett Show; Skinflint; The Gossip Columnist.
With USO during WW II, toured South Viet Nam annually as both nurse and entertainer during Viet Nam conflict.
(Jean Hersholt Humanitarian Award 1968).

RAYMOND, Gene (Raymond Guion): Act. b. NYC, Aug 13, 1908. H of late Jeanette MacDonald. Films inc: Personal Maid; Zoo In Budapest; Smilin' Through; Red Dust; If I Had a Million; Flying Down To Rio; The House on 56th Street; Seven Keys to Baldpate; The Woman in Red; The Life of the Party; The Locket; Hit the Deck; I'd Rather Be Rich; The Best Man.
TV inc: Climax; Playhouse 90; Uncle; Girl from Uncle; Laredo; Ironsides; Julia; Judd; McNaughton's Daughter.
Bway inc: The Potters; Cradle Snatchers; Young Sinners; Shadow of My Enemy; The Best Man (nat'l co).

READ, Sir John: Exec. b. Brighton, Eng, 1918. Joined EMI Jan, 1965; apptd to board in Dec; in 1966 became dep man dir (UK); in 1967 apptd jnt man dir; exec dir Associated British Picture Corp (now EMI film and Theatre Corp); apptd chf exec and group man dir in 1969; appt chmn EMI in 1974.

READ, Timothy Philip: Prod. b. Hamilton, Bermuda, Jul 26, 1941. Head of prodn, Film Australia. Films inc: Stirring; When Will the Birds Return?; Do I Have to Kill My Child? N S W Chmn Film Edtrs Guild of Australia; vice chmn Australian Film Council; VP Producers & Directors Guild of Australia; dir Australian Film Institute.

REAGAN, Ronald: Act. b. Tampico, IL, Feb 6, 1911. Governor of California, 1968-1975; Elected President of United States, 1980. Screen debut, 1937, Love Is On the Air. Films inc: Cowboy From Brooklyn; Boy Meets Girl; Brother Rat; Dark Victory; Knute Rockne-All American; Kings Row; Desperate Journey; This Is The Army; The Killers; That Hagen Girl; Stallion Road; The Voice of the Turtle; John Loves Mary; Girl From Jones Beach; The Hasty Heart; Storm Warning; She's Working Her Way Through College; Law and Order; Hellcats of the Navy; Bombs Over China.
TV inc: Death Valley Days (host); GE Theatre (host).

REASONER, Harry: TV Newsman. b. Dakota, IA, Apr 17, 1923. e. Stanford U, U of MN. Began as reporter, Minneapolis Times, 1941-43. US Army, WW II. Drama critic Minneapolis Times 1946-48; radio newswriter, 1950-51; writer U.S. Information Agency, Manila, 1951-54; news-dir, KEYD-TV (now KMSP-TV), Minneapolis 1954. Joined CBS News, NY, 1956; joined ABC News 1970 (Emmy-outstanding news broadcast-1974); returned to CBS, Aug 1978.
TV inc: What About Ronald Reagan (Emmy-1968); American Dream, American Nightmare; Boys and Girls Together; The Trouble With Women; Gay Power-Gay Politics.

REDDY, Helen: Act. b. Melbourne, Australia, Oct 25, 1941. Night club and recording artist. Came to US at age 15. Films inc: Airport 1975; Pete's Dragon.
TV inc: Midnight Special; Tonight Show; American Music Awards Show; American Song Festival.
(Grammy-pop vocal-1972).

REDEKER, Quinn: Act. b. Woodstock, IL, May 2, 1936. Films inc: The Candidate; Airport; The Andromeda Strain; Rollercoaster; The Electric Horseman; The Deer Hunter (story); Coast to Coast; Ordinary People.

REDFORD, Robert: Act. b. Santa Monica, CA, Aug 18, 1937. e. AADA. Films inc: Warhunt; Barefoot in the Park; The Chase; Butch Cassidy and the Sundance Kid; Downhill Racer; The Candidate; The Way We Were; The Sting; The Great Gatsby; The Days of the Condor; All The President's Men; A Bridge Too Far; The Electric Horseman; Brubaker; Ordinary People (dir).
Bway inc: Tall Story; Sunday in New York; Barefoot in the Park.
TV inc: In the Presence of Mine Enemies; Moment of Fear; The Iceman Cometh; Black Monday.

REDGRAVE, Lynn: Act. b. London, Mar 8, 1943. D of Sir Michael Redgrave. Films inc: Tom Jones; Georgy Girl; Girl with the Green Eyes; The Virgin Soldier; Every Little Crook and Nanny; Everything You Always Wanted to Know About Sex; Don't Turn the Other Cheek; The Happy Hooker; The Big Bus; Sunday Lovers.
TV inc: Pretty Polly; The Power and the Glory; The End of the Tunnel; What's Wrong With Humpty Dumpty?; Pygmalion; Turn of the Screw; Daft As A Brush; Not For Women Only; Centennial; Sooner or Later; Beggarman, Thief; Gauguin the Savage; The Seduction of Miss Leona; To Tell the Truth (panelist); House Calls; Linda In Wonderland.
Thea inc: (London) Various Shakespearean roles; Saint Joan; The Recruiting Officer; Hay Fever; The Two Of Us; Born Yesterday. (Bway): Black Comedy; My Fat Friend; Mrs. Warren's Profession; Saint Joan.

REDGRAVE, Sir Michael: Act. b. Bristol, Eng, Mar 20, 1908. F of Vanessa and Lynn Redgrave. Screen debut, 1938, The Lady Vanishes. Films inc: The Browning Version; The Importance of Being Earnest; The Dam Busters; The Quiet American; Mourning Becomes Electra; Shake Hands With The Devil; The Wreck of the Mary Deare; The Innocents; Young Cassidy; The Hill; The Heroes of Telemark; The Battle of Britain; Goodbye, Mr. Chips; Oh What A Lovely War; The Go-Between; Nicholas and Alexandra.

Thea inc: (London) Various Shakespearean roles: Beggar's Opera; Jacobowsky and the Colonel; Tiger at the Gates; The Sleeping Prince; A Touch of the Sun; The Complaisant Lover; Voyage Round My Father; Hobson's Choice; The Master Builder; Close of Play. (Bway) Macbeth; Tiger At The Gates; The Sleeping Prince.

REDGRAVE, Vanessa: Act. b. London, Jan 30, 1937. D of Sir Michael Redgrave. Films inc: Morgan; A Suitable Case for Treatment; A Man for All Seasons; Blow-up; Red and Blue; Camelot; Charge of the Light Brigade; The Loves of Isadora; Oh! What a Lovely War; The Seagull; The Devils; The Trojan Women; Mary, Queen of Scots; Murder on the Orient Express; Out of Season; Seven-per-cent Solution; Julia (Oscar-supp-1977); Agatha; Yanks; Bear Island.

Thea inc: (London) A Touch of the Sun; Major Barbara; Cato Street; The Threepenny Opera; Twelfth Night; As You Like It; The Taming of the Shrew; Cymbeline; The Sea Gull; The Prime of Miss Jean Brodie; Anthony & Cleopatra; Design for Living; Macbeth. (Bway) Lady from the Sea.

TV inc: A Farewell to Arms; Katherine Mansfield; As You Like It; Playing For Time.

REDMAN, Joyce: Act. b. Ireland, 1918. e. RADA. Films inc: Tom Jones; Othello. Thea inc: (London) Affairs of State; The Merry Wives of Windsor; The Long Echo; The Party; The Rape of the Belt; The Dutch Courtesan; The Crucible; Dear Antoine; The Undiscovered Country; The Fruits of Enlightenment.

REDMOND, Liam; Act. b. Limerick, Ireland, Jul 27, 1913. e. National U. Started as an Abbey Player, appearing in over 50 plays at the Abbey Theatre. Thea inc: (London) The White Steed; Happy as Larry; The Playboy of the Western World; The Anatomist; The King of Friday's Men; The Devil Came From Dublin; It's the Geography That Counts; The Doctor's Dilemma; On the Rocks. (Bway) The White Steed; The Wayward Saint; The Loves of Cass Maguire; Loot.

Films inc: I See a Dark Stranger; Captain Boycott; High Treason; The Gentle Gunman; The Divided Heart; The Boy and the Bridge; The Ghost and Mr Chicken; Tobruk; The Twenty-Fifth Hour; The Last Safari.

REDMOND, Moira: Act. b. Eng. London stage debut 1957 in Titus Andronicus. Thea inc: Verdict; Detour After Dark; The Winter's Tale; Horizontal Hold; The Trojan Women; Journey of the Fifth Horse; Early Morning; The Watched Pot; The Widowing of Mrs Holroyd; The Three Arrows; Night Watch; The National Health; Hearthbreak House; Habeas Corpus. Films inc: Doctor in Love; Nightmare; Jigsaw; The Limbo Line.

REDSTONE, Sumner M: Exec. b. Boston, MA, May 27, 1923. e. Harvard, BA, LLB. Legal career inc spec asst to US Atty-gen; 1961, exec vp New England Drive In Theatres; 1967, P New England Theatre Corp.

REED, Alan Jr: Act. b. NYC, May 10, 1936. e. UCLA, BA. Films inc: Rock, Pretty Baby; Peyton Place; Going Steady; The New Interns.

REED, Donna (nee Mullenger): Act. b. Denison, IA, Jan 27, 1921. Screen debut, 1941, The Get-Away. Films inc: The Human Comedy; The Courtship of Andy Hardy; Calling Dr. Gillespie; Thousands Cheer; See Here, Private Hargrove; The Picture of Dorian Gray; They Were Expendable; Green Dolphin Street; Saturday's Hero; From Here To Eternity (Oscar-supp-1953); The Last Time I Saw Paris; The Benny Goodman Story; Ransom; Backlash; Pepe.

TV inc: The Donna Reed Show; The Best Place to Be.

REED, Jerry: Sngwri-Singer-Act. b. Mar 20, 1937. Started as backup guitarist for Nashville recording sessions; later teamed with Chet Atkins on album Me and Jerry (Grammy-country inst-1970); solo album When You're Hot You're Hot (Grammy-country vocal-1971).

Songs inc: Amos Moses; Guitar Man; U.S. Male; That's All You Gotta Do; Remembering; A Thing Called Love; Eastbound and Down.

Films inc: W.W. and the Dixie Dancekings; Gator; Smokey and the Bandit (& mus); High-Ballin' (& mus); Hot Stuff (& mus); Smokey and the Bandit II.

TV inc: Nashville 99; The Concrete Cowboys.

REED, Marshall: Prod-Dir-Wri-Act. b. Englewood, CO, May 28, 1917. Began acting in teens at Ehrlich Gardens, Denver later toured Colorado with own company before going to Hollywood.

Films inc: Spy Smasher (serial); The Texas Kid; Haunted Harbor (serial); The Chicago Kid; Drifting Along; Gentleman Joe Palooka; Angel and the Badman; Purple Heart Diary; The Longhorn; Sound Off; Kansas Territory; The Hard Ride; The Lineup.

TV inc: The Lineup; The Cisco Kid; The Roy Rogers Show; The Gene Autry Show.

(Died April 15, 1980).

REED, Oliver: Act. b. Wimbledon, Eng, Feb 13, 1938. Films inc: Oliver!; The Prince and the Pauper; Tommy; Great Scout and Cathouse Thursday; Burnt Offerings; Sell Out; The Three Musketeers; The Four Musketeers; The Big Sleep; Crossed Swords; Maniac; The Brood; The Class of Miss MacMichael; Dr. Heckyl and Mr. Hype.

TV inc: Richard III; It's Dark Outside.

REED, Pamela: Act. b. Tacoma, WA. Thea inc: Best Little Whorehouse in Texas; Seduced.

Films inc: The Long Riders; Melvin and Howard.

TV inc: Mugsy; The Andros Targets; Spencer's Pilots.

REED, Robert (John Robert Rietz): Act. b. Highland Park, IL, Oct 19, 1932. e. Northwestern U. Films inc: Hurry Sundown; Star!; The Maltese Bippy.

TV inc: The Defenders; The Brady Bunch; Love's Savage Fury; Mandrake; The Seekers; Scruples; Nurse; Casino.

Bway inc: Barefoot in the Park; Avanti.

REED, Susan: Singer. b. Columbia, SC, 1927. Folk Song recording artist. Appeared in niteries, NY's Town Hall, concert halls throughout US, TV, radio; plays Irish harp, zither.

REESE, Della (Deloreese Patricia Early): Singer. b. Detroit, MI, Jul 6, 1932. Recording artist; niteries. Films inc: Let's Rock; Psychic Killer.

TV inc: Della; Sanford and Son; Chico and the Man; God In The Dock.

REEVE, Christopher: Act. b. NYC, Sep 25, 1952. e. Cornell, BA. Films inc: Gray Lady Down; Superman, I & II; Somewhere In Time.

Bway inc: The Irregular Verb To Love; A Matter of Gravity; The Fifth of July.

TV inc: Love of Life.

REEVES, Steve: Act. b. Glasgow, MT, Jan 21, 1926. Mr. America of 1947. Films inc: Athena; Hercules; Goliath and the Barbarian; The Giant of Marathon; Hercules Unchained; The Last Days of Pompeii; The Thief of Bagdad; The Trojan Horse; Duel of the Titans; The Slave; The Pirate Prince; The Long Ride From Hell.

REGGIANI, Serge: Act. b. France, 1922. Films inc: Les Portes de la Nuit; Manon; Le Ronde; Secret People; Casque d'or; The Wicked Go To Hell; Les Miserables; Paris Blues; The Leopard; The 25th Hour; Les Aventuriers; Day of the Owl; The Good and the Bad; Cat and Mouse; The Terrace; The Imprint of Giants; Fantastica.

REHME, Robert G: Exec. b. Cincinnati, OH, May 5, 1935. Pres B & R Theatres, 1975; vp April Fools Films, Inc, 1976; vp New World Pictures, 1977; Pres Avco Embassy Pictures, Jan 1980.

REID, Beryl: Act. b. Hereford, Eng, Jun 17, 1920. Started in radio. London stage debut, 1951, in the revue After the Show. Thea inc: (London) Rockin' the Town; The Killing of Sister George; Spring Awakening; Campiello; Counting the Ways; Born in the Gardens. The Killing of Sister George (Tony-1967).

Films inc: The Belles of St Trinian's; The Extra Day; Star!; Inspector Clousseau; The Assassination Bureau; The Killing of Sister George; The Beast in the Cellar; Psychomania; Father Dear Father; No Sex Please, We're British; Joseph Andrews; Carry On Emmanuelle.

REID, John A: Exec. b. Sydney, Australia, Mar 24, 1932. GM, chief exec, G U O Film Dist, PTY Ltd. Formerly M-dir, UA (Aust).

REID, Kate: Act. b. London, Nov 4, 1930. Performed in stock in Canada, Bermuda. Joined The Stratford Shakespeare Festival in Canada, remained for seven seasons playing a variety of major roles. Films inc: This Property Is Condemned; The Side Glances of a Pigeon Kicker; The Andromeda Strain; A Delicate Balance; Equus; Death Ship; Double Negative; Plague; Circle of Two; Atlantic City, USA.

Bway inc: Dylan; Slapstick Tragedy; Cat On A Hot Tin Roof; The Freedom of the City; Bosoms and Neglect. TV inc: Nellie McClung; Crossbar.

REID, Tim: Act. b. Norfolk, VA, Dec 19, 1944. e. Norfolk State College. Originaly standup comic Chicago niteries.

Films inc: Mother, Jugs and Speed; Uptown Saturday Night; The Union.

TV inc: The Marilyn McCoo and Billy Davis Jr Show; The Frankie Avalon Summer Show; That's My Mama; What's Happening; Fernwood 2Night; You Can't Take It With You; WKRP in Cincinnati.

REILLY, Charles Nelson: Act. b. NYC, Jan 13, 1931. e. U of CT. Bway inc: Best Foot Forward; The Saintliness of Margery Kempe; Lend an Ear; The Billy Barnes Revue; The Inspector General; How to Succeed in Business Without Really Trying (Tony-supp-1962); Hello, Dolly; God's Favorite; The Belle of Amherst (dir); Charlotte; Break A Leg (dir).

Films inc: A Face in the Crowd; Two Tickets to Paris; The Tiger Makes Out.

TV inc: The Broadway of Lerner and Lowe; The Ghost and Mrs Muir; The Dean Martin Show.

REINER, Carl: Act-Wri-Dir. b. NYC, Mar 20, 1922. Films inc: (act) Happy Anniversary; The Gazebo; Gidget Goes Hawaiian; It's a Mad, Mad, Mad, Mad World; The Art of Love (& sp); The Russians Are Coming; A Guide for the Married Man; The Comic (sp-dir); Where's Poppa? (dir only); Oh, God (dir only); The End; The One And Only; (dir only); The Jerk (& dir).

TV inc: Caesar's Hour (Emmy Awards-supp-1956, 1957); Dick Van Dyke Show (Emmys-wri-1962, 1963, 1964; Prod 1965, 1966); Sid Caesar, Imogene Coca Special (Emmy-wri-1967); Comedy Is Not Pretty; 30 Years of TV Comedy's Greatest Hits (co-host).

Bway inc: (act) Call Me Mister; Inside USA; Alive and Kicking; The Roast (dir).

Recordings inc: (with Mel Brooks) The 2000 Year Old Man; The 2001 Year Old Man; The 2013 Year Old Man.

REINER, Rob: Act. b. NYC, Mar 6, 1945. S of Carl Reiner. Apprentice, Bucks County Playhouse, New Hope, PA. Wrote for The Summer Brothers Smothers Show; The Smothers Brothers Comedy Hour. Films inc: Fire Sale; Enter Laughing; Hall of Anger; Where's Poppa.

TV inc: All In The Family; (Emmys-supp-1974, 1978); The Partridge Family; That Girl; Gomer Pyle-USMC; Headmaster.

Bway inc: The Roast.

REINKING, Ann: Act. b. Nov 10, 1949. Bway inc: Cabaret; Pippin; Chicago; Over Here; Goodtime Charlie; A Chorus Line; Dancin'.

TV inc: Julie Andrews' Invitation to the Dance With Rudolf Nureyev.
Films inc: Movie Movie; All That Jazz.

REISCH, Walter: Wri-Dir. b. Vienna, Austria, May 23, 1903. European screenplays inc: Two Hearts in 3/4 Time; The Song Is Ended; Men Are Not Gods. US screenplays: The Great Waltz; Ninotchka; Gaslight; Comrade X; Journey to the Center of the Earth; The Girl on the Red Velvet Swing; The Mating Season; Titanic (Oscar-story and sp-1953); Niagara.

REISFELD, Bert: Comp. b. Vienna, Dec 12, 1906. e. Conservatory of Music, Vienna. Comp. films scores, Berlin, Paris. To US, 1938. Songs inc: Call Me Darling; You Rhyme with Everything that's Beautiful; The Three Bells; California Concerto for Piano.

REISNER, Allen: Dir. b. NYC. Films inc: The Day They Gave Babies Away; St. Louis Blues; All Mine to Give.

TV inc: The Untouchables; Mary Jane Harper Cried Last Night; The Captains and the Kings; Your Money or Your Wife; To Die in Paris; The Cliff; Climax; Hawaii 5-0; Kojak; Streets of San Francisco; Gunsmoke; The Love Tapes.

REISZ, Karel: Dir. b. Czechoslovakia, 1926. Wrote Technique of Film Editing for British Film Academy. Worked with British Film Institute and National Film Library. Films inc: Momma Don't Allow; Every Day Except Christmas; We Are the Lambeth Boys; Saturday Night and Sunday Morning; This Sporting Life; Night Must Fall; Morgan; Isadora; The Gambler; Who'll Stop the Rain.

TV inc: On the Road.

REITMAN, Ivan: Prod. b. Czechoslovakia, Oct 26, 1946. e. McMaster U. Films inc: Foxy Lady; Cannibal Girls; Shivers; Death Weekend; Blackout; Animal House; Meatballs (& dir).

Bway inc: The Magic Show; The National Lampoon Show.

TV inc: The Delta House.

RELPH, Michael: Prod-Dir. b. Eng, 1915. Films inc: The Captive Heart; Frieda; Saraband for Dead Lovers; The Blue Lamp; The Rainbow Jacket; Davy; Rockets Galore; Sapphire; The League of Gentlemen; Victim; Life for Ruth; The Mind Benders; Woman of Straw; Masquerade; The Assassination Bureau; The Man Who Haunted Himself; Scum (exec prod).

RELYEA, Robert: Prod. b. Santa Monica, CA, May 3, 1930. e. UCLA, BA. VP, Melvin Simon Prdctns, Inc. Films inc: Bullitt; The Reivers; Le Mans; Adam at Six A M; Day of the Dolphin; Seven (act).

REMBUSCH, Trueman T: Exhb. b. Shelbyville, IN, Jul 27, 1909. S of Frank Rembusch. Pioneer exhib and inventor of Glass Mirror Screen; left Notre Dame to install snd eqpt in his father's circuit; became mgr 1932; on bd dir Allied Theatre Owners of Ind IN., 1932-39; P 1945-1951; named by Allied as one of triumvirate heading COMPO 1952; chmn joint comm on toll tv 1954; currently P Syndicate Theatres Inc.

REMICK, Lee: Act. b. Boston, Dec 14, 1937. Began in summer stock. Toured in Jenny Kissed Me; The Seven Year Itch. Bway stage debut at 16 in Be Your Age. Screen debut, 1957, A Face in the Crowd.

Films inc: The Long Hot Summer; Anatomy of a Murder; Experiment in Terror; The Days of Wine and Roses; The Detective; A Delicate Balance; The Omen; Telefon; The Medusa Touch; The Europeans; Tribute.

TV inc: The Blue Knight; Jennie; QB VII; Torn Between Two Lovers; Ike; Haywire; The Women's Room.

Thea inc: (London) Bus Stop.

REMSEN, Bert: Act. b. Glen Cove, NY, Feb 25, 1925. e. Ithaca Coll. Films inc: Pork Chop Hill; Kid Galahad; Moon Pilot; Brewster McCloud; Thieves Like Us; Baby Blue Marine; McCabe and Mrs. Miller; Sweet Hostage; Nashville; The Awakening Land; California Split; Tarantulas; A Wedding; Buffalo Bill and the Indians; The Rose; Uncle Joe Shannon; Carny; Borderline; Second Hand Hearts; Joni; Inside Moves.

TV inc: Love for Rent.

RENALDO, Duncan (Renault Renaldo Duncan): Act-Prod. b. Spain, Apr 23, 1904. Appeared on NY stage in My Son. Films inc: Fifty-Fifty; Marchetta; Bridge of San Luis Rey; Trader Horn; Rose of the Rio Grande; Spawn of the North; Secret Service in Darkest Africa (serial); For Whom the Bell Tolls; The Cisco Kid (series); The Fighting Seabees; The Cisco Kid Returns; Sword of the Avenger; The Daring Caballero; Zorro Rides Again.

TV inc: The Cisco Kid.

Died Sep 4, 1980).

RENOIR, Jean: Wri-Dir. b. Paris, Sep 15, 1894. Began screen writing and dir in France, 1924. Films inc: La Fille de L'Eau; Nana; Charleston; The Little Match Girl; Toni; Madame Bovary; Le Crime de Monsieur Lange; La Grande Illusion; Swamp Water; This Land is Mine; The Southerner; Diary of a Chambermaid; The Woman on the Beach; The River; The Golden Coach; French Can Can; Lunch on the Grass; The Vanishing Corporal; C'est la Revolution. (Honorary Oscar-1974).

TV inc: Dr Cordelier; The Petit Theatre de Jean Renoir.

Thea inc: Julius Caesar; Orvet; Carola.

(Died Feb 12, 1979).

REO Speedwagon: Band. Members are Kevin Cronin, lead voc; Gary Richrath, guitar; Neil Doughty, piano; Alan Gratzer, drums; Bruce Hall, bass. Albums inc: REO Speedwagon; REO Two; Ridin' The Storm Out; Lost In A Dream; This Time We Mean It; REO; You Get What You Play For; You Can Tune a Piano, but You Can't Tuna Fish; 9 Lives; A Decade of Rock 'N' Roll; Hi InFidelity.

RESNAIS, Alain: Dir. b. Vannes, France, Jun 3, 1922. Made several shorts, beginning 1948; inc: Van Gogh, Gauguin; Guernica; Statues Also Die; Toute la Memoire du Monde.

Films inc: Hiroshima Mon Amour; Last Year at Marienbad; Muriel; The War Is Over; Je n'Aime, Je t'Aime; Stavisky; Providence; My Uncle in America.

RESNICK, Patricia: Wri. b. Miami, FL, 1953. e. USC, BA. AFI Intern grant to work with Robert Altman on Buffalo Bill and the Indians; The Late Show; Three Women; Wrote sketches for Lily Tomlin's Appearing Nitely on Bway.

Films inc: A Wedding (& act); Quintet; Nine to Five.

TV inc: Ladies in Waiting.

REVERE, Anne: Act. b. NYC, Jun 25, 1907. On screen from 1940. Films inc: Double Door; One Crowded Night; The Howards of Virginia; Men of Boys Town; Star Spangled Rhythm; The Song of Bernadette; Dragonwyck; National Velvet (Oscar-supp-1945); Body and Soul; Forever Amber; Gentleman's Agreement; A Place in the Sun; The Great Missouri Raid; Tell Me That You Love Me, Junie Moon; Birch Interval. Bway inc: The Great Barrington; The Lady With A Lamp; Wild Waves; Double Door; The Children's Hour; Three Sisters; Toys in the Attic (Tony-supp-1960).

REVIER, Dorothy: Act. b. San Francisco, Apr 18, 1904. Films inc: The Wild Party; Rose of Paris; Just a Woman; Poker Faces; Red Dance; Drop Kick; Beware of Blondes; The Siren; The Iron Mask; The Donovan Affair; Father and Son; Burlesque; The Black Camel; Unknown Blonde; The Lady in Scarlet; Light Fingers; The Cowboy and the Kid. Ret 1936.

REVILL, Clive: (nee Selsby): Act. b. Wellington, NZ, Apr 18, 1930. e. Rongotai Coll, Victoria U. Films inc: Bunny Lake is Missing; Modesty Blaise; A Fine Madness; The Double Man; Fathom; Nobody Runs Forever; A Severed Head; Avanti; The Legend of Hell House; The Black Windmill; One of Our Dinosaurs Is Missing; Galileo; The Empire Strikes Back.

TV inc: Chicken Soup With Barley; Volpone; Bam, Pow, Zapp; Candida; A Bit of Vision; The Piano Player; Licking Hitler; Centennial; She's Dressed to Kill; Moviola (The Scarlett O'Hara War); The Diary of Anne Frank.

Thea inc: (London) Irma La Douce; The Mikado; Oliver!; Marat/Sade.

Bway inc: Irma La Douce; Oliver; Sherry; The Incomparable Max; Sherlock Holmes.

REY, Alejandro: Act-Dir. b. Buenos Aires, Argentina, Feb 8, 1913. Films inc: Solomon and Sheba; The Battle of Bloody Beach; Blindfold; Synanon; Mr. Majestyk; Breakout; The Swarm; Sunburn; Cuba; The Ninth Configuration.

TV inc: Stunts Unlimited.

REY, Fernando: Act. b. Spain, Sep 20, 1915. Films inc: Welcome Mr Marshall; The Adventurers; The French Connection; The Discreet Charm of the Bourgeoisie; French Connection II; A Matter of Time; Desert of the Tartars; Elisa My Love; The Second Power; The Assignment; La Grande Bourgeoisie; That Obscure Object of Desire; The Last Romantic Lover; Memoirs of Leticia Valli; Quintet; L'ingorgo; The Cuenca Crime.

REYNOLDS, Burt: Act. b. Waycross, GA, Feb 11, 1936. e. FL State U. Bway debut, revival of Mister Roberts. Worked as film stunt man. Films inc: Armored Command; Angel Baby; Operation CIA; Navajo Joe; Shark; 100 Rifles; Fade-In; Skullduggery; Everything You Always Wanted To Know About Sex; Fuzz; Silent Movie; Deliverance; Shamus; White Lightning; The Man Who Loved Cat Dancing; The Longest Yard; WW & The Dixie Dancekings; At Long Last Love; Hustle; Lucky Lady; Gator; Nickleodeon; Smokey and the Bandit; Semi-Tough; The End; Hooper; Starting Over; Rough Cut; Smokey and the Bandit II.

TV inc: Gunsmoke; Riverboat; Hawk; Dan August.

REYNOLDS, Debbie: Act. b. El Paso, TX, Apr 1, 1932. Screen debut, 1948, June Bride. Films inc: The Daughter of Rosie O'Grady; Three Little Words; Singing in the Rain; Susan Slept Here; Tender Trap; Catered Affair; Bundle of Joy; Tammy and the Bachelor; The Mating Game; It Started With a Kiss; The Gazebo; How The West Was Won; Goodbye Charlie; The Unsinkable Molly Brown; The Singing Nun; What's The Matter With Helen; That's Entertainment.

Bway inc: Irene; Annie Get Your Gun.

TV inc: The Debbie Reynolds Show.

REYNOLDS, Frank: TV Newscaster. b. East Chicago, IN, Nov 29, 1923. e. IN U; Wabash College. Reporter with WJOB, Hammond IN, 1947; WBKB-TV, Chicago, 1950; WBBM, Chicago 1951; ABC corr Chicago 1963; Washington corr 1965; anchor World News Tonight, 1978.

REYNOLDS, Gene: Prod-Dir-Act. b. Cleveland, OH, Apr 4, 1925. Began as child radio actor, Detroit; on screen from 1934 in Our Gang comedies and Babes in Toyland. Films inc: In Old California; Sins of Man; Captains Courageous; Thank You, Jeeves; Madame X; Heidi; In Old Chicago; Boys Town; Love Finds Andy Hardy; They Shall Have Music; Edison the Man; The Mortal Storm; 99 River Street; The Country Girl; The Bridges of Toko-Ri; Diane.

TV inc: (as dir-prod) Room 222 (Emmy-prod-1970); M*A*S*H (Emmy-prod-1974; dir-1975, 1976); in 1976, became exec prod of M*A*S*H; The Ghost and Mrs Muir (prod & dir); Anna and the King (exec prod of pilot); Roll Out! (co-prod-dir); Karen (exec prod); Hogan's Heroes; My Little Margie; My Three Sons; Father of the Bride; The Andy Griffith Show; Lou Grant (Emmys-exec prod-1979, 1980).

REYNOLDS, William H: Flm Ed. e. Princeton U, BA. Films inc: The Day the Earth Stood Still; Three Coins in the Fountain; Desiree; Daddy Longlegs; Love Is A Many Splendored Thing; Carousel; Bus Stop; South Pacific; Compulsion; Beloved Infidel; Fanny; Tender Is The Night; The Sound of Music; (Oscar-1965); The Sand Pebbles; Star; Hello, Dolly; The Godfather; The Sting (Oscar-1973); The Great Waldo Pepper; The Seven Percent Solution; The Turning Point; Old Boyfriends; A Little Romance; Nijinsky; Heaven's Gate.

RHINE, Larry: Wri. b. San Francisco. TV inc: Duffy's Tavern (& radio); Brady Bunch; Mr. Ed; Red Skelton Show; Lucy; Bob Hope Show; All in the Family.

RHOADES, Barbara: Act. b. Poughkeepsie, NY, 1948. Bway inc: Funny Girl.

Films inc: Don't Just Stand There; Shakiest Gun in the West; The Choir Boys;

TV inc: The Day The Women Got Even. The Goodbye Girl; Serial.

RHODEN, Elmer C: Exec. b. Le Mars, IA, May 15, 1893. e. Nebraska U. Started in film industry with General Film Co. Omaha 1912; organized Midwest Film Distributors 1920; organized Midwest Theatre Co, 1927, served as P until 1929; moving div mgr Midwest Theatres 1929; P National Theatres Inc 1954-58; bd chmn 1958-59; bd chmn Commonwealth Theatres Inc 1959-1977; chmn exec comm Commonwealth Theatres.

RHODES, Mike (Michael Ray Rhodes): Prod-Dir. b. Estherville, IA, Jul 11, 1945. e. Yale, BA; Pacific School of Religion, M Div; USC, MFA (film). Films inc: The Bus Is Coming (Cin); Bloomin' Human (series of 16 shorts).
TV inc: Capital Cities Family Theatre; Insight/This Side of Eden; This One For Dad; Chicken; Insight/Holy Moses; Insight/Checkmate; Princess (dir); God In The Dock; 17 Going Nowhere; The Long Road Home.

RHUE, Madlyn (Madeline Roche): Act. b. Washington, DC, 1934. Films inc: Operation Petticoat; Escape from Zahrain; It's a Mad, Mad, Mad, Mad World; He Rides Tall; Stand Up and Be Counted.
TV inc: Bracken's World; Executive Suite; The Best Place To Be; Goldie and the Boxer.
Bway inc: Two for the Seesaw; The Best Laid Plans.

RIBMAN, Ronald: Plywri. b. NYC, May 28, 1932. e. U Pittsburgh, BA, MA, PhD. Former English prof. Plays inc: Harry, Noon and Night; Journey of the Fifth Horse; The Ceremony of Innocence; Passing Through from Exotic Places; Fingernails Blue as Flowers; A Break in the Skin; The Poison Tree; The Angel Levine.
TV inc: The Final War of Olly Winter.

RICE, Tim: Lyr. b. Amersham, Bucks, Eng, Nov 10, 1944. Thea inc: The Amazing Technicolour Dreamcoat; Jesus Christ Superstar; Evita (*Tonys*-book & lyr-1980).
Films inc: Gumshoe; The Odessa File.
TV inc: Musical Triangles; Disco.

RICH, Buddy (Bernard Rich): Mus. b. Brooklyn, NY, Jun 30, 1917. In vaude as child with family act (Wilson & Rich); on Bway in Pinwheel at 4; toured Australia at 6. With various bands inc Joe Marsala; Bunny Berigan; Artie Shaw; Tommy Dorsey; Benny Carter before forming own band to tour with Jazz at the Philharmonic; later with Harry James.
Albums inc: Bird and Diz; Jazz on the Air; Jam Session; Jazz Scene; Stick It; Roar of 74; A Different Drummer; Take It Away.

RICH, Charlie: Singer-Comp. b. Forrest City, AR, Dec 14, 1932. e. U of AR. Country mus recording artist. (*Grammy*-country voc-1973).

RICH, David Lowell: Dir. b. NYC, Aug 31, 1920. Began career in NY in live TV; worked on Studio One; Big Town; The Big Story; Playhouse 90. In 1957 moved to Hollywood; dir Naked City; Route 66; Arrest and Trial; The Sex Symbol; The Defection of Simas Kudirka (*Emmy*-1978); Little Women; Nurse; Enola Gay--The Men, The Mission, The Atomic Bomb.
Films inc: Senior Prom; Hey Boy, Hey Girl; Have Rocket Will Travel; Madame X; The Plainsman; Rosie; A Lovely Way to Die; Eye of the Cat; Concorde-Airport '79.

RICH, Irene (nee Luther): Act. b. Buffalo, NY, Oct 13, 1897. On radio, Dear John, several years. Films inc: Stella Maris; Beau Brummel; So This Is Paris; Craig's Wife; Lady Windermere's Fan; Shanghai Rose; That Certain Age; The Lady in Question; This Time for Keeps; Angel and the Badman; Fort Apache; New Orleans; Joan of Arc.
Bway inc: Seven Keys To Baldpate; As The Girls Go.

RICH, John: Prod-Dir. b. Rockaway Beach, NY, Jul 6, 1925. e. U of MI, MA. Films inc: Boeing-Boeing; The New Interns; Wives and Lovers; Roustabout; Easy Come, Easy Go.
TV inc: The Dick Van Dyke Show (*Emmy*-dir-1963); All in the Family (*Emmy*-dir-1972; prod-1973).

RICH, Lee: Exec prod. b. Cleveland, OH. Adv exec, resigned as sr tv vp Benton & Bowles to become P Mirisch-Rich TV 1965; Prod Rat Patrol; The Good Life; resigned 1967 to join Leo Burnett Agency; resigned 1969 to form Lorimar Productions.
TV inc: (exec prod) Helter Skelter; The Waltons (*Emmy*-exec prod-1973); Sybil; Eric; Green Eyes; The Blue Knight; The Long Journey Back; Kaz; Eight Is Enough; Dallas; Some Kind of Miracle; Mr. Horn; Studs Lonigan; A Man Called Intrepid; Big Shamus, Little Shamus; Young Love, First Love; Mary and Joseph--A Story of Faith; Knots Landing; Skag; Flamingo Road; Reward; Willow B--Women in Prison; Joshua's World; A Perfect Match; Secret of Midland Heights.
Films inc: (exec prod) The Man; Who Is Killing the Great Chefs of Europe?; Marriage is Alive and Well; The Big Red One.

RICHARD, Cliff: Act-Singer. b. India, Oct 14, 1940.
Films inc: Serious Charge; Expresso Bongo; The Young Ones; Summer Holiday; Wonderful Life; Finders Keepers; Two A Penny; His Land; Take Me High.
TV inc: Cliff Richard Show; Sunday Night at the London Palladium; Oh, Boy.

RICHARD, Pierre: Act. b. France, Aug 16, 1934. Films inc: Alexandre le Bienheureux; La Coqueluche; The Tall Blond Man with One Black Shoe; La Raison du plus fou; Juliette and Juliette; Un nuage entre les dents; Return of the Tall Blond Man; La Course a l'echalote; The Bottom Line; We've Seen Everything; The Castaways of Turtle Island; The Toy; The Wild Goose Chase; Le Coup du Parapluie (The Umbrella Coup). (Dir) Le Distrait (& wri-act); Les Malheurs d'Alfred (& wri-act); Je Ne Sais Rien, Mais Je Dirais Tout (& wri-act); The Daydreamer (& wri-act); I'm Timid But I'm Treating It (& co-sp-act).

RICHARDS, Beah: Act-Plywri. b. Vicksburg, MS. e. Dillard U. Bway inc: The Miracle Worker; Purlie Victorious; A Raisin in the Sun; Macbeth.
Films inc: Take a Giant Step; The Miracle Worker; Guess Who's Coming To Dinner?; Heat of the Night; Hurry Sundown; Great White Hope; Mahogany.
TV inc: One Angry Man; A Dream for Christmas; Just An Old Sweet Song; Kinfolk; A Black Woman Speaks; Roots II--The Second Generation; A Christmas Without Snow.

RICHARDS, Dick: Dir. b. 1936. Films inc: Farewell My Lovely; Rafferty and the Gold Dust Twins; March or Die (& prod-wri).

RICHARDS, Kim: Act. b. Long Island, NY, Sep 19, 1964. Films inc: Escape to Witch Mountain; No Deposit, No Return; Anderson's Alamo; Special Delivery; Kotch; The Car; Return from Witch Mountain.
TV inc: Nanny and the Professor; Here We Go Again; Raid on Entebbe; Ben Franklin in Paris; Portrait of Dorian Gray; The Horrible Honchos; Angel's Nest; Death Trap; James at 15.

RICHARDS, Martin: Prod. H of Mary Lea Johnson. Off-Bway inc: Dylan. Bway inc: The Norman Conquests; Chicago; On The Twentieth Century; Sweeney Todd (*Tony*-1979).
Films inc: The Shining; The Boys From Brazil.

RICHARDSON, Don: Dir. b. NYC, Apr 30, 1918. e. AADA. TV inc: I Remember Mama: The Elgin Hour: The 13 Clocks; The Defenders; Mission Impossible; Bonanza; Get Smart; The Virginian; High Chaparral; Arnie; The Lancers; One Day at a Time.

RICHARDSON, Ian: Act. b. Edinburgh, Scotland, Apr 7, 1934. e. Glasgow Coll Dramatic Art. With Birmingham Repertory; Royal Shakespeare Company. Thea inc: (London) The Duchess of Malfi; Much Ado About Nothing; The Taming of the Shrew; Comedy of Errors; The Representative; The Miracles; King Lear; Marat/Sade; The Jew of Malta; The Merry Wives of Windsor; The Revenger's Tragedy; Coriolanus; Measure for Measure; The Tempest; Trelawney of the Wells; Love's Labour's Lost; Richard III. (Bway) The Comedy of Errors; Marat/Sade; My Fair Lady.
Films inc: The Darwin Adventure; Man of La Mancha.

RICHARDSON, Sir Ralph: Act. b. Cheltenham, Gloucestershire, Eng, Dec 19, 1902. Stage debut 1921 The Merchant of Venice; recent thea inc: Separate Tables; The Sleeping Prince; The Waltz of the Toreadors; Flowering Cherry; The School for Scandal; Six Characters in Search of an Author; What the Butler Saw; Home; No Man's Land; The Kingfisher; The Cherry Orchard; Alice's Boys; The Fruits of Enlightenment; Early Days.

Screen debut, 1933, The Ghoul.

Films inc: The Return of Bulldog Drummond; Things to Come; The Man Who Could Work Miracles; The Citadel; Four Feathers; The Avengers; Anna Karenina; The Heiress; The Fallen Idol; An Outcast of the Islands; Breaking the Sound Barrier; The Holly and the Ivy; Richard III; Oscar Wilde; Our Man in Havana; Exodus; Long Day's Journey Into Night; Doctor Zhivago; Khartoum; The Midas Run; The Battle of Britain; Oh! What a Lovely War; Eagle in a Cage; Lady Caroline Lamb; Tales From the Crypt; A Doll's House; O Lucky Man; Rollerball; Watership Down (voice).

TV inc: Hedda Gabler; Twelfth Night; Blandings Castle.

RICHARDSON, Tony: Dir-Prod-Wri. b. Shipley, Eng, Jun 5, 1928. e. Oxford. Films inc: Look Back in Anger; The Entertainer; Sanctuary; A Taste of Honey; The Loneliness of the Long Distance Runner; Tom Jones (Oscar-1963); The Loved One; Red and Blue; The Charge of the Light Brigade; Laughter in the Dark; Hamlet; Ned Kelly; A Delicate Balance; Dead Cert; Joseph Andrews (& wri).

RICHMAN, Peter Mark: Act. b. Philadelphia, 1927. e. Philadelphia Coll of Pharmacy and Science, BS. Films inc: Friendly Persuasion; The Black Orchid; The Dark Intruder; Agent for H.A.R.M.; For Singles Only.

TV inc: Cain's Hundred; Longstreet; Blind Ambition; Greatest Heroes of the Bible.

Bway inc: End as a Man; Masquerade; The Zoo Story; Detective Story; Rose Tattoo.

RICHMOND, Bill: Wri-Prod. b. Central City, KY, Dec 19, 1921. e. U of IL. Films inc: The Ladies Man; The Errand Boy; The Nutty Professor; The Patsy; The Family Jewels; The Big Mouth.

TV inc: The Jerry Lewis Show; Diahann Carrol Show; The Singers; Laugh In; The Carol Burnett Show (Emmys-wri-1974, 1975 & 1978); Tim Conway Special; Welcome Back Kotter (prod); Three's Company (prod); The Tim Conway Show (prod-wri).

RICHMOND, Ted: Prod. b. Norfolk, VA, Jun 10, 1912. e. MIT. Films inc: So Dark the Night; The Milkman; Smuggler's Island; The Strange Door; Desert Legion; Francis Joins the WACS; Forbidden; Count Three and Pray; Nightfall; Abandon Ship; Solomon and Sheba; Bachelor in Paradise; Advance to the Rear; Return of the Seven; Villa Rides; Red Sun; Papillon; The Fifth Musketeer.

RICHTER, Richard: Prod. Began as reporter on Newsday; NY World Telegram Sun before joining CBS 1959 as wri-news editor; 1960 won CBS Fellowship for advanced study at Columbia U; 1963-1967 with Peace Corps; joined ABC 1969 as prod Evening News; 1976 senior prod ABC Evening News; 1978 senior prod ABC News Doc unit.

TV inc: The American Army--a Shocking State of Readiness; Youth Terror--The View from Behind the Gun; Youth Terror--Is There an Answer?; Asbestos--The Way to a Dusty Death; Arson! Fire For Hire!; The Police Tapes; Terror in the Promised Land; Politics of Torture; The Killing Ground; The Shooting of a Big Man--Anatomy of a Criminal Case; Infinite Horizons--Space After Apollo; This Shattered Land; Lights, Camera. . .Politics; The Apocalypse Game; The Shattered Bridge;; A Matter of Survival.

RICKERT, John F: Exec. b. Kansas City, MO, Oct 29, 1924. e. USC, BS. In film industry since 1950. P, CineWorld Corp.

RICKLES, Don: Act. b. NYC, May 8, 1926. e. AADA. Films inc: Run Silent, Run Deep; The Rabbit Trap; The Rat Race; Enter Laughing; Where It's At; Kelly's Heroes.

TV inc: The Don Rickles Show; CPO Sharkey; For The Love of It.

RIDDLE, Nelson: Comp-Cond. b. Hackensack, NJ, 1921. Film scores inc: A Kiss Before Dying; St Louis Blues; Ocean's Eleven; Lolita; L'il Abner; Can Can; Robin and the Seven Hoods; Marriage on the Rocks; El Dorado; Paint Your Wagon; The Great Gatsby (Oscar-1974); Fugitive Girls (perf); Guyana-Cult of the Damned.

TV inc: The Carpenters-Music, Music, Music.

(Grammy-composition-1958).

RIEFENSTAHL, Leni: Dir. b. Berlin, 1902. Former dancer who made Nazi propaganda films for Hitler. Films inc: Peaks of Destiny (act only); The Blue Light (& act); Triumph of the Will; Olympische Spiele 1936; Tiefland; SOS Iceberg (act); Stuerme Uber Dem Mount Blanc (act); Der Weisse Rauch (act).

RIGG, Diana: Act. b. Doncaster, Yorks, Eng, Jul 20, 1938. e. RADA. London stage debut, 1961, Ondine. Thea inc: (London) The Devils; Becket; The Physicists; Jumpers; Macbeth; Pygmalion; Phaedra Britannica; Abelard and Heloise; The Guardsman. (Bway) King Lear; Abelard and Heloise.

Films inc: Assassination Bureau; On Her Majesty's Secret Service; Julius Caesar; The Hospital; Theatre of Blood; A Little Night Music.

TV inc: The Avengers; Comedy of Errors; The Diana Rigg Show; In This House of Brede; The New Avengers.

RILEY, Jeanie C (nee Stephenson): Singer-Sngwri. b. Stamford, TX, Oct 19, 1945. Songs inc: Harper Valley PTA (Grammy-country voc-1968).

RINTELS, David W: Wri-Prod. b. Boston, MA. e. Harvard. Joined NBC 1961 as researcher, began freelance writing. TV inc: The Defenders; Run for Your Life; Slattery's People; The Invaders; The Young Lawyers; A Continual Roar of Musketry (The Senator); Clarence Darrow (Emmy-1975); Fear on Trial (Emmy-1976); The Oldest Living Graduate (exec prod); Gideon's Trumpet (& prod).

RIOMFALVY, Paul H: Prod. b. Budapest, Hungary, Dec 24, 1924. To Australia, 1949. Prod over 60 plays, musicals and revues, inc: A Cup of Tea; Is Australia Really Necessary?; Beyond the Fringe; Canterbury Tales; Private Lives; The Boyfriend; Anything Goes; A Severed Head; Godspell; The Private Ear and Public Eye. Chmn, Interim Film Commission; chmn, New South Wales Film Corp; chmn, Australian Film Office Inc.

RISI, Dino: Dir. b. Italy. Films inc: The Sign of Venus; Poveri ma Belli; Il Sorpasso; Scent of Woman (& wri); Viva Italia!; I'm Photogenic; Sunday Lovers.

RISSNER, Danton: Exec. b. Brooklyn, Mar 27, 1940. Started as agent with Ashley Famous, later International Famous; joined WB 1969, vp chg European Prodn; 1972 UA vp chg European prodn; 1974, vp chg East Coast & European prodn; 1978 sr vp in chg West Coast prodn; resigned Sept 1978 to enter ind prodn; July 1980 named vp Motion Pictures, Marble Arch Prodns.

Films inc: Up the Academy.

RITCHIE, Clint: Act. b. Grafton, ND, Aug 9. Films inc: The St. Valentine's Day Massacre; Bandolero; Patton; A Force of One.

TV inc: Wild Wild West; Centennial; Thunder; One Life to Live.

RITCHIE, Michael: Dir. b. Waukesha, WI, 1938. e. Harvard U. TV inc: asso prod, later dir on Ford Foundation's Omnibus TV series; The Man From U.N.C.L.E.; Dr. Kildare; Run For Your Life.

Films inc: Downhill Racer; Prime Cut; The Candidate; Smile; The Bad News Bears; Semi-Tough; The Bad News Bears Go to Japan (prod); An Almost Perfect Affair (& sp); The Island; Divine Madness (& prod).

RITT, Martin: Dir. b. NYC, Mar 2, 1919. Films inc: Edge of the City; No Down Payment; The Long Hot Summer; The Sound and the Fury; Paris Blues; Hemmingway's Adventures of a Young Man; Hud; The Outrage; The Spy Who Came in from the Cold; Hombre; The Brotherhood; The Molly Maguires; The Great White Hope; Sounder; Pete 'n Tillie; Conrack; The Front; Casey's Shadow; Norma Rae; End of the Game (perf); Hollywood on Trial (perf).

TV inc: Danger.

Bway inc: (act) Golden Boy. (Dir) The Man; Set My People Free; A View From the Bridge.

RITTENBERG, Saul N: Atty. b. Chicago, Aug 4, 1912. e. UCLA, BA Northwestern Law School, JD. Partner Loeb and Loeb law firm. Asst sec MGM 1956-70; Board Trustees, Directors Guild Pension & Health and Welfare Plans, 1960-70; Director, Association of Motion Picture and TV Producers, 1956-70.

RITTER, John: Act. b. Burbank, CA, Sep 17, 1948. e. USC, BA. S of the late Tex Ritter. TV inc: The Waltons; Three's Company; Leave Yesterday Behind; Completely Off The Wall; That Thing on ABC; The Comback Kid; Echoes of the 60's (host); John Ritter, Being of Sound Mind and Body.

Films inc: The Barefoot Executive; The Other; The Stone Killer; Nickelodeon; Breakfast in Bed; Americathon; Hero at Large.

RITZ BROTHERS (nee Joachim): Comedians. Al (1901-65), Jim (1903-), and Harry (1906-). Zany nitery comedians. Films inc: Sing, Baby, Sing; One in a Million; On the Avenue; You Can't Have Everything; The Goldwyn Follies; Straight, Place and Show; The Three Musketeers; The Gorilla; Argentine Nights; Behind the Eight Ball; Hi Ya chum; Never a Dull Moment; Won Ton Ton the Dog That Saved Hollywood; Blazing Stewardesses; Real Life.

RIVA, Emmanuelle: Act. b. Chenimenil, France, 1932. Films inc: Hiroshima Mon Amour; Hungry for Love; Kapo; Leon Morin Priest; Climats; Therese Desqueyroux; Soledad; L'Homme de Desir; La Modification.

RIVERA, Chita (Concita del Rivero): Act. b. Washington, DC, Jan 23, 1933. Bway debut 1952, Call Me Madam. On stage in: Guys and Dolls; Can-Can; Seventh Heaven; Mr. Wonderful; West Side Story; Bye Bye Birdie; Bajour; The Three Penny Opera; Flower Drum Song; Zorba; Sweet Charity; Born Yesterday; Jacques Brel Is Alive and Well and Living in Paris; Sondheim: A Musical Tribute; Kiss Me Kate; Ivanhoe; Father's Day; Chicago.

Films inc: Sweet Charity.

TV inc: The New Dick Van Dyke Show.

RIVERA, Geraldo: TV newsman. b. NYC, Jul 4, 1943. e. U AZ, BS. TV inc: Reporter WABC-TV, 1968; Goodnight America (host) 1974; corr Good Morning America, 1976; corr ABC News & 20/20 since 1977.

RIVERS, Joan: Act-Wri-Dir. b. NYC, 1937. Mostly TV, niteries. Films inc: The Swimmer; Rabbit Test (dir-wri-act).

RIVETTE, Jacques: Dir. b. Rouen, France, 1928. Films inc: Le Coup de Berger; Paris Nous Appartient; La Religieuse (& sp); L'Amour Fou (& sp); Out One: Spectre; Celine and Julie Go Boating.

RIVKIN, Allen: Wri-Edtr. b. Hayward, WI, Nov 20, 1903. e. U of MN, BA. Films inc: 70,000 Witnesses; Madison Square Garden; Headline Shooter; Picture Snatcher; Meet the Baron; Dancing Lady; Cheating Cheaters; Your Uncle Dudley; Half Angel; Love Under Fire; Straight, Place and Show; Let Us Live; Typhoon; Joe Smith, American; The Kid Glove Killer; Till the End of Time; The Thrill of Brazil; Dead Reckoning; The Farmer's Daughter; My Dream is Yours; Grounds for Marriage; Battle Circus; Timberjack; Prisoner of War; The Eternal Sea; Big Operator.

TV inc: M-Squad; Small Explosion; Troubleshooters; Beginning of the End; Billion Dollar Swindle; Saints and Sinners.

RIX, Brian: Act. b. Yorkshore, Eng, 1924. Films inc: Reluctant Heroes; What Every Woman Wants; Up to His Neck; Dry Rot; The Night We Dropped a Clanger; And the Same to You; Nothing Barred; Don't Just Lie There, Say Something!

Thea inc: A Bit Between the Teeth (& prod); Jack the Ripper (prod); Beatlemania.

ROACH, Hal E: Prod. b. Elmira, NY, Jan 14, 1892. Film career started with Universal as stock cowboy; met Harold Lloyd and the two made a picture that sold for $850. Opened Roach Studio at Edendale, then moved to Santa Monica Blvd, where Lonesome Luke Comedies were made; final quarters at Culver City where studio was built in 1919. Specialized in comedy shorts inc Our Gang Comedies and early Laurel & Hardy Shorts.

Films inc: The Music Box (Oscar-short-1931); Bored of Education (Oscar-short-1936).

ROBARDS, Jason: Act. b. Chicago, Jul 26, 1922. e. AADA. Stage debut at the Children's World Theatre 1947, as the rear end of The Cow in Jack and the Beanstalk. Bway credits inc: The Iceman Cometh; Long Day's Journey Into Night; The Disenchanted (Tony-1959); Toys in the Attic; After the Fall; Hughie; We Bombed in New Haven; A Moon for the Misbegotten; A Touch of the Poet.

Screen debut 1958, The Journey. Films inc: By Love Possessed; Tender Is the Night; Long Day's Journey Into Night; A Thousand Clowns; A Big Hand for the Little Lady; Any Wednesday; The St. Valentine's Day Massacre; The Night They Raided Minsky's; The Loves of Isadora; The Ballard of Cable Hogue; Johnnie Got His Gun; The War Between Men and Women; Pat Garrett and Billy the Kid; Play It As It Lays; A Boy and His Dog; Mr. Sycamore; All the President's Men (Oscar-supp-1976); Julia (Oscar-supp-1977); Comes a Horseman; Hurricane; Raise The Titanic; Melvin and Howard.

TV inc: The Iceman Cometh; The Doll's House; For Whom the Bell Tolls; The Easter Promise; A Christmas to Remember; Haywire; For the Last Year.

ROBB, Jillian Claire: Prod. b. London. Films inc: Skippy the Bush Kangaroo; They're a Weird Mob; Wake in Fright; Contra Bandits. Marketing and dist m for the South Australian Film Corp; chief exec, Victorian Film Corp.

ROBBE-GRILLET, Alain: Wri-Dir. b. Brest, France, Aug 18, 1922. Films inc: Last Year at Marienbad; L'Imortelle (sp & dir); Trans Europ Express (sp & dir); L'Homme qui ment; L'Eden et Apres; Glissements progressifs du plaisir; Le Jeu avec le feu; Piege a Fourrure.

ROBBIE, Seymour Mitchell: Dir. TV inc: Omnibus; Jackie Gleason Show; The Man from U.N.C.L.E.; F. Troop; Mr. Roberts; Lost in Space; Name of the Game; It Takes a Thief; Mannix; Mission-Impossible; Cannon; Mod Squad; Streets of San Francisco; Kojak; Moving On; The New Adventures of Wonder Woman.

Films inc: C.C. & Company; Marco.

ROBBINS, Gale: Act. b. Chicago, IL, May 7, 1924. On radio as teenager; to Hollywood 1944 as singing actress. Films inc: My Dear Secretary; Oh, You Beautiful Doll; Girl on the Red Velvet Swing; Barkleys of Broadway; Three Little Words; Belle of New York; My Girl Tiza; Strictly Dishonorable; Fuller Brush Girl; Race Street; Double Jeopardy; Quantrill's Raiders.

TV inc: Gale Robbins Show; numerous guest appearances on Bob Hope Show; Red Skelton Show; George Jessel Show, etc; numerous segs.

Played all top niteries, toured with Frank Sinatra; Bob Hope; did one woman show in Far East, Caribbean and Mediterranean.

(Died Feb 18, 1980).

ROBBINS, Jerome (nee Rabinowitz): Dancer-Chor. b. NYC, Oct 11, 1918. Bway inc: Billion Dollar Baby; High Button Shoes; Look Ma, I'm Dancin'; Miss Liberty (& dir); Call Me Madam (& dir); Bells Are Ringing (& dir); West Side Story (& dir) *(Tony*-chor-1958); Gypsy (& dir); Fiddler on the Roof *(Tonys*-(2)-dir & chor-1966); also chor for many ballet cos inc: Ballet Russe; The Royal Danish Ballet; New York City Ballet; and his own co, Ballet USA.

Films inc: The King and I; West Side Story *(Oscar*-co-dir-1961); Honorary Oscar 1961 "for his brilliant achievements in the art of choreography on film."

TV inc: Peter Pan, 1956 & 1960 *(Emmy*-1956).

ROBBINS, Marty: Singer-Sngwri. b. Glendale, AZ, Sep 26, 1925. C&W recording artist. On radio, TV; became regular on Grand Ole Opry; toured US, many foreign nations. *(Grammys*-country perf-1960; country song-1970).

ROBBINS, Matthew: Wri-Dir. e. USC. Writes in collab with Hal Barwood. Films inc: The Sugarland Express; The Bingo Long Traveling All-Stars and Motor Kings; Corvette Summer (& dir).

ROBERT, Yves: Act-Dir-Prod. b. Saumur, France, Jun 19, 1920. H of Daniele Delorme. Films inc: (act) Les Dieux de dimanche; Trois telegrammes; La Rose rouge; Deux sous de violette; Suivez cet homme; Nina; La Francaise et l'amour; La Brune que voila; Cleo de 5 a7; Le Voyou; La distrait; Chere Louise; The Judge and the Assassin. (Dir) Les Hommes ne pensent qu'a ca; Signe Arsene Lupin; The War of the Buttons; Bebert et l'omnibus; Les Copains; Monnaie de singe; Very Happy Alexander; Clerambard; The Tall Blond Man With One Black Shoe; Salut l'artiste; The Return of the Tall Blond; Pardon mon affaire; We Will All Meet in Paradise; Courage, Fuyons; A Bad Son.

ROBERTS, Ben (nee Eisenberg): Wri-Prod. b. NYC, Mar 23, 1916. e. NYU. Films inc: White Heat; Goodbye My Fancy; Captain Horatio Hornblower; Come Fill the Cup; White Witch Doctor; Green Fire; Serenade; Midnight Lace; Portrait in Black; Man of a Thousand Faces.

TV inc: The Rogues; Charlie's Angels; Mannix; Time Express.

ROBERTS, Doris: Act. b. St Louis, MO, Nov 4, 1930. e. NYU. Bway inc: The Death of Bessie Smith; Desk Set; The Office; The Natural Look; Last of the Red Hot Lovers; The Secret Affairs of Mildred Wild; Cheaters.

Films inc: Something Wild; A New Leaf; No Way to Treat a Lady; The Honeymoon Killers; A Lovely Way to Die; Little Murders; Such Good Friends; The Taking of Pelham 1,2,3; Heartbreak Kid; Hester Street; Once In Paris; Good Luck Miss Wyckoff; The Rose; Rabbit Test.

TV inc: Look Homeward, Angel; The Neil Simon Comedy Hour; Angie; The Diary of Anne Frank.

ROBERTS, James M: Exec. b. Canada, 1923. Exec dir Academy of Motion Picture Arts and Sciences.

ROBERTS, Pernell: Act. b. May 18, 1930. Films inc: Desire Under the Elms; The Sheepman; Ride Lonesome; The Errand Boy; Four Rode Out; The Magic of Lassie.

TV inc: Bonanza; The Silent Gun; Centennial; The Immigrants; The Night Rider; Hot Rod; Trapper John; High Noon Part II--The Return of Will Kane.

ROBERTS, Rachel: Act. b. Llanelli, Wales, Sep 20, 1927. e. U of Wales, BA, RADA. Joined the Shakespeare Memorial Theatre, Stratford-on-Avon, 1951. Thea inc: (London) The Buccaneer; Numerous Shakespearean roles; Oh! My Papa; Keep Your Hair On; A Clear Kill; Platonov; August for the People; The Three Musketeers Ride Again; The Effect of Gamma Rays on Man-in-the-Moon Marigolds; This Sporting Life; Habeas Corpus; Once a Catholic. (Bway) The Visit; Chemin de Fer; Habeas Corpus.

Films inc: Valley of Song; The Good Companions; Our Man in Havana; Saturday Night and Sunday Morning; The Sporting Life; A Flea in Her Ear; O Lucky Man; The Belstone Fox; Murder on the Orient Express; Foul Play; When a Stranger Calls; Picnic at Hanging Rock; Yanks.

TV inc: Our Mutual Friend; A Circle of Children; Release; The Hostage Tower.

(Died Nov 26, 1980).

ROBERTS, Tanya: Act. b. Bronx, NY, Oct 15. Studied with Herbert Berghof; Lee Strasberg. TV inc: Pleasure Cove; Zuma Beach; Vega$; Charlie's Angels.

ROBERTS, Tony: Act. b. NYC, Oct 22, 1939. e. Northwestern U, BS. Films inc: Million Dollar Duck; The Star Spangled Girl; Play it Again, Sam; Serpico; The Taking of Pelham, One, Two, Three; Lovers Like Us; Annie Hall; Just Tell Me What You Want; Stardust Memories.

Bway inc: Play It Again, Sam; How Now, Dow Jones; Promises, Promises; Barefoot in the Park; The Last Analysis; Absurd Person Singular; Sugar.

TV inc: Messiah on Mott Street; The Lindbergh Kidnapping Case; Rosetti and Ryan; The Girls in the Office; If Things Were Different.

ROBERTSON, Cliff: Act. b. La Jolla, CA, Sep 9, 1925. Screen debut 1956, Picnic. Films inc: Autumn Leaves; The Naked and the Dead; Battle of the Coral Sea; Gidget; The Interns; My Six Loves; PT-109; The Honey Pot; The Devil's Brigade; Charly *(Oscar*-1968); Too Late the Hero; Three Days of the Condor; Midway; Shoot.

TV inc: The Man Without a Country; The Game *(Emmy*-1966); Overboard; Washington Behind Closed Doors.

Bway inc: The Wisteria Tree; Mr. Roberts; Late Love; The Lady and the Tiger; Orpheus Descending.

ROBERTSON, Dale: Act. b. Oklahoma City, OK, Jul 14, 1923. Films inc: Fighting Man of the Plains; Caribou Trail; Two Flags West; Return of the Texan; Outcasts of Poker Flats; The Farmer Takes a Wife; The Gambler from Natchez; Blood on the Arrow; The Walking Major.

TV inc: Wells Fargo; The Iron Horse; Death Valley Days; Kansas City Massacre; The Last Ride of the Dalton Gang.

ROBIN, Leo: Lyr. b. Pittsburgh, Apr 6, 1900. e. U of Pittsburgh Law School, Carnegie Tech Drama School. Films scores inc: Innocents in Paris; Little Miss Marker; Big Broadcast of 1935, '37 & '38 *(Oscar*-best song-Thanks for the Memories-1938); Paris Honeymoon; Gulliver's Travels; My Gal Sal; The Time, the Place and the Girl; Meet Me After the Show; Latin Lovers; Hit the Deck; My Sister Eileen.

Bway inc: Girl in Pink Tights; Hit the Deck; Greenwich Village Follies; Judy; Bubbling Over.

Songs inc: Hallelujah; Love in Bloom; June in January; Louise; Prisoner of Love; So in Love; Beyond the Blue Horizon; My Ideal; For Every Man There's a Woman.

ROBINSON, Casey: Wri-Prod. b. Logan, UT, Oct 17, 1903. Films inc: Captain Blood; Yes, My Darling Daughter, Dark Victory; All This and Heaven Too; Now Voyager; The Corn is Green; This is the Army; Kings Row; Saratoga Trunk; Passage to Marseilles; Casablanca; The Macomber Affair; Under My Skin; Two Flags West; Diplomatic Courier; The Snows of Kilimanjaro; The Egyptian; While the City Sleeps; This Earth is Mine.

(Died Dec 6, 1979).

ROBINSON, Charles: Wri. b. 1910. Asst to Daniel Frohman on Bway; wrote and prod Lighted Windows and Big Town series.

Plays inc: Sailor, Beware; Apple of His Eye; Mahogany Hall; Swing Your Lady; The Flying Gerardos.

Films inc: Taxi.

(Died Jun 4, 1980).

ROBINSON, Chris: Act. b. Nov 5, 1938. Films inc: Birdman of Alcatraz; The Hawaiians; 13 West Street; Because They're Young; Young Savages; Darker than Amber.

TV inc: 12 O'Clock High; Deep Lab; Alvin Karpis, F B I; Busters; Cabot Connection; The Wilds of 10,000 Islands; Travis Logan, D A; Men From Shiloh; The Intruder; The Dream Merchants.

ROBINSON, Earl: Comp-Cond-Act. b. Seattle, WA, Jul 2, 1910. e. U of WA. Began as folk singer in the 40's. Films scores inc: California; A Walk in the Sun; The Romance of Rosy Ridge; Man from Texas; The Roosevelt Story; also Army films.

Cantatas inc: Ballard for Americans; Battle Hymn; The Lonesome Train; The Town Crier. Ballet: Bouquet for Molly.

Songs inc: Joe Hill; Abe Lincoln; The House I Live In *(Special Oscar*-1945); Free and Equal Blues; Molly O'.

ROBINSON, Jay: Act. b. 1930. Films inc: The Robe; Demetrius and the Gladiator; The Virgin Queen; My Man Godfrey; Bunny O'Hare; Shampoo; Nightmare Honeymoon; Born Again; The Man With Bogart's Face.

ROBINSON, Madeleine (nee Svoboda): Act. b. France, 1916. Films inc: Soldiers Without Uniforms; Douce;Une Si Jolie Petite Plage; Dieu a Besoin des Hommes; Le Garcon Sauvage; The She Wolves; A Double Tour; The Trial; A Trap For Cinderella; A New World; Le Petit Matin; A Simple Story; Body to Heart.

ROBINSON, Roger: Act. b. Seattle, WA, May 2, 1940. Films inc: Believe In Me; Willie Dynamite; Newman's Law; Silver Bears; It's My Turn.

Bway inc: Does a Tiger Wear a Necktie? TV inc: Only the Pretty Girls Die.

ROBINSON, Smokey: Singer-Comp. b. Detroit, MI, Feb 19, 1940. Formed Smokey Robinson and the Miracles 1957; co-founder Tamla Records 1959.

Recordings inc: (with Miracles) Sweet Harmony; Virgin Man; Agony and the Ecstasy; Quiet Storm; Open; There Will Come A Day. (Solo) Smokey; Smokey's Family Robinson; Deep In My Soul.

ROBSON, Flora, Dame: Act. b. South Shields, Eng, Mar 28, 1902. e. RADA. On screen from 1931. Films inc: Dance Pretty Lady; Catherine the Great; Fire Over England; Wuthering Heights; We Are Not Alone; The Sea Hawk; Saratoga Trunk; Bahama Passage; Caesar and Cleopatra; Black Narcissus; 55 Days in Peking; Those Magnificent Men in Their Flying Machines; Fragment of Fear; The Beast in the Cellar; The Beloved.

Thea inc: Black Chiffon; The Importance of Being Ernest; Ring Around the Moon.

TV inc: The Corn is Green; A Message for Margaret; The Untouchables; David Copperfield; Heidi; A Man Called Intrepid; Les Miserables; Gauguin the Savage; A Tale of Two Cities.

ROCCO, Alex: Act. b. Cambridge, MA, Feb 29, 1936. Films inc: The Godfather; Slither; Freebie and the Bean; Three the Hard Way; Rafferty and the Gold Dust Twins; Voices; The Stuntman; House Calls; Rabbit Test; Herbie Goes Bananas.

TV inc: Three for the Road.

ROCHE, Eugene: Act. b. Boston. e. Emerson Coll. Films inc: The Happening; Cotton Comes to Harlem; Slaughterhouse Five; Newman's Law; Mr. Ricco; The Late Show; Corvette Summer; Foul Play; Voices.

TV inc: The Murderers; Winter Kill; Crawl Space; People Like Us; Crime Club; Possessed; Ghost of Flight 401; You Can't Take It With You; Soap; Corner Bar; Love for Rent; Good Time Harry; Rape and Marriage--The Rideout Case.

Bway inc: Blood Sweat and Stanley Poole; Great Day in the Morning; Time for the Barracudas; All In Good Time; In the White House; Mother Courage; The Price.

ROCHEFORT, Jean: Act. b. Paris, 1930. Films inc: Une balle dans le canon; 20,000 lieues sur la terre; Cartouche; The Man in the Iron Mask; Symphony for a Massacre; Les Pieds nickeles; Angelique, Mariquise of the Angels; Up to his Ears; Angelique et le Roy;The Devil by the Tail; Le temps de mourir; Celeste; The Tall Blond Man with One Black Shoe; The Inheritor; Bel Ordure; The Clockmaker; The Phantom of Liberty; Let Joy Reign Supreme; Dirty Hands; Till Marriage Do Us Part; Les Magiciens; Pardon Mon Affaire; Femmes Fatales; We Will All Meet in Paradise; Who is Killing the Great Chefs of Europe?; French Postcards; Les Gradissou; Courage Fuyons; Chere Inconnu.

ROCHIN, Aaron: Sound. b. LA, Jun 25, 1935. Films inc: The Dirty Dozen; Point Blank; Candy; Alfred the Great; Castle Keep; Shaft; Soylent Green; That's Entertainment, Part I; That's Entertainment, Part II; The Wind and the Lion; King Kong; Telefon; Audrey Rose; Coma; Corvette Summer; Voices; The Champ; Grease; The Deer Hunter (Oscar-1978); The Villain.

RODDENBERRY, Gene: Wri-Prod. b. El Paso, TX, Aug 19, 1921. Former airline pilot and LAPD sergeant.

TV inc: Star Trek (crea-prod); Questor; The Lieutenant; Genesis 2.

Films inc: Pretty Maids All In A Row (wri-prod); Star Trek--The Motion Picture.

RODGERS, James Charles (Jimmy): Act. b. Camas, WA, 1933. Recording artist. Films inc: The Little Shepherd From Kingdom Come; Back Door to Hell.

RODGERS, Richard: Comp. b. NYC, Jun 28, 1902. e. Columbia U, Juilliard School of Music. Collaborated with the late Lorenz Hart; later with late Oscar Hammerstein II, for both stage, screen. First published song, Auto Show Girl, was written at age 15. From 1919 until Hart's death in 1943, collaborated on 28 stage musicals, one night club review, eight film musicals, one non-musical play. From 1943 until Hammerstein's death in 1960 wrote nine stage musicals, one film musical, one TV musical. In addition they produced six plays and one musical that they did not write. Film versions have been made of 13 stage musicals Rodgers wrote with Hart and six that he wrote with Hammerstein. Plays inc: (with Hart) Poor Little Ritz Girl; The Garrick Gaieties; Dearest Enemy; A Connecticut Yankee; Present Arms; Heads Up!; Jumbo; On Your Toes; Babes in Arms; I'd Rather Be Right; I Married an Angel; The Boys from Syracuse; Higher and Higher; Pal Joey; By Jupiter.

Plays with Hammerstein inc: Oklahoma! (Pulitzer Prize-1943); Carousel; Allegro; South Pacific (also prod w. Leland Hayward & Joshua Logan) (Pulitzer Prize-1950) The King and I (Tony-1951); Me and Juliet; Pipe Dream; Flower Drum Song; The Sound of Music (Tony-1959), the last musical by the pair. 1960, Rodgers wrote both words and music for No Strings, a Broadway Musical (Tony-1962); in 1962 lyricist Stephen Sondheim and librettist Arthur Laurents joined Rodgers to write Do I Hear a Waltz?; Rodgers served as own lyricist again in 1967 when he created score for TV adaptation Bernard Shaw's Androcles and the Lion. In 1970 he teamed with librettist Peter Stone and lyricist Martin Charnin for the Broadway Two By Two, starring Danny Kaye. His last musical was Rex, 1976. Rodgers and Hammerstein prodns of works by other writers inc: I Remember Mama; Annie Get Your Gun; Happy Birthday; John Loves Mary; The Happy Time; a touring version of Show Boat, which Hammerstein had written with Jerome Kern.

Films inc: Love Me Tonight; Hallelujah, I'm a Bum; Mississippi; State Fair (Oscar-1945-for song It Might as Well Be Spring).

TV inc: (score) Victory at Sea (Emmy-1952); Winston Churchill-The Valiant Years (Emmy-1960); Cinderella. (Special Tony-1962). Lawrence Langner Award 1979.

(Died Dec 30, 1979).

RODRIGUES, Percy: Act. b. Canada, 1924. Films inc: The Sweet Ride; The Plainsman; The Heart is a Lonely Hunter; Come Back Charleston Blue; Hugo the Hippo (voice).

TV inc: Peyton Place; Sanford and Son; Silent Force; Executive Suite; Genesis II; The Lives of Jenny Dolan; Last Survivor; The Night Rider.

Bway inc: Blues for Mr. Charlie.

ROE, David: Exec. b. Perth, Australia, Dec 1949. Prodn, mktg consultant, New South Wales Film Corp; exec consultant, Australian Film Institute.

ROEG, Nicholas: Dir. b. London, 1928. Started as cin. Films inc: Far From the Madding Crowd; Fahrenheit 451; Judith; A Funny Thing Happened on the Way to the Forum; Petulia. (Dir) Walkabout; Don't Look Now; Performance; The Fan Club; The Man Who Fell to Earth; Bad Timing.

ROEMHELD, Heinz: Cond-Comp. b. Milwaukee, WI, May 1, 1901. e. WI Coll of Music. Film scores inc: Ruby Gentry; Valentino; The Moonlighter; Strawberry Blonde; Yankee Doodle Dandy (Oscar-1942).

ROGELL, Albert S: Dir. b. Oklahoma City, OK, Aug 21, 1901. e. WA State College. Began as cin, later title wri for silents; film edtr. Prod more than 2000 films.
Films inc: Mamba; Shepherd of the Hills; Riders of Death Valley; Argentine Nights; The Black Cat; Tight Shoes; In Old Oklahoma; Heaven Only Knows; Magnificent Rogue; Earl Carroll's Sketchbook; Northwest Stampede; The Admiral Was A Lady; Shadow of Fear.

ROGERS, Anne: Act. b. Liverpool, Eng, Jul 29, 1933. Theatre inc: My Fair Lady; Zenda; She Loves Me; Walking Happy; I Do! I Do!; A Shot in the Dark; No, No, Nanette; The Turning Point; Camelot.
TV inc: Birds on the Wing; Song of Songs.

ROGERS, Charles (Buddy): Act. b. Olathe, KS, Aug 13, 1904. H of late Mary Pickford. On screen from 1926 in Fascinating Youth. Films inc: Wings; My Best Girl; Abie's Irish Rose; Half Way to Heaven; Young Eagles; Best of Enemies; Sing for Your Supper; The Mexican Spitfire; An Innocent Affair; The Parson and the Outlaw.

ROGERS, Fred: Prod-Wri-TV pers. b. Latrobe, PA, Mar 20, 1928. e. Rollins Coll, B Mus; Pittsburgh Theological Seminary, M Div. Joined NBC-TV 1951 as asst prod The Voice of Firestone; NBC Television Opera Theatre; later supv Lucky Strike Hit Parade; joined WQED, Pittsburgh, 1953 to set up pgm sched. TV inc: Children's Corner; Misterogers; Mister Rogers Neighborhood; Mister Rogers Goes to School *(Emmy-*1980); Old Friends. . .New Friends.

ROGERS, Ginger (Virginia Katherine McMath): Act. b. Independence, MO, Jul 10, 1911. On screen from 1930. Films inc: Young Man of Manhattan; Flying Down to Rio; 42nd Street; Gold Diggers of 1933; Roberta; Top Hat; Shall We Dance; Bachelor Mother; The Story of Vernon and Irene Castle; Kitty Foyle *(Oscar-*1940); Roxie Hart; The Barkleys of Broadway; Monkey Business; Let's Get Married.
Bway inc: Oh Men! Oh Women!; Hello, Dolly; Coco; Auntie Mame.

ROGERS, Kenny: Singer-Songwri. b. Crockett, TX, Aug 21, 1938. C & W singer. TV inc: Kenny Rogers and the American Cowboy; A Christmas Special With Love from Mac Davis; Lynda Carter's Special; Kenny Rogers as the Gambler.
Albums inc: Ten Years of Gold; The Gambler; Kenny; Gideon; Greatest Hits.
*(Grammys-*Country Vocal-1977, 1980).

ROGERS, Roy (Leonard Slye): Act. b. Cincinnati, OH, Nov 5, 1912. Started as radio singer. On screen from 1935. Films inc: The Old Corral; Under Western Stars; Frontier Pony Express; Robin Hood of the Pecos; Silver Spurs; My Pal Trigger; Heart of the Rockies; Son of Paleface; Mackintosh and T.J.
TV inc: Numerous shows with wife, Dale Evans.

ROGERS, Wayne: Act. b. Birmingham, AL, Apr 7, 1933. e. Princeton U, BA. Films inc: Odds Against Tomorrow; The Glory Guys; Chamber of Horrors; Cool Hand Luke; Astro Zombies; WUSA; Pocket Money; Once in Paris.
TV inc: Edge of Night; Stagecoach West; M*A*S*H; City of Angels; Attack on Terror; Mitzi Zings Into Spring; It Happened One Christmas; Making Babies II; House Calls; The Top of the Hill.

ROGERS, Will Jr: Act. b. NYC, Oct 20, 1912. e. Stanford U. On screen from 1949 in Look for the Silver Lining. Films inc: The Story of Will Rogers; The Eddie Cantor Story; The Boy from Oklahoma; Wild Heritage. Toured West with solo stage show: My Father's Humor.

ROGOSIN, Joel: Prod-Wri. b. Boston, Oct 30, 1932. e. Stanford U, AB. TV inc: Hawaiian Eye; Surfside 6; 77 Sunset Strip; The Bold Ones; Destry; Ironside; The Virginian; Longstreet; Ghost Story; Circle of Fear; Jerry Lewis Labor Day Telethon (1972-73); The Blue Knight; The Gift; The Gathering, Part II.

ROHMER, Eric (Jean Maurice Scherer): Dir-Wri. b. France, 1920. Films inc: Le Signe du Lion; La Collectioneuse; My Night at Maude's; Claire's Knee; Chloe in the Afternoon; The Marquise of O. . .; Perceval.
TV inc: Don Quixote; Edgar Poe; Pascal; Louis Lumiere.

ROKER, Rennie: Act. b. NYC, Sep 6. e. Inter-American U, Puerto Rico. Worked as record promoter, later exec with Liberty Records, UA Records while acting in little theatres. Films inc: Skidoo; Brothers.
TV inc: Gomer Pyle, USMC; My Friend Tony; Nobody's Perfect.

ROKER, Roxie: Act. b. Miami, FL, Aug 28, 1929. e. Howard U, BA; postgrad work at Skakespeare Institute, Englad on Hattie M. Strong Fellowship. Bway inc: Rosalee Pritchet; The River Niger.
TV inc: Roots; Billy--Portrait of a Street Kid; The Jeffersons.

ROLAND, Gilbert (Luis Antonio Damasco De Alonso): Act. b. Juarez, Mexico, Dec 11, 1905. On screen from the 20s. Films inc: Camille; The Last Train from Madrid; The Sea Hawk; Captain Kidd; The Bullfighter and the Lady; My Six Convicts; The Big Circus; Run Wild; Islands in the Stream.

ROLAND, Rita: Film edtr. Films inc: A Patch of Blue; Justine; To Find A Man; Where Were You When the Lights Went Out?; Penelope; The Betsy.
TV inc: The Lindbergh Kidnaping Case; Sybil; Eleanor and Franklin *(Emmy-*1977).

ROLLE, Esther: Act. b. Pompano Beach, FL, Nov 8. Films inc: Cleopatra Jones; I Know Why the Caged Bird Sings. One of the original members of the Negro Ensemble Co.
Bway inc: The Amen Corner; Blues for Mister Charlie; Don't Play Us Cheap; Macbeth; Horowitz and Mrs. Washington.
TV inc: One Life to Live; Maude; Good Times; Summer of My German Soldier *(Emmy-*supp-1979).

THE ROLLING STONES: Group. Originally formed 1962. Members are Mick Jagger; Keith Richards, Ron Wood, Bill Wyman, Charlie Watts. Films inc: Gimme Shelter; No Nukes.
Albums inc: Rolling Stones I; Rolling Stones II; Rolling Stones Now; Out Of Our Heads; Aftermath; Between the Buttons; Their Satanic Majesties Request; Beggar's Banquet; Let It Bleed; Sticky Fingers; Exile on Main Street; Black and Blue; Some Girls; Emotional Rescue.

ROMAIN, Yvonne: Act. b. France, 1938. Films inc: The Baby and the Battleship; Seven Thunders; Corridors of Blood; Chamber of Horrors; Curse of the Werewolf; Devil Doll; The Swinger; Double Trouble; The Last of Sheila.

ROMAN, Joseph: Act. b. S Philadelphia, May 23. Films inc: St. Ives; The White Buffalo; Love and Bullets.
TV inc: Quincy.
Bway inc: Mr. Roberts; Twilight Walk; Child of the Morning.

ROMAN, Ruth: Act. b. Boston, MA, Dec 23, 1923. On screen from 1943 in Stage Door Canteen. Films inc: Champion; The Window; Beyond the Forest; Three Secrets; Dallas; Strangers on a Train; Mara Maru; The Far Country; Bottom of the Bottle; Bitter Victory; Love Has Many Faces; A Knife for the Ladies; Want a Ride, Little Girl?
TV inc: Medical Center; Cannon; Marcus Welby; The Long Hot Summer; Go Ask Alice; Willow B--Women In Prison.

ROMERO, Cesar: Act. b. NYC, Feb 15, 1907. On screen from 1934. More than 100 films inc: Metropolitan; Wee Willie Winkie; Cisco Kid (series); The Gay Caballero; The Thin Man; Clive of India; The Devil Is a Woman; Diamond Jim; Weekend in Havana; Tales of Manhattan; The Captain from Castile; Vera Cruz; Villa; Ocean's 11; Donovan's Reef; Marriage on the Rocks; Batman; The Spectre of Edgar Allen Poe; Crooks and Coronets; The Midas Run; The Strongest Man in the World; Carioca Tiger; Target-Harry.

RONET, Maurice: Act. b. France, Apr 13, 1927. Films inc: Rendezvous de Juillet; He Who Must Die; Lift to the Scaffold; Carve Her Name with Pride; Plein Soleil; La Ronde; Three Weeks in Manhattan; Lost Command; La Scandale; The Road to Corinth; How Sweet It Is; The Marseilles Contract; Sidney Sheldon's Bloodline.

RONSTADT, Linda: Singer. b. Tucson, AZ, Jul 15, 1946. Recording artist. Toured niteries, colleges with own band. Recordings inc: I Can't Help It If I'm Still In Love With You (Grammy-country voc-1975); Hasten Down The Wind (Grammy-pop vocal-1976); Greatest Hits; Simple Dreams; Living In the U.S.A.; Mad Love.

TV inc: The Unbroken Circle--A Tribute to Mother Maybelle Carter; The Women's Room (song).

ROONEY, Andy (Andrew Aitken Rooney): Wri-Dir-Act. b. Albany, NY, Jan 14, 1920. e. Colgate U. Began as wri for Arthur Godfrey; Garry Moore; Sam Levenson; Victor Borge; Perry Como; Harry Reasoner. Later prod-dir-perf in doc essays inc: Black History-Lost, Strayed or Stolen (Emmy-wri-1969); An Essay on War; An Essay on Churches; In Praise of New York City--The Colleges; Mr Rooney Goes to Washington; The Great American Dream Machine; Mr. Rooney Goes To Dinner; Mr. Rooney Goes To Work; 60 Minutes.

ROONEY, Mickey (Joe Yule): Act. b. NYC, Sep 23, 1920. In vaudeville during infancy with parents. From age 5 to 12 created screen version of newspaper comic character Mickey McGuire in series of shorts; took name of Mickey Rooney, returned to vaudeville; resumed screen career 1934. (Special Oscar-1938) "for setting a high standard of ability and achievement" as a juvenile actor. Films inc: Fast Companions; My Pal, the King; Chained; The Devil Is a Sissy; A Family Affair (and 15 other Andy Hardy films); Boys Town; Stablemates; Babes in Arms; Young Tom Edison; A Yank at Eton; Girl Crazy; The Human Comedy; National Velvet; Killer McCoy; Summer Holiday; Quicksand; Off Limits; Drive a Crooked Road; The Bridges of Toko-Ri; The Bold and the Brave; The Last Mile; King of the Roaring 20's; Breakfast at Tiffany's; It's a Mad, Mad, Mad, Mad World; The Secret Invasion; The Extraordinary Seaman; The Comic; The Cockeyed Cowboys of Calico County; Skidoo; Pulp; Richard; B.J. Presents; That's Entertainmen; The Domino Principle; Pete's Dragon; The Magic of Lassie; The Black Stallion; Arabian Adventure.

TV inc: Playhouse 90; Pinocchio; The Dick Powell Theater; The Mickey Rooney Show; Name of the Game; Evil Roy Slade; Night Gallery; Donovan's Kid; Rudolph and Frosty's Christmas in July (voice); From Raquel With Love; My Kidnapper, My Love.

Bway inc: Sugar Babies.

ROONEY, Pat: Prod-Wri. b. NE. e. Marquette U, UCLA. Started in vaudeville, niteries. Formed Pat Rooney Prodns, 1962. Films inc: Dime With a Halo; Danger Pass; Caged; Law of the Lawless; Requiem for a Gunfighter; Bounty Killer; Young Once; Fools; Christmas Couple; Black Eye; Deadmans Curve.

ROOS, Fred: Prod. b. Santa Monica, CA, May 23, 1934. e. UCLA, BA. Started as a casting dir. Films inc: The Conversation; The Godfather Part 2 (Oscar-1974); Apocalypse Now; The Black Stallion.

ROOT, Wells: Wri. b. Buffalo, NY, Mar 21, 1900. e. Yale, BA. Films inc: I Cover the Waterfront; Tiger Shark; The Prisoner of Zenda; The Magnificent Obsession; Texas Across the River. TV inc: Ford Theatre;

TV inc Ford Theatre; G.E. Theatre; Fireside Theatre; Cheyenne; Four Star Theatre; The Rogues; Maverick.

Author: Writing the Script.

RORKE, Hayden: Act. b. NYC, Oct 24, 1910. e. Villanova Coll, AADA. Toured with Walter Hampden Repertory: Cyrano; Hamlet; Macbeth; Richelieu. Films inc: Pillow Talk; Spencer's Mountain; The Law and the Lady; An American in Paris; Midnight Lace; The Nightwalker.

TV inc: I Love Lucy; The Jack Benny Show; Dr. Kildare; Cannon; The Legend of Lizzie Borden; The Money Changers; etc.

Bway inc: Three Men on a Horse; The Philadelphia Story; Personal Appearance; The Iceman Cometh; Dream Girl.

ROSE, Alex (Alexandra): Prod. b. 1946. e. U of WI, BS. In dist, 1970 with Medford Films; asst sls mgr New World Pictures; teamed with Tamara Assayev to prod Drive-In; I Wanna Hold Your Hand; Big Wednesday; Norma Rae.

ROSE, David: Comp-Cond. b. London, Jun 24, 1910. e. Chicago College of Music. To US 1914. Pianist in dance orchs inc: Ted Fiorito; formed 1st orch. 1936; staff arr radio; 1938, music dir Mutual Network, Hollywood. While in USAAR, WW II, comp & dir music for Winged Victory. Music Dir MGM.

Films inc: The Princess and the Pirate; Rich, Young and Pretty; The Clown; Operation Petticoat; Please Don't Eat the Daisies; Jupiter's Darling; Port Afrique.

TV inc: Red Skelton Show; An Evening with Fred Astaire (Emmy-1959); Bonanza (Emmy-1971); Suddenly Love; Little House on the Prairie (Emmy-1979).

Songs inc: Holiday for Strings; Our Waltz; Manhattan Square Dance; Never Too Late.

ROSE, George: Act. b. Bicester, England, Feb 19, 1920. With Old Vic Company 1944-1948. Thea inc: (London) The Government Inspector; People Like Us; A Penny for a Song; The Square Ring; The Apple Cart; My Three Angels; The Chalk Garden; Living for Pleasure; The Visit; A Man for All Seasons. (Bway) The Government Inspector; Much Ado About Nothing; A Man For All Seasons; Hamlet; Slow Dance on the Killing Ground; Royal Hunt of the Sun; Walking Happy; Loot; Coco; Wise Child; Sleuth; My Fat Friend; My Fair Lady (rev) (Tony-1976).

Films inc: Pickwick Papers; Grand National Night; The Sea Shall Not Have Them; The Night My Number Came Up; Brothers In Law; A Night To Remember; Jack the Ripper; The Flesh and the Fiends; Hawaii; A New Leaf; No Love for Johnnie; From the Mixed-Up Files of Mrs. Basil E Frankweiler.

ROSE, Jack: Prod. b. Chicago, Jul 4, 1939. Films inc: Moonshine; Forever My Love; Sniper; Starhops; Other Roads; The Warrior.

ROSE, Jack: Wri. b. Warsaw, Poland, Nov 4, 1911. e. OH U, BA. Films inc: (mostly in collab with Mel Shavelson) Ladies Man; Sorrowful Jones; The Great Lover; Pale Face; The Road to Rio; Daughter of Rosie O'Grady; Always Leave Them Laughing; On Moonlight Bay; I'll See You in My Dreams; April in Paris; The Seven Little Foys; Houseboat; The Five Pennies; Beau James; It Started in Naples; Double Trouble; Papa's Delicate Condition; Who's Got the Action; Who's Been Sleeping in My Bed?; A Touch of Class; The Duchess and the Dirtwater Fox; Lost and Found.

ROSE, Peter N C H: Mktg Exec. b. Rawalpindi, India, Aug 1, 1947. Merchandising m, Hoyts Theatres Ltd; mktg m, South Australian Film Corp.

ROSE, Philip (nee Rosenberg): Prod. b. NYC, Jul 4, 1921. Bway inc: A Raisin in the Sun; Semi-Detached; Purlie Victorious; Bravo, Giovanni; Nobody Loves an Albatross; Cafe Crown; The Owl and the Pussycat; Nathan Weinstein; Mystic, Connecticut; The Ninety-Day Mistress; Does a Tiger Wear a Necktie?; Purlie; Shenandoah (Tony-co-author-1975); Angel; Comin' Uptown (& book).

ROSE, Reginald: Wri-Prod. b. NYC, Dec 10, 1920. Films inc: Crime in the Streets; The Man in the Net; Man of the West; Twelve Angry Men; Baxter; Somebody Killed Her Husband; The Wild Geese; The Sea Wolves.

TV inc: The Remarkable Incident at Carson Corners; Thunder on Sycamore Street; A Quiet Game of Cards; The Cruel Day; The Sacco-Vanzetti Story; Twelve Angry Men (Emmy-1954); The Defenders (2 Emmys-1962 & 1963); Tragedy in a Temporary Town; Black Monday; Dear Friends; Studs Lonigan.

ROSE, William: Wri. b. Jefferson City, MO, 1918. Films inc: Once a Jolly Swagman; The Gift Horse; Genevieve; The Maggie; The Lady Killers; The Smallest Show on Earth; It's a Mad, Mad, Mad, Mad World; The Russians Are Coming; The Flim Flam Man; Guess Who's Coming to Dinner (Oscar-1967); The Secret of Santa Vittoria.

ROSE MARIE (nee Mazzetta): b. NYC, Aug 15. Child actress as Baby Rose Marie. Films Inc: Cheaper To Keep Her.

TV inc: Dick Van Dyke Show; Robert Cummings Show; Doris Day Show; regular on Hollywood Squares.

Bway inc: Top Banana.

ROSEMONT, Norman: Prod. b. NYC, Dec 12, 1924. TV inc: Brigadoon; Carousel; Kiss Me Kate; Kismet; Stiletto; The Man Without a Country; Miracle on 34th Street; A Tree Grows in Brooklyn; The Red Badge of Courage; The Count of Monte Cristo; The Man in the Iron Mask; The Mad Mad Mad Mad World of the Super Bowl; Captains Courageous; The Court Martial of George Armstrong Custer; The Four Feathers; Les Miserables; All Quiet on the Western Front; Pleasure Palace; Little Lord Fauntleroy; A Tale of Two Cities.

ROSEN, Arnie: Wri-Prod. b. 1922. TV inc: Phil Silvers Show (*Emmys*-wri-1955, 1956, 1957); Carol Burnett Show (*Emmys*-wri-prod-1972); Garry Moore Show; Get Smart; CPO Sharkey.
(Died Jan 30, 1980).

ROSEN, Robert Lewis: Prod. b. NYC, Oct 7, 1935. e. Lehigh U, BSC. TV inc: Puff The Magic Dragon; The Little Rascals Christmas Special; Seiko World Tennis Tournament; The World of Strawberry Shortcake; Puff The Magic Dragon in the Land of Living Lies; NCAA Japan Bowl; Thanksgiving in the Land of Oz.

ROSENBERG, Aaron: Prod. b. NYC, Aug 26, 1912. e. USC, 1934 (All-American, football). Asst dir under Sol Wurtzel, Fox, 1934-42. Joined UI after war. First production 1949, Johnny Stool Pigeon. Films inc: Outside the Wall; The Story of Molly X; Air Cadet; Cattle Drive; Iron Man; Here Come the Nelsons; Winchester '73; Bend of the River; Gunsmoke; Thunder Bay; All-American; Wings of the Hawk; The Glenn Miller Story; Six Bridges to Cross; Man Without a Star; The Benny Goodman Story; To Hell and Back; Backlash; The World in My Corner; Walk the Proud Land; The Great Land; Night Passage; It Started with a Kiss; Fate is the Hunter; The Saboteur; The Badlanders; Move Over Darling; Do Not Disturb; Caprice; Mutiny on the Bounty; The Reward; Tony Rome; The Lady in Cement; The Detective; The Boy Who Cried Werewolf.
TV inc: (exec prod) Daniel Boone; Virginia Hill; Reflections of Murder.
(Died Sep 1, 1979).

ROSENBERG, Frank P: Prod-Wri. b. NYC, Nov 22, 1913. Joined Columbia Pictures, NY, as office boy, 1929. Promoted to publicist, became national dir adv, publicity, exploitation, 1944. Resigned 1947 to enter prodn. Films inc: Man Eater of Kumaon; Where the Sidewalk Ends; Secret of Convict Lake; Return of the Texan; The Farmer Takes a Wife; King of the Khyber Rifles; Miracle in the Rain; The Girl He Left Behind; One-Eyed Jacks; Critic's Choice; Madigan; The Steagle; The Reincarnation of Peter Proud; Gray Lady Down (adapt only).
TV inc: Exec prod and prod for Schultz Playhouse programs during 1957-58; exec prod Arrest and Trial, 1963-64; exec prod Kraft Suspense Theatre, 1964-65.

ROSENBERG, Mark: Exec. b. 1948. e. U WI. Ed University Review; ad exec, Seiniger & Associates; agent with ICM, Adams, Ray & Rosenberg; joined WB 1975 as vp prodn; 1980 sr vp prodn.

ROSENBERG, Meta: Prod-Former Agent. TV inc: The Rockford Files (*Emmy*-exec prod-1978).

ROSENBERG, Rick: Prod. b. LA. e. UCLA. Asst film edtr, later asst to prod Jerry Bresler. Films inc: The Reivers (asso prod); Adam At 6 A.M.; Hide in Plain Sight. TV inc: Suddenly Single; The Glass House; A Brand New Life; The Autobiography of Miss Jane Pittman (*Emmy*-1974); I Love You...Goodbye; Queen of the Starlight Ballroom; A Death in Canaan; Strangers--The Story of a Mother and Daughter.

ROSENBERG, Stuart: Dir-Prod. b. NYC, 1928. e. NYU. Films inc: Murder Inc; Question 7; Cool Hand Luke; April Fools; Move; W U S A; Pocket Money; The Laughing Policeman; The Drowning Pool; Voyage of the Damned; The Amityville Horror; Love and Bullets; Brubaker.
TV inc: The Untouchables; Naked City; The Defenders (*Emmy*-dir-1953); Espionage; Run for Your Life.

ROSENFELT, Frank E: Exec. b. Peabody, MA, Nov 15, 1921. e. Cornell U, BS, LLB. Served as atty for RKO before joining MGM in 1955. Named VP, gen. counsel 1969; pres. in 1973. Also CEO, 1974.

ROSENFIELD, Jonas Jr: Exec. b. Dallas, TX, Jun 29, 1915. e. U of Miami, BA. VP, worldwide adv., publicity & promo Italian Films Export, 1950-55; same post at Columbia Pictures, 1960-63; same with 20th Century-Fox, 1963-77. Formed own marketing consultant company, 1977; Sr vp worldwide mktg Melvin Simon Prodns 1978.

ROSENMAN, Howard: Prod. b. Brooklyn, NY. Worked as asst to Sir Michael Benthall on Bway prodns; became prod Benton & Bowles agcy; with ABC TV; RSO Prodns before becoming indie prod. TV inc: Virginia Hill; The Bees.
Films inc: The Main Event; Resurrection.

ROSENMAN, Leonard: Comp. b. NYC, Sep 7, 1924. Film scores inc: East of Eden; Cobweb; Rebel Without a Cause; Edge of the City; The Savage Eye; The Chapman Report; Fantastic Voyage; Hellfighters; Beneath the Planet of the Apes; Barry Lyndon (*Oscar*-1975); The Car; September 30, 1955; Promises In the Dark; Prophecy; Hide in Plain Sight; The Jazz Singer.
TV inc: Sybil (*Emmy*-1977); Friendly Fire (*Emmy*-1979); City in Fear.

ROSHKIND, Michael: Exec. b. NYC, Oct 4, 1921. e. Northwestern U, BS. Joined NBC 1941 as news ed; 1942 dir news & spec events ABC; 1948, exec vp Weintraub Adv agcy; 1950, exec vp AA Schechter Public Relations; 1960, partner Strauss Public Relations; 1966, vp & COO Motown.

ROSS, Diana: Singer-Act. b. Detroit, MI, Mar 26, 1944. Member of Supremes as teenager. Over period of 10 years the trio had 15 consecutive hit records. Went solo in 1969, appearing in niteries, TV. Screen debut 1973, Lady Sings the Blues. Films inc: Mahogany; The Wiz. (*Special Tony*-1977).

ROSS, Frank: Prod. b. Boston, Aug 12, 1904. e. Exeter, Princeton. Films inc: Of Mice and Men; The Devil and Miss Jones; The More the Merrier (sp only); The Robe; The Rains of Ranchipur; Kings Go Forth; Mister Moses; Where It's At.

ROSS, Herbert: Dir. b. NYC, May 13, 1927. H of Nora Kaye. Bway inc: (chor) On a Clear Day You Can See Forever; A Tree Grows in Brooklyn; House of Flowers; I Can Get It For You Wholesale; Anyone Can Whistle. (Dir): Chapter Two; I Ought To Be In Pictures. Later became resident choreographer for American Ballet Theatre, staging Caprichos; The Maids. Film debut as choreographer/musical sequence dir. Inside Daisy Clover, 1966. Also Dr. Dolittle; Funny Girl. Films Dir: Goodbye Mr. Chips; The Owl and the Pussycat; T.R. Baskin; Play It Again, Sam; The Last of Shelia; Funny Lady; The Sunshine Boys; The Seven Per Cent Solution; The Turning Point; The Goodbye Girl; California Suite; Nijinsky.
TV inc: The Bell Telephone Hour; Fred Astaire Special.

ROSS, Katharine: Act. b. LA, Jan 29, 1943. Screen debut, 1965, Shenandoah. Films inc: Mister Buddwing; The Singing Nun; Games; The Graduate; The Ski Bums; A Nice Girl Like Me; Bullitt; Hellfighters; Butch Cassidy and the Sundance Kid; Tell Them Willie Boy Is Here; Fools; They Only Kill Their Masters; The Stepford Wives; Voyage of the Damned; The Betsy; The Swarm; The Legacy; The Final Countdown.
TV inc: Sam Benedict; Doctors at Work; The Longest Hundred Miles; Ben Casey; The Bob Hope-Chrysler Theatre; The Virginian; Wagon Train; The Road West; Rodeo Girl.

ROSS, Marion: Act. b. Albert Lea, MN, Oct 25, 1928. e. San Diego State Coll. Films inc: Forever Female; The Glenn Miller Story; Sabrina; The Proud and the Profane; Operation Petticoat; Teacher's Pet; Lust for Life; Colossus: The Forbin Project; Airport; Honkey; Grand Theft Auto.
TV inc: Life with Father; Paradise Bay; Happy Days; Pear; Skyward.
Bway inc: Edwin Booth.

ROSSON, Hal: Cin. b. 1895. Started in silent films. Films inc: Manhandled; Gentlemen Prefer Blondes; Tarzan of the Apes; The Scarlet Pimpernel; The Ghost Goes West; The Garden of Allah (*Honorary Oscar*-1936); The Wizard of Oz; Johnny Eager; The Hucksters; On the Town; The Red Badge of Courage; Singin' in the Rain; The Bad Seed; No Time for Sergeants; El Dorado.

ROSTEN, Irwin: Wri-Prod. b. NYC, Sep 10, 1924. Started as newsman with Dumont Network; 1954 wri-prod news, pub aff KNXT, LA; 1960 news dir KTLA; 1963 wri-prod Wolper Prodns; 1967-1972 chief of doc dept MGM; then indie.

TV inc: Grizzly!; The Incredible Machine; The Volga; The Legacy of LSB Leakey; Gold!; Mysteries of the Mind; Trial by Wilderness; Hollywood--The Dream Factory; Kifaru--The Black Rhinocerous.

ROTA, Nino: Comp. b. Italy, 1911. Film scores inc: My Son the Professor; Flight into France; The Glass Mountain; War and Peace; La Dolce Vita; Plein Soleil; Boccaccio; Eight and a Half; Juliet of the Spirits; The Abdication; The Godfather Part II *(Oscar-*1974*)*; Death on the Nile; Hurricane.

(Died Apr 10, 1979).

ROTH, Ann: Cos dsgn. Bway inc: Maybe Tuesday; Make a Million; The Cool World; Face of a Hero; Purlie Victorious; This Side of Paradise; A Portrait of the Artist as a Young Man; Children From Their Games; A Case of Libel; In the Summer House; Slow Dance On a Killing Ground; I Had a Ball; The Odd Couple; Star Spangled Girl; The Deer Park; Play It Again Sam; Tiny Alice; Father's Day; Fun City; 6 Rms Riv Vu; Enemies; Seesaw; The Royal Family; The Crucifer of Blood; They're Playing Our Song; Lunch Hour.

Films inc: Up the Down Staircase; Pretty Poison; Midnight Cowboy; The Owl and the Pussycat; Klute; They Might Be Giants; The Pursuit of Happiness; Law and Disorder; The Valachi Papers; The Goodbye Girl; California Suite; Coming Home; Nunzio; Hair; Promises in the Dark; Nine to Five.

ROTH, Lillian: Act. b. Boston, Dec 13, 1910. Child star in vaudeville, nieteries. Films inc: The Vagabond King; The Love Parade; Honey; Sea Legs; Ladies They Talk About; Madame Satan; Animal Crackers; Alice, Sweet Alice; The Boardwalk.

Bway inc: Penrod; The Betrothal; Shavings; Vanities; Midnight Frolics; I Can Get It for You Wholesale.

TV inc: Outcast.

(Died May 12, 1980).

ROTH, Richard: Prod. b. Chicago, Sep 16, 1940. e. Stanford U Law School. Films inc: Summer of '42; Our Time; The Adventures of Sherlock Holmes' Smarter Brother; Julia.

ROTHMAN, Mo: Exec. b. Montreal, Jan 14, 1919. Worldwide rep for Edward Small, 1950; int'l sls dept UA, 1952; sls mgr, Continent, Near East, 1955; Cont'l mgr 1957; VP int'l ops, 1960; Exec VP Col Pict Int'l, 1960; VP world distrib 1966; distrib, Chaplin Pictures, 1971. Films inc: ffolkes (exec prod).

ROTHSCHILD, Eileen: Prod Coord. b. NYC, Mar 3, 1947. e. Brooklyn Coll. Bway inc: Jesus Christ Superstar. Films inc (Prod exec): Tommy; Survive.

ROTUNNO, Giuseppe: Cin. b. Italy. Films inc: Scandal in Sorrento; Anna of Brooklyn; White Nights; The Naked Maja; The Angel Wore Red; Rocco and His Brothers; The Best of Enemies; The Leopard; Yesterday, Today and Tomorrow; Anzio; The Secret of Santa Vittoria; Fellini's Satyricon; Sunflower; Carnal Knowledge; Man of La Mancha; Amarcord; Divine Creature; The End of the World In Our Usual Bed in a Night Full of Rain; Orchestra Rehearsal; All That Jazz; City of Women; Popeye.

ROUNDTREE, Richard: Act. b. New Rochelle, NY, Jul 9, 1937. e. Southern IL U. Films inc: Shaft; Shaft's Big Score; Shaft in Africa; Charley One-Eye; Earthquake; Man Friday; Diamonds; Escape to Athena.

TV inc: Shaft; Firehouse; Roots.

ROUSE, Russel: Dir-Wri. b. NYC, 1916. Films inc: D O A; The Well; The Thief; New York Confidential; The Fastest Gun Alive; Pillow Talk *(Oscar-*1959*)*; Thunder in the Sun; A House is Not a Home; The Oscar; Caper of the Golden Bull.

ROUTLEDGE, Patricia: Act. b. Birkenhead, Cheshire, Eng, Feb 17, 1929. e. U of Liverpool. Thea inc: (London) The Duenna; Zuleika; The Love Doctor; Follow That Girl; Little Mary Sunshine; How's the World Treating You?; Darling of the Day; The Country Wife; The Magistrate; First Impressions; And A Nightgale Sang. (Bway) Darling of the Day *(Tony-*1968*)*; 1600 Pennsylvania Ave; On Approval.

TV inc: Sense and Sensibility; Tartuffe; David Copperfield.

ROVINA, Hanna: Act. b. Russia, circa 1900. Studied with Stanlislavsky, helped found Habimah Theatre in Moscow 1918, presenting plays in Hebrew. Company toured Europe and US 1926-1928 then moved to Palestine (now Israel) where it was established as the National Theatre.

(Died Feb 2, 1980).

ROWAN, Dan: Act. b. Beggs, OK, 1922. Performed in niteries with Dick Martin. On TV in Rowan & Martin's Laugh-In, NBC, 1967-73 *(Emmys-*1968 & 1969*)*. Films inc: Once Upon a Horse; The Maltese Bippy.

ROWLANDS, Gena: Act. b. Cambria, WI, Jun 19, 1936. e. U of WI, AADA. W of John Cassavetes. Bdwy debut as understudy and then succeeded to role of the Girl in The Seven Year Itch. Screen debut, 1958, The High Cost of Living. Films inc: Lonely Are the Brave; The Spiral Road; A Child Is Waiting; Tony Rome; Faces; Minnie and Moskowitz; A Woman Under the Influence; Two Minute Warning; Gloria.

TV inc: The Philco Playhouse; Studio One; Alfred Hitchcock Presents; Dr. Kildare; Bonanza; The Kraft Mystery Theatre; Strangers--The Story of a Mother and Daughter.

Bway inc: The Middle of the Night.

ROYCE, Riza: Act-Wri. b. 1908. Twice married to late Josef von Sternberg. Film inc: The Blue Angel; A Star is Born; House of Wax; Wives and Lovers; Good Neighbor Sam; Myra Breckenridge; The Great White Hope.

Bway inc: The Searching Wind; O Mistress Mine; Pickup Girl; The Soldier's Wife.

TV inc: Jackie Gleason Show; Studio One; Kraft Theatre.

(Died Oct 20, 1980).

ROYER, Robb: Comp-Wri. b. LA, Dec 6, 1942. Songs for films inc: (w. Fred Karlin) Cover Me Babe; Lovers and Other Strangers *(Co-Oscar-*song*-*1970*)*; California Dreaming.

TV inc: Awakening Land; Roll of Thunder.

ROZSA, Miklos: Comp. b. Budapest, Apr 18, 1907. e. Leipsig Cons. Film scores inc: The Four Feathers; The Thief of Badgad; Lady Hamilton; Sundown; Lydia; Jungle Book; Five Graves to Cairo; Double Indemnity; The Lost Weekend; Spellbound *(Oscar-*1945*)*; The Killers; Brute Force; A Double Life *(Oscar-*1947*)*; Adam's Rib; The Asphalt Jungle; Quo Vadis; Ivanhoe; Julius Caesar; Lust for Life; Ben Hur *(Oscar-*1950*)*; King of Kings; El Cid; Sodom and Gomorrah; The VIPs; The Power; The Green Berets; Providence; Fedora; Last Embrace; Time After Time.

RUBAN, Al: Prod. b. NYC, Nov 4, 1934. Films inc: Faces; Husbands; Minnie and Moskowitz; Opening Night (& cin); The Big Fix (act).

RUBIN, Benny: Act. b. Boston, 1899. On screen from 1929. Films inc: Naughty Baby; Marianne; George White's Scandals of 1935; Here Comes Mr. Jordan; Yankee Pasha; Meet Me in Los Vegas; A Hole in the Head; A Pocketful of Miracles; The Patsy; That Funny Feeling; Thoroughly Modern Millie; Airport; Won Ton Ton, the Dog Who Saved Hollywood; Coma.

RUBIN, Mann: Wri. b. NYC, Dec 11, 1926. e. NYU. TV inc: Philco Playhouse; Studio One; Climax; Playhouse 90; Armstrong Circle Theatre; Mod Squad; The Rookies; Mannix; Barnaby Jones; Quincy; See the Man Run.

Films inc: The Best of Everything; Brainstorm; An American Dream; Warning Shot; Once You Kiss a Stranger; The First Deadly Sin.

RUBIN, Stanley: Wri-Prod. b. NYC, Oct 8, 1917. e. UCLA. Films inc: The Narrow Margin; My Pal Gus; Destination Gobi; River of No Return; Destry; Promise Her Anything; The President's Analyst; The Take.

TV inc: Channing; The Ghost and Mrs. Muir; Bracken's World; The Man and the City; Executive Suite; Babe; And Your Name Is Jonah.

RUBINSTEIN, Artur: Classical pianist. b. Lodz, Poland, 1887. Films inc: Follow the Boys; Carnegie Hall; Night Song; Of Men and Music.

TV inc: Artur Rubinstein (Emmy-1970).

(Grammys-(10)-classical performance 1959, 1963, 1965, 1977; chamber music-1959, 1974, 1975; instrumental solo-1972, 1976; classical album of the year-1976).

RUBINSTEIN, John: Act-Comp. b. Dec 8, 1946. S of Artur Rubinstein. Films inc: (act) Zachariah; Journey to Shiloh; Getting Straight; The Wild Pack; The Car; The Boys From Brazil; In Search of Historic Jesus. (Score) Paddy; The Candidate; Jeremiah Johnson; Kid Blue.

TV inc: A Howling in the Woods; All Together Now; God Bless the Children; Something Evil; Jack and the Princess; Family (& theme song); The Gift of the Magi; She's Dressed to Kill; Make Me An Offer; Amber Waves; Moviola (The Silent Lovers).

Bway inc: Pippin; On a Clear Day You Can See Forever; Metamorphoses; Children of a Lesser God (Tony-1980).

RUBY, Harry: Comp-lyr. b. NYC, Jan 27, 1895. Pianist, song plugger; also played vaudeville, cafes. Bway inc: Helen of Troy, New York; The Ramblers; Lucky; The Five O'Clock Girl; Animal Crackers; Top Speed.

Films inc: Check and Double Check; The Cuckoos; Horsefeathers; The Kid from Spain; Look for the Silver Lining; Bright Lights; Duck Soup.

Songs inc: Daddy Long Legs; A Kiss to Build A Dream On; Who's Sorry Now?; I Wanna Be Loved by You; Watching the Clouds Roll By; Three Little Words.

RUDD, Hughes: TV newsman. b. Wichita, KS, Sep 14, 1921. With Kansas City Star, Minneapolis Tribune before joining CBS 1959 as corr; 1965 chf Moscow Bureau; 1966, Bonn Bureau; 1974 anchorman Morning News; 1979 to ABC-TV as spec corr.

RUDDY, Albert: Prod. b. Montreal, Mar 28, 1934. e. USC, BS. Films inc: The Wild Seed; Little Fauss and Big Halsey; Making It; The Godfather (Oscar-1972); The Longest Yard; Coonskin; Matilda.

TV inc: The Macahans.

RUEHMANN, Heinz: Act. b. Germany, 1902. Films inc: Drei von der Tankstelle; Man Braucht Kein Geld; If We Were All Angels; Captain From Kopenick; It Happened in Broad Daylight; The Judge and the Sinner; Ship of Fools; The Chinese Miracle; Scrounged Meals; On A Silver Platter.

RUGOLO, Pete: Comp. b. Sicily, Dec 25, 1915. e. St Francis State College. To US 1919. Pianist; arranger for orchs. Films inc: The Strip; Skirts Ahoy; Glory Alley; Latin Lovers; Easy to Love; Jack the Ripper.

TV inc: Run for Your Life; The Fugitive; The Challengers (Emmy-1970); The Bold Ones (Emmy-1972); Alias Smith & Jones; The Virginian; Jig Saw John; Carter Country; Family; The Home Front.

RULE, Elton H: Exec. b. Stockton, CA, Jun 13, 1917. e. Sacramento Coll. VP and gen mgr, KABC-TV, LA, 1961-68; pres, ABC TV Network, 1968-70; pres ABC (broadcast division), 1970-72; member board of directors, ABC, Inc, since 1972; pres ABC, Inc, since 1972.

RULE, Janice: Act. b. Cincinnati, OH, Aug 15, 1931. Films inc: Starlift; Holiday for Sinners; Rogue's March; Woman's Devotion; Gun for a Coward; Subterraneans; Invitation to a Gunfighter; The Chase; Welcome to Hard Times; The Ambushers; Kid Blue; Three Women.

Bway inc: Picnic; The Flowering Peach; Princess in a Carefree Tree; Night Circus; Happiest Girl in the World.

RUSH, Barbara: Act. b. Denver, CO, Jan 4, 1930. On screen from 1951. Films inc: The First Legion; Molly; When Worlds Collide; It Came From Outer Space; Magnificent Obsession; Bigger than Life; Oh Men! Oh Women!; No Down Payment; The Young Philadelphians; Bramble Bush; Strangers When We Meet; Come Blow Your Horn; Robin and the 7 Hoods; Hombre; Airport; Superdad; Can't Stop the Music.

TV inc: Death Car on the Freeway; The Seekers; Flamingo Road.

RUSH, Herman: TV Exec. b. Philadelphia, Jun 20, 1929. e. Temple U. 1957-60 P Flamingo Telefilms Inc; 1960-71 P TV division of Creative Mgt Asso; 1971-77 P Herman Rush Asso Inc; 1977-78 chmn bd Rush-Flaherty Agency Inc; 1979 P Marble Arch TV; 1980 P Col TV.

TV inc: Touch of Grace; Love Thy Neighbor; DHO; Death Stalk; Celebration-The American Spirit.

RUSH, Richard: Prod-Dir-Wri. b. NYC. e. UCLA. Films inc: Too Soon to Love; Of Love and Desire (dir-sp); A Man Called Dagger (dir); The Fickle Finger of Fate (dir); Thunder Alley (dir); Hells's Angels on Wheels (dir); Psych-Out (dir-wri); Savage Seven (dir); Getting Straight (dir-prod); Freebie and the Bean (dir-prod); The Stunt Man (dir-prod).

RUSSEL, Del: Act. b. Pasadena, CA, Sep 27, 1952. Films inc: Tammy Tell Me True; Cleopatra. TV inc: Men into Space; Arnie.

RUSSELL, Harold: Act. b. MA, 1914. Handless ex-paratrooper. Acted in one film, The Best Years of Our Lives (Oscars-(2)-supp & honorary-1946).

RUSSELL, Jane: Act. b. Bemidji, MN, Jun 21, 1921. Films inc: The Outlaw; The Paleface; Son of Paleface; Maccao; Montana Belle; His Kind of Woman; The Las Vegas Story; Gentlemen Prefer Blondes; Underwater; Gentlemen Marry Brunettes; Foxfire; Hot Blood; The Tall Men; The Revolt of Mamie Stover; The Fuzzy Pink Nightgown; Waco; Darker than Amber.

RUSSELL, John: Act. b. LA, Jan 3, 1921. e. U of CA. Films inc: Frameup; Story of Molly X; Slattery's Hurricane; Yellow Sky; Sitting Pretty; Forever Amber; Bell for Adano; Barefoot Mailman; Hoodlum Empire; Fair Wind to Java; Jubilee Trail; Last Command; Rio Bravo; Yellowstone Kelly; Fort Utah; Outlaw Josie Wales. TV inc: Lawman; Soldiers of Fortune; Jason and the Star Command; How the West Was Fun.

RUSSELL, Ken: Dir. b. Southampton, Eng, 1927. Early career as dancer, actor, still photog, doc prod for BBC. Feature films inc: French Dressing; Billion Dollar Brain; Women in Love; The Music Lovers; The Devils; The Boy Friend; Mahler; Tommy; Lisztomania; Valentino; Altered States.

RUSSELL, Nipsey: Act. b. Atlanta, GA, Oct 13, 1925. Performs on TV, nightclubs, stage, summer stock appearance in The Odd Couple; Cabin in the Sky. Bway credits inc: Tambourines to Glory.

Films inc: The Wiz.

TV inc: Fame; Uptown-A Tribute to the Apollo Theatre; A Funny Thing Happened On the Way to the White House (cable tv).

RUSSELL, Theresa: Act. b. Burbank, CA. Films inc: The Last Tycoon; Straight Time; Bad Timing.

TV inc: Blind Ambition.

RUTHERFORD, Ann: Act. b. Toronto, 1920. On screen from 1935. Appeared in 17 Andy Hardy pictures. Other films inc: Gone With The Wind; Pride and Prejudice; Whistling in the Dark; Bermuda Mystery; Bedside Manner; Murder in the Music Hall; The Secret Life of Walter Mitty; Adventures of Don Juan; Operation Haylift; They Only Kill Their Masters.

RUTTENBERG, Joseph H: Cin. b. Russia, Jul 4, 1889. Films inc: Over the Hill; Fury; The Great Waltz (Oscar-1938); Broadway Melody; Waterloo Bridge; The Philadelphia Story; Comrade X; Dr. Jekyll and Mr. Hyde; Mrs. Miniver (Oscar-1942); Madame Curie; Adventure; Gaslight; BF's Daughter; The Forsythe Saga; The Great Caruso; Kind Lady; Prisoner of Zenda; Julius Caesar; The Last Time I Saw Paris; The Swan; Somebody Up There Likes Me (Oscar-1956); Until They Sail; Gigi (Oscar-1958); The Reluctant Debutante; Butterfield 8; Who's Been Sleeping in My Bed?; Sylvia; Harlow; Love Has Many Faces; The Oscar; Speedway. (Ret.)

RYAN, Mitchell: Act. b. Cincinnati, OH, Jan 11, 1934. Started on stage with Barter Theatre, Abingdon, VA; then off-Bway, Bway. Films inc: Monte Walsh; The Hunting Party; The Old Man's Place; High Plains Drifter; Magnum Force; Electroglide in Blue; Friends of Eddie Coyle; Labrynth.

TV inc: Bonanza; High Chaparral; O'Hara, US Treasury Agent; Cannon; Chase; Executive Suite; Flesh and Blood; The Chisholms; Angel City.

RYAN, Natasha: Act. b. LA, May 14, 1970. TV inc: Days of Our Lives (since 1974); Sybil; Mary Jane Harper Cried Last Night; Good Against Evil; Sex and the Single Parent; Honor Thy Father; The Pirate; Ladies' Man.

Films inc: Fatso; Kingdom of the Spiders; Boulevard Nights; The Amityville Horror; The Day Time Ended.

RYAN, Peggy: Act. b. Long Beach, CA, Aug 28, 1924. Films inc: Top of the Town; Give Out Sisters; Top Man; The Merry Monahans; Bowery to Broadway; That's the Spirit; On Stage Everybody; All Ashore.

TV inc: Hawaii Five-0; Pleasure Palace.

RYDELL, Mark: Dir-Prod. b. Mar 23, 1934. e. Juilliard School of Music. Films inc: The Fox; The Reivers; The Cowboys (& prod); Cinderella Liberty (& prod); Harry and Walter Go to New York; The Rose.

RYDER, Alfred (Alfred Jacob Corn): Act-Dir. b. NYC, Jan 5, 1919. H of Kim Stanley. As child actor played Sammy in radio show The Rise of the Goldbergs, 1930-33. Bway inc: (as Alfred Corn) East of Broadway; Another Love; Come What May. (As Ryder) Our Town; Medicine Show; Winged Victory; The Tower Beyond Tragedy; One More River; A Far Country (dir); Rhinocerous; Hey You; Light Man! (& dir); Windows (dir); The Exercise (dir).

Films inc: Winged Victory; T-Men; Story on Page One; Invitation to a Gunfighter; Hotel; The Stone Killer; Who Fears the Devil. TV inc: Lago; Tiberius; Mark Antony; John Wilkes Booth; I Rise in Flames, Cried the Phoenix; The Lady of Larkspur Lotion; Bogie.

RYDER, Loren: Exec. b. Pasadena, CA, Mar 9, 1900. e. UC Berkeley, BA. Research engr Telephone Co, 1924-25; radio importer Sherman-Clay Co, 1926-28; snd dir. Paramount Pictures, 1929-45; chief engr Paramount, 1945-48; President Ryder Sound Services, 1948-76; gen mgr Nagra Magnetic Recorders, Inc, NYC, 1967-78. (Oscars-1938, 1941, 1945, 1949, 1950, 1953, 1955 for technical and scientific achievement).

RYDGE, Sir Norman CBE: Exec. b. Sydney, Australia, Oct 18, 1900. Chmn Carlton Hotel Ltd; Carlton Investments Ltd; Amalgamated Holdings Ltd; Manly Hotels Pty, Ltd; Greater J D Williams Amusement Co Ltd; Hon Pres & Chmn Greater Union Organisation Pty.

RYSKIND, Morrie: Wri. b. 1895. Films inc: Animal Crackers; Palmy Days; A Night at the Opera; My Man Godfrey; Stage Door; Room Service; Man About Town; Penny Serenade; Where Do We Go from Here?; Heartbeat.

Bway inc: Of Thee I Sing (Pulitzer Prize-1932); Animal Crackers; Louisiana Purchase.

SACCHI, Robert: Act. b. 1941. Thea inc: Play It Again, Sam (Bway); Bogey's Back (One-man show on tour).

Films inc: The Man With Bogart's Face.

SACKHEIM, William B: Wri-Prod. b. Gloversville, NY, Oct 31, 1921. e. UCLA. Sr vp, Rastar Films. Films inc: Smart Girls Don't Talk; One Last Fling; Yank in Korea; Paula; Reunion in Reno; Border River; Tanganyika; Chicago Syndicate; Art of Love; The In-Laws; The Competition.

TV inc: Alcoa-Goodyear Presents (Emmy-1959); Gidget; The Neon Ceiling; A Clear and Present Danger; The Impatient Heart; The Harness; The Law (Emmy-1975).

SAFER, Morley: TV Newsman. b. Toronto, 1931. e. U of Western Ontario. CBS London Bureau Chief, 1967-70. Co-edtr 60 Minutes since 1970.

SAFRAN, Henri: Dir-Prod. b. Paris, Oct 7, 1932. TV inc: The Trouble Shooters; Softly Softly; Somerset Maugham; The Inheritors; Elephant Boy; Storm Boy; Listen to the Lion.

SAGAL, Boris: Dir. b. USSR, Oct 18, 1923. e. UCLA, BA, Harvard Law, Yale School of Drama, MFA. H of Marge Champion. Films inc: Dime with a Halo; Twilight of Honor; Girl Happy; Made in Paris; The Thousand Plane Raid; Mosquito Squadron; The Omega Man.

TV inc: T.H.E. Cat (exec prod); Destiny of a Spy; Case of Rape; Rich Man, Poor Man; The Money Changers; Awakening Land; Ike; The War Years; The Diary of Anne Frank.

SAGAN, Carl Edward: Astronomer-TV Pers. b. NYC, Nov 9, 1934. e. U Chicago, BS, MS, PhD, ScD. Created Murmurs of Earth recording for Voyager space probe. TV inc: Cosmos (wri-host).

SAGAR, Ramanand: Dir. b. India, Dec 29, 1917. e. U of Lahore. Films inc: Mehman (The Guest); The Message; Aarzoo; The Eyes; The Song; Lalkar; Hamrahi; Charas.

SAGE, Liz: Wri. b. South Bend, IN, Nov 23, 1953. e. LA City College. TV inc: The Carol Burnett Show (Emmy-1978); exec story cons Welcome Back Kotter; exec story cons Dorothy.

SAGER, Carole Bayer: Lyr. b. Mar 8, 1946. Films inc: The Spy Who Loved Me; Nobody Does It Better; Paradise Alley; Ice Castles; Starting Over.

Bway inc: They're Playing Our Song.

Songs inc: Through the Eyes of Love; I'd Rather Leave While I'm In Love; Come In From The Rain; Break It To Me Gently; I Don't Wanna Go.

SAHL, Mort: Act. b. Montreal, 1927. TV, niteries. Films inc: In Love and War; All the Young Men; Don't Make Waves; Doctor You've Got to be Kidding.

SAINT, Eva Marie: Act. b. Newark, NJ, Jul 4, 1924. Screen debut, On the Waterfront (Oscar-1954), Films inc: That Certain Feeling; Raintree County; A Hatful of Rain; North by Northwest; Exodus; All Fall Down; Grand Prix; The Stalking Moon; Loving; Cancel My Reservation.

TV inc: One Man's Family; Philco Playhouse; Kraft Theatre; Omnibus; Producers Showcase; How the West Was Won; A Christmas to Remember; When Hell Was in Session; The Curse of King Tut's Tomb.

Bway inc: Trip to Bountiful; First Monday In October.

ST JACQUES, Raymond (James Johnson): Act-Dir. b. 1930. Films inc: Black Like Me; Mister Moses; Mister Buddwing; The Comedians; The Green Berets; If He Hollers Let Him Go; Uptight; Change of Mind; Cotton Comes to Harlem; The Book of Numbers (& prod-dir); Lost in the Stars; Cuba Crossing.

Thea inc: The Blacks; Night Life; The Cool World; Seventh Heaven. TV inc: The 416th.

ST JAMES, Susan (nee Miller): b. LA, Aug 14, 1946. e. CT Coll for Women. Films inc: What's So Bad About Feeling Good?; Jigsaw; P J; Where Angels Go. . .Trouble Follows; Outlaw Blues; Love At First Bite; How to Beat the High Cost of Living.

TV inc: The Name of the Game (Emmy-1969); McMillan & Wife; Magic Carpet; The Girls in the Office; Sex and the Single Parent; S.O.S. Titanic; How to Beat the High Cost of Living.

SAINTE-MARIE, Buffy: Singer-Sngwri. b. Canada (or Sebago Lake, ME), Feb 20, 1941. Folk singer; toured US, Canada concert halls; recordings inc the controversial The Universal Soldier, 1963.
TV inc: Perry Como's Christmas In New Mexico.

ST JOHN, Jill (nee Oppenheim): Act. b. LA, Aug 10, 1940. On radio series One Man's Family. Tv debut 1948, A Christmas Carol. Film debut 1957 Summer Love. Films inc: The Remarkable Mr. Pennypacker; Holiday for Lovers; The Roman Spring of Mrs. Stone; Tender Is the Night; Come Blow Your Horn; Who's Been Sleeping In My Bed?; Honeymoon Hotel; The Oscar; Banning; Tony Rome; Diamonds Are Forever.
TV inc: Fame is the Name of the Game; Dupont Theatre; How I Spent My Summer Vacation; Fireside Theatre; Brenda Starr.

ST JOHNS, Adela Rogers: Wri. b. LA, May 20, 1894. Newspaperwoman, first female sportswriter. Author of books, articles on Hollywood. Films inc: A Free Soul; Single Standard.

ST JOHNS, Richard Rogers: Prod-OExec. b. LA, Jan 30, 1929. e. Stanford U, BA; Stanford Law School, JD. S of Adela Rogers St. Johns and Richard Hyland. On graduation joined O'Melveny & Myers, specializing in entertainment law; 1963 became partner; 1968 sr. vp Filmways, Inc.; 1969 P, CEO Filmways; 1972 formed ind packaging firm; 1975 formed Guinness Film Group.
Films inc: (prod or exec prod) Circle of Iron; Nightwing; The Wanderers; The Mountain Men; Matilda; The Final Countdown; A Change of Seasons.

SAITO, Bill: Act. b. Oklahoma City, Dec 22, 1936. e. UCLA, BS. Films inc: Sand Pebbles; Too Late the Hero; The Wrecking Crew; Yakuza; Sidewinder One; Rollercoaster.
TV inc: The Wackiest Ship in the Army; That Girl; Get Smart; Hawaii Five-O; Six Million Dollar Man; The Hardy Boys.

SAKS, Gene: Dir-Act. b. NYC, Nov 8, 1921. e. Cornell U. H of Bea Arthur. Films inc: (dir) Barefoot in the Park; The Odd Couple; Last of the Red Hot Lovers; Mame; Cactus Flower; (act) A Thousand Clowns; Prisoner of Second Avenue; The One and Only.
Bway inc: (dir) Enter Laughing; Nobody Loves an Albatross; Generation; Half a Sixpence; Mame (act); Middle of the Night; Howie; The Tenth Man; A Shot in the Dark; A Thousand Clowns; Same Time, Next Year; I Love My Wife (Tony-dir-1977).

SALANT, Richard S: Exec. b. NYC, Apr 14, 1914. e. Harvard LLB. Originally an attorney, joined CBS in 1952 as vp, general exec. Named head of CBS News 1961, first non-journalist ever named to such a network post. P CBS News 1961-1964; special asst to CBS prexy 1964-1966; resumed P CBS News 1966, remained there until forced out by network's mandatory retirement policy at 65. Two weeks later became V ChmnB NBC with overall responsibility for NBC News.

SALE, Richard: Wri-Prod-Dir. b. NYC, Dec 17, 1911. Pres Voyager Films Inc; VP Libra Productions, Inc Films inc: Find the Witness; Shadows Over Shanghai; Strange Cargo; Rendezvous with Annie; Mother Is a Freshman; Mr. Belvedere Goes to College; Father Was a Fullback; Driftwood; I'll Get By; A Ticket to Tomahawk; When Willie Comes Marching Home; Meet Me After the Show; My Wife's Best Friend; Let's Make It Legal; The Girl Next Door; A Woman's World; French Line; Let's Do It Again; Lady at Midnight; Suddenly; Fire Over Africa; Half-Angel; Gentlemen Marry Brunettes; Abandon Ship; The Oscar; The White Buffalo.
TV inc: Yancy Derringer Series (wri-prod-dir); High Chapparal; Wackiest Ship in the Army; Bewitched; Please Don't Eat the Daisies; Everywhere a Chick-Chick; Legend of Custer; The FBI.

SALES, Soupy: Act. b. Franklinton, NC, Jan 8, 1926. TV inc: Soupy Sales Show; What's My Line; To Tell the Truth.
Films inc: The Two Little Bears; Birds Do It.

SALINGER, Pierre: TV news. b. San Francisco, CA, Jun 14, 1925. e. U San Francisco, BS. Reporter, later night city edtr San Francisco Chronicle; 1955 West Coast edtr Colliers; 1956 Contributing edtr; 1959 press sec to Sen John F Kennedy, became Kennedy's presidential press sec; press sec Pres Lyndon B Johnson until March 1964; 1965 vp National General Corp; 1968 P Fox Overseas Theatres Corp; 1976 roving corr ABC Olympics coverage; 1977 contributing corr for ABC News, based in Paris.

SALKIND, Alexander: Prod. Films inc: Three Musketeers; Light at The Edge of the World; The Prince and the Pauper; Superman (Oscar-special achievement-1978).

SALKIND, Ilya: Prod. b. Mexico City, 1948. S of Alexander Salkind. Films inc: Crossed Swords; Superman; Superman II.

SALKOWITZ, Sy: Exec. b. Philadelphia, Apr 21, 1926. e. Yale U, BA. TV inc: Sr wri Ironside series; same position for Police Story. Joined Fox TV, July 1974, as vp dev; then vp primetime pgm; p FOX TV, July 1976-March 1979.

SALMI, Albert: Act. b. 1928. Films inc: The Brothers Karamazov; The Unforgiven; Wild River; The Ambushers; The Deserter; Lawman; The Take; Black Oak Conspiracy; Empire of the Ants; Moonshine County Express; Viva Knievel!; Love and Bullets; Cuba Crossing; Cloud Dancer; Brubaker; Caddyshack; Steel.
TV inc: Greatest Heroes of the Bible; Undercover with the KKK; The Great Cash Giveaway Getaway; Portrait of a Rebel--Margaret Sanger.

SALT, Jennifer: Act. b. LA, Sep 14. e. Sarah Lawrence Coll. D of Waldo Salt. Films inc: Midnight Cowboy; Sisters; Hi, Mom!; The Revolutionary; Brewster McCloud; Play it Again, Sam; It's My Turn.
TV inc: Family; The Great Niagara; Gargoyles; Soap.
Bway inc: Father's Day; Water Color.

SALT, Waldo: Wri. b. Chicago, Oct 18, 1914. e. Stamford U, AB. Films inc: The Shopworn Angel; Tonight We Raid Calais; Mr Winkle Goes to War; Rachel and the Stranger; The Flame and the Arrow; Taras Bulba; Flight from Ashiya; Wild and Wonderful; Midnight Cowboy (Oscar-1969); The Gang That Couldn't Shoot Straight; Serpico; The Day of the Locust; Coming Home (Oscar-1978).

SALTER, Hans J: Comp-Mus dir. b. Vienna, Jan 14, 1896. e. U of Vienna. Films inc: Beau Geste; Bedtime Story; Autumn Leaves; Don't Trust Your Husband; The Oklahoman; Hold Back the Night; The Spoilers; Ghost of Frankenstein; It Started with Eve; The Amazing Mrs. Halliday; Christmas Holiday; Can't Help Singing; The Merry Monahans; This Love of Ours; Love from a Stranger; Phantom Lady.
TV inc: Maya; Wagon Train; Laramie; The Law and Mr. Jones; Dick Powell; Lost in Space.

SALTMAN, Sheldon A: Prod. b. Newton, MA, Aug 17, 1930. e. U of MA, BA; Boston U, SPRC; Boston Coll, LLD. Pub-promo dir for all Star Baseball; World Series; promo dir WBZ-TV; promo dir WJW-TV; vp pub-ad-promo MCA-TV; formed Barnaby Records; vp-gm 20th Fox Telecommunications; vp-gm 20th Fox Sports; resd Dec 1980 to form own firm.
TV inc: Challenge of the Sexes (co-crea); Celebrity Superstars; Pro Fan; Fights of the 70's.

SALTZMAN, Harry: Prod. b. St John, NB, Oct, 1915. Films inc: The Iron Petticoat; Look Back in Anger; The Entertainer; Saturday Night, Sunday Morning; Call Me Bwana; Dr No; From Russia with Love; Goldfinger; The Ipcress File; Thunderball; Funeral in Berlin; You Only Live Twice; The Billion Dollar Brain; Play Dirty; Battle of Britain; On Her Majesty's Secret Service; The Man with the Golden Gun; Nijinsky.
TV inc: Robert Montgomery Show; Capt Gallant of the Foreign Legion.

SALTZMAN, Philip: Exec-Prod-Wri. b. Mexico, Sep 19, 1928. e. UCLA, BA, MA. TV inc: (wri) Rifleman; Fugitive; Dr. Kildare; Perry Mason. (Asso prod) Twelve O'Clock High. (Prod) Felony Squad; The FBI; Barnaby Jones; Alvin Karpis; Brinks; The Great Robbery; Attack on Terror; Crossfire (& prod). (Exec prod) Barnaby Jones; Escapade; Paradise Connection; A Man Called Sloan; The Aliens Are Coming; Freebie and the Bean.

Films inc: (wri) The Swiss Conspiracy.

SALVATORI, Renato: Act. b. Forte dei Marmi, Italy, Mar 20, 1934. Films inc: The Girls on the Spanish Steps; Big Deal on Madonna Street; Rocco and His Brothers; Two Women; Smog; The Organizer; One Out of Three; The Harem; Queimada, Z; State of Siege; The Burglars; Suspicion; The Lighthouse at the End of the World; Todo Modo; Flic Story; The Gypsy; Armageddon; Ernesto; Luna; Oggetti Smaritti (Lost and Found).

SAMOILOVA, Tatyana: Act. b. Russia, May 4, 1934. e. Shchukin Drama School. Films inc: The Mexican; The Cranes Are Flying; An Unposted Letter; Leon Garros is Looking for His Friend; They Headed For the East; Anna Karenina; Long Journey Into a Short Day; The Ocean; No Return.

SAMPSON, Will: Act. b. Okmulgee, OK, 1935. Screen debut, 1975, One Flew Over the Cuckoo's Nest. Films inc: Buffalo Bill and The Indians or Sitting Bull's History Lesson; The Outlaw Josey Wales; The White Buffalo; Fishhawk. TV inc: Alcatraz--The Whole Shocking Story.

SAMUELS, Lesser: Wri. b. Pittsburgh, PA, 1894. e. Carnegie Tech. Scriptwriter in England during early 30's to Hollywood 1939 under contract to MGM. Films inc: Strange Cargo; The Earl of Chicago; Bitter Sweet; Great Day in the Morning; The Long Wait; Darling, How Could You!; Adventure in Baltimore; Tonight and Every Night; The Hour Before the Dawn; Gangway; No Way Out; Ace in the Hole; You're in the Army Now; The Silver Chalice; It's Love Again; OHMS.

(Died Dec 22, 1980).

SAMUELSON, David Wylie: Exec. b. London, Eng, Jul 6, 1924. S of Pioneer prod G B Samuelson. Cin for British Movietone News 1941-1960 inc svs as RAF photographer; freelance cin; joined family firm, Samuelson Service Ltd.

SAMUELSON, Sydney CBE: Exec. b. London, Dec 7, 1925. Entered film ind age 14 as projection asst; became cin & dir of documentaries after World War II; founded Samuelson Film Service 1955; currently Chmn & CEO.

SAND, Paul (nee Sanchez): b. LA, Mar 5, 1944. Films inc: Viva Max!; The Hot Rock; The Second Coming of Suzanne; The Main Event; Wholly Moses!; Can't Stop The Music.

TV inc: Brothers Grimm; Friends and Lovers; The Legend of Sleepy Hollow.

Bway inc: Star Spangled Girl; Second City; Festival of Two Worlds; Story Theatre (Tony-supp-1971).

SANDA, Dominique (nee Varaigne): Act. b. Paris, 1948. Films inc: A Gentle Woman; The Conformist; The Garden of the Finzi-Continis; Without Apparent Motive; The Impossible Object; Steppenwolf; The Inheritance; Bertolucci's 1900; Damnation Alley; Le Voyage en Douce.

SANDBERG, Anders: Prod-Dist Exec. b. Denmark, May 7, 1945. Happy Film, Copenhagen.

SANDBERG, Henrik W: Prod-Dist Exec. b. Denmark, May 15, 1919. Merry Film Prodns, Copenhagen.

SANDERS, Denis: Prod-Dir-Wri. b. NYC, Jan 21, 1929. e. UCLA, MA. Films inc: A Time Out of War (Oscar-ss-1954); The Naked and the Dead; Crime and Punishment; Shock Treatment; War Hunt; One Man's Way; Elvis, That's the Way it Was; Czechoslovakia, 1968 (Oscar-doc-1969); Soul to Soul; Invasion of the Bee Girls.

TV inc: The Day Lincoln was Shot; Alcoa Premiere; Route 66; Defenders; Naked City; Mannix; Trial; City and County of Denver vs Laureen Watson; American West of John Ford;   In Search of. . .

Docs & edu films inc: West Point; Adlai Stevenson; Subject: Narcotics; Me, An Alcoholic?; A Declaration; The Right to Eat; Arbitration: The Truth of the Matter.

SANDERS, Marlene: TV news. b. Cleveland, OH, Jan 10, 1931. e. OH State U. Wri-prod WNEW-TV 1955; pgm dir Westinghouse, NY, 1960; retd to WNEW 1962 as asst dir news & pub aff; 1964 corr ABC-TV; 1971, doc prod; 1976 VP TV Doc ABC News; 1978, corr-prod CBS Doc; corr CBS Reports.

TV inc: Up-Date--Since Gary Gilmore; Promise Now, Pay Later; Taiwan Dilemma; Going, Going, Gone; Whatever Happened to Civil Defense; How Much for the Handicapped?

SANDERS, Richard: Act. b. Harrisburg, PA, Aug 28, 1940. e. Carnegie Tech, BFA. Dir at State Theatre, Paraiba, Brazil, while with Peace Corps. Bway inc: Raisin.

TV inc: Ruby and Oswald; Alexander; Good Against Evil; Victory at Entebbe; They've Killed President Lincoln; Surrender at Appomattox; Stop Thief; WKRP in Cincinnati.

SANDERS, Terry Barrett: Prod-Dir-Wri. b. NYC, Dec 20, 1931. e. UCLA. Freelance doc film maker; co-prod-cin A Time Out of War (Oscar-ss-1954); The Naked and the Dead (sp); Portrait of Zubin Mehta (prod-dir).

TV inc: The Day Lincoln Was Shot (wri); Hollywood and the Stars (prod-dir); The Legend of Marilyn Monroe; National Geographic specials.

SANDRICH, Jay: Dir. b. LA, Feb 24, 1932. e. UCLA. TV inc: He and She; Mary Tyler Moore Show (Emmy-1971, 1973); Soap; Phyllis (pilot); Tony Randall Show (pilot); Bob Newhart Show (pilot); Benson (pilot); Insight/This Side of Eden; Packy; Insight/Checkmate.

Films inc: Seems Like Old Times.

SANDS, Dorothy: Act. b. Cambridge, MA, Mar 5, 1893. e. Radcliffe. Studied with George Pierce Baker's Harvard playwriting course.

Bway inc: Catskill Dutch; The Seagull; Half-Gods; The Royal Family; Papa Is All; All The Comforts of Home; Tomorrow The World; A Joy Forever; Misalliance; Time Remembered; Once for the Asking; My Fair Lady (rev); Come Summer; Paris is Out; Right You Are, if You Think You Are. Also toured extensively in one-woman shows and for State Department overseas in American Theatre Highlights.

(Died Sep 11, 1980).

SANDS, Tommy: Act. b. Chicago, Aug 27, 1937. Films inc: Sing Boy Sing; Mardi Gras; Love in a Goldfish Bowl; Babes in Toyland; The Longest Day; None But the Brave.

SANDY, Gary: Act. b. Dayton, OH, Dec 25, 1945. e. AADA. Films inc: Some of My Best Friends Are; Hail to the Chief; Last of the Cowboys.

TV inc: As The World Turns; Somerset; The Secret Storm; Melvin Purvis--The Kansas City Masscare; The Shell Game; All That Glitters; WKRP in Cincinnati.

SANFORD, Donald S: Wri. b. Mar 17, 1920. Films inc: Thousand Plane Raid; Mosquito Squadron; Submarine X One; Midway; The Ravagers.

SANFORD, Isabel: Act. b. NYC, Aug 29, 1917. Films inc: Guess Who's Coming to Dinner; Pendulum; Stand Up and Be Counted; The New Centurions; Love at First Bite. TV inc: The Carol Burnett Show; The Great Man's Whiskers; The Jeffersons; The Sensational, Shocking Wonderful Wacky 70's.

Bway inc: The Amen Corner.

SANGSTER, Jimmy: Wri-Prod-Dir. b. England, Dec 2, 1927. Films inc: The Trollenberg Terror; The Curse of Frankenstein; Dracula; The Mummy; Jack the Ripper; Brides of Dracula; Taste of Fear (& prod); Maniac (& prod); Hysteria (& prod); The Nanny (& prod); Deadlier than the Male; The Anniversary (& prod); Horror of Frankenstein (& prod-dir); Lust for a Vampire (& dir); Fear in the Night (& prod-dir); Phobia (wri).

TV inc: Motive for Murder; The Assassins; I Can Destroy the Sun; Murder in Music City; The Billion Dollar Threat (wri); Ebony, Ivory & Jade; The Concrete Cowboys (wri); Once Upon A Spy (wri).

SANTON, Penny (Pierina della Santina): Act. b. NYC, Sep 2, 1916. Films inc: Interrupted Melody; Full of Life; Dino; West Side Story; Cry Tough; Love With the Proper Stranger; Captain Newman, M.D.; Don't Just Stand There; Funny Girl; Kotch.

SANTOS, Joe: Act. b. NYC, Jun 9. Films inc: Panic in Needle Park; The Gang that Couldn't Shoot Straight; Shamus; Zandy's Bride.

TV inc: The Blue Knight; The Rockford Files; Man Undercover; Power; Me and Maxx; The Hustler of Muscle Beach.

SARAFIAN, Richard: Dir. b. NYC, Apr 28, 1932. Films inc: Andy; Run Wild, Run Free; Fragment of Fear; Vanishing Point; Man in the Wilderness; The Man Who Loved Cat Dancing; Lolly Madonna XXX; Sunburn.

TV inc: Bronco; Maverick; Hawaiian Eye; Roaring 20's; 77 Sunset Strip; Bonanza; Ben Casey; Twilight Zone; Disaster on the Coastline; The Golden Moment-An Olympic Love Story.

SARANDON, Chris: Act. b. 1942. Films inc: Dog Day Afternoon; Lipstick; The Sentinel; Cuba; Atlantic City, USA.

TV inc: You Can't Go Home Again; The Day Christ Died; A Tale of Two Cities.

Bway inc: Censored Scenes From King Kong.

SARANDON, Susan (nee Tomaling): Act. b. NYC, 1946. Films inc: The Front Page; The Great Waldo Pepper; Dragonfly; The Other Side of Midnight; Pretty Baby; Checkered Flag or Crash; The Great Smoky Road Block; King of the Gypsies; Something Short of Paradise; Loving Couples.

SARGENT, Alvin: Wri. Films inc: The Stalking Moon; Gambit; The Sterile Cuckoo; The Effect of Gamma Rays on Man-in-the-Moon Marigolds; Love and Pain and the Whole Damn Thing; Julia *(Oscar-*1977); Bobby Deerfield; Straight Time; Ordinary People.

SARGENT, Herb: Wri. TV inc: Annie--The Women in the Life of A Man *(Emmy-*1970); Jack Lemmon Special; Burt Bacharach Specials; Lily (& prod) *(Emmys-*prod-wri-1974); Alan King Specials; George Siegel Show; Funny Girl to Funny Lady; Saturday Night Live *(Emmys-*1976-1977); Inaugural Eve Gala Performance.

SARGENT, Joseph Daniel (Giuseppe Danielle Sorgente): Dir. b. Jersey City, NJ, Jul 25, 1925. Films inc: The Man; White Lightning; The Taking of Pelham 1-2-3; MacArthur; Golden Girl; Coast to Coast

TV inc: Tribes; Maybe I'll Come Home in the Spring; The Marcus-Nelson Murders *(Emmy-*1973); Sunshine; Hustling; Friendly Persuasion; The Night That Panicked America; Amber Waves.

SAROYAN, William: Wri. b. Fresno, CA, Aug 31, 1908. Films inc: The Human Comedy *(Oscar-*1943); The Time of Your Life.

Plays inc: My Heart's in the Highlands; The Time of Your Life *(Pulitzer Prize-*1940); Love's Old Sweet Song; Hero of the World; Something About a Soldier; The Cave Dwellers; Ever Been in Love with a Midget?

SARRAZIN, Michael: Act. b. Quebec, Canada, May 22, 1940. Began career at 17 on CBC-TV. Screen debut, 1967, Gunfight in Abilene. Films inc: The Flim-Flam Man; The Sweet Ride; Journey to Shiloh; A Man Called Gannon; Eye of the Cat; In Search of Gregory; They Shoot Horses, Don't They?; The Pursuit of Happiness; Sometimes a Great Notion; Believe In Me; The Groundstar Conspiracy; The Reincarnation of Peter Proud; The Loves and Times of Scaramouche; The Gumball Rally; Caravans; Double Negative.

TV inc: Chrysler Theatre; The Virginian; The Doomsday Flight; Beulah Land.

SARSON, Christopher: Prod-Dir-Wri. TV inc: Elizabeth R *(Emmys-*exec prod series & new series-1972); Zoom *(Emmys-*prod-1973, 1974).

SARTRE, Jean-Paul: Wri. b. Paris, Jun 5, 1905. Plays inc: The Flies; No Exit; Vicious Circle; Men Without Shadows; The Respectable Prostitute; Crime Passionel; Nekrassov; The Condemned of Altona; Kean.

Films inc: The Proud and the Beautiful.

(Died April 15, 1980).

SATLOF, Ron: Dir. TV inc: Benny and Barney; From Here to Eternity; Barnaby Jones; Salvage; Dukes of Hazzard; Capra; Quincy; Hawaii 5-0; Class of 65 (& prod); Get Christie Love (& prod); Spiderman (& prod); McCloud; From Here to Eternity--The War Years; Battles--The Murder that Wouldn't Die; Waikiki.

SAUNDERS, Peter: Prod. b. London, Nov 23, 1911. Thea inc: (London) Fly Away Peter; The Perfect Woman; Breach of Marriage; My Mother Said; The Mousetrap; Witness for the Prosecution; Spider's Web; The Bride and the Bachelor; Subway in the Sky; The Trial of Mary Dugan; A Day in the Life Of. . .; And Suddenly It's Spring; Alfie; On a Foggy Day; Cockie; Double Edge; The Reluctant Peer; The Jockey Club Stakes; A Murder Is Announced.

SAURA, Carlos: Dir. b. Huesca, Spain, Jan 4, 1932. Films inc: Sunday Afternoon; Riffraff; Lament for a Bandit; The Hunt; Peppermint Frappe; Stress is Three, Three; The Honeycomb; The Garden of Delights; Ana and the Wolves; Cousin Angelica; Dear Ravens; Cria Cuervos; Elsa, Vida Mia; Mom's 100 Years Old (& wri); Blindfolded Eyes.

SAUTET, Claude: Dir. b. Paris, Feb 23, 1924. e. Ecole des Arts Decoratifs. Dir 1st film 1951, a short, Nous n'irons plus au bois. Films inc: The Big Risk; Guns for the Dictator; The Things of Life; Max et les Ferrailleurs; Cesar and Rosalie; Vincent, Francois, Paul et les Autres; Mado; A Simple Story; A Bad Son (& wri).

SAVAGE, John: Act. b. Old Bethpage, NY, Aug 25. Films inc: Bad Company; The Killing Kind; Steelyard Blues; No Deposit, No Return; The Deer Hunter; Hair; The Onion Field; Inside Moves.

Bway inc: Fiddler on the Roof; Ari; Dance on a Country Grave; American Buffalo.

TV inc: Cade's County; Eric (& wrote theme song); Gibbsville.

SAVALAS, George: Act. b. NYC, Dec 5. B of Telly Savalas. Films inc: Kelly's Heroes; The Greatest Story Ever Told; The Silent Thread; RPM; Johnny Cool; Genghis Khan; The Outfit; Good Neighbor Sam.

TV inc: Kojack.

SAVALAS, Telly (Aristotle Savalas): Act. b. Garden City, NY, Jan 21, 1924. e. Columbia U, BS. Joined Information Services, State Dept; made exec dir. Then named sr. dir of news, special events for ABC where created Your Voice of America series. Acting career began with debut in Bring Home a Baby on Armstrong Circle Theatre TV. Films inc: Birdman of Alcatraz; Young Savages; Cape Fear; The Man from the Diner's Club; Battle of the Bulge; The Greatest Story Ever Told; Beau Geste; The Dirty Dozen; Crooks and Coronets; Kelly's Heroes; On Her Majesty's Secret Service; Killer Force; Lisa and the Devil; Capricorn One; Beyond the Poseidon Adventure; Escape to Athena; The Muppet Movie.

TV inc: Mongo's Back in Town; Visions; The Marcus-Nelson Murders; Kojak *(Emmy-*1974); The French-Atlantic Affair; Alcatraz--The Whole Shocking Story.

SAVILLE, Victor: Dir. b. Birmingham, Eng, 1897. Films inc: The Arcadian; Roses of Picardy; Woman to Woman; The Good Companion; I Was a Spy; Friday the Thirteenth; Evergreen; Dark Journey; Storm in a Teacup; South Riding; The Citadel (prod only); Goodbye Mr Chips (prod only); Bitter Sweet (& prod); Dr Jekyl and Mr Hyde (& prod); White Cargo (& prod); The Green Years (& prod); If Winter Comes; The Conspirator; Kim; The Long Wait (& prod); The Silver Chalice (& prod); Kiss Me Deadly (prod only); The Greengage Summer (prod only).

(Died May 8, 1979).

SAWYER, Gordon: Snd dir. b.Santa Barbara, CA, 1905. e. UCLA. Worked as elec eng building radio stations in the 20's, came to Hollywood with advent of sound films, became lab control man at Goldwyn, 1928; promoted to sound dir following year, remained that position until retirement 1970; Goldwyn sound dept under his direction achieved int'l reputation, with other studios and indies frequently making use of facilities and Sawyer's expertise.

Films inc: The Hurricane; The Cowboy and the Lady (Both Oscar winners for dept); Wonder Man; The Best Years of Our Lives; I Want You; Hans Christian Anderson; Friendly Persuasion; Witness for the Prosecution; I Want to Live; The Alamo *(Oscar-*1960); Porgy and Bess; West Side Story *(Oscar-*1961); It's A Mad, Mad, Mad, Mad World; Hawaii. *(Special Oscar-*1977).

(Died May 15, 1980).

SAXON, John (Carmine Orrico): Act. b. NYC, Aug 5, 1936. Films inc: Running Wild; Rock Pretty Baby; The Reluctant Debutante; Cry Tough; The Big Fisherman; Portrait in Black; The Unforgiven; War Hunt; Mr. Hobbs Takes a Vacation; The Cardinal; The Appaloosa; Winchester 73; For Singles Only; Death of a Gunfighter; Black Christmas; Mitchell; The Swiss Conspiracy; The Bees; The Electric Horseman; Fast Company; Beyond Evil; Battle Beyond The Stars.

TV inc: The Bold Ones; Raid on Entebbe; Moonshine County Express; Shalimar; Killer Bees; The Glove; Greatest Heroes of the Bible; The Immigrants.

SAYER, Leo: Singer-Sngwri. b. Brighton, Eng, May 21, 1948. Vocalist; recording artist. *(Grammy-*R&B Song-1977).

TV inc: Lynda Carter's Special. Films inc: The Missing Link (songs).

SCAGGS, Boz (nee William Royce Scaggs): Mus-Sngwri. b. OH, Jun 8, 1944. With Steve Miller band; formed own R&B group, The Wigs; rejoined Miller, then solo.

Recordings inc: Boz Scaggs; Moments; Boz Scaggs and Band; My Time; Slow Down; Silk Degrees; Down Two, Then Left.

*(Grammy-*R&B song-1976).

SCAIFE, Ted: Cin. b. England, 1912. Films inc: Bonnie Prince Charlie; An Inspector Calls; Sea Wife; Night of the Demon; Khaartoum; The Dirty Dozen; Play Dirty; Sinful Davey; Forbush and the Penguins; Hannie Caulder; Catlow.

SCALI, John: TV news. b. Canton, OH, Apr 27, 1918. e. Boston U, BSJ. Reporter Boston Herald; Boston Bureau United Press; Washington Bureau Associated Press; war corr, AP; postwar traveling corr until 1961 when joined ABC as State Dept & diplomatic corr; in 1963 backstage role as negotiator credited with helping avert possible war during Cuban missile crisis; 1971 apptd special consultant foreign aff and communications by Pres. Nixon; 1973 became permanent US rep to UN; 1975 retd to ABC as senior corr.

SCARDINO, Don: Act. b. Canada. Bway inc: Godspell; Angel; The Unknown Soldier and His Wife: King of Hearts; Johnny No Trump; The Sorrows of Stephen; As You Like It; I'm Getting My Act Together; Boy Meets Girl.

Films inc: The People Next Door; Homer; Squirm; Cruising; He Knows You're Alone.

TV inc: Guiding Light.

SCARWID, Diana: Act. b. Savannah, GA. e. AADA, Pace U. TV inc: Gibbsville; Forever; Battered; Kingston Confidential.

Films inc: Pretty Baby; Inside Moves.

SCHAEFER, George: Dir-Prod. b. Wallingford, CT, Dec 16, 1920. e. Lafayette Coll, Yale Drama School. Films inc: Once Upon a Scoundrel; Generation; Doctors' Wives; Pendulum;

TV inc: Hamlet; One Touch of Venus; Alice in Wonderland; The Devil's Disciple; The Corn Is Green; The Good Fairy; Born Yesterday; Man and Superman; The Little Foxes; Green Pastures; On Borrowed Time; Little Moon of Alban *(Emmy-*dir-1959); Dial M for Murder; Victoria Regina; Macbeth *(Emmy-*dir-1961); Harvey; Gift of the Magi; Johnny Belinda; The Magnificent Yankee *(Emmy-*prod-1965); Kiss Me Kate; Green Pastures; Elizabeth the Queen *(Emmy-*prod-1968); The Cradle Song; A Doll's House; Pygmalion; F Scott Fitzgerald; Sandburg's Lincoln; Truman at Potsdam; The Last of Mrs Lincoln; Amelia; Our Town; A War of Children *(Emmy-*prod-1973); First You Cry; Sad Figure Laughing; Who Will Save Our Children; Enemy of the People; Blind Ambition; Mayflower-The Pilgrim's Adventure; Barry Manilow-One Voice.

Bway inc: Darling, Darling, Darling; The Linden Tree; Man and Superman; She Stoops to Conquer; The Corn is Green; The Heiress; Idiot's Delight; The Male Animal; Tovarich; The Teahouse of the August Moon *(Tony-*co-prod-1954); To Broadway with Love; Write Me a Murder; Mixed Couples.

SCHAFER, Natalie: Act. b. Rumson, NJ, Nov 5. Widow of Louis Calhern. On screen from 1944. Films inc: Marriage Is a Private Affair; Keep Your Powder Dry; Dishonored Lady; Secret Beyond the Door; Time of Your Life; Snake Pit; Oh Men, Oh Women; Anastasia; Bernardine; Back Street; Susan Slade; Forty Carats; Day of the Locust.

Bway inc: Lady in the Dark; Doughgirls; A Joy Forever; Susan and God; Romanoff & Juliet; The Highest Tree.

TV inc: Kraft Theatre; Philco Playhouse; Topper; Gilligan's Island; Three's Company; Doctor's Private Lives.

SCHAFFNER, Franklin: Dir. b. Tokyo, Japan, May 30, 1920. e. Franklin Marshall Coll, BA. Films inc: The Stripper; The Double Man; The Best Man; Planet of the Apes; Patton *(Oscar-*1970); Nicholas and Alexandra; Papillon; Islands in the Stream; The Boys From Brazil. TV inc: Person to Person; Studio One; Playhouse 90; Kaiser Aluminum Hour (& prod); DuPont Show of the Week (& prod); Twelve Angry Men *(Emmy-*1954); Caine Mutiny Court Martial *(Emmys-*dir-wri-1955); The Defenders *(Emmy-*1962).

SCHALLERT, William: Perf. b. LA, Jul 6, 1922. e. UCLA; Fulbright Fellowship, Eng. Films inc: The Man from Planet X; Flat Top; The Red Badge of Courage; Riot in Cell Block 11; Written on the Wind; Friendly Persuasion; Cry Terror; Pillow Talk; In the Heat of the Night; Colossus; Will Penny; The Computer Wore Tennis Shoes; The Strongest Man in the World; Charley Varrick; Hangar 18. TV inc: Dobie Gillis; Nancy Drew Mysteries; Little Women; Ike; Blind Ambition.

SCHARF, Walter: Comp-Cond-Arr. b. NYC, Aug 1. Accomp to Kate Smith; accomp, arr, Rudy Vallee; mus dir, Phil Harris-Alice Faye radio show. Films inc: Mercy Island; Hit Parade; The Fighting Seabees; Dakota; The Saxon Charm; Brazil; Hans Christian Anderson; Living It Up; Hollywood or Bust; A Pocketful of Miracles; Where Love Has Gone; Pendulum; The Cheyenne Social Club; Willy Wonka and the Chocolate Factory; Funny Girl; Ben; Final Chapter-Walking Tall; Gasp.

TV inc: The Tragedy of the Red Salmon *(Emmy-*1971); Beneath the Frozen World *(Emmy-*1974); From Here to Eternity-The War Years; The Long Days of Summer.

SCHARY, Dore: Wri-Prod-Dir. b. Newark, NJ, Aug 31, 1905. Exec prod MGM, 1942; p & chief exec ofcr Schary Prodns Inc, 1973. Films inc: Boys Town *(Oscar-*wri, 1938); Journey for Margaret; The War Against Mrs. Hadley; Lassie Come Home; Joe Smith, American; Lost Angel; Bataan; I'll Be Seeing You; Till the End of Time; The Spiral Staircase; The Farmer's Daughter; Mr Blanding Builds His Dream House; The Window; Crossfire; Bad Day at Black Rock; The Swan; Designing Woman; Sunrise at Campobello; Act One (sp, prod, dir).

Plays inc: Sunrise at Campobello *(Tony-*1958); The Highest Tree; The Unsinkable Mollie Brown; The Devil's Advocate; Something About a Soldier; The Zulu and the Zayda.

(Died July 7, 1980).

SCHATZBERG, Jerry: Dir. Former fashion photog. Films inc: Panic in Needle Park; Puzzle of a Downfall Child; Scarecrow; Dandy, The All American Girl; Sweet Revenge (& prod); The Seduction of Joe Tynan; Honeysuckle Rose.

SCHEERER, Robert: Dir. b. Santa Barbara, CA. Originally act-singer-dancer. Bway inc: (Act) Lend An Ear; Top Banana; The Boy Friend.
 Films inc: (Dir) Adam at Six A.M.; The World's Greatest Athlete; How to Beat The High Cost of Living.
 TV inc: (Dir) Dick Van Dyke Show (Emmy-1964); Mary Tyler Moore Show; Barbra Streisand Special; Frank Sinatra Special; Perry Como Special; AFI Tribute to John Ford; AFI Tribute to Bette Davis; Andy Williams Show; Supershow; Superbowl Special; Number 96.

SCHEIDER, Roy: Act. b. Orange, NJ, Nov 10, 1932. e. Franklin Marshall College. Films inc: Loving; Paper Lion; Klute; The French Connection; The Outside Man; The Seven Ups; Jaws; Sorcerer; Jaws II; Last Embrace; All That Jazz.
 TV inc: Hallmark Hall of Fame; Studio One.
 Bway inc: Betrayal.

SCHELL, Maria: Act. b. Vienna, 1926. Films inc: The Angel with the Trumpet; The Magic Box; So Little Time; The Heart of the Matter; The Last Bridge; White Nights; The Brothers Karamazov; Cimarron; The Mark; Women; The Odessa File; The Twist (Folies Bourgeoises); Superman; Just a Gigolo; Die Erste Polka.
 TV inc: Christmas Lilies of the Field; The Martian Chronicles.
 Bway inc: Poor Murderer.

SCHELL, Maximilian: Act-Prod-Dir. b. Vienna, Dec 8, 1930. Stage debut at age 11, Zurich. Films inc: (act) The Young Lions; Judgment at Nuremberg (Oscar-1961); Reluctant Saint; The Condemned of Altona; Return from the Ashes; The Deadly Affair; Counterpoint; Five Finger Exercise; Topkapi; Krakatoa; Simon Bolivar; The Castle (& prod); First Love (& dir); The Odessa File; The Pedestrian; Man in the Glass Booth; The Assassination at Sarajevo; End of the Game (prod-dir); Cross of Iron; A Bridge Too Far; Julia; Avalanche Express; Players; The Black Hole; Tales From the Vienna Woods; Amo non Amo.
 TV inc: Judgment at Nuremberg; The Fifth Column; Turn the Key Deftly; The Diary of Anne Frank.
 Bway inc: A Patriot for Me; Tales from the Vienna Woods (dir).

SCHELL, Ronnie: Comedian-Act. b. Richmond, CA, Dec 23. e. San Francisco State College. Started as nitery comic. TV inc: Gomer Pyle, USMC; Good Morning, World; The Jim Nabors Hour; The Impostor; Honeymoon Suite; The Shape of Things; Hellzapoppin Special; 2d annual CBS Super Comedy Bowl; Friends and Nabors Special; California Fever.
 Films inc: The Cat From Outer Space; The Shaggy D.A.; Gus; The Strongest Man in the World; Love at First Bite; How to Beat the High Cost of Living.

SCHENKEL, Chris: Sportscaster. b. Bippus, IN, 1924. e. Purdue U. Covers a variety of sporting events for ABC's Wide World of Sports. Films inc: Dreamer.

SCHEPISI, Fred: Prod-Dir-Wri. b. Melbourne, Australia, Dec 26, 1939. Films inc: The Devil's Playground; The Chant of Jimmie Blacksmith.

SCHERICK, Edgar J: Prod. b. NYC. e. Harvard, BA. Conceived and developed Wide World of Sports for ABC-TV through his company, Sports Programs, Inc. In June 1963, named vp in charge of programming for ABC-TV. Left ABC Jan 1, 1967 to form Palomar Pictures Int'l. Films inc: For Love of Ivy; The Birthday Party; Ring of Bright Water; Take the Money and Run; They Shoot Horses, Don't They?; The Killing of Sister George; Sleuth; The Heartbreak Kid; Law and Disorder; The Stepford Wives; The Taking of Pelham One, Two, Three; I Never Promised You a Rose Garden; The American Success Company.
 TV inc: A Circle of Children (exec prod); Raid on Entebbe (exec prod); Mother and Daughter-The Loving War (exec prod); The Seduction of Miss Leona; Revenge of the Stepford Wives.

SCHICK, Elliot: Prod. b. NYC, Dec 24, 1924. e. Brooklyn Coll, BA. Films inc; Sugar Hill; Return to Macon County; Futureworld; The Island of Dr Moreau; Deerhunter (exec in charge of prodn); The Earthling.

SCHIEFFER, Bob: Newscaster. b. Austin, TX. e. TCU, BA. With CBS News since 1969. Member of the Emmy Award-winning team that reported the war in Indochina for CBS, 1972. named anchorman of the Saturday edition of the CBS Evening News, 1976. TV inc: The Air War (Emmy-1972); Watergate-The White House Transcripts (Emmy-1974).

SCHIFRIN, Lalo: Comp-Cond. b. Buenos Aires, 1932. e. Paris Conservatoire of Music. Films inc: Rhino; Once a Thief; Cincinnati Kid; Cool Hand Luke; Bullitt; The Fox; The Brotherhood; Dirty Harry; Enter the Dragon; Magnum Force; The Four Musketeers; Voyage of the Damned; The Eagle Has Landed; Rollercoaster; Telefon; Nunzio; The Cat From Outer Space; The Manitou; Return From Witch Mountain; Boulevard Nights; The Amityville Horror; The Concorde-Airport '79; Love and Bullets; Serial; When Time Ran Out; The Nude Bomb; Brubaker; The Big Brawl; The Competition.
 TV inc: T.H.E. Cat; Mission Impossible; Rise and Fall of the Third Reich; Mannix; The Making of the President, 1964; Medical Center; The World of Jacques Cousteau; The Young Lawyers; Starsky & Hutch; Bronk; Most Wanted.
 (Grammys-Jazz comp-1964, 1965; Inst Theme-1967; Orig TV score-1957).

SCHILLER, Bob: Wri-Prod. b. San Francisco, Nov 8, 1918. e. UCLA, BA. Wrote for radio 1946-49; Ozzie & Harriet; Mel Blanc; Jimmy Durante; Abbott & Costello; Duffy's Tavern. TV inc (writes with Bob Weiskopf): Ed Wynn; Danny Thomas; I Love Lucy; Phyllis Diller; Carol Burnett; Flip Wilson Show (Emmy-1971); Maude (& prod.); All's Fair (& prod., creator); All in the Family (& script consultant). (Emmy-wri-1978).

SCHILLER, Lawrence: Prod. b. NYC, Dec 28, 1936. Originally still photog. TV inc: The Winds of Kitty Hawk; Hey, I'm Alive (& dir); The Trial of Lee Harvey Oswald; A Place For Noah; Marilyn--The Untold Story (& dir).

SCHILLER, Tom: Wri. TV inc: Staff Saturday Night Live (Emmys-1976, 1977).

SCHINE, G David: Prod. b. Gloversville, NY, Sep 11, 1927. e. Harvard U, BA. Pres., GM Schine Hotels. Films inc: The French Connection (exec prod); That's Action (prod-dir-wri).

SCHISGAL, Murray: Wri. b. NYC, Nov 25, 1926. e. Brooklyn Law School, LLB. Plays inc: The Typists and the Tiger; Ducks and Lovers; Knit One, Purl Two; Jimmy Shine; The Chinese & Doctor Fish; An American Millionaire; All Over Town.
 TV inc: The Love Song of Barney Kempinski; Natasha Kovolina Pipshinsky.
 Film inc: The Tiger Makes Out.

SCHLATTER, George: Prod-Dir-Wri. b. Dec 31, 1932. e. George Pepperdine College. TV inc: Laugh-In (Emmys-(2)-series & program-1968); Shirley MacLaine Specials; Great American Laugh-Off; Just For Laughs; Laugh-In Specials; Goldie Hawn Special; Goldie And Liza Together; Speak Up, America!.

SCHLESINGER, John Richard: Dir. b. London, Feb 16, 1926. e. Oxford. Films inc: A Kind of Loving; Billy Liar; Darling Far From the Madding Crowd; Midnight Cowboy (Oscar-1969); Sunday, Bloody Sunday; The Day of the Locust; Marathon Man; Yanks.
 Thea inc: No Why; Timon of Athens; Days in the Trees; I and Albert; Heartbreak House; Julius Caesar.

SCHLONDORFF, Volker: Dir. b. Wiesbaden, Ger, 1939. Films inc: Young Torless; Der Rebell; Baal; The Sudden Fortune of the Poor People of Kombach; The Moral of Ruth; Summer Lightning; The Coup de Grace; The Tin Drum. (Oscar-Foreign Film-1979).

SCHLOSSER, Herbert S: Exec. b. Atlantic City, NJ. e. Princeton U, Yale U. Atty, Calif Nat'l Prodns (subsid NBC); VP, GM, 1960; dir talent & program admin, NBC TV, 1961; vp talent & pgm admin, 1962; VP pgms, west coast, 1966-72; exec vp, NBC-TV, 1972; p, NBC-TV, 1973; P & COO, 1974-76; P & CEO, 1977.

SCHNABEL, Stefan: Act. b. Berlin, Feb 2, 1912. e. Bonn U. Bway 1937, Julius Caesar. Plays inc: Shoemaker's Holiday; Glamour Preferred; Everyman; Land of Fame; The Cherry Orchard; Around the World in 80 Days; Faust; The Love of Four Colonels; Plain and Fancy; Small War on Murray Hill; In the Matter of J Robert Oppenheimer; Older People; Enemies; Rosmersholm; Little Black Sheep; Passion of Dracula; Teibele and Her Dream.

Films inc: Journey Into Fear; The Iron Curtain; Diplomatic Courier; The Great Houdini; The Twenty-Seventh Day; The Ugly American; The Counterfeit Traitor; Two Weeks in Another Town; Rampage. .

TV inc: The Guiding Light.

SCHNEER, Charles: Prod. b. Norfolk, VA, May 5, 1920. e. Columbia Coll. Films inc: The Seventh Voyage of Sinbad; The Three Worlds of Gulliver; 20 Million Miles to Earth; Good Day For A Hanging; I Aim at the Stars; Mysterious Island; Jason and the Argonauts; The First Men in the Moon; You Must be Joking; Landraiders; Half a Sixpence; The Executioner; Sinbad's Golden Voyage; Sinbad and the Eye of the Tiger.

SCHNEIDER, Alan: Dir. b. Kharkov, Russia, Dec 12, 1917. e. U WI, BA; Cornell U, MA; Johns Hopkins U. Dir plays at Catholic University Theatre, Washington, prior to Bway; dir drama division Juillard.

Bway inc: Storm Operation (act only); A Long Way From Home; The Remarkable Mr. Pennypacker; All Summer Long; Anastasia; Tonight in Samarkand; Miss Lonelyhearts; Endgame; The American Dream; The Ballad of the Sad Cafe; Who's Afraid of Virginia Woolf? (Tony-1963); Happy Days; A Delicate Balance; You Know I Can't Hear You When the Water's Running; The Birthday Party; I Never Sang for My Father; Krapp's Last Tape; The Sign in Sidney Brustein's Window; Zalmen, or the Madness of God; The Lady from Dubuque.

Films inc: Samuel Beckett's Film.

TV inc: Pullman Car Hiawatha; Oedipus the King; The Life of Samuel Johnson; Waiting for Godot; The Years Between.

SCHNEIDER, John: Act-Singer. b. Mt. Kisco, NY, Apr 8. Started as fashion model; worked summer stock, off-Bway.

Films inc: Smokey and the Bandit.

TV inc: The Million Dollar Dixie Delivery; The Dukes of Hazzard; John Schneider--Back Home. Barbara Mandrell and the Mandrell Sisters.

SCHNEIDER, Romy (Rosemarie Albach-Retty): Act. b. Vienna, Sep 23, 1938. Films inc: The Story of Vicki; Forever My Love; Boccaccio 70; The Cardinal; The Trial; The Victors; Good Neighbor Sam; What's New Pussycat?; 10:30 P.M. Summer; Triple Cross; Don't You Cry; Bloomfield; The Assassination of Trotsky; The Infernal Trio; Dirty Hands; Mado; Group Portrait With Lady; A Woman At Her Window; Clair De Femme; Sidney Sheldon's Bloodline; A Simple Story; Death Watch; La Banquiere (The Woman Banker).

SCHOENFELD, Joe: Exec. b. NYC, Jun 2, 1907. Reporter in NY before joining Variety, 1932; resd 1943 to join William Morris Agency on coast as exec; 1950 became edtr Daily Variety; 1959 retd to William Morris; resd 1974 to open consltnt office; 1978 joined Ted Mann Prodns as prodn exec.

SCHORR, Daniel L: TV newsman. b. NYC, Aug 31, 1916. e. CCNY, BSS. With various news services and newspapers before joining CBS in 1953 on special assignment; 1955 reopened CBS Bureau, Moscow; 1958-1960 on roving assignment; 1960-1966 chief German Bureau; 1966-1976, chief of Washington Bureau; 1979 Public Radio and TV; 1980 Cable News Network.

TV inc: The Watergate Affair (Emmy-1973); Watergate--The White House Transcripts (Emmy-1974); The Senate and the Watergate Affair (Emmy-1974).

SCHRADER, Paul Wri. b. Grand Rapids, MI, Jul 22, 1946. e. Calvin Coll, BA, UCLA, MA. Films inc: Obsession; The Yakuza; Taxi Driver; Rolling Thunder; Blue Collar; Hardcore; Old Boyfriends; American Gigolo (& dir); Raging Bull.

SCHREIBER, Avery: Act. b. Chicago, IL, Apr 9, 1935. With Second City troupe; teamed with Jack Burns in comedy act; then solo. Bway inc: How To Be a Jewish Mother (dir); Ovid's Metamorphoses; Dreyfus in Rehearsal.

TV inc: My Mother The Car; Burns and Schreiber Comedy Hour; Sammy Davis & Friends; Ben Vereen Summer Show; Harlem Globetrotter's Popcorn Machine; Second City Comedy Show (host); Flatbed Annie and Sweetiepie--Lady Truckers; All Commercials; More Wild Wild West.

Films inc: Swashbuckler; The Last Remake of Beau Geste; Scavenger Hunt; Concorde--Airport '79; Silent Scream; Galaxina.

SCHRODER, Ricky: Act. b. Staten Island, NY, Apr 13, 1970. Began modeling at four months; did scores of commercials before film debut in The Champ. Films inc: The Last Flight of Noah's Ark; The Earthling.

TV inc: Little Lord Fauntleroy.

SCHUCK, John: Act. b. Boston, Feb 4. e. Denison, BA. Films inc: M*A*S*H; Brewster McCloud; McCabe and Mrs Miller; Thieves Like Us; Butch and Sundance-The Early Days; Just You and Me Kid.

TV inc: McMillan and Wife; Holmes and YoYo; The Halloween That Almost Wasn't; Turnabout.

SCHUDSON, Hod David: Comp. b. Milwaukee, WI, Oct 29, 1942. e. Northwestern U. Member of Hod & Marc recording team in early 70's before moving to LA to do film-tv scoring, composing. Partner, 1980, Great Plains Entertainment Corp. TV inc: Lou Grant; Friends; ABC Afternoon Specials (Emmy-1978).

(Died Nov 17, 1980).

SCHUENZEL, Dr Rolf G: Prod-Dist. b. Dresden, Germany, Dec 24, 1934. e. U of WI, EE, PhD. Founded Profilm, 1967; Viva-Film, 1972; Look Filmverleih, 1978; all in Munich. Film distributor with 5 offices in Germany.

SCHULBERG, Budd Wilson: Wri. b. NYC, Mar 27, 1914. e. Dartmouth College. S of Ad and B P Schulberg. Publicist, Paramount Pictures, 1931. Screenwriter from 1932. Films inc: A Star Is Born (add dial); Little Orphan Annie; Winter Carnival; Weekend for Three; City Without Men; On the Waterfront (Oscar-Story, sp-1954); A Face In The Crowd; Wind Across The Everglades. Bway inc: The Disenchanted; What Makes Sammy Run?

TV inc: The Angry Voice of Watts (Emmy-special-1966).

SCHULBERG, Stuart: Prod. b. LA, Nov 17, 1922. B of Budd Schulberg. With NBC since 1961. TV shows inc: David Brinkley's Journal; NBC Sports in Action; The Angry Voices of Watts; The Air of Disaster; Loosers Weepers; The New Voices of Watts; Somehow It Works; for eight years (1968-76) prod Today Show (Emmys-1970, 1971); College Sports; Big Money On Campus; The American Family: An Endangered Species.

Films inc: No Way Back; Wind Across the Everglades; Special Delivery.

(Died June 28, 1979).

SCHULMAN, Arnold: Wri. b. Philadelphia, Aug 11, 1925. e. U of NC, American Theatre Wing, Actor's Studio. Films inc: Wild in the Wind; A Hole in the Head; Love with the Proper Stranger; The Night They Raided Minsky's; Goodbye, Columbus; Funny Lady; Players (& prod).

SCHULTZ, Michael A: Dir. b. Milwaukee, WI, Nov 10, 1938. e. U of WI, Marquette U. Thea inc: Song of the Lusitanian Bogey; Kongi's Harvest; God Is A (Guess What?); Does a Tiger Wear a Necktie?; Every Night When the Sun Goes Down; What the Winesellers Buy.

Films inc: To Be Young, Gifted and Black; Sgt Pepper's Lonely Hearts Club Band; Scavenger Hunt.

TV inc: To Be Young, Gifted and Black; Ceremonies In Dark Old Men.

SCHULZ, Charles Monroe: Cartoonist-Wri. b. Minneapolis, MN, Nov 26, 1922. Created comic strip Peanuts in 1950; strip has been the basis for books, plays, films, tv.
Films inc: Bon Voyage, Charlie Brown and Don't Come Back.
TV inc: A Charlie Brown Christmas (*Emmy*-wri-1966); A Charlie Brown Thanksgiving (*Emmy*-wri-1974); Happy Birthday, Charlie Brown; You're the Greatest, Charlie Brown; She's a Good Skate, Charlie Brown; The Fantastic Funnies; Life Is A Circus, Charlie Brown.

SCHUMACHER, Joel: Wri. b. NYC, 1942. Before turning to screenplays, held jobs as art dir, costume designer. Created designs for The Last of Sheila; Blume in Love; Sleeper. Film scripts inc: Car Wash; Sparkle; The Wiz.
TV inc: Virginia Hill; Amateur Night at the Dixie Bar & Grill.

SCHWARTZ, Al: Prod-Dir. b. Chicago, Jan 3, 1932. e. U of WI, BA. TV inc: Women in Prison; The Unwed Mother; Many Moods of Ravinia; The World of Andrew Wyeth; Child's Garden of Pollution; Cinderella; Canterville Ghost; Cousteau's People of the Sea; Donny and Marie Special; Dick Clarke's Good Ol Days; My Three Sons; The Partridge Family; Dick Clarke's Good Ol Days II; The Man in the Santa Claus Suit; The Sensational, Shocking, Wonderful Wacky 70's.

SCHWARTZ, Arthur: Comp. b. NYC, Nov 25, 1900. e. NYC, AB, JD, Columbia U, MA. Bway inc: The Little Show; Princes Charming; the Second Little Show; Three's A Crowd; The Band Wagon; Flying Colors; Revenge With Music; At Home Abroad; Virginia; Stars in Your Eyes; American Jubilee; Park Avenue; Inside U.S.A. (& prod); A Tree Grows in Brooklyn; The Gay Life; Jennie; That's Entertainment; Nicholas Nickleby.
Films inc: Under Your Spell; That Girl from Paris; Navy Blues; Thank Your Lucky Stars; The Time, the Place and the Girl; Excuse My Dust; Dangerous When Wet; The Band Wagon; You're Never Too Young; Cover Girl (prod); Night and Day (prod).
Songs inc: Dancing in the Dark; I See Your Face Before Me; You and the Night and the Music; That's Entertainment; I Guess I'll Have to Change My Plans; Something To Remember You By; I Love Louisa; They're Either Too Young or Too Old.

SCHWARTZ, Stephen: Comp-Lyr. b. NYC, Mar 6, 1948. e. Carnegie-Mellon U, BFA, Juilliard. Bway inc: Butterflies Are Free (title song); Godspell; Mass; Working; Pippin; The Magic Show; Straws in the Wind; The Baker's Wife.
Films inc: Godspell.
(*Grammys*-comp & prod-1971).

SCHWARTZMAN, Jack: Exec. b. NYC, Jul 22, 1932. e. UCLA, BS, UCLA Law School, LLB. Films inc: Being There (exec prod). Exec vp, Lorimar Productions, Inc.

SCHWARZENEGGER, Arnold: Act. b. Graz, Austria, Jul 30, 1947. Former Mr Universe. Films inc: Stay Hungry; Pumping Iron (doc); The Villain. TV inc: The Jayne Mansfield Story.

SCHYGULLA, Hanna: Act. b. Kattowitz, Germany, Dec 25, 1943. Worked with Rainer Werner Fassbinder in Munich's Action-Theater; one of the founders of the 'anti-teater' group. Films inc: Love Is Colder Than Death; Katzelmacher; Gods of the Plague; The Bridegroom, The Comedienne and the Pimp; Hunting Scenes From Bavaria; Baal; Rio Das Mortes; Whity; Niklashauser Fahrt; Beware of a Holy Whore; Pioneers in Ingolstadt; Mathias Kneissl; The Merchant of Four Seasons; Jacob Von Gunten; The Bitter Tears of Petra Von Kant; The House By the Sea; Jail Bait; The Wrong Move; Effi Briest; The Third Generation; The Clown; The Marriage of Maria Braun; Berlin Alexanderplatz.

SCOFIELD, Paul: Act. b. Hurstpierpoint, Eng, Jan 21, 1922. Films inc: That Lady; Carve Her Name with Pride; The Train; A Man for All Seasons (*Oscar*-1966); King Lear; Bartleby; Scorpio; A Delicate Balance.
Bway inc: A Man for All Seasons (*Tony*-1962); King Lear.
London Thea inc: Desire Under the Elms; numerous Shakespearean roles; Pericles (& prod); A Question of Fact; Time Remembered; The Power and the Glory; Expresso Bongo; A Man for All Seasons; The Government Inspector; Staircase; Hotel in Amsterdam; Dimetos; The Madras House; Amadeus.
TV inc: Male of the Species (*Emmy*-1969); The Curse of King Tut's Tomb (narr).

SCORSESE, Martin: Wri-Dir. b. NYC, 1942. While attending NYU produced two award winning film shorts, What's A Girl Like You Doing in A Place Like This?; It's Not Just You, Murray.
Films inc: Woodstock (supv ed); Who's That Knocking At My Door; Boxcar Bertha; Alice Doesn't Live Here Anymore; Taxi Driver; New York, New York; Raging Bull.

SCOTT, Brenda (nee Smith): Act. b. Cincinnati, OH, Mar 15, 1943. Films inc: Johnny Tiger; Journey to Shiloh; This Savage Land; Simon, King of the Witches.
TV inc: Window on Main Street; The Road West; Donovan's Kid.

SCOTT, Debralee: Act. b. Elizabeth, NJ, Apr 2. Films inc: American Graffiti; The Candidate; Dirty Harry; Superdad; Our Time; Crazy World of Julius Vrooder; Reincarnation of Peter Proud; Just Tell Me That You Love Me.
TV inc: Lisa, Bright and Dark; Summer Without Boys; Senior Year; Earthquake; Sons and Daughters; Welcome Back Kotter; Mary Hartman, Mary Hartman; Forever Fernwood; Angie.

SCOTT, Eric: Act. b. LA, Oct 20, 1958. TV inc: Norman Rockwell's America; The Clowns; The Waltons.

SCOTT, George C: Act. b. Wise, VA, Oct 18, 1927. On screen from 1959. Films inc: The Hanging Tree; Anatomy of A Murder; The Hustler; The Power and the Glory; The List of Adrian Messenger; Dr. Strangelove; The Bible; The Flim Flam Man; Patton (*Oscar*-1970, refused to accept); They Might Be Giants; Hospital; New Centurions; Oklahoma Crude; The Day of the Dolphin; The Hindenburg; Islands in the Stream; Crossed Swords; Movie Movie; Hard Core; Arthur Miller on Home Grounds; The Changeling; The Formula.
Bway inc: Comes a Day; The Andersonville Trial; The Little Foxes; Plaza Suite; Uncle Vanya; Death of a Salesman (& dir); Sly Fox; Tricks of the Trade.
TV inc: The Crucible; Jane Eyre; The Price (*Emmy*-1971); Fear on Trial; Beauty and the Beast.

SCOTT, Gordon (nee Werschkul): Act. b. Portland, OR, Aug 3, 1927. e. OR U. Screen debut, Tarzan's Hidden Jungle, 1955. Films inc: Tarzan and the Lost Safari; Tarzan's Greatest Adventure; The Tramplers; Arm of Fire.

SCOTT, Hazel: Pianist-Singer. b. Trinidad, 1920. Nitery and concert performer. Films inc: Something to Shout About; I Dood It; The Heat's On; Broadway Rhythm; Rhapsody in Blue; Night Affair.
TV inc: One Life to Live; The Bold Ones.

SCOTT, Janette: Act. b. Morecambe, Eng, Dec 14, 1938. Films inc: Went the Day Well?; No Place for Jennifer; No Highway; The Magic Box; As Long as They're Happy; Now and Forever; The Good Companions; The Devil's Disciple; The Old Dark House; The Beauty Jungle; Crack in the World.

SCOTT, Lizabeth: Act. b. Scranton, PA, 1922. On screen from 1945. Films inc: The Strange Love of Martha Ivers; Dead Reckoning; I Walk Alone; Desert Fury; Pitfall; Too Late for Tears; Paid in Full; Bad for Each Other; Quantrill's Raiders; Pulp.

SCOTT, Margaretta: Act. b. London, Feb 13, 1912. Films inc: Dirty Work; Things to Come; Quiet Wedding; Sabotage at Sea; Fanny by Gaslight; The Man from Morocco Idol of Paris; Where's Charley?; Town on Trial; The Last Man to Hang; A Woman Possessed; An Honourable Murder; Crescendo; Percy.

Thea inc: Confrontation; Country Wife; Alien Corn; Oedipus Rex; A Woman of No Importance; Equus.

SCOTT, Martha: Act. b. Jamesport, MO, Sep 22, 1916. Began in summer stock, radio. Screen debut, 1940, Our Town. Films inc: The Howards of Virginia; One Foot in Heaven; So Well Remembered; Strange Bargain; The Desperate Hours; The Ten Commandments; Sayonara; Ben-Hur; Airport 1975.

TV inc: The Bob Newhart Show; Route 66; The Nurses; The Word; Charleston; Married--The First Year; Beulah Land; Father Figure; Secret of Midland Heights.

Bway inc: Soldier's Wife; Voice of the Turtle; The Male Animal; The Remarkable Mr. Pennypacker; The Skin of Our Teeth.

SCOTT, Randolph: Act. b. Orange Co, VA, Jan 23, 1903. e. U of NC On screen from 1929. Films inc: Far Call; Island of Lost Souls; To The Shores of Tripoli; Bombardier; The Spoilers; Captain Kidd; My Favorite Wife; Badman's Territory; Virginia City; Belle Starr; Pittsburgh; Albuquerque; Colt '45; Man in the Saddle; The Bounty Hunter; Decision at Sundown; Comanche Station; Ride the High Country.

SCOTTI, Vito: Act. b. San Francisco, Jan 26, 1918. Films inc: Where the Boys Are; The Explosive Generation; Two Weeks in Another Town; Captain Newman, M.D.; Rio Conchos; The Pleasure Seekers; Von Ryan's Express; What Did You Do in the War, Daddy?; The Caper of the Golden Bulls; The Secret War of Harry Frigg; How Sweet It Is; Head; Cactus Flower; The McCullochs.

TV inc: Playhouse 90; Climax; To Rome With Love; The Flying Nun; Barefoot in the Park; The Bionic Woman; Colombo; The Ghosts of Buxley Hall.

SCOTTO, Renata: Soprano. b. Savona, Italy, Feb 1936. Won nat'l competition for young artists, debuted 1953 Milan's Teatro Nuovo; 1954 La Scala debut; guest artist Buenos Aires; Moscow; Tokyo; Covent Garden; 1966 Metropolitan opera debut; 1976 became first soprano in Met history to sing all three heroines in Puccini's trilogy, Il Trittico.

TV inc: La Boheme; Renata Scotto, Prima Donna.

SCOURBY, Alexander: Act. b. NYC, Nov 13, 1913. e. U of WV. Films inc: Affair in Trinidad; The Big Heat; The Silver Chalice; Giant; Seven Thieves; The Big Fisherman; Confessions of a Counterspy.

TV inc: (narr) The World of Maurice Chevalier; The World of Jacqueline Kennedy; The World of Bob Hope; The World of Sophia Loren; The World of Benny Goodman; The Death of the Hired Man; Project 20; The Superliners-Twilight of an Era; The Body Human, The Body Beautiful; The Body Human--The Sexes II.

Bway inc: Hamlet; The Deputy of Paris; Crime and Punishment; Detective Story; Darkness at Noon; Saint Joan; An Inspector Calls.

SCRUGGS, Earl: Singer-Mus. b. Cleveland County, NC, Jan 6, 1924. With partner Lester Flatt became the undisputed kings of Bluegrass music during the 50s and 60s. With their Foggy Mountain Boys, Flatt & Scruggs were regular cast members of the Grand Ole Opry until they split up in early 1969. Team won (Grammy-1968). (See also FLATT, Lester).

SCULLY, Vin: Sportscaster. b. NYC, Nov 29, 1927. e. Fordham U. Joined CBS sports 1975. Hosts The Challenge of the Sexes. Has been associated with the Dodgers baseball club since 1950. Still handles Dodger broadcasts along with CBS sports assignments.

SEAL, Elizabeth: Act. b. Genoa, Italy, Aug 28, 1933. e. Royal Academy of Dancing

Thea inc: (London) The Pajama Game; Camino Real; Irma La Douce; Cat Among the Pigeons; The Recruiting Officer; Cabaret; Fajeon Reviewed; Salad Days. Bway inc: Irma La Douce (Tony-1961).

Films inc: Town on Trial; Cone of Silence; Vampire Circus.

TV inc: Trelawney of the Wells; Philby, Burgess and MacLean.

SEALS AND CROFTS: (See CROFTS, Dash and SEALS, James).

SEALS, James: Mus-Singer. b. Sidney, TX. With The Champs, The Dawnbreakers before teaming with Dash Crofts. Albums inc: Seals and Crofts I and II; Year of Sunday; Summer Breeze; Diamond Girl; Unborn Child; I'll Play for You; Greatest Hits; Get Closer; Sudan Village; Takin' It Easy.

SEARS, Sally: Thea Prod. b. NYC, Nov 13, 1937. P, Primavera Productions, Ltd 1962-63, special Asst The Washington Ballet; 1965, Co-Dir Manhattan Festival Ballet. VP, Continental Concert Service; advisory board, Performance Theatre Center & School, Ltd

Thea inc: (prod) Please Don't Cry and Say No (off-Bdwy) Nellie Toole & Co. (off-Bdwy); Summer Brave; The Royal Family; Tickles by Tucholsky; The Night of the Tribades; An Almost Perfect Person.

SEATON, George: Wri-Dir-Prod. b. South Bend, IN, Apr 17, 1911. Started as actor, played Lone Ranger on radio.

Films inc: A Day at the Races (co-sp); The Song of Bernadette (sp); Diamond Horseshoe (dir); Junior Miss (& dir); The Shocking Miss Pilgrim (& dir); Miracle on 34th Street (& dir) (Oscar-Sp-1947); The Big Lift (& dir); For Heaven's Sake (& dir); Anything Can Happen (& dir); Little Boy Lost (& dir); The Country Girl (& dir) (Oscar-sp-1954); and Profane (& dir); The Tin Star (prod); Teacher's Pet (dir); The Pleasure of His Company (dir); The Counterfeit Traitor (sp & dir); Thirty-Six Hour (sp & dir); What's So Bad about Feeling Good? (sp, dir, prod); Airport (sp & dir); Showdown (sp, dir, prod).

Jean Hersholt Humanitarian Award 1961.

(Died July 28, 1979).

SEBERG, Jean: Act. b. Marshalltown, IA, Nov 13, 1938. Won contest at age 17 for role of Preminger's Saint Joan. Films inc: Bonjour Tristesse; The Mouse that Roared; Breathless; Playtime; In the French Style; Lilith; Moment to Moment; Estouffade a la Caraibe; The Road to Corinth; Pendulum; Paint Your Wagon; Airport; Macho Callahan; Behind the Shutters; The Wild Duck.

TV inc: Mousey.

(Died Sep 8, 1979).

SEDAKA, Neil: Singer-Sngwri. b. Mar 13, 1939. e. Juilliard. Songs inc: Stupid Cupid; Calendar Girl; Oh, Carol; Stairway to Heaven; Happy Birthday, Sweet 16; Laughter in the Rain; Bad Blood; Love Will Keep Us Together; Lonely Night; Breaking Up Is Hard To Do.

Albums inc: Sedaka's Back; Hungry Years; Stepping Out; All You Need Is Music.

SEDAN, Rolfe: Act. b. NYC, Jan 20, 1896. Started in vaudeville, 1912. Films inc: The Golden Goose; The Spy; April in Paris; Mississippi Gambler; Ninotchka; The Story of Vernon and Irene Castle; Young Frankenstein; Chinatown; Art of Love; Murder at the Rue Morgue; 36th Hour; The Iron Mask; The World's Greatest Lover; The Happy Hooker Goes to Washington; The Hindenberg; Love at First Bite; The Frisco Kid.

Thea inc: A Bell for Adano; All Men Are Alike; Would-Be Gentlemen; On the House; The Web and the Rock.

SEEGER, Pete: Singer-Comp. b. NYC, May 3, 1919. Developed into an authority on folk music. Founded the Almanac Singers, 1940; later was one of the founders of The Weavers; indicted 1955 after refusing to testify before House Un-American Activities Committee; charges dismissed in 1962. Gave concerts throughout the world on American Folk Music and its origins.

Songs inc: Where Have All the Flowers Gone; If I Had a Hammer; Kisses Sweeter Than Wine.

TV inc: Smothers Brothers Comedy Hour; Rainbow Quest (educational).

SEGAL, Erich: Wri. b. Brooklyn, NY, Jun 16, 1937. e. Harvard. Films inc: Yellow Submarine; The Games; Love Story; RPM; Oliver's Story; A Change Of Seasons.

TV inc: The Ancient Games (wri-narr); Mourning Becomes Electra (narr); 1972, 1976, 1980 Olympic Games (Commentator).

SEGAL, George: Act. b. Great Neck, NY, Feb 13, 1934. e. Columbia U, BA. On screen from 1961. Films inc: The Young Doctors; The Longest Day; Act One; The New Interns; Invitation to a Gunfighter; Ship of Fools; King Rat; The Lost Command; Who's Afraid of Virginia Woolf?; The Quiller Memorandum; The St. Valentine's Day Massacre; Bye Bye Braverman; No Way to Treat a Lady; The Southern Star; The Bridge at Remagen; The Girl Who Couldn't Say No; Loving; The Owl and the Pussycat; Where's Poppa?; Born to Win; The Hot Rock; A Touch of Class; Blume in Love; The Terminal Man; California Split; The Black Bird; Russian Roulette; The Dutchess and the Dirtwater Fox; Fun with Dick and Jane; Rollercoaster; Who is Killing the Great Chefs of Europe?; Lost and Found; Last Married Couple in America.

TV inc: Death of a Salesman; Of Mice and Men; The Desperate Hours.

Bway inc: The Iceman Cometh (revival); Antony and Cleopatra; Leave It to Jane; The Premise; Rattle of a Simple Man; The Knack.

SEGAL, Jonathan: Act. b. NYC, Jul 8, 1953. TV inc: The Lie; Quincy; The Paper Chase; Brave New World.

SEGAL, Vivienne: Act. b. Philadelphia, PA, 1897. Bway inc: The Blue Paradise; My Lady's Glove; Miss 1917; Oh! Lady, Lady!; The Little Whopper; The Yankee Princess; Ziegfeld Follies; Florida Girl; Castles In The Air; The Desert Song; The Chocolate Soldier; The Three Musketeers; Music in the Air; I Married An Angel; Pal Joey; A Connecticut Yankee; Forever Is Now.

On screen from 1930. Films inc: Song of the West; Bridge of the Regiment; Golden Dawn; Viennese Nights; The Cat and the Fiddle.

SEGELSTEIN, Irwin: Exec. b. NYC. e. CCNY. With Benton & Bowles Advertising agency for 18 years before joining CBS in 1965. Left CBS-TV in 1973 to become pres, CBS Records Division; joined NBC in 1976 as exec vp, programs; appointed exec vp, Broadcasting, NBC, Jun 9, 1978; Pres June 1980.

SEGOVIA, Andres: Guitarist. b. Linares, Spain, Feb 18, 1894. Debut, Granada 1909; has toured world extensively; made NY debut 1928 at Town Hall.

(*Grammy*-Classical Inst-1959).

SEIZER, Bob: Wri-Prod. b. Des Moines, IA, May 13, 1931. TV inc: Challenge Golf; Big Three Golf; Winter Olympic Games, 1972; Challenge of the Sexes; Three on Three Basketball; Walter Alston-The Quiet Man; World Team Tennis; Memories of Elvis; Rock 'N Roll Sports Classic.

SEKELY, Steve: Dir. b. Budapest, Hungary, Feb 25, 1899. Directed films in Germany, Budapest before coming to US in 1938. Films inc: Miracle on Main Street; Behind Prison Walls; Women in Bondage. In 1945 org. Star Pictures, served as pres.; prod.: Lady in the Death House; Waterfront; My Buddy; The Fabulous Suzannne; Hollow Triumph; The Scar; Cartouche; The Sinner; The Day of the Triffids; Kenner; The Girl Who Loved Purple Flowers.

TV inc: Orient Express; New York Confidential; Assignment; Underwater.

(Died March 9, 1979).

SELANDER, Lesley: Dir. b. LA, May 26, 1900. Approximately 150 feature pictures since 1936, inc: Cattle Pass; The Round-Up; Belle Starr's Daughter; 25 Hopalong Cassidy films; I Was an American Spy; The Highwayman; Tall Man Riding; The Lone Ranger and the Lost City of Gold; Town Tamer; Fort Utah; Arizona Bushwackers.

TV inc: 60 Lassie episodes; 40 Laramie episodes; 30 Cannonball episodes.

(Died Dec 5, 1979).

SELDEN, Albert W: Prod-Comp. b. NYC, Oct 20, 1922. e. Yale U. Bway inc: Small Wonder (comp); Grey-Eyed People; A Month of Sundays (comp); His and Hers; Waiting for Gilliam; Body Beautiful; The Amazing Adele (prod-comp-lyr); Hallelujah Baby (*Tony*-1968); Girls Against the Boys; Man of La Mancha (*Tony*-1972); What Do You Really Know About Your Husband; Portrait of a Queen; Come Summer; The Lincoln Mask; Irene; Comin' Uptown.

SELDES, Marian: Act. b. NYC, Aug 23, 1928. Bway inc: Medea; Crime and Punishment; That Lady; Come of Age; The High Ground; Ondine; The Chalk Garden; The Wall; A Gift of Time; The Milk Train Doesn't Stop Here Anymore; A Delicate Balance (*Tony*-1967); Father's Day; Equus; The Merchant; Deathtrap.

Films inc: Mr Lincoln; The Big Fisherman; The Greatest Story Ever Told; Fingers.

TV inc: Macbeth. Radio: Mystery Theatre.

SELF, William: Exec. b. Dayton, OH, Jun 21, 1921. e. U of Chicago, BS. TV inc: (Prod) Schlitz Playhouse of Stars, CBS 1952-56; Frank Sinatra Show, 1957-58; exec. prod. CBS TV Network, 1959; exec. prod. 20th Century-Fox-TV, 1960-61; VP in charge of prod., 20th Century-Fox-TV, 1961-69; pres., 20th Century-Fox-TV, 1969-74; Frankovich-Self Prods, 1975; VP, programs, CBS-TV, 1976-77; VP, motion pictures and Mini-series CBS Entertainment Division, 1978.

SELLECK, Tom: Act. b. Detroit, MI, Jan 29. e. USC. Films inc: Myra Breckenridge; Seven Minutes; Coma.

TV inc: Bracken's World; Countdown at the Superbowl; The Sacketts; Gypsy Warriors; Boston and Kilbride; The Concrete Cowboys; Magnum, P.I.

SELLERS, Arlene: Prod. b. Sep 7, 1921. e. UC Berkeley, BA, LLB, JD. Films inc: Silver Bears; Cross of Iron; End of the Game; The Lady Vanishes; The Seven-Per-Cent Solution; House Calls; Cuba.

SELLERS, Elizabeth: Act. b. Glasgow, Scotland, May 6, 1923. Films inc: Floodtide; Madeleine; Cloudburst; The Gentle Gunman; The Barefoot Contessa; Three Cases of Murder; The Shiralee; The Day They Robbed the Bank of England; The Chalk Garden; The Mummy's Shroud; The Hireling.

Thea (London) The Remarkable Mr Pennypacker; South Sea Bubble; Tea & Sympathy; The Sound of Murder.

TV inc: Too Late for the Mashed Potato; The Happy Ones; R 3.

SELLERS, Peter: Act. b. Southsea, Eng, Sep 8, 1925. Began career in theatre, radio as a mimic. Screen debut, 1950, Orders Are Orders. Films inc: John and Julie; The Ladykillers; The Naked Truth; Up the Creek; Tom Thumb; The Mouse That Roared; I'm All Right, Jack; Two Way Stretch; Lolita; Only Two Can Play; Trial and Error; The World of Henry Orient; The Pink Panther; A Shot in the Dark; What's New Pussycat?; The Wrong Box; Casino Royale; The Bobo; The Party; I Love You Alice B. Toklas; The Magic Christian; There's a Girl in My Soup; Where Does It Hurt?; Alice in Wonderland; The Optimists of Nine Elms; Soft Beds, Hard Battles; Return of the Pink Panther; Ghost in the Noonday Sun; Murder by Death; The Pink Panther Strikes Again; Revenge of the Pink Panther; The Prisoner of Zenda; Being There; The Fiendish Plot of Dr. Fu Manchu.

TV inc: Gently Bentley; Idiot Weekly; A Show Called Fred; Son of Fred; The Cathode Ray Tube Show.

(Died July 23, 1980).

SELLIER, Charles E Jr: Prod. Films inc: The Adventures of Frontier Fremont (& wri); In Search of Noah's Ark (& wri); The Lincoln Conspiracy (& wri); Beyond and Back; The Bermuda Triangle; In Search of Historic Jesus; Hangar 18.

TV inc: The Deerslayer; Greatest Heroes of the Bible; The Life and Times of Grizzly Adams; Mark Twain's America--Tom Edison, Lightning Slinger; Mark Twain's America--Abe Lincoln, Freedom Fighter; The Legend of Sleepy Hollow.

SELTZER, Leo: Prod-Dir-Wri. b. Montreal, Mar 13, 1913. e. U of MA, BA. Prod & dir docs, informational, theatrical, TV films for various private and governmental orgs. Films inc: Day in Malaysia; Summit; Sinews of Freedom; Traditional Chinese Opera.

SELTZER, Walter: Prod. b. Philadelphia, Nov 7, 1914. e. U of PA. Pub for WB Theatres, Philadelphia; Fox West Coast Theatres; to Hollywood with MGM 1936-39. Col 1940-41; USMC 1941-44. Pub dir, Hal Wallis, 1945-54; vp in chg adv & pub; Hecht-Lancaster 1954-55; partner Glass-Seltzer PR firm; & Glass-Seltzer Prodns; vp & exec prod Pennebaker Prodns. Films inc: The Boss (asso prod); One-Eyed Jacks; Shake Hands With the Devil; Paris Blues; The Naked Edge; Man in the Middle; Wild Seed; War Lord; Beau Geste; Will Penny; Number One; Darker Than Amber; The Omega Man; Skyjacked; Soylent Green; The Cay; The Last Hard Men.

SELVIN, Ben: Exec. b. NYC, 1898. Started as bandleader at age 19 at Moulin Rouge, NYC; led various orchestras over the next two decades, his sidemen included such musicians as Benny Goodman, Glenn Miller, Tommy and Jimmy Dorsey. A pioneer in the field of electrical transcriptions, he became an exec with various recording companies and made more than 9,000 recordings.
(Died July 15, 1980).

SELZNICK, Irene Mayer: Prod. b. NYC, Apr 2, 1910. D of the late Louis B Mayer; ex-wife late David O Selznick. Exec with Selznick Int'l 1936-40; Vanguard Films, 1941-49. Formed own company, NY, 1949.
Bway inc: Streetcar Named Desire; Bell, Book and Candle; Flight Into Egypt; The Chalk Garden; The Complaisant Lover. (London): The Last Joke.

SELZNICK, Joyce: Exec. b. LA, Feb 12, 1928. Began as apprentice writer, WB, switched to cast dept; 1936 pub dept Col; 1944, Eastern Talent Head; later became story head; 1967 named head wldwde talent & story depts Par; became ind cast dir, packager.

SEMEL, Terry: Exec. b. NYC, Feb 24, 1943. e. CCNY, MBA. Originally a CPA, joined WB 1966 working NY, Cleveland, LA; 1971, domestic sls mgr CBS Cinema Center Films; 1973, vp-gen sls mgr Buena Vista; 1975 retd to WB as vp-gen sls mgr; 1978, exec vp, COO.

SEMPLE, Lorenzo Jr: Wri. Films inc: Pretty Poison; Marriage of a Young Stockbroker; The Drowning Pool; Three Days of the Condor; King Kong; Hurricane; Flash Gordon.

SENENSKY, Ralph: Dir. b. Mason City, IA, May 1, 1923. e. Northwestern U. TV inc: Dr. Kildare; Twilight Zone; Route 66; Naked City; Arrest and Trial; The Fugitive; Twelve O'Clock High; Star Trek; Mission Impossible; Ironside; Mannix; The Name of the Game; The Courtship of Eddie's Father; Dan August; Night Gallery; The Rookies; Barnaby Jones; The Waltons; The New Adventures of Heidi.

SERKIN, Peter: Concert pianist. b. NYC, Jul 24, 1947. e. Curtis Inst of Music. S of Rudolf Serkin. Recitals major cities; guest soloist with NY Philharmonic; Cleveland Symphony; London Symphony.
(*Grammy*-New class artist-1965).

SERKIN, Rudolf: Concert pianist. b. Eger, Bohemia, Mar 28, 1903. Child prodigy at 4, guest artist with Vienna Symphony at 12. Began concert career Europe 1920; US debut 1933 Coolidge Festival, Washington; with Toscanini 1936. Guest artist major world orchestras in series of annual tours.
TV inc: America Entertains Vice Premier Teng Hsiao-Ping.

SERNA, Pepe: Act. b. Corpus Christi, TX, Jul 21, 1944. Films inc: Red Sky at Morning; Shootout; Hangup; Car Wash; Honeysuckle Rose; Inside Moves.
TV inc: The Deadly Tower; City in Fear.

SERRAULT, Michel: Act. b. France. Films inc: L'Argent des Autres; Get Out Your Handkerchiefs; The Associate; La Cage Aux Folles; La Gueule de l'autre; Heads or Tails; La Cage Aux Folles II.

SEVAREID, Eric: News Commentator. b. Velva, ND, Nov 26, 1912. e. U of MN. Started career as reporter Minneapolis Journal, Paris Herald Tribune, United Press. Joined CBS radio news staff in Paris at outbreak of WW II. Later natl correspondent with CBS. TV inc: LBJ-The Man and the President (*Emmy*-1973). Ret, 1977.

SEVAREID, Michael: Exec. b. Paris, Apr 25, 1940. e. Middlebury Coll, BA. S of Eric Sevareid. Actor 1960-1971. Films inc: The Shoot Horses, Don't They?; Airport; They Call Me Mr. Tibbs; Raid on Rommel.
TV inc: numerous segs as actor. Exec prod, CBS-TV, 1970-79. Named VP prodn, MGM, Sept 1979.

SEVEN, Johnny (John Anthony Fetto): Act-Prod-Dir. b. NYC, Feb 23, 1930. Films inc: Never Steal Anything Small; Sweet Smell of Success; The Last Mile; Guns of the Timberlane; The Apartment; Johnny Gunman; The Greatest Story Ever Told; Navajo Run (prod. & dir.); What Did You Do in the War, Daddy?; Gunfight in Abilene; The Destructors; The Love God.
TV inc: Ironside; Switch; CHiPs; Rockford Files; Police Woman; The New Terror (doc., prod. & dir.).
Bway inc: The Story Teller; Rose Tattoo.

SEVERINSEN, Carl H (Doc): Comp-Cond. b. Arlington, OR, Jul 7, 1927. Trumpeter in orchs inc Ted Fiorito; Benny Goodman; Charlie Barnet; Tommy Dorsey; Vaughn Monroe.
TV inc: Tonight Show (cond); Uptown-A Tribute to the Apollo Theatre.

SEVERN, Maida: Act. b. Aug 6, 1902. Films inc: Loving You; Marjorie Morningstar; Imitation of Life; Bells Are Ringing; Back Street; Mr. Hobbs Takes a Vacation; Story of Ruth; Dear Brigitte; Airport 1975; Young Frankenstein; Wonder Woman.
TV inc: General Hospital; Divorce Court; Ellery Queen.

SEYLER, Athene, CBE: Act. b. London, May 31, 1889. e. Bedford Coll. Stage debut 1909 in The Truants. Thea (London) The Dover Road; The Corn Is Green; The Cherry Orchard; Watch on the Rhine; The Last of Mrs Cheyney; Lady Windermere's Fan; Harvey; Who Is Sylvia; First Person Singular; Bell, Book and Candle; The Iron Duchess; Breath of Spring; The Gentleman Dancing Master; The Dark Stranger; The Reluctant Peer; Too True to be Good; Arsenic And Old Lace.
Films inc: This Freedom; The Perfect Lady; The Citadel; Quiet Wedding; Dear Octopus; Nicholas Nickleby; Queen of Spades; Young Wives' Tale; Pickwick Papers; Yield to the Night; Campbell's Kingdom; The Inn of the Sixth Happiness; Make Mine Mink; Nurse on Wheels.

SEYMOUR, Anne (nee Eckert): Act. b. NYC, Sep 11, 1909. On radio, about 5000 network programs inc: Grand Hotel; Story of Mary Marlin.
Bway inc: School for Scandal; Sunrise at Campobello; Ring Around the Moon.
Films inc: All the King's Men; The Whistle at Eaton Falls; Man on Fire; Pollyanna; Desire Under the Elms; Gift of Love; Home from the Hill; Misty; Good Neighbor Sam; Mirage; How To Succeed In Business Without Really Trying; Fitzwilly; Stay Away, Joe; Hearts of the West.
TV inc: Empire; I Never Said Goodbye; The Last Survivors; General Hospital; Sandburg's Lincoln; James at 15; Studs Lonigan; The Miracle Worker; Angel on My Shoulder.

SEYMOUR, Jane (Joyce Frankenberg): Act. b. England, Feb 15, 1951. With London Festival Ballet at age 13 before act. Films inc: Live and Let Die; Sinbad and the Eye of the Tiger; Battlestar Galactica; Oh, Heavenly Dog; Somewhere In Time.
TV inc: Captains and the Kings; Four Feathers; The Dallas Cowboy Cheerleaders.
Bway inc: Amadeus.

SEYRIG, Delphine: Act. b. Beirut, 1932. Formal dramatic training in Paris, later Actors Studio NY. Films inc: Pull My Daisy; Last Year in Marienbad; Muriel; La Musica; Accident; Mr. Freedom; Stolen Kisses; Daughters of Darkness; Milky Way; Peau d'Ane; The Discreet Charm of the Bourgeoisie; The Day of the Jackal; The Black Windmill; Aloise; Doll's House; Dear Michael; Le Dernier Cri; India Song; Faces of Love; Utkozben; Chere Inconnue; Le Chemin Perdu (The Lost Way).
Thea inc: The Lover; The Seagull; Old Times; The Garden of Delight; The Bitter Tears of Petra Von Kant.

SHACKELFORD, Ted: Act. b. Oklahoma City, OK, Jun 23, 1946. e. U Denver. TV inc: Another World; The Defection of Simas Kudirka; The Jordan Chance; Knots Landing.

SHAFFER, Anthony: Wri. b. Liverpool, Eng, May 15, 1926. e. Cambridge. B of Peter Shaffer. Films inc: Forbush and the Penguins; Frenzy; The Wicker Man; Death on the Nile.
 Plays inc: The Savage Parade; Sleuth (Tony-1971); The Case of Oily Levantine.
 TV inc: Pig in the Middle.

SHAFFER, Louise: Act. b. New Haven, CT, Jul 5. e. CT College for Women; Yale Drama School. Bway inc: First One Asleep, Whistle; We Have Always Lived In The Castle; Keep It In The Family; The Women.
 TV inc: Autumn Garden; All That Glitters; Search For Tomorrow; Where The Heart Is; Edge of Night; Ryan's Hope.

SHAFFER, Paul: Comp-Wri-Act. b. Thunder Bay, Ont, Canada. Played with Canadian jazz group; became mus dir Toronto company of Godspell.
 Bway inc: The Magic Show (cond); Godspell (cond); Gilda Radner--Live from NY (wri-act).
 Films inc: Gilda Live (wri-act).
 TV inc: Saturday Night Live (wri); A Year at the Top (act).

SHAFFER, Peter: Wri. b. Liverpool, Eng, May 15, 1926. e. Cambridge. D of Anthony Shaffer. Plays inc: Five Finger Exercise; The Private Ear and the Public Eye; The Merry Roosters Panto; The Royal Hunt of the Sun; The Battle of Shrivings; Equus (Tony-1975).
 Films inc: The Lord of the Flies; Equus; Amadeus.
 TV inc: The Salt Land; Balance of Terror.

SHAGAN, Steve: Wri. b. NYC, Oct 25, 1927. Films inc: Save the Tiger (& prod); Hustler; Voyage of the Damned; Nightwing; The Formula (& prod).
 TV inc: River of Mystery (& prod); Spanish Portrait (& prod); Sole Survivor (& prod); A Step Out of Line (& prod); The House on Garibaldi Street (& exec prod).

SHAH, Krishna: Wri-Dir. b. May 10, 1938. Films inc: Rivals; River Niger; Shalimar; Cinema Cinema.
 TV inc: Ironside; Six Million Dollar Man; Love American Style; Man from U N C L E; The Flying Nun; Maya.

SHAKESPEARE, Frank: Exec. b. NYC, Apr 9, 1925. e. Holy Cross, BS. Started with WCBS-TV, NY became vp-gm then moved to CBS net as sr vp; P CBS-TV Services; resd 1969 to become dir US Information Agency; 1973, exec vp Westinghouse; 1975 P, RKO General.

SHALIT, Gene: TV pers. b. NYC, 1932. e. U of IL. With NBC Radio Network. In Jan., 1973 became regular film critic NBC-TV Today Show.
 TV inc: Mystery! (host).

SHA NA NA: Rock group. Members are Scott Powell (Santini); Jon Bauman (Bowzer); Denny Greene; Johnny Contardo; Jocko Marcellino; Screamin' Scott Simon; Donny York; Chico Ryan; Lennie Baker.
 Films inc: Grease.
 TV inc: Sha Na Na.

SHAPIRO, Arnold: Prod-Exec. b. LA, Feb 1, 1941. e. UCLA, BA. VP for tv TAT Communications Co. Began as doc wri, prod. TV inc: (Prod-wri) Medix series; The Feminine Mistake; The Science Fiction Film Awards (prod); Scared Straight (& dir) (Emmy-1979); Gene Autry--An American Hero; The Real Rookies; Scared Straight--Another Story.
 Films inc: Scared Straight (Oscar-doc-1978).

SHAPIRO, Dan: Wri. b. NYC, Jan 3, 1910. Wrote TV, night club material for Milton Berle; Bob Hope; Jackie Gleason; Eddie Cantor; Joe E. Lewis. Bway inc: Artists and Models; Follow the Girls; Peep Show; Ankles Aweigh. Songs: I Wanna Get Married; The Next Time Around; You Are Romance.

SHAPIRO, Irvin: Exec. e. George Washington U. P Films Around the World, Inc; P Filmworld Export Corp.

SHAPIRO, Ken: Prod. b. NJ, 1943. e. Bard Coll. Films inc: The Groove Tube.

SHAPIRO, Robert W: Exec. b. Brooklyn, Mar 1, 1938. e. USC. Started with William Morris Agency 1960; vp & m-dir William Morris (UK) Ltd. 1968-74; vp in charge intl mp dept 1974-77; formed Robert W Shapiro Prodns; named exec vp in charge worldwide prodn WB May 1977; Nov 1980, P WB prodn.

SHAPIRO, Stanley: Wri-Prod. b. NYC, Jul 16, 1925. Wrote for Fred Allen's radio show; also wrote for Burns & Allen, TV. Screenwriting debut, 1958, The Perfect Furlough. Films inc: Pillow Talk (Oscar-co-sp-1959); Operation Petticoat; Come September; Lover Come Back; That Touch of Mink; Bedtime Story (& prod); How to Save a Marriage (prod only); For Pete's Sake (co prod-co sp); Seniors.

SHARAFF, Irene: Cos Dsgn. b. 1910. Films inc: B.F.'s Daughter; An American in Paris (Oscar-1951); Brigadoon; A Star Is Born; Guys and Dolls; The King and I (Oscar-1956); Porgy and Bess; Can Can; Flower Drum Song; West Side Story (Oscar-1961); Cleopatra (Oscar-1963); Who's Afraid of Virginia Woolf? (Oscar-1966); Call Me Madam; Taming of the Shrew; Hello, Dolly!; The Other Side of Midnight.
 Bway inc: The King and I (Tony-1952); The Flower Drum Song; The Girl Who Came To Supper; Sweet Charity.

SHARIF, Omar (Michel Shahoub): Act. b. Alexandria, Egypt, Apr 10, 1932. On screen from 1953 in The Blazing Sun (Egyptian). Films inc: Lawrence of Arabia; Genghis Khan; The Fall of the Roman Empire; The Yellow Rolls-Royce; Behold a Pale Horse; Doctor Zhivago; Night of the Generals; More Than a Miracle; MacKenna's Gold; Che!; Funny Girl; The Appointment; Mayerling; The Horsemen; The Burglars; The Tamarind Seed; The Mysterious Island of Captain Nemo; Juggernaut; Funny Lady; Crime and Passion; The Baltimore Bullet; Ashanti; Oh Heavenly Dog.
 TV inc: S*H*E*; Pleasure Palace.

SHARKEY, Ray: Act. Films inc: Stunts; Paradise Alley; Who'll Stop the Rain; Willie & Phil; The Idolmaker.

SHARP, Phil: Wri. b. Chicago, Feb 6, 1919. e. U of Chicago. Radio: Duffy's Tavern; Alan Young Show; December Bride; Life with Luigi; The Aldrich Family.
 TV inc: Ed Wynn Show; Danny Thomas; Saturday Night Revue; Joan Davis Show (pilot); Sid Caesar Hour; The Phil Silvers Show (Emmy-1957); Bob Newhart Show; Andy Williams Show; Doris Day Show; Hogan's Heroes; Maude; All in the Family.

SHARPSTEEN, Benjamin: Ani Prod-Dir. b. 1895. Cartoonist with Oakland Tribune; joined Disney in 1929; later worked with Max Fleischer; Walter Lantz. Films inc: Fantasia; Pinocchio; Dumbo; Cinderella.
 (Died Dec 20, 1980).

SHATNER, William: Act. b. Montreal, Mar 22, 1931. e. McGill U. Toured Canada in various stock, repertory companies. Bway debut, 1956, Tamburlaine the Great. Bway inc: The Merry Wives of Windsor; Henry V; The World of Suzie Wong; A Shot in the Dark; Remote Asylum.
 Films inc: The Brothers Karamazov; Judgment at Nuremberg; The Explosive Generation; The Intruder; The Outrage; Big Hot Mama; Dead of Night; The Devil's Rain; Kingdom of the Spiders; Star Trek-The Motion Picture; The Kidnapping of the President.
 TV inc: Star Trek; The Statesman; The Bastard; Disaster on the Coastline; The Baby Sitter.

SHAVELSON, Melville: Wri-Dir-Prod. b. NYC, Apr 1, 1917. e. Cornell U, AB. Started as radio writer: We the People; Bicycle Party; Bob Hope Show; then screen writer, prod., WB.
 Films inc: The Princess and the Pirate; Always Leave Them Laughing; Room for One More; The Seven Little Foys (& dir.); Beau James (& dir.); Houseboat (& dir.); The Five Pennies (& dir.); The Pigeon that Took Rome (& dir., prod.); A New Kind of Love (& dir., prod.); Cast a Giant Shadow (& dir., prod.); The War Between Men and Woman (co-sp & dir.); Mixed Company.
 TV inc: Creator of Emmy-winning series: Make Room for Daddy; My World and Welcome to It; The Legend of Valentino; The Great Houdini; Ike.

SHAVER, Helen: Act. b. St. Thomas, Ont, Canada. e. U of Alberta. Films inc: Christina; High-Ballin'; Starship Invasions; In Praise of Older Women; Who Has Seen the Wind; The Amityville Horror; The Dogs of War.
TV inc: United States.

SHAW, Artie: Orch Ldr. b. NYC, May 23, 1910. Started as clarinetist with various orchestras. Organized own orchestra in 1936. Films inc: Dancing Co-Ed; Second Chorus.

SHAW, Irwin: Wri. b. NYC, Feb 2, 1913. Films inc: Talk of the Town; I Want You; Fire Down Below; The Young Lions; Tip on a Dead Jockey.
Plays inc: Bury the Dead; Siege; Quiet City; The Gentle People; Retreat to Pleasure; The Assassin; The Survivors.

SHAW, Lachlan Charles: Exec. b. Forbes, Australia, Nov 15, 1932. Dir, Creative Dev Branch, Australian Film Commission. Former dir Current Affairs, Australian Broadcasting Commission & dir, Film, Radio & Television Board, Australian Council.

SHAW, Lou: Wri-Prod. b. St Paul, MN, Apr 29, 1926. TV inc: Nancy Drew; McCloud; Quincy (pilot); Pleasure Cove (Pilot); Beyond Westworld (Wri-prod of pilot & exec prod of series).

SHAW, Reta: Act. b. S. Paris, ME, Sep 13, 1912. (ret). Films inc: Pollyanna; Mary Poppins; Escape To Witch Mountain.
Bway inc: Pajama Game; Picnic; Gentlemen Prefer Blondes; It Takes Two.

SHAW, Rose Tobias: Casting Dir. b. Germany. Films inc: Equus; A Little Night Music; The Greek Tycoon; The Seven Per Cent Solution; The Last Remake of Beau Geste.
TV inc: The Word; The Corn Is Green; A Man Called Intrepid; Lady Oscar; Brass Target.

SHAWN, Dick (Richard Schulefand): Act. b. Buffalo, NY, Dec 1, 1928. e. U of Miami. Films inc: The Opposite Sex; It's A Mad, Mad, Mad, Mad World; The Wizard of Bagdad; Wake Me When It's Over; What Did You do in the War, Daddy; Penelope; Way Way Out; The Producers; The Happy Ending; Love at First Bite.
Bway inc: For Heaven's Sake, Mother!; The Egg; A Funny Thing Happened on the Way to the Forum; Peterpat; Fade Out--Fade In; I'm Solomon; A Musical Jubilee.
TV inc: Fast Friends; Mr and Mrs Dracula.

SHEA, Jack: Dir-Prod-Wri. b. NYC, Aug 1, 1928. e. Fordham U, BA. TV inc: Insight; Hawaii 5-0; Calucci's Dep't (pilot); Glen Campbell Goodtime Hour; Sanford & Son; We'll Get By; The Waltons; The Jeffersons.

SHEAR, Barry: Prod-Dir. b. NYC, Mar 23, 1923. e. U of WI. Films inc; Wild in the Street; Across 110th Street; Skipper; The Five Women Affair; The Deadly Trackers.
TV inc: Name of the Game; Night Gallery; It Takes a Thief; Ironside; Ernie Kovacs Show; Here's Edie; The Billion Dollas Threat; Power.
(Died June 13, 1979).

SHEARER, Moira: Ballerina. b. Scotland, 1926. Joined Sadler's Wells (The Royal Ballet now) at age 16. Screen debut, 1948, The Red Shoes.
Films inc: Tales of Hoffman; The Story of Three Loves; The Man Who Loved Redheads; Peeping Tom; Black Tights.
Thea inc: Man and Wife.

SHEARER, Norma: Act. b. Montreal, 1904. On screen from 1920. Films inc: The Stealers; The Divorcee (Oscar-1929/30); Their Own Desire; A Free Soul; The Barretts of Wimpole Street; Romeo and Juliet; Marie Antoinette; The Student Prince; The Actress; The Trial of Mary Dugan; Private Lives; Smilin' Through; Strange Interlude; Riptide; Idiot's Delight; Her Cardboard Lover (last film made in 1942).

SHEARING, George: Mus-Comp. b. London, England, Aug 13, 1919. Blind since birth. Studied class mus but moved to jazz while in his teens. Began playing piano in pub, later with Frank Wier Quartet; Claude Bampton All-Blind Band; became arr for various bands inc Ted Heath; nitery, recording star in US since 1941 appearing all top clubs, Carnegie Hall; appeared with major symphonies. Composer Lullaby of Birdland.
Recordings inc: September in The Rain; Cherokee; I'll Remember April. Albums inc: The Best of George Shearing; Light, Airy and Swinging; The Way We Are; As Requested.

SHEEN, Fulton J, Archbishop: Educator-TV pers. b. El Paso, IL, May 8, 1895. A Roman Catholic Priest, he became a radio personality in the 1930's on The Catholic Hour; widely known for converting hundreds to the Catholic faith; began tv series Life is Worth Living in 1951 (Emmy-1952 as Outstanding TV Personality); prod tv series Life of Christ; Quo Vadis America; narr story of the Vatican (March of Time doc).
(Died Dec 10, 1979).

SHEEN, Martin (Ramon Estevez): Act. b. Dayton, OH, Aug 3, 1940. On screen from 1967. Films inc: The Incident; The Subject Was Roses; Catch 22; No Drums, No Bugles; Badlands; The Little Girl Who Lives Down the Lane; The Cassandra Crossing; Apocalypse Now; The Eagle's Wing; The Final Countdown.
TV inc: That Certain Summer; Letters for Three Lovers; The Execution of Private Slovik; The Missiles of October; Sweet Hostage; Third Annual Circus of the Stars; Blind Ambition; The Long Road Home.
Bway inc: The Subject Was Roses.

SHEINBERG, Sid (Sidney J Sheinberg): Exec. b. Corpus Christi, TX, Jan 14, 1935. e. Columbia College; Columbia Law School. H of Lorraine Gary. Joined legal dept Revue Prodns (prodn arm of MCA before divorcement of agency operation) 1959; vp in chg prodn U-TV, 1968; P U-TV & exec VP MCA Inc, 1970; P & COO of MCA Inc, June 1973.

SHELDON, James (nee Schleifer): Dir. b. NYC, Nov 12. e. U of NC, AB. TV inc: Armstrong Circle Theatre; Studio One; Robert Montgomery Presents; Mr Peppers; Twilight Zone; Naked City; The Virginian; My World and Welcome to It; Love, American Style; Room 222; Insight; Sanford and Son; Rich Man, Poor Man; Love Boat; Family; The Gossip Columnist.

SHELDON, Sidney: Wri. b. Feb 11, 1917. Films inc: The Bachelor and the Bobbysoxer (Oscar-1947); Dream Wife (& dir); You're Never Too Young; Pardners; The Buster Keaton Story (& prod-dir); Jumbo; The Other Side of Midnight (sp).
Bway inc: Redhead (Tony-1959).

SHELLEY, Carole: Act. b. London, Aug 16, 1939. e. RADA. London stage debut 1955 in Simon and Laura. Thea inc: (London) The Art of Living; New Cranks; Boeing Boeing; Mary, Mary. (Bway) The Odd Couple; The Astrakhan Coat; Loot; Sweet Potato; Little Murders; Absurd Person Singular; The Norman Conquests; Elephant Man (Tony-1979).
Films inc: Little Nell; The Man from Morocco; It's Great to be Young; Give Us This Day; The Odd Couple; The Boston Strangler; Robin Hood and the Aristocrats (voice).
TV inc: The Odd Couple.

SHENSON, Walter: Prod. b. San Francisco, CA. e. Stanford. Started in trailer dept., Col, later in pub dept; to London 1955 as pub supv European prodn before becoming prod.
Films inc: The Mouse That Roared; A Matter of WHO; The Mouse on the Moon; A Hard Day's Night; Help!; 30 is a Dangerous Age; Don't Raise the Bridge, Lower the Water; A Talent for Loving; Welcome to The Club; The Chicken Chronicles.

SHEPARD, Sam: Wri-Act. b. Fort Sheridan, IL, Nov 5, 1943. Plays inc: Cowboys; Rock Garden (a short play later included in the revue Oh! Calcutta!); La Turista; Forensic and the Navigators; Melodrama Play; Tooth of Crime; Operation Sidewinder; 4-H Club; The Unseen Hand; Mad Dog Blues; Shaved Splits; Curse of the Starving Class; Buried Child (Pulitzer Prize-1979).
  Films inc: (act) Days of Heaven; Renaldo and Clara; Resurrection.

SHEPHARD, Harvey: Exec. b. NYC, 1937. e. CCNY. Started with Lennen & Newell ad agcy; joined CBS 1967 as mgr Audience Measurement; 1969, mgr audience measurement-tv network research; 1973, dir pgm projects; 1975, vp pgm planning; March 1977, vp-pgms, NY; Oct 1977, vp-pgms, NY, CBS Entertainment; 1978, vp-pgm administration; 1980, vp pgms.

SHEPHERD, Cybill: Act. b. Memphis, TN, Feb 18, 1950. Former model. Films inc: The Last Picture Show; Daisy Miller; Taxi Driver; Special Delivery; The Silver Bears; The Lady Vanishes.

SHEPHERD, Richard: Exec. b. Kansas City, MO, Jun 4, 1927. e. Stanford U. Began career 1948 at MCA; 1956 Head of Talent, Col; 1962 joined CMA talent agency, serving as exec VP; to WB 1972-1974 as exec. VP, prod; 1974-76; ind prod; 1976 named MGM sr. VP & worldwide head of prod; resigned May 1980 to return to ind prodn.
  Films inc: Twelve Angry Men; The Hanging Tree; The Fugitive Kind; Breakfast at Tiffany's; Robin and Marion; Alex and the Gypsy.

SHEPITKO, Larissa: Dir. b. Ukraine, 1939. e. Moscow Film School. Films inc: Heat; Wings; Homeland of Electricity (doc); You and I; The Ascent.
  (Died July 26, 1979.)

SHER, Jack: Wri-Prod-Dir. b. Minneapolis, MN, 1913. Films inc: My Favorite Spy; Off Limits; Shane; Kathy 'O; The Wild and the Innocent; The Three Worlds of Gulliver; Paris Blues; Critic's Choice; Move Over, Darling.
  Plays inc: The Perfect Setup.
  TV inc: The Kid from Left Field.

SHERA, Mark (nee Shapiro): Act. b. Bayonne, NJ, Jul 10, 1949. e. Boston U, BFA. TV inc: Nicky's World; S.W.A.T.; Barnaby Jones.
  Bway inc: Godspell.

SHERDEMAN, Ted (AKA John Elton): Wri-Prod-Dir. b. Lincoln, NE, Jun 21, 1909. Films inc: Lust for Gold; Breakthrough; Scandal Sheet; Retreat Hell!; The Winning Team; The Eddie Cantor Story; The McConnell Story; From Hell to Eternity; Away All Boats; Toy Tiger; Maracaibu; St. Louis Blues; Dog of Flanders; Misty; The Big Show; Island of the Blue Dolphins; And Now Miguel; My Side of the Mountain; Latitude Zero; Nocturne for Nero; The Day the Band Played.
  TV inc: Wagon Train; Californians; Astronaut; Hazel; Men Into Space; My Favorite Martian; Bewitched; Family Affair; The Monroes; Flying Nun.

SHERIDAN, Dinah: Act. b. Hampstead, London, Eng, Sep 17, 1920. Thea inc: Let's All Go Down to the Strand; A Boston Story; The Gentle Hook; The Pleasure of His Company; In the Red; A Murder Is Announced.
  Films inc: Irish and Proud of It; Where No Vultures Fly; Sound Barrier; Genevieve; The Railway Children; The Mirror Crack'd.

SHERIN, Edwin: Dir-Act. b. Harrisburg, PA, Jan 15, 1930. e. Brown U. Thea inc: (act) Romeo and Juliet; As You Like It; A Desert Incident. (Dir) Joan of Lorraine; Mister Roberts; The Wall; The Inspector General; The Iceman Cometh; The Lonesome Train; The Great White Hope; Look at Any Man; Hallelujah!; Nourish the Beast; Find Your Way Home; Of Mice and Men; Eccentricities of a Nightingale; Rex; First Monday in October; Goodbye, Fidel.
  Films inc: Valdez Is Coming; My Old Man's Place.
  TV inc: Deirdre of the Sorrows; King Lear; An American Christmas.

SHERMAN, Edward: Pers mgr. b. Russia, Jan 12, 1903. An agent in the 1920's, formed own agency 1941; long-time personal mgr for Abbott and Costello; pioneered films-to-tv field, creating MPM Corp 1947; 1952 Globe TV Corp.
  (Died Feb 20, 1980).

SHERMAN, George: Prod-Dir. b. NYC, 1908. Films inc: Sword in the Desert; Target Unknown; Against All Flags; The Lone Hand; Dawn At Socorro; Johnny Dark; Count Three And Pray; Comanche; Reprisal; Panic Button; Joaquin Murieta; Smokey; Big Jake; For The Love of Mike.
  TV inc: Little Mo; Daniel Boone; Sam.

SHERMAN, Harry R: Prod. b. LA, Sep 21, 1927. e. UCLA. Worked For Directors Guild America; toured world as prodn mgr Wonderful World of Gulf; exec in chg prodn for Talent Associates.
  TV inc: Eleanor and Franklin (Emmy-1976); Eleanor and Franklin-The White House Years (Emmy-1977); The Gathering (Emmy-1978); Studs Lonigan; This Man Stands Alone.

SHERMAN, Hiram: Act. b. Boston, MA, Feb 11, 1908. e. U of IL. Bway inc: Horse Eats Hat; The Cradle Will Rock; The Shoemaker's Holiday; Sing Out the News; Mum's The Word; The Alchemist; Brigadoon; Two's Company (Tony-supp-1953); Goodbye Again; Measure for Measure; The Merry Widow; The Killer; Troilus and Cressida; Mary, Mary; How Now Dow Jones (Tony-supp-1968); Anne of Green Gables.
  Films inc: One Third of a Nation; The Solid Cadillas; Mary, Mary; O Dad, Poor Dad, Mama's Hung You in the Closet and I'm Fellin' So Sad.

SHERMAN, Richard M: Comp-Lyr. b. NYC, Jun 12, 1928. e. Bard Coll, BA. Films (collab. with brother, Robert) Parent Trap; Bon Voyage; In Search of the Castaways; Moon Pilot; Sword in the Stone; Summer Magic; Mary Poppins (2 Oscars-1964-best score & best song, Chim Chim Cher-ee); The One and Only Genuine Original Family Band; Bedknobs and Broomsticks; Huckleberry Finn (& sp); The Slipper and the Rose; The Magic of Lassie.
  Bway inc: Victory Canteen; Over Here!
  TV inc: Wonderful World of Color; Bell Telephone Hour.
  Songs inc: It's a Small World; You're Sixteen; Let's Get Together; A Spoonful of Sugar. (Grammy-Film Score-1964).

SHERMAN, Robert B: Comp-Lyr. b. NYC, Dec 19, 1925. e. Bard Coll, BA. All work in collab. with brother. See Richard M. Sherman.

SHERMAN, Robert M: Prod-Exec. S of late Edward Sherman. Started as agent with MCA; later publ; ret to agency biz with CMA, serving as vp film div in London; became prod 1972; named prodn vp Fox 1974; 1977 joined MGM as vp; 1978 joined newly-formed Orion Pictures as sr vp prod. Films inc: (Prod) Scarecrow; Night Moves; Missouri Breaks; Convoy; Blockbusters.

SHERMAN, Vincent (Abram Orovitz): Dir. b. Vienna, GA, Jul 16, 1906. e. Oglethorpe U, AB, Atlanta Law School, LLB. Actor, writer then dir. Films inc: Return of Dr. X; Saturdays Children; Man Who Talked Too Much; Underground; All Thru the Night; The Hard Way; Old Acquaintance; In Our Time; Mr. Skeffington; Pillow to Post; Janie Gets Married; Unfaithful; Nora Prentiss; Adventures of Don Juan; The Hasty Heart; Harriet Craig; Goodbye, My Fancy; Affair in Trinidad; The Young Philadelphians; The Naked Earth; The Second Time Around; The Young Rebel.
  TV inc: Medical Center; The Waltons; Baretta; Executive Suite; Doctors Hospital; The Last Hurrah; Hagen; Bogie; The Dream Merchants; Trouble in High Timber Country.

SHERRIN, Ned: Prod-Dir-Plywri. b. Low Ham, Somerset, England, Feb 18, 1931. e. Oxford; Gray's Inn. Former barrister who turned to playwriting; became performer, later BBC prod.

Thea inc: (wri) No Bed For Bacon; Cindy-Ella or I Gotta Shoe; The Spoils; Nicholas Nickleby; Sing a Rude Song; Fish Out of Water; Come Spy With Me (dir); Side By Side With Sondheim (dir-act); Beecham.

Films inc: (prod) The Virgin Soldier; Every Home Should Have One; Girl Stroke Boy; Up Pompeii; Rentadick; Up the Chastity Belt; The Alf Garnett Saga.

TV inc: That Was The Week That Was; Not So Much A Program; Benbow Was His Name; We Interrupt This Week; The Great Inimitable Mr. Dickens.

SHERWOOD, Madeleine Thornton: Act-Dir. b. Montreal, Canada, Nov 13, 1922. Bway inc: The Crucible; Cat on a Hot Tin Roof; Sweet Bird of Youth; Invitation to a March; All Over; Inadmissible Evidence; Do I Hear a Waltz; Hey, You, Light, Man!

Films inc: Baby Doll; Cat on a Hot Tin Roof; Sweet Bird of Youth; The 91st Day; Hurry Sundown; Pendulum; Wicked, Wicked.

TV inc: The Flying Nun; Rich Man, Poor Man.

SHEVELOVE, Burt: Dir. b. Newark, NJ, Sep 19, 1915. e. Brown U, AB. Plays inc: Kiss Me Kate (revival); A Funny Thing Happened on the Way to the Forum (Tony-1962); The Butter and Egg Man; Hallelujah, Baby; Rockefeller and the Red Indians; Sondheim: A Musical Tribute; No, No Nanette; Rodgers and Hart. (London) The Traveling Music Show.

TV inc (prod & dir): Art Carney Specials; The Bell Telephone Hour; The Judy Garland Show; The Jack Paar Show; Victor Borge Show; An Evening with Richard Rodgers.

SHIELDS AND YARNELL (Robert Shields and Lorene Yarnell): Mime Duo. Started as street mimes in San Francisco; won first place in Ted Mack amateur contest, signed for Las Vegas show Doo Dah Daze; worked niteries, concerts. TV inc: Toys on the Town (& wri); Dean Martin Christmas Special 1975; Mac Davis Show; Sonny and Cher Show; American Moments; Bob Hope on the Road to China; The Wild Wild West Revisited.

Films inc: The Conversation.

SHIELDS, Brooke: Act. b. NYC, May 31, 1965. Films inc: Alice, Sweet Alice; King of the Gypsies; Pretty Baby; Just You and Me, Kid; Wanda Nevada; Tilt; The Blue Lagoon.

TV inc: The Prince of Central Park; After the Fall.

SHIGETA, James: Act. b. HI, 1933. Films inc: The Crimson Kimona; Cry for Happy; Walk Like a Dragon; Bridge to the Sun; Flower Drum Song; Paradise Hawaiian Style; Nobody's Perfect; Lost Horizon; Midway; Enola Gay--The Men, The Mission, The Atomic Bomb.

TV inc: Samurai.

SHIMKIN, Arthur: Exec. b. NYC, Oct 8, 1922. e. Columbia, BA. Started with Simon & Schuster; 1951-55, exclusive publ of Disney Books and Records; later, dir of all CBS Children's Book and Record Publications; 1973-76, p Children's Records of America Inc; 1977 p, Sesame Street Records; merged co with Children's Television Workshop.

SHIMODA, Yoki: Act. Bway inc: Pacific Overtures. Films inc: Auntie Mame; A Majority of One; The Horizontal Lieutenant; Once A Thief; MacArthur; The Last Flight of Noah's Ark; The Octagon.

TV inc: Farewell to Manzanar; The Immigrants.

SHIRE, David: Comp. b. Buffalo, NY, Jul 3, 1937. e. Yale, BA. Films inc: Two People; Conversation; The Taking of Pelham 1-2-3; Farewell, My Lovely; The Hindenburg; All the President's Men; Saturday Night Fever; Straight Time; Old Boyfriends; Norma Rae (Oscar-song-1979); Fast Break; The Promise.

TV inc: Tell Me Where It Hurts; Raid on Entebbe; The Defection of Simas Kudirka.

Bway inc: Sap of Life; Graham Crackers; Unknown Soldier and His Wife; How Do You Do, I Love You; Love Match.

Recordings inc: Saturday Night Fever (Grammys-Artist & Prod-1978).

SHIRE, Talia: Act. b. Long Island, NY, Apr 25, 1946. Sis of Francis Ford Coppola. Films inc: The Dunwich Horror (as Talia Coppola); Gas-s-s; The Christian Licorice Store; The Outside Man; The Godfather; The Godfather, Part II; Rocky; Rocky II; Old Boyfriends; Prophecy; Windows.

TV inc: Rich Man, Poor Man; Kill Me If You Can.

SHIRLEY, Anne (Dawn Evelyeen Paris): Act. b. NYC, 1918. On screen from 1934. Films inc: Steamboat Round the Bend; Make Way for a Lady; Law of the Underworld; Mother Carey's Chickens; A Man to Remember; Stella Dallas; West Point Widow; All That Money Can Buy; Bombardier; The Powers Girl; The Man from Frisco; Music in Manhattan.

SHOEMAKER, Ann: Act. b. NYC, Jan 10, 1891. Bway inc: The Noose; The Ladder; We All Do; The Novice and the Duke; The Rich Full Life; The Bad Seed; The Importance of Being Earnest; Half-a-Sixpence.

Films inc: A Dog of Flanders; Alice Adams; Stella Dallas; Babes in Arms; Conflict; A Woman's Secret; Sunrise at Campobello; The Fortune Cookie.

TV inc: Omnibus; Roberta.

SHORE, Dinah (Frances Rose Shore): Singer-TV Pers. b. Winchester, TN, Mar 1, 1917. e. Vanderbilt, BA. Began as singer on WSM, Nashville while attending college. Radio and thea appearances in NYC led to first recordings with Xavier Cugat. Radio inc: Chamber Music Society of Lower Basin Street; Ben Bernie; Eddie Cantor; into TV 1951 with Chevy Show.

TV inc: Dinah Shore Show (Emmy-singer, 1954, 1955, 1957, 1959; personality 1956); Dinah Shore Specials; Dinah's Place (Emmys-1973, 1974); Dinah! (Emmy-1976); Death Car on the Freeway; Pat Boone and Family Christmas Special.

Films inc: Thank Your Lucky Stars; Up In Arms; Belle of the Yukon; Follow the Boys; Make Mine Music; Till the Clouds Roll By; Fun and Fancy Free; Aaron Slick from Punkin Crick.

SHORT, Bobby: Singer-Mus. b. Danville, IL, Sep 15, 1924. Performs in concert, niteries. At Cafe Carlyle, NYC, since 1968.

TV inc: Hardhat & Legs.

SHOWALTER, Max (formerly known as Casey Adams): Act. b. Caldwell, KS, Jun 2, 1917. Films inc: Always Leave Them Laughing; With a Song in My Heart; Bus Stop; The Naked and the Dead; Elmer Gantry; Bon Voyage; Fate Is the Hunter; The Moonshine War; The Anderson Tapes; Sgt. Pepper's Lonely Hearts Club Band; 10.

Bway inc: Knights of Song; Very Warm for May; My Sister Eileen; Showboat; John Loves Mary; Make Mine Manhattan; Lend An Ear.

TV inc: The Stockard Channing Show.

SHROYER, Sonny: Act. b. Valdosta, GA, Aug 28. e. U GA. Films inc: Payday; Like a Crow on a June Bug; The Longest Yard; Smokey and the Bandit; Greased Lighting; The Devil and Max Devlin.

TV inc: The Million Dollar Dixie Deliverance; Freedom Road; The Summer of My German Soldier; King; The Lincoln Conspiracy; The Dukes of Hazzard; Enos.

SHRYACK, Dennis: Wri. b. Duluth, MI, Aug 25, 1936. e. U of MN. Films inc: The Good Guys and the Bad Guys; Rise Up in Anger; The Car; The Gauntlet.

SHULER, Lauren: Prod. b. Cleveland, OH, Jun 23, 1949. e. Boston U. Dir creative affairs, Motown Prodns; assoc prod, Thank God It's Friday.

TV inc: Amateur Night at the Dixie Bar and Grill.

SHULMAN, Max: Wri. b. St Paul, MN, Mar 14, 1919. e. U of MN, BA. Films inc: Always Leave Them Laughing; Confidentially Connie; Affairs of Dobie Gillis; Half a Hero.

Bway inc: Barefoot Boy with Cheek; The Tender Trap; House Calls.

TV inc: The Many Loves of Dobie Gillis; House Calls.

SHUMLIN, Herman E: Prod-Dir. b. Atwood, CO, Dec 1898. Originally a reporter, became thea press agent then manager (1927) for prod Jed Harris. Became prod. Bway inc: (Prod) Celebrity; The Command Performance; Tonight at Twelve; Button, Button; The Last Mile; Grand Hotel; Merchant of Yonkers; The Corn is Green; Daphne Laureola; Lace on Her Petticoat; Soldiers. (Prod-dir) Clear All Wires; Bride of Torozko; Children's Hour; Days to Come; The Little Foxes; The Male Animal; Watch on the Rhine; The Great Big Doorstep; The Visitor; To Dorothy a Son; Inherit the Wind; Only in America; The Searching Wind; Bicycle Ride to Nevada; The Deputy; Transfers; Flowers. (Dir only) Wine of Choice; Kiss Them for Me; The Biggest Thief in Town; The High Ground; Candida; The Gambler; Regina; Wedding Breakfast; Tall Story; Little Moon of Alban; Dear Me, the Sky is Falling; Spofford (& wri). Films inc: (dir) Watch on the Rhine; The Confidential Agent.

(Died Jun 14, 1979).

SHYER, Charles: Wri. b. LA, Oct 11, 1941. e. UCLA. Worked as film AD, prodn mgr before writing career. TV inc: Lily Tomlin; The Odd Couple.

Films inc: Smokey and the Bandit; Goin' South; House Calls; Private Benjamin (& prod).

SHYRE, Paul: Plywri-Prod-Dir-Act. b. NYC, Mar 8, 1929. e. U FL, AADA. Plays: USA; Pictures in the Hallway; I Knock at the Door; Drums Under the Windows; The Child Buyer; An Unpleasant Evening; Will Rogers USA; Blasts and Bravos--an Evening with H.L. Mencken.

Bway inc: I Knock at the Door (prod-dir-act); USA (dir); A Fair Game for Lovers; Blasts and Bravos (dir-act); Will Rogers' USA (dir); Absurd Person Singular (act).

(*Tony*-Special-1957).

SIDARIS, Andy: Prod-Dir. b. Chicago, Feb 20, 1932. e. Southern Methodist U, BA. Films inc (dir): Stacey; The Racing Scene; M*A*S*H (football sequence); Seven.

TV inc (dir): The Racers/Mario Andretti/Joe Leonard/Al Unser; ABC's Championshop Auto Racing; ABC's NCAA Game of the Week; 1968 Summer Olympics (*Emmy*-1969); Wide World of Sports; The Racers/Craig and Lee Breedlove; XII Winter Olympics (*Emmy*-1976).

SIDARIS, Arlene T (nee Smilowitz): Prod-Wri. b. NYC, Apr 21. W of Andy Sidaris. TV inc: Hardy Boys/Nancy Drew Mysteries (prod-wir); Missiles of October (asst prod); Glen Campbell Variety Hour (asst prod).

SIDNEY, George: Dir-Prod. b. NYC, Oct 4, 1916. Shorts dir, MGM, 1932. Pres Hanna-Barbera Prodns, 1961-66. Films inc: Free and Easy; Pacific Redezvous; Pilot No. 5; Thousands Cheer; Bathing Beauty; Anchors Aweigh; The Harvey Girls; Cass Timberlane; The Three Musketeers; Red Danube; Annie Get Your Gun; Holiday in Mexico; Showboat; Scaramouche; Young Bess; Kiss Me Kate; Jupiter's Darling; The Eddy Duchin Story; Jeanne Eagles; Pal Joey; Pepe; Bye Bye Birdie; Viva Las Vegas; Who Has Seen The Wind?; The Swinger; Half a Sixpence.

SIDNEY, Sylvia: Act. b. NYC, Aug 8, 1910. e. Theatre Guild School. On stage, then screen debut in Through Different Eyes, 1929. Films inc: City Streets; An American Tragedy; The Miracle Man; If I Had a Million; The Trail of the Lonesome Pine; Fury; You Only Live Once; Dead End; The Searching Wind; Les Miserables; Violent Saturday; Behind the High Wall; Summer Wishes, Winter Dreams; God Told Me To; Damien-Omen II.

TV inc: Do Not Fold, Spindle or Mutilate; Death at Love House; Raid on Entebbe; The Gossip Columnist; FDR-The Last Year; The Shadow Box.

Bway inc: Crossroads; To Quito and Back; The Gentle People; The Fourposter; Enter Laughing.

SIEBERT, Charles: Act. b. Kenosha, WI, May 9. e. Marquette U. Studied at London Academy of Music and Dramatic Art, later taught there.

TV inc: Search for Tomorrow; As the World Turns; Another World; Husbands, Wives and Lovers; One Day at a Time; The Blue Knight; The Miracle Worker; The Seeding of Sarah Burns; Willow B: Women in Prison; Trapper John.

Films inc: Deadly Hero; Blue Sunshine; The Other Side of Midnight. Bway inc: Jimmy Shine.

SIEGEL, Don: Dir. b. Chicago, IL, Oct 26, 1912. Joined Warner Bros. as asst. film librarian, 1934. Became asst. cutter. Organized montage dept. Started dir shorts inc Oscar winning Hitler Lives and Star in the Night.

Features inc: The Verdict; Annapolis Story; Big Steal; No Time for Flowers; China Venture; Private Hell 36; Riot in Cell Block 11; Madigan; Coogan's Bluff; Two Mules for Sister Sara; Dirty Harry; The Shootist (& act); Telefon (& act); Invasion of the Body Snatchers (act); Escape From Alcatraz (prod-dir); Rough Cut.

SIEGEL, Larry: Wri. b. NYC, Oct 29, 1925. e. U of IL, AB. TV inc: Bob Newhart Show; That Was the Week That Was; Laugh-In; The Carol Burnett Show (*Emmys*-1971, 1973, 1978).

SIEGEL, Sol C: Prod. b. NYC, Mar 30, 1903. e. Columbia U. Joined Republic 1934 as exec prod; 1940 to Par as unit exec prod; 1944 resd to enter indie prodn; retd to Par 1945 as prod; to Fox 1946; retd to indie prodn; 1958 became vp in chg prodn MGM; resumed indie prod 1964.

Films inc: Letter To Three Wives; House of Strangers; I Was A Male War Bride; Panic in the Streets; Prince of Foxes; My Blue Heaven; Fourteen Hours; Deadline USA; What Price Glory; Dream Boat; Monkey Business; Call Me Madam; Gentlemen Prefer Blondes; Three Coins in a Fountain; There's No Business Like Show Business; High Society; Les Girls; Merry Andrew; Some Came Running; The World, The Flesh and the Devil; Alvarez Kelly; Walk Don't Run; No Way To Treat A Lady.

SIEGLER, Scott Merrill: Exec. b. Cleveland, OH, Feb 15, 1948. e. Union Coll, BA. Prod numerous docs for PBS, NBC. April 1980 named vp dramatic dvlpmnt CBS.

Films inc: The Manitou (asst prod); Cloud Dancer (asst prod).

SIGNORET, Simone (nee Kaminker): Act. b. Weisbaden, Germany, Mar 21, 1921. W of Yves Montand. On screen from 1938. Films inc: The Living Corpse; Bolero; Macadam; Dedee; The Cheat; La Ronde; Diabolique; Room at the Top (*Oscar*-1958); Witches of Salem; The Sleeping Car Murders; Term of Trial; Is Paris Burning?; The Deadly Affair; Games; The Sea Gull; Ship of Fools; The Confession; Police Python 357; Madame Rosa; L'Adolescente; Chere Inconnu.

TV inc: A Small Rebellion (*Emmy*-1966).

SILLIPHANT, Stirling: Wri-Prod. b. Detroit, Jan 16, 1918. e. USC, BA. Films inc: The Joe Louis Story (sp); Five Against the House (sp, co-prod); Nightfall (sp); Damn Citizen (sp); The Slender Thread (sp); In the Heat of the Night (*Oscar*-sp-1967); Shaft (prod); Shaft in Africa (sp); The New Centurions (sp); The Poseidon Adventure (sp); The Towering Inferno (sp); The Killer Elite (sp); The Enforcer (sp); Telefon (sp); Circle of Iron; When Time Ran Out (sp).

TV inc: Pearl (exec prod-wri); Salem's Lot (exec prod).

SILLMAN, Leonard: Prod-Dir-Act. b. Detroit, MI, May 9, 1908. In Vaude 1924 as singer-dancer in act with Lew Fields; NY debut at Palace 1926 in act with Imogene Coca.

Thea inc: Merry-Go-Round; Temptation of 1930; Hullaballoo; Low and Behold (& prod).

Bway inc: 13 editions (starting in 1934) of Leonard Sillman's New Faces; since then concentrated on producing with occasional appearances; They Knew What They Wanted; Journey's End; Happy as Larry; Hay Fever; Come as You Are.

Films inc (act): Goldie Gets Along; Whistling in the Dark; Bombshell; (prod) Angel Comes to Broadway; New Faces of 1954.

TV inc: The Best of New Faces.

SILLS, Beverly (Belle Silverman): Soprano. b. NYC, May 25, 1929. e. Professional Childrens School. On radio at age 3; won Major Bowes Amateur contest at age 6; as child made film shorts with Willie Howard; appeared in musicomedys on road; starred in radio show Our Gal Sunday; debut with NYC Opera 1955; LaScala 1969; Metropolitan Opera 1975; retired 1980 to become dir NYC Opera.

TV inc: NY Philharmonic Young People's Concerts; A Conversation with Beverly Sills; Profile in Music (*Emmy*-1975); In Performance at Wolf Trap; Dean Martin Christmas Special 1980.

(*Grammy*-Class voc-1976).

SILVA, Henry: Act. b. Puerto Rico, 1928. Films inc: Viva Zapata; Crowded Paradise; A Hatful of Rain; The Bravados; Green Mansions; Cinderfella; The Manchurian Candidate; Johnny Cool; The Return of Mr Moto; The Reward; The Plainsman; The Hills Ran Red; Never a Dull Moment; Five Savage Men; Shoot; Buck Rogers In The 25th Century; Love and Bullets; Thirst; Virus; Almost Human; Alligator.

SILVER, Franelle: Wri. b. Toronto, Canada, Sep 12, 1952. TV inc: Excuse My French; David Steinberg Show; Custard Pie; The Carol Burnett Show *(Emmy-*1978); Donny & Marie; Three's Company; The Kristy & Jimmy McNichol Special; The Tim Conway Special.

SILVER, Joan Micklin: Dir-Wri. b. Omaha, NE, May 24, 1935. e. Sarah Lawrence Coll. Films inc: Limbo (sp); Hester Street (sp & dir); Bernice Bobs Her Hair (sp & dir); Between the Lines (dir only); On the Yard (prod); Head Over Heels (sp & dir).

SILVER, Joe: Act. b. Chicago, Sep 28, 1922. Films inc: Diary of a Bachelor; Move; They Came from Within; The Apprenticeship of Duddy Kravitz; Rabid; Rhinoceros; You Light Up My Life; Boardwalk.
Bway inc: Tobacco Road; Doughgirls; Nature's Way; Heads or Tails; You Know I Can't Hear You When the Water's Running; Lenny.

SILVER, Raphael D: Prod-Dir. H of Joan Micklin Silver. Films inc: Hester Street (prod); Between the Lines (prod); On the Yard (dir).

SILVER, Ron: Act. b. NYC, Jul 2. e. St. Johns U, U of Valencia in Spain. Films inc: Tunnelvision; Welcome to LA.
TV inc: Rhoda; Betrayal; The Stockard Channing Show.

SILVERHEELS, Jay: Act. b. Canada, 1920. Films inc: The Prairie; Fury at Furnace Creek; Broken Arrow; War Arrow; The Lone Ranger; Indian Paint; The Phynx; Santee.
TV inc: The Lone Ranger.
(Died March 5, 1980).

SILVERMAN, Fred: Exec. b. NYC, 1938. e. OH State U. Started at CBS at age 25 as dir of daytime programs; later served as VP, programs, at CBS-TV for five years; 1975 P, ABC Entertainment; To NBC 1978 as P, & CEO.

SILVERMAN, Ron: Prod. b. LA, Jun 13, 1933. e. UCLA, U of AZ. Daily Variety staff, 1957-61; then asst to Mark Robson; later vp Daystar Prodns; vp Ted Mann Prodns.
Films inc: Buster and Billie; Lifeguard; Brubaker.
TV inc: Stoney Burke; O.K. Crackerby.

SILVERMAN, Syd: Publ-Edtr. b. NYC, Jan 23, 1932. e. Princeton U. S Sidne Silverman, grandson of Sime Silverman. Publisher, exec ed Variety; P, Daily Variety.

SILVERS, Phil: Act. b. NYC, May 11, 1912. In vaudeville as boy tenor, later comedian in burlesque, then on Bway. Screen debut, 1940, The Hit Parade. Films inc: You're In the Army Now; Diamond Horseshoe; Something for the Boys; Lady Be Good; Roxie Hart; My Gal Sal; Cover Girl; Top Banana; 40 Pounds of Trouble; It's a Mad, Mad, Mad, Mad World; A Guide for the Married Man; The Strongest Man in the World; The Chicken Chronicles; Won Ton Ton; The Cheap Detective; The Happy Hooker Goes to Washington; There Goes The Bride.
TV inc: The Phil Silvers Show (Sgt. Bilko) *(Emmy-*1955); also Best Comedian-1955); Goldie and the Boxer.
Bway inc: Yokel Boy; High Button Shoes; Top Banana *(Tony-*1952); Do Re Mi; How the Other Half Loves; A Funny Thing Happened on the Way to the Forum (rev.) *(Tony-*1972).

SILVERSTEIN, Elliot: Dir. b. Boston, MA. e. Boston Coll, BS; Yale, MFA. Films inc: Cat Ballou; The Happening; A Man Called Horse; Deadly Honeymoon; The Car.

SIMMONS, Jean: Act. b. London, Jan 31, 1929. Screen debut, 1944, Give Us the Moon. Films inc: Hamlet; Caesar and Cleopatra; The Way to the Stars; Great Expectations; Hungry Hill; Black Narcissus; The Woman in the Hall; Blue Lagoon; Hamlet; Adam and Evalyn; Trio; So Long at the Fair; Cage of Gold; The Clouded Yellow; Androcles and the Lion (US film debut); Angel Face; Young Bess; Affair with a Stranger; Kiss the Boys Goodbye; The Actress; The Egyptian; Desiree; Footsteps in the Fog; Guys and Dolls; Hilda Crane; This Could Be the Night; Until They Sail; Home Before Dark; Spartacus; The Grass Is Greener; All the Way Home; Elmer Gantry; Divorce American Style; Rough Night in Jericho; The Happy Ending; Say Hello to Yesterday.
TV inc: Beggarman, Thief; The Easter Promise; The Dain Curse; The Home Front.

SIMMONS, Matty: Prod. b. Oct 3, 1926. Bd Chmn Nat'l Lampoon Inc. Prod Nat'l Lampoon Radio Hour; Nat'l Lampoon Lemmings; Nat'l Lampoon Show. Films inc: That's Not Funny, That's Sick!; Nat'l Lampoon's Animal House.
TV inc: Delta House.

SIMMONS, Richard Alan: Wri. TV inc: Trials of O'Brien; The Price of Tomatoes *(Emmy-*1961); Doyle Against the House; Wichita Town; Adventures in Paradise; Columbo (prod); Mrs. Columbo.
Films inc: Woman on the Beach; Bengal Brigade; Tanganyika; Looters; The Private War of Major Benson; King and Four Queens; Tarawa Beachhead; Istanbul; The Trap; Juggernaut; The Island of Dr. Moreau; The Sentinel.

SIMON & GARFUNKEL: See SIMON, Paul & GARFUNKEL, Art.

SIMON, Carly: Singer-Comp. b. Jun 25. Studied with Pete Seeger. Films inc: No Nukes.
Albums inc: Carly Simon *(Grammy-*New Artist-1971); Playing Possum; The Best of Carly Simon; Another Passenger; The Boys in the Trees.

SIMON, Danny: Wri-Dir. b. NYC, Dec 18, 1920. Wrote in collab with brother, Neil, from 1947-56.
TV inc: Kraft Music Hall; What's Happening (dir).
Thea inc: Sunshine Boys (dir London prod).

SIMON, Melvin: Exec. b. NYC. e. CCNY. After WW2 service worked as salesman for shopping center development company; formed own firm, developed more than 80 centers; became interested in film industry, formed Mel Simon Productions to function as production firm to attract independent filmakers.
Films (as exec prod) When a Stranger Calls; The Runner Stumbles; Scavenger Hunt; Cloud Dancer; The Stunt Man; My Bodyguard.

SIMON, Neil: Plywri. b. NYC, Jul 4, 1927. Wrote comedy for radio with brother, Danny. supplied sketches, other material for Phil Silvers Arrow Show for TV, 1948; wrote material for Tallulah Bankhead Show; contributed sketches to Broadway show Catch a Star; New Faces of 1956. Wrote first full-length Broadway show, Come Blow Your Horn, 1961; also wrote for Garry Moore Show; The Sid Caesar Show; Jackie Gleason; Red Buttons. Plays: Barefoot in the Park;
Plays: Barefoot in the Park; The Odd Couple *(Tony-*1965); Sweet Charity; The Star Spangled Girl; Plaza Suite; Promises, Promises; Last of the Red Hot Lovers; The Prisoner of Second Ave; The Sunshine Boys; God's Favorite; The Gingerbread Lady; Chapter Two; California Suite; I Ought to Be in Pictures; They're Playing Our Song. *(Special Tony-*1975).
Films inc: Barefoot in the Park; The Odd Couple; Sweet Charity; The Out-of-Towners; Plaza Suite; The Sunshine Boys; Murder by Death; The Goodbye Girl; The Cheap Detective; Chapter Two; Seems Like Old Times.

SIMON, Paul: Singer-Comp. b. Newark, NJ, Nov 8, 1942. Sngwri half of the Simon and Garfunkel (Art) duo. The vocal and instrumental duo split in 1970 to embark on separate careers. Prior to breaking up they appeared in concerts inc Carnegie Hall.

Films inc: The Graduate (songs); Annie Hall (act); One-Trick Pony (wri-act-comp).

TV inc: The Paul Simon Special (*Emmy*-wri-1978).

(*Grammys*-(9)-Song of Year-1970; Record of Year-1968, 1970; Album of Year-1970, 1975; Arr Accomp Vocalist-1970; Contemporary Song-1970; Pop Voc-1975; Film Score-1968).

SIMONE, Simone: Act. b. Marseilles, France, Apr 23, 1914. On screen from 1931 in France. Films in U.S. inc: Seventh Heaven; Love and Hisses; Josette; The Human Beast; All That Money Can Buy; The Cat People; Johnny Doesn't Live Here Anymore; Mademoiselle Fifi; Curse of the Cat People; Le Ronde; Pit of Loneliness; Double Destiny; The Extra Day.

SIMPSON, Donald C: Exec. b. Anchorage, AK, Oct 29,1945. e. U of OR; BA,MA. 1969 With Jack Woodell Agency as acct exec handling WB; 1971 joined WB as ad-mktg exec; 1975 to Par as prodn exec; 1977 prodn vp; 1978 top prodn vp; 1980 SR vp chg wldwde prodn.

SIMPSON, O J (Orenthal James Simpson): Act. b. San Francisco, CA, Jul 1947. e. USC. Star collegiate and professional football player; Heisman Trophy Winner 1968; Films inc: The Towering Inferno; The Klansman; Killer Force; Cassandra Crossing; Capricorn 1; Firepower.

TV inc: A Killing Affair; Roots; Goldie and the Boxer (& exec prod); Detour to Terror (& exec prod); The Golden Moment-An Olympic Love Story.

SINATRA, Frank: Perf. b. Hoboken, NJ, Dec 12, 1915. Singer on radio; joined Harry James orch., later Tommy Dorsey. On screen 1943, Higher and Higher. Films inc: Step Lively; Anchors Aweigh; Words and Music; It Happened in Brooklyn; Miracle of the Bells; The Kissing Bandit; Take Me Out to the Ball Game; On the Town; Double Dynamite; From Here to Eternity (*Oscar*-supp-1953); Suddenly; Young at Heart; Not as a Stranger; Guys and Dolls; Johnny Concho; High Society; The Pride and the Passion; The Joker Is Wild; Pal Joey; Kings Go Forth; Some Came Running; A Hole in the Head; Never So Few; Ocean's 11; The Devil at Four O'Clock; Sergeants 3; The Manchurian Candidate; Come Blow Your Horn; Robin and the Seven Hoods; None But the Brave (dir); Von Ryan's Express; Assault on a Queen; The Naked Runner; Tony Rome; The Detective; Lady in Cement; Dirty Dingus Magee; That's Entertainment; The First Deadly Sin (& exec prod).

TV inc: Frank Sinatra-A Man and His Music (*Emmy*-1966); The Frank Sinatra Show; Contract on Cherry Street; Sinatra-The First 40 Years.

(*Grammys*-(7)-Album of the Year-1959, 1965, 1966; Vocal-1959, 1965, 1966; Record of the Year-1966).

(*Oscar*-special-1945). (Jean Hersholt Humanitarian Award-1970).

SINATRA, Frank Jr: Singer-Act. b. Jersey City, NJ, Jan 10, 1944. Performs in niteries. Films inc: A Man Called Adam. TV inc: Confessions of a Lady Cop.

SINATRA, Nancy Jr: Act. b. Jersey City, NJ, Jun 8, 1940. D of Frank Sinatra, Sr. On screen from 1964. Films inc: For Those Who Think Young; Marriage on the Rocks; Get Yourself a College Girl; Last of the Secret Agents?; The Ghost in the Invisible Bikini; The Wild Angels; Speedway.

SINATRA, Ray: Comp-Cond-Arr. b. Gergenti, Sicily, Nov 1, 1904. Child prodigy on the piano; gave first recital, Symphony Hall, Boston, age 13; arr-cond for various New England bands; cond NBC and CBS (radio) house orchs; cond opening season Greek Theatre, LA; cond for opening Sands Hotel, Las Vegas; later moved to Riviera, then Tropicana, Landmark, Stardust hotels. Ret 1975.

Bway inc: Banjo Eyes; Panama Hattie; One Touch of Venus; Du-Barry Was A Lady; Star and Garter.

Films inc: The Thin Man; After the Thin Man; Fiesta.

(Died Nov 1, 1980).

SINCLAIR, Madge: Act. b. Kingston, Jamaica, Apr 28, 1938. e. Shortwood Teacher Training College, Jamaica. School teacher for six years. Films inc: Leadbelly; I Will, I Will. . .for Now; Conrack; Convoy; Uncle Joe Shannon.

TV inc: The Mad Messiah; Jimmy B and Andre; I Know Why the Caged Bird Sings; Roots; The Autobiography of Miss Jane Pitman; Trapper John.

SINDEN, Donald: Act. b. Plymouth, Eng, 1923. In repertory; joined Shakespeare Memorial Theatre; then Old Vic Company. Thea inc: London Assurance; Haebeas Corpus; Shut Your Eyes and Think of England.

Films inc: The Cruel Sea; Doctor in the House; Simba; Eyewitness; Doctor at Large; Decline and Fall; The National Health; The Day of the Jackal; The Island at the Top of the World; That Lucky Touch.

SINGER, Carla: Exec. b. Winnipeg, Canada, Mar 4, 1945. e. Brandeis U, BA; Hebrew University, MA. Started 1970 as asst dir CTV Network, Toronto; 1972, dir City-TV, Toronto; 1973, dir-wri BBC-TV, London; 1976, exec prod Westinghouse TV; prod PM Magazine, Everyday; Dir dvlpmt & crea Hour Magazine; Jun 1980, dir dramatic dvlpmt CBS-TV.

SINGER, Robert: Exec. b. Nyack, NY. e. NYU, BS. TV prodns inc: Lacy and the Mississippi Queen; Dog and Cat series; Night Stalker; 7 Wide World of Entertainment Specials. Named vp, drama development, NBC Entertainment on Sep 26, 1978.

SINGLETON, Penny (Dorothy McNulty): Act. b. Philadelphia, PA, Sep 15, 1908. On screen from 1930 as Dorothy McNulty in: Love in the Rough; Good News; After the Thin Man; as Penny Singleton from 1938 in Swing Your Lady; Men Are Such Fools; Boy Meets Girl; The Chump; The Mad Miss Manton: Blondie (series of 28); Go West Young Lady; Young Widow; The Best Man.

Bway inc: No, No, Nanette; Follow Through; Hey Nonny Nonny.

SJOBERG, Alf: Dir-Act. b. Stockholm, 1903. e. Dramaten Drama School (Royal Dramatic Theatre) went on stage, later directing. Most of career spent at the Dramaten Theatre. Films inc: Den Starkaste; Den Blomstertid; Hem fran Babylon; The Road to Heaven; Kungajakt; Frenzy; Only a Mother; Miss Julie; Barabbas; Karin Mansdotter; Wild Birds; Sister Paret ut; The Judge; The Island. (Died April 17, 1980).

SJOBERG, Tore: Prod. b. Stockholm, 1915. Began as dist for U S films during WW2; imported censored films (like Chaplin's Great Dictator) for club audience screening; P Nordisk Tone Film 1944-47; became prod 1958. Films inc: Mein Kampf (doc); Fanny Hill; The Snake; Adamson. (Died May 29, 1980).

SJOMAN, Vilgot: Dir. b. Sweden, 1924. Films inc: 491; I Am Curious: Blue; I Am Curious: Yellow; Blushing Charlie; Linus (& wri).

SKALA, Lilia: Act. b. Vienna. Films inc: Call Me Madam; Lilies of the Field; Ship of Fools; Caprice; Charly; Deadly Hero; Roseland; Heartland.

TV inc: Search for Tomorrow; Guiding Light; Secret Storm; Valiant Lady; Eleanor and Franklin; Sooner or Later.

Bway inc: Letters to Lucerne: With a Silk Thread; Call Me Madam; Diary of Anne Frank; Zelda; Forty Carats; Medea and Jason.

SKELTON, Red (Richard): Act. b. Vincennes, IN, 1913. Joined medicine show at age 10. Later in showboat, stock, minstrel shows, vaudeville, burlesque, circus. On radio from 1936, TV from 1950. Screen debut, 1939, Having Wonderful Time.

Films inc: Lady be Good; Dr. Kildare's Wedding Day; Whistling in the Dark; Ship Ahoy!; Panama Hattie; Merton of the Movies; The Fuller Brush Man; A Southern Yankee; The Clown; Public Pigeon No. 1; Those Magnificent Men in Their Flying Machines.

TV inc: The Red Skelton Show (*Emmy*-Comedian-1952; wri-1961).

SKERRIT, Tom: Act. b. Detroit, MI, Aug 25, 1933. Films inc: M*A*S*H; Fuzz; Turning Point; Ice Castles; Alien.

SKINNER, Cornelia Otis: Act. b. Chicago, IL, 1901. On screen from 1943. Films inc: Stage Door Canteen; The Uninvited; The Girl in the Red Velvet Swing; The Swimmer.

Bway inc: Blood and Sand; The Wild Westcotts; White Collars; toured for many years (U.S. & England) in one-woman show; Major Barbara; The Pleasure of His Company (& co-wri); Paris 90 (& wri).

(Died July 9, 1979).

SKIRBALL, Jack H: Prod. b. Homestead, PA, Jun 23, 1896. e. Western Res U, BA, Hebrew Union College, LLD. Gen. Mgr charge Prod. Educational Films, NY, 1939-39; Ind. film producer, Hollywood, 1933-46; Pres, Skirball-Manning Prods, 1946-54;

Films inc: The Howards of Virginia (asso prod); Half a Sinner; Miracle on Main Street; The Lady from Cheyenne; This Woman Is Mine; Saboteur; Shadow of a Doubt; It's in the Bag; Guest Wife; So Goes My Love; The Secret Fury; Payment on Demand; A Matter of Time.

SKOLIMOWSKI, Jerzy: Dir. b. Poland, 1938. Films inc: The Barrier; The Departure; Hands Up; Dialogue; The Adventures of Gerard; Deep End; King, Queen, Knave; The Shout.

SKOLSKY, Sidney: Columnist-Prod. b. NYC, May 2, 1905. e. NYU. Bway press agent before becoming columnist for NY Sun, later NY Daily News; NY Mirror; United Feature Syndicate. Films inc: The Daring Young Man (wri); The Jolson Story (prod); The Eddie Cantor Story (prod).

TV inc: Hollywood--The Golden Era (prod).

SKOURAS, Plato A: Prod. b. NYC, Mar 7, 1930. e. Yale BA. S of late Spyros P Skouras. In theatre mgt 1952-54 with Skouras Theatres; joined Fox 1954 in story dept, later prodn asst; wrote narr for (short) Gods of the Road.

Films inc: Apache Warrior; Under Fire; Sierra Baron; Villa!; Frances of Assisi.

SLADE, Bernard (B S Newbound) Wri. b. Canada, May 2, 1930. Films inc: Stand Up and Be Counted; Same Time, Next Year; Tribute.

Plays inc: Simon Says Get Married; A Very Close Family; Same Time, Next Year; Tribute; Romantic Comedy.

TV inc: Bewitched; Love on a Rooftop; The Flying Nun; The Partridge Family; Mr Deeds Goes to Town; The Bobby Sherman Show; The Girl with Something Extra; Everything Money Can't Buy.

SLATE, Jeremy: Act. Films inc: Wives and Lovers; I'll Take Sweden; The Sons of Katie Elder; Devil's Brigade. TV inc: Mr. Horn.

SLAVIN, George F: Wri. b. Newark, NJ, Mar 2, 1918. e. Bucknell U, Yale U. Films inc: Intrigue; The Nevadan; Mystery Submarine; Peggy; Red Mountain; City of Bad Men; Weekend with Father; Thunder Bay; Rocket Man; Smoke Signal; Uranium Boom; Desert Sands; The Halliday Brand; Son of Robin Hood.

SLEZAK, Erika: Act. b. LA, Aug 5, 1946. D of Walter Slezak. Member of the Milwaukee Repertory Co. TV inc: One Life to Live.

SLEZAK, Walter: Act. b. Vienna, Austria, May 3, 1902. Hollywood debut 1942, Once Upon a Honeymoon.

Films inc: This Land Is Mine; Cornered; The Fallen Sparrow; Lifeboat; The Pirate; The Princess and the Pirate; The Yellow Cab Man; Salome; Riffraff; Sinbad the Sailor; Call Me Madam; The Miracle; The Gazebo; Come September; Emil and the Detectives; The Wonderful World of the Brothers Grimm; Dr. Coppelius; Black Beauty; The Mysterious House of Dr. C.

Bway inc: Meet My Sister; Music in the Air; Ode to Liberty; May Wine; I Married an Angel; My Three Angels; Fanny (Tony-1955); The Gazebo.

Opera inc: La Perichole; The Gypsy Baron; Die Fledermaus.

SLICK, Grace: Singer. b. Chicago, IL, Oct 30, 1939. e. U Miami. With Great Society; Jefferson Airplane; Jefferson Starship before solo.

SLOAN, Michael: Prod-Wri. b. NYC, Oct 14, 1946. e. Arts Educational Trust, England. S of Paula Stone and Mike Sloan. Films inc: Hunted; Assassin; Moments. TV inc: Colombo (wri); Switch (wri); McCoy (wri); Harry-O (wri); McCloud; Quincy; Hardy Boys Mysteries; Nancy Drew Mysteries; Evening in Byzantium; Sword of Justice; B J and the Bear (wri-exec prod).

SMALL, William J: News exec. b. Chicago, IL, Sep 20, 1926. e. U Chicago, MA. News dir WLS Chicago, 1951; News dir WHAS AM-TV, Louisville, 1956; news dir & Washington bureau chief CBS 1962; sr vp CBS News 1974; VP CBS Inc., 1978; Pres NBC News, 1979.

SMIGHT, Jack: Dir. b. Minneapolis, MN, Mar 9, 1926. e. U of MN, BA. Began as disc jockey; into tv as Dir One Man's Family 1953. TV inc: Eddie (Emmy-1959); Banacek; Columbo; Roll of Thunder, Hear My Cry. Film dir debut, I'd Rather Be Rich. Films inc: The Third Day; Harper; Kaleidoscope; The Secret War of Harry Frigg; No Way to Treat a Lady; Strategy of Terror; The Illustrated Man; The Traveling Executioner; Rabbit Run; Dr. Frankenstein; Frankenstein--The True Story; Airport 1975; Midway; Damnation Alley; Fast Break; Loving Couples.

SMITH, Alexis: Act. b. Penticton, Canada, Jun 8, 1921. On screen from 1941 in Dive Bomber; Gentleman Jim; The Animal Kingdom; The Constant Nymph; Night and Day; Of Human Bondage; Any Number Can Play; Split Second; The Sleeping Tiger; The Young Philadelphians; Once Is Not Enough; The Little Girl Who Lives Down the Lane; Casey's Shadow.

Bway inc: Follies (Tony-1972); Summer Brave; Platinum.

SMITH, Connie: Singer. b. Elkhart, IN, Aug 14, 1941. C&W recording artist. Regular with the Grand Ole Opry.

Films inc: Road to Nashville; Las Vegas Hillbillies; Second Fiddle to a Steel Guitar.

SMITH, Ethel: Organist. b. Pittsburgh, PA, 1921. Theatre, nitery performer. Films inc: Bathing Beauty; George White's Scandals; Twice Blessed; Easy to Wed; Cuban Pete; Melody Time; C'mon, Let's Live a Little; Pigeons.

SMITH, Gary: TV prod. b. NYC, Jan 7, 1935. e. Carnegie-Mellon U. Former art dir. TV inc: Kraft Music Hall (Emmy-Art Dir-1962); (as prod) Herb Alpert and the Tijuana Brass; Judy Garland Show; Singer Presents Burt Bacharach (Emmy-1971); James Paul McCartney: Wings; Steve and Eydie - Our Love Is Here To Stay; Barbra Streisand and other Musical Instruments; Merry Christmas, Fred. . .from the Crosbys; Ann-Margret Smith; Peter Pan; America Salutes Richard Rodgers; Neil Diamond Special; Mac Davis Christmas Special; Ben Vereen. . .His Roots; Elvis in Concert; Steve and Eydie - From This Moment On; Bette Midler - Ole Red Hair Is Back (Emmy-1978); Rockette - A Holiday Tribute to the Radio City Music Hall; Shirley MacLaine at the Lido; Steve and Eydie Celebrate Irving Berlin (Emmy-1979); An American Christmas Carol; Baryshnikov on Broadway (Emmy-1980); The Cheryl Ladd Special; Merry Christmas From Grand Ole Opry House; Kraft Salutes Disneyland's 25th Anniversary; Ann-Margret---Hollywood Movie Girls; Shirley MacLaine-Every Little Movement (& dir); Uptown-A Tribute to the Apollo Theatre; Linda In Wonderland.

SMITH, Howard K: News Commentator. b. Ferriday, LA, May 12, 1914. e. Tulane U, Heidelberg U, Oxford U, Rhodes Scholarship. United Press, London, 1939; UP, Copenhagen; UP, Berlin. Joined CBS News, Berlin corr., 1941; covered Nuremberg trials, 1946; returned to US, moderator, commentator or reporter. Joined ABC News, Jan. 1962, anchorman and commentator. TV inc: The Population Explosion (Emmy-wri-1960); Is Congress Out of Date?

SMITH, Jaclyn: Act. b. Houston, TX, Oct 26, 1947. Films inc: Bootleggers; Adventurers.

TV inc: Charlie's Angels; Escape From Bogen County; Nightkill.

SMITH, Jacqueline: Exec. b. Phila, May 24, 1933. e. Antioch Coll. Wrote and prod more than 100 children's shows for KPIX-TV, San Francisco; in 1963 appointed exec prod, daytime programs, CBS-TV; dir of special projects, Warner Bros; vp, daytime programs, ABC Entertainment since 1977.

SMITH, Kate: Singer. b. Greenville, VA, May 1, 1909. Performed on Broadway in musicals, Honeymoon Lane; Hit the Deck; Flying High. Joined the late Ted Collins for radio programs 1931. Later on NBC-TV in own show.
Films inc: Hello, Everybody!; This Is the Army.

SMITH, Keely: Singer. b. Norfolk, VA, 1935. Performs in niteries. On screen in: Senior Prom; Thunder Road; Hey Boy! Hey Girl! *(Grammy-vocal group-1958).*

SMITH, Kent: Act. b. NYC, Mar 19, 1907. Films inc: Cat People; Hitler's Children; This Land Is Mine; The Spiral Staircase; Nora Prentiss; The Fountainhead; The Damned Don't Cry; Comanche; Strangers When We Meet; Moon Pilot; A Distant Trumpet; The Trouble With Angels; Death of a Gunfighter; Pete 'n Tillie; Cops and Robbers.
TV inc: Peyton Place; Outer Limits; Profiles in Courage.
Bway inc: Measure for Measure; Sweet Love Remembered; The Best Man; Ah, Wilderness.

SMITH, Maggie: Act. b. Ilford, Eng, 1934. On screen from 1957. Films inc: Nowhere to Go; The V.I.P.s; Young Cassidy; Othello; The Honey Pot; Hot Millions; The Prime of Miss Jean Brodie *(Oscar-1969);* Oh What a Lovely War; Love and Pain; Travels With My Aunt; Murder by Death; California Suite *(Oscar-supp-1978);* Death on the Nile.
Thea inc: Twelfth Night; Share My Lettuce; The Double Dealer; As You Like It; Richard II; The Merry Wives of Windsor; The Private Ear; The Public Eye; Mary, Mary; The Three Sisters; Snap; Private Lives.
TV inc: Much Ado About Nothing; Man and Superman; On Approval; Home and Beauty.

SMITH, Malcolm Neil: Prod. b. London, Jun 6, 1941. Joined Film Australia, 1966. Freelance filmmaker, mainly on documentary films, 1971-72; edited feature film Shirleen Thompson Versus the Aliens; exec prod South Australian Film Corp, responsible for edu pgms and doc, 1973-77.

SMITH, Oliver: Dsgn. b. Wawpawn, WI, Feb 13, 1918. e. PA State U, BA. Bway inc: Rosalinda; The New Moon; On the Town (& co-prod); Billion Dollar Baby (& co-prod); No Exit (& co-prod); Beggar's Holiday; Brigadoon; High Button Shoes; Topaze; Look Ma, I'm Dancin'!; Me and Molly; Gentlemen Prefer Blondes (& co-prod); Paint Your Wagon; Pal Joey; Carnival in Flanders; On Your Toes; Mr. Wonderful; My Fair Lady *(Tony-1957);* Auntie Mame; Candide; Visit to a Small Planet (& co-prod); West Side Story *(Tony-1958);* Destry Rides Again; The Sound of Music *(Tony-1960);* Five Finger Exercise; Camelot *(Tony-1961);* Becket *(Tony-1961);* Barefoot in the Park; Hello, Dolly! *(Tony-1964);* Baker Street *(Tony & Special Tony-1965);* How Now Dow Jones; Plaza Suite; Last of the Red Hot Lovers; Gigi; Endgame; Mixed Couples.
Films inc: Band Wagon; Oklahoma; Guys and Dolls; Porgy and Bess.
Also des Ballets for American Ballet Theatre and Opera for The Met.

SMITH, Paul J: Comp-Cond. b. Calumet, MI, Oct 30, 1906. e. UCLA, BA, Juilliard. Films inc: Snow White and the Seven Dwarfs; Pinocchio *(Oscar-1940);* Saludos Amigos; Victory Through Air Power; Three Caballeros; Song of the South; Cinderella; Perri; 20,000 Leagues Under the Sea; The Parent Trap.

SMITH, Pete: Prod-Narr. b. NYC, Sep 4, 1892. Began as reporter, movie critic; then publicity dir., Paramount Pictures; joined MGM, 1925, as dir. publicity; turned to writing and narrating MGM Oddities; from 1935 produced & narrated various MGM shorts; then prod. and narrator Pete Smith Specialties. Shorts inc: Penny Wisdom *(Oscar-1939);* Quicker 'n a Wink *(Oscar-1941). (Special Oscar-1953,* "for his witty and pungent observations on the American scene in his series of Pete Smith Specialties").
(Died Jan 12, 1979).

SMITH, Roger: Act. b. South Gate, CA, Dec 18, 1932. e. U AZ. H of Ann-Margret. With Meglin Kiddies while in grade school. Films inc: No Time To Be Young; Crash Landing; Operation Madball; Man of a Thousand Faces; Never Steal Anything Small; Auntie Mame; Rogues Gallery. TV inc: (Act) 77 Sunset Strip; Mister Roberts. (Prod) Ann-Margret Olsson; Ann-Margret Smith; Ann-Margret--Rhinestone Cowgirl.

SMITHERS, Jan: Act. b. North Hollywood, CA, Jul 3, 1949. Films inc: Where the Lilies Bloom; Our Winning Season.
TV inc: WKRP in Cincinnati; The Love Tapes.

SMOTHERS, Dick: Act. b. NYC, Nov 20, 1939. Part of comedy team with brother Tom. TV inc: The Smothers Brothers Comedy Hour; Tom and Dick Smothers Brothers Special I (& exec prod).

SMOTHERS, Tom: Act. b. NYC, Feb 2, 1937. Appeared with brother Dick on The Smothers Brothers Comedy Hour; Tom and Dick Smothers Brothers Special I (& exec prod).
Films inc: Get to Know Your Rabbit; Silver Bears; The Kids Are Alright; Serial; There Goes The Bride.
TV inc: The Bear Who Slept Through Christmas (voice).

SNODGRESS, Carrie: Act. b. Park Ridge, IL, Oct 27, 1946. e. Northern IL U. Bway inc:: All the Way Home; Oh What a Lovely War; Caesar and Cleopatra; Tartuffe.
Films inc: Rabbit Run; Diary of a Mad Housewife; Fast Friends; The Fury.
TV inc: The Forty-Eight Hour Mile; Silent Night, Lonely Night; The Whole World Is Watching; The Solitary Man.

SNOW, Hank: Singer. b. Liverpool, Nova Scotia, Can, May 9, 1914. C&W recording artist. Joined the Grand Ole Opry 1950. Originally known as Hank, the Singing Ranger.

SNYDER, Tom: TV pers. b. Milwaukee, WI, May 12, 1936. Newscaster-anchorman WSAV, Savannah, GA.; KTLA, LA; KYW-TV, Philadelphia; KNBC-TV, LA before starting Tomorrow Show 1973. *(Emmy-host-1974).* Other TV inc: The Legionaires Disease; The National Disaster Survival Test; The National Love, Sex and Marriage Test.

SNYDER, William L: Prod. b. Baltimore, MD, Feb 14, 1920. e. Johns Hopkins U, BA. Cartoons inc: Tom and Jerry; Popeye; Krazy Kat; Munro *(Oscar-1960).* Short subjects: Self Defense for Cowards; The Game; How to Avoid Friendship; Nudnik. Cartoon features: Alice in Paris; I Am a Woman II; The Daughter.

SOBIESKI, Carol: (nee O'Brien): Wri. b. Chicago, Mar 16, 1939. e. Smith Coll, BA, Trinity Coll. TV inc: Mr Novak; Peyton Place; Neon Ceiling; Dial Hot Line; A Little Game; Reflections of Murder; Sunshine, Sunshine; Amelia; Harry Truman: Plain Speaking; Where the Ladies Go; The Women's Room.
Films inc: Casey's Shadow; Honeysuckle Rose.

SOFAER, Abraham: Act. b. Rangoon, Burma, Oct 1, 1896. London stage debut 1925 in Gloriana. Thea inc: (London) Scotch Mist; Black Velvet; The Man in Dress Clothes; Before Midnight; The Matriarch; Twelfth Night; Hamlet; Street Scene; The Mask and the Face; Victoria Regina; The Witch; The Flies; Skipper Next to God; A Doll's House.
Bway inc: The Matriarch; Victoria Regina; In the Matter of J Robert Oppenheimer.
Films inc: His Majesty O'Keefe; Elephant Walk; The Naked Jungle; Out of the Clouds; Bhowani Junction; Sinbad; King of Kings; Head.

SOKOLOW, Diane (nee Schwartz): Exec. b. NYC. e. Temple, BS. W of Mel Sokolow. VP east coast ops Lorimar Prodns 1975; vp east coast prodn WB 1977; resd 1980, formed Sokolow Company with husband to make films for WB release.

SOKOLOW, Mel: Exec. b. NYC, Jan 2, 1934. VP Warner Books 1971; exec vp Casablanca Filmworks 1977; Pres Mel Sokolow & Associates 1977; formed Sokolow Company with wife 1980 to make films for WB release.

SOLO, Robert H: Prod. b. Waterbury, CT, Dec 4, 1932. e. U of CT, BA. VP Foreign Prodn WB 1971-1974; exec VP prodn WB 1974-1975. Ind prodn 1976. Films inc: Scrooge; The Devils; Invasion of the Body Snatchers; The Awakening.

SOLOW, Herbert: Prod-Dir-Wri. b. NYC, Dec 14, 1930. e. Dartmouth. With William Morris Agency as packager; dir pgms NBC; dir daytime pgmg NBC; dir daytime pgmg CBS; vp tv pgmg Par; vp prodn Desilu Studios; tv prodn head MGM, later vp motion picture and tv prodn; P Solow Prodn Co. TV inc: Killdozer; Heatwave.

SOLOW, Sidney Paul: Exec. b. Jersey City, NJ, Sep 15, 1910. e. NYU, BS. Chief chemist, Consolidated Film Industries, 1932-36; plant supt, 1937-42; gen mgr, 1942; pres, 1954; chmn, exec committee Consolidated Film Industries. (*Oscar*-tech-1964).

SOLT, Andrew: Prod-Wri-Dir. b. London, Dec 13, 1947. e. UCLA, BA. Films inc: The Explorers; The Roy Campanella Story; Pioneer Woman; Where Have All the People Gone?; The Cousteau Odyssey Specials; Heroes of Rock 'N Roll.

SOLTI, Sir Georg: Cond. b. Budapest, Hungary, Oct 21, 1912. Mus asst Budapest Opera House 1930-1939; pianist, Switzerland 1939-1945; Gen mus dir Munich State Opera, 1946-1952; Frankfurt City Opera 1952-1960; mus dir Royal Opera House Covent Garden 1961-1971; cond Chicago Symphony 1969-1972; Orchestre de Paris 1972-1975; guest cond London Philharmonic; NY Philharmonic; Vienna Philharmonic; London Symphony; Los Angeles Philharmonic; Salzburgh Festival; Edinburgh Festival; Ravinia Festival; Vienna Staadtsopera; Concertgebouw, Amsterdam.

(*Grammys*)-(15)-Opera Rec-1962, 1966, 1974; Class Perf Orch-1972, 1974, 1976, 1979; Choral Perf-1972, 1977, 1978, 1979; Class Album of Year-1972, 1974, 1975, 1979).

SOMERS, Suzanne (nee Mahoney): Act. b. San Bruno, CA, Oct 16, 1946. Films inc: Daddy's Gone A-Hunting; American Graffiti; Bullitt; Magnum Force; Yesterday's Hero; Nothing Personal.

TV inc: Three's Company; Zuma Beach; Paul Anka In Monte Carlo; The Princess and the Lumberjack; Ants; High Rollers (Host); It Happened at Lake Wood Manor; Jack and the Princess; John Ritter, Being of Sound Mind and Body.

SOMMARS, Julie: Act. b. Fremont, NE, Apr 15. Named dir dvlpt Montanus Prodns 1980. TV inc: Harry O; The Rockford Files; Three for the Road; The Governor and J J: The Harness; Shirley; Centennial; Sex and the Single Parent.

SOMMER, Elke: Act. b. Berlin, 1941. Screen debut in Germany, 1958. Films inc: Don't Bother to Knock; The Money Trap; Love the Italian Way; The Venetian Affair; Deadlier Than the Male; The Corrupt Ones; They Came to Rob Las Vegas; The Wrecking Crew; Zeppelin; Ten Little Indians; Lisa and the Devil; On a Dead Man's Chest; It's Not the Size That Counts; The Swiss Conspiracy; The Prisoner of Zenda; The Net; The Double McGuffin; Exit Sunset Boulevard.

TV inc: Stunt Seven; The Top of the Hill.

SONDERGAARD, Gale: Act. b. Litchfield, MN, 1900. Films inc: Anthony Adverse (*Oscar*-supp-1936); Maid of Salem; The Life of Emile Zola; Juarez; The Cat and the Canary; The Mark of Zorro; The Letter; A Night to Remember; Sherlock Holmes and the Spider Woman; The Invisible Man's Revenge; Anna and the King of Siam; The Time of Their Lives; The Return of a Man Called Horse; Pleasantville.

Bway inc: The Crucible; A Family and a Fortune; Goodbye, Fidel.
TV inc: Medical Center; The Cat Creature; Centennial.

SONDHEIM, Stephen: Comp-Wri. b. NYC, Mar 22, 1930. e. Williams Coll. Bway inc: West Side Story; Gypsy; A Funny Thing Happened on the Way to the Forum; Anyone Can Whistle; Do I Hear a Waltz?; Company (*Tony*-score & lyrics-1971); Follies (*Tony*-score & lyrics-1972); A Little Night Music (*Tony*-score-1973); Candide; Pacific Overtures; Sweeney Todd (*Tony*-score & lyrics-1979).

TV inc: Topper (wri).
Films inc: The Last of Sheila (sp); Stavisky (score); A Little Night Music.

(*Grammys*)-(4)-cast albums-1970, 1973, 1980; Song of Year-1975).

SONTAG, David: Prod-Wri. b. NYC, Aug 17, 1934. e. NC State, BS. From 1955 served in various capacities with NBC, CBS and ABC. TV inc: A Christmas Memory; The Love Song of Barney Kempinsky; Shindig; The Las Vegas Show; In Concert; My Father's House; R I P; The Beaks of Eagles; Billy Liar; Phantom of the Open Hearth; Courthouse; The Texans; Mother, Juggs & Speed; Hunter's Moon; Trapper John, MD; sr vp, crea affairs, Fox TV since 1976.

SOO, Jack: Act. b. San Francisco, Oct 28. Films inc: Flower Drum Song; Who's Been Sleeping in My Bed?; The Oscar; Thoroughly Modern Millie; The Green Berets; Return From Witch Mountain.

TV inc: Valentine's Day; She Lives; Barney Miller.
(Died Jan 11, 1979).

SOREL, Louise: Act. b. LA, Aug 6. e. Neighborhood Playhouse, NY. D of Albert H Cohen. Bway inc: Take Her, She's Mine; Lorenzo; Philadelphia, Here I Come!; The Dragon; The Sign in Sidney Brustein's Window; The Lion in Winter; Man and Boy.

Films inc: The Party's Over; Plaza Suite; P S I Love You; Every Little Crook and Nanny.

TV inc: Cliffhangers; The Survivors; Don Rickles Show; When Every Day Was The Fourth of July; The Girl Who Came Gift-Wrapped; Mr Deeds Goes to Town; Ladies Man.

SORVINO, Paul: Act. b. NYC, 1939. Films inc: Where's Poppa?; The Gambler; A Touch of Class; Day of the Dolphin; Made for Each Other; I Will, I Will, For Now; Oh, God!; Slow Dancing in The Big City; Bloodbrothers; The Brink's Job; Shoot It Black, Shoot It Blue!; Lost and Found; Cruising.

TV inc: Bert D'Angelo, Superstar; We'll Get By; Seventh Avenue; Tell Me Where It Hurts; Dummy; A Friend In Deed.

Bway inc: Bajour; An American Millionaire; The Mating Dance; Skyscraper; King Lear.

SOSNIK, Harry: Comp-Cond. b. Chicago, IL, Jul 13, 1906. Quit engineering studies at age 17 to enroll in American Conservatory of Music; pioneer radio mus adv & arr with CBS Chicago; mus dir Decca Records 1937-1944; in Hollywood as film comp-cond and cond-arr-comp for network radio shows; vp chg music ABC-TV 1967-1976, scores inc Producers Showcase, Philco Playhouse.

Songs inc: You Stole My Heart; Lazy Rhapsody; Gayety; Out of the Night; Who Are We To Say; I'd Like to Fall In Love Again; Night Time in Rio.

SOTHERN, Ann (Harriet Lake): Act. b. Valley City, ND, Jan 23, 1911. On screen from 1929. Films inc: Let's Fall in Love; Kid Millions; The Girl Friend; Don't Gamble with Love; Trade Winds; Maisie (series of nine); Dulcy; Panama Hattie; Cry Havoc; April Showers; A Letter to Three Wives; The Judge Steps Out; Blue Gardenia; Chubasco; The Killing Kind; Golden Needles; Crazy Mama; The Manitou; The Little Dragons.

TV inc: Private Secretary; The Ann Sothern Show; Captains and the Kings.

SOUL, David (nee Solberg): Act. b. Chicago, Aug 28, 1943. Films inc: Johnny Got His Gun; Magnum Force; Dog Pound Shuffle.

TV inc: Starsky and Hutch; Salem's Lot; A Country Christmas; Swan Song (& prod); Homeward Bound.

SOULE, Olan: Act. b. La Harpe, IL, Feb 28, 1909. Started on radio 1933; then TV. Films inc: Cuban Fireball; Call Me Madam; Dragnet; Prince of Players; Queen Bee; Daddy Long Legs; Girl Happy; The Destructors; The Seven Minutes; The Towering Inferno.

SPAAK, Catherine: Act. b. Belgium, 1945. Films inc: La Trou; The Easy Life; Of Wayward Love; The Little Nuns; The Empty Canvas; Circle of Love; Weekend at Dunkirk; Made In Italy; The Man With the Balloons; Libertine; Take A Hard Ride; Cat O' Nine Tails; The Precarious Bank Teller.

SPACEK, Sissy (Mary Elizabeth Spacek): Act. b. Quitman, TX, Dec 25, 1950. Photographer's model. Films inc: Prime Cut; Ginger in the Morning; Badlands; Carrie; Welcome to L.A. Three Women; Coal Miner's Daughter.

TV inc: The Girls of Huntington House; Verna--USO Girl; The Migrants; Katherine.

SPARKS, Randy: Act-Comp-Prod. b. Leavenworth, KS, Jul 29, 1933. e. UC Berkeley. Toured college campusus, recorded folk mus during the 50s. In 1961, formed his own folk group, the New Christy Minstrels. In 1962 Sparks retired from performing to concentrate on group's business affairs. In 1964, he sold the group to the management firm of Greif-Harris for $2.5 million. After leaving the Minstrels, Sparks founded the Back Porch Majority and the New Society.

Films inc: Advance to the Rear (score); The Singing Nun (score & lyr).

SPARKS, Robert F: Cin. b. Hollywood, CA, Jan 9, 1930. Films inc: The Hard Ride; Starbird and Sweet William.

TV inc: Lassie; Wonderful World of Disney; Death Stalk; The Honorable Sam Houston; Shazam; Isis; Ark II; The Return of Jimmy Valentine; My Dear Uncle Sherlock; CHiPs.

SPARV, Camilla: Act. b. Stockholm, 1943. Started as a fashion model. Films inc: The Trouble With Angels; Murderers' Row; Dead Heat on a Merry-Go-Round; Assignment K; The High Commissioner; Downhill Racer; Greek Tycoon; Winter Kills.

SPELLING, Aaron: Exec. b. Dallas, Apr 22, 1928. e. Sorbonne; SMU, BA. Act-wri before producing TV series Johnny Ringo, which he created; prod. on Zane Grey Theatre and The Dick Powell Show; partner for 3 years with Danny Thomas in Thomas-Spelling Prods; had own prod co, filming 57 MOW films; joined forces with Leonard Goldberg to form Spelling/Goldberg Prods, 1972-76; pres. Aaron Spelling Prods, Inc, 1977.

TV inc: Mod Squad; The Rookies; Starsky and Hutch; Family; The Beach Bums; The Love Boat; Charlie's Angels; Beach Patrol; Return of the Mod Squad; Love's Savage Fury; The Power Within; Hart to Hart; The French Atlantic Affair; B.A.D. Cats; Waikiki; Murder Can Hurt You; Casino.

SPELMAN, Sharon: Act. b. LA, May 1. e. U of IA, BA. TV inc: Search for Tomorrow; Friends and Lovers; The Cop and the Kid; Deadly Game; The Girl in the Empty Grave; Angie; Number 96.

SPENCER, Dorothy: Film edtr. b. Covington, KY, Feb 2, 1909. Has edited 74 films inc: Stagecoach; To Be Or Not-To Be; Lifeboat; A Tree Grows In Brooklyn; My Darling Clementine; The Snake Pit; Down To the Sea In Ships; Decision Before Dawn; Man in the Gray Flannel Suit; A Hatful of Rain; The Young Lions; The Journey; From The Terrace; Cleopatra; Von Ryan's Express; Lost Command; Valley of the Dolls; Earthquake; Concorde--Airport '79.

SPENGLER, Pierre: Prod. b. Paris, 1947. Films inc: Satan's Brew (act); Chinese Roulette; The Prince and the Pauper; Superman; Superman II.

SPERLING, Milton: Wri-Prod. b. NYC, Jul 6, 1912. e. CCNY. Films inc: (as wri): Sing Baby Sing; Happy Landing; Thin Ice; I'll Give a Million; Here I Am a Stranger; The Story of Alexander Graham Bell; The Great Profile; Four Sons; (prod): Sun Valley Serenade; Rings on Her Fingers; I Wake Up Screaming; To the Shores of Tripoli; Hello, Frisco, Hello; Crash Dive; Cloak and Dagger; Pursued; My Girl Tisa; Three Secrets; Distant Drums; The Court Martial of Billy Mitchell (& sp); Marjorie Morningstar; The Enforcer; Top Secret Affair; The Bramble Bush; The Battle of the Bulge (& sp); Capt. Apache.

TV inc: Brave New World; The Dream Merchants.

SPEWACK, Bella: Wri. b. Hungary, 1899. W of late Sam Spewack. Wrote mostly in collab with husband. Films inc: Clear All Wires; Boy Meets Girl; Cat and the Fiddle; Rendezvous; The Nuisance; Three Loves of Nancy; My Favorite Wife; When Ladies Meet; Weekend at the Waldorf; Move Over Darling; We're No Angels.

TV inc: Mr Broadway; Kiss Me Kate; My Three Angels; The Enchanted Nutcracker.

Plays inc: Solitaire Man; Poppa; Clear All Wires; Spring Song; Boy Meets Girl; Leave It to Me; Kiss Me Kate (Tony-1949); My Three Angels; Festival.

SPIEGEL, Sam: Prod. b. Poland, Nov 11, 1903. e. U of Vienna. Films inc: Tales of Manhattan; The Stranger; We Were Strangers; The Prowler; When I Grow Up; The African Queen; Melba; On the Waterfront (Oscar-Best picture-1954); The Strange One; The Bridge on the River Kwai (Oscar-Best picture-1957); Suddenly Last Summer; Lawrence of Arabia (Oscar-Best picture-1962); The Chase; The Night of the Generals; The Happening; The Swimmer; Nicholas and Alexander; The Last Tycoon.

(Irving Thalberg Award-1963).

SPIELBERG, David: Act. b. Weslaco, TX, Mar 6, 1939. Films inc: Choirboys; The Effect of Gamma Rays on Man-in-the-Moon Marigolds; Newman; Law and Disorder; Hustle; Real Life.

TV inc: The Rosenberg Trial; American Girls; Bob & Carol & Ted & Alice; The Practice; The Lindbergh Kidnapping Case; King; Wheels; In the Matter of Karen Quinlan; Air Force vs Matlovitch; From Here to Eternity; One Day at a Time; Henderson Monster; Act of Love.

Bway inc: Trial of the Catonsville Nine; Black Angel; Thieves; Macbird; After the Fall.

SPIELBERG, Steven: Dir. b. Cincinnati, OH, Dec 18, 1947. e. CA State Coll. Made home movies as child. First professional work, Amblin', a 20-minute short, impressed Universal enough to sign him to contract. Films inc: The Sugarland Express; Jaws; Close Encounters of a Third Kind (dir. & sp); I Wanna Hold Your Hand; 1941; The Blues Brothers (act); Used Cars (exec prod).

TV inc: Night Gallery; Something Evil; The Name of the Game; The Psychiatrist; Marcus Welby, M.D.; Duel.

SPIGELGASS, Leonard: Wri. b. NYC, Nov 26, 1908. e. NYU. Started as reader and story ed., 1930. Films inc: Princess O'Hara; Letter of Introduction; The Boys from Syracuse; Tight Shoes; Butch Minds the Baby; All Through the Night; The Perfect Marriage; So Evil, My Love; I Was a Male War Bride; Mystery Street; Because Your Mine; Athena; Deep In My Heart; Silk Stockings; 10,000 Bedrooms; Pepe; A Majority of One; Gypsy.

TV inc: Eloise; The Helen Morgan Story.

Plays inc: A Majority of One; Dear Me, the Sky is Falling; A Remedy for Winter; The Wrong Way Light Bulb; Look to the Lillies; Mack and Mabel.

SPIKINGS, Barry: Prod. b. Boston, Eng, Nov 23, 1939. Chmn & CEO EMI Film & Theatre Corp; Chmn Elstree Studios; relocated hq to LA, Jan 1981. Films inc: Conduct Unbecoming; The Man Who Fell to Earth; Convoy; The Deer Hunter (Oscar-1978).

SPINETTI, Victor: Act. b. Monmouthshire, England, Sep 2, 1933. e. Coll of Music and Drama, Cardiff. Thea inc (London): Expresso Bongo; Candide; Make Me An Offer; Oh, What A Lovely War!; Merry Roosters pantomime (matinees); The Odd Couple; In His Own Write (& co-adapt, dir); Cat Among the Pigeons. (Dir) Shirley Abicair's Evening; Off The Peg (& devised); Let's Get Laid; Deja Revue; Come Into My Bed; The Biograph Girl.

(Bway) Oh, What A Lovely War! (Tony-supp-1965); La Grosse Valise; The Philanthropist.

Films inc: Hard Day's Night; The Wild Affair; Help!; The Taming of the Shrew; Hieronymous Merkin; Under Milkwood; The Return of the Pink Panther.

SPINNER, Anthony: Prod. b. NYC, Apr 4, 1930. e. Hofstra U, BA. VP pgm dvlpt 20th Fox TV May 1979; crea aff vp June 1980; Sep 1980 Sr prodn vp Playboy Prodns. TV inc: Dakotas; Invaders; Man from U.N.C.L.E.; Dan August; Mod Squad; Search; F.B.I.; Cannon; Caribe; Baretta; Roger and Harry; Return of the Saint; Supertrain.

SPIRES, John B: Exec. b. NYC. Worked as asst thea mgr, in Par lab prior to WW 2; 1946, European rep RKO; 1947, asst foreign mgr United World Films; 1949 in chg 16m foreign ops U; 1950, asst to GM, U-I; 1955. European GM, U-I; 1958, GM foreign film sales MCA-TV; 1961, dir TV sls Europe, MGM-TV; 1964, dir Int'l TV sls MGM-TV; 1973, vp MGM-TV; 1978, sr vp MGM-TV; 1980, formed Phoenix Int'l Associates.

SPIVACK, Murray: Sound Eng. b. NYC, Sep 6, 1903. e. CCNY. Films inc: King Kong; Around the World in 80 Days; West Side Story; My Fair Lady; The Sound of Music; Sand Pebbles; South Pacific; Tora! Tora! Tora!; Hello, Dolly! *(Oscar*-1969); Patton.

SPIVAK, Lawrence: TV Pers. b. NYC, 1900. e. Harvard. Prod, panel member, TV inc Meet the Press; A Day For History-The Supreme Court and the Pentagon Papers *(Emmy*-exec prod-1972).

SPRADLIN, G D: Act. Films inc: Will Penny; Zabriskie Point; Tora! Tora! Tora!; Number One; Monte Walsh; Hell's Angels; The Hunting Party; The Godfather--Part 2; Apocalypse Now; North Dallas Forty.
TV inc: The Jayne Mansfield Story.

SPRINGSTEEN, Bruce: Mus-Sngwri. b. Freehold, NJ, Sep 23, 1949. With various local groups around NJ; formed E Street Band for concert, recording dates. Songs inc: It's Hard to be A Saint in the City; Blinded by the Light; Born to Run.
Albums inc: Greetings from Asbury Park; The Wild, The Innocent and the E Street Shuffle; Born to Run; Darkness on the Edge of Town.
Films inc: No Nukes.

STABILE, Dick: Bandleader. b. 1909. Sideman with Ben Bernie before forming own band, played at NY World's Fair prior to WW2 service; in LA cond house orchs Cocoanut Grove, Slapsy Maxie, Ciro's; became cond for Martin & Lewis, when team split stayed with Martin as cond for Dean Martin tv series; opened Circus Lounge of Sheraton Universal Hotel, LA, 1969; cond Fairmount Hotel, New Orleans, 1947.
(Died Sep 25, 1980).

STACK, Robert: Act. b. LA, Jan 13, 1919. On screen from 1939. Films inc: First Love; The Mortal Storm; To Be or Not To Be; A Date with Judy; The Bullfighter and the Lady; The High and the Mighty; Written on the Wind; The Tarnished Angels; John Paul Jones; The Last Voyage; The Caretakers; Is Paris Burning?; The Corrupt Ones; Story of a Woman; A Second Wind; 1941; Airplane.
TV inc: The Untouchables *(Emmy*-1960); Name of the Game; Most Wanted; Undercover With the KKK (narr).

STACY, James (Maurice W Elias): Act. b. LA, Dec 23, 1936. TV inc: Gunsmoke; Sayonara; Ozzie & Harriet; Lancer; My Kidnapper, My Love (& prod).

STADLEN, Lewis J: Act-Prod-Dir. b. NYC, Mar 7, 1947. Films inc: Parades; Savages; Portnoy's Complaint; Serpico; Between the Lines; Harvest Home.
Bway inc: (act) Minnie's Boys; The Time of Your Life; Play it Again Sam; The Sunshine Boys; An Evening with Groucho Marx; Candide.
TV inc: George M; Feeling Good; Judge Horton and the Scottsboro Boys; Hot L Baltimore; One Day At A Time.

STAFFORD, Jim: TV Pers-Singer. b. Eloise, FL, Jan 16. With rock groups, guitarist for Grand Ole Opry before going solo; opening act for Muddy Waters, Freda Payne, others. Albums inc: Jim Stafford; Not Just Another Pretty Foot.
TV inc: The Jim Stafford Show; Those Amazing Animals (host).

STAFFORD, Jo: Singer. b. Coalinga, CA, 1918. W of Paul Weston. Started with Stafford Sisters singing act, then joined Pied Pipers singing group with Tommy Dorsey; featured soloist with Dorsey before going single 1943, began recording for Capitol, did comedy singing character Cinderella Q Stump on Red Ingles recording Timtayshun; later with Paul Weston created Jonathan and Darlene Edwards recordings *(Grammy*-comedy-1960).
Radio inc: The Chesterfield Supper Club. TV inc: The Jo Stafford Show.
Recordings inc: (With Pied Pipers) I'll Never Smile Again; There Are Such Things; Street of Dreams. (Solo) Tumbling Tumbleweeds; Shrimp Boats; You Belong to Me; Jambalaya.

STAHL, Lesley: TV newscaster. b. Lynn, MA, Dec 16, 1941. e. Wheaton. Began as wri-researcher for NBC 1968 election unit; 1969, re-searcher Huntley-Brinkley report from London; 1970, prod-reporter WHDH, Boston; 1972, Washington corr CBS; 1977 co-anchor CBS Morning News.

STALLONE, Sylvester: Act-Wri. b. NYC, Jul 6, 1946. Films inc: The Lords of Flatbush; Capone; Death Race 2000; Rocky (& sp); F.I.S.T. (& sp); Paradise Alley (& dir-sp); Rocky II (& dir-sp).

STAMP, Terence: Act. b. Stepney, Eng, Jul 22, 1939. Films inc: Billy Budd; Term of Trial; The Collector; The Thief of Baghdad; Modesty Blaise; Far From the Maddening Crowd; Poor Cow; Blue; Theorem; The Mind of Mr. Soames; Divine Creature; Meetings with Remarkable Men; Amo Non Amo; Superman; Superman II.

STAMPLEY, Joe: Act. b. Jun 6, 1943. Singer; recording artist.

STANDER, Lionel: Act. b. NYC, Jan 11, 1908. On screen from 1935. Films inc: The Scoundrel; We're in the Money; Mr. Deeds Goes to Town; The Music Goes Round; The Milky Way; Soak the Rich; A Star Is Born; Guadalcanal Diary; Spectre of the Rose; Call Northside 777; St. Bennie the Dip; The Black Hand; The Gang That Couldn't Shoot Straight; Pulp; The Loved One; The Black Bird; The Cassandra Crossing; New York, New York; The Sensual Man; 1941; The Squeeze.
TV inc: Hart to Hart.

STANFILL, Dennis: Exec. b. Centerville, TN, Apr 1, 1927. e. Annapolis, Oxford U, MA. Entered film industry 1969 as exec vp, finance, Fox & member of Fox board & exec committee; named p, Fox in March, 1971; named chmn, CEO, Sept, 1971.

STANG, Arnold: Act. b. Chelsea, MA, Sep 28, 1927. Performed on radio, TV, Broadway. Films inc: Seven Days' Leave; So This Is New York; Two Gals and a Guy; The Man with the Golden Arm; Dondi; The Wonderful World of the Brothers Grimm; It's a Mad, Mad, Mad, Mad World; Skidoo!; Hello Down There; The Gang That Couldn't Shoot Straight.
TV inc: Milton Berle; Danny Thomas; Perry Como; Ed Sullivan; Red Skelton; Bob Hope; Danny Kaye; Jackie Gleason; Feeling Good; Chico & the Man; Supersaws & Catfish.

STANLEY, Hal: Sngwri-Prod. b. 1913. TV inc: The Lord Don't Play Favorites; The Pied Piper of Hamelin; Mr. Smith Goes to Washington.
(Died Feb 17, 1980).

STANLEY, Kim (Patricia Reid): Act. b. Tularosa, NM, Feb 11, 1921. e. TX State U, U of NM. Films inc: The Goddess; Seance on a Wet Afternoon.
Bway inc: Yes is for a Very Young Man; Montserrat; Seance on a Wet Afternoon; The Chase; The Great Dreamer; Bus Stop; A Clearing in the Woods; Natural Affection; Picnic.
TV inc: Clash by Night; The Travelling Lady; A Cardinal Act of Mercy *(Emmy*-1963); You Are There.

STANTON, Dr Frank Nicholas Exec. b. Muskegon, MI, Mar 20, 1908. e. OH Wesleyan, BA, OH State U, PHD. Entered broadcasting in 1934 with CBS, became research dir 1938; named vp, gm CBS 1945; became pres 1946 when William S Paley resigned; vice chmn and chief operating officer 1971-1973 when he retired under company's mandatory policy at age 65; invented first automatic recording device designed to measure radio listenting; made two short (silent) films, Some Physiological Reactions to Emotional Stimuli (1932) and Factors in Visual Depth Perception (1936). *(Special Emmy Awards*-1960, 1972).

STANTON, Harry Dean: Act. b. KY, Jul 14, 1926. e. Pasadena Playhouse. Films inc: The Proud Rebel; The Adventures of Huckleberry Finn; Pat Garret and Billy the Kid; Rancho Deluxe; Cool Hand Luke; Missouri Breaks; Straight Time; Renaldo and Clara; Wise Blood; Alien; The Rose; Private Benjamin.

STANWYCK, Barbara (Ruby Stevens): Act. b. NYC, Jul 6, 1907. On screen from 1929. Films inc: The Locked Door; Ladies of Leisure; Ten Cents a Dance; So Big; Shopworn; The Bitter Tea of General Yen; A Message to Garcia; Stella Dallas; Union Pacific; Golden Boy; Meet John Doe; Two Mrs. Carrolls; Ball of Fire; Double Indemnity; Sorry, Wrong Number; The Mad Miss Manton; B.F.'s Daughter; Titanic; Executive Suite; The Maverick Queen; Walk on the Wild Side; The Night Walker.
TV inc: The Barbara Stanwyck Show *(Emmy*-1961); The Big Valley *(Emmy*-1966).

STAPLETON, Damien: Union Exec. b. Australia, Oct 8, 1946. e. Harvard U. Trade Union Secy, Australian Theatrical and Amusement Employees Assn.

STAPLETON, Jean: Act. b. NYC, Jan 19, 1925. Bway inc: In The Summer House; Damn Yankees; Juno; Bells Are Ringing; Rhinoceros; Funny Girl.
Films inc: Damn Yankees; Bells Are Ringing; Something Wild; Up the Down Staircase; Cold Turkey; Klute.
TV inc: All in the Family (Emmys-1971, 1972, 1978); Cher; Sammy & Co; The Carol Burnett Show; Aunt Mary.

STAPLETON, Maureen: Act. b. Troy, NY, Jun 21, 1925. Films inc: Lonely Hearts; The Fugitive Kind; A View from the Bridge; Bye Bye Birdie; Trilogy; Airport; Plaza Suite; Interiors; Lost and Found; The Runner Stumbles; Arthur Miller on Home Ground.
TV inc: For Whom the Bell Tolls; All the King's Men; Among the Paths to Eden (Emmy-1968); Queen of the Stardust Ballroom; Cat on a Hot Tin Roof; Letters From Frank; The Gathering Part 2.
Bway inc: The Playboy of the Western World; The Rose Tattoo (Tony-1951); The Crucible; Richard III; The Seagull; Toys in the Attic; Plaza Suite; Norman Is That You?; The Gingerbread Lady (Tony-1971); The Glass Menagerie.

STARGER, Martin: Exec Prod. b. NYC, May 8, 1932. e. CCNY, BS. P ABC Entertainment, 1972-75; p & CEO Marble Arch Prodns. Films inc: Nashville; The Domino Principle (prod); Movie Movie; The Muppet Movie; Saturn 3; Borderline; From the Life of the Marionettes; Raise the Titanic.
Bway inc: The Sly Fox (prod).
TV inc: (prod) Jennifer; Friendly Fire (Emmy-1979); All Quiet on the Western Front; Rodeo Girl.

STARK, Ray: Prod. b. circa 1914. e. Rutgers U. Started as literary agent; joined Famous Artists Agency, where he represented Marilyn Monroe, Lana Turner, Ava Gardner, William Holden, Kirk Douglas and Richard Burton. Resd in 1957 to form indy prodn co which became Seven Arts Prodns; formed Raystar Prodns in 1966.
Films inc: The World of Suzie Wong; Oh Dad, Poor Dad; The Night of the Iguana; This Property is Condemned; Funny Girl; Reflections in a Golden Eye; The Way We Were; Funny Lady; The Owl and the Pussycat; Fat City; Summer Wishes, Winter Dreams; For Pete's Sake; The Sunshine Boys; The Goodbye Girl; The Cheap Detective; California Suite; The Electric Horseman; Chapter Two; Seems Like Old Times.
(Irving Thalberg Award-1979).
Bway inc: Funny Girl.

STARR, Ringo (Richard Starkey): Singer-Mus-Sngwri. b. Liverpool, England, Jul 7, 1940. Member of The Beatles (see group listing).
Individual film credits inc: (act) The Last Waltz; Sextette; The Kids Are Alright.
(Grammys-(2)-(in addition to group Awards) Film soundtrack, 1970; Album of the Year, 1972).

STARRETT, Jack: Dir-Wri-Act. b. Refugio, TX, Nov 2, 1936. e. U of the South. Films inc: Run Angel Run; The Losers; Cleopatra Jones; The Gravy Train; Race with the Devil; A Small Town in Texas.
TV inc: Mr. Horn; The Survival of Dana.

STATLER BROTHERS: C&W group. Members are Harold Reid, Lew Dewitt, Don Reid, Phil Balsley.
(Grammys-(3)-Contemp Rock n' Roll group & New C&W artist-1965; country voc group-1972).

STEEL, Anthony: Act. b. London, May 21, 1920. e. Cambridge. Films inc: Saraband for Dead Lovers; Marry Me; The Wooden Horse; Laughter in Paradise; The Malta Story; Albert RN; The Sea Shall Not Have Them; Storm over the Nile; The Black Tent; Checkpoint; A Question of Adultery; Harry Black; Honeymoon; The Switch; Hell is Empty; Anzio; Massacre in Rome; The World Is Full of Married Men; The Mirror Crack'd.

STEELE, Tommy (nee Hicks): Act. b. London, Dec 17, 1936. Thea inc: Cinderella; She Stoops to Conquer; Half-a-Sixpence; The Servant of Two Masters; Dick Whittington; Meet Me in London; Hans Anderson; An Evening With Tommy Steele.
Films inc: Kill Me Tomorrow; The Tommy Steele Story; The Duke Wore Jeans; Tommy the Toreador; Light Up the Sky; It's All Happening; The Happiest Millionaire; Half A Sixpence; Finian's Rainbow; Where's Jack?
TV inc: Off the Record; The Tommy Steele Spectaculars; Twelfth Night; Tommy Steele In Search Of Charlie Chaplin; Quincy's Quest.

STEELY DAN: Band. Regular members are Walter Becker, bass; Donald Fagen, vocals-keyboards. Use various sidemen for recording dates. Albums inc: Can't Buy A Thrill; Countdown to Ecstasy; Pretzel Logic; Katy Lied; The Royal Scam; Aja; Greatest Hits.

STEENBURGEN, Mary: Act. b. Newport, AR. Films inc: Goin' South; Rabbit Test; Time After Time; Melvin and Howard.

STEIGER, Rod: Act. b. Westhampton, NY, Apr 14, 1925. Films inc: Teresa; On The Waterfront; Oklahoma!; The Big Knife; The Court Martial of Billy Mitchell; The Harder They Fall; Back From Eternity; Run of the Arrow; Across the Bridge; Cry Terror; Al Capone; Seven Thieves; The Mark; Reprieve; 13 West Street; The Longest Day; The Pawnbroker; The Loved One; Dr. Zhivago; In the Heat of the Night (Oscar-1967); The Girl and the General; No Way to Treat a Lady; And There Came a Man; The Illustrated Man; Three Into Two Won't Go; Waterloo; Duck! You Sucker; Happy Birthday, Wanda June; The Lolly-Madonna War; Lucky Luciano; Hennessy; W.C. Fields and Me; F.I.S.T; Dirty Hands; Breakthrough; The Amityville Horror; Love and Bullets; Klondike Fever; The Lucky Star.
TV inc: Marty; You Are There; The Lonely Wizard; Jesus of Nazareth.

STEIN, James R: Wri. b. Chicago, Jan 9, 1950. e. USC, BA. TV inc: The New Bill Cosby Show; Lily (Emmy-1974); The John Denver Special; Phyllis Diller's 102nd Birthday Party; The Smothers Brothers Show; The Captain & Tennille; Fernwood 2 Night; Dick Clark's Good Ol' Days; Peeping Times; The Carol Burnett Show (Emmy-1978); The Helen Reddy Special; Steve Allen Comedy Hour.

STEIN, Joseph: Wri. b. NYC, May 30, 1912. e. CCNY, Columbia U. Bway inc: Inside USA; Plain and Fancy; Mr Wonderful; The Body Beautiful; Take Me Along; Fiddler on the Roof (Tony-1965); Zorba; We Bombed in New Haven (co-prod); So Long, 174th St.
Films inc: Enter Laughing; Fiddler on the Roof.
TV inc: NBC Comedy Hour; Your Show of Shows; The Sid Caesar Show.

STEIN, Jules: Exec. b. South Bend, IN, Apr 26, 1896. e. U of WV, PhB; U of Chicago, MD; Rush Medical College, Chicago; Post Grad. Dye Clinic, U of Vienna. Resident opthalmologist, Cook County Hosp, Chicago. Founder-Pres Music Corp of America (MCA) 1924-46; Chmn B 1946-73; Chmn Emeritus 1973.
(Jean Hersholt Humanitarian Award-1976).

STEIN, Ronald: Comp-Cond. b. St Louis, MO, Apr 12, 1930. e. WA U, AB, Yale U Music School, USC. Pres US Educational Films; Music Dir. Films inc: Apache Woman; Gunslinger; Thunder Over Hawaii; Invasion of the Saucer Men; Sorority Girl; Jet Attack; Suicide Battalion; The Littlest Hobo; Legend of Tom Dooley; Dinosaurus!; The Bashful Elephant; Lost Battalion; Of Love and Desire; The Young and the Brave; Boy On Horseback; The Bounty Killer; Requiem for a Gunfighter; Blood Bath; Portrait In Terror; Curse of the Swamp Creatures; Psych-Out; The Rain People; Getting Straight; Prisoners.
TV inc: Julius Caesar; Galileo Galilei; Nefertiti; Hernan Cortes; Socrates; Dateline Yesterday. Los Angeles Music Theatre Co.

STEINBERG, Herb: Exec. b. NYC, Jul 3, 1921. e. CCNY. In U.S. Army during WW II; joined Paramount Pictures, NY, 1947, as publicity mgr; later national exploitation dir. To LA 1956 as studio publicity and adv dir, Para Joined MCA Inc, 1963: was one of planning team of Studio Tour program: currently VP of MCA Recreation Services, in charge of marketing and promotion.

STEINBERGER, Bert: Exec. b. Brooklyn, Jul 11, 1938. Pgm exec ABC entertainment.

STEINER, Fred: Comp-Cond. b. NYC, Feb 24, 1923. e. Oberlin Conservatory of Music, BM, USC. Films inc: First to Fight; Hercules; The Man from Del Rio; St. Valentine's Day Massacre; Time Limit; The Sea Gypsies.

TV inc: Andy Griffith; Danny Thomas; Gunsmoke; Have Gun Will Travel; Hogan's Heroes; Rawhide; The Bullwinkle Show; Hawaii Five-O.

Songs: Perry Mason Theme; Navy Log March.

STELLING, Joseph: Dir-Prod. b. Utrecht, The Netherlands, Jul 16, 1945. Films inc: Mariken Van Nieumeghen; Elckerlijc; Rembrandt Fecit 1669.

STEN, Anna (Anjuschka Stenski Sujakevitch): Act. b. Russia, 1908. Films inc: Storm over Asia; Trapeze; The Brothers Karamazov; Nana; We Live Again; The Wedding Night; A Woman Alone; So Ends Our Night; They Came to Blow Up America; She Who Dares; Let's Live a Little; Soldier of Fortune; The Nun and the Sergeant.

STEPHEN, Susan: Act. b. London, Jul 16, 1931. e. RADA. Films inc: His Excellency; Stolen Face; Treasure Hunt; Father's Doing Fine; The Red Beret; Private Man; For Better, For Worse, as Long as They're Happy; Value for Money; Barretts of Wimpole Street; Carry on Nurse.

TV inc: Little Women; No Hero; Pillars of Midnight.

STEPHENS, James: Act. b. Mount Kisco, NY, May 18, 1951. TV inc: How the West Was Won; The Paper Chase; True Grit; Only the Pretty Girls Die; The Death of Ocean View Park.

STEPHENS, Laraine: Act. b. Oakland, CA. TV inc: Bracken's World; Eischeid; Dallas Cowboys Cheerleaders; Powers; Women in White.

Films inc: None But the Brave.

STEPHENS, Robert: Act. b. Bristol, England, Jul 14, 1931. Thea inc: (London) The Crucible; The Good Woman of Setzuan; The Country Wife; The Apollo de Bellac; Yes--And After; The Waters of Babylon; The Entertainer; Epitaph for George Dillon; Look After Lulu; The Wrong Side of the Park; Saint Joan; The Recruiting Officer; Royal Hunt of the Sun; Armstrong's Last Goodnight; Trelawny of the Wells; The Beaux Stratagem; Apropos of Falling Sleet (& dir); Murderer. (Bway) Epitaph for George Dillon; Sherlock Holmes.

Films inc: Circle of Deception; Pirates of Tortuga; A Taste of Honey; The Inspector; Cleopatra; Morgan; Romeo and Juliet; The Prime of Miss Jean Brodie; The Private Life of Sherlock Holmes; Travels With My Aunt; The Duellists; The Shout.

STERLING, Jan (nee Adriance): Act. b. NYC, Apr 3, 1923. Films inc: Johnny Belinda; Appointment with Danger; Mating Season; Union Station; Caged; Rhubarb; Flesh and Fury; Pony Express; The Vanquished; The High and the Mighty; Women's Prison; Man with the Gun; 1984; The Harder they Fall; Love is a Goldfish Bowl; The Incident; The Minx.

Bway inc: Bachelor Born; Panama Hattie; John Loves Mary; Front Page; Over 21; Born Yesterday; The November People.

TV inc: Backstairs at the White House; My Kidnapper, My Love.

STERLING, Robert (William Sterling Hart): Act. b. Newcastle, PA, Nov 13, 1917. e. U of Pittsburgh. Films inc: Only Angels Have Wings; I'll Wait for You; Somewhere I'll Find You; The Secret Heart; Bunco Squad; Thunder in the Dust; Column South; Return to Peyton Place; Voyage to the Bottom of the Sea.

TV inc: Topper; Ichabod and Me; Beggarman, Thief.

STERN, Isaac: Violinist. b. Russia, Jul 21, 1920. e. San Francisco Consvervatory. Debut with the San Francisco Symphony. Has performed in concert, as guest soloist with leading orchs. Film soundtracks inc: Humoresque; Fiddler on the Roof. Appeared in films Tonight We Sing; Journey to Jerusalem.

(Grammys-(5)-Class solo-1961, 1962, 1964; chamber mus perf-1970; class album of year-1977).

STERN, Leonard B: Wri-Prod. b. Dec 23, 1923. TV inc: The Honeymooners; The Bilko Show (Emmy-wri-1956); Get Smart (Emmy-wri-1967). (Exec prod): The Governor and JJ; Diana; Faraday & Company; The Snoop Sisters; MacMillan and Wife; Holmes and Yo Yo; Lannigan's Rabbi; Rosetti and Ryan; Operation Petticoat; Windows, Doors & Keyholes.

Films inc: Just You and Me Kid; The Nude Bomb.

STERN, Sandor: Wri-Dir. b. Timmins, Ont, Canada, Jul 13, 1936. e. U of Toronto. TV inc: The Bold Ones; Ironside; Longstreet; All in the Family; Say Goodbye Maggie Cole; Mod Squad (prod); The Strange and Deadly Occurrence (prod & wri); Where Have All the People Gone; Red Alert; Killer on Board; True Grit: A Further Adventure; The Seeding of Sarah Burns; Mysterious Island of Beautiful Women; To Find My Son.

Films inc: Fast Break (sp); The Amityville Horror (sp).

STERN, Steven H: Dir-Wri. b. Ontario, Can, Nov 1, 1937. e. Ryerson Institute of Technology. Films inc: B.S. I Love You; Harrod Summer; Running.

TV inc: Ghost of Flight 401; Getting Married; Anatomy of a Seduction; A Boy and a Girl; Fast Friends; Young Love, First Love; Portrait of an Escort.

STERN, Stewart: Wri. b. NYC, Mar 22, 1922. e. U of IA. Films inc: Teresa; Rebel Without a Cause; The Rack; The James Dean Story; The Outsider; The Ugly American; Rachel, Rachel; The Last Movie; Summer Wishes - Winter Dreams; Benjy.

TV inc: Crip; And Crown Thy Good; Thunder of Silence; Heart of Darkness; Sybil (Emmy-1977); A Christmas to Remember.

STERNHAGEN, Frances: Act. b. Washington, DC, Jan 13, 1930. e. Vassar, BA. Films inc: Up the Down Staircase; The Tiger Makes Out; The Hospital; Two People; Fedora; Starting Over.

TV inc: Love of Life; Doctors; Enemies; Mother and Daughter-The Loving War.

Bway inc: The Skin of Our Teeth; The Carefree Tree; The Country Wife; The Chalk Garden; Great Day in the Morning; Cock-a-Doodle Dandy; Great Day in the Morning; The Right Honorable Gentleman; The Playboy of the Western World; The Sign in Sidney Brustein's Window; Enemies; The Good Doctor (Tony-1974); Equus; Angel; On Golden Pond; Peter Pan.

STEVENS, Andrew: Act. b. Memphis, TN, Jun 10 1955. Films inc: Shampoo; Vigilante Force; Massacre at Central High; Las Vegas Lady; The Boys of Company C; Day of the Animals; The Fury.

TV inc: The Last Survivors; Secrets; Once an Eagle; The Bastard; The Oregon Trail; The Rebels; Women at West Point; Topper (& exec prod); Beggarman, Thief.

STEVENS, Cat (Stephan Demetri Georgiou): Mus-Singer. b. London, Jul 21, 1948. Recording artist. Bway inc: Dancin.

STEVENS, Connie (Concetta Rosalie Ann Ingolia): Act. b. Brooklyn, Aug 8, 1938. Films inc: Eighteen and Anxious; Young and Dangerous; Drag Strip Riot; Rock-A-Bye Baby; Susan Slade; Palm Springs Weekend; Cruise-A-Go-Go; The Grissom Gang; Last Generation.

TV inc: Hawaiian Eye; Wendy and Me; Sex Symbol; Love's Savage Fury; Scruples; Murder Can Hurt You.

Bway inc: Star Spangled Girl.

STEVENS, Craig (Gail Shekles): Act. b. Liberty, MO, 1918. H of Alexis Smith. Films inc: Affectionately Yours; Since You Went Away; The Lady Takes a Sailor; The French Line; Abbott and Costello Meets Dr Jekyll and Mr Hyde; Gunn; The Limbo Line.

TV inc: The Snoop Sisters; Rich Man, Poor Man; Peter Gunn; Man of the World; Mr Broadway; The Home Front.

STEVENS, George Jr: Prod-Dir. b. LA, Apr 3, 1932. e. Occidental College, BA. Started in films as asst to his father on A Place in the Sun; Shane; 1962 named head motion picture div U.S. Information Agency; 1967 helped found, was first dir American Film Institute; 1980 became co-chmn AFI.

Films inc: (Asso prod) The Greatest Story Ever Told; The Diary of Anne Frank (& dir location sequences). (Prod) John F. Kennedy--Years of Lightning, Days of Drums; America at the Movies.

TV inc: (prod) The Stars Salute America's Greatest Movies; AFI Salute to James Cagney *(Emmy*-prod-1975); AFI Salute to Orson Welles; AFI Salute to John Ford; AFI Salute to Henry Fonda; The Kennedy Center Honors--A Celebration of the Performing Arts, 1979; The Kennedy Center Honors, 1980 (& wri). (Dir) Peter Gunn; Alfred Hitchcock Presents.

STEVENS, Jeremy: Wri. TV inc: The Electric Company *(Emmy*-1973); Mac Davis Specials; Diahann Carroll Show; Fernwood 2night; Richard Pryor Show; What's Happening; America 2night; Barbara Mandrell Show; Steve Allen Comedy Hour.

STEVENS, Leslie: Wri-Prod-Dir. b. Washington, DC, Feb 3, 1924. e. Yale Drama School. Films inc: The Left-Handed Gun; Private Property (& prod-dir); The Marriage-Go-Round; Hero's Island (& prod-dir); Buck Rogers in the 25th Century (wri).

TV inc: Stony Burke (crea, prod-dir); The Outer Limits; It Takes a Thief; McCloud; Men from Shiloh; Name of the Game.

Thea inc: Champagne Complex; The Lovers; The Marriage-Go-Round; The Pink Jungle.

STEVENS, Mark (Richard Stevens): Act. b. Cleveland, OH, Dec 13, 1916. On stage and radio in Canada before Hollywood. Early films as Stephen Richards inc Two Faced Woman; Passage to Marseilles; The Doughgirls; Objective Burma; Pride of the Marines.

Films (as Stevens) Within These Walls; From This Day Forward; The Dark Corner; God Is My Co-Pilot; I Wonder Who's Kissing Her Now; Reunion in Reno; Mutiny; The Big Frame; The Street With No Name; The Snake Pit; Jack Slade; Torpedo Alley; Cry Vengeance (& prod-dir); Timetable (& prod-dir); September Storm; Fate is the Hunter; Sunscorched.

TV inc: Martin Kane; Big Town.

STEVENS, Morton: Comp-Cond. b. Newark, NJ, Jan 30, 1929. e. Juilliard. Arr-cond for Sammy Davis Jr in concerts, niteries before turning to scoring. TV inc: 87th Precinct; Wild and Wonderful; Wheels; A Thousand Pardons, You're Dead *(Emmy*-1970); Hawaii 5-0 *(Emmy*-1974); Policewoman; Apple's Way; Backstairs at the White House; Lucy Moves to NBC; Detour to Terror; Fugitive Family.

STEVENS, Rise: Mezzo-Soprano. b. NYC, 1913. Gave up singing career in 1964, to serve as co-general manager of the Metropolitan Opera National Company for two years. Later a voice coach and tutor. Films inc: The Chocolate Soldier; Going My Way; Carnegie Hall.

STEVENS, Roger L: Prod. b. Detroit, Mar 12, 1910. e. U of MI. Bway inc: Twelfth Night; The Cellar and the Well; Peter Pan; Peer Gynt; The Fourposter; Barefoot in Athens; Tea and Sympathy; The Remarkable Mr Pennypacker; Sabrina Fair; Ondine; Bus Stop; Cat on a Hot Tin Roof; Tiger at the Gates; Separate Tables; A Clearing in the Woods; The Waltz of the Toreadors; Orpheus Descending; A Hole in the Head; West Side Story; Nude with Violin; The Pleasure of His Company; Five Finger Excercise; Under the Yum Yum Tree; The Caretaker; A Man for All Seasons; *(Tony*-1962); Sheep on the Runway; Conduct Unbecoming; Lost in the Stars; Leonard Bernstein's Mass; Jumpers; A Matter of Gravity; 1600 Pennsylvania Avenue; Betrayed; Bedroom Farce; Lunch Hour. *(Special Tony*-1971).

STEVENS, Ronnie: Act. b. London, England, Sep 2, 1925. Thea inc: Ad Lib; High Spirits; Intimacy at 8:30; For Amusement Only; The Lily White Boys; The Billy Barnes Revue; Rose Marie; The Lord Chamberlain Regrets; Round Leicester Square; The Man of Mode; Twelfth Night; The Bird Watcher; Two Gentlemen of Verona; The Merchant of Venice; Much Ado About Nothing; Ruling The Roost; Royal Hunt of the Sun; The Caretaker; Joseph and the Amazing Technicolor Coat; The Owl and the Pussycat; The Tempest; Sgt. Musgrave's Dance; Habeas Corpus; Hard Times; Dry Rot.

Films inc: I'm Alright Jack; A Home of Your Own; Goodbye Mr. Chips.

STEVENS, Stella: Act. b. Hot Coffee, MS, Oct 1, 1938. Began as model. On screen from 1959. Films inc: Say One for Me; Li'l Abner; Too Late Blues; The Courtship of Eddie's Father; Synanon; Sol Madrid; The Poseidon Adventure; Slaughter; Las Vegas Lady; Nickelodeon; The Manitou.

TV inc: Ben Casey; The Jordan Chance; The French Atlantic Affair; Friendships, Secrets and Lies; Make Me An Offer; Flamingo Road; Children of Divorce.

STEVENSON, Margot: Act. b. NYC, Feb 8, 1914. Bway inc Firebird; The Barretts of Wimpole Street; Stage Door; You Can't Take It With You; The Male Animal; The Rugged Path; Sweet Peril; The Seven Year Itch; The Happiest Millionaire; The Sea Gull; Hostile Witness; End of Summer; The Royal Family.

Films inc: Smashing the Money Ring; Castle on the Hudson; Valley of the Dolls; The Brotherhood; Rabbit Run.

STEVENSON, McLean: Act. b. Normal, IL, Nov 14, 1929. e. Northwestern U. TV inc: That Was the Week That Was (& wri); The Smothers Brothers Comedy Hour (wri); The Doris Day Show; The Tim Conway Comedy Hour; M*A*S*H*; In The Beginning; Hello, Larry; Alan King's Thanksgiving Special--What Do We Have To Be Thankful For.

STEVENSON, Parker: Act. b. Philadelphia, PA, Jun 4. Films inc: A Separate Peace; Lifeguard. TV inc: Hardy Boys Mysteries; The Mike Douglas Show (co-host).

STEVENSON, Robert: Dir. b. London, 1905. e. Cambridge U. Films inc: King Solomon's Mines; Tom Brown's Schooldays; Back Street; Jane Eyre; To the Ends of the Earth; The Las Vegas Story; Old Yeller; Kidnapped; The Absent Minded Professor; Son of Flubber; Mary Poppins; That Darn Cat; Blackbeard's Ghost; The Love Bug; Bedknobs and Broomsticks; Herbie Rides Again; One of Our Dinosaurs is Missing; The Shaggy DA.

STEWART, Alexandra: Act. b. Canada, 1939. Films inc: Exodus; Le Feu Follet; Dragees au Poivre; The Bride Wore Black; The Man Who Had Power Over Women; The Marseilles Contract; Zeppelin; Day for Night; Because of the Cats; Black Moon; The Little Girl In Blue Velvet; In Praise of Older Women; Le Soleil en Face (Face to the Sun); Phobia; Final Assignment.

TV inc: Separation.

STEWART, Don: Act-Singer. b. Staten Island, NY, Nov 14, 1935. e. Hastings Coll. Sang with American Choral Society; Schola Cantorum; Radio City Chorus. Thea inc: The Fantasticks; Jo; Babes in the Woods. TV inc: Guiding Light (since 1968).

STEWART, Donald Ogden: Wri. b. Columbus, OH, Nov 30, 1894. e. Yale, BA. Magazine writer and humorist. Appeared on Bway in Holiday.

Plays inc: Rebound (& act); Fine and Dandy, How I Wonder.

Films inc: Laughter; Finn and Hattie; Tarnished Lady; Smiling Through; White Sister; Going Hollywood; Another Language; Dinner at Eight; Barretts of Wimpole Street; No More Ladies; Prisoner of Zenda; Marie Antoinette; Love Affair; Night of Nights; The Philadelphia Story *(Oscar*-1940) Kitty Foyle; That Uncertain Feeling; A Woman's Face; Tales of Manhattan; Keeper of the Flame; Without Love; Life With Father; Cass Timberlane; Edward, My Son.

(Died Aug 2, 1980).

STEWART, Elaine: Act. b. Montclair, NJ, May 31, 1929. Films inc: Sailor Beware; The Bad and the Beautiful; Young Bess; Brigadoon; The Tattered Dress; The Adventures of Hajji Baba; The Rise and the Fall of Legs Diamond; The Most Dangerous Man Alive.

STEWART, James: Act. b. Indiana, PA, May 20, 1908. On screen from 1935. Films inc: Murder Man; Rose Marie; Wife vs. Secretary; Next Time We Love; Born to Dance; Seventh Heaven; You Can't Take it With You; Mr. Smith Goes to Washington; The Philadephia Story *(Oscar-*1940); It's a Wonderful World; Destry Rides Again; The Shop Around the Corner; It's a Wonderful Life; Magic Town; Call Northside 777; Rope; You Gotta Stay Happy; The Stratton Story; Malaya; Winchester '73; Broken Arrow; Harvey; The Jackpot; No Highway in the Sky; The Greatest Show on Earth; Carbine Williams; Bend of the River; Thunder Bay; The Glenn Miller Story; Far Country; The Rear Window; Strategic Air Command; The Man from Laramie; The Man Who Knew Too Much; The Spirit of St. Louis; Night Passage; Vertigo; Bell, Book and Candle; The FBI Story; Two Rode Together; The Man Who Shot Liberty Valance; Mr. Hobbs Takes a Vacation; How the West Was Won; Take Her, She's Mine; Dear Brigitte; Shenandoah; The Rare Breed; The Flight of the Phoenix; Fire Creek; Bandolero; The Cheyenne Social Club; Fool's Parade; That's Entertainment!; The Shootist; Airport '77; The Big Sleep; The Magic of Lassie.

Bway inc: Spring in Autumn; All Good Americans; Yellow Jack; Journey at Night; Harvey.

TV inc: Jimmy Stewart Show; Hawkins on Murder.

STEWART, Michael (nee Rubin): Plywri. b. NYC, Aug 1, 1929. e. Yale, MFA. Contributed material to Sid Caesar hour.

Bway inc: Shoestring Revue; Shoestring '57; Bye Bye Birdie *(Tony-*1961); Hello, Dolly! *(Tony-*1964); Those That Play the Clowns; George M!; Mack and Mabel; Barnum; 42d Street.

STEWART, Paul (nee Sternberg): Act-Dir. b. NYC, Mar 13, 1908. Appeared on approximately 5,000 radio shows between 1933 and 1944; also prod Mercury Theatre of the Air and dir daytime serials.

Bway inc: Subway Express; Wine of Choice; Native Son; Mr. Roberts.

Films inc: Citizen Kane; Johnny Eager; Mr. Lucky; Champion; The Window; 12 O'Clock High; A Child is Waiting; The Greatest Story Ever Told; In Cold Blood; F For Fake; Opening Night; Revenge of the Pink Panther.

TV inc: (Dir) The Defenders; Twilight Zone; Peter Gunn; Checkmate; M-Squad; Hawaiian Eye. (Act) The Nativity; The Dain Curse; Power.

STEWART, Rod: Mus-Singer. b. London, Jan 10, 1945. With Jeff Beck Group 1965-1968; Faces 1968-1970 before solo.

Albums inc: Rod Stewart; Gasoline Alley; Every Picture Tells A Story; Never A Dull Moment; A Night on the Town; Atlantic Crossing; Smiles; Foot Loose and Fancy Free; Blondes Have More Fun; Do Ya Think I'm Sexy; Rod Stewart's Greatest Hits.

STEWART, Trish: Act. b. Hot Springs, AR, Jun 14. Films inc: Time Travelers; Mansion of the Doomed People.

TV inc:The Young and the Restless; Salvage; Breaking Up Is Hard To Do; Wild Times.

STICKNEY, Dorothy: Act. b. Dickinson, ND, Jun 21, 1900. Widow of Howard Lindsay. Bway inc: The Squall; March Hares; The Front Page; The County Chairman; The Small Hours; Kind Sir; A Lovely Light; Pippin.

Films inc: Working Girls; The Little Minister; What a Life; The Remarkable Mr Pennypacker; I Never Sang for My Father.

TV inc: Arsenic and Old Lace; Cinderella; A Lovely Light.

STIERS, David Ogden: Act. b. Peoria, IL, Oct 31, 1942. Films inc: Drive, He Said; THX 1138; Oh, God!; The Cheap Detective; Magic.

TV inc: The Mary Tyler Moore Show; Doc; A Circle of Children; M*A*S*H; Breaking Up Is Hard To Do; The Oldest Living Graduate; Damien. . .The Leper Priest.

Bway inc: The Magic Show; Ulysses in Nighttown; The Three Sisters; The Beggar's Opera; Measure for Measure.

STIGWOOD, Robert C: Prod. b. Adelaide, Australia, 1934. Talent agent London 1962; became ind record prod; co-m dir NEMS Enterprises, which controlled Beatles, Jan 1967; formed Robert Stigwood Organization Nov 1967; prod in London: Hair; Oh! Calcutta!; Pippin; Sweeney Todd; acquired British tv shows Till Death Do Us Part and Steptoe and Son, sold U.S. rights to Norman Lear to provide basis for All in the Family and Sanford and Son.

Bway inc: Jesus Christ Superstar; Joseph and the Amazing Technicolor Dreamcoat; John, Paul, George, Ringo. . .and Bert; Happy End; Evita *(Tony-*1980).

Films inc: Jesus Christ Superstar; Tommy; Saturday Night Fever; Grease; Sergeant Pepper's Lonely Hearts Club Band; Moment by Moment; Times Square.

TV inc: Beacon Hill; The Prime of Miss Jean Brodie.

STILLER, Jerry: Act. b. NYC, Jun 8, 1929. e. Syracuse U, BS. H of Anne Meara. Films inc: The Taking of Pelham 1-2-3; The Ritz; Nasty Habits.

TV inc: Joe and Sons.

Bway inc: Member Joseph Papp's Shakespeare Co; The Ritz; Unexpected Guests; Passione; toured in comedy act with wife.

STITT, Milan: Wri. b. Detroit, MI, Feb 9, 1941. e. U of MI, BA; Yale, MFA. Bway inc: The Runner Stumbles.

Films inc: The Runner Stumbles.

TV inc: Between the Lions (& host-moderator); Ephraim McDowell's Kentucky Ride (pilot for Tales of Medical Life series).

STIX, John: Dir. b. St Louis, MO, Nov 14, 1920. e. Yale U, MFA. Bway inc: Mary Rose; Take A Giant Step; The Wisteria Trees; What Every Woman Knows; Too Late The Phalarope; The Price (revival).

Film inc: The Great St Louis Bank Robbery.

TV inc: Omnibus (10 segs).

STOCKWELL, Dean: Act. b. LA, Mar 5, 1936. Former child star. On screen from 1945. Films inc: Anchors Aweigh; Home Sweet Homicide; The Romance of Rosy Ridge; Song of the Thin Man; Gentleman's Agreement; The Boy with Green Hair; Down to the Sea in Ships; Stars in My Crown; Kim; Gun for a Coward; Compulsion; Sons and Lovers; Long Day's Journey Into Night; Psych-Out; The Dunwich Horrors; Win Place or Steal; The Pacific Connection.

TV inc: Greatest Heroes of the Bible.

STODDARD, Brandon: Exec. b. Cannan, NY, Mar 31, 1937. e. Yale U, Columbia Law School. With BBD&O before joining Grey Advertising; joined ABC 1970; named vp daytime programs for ABC entertainment, 1972; vp children's programs, 1973; named vp motion pictures for TV, 1974; in 1976 named vp dramatic programs and motion pictures for TV; in 1979 appointed P of new ABC motion picture unit.

STODDARD, Haila: Thea Prod-Act. b. Great Falls, MT, Nov 14, 1913. e. USC. Bway inc: (Act): Merrily We Roll Along; Tobacco Road; Yes, My Darling Daughter; The Moon Vine; Rip Van Winkle; Joan of Lorraine; The Voice of the Turtle; Her Cardboard Lover; Glad Tidings; Lunatics and Lovers; Who's Afraid of Virginia Woolf?; Dark Corners. (Prod) A Thurber Carnival; Sail Away; The Affair and The Hollow Crown; The Birthday Party; The Last Sweet Days of Isaac; The Lemon Sky; The Survival of St Joan; Lady Audley's Secret.

TV inc: Secret Storm (act); adapted Men, Women and Less Alarming Creatures From Thurber's works for tv series.

STOLL, George E: Mus Dir. b. Minneapolis, MN, May 7, 1905. Film scores inc: Babes in Arms; Strike Up the Band; For Me and My Gal; Meet Me in St Louis; Anchors Aweigh *(Oscar-*1945); Love Me or Leave Me; Meet Me in Las Vegas; Jumbo.

STOLLER, Morris: Exec. b. NYC, Nov 22, 1915. e. CCNY, BBA; NYU, CPA; Brooklyn Law School, LLB. Joined William Morris Agency, NY in 1937; shifted to Coast office 1947; named vp, later exec-vp & treas; Dec 1980 named bd chmn.

STOLOFF, Morris: Comp-Cond. b. Philadelphia, Aug 1, 1898. Concert violinist; mem. LA Philharmonic; gen music dir Columbia Pictures. Films inc: Cover Girl *(Oscar-*1944); The Jolson Story *(Oscar-*1946); Jolson Sings Again; The Eddie Duchin Story; Song Without End *(Oscar-*1960); They Came to Cordura; Gidget; The Last Angry Man.

Songs: A Song to Remember; Love of a Gypsy; My Consolation; Dream Awhile With Me; Love Comes but Once in a While; To You, Sweetheart; Song Without End; Fanny.

(Died April 16, 1980).

STOLOFF, Victor: Prod-Wri-Dir. b. Mar 17, 1913. e. French Law U. Films inc: Why?: Intimacy; Of Love and Desire.

TV inc: Israel Is Real; Hawaii 5-0; High Adventure with Lowell Thomas; Volcano; Sinner; Desert Boy; Little Isles of Freedom; Woman of Iran; Ballet Gayane.

STONE, Andrew L: Prod-Dir. b. Oakland, CA, Jul 16, 1902. Films inc: Hi Diddle Diddle; Sensations of 1945; Bedside Manner; Highway 301; Confidence Girl; Steel Trap; Blueprint for Murder; Bachelor's Daughter; Fun on a Weekend; Night Holds Terror; Julie; Cry Terror; The Decks Ran Red; The Last Voyage; Ring of Fire; Password Is Courage; Never Put It In Writing; Secret of My Success; Song of Norway; The Great Waltz.

STONE, Cliffie: Mus-Exec. b. Burbank, CA, Mar 1, 1917. C&W disc jockey 1935; formed own band; 1946 Capital Records consultant on folk artists. Radio inc: Hollywood Barn Dance. TV inc: Hometown Jamboree.

STONE, Ezra (nee Feinstone): Prod-Dir-Wri-Act. b. New Bedford, MA, Dec 2, 1917. e. AADA. Child Actor on radio; crea Henry Aldrich role. Bway inc: (Act) Parade; Ah, Wilderness; Oh, Evening Star; Three Men on a Horse; Brother Rat; What a Life (origin of Aldrich character); Pal Joey; Best Foot Forward; Boys From Syracuse. (Dir) See My Lawyer; Reunion in New York; This Is The Army; January Thaw; Me and Molly; At War With the Army; The Man That Corrupted Hadleyburg; Count Your Blessings; The Blue Danube; The Pink Elephant.

Films inc: Those Were The Days; This Is The Army; Tammy and The Millionare (dir).

TV inc: (Act) The Aldrich Family; Danny Thomas Show; Life With Father; The Hathaways; The Eternal Light; Actor; The 40 Million (& prod-dir). (Dir) I Married Joan; Bachelor Father; The Munsters; Petticoat Junction; Lost in Space; The Flying Nun; Please Don't Eat the Dasies; My Living Doll.

Dir more than 150 docs, staged 45 conventions for IBM.

STONE, Milburn: Act. b. Burrton, KS, Jul 5, 1904. Films inc: The Milky Way; China Clipper; Federal Bullets; Mr. Boggs Steps Out; Young Mr. Lincoln; Reap the Wild Wind; Gung Ho!; Calamity Jane and Sam Bass; Branded; The Atomic City; The Long Gray Line; The Private War of Major Benson.

TV inc: Gunsmoke *(Emmy-*1968).

Bway inc: Jaywalker; Around the Corner.

(Died June 12, 1980).

STONE, Oliver (William Oliver Stone): Wri. b. NYC, Sep 15, 1946. e. NYU, BFA. Films inc: Seizure (& dir); Midnight Express *(Oscar-*1978).

STONE, Peter: Wri. b. LA, Feb 27, 1930. e. Yale U, MA. Films inc: Charade; Father Goose *(Oscar-*co-sp-1964); Mirage; Arabesque; The Secret War of Harry Frigg; Sweet Charity; Skin Game; 1776; Taking of Pelham 1-2-3; Why Would I Lie?.

Plays inc: Kean; Skyscraper; 1776 *(Tony-*1969); Sugar; Two by Two; Full Circle.

TV inc: The Defenders; Adam's Rib; Happy Endings; Androcles.

STONE, Virginia Lively: Prod-Dir. b. Miami Beach, FL, May 3, 1931. Films inc: Blueprint for Murder; Steel Trap; The Night Holds Terror; Julie; Cry Terror; The Decks Ran Red; The Last Voyage; Ring of Fire; The Password is Courage; Song of Norway; Jamaica Reef; Evil in the Deep; Daddy's Girl.

STOPPARD, Tom: Wri. b. Czechoslovakia, Jul 3, 1937. Former journalist. Plays inc: Rosencrantz and Guildenstern Are Dead *(Tony-*1968); Enter a Free Man; The Real Inspector Hound; If You're Glad I'll Be Frank; After Magritte, Where Are They Now?; Jumpers; Travesties; Dirty Linen and New Found Land; Night and Day; Every Good Boy Deserves Favor (& dir).

Films inc: Despair; The Human Factor.

STORCH, Arthur: Act-Dir. b. NYC, Jun 29, 1925. e. Brooklyn Coll, New School for Social Research. NY stage debut, 1953, in End as a Man.

Bway inc: Time Limit!; Girls of Summer; The Long Dream; (as dir); Two By Saroyan; Three By Three; The Typists; The Tiger; The Owl and the Pussycat; The Impossible Years; Under the Weather; Golden Rainbow; 42 Seconds from Broadway.

Films inc: The Strange One; The Mugger; The Girl of the Night.

TV inc: (dir) Harry Belafonte Special; 100 Years of Laughter; George Washington Crossing the Delaware.

STORCH, Larry: Act. b. NYC, 1925. Nitery comedian and impressionist before Bway appearance in Who Was That Lady I Saw You With. Repeated role in film version. Other films inc: The Prince Who Was a Thief; Who Was That Lady?; 40 Pounds of Trouble; Captain Newman, MD; Sex and the Single Girl; That Funny Feeling; Bus Riley's Back in Town; The Great Bank Robbery; The Happy Hooker Goes to Washington; Without Warning.

TV inc: The Larry Storch Show; My World and Welcome To It; F Troop; Better Late Than Never; Jack Frost (voice); The Great American Traffic Jam.

STRACHAN, Alan: Dir. b. Dundee, Scotland, Sep 3, 1946. e. Oxford. Thea inc: (London) OK for Sound; The Watched Pot; John Bull's Other Island; Children; Confusions; Yahoo.

STRADLING, Harry Jr: Cin. b. NYC, Jan 7, 1925. Films inc: Welcome to Hard Times; support Your Local Sheriff; Something Big; Fool's Parade; 1776; The Way We Were; Bite the Bullet; Airport 77; Midway; The Big Bus; Born Again; Convoy; Go Tell the Spartans; Prophecy.

STRAIGHT, Beatrice: Act. b. Old Westbury, NY, Aug 2, 1918. Bway debut, 1935, Bitter Oleander. On screen from 1952.

Films inc: Phone Calls From a Stranger; Patterns; The Silken Affair; The Nun's Story; Network *(Oscar-*supp-1976); The Promise; Sidney Sheldon's Bloodline; The Formula.

Bway inc: Eastward in Eden; Macbeth; The Heiress; Heartbreak House; The Crucible *(Tony-*supp-1953); Sing Me No Lullaby; The River Line; Phedre; Everything in the Garden.

TV inc: Beacon Hill; Mission Impossible; Felony Squad; Matt Lincoln; The Dain Curse.

STRANGIS, Greg: Wri-Prod. b. LA, Jan 5, 1951. e. UCLA. TV inc: Love American Style (story ed); Eight is Enough (story ed, later prod); Rainbow (exec prod); Better Late Than Never (wri-exec prod); Shirley (wri-exec prod); The Great American Traffic Jam (exec prod).

STRANGIS, Sam: Prod. b. Tacoma, WA, Jun 19, 1929. e. Loyola U. Pgm prodn vp Par TV 1974-1976; P & exec prod Ten/Four Prodns. TV inc: Nikie; $6 Million Man; The Great American Traffic Jam.

STRASBERG, Lee: Act. b. Budanov, Austria-Hungary, Nov 17, 1901. F of Susan Strasberg. Co-founder-dir Actors Studio. Films inc: The Godfather, Part II; The Cassandra Crossing; And Justice For All; Boardwalk; Going In Style.

TV inc: To Be An Actor.

STRASBERG, Susan: Act. b. NYC, 1938. Performed off-Broadway. On Broadway in The Diary of Anne Frank.

Films inc: Picnic; Stage Struck; Scream of Fear; Hemingway's Adventures of a Young Man; Chubasco; The Name of the Game Is Kill; The Brotherhood; Rollercoaster; The Manitou; In Praise of Older Women.

TV inc: The Marriage; The Duchess and the Smugs; Catch a Falling Star; The Immigrants; Beggarman, Thief.

STRASSER, Robin: Act. b. NYC, May 7, 1945. e. Yale Drama School. Bway inc: Shadow Box; Chapter II. TV inc: Another World; All My Children; This Child is Mine; The Bones Came Together; Murder-Impossible; One Life to Live.

STRASSMAN, Marcia: Act. b. NYC, Apr 28, 1948. Debut age 15 in off-Bway prodn Best Foot Forward; appeared stock, off-Bway. TV inc: M*A*S*H; Welcome Back Kotter; Brave New World; Nightengales; Once Upon A Family; Good Time Harry.

STRATTON, David: Exec. b. Trowbridge, Eng, Sep 10, 1939. e. Bradfield Coll, Oxford. Film festival dir. Founded Newbury Film Society, England, Dir, Sydney Film Festival, from 1966. Programme advisor to London, LA, Chicago Film Festivals.

STRAUB, Jean-Marie: Dir. b. Metz, France, 1933. Films inc: Machorka Muff; Nicht Versohnt; The Chronicle of Anna-Magdalena Bach; Othon; History Lessons; Moses and Aaron.

STRAUSS, Helen M: Exec-Wri. b. NY. e. Columbia U. Assoc story ed, Paramount; NY rep for Walter Wanger; literary agent; vp WB 7 Arts; vp U-MCA; in chg motion pictures, Readers Digest.
Films inc: Mr Quilp; Incredible Sarah. Autobiography: A Talent for Luck.

STRAUSS, Peter: Act. b. Croton-on-Hudson, NY, Feb 20, 1947. Screen debut, 1969, Hail, Hero!. Thea inc: Dance Next Door; The Dirty Man.
Films inc: Soldier Blue; The Trial of the Catonsville Nine; The Last Tycoon.
TV inc: The Man Without a Country; Attack on Terror; Rich Man, Poor Man; The Forgotten Kennedy; The Jericho Mile (Emmy-1979); Angel On My Shoulder.

STRAUSS, Theodore: Wri. TV inc: Four Days in November; The Legend of Marilyn Monroe; They've Killed President Lincoln (Emmy-1971); The Rise and Fall of the Third Reich; Appointment With Destiny; I Will Fight No More Forever; America at the Movies; America Salutes Richard Rodgers--The Sound of His Music (Emmy-1977); National Geographic Series; Cousteau Odysseys.

STREEP, Meryl: Act. b. Bernardsville, NJ, Apr 22, 1949. e. Vassar, Yale Drama School, MFA. Films inc: Julia; The Deer Hunter; Manhattan; The Seduction of Joe Tynan; Kramer vs Kramer (Oscar-supp-1979). TV inc: The Deadliest Season; Holocaust (Emmy-1978).
Bway inc: Trelawny of the Wells; 27 Wagons Full of Cotton; Memory of Two Mondays; Secret Service; The Cherry Orchard; Happy End.

STREISAND, Barbra: Act. b. NYC, Apr 24, 1942. Broadway inc: I Can Get It for You Wholesale; Funny Girl.
Films inc: Funny Girl (Oscar-1968); Hello Dolly; On a Clear Day You Can See Forever; The Owl and the Pussycat; What's Up Doc?; The Way We Were; Funny Lady; A Star Is Born; Main Event.
TV inc: My Name Is Barbra (Emmy-1965); Color Me Barbra; Belle of 14th Street; A Happening in Central Park.
Albums inc: A Star Is Born; Superman; Songbird; Barbra Streisand's Greatest Hits, Vol II; Wet; Guilty. (Grammys-Vocal Perf 1963, 1964, 1965, 1977; Album of Year 1963; Song of Year-1977).

STRICK, Joseph: Dir. b. Braddock, PA, Jul 6, 1923. e. UCLA. Films inc: Muscle Beach; The Savage Eye; The Balcony; Ulysses; Tropic of Cancer; Interviews with My Lai Veterans; (Oscar-Doc-1970); Road Movie; A Portrait of the Artist as a Young Man; The Space Works.

STRICKLAND, Gail: Act. b. Birmingham, AL, May 18. e. FL State U. Studied with Sanford Meisner. Bway inc: Status Quo Vadis. TV inc: Letters From Frank; The Gathering; The President's Mistress; Ski Lift to Death; King Crab; Rape and Marriage--The Rideout Case.
Films inc: The Drowning Pool; Bittersweet Love; Bound for Glory; One on One; The Dog Soldiers; Who'll Stop the Rain; Norma Rae.

STRITCH, Elaine: Act. b. Detroit, MI, 1928. On screen from 1956. Films inc: The Scarlet Hour; Three Violent People; A Farewell to Arms; The Perfect Furlough; Kiss Her Goodbye; Who Killed Teddy Bear?; Pigeons; Providence.
TV inc: Two's Company.

STROCK, Herbert L: Prod-Wri-Dir. b. Boston, Jan 13, 1918. e. USC, BA. Films inc: Storm Over Tibet; Magnetic Monster; Riders to the Stars; The Glass Wall; Gog; Battle Taxi; Donovan's Brain; Rider on a Dead Horse; Devil's Messenger; Brother on the Run; One Hour of Hell.
TV inc: Highway Patrol; Harbor Command; Men of Annapolis; I Led Three Lives; The Veil; Dragnet; 77 Sunset Strip; Maverick; Cheyenne; Bronco; Sugarfoot; Bonanza; The Small Miracle; Hans Brinker; What Will We Say to a Hungry World (Telethon); The Search for Survival.

STROMBERG, Gary: Prod. b. LA, May 14, 1942. Films inc: Car Wash; The Fish that Saved Pittsburgh.

STRONG, Michael: Act. b. NYC. Films inc: Detective Story; Dead Heat on a Merry-Go-Round; Point Blank; Patton.
TV inc: Queen of the Stardust Ballroom; The Ascent of Mt. Fuji; Paradise Lost.
Bway inc: The American Way; Spring Again; Counter-Attack; Eve of St. Mark; I'll Take the High Road; It's a Gift; An Enemy of the People; The Emperor's Clothes; Detective Story; Anastasia; A Month in the Country; A Far Country; Rhinoceros.
(Died Sep 17, 1980).

STROSS, Raymond: Prod. b. Leeds, Eng, May 22, 1916. e. Oxford. H of Anne Heywood. Films inc: As Long as They're Happy; An Alligator Named Daisy; The Flesh is Weak; A Question of Adultery; The Angry Hills; A Terrible Beauty; The Mark; The Very Edge; The Leather Boys; Ninety Degrees in the Shade; The Fox; The Midas Run; I Want What I Want; The Woman Who Rode Away; Good Luck Miss Wyckoff.

STROUD, Don: Act. b. 1937. Films inc: Madigan; Games; What's So Bad about Feeling Good; Coogan's Bluff; Bloody Mama; Explosion; Von Richtofen and Brown; Tick Tick Tick; Joe Kidd; Scalawag; The Killer Inside Me; The Choirboys; The House by the Lake; The Buddy Holly Story; The Amityville Horror.
TV inc: Supertrain; God In The Dock.

STRUDWICK, Shepperd: Act. b. Hillsboro, NC, Sep 22, 1907. e. U of NC, BA. Bway inc: Yellow Jacket; Both Your Houses; Biography (tour); Let Freedom Ring; End of Summer; As You Like It; The Three Sisters; Christopher Blake; Affairs of State; Ladies of the Corridor; Night Circus; Only in America; Who's Afraid of Virginia Woolf? (matinees & tour); Last Days of Lincoln; Galileo; In the Matter of J. Robert Oppenheimer; The Desert Song; The Eccentricities of a Nightingale.
Films inc: (from 1941-1947 billed as John Shepperd) Congo Maisie; Fast Company; Flight Command; Remember The Day; Joan of Arc; Enchantment; The Red Pony; All the King's Men; A Place in the Sun; Eddie Duchin Story; Autumn Leaves; Psychomania; The Daring Game; The Sad Sack; Cops and Robbers.
TV inc: Julius Caesar; Love of Life.

STRUTHERS, Sally: Act. b. Portland, OR, 1948. Films inc: The Phynx; Charlotte; Five Easy Pieces; The Getaway.
TV inc: The Summer Brothers Smothers Show; The Tim Conway Comedy Hour; The Great Houndinis; Aloha Means Goodbye; Hey, I'm Alive; All in the Family (Emmys-supp-1972 & 1979).

STUART, Malcolm: Prod-Exec. Started 1950 as agent, MCA; 1955 formed own literary agency with Ingo Preminger; sold to GAC 1962, he remained with GAC until 1965 when entered indie prodn; became agent with IFA (now ICM); 1972 vp chg dvlpmt Metromedia Producers Corp; 1974 vp dvlpmt Charles Fries Prodns; 1976 vp crea aff; 1980 vp chg vidpix, miniseries Lorimar Prodns. TV inc: Delaney; Call of the Wild; The Home Front; The Children of An Lac; High Noon, Part II--The Return of Will Kane.

STUART, Mary: Act. b. Miami, FL, Jul 4. Films inc: The Adventures of Don Juan; Thunderhoof; Caribou Trail. TV inc: Search for Tomorrow (since 1951); After Hours; From Janice, John, Mary and Michael, with Love.

STUART, Maxine (nee Shlivek): Act. b. Elberon, NJ. e. AADA. Films inc: Days of Wine and Roses; Dear Heart; Winning; Prisoner of Second Avenue; Fun With Dick & Jane; Coast to Coast.
Thea inc: Tunnel of Love; At War with the Army; A Goose for the Gander; Sun-Up to Sundown; Cry Havoc.
TV inc: Kill Me If You Can; Executive Suite; Doctor's Hospital.

STUART, Mel: Dir. b. Sep 2, 1928. Films inc: The White Lions; If It's Tuesday, This Must Be Belgium; Willie Wonka and the Chocolate Factory; One Is A Lonely Number; I Love My Wife; Wattstax.
TV inc: China, The Roots of Madness (Emmy-prod-1967); The Making of the President, 1960, 1964, 1968 (Emmy-prod-1970); Rise and Fall of the Third Reich; Life Goes to the Movies; The Triangle Factory Fire Scandal; The Chisholms; Sophia Loren--Her Own Story.

STUART, William Victor: Exec. b. Glendale, CA, Dec 29, 1946. e. College of Switzerland, Emerson Coll. Trainee Mgr, Fox, Amsterdam, 1973-75; asst European sls Mgr, inc Near and Far East. Fox, 1975-77; M-dir, Fox, Madrid and supervisor of Portugal, 1977-78; M dir, UA (A/Asia), 1978.

STUBENHAUS, Neil: Bassist. b. Bridgeport, CT, Jul 18, 1953. See Blood, Sweat & Tears.

STULBERG, Gordon: Exec. b. Toronto, Cana, Dec 17, 1923. e. U of Toronto, BA; Cornell, LLD. With Law firm of Pacht, Ross, Warne and Bernhard specializing in film law; Joined Col as exec asst to vp 1956; vp & chief admn officer 1960; P Cinema Center Films 1967; P 20th Century-Fox 1971; returned to law practice 1975; named P Polygram Pictures (former Casablanca Records and Filmworks), March 18,- 1980.

STUMPF, Richard J: Snd eng. b. Glendale, CA, Oct 15, 1926. e. UC Berkeley, BS. With NBC in tv eng dept; 1959 proj coord for Project Mercury (first man-in space program); 1961 to RCA where he created first digitally controlled automatic sound mixdown system; 1968 to U; 1973 head of Sound & Electronics Dept; principal co-inventor Sensurround (Oscar-scientific-1974).

STURGES, John: Dir. b. Oak Park, IL, Jan 3, 1911. Films inc: The Man Who Dared; Shadowed; Keeper of the Bees; The Best Man Wins; The Sign of the Ram; The Magnificent Yankee; Kind Lady; Right Cross; The People Against O'Hara; The Girl in White; Jeopardy; Escape from Fort Bravo; Bad Day At Black Rock; Underwater; Gunfight at the OK Corral; The Law and Jake Wade; Never So Few; The Magnificent Seven; By Love Possessed; Sergeants Three; The Great Escape; The Old Man and the Sea; The Satan Bug; The Hallelujah Trail; The Hour of the Gun; Ice Station Zebra; Marooned; Joe Kidd; McQ; The Eagle Has Landed.

STYNE, Jule (nee Stein): Comp-Prod. b. London, Dec 31, 1905. e. Northwestern U, Chicago Musical Coll. Child prodigy as a pianist, appearing with Chicago Symphony at age 8.
Bway inc: (scores) High Button Shoes; Gentlemen Prefer Blondes; In Any Language; Hazel Flagg; Peter Pan; Say Darling; Bells Are Ringing; Gypsy; Do Re Mi; Subways Are For Sleeping; Funny Girl; Fade Out-Fade In; Hallelujah Baby (Tony-1967); Darling of the Day; Sugar; Peter Pan. (Prod) Make A Wish; Pal Joey; Will Success Spoil Rock Hunter; Mr. Wonderful; Teibele and Her Demon.
Films inc: Sailors on Leave; Follow the Boys; The Kid From Brooklyn; The West Point Story; Anchors Aweigh; Tars and Spars; Three Coins in the Fountain (Oscar-1954-title song); My Sister Eileen.
TV inc: Ruggles of Red Gap; Mr. Magoo's Christmas Carol; The Dangerous Christmas of Red Riding Hood. . .or Oh Wolf, Poor Wolf. (Prod) Anything Goes; Panama Hattie; The Best of Broadway; The Eddie Fisher Show.
Songs inc: I've Heard That Song Before; I'll Walk Alone; I Fall in Love Too Easily; It's Magic; Let it Snow. (Grammy-cast album-1964).

SUBOTSKY, Milton: Wri-Prod. b. NYC, Sep 27, 1921. Films inc: Rock, Rock, Rock; The Last Mile; Laugh Parade; The World of Abbott and Costello; City of the Dead; Dr Terror's House of Horrors; The Skull; The Deadly Bees; Dr. Who and the Daleks; The Psychopath; Daleks Invasion Earth; 2150 AD; Torture Garden; The House That Dripped Blood; Tales from the Crypt; Asylum; Madhouse; The Land that Time Forgot; The Mind of Mr. Soames; Scream and Scream Again; At the Earth's Core; The Uncanny; Dominique.
TV inc: The Martian Chronicles.

SUGAR, Joseph M: Exec. b. NYC, Jun 4, 1916. e. NYU. In contract dept Republic 1938. After military service World War II, joined Producers Releasing Corp as asst contract mgr, later mgr; following merger with Eagle Lion became exec asst to distribution vp; 1953 UA NY exchange; 1959 sales vp Magna Theatres Corp; joined 20th Fox 1962 as road show mgr, became vp domestic dist following year; 1967, exec vp Warner-Seven Arts; 1968 P Cinerama Releasing Corp; 1975 P Gamma III Distributing Co; from 1976-78 operated own firm; 1978 joined AIP as exec vp worldwide sls, P AIP Distributing Co; when AIP merged with Filmways, became exec vp parent company.

SUGARMAN, Burt: Prod. b. LA. e. USC. TV inc: The Midnight Special; Celebrity Sweepstakes; Bob Dylan Special.

SUKMAN, Harry: Comp-Cond-Pianist. b. Chicago, Dec 2, 1912. Film scores inc: Song without End (Oscar-1960); Fanny; The Singing Nun; The Naked Runner; A Thunder of Drums; Welcome to Hard Times; A Bullet for Joey; Screaming Eagles; If He Hollers, Let Him Go; Riders to the Stars; Gog; Battle Taxi; Verboten.
TV inc: Dr. Kildare; Eleventh Hour; High Chaparral; Bonanza; Gentle Ben; The Family Kovak; The Monroes.
Songs: You Are There; My Consolation; I Love Your Gypsy Heart; The Gentle Ben Theme.

SULLIVAN, Barry (Patrick Barry): Act. b. NYC, Aug 29, 1912. Summer stock, NY stage. On screen from 1942. Films inc: We Refuse to Die; High Explosives; Lady in the Dark; Rainbow Island; And Now Tomorrow; Suspense; The Gangster; Any Number Can Play; The Great Gatsby; A Life of Her Own; Payment on Demand; Bad and the Beautiful; Jeopardy; Strategic Air Command; Julie; Light in the Piazza; A Gathering of Eagles; My Blood Runs Cold; An American Dream; Tell Them Willie Boy Is Here; Earthquake; Take a Hard Ride; The Human Factor; Oh, God!; Caravan.
Bway inc: The Man Who Came to Dinner; Brother Rat; Idiot's Delight; The Land Is Bright; The Caine Mutiny Court Martial.
TV inc: Cool Million; Sixth Sense; The Immigrants; Backstairs at the White House; The Bastard; The Secret of Lost Valley; Casino.

SULTZMAN, Phillip: Exec prod-Wri. b. Mexico, Sep 19, 1928. e. UCLA, BA, MA. TV inc: (wri) Rifleman; Fugitive; Dr Kildare; Perry Mason. (Asso prod) Twelve O'Clock High. (Prod) Felony Squad; The FBI; Barnaby Jones; Alvin Karpis; Brinks--The Great Robbery; Attack on Terror.

SUMMER, Donna: Singer-Act. b. Boston, MA, Dec 31, 1948. Appeared in German prodns of Hair; Godspell; The Me Nobody Knows; Vienna folkopera prodns of Showboat; Porgy & Bess.
Albums inc: Love To Love You, Baby; A Love Trilogy; The Four Seansons of Love; I Remember Yesterday; Once Upon a Time; Live & More; Thank God It's Friday; Hot Stuff; Bad Girls; Greatest Hits on the Radio, Vol 1 & 2.
(Grammys-(2)-R&B vocal 1978; rock vocal 1979).
Films inc: The Deep (mus); Thank God It's Friday (act).
TV inc: The Donna Summer Special.

SUMMERALL, Pat: Sportscaster. b. 1932. e. U of AR. Former pro football player. Covers various sports for CBS; host of CBS Sports Spectacular.

SUMMERFIELD, Eleanor: Act. b. London, Mar 7, 1921. Films inc: London Belongs to Me; Scrooge; It's Great to be Young; Dentist in the Chair; The Running Man; The Yellow Hat; Private Eye; Some Will, Some Won't.
TV inc: The Two Charles; The Rather Reassuring Show; You're Lovely in Black; Murder at the Panto; Husband of the Year; Madly in Love.

SUMMERS, Hope: Act. b. Chicago, 1901. Performed in radio during the 1940s-50s. Films inc: Parrish; Spencer's Mountain; The Hallelujah Trail; Rosemary's Baby.
TV inc: The Rifleman; The Andy Griffith Show.
(Died July 22, 1979.)

SUMNER, Gabe: Exec. b. NYC, Apr 20, 1929. e. NYU BA. Joined Par pub dept 1950; ass't pub dir Schine Theatre Circuit 1951-53; Par 1953-55; ind agcy 1955-1960; to UA 1960; named sr vp, prodn head 1977; Orion Pictures Co 1979 as sr vp sales-ad-pub.

SURTEES, Bruce: Cin. b. LA. S of Robert Surtees. Films inc: Play Misty for Me; Dirty Harry; The Great Northfield Minnesota Raid; The Beguiled; High Plains Drifter; Blume In Love; Joe Kidd; Lenny; Leadbelly; Sparkle; Three Warriors; Big Wednesday; Movie Movie; Dreamer; Escape From Alcatraz.

SURTEES, Robert: Cin. b. Covington, KY, Aug 9, 1906. Films inc: Thirty Seconds Over Tokyo; Act of Violence; Intruder in the Dust; King Solomon's Mines *(Oscar*-1950); Quo Vadis; The Bad and the Beautiful *(Oscar*-1952); Trial; Oklahoma!; Raintree County; Ben Hur *(Oscar*-1959); The Collector; The Satan Bug; Doctor Dolittle; The Graduate; Sweet Charity; Summer of '42; The Last Picture Show; Oklahoma Crude; The Sting; The Great Waldo Pepper; The Hindenberg; A Star is Born; The Turning Point; Bloodbrothers; Same Time Next Year.

SUSSKIND, David: Prod-TV pers. b. NYC, Dec 1920. Films inc: Edge of the City; A Raisin in the Sun; Requiem for a Heavyweight; All the Way Home; Lovers and Other Strangers; Loving Couples.
TV inc: Ages of Man *(Emmy-*1966); Blind Ambition; Transplant; Sex and the Eleanor and Franklin *(Emmy-*Exec Prod-1976); Eleanor and Franklin-The White House Years *(Emmy-*Exec Prod-1977); Sex and the Single Parent; The Family Man; The Plutonium Incident; Father Figure; Mom, The Wolfman and Me.
Bway inc: Mister Lincoln.

SUTHERLAND, Donald: Act. b. St John, NB, Canada, Jul 17, 1935. e. U of Toronto, BA. Films inc: The Castle of the Living Dead; Die, Die My Darling; The Bedford Incident; Oedipus Rex; M*A*S*H; Kelly's Heroes; Johnny Get Your Gun; Klute; Steelyard Blues; The Day of the Locust; The Disappearance; Blood Relatives; The Invasion of the Body Snatchers; The Eagle Has Landed; Fellini's Casanova; The Great Train Robbery; Nat'l Lampoons Animal House; Murder By Decree; A Man, A Woman and a Bank; Bear Island; Nothing Personal; Ordinary People.
TV (British): Marching to the Sea; The Death of Bessie Smith; Hamlet at Elsinore.
Thea inc: On a Clear Day You Can See Canterbury; The Shewing Up of Blanco Posnet; The Spoon River Anthology.

SUTHERLAND, Joan: Coloratura Soprano. b. Sydney, Australia, Apr 7, 1926. Concert and oratorio artist. Opera debut Covent Gardens 1952 in the Magic Flute; guest appearances La Scala; Metropolitan Opera; Lyric Opera of Chicago; Melbourne Opera; Carnegie Hall.
*(Grammy-*Class vocal-1961).

SUZMAN, Janet: Act. b. Johannesburg, S Africa, Feb 9, 1939. e. Kingsmead Coll, U of Witwatersrand. Joined the Royal Shakespeare Company 1962. London stage debut in The Comedy of Errors. Thea inc: The Greeks.
Films inc: A Day in the Death of Joe Egg; Nicholas and Alexandra; The Black Windmill; Nijinsky.
TV inc: The Three Sisters; Hedda Gabler; The House on Garibaldi Street.

SVENSON, Bo: Perf. b. Sweden, Feb 13, 1941. Films inc: Maurie; The Great Waldo Pepper; Walking Tall, Part II; Breaking Point; Special Delivery; Walking Tall--Final Chapter; Jim Buck; The Unglorious Bastard; Our Man in Mecca; Son of the Sheik; Night Flight; North Dallas Forty; Virus.

SWANSON, Glen: Dir. TV inc: Sports Challenge; Movie Game; The Way It Was; Grease-Pay; Dinah's Place; Make Me Laugh; Dinah Salutes Broadway *(Emmy-*1975); Dinah Salutes Tony Orlando and Dawn on their Fifth Birthday *(Emmy-*1976); Dinah!.

SWANSON, Gloria: Act. b. Chicago, Mar 27, 1899. On screen from 1913 in The Romance of an American Duchess. Appeared in many silent films inc Mack Sennett comedies. In 1926 became producer-star as an owner-member of United Artists.
Films inc: Don't Change Your Husband; For Better, For Worse; Male and Female; Zara; Manhandled; Wages of Virtue; The Love of Sunya; Sadie Thompson; The Trespasser; What a Widow; Indiscreet; Tonight or Never; Music in the Air; Father Takes a Wife; Sunset Boulevard; 3 for Bedroom C; Nero's Mistress; Airport 1975.
Bway inc: Twentieth Century; Nina; Butterflies Are Free.
TV inc: Killer Bees.

SWAYZE, John Cameron: Broadcaster. b. Wichita, KS, Apr 4, 1906. Reporter and editor Kansas City, MO, Journal-Post; news dept. KMBC, Kansas City; head of News, NBC western network, Hollywood; NBC radio news, NYC; TV, 1948-52. TV inc: News Caravan; Who Said That; Watch the World; Sightseeing with the Swayzes; Circle Theatre; To Tell the Truth.

SWEET, Blanche: Act. b. Chicago, Il, Jun 18, 1896. Silent screen star, made her debut in 1909 in The Rocky Road.
Films inc: Was He a Coward?; A Country Cupid; The Eternal Mother; The Making of a Man; The Painted Lady; The Lesser Evil; Broken Ways; Judith of Bethulia; The Battle of Elderberry Gulch; The Storm; Quincy Adams Sawyer; Tess of the D'Urbervilles; Anna Christie; The Sporting Venus; Bluebeard's Seven Wives; Diplomacy; The Silver Horde; The Five Pennies.

SWENSON, Inga: Act. b. Omaha, NE, Dec 29, 1934. e. Northwestern U. Bway inc: Twelfth Night; New Faces of 1956; The First Gentleman; 110 Degrees in the Shade; Baker Street.
Films inc: The Miracle Worker; Advise and Consent; The Betsy; Wind River.
TV inc: Playhouse 90; U S Steel Hour; Soap; Androcles and the Lion; Testimony of Two Men; Benson.

SWERLING, Jo: Wri. b. Russia, Apr 8, 1897. Newspaper and mag wr; auth vaudeville sketches; co-author plays, The Kibitzer; Guys and Dolls *(Tony*-1951).
Films inc: The Kibitzer; The Pride of the Yankees; Guys and Dolls; Platinum Blonde; Washington Merry-Go-Round; Dirigible; No Greater Glory; Pennies from Heaven; Made for Each Other; Confirm or Deny; Blood and Sand; The Lady Takes a Chance; Crash Dive; Lifeboat; Leave Her to Heaven; Thunder in the East.
TV: The Lord Don't Play Favorites.

SWERLING, Jo Jr: Prod. b. LA, Jun 18, 1931. e. UCLA. Joined Revue Prodns 1957 as prodn coord; became asso prod, later prod Kraft Suspense Theatre. TV inc: (Prod) Run For Your Life; The Bold Ones; Drive Hard, Drive Fast; The Lonely Profession; The Whole World is Watching; The Sound of Anger; How to Steal an Airplane; Cool Million; Toma; The Story of Pretty Boy Floyd; This is the West That Was; Baretta; Captains and the Kings; The 3,000 Mile Chase; Aspen; The Jordan Chance; Pirate's Key. (Exec Prod) Target Risk; City of Angels; Hazard's People; The Invasion of Johnson County; The Last Convertible (& dir). The Rockford Files (asso exec prod of pilot, supv prod series).

SWIFT, Lela: Dir. TV inc: Studio One; Dupont Show of the Week; Norman Corwin Presents; Years Without Harvest; A Gift of Terror *(Emmy-*1973); Purex Specials for Women; Ryan's Hope *(Emmys-*1977, 1979, 1980).

SWIFT, Susan: Act. b. Houston, TX, Jul 21, 1964. Films inc: Audrey Rose; Harper Valley PTA.

SWINK, Robert E: Film Ed-Dir. b. Rocky Ford, CO, Jun 3, 1918. Films inc: Detective Story; Carrie; Roman Holiday; Desperate Hours; Friendly Persuasion; The Diary of Anne Frank; The Children's Hour; The Best Man; How to Steal a Million; Flim Flam Man; Funny Girl; The Cowboys; Skyjacked; Papillon; Three the Hard Way; Rooster Cogburn; Midway; Islands in the Stream; Gray Lady Down; The Boys From Brazil; The In-Laws.

SWIT, Loretta: Act. b. Passaic, NJ, Nov 4, 1937. Films inc: Stand Up and be Counted; Freebie and the Bean; Race with the Devil.
TV inc: M*A*S*H (Emmy-supp-1980); Shirts/Skin; Coffeeville; Friendships, Secrets and Lies; The Love Tapes; Bob Hope All-Star Comedy Christmas Special.
Bway inc: Same Time, Next Year.

SWOFFORD, Ken: Act. b. DuQuoin, IL, Jul 25. Films inc: Captain Newman, M.D.
TV inc: Rich Man, Poor Man II; Ellery Queen; Switch; Capra; Sultan and the Rock Star; All God's Children.

SWOPE, Mel: Prod-Dir. TV inc: (Dir) Tennessee Ernie Ford Show; Partridge Family; Land of Tinkerdee (Muppets pilot); Everything Money Can't Buy (& prod). (Prod) California Fever; Man Undercover; Paradise Cove; Police Story; The Girl With Something Extra (pilot); The Night The City Screamed; Walking Tall.

SYBERBERG, Hans-Jurgen: Dir-Cin. b. E Germany, Dec 8, 1935. Worked with Brecht and the Berliner Ensemble as cin. Films inc: Fritz Kortner Rehearses Schiller's "Kabale und Liebe" (doc); Romy--Anatomy of a Face (doc); Kortner Speaks Monologs for a Record (doc); Count Pocci (doc); Scarabea--How Much Earth Does Man Need?; Sex Business Made in Passin (doc); San Domingo; After My Last Move (doc); Ludwig--Requiem for a Virgin King; Theodor Hiernies--Or How To Become the Cook of the Court; Karl May; Winifried Wagner and the story of the "Haus Wahnfried" (doc); Our Hitler--A Film From Germany.

SYLBERT, Anthea: Exec. b. NYC, Oct 6, 1939. e. Barnard College; Parsons School of Design. Started as costume desgn; 1977 vp special projects WB; 1978 vp prodn; 1980, vp prodn UA.
Films inc: (dsgn) Rosemary's Baby; A New Leaf; Carnal Knowledge; The Heartbreak Kid; Chinatown; Shampoo; The Fortune; Julia; F.I.S.T. (part).

SYLBERT, Paul: Dsgn-Dir. Films inc: (Dsgn) The Steagle (& wri-dir); The Drowning Pool; One Flew Over the Cuckoo's Nest; Hardcore; Heaven Can Wait (Oscar-1978); Kramer vs. Kramer; Resurrection.
TV inc: (Dsgn) Studio One; Suspense; Ed Sullivan Show. (Dir) The Defenders; The Nurses.
Has also dsgn for NY City Opera Company.

SYLBERT, Richard: Art Dir. b. NYC, Apr 16, 1928. e. Temple U. VP prod. Paramount Pictures Corp, 1975-76. Films inc: Baby Doll; Splendor in the Grass; Walk on the Wild Side; The Manchurian Candidate; How to Murder Your Wife; The Pawnbroker; Who's Afraid of Virginia Woolf (Oscar-1966); Rosemary's Baby; Catch 22; Carnal Knowledge; Chinatown; Shampoo; The Fortune; Players.

SYMS, Sylvia: Act. b. London, Dec 3, 1934. Films inc: My Teenage Daughter; No Time for Tears; Birthday Present; Ice Cold in Alex; The Devil's Disciple; Moonraker; Ferry to Hong Kong; Expresso Bongo; The World of Suzie Wong; Flame in the Streets; The Quare Fellow; The World Ten Times Over; East of Sudan; The Eliminator; Operation Crossbow; Hostile Witness; The Marauders; Run Wild, Run Free; The Tamarind Seed; Give Us This Day.
TV inc: The Human Jungle; Bat Out of Hell; Depart in Terror; Friends and Romans; The Root of All Evil; My Good Woman; Love and Marriage; There Goes the Bride.

SZWARC, Jeannot: Dir. b. Paris, Nov 21, 1939. Films inc: Extreme Close-up; Bug; Jaws 2; Somewhere In Time.
TV inc: Ironside; To Catch A Thief; Kojak; Columbo; Night Gallery; Crime Club.

TABORI, George: Wri. b. Budapest, Hungary, May 24, 1914. Plays inc: Flight Into Egypt; The Emperor's Clothes; Brouhaha; Brecht on Brecht; Demonstration, and Man and Dog (one-acters); The Cannibals; Pinkville.
Films inc: Young Lovers; I Confess; The Journey; No Exit; Secret Ceremony; Parades.

TABORI, Kristofer: Act. b. 1955. S of Viveca Lindfors and Don Siegel. Films inc: Weddings and Babies; Making It; Journey Through Rosebud; Girlfriends.
TV inc: The Greatest Heroes of the Bible; Brave New World.
Bway inc: Habeas Corpus.

TAHSE, Martin: Prod. TV inc: Exec prod ABC Afternoon Specials (Emmy-Very Good Friends-1980).

TAIT, Don: Wri. Films inc: The Castaway Cowboy; The Apple Dumpling Gang; Treasure of the Matecumbe; The Shaggy D A; The North Avenue Irregulars; The Apple Dumpling Gang Rides Again; Unidentified Flying Oddballs; Herbie Goes Bananas (& co-prod).
TV inc: The Green Hornet; The Iron Horse; The Outcasts; The Virginian; Here Come the Brides; The Bold Ones.

TAKA, Miiko: Act. Films inc: Cry for Happy; Hell to Eternity; A Girl Called Tamiko; Operation Bottleneck; A Global Affair; The Art of Love; Walk, Don't Run; Lost Horizon; Paper Tiger; The Big Fix.
TV inc: Shogun.

TAKEI, George: Act. Films inc: Ice Palace; Red Line 7000; Walk Don't Run; The Green Berets; Which Way to the Front; Star Trek--The Motion Picture.
TV inc: Star Trek.

TALBOT, Lyle (Lysle Henderson): Act. b. Pittsburgh, PA, Feb 8, 1904. Screen debut, 1932, Love Is a Racket.
Films inc: Up in Arms; One Body Too Many; Vicious Circle; Sky Dragon; The Jackpot; Oil for the Lamps of China; 20,000 Years in Sing Sing; The Life of Jimmy Dolan; White Lightning; The Great Man; Sunrise at Campobello; Adventures of Batman and Robin.

TALBOT, Nita (Anita Sokol): Act. b. NYC, Aug 8, 1930. Films inc: Bundle of Joy; I Married a Woman; Once Upon a Horse; Who's Got the Action?; A Very Special Favor; That Funny Feeling; Girl Happy; The Cool Ones; Buck and the Preacher; The Manchu Eagle; The Sweet Creek County War.
TV inc: Stage Door; Here We Go Again; The Movie Murderer.
Thea inc: Never Say Never; The Fifth Season; Uncle Willie; Zelda.

TALLAS, Gregory: Prod-Dir-Edtr. b. Athens, Greece, Jan 25, 1915. e. Princeton. Films inc: (edtr) Shanghai Gesture; Three Russian Girls; Summer Storm; The Southerner; Whistle Stop; Night in Casablanca; Without Honor; Flight to Nowhere; Captain Apache. (Dir) Siren of Atlantis; Red Rock Outlaw; Prehistoric Women; Barefoot Battalion; Bed of Grass; Forbidden Love; Bikini Paradise; S-007; Espionage in Tangiers; Love is Out; Cataclysm.
TV inc: (dir) Ford Theatre; Rheingold Theatre; You Be The Jury.

TALLCHIEF, Maria: Dancer. b. Fairfax, OK, 1925. Generally regarded as the first great American prima ballerina. With the Ballet Russe de Monte Carlo; New York City Ballet; guest prima ballerina American Ballet Theatre; last danced profesionally in 1965; founder, artistic dir Lyric Opera Ballet, Chicago; in 1980 group renamed Chicago City Ballet while retaining ties to Lyric Opera. Films inc: Million Dollar Mermaid.

TAMBLYN, Russ: Act. b. LA, Dec 30, 1934. Films inc: Father of the Bride; Father's Little Dividend; Seven Brides for Seven Brothers; Hit the Deck; Don't Go Near the Water; Peyton Place; Tom Thumb; Cimarron; West Side Story; The Wonderful World of the Brothers Grimm; The Haunting; Son of a Gunfighter; Blood of Frankenstein; The Last Movie; Win, Place or Steal.

TAMBOR, Jeffrey: Act. b. San Francisco, CA, Jul 8. e. San Francisco State, BA; Wayne State, MA. Worked with Seattle Repertory; Old Globe Theatre San Diego; Louisville Actors Theatre. Bway inc: Sly Fox; Measure for Measure.
TV inc: The Ropers; Alcatraz--The Whole Shocking Story.
Films inc: And Justice for All.

TANAKA, Tomoyuki: Prod. b. Osaka, Japan, 1910. P of Toho Pictures, Inc. Has prod more than 200 films since joining Toho 1944. Films inc: Godzilla; The Rickshaw Man; The Bad Sleep Well; Yojimbo; Sanjuro; High and Low; Red Beard; The Emperor and the General; The Submersion of Japan; Mount Hakkoda; Kagemusha.

TANDY, Jessica: Act. b. London, Eng, Jun 7, 1909. W of Hume Cronyn. Thea inc: (London) The Rumour; Theatre of Life; Water; The Unknown Warrior; Autumn Crocus; Juarez and Maximilian; Children In Uniform; Lady Audley's Secret; various Shakespearean roles. (Bway) The Matriarch; The Last Enemy; Time and the Conways; The White Steed; Geneva; Jupiter Laughs; A Streetcar Named Desire *(Tony*-1948); The Little Blue Light; Hilda Crane; The Fourposter; Madame Will You Walk; The Man in the Dog Suit; Five Finger Exercise; The Physicists; A Delicate Balance; All Over; Noel Coward in Two Keys; The Many Faces of Love; The Gin Game *(Tony*-1978).

Films inc: The Indiscretions of Eve; The Green Years; Forever Amber; The Seventh Cross; Dragonwyck; Valley of Decision; September Affair; The Four Poster; The Desert Fox; Butley; A Light in the Forest; The Birds.

TANEN, Ned: Exec. b. LA. e. UCLA. Joined MCA, Inc, 1954; app'd VP, 1968. Bought Uni Records, since absorbed by MCA Records. Became active in film prod, 1972. In 1976 named P Universal Theatrical Motion Pictures.

TANNENBAUM, Tom: Exec. Started as asst in MGM casting dept; with Famous Artists as agent, co-head tv dept; exec asst to Ray Stark at Seven Arts; vp David Wolper Prodns; sr vp Paramount TV; sr VP U-TV; Nov 1978, exec vp Columbia Pictures TV; May 1980 P MGM-TV.

TANNER, Pearl King: Act. b. CA, 1880. After several years of stage work, entered radio and starred on an early soap, Hawthorne House. (Died July 16, 1980).

TAPLIN, Jonathan L: Prod. b. Cleveland, OH, Jul 18, 1947. e. Princeton U, BA. Concert mgr for Judy Collins; The Band; The Concert for Bangladesh.
Films inc: Mean Streets; The Last Waltz; Carny.

TARADASH, Daniel: Wri-Dir. b. Louisville, KY, Jan 29, 1913. e. Harvard Coll, AB, Harvard Law School, LLB. Films inc: Golden Boy; A Little Bit of Heaven; Knock On Any Door; Don't Bother to Knock; Rancho Notorious; From Here To Eternity *(Oscar*-1953); Picnic; Desiree; Storm Center (& dir); Bell Book and Candle; Hawaii; Castle Keep; Doctor's Wives; The Other Side of Midnight. Plays: American adaptation, Red Gloves; There Was a Little Girl.
TV inc: Bogie.

TARKENTON, Fran: TV pers. b. Richmond, VA, Feb 3, 1940. e. U GA. Former pro football QB with Vikings 1961-1967, 1972-1979; Giants 1967-1972. TV inc: Monday Night Football; That's Incredible (host).

TARKOVSKY, Andrei: Dir. b. Russia, Apr 4, 1932. e. Moscow Film Institute. Films inc: The Roller and the Violin (short) (& sp); Ivan's Childhood; Andrei Rublev (& co-sp); Solaris (& co-sp); The Mirror (& co-sp); Stalker (& co-sp, sets).

TARLOFF, Frank: Wri. Films inc: Father Goose *(Oscar*-1964); The Secret War of Harry Frigg; Once You Kiss A Stranger.
TV inc: Shirley MacLaine Show (crea); The Jeffersons; A Guide for the Married Woman.

TARNOFF, John B: Exec. b. NYC, Mar 3, 1952. e. Amherst Coll, BA. With Billy Jack Enterprises, 1974: literary agent, Bart-Levy Assoc, 1975-77; head of tv dept, Kohner-Levy Assoc; vp motion picture devlpmnt, MGM, 1979; sr vp in chg prodn & devlpmt Dec. 1980.

TARTIKOFF, Brandon: Exec. b. NY, 1949. e. Yale U, BA. Joined ABC-TV in 1976 as m, dramatic development; moved to NBC Entertainment in Sep 1977, as dir, comedy programs; apptd vp, programs, West Coast NBC Entertainment, July 1978; P NBC Entertainment, July 1980.

A TASTE OF HONEY: Group. Members are Don Johnson, Perry Kibble, Hazel Payne, Janice Johnson. Albums inc: A Taste of Honey *(Grammy*-new art-1978).

TATI, Jacques (nee Tatischeff): Mime-Dir-Wri. b. Le Pecq, France, 1908. Films inc: Jour de Fete; Monsieur Hulot's Holiday; Mon Oncle; Playtime; Traffic.

TATUM, Donn B: Exec. b. LA, Jan 9, 1913. e. Stanford, Oxford. Chmn Bd & CEO of Walt Disney Productions. With company since 1956 when he left ABC to become Disney's prodn business mgr.

TAUROG, Norman: Dir. b. Chicago, Feb 23, 1899. After short career as actor, to Hollywood as property man; dir of two-reel comedies. Dir first feature, The Farmers Daughter, 1928.
Films inc: Sunny Skies; Skippy *(Oscar*-1930-31); Finn and Hattie; If I Had a Million; Huckleberry Finn; Sooky; Bedtime Story; Mrs. Wiggs of the Cabbage Patch; College Rhythm; The Big Broadcast of 1936; You Can't Have Everthing; The Adventures of Tom Sawyer; Boys Town; A Yank at Eton; Presenting Lily Mars; The Hoodulum Saint; Words and Music; The Toast of New Orleans; Mrs. O'Malley and Mr. Malone; Jumping Jacks; The Stars Are Singing; The Caddy; You're Never Too Young; The Birds and the Bees; The Fuzzy Pink Nightgown; Onionhead; Don't Give Up the Ship; Visit to a Small Planet; Blue Hawaii; Girls, Girls, Girls; It Happened at the World's Fair; Palm Springs Weekend; Dr. Goldfoot and the Bikini Machine; Spinout; Double Trouble; Speedway; Live a Little, Love a Little.

TAVEL, Ronald: Wri. b. NYC, May 1941. e. U of WY. Plays inc: Tarzan of the Flicks; Screen Test; The Life of Juanita Castro; Shower; The Life of Lady Godiva; Gorilla Queen; Boy on the Straight-Back Chair; How Jacqueline Kennedy Became Queen of Greece.

TAVERNIER, Bertrand: Wri-Dir. b. Lyons, France, Apr 25, 1941. Originally a film publicist, he studied techniques of prods with whom he worked; debuted as dir with one of five episodes in Les Baisers; later contributed episode to La Chance et L'Amour.
Films inc: (wri) Coplan Ouvre le feu a Mexico; Capitaine Singrid. (Wri-dir) The Clockmaker of Saint Paul; Let Joy Reign Supreme; The Judge and the Assassin; Spoiled Children; Deathwatch (co-prod, dir, co-sp); Une Semaine De Vacances (wri-dir).

TAYBACK, Vic: Act. b. NYC. Films inc: Bullitt; Papillon; The Gambler; Report to the Commissioner; The Big Bus; The Shaggy D A; Alice Doesn't Live Here Anymore; The Choirboys; Special Delivery; The Cheap Detective.
TV inc: MacKenzie's Raiders; Honor Thy Father; Getting Married; Alice; Moviola (This Year's Blonde); The Great American Traffic Jam; The Night the City Screamed.
Thea inc: The Diary of Anne Frank; Death of a Salesman; Stalag 17.

TAYLOR, Don: Act-Dir. b. Freeport, PA, Dec 13, 1920. Films inc: (act) Naked City; For the Love of Mary; Ambush; Father of the Bride; Submarine Command; The Blue Veil; Stalag 17; Men of Sherwood Forest; I'll Cry Tomorrow. (Dir) The Savage Guns; Ride the Wild Surf; Jack of Diamonds; Five Man Army; Escape from the Planet of the Apes; Tom Sawyer; Echoes of a Summer; The Great Scout and Cathouse Thursday; The Island of Dr Moreau; Damien-Omen II; The Final Countdown.
TV inc: (dir) The Gift; The Promise of Love.

TAYLOR, Elizabeth: Act. b. London, Feb 27, 1932. Danced before Princess Elizabeth & Princess Margaret at age 3. Came to US at outbreak WW II. Screen debut, 1943, Lassie Come Home.
Films inc: National Velvet; Life With Father; Cynthia; Courage of Lassie; Little Women; The White Cliffs of Dover; Jane Eyre; Father of the Bride; Father's Little Dividend; A Place in the Sun; Ivanhoe; The Girl Who Had Everything; Elephant Walk; Beau Brummell; The Last Time I Saw Paris; Giant; Raintree Country; Cat on a Hot Tin Roof; Suddenly, Last Summer; Butterfield 8 *(Oscar*-1960); Cleopatra; The V.I.P.'s; The Night of the Iguana; Who's Afraid of Virginia Woolf? *(Oscar*-1966); The Taming of the Shrew; The Sandpiper; Doctor Faustus; Reflections in a Golden Eye; The Comedians; The Only Game in Town; X, Y, and Zee; Hammersmith Is Out; Night Watch; Ash Wednesday; That's Entertainment!; The Driver's Seat; The Blue Bird; A Little Night Music; The Mirror Crack'd.

TAYLOR, James: Comp-Mus. b. Boston, MA, Mar 12, 1948. Albums inc: Sweet Baby James; Mud Slide; Slim and the Blue Horizon; One Man Dog; Walking Man; Gorilla; In the Pocket; J.T.; James Taylor's Greatest Hits; Flag. Singles inc: You've Got a Friend *(Grammy*-pop male voc-1971); Handy Man *(Grammy*-pop male vocal-1977).

TAYLOR, Jud: Dir. b. Feb 25, 1940. TV inc: Hawkins; Winter Kill; Sara; Future Cop; Return to Earth; Tail Gunner Joe; Mary White; Circle of Children II; Lovey; The Last Tenant; Flesh and Blood; Act of Love.

TAYLOR, Kent (Louis Weiss): Act. b. Nashua, IA, May 11, 1907. On screen from 1931. Films inc: Road to Reno; The Devil and the Deep; Blonde Venus; Death Takes a Holiday; Mrs. Wiggs of the Cabbage Patch; David Harum; Ramona; Mississippi Gambler; Roger Touhy-Gangster; Payment on Demand; Brides of Blood; Girls for Rent.

TAYLOR, Noel: Cos Dsgn. b. Youngstown, OH, Jan 17, 1917. Bway inc: Alice in Wonderland; Twentieth Century; Stalag 17; One Bright Day; Dial M for Murder; Teahouse of the August Moon; Ladies of the Corridor; In the Summer House; Festival; No Time for Sergeants; Time Limit; Auntie Mame; The Body Beautiful; Tall Story; Write Me a Murder; Night of the Iguana; Desire Under the Elms; One Flew Over the Cuckoo's Nest; What Makes Sammy Run?; The White Devil; We Have Always Lived in the Castle; We Bombed in New Haven; A Funny Thing Happened on the Way to the Forum; The Last of Mrs Lincoln; The Norman Conquests; Mixed Couples.

Films inc: Rhinoceros.

TV inc: The Hallmark Hall of Fame; NBC Opera; Dupont Show of the Week; Turn of the Screw.

TAYLOR, Renee: Act-Plywri. b. Mar 19, 1945. W of Joseph Bologna. (Writes in collaboration with husband). Bway inc: Luv; Agatha Sue I Love You; Lovers and Other Strangers (& wri).

Films inc: The Last of the Red Hot Lovers; The Errand Boys; The Detective; The Producers; The New Leaf; Lovers and Other Strangers (& wri); Made for Each Other (& wri).

TV inc: (wri) Acts of Love and Other Comedies *(Emmy*-1973); Paradise; Calucci's Department (created); The American Dream Machine; Drink, Drank, Drunk.

TAYLOR, Rod: Act. b. Sydney, Australia, Jan 11, 1929. e. Fine Arts Coll. Originally an artist. Screen debut, 1955, Long John Silver. Films inc: The Virgin Queen; Giant; Separate Tables; Step Down to Terror; The V.I.P.s; The Birds; Young Cassidy; A Gathering of Eagles; 36 Hours; The Glass Bottom Boat; Hotel; Chuka; The Train Robbers; Blondy; Trader Horn; On a Dead Man's Chest; Hell River.

TV inc: Cry of the Innocent.

TAYLOR, Ron: Cin-Prod. b. Sydney, Australia, Mar 8, 1934. Underwater photography for Blue Water White Death; live shark footage for Jaws; Jaws II; Orca. Films inc: Sharks (prod); Sharks, The Death Machine (cin).

TAYLOR, Samuel A: Plywri. b. Chicago, Jun 13, 1912. Plays inc: The Happy Time; Sabrina Fair; The Pleasure of His Company; First Love; No Strings; Beekman Place: Avanti; A Touch of Spring; Legend; Perfect Pitch; Gracious Living.

Films inc: Sabrina.

TAYLOR-YOUNG, Leigh: Act. b. 1944. Films inc: I Love You Alice B. Toklas; The Big Bounce; The Adventurers; The Buttercup Chain; The Horsemen; The Gang That Couldn't Shoot Straight; Soylent Green; Can't Stop the Music.

TV inc: Peyton Place; Marathon.

TEASDALE, Verree: Act. b. Spokane, WA, Mar 15, 1906. Films inc: Syncopation; The Sap from Syracuse; Luxury Liner; Roman Scandals; Madame Du Barry; A Midsummer Night Dream; The Milky Way; Topper Takes a Trip; I Take This Woman; Love Thy Neighbor; Come Live With Me.

TEBALDI, Renata: Lyric soprano. b. Pesaro, Italy, Jan 2, 1922. Debut La Scala, 1946; sang with opera companies in Naples, Rome, Venice, Bologna, Turin before US debut 1950 with San Francisco Opera Company; Metropolitan Opera debut 1955. Best known roles in Aida; Othello; La Boheme; Madame Butterfly; Tosca.

(Grammy-Class vocal-1958).

TEBET, David W: Exec. b. Dec 27, 1920. Sr VP, NBC-TV 22 years; joined Marble Arch Prods as talent consultant March 1979.

TECHINE, Andre: Wri-Dir. b. France, 1943. Critic for Cahiers de Cinema. Teacher at IDHEC. Films inc: Pauline s'en va; French Provincial; Barocco; The Bronte Sisters.

TEDROW, Irene: Act. b. Denver, Aug 3, 1907. e. Carnegie Tech, BA. Radio-Corliss Archer, 11 years.

Films inc: They Won't Forget; Cheers for Mrs. Bishop; Journey Into Fear; The Moon and Sixpence; They Won't Believe Me; A Lion in the Streets; Not as a Stranger; The Ten Commandments; Never So Few; Please Don't Eat the Daisies; The Parent Trap; The Greatest Story Ever Told; The Cincinnati Kid; The Comic; Getting Straight; Midnight Madness.

TV inc: Father of the Bride; Dennis The Menace; Eleanor and Franklin; Special Olympics; Quincy; James at 16; Mary Tyler Moore; Little House on the Prairie; Rockford Files. Never Say Never; The Two Worlds of Jenny Logan.

Thea inc: Look Homeward Angel; Skin of Our Teeth; Camino Real; Our Town; Children of the Wind; Hot L Baltimore.

TEITELBAUM, Pedro: Exec. b. Brazil, Nov 21, 1922. Started 1939 with Col; 1943, WB; 1948 Latin-American supv Republic; 1957 became prod-dist-exhb in Brazil; 1968, area supv UA; 1973 vp Intl sls; 1975, vp intl sls & dist; 1977 sr exec vp CIC; July 1977, P CIC; 1980 P Filmcrest International Corp.

TEMPLE, Shirley: Act. b. Santa Monica, CA, Apr 23, 1927. On screen at age 3 in short films. Feature debut 1932 Red Haired Alibi. After film career entered public life, served as U.S. Ambassador to Ghana 1974-76.

Films inc: To the Last Man; Out All Night; Carolina; Mandalay; Stand Up and Cheer; Now I'll Tell; Change of Heart; Little Miss Marker; Baby Take a Bow; Now and Forever; Bright Eyes; The Little Colonel; Our Little Girl; Curly Top; The Littlest Rebel; Captain January; Poor Little Rich Girl; Dimples; Stowaway; Wee Willie Winkie; Heidi; Rebecca of Sunnybrook Farm; Little Miss Broadway; Just Around the Corner; The Little Princess; Susannah of the Mounties; The Blue Bird; Young People; Kathleen; Miss Annie Rooney; Since You Went Away; I'll Be Seeing You; Kiss and Tell; Honeymoon; The Bachelor and the Bobby Soxer; That Hagen Girl; Fort Apache; Mr. Belvedere Goes to College; Adventure in Baltimore; A Kiss for Corliss; The Story of Seabiscuit.

TV inc: Shirley Temple Storybook.

(Oscar-honorary-1934).

TEMPLETON, Olive: Act. b. 1883. Stage debut 1899, Peer Gynt. Films inc: Damaged Goods.

TV inc: Mr Peepers.

(Died May 29, 1979.)

TENNILLE, Toni: Singer-Mus. b. Montgomery, AL, May 8. Co-wrote rock-ecology musical Mother Earth for which Daryl Dragon was hired as pianist between tours of Beach Boys group with which he worked. Tennille joined group briefly before she and Dragon married and teamed as Captain and Tennille.

(Grammy-record of the year-1975).

TV inc: The Captain and Tennille; The Toni Tennille Show.

TER-ARUTUNIAN, Rouben: Dsgn. b. Tiflis, USSR, Jul 24, 1920. e. Friedrich Wilhelm U, U of Vienna, Ecole des Beaux Arts. First des in US were for TV, 1951; since then has designed scenery and costumes for American Shakespeare Festival; NYC Opera; NYC Ballet & most ballet and dance companies in US and Europe.

Bway inc: New Girl in Town; Who Was That Lady I Saw You With?; Redhead *(Tony-*1959) The Milk Train Doesn't Stop Here Anymore; The Lady From Dubuque; Goodbye, Fidel.

TV inc: The Would-Be Gentleman; Ariadne auf Naxon; The Magic Flute; Antigone; The Taming of the Shrew; The Flood; Twelfth Night *(Emmy-*1957).

TERRY, Alice (nee Taafe): Act. b. Vincennes, IN, Jul 24, 1901. W of Rex Ingram. On screen from 1916 in Not My Sister. Film inc: The Four Horsemen of the Apocalypse; The Prisoner of Zenda; Mare Nostrum; The Garden of Allah; The Three Passions.

TERRY, Megan: Plywri. b. Seattle, WA, Jul 22, 1932. e. U WA; U Alberta; Yale. Plays inc: Ex-Miss Copper Queen on a Set of Pills; The Magic Realist; People vs. Ranchman; The Gloaming; O My Darling; Calm Down; Keep Tightly Closed In a Cool, Dry Place; Viet Rock; Comings and Goings; Jack-Jack; The Key Is on the Bottom; The Tommy Allen Show; One More Little Drinkie; Approaching Simone; Choosing a Spot on the Floor; Grooving; Fado; Madwoman With Carrot; Nightwalk; Hothouse; Attempted Rescue on Avenue B; The Mother Jones and Mollie Bailey Family Circus.

TERRY, Phillip: Act. b. San Francisco, Mar 7, 1909. e. Stanford U, RADA. Films inc: Navy Blue and Gold; Mannequin; Balalaika; The Parson of Panamint; Wake Island; The Lost Weekend; Seven Keys to Baldpate; The Leech Woman; The Navy vs the Night Monsters.

TERRY-THOMAS (Thomas Terry Hoar-Stevens): Act. b. London, Jul 14, 1911. Professional debut London nitery as impressionist. In British films since 1948. Hollywood debut 1961.

Films inc: Private's Progress; The Naked Truth; Carleton Browne of the FO; I'm All Right, Jack; School for Scoundrels; The Wonderful World of the Brothers Grimm; It's a Mad Mad Mad Mad World; Those Magnificent Men in Their Flying Machines; How to Murder Your Wife; Kiss the Girls and Make Them Die; The Perils of Pauline; Where Were You When the Lights Went Out?; 2000 Years Later; The Abominable Dr. Phibes; Vault of Horror; Spanish Fly; The Last Remake of Beau Geste; Hound of the Baskervilles.

TESHIGAHARA, Hiroshi: b. Tokyo, Japan, 1927. Films inc: (Doc) Hokusai; Sofu Teshigahara; Jose Torres; Otoshi Ana. (Features) Woman in the Dunes; The Face of Another; Bakuso; The Man Without A Map; Summer Soldiers.

TETZLAFF, Ted: Dir. b. LA, Jun 3, 1903. Films inc: (cin) Enchanted Cottage; Notorious; (dir) World Premiere; Riffraff; Fighting Father Dunne; Johnny Allegro; Dangerous Profession; Gambling House; White Tower; Under the Gun; Treasure of Lost Canyon; Terror on a Train; Son of Sinbad.

TEWES, Lauren: Act. b. Trafford, PA, Oct 26. TV inc: Love Boat; The Dallas Cowboys Cheerleaders.

TEWKESBURY, Joan: Wri-Chor-Dir. b. Redlands, CA, 1937. Films inc: Thieves Like Us (co-sp); Nashville (sp); Old Boyfriends (dir).

TV inc: The Tenth Month.

THACHER, Russell: Prod-Wri. b. Hackensack, NJ, May 29. e. Bucknell U, AB. Exec story edtr MGM, 1963-72. Films inc: (Prod) Travels with My Aunt; Soylent Green; The Last Hard Men.

TV inc: The Cay (& wri).

THARP, Twyla: Dancer-Chor. b. Portland, IN, Jul 1, 1941. e. Barnard; American Ballet Theatre School. With Paul Taylor Dance Co., 1963; joined Joffrey Ballet, American Ballet Theatre 1965; chor Tank Dive; Re-Moves; Forevermore; Generation; Eight Jelly Rolls; The Raggedy Dances; As Time Goes By; Push Comes to Shove; Mud; Baker's Dozen.

Films inc: Hair.

THATCHER, Torin: Act. b. Bombay, Jan 15, 1905. e. RADA. Films inc: Major Barbara; The Captive Heart; Great Expectations; The Robe; Love is a Many Splendored Thing; Witness for the Prosecution; The Canadians; Jack the Giant Killer; The Sandpiper; Hawaii; The King's Pirate.

Thea inc: Billy Budd; Edward My Son; That Lady; The Firstborn; The Miracle Worker; Write Me a Murder.

THAU, Benjamin: Exec. b. Dec 15. Started with Keith vaude booking office; head booker Orpheum Circuit; when Keith and Orpheum Circuits merged in 1927, resd to become booker for Loew's Inc; 1932 casting dir MGM; 1940 named asst to Louis B Mayer; 1944, vp Loew's Inc; 1956 became administrative head MGM Studios. Ret.

THAXTER, Phyllis: Act. b. Portland, ME, Nov 20, 1921. Films inc: 30 Seconds Over Tokyo; Weekend at the Waldorf; Bewitched; Tenth Avenue Angel; Blood on the Moon; Come Fill the Cup; Springfield Rifle; Women's Prison; The World of Henry Orient.

TV inc: Wagon Train; The Fugitive.

Thea inc: What a Life; There Shall Be No Night; Claudia; Take Her She's Mine.

THINNES, Roy: Act. b. Chicago, 1938. Films inc: Journey to the Far Side of the Sun; Charlie One-Eye; Airport 75; The Hindenberg.

TV inc: The Long Hot Summer; The Invaders; The Psychiatrist; The Horror at 37,000 Feet; The Norliss Tapes; Return Of The Mod Squad; From Here To Eternity-The War Years; Stone.

THOM, Robert: Wri. b. 1929. Films inc: The Subterraneans; All the Fine Young Cannibals; The Legend of Lylah Clare; Wild in the Streets; Angel, Angel, Down We Go (& dir).

TV inc: The Defenders *(Emmy-*1963).

(Died May 8, 1979).

THOMAS, B J: Singer. b. Houston, TX, 1942. *(Grammys*(3)-inspirational perf-1977, 1978, 1979).

THOMAS, Bill: Cos Dsgn. b. Chicago, Oct 13, 1921. e. USC, AB. Films inc: High Time; Beloved Infidel; By Love Possessed; Babes in Toyland; Spartacus *(Oscar-*1960); Seven Thieves; Bon Voyage; Toys in the Attic; Inside Daisy Clover; The Happiest Millionaire; The Hawaiians; The Children of Sanchez.

THOMAS, Danny (Amos Jacobs): Act. b. Deerfield, MI, Jan 6, 1914. Performed in niteries, radio, TV. Films inc: Unfinished Dance; Big City; Call Me Mister; I'll See You in My Dreams; The Jazz Singer.

TV inc: (act) Make Room For Daddy, *(Emmy-*1954); Make Room for Grandaddy; The Practice; I'm A Big Girl Now. (Exec prod) The Return Of The Mod Squad; Samurai; The Unbroken Circle-A Tribute to Mother Maybelle Carter.

THOMAS, Lowell: Commentator. b. Woodington, OH, Apr 6, 1892. e. Northern IN U, Denver U, Princeton U, Kent Coll of Law. Instructor Eng Lit, Princeton, 1914. Lecturer, biographer, historian, film prod until 1930. Broadcaster for CBS; commentator on first TV news program for NBC, 1939 and on first daily TV program, 1940; foreign commentator during WW II. Chman bd, then vice chmn, Cinerama Prod Corp, 1952; p, 1953-54; co-founder, Capital Cities Broadcasting Corp.

TV inc: (exec prod) High Adventure; The World of Lowell Thomas.

THOMAS, Mark (Ernest Tumolillo): Act. b. Brooklyn, NY, Jun 19, 1941. e. St John's U. Films inc: St Ives; 9/30/55; Rollercoaster; Final Countdown.

TV inc: General Hospital; Panic on the 522; Black Market Baby; The Night the City Screamed.

THOMAS, Marlo: Act. b. Detroit, MI, Nov 21, 1938. e. USC. D of Danny Thomas. Thea inc: Barefoot in the Park (London); Thieves.

TV inc: That Girl; Free To Be--You And Me *(Emmys-*as prod & star-1974).

Films inc: Jenny; Thieves.

THOMAS, Richard: Act. b. NYC, Jun 13, 1951. TV inc: The Waltons (Emmy-1973); No Other Love; All Quiet on the Western Front; To Find My Son.

Films inc: Winning; Last Summer; The Todd Killings; Red Sky At Morning; You'll Like My Mother; September 30, 1955; Battle Beyond The Stars.

Thea inc: Merton of the Movies; St. Joan; Everthing in the Garden.

THOME, Karin: Wri-Dir-Prod-Act. b. Tubingen, W Germany, Sep 16, 1943. e. Leicester Coll of Art, England. Films inc: Emigration (sp, dir, prod); The Joint (sp, dir, prod); Crash Theo (sp, dir, prod, act); Blinker (prod, act); The Pretty Things (sp, dir, prod); Supergirl (co-prod); Amerika (sp, dir, act); Willi and the Chinese Cat (sp, prod, dir).

THOMOPOULOS, Anthony D: Exec. b. Mt Vernon, NY, Feb 7, 1938. e. Georgetown U. Started at NBC, 1959. Dir Foreign Sales RCA SelectaVision, 1964; named vp, 1965; to ABC as vp, prime-time programs, 1973; vp, prime time TV Creative Operations, 1974; p of ABC Entertainment, 1978.

THOMPSON, Eric: Act-Dir. b. Sleaford, Lincs, Eng, Nov 9, 1929. Thea inc: (Act) The Merchant of Venice; Othello; The Alchemist. (Dir) Journey's End; Time and Time Again; My Fat Friend; Absurd Person Singular; Jeeves; Absent Friends; Same Time Next Year.

Films inc: One Day in the Life of Ivan Denisovitch (dir).

THOMPSON, Hank: Singer-Sngwri. b. Waco, TX, Sep 3, 1925. C&W recording artist. Formed his own band, the Brazos Valley Boys, 1946.

THOMPSON, J Lee: Dir. b. Eng, 1914. Films inc: An Alligator Named Daisy; Tiger Bay; Northwest Frontier; I Aim at the Stars; The Guns of Navarone; Cape Fear; Taras Bulba; Kings of the Sun; What a Way to Go; John Goldfarb Please Come Home; Eye of the Devil; MacKenna's Gold; Before Winter Comes; The Chairman; Conquest of the Planet of the Apes; Huckleberry Finn; The Reincarnation of Peter Proud; The White Buffalo; The Greek Tycoon; The Passage.

THOMPSON, Jack: Act. b. Sydney, Australia, Aug 31, 1940. e. Queensland U. Films inc: Outback; Libido; Sunday Too Far Away; Scobie Malone; Caddie; Mad Dog; Because He's My Friend; Jock Peterson; Breaker Morant; The Earthling; The Club.

THOMPSON, Robert C: Prod. b. Palmyra, NY, May 31, 1937. e. Ithaca Coll, BS. Joined U 1961 in talent dept, later heading dept; 1968 head talent & creative affairs Cinema Center Films; 1972 formed Thompson-Paul Prodns. TV inc: (prod) Paper Chase (& dir); Lanigan's Rabbi; The Mark of Zorro; Bud and Lou (& dir).

THOMPSON, Robert E: Wri. Films inc: They Shoot Horses Don't They? TV inc: Sherlock Holmes; Jigsaw (crea); Footsteps; Children of God; A Case of Rape; Niagara; DA's Investigator (pilot); The Francis Gary Powers Story; Childhood of Lee Harvey Oswald; Brave New World; The $5.20 an Hour Dream.

THOMPSON, Sada: Act. b. Des Moines, IA, Sep 27, 1929. e. Carnegie Tech. Films inc: You are Not Alone; The Pursuit of Happiness; Desperate Characters.

Bway inc: Under Milkwood; The Effect of Gamma Rays on Man-in-the-Moon Marigolds; Morning Becomes Electra; Twigs (Tony-1972); The Cherry Orchard; Saturday, Sunday, Monday.

TV inc: Sandburg's Lincoln; The Entertainer; Our Town; Family (Emmy-1978).

THOMSON, Virgil: Comp. b. Kansas City, MO, Nov 25, 1896. e. Harvard, AB. Film scores inc: The Plough That Broke the Plains; The River; Louisiana Story (Pulitzer Prize-1949); The Goddess.

Thea inc: Four Saints in Three Acts; Negro Macbeth; Filling Station; The Mother of Us All; Lord Byron; Measure for Measure; Parson Weems and the Cherry Tree.

TV inc: Virgil Thomson--Composer.

THORPE, Jerry: Dir. b. 1930. Films inc: The Venetian Affair; The Day of the Evil Gun (& prod).

TV inc: Kung Fu (Emmy-1973); A Question of Love; Fast Lane Blues; The Lazarus Syndrome; All God's Children (& prod).

THORPE, Richard: Dir. b. Hutchinson, KS, Feb 24, 1896. Act, wri, flm ed, studio exec before becoming a dir. Now retired.

Films inc: Double Wedding; The Crowd Roars; Earl of Chicago; Huckleberry Finn; White Cargo; Two Girls and a Sailor; Malaya; Three Little Words; The Great Caruso; It's a Big Country; Ivanhoe; Carbine Williams; The Prisoner of Zenda; All the Brothers Were Valiant; Knights of the Round Table; Student Prince; Athena; The Prodigal; The Tartars; The Honeymoon Machine; The Horizontal Lieutenant; Follow the Boys; The Truth About Spring; That Funny Feeling; The Scorpio Letters; Last Challenge.

THRELKELD, Richard: TV newsman. b. Cedar Rapids, IA, Nov 20, 1937. e. Ripon College, BA; Northwestern U, BSJ; Columbia School Int'l Affairs. Wri-prod WHAS-TV, Louisville, KY.; newsman WMT-AM-TV, Cedar Rapids; joined CBS News 1966; corr Viet Nam; 1970, San Francisco bureau chief; April 1977, Rome bureau; Nov 1977, co-anchor CBS Morning News.

THULIN, Ingrid: Act. b. Sollefteå, Sweden, Jan 27, 1929. Films inc: Foreign Intrigue; Wild Strawberries; So Close to Life; The Face; The Four Horsemen of the Apocalypse; Winter Light; The Silence; Return from the Ashes; The War Is Over; Night Games; The Damned; The Rite; Cries and Whispers; Moses; The Cassandra Crossing; Madame Kitty; The Voyage Into The Whirlpool Has Begun.

Thea inc: Of Love Remembered.

THURN-TAXIS, Alexis: Prod-Dir. b. Austria, 1891. Films inc: Night for Crime; The Yanks Are Coming; Man of Courage; Slightly Terrific; Hollywood and Vine; Rough, Tough and Ready; Girl of the Limberlost; Prison Ship; The Gentleman Misbehaves.

(Died July 26, 1979.)

TIDYMAN, Ernest: Wri. b. Cleveland, Jan 1, 1928. Started as newspaperman; turned to writing fiction at age 42.

Films inc: The French Connection (Oscar-Sp-1971); Shaft; Shaft's Big Score; High Plains Drifter; Report to the Commissioner; A Force of One; Street People.

TV inc: To Kill a Cop; Dummy (& dir); Power; Guyana Tragedy - The Story of Jim Jones; Alcatraz--The Whole Shocking Story (& co-prod).

TIERNEY, Gene: Act. b. NYC, Nov 20, 1920. On screen from 1940 in The Return of Frank James. Films inc: Tobacco Road; Belle Starr; Son of Fury; Heaven Can Wait; Laura; A Bell for Adano; Leave Her to Heaven; Dragonwyck; The Razor's Edge; The Ghost and Mrs. Muir; Whirlpool; Close to My Heart; Never Let Me Go; The Egyptian; The Black Widow; Left Hand of God; Advise and Consent; The Pleasure Seekers.

TV inc: Daughter of the Mind; Scruples.

TIERNEY, Lawrence: Act. b. NYC, Mar 15, 1919. Films inc: The Ghost Ship; Dillinger; Step by Step; San Quentin; The Devil Thumbs a Ride; Shakedown; The Hoodlum; A Child is Waiting; Custer of the West; Such Good Friends; Andy Warhol's Bad.

TIFFIN, Pamela: Act. b. Oklahoma City, OK, Oct 13, 1942. On screen from 1961 in Summer and Smoke. Films inc: One, Two, Three; State Fair; Come Fly With Me; For Those Who Think Young; The Pleasure Seekers; Harper; The Protagonists; Paranoid; Kiss the Other Sheik; Viva Max;

Thea inc: Dinner at Eight.

TIKHONOV, Vyacheslav: Act. b. Feb 8, 1928. e. Moscow Film Institute. Films inc: The Young Guard; Peace Time; Maximka; It Must Not Be Forgotten; Stars on the Wings; The Heart Beats Anew; It Happened in Penkovo; An Extraordinary Event; Midshipman Panin; Two Lives; Seven Winds; An Optimistic Tragedy; War and Peace; We'll Get By Till Monday; The Man From the Other Side; Front Without Flanks; They Fought for Their Country; White Bim with Black Ear.

TV inc: Seventeen Moments of Spring.

TILLER, Nadja: Act. b. Austria, 1929. Films inc: Rosemary, Portrait of a Sinner; The World in My Pocket; And So to Bed; The Upper Hand; The Making of a Lady.

TILLIS, Mel: Mus-Singer-Sngwri. b. Aug 8, 1932. Films inc: The Villain; Smokey and the Bandit II. TV inc: Dean Martin's Christmas in California; Skinflint; Dean Martin Christmas Special 1980.

TILLMAN, Floyd: Singer-Sngwri. b. Ryan, OK, Dec 8, 1914. C&W recording artist. Played guitar, mandolin, banjo with various groups.

TILLSTROM, Burr: Act. b. Chicago, Oct 13, 1917. e. U of Chicago. Traveled with puppet, marionette, stock shows. Created puppet troupe headed by Kukla and Ollie; TV: started Kukla, Fran and Ollie Show 1947 (*Emmy*-1971); That Was The Week That Was (*Emmy*-1967-spec); Happy Birthday, Beulah Witch.

TILTON, Charlene: Act. b. San Diego, CA, Dec 1, 1958.
TV inc: Go Ask Alice; Dallas. Films inc: Freaky Friday; Big Wednesday; Sweater Girl; The New Centurions.

TINKER, Grant: Exec. b. Stamford, CT, Jan 11, 1926. e. Dartmouth Coll. Joined NBC radio program dept in 1949; with McCann-Erickson ad agency, TV dept, 1954; in 1958, joined Benton & Bowles, TV dept; from 1961-65 with NBC, vp programs, West Coast; vp in chg of programming, NY, 1966-1967; joined Universal TV as vp, 1968-1969; Fox vp, 1969-1970; p MTM Enterprises, Inc, 1970.

TIOMKIN, Dimitri: Comp. b. Russia, May 10, 1899. e. St Petersburg Conservatory of Music. Came to America 1925; debut as concert pianist, Town Hall, NY, 1926; introduced Gershwin's music to Europe, 1928; first film score 1931.
Films inc: Lost Horizon; The Moon and Sixpence; Shadow of a Doubt; Dark Mirror; Duel in the Sun; Red River; Portrait of Jennie; Champion; Home of the Brave; Cyrano de Bergerac; The Big Sky; High Noon (2 *Oscars*-1952-score & best song, Do Not Forsake Me); Happy Time; Strangers on a Train; Fourposter; Jeopardy; The High and the Mighty (*Oscar*-1954); A Bullet Is Waiting; Land of the Pharaohs; Court Martial of Billy Mitchell; The Old Man and the Sea (*Oscar*-1958); Dial M for Murder; Rio Bravo; Friendly Persuasion; The Unforgiven; Wild Is the Wind; Giant; The Sundowners; The Guns of Navarone; 55 Days at Peking; The Fall of the Roman Empire; 36 Hours; The War Wagon; Great Catherine; Tchaikovsky (& prod).
(Died Nov 11, 1979).

TIPTON, George Aliceson: Comp. b. Huntington Park, CA, Jan 23, 1932. Films inc: Phantom of the Paradise; Badlands; Skidoo; Griffin and Phoenix; Hit Lady.
TV inc: The Courtship of Eddie's Father; The Gift; Soap; Benson; The Yeagers; Trouble in High Timber Country; It's A Living; I'm a Big Girl Now.

TISCH, Laurence A: Exec. b. Brooklyn, NY, Mar 5, 1923. e. NYU; Harvard Law School. Chmn, CEO Loew's Corp.

TISCH, Preston Robert: Exec. b. Brooklyn, NY, Apr 29, 1926. e. Bucknell; U of MI. Chmn Exec Comm Loew's Theatres, Chmn & CEO, Loew's Hotels.

TISCH, Steve: Prod. b. Lakewood, NJ, 1949. e. Tufts U. S of Preston Tisch. Films inc: Outlaw Blues; Almost Summer; Coast to Coast; Homeward Bound.
TV inc: No Other Love.

TOBIAS, George: Act. b. NYC, 1901. On screen from 1939. Films inc: Ninotchka; Maisie; Balalaika; They Drive By Night; Sergeant York; My Sister Eileen; Yankee Doodle Dandy; Air Force; Mission to Moscow; The Mask of Dimitrios; Mildred Pierce; My Wild Irish Rose; Rawhide; Ten Tall Men; The Glenn Miller Story; Silk Stockings; Marjorie Morningstar; Bullet for a Bad Man; The Glass Bottom Boat; The Phynx.
Thea inc: The Hairy Ape; What Price Glory; Road to Rome; Paths of Glory; You Can't Take It With You. TV inc: Bewitched; Medical Center.
(Died Feb 27, 1980).

TOBIAS, Harry: Sngwri-Music publisher. b. NYC, Sep 11, 1895. To Hollywood, 1929; wrote for films. Chief collaborators: Chas. Tobias, Henry Tobias (brothers). Songs: Sweet and Lovely; Miss You; It's a Lonesome Old Town; Sail Along, Silv'ry Moon; No Regrets; At Your Command; I'm Sorry Dear; The Daughter of Peggy O'Neill; When It's Harvest Time; Somebody Loves Me; The Broken Record; Girl of My Dreams; I Want You to Want Me; Oh, Bella Mia; May I Have the Next Dream With You; If I Knew Then What I Know Now; Moonlight Brings Memories; In God We Trust; Star of Hope.

TOBIN, Michele: Act. b. Chi, Jan 25, 1961. Films inc: Yours, Mine and Ours; The One and Only, Genuine, Original Family Band; The Happy Ending; Eighty Steps to Jonah; Freaky Friday. TV inc: Imagination; The Fitzpatricks.

TODD, Ann: Act. b. England, 1909. On screen from 1931. Films inc: Keepers of Youth; The Ghost Train; Ships With Wings; The Seventh Veil; Daybreak; So Evil My Love; Madeleine; Breaking the Sound Barrier; Taste of Fear; Son of Captain Blood; Beware of the Brethren; The Human Factor.
Thea inc: When Ladies Meet; Man in Half-Moon Street; Peter Pan.
TV inc: The Vortex; The Door; The Snows of Kilimanjaro; The Last Target. Produces travelogues.

TODD, J Hunter: Flm Festival Exec. b. New Orleans, Aug 9, 1938. e. U of VA, William & Mary Coll. Atlanta Intl Film Fest, 1968-74; Virgin Islands Intl Film Fest, 1975-77; Miami Intl Film Fest, 1978. Prod doc films, shorts.

TODD, Richard: Act. b. Dublin, Jan 11, 1919. In repertory, 1937. On screen from 1948. Films inc: For Them That Trespass; Stage Fright; Lightning Strikes Twice; The Story of Robin Hood; The Assassin; A Man Called Peter; The Hasty Heart; The Virgin Queen; D-Day, the Sixth of June; The Longest Day; The Love-Ins; Dorian Gray; Asylum; The Sky Is Falling; The Big Sleep.
Thea inc: An Ideal Husband; Roar Like a Dove; The Marquise; Sleuth; Thunder By Numbers; On Approval; Quadrille.

TODMAN, Howard: Exec. b. NYC, Nov 24, 1920. e. Hamilton Coll. Dir. business affairs, Goodson-Todman Productions; treas. Goodson-Todman Associates, Inc; VP & treas, Goodson-Todman Enterprises, Ltd; treas, Peak Prods, Inc.

TODMAN, William: Prod. b. NYC, Jul 31, 1916. e. Johns Hopkins U. Partner, Goodson-Todman Productions. TV programs inc: What's My Line; To Tell the Truth; Password; The New Price Is Right; Match Game '74; Concentration; Tattletales; Now You See It.
(Died July 29, 1979).

TOEPLITZ, Jerzy: Film Historian. b. Kharkov, USSR, Nov 24, 1909. e. U of Warsaw. 1945, secy gen Polish Film; 1948, dir, Foreign Dept Polish Film; dir, Polish Film School, Lodz; 1949-72, Head of Film Dept, Inst of Art, Polish Academy of Science; 1972-73, visiting professor, La Trobe U, Melbourne; 1973, foundation dir, The Australian Film and Television School, Sydney. Author: History of Cinematographic Art, vols 1-5.

TOGNAZZI, Ugo: Act. b. Italy, 1922. Films inc: His Woman; The Fascist; Queen Bee; The Magnificent Cuckold; An American Wife; A Question of Honor; Barbarella; Blowout; Duck in Orange Sauce; Goodnight Ladies and Gentlemen; Bishop's Bedroom; Viva Italia!; La Cage Aux Folles; L'Ingorgo; Dove Va in Vacanza?: First Love; The Terrace; Casotto; Sunday Lovers; La Cage Aux Folles II.

TOKAR, Norman: Prod-Dir. b. Newark, NJ, Nov 25, 1919. Played Henry Aldrich on radio; wri Henry Aldrich radio and TV shows. TV inc: Life with Luigi; Alan Young Show; Claudette Colbert Show; Leave it to Beaver; Donna Reed Show.
Films inc: Big Red; Savage Sam; Sammy the Way Out Seal; A Tiger Walks; Those Calloways; Follow Me Boys; The Ugly Dachshund; The Happiest Millionaire; The Horse in the Grey Flannel Suit; Rascal; Snowball Express; The Apple Dumpling Gang; Candleshoe; The Cat From Outer Space.
(Died Apr 6, 1979).

TOKOFSKY, Jerry: Prod. b. NYC, Apr 14, 1936. e. NYU, BS. Exec VP prodn Columbia 1963-70. Into ind prodn 1970. Films inc: Where's Poppa; Born to Win.

TOLKIN, Mel: Wri. b. Russia, Aug 3, 1913. TV inc: Your Show of Shows; Caesar's Hour; The Sid Caesar, Imogene Coca, Carl Reiner, Howard Morris Special *(Emmy*-1967); Danny Kaye Show; Bob Hope; All in the Family (co-story edtr).

TOLKSDORF, Gittana (Formerly known as Birgitta Tolksdorf): Act. b. Osnabruck, W Germany, Dec 9, 1947. In stock and repertory. Thea inc: The Secretary Bird.
TV inc: Love of Life.

TOMLIN, Lily: Act. b. Detroit, MI, 1939. Performed in cafes and niteries. In December, 1969, first appeared on Laugh-In, TV series. Films inc: Nashville; The Late Show; Moment By Moment; Nine To Five.
TV inc: Lily; The Lily Tomlin Show *(Emmys*-wri & star-1974); The Paul Simon Special *(Emmy*-wri-1978).
Thea inc: Appearing Nightly (dir-wri-act). *(Tony*-Special-1977). *(Grammy*-Comedy-1971).

TOMLIN, Pinky: Comp-Singer. b. Eureka Springs, AR, Sep 9, 1907. e. U of OK. While in college organized own dance band, played quitar and sang. Wrote song Object of My Affections which led to professional career.
Films inc: Times Square Lady; King Solomon of Broadway; Paddy O'Day; Don't Get Personal; Down in Arkansas; Here Comes Elmer.

TOMLINSON, David: Act. b. Henley-on-Thames, England, May 7, 1917 Thea inc: (London) The Little Hut; All for Mary; Dear Delinquent; The Ring of Truth; Boeing Boeing; Mother's Boy (& dir); A Friend Indeed; The Impossible Years; The Turning Point (& dir).
Films inc: Quiet Wedding; Journey Together; The Way to the Stars; Master of Bankdam; Pimpernel Smith; Miranda; Sleeping Car to Trieste; The Chiltern Hundreds; Hotel Sahara; Three Men in a Boat; Up the Creek; Follow That Horse; Tom Jones; Mary Poppins; The Truth About Spring; The Liquidator; The Love Bug; Bedknobs and Broomsticks; From Hong Kong with Love: The Waterbabies; The Fiendish Plot of Dr. Fu Manchu.

TOMPKINS, Angel: Act. b. Albany, CA, Dec 20, 1943. Began as a model before TV appearances in Dragnet; The Wild, Wild West; Hang Your Hat On The Wind.
Films inc: I Love My Wife; Kansas City Prime; How To Seduce A Woman; The Don Is Dead; The Bees.

TOMS, Carl, OBE: Dsgn. b. England, May 29, 1927. e. Royal College of Art; Old Vic School. First head of dsgn for Young Vic; dsgd operas and ballets for Sadlers Wells, Covent Garden. Thea inc: (London) The Apollo de Bellac; Beth; Something to Hide; The Complaisant Lover; The Merry Wives of Windsor; New Cranks; Camille; Write Me a Murder; A Time To Laugh; Who'll Save the Plowboy?; A Singular Man; The Burglar; Fallen Angels; The Magistrate; Sleuth; Vivat! Vivat Regina!; The Beheading; Sherlock Holmes; The Waltz of the Toreadors; Travesties. (Bway) Sleuth; Sherlock Holmes *(Tony*-1975); Travesties.

TOOMEY, Regis: Act. b. Pittsburgh, PA, Aug 13, 1902. e. U of Pittsburgh, Carnegie Inst of Technology (drama). On NY and London stage. Screen debut, Alibi, 1929. Films inc: Spellbound; The Big Sleep; Magic Town; The Bishop's Wife; The Boy With Green Hair; Mighty Joe Young; Cry Danger; Union Pacific; Come to the Stable; Northwest Passage; The High and the Mighty; Guys and Dolls; Warlock; Man's Favorite Sport?; Gunn; Change of Habit; The Carey Treatment; C.H.O.M.P.S.
TV inc: December Bride; Hey Mulligan; Dodsworth; Richard Diamond; Burke's Law; Petticoat Junction.

TOONE, Geoffrey: Act. b. Dublin, Ireland, Nov 15, 1910. e. Christ's College, Cambridge. Student at Old Vic, played various Shakespearean roles; appeared in repertory. Thea inc: (London) A Man's House; Dodsworth; Watch on the Rhine; The End of Summer; Quality Street; Lady Windermere's Fan; The Little Hut; Auntie Mame; The Rivals; Hedda Gabler; Conduct Unbecoming.
Films inc: Sword of Honor; The King and I; Zero Hour; The Entertainer; Once More With Feeling.

TOPOL (Chaim Topol): Act. b. Israel, 1935. Films inc: Cast a Giant Shadow; Sallah; Before Winter Comes; Fiddler on the Roof; Follow Me; Galileo; Flash Gordon.
Thea inc: Fiddler on the Roof.
TV inc: The House on Garibaldi Street.

TOPPER, Burt: Wri-Dir-Prod. b. NYC, Jul 31, 1928. Films inc: Hell Squad; Tank Command; Diary of a High School Bride; War Is Hell; The Strangler; Sex and the Teenager; Thunder Alley; Devils Angels; Fireball 500; Wild in the Streets; Devils Eight; The Hard Ride.
TV inc: Taggart; First Woman in Space.

TORME, Mel: Singer. b. Chicago, IL, Sep 13, 1925. Started in vaudeville, radio. On screen from 1943. Films inc: Higher and Higher; Pardon My Rhythm; Let's Go Steady; Good News; Words and Music; Girls' Town; Walk Like a Dragon; A Man Called Adam.

TORN, Rip: Act. b. Temple, TX, Feb 6, 1931. e. TX A & M; U of TX. Films inc: Time Limit; The Cincinnati Kid; Beach Red; Sol Madrid; Tropic of Cancer; Crazy Joe; The Man Who Fell To Earth; Nasty Habits; Coma; The Seduction of Joe Tynan; Heartland; One-Trick Pony; First Family.
TV inc: Betrayal; Blind Ambition; Steel Cowboy; A Shining Season; Sophia Loren--Her Own Story; Rape and Marriage--The Rideout Case.
Bway inc: Cat On A Hot Tin Roof; Sweet Bird of Youth; Daughter of Silence; Strange Interlude; Blues for Mr. Charlie; The Cuban Thing; Dance of Death; Mixed Couples.

TORRE-NILLSON, Leopoldo: Dir. b. Argentina, 1924. Films inc: The House of the Angel; The Fall; Hand In a Trap; Summer Skin; Four Women for One Hero; The Roof Garden; The Eavesdropper; Monda's Child; Martin Fierro; Mafia; Painted Lips; The Jewish Gauchos.

TORS, Ivan: Wri-Prod-Dir. b. Budapest, Hungary, Jun 12, 1916. e. U of Budapest, Fordham U. In Hollywood from 1941. Films inc: Song of Love (sp); The Forsyte Saga (sp); Storm Over Tibet (sp & prod); The Magnetic Monster (sp & prod); Gog (sp & prod); Return to the Stars (prod); Battle Taxi (prod); Flipper (prod); Rhino (prod & dir); Zebra in the Kitchen (sp); Escape from Angola (exec prod); Galyon File (exec prod).
TV inc: (as prod) The Man and the Challenge; Sea Hunt; Daktari; Gentle Ben; Flipper; Primus.

TOSI, Mario: Cin. Films inc: Some Call It Loving; Buster and Billie; Hearts of the West; The Killing Kind; Report to the Commissioner; Carrie; MacArthur; The Betsy; The Main Event; The Stunt Man; Coast to Coast.

TOTTEN, Robert: Dir-Wri-Act. b. LA, Feb 5, 1937. Films inc: The Quick and the Dead (sp & dir); The Wild Country (dir).
TV inc: Gunsmoke (dir-wri-act); The Red Pony (wri-dir); The Sacketts (dir).

TOTTER, Audrey: Act. b. Joliet, IL, 1919. Films inc: Main Street After Dark; Her Highness and the Bellboy; The Postman Always Rings Twice; Lady in the Lake; The Saxon Charm; A Bullet for Joey; The Carpetbaggers; Chubasco; The Apple Dumpling Gang Rides Again.
TV inc: Medical Center; Our Man Higgins; Nativity; The Great Cash Giveaway Getaway.

TOVROV, Orin: Wri. b. Chicago, IL, 1911. Mgr WCCO Minneapolis 1935; prod-dir-wri WLW, Cincinnati 1936; 1937 became wri for radio soap Ma Perkins, continued except for war service, until program went off the air 1960; also wrote The Brighter Day on radio from 1948-1954; first pres Radio Writers Guild.
TV inc: The Doctors (& crea); The Brighter Day.
(Died Aug. 16, 1980).

TOWERS, Constance: Act. b. Whitefish, MT, May 20, 1933. e. Juilliard School of Music. Thea inc: Anya; Show Boat; Carousel; The Sound of Music; Dumas & Son; The King and I; I Do! I Do!; The Desperate Hours.
Films inc: Horse Soldiers; Sergeant Rutledge; Fate Is the Hunter; Shock Corridor; Naked Kiss; The Spy.
TV inc: Love Is a Many Splendored Thing; Once in Her Life.

TOWERS, Harry Alan: Exec Prod. b. London, 1920. Films inc: Victim Five (& sp); Mozambique (& sp); The Face of Fu Manchu; Ten Little Indians; Our Man in Marrakesh (Bang, Bang, You're Dead); The Brides of Fu Manchu; Rocket to the Moon; Treasure Island; Call of the Wild; Count Dracula; The Shape of Things to Come.

TOWNE, Robert: Wri. Films inc: Villa Rides; The Tomb of Ligeia; The Last Detail; Chinatown (Oscar-1974); Shampoo (co-sp); The Yakuza (co-sp).

TOWNES, Harry: Act. b. Huntsville, AL, Sep 18, 1914. Films inc: Operation Manhunt; The Brothers Karamazov; The Screaming Mimi; Cry Tough; Sanctuary; The Bedford Incident; Fitzwilly; Heaven with a Gun; In Enemy Country; Strategy of Terror; Casino.
Thea inc: Tobacco Road; Mr. Sycamore; Twelfth Night; Finian's Rainbow; Gramercy Ghost; In the Matter of J. Robert Oppenheimer.
TV inc: The Immigrants.

TOWNSEND, Claire: Exec. b. NYC, Feb 20, 1952. e. Princeton, BA. Worked with Ralph Nader, authored book Old Age; The Last Segregation. Entered film ind as reader, researcher for Martin Ransohoff; West Coast story edtr Frank Yablans Presentations; 1976 West Coast Story edtr Fox; Feb 1978, crea aff vp; Oct 1978 vp-prodn UA; Jan 1980 returned to Fox as prodn VP.

TOWNSEND, Leo: Wri. b. Faribault, MN, May 11, 1908. e. MN U. Films inc: It Started with Eve; The Amazing Mrs Holliday; Chip off the Old Block; Night and Day; The Black Hand; Port of New York; Southside 1-1000; A Life in the Balance; White Feather; Running Wild; Fraulein; Bikini Beach; How to Stuff a Wild Bikini; Fireball 500; I'd Rather be Rich.
TV inc: Beulah; Wagon Train; Dinah Shore Chevy Show; Maverick; Roaring Twenties; Destry; Bachelor Father; The Eve Arden Show; Shirley Temple Show; Death Valley Days; Patty Duke Show; The Munsters; Batman; Andy Griffith Show; Bewitched.

TOWNSHEND, Peter: Mus-Comp. b. London, England, May 19, 1945. Member The Who. Films inc: Tommy (mus-lyr); The Kids Are Alright (act).

TOYE, WENDY: Dancer-Dir-Chor-Act. b. London, May 1, 1917. Appeared as dancer at Royal Albert Hall at age 4; prod ballet at Palladium at age 10; at 13 joined Ninette de Valois' Old Vic-Sadlers Wells Ballet Co.
Thea inc: (dancer) The Golden Toy; toured with Anton Dolin, later with Dolin and Alicia Markova; Aladdin; Camargo Society Ballet. (Chor) Mother Earth; The Legend of the Willow Pattern; all George Black prodns between 1937-1945; Gay Rosalinda; Concerto for Dancers; Robert and Elizabeth. (Act) Toad of Toad Hall; Hiawatha; The Miracle; Tulip Time; Love and How To Cure It; Simple Simon; Annie Get Your Gun. (Dir) Tough at the Top; And So To Bed; Second Threshold; Wild Thyme; Lady at the Wheel; Fledermaus; As You Like It; A Majority of One; Orpheus in the Underworld; The Great Waltz; The Soldier's Tale; Show Boat; Colette.
Films inc: (Dir) The Stranger Left No Card (short); On the 12th Day (short); Three Cases of Murder; All For Mary; True as a Turtle; We Joined the Navy; The King's Breakfast;
TV inc: (Dir) Esme Divided; Cliff in Scotland; Girls Wanted; Chelsea at Nine; Orpheus in the Underworld; Girls, Girls, Girls; Istanbul; A Goodly Manor for a Song.

TRAKTMAN, Peggy Simon: Wri-Dir-Prod. b. NYC, Jul 19, 1932. e. Columbia School of Dramatic Arts, BFA. Wri-dir Maximillion Prodns, 1962-78. Dir Village Green Summer Prodns.

TRAPNELL, Coles (Valentine C Trapnell): Wri-Prod-Story ed. b. NYC, Aug 2, 1910. e. VMI, NYU. Story ed 1945, Within These Walls. TV inc: Prod 1954-58, Four Star TV; Maverick (prod-wri); Lawman (prod); 12 O'Clock High (wri). Exec story consl, Universal, 1967-77. Author: Teleplay: An Introduction to Television Writing.

TRAUBE, Shepard: Prod-Dir. b. Malden, MA, Feb 27, 1907. Plays inc: No More Frontier; A Thousand Summers; The Sophistocrats; Angel Street; Winter Soldiers; Patriots; Bell, Book and Candle; The Girl In Pink Tights; Goodbye Again; Holiday for Lovers; The Tunnel of Love; Venus at Large; Memo; Undercover Man; Children of the Wind.
Films inc: Goose Step; Street of Memories; The Bride Wore Crutches.

TRAUNER, Alexander: Art Dir. b. France, 1906. Films inc: Les Enfants du Paradis; Les Portes de la Nuit; Maneges; Othello; Love in the Afternoon; The Nun's Story; The Apartment (Oscar-1960); One, Two, Three; Irma La Douce; The Night of the Generals; A Flea in Her Ear; Mr Klein; The First Time; Fedora; The Fiendish Plot of Dr. Fu Manchu.

TRAVALENA, Fred: Act. b. NYC, Oct 6, 1942. Singer-impressionist in niteries.
TV inc: The Funny World of Fred and Bunni; numerous segs.
Films inc: The Buddy Holly Story.

TRAVERS, Ben: Wri. b. London, 1886. Plays inc: Rookery Nook; A Cuckoo; Thark; Plunder; Banana Ridge; Bed Before Yesterday.
Films inc: Fighting Stock; Just My Luck; Uncle Silas.
(Died Dec 18, 1980).

TRAVERS, Bill: Act. b. England, 1922. Films inc: The Square Ring; Geordie; Bhowani Junction; The Barretts of Wimpole Street; The Smallest Show on Earth; The Seventh Sin; The Bridal Path; Gordo; Two Living, One Dead; Born Free; Duel at Diablo; A Midsummer Night's Dream; Ring of Bright Water; The Belstone Fox.
TV inc: Jane Goodall and the World of Animal Behavior (Emmy-1973).

TRAVILLA (William Travilla): Cos dsgn. b. Avalon, CA, Mar 22, 1925. Films inc: Adventures of Don Juan (Oscar-1949); Viva Zapata; Gentlemen Prefer Blondes; Don't Bother To Knock; How to Marry a Millionaire; The Stripper; River of No Return; Seven Year Itch; Bus Stop.
TV inc: Moviola (Emmy-1980).

TRAVIS, Merle: Singer-Sngwri. b. Rosewood, KY, Nov 29, 1917. Folk singer, C&W recording artist; performed with Grand Ole Opry; wrote such classics as Sixteen Tons; Dark As a Dungeon; So Round, So Firm, So Fully Packed. (Grammy-Country Inst-1974).

TRAVIS, Richard (William Justice): Act. b. Carlsbad, NM, Apr 17, 1913. Films inc: The Man Who Came to Dinner; The Big Shot; Buses Roar; Jewels of Brandenberg; Alaska Patrol; Skyliner; Operation Haylift; Mask of the Dragon; Fingerprints Don't Lie; City of Shadows.
TV inc: Treasury Men in Action; Pride of the Family; The Falcon; Missile to the Moon.

TRAVOLTA, John: Act. b. Englewood, NJ, Feb 18, 1955. Stage debut in Who Will Save the Plowboy?. On Broadway in Grease; Over Here.
Films inc: Carrie; Saturday Night Fever; Grease; Moment By Moment; Urban Cowboy.
TV inc: Emergency; Owen Marshall; The Rookies; Medical Center; Welcome Back, Kotter; The Boy in the Plastic Bubble.

TRBOVICH, Thomas E (Tom): Dir. TV inc: United Cerebral Palsy Telethon; Ontario 500; Long Beach Grand Prix; Orange Bowl; Fun Factory; Phyllis Diller Special; Andy Kaufman Special; Vic Damone Show; Manhattan Transfer; This Is Burlesque; Hot Hero Sandwich; Sugartime; Archie Special; Sirota's Court; Bette Midler Live; 34th Golden Globe Awards; 29th Emmy Awards; Waylon, Starring Waylon Jennings; The Mouseketeer Reunion; I'll Be Home for Christmas.

TREBEK, Alex: Act. b. Sudbury, Ontario, Canada, Jul 22, 1940. TV inc: High Rollers; The $128,000 Question; The New High Rollers.

TREBITSCH, Gyula: Prod. b. Budapest, Hungary, Nov 3, 1914. Films inc: The Captain of Kopenick. Pres, Trebitsch Productions Int.

TREMAYNE, Les: Act. b. London, Apr 16, 1913. Films inc: The Racket; The Blue Veil; It Grows on Trees; War of the Worlds; A Man Called Peter; The Perfect Furlough; North by Northwest; The Gallant Hours; The Story of Ruth; The Fortune Cookie.

Thea inc: Woman in My House; Errand of Mercy; One Man's Family; Heads or Tails; Detective Story.

TV inc: Perry Mason; Adventures of Ellery Queen; Raggedy Ann & Andy in the Pumpkin Who Couldn't Smile.

TREVOR, Claire: Act. b. NYC, 1909. e. AADA. On screen from 1933. Films inc: Life in the Raw; Stagecoach; Allegheny Uprising; Murder, My Sweet; Johnny Angel; Crack-Up; Key Largo (Oscar-supp-1948); Hoodlum Empire; The High and the Mighty; Dead End; The Babe Ruth Story; Lucy Gallant; Marjorie Morningstar; Two Weeks in Another Town; The Stripper; How to Murder Your Wife; Capetown Affair.

TV inc: Dodsworth (Emmy-1956).

TRIKONIS, Gus: Dir. b. NYC. Started in chorus West Side Story Bway. Later act before turning dir. Films inc: Moonshine County Express; Nashville Girl; The Evil; Touched By Love.

TV inc: The Darker Side of Terror; The Last Convertible; She's Dressed to Kill; Flamingo Road.

TRINDER, Tommy: Act. b. London, Mar 24, 1909. Thea inc: Tune In; In Town Tonight; Band Wagon; Top of the World; Gangway; Best Bib and Tucker; Happy and Glorious; Here, There and Everywhere; Cinderella; Puss in Boots; several command performances.

Films inc: Almost a Honeymoon; Laugh It Off; Sailors Three; The Foreman Went to France; Champagne Charlie; Fiddlers Three; Bitter Springs; You Lucky People.

TV inc: Master of Ceremonies; Sunday Night at the London Palladium; My Wildest Dream; The Trinder Box.

TRINTIGNANT, Jean-Louis: Act. b. Pont-Saint-Esprit, France, Dec 11, 1930. Films inc: Race for Life; And God Created Woman; Austerlitz; Chateau en Suede; Mata Hari; Angelique; A Man and a Woman; Trans-Europe Express; The Sleeping Car Murders; Is Paris Burning?; The Libertine; Les Biches; Z; Ma Nuit Chez Maud; The American; The Conformist; The Crook; Without Apparent Motive; The Outside Man; The French Conspiracy; Simon the Swiss; Aggression; Sunday Woman; The Honeymoon Trip; Desert of the Tartars; Les Violins du Bal; Faces of Love; Melancholy Baby; Les Argent de Autres; La Terrazza; La Banquiere.

TROELL, Jan: Wri-Dir. b. Sweden, 1931. Films inc: Stay in the Marshland; Here is Your Life; Eeny, Meeny, Miny, Mo; The Emigrants; The New Land; Zandy's Bride; Hurricane.

TROUP, Bobby: Act. b. Harrisburg, PA, Oct 13, 1918. e. U of PA. H of Julie London. Comp, singer, recording artist. Films inc: Bop Girl; The Five Pennies; The High Cost of Loving; The Gene Krupa Story; First to Fight; Number One; M*A*S*H.

TV inc: Emergency; The Rebels.

TRUDEAU, Garry: Wri. b. NYC, 1948. e. Yale and Yale School of Art & Architecture. Crea cartoon strip Doonesbury. TV inc: A Doonesbury Special.

TRUEMAN, Paula: Act. b. NYC, Apr 25, 1907. e. Neighborhood Playhouse. Debut as teenage dancer in Michael Fokine's The Thunderbird; appeared in six editions of Grand Street Follies from 1924 to 1929. Bway inc: Lovers and Enemies; If; Love Nest; Maya; Sweet and Low; Ladies of Creation; Midsummer Night's Dream; Merchant of Venice; A Woman in Panic; You Can't Take It With You; George Washington Slept Here; Kiss and Tell; For Love or Money; Gentlemen Prefer Blondes; Wake Up, Darling; A Family Affair; Wonderful Town; The Sunday Man; The Long Christmas Dinner; Sherry!; Postcards; Dr Fish.

Films inc: Crime and Punishment; One Foot in Heaven; Paint Your Wagon; The Anderson Tapes; On A Clear Day You Can See Forever; Homebodies; The Outlaw Josey Wales; Annie Hall.

TV inc: Better Late Than Never; Breaking Away.

TRUFFAUT, Francois: Dir-Wri. b. Paris, Feb 6, 1932. Worked as journalist, becoming France's most controversial film critic. Directorial debut 1957 with Les Mistons, a short subject.

Films inc: The Four Hundred Blows; Shoot the Piano Player; Soft Skin; The Bride Wore Black; Stolen Kisses; Mississippi Mermaid; The Wild Child; Bed and Board; Two English Girls; Such a Gorgeous Kid Like Me; Day for Night; The Story Of Adele H; Small Change; The Man Who Loved Women; The Green Room; Love on the Run; Close Encounters of the Third Kind (act); The Last Metro.

TRUMBULL, Douglas: Dir-Wri-Cin. Crea sfx for Silent Running; 2001, A Space Odyssey; The Andromeda Strain; Close Encounters of the Third Kind.

TRYON, Tom: Act-Wri. b. Hartford, CT, Jan 14, 1926. e. Yale U. Films inc: The Scarlet Hour; Three Violent People; I Married a Monster from Outer Space; Moon Pilot; Marines Let's Go; The Cardinal; In Harm's Way; The Glory Guys; The Horsemen.

Thea inc: Wish You Were Here; Cyrano de Bergerac; Richard III.

Books inc: The Other; Crowned Heads.

TUBB, Ernest: Singer-Comp. b. Crisp, TX, Feb 9, 1914. Country mus recording artist. Became a regular on Grand Ole Opry. Elected to Country Music Hall of Fame, 1965. Films inc: Fighting Buckaroo; Ridin' West; Jamboree; Hollywood Barn Dance. Appeared at Carnegie Hall.

TUCCI, Maria: Act. b. Florence, Italy, Jun 19, 1941. e. Actors Studio. Bway inc: The Jackhammer; The Milk Train Doesn't Stop Here Anymore; The Deputy; The Rose Tattoo; The Cuban Thing; The Little Foxes; School For Wives; A Lesson From Aloes.

TUCHNER, Michael: Dir. b. England. Films inc: Villain; Fear Is The Key; Mr Quilp; Likely Lads.

TV inc: The One and Only Phyllis Dixie; Summer of My German Solider; Haywire.

TUCKER, Forrest: Act. b. Plainfield, IN, Feb 12, 1919. Screen debut, 1940, The Westerner. Films inc: New Wine; Canal Zone; Keeper of the Flame; Renegades; The Yearling; Hellfire; Sands of Iwo Jima; Bugles in the Afternoon;

TV inc: F Troop; Crunch and Des; A Real American Hero; The Rebels; Trouble in the Glen; Auntie Mame; The Night They Raided Minsky's; Cancel My Reservation; Music Man; Fair Game for Lovers; Pottsville. The Wild McCullochs.

TUCKER, Melville: Prod. b. NYC, Mar 4, 1916. e. Princeton. Started in mailroom at Consolidated Labs, NY, became asst purchasing agent; to Hollywood as edtr Republic, later AD; after war service became prod; 1956 to 1970, prodn exec-vp U. Films inc: The Missourians; Thunder in God's Country; The Rodeo King and the Senorita; Utah Wagon Train; Drums Across the River; Black Shield of Falworth; A Warm December; Uptown Saturday Night; Let's Do It Again; A Piece of the Action; Stir Crazy.

TUCKER, Tanya: Singer-Act. b. Seminole, TX, Oct 10, 1958. Films inc: Jeremiah Johnson.

TV inc: Amateur Night at the Dixie Bar and Grill; The Rebels; Georgia Peaches; A Country Christmas.

Albums inc: Delta Dawn; What's Your Mama's Name; Greatest Hits; Here's Some Love; Tanya Tucker; Lovin' and Learnin'; Ridin' Rainbows.

TUMARIN, Boris (nee Tumarinson): Act-Dir. b. Riga, Latvia, Apr 4, 1910. e. Academy of Arts Berlin. Came to the US in 1939. Thea inc: The Emperor's New Clothes; Winter Soldiers; A Checkov Carnival; Paths of Glory; He Who Gets Slapped; Venus at Large; Whisper into My Good Ear; The Tenth Man; The Three Sisters (dir).

TV inc: The Great Sebastian; Ninotchka; The Eternal Light.

TUNBERG, Karl: Wri. b. Spokane, WA, 1908. Films inc: My Lucky Star; Down Argentine Way; Tall, Dark and Handsome; You Gotta Stay Happy; The Scarlet Coat; Ben Hur; Libel; Taras Bulba; Harlow; Where Were You When the Lights Went Out.

TUNICK, Eugene: Exec. b. Cincinnati, OH, Oct 21, 1920. e. U of Cincinnati. Started as shipping clerk with RKO Cincinnati. On return from military service became booker; Office mgr 1946; Salesman 1948; sales mgr 1949; sales mgr Eagle Lion 1949-51; branch mgr Indianapolis 1951-52; Lippert branch mgr, franchise holder 1951-53; branch mgr UA, Philadelphia 1957; district mgr 1961; Eastern and Canadian division mgr 1968; joined National General Pictures as vp-gen sales mgr 1970, became exec vp following year; exec vp National Amusements 1975; western vp General Cinema 1977; joined American International as vp special projects 1978, became VP gen sales mgr after merger with Filmways.

TUNICK, Jonathan: Comp-Cond-Arr. Bway inc: (arr) A Little Night Music; Company; Follies; Pacific Overtures; A Chorus Line; Ballroom; Sweeney Todd.
Films inc: A Little Night Music (Oscar-adapt-1977).
TV inc: (comp) Swan Song; Blinded by the Light.

TURKEL, Ann; Act. W of Richard Harris. Films inc: Paper Lion; 99 44/100ths % Dead; The Cassandra Crossing; Ravagers; Humanoids From the Deep; The Shining.
TV inc: Greatest Heroes of the Bible.

TURMAN, Lawrence: Prod. b. LA, 1926. e. UCLA. Started as agent, 1960, partnered with Stuart Miller on The Young Doctors; I Could Go On Singing; Stolen Hours; The Best Man. Solo Prod: The Flim-Flam Man; The Graduate; Pretty Poison; The Great White Hope; Marriage of a Young Stockbroker. Partnered with David Foster on The Drowning Pool; Heroes; Walk Proud; Tribute.

TURNBULL, Dale: Exh exec. b. Melbourne, Australia, Nov 19, 1927. GM Hoyts Theatres Ltd & GM Fox Film Corp, Australia; m dir Hoyts Theatres Ltd; p The Old Tote Theatre Co.

TURNER, Ike: Mus-Singer. b. Clarksdale, MS, 1934. Formed Ike Turner Kings of Rhythm; Ike and Tina Turner Revue. Concerts, world tours. Recordings inc: Proud Mary (Grammy-R&B voc group-1971).
Films inc: Gimme Shelter; Soul to Soul.

TURNER, Lana: Act. b. Wallace, ID, Feb 8, 1920. On screen from 1937 in They Won't Forget. Films inc: The Great Garrick; The Adventures of Marco Polo; Love Finds Andy Hardy; Rich Man, Poor Girl; Dancing Coed; Ziegfeld Girl; Dr. Jekyll and Mr. Hyde; Honky Tonk; Johnny Eager; Somewhere I'll Find You; Marriage Is a Private Affair; Weekend at the Waldorf; The Postman Always Rings Twice; Green Dolphin Street; Cass Timberlane; A Life of Her Own; The Merry Widow; The Sea Chase; Diane; Peyton Place; Imitation of Life; Portrait in Black; Bachelor in Paradise; By Love Possessed; Who's Got the Action?; Madame X; The Big Cube; Persecution; Bittersweet Love.
TV inc: The Survivors.
Thea inc: Forty Carats; Legendary Ladies; The Pleasure of His Company.

TURNER, Ted (Robert Edward Turner 3rd): Exec. b. Cincinnati, OH, Nov 19, 1938. e. Brown U. Owner WTBS (Atlanta, Ga, tv "superstation"); owner-founder of of Cable News Network. Also owns Atlanta Braves baseball team; Atlanta Hawks basketball team.

TURNER, Tina (Annie Mae Bullock): Singer. b. Brownsville, TX, Nov 25, 1941. W of Ike Turner. Appeared with him in Ike Turner King of Rhythm; Ike and Tina Turner Revue. Recs inc: Proud Mary (Grammy-R&B voc group-1971).
Films inc: Gimme Shelter; Soul to Soul; Tommy.

TURTELTAUB, Saul: Wri-Prod. b. Teaneck, NJ, May 5, 1932. e. Columbia Coll, BA, Columbia Law School, JD. TV inc: (Wri) Shari Lewis Show; Candid Camera; That Was the Week That Was; The Les Crane Show; The Steve Lawrence Show; The Jackie Gleason Show; The Pat Boone Show; The Carol Burnett Show. (Prod) That Girl; The New Dick Van Dyke Show; A Touch of Grace; Love American Style; Sanford and Son; What's Happening; Carter Country; One In A Million.

TUSHINGHAM, Rita: Act. b. Liverpool, Eng, Mar 14, 1942. Films inc: A Taste of Honey; The Leather Boys; The Girl with Green Eyes; The Knack; Dr Zhivago; The Trap; Smashing Time; Diamonds for Breakfast; The Guru; The Bed-Sitting Room; Straight On Till Morning; The Human Factor.
Thea inc: The Giveaway; Lorna and Ted; Mistress of Novices; The Undiscovered Country; Mysteries.

TUTIN, Dorothy: Act. b. London, Apr 8, 1930. e. RADA. Thea inc: The Thistle and the Rose; As You Like It; Captain Carvallo; The Provoked Wife; The Merry Wives of Windsor; Thor With Angels; The Living Room; Othello; The Cherry Orchard; The Hollow Crown; The Beggar's Opera; Old Times; What Every Woman Knows; A Month in the Country; Anthony and Cleopatra; Reflections; The Provok'd Wife.
Films inc: The Importance of Being Earnest; The Beggar's Opera; A Tale of Two Cities; Cromwell; Savage Messiah.
TV inc: Six Wives of Henry VIII; South Riding; Willow Cabins.

TUTTLE, Lurene: Act. b. Pleasant Lake, IN, Aug 29, 1907. e. USC. On stage, radio. Films inc Heaven Only Knows; Mr. Blandings Builds His Dream House; Goodbye, My Fancy; Don't Bother to Knock; Niagara; The Affairs of Dobie Gillis; The Glass Slipper; Sweet Smell of Success; Psycho; Critic's Choice; The Fortune Cookie; The Ghost and Mr. Chicken; The Horse in the Gray Flannel Suit; Walking Tall; Walking Tall, Part II; Nutcracker Fantasy; The Manitou; Parts-The Clonus Horror.
Radio inc: Sam Spade; Hollywood Hotel.
TV inc: Life With Father; Julia; White Mama; For The Love Of It; Thanksgiving In the Land of Oz (voice).

TWEED: Group. Members inc: Wendell Harrold, b. Tulsa, OK, Aug 12, 1951; Rick Gomez, b. Tulsa, OK, Sep 13, 1949; Charlie Davis, b. Carthage, MO, Aug 11, 1951; Connie Denise Hensley, b. Wichita Falls, TX, Mar 3, 1954; Jimmy Thomas Ray, b. Tulsa, OK, Aug 20, 1950.

TWIGGY (Leslie Hornby): Act. b. London, Sep 19, 1949. Former model. Films inc: The Boy Friend; The Blues Brothers; There Goes The Bride.

TWITTY, Conway: Singer-Sngwri. b. Friarspoint, MS, Sep 1, 1933. Rock 'n' roll singer 1965 to 1969 then switched to C&W. Songs inc: It's Only Make Believe; Hello Darlin'.
(Grammy-C&W group-1971).

TYNAN, Kenneth: Wri. b. Birmingham, England, Apr 2, 1927. e. Magdalen College Oxford. Started career in theatre as dir of Lichfield Repertory Company. Thea inc: (London) Man of the World (dir); Othello (dir); Hamlet (act); Soldiers (co-presenter); became drama critic The Spectator, Later for Evening Standard; Daily Sketch; Observer; New Yorker; appointed literary mgr Britain's National Theatre by Laurence Olivier; "devised" the review Oh! Calcutta!. Also served as script ed Ealing Studios, 1956-58 and ed of tv program Tempo. (Died July 26, 1980).

TYNE, George (Martin Yarus): Act-Dir. b. Philadelphia, Feb 6, 1917. Films inc: (act) A Walk in the Sun; Objective Burma; Call Northside 777; Sands of Iwo Jima; Decision before Dawn; Not With My Wife You Don't; Don't Make Waves; Willie Boy; Marlowe; Skin Game; Ricco; The Boston Strangler; Guide for a Married Man; Fun and Games.
TV inc: (dir) Good Morning World; Governor and JJ; The Odd Couple; Love American Style; Sanford and Son; The Brady Bunch; Mary Tyler Moore Show; The Ghost and Mrs Muir; M*A*S*H; Miss Winslow and Son (pilot); Friends; Love Boat; Fighting Nightingales (pilot); The 416th; Fun and Games.
Thea inc: (act) Romanoff and Juliet; Three Penny Opera; Hotel Paradiso; Too Late the Phalarope.

TYRRELL, Susan: Act. b. San Francisco, 1946. Films inc: The Steagle; Fat City; Catch My Soul; The Killer Inside Me; Islands in the Stream; I Never Promised You A Rose Garden; Andy Warhol's Bad; Another Man, Another Chance; September 30, 1955; Forbidden Zone.
TV inc: Lady of the House; Willow B-Women In Prison.
Thea inc: Father's Day.

TYSON, Cicely: Act. b. NYC, Dec 19, 1933. Films inc: A Man Called Adam; The Comedians; The Heart Is a Lonely Hunter; Sounder; A Hero Ain't Nothin' But a Sandwich; The Concorde-Airport '79.

TV inc: The Autobiography of Miss Jane Pittman (*Emmys*-1974 & actress of year); Roots; East Side, West Side; A Woman Called Moses; King.

UGGAMS, Leslie: Singer-Act. b. NYC, May 25, 1943. e. Professional Children's School, Juilliard. Began singing career at age 5; TV debut, age 7, Johnny Oleson's TV kids.

Bway inc: Hallelujah Baby (*Tony*-1968).

Radio: Peter Lind Hayes-Mary Healy Show; Milton Berle; Arthur Godfrey; Star Time.

TV inc: Milton Berle Show; Name That Tune; Sing Along With Mitch; Backstairs at the White House.

ULLMAN, Daniel: Wri-Dir. b. NYC, Oct 18, 1921. e. UCLA, BA. Films inc: The Maze; Seven Angry Men; Annapolis Story; Wichita; At Gunpoint; Good Day for a Hanging; Battle of the Coral Sea; Mysterious Island.

TV inc: Bonanza; Jim Bowie; The Fugitive; Mannix; Outer Limits; Big Valley; The Invaders; Police Woman; Charlie's Angels; Fantasy Island.

(Died Oct 23, 1979).

ULLMANN, Liv: Act. b. Tokyo, 1939. Films inc: Persona; A Passion; Pope Joan; Cries and Whispers; The Emigrants; Face To Face; A Bridge Too Far; Autumn Sonata; Leonor; Richard's Things.

Thea inc: I Remember Mama; Anna Christie.

UMEKI, Miyoshi: Act. b. Japan, 1929. Films inc: Sayonara (*Oscar*-supp-1957); Cry for Happy; Flower Drum Song; The Horizontal Lieutenant; A Girl Named Tamiko.

UNGER, Anthony B: Prod. b. NYC, Oct 19, 1940. e. Duke U, USC. Films inc: (asso prod) The Desperate Ones; The Madwoman of Chaillot. (Exec prod) The Battle of Neretva; The Magic Christian; Julius Caesar; The Devil's Widow; Don't Look Now; Force 10 From Navarone.

UNGER, Daniel: Prod. b. Tel Aviv, Apr 6, 1948. Films inc: Puppet on a Chain; Pope Joan.

UNGER, Kurt: Prod. b. Berlin, Jan 10, 1922. Dir RoadShow Prodns, Ltd London. Films inc: Judith; Best House in London; Puppet on a Chain; Pope Joan.

UNGER, Oliver A: Exec. b. Chicago, IL, Aug 28, 1914. e. Syracuse U. 1937, vp Hoffberg Prodns; 1945, P Distinguished Films; 1950, vp Snader Telescription Sales; 1952 P, Television Exploitation; 1957, exec vp National Telefilm Associates; 1964, Unger Prodns; 1965 exec vp Commonwealth-United; 1969, vice chmn, CEO Commonwealth-United; 1975 p Hotel Film Intl.

Films inc: (prod) The Day That Shook the World; Force 10 from Navarone.

UNGER, Stephen A: Exec. b. NYC, May 31, 1946. e. Syracuse U, BA; NYU Film School. S of Oliver Unger. vp Intl Sls, U; 1980, sr vp Filmways Pictures Inc; Dec 1980, VP foreign sls CBS Theatrical Films. TV inc: (co-prod) Verna--USO Girl.

URICH, Robert: Act. b. Toronto, OH, Dec 19. e. FL State U, BA. Films inc: Magnum Force.

TV inc: Bob and Carol and Ted and Alice; S.W.A.T.; Soap; Tabitha; Vega$; Merry Christmas From the Grand Ole Opry House; A Christmas Special With Love-Mac Davis; The Starmakers; Fighting Back.

USTINOV, Peter: Act-Wri-Dir. b. London, Apr 16, 1921. On Brit. stage from 1937. Screen debut 1940, Mein Kampf. Films inc: (act) Quo Vadis; Hotel Sahara; Beau Brummell; We're No Angels; An Angel Flew Over Brooklyn; Spartacus (*Oscar*-supp-1960); The Sundowners; Romanoff and Juliet (& wri-prod-dir); Billy Budd (& dir-prod); Topkapi (*Oscar*-supp-1964); John Goldfarb, Please Come Home; Lady L. (prod-dir); Blackbeard's Ghost; The Comedians; Hot Millions (& sp); Viva Max; Hammersmith Is Out (& dir); Big Truck; Poor Clare; One of Our Dinosaurs Is Missing; Logan's Run; Treasure of Matecumbe; The Purple Taxi; Last Remake of Beau Geste; Death on the Nile; The Mouse and His Child; Nous Maigrirons Ensemble; Ashanti.

TV inc: The Life of Samuel Johnson (*Emmy*-1958); Barefoot in Athens (*Emmy*-1967); A Storm in Summer (*Emmy*-1970); Omnibus; Babar the Elephant; Hallmark Hall of Fame; The Thief of Bagdad.

Thea inc: Romanoff and Juliet; Photo Finish; Halfway Up the Tree; The Unknown Soldier and His Wife; Who's Who in Hell.

(*Grammy*-childrens-1959).

VACCARO, Brenda: Act. b. NYC, Nov 18, 1939. Bway inc: Everybody Loves Opal; The Affair; Cactus Flower; toured in Tunnel of Love.

Films inc: Midnight Cowboy; I Love My Wife; Summertree; Going Home; Once Is Not Enough; Airport '77; House by the Lake; Capricorn One; Fast Charlie the Moonbeam Rider; The First Deadly Sin.

TV inc: The FBI; The Name of the Game; The Helen Reddy Show; The Shape of Things (*Emmy*-1974); Sunshine; Guyana Tragedy-The Story of Jim Jones.

VADIM, Roger (R V Plemiannikov): Dir. b. Paris, 1928. Films inc: Futures Vedettes; And God Created Woman; Heaven Fell That Night; Les Liaisons Dangereuses; Warrior's Rest; Vice and Virtue; La Ronde; Nutty Naughty Chateau; The Game Is Over; Histoires Extraordinaires; Barbarella; Pretty Maids All in a Row; Don Juan; Night Games; A Faithful Woman.

VALE, Eugene: Wri. b. Zurich, Apr 11, 1916. Films inc: A Global Affair; Francis of Assisi; The Second Face; The Bridge of San Luis Rey.

TV inc: Four Star Playhouse; Fireside Theatre; Schlitz Playhouse; Crusader; Lux Video Theatre; Danger; Chevron Theatre; Waterfront; Christophers; Cavalcade of America; Hallmark Hall of Fame.

Plays inc: Devils Galore; The Buffoon; Of Shadows Cast by Men.

Author: Technique of Screenplay Writing; Some State of Affairs; The Children's Crusade.

VALENTEE, Renee: Prod. Started as sec with David Susskind, later becoming story ed, asso prod; 1963 to Col in casting; 1964 to Screen Gems as prod; 1973 talent vp; 1976, vp telepix & longform; resd 1977 to enter indie prodn.

TV inc: (exec prod) Contract on Cherry Street; Kill Me If You Can; The Last Hurrah. Blind Ambition; Swan Song. Films inc: Loving Couples.

VALENTI, Jack J: Exec. b. Houston, TX, Sep 5, 1921. e. U of Houston, BA, Harvard, MBA. Air Force pilot, WW II. Special asst and advisor to p Lyndon B Johnson, 1963-66; p, MPAA; elected p, AMPTP, June, 1966.

VALENTINE, Karen: Act. b. Sebastopol, CA, May 25, 1947. Films inc: Forever Young, Forever Free; Hot Lead and Cold Feet; The North Avenue Irregulars.

TV inc: Room 222 (*Emmy*-supp-1970); Karen; My Friend Tony; Hollywood Squares; Laugh-In; The Bold Ones; Sonny and Cher; Gidget Grows Up; Daughters of Joshua Cabe; The Girl Who Came Gift Wrapped; Murder at the World Series; Having Babies; America 2100; Only the Pretty Girls Die.

Thea inc: Stop the World, I Want to Get Off;The Moon Is Blue; Born Yesterday; Bus Stop.

VALLEE, Rudy (Hubert Prior Vallee): Singer-Mus-Act. b. Island Point, VT, Jul 28, 1901. e. U of ME, Yale U. Org. own band, Connecticut Yankees. Later featured on radio, various NY musicals. On screen from 1929. Films inc: The Vagabond Lover; George White's Scandals; The Palm Beach Story; I Remember Mama; The Helen Morgan Story; Live a Little, Love a Little; The Phynx.

VALLI, Alida (nee von Altenburger): Act. b. Pola, Italy, May 31, 1921. Films inc: Vita Ricomincia; Giovanna; The Paradine Case; Miracle of the Bells; The Third Man; Walk Softly Stranger; White Tower; Lovers of Toledo; Stranger's Hand; The Castilian; Ophelia; Spider's Stratagem; The Cassandra Crossing; Suspiria; 1900; The Tempter; Luna; Ce Cher Victor; The Bailiff of Griefensee; That House in the Outskirts.

VALLONE, Raf: Act. b. Turin, Italy, 1916. Films inc: Bitter Rice; Vendetta; Anna; The Beach; The Sign of Venus; El Cid; A View from the Bridge; Phaedra; The Cardinal; Harlow; Beyond the Mountains; The Italian Job; Cannon for Cordoba; A Gunfight; Rosebud; The Human Factor; The Other Side of Midnight; The Greek Tycoon; An Almost Perfect Affair; Arthur Miller on Home Ground; Return to Marseilles.
 TV inc: Fame.

VAN, Bobby (Robert King): Dancer-Singer-Act. b. NYC, 1930. Bway inc: Alive and Kicking; On Your Toes; No, No, Nanette; Doctor Jazz.
 Films inc: Because You're Mine; Skirts Away; Small Town Girl; Dobie Gillis; Kiss Me Kate; The Night Crawlers; The Lost Flight; Lost Horizon.
 TV inc: Shiwiffs; Fun Factory; Make Me Laugh!; Mrs. America Pageant; The Hustler of Muscle Beach.
 (Died July 31, 1980).

VAN ARK, Joan: Act. b. NYC, Jun 16. e. Yale U. Films inc: The Frogs.
 TV inc: We've Got Each Other; Knott's Landing.
 Theatre inc: Barefoot in the Park; School for Wives; Cyrano de Bergerac; Ring Around the Moon; Chemin de Fer; As You Like It.

VANCE, Leigh: Wri-Prod. b. Harrogate, Eng, Mar 18, 1922. e. Shrewsbury Coll. Films inc: The Flesh Is Weak; Heart of a Child; The Shakedown; The Frightened City; It's All Happening; Dr Crippen; Walk Like a Man; Cross Plot; The Black Windmill.
 TV inc: Mannix; Mission Impossible; The Avengers; Cannon; Caribe; Bronk; Baretta; Switch.

VANCE, Vivian: Act. b. Cherryvale, KS, Jul 26, 1912. Films inc: The Secret Fury; The Blue Veil; The Great Race.
 TV inc: I Love Lucy (*Emmy*-supp-1953); The Lucy Show.
 Thea inc: Music in the Air; Anything Goes; Red, Hot and Blue; Kiss the Boys Goodbye; Skylark; Let's Face It; Voice of the Turtle.
 (Died Aug 17, 1979).

VAN CLEEF, Lee: Act. b. Somerville, NJ, Jan 9, 1925. Films inc: High Noon; Arena; Yellow Tomahawk; A Man Alone; Joe Dakota; Guns, Girls and Gangsters; The Man Who Shot Liberty Valance; For a Few Dollars More; Day of Anger; The Good, the Bad and the Ugly; Death Rides a Horse; Sabata; Barquero; El Condor; Captain Apache; Bad Man's River; The Magnificent Seven Ride; Take a Hard Ride; The Squeeze; The Octagon.

VANDERBES, Romano R: Exec. b. Amsterdam, The Netherlands, Jan 16, 1938. e. U of Amsterdam, Yale U, UCLA. P, wri-dir-prod Pace Productions, Inc, 1961-68; P-American-European Films, Inc, New York, Paris, Madrid; P, IFM Releasing Corps, NY.

VAN De VEN, Monique: Act. b. Holland, Jul 28, 1952. e. Acad Dramatic Arts. W of Jan DeBont. Films inc: Turkish Delight; Lost Monday; Dakota; Syl, the Beachcomber; Anita; Keetje Tippel; Doctor Vlimmen; Farewell Doctor; A Woman Like Eve; Separation.

VAN DEVERE, Trish: Act. b. Tenafly, NJ, 1943. W of George C Scott. Films inc: Where's Poppa?; The Last Run; One Is a Lonely Number; The Day of the Dolphin; The Savage is Loose; Fifty-Two Pickup; Movie Movie; The Changeling; The Hearse.
 TV inc: Mayflower-The Pilgrim Adventure; All God's Children.
 Thea inc: Sly Fox; Tricks of the Trade.

VAN DOREN, Mamie (Joan Lucille Olander): Act. b. Rowena, SD, Feb 6, 1933. Prof. debut as singer with Ted Fio Rita orch. Appeared in stock. Films inc: Forbidden; All American; Yankee Pasha; The Girl in Black Stockings; Teacher's Pet; Born Reckless; The Beat Generation; Four Nuts in Search of a Bolt; You've Got to be Smart.

Van DREELEN, John (Jacques Van Dreelen Gimberg): Act. b. Amsterdam, Netherlands, May 5, 1922. Debut with Royal Theatre, The Hague; on stage in Europe before coming to US. Bway inc: Daphne Laureola; The Sound of Music; The Deputy; Private Lives; Marriage-Go-Round; Write Me a Murder.
 Films inc: A Time To Live, A Time To Die; Monte Carlo Baby; Von Ryan's Express; Madame X; Dirty Business; Topaz; Flying Fontaines; Too Hot To Handle; The Formula.
 TV inc: The Great Wallendas; The Clone Master; The Word; The Ultimate Impostor; Swan Song.

VANDROSS, Luther: Singer-Sngwri. b. NYC, Apr 20, 1951. Sang back-up vocals on LP's by Ringo Starr; Carly Simon; David Bowie; Bette Midler; Cat Stevens; Roberta Flack; Martha Reeves. Songs inc: Brand New Day; Fascination.

VAN DYKE, Dick; Act. b. West Plains, MO, Dec 13, 1925. Films inc: Bye Bye Birdie; What a Way to Go!; Mary Poppins; The Art of Love; Chitty Chitty Bang Bang; Some Kind of Nut; The Comic; Cold Turkey; The Runner Stumbles.
 Thea inc: The Girls Against the Boys; Bye Bye Birdie (*Tony*-1961); The Music Man (rev).
 TV inc: The Merry Mute Show; The Music Shop; The Dick Van Dyke Show (*Emmys*-1964,1965,1966); Dick Van Dyke & Company (*Emmy*-1977); Carol Burnett Show; How to Survive the 70's and Maybe Even Bump into Happiness; 30 Years of TV Comedy's Greatest Hits (co-host).

VAN DYKE, Jerry: Act. b. Danville, IL, Jul 27, 1931. TV inc: My Mother the Car; The Judy Garland Show; Accidental Family; Headmaster.

VANE, Edwin T: Exec. b. NYC, Apr 29, 1927. e. Fordham, BA; NYU, MBA. Joined ABC 1964 as dir daytime pgm East Coast; 1966 VP chg daytime pgm; 1969, primetime prodn ABC Entertainment; 1972 VP & net pgm dir; 1979, VP net pgm aff; 1979 P & CEO Group W Productions.

VAN ENGER, Charles J Sr: Cin. b. 1891. Started as a lab worker, became cinematographer shortly after WW1.
 Films inc: The Phantom of the Opera; Lady Windermere's Fan; A Doll's House; Salome; Hunchback of Notre Dame; Fox Movietone Follies of 1929; Words and Music; I Was a Spy (in Britain while a Gaumont-British exec); Never Give a Sucker an Even Break; several films in the Abbott and Costello series and the Sherlock Holmes series; Lorna Doone; Sitting Bull.
 TV inc: Lassie; Many Loves of Dobie Gillis; Betty Hutton Show; Big Town; Bat Masterson; Man Without a Gun; Decision; My Mother, the Car.
 Ret 1969. (Died July 4, 1980).

VAN FLEET, Jo: Act. b. Oakland, CA, 1922. Films inc: East of Eden (*Oscar*-supp-1955); The Rose Tattoo; I'll Cry Tomorrow; The King and Four Queens; Gunfight at the O.K. Corral; Wild River; Cool Hand Luke; I Love You Alice B. Toklas!; The Gang That Couldn't Shoot Straight; The Tenant.
 Thea inc: Winter's Tale; The Whole World Over; King Lear; Flight into Egypt; Camino Real; Trip to Bountiful (*Tony*-1954); Look Homeward Angel; The Glass Menagerie.
 TV inc: Power.

VAN HALEN: Rock Group. Members are Eddie Van Halen guitar; David Lee Roth, guitar; Alex Van Halen, drums; Michael Anthony, bass.
 Albums inc: Van Halen; Van Halen II; Women and Children First.

VAN HEUSEN, James (Edward Chester Babcock): Comp-Pianist. b. Syracuse, NY, Jan 26, 1913. Films inc: Love Thy Neighbor; Road to Zanzibar; Road to Morocco; Dixie; Going My Way; And the Angels Sing; Road to Utopia; Road to Rio; A Connecticut Yankee in King Arthur's Court; Road to Bali; Road to Hong Kong; Bells of St Mary's; Little Boy Lost.

Songs inc: All This and Heaven Too; Moonlight Becomes You; Suddenly It's Spring; Swinging on Star *(Oscar-*1944); Love and Marriage *(Emmy-*1955); All the Way *(Oscar-*1957); Come Fly with Me; High Hopes *(Oscar-*1959); The Second Time Around; Call Me Irresponsible *(Oscar-*1963); My Kind of Town.

Film title songs inc: The Tender Trap; Indiscreet; Pocketful of Miracles; Come Blow Your Horn.

Thea inc: Swingin' the Dream; Nellie Bly; Carnival in Flanders; Skyscraper.

VAN NIE, Rene: Prod-Dir-Wri. b. Amsterdam, Netherlands, Oct 1, 1939. Films inc: Anna, Child of the Daffodils; Silent Love; The Deadly Sin.

VANOCUR, Sander: TV News Pers. b. Cleveland, OH. e. Northwestern U, BA. Started as journalist in London. Joined NBC, 1957; hosted First Tuesday Series; resigned 1971, to become correspondent of the National Public Affairs Center for PBS; June 1977 joined ABC News as vp, special reporting units.

VANOFF, Boris: Prod. b. Buffalo, NY, Dec 7, 1939. Cameraman, ABC-TV; talent coordinator; prodn m. TV inc: King Family; Milton Berle Show. Record prod, Nico records; M & L Records; Sunburst Records; Capitol records. Pres Boris Music Inc.

VANOFF, Nick: Prod. b. Greece, Oct 25, 1929. e. McCune School of Music and Art, Salt Lake City. Began career with Charles Weidman Dance Theatre; brief career as dancer on tv, Bway; now owner, with Saul Pick, Sunset-Gower Studios.

TV inc: Perry Como Show (asso prod); Steve Allen Tonight Show; Perry Como Kraft Music Hall; The Milton Berle Show; The King Family; Hollywood Palace; The Julie Andrews Hour *(Emmy-*1973); The Don Knotts Show; Hee Haw; Swing Out, Sweet Land; Perry Como Christmas Show; The Sonny and Cher Show; The Kennedy Center Honors, 1979; The Big Show; The Kennedy Center Honors, 1980.

VAN PALLANDT, Nina: Singer-Act. b. Copenhagen, Denmark, Jul 15, 1932. e. USC, Sorbonne. Films inc: The Long Goodbye; Assault on Agathon; Quintet; A Wedding; American Gigolo.

VAN PATTEN, Dick: Act. b. NYC, Dec 9, 1928. Bway debut age 7 as Melvyn Douglas' son in Tapestry and Gray; 27 other Bway plays inc: On Borrowed Time; The American Way; The Skin of Our Teeth; Kiss and Tell; The Wind is 90; O Mistress Mine; Mr. Roberts; The Male Animal; Have I Got a Girl for You; Thieves.

Films inc: Charly; Zachariah; Joe Kidd; Snowball Express; Dirty Little Billy; Westworld; Soylent Green; Super Dad; Strongest Man in the World; Gus; Shaggy D.A.; Treasure of the Matecumbe; High Anxiety; Nutcracker Fantasy.

TV inc: I Remember Mama (8 years); The Dick Van Dyke Show; The Partners; Arnie; When Things Were Rotten; Eight is Enough; Diary of a Teen-Age Hitchhiker; Alan King's Thanksgiving Special--What Do We Have to be Thankful For?

VAN PATTEN, Joyce: Act. b. Queens, NY, Mar 9, 1934. Films inc: The Goddess; I Love You Alice B Toklas; Something Big; Thumb Tripping; Mikey and Nicky. TV inc: The Bravos; Shadow of Fear; Mary Tyler Moore Hour; A Christmas for Boomer; The Martian Chronicles.

Thea inc: I Ought to be in Pictures.

VAN PEEBLES, Melvin: Dir-Wri-Comp. Films inc: The Story of a Three-Day Pass; Watermelon Man; Sweet Sweetback's Baadasssss Song.

Plays inc: Aint Supposed to Die a Natural Death; Don't Play Us Cheap; Reggae.

TV inc: Just an Old Sweet Song.

VAN VLEET, Richard: Act. b. Denver, CO, Jan 19. e. Western State College; AADA. Films inc: Airport; Ben. TV inc: All My Children.

VARDA, Agnes: Wri-Dir. b. 1928. Began as still photog for Theatre National Populaire. Launched herself as a filmmaker with La Pointe Courte, regarded as a forerunner of the French new wave. Other films inc: O Saisons, O Chateaux (short); L'Opera Mouffe (short); Du Cote de la Cote (short); Cleo de 5 a 7; Salut Les Cubains (short); Le Bonheur; Les Creatures; Uncle Yanco (short) (& prod); Black Panthers (short) (& prod); Lions Love (& prod); Last Tango in Paris (dialog credit only); Daguerreotypes (& prod); One Sings, The Other Doesn't; Lady Oscar (prod only).

VARSI, Diane: Act. b. San Francisco, 1938. Films inc: Peyton Place; Ten North Frederick; From Hell to Texas; Compulsion; Sweet Love, Bitter; Wild in the Streets; Killers Three; Bloody Mama; Johnny Got His Gun; I Never Promised You a Rose Garden.

VAUGHAN, Sarah: Singer. b. Newark, NJ, Mar 27, 1924. Recording artist; sang with bands, niteries.

TV inc: Uptown-A Tribute to the Apollo Theatre.

VAUGHN, Robert: Act. b. NYC, 1932. Films inc: Hell's Crossroads; No Time to be Young; Unwed Mother; Good Day for a Hanging; The Young Philadelphians; The City Jungle; The Magnificent Seven; The Big Show; The Caretakers; To Trap a Spy; The Spy with My Face; One Spy Too Many; The Venetian Affair; How to Steal the World; Bullitt; The Bridge at Remagen; The Mind of Mr. Soames; If It's Tuesday, This Must Be Belgium. Julius Caesar; The Statue; The Clay Pigeon; The Towering Inferno; Brass Target; Starship Invasions; Good Luck Miss Wyckoff; Virus; Cuba Crossing; Battle Beyond the Stars; Hangar 18.

TV inc: The Man From U.N.C.L.E.; Washington--Behind Closed Doors *(Emmy-*1978); One of Our Spies Is Missing (Brit. TV); The Spy in the Green Hat (Brit. TV); Greatest Heroes of the Bible; Centennial; The Rebels; Dr. Franken; The Gossip Columnist; City in Fear.

VEITCH, John: Exec. b. NYC, Jun 22, 1920. Under contract to David O Selznick as actor, switched to asst dir

Films inc: The Greatest Story Ever Told; Ship of Fools; Major Dundee; Horse Soldiers (prodn mgr); Magnificent Seven (Prodn mgr); Some Like It Hot (prodn mgr). 1961 exec asst prodn mgr Col; 1963 exec prodn mgr; 1966 vp-exec prodn mgr; 1977 exec vp-exec prodn mgr; 1979 P Col Pictures Productions.

VELDE, James R: Exec. b. Bloomington, IL, Nov 1, 1913. e. IL Wesleyan U. Started as night shipper, PAR, 1934; then city salesman; office mgr and branch mgr for Selznick, Eagle Lion Classics and to UA in 1951 as West Coast dist mgr; gen sales mgr in 1956; vp in 1958; dir UA in 1968; sr vp 1972; retired 1977; joined Rastar as sr vp in charge of distribution in May, 1979.

VELLA, Lawrence Kay: Exec. b. Auckland, NZ, Aug 26, 1932. GM Kerridge Odeon; member NZ Film Trade Industry Bd.

VENTURA, Lino: Act. b. Parma, Italy, Jul 14, 1919. Films inc: Touchez Pas au Grisbi; Marie Octobre; Crooks in Clover; Les Aventuries; The Valachi Papers; Wild Horses; La Bonne Annee; A Butterfly on the Shoulder; The Medusa Touch; Sunday Lovers.

VENUTA, Benay: Act. b. San Francisco, 1912. Films inc: Trail of 98; Kiki; Repeat Performance; Jane Doe; Annie Get Your Gun; Call Me Mister; Richochet Romance; The Fuzzy Pink Nightgown.

Thea inc: Dear Me, The Sky Is Falling; A Quarter for the Ladies Room; Nanus.

VENZA, Jac: Prod-Exec. b. Dec 23, 1926. e. Goodman Theatre Chicago Art Institute. Started as dsgn; later exec producer N.E.T.; head of drama N.E.T.

TV inc: 24 Hours in the Life of a Woman *(Emmy-*art dir-1961); Five Ballets of the Five Senses *(Emmy-*prod-1968); N.E.T. Playhouse *(Emmy-*exec prod-1971); The Adams Chronicles *(Emmys-*exec prod-1976, 1977); Classical Dance in America--City Centre Joffrey Ballet *(Emmy-*exec prod); The Martha Graham Dance Company *(Emmy-*exec prod-1977); Billy The Kid--The American Ballet Theatre; American Ballet Theatre *(Emmy-*exec prod-1977); Artur Rubinstein at 90; Balanchine--Dance in America (I, II, III, IV) *(Emmy-*exec prod-1979); Fred Astaire--Change Partners and Dance With Me *(Emmy-*exec prod-1980); Big Blonde.

VERA-ELLEN: Act. b. Cincinnati, OH, 1920. Films inc: Wonder Man; The Kid from Brooklyn; Three Little Girls in Blue; Carnival in Costa Rica; Words and Music; On the Town; Three Little Words; The Belle of New York; Call Me Madam; White Christmas; Let's Be Happy; Web of Violence.

VERDON, Gwen: Act. b. LA, 1926. On screen from 1951. Films inc: On the Riviera; David and Bathsheba; Mississippi Gambler; Meet Me After the Show; The Farmer Takes a Wife; Damn Yankees.
    Bway inc: Can Can *(Tony*-1954); Damn Yankees *(Tony*-1956); Redhead *(Tony*-1959); Chicago.

VEREEN, Ben: Singer-Act-Dancer. b. Miami, FL, 1946. Films inc: Gas-sss; Funny Lady; All That Jazz.
    TV inc: Roots; Ben Vereen--His Roots; Ten Speed and Brown Shoe; Uptown-A Tribute to the Apollo Theatre.
    Bway inc: Sweet Charity; No Place to be Somebody; Jesus Christ Superstar; Pippin *(Tony*-1973).

VERHOEVEN, Michael: Dir-Prod-Wri. b. Berlin, Jul 13, 1938. Films inc: Dance of Death; Sonja Gets Rid of Reality; Killing Them Softly; On Silver Platter; Sunday's Children.

VERNEUIL, Henri: Dir. b. Turkey, Oct 15, 1920. Films inc: La Table Aux Creves; Forbidden Fruit; Public Enemy Number One; The Sheep Has 5 Legs (sp); Paris Palace Hotel; The Cow and I; Weekend at Dunkirk; The Big Snatch; Guns for Sebastian; The Burglars; The Sicilian Clan; The Serpent; The Night Caller; Le Corps de Mon Ennemi; I Comme Icarus (& sp-prod).

VERNON, Anne (Edith Vignaud): Act. b. Paris, Jan 24, 1925. Films inc: Le Mannequin Assassine; Warning to Wantons; Shakedown; Edward and Caroline; The Love Lottery; Time Bomb; The Umbrellas of Cherbourg.

VERNON, John: Act. b. Canada, 1936. e. Banff School of Fine Arts; RADA. TV inc: Wojeck; Three Sisters; Uncle Vanya; Wild Duck; Mary Jane Harper Cried Last Night; The Sacketts.
    Films inc: Point Blank; Justine; Topaz; One More Train to Rob; Dirty Harry; Charlie Varrick; The Black Windmill; Fear is the Key; Cat and Mouse; Brannigan; The Outlaw Josey Wales; Angela; A Special Day; National Lampoon's Animal House; Fantastica; Crunch; Herbie Goes Bananas.

VERONA, Stephen F: Prod-Dir. Started as dir of commercials. Films inc: The Rehearsal (short); Pipe Dreams; Boardwalk.

VERSINI, Marie: Act. b. Paris, Oct 8, 1939. Films inc: Tale of Two Cities; Le Chien de Pique; Paris Blues; The Young Racers; Is Paris Burning; Liebesnachte in der Taiga.
    TV inc: Il ne Faut Jurer de Rien; Britannicus; Cinq Mars; Inferno; La Foire; Les Pieds.
    Thea inc: Tessa; Romeo and Juliet; Les Rustres.

VERSOIS, Odile: Act. b. Paris, Jun 15, 1930. Films inc: Into the Blue; A Day to Remember; Young Lovers; To Paris With Love; Checkpoint; Ruler Without Crown; Passport to Shame; Docks; Nude in a White Car.
    (Died June 23, 1980).

VERSTAPPEN, Wim: Dir-Wri-Prod. b. Holland, Apr 5, 1937. e. Dutch Film Academy. Films inc: Joszef Katus; Confessions of Loving Couples; Drop Out; Blue Movie; VD; Dakota; Alicia; Learning from Las Vegas; Pastorale; Rubia's Jungle; Frank and Eva; Living Apart Together; My Nights with Susan; Olga, Julie, Bill and Sandra.

VERTUE, Beryl: Prod. b. Mitcham, Surrey, Eng, Apr 8, 1931. Worldwide head of TV for Robert Stigwood Organisation.
    Films inc: The Spy With a Cold Nose; Tommy; Till Death Us Do Part; Pompeii; Up the Chastity Belt.
    TV inc: Beacon Hill; Almost Anything Goes; The Entertainer; Dominick Ayres; All Star Anything Goes; The Prime of Miss Jean Brodie (exec prod); Charleston; Steptoe & Son; The Plank.

VETTER, Richard: Exec. b. San Diego, CA, Feb 24, 1928. e. Pepperdine Coll, BA, San Diego State Coll, MA, UCLA, PhD. VP United Artists Theatres. Oscar (Class III) for development of Todd-AO 35 widescreen system, 1973.
    Films inc: (tech dir) The Bible; Patton; Macbeth; Junior Bonner; The Getaway; Logan's Run.

VICAS, George A: Prod-Dir-Wri. b. Berlin, May 12, 1926. e. Harvard, AB; Columbia, MA. TV inc: Berlin--The End of the Line; Money and the Next President; The Great Holiday Massacre; The Trials of Charles de Gaulle; Germany--Fathers and Sons; Britain--The Changing Guard; The Kremlin; The French Revolution; The Middle Ages; The Spanish Armada; The Reformation; An Austrian Affair; Leningrad; The French Army; Siberia--A Day In Irkutsk; The Soviets in Space; The Aviation Revolution; The Pope and the Vatican; A Young American in Paris; Paris--A Story of High Fashion; The Whale Hunters of Fayal; Artur Rubinstein *(Emmy*-prod-1970); The Last of the Vikings; The Methadone Connection.

VICAS, Victor: Prod-Dir-Wri. b. Moscow, Mar 25, 1918. Films inc: No Way Back; Double Destiny; Master Over Life and Death; Back To Kandara; The Wayward Bus; Count Five and Die; Les Disparus; La Donna Dell'Altro; Zwei Unter Millionen; The Third Front; The Camp Followers; The Middle Ages; The Bonapartes; The Hapsburgs; Tolstoy; The Indians; The Bourbons; The Romanoffs; The Hohenzollerns; The Sons of the Queen of Sheba; A Young American in Paris; Passport to Prague; Color Me German; The Crusades; The French Revolution; Charlemagne; The Making of a Dictator; L'Attentat de la rue St Nicaise; Johan-Sebastian Bach; Rallye; Le Calvaire d'un Jeune Homme Impeccable; Portrait d'une Femme sans Pieds.
    TV inc: Aux Frontieres du Possible; Les Brigades du Tigre; Rainer; Mission To Israel.

VICTOR, David: Prod-Wri. b. Odessa, Russia. e. Columbia U. NYC Newspaperman, began wri scripts for radio. VP Arena Prodns 1966; TV vp Filmways 1967 before joining U as prod.
    TV inc: Junior Miss (wri); Date With Judy (wri); Gunsmoke (wri); Restless Gun (wri); The Rebel (& asso prod); The Man From Uncle (prod); Dr Kildare (prod); Little Women; Lucas Tanner; Women In White; The Thirteenth Day--The Story of Esther.

VIDAL, Gore: Wri. b. West Point, NY, Oct 3, 1925. Plays inc: A Visit to a Small Planet; The Best Man; Romulus; Weekend; An Evening with Richard Nixon and . . . Films inc: The Catered Affair; I Accuse; The Scapegoat; Suddenly Last Summer.
    TV inc: Omnibus; Studio One; Philco Playhouse.

VIDOR, King Wallis: Dir. b. Galveston, TX, Feb 8, 1896. Films inc: Turn in the Road; La Boheme; The Crowd; The Big Parade; Hallelujah; Billy the Kid; Street Scene; The Champ; Bird of Paradise; Stella Dallas; The Citadel; Northwest Passage; H.M. Pulham, Esq.; Duel in the Sun; Fountainhead; Ruby Gentry; Man Without a Star; War and Peace; Solomon and Sheba. *(Honorary Oscar*-1978).

VIGODA, Abe: Act. b. NYC, Feb 24, 1921. e. NY School of Dramatic Arts, American Theatre Wing. Films inc: The Godfather; The Godfather, Part II; The Cheap Detective.
    Thea inc: NY Shakespeare Festival; Inquest; The Man in the Glass Booth; Tough to Get Help.
    TV inc: Barney Miller; Fish; Death Car on the Freeway; The Great American Traffic Jam.

VILLAGE PEOPLE: Group. Members are David Hodo; Randy Jones; Alexander Briley; Glenn Hughes; Felipe Rose; Ray Simpson. Formed 1977. Albums inc: Village People; Macho Man; Cruisin'; Live and Sleazy; Can't Stop the Music.
    Films inc: Je Ne Tiens, Tu Me Tiens par la Barbichette; Can't Stop the Music.

VILLECHAIZE, Herve: Act. b. Paris, Apr 23, 1943. Films inc: Guitar; Hollywood Blvd No 2; Hot Tomorrow; Man with the Golden Gun; Crazy Joe; The Gang That Couldn't Shoot Straight; Seizure; The One and Only; Forbidden Zone.
    TV inc: Fantasy Island.
    Theatre inc: Elizabeth the First; Gloria Esperenza.

VINCENT, Jan-Michael: Act. b. Denver, CO, Jul 15, 1944. Films inc: The Undefeated; Going Home; The Mechanic; The World's Greatest Athlete; Buster and Billie; Bite the Bullet; White Line Fever; Baby Blue Marine; Vigilante Force; Shadow of the Hawk; Damnation Alley; Big Wednesday; Hooper; Defiance.

TV inc: Tribes; Sandcastles; The Catcher; The Survivors; The Banana Splits.

VINNICOF, Cecil: Exh. b. LA, Jun 24, 1914. e. USC, LLB. P, Vinnicof Theatre Circuit (California).

VINSON, Helen: Act. b. Beaumont, TX, 1907. On screen from 1932. Films inc: Jewel Robbery; Two Against the World; I Am a Fugitive from a Chain Gang; The Power and the Glory; Broadway Bill; Private Worlds; In Name Only; Are These Our Parents; The Thin Man Goes Home (last film, 1945).

VINTON, Bobby: Singer. b. Canonsburg, PA, Apr 16, 1935. e. Duquesne U. Recording artist. Films inc: Big Jake; Train Robbers.

TV inc: The Gossip Columnist.

VISCUSO, Sal: Act. b. Brooklyn, NY, Oct 5. e. U of CA Davis, BA; NYU, MFA. Films inc: The Taking of Pelham 1-2-3. TV inc: Mary Hartman, Mary Hartman; The Montefuscos.

VITTI, Monica (Monica Luisa Ceciarelli): Act. b. Italy, 1933. Films inc: L'avventura; La Notte; L'Eclipse; Dragees du Poivre; The Nutty Naughty Chateau; The Red Desert; Modesty Blaise; The Chastity Belt; Girl With a Pistol; The Pacifist; Duck in Orange Sauce; An Almost Perfect Affair; The Mystery of Oberwald.

VLADY, Marina (Marina de Poliakoff-Baidaroff): Act. b. Clichey-la-Garenne, France, 1938. Films inc: Orage d'Ete; Avant le Deluge; The Wicked Go to Hell; Crime and Punishment; Toi le Venin; La Steppa; Climats; Enough Rope; Dragees au Poivre; Queen Bee; Chimes at Midnight; Sapho; The Two of Them; Women; The Hypochondriac; L'oeil du Maitre.

TV inc: The Thief of Baghdad.

VOELPEL, Frank: Dsgn. b. Sep 23, 1927. e. Yale, MFA. Thea inc: Fallout; From A to Z; The Alligators; Rosemary; Young Abe Lincoln; Hang Down Your Head and Die; Tiger at the Gates; Spitting Image; Oh! Calcutta!; Blueprints; No Strings; The Critic; The Effect of Gamma Rays on Man-in the-Moon Marigolds; Her Ten Stout-Hearted Men; And Miss Reardon Drinks a Little; Small Craft Warnings; Hurry, Hurry; The Little Theatre of the Deaf; Smith; The Beauty Part; Dybbuk; Priscilla, Very Good Eddie.

VOGEL, Jesse: Wri-Prod. b. NYC, Oct 24, 1925. e. CCNY, Paris Conservatory of Music. Films inc: Carmen, Baby (sp); Therese & Isabelle (sp); Who's Harriet? (prod); My Pleasure Is My Business (prod).

VOGEL, Virgil W: Dir-Prod. b. Peoria, IL. Films inc: The Mole People; Land Unknown; Ma and Pa Kettle; Animal People; Sword of Ali Baba.

TV inc: Cannon; Barnaby Jones; Super Cop; Bonanza; Big Valley; Wagon Train; Police Story; Law of the Land; Centennial; Power; Portrait of a Rebel-Margaret Sanger; Beulah Land.

VOIGHT, Jon: Act. b. Yonkers, NY, Dec 29, 1938. Films inc: The Hour of the Gun; Fearless Frank; Out of It; Midnight Cowboy; The Revolutionary; The All American Boy; Catch 22; Deliverance; Conrack; The Odessa File; Coming Home (Oscar-1978); The Champ.

TV inc: The Dwarf; Cimarron Strip; Centennial.

Thea inc: The Sound of Music; A View From the Bridge; Romeo and Juliet; That Summer, That Fall.

VOLONTE, Gian-Maria: Act. b. Italy, 1930. Films inc: A Fistful of Dollars; For a Few Dollars More; We Still Kill the Old Way; Investigation of a Citizen Above Suspicion; Sacco & Vanzetti; Lucky Luciano; Christ Stopped At Eboli; Ogro; Todo Modo.

VON FURSTENBERG, Betsy: Act. b. Neiheim Heusen, Germany, Aug 16, 1933. Thea inc: Second Threshold; Dear Barbarians; The Petrified Forest; The Secret Man; Oh, Men! Oh, Women!; The Chalk Garden; What Every Woman Knows; Wonderful Town; Mary, Mary; The Paisley Convertible; The Gingerbread Lady; Absurd Person Singular.

Films inc: Women Without Names.

TV inc: The Fifth Column.

von KARAJAN, Herbert: Cond. b. Salzburg, Austria, Apr 5, 1908. e. Vienna College of Music. Cond debut 1929, Ulm, Germany; cond Ulm Opera, 1929-1934; gen dir Aachen Opera 1935; debut with Vienna Staadstopera 1937; artistic dir Berlin State Opera 1938; founder London Philharmonic 1948; permanent cond since 1950.

(Grammys-(3)-opera recording-1964, 1969; classical orch-1978).

VONNEGUT, Kurt Jr: Wri. b. Indianapolis, IN, Nov 11, 1922. Author of several novels. Plays inc: Happy Birthday, Wanda June.

TV inc: Between Time and Timbuktu; Breakfast of Champions; Life On the Mississippi (host).

VON SYDOW, Max: Act. b. Lund, Sweden, Apr 10, 1929. Films inc: Miss Julie; The Seventh Seal; Wild Strawberries; The Face; The Virgin Spring; Through a Glass Darkly; The Mistress; The Greatest Story Ever Told; The Reward; Hawaii; The Quiller Memorandum; Hour of the Wolf; The Shame; The Kremlin Letter; The Touch; The Emigrants; The Exorcist; Foxtrot; Three Days of the Condor; Desert of the Tartars; Exorcist II-The Heretic; March or Die; Brass Target; Hurricane; Deathwatch; Flash Gordon.

VON ZELL, Harry: Radio announcer. b. Indianapolis, IN, Jul 11, 1906. Started at radio station KMPC, LA, 1927. Joined CBS, NY. Network announcer for Eddie Cantor; Fred Allen; Phil Baker; Dinah Shore; Burns & Allen; Joan Davis. On screen from 1945. Films inc: It's in the Bag; Til the End of Time; The Guilt of Janet Ames; The Saxon Charm; Dear Wife; Where the Sidewalk Ends; Two Flags West; Call Me Mister; You're in the Navy Now; I Can Get it for You Wholesale; Boy, Did I Get a Wrong Number!

VOSKOVEC, George: Act-Prod-Dir-Wri. b. Sazava, Czechoslovakia, Jun 19, 1905. e. U of Dijon, BA. First appearance on stage in Prague, 1922; formed a partnership with Jan Werich and for next 11 years they wrote, prod & perf in 26 prodns for The Liberated Theatre of Prague.

Bway inc: The Tempest; Love of Four Colonels; His and Hers; Brecht on Brecht; Player King; The Tenth Man; Big Fish, Little Fish; A Call on Kuprin; The Penny Wars; All Over; The Cherry Orchard; Agamemnon.

Films inc: Affair in Trinidad; Twelve Angry Men; Butterfield 8; The Bravados; The Spy Who Came in from the Cold; The Boston Strangler; The Iceman Cometh; The Man on a Swing; Somewhere in Time.

TV inc: The Nativity; Skag; Great Performances (Happy Days).

VREELAND, Byron: Exec. b. Bozeman, MT, Jun 1, 1900. e. MT State Coll. Carpenter MGM Studios, 1917; grip Hal Roach studios, 1921; head grip, 1927; studio supt, 1937; studio mgr, 1946-62; coord, TV series, Fugitive. Retired 1968.

WAGENHEIM, Charles: Act. b. Newark, NJ, Feb 21, 1906. Films inc: Charlie Chan at the Wax Museum; Two Girls on Broadway; Meet Boston Blackie; Summer Storm; The House on 92nd Street; The Dark Corner; The House on Telegraph Hill; The Prodigal; Tunnel of Love; The Baby Maker; The Missouri Breaks.

(Died Mar 12, 1979).

WAGER, Michael (Mendy Weisgal): Act-Dir-Prod. b. NYC, Apr 25, 1929. e. Harvard, AB, MA. Bway inc: A Streetcar Named Desire; Small Hours; Bernardine; The Merchant of Venice; Misalliance; Six Characters in Search of an Author; Saint Joan; Firstborn; Noontide; Brecht on Brecht; The Three Sisters; Where's Daddy (prod); Sunset; Cuban Thing; Trelawney of the Wells; The Interview; Visions of Kerouack; The Dream; Songs at Twilight.

Films inc: Hill 24 Does Not Answer; Exodus; King of Kings; Jane Austen In Manhattan.

WAGGONER, Lyle: Act. b. Kansas City, KS, Apr 13. TV inc: The Carol Burnett Show; host of game show, It's Your Bet; Sonny and Cher Show; Once Upon a Mattress; The Love Boat II; The New Adventures of Wonder Woman; The Gossip Columnist; The Ugily Family; The Great American Traffic Jam.
Films inc: Love Me Deadly; Journey to the Center of Time; Catalina Caper.

WAGNER, Jane: Wri-Dir. b. Morristown, TN, Feb 2, 1935. Bway inc: Appearing Nitely. TV inc: Lily *(Emmy*-Wri-1974); Lily Tomlin *(Emmy*-Wri-1976) J.T.; Earthwatch; People.
Films inc: Moment by Moment.

WAGNER, Lindsay: Act. b. LA, Jun 22, 1949. Sang with rock group. Screen debut, 1973, Two People. Films inc: Paper Chase; Second Wind.
TV inc: The F.B.I.; Owen Marshall; Counselor at Law; Night Gallery; The Bold Ones; Marcus Welby, M.D.; The Rockford Files; The Six Million Dollar Man; The Bionic Woman *(Emmy*-1977); The Incredible Journey of Dr Meg Laurel; The Two Worlds of Jennie Logan; Scruples.

WAGNER, Robert: Act. b. Detroit, MI, Feb 10, 1930. Films inc: Halls of Montezuma; With a Song in My Heart; Titanic; Prince Valiant; Broken Lance; White Feather; The Mountain; A Kiss Before Dying; The Hunters; Say One For Me; All The Fine Young Cannibals; The Longest Day; The War Lover; The Condemned of Altona; Harper; Banning; Don't Just Stand There; Winning; The Towering Inferno; Midway; Concorde--Airport 79.
TV inc: It Takes a Thief; Cat on a Hot Tin Roof; Colditz; Death at Lovehouse; Pearl; Switch; Hart to Hart.

WAGNER, Robin: Dsgn. b. San Francisco, Aug 31, 1933. Thea inc: And the Wind Blows; The Prodigal; Between Two Thieves; A Worm in Horseradish; A View from the Bridge; An Evening's Frost; The Condemned of Altona; The Trial of Lee Harvey Oswald; Hair; Lovers and Other Strangers; The Cuban Thing; The Great White Hope; Promises, Promises; The Watering Place; The Engagement Baby; Jesus Christ Superstar; Seesaw; Full Circle; Mack and Mabel; Sergeant Pepper's Lonely Hearts Club Band on the Road; A Chorus Line; On the 20th Century *(Tony*-1978); 42d Street.
Films inc: Glory Boy.

WAGONER, Porter: Singer. b. West Plains, MO, Aug 12, 1930. C&W recording artist; regular member of the Grand Ole Opry; on radio, TV with own show. *(Grammys*-(with Blackwood Bros.)-Sacred Recording-1966; Gospel Perf-1967, 1969).

WAGSTAFF, Stuart: Act-Prod. b. Salisbury, Eng, Feb 13, 1925. Repertory in England, then Australia. Host TV shows Channel 7 Sydney.
TV inc: Blankety Blanks; Showcase. Formed Stuart Wagstaff Enterprises Ltd, Sydney.

WAIN, Bea: Singer-Bcst pers. b. NYC. W of Andre Baruch. Featured singer with Larry Clinton Band; radio-tv inc: Your Hit Parade; Your All-Time Hit Parade; The Bea and Andre Show; recordings, concerts.

WAINWRIGHT, James: Act. b. Danville, IL, Mar 5, 1938. TV inc: Daniel Boone; Jigsaw; The President's Plane is Missing; Man On the Move; Killdozer; A Woman Called Moses; Freedom Riders; Beyond Westworld.
Films inc: Joe Kidd; Hooper; Mean Dog Blues.

WAISSMAN, Kenneth: Prod. b. NYC, Jan 24, 1943. e. U of MD, NYU. Plays inc: Grease; Over Here!; And Miss Reardon Drinks a Little.

WAITE, Ralph: Act. b. White Plains, NY, Jun 22, 1928. e. Bucknell U, BA, Yale U, divinity degree. Films inc: A Lovely Way to Die; Five Easy Pieces; Lawman; The Grissom Gang; Dime Box; Sporting Club; On The Nickel (prod-dir-wri).
TV inc: The Waltons; Red Alert; Roots; OHMS; Angel City.
Thea inc: Hogan's Goat; Watering Place; The Trial of Lee Harvey Oswald; Blues for Mister Charlie.

WAJDA, Andrzej: Prod-Dir. b. Suwalki, Poland, Mar 6, 1926. e. Polish Film School. Films inc: Generation; Dunikowski; Kanal; Ashes and Diamonds; Lot A; The Innocent Charmers; Samson; Love at Tventies; Siberian Lady Macbeth; Ashes; Gates of Paradise; Roly Poly; Hunting Flies; Landscape after Battle; The Birch Wood; Pilate and Others; The Wedding; Land of Promise; The Man of Marble; Invitation to the Interior; Without Anaesthesia; Young Ladies from Wilno; Drygent (The Orchestra Conductor).
TV inc: Interview with Ballmayer; Another Wife; Macbeth; November Night.

WAKELY, Jimmy: Singer-Act. b. Mineola, AR, Feb 16, 1914. Started as C&W singer, recording artist. Screen debut 1939, Saga of Death Valley. Films inc: The Tulsa Kid; Heart of the Rio Grande; Deep in the Heart of Texas; Song of the Range; Moon Over Montana; Cowboy Cavalier; Across the Rio Grande; The Silver Star.

WALBERG, Garry: Act. b. Buffalo, NY, Jun 19. TV inc: The Odd Couple; Quincy.

WALCH, Reiner: Prod. b. Berlin, May 30, 1932. e. Berlin U. Films inc: The Second Spring; Fort Travis.

WALD, Malvin: Wri-Prod. b. NYC, Aug 8. e. Brooklyn Coll, BA, Woodland U, JD. Films inc: The Naked City; Behind Locked Doors; The Dark Past; Ten Gentlemen from West Point; The Powers Girl; Two in a Taxi; Undercover Man; Outrage; Battle Taxi; Man on Fire; Al Capone; Venus in Furs; In Search of Historic Jesus.
TV inc: (wri) Hollywood; The Golden Years; The Rafer Johnson Story; D-Day; Project: Man in Space; Climax; Shirley Temple Storybook; Peter Gunn; Perry Mason; Dobie Gillis; Combat; Daktari; The Legend of Sleepy Hollow. (Asso prod) Primus; California Tomorrow. (Prod): Mod Squad; Untamed World; Around the World of Mike Todd; The Billie Jean King Show; Mark Twain's America-Abe Lincoln, Freedom Fighter.

WALD, Richard C: Exec. b. NYC, 1931. e. Columbia Coll, BA; Columbia U, MA; Clare Coll, Cambridge (England) BA. Corr for NY Herald-Tribune while in college, joined paper after college, serving as religion edtr, political reporter, foreign corr in London and Bonn, asso edtr, managing edtr; 1967, exec vp Whitney Communications; 1968 vp news NBC; 1973, P NBC News; 1977, asst to bd chmn Times-Mirror Co; 1978, sr vp ABC News.

WALDEN, Robert (nee Wolkowitz): Act. b. NYC, Sep 25, 1943. e. CCNY. Films inc: Bloody Mary; Pigeons; New York, New York; Capricorn One; Rage; Audrey Rose; All The President's Men.
TV inc: The Great Ice Rip-Off; Larry; The Marcus-Nelson Murders; Lou Grant; Enola Gay--The Men, The Mission, The Atomic Bomb.

WALKEN, Christopher: Act. b. NYC, Mar 31, 1943. e. Hofstra U. Films inc: The Anderson Tapes; The Happiness Cage; Next Stop Greenwich Village; Roseland; The Sentinel; Annie Hall; The Deer Hunter *(Oscar*-supp-1978); Last Embrace; Heaven's Gate; The Dogs of War.
Thea inc: JB; High Spirits; Baker Street; West Side Story (road tour); The Lion In Winter; Kid Champion; The Rose Tattoo (rev); The Unknown Soldier and his Wife; Sweet Bird of Youth.

WALKER, Cardon E (Card): Exec. b. Rexburg, ID, Jan 5, 1916. e. UCLA, BA. Joined the Disney organization as a traffic boy, 1938. Subsequently unit manager on short subjects, eventually handled budget control for short subjects. After service in WW II, returned to Disney, receiving a number of promotions until in December, 1971, he was elected P, COO; Jun 1980, P & CEO.

WALKER, Clint: Act. b. Hartford, IL, May 30, 1927. First film job as extra in The Ten Commandments.
Films inc: The Great Bank Robbery; The Dirty Dozen; More Dead Than Alive; The White Buffalo; Bakers Hawk.
TV inc: Cheyenne.

WALKER, Jimmie: Act. b. NYC, Jun 25. Films inc: Let's Do It Again; The Greatest Thing That Almost Happened; Rabbit Test; Concorde-Airport '79.
TV inc: Good Times; B.A.D. Cats; Murder Can Hurt You.

WALKER, Nancy: Act. b. Philadelphia, PA, May 10, 1922. D of the Vaudeville team Barto and Mann. Singer, comedienne. Films inc: Girl Crazy; Stand Up And Be Counted; Murder By Death; Can't Stop The Music (dir).

Thea inc: Best Foot Forward; Look Ma, I'm Dancing; Pal Joey; Wonderful Town; The Cherry Orchard; A Funny Thing Happened On The Way to the Forum.

TV inc: The Danny Kaye Show; Family Affair; The Mary Tyler Moore Show; Rhoda; MacMillan and Wife; The Nancy Walker Show; Blansky's Beauties.

WALLACE, Irving (nee Wallechinsky): Wri. b. Chicago, Mar 19, 1916. e. Williams Inst., Berkeley. Best-selling author, many of whose books have been filmed. Sp inc: The West Point Story; Meet Me at the Fair; Desert Legion; Gun Fury; Split Second; The Burning Hills; Bombers B-25.

WALLACE, Jean (nee Wallasek): Act. b. Chicago, Oct 12, 1923. W of Cornel Wilde. Films inc: You Can't Ration Love; Jigsaw; The Good Humor Man; Song of India; Sudden Fear; The Big Combo; Maracaibo; Lancelot and Guinevere; Beach Red; No Blade of Grass.

WALLACE, Mike: TV Commentator. b. Brookline, MA, May 9, 1918. e. U of MI. Night Beat, WABD, NY; The Mike Wallace Interview, ABC; newspaper col, NY Post, 1957-58; News Beat, WNTA-TV, 1959-61; correspondent, CBS News, 1963. TV inc: Mike Wallace at Large; co-edtr, 60 Minutes *(Emmys*-1971, 1972, 1973); The Selling of Colonel Herbert *(Emmy*-1973).

WALLACH, Eli: Act. b. NYC, Dec 7, 1915. e. U of TX; CCNY; Neighborhood Playhouse. Studied with Lee Strasberg. Bway inc: Yellowjack; Antony and Cleopatra; Mister Roberts; The Rose Tattoo *(Tony*-supp-1951); Camino Real; Teahouse of the August Moon; Major Barbara; The Cold Wind and the Warm; Rhinocerous; Luv; Saturday, Sunday and Monday; Every Good Boy Deserves Favor.

Films inc: Baby Doll; The Misfits; The Magnificent Seven; How the West Was Won; Nasty Habits; The Domino Principle; The Sentinel; Movie, Movie; Girlfriends; Circle of Iron; Firepower; Winter Kills; The Hunter.

TV inc: The Poppy Is Also A Flower *(Emmy*-1967); The Pirates; Fugitive Family.

WALLIS, Hal B: Prod. b. Chicago, Sep 14, 1898. H of Martha Hyer. Started as thea mgr in LA; pub dept WB before becoming prod. Has made approximately 300 films.

Films inc: Little Caesar; Five Star Final; Dawn Patrol; Midsummer Night's Dream; Story of Louis Pasteur; Anthony Adverse; King's Row; Sergeant York; Yankee Doodle Dandy; Now, Voyager; Casablanca; Saratoga Trunk; Strange Love of Martha Ivers; Sorry, Wrong Number; My Friend Irma; The Stooge; Sailor Beware; Come Back, Little Sheba; Rose Tattoo; The Rainmaker; Gunfight at the OK Corral; Visit to a Small Planet; Summer and Smoke; Becket; The Sons of Katie Elder; Boeing-Boeing; True Grit; Norwood; Anne of the Thousand Days; Red Sky at Morning; Shoot Out; Mary Queen of Scots; Bequest to the Nation.

Irving Thalberg Awards 1938 and 1943.

WALSH, David M: Cin. b. Cumberland, MD. Films inc: Monte Walsh; I Walk the Line; Everything You Always Wanted to Know About Sex and Were Afraid to Ask; The Laughing Policeman; The Other Side of the Mountain; W.C. Fields; Murder by Death; The Sunshine Boys; Rollercoaster; The Goodbye Girl; Foul Play; House Calls; California Suite; The In-Laws; Private Benjamin; Seems Like Old Times.

TV inc: Queen of the Stardust Ballroom *(Emmy*-1975).

WALSH, Raoul: Dir. b. NYC, Mar 11, 1892. e. Seaton Hall U, NYC. On stage, 1910. On screen with Biograph Players, 1912. Dir more than 100 films inc: The Thief of Bagdad; East of Suez; Sadie Thompson; What Price Glory?; Manpower; They Died with Their Boots On; Desperate Journey; Gentleman Jim; The Horn Blows at Midnight; Pursued; Cheyenne; One Sunday Afternoon; White Heat; Along the Great Divide; Capt. Horatio Hornblower; Distant Drums; Saskatchewan; Battle Cry; Revolt of Mamie Stover; The Naked and the Dead; The Sheriff of Fractured Jaw; Marines, Let's Go; A Distant Trumpet.

(Died Dec 31, 1980).

WALSTON, Ray: Act. b. New Orleans, LA, Nov 2, 1917. Films inc: Kiss Them for Me; South Pacific; Damn Yankees; The Apartment; Tall Story; Convicts Four; Wives and Lovers; Who's Minding the Store?; Kiss Me, Stupid!; Caprice; Paint Your Wagon; Viva Max!; The Sting; Silver Streak; The Happy Hooker Goes to Washington; Popeye.

TV inc: There Shall Be No Night; My Favorite Martian; Institute for Revenge.

Bway inc: Damn Yankees *(Tony*-1956).

WALTER, Jessica: Act. b. NYC, Jan 31, 1944. Films inc: Lilith; The Group; Grand Prix; Bye Bye Braverman; Number One; Play Misty for Me.

TV inc: Amy Prentiss *(Emmy*-1975); Vampire; She's Dressed to Kill.

Thea inc: Advise and Consent; Photo Finish; Night Life; A Severed Head.

WALTERS, Barbara: TV pers. b. Boston, MA, Sep 25, 1931. e. Sarah Lawrence Coll. Started in TV after graduation. Joined Today Show in 1961 as writer, occasionally on-camera; 1963 full-time on camera. In April, 1974, named permanent co-host *(Emmy*-1975). In 1976 joined ABC-TV as first female anchor on a network newscast and highest-paid news personality in TV with a five-year contract guaranteeing $1 million a year.

WALTERS, Charles: Dir. b. Pasadena, CA, Nov 17, 1911. e. USC. Former dancer. Films inc: (dir dance sequences) Seven Days' Leave; Presenting Lily Mars; Girl Crazy; Meet Me in St Louis; Abbott and Costello in Hollywood; Ziegfeld Follies (dir); Good News; Easter Parade; Barkleys of Broadway; Summer Stock; Three Guys Named Mike; Belle of New York; Torch Song; Easy to Love; Tender Trap; High Society; Don't Go Near the Water; Please Don't Eat the Daisies; Jumbo; The Unsinkable Molly Brown; Walk, Don't Run.

TV inc: Here's Lucy; The Governor and J J; Lucille Ball Specials.

Thea inc: Let's Face It; Banjo Eyes.

WALTON, Kip: Dir. TV inc: Perry Como Special; Diana Ross Special; Johnny Mathis Christmas Hour; In Session with Sarah Vaughn; In Session with Seals and Crofts; In Session with Aretha Franklin; Touch of Gold; Split Second; Coliseum Concert; Jackson Five Special; Miss America Teenager Pageant; Almost Anything Goes; Paul Williams Special; Hot City; Teddy Pendergrass at the Greek; Hope for President.

WALTON, Tony: Dsgn. b. Walton-on-Thames, Surrey, Eng, Oct 24, 1934. e. Radley Coll. Thea inc: Fool's Paradise; The Pleasure of His Company; The Ginger Man; Pieces of Eight; Most Happy Fella; Once There Was a Russian; A Funny Thing Happened on the Way to the Forum; Caligula; Golden Boy; The Apple Tree; Pippin *(Tony*-1973); The Good Doctor; Uncle Vanya; Bette Midler's Clams on the Half Shell Revue; Chicago; Streamers.

Films inc: Mary Poppins; Farenheit 451; The Seagull; The Boy Friend; Murder on the Orient Express; The Wiz; All That Jazz *(Oscar-*art dir-1979).

WALTON, Sir William: Comp. b. England, 1902. Films inc: Henry V; Hamlet; Richard III.

WAMBAUGH, Joseph: Wri. b. East Pittsburgh, PA, Jan 22, 1937. e. CA State College, BA. LA policeman from 1960-1974. Created Police Story TV series.

Films inc: The Onion Field; The Black Marble.

WANAMAKER, Sam: Act-Prod-Dir. b. Chicago, Jun 14, 1919. e. Drake U. Films inc: My Girl Tisa; Give Us This Day; Taras Bulba; The Man in the Middle; Those Magnificent Men in Their Flying Machines; The Spy Who Came in from the Cold; Warning Shot; The Day the Fish Came Out; The Executioner (dir); Catlow (dir); The Sell Out; Billy Jack Goes to Washington; Sinbad and the Eye of the Tiger (dir); Death on the Nile; From Hell to Victory; Private Benjamin; The Competition.

TV inc: Mousey; Espionage; Outer Limits; The Holocaust (& dir); Dark Side of Love; Man Undercover; Hart to Hart; Jimmy Breslin's Neighborhood; My Kidnapper, My Love (dir).

Thea inc: This, Too, Shall Pass; Joan of Lorraine; A Hatful of Rain (& dir); Ding Dong Bell (dir); A Case of Libel (dir).

WANNBERG, Kenneth: Mus ed-Comp. b. Inglewood, CA, Jun 28, 1930. Films inc: (mus edtr) Hello, Dolly!; Patton; Tora Tora Tora; At Long Last Love; French Connection I & II; The Last Waltz; Star Wars; Close Encounters of the Third Kind. (Comp): Four Deuces; Lepke; Bitter Sweet Love; Tribute.
TV inc: (comp) Silent Partner; Remember My Name.

WARD, David S: Wri. b. Oct 24, 1945. e. Pomona Coll, UCLA. Films inc: Steelyard Blues; The Sting (Oscar-1973).

WARD, Douglas Turner: Act-Wri-Dir. b. Burnside, LA, May 5, 1930. e. Wilberforce U, U of MI. Thea inc: (act) The Iceman Cometh; Lost in the Stars; A Raisin in the Sun; Pullman Car Hiawatha; One Flew Over the Cuckoo's Nest; Coriolanus; Happy Ending; Day of Absence. (Wri-prod) Brotherhood; Happy Ending; Day of Absence.
Films inc: Man and Boy.
TV inc: The First Breeze of Summer; Ceremonies In Dark Old Men.

WARD, Simon: Act. b. Beckenham, Eng, Oct 19, 1941. Films inc: Frankenstein Must be Destroyed; Start Counting; Young Winston; Hitler-The Last 10 Days; The Three Musketeers; The Four Musketeers; The Battleflag; Deadly Strangers; All Creatures Great and Small; Aces High; Zulu Dawn; La Sabina.
TV inc: Spoiled; Chips with Everything; All Creatures Great and Small; Dracula; The Last Giraffe.
Thea inc: Hamlet; The Rear Column.

WARDEN, Jack: Act. b. Newark, NJ, 1925. Films inc: From Here to Eternity; Twelve Angry Men; Run Silent, Run Deep; Mirage; Shampoo; All The President's Men; The White Buffalo; Heaven Can Wait; Death on the Nile; Dreamer; Beyond the Poseidon Adventure; The Champ; And Justice for All; Being There; Used Cars.
TV inc: The Wackiest Ship in the Army; N.Y.P.D.; Brian's Song (Emmy-1972); Bad News Bears; Topper; A Private Battle.
Bway inc: Stages.

WARDROPE, Alan J: Exec. b. Australia, Aug 8, 1912. Ad-pub M, Par, 1958-67; CBS (Cinema Center Films). Dir, Australia, New Zealand, Far East, 1968-72; CIC Int'l Sls, London & Singapore, 1972-75; Australian Film Commission. mktg,

WARHOL, Andy: Dir-Prod. b. Pittsburgh, PA, 1928. Films inc: Sleep; Blow Job; Harlot; The Chelsea Girls; Blue Movie; Trash (prod only); Flesh (prod only); Bad; L'Amour; C S Blues.

WARING, Fred: Mus. b. Tyrone, PA, Jun 9, 1900. Inventor of Waring Blender. Launched his band, The Pennsylvanians, in the early thirties, still does concert, recording dates. Began on radio in 1935. Sponsors music education through Waring Music Workshop and Shawnee Press music pubbery. Films inc: Variety Show.

WARNER, David: Act. b. Manchester, Eng, Jul 29, 1941. e. RADA. London stage debut, 1962, A Midsummer Night's Dream. Thea inc: Afore Night Come; The Tempest; The Wars of the Roses; The Government Inspector; Twelfth Night; I, Claudius.
Films inc: Tom Jones; Morgan; Work Is a Four Letter Word; The Bofors Gun; The Ballad of Cable Hogue; Straw Dogs; A Doll's House; Tales from the Crypt; Providence; Cross of Iron; The Omen; Silver Bears; The 39 Steps (remake); Time After Time; Concorde-Airport '79; Nightwing; The Island.
TV inc: Holocaust; SOS Titanic.

WARNER, Jack (nee Waters): Act. b. London, Oct 24, 1894. Films inc: The Dummy Talks; The Captive Heart; It Always Rains on Sunday; Here Come the Huggetts; The Blue Lamp; Valley of the Eagles; Scrooge; Home and Away; Carve Her Name with Pride; Jigsaw.
TV inc: Dixon of Dock Green.

WARREN, Charles Marquis: Wri-Dir-Prod. b. Baltimore, MD, Dec 16, 1917. e. Baltimore City Coll. Films inc: Only the Valiant (wri); Little Big Horn (wri-prod-dlr); Hellgate (wri-prod-dir); Springfield Rifle (wri); Pony Express (wri); Arrowhead (wri-dir); Flight to Tangier (wri-dir); Seven Angry Men (wri-dir); Tension at Table Rock (dir); Black Whip (prod-dir); Trooper Hawk (wri-dir); Charro! (wri-prod-dir); Down to the Sea (wri-prod-dir); Hunter (wri).
TV inc: Gunsmoke; Rawhide; Gunslinger; The Virginian; Iron Horse.

WARREN, Eda: Film ed. b. 1904. One of the original founders of the American Cinema Editors, began in silent film, worked mostly at Paramount.
Films inc: (silents) Peter Pan; Hula; Abie's Irish Rose; Wolf Song. (Sound) So Red the Rose; The General Died at Dawn; The Big Broadcast; I Married a Witch; Strategic Air Command and 11 John Farrow films during the 1940's.
(Died July 15, 1980).

WARREN, Gene: SFX Prod-Dir. b. Denver, CO, Aug 12, 1916. e. LA Art Center School. Films inc: The Monster From the Green Hell; Jack the Giant Killer; The Lost Balloon; Atlantis, the Lost Continent; Around the World Under the Sea; Tom Thumb; The Time Machine (Oscar-1960); Wonderful World of the Brothers Grimm; The Seven Faces of Dr. Lao; The Power; My Name is John; Black Sunday; Avalanche.
TV inc: Twilight Zone; Outer Limits; Star Trek; Man from Atlantis.

WARREN, Harry: Comp. b. NYC, Dec 24, 1893. Bway inc: The Laugh Parade; Crazy Quilt; 42d Street.
Films inc: 42nd street; Gold Diggers (1933, 1935, 1937); Roman Scandals; Footlight Parade; Wonder Bar; Dames; Go Into Your Dance; Shipmates Forever; Going Places; Naughty but Nice; Down Argentine Way; That Night in Rio; Springtime in the The Singing Marine; Garden of the Moon; Rockies; The Harvey Girls; Summer Holiday; The Barkleys of Broadway; The Belle of New York; Cinderfella.
Songs inc: Lullaby of Broadway (Oscar-1935); Jeepers Creepers; Down Argentine Way; Chattanooga Choo Choo; I've Got a Gal in Kalamazoo; You'll Never Know (Oscar-1943); On the Atchison, Topeka and Santa Fe (Oscar-1946); Zing a Little Zong; That's Amore; An Affair to Remember.

WARREN, Jennifer: Act. Films inc: Night Moves; Another Man, Another Chance; Slap Shot; Ice Castles.
TV inc: First You Cry; Steel Cowboy; Champions, A Love Story; Angel City.

WARREN, Madeline: Exec. b. Greenport, NY, Sep 10, 1949. e. NYU, BA, MA. Worked as story edtr before becoming dir dvlpmt The Fields Co; vp prodn-dvlpt Begelman-Fields Co; Jan 1980 to MGM as prodn exec; Dec 1980, vp prodn MGM.

WARREN, Michael: Act. b. South Bend, IN, 1946. e. UCLA. Films inc: Drive, He Said; Cleopatra Jones; Butterflies Are Free; Norman. . .Is That You?; Fast Break.
TV inc: Days of Our Lives; Sierra.

WARRICK, Ruth: Act. b. St Louis, MO, Jun 29, 1915. On screen from 1941. Films inc: Citizen Kane; The Corsican Brothers; Journey Into Fear; The Iron Major; Perilous Holiday; Daisy Kenyon; The Great Dan Patch; The Great Bank Robbery.
TV inc: Peyton Place; All My Children.
Thea inc: Conditions of Agreement; Irene.

WARTLIEB, Jack: Exec. b. Chicago, IL, Feb 7, 1930. e. Columbia College, BA. TV prodn mgr on CBS remotes; prodn mgr David Frost Show; Merv Griffin Show; Norman Corwin Presents; vp chg prod Westinghouse in chg of Mike Douglas Show; Peter Marshall Show; Every Day; May 1980 prodn-ops vp Golden West Broadcasters.

WARWICK, Dionne: Singer. b. East Orange, NJ, Dec 12, 1941. Albums inc: Here Where There Is Love; Golden Hits; Valley of the Dolls; A Decade of Gold; I'll Never Fall In Love Again (*Grammy*-contemporary voc-1970); Dionne.

Singles inc: I Say A Little Prayer; Do You Know the Way to San Jose? (*Grammy*-contemporary voc -1968); Then Came You; I'll Never Love This Way Again (*Grammy*-pop vocal-1979); Deja Vu (*Grammy*-R&B vocal-1979)

TV inc: Dionne Warwick Special: History of Jazz; Solid Gold (cohost); Barry Manilow--One Voice; Crystal.

WASHBOURNE, Mona: Act. b. Birmingham, Eng, Nov 27, 1903. Theatre inc: Mourning Becomes Electra; Blithe Spirit; The Winslow Boy; Honour and Obey; The Foolish Gentlewoman; The Mortimer Touch; Mornings at Seven; Nude With Violin; Billy Liar; Semi Detached; The Anniversary; Misalliance; Home; Getting On.

Films inc: The Winslow Boy; The Good Companions; Billy Liar; Night Must Fall; My Fair Lady; The Collector; Quilp; The Bluebird; Stevie.

TV inc: A Hundred Years Old; Dear Petitioner; Homecoming.

WASILEWSKI, Vincent T: Exec. b. Athens, IL, Dec 17, 1922. e. U IL, BA, JD. 1949 joined legal staff National Ass'n Broadcasters; 1953, chief counsel; 1955 Mgr Govt relations; 1960 VP Govt Aff; 1961, exec VP; 1965, Pres.

WASS, Ted: Act. b. Lakewood, OH, Oct 27. TV inc: Family; Handle with Care; Loves Me, Loves Me Not; Daughters; Soap; The Triangle Factory Fire Scandal.

WASSERMAN, Dale: Wri. b. Rhinelander, WI, Nov 2, 1917. Started as theatrical lighting dsgn, later a dir and prod. Became wri during era of live tv.

TV inc: Elisha and the Long Knives; Collision; The Man That Corrupted Hadleyburg; The Citadel; Long After Summer; The Fog; Brotherhood of the Bell; The Blue Angels; The Power and the Glory; Stranger; I, Don Quixote; The Lincoln Murder Case; Eichmann--Engineer of Death; The Luck of Roaring Camp; Circle of Death; The Fool Killer.

Plays inc: 998; Livin' The Life; Beggar's Holiday (prod); Man of La Mancha; Pencil of God; One Flew Over the Cuckoo's Nest.

Films inc: The Power and the Glory; Quick Before It Melts; Mister Buddwing; Doctor, You've Got to Be Kidding; A Walk With Love and Death (& asso prod); Man of La Mancha.

WASSERMAN, Lew R: Exec. b. Cleveland, OH, Mar 15, 1913. Joined MCA on Dec. 12, 1936, and 10 years later to the day was named President of the Corporation. Currently Chairman of the Board, CEO.

Jean Hersholt Humanitarian Award, 1973.

WATERHOUSE, Keith: Wri. b. Leeds, England, Feb 6, 1929. Plays inc: Billy Liar; Celebration; England, Our England; All Things Bright and Beautiful; Come Laughing Home; Say Who You Are; Children's Day; Who's Who; Saturday, Sunday, Monday (adapt); Filomena (adapt).

Films inc: Whistle Down the Wind; A Kind of Loving; Billy Liar; Man in the Middle; Pretty Polly; Lock Up Your Daughters; The Valiant.

WATERSTON, Sam: Act. b. Cambridge, MA, Nov 15, 1940. Films inc: A Time for Giving; A Delicate Balance; The Great Gatsby; Rancho de Luxe; Capricorn One; Interiors; Sweet Revenge; The Eagles Wing; Sweet William; Hopscotch; Heaven's Gate.

TV inc: Friendly Fire.

Thea inc: Hamlet; Lunch Hour.

WATSON, Mills: Act. b. Oakland, CA, Jul 10, 1940. e. RADA. Films inc: The Midnight Man; Dracula's Castle; Charlie and the Angel; Cheech and Chong's Up in Smoke.

TV inc: The Migrants; Amy Prentiss; The Misadventures of Sheriff Lobo; I'll Be Home For Christmas.

WAYNE, David (Wayne McKeekan): Act. b. Travers City, MI, Jun 30, 1916. Bway inc: Park Avenue; Finian's Rainbow (*Tony*-Supp-1947); Mister Roberts; Teahouse of the August Moon (*Tony*-1954).

Films inc: Portrait of Jennie; Adams Rib; The Reformer and the Redhead; My Blue Heaven; Stella; M; Up Front; As Young as You Feel; With a Song in My Heart; Wait 'Til the Sun Shines, Nellie; Down Among the Sheltering Palms; We're Not Married; Tonight We Sing; How to Marry a Millionaire; Hell and High Water; The Tender Trap; The Last Angry Man; The Big Gamble; The Andromeda Strain; The African Elephant (narr); Huckleberry Finn; The Front Page; The Apple Dumpling Gang; The Prize Fighter.

TV inc: Arsenic and Old Lace; The World of Disney; Matt Lincoln; The Name of the Game; The Good Life; Cade's Country; Streets of San Francisco; The Gift of Love; The Statesman (Benjamin Franklin); The Girls in the Office; House Calls.

WAYNE, Jerry (Jerome Marvin Krauth): Prod-Wri. b. Buffalo, NY, Jul 24, 1926. e. U of Buffalo, OH State Dental. Began as singer; recording artist. On stage in Guys and Dolls; Pajama Game; Silk Stockings.

Plays inc: (prod-wri) Two Cities (London); King's Mare (London).

WAYNE, John (Marion Michael Morrison): b. Winterset, IA, May 26, 1907. e. USC. Backlot worker during and after college, given acting break by John Ford. Appeared in 120 features, including several in series The Three Mesquiteers, and two serials.

Films inc: The Big Trail; Range Feud; Hurricane Express (Serial); Shadow of the Eagle (serial); Maker of Men; Two Fisted Law; Lady and the Gent; Haunted Gold; Baby Face Harrington; Baby Face; Randy Rides Alone; The Star Packer; Neath Arizona Skies; The Lawless Frontier; Lawless Range; Rainbow Valley; The Dawn Rider; The Lawless Nineties; King of the Pecos; The Oregon Trail; Spoilers of the Sea; Idol of the Crowds; Stagecoach; Nightriders; Wyoming Frontier; Dark Command; Three Faces West; The Long Voyage Home; Seven Sinners; A Man Betrayed; The Lady From Louisiana; Shepherd of the Hills; Lady For a Night; Reap the Wild Wind; The Spoilers; In Old California; Flying Tigers; Pittsburgh; In Old Oklahoma; The Lady Takes a Chance; The Fighting Seabees; Tall in the Saddle; Back To Bataan; Flame Of the Barbary Coast; They Were Expendable; Without Reservations; Angel and the Badman; Fort Apache; Red River; Three Godfathers; Wake of the Red Witch; She Wore a Yellow Ribbon; Sands of Iwo Jima; Flying Leathernecks; Big Jim McLain; The Quiet Man; Hondo; The High and the Mighty; The Sea Chase; The Conqueror; The Searchers; The Barbarian and the Geisha; Rio Bravo; The Horse Soldiers; The Alamo (& prod-dir).

The Comancheros; The Man Who Shot Liberty Valance; The Longest Day; Hatari; How the West Was Won; McLintock; The Greatest Story Ever Told; In Harm's Way; The Sons of Katie Elder; Cast a Giant Shadow; El Dorado; The War Wagon; The Green Berets (& dir); Hell Fighters; The Undefeated; True Grit (*Oscar*-1969); Chisum; Rio Lobo; The Cowboys; The Train Robbers; McQ; Brannigan; Rooster Cogburn; The Shootist.

(Died Jan. 11, 1979).

WAYNE, Michael: Exec. b. LA, Nov 23, 1934. e. Loyola U, BBA. S of late John Wayne. Worked as asst dir, became P Batjac Prodns (Wayne indie). Films inc: China Doll; Escort West; The Alamo; McClintock; Cast A Giant Shadow; The Green Berets; Chisum; Big Jake; The Train Robbers; Cahill, US Marshall; McQ; Brannigan.

WAYNE, Patrick: Act. b. LA, Jul 15, 1939. S of John Wayne. Screen debut at age 11, Rio Grande. Films inc: The Searchers; The Alamo; The Comancheros; McLintock!; The Bears and I; Mustang Country; Sinbad and the Eye of the Tiger; The People That Time Forgot.

TV inc: Shirley; The Rounders; Flight To Holocaust; Yesterday's Child; The Last Hurrah; The Monte Carlo Show (host).

WAYNE, Sid: Lyr-Comp. b. NYC, Jan 26, 1923. Entertainer in niteries; wrote songs for Bway musicals inc: Ziegfeld Follies; Thirteen Daughters.
   TV inc: Victor Borge; Peter Lind Hayes & Mary Healy.
   Films inc: G.I. Blues; From Hell to Borneo; Cleopatra; Only Once in a Lifetime.
   Songs inc: It's Impossible; I'm Gonna Knock On Your Door; Two Different Worlds; I Need Your Love Tonight; Mangos; Winner Take All; 99 Years in the Penitentiary; My Love For You; First Anniversary. Also songs for 30 Elvis Presley films.

WEATHER REPORT: Group. Members are Josef Zawinul, Wayne Shorter, Jaco Pastorius, Peter Erskine, Robert Thomas Jr. Albums inc: Weather Report; I Sing the Body Electric; Sweetnighter; Mysterious Traveler; Tale Spinnin'; Black Market; Heavy Weather; Mr. Gone; 8:30 (Grammy-jazz fusion-1979).

WEATHERSTONE, Roger Seddon: Exec-TV prod. b. Gunning NSW, Australia, May 29, 1943. M Mobbs Lane Prodns for ATW, 1976-77; gm Vidio Tape Corp, Sydney.

WEAVER, Dennis: Act. b. Joplin, MO, Jun 4, 1924. e. U of OK. TV inc: Gunsmoke (Emmy-supp-1959); Kentucky Jones; Gentle Ben; McCloud; Intimate Strangers; Ishi; Pearl; The Islander; The Ordeal of Patty Hearst; A Cry for Justice; Stone; Amber Waves; The Ordeal of Dr. Mudd; Country Gold--The First Fifty Years.
   Films inc: Dragnet: The Bridges at Toko-Ri; Ten Wanted Men; Seven Angry Men.

WEAVER, Fritz: Act. b. Pittsburgh, PA, Jan 19, 1926. e. U of Chicago, BA. Thea inc; Chalk Garden; Protective Custody; Miss Lonely Hearts; Loreno; All American; Shot in the Dark; Absurd Person Singular; Baker Street; Child's Play (Tony-1970); The Price.
   Films inc: Demon Seed; Marathon Man; Black Sunday; The Day of the Dolphin; The Guns of August; The Big Fix.
   TV inc: The Legend of Lizzie Borden; Holocaust; The Martian Chronicles; Children of Divorce; Nightkill.

WEAVER, Marjorie: Act. b. Grossville, TN, Mar 2, 1913. On screen from 1936. Films inc: China Clipper; This Is My Affair; Second Honeymoon; The Cisco Kid and the Lady; You Can't Ration Love; Fashion Model; We're Not Married.

WEAVER, Sylvester J (Pat): Exec. b. LA, Dec 21, 1908. e. Dartmouth Coll. Young & Rubicam adv agency, 1935-38; American Tobacco Co, adv mgr, 1938-47; VP Y&R, 1947-49. Joined NBC as VP charge of TV, 1949; appt'd VP chg. NBC Radio & TV networks, 1952; vice chmn bd, NBC, 1953; p NBC, Dec, 1953; bd chmn, Dec, 1955; resigned 1956, formed own broadcast company and then became advertising exec with McCann-Erickson. From 1963-66 he headed Subscription Television Inc. (Emmy-Trustees Award-1968). Returned to advertising field as cnsltnt to the Wells, Rich, Greene agency.

WEBB, Alan: Act. b. York, Eng, Jul 2, 1906. e. Osborne, Dartmouth. Thea inc: The Devil's Disciple; This One Man; Tonight at 7:30; She, Too, Was Young; Blithe Spirit; Pygmalion; The Night of the Iguana; The Physicists; The Chinese Prime Minister; We Have Always Lived in the Castle; The Three Sisters; The Kingfisher.
   Films inc: Chimes at Midnight; Tha Taming of the Shrew; Women in Love; Nicholas and Alexandra; The Duellists; The Great Train Robbery.

WEBB, Jack: Prod-Dir. b. Santa Monica, CA, Apr 2, 1920. Began radio career, San Francisco, 1945, announcer, writer, actor. After career as an actor (the 1952 Dragnet series, which he also directed), formed an independent production company, Mark VII Ltd. TV series inc: Dragnet; Adam-12; Emergency; The D.A.; The Rangers; O'Hara, U.S. Treasury; Hec Ramsey; Mobile One.

WEBB, Roy: Comp. b. NYC, Oct 3, 1888. Charter member of ASCAP, 1914. Films inc: Quality Street; My Favorite Wife; I Married a Witch; Joan of Paris; The Fallen Sparrow; The Fighting Seabees; Enchanted Cottage; Mr Lucky; Kitty Foyle; Stage Door; The Track of the Cat; Teacher's Pet; Marty.

WEBBER, Andrew Lloyd Comp. b. London, Eng, Mar 22, 1948. Had first comp published at age eight. Thea inc: Jesus Christ, Superstar; Evita (Tony-score-1979). Films inc: Jesus Christ, Superstar. TV inc: Tell Me On Sunday (wri).

WEBBER, Robert: Act. b. Santa Ana, CA, Oct 14, 1928. Films inc: Highway 301; Twelve Angry Men; The Stripper; Hysteria; The Sandpiper; The Third Day; No Tears for a Killer; Harper; The Silencers; The Dirty Dozen; Dollars; Bring Me the Head of Alfredo Garcia; Midway; The Choirboys; Pacific Challenge (& narr); Madame Claude; Casey's Shadow; Revenge of the Pink Panther; 10; Courage, Fuyons; All Stars; Private Benjamin; Sunday Lovers.

WEBSTER, Nicholas: Dir. b. Spokane, WA, Jul 24. e. LA City Coll. TV inc: Apple's Way; Mannix; Bracken's World; Get Smart; Bonanza; Johnny Cash Ridin' the Rails; The Great American Train Story; Appointment with Destiny; Showdown at OK Corral; Last Days of John Dillinger; Long Childhood of Timmie; Walk in My Shoes; Violent World of Sam Huff; Purlie Victorious.

WEBSTER, Paul Francis: Sngwri. b. NYC, Dec 20, 1907. e. Cornell U, NYU. To Hollywood 1935; under contract to 20th Century-Fox to write for Shirley Temple; then freelance. Films inc: Minstrel Man; Hit the Ice; Calamity Jane; Rose Marie; The Merry Widow; Tender Is the Night; Marjorie Morningstar; Student Prince; The Great Caruso; 55 Days at Peking; April Love.
   Thea inc: Casino de Paree; Jump for Joy; Windy City; Christine.
   Songs inc: Masquerade; Two Cigarettes in the Dark; How Green Was My Valley; Rainbow on the River; The Lamplighter's Serenade; I Got It Bad and That Ain't Good; The Loveliest Night of the Year; Merry Widow Waltz; Tender Is The Night; Secret Love (Oscar-1953); Love Is A Many-Splendored Thing (Oscar-1955); The Twelfth of Never; There's Never Been Anyone Else But You; Giant; Anastasia; Friendly Persuasion; The Shadow of Your Smile (Oscar-1965); Somewhere My Love.
   TV title song: Maverick; Sugarfoot.

WECHSLER, Lazar: Prod. b. Poland, Jun 28, 1896. e. U of Zurich. Set up first film co in Switzerland. Films inc: Wings Over Ethiopia; This Is China; Marie Louise; The Last Chance; The Search; Four in a Jeep; The Village; Heidi; Heidi and Peter; It Happened in Broad Daylight; The Marriage of Mr Mississippi; Shadows Growing Longer; The Right to be Born.

WECHTER, David: Wri-Dir. b. LA, Jun 27, 1956. e. USC, BA. S of Julius Wechter. Films inc: Gravity (short); Junior High School (short); Midnight Madness.

WECHTER, Julius: Band ldr-Comp. b. Chicago, May 10, 1935. Played vibes with Martin Denny; comp and played with Herb Alpert and the Tia Juana Brass, 1962; then leader of the Baja Marimba Band.
   Film scores inc: Midnight Madness.
   Songs inc: Spanish Flea; Brasilia.

WEDEMEYER, Herman: Act. b. Hilo, HI, May 20, 1924. e. St. Mary's College. TV inc: Hawaii Five-O.

WEDGEWORTH, Ann: Act. b. Abilene, TX, Jan 21. e. SMU. Bway inc: Thieves; Make a Million; Blues for Mr. Charlie; The Last Analysis; Chapter Two (Tony-supp-1978).
   TV inc: The Edge of Night; Another World; Somerset; All That Glitters; The War Between the Tates; Three's Company.
   Films inc: Handle With Care; Thieves; Bang the Drum Slowly; Scarecrow; Law and Disorder; Dragon Fly; The Birch Interval.

WEIDMAN, Jerome: Wri. b. NYC, Apr 4, 1913. e. CCNY, NYU Law School. Plays inc: Fiorello! (Pulitzer Prize & Tony-1959); Tenderloin; I Can Get It For You Wholesale; Cool Off!; Pousse-Cafe; Ivory Tower; The Mother Lover.
   Films inc: The Damned Don't Cry; House of Strangers; I Can Get It For You Wholesale.
   TV inc: The Reporter (series).

WEILEY, John Francis: Wri-Dir-Prod. b. Grafton NSW, Australia, Jan 28, 1942. e. Sydney U. Films inc: Journey Among Women; Third Person Plural; Dimboola.
TV inc: Autopsy on a Dream; Tomorrows World; The Controllers; Sob Sisters; Horizon; The Total War Machine.

WEILL, Claudia: Dir. b. NYC, 1947. e. Radcliffe. Worked as prodn asst on doc Revolution; later made doc shorts inc This is the Home of Mrs. Levant Grahame; Roaches' Serenade. Films inc: Girlfriends; It's My Turn.
TV inc: Joyce at 34; Sesame Street; The Other Half of the Sky--a China Memoir.

WEINBERGER, Ed (Edwin B. Weinberger): Wri. TV inc: The Bill Cosby Specials; The Dean Martin Show; Hey, Hey It's Fat Albert; Mary Tyler Moore Show (& prod) *(Emmys-prod-1975, 1976, 1977; Wri-1975, 1977)*; Phyllis; Doc; Betty White Show; Cindy; Taxi (& prod-crea) *(Emmy-exec prod-1979, 1980)*; The Associates (& prod-crea).

WEINBLATT, Mike: Exec. e. Syracuse U. Joined NBC in 1957. Serving in various capacities, he has been exec vp and gm of the NBC TV Network Aug, 1977; P of NBC Entertainment Sep 6, 1978; P NBC Enterprises Div Jan 15, 1980; resigned May 29, 1980 to become P of Showtime.

WEINGARTEN, Lawrence: Exec. b. Chicago, IL. Started as publicist for Thomas Ince; became prod 1920. Films inc: Buster Keaton films; Marie Dressler-Polly Moran series; Broadway Melody; A Day at the Races; Libeled Lady; I Love You Again; When Ladies Meet; Escape; Adam's Rib; Invitation; Pat and Mike; The Actress; Tender Trap; I'll Cry Tomorrow; Don't Go Near The Water; Cat On a Hot Tin Roof; The Gazebo; Period of Adjustment; Unsinkable Molly Brown.
(Irving Thalberg Award-1973).

WEINSTEIN, Hannah: Prod. b. NYC. e. NYU, BA. M of Paula Weinstein. Films inc: Escapade; Claudine; Greased Lightnin'; Stir Crazy.
TV inc: Robin Hood; Buccaneers; Sword of Freedom; Scotland Yard.

WEINSTEIN, Henry T: Exec prod. b. NYC, Jul 12, 1924. e. CCNY, Carnegie Tech. Worked with various rep groups, stock companies; 1970, exec in chg prodn American Film Theatre; 1975, became ind prod. Films inc: Tender Is The Night; Joy in the Morning; Cervantes; Madwoman of Chaillot; The Battle of Neretva; A Delicate Balance; The Homecoming; The Iceman Cometh; Lost in the Stars; Butley; Luther; Rhinoceros; Galileo; The Man In the Glass Booth; In Celebration.

WEINSTEIN, Paula: Exec. b. Nov 19, 1945. e. Columbia U. Started as publicist; then film ed; agent William Morris; vp prod, Warner Bros; studio exec, sr vp worldwide prodn, Fox; prodn vp The Ladd Co, 1980.

WEINSTOCK, Lew: TV prod-Dir. b. LA, Jun 2, 1945. Prodn dir for numerous concerts, festivals and fairs.
TV inc: The Grant Griffin Special; Total Environment Concert Special; In Concert/California Jam; California Jam II; Canada Jam.
Films inc: Symphony in Glass; That Tender Touch (prodn cnsltnt).

WEINTRAUB, Fred: Prod. b. NYC, Apr 27, 1928. e. U of PA. Formed Weintraub-Heller Productions, 1974. Films inc: Enter the Dragon; Rage; Black Belt Jones; The Ultimate WArrior; Dirty Knights Work; Checkered Flag or Crash; The Pack; Outlaw Blues; The Promise (& sp); Die Laughing; The Big Brawl; Tom Horn.

WEINTRAUB, Jerry: Prod. b. NYC, Sep 26, 1937. Films inc: Nashville; Oh, God!; Sept 30, 1955.
TV inc: John Denver's Rocky Mountain Christmas *(Emmy-1974)*; An Evening With John Denver *(Emmy-1975)*; Sinatra-The Main Event; Good Night, America; The Higher We Fly; Blue Jeans.

WEINTRAUB, Sy: Exec. b. NYC, 1923. e. U Mo. Formed Flamingo Films, tv synd firm, 1949, created Superman and Grand Ole Opry tv series; bought Sol Lesser's rights to Tarzan films 1958, creating Banner Films which prod several new Tarzan adventures; 1965 purchased Panavision, later acquired Nassour Studios; 1967 sold Banner Prodns to National General Corp, becoming P National General's tv arm; 1978 became chmn Columbia Pictures Entertainment; 1979 became chmn exec committee of Columbia Pictures Industries and member of three-man office of chief exec.

WEIR, Bob: Mus. b. Oct 16, 1947. Founder-member of The Grateful Dead. Occasionally records with other musicians. Albums inc: Ace; Heaven Help The Fool.
(See The Grateful Dead for group credits).

WEIR, Peter: Dir. b. Sydney, Australia, Aug 8, 1944. Films inc: Homesdale; The Cars that Ate Paris; Picnic at Hanging Rock; The Last Wave (& sp); The Plumber (& sp).

WEIS, Don: Dir. b. Milwaukee, WI, May 13, 1922. e. USC. Films inc: (dial dir) Body & Soul; Home of the Brave; Champion; The Men. (Dir): Letter from a Soldier; sequence in It's a Big Country; Bannerline; Just This Once; You for Me; I Love Melvin; Remains to be Seen; A Slight Case of Larceny; Half a Hero; Affairs of Dobie Gillis; Adventures of Hajji Baba; Ride the High Iron; Catch Me If You Can; The Gene Krupa Story; Critic's Choice; Looking for Love; The King's Pirate.
TV inc: Dear Phoebe; The Longest Hundred Miles; It Takes a Thief; Ironside; M*A*S*H; Happy Days; Planet of the Apes; Bronk; Petrocelli; The Magician; Mannix; Night Stalker; Barbary Coast; The Courtship of Eddie's Father; Starsky & Hutch; Andros Targets; Kingston Confidential; Hawaii Five-O; The Millionaire.

WEISBORD, Sam: Exec. b. NYC, Sep 21, 1911. Joined William Morris Agency 1929; moved to West Coast office 1945; named sr exec vp 1965; became pres 1975.

WEISKOPF, Bob: Wri. Writes with Bob Schiller. TV inc: I Love Lucy; Red Skelton Show *(Emmy-1971)*; Flip Wilson Show; Maude; All's Fair (crea); All in the Family *(Emmy-1978)*; Archie Bunker's Place; Living in Paradise (pilot).

WEISMAN, Ben: Comp-Arr. b. Providence, RI, Nov 16, 1921. e. Juilliard School of Music. Films inc: Jailhouse Rock; It Happened at the World's Fair; The Trouble with Girls; G.I. Blues; Blue Hawaii; Roustabout; Frankie and Johnnie; Wild in the Country; Change of Habit; Tickle Me; The Young Americans; Wild Honey.
TV inc: Dick Tracy; Joey Bishop.
Songs inc: The Night Has a Thousand Eyes; Lonely Boy Blue; Got a Lot of Livin' to Do; Pocketful of Rainbows; Summer Kisses, Winter Tears; Frankie and Johnnie; When I Am With You.

WEISSMULLER, Johnny: Act. b. Chicago, IL, Jun 2, 1904. e. Chicago U. Champion swimmer. Screen debut in Tarzan, the Ape Man, 1932. Played Tarzan in 12 films. Other pictures inc: Jungle Jim; Swamp Fire; The Lost Tribe; Pygmy Island; Captive Girl; Savage Mutiny; Cannibal Attack; Jungle Man-Eater; The Phynx.

WEITMAN, Robert M: Exec. b. NYC, Aug 18, 1905. e. Cornell U, BS. M, Paramount Theatres, Greater NY, 1933-35; M dir NY Para, 1935-53, instituted big-name personality and big-band policy; VP-programming and talent, ABC-TV when United Paramount Theatres merged with ABC, 1953-56; VP-program development, CBS-TV, 1956; VP, TV prodn, MGM, 1960; VP-all prodn, feature and TV for MGM; elected to MGM bd. of directors, 1963-68; VP, Motion Picture Prodn, Columbia Pictures, 1968-70; appointed 1st VP in charge of all prodn, 1969; 1970 ret to Ind Prodn.
Films inc: The Anderson Tapes; Shamus.
TV inc: Shamus; A Matter of Wife. . .and Death.

WEITZMAN, Bernard: Exec. b. Springfield, MA. e. Southwestern U School of Law, U of Alabama, USC. Dir of business affairs, CBS-TV, 1948-54; Desilu Productions, vp & board member, 1954-67; MCA. VP, 1961-72; pres, Cinemobile Systems/Taft Broadcasting, 1972-74; vp, MGM, 1974-77; Lorimar Productions, exec vp since 1977.

WEITZNER, David A: Exec. b. NYC, Nov 13, 1938. e. MI State U. Entered film industry 1960 in Columbia adv dept. Subsequently with Donahue & Coe Agency, Loew's Theatres, Embassy Pictures in adv dept; dir adv-expl Palomar Pictures; Ad-Pub-Expl vp ABC Pictures Corp; vp entertainment & leisure div Grey Advertising; vp worldwide adv 20th Fox, Feb 1977; Exec vp ad-pub-expl Universal Jan 1980.

WELCH, Ken: Wri-Lyr-Comp. b. Kansas City, MO, Feb 4, 1926. e. Carnegie-Mellon. H of Mitzie Welch. Spec material wri, teamed with Mitzie Cottle writing spec material for Carol Burnett, others; worked niteries as team.

TV inc: The Garry Moore Show; Julie and Carol at Carnegie Hall; Carol and Company; Carol Plus Two; The Entertainers; Kraft Music Hall; Burt Bacharach specials; Petula Clark special; Julie and Carol at Lincoln Center; Barbra Streisand and other Musical Instruments (*Emmy*-mus-dir-1974; also musician of year); Duke Ellington Special; Bing Crosby and Friends; Olivia Newton-John Special; Sills and Burnett at the Met; Carol Burnett Show (*Emmy*-song-1976) Ben Vereen--His Roots (*Emmy*-song-1978); Hope for President (& prod); Linda in Wonderland (& prod).

WELCH, Mitzie (Marilyn Cottle): Wri-Lyr-Comp. b. McDonald, PA, Jul 25. e. Carnegie-Mellon. W of Ken Welch. Singer at Pittsburgh Playhouse, vocalist with Benny Goodman at Waldorf-Astoria, NY; teamed with Welch writing spec material for Carol Burnett, others; worked niteries as team. Bway inc: (act) Student Gypsy; Fade Out, Fade In; Do I Hear A Waltz; Second City.

TV inc: The Garry Moore Show; Julie and Carol at Carnegie Hall; Carol and Company; Carol Plus Two; The Entertainers; Kraft Music Hall; Burt Bacharach Specials; Petula Clark Specials; Julie and Carol at Lincoln Center; Barbra Streisand and Other Musical Instruments (*Emmy*-mus-dir-1974); also musician of year); Duke Ellington Special; Bing Crosby and Friends; Olivia Newton-John Special; Sills and Burnett at the Met; Carol Burnett Show (*Emmy*-song-1976); Ben Vereen--His Roots (*Emmy*-song-1978); Hope for President (& prod) Linda in Wonderland (& prod).

WELCH, Raquel (nee Tejada): Act. b. Chicago, IL, 1942. Fashion and photographic model. Co-Hostess, Hollywood Palace. Screen debut in Roustabout, 1964. Films inc: A House Is Not a Home; Fantastic Voyage; Our Man Flint; One Million Years B.C.; Lady in Cement; 100 Rifles; Myra Breckinridge; Kansas City Bomber; The Wild Party; Mother, Jugs and Speed; Crossed Swords.

TV inc: From Raquel With Love (& wri).

WELCH, Robert L: Prod-Wri. b. Chicago, IL, Nov 23, 1910. e. Northwestern, U of IL. In stock with Hedgerow Theatre, Pasadena Playhouse. In radio as wri-prod Kate Smith Show, Fred Allen Show; Jack Benny Show; Henry Aldrich Shows; US Armed Forces Radio Shows during WW 2.

Films inc: Variety Girl; Paleface; Sorrowful Jones; Top O' The Morning; Fancy Pants; Mr. Music; The Lemon Drop Kid; Son of Paleface.

WELD, Tuesday (nee Susan Weld): Act. b. NYC, Aug 27, 1943. On screen from 1956. Films inc: Rock, Rock, Rock; Rally Round the Flag, Boys!; The Five Pennies; The Private Lives of Adam and Eve; Return to Peyton Place; Wild in the Country; Bachelor Flat; Soldier in the Rain; The Cincinnati Kid; Pretty Poison; I Walk the Line; A Safe Place; Play It As It Lays; Looking for Mr. Goodbar; Dog Soldiers; Who'll Stop the Rain; Serial.

TV inc: The Many Loves of Dobie Gillis; Dupont Show of the Month; The Greatest Show on Earth; Mr. Broadway; Fugitive; The Crucible; Cimarron Strip; Mother and Daughter-The Loving War.

WELK, Lawrence: Orch Ldr. b. Strasburg, ND, Mar 11, 1903. Played hotels, ballrooms. 1951 started weekly TV show from Aragon Ballroom, Pacific Ocean Park, CA. Champagne Music Makers, ABC-TV, July, 1955; The Lawrence Welk Show, ABC; signed lifetime contract, Hollywood Palladium, July 1961; Syndicated network show started 1971.

WELLES, Orson: Prod-Dir-Wri-Act. b. Kenosha, WI, 1915. Started in radio: March of Time; The Shadow; War of the Worlds; Campbell Playhouse; co-prod: Julius Caesar; Doctor Faustus; Macbeth; Heartbreak House.

Films inc: (act) Citizen Kane (also prod, dir & co-sp) (*Oscar*-co-sp-1941); Magnificent Ambersons (sp & dir only); Journey into Fear; Jane Eyre; Follow the Boys; Tomorrow Is Forever; The Stranger (& dir); The Lady from Shanghai (& dir); Macbeth (& dir); Prince of Foxes; The Third Man; Othello (& dir); Trouble in the Glen; Napoleon; Moby Dick; Touch of Evil (& dir); The Long Hot Summer; David and Goliath; Compulsion; The Mongols; Lafayette; The Trial (& dir); Is Paris Burning?; A Man for All Seasons; I'll Never Forget Whatshisname; Casino Royale; Start the Revolution Without Me; The Kremlin Letter; Catch 22; Necromancy; Treasure Island; Ten Days Wonder; The Other Side of the Mountain; The Late, Great Planet Earth; The Muppet Movie; The Shah of Iran (doc-narr); The Secret of Nikola Tesla. (*Special Oscar*-1970-for "superlative artistry and versatility in the creation of motion pictures.")

TV inc: The Man Who Came to Dinner; Shogun (narr). (*Grammy*-spoken word-1976, 1979).

WELLMAN, William Jr: Act. b. LA, Jan 20, 1937. e. Duke U, UCLA. Films inc: Darby's Rangers; Sayonara; The Horse Soldiers; Pork Chop Hill; Dondi; How the West Was Won; The Errand Boy; Rebel in the Ring; The Disorderly Orderly; A Swinging Summer; Winter A-Go-Go; The Happiest Millionaire; Which Way to the Front; The World Within; Billy Jack Goes to Washington; MacArthur; Private Files of J. Edgar Hoover.

TV inc: U.F.O.; Fire in the Sky; Midway; The Eleanor and Lou Gehrig Story; Logan's Run; Hunter.

WELLS, Frank G: Exec. b. Mar 4, 1932. e. Pomona College; Rhodes Scholar at Oxford (Jurisprudence); Stanford Law School. Joined Hollywood law firm of Gang, Tyre & Brown, 1959; became partner three years later; 1969, vp WestCoast, WB; 1972, P; 1975 became chmn, CEO when Ted Ashley stepped out; reverted to presidency year later with Ashley's return; Nov 1980, co-chmn & CEO.

WELLS, George: Wri. b. 1909. Films inc: Take Me Out to the Ball Game; Three Little Words; Everything I Have is Yours (& prod); Jupiter's Darling (prod); Designing Woman (*Oscar*-sp-1957); Ask Any Girl; The Honeymoon Machine; The Horizontal Lieutenant; Penelope; The Impossible Years.

WELLS, Kitty (Muriel Deason): Singer-Sngwri. b. Nashville, TN, Aug 20, 1919. Country mus recording artist. Performed with Grand Ole Opry.

WENDERS, Wim: Dir. b. Dusseldorf, Germany, 1945. Films inc: Summer in the City; Di Angst Des Tomanns Beim Elfmeter; The Scarlet Letter; Aus Der Familie Der Panzerechsen; Falsche Bewegung; Alice in the Cities; The Goalie's Anxiety at the Penalty Kick; Kings of the Road; In the Course of Time; The American Friend; Long Shot (act); Radio On; Lightning Over Water (Nick's Movie) (& act).

WENDKOS, Paul: Dir. b. 1922. Films inc: The Burglar; Tarawa Beachhead; Gidget; Face of a Fugitive; Because They're Young; Angel Baby; Gidget Goes to Rome; Miles to Terror; Guns of the Magnificent Seven; Cannon for Cordova; The Mephisto Waltz; Special Delivery.

TV inc: Haunts of the Very Rich; Honor Thy Father; Betrayal; The Legend of Lizzie Borden; A Woman Called Moses; The Ordeal of Patty Hearst; Act of Violence; The Ordeal of Doctor Mudd.

WERBLIN, David (Sonny): Exec. b. Brooklyn, Mar 17, 1910. Joined MCA in 1932 as band mgr, later agent; P MCA-TV 1951, regarded as father of package deals which brought name stars to tv; in 1963 bought NY Titans Football Team, re-named it the Jets; resigned MCA Jan 1, 1965 to devote full-time to sports; sold Jets 1968 formed (with Johnny Carson) Raritan Enterprises with real estate, showbiz holdings and prod, for a period, the Tonight Show starring Carson; returned to sports 1971 as Chairman NJ Sports and Exposition Authority; resigned Dec, 1977, became P, CEO of Madison Square Garden.

WERNER, Oskar: Act-Dir-Prod. b. Vienna, Nov 13, 1922. Began as apprentice with Burgtheater, Vienna, later with Josefstadt Theater, Volkstheater; formed own theatre company 1959; dir at Salzburg Festival. Films inc: Angel With the Trumpet; Eroica; A Wonder of Our Days; Decision Before Dawn; The Last Act; Lola Montes; One Named Judas (& dir); Jules and Jim; Ship of Fools; The Spy Who Came in from The Cold; Fahrenheit 451; Interlude; Shoes of the Fisherman; Voyage of the Damned.

WERNER, Peter: Prod. b. NYC, Jan 17, 1947. e. Dartmouth Coll, BA. Films inc: In the Region of Ice (Oscar-ss-1976).
TV inc: Battered; Barnburning; Learning in Focus; Aunt Mary (dir).

WERNER, Theo M: Prod-Dir. b. Munich, May 15, 1926. M-dir Neue Regina Film.

WERRIS, Snag: Wri-Act. b. NYC, Nov 19, 1915. e. CCNY. In vaudeville, burlesque; then started writing material for comedians, inc: Bert Wheeler, Bert Lahr, Alan Young, Vilma & Buddy Ebsen, Phil Silvers. In radio wrote for: Dinah Shore, Frank Sinatra, Bing Crosby, Colonel Stoopnagle, Ben Bernie, Rudy Vallee, Abbott & Costello. In TV for: Fred Allen, Ritz Bros., Ben Blue, Judy Canova, Perry Como, Martin & Lewis, Ken Murray, Jack Carter, Jerry Lester, Eddie Albert, Ed Wynn, Jackie Gleason.

WERTMULLER, Lina: Dir. b. Rome, Aug 14, 1928. Worked as an Asst Dir in legitimate theatre; wrote plays and musicals. Dir 1st feature film, 1963, The Lizards. Films inc: This Time Lets's Talk About Men; Rita the Mosquito; The Seduction of Mimi; Love and Anarchy; All Screwed Up; Swept Away; Seven Beauties (& sp); The End of the World in Our Usual Bed in a Nightful of Rain (& sp); Revenge (& sp).

WESKER, Arnold: Plywri. b. London, England, May 24, 1932. Plays inc: Chicken Soup With Barley; Roots; The Kitchen; I'm Talking About Jerusalem; Chips With Everything; Their Very Own and Golden City; The Four Seasons; The Friends; The Old Ones; The Merchant.
TV inc: Menace.
Films inc: The Kitchen.

WESNES, Hans: Prod-Dist. b. Berlin, Apr 12, 1950. Chmn of Luxmeta Filmveleih Dist Co. Films inc: Youth's Blues; Belcanto.

WEST, Adam (William Anderson) b. 1929. Films inc: The Young Philadelphians; Robinson Crusoe on Mars; Mara of the Wilderness; Batman; The Girl Who Knew Too Much; Marriage of a Young Stockbroker; The Specialist; Partisans; Hell River; Hooper.
TV inc: The Detectives; Batman; For the Love of It.

WEST, Dottie: Singer-Sngwri. b. McMinnville, TN, Oct 11, 1932. e. TN Technological U. Country mus recording artist. Performed on Grand Ole Opry. Films inc: Second Fiddle to a Steel Guitar; There's a Still on the Hill. (Grammy-C&W voc-1964).

WEST, Mae: Act-Wri. b. Brooklyn, NY, Aug 17, 1892. On stage as child; in vaude; with stock companies. Bway inc: A La Broadway; Vera Violetta; A Winsome Widow; Demitasse Revue. Beginning with Sex in 1926 thereafter only appeared on Bway in her own plays inc: The Wicked Age; The Drag; Diamond Lil; Pleasure Man; The Constant Sinner; I'm No Angel; Catherine Was Great; Sextet.
Films inc: Night After Night; She Done Him Wrong; I'm No Angel; Going to Town; Belle of the Nineties; Klondike Annie; Go West Young Man; Every Day's a Holiday; My Little Chickadee; The Heat's On; Myra Breckenridge; Sextette.
(Died Nov. 22, 1980).

WESTCOTT, Helen (Myrthas Helen Hickman): Act. b. LA, 1929. Former child actress. Films inc: A Midsummer Night's Dream; The New Adventures of Don Juan; The Gunfighter; With a Song in My Heart; The Charge at Feather River; Hot Blood; The Last Hurrah; I Love My Wife.

WESTIN, Av (Avram Robert Westin): b. NYC, Jul 29, 1929. e. NYU, BA; Columbia U, MA. Started 1950 as wri, CBS News; 1951, reporter CBS; 1953 news edtr CBS; 1955, dir; 1958, prod-dir; 1961 CBS news prod in Europe; 1965 exec prod CBS News; 1967 exec prod-dir Columbia Broadcast Lab; 1968 dir Public Broadcast Lab; 1969, exec prod ABC news; 1973vp news docs; 1977 vp news; 1979 vp pgm dvlpt, exec prod World News Tonight.
TV inc: The Ruble War; The Arab Tide; Jordan--Key to the Middle East; Moonshot; Where They Stand--Part 2; Hawaii--The 50th State; The Population Explosion (Emmy-wri-1960); Hungary--Five Years Later; Germany--Red Spy Target; Pres. Nixon's China Trip (Emmy-exec prod-1972); Heros and Heroin; The National Citizen Test; We Will Freeze in the Dark.

WESTON, Jack: Act. b. 1915. Films inc: Stage Struck; Please Don't Eat the Daisies; All in a Night's Work; The Honeymoon Machine; The Incredible Mr Limpet; Mirage; The Cincinnati Kid; The Thomas Crown Affair; The April Fools; Cactus Flower; A New Leaf; Fuzz; Marco; Gator; The Ritz; Cuba; Can't Stop the Music.
TV inc: Rod Browning of the Rocket Rangers; numerous segs.
Bway inc: Season in the Sun; South Pacific; Crazy October; The Ritz; California Suite; Cheaters; Break A Leg.

WESTON, Jay: Prod. b. NYC, Mar 9, 1929. e. NYU, BA. Former publicist. In 1967, prod exec, Palomar-ABC Pictures; p Jay Weston Productions Inc.
Films inc: For Love of Ivy; Lady Sings the Blues; W.C. Fields and Me; Night of the Juggler.
Thea inc: Does a Tiger Wear a Necktie? (co-prod.).

WESTON, Paul (nee Wetstein): Mus-Comp. b. Springfield, MA, Mar 12, 1912. e. Dartmouth, BA; Columbia. H of Jo Stafford. Arr for Rudy Vallee; Tommy Dorsey; Bob Crosby; arr-cond for top girl singers inc Connee Boswell, Lee Wiley; Ella Fitzgerald; Doris Day; Dinah Shore; Kate Smith; Sarah Vaughan; Jo Stafford; A&R dir Capitol Records when it was organized 1943; A&R dir Columbia 1950; retd to Capitol 1958; regarded as creator of mood music albums; later, with Stafford, created Jonathan and Darlene Edwards recordings (Grammy-comedy-1960).
TV inc: The Chevy Show; The Danny Kaye Show; Jim Nabors Show.
Comps inc: I Should Care; Day By Day; Shrimp Boats; Mr. Postman; No Other Love; Autumn in Rome; Cresent City Suite; Mass for Three Voices; Memories of Ireland.

WEXLER, Haskell: Cin. b. Chicago, 1926. Films inc: Allende (doc); Undergound (doc); The Best Man; Angel Baby; Stakeout on Dope Street; The Savage Eye; Who's Afraid of Virginia Woolf? (Oscar-1966); In the Heat of the Night; The Thomas Crown Affair; American Graffiti; One Flew Over the Cuckoo's Nest; Bound for Glory (Oscar-1976); Coming Home; No Nukes; Second Hand Hearts.

WEXLER, Peter: Dsgn. b. NYC, Oct 31, 1936. e. U of MI, Yale U. NY debut as dsgn decor, costumes, light of the NY Shakespeare Festival prodn of Antony and Cleopatra, 1959. Thea inc: The Big Knife; Brecht on Brecht; The Curate's Play; Portrait of the Artist as a Young Man; The Taming of the Shrew; Abe Lincoln in Illinois; On a Clear Day You Can See Forever (tour); The Happy Time; Uncle Vanya; The Trial of the Catonsville Nine; The Trial of A Lincoln; The Web and the Rock.
Films inc: Andy; Watch the Birdie; The Trial of the Catonsville Nine.

WEXLER, Yale: Prod-Act. b. Chicago, Feb 6, 1930. e. Carnegie Tech, BFA. B of Haskell Wexler. Thea inc: Tea and Sympathy; The Best House in Naples; Once Over Lightly (coprod); A Sound of Hunting. TV inc: You Are There; Stakeout; Time Limt.

WHEATLEY, Glenn: Mus publ. b. Nambour, Australia, Jan 23, 1948. Dir Tumbleweed Mus Pty Ltd & Antipodes Mus P/L; The Little River Band.

WHEDON, Peggy (Margaret Brunssen): TV prod. b. NYC. e. U Rochester, BA; Hunter College. Prod ABC Issues and Answers since 1960.

WHEELER, Hugh: Wri. b. London, 1912. e. London U. Plays inc: Big Fish, Little Fish; Look, We'e Come Through; We Have Always Lived in the Castle; A Little Night Music *(Tony-*book-1973); Candide *(Tony-*book-1974); Love for Love; Sweeney Todd *(Tony-*book-1979).

Films inc: Something for Everyone; Travels with My Aunt; Cabaret; Nijinsky.

TV inc: The Snoop Sisters.

WHELCHEL, Lisa: Act. b. Fort Worth, TX, May 29, 1963. Professional debut as Mousketeer on New Mickey Mouse Club. TV inc: The Healer; The Facts of Life.

Films inc: The Magician of Lublin; The Double McGuffin.

WHERRETT, Richard: Thea Dir. b. Sydney, Australia, Dec 10, 1940. e. U of Sydney, BA. Dir: Lincoln Theatre Royal; Manchester Library Theatre; ADA; LAMDA, 1968-70; asso dir: Old Tote Theatre, 1970-72; co-artistic dir Nimrod Theatre, 1974-78.

WHITAKER, Jack: Sportscaster. b. Philadelphia, May 18, 1924. Started in radio 1947. In 1961 took over as host of CBS Sports Spectacular. Also host announcer on horse-racing programs and golf tournaments.

WHITE, Betty: Act. b. Oak Park, IL, Jan 17, 1924. W of Allen Ludden. Began on radio in Blondie; The Great Gildersleeve; This is Your FBI. Moved into TV with live local show, LA.

TV inc: Life With Elisabeth *(Emmy-*female personality-1953); Tonight Show; Mary Tyler Moore Show *(Emmys-*supp-1975, 1976); The Pet Set; annual Rose Parade; Macy's Thanksgiving Parade; The Betty White Show; The Best Place to Be; The Gossip Columnist.

WHITE, Joan: Act-Prod-Dir. b. ALexandria, Egypt, Dec 3, 1909. e. RADA. London stage debut, 1931, in Betrayal. Thea inc: The Black Eye: The Luck of the Devil; Junior Miss; Ten Shilling Doll; The Romantic Young Lady; A London Actress; The Happiest Days of Your Life; The Cocktail Party; The School for Scandal; Love's Labours Lost.

TV inc: The Citadel; Vanity Fair; The Invincible Mr Disraeli.

WHITE, Jules J: Prod-Dir. b. Budapest, Hungary, Sep 17, 1900. Started as child actor, then edtr, cin. Prod-dir-cowri of more than 700 shorts while under contract MGM 1922-1933; Columbia 1933-1959. Prod approx 200 Three Stooges shorts and two-reel series starring Billie Burke; Buster Keaton; Harry Langdon; Bert Wheeler; Leon Errol; Chester Conklin; Pete Smith; co-dir Keaton feature Sidewalks of New York; dir Three Stooges feature Stop Look and Laugh.

TV inc: Oh, Those Bells (co-prod).

WHITE, Lawrence R (Larry): Prod. b. 1926. e. Syracuse, U. Started with Dumont TV in 1948 as prod-dir; 1951 Benton & Bowles dir pgmg; 1959 vp daytime pgmg CBS-TV; 1963 dir pgm dvlpt; 1965 vp daytime pgms NBC-TV; 1969 vp pgms east coast; 1972 vp pgms; 1972 into ind prodn for Col Pictures-TV; 1976 vp Col Pictures-TV; 1978, Pres; 1980 resd to return to ind prod.

WHITE, Maurice: Singer-Mus. b. Chicago, Dec 19, 1941. Founder, lead voc, percussionist Earth, Wind and Fire. See group listing.

(Grammy-(in addition to group awards)-arr accomp voc-1978).

WHITE, Michael Simon: Prod. b. Scotland, Jan 16, 1936. e. Sorbonne. Thea inc: The Connection; The Secret of the World; The Scatterin'; Jungle of the Cities; The Voices of Shem; Cambridge Circus; Saint's Day; Saturday Night and Sunday Morning; Hogan's Goat; Sleuth *(Tony-*1971); A Doll's House; The Championship Season; Too True to be Good; The Chairman; Carte Blanche; Annie; Censored Scenes from King Kong.

Films inc: Moviemakers; Monty Python and the Holy Grail; The Rocky Horror Picture Show.

WHITE, Miles: Cos Dsgn. b. Oakland, CA, Jul 27, 1914. Thea inc: Right This Way; Best Foot Forward; The Pirate; Ziegfeld Follies; Oklahoma!; Bloomer Girl: Carousel; The Duchess of Malfi; High Button Shoes; Gentlemen Prefer Blondes; Bless You All *(Tony-*1951); Pal Joey; Hazel Flagg *(Tony-*1953); The Girl in Pink Tights; Strip for Action; Oh Captain; Bye, Bye Birdie; The Unsinkable Molly Brown; Song of Norway; A Quarter for the Ladies Room; Sleeping Beauty (American Ballet Theatre).

Films inc: Up in Arms; The Kid from Brooklyn; The Greatest Show on Earth; There's No Business Like Show Business; Around the World in 80 Days.

WHITE, Onna: Chor. b. Nova Scotia, Canada. Films inc: The Music Man; Bye Bye Birdie; Oliver *(Special Oscar-*1968); 1776; The Great Waltz; Mame; Pete's Dragon.

Bway inc: Carmen Jones; The Music Man; Take Me Along; Irma La Douce; Gantry; Girls; Gigi; Goodtime Charley; I Love My Wife; Working.

WHITE, Peter: Act. e. Northwestern U; Yale Drama School. Bway inc: The Boys in the Band; P.S. Your Cat is Dead. Films inc: The Boys in the Band. TV inc: Another World; Secret Storm; The Nurses; Love Is A Many Splendored Thing; All My Children.

WHITE, Theodore H: Wri. b. Boston, MA, May 6, 1915. e. Harvard, AB. China Bureau Time Mag 1939-1945; edtr New Republic Magazine; author of books The Making of the President.

TV inc: The Making of the President 1960 *(Emmy-*1964); China--The Roots of Madness *(Emmy-*1977).

WHITEHEAD, Robert: Prod. b. Montreal, Mar 3, 1916. e. Trinity Coll. Thea inc: Medea; Crime and Punishment; Desire Under the Elms; Mrs McThing; Golden Boy; Four Saints in Three Acts; The Time of the Cuckoo; The Remarkable Mr Pennypacker; The Confidential Clerk; Bus Stop; Separate Tables; The Waltz of the Toreadors; A Hole in the Head; Orpheus Descending; The Visit; A Touch of the Poet; A Man for All Seasons *(Tony-*1962); The Changeling; The Prime of Miss Jean Brodie; Sheep on the Runway; The Creation of the World and Other Business; A Matter of Gravity; 1600 Pennsylvania Avenue; Bedroom Farce; Betrayal; Lunch Hour.

TV inc: The Skin of Our Teeth.

WHITELAW, Arthur: Prod. Thea inc: Best Foot Forward; Cabin in the Sky; A Woman and the Blues; You're a Good Man, Charlie Brown; Butterflies Are Free; Minnie's Boys; 70, Girls, 70; Children! Children!; Thoughts; Snoopy!!! (& dir).

WHITELAW, Billie: Act. b. Coventry, Eng, Jun 6, 1932. London debut, 1956, Hotel Paradiso. On screen from 1955 in No Love for Johnnie; Mr. Topaze; Hell Is a City; Payroll; Charlie Bubbles; The Adding Machine; Twisted Nerve; Start the Revolution; Without Me; Leo the Last; Eagle in a Cage; Gumshoe; Frenzy; Nightwatch; The Omen; Leopard in the Snow; The Water Babies.

Thea inc: Progress to the Park; A Touch of the Poet; Othello; Trelawney of the Wells; After Haggerty; Not I; Alphabetical Order; Footfalls; The Greeks; Happy Days.

TV inc: No Trains to Lime Street; Lady of the Camelias; Resurrection; The Pity of it All; You and Me; A World of Time; Dr. Jekyll and Mr. Hyde; Poet Game Wessex Tales; The Fifty Pound Note.

WHITLOCK, Albert: Special effects. b. London, 1915. Started in British film industry, 1929. Painted signs, scenery, ran errands. One of 1st assignments at age 19 was painting all the signs for Alfred Hitchcock's The 39 Steps. Came to US in 1954. Worked for Walt Disney Studios; designed the titles for 20,000 Leagues Under the Sea. Left Disney 1961 to freelance.

Films inc: The Birds; Marnie; Ship of Fools; Torn Curtain; Tobruk; Diamonds Are Forever; Frenzy; Earthquake *(Oscar-*1974); The Hindenburg *(Oscar-*1975); Bound for Glory; Airport '77; The Car; MacArthur; The Last Remake of Beau Geste; High Anxiety.

WHITMAN, Stuart: Act. b. San Francisco, Feb 1, 1936. Films inc: When Worlds Collide; The Day the Earth Stood Still; China Doll; Johnny Trouble; Hell Bound; No Sleep 'Till Dawn; Ten North Frederick; Three Thousand Hills; The Deck Ran Red; The Sound and the Fury; The Story of Ruth; Murder, Inc.; Francis of Assisi; The Fiercest Heart; The Mark; The Comancheros; Reprieve; The Day and the Hour; Signpost to Murder; Rio Conchos; Last Escape; Last Generation; Night of the Lepus; Crazy Mama; Call Him Shatter; Las Vegas Lady; Strange Shadows in an Empty Room; The White Buffalo; Maniac; Woman From the Torrid Land; Run for the Roses; Guyana-Cult of the Damned; Cuba Crossing.

TV inc: The Crowd Pleaser; Highway Patrol; Dr. Christian; Hangman's Noose; Women in White; The Last Convertible; The Seekers.

WHITMORE, James: Act. b. White Plains, NY, Oct 1, 1921. e. Yale U. Bway debut 1947 Command Decision. On screen from 1949. Films inc: The Undercover Man; The Asphalt Jungle; Kiss Me, Kate; Across the Wide Missouri; Battle Cry; The McConnell Story; Oklahoma; Planet of the Apes; Madigan; Give 'Em Hell, Harry; The Split; The Harrad Experiment; Bully; The First Deadly Sin.

TV inc: The Law and Mr. Jones; Give 'Em Hell, Harry; The Word; The Golden Honeymoon; Mark, I Love You.

Thea inc: Give 'Em Hell, Harry; Will Rogers, USA. *(Special Tony-1948).*

WHITTINGHILL, Dick: Act. b. Helena, MT, Mar 5, 1913. e. U of MT. Founded the Pied Pipers, singing group featured with Tommy Dorsey Band, in 1936. Spent more than 25 years as deejay with radio KMPC, Los Angeles. Appeared in more than 59 films, also in numerous TV segs. Retired from KMPC in 1979.

WICKES, Mary (Mary Isabelle Wickenhauser): Act. b. St Louis, Jun 13. e. WA U, BA. Films inc: The Man Who Came to Dinner; Now Voyager; My Kingdom for a Cook; Higher and Higher; Anna Lucasta; The Petty Girl; On Moonlight Bay; The Story of Will Rogers; By the Light of the Silvery Moon; White Christmas; Good Morning, Miss Dove; Don't Go Near the Water; The Music Man; Fate Is the Hunter; How to Murder Your Wife; The Trouble with Angela; Where Angels Go, Trouble Follows; Snowball Express; Touched By Love.

TV inc: Doc; Dennis the Menace; Mary Poppins; Make Room for Daddy; Julia; The Halls of Ivy; Annette; Willa.

Thea inc: The Farmer Takes a Wife; Stage Door; The Cat and the Canary; The Constant Nymph; The Good Fairy; You Can't Take It With You; The Man Who Came to Dinner; Wonderful Town; The Great Sebastian; Oklahoma! (rev).

WICKI, Bernhard: Act-Dir. b. St Polten, Switzerland, Oct 18, 1919. e. Academy of Fine Arts, Vienna. Films inc: (act) The Last Bridge; Kinder, Mutter und ein General; Jackboot Mutiny; The Face of the Cat; La Notte; Despair; (dir) The Bridge; The Miracle of Malachias; The Longest Day; The Visit; Morituri; The False Weight; The Career of Mr Karpf; The Left Handed Woman; The Conquest of the Citadel.

WIDENER, Don: Wri-Prod. b. Holdenville, OK, Mar 13, 1930. e. Compton Coll. TV inc: Slow Guillotine (doc); A Sea of Trouble (doc); Timetable for Disaster (doc); Power and the People (doc); Plutonium; Element of Risk.

WIDERBERG, Bo: Dir-Wri. b. Sweden, 1930. Films inc: Raven's End; Karleck; Thirty Times Your Money; Elvira Madigan; Adalen 31; The Ballad of Joe Hill; The Man on the Roof; Victoria.

WIDMARK, Richard: Act. b. Sunrise, MI, Dec 26, 1914. e. Lake Forest U. Started on radio. Bway debut Kiss and Tell. Screen debut, 1947, Kiss of Death.

Films inc: Street With No Name; Slattery's Hurricane; Yellow Sky; Halls of Montezuma; Panic in the Streets; Destination Gobi; Warlock; The Long Ships; Madigan; The Alamo; How the West Was Won; Broken Lance; Judgement at Nuremberg; Murder on the Orient Express; To The Devil A Daughter; The Sellout; Twilight's Last Gleaming; The Domino Principle; Roller Coaster; Coma; The Swarm; Bear Island.

TV inc: Madigan; Mr. Horn; All God's Children.

WIENER, Jack: Prod. b. Paris, Jun 8, 1926. Started as U.S. field publicist with MGM; 1956 to Paris as continental pub mgr Col; 1966 vp Col Int'l; 1968 continental prodn exec; 1970 vp Col Pictures Corp; 1970 became ind prod. Films inc: Vampire; The Eagle Has Landed; Escape To Athena.

WIESEN, Bernard: Prod-Dir. b. NYC, Oct 6, 1922. e. CCNY, BBA. Films inc: (asst dir) The King and I; The Left Hand of God; The Rains of Ranchipur; To Catch a Thief; The Trouble with Harry; (prod & dir); Fear No More. TV inc: Executive Suite; The Jimmy Stewart Show; Julia; Valentine's Day; Three on an Island; Cap'n Ahab; Sally and Sam. Plays inc: (co-prod) Tribute to the Lunts; First Monday in October. (Dir): Under the Yum Yum Tree; Toys in the Attic; Trojan Woman; Once Upon a Christmas.

WILBUR, Richard: Lyr-Poet. b. NYC, Mar 1, 1921. e. Amherst Coll, Harvard U. Wrote lyrics for Leonard Bernstein's operetta Candide. Thea inc: translations of most of Moliere's plays. Books of poetry inc: Things of This World *(Pulitzer Prize-1956).*

WILCOX, Larry: Act. b. San Diego, CA, Aug 8.

TV inc: Police Story; Death Stalk; Sorority Kill; CHiPs; The Raid on Coffeyville; The Last Ride of the Dalton Gang; The Love Tapes.

WILCOXON, Henry: Act-Prod. b. British West Indies, Sep 8, 1905. On London stage from 1925. Films inc: The Perfect Lady; The Flying Squad; Cleopatra; The Crusades; The Last of the Mohicans; Mrs Miniver; Samson and Delilah; Scaramouche; The Greatest Show on Earth; The Ten Commandments (& coprod); The Buccaneer (& prod); The Private Navy of Sergeant O'Farrell; Man in the Wilderness; Against a Crooked Sky; Pony Express Rider; F.I.S.T.; The Man with Bogart's Face; Caddyshack.

TV inc: When Every Day was the 4th of July; Married; The Two Worlds of Jennie Logan.

WILD, Jack: Act. b. England, 1952. Films inc: Oliver!; Pufnstuf; Melody; Flight of the Doves; The Pied Piper; The Fourteen.

TV inc: Pufnstuf; Our Mutual Friend; The Government Inspector.

WILDE, Cornel: Act-Prod-Dir-Wri. b. NYC, Oct 13, 1915. e. CCNY, Columbia College of Physicians. Films inc: Lady with Red Hair; High Sierra; The Perfect Snob; Wintertime; A Song to Remember; A Thousand and One Nights; The Bandit of Sherwood Forest; The Homestretch; Centennial Summer; Forever Amber; Two Flags West; The Greatest Show on Earth; Walls of Jericho; Woman's World; Storm Fear (& prod-dir); The Devil's Hairpin (& prod-dir-co-wri); The Naked Prey (& prod-dir); Beach Red (& prod-dir, co-wri sp); No Blade of Grass (prod-dir-sp); Shark's Treasure (& prod-dir-sp); The Norsemen; The Fifth Musketeer.

TV inc: Gargoyles.

WILDER, Alec: Comp. b. Rochester, NY, Feb 16, 1907. e. Eastman School of Music. Wrote songs for Mildred Bailey, Bing Crosby, Ethel Waters, Frank Sinatra; later turned to writing chamber music; hosted Public radio program honoring great America composers.

Songs inc: It's So Peaceful in the Country; A Child is Born; Soft as Spring; I'll Be Around; Who Can I Turn To?; While We're Young; Where Do You Go; Where Is The One?; I See It Now.

(Died Dec 24, 1980).

WILDER, Billy: Prod-Dir-Wri. b. Austria, Jun 22, 1906. Worked as reporter, Vienna, Berlin; then turned to screen writing. To Hollywood, 1934. Films inc: Bluebeard's Eighth Wife; Ninotchka; Arise My Love; Hold Back the Dawn; The Major and the Minor; Five Graves to Cairo; Double Indemnity; The Emperor Waltz; A Foreign Affair; Lost Weekend *(2 Oscars-sp & dir-1945);* Sunset Boulevard *(Oscar-story and sp-1950);* The Big Carnival; Stalag 17; Sabrina; Love in the Afternoon; Some Like It Hot; The Apartment *(3 Oscars-sp-dir-prod-1960);* One, Two, Three; Irma La Douce; Seven Year Itch; Spirit of St. Louis; Witness for the Prosecution; The Fortune Cookie; The Private Lives of Sherlock Holmes; Avanti; The Front Page; Fedora; Portrait of a 60% Perfect Man (doc on Wilder).

WILDER, Clinton: Prod. b. Irvine, PA, Jul 7, 1920. e. Princeton U, BA. Stage mgr for Arthur Laurents' Heartsong 1947; A Streetcar Named Desire; since then prod or co-prod following plays: Regina; The Tender Trap; Six Characters in Search of an Author; A Visit to a Small Planet; The World of Suzie Wong; The American Dream; Bartleby; The Death of Bessie Smith; Gallows Humor; Happy Days; Who's Afraid of Virginia Woolf? *(Tony*-1963); The American Dream; The Zoo Story; The Giant's Dance; Hunting the Jingo Bird; The Long Christmas Dinner; The Butter and Egg Man; Match Play; A Party for Divorce; A Delicate Balance; The Party on Greenwich Avenue; Johnny No Trump; How Much, How Much?; The Enclave; Seascape.

WILDER, Gene (Jerry Silberman): Act. b. Milwaukee, Jun 11, 1939. e. U of IA. Thea inc: One Flew Over the Cuckoo's Nest; The Complaisant Lover; The White House; Luv; Mother Courage.
    Films inc: Bonnie and Clyde; The Producers; Start the Revolution Without Me; Quackser Fortune Has an Uncle in the Bronx; Willie Wonka and the Chocolate Factory; Everything You Always Wanted to Know About Sex; Blazing Saddles; Rhinoceros; Young Frankenstein; The Little Prince; Adventures of Sherlock Holmes Smarter Brother (& sp, dir); Silver Streak; The World's Greatest Lover (& sp, dir); The Frisco Kid; Stir Crazy; Sunday Lovers.

WILDER, John (Keith Magaurn): Prod. b. Tacoma, WA, 1936. e. UCLA. Child actor on radio; story ed Branded; wrote 134 episodes Peyton Place before becoming prod. TV inc: Paris 7-000; Streets of San Francisco; Most Wanted; Law of the Land; The City (& wri); Quinn Martin's Tales of the Unexpected; Centennial.

WILDER, Yvonne: Act. b. NYC, Sep 20. e. RADA. Films inc: West Side Story; Silent Movie; High Anxiety; Bloodbrothers; Seems Like Old Times.
    TV inc: Operation Petticoat.
    Thea inc: The Princess and the Pea; The Body Beautiful; West Side Story.

WILDING, Michael: Act. b. Westcliff, Essex, Eng, Jul 23, 1912. London stage debut 1933, Chase the Ace. On screen from 1935. Films inc: Wedding Group; Convoy; In Which We Serve; An Ideal Husband; Under Capricorn; The Law and the Lady; Maytime in Mayfair; The Egyptian; The Glass Slipper; The World of Suzie Wong; The Naked Edge; Waterloo; The Sweet Ride; Lady Caroline Lamb.
    Thea inc: Victoria Regina; Nude with Violin; The Geese Are Getting Fat; Mary Mary.
    (Died July 7, 1979).

WILKOF, Lee: Act. b. Canton, OH, Jun 25. e. Temple U, U of Cincinnati. TV inc: W.E.B.; The Girl Who Saved Our America.
    Thea inc: Diary of a Scoundrel; The Last Straw; The Dybbuk.

WILLENS, Rita Jacobs: Exec. b. Chicago, Jun 13, 1927. Co-founder WFMT, Chicago; prod Gamut Productions; Shows inc: Gamut-The Great Ideas of Man; Follies of 1952; Raisins with Almonds.

WILLIAM, David (nee Williams): Act-Dir. b. London, Jun 24, 1926. e. Oxford. Thea inc: Hamlet; King John; A Man for All Seasons; Peer Gynt; Naked (dir); Queen B (dir); The Canker and the Rose (dir); Saint's Day; Studies of the Nude (dir); What the Butler Saw (dir); The Way of the World (dir); Robin Red Breast; Sentenced to Life (dir).
    TV inc: An Age of Kings; The Cruel Neccessity; Troubleshooters.

WILLIAMS, Andy: Act. b. Wall Lake, IA, 1930. Recording artist. Niteries. Films inc: Something in the Wind (as part of the singing Williams Brothers); I'd Rather Be Rich.
    TV inc: Tonight Show (3 years); Andy Williams In Music from Shubert Alley; The Andy Williams Show *(Emmy*-1966); The Andy Williams Christmas Show; The Andy Williams Special.

WILLIAMS, Anson: Act. b. LA, Sep 25. In summer stock; later in niteries as singer. Films inc: Money Tree; Heed the Call.
    TV inc: Anson Williams at Sea World; The Paul Lynde Show; Happy Days; Greatest Heroes of the Bible; Skyward (prod).

WILLIAMS, Billy Dee: Act. b. NYC, Apr 6, 1937. Acting debut age 7, The Firebrand. Adult Broadway debut, The Cool World. Films inc: The Last Angry Man; Lady Sings The Blues; Mahogany; The Bingo Long Traveling All-Stars; Scott Joplin; The Empire Strikes Back.
    TV inc: Brian's Song; The Glass House; Mission Impossible; Mod Squad; Christmas Lilies of the Field; The Hostage Tower; Children of Divorce.
    Thea inc: A Taste of Honey; Hallelujah, Baby.

WILLIAMS, Cara (Bernice Kamiat): Act. b. NYC, 1925. e. Hollywood Professional School. Film inc: The Happy Land; Don Juan Quilligan; Boomerang; Something for the Boys; Meet Me In Las Vegas; Sitting Pretty; Never Steal Anything Small; The Girl Next Door; The Defiant Ones; The Man From the Diner's Club; The White Buffalo; Doctor's Wives.
    TV inc: Pete and Gladys; The Cara Williams Shows.

WILLIAMS, Cindy: Act. b. Van Nuys, CA, Aug 22, 1948. Beware the Blob; Drive, He Said; American Graffiti; Travels with My Aunt; The Conversation; More American Graffiti.
    TV inc: Room 222; Nanny and the Professor; Suddenly, Love; Donny and Marie Christmas Special.

WILLIAMS, Elmo: Film Edtr-Prod. b. Oklahoma City, OK, Apr 30, 1915. Worked as film edtr British & Dominion Studios; RKO. VP wldwde prodn Fox 1971; P Ibex films 1974.
    Films inc: High Noon *(Oscar*-edit-1952); The Tall Texan (& dir); The Cowboy (& prod-dir); 20,000 Leagues Under The Sea; Apache Kid (dir); The Vikings; The Big Gamble. (Asso prod) The Longest Day. (Prod) Tora! Tora! Tora!; Sidewinder One; Caravans. (Exec prod) Those Magnificent Men in Their Flying Machines; The Blue Max; Zorba the Greek.

WILLIAMS, Emlyn: Wri-Dir-Act. b. Mostyn, Flintshire, Wales, Nov 26, 1905. e. Oxford. On stage since 1927. Thea inc: (act) And So to Bed; The Pocket-Money Husband; Glamour; Night Must Fall; He Was Born Gay; Bleak House; A Boy Growing Up; The Deputy; A Month In the Country. Plays inc: Full Moon; The Late Christopher Bean; Vessels Departing; The Corn Is Green; The Wind of Heaven; Spring 1600; Trespass; Accolade; Beth; Dylan Thomas Growing Up. Dir many of his own plays.
    Films inc: (act) The Case of the Frightened Lady; Men of Tomorrow; Friday the Thirteenth; Sally Bishop; Broken Blossoms; The Citadel; The Stars Look Down; Major Barbara; Hatter's Castle; The Last Days of Dolwyn (& sp-dir); Three Husbands; Ivanhoe; The Deep Blue Sea; I Accuse; Beyond This Place; The L-Shaped Room; Eye of the Devil; The Walking Stick; David Copperfield.

WILLIAMS, Esther: Act. b. LA, Aug 8, 1923. e. USC. Professional swimmer, appeared in Aquacade, SF World's Fair; professional model before act. Screen debut 1942 Andy Hardy Steps Out. Films inc: A Guy Named Joe; Bathing Beauty; The Thrill of A Romance; This Time for Keeps; Ziegfeld Follies; Easy to Wed; Fiesta; Hoodlum Saint; On an Island With You; Neptune's Daughter; Pagan Love Song; Duchess of Idaho; Texas Carnival; Skirts, Ahoy!; Million Dollar Mermaid; Dangerous When Wet; Easy to Love; Jupiter's Darling; The Big Show.

WILLIAMS, John: Act. b. Chalfont St Giles, Bucks, Eng, Apr 15, 1903. e. Lansing Coll. Films inc: Next of Kin; A Woman's Vengeance; Dial M for Murder; Sabrina Fair; To Catch a Thief; The Solid Gold Cadillac; Island in the Sun; Witness for the Prosecution; Visit to a Small Planet; The Secret War of Harry Frigg; A Flea in Her Ear; Coming Home; Hot Lead and Cold Feet; The Swarm.
    TV inc: The Hound of the Baskervilles.
    Thea inc: Numerous perf dating back to 1916; recent perfs inc: The Velvet Glove; Venus Observed; Dial M for Murder *(Tony*-supp-1953); The Dark Is Light Enough; The Chinese Prime Minster; Hay Fever.

WILLIAMS, John T: Comp. b. NYC, Feb 8, 1932. e. UCLA, Juilliard. Succeeded late Arthur Fiedler as conductor of Boston Pops, Jan 1980. Film scores inc: I Passed for White; Diamond Head; Gidget Goes to Rome; John Goldfarb Please Come Home; The Rare Breed; The Plainsman; Not With My Wife You Don't; A Guide for the Married Man; Valley of the Dolls; Goodbye Mr Chips; The Reivers; Fiddler on the Roof *(Oscar-*1971); Images; The Poseidon Adventure; The Paper Chase; The Sugarland Express; Earthquake; The Towering Inferno; Jaws *(Oscar-*1975); Family Plot; Midway; Black Sunday; Star Wars *(Oscar-*1977); Close Encounters of the Third Kind; The Fury; Jaws II; Meteor; Quintet; Superman; Dracula; 1941; The Empire Strikes Back.

TV inc: Once Upon a Savage Night; Sergeant Ryker; Heidi *(Emmy-*1969); Jane Eyre *(Emmy-*1972).

(Grammys-(8)-original score film-1975, 1977, 1979; soundtrack album-1978; pop inst perf-1977; inst comp-1977, 1978, 1979).

WILLIAMS, Lenny: Act-Sngwri. b. Little Rock, AR, 1945. Recording artist.

WILLIAMS, Mason: Comp-Mus-Wri. b. Abilene, TX, 1938. TV inc: (wri) Smothers Brothers Show *(Emmy-*1968); Andy Williams Show; Petula Clark Show; Glen Campbell Show; Pat Paulsen Show.

Comp: Classical Gas *(Grammys-*inst theme, contemp inst perf-1968). Recs inc: Mason Williams Phonograph Record; Ear Show; Music; Hand Made; Share Pickers; Fresh Fish.

WILLIAMS, Michael George: Prod. b. London, Sep 8, 1938. Member Queensland Film Corp; consultant, Australian Film TV School. Films inc: Final Cut.

WILLIAMS, Patrick: Comp. b. Bonne Terre, MO, Apr 23, 1939. e. Duke U, BA. Films inc: The One and Only; Casey's Shadow; The Cheap Detective; Cuba; Breaking Away; Butch and Sundance--The Early Years; Hero At Large; Used Cars; Wholly Moses; It's My Turn.

TV inc: Bob Newhart Show; Streets of San Francisco; The Mary Tyler Moore Show; Lou Grant *(Emmy-*1980)

*(Grammy-*Inst arr-1974).

WILLIAMS, Paul: Lyr-Comp-Act. b. Omaha, NE, Sep 19, 1940. Began as set painter and stunt parachutist. Played bit and character parts in commercials. Seen briefly in The Chase and The Loved One. Became sngwri, collaborating briefly with Biff Ross and later with Roger Nichols.

Songs inc: You're So Nice to be Around; We've Only Just Begun; Rainy Days and Monday; Just an Old Fashioned Love Song; Evergreen *(Oscar-*1976), *(Grammy-*1976).

Films inc: Cinderella Liberty (score); Phantom of the Paradise (score & act); Bugsy Malone (score); A Star Is Born (score); Smokey and the Bandit (act); One on One (score); The Cheap Detective (act); The End (score); Grease (title song); Agatha (score); The Muppet Movie (act); Stone Cold Dead (act); Smokey and the Bandit II (act).

TV inc: The Wild Wild West Revisited (act); Emmet Otter's Jug-Band Christmas (mus-lyr).

WILLIAMS, Robin: Act. b. Chicago, IL, Jul 21. Performed in nileries. TV inc: Laugh In; The Great American Laugh Off; Ninety Minutes Live; The Alan Hamel Show; Mork & Mindy.

Films inc: The Last Laugh; Popeye. *(Grammy-*comedy rec-1979).

WILLIAMS, Roger: Pianist. b. Omaha, NE, 1926. e. Drake U, ID State Coll. Public debut on TV's Arthur Godfrey Talent Scout and Chance of a Lifetime. Other TV appearances inc: Ed Sullivan; Hollywood Palace; Kraft Summer Series; Celanese Special. Tours in addition to US: Australia; Japan; Mexico; South Africa. Recording artist. Guest artist several films.

WILLIAMS, Simon: Act. b. London, England. Thea inc: (London) A Friend Indeed; The Last of Mrs. Cheyney.

Films inc: The Fiendish Plot of Dr. Fu Manchu.

TV inc: His, Hers and Theirs; Upstairs, Downstairs.

WILLIAMS, Tennessee (Thomas Lanter Williams): Plywri. b. Columbus, MI, Mar 26, 1914. e. U of MO, 1931-33; WA U, St. Louis, 1936-37; U of IA, AB, 1938. Plays inc: Battle of Angels; The Glass Menagerie; You Touched Me; Streetcar Named Desire *(Pulitzer Prize-*1948); Cat On a Hot Tin Roof *(Pulitzer Prize-*1955); Camino Real; Summer and Smoke; Rose Tattoo *(Tony-*1951); Orpheus Descending; Sweet Bird of Youth; Period of Adjustment; Small Craft Warnings; Red Devil Battery Sign; Vieux Carre.

Films inc: The Glass Menagerie; Streetcar Named Desire; Baby Doll; Rose Tattoo; Night of the Iguana.

TV inc: The Kennedy Center Honors: A Celebration of the Performing Arts.

WILLIAMS, Tex: Act-Sngwri. b. Ramsey, Fayette County, IL, Aug 23, 1917. C&W recording artist. Formed band, The Western Caravan, in 1946; toured US, appeared with Grand Ole Opry; various TV shows.

WILLIAMS, Tony: Dir-Prod. b. New Zealand, May 31, 1942. e. Victoria U. TV inc: Freedom; Deciding; Rally; Getting Together; Lost in the Garden of the World; Solo (co-prod, co-wri).

WILLIAMS, Treat: Act. Bway inc: Over Here!; Grease; Danny Zuko.

Films inc: The Ritz; The Eagle Has Landed; Hair; Why Would I Lie?

WILLIAMSON, Fred: Act. b. Gary, IN, Mar 5, 1938. Films inc: M*A*S*-H; The Legend of Nigger Charley; Hammer; Black Caesar; Crazy Joe; That Man Bolt; Boss Nigger; Darktown; Take a Hard Ride; No Way Back (& prod-dir-wri); Death Journey (& prod-dir); Fist of Fear, Touch of Death.

TV inc: Julia; Police Story; Monday Night Football.

WILLIAMSON, Nicol: Act. b. Hamilton, Scotland, Sep 14, 1938. Joined Dundee Repertory Theatre, 1960. London debut, 1961, That's Us. On screen from 1964. Films inc: Six-Sided Triangle; The Bofors Gun; Laughter in the Dark; The Reckoning; The Jerusalem File; The Wilby Conspiracy; Robin and Marian; The Seven-Per-Cent Solution; The Cheap Detective; The Human Factor.

TV inc: Of Mice and Men; Arturo Ui; I Know What I Meant; Terrible Jim Fitch; The Word.

Thea inc: Awakening; Kelly's Eye; The Ginger Man; Inadmissable Evidence; A Cuckoo In the Nest; Waiting For Godot; The Diary of a Madman; Uncle Vanya; Coriolanus; Macbeth; Twelfth Night; Rex.

WILLINGHAM, Calder: Wri. b. Atlanta, GA, Dec 23, 1922. e. The Citadel, U VA. Plays inc: End As A Man.

Films inc: End As A Man; Paths of Glory; The Vikings; One-Eyed Jacks; Little Big Man; The Graduate; Thieves Like Us.

WILLIS, Bob: Singer-Sngwri. b. Hall County, TX, Mar 6, 1905. C&W recording artist. Elected to Country Music Hall of Fame, 1968. Formed the Texas' Playboys, which grew from a small unit to 25 musicians. In addition to radio shows band also was featured in several movies.

WILLIS, Gordon: Cin. Films inc: End of the Road; Loving; The Landlord; Little Murders; Bad Company; Klute; Up the Sandbox; The Paper Chase; The Godfather; The Parallax View; The Godfather Part 2; All The President's Men; Sept. 30, 1955; Annie Hall; Comes a Horseman; Interiors; Manhattan; Windows (& dir); Stardust Memories.

WILLIS, Larry: Mus. b. NYC, Dec 20, 1942. See Blood, Sweat & Tears.

WILLIS, Ted, Lord: b. Tottenham, Middlesex, England, Jan 13, 1918. Films inc: Holiday Camp; The Blue Lamp; It's Great to Be Young; Woman in a Dressing Gown; No Trees in the Street; Bitter Harvest.

Plays inc: Buster; No Trees in the Street; The Lady Purrs; The Blue Lamp; The Magnificent Moodies; Kid Kenyon Rides Again; Doctor in the House; Hot Summer Night; God Bless the Guvnor; Brothers-in-Law; The Eyes of Youth; Doctor at Sea; Woman in a Dressing Gown; A Slow Roll of Drums; A Murder of Crows; Queenie; A Fine Day for Murder; Dead on Saturday.

TV inc: Dixon of Dock Green; Mrs. Thursday; Crimes of Passion; Hunter's Walk; The Young and the Guilty; Strictly for Sparrows; Four Seasons of Rosie Carr; Look in any Window.

Life peerage created 1963.

WILLMAN, Noel: Dir-Act. b. Londonderry, Northern Ireland, Aug 4, 1918. Thea inc: (act) Adventure Story, Accolade, The Prisoner, Legend of Lovers, Isle of Children, The Devil's Disciple (& dir); Saint Joan. (Dir); The White Carnation; Someone Waiting; A Man For All Seasons (*Tony*-1961); The Lion In Winter; A Matter of Gravity.

Films inc: (act) The Cone of Silence; Dr Zhivago;

TV inc: The Green Bay Tree; Strange Interlude; The Crucible.

WILLSON, Meredith: Comp-Lyr-Cond. b. Mason City, IA, May 18, 1902. e. Damrosch Inst. Solo flutist with John Philip Sousa Band; NY Philharmonic, mus dir western division ABC Network.

Bway inc: Music Man (*Tonys*-(3) musical, book, score-1958); Unsinkable Molly Brown; Here's Love.

Films scores inc: The Great Dictator; The Little Foxes.

Songs inc: You and I; May the Good Lord Bless and Keep You; 76 Trombones.

(*Grammy*-cast album-1958).

WILSON, Daniel: Prod. b. Chicago, 1931. Started with ad agency writing, prod-dir commercials.

TV inc: Discovery; The Great Wallendas; Rookie of the Year (*Emmy*-1974); Me and Dad's New Wife; Hewitt's Just Different (*Emmy*-1978); Mom and Dad Can't Hear Me; Henry Winkler Meets William Shakespeare: The Secret of Charles Dickens; New York City Too Far From Tampa Blues; The Terrible Secret; The Sophisticated Gents; The Late Great Me--Story of a Teenage Alcoholic (*Emmy*-1980); The House at 12 Rose St; Here's Boomer.

WILSON, Dave: Dir. TV inc: The Bob and Ray Special; The Paul Simon Special; NBC Saturday Night Live (*Emmy*-1976).

WILSON, Elizabeth: Act. b. Grand Rapids, MI, Apr 4, 1925. NY stage debut, 1953, Picnic. Bway inc: The Desk Set; The Tunnel of Love; Yes is for a Very Young Man; Little Murders; Sheep on the Runway; Dark of the Moon; Sticks and Bones (*Tony*-supp-1972); The Secret Affairs of Mildred Wild; Uncle Vanya; Morning's at Seven (rev).

Films inc: Little Murders; Day of the Dolphin; Man on the Swing; Nine To Five.

TV inc: Doc.

WILSON, Flip (Clerow Wilson): Act. b. Jersey City, NJ, 1933. Performed in niteries. TV inc: The Flip Wilson Show (*Emmy*-1971); Uptown-A Tribute to the Apollo Theatre.

Films inc: Uptown Saturday Night; Skatetown USA; The Fish That Saved Pittsburgh.

WILSON, Lanford: Plywri. b. Lebanon, MO, Apr 13, 1937. e. U of Chicago. Plays inc: So Long at the Fair; Home Free !; No Trespassing; Sand Castle; The Madness of Lady Bright; Ludlow Fair; Balm in Gilead; This is the Rill Speaking; Sex Is Between Two People; Wandering; The Gingham Dog; Lemon Sky; Serenading Louie; The Family Continues; Hot L Baltimore; Talley's Folly (*Pulitzer Prize*-1980) The Fifth of July.

TV inc: This is the Rill Speaking; The Sandcastle; Stoop.

WILSON, Nancy: Singer. b. Chillicothe, OH, Feb 20, 1931. Worked small clubs in the Columbus area, then joined Rusty Bryant band. Began recording for Capitol in 1960.

(*Grammy*-R&B recording-1964).

WILSON, Richard: Prod-Dir-Wri. b. McKeesport, PA, Dec 25, 1915. e. Denver U. Started as radio act, joined Orson Welles' Mercury Theatre group, asso with all Mercury films through 1951.

Films inc: Lady From Shanghai; Macbeth; Ma and Pa Kettle on Vacation; Redhead from Wyoming; Ma and Pa Kettle at Home; Golden Blade; Man With a Gun; Ma and Pa Kettle in the Ozarks; The Big Boodle; Raw Wind in Eden; Al Capone; Pay or Die; Invitation to a Gunfighter; Three in an Attic.

WILSON, Theodore: Act. b. NYC, Dec 10, 1943. e. Florida A&M. Worked with Negro Ensemble Company, Arena Stage before Hollywood.

Films inc: The River Niger; Come Back, Charleston Blue; The Greatest.

TV inc: The Partridge Family; The Waltons; Roll Out; That's My Mama; The Sanford Arms.

WINANT, Ethel Wald: Exec. b. Worcester, MA, Aug 5. e. UC Berkeley. Started as prodn asst Bway; 1953, cast dir Talent Associates; 1956 cast dir-asso prod Playhouse 90; Twilight Zone; 1963 Great Adventure (prod); 1963 asso dir pgm dvlpt CBS-TV; 1965, talent dir; 1975, Childrens TV Workshop, prod Best of Families; 1978, vp talent CTW. 1978 talent vp NBC-TV; 1980 vp miniseries & novels for tv.

WINCELBERG, Shimon: Wri. b. Kiel, Germany, Sep 26, 1924. e. Providence Coll. Short stories: New Yorker; Harper's Bazaar; Punch.

TV inc: Naked City; Have Gun Will Travel; Gunsmoke; Mannix; Star Trek; Police Woman.

WINCHELL, Paul: Ventriloquist. b. NYC, 1924. At 13 won first prize on Major Bowes Radio Amateur Hour. Films inc: Stop! Look! and Laugh!; Which Way to the Front? TV inc: Paul Winchell-Jerry Mahoney Show.

WINDOM, William: Act. b. NYC, 1923. Films inc: To Kill a Mockingbird; Cattle King; One Man's Way; The Americanization of Emily; The Detective; The Gypsy Moths; The Man; Echoes of a Summer.

TV inc: My World and Welcome To It (*Emmy*-1970); Blind Ambition; Thurber; Portrait of a Rebel: Margaret Sanger; Landon, Landon and Landon.

Thea inc: Thurber.

WINDSOR, Marie (Emily Marie Bertelsen): Act. b. Marysvale, UT, Dec 11, 1921. Films inc: Abbott & Costello Meet the Mummy; Force of Evil; Outpost in Morocco; The Beautiful Blonds from Bashful Bend; The Fighting Kentuckian; Dakota Lil; Hellfire; The Showdown; Frenchie; Little Big Horn; Two Dollar Bettor; Support Your Local Sheriff; Japanese War Bride; The Sniper; The City That Never Sleeps; Hell's Half Acre; The Bounty Hunter; No Man's Woman; The Parson & the Outlaw; The Killing; Stars in the Backyard; Island Women; Hurricane Island; Mail Order Bride; One More Train to Rob; Cahill, US Marshal; Hearts of the West; Freaky Friday. TV inc: Alias Smith and Jones; Hec Ramsey; Man Hunter; Barnaby Jones; Police Story; Salem's Lot.

WINFIELD, Paul: Act. b. 1941. Films inc: The Lost Man; RPM; Brother John; Sounder; Gordon's War; Conrack; Hustle; Damnation Alley; The Greatest; A Hero Ain't Nothin' But a Sandwich; Twilight's Last Gleaming.

TV inc: King; Backstairs at the White House; Angel City.

WINITSKY, Alex: Prod. b. NYC, Dec 27, 1924. e. NYU, BS, LLB, JD. Films inc: The Seven-Per-Cent Solution; Cross of Iron; End of the Game; House Calls; Silver Bears; The Lady Vanishes; Breakthrough; Cuba.

WINKLER, Henry: Act. b. NYC, Oct 30, 1946. e. Emerson Coll, Yale School of Drama. Yale Repertory Co; in radio; TV commercials.

Films inc: The Lords of Flatbush; Crazy Joe; Nickelodeon; Heroes; The One and Only.

TV inc: The Great American Dream Machine; Masquerade; The Mary Tyler Moore Show; Rhoda; Happy Days; Laverne & Shirley; Katherine.

WINKLER, Irwin: Prod. b. NYC. e. NYU, BS. Films inc: Double Trouble; Point Blank; The Split; They Shoot Horses Don't They?; The Strawberry Statement; Believe in Me; The Gang That Couldn't Shoot Straight; The New Centurions; Up the Sandbox; The Mechanic; Busting; SPY's; The Gambler; Breakout; Rocky (Oscar-1976); Nickelodeon; New York, New York; Valentino; Comes A Horseman; Uncle Joe Shannon; Rocky II; Raging Bull.

WINNER, Michael Robert: Prod-Dir-Wri. b. London, Oct 30, 1935. e. Cambridge U. Wrote, prod & dir docs and short films, 1955-61. Feature film inc: Man with a Gun; Shoot to Kill; Play It Cool; The Cool Mikado; The Girl Getters; You Must Be Joking; I'll Never Forget What'sIsname; Hannibal Brooks; The Games; Lawman; The Nightcomers; Chato's Land; The Mechanic; Scorpio; The Stone Killer; Death Wish; Won Ton Ton, the Dog Who Saved Hollywood; The Sentinel; The Big Sleep; Firepower.

WINTER, Edward: Act. b. Ventura, CA. e. U of OR. Bway inc: Cabaret; Promises, Promises; The Birthday Party; Night Watch.
TV inc: Somerset; Karen; Adam's Rib; Eleanor and Franklin; Project UFO; M*A*S*H; The Second Time Around.
Films inc: A Change of Seasons.

WINTER, Vincent: Act. b. England, 1947. Started as child actor. Films inc: The Kidnappers (Special Oscar-1954); The Dark Avenger; Time Lock; Beyond This Place; Gorgo; Greyfriars Bobby; Almost Angels; The Three Lives of Thomasina; The Horse Without a Head.

WINTERS, David (nee Weizer): Dir-Chor-Prod. b. London, Apr 5, 1939. TV inc: Dr Jekyll and Mr Hyde; The London Bridge Special; Raquel Welch Special; Once Upon a Wheel; 2 Ann-Margret Specials; The Monkees; Lucy in London; Moving with Nancy; The Big Show.
Thea inc: Of Love Remembered.
Films inc: A Star is Born.

WINTERS, Jerry: Prod-Dir. b. Waterbury, CT, Aug 18, 1917. e. Antioch Coll. Films inc: (shorts) Herman Melville's Moby Dick; Central Park; Speak to Me Child; Renoir. Specialist in preparing foreign films for US import inc Seventh Continent; The Loves of Liszt; The Lost Talisman; A Look At Liv.

WINTERS, Jonathan: Act. b. Dayton, OH, Nov 11, 1925. Deejay, Dayton, Columbus stations; niteries. On screen from 1963. Films inc: It's a Mad, Mad, Mad, Mad World; The Loved Ones; Penelope; The Russians Are Coming, The Russians Are Coming; Eight on the Lam; Oh Dad, Poor Dad, Mama's Hung You in the Closet and I'm Feeling So Sad; Viva Max!; The Fish That Saved Pittsburgh.
TV inc: Jonathan Winters Show, NBC; More Wild Wild West; Hope For President.

WINTERS, Marian: Act-Wri. b. NYC, Apr 19, 1924. e. Brooklyn Coll. Thea inc: The Dream Girl; I Am A Camera (Tony-supp-1952); Sing Me No Lullaby; The Dark Is Light Enough; Medea; The Cherry Orchard; Nobody Loves An Albatross; Mating Dance; King John. Plays inc: Animal Keepers; A is for All; All Saint's Day; All Is Bright.

WINTERS, Roland: Act. b. Boston, MA, Nov 22, 1904. In stock cos, radio around Boston, later on West Coast before entering films. Films inc: 13 Rue Madeleine; Return of October; series of Charlie Chan films for Monogram; West Point Story; Follow the Sun; Inside Straight; She's Working Her Way Through College; Jet Pilot; So Big.
TV inc: You Can't Go Home Again.

WINTERS, Shelley (Shirley Schrift): Act. b. St Louis, MO, Aug 19, 1922. Started in vaude. Screen debut 1944. Films inc: Nine Girls; Sailor's Holiday; Larceny; Take One False Step; Johnny Stool Pigeon; My Man and I; Executive Suite; Saskatchewan; Playgirl; Night of the Hunter; The Big Knife; The Great Gatsby; South Sea Sinner; Winchester '73; A Place in the Sun; I Am a Camera; The Treasure of Pancho Villa; I Died a Thousand Times; Cash on Delivery; The Diary of Anne Frank (Oscar-supp-1959); The Young Savages; Lolita; The Chapman Report; A House Is Not a Home; A Patch of Blue (Oscar-supp-1966); Alfie; Enter Laughing; The Scalphunters; Wild in the Streets; Buena Sera Mrs. Campbell; Bloody Mama; What's the Matter With Helen?; The Poseidon Adventure; Cleopatra Jones; Something to Hide; Blume in Love; Diamonds; Next Stop Greenwich Village; The Tenant; An Average Man; Tentacles; City on Fire; Magician of Lublin; The Visitor.
Bway inc: A Hatful of Rain; Girls of Summer; Minnie's Boys; The Effect of Gamma Rays on Man-In-The-Moon-Marigolds (rev).
TV inc: Sorry, Wrong Number; The Woman; Wagon Train; Two Is the Number (Emmy-1964); A Death of Innocence; The Adventures of Nick Carter; Elvis; The French Atlantic Affair; Rudolph & Frosty's Christmas in July (voice).

WINTLE, Julian: Prod. b. Liverpool, England, 1913. Started as film edtr; joined Two Cities Films as prod; co-founder Independent Artists. Films inc: Waltz of the Toreadors; This Sporting Life; Bitter Harvest; Madame Sin; Circus of Horrors; Tiger Bay; Belstone Fox.
TV inc: The Avengers; The Human Jungle.
(Died Nov. 8, 1980).

WISBERG, Aubrey: Wri-Prod. b. London, Oct 20, 1909. e. Columbia U. Films inc: (sp only) Submarine Raider; Escape in the Fog; Just Before Dawn; Power of the Whistler; After Midnight; So Dark the Night; The Wreck of the Hesperus; Treasure of Monte Cristo; The Big Fix; Son of Sinbad; At Sword's Point; They Came to Blow Up America. Bomber's Moon; The Lady in the Iron Mask; The Horn Blows at Midnight; The Snow Devils; Casanova's Big Night; Mission: Mars. (sp & prod): The Man from Planet X; Captive Women; Sword of Venus; Port Sinister; The Neanderthal Man; Capt. John Smith & Pocahontas; Return to Treasure Island; Capt. Kidd & the Slave Girl; Problem Girls; Murder is My Beat; The Women of Pitcairn Island; Hercules in New York.

WISDOM, Norman: Act. b. London, Feb 4, 1920. Films inc: Trouble in Store; One Good Turn; Up in the World; Just My Luck; The Square Peg; Follow a Star; There Was a Crooked Man; A Stitch in Time; The Early Bird; The Sandwich Man; The Night They Raided Minsky's; What's Good for the Goose.
Thea inc: Walking Happy; Not Now Darling; A World of Wisdom.

WISE, Ernie (Ernest Wiseman, OBE): Comedian. b. England, Nov 27, 1925. Teamed with Eric Morecambe since 1941. On radio, tv with Morecambe and Wise Shows. Films inc: The Intelligence Man; That Riviera Touch; The Magnificent Two.

WISE, Herbert (nee Weisz): Dir. b. Vienna, Aug 31, 1924. Thea inc: While The Sun Shines; So What About Love; I Want To Marry a Goldwyn Girl.
TV inc: Vienna 1900--Games With Love and Death; I Claudius.

WISE, Robert E: Dir-Prod. b. Winchester, IN, Sep 10, 1914. Started in cutting dept RKO, 1933; film ed, 1939; edited Citizen Kane; dir, 1943; ind prod 1959; partner Filmakers Group, The Tripar Group.
Films inc: (dir) Curse of the Cat People; Mademoiselle Fifi; The Set-Up; Two Flags West; The Day the Earth Stood Still; The Desert Rats; Executive Suite; Helen of Troy; Somebody Up There Likes Me; Run Silent; Run Deep; I Want to Live!. (Prod-dir) Odds Against Tomorrow; West Side Story (2 Oscars-dir & prod-1961); Two for the Seesaw; The Haunting; The Sound of Music (2 Oscars-dir & prod-1965); The Sand Pebbles; Star!; The Andromeda Strain; Two People; The Hindenburg Audrey Rose; Star Trek-The Movie.
(Irving Thalberg Award-1966).

WISEMAN, Frederick: Prod-Dir. b. Boston, MA, Jan 1, 1930. e. Williams College, BA; Yale Law School; U of Paris. Taught law for two years. Founded Zipporah Films to enter film ind as prod of doc The Cool World. Since then has pro & dir. Films inc: Titicut Follies; High School; Manoeuvre.

TV inc: Law and Order (*Emmy*-1969); Hospital (*Emmys*-prod & dir-1970); Basic Training; Essene.

WISEMAN, Joseph: Act. b. Montreal, May 15, 1918. Films inc: Detective Story; Viva Zapata; Les Miserables; The Prodigal; The Garment Jungle; The Unforgiven; Dr No; The Night They Raided Minsky's; Bye, Bye, Braverman; Stiletto; The Valachi Papers; The Apprenticeship of Duddy Kravitz; Homage of Chagall (narr); The Betsy; Buck Rogers in the 25th Century; Jaguar Lives.

Thea inc: King Lear; Golden Boy; The Diary of Anne Frank; Uncle Vanya; The Last Analysis; Enemies.

WITHERS, Googie (Georgette Lizette Withers): Act. b. Karachi, India, Mar 12, 1917. Stage debut, 1929, The Windmill Man. Thea inc: Hand in Glove; The Deep Blue Sea; Janus; The Complaisant Lover; Woman in a Dressing Gown; Exit the King; Beekman Place; Getting Married; The Cherry Orchard; An Ideal Husband; The Circle.

Films inc: Girl in the Crowd; Accused; Strange Boarders; The Lady Vanishes; One of Our Aircraft Is Missing; On Approval; It Always Rains on Sunday; Miranda; White Corridors; Derby Day; Devil on Horseback; Port of Escape; The Nickel Queen.

WITHERS, Jane: Act. b. Atlanta, GA, 1927. On screen as a child from 1933. Films inc: Bright Eyes; Ginger; North Star; Johnny Doughboy; My Best Girl; Dangerous Partners; Affairs of Geraldine; Giant; The Right Approach; Captain Newman, M.D.

TV inc: All Together Now (First appearance after 12 years as Comet Cleanser's TV character Josephine the Plumber.)

WITT, Paul Junger: Prod-Dir. b. NYC, Mar 20, 1943. e. U of VA, BA. Asso prod-dir Screen Gems, 1965; prod-dir 1967; prod Spelling-Goldberg 1972; P-exec prod Danny Thomas Prodns 1973; founder exec prod Witt/Thomas Prodns 1975.

TV inc: The Rookies; Brian's Song (*Emmy*-prod-1972); Griffin and Phoenix; Trouble In High Timber Country; The Yeagers (exec prod); It's A Living; I'm A Big Girl Now.

WITTOP, Freddy (nee Koning): Cos dsgn. b. Bussum, Holland, Jul 26. Originally a dancer, toured with Argentinita as Frederico Rey; Bway inc: Heartbreak House; Carnival; Subways Are for Sleeping; Toured US & Europe with own dance co from 1951-1958. Hello, Dolly! (*Tony*-1964); To Broadway With Love; Bajour; The Roar of the Greasepaint-The Smell of the Crowd; Pleasures and Palaces; On a Clear Day You Can See Forever; I Do! I Do!; The Happy Time; George M!; Dear World; A Patriot for Me; Lovely Ladies, Kind Gentlemen.

WIZAN, Joe: Prod. b. LA, Jan 7, 1935. e. UCLA. Films inc: Jeremiah Johnson; Junior Bonner; Prime Cut; 99 44/100% Dead; The Last American Hero; Audrey Rose; Voices; And Justice for All.

TV inc: The Two Worlds of Jennie Logan.

WOLF, Emanuel: Exec. b. NYC, May 27, 1927. e. Syracuse U, BA, MA. Named director Allied Artists Pictures Corp 1963. Became Pres & bd chmn 1968.

WOLF, Fred: Prod-Dir-Ani. b. Brooklyn, NY, Mar 27, 1933. Pres Murakami-Wolf-Swenson Films. Films inc: The Bird; The Box (*Oscar*-cartoon-1967); The Mouse and His Child.

TV inc: The Point; Carlton Your Doorman; Puff The Magic Dragon in the Land of the Living Lies; Thanksgiving in the Land of Oz.

WOLF, Harry L: Cin. b. San Francisco, Jun 20, 1912. TV inc: Hennessy; Beverly Hillbillies; Sunshine; Devil and Miss Sarah; Get Smart; What's a Nice Girl Like You; Hound of the Baskervilles; Little Mo; Columbo (*Emmy*-1974); Baretta (*Emmy*-1975); Brave New World.

WOLF, Herbert: Prod. b. NYC, Jul 11, 1917. e. NYU. Radio, TV prod, Wolf Presentations, Inc. TV inc: Masquerade Party; Break the Bank; Hold That Note; Keep Talking; Window Shopping.

WOLF, Richard A: Prod-Wri. b. NYC, Dec 20, 1946. e. U of PA. Films inc: Skateboard (sp, prod).

WOLFE, Digby: Wri-Prod-Dir. b. Eng, Jun 4, 1932. e. Thurlestone Coll. TV inc: (Eng) Chelsea At Nine; I've Got A Secret; Wolfe at the Door; Saturday Spectacular; (U.S.): Laugh-In (*Emmy*-wri-1968); The Doris Day Special; The Tennessee Ernie Ford Special; Diana Ross; Opryland USA; John Denver & Friend; The Cher Series; The New Bill Cosby Variety Series; Lampoon; Li'l Abner; The Goldie Hawn Special; The Flip Wilson Special; The Wayne Newton Special; The Tammy Awards Show; Real People.

WOLFE, Robert L: Film Edtr. b. LA, Jul 5, 1928. Films inc: The Wild Bunch; Straw Dogs; The Getaway; The Wind and the Lion; Terminal Man; Junior Bonner; Pat Garrett and Billy the Kid; The Deep; All The President's Men; Big Wednesday; The Rose; The Hunter.

WOLFF, Lother: Prod-Dir. b. Bromberg, Germany, 1909. Asst prod, The March of Time; VP & prod, Louis de Rochemont Assoc. Films inc: Lost Boundaries; Martin Luther; Windjammer; Question Seven; Fortress of Peace.

WOLFMAN JACK (Bob Smith): Act. b. NYC, Jan 21. Films inc: The Seven Minutes; American Graffiti; More American Graffiti; Motel Hell.

TV inc: The Midnight Special.

WOLPER, David L: Exec. b. NYC, Jan 11, 1928. e. Drake U, USC. In 1949, partnered in Flamingo Films, a TV dist co; merged with Associated Artists 1951 and became known as Motion Pictures for Television, Inc; formed Wolper Productions, Inc, 1958. Docs inc: Race for Space; Hollywood-The Golden Years; Hollywood-The Fabulous Era; Project--Man In Space; Biography of a Rookie; The Rafer Johnson Story; D-Day; The Making of the President, 1960; 39 half-hour programs titled The Story Of. . .; Escape to Freedom; The Legend of Marilyn Monroe; Berlin: Kaiser to Khrushchev; The Battle of Britain; Trial at Nuremberg; Korea: The 38th Parallel; Four Days in November; The Teenage Revolution; Pro Football: Mayhem On a Sunday Afternoon; National Geographic Society Specials; The World of Animals; The Undersea World of Jacques-Yves Cousteau.

Feature films inc: I Love My Wife; The Devil's Brigade; It It's Tuesday, This Must Be Belgium; The Bridge At Remagen; The Confessions of Nat Turner; Couples; King, Queen, Knave; Blessed McGill; The Great Cowboy Race; Willy Wonka and the Chocolate Factory; Visions of Eight; Birds Do It, Bees Do It.

TV inc: Get Christie Love!; Chico and the Man; Sandburg's Lincoln; Welcome Back, Kotter; Roots (*Emmy*-exec prod-1977); Roots - The Next Generations (*Emmy*-exec prod-1979); Moviola.

WOLSK, Eugene V: Prod. b. NYC, Aug 16, 1928. e. Allegheny Coll, BA, Yale U Drama School, NYU. Bway inc: The Father; Chaparral; The Lion in Winter; Mark Twain Tonight!; The Investigation; Something Different; Aint Supposed to Die a Natural Death; The Sunshine Boys; The Good Doctor; Scapino; Miss Moffat; God's Favorite; Charlotte.

TV inc: The Investigation.

WOLSKY, Albert: Cos Dsgn. b. Paris, France, Nov 24, 1930. Films inc: The Heart Is a Lonely Hunter; Where's Poppa?; Harry and Tonto; Lenny; Beauty and the Beast; An Unmarried Woman; The Turning Point; Grease; Manhattan; All That Jazz (*Oscar*-1979); The Jazz Singer.

Bway inc: Tricks of the Trade.

WONDER, Stevie: (nee Steveland Morris): Singer-Mus-Sngwri-Rec prod. b. Saginaw, MI, May 13, 1950. Blind since birth. A natural mus, began writing, recording songs as a child; first gold album, Fingertips, at age 13 (billed as Little Stevie Wonder). Writes own material, produces own records.

Songs inc: Purple Raindrops; Someday at Christmas; I'm Wondering; Every Time I See You I Go Wild; Shoo Be Doo Be Doo Da Day; My Girl; For Once in My Life; My Cherie Amour; Yester Me Yester You, Yester Day; Never Had A Dream Come True; Superstition *(Grammys-R&B song & R&B voc-1973)*; You Are The Sunshine of My Life *(Grammy-pop vocal-1973)*; Boogie on a Reggae Woman *(Grammy-R&B voc-1974)*; Living For the City *(Grammy-R&B song-1974)*; You Haven't Done Nothin'; High Ground; I Wish *(Grammy-R&B voc-1976)*.

Albums inc: 12-year-old Genius; Tribute To Uncle Ray; Jazz Soul; With A Song in My Heart; Uptight; Down to Earth; I Was Made to Love Her; Stevie Wonder's Greatest Hits; Music on My Mind; Innervisions *(Grammys-artist & prod-1973)*; Fullfillingness First Finale *(Grammys-artist-prod-pop voc-1974)*; Songs in the Key of Life *(Grammys-artist, pop vocal, prod also prod of year-1976)*.

Films inc: Bikini Beach; Muscle Beach Party; CS Blues.

WOOD, John: Act. b. Derbyshire, England. e. Jesus College, Oxford. Thea inc: (London) various Shakespearean roles with Old Vic; Camino Real; The Making of Moo; Brouhaha; The Fantasticks; Exiles; Enemies; The Man of Mode; Collaborators; A Lesson in Blood and Roses; Sherlock Holmes; Travesties; The Devil's Disciple; Ivanov; The Provok'd Wife. (Bway) Rosencrantz and Guildenstern Are Dead; Sherlock Holmes; Travesties *(Tony-1976)*.

Films inc: Nicholas and Alexandra; Slaughterhouse Five; Somebody Killed Her Husband.

WOOD, Natalie (Natasha Gurdin): Act. b. San Francisco, 1938. W of Robert Wagner. Screen debut, 1946, Tomorrow is Forever. Films inc: Miracle on 34th Street; The Ghost and Mrs. Muir; Driftwood; The Bride Wore Boots; Green Promise; One Desire; Scudda-Hoo, Scudda Hay; Chicken Every Sunday; Father Was a Fullback; No Sad Songs for Me; The Jackpot; Never a Dull Moment; Blue Veil; The Star; Rebel Without a Cause; Cry In the Night; The Searchers; Burning Hills; Bombers B-52; Marjorie Morningstar; Kings Go Forth; Cash McCall; Splendor in the Grass; West Side Story; Gypsy; Love With a Proper Stranger; Sex and the Single Girl; Inside Daisy Clover; This Property is Condemned; Penelope; Bob and Carol and Ted and Alice; Peeper; Meteor; The Last Married Couple in America; Willie and Phil.

TV inc: Cat on a Hot Tin Roof; From Here to Eternity; The Cracker Factory; The Memory of Eva Ryker.

WOOD, Peter: Dir. b. Colyton, Devon, Eng, Oct 8, 1927. e. Cambridge. Resident dir Arts Theatre, London, 1956. Thea inc: No Laughing Matter; The Iceman Cometh; The Birthday Party; Who's Your Father?; Five Finger Excercise; The Winter's Tale; The Devil; Hamlet; The Private Ear and the Public Eye; The Master Builder; Poor Richard; Love for Love; Design for Living; Jumpers; Travesties; Night and Day; The Provok'd Wife.

Films inc: In Search of Gregory.

TV inc: Song for Songs; Long Day's Journey Into Night; Dear Love.

WOOD, Robert D: Exec. b. Boise, ID, Apr 17, 1925. e. USC, BS. Joined KNX (CBS Radio) as slsmn; 1951 account exec KTTV-TV; 1952 account exec KNXT (CBS TV); 1954 account exec CBS TV natl sales dept, NY; 1955 gen sls mgr KNXT; 1960 vp-gm KNXT; 1966 exec vp CBS tv stations div; 1967 P; 1969 P CBS-TV; 1976 resd to enter ind prodn; 1980 P Metromedia Producers Corp.

TV inc: The Cheap Show; Maneaters Are Loose!; Gauguin the Savage.

WOODARD, Bronte: Wri. b. GA, 1941. e. GA State U. Films inc: Grease; Can't Stop the Music.

(Died Aug 6, 1980).

WOODFIELD, William R: Wri-Prod. b. San Francisco, Jan 21, 1928. e. U of CA, BA. TV inc: (wri) Sea Hunt: Voyage to the Bottom of the Sea; Time Tunnel; (wri-prod): Mission Impossible; San Francisco International Airport; Shaft; Earth II; Satan's Triangle.

WOODWARD, Charles: Prod. b. Niagara Falls, NY, Oct 14, 1923. e. U of PA, BS. Thea inc: Johnny No-Trump; The Boys in the Band; The Front Page; What the Butler Saw; The Last of Mrs. Lincoln; All Over; Drat!; The Grass Harp; Noel Coward in Two Keys; Seascape; P.S. Your Cat Is Dead!; Sweeney Todd *(Tony-1979)*.

WOODWARD, Edward: Act. b. Surrey, England, Jun 1, 1930. e. RADA. Thea inc: (London) Where There's A Will; A Girl Called Jo; Doctor in the House; The Queen and the Welshman; with Shakespeare Memorial Theatre, 1958 playing various roles and appearing with company during Russian tour; The Art of Living; The Little Doctor; Scapa; Rattle of a Simple Man; The High Bid; Two Cities; Cyrano; The Wolf; The Male of the Species; On Approval. (Bway) Rattle Of a Simple Man; The Best Laid Plans.

Films inc: Becket; Young Winston; Sitting Target; The Wicker Man; Breaker Morant.

TV inc: Callan; Major Barbara; A Dream Divided; Edward Woodward Specials.

WOODWARD, Joanne: Act. b. Thomasville, GA, Feb 27, 1930. e. LA State U; Neighborhood Playhouse, Actor's Studio, NY. W of Paul Newman. On screen from 1955 in Count Three and Pray. Films inc: A Kiss Before Dying; The Three Faces of Eve *(Oscar-1957)*; No Down Payment; The Long Hot Summer; Rally Round the Flag Boys; The Sound and the Fury; From The Terrace; The Fugitive Kind; Paris Blues; The Stripper; A New Kind of Love; Signpost to Murder; A Big Hand for the Little Lady; Rachel, Rachel; Winning; WUSA; The Effect of Gamma Rays on Man-in-the-Moon Marigolds; Summer Wishes, Winter Dreams; The Drowning Pool; The End; Angel Dust (doc-narr).

Thea inc: Picnic.

TV inc: Robert Montgomery Presents; US Steel Hour; G.E. Theatre; Studio One; Four Star Playhouse; Playhouse 90; Hallmark Hall of Fame; Sybil; See How She Runs *(Emmy-1978)*; A Christmas To Remember; The Streets of L. A.; Fred Astaire-Putting On His Top Hat (narr); Fred Astaire-Change Partners and Dance (narr); The Shadow Box.

WOOLERY, Chuck: Act. b. Ashland, KY, Aug 22. Films inc: Treasure of Jamaica Reef.

TV inc: The Jimmy Dean Show; Your Hit Parade; Wheel of Fortune (host).

WOOLEY, Sheb: Singer-Sngwri. b. Erick, OK, Apr 10, 1921. C&W recording artist. Films inc: Rocky Mountain; The Boy From Oklahoma; High Noon; Giant; Little Big Horn.

TV inc: Rawhide.

WOOLF, John: Exec. b. England, 1913. Films inc: Pandora and the Flying Dutchman; The African Queen; Moulin Rouge; Beat the Devil; Carrington V.C.; I Am a Camera; Sailor Beware; Three Men in a Boat; The L-Shaped Room; Life at the Top; Oliver! *(Oscar-1968)*; The Day of the Jackal; The Odessa File.

WORLEY, JoAnne: Act. b. Lowell, IN, 1942. Films inc: Moon Pilot; Nutcracker Fantasy.

TV inc: Laugh-In; Love American Style; The Gift of the Magi.

WOROB, Malcolm: Dir-Prod. b. Newark, NJ, Oct 17, 1944. e. Rochester Institute of Technology. Films inc: The Sister-In-Law; Panic Rock.

WORTH, Irene: b. NE, Jun 23, 1916. e. UCLA. Films inc: One Night with You; Secret People; Orders to Kill; Seven Seas to Calais; King Lear; Nicholas and Alexandra; Rich Kids.

Thea inc: Tiny Alice *(Tony-1965)*; A Song at Twilight; Come into the Garden; Heartbreak House; Sweet Bird of Youth *(Tony-1976)*; The Lady From Dubuque; John Gabriel Borkman.

TV inc: Stella in the Lake; The Lady from the Sea; The Duchess of Malfi; Prince Orestes; Happy Days.

WORTH, Marvin: Prod. b. Brooklyn, NY. Originally jazz promoter and mgr before becoming wri of special material for Alan King; Buddy Hackett; Joey Bishop. TV inc: Steve Allen Show; Jackie Gleason Show; Milton Berle Show; Colgate Comedy Hour; Judy Garland; Where's Poppa.

Films inc: (wri) Boys Night Out; Three on a Couch; Promise Her Anything. (Prod) Where's Poppa? Lenny: Fire Sale; The Rose; Up the Academy.

WRATHER, Jack: Prod. b. Amarillo, TX, May 24, 1918. H of Bonita Granville. Co-ownr, KFMB-TV, San Diego; KERO-TV, Bakersfield, CA; Muzak Corp; Lone Ranger, Inc, Lassie Programs, Inc; ownr, Disneyland Hotel; P, Wrather Corp; dir, TelePromTer.

Films inc: The Guilty; High Tide; Perilous Waters; Strike It Rich; Guilty of Treason; Lone Ranger; The Lone Ranger and the Lost City of Gold; The Magic of Lassie.

TV inc: Lassie; Sgt Preston of the Yukon; Lone Ranger.

WRAY, Fay: Act. b. Alberta, Canada, Sep 10, 1907. On screen from 1928. Films inc: The Legion of the Condemned; The Four Feathers; Dirigible; Doctor X; The Countess of Monte Cristo; Viva Villa!; King Kong; Alias Bulldog Drummond; Adam Had Four Sons; The Cobweb; Summer Love.

TV inc: Gideon's Trumpet.

WRIGHT, Amy: Act. b. Chicago, IL. e. Beloit Coll. Started teaching career before act. Bway inc: Hamlet; Fifth of July.

Films inc: Not A Pretty Picture (doc); Girlfriends; The Deer Hunter; The Amityville Horror; Breaking Away; Wise Blood; Inside Moves.

WRIGHT, Norman H: Wri-Dir-Prod. b. Redlands, CA, Jan 8, 1910. e. USC. Field prod for Wonderful World of Disney. TV inc: Pancho the Fastest Paw in the West; Cristobalito the Calypso Colt; Chandar, Black Leopard of Ceylon; Deacon the High Noon Dog (& wri-dir); Saving of Sam the Pelican (wri); Golden Dog (wri); Grizzly (wri).

Films inc: Fantasia (story dir); Bambi (sequence dir).

WRIGHT, Samuel E: Act. b. Camden, SC, Nov 20, 1948. e. SC State; C W Post Coll. Bway inc: Jesus Christ Superstar; Two Gentlemen of Verona; Over Here; Pippin. Other thea inc: Downriver (Off-Bway); Georgie Porgie (Off-Bway); Mushroom (Off-Bway); Two Gentlemen of Verona (London).

TV inc: Ed Sullivan's Broadway; Patchwork Family; Positively Black; Ball Four; Enos.

WRIGHT, Teresa: Act. b. NYC, Oct 27, 1919. On screen from 1940. Films inc: The Little Foxes; Mrs. Miniver (Oscar-supp-1942); The Pride of the Yankees; Casanova Brown; The Best Years of Our Lives; The Steel Trap; Track of the Cat; The Search for Bridie Murphy; The Restless Years; Hail Hero!; The Happy Ending; Somewhere In Time.

Thea inc: Death of a Salesman; Ah Wilderness!; I Never Sang for My Father; The Master Builder; Morning's At Seven (rev).

TV inc: The Margaret Bourke-White Story; The Miracle Worker; The Golden Honeymoon.

WRIGHT, William H: Prod-Wri. b. Lawrenceburg, IN, Apr 29, 1902. e. IN U, AB. Films inc: Blonde Fever; A Letter for Evie; Three Wise Fools; The Bride Goes Wild; Act of Violence; Stars in My Crown; Black Hand; The Skipper Surprised His Wife; Mrs. O'Malley and Mr. Malone; Love Is Better Than Ever; The People Against O'Hara; Shadow in the Sky; Young Man with Ideas; The Naked Spur; The Clown; Dead Ringer; A Distant Trumpet; The Sons of Katie Elder (sp).

TV inc: (prod) Adventures of Jim Bowie; Barbara Stanwyck Theatre; Follow The Sun Co-creater NBC series Kentucky Jones. (Wri): The Californians; Family Affair; Bonanza; Daniel Boone; Kentucky Jones; Burke's Law; Amos Burke; Secret Agent; Mannix.

(Died July 23, 1980).

WRYE, Donald: Dir. TV inc: The Man Who Could Talk To Kids; Death Be Not Proud (& prod-wri); It Happened One Christmas.

Films inc: Ice Castles (& wri).

WYATT, Jane: Act. b. NYC, Aug 10, 1913. On screen from 1934. Films inc: One More River; Great Expectations; Lost Horizon; None but the Lonely Heart; Boomerang; Gentleman's Agreement; Pitfall; Never Too Late; Treasure of Matecumbe.

Thea inc: The Autumn Garden; The Bishop Misbehaves; Conquest; The Mad Hopes.

TV inc: Father Knows Best (Emmys-1957, 1959, 1960); The Virginian; Wagon Train; My Luke and I; Amelia Earhart; The Nativity; The Millionaire.

WYENN, Than: Act. b. NYC, May 2, 1919. Films inc: Pete Kelly's Blues; Beginning of the End; The Invisible Boy; Imitation of Life; The Boy and the Pirates; Thunderbolt; Black Sunday; The Other Side of Midnight.

TV inc: Six Million Dollar Man; Switch; Barnaby Jones; The Lou Grant Show; Quincy; Victory at Entebbe; Power.

WYLER, Gretchen (nee Wienecke): Act. b. Bartlesville, OK, Feb 16, 1932. Thea inc: Where's Charley; Silk Stockings; Damn Yankees; Sweet Charity (London); Sly Fox.

TV inc: Step This Way; Somerset; On Our Own; Portrait of an Escort.

Films inc: Devils's Brigade.

WYLER, William: Prod-Dir. b. Mulhouse, France, Jul 1, 1902. e. Coll of Paris. Became asst dir Hollywood, 1920, then dir. Later partnered with Frank Capra, George Stevens in Liberty Films Inc. Films inc: Anybody Here Seen Kelly; Hell's Heroes; Counsellor At Law; Dodsworth; Dead End; Jezebel; Wuthering Heights; The Letter; The Little Foxes; Mrs. Miniver (Oscar-1942); The Best Years of Our Lives (Oscar-1946); The Heiress; Detective Story; Carrie; Roman Holiday; Desperate Hours; Friendly Persuasion; Ben Hur (Oscar-1959); The Big Country; The Children's Hour; The Collector; How to Steal a Million; Funny Girl; The Liberation of L.B. Jones.

(Irving Thalberg Award 1965.)

WYMAN, Jane (Sarah Jane Fulks): Act. b. St Joseph, MO, Jan 4, 1914. On screen from 1935. Films inc: My Man Godfrey; The Crowd Roars; Crime By Night; Lost Weekend; One More Tomorrow; Johnny Belinda (Oscar-1948); Here Comes the Groom; The Yearling; Blue Veil; The Story of Will Rogers; So Big; Magnificent Obsession; Lucy Gallant; All that Heaven Allows; Miracle in the Rain; Holiday for Lovers; How to Commit Marriage; Bon Voyage.

TV inc: The Incredible Journey of Doctor Meg Laurel.

WYNETTE, Tammy (Virginia Wynette Pugh): Act. b. Red Bay, MS, May 5, 1942. C&W recording artist.

(Grammys-country voc-1967, 1969).

WYNGARDE, Peter: Act. b. Marseilles, France. Thea inc: (London) With Bristol Old Vic in various Shakespearean roles and dir Long Day's Journey Into Night; The Good Woman of Setzuan; Duel of Angels; The Duel; The King and I; Present laughter (& dir); Anastasia (& dir). (Bway) Duel of Angels.

Films inc: The Siege of Sidney Street; Night of the Eagle; Flash Gordon.

TV inc: Departmet S; Jason King.

WYNN, Keenan: Act. b. NYC, Jul 27, 1916. S of late Ed Wynn. On screen from 1942. Films inc: See Here, Private Hargrove; Marriage Is a Private Affair; Without Love; The Clock; Easy to Wed; The Hucksters; Neptune's Daughter; Annie Get Your Gun; Kiss Me Kate; The Great Man; Don't Go Near the Water; The Great Race; Welcome to Hard Times; Finian's Rainbow; The Devil's Rain; Nashville; The Killer Inside Me; The Shaggy D.A.; Coach; Laserblast; Piranha; The Dark; Sunburn; Parts - The Clonus Horror; Just Tell Me What You Want.

TV inc: Dallas; The Bastard; The Billion Dollar Threat; Mom, The Wolfman and Me.

WYNN, Tracy Keenan: Wri. b. LA, Feb 28, 1945. e. Switzerland, UCLA. S of Keenan Wynn. Films inc: The Longest Yard; The Deep.

TV inc: The Glass House; Tribes (Emmy-1971); The Autobiography of Miss Jane Pittman (Emmy-1974); The Drowning Pool; Quest.

WYNTER, Dana (Dagmar Wynter): Act. b. London, Jun 8, 1930. Launched career on TV, Robert Montgomery Presents series.

Films inc: The View from Pompey's Head; Invasion of the Body Snatchers; D-Day; The Sixth of June; Something of Value; Fraulein; Shake Hands with the Devil; In Love and War; Sink the Bismark!; The List of Adrian Messenger; If He Hollers, Let Him Go; Airport.

TV inc: My Three Sons; Twelve O'Clock High; The Rogues; Wild, Wild West; Companions in Nightmare; Any Second Now; Owen Marshall; The Man Who Never Was; Backstairs At The White House; M-Station Hawaii; Dana Wynter In Ireland.

YABLANS, Frank: Prod. b. NYC, Aug 27, 1935. Started as WB booker, 1957; eastern sls mgr, 1967; sls mgr, 1967; sls vp, 1968; vp, gen sls mgr, Par, 1969; vp, dist, 1970; exec vp, 1971; named p, 1971. In 1975 became independent prod, (Frank Yablans Presentations Inc).

Films inc: Silver Streak; The Other Side of Midnight; The Fury; North Dallas Forty (& wri).

YABLANS, Irwin: Exec-Prod. b. NYC, Jul 25, 1934. P, Irwin Yablans Co. Film salesman before joining Paramount 1962 as Los Angeles Mgr; western sales Mgr 1964; Films inc: Badge 373 The Education of Sonny Carson; Halloween; Roller Boogie; Fade To Black.

YANNE, Jean (nee Gouille): Act. b. Brittany, Jul 18, 1933. Films inc: La Vie a L'Envers; L'Amour a la Chaine; La Saint Contre; Bang Bang; Weekend; Erotissimo; Le Boucher; Le Saut de L'Ange; The Accuser; State Reason; Je Te Tiens, Tu Me Tiens par la Barbichette. TV inc: Les Grands Enfants.

YARROW, Peter: Comp-Singer. b. NYC, May 31, 1938. e. Cornell U. Member, Peter, Paul and Mary Trio. Songs inc: Puff, The Magic Dragon; A-Soulin'.

TV inc: Puff The Magic Dragon in the Land of Living Lies (& prod).

YATES, Peter: Dir. b. Eng, 1929. Films inc: Summer Holiday; One Way Pendulum; Robbery; Bullitt; John and Mary; Murphy's War; The Hot Rock; The Friends of Eddie Coyle; For Pete's Sake; Mother Jugs and Speed; The Deep; Breaking Away (& prod).

TV inc: The Saint; Danger Man; Breaking Away (exec prod).

YATES, William Robert: Prod-Exec. b. Glendale, CA, 1930. e. U IL, BA; Columbia, LLD. 1955, publicist KNXT; 1959, story ed Studio One, Camera Three; 1961, Dir Pgm Dvlpmnt ABC-TV; 1963 retd to KNXT as dir Repertoire Workship; 1967 dir pgm dvlpmnt Selmur Prodns; 1970 to Disney writing Wonderful World of Disney; 1973, exec story cnsltnt Streets of San Francisco; 1975 prod; 1978 vp crea aff Quinn Martin Prodns, prod Tales of the Unexpected; The Runaways; 1979 vp tv prodn Disney.

TV inc: Lefty.

YAWITZ, Paul: Wri. b. St Louis, MO, Feb 5, 1905. Publicist; Bway columnist, NY Mirror.

Films inc: She Has What It Takes; They Knew What They Wanted; The Affairs of Annabelle; Go Chase Yourself; The Chance of a Lifetime; The Racket Man; Breakfast for Two; A Close Call for Boston Blackie; Walk Softly; Models, Inc.; The Black Scorpion.

YORDAN, Philip: Wri. b. Chicago, 1913. e. U of IL, BA, Kent Coll Law, LLD. Films inc: Syncopation; Dillinger; House of Strangers; Detective Story; Johnny Guitar; El Cid; Broken Lance (Oscar-1954); 55 Days at Peking; The Fall of the Roman Empire; (& prod): The Harder They Fall; Men in War; God's Little Acre; Day of the Outlaw; Studs Lonigan; The Day of the Triffids; The Thin Red Line; The Battle of the Bulge; Captain Apache.

YORK, Michael: Act. b. Fulmer, England, Mar 27, 1942. e. Oxford U. With Dundee Repertory Theatre. Thea inc: Any Just Cause; Hamlet; Outcry. On screen from 1967. Films inc: The Taming of the Shrew; The Strange Affair; Romeo and Juliet; The Guru; Zepplin; Cabaret; Lost Horizon; The Three Musketeers; The Four Musketeers; Murder on the Orient Express; Conduct Unbecoming; Logan's Run; Seven Nights in Japan; The Last Remake of Beau Geste; The Island of Dr. Moreau; Fedora; Riddle of the Sands; Final Assignment.

TV inc: The Forsyte Saga; Revel in the Grave; Great Expectations; Jesus of Nazareth; A Man Called Intrepid.

YORK, Susannah: Act. b. London, Jan 9, 1942. TV inc: The Crucible; The Rebel and the Soldier; The First Gentleman; The Richest Man in the World; The Golden Gate Murders.

Films inc: Tunes of Glory; There Was a Crooked Man; Freud; Tom Jones; Loss of Innocence; A Man for All Seasons; Lock Up Your Daughters; The Killing of Sister George; They Shoot Horses, Don't They?; Images; Conduct Unbecoming; Heaven Save Us From Our Friends; Sky Riders; The Shout; Mrs Eliza Fraser; Superman; The Silent Partner; The Awakening; Falling In Love Again (& wri); Superman II.

Thea inc: A Cheap Bunch of Flowers; Wings of the Dove; A Singular Man; Man and Superman.

YORKIN, Alan (Bud): Prod-Dir-Wri. b. Washington, PA, Feb 22, 1926. e. Carnegie Tech. Started in tv on NBC engineering staff; became asso dir Colgate Comedy Hour; partnered with Norman Lear in Tandem Productions; with Saul Turtletaub and Bernie Orenstein in Toy Productions.

TV inc: (dir) Martin & Lewis Show; Dinah Shore Show; The Tony Martin Show; Ernie Ford Show; George Gobel Show; An Evening With Fred Astaire (Emmys-dir-wri-1959); Another Evening With Fred Astaire; Jack Benny Specials (Emmy-1960); We Love You Madly; Duke Ellington Special; All in the Family; Sanford and Son; Good Times; Maude; Carter Country.

Films inc: Come Blow Your Horn; Never Too Late ; Divorce American Stye; Inspector Clouseau; Start the Revolution Without Me (& prod); Cold Turkey (exec prod); The Thief Who Came to Dinner (& prod).

YOUNG, Alan: Act. b. Northumberland, Eng, Nov 19, 1919. Films inc: Margie; Chicken Every Sunday; Mr Belvedere Goes to College; Aaron Slick from Punkin Crick; Androcles and the Lion; Gentlemen Marry Brunettes; Tom Thumb; Time Machine; Bakers Hawk; The Cat from Outer Space.

TV inc: The Alan Young Show (Emmy-1950); Mister Ed; The Gift of the Magi; Scruffy (voice).

YOUNG, Buddy: PR exec. b. NYC, Jun 15, 1935. e. CCNY. Joined UA publicity dept, 1952; asst pub mgr, 1963; west coast dir of adv, pub; in 1975 dir worldwide of adv, pub, exp col; 1976 named MGM adv, pub coordinator MGM; 1977: VP ad, pub, promo, U; formed ind pub marketing firm with Charles Powell, Jan 1980.

YOUNG, Burt: Act-Wri. Films inc: Cinderella Liberty; The Gambler; The Killer Elite; Chinatown; Rocky; The Choirboys; Convoy; Uncle Joe Shannon (& sp); Rocky II.

TV inc: MASH; Murder Can Hurt You.

YOUNG, Collier Hudson: Wri-Prod. b. Ashville, NC, Aug 19, 1908. e. Dartmouth Coll, BA. Films inc: (prod-sp) The Hitchhiker; The Bigamist; Private Hell 36; The Young Lovers; Not Wanted (prod); Hard, Fast, and Beautiful; Mad at the World; Huk!; The Halliday Brand; The Man; On the Loose; (Orig stories): Act of Violence; Keeper of the Flame.

TV inc: (series creator) Mr Adam and Eve; Crime and Punishment; Ironside. (Prod): The Rogues; The Joseph Cotten Show; On Trial; One Step Beyond. Ironside; Night Chase; Horatio Hornblower; The Next Step Beyond.

(Died Dec 25, 1980).

YOUNG, Dalene: Wri. TV inc: Dawn--Portrait of a Runaway; Christmas Coal Mine Disaster; Dead Man's Curve; Can You Hear the Laughter--The Story of Freddie Prinze; Plutonium, Inc; Marilyn--The Untold Story.

Films inc: Little Darlings.

YOUNG, Faron: Singer-Sngwri. b. Shreveport, LA, Feb 25, 1932. Country music recording artist; regular on Grand Ole Opry. Films inc: Country Music Holiday; Daniel Boone; Hidden Guns.

YOUNG, Frederick: Cin. b. England, 1902.
Films inc: Bitter Sweet; Nell Gwyn; When Knights Were Bold; Goodbye Mr Chips; The Young Mr Pitt; Edward My Son; Treasure Island; Ivanhoe; Lust for Life; Invitation to the Dance; Island in the Sun; Lawrence of Arabia (Oscar-1962); Lord Jim; Doctor Zhivago (Oscar-1965); The Deadly Affair; You Only Live Twice; The Battle of Britain; Ryan's Daughter (Oscar-1970); Nicholas and Alexandra; The Tamarind Seed; Permission to Kill; Stevie; Sidney Sheldon's Bloodline; Rough Cut; Richard's Things.
TV inc: Ike.

YOUNG, Loretta (Gretchen Young): Act. b. Salt Lake City, UT, Jan 6, 1913. On screen from 1928. Films inc: Laugh, Clown, Laugh; Man's Castle; The House of Rothschild; Bulldog Drummond Strikes Back; Clive of India; The Farmer's Daughter (Oscar-1947); Suez; Kentucky; Bedtime Story; The Bishop's Wife; Come to the Stable; Half Angel; Because of You; It Happens Every Thursday.
TV inc: A Letter to Loretta, 1953; The Loretta Young Show, 1954-60 (Emmys-1954, 1956, 1959); The New Loretta Young Show, 1962.

YOUNG, Neil: Mus-Sngwri. b. Toronto, Canada, Nov 12, 1945. Formed Buffalo Springfield with Stephen Sills; went solo 1968 then rejoined Crosby, Stills & Nash. Films inc: Journey Through the Past (wri-dir-act); Rust Never Sleeps (wri-dir-act); Where the Buffalo Roam (score).
Albums inc: Everybody Knows This Is Nowhere; After the Goldrush; Harvest; Journey Through the Past (soundtrack); Time Fades Away; On the Beach; Tonight's The Night; Zuma; American Stars 'n' Bars; Rust Never Sleeps.

YOUNG, Robert: Act. b. Chicago, IL, Feb 22, 1907. On screen from 1931. Films inc: Lullaby; The Black Camel; The Sin of Madelon Claudet; Strange Interlude; Tugboat Annie; The House of Rothschild; Stowaway; Married Before Breakfast; The Bride Wore Red; Northwest Passage; Western Union; H M Pulham, Esq; Joe Smith, American; Claudia; The Searching Wind; The Half Breed; Secret of the Incas.
TV inc: Father Knows Best (Emmys-1956, 1957); Marcus Welby, MD (Emmy-1970); Little Women.

YOUNG, Robert M: Dir. b. NYC, Nov 22, 1924. e. Harvard U.
Films inc: Nothing But A Man; Short Eyes; Rich Kids; The World Is Full of Married Men; One-Trick Pony.
TV inc: Eskimo-Fight for Life. (Emmy-1971).
Thea inc: Gaslight.

YOUNG, Terence: Dir. b. Shanghai, China, Jun 20, 1915. e. Cambridge U.
Films inc: Corridor of Mirrors; They Were Not Divided; The Tall Headlines; The Red Beret; Zarak; Too Hot to Handle; Doctor No; From Russia With Love; The Amorous Adventures; Thunderball; The Poppy is Also a Flower; Wait Until Dark; Mayerling; The Christmas Tree; Grand Slam; Cold Sweat; Red Sun; The Valachi Papers; War Goddess; The Klansman; Jackpot; Sidney Sheldon's Bloodline.

YOUNG, Tony: Act. b. 1932. Films inc: He Rides Tall; Taggart; Charroi; Chrome and Hot Leather; A Man Called Sledge; The Outfit; Policewomen; Act of Vengeance.
TV inc: Gunslinger.

YOUNGERMAN, Joseph C: Exec. b. Chicago, May 1, 1906. Started as prop man, Par, 1926; second asst dir 1928; first asst unit prodn mgr, second unit dir, 1930; dir US Signal Corps under Darryl F Zanuck, 1940-45; asst to VP, Par Pictures, 1945-50; National exec sec, Directors Guild of America, 1950-78; Board of Trustees, Motion Picture Television Fund.

YOUNGMAN, Henny: Comedian-Act. b. Liverpool, Eng, 1906. On screen in: A WAVE, A WAC and a Marine; Nashville Rebel; Won Ton Ton, the Dog Who Saved Hollywood; The Silent Movie.

YOUNGSTEIN, Max E: Exec. b. NYC, Mar 21, 1913. e. Fordham Law School, LLB, Brooklyn Law School, LLM. 1942-43, dir ad-pub-expl, Fox; 1945, VP & GM, Stanley Kramer Prodns; 1946, dir ad-pub-expl Eagle-Lion; 1949, dir ad-pub-expl, member exec comm Par Pictures; 1950, vp & dir Paramount Film Distrib Corp; 1955, vp & member of board UA; 1957-62, founder, p, UA Records, UA Music; 1962, exec vp Cinerama, Inc; 1962, independent prod, p, Max Youngstein Enterprises; 1972, vp, Todd-A O Corp; 1973, P, Taylor-Laughlin Distributing Co; sr VP, Billy Jack Prodns & National Student Film Corp; VP Billy Jack Records and Publishing, 1974-75; 1975-78 cnsltnt to various ind prodn firms, studios; gen film cnsltnt to Reader's Digest; co-exec prod-Diahann Carrol TV specials. Films inc: Best of Cinerama; Man in the Middle; Fail Safe; The Money Trap; Young Billy Young; co-prod. The Dangerous Days of Kiowa Jones; Welcome to Hard Times.

YULIN, Harris: Act. Films inc: Doc; The Midnight Man; Night Moves; Steel. TV inc: The Thirteenth Day--The Story of Esther; When Every Day Was The Fourth of July; Last Ride of the Dalton Gang.
Bway inc: Watch on the Rhine (rev); A Lesson From Aloes.

YUTKEVICH, Sergei: Dir-Wri. b. Russia, Dec 28, 1904. Films inc: (Silent) Radio Now!; Lace; The Black Sail (Dir). (Sound) Mountains of Gold; The Counter-Plan (Co-dir & Sp); Miners (dir); The Man With A Rifle (dir); New Adventures of Schweik (dir); Othello; The Bathhouse (Ani); Lenin in Poland; A Plot for a Short Story (dir); Mayakovsky Laughs. (Doc) Ankara--Heart of Turkey (dir); Liberated France; Young Years of Our Country; Yves Montand Sings; Meeting With France.

ZADAN, Craig: Prod-Dir-Wri. b. Miami, FL, Apr 15, 1949. e. Hofstra. Dir spec proj for Joseph Papp's Shakespeare Festival; co-prod Sondheim-A Musical Tribute; crea vp Casablanca Filmworks (later Polygram); 1980, vp crea aff UA.

ZAENTZ, Saul: Prod. b. Passaic, NJ.
Films inc: One Flew Over the Cuckoo's Nest (Oscar-1975); Three Warriors; The Lord of the Rings.

ZAMPA, Luigi: Dir. b. Rome, 1905. Films inc: American on Vacation; To Live in Peace; Difficult Years; Angelina; The White Line; City on Trail; Two Gentlemen in a Carriage; His Last 12 Hours; We Women; Woman of Rome; Art of Getting Along; Girl in Australia.

ZANUCK, Darryl F: Exec-Prod-Wri. b. Wahoo, NE, Sep 5, 1902. Prod exec Warners, 1929-30; gen prod chief, 1931; chief exec in charge prodn WB and First National; VP WB Pictures, Inc; resigned 1933 to form 20th Century Productions with Joseph M Schenck. Prod films inc: The Bowery; Moulin Rouge; The House of Rothschild; Bulldog Drummond Strikes Back; The Mighty Barnum; Clive of India; Folies Bergere; Call of the Wild; Les Miserables. In 1935 elected VP in charge of prodn when 20th Century merged with Fox. During WW2 commissioned Lt Col US Signal Corps, supervised prodn US Army training films; resd Army commission to return to 20th Century Fox as prodn chief 1943; Awarded Legion of Merit. Pres Darryl F Zanuck Prodns. Pres 20th Century-Fox Film Corp, 1962; chmn, CEO, 20th Century-Fox Film Corp, 1969. Resd, 1971.
Films inc: Wilson; Winged Victory; Dragonwyck; Anna and the King of Siam; The Razor's Edge; Gentleman's Agreement (Oscar-1947); Twelve O'Clock High; All About Eve (Oscar-1950); Viva Zapata; Snows of Kilimanjaro; The Egyptian; Man in the Gray Flannel Suit; Island in the Sun; The Longest Day.
(Irving Thalberg Award-1937,1944,1950).
(Died Dec 22, 1979).

ZANUCK, Richard Darryl: Exec. b. LA, Dec 13, 1934. e. Stanford U. S of Darryl Zanuck. Story dept 20th Century-Fox, 1954; NY pub dept, 1955; asst to prod, Island in the Sun, 1957; vp, Darryl F Zanuck Prod, 1958; prod, Compulsion, 1959; Sanctuary, 1961; The Chapman Report, 1962; asst to prod, The Longest Day, 1962; president's prod rep, 20th Century Fox Studio 1963; vp charge of prod 20th Fox; p, 20th Fox TV; exec vp charge prod, 20th Fox, 1967; P, 1969; joined WB, Mar 1971, as sr exec vp; resigned July 1972, to form (with David Brown) Zanuck/Brown Prodns.
Films inc: Sssssss; The Sugarland Express; Willie Dynamite; The Sting (Oscar-1973); The Black Windhill; The Girl from Petrovka; Jaws; MacArthur; Jaws 2; The Island.

ZAPATA, Carmen: Act. Films inc: Hail Hero; I Will, I Will. . .For Now; Rabbit Test; How To Beat the High Cost of Living; There Goes the Bride.
TV inc: Hagen; One Last Ride; Homeward Bound; Children of Divorce.

ZAPPA, Frank: Comp. b. Baltimore, MD, Dec 21, 1940. Film scores inc: Freak Out; 200 Motels; Burnt Weenie Sandwich; A Token of His Extreme; Baby Snakes (Musical Doc) (& prod-dir-ed-act); Sheik Yerbouti.

ZARKHI, Alexander: Wri-Dir. b. Russia, Feb 18, 1908. Began as a writer, collaborating with Iosif Heifits while both were students at Leningrad Film Factory; after two films, The Moon on Your Left and Fiery Transport, they began directing in tandem and turned out a dozen films inc: Wind In the Face; Midday; My Homeland; Those Were the Days!; The Baltic Deputy; Member of the Government; His Name is Sukhe-Bator; Precious Grains; The Lights of Baku. Solo dir inc: Height; People on The Bridge; My Younger Brother (& co-sp); Anna Karenina (& co-sp); Cities and Times (& co-sp). Story About an Unknown Actor (& co-sp).

ZASLOW, Michael: Act. b. Inglewood, CA, Nov 1, 1942. e. UCLA.
Films inc: You Light Up My Life; Meteor; There's a Girl in My Soup.
TV inc: Love is a Many Splendored Thing; Search for Tomorrow; Guiding Light; Star Trek.
Thea inc: Fiddler on the Roof; Cat on a Hot Tin Roof (rev); Boccaccio.

ZASTUPNEVICH, Paul: Cos Dsgn. b. Homestead, PA, Dec 24, 1931. e. Duquesne, B Ed; U of Pittsburgh, M Ed; Pasadena Playhouse, MA; Louise Salinger School Dress Design. Films inc: The Big Circus; The Lost World; Voyage to the Bottom of the Sea; Five Weeks In a Balloon; The Poseidon Adventure; The Towering Inferno; The Swarm; Beyond the Poseidon Adventure; When Time Ran Out.
TV inc: Voyage to the Bottom of the Sea; Swiss Family Robinson; Lost In Space; The Time Tunnel; Land of the Giants; City Beneath the Sea; Flood; Fire; Adventures of the Queen; The Return of Captain Nemo; Hanging By a Thread; The Memory of Eva Ryker.

ZAVATTINI, Cesare: Wri. b. Italy, 1902.
Films inc: Shoeshine; Bicycle Thieves; Miracle in Milan; First Communion; Umberto D; Gold of Naples; The Roof; Two Women; Marriage Italian Style; A Brief Vacation; The Children of Sanchez; Ligabue.

ZEFFIRELLI, Franco: Dir. b. Italy, Feb 12, 1923.
Films inc: The Taming of the Shrew; Romeo and Juliet; Brother Sun, Sister Moon; The Champ.
Thea inc: Saturday, Sunday and Monday; Filumena (& prod). (*Tony*-special-1962).

ZEITMAN, Jerome M: Prod. Started as agent in band dept MCA, later tv packaging vp; when MCA agency dissolved, moved to William Morris; became prod when he became partner on Playboy Prodms. Films inc: Damnation Alley; Just You and Me Kid; How to Beat the High Cost of Living.
TV inc: My Old Man; Devil Dog/Hound of Hell.

ZEMAN-KAUFMAN, Jackie: Act. b. Englewood, NJ, Mar 6. e. NYU on dance scholarship. Dancer and model before turning to act. Films inc: The Groove Tube; The Day The Music Stopped.
TV inc: One Life to Live; General Hospital.

ZEMECKIS, Robert: Wri-Dir. b. Chicago, 1952. e. USC.
Films inc: I Wanna Hold Your Hand; 1941; Used Cars.
TV inc: The Nightstalker.

ZERBE, Anthony: Act.
Films inc: Will Penny; The Liberation of L B Jones; Cotton Comes to Harlem; Farewell My Lovely; Rooster Cogburn; Who'll Stop The Rain; The First Deadly Sin.
TV inc: Harry O (*Emmy*-supp-1976); The Statesman (Benjamin Franklin); Centennial; Attica; The Seduction of Miss Leona.

ZETTERLING, Mai: Act-Dir. b. Sweden, May 24, 1925. Screen debut in Sweden in Frenzy.
Films inc: Torment; Frieda; Quartet (The Facts of Life episode); The Bad Lord Byron; Hell Is Sold Out; Desperate Moment; Knock on Wood; A Prize of Gold; Abandon Ship; The Truth About Women; Only Two Can Play; Night Is My Future; The Bay of St Michel. In 1965-66 wrote, dir Loving Couples; Night Games; 1968; Dr Glas; The Girls. Since 1969 dir doc for BBC and in Sweden.

ZIEFF, Howard: Dir. b. LA, 1943. While in Navy enrolled in Photographic School, made film, A Day in the Life of a Cadet; after service became tv newsreel cin; directorial debut Slither. Films inc: Hearts of the West; House Calls; The Main Event; Private Benjamin.

ZIMBALIST, Efrem, Jr: Act. b. NYC, Nov 30, 1923.
Bway debut 1946, The Rugged Path. On screen from 1949.
Films inc: House of Strangers; Bombers B-52; Band of Angels; Too Much, Too Soon; Home Before Dark; By Love Possessed; The Chapman Report; Wait Until Dark; Airport 1975; Harlow.
TV inc: Maverick; 77 Sunset Strip; The FBI; The Black Dahlia; Terror Out Of The Sky; The Best Place To Be; The Gathering, Part II; A Family of Winners; Scruples.

ZIMBALIST, Stephanie: Act. b. Encino, CA, Oct 6, 1956. D of Efrem Zimbalist, Jr. Films inc: Lassie, My Lassie; The Magic of Lassie; The Awakening.
TV inc: Forever; The Gathering; In the Matter of Karen Ann Quinlan; Yesterday's Child; The Best Place To Be; Long Journey Back; The Triangle Factory Fire Scandal; The Golden Moment-An Olympic Love Story; The Baby Sitter.

ZINBERG, Michael: Exec. b. San Antonio, TX. e. U of TX. With Mary Tyler Moore Productions for eight years as a wri-dir-prod. Joined NBC in June 1979 as vp, comedy development, West Coast, NBC Entertainment; resd Oct 1980 to ret to prodn.
TV inc: Bob Newhart Show; Mary Tyler Moore Show; Tony Randall Show; Rhoda.

ZINDEL, Paul: Plywri. b. Staten Island, NY, May 15, 1936. e. Wagner College. Plays inc: The Effect of Gamma Rays on Man-In-The-Moon Marigolds (*Pulitzer Prize*-1971); And Miss Reardon Drinks A Little; The Secret Affairs of Mildred Wild; Ladies at the Alamo.
TV inc: Let Me Hear You Whisper.

ZINNEMANN, Fred: Dir. b. Vienna, Austria, Apr 29, 1907. e. Vienna U. Studied photographic technique, lighting & mechanics (Paris); cam 1 yr (Berlin). Came to US 1929; extra in All Quiet on the Western Front, 1930; asst to dir Berthold Viertel; asst to Robert Flaherty, 1931; dir Mexican doc The Wave; short subjects dir, MGM, winning Oscar, 1938, That Mothers Might Live. Feature dir, 1941.
Films inc: The Seventh Cross; The Search; The Men; Teresa; High Noon; Benjy (short for LA Orthopedic Hospital, for which Oscar best doc short, 1951); Member of the Wedding; From Here to Eternity (*Oscar*-1953); Oklahoma; A Hatful of Rain; The Nun's Story; The Sundowners; Behold a Pale Horse; A Man for All Seasons (& prod) (*2 Oscars*-dir & picture-1966); Day of the Jackal; Julia.

ZINNER, Peter: Flm ed. b. Vienna, Austria, Jul 24, 1919.
Films inc: The Professionals; Changes; Darling Lili; Peter Gunn; In Cold Blood; The Red Tent; Godfather; Valdez' Horses; Crazy Joe; Godfather II; Mahogany; A Star is Born; Fox Trot; The Deer Hunter (*Oscar*-1978); Foolin' Around; Tintorera.

ZIPPRODT, Patricia: Cos dsgn. Bway inc: The Potting Shed; Visit To a Small Planet; The Virtuous Island; The Apollo of Bellac; Miss Lonelyhearts; The Rope Dancers; The Crucible; Back to Methusaleh; The Night Circus; Our Town; Camino Real; Period of Adjustment; The Blacks; Sunday in New York; Oh Dad, Poor Dad, Mama's Hung You In the Closet and I'm Feeling So Sad; Step On a Crack; The Dragon; She Loves Me; Fiddler on the Roof (*Tony*-1965); Anya; Pousse-Cafe; Cabaret; The Little Foxes; Plaza Suite; Zorba; Georgy; Pippin; Dear Nobody; Mack and Mabel.
Films inc: The Graduate; Last of the Mobile Hotshots.

ZORINA, Vera (Brigitta Hartwig): Dancer-Act. b. Berlin, Germany, 1917. On screen from 1938.

Films inc: The Goldwyn Follies; On Your Toes; I Was an Adventuress; Louisiana Purchase; Follow the Boys; Lover Come Back.

ZSIGMOND, Vilmos: Cin. b. Czeged, Hungary, Jun 16, 1930. e. U of Film and Theatre Art, Budapest.

Films inc: Hired Hand; Red Sky at Morning; McCabe and Mrs Miller; Deliverance; Images; The Long Goodbye; Scarecrow; Sugarland Express; Cinderella Liberty; The Girl from Petrovka; Obsession; Close Encounters of the Third Kind (*Oscar*-1977); The Deer Hunter; The Last Waltz; Sweet Revenge; Winter Kills; The Rose; Heaven's Gate.

TV inc: Flesh and Blood.

ZUGSMITH, Albert: Prod. b. Atlantic City, NJ, Apr 24, 1910. e. U of VA. Newspaper exec before turning to pictures.

Films inc: Written on the Wind; Man in the Shadow; Red Sundown; Star in the Dust; The Incredible Shrinking Man; The Girl in the Kremlin; Touch of Evil; Captive Women; Sword of Venus; Invasion USA; Top Banana; Slaughter on Tenth Avenue; The Beat Generation; Private Lives of Adam and Eve; Dondi; Fanny Hill; The Rapist!.

ZUKOR, Eugene J: Exec (ret). b. Chicago, Oct 25, 1897. S of late Adolph Zukor. With Par from 1916, pub and adv dept to asst treas, member of Par board of dir.

DISTRIBUTOR CODE

These abbreviations refer to the distributor designation found at the beginning of each film credit. Where the letter X appears, the distributor is unknown.

The code also is used in indicating distributors of Oscar-nominated films.

DISTRIBUTOR CODES

AA Allied Artists
AB A & B Distributors
ABX ABC Pictures Corp.
ACR Artists Creations & Associates Inc.
ACV Arge Fi/Li/Po-Cinecoop Film (Vienna)
ADS Art Du Siecle (France)
ADT Aditec (France)
AEF Actueelfilm
AES Aries (Argentina)
AFC Associated Film Distributing Corp.
AFD Archway Film Distributors
AFI Art Films International
AFT American Film Theatre
AGI Angelopolous-INA (Greece)
AHD Arthur Davis
AIC AIC
AIP American International Pictures
AIT Australian Film Institute
ALA Albanian Film
ALB Albina Prodns.
ALG Office Des Actualities Algeriennes
ALP Alpha (German)
ALX Alix Films (Greece)
AMB Ambassador
AMC American Cinema
AMLF AMLF
AMP Alaminos Films (Philippines)
AMQ Amolrat Films (Thailand)
AMX Ambar
ANL Angle Films
ANO Anonymous Releasing Triumvirate
ANY Analysis Films
AOJ Argos-Oshima-Shimbata
APF April Films
APH Alpherat (Italy)
APR April Fool Films
APV Amos Poe Visions
APX Adpix
AQU Aquarius
ARB Artemis (Britain)
ARG Argentine Sono Films

ARK Artkino (USSR)
ARQ Arquebuse (France)
ARS Argos
ARX Arandano (Spain)
ARZ Artco Film (Switzerland)
ASD Asa Films (Denmark)
AST Astral Films (Canada)
ASV Asvin Pictures (Thailand)
ASX ASOM Distributing Co.
ATF Atlas Films
ATG ATG
ATL Atlantic
ATP Atienza (Philippines)
AUD Audubon
AUE Aurore Edition (France)
AUR Aurora
AVE Avco Embassy
AXT Apex Prodns. (Thailand)
AYT Athit Taya Films (Thailand)
AZT Azteca Films
AZZ Arzu Films (Turkey)
BAB Babylone Films
BAI Baires (Argentina)
BBZ Bruno Bozzetto (Italy)
BCR BAC-RTE (Ireland)
BDD Buddadeb Dasgupta (India)
BDV Barrandov
BED Belladonna Films
BEF British Empire Films
BEG Bel Air-Gradison
BFI British Film Institute
BGA Belga Films (Belgium)
BGK Bangkok Films (Thailand)
BGO Bulgaro Films (Bulgaria)
BHF Blueberry Hill Films
BIH Bioscop (Hungary)
BIM Biomed Arts Associates
BKF Bangkok Karn Films (Thailand)
BLI British Lion
BLO Blossom Pictures
BLZ Blaze Enterprises (India)

BMM Bhadra Movie Makers Prodn. Co. (India)
BND Bangladesh Film
BNG Bang Bang Films Co. Ltd.
BOR Borde
BPC Blue Pacific Corp.
BQT Betancourt, Quintana (Venezuela)
BRE Brenner
BRI Brian Distributing
BRU Brut
BSG Basis Film (Germany)
BTN Bryanston
BUI Buffalo Films-INA (France)
BV Buena Vista
BVA Bavaria Atelier
BXX Burbank Int'l. Pictures
CAF Camera Films
CAL Carolyn Films
CAM Cambist
CAN Cannon
CAP Capitol
CAW Cal Am Releasing
CAX Cine Artists Pictures Corp.
CAY Catalyst Prodns. Inc.
CBB C. B. Bartell
CBF CB Films
CBT Co Brothers Films (Thailand)
CBZ Columbus Films (Switzerland)
CCD Concord
CCF CCFC
CCI COFCI
CCR Capricorno Films (Italy)
CCU Contracuardo (Argentina)
CCZ Cactus Films (Switzerland)
CDB CDEC (Belgium)
CDE Conde
CDK Cinema Film (Denmark)
CDV Campbell-Devon
CED CEIAD
CEK Ceskoslovensky
C11 Cinema 11

DISTRIBUTOR CODES

CEN Centaur
CFA China Film Agency
CFC CFCC
CFD Compagnie Francaise du Cinema
C5 Cinema 5
CFN Children's Film Foundation (Britain)
CFS Compass Film Sales
CFZ Coliseum Films (Thailand)
CGS Cinematograph (Sweden)
CHB Churubusco
CHT Chao Poj Films (Thailand)
CHY Chaiyo Films (Thailand)
CHZ Cherdchai Prodns. (Thailand)
CIA Cine Art
CIC Columbia In Canada
CID CIDIF
CIG Cine-Int'l. (Germany)
CII Cinema Int'l. Corp.
CIM Cimex
CIR Circuit Films
CIT Citel
CIX Capi Films-INA (France)
CIZ Cite Films
CKI Cinak-Filmoblic-INA (France)
CLA Classic Festival
CLK Clark Films
CLP Calliope
CLU Clouds Prodns.
CLZ Chan Lin Kang (Thailand)
CM CineMasters (Italy)
CMA Cinemation
CMI Cine America
CMJ Cinemanjali (Sri Lanka)
CMO Centre Cinematographique Morocain
CMR Camera One
CMT Central Motion Picture Co. (Taiwan)
CMY Cine Manifest
CMZ Cine-Media Int'l.
CN Cinema National
CNE Cineastes Animaliers Associes
CNG Cinegate (Britain)

C9 Cinema 9 (France)
CNW CineWorld Pictures Int'l.
CNZ Cineriz
COH Contrechamp (France)
COI Coliseum Films Ltd. (Italy)
COL Columbia
CON Continental
COX Conacine (Mexico)
COZ Coline (France)
CPI Cinemanila (Philippines)
CPM Claude Antoine-Polifilm
CPQ Compass Int'l.-Manson Int'l.
CPR Chayabani Private (India)
CPX Cinepix
CPZ Cine-Pro (Germany)
CQC Films Coute Que Coute (France)
CQD Films Coute Que Coute-Cafe de la Gare (France)
CRC Cinerama Releasing Corp.
CRG Cemp-Regent (Australia)
CRL Carle (Canada)
CRQ Chronos Films
CRV Cinerama (Germany)-Rialto (Austria)
CRX Creswin Films (Canada)
CSH Cinema Shares
CTB Cinematic Releasing
CTD City Film (Netherlands)
CTE Cinetel
CTG CTGE
CTP Cinema Artists (Philippines)
CTT Constantin
CTW Cinema 2000 (Spain)
CTY Contemporary Films
CUI Calcutta Films (India)
CUT SATPEC (Secretary of Cultural Affairs & Information, Tunisia)
CVG Cine Vog
CVT Cinevest Int'l.
CWN Crown
CWR Cinema World Releasing
CXP Cine Export (France)
CYF City Life Films

CYT Cythere (France)
CZC Cinema Diez-Conacine (Mexico)
CZS Czech State Film
DAG Dagmar Distribution (Denmark)
DAI Dan-Ima Films (Denmark)
DAM Damiani
DD Day and Date Int'l.
DDY Doty-Dayton
DEB Debara (Canada)
DEE DEFA (East Germany)
DEP Derio Prodns.
DET Duangkamol Entertainment (Thailand)
DFJ Dokoritsu Film Center (Japan)
DFM Distrifilm (Argentina)
DGF Diagonale Films (France)
DIF Difilm (Brazil)
DIM Dimension
DIX Distribuidora Internacional de Peliculas
DKF Dokdin Kanyaman Films (Thailand)
DLT Delta
DNS Dansk-Svensk Films
DOA Double Head Prodns.
DOV Dovidis
DPA Disprofilm (Argentina)
DPC Dpica Prodn. Co. (India)
DPO DPFN-ONC (Algeria)
DPX Distribpix
DRF D/R Films
DRO Dragon One Films
DRV Domirev (Senegal)
DSC Discopat
DSM DNS Munich Films (West Germany)
DSS Dolin Siam Film (Thailand)
DYN Dynamite Entertainment
EF Exportfilm
EGC Egyptian Cinema Organization
EI Euro-Int'l.
ELG Eleftheroudakis (Greece)
ELL Ellman
ELN Elan Films
EM Emco

DISTRIBUTOR CODES

EME Emerson
EMF Earle Mack Films
EMI EMI (Britain)
EMQ Entertainment Mktg. Corp.
EMR Empire
EMZ Embrafilms (Brazil)
ENZ Endeavour Prodns.-New Zealand Film Commission
EOS EOS Film-SSR (Switzerland)
EPI Enterprise Pictures Ltd.
EPN European Film
EPO EPOH
EPP Emperor Films (Philippines)
ERE ERE Films (Brazil)
ESX Essex
ETE Eternal Film (Hong Kong)
ETQ ETC (Iraq)
EUP Europea Film
EV Entertainment Ventures
EVO Evolution Enterprises
EVT Evart Releasing
EXB Exportfilm Bischoff
EXT Extravagant
FAA Fania
FAL Falcon
FAN Fanfare
FAP Filmhouse Australia
FAS First Artists
FAW Films Around the World
FBE Films de la Boetie (France)
FBK Fred Baker
FBU Films Bulgaria
FCD Film Consortium of Canada
FCM FFCM (France)
FCO Filmoblic-Open Film (France)
FCS Faces Int'l.
FCT Filmcentralen
FCU Film Cuatro (Argentina)
FDA Filmverlag Der Autoren
FDD Fernsehen DDR (West Germany)
FDL Films de Losange (France)

FDM Filmverlag Der Autoren (Germany)-Les Films Oli (France)
FDP Films de Plateau (France)
FDT Films du Tamonoir (France)
F8 Les Films 88
FEL Fox/Lira
FFA Films Armorial
FFF First Films (China)
FFG Films Finance Group (India)
FFP Forum Film Prodns.
FFT Focus Films (Turkey)
FFU First American Films
FGG Films Galatee/Gaumont (France)
FGR Francos Film-Films Ege-Rapid Film (France)
FGU Film League, Inc.
FHB Films Hans-Bobwin
FI Films Int'l.
FIA FIDA
FII Filmalpha (Italy)
FIM Films Mutuels
FIS Finos Films
FJL Films Jacques Leitienne
FKC Fish Hawk Co.-CFDC (Canada)
FKY Funky Films
FKZ Filmkollektiv Zurich (Switzerland)
FLG Filmologies (France)
FLN Flan Film
FLY Filmityo Oy
FMG Filmalpha-Megavision (Italy)
FOG First Organization
FPH Filmel-PHPG (France)
FPJ FPJ (Philippines)
FPL Filmpeople, Inc.
FPZ Filmpool Zurich (Switzerland)
FR FR3 Lyon (France)
FRK Fox-Rank (Britain)
FRM Framo
FRT Franco Roma & Adriatica Film (Italy)
FSF First Scope Films (China)
FSH Friendship Motion Picture Co. (Nigeria)
FSI Film Saturation Inc.

FST Five Stars Prodns. (Thailand)
F13 Films 13
FUJ Fuji Films (Japan)
FVA Film Valas (India)
FVI Film Ventures Int'l.
FWG Filmwelt Munich (West Germany)
FWS Filmways
FXC Fox-Columbia
FXE Fox Europe
FXG Flaxfold Prodns.
FXN Fox Netherlands
FXS Fox Stockholm
FYF Fantasy Films
GAG Joe Gage Films
GAP Gaia Prodns. (France)
GAU Gaumont
GB Gaumont British
GBF Globe Film Co.
GCC GEF-CCFC (France)
GDA Gendai
GDG Goldig Films (Hong Kong)
GDN Golden Films
GDR Robert Gardner Representative (Switzerland)
GDW Goodwill (Philippines)
GEM Gemini
GEX Great Expectations
GFE GEF
GFF Griffifilms (Greece)
GGC GGC Communications
GHV Golden harvest
GIR Giriraj Pictures (India)
GKF Greek Film Centre
GKN Gulkin Prodns. (Canada)
GLA Gloria Films
GLI General Pictures (India)
GMA Gamma
GMF GMF (France)
GNX General National Enterprises
GOI Gold (Italy)
G 1 Group 1 Films

DISTRIBUTOR CODES

GOS Goskino (USSR)
GOY Goya Film (Spain)
GP Grove Press
GPP G P Film Promotions (Thailand)
GRO Jerrry Gross Organization
GSB Golden Star Barbad (Singapore)
GST Guest Prodns. (South Africa)
GTM Good Time Movies
GUC Gaumont-Coline (France)
GUD Gaumont-Cerito Rene Chateau (France)
GUI Gueney Films (Turkey)
GUN GUNRO (Japan)
GUO Greater Union Film Distributors (Australia)
HA Harris
HAP Hapdong Films (Korea)
HBD Eginhart Hillebrand
HBH H B Halicki Int'l.
HDF Hound Dog Films
HDS Henderson Films
HEL Helios Films (Switzerland)
HFT Hollywood Films (Thailand)
HI Hollywood Int'l.
HIT Hitimarama Films (Tahiti)
HMD Hemdale Film Distributors
HND Handinhand
HOW Howco
HOY Hoyt's (Australia)
HPP Harsha Pictures Prodns. (India)
HSM Hasam Films (Iran)
HTM HTM Films (Denmark)
HTR Hamster (France)
HU Hungarofilm
HWK Hawk Serpent Prodns.
HWT Hawthorne Int'l.
IAA International Aries Angkasa Films (Indonesia)
IAM International Amusement
IAP Ian Film Prodns. (Philippines)
ICA International Cinema
ICI ICAIC
ICR Intercontinental

IDI Idi Cinematografica
IDP IDP (Cuba)
IFS Ideal Film (Switzerland)
IFX Ifex (Britain)
IGI Integrated Film (India)
IGR Italnoleggio-RAI (Italy)
IHA International Harmony
IID INA-ISKA-Dovidis (France)
IIP Independent Int'l.
IIT Iris Films-International Tropic Films
ILZ ILA Film Prodns. (New Zealand)
IMA Imperia
IMX Impexfilm
INA Internation Film Ass'n.
INS Incine (Spain)
INZ INA (France)
IOS Inter Ocean Film Sales Ltd. (Canada)
IPD IPDC (Portugal)
IR Iran Film
IRQ Iraqui General Organization For Cinema
ISC IFI-Scope III
ISM Isram Film Corp. (Israel)
ISR Isfilm (Iceland)
ITC ITC Releasing
ITF Interfilm
ITG Italnoleggio (Italy)
ITI Italian Int'l.
ITP International Picture Show
ITR Intercine
ITV International TV Trading Corp.
IUS Imus (Philippines)
JAN Janus
JAT Jaturamit (Thailand)
JCI Jayasarathy Combine (India)
JDJ Joden Distributing (Jamaica)
JEL Joseph E Levine
JEP JE (Philippines)
J-5 J-5 Prodns. (Thailand)
JIR Jirabanterng Films (Thailand)
JOD Jorn Donner Prodns. (Finland)
JOG Joseph Green Prodns.

JUG Jugendfilm (West Germany)
JVA Jarva
JWJ Jin Woo Jung Films (South Korea)
K-J Kelly Jordan
KDK Kodiak
KEX Kemal Enterprises
KFF Key Films (France)
KGS Kogei-Sha (Japan)
KHU King Hu
KID Kino Films (Denmark)
KKC Krung Kasem Films (China)
KKW Keung Keow Films (Thailand)
KLF Ken Lane Films
KNS Kinesis Ltd.
KOM Kommunes Filmcentral
KSH Kshirgar (India)
KTD K-Tell Distributors
KTQ Kartemquin Films
KYH Koo Yong Hua (China)
KYI Key Int'l. Films
L-P Levitt Pickman
LAD Lademann Films (Denmark)
LAU Taylor-Laughlin
LBR Libra Films
LDS LDS Films (Britain)
LFA Leonard Franklin Associates
LGT Lighthouse Prodns.
LH Lo and Hu (Hong Kong)
LIG Lionsgate
LII Lissar Film Group (Iran)
LIO Lion Int'l.
LIR Lira Film
LKN Lakshmipathy-Narayan (India)
LKS Lakshmipathy-Swan Movies (India)
LML Les Films Moliere (France)
LNF Lenefilm
LOR Lorimar Prodns.
LOS Lone Star
LST Lustig Prodns.
LUF Lusofrance
LUG Lugo Films (France)

LWM Low Wei Motion Picture Co. (China)
LXM Luxmeta (West Germany)
LYC Lycouressis (Greece)
LYN Greg Lynch Film Distributors (Australia)
MA Mayleys
MAH Mahler
MAL Mallia Films (France)
MAM Mammoth
MAN Manson
MAR Marvin
MAS Master Art & Mastermind
MAT Mature
MAV Maverick Pictures Int'l.
MBC MBC (Argentina)
MCA Melbourne Co-op Cinema (Australia)
MCH March Films (Canada)
MDM Michele Dimitri Films (France)
MDN Mediane Films (France)
MDU Medusa
MDW Midwest Film Prodns. Inc.
MEH Metanee Films (Thailand)
MFM Melbourne
MFN Marcusfilm (Norway)
MFR Mayfair
MGF Mongofilm
MGM Metro Goldwyn Mayer
MHT Chokchai Mahasombat (Thailand)
MIS Mishkin
MJS Majestic Sa (Switzerland)
MK MK2 (France)
MKA McKinley Prodns./Media America
MLB Mulberry Square
MMI Mohan Mohammed Films Prodn. Co. (India)
MMK Multicine-MK2 (France)
MNF Minerva Films
MNP Monopole Pathe Films (Switzerland)
MNR Monarch
MNY Monarch-Noteworthy
MOS Mostest
MRD M & R Distributors

MRG Munstergasse (Switzerland)
MRH Marathon Films
MRK Mairik (Philippines)
MRR Merry Films
MRS Miraleste Co.
MRX Miramax
MSF Mosfilm (USSR)
MSP Mrinal Sen Prodns. (India)
MSV Mauel Salvador (Spain)
MSY M. Shuffey Associates
MTF Metronome Films (Denmark)
MTL Mitchell
MUT Mutual Films (Canada)
MVS Moving Picture Co. (Thailand)
MVT Movietime Films
MWE Midwest Enterprises
MXF Maxifilm (Argentina)
MXM Max Mambru
NA North American
NAE National-American Entertainment Corp.
NAI NAI Entertainment
NCF NEF-CFDC
NCH Nachson Films (Israel)
NCS National Cinema Organization (Syria)
NCT Neue Constantin Film (West Germany)
NDF New Day Films
NEF Neue Filmform
NFC National Film Board (Canada)
NFL Norfolk Int'l. Pictures
NFT New Five Star Prodns. (Thailand)
NHN Nahoun (France)
NIK Nikkatsu (Japan)
NIP Nippon Herald (Japan)
NJI Nachiket Jayoo (India)
NKP Nakorn Ping Films (Thailand)
NL New Line Films
NNT Nine Network
NOA Noah Film
NOR Nordisk
NPF NPF
NPP Narong Poomin Prodns. (Thailand)

NPT Napasiri Papiyon (Thailand)
NRH Nirmithi Films (India)
NRP New Realm Pictures
NSF New Star Film Co.
NSK Norsk Film
NSW New South Wales Film Corp. (Australia)
NTC National Cinema
NTK Nantanakorn Films (Thailand)
NUI Nu-Image Films
NVA Navarro Prodns.
NVP N V Prodns.
NVR Nouveau Reseau (Canada)
NW New World
NWA New American Cinema
NWI New Int'l. Cinema (West Germany)
NY New Yorker
OBL Obel
OCM Ocinam (Mali)
ODY Odyssey
OFF Orion Films (France)
OH Ohio River
OMF Omnifilms
OMN Omnia
ONC ONCIC (Algeria)
ONS ONC (Syria)
OPC Open Circle Cinema (Canada)
OPH Orpham
ORF ORTF
OSM Osmond Distribution Co.
OSP Osprey Films (Britain)
OZA O-Zali Films (Canada)
PAL Palladium
PAR Paramount
PCI PAC (Italy)
PCN Pan Canadian Film Distribution
PCX Procinex
PCY Public Cinema Organization (Libya)
PDI Production Co. (India)
PDP Producciones Del Plata (Argentina)
PDS Prodis
PEA PEA (Italy)

PEN Pennapacker
PEP Penland Prodns.
PES Peries Prodns. (Sri Lanka)
PEX Pelimex
PF Paris Film
PFC Parafrance
PFE PFE
PFP Parindah Films (Pakistan)
PGS Pathe-Gaumont-Sirius (France)
PHI Pethurst Int'l. (Britain)
PHK Pearl City Films (Hong Kong)
PHU Pathe-CFDC-Sirius (France)
PHZ Production Co. Hamzu (India)
PI Phoenix Int'l.
PIC PIC (Italy)
PIE Pires
PIF Pari Films (France)
PII Producciones Inca Films (Peru)
PKN Parker National
PKT Park Films (Thailand)
PLF Planfilm
PLL Parallel
PLS Pallas Film
PMA Producciones Imperial (Argentina)
PMB Promofilms (Belgium)
PML Promotional Films
PMP Premiere Prodns. (Philippines)
PMR Poolemar
PNB Pennebaker
PNR Panorama
PNS Planfilm-Sirius (France)
PNT Penthouse Prodns.
POF Polish Corp. for Film
POI Pro-International
POL Polski Film
PON Prodis-Oceanic (France)
PPFC PPFC
PPY Peter Perry Pictures
PRG Progress
PRI Prisma
PRO Pros Releasing Organization

PRS Profilmes (Spain)
PSD Panorama-Asa (Denmark)
PSP Prospectable (France)
PTS Prentiss Prodns.
PTV Poltel (Poland)
PXA Perucinex-Mario Abate
PYO Proyecto (Venezuela)
PYR Pyramid Films
QBY Queensbury Films (Canada)
QDC Quadrant Films (Canada)
QRT Quartet Films
RBS Robson Street Prodns.
RCR R. C. Riddell & Associates
RDB R. D. Bansal
RDP Roadshow Distributors (Australia)
RGR Roger Grod Prodns.
RHM RHM Distributors
RIA Rialto Films
RIG Riga Studios (Latvia)
RIN Ray (India)
RIZ Rizzoli (Italy)
RMN Romania Film
RMX Rio Mexcoac (Mexico)
RMY R M Films Int'l.
RNK Rank
ROD Roda Films
ROL Rochelle Films
ROX Roxy Int'l.
RPA Republic Arts
RRX Reel to Reel
RSH Rush Prodns. (France)
RSS Roissy Films (France)
RTA RTA (Algeria)
RTI RAI-Radiotelevision Italy
RTS RAI-Sacis (Italy)
RVD Raven-Doyon
RVR Raviraj Int'l. (India)
RXF Rex-Film
RYK Royal Oak Film Corp.
SAA Salt-Pan Films (Australia)
SAF South Australian Film Corp.

SAH Saha Mongkol Films (Thailand)
SAI Sarinande (Indonesia)
SAL Saliva Films
SAT Sanam Suansujarit (Thailand)
SAY Sayawan Motion Picture Co. (Thailand)
SBD SBD (France)
SBV Les Films de la Seine-Bavaria Atelier
SCB State Establishment for Cinema & Theatre (Iraq)
SCI Sacis (Italy)
SDK Sudarsky Film
SDN Stand'art-INA (France)
SEH Seasonal Films (Hong Kong)
SEI Seine Prodns. (France)
SEJ Seirinsha (Japan)
722 722 Investments
77 77 Cinematographica (Italy)
SFC Sofac
SFI Selected Films Inc.
SFK Statens Filmcentral-Kollektiv Film (Denmark)
SFO Stefano (Italy)
SFT Sibunruang Films (Thailand)
SGY Saguenay Films (Canada)
SHA Shanghai Animation Studios
SHD Sunchild (France)
SHF Shaw Film Distributors (Hong Kong)
SHO Shibata Organization (Japan)
SHP Shapira Films (Israel)
SHS Udaya Shaskar Int'l. (India)
SHW Shaw Ltd. (Singapore)
SI Scotia Int'l.
SIA Sino-American Corp.
SJS Sippang Jaya Sakti Films (Indonesia)
SKU Shochiku (Japan)
SKY Seven Keys (Australia)
SLG Silenes-Lugo Films (France)
SLN Silenes (France)
SMB Summer Brown
SNA Sandrew
SNC SNC
SND Sand Film

SNM SNC-Imperia
SNX SND (France)
SOC Sofracima
SOE Southern Pictures (Britain)
SOG Societe Generale de Production
SON Soho Cinema (Britain)
SOV Sovexport (USSR)
SP Sun Prodns.
SPB Spiegel-Bergman
SPV Special Event Entertainment
SPZ Spencer Prodns.
SRI Sanrio Films
SRS Sri Syarm Prodns. (Thailand)
SRT Sri Boonliang Film (Thailand)
SSF Sun Child-Saga (France)
SSH Sunshine Artists (Philippines)
SSI S. Sainath Prodns. (India)
SSU Schick Sunn Classics
STC Santisucha Prodns. (Thailand)
STH Saha Thai Prodns. (Thailand)
STK Stockholm Film
STW Star-Film
SUN Sun Int'l.
SUS Susetz (Israel)
SUW Suwannit Prodns. (Thailand)
SVE Svensk Filmindustri (Sweden)
SVF Svensk Filminstitutet (Sweden)
SVO Svenska Ord (Sweden)
SVS Swedish Filminstitutet-Svensk Films (Sweden)
SWI Swairi Films (India)
SWN Swan Diffusion
SYG Sygma (France)
TA Transamerican (AIP Subsidiary)
TAL Talar (Argentina)
TBS TBS Distributing Corp. (Britain)
TCF Tricontinental Films
TCK Tai Cheng Enterprises (Korea)
TCZ Telecinez
TDB Trident Barber (Britain)
TDD Theatre D'Orsay-Duras (France)

TEF Thuering-Engstrom Film Prodns.
TEG Team Film (West Germany)
TER Terra
TFI Telefilm (Iran)
TFK Teatrenes Filmkontor (Denmark)
TGO Tango Films
TGT Target Int'l. Films
THB Thomas Brothers Film Studio
THT Theh Prasin Pictures (Thailand)
THW Toho-Towa (Japan)
TII Tagalog Ilang-Ilang
TIY Tarik Film Distributors
TLF Tele Film (Greece)
TMK Trimek Films (Thailand)
TOE Toei (Japan)
TOH Toho (Japan)
TPF Top Film (Austria)
TPZ Topaz (Philippines)
TRO Transocean
TSU Tronsue Pictures Corp.
TSZ Television Suisse-Zurich (Switzerland)
TTV Theatre Television
TUR Turtle Releasing Organization
TUS Tuschinski Film Distribution (Netherlands)
TVA Televisa
TVD Trivandrum (India)
TW Trans World
TWA Towa (Japan)
TYL Taylor-Laughlin
TYW Tsai Yu Wen (Taiwan)
U Universal
UA United Artists
UAZ Ursuline & AZ Distribution (France)
UCC UGC-CFDC (France)
UCS UGC-CFDC-Sirius (France)
UF United Film
UGC UGC (France)
UGP UGC-Parafrance (France)
UIP United Int'l. Pictures
UMU Umut Sanat Urunleri (Turkey)

UNF Unifilms
UNI Unique
UPR Universal-Paramount
UT Unite Trois (France)
UZF UZ (France)
VAL Valoria Films
VBX Video Box
VDE Vides (Italy)
VDI Venture Distribution Inc.
VF Variety Films
VFT Virasak Films (Thailand)
VGD Vanguard
VIB Viba Films (Yugoslavia)
VIE Vietnam Feature Film Studio
VLS Valois
VMB Visit Mingwattanaboon (Thailand)
VO V.O. Films (Portugal)
VPF Ventania Producoes Cinematograficas-PC R.F. Farias
VPS Visual Programme Systems Ltd. (Britain)
VRA Varia Film Prodns. (Malaysia)
VSI V.I.S. (Italy)
V3 Virgo 3 Films
WB Warner Brothers
WBC Warner Bros.-Columbia
WBL Warner Bros.-Lademan
WBO Warner Bros.-Orion
WBS Warner Bros. Spain
WCT Warner Bros.-Constantin
WDR WDR (West Germany)
WHP Whitepal
WKD Weekend
WKR Brent Walker (Britain)
WMF World Marketing Film (France)
WNO World-Northal
WOR World Entertainment
WW Worldwide
WWP Western World Prodns.
X (Distributor Unknown)
YAB Irwin Yablans
YBK Yung Bang Films (South Korea)

YFR Yugoslav Film Releasing

YMT Yamamoto (Japan)

ZAG Zagreb Film (Yugoslavia)

ZDF Zweites Deutsches Fernsehen (TV 2 West Germany)

ZFB Zeno Films (Belgium)

ZOD Zodiac

ZPF Z Prodns. (France)

ZSP Zoetrope Studios (Philippines)

FILM CREDITS

Jan. 1, 1976–Dec. 31, 1980

NOTE: Foreign films are listed by their original titles and cross-indexed by U.S. titles wherever possible. However, many foreign films are reviewed at festivals where temporary English-language titles, usually direct translations of the original, are used. When such films are subsequently picked up for U.S. release, distributors frequently create a different title. While every effort has been made to keep these English-language titles up to date, some discrepancies are inevitable.

A Bad Son: SEE Un Mauvais Fils

A Bridge Too Far
(Britain)
UA. Joseph E Levine prodn. Prods, Joseph E Levine, Richard P Levine. Dir, Richard Attenborough. Sp, William Goldman, based on book by Cornelius Ryan; cam, Geoffrey Unsworth; co-prod, Michael Stanley-Evans; asso prod, John Palmer; edtr, Anthony Gibbs; snd, Simon Kaye; art dirs, Roy Stannard, Stuart Craig; prodn des, Terry Marsh; sfx, John Richardson; mus, John Addison; stunt coord, Alf Joint; asst dir, David Tomblin. (MPAA rating: PG). 175.
Dirk Bogarde, James Caan, Michael Caine, Sean Connery, Edward Fox, Elliott Gould, Gene Hackman, Anthony Hopkins, Hardy Kruger, Laurence Olivier, Ryan O'Neal, Robert Redford, Maximilian Schell, Liv Ullman, Arthur Hill, Wolfgang Preiss, Siem Vroom, Eric Van't Wout, Mary Smithuysen, Marlies Van Alcmaer, Nicholas Campbell, Christopher Good, Keith Drinkel, Peter Faber.
06/08/77

A Butterfly on the Shoulder:
SEE Un Papillon Sur L'Epaule

A Chacun Son Enfer
(To Each His Hell)
(France)
LUG. Paris-Cannes Prodn-Cinema 77 prodn. Dir, Andre Cayatte. Sp, Cayatte, Jean Curtelin; cam (Eastmancolor), Maurice Fellous; edtr, Paul Cayatte; prod, Sergio Gobbi. 100.
Annie Girardot, Stephane Hillel, Hardy Kruger, Bernard Fresson, Fernand Ledoux.
02/16/77

A Change of Seasons
FOX. Film Finance Group Ltd/Martin Ransohoff prodn. Exec prod, Richard R St Johns. Prod, Ransohoff. Dir, Richard Lang. Sp, Erich Segal, Ronni Kern, Fred Segal, from a story by Erich Segal, Ransohoff; cam (Deluxe Color), Philip Lathrop; 2d unit cam, Dick Kratina, Rexford Metz, Joe Jackman; ski photographer, Scott Miller; mus, Henry Mancini; song, "Where Do You Catch The Bus For Tomorrow?"; Alan & Marilyn Bergman, Mancini; edtr, Don Zimmerman; prodn des, Bill Kenney; set decor, Rick T Gentz; snd, Richard Gragg, Robert Knudson, Don MacDougall, Robert Glass; asso prod, Cathleen Summers; 2d unit dir, Michael Moore; asst dirs, Donald Heitzer, James Weatherill. (MPAA rating: R). 102.
Shirley MacLaine, Anthony Hopkins, Bo Derek, Michael Brandon, Mary Beth Hurt, Ed Winter, Paul Regina, K Callan, Rod Colbin, Steve Eastin, Christopher Coffey.
12/24/80

A Child in the Crowd: SEE Un Enfant Dans La Foule

A Child Is A Wild Thing
SDK. Wri-dir-lensed-co-edtr, Peter Skinner. Edtrs, Skinner, Vincent Suprynowicz, Sidney Katz; mus, Derek Wadsworth. 88.
Marie Antoinette Skinner, Adam, George S Irving.
09/15/76

A Commuter Kind of Love:
SEE Kjaerleikens Ferjreiser

A Confederacao-O Povo E Que Faz A Historia
(The Confederation-The People Make History)
X. Cinequanon prodn, financed by Institut Portuges de Cinema and Calouste Gulbenkian. Dir, Luis Galvao Teles. Sp, Amadeu Lopes Sabibo, Luis Galvao Teles; cam, Elso Roque; mus, Sergio Godinho-Fausto, Jose Maria Branco; edtr, Glara Diaz-Berrio. 105.
Margarida Carpinteiro, Carlos Cabral, Irene Ruivo, Jorge Cortes, Luis Santos,
10/10/79 Jorge Vale, Artur Semedo, Santos Manuel, Ricardo Pais, Orlando Costa.
(16m)

A Culpa
(The Fault)
(Portugal)
X. Antonio Victorino d'Aleida, Vindobona Film prodn, Lisbon. Wri-dir-mus, Antonio Victorino d'Almeida; cam, Hanus Polak; edtrs, Daniela Klein, Victor Silva. 140.
Sinde Filipe, Mario Viegas, Estrela Novais, Lia Gama, Paula Guedes.
10/15/80

A Dead End: SEE Peruvaziambalan

A Decent Life: SEE Ett anstaendigt liv

A Different Story
AVE. Prod, Alan Belkin; exec prod, Michael F Leone. Dir, Paul Aaron. Sp, Henry Olek; cam (CFI color), Philip Lathrop; 2d unit camera, Michael Werk; edtr, Lynn McCallon; mus, David Frank; songs, Bob Wahler; set decor, Lee Poll; snd, William Teague, Thomas Dodington; cos-ward, Robert Demora, Agnes Lyon. (MPAA rating: R). 106.
Perry King, Meg Foster, Valerie Curtin, Peter Donat, Richard Bull, Barbara Collentine, Guerin Barry, Doug Higgins, Lisa James, Eugene Butler.
04/19/78

A Difficult Transport: SEE Nje Udhetimi I Veshtire

A Dirty Story: SEE Une Sale Histoire

A Distant Cry From Spring:
SEE Harukanaru Yama No Yobigoe

A Dream Of Passion
(Greece)
SNC. Brenfilm-Melina Film prodn. Dir-prod-wri, Jules Dassin. Cam (Eastmancolor), George Arvanitis; edtr, George Klotz; art dir, Dionysis Fotopoulos; mus, Iannis Markpopoulos. 110.
Melina Mercouri, Ellen Burstyn, Andreas Voutsinas, Despo Diamantidou, Dimitris Papamicahel, Yannis Voglis, Phedon Georgitsis, Betty Valassi.
(English and Greek soundtrack)
05/24/78

A Faithful Woman: SEE Une Femme Fidele

A Few Days In The Life Of I I Oblomov
(USSR)
SOV. Mosfilm prodn. Dir, Nikita Mikhalkov. Sp, Mikhalkov, Alexandre Adabachiane from book by Ivan Gontcharov; cam (Sovcolor), Pavel Lebechev. 150.
Oleg Tabakov, Elena Soloyei, Andrei Popov, Youri Bogatyrev.
05/28/80

A Flor Da Pele
(Touchy)
(Brazil)
X. Oca Cinematografic prodn (Sao Paulo). Dir, Francisco Ramalho Jr. Prods, A Palacios, A P Galante. Sp, Francisco Ramalho Jr from a play by Consuelo de Castro; cam (Eastmancolor), Lucio Kodato; edtr, Mauricio Wilke; mus, Eduardo Gudin. 100.
Juca de Oliveira, Denise Bandeira, Beatriz Segall, Ewerton de Castro, Sergio Hingst.
09/29/76

A Force of One
AMC. Exec prod, Michael F Leone. Prod, Alan Belkin. Dir, Paul Aaron. Sp, Ernest Tidyman, from a story by Pat Johnson, Ernest Tidyman; cam (CFI color), Roger Shearman; edtr, Bert Lovitt; mus, Dick Halligan; asso prod, Jonathan Sanger; art dir, Norman Baron; asst dir, Jerald Sobul; snd, Marty Bolger. (MPAA rating: PG). 90.
Jennifer O'Neill, Chuck Norris, Clu Gulager, Ron O'Neal, James Whitmore Jr, Clint Ritchie, Pepe Serna, Ray Vitte, Taylor Lacher, Chu Chu Malave, Kevin Geer, Eugene Butler, James Hall, Charles Cyphers, Bill Wallace, Eric Laneuville.
07/04/79

A Girl Fit To Be Killed: SEE Holka Na Zabiti

A Girl Named Poo Lom: SEE Poo Lom

A Great Bunch of Girls
X. Cowgirls Prodn. Prods-dirs, Tracy Tynan, Mary Ann Braubach. Prodn supv, Karl Epstein. Cam, Eric Saarinen; edtr, Anne Goursaud Epstein. 58.
Dallas Cowboy Cheerleaders.
(DOC) (16m)
09/26/79

A Guy Like Me Should Never Die: SEE Un Type Comme Moi Ne Devrait Jamais Mourir

A Hell of a Life: SEE Ein Verdammt Gutes Leben

A Hero Ain't Nothin' But A Sandwich
NW. Radnitz/Mattel prodn. Prod, Robert B Radnitz. Dir, Ralph Nelson. Sp, Alice Childress, based on her novel; cam (CFI Color), Frank Stanley; edtr, Fred Chulack; mus, Tom McIntosh; prodn des, Walter Scott Herndon; set decor, Cheryal Kearney; snd, Bill McCaughey; cos-ward, Nedra Watt; asst dir, Reuben Watt. (MPAA rating: PG.) 107.
Cicely Tyson, Paul Winfield, Larry B Scott, Helen Martin, Glynn Turman, David Groh, Kevin Hooks, Kenneth Green, Harold Sylvester, Erin Blunt, Claire Brennen, Arthur French, Bill Cobbs, Sheila Wills, Arnold Johnson, Barbara Alston, Keny Long, Hartwell Simms.
12/14/77

A Hole in the Wall: SEE Jarha Fi Lhaite

A Hunting Accident: SEE Moi Laskoviy I Niejnie Zver

A Idade Da Terra
(The Age of the Earth)
(Brazil)
EMZ. Embrafilme, Glauber Rocha Communicacoes Artisticas prodn. Wri-dir, Glauber Rocha; cam, Roberto Pires; edtrs, Carlos Cox, Raul Soares, Ricardo Miranda; mus, Rogerio Duarte. 158.
Mauricio Do Valle, Jece Valadado, Norma Benguel, Tarcisio Meira, Antonio D'El Rey, Danuza Leao, Carlos Petrovich.
09/17/80

A Journey into Spring: SEE Udhetim Ne Pranvere

A Kard
(The Sword)
(Hungary)
X. Budapest Studio prodn. Dir, Janos Domolky. Sp, Istvan Csurka, Janos Domolky, based on a poem by Zoltan Jekely; cam (Eastmancolor), 80.
Peter Haumann, Mari Szemes.
03/09/77

A Kedves Somszed
(The Nice Neighbor)
(Hungary)
HU. Mafilm Objectiv Studio prodn. Dir, Zsolt Kezdi-Kovacs; sp, Geza Bermenyi, Kezdi-Kovacs; cam (Eastmancolor), Janos Zsombolyai. 102.
Laszlo Szabo, Lajos Szabo, Margit Dayka, Agi Margittay, Gyongi Vigh, Bertanal Solti, Agi Kakasi.
02/28/79

A Kiralylany Zsamolya
(Kneeler Peak)
(Hungary)
X. Budapest Studio prodn. Dir, Tamas Fejer. Sp, Impre Dobozy; cam (Eastmancolor), Istvan Hildebrand; mus, Geza Berki. 86.
Lajos Balazsovits, Istvan O Szabo, Tibor Molnar, Mari Kiss, Peter Barbinek, Karoly Safranek, Attila Balogh-Bodor, Bela Turpinszky, Albert Harmath.
03/02/77

A Kis Valentino
(The Little Valentino)
(Hungary)
HU. Mafilm Hunnia Studios prodn. Wri-dir, Andras Jeles. Cam (b&w), Sandor Kardos; mus of Schubert arranged by M Miklos. 92.
Janos Opoczki, Mrs. Sekacs, Mrs. Levai, Istvan Ivanyi, Jozsef Farkas.
(B & W)
02/28/79

A Labor of Love
FXG. Dirs-prods-edtrs, Robert Flaxman, Daniel Goldman, Cam, Flaxman; snd, Goldman and David Tekler; asso prods, Jack Behrend, John Iltis; snd mix, William Reis. (Self-imposed X rating). 70.
Henry Cheharbaschi, Deborah Dan, Ronald Dean, Peter Belden, Len Ozwald, Jerry Goodman, Anna Welch, Alex Boas.
(DOC)
02/18/76

A Lenda De Ubirajara
(The Legend of Ubirajara)
(Brazil)
X. Alo Filmes prodn. Wri-prod-dir, Andre Luiz. Cam, Mario Cravo Neto; edtr, Amauri Alves; mus, Tuze de Abreu. 110.
Tatau, Taise Costa, Robert Bomfim, Ana Maria Miranda.
04/07/76

A Letter to Nazim Hikmet: SEE Gramma Ston Nazim Hikmet

A Little Affair: SEE Chotisi Baat

A Little Godard: SEE Der Kleine Godard

A Little Night Music
(Austria - US - Germany)
NW. Sascha Wien, Elliott Kastner prodn; exec prod, Heinz Lazek. Dir, Hal Prince. Sp, Hugh Wheeler, based on a film "Smiles of a Summer Night" by Ingmar Bergman; mus-lyrs, Stephen Sondheim; cam (Eastmancolor), Arthur Ibbetson; edtr, John Jumpson. (MPAA rating: PG). 124.
Elizabeth Taylor, Diana Rigg, Len Cariou, Hermione Gingold, Lesley-Ann Down, Laurence Guittard, Christopher Guard, Lesley Dunlop, Chloe Franks, Heinz Marecek.
(MUSICAL)
09/21/77

A Little Romance
(USA - France)
WBO. Pan Arts (George Roy Hill)-Trinacra (Yves Rousset-Rouard) co-prodn. Exec prod, Patrick Kelley. Prods, Yves Rousset-Rouard, Robert L Crawford. Dir, Hill. Sp, Allan Burns; cam, Pierre William Glenn; edtr, William Reynolds; prodn des, Henry Bumstead; art dir, Francois De Lamthoe; ward des, Rosine Delamare; snd, Michel Desrois, asst dir, Carlo Lastricati. (MPAA rating: PG). 108.
Laurence Olivier, Arthur Hill, Sally Kellerman, Diane Lane, Thelonious Bernard, Broderick Crawford, David Dukes, Andrew Duncan, Claudette Sutherland, Graham Fletcher-Cook, Ashby Semple, Claude Brosset.
04/04/79

A Look at Liv
X. Win-Kap Prodns film. Prods, Jerry Winters, Richard Kaplan. Dir-interviewer, Kaplan; sp, Winters, Kaplan; cam, Peter Beil, Marcel Broekman, John Dildine, Gerhard Fromm, Bill Gidsey, Svein Johansen, Asmund Revold, Heinz Sottung, Sol Tabachnick, Rick Spalla Video Prodns; edtr, Howard Kuperman. 67.
(DOC)
12/07/77

A Lost Life: SEE Verlorenes Leben

A Man, A Woman and a Bank: SEE A Very Big Withdrawal

A Man Called Autumn Flower: SEE Un Hombre Llamado Flor De Otono

A Man on the Run: SEE Un Homme en fuite

A Man, Some Women: SEE Sey Seyeti

A Matter of Time
(Italy - US)
AIP. Prods, Jack H Skirball, J Edmund Grainger; exec prods, Samuel Z Arkoff, Giulio Sbarigia. Dir, Vincente Minnelli. Sp, John Gay, based on novel, "The Film Of Memory," by Maurice Druon; cam (Movielab Color), Geoffrey Unsworth; edtr, Peter Taylor; mus, Nino Oliviero; songs, Fred Ebb, John Kander, George Gershwin, B G DeSilva; prodn des, Colasanti and Moore; set decor, Arrigo Breschi; snd, Basil Fenton Smith; asst dir, Luciano Sacripanti. (MPAA rating: PG). 99.
Liza Minnelli, Ingrid Bergman, Charles Boyer, Spiros Andros, Tina Aumont, Gabriele Ferzetti, Orso Maria Guerrini, Amedeo Nazzari, Fernando Rey, Isabella Rossellini, Geoffrey Coppleston, Dominot, Jean Mas.
10/06/76

A Mess In The House: SEE Luda Kuca

A Necessary Action: SEE
Black Sun

A Night Over Chile: SEE Nochi
Nad Chili

A Non-Matrimonial Story:
SEE Dulscy

A Nous Deux
(Us Two)
(France)
AMLF. Les Films 13-Cinevideo prodn. Wri-dir, Claude Lelouch. Cam (Eastmancolor), Bernard Zitzermann; edtr, Sophie Bhaud, Hugues Darmois; mus, Francis Lai. 110.
Catherine Deneuve, Jacques Dutronc, Jacques Villeret, Paul Preboist, Bernard Crommbey.
06/06/79

A Nous Les Petites Anglaises
(Let's Get Those English Girls)
(France)
CCF. Les Films Galaxie prodn. Wri-dir, Michel Lang. Cam (Eastmancolor), Daniel Gaudry; edtr, Thierry Derocles; mus, Mort Shuman. 110.
Remi Laurent, Stephane Hillel, Veronique Delbroug, Sophie Barjac, Brigitte Bellac, Michel Melki.
01/14/76

A Page Of Love: SEE Une Page
D'Amour

A Perfect Couple
FOX. Lion's Gate film. Exec prod, Tommy Thompson. Prod-dir, Robert Altman. Sp, Altman, Allan Nicholls; cam, Edmond L Koons; edtr, Tony Lombardo; snd, Robert Gravenor, Don Merritt; mus prodn, Nicholls; asst dir, Thompson. (MPAA rating: PG). 110.
Paul Dooley, Marta Heflin, Titos Vandis, Belita Moreno, Henry Gibson, Dimitra Arliss, Allan Nicholls, Ann Ryerson, Mona Golabek, Ted Neeley, Heather MacRae, Tomi-Lee Bradley, Steven Sharp.
04/04/79

A Personal Opinion: SEE
Sobstvennoie Minienie

A Piano in Mid-Air: SEE
Zongora A Levegoben

A Piece Of The Action
WB. First Artists presentation. Prod, Melville Tucker. Dir, Sidney Poitier. Sp, Charles Blackwell, from a story by Timothy March; cam (Metrocolor), Donald H Morgan; edtr, Pembroke J Herring; mus, Curtis Mayfield; prodn des, Alfred Sweeney; set decor, William J McLaughlin; snd, Willie D Burton, William McCaughey; cos-ward, David Rawley, Marie V Brown; asst dir, Dwight Williams; 2d unit dir, Malcolm Atterbury; stunt coord, Henry Kingi. (MPAA rating: PG). 134.
Sidney Poitier, Bill Cosby, James Earl Jones, Denise Nicholas, Hope Clarke, Tracy Reed, Titos Vandis, Frances Foster, Jason Evers, Marc Lawrence, Janet DuBois.
10/05/77

A Portrait of Shunkin: SEE
Shunkin Sho

A Portrait of the Artist As a Young Man
MAH. Ulysses Film Company Ltd prodn. Dir, Joseph Strick. Asso prods, Richard Hallinan, Betty Botley. Sp, Judith Rascoe. Based on the novel by James Joyce; cam, Stuart Hetherington; edtr, Lesley Walker; mus, Stanley Myers; snd, Pat Hayes; cos, Judy Nolan. 98.
Boscoe Hogan, T P McKenna, Sir John Gielgud, Rosaleen Linihan, Maureen Potter, Cecil Sheehan, Niall Buggy, Brian Murray, Terence Strick, Luke Johnston.
04/25/79

A Priceless Day: SEE Ajandek
Ez A Nap

A Queda
(The Fall)
(Brazil)
X. Zoom Cinematografica prodn. Prod, Nei Sroulevich. Dir, Ruy Guerra, Nelson Xavier. Sp, Guerra, Xavier; cam, Edgar Moura; edtr, Ruy Guerra; art dir, Carlos Prieto; mus, Milton Nascimento, Ruy Guerra. 120.
Nelson Xavier, Lima Duarte, Isabel Ribeiro, Maria Silvia, Hugo Carvana.
04/05/78

A Queen's Ransom
(Hong Kong)
GHV. Dir, Ting Shan-si. 90.
Jimmy Wang Yu, Ko Chun-hsuing, George Lazenby, Angela Mao Ying, Tien Ni, Hsing Hwa-chiang, Judy Brown.
(English subtitles)
10/13/76

A Quite Ordinary Life: SEE
Ket Elhatarozas

A Ray of Sunlight: SEE Kratko
Sluntze

A Rich Man: SEE En rig mand

A Roof: SEE Pokriv

A Room With A View On The Sea: SEE Pokoj Z Widkiem
Na Morze

A Santa Alianca
(The Holy Alliance)
(Portugal)
X. Portuguese Cinema Institute Prodn, Lisbon. Wri-dir-edtr, Eduardo Geada. Cam, Manuel Costa e Silva; mus, Pedro Osorio. 110.
Io Apollini, Lia Gama, Henrique Viana, Helena Isabel, Paulo Duarte, Jose De Castro, David Silva.
06/28/78

A Scream from Silence: SEE
Mourir a Tue-Tete

A Sea Urchin In The Pocket: SEE Un Oursin Dans La
Poche

A Second Wind: SEE Un
Second Souffle

A Sentimental Story: SEE
Sentimentalnyi Roman

A Simple Heart: SEE Un Cuore
Semplice

A Simple Story: SEE Une
Histoire Simple

A Small Circle of Friends
UA. Tim Zinnemann prodn. Prod, Tim Zinnemann. Dir, Rob Cohen. Sp, Ezra Sacks; cam (Technicolor), Michael Butler; prodn des, Joel Schiller; edtr, Randy Roberts; mus comp, Jim Steinman; mus arr, Steven Morgoshes; asst dir, Michael Haley; set des, Al Kemper, Nicholas Laborczy; set decor, Rick Simpson; snd edtr, Victoria Rose Sampson; sfx, Larry Cavanaugh, Joe Lombardi, Rudy Lisczak; (MPAA rating: R). 112.
Brad Davis, Karen Allen, Jameson Parker, Shelley Long, John Friedrich, Gary Springer, Craig Richard Nelson, Harry Caesar, Nan Martin, Dan Stern, Jason Laskay, Jamie Squire, Mary Margaret Amato, David Hollander, Frank Rich, Pamela Cresant, Nick Kairis, Severn Darden, Jonathan Moore, Nancy Penoyer, Deborah Offner, John Peters, Doug Llewelyn.
03/05/80

A Small Town in Texas
AIP. CoCaCo Service Co film, prod, Joe Solomon; exec prod, Louis S Arkoff. Dir, Jack Starrett. Sp, William Norton; cam (Movielab Color), Bob Jessup; 2d unit cam, Paul vom Brack; edtrs, John C Horger, Larry L Mills, Jodie Copelan; mus, Charles Bernstein; art dir, Elayne Ceder; snd, Seymor S Klein; asst dir, Thomas B McCrory; stunt coord-2d-unit dir, Paul Knuckles. (MPAA rating: PG). 95.
Timothy Bottoms, Susan George, Bo Hopkins, Art Hindle, John Karlen, Morgan Woodward, Patrice Rohmer, Hank Rolike, Buck Fowler, Clay Tanner.
06/09/76

A Special Day: SEE Una
Giornata Speciale

A Spiral of Mist: SEE Una
Spirale Di Nebbia

A Star Is Born
WB. Prod, Jon Peters; exec prod, Barbra Streisand. Dir, Frank Pierson. Sp, John Gregory Dunne, Joan Didion, Pierson, based on a story by William Wellman, Robert Carson; cam (Metrocolor), Robert Surtees; edtr, Peter Zinner; mus, Paul Williams, Kenny Ascher, Rupert Holmes, Kenny Loggins, Alan and Marilyn Bergman, Leon Russell, Streisand; prodn des, Polly Platt; art dir, William Hiney; set decor, Ruby Levitt; snd, Dan Wallin, Tom Overton; cos-ward, Shirley Strahm, Seth Banks; asst dir, Stu Fleming. (MPAA rating: R). 140.
Barbra Streisand, Kris Kristofferson, Paul Mazursky, Gary Busey, Oliver Clark, Vanetta Fields, Clydie King, Marta Heflin, M G Kelly, Sally Kirkland, Joanne Linville, Uncle Rudy. (MUSICAL)
12/22/76

A Strait-Laced Girl: SEE Une Fille Cousue De Fil Blanc

A Strange Role: SEE Herkulesfurdoi Emlek

A Strange Woman: SEE Strannaya Zhenshina

A Summer Of Love: SEE En kaerleks sommar

A Summer Rain: SEE Chuvas de Verao

A Sunday in October: SEE Oktoberi Vasarnap

A Terrific Scent of Fresh Hay: SEE Ein Irrer Duft Von Frischem Heu

A Trombitas
(The Trumpeter)
(Hungary)
HU. Mafilm Objectiv Studio, Hunnia Studio, Magyar TV prodn. Dir, Janos Rosza. Sp, Istvan Kardos; cam (Eastmancolor), Elemer Ragalyi; mus, Levente Szorenyi. 102.
Zoltan Czoma, Ferenc Fabian, Ferenc Bencze, Robert Koltai, Ferenc Baks.
02/28/79

A Un Dios Desconocido
(To an Unknown God)
(Spain)
X. Elias Querejeta PC prodn; dir, Jaime Chavarri. Sp, Querejeta, Chavarri; cam (Eastmancolor), Teo Escamilla; edtr, Pablo G del Amo; mus, Luis de Pablo; sets, Rafael Palmero. 108.
Hector Alterio, Javier Elorriaga, Maria Rosa Salgado, Rosa Valenty, Angela Molina, Margarita Mas, Mercedes San Pietro, Jose Joaquin Boza, Emilio Siegrist.
09/28/77

A Very Big Withdrawal
(A Man, A Woman and a Bank)
(Canada)
AVE. Bennett Films in asso with McNichol presentation. Exec prod, Frederick W Field. Prods, Peter Samuelson, John B Bennett. Dir, Noel Black. Sp, Raynould Gideon, Bruce A Evans from a story by Gideon and Evans; cam, Jack Cardiff; edtr, Carl Kress. 100.
Donald Sutherland, Brooke Adams, Paul Mazursky, Allan Magicovsky, Leigh Hamilton, Nick Rice.
05/23/79

A Very Moral Night: SEE Egy Erkolcsos Ejszaka

A Walk in the Sun: SEE En vandring i solen

A Wedding
FOX. Lion's Gate Films Prodn. Prod-dir, Robert Altman; exec prod, Tommy Thompson. Sp, John Considine, Patricia Resnick, Allan Nicholls, Altman from a story by Altman and Considine; cam (DeLuxe Color), Charles Rosher; edtr, Tony Lombardo; snd, Jim Webb, Chris McLaughlin, Jim Bourgeois, Jim Stuebe; re-recording, Richard Portman; asso prods, Robert Eggenweiler, Scott Bushell; asst dir, Tommy Thompson; mus supv, Tom Walls. (MPAA rating: PG). 125.
Carol Burnett, Paul Dooley, Amy Stryker, Mia Farrow, Dennis Christopher, Gerald Busby, Peggy Ann Garner, Lillian Gish, Nina Van Pallandt, Vittorio Gassman, Desi Arnaz Jr, Dina Merrill, Pat McCormick, Howard Duff, John Cromwell, Geraldine Chaplin, John Considine, Lauren Hutton, Viveca Lindfors, Robert Fortier, Bert Remsen, Ellie Albers.
09/06/78

A Week's Vacation: SEE Une Semaine De Vacances

A Woman: SEE Phooying

A Woman and a Woman: SEE Kobieta I Kobieta

A Woman at Her Window: SEE Une Femme A Sa Fenetre

A Woman Between Dog and Wolf: SEE Een Vrouw Tussen Hond en Wolf

A Woman Like Eve: SEE Een Vrouw Als Eva

A Woman, One Day: SEE Une Femme, Un Jour

A Woman with Responsibilities: SEE Eine Frau Mit Verantwortung

A Year of School: SEE Un Anno Di Scuola

A Yellow Handkerchief Of Happiness: SEE Siawase No Cakusoku Hankeci

ABBA - The Movie
(Sweden - Australia)
SVE. Polar Music Int'l AB (Sweden)/Reg Grundy Prodns (Australia) prodn. Prods, Stig Anderson, Reg Grundy. Dir, Lasse Hallstroem. Orig story-sp, Lasse Hallstroem, Bob Caswell; cam (Eastmancolor), Jack Churchill, Paul Onorato; edtrs, Lasse Hallstroem, Malou Hallstroem, Ulf Neidemar; cos des, Ing-Marie Nilsson; mus, Benny Andersson, Bjoern Ulvaeus, Stig Anderson. 94.
Anni-Frid Lyngstad, Agneta Faeltskog, Benny Andersson, Bjoern Ulvaeus, Bruce Barry, Robert Hughes, Tom Oliver, Stig Angerson.
12/14/77

Abu Raihan Beruni
(USSR)
SOV. Uzbekfilm Studio Production, Tashkent, Uzbekistan Republic, Soviet Union. Dir, Shukhrat Abbasov; sp, Pavel Bulgakov, Abbasov; cam, Khatam Faisiev. 150.
Pulat Saidkasymov, Bikhtiar Shukurov, Razzak Khamraev, Bimbulat Vataev.
06/18/80

The Accuser: SEE L'Imprecateur

AC/DC: Let There be Rock
(France)
X. High Speeds Prodn film. Dirs, Eric Dionysius, Eric Mistler; cam, Jean Francis Gorde. 95.
Angus Young, Malcolm Young, Bon Scott, Phill Rudd, Cliff Williams.
10/01/80

Aces High
(Britain)
EMI. S Benjamin Fisz prodn, prod, S Benjamin Fisz. Dir, Jack Gold. Sp, Howard Barker (inspired by R C Sheriff's play, "Journey's End"); cam (Technicolor), Gerry Fisher; aerial pho, Peter Allwork; edtr, Anne Coates; mus, Richard Hartley; set decor, Syd Caine; sfx, Derek Meddings; asso prod, Basil Keys; asst dir, Derek Cracknell; tech advs, Air Commodore Alan Wheeler, Group Capt Dennis David. (MPAA rating: PG). 114.
Malcolm McDowell, Christopher Plummer, Simon Ward, Peter Firth, John Gielgud, Trevor Howard, Richard Johnson, Ray Milland, David Wood, David Daker, Elliott Cooper, Pascale Christophe, Jeanne Patou.
05/26/76

Achalta Ota
(You've Been Had...You Turkey!)
(Israel)
X. Candid Prodn. Prod, Yehuda Barkan. Dirs, Yehuda Barkan, Igal Shilon. Sp, Shimon Israeli, Yehuda Barkan. Cam, Gadi Danzig, Beni Carmeli; mus, Ilan Mochiach; edtr, Zion Avramian. 90.
Yehuda Barkan, Karolin Langford, Arie Moskuna, Dvora Bakon, Uri Gross.
05/28/80

Achilleshaelen er mit vaaben
(The Achilles Heel Is My Weapon)
(Denmark)
DAG. Danish Film Studio/Danish Film Institute prodn. Wri-dir, Jytte Rex. Cam (Eastmancolor), Dirk Bruel, Alexander Gruszynski, Jytte Rex; mus, quotes from classical and traditional recordings; edtr, Grethe Moldrup; prodn mgr, Nina Crone. 92.
Clemens Hildebrandt, Helle Ryslinge.
03/28/79

The Acrobat: SEE L'Acrobate

Act of Violence: SEE Ato de Violencia

Actas De Marusia
(Letters from Marusia)
(Mexico)
CIM. Conacine - Arturo Feliu prodn. Wri-dir, Miguel Littin. Cam (Technicolor), Jorge Stahl Jr; mus, Mikis Theodrakis. 115.
Gian Maria Volonte, Claudio Obregon, Diana Brachem, Eduardo Lopez Rojas.
05/19/76

Action
(Italy)
CID. Ars Cinematografica prodn. Dir, Giovanni Tinto Brass. Sp, Giancarlo Fusco, Roberto Lerici, Tinto Brass; cam (Eastmancolor), Silvano Ippoliti; art dir, Claudio Cinini; edtr, Tinto Brass; mus, Riccardo Giovannini. 123.
Luc Merenda, Adriana Asti, Susanna Javicoli, Alberto Sorrentino.
(16m blown up)
02/20/80

Adela Jeste Nevecerela
(Adele Hasn't Had Her Supper Yet)
(Czechoslovakia)
CZS. Czechoslovak Film Prodn, Barrandov Studios, Prague. Dir, Oldrich Lipsky. Sp, Jiri Brdecka; cam (Eastmancolor), Jaroslav Kucera; sets, Vladimir Labsky, Milan Nejedly; sfx, Jan Svankmaier; mus, Lubos Fiser. 100.
Michal Docolomansky, Rudolf Hrusinsky, Milos Kopecky, Ladislav Pesek, Nada Konvalinkova, Martin Ruzek, Vaclav Lohnisky, Olga Schoberova, Kveta Fialova.
06/21/78

Adios Alicia
(Good-Bye Alicia)
(Venezuela)
X. Nostromo Cine-Films 71 (Venezuela) and El Iman (Madrid) prodn. Prod-dir, Liko Perez, Santiago San Miguel; sp, San Miguel; cam (Eastmancolor), Jose Luis Alcaine; edtr, Jose Salcedo; sets, Martha Trubint; mus, Vytas Brenner. 77.
Carlos Marquez, Cecilia Villarreal, Isabel Mestres, Nelida Quiroga, Xiomara Perez.
09/28/77

Adios Amigo
ATF. Po' Boy prodn. Wri-prod-dir, Fred Williamson. Exec prod, Lee W Winkler. Cam (Eastmancolor), Tony Palmieri; edtrs, Gene and Eva Ruggiero; mus com-cond, Luici de Jesus, performed by The Blue Infernal Machine. (MPAA rating: PG). 87.
Fred Williamson, Richard Pryor, James Brown, Robert Phillips, Mike Henry, Suhalia Farhat, Victoria Jee, Lynne Jackson, Heidi Dobbs, Liz Treadwell, Joy Lober, Thalmus Rasulala.
01/14/76

The Adolescent: SEE L'Adolescente

The Adolescents: SEE Los Adolescentes

Adolf & Marlene
(W Germany)
X. Albatros prodn, Munich, Trio Film, Duisburg, co-prodn. Wri-dir, Ulli Lommel. Cam, Michael Ballhaus; edtr, Thea Eymes; mus, Wagner, Liszt; set des, Curd Melber. 92.
Kurt Raab, Margit Carstensen, Ila von Hasperg, Harry Baer, Ulli Lommel, Andrea Schober, Brigitte Mira, Alexander Allerson.
06/01/77

The Adoption: SEE L'Adoption

Adrien's Story: SEE Histoire D'Adrien

The Advantage: SEE Avantazh

Adventures of a Dentist
(USSR)
GOS. Mosfilm Prodn, Moscow. Dir, Elem Klimov. Sp, Alexander Volodin; cam (b&w), S Rubashkin; sets, V Kamsky, B Blank; mus, A Shnitke. 90.
Andrei Miagkov, B Vasilyeva, A Freyndlikh, P Krymov, I Kvasha.
(B & W)
07/05/78

The Adventures of Baron Muenchhausen: SEE Muenchhausen

The Adventures of Picasso: SEE Picassos aeventyr

The Adventures of the Wilderness Family
PIE. Arthur R Dubs prodn. Wri-dir, Stewart Raffil. Color by CFI; score, Gene Kauer, Douglas Lackey. (MPAA rating: G). 94.
Robert F Logan, Susan Damante Shaw, Hollye Holmes, Ham Larsen.
01/14/76

Advokatka
(The Lawyer)
(Czechoslovakia)
CZS. Czechoslovak Film Prodn, Koliba Studios, Bratislava. Dir, Andrej Lettrich. Sp, J A Tallo, Lettrich, based on a story by Tallo; cam, Alojz Hanusek; mus, Svetozar Strachina. 90.
Emilia Vasaryova-Horska, Svatopluk Matyas, Hana Packertova, Julius Vasek, Jaroslava Obermayerova, Lubo Roman, Lotar Radvanyi, Viliam Zaborsky, Dana Medricka, Anton Korenci, Frantisek Filipovsky, Jozef Adamovic, Igor Hrabinsky.
08/02/78

Affaeren I Moelleby
(The Moelleby Affair)
(Denmark)
NOR. Dir, Tom Hedegaard. Sp, Henning Bahs, Erik Balling, Hedegaard, based on Morten Korch novel. Cam (Eastmancolor), Claus Loof; mus, Bent Fabiricius-Bjerre; edtr, Ole Steen Nielsen; exec prod, Bo Christensen; prodn mgr, Jan Lehmann. 92.
Poul Reichhardt, Ove Sprogoe, Dick Kaysoe, Inger Margrete Svendsen.
01/12/77

Affair at Akitsu: SEE Akitsu Onsen

Affairs
(Hong Kong)
X. Sino-Great Wall prodn. Prod, Fu Chi. Exec prod, Patrick Lui. Dir, Stephen Shin. Sp, Mok Song; cam, Danny Tsang, Yeung Wor-Leung; edtr, Li Yu-Huai, Koo Chi-Wai; mus, Joseph Koo. 112.
Shih Hui, Fu Chi, Gigi Wong, Ivan Ho.
(Cantonese soundtrack with English subtitles)
08/22/79

Affinita Elettive
(Elective Affinities)
(Italy)
X. RAI-Instituto Luce-prodn. Dir, Gianni Amico. Sp, Amico, Marco Melani, Alighiero Chiusano, from the novel by Johann Wolfgang von Goethe; cam, Tonino Nardi; edtr, Roberto Perpignani; snd, Claudio Maielli, Mario Bramonti, Remo Ugonelli; mus, Nicola Samale, Giuseppe Mazzuca; art dir, Giorgio Bertolini; cos, Lina Nerli Taviani. 135.
Francesca Archibugi, Paolo Graziosi, Nino Castelnuovo, Veronica Lazar, Edoardo Torricella, Federic Pacifici, Ellis Dona, Luana Potrich, Lucia Poli, Bruno Cattaneo.
10/04/78

Aftenlandet
(Evening Land)
(Denmark)
PSD. 1980 Film ApS prodn (Ebbe Preisler, Jeff McBride, Steen Herdel). Dir, Peter Watkins. Story-sp, Carsten Clante, Poul Martinsen, Watkins; cam (Eastmancolor), Joan Churchill; edtr, Watkins; mus, Anders Koppel; prodn mgr, Ebbe Preisler. 104.
03/02/77

After The Rain: SEE Fah Larng Fon

Agatha
(Britain)
WB. Sweetwal prodn in asso with Casablanca FilmWorks. Prods, Jarvis Astaire, Gavrik Losey. Dir, Michael Apted. Sp, Kathleen Tynan, Arthur Hopcraft, based on a story by Tynan; cam (Technicolor), Vittorio Storaro; edtr, Jim Clark; mus, Johnny Mandel; prodn dsgn, Shirley Russell; art dir, Simon Holland; snd, Christian Wangler; asst dir, Jonathan Benson. (MPAA rating: PG). 98.
Dustin Hoffman, Vanessa Redgrave, Timothy Dalton, Helen Morse, Celia Gregory, Paul Brooke, Yvonne Gilan, David Hargreaves.
02/14/79

Agaton Sax Och Bykoebings Gaestabud
(Agaton Sax and the Bykoebing Village Festival)
(Sweden)
SVE. Team Film/Svensk Filmindustri AB/Swedish Film Institute prodn, Based on Nils-Olaf Franzen novel. Wri-dir, Stig Lasseby. Chief des, Jann Gissberg; cam, Eberhard Fehmers; sfx, Hans-Walter Kramski; mus, Charles Redland; exec prod, Bengt Forslund. 77.
Olof Thunberg, Stig Grybe, Per Sjoestrand, Leif Liljeroth, Stig Lasseby.
   Singer, Annika Risberg.
(ANI)
12/08/76

The Age of the Earth: SEE A Idade Da Terra

Agee
X. James Agee Film Project prodn. Prod-dir-wri, Ross Spears; cam, Anthony Forma; mus, Kenton Coe; asso prod, Jude Cassidy. 98.
Jimmy Carter, Father James Flye, Robert Saudek, Olivia Wood, Dwight MacDonald, Robert Fitzgerald, Elizabeth Tingle, Mae Burroughs, Alma Neuman, Mia Agee, John Huston, Earl McCarroll, voice of Walker Evans.
(DOC) (COLOR & B & W) (16m)
09/24/80

Agent 69 Jensen i Skorpionens Tegn
(Agent 69 Jensen in the Sign of Scorpio)
(Denmark)
DNS. Merry Film (Anders Sandberg) prodn. Story, Edmondt Jensen. Wri-dir, Werner Hedman. Cam (Eastmancolor), Rolf Roenne; prodn co-ord, Vibeke Windeloev; edtr, May Soya; mus, Bertrand Bech. 90.
Anna Bergman, Gina Janssen, Ole Soeltoft, Soeren Stroemberg.
07/27/77

Agent 69 Jensen Skyttens Tegn
(Agent 69 Jensen In The Sign Of Sagittarius)
(Denmark)
EUR. Happy Film (Anders Sandberg) prodn. Story, Edmondt Jensen. Sp-dir, Werner Hedmann. Cam (Eastmancolor), Rolf Roenne, Gerhard Petersen; mus, Bent Fabricius-Bjerre; edtr, Maj Soya; prodn des, Erling Joergensen; cos, Keld Rex Holm. 90.
Gina Janssen, Anna Bergman, Ole Soeltoft, Lee Fong Wong, Andre Chazel, Soeren Stroemberg.
08/02/78

Agenzia Riccardo Finzi...Praticamente Detective
(Detective Riccardo Finzi)
(Italy)
TIT. Prod, Galliana Juso for Cinemaster film prodn. Dir, Bruno Corbucci. Sp, Bruno Corbucci, Mario Amendola; cam (Technicolor), Giovanni Ciarlo; art dir, Claudio Cinnini; edtr, Daniele Anabiso; mus, Guido and Maurizio De Angelis. 94.
Renato Pozzetto, Silvano Tranquilli, Olga Karlatos, Enzo Cannavale.
02/20/80

Agraharathil Kazhuthai
(Donkey in a Brahmin Village)
(India)
NRH. Wri-dir, John Abraham. Cam (b&w), Ramachandrabub; mus, M B Srinivasan. 95.
Swathi, Veeraraghavan, Krishnaraj.
(B & W)
01/31/79

Aguila
(Eagle)
(Phillipines)
X. Bancom Audiovision Corporation prodn. Wri-dir, Eddie Romero. Cam, Mike de Leon, Rody Lacap; edtr, Ben Barcelon; mus, Ryan Cayabyab; art dir, Mel Chionglo. 210.
Fernando Poe, Jr, Charo Santo, Christopher de Leon, Eddie Garcia, Amalia Fuentes, Elizabeth Oropesa, Jay Ilagan.
06/25/80

Ah! Nomugi Toge
(Nomugi Pass)
(Japan)
YMT. Dir, Satsuo Yamamoto; sp, Yoshi Hatori, Shigemi Yamamoto; cam (Fujicolor), Setsuo Kobayashi; mus, Masaru Sato. 145.
Shinobu Otake, Mieko Harada, Chikako Yuri, Yuko Kotegawa, Takeo Jii, Akira Ninishimura.
07/30/80

Ai Kruie
(Bloody Life)
(Thailand)
SAH. Prod-dir-wri-edtr, Rungsiri Lim-aksorn. Exec prod, Seepratha Lim-aksorn. Cam-light, Sophon Jaenphanit; mus-cos, J-5; snd recording, King Sound Studio; color processing, Union Lab (Hong Kong); prodn asst, Terry Wong. Theme song, "Chiwit" (Life), orig comp-lyr, Rungsiri Lim-aksorn, sung by Srisarai Suchartboot. 125.
Sombat Metanee, Somkiat Sayanont, Aranya Namwong, Piathip Kumvongse, Mayurachat Muenpasitiwet, Tarika Tarathit, Choosri Misomon, Tasawin Ratanapracha, Vilaiwan Wattanaphanit.
02/23/77

Ai Kwai Legg
(The Iron Buffalo)
(Thailand)
CHT. Prods, Rachaniwan Kanitasen, Somchai Kitiparaporn. Dir, Pornphote Kanitasen. Story, Somchai Kitiparaporn; sp, Supaksorn; cam Pisan Prasingh, Manat Topoyat; asst cam, Somwang Nemcharoen; mus, Seksan Sonimsart; snd, Maitree Janjarasskul; color processing, Siam Pattana Lab; light, Dong; edtr, Prawit Lilawai; art dir, Ulai Srisombat; cos, Sampan Kambangpai; prodn mgrs, Preeda Teosiri, Wanchai Termjitaree; asst dir, Apichat Pornpairoj. 135.
Sombat Metanee, Pisamai Wilaisak, Sorapong Chatri, Nawarat Yukthanan, Yodchai Megsuan, Niroot Sirichanya, Chumporn Tepitak, Dekchai Eh, Lak Apichat, Bu Vibulnan, Pipop Pupinyo, Somsak Chaisongkram, Terd Daotai.
08/24/77

Ai No Borei
(Phantom Love)
(Japan - France)
ARS. Oshima Prodns Ltd-Argos Films prodn. Dir, Nagisa Oshima. Sp, Oshima from the book by Itoko Nakamura; cam (Eastmancolor), Yoshio Miyajima; edtr, Keiichu Uraoka; art dir, Jusho Toda; mus, Toru Takemitsu; prodn coord, Shibata Org. Inc. 108.
Kazuko Yoshiyuki, Tatsuya Fuji, Takashiro Tamura, Takuzo Kawatani, Akiko Koyama, Taiji Tonoyama.
05/24/78

Ai No Corrida
(Corrida of Love)
(Japan - France)
AOJ. Argos Films (Paris)-Oshima Productions (Tokyo)-Shibata Organization (Tokyo) prodn. Wri-dir, Nagisa Oshima. Cam (Eastmancolor), Hideo Ito; edtr, Keiichi Uraoka; art dir, Jusho Toda; mus, Minoru Miki. 105.
Eiko Matsuda, Tatsuya Fuji.
02/25/76

Aika Hyva Ihmiseksi
(Pretty Good For A Human)
(Finland)
X. Finnish Film Prodn. Dir, Rauni Mollberg. Sp, Mollberg, Veikko Korpala, Seppo Heinonen; cam, Hannu Peltomaa; mus, Harri Tuominen. 100.

Martti Kainulainen, Raili Veivo, Toivo Makela, Asko Sarkola, Sirkka Metsasaariova, Gustav Wiklund.
08/09/78

Airplane
PAR. Howard W Koch prodn. Prod, Jon Davison. Exec prod-dir-wris, Jim Abrahams, David Zucker, Jerry Zucker. Cam (Metrocolor), Joseph Biroc; edtr, Patrick Kennedy; mus, Elmer Bernstein; prodn des, Ward Preston; set des, Joe Hubbard; set decor, Anne D McCulley; cos des, Rosanna Norton; snd, Tom Overton; asst dir, Aren Schmidt. (MPAA rating: PG). 88.
Robert Hays, Julie Hagerty, Kareem Abdul-Jabbar, Lloyd Bridges, Peter Graves, Leslie Nielsen, Lorna Patterson, Robert Stack, Stephen Stucker.
07/02/80

Airport '77
U. Prod, William Frye; exec prod, Jennings Lang. Dir, Jerry Jameson. Sp, Michael Scheff, David Spector, from a story by H A L Craig, Charles Kuenstle, inspired by the film "Airport" based on the novel by Arthur Hailey; cam (Technicolor), Philip Lathrop; special visual effects, Albert Whitlock; 2d unit cam, Rexford Metz; edtrs, J Terry Williams, Robert Watts; mus, John Cacavas; song, Tom Sullivan; prodn des, George C Webb; set decor, Mickey S Michaels; snd, Charles D Knight, Robert Knudson; cos-ward, Edith Head, Burton Miller, John Anderson, Sheila Mason; asst dir, Wilbur Mosier; 2d unit dir, Michael Moore; stunt coord, Stan Barrett. (MPAA rating: PG). 113.
Jack Lemmon, Lee Grant, Brenda Vaccaro, Joseph Cotten, Olivia de Havilland, Darren McGavin, Christopher Lee, Robert Foxworth, Robert Hooks, George Kennedy, James Stewart, Monte Markham, Kathleen Quinlan, Gil Gerard, James Booth, Monica Lewis, Maidie Norman, Pamela Bellwood, Arlene Golonka, Tom Sullivan, M Emmet Walsh, Michael Richardson, Michael Pataki, George Furth, Richard Vanture.
03/23/77

Ajandek Ez A Nap
(A Priceless Day)
(Hungary)
HU. Mafilm-Budapest Studio prodn. Wri-dir, Peter Gothar from an idea by Peter Zimre. Cam (Eastmancolor), Lajos Koltai; mus, Gyorgy Selmeczi. 87.
Cecilia Estergalyos, Pal Hetenyi, Judit Pogany, Lajos Szabo, Janos Dersi.
02/27/80

Ajuricaba
(Brazil)
EMZ. Ipanema-Caldeira prodn. Dir, Oswaldo Caldeira. Sp, Caldeira, Almir Muniz; cam (Eastmancolor), Edison Santos; edtr, Carlos Brajsbat; mus, Airton Barbosa. 97.
Paulo Villaca, Rimaldo Genes, Emmanuele Cavalcanti, Nildo Parente, Sura Berditchewsky, Fregolente.
08/31/77

Akcija Stadion
(Operation Stadium)
(Yugoslavia)
YFR. Zagreb Film-Zagreb Kinematografi-Dunav Film prodn. Dir, Dusan Vukotic. Sp, Slavko Goldstein, Vukotic; cam (Eastmancolor), Ivica Rajkovic; mus, Tomica Simovic. 90.
Igor Galo, Zvonimir Crnko, Franjo Majetic, Bozidar Alic, Zvonko Lepetic, Darko Srica, Natasa Hrzic, Jadranka Stilin, Zaltko Mudinic.
08/17/77

A Kenguru
(The Kangaroo)
(Hungary)
HU. Hunnia Studio prodn. Dir, Janos Zsombolyai. Sp, Bulcsu Bertha. Zsombolyai from the book by Bertha; cam (Eastmancolor), Zsombolyai. 98.
Laszlo Galffy, Eva Vandor, Robert Koltai, Erzsi Pasztor.
07/28/76

Akibiori
(End Of Autumn)
(Japan)
PIF. Shochiku prodn. Dir, Yasujiro Ozu. Sp, Kogo Nodo, Ozu; cam (Agfacolor), Yuji Atsuda; mus, Kojan Saito. 131.
Chishu Ryu, Nobuo Nakamura, Teruo Oshida.
07/26/78

Akitsu Onsen
(Affair at Akitsu)
(Japan)
SKU. Exec prod, Masao Shirai; planned by Mariko Okada. Dir-sp, Yoshishige Yoshida, from a story by Shinji Fujiwara; cam, Toichiro Narushima; mus, Hikaru Hayashi; art dir, Tatsuo Hamada; cos, Mariko Okada. 113.
Mariko Okada, Hiroyuki Nagato, Sumiko Hidaka, Taiji Tonoyama, Masako Nakamura, Jinkichi Uno, Eijiro Tono, Fukuko Sayo, Teruo Yoshido.
(MADE IN 1962)
11/19/80

Akramana
(The Conquest)
(India)
SSI. Dir, Girish Kasaravalli. Sp, G S Sadashiv; cam, S Ramahchandra; mus, B V Karanth. 121.
Vijaya Kashi, Vaishali Kasaravilli.
02/06/80

Aktorzy Prowincjonalni
(Provincial Actors)
(Poland)
POL. Group "X," Warsaw. Dir, Agnieszka Holland. Sp, Holland, Witold Zatorski; cam, Jacek Petrcki; mus, Andrzej Zarycki; asst dir, Bogdan Soelle. 108.
Halina Labonarska, Tadeusz Huk, Iwona Biernacka, Ewa Dalkowska, Slawa Kwasniewska, Kazimierz Nogajowna, Janina Ordezanka, Krystyna Wachelko, Zaleska.
05/21/80

Al Aswar
(The Walls)
(Iraq)
ETQ. ETC prodn. Dir, Muhammad Shoukri Jamil. Sp, Sabry Moussa, Fawaz Mouaffar Khidr from a book by Abd-er Rahmane Rabi; cam (Eastmancolor), Rifate Abdelhamid; Amer Arakoushi, Jamil. 94.
Ibrahim Jalal, Abdel Hamio, Saadiya Zobeydi, Tou'ma Tamini.
07/25/79

Al Hayatt Al Yawmiyah Fi Qariah Suriyah
(Everyday Life in a Syrian Village)
(Syria)
X. Syrian General Organization for Film prodn. Dir, Omar Amiralay. Sp, Sadala Wannous; cam (b&w), Hazem Bay'a, Abdo Hamze; edtr, Kaiss Zoubaydi. With participation of the villagers of Al Mouwayleh. 90. (DOC)
07/07/76

Al Kautsar
(Indonesia)
SJS. Prod, Chan Pattiumura. Dir, Chaerul Umam. Sp, Asrul Sani; cam, Kasiyo; edtr, Yanis Badar; mus, Thoifur; art dir, Lily Delia Fatma. 100.
Wahab Abdi, W.S Rendra, Julinar Firdaus, Henny Kundalini, Soultan Saladin.
12/14/77

Al Raas
(The Head)
(Iraq)
IRQ. Iraqi General Organization for Cinema prodn, Baghdad. Wri-dir, Faisal Al Yassiry. Cam, Majid Kamil. 100.
Kasim Mohammed, Kaid Al Nomani, Sami Kafan, Z Al Rubain.
02/06/80

Al Servicio De La Mujer Espanola
(At the Service of Spanish Womanhood)
(Spain)
X. Exclusivas Molpeceres SA prodn. Wri-dir, Jaime de Arminan. Exec prod, Miguel Gomez. OCam (Eastmancolor), Domingo Solano; edtr, J Luis Matesanz; mus, Mari Carmen Santoja; sets, Eduardo de la Torre. 109
Marilina Ross, Adolfo Marsillach, Mari Carrillo, Amparo Baro, Emilio Gutierrez Caba.
10/04/78

Al Tejruba
(The Experiment)
(Iraq)
IRQ. Iraqi General Organization for Cinema prodn. Wri-dir, Fuad al Tohami. Cam, L Salih. 90.
Salima Khudhair, Semar Mohammed, Sami Kaftan.
02/06/80

Al Tish'ali Im Ani Ohev
(Don't Ever Ask Me If I Love)
(Israel)
X. Forum Films Presentation of a K R A K Prodn. Prod, Amos Kolek, Rafi Reibenbach. Dir, Barbara Noble. Sp, Kolek, Mark Dickerman, based on novel by Kolek; cam, David Gurfinkel; edtr, Alain Jakobowitz; mus, Niruth Hirsch. Songs perf by David Broza, Sherri and Josy Katz. 94.
Amos Kolek, Shelby Leverington, Joe Cortez, Yossi Yadin, Shraga Harpaz, Lya Koenig, Yossi Polak, Lea Orsher, Gidi Gov.
04/18/79

Alakdang Gubat
(Scorpion Woods)
(Philippines)
X. FPJ Production presentation. Dir, Armando Herrera. Sp, Fred Navarro; story, Pablo S Gomez; cam, Sergio Lobo; mus, Ernani Cuenco. 100.
Fernando Poe Jr, Marianne De La Riva, Paquito Diaz, Perla Bautista, Dencio Padilla, Jose Romulo, Andy Poe, Max Laurel, Dave Brodett.
06/23/76

Alambrista
(The Illegal)
FHB. Film Hans-Bobwin Prod-Michael Hausman and Irwin Young prodn. Wri-dir-cam, Robert Young. Edtr, Paul Jaeger. 90.
Domingo Ambriz, Trinidad Silva, Linda Gillin, Ludevina Salazar, Ned Beatty.
05/24/78

Albert - Warum?
(Albert - Why?)
(W Germany)
X. Munich Film & Television Academy diploma film. Wri-dir, Josef Roedl. Cam, Karlheinz Gschwind; snd, Hans Roedl; asst, Angela Kifmann. 115.
Fritz Binner, Michael Eichenseer, Georg Schiessl, Elfriede Bleisteiner.
(B & W) (16m)
01/17/79

Alcool
(Alcohol)
(Italy)
X. Prod, Augusto Tretti for Province of Milan. Wri-dir, Augusto Tretti, with the consultation of Dario De Martis; cam, Maielli. 110.
Mario Grazioni.
09/24/80

Aleluia, Gretchen
(Brazil)
EMZ. Silvio Back prodn. Wri-dir, Back. Addl dial, Manoel Carlos Karam, Oscar Milton Volpini; cam (Eastmancolor), Jose Madeiros; art dirs, Ronald Rego Leao, Marcos Carrilho; edtr, Inacio Araujo; cos, Luis Afonso Burigo; asst dir, Manoel Carlos Karam. 109.
Carlos Vereza, Miriam Pires, Lilian Lemmertz, Sergio Hingst, Kate Hansen, Selma Egrei, Jose Maria Santos, Mauricio Tavora, Lala Schneider, Lauro Hanke, Edson D'Avila, Joel de Oliveira, Rafael Pacheco, Abilio Mota, Lorival Gipiella, Narciso Assumpcao.
06/15/77

Alex & The Gypsy
FOX. Prod, Richard Shepherd. Dir, John Korty Sp, Lawrence B. Marcus, based on the novella, "The Bailbondsman," by Stanley Elkin; cam (DeLuxe Color), Bill Butler; edtr, Donn Cambern; mus, Henry Mancini; prodn des, Bill Malley; set decor, John H Anderson; snd, Theodore Soderberg, Bill Teague; asst dir, Irby Smith. (MPAA rating: R). 99.
Jack Lemmon, Genevieve Bujold, James Woods, Gino Ardito, Robert Emhardt, Joseph X Flaherty, Todd Martin.
09/29/76

Alexander The Great: SEE O Megalexandros

Alexandria. . .Why?: SEE Iskindiria. . .Leh?

Alice in Spanish Wonderland: SEE Alicia En La Espana De Las Maravillas

Alice In Wonderland
GNX. Cruiser Prodns prodn. Prod, Bill Osco. Dir, Bud Townsend. Sp, B A Fredericks; cam, Joseph Barlo; score, Bucky Searles; arrconds, Jack Stearn, Peter Matz. (Self-applied X Rating). 88.
Kristine De Bell, Larry Gelman, Allan Novak, Terry Hall, Jason Williams, Bree Anthony.
09/08/76

Alice Ou La Derniere Fugue
(Alice or the Last Escapade)
(France)
FPH. Wri-dir, Claude Chabrol. Cam (Eastmancolor), Jean Rabier; edtr, Monique Fardoulis; mus, Pierre Jansen. 93.
Sylvia Kristel, Charles Vanel, Jean Carmet, Andre Dussollier, Fernand Ledoux, Thomas Chabrol, Bernard Rousselet.
01/12/77

Alice, Sweet Alice: SEE Communion

Alicia En La Espana De Las Maravillas
(Alice in Spanish Wonderland)
(Spain)
X. Roda Films (Barcelona) prodn. Dir, Jorge Feliu. Sp, Jordi Feliu, Jesus Borras, Antoni Colomer; sets, Elisa Ruiz; mus, Juan Pineda; edtrs, Teresa Alcocer, Guillermo Maldonado; cam (Eastmancolor), Raul Perez Cubero; exec prod, Isabel Fabra. 86.
Mireia Ros, Silvia Aguilar, Montserrat Mostoles, Concha Bardem, Pau Bizarro, Alfredo Lucchetti.
05/24/78

Alien
FOX. Brandywine-Ronald Shusett prodn. Prods, Gordon Carroll, David Giler and Walter Hill. Dir, Ridley Scott. Exec prod, Ronald Shusett. Sp, Dan O'Bannon. Cam (Eastmancolor), Derek Vanlint; edtr, Terry Rawlings; snd, Derrick Leather; prodn des, Michael Seymour; art dir, Les Dilley, Roger Christian; sfx, Brian Johnson, Nick Allder; cos, John Mollo; asst dir, Paul Ibbetson; mus, Jerry Goldsmith. (MPAA rating: R). 124.
Tom Skerritt, Sigourney Weaver, Veronica Cartwright, Harry Dean Stanton, John Hurt, Ian Holm, Yaphet Kotto.
05/23/79

The Alien: SEE De Plaats van de Vreemdeling

Alison's Birthday
(Australia)
FWS. Australian Film Commission-Fontana Films presentation of the David Hannay Prodn. Prod, David Hannay. Wri-dir, Ian Coughlan. Exec prods, Ric Kabriel, John Sturzaker; cam, Kevan Lind; light dir, Brian Bansgrove; edtr, Timothy Street; snd, Phil Judd; mus, Brian King, Alan Oloman; prodn des, Robert Hildritch; asst dir, Michael Falloon. 95.
Joanne Samuel, Margie McCrae, Martin Vaughan, Rosalind Speirs, Robyn Gibbes, Lou Brown, Ian Coughlan, Bunney Brooke, John Bluthal, Ralph Cotterill, Marion Johns, George Carden, Belinda Giblin, Vincent Ball, Lisa Peers, Eric Oldfied, Sonia Peat.
10/17/79

The All-Around Reduced Personality-Outtakes: SEE Die Allseitig Reduzierte Persoenlichkeit-Re

All Is Love: SEE Vsichko e Lyubov

All Stars: SEE Tous Vedettes

All That Jazz
FXC. Prod, Robert Alan Aurthur. Dir, Bob Fosse; sp, Fosse, Robert Alan Aurthur; exec prod, Daniel Melnick; cam (Technicolor), Giuseppe Rotunno; edtr, Alan Heim; prodn des, Philip Rosenberg; cos, Albert Wolsky; mus, Ralph Burns; chor, Bob Fosse. (MPAA rating; R). 123.
Roy Scheider, Jessica Lange, Ann Reinking, Leland Palmer, Cliff Gorman, Ben Vereen, Erzsebet Foldi, Michael Tolan, Max Wright, William Le Massena, Chris Chase, Deborah Geffner, Kathryn Doby, Anthony Holland, Robert Hitt, David Margulies, Sue Paul, Keith Gordon, Frankie Man, Alan Heim, John Lithgow.
12/12/79

All The President's Men
WB. Prod, Walter Coblenz. Dir, Alan J Pakula. Sp, William Goldman, based on the book by Carl Bernstein, Bob Woodward; cam (Technicolor), Gordon Willis; edtr, Robert L. Wolfe; mus, David Shire; prodn des, George Jenkins; set decor, George Gaines; snd, Art Piantadosi, Les Fresholtz, Dick Alexander, Jim Webb; asst dirs, Bill Green, Art Levinson. (MPAA rating: PG). 138.
Dustin Hoffman, Robert Redford, Jack Warden, Martin Balsam, Hal Holbrook, Jason Robards, Jane Alexander, Stephen Collins, Meredith Baxter, Ned Beatty, Penny Fuller, John McMartin, Robert Walden, Frank Wills, Allyn Ann McLerie, Polly Holiday.
03/31/76

All This and World War II
FOX. Prods, Sandy Lieberson, Martin J Machat; exec prod, Russ Regan. Dir, Susie Winslow. Research, Tony Palmer; edtr, Colin J Berwick; mus dir, Lou Reizner; songs, John Lennon, Paul McCartney; arr, Wil Malone. (MPAA rating: G). 88.
Vocals: Ambrosia, The Bee Gees, The Brothers Johnson, Richard Cocciante, Lynsey De Paul, David Essex, Bryan Ferry, The Four Seasons, Peter Gabriel, Henry Gross, Elton John, Frankie Laine, Jeff Lynne, Wil Malone, Keith Moon, Helen Reddy, Lou Reizner, Leo Sayer, Status Quo, Rod Stewart, Tina Turner, Frankie Valli, Roy Wood, London Symphony Orchestra, Royal Philharmonic Orchestra. (CLIPS)
11/17/76

Allegro Non Troppo
(Italy)
BBZ. Wri-dir, Bruno Bozzeto. Color by Technicolor. 85. (ANI)
12/08/76

Aller Retour
(Round Trip)
(Yugoslavia)
YFR. Danas Film prodn. Dir, Aleksandar Petkovic. Sp, Dragoslav Mihailovic; cam (Eastmancolor), Tomislav Pinter; mus, Kornelije Kovao. 93.
Dusan Janicijevic, Milena Dravic, Slavko Simac, Ljubisa Samardzic.
08/16/78

Alligator
G1. Prod, Brandon Chase. Exec prod, Robert S Bremson. Dir, Lewis Teague. Sp, John Sayles; cam (Deluxe), Joseph Mangine. (MPAA rating: R). 94.
Robert Forster, Robin Riker, Michael Gazzo, Perry Lang, Jack Carter, Henry Silva, Bart Braverman, Dean Jagger.
11/19/80

Almost A Love Story: SEE
Pochti Lyubovna Istorya

Almost Human: SEE Milano
Odia: La Polizia non puo'Sparare

Almost Summer
U. Motown Prodn. Prod, Rob Cohen; exec prod, Steve Tish. Dir, Martin Davidson; sp, Judith Berg, Sandra Berg, Davidson, Marc Reid Rubel; cam (Technicolor), Stevan Larner; edtr, Lynzee Klingman; mus, Charles Lloyd, Ron Altbach; art dir, William M Hiney; set decor, Mary Ann Biddle; snd, Jim Alexander, Bill Varney; cos-ward, Sandra Davidson; asst dir, Gary Daigler; stunt coord, Conrad Palmisano. (MPAA rating: PG). 88.
Bruno Kirby, Lee Purcell, John Freidrich, Didi Conn, Thomas Carter, Tim Matheson, Petronia Paley, David Wilson, Sherry Hursey, Harvey Lewis.
04/26/78

Almost Transparent Blue:
SEE Kagirinaku Tomei Ni Chikai Buruu

Alone: SEE Sola

Alone At Daybreak: SEE Solos En La Madrugada

Alpenbaringen
(The Revelation)
(Norway)
X. Norsk Film Prodn, Oslo. Dir, Vibeke Loekkeberg. Sp, Loekkeberg, Terje Kristiansen; cam, Paul Rene Roestad. 81.
Marie Rakvam, Wilfred Briestrand, Bonne Gauguin, Wilhelm Lunds, Vibeke Loekkeberg, Terje Kristiansen.
01/10/79

Also Es War So. . .
(Willie and the Chinese Cat)
(W Germany - Austria)
NWI. Karin Thome Film prodn, Munich, in collab with Kuratorium Junger Deutscher Film, Zweites Deutsches Fernsehen (ZDF), Mainz, Sasbha Film, Vienna, and SWK Schutzgemeinschaft. Wri-prod-dir, Karin Thome. Cam, Michael Ballhaus, Lothar Elias Stickelbrucks; edtrs, Josef Jovancic, S Geiger-Haas; des-cos, Johannes Schuetz, Marlies Paul Bacquer, Erhard Stiefel, Marlies von Soden; mus, Heinz Loenhardsberger. 90.
Giovani Widmann, Anna Karina, Ulli Lommel, Little Columbine.
06/01/77

Alt paa et braet
(Going for Broke)
(Denmark)
DNS. Merry Film prodn. Dir, Gabriel Axel. Sp, Axel, Ole Boje, based on Jean Halain and Jacques Besnard's Trinacra (Paris) prodn of "C'est pas parce qu' on a rein a dire qu'il faut fermer sa gueule"; cam (Eastmancolor), Rolf Roenne; mus, Joern Grauengaard. 88.
Dirch Passer, Joergen Ryg, Preben Kaas, Lily Broberg, Peter Steen.
03/02/77

Altars of the World
X. All State Productions, Inc presentation. Prod-dir-pho-edtr, Lew Ayres. 150. (RELIGIOUS DOC)
01/21/76

Altered States
WB. Prod, Howard Gottfried. Exec prod, Daniel Melnick. Dir, Ken Russell. Sp, Sidney Aaron; novel, Paddy Chayefsky; cam (Technicolor), Jordan Cronenweth; edtr, Eric Jenkins; mus, John Corigliano; prodn des, Richard McDonald; asso prod, Stuart Baird; asst dir, Gary Daigler; snd (Dolby) cnsltnt, Stephen Katz; sfx, Chuck Gaspar; special visual effects, Bran Ferren; special optical effects, Robbie Blalack, Jamie Shourt; time-lapse pho, Lou Schwartzberg; cos, Ruth Myers; make-up, Dick Smith. (MPAA rating: R). 102.
William Hurt, Blair Brown, Bob Balaban, Charles Haid, Thaao Penghlis, Miguel Godreau, Dori Brenner, Peter Brandon, Charles White Eagle, Drew Barrymore, Megan Jeffers, Jack Murdock, Frank McCarthy, Deborah Baltzell, Evan Richards, Hap Lawrence, John Walter Davis, Cynthia Burr, Susan Bredhoff, John Larroquette.
12/10/80

The Alternative Miss World
(Britain)
X. James Street Ltd prodn. Prod-dir, Richard Gayer. Cam, Mike Davis, Mike Dodds, Nick Knowland, Mike Lensvelt, Bob Smith, Clive Tickner; snd, Malcolm Stuart; edtr, Rob Small; lighting, Stephen Goldblatt; asso prods, Michael Davis, Simon Mallin, Toni Tye Walker; exec prod, Judy McDonald. 114.
Divine, Andrew Logan, Sophia Parkin, Nigel Adey, Riccardo de Velasco, John Thomas, Rosemary Gibb, Rebecca du Pont de Bie, Jenny Runacre, Stevie Hughes, James Birch, Sarah Parkin, Golinda Von Regensburg, Joanie de Vere Hunt, Jill Bruce, John Maybury, Emma Harrison, William Waldron, Janet Slee, John Hopwood, Stephen Holt, Bob Anthony, Maruice, Bobby Claridge, Lynn O'Liam. (DOC)
11/26/80

Always For Pleasure
X. Les Blank prodn. Prod-dir, Blank. Cam, Blank, Maureen Gosling; edtrs, Blank, Gosling; snd, Gosling; paintings, Bruce Brice. 58.
"Blue Lu" Barker, Professor Longhair, Kid Thomas Valentine, Irma Thomas, Allen Toussaint, The Wild Tchoupitoulas with the Neville Brothers. (DOC)
01/17/79

Always With Me
(USSR)
SOV. Lenfilm prodn. Dir, Solomon Chouster. Sp, Leonid Zorine. 100.
Vladislav Strjeltchik, Alissa Freindikh.
12/01/76

Alzire oder der neue Kontinet
(Alzire or the New Continent)
(Switzerland)
X. Filmkollektiv Zurich/Thomas Koerfer Film prodn. Dir, Koerfer; sp, Dieter Feldhausen; cam, Renato Berta; edtr, Georg Janett. 108.

Francois Simon, Roger Jendly, Rudiger Vogler.
(16m)
04/11/79

Amada Amante
(Beloved Lover)
(Brazil)
X. Prod, Luis Carlos Barreto. Dir, Bruno Barreto. Sp, Jose Louziero, Leopoldo Serran; cam, Lauro Escorel Filho; edtr, Raimundo Higino; mus, Guto Graca Mello.   98.
Paulo Gracindo, Cristina Ache, Paulo Guarnieri, Ligia Diniz, Flavio Sao Thiago.
03/28/79

Amator
(Camera Buff)
(Poland)
POL. Film Polski Prodn, Film Unit Tor, Warsaw. Dir, Krzysztof Kieslowski. Sp, Kieslowski, Stuhr; cam, Jacek Petrycki; mus, Krzysztof Knittel; sets, Rafal Waltenburger; prodn mgr, Wielislawa Piotrowska.   112.
Jerzy Stuhr, Malgorzata Zabkowska, Ewa Pokas, Stefan Czyzewski, Jerzy Nowak, Tadeusz Bladecki, Marek Litewka, Buguslaw Sobczuk.
09/05/79

The Amazing Dobermans
GDN. Prod, David Chudnow; exec prod, Don Reynolds. Dir, Byron Chudnow. Sp, Michael Kraike, William Goldsten, Richard Chapman, from a story by Kraike, Goldstein; cam (CFI Color), Jack Adams; edtr, James Potter; mus, Alan Silvestri; (MPAA rating: G).   96.
Fred Astaire, James Franciscus, Barbara Eden, Jack Carter, Billy Barty, Parley Baer.
12/01/76

The Ambassadors: SEE Les Ambassadeurs

Amendment to the Law for the Defence of the State: SEE Dopalnenie Kan Zakona Za Zaschitita Na Darjavata

America at the Movies
X. American Revolution Bicentennial presentation of an American Film Institute prodn. Prod, George Stevens Jr; film des, James R Silke; narr wri, Theodore Strauss; spoken by Charlton Heston; asso prod, Harrison Engle; edtr, David Saxon; title mus arr-cond, Nelson Riddle; historical cnslnt, Arthur Schlesinger Jr; des cnslnt, Ivan Chermayeff; for ARBA: admn, John W Warner; project dir, Jack Masey. (MPAA rating: PG).   116.
07/14/76

America Lost And Found
X. Prodn of Media Study/Buffalo, American Portrait Unit. Project dir, Dr Gerald O'Grady; prod, Tom Johnson; dir, Lance Bird; sp, John Crowley; narr, Pat Hingle; edtr, Kate Hirson; mus prodn, Arthur Gorson.   65.
(DOC)
11/07/79

The American Dream: SEE Droemmen om Amerika

The American Friend: SEE Der Amerikanische Freund

The American Game
WNO. Prod, Anthony Jones. Wri-dirs, Jay Freund, David Wolf. Cam-location dirs, Robert Elfstrom, Peter Powell; co-prods, Powell, Robby Kenner; asso prod, Grania Gurievitch; edtrs, Freund, Nancy Baker; contributing edtrs, Michael Steinfeld, Kenneth Eluto, Judith Guerra; snd edtr, Al Nahmias.   85.
(DOC)
04/18/79

American Gigolo
PAR. Freddie Fields prodn. Exec prod, Freddie Fields. Prod, Jerry Bruckheimer. Wri-dir, Paul Schrader. Cam (Metrocolor), John Bailey; art dir, Ed Richardson; edtr, Richard Halsey; mus, Giorgio Moroder; set decor, George Gaines; snd, Barry Thomas; snd fx edtrs, Ray Alba, Bert Schoenfeld; asst dir, Peter Bogart. (MPAA rating: R).   117.
Richard Gere, Lauren Hutton, Hector Elizondo, Nina Van Pallandt, Bill Duke, Brian Davies, K Callan, Tom Stewart, Patti Carr, David Cryer, Carole Cook, Carol Bruce, Frances Bergen, Macdonald Carey, William Dozier, Peter Turgeon, Robert Wightman, Richard Derr, Jessica Potter.
01/30/80

American Hot Wax
PAR. Prod, Art Linson. Dir, Floyd Mutrux. Sp, John Kaye; cam, William A Fraker; edtrs, Melvin Shapiro, Ronald J Fagan; mus supv, Kenny Vance; art dir, Elayne Barbara Ceder; set decor, George Gaines; snd, Robert Knudsen, Thomas Overton; cos-ward, Robert DeMora, Don Vargas, Mina Mittelman; asst dir, Joe Wallenstein. (MPAA rating: PG).   91.
Tim McIntire, Fran Drescher, Jay Leno, Laraine Newman, Carl Earl Weaver, Al Chalk, Sam Harkness, Arnold McCuller, Jeff Altman, Moosie Drier, John Lehne, Chuck Berry, Jerry Lee Lewis, Screamin' Jay Hawkins, Kenny Vance.
03/15/78

American Nitro
X. K B prodn. Prods, Jim Kimberlin, Tim Geideman. Dir-edtr, Bill Kimberlin. Cam, Kimberlin, Geideman; mus, Art Twain.   75.
(DOC) (16m)
03/28/79

American Odyssey
MKA. Exec prod, Suzanne Beffa. Wri-dir, Ambrose Salmini. Cam, Salmini, Steve Marts, Peter Salmini, Norv Knight; edtr, Ambrose Salmini; snd, Kathy Emerick; narr, Gerard Bocker; asso prod, Peter Salmini.   87.
Melody Mayer, Todd Gay, Leon Henderson, Linda Macias.
(DOC) (16m)
11/05/80

The American Success Company
COL. Edgard J Scherick/Daniel H Blatt prodn. Prod, Daniel H Blatt, Edgar J Scherick. Dir, William Richert; sp, William Richert, Larry Cohen. Based on a story by Cohen. Cam, Anthony Richmond; edtr, Ralph E Winters; mus, Maurice Jarre; prodn des, Rolf Zehetbauer; art dir, Werner Achmann; cos des, Robert De Mora, Helga Pinnow; snd, Gordon Everett; asso prod, Pia I Arnold; asst dirs, Dietmar Siegert, Marijan Vajda. (MPAA rating: PG).   94.
Jeff Bridges, Belinda Bauer, Ned Beatty, Steven Keats, Bianca Jagger, John Glover, Mascha Gonska, Michael Durrell, Eva-Maria Meineke, Gunter Meisner, David Brooks.
11/28/79

American Torso: SEE Amerikai Anzix

America's Fat: SEE El Gordo de America

Americathon
UA. Lorimar prodn. Prod, Joe Roth. Exec prod, Edward Rosen. Dir, Neil Israel. Sp, Michael Mislove, Monica Johnson, from story by Israel, Peter Bergman, Philip Proctor; cam (Technicolor) Gerald Hirschfield; edtr, John C Howard; prodn des, Stan Jolley; set des, Mark L Fabus; cos des, Daniel Paredes; Jim La Rue; asst dir, Jack Baran. (MPAA rating: PG).   85.
Peter Riegert, Harvey Korman, Fred Willard, Zane Buzby, Nancy Morgan, John Ritter, Richard Schaal, Chief Dan George, Meat Loaf, Terry McGovern.
08/15/79

Amerikai Anzix
(American Torso)
(Hungary)
HU. Bela Balazs Studio prodn. Dir-sp, Gabor Body, based on short story by Ambrose Bierce. Cam, Istvan Lugossy, Gabor Body, Peter Timar.   104.
Sandor Csutoros, Gyorgy Cserhalmi, Andras Fekete.
(B & W)
03/02/77

The Amityville Horror
AIP. Prods, Ronald Saland, Elliot Geisinger. Exec prod, Samuel Z Arkoff. Dir, Stuart Rosenberg. Sp, Sandor Stern, based on book by Jay Anson; cam, Fred J Koenekamp; edtr, Robert Brown; art dir, Kim Swados; visual effects des, William Cruse; sfx, Delwyn Rheaume; mus, Lalo Schifrin. (MPAA rating: R).   117.
James Brolin, Margot Kidder, Rod Steiger, Don Stroud, Natasha Ryan, K C Martel, Meeno Peluce, Michael Sacks, Helen Shaver, Val Avery, Amy Wright, Murray Hamilton, John Larch, Irene Dailey.
08/01/79

Amo non Amo
(I Love You, I Love You Not)
(Italy)
TIT. Prods, Valerio De Paolis, Gianni Bozzacchi for Compagnia Europea Cinematografica. Dir, Armenia Balducci. Sp, Armenia Balducci, Ennio De Concini; cam (Technicolor); Carlo di Palma; art dir, Maria Paola Maino; mus, Goblin Bixio-Cemsa. 100.
Jacqueline Bisset, Maximilian Schell, Terence Stamp, Monica Guerritore.
03/07/79

Among People: SEE Sredi Ludei

Amor Der Perdicao
(Love Of Perdition)
(Portugal)
X. Portuguese Film Institute prodn, Lisbon. Wri-dir, Manoel de Oliveira, adapted from the novel with the same title by Camilo Castelo Branco; cam, Manuel Costa e Silva; mus, Jaoa Paes, Handel. 260.
Cristina Hauser, Antonio Sequeira Lopes, Elsa Wallenkamp, Antonio J Costa, Henrique Viana, Maria Dulce.
10/15/80

The Amorous Adventures Of Don Quixote & Sancho Panza
(The Erotic Adventures of Super Knight)
BXX. Dalia Prods film, prod-dir, Raphael Nussbaum; exec prod, Roberta Reeves. Sp, Nussbaum, Ed Woodworth, with addt dial by Al Bukzin; cam (CFI Color), Bill de Diego; edtr, Dick Brummer; mus, Don Great; songs, Bukzin, Great; art dir, Joel Leonard; snd, Bob Dietz; asst dir, Henning Schellerup; stunt coord, Peter Horak. (MPAA rating: R). 127.
Corey John Fischer, Hy Pyke.
04/21/76

Amsterdam Kill
(Hong Kong)
GHV. Exec prod, Raymond Chow. Prod, Andre Morgan. Dir, Robert Clouse. Sp, Clouse, Gregory Tiefer; cam, Alan Hume; snd, Peter Davies, Charles McFadden; edtr, Alan Holtzman; sfx, Gene Grigg. (MPAA rating: R). 93.
Robert Mitchum, Bradford Dillman, Richard Egan, Leslie Nielsen, Keye Luke, George Cheung, Chan Sing, Stephen Leung.
(English soundtrack)
05/11/77

An Almost Perfect Affair
PAR. Prod, Terry Carr; dir, Michael Ritchie; sp, Walter Bernstein, Don Peterson, based on a story by Ritchie and Peterson; cam (Deluxe Color), Henri Decae; edtr, Richard A Harris; art dir, Willy Holt; mus, Georges Delerue; snd, Bernard Bats; asst dir, Marc Monnet. (MPAA rating: PG.) 93.
Keith Carradine, Monica Vitti, Raf Vallone, Christian De Sica, Dick Anthony Williams, Henri Garcin, Anna Maria Horsford.
04/11/79

An Average Man: SEE Un Borghese Piccolo Piccolo

An Elephant Can Be Extremely Deceptive: SEE Un Elephant Ca Trompe Enormement

An Enemy of the People
WB. First Artists (Solar) Prodn. Prod-dir, George Schaefer; exec prod, Steve McQueen. Sp, Alexander Jacobs, based on adaptation of the Henrik Ibsen play by Arthur Miller; cam (Metrocolor), Paul Lohmann; edtr, Sheldon Kahn; mus, Leonard Rosenman; prodn des, Eugene Lourie; set decor, Anthony Mondello; cos, Noel Taylor; snd, Michael J Kohut; asst dir, Jack Aldworth. (MPAA rating: G). 103.
Steve McQueen, Charles Durning, Bibi Andersson, Eric Christmas, Michael Cristofer, Richard A Dysart, Michael Higgins, Richard Bradford, Ham Larsen, John Levin, Robin Pearson Rose.
08/30/78

An Old Woman: SEE Wai Tok Kra

An Uncompromising Man: SEE O Asymvivastos

An Unmarried Woman
FOX. Prods, Tony Ray, Paul Mazursky. Sp-dir, Mazursky. Cam (Movielab Color), Arthur Ornitz; edtr, Stuart H Pappe; mus, Bill Conti; prodn des, Pato Guzman; set decor, Edward Stewart; snd, Arthur Piantadosi, Dennis Maitland; cos-ward, Albert Wolsky, Max Solomon, Beverly Cycon; asst dir, Terry Donnelly. (MPAA rating: R). 124.
Jill Clayburgh, Alan Bates, Michael Murphy, Cliff Gorman, Pat Quinn, Kelly Bishop, Lisa Lucas, Linda Miller, Andrew Duncan, Daniel Seitzer, Matthew Arkin, Penelope Russianoff, Novelle Nelson, Raymond J Barry, Paul Mazursky, Ultra Violet.
02/15/78

An Untypical Story: SEE Netepichnaja Istoria

An Unusual Girl: SEE Une Fille Unique

Anastasia Passed By: SEE Duios Anastasia Trecea

Anatoliki Periferia
(Eastern Territory)
(Greece)
X. Vassilis Vafeas prodn. Wri-dir, Vafeas; cam, George Kavayas; sets-cos, Damianos Zarifis; edtr, George Korras; snd, Thanassis Georgiades. 77.
Menas Hatzisavas, Nelli Anguelidou, Yannis Goumas.
(B & W)
11/28/79

Anatomie D'Un Rapport
(Anatomy of a Relationship)
(France)
AUE. Moullet Et Cie prodn. Wri-dirs, Luc Moullet, Antonietta Pizzorno. Cam, Michel Fournier; edtr, Genevieve Dufour. 82.
Luc Moullet, Christine Herbert, Antonietta Pizzorno, Viviane Barthhommier.
(B & W) (16m)
09/29/76

The Anchorite: SEE El Anacoreta

...And Justice For All
COL. Prods, Norman Jewison, Patrick Palmer. Dir, Jewison. Exec prod, Joe Wizan. Sp, Valerie Curtin, Barry Levinson; cam, Victor J Kemper; edtr, John F Burnett; mus, Dave Grusin; prodn des, Richard MacDonald; snd, Robert Henderson; art dir, Peter Samish; asst dir, Win Phelps. (MPAA rating: R). 120.
Al Pacino, Jack Warden, John Forsythe, Lee Strasberg, Jeffrey Tambor, Christine Lahti, Sam Levene, Robert Christian, Thomas Waites, Larry Bryggman, Craig T Nelson, Dominic Chianese, Victor Arnold.
09/19/79

And Long Live Liberty: SEE Et Vive La Liberte

And Quiet Rolls the Day: SEE Ekdin Pratidin

...And the Third Year, He Resuscitated: SEE ...Y Al Tercer Ano Resucito

And They Lived Happily Ever After: SEE Colorin, Colorado

The Andes Odyssey: SEE La Odisea De Los Andes

Ang Boyfriend Kung Badoy
(The Stupid Boyfriend)
(Philippines)
X. Jessalee Film prodn. Exec prod, Jess Cabalza. Dir, Joey Gosienfiao. Sp, Toto Belano from story by Luciano Carlos; edtr, Rogelio Salvador; mus, Demet Velasquez. 100.
Amalia Fuentes, Gina Parino, Barbara Perez, Orestes Ojeda, Helen Gamboa, Greg Lozano, Sandy Garcia, Alona Alegre, Dante Ramirez models.
04/07/76

Ang Leon At Ang Daga
(The Lion and the Rat)
(Philippines)
X. F P J prodn. Dir, Armando Herrera. Sp, Fred Navarro; cam, Sergio Lobo; mus, Ernami Cunenco. 106.
Fernando Poe Jr, Marianne de la Riva, Nino Muhlach, Paquito Diaz,

Dencio Padilla, Vic Varrion, the Thunder Stuntmen and S O S Daredevils.
05/05/76

Angel and Woman: SEE L'Ange et La Femme

Angel Mine
(New Zealand)
ILZ. Prods, David Blyth, Warren Sellers. Wri-dir, Blyth. Cam, John Earnshaw; snd, Mike Westgate; edtr, Phillip Howe; mus, Mark Nicholas, played by Auckland Youth Orchestra, Charisma, Urban Road, Suburban Reptiles. 72.
Derek Ward, Jennifer Redford.
01/10/79

Angela Davis, L'Enchainement
(Angela Davis, The Sequence Of Events)
(France)
SDN. Dir, Jean-Daniel Simon. Conceived by Simon, Angela Davis, Claude May, Jacqueline Meppiel. Cam, Jacques Boumendil; edtr, Simon. 95.
(DOC)
12/28/77

Angels
X. Jape Ltd prodn, prod, Denis Rubin. Dir, Spencer Compton. Sp, Drew Abrams, Richard Power, Compton, Ed Margulies; cam, Rob Hahn, Michael Parker; edtr, Gary Gasgarth; mus, Olubji Adetoye. (MPAA rating: R). 90.
Vincent Schiavelli, Keith Berger, Marquita Callwood, David Bryant, Mark Suben, Dan McCarthy.
04/07/76

Angi Vera
(Vera's Training)
(Hungary)
HU. Mafilm Objectiv Studio prodn. Wri-dir, Pal Gabor from a book by Endre Veszi; cam (Eastmancolor), Lajos Koltai; mus, Gyorgy Selmeczi. 96.
Veronika Papp, Erszi Pasztor, Tamas Dunai, Eva Szabo.
02/28/79

The Angry Man: SEE L'Homme En Colere

Angst
(Anguish)
(Norway)
MFN. Dir, Oddvar Bull Tuhus. Sp, Lass Glomm, Tuhus; 85.
Svein Scharrfenberg, Eva Sevaldson, Thea Stagel, Alf Nordhus.
08/25/76

Angst Haben Und Angst Machen
(To Be Afraid and Make Others Afraid)
(W Germany)
X. AST prodn, Berlin, in collab with Zweites Deutsches Fernsehen, Mainz. Wri-dir, Wolfram Zobus. Cam (b&w), Joerg Jeschel; snd, Helmut Roettgen; edtr, Christine Wolf. 95.
(DOC) (B & W)
09/22/76

Angst Vor Der Angst
(Fear of Fear)
(W Germany)
X. Westdeutscher Rundfunk prodn. Exec prod, Peter Marthesheimer. Dir-sp, Rainer Werner Fassbinder. Cam, Jurgen Jurges, Ulrich Prinz; snd, Manfred Oelschlegel, Hans Pampuch; edtrs, Liesgrett Schmitt-Klink, Beate Fischer-Weiskirch; mus, Peer Raben. 88.
Margit Carstensen, Ulrich Faulhaber, Brigitte Mira, Irm Hermann, Amin Meier, Adrian Hoven, Kurt Raab, Ingrid Caven, Lilo Pempeit.
(16m)
10/20/76

Anguish: SEE Angst

Ani Imouto
(Mon and Ino)
(Japan)
TOH. Dir, Tadashi Imai. Cam (Eastmancolor), Kazutami Haia. 90.
Kimiko Akiosha, Masao Kusahaii, Kimuko Ikegani.
01/26/77

Anima Persa
(The Forbidden Room)
(France - Italy)
FOX. Dear Film (Rome) and Fox-Europa (Paris). Prods, Pio Angeletti, Adriano De Micheli. Dir, Dino Risi. Sp, Bernardino Zapponi, Risi from novel by Giovanni Arpino; cam (Technospes), Tonino Delli Colli; edtr, Alberto Gallitti; mus, Francis Lai; prods, Pio Angeletti, Adriano De Micheli. 102.
Vittorio Gassman, Catherine Deneuve, Danilo Mattei, Anicee Alvina, Ester Carloni, Michele Capnist, Gino Cavalieri.
01/26/77

The Animal: SEE L'Animal

Anita Droegemoeller Und Die Ruhe An Der Ruhr
(Anita Droegemoeller and Quiet on the Ruhr)
(W Germany)
X. CTV 72-Prodn, Horst Haechler, Munich. Terra-Filmkunst, Berlin, prodn. Dir, Alfred Vohrer. Sp, W P Zibaso, based on novel of same title by Juergen Lodemann; cam, Ernst W Kalinke; edtr, Ingeborg Taschner. 87.
Monique van de Ven, Harald Leipnitz, Helga Anders, Alf Marholm, Dick Galuba, Reiner Schoene, Rudolf Schuendler, Brigitte Mira, Walter Buschhoff, Juergen Draeger.
04/27/77

Annie Hall
UA. Jack Rollins-Charles H Joffe prodn, prod, Joffe; exec prod, Robert Greenhut. Dir, Woody Allen. Sp, Allen, Marshall Brickman; cam (DeLuxe color), Gordon Willis; edtr, Ralph Rosenblum; songs, "Seems Like Old Times," Carmen Lombardo and John Jacob Loeb, and "It Had To Be You," Isham Jones and Gus Kahn; art dir, Mel Bourne; set decor, Robert Drumheller, Justin Scoppa Jr, Barbara Kreiger; cos-ward, Ruth Morley, George Newman, Marilyn Putnam, Ralph Lauren, Nancy McArdle; snd, Jack Higgins, James Sabat, James Pilcher; asst dir, Fred T Gallo. (MPAA rating: PG). 93.
Woody Allen, Diane Keaton, Tony Roberts, Carol Kane, Paul Simon, Colleen Dewhurst, Janet Margolin, Shelley Duvall, Christopher Walken, Donald Symington, Mordecai Lawner, Joan Newman, Jonathan Munk, Ruth Volner, Martin Rosenblatt, Marshall McLuhan, Dick Cavett.
03/30/77

Anno Domini 1573
(Yugoslavia)
X. Jadran Film Production, Zagreb. Sp-dir, Vatroslav Mimica. Exec prod, Suleiman Kapic; cam, Branko Blazina; art dir, Vljko Despotovic; cos, Ferninand Kulmer; edtr, Vuksan Lukovac; mus, Alfi Kabiljo. 150.
Fabijan Sovagovic, Velimir Zivojinovic, Pavle Vujisic, Franjo Majetic, Srdjan Mimica, Marina Nemet, Zvonimir Crnko, Zdenka Hersak, Djuro Utjesinovic, Stole Arandjelovic, Boris Festini, Ivica Pajer, Adam Cejvan, Aco Jovanovski, Miodrag Krivakapic, Zdenka Trach, Ilija Ivezic, Natasa Maricic, Charles Millot, Lojze Rozman, Minja Nikolic, Julije Perlaki, Petar Dobric, Zaim Muzaferija, Vladimir Medar, Edo Perocevic, Mato Ergovic, Ivica Kunej, Fahro Konjhodzic, Mladen Vasari.
03/17/76

Another Day: SEE Yawmun Akher

Another Man, Another Chance: SEE Un Autre Homme, Une Autre Chance

Anschi Und Michael
(Anschi and Michael)
(W Germany)
X. Bayerischer Rundfunk TV prodn, Munich. Wri-dir, Ruediger Nuechtern; cam, Hans Osterrieder; mus, Joerg Evers; edtr, Vera Grund. 108.
Gaby Rubner, Michael Bentele, Joerg Hube, Helga Endler, Peter Gebhardt, Edith Kunze-Krueger, Klaus Krueger.
(16m)
11/16/77

Ansichten Eines Clowns
(The Clown)
(W Germany)
CTT. Heinz Angermeyer prodn, in collab with MFG-Film/Filmaufbau. Prods, Heiner Angermeyer, Maximilian Schell. Dir, Vojtech Jasny. Sp, Jasny, Heinrich Boell, based on novel of same name by Boell; cam, Walter Lassally; mus, Berhard Schoener; edtr, Dagmar Hirtz. 120.
Helmut Griem, Hanna Schygulla, Eva-Maria Meineke, Gustav Rudolf Sellner, Hans Christian Blech, Alexander May, Jan Niklas, Rainer Basedow, Helga Anders, Claudia Butenuth, Ben Hecker, Wolfram Koch, Susanne Seidler, Heinrich von Busch.
03/17/76

Anti-Clock
(Britain)
IFX. Kendon Film (Boyd's Co) presentation of a Jack Bond prodn. Prod, Bond; dirs, Jane Arden, Bond; sp-songs, Arden; cam, Mike Davis, Nic Knowland; mus, Mihai Dragutescu; video concepts, Robert Parker; exec prod, Don Boyd; asso prod, Louise Temple. 97.
Sebastian Saville, Liz Saville, Suzan Cameron, Louise Temple, Tom Gerrard.
(COLOR - B & W - VIDEO)
09/17/80

Anton Der Zauberer
(Anton The Magician)
(E Germany)
DEE. DEFA Film Prodn, Group Johannisthal. Dir, Guenter Reisch. Sp, Karl Georg Egel; cam, Guenter Haubold; sets, Hans Jorg Mirr; mus, Wolfram Heicking; edtr, Baerbel Weigel. 95.
Ulrich Thein, Anna Dymna, Erwin Geschonneck, Barbara Dittus, Marina Krogull, Eric S Klein, Marianne Wuenscher, Jessy Rameik, Ralph Borgwardt, Gerry Wolf, Werner Godemann, Grigori Grigoriu, Dezso Garas, Leon Niemzcyk, Alfred Struwe.
06/28/78

Antonio Gramsci-I Giorni Del Carcere
(Antonio Gramsci-The Days of Prison)
(Italy)
ITG. Cooperative Nuovi Schermi prodn. Dir, Lino Del Fra. Sp, Cecilia Mangini, Piero Anchisi, Del Fra; cam, Gabor Pogany; edtr, Ailvano Agosti; mus, Egisto Macchi. 127.
Riccardo Cucciolla, Paolo Bonacelli, Lea Massari, Mimsy Farmer, Pier Paolo Capponi, Jacques Herlin, Franco Graziosi.
(B & W)
08/31/77

Antti Puuhaara
(Antti the Treebranch)
(Finland)
X. Partanen, Rautoma prodn. Dirs, Heikki Partanen, Ruta Rautoma, Katarina Lahti. Sp, Erkki Myakinen; cam, Markki Lehkmuskallio, Raimo Paananen; cos, Sari Salmela; mus, Kari Ryudman. 100.
07/27/77

Anugraham
(The Boom)
(India)
RVR. Dir, Shyam Benegal. Sp, Satyadev Dubey; cam (Eastmancolor), Govind Nihalani; mus, Vanraj Bhatia. 132.
Vanishree, Anant Nag, Smita Patil, N T Rama Rao, Amrish Puri.
01/31/79

Anxious to Return: SEE Gui Xin Shi Jian

Any Which Way You Can
WB. Prod, Fritz Manes. Exec prod, Robert Daley. Dir, Buddy Van Horn. Sp, Stanford Sherman, based on characters created by Jeremy Joe Kronsberg; cam (DeLuxe), David Worth; edtrs, Ferris Webster, Ron Spang; mus supv, Snuff Garrett; prodn des, William J Creber; set decor, Ernie Bishop; cos supv, Glenn Wright; snd, Bert Hallberg; asst dir, Tom Joyner. (MPAA rating: PG). 116.
Clint Eastwood, Sondra Locke, Geoffrey Lewis, William Smith, Harry Guardino, Ruth Gordon, Michael Cavanaugh, Barry Corbin, Roy Jenson, Bill McKinney, William O'Connell, John Quade, Al Ruscio, Dan Vadis, Camila Ashlend.
12/17/80

Apam Nehany Boldog Eve
(My Father's Happy Years)
(Hungary)
X. Hungarofilm, Budapest, prodn, Hunnia Studio. Sp-dir, Sandor Simo. Cam (Eastmancolor), Tamas Andor; edtr, Eva Karmento; sets, Jozsef Romvary; mus, Zdenko Tamassy. 98.
Lorand Lohinszky, Eszter Szakacs, Peter Hollo, Judit Meszleri, Jozsef Madaras, Istvan Bujtor, Irma Patkos, Gyorgyi Tarjan.
03/29/78

Ape
(Korea)
WW. Presentation by Jack Harris via Lee Ming Film Company. Prods, K M Yeung, Paul Leder; dir, Leder. 87.
Rod Arrants, Joanne De Verona, Alex Nicol.
(3-D)
12/15/76

Aphonya
(USSR)
SOV. Mosfilm prodn. Dir, Georgy Danelia. Sp, Alexander Borodiansky; cam (Sovocolor), Serguei Vronsky; mus, Moisey Vienberg. 90.
Leonid Kuravlev, Evgfueny Leonov, Eugenia Simonova.
08/25/76

Apocalypse Now
UA. Francis Coppola prodn. Prod-dir, Francis Coppola. Co-prod, Fred Roos, Gray Frederickson. Sp, John Milius, Francis Coppola, based on Joseph Conrad's "Heart of Darkness"; cam (Technicolor), Vittorio Storaro; edtr, Barry Malkin; prodn des, Dean Tavoularis; art dir, Angelo Graham; set decor, Bob Nelson; snd, Jacob Jacobsen; asst dir, Tony Brandt. 139.
Marlon Brando, Martin Sheen, Robert Duvall, Fred Forrest, Sam Bottoms, Albert Hall, Larry Fishborne, Dennis Hopper, Harrison Ford, G D Spradlin, Bill Graham, Cynthia Wood, Francis Coppola.
05/16/79

The Apple
(US - Germany)
CAN. N F Geria III Prodn. Prods, Menahem Golan, Yoram Globus. Wri-dir, Menahem Golan. Story, Iris and Coby Recht; cam, David Gurfinkel; prodn des, Jurgen Kiebach; cos, Ingrid Zore; edtr, Alain Jacubowicz; mus, Coby Recht; lyrs, Iris Recht, George Clinton; chor, Nigel Lythgoe. 90.
Catherine Mary Stewart, George Gilmour, Joss Ackland, Gladek Sheybal, Grace Kennedy, Allan Love, Ray Shell.
05/28/80

The Apple Dumpling Gang Rides Again
BV. Walt Disney prodn. Prods, Ron Miller, Tom Leetch. Dir, Vincent McEveety. Sp, Don Tait, based on characters created by Jack M Bickham; cam (Technicolor), Frank Phillips; edtr, Gordon D Brenner; art dir, Norman Rockett; sfx, Art Cruickshank, Danny Lee; snd, Henry A Maffett; asst dir, Robert W Webb. (MPAA rating: G). 88.
Tim Conway, Don Knotts, Tim Matheson, Kenneth Mars, Elyssa Davalos, Jack Elam, Robert Pine, Harry Morgan, Ruth Buzzi, Audrey Totter, Richard X Slattery, John Crawford, Cliff Osmond, Ted Gehring, Morgan Paull.
06/20/79

The Apprentice Heel: SEE L'Apprenti Salaud

The Apprentice Sorcerers: SEE Les Apprentis Sorciers

April Has 30 Days: SEE Ein April Hat 30 Tage

Aquella Casa En Las Afueras
(That House In The Outskirts)
(Spain)
X. Kalender Films International S A K prodn. Dir, Eugenio Martin. Sp, Manuel Summers, Antonio Cuevas, Jose G Castrillo, Eduardo Alvarez, Eugenio Martin, Manuel Matji; cam (Eastmancolor), Manuel Rojas; exec prod, Antonio Cuevas; mus, Carmelo Bernaola; edtr, Pablo G del Amo; sets, Jose Maria Alarcon. 101.
Javier Escriva, Silvia Aguilar, Alida Valli, Mara Goyanes, Carmen Maura.
11/19/80

Aquella Larga Noche
(That Long Night)
(Cuba)
X. Prod, Instituto Cubano del Arte y la Industria Cinematografica. Dir, Enrique Pineda Barnet. Sp, Ambrosio Fornet, Enrique Pineda; cam, Raul Rodriguez; mus, Carlos Farinas; edtr, Gloria Arguelles; prod, Rolindo Diaz Reyes; sets, Luis Lacosta. 100.

Raquel Revuelta, Maria Eugenia Garcia.
09/26/79

Arabian Adventure
(Britain)
WBO. EMI Films presentation of a John Dark prodn. Dir, Kevin Connor. Sp, Brian Hayles; cam, Alan Hume; mus, Ken Thorne; edtr, Barry Peters; prodn des, David Harris; snd, Jim Atkinson. 98.
Christopher Lee, Milo O'Shea, Oliver Tobias, Emma Samms, Puneet Sira, Peter Cushing, Capucine, Mickey Rooney, John Wyman, Shane Rimmer, John Ratzenberger, Elizabeth Welch, Michael Watkins.
05/30/79

Arabische Naechte
(Arabian Nights)
(W Germany)
ATF. Albatros-Production Michael Fengler, Munich, in co-prodn with Popular-Film, Stuttgart, and Trio-Film, Duisburg. Wri-dir, Klaus Lemke. Cam, Ruediger Meichsner; edtr, Inez Regnier; mus, Juergen Kniepor; exec prod, Christian Hohoff. 94.
Cleo Kretschmer, Wolfgang Fierek, Dolly Dollar, Michael Lampert, Horatius Haeberle, Jonny Badr, Zora Z, King Herbert, Guenni, El Hodjem.
06/04/80

Aran
(France)
FDP. Dir, Georges Combe. Cam, Guy Marconnier; edtr, Philipe Baudart; snd, Claude Joly; mus, traditional airs specially recorded by Combe. 60.
Maggie Dirranne and the inhabitants of the Aran Islands.
(DOC) (16m)
09/05/79

Aria Dla Atlety
(Aria for an Athlete)
(Poland)
POL. Film Polski Prodn, Film Unit Tor, Warsaw. Wri-dir, Filip Bajon. Cam, Jerzy Zielinski; mus, Zdzislaw Szostak. 108.
Krysztof Majchrzak, Pola Raksa, Roman Wilhelmi, Bogusz Bilewski, Wojciech Pszoniak, Ryszard Pietruski, Zdzislaw Wardejn.
06/25/80

Arkadas
(The Friend)
(Turkey)
X. Guney Film Prodn, Istanbul. Wri-dir, Yilmaz Guney. Cam, Cetin Tunca. 90.
Yilmaz Guney, Melike Demirag, Kerim Afsar, Azra Balkan, Ahu Tugbay.
08/02/78

Armaguedon
(France - Italy)
AMLF. Lira Films, Adel Prodns, Filmes prodn. Wri-dir, Alain Jessua; book, David Lippincott. Cam (Eastmancolor), Jacques Robin; edtr, Helen Plemiannikov. 95.
Alain Delon, Jean Yanne, Renato Salvatore, Michel Duchaussoy.
03/23/77

Armee der Liebenden Oder Aufstand der Perversen
(Army of Lovers Or Revolt of the Perverts)
(W Germany)
X. Prod-dir-wri-edtr, Rosa von Praunheim, assisted by Mike Shephard. Cam, Von Praunheim, Lloyd Williams, Juliana Wang, Michael Oblovitz, Ben van Meter, Nickolai Ursin, John Rome, Bob Schub, Werner Schroter. 107.
(DOC)
03/21/79

Arrebato
(Rapture)
(Spain)
X. Nicolas Astiarraga P C prodn. Wri-dir, Ivan Zulueta; cam (Eastmancolor), Angel Luis Fernandez; edtr, Jose Luis Pelaez; sets, Ivan Zulueta, Carlos Astiarraga, Eduardo Eznarriaga; mus, Ivan Zulueta. 115.
Eusebio Poncela, Cecilia Roth, Will More, Marta Fernandez-Muro.
10/15/80

Arriba Hazana
(Long Live Hazana)
(Spain)
X. Sabre Films prodn. Dir, Jose Maria Gutierrez. Sp, Jose Samano, Gutierrez based on novel by Jose Maria Vaz de Soto, "El Infierno y la Brisa"; exec prod, Jose Samano; cam (Eastmancolor), Magi Torruella; mus, Eduardo Aute; edtr, Rosa Salgado. 97.
Fernando Fernan Gomez, Hector Alterio, Jose Sacristan, Gabriel Llopart, Lola Herrera, Andres Isbert, Jose Luis Perez, Emilio Siefrist, Quique San Francisco, Agustin Navarro, Inaki Marimon, Hans Isbert.
06/21/78

Arrive Before Breakfast: SEE Stici Pre Svitanja

Art of Killing
(Japan)
AHD. Arthur Davis Organization Japan Inc presentation. Exec prod, Arthur Davis; asso prod, Miyako Ejiri; prod, Hisao Masudo. Wri-dir, Masayoshi Nemoto. Cam, Ryo Yano, Yoshiaki Kato; mus, Stomu Yamashta; snd, Tetsuo Sagawa; edtr, Koichi Atsumo; prodn mgr, Hiroshi Sakano; narrator, Harry J Quini. 90.
11/22/78

Arthur Miller On Home Ground
(Canada)
X. Prodn of the Canadian Broadcasting Corp. Prod-dir-wri, Harry Rasky. Cam, Hideaki Kobayashi, Kenneth Gregg, Edmund Long; edtr, Arla Saare. 90.
Marilyn Monroe, Clark Gable, Burt Lancaster, Faye Dunaway, Lee J Cobb, Colleen Dewhurst, George C Scott, Maureen Stapleton, Raf Vallone, Mildred Dunnock, Christopher Plummer.
(DOC) (16m)
09/05/79

Arvacska
(No Man's Daughter)
(Hungary)
X. HungaroFilm prodn. Dir, Laszlo Ranody. Sp, Judith Elek, Laszlo Ranody, based on a novel by Zsigmond Moricz; cam, Sandor Sara; mus, Rudolf Maros. 87.
Zsuzsa Czinkoczi, Anna Nagy, Sandor Horvath, Jozsef Bihari, Adam Szirtes, Marian Moor.
05/26/76

Arven
(The Heritage)
(Norway)
NSK. Orig story and script by Anja Breien, Oddvar Bull Tuhus and Lasse Glomm. Dir, Anja Breien. Cam (Eastmancolor), Erling Thurmann-Andersen; edtrs, Henning Carlsen, Christian Hartkopp; exec prod, Harald Ohrvik; prodn mgrs, Laila Mikkelsen, Hans Lindgren prodn des, Lubos, Madla Hruza; cos, Siri Bryhni; mus, Mozart and other recordings. 90.
Espen Skjoenberg, Anita Bjoerk, Haege Juve, Jan Haarstad, Eva Opaker.
05/23/79

As A Turtle On Its Back: SEE La Tortue Sur Le Dos

As Easy As Pie: SEE Comme Sur Des Roullettes

As Far As The Eye Sees: SEE So Weit Das Auge Reicht

As Horas De Maria
(Maria's Hours)
(Portugal)
X. Cinequanon prodn. Wri-dir, Antonio de Macedo. Cam, Elso Roque. 105.
Cecilia Giumaraes, Eugenia Bettencourt, Joao d'Avila.
(16m)
10/10/79

As the Moon: SEE Comme La Lune

The Ascent: SEE Voshojdenie

The Ascent: SEE Kodiyettom

Ashanti
COL. Georges-Alain Vuille prodn. Exec prod, Luciano Sacripanti. Prod, Georges-Alain Vuille. Dir, Richard Fleischer. Sp, Stephen Geller (based on novel, "Ebano," by Alberto Vasquez-Figueroa); cam, Aldo Tonti; prodn des, Aurelio Crugnola; art dir, Kuli Sander; snd, David Hildyard; asso prod, John C Vuille. 117.
Michael Caine, Peter Ustinov, Beverly Johnson, Kabir Bedi, Omar Sharif, Rex Harrison, William Holden, Zia Mohyeddin, Winston Ntshona, Tariq Yunus, Tyrone Jackson, Jean-Luc Bideau, Johnny Sekka.
02/07/79

Ashwathama
(Wandering Soul)
(India)
MMI. Dir, K R Mohaman. Sp, P Raman Nair from book by Madampu Kunjukuttan; cam, Madhu Ambat; mus, A Padmanabhan. 120.
Madampu Kunjukuttan, Vidhubala, Vatsala, Ravi Menon.
(B & W)
02/13/80

Asignatura Pendiente
(Flunking Out)
(Spain)
X. Jose Luis Tafur prodn. Dir, Jose Luis Garcia. Sp, Jose Maria Gonzalez Sinde, Garcia; cam, Manuel Rojas; mus, Jesus Gluck. 105.
Jose Sacristan, Fiorella Flatoyano, Antonio Gamero, Silvia Tortosa, Hector Alterio, Simon Andreu, Covadonga Cadenas, Maria Casanova.
08/17/77

Asphaltnacht
(Asphalt Night)
(W Germany)
X. Tura-Film prodn, Munich, in collab with ZDF, Wiesbaden-Mainz. Wri-dir, Peter Fratzcher; cam, Bernd Heinl; mus, Lothar Meid; edtr, Fratzcher; TV-edtr, Sibylle Hubatschek-Rahn; prod, Alena Rimbach. 90.
Gerd U Heinemann, Thomas Davis, Ralf Herrmann, Charly Wierczejewsky, Michael Zens, Herbert "Rim" Rimbach, Debbie Neon, Gabriele Helene Ruttmann, Christiane Plate, Clemens Schkorski.
10/08/80

Assassination: SEE Attentat

Assassination in Sarajevo:
SEE Atentat U Sarajevu

Assault On Agathon
NNT. Jensen Int'l Film Company prodn. Prod, Nico Minardos. Dir, Laslo Benedek. Sp, Alan Caillou, based on his novel of same name; co-prods, Igo Kantor, Kjell Qvale; cam, George Arvanitis, Aris Stavrou; mus, Ken Thorne; song "Sooner Than We Know" by Ken Thorne, Hal Shaper, sung by Diane Solomon. (MPAA rating: PG). 96.
Nico Minardos, Nina Van Pallandt, John Woodvine, Marianne Faithfull, Kostas Baladimas, George Moussou, Dimitri Aronis, Takis Kavouras, Tina Spathi, Walter Heissig.
10/13/76

Assault On Precinct 13
TUR. CKK prodn; prod, J S Kaplan. Wri-dir, John Carpenter. Cam (Metrocolor), Douglas Knapp; mus, Carpenter; edtr, John T Chance; art dir, Tommy Wallace; snd, William Cooper; asst dir, James Nichols; cos-ward, Louise Kyes. (MPAA rating: R). 91.
Austin Stoker, Darwin Joston, Laurie Zimmer, Martin West, Tony Burton, Charles Cyphers, Nancy Loomis, Peter Bruni, John J Fox.
11/17/76

The Assignment
(Sweden)
SVF. Nordisk Tonefilm/AB Svensk Filmindustri/Swedish Film Institute prodn. Dir, Mats Arehn. Sp, Lars Magnus Jansson, Ingemar Ejve, Mats Arehn, based on Per Wahloo novel; dial trans into English and asst dir, George Bisset; cam (Eastmancolor), Lennart Carlsson; edtr-exec prod, Ingemar Ejve; mus, Allan Petterson's 7th Symphony; cos, Ulla Britt Soederlund. 97.
Thomas Hellberg, Christopher Plummer, Carolyn Seymour, Fernando Rey, Per Oscarsson.
(English soundtrack)
05/25/77

The Associate: SEE L'Associe

Asya's Happiness: SEE Istoriya As: Klyachimol

At Dere Tor!
(Stop It!)
(Norway)
X. Marcusfilm A/S prodn. Dir, Lasse Glomm. Sp, Glomm, based on novel by Espen Haavardsholm; cam, Erling Thurmann-Andersen. 100.
Eirik Kvale, Ole Moystad, Eindride Eidsvold, Wenche Bjornstad, Kristin Hauge, Karen Randers-Pherson.
11/19/80

At Night All Cats Are Gray:
SEE La Nuit Tous Les Chats Sont Gris

At the Beginning of Summer: SEE Ne Fillim Te Veres

At the Brink of the Brink of the Bench: SEE Au Bout du Bout du Banc

At The Earth's Core
(Britain)
AIP. Amicus (Max J Rosenberg and Milton Subotsky) prodn, prod, John Dark; exec prod, Harry N Blum. Dir, Kevin Connor. Sp, Subotsky, from the novel by Edgar Rice Burroughs; cam (Movielab Color), Alan Hume; edtrs, John Ireland, Barry Peters; mus, Mike Vickers; prodn des, Maurice Carter; art dir, Bert Davey; set decor, Michael White; snd, George Stephenson, Ken Barker; asst dir, Jack Causey. (MPAA rating: PG). 89.
Doug McClure, Peter Cushing, Caroline Munro, Cy Grant, Godfrey James, Sean Lynch, Keith Barron, Helen Gill, Anthony Verner, Robert Gillespie, Michael Crane, Bobby Parr, Andee Cromarty.
06/23/76

At the Service of Spanish Womanhood: SEE Al Servicio De La Mujer Espanola

At Your Own Request: SEE Na Wlasna Prosbe

At Ziji Duchove!
(Long Live Ghosts!)
(Czechoslovakia)
CZS. Czechoslovak Film prodn, Studio Barrandov, Prague. Dir, Oldrich Lipsky. Sp, Zdenek Sverak from a story by Jiri Melisek; cam, Jan Nemecek; mus, Jaroslav Uhlir; sets, Vladimir Labsky. 92.
Jiri Sovak, Dana Vavarova, Jiri Prochazka, David Vlcek, Tomas Holly, Igor Broz, Petr Stary, Igor Nachtigal Vladimir Brodsky, Lubomir Lipsky.
02/28/79

Ate a ultima gota
(To The Last Drop)
(Brazil)
X. Mariza Leao prodn. Dir-sp, Sergio Rezende. Cam (Eastmancolor), Jose Joffily; edtr, Vera Freire; mus, Paul de Castro; narr, Hugo Carvana. 70.
(DOC)
05/28/80

Atentat U Sarajevu
(Assassination in Sarajevo)
(Yugoslavia - Czechoslovakia)
YFR. Jadran Film-Kinema Sarajevo-Barrandov Studios prodn. Dir, Veljko Bulajic. Sp, Stevan Bulajic, Vladimir Bor, Paul Jarrico; cam (Eastmancolor), Jan Curk; art dir, Vlado Bankovic, Bohumil Pokorny; mus, Ljubas Fiser. 136.
Christopher Plummer, Florinda Bolkan, Maximilian Schell, Irfan Mensur, Rados Bajic.
08/18/76

Atlantic City, U.S.A.
(Canada - France - US)
PLF. Selta Films-Elie Kfouri-Cine Neighbor Inc.-FR3-SDICC prodn. Dir, Louis Malle; sp, John Guare; cam, Richard Ciupka; edtr, Suzanne Baron; mus, Michel Legrand; song "Atlantic City, My Old Friend" by Paul Anka; prods, Dennis Heroux, Gabriel Boustani. 104.
Burt Lancaster, Susan Sarandon, Kate Reid, Michel Piccoli, Hollis MacLaren, Robert Joy, Al Waxman, Robert Goulet.
09/03/80

The Atlantic Swimmers: SEE Die Atlantikschwinner

Ato de Violencia
(Act of Violence)
(Brazil)
EMZ. Linxfilm/Embrafilme prodn. Prod, Cesar Memolo Jr. Dir, Eduardo Escorel. Sp, Escorel, Roberto Machado; cam (Eastmancolor), Lauro Escorel Filho; mus, Egberto Gismonti; edtr, Gilberto Santeiro; snd, Victor Raposeiro; art dir, Paulo Chada; vocal, Pepe Castro Neves. 112.
Nuno Leal Maia, Selma Egrei, Renato Consorte, Eduardo Abbas, Liana Duval, Antonio Petrin, Oscar Felipe, Luis Serra, Ruthnea de Morais, Chico Martins, Abrahao Farc.
12/24/80

Attack of The Killer Tomatoes
NAI. Four Square prodn. Prods, Steve Peace, John De Bello. Dir, De Bello. Sp, Costa Dillon, Peace, De Bello; cam, John K Culley; edtr, De Bello; snd, Paul Wear; mus, Gordon Goodwin, Paul Sundfor; sfx, Greg Auer. (MPAA rating: PG).   87.
David Miller, George Wilson, Sharon Taylor, Jack Riley, Rock Peace, Eric Christmas, Al Sklar, Ernie Meyers, Jerry Anderson, Ron Shapiro.
01/31/79

Attentat
(Assassination)
(Denmark)
ASD. A/S Panorama (Just Betzer) prodn. Story-sp, Poul-Henrik Trampe, based on his novel. Dir, Bent Christensen; prodn mgr, John Hilbard; cam (Eastmancolor), Erik Wittrup Willumsen; edtr, Maj Soya; prodn des, Palle Arestrup, Viggo Bentzon; mus, Ole Hoeyer; stunt action, Jen Sheppard, Stunt Inc, England.   88.
Jesper Langberg, Bent Mejding, Claus Strandberg, Joern Fauerschou, Peter Eszterhas, Anne-Lise Gabold, Susanne Heinrich.
09/10/80

Attention, Les Enfants Regardent
(Attention, The Kids Are Watching)
(France)
UA. Adel Prodns-UA prodn. Dir, Serge Leroy; sp, Christopher Frank, Leroy, from a book by Laird Koenig, Peter Dixon; cam (Eastmancolor), Claude Renoir; edtr, Fernand Cespi.   100.
Alain Delon, Francoise Brion, Richard Constantini, Sophie Renoir, Thierry Torchet, Tiphaine Leroux, Henri Vilbert, Marco Perrin.
04/26/78

Attention Les Yeux
(Watch Out for the Eyes)
(France)
CCF. Attention Les Yeux, Films Du Jeudi prodn. Dir, Gerard Pires. Sp, Nicole de Buron, Pires; cam (Eastmancolor), Michel Serrezin; edtr, Jacques Wita.   80.
Claude Brasseur, Andre Pousse, J P Darras, Nicole Courval, Guy Marchand.
03/03/76

Au Bout du Bout du Banc
(At the Brink of the Brink of the Bench)
(France)
PLF. Films de la Drouette/Films de la Tour co-prod. Prod, Victor Lanoux. Dir, Peter Kassovitz. Sp, Kassovitz, Elie Pressman, Chantal Remy; cam (Eastmancolor-Panavision), Etienne Szabo; mus, Georges Moustaki; edtr, Chantal Remy.   105.
Victor Lanoux, Jane Birkin, Georges Wilson, Henri Cremieux, Matthieu Kassovitz.
07/11/79

Au Nom du Fuhrer
(In the Name of the Fuhrer)
(Belgium)
ADT. Films Lyda prodn. Sp, Frans Buyen, Lydia Chagoll. Dir-edtr, Chagoll. Cam (b&w), Fernand Tack, Andre Geoffers; mus, Arsene Souffriau; voice-over, Marcel Dossogne, Anne Marev.   87.
(DOC) (B & W)
03/07/79

Au Revoir. . .A Lundi
(Goodbye . . .See You Monday)
(France - Canada)
UA. Fildebroc CAPAC (Paris)/Sommerville House (Montreal) co-prodn. Dir, Maurice Dugowson. Sp, Jacques and Maurice Dugowson, Roger Fournier, from novel, "Moi, Mon Corps, Mon Ame, Montreal, etc." by Fournier; cam, Francois Protat; mus, Lewis Furey, Jean-Daniel Mercier; edtr, Jean-Bernard Bonis; art dir, Michel Proulx; snd, Henri Blondeau.   110.
Carole Laure, Miou-Miou, Claude Brasseur, David Birney, Frank Moore, Alain Montpetit.
09/05/79

Audrey Rose
UA. Prods, Joe Wizan, Frank De Felitta. Dir, Robert Wise. Sp, De Felitta, based on his novel; cam (DeLuxe Color), Victor J Kemper; edtr, Carl Kress; mus, Michael Small; prodn des, Harry Horner; set decor, Jerry Wunderlich; snd, Tom Overton, William McCaughey, Aaron Rochin, Michael J Kohut; cos-ward, Dorothy Jeakins, Sheldon Levine, Shirlee Strahm; asst dir, Art Levinson. (MPAA rating: PG).   112.
Marsha Mason, Anthony Hopkins, John Beck, Susan Swift, Norman Lloyd, John Hillerman, Robert Walden, Philip Sterling, Ivy Jones, Stephen Pearlman, Aly Wassil, Mary Jackson.
04/06/77

Auf Biegen Oder Brechen
(By Hook or By Crook)
(W Germany)
X. City Film-Maran Film-Big Sky Film prodn. Wri-dir, Hartmut Bitomsky. Cam, Bernd Fiedler; snd, Hans Beringer; mus, Juergen Knieper; edtr, Sybille Windt.   94.
Jo Bolling, Christine Kaufmann, Lisa Kreuzer, Harry Baer.
09/01/76

Auf Der Insel
(On the Island)
(W Germany)
X. Literarische Colloquium Berlin prodn, in collab with Zweites Deutsches Fernsehen. Exec prod, Christoph Holch. Dir, Wolfram Zobus. Sp, Etta Lubowski; cam, Joerg Jeshel.   67.
Erika Skrotzki, Peter Schiff, Ilse Trautschold, Peter Schlesinger, Ulrich Gressieker, Barbara Ratthey.
(B & W) (16m)
06/01/77

Aufwind
(Up Wind)
(W Germany)
CIG. Rudolf Steiner Film Prodn. Dir, Rudolf Steiner. Sp, Renate Cesar; cam, H V Moennling; mus, Charles Orieux.   90.
Ingolf Gorges, Uschi Bour, Tatjana Blacher.
05/23/79

Augh! Augh!
(Italy)
X. Prod, Kronos Film prodns. Dir, Marco Toniato. Sp, Lucio Manlio Battistrada, Toniato; cam, Cristiano Pogany; art dir, Paolo Montesi; edtr, Raimondo Crociani; mus, Pino Donaggio.   90.
Andrea Occhipinti.
10/01/80

The August Star: SEE Sao Thang Tam

Aulad El Rih
(Children of the Wind)
(Algeria)
DPO. Wri-dir, Brahim Tsaki; cam (Eastmancolor), Mustapha Beimihoub; edtr, Rachid Soufi; mus, Djilali Detto Carlos.   79.
Djamel Youbi, Bennani Broualem, Si-Ahmed, Si-El Hadj De Hassi.
09/10/80

Aunt Clara: SEE Doda Clara

Aus Der Ferne Sehe Ich Dieses Land
(I See This Land from Afar)
(W Germany)
BSG. Basis-Film Verleih Prodn, Berlin, in collab with WDR-TV, Cologne. Prodn mgrs, Clara Burckner, Joachim von Mengershausen. Dir, Christian Zeiwer. Sp, Antonio Skarmeta, Ziewer, based on Skarmeta's story, "Nix passiert"; cam, Gerard Vandenberg; mus, Andariegos, Dance Group "Victor Jara," Omero Caro; art dir, Juergen Herze; edtr, Stefanie Wilke.   98.
Pablo Lira, Anibal Reyna, Valeria Villarroel, Raul Becerra, Daniel.
10/11/78

Auschwitz Street: SEE Lagerstrasse Auschwitz

Authorized Instructor: SEE Educatore Autorizzato

The Autobiography of a Flea
MTL. Prods, James and Arthur Mitchell. Dir, Sharon McNight. Sp, McNight, William Boyer; cam, Jon Fontana; snd, Jay Benton; art dir, Gerd Mairandres; prodn supv, Robert Cecchini. (Self-applied X Rating).   90.
Jean Jennings, Paul Thomas, John Holmes, John Leslie, Warren Pierce, Annette Haven, Mitch Mandell, Dale Meador.
02/09/77

Autopsie D'Un Complot
(Autopsy Of A Conspiracy)
(Algeria)
X. Algerian Film Prodn. Dir, Mohamed Slim Riad. Sp, Etienne Rolo; cam, Dahn Bukersh. 90.
08/02/78

Autopsy
(Italy)
BRE. Prod, Leonardo Pescarolo. Dir, Armando Crispini. Cam, Carlo Carlini. (MPAA rating: R). 125.
Mimsy Farmer, Barry Primus, Ray Lovelock, Angela Goodwin.
10/04/78

Autopsy Of A Conspiracy:
SEE Autopsie D'Un Complot

Autumn Marathon: SEE
Osenny Maraphon

Autumn Sonata
(Sweden)
NW. Lord Lew Grade (ITC) and Martin Starger presentation of a Personafilm GmbH (Munich) prodn. Dir, Ingmar Bergman (no wri credit but probably Bergman). Cam, Sven Nykvist; set des, Anna Asp;; snd, Owe Svensson; edtr, Sylvia Ingmarsdotter; asst dir, Peder Langenskiold. 97.
Ingrid Bergman, Liv Ullmann, Lena Nyman, Halvar Bjork, Georg Lokkeberg, Knut Wigert, Eva Von Hanno, Erland Josephson, Linn Ullmann, Arne Bang-Hansen, Gunnar Bjornstrand, Marianne Aminoff, Mimi Pollak.
(English subtitles)
09/13/78

Avalanche
NW. Prod, Roger Corman. Dir, Corey Allen. Exec prod, Paul Rapp; sp, Claude Pola, Allen; cam (Metrocolor), Pierre-William Glenn; edtrs, Stuart Schoolnik, Larry Bock; snd, David Schneiderman; mus, William Kraft; prodn des, Sharon Compton; art dir, Phillip Thomas; asst dir, Russell Vreeland; avalanche sequences (dir-edtr), Lewis Teague; stunt coord, Robert Bralver. (MPAA rating: PG). 91.
Rock Hudson, Mia Farrow, Robert Forster, Jeanette Nolan, Rick Moses, Steve Franken, Barry Primus, Cathey Paine, Peggy Browne.
09/06/78

Avalanche Express
FOX. Lorimar prodn. Prod-dir, Mark Robson. Sp, Abraham Polonsky, based on the novel by Colin Forbes; cam, Jack Cardiff; edtr, Garth Craven; prodn des, Fred Tuch; snd, George Stevenson; cos, Mickey Shirrard; asso prod, Lynn Guthrie; in chg of prodn, Harry Caplan; Bavaria prodn exec, Willy Egger; sfx (miniatures) dir, John Dykstra; cam, (min), Bruce Logan; boat battle sequence dir, Allan Gibbs; sfx (boat), Ross Hahn; mus, Allyn Ferguson; asst dir, Wieland Liebske. 88.
Robert Shaw, Lee Marvin, Linda Evans, Maximilian Schell, Mike Connors, Joe Namath, Horst Buchholz, David Hess, Arthur Brauss, Kristine Nel, Sylva Langover.
07/25/79

Avantazh
(The Advantage)
(Bulgaria)
FBU. Dir, Georgi Dyulgerov. Sp, Roussi Chanev, Dyulgerov; cam, Radoslav Spassov; sets, Roussi Doundakov, Georgi Todorov; mus, Bozhidar Petrov. 142.
Roussi Chanev, Maria Statulov, Plamena Getova, Radosvet Vassileva, Plamen Donchev, Dimiter Ganev, Velyo Goranov, Stepan Popov.
02/22/78

The Awakening
WBO. Robert Solo prodn. Prods, Robert Solo, Andrew Scheinman, Martin Shafer; dir, Mike Newell; sp, Allan Scott, Chris Bryant, Clive Exton, based on novel "The Jewel Of Seven Stars" by Bram Stoker; cam (Technicolor), Jack Cardiff; edtr, Terry Rawlings; mus, Claude Bolling; prodn des, Michael Stringer; art dir, Lionel Couch; cos des, Phyllis Dalton; snd (Dolby), Brian Simmons; asso prod, Harry Benn; asst dir, Neill Vine-Miller. (MPAA rating: R). 102.
Charlton Heston, Susannah York, Jill Townsend, Stephanie Zimbalist, Patrick Drury, Bruce Myers, Nadim Sawalha, Ian McDiarmid.
09/17/80

Awans
(Long Live Progress)
(Poland)
POL. Dir, Janusz Zaorski. Sp, Edward Redlinski; cam (Eastmancolor), Jan Hesse; mus, Adam Slawinski. 91.
Marian Opania, Bozena Duriel, Joszef Nalberczak, Gustaw Lutkiewicz.
08/25/76

Az Erod
(The Fortress)
(Hungary)
HU. Mafilm Budapest Studio prodn. Dir, Miklos Szinetar. Sp, Gyula Hernadi, Szinetar; cam (Eastmancolor), Miklos Biro. 119.
Bella Tanai, Sandor Oszter, Adam Rajhona, Ferenc Bencze.
02/28/79

Az Otodik Pecset
(The Fifth Seal)
(Hungary)
X. Budapest Studio prodn. Dir, Zoltan Fabri. Sp, Fabri, based on novel by Ferenc Santa; cam (Eastmancolor), Gyorgy Illes; mus, Gyorgy Vukan. 116.
Lajos Oze, Sandor Horvath, Laszlo Markus, Ferenc Bencze, Istvan Degi, Zoltan Latinovits.
03/02/77

Aziza
(Tunisia - Algeria)
X. SATPEC, Tunisia, co-prodn with Radio Television Algeria and LATIF; prod, Hassen Daldoul. Dir, Abdel Latif Ben Ammar. Sp, Ben Ammar, Tawfik Jebali; cam, Youssef Sharaqui; edtr, Moufida Tlatli; mus, Ahmed Malek; prod mgr, Lotfi Layouni. 90.
Yasmine Khlat, Raouf Ben Amor, Dalila Rames, Mohamed Zinet, Tawfik Jebali, Mouna Nourredine.
06/25/80

Azonositas
(Man Without a Name)
(Hungary)
X. Hungarofilm prodn. Dir, Laszlo Lugossy. Sp, Istvan Kardos; cam, Jozsef Lorinc; mus, Emil Petrovics. 91.
Gyorgy Cserhalmi, Jozsef Madaras, Lili Monori, Robert Koltai, Ludovit Gresso.
07/14/76

Baara
(The Porter)
(Mali)
OCM. Suleyman Cisse prodn. Wri-dir, Suleyman Cisse. Cam (Eastmancolor), Etienne Carton De Grammont, Abdoulaye Sidibe; edtr, Andree Devanture; mus, Lamin Konte. 90.
Balla Moussa Keita, Bana Naire, Boubacar Keita, Oumou Diarra, Oumou Kone, Ismalia Sarr.
08/23/78

Babatu
(Nigeria)
X. IRSH - SERDAV - SCC - Musee De L'Homme prodn. Dir, Jean Rouch. Sp, Boubou Hama; cam, Rouch, Moustapha Alassane; edtr, Christine Lefort; mus, Dyeliba Badye, Daouda Kante. 92.
Doulde Laya, Moustapha Alassane, Oumarou Ganda, Baba Nore.
05/26/76

Babek
(USSR)
SOV. Azerbaidzhanfilm Studio Production, Baku, Azerbaidzhan Republic, Soviet Union. Dir, Eldar Kuliev. Sp, Anver Mamedkhanli. 120.
Rasim Belaev, Amalia Panakhova, Tamara Yandieva.
07/02/80

Baby Blue Marine
COL. Prod, Aaron Spelling, Leonard Goldberg. Dir, John Hancock. Sp, Stanford Whitmore; cam (Metrocolor), Laszlo Kovacs; edtr, Marion Rothman; mus, Fred Karlin; prodn des, Walter Scott Herndon; set decor, Marvin March; snd, Tex Rudloff, Glenn Anderson; asst dir, Michael Daves. (MPAA rating: PG). 90.
Jan-Michael Vincent, Glynnis O'Connor, Katherine Helmond, Dana Elcar, Bert Remsen, B Kirby Jr, Richard Gere, Art Lund, Michael Conrad, Allan Miller, Michael Le Clair, Will Seltzer, Kenneth Tobey.
04/28/76

Baby Rosemary
ESX. Prod, Bill Steele. Dir, Harold Perkins. Cam, John Lyons; sp, Ruth Price, Virgil Rom; edtr, Luke Porun. (Self-applied X rating). 80.
Sharon Thorpe, John Leslie Dupree, Leslie Bovee, Ken Cotton.
08/11/76

Baby Snakes

X. Intercontinental Absurdities Presentation. Prod-dir-edtr, Frank Zappa; mus, Zappa; cam (Deluxe), Robert Leacock, Richard Pearce, Phil Parmet; asst edtr, Laura Whipple. (MPAA rating: R).   166.

Frank Zappa, Adrian Belew, Tommy Mars, Terry Bozzio, Kerry McNabe, Ron Delsener, Bruce Bickford, Rob Leacock, Ed Mann, Warren Cucurullo, Chris Martin, Klaus Hundsbichler, French The Poodle, Ms Pinky's Larger Sister, Roy Estrada, John Smothers, David Ditkowich, New York's Finest Crazy Persons, Bill Harrington, Patrick O'Hearn, Phil Parmet, Peter Wolf, Dick Pearce, Angel, Janet The Planet, Donna U Wanna, Phil Kaufman, Tex Abel, Dale Bozzio, Diva, John, Chris, Nancy, Brian Rivera, Joey Psychotic.
12/26/79

Babylon
(Britain)

X. Diversity Music prod, in association with the National Film Finance Corp, Chrysalis Group, Lee (Electric) Lighting. Prod, Gavrik Losey. Dir, Franco Rosso. Sp, Martin Stellman, Franco Rosso; cam, Chris Menges; edtr, Thomas Schwalm; mus, Denis Bovell, Aswad; art dir, Brian Savegar; snd, Ed Pise; asso prod, Stellman; prod mgr, Ray Corbett; asst dir, Raymond Day.   95.

Brinsley Forde, Karl Howman, Trevor Laird, Brian Bovell, Victor Romero Evans, David N Haynes, Archie Pool, T Bone Wilson, Mel Smith, Beverly Michaels, Maggie Steed, Bill Moody, Stephan Kaliphi, Beverley Dublin, Granville Garner, Mark Monero, David Cunningham, Kosmo Laidlaw.
05/14/80

Babylone - XX
(USSR)

SOV. Alexander Dov-Zhenko Studio prodn. Dir, Ivan Mikolaitchouk; sp, Vassili Zemliak, Mikolaitchouk; book, Zemliak; cam (Sovcolor-b&w), Youri Gartman.   98.

Lubov Politchchouk, Ivan Mikolaitchouk, Les Surdak, Yaraslov Gavriluk, Ivan Taissia Litvinenko, Raissa Nedachkovskaia.
09/03/80

Bach: H-Moll Messe
(Bach: B-Minor Mass)
(W Germany)

HBD. Artfilm Pitt Koch prodn, Munich, in collab with Second German Television (ZDF), Wiesbaden. Wri-dir, Klaus Kirschner. Cam (b&w), Dietrich Lohmann; mus, Johann Sebastian Bach's "B-Minor Mass"; mus prodn, CBS Records, prod, Hans Joachim Daub; snd engineer, Richard Hauck.   150.

Ana Torrent, Arleen Auger, Julia Hamari, Adalbert Kraus, Siegmund Nimsgern, Wolfgang Schoene, Helmuth Rilling, Gaechinger Kantorei Stuttgart, Bach Kollegium, extras from Montbard.
(B & W)
04/25/79

Back of the Store: SEE La Trastienda

Bad

NW. Prod, Jeff Tornberg; exec prod, Fred Hughes. Dir, Jed Johnson. Sp, Pat Hackett, George Abagnalo; cam (Movielab color), Allan Metzger; edtrs, Franca Silvi, David McKenna; mus, Mike Bloomfield; art dir, Eugene Rudolph; set decor, Fred C Weiler; snd, Chris Newman; cos-ward, John Boxer, Elisabeth Seley, Bill Christians; asst dir, Bob Colesberry. (MPAA rating: X).   105.

Carroll Baker, Perry King, Susan Tyrrell, Stefania Cassini, Cyrinda Foxe, Mary Boylan, Charles McGregor, Tere Tereba, Brigid Polk, Susan Blond, Maria Smith, Geraldine Smith, Lawrence Tierney, Joe Lamba, Renee Paris, John Starke, Gordon Oasheim, Barbara Allen.
03/30/77

The Bad Guys: SEE Rosszemberek

The Bad News Bears

PAR. Prod, Stanley R Jaffe. Dir, Michael Ritchie. Sp, Bill Lancaster; cam (Movielab Color), John A Alonzo; edtr, Richard A Harris; mus, Jerry Fielding; prodn des, Polly Platt; set decor, Cheryal Kearney; snd, John Wilkinson, Gene Cantamessa; asst dir, Jack Roe. (MPAA rating: PG).   102.

Walter Matthau, Tatum O'Neal, Vic Morrow, Joyce Van Patten, Ben Piazza, Jackie Earle Haley, Alfred W Lutter, Brandon Cruz, Shari Summers, Joe Brooks, Maurice Marks, Quinn Smith, Gary Lee Cavagnaro, Erin Blunt, Jaime Escobedo, George Gonzales, David Pollock, Chris Barnes, David Stambaugh, Scott Firestone, Brett Marx.
04/07/76

The Bad News Bears Go To Japan

PAR. Michael Ritchie prodn. Prod, Michael Ritchie. Dir, John Berry. Wri, Bill Lancaster; cam (Movielab Color), Gene Polito (USA), Kozo Okazaki (Japan); edtr, Richard A Harris; prodn des, Walter Scott Herndon; snd, Gene Cantamesa; mus, Paul Chihara; cos, Tommy Welsh, Nancy Martinelli; asst dir, Jerry Ziesmer. (MPAA rating: PG).   91.

Tony Curtis, Jackie Earle Haley, Tomisaburo Wakayama, Hatsune Ishihara, George Wyner, Lonny Chapman, Matthew Douglas Anton, Erin Blunt, George Gonzales, Brett Marx, David Pollock, David Stambaugh, Jeffrey Louis Starr, Scoody Thornton.
06/14/78

The Bad News Bears In Breaking Training

PAR. Prod, Leonard Goldberg. Dir, Michael Pressman. Sp, Paul Brickman, based on characters created by Bill Lancaster; cam (Movielab Color), Fred J Koenekamp; edtr, John W Wheeler; mus, Craig Safan; song lyr, Norman Gimbel; art dir, Steve Berger; set decor, Fred R Price; snd, John K Wilkinson, Nick Gaffey; cos-ward, Jack Martell; asst dir, Michael Daves. (MPAA rating: PG).   99.

William Devane, Clifton James, Jackie Earle Haley, Jimmy Baio, Chris Barnes, Erin Blunt, Jaime O Escobedo, George Gonzales, Alfred Lutter, Brett Marx, David Pollock, Quinn Smith, David Stambaugh, Jeffrey Louis Starr, Fred Stuthman, Dolph Sweet, Lane Smith, Pat Corley.
07/27/77

Bad Sorts: SEE Warui Yatsura

The Bad Spirits Of The Euphrates: SEE Firatin Cinleri

The Bad Starters: SEE Les Mal Partis

Bad Timing
(Britain)

WNO. Recorded Picture Co prodn. Prod, Jeremy Thomas. Dir, Nicolas Roeg. Sp, Yale Udoff; cam, Anthony Richmond; edtr, Tony Lawson; mus dir, Richard Hartley; art dir, David Brockhurst; snd, Tony Jackson; asso prod, Tim Van Rellim; prodn mgr, Aivar Kaulins; asst dir, Niel Vine-Miller. (MPAA rating: X; later withdrawn from rating).   123.

Art Garfunkel, Theresa Russell, Harvey Keitel, Denholm Elliott, Daniel Massey, Dana Gillespie.
02/20/80

Badi Blagoslovena
(Be Blessed)
(Bulgaria)

BGO. BulgaroFilm prodn, Mladost Group, Sofia. Dir, Alexander Obreshkov. Sp, Kiril Topalov; cam, Kroum Kroumov; art dir, Konstantin Roussakov; mus, Dimiter Griva.   90.

Marianna Dimitrova, Dorothea Toncheva, Evgenia Barakova, Maria Statoulova.
05/31/78

Baghe Sangui
(The Garden of Stones)
(Iran)

X. N I R T prodn. Wri-dir, Parviz Kimiavi. Cam, Freydoun Ghovaniou.   84.

Darvich Khan, his family, and villagers of Balvarad.
07/14/76

The Bailiff of Griefensee: SEE Der Landvogt von Griefensee

Bajecni Muzi S Klikou
(Those Wonderful Men with a Crank)
(Czechoslovakia)

X. Czechoslovak Film prodn, Studio Barrandov, Prague. Dir, Jiri Menzel. Sp, Oldrich Vlcek, Menzel, based on a story by Vlcek; cam, Jaromir Sofr; sets, Zbynek Holoch; mus, Jiri Sust.   90.

Rudolf Hrusinsky, Jiri Menzel, Blazena Holisova, Vlasta Fabianova, Vladimir Mensik, Jaromira Milova, Hana Buresova, Oldrich Vlcek, Josef Kemr.
02/07/79

The Baker's Bread: SEE Das Brot Des Baeckers

Baker's Hawk
DDY. Prod-dir, Lyman D Dayton. Sp, Dan Greer, Hal Harrison Jr, from novel by Jack Bickham; cam (DeLuxe Color), Bernie Abramson; edtr, Parkie Singh; mus, Lex De Azevedo; prodn des, Bill Kenney; set dir, Tony Montenaro; set des, Sig Tinglof; cos, Tom Dawson; snd, Bob Miller; asst dir, Bill Lukather. (MPAA rating: G).   98.
Clint Walker, Burl Ives, Diane Baker, Lee H Montgomery, Alan Young, Taylor Lacher, Bruce M Fischer, Cam Clarke, Phil Hoover, Danny Bonaduce, Brian Williams, Burt Mustin, Martin Eric.
01/12/77

Bako, L'Autre Rive
(Bako, The Other Shore)
(Senegal - France)
OPH. Dir, Jacques Champreux. Sp, Champreux, Cheik Doukoure; cam (Eastmancolor), Jacques Ledouz; edtr, Andree Devanture. 105.
Sidiki Bakaba, Doura Mane, Cheik Doukoure, Guilaume Korrea, Martin Trevieres.
08/23/78

Balint Fabian Meets God:
SEE Fabian Balint Talalkozasa Istennel

Ballad of Tara
(Iran)
LII. Wri-dir, Bahram Beiz'i. Cam, Mehrdad Fakhimi; edtr, Beiz'i.   103.
Sussan Taslimi, Manoutchehr Farid, Reza Babak, Siamak Atlassi.
05/28/80

The Ballad of the Daltons:
SEE La Ballade Des Daltons

Ballet Gayane
SPV. Prod, Victor Stoloff. Dir, Horace King. Exec prods, Ed Rood Sr, Saul Barnett. Cam, Paul Beeson; edtr, H G Ink; snd, Ray Prickett; cos, Biruta Gage.   110.
Larisa Tuisova, Alexander Rumyantsev, Genadi Barbanyov, Maris Koristin.
(BALLET)
12/27/78

The Baltimore Bullet
AVE. Prod, John F Brascia. Dir, Robert Ellis Miller. Exec prods, William D Jekel, Norman G Rudman. Wris, Brascia, Robert Vincent O'Neill; Cam (Eastmancolor), James A Crabe; edtr, Jerry Brady; snd, Jacque Nosco; prodn des, Herman Blumenthal; art dir, Adrian Gortoux; mus, Johnny Mandel; cos, Patricia Ann Norris. (MPAA rating: PG).   103.
James Coburn, Omar Sharif, Bruce Boxleitner, Ronee Blakely, Jack O'Halloran, Calvin Lockhart, Michael Learner, Paul Barselou, Cisse Cameron, Jeff Temkin, Willie Mosconi.
02/27/80

Bandera Rota
(Broken Flag)
(Mexico)
RMX. Dir, Gabriel Retes. Sp, Retes, Ignacio Retes; cam (Eastmancolor), Genaro Hurtado; edtr, Eufemio Rivera; mus, Raoul Lavista. 95.
Manolo Fabregas, Luis Iriarte, Tina Romero, Jorge Humberto Robles, Jorge Santoyo, Ignacio Retes, Abel Woolrich.
09/05/79

Bang
(Sweden)
SVF. Swedish Film Institute (prod Bengt Forslund)/AB Svensk Filmindustri prodn. Diredtr-pho (Eastmancolor), Jan Troell; based on Sven Christer Swahn story; sp, Troell, George Oddner, Sven Christer Swahn; mus, K E Welin, Dvorak, Fats Waller; prodn des, Carl Johan de Geer; prodn mgr, Goeran Setterberg.   105.
Hakan Serner, Yvonne Lombard, Eva von Hanno, Susan Hampshire, Beate Oerskov.
05/25/77

Banished: SEE Hanare Goze Orin

Bao Feng Chou Yu
(Hurricane)
(People's Republic of China)
X. Peking Film Studio Prodn. Dir, Hsie Tie-Li. Sp, Lin Lan, based on the novel with the same name by Chou Li-Po; cam (b&w), Wu Shen-Han; mus, Li Huan-Chi; snd, Shen Jie-Hsi. 130.
You Yank, Yu Ping, Li Bai-Wan, Wu Su-Chin, Liu Chi-Yun.
(B & W)
01/17/79

Baranski
(W Germany)
X. Munich Film & TV Academy Prodn. Dir, Werner Masten. Sp, Klaus Eichhammer, Masten, Michael Breining; cam (b&w), Eichhammer; sets, Andrea Oechsner; mus, Breining. 68.
Jan Groth, Nikolaus Pichler, Rick Schulz, Thussy Marini, Wolf Ackva, Edgar Wenzel, Werner Masten, Mark Pouliv, Jadwiga Czerwinska, Albert Sandner.
(16m) (B & W)
04/02/80

Bare Knuckles
ICR. Prod-wri-dir, Don Edmonds. Cam (Metrocolor), Dean Cundey; edtr, Robert Freeman; asst dir, Buck Flower; mus, Vic Caesar; prodn des, Michael Riva; snd, Al Ramierez; stunt coord, Jim Winburn. (MPAA rating: R). 90.
Robert Viharo, Sherry Jackson, Michael Heit, Gloria Hendry, John Daniels.
02/08/78

Barefooted Gen: SEE Hadashi No Gen

Barierata
(Barrier)
(Bulgaria)
FBU. Bulgarian Film Prodn, Mladost Film Group, Sofia. Dir, Christo Christov. Sp, Pavel Vezhinov, based on his novella of same title; cam, Atanas Tassev; art dir, Stefan Savov; mus, Kiril Tsiboulka.   90.
Innokenti Smoktunovsky, Venya Tsvetkova, Maria Dimcheva.
07/18/79

Barna fran Blasjofjaellet
(The Children From Blue Lake Mountain)
(Sweden)
SVF. Moviemakers/Sandrews/Film Institute prodn. Script, Bjoern Norstroem, Jonas Sima, based on their book. Dir, Sima. Cam (Fujicolor), Rune Erickson; prodn mgr, Gustav Wiklund; edtr, Lasse Lundberg; mus, Bernt Rosengren; title song, Torgny Bjoerk. 92.
Anders Edvinsson, Carina Linder, Yvonne Danielsson, Kent Ivar Frederiksson, Martin Isaksson, Lova Sima.
12/24/80

Barney
(Australia)
COL. David S Waddington prodn. Prod-dir, Waddington. Co-prod, John Williams. Sp, Colin Drake; mus, Tommy Tycho; cam, Richard Wallace; edtr, Rod Hay; cos, Carol Berry; snd, Ken Hammond; 2d unit dir, Ross Nichols; set decor, Ray Frost.   87.
Brett Maxworthy, Sean Kramer, Lionel Long, Spike Milligan, Jack Allen, Robert Quilter, Shirley Cameron, Jackie Rees, Rob Steele, Danny Adcock, Mike Preston, Terry Redell, Jim Clifford, Ron Ratcliff, Judy Connelli, Herbie Nelson, Al Thomas, Larry McGarry, Andy Clark, Jerry Thomas, Dieter Chidel, Alex Pope.
01/12/77

Barnfoerbjudet
(Not For Children)
(Sweden)
SNA. Swedish Film Institute with HB Three Leaf Clover prodn. Orig story-sp-dir, Marie-Louise de Geer Bergenstrahle; cam (Eastmancolor), Lars Svanberg, Ronald Sterner; exec prod, Anna-Lena Wibom; prodn management, Peter Hald, Britta Werkmaester; mus, quotes from E Kalman, F Lehar; prodn des, Carl Johan de Geer.   76.
Ann Smith, Bibi Andersson, Rolf Skoglund, Annalisa Ericson.
01/02/80

Barocco
(France)
FBE. Films La Boetie-Sara Fims prodn. Dir, Andre Techine. Sp, Techine, Marilyn Goldin; cam (Eastmancolor), Bruno Nuytten; edtr, Claudine Merlin; mus, Philippe Sarde. 102.
Isabelle Adjani, Gerard Depardieu, Marie-France Pisier, Jean-Claude Brialy, Julien Guiomar, Helene Surgere, Claude Brasseur.
12/01/76

Barra Pesada
(Heavy Trouble)
(Brazil)
EMZ. Wri-dir, Reginaldo Faria, based on a story by Plinio Marcos. Exec prod, Rivanides Faria; cam (Eastmancolor), Fernando Durante, Jose Medeiros, Reginaldo Faria; mus, Edu Lobo; edtr, Waldemar Noya. 110.
Stepan Nercessian, Cosme dos Santos, Milton Moraes, Itala Nandi, Marcos Vinicius, Ivan Candido, Wilson Grey, Katia D'Angelo, Lutero Luis, Haroldo de Oliveira.
11/16/77

The Barricade At Point Du Jour: SEE La Barricade Du Point Du Jour

Barrier: SEE Barierata

Barwy Orchronne
(Camouflage)
(Poland)
POL. Film Polski, Warsaw, prodn, Tor unit. Wri-dir, Krzystof Zanussi. Cam, Edward Klosinski; mus, Wojciech Kilar; art dirs, Tadeusz Wybult, Maciej Putowski, Ewa Braun, Joanna Lelanow. 106.
Piotr Garlicki, Zbigniew Zapasiewicz, Christine Paul, Mariusz Dmochowski.
05/18/77

The Base Of The Air Is Red: SEE Le Fond De L'Air Est Rouge

Basseinut
(The Swimming Pool)
(Bulgaria)
X. Bulgaro Film prodn, Sofia. Dir, Binka Zhelyazkova. Sp, Christo Ganev; cam, Ivailo Trenchev; art dir, Marie-Therese Gospodinova; mus, Simeon Pironkov. 140.
Yanina Kasheva, Kosta Tsonev, Kliment Denchev, Tsvetana Maneva, Peter Slabakov.
08/03/77

Bastien, Bastienne
(France)
LML. L'Agence D'Images, FR3 prodn. Wri-dir, Michel Andrieu. Cam (Eastmancolor), Rennan Plles; edtr, Chantale Colomer. 106.
Juliet Berto, Anna Prucnal, Orane Demazis, Beatrice Bruno, Emmanuel Prat, Serge Dambrine, Mathieu Lacaille.
09/19/79

Battle Beyond the Stars
NW. Prod, Ed Carlin; exec prod, Roger Corman. Dir, Jimmy T Murakami; Sp, John Sayles based on story by Sayles, Anne Dyer; cam, Daniel Lacambre; score, James Horner; set dec, John Zabrucky; cos, Durinda Rice Wood; light supv, Paul Turner; miniature pho effects, C Comisky; miniatures des, Mary Schallock. (MPAA Rating; PG) 104.
Richard Thomas, Robert Vaughn, Darlanne Fleugel, George Peppard, Sybil Danning, Sam Jaffe, Morgan Woodward, Steve Davis, Earl Boen, John McGowans, Larry Meyers, Laura Cody, Lynne Carlin, Jeff Corey, Julia Duffy, Eric Morris, Marta Kristen, Doug Carleson, Ron Ross, Terrence McNally, Don Thompson, Daniel Carlin, Ansley Carlin.
07/30/80

Battle For The Railway: SEE Dvoboj Za Juznu Prugu

The Battle of Chile, II: The Coup d'Etat: SEE La Batalla De Chile, II: El Golpe De Estado

The Battle Of Chile, Part III: The Power Of The People: SEE La Battala de Chile - III

Battleflag: SEE Die Standarte

The Bawdy Adventures of Tom Jones
(Britain)
U. Robert Sadoff prodn. Dir, Cliff Owen. Sp, Jeremy Lloyd, based on legit musical, "Tom Jones," wri by Don MacPherson; mus-lyrs, Paul Holden; adapt from Henry Fielding's novel, "Tom Jones"; cam (Technicolor), Douglas Slocombe; art dir, Jack Shampan; edtr, Bill Blunden; cos, Beatrice Dawson; score, Ron Grainer, with songs by Paul Holden, David Matthews, Michael Guilgud, Annie and Christopher Gunning; snd, Claude Hitchcock, Gordon K McCallum; prodn mgr, Frank Sherwin Green; asst dir, Anthony Wayne; dubbing edtr, Peter Keen. (MPAA rating: R). 94.
Nicky Henson, Trevor Howard, Terry-Thomas, Arthur Lowe, Georgia Brown, Joan Collins, William Mervyn, Murray Melvin, Madeline Smith, Geraldine McEwan, Jeremy Lloyd, Janie Greenspun, Michael Bates, Hilda Fenemore, Patricia MacPherson, Isabel Dean, James Hayter, Frank Thornton, Gladys Henson, Joan Cooper, Maxine Casson, Judy Buxton, Arthur Howard, John Forrest, Arnold Diamond, Claire Davenport, Griffith Davies, Christine Ozanne, Tricia Newby, Erik Chitty, Roy Evans, Michael Burrell, John Hartley, Bart Allison, Peter Forbes Robertson, Susan Shaper, Angela Crow, Jeannie Collings, Penny Irving, Zena Clifton, Patrick Westwood, Donald Bisset, Max Faulkner, Jean Gilpin, Colin Cunningham, Eric Longworth, Terence Sewards, Maggy Maxwell, Patsy Smart, Rosamund Greenwood.
09/08/76

Baxter, Vera Baxter
(France)
SHD. Sunchild-INA prodn. Wri-dir, Marguerite Duras. Cam (Eastmancolor), Sacha Vierny; edtr, Dominique Auvray; mus, Carlos D'Alessio. 90.
Claudine Gabay, Delphine Seyrig, Gerard Depardieu, Noelle Chatelet, Claude Aufort, Nathalie Nell.
06/22/77

Be Blessed: SEE Badi Blagoslovena

The Beach Guard in Winter: SEE Cuvar Plaze U Zimskom Periodu

The Beach Hotel: SEE L'Hotel De La Plage

The Beach House: SEE Il Casotto

The Beads of One Rosary: SEE Paciorki Jednego Rozanca

Bear Island
(Britain - Canada)
COL. Selkirk Films presentation. Prod, Peter Snell. Dir, Don Sharp. Sp, Sharp, David Butler, Murray Smith (based on novel by Alistair MacLean); cam, Alan Hume; edtr, Tony Lower; art dirs, Kenneth Ryan, Peter Childs; sfx, David Harris, Thomas Clark, Paul Whybrow; stunt coord, Vic Armstrong; asst dirs, Stuart Freeman, Don Brough, Roy Stevens, Jerry Daly; asso prod, Bill Hill. (MPAA rating: PG). 118.
Donald Sutherland, Vanessa Redgrave, Richard Widmark, Christopher Lee, Barbara Parkins, Lloyd Bridges, Lawrence Dane, Patricia Collins, Michael Reynolds, Nicholas Cortland, August Schellenberg, Candace O'Conner, Joseph Golland, Bruce Greenwood, Hagen Beggs, Michael Collins, Terry Kelly, Terry Waterhouse.
01/23/80

The Beast
(Hong Kong)
PHK. Exec prod, Teddy Robin Kwan. Prod, Wallace Cheung. Dir, Dennis Yu. Cam, Bob Thomson. 90.
Patricia Chong, Paul Chung, Wong Ching, Eddie Chang, Juk Sze, Chan Sing.
(Cantonese with English subtitles)
12/24/80

Beasts: SEE Bestije

Beauty and the Beast
(Czechoslovakia)
CZS. Czechoslovak Film, prodn, Studio Barrandov, Prague. Dir, Juraj Herz. Sp, Ota Hoffmann. 90.
Zdena Studenkova, Vlastimil Harapes, Vaclav Vosko, Jana Brejchova, Zuzana Kocurikova.
02/07/79

Bedniyat Louka
(Poor Lucas)
(Bulgaria)
FBU. Bulgarian Film Prodn, Mladost Unit, Sofia. Dir, Yakim Yakimov. Sp, Ivan Stanev, based on novella with same title by Dobri Nemirov; cam, Ivan Velchev; art dir, Bogoya Sapoundjiev; mus, Kiril Tsiboulka. 90.
Naoum Shopov, Katya Paskaleva.
07/18/79

Bedside Sailors: SEE Soemaend paa sengekanten

Beer Chase: SEE Bierkampf

The Bees
NW. Bee One/Panorama Films Prodn; prod-dir-wri, Alfredo Zacharias. Cam (CFI Color), Leon Sanchez; edtr, Sandy Nervis; art dir, Jose Rodriguez Granada; sfx, Jack Rabin; asso prod, Teri Schwartz; asst dirs, Joe B Carles, Michael Moore. (MPAA rating: PG). 83.
John Saxon, Angel Tompkins, John Carradine, Claudio Brook, Alicia Encinias.
11/15/78

Beethoven-Days in a Life:
SEE Beethoven-Tage Aus Einem Leben

Beethoven "Fidelio"
(France)
GAU. Sunchild - F R 3 - Radio France - OCAV - Dept of Culture and Communication co-prodn. Prod, Stephane Tchalgadjieff. Dir, Pierre Jourdan. Israeli Philharmonic Orchestra and the London New-Philharmonic Choir under the dir of Zubin Mehta. 130.
Gundula Janovitz, Jon Vickers, Theo Adams, William Wildermann, Stella Richmond, Misha Raitzin.
(Opera performed in German)
03/21/79

Beethoven-Tage Aus Einem Leben
(Beethoven-Days in a Life)
(E Germany)
X. DEFA-Studio prodn, East Berlin, in collab with Gruppe "Babelsberg." Dir, Horst Seemann. Sp, Seemann, Guenter Kunert; cam, Otto Hanisch; art dir, Hans Poppe; cos, Inge Kistner; edtr, Baerbell Weigel; prodn chief, Manfred Renger. With mus, Beethoven. 110.
Donatas Banionis, Stefan Lisewski, Hans Teuscher, Renate Richter, Fred Delmare.
12/15/76

Before Dan: SEE Pratyusha

Before Hindsight
(Britain)
X. Prod, Elizabeth Taylor-Mead. Dir-edtr, Jonathon Lewis. Res-Elizabeth Taylor-Mead. 78.
(DOC) (16m)
11/16/77

Before Silence Came
(Romania)
RMN. Wri-dir, Aleka Visarion, based on Ion Luca Caragiale's short story, "In Time of War"; cam, Nicu Stan; sets, Vittorio Holtier, Sava Cuzmin; edtr, Maria Neagu. 103.
Liviu Rozovea, Valeria Seciu, Ion Caramitru, Mircea Diaconu, Florin Zamfirescu, Gilda Petrican, Adriana Trandafir. Marinescu, Vasile Muresan, Nicolas Praida, Cornel Dumitras, Elisabeta Jar-Rozovea, Constantin
02/28/79

Before the Day Breaks: SEE
Zanim Nadejdzie Dzien

Begging the Ring
(Britain)
X. Colin Gregg Films prodn. Prod-dir-edtr, Colin Gregg. Sp, Gregg, Hugh Stoddart; cam, John Metcalfe. 55.
Danny Simpson, Jon Croft, Janette Legge, Kenneth Midwood, Terence Conoley, Alan Penn, Brian Capron.
(16m)
03/21/79

Behinderte Liebe
(Handicapped Love)
(Switzerland)
FKZ. Marlies Graf prodn. Wri-dir, Graf. Cam (Kodacolor), Werner Zuber; snd, Florian Eidenbenz, Urs Kohler, Hugo Sigrist; edtr, Graf; mus (Recordings), Keith Jarrett, Fly Orchestra Zurich, Sero-Sextett Oberhofen. 120.
Therese Zemp, Jules Burgener, Christoph Eggli, Ursual Eggli, Paolo Poloni, Wolfgang Suttner.
(DOC)
05/30/79

Being There
UA. Andrew Braunsberg prodn for Lorimar. Prod, Andrew Braunsberg. Dir, Hal Ashby; exec prod, Jack Schwartzman; sp, Jerzy Kosinski, based on his novel; cam (Technicolor), Caleb Deschanel; edtr, Don Zimmerman; mus, John Mandel; prodn des, Michael Haller; art dir, James Schoppe; set decor, Robert Benton; cos des, May Routh; snd, Jeff Wexler; asso prod, Charles Mulvehill; asst dir, David S Hamburger. (MPAA rating: PG). 130.
Peter Sellers, Shirley MacLaine, Melvyn Douglas, Jack Warden, Richard Dysart, Richard Basehart, Ruth Attaway, Dave Clennon, Fran Brill, Denise DuBarry.
12/19/79

Belfer
(Israel)
NCH. Prods, Izkah Shani, Josef Dimant. Dir, Igal Burstein. Sp, Burstein, based on orig story, Yossi Birstein; cam, Adam Greenberg; edtrs, Alain Jakobowitz; sets, Eytan Levy; mus, Roni Weiss; title song performed by Sherri. 87.
Talia Shapira, Avner Hizkiahu, Hana Laszlo, Rafael Klatchkin, Jacques Cohen.
01/10/79

Beli Bim-Chornoye Ukho
(White Bim With Black Ear)
(USSR)
GOS. Gorky Film Studios Prodn, Moscow. Dir, Stanislas Rosototzki. Sp based on novel by Gavril Troepolsky. 90.
Viatcheslav Tikhonov.
07/05/78

The Bell Jar
AVE. Larry Peerce/Robert A Goldston prodn. Prods, Jerrold Brandt Jr, Michael Todd Jr. Dir, Larry Peerce. Sp, Marjorie Kellogg, based on the novel by Sylvia Plath; cam, Gerald Hirschfeld; prodn des, John Robert Lloyd; cos, Donald Brooks; mus, Gerald Fried; edtr, Marvin Wallowitz; set decor, Don Holtzman and Paul Heffernan; asst dir, Steve Barnett. 107.
Marilyn Hassett, Julie Harris, Anne Jackson, Barbara Barrie, Robert Klein, Donna Mitchell, Mary Louise Weller, Scott McKay, Jameson Parker, Thaao Penghlis, Carlo Monferdini, Debbie McLeod, Meg Mundy, Elizabeth Hubbard, Karen Howard.
03/21/79

Belle Trave
(White Grass)
(Yugoslavia)
YFR. Viba Film prodn. Dir, Bostjan Hladnik. Sp, Branko Soemen; cam (Eastmancolor), Jure Pervande; mus, Bojan Adamic. 95.
Joze Hrovat, Marina Urbanic, Ljubisa Samardzic, Barbara Jakopic.
08/25/76

Bells Of Autumn
(USSR)
SOV. Maxim Gorky Studios prodn. Dir, Vladimir Gorikker. Sp, Alexander Volodin, based on the poem by Alexander Pushkin; cam, Lev Rogozin; mus, A Kogan; snd, A Izbutsky. 77.
Irina Alferova, Alexander Kirillov, Ludmilla Drebneva, Natalia Saiko.
(English subtitles)
03/26/80

Beloved Love: SEE Ljubavni
Zivot Budmira Trajkovica

Beloved Lover: SEE Amada
Amante

Below The Belt
ATL. Aberdeen/RLF/Tom-Mi Prods film. Exec prod, Joseph Miller. Prod-dir, Robert Fowler. Sp, Fowler, Sherry Sonnett, from the novel "To Smithereens" by Rosalyn Drexler; cam (TVC), Alan Metzger, with additional pho, Misha Suslov; edtr, Stephen Zaillion; mus, Jerry Fielding; lyr, Fielding, David MacKechnie. (MPAA rating: R). 91.
Regina Baff, Mildred Burke, John C Becher, Annie McGreevey, Jane O'Brien, Sierra Pecheur, Frazer Smith, Shirley Stoler, Dolph Sweet, Ric Mancini, K C Townsend, and the voices of the Firesign Theatre.
12/17/80

Beloy and the Kid
(Philippines)
X. D'Wonder Films and A M Productions presentation. Dir, Romy Villaflor. Story-sp, Ben Feleo; cam, Loreto U Usleta. 97.
Vic Vargas, Nino Muhlach, Panchito, Paquito Diaz, Josephine Garcia, Subas Herrero, Angie Ferro, Venchito Galvez.
06/23/76

Belyi Parohod
(The White Ship)
(USSR)
X. Kirgizfilm Studio prodn, Kirghizia. Dir, Bolot Shamshiev. Sp, Shamshiev, based on novel by Genghis Aitmatov; cam, Manas Mussajev; mus, Alfred Schnittke. 99.
Nurgasy Sydygalijev, Assankul Kuttubajev, Orosbek Kutmanalijev.
07/14/76

Ben et Benedict
(France)
NEF. NEF Diffusion-SFP-Hamster Films prodn. Prod, Claude Nedjar. Wri-dir, Paule Delsol. Cam (Eastmancolor), Claude Beausoleil; edtr, Francoise Collin; mus, Larry Martin. 92.
Francoise Lebrun, Andre Dussolier, Daniel Duval, Jacqueline Staup, Pierre Brechignac.
04/27/77

Beneath the Valley of the Ultravixens
04/18/79
RMY. Russ Meyer prodn. Prod-cam-dir-edtr, Meyer. Sp, R Hyde, B Callum from a story by Meyer. 93.
Francesca (Kitten) Natividad, Anne Marie, Ken Kerr, June Mack, Lola Langusta, Pat Wright, Michael Finn, Steve Tracy, Sharon Hill, Henry Rowland, Robert E Pearson, De Forest Covan, Don Scarbrough, Aram Katcher, Uschi Digard, Mary Gavin, Stuart Lancaster.

The Beneficiary
(Britian)
X. National Film School (UK) prodn. Dir-sp, Carlo Gebler, based on the Anton Chekhov story, "In The Ravine;" cam, Pascoe Macfarlaine; edtr, Alan Tyrer; mus-snd, Trevor Jones; art dir, Celia Barnett; asst dir, Maggie Brooks. 47.
Marian Richardson, Desmond Fenell.
(16m) (B & W)
03/12/80

Bereketli Topraklar Uzerinde
(On the Fertile Land)
(Turkey)
FFT. Doga Film, Polar Film prodn. Dir-sp, Erden Kiral; story, Orhan Kemal; cam, Jan Perhson. 130.
Tuncel Kurtiz, Erkan Yucel, Yaman Okay, Nur Surer, Meanderes Samanci, Ozcan Ozgur, Selcuk Ulyerguven.
09/03/80

Bergado
(Terror of Cavite)
(Philippines)
IUS. Dir, Jose Yandoc. Sp, Jose Yandoc, Felix Dalay, Larry de Mesa; cam, Nong Rasca. 99.
Lotis Key, Johnny Delgado, Nick Romano, Renato Robles, Marissa Delgado, Charlie Davao, Paquito Diaz, Ramon Rivella Jr, Van de Leon, Chona Castillo, Anita Linda, Katy de la Cruz, Marlon Bautista.
05/05/76

Berlin - Dein Filmgesicht
(Berlin - Your Film Profile)
(Germany)
Film Collage on the History of the German Sound Film from 1929 to 1979, prods, Kaeguruh-Film, Hans-Henning Borgelt, Detlef Gumm, Hans Georg Ullrich; wri-dir, Hans Borgelt, in collab with Edmund Luft. 95.
(DOC) (COLOR & B & W)
08/20/80

Berlin Alexanderplatz
(W Germany - Italy)
BVA. Bavaria Atelier, RAI-TV2 prodn. Wri-dir, Rainer Werner Fassbinder from book by Alfred Doblin in 13 episodes for TV. Cam, Xaver Schwarzenberger; edtr, Juliane Lorenz; mus, Peer Raben; art dir, Barbara Baum. 975.
Gunter Lamprecht, Hanna Schygulla, Franz Buchrieser, Gottfried John, Barbara Sukowa, Claus Holm, Elisabeth Trissenaar, Brigitte Mira, Roger Frotz, Volker Spengler, Ivan Desny.
(MADE FOR TV - 13 75-MIN EPISODES)
09/17/80

Berliner Bettwurst
(W Germany)
X. Rosa von Praunheim prodn, Berlin, in collab with Sender Freies Berlin (SFB). Wri-dir-pho, Rosa von Praunheim. Tech asst, Bernd Upnmoor. 90.
Luzi Kryn, Dietmar Kracht, Berryt Bohlen, Lou van Burg, Wolfgang Macke.
02/16/77

Berlinger
(The Outsider)
(W Germany)
EXB. ABS-Filmproduktion/Independent Film Heinz Angermeyer prodn, Munich. Wri-dirs, Bernhard Sinkel, Alf Brustellin. Cam, Dietrich Lohmann; edtr, Heidi Genee; mus, Joe Haider. 120.
Martin Benrath, Hannelore Elsner, Peter Ehrlich, Tilo Prueckner, Martin Luettge, Elisabeth Volkmann, Max Mairich.
07/14/76

The Bermuda Triangle
SSU. Charles E Sellier Jr and James L Conway prodn. Dir, Richard Friedenberg. Sp, Stephen Lord, from book by Charles Berlitz; cam (Technicolor), Henning Schellerup; edtr, John Link; art dir, Charles Bennett; mus, John Cameron; stunt coord, Alan Gibbs; asst dir, Jeff Richard; snd, Robert Eber; sfx, Doug Hubbard; set decor, Freddie Mullis; narr, Brad Crandall. (MPAA rating: G). 93.
(DOC)
01/17/79

Beschreibung Einer Insel
(Description of an Island)
(W Germany)
X. Moana Film prodn. Dirs, Rudolf Thome, Cynthia Beatt. 192.
Gabrielle Baur, Brian Beatt, Cynthia Beatt, Susanne Christmann, Otto Kayser, Edda Loechl, and inhabitants of the island of Ureparapara.
(16m) (DOC)
08/15/79

Best Boy
X. Wri-prod-dir-conceived-edtr, Ira Wohl. Cam, Tom McDonough. 110. (DOC)
(16m)
09/19/79

The Best Way To Get Along: SEE La Meilleure Facon De Marcher

Bestije
(Beasts)
(Yugoslavia)
YFR. CFS Kosutnjak-Avala Film, Filmski Studio-Dunav Film-Zeta Film prodn. Dir, Zivko Nikolic. Sp, Nikolic, Dusan Kovacevic; cam (Eastmancolor), Bozidar Nikolic; mus, Boro Tamindzic. 90.
Rados Bajic, Bata Zivojinov, Gidra Bojanic, Eva Ras, Viktor Starcic.
08/17/77

Bete Mais Discipline
(Dumb But Disciplined)
(France)
AMLF. Christian Fechner Films prodn. Prod, Bernard Artigues. Wri-dir, Claude Zidi. Cam, Jean-Paul Schwartz; art dir, Jacques Bufnoir; edtr, Georges Klotz. 95.
Jacques Villeret, Kelvine Dumour, Celeste Bollack, Michel Aumont.
09/26/79

The Betsy
AA. Allied Artists Harold Robbins Intl prodn. Prod, Robert R Weston. Dir, Daniel Petrie. Sp, William Bast, Walter Bernstein, based on the novel by Harold Robbins; cam (Technicolor), Mario Tosi; edtr, Rita Roland; prodn des, Herman A Blumenthal; mus, John Barry; cos des, Dorothy Jeakins; set decors, James Payne, Sal Blydenburgh; asso prod, Jack Grossberg; asst dir, Wolfgang Glattes; snd, Lee Alexander, Rimas Tumasonis; stunt coord, William Couch. (MPAA rating: R). 125.
Laurence Olivier, Robert Duvall, Katharine Ross, Tommy Lee Jones, Jane Alexander, Lesley-Ann Down, Joseph Wiseman, Kathleen Beller, Edward Herrmann, Paul Rudd, Roy Poole, Richard Venturo, Titos Vandis, Clifford David, Inga Swenson, Whitney Blake, Carol Williard, Read Morgan, Charlie Fields.
02/15/78

Betty Blokk-Buster Follies
(Australia)
Roadshow. Reg Livermore Film Prodn prodn. Exec prod, Eric Dare. Dir, Peter Baty. Prod, Doug Livermore. Mus dir, Mike Wade. 120.
Reg Livermore, Baxter Funt, The Reginas.
08/18/76

Between Fear and Duty: SEE Med Strahom In Dolznostjo

Between Heaven and Hell: SEE Nasa Lupa Ang Langit At Impiyerno

Between Men
OH. Prod-dir, Will Roberts. Cam, Steogehen Lighthill, Josh Hanig, Robert Ellis; snd, Nelson Stoll, Marie Ashton, Peter Entell; edtrs, Roberts, Joe Gray, Charles Miller, Matt Hausle. 57.
(DOC)
05/23/79

Between The Lines
MDW. Raphael D Silver prodn. Dir, Joan Micklin Silver. Sp-story, Fred Barron; cam, Kenneth Van Sickle; prodn des, Stuart Wurtzel; edtr, John Carter; snd, Nigel Noble; mus, Southside Johnny and the Asbury Jukes; addl mus, Michael Kamen. (MPAA rating: R). 101.
John Heard, Lindsay Crouse, Jeff Goldblum, Jill Eikenberry, Bruno Kirby, Gwen Welles, Stephen Collins, Lewis J Stadlen, Michael J Pollard, Lane Smith, Marilu Henner, Susan Haskins, Ray Barry, Douglas Kenney, Jon Korkes, Joe Morton, Richard Cox, Gary Springer, Charles Levin, Guy Boyd.
04/20/77

Beyond and Back
SSU. Prod, Charles E Sellier Jr. Dir, James L Conway. Sp, Stephen Lord, based in part on the book by Ralph Wilkerson. Cam (Technicolor), Henning Schellerup; edtr, James D Wells; mus, Bob Summers; art dir, Charles Bennett; asst dir, Jerry Fleck; snd, Robert Eber; sfx, Doug Hubbard; stunt coord, Alan Biss. (MPAA rating: G). 93.
Brad Crandall, Vern Adix, Linda Bishop, Janet Bylund, Richard Cannaday, Maxilyn Capell, Bill Carroll, David Chandler, Hyde Clayton, Elaine Daniels, Lori Davis, Stewart Falconer.
02/08/78

Beyond Evil
ISC. Prods, David Baughn, Herb Freed. Exec prod, Roven Akiba. Dir, Herb Freed. Sp, Freed, Paul Ross based on a story by David Baughn; cam (Metrocolor), Ken Plotin; edtr, Rick Westover. (MPAA rating: R). 94.
John Saxon, Lynda Day George, Michael Dante, Mario Milano, Janice Lynde, David Opatoshu, Anne Marisse, Zitto Kazaan.
05/07/80

Beyond Good and Evil: SEE Oltre Il Bene E Il Male

Beyond Reasonable Doubt
(New Zealand)
X. Endeavor Prodns. Prod, John Barnett. Dir, John Laing. Sp, David Yallop, based on his book "Beyond Reasonable Doubt." Edtr, Michael Horton; cam (Eastmancolor), Alun Bollinger; mus, Dave Fraser; art dir, Kai Hawkins. 127.
David Hemmings, John Hargreaves, Martyn Sanderson, Grant Tilly, Diana Rowan, Ian Watkin, Terence Cooper, Marshall Napier, John Bach, Bruce Allpress, Bruno Lawrence, Peter Hayden.
10/01/80

Beyond the Bridge: SEE Dincolo De Pod

Beyond The Poseidon Adventure
WB. Irwin Allen prodn. Prod-dir, Irwin Allen. Sp, Nelson Gidding, based on the novel by Paul Gallico; cam, Joseph Biroc; edtr, Bill Brame; prodn des, Preston Ames; mus, Jerry Fielding; cos des, Paul Zastupnevich; special pho effects, Harold Wellman; snd, Herman Lewis; asst dir, Mike Salamunovich. 122.
Michael Caine, Sally Field, Telly Savalas, Peter Boyle, Jack Warden, Shirley Knight, Shirley Jones, Karl Malden, Slim Pickens, Veronica Hamel, Angela Cartwright, Mark Harmon.
05/30/79

Bez Milosci
(Without Love)
(Poland)
POL. Film Polski prodn, Iluzion Film Unit Warsaw. Wri-dir, Barbara Sass. Cam, Wieslaw Zdort; sets, Roman Rozycki; mus, Seweryn Krajewski; prodn mgr, Ryszard Straszewski. 103.
Dorota Stalinska, Wladyslaw Kowalski, Malgorzata Zajaczkowska, Zdzislaw Wardjn, Malgorzata Pritulak, Jadwiga Polanowska, Emilian Kaminski.
10/01/80

Bez Znieczulenia
(Without Anaesthetic)
(Poland)
X. Film Polski prodn, Warsaw, Film Unit X. Dir, Andrzej Wajda. Sp, Agnieszka Holland, Wajda; cam, Edward Klosinski; mus, Jerzy Derfel, Wojciech Mlynarski; sets, Allan Starski; prodn mgr, Barbara Pec-Slesicka. 131.
Zbigniew Zapasiewicz, Ewa Dalkowska, Andrzej Seweryn, Krystyna Janda, Roman Wilhelmi, Emilia Krakowska, Kazimierz Kaczor, Magda Teresa Wojcik, Jerzy Stuhr.
02/07/79

Bhumika
(The Role)
(India)
X. Blaze Film Enterprises, PVT Ltd Prodn. Prod, Lalit M Bijlani, Freni M Variava. Dir, Shyam Benegal. Sp, Benegal; edtr, Bhanudas; cam, Govind Nihalani; mus, Vanraj Bhatia; lyr, Majrooh Sultanpuri, Vasanth Dev; dialog, Pt Staya Dev Dubey. 160.
Smita Patil, Anant Nag, Amrish Puri, Naseerudding Shah, Sulabha Deshpande, Kulbhushan Kharbanda, Baby Rukhshana, Amol Palekar.
11/15/78

The Biassoli Embers: SEE La Brace Dei Biassoli

Bierkampf
(Beer Chase)
(W Germany)
X. Herbert Achternbusch prodn. Dir-wri, Achternbusch. Cam (Eastmancolor), Joerg Schmidt-Reitwein; edtr, Christl Leyrer. 85.
Herbert Achternbusch, Annamirl Bierbichler, Sepp Bierbichler, Heinz Braun.
(16m)
07/13/77

Big and Little: SEE Gross Und Klein

Big Bad Sis
(Hong Kong)
SHW. Run Run Shaw prodn. Dir, Sun Chung. Sp, Szu Tu An; cam, Lan Nai-tsai; prodn mgr, Liu Tsu-wei; art dir, Chen Ching-shen; edtr, Chiang Hsing-lung; martial arts, Tang Chia, Huang Pei-chi. 105.
Chen Kuan-tai, Chen Ping, Wang Chung, Shaw Yin-yin, Chuang Li, Wang Hsieh, Ku Kuan-chung, Chiang Nan, Hsia Ping.
10/27/76

Big Banana Feet
(Britain)
X. VizUnicorn Enterprises documentary prodn with Billy Connolly. Prods, Murray Grigor, Patrick Higson. Dir, Murray Grigor; cam, David Peat; edtr, Patrick Higson; snd, Ian Leslie. 77.
(DOC)
12/08/76

The Big Brawl
WB. Golden Harvest presentation. Exec prod, Raymond Chow; prods, Fred Weintraub, Terry Morse Jr; dir-sp, Robert Clouse; story, Clouse, Weintraub; cam (Technicolor), Robert Jessup; mus, Lalo Schifrin; edtr, George Grenville; art dir, Joe Altadonna; set decor, Jack Marty; snd, Bob Wald, Bob Litt; stunt coord, Pat Johnson; asst dir, Craig Huston. (MPAA rating: R). 95.
Jackie Chan, Jose Ferrer, Kristine De Bell, Mako, Ron Max, David Sheiner, Rosalind Chao, Lenny Montana, Pat Johnson, Mary Ellen O'Neill, H B Haggerty, Chao-Li Chi, Joycelyne Lew.
08/27/80

The Big Bus
PAR. Wri-prods, Fred Freeman, Lawrence J Cohen; exec prods, Michael, Julia Phillips. Dir, James Frawley. Cam (Movielab Color), Harry Stradling Jr; edtr, Edward Warschilka; mus, David Shire; prodn des, Joel Schiller; set decor, Barbara Krieger; snd, Doc Wilkinson, Al Overton Jr; asst dirs, Mel Efros, Chris Christenberry. (MPAA rating: PG). 88.
Joseph Bologna, Stockard Channing, John Beck, Rene Auberjonois, Ned Beatty, Bob Dishy, Jose Ferrer, Ruth Gordon, Harold Gould, Larry Hagman, Sally Kellerman, Richard Mulligan, Lynn Redgrave, Richard B Shull, Stuart Margolin, Howard Hesseman, Mary Wilcox, Walter Brooke, Vic Tayback, Murphy Dunne, Raymond Guth, Miriam Byrd-Nethery, Dennis Kort, James Jeter.
06/23/76

The Big Fix
U. Prods, Carl Borack, Richard Dreyfuss. Dir, Jeremy Paul Kagan. Sp, Roger L Simon, based on his novel; cam, Frank Stanley; prodn des, Robert F Boyle; edtr, Patrick Kennedy; cos, Edith Head; mus, Bill Conti; art dir, Raymond Brandt; set decor, Mary Ann Biddle; snd, David Ronne; asst dir, Jon C Andersen. (MPAA rating: PG). 108.
Richard Dreyfuss, Susan Anspach, Bonnie Bedelia, John Lithgow, Ofelia Medina, Nicolas Coster, F Murray Abraham, Fritz Weaver, Jorge Cervera Jr, Michael Hershewe, Rita Karlin.
10/04/78

Big Mamma: SEE II
Mammasantissima

The Big Night: SEE Le Grand Soir

The Big Operator: SEE Le Grand Escogriffe

The Big Red One
UA. Lorimar prodn. Prod, Gene Corman. Dir-sp, Samuel Fuller. Exec prods, Merv Adelson, Lee Rich. Cam, Adam Greenberg; supv flm ed, David Breatherton; edtr, Morton Tubor; mus, Dana Kaproff; art dir, Peter Jamison; snd, Cyril Collick; asst dir, Arne Schmidt; 2nd unit dir, Lewis Teague. (MPAA rating: PG). 111.
Lee Marvin, Mark Hamill, Robert Carradine, Bobby DiCicco, Kelly Ward, Stephane Audran, Siegfried Rauch, Serge Marquand, Charles Macaulay, Alain Doutey, Maurice Marsac, Colin Gilbert.
05/14/80

The Big Sleep
(Britain)
UA. Prod, Elliott Kastner, Michael Winner. Adapted-dir, Winner. Based on the novel by Raymond Chandler; cam (DeLuxe Color), Robert Paynter; edtr, Freddie Wilson; mus, Jerry Fielding; prodn des, Harry Pottle; art dir, John Graysmark; snd, Hugh Strain, Brian Marshall; cos-ward, Ron Beck; asst dir, Michael Dryhurst. (MPAA rating: R). 99.
Robert Mitchum, Sara Miles, Richard Boone, Candy Clark, Joan Collins, Edward Fox, John Mills, James Stewart, Oliver Reed, Harry Andrews, Colin Blakely, Richard Todd, Diana Quick, James Donald, John Justin, Simon Turner, Martin Potter, David Savile, Dudley Sutton, Don Henderson, Nik Forster, Joe Ritchie, Patrick Durkin, Derek Deadman.
03/15/78

Big Thumbs
FPL. Richard Lipton prodn. Prod-dir, Lipton. Sp, Carl Stone, David Newburge; cam (Eastmancolor), Pierre Schwartz II; edtr, St. Marks Place; snd, Sonny Heiser; mus, Roger Joyce. (Self-imposed X rating). 80.
Janette Sinclair, Jamie Gillis, David Lipman, Jason Dean, Crystal Field, George Bartenieff, Arthur Williams, Theo Barnes, Ras Kean, Jennifer Jordan, Sonny Landham, Eric Edwards, Val Oisteanu, Denny Davis, Terrick McCarthy, Larry Paster, Harvey Atwater, Jacob Pomerantz.
08/17/77

Big Wednesday
WB. A-Team prodn. Prod, Buzz Feitshans; exec prods, Alex Rose, Tamara Asseyev. Dir, John Milius. Sp, Milius, Dennis Aaberg; cam (Metrocolor), Bruce Surtees; prodn des, Charles Rosen; edtrs, Robert L Wolfe, Tim O'Meara; mus, Basil Poledouris; 2d unit dir, Terry Leonard; asst dir, Richard Hashimoto; snd, Harlan Riggs; set decor, Ira Bates; art dir, Dean Mitzner; sfx, Joe Unsinn; surfing sequences prod, Greg MacGillivray. (MPAA rating: PG). 126.
Jan-Michael Vincent, William Katt, Gary Busey, Patti D'Arbanville, Lee Purcell, Sam Melville, Robert Englund, Barbara Hale, Fran Ryan, Reb Brown.
05/24/78

Bilbao
(Spain)
X. Figaro-Ona Films (Barcelona) co-prodn. Exec prod, Pepon Coromina. Wri-dir, J J Bigas Luna. Cam (Eastmancolor), Pedro Aznar; edtr, Anastasio Rinos; sets, Carlos Riart; mus, Iceberg. 90.
Angel Jove, Maria Martin, Isabel Pisano, Francisco Falcon, Pepita Llunell, Jordi Torras.
05/24/78

Bildnis Einer Trinkerin
(Portrait of a Female Drunkard)
(W Germany)
X. Autoren-Film Prodn, Berlin; prodn mgr, Marianne Gassner. Wri-dir-pho, Ulrike Ottinger. Edtr, Ila von Hasperb; cos-asst dir, Tabea Blumenschein; mus, Peel Raben; snd, Margit Eschenbach. 108.
Tabea Blumenschein, Lutze, Magdalena Montezuma, Orpha Termin, Monika von Cube, Paul Glauer, Nina Hagen, Guenter Meisner, Kurt Raab, Volker Spengler, Eddie Constantine, Ginka Steinwachs, Mercedes Vostell, Wolf Vostell.
03/12/80

Bilitis
(France)
SNC. Films 21, MIP, Ectafilms prodn. Dir, David Hamilton. Sp, Robert Boussinot, Jacques Nahum, Catherine Breillat; book, Pierre Louys; cam, Bernard Daillencourt; tech counseller, Henri Colpi; edtr, Colpi; mus, Francis Lai; prods, Sylvio Tabet, Jacques Nahum. 95.
Patti D'Arbanville, Mona Kristensen, Bernard Giraudeau, Gilles Kohler, Mathieu Carriere.
04/06/77

The Billion Dollar Hobo
ITP. Prod, Lang Elliott; exec prods, Lloyd N Adams Jr, Dorrell McGowan. Dir, Stuart E McGowan. Sp, McGowan, Tim Conway, Roger Beatty; cam (DeLuxe Color), Irv Goodnuff; mus, Michael Leonard. (MPAA rating: G). 96.
Tim Conway, Will Geer, Eric Weston, Sydney Lassick, John Myhers, Frank Sivero, Sharon Weber, Sheela Tessler, Victoria Carroll.
06/21/78

Billy In The Lowlands
X. Theatre Co of Boston-FTF Inc prodn. Exec prod, Rikk Larsen. Prod, Nick Egleson. Wri-dir, Jan Egleson. Cam, D'Arcy Marsh; edtrs, Jan Egleson, D'Arcy Marsh; snd, Adrienne Linden; mus, The Nighthawks. 88.
Henry Tomaszewski, Paul Benedict, David Morton, David Clennon, Ernie Loew, Genevieve Reale, Bronia Wheeler, Robert Owczarek.
01/17/79

Billy Jack Goes To Washington
LAU. Prod, Frank Capra Jr. Exec prod, Delores Taylor. Dir, T C Frank (Tom Laughlin). Sp, Frank and Teresa Cristina (Tom Laughlin and Delores Taylor), from sp, "Mr Smith Goes To Washington" Sidney Buchman, based on a story by Lewis R Foster; cam, Jack Merta; mus, Elmer Bernstein; art dir, Hilyard Brown. 155.
Tom Laughlin, Delores Taylor, E G Marshall, Teresa Laughlin, Sam Wanamaker, Lucie Arnaz, Dick Gautier, Pat O'Brien.
04/20/77

Bim
(Trinidad)
X. Sharc Prods Ltd film, prods, Hugh A Robertson, Suzanne C Robertson. Dir, Robertson. Sp, Raoul Pantin, from idea by Suzanne C Robertson; cam (TVC Color), Bruce G Sparks; edtr, Paul L Evans; mus, Andre Tanker; theme song, Andrew Beddoe; asst dir, Wilbert Holder. 100.
Ralph Maharaj, Hamilton Parris, Wilbert Holder, Joseph Gilbert, Lawrence Goldstraw, Anna Seerattan.
03/31/76

Binge: SEE Parranda

The Bingo Long Traveling All-Stars and Motor Kings
U. Motown-Pan Arts prodn, prod, Rob Cohen; exec prod, Berry Gordy. Dir, John Badham. Sp, Hal Barwood, Matthew Robbins, based on the novel by William Brashler; cam (Technicolor), Bill Butler; edtr, David Rawlins; mus, William Goldstein; songs, Ron Miller, Goldstein, Gordy; prodn des, Lawrence G Paull; set decor, Leonard A Mazzola; snd, Robert Hoyt, Willie D Burton; asst dir, Tom Joyner; stunt coord, Jophery Brown. (MPAA rating: PG). 110.
Billy Dee Williams, James Earl Jones, Richard Pryor, Rico Dawson, Sam (Birmingham) Brison, Jophery Brown, Leon Wagner, Tony Burton, John McCurry, Stan Shaw, De Wayne Jessie, Ted Ross, Mabel King, Sam Laws, Alvin Childress, Ken Force, Carl Gordon, Ahna Capri, John R McKee, Brooks Clift.
05/19/76

Birch Interval
GMA. Radnitz/Mattel prodn, prod, Robert B Radnitz. Dir, Delbert Mann. Sp, Joanna Crawford, based on her novel; cam (Movielab Color), Urs B Furrer; edtr, Robbe Roberts; mus, Leonard Rosenman; prodn des, Walter Scott Herndon; set decor, Marvin March; snd, John Wilkinson, Jack Finlay, Fred Faust; asst dir, Terry Nelson. (MPAA rating: PG). 103.
Eddie Albert, Rip Torn, Ann Wedgeworth, Susan McClung, Brian Part, Jann Stanley, Bill Lucking, Margaret Leary, Anne Revere, Robin Storsnider, George Ebeling, Eunice Lehman, Joanna Crawford.
03/24/76

The Birds of Baden-Baden:
SEE Los Pajaros De Baden-Baden

Birjuk
(Lone Wolf)
(USSR)
X. Dovzhenko Film Studio prodn, Kiev. Prods, Leonid Korezski, Valentina Grishokin. Dir, Roman Balaian. Sp, Balaian, Ivan Mikolaitchuk, based on a story by Ivan Sergeyevich Turgenev; cam, Vilen Kaliuta; edtr, E Lukasheiko; sets, Vitali Kaliuta; mus, V Guba; snd, S Sergijenko. 77.
Michael Golubovich, Oleg Tabakov, Lana Chrol, Juri Dubrovin, Alexei Saizev.
03/01/78

The Birthday: SEE Urodziny Mlodego Warszawiaka

Bis Dass Der Tod Euch Scheidet
(Until Death Do Us Part)
(E Germany)
DEE. DEFA-Film Prodn, Babelsberg Group, Berlin, GDR; dir, Heiner Carow. Sp, Guenther Ruecker; cam, Juergen Brauer; sets, Harry Leupold; mus, Peter Gotthardt; prodn mgr, Erwin Albrecht. 100.
Karin Sass, Martin Seifert, Renate Kroessner, Angelika Domroese, Peter Zimmermann, Horst Schulze, Werner Godemann.
07/30/80

Bishop's Bedroom: SEE La Stanza Del Vescovo

The Bit Between the Teeth: SEE Le Mors Aux Dents

The Bitch
(Britain)
722. Brent Walker prodn. Prod, John Quested. Exec prods, Edward D Simons, Ronald S Kass, Oscar S Lerman. Dir, Gerry O'Hara. Sp, Gerry O'Hara, based on story by Jackie Collins; cam, Denis Lewiston; snd, David Crozier; art dir, Malcolm Middleton; asst dirs, Redmond Morris, Terry Pearce, Michael Zimbrich. (MPAA rating: R). 90.
Joan Collins, Michael Coby, Kenneth Haigh, Ian Hendry, Carolyn Seymour, Sue Lloyd, Mark Burns, John Ratzenberger, Pamela Salem, Anthony Heaton, Maurice O'Connell, Peter Wight.
10/03/79

Bitter Morsel: SEE Neem Annapurna

Bittersweet Love
AVE. Zappala-Slott prodn. Prods, Joseph Zappala, Gene Slott, Joel B Michaels. Dir, David Miller. Sp, Adrian Morrall, D A Kellogg; cam (Deluxe Color), Stephen Katz; edtr, Bill Butler; mus, Ken Wannberg; art dir, Vince Cresciman; snd, Hal Watkins, Lyle Burbridge, Curt Price, Michael Evje. (MPAA rating: R). 90.
Lana Turner, Robert Lansing, Celeste Holm, Robert Alda, Scott Hylands, Meredith Baxter Birney, Gail Strickland, Richard Masur, Denise DeMirjian, John Friedrich, Amanda Gavin, Jerome Guardino.
10/27/76

Bizalom
(Confidence)
(Hungary)
HU. Mafilm-Objektiv Studio Prodn. Wri-dir, Istvan Szabo from a story by Erika Szanto, Szabo; cam (Eastmancolor), Lajos Koltai. 117.
Ildiko Bansagi, Peter Andorai.
02/20/80

Black and White Like Days and Nights: SEE Schwarz Und Weiss Wie Tage Und Naechte

The Black Banana
(Israel)
X. Black Banana Co. Ltd. feature. Prod-dir-co-sp-co-edtr, Ben Hayeem. Cam, Emil Knebel; mus, P.C Usherovici, Ed Thomas, N Rapp. 74.
12/07/77

Black Bird Descending: Tense Alignment
(Britain)
X. Malcolm LeGrice/Arts Council of Great Britain prodn. Prod-dir-wri-cam, (b&w), Malcolm LeGrice; prod-edtrs, Malcolm LeGrice, Jack Murray; prodn assts, Tim Bruce, David Crosswaite, Marilyn Halford, Jane Jackson, Judith LeGrice, Oliver LeGrice, Jack Murray, William Raban, Liz Rhodes. 110.
Tessa Adams, Josephine LeGrice, Jack Murray, Liz Rhodes.
11/16/77

The Black Diamond: SEE Fekete Gyemantok

The Black Hand: SEE La Mano Negra

The Black Hole
BV. Walt Disney Prodns film. Prod, Ron Miller. Dir, Gary Nelson; sp, Jeb Rosebrook, Gerry Day from a story by Rosebrook, Bob Barbash, Richard Landau; cam (Technicolor), Frank Phillips; mus comp-cond, John Barry; prodn des, Peter Ellenshaw; art dirs, John B Mansbridge, Al Roelofs, Robert T McCall; edtr, Gregg McLaughlin; dir-min pho, Art Cruickshank; min effects, Peter Ellenshaw; set decors, Frank R McKelvy, Robert M Shook; asst dir, Tom McCrory. (MPAA rating: PG). 97.
Maximilian Schell, Anthony Perkins, Robert Forster, Joseph Bottoms, Yvette Mimieux, Ernest Borgnine, Tommy McLoughlin.
12/19/79

Black Jack
(Britain)
X. Kestrel Films prodn in asso with the Nat'l Film Finance Corp. Prod, Tony Garnett. Dir, Kenneth Loach. Sp, Loach, from the novel by Leon Garfield; cam, Chris Menges; edtr, Bill Shapter; des, Martin Johnson; cos, Sally Nieper; mus, Bob Pegg; asst dir, Raymond Day. 106.
Jean Franval, Stephen Hirst, Louise Cooper, Andrew Bennett, Packie Byrne, Pat Wallis, John Young, William Moore, Russell Waters.
09/12/79

Black Joy
(Britain)
X. Elliott Kastner, Arnon Milchan prodn. Dir, Anthony Simmons. Sp, Jamal Ali, Simmons; from play by Ali; cam (Eastmancolor), Philip Mehuex; edtr, Terry Tom Noble. 110.
Norman Beaton, Trevor Thomas, Dawn Hope, Floella Benjamin, Oscar James, Paul Medford.
06/01/77

Black Litter: SEE Camada Negra

Black Magic 2
(Singapore)
SHW. Prod, Run Run Shaw. Dir, Ho Menghua. Sp, Yi Kuang; cam, Tsao Hui-chi; edtr, Chiang Hsing-lung; mus, Chan Yang Yu; art dir, Chen Ching-shen; snd, Wang Yung-hua; martial arts instructor, Yuan Hsiang-jen; make-up, Wu Hsu-ching. 95.
Ti Lung, Tanny, Lo Lieh, Terry Liu, Lily Li, Frankie Wei, Yang Ai-ling, Lin Wei-tu, Yang Chih Chung, Lin Feng, Ou Chia-li.
12/14/77

The Black Marble
AVE. Prod, Frank Capra Jr. Dir, Harold Becker. Sp, Joseph Wambaugh, from his novel; cam (DeLuxe Color), Owen Roizman; edtr, Maury Winetrobe; snd, Jeff Wexler; prodn des, Alfred Sweeney; asst dir, Tom Mack; mus, Maurice Jarre. (MPAA rating: PG). 113.
Robert Foxworth, Paula Prentiss, Harry Dean Stanton, Barbara Babcock, John Hancock, Raleigh Bond, Judy Landers, Pat Corley, Paul Henry Itken, Richard Dix, James Woods.
02/27/80

Black Oak Conspiracy

NW. Prods, Jesse Vint, Tom Clark. Dir, Bob Kelljan. Sp, Hugh Smith, Jesse Vint, from a story by Hugh Smith. Exec prod, Gail Clark; mus, Don Peake; cam, Chris Ludwig; edtr, Jerry L Garcia; asst dir, Dennis Jones; stunt coord, Ted White. (MPAA rating: R).   92.
Jesse Vint, Karen Carlson, Albert Salmi, Seymour Cassel, Douglas V Fowley, Robert F Lyons, Mary Wicox, James Gammon, Janus Blyth, Will Hare, Jeremy Foster, Peggy Stewart, Jo Anne Strauss, Vic Perrin, Darby Hinton, Dana Derfus, Bill Cross.
04/13/77

The Black Panther
(Britain)
X. Impics prodn. Prod-dir, Ian Merrick. Sp, Michael Armstrong; orig treatment, Joanne Leighton; cam, Joe Mangine; edtr, Teddy Darvas; mus, Richard Arnell; art dir, Carlotta Barrow.   102.
Donald Sumpter, Debbie Farrington, Marjorie Yates, Sylvia O'Donnell, Andrew Brut, Alison Key, Ruth Dunning, David Swift.
12/21/77

The Black Pirate: SEE *Il Corsaro Nero*

Black River: SEE *Rio Negro*

Black Shampoo
DIM. Greydon Clark prodn. Prod, Alvin L Fast. Dir, Greydon Clark. Wris, Fast and Clark. Edtr, Earl Watson Jr; mus, Gerald Lee. (MPAA rating: R).   83.
John Daniels, Tanya Boyd, Joe Ortiz, Skip Lowe.
06/02/76

The Black Sheep: SEE *Le Mouton Noir*

The Black Stallion
UA. Prods, Fred Roos, Tom Sternberg; exec prod, Francis Coppola. Dir, Carroll Ballard. Sp, Melissa Mathison, Jeanne Rosenberg, William D Wittliff, based on the novel by Walter Farley; cam (Technicolor), Caleb Deschanel; edtr, Robert Dalva; mus, Carmine Coppola; art dirs, Aurelio Crugnola, Earl Preston; asst dir, Doug Claybourne.   118.
Kelly Reno, Mickey Rooney, Teri Garr, Clarence Muse, Hoyt Axton, Michael Higgins, Ed McNamara, Dogmi Larbi, John Burton, John Buchanan, Kristen Vigard, Fausto Tozzi, Cass-ole.
10/17/79

Black Sun
(A Necessary Action)
(Sweden - Yugoslavia)
X. Stockholm Film prodn in collab with Jadran Film, Zagreb. Exec prod, Jorn Donner. Dir, Arne Mattson. Sp, Wahloo, Mattson, based on Per Wahloo's novel "The Lorry" Edtr, John Trumper; mus, Wilfred Josephs; cam (Eastmancolor), Tony Forsberg. 100.
Helmut Griem, Slobodan Dimitrijevic, John Hamill, Gunnel Fred, Richard Warwick.
(English soundtrack)
05/31/78

Black Sunday
PAR. Prod, Robert Evans; exec prod, Robert L Rosen. Dir, John Frankenheimer. Sp, Ernest Lehman, Kenneth Ross, Ivan Moffat, based on the novel by Thomas Harris; cam (Movielab Color), John A Alonzo; edtr, Tom Rolf; mus, John Williams; art dir, Walter Tyler; set decor, Jerry Wunderlich; snd, John K Wilkinson, Gene Cantamessa; cos-ward, Ray Summers; asst dir, Jerry Ziesmer; stunt coord, Everett Creach; 2d unit dir, Marc Monnet. (MPAA rating: R).   143.
Robert Shaw, Bruce Dern, Marthe Keller, Fritz Weaver, Steven Keats, Bekim Fehmiu, Michael V Gazzo, William Daniels, Walter Gotell, Victor Campos, Walter Brooke, James Jeter, Clyde Kusatsu, Tom McFadden, Robert Patten, Than Wyenn, Joseph Robbie, Robert Wussler, Pat Summerall, Tom Brookshier.
03/30/77

Black Victory: SEE *La Victoire En Chantant*

Blacks Britannica
(Britain)
X. David Koff/Musindo Mwinyipembe prodn. Prods, Koff, Mwinyipembe. Dir, Koff. Cam, William Brayne, Mike Davis, Charles Stewart; edtr, Tom Scott Robson; mus, Steel Pulse.   57.
(DOC) (16m)
03/28/79

Blind Makker
(Blind Is Beautiful)
(Denmark)
WCT. Crone Film (Nina Crone) prodn. Sp, Hans Hansen, Hans Kristensen. Dir, Kristensen. Cam (Eastmancolor), Dirk Bruel; mus, Fuzzy; edtr, Lizzi Weischenfeld; in charge of prodn, Joergen Hinscch; prodn des, Peter Hoejmark; asst dir, Gert Fredholm. 93.
Ole Ernst, Lisbeth Dahl, Claus Nissen, Jesper Klein.
09/15/76

Blinders: SEE *Kara Kafa*

Blindfolded Eyes: SEE *Los Ojos Vendados*

Blizna
(The Scar)
(Poland)
POL. Dir, Kryzysztof Kieslowski. Based on story by Romuald Karas and Kieslowski; cam, Slawomir Idziak; mus, Stanislaw Radwan. 112.
Franciszek Pieczka, Mariusz Dmochowski, Jerzy Sztuhr, Michal Tarkowski.
02/02/77

Blomstrande tider
(Flourishing Times)
(Sweden)
EUR. Swedish Film Institute/Drakfilm/Three Leaf Clover prodn. Wri-dir, John Olsson. Cam (Eastmancolor), Hanno Fuchs; exec prod, Hans Iveberg; edtr, Christin Loman; mus, Bjoern Isfaelt.   98.
Kristen Henriksson, Carl-Gustaf Lindstedt, Halvar Bjoerk, Keve Hjelm, Essy Persson.
02/20/80

Blondy
(France)
LUG. Paris Cannes Production-TIT Film Produktion prodn. Dir, Sergio Gobbi. Sp, Lucio Attinelli, Catherine Arley from the book by Arley; cam (Eastmancolor), Jean Badal; edtr, Gabriel Rongier.   90.
Catherine Jourdan, Bibi Andersson, Rod Taylor, Hans Meyer.
01/28/76

Blood And Guts
(Canada)
AMB. Quadrant Films presentation of a Peter O'Brian Independent Pictures prodn. Exec prod, David Perlmutter. Prod, Peter O'Brian. Co-prod, John Hunter. Dir, Paul Lynch. Sp, Joseph McBride, William Gray, John Hunter from orig story by McBride; cam, Mark Irwin; edtr, William Gray; mus, Milton Barnes; art dir, Reuben Freed; cos, Delphine White; casting, Karen Hazzard Ltd.; wrestling supv, Reg Love.   92.
William Smith, Micheline Lanctot, Henry Beckman, Brian Patrick Clark, John McFadyen, Ken James.
09/20/78

Blood in the Streets
(Italy - France - W Germany)
IIP. Ugo Santalucia prodn. Dir, Sergio Sollima. Sp, Arduino Maiuri, Massimo De Rita, Sollima; cam (De Luxe Color), Aldo Scayarda; art dir-set dir, Carlo Simi; edtr, Sergio Montanara; mus, Ennio Morricone; cond, Bruno Nicolai. (MPAA rating: R).   111.
Oliver Reed, Agostina Belli, Fabio Testi, Paola Pitagora, Frederic De Pasquale, Marc Mazza, Rene Koldehoff, Peter Berlin, Gunnar Warner, Daniel Baretta.
(Dubbed English soundtrack)
01/14/76

The Blood Of Hussain
(Pakistan)
PFP. Wri-dir-edtr, Jamil Dehlavi. Cam, Walter Lassally, Dehlavi.   112.
Kika Markham, Salman Peerzada, Jamil Dehlavi.
05/14/80

Blood of the Railroad Workers: SEE *Rallarblod*

Blood Relatives: SEE *Les Liens De Sang*

Bloodbrothers
WB. Stephen Friedman-Kings Road prodn. Prod, Stephen Friedman. Dir, Robert Mulligan; sp, Walter Newman, based on novel by Richard Price; cam (Techncolor), Robert Surtees; edtr, Shelly Kahn; mus, Elmer Bernstein; prodn des, Gene Callahan; snd, Charles Knight; prodn mgr, John Coonan; asst dirs, Howard Roessel, Robert Hargrove. (MPAA rating: R).   116.
Paul Sorvino, Tony Lo Bianco, Richard Gere, Lelia Goldoni, Yvonne Wilder, Kenneth

McMillan, Floyd Levine, Marilu Henner, Michael Hershewe.
09/20/78

Bloodeaters
PKN. CM prodn. Prod-dir-sp, Chuck McCrann; cam (Movielab color), David Sperling; edtrs, McCrann, Sperling; mus, Ted Shapiro; prodn mgr, C A Harris; snd, James McGonigal Jr; asst dir, Jenny Lee; make-up, Craig Harris, Gerald Cullen. (MPAA rating: R). 84.
Charles Austin, Beverly Shapiro, Dennis Helfend, Paul Haskin, John Amplas.
10/29/80

Bloodline
PAR. Geria prodn. Prod, David V Picker, Sidney Beckerman. Dir, Terence Young. Sp, Laird Koenig, based on the novel by Sidney Sheldon; cam (Movielab color), Freddie Young; edtr, Bud Molin; mus, Ennio Morricone; prodn des, Ted Haworth; asso prod, Richard McWhorter; cos des, Enrico Sabbatini; asst dirs, John Longmuir, Gianni Cozzo; snd, Gordon Everett. 116.
Audrey Hepburn, Ben Gazzara, James Mason, Claudia Mori, Irene Papas, Michelle Phillips, Maurice Ronet, Romy Schneider, Omar Sharif, Beatrice Straight, Gert Frobe, Wolfgang Preiss, Marcel Bozzuffi, Pinkas Braun, Wulf Kessler.
07/04/79

Bloody Life: SEE Ai Kruie

Blowdry
GEX. Prod, Joey Vincent. Dir, Laser Scepter. Sp, Sam Kitt; mus, Bill Dern, Joel Mofsenson. (Self-applied X rating). 75.
Pepe, Helen Madigan, Peonies Jong, Michael Gaunt, Ultra Max, Richard Bolla, Crystal Sync, Jamie Gillis, Marie Roberts, Eddie Haskell.
11/10/76

The Blue Bird
(US - USSR)
FOX. Prod, Paul Maslansky; exec prod, Edward Lewis; co-prods, Lee Savin, Paul Radin. Dir, George Cukor. General dir of prodn, Aleksandr Arshansky. Sp, Hugh Whitemore, Alfred Hayes (USA), Alexei Kapler (USSR); based on novel by Maurice Maeterlinck; cam (DeLuxe Color), Freddie Young, Ionas Gritzus; edtrs, Ernest Walter, Tatyana Shapiro, Stanford C Allen; mus, Irwin Kostal, Lionel Newman; lyr, Tony Harrison; prodn des, Brian Wildsmith; art dir, Valery Urkevich; set decors, Yevgeny Starikovitch, Edward Isaev, Tamara Polyanskaya; snd, Theodore Soderberg, Gordon Everett, Gregory Elbert, John Bramall; asst dirs, Mike Gowans, Yevgeny Tatarsky, Liliana Markova, Stirling Harris. (MPAA rating: G). 100.
Elizabeth Taylor, Jane Fonda, Ava Gardner, Cicely Tyson, Robert Morley, Harry Andrews, Todd Lookinland, Patsy Kensit, Will Geer, Mona Washbourne, George Cole, Richard Pearson, Nadejda Pavlova, George Vitzin, Margareta Terechova, Oleg Popov, Leonid Nevedomsky, Valentina Ganilaee Ganibalova, Yevgeny Scherbakov, Pheona McLellan.
05/12/76

Blue Collar
U. T A T Communications Co prodn. Exec prod, Robin French. Prod, Don Guest. Dir, Paul Schrader. Sp, Paul Schrader, Leonard Schrader, based on source material by Sydney A Glass; cam (Technicolor), Bobby Byrne; mus, Jack Nitzsche; edtr, Tom Rolf; prodn des, Lawrence G Paull; set decor, Peggy Cummings; snd, Willie Burton, Marvin Lewis, Winfred Tennison; special mus arr, Ry Cooder. (MPAA rating: R). 110.
Richard Pryor, Harvey Keitel, Yaphet Kotto, Ed Begley Jr, Harry Bellaver, George Memmoli, Lucy Saroyan, Lane Smith, Cliff De Young, Borah Silver, Chip Fields, Harry Northrup, Leonard Gaines, Milton Selzer, Sammy Warren, Kimmy Martinez, Jerry Dahlmann, Denny Arnold, Rock Riddle, Stacey Baldwin, Steve Butts, Stephen P Dunn, Speedy Brown, Davone Florence, Eddie Singleton, Rya Singleton, Vermettya Royster, Jaime Carreire.
02/08/78

The Blue Country: SEE Le Pays Bleu

The Blue Ferns: SEE Les Fougeres Bleues

Blue Fin
(Australia)
RDP. South Australian Film Corp-McElroy and McElroy Prodn. Prod, Hal McElroy. Dir, Carl Schultz. Exec prod, Matt Carroll. Sp, Sonia Borg, from novel, "Blue Fin," by Colin Theile; story edtr, Harold Lander; art dir, David Copping; cam, Geoff Burton; edtr, Rod Adamson; mus, Michael Carlos; asst dir, Pat Clayton; ward, Annie Bleakley; snd, Don Connolly; sfx, Chris Murray. 90.
Hardy Kruger, Greg Rowe, Elspeth Ballantyne, Liddy Clark, John Jarratt, Hugh Keays-Byrne, Ralph Cotterill, George Spartels, Alfred Bell, Wayne Rodda, John Thompson, John Godden, Kelly Aitken, Terry Camilieri, Graham Rouse, Peter Crossley, Rob George, John Frawley, Anne Mullinar, Brian Moore, Max Cullen.
11/15/78

Blue Fire Lady
(Australia)
X. Blue Fire Prodns Pty Ltd picture for Australia Int'l Film Corp. Prod, Antony I Ginnane. Dir, Ross Dimsey. Sp, Bob Manumii; cam (Eastmancolor), Vincent Monton; edtr, Tony Patterson; art dir, John Powditch; snd, Gary Wilkins; ward, Terry Ryan; asst dir, Geoff Morrow. 95.
Cathryn Harrison, Mark Holden, Peter Cummins, Marion Edward, Lloyd Cunnington, Anne Sutherland, Gary Waddell, John Wood, John Ewart, Rollo Roylance, John Murphy, Telford Jackson.
05/10/78

Blue Lagoon
COL. Prod-dir, Randal Kleiser. Sp, Douglas Day Stewart, based on the novel by Henry DeVere Stacpoole; cam (Colorfilm), Nestor Almendros; edtr, Robert Gordon; snd, Paul Clark; art dir, Jon Dowding; cos, Jean-Pierre Dorleac; asst dir, Peter Bogart; underwater pho, Ron Taylor, Valerie Taylor; mus, Basil Poledouris. (MPAA rating: R). 102.
Brooke Shields, Christopher Atkins, Leo McKern, William Daniels, Elva Josephson, Glenn Kohan.
06/11/80

Blue Suede Shoes
(Britain)
X. Kendon Films prodn. Exec prod, Don Boyd. Prod, Penny Clark. Dir, Curtis Clark. Cam, Roger Deakins; edtr, Hugh Newsam, snd, Doug Turner, Ron Fawcus; prodn mgr, Vivien Pottersman. 97.
Bill Haley, Ray Campi and the Rockabilly Rebels, Freddie Fingers Lee, Flying Saucers, Crazy Cavan and the Rhythm Rockers, Matchbox.
(DOC)
02/13/80

The Blues Brothers
U. Prod, Robert K Weiss; exec pro, Bernie Brillstein; dir, John Landis; sp, Dan Aykroyd, John Landis; cam (Technicolor), Stephen M Katz; edtr, George Folsey Jr; prodn des, John J Lloyd; art dir, Henry Larrecq; set decor, Hal Gausman, Leslie McCarthy-Frankenheimer; cos des, Deborah Nadoolman; snd, Bill Kaplan; asso prods, George Folsey Jr, David Sosna; asst dirs, David Sosna, Jerram Swartz. (MPAA rating: R). 133.
John Belushi, Dan Aykroyd, James Brown, Cab Calloway, Ray Charles, Carrie Fisher, Aretha Franklin, Henry Gibson, John Candy, Murphy Dunne, Steve Cropper, Donald "Duck" Dunn, Willie Hall, Tom Malone, Lou Marini, Matt Murphy, Frank Oz, Kathleen Freeman, Armand Cerami, Steve Williams, Charles Napier, Steve Lawrence, Twiggy, Steven Spielberg.
06/18/80

Bluff Stop
(Sweden)
SVF. Sp-dir, Jonas Cornell. Cam (Eastmancolor), Lars Svanberg; prodn mgr, Jutta Ekman; exec prod, Jorn Donner. 104.
Bjoern Andresen, Barbro Skarp, Keve Hjelm, Maj-Britt Nilsson, Agneta Ekmanner, Jan Malmsjoe.
03/29/78

Boardwalk
ATL. Gerald T Herrod prodn. Dir, Stephen Verona; sp, Verona, Leigh Chapman; exec prod, Gerry Herrod; prod, George Willoughby; cam, Billy Williams. 98.
Ruth Gordon, Lee Strasberg, Janet Leigh, Joe Silver, Eli Mintz, Eddie Barth, Merwin Goldsmith, Kim Delgado, Michael Ayr, Forbesy Russell.
11/14/79

Bobbie Jo And The Outlaw
AIP. Prod-dir, Mark L Lester. Sp, Vernon Zimmerman; cam (Movielab Color), Stanley Wright; edtr, Michael Luciano; mus, Barry DeVorzon; art dir, Mike Levesque; snd, Lee Alexander; asst dir, Dennis Jones; stunt coord, Speed Sterns. (MPAA rating: R). 88.
Marjoe Gortner, Lynda Carter, Jesse Vint, Merrie Lynn Ross, Belinda Balaski, Gene Drew, Peggy Stewart, Gerrit Graham, John Durren, Virgil Frye, Joe Toledo.
04/07/76

Bobby Deerfield
COL. Prod-dir, Sydney Pollack; exec prod, John Foreman. Sp, Alvin Sargent, based on novel, "Heaven Has No Favorites," by Erich Maria Remarque; cam (Metrocolor), Henri Decae; Gerard Hernandez. addl racing pho, Tony Maylam; edtr, Fredric Steinkamp; mus, Dave Grusin; prodn des, Stephen Grimes; art dir, Mark Frederix; set decor, Gabriel Bechir; snd, Arthur Piantadosi, Les Fresholtz, Mike Minkler; cos-ward, Basil Fenton Smith; cos-ward, Bernie Pollack, Annalisa Masalli Rocca; asst dir, Paul Feyder; 2d unit dir, Stephen Grimes; stunt coord, Remy Julienne. (MPAA rating: PG). 124.
Al Pacino, Marthe Keller, Anny Duperey, Walter McGinn, Romolo Valli, Stephan Meldegg, Jaime Sanchez, Norman Nielsen, Mickey Knox, Dorothy James, Guido Alberti, Aurora Maris,
09/14/77

Bobo, Jacco
(France - Belgium - Tahiti)
PLF. Belstar-AMS-Cathala-Tour Films-Pacific Business Group (Tahiti)-Sodep-Belga Films (Belgium) co-prodn. Prods, Jacques Dorfmann, Laurent Meyniel, Norbert Saada. Wri-dir, Walter Bal; cam (Fujicolor), Pascal Gennesseau; snd, Alain Curnelier; edtr, Michel Lewin; mus, Jacques Revaux. 92.
Laurent Malet, Annie Girardot, Michel Montanary, Evelyne Bouix, Jean-Claude Brialy.
11/21/79

The Body of My Enemy: SEE Le Corps De Mon Ennemi

Body to Heart: SEE Corps a Coeur

The Bodyguard
(USSR)
SOV. Tadzhikfilm Studio Prodn, Dushanbe, Tadzhik Republic, Soviet Union; dir, Ali Khamraev. 90.
Alexander Kaidanovsky, Anatoly Solonitsyn, Gula Khamrayova.
07/30/80

Bogeyman: SEE Kummatty

Bomber Und Paganini
(Bomber And Paganini)
(W Germany)
X. Joachim von Vietinghoff/Nicos Perakis Filmproduktion (Munich) in collab with Zweites Deutsches Fernsehen (ZDF) (Wiesbaden). Christoph Holch, prodn mgr. Dir, Nicos Perakis. Sp, Perakis, Joe Hembus, Uli Greiwe; cam, Dietrich Lohmann; mus, Nicos Mamangakis. 114.
Mario Adorf, Tilo Prueckner, Barbara Valentin, Margot Werner, Hannelore Schroth, Heinrich Schweiger, Otto Tausig, Rainer Artenfels, Hark Bohm, Hannelore Eisner.
02/02/77

Bomsalva
(Misfire)
(Sweden)
EUR. Svenska Filminstitutet/Europa Film prodn. Sp-dir, Lars Molin. Cam (Eastmancolor), Hans Welin, Roland Sterner; exec prods, Bo Jonsson, Per Berglund; mus, Kaj Chydenius; edtr, Wic Kjellin. 106.
Lars Hjelt, Gunnel Lindblom, Folke Asplund, Carl-Axel Heiknert.
03/22/78

Bon Bast
(The Dead-End)
(Iran)
X. New Film Group prodn. Wri-dir, Parviz Sayyad. Cam, Houshang Baharlou. 90.
Mary Apik, Parviz Bahadour, Bahman Zarinpour, Apik Yousefian.
07/27/77

Bon Voyage, Charlie Brown (And Don't Come Back)
PAR. Lee Mendelson-Bill Melendez prodn. Prods, Lee Mendelson, Bill Melendez. Dir, Melendez; co-dir, Phil Roman. Sp, Charles M Schulz, based on his "Peanuts" characters; cam (Movielab color, Nick Vasu Inc); mus, Ed Bogas, Judy Munsen; ani, Sam Jaimes, Hank Smith, Al Pabian, Joe Roman, Ed Newmann, Bill Littlejohn, Bob Carlson, Dale Baer, Spencer Peel, Larry Leichliter, Sergio Bertolli; snd, Producers' Sound Service. (MPAA rating: G). 75.
Voices of Daniel Anderson, Scott Beach, Casey Carlson, Debbie Muller, Patricia Patts, Laura Planting, Arrin Skelley, Bill Melendez, Annalisa Bortolin, Roseline Rubens, Pascale De Bardlet.
(ANI)
05/28/80

The Boogey Man
GRO. Prod-dir-wri, Ulli Lomel. Exec prod, Wolf Schmidt. Cam (Metrocolor), David Sperling, Jochen Beitenstein. (MPAA rating: R). 79.
Suzanna Love, Ron James, John Carradine.
11/19/80

The Boom: SEE Anugraham

Boomerang
(Bulgaria)
BGO. Bulgarian Film prodn, Sofia. Dir, Ivan Nichev. Sp, Svoboda Bucharova, Jenny Radeva, Nichev; cam, Victor Chichov; art dir, Anghel Ahryanov; mus, Kiril Tsiboulka. 90.
Lyuben Chatalov, Yavor Spassov, Nikolai Binev, Katya Paskaleva, Krassimira Damyanova, Anzhela Atanassova, Velya Goranov.
02/07/79

Borderline
ITC. Exec prod, Martin Starger. Prod, James Nelson. Dir, Gerrold Freedman. Sp, Steve Kline, Freedman; cam, Tak Fujimoto; edtr, John Link; art dir, Michael Levesque; mus, Gil Melle; snd, Gene Cantamessa; prodn mgr, Christopher Seiter; asst dir, Chuck Myers. (MPAA rating: PG). 97.
Charles Bronson, Bruno Kirby, Karmin Murcelo, Bert Remsen, Enrique Castillo, A Wilford Bramley, Michael Lerner, Ed Harris, Norman Alden, John Ashton, Larry Casey, Panchito Gomez.
07/23/80

Born Again
AVE. Robert L Munger Prodn. Prod, Frank Capra, Jr; exec prod, Robert L Munger. Dir, Irving Rapper. Sp, Walter Bloch; cam (Technicolor), Harry Stradling Jr; edtr, Axel Hubert; mus, Lex Baxter; asso prod, Paul Temple; prodn des, William J Kenney; set des, Mark Poll; snd, Berg Hallberg; set decor, Rick Gentz; asst dir, Bob Bender. (MPAA rating: PG). 110.
Dean Jones, Anne Francis, Jay Robinson, Dana Andrews, Raymond St Jacques, George Brent, Sen Harold Hughes, Harry Spillman, Christopher Conrad, Stuart Lee, Alicia Fleer, William Zuckert.
09/06/78

Born of Fire: SEE Im Feuer Bestanden

The Boscop Diagram: SEE Le Graphique De Boscop

Bosko Buha
(Yugoslavia)
YFR. Centar Film prodn. Dir, Branko Bauer. Sp, Bosko Matic, Dusan Perkovic; cam (Eastmancolor), Branko Bazina; mus, Zoran Simjanovic. 120.
Marko Nicolic, Zarko Radic, Ljubisa Samardzic, Miroljub Leso, Milena Dapevic, Milan Strljic, Ljiljana Blagojevic.
08/15/79

The Boss' Son
NWA. The Boss' Son Prodns. Wri-dir, Bobby Roth. Cam (Metrocolor), Alfonso Beato; edtr, John Carnochan; mus, Richard Markowitz; exec prod, Robert Estrin; prod, Jeffrey White. 101.
Asher Brauner, Rudy Solari, Rita Moreno, Henry G Sanders, James Darren, Richie Havens, Michelle Davison, Gammy Burdett.
09/20/78

Boszka Ema
(Divine Ema)
(Czechoslovakia)
CZS. Barrandov Studio prodn. Dir, Jiri Krejcik. Sp, Zdenek Mahler, Krejcik; cam (Eastmancolor), Miroslav Ondricek; art dir, Jindrich Goets; mus, Zdenek Liska. 110.
Bozidara Turzonovova, Juraj Kukura, Milos Kopecky, Jiri Adamira, Joszef Somr.
07/23/80

Botschaft Der Goeter
(Miracles of the Gods)
(W Germany)
EXB. A R von Hirschberg, Rudolf Kalmowicz prodn. Dir, Harald Reinl; cam, Bernd Elstner, Edgar Scholz; mus, Peter Thomas; commentary, Manfred Barthel, based on Erich von Daeniken's "The Chariots of the Gods." 97.
(DOC)
05/26/76

The Bottleneck: SEE L'Ingorgo

Bou Posleden
(The Last Battle)
(Bulgaria)
X. Bulgarian Film prodn. Dir, Zako Heskia. Sp, Heskia, Svoboda Batchvarova, Nicolas Roussev; cam, Victor Tchitchov; art dir, Stefan Savov. 150.
Ivan Bourgev, Ilya Karaivanov, Vassil Banov, Mimosa Bazova, Yuri Angelov, Anasthase Madjarov, Maria Slavtcheva, Ivan Zlatarov.
11/17/76

Boulevard Nights
WB. Tony Bill-Bill Benenson prodn. Exec prod, Tony Bill. Prod, Bill Benenson. Dir, Michael Pressman. Sp, Desmond Nakano; cam, John Bailey; edtr, Richard Halsey; mus, Lalo Schifrin; prodn des, Jackson DeGovia; snd, Robert Gravenor, Kenneth Isley; asst dir, Ramiro Jaloma (MPAA rating: R). 102.
Richard Yniguez, Danny De La Paz, Marta Du Bois, James Victor, Betty Carvalho, Carmen Zapata, Gary Cervantes, Victor Millan, Roberto Covarrubias.
03/21/79

Bound For Glory
UA. Prod, Robert F Blumofe, Harold Leventhal. Dir, Hal Ashby. Sp, Robert Getchell, based on autobiography of Woody Guthrie; cam (DeLuxe Color), Haskell Wexler; edtrs, Robert Jones, Pembroke J Herring; mus supv, Leonard Rosenman; prodn des, Michael Haller; art dirs, William Sully, James H Spencer; set decor, James Berkey; snd, Robert Knudson, Dan Wallin, Robert Glass, Donald E Parker, Jeff Wexler; asst dir, Charles A Myers; stunt coord, Buddy Joe Hooker. (MPAA rating: PG). 147.
David Carradine, Ronny Cox, Melinda Dillon, Gail Strickland, John Lehne, Ji-Tu Cumbuka, Randy Quaid, Elizabeth Macey, Allan Miller.
10/27/76

Bourlive Vino
(Stormy Wine)
(Czechoslovakia)
Barrandov Studio prodn. Dir, Vaclav Vorlicek. Sp, Jan Kozak, Milos Marcourek, Vorlicek; cam (Eastmancolor), Josef Illik; mus, Karel Svoboda. 123.
Josef Hrdlicka, Vladimir Mensik, Bozidara Turzokovova, Zdenek Kryzanek.
07/28/76

The Boxer
(Japan)
TOE. Dir, Shuji Terayama. Sp, Shiro Ishimori, Rio Kishida, Terayama; cam (Eastmancolor), Tatsuo Susuki; mus, J.A Seazer. 95.
Bunta Sugawara, Kentaro Shimizu.
11/16/77

Boys: SEE Drenge

The Boys From Brazil
FOX. A Producer Circle Prodn. Prod, Martin Richards, Stanley O'Toole. Exec prod, Robert Fryer. Dir, Franklin J Schaffner. Sp, Heywood Gould, based on novel by Ira Levin; cam, Henri Decae; edtr, Robert E Swink; snd, Derek Ball; mus, Jerry Goldsmith; prodn des, Gil Parrondo; art dir, Peter Lamont; asst dir, Jose Lopez Rodero; cos, Anthony Mendleson. (MPAA rating: R). 123.
Gregory Peck, Laurence Olivier, James Mason, Lilli Palmer, Uta Hagen, Steven Guttenberg, Denholm Elliott, Rosemary Harris, John Dehner, John Rubinstein, Anne Meara, Jeremy Black, David Hurst, Bruno Ganz, Michael Gough.
09/27/78

The Boys In Company C
(USA - Hong Kong)
COL. Golden Harvest prodn. Prod, Andre Morgan; exec prod, Raymond Chow. Dir, Sidney J Furie. Sp, Rick Natkin, Furie; cam (Technicolor), Godfrey A Godar; edtrs, Michael Berman, Frank J Urioste, Alan Pattillo, James Benson; mus, Jaime Mendoza-Nava; song, Craig Wasson; prodn des, Robert Lang; art dir, Laida Perez; snd, Bob Litt, Danny Daniel; cos-ward, Erwin Arenas; asst dirs, Fred Slark, Hernan Robles. (MPAA rating: R). 125.
Stan Shaw, Andrew Stevens, James Canning, Michael Lembeck, Craig Wasson, Scott Hylands, James Whitmore Jr, Noble Willingham, Lee Ermey, Santos Morales, Drew Michaels, Karen Hilger, Peggy O'Neal, Jose Avellana, Vic Diaz.
01/25/78

Brand-Boerge Rykker Ud
(Flamin' Fire-Chief)
(Denmark)
ASD. Just Betzer (Panorama) prodn. Dir, Ib Mossin. Sp, Sven Methling; cam (Eastmancolor), Erik Wittrup Willumsen; mus, Ole Hoeyer; edtr, Maj Soya. 81.
Axel Stroebye, Kaj Loevring, Sonja Oppenhagen.
03/03/76

Brandstellen
(Scenes of Fire)
(E Germany)
DEE. DEFA Film Prodn, Group "Berlin". Dir, Horst E Brandt. Sp, Gerhard Bengsch; based on novel of same name by Franz Josef Degenhardt; cam, Rolf Sohre; sets, Christoph Schneider; mus, Peter Gotthardt, Reiner Gaebler; theme mus, Lokomotive Kreuzberg; edtr, Karisch Kusche. 90.
Dieter Mann, Heidemarie Wenzel, Wolfgang Dehler, Eduard Haussmann, Petra Hinze, Dietmar Richter-Reinick, Berko Acker, Thomas Wolf, Dieter Wien, Annekathrin Buerger.
06/28/78

Brass Target
UA. MGM film. Exec prod, Berle Adams. Prod, Arthur Lewis. Dir, John Hough. Sp, Alvin Boretz, based on the novel, "The Algonquin Project," by Frederick Nolan; cam, Tony Imi; edtr, David Lane; prodn des, Rolf Zehetbauer; mus, Laurence Rosenthal; cos des, Monika Bauert; snd, Peter Beil; sfx, Karl Baumgartner; asst dir, Bert Batt. (MPAA rating: PG). 111.
Sophia Loren, John Cassavetes, George Kennedy, Robert Vaughn, Patrick McGoohan, Bruce Davison, Edward Herrman, Max Von Sydow, Ed Bishop, Lee Montague.
12/13/78

Bravo Maestro
(Yugoslavia)
YFR. Jadran Film prodn. Dir, Rajko Grlic. Sp, Grlic, Srdan Karanovic; cam (Eastmancolor), Zivko Zalar; edtr, Zivka Toplak; mus, Branislav Zivkobvic. 99.
Rade Serbezija, Aleksander Bercek, Bozidar Boban, Mladen Budiscak, Koraljka Krs, Zvonko Lepetic.
06/07/78

Bread and Stones: SEE Brot und Steine

Break Away: SEE Przed Odlotem

Break Of Day
(Australia)
GUO. Clare Beach Films prodn; prod, Pat Lovell. Exec prod, Tom Haydon. Dir, Ken Hannam; sp, Cliff Green; cam (Eastmancolor), Russel Boyd; des, Wendy Dickson. 106.
Sara Kestelman, Andrew McFarlane, Ingrid Mason, Tony Barry, Eileen Chapman, Ben Gabriel, Maurie Fields, Malcolm Phillips, John Bell, Dennis Olsen, Sean Myers, Kate Ferguson, Geraldine Turner.
01/12/77

Break Up: SEE Eutanasia Di Un Amore

Breakdown: SEE Kvar

Breaker, Breaker
AIP. Paragon Films prodn. Prod-dir, Don Hulette. Exec prods, Samuel Schulman, Bernard Tabakin. Sp, Terry Chambers; cam, Mario DiLeo; edtr, Steven Zaillian; mus, Don Hulette; art dir, Thomas Thomas; stunts, Ran Saniger; trucking cnsltnt, Russell Chambers; asst dir, Doron Kauper. (MPAA rating: PG). 86.
George Murdock, Terry O'Connor, Don Gentry, John Difusco, Ron Cedillos, Michael Augenstein, Dan Vandergrift, Douglas Stevenson.
04/27/77

Breaker Morant
(Australia)
X. South Australian Film Corporation presentation. Prod, Matt Carroll. Dir, Bruce Beresford. Sp, Beresford, Jonathon Hardy, David Stevens, based on a play by Kenneth Ross; cam (Eastmancolor, Panavision), Don McAlpine; snd, Gary Wilkins; edtr, William Anderson; prodn mgr, Pamela Vanneck; asst dir, Mark Edgerton; art dir, David Copping; cos des, Anna Senior; sfx, Monty Fieguth, Chris Murray; mus, Phil Cunneen; stunts, Heath Harris, Tony Smart. (MPAA rating: PG). 106.
Edward Woodward, Jack Thompson, John Waters, Bryan Brown, Rod Mullinar, Lewis Fitz-Gerald, Charles Tingwell, Terence Donovan, Vincent Ball, Frank Wilson, Alan Cassell, Russell Kiefel, Judy Dick, Barbara West.
04/23/80

Breakfast In Bed
X. William Haugse prodn. Prod, Catherine Coulson. Sp-dir-edtr, William Haugse. Cam (Metrocolor), Frederick Elmes; mus, Tom Grant. 56.
Jenny Sullivan, John Ritter, V Phipps-Wilson, Mitchell Breit, Timothy Near, Buckline Beery. (16m)
04/12/78

Breakheart Pass
UA. Jerry Gershwin-Elliott Kastner prodn, prod, Gershwin. Exec prod, Kastner. Dir, Tom Gries. Sp, Alistair MacLean (based on his novel); cam (Deluxe Color), Lucien Ballard; edtr, Buzz Brandt; prodn des, Johannes Larsen; mus, Jerry Goldsmith; set des, Herbert S Deverill, Richard G Clayton; snd, Gene Cantamessa; 2d unit dir, Yakima Canutt; asst dirs, Ronald L Schwary, Ron Wright, Peter Gries. 95.
Charles Bronson, Ben Johnson, Jill Ireland, Richard Crenna, Charles Durning, Roy Jenson, Casey Tibbs, Archie Moore, Joe Kapp, Ed Lauter, Read Morgan, Robert Rothwell, Rayford Barnes, Scott Newman, Eldon Burke, David Huddleston, William McKinney, Eddie Little Sky, Robert Tessier, Doug Atkins, Irv Faling, Bill Klem, John Mitchum, Keith McConnell.
02/04/76

Breaking Away
FOX. Prod-dir, Peter Yates. Sp, Steve Tesich; cam (Deluxe Color), Matthew F Leonetti; edtr, Cynthia Scheider; snd, Bud Alper; art dir, Patrizia von Brandenstein; asst dir, Mike Grillo; mus, Patrick Williams. (MPAA rating: PG). 100.
Dennis Christopher, Dennis Quaid, Daniel Stern, Jackie Earle Haley, Barbara Barrie, Paul Dooley, Robyn Douglass, Hart Bochner, Amy Wright.
07/11/79

Breaking Glass
(Britain)
PAR. Allied Stars presentatiion of a Film & General Prodn. Exec prod, Dodi Fayed. Prod, Davina Belling, Clive Parsons. Dir-sp, Brian Gibson; cam, Stephen Goldblatt; edtr, Michael Bradsell; orig songs, Hazel O'Connor; mus dir, Tony Visconti; snd, Bruce White; art dir, Evan Hercules; chor, Eric G Robarts; prodn supv, John Comfort; asst dir, Roger Simons. 104.
Phil Daniels, Hazel O'Connor, Jon Finch, Jonathan Pryce, Peter-Hugo Daly, Mark Wingett, Gary Tibbs, Charles Wegner, Mark Wing-Davey, Hugh Thomas, Nigel Humphreys, Ken Campbell, Peter Tilbury, Gary Holton, Derek Thompson, Janine Duvitski, Lowri Ann Richards, Gary Olsen.
05/28/80

Breaking Point
(Canada)
FOX. Astral Bellevue-Pathe/20th film, prods, Claude Heroux, Bob Clark; exec prods, Harold Greenberg, Alfred Pariser. Dir, Bob Clark. Sp, Roger E Swaybill, Stanley Mann, from story by Swaybill; cam (DeLuxe Color), Marc Champion; edtr, Stan Cole; mus, David McLey; art dir, Wolf Kroeger; set des, Dave Deyell; snd, Russ Heisse, Mel Lovell; asst dir, Tony Thatcher; 2d unit dir, Bud Cardos; stunt coord, Dwayne McLean. (MPAA rating: R). 92.
Bo Svenson, Robert Culp, John Colicos, Belinda J Montgomery, Stephen Young, Linda Sorenson, Jeffrey Lynas, Gerry Salsberg, Richard M Davidson, Jonathon White, Alan McRae, Dwayne McLean, Doug Lennox, Jim Hunter, Bud Cardos, Joanna Noyes, Ken Camroux, Ken James, Bill Kemp, David Mann.
06/02/76

Breaking With Old Ideas
(Peoples Republic of China)
X. Peking Film Studio prodn. Dir, Li Wen-hua. Sp, Chun Chao, Chou Chieh; cam, Cheng Li-yuan, Lo Teh-an; mus, Lu Yuan, Tang Ke. 110.
Kuo Chen-ching, Wang Su-ya, Wen Su-ya, Wen Hsi-ying, Chang Cheng.
07/07/76

Breakthrough
(Sergeant Steiner)
(W Germany)
X. Palladium (Hubert Lukowski)-Rapid Film prodn, Munich. Exec prods, Wolf C Hartwig, Ted Richmond. Prods, Arlene Sellers, Alex Winitsky. Dir, Andrew V McLaglen. Sp, Tony Williamson; cam (Eastmancolor, Panavision), Tony Imi; mus, Peter Thomas; snd, David Hildyard, Peter Horrocks; edtr, Raymond Poulton; asst dir, Burt Batt; sfx, Sass Bedig; prodn des, Gerhard Janda; military advisors, Maj Gen Bernadiner and Lt Col (ret) Sam Magill. 115.
Richard Burton, Rod Steiger, Robert Mitchum, Curt Jurgens, Helmuth Griem, Michael Parks, Klaus Loewitsch, Veronique Vendell, Joachim Hansen.
03/21/79

The Bricklayers: SEE Los Albaniles

Brigade Mondaine
(Vice Squad)
(France)
PLF. FranCos Films prodn. Dir, Jacques Scandelari. Sp, Jacques Robert from book by Gerard De Villiers; cam (Eastmancolor), Francois About; edtr, Catherine Snopko; mus, Cerrone. 90.
Patrice Valota, Odile Michel, Florence Cayrol, J P Brissart, Jacques Berthier, Patrick Oliver.
09/20/78

The Brink's Job
U. Dino de Laurentiis presentation. Prod, Ralph Serpe. Dir, William Friedkin. Sp, Walon Green, based on book by Noel Behn; cam, A Norman Leigh; edtrs, Bud Smith, Robert K Lambert; snd, Jeff Wexler; prodn des, Dean Tavoularis; asst dir, Terence A Donnelly; art dir, Angelo Graham; mus, Richard Rodney Bennett. (MPAA rating: PG). 103.
Peter Falk, Peter Boyle, Allen Goorwitz, Warren Oates, Gena Rowlands, Paul Sorvino, Sheldon Leonard, Gerard Murphy, Kevin O'Connor, Claudia Peluso.
12/13/78

Broederna Lejonhjaerta
(The Brothers Lionheart)
(Sweden)
SVF. Exec prods, Olle Hellbom, Olle Nordemar. Dir, Hellbom. Sp, Astrid Lindgren from her novel. Prodn mgr, Waldemar Bergendahl. Cam (Eastmancolor), Rune Ericsson. Prodn des, Lotta Melanton, P A Lundgren. Cos, Gunilla Norlund. 101.
Staffan Goetestam, Lars Soederdahl, Allan Edwall, Gun Wallgren, Per Oscarsson.
10/05/77

Broken Comedy: SEE Comedia Rota

Broken Flag: SEE Bandera Rota

Bronco Billy
WB. Prods, Dennis Hackin, Neal Dobrofsky. Exec prod, Robert Daley. Dir, Clint Eastwood. Sp, Dennis Hackin; cam (Deluxe Color), David Worth; edtrs, Ferris Webster, Joel Cox, snd, Bert Hallberg; art dir, Gene Lourie; asso prod, Fritz Manes; asst dir, Tom Joyner; mus, Snuff Garrett. (MPAA rating: PG). 119.
Clint Eastwood, Sondra Locke, Geoffrey Lewis, Scatman Crothers, Bill McKinney, Sam Bottoms, Dan Vadis, Sierra Pecheur, Walter Barnes, Woodrow Parfrey, Beverlee McKinsey, William Prince, Tessa Richarde, Tanya Russell.
06/11/80

The Bronte Sisters: SEE Les Soeurs Bronte

The Brood
(Canada)
NW. Exec prods, Pierre David, Victor Solnicki. Prod, Claude Heroux. Dir-wri, David Cronenberg. Cam, Mark Irwin; edtr, Alan Collins; mus, Howard Shore; art dir, Carol Spier; snd, Bryan Day. (MPAA rating: R). 91.
Oliver Reed, Samantha Eggar, Art Hindle, Cindy Hinds, Nuala Fitzgerald, Henry Beckerman, Susan Hogan, Michael McGhee, Gary McKeehan, Bob Silverman, Joseph Shaw, Felix Silla, Larry Solway, Rainer Schwartz, Nicholas Campbell.
06/06/79

Brot und Steine
(Bread and Stones)
(Switzerland)
MJS. Logos-Film Zurich (Claude M Beck) prodn. Dir, Mark M Rissi. Sp, Walther Kauer, from an idea by Otto Locher; cam, Edwin Horak; edtr, Evelyne von Rabenau; mus, Martin Boettcher, Veronique Muller, Trio Eugster; lyr, Muller, Max Rueger. 95.
Liselotte Pulver, Henrik Rhyn, Beatrice Kessler, Walo Luond, Sigfrit Steiner, Hans Gaugler, Peter Leu.
05/30/79

Brotherhood
(Hong Kong)
SHW. Run Run Shaw prodn. Dir, Hua Shan. Cam, Chang Te-Wei; edtr, Chang Hsing-lung; art dir, Wang Yung-hua; snd, Wang Yung-hau. 100.
Liu Yung, Hu Chin, Lily Li, Ching Miao, Yang Tse-lin, Liang Shang-yun, Ai Frei, Wang Hsieh, Shih Chung-tien, Chiang Tao.
08/18/76

Brothers
WB. Soho Assos prodn, prod-wri, Edward and Mildred Lewis. Exec prod, Lee Savin. Dir, Arthur Barron. Cam (MetroColor), John Morrill; edtr, William Dornisch; mus, Taj Mahal; art dir, Vince Cresciman; snd, Kirk Francis; asst dirs, Michael Blum, Kim Kurumada. (MPAA rating: R). 105.
Bernie Casey, Vonetta McGee, Ron O'Neal, Renny Roker, Stu Gilliam, John Lehne, Owen Pace.
03/23/77

The Brothers: SEE Die Brueder

Brothers And Sisters
(Britain)
British Film Institute prodn. Exec prod, Peter Sainsbury; prod, Keith Griffiths; dir, Richard Woolley; sp, Woolley, Tammy Walker; cam, Pascoe Macfarlane; edtr, Mick Audsley; mus, Trebor Jones; art dir, Miranda Melville; snd, Alf Bower; prodn supv, Jim Pearse. 96.
Carolyn Pickles, Sam Dale, Robert East, Elizabeth Bennett, Jenifer Armitage, Barry McCarthy, Barrie Shore, Norman Claridge, Mavis Pugh, Fred Gaunt, Nick Jensen, Jack Platts, Mary Wray, David Theakston, Nelson Fletcher.
09/17/80

The Brothers Lionheart: SEE Broederna Lejonhjaerta

Brubaker
FOX. Prod, Ron Silverman; exec prod, Ted Mann; dir, Stuart Rosenberg; sp, W D Richter; cam (Deluxe Color), Bruno Nuytten; edtr, Robert Brown; snd, Charles Wilborn; art dir, J Michael Riva; asst dir, Jon C Andersen; asso prod, Gordon Webb; mus, Lalo Schifrin. (MPAA rating: R). 130.
Robert Redford, Yaphet Kotto, Jane Alexander, Murray Hamilton, David Keith, Morgan Freeman, Matt Clark, Tim McIntire, Richard Walsh, Jon Van Ness, M Emmet Walsh, Albert Salmi, Linda Haynes, Everett McGill, Val Avery.
06/18/80

Bruce Lee and I
(Hong Kong)
SHW. Ting Pei Motion Picture presentation. Dir, Lo Mar. Shot in Eastmancolor. 106.
Betty Ting Pei, Li Hsiu Hsien.
01/28/76

Bruce Lee-True Story
(Hong Kong)
ETE. A Pal Ming prodn. Dir-sp, Ng See Yuen. Cam, Chang Chee; edtr, Sung Ming; mus, Chow Fu Liang; boxing dir, Kiang Siao Sung. 100.
Ho Chung Tao, Unicorn Chan, Lia Siao Sung, Donnie William, David Chow, Roberta Ciappi, Mario Viadiano, Sham Chien Po, Tisui Chung Shun.
(English Subtitles)
12/08/76

Brussels-Transit
(Belgium)
X. Paradise Films prodn. Wri-dir, Samy Szlingerbaum. Cam, Michael Houssiau; edtr, Eva Houdova. 80.
Helene Laplower, Boris Lehman, Jeremy Wald, Micha Wald.
(16m) (B & W)
12/17/80

Brutes and Savages
AHD. Arthur Davis Organization presentation. Prod-dir, Davis. Asso prod, Miyako Ejiri; edtr, Alan J Cummer-Price; narration written by Jenny Craven; spoken by Richard Johnson; cam, Natives; mus, Riz Ortolani. 94.
(DOC)
11/22/78

Brutti, Sporchi E Cattivi
(Ugly, Dirty and Bad)
(Italy)
GOI. Carlo Ponti prodn for Compagnia Cinematografica Champion. Dir, Ettore Scola; sp, Ruggero Maccari, Scola; cam (Technicolor), Dario Di Palma; art dir, Luciano Ricceri, Franco Velchi; edtr, Raimondo Crociani; mus, Armando Trovaioli. 115.
Nino Manfredi.
06/02/76

Brutus
(Philippines)
X. RVQ prodn. Wri-dir, Ading Fernando. Based on Jun Fernandez comics serial; cam, Manuel Bulotano; mus, Dominic Salustiano. 100.
Panchito and Rez Cortez, Teroy de Guzman, Bert Marcelo, Rebecca Gonzales, Joaquin Fajardo, Golay, Nieves Manuel, Metring David, Georgie Quizon.
05/26/76

The Bubble: SEE La Bulle

Buck Rogers
U. Glen A Larson prodn. Prod, Richard Caffey. Exec prod, Glen A Larson. Dir, Daniel Haller. Sp, Larson and Leslie Stevens; cam (Technicolor), Frank Beascoechea; edtr, John J Dumas; snd, Andy Gilmore, John Carter, Clyde Sorenson; art dir, Paul Peters; set decor, Richard Reams; asst dirs, Phil Bowles, Jerry Sobul; cos, Jean-Pierre Dorleac; sfx, Bud Ewing, Jack Faggard; mus, Stu Phillips. (MPAA rating: PG). 89.
Gil Gerard, Pamela Hensley, Erin Gray, Henry Silva, Tim O'Connor, Joseph Wiseman, Duke Butler, Felix Silla, Mel Blanc.
04/04/79

Budapesti Mesek
(Budapest Tales)
(Hungary)
X. Hunnia Studio prodn. Wri-dir, Istvan Szabo. Cam (Eastmancolor), Sandor Sara; mus, Zdenko Tamassy. 91.
Maya Komorowska, Agi Meszaros, Ildiko Bansagi, Andras Balint, Frantiszek Pieczka, Karoly Kovacs.
03/02/77

Buddies: SEE Polare

Budding Love: SEE L'Amour En Herbe

The Buddy Holly Story
COL. Innovisions-ECA prodn. Prod, Fred Bauer; exec prods, Edward H Cohen, Fred T Kuehnert. Dir, Steve Rash. Sp, Robert Gittler, based on story by Alan Swyer; cam, Stevan Larner; edtr, David Blewitt; mus dir, Joe Renzetti; dir of special audio, Joel Fein; prodn des, Joel Schiller; asst dir, Carol Himes; snd, Willie Burton. (MPAA rating: PG). 113.
Gary Busey, Don Stroud, Charles Martin Smith, Bill Jordan, Maria Richwine, Conrad Janis, Albert Popwell, Amy Johnston, Fred Travalena, Dick O'Neil, Gloria Irricari.
(MUSICAL)
05/17/78

Buek
(Happy New Year)
(Hungary)
HU. Mafilm Objectiv Studio prodn. Dir, Rezso Szoreny. Sp, Peter Modos, Szoreny; cam, (Eastmancolor), Janos Zsombolyai. 84.
Istvan Bujtor, Erika Bodnar, Andras Balint, Cecilia Esztergalyos, Judit Meszieri, Erika Horineczi.
02/28/79

Buffalo Bill and the Indians, Or Sitting Bull's History Lesson
UA. Dino De Laurentiis presentation. Prod-dir, Robert Altman; exec prod, David Susskind. Sp, Alan Rudolph, Altman, based on the play, "Indians," by Arthur Kopit; cam (DeLuxe Color), Paul Lohmann; edtrs, Peter Appleton, Dennis Hill; mus, Richard Baskin; prodn des, Tony Masters; art dir, Jack Maxsted; snd, Richard Portman, Jim Web, Chris McLaughlin; asst dir, Tommy Thompson. (MPAA rating: PG). 123.
Paul Newman, Joel Grey, Kevin McCarthy, Harvey Keitel, Allan Nicholls, Geraldine Chaplin, John Considine, Frank Kaquitts, Will Sampson, Burt Lancaster, Robert Doqui, Mike Kaplan, Bert Remsen, Denver Pyle, Bonnie Leaders, Noelle Rogers, Evelyn Lear, Pat McCormick, Shelley Duvall.
06/30/76

Buffet Froid
(Cold Cuts)
(France)
PFC. Sara Films/Antenne 2 co-prodn. Prod, Alain Sarde; wri-dir, Bernard Blier; cam (Eastmancolor), Jean Penzer; edtr, Claudine Merlin; art dir, Theo Meurisse; cos, Michele Cerf; snd, Jean-Pierre Ruh; mus, Johannes Brahms. 95.
Gerard Depardieu, Bernard Blier, Jean Carmet, Genevieve Page, Denise Gence, Carole Bouquet, Jean Benguigui.
01/02/80

Bugsy Malone
(Britain)
Bugsy Malone Productions Ltd. in ass'n with the National Film Finance Corp. A Goodtimes prodn of Alan Parker's film. Wri-dir, Alan Parker; prod, Alan Marshall; exec prod, David Puttnam; words-mus, Paul Williams; cam, Michael Seresin, Peter Biziou; edtr, Gerry Hambling; prodn des, Geoffrey Kirkland; dances, Gillian Gregory; cos, Monica Howe. (MPAA rating: G). 93.
Scott Baio, Jodie Foster, Florrie Dugger, John Cassisi, Martin Lev, Paul Murphy, "Humpty" Albine Jenkins, Davidson Knight, Sheridan Earl Russell, Paul Chirelstein, Dexter Fletcher, Vivienne McKonne, Helen Corran, Andrew Paul.
06/09/78

Buhay At Pag-Ibig Ni Boy Zapanta
(Life and Love of Boy Zapanta)
(Philippines)
X. Pentagon Films prodn. Wri-dir, Armando Ruiz David. Asso prods, Manuel D Barretto, Lt Col Juanito E Fernando; cam, Felizardo Bailen; exec prod, Augusto Bernarte. 103.
George Estregan, Philip Gamboa, Fe Galvez, Elizabeth Perez, Joseph Estrada, Paquito Diaz.
08/25/76

Build A House, Plant A Tree: SEE Postav Dom, Zasad Strca

Bully
EME. Maturo, Image Corp presentation. Prods, Sam Maturo, Mel Marshall. Dir, Peter H Hunt. Sp, Jerome Alden; cam, Ken Pailus; edtr, Terry Green; snd, Larry Stevens; set, cos des, John Conklin. (MPAA rating: PG). 120.
James Whitmore.
(FILMED STAGE PRESENTATION)
10/04/78

Buna Seara, Irina
(Good Evening, Irina)
(Rumania)
RMN. Romaniafilm Prodn, Bucharest. Dir, Tudor Marascu. Sp, Timotei Ursu; cam, Mirian Iordache, Duntitru Truica. 90.
Valeria Seciu, Stefan Iordache, Emil Hossu, Radu Panamerenco, Bogdan Carp.
07/23/80

Buone Notizie
(Good News)
(Italy)
MDU. Prod, Elio Petri, Giancarlo Giannini. Wri-dir, Elio Petri; cam (Eastmancolor), Antonio Nardi; art dirs, Amadeo Fago, Franco Pellecchia; edtr, Ruggero Mastroianni; mus, Ennio Morricone. 110.
Giancarlo Giannini, Angela Molina, Aurore Clement, Paolo Bonacelli, Ombretta Colli.
12/19/79

The Burgos Trial: SEE El Proceso De Burgos

The Burned City: SEE La Ciudad Cremada

Burning: SEE Usijanje

The Burning Years: SEE Gli Anni Struggenti

Burnt Offerings
UA. PEA Films Inc film, prod-dir, Dan Curtis. Sp, William F Nolan, Curtis, from the novel by Robert Marasco; cam (DeLuxe Color), Jacques Marquette, Stevan Larner; edtr, Dennis Virkler; mus, Robert Cobert: prodn des, Eugene Lourie; set decor, Solomon Brewer; snd, David Ronne'; asst dir, Howard Grace. (MPAA rating: PG). 116.
Karen Black, Oliver Reed, Burgess Meredith, Eileen Heckart, Lee Montgomery, Dub Taylor, Bette Davis, Anthony James, Orin Cannon, James T Myers, Todd Turquand, Joseph Riley.
08/25/76

The Bus
(Switzerland)
HEL. Dir-wri, Bay Okan. Cam (Eastmancolor), Gunash Karabuda; edtr, Okan; mus, Omar Zulfu, Pierre Leon Francioli. 66.
Bay Okan, Bjorn Gedda, Tuncel Kuritz, Aras Oren, Orguz Arlas.
08/25/76

Bushkhugin Ulger
(The Story of a Good Guy)
(Mongolia)
MGF. Mongolian Film Prodn, Ulan Bator; wri-dir-art dir, Purev Tsogzol. Cam, L Sharadorzh; mus, T Namsraizhav. 90.
O Ganbat, S Gedzhen, T Sainsana, N Daiyrane, N Suvda, D Dolgorsuren.
07/30/80

But Aren't You Ever Going To Change, Margarita?: SEE Pero No Vas A Cambiar Nunca Margarita?

But What Do They Want?: SEE Mais Qu'Est-Ce Qu'Elles Veulent?

Butch and Sundance
FOX. Pantheon William Goldman prodn. Prods, Gabriel Katzka, Steven Bach. Dir, Richard Lester. Sp, Allan Burns, based on characters created by William Goldman; cam, Laszlo Kovacs; edtrs, Antony Gibbs, George Trirogoff; mus, Patrick Williams; prodn des, Brian Eatwell; art dir, Jack DeGovia; cos des, William Theiss; snd, David Ronne; stunt coord, Loren Janes; asst dir, Jack Frost Sanders. (MPAA rating: PG). 110.
William Katt, Tom Berenger, Jeff Corey, John Schuck, Michael C Gwynne, Peter Weller, Brian Dennehy, Chris Lloyd, Jill Eikenberry, Arthur Hill, Vincent Schiavelli.
06/06/79

Butterfly Cloud: SEE Leptirov Oblak

The Butterfly Murders
(Hong Kong)
SEH. Dir, Hark Tsui. Sp, Lum Chi-Ming; cam, Fan Ching-Yu; action dir, Wong Shih-Tong; story, Hark Tsui. 100.
Lau Siu-Ming, Wong Shih-Tong, Michelle Mee, Jo Jo Chan, Tino Wong, Koh Hung, Ching Kwok-Chu.
(English subtitles)
08/01/79

By Hook or By Crook: SEE Auf Biegen Oder Brechen

By the Tennis Courts: SEE Du Cote Des Tennis

Bye-Bye Bavaria: SEE Servus Bayern!

Bye Bye Brazil
(Brazil - France)
GAU. Aries Cinematografica, Luiz Barreto, Lucy Barreto, Gaumont prodn. Wri-dir, Carlos Diegues. Cam (Eastmancolor), Lauro Escorel Filho; edtr, Mair Tavares; mus, Chico Buarque, Roberto Menescal, Dominguinhos. 100.
Betty Faria, Jose Wilker, Fabio Junior, Zaira Zambelli.
05/21/80

Bye Bye Monkey
(Italy - France)
GAU. 18 Dicembre-Prospectacle-Action Film prodn. Dir, Marco Ferreri. Sp, Ferreri, Gerard Brach, Rafael Azcona; cam (Eastmancolor), Luciano Tavoli; edtr, Ruggero Mastroianni; mus, Philipe Sarde. 114.
Gerard Depardieu, Marcello Mastroianni, James Coco, Gail Lawrence, Geraldine Fitzgerald, Avon Long.
(English soundtrack)
05/24/78

Bzlet
(The Takeoff)
(USSR)
SOV. Mosfilm prodn. Dir, Savva Kulish. Sp, Oleg Osetinsky; cam (Sovcolor), Vladimir Klimov; art dir, Vladimir Aronin; mus, Oleg Karavaichuk. 148.
Yevgeny Yevtushenko, Albert Filozov, Elena Finogenova, Kiril Arbuzov, Vadim Aleksandrov, Georgy Burkov.
09/05/79

Cabaret Mineiro
(Mineiro Cabaret)
(Brazil)
EMZ. Cinematografica Montesclarense prodn with Zoom Cinematografica, Corisco Filmes and Embrafilme. Wri-dir, Carlos Alberto Prates Correia. Cam (Eastmancolor), Murilo Salles; art dir-cos des, Carlos Wilson; mus, Tavinho Moura; snd, Walter Goulart; edtr, Ide Lacreta; exec prods, Lacreta, Paulo Henrique Souto. 90.
Nelson Dantas, Tamara Taxman, Tania Alves, Helber Rangel, Louise Cardoso, Eliete Narduci, Dora Pellegrino, Luiza Clotilde, Carlos Wilson, Maria Silvia, Saira Zambelli, Thelma Reston, Nildo Parente, Paschoal Villaboim, Sonia Santos, Nena Ainhoren, Celia Maracaja.
10/22/80

Cadaveri Eccellenti
(The Context)
(Italy)
UA. Produzioni Europee Associates Film, prod, Alberto Grimaldi. Dir, Francesco Rosi. Sp, Rosi, Tonino Guerra, Lino Jannuzzi; cam (Technicolor), Pasqualino De Santis; edtr, Ruggero Mastroianni; mus, Piero Piccioni; art dir, Andrea Crisanti; asst dir, Gianni Arduini. 110.
Lino Ventura, Alain Cuny, Paolo Bonacelli, Marcel Bozzuffi, Tina Aumont, Max Von Sydow, Fernando Rey, Charles Vanel.
(English subtitles)
03/31/76

Caddie
(Australia)
RDP. Anthony Buckley Productions film. Prod, Tony Buckley. Dir, Donald Crombie. Sp, Joan Long; cam (Panavision-color), Peter James; art dir, Owen Williams; cos, Judith Dorsman; edtr, Tim Wellburn; snd, Peter Fenton, mus, Patrick Flynn. 107.
Helen Morse, Takis Emmanuel, Jack Thompson, Jacki Weaver, Melissa Jaffer, Ron Blanchard, Drew Forsythe, Kirrili Nolan, Lynette Currin, Phillip Hinton, Simon Hinton, Sean Hinton, Deborah Kounnas, Marianne Howard, Mary Mackay, Lucky Grills, Robyn Nevin, Pat Evison, June Salter, Joy Hruby, Jan Adele, Johnny Garfield, Shirley Cameron, Frank Lloyd, Sid Heylan, Pat Rooney, Roy Corbett, Norman Erskine, Ray Marshall.
04/14/76

Caddyshack
WBO. Jon Peters Prodn. Prod, Douglas Kenney. Exec prod, Jon Peters. Dir, Harold Ramis. Wris, Brian Doyle-Murray, Ramis, Kenney. Cam (Technicolor), Steven Larner; edtr, William Carruth; supv edtr, David Bretherton; prodn des, Stan Jolley; mus, Johnny Mandel; sngwri, Kenny Loggins. (MPAA rating: R). 90.
Chevy Chase, Rodney Dangerfield, Ted Knight, Michael O'Keefe, Bill Murray, Sarah Holcomb, Scott Colomby, Cindy Morgan, Dan Resin, Henry Wilcoxon, Elaine Aiken, Albert Salmi.
07/23/80

Cafe Express
(Italy)
X. Vides Cinematrogafica SpA prodn. Prods, Franco Cristaldi, Nicola Carrao; dir, Nanni Loy; sp, Nino Manfredi, Loy, Elvio Porta; cam (Technicolor), Claudio Cirillo; score, Giovanna Marini. 105.
Nino Manfredi, Adolfo Celi, Vittorio Mezzogiorno, Marzio C Honorato, Gigi Reder, Luigi Basagaluppi, Marisa Laurito, Vittorio Marsiglia, Vittorio Caprioli.
09/10/80

Calamity: SEE Urgia

California Dreaming
AIP. Taft Organization-Whittaker prodn. Exec prod, Louis S Arkoff. Prod, Christian Whittaker. Dir, John Hancock. Sp, Ned Wynn; cam (Movielab Color), Bobby Byrne; edtrs, Sid Leven, Herb Dow, Roy Peterson; mus, Fred Karlin; prodn des, Bill Hiney; snd, Howard Steele. (MPAA rating: R). 92.
Glynnis O'Connor, Seymour Cassel, Dorothy Tristan, Dennis Christopher, John Calvin, Tanya Roberts, Jimmy Van Patten, Todd Susman, Alice Playten, Ned Wynn, John Fain, Marshall Efron.
04/04/79

The California Reich
CYF. Prod-dir-pho-edtrs, Walter Parkes, Keith Critchlow. Mus, Craig Safan. (MPAA rating: PG). 58.
(DOC)
03/31/76

California Suite
COL. Ray Stark prodn. Prod, Stark. Dir, Herbert Ross. Sp, Neil Simon, based on his play; cam, David M Walsh; edtr, Michael A Stevenson; supv edtr, Margaret Booth; prodn des, Albert Brenner; cos des, Patricia Norris; mus, Claude Bolling; snd, Al Overton Jr; asso prod, Ronald L Schwary; asst dir, Jack Roe. (MPAA rating: PG). 103.
Alan Alda, Michael Caine, Bill Cosby, Jane Fonda, Walter Matthau, Elaine May, Richard Pryor, Maggie Smith, Gloria Gifford, Sheila Frazier, Herbert Edelman.
12/13/78

Caligula
(Italy - USA)
PCI. Prods, Bob Guccione, Franco Rossellini for Penthouse Films International and Felix Cinematografica. Scenes dir, Giovanni Tinto Brass from an uncredited sp adapt from the story by Gore Vidal. Cam (Eastmancolor), Silvano Ippoliti; prodn des, Danilo Donati; edtng cnslt, Nino Baragli; mus, Paul Celmente. 150.
Malcolm McDowell, Teresa Ann Savoy, Helen Mirren, Peter O'Toole, John Steiner, Guido Mannari, Paolo Bonacelli, Giancarlo Badessi, Adriana Asti, John Gielgud, Leopoldo Trieste.
11/21/79

Call Him Mr. Shatter
(Hong Kong)
AVE. Hammer Films prodn. Prods, Michael Carreras, Vee King Shaw. Dir, Carreras. Sp, Don Houghton; cam, Brian Probyn, John Wilcox, Roy Ford; edtr, Eric Boyd-Perkins; mus, David Lindup; art dir, Johnson; asst dir, Geoffrey Ho. (MPAA rating: R). 90.
Stuart Whitman, Ti Lung, Lily Li, Peter Cushing, Anton Diffring, Yemi Ajibade, Liu Ka Yong, Huang Pei Chi, Liu Ya Ying, Lo Wei, James Ma, Chiang Han, Kao Hsiung.
01/14/76

Call Me From Afar: SEE Posowi Mnja W Dal Swjet Luju

The Call Of Spring: SEE Praznovanje Pomladi

The Call of the Front: SEE Tieng Goi, Phiatruoc

The Call-Up: SEE Repmanad

Calmos
(Cool, Calm and Collected)
(France)
AMLF. Films Christian Fechner-Renn Productions prodn. Dir, Bertrand Blier. Sp, Blier, Philippe Dumarcay; cam (Eastmancolor), Claude Renoir; edtr, Claudine Merlin; mus, Georges Delerue. 107.
Jean-Pierre Marielle, Jean Rochefort, Bernard Blier, Brigitte Fossey, Claude Pieplu, Micheline Kahn, Dora Doll.
02/11/76

Camada Negra
(Black Litter)
(Spain)
X. El Iman prodn; dir, Manuel Gutierrez Aragon. Sp, Manuel Gutierrez, Jose Luis Borau; cam (Eastmancolor), Magi Torruella; mus, Jose Nieto; sets, Wolfgang Burman; edtr, Jose Salcedo; cos, Maiki Marin. 82.
Jose Luis Alonso, Maria Luisa Ponte, Angela Molina, Joaquin Hinojosa, Manuel Fadon, Emilio Fornet, Petra Martinez.
05/11/77

Cambio De Sexo
(I Want To Be A Woman)
(Spain)
X. Impala S A and Morgana Films S A prodn. Dir, Vicente Aranda. Sp, Joaquin Jorda, Arnada, based on idea by Carlos Duran; cam (Eastmancolor), Nestor Almendros; mus, Ricardo Miralles; edtr, Maricel; chor, Margot Leargo. 108.
Victoria Abril, Lou Castel, Fernando Sancho, Rafaela Aparicio, Montserrat Carulla, Daniel Martin, Maria Elias, Rosa Morata, Bibi Anderssen.
06/01/77

Camera Buff: SEE Amator

Camouflage: SEE Barwy
Orchronne

Can I Do It. . .Til I Need Glasses?
NAE. Dauntless Prodn. Exec prods, Edward Colarik, Hal Wasserman; dir, I Robert Levy; prod, Mike Callie; sp, Mike Callie based on an orig story by Callie, Levy, Mike Price; cam, Craig Green; edtr, Steven Schoenberg; mus, Bob Jung; art dir, Robert W Zentis. (MPAA rating: R.) 73.
Roger & Roger, Jeff & Ernst, Victor Dunlap, Moose Carlson, Pat Wright, Joey Camen, Walter Oklewicz Saba, Ollie Prater, Ann Collier, Deborah Klose, Robin Williams, Ann Kellogg.
11/14/79

The Canal: SEE Kanal

Canal Zone
X. Zipporah Film presentation. Prod-dir-sp-edtr, Frederick Wiseman. Cam, William Brayne; asst dir, Oliver Kool. 175.
(DOC)
12/07/77

Can-Cannes
(Italy)
X. Prods, Franco Scepi, Mario Battistoni, Andrea De Micheli, Pierluigi Ronchetti for Monolite Cinematografica Milano prodns. Wri-dir, Franco Scepi. Cam, Mario Battistoni; edtr, Lucio Tomaz; mus, Detto Mariano; ani, Guido Manuli. 90.
Andrea De Micheli, Franco Scepi, Massimo De Rossi.
10/01/80

The Candidate: SEE Der
Kandidat

Candleshoe
BV. Walt Disney prodn. Prod, Ron Miller. Dir, Norman Tokar; sp, David Swift, Rosemary Anne Sisson, based on book, "Christmas at Candleshoe," by Michael Inness; asso prod, Hugh Attwooll; cam (Technicolor), Paul Beeson; edtr, Peter Boita; mus, Ron Goodwin; art dir, Albert Witherick; cos des, Anthony Squire, Julie Harris; prodn mgr, Robin Douet; sfx, Cliff Culley; stunt arranger, Bob Anderson; asst dir, Jack Causey. (MPAA rating: G). 101.
David Niven, Helen Hayes, Jodie Foster, Leo McKern, Veronica Quilligan, Ian Sharrock, Sarah Tamakuni, David Samuels, John Alderson, Mildred Shay, Michael Balfour, Sydney Bromley, Michael Segal, Vivian Pickles.
12/21/77

Caniche
(Poodle)
(Spain)
X. Figaro Films prodn. Exec prod, Pepon Coromina. Wri-dir, Bigas Luna. Cam (Eastmancolor), Predro Aznar; edtr, Anastasi Rinos; sets, Carlos Riart. 90.
Angel Jove, Consol Tura, Linda Perez Gallardo, Cruz Tobar, Sara Grey, Marta Molins.
05/16/79

Cannonball
(US - Hong Kong)
NW. Prod, Samuel W Gelfman; exec prods, Run Run Shaw, Gustave Berne. Dir, Paul Bartel. Sp, Bartel, Donald C Simpson; cam (Metrocolor), Tak Fujimoto; stunt coord, Alan Gibbs; edtr, Morton Tubor; mus, David A Axelrod; art dir, Michel Levesque; snd, Alex Vandercar; asst dir, Cathy McCabe. (MPAA rating: PG). 93.
David Carradine, Bill McKinney, Veronica Hamel, Gerrit Graham, Robert Carradine, Belinda Balaski, Judy Canova, Carl Gottlieb, Archie Hahn, Martin Scorsese.
07/21/76

Canoa
(Mexico)
COX. Dir, Felipe Cazals. Sp, Tomas Perez Turrent; cam, Alex Philips Jr. 115.
Enrique Lucero, Salvador Sanchez, Ernesto Gomez Cruz, Arturo Alegro, Jaime Garza, Carlos Chavez, Roberto Sisa; Gerardo Vigil, Rodrigo Puebla, Malena Doria, Flor Trujillo.
07/14/76

Can't Stop The Music
AFD. Allan Carr prodn. Prods, Allan Carr, Jacques Morali, Henri Belolo. Dir, Nancy Walker. Sp, Bronte Woodard, Allan Carr; cam (Panavision-Metrocolor), Bill Butler; mus, Jacques Morali; mus staging-chor, Arlene Phillips; cos, Jane Greenwood; art dir, Harold Michelson; edtr, John F Burnett; asst dir, Bill Beasley; set decors, Marvin March, Victoria Hugo; sfx, Michael Sullivan; mus arr, Horace Ott. (MPAA rating: PG). 118.
Ray Simpson, David Hodo, Felipe Rose, Randy Jones, Glenn Hughes, Alex Briley, Valerie Perrine, Bruce Jenner, Steve Guttenberg, Paul Sand, Tammy Grimes, June Havoc, Barbara Rush, Altovise Davis, Marilyn Sokol, Russell Nype, Jack Weston, Leigh Taylor-Young, Dick Patterson, Bobo Lewis, Paula Trueman, Portia Nelson.
(MUSICAL)
06/04/80

Cantata De Chile
(Cuba)
ICI. Wri-dir, Humberto Solas with help on script from Patricio Manns, Alberto Santana, Manuel Payan, Orlando Rojas, Jorge Herrera. Cam (Eastmancolor), Alberto Menendez; edtr, Nelson Rodriguez. 119.
07/28/76

Capricorn One
WB. GFD prodn. Prod, Paul N Lazarus 3d. Wri-dir, Peter Hyams. Cam (CFI Color), Bill Butler; mus, Jerry Goldsmith; edtr, James Mitchell; prodn des, Albert Brenner; art dir, David M Haber; set decor, Rick Simpson; cos des, Patricia Norris; asso prod, Michael Rachmil; asst dir, Irby Smith; snd, Jerry Jost. (MPAA rating: PG). 127.
Elliott Gould, James Brolin, Brenda Vaccaro, Sam Waterston, O J Simpson, Hal Holbrook, David Huddleston, David Doyle, Denise Nicholas, Robert Walden, Lee Bryant, Alan Fudge, Karen Black, Telly Savalas.
06/07/78

Captain Kreutzer: SEE
Hauptmann Kreutzer

Captain Lust
ANO. Tantric Pictures prodn. Prod-dir, Beau Buchanan. Sp, Steven Barry, Buchanan; cam, Joe Mangine; edtr, B E Bangsberg; mus, Fred Schminke; snd, C W Cressler, Paul Blank. (Self-imposed X Rating). 82.
Nancy Dare, Justine Fletcher, Jamie Gillis, Verry Knotty, Sharon Mitchell, Wade Nichols, Ming Toy, Jake Teague.
03/30/77

The Car
U. Prods, Marvin Birdt, Elliot Silverstein. Dir, Silverstein. Sp, Dennis Shryack, Michael Butler, Lane Slate; story, Shryack, Butler; cam (Technicolor), Gerald Hirschfield; edtr, Michael McCroskey; mus, Leonard Rosenman; art dir, Loyd S Papez; set decor, John McCarthy; snd, Jim Alexander, Kevin F Cleary; asst dir, Gary Daigler; stunt coord, Everett Creach. (MPAA rating: PG). 98.
James Brolin, Kathleen Lloyd, John Marley, R G Armstrong, John Rubinstein, Elizabeth Thompson, Roy Jenson, Kim Richards, Kyle Richards, Kate Murtagh, Robert Phillips, Doris Dowling, Henry O'Brien, Ronny Cox, Melody Thomas, Bob Woodlock.
05/11/77

Car Wash
U. Prod, Art Linson, Gary Stromberg. Dir, Michael Schultz. Sp, Joe Schumacher; cam (Technicolor), Frank Stanley; edtr, Christopher Holmes; mus, Norman Whitfield; art dir, Robert Clatworthy; set decor, A C Montenaro; snd, Willie D Burton, Robert L Hoyt; asst dir, Phil Bowles. (MPAA rating: PG). 97.
Franklyn Ajaye, Sully Boyar, Richard Brestoff, George Carlin, Prof Irwin Corey, Ivan Dixon, Bill Duke, Antonio Fargas, Michael Fennell, Arthur French, Lorraine Gary, Darrow Igus, Leonard Jackson, DeWayne Jessie, Lauren Jones, Jack Kehoe, Henry Kingi, Melanie Mayron, Garrett Morris, Clarence Muse, Leon Pinkney, The Pointer Sisters, Richard Pryor, Tracy Reed, Pepe Serna, James Spinks, Ray Vitte, Ren Woods.
09/01/76

Cara Sposa
(Dear Wife)
(Italy)
TIT. Prod, Laser Film (Italy). Dir, Pasquale Festa Campanile. Sp, Franco Verucci. Cam (Eastmancolor), Giuseppe Ruzzolini; art dir, Giantito Burchiellaro; edtr, Mario Morra. 107.
Johnny Dorelli, Agostina Belli, Enzo Cannavale.
10/12/77

Caravans
(USA - Iran)
U. Ibex Films - FIDCI prodn. Dir, James Fargo. Sp, Nancy Voyles Crawford, Thomas A McMahon, Lorraine Williams, based on the James Michener novel; cam (Technicolor), Douglas Slocombe; mus, Mike Batt; edtr, Richard Marden; cos, Renie Conley; set-tech suprv, Fereydoun Razavi; asst dirs, Anthony Waye, Bozorgmehr Rafia; title song sung by Barbara Dickson; art dirs, Ted Tester, Peter Williams, Peter James; 2d unit cam, Gordon Meagher, snd edtr, Mike Le Mare; sfx, Karli Baumgartner; stunt coord, John Sullivan. (MPAA rating: PG). 127.
Anthony Quinn, Michael Sarrazin, Jennifer O'Neill, Christopher Lee, Joseph Cotten, Behrooz Vosoughi, Barry Sullivan, Jeremy Kemp, Duncan Quinn, Behrooz Gueramian, Mohammad Ali Keshavarz, Parviz Gharib-Afshar, Fahimeh Amouzandeh, Khosrow Tabatabai, Mohammad Kahnemout, Susan Vaziri, Parviz Jafari, Mohammad Poursattar, Hamid Lighvani, Djamshid Sadri, Shahnaz Pakravan, Parviz Shahinkhoo, Ahmad Kashani, Eskandar Rafii, Firooz Bahjat Mohamadi, Sami Tahasonee, Ali Zandi, Bozorgmeh Rafia.
11/08/78

Cardena Perpetua
(Vicious Circle)
(Mexico)
COX. Dir, Arturo Ripstein; sp, Vicento Lenaro, Ripstein; cam, Jorge Stahl; mus, Miguel Pons. 90.
Pedro Armendariz Jr, Narciso Busquets, Ernesto Gomez Cruz, Ana Martin, Angelica Chain, Ana Ofelia Marguia, Roberto Cobo.
07/30/80

Carny
UA. Prod, Robbie Robertson. Exec prod, Jonathan Taplin. Dir, Robert Kaylor. Sp, Thomas Baum, based on a story by Phoebe Kaylor, Robert Kaylor, Robbie Robertson; cam (Technicolor), Harry Stradling Jr; mus, Alex North; edtr, Stuart Pappe; prodn des, William J Cassidy; art dir, Josan F Russo; set decor, Ray Molyneaux, Charles R Pierce; snd, Bill Kaplan; asst dir, William Scott; 2nd unit dir, Garth Craven. (MPAA rating: R). 105.
Gary Busey, Jodie Foster, Robbie Robertson, Meg Foster, Kenneth McMillan, Elisha Cook, Theodore Wilson, John Lehne, Tina Andrews, Bert Remsen, Alan Braunstein, Bill McKinney, Woodrow Pargrey, Craig Wasson.
05/21/80

Caro Michele
(Dear Michael)
(Italy)
CNZ. FLAG (Gianni Hecht Lucari) prodn. Dir, Martio Monicelli; sp, Suso Cecchi D'Amico, Tonino Guerra, based on Natalia Ginzburg novel; cam, Tonino Delli Colli; mus, Nino Rota. 108.
Mariangela Melato, Delphine Seyrig, Aurore Clement, Marcella Michelangeli, Lou Castel, Fabio Carpi.
07/14/76

Caro Papa
(Dear Papa)
(Italy)
AMLF. Dir, Dino Risi. Sp, Bernardino Zapponi, Marco Risi. Cam, Tonino Delli Colli; mus, Manuel De Sica. 110.
Vittorio Gassman, Aurore Clement, Andre Lachapelle, Stefano Madia, Julien Guiomar.
05/23/79

Carrie
UA. Prod, Paul Monash. Dir, Brian De Palma. Sp, Lawrence D Cohen, based on novel by Stephen King; cam (DeLuxe Color), Mario Tosi; edtr, Paul Hirsch; mus, Pino Dinaggio; art dir, William Kenny, Jack Fisk; set decor, Robert Gould; cos des, Rosanna Norton; snd, Dick Vorisek, Bertil Hallberg; stunt coord, Richard Weiker; asst dir, Donald Heitzer. (MPAA rating: R). 97.
Sissy Spacek, Piper Laurie, Amy Irving, William Katt, John Travolta, Nancy Allen, Betty Buckley, B J Soles, Sydney Lassick, Stefan Gierash, Priscilla Pointer, Michael Talbot, Cameron De Palma.
11/03/76

The Carrot Queen: SEE Reina Zanahoria

Carry On Emmannuelle
(Britain)
HMD. Thirtieth Film Prodns Limited prodn. Prod, Peter Rogers. Dir, Gerald Thomas. Sp, Lance Peters; cam, Alan Hume; edtr, Peter Boita; art dir, Jack Shampan, cos, Courtenay Elliott; mus, Eric Rogers; song, "Love Crazy," composed by Kenny Lynch, sung by Masterplan; prodn mgr, Roy Goddard; asst dir, Gregory Dark; snd, Danny Daniel. 88.
Suzanne Danielle, Kenneth Williams, Kenneth Connor, Jack Douglas, Joan Sims, Peter Butterworth, Larry Dann, Beryl Reid, Henry McGee, Howard Nelson, Albert Moses.
12/06/78

Carry on England
(Britain)
FRK. Peter Rogers prodn. Dir, Gerald Thomas. Sp, Jack Seddon, David Pursall; cam (Technicolor), Ernest Steward; edtr, Richard Marden. 89.
Kenneth Connor, Windsor Davies, Patrick Mower, Judy Geeson, Jack Douglas, Diane Langton, Melvyn Hayes, Joan Sims, Peter Jones, Peter Butterworth, David Lodge, Julian Holloway, Linda Hooks, Patricia Franklin, Vivienne Johnson, Barbara Rosenblat, Johnny Briggs, Brian Osborne, Larry Dann, Jeremy Connor, Barbara Hampshire, Tricia Newby, Jeannie Collings, Louise Burton, Linda Regan, Billy J Mitchell, Richard Bartlett, Peter Banks, Peter Quince, Richard Olley, Paul Toothill.
11/03/76

Casanova
(Italy)
TIT. Prod, Alberto Grimaldi for PEA. Dir, Federico Fellini. Sp, Fellini, Bernardino Zappone; cam (Eastmancolor), Giuseppe Rotunno; prodn des, Fellini; art dir, Danilo Donati; edtr, Ruggiero Mastroianni; mus, Nino Rota. 166.
Donald Sutherland, Tina Aumont, Cicely Browne, Olimpia Carlisi, Adele Angela Lojodice.
12/22/76

Casanova & Co.
(W Germany - Austria - Italy - France)
CRV. Neue Delta (Vienna)-Pan-Film (Vienna) - Panther Cinematografica (Rome) - COFCI (Paris) - TV 13 (Munich) film. Dir, Francois Legrand (Franz Antel). Prods, Antel, Carl Szokoll. Sp, Joshua Sinclair, Tom Priman; cam, Hans Matula; edtr, Michel Lewin; mus, Riz Ortolani. 100.
Tony Curtis, Marisa Berenson, Hugh Griffith, Marisa Mell, Britt Ekland, Jean Lefebvre, Andrea Ferreol, Umberto Orsini, Sylva Koscina, Victor Spinetti, Lillian Mueller, Werner Pochath, Olivia Pascal.
03/09/77

Cascabel
(The Rattlesnake)
(Mexico)
PEX. Conacine-Dasa Film prodn. Dir, Raul Araiza. Sp, Araiza, Jorge Patino, Antonio Monsel; cam (Eastmancolor), Rosalio Solano; edtr, Reynaldo Portillo. 108.
Ernesto Gomez Cruz, Paul Ramirez, Aaron Hernan, Sergio Jiminez, Hector Gomez, Norma Herrera.
08/31/77

Casey's Shadow
COL. Prod, Ray Stark; exec prod, Michael Levee. Dir, Martin Ritt. Sp, Carol Sobieski, based on short story, "Ruidoso", by John McPhee; cam (Metrocolor), John A Alonzo; edtr-2d unit dir, Sidney Levin; mus, Patrick Williams; prodn des, Robert Luthardt; set decor, Charles Pierce; snd, Al Overton Jr; cosward; Moss Mabry, Michael Harte, Gail Viola; asst dir, Ronald L Schwary. (MPAA rating: PG). 116.
Walter Matthau, Alexis Smith, Robert Webber, Murray Hamilton, Andrew A Rubin, Stephen Burns, Susan Myers, Michael Hershewe, Harry Caesar, Joel Fluellen, Whit Bissell.
03/08/78

The Cassandra Crossing

AVE. Associated General Films prodn; prod, Carlo Ponti; exec prod, Giancarlo Pettini. Dir, George Pan Cosmatos. Sp, Tom Mankiewicz, Robert Katz, Cosmatos, from a story by Katz, Cosmatos; cam (CFI Color), Ennio Guarnieri; special pho, Tazio Secciaroli; edtrs, Francois Bonnot, Roberto Silvi; mus, Jerry Goldsmith; art dir, Aurelio Crugnola; snd, Carlo Palmieri; cos-ward, Andriana Berselli, asst dir, Antonio Gabrielli. (MPAA rating: R). 126.
Sophia Loren, Richard Harris, Ava Gardner, Burt Lancaster, Martin Sheen, Ingrid Thulin, Lee Strasberg, John Philip Law, Ann Turkel, O J Simpson, Lionel Stander, Raymond Lovelock, Alida Valli, Lou Castel, Stefano Patrizi, Carlo De Majo, Fausta Avelli.
02/02/77

The Castaways of Turtle Island: SEE Les Naufrages De L'Ile De La Tortue

The Cat and the Canary
(Britain)
CSH. Prod, Richard Gordon. Dir, Radley Metzger. Sp, Metzger, based on John Willard play; asso prod, Ray Corbett; cam, Alex Thompson; edtr, Roger Harrison. 90.
Honor Blackman, Michael Callan, Edward Fox, Wendy Hiller, Olivia Hussey, Carol Lynley, Peter McEnery, Wilfrid Hyde-White.
11/22/78

The Cat From Outer Space

BV. Walt Disney Prodn. Prod, Ron Miller. Dir, co-prod, Norman Tokar. Sp, Ted Key; cam (Technicolor), Charles F Wheeler; edtr, Cotton Warburton; snd, Bud Maffett; mus, Lalo Schifrin; art dir, John B Mansridge, Preston Ames; asst dir, Gene Sultan; stunt coord, Richard Warlock; sfx, Eustace Lycett, Art Cruickshank, Danny Lee. (MPAA rating: G). 103.
Ken Berry, Sandy Duncan, Harry Morgan, Roddy McDowall, McLean Stevenson, Jesse White, Alan Young, Hans Conried, Ronnie Schell, James Hampton, Howard T Platt, William Prince.
06/21/78

Cat Murkil and the Silks
(Cruisin' High)
GMA. Pine-Thomas prodn. Prod, William C Thomas. Dir, John Bushelman. Sp, Thomas; cam, Bruce Logan; edtr, Jeff Bushelman; mus, Bernie Kaai Lewis. (MPAA rating: R). 102.
David Kyle, Steve Bond, Kelly Yaegermann, Rhodes Reason, Meegan King, Don Carter, Derrel Maury, Joe Reteria, Ruth Manning.
06/16/76

Catalan Cuckold: SEE Salut I Forca Al Canut

Catherine and Her Daughters: SEE Katerina A Jeji Deti

Cathy's Child
(Australia)
RDP. C B Films prodn. Prods, Pom Oliver, Errol Sullivan. Dir, Donald Crombie. Sp, Ken Quinnell from a book by Dick Wordley; cam, Gary Hansen; prodn des, Ross Major; snd, Tim Lloyd; edtr, Tim Wellburn; asst dirs, Mark Egerton, Mark Turnbull. 89.
Michelle Fawdon, Alan Cassell, Bryan Brown, Harry Michael, Anna Hruby, Bob Hughes, Sophia Haskas, Sarah McKenzie, Judy Stevenson, Bobbie Ward, Gerry Gallagher, Annibale Migliucci, Arthur Dignam, Willie Fennell.
05/02/79

Cauchmars
(Nightmares)
(France)
DGF. Wri-dir, Noel Simsolo. Cam (Eastmancolor), Armon Suarez; edtr, Khadicha Barha. 98.
Pierre Clementi, Helene Surgere, Beatrice Bruno, Dominique Erlanger, Monique Melinand, Andre Thorent.
05/14/80

Caudillo
(Spain)
X. Retasa prodn. Dir, Basilio Martin Patino. Cam, Alfredo F Mayo; edtr, Jose Luis Pelaez, Patino; mus, songs of the Spanish Civil War (sung by Franz Heiler, Pete Seeger, Charles Heden). 110.
(DOC)
07/06/77

Causa Kralik
(The Rabbit Case)
(Czechoslovakia)
CZS. Barrandov Studios prodn. Dir, Jaromil Jires. Sp, Jaroslav Dietl; cam (Eastmancolor), Jaromir Sofr; mus, Vadim Petrov. 85.
Milos Kopecky, Alena Vranova, Zlata Adamovska, Marie Brozova, Jaroslav Satoransky, Martin Ruzek.
05/28/80

Caution To The Wind: SEE Con El Culo Al Aire

The Cayman Triangle

X. Hefalump Pictures Inc. of Coral Gables feature. Prod-dir, Anderson Humphreys, asst, Ralph Clemente. sp, Humphreys, Clemente. Cam, Ed Paveitti, Tom Rooester, Egon Stephan; snd, Henri Lopez. (No MPAA Rating). 92.
Reid Dennis, John Morgan, Anderson Humphreys, Ed Beheler, Jules Kreitzer, Dale Reeves, Dick Barker, Mary Gillooly, Arek Joseph, Ryhal Gallagher, Ron Sinclair, Brian Uzzell, Bob Ankrom, Steve Foster, Tian Giri, Noel Spencer-Barnes, Michael Blackie, Emily Hector.
12/07/77

Ceddo
(Outsiders)
(Senegal)
DRV. Wri-dir, Ousmane Sembene. Cam (Eastmancolor), Georges Caristan; edtr, Florence Eymon; mus, Manu Dibango. 120.
Tabara Ndiaye, Moustapha Yade, Amadou Diagne Ndiaye.
06/01/77

Celestina
(Mexico)
PEX. Televisa prodn. Wri-dir, Miguel Sabido. Cam, Miguel Garson; edtr, Federico Landeros; mus, Marcos Lipshitz. 88.
Isela Vega, Ofelia Guilmain, Jose Galvez, Luigi Montefiore, Marcela Lopez Rey, Ana de Sade, Rosa Furman.
08/04/76

Cerromaior
(Portugal)
X. Prole Films prodn, Lisbon. Wri-dir, Luis Filipe Rocha, based on a novel by Manuel da Fonseca; cam, Joao Abel Aboim; mus, Constanca Capdeville; edtr, Jose Nascimento. 90.
Carlos Paulo, Santos Manuel, Clara Joana, Rui Fortado, Titus Faria, Elsa Wallenkamp.
10/15/80

C'Est La Vie!
(That's Life)
(France)
MK. Diagonale Productions prodn. Wri-dir, Paul Vecchiali; cam (Eastmancolor), Georges Strouve; mus, Roland Vincent. 90.
Chantal Delsaux, Jean-Christophe Bouvet, Cecile Clairval, Ingrid Bourgoin, Helene Surgere, Beatrice Bruno, Michel Delahaye.
09/03/80

C'Est La Vie Rose
(W Germany)
X. Distelfilm Berlin prodn, in collab with Second Television (ZDF), Mainz. Wri-dir, Hans-Christian Stenzel, with dialog by Joerg Fauser; cam, Lothar E Stickelbrucke; snd-edtr, Rosemarie Stenzel-Quast. 81.
I Sa Lo, Kurt Kalb, Hannah Wilke, John Cage, Jean Halbert, Hal James.
03/02/77

C'est pas moi c'est lui
(It's Not Me, It's Him)
(France)
CCF. Fideline Films prodn. Dir, Pierre Richard. Sp, Richard, Alain Godard; cam (Fujicolor), Claude Agostini; mus, Vladimir Cosma; edtr, Noelle Boisson; art dir, Jean-Baptiste Poiret; snd, Bernard Bats. 90.
Pierre Richard, Aldo Maccione, Valerie Mairesse, Henri Gardin.
02/27/80

Cet Age Sans Pitie
(This Age Without Pity)
(France)
RSH. Wri-dir, Edouard Niermans. Cam (Eastmancolor), Bernard Lutic; edtr, Yves Deschamp; mus, Alain Jomy. 90.
Bruno Cremer, Jean Bouise, Roland Bertin, Jean-Paul Dubois, Jerome Zucca.
05/14/80

Cet Obscure Objet Du Desir
(That Obscure Object of Desire)
(France)
GCC. Greenwich Films-Les Films Galaxie-In Cine prodn. Dir, Luis Bunuel. Sp, Bunuel, with collab of Jean-Claude Carriere; book, Pierre Louys; cam (Eastmancolor), Edmond Richard; edtr, Helene Plemiannikov; prod, Serge Silberman. (MPAA rating: R). 100.
Fernando Rey, Carole Bouquet, Angele Molina, Julien Bertheau, Andre Weber, Milena Vukotic, Pieral.
08/31/77

Cetiri Dana Do Smrti
(Four Days to Death)
(Yugoslavia)
YFR. Telefilm-Jadran Film-Viba Film prodn. Dir, Miroslav Jokic. Sp, Jokic, Ivan Potrc, Dejan Djurkovic, Slobodan Stojanovic; cam (Eastmancolor), Zivorad Milic; mus, Radomir Petrovic. 88.
Bert Sotlar, Predrag Ejdus, Fabijan Sovagovic, Ljuba Tadic.
08/25/76

Chain Reaction
(Australia)
HOY. Palm Beach Picture. Prod, David Elfick. Wri-dir, Ian Barry. Asso prods, George Miller, Ross Matthews. Prodn mgr, Lynn Gailey; asst dirs, Ross Matthews, Chris Maudson, P J Jones; cam, Russell Boyd; underwater pho, George Greenough; snd, Lloyd Carrick; art dir, Graham Walker; stunt coord, Max Aspin; edtr, Tim Tim Wellburn; mus, Andrew Thomas Wilson. 87.
Steve Bisley, Arna-Maria Winchester, Ross Thompson, Ralph Cotterill, Patrick Ward, Laurie Moran, Richard Moir, Hugh Keays-Byrne, Michael Long, Lorna Lesley.
04/23/80

Chajrchan Ondor Chaana Bajna
(Discover Turquoise Mountain)
(Mongolia - Czechoslovakia)
X. Mongolian-Czechoslovak Co-prodn. Dir, Najdangin Hjamdava and Ivo Toman. Sp, S Dashdorov, based on a story by Zdenek Braunschlaeger; cam, Josef Illik, D Batulga; mus, L Mordordzh. 90.
Josef Langmiler, D Elbegsajchan, Karel Hlusicka, D Dzanabadzar, S Ceceg, Slavka Budinova, Josef Vetrovec, Jan Kanyza.
08/16/78

The Challenge Of Greatness
IMX. Worldview Prodn prodn. Conceived-dir-prod, Herbert Kline. Commentary wri, Pierre Schneider, spoken by Orson Welles; cam (Eastmancolor), Derrett Williams, Arnold Eagle; mus, Michel Michelet. 140.
(DOC)
09/15/76

Chameleon
X. Jon Jost, Rising Sun Prodns prodn. Dir, Jon Jost. Sp, Bob Glaudini, Jost; cam, Jost. 90.
Bob Glaudini, Kathleen McKay, Ellen Blake, Lee Kissman.
09/20/78

The Champ
UA. MGM film. Prod, Dyson Lovell. Dir, Franco Zeffirelli. Sp, Walter Newman, based on a story by Frances Marion; cam (Metrocolor), Fred J Koenekamp; edtr, Michael J Sheridan; prodn des, Theoni V Aldredge; snd, Jerry Jost, William McCaughey, Aaron Rochin, Michael J Kohut; mus, Dave Grusin; asst dir, David Silver. (MPAA rating: PG). 121.
Jon Voight, Faye Dunaway, Ricky Schroder, Jack Warden, Arthur Hill, Strother Martin, Joan Blondell, Mary Jo Catlett, Elisha Cook.
03/28/79

Chance: SEE Szansa

Chance Meeting on the Ocean: SEE Spotkanie Na Atlantyku

The Changeling
(Canada)
AFD. Prods, Joel B Michaels, Garth H Drabinsky. Exec prods, Mario Kassar, Andrew Vajna. Dir, Peter Medak. Sp, William Gray, Diana Maddox, from a story by Russell Hunter; cam (Panavision), John Coquillon; prodn des, Trevor Williams; art dir, Reuben Freed; mus, Rick Wilkins; edtr, Lilla Ledersen; snd, Patrick Drummond, Dennis Drummond, Robert Grieve; sfx, Gene Grigg; asst dir, Irby Smith. (MPAA rating: R). 107.
George C Scott, Trish Van Devere, Melvin Douglas, John Colicos, Jean Marsh, Barry Morse, James Douglas, Madeleine Thornton-Sherwood, Roberta Maxwell, Bernard Behrens, Frances Hyland, Ruth Springford, Helen Burns, Eric Christmas.
02/20/80

The Chant Of Jimmie Blacksmith
(Australia)
FAP. Wri-dir-prod, Fred Schepisi from the book by Thomas Keneally. Cam (Eastmancolor-C'scope), Ian Baker; edtr, Brian Kavanaugh. 122.
Tommy Lewis, Freddy Reynolds, Ray Barrett, Jack Thompson, Peter Carroll, Elizabeth Alexander.
05/31/78

Chantons Sous L'Occupation
(Singing During the Occupation)
(France)
ARS. Argos Films-Les Films Armorial-INA prodn. Conceived-dir, Andre Halimi. Addl cam (Eastmancolor), Jean Rouch; edtr, Henri Colpi; commentary, Halimi spoken by Pascal Mazzoti. 87.
(DOC)
04/14/76

Chapeau Claque
(Top Hat)
(W Germany)
GLA. Baerenfilm prodn, Berlin. Wri-dir, Ulrich Schamoni. Cam, Igor Luther; snd, Christian Moldt, Reiner Lorenz; edtr, Regine Heuser; art dir, Gyorgy Janoschka; prodn mgr, Regina Ziegler. 90.
Ulrich Schamoni, Anna Henkel, Juergen Barz, Alix Buchen, Karl Dall, Peter Ehlebracht, Ingo Insterburg, Wolfgang Neuss, Peter Schlesinger, Erika Skrotzki, Rudi Unger, Ben Wargin, Rolf Zacher.
02/16/77

Chapter Two
COL. Ray Stark prodn. Dir, Robert Moore; sp, Neil Simon, based on his play; cam, David M Walsh; exec prod, Roger M Rothstein; mus, Marvin Hamlisch; lyr, Carole Bayer Sager; prodn des, Gene Callahan; edtr, Michael A Stevenson; asst dir, Jack Roe; art dir, Pete Smith; set decor, Lee Poll; sfx, Sam Dockrey; unit pa, Scott McDonough. (MPAA rating: PG). 124.
James Caan, Marsha Mason, Joseph Bologna, Valerie Harper, Judy Farrell, Debra Mooney, Isabel Cooley, Imogene Bliss, Larry Michlin, Ray Young, George Rondo, Cheryl Bianchi, Greg Zadikov, Paul Singh, Elizabeth Farley, Sunday Brennan, Danny Gellis, Carl Jones, Henry Sutton, D Miller, Howard Jeffrey, Marie Reynolds.
012/12/79

Charles et Lucie
(France)
CYT. Cythere Films/Films de la Chouette/Antenne 2/Tele Europe co-prodn. Prod, Claude Makovski. Dir, Nelly Kaplan. Sp, Kaplan, Jean Chapot, Makovski; cam (Eastmancolor), Gilbert Sandoz; edtr, Gerard Le Du; snd, Guy Villette; mus, Pierre Perret. 97.
Daniel Ceccaldi, Ginette Garcin, Belen (Nelly Kaplan), Jean-Marie Proslier.
09/26/79

Charleston
(Italy)
ANY. Prod, Elio Scardamaglia. Dir, Marcello Fondato. Sp, Scardamaglia, Fondato; mus, Guido & Maurizio De Angelis; US snd, Fred De Croce. 77.
Bud Spencer, Herbert Lom, James Coco.
12/20/78

Charlie Bravo
(France)
GAU. Shagrila Productions/Gaumont co-prodn. Dir, Claude Bernard-Aubert; sp, Bernard-Aubert, Pascal Jardin; cam (Eastmancolor), Pierre Fattori; edtr, Gabriel Rongier, Robert Rongier; snd, Lucien Yvonnet; mus, Alain Goraguer. 104.
Bruno Pradal, Jean-Francois Poron, Karine Verlier, Gerard Boucaran, Georges Chelon.
07/30/80

Charlotte Loewenskoeld
(Charlotte Lionshield)
(Switzerland)
SNA. Swedish TV Channel Goetenburg/AB Sandrew Film & Teater prodn. Based on Selma Lagerloef's novels "Charlotte Lionshield" and "Anna Svaerd". Sp, Begt Bratt; dir, Jackie Soederman; cam (Eastmancolor), Rune Ericson; exec prod, Bo Berndtson; edtr, Leif Gummesson; prodn des, Ingemar Wiberg; mus, Eskil Hemberg. 119.
Ingard Janbell, Lars Green, Gunnel Brostroem, Gunnar Bjoernstrand, Sickan Carlsson,

Sven Wollter, Arja Saijonmaa, Christina Stenius.
12/26/79

Charly og Steffen
(Charly and Steffen)
(Denmark)
EUR. Merry prodn. Story-sp, Bent Rasmussen, Henning Kristiansen; dir, Kristiansen; cam (Eastmancolor), Peter Klitgaard; prodn des, Sven Wickman; edtrs, Kristiansen, Sven Methling, Merete Brunsendorff; mus, Jacob Groth. 83.
Kim E Larsen, Allan Olsen, Ghita Noerby, Pia Rosenbaum, Lone Kellermann.
12/26/79

The Charter Trip: SEE
Saellskapsresan

Chatter-Box
AIP. Lips Prodn. Prod, Bruce Cohn Curtis. Dir, Tom De Simone. Sp, Mark Rosin, Norman Yonemoto, from story by De Simone; asso prod, John Williams; cam, Tak Fujimoto; mus, scored-cond, Fred Karger; songs, Michael Hazlewood; edtr, William Marlin. (MPAA rating: R). 73.
Candice Rialson, Larry Gelman, Jane Kean, Perry Bullington, Arlene Martell, Michael Taylor, Cynthia Hoppenfield, Robert Lipton, Rip Taylor, Professor Irwin Corey, Sandra Gould, Trent Dolan.
02/23/77

Chaussette Surprise
(Surprise Sock)
(France)
GCC. Clap 7, SFP, Pebby Guisez prodn. Prod-dir, Jean-Francois Davy. Sp, Davy, Jean-Claude Carriere; cam (Eastmancolor), Jacques Guerin; edtr, Thierry Derocles; mus, Marie-Paule Belle. 95.
Bernadette Lafont, Anna Karina, Christine Pascal, Michel Galabru, Bernard Haller, Rufus, Claude Pieplu.
06/21/78

The Cheap Detective
COL. Dir, Robert Moore. Sp, Neil Simon; cam (Metrocolor), John A Alonzo; edtrs, Sidney Levin, Michael A Stevenson; mus, Patrick Williams; prodn des, Robert Luthardt; art dir, Phillip Bennett; set decor, Charles Pierce; snd, Bill McCaughey, Mike Kohut, Lyle Burbridge, Al Overton Jr; cos-ward, Theoni V Aldredge, John A Anderson, Agnes G Henry; asst. dir, John C Chulay. (MPAA rating: PG). 92.
Peter Falk, Ann-Margaret, Eileen Brennan, Sid Caesar, Stockard Channing, James Coco, Dom DeLuise, Louise Fletcher, John Houseman, Madeline Kahn, Fernando Lamas, Marsha Mason, Phil Silvers, Abe Vigoda, Paul Williams, Nicol Williamson, Emory Bass, Carmine Caridi, Scatman Crothers, Vic Tayback.
06/07/78

Cheaper To Keep Her
AMC. Prod, Lenny Isenberg; dir, Ken Annakin; prod, Jerry Frankel; sp, Timothy Harris, Herschel Weingrod; cam (Metrocolor), Roland (Ozzie) Smith; edtr, Edward Warschilka; snd (Fast) Eddie Mahler; mus, Dick Halligan; set decor, Charles Rutherford; asst dir, Rafael Elortegui. (MPAA rating: R). 92.
Mac Davis, Tovah Feldshuh, Art Metrano, Ian McShane, Priscilla Lopez, Rose Marie, Jack Gilford, J Pat O'Malley.
09/24/80

Check to the Queen: SEE
Jacque A La Dama

Cheech And Chong's Next Movie
U. C&C Brown Prodn film. Prod, Howard Brown. Dir, Thomas Chong. Sp, Chong, Cheech Marin; cam (Technicolor), King Baggot; edtr, Scott Conrad; mus, Mark Davis; prodn des, Fred Harpman; set decor, Bob Benton; snd, Darin Knight, Bill McCaughey, Bob Harman; asst dir, Newton Arnold; spec visual effects, Albert Whitlock; ani des, Paul Power; asso prod, Peter MacGregor-Scott. (MPAA rating: R). 99.
Richard Marin, Thomas Chong, Evelyn Guerrero, Betty Kennedy, Sy Kramer, Rikki Marin, Bob McClurg, Edie McClurg, Paul Reubens.
07/23/80

Cheech and Chong's Up In Smoke: SEE *Up In Smoke*

Chelsia My Love
(Hong Kong)
GHV. Dir, Sung Cheng Shou. 96.
Chelsia Chan, Kenny Bee.
09/22/76

Chere Inconnue
(I Sent A Letter To My Love)
(France)
GAU. Cineproduction prodn. Prods, Lise Fayolle, Giorgio Silvagni. Dir, Moshe Mizrahi. Sp, Mizrahi, Gerard Brach, based on the novel "I Sent A Letter To My Love" by Bernice Rubens. Cam, Ghislain Cloquet. Edtr, Francoise Bonnot. Mus, Philippe Sarde. Snd, Michel Vionnet, Claude Villand. Art dir, Bernard Evein. 96.
Simone Signoret, Jean Rochefort, Delphine Seyrig, Genevieve Fontanel, Dominique Labourier.
05/21/80

The Chess Player: SEE
Shatranj Ke Khilari

Chevelok Ukhodit Za Ptitsami
(The Man Who Loves the Birds)
(USSR)
SOV. Uzbekistan Studios prodn. Dir, Ali Khamraev. Sp, Timur Zulfikarov; cam (Sovcolor), Yuri Klimenko. 88.
D Kambarova, N Avazova, M Abzalov.
01/26/77

Chez Nous
(Sweden)
SNA. Swedish Film Institute (prodn head Bengt Forslund)/HB Three Leaf Clover prodn. Dir, Jan Halldoff. Story-script, based on their own stage play, Anders Ehnmark, P O Enquist; cam (Eastmancolor), Jack Churchill; prodn des, Anders Barreus; mus, quotes from the classics; edtr, Wic Kjellin; exec prod, Jutta Ekman. 95.
Ewa Froling, Ernst Gunther, Sven Lindberg, Ernst-Hugo Jaeregard, Ingvar Kjellson, Lis Nilheim.
09/20/78

Chhatrabhang
(The Divine Plan)
(India)
X. Asha Sheth prodn, with support of the Vashketu Foundation. Prod, Nina Shivdasani; prodn head, Naaz Rovshen. Wri-dir-edtr, Nina Shivdasani; cam, Apurba Kishore Bir; mus, Edgar Varese; snd, Hitendra Ghosh. Commentary written by Vinay Shukla, spoken by Amrish Puri. 80.
(DOC)
07/14/76

KTQ. Sp-dir-edtr, Jerry Blumenthal, Suzanne Davenport, Sharon Karp, Jennifer Rohrer, Gordon Quinn; cam (b&w), Quinn, Rohrer, Davenport; commentator, Rohrer. 60.
Beatrice Tucker, personnel of the Chicago Maternity Center, members of WATCH (Women Act to Control Healthcare), Scharene Miller and her family and friends.
(DOC) (B & W) (16m)
05/02/79

The Chicken Chronicles
AVE. Prod, Walter Shenson. Dir, Francis Simon. Sp, Paul Diamond, based on his novel; cam (CFI Color), Matthew F Leonetti; edtr, George Folsey Jr; mus, Kan Lauber; art dir, Ray Markham; snd, William McCaughey, Aaron Rochin, Michael J Kohut, Carey Lindley; cos-ward, Richalene Kelsay, Sandra Burke; asst dir, Jack Baran. (MPAA rating: PG). 92.
Phil Silvers, Ed Lauter, Steven Guttenberg, Lisa Reeves, Meredith Baer, Branscombe Richmond, Will Seltzer, Kutee, Gino Baffa, Robert Resnick, Joe Medalis, Robin T Williams.
10/19/77

Chiedo Asilo
(My Asylum)
(Italy)
GAU. Prod, 23 June-ASM Productions-Best Int'l Film. Dir, Marco Ferreri; sp, Gerard Brach; cam (Eastmancolor), Pasquale Rachini; art dir, Enrico Manelli; edtr, Mauro Bonanni; mus, Philippe Sarde. 105.
Robert Benigni, Dominique Laffin.
01/16/80

Chikuzan Hitori Tabi
(The Life of Chikuzan)
(Japan)
TOH. Kindai Eiga Kyokai prodn. Exec prods, Susumu Takashima, Sadaki Sato, Setsuo Noto, Manabu Akashi. Wri-dir, Kaneto Shindo. Cam, Kiyomi Kuroda; mus, Hikaru Hayashi. 122.

Chikuzan Takahashi, Ryuzo Hayashi, Nobuko Otowa, Dai Kanai, Mitsuko Baisho, Yoshie Shimamura, Hideo Kanze, Takuzo Kawatani, Mutsuhiro Toura, Taiji Tonoyama, Hosei Komatsu, Hiroko Isayama, Kei Sato.
07/27/77

Child of the Night: SEE L'Enfant De La Nuit

The Child Woman: SEE La Femme-Enfant

The Children
WNO. Albright Films prodn. Prod, Carlton J Albright; co-prod-dir, Max Kalmanowicz. Sp, Albright, Edward Terry; cam, Barry Abrams; edtr, Nikki Wessling; mus, Henry Manfredini; snd, W A Grive-Smith; make-up, Carla White; asst dir, William Medsher. (MPAA rating: R) 90.
Martin Shakar, Gil Rogers, Gale Garnett, Jessie Abrams, Tracy Griswold, Joy Glaccum, Suzanne Barnes, Rita Montone, Michell Le Mothe, Shannon Bolin, Clara Evans, Jeptha Evans, Sarah Albright, Nathanael Albright, Julie Carrier, Edward Terry.
07/09/80

The Children From Blue Lake Mountain: SEE Barna fran Blasjofjaellet

The Children from No. 67: SEE Die Kinder Aus No. 67

Children of Agony: SEE Smertens Boern

Children Of Babylon
(Jamaica)
JDJ. Rainbow Prodns Ltd prodn. Prod-dir-sp-edtr-lyr, Lennie Little-White. cam, Franklyn St Juste; mus, Harold Butler; lyr, Little-White; prodn mgr, Peter Packer; snd, Oscar Lawson. 122.
Tobi, Don Parchment, Bob Andy, Leonie Forbes, Elizabeth de Lisser.
10/08/80

Children of Labor
X. CD Film Workshop presentation. Dir-sp-cam-edtrs, Noel Buckner, Mary Dore, Richard Broadnan, Al Gedricks. 58.
(DOC)
09/28/77

The Children of Oblivion: SEE Les Enfants de L'Oubli

The Children of Sanchez
(US - Mexico)
LOS. Hall Bartlett Films prodn. Dir, Hall Bartlett; sp, Cesare Zavattini, Bartlett from the book by Oscar Lewis; cam, Gabriel Figueroa; mus, Chuck Mangione. 126.
Anthony Quinn, Lupita Ferrer, Dolores Del Rio, Stathis Giallelis, Lucia Mendez, Duncan Quinn, Katy Jurado.
09/20/78

Children of the Warriors: SEE Krigernes Boern

Children of the Wind: SEE Aulad El Rih

The Children Of Theatre Street
(US - USSR)
EMF. Dir, Robert Dornhelm. Asso prod, Jean Dalrymple. Artistic dir, Oleg Briansky; edtr, Tina Frese. Narr-wri, Beth Gutcheon, spoken by Princess Grace of Monaco. (MPAA rating: G). 100.
Angelina Armelskaya, Alex Timoushin, Lena Voronzova, Michaela Cerna, Galina Messenzeva, Konstantine Zaklinsky, students and faculty of the Vaganova Choreographic Institute.
(DOC)
04/27/77

The Children Song Festival - The Movie: SEE Hasereth Festival Hayeladim

Chin Chin El Teporocho
(Chin Chin, the Drunken Bum)
(Mexico)
CIM. Conacine, STPC, RM prodn. Dir, Gabriel Retes. Sp, Armando Ramirez; cam (Eastmancolor), Daniel Lopez; edtr, Eufemio Rivera; mus, Manuel Esperon. 107.
Carlos Chavez, Jorge Santoyo, Jorge Balzaretti, Abel Wollrich, July Furlong, Diana Bracho.
08/25/76

China 9, Liberty 37
(Italy)
TIT. CEA prodn. Prods, Gianni Bozzacchi, Valerio de Paolis. Dir, Monte Hellman. 94.
Fabio Testi, Warren Oates, Jenny Agutter.
08/23/78

The China Syndrome
COL. Michael Douglas/IPC Films prodn. Exec prod, Bruce Gilbert. Prod, Michael Douglas. Dir, James Bridges. Sp, Mike Gray, T S Cook, Bridges; cam (Metrocolor), James Crabe; prodn dsgn, George Jenkins; edtr, David Rawlins; set decor, Arthur Jeph Parker; snd, Willie Burton; cos, Donfeld; sfx, Henry Millar Jr; asst dir, Kim Kurumada. (MPAA rating: PG). 122.
Jane Fonda, Jack Lemmon, Michael Douglas, Scott Brady, James Hampton, Peter Donat, Wilford Brimley, Richard Herd, Daniel Valdez, Stan Bohrman, James Karen.
03/07/79

Chinatown Kid
(Hong Kong)
SHW. Run Run Shaw prodn. Exec prod, Chen Lieh. Prod, Mona Fong. Dir, Chang Cheh. Sp, Yi Kuang, James Wong, Chang Cheh; cam, Kung Mo To; edtr, Chiang Hsing-lung; art dir, Tsao Chuang sheng. 100.
Alexander Fu Sheng, Shirley Yu, Shaw Yin-yin, Kuo Chue, Sun Chien, Lo Meng, Tsai Hung.
12/07/77

The Chinese Miracle: SEE Das Chinesische Wunder

Chinesisches Roulett
(Chinese Roulette)
(W Germany)
LML. Films Du Losange-Alabatross Produktion-Multicine prodn. Wri-dir, Rainer Werner Fassbinder. Cam (Eastmancolor), Michael Ballhaus; edtr, Ila Von Hasperg; mus, Peer Raben. 96.
Margit Carstensen, Ulli Lommel, Anna Karina, Alexander Allerson, Andrea Schober, Macha Meril, Brigitte Mira, V Spengler.
12/01/76

Chinois, Encore un Effort Pour Etre Revolutionaires
(Peking Duck Soup)
(France)
X. Films des Iles/Edo Elga prodn. Dir, Rene Vienet, Ji Qing-ming. Mao Tse-Tung, Chiang Ch'ing, Lin Pao. 120.
(DOC)
11/16/77

Chitegu Chinte
(The Restless Corpse)
(India)
LKS. Dir, M S Sathyu. Sp, Javed Siddiqui; cam (Eastmancolor), Ashok Gunjal; edtr, Chakraborty; mus, G K Venkstesh. 129.
C R Simha, Manjula, Ram Prakash.
01/31/79

Chiwit Batsop
(Stupid Life)
(Thailand)
MVS. Prods, Permpon Choyaroon, Choosung Sonimsart. Wri-dir-pho-edtr, Permpon Choyaroon. Exec prod, Patpong Choyaroon. Art dir, Pakorn Pomwitat; snd recordng, Siam Pattana Lab; cos, Sawet Parichat; mus dir, Seksan Sominsat; title song, "Chiwit Batsop," mus-lyrics, Seksan Sominsat, sung, Suda Chuenban. 125.
Sorapong Chatri, Piathip Kumvongse, Tongta Ratanapanoo, Pinyo Panui, Rachan Rajanamak, Tolap Kampusiri, Somchai, Matta Puaphan, Panit Mama, Somchai Srikrung, Supong Tangtongmit, Pramuan Issarapoonchai.
06/22/77

Chocolate Eclair: SEE Eclair au Chocolat

The Choice: SEE Le Choix

The Choirboys
U. Lorimar-Airone prodn. Prods, Merv Adelson, Lee Rich; exec prods, Pietro and Mario Bregni, Mark Damon. Dir, Robert Aldrich. Sp, Christopher Knopf, based on the novel by Joseph Wambaugh; cam (Technicolor), Joseph Biroc; edtrs, Maury Winetrobe, William Martin, Irving Rosenblum; mus, Frank DeVol; prodn des, Bill Kenney; set decor, Raphael Bretton; snd, William McCaughey, James Contreras; cos-ward, Tom Dawson, Yvonne Kubis; asst dir, Malcolm Harding. (MPAA rating: R). 119.
Charles Durning, Louis Gossett Jr, Perry King, Clyde Kusatsu, Stephen Macht, Tim McIntyre, Randy Quaid, Chuck Sacci, Don Stroud, James Woods, Burt Young, Robert Webber,

Jeanie Bell, Blair Brown, Michele Carey, Charles Haid, Joe Kapp, Barbara Rhoades, Jim Davis, Phyllis Davis, Jack DeLeon, George Di Cenzo, David Spielberg, Vic Tayback, Michael Wills, Susan Batson, Claire Brennen.
12/21/77

Chomana Dudi
(Choma's Drum)
(India)
X. Dir, B V Karanth. 120.
Vasudeva Rao.
(B & W)
07/28/76

Chomps
AIP. Hanna-Barbera/AIP Prodn. Prod, Joseph Barbera. Dir, Don Chaffey; exec prod, Samuel Z Arkoff; sp, Dick Robbins, Duane Poole, Joseph Barbera from a story by Barbera; cam, Charles F Wheeler; edtr, Waner Leighton, Dick Darling; mus, Hoyt Curtin; set decor, Tony Montenaro; snd, Keith Wester; asst dir, Al Nicholson. (MPAA rating: G). 89.
Wesley Eure, Valerie Bertinelli, Conrad Bain, Chuck McCann, Red Buttons, Larry Bishop, Hermione Baddeley, Jim Backus, Robert Q Lewis, Regis Toomey.
12/26/79

The Chosen One: SEE El Elegido

Chotisi Baat
(A Little Affair)
(India)
X. B R Films prodn; prod, B R Chopra. Dir, Basu Chatterji. Sp, Chatterji. Cam, K K Mahajan. 120.
Ashok Kumar, Amol Palekar, Vidya Sinha, Asrani, Nandita Thakur, Rajan, Haksar.
01/19/77

Chrissomaloussa
(The Girl with Golden Hair)
(Greece)
LYC. Dir, Tony Lycouressis. Sp, Stratis Karras, Lycouressis; cam (Eastmancolor), Andreas Bellis; edtr, George Triandafillou. 98.
Anotonis Katsaris, Vera Krouska, Vangelis Kazan, T A Velloudios.
05/23/79

Christ Stopped at Eboli: SEE Cristo si e fermato a Eboli

Christian the Lion
(Britain)
Sl. Bill Travers-James Hill prodn. Wri-prod-dir, Travers and Hill. Cam, Simon Trevor; edtr, Andrew Borthwick; narrs, Travers, Virginia McKenna; mus, Pentangle. (MPAA rating: G). 89.
Bill Travers, Virginia McKenna, George Adamson, Terence Adamson, Anthony Bourke, John Rendall.
12/15/76

Christiania
(Denmark)
DAI. Filmpol I/S (with State Film Institute support) prodn. Dirs, Ove Nyholm Christiansen, Fleming Colstrup. Cam, Dirk Bruel. Cartoon sequence des and ani, Solvognen, Arne Wurgler; mus, Gasolin, Hanegal; edtr, Soeren Christensen. 103.
Teit Jorgensen, Gregers Nielsen, Frank Paulsen, Anders Soerensen, Sv. Christensen, Rene Jalford, Linda Nysted, Marianne Troutman.
(DOC) (16m)
06/01/77

Chronicle of a Latin-American Subversive: SEE Cronica De Un Subversivo Latino-Americano

Chronicle Of An Industrialist: SEE Cronica de Um Industrial

Chuen Chulamoon
(Happy Confusion)
(Thailand)
NFT. Prod, Kiat lampungporn. Dir-edtr, Piac Poster. Story, Boonyarat; sp, Vitsanusit; cam, Chone Bunnag; snd, Maitree Janjarasskul; mus, 110.
Pairoj Sangborivutr, Lalana Sulawan, Chandra Napaporn, Somkuan Krajamsart, Somkid Sapsamluay, Jirasak Issarangkul Na Ayudhya, Prasert Srisomsak.
09/06/78

Chui Petela
(Hark to the Cock)
(Bulgaria)
BGO. BulgaroFilm prodn, Sredets Group, Sofia. Dir, Stefan Dimitrov. Sp, Konstantin Pavlov; cam, Emil Wagenstein; art dir, Nikolai Surchadjiev; mus, Georgi Genkov. 90.
Nikolai Binev, Nevena Kokanova, Ivan Tsvetarski, Elena Kuneva.
05/31/78

Chuquiago
(Bolivia)
X. Ukamau Prodn. Dir, Antonio Eguino. Sp, Oscar Soria; cam, Fuguino, Julio Lencina; edtrs, Deborah Shaffer, Susane Fern. 87.
Nestor Yulra, Edmundo Villarreoi, David Santalla, Taliana Aponte.
11/08/78

Churning: SEE Manthan

Chuvanna Vithukal
(Red Seedlings)
(India)
PDI. Wri-dir, P A Backer. Cam (b&w), Vipin Das; edtr, Ravi; mus, Devera Jan. 88.
Rehamn, Shanta Kumari, Zeenath, Nilambur Ayesha.
01/31/79

Chuvas de Verao
(A Summer Rain)
(Brazil)
X. Alter Filmes prodn. Prod, Luis Fernando Goulart. Dir-wri, Carlos Diegues. Cam, Jose Meteiros; edtr, Mair Tavares. 87.
Jofre Soares, Rodolfo Arena, Cristina Ache, Luiz Antonio, Paolo Cesar Pereio.
(Portuguese soundtrack; English subtitles)
03/26/80

Ciao, Les Mecs
(Ciao, You Guys)
(France)
SLN. Alpes Cinema-Paris-Cannes Prodn-Ginis Film prodn. Dir, Sergio Gobbi. Sp, Enrico Oldoini. Cam (Eastmancolor), Jean Badal; snd, Paul Habans; edtr, Gabriel Rongier; mus, Paul-Jean Borowsky. 100.
Gerard Herold, Anne Lonnberg, Charles Aznavour, Jean Piat, Dany Saval, Michel Galabru, Roland Dubillard.
05/16/79

Cinco Tenedores
(Five Forks)
(Spain)
X. Bridas S A prodn for Izaro Films. Dir, Fernando Fernan Gomez. Sp, Esmeralda Adam, Manuel Ruiz Castillo; cam (Eastmancolor), Carlos Suarez; mus, Anton Garcia Abril; edtr, Rosa Salgado. Exec prod, Juan L Isasi. 95.
Concha Velasco, Jose Sazatornil, Rafael Alonso, Agustin Gonzalez, William F Sully, Manuel de Benito, Alicia Sanchez, Manuel de Blas, Maribel Ayuso, Ana Frigola.
03/05/80

Cinderella
G1. Prod, Charles Band. Dir, Michael Pataki. Exec prods, Lenny Shabes, Ronald Domont; sp, Frank Ray Perilli; edtr, Laurence Jacobs; cam, Joseph Mangine; mus, Andrew Belling; lyr, Lee Arries; chor, Russell Clark. (MPAA rating: X). 94.
Cheryl Smith, Kirk Scott, Brett Smiley, Sy Richardson, Yana Nirvana, Marilyn Corwin. Jennifer Doyle, Buckley Norris, Pamela Stonebrook.
06/08/77

Cine Follies
(France)
FLG. Conceived-dir, Philippe Collin. Edtr, Jocelyne Triquet; prod, Bernard Marescot. 90.
(B & W)
02/16/77

Cinema Cinema
(USA - France)
X. Shahab International Prodn Assoc presentation. Prod, Shahab Ahmed. Dir, Krishna Shah; sp, Krishna Shah; Hindi script, Kamleshwar; cam, K K Mahajan; mus, Vijay Raghav Rao; edtr, Amit Bose; snd, Minno Tampal; set des, Ram Mohan; res cnslts, B D Garga, P K Nair, Chindananda Das Gupta; exec prod, Bhupendra Shah. 102.
Dharmendra, Hema Malini, Amitabh Bachchan, Zeenat Aman, Kim, Mushtaque Merchant, Dinyar Contractor, Hoshidar Kambhatta, Kanchan Mattu, Sharad Bhagtani, Amar Sneh,

Bishan Khanna, Hriday Lani, Momin Khan, Bobby Grewal, Phonsuk, Dharam Veer, Manmauji, Payal Paryez, Babu, Shyam Awasthe, Dev Sharma, Nandu.
11/28/79

Circle Of Iron
AVE. Sandy Howard/Richard St Johns prodn. Exec prod, St Johns. Prods, Paul Maslansky, Howard. Dir, Richard Moore. Sp, Stirling Silliphant, Stanley Mann, based on a story by Bruce Lee, James Coburn, Silliphant; cam (CFI color), Ronnie Taylor; edtr, Ernie Walter; prodn des, Johannes Larsen; cos des, Lilly Fenichel; snd, Cyril Collick; tech advisor, Kam Yuen; asst dir, Nissim Levy. (MPAA rating: R). 102.
David Carradine, Jeff Cooper, Roddy McDowall, Eli Wallach, Erica Creer, Christopher Lee, Anthony De Longis, Earl Maynard.
01/24/79

Circle Of Two
(Canada)
FCD. In asso with Jerome Simon and Milton Zysman prodns. Prod, Henk Van der Kolk. Dir, Jules Dassin. Exec prod, Bill Marshall. Sp, Thomas Hedley, based on "A Lesson in Love" by Marie Terese Baird; cam, Lazlo George; prodn des, Claude Bonniere; art dir, Francois de Lucy; edtr, David Nichols; snd, Owen Langevin; mus, Paul Hoffert; asst dir, Timothy Rowse. 105.
Richard Burton, Tatum O'Neal, Nuala FitzGerald, Robin Gammell, Patricia Collins, Kate Reid, Donann Cavin, Michael Wincott, Norma Dell'Agnese.
05/28/80

Circles: SEE Ma'Agalim

The Circus Tent: SEE Thampu

Citizens Band
PAR. Fields Company prodn. Exec prod, Shep Fields. Dir, Jonathon Demme. Sp, Paul Brickman; cam (Movielab Color), Jordon Cronenweth; edtr, John F Link II; mus, Bill Conti; prodn des, Bill Malley; set decor, Ira Bates; snd, John K Wilkinson, Gene Cantamesse; cos, Jodie Lynn Tillen; asst dir, Charles Okun. 98.
Paul Le Mat, Candy Clark, Ann Wedgeworth, Bruce McGill, Marcia Rodd, Charles Napier, Alix Elias, Roberts Blossom, Richard Bright, Ed Begley Jr, Michael Rothman, Michael Mahler, Harry Northrup, Will Seltzer.
04/20/77

City of My Dreams: SEE Mina droemmars stad

City of Women: SEE La Citta' Delle Donne

City On Fire
(Canada)
AST. Astral Bellevue Pathe prodn. Exec prods, Sandy Howard, Harold Greenberg. Prod, Claude Heroux. Dir, Alvin Rakoff. Sp, Jack Hill, David P Lewis, Celine LaFreniere; cam, Rene Verzier; mus, William McCauley, Matthew McCauley; edtr, Jean-Pol Passet, Jacques Clairoux; snd, Patrick Rousseau. 104.

Barry Newman, Susan Clark, Shelley Winters, Leslie Nielsen, James Franciscus, Ava Gardner, Henry Fonda, Jonathan Welsh.
05/23/79

Clair de Femme
(Womanlight)
(France - Italy - Germany)
GAU. Films Gibe-Films Corona (Paris)/Parva Cinematografica (Rome)/Film Produktion Janus (Frankfurt) co-prodn. Prod, Georges-Alain Vuille. Wri-dir, Constantine Costa-Gavras, based on the novel by Romain Gary. Cam, Ricardo Aranovich; art dirs, Mario Chiari, Eric Simon; snd, Pierre Gamet; mus, Jean Musy; edtr, Francoise Bonnot. 105.
Romy Schneider, Yves Montand, Romolo Valli, Lila Kedrova, Heinz Bennent.
09/26/79

Clan of the White Lotus
(Hong Kong)
SHF. Prod, Run Run Shaw. Exec prod, Mona Fong. Dir, Lo Lieh. Sp, Wong Tien; cam, Ao Chin-chin; edtrs, Chiang Hsing-lung, Li Yinhoi, mus, Eddie Wang; art dir, Johnson Tasao; martial arts instructor, Liu Chia-liang; make-up, Wu Hsu-ching. 95.
Liu Chia-hui, Lo Lieh, Hui Ying-hung, Huang Lung-wei, Lin Hui-huang, Ching Chu, Li Baihsiang.
06/11/80

Clans of Intrigue
(Hong Kong)
SHW. Runme Shaw prodn. Dir-Chu Yuan. Sp, Ku Lung; cam, Huang Chieh; martial arts instructor, Tang Chia; edtr, Ching Hsing-lung; art dir, Chen Ching-shen. 100.
Tien Ching, Ti Lung, Yueh Hua, Nora Miao, Liu Hui-ling, Pei Ti, Li Ching, Ling Yun, Yen Nan-hsi.
04/20/77

Clarence and Angel
GDR. Robert Gardner Representative-Clarence and Angel Productions prodn. Wri-dir, Robert Gardner; cam, Doug Harris; edtr, Jonathan Weld; mus, Philip Wilson. 72.
Darren Brown, Mark Cardova.
(16m)
08/20/80

Clark
(Denmark)
CTT. Steen Herdel prodn. Dir, Poul Martinsen. Wri, Martinsen in collab with Clark Olofsson; cam (Eastmancolor), Dirk Bruel, Morten Brugs, Michael Christensen, Dan Holmberg, Jan Weincke; edtrs, Henrik Carlsen, Niels Arild; mus, Gunner Moeller Pedersen. 113.
09/21/77

The Class of Miss MacMichael
(Britain - USA)
BRU. Kettledrum-Brut prodn. Exec prod, George Barrie. Dir, Silvio Narizzano. Prod-sp, Judd Bernard from the book by Sandy Hutson; cam (Technicolor), Alex Thomason; edtr, Max Benedict; mus, Stanley Myers. (MPAA rating: R). 100.
Glenda Jackson, Oliver Reed, Michael Murphy, Rosalind Cash, John Standing,

Riba Akabusi, Phil Daniels, Patrick Murray, Silvia O'Donnel.
09/13/78

Claude Francois: Le Film de Sa Vie
(Claude Francois; The Film Of His Life)
(Belgium - France)
ELN. Elan Films (Brussels) S N D (Saint Ouen) co-prodn. Wri-dir, Samy Pavel. Asst dir, Alain Cohen; cam (Eastmancolor), Ramon Suarez; edtrs, Pierre Didier, Eloise Cohen; snd, Pierre Daventure. 90.
(DOC)
05/30/79

The Claudia Case: SEE O Caso Claudia

Clear Horizons: SEE Horizonte Te Hapura

Clinch: SEE Klincz

Clipa
(The Moment)
(Romania)
RMN. Romaniafilm Prodn, Bucharest. Dir, Gheorghe Vitanidis. Sp, Dinu Sararu; cam, Nicu Stan; snd, Dan Ionescu; sets, Guta Stirbu; cos, Gabriela Ricsan; edtr, Maria Chise. 138.
Gheorghe Cozorici, Ion Dichiseanu, Octavian Andrei, Sebastian Papaiani, Emanoil Petrut, Mitica Popescu, Octavian Cotescu, Leopoldina Balanuta, Rodica Tapaaga, Olga Tudorache, Margareta Pogonat, Valeria Seciu, Sandu Simionica, Amza Pellea, Vasile Nitulescu.
09/05/79

Close Encounters of The Third Kind
COL. Prods, Julia and Michael Phillips. Sp-dir, Steve Spielberg. Cam (Metrocolor), Vilmos Zsigmond, Douglas Trumbull, William A Fraker, Douglas Slocombe, John Alonzo, Laszlo Kovacs, Richard Yuricich, Dave Stewart, Robert Hall, Don Jarel, Dennis Muren; 2d unit cam, Steve Poster; edtr, Michael Kahn; mus, John Williams; prodn des, Joe Alves; art dir, Dan Lomino; set decor, Phil Abramson; snd, Buzz Knudson, Don MacDougall, Robert Glass, Gene Cantamesse, Steve Katz; cosward, Jim Linn; asst dir, Chuck Myers; stunt coord, Buddy Joe Hooker. (MPAA rating: PG). 135.
Richard Dreyfuss, Francois Truffaut, Teri Garr, Melinda Dillon, Cary Guffey, Bob Balaban, J Patrick McNamara, Warren Kemmerling, Roberts Blossom, Philip Dodds, Shawn Bishop, Adrienne Campbell, Justin Dreyfuss, Lance Hendricksen, Merrill Connally, George Dicenzo.
11/09/77

The Closet Children: SEE Les Enfants Du Placard

Cloud Dancer

BLO. Melvin Simon Production. Prod-dir, Barry Brown. Exec prod, Melvin Simon. Sp, William Goodhart, based on a story by Brown, Daniel Tamkus, Goodhart; cam (MGM Color), Travers Hill; edtr, Marshall Borden; snd, Michael Evje; tech adv-chief pilot, Tom Poberezny; flying sequences conceived-created, Brown; mus, Fred Karlin; asst dir, Don Klune. (MPAA rating: PG). 108.
David Carradine, Jennifer O'Neill, Joseph Bottoms, Colleen Camp, Albert Salmi, Salome Jens, Arnette Jens Zerbe, Norman Alden, Nina Van Pallandt.
06/11/80

The Clown: SEE Ansichten Eines Clowns

The Clown Murders
(Canada)
AST. Magnum Int'l Prodns presentation. Prod, Christopher Dalton; exec prod, J Stephen Stohn. Wri-dir, Martyn Burke. 94.
Stephen Young, Susan Keller, Lawrence Dane, John Candy, Gary Reineke, John Bayliss, Al Waxman, Michael Magee, Cec Linder.
10/06/76

The Club
(Australia)
RDP. South Australian Film Corporation and New South Wales Film Corporation prodn of David Williamson's "The Club". Prod, Matt Carroll; dir, Bruce Beresford; sp, David Williamson; asso prod, Moya Iceton; cam (Color-Panavision), Don McAlpine; art dir, David Copping; snd, Gary Wilkins; edtr, William Anderson; mus, Mike Brady. 99.
Jack Thompson, Graham Kennedy, Frank Wilson, Harold Hopkins, John Howard, Alan Cassell, Maggie Doyle.
10/08/80

Cma
(The Moth)
(Poland)
POL. Film Polski prodn, Film Unit Warsaw. Wri-dir, Tomasz Zygadlo. Cam, Jacek Zygadlo; sets, Janusz Sosnowski; mus, Jan Kanty Pawluskiewicz; prodn mgr, Andrzej Smulski. 103.
Roman Wilhelmi, Anna Seniuk, Iwona Bielska, Nela Obarska, Jerzy Trela, Grzegorz Herominski, Marek Probosz, Piotr Fronczewski, Jerzy Stuhr, Inez Fichna.
(B & W)
10/01/80

Coach
CWN. Prod, Mark Tenser; exec prod, Newton P Jacobs. Dir, Bud Townsend. Sp, Stephen Bruce Rose, Nancy Larson, based on an idea by Mark Tenser; cam (Metrocolor), Mike Murphy; edtr, Bob Gordon; art dir, Ken Hergenroeder; mus, Anthony Harris; prodn mgr-asst dir, Mike Castle. (MPAA rating: PG). 100.
Cathy Lee Crosby, Michael Biehn, Keenan Wynn, Steve Nevil, Channing Clarkson, Jack David Walker, Meredith Baer, Myron McGill, Robyn Pohle, Kristine Greco.
03/08/78

The Coach: SEE Trener

Coal Miner's Daughter
U. Bernard Schwartz prodn. Dir, Michael Apted. Exec prod, Bob Larson. Sp, Tom Rickman, based on the autobiography by Loretta Lynn with George Vescey; cam, Ralf D Bode; edtr, Arthur Schmidt; prodn des, John D Bode; mus, Owen Bradley; snd, Jim Alexander; set decor, John M Dwyer; asst dir, Dan Kolsrud. (MPAA rating: PG). 125.
Sissy Spacek, Tommy Lee Jones, Bevery D'Angelo, Levon Helm, Phyllis Boyens, William Sanderson, Robert Elkins, Bob Hannah, Bill Anderson Jr, Foister Dickerson, Malla McCown, Pamela McCown, Kevin Salvilla, Sissy Lucas, Pat Patterson, Brian Warf, Elizabeth Watson, David Gray.
02/20/80

Coast to Coast
PAR. Exec prod, Terry Carr; prods, Steve Tisch, Jon Avnet; dir, Joseph Sargent; sp, Stanley Weiser; cam (Movielab Color), Mario Tosi; 2d-unit cam, Joel King; edtr, George Jay Nicholson; mus, Charles Bernstein; art dir, Hilyard Brown; set decor, Ira Bates; snd, Gene S Cantamessa, John T Reitz, David Campbell, David Hudson; asso prod, Vince Cannon; asst dir, Michael Daves. (MPAA rating: PG). 95.
Dyan Cannon, Robert Blake, Quinn Redeker, Michael Lerner, Maxine Stuart, Bill Lucking, Ellen Gerstein, Patricia Conklin, David Moody, Rozelle Gayle, Martin Beck, Karen Rushmore.
10/08/80

Cocktail Molotov
(France)
AMLF. Alexandre Films/Antenne 2 co-prodn. Dir, Diane Kurys. Wris, Kurys, Philippe Adrien, Alain Le Henry; cam, Philippe Rousselet; snd, Bernard Aubouy; art dirs, Hilton McConnico, Tony Egry; edtr, Joelle Van Effenterre; mus, Yves Simon; sngs perf by Murray Head. 100.
Elise Caron, Philippe Lebas, Francois Cluzet.
02/27/80

Coco La Fleur, Candidat
(Coco-the-Flower, Candidate)
(France)
RSH. Rush prodn-Claude Geudj prodn. Prod, Claude Guedj. Wri-dir, Christian Lara. Cam (Panavision-Eastmancolor), Jean-Claude Couty; mus, Experience 7; edtr, Gerard Kikoine; snd, Jack Jullian; art dir, Traute Sigel. 85.
Robert Liensol, Jennifer, Greg Germain, Guy Pierre Mineur, Felix Marten, Jean-Jacques Moreau, Lucrece Saintol, Lucien Gerville-Reache.
02/28/79

The Coffin Affair: SEE L'Affaire Coffin

Cold Cuts: SEE Buffet Froid

The Cold Heart: SEE Le Coeur Froid

Cold Homeland: SEE Kalte Heimat

Collections Privees
(Private Collections)
(France - Japan)
UGC. Films du Jeudi-French Movies (Paris)-Toei Company (Tokyo) co-prodn. Prod, Pierre Braunberger; dirs, Just Jaeckin, Shuji Terrayama, Walerian Borowczyk.
"L'Ile Aux Sirenes"-(Jaeckin); sp, Jean-Michel Ribes; cam, Robert Fraisse; edtr, Michelle Boehm, Michelle Ansellem; mus, Pierre Bachelet.
"Le Labyrinthe d'Herbes"-(Terayama); sp, Terayama, Rio Kishida, based on the novel by Kyoka Izumi; cam, Tatsuo Suzuki; snd, Katsuhide Kamura; edtr, Tomoyo Oshima; art dir, Isao Yamada; mus, J A Seazer.
"L'Armoire"-(Borowczyk); sp, Borowczyk, from story by Guy de Maupassant; cam, Noel Very; edtr, Khadicha Bariha; snd, Jean-Charles Ruault; cos, Piet Bolscher. 105.
Robert Blanche, Laura Gemser, Catherine Gadois, Marpessa Dawn, Edwige Thabouis.
Hiroshi Mikami, Takeshi Wakamatsu, Keiko Niitaka, Juzo Itami.
Marie-Catherine Conti, Yves Marie.
07/11/79

The Colonel and the Werewolf: SEE O Coronel e O Lobisomem

Colorin, Colorado
(And They Lived Happily Ever After)
(Spain)
X. Eco Films SA and Luis Megino PC prodn (Madrid). Dir, Jose Luis Garcia Sanchez. Sp, Juan Miguel Lamet; mus, Victor Manuel; cam (Eastmancolor), Magi Torruella; sets, Rosa German; edtr, Eduardo Biurrum. 94.
Jose Sazatornil, Mari Carrillo, Teresa Rabal, Juan Diego, Fiorella Faltoyano, Antonio Gamero, Maria Massip.
09/29/76

Coma
UA. MGM picture. Prod, Martin Erlichman. Sp-dir, Michael Crichton, based on the novel by Robin Cook. Cam (Metrocolor), Victor J Kemper, Gerald Hirschfield; edtr, David Bretherton; mus, Jerry Goldsmith; prodn des, Albert Brenner; set decor, Rick Simpson; snd, Bill Griffith, William McCaughey, Michael J Kohut, Aaron Rochin; cos-ward, Eddie Marks, Yvonne Kubis; asst dirs, William McGarry, Ron Grow. (MPAA rating: PG). 113.
Genevieve Bujold, Michael Douglas, Elizabeth Ashley, Rip Torn, Richard Widmark, Lois Chiles, Harry Rhodes, Gary Barton, Frank Downing, Richard Doyle, Alan Haufrect, Lance Le Gault, Michael MacRae, Betty McGuire, Tom Selleck, Charles Siebert, William Wintersole.
01/25/78

Come Perdere Una Moglie E Trovare Un'Amante
(How to Lose a Wife and Find a Lover)
(Italy)
TIT. Cinematografica Alex prodn. Dir, Pasquale Festa Campanile. Prod, Luigi Borghese; cam (Kodak), Giuseppe Ruzzolini; mus, Gianni Ferrio. 100.
Johnny Dorelli, Barbara Bouchet, Carlo Bagno, Elsa Vazzoler, Felice Andreassi.
12/13/78

Comedia Rota
(Broken Comedy)
(Argentina)
X. Nuevo Cine productores Cinematografices Asociados film. Wri-dir, Oscar Barney Finn, based on story by Julia Von Grolman. Cam, Alberto Basail; sets, Aldo Guglielmone; edtr, Antonio Ripoli. 114.
Julia Von Grolman, Gianni Lunadel, Elsa Daniel, Ignacio Quiros, Darwin Sanchez, Elena Tasito, Monica Escudero.
10/10/79

The Comedy Harmonists:
SEE Die Comedien Harmonists

Comes A Horseman
UA. Robert Chartoff-Irwin Winkler prodn; prods, Gene Kirkwood, Dan Paulson; exec prods, Robert Chartoff, Irwin Winkler. Dir, Alan J Pakula. Sp, Dennis Lynton Clark; cam, Gordon Willis; prodn des, George Jenkins; edtr, Marion Rothman; mus, Michael Small; set decor, Arthur Jeph Parker; snd, Chris Newman; cos, Luster Bayless; stunt coord, Walter Scott; asso prod, Ronald Caan; asst dir, Paul Helmick. (MPAA rating: PG). 118.
James Caan, Jane Fonda, Jason Robards, George Grizzard, Richard Farnsworth, Jim Davis, Mark Harmon, Macon McCalman, Basil Hoffman, James Kline, James Keach, Clifford A Pellow.
10/11/78

Coming Home
UA. Prod, Jerome Hellman. Dir, Hal Ashby. Sp, Waldo Salt, Robert C Jones, based on a story by Nancy Dowd; cam (DeLuxe Color), Haskell Wexler; edtr, Don Zimmerman; prodn des, Mike Haller; set decor, George Gaines; snd, Buzz Knudson; cos-ward, Ann Roth, Mike Hoffman, Silvio Scarano, Jennifer Parson; asst dir, Chuck Myers. (MPAA rating: R). 126.
Jane Fonda, Jon Voight, Bruce Dern, Robert Ginty, Penelope Milford, Robert Carradine.
02/15/78

Comme La Lune
(As the Moon)
(France)
AMLF. Coquelicot Films-Sara Films prodn. Wri-dir, Joel Seria. Cam (Eastmancolor), Marcel Combes; edtr, Claudine Bouche; mus, Philippe Sarde. 88.
Jean-Pierre Marielle, Sophie Daumier, Dominique Lavanant, Anna Gaylor, Marco Perrin.
09/14/77

Comme Sur Des Roullettes
(As Easy As Pie)
(France)
SNC. Cinemag, SFP, SNC, AZ prodn. Wri-dir, Nina Companeez. Cam (Eastmancolor), Pierre Marechal; edtr, Jacqueline Aubery. 95.
Evelyne Buyle, Mathe Souverbie, Francis Huster, Andre Batisse.
04/20/77

Comme Un Boomerang
(Like A Boomerang)
(France)
FEL. Lira Films (Raymond Danon)-Adel Prodns (Alain Delon) Filmes prodn. Dir, Jose Giovanni. Sp, Giovanni, Delon; cam (Eastmancolor), Pierre William Glenn; edtr, Francois Chauet. 100.
Alain Delon, Charles Vanel, Carla Gravina, Louis Julien, Dora Doll, Suzanne Flon.
09/01/76

Comment Yukong Deplace Les Montagnes
(How Yukong Moved Mountains)
(France)
CIX. Conceived-dir, Joris Ivens with the collab of Marcelline Loridan, Jean Bigiaoui. Cam, Li Tse-Hsiang. 720.
(DOC)
03/17/76

The Commitment
X. Commitment Co film, prod, Elliott Brandes. Dirs, Richard Grand, Louis A Shaffner. Sp, Andrew Laskos, Shaffner, Grand, from story by Barbara Grand; cam, Shaffner; edtr, Elen Orson; mus, Dobie Gray, John D'Andrea; songs, Gray, Troy Seals, Eddie Setser, Max D Barns, Will Jennings, Barry Goldberg, all sung by Gray; art dir, Karen Shaffner, Janice Orson; snd, Don Sanders, Dick Damen. 88.
Richard Grand, Barbara Graham, Joseph Turkel, Diane Vincent, Jon Ian Jacobs, Tom Bower, Bruce Kirby, Richard Adams, Frank Arata, Mimi Davis, Cal Haynes, Esther Sutherland, Jeremiah Gorwitz, Syl Words, Peg Shirley; John Kirby, Joe Valino, Carol McGinnis, Allen Garfield.
02/04/76

Communion
(Alice, Sweet Alice)
(Britain)
HMD. Harristown Funding Ltd (Richard K Rosenberg) prodn. Dir, Alfred Sole. Sp, Rosemary Ritvo, Sole; cam, John Friberg, Chuck Hall; edtr, Edward Sallier; mus, Stephen Lawrence; asst dir, Adrienne Hamalian; prodn des, John Lawless; cos, Michelle Cohen; snd, Mark Salwasser. (MPAA rating: R). 108.
Linda Miller, Mildred Clinton, Paula Sheppard, Niles McMaster, Rudolph Willrich, Jane Lowry, Alphonse De Noble, Brooke Shields, Kathy Rich, Tom Signorelli, Lillian Roth.
09/21/77

Companero De Viaje
(Travelling Companion)
(Venezuela)
BQT. Dir, Clemente De La Cerda. Sp, Rodolfo Santana, Orlando Abrauyo. 110.
Toco Gomez, Maria Escalona, Julio Motta.
09/05/79

Companys, Proces A Catalunya
(Companys, Catalonia On Trial)
(Spain)
X. Produccions Zeta S A-La Llanterna Films and P C Teide co-prodn. Dir, Josep Maria Forn. Exec prod, J A Perez Giner; sp, Josep Maria Forn, Antoni Freixas; cam (Eastmancolor), Cecilio Paniagua; sets, Josep Maria Espada, Josep Maria Segarr; edtr, Emilio Rodriguez. 103.
Luis Iriondo, Marta Angelat, Montserrat Carulla, Xabier Elorriaga, Pau Garsaball, Agustin Gonzalez, Alfred Luchetti, Carlos Lucena, Marta May, Biel Moll, Ovidi Montllor, Jordi Serrat.
(Soundtrack in Catalan and Castilian)
05/16/79

The Competition
COL. Rastar-William Sackheim prodn, exec prod, Howard Pine. Prod, Sackheim. Dir-sp, Joel Oliansky; story, Oliansky, Sackheim; cam (Metrocolor), Richard H Kline; orig mus, Lalo Schifrin; song, "People Alone," by Schifrin, Wilbur Jennings; mus, Ginastera, Brahms, Chopin, Prokofiev, Beethoven; performed by Eduardo Delgado, Ralph Grierson, Lincoln Mayorga, Daniel Pollack, Chester B Swiatowski and the L A Philharmonic Orchestra; edtr, David Blewitt; prodn des, Dale Hennesy; set decor, James Payne; set des, Dianne Wager; snd, John Speak, Les Fresholtz, Tex Rudloff, Asron Rochin; piano instr-mus cnsltnt, Jean Evensen Shaw; asst dir, Jon C Anderson. (MPAA rating: PG). 129.
Richard Dreyfuss, Amy Irving, Lee Remick, Sam Wanamaker, Joseph Cali, Ty Henderson, Vickie Kriegler, Adam Stern, Bea Silvern, Philip Sterling, Gloria Strook, Delia Salvi, Priscilla Pointer.
12/03/80

The Computer Superman:
SEE Yod Manoot Computer

Comrade Nikanorova Awaits You:
SEE Was Oshidajet Grashdanka Nikanorova

Con El Culo Al Aire
(Caution To The Wind)
(Spain)
GBF. Ascle-Globe-Andro prodn. Prod, Juan Andreu. Dir-sp, Carlos Mira. Cam, Hans Burmann; edtr, Pablo del Amo; art dir, Alejandro Soler; mus, Juan C Senante. 97.
Ovidi Montllor, Eva Leon, Maria Jose Arenos, Juan Monleon, Juan Carlos Serante, Antonio Morant, Rosita Amores, Jorge Segujj.
10/29/80

Con Fusione
(Con-fusion)
(Italy)
GAU. Gaumont Italia film, prod by Azione Cinematografica. Wri-dir, Piero Natoli; cam, Giuseppe Lanci, edtr, Anna Napoli; mus, Arturo Annecchion.   100.
Carlotta Natoli, Piero Natoli, Luisa Maneri.
09/17/80

Con Mucho Carino
(With Lots Of Love)
(Spain)
X. Z-Gora prodn. Wri-dir, Gerardo Garcia. Cam (Eastmancolor), Roberto Gomez; edtr, Rafael de la Cueva; mus, Fermin Gurbindo; sets, Ignacio Inchaurbe.   81.
Jose A. Garido, Ana Maria Simon, Almudena Cotos, Ana Maria Granda, Concha Gregori, Fernando Tejadas, Elvira Quintilla.
09/12/79

Concert at the End of Summer: SEE Koncert Na Konci Leta

Concert for Mourners: SEE Koncert Pre Pozostalych

The Concorde--Airport '79
U. Jennings Lang prodn. Prod, Lang. Dir, David Lowell Rich. Sp, Eric Roth, from a story by Lang, inspired by the film "Airport," based on the novel by Arthur Hailey; cam, Philip Lathrop; edtr, Dorothy Spencer; prod des, Henry Bumstead; mus, Lalo Schifrin; cos des, Burton Miller; set decor, Marry Ann Biddle, Mickey S Michaels;
08/01/79 snd, Jim Alexander; special photographic effects, Universal Hartland; special visual effects, Abe Milrad; stunt coord, George Sawaya; asst dir, Newton Arnold. (MPAA rating: PG).   123.
Alain Delon, Susan Blakely, Robert Wagner, Sylvia Kristel, George Kennedy, Eddie Albert, Bibi Andersson, Charo, John Davidson, Andrea Marcovicci, Martha Raye, Cicely Tyson, Jimmie Walker, David Warner, Mercedes McCambridge, Avery Schreiber, Sybil Danning, Monica Lewis, Nicolas Coster, Robin Gammell, Jon Cedar.

Condemned: SEE Skazany

The Confederation-The People Make History: SEE A Confederacao-O Povo E Que Faz A Historia

Confession of Love: SEE Objasnenie W Lubwi

Confessions From a Holiday Camp
(Britain)
COL. Swiftdown prodn. Prod, Greg Smith. Exec prod, Michael Klinger. Dir, Norman Cohen. Sp, Christopher Wood (Timothy Lea), based on novel by Timothy Lea; cam, Ken Hodges, art dir, Harry Pottle; edtr, Geoffrey Foot; snd, Dennis Whitlock.   88.
Robin Askwith, Anthony Booth, Doris Hare, Bill Maynard, Sheila White, Colin Crompton, Liz Frazer, Linda Hayden, John Junkin, Lance Percival, Nicholas Owen, Janet Edis, Mike Savage.
08/17/77

The Confessions of Amans
X. Prod-dir-pho, Gregory Nava. Sp, Nava, Anna Thompson.   88.
William Bryan, Michael St John, Susahnna Macmillan.
(16m)
12/08/76

The Confessions of Winifred Wagner: SEE Winifried Wagner Und Die Geschichte Des Hauses Wahnfried 1914-1975

Confidence: SEE Bizalom

Confidences Pour Confidences
(Confidences For Confidences)
(France)
GCC. Albina Production TFI prodn. Dir, Pascal Thomas. Sp, Thomas, Jacques Lourcelles; cam (Eastmancolor), Renan Polles; edtr, Nathalie Lafaurie; mus, Vladimir Cosma.   110.
Daniel Ceccaldi, Laurence Ligneres, Michel Galabru, Anne Caudry, Carole Jacquinot, Elisa Servier, Ogor Lafaurie.
12/27/78

Confused Feelings: SEE Smyateniye Chuvstv

Con-fusion: SEE Con Fusione

The Congressman: SEE El Diputado

The Conquest of the Citadel: SEE Die Eroberung Der Zitadelle

The Conquest: SEE Akramana

The Consequence: SEE Die Konsequenz

Constancy: SEE Constans

Constans
(Constancy)
(Poland)
POL. TOR Unit prodn. Wri-dir, Krzysztof Zanussi. Cam (Eastmancolor), Slawomir Idziak; edtr, Wieslawa Dembinska.   92.
Tadeusz Bradecki, Zofia Morzowska, Malgorzata Zajaczowska, Cezary Morawaski.
05/21/80

Contes Pervers
(Perverse Tales)
(France - Italy)
UGC. Belstar/Cathala/New Movie (Rome) co-prodn. Wri-dir, Regine Deforges; cam (Fujicolor), Alain Derobe, edtr, Michel Valio; snd, Alain Curvelier; mus, Martial Carceles.   90.
Francoise Gayat, Beatrice, Carina Barone, Genevieve Omini, Salima Bahloul, Gerard Lauzier.
07/30/80

The Context: SEE Cadaveri Eccellenti

Contos Eroticos
(Erotic Stories)
(Brazil)
X. Lynxfilm e Editora Tres prodn. Dirs, Roberto Santos, Roberto Palmari, Eduardo Escorel, Joaquim Pedro de Andrade. Sp, Sergio Toni, Yara Ramos Ribeiro, Aercio Flavio Consolin, Pedro Maia Soares; cam, Marcelo Primavera, Geraldo Gabriel, Miguel Parente, Kimihiko Kato.   100.
Joana Fomm, David Jose, Carmen Silva, Lima Duarte, Liza Vieira, Castro Gonzaga, Claudio Cavalcanti, Christina Ache, Carlos Galhardo.
(Portuguese Soundtrack)
10/17/79

The Contract
(Hong Kong)
GHV. Prod, Raymond Chow. Dir-sp Michael Hui. Cam, Tom Lau; art des, David Chan; edtr, Chang Yao Chung; mus, Samuel Hui.   90.
Michael Hui, Sam Hui, Ricky Hui, Tiffany Bao, Ellen Lau, Yeung Wei, Cheng Fu Hsiung, Russell Cawthorne, Chan King Chang, Chen Sau Ping, Louis Kwong.
(English subtitles)
08/09/78

Contract: SEE Kontrakt

The Convict Killer
(Hong Kong)
SHF. Prod, Run Run Shaw. Dir, Chu Yuan. Exec prod, Mona Fong; story, Chu Yu; sp, Chin Yu; cam, Wang Cheh; edtrs, Chiang Hsing Lung, Yu Hsiao Feng; snd-mus dir, Eddie Wang; art dir, Chiang Hsing Lung; martial art instructors, Tang Chia, Huang Pei Chi; make-up, Wu Hsu Ching.   95.
Ti Lung, Pai Piao, Liu Yung, Ching Li, Chen Man Na, Ching Miao, Ku Kuan Chung, Ai Fei.
05/21/80

Convoy
UA. Prod, Robert M Sherman; exec prods for EMI, Michael Deeley, Barry Spikings. Dir, Sam Peckinpah. Sp, B W L Norton, based on the song by C W McCall; cam (DeLuxe Color), Harry Stradling Jr; 2d unit cam, Richard Kelley; edtrs, Graeme Clifford, John Wright, Garth Craven; mus, Chip Davis; sng lyr, Bill Fries; prodn des, Fernando Carrere; art dir, J Dennis Washington, Francis Lombardo; snd, Don Mitchell, Bob Litt, Steve Maslow, Bill Randall; cos-ward, Kent James, Carol James; asst dirs, Tom Shaw, Richard Wells, Pepi Lenzi, John Poer, Cliff Coleman, Newton Arnold; 2d unit dirs, Walter Kelley, James Coburn. (MPAA rating: PG). 110.
Kris Kristofferson, Ali MacGraw, Ernest Borgnine, Burt Young, Madge Sinclair, Franklyn Ajaye, Brian Davies, Seymour Cassel, Cassie Yates, Walter Kelley.
06/28/78

Cool, Calm and Collected: SEE Calmos

Cop: SEE Stroemer

Cop or Hood: SEE Flic ou Voyou

Copculer Krali
(The King Of The Street Cleaners)
(Turkey)
X. Arzu Film Prodn, Istanbul. Dir, Zeki Okten. Sp, Umor Bugay; cam, Erdogan Engin. 88.
Kemal Sunal, Sener Sen, Aysen Gruda.
08/02/78

Cordelia
(Canada)
MUT. National Film Board of Canada prodn. Prod, Jean-Marc Garand. Dir, Jean Beaudin. Sp, Beaudin, Marcel Sabourin, from "La Lampe dans la Fenetre" by Pauline Cadieux; cam, Pierre Mignot; edtr, Jean Beaudin; art dirs, Denis Boucher, Vianney Gauthier; snd, Jacques Blain; mus, Maurice Blackburn. 118.
Louise Portal, Gaston Lepage, Pierre Gobeil, Gilbert Sicotte, Raymond Cloutier, Jean-Louis Roux, James Blendick, Rolland Bedard.
02/27/80

Corleone
(Italy)
CNZ. Prod, Mario Cecchi Gori for Capital Film. Dir, Pasquale Squitieri. Sp, Barrese, De Rita, Maiuri, Squitieri; cam (Kodak), Eugenio Bentivoglio; art dir, Umberto Turco; edtr, Mauro Bonanni; mus, Ennio Morricone. 111.
Giuliano Gemma, Claudia Cardinale, Francisco Rabal, Stefano Satta Flores, Michele Placide.
12/06/78

Corps a Coeur
(Body to Heart)
(France)
07/25/79
PFC. Diagonale prodn. Prod-wri-dir, Paul Vecchiali. Cam, Georges Strouve; snd, J Francois Chevalier; edtr, Vecchiali; mus, Gabriel Faure. 126.
Nicolas Silberg, Helen Surgere, Madeleine Robinson, Myriam Mezieres, Beatrice Bruno, Christine Murillo.

Corpus
(Greece)
X. Stefi Film and Thanasis Rentzis prodn. Dir, Thanassis Rentzis. Sp, Gay Angueli, Rentzis; cam (b&w), Vittorio Pietra, Elias Papageorgopoulos; mus, George Kouroupos, Stefanos Vassilliades, Vaguelis Katsoulis, Demetris Lecas, Theodre Katelanos; edtr, Thanassis Rentzis; narr, Costa Tsoumas. 80.
(DOC)
10/31/79

Corrida of Love: SEE Ai No Corrida

Corvette Summer
UA. MGM picture. Prod, Hal Barwood. Dir, Matthew Robbins. Sp, Barwood, Robbins; cam (Metrocolor), Frank Stanley; 2d unit cam, Rexford Metz; edtr, Amy Jones; mus, Craig Safan; art dir, James Schoppe; set decor, Richard Spero; snd, Willie D Burton, William McCaughey, Aaron Rochin, Michael J Kohut; cos-ward, Aggie Guerard Rodgers; asst. dir, Jim Bloom; 2d unit dir, Buddy Joe Hooker; stunt coord, Bobby Bass. (MPAA rating: PG). 105.
Mark Hamill, Annie Potts, Eugene Roche, Kim Milford, Richard McKenzie, William Bryant, Philip Bruns, Danny Bonaduce, Jane A Johnston, Albert Insinnia, Isaac Ruiz Jr, Stanley Kamel, Jason Ronard, Brion James.
05/24/78

Cosi Come Sei
(Stay As You Are)
(Italy)
CED. San Francisco Film prodn. Prod, Giovanni Bertolucci. Dir, Alberto Lattuada. Sp, Enrico Oldoini, Lattuada; cam, Luis Alcaine; mus, Ennio Morricone. 118.
Marcello Mastroianni, Nastassja Kinski, Francisco Rabal, Anja Pieroni, Giuliana Calandra.
12/20/78

Could We Maybe: SEE Maaske Ku' Vi

Count Dracula And His Vampire Bride
(Britain)
DYN. Hammer Film prodn. Prod-dir, Alan Gibson. Sp, Don Houghton; cam, Brian Probyn; art dir, Lionel Couch; edtr, Chris Barnes; snd, Claude Hitchcock; mus, John Cacavas; asso prod, Houghton; asst dir, Derek Whithurst. (MPAA rating: R). 87.
Christopher Lee, Peter Cushing, Michael Coles, William Franklyn, Freddie Jones, Joanna Lumley, Richard Vernon, Patrick Barr, Barbara Yu Ling, Richard Mathews, Lockwood West, Maurice O'Connell, Valerie Van Ost.
12/06/78

Count of Monte Cristo
(Britain)
ITC. Norman Rosemont prodn. Prod, Norman Rosemont. Dir, David Greene. Sp, Sidney Carroll (based on the novel by Alexandre Dumas); cam (Eastmancolor), Aldo Tonti; edtr, Gene Milford; mus, Allyn Ferguson; prodn des, Walter Patriarca; asst dir, Gianni Cozzo. 103.
Richard Chamberlain, Tony Curtis, Trevor Howard, Louis Jourdan, Donald Pleasence, Kate Nelligan, Angelo Infanti, Taryn Power, Harold Bromley, Carlo Puri, Alessio Orano, Domenic Guard, Isabelle De Valvert, Ralph Michael, Dominic Barto, Harry Baird, George Willing, David Mills, Anthony Dawson.
06/02/76

Count the Ways
EVO. Prod-dir-wri, Ann Perry. Cam (Eastmancolor), Ken Gibb; mus, Dan Samuels; edtr, Bob Freeman; (Self-imposed X rating). 84.
Tyler Horn, Yvonne Green, Charla, Deseree, Joe Summer, Jason Wells.
12/15/76

Countdown At Kusini
(US - Nigeria)
COL. DST Telecommunications Inc presentation, prod, Ladi Ladebo in association with Tan Int'l Ltd of Nigeria-Glipp Productions Inc, Arnold Stone, Bruce Graham. Dir, Ossie Davis. Sp, Davis, Ladebo, Al Freeman Jr; orig story, screen treatment, John Storm Roberts; cam (Metrocolor), Andrew Laszlo; mus, Manu Dibango; snd, Lee Bost; asst dirs, Dwight Williams, Joseph Ray Johnson. (MPAA rating: PG). 99.
Ruby Dee, Ossie Davis, Greg Morris, Tom Aldredge, Michael Ebert, Thomas Baptiste, Jab Adu, Elsie Olusola, Funso Adeolu.
04/07/76

The Country Is Calm: SEE Es Herrscht Ruhe Im Land

The Coup De Grace: SEE Der Fangschuss

Coup d'Etat: SEE Zamach Stanu

Coup de Tete
(Hot Head)
(France)
GAU. Gaumont-S F P prodn. Prod by Alain Poire. Dir, Jean-Jacques Annaud. Sp, Francis Veber, from an original idea by Alain Godard; cam, Claude Agostini; snd, Francois Soler; mus, Pierre Bachelet; edtr, Noelle Boisson; art dir, Alain Maunoury. 90.
Patrick Dewaere, France Dougnac, Jean Bouise, Michel Aumont, Paul Le Person, Michel Fortin, Dorothee Jemma, Patrick Floersheim.
03/07/79

Courage Fuyons
(Courage, Let's Run For It)
(France)
GAU. La Gueville/Gaumont Int'l co-prodn. Prods, Alain Poire, Yves Robert. Dir, Yves Robert. Sp, Robert, Jean-Loup Dabadie; cam; Yves Lafaye; edtr, Pierre Gillette; snd, Alain Sempe; art dir, Jean-Pierre Kohut Svelko; cos, Christian Gasc; artistic collab, Frantz Salieri, Laurent Petitgirard. 98.
Jean Rochefort, Catherine Deneuve, Phillippe Leroy-Beaulieu, Robert Webber.
10/24/79

Cours Apres Moi Que Je T'Attrape
(Run After Me Until I Catch You)
(France)
FBE. Les Films 21 - Les Films Monfort-FR3-SFP-Axe Films-Films La Boetie prodn. Dir, Robert Pouret. Sp, Nicole De Buron, Pouret; cam (Eastmancolor), Guy Durban; edtr, Armand Psenny. 91.
Annie Girardot, Jean-Pierre Marielle, Marilu Tolo, Genevieve Fontanel, Sylvain Rougerie, Christine Laurent, Daniel Prevost.
09/15/76

Court Martial: SEE Prijeki Sud

Covert Action: SEE Sono Stato Un Agente Cia

Covjek Koga Treba Ubiti
(The Man to Kill)
(Yugoslavia)
YFR. Jadran Film-Croatia Film-Filmski Studio Titograd prodn. Dir, Veljko Bulajic. Sp, Bruni Di Geronimo, Ratko Durovic, Bulajic Cam (Eastmancolor), Branko Ivatovic; art dir, Veljko Despotovic; mus, Jose Privsek. 100.
Zvonimir Crnko, Vladimir Popovic, Charles Millot, Ranko Kovacevic, Tanja Boskovic, Duscia Zegarac, Tanasije Uzunovic, Mato Ergovic.
08/15/79

The Crab Drum: SEE Le Crabe-Tambour

Cracking Up
AIP. Comedy Jam prodn, prod, C D Taylor and Rick Murray. Exec prod, Joe Roth. Dirs, Rowby Goren, Chuck Staley. Art dir, C D Taylor; edtr, Roger Parker; title ani, Linda Taylor; mus, Ward Jewel, the Tubes. (MPAA rating: R). 69.
Phil Proctor, Peter Bergman, Michael Mislove, Fred Willard, Paul Zegler, Steve Bluestein, The Credibility Gap, Harry Shearer, Michael McCane, David Lander, the Graduates, Jim Fisher, Jim Staahl, Gino Insana, "Kansas City" Bob McClurg, Leslie Ackerman, Rowby Goren, Neil Isreal, Rick Murray, C D Taylor, Edie McClurg, Mary McCusker, Cris Pray, Ron Prince, Lynn Marie Stuart, Steven Stucker, Kurt Taylor, Paul Willson, Fee Waybill.
07/27/77

Cramp: SEE Krc

Crazy Days: SEE Ludi Dani

Crazy-Horse Paris-France
(France)
SNC. Crazy Horse Prodns prodn. Sp-dir, Alain Bernardin. Cam (Eastmancolor), Roland Pontoizeua; edtr, Yvonne Martin; tech advisor, Michel Bernheim; mus, Jacques Morali; chor, Victor Upshaw, Bernardin. 95.
John Lennox, Alain Bernardin.
11/02/77

Crazy Sex
(Hong Kong)
X. Prod, Runme Shaw. Dir, Li Han-hsiang. Sp, Li Han-hsiang; cam, Lin Chao; edtr, Ching Lung; mus, Chen Yung Yu. 102.
Shirley Yu, Hu Ching, Chen Ping, Kang Kai.
08/04/76

Crazy Women: SEE Las Locas

The Creature: SEE La Criatura

Crecer De Golpe
(Growing Up Suddenly)
(Argentina)
X. Productores Americanos prodn; dir, Sergio Renan; exec prod, Emilio Spitz; sp, Sergio Renan, Aida Bortnik based on novel by Jaroldo Conti "Alrededor de la Jaula"; cam (Eastmancolor), Leonardo Rodriguez Solis; edtr, Miguel Perez; sets, Miguel Angel Lumaldo; mus, Rololfo Mederos. 83.
Ubaldo Martinez, Olga Zubarry, Miguel Angel Sola, Cecilia Toth, Tincho Zabala.
09/28/77

The Crew: SEE Eqipaj

Crew Cut
(Holland)
RSS. Prod, Gerrit Visscher. Dir, Guido Pieters. Sp, Pieters, Karin Loomans; cam, Eduard Van Der Enden. 105.
Derek De Lint, Tingue Dongelmans, Cristel Braak, Guus Oster.
11/26/80

Cria Cuervos
(Raise Ravens)
(Spain)
X. Elias Querejeta prodn. Dir-wri, Carlos Saura. Edtr, Pablo G del Amo; cam (Eastmancolor), Teodoro Escamilla; sets, Rafael Palmero; prodn chief, Primitivo Alvaro; snd, Bernardo Menz. 97.
Ana Torrent, Geraldine Chaplin, Monica Randall, Florinda Chico, Hector Alterio, German Cobos, Mirta Miller, Josefina Diaz, Conchita Perez, Maite Sanchez Almendros.
02/04/76

Cricket in the Ear: SEE Shtourets V Ouhoto

Crime and Passion
(US - W Germany)
AIP. Gloria Films prodn, prod, Robert L Abrams; exec prod, Barney Bernhard. Dir, Ivan Passer. Sp, Jesse Lasky Jr, Pat Silver, based on the novel, "An Ace Up Your Sleeve", by James Hadley Chase; cam (Technicolor), Denis C Lewiston; stunt cam, Karl Kases; edtrs, John Jympson, Bernard Gribble; art dir, Herta Pischinger; snd, Robi Guever, Bill Rowe; asst dir, Wieland Liebske. (MPAA rating: R). 92.
Omar Sharif, Karen Black, Joseph Bottoms, Bernhard Wicki, Heinz Ehrenfreund.
02/25/76

Crime At Porta Romana: SEE Delitto A Porta Romana

Criminal Conversation
(Ireland)
BCR. Dir, Kieran Hickey. Sp, Philip Davison, Hickey; cam, Sean Corcoran; edtr, J Patrick Duffner. 61.
Emmet Bergin, Deirdre Donnelly, Peter Caffrey, Leslie Lalor, Kate Thompson, Garrett Keogh.
(16m)
10/29/80

Cristo si e fermato a Eboli
(Christ Stopped at Eboli)
(Italy - France)
TIT. Prods, Franco Cristaldi, Nicola Carraro for RAI-TV 2 and Vides Cinematografica (Rome)-Action Films (Paris). Dir, Francesco Rosi. Sp, Rosi, Tonino Guerra, Raffaele La Capria, from a novel by Carlo Levi; cam, Pasqualino De Santis; art dir, Andrea Crisanti; edtr, Ruggero Mastroianni; mus, Piero Piccioni. 150.
Gian Maria Volonte, Paolo Bonacelli, Alain Cuny, Lea Massari, Irene Papas, Francois Simon.
03/21/79

Cronica de Um Industrial
(Chronicle Of An Industrialist)
(Brazil)
X. Prods, Luis Rosemberg Filho, Renator Coutinho. Dir, Rosemberg. Sp, Rosemberg; cam, Luis; edtr, Ricardo Miranda. 100.
Renato Coutinho, Ana Maria Miranda, Wilson Grey.
05/30/79

Cronica De Un Subversivo Latino-Americano
(Chronicle of a Latin-American Subversive)
(Venezuela)
X. Alfa Films Int'l prodn. Dir, Mauricio Walerstein. Sp, Jose Ignacio Cabrujas, Luis Correa, Walerstein. Cam, Abigail Rojas; edtr, Alberto Torrija; mus, Miguel Angel Fuster. 102.
Miguel Angel Landa, Claudio Brook, Orlando Urdaneta, Maria Eugenia Dominguez, Pedro Laya, Perla Wonasheck, Eva Mondolfi, Oscar Mendoza, Lucio Bueno, Asdrubal Melendez, Julio Mota.
11/17/76

Cross Of Iron
(Britain - W Germany)
EMI. Arlene Sellers & Alex Winitsky presentation of an EMI Prodns Ltd and Rapid Film GmbH (Munich)-Terra Film Kunst (Berlin) prodn. Prod, Wolf C Hartwig. Dir, Sam Peckinpah. Sp, Julius J Epstein, Herbert Asmodi based on the book "Das geduldige Fleisch" (Cross of Iron), Willi Heinrich; cam (Technicolor), Ted Haworth, Brian Ackland Snow; edtrs, Tony Lawson, Mike Ellis, Herbert Taschner; snd, Rodney Holland; sfx, Richard Richtsfeld, Robin Cutteridge; Helmuth Klee; asst dir, Bert Batt. (MPAA rating: R). 130.
James Coburn, Maximilian Schell, James Mason, David Warner, Klaus Lowitsch, Roger Fritz, Vadim Glowna, Fred Stillkrauth, Burkhardt Driest, Dieter Schidor, Michael Nowka, Veronique Vendell, Arthur Brauss, Slavco Stimac, Senta Berger.
02/09/77

The Crown of Sonnets
(USSR)
SOV. Bielorousfilm prodn. Dir, Valeri Roubintchik. Sp, Viktor Mouratov; cam, Tatiana Loghinova. 90.
Igor Merkoulov, Sacha Joukovski, Ira Zelenko, Gheorgi Stil.
(B & W)
08/31/77

Crown Prince: SEE Kronprinsen

Cruel Love: SEE Kruta Lubost

Crueldade Mortal
(Deadly Cruelty)
(Brazil)
EMZ. SNCRO - Embrafilme - Sincrogne prodn. Wri-dir, Luis Paulino Dos Santos. Cam (Eastmancolor), Helio Silva; edtr, Joao De Mello. 90.
02/02/77

The Cruise: SEE Rejs

Cruisin' High: SEE Cat Murkil and the Silks

Cruising
UA. Lorimar presentation. Prod, Jerry Weintraub. Wri-dir, William Friedkin, based on the novel by Gerald Walker. Cam, James Contner; mus, Jack Nitzsche, perf by The Cripples; prodn des, Bruce Weintraub; art dir, Edward Pisoni; edtr, Bud Smith; asst dir, Alan Hopkins. (MPAA rating: R). 106.
Al Pacino, Paul Sorvino, Karen Allen, Richard Cox, Don Scardino, Joe Spinell, Jay Acovone, Randy Jurgensen, Barton Heyman, Gene Davis, Sonny Grosso.
02/13/80

Cry for Cindy
X. Prod, Henry Locke. Dir, Wendy Lions. Sp, Dean Rogers; cam, Casey Maxwell. (Self-imposed X rating). 90.
Amber Hunt, Maryanne Fisher, Mitzi Fraser, Fred James, Mark McGuire.
05/26/76

The Crying Woman: SEE La Femme Qui Pleure

CS Blues
X. Rolling Stones presentation. Prod, Marshall Chess. Dir, Robert Frank, Daniel Seymour. Edtrs, Susan Steinberg, Paul Justman. 95.
The Rolling Stones, Marshall Chess, Stevie Wonder, Andy Warhol, Truman Capote, Dick Cavett, Terry Southern, Lee Radziwill, Tina Turner, Bianca Jagger, Bobby Keyes, Jim Price, Nicky Hopkins.
(DOC) (16m)
05/02/79

Cseplo Gyuri
(Hungary)
HU. Hunnia-Bela Balasz Studio prodn. Dir, Pal Schiffer. Sp, Istvan Kameny, Schiffer; cam (Eastmancolor), Tamas Andro. 96.
08/23/76

Cu Minile Curate
(With Clean Hands)
(Romania)
RMN. Rumaniafilm Prodn, Bucharest. Dir, Sergiu Nicolaescu. Sp, Titus Popovici, Petre Salcudeanu; cam, Alexandru David; mus, Richard Oschanitzky. 95.
Ilarion Ciobanu, Sergiu Nicolaescu, Alexandru Dobrescu, Gheroghe Dinica, George Constantin, Sebastian Papaiani.
06/14/78

Cuba
UA. Alex Winitsky-Arlene Sellers prodn. Prods, Sellers, Winitsky. Dir, Richard Lester; sp, Charles Wood; exec prod, Denis O'Dell; cam, David Watkin; edtr, John Victor Smith; mus, Patrick Williams, prodn des, Gil Parrondo; art dir, Denis Gordon Orr; cos des, Shirley Russell; snd, Roy Charman; asst dir, David Tringham. (MPAA rating: R). 122.
Sean Connery, Brooke Adams, Jack Weston, Hector Elizondo, Denholm Elliott, Martin Balsam, Chris Sarandon, Alejandro Rey, Lonette McKee, Danny De La Paz, Louisa Moritz.
12/19/79

Cuba Crossing
X. Key West Prodn. Prod, Peter J Barton. Wri-dir, Chuck Workman. 90.
Stuart Whitman, Robert Vaughn, Raymond St Jacques, Caren Kaye, Woody Strode, Sybil Danning, Mary Lou Gassen, Albert Salmi, Michael Gazzo, Monty Rock III.
02/13/80

The Cuenca Crime: SEE El Crimen De Cuenca

Cuore Di Cane
(Dog's Heart)
(Italy)
ITG. Prods, Mario Gallo, Alberto Lattuada for Filmalpha, and Corona (Munich). Dir, Alberto Lattuada. Sp, Alberto Lattuada, Viveca Melander from the novel by Michail Bulgakov. Cam (Eastmancolor), Lamberto Caimi; art dir, Vincenzo Del Prato; edtr, Sergio Montanari; mus, Piero Piccioni. 109.
Max Von Sydow, Cochi Ponzoni, Eleonora Giorgi, Mario Adorf.
03/17/76

Cursa
(The Long Drive)
(Romania)
RMN. Rumaniafilm Prodn, Group One, Bucharest. Dir, Mircea Daneliuc. Sp, Timotei Ursu, from an idea by Petru Vintila; cam, Florin Mihailescu; mus, Lucian Metianu; setscos, Dumitru Georgescu. 90.
Mircea Ablulescu, Tora Vasilescu, Constantin Diplan, Olga Bucataru, Paul Lavric, Angela Costache, Teofil Caliman, Constanta Comanoiu, Mircea Daneliuc.
06/14/78

Cuvar Plaze U Zimskom Periodu
(The Beach Guard in Winter)
(Yugoslavia)
X. Center FRZ prodn, Belgrade. Dir, Goran Paskaljevic. Sp, Gordan Mihic; cam, Aleksandar Petkovic; mus, Zoran Hristic; art dir, Dragoljub Ivkov. 90.
Irfan Mensur, Gordana Kosanovic, Danilo-Bata Stojkovic, Dara Calenic, Mira Banjac, Ruzica Sokic.
07/07/76

Cyclops: SEE Tsekloput

Cyprus
(Greece)
X. George Papalios prodn. Wri-dirs, Thekla Kittou, Lambros Papademetrakis. Cam, Stavros Hassapis. 115.
(DOC)
10/27/76

Czlowiek Z Marmuru
(Man of Marble)
(Poland)
POL. Film Polski prodn, Warsaw, undertaken by Zespoly Filmowe Group X. Dir, Andrzej Wajda. Sp, Aleksander Sciber-Rylski; cam, Edward Klosinski; mus, Andrzej Korzynski; art dir, Allan Starski; prodn mgr, Barbara Pec-Slesicka. 161.
Jerzy Radziwilowicz, Krystyna Janda, Tadeusz Lomnicki, Jacek Lomnicki, Michal Tarkowski, Piotr Cieslak, Wieslaw Wojcik, Krystyna Zachwatowicz, Magda Teresa Wojcik, Boguslaw Sobczuk, Leonard Zajaczkowski, Jacek Domanski, Irena Laskowska, Zdzislaw Kozien, Wieslaw Drzewicz, Kazimierz Kaczor, Ewa Zientek.
06/01/77

Czontvary
(Hungary)
HU. Hunnia prodn. Dir, Zoltan Huszarik. Sp, Istvan Csaszar; cam (Eastmancolor), Peter Jankura. 110.
Ichak Fintzi, Istvan Holl, Andrea Drahota, Margit Dayka, Agnes Bantalvi.
02/27/80

Da Lang Tao Sha
(Great Waves Purify the Sand)
(People's Republic of China)
X. Pearl River Studio Film Prod, Canton. Dir, Yi Lin. Sp, Chu Tao-Nan, Yu Pin Kuen, Yi Lin; cam, Liu Tsin-Tang; sets, Tiang Tsin; edtr, Tan King-Long; mus, Che Ming; snd, Li Lie-Hung. 120.
Tsin Kung Cho, Yu Yang, Ku Ta-Ming, Tien Jui Chao, Yang Ju-Kuan.
(B & W)
01/10/79

Da Svante forsvandt
(When Svante Disappeared)
(Denmark)
DAG. Henning Carlsen prodn. Dir, Henning Carlsen. Sp, Benny Andersen, Carlsen; cam (Eastmancolor), Henning Kristiansen; mus, Benny Andersen; edtr, Christian Hartkopp. 85.
Benny Andersen, Benny Holst, Fritze Hedemann.
01/14/76

Daag
(The Stain)
(India)
X. Trimurti/Yash Raj Film, prod-dir, Yash Chopra. Sp, Chopra; cam, Kay Gee, Romesh Bhalla; chor, Suresh Blatt. 147.
Rajesh Khanna, Sharmila Tagore, Raakhee.
02/02/77

Daddy's War: SEE La Guerra De Papa

Dagny
(Poland - Norway)
POL. Film Polski prodn, Warsaw, "Zespoly Filmowe" and "Pryzmat" units, in co-prodn with Norsk Film, Oslo. Dir, Haakon Sandy. Sp, Aleksander Scibor-Rylski; cam, Zygmunt Samosuik; mus, Arne Nordhein; art dirs, Teresa Barska, Tadeusz Rypski, Hans Poppe, Odd Danielsen; prodn mgrs, Jerzy Nitecki, Jerzy Rutowicz, Jerzy Laskowski, Sverre Gran. 88.
Lise Fjeldstad, Daniel Olbrychski, Per Oscarsson, Nils Ole Oftebro, Maciej Englert, Olgierd Lukaszewicz, Jerzy Binczycki, Barbara Wrzesinska.
06/01/77

Dahana-Aranja
(The Middleman)
(India)
RIN. Wri-dir, Satyajit Ray. Cam, Soumendu Roy. 122.
Pradio Mukerji, Utpal Dutt, Lily Chakavarti.
(B & W)
07/28/76

Daj Sto Das
(Whatever You Can Spare)
(Yugoslavia)
YFR. Jadran Film-Croatia Film release. Dir, Bogdan Zizic; sp, Kruno Quien, Zizic; cam (Eastmancolor), Zeljko Guberobid; mus, Ozren Depolo. 96.
Sreten Mokrovic, Slobodan Milovanovic, Zonvko Lepetic, Vjera Zagar, Nardelli, Fabian Sovagovic.
08/27/80

Daluyong At Habagat
(Tidal Wave and West Wind)
(Philippines)
X. The Associates and Celso Ad Castillo Company prodn. Dir, Celso Ad Castillo. Cam, Ricardo David; edtr, Augusto Salvador; mus, Ernani Cuenco. 106.
Vic Vargas, Pinky de Leon, Ricky Belmonte, Lito Anzures, Rey Cortez, Alma Moreno, Joone Gamboa.
06/23/76

Damien - Omen II
FOX. Prod, Harvey Bernhard; co-prod, Charles Orme. Dir, Don Taylor. Sp, Stanley Mann, Michael Hodges; cam, Bill Butler; edtr, Robert Brown, Jr; mus, Jerry Goldsmith; prodn des, Philip M Jefferies, Fred Harpman; snd, Al Overton; asst dirs, Al Nicholson, Jerry Ballew. (MPAA rating: R). 109.
William Holden, Lee Grant, Jonathan Scott-Taylor, Robert Foxworth, Lucas Donat, Nicholas Pryor, Lew Ayres, Sylvia Sidney, Lance Henriksen, Elizabeth Shepherd, Alan Arbus, Fritz Ford, Meshach Taylor.
06/07/78

Damnation Alley
FOX. Landers-Roberts-Zeitman prodn. Prods, Jerome M Zeitman, Paul Maslansky; exec prods, Hal Landers, Bobby Roberts. Dir, Jack Smight. Sp, Alan Sharp, Lukas Heller, from novel by Roger Zelanzny; cam (Deluxe Color), Harry Stradling Jr; edtr, Frank J Urioste; snd, Bruce Bisenz; mus, Jerry Goldsmith; prodn des, Preston Ames; art dir, William Cruse; asst dir, Donald Roberts; sfx, Milt Rice; stunt coord, Dean Jeffries. (MPAA rating: PG). 95.
Jan-Michael Vincent, George Peppard, Dominique Sanda, Paul Winfield, Jackie Earle Haley, Kip Niven.
10/26/77

Damned Be Those Who Cry
(Iran)
X. Iranian Film Prodn, Teheran. Dir, Mohammad-Ali Najafi. Sp, Najafi, Mahmud Ostad Mohamad. 90.
F Gharibian, R Ale Payyam, G Lofti.
(B & W)
09/05/79

The Dancing Hawk: SEE Tanczacy Jastrzab

Dandy, The All American Girl
UA. MGM picture, prod-dir, Jerry Schatzberg. Sp, B J Perla, Marilyn Goldin, from a story by Perla; cam (Metrocolor), Vilmos Zsigmond; edtrs, Evan Lottman, Richard Fetterman; mus, Paul Chihara; art dir, Bill Kenney; set decor, Rick T Gentz; snd, Bertil G Hallberg, Hal Watkins; asst dir, John Nicolella; stunt coord, Ted Duncan. (MPAA rating: PG). 89.
Stockard Channing, Sam Waterston, Richard Doughty, Norman Matlock, Franklyn Ajaye, Ed E Villa, Evan Lottman.
05/26/76

Dangerous Girl: SEE I Sao Untarai

Dani Od Snova
(Days of Dreams)
(Yugoslavia)
YFR. Centar, Dan/Tana Productions prodn. Wri-dir, Vlatko Gilic. Cam (Eastmancolor), Branko Ivatovic; mus, Ksenija Zecevic. 92.
Vladislava Milosavljevic, Boris Komnenic, Ljiljana Krstic.
05/28/80

Danmark er lukket
(Denmark Closed Down)
(Denmark)
NOR. Focus Film prodn. Based on Benny Andersen's stage play "Orfeus In The Underground". Sp, Andersen, Dan Tschernia; dir, Tschernia; cam (Eastmancolor), Claus Loff; prodn mgrs, Erik Overbye, Erik Nissen; edtr, Anker; mus-lyr, Benny Andersen. 85.
Christoffer Bro, Anne Linnet, Claus Ryskjaer, Paul Hagen, Jess Ingerslev, Ove Sprogoe, Olaf Ussing, Peter Steen.
10/15/80

Dante, akta're foer Hajen
(Dante, Mind the Shark)
(Sweden)
EUR. Gunnar Hoglund Film Prodns AB/AB Europa Film prodn. Sp, Linder, Gunnar Hoglund, based on Bengt Linder novel. Dir, Hoglund. Cam (Eastmancolor), Kalle Bergholm; mus, Bjoern Jason Lind, Lasse Berghagen; exec prod, Stig Skoglund; prodn mgr, Michael Hoglund; edtr, Gunnar Hoglund. 100.
Jan Ohlsson, Ulf Hasselkorp, John Harrison, Carli Tornehave, Lillemor Ohlsson.
01/10/79

Dao Ruang
(The Yellow Flower)
(Thailand)
SAH. Prod, Somsak Techaratanaprasert. Exec Prod, Primprapai Galasnimee. Dir, Neramitr. Sp, Tomayanti, Tananya Prapasalobon; cam, Anant Inlaord; mus, Universal Lab; snd, Kasem Militachinda; edtr and lighting, Piyakul Sudpranond; prodn des, Saard Guptarak; continuity, Chaluay Sriratana. 120.
Lalana Sulawan, Tirayuth Silapirat, Jamroon Nuatjim, Adinan Singhilan, Suphan Buranaphim, Cheng Chomaduah, Sayant Chantrawiboon, Bu Vibulnan.
05/23/79

Daredevil's Time: SEE Hajducka Vremena

The Dark
FVI. Edward L Montoro-Dick Clark presentation. Exec prod, Derek Power. Prods, Dick Clark, Edward L Montoro. Asso prod, Igo Kantor. Dir, John (Bud) Cardos. Sp, Stanford Whitmore; cam (Deluxe Color, Panavision), John Morrill; edtr, Martin Dreffke; mus, Roger Kellaway; art dir, Rusty Rosene; snd, Robert Dietz. (MPAA rating: R). 92.

William Devane, Cathy Lee Crosby, Richard Jaeckel, Keenan Wynn, Jacquelyn Hyde, Warren Kemmerling, Biff Elliot, Vivian Blaine, Casey Kasem.
05/02/79

Dark Sun: SEE Temne Slunce

The Dark-Veiled Bride: SEE Kara Carsafli Gelin

Das Andere Laecheln
(The Other Smile)
(W Germany)
LXM. Robert Van Ackeren Film, Berlin, in coprodn with Bavaria Atelier, Munich. Prod, Peter Maerthesheimer. Dir, Robert Van Ackeren. Sp, Van Ackeren, Joy Markert, Peter Stripp; cam, Janken Janssen; edtr, Hannes Nikel. 115.
Katja Rupe, Elisabeth Trissenaar, Heinz Ehrenfreund, Anja Muessiggang.
06/21/78

Das Brot Des Baeckers
(The Baker's Bread)
(W Germany)
X. Artus-Film prodn in collab with Zweites Deutsches Fernsehen (ZDF), Wiesbaden. Dir, Erwin Keusch. Sp, Keusch, Karl Saurer; cam (Eastmancolor), Dietrich Lohmann; mus, Condor; art dirs, Peter Herrmann, Joerg Schmidner; edtr, Lilo Krueger; snd, Peter Wagner. 117.
Bernd Tauber, Guenter Lamprecht, Maria Lucca, Sylvia Reize, Anita Lochner, Manfred Seipold, Gerhard Acktun, Krystian Martinek, Ronald Nitschke.
04/27/77

Das Chinesische Wunder
(The Chinese Miracle)
(W Germany)
TRO. Cinema 77 - Hans Pflueger, prodn. Dir, Wolfgang Liebeneiner. Sp, Manfred Barthel, Kurt Nachmann; cam, Goetz Neumann. 94.
Heinz Ruehmann, Senta Berger, Christian Kohlund, Harald Leipnitz, Peter Pasetti.
02/09/77

Das Ende Des Regenbogens
(The End of the Rainbow)
(W Germany)
BSG. Basis-Film prodn, Berlin, with Westdeutscher Rundfunk (WDR). Wri-dir, Uwe Friessner. Cam, Frank Bruehne; edtr, Stefanie Wilke; mus, Alexander Kraut, Klaus Krueger, Michael Nuschke, Matthias Kaebs; sets, Edwin Wengoborski, Martin Mohr. 107.
Thomas Kufahl, Slavica Rankovic, Henry Lutze, Udo Samuel, Heinz Hoenig, Sabine Baruth.
10/31/79

Das Fuenfte Gebot
(The Fifth Commandment)
(W Germany)
NCT. Oase-Film Prodn. Jelka Naber. Dir, Duccio Tessari; sp, Michael Lentz, Tessari; cam, Jost Vacano; edtr, Eugenio Alabiso; sets, Bernhard Sauter; mus, Armando Trovaioli. 113.
Helmut Berger, Peter Hooten, Udo Kier, Heinrich Giskes.
05/23/79

Das gefrorene Herz
(The Frozen Heart)
(Switzerland - W Germany - Austria)
CBZ. Fernsehen DRS (Swiss TV), ZDF (2nd German TV) and ORF (Austrian TV) coprodn. Prod, Cine Group Zurich. Wri-dir, Xavier Koller, from a short story by Meinrad Inglin. Cam (Eastmancolor), Hans Liechti; mus, Hardy Hepp; edtr, Fee Liechti; art dir, Rolf Engler; cos, Sylvia de Stoutz. 108.
Sigfrit Steiner, Emilia Krakowska, Paul Buehlmann, Otto Maechtlinger, Heinz Buehlmann, Erwin Kohlund, Giovanni Frueh, Volker Prechtel, Guenter Lamprecht, Vera Schweiger, Herbert Leiser.
02/20/80

Das Licht Auf Dem Galgen
(The Light on the Gallows)
(E Germany)
DEE. VEB DEFA prodn, Berlin Group Roter Kreis. Wri-dir, Helmut Nitzschke. Cam (Orwocolor), Claus Neumann; art advisor, Thea Richter; art dir, Heinz Roeske; mus, Karl-Ernst Sasse; prodn mgr, Dorothea Hildebrandt. 90.
Alexander Lang, Amza Pelea, Juergen Holtz, Erwin Geschonneck, Szymon Szurmiej, Volkmar Kleinert, Samuel Klaxton, Tito Junco.
06/01/77

Das Netz
(The Net)
(W Germany)
COL. Luggi Waldleitner prodn for Roxy-Film, Munich. Based on Hans Habe novel. Wri-dir, Manfred Purzer; cam, Charly Steinberger; mus, Klaus Doldinger, Vivaldi. 100.
Mel Ferrer, Klaus Kinski, Heinz Bennent, Elke Sommer, Andrea Rau, Susanne Uhlen, Carlo de Mejo, Claudio Gora, Franz Rudnick, Willi Rose, Sabine von Maydell, Maria d'Incoronato, Giovanella Grifeo.
(English soundtrack)
04/07/76

Das Versteck
(The Hiding Place)
(E Germany)
DEE. DEFA, Group Johanisthal Film Prodn, in collab with der Fernsehen der DDR. Dir, Frank Beyer. Sp, Jurek Becker; cam, Juergen Brauer; mus, Guenther Fischer. 101.
Jutta Hoffman, Manfred Krug, Dieter Mann, Alfred Mueller, Marita Boehme.
03/12/80

Das Zweite Erwachen Der Christa Klages
(The Second Awakening of Krista Klages)
(W Germany)
FDA. Bioskop-Film, Munich, prodn in collab with Westdeutscher Rundfunk, Cologne. Dir, Margarethe von Trotta. Sp, von Trotta, Luisa Francia; cam, Franz Rath; snd, Vladimir Vizner; mus, Klaus Doldinger; edtr, Anette Dorn; exec prod, Eberhard Junkersdorf. 93.
Tina Engel, Silvia Reize, Katharina Thalbach, Marius Muller-Westernhagen, Peter Schneider.
06/21/78

The Daughter-In-Law: SEE Snaha

David
(W Germany)
FDA. Vietinghof Filmproduktion, Pro-Ject Film Produktion, Filmverlag Der Autoren, ZDF, Dedra Pictures prodn. Dir, Peter Lilienthal. Sp, Jurek Becker, Ulla Zieman, Lilienthal from the book by Joel Konig; cam (Eastmancolor), Al Ruban; edtr, Siegrun Jager; mus, Wojiech Kilar. 125.
Walter Taub, Irena Vrkljan, Eva Mattes, Mario Fischel, Dominique Horwitz.
03/07/79

Dawn
(Australia)
HOY. Aquataurus Film Productions presentation in asso with the South Australian Film Corporation. Prod, Joy Cavill. Dir, Ken Hannam. Sp, Cavill; cam, Russell Boyd; edtr, Max Lemon; snd, Ken Hammond; art dir, Ross Major; asst dirs, Mark Egerton, Penny Chapman, Scott Hicks. 111.
Bronwyn Mackay-Payne, Tom Richards, John Diedrich, Bunney Brooke, Ron Haddrick, Gabrielle Hartley, Ivar Kantz, David Cameron, Kevin Wilson, Lyndall Barbour, John Clayton, Margaret Gerard, Don Barkham, Joan Evatt, Go Mikami, Carmelina Caterina.
04/25/79

Dawn of the Dead
UF. Laurel Group-Alfredo Cuomo and Claudio Argento prodn, presented by Herbert Steinmann and Billy Baxter. Prod, Richard Rubinstein. Dir, George Romero. Sp, Romero; cam (Technicolor), Michael Gornick; script consultant, Dario Argento; edtrs, Romero, Kenneth Davidow; make-up-sfx, Tom Savini; snd, Tony Buba; lighting, Carl Augenstein; cos, Josie Caruso; asst dir, Christine Forrest. 125.
David Emge, Ken Foree, Scott Reiniger, Gaylen Ross.
04/18/79

The Day Elvis Came To Bremerhaven: SEE Der Tag, An Dem Elvis Nach Bremerhaven Kam

Day for My Love: SEE Den Pro Mou Lasku

The Day of Glory: SEE Le Jour De Gloire

Day Of The Animals
FVI. Prod, Edward L Montoro. Dir, William Girdler. Sp, William Norton, Eleanor E Norton; cam (DeLuxe Color), Bob Sorrentino; edtrs, Bub Asman, James Mitchell; mus, Lalo Schifrin. (MPAA rating: PG). 95.
Christopher George, Leslie Nielson, Lynda Day George, Richard Jaeckel, Michael Ansara, Ruth Roman, Jon Cedar, Paul Mantee, Walter Barnes, Susan Backlinie.
06/08/77

The Day of the Vistula: SEE Dzien Wisly

Day of the Woman
X. Cinemagic Pictures Inc. Prods, Joseph Zbeda, Meir Zarchi. Dir-sp, Zarchi; cam, Youri Haviv; edtr, Zarchi. (MPAA rating: R). 101.
Camille Keaton, Eron Tabor, Richard Pace, Anthony Nichols.
11/22/78

The Day Time Ended
CPQ. Vortex prodn. Prods, Wayne Schmidt, Steve Neill. Exec prod, Charles Band. Dir, John (Bud) Cordos. Sp, Schmidt, J Larry Carroll, David Schmoeller; cam (Metrocolor), John A Morrill; edtr, Ted Nicolaou; mus, Richard Band; asst dir, Bob Shug; art dir, Rusty Rosene; special visual effects, Paul W Gentry, David Allen, Randy Cook; ani effects supv, Pete Kuran; "City of Light" visual effects, Jim Danforth; stop-motion ani, Lyle Conway; models des, Lain Liska; models execution, Greg Jein. (MPAA rating: PG). 79.
Jim Davis, Christopher Mitchum, Dorothy Malone, Mercy Lafferty, Scott Kolden, Natasha Ryan, Roberto Contreras.
11/19/80

Dayereh Cycle
(The Mina Cycle)
(Iran)
TFI. Dir, Dariush Mehrjui. Sp, G H Sahedi, Mehrjui; cam (Eastmancolor), Houshang Baharlou; edtr, Talat Mirfenderski. 95.
E Entezani, Fourouzan, Ali Nassirian, Said Kangarani.
11/16/77

The Days Are Passing: SEE Zemaljski Dani Teku

Days of Dreams: SEE Dani Od Snova

Days Of Heaven
PAR. O P prodn. Prods, Bert and Harold Schneider; exec prod, Jacob Brackman. Wri-dir, Terrence Malick. Cam (Metrocolor), Nestor Almendros; additional pho, Haskell Wexler; art dir, Jack Fisk; edtr, Billy Weber; mus, Ennio Morricone; cos, Patricia Norris; addl mus, Leo Kottke; snd mixers, George Ronconi, Barry Thomas; Dolby consultants, Steve Katz, Philip Boole, Clyde McKinney; spec snd effects, James Cox; sfx, John Thomas, Mel Merrells; second unit dir, Jacob Brackman; second unit pho, Paul Ryan; set decor, Robert Gould; asst dir, Skip Cosper. (MPAA rating: PG). 95.
Richard Gere, Brooke Adams, Sam Shepard, Linda Manz, Robert Wilke, Jackie Shultis, Stuart Margolin, Tim Scott, Gene Bell, Doug Kershaw.
09/13/78

Days of the Past: SEE Los Dias Del Pasado

De Fresa, Limon Y Menta
(Strawberry, Lemon and Mint)
(Spain)
X. Zeppo Films (Madrid) prodn; dir, Miguel Angel Diez; sp, Fernando Colomo, Diez; cam (Eastmancolor), Miguel Angel Trujillo; sets, Antonio de Miguel; edtr, Julio Pena; exec prod, Imanol Uribe. 90.
Emilio Gutierrez Caba, Kiti Manver, Carmen Maura, Miguel Arribas, Felix Rotaeta, Maria Luisa Ponte, Maria Paz Ballesteros.
09/28/77

De 141 Dage
(The 141 Days)
(Denmark)
X. BT-Klubben prodn. Dir, Ib Makwarth. Edtr, typesetters and film technicians under Toerk Haxtausen's supv; cam (Eastmancolor), Peter Klitgard, Gregers Nielsen, Frank Paulsen, Peter Roos, Philip Sadolin, Tonni Nielsen, Joergen Nielsen; mus, Andy Sundstroem, Jan Toftlund, Faellesakkorden, Den Roede Lue. 101.
(DOC)
09/14/77

De Plaats van de Vreemdeling
(The Alien)
(Holland)
X. Movies Filmproductions B V prodn. Dir, Rudolf van den Berg. Cam, Theo van de Sande; edtr, Tom de Graaf; mus, Louis Andriessen. 89. (DOC) (16m) (English subtitles)
03/26/80

De Verworking van Herman Durer
(The Demise of Herman Durer)
(Holland)
X. Virginia Films B V prodn. Prod, Hans Klap. Dir-sp, Rene Seegers, Jean van de Velde, Leon de Winter, based on a novel by de Winter; cam, Sjoerd Jansen; edtr, Rene Seegers; mus, Angelo Branduardi; snd, Jan Musch. 108.
Felix-Jan Kuipers, Alma, Albert Abspoel, Ed van Gils, Miek Smit, Vivan Lampe.
(Dutch soundtrack - English subtitles)
03/26/80

De Witte Van Sichem
(Whitey)
(Belgium)
NSF. New Star-Visie prodn. Prods, Henk Van Soom, Roland Verhavert. Dir, Robbe de Hert. Sp, Fernand Auwera, Robbe de Hert, Gaston Durnez, Louis-Paul Boon, based on work of Ernest Claes; cam (Eastmancolor), Walter Van den Ende, Theo van de Sande; edtr, Ton de Graaf; snd, Andre Patrouille; art dir, Philippe Graff; cos, Ann Verhoeven. Set decor, Andre Fonteyne; mus, Jurgen Knieper; songs, Wannes van de Velde, Walter Heynen. 106.
Eric Clerckx, Paul S Jongers, Blanka Heirman, Jos Verbist, Magda De Winter, Ralf Troch, Luc Philips, Martha Dewachter, Paul-Emiel Van Royen, Bert Struys.
06/25/80

The De Yongs
(Yugoslavia)
YFR. Center FRZ Belgrade prodn. Dir, Mica Milosevic. Sp, Milosevic, A Dragojevic; cam (Eastmancolor), Dj. Nikolic. 70.
(DOC)
09/22/76

The Dead-End: SEE Bon Bast

Dead Man's Float
(Australia)
LYN. Andromedia Prodn. Prod, Tom Broadbridge; dir, Peter Sharp; sp, Roger Carr, based on his novel; cam, David Eggby; asst dir, Michael McKeag; snd, Gary Wilkins; edtr, Clifford Hayes. 75.
Sally Boyden, Greg Rowe, Jacqui Gordon, Rick Ireland, Bill Hunter, Sue Jones, John Heywood, Gus Mercurio, Brian Hannan, Marcel Cugola, Ernie Sigley, Bunney Brooke, Chris Hayward.
08/20/80

Dead or Alive: SEE Elve Vagy Halva

The Dead Pay the Price for Death: SEE Tsenu Smerti Sprosi u Miortvykh

Dead Times: SEE Temps Morts

Deadly Cruelty: SEE Crueldade Mortal

The Deadly Females
(Britain)
X. Donwin prodn. Prod-wri-dir, Donovan Winter. Cam (Eastmancolor), Austin Parkinson. 105.
Tracy Reed, Bernard Holley, Scott Fredericks, Heather Chasen, Brian Jackson, Roy Purcell, Jean Harrington, Olivia Munday, Jean Rimmer, Raymond Young, Lans Travers, Angela Jay, Gennie Nevison, Graham Ashley, Rula Lenska.
12/01/76

Deadly Hero
AVE. Prod, Thomas J McGrath; exec prods, Robert Liberman, Stanley Plotnick. Dir, Ivan Nagy. Sp, George Wislocki; cam (Movielab Color), Andrzej Bartkowiak; edtr, Susan Steinberg; mus, Brad Fiedel, Tommy Mandel; art dir, Alan Herman; snd, Al Gramaglia, Nigel Nobel; asst dir, Jack Baran. (MPAA rating: R). 99.
Don Murray, Diahn Williams, James Earl Jones, Lilia Skala, George S Irving, Treat Williams, Charles Siebert, Hank Garrett, Dick A Williams, Mel Berger, Virginia Sandifur, Ronald Weyand.
08/11/76

Deal
X. Schott-Vaughn prodn presented by Document C B. Prod, E J Vaughn. Dir, John Schott, Vaughn in collab with Robert M Young. Conceived by Robert Horvitz, Schott, Vaughn. Cam, Young, Tom McDonough; edtr, Schott; snd, Larry Loewinger, Vic Losick. 95. (DOC)
02/01/78

Dear Boys: SEE Lieve Jongens

Dear Comrades: SEE Queridos Companeros

Dear Fatherland, Be at Peace: SEE Lieb Vaterland, Magst Ruhig Sein

Dear Friends: SEE Queridas Amigas

Dear Michael: SEE Caro Michele

Dear Papa: SEE Caro Papa

Dear Wife: SEE Cara Sposa

Dearest Executioners: SEE Queridisimos Verdugos

Death at an Old Mansion: SEE Honjin Satsujin Jiken

Death at Dawn: SEE Muerte Al Amanecer

Death At Work: SEE La Morte Al Lavoro

Death Collector
EPO. Goldstone Film Enterprise prodn. Prod, William Panzer; exec prod, Peter S Davis. Wri-dir, Ralph De Vito. Cam, Bob Bailan. (MPAA rating: R). 85.
Joseph Cortese, Lou Criscuola, Joseph Pesci, Anne Johns, Keith Davis.
02/02/77

Death Duel
(Hong Kong)
SHW. Runme Shaw and Mona Fong prodn. Exec prod, Chen Lieh. Dir, Chu Yuan. Cam, Huang Chieh; edtr, Chiang Hsing-lung; martial arts instructors, Tang Chia, Huang Peichi. 92.
Ling Yun, Chen Ping, Erh Tung Sheng, Fan Mei Sheng, Yu Ann An, Ku Feng.
(Mandarin soundtrack; English subtitles)
07/27/77

Death Game
L-P. Larry Spiegel & Mel Bergman presentation. Exec prods, Bergman, William Duffy. Prods, Spiegel, Peter Traynor. Dir, Traynor; sp, Anthony Overman, Michael Ronald Ross; cam, David Worth; mus, Jimmie Haskell. (MPAA rating: R). 89.
Sondra Locke, Colleen Camp, Seymour Cassel, Beth Brickell, Michael Kalmansohn, Ruth Warshawsky.
04/27/77

Death Has No Mercy
(Philippines)
07/25/79
MRK. Prod, Jesse Chua. Wri-dir, Cesar Gallardo. Cam, Rey Lapid; mus, Ernanie Cuenco; snd, Rolly Rota; cos-make-up, Rhoda Perez. 120.
Lito Lapid, Marian de la Riva, Eddie Garcia, Rosemarie Gil, Nello Nayo.

Death Is My Trade
(W Germany)
X. WDR-Cologne and Iduna Film (Munich) prodn. Dir-wri, Theodor Kotulla. Cam (Eastmancolor), Dieter Naujeck; exec prods, Volker Canaris, Nils Nillson, based on novel, "La Mort est Mon Metier," by Robert Merle; edtr, Wolfgang Richter; sets, Wolfgang Schuenke; cos, Uta Wilhelm. 139.
Goetz George, Elisabeth Schwarz, Kai Taschner, Sigurd Fitzek, Peter Franke, Wilfried Elste, Hans Korte, Matthias Fuchs.
07/27/77

Death Magazine or How To Become a Flowerpot: SEE Todesmagazin order Wie werde ich ein Blumentopf

Death of a Cameraman: SEE Morte Di Un Operatore

Death Of A Corrupt Man: SEE Mort D'Un Pourri

The Death of the Fisherman Marc Leblanc: SEE Der Tod Des Fischers Marc Leblanc

Death of the President: SEE Zmierc Prezydenta

Death of the Water Carrier: SEE Essakamat

Death On The Nile
(Britain)
PAR. John Brabourne, Richard Goodwin prodn. Dir, John Guillermin. Sp, Anthony Shaffer; cam, Jack Cardiff; prodn des, Peter Murton; edtr, Malcolm Cooke; cos, Anthony Powell; mus, Nino Rota; asso prod, Norton Knatchbull; asst dir, Ted Sturgis. (MPAA rating: PG). 140.
Peter Ustinov, Jane Birkin, Lois Chiles, Bette Davis, Mia Farrow, Jon Finch, Olivia Hussey, George Kennedy, Angela Lansbury, Simon MacCorkindale, David Niven, Maggie Smith, Jack Warden, Harry Andrews, I S Johar.
09/27/78

Death Or Freedom: SEE Tod Ode Freiheit

Death Play
NL. Prods, Norman I Cohen, Joseph Lyttle. Dir, Arthur Storch. Sp, Jeff Tamborino; cam, Gerald Cotts; edtr, Arthur Williams; mus, Rupert Holmes; snd, John Bolz; cos, Francine Tint. (MPAA rating: PG). 86.
Karen Leslie, Michael Higgins, James Keach, Hy Anzel, James Catusi, Elizabeth Farley, Don Fellows, Jack Hollander, Robert Jackson, Zina Jasper, Virginia Kiser, James Noble, Nancy R Pollock, Stephen Strimpell.
09/08/76

Death Ship
(Canada)
AVE. Astral Bellevue-Pathe-Bloodstar prodn. Prods, Derek Gibson, Harold Greenberg. Dir, Alvin Rakoff. Exec prod, Sandy Howard. Sp, John Robins; cam (CFI), Rene Verzier; edtr, Mike Campbell; art dirs, Chris Burke, Michel Proulx; sfx, Mike Albrechtsen; snd, Henri Blondeau; asst dir, Charles Braive. (MPAA rating: R). 91.
George Kennedy, Richard Crenna, Nick Mancuso, Sally Ann Howes, Kate Reid, Victoria Burgoyne, Jennifer McKinney, Danny Higham, Saul Rubinek.
04/16/80

Death Weekend
(The House By the Lake)
(Canada)
CPX. Prod, Ivan Reitman; exec prods, John Dunning, Andre Link. Dir, William Freut. Sp, Freut; cam, Robert Saad; edtrs, Jean LaFleur, Debbie Karjala; art dir, Roy Forge Smith; mus supv, Reitman; snd, Dan Goldberg, Joe Grimaldi. (MPAA rating: R). 94.
Brenda Vaccaro, Don Stroud, Chuck Shamata, Richard Ayres, Kyle Edwards, Don Granbery, Ed McNamara.
10/06/76

Deathcheaters
(Australia)
RDP. Brian Trenchard Smith Prodns and D L. Taffner/Australia prodn. Prod-dir, Brian Trenchard Smith. Exec prod, Richard Brennan. Sp, Michael Cove; story, Brian Trenchard Smith; cam, John Seale; mus, Peter J Martin; art dir, Darrel Lass; ward, Jenni Campbell; stunt coord, Grant Page; edtr, Ron Williams; makeup, Jill Porter. 96.
John Hargreaves, Grant Page, Margaret Gerard, Noel Ferrier, Judith Woodroffe,

Ralph Cotterill, John Kummel, Drew Forsythe, Brian Trenchard Smith, Michael Aitkens, Roger Ward, Wallas Eaton, Dale Aspin, Peter Collingwood, Chris Hayward, Ann Semler, Max Aspin, David Bracks.
12/22/76

Deathsport
NW. Prod, Roger Corman. Dirs, Henry Suso, Allen Arkush. Sp, Suso, Donald Stewart, from a story by Francis Doel; cam (Metrocolor), Gary Graver; edtr, Larry Bock; mus, Andrew Stein; art dir, Sharon Compton; sfx, Jack Rabin; asst dirs, Tom Jacobson, Jim Burnett; snd, Paul Hunt. (MPAA rating: R). 83.
David Carradine, Claudia Jennings, Richard Lynch, William Smithers, Will Walker, David McLean, Jesse Vint, H B Haggerty, John Himes.
04/26/78

Deathwatch
(France - W Germany)
PLF. Selta Films-Little Bear-Antenne 2-Sara Films-Gaumont-SFP-TV 13 (Munich) co-prodn. Prods, Gabriel Boustani, Janine Rubeiz. Co-prod-dir, Bertrand Tavernier. Wris, Tavernier, David Rayfiel, based on novel, "The Continous Katherine Mortenhoe" (U S title: "The Unsleeping Eye"), by David Compton; cam (Panavision-Fujicolor), Pierre-William Glenn; mus, Antoine Duhamel; edtrs, Armand Psenny, Michael Ellis; art dir, Tony Pratt; snd, Michel Desrois. 128.
Romy Schneider, Harvey Keitel, Harry Dean Stanton, Therese Liotard, Max Von Sydow.
(English-language version)
02/06/80

Dedicatoria
(Dedicated To. . .)
(Spain)
X. Elias Querejeta prodn. Dir, Jaime Chavarri. Sp, Elias Querejeta, Jaime Chavarri; cam (Eastmancolor), Teo Escamilla; edtr, Pablo G del Amo; sets, Antonio Belison; snd, Bernardo Menz. 99.
Jose Luis Gomez, Amparo Munoz, Patricia Adriani, Francisco Casares, Luis Politti, Helene Peycherand, Marie Mansart, Claude Legros.
05/28/80

The Deep
COL. Col-EMI presentation, prod, Peter Guber. Dir, Peter Yates. Sp, Peter Benchley, Tracy Keenan Wynn, from Benchley's novel; cam (Metrocolor), Christopher Challis; 2d-unit (underwater) dir-cam, Al Giddings, Stan Waterman; supv edtr, Robert L Wolfe; edtr, David Berlatsky; mus, John Barry; prodn des, Tony Masters; art dir, Jack Maxted; underwriter art dir, Terry Ackland-Snow; set decor, Vernon Dixon; cos-ward, Ron Talsky, Tom Bronson; snd, Hal Landaker, Fred Brown, Ross Taylor, Robin Gregory, Dana Wood; stunt coords, Howard Curtis, Bob Minor, Jim Nickerson, Richard Washington; asst dir, Derek Cracknell. (MPAA rating: PG). 124.
Robert Shaw, Jacqueline Bisset, Nick Nolte, Louis Gossett, Eli Wallach, Robert Tessier, Earl Maynard, Dick Anthony Williams, Bob Minor, Teddy Tucker, Lee McClain.
06/22/77

Deep Jaws
CDE. TFC1 prodn. Exec prod, Charles Teitel. Dir, Perry Dell. Sp, Walt Davis, based on story, Teitel; cam, Manuel S Conde; edtr, Andrew Herbert; developed for the screen by Conde; prodn mgr, Buck Buckalew; asst prodn mgr, Loretta Samaniego; mus and vocals, Jack Millman; snd, Manny Conde Jr. (Self-imposed X rating). 89.
David Kelly, Anne Gaybis, Gordon Herigstadt, Candy Samples, Sandra Casey, Rhiannon Vaughan, Richard Nathan, Byron Cole, Gordon Freed, Adrianna Bijou, Mickel Van Scott, Earl Karpen, Lady Diana, Suzanne Delor, Wilma Shock.
05/05/76

Deep Red: SEE Profondo Rosso

The Deer Hunter
U. U-EMI Films prodn. Prod, Barry Spikings, Michael Deeley, Michael Cimino, John Peverall. Dir, Cimino. Sp, Deric Washburn, from a story by Cimino, Washburn, Louis Garfinkle and Quinn K Redeker; cam, Vilmos Zsigmond; art dirs, Ron Hobbs, Kim Swados; edtr, Peter Zinner; mus, Stanley Myers; set decors, Dick Goddard, Alan Hicks; asso prods, Marion Rosenberg, Joann Carelli; snd, Darrin Knight; asst dir, Charles Okun. (MPAA rating: R). 183.
Robert DeNiro, John Cazale, John Savage, Christopher Walken, Meryl Streep, George Dzundza, Chuck Aspegren, Shirley Stoler, Rutanya Alda, Pierre Segui, Mady Kaplan.
11/29/78

Deewar
(The Wall)
(India)
X. Trimurti Film prod, Gulshan Rai. Dir, Yash Chopra. Sp, Salim-Javed; cam, Kay Gee, Romesh Bhalla. 168.
Shashi Kapoor, Amitabh Bachan, Neetu Singh, Parveen Babi, Nirupa Roy.
01/19/77

The Defense Takes the Floor: SEE Slovo Dlia Zaschity

Defiance
AIP. Necta film prodn. Prods, William S Gilmore Jr, Jerry Bruckheimer. Dir, John Flynn. Exec prod, Robert J Wunsch. Sp, Thomas Michael Donnelly based on a story by Donnelly and Mark Tulin. Cam, Ric Waite; edtr, David Finfer; prodn des, Bill Malley; mus, Basil Poledouris; orig sngs and addl score, Gerard McMahon; set decor, Rick T Gentz; cos, Ellis Cohen; snd, William Nelson; asst dir, Peter Bogart. (MPAA rating: PG). 102.
Jan Michael Vincent, Theresa Saldana, Fernando Lopez, Danny Aiello, Art Carney, Santos Morales, Don Blakely, Frank Pesce, Rudy Ramos, Lee Fraser, Randy Herman, Alberto Vazquez, Church Ortix, East Carlo, Lenny Montana.
03/12/80

Defiant Delta: SEE Prkosna Delta

Delirium
07/25/79
ODY. Worldwide Prodn (Delirium Associates). Prods, Sunny Vest, Peter Maris. Exec prod, Mark Cusumano. Dir, Peter Maris. Sp, Richard Yalem; story, Yalem, Eddie Krell, Jim Loew; mus, David Williams; cam, John Huston, Bill Mensch; edtr, Dan Perry; sfx, Bob Shelly. (MPAA rating: R). 90.
Debi Chaney, Turk Cekovsky, Terry Ten Broeck, Barron Winchester, Nick Panouzis, Bob Winters, Garrett Bergfeld, Harry Gorsuch, Chris Chronopolis, Lloyd Schattyn, Jack Garvey, Mike Kalist, Myron Kozman.

Delitto A Porta Romana
(Crime At Porta Romana)
(Italy)
TIT. Prod, Giovanni Di Clemente for Cleminternazionale Prodns. Dir, Bruno Corbucci. Sp, Mario Amendola, Corbucci; cam (Technicolor), Giovanni Ciarlo; art dir, Claudio Cinini; edtr, Daniele Alabiso; mus, Franco Miccolizzi. 94.
Tomas Milian, Olimpia Di Nardo, Nerino Montagnai, Bombolo.
12/17/80

Deliver Us from Evil: SEE Szabadits Meg A Gonosztol

Demain les Momes
(Tomorrow's Children)
(France)
X. Unite Trois prodn. Dir, Jean Pourtale. Sp, Pourtale, Franck Vialle, Raymond Lepoutre; cam, Jean-Jacques Rochut; edtr, Philippe Gosselet; snd engr, Roger Lettellier; cos-sets, Michel Farge; makeup, Jose Denizot; coord, Mireille Merx Tanguy; mus, Eric De Marsan; prodn dir, Alain Dahan. 95.
Niels Arestrug, Michel Esposito, Brigitte Rouan, Emmanuelle Beart.
11/10/76

The Demise of Herman Durer: SEE De Verworking van Herman Durer

Demon Lover Diary
X. A film by Joel DeMott. 90.
(DOC) (16m)
02/13/80

Demon Pond: SEE Yashaga Ike

Demon Seed
UA. MGM picture, prod, Herb Jaffe. Dir, Donald Cammell. Sp, Robert Jaffe, Roger O Hirson, based on the novel by Dean R Koontz; cam (Metrocolor), Bill Butler; edtr, Francisco Mazzola; mus, Jerry Fielding; prodn des, Edward C Carfagno; set decor, Barbara Kreiger; snd, Jerry Jost, William McCaughey; cos-ward, Sandy Cole, Bucky Rous, Joie Hutchinson; asst dir, Edward A Teets. (MPAA rating: R). 94.
Julie Christie, Fritz Weaver, Gerrit Graham, Berry Kroeger, Lisa Lu, Larry J Blake, Dana Laurita, Robert Vaughn.
03/30/77

Demons du midi
(Demons of the South)
(France - Spain - Belgium)
GAU. C P Prodn (France)/2000 Prodn (Belgium)/Imago International (Spain) co-prodn. Prod-dir, Christian Paureilhe. Sp, Paureilhe, Sylvie Coste; cam (Eastmancolor), Georges Barsky, Lionel Legros; edtr, Delphine Desfons; mus, Michel Berno'hc.   103.
Pierre Mondy, Micheline Presle, Sylvie Coste.
02/06/80

Den allvarsamme Leken
(The Serious Game)
(Sweden - Norway)
SVF. Swedish Film Institute-AB Sandrews-AS Norsk Film (Oslo) prodn. Dir, Anja Breien. Sp, Breien, Per Blom, Bengt Forslund, based on Hjalmar Sohderberg novel; cam (Eastmancolor), Erling Thurmann-Andersen; exec prod, Bengt Forslund; edtr, Edith Thoreg; prodn des, Ulf Axen, Eva Renman; mus, excerpts from Beethoven, Dvorak, Mozart, Chopin, Friedrich von Flotow.   102.
Stefan Ekman, Lil Terselius, Allan Edwall, Katarina Gustafsson.
08/31/77

Den attonde dagen
(The Eight Day)
(Sweden)
SVE. Based on novel by Rose Lagerkrantz. Wri-dir, Anders Groenros. Exec prod, Olle Hellbom. Cam (Eastmancolor), Joergen Persson, Rolf Lindstroem; edtr, Yolanda Knobel; mus, Keith Jarrett.   92.
Susanna Radoe, Benny Feher, Bo-Patrik Gusterman, Tin-Tin Andersson, Per Leonstroem.
08/15/79

Den Dobbelte Mand
(The Double Man)
(Denmark)
KID. Steen Herdel/Franz Ernst prodn. Dir, Franz Ernst. Orig story-sp, Kirsten Thorup, Franz Ernst; cam (Eastmancolor), Dirk Bruel; edtr, Christian Hartkopp; mus, Fuzzy.   80.
Erik Wedersoe, Peter Belli, Inge Margrethe Svendsen, Lane Lind.
04/07/76

Den enes doed. . .
(One Man's Loss. . .)
(Sweden)
SVF. Movie Makers Sweden AB/Europa AB/Swedish Film Institute prodn. Wri-dir, Stellan Olsson. Based on Poul Oerum's novel "The Unforgiving"; cam (Fuji color), Odd Geir Saether, Torbjoern Andersson; edtr, Lasse Lundberg; mus, Christer Boustedt; exec prod, Bert Sundberg; prod mgr, Gustav Wiklund.   106.
Jan Waldecranz, Agneta Ekmanner, Christer Boustedt, Anders Granstroem, Gunnar Oehlund.
06/04/80

Den Korte Sommer
(That Brief Summer)
(Denmark)
WCT. Crone Film/Edward Fleming prodn. Wri-dir, Edward Fleming. Cam (Eastmancolor), Henning Kristiansen; mus, Ole Hoyer, Edward Fleming; edtr, Lizzie Weichenfeldt; in charge of prodn, Joergen Hinch; prodn des, Erik Bjoerck.   88.
Casper Bjoerck, Ghita Noerby, Bodil Udsen, Ove Sprogoe, Ole Larsen, Lone Hertz.
01/28/76

Den Pro Mou Lasku
(Day for My Love)
(Czechoslovakia)
X. Czech Film prodn (Prague), Barrandov Studios. Dir, Juraj Herz. Sp, Marketa Zinnerova; cam (Eastmancolor), Jiri Machane; mus, Petr Hapka.   90.
Marta Vancurova, Vlastimil Harapes, Jirina Sejbalova, Dana Medricka, Eva Pichova, Lubomir Cernik, Zofie Vesela, Jan Hartl, Ema Cerna, Eva Svobodova.
03/09/77

Dendang Perantau
(Stranger's Melody)
(Malaysia)
07/25/79
VRA. Prod, Mustafa Haji Ton. Wri-dir, Jamil Sulong. Cam, Abdul Rackman; lighting, Roger Idris; mus, Kasem Masdoor; snd, Peter Lim of Perfima Studio, Kuala Lumpur; edtr, Salehan; cos-make-up, Yurni Mastafa.   100.
Rathip Ibrahim, Uji Raschid, Hali Amir, Deh Farida, Urni Ka Isuk, Rurnaino.

Denmark Closed Down: SEE
Danmark er lukket

Der Amerikanische Freund
(The American Friend)
(W Germany - France)
FDM. Road Movies Filmproduktion-Les Films Du Losange-Wim Wenders Produktion-Westdeutsche Rundfunk prodn. Wri-dir, Wim Wenders, from book, "Ripley's Game," by Patricia Highsmith. Cam (Eastmancolor), Bobby Muller; edtr, Peter Przygodda; mus, Jurgen Knieper.   127.
Dennis Hopper, Bruno Ganz, Lisa Kreuzer, Gerard Blin, Nicholas Ray, Sam Fuller, Peter Lilienthal, Daniel Schmidt, Lou Castel.
06/08/77

Der Aufrechte Gang
(Walking Upright)
(W Germany)
X. Basis Film Verleih prodn in collab with Westdeutsches Rundfunk (WDR). Wri-dir, Christian Ziewer, with story advice by Klaus Wiese. Cam, Ulli Heiser; edtr, Stephanie Wilke; mus, Erhard Grosskopf.   115.
Claus Eberth, Antje Hagen, Wolfgang Liere, Walter Pruessing, Rainer Pigulla, Mathias Eberth, Martina Hennig.
06/30/76

Der Aufstand
(The Uprising)
(W Germany)
X. Istmo Film Production, in co-prodn with Provobis, von Vietinghoff Film, and Zweites Deutsches Fernsehen (ZDF), Munich-Berlin, San Jose (Costa Rica). Dir, Peter Lilienthal. Sp, Lilienthal, Antonio Skarmeta; cam, Michael Ballhaus.   90.
Carlos Catania, Oscar Castillo, Guido Saenz, Agustin Pereira.
07/02/80

Der Comanche
(W Germany)
X. Herbert Achternbusch Film Prodn, Munich, in collab with Second German Television (ZDF), Wiesbaden-Mainz. Prod-wri-dir, Herbert Achternbusch. Cam, Joerg Schmidt-Reitwein; edtr, Heidi Handorf.   90.
Annamirl Bierbichler, Barbara Gass, Heinz Braun, Brigitte Kramer, Franz Baumgaretner, Herbert Achternbusch, Sepp Bierbichler.
09/19/79

Der Durchdreher
(It Can Only Get Worse)
(W Germany)
ATF. Helmut Dietl Film Prodn, prod, Balance Film, Munich. Wri-dir, Helmut Dietl. Cam, Fred Tammes, Hermann Fahr, Lothar-Elias Stickelbrucks; snd, Ed Parente; sets, Jochen O Schmidt, Peter Grundke; cos, Bernd Stockinger; edtr, Thea Exmess.   95.
Towje Kleiner, Mo Schwarz, Helmut Fischer, Ilse Neubauer, Herb Andress, Dieter Augustin, Toni Berger, Lambert Hamel, Kurt Huebner, Christine Kaufmann, Karl Lieffen, Alexander May, Richard Muench, Rolf Olsen, Barbara Valentin, Helen Vita.
05/23/79

Der Erfinder
(The Inventor)
(Switzerland)
RXF. Kurt Gloor prodn in collab with ZDF (2d German TV), Swiss TV, Jean Frey AG and Dr A Eric Scotom. Wri-dir, Gloor, from a play by Hansjoerg Schneider. Cam (Fujicolor), Franz Rath; edtr, Stefanie Wilke; mus, Jonas C Haefeli; snd, Hans Kuenzi; art dir, Bernhard Sauter; cos, Regina Baetz.   97.
Bruno Ganz, Walo Luond, Verena Peter, Oliver Diggelmann, Thomas S Ott, Klaus Knuth, Babett Areans, Inigo Gallo, Erwin Kohlund, Klaus Steiger, Walter Ruch, Mathias Gnaedinger, Ettore Cella, Margrit Rainer, Guido Bachmann, Rene Scheibli, Michael Gempart, Ernst Stiefel.
11/19/80

Der Erste Walzer
(The First Waltz)
(W Germany)
X. Doris Doerrie Film, Munich, in collab with the Munich Film School and Bavarian TV. Dir, Doris Doerrie. Sp, Doerrie, W A Reimann; cam, Peter Fauhe; snd, Jan Christian Martens; edtr, Raimund Barthelmes; prodn mgr, Franz X Gernstl.   58.
Christopher Thomas, Katharina Hembus, Jutta Mueller-Schwarz, Louise Francia, Sepp Bierbichler.
01/17/79

Der Fangschuss
(The Coup De Grace)
(W Germany - France)
CII. Bioskop - HR - Argos Film prodn. Dir, Volker Schloendorff. Sp, Genevieve Formann, Von Trotta, Jutta Bruckner, from book by Marguerite Yourcenar; cam, Igor Luther; mus, Stanley Myers. 95.
Margarethe Von Trotta, Matthieu Habich, Rudiger Kirschstein, Matthieu Carriere.
(B & W)
08/25/76

Der Gehulfe
(The Handyman)
(Switzerland)
X. Thomas Koerfer Film AG prodn. Dir, Thomaas Koerfer. Sp, Dieter Feldhausen, Koerfer from book by Robert Walser; cam (Eastmancolor), Renato Berta; edtr, Frederic Gonseth. 122.
Paul Burian, Ingold Wildenauer, Verena Buss, Tobi Mettler, Nicole Heri, Nikola Weisse, Wolfran Berger, Hannelore Hoger.
05/19/76

Der Gelbe Stern
(The Yellow Star)
(W Germany)
CRO. Wri-dir, Dieter Hildebrandt. Research cnsltnt, Gerhard Schoenberner; asst dir, Manfred Helling; compilation edtr, Helga Kruska; cam sequences, Nicolas Joray; narrs, Friedhelm Ptok, Heidemarie Theobald, Heinz Rabe. 90.
(DOC) (B & W)
12/10/80

Der Hauptdarsteller
(The Main Actor)
(W Germany)
FDA. Bioskop-Film (Munich) prodn in collab with Westdeutcher Rundfunk (WDR) Cologne. Wolf-Dietrich Bruecker, TV edtr. Dir, Reinhard Hauff. Sp, Christel Buschmann, Hauff; cam (Metrocolor), Frank Bruehne; sets, Winfried Hennig; edtr, Stefanie Wilke; mus, Klaus Doldinger. 88.
Mario Adorf, Vadim Glowna, Michael Schweiger, Hans Brenner, Rolf Zacher, Akim Ahrens, Karl Obermayr, Carola Wittmann.
12/28/77

Der Junge Moench
(The Young Monk)
(W Germany)
X. Herbert Achternbusch Prodn, Munich. Prod-wri-dir, Herbert Achternbusch. Cam, Joerg Jeshel; snd, Peter van Anft; edtr, Christl Leyrer; prodn mgr, Dietmar Schneider. 84.
Heinz Braun, Branko Samarovski, Karolina Herbig, Herbert Achternbusch.
01/17/79

Der Kandidat
(The Candidate)
(W Germany)
FDA. Pro-ject Film in Filmverlag der Autoren, Bioskop-Film, and Kairos-Film Prodn. Dirs, Stefan Aust, Alexander von Eschwege, Alexander Kluge, Volker Schloendorff. Cam, Igor Luther, Werner Luering, Joerg Schmidt-Reitwein, Thomas Mauch, Bodo Kessler; edtrs, Inge Behrens, Beate Mainka-Jellinghaus, Jane Sperr, Mulle Goetz-Dickopp; snd, Manfred Meyer, Vladimir Vizner, Anke Apelt, Martin Mueller. 129.
(DOC)
05/21/80

Der Kleine Godard
(A Little Godard)
(W Germany)
X. Toulouse-Lautrec-Institute, Hellmuth Costard, Hamburg, in collaboration with "Das kleine Fernsehspiel" of Second German Television (ZDF), Eckhart Stein, prodn chief, Wiesbaden. Dir, Hellmuth Costard. Cam, Bernd Upnmoor, Hans-Otto Walter, Hanno Hart, Costard; snd, Herbert Jeschke, Marcia Bronstein; edtr, Susanne Paschen; blow-up advisors, Helmut Rings, Helmut Herbdt. 81.
Jean-Luc Godard, Rainer Werner Fassbinder, Mark Bohm.
(16m)
11/22/78

Der Landvogt von Griefensee
(The Bailiff of Griefensee)
(Switzerland)
X. Condor Film, Zurigo prodn. Dir, Wilfried Bolliger. Wris, Bolliger and Gerold Spaeth from the novel by Gottfried Keller. Sets, Mario Garbuglia; cam, Armando Nannuzzi; mus, Arie Dzierlatka; edtrs, Johnny Dubach, Usci Meier. 100.
Christian Quadflieg, Laura Trotter, Silvia Dionisio, Adelheid Arndt, Pauline Larrieu, Alida Valli.
08/29/79

Der Lange Jammer
(The Long Lament)
(W Germany)
BSG. Basis-Film, Berlin/News & Documentary Film, Wiesbaden, prodn. Dir, Max D Willutzki. Sp, Willutzki, Horst Lange, Aribert Weis; cam, Rolf Deppe, Rene Perraudin; snd, Stefan van Ballaer, Gerd Bluhm; edtr, Regine Heuser; mus, "Die Conrads." 94.
01/26/77

Der Letzte Schrei
(The Last Cry)
(W Germany)
CTT. Inter-West-Film/Robert van Ackeren prodn, Berlin. Dir, Robert van Ackeren. Sp, van Ackeren, Iris Wagner, Joy Markert; cam, Dietrich Lohmann; mus, Cham (Rome); edtr, Clarissa Ambach. 96.
Barry Foster, Delphine Seyrig, Peter Hall, Kirstie Pooley.
02/02/77

Der Lieberschuler
(Julia)
(W Germany)
CMZ. Lisa Films prodn. Exec prod, Erich Tomak. Dir, Sigi Rothemund. Sp, Wolfgang Bauer; cam (Technicolor), Heinz Holscher; edtr, Eva Zeyn; mus, Gerhard Heinz; art dir, Robert Fabiankovich; asst dir, Ulrich Strobel. (MPAA rating: R). 83.
Sylvia Kristel, Jean-Claude Bouillon, Terry Torday, Ekkehardt Belle, Gisela Hahn, Peter Berling, Rose-Renee Roth, Christine Glasner, Alois Mittermayer, Dominique del Pierre, Manfred Spies.
(English dubbed soundtrack)
01/21/76

Der Madchenkrieg
(The Maiden's War)
(W Germany)
CTT. Prodn of Independent-Film Heinz Angermayer/ABS Filmproduktion/Maran-Film and Terra-Filmkunst, Berlin. Prod, Heiner Angermeyer. Wri-dir, Alf Brustellin, Bernhard Sinkel, based on novel by Manfred Bieler. Cam, Dietrich Lohmann; mus, Nicos Mamangakis; songs sung by Lena Valaitis; edtr, Dagmar Hitz; art dir, Hans Gailling, Karel Vacek. 150.
Adelheid Arndt, Katherine Hunter, Antonia Reininghaus, Matthias Habich, Hans Christian Blech, Dominik Graf, Christian Berkel, Eva Maria Meineke, Walter Taub, Svatopluk Benesch, Jan Triska, Jan Medricka, Vaclav Postranecky, Karel Hermanek.
09/14/77

Der Pfingstausflug
(The Pentecost Outing)
(W Germany)
X. Ottokar Runze Film Prodn, Hamburg, in collab with Second German Television (ZDF) and SRG. Wri-dir, Michael Guenther, based on an idea by Peter Albrechtsen. Cam, Michael Epp; mus, Hans-Martin Majewski. 90.
Elisabeth Bergner, Martin Held, Brigitte Groohum, Edda Seippel, Gaby Gasser, Dagmar Biener, Simone Rethel, Ewald Wenck, Otto Czarski, Horst Poenichen, Friedhelm Ptok, Klaus Sonnenschein.
04/18/79

Der Preis Fuers Ueberleben
(The Price for Survival)
(W Germany)
X. DNS Film-Popular Film-Les Films 66 Prodn in collab with Bayerischer Rundfunk, Munich. Prod, Veith von Fuerstenberg. Wri-dir, Hans Noever. Dial, Noever, Christian Watton, Patrick Roth; cam, Walter Lassally; mus, Joe Haider; set, Toni Luedi; edtr, Christa Wernicke. 107.
Michel Piccoli, Martin West, Marilyn Clark, Suzie Galler, Daniel Rosen, Ben Dova, Kurt Weinzierl, Michael Stumm, Roger Burget, Al Christy, William Kuhlke, Charles Jones, Henry Effertz, Leonard Belove, John Haseltine, Charles Devault, Paul Murphy.
(English soundtrack)
02/13/80

Der Rote Strumpf
(The Red Stocking)
(W Germany)
X. Aspekt Telefilm Produktion, Markus Trebitsch, prod, Berlin, in collab with Zweites Deutsches Fernsehen (ZDF), Martin Buettner, Redakteur, Mainz. Dir, Wolfgang Tumler. Sp, Elfie Donnelly; cam, Petrus Schloemp; snd, Gunther Kortwich; mus, Eberhard Weber, Rainer Brueninghaus; edtr, Peter Przygodda. 92.
Inge Meysel, Julie Tumler, Ulrike Bleifert, Peter Bauer, Inge Wolffberg, Dorothea Moritz.
12/31/80

Der Schneider Von Ulm
(The Tailor From Ulm)
(W Germany)
FDA. Edgar Reitz/Peter Genee Film Prodn, in collab with Second German Television (ZDF), Wiesbaden. Dir, Edgar Reitz. Sp, Petra Kiener, Reitz; cam (Eastmancolor), Dietrich Lohmann; mus, Nikos Mamangakis; edtr, Siegrun Jaeger; sets, Winfried Hennig. 115.
Tilo Prueckner, Vadim Glowna, Harald Kuhlmann, Dieter Schidor, Rudolf Wessely, Herbert Prikopa, Marie Colbin, Otto Kackovic, Michael Hoffbauer, Ivan Vyskocil, Karel Augusta, Bronislav Poloczek, Hannelore Elsner.
05/30/79

Der Sprung von der Bruecke
(The Leap from the Bridge)
(Switzerland)
STW. Blackbox A G Zurich (John Winistoerfer) prodn. Wri-dir, Adrian Baenninger. Cam, Pio Corradi; edtr, Franziska Wirz; snd, Robert Jansa; mus, Markus Fischer; art dirs, Catherine Scholz, Rolf Engeler, Edith Peyer. 95.
Bruno Signer, Stefan Rainer, Sammy Ruegsegger, Benedict Freitag, Nicole Pozzi, Christa Ettlin, Lea Joannidis, Bruno Eberle, Beneo Abbuehl, Mike Zweifel, Otto Dornbierer, Rene Scheibli, Franziskus Abottspon, G P Huber, Hans Suter, Ruth Bannwart, Maria Dornberger, Guenter Gube, Monika Imhof, Rudi Nater.
05/21/80

Der Starke Ferdinand
(Strong Ferdinand)
(W Germany)
CTT. Kairos/Reitz prodn. Dir-sp, Alexander Kluge. Cam, Thomas Mauch; art dir, Traudi Kurz; snd, Heiko Hinderks. 98.
Heinz Schubert, Verena Rudolph, Joachim Hackethal, Gert Guenther Hoffmann, Heinz Schimmelpfennig, Siegfried Wischnewski, Erich Kleiber, Daphne Wagner, Hans Faber.
05/26/76

Der Stumme
(The Mute)
(Switzerland)
TSZ. Wri-dir, Gaudenz Meili; book, Otto F Walter. Cam, Pio Corradi; mus, Jonas C Hasfeli. 115.
Wolf Kaiser, Uli Krohm, Ingold Wildernauer.
(16m)
08/25/76

Der Sturz
(The Fall)
(W Germany)
FDA. Independent Film Heinz Angermeyer prodn, Munich, in collab with ABS/Maran/von Vietinghoff Film, Munich. Dir, Alf Brustellin. Sp, Brustellin, Bernhard Sinkel, based on the novel of same name by Martin Walser; cam, Dietrich Lohmann; sets, Winfried Hennig; mus, Klaus Doldinger. 101.
Franz Buchrieser, Hannelore Eisner, Wolfgang Kieling, Eva Maria Meineke, Klaus Pohl, Carl Fox-Duering, Mady Rahl.
02/07/79

Der Tag, An Dem Elvis Nach Bremerhaven Kam
(The Day Elvis Came To Bremerhaven)
(W Germany)
X. Tura-Film prodn, Munich, in collab, with Westdeutscher Rundfunk (WDR), Cologne. Dir, Peter F Bringmann; sp, Horst Konigstein; cam, Axel Block; edtr, Stefan Arnsten; sets, Goetz Heymann. 103.
Wolfgang Drygalla, Petra Bigaj, Michael Shelley, Margret Homeyer, Michael Rehberg, Hannelore Hoger, Susanne Schnur, Marcus Mueller.
09/17/80

Der Tod Des Fischers Marc Leblanc
(The Death of the Fisherman Marc Leblanc)
(W Germany)
X. Christian Rischert Film prodn, Munich. Wri-dir, Christian Rischert. Cam, Kurt Lorenz, Lothar Elias Stickelbrucks; edtr, Gudrun Keyser-Mochert; mus, Franz Schubert. 121.
(DOC)
04/27/77

Der Umsetzer
(The Evictor)
(W Germany)
BSG. Benno Trautmann, Brigitte Toni Lerch Film prodn, Berlin. Dirs, Trautmann and Lerch. Sp, Trautmann; cam, Aribest Weis; edtr, Regine Heuser; mus, Dieter Wilhelm Siebert; snd, Detlev Fichter, Gerd Bluhm; art dir, Horst Lange. 75.
Klaus Jepsen, Charles H Vogt, Charlott Adami, Peter Schlesinger, Hildegard Wensch, Friedhelm Lehmann, Till Hoffmann.
(B & W) (16m)
05/11/77

Der Unanstaendige Profit
(The Dishonest Profit)
(W Germany)
X. Regina Ziegler prodn, Berlin, in collab with Zweites Deutsches Fernsehen (ZDF), Wiesbaden. Dir, Thomas Mitscherlich. Sp, Detlef Michel, Mitscherlich; cam, David Slama; edtr, Susann Lahaye; mus, Erhard Grosskopf; art dir, Sergio Donini. 75.
Peter Fitz, Dorothea Moritz, Grischa Huber, Heinz Diesing, Nikolaus Dutsch, Dietrich Frauboes, Helmut Wildt, Joachim Nottke, Henning Gissel, Wolfgang Immenhausen, Gerd Holtenau.
04/27/77

Der Verlorene Engel
(The Lost Angel)
(E Germany)
DEE. DEFA Film prodn, East Berlin. Dir, Ralf Kirsten; sp, Kirsten, Manfred Freitag, Joachim Nestler based on novel, "Das Schlimme Jahr" (The Terrible Year), by Franz Fuchmann; cam, Claus Neumann; mus, Andre Asriel; sets, Hans Poppe, dramatic advisor, Klaus Wischnewski. 59.
Fred Dueren, Erika Polikowsky, Erik S Klein, Walter Lendrich, Agnes Kraus, Heidemarie Wenzel, Frank Schenk.
(B & W)
10/01/80

Der Willi Busch Report
(The Willi Busch Report)
(W Germany)
X. Visual Film Prodn, (Elke Haltaufderheide), Munich. Wri-dir, Niklaus Schilling; cam, Wolfgang Dickmann; sets, Christa Molitor; mus, Patchwork, BSW-Combo, Fanfarenzug Wanfried; edtr, Schilling. 118.
Tilo Prueckner, Dorothea Moritz, Kornelia Boje, Karen Frey, Jenny Thelen, Hannes Kaetner, Klaus Hoser, Hildegard Friese, Wolfgang Groenebaum, Christoph Lindert.
11/28/79

Derniere Sortie Avant Roissy
(Last Exit Before Roissy)
(France)
LML. Z Prod-Francina-Orphee Arts prodn. Dir, Bernard Paul. Sp, Michel Piedoue, Paul; cam (Eastmancolor), William Lubschansky; edtr, Christian Lacq; mus, Eric De Marsan. 100.
Pierre Mondy, Anne Jousset, Herve Bellon, Roseline Villaume, Francoise Arnoul.
09/07/77

Deryne, Hol Van?
(Mrs. Dery, Where Are You?)
(Hungary)
HU. Hunnia Studio prodn. Wri-dir, Gyula Maar, based on the memoirs of Roza Dery. Cam (Eastmancolor), Lajos Koltai. 102.
Mari Torcsik, Ferenc Kallai, Maria Sulyok, Tamos Major.
05/26/76

Des Enfants Gates
(Spoiled Children)
GAU. Film 66-Little Bear, Sara Film-Gaumont prodn. Dir, Bertrand Tavernier. Sp, Christine Pascal, Charlotte Dubreuil, Tavernier; cam (Eastmancolor), Alain Levent; edtr, Armand Psenny, Ariane Boeglin; mus, Philippe Sarde. 113.
Michel Piccoli, Christine Pascal, Michel Aumont, Gerard Jugnot, Arlette Bonnard, Georges Riquier, Gerard Zimmerman.
09/14/77

Des Journees Entieres Dans Les Arbres
(Entire Days in the Trees)
(France)
TDD. Wri-dir, Marguerite Duras from her play. Cam, Nestor Almendros; mus, Carlo D'Alessio.   95.
Madeleine Renaud, Jean-Pierre Aumont, Bulle Ogier.
(16m)
10/20/76

Des Morts
(Of Death and Deads)
(Belgium - France)
X. Zeno Films (Brussels) and Films du Losange (Paris) prodn. Dirs, Jean-Pol Ferbus, Dominique Garny, Thierry Zeno. Cam (Eastmancolor), Terry Stegner, Zeno; snd, Ferbus, Garny; edtrs, Zeno, Roland Grillon; mixing, Dominique Hennequin; mus, Alain Pierre. 106. (DOC)
02/07/79

Description of an Island:
SEE Beschreibung Einer Insel

Desde El Abismo
(From The Abyss)
(Argentina)
AES. Prods, Hector Olivera, Luis Repetto. Dir, Fernando Ayala. Sp, Eduardo Gudino Kieffer, Ayala, based on Teresa Gondra's memoirs, "Desde la Septima Tiniebla" (From the Seventh Shadow), cam, Victor Hugo Caula; edtr, Carlos Piaggio; snd, Norberto Castronuovo; sets, Emilio Basaldua; asst dirs, Americo Ortiz de Zarata, Alberto Lecchi; Vidal Rivas; mus, Oscar Cardozo Ocampo.   100.
Thelma Biral, Alberto Argibay, Hector Pellegrini, Adriana Parets, Raul Rizzo, Olga Zubarry, Marta Albertini, Nestor Hugo Rivas, Cristina Murta, Boy Olmi, Luis Garparini, Cristina Fernandez, Betty Couceiro, Analia Agullo, Estela de la Rosa.
04/23/80

Dese Nise
(The Eyes)
(Sri Lanka)
PES. Dir, Lester James Peries. Sp, Primasiri Kemadase; cam (b&w), Sumite Amarasingn. 88.
Do Abejvikreme, Srijani Amarasane, D M Denawake Haminava, Ravendre Randenija.
(B & W)
07/28/76

The Desert of the Tartars:
SEE Le Desert Des Tartares

Desideria, La Vita Interiore
(Desire, the Interior Life)
(Italy - W Germany)
CM. Prod, Galliano Juso for Cinemaster (Rome), Medusa Cinematografica (Rome) and Lisa Film (Munich). Dir, Gianni Barcelloni; sp, Enzo Ungari, Barcelloni, from the novel by Alberto Moravia; cam (Eastmancolor), Claudio Cirillo; art dir, Ferdinando Giovanoni; edtr, Daniele Alabiso; mus, Pino Donaggio.   105.
Rosana Marra, Lara Wendel, Stefani Sandrelli, Klaus Lowitsch, Vittorio Mezzogiorno.
10/15/80

Desiderium: SEE Sutedelan

Desire, the Interior Life: SEE
Desideria, La Vita Interiore

Despair
(W Germany)
SWN. Bavaria Atelier-SFP-Geria prodn. Dir, Rainer Werner Fassbinder. Sp, Tom Stoppard from novel by Valdimir Nabokov; cam (Eastmancolor), Michael Ballhaus; edtrs, Juliane Lorenz, Franz Walsch; mus, Peer Raben; art dir, Rolf Zehetbauer.   119.
Dirk Bogarde, Andrea Ferreol, Volker Spengler, Klaus Lowitsch.
(English soundtrack)
05/24/78

Desperate Living
NL. Prod-dir-sp-cam, John Waters. Thomas Loizeaux; edtr, Charles Roggero; snd, Robert Maier; mus, Chris Lobinger, Allen Yarus; sets, Vincent Peranio; cos-makeup, Van Smith. (Rating: self-imposed X).   90.
Liz Renay, Mink Stole, Susan Lowe, Edith Massey, Mary Vivian Pearce, Jean Hill, Cookie Mueller, Marina Melin, Sharon Niesp, Ed Peranio, Steve Butow, Channing Wilroy, George Stover, Turkey Joe, Roland Hertz, Pirie Woods, H C Kliemisch, George Figgs, Pat Moran, Dolores Deluxe, Peter Koper, Steve Parker, Chuck Yeaton, Pete Denzer, Ralph Crocker, David Klein.
10/26/77

Destinies: SEE Sudbine

Det Andre Skiftet
(The Second Shift)
(Norway)
X. Marcusfilm A/S prodn. Prod, Oddvar Bull Tuhus. Dir-sp, Lasse Glomm, from story by Espen Hraavardsholm; cam, Erling Thurmann-Andersen; edtrs, Fred Sassebo, Christian Hartkopp; mus, Arne Garvang; art dir, Frode Krogh; asst dir, Aamund Johannesen. 78.
Mona Malm, Gunnar Enerkjaer, Nils Gaup, Frode Rasmussen, Rolf Nielsen.
11/12/80

Detective Riccardo Finzi:
SEE Agenzia Riccardo
Finzi. . .Praticamente Detective

Deutscher Fruehling
(German Spring)
(Austria - W Germany - Switzerland)
X. ORF (Austrian Broadcasting Corp) prodn. Dir, Dieter Berner. Sp, Peter Turrini, Wilhelm Pevny, Berner; cam, Michael Ballhaus; edtr, Erika Geiger; art dirs, Herta Fischinger-Hareiter, Fritz Hollergschwandtner; snd, Rolf Schmidt-Gentner, Kurt Schwartz; asst dirs, Burgl Mattuschka, Markus Heltschl; mus, Peer Raben.   105.
Elisabeth Stepanek, Manfred Lukas-Luderer, Karl Kroepfl, Bernd Spitzer, Hans Thimin, Paola Loew.
(16m)
04/09/80

Deutschland Bleiche Mutter
(Germany, Pale Mother)
(W Germany)
X. Helma Sanders Film Prodn in co-prodn with Literarisches Colloquium, Berlin, and Westdeutscher Rundfunk (WDR), Cologne; prod, Ursula Ludwig. Wri-dir, Helma Sanders-Brahams. Cam, Juergen Juerges; sets, Goetz Heymann; mus, Juergen Knieper; edtrs, Elfi Tillack, Uta Perignelli.   130.
Eva Mattes, Ernst Jacobi, Elisabeth Stepanek, Angelika Thomas, Reiner Friedrichsen, Gisela Stein, Fritz Lichtenhahn, Anna Sanders, Sonja Lauer, Miriam Lauer.
03/05/80

Deutschland Im Herbst
(Germany In Autumn)
(W Germany)
FDA. Projekt Film Prodn in Filmverlag der Autoren, Munich, together with Hallelujah-Film, Munich, and Kairos-Film, Munich. Prods, Theo Hinz, Eberhard Junkersdorf. Dir (as Omnibus Film), Alf Brustellin, Bernhard Sinkel, Rainer Werner Fassbinder, Alexander Kluge, Beate Mainka-Jellinghaus, Maximiliane Mainka, Peter Schubert, Edgar Reitz, Katja Rupe, Hans Peter Cloos, Volker Schloendorff. Sp, Heinrich Boell, Peter Steinbach; cam, Michael Ballhaus, Juergen Juerges, Bodo Kessler, Dietrich Lohmann, Colin Mounier, Joerg Schmidt-Reitwein; edtrs, Heidi Genee, Mulle Goetz-Dickopp, Tanja Schmidbauer, Christina Warnick; sets, Winfried Henning, Henning von Gierke, Toni Luedi; snd, Roland Hentschke, Martin Mueller, Guenther Stadelmann; prodn mgr, Heinz Badewitz, Karl Helmer, Herbert Kerz. 134.
Caroline Chaniolleau, Hildegard Friese, Petra Kiener, Lisi Mangold, Eva Meier, Katja Rupe, Franziska Walser, Angela Winkler, Wolfgang Baechler, Heinz Bennent, Wolf Biermann, Joachim Bissmeyer, Hans Peter Cloos, Otto Friebel, Michael Gahr, Vadim Glowna, Helmut Griem, Horatius Heberle, Hannelore Hoger, Dieter Laser, Horst Mahler, Enno Patalas, Franz Priegel, Werner Possardt, Leon Rainer, Walter Schmiedinger, Gerhard Schneider, Eric Vilgertshofer, Manfred Zapatka, Joey Buschmann, and the Collective "Rote Ruebe".
03/29/78

Deux Lions Au Soleil
(Two Lions in the Sun)
(France)
GAU. Basta Films, FR3 prodn. Wri-dir, Claude Faraldo; cam (Eastmancolor), Bernard Lutic; edtr, Dominique Gallieni; mus, Albert Marcoeur, Francois Ovide.   110.
Jean-Pierre Sentier, Jean-Francois Stevenin, Catherine Lachens, Martine Sarcey, Michel Robin, Valerie Kling, Alain Doutey, Jean-Pierre Tailhade.
09/03/80

Deux Super Flics
(Two Super Cops)
(Italy)
WBC. Triton Cinematografica prodn. Prod, Salvatore Alabiso. Sp-dir, E B Clucher (Enzo Barboni). Cam, Laudio Cirillo; mus, Guido and Maurizio DeAngelis. 115.
Terence Hill, Bud Spencer, Laura Gemser, Luciano Catenacci.
02/08/78

The Devil in the Box: SEE Le Diable Dans La Boite

The Devil in the Heart: SEE Le Diable Au Coeur

The Devil Is Beating His Wife: SEE Veri Az Ordog A Feleseget

The Devil, Probably: SEE Le Diable Probablement

The Devil Within Her
(Britain)
AIP. Unicapital prodn. Dir, Peter Sasdy. Exec prod, Nato de Angeles. Sp, Stanley Price, from story by de Angeles; cam, Kenneth Talbot; edtr, Keith Palmer; prodn supv, Christopher Sutton; art dir, Roy Stannard; chor, Mia Nadasi; first asst dir, David Bracknell; snd recording, Kevin Sutton; snd edtr, Don Challis; sfx, Bert Luxford; mus, Ron Grainer. (MPAA rating: R). 90.
Joan Collins, Eileen Atkins, Donald Pleasance, Ralph Bates, Caroline Munro, Hilary Mason, John Steiner, Janet Key, George Claydon, Judy Buxton, Derek Benfield, Stanley Lebor, John Moore, Phyllis McMahon, Andrew Secombe, Susan Richards.
02/18/76

Devil's Island: SEE Die Teufelsinsel

The Devil's Playground
(Australia)
X. Film House prodn, with assistance from Australian Film Commission. Prod-dir-sp, Fred Schepisi. Cam, Ian Baker; mus, Bruce Smeaton; edtr, Brian Kavanagh. 107.
Arthur Dignam, Nick Tate, Simon Burke, Charles McCallum, John Frawley, Jonathon Hardy, Gerry Duggan, Peter Cox, John Diedrich, Thomas Keneally, Sheila Florance, Anne Phelan, Jillian Archer, Gerda Nicholson, John Proper.
03/10/76

Di Dao Chan
(Tunnel Warfare)
(China)
X. Peking Film Studio Prodn. Prod, Army Propaganda Unit. 90.
01/17/79

Diabolo Menthe
(France)
GAU. Les Films de L'Alma-Alexandre Films prodn. Wri-dir, Diane Kurys. Cam (Eastmancolor), Philippe Rousselot; edtr, Joelle Van Effenterre; mus, Yves Simone. 97.
Eleonore Klarwein, Odile Michel, Coralie Clement, Marie-Veronique Maurin, Valerie Stand, Anouk Ferjac.
12/21/77

Diadicassia
(Proceedings)
(Greece)
X. Yannis Stefanis prodn. Wri-dir, Demosthenes Theos. Cam, Georges Arvanits, Aris Stavrou; mus, Christodoulos Halaris; sets, T Ioannou; cos, T Katolianou. 115.
Costas Sfecas, Heleni Maniati.
10/27/76

Dialogue With a Woman Departed
X. Leo Hurwitz Prodns. Prod-wri-dir-edtr-cam (color & b&w), Leo Hurwitz. 270.
(DOC) (16m) (COLOR - B & W)
12/17/80

Diamante Bruto
(Rough Diamond)
(Brazil)
EMZ. Pilar Films prodn. Wri-dir, Orlando Senna from the novel by Afranio Pexioto. Cam (Eastmancolor), Joao Carlos Horta; edtr, Roberto Pires. 114.
Jose Wilker, Gilda, Conceicao Senna, Wilson Melo, Ademario Rufino, Flora, Filma Natalia.
08/23/78

The Diary: SEE Tagebuch

Diary of a Lover: SEE Tagebuch Eines Liebenden

Diary of a Moonlighter
X. Prod-dir-edtr, Gar LaSalle. Cam, Kris Malkiewics. 70.
(DOC)
03/28/79

Did Somebody Laugh?: SEE Hoer, var der ikke en, som lo?

Die Abfahrer
(On the Move)
(W Germany)
FDA. Adolf Winkelmann Film Prodn, Dortmund, in collab with Westdeutsche Rundfunk (WDR), Cologne. Dir, Adolf Winkelmann. Sp, Winkelmann, Gerd Weiss; cam, David Slama; edtr, Helga Schnurre; sets, Gerlinde Feddeler, Bernd Twardy; mus, "Die Schmetterlinge." 94.
Detlev Quandt, Ludger Schneider, Anastasios Avgerlis, Beate Brockstedt, Josefine Carree, Manfred Doenicke, Martha Dors, Betti Eiermann, Freddy Garber, Harald Hampe, Gerd Hohmann, Hermann Lause, Gertrud von Linteln, Regina Mueller, Edzard Obendiek, Eduard Schalow, Tana Schanzara, Otto Schnelling, Dagmar Schulz, Wolf Sesemann, Irmgard Thielebeule, Willi Wagener, Gerd Weiss.
05/23/79

Die Allseitig Reduzierte Persoenlichkeit-Redupers
(The All-Around Reduced Personality-Outtakes)
(W Germany)
X. Helke Sander Film, Berlin, prod, Basis-Film Verleih, Berlin, in co-prodn with Zweites Deutsches Fernsehen, Wiesbaden. Wri-dir, Helke Sander; cam (b&w), Katia Forbert; edtr, Ursula Hoef; phos, Abisag Tuellmann; snd, Gunther Kortwich; prodn mgr, Clara Burckner. 98.
Helke Sander, Joachim Baumann, Frank Burckner, Eva Gagel, Ulrich Gressieker, Beate Kopp, Andrea Nabakowski, Helga Storck, Gesine Strempel, Ronny Tanner, Abisag Tuellmann, Ulla Ziemann, Gisela Zies.
(B & W)
06/28/78

Die Anstalt
(The Institution)
(W Germany)
BSG. Common Film Prodn. Wri-dir, Hans-Ruediger Minow. Cam, Bernd Fiedler; mus, Andi Brauer; edtr, Hanne Huxoll; snd, Heiko von Swieykowski; sets, Renate Pfab; prodn mgr, Helmut Wietz. 90.
Susanne Ganzler, Wolfgang Preiss, Gerd Baltus, Wolfgang Ransmayr, Ursula Roche, Hans-Peter Korff, Dieter Prochnow, Christiane Bruhn, Eva Dreyer-Eschenbach, Carin Braun, Rolf Beuckert, Walter Ladengast, Peter Petran, Gertrud Hinz, Friedrich W Rasch, Guenter Keutemeyer, Til Kiwe.
(B & W)
01/17/79

Die Atlantikschwinner
(The Atlantic Swimmers)
(W Germany)
X. Herbert Achternbusch prodn. Wri-prod-dir, Achternbusch. Cam, Joerg Schmidt-Reitwein; edtr, Karin Fischer; snd, Peter van Anft. 81.
Heinz Braun, Herbert Achternbusch, Alois Hitzenbichler, Sepp Bierbichler, Ingrid Gailhofer, Barbara Gass, Gunter Freyse, Margarethe von Trotta.
07/07/76

Die Blechtrommel
(The Tin Drum)
(W Germany - France - Yugoslavia - Poland)
UA. Franz Seitz Film/Bioskop-Film/Artemis Film/Hallelujah-Film/GGB 14.KG/Argos Films Paris prodn in collab with Jadran Film Zagreb and Film Polski Warsaw. Prod, Franz Seitz. Dir, Volker Schloendorff. Sp, Jean-Claude Carriere, Schloendorff. Seitz; extra dialogue, Guenter Grass based on the Guenter Grass novel of the same name; cam (Eastmancolor), Igor Luther; art dir, Nicos Perakis; edtr, Suzanne Baron; mus, Friedrich Meyer; prodn mgr, Eberhard Junkersdorf. 150.
Mario Adorf, Angela Winkler, David Bennent, Daniel Olbrychski, Katharina Thalbach, Heinz Bennent, Fritz Hakl, Mariella Oliveri, Tina Engel, Berta Drews, Roland Teubner,

Ernst Jacobi, Werner Rehm, Ilse Page, Otto Sander, Andrea Ferreol, Charles Aznavour.
05/16/79

Die Brueder
(The Brothers)
(W Germany)
CII. Regina Ziegler prodn, Berlin, of a Wolf Gremm film. Wri-dir, Gremm, with motifs taken from short stories, "The Little Girl Eater," by Septimus Dale. Cam (Eastmancolor), Jost Vacano; art dir, Will Kley, Rolf Kaden, Bernhard Frey; mus, Guido and Maurizio des Angelis; edtr, Siegrun Jaeger; asst dir, Claudia Holldack; prodn asst, Michael Boehme. 100.
Erika Pluhar, Klaus Loewitsch, Georges Wilson, Doris Kunstmann, Peter Sattmann, Christian Bzik.
12/15/76

Die Comedien Harmonists
(The Comedy Harmonists)
(W Germany)
X. Norddeutscher Rundfunk (NDR), Hamburg, prodn. Exec prod, Dieter Meichsner. Wri-dir, Eberhard Fechner. Cam, Rainer Schaeffer; edtr, Brigitte Kirsche; mus, Comedien Harmonists; ani, Hans-Ulrich Kaulbarsch; prodn mgr, Karl Heinz Knippenberg. 191.
Robert Biberti, Erwin Bootz, Roman Cycowski, Ari Leschnikoff, Annemarie Collin, Fernande Currie, Mary Cycowski, Marion Kiss, Erika von Spath.
(DOC) (B & W)
04/27/77

Die Dritte Generation
(The Third Generation)
(W Germany)
FDA. Tango Film-Filmverlag Der Autoren prodn. Wri-dir, lensed (Eastmancolor), Rainer Werner Fassbinder. Edtr, Juliane Lorenz; mus, Peer Raben. 111.
Rudolf Mann, Margit Carstensen, Eddie Constantine, Hanna Schygulla, Volker Spengler, Gerhard Gast, Udo Kier.
05/23/79

Die Ehe der Maria Braun
(The Marriage of Maria Braun)
(W Germany)
UA. Albatros Film (M Fengler) - Trio Film - WDR - Filmerlog Der Autoren prodn. Dir, Rainer Werner Fassbinder. Sp, Peter Marthesheimer, Pia Frolich; dialog, Fassbinder; cam (Fujicolor), Michael Ballhaus; edtr, Juliane Lorenz. 120.
Hanna Schygulla, Klaus Lowitsch, Ivan Desny, Gottfried John, Gisela Uhlen, George Byrd, Elisabeth Trissenaar.
02/28/79

Die Elixiere Des Teufels
(The Elixirs of the Devil)
(W Germany)
X. Luggi Waldleitner prodn of Roxy-Divina Film and Bayerischer Rundfunk. Dir, Manfred Purzer. Sp, Purzer, based on novel by E T A Hoffmann; cam (Eastmancolor), Charly Steinberger; edtr, Wolfgang Schacht; mus, Hans-Martin Majewski; sets, Peter Rothe; cos, Charlotte Flemming. 113.

Dieter Laser, Sylvia Manas, Christine Buchegger, Peter Brogle, Rudolf Fernau, Karl Maria Schley, Heinrich Schweiger.
07/27/77

Die Eroberung Der Zitadelle
(The Conquest of the Citadel)
(W Germany)
X. Scorpion Film prodn for Westdeutsche Radio. Dir, Bernhard Wicki; sp, Wicki, Gunther Witte, based on short story by Gunter Herburger; cam (Eastmancolor), Igor Luther; edtr, Jane Seitz; mus, George Gruntz. 139.
Andreas Fricsay, Armando Brancia, Dieter Kirchlechner, Vittoria di Silverio, Ivan Desny, Antonia Reininghaus, Assunta and Elena de Maggi, Costas Papanastasiou, Kurt Mergenthal.
07/13/77

Die Erste Polka
(The First Polka)
(W Germany)
BVA. NDF/Bavaria Atelier prodn. Dir, Klaus Emmerich. Sp, Helmut Krapp from the book by Von Horst Bienek; cam (Eastmancolor), Michael Ballhaus; edtr, Hannes Nikel; mus, Edward Aniol. 105.
Maria Schell, Erland Josephson, Guido Wieland, Ernst Stankovski, Marco Kruger, Miriam Geissler, Eva Maria Bauer, Marcus Stolberg.
03/14/79

Die Farbe des Himmels
(Milk War in Bavaria)
(W Germany)
X. Infafilm Manfred Korytowski, Berlin/Munich, Film Prodn in collab with Second Channel Television (ZDF), Mainz. Wri-dir, Thomas Hartwig. Cam, Horst Schlier; edtr, Elfriede Boettrich; mus, Birger Heymann; snd, Peter Beil; sets, Ingo Toegel; asst, Anke Becker; prodn mgr, Manfred Korytowski. 110.
Hans Brenner, Ruth Drexel, Peter Kaufmann, Guenther Ziessler, Gustl Weishappel, Anton Rattinger, Helmut Fischer, Elisabeth Karg, Rudolf Lenz, Nino Korda, Robert Fackler, Peter Boehlke.
06/13/79

Die Faust in der Tasche
(Fist in the Pocket)
(W Germany)
X. Basis Film Prodn. West Berlin. Wri-dir, Max Willutzki. Cam, Mario Masini; edtr, Ola Hoef; sets, Goetz Heymann; mus, Satin Whale; asst dir, Claudia Holldack. 106.
Ernst Hannawald, Ursela Monn, Manfred Krug, Jakobeit Benz, Tommi Piper, Inge Wolffberg, Gerd Holtenau, Albet Venohr, Friedhelm Lehmann, Horst Pinnow, Isolde Chalpek.
05/23/79

Die Flucht
(The Flight)
(E Germany)
DEE. DEFA Film Prodn, Roter Kreis Group. Dir, Roland Graef. Sp, Hannes Huettner, Graef; cam, Claus Neumann; sets, Georg Wratsch; mus, Guenther Fischer; edtr, Monika Schindler. 90.
Armin Mueller-Stahl, Jenny Groellmann, Erika Pelikowsky, Wilhelm Koch-Hooge, Karin Gregorek, Simone von Zglinicki, Rolf Hoppe, Wilfried Glatzeder, Gerhard Bienert.
06/28/78

Die Flucht
(The Escape)
(W Germany)
OMN. CCC Kunstfilm prodn with Avala Film, Belgrade. Dir, Edwin Zbonek. Sp, Sigmund Bendkover, Al Bronsowy. Based on idea by Robert Azderball; cam, Nenad Jovicic. 80.
Gunther Ungeheuer, Goetz George, Helmut Oeser, Alexander Allerson, Katinka Hoffmann, Helmut Sobotka.
(B & W)
07/02/80

Die Frau Gegenuber
(The Woman Across The Way)
(W Germany)
DSM. Dir, Hans Noever. Sp, Noever, Elvira Del Boca; cam (b&w), Walter Lassally; edtr, Crista Wernicke, mus, Robert Eliscu. 90.
Petra Maria Gruhn, Franciszek Piecza, Jody Buchmann, Agnes Dunneisen, Brigitte Mira, Herbert Weihbach, Madeleine Kristl, Horst Nowack.
(B & W)
05/24/78

Die Glaeserne Zelle
(The Glass Cell)
(W Germany)
FDA. Roxy/Solaris Film Prodn, Munich, in collab with Bayerischer Rundfunk. Dir, Hans C Geissendoerfer. Sp, Geissendoerfer, Klaus Baedekerl, based on novel "The Glass Cell" by Patricia Highsmith; cam (Eastmancolor), Robby Mueller; mus, Niels Walen, sets, Heidi Luedi, edtr, Peter Przygodda; prodn mgrs, Bernd Eichinger, Luggi Waldleitner. 100.
Helmut Griem, Brigitte Fossey, Dieter Laser, Walter Kohut, Claudius Kracht, Guenther Strack, Klaus Muenster, Hans Guenther Martens, Christa-Maria Netsch, Gerlinde Egger, Bernhard Wicki.
06/21/78

Die Hamburger Krankheit
(The Hamburg Syndrome)
(W Germany - France)
FDA. Hallelujah Film, Munich, Prodn, in collab with Michel Gast SND, Paris, ZDF, Mainz, Terra-Film, Coleidon Film, Munich. Dir-edtr, Peter Fleischmann. Sp, Fleischmann, Roland Topor, Otto Jaegersberg; cam, Colin Mounier; mus, Erich Fersti, Die Gaichinger Pfeiffer, Esteban; sets, Luigi de Luca; TV-edtr, Willi Segler. 130.
Helmut Griem, Fernando Arrabal, Carline Selser, Tilo Pruechner, Ulrich Wildgruber,

Rainer Langhans, Romy Haag, Evelyn Kuenneke, Peter von Zah.
10/31/79

Die Herren Machen Das Selber, Dass Ihnen Der Arme Mann Feyndt Wird
(It's The Rich Man's Fault That The Poor Man Is His Enemy)
(W Germany)
X. Wendlaendische Filmkooperative, Marleben, Prodn. Dir-snd-edtng, Roswitha Ziegler, Niels-Christian Bolbrinker, Bernd Westphal, in collab with Thomas Wittenberg. Cam, Bolbrinker. 126.
(DOC) (16m)
03/26/80

Die Kinder Aus No. 67
(The Children from No. 67)
(W Germany)
X. Road Movies Film Prodn, Berlin, Renee Gundelach, in collab with Zweites Deutsches Fernsehen (ZDF), Wolfgang Patzschke, and support from Kuratorium Junger Deutscher Film and the Stiftung Deutsche Jugendmarke. Wri-dirs, Usch Barthelmess-Weller, Werner Meyer. Cam, Juergen Juerges, Hans-Guenther Buecking; sets, Maciej Putowski, Thomas Irmscher; edtrs, Helga Borsche, Thorsten Naeter; mus, Andi Brauer. 103.
Elfriede Irall, Tilo Prueckner, Bernd Riedel, Martina Krauel, Peter Franke, Rene Schaaf, Rainer-Goetz Otto.
02/27/80

Die Kleine Welt
(The Small World)
(W Germany)
X. German Film and Television Academy Berlin (DFFB) prodn. Wri-dir-pho-edtr, Rene Perraudin. Team assts, Reiner Heinzelmann, Randolf Goldbach, Luc Perraudin; mus, Ligeti, Handel, Sonny & Cher. 52.
Joachim Tennstedt, Gabi Rummel.
(16m)
02/09/77

Die Konsequenz
(The Consequence)
(W Germany)
X. Solaris Film prodn in collaboration with Westdeutscher Rundfunk (WDR). Bernd Eichinger, prod, and Gunther Witte, Redakteur for WDR. Dir, Wolfgang Petersen. Sp, Alexander Ziegler, Petersen, based on Ziegler's novel of same name; cam (b&w), Joerg-Michael Baldenius, Ernst Schmid, Bernd Elstner; sets, O Jochen Schmidt; edtr, Johannes Nikel, Evi Seyfried; mus, Nils Sustrate. 95.
Juergen Prochnow, Ernst Hannawald, Werner Schwuchow, Hans Michael Rehberg, Hans Putz, Elisabeth Fricker, Erwin Kohlund, Walo Lueoend, Edith Volkmann.
(B & W)
11/16/77

Die Langen Ferien Der Lotte H Eisner
(The Long Vacation of Lotte H Eisner)
(W Germany)
X. Prod-dir-wri, Sonrab Shahid-Saless, in collab with Lotte H Eisner. 60. (DOC) (B & W) (16m)
12/19/79

Die Laughing
WBO. Jon Peters prodn. Prods, Mark Canton, Robby Benson. Exec prod, Jon Peters. Dir, Jeff Werner. Sp, Jerry Segal, Robby Benson, Scott Parker, based on a story by Parker; cam (Technicolor), David Myers; edtr, Neil Travis; orig mus, Robby Benson, Jerry Segal; mus scoring, Craig Safan; prodn des, James H Spencer; set decor, Doug Von Koss; cos, Nancy McArdle; snd, David McMillan; asst dir, David Whorf. (MPAA rating: PG). 108.
Robby Benson, Linda Grovenor, Charles Durning, Elsa Lanchester, Bud Cort, Rita Taggart, Marty Zagon, Larry Hankin, Sammuel Krachmalnick.
03/26/80

Die Leiden Des Jungen Werther
(The Sorrows of Young Werther)
(E Germany)
X. DEFA-Studios prodn in collab with Gruppe "Bablesberg" and DDR Television. Dir, Egon Guenther. Sp, Guenther, Helga Schuetz; cam, Erich Gusko; art dir, Harald Horn; cos, Christiane Dorst; mus, Siegfried Matthus (with Mozart's violin concerto in G-Major); prodn chief, Erich Kuehne; edtr, Rita Hiller. 100.
Hans-Juergen Wolf, Katharina Thalbach, Hilmar Baumann, Heinz Dieter Knaup, Herwart Grosee, Dieter Mann, Barbara Dittus, Angelika Mann, Juliane Koren, Irmhild Wagner, Bob Kraemer, Stefan Lisewski, Klaus Piontek, Kurt Goldstein, Peter Hladik, Gerhard Bienert, Anita Herbst.
12/15/76

Die Letzten Jahre Der Kindheit
(The Last Years of Childhood)
(W Germany)
FDA. FEAT Film Prodn, Munich. Wri-dir, Norber Kueckelmann; cam, Juergen Juerges; edtr, Jane Sperr; mus, Markus Urchs. 110.
Gerhard Gundel, Dieter Mustafoff, Lissy Zimmermann, Leopoldine Schwankel, Thomas Wommer, Manfred Rendl, Wilfried Klaus, Eggert Langmann.
(16m)
10/31/79

Die Linkshaendige Frau
(The Left-Handed Woman)
(W Germany)
X. Road Movies Film prodn (Berlin) with Wim Wenders (Munich). Wri-dir, Peter Handke, based on his novel of the same name. Cam, Robby Mueller; edtr, Peter Przygodda; snd, Ulrich Winkler; prodn mgr, Renee Gundelach. 119.
Edith Clever, Markus Muehleisen, Bruno Ganz, Michel Lonsdale, Angela Winkler, Ines de Longchamps, Philippe Caizergues, Gerard Depardieu, Bernhard Wicki, Nicolas Novikoff, Janine Holt, Bernard Minetti, Ruediger Vogler.
11/16/77

Die Macht Der Maenner Ist Die Geduld Der Frauen
(The Power of Men Is the Patience of Women)
(W Germany)
BSG. Sphinx-Film prodn, Berlin. Wri-dir, Cristina Perincioli; cam, Katia Forbert Petersen; edtr, Helga Schnurre; mus, Flying Lesbians. 75.
Elisabeth Walinski, Eberhard Feik, Dora Kuerten, Christa Gehmann, Hilde Hessmann, Barbara Stanek.
(16m)
09/17/80

Die Moral Der Banditen
(Outlaw Morality)
(E Germany)
DEE. Dir, Erwin Stranka. Sp, Horst Bastian, Stranka; cam (Orwocolor), Peter Brand; mus, Uve Schikora. 90.
Jorge Braune, Karole Kostel, Reiner Wilhelm, Harry Hubschen.
07/28/76

Die Nacht Mit Chandler
(The Night with Chandler)
(W Germany)
X. Olga-Film Prodn, Munich in collab with Bayerischer Rundfunk, Munich. Wri-dir, Hans Noever. Cam, Kurt Lorenz; edtr, Helga Beyer; mus, Tom Steine, Sherben, Rio Reiser; snd, Vladimir Vizner; prodn mgr, Elvira Senft. 87.
Agnes Dueneisen, Rio Reiser, Thomas Schuecke, Vania Vlers, Ray Verhaege, Tommy Wieghand, Remy Eyssen.
(16m)
03/12/80

Die Ortliebschen Frauen
(The Ortlieb Women)
(W Germany)
X. Solaris/von Vietinghoff Film Prodn in co-prodn with Pia Frankenberg Music and Film Prodn, Hamburg, Westdeutscher Rundfunk (WDR), Cologne. Dir, Luc Bondy. Sp, Bondy, Libgart Schwarz, based on motifs in Franz Nabl's novel, "The Grave of the Living;" cam, Ricardo Arnovich; mus, Peer Raben. 106.
Edith Heedegen, Libgart Schwarz, Elisabeth Stepanek, Klaus Pohl.
03/05/80

Die Patriotin
(The Patriot)
(W Germany)
X. Kairos-Film Prodn, Alexander Kluge, Munich. Dir, Alexander Kluge. Sp, Willi Segler, Hans-Dieter Mueller, Dagmar Steurer, Christel Buschman, Helga Sander, Juergen Habermas, Oskar Negt, Karen and Bion Steinborn. Cam, Guenter Hoermann, Werner Luering, Thomas Mauch, Joerg Schmidt-Reitwein; edtr, Beate Mainka-Jellinghaus. 121.

Hannelore Hoger, Dieter Mainka, Alfred Edel, Alexander von Eschwege, Beate Holle, Kurt Juergens, Willi Muench, Mairus Mueller-Westernhagen, Guenther Keidel, Hans Heckel, Wolf Hanne.
10/31/79

Die Ploetzliche Einsamkeit Des Konrad Steiner
(The Sudden Loneliness of Konrad Steiner)
(Switzerland)
X. Kurt Gloor Film prodn, Zurich. Wri-dir, Gloor; cam, Franz Rath; mus, Peter Jacques. 102.
Sigfrit Steiner, Silvia Jost, Helmut Foernbacher, Gretel Mathis, Lilian Westphal.
07/07/76

Die Reinheit Des Herzens
(Purity Of Heart)
(W Germany)
FDA. Bavaria Atelier Prodn with Project Film Prodn. Wri-dir, Robert Van Ackeren. Cam, Dietric Lohmann; sets, O Jochen Schmidt; cos, Janken Janssen; edtr, Hannes Nikel, Eva Seyfried; mus, Peer Raben; prod, Peter Maerthesheimer. 104.
Elisabeth Trissenaar, Mathias Habich, Heinrich Giskes, Marie Colbin, Herb Andress, Isolde Barth.
05/14/80

Die Schattengrenze
(Frontiers of Darkness)
(W Germany)
X. CCC-Television Prodn, West Berlin for Second German Television (ZDF), Wiesbaden. Dir, Wolf Gremm. Sp, Dieter Wellershoff, based on his novel; cam, Juergen Wagner; sets, Herbert Schaefer; cos, Uschi Welter; TV edtr, Willi Segler. 105.
Guenter Lamprecht, Antje Hagen, Friedrich W Bauschulte, Dieter B Gerlach, Ulli Kinalzik, Carlos M Bravo, Roman A N Gonzales, Ayten Erten, Dorothea Moritz, Andreas Mannkopf, Englebert von Nordhausen.
05/30/79

Die Schweizermacher
(The Swissmakers)
(Switzerland)
RXF. T & C Film AG Zurich prodn. Wri-dir, Rolf Lyssy. Script collaboration, Christa Maerker, Georg Janett, Martin Schmassmann, Pierre Lachat. Prod, Marcel Hoehn; prodn mgr, Rudolf Santschi; cam (Eastmancolor), Fritz E Maeder; art dirs, Edith Peier, Bernhard Sauter; cos, Greta Roderer; snd, Hans Kuenzi; lights, Max Isler, Andre Simmen; mus, Jonas C Haefeli; edtr, Georg Janett; chor, Juerg Burth. 104.
Walo Luond, Emil Steinberger, Beatrice Kessler, Wolfgang Stendar, Hilde Ziegler, Silvia Jost, Bettina Lindtberg.
11/29/78

Die Standarte
(Battleflag)
(W Germany)
X. Ottokar Runze Film prodn, Hamburg. Dir, Ottokar Runze. Sp, Herbert Asmondi, based on novel by Alexander Lernet-Holenia; cam, Michael Epp; mus, Hans-Martin Majewski; edtr, Tamara Epp. 120.
Simon Ward, Siegfried Rauch, Viktor Staal, Veronica Forque, Gerd Boeckmann, Robert Hoffmann, Wolfgang Preiss, Peter Cushing, Lil Dagover, Maria Perschy, Friedrich von Ledebur, Werner Fuetterer, Rudolf Prack.
05/25/77

Die Tannerhuette
(The Tanner Steel Mill)
(W Germany)
X. Westdeutscher Rundfunk (WDR) prodn, Cologne, prod, Wolf-Dietrich Bruecker. Dirs, Marianne Leudcke, Ingo Kratisch. Sp, Peter Stripp, based on Felix Pinner's novel; cam, Kratisch/Luedcke; art dir, Wolfgang Schuenke; cos, Dela Fredrich; mus, Peter Fischer; edtr, Wolfgang Richter; prodn chief, Fred Ilgner. 100.
Christoph Felsenstein, Grischa Huber, Margret Homeyer, Willy Semmelrogge, Hans-Georg Panczak, Paul Dahlke, Karlheinz Boehm, Walter Rilla, Peter Franke, Hermann Guenther, Karlheinz Vosgerau, Traugott Buhre.
12/29/76

Die Teufelsinsel
(Devil's Island)
(E Germany)
X. Studio Heynowski & Scheumann prodn, East Germany. Wri-dir, Walter Heynowski, Gerhard Scheumann. Cam and documentation, Peter Hellmich, Horst Donth, Winfrid Goldner; mus, Sergio Ortega; edtr, Ilse Radtke. 61.
(DOC)
09/22/76

Die Unverbesserliche Barbara
(The Incorrigible Barbara)
(E Germany)
X. Gruppe Babelsberg DEFA, Berlin, prodn. Wri-dir, Lothar Warneke. Cam (Orwo-color), Juergen Lenz; art dir, Dieter Adam; literary advisor, Christel Graef; prodn mgr, Wolfgang Rennebarth. 90.
Cox Habbema, Peter Aust, Werber Godemann, Herta Thiele, Monika Hildebrandt, Eberhard Esche, Petra Hinze.
05/11/77

Die Verlobte
(The Fiancee)
(E Germany)
DEE. Co-prodn between DEFA-Studio for Feature Films and GDR-Television; dirs, Guenter Reisch, Guenther Ruecker. Sp, Ruecker, based on the novel trilogy, "The House with the Heavy Doors" by Eva Lippold; cam, Juergen Brauer; art dir, Dieter Adam; mus, Karl-Ernst Sasse; edtr, Erika Lemphul; artistic mgr, Hans Muencheberg. 105.
Jutta Wachowiak, Regimantas Adomaitis, Slavka Budinova, Christine Gloger,
Inge Keller, Kaethe Reichel, Hans-Joachem Hegewald, Barbara Zinn, Katrin Sass, Ewa Zieteck, Ursula Braun, Katrin Martin, Reinhard Straube, Friedrich Richter, Johannes Wieke, Rolf Ludwig.
07/23/80

Die Vertreibung Aus Dem Paradies
(The Expulsion from Paradise)
(W Germany)
FDA. Visual KW Film & TV prodn, Munich. Wri-dir, Niklaus Schilling. Cam (Eastmancolor), Ingo Hamer; snd, Francis Quinton; art dir, Christa Molitor; cos, Anna Banfield; edtr, Schilling; mus, archive (adapted from known mus, arrangements and compositions). 119.
Herb Andress, Elke Haltaufderheide, Ksenija Protic, Jochen Busse, Andrea Rau, Herbert Fux, Elisabeth Bertram, Caterina Conti, Wolfgang Lukschy, Rudolf Lenz, Nino Korda, Willy Schultes, Eudolf Schuendler, Jean-Pierre Zola, Herta Stal, Herbert Tiede.
04/20/77

Die Wildente
(The Wild Duck)
(W Germany - Austria)
X. Solaris-Film prodn, prod, Bernd Eichinger, in collab with Sascha-Film, Vienna, and Westdeutscher Rundfunk, Cologne. Wri-dir, Hans W Geissendoerfer; cam, Robby Mueller; mus, Nils Janette Walen; snd, James Mack; cos, Edith Almoslino-Assmann, Lambert Hofer; edtr, Jutta Brandstaetter. 100.
Jean Seberg, Peter Kern, Bruno Ganz, Anne Bennent, Martin Floerchinger, Heinz Bennent, Heinz Moog, Sonja Sutter, Robert Werner, Guido Wieland.
09/08/76

Die Wunderbaren Jahre
(The Wonderful Years)
(W Germany)
X. Franz Seitz Film Production, Munich, Caro-Film, Starnberg. Wri-dir, Rainer Kunze. Cam, Wolfgang Treu; mus, Rolf Wilhelm; edtr, Barbara von Weitershausen. 90.
Rolf Boysen, Dietrich Mattausch, Christine Wlodetzky, Gabi Marr, Martin May.
06/11/80

Dieu le veut
(God Wills It So)
(France)
X. Prodifilm Europe (Claude Michiels) prodn. Dir-wri, Luc Monheim. Exec prod, Andre Thomas. Cam (Gevacolor), Michiels; snd, Roger Defays (Studio l'Equipe); edtrs, Luc Monheim, Michiels; asst dir, Dirk Van Den Eyden; cos, Frieda Verhees, Jacotte Piroton; edtng asst, Ludmila Tchorbadjiiska; decors, Wally Van Looy, Luc Peeters. 93.
Liliane Becker, Lucien Charbonnier, Jean Decraux, Andre Desramaux, Robert Delieu, Frederique Hender, Claudine Laroche, Albert-Andre Lheureux, Yvette Merlin, Gerard Vivane.
12/15/76

Dikaia Okhota Korolia Stakha
(Wild Hunting of King Stakh)
(USSR)
SOV. Studios Bielarousfilm prodn. Dir, Valeri Roubinchik; sp, Vladimir Korotkevitch; cam, Tatiana Loguinova. 135.
Boris Plotnikov, Elena Dimitrova, Boris Khmelnitski, Valentina Chendrikova.
08/27/80

Dimboola
(Australia)
GUO. Pram Factory Pictures prodn, with the Victorian Film Corporation and the New South Wales Film Corporation. Prod, John Weiley. Dir, John Duigan. Sp, Jack Hibberd, from his play; cam (Panavision, Eastmancolor), Tom Cowan; edtr, Tony Paterson;, mus, George Dreyfus; snd, Lloyd Carrick; art dir, Larry Eastwood. 89.
Bruce Spence, Natalie Bate, Max Gillies, Bill Garner, Kerry Dwyer, Chad Morgan, Tim Robertson, Barry Barkla, Jack Perry, Claire Binney, John Murphy, Max Cullen, Helen Sky, Dick May, Irene Hewitt, Alan Rowe, Esme Melville, Terry McDermott, Paul Hampton, Evelyn Krape, Val Jellay, Sue Ingleton, Laurel Frank, Claire Dobbin, John Murphy, Fay Mokotow, Max Fairchild, Phil Motherwell, Matt Burns, Frankie Raymond, Sandra Evans, Matchbox.
05/16/79

Dimenticare Venezia
(To Forget Venice)
(Italy - France)
QRT. Robert A McNeil presentation. Rizzoli Film (Rome)-Action Films (Paris) co-prodn. Dir, Franco Brusati. Sp, Franco Brusati, Jaja Fiasti, based on a story by Brusati; cam, Romano Albani; mus, Benedetto Ghighlia; art dir, Luigi Scaccianoce; cos, Luca Sabatelli; edtr, Ruggero Mastroianni. 110.
Erland Josephson, Mariangela Melato, Eleanora Pontremoli, Hella Petri, Fred Personne.
(Italian with English subtitles)
01/23/80

Dimri I Fundit
(The Last Winter)
(Albania)
ALA. Albfilm Prodn, Tirana. Dirs, Ibrahim Mucaj, Kristaq Mitro. Sp, Nexhat Tafa, based on motifs in A Kondo's story, "The Women of My Village"; cam (b&w), Ilia Terpini; art dir, Shyqyri Sako; mus, Aleksander Lalo. 90.
Liza Laska, Margarita Xhepa, Agim Qirjaqi, Gulielm Radoja, Rajmonda Bulku.
(B & W)
01/17/79

Dincolo De Pod
(Beyond the Bridge)
(Romania)
RMN. Romaniafilm prodn, Bucharest. Wri-dir, Mircea Veroiu, based on the novel "Mara" by Ioan Slavici. Cam, Calin Ghibu; mus, Romeo Chelaru; art dir, Nicolae Dragan; cos, Hortensia Georgescu. 100.
Leopoldina Balanuta, Maria Ploae, Andrei Finti, Mircea Albulescu, Florin Zamfirescu, Ion Caramitru, Irina Petrescu, Ovidiu Iuliu Moldovan, Florina Cercel, Petre Gheorghiu, Jean Reder, Monica Ghiuta.
06/02/76

Dios Bendiga Cada Rincon De Esta Casa
(God Bless Each Corner of This Room)
(Spain)
X. Daga Films prodn (Paraguas Films and Kalender Films Int'l, Madrid); dir, Chumy Chumez. Exec prod, Antonio Cuevas; cam (Eastmancolor), Jose Luis Alcaine; edtr, Pablo G del Amo; mus, Carlos Vizzuello; sets, Wolfgang Burman. 87.
Lola Gaos, Blanca Estrada, Sergio Mendizabel, Jorge Nieto.
09/28/77

Dirt
AMC. Pacific Films-Sports VIP prodn. Exec prods, Michael F Leone, Roger Riddell. Prod, Allan F Bodoh, John Patrick Graham. Dir, Eric Karson, Cal Naylor. Sp, S S Schweitzer, Bud Freidgen, Tom Madigan; mus, Dick Halligan; edtr, asso prod, Skeeter McKitterick. (MPAA rating: PG). 95.
R R Young, Parnelli Jones, Rick Mears, Mickey Thompson, Bobby Ferro, Malcolm Smith.
03/21/79

Dirty Dreamer: SEE Sale Reveur

The Dirty Seven: SEE Neung Toh Jet

Disappearance
(Canada)
X. Prods, David Hemmings, James Mitchell, Gerry Arbeid. Dir, Stuart Cooper; cam (Eastmancolor), John Alcott; sp Paul Mayersberg, based on novel "Echoes of Celandine" by Derek Marlowe. 100.
Donald Sutherland, Francine Racette, David Hemmings, Virginia McKenna, Christopher Plummer.
09/28/77

The Disco of Love: SEE La Discoteca Del Amor

Discover Turquoise Mountain: SEE Chajrchan Ondor Chaana Bajna

The Disenchantment: SEE El Desencanto

The Dishonest Profit: SEE Der Unanstaendige Profit

Disorder and Early Torment: SEE Unordnung Und Fruehes Leid

Distance: SEE Dooratwa

Disturbance: SEE Poloh **Dites Lui Que Je L'Aime**
(Tell Him I Love Him)
(France)
AMLF. Prospectacle, Filmoblic, FR3 prodn. Dir, Claude Miller. Sp, Miller, Luc Beraud from the book "Sweet Sickness" by Patricia Highsmith; cam (Eastmancolor), Pierre Lhomme; mus, Alain Jonny; edtr, Jean-Bernard Bonis. 107.
Gerard Depardieu, Miou-Miou, Claude Pieplu, Jacques Denis, Dominique Laffin, Christian Clavier.
10/05/77

Diversions
(Britain)
ARB. Blackwater Film prodn. Prod, Valerie Ford. Dir-wri, Derek Ford. Cam, Geoffrey Glover; edtr, Pat Foster; mus, De Wolfe. (Self-imposed X rating). 87.
Heather Deeley, Jeffrey Morgan, Tim Blackstong, James Lister, Tim Burr, Terry Walsh, Christopher Gilbert, Tony Kenyon, Gilly Sykes, Jacky Rigby, Derek Martin.
03/17/76

Divina Creatura
(Divine Creature)
(Italy)
TIT. Filmarpa prodn. Exec prod, Raimondo Castelli. Dir, Giuseppe Patroni Griffi. Sp, Griffi, A Valdarnini, based on novel, "La Divina Fanciulla" by Luciano Zuccoli. Cam (Technicolor), Giuseppe Rotunno; mus, Ennio Morricone. 114.
Laura Antonelli, Terence Stamp, Marcello Mastroianni, Michele Placido, Duilio Del Prete, Ettore Manni, Carlo Tamberlani, Cecilia Polizzi, Piero di Jorio, Marina Berti, Doris Duranti.
07/14/76

Divine Ema: SEE Boszka Ema

Divine Madness
WB. Ladd Company release. Exec prod, Howard Jeffrey; prod-dir, Michael Ritchie; wris, Jerry Blatt, Midler, Bruce Vilanch; cam (Technicolor), William A Fraker; addl pho, Bobby Byrne; concert light, E H B ("Chip") Monck; edtr, Glenn Farr; mus arr-supv, Tony Berg, Randy Kerber; chor, Toni Basil; addl chor, Marla Blakey; prodn des, Albert Brenner; snd, Don Rush, Billy Youdelman, Bill Darlington, Bob Litt, Steve Maslow, Elliot Tyson; asst dir, Jack Roe. (MPAA rating: R). 94.
Bette Midler, Jocelyn Brown, Ula Hedwig, Diva Gray, Irving Sudrow, Tony Berg, Jon Bonine, Joey Carbone, Randy Kerber.
(CONCERT FILM)
09/17/80

The Divine Plan: SEE Chhatrabhang

Dizengoff 99
(Israel)
SHP. Shapira Films Presentation of an Arnon Milchan, David Shapira and Roni Yaakov Prodn. Wri-dir, Avi Nesher. Cam, Jean Boffety; edtr, Izhak Zhayek; art dir, Dita Abayov, Ben Lam; snd, Eli Yarkoni; mus, Koby Oshrath, Yorik Ben-David, Dori Ben-Zeev, David Broza, Igal Bashan, Rikki Gal, Beny Nagari, Eric Sinai, Dany Litani, Gali Attari, Rami Fortis, Zvika Pik, Izhak (Churchill) Klefter, Judith Ravitz, Yoni Rechter and Eric Rudich. 110.
Gidi Gov, Anath Azmon, Gali Attari, Meir Suissa, Heli Goldberg.
06/13/79

Djungelaeventyret Campa-Campa
(Jungle Adventure Campa Campa)
(Sweden)
X. Krister Hageus/Allboksfoerlaget (Stockholm) prodn. Wri-dir, Torgny Anderberg. Cam (Eastmancolor), Mogens Frendel; prodn mgr, Daniel Pacheco; edtr, Carl-Olov Skeppstedt; mus, Sven Olof Walldoff. 92.
Gunnar Hellstroem, Hugo Alvarez, Amadeo Barboza, Myriam Reategui.
06/09/76

Do We Start Off With A Dance: SEE Skal vi danse foerst

Do You Know Pavla Plesa: SEE Poznajete Li Pavla Plesa

Dobro Poshalovat
(Welcome)
(USSR)
GOS. Mosfilm Prodn, Moscow. Dir, Elem Klimov. Sp, Semyon Lunghin, Ilya Nussinov; cam, Anatoli Kuznetsov; sets, V Kamsky, B Blank; mus, M Tariverdiev. 85.
Arina Aleynikova, Lydia Smirnova, Yevgheni Yevstigneyev, Vitya Kosykh, I Rutberg.
(B & W)
07/05/78

Dr. Black Mr. Hyde
DIM. Charles Walker-Manfred Bernhard prodn, prod, Walker. Dir, William Crain. Sp, Larry LeBron; cam (Technicolor), Tak Fujimoto; mus, Johnny Pate; edtr, Jack Horger. (MPAA rating: R). 87.
Bernie Casey, Rosalind Cash, Marie O'Henry, Ji-Tu Cumbuka, Milt Kogan, Stu Gilliam.
01/21/76

Dr. Heckyl & Mr. Hype
CAN. Golan-Globus prodn. Prods, Menahem Golan, Yoram Globus. Dir-sp, Charles B Griffith. Cam (Metrocolor), Robert Carras; edtr, Skip Schoolnik; mus, Richard Band; prodn des, Maxwell Mendes; art dir, Bob Ziembiki; set decor, Maria Delia Javier; snd, Rob Newell; asst dir, Peter Manoojian. (MPAA rating: R). 99.
Oliver Reed, Sunny Johnson, Maia Danziger, Mel Welles, Virgil Frye, Kedrick Wolfe, Jackie Coogan, Corinne Calvet.
07/02/80

Doctor Judym
(Poland)
POL. Pryzmat Unit prodn. Dir, Wlodzimierz Haupe. Sp, Andrzej Szcypiorski from the novel by Stefan Zeronski; cam (Eastmancolor), Maciej Kijowski; mus, Andrezej Korzynski. 94.
Jan Englert, Anna Nerhebecka, Jerzy Kamas.
07/28/76

Dr Norman Bethune
(China)
X. Peking Film Prodn. Wri-dir, Chang Chunhsiang. Cam, Ma Li-fa; art dir, Hang Sanyi; edtr, Chu Chao-seng; mus, Liu Qiming; snd, Wu Chang-hai. 115.
Tain Nin-pang, Chun Li, Yin Ruo-cheng, Wu Shiu.
06/06/79

Dr Plern: SEE Plern

Doctor Poenaru
(Romania)
RMN. Rumaniafilm Prodn, Group One, Bucharest. Wri-dir, Dinu Tanase. Cam, Mihai Popescu; mus, Adrian Enescu; sets Florin Gabrea; cos, Ileana Mirea. 107.
Victor Rebengiuc, Stefan Iordache, Elena Dacian, Vasile Nitulescu, Gheorghe Dinica, Gheorghe Metzenrath, Dionisie Vitcu, Victor Strengaru, Adrian Georgescu, Ion Vilcu.
06/14/78

Doctor Vlimmen
(Holland - Belgium)
X. Cinecentrum (Amsterdam)-Kunst en Kino (Brussels) prodn. Prods, Gerrit Visscher, Jef Vliegen, Jan Van Raemdonck. Dir, Guido Pieters. Sp, Guido Pieters, Ben Verbong, from novel by A Roothaert; cam (Kodacolor), Theo van de Sande; edtr, Ton Ruys; mus, Pim Koopman; art dir, Dick Schillemans; asst dir, Eefje Cornelis. 70.
Peter Faber, Roger Van Hool, Chris Lomme, Brigitte de Man, Mattijn Hallers, Erik van't Wout, Helmert Woudenberg, Leo Beyers, Manfred de Graaf, Serge Henri Valcke, Reinhilde Decleir, Frans Vorstman, Tim Beekman, Yolande Bertsch, Cox Habbema, Monique van de Ven, Hein Fentener van Vlissingen, Guy Lavreysen, Michel van Rooy, Dorien van der Klei.
03/22/78

Doda Clara
(Aunt Clara)
(Israel)
APF. Wri-dir, Avram Heffner. Cam (Eastmancolor), David Gurfinkel; edtr, Avi Cohen. 93.
Hana Maron, Schmuel Rodenski, Edna Fliedel, Ruth Segal.
08/31/77

The Dog: SEE El Perro

The Dog That Liked Trains: SEE Pas Koji Je Voleo Vozove

The Dogs: SEE Les Chiens

Dog's Heart: SEE Cuore Di Cane

The Dogs Of War
(Britain)
UA. Norman Jewison/Patrick Palmer prodn. Dir, John Irvin. Sp, Gary DeVore, George Malko, based on novel by Frederick Forsyth; cam (Panavision-Technicolor), Jack Cardiff; prodn des, Peter Mullins; edtr, Antony Gibbs; first asst dirs, Candace Suerstedt-Rehmet, Michelle Marx; mus, Geoffrey Burgon; cos, Emma Porteous; art dir, John Siddall, Bert Davey; sfx, Larry Cavanaugh, Rudi Liszczak, Steve Lombardi, Mike Collins. (MPAA rating: R). 122.
Christopher Walken, Tom Berenger, Colin Blakely, Hugh Millais, Paul Freeman, Jean-Francois Stevenin, JoBeth Williams, Robert Urquhart, Winston Ntshona, Pedro Armendariz, Harlan Cary Poe, Ed O'Neill, Isabel Grandin, Ernest Graves, Kelvin Thomas, Shane Rimmer, Father Joseph Konrad, Bruce McLane, George W Harris, David Schofield, Terence Rigby, Tony Mathews.
12/10/80

Dokter Pulder Zaait Papavers
(When the Poppies Bloom Again)
(The Netherlands)
X. Bert Haanstra Films prodn. Dir, Bert Haanstra; sp, Anton Koolhaas; cam, Anton van Munster; mus, Otto Ketting. 105.
Kees Brusse, Henny Orri, Ton Lensink, Dora van der Groen, Manon Alving, Karin Loeb, Peter Roemer, Sacco van der Made.
07/07/76

Dolly Kaputt: SEE Puppe Kaputt

Dolphin
X. Michael Wiese Film Prodns presentation. Prod, Wiese. Dir, Hardy Jones, Wiese. Sp, Jones. Cam, John Knoop; edtr, John V Fanto; mus, Basil Poledouris. 75.
(DOC)
07/04/79

The Domino Principle
AVE. ITC Entertainment-Asso General Films prodn, prod-dir, Stanley Kramer; exec prod, Martin Starger. Sp, Adam Kennedy, based on his novel; cam (CFI Color), Fred Koenekamp, Ernest Laszlo; edtr, John Burnett; mus, Billy Goldenberg; prodn des, William Greber; art dir, Ron Hobbs; sets, Andy Szolosi, Raphael Bretton; snd, Richard Portman, David Ronne; cos-ward, Rita Riggs, Laurie Riley; asst dir, Michael S Glick; stunt coord, Bear Hudkins. (MPAA rating: R). 97.
Gene Hackman, Candice Bergen, Richard Widmark, Mickey Rooney, Edward Albert, Eli Wallach, Ken Swofford, Neva Patterson, Jay Novello.
03/23/77

Don Giovanni
(France - Italy - Germany)
GAU. Gaumont-Camera One-Opera Film Produzione-Janus Film-Antenne 2 co-prodn. Prod, Michel Seydoux. Dir, Joseph Losey. Based on the opera by W A Mozart and Lorenzo Da Ponte; cinematic conception by Rolf Liebermann; adaptation, Patricia and Joseph Losey, Frantz Salieri; cam (Color-Panavision), Gerry Fisher; art dir, Alexandre Trauner; cos, Marthe Mikon; snd, Jean-Louis Ducarme, Jacques Maumont, Michele Neny; edtr, Reginald Beck; prodn mgr, Pierre Saint-Blancat; Orchestra and Choir of the Paris Opera under the dir of Lorin Maazel; mus advisor and harpsichordist, Janine Reiss. 184.
Ruggero Raimondi, John Maccurdy, Edda Moser, Kiri Te Kanawa, Kenneth Riegel, Jose Van Dam, Teresa Berganza, Malcolm King, Eric Adjani.
(OPERA)
10/24/79

The Don of Japan-Big Schemes: SEE Nippon No Don-Yabohen

Dona Flor E Seus Dois Maridos
(Dona Flora and Her Two Husbands)
(Brazil)
GUC. Luis Carlos Barreto-Newton Rique-Cia Serrador prodn. Wri-dir, Bruno Parreto; book, Jorge Amado. Cam (Eastmancolor), Maurilo Salles; edtr, Raimondo Higino; mus, Chico Buarque. (MPAA rating: R). 106.
Sonia Braga, Jose Wilker, Mauro Mendonca, Dinorah Brillanti, Nelson Xavier, Arthur Costa Filho, Rui Rezende.
09/14/77

Dona Perfecta
(Spain)
X. Azor Films S A prodn. Wri-dir, Cesar Ardavin, based on novel by Benito Perez Galdos. Cam (Eastmancolor), Jose F Aguayo; mus, Angel Arteaga; sets, Eduardo Torre de la Fuente; edtr, Jose Luis Matesanz. 104.
Jose Luis Lopez Vazquez, Julia Gutierrez Caba, Victoria Abril, Manuel Sierra, Emilio Gutierrez Caba, Jose Orjas, Roberto Camardiel, Maria Kosti, Jorge Rigaud, Mirtha Miller, Monserrat Julio.
11/09/77

Donkey in a Brahmin Village: SEE Agraharathil Kazhuthai

Don's Party
(Australia)
DOA. Prod, Philip Adams. Dir, Bruce Beresford. Sp, David Williamson, (based on his play); cam (Panavision 200 Color), Don McAlpine; edtr, Bill Anderson; snd, Des Bone; set des, Rhoisin Harrison; cos, Anna Senior. 90.
Ray Barrett, Claire Binney, Pat Bishop, Graeme Blundell, Jeannie Drynan, John Gorton, John Hargreaves, Harold Hopkins, Graham Kennedy, Veronica Lang, Candy Raymond, Kit Taylor.
10/06/76

Don't Answer The Phone
CWN. Scorpion prod. Prod-sp, Robert Hammer, Michael Castle. Dir, Hammer. Exec prod, Michael Towers; cam (Metrocolor), James Carter; edtr, Joseph Fineman; mus, Byron Allred; art dir, Kathy Cahill; snd, Jan Brodin; asst dir, David Osterhout. (MPAA rating: R). 94.
James Westmoreland, Flo Gerrish, Ben Frank, Nicholas Worth, Stan Haze, Gary Allen, Pamela Bryant.
04/16/80

Don't Bite, We Love You:
SEE Mords Pas On T'Aime

Don't Count On Us: SEE Non Contate Su Di Noi

Don't Cry: SEE Ne Pleure Pas

Don't Ever Ask Me If I Love:
SEE Al Tish'ali Im Ani Ohev

Don't Go Away: SEE Ne Si Otivai

Don't Go In The House
FVI. Turbine Films prodn. Prod, Ellen Hammill. Dir, Joseph Ellison; sp, Ellison, Hammill, Joseph Masefield; cam (Deluxe), Oliver Wood; edtr, Jane Kurson; mus, Richard Einhorn. (MPAA rating: R). 82.
Dan Grimaldi, Robert Osth, Ruth Dardick.
06/11/80

Don't Lean Out The Window: SEE Kihajolni Veszelyes

Don't Lean Out the Window:
SEE Ne Naginji Se Van

The Doom: SEE Osinda

Doomed Souls: SEE Ossudeni Doushi

Dooratwa
(Distance)
(India)
BDD. Wri-dir, Buddhadeb Dasgupta. Cam (b&w), Ranjit Roy; edtr, Mrinmoy Chakabarty; mus, Ain Rasheed. 96.
Mamata Shankar, Pradip Mukherjee, Bijon Bhattacharya, Niranjan Roy, Singdha Bannerjee.
01/31/79

Dopalnenie Kan Zakona Za Zaschitita Na Darjavata
(Amendment to the Law for the Defence of the State)
(Bulgaria)
BGO. Dir, Lyudmil Staikov. Sp, Angel Wagenstein; cam (Eastmancolor), Boris Yanakiev; mus, Simeon Pironkov; art dir, Petko Bontchev; cos, Venera Naslednikova. 150.
Stefan Getsov, Ivan Kondov, Georgi Georgiev-Getz, Violetta Doneva, Kosta Tsonev, Nevena Kokanova, Georgi Cherkelov, Naoum Shopov.
11/10/76

Doppio Delitto
(Double Murder)
(Italy - France)
PIC. Prod, Roberto Infascelli for Primex (Rome) and PECF (Paris). Dir, Steno. Sp, Age-Scarpelli-Steno; cam (Eastmancolor), Luigi Kuveiller; art dir, Mario Ambrosino; edtr, Antonio Siciliano; mus, Riz Ortolani. 113.
Marcello Mastroianni, Agostina Belli, Ursula Andress, Peter Ustinov, Jean-Claude Brialy, Gianfranco Barra, Mario Scaccia.
01/11/78

Dora Et La Lanterne Magique
(Dora and the Magic Lantern)
(France)
C9. Dir, Pascal Kane. Sp, Kane, Raoul Ruiz; cam (Eastmancolor), Gilberto Azvedo; edtr, Martine Giordano; mus, Daniel Vangarde. 100.
Valerie Maitresse, Nathalie Manet, Rita Maiden, Gerard Boucaron, Alain David, Fabrice Herrero, Michel Peyrelon.
03/01/78

Doramundo
(Brazil)
ERE. Eve Films prodn. Dir, Joao Batista De Andrade. Sp, De Andrade, David Jose, Alain Fresnot; cam (Eastmancolor), Antonio Meliande; edtr, Glauco Mirko Laurelli; mus, Alemdo Prado. 100.
Rolando Boldrin, Antonio Fagundes, Armando Bogus, Irene Revache, Rodrigo Santiago, Oswaldo Camposana.
10/25/78

The Double: SEE Dvoynikat

The Double: SEE Kagemusha

The Double-Crossers
(Hong Kong - Indonesia)
GHV. Co-prodn of Golden Harvest (Hong Kong)-Isetase Films (Jakarta). Prod, Raymond Chow. Dir, Chung Chang-wha. 90.
Shin Il-lung, Chen Hsing, Tuty Kirana, Chen Hui-ming, Soekarno Noor.
09/29/76

The Double Exposure of Holly
X. Prods, Ronan O'Casey, Bernard Stone. Dir, Bob Gill. Sp, O'Casey; score, Stan Free. (Self-applied X rating). 77.

Catherine Earnshaw, Ronan O'Casey, Terri Hall, Jamie Gillis, Con Peterson, Robert Maroff, Annie Sprinkle, Bree Anthony, Tony Blue, Bobby Astyr, Sol Weiner, Tina Mira, Steve Lincoln, Cecilia Gardner, Darryl Speer, Ed Dowling, Turk Turpin, Roy Palladino.
10/13/76

The Double Man: SEE Den Dobbelte Mand

The Double McGuffin
MLB. Prod-dir-wri, Joe Camp. Story, Camp, Richard Baker; cam, Don Reddy; edtr, Leon Seith; mus, Euel Box; prodn des, Harland Wright; art dir, Ed Richardson; asso prod, Dan Witt; asst dir, Terrence A Donnelly; snd, Jim Sabat. (MPAA rating: PG). 101.
Ernest Borgnine, George Kennedy, Elke Sommer, Ed (Too Tall) Jones, Lyle Alzado, Rod Browning, Dion Pride, Lisa Whelchel, Jeff Nicholson, Michael Gerard, Greg Hodges, Vinnie Spano.
06/13/79

Double Murder: SEE Doppio Delitto

Double Negative
(Canada)
QDC. Prods, Jerome Simon, David Main. Dir, George Bloomfield; exec prod, David Perlmutter; sp, Thomas Hedley Jr, Charles Dennis, Janis Allen, based on "The Three Roads" by Ross Macdonald. Cam, Rene Verzier; edtr, George Appleby; art dir, Mary Kerr; snd, Douglas Ganton; mus, Paul Hoffert. 96.
Michael Sarrazin, Susan Clark, Anthony Perkins, Howard Duff, Kate Reid, Al Waxman, Elizabeth Shepherd, Kenneth Welsh, Rawlins.
05/28/80

Double Nickels
X. Smokey Prodns presentation, prod-dir, Jack Vacek. Exec prod, John Vacek Sr. Sp, Jack Vacek, Patrice Schubert; cam (Eastmancolor), Tony Syslo, Ron Sawade; asso prod, Mick Brennan; edtrs, Vacek, Brennan, Sawade, Syslo; snd, Mark Hanes. (MPAA rating: PG). 89.
Jack Vacek, Ed Abrams, Patrice Schubert, George Cole, Heidi Schubert.
05/25/77

Double Suicide of Sonezaki
(Japan)
X. Kodosha-Kimura-ATG co-prodn. Prods, Hiroaki Fiujii, Motoyasu, Takahei Nishimura. Dir, Yasuzo Masumura. Sp, Yoshio Shirasaka, Masumura, based on orig story by Monzaemon Chikamatsu. Cam, Setsuo Kobayashi; snd, Rokubin Ota, Mitsutake Miyashita; art dir, Shigeo Mano; edtr, Tatsuji Nakano; cos, Toshiaki Maki; mus, Ryudo Uzaki, played by Down Town Boogie Woogie Band. 112.
Meiko Kaji, Ryudo Uzaki, Hiashi Igawa, Sachiko Hidari, Isao Hashimoto, Gen Kimura.
(French subtitles)
09/06/78

Doubles
CWR. Doppleganger Prodn Associates prodn in ass'n with Skylight prodns. Prod-sp-dir, Bruce Wilson. Story cnsltnt, Ed Leimbacher; cam (Eastmancolor), P Kip Anderson; mus, Jim Bredouw, Martin Lund; edtrs, Art Coburn, Skeets McGrew; asst dir-prodn mgr, Pat Fay; script supv, Karen Thorndike. 90.
Ted D'Arms, Martin La Platney, Ann Bowden, Dean Melang, Peggy Nielsen, Glen Mazen, Sally Pritchard, Niles Brewster.
03/22/78

Dove Vai In Vacanza?
(Where Are You Going on Holiday?)
(Italy)
CNZ. Rizzoli film. Prod, Gianni Hecht Lucari. Dirs, Mauro Bolognini, Luciano Salce, Alberto Sordi. Sp, Ruggero Maccari, Jaja Fiastri, Furio Scarpelli, Sandro Continenza, Roberto Sonego and Alberto Sordi; cam (Eastmancolor), Luciano Tovoli, Danilo Desideri, Sergio D'Offizi. 167.
"Saro tutta per te"- Ugo Tognazzi, Stefania Sandrelli
"Si buana"- Paolo Villaggio, Anna Maria Rizzoli
"Le vacanze intelligenti"- Alberto Sordi, Anna Longhi.
01/10/79

Doverie
(Trust)
(USSR - Finland)
GOS. Lenfilm, Leningrad, prodn, in collab with Finland. Dirs, Victor Tregubovich, Edvin Laine. Sp, Mihail Schatrov, Vladlen Loginov; cam, Dmitrii Meshiev. 90.
Kirill Lavrov, Margareta Terehova, Anatolii Solonitzin, Antonina Schuranova.
01/19/77

Dracula
U. Prod, Walter Mirisch. Dir, John Badham. Exec prod, Marvin E Mirisch. Sp, W D Richter, based on stage play by Hamilton Deane, John L Balderston, from novel by Bram Stoker; cam (Technicolor), Gilbert Taylor; edtr, John Bloom; snd (Dolby Stereo), Robin Gregory; prodn des, Peter Murton; art dir, Brian Ackland-Snow; cos, Julie Harris; special visual, Albert Whitlock; asst dir, Anthony Waye; asso prod, Tom Pevsner; sfx, Roy Arbogast; models, Brian Smithies; mus, John Williams. (MPAA rating: R). 109.
Frank Langella, Laurence Olivier, Donald Pleasence, Kate Nelligan, Trevor Eve, Jan Francis, Janine Duvitski, Tony Haygarth, Teddy Turner.
07/04/79

Dracula Pere et Fils
(Dracula Father And Son)
(France)
GAU. Gaumont-Int'l-Prodn 2000 prodn. Dir, Edouard Molinaro. Sp, Molinaro, Jean-Marie Poire, Alain Godard from book by Claude Klotz; cam (Eastmancolor), Alain Levent; edtr, Robert Isnardon; mus, Vladimir Cosma. 96.
Christopher Lee, Bernard Menez, Marie-Helene Breillat, Catherine Breillat, Anna Gael, Jean-Claude Dauphin.
09/29/76

Dracula's Dog
CWN. Prods, Albert Band, Frank Ray Perilli. Dir, Band. Sp, Perilli; cam (DeLuxe Color), Bruce Logan; edtr, Harry Keramidas; mus, Andrew Belling. (MPAA rating: R). 90.
Michael Pataki, Reggie Nalder, Jose Ferrer, Jan Shutan, Libbie Chase, John Levin, Cleo Harrington, Simmy Bow, Jojo D'Amore.
06/21/78

The Dragon Lives
(Hong Kong)
FVI. Herman Cohen presentation. Prod, C H Wong. Dir, Singloy Wang. Sp, Wang, Yi Kwan; cam, Chen Wing, Li Wom Chung; edtr, Mike Harris. (MPAA rating: R). 90.
Bruce Li, Caryn White, Betty Chen, Ernest Curtis.
10/04/78

Dragonfly
AIP. Prod-dir, Gilbert Cates; exec prod, Samuel Z Arkoff. Sp, N Richard Nash; cam (Movielab Color), Gerald Hirschfeld; edtr, Barry Malkin; mus, Stephen Lawrence; set decor, Dick Merrell; snd, Dennis L Maitland; asst dir, Alex Hapsas. (MPAA rating: PG). 95.
Beau Bridges, Susan Sarandon, Mildred Dunnock, Michael B Miller, Linda Miller, Martin Burke, James Otis, James Noble, Ann Wedgeworth, Fredrick Coffin, Harriet Rogers.
02/18/76

The Dream: SEE Moemoea

Dreamer
FOX. Michael Lobell prodn. Prod, Michael Lobell. Dir, Noel Nosseck. Sp, James Proctor, Larry Bischof; cam (Deluxe Color), Bruce Surtees; edtr, Fred Chulack; mus, Bill Conti; art dir, Archie Sharp; set decor, Bruce Kay; cos, Guy Verhille; asso prod, James Herbert; asst dir, William Hole. (MPAA rating: PG). 90.
Tim Matheson, Susan Blakely, Jack Warden, Richard B Shull, Barbara Stuart, Owen Bush, Marya Small, Matt Clark, John Crawford, Chris Schenkel, Nelson Burton Jr, Morgan Farley, Pedro Gonzalez Gonzalez, Speedy Zapata, Jobe Cerny, Azizi Johari, Dick Weber.
04/25/79

Dreams, Life, the Death of Filip Filipovic: SEE Snovi, Zivot, Smrt Filipa Filipovic

Dreams Make No Noise When They Die: SEE Droemme stoejer ikke, naar de doer

Drenge
(Boys)
(Denmark)
KID. Steen Herdel/EBC Film/Nils Malmros prodn. Dir, Nils Malmros. Story-sp, Malmros, Frederick Cryer; cam, Dirk Bruel, Morten Bruus, Morten Arnfred; edtr, Janus Billeskov Jansen; mus, Gunner Moeller Pedersen. 86.
Mads Ole Erhardsen, Lars Junggren.
03/09/77

Dressed To Kill
FWS. Samuel Z Arkoff presentation of a Cinema 77 film. Prod, George Litto. Wri-dir, Brian De Palma, cam (Technicolor), Ralf Bode; edtr, Jerry Greenberg; mus comp, Pino Donaggio, mus cond, Natalie Massara; prod des, Gary Weist; cos, Ann Roth; cos des, Gary Jones. (MPAA rating: R). 105.
Michael Caine, Angie Dickinson, Nancy Allen, Keith Gordon, Dennis Franz, David Margulies, Ken Baker, Brandon Maggart, Susanna Clemm.
07/23/80

Drevo Jelania
(The Miracle Tree)
(USSR)
X. Grusiafilm Prodn, Tbilisi. Dir, Tengiz Abuladze. Sp, Revas Inanishvili, Abuladze, based on a story by Georgi Leonidze; cam, Lomer Ahvlediani; sets, Revas Mirashvili; cos, Achab Abakarov; mus, Bidsina Kvernadze, Jakov Bobochidze; edtr, G Omadso; snd, T Naobachvili. 108.
Lika Davtaradze, Sosso Dchatchvliani, Sasa Kolelichvili, Kote Dauchvili, Sofiko Chiaureli, Kachi Kawsadze, Erosi Mandchgaladze, Otar Megvinetuchuzesi, Ramas Chikwadze, Georgi Gegetchkori, Cecilia Takaichvili, Georgi Chobua, Dchemal Gaganidze, Boris Zipuria, Ija Chobua, Msia Machvladze, Termina Tuajeva, Dato Abachidze, Tina Burbutachvili, Chota Chirtladze.
06/21/78

Driller Killer
ROL. Navaron Film prodn. Exec prod, Rochelle Weisberg. Dir, Abel Ferrara. Sp, Nicholas St John; cam, Ken Kelsch; snd, J P MacIntyre; mus, Joseph Delia. 90.
Carolyn Marz, Jimmy Laine, Baybi Day, Bob De Frank, Peter Yellen, Harry Schultz, Tony Coca Cola and the Roosters.
07/04/79

Drive-In
COL. Prods, Alex Rose, Tamara Asseyev; exec prod, George Litto. Dir, Rod Amateau. Sp, Bob Peete; cam (Metrocolor), Robert Jessup; edtrs, Bernard F Caputo, Guy Scarpitta; set decor, Jack Marty; snd, Robert Knudson, Bob Wald; asst dir, Robert Greene. (MPAA rating: PG). 96.
Lisa Lemole, Glenn Morshower, Gary Cavagnaro, Billy Milliken, Trey Wilson, Gordon Hurst, Louis Zito, Linda Larimer, Kent Perkins, Ashley Cox, Lee Newsom, Andy Parks, Reagan Kee, David Roberts, Phil Ferrell, Joe Flower, Bill McGhee, Gloria Shaw, Jessie Lee Fulton, Robert Valgova, Jack Isbell, Michelle Franks, Dejah Moore, Curtis Posey, Billy Vance White, Carla Palmer, Carrie Jessup, Barry Gremillion.
05/26/76

The Driver
FOX. Lawrence Gordon prodn. Prod, Lawrence Gordon. Wri-dir, Walter Hill; cam (DeLuxe Color), Philip Lathrop; prodn des, Harry Horner; mus, Michael Small; edtrs, Tina Hirsch, Robert K Lambert; stunt coord, Everett Creach; art dir, David Haber; set decor, Darrel Silvera; sfx, Charley Spurgeon; asso prod, Frank Marshall; asst dir, Pat Kehoe; snd, Richard Wagner. (MPAA rating: R). 91.
Ryan O'Neal, Bruce Dern, Isabelle Adjani, Ronee Blakley, Matt Clark, Felice Orlandi, Joseph Walsh, Rudy Ramos, Denny Macko, Frank Bruno, Will Walker.
07/26/78

Droemme stoejer ikke, naar de doer
(Dreams Make No Noise When They Die)
(Denmark)
DAG. Det Danske Filmstudio 1979 prodn. Wri-dir, Christian Braad Thomsen. Cam (Eastmancolor), Dirk Bruel; edtr, Grete Moeldrup; mus, various recording by Bob Wills & The Texas Playboys, Albert Ayler, Ivan Leth and others; prodn mgr, Per Arman. State Film Institute prodn aid granted by Counselor Frits Raben. 80.
Kaj Holm, Asta Esper Andersen, Jon Bang Carlsen, Irm Hermann.
05/16/79

Droemmen om Amerika
(The American Dream)
(Sweden)
SVE. Cinema Art/Swedish Film Institute/Public Motion Picture prodn. Story, based on authentic case history; sp, Niels Halding, Christer Abrahamsen, Tom Lazarus. Dir, Christer Abrahamsen. Exec prod, Joern Donner. Cam (Eastmancolor), Jack Churchill; edtr, Thomas Holewa; prodn des, Stig Boquist, P A Lundgren; cos, Ulla-Britt Soederlund; mus, David Clayton-Thomas, Doug Riley. 94.
Hans Klinga, Janne Carlsson.
12/08/76

Drug Connection
(Hong Kong)
SHW. Runme Shaw prodn. Dir, Sun Chung. Sp, Yi Kuang; cam, Lan Nai-tsai; art dir, Chen Ching-shen; snd, Wang Yung-hua; edtr, Chiang Hsing-lung. 120.
Yueh Hua, Chen Ping, Szu Wei, Tien Ching, Wang Hsieh.
03/24/76

Drugarcine
(The Pals)
(Yugoslavia)
YFR. Avala Film prodn. Dir, Mica Milosevic. Sp, Vlasta Radonovic; cam (Eastmancolor), Bozidar Nikolic; mus, Vojislav Kostic. 95.
Milan Gutovic, Beba Loncar, Erol Kadic, Ratko Miletic, Zeljka Basic, Pavle Vujisic.
08/15/79

Drum
UA. Dino De Laurentiis prodn, prod, Ralph Serpe. Dir, Steve Carver. Sp, Norman Wexler, based on novel by Kyle Onstott; cam (Metrocolor), Lucien Ballard; edtr, Carl Kress; mus, Charlie Smalls; prodn des, Stan Jolley; art dir, Bill Kenney; set decor, John McCarthy; snd, Bill Varney, Robert Gravenor; asst dir, Peter Bogart; stunt coord, Eddie Smith. (MPAA rating: R). 100.
Warren Oates, Isela Vega, Ken Norton, Pamela Grier, Yaphet Kotto, John Colicos, Fiona Lewis, Paula Kelly, Royal Dano, Lillian Hayman, Rainbeaux Smith, Alain Patrick, Brenda Sykes.
08/04/76

Drunken Monkey In A Tiger's Eye
(Hong Kong)
SEH. Wri-dir, Ng Si Yuen. 100.
(English subtitles)
11/29/78

Du aer inte klok, Madicken
(You're Out Of Your Mind, Maggie)
(Sweden)
SVE. SF Artfilm prodn. Story-sp, Astrid Lindgren; based on her story collections, "Madicken" and "Madicken och Junibackens Pims." Dir, Goeran Graffman; exec prods, Olle Hellbom, Olle Nordemar; cam (Eastmancolor), Joergen Persson; mus, Bengt Hallberg; edtr, Jan Persson. 97.
Jonna Liljendahl, Liv Alsterlund, Monica Nordquist, Bjoern Granath, Lis Nilheim, Allan Edwall, Birgitta Andersson, Sebastian Haakansson, Yvonne Lombard.
01/02/80

Du Bout Des Levres
(On the Tip of the Tongue)
(Belgium)
ELN. Pierre Films prodn. Prod, Jacqueline Pierreux. Wri-dir, Jean-Marie Degesves. Cam (Gevacolor), Walther Vanden Ende, Rufus Bohez; edtr, Michele Maquet; snd, Jean-Claude Boulanger; prodn mgr, Tom Coene; mus, Frederic Devreese, Chopin; asst dirs, Jacques Raket, Dominique Janne, Anita Haccuria. 87.
Marie Dubois, Olivier de Seadeleer, Georges Aubrey, Francine Blistin, Martine Regnier, Gabriel Discry, Rene Hainaux, Maurice Sevenant, Leopold Chaudiere, Pierre Crelot, Veronique Bailly, Thierry Luthers, Marcel Buelens, Frederic Bien, Patrick Courtois.
01/28/76

Du Cote Des Tennis
(By the Tennis Courts)
(France)
PLF. Camera One-Semeion Films prodn. Wri-dir, Madeleine Hartmann-Clausset. Cam (Eastmancolor), Michel Duverger; edtr, Francois Berthe. 90.
Marie-Christine Barrault, Claude Lemaire, Bernadette Clauzel, Madeleine Monteil, Joelle Rault, Siglinde Haas, Colette Jan.
11/10/76

The Duchess And The Dirtwater Fox
FOX. Prod-dir, Melvin Frank. Sp, Frank, Barry Sandler, Jack Rose, from a story by Sandler; cam (DeLuxe Color), Joseph Biroc; 2d unit cam, Joe Jackman; edtrs, Frank Bracht, William Butler; mus, Charles Fox; lyr, Frank, Sammy Cahn; art dirs, Trevor Williams, Robert Emmet Smith; set decor, Dennis Peeples; snd, Theodore Soderberg, Dick Wagner; 2d unit dir, Max Kleven; stunt coord, Jerry Gatlin. (MPAA rating: PG).   104.
George Segal, Goldie Hawn, Roy Jenson, Thayer David, Pat Ast, Sid Gould, Conrad Janis, Bob Hoy, Bennie Dobbins, Walter Scott, Jerry Gatlin.
03/17/76

Duck in Orange Sauce: SEE L'Anatra All'Arancia

Due Pezzi di Pane
(Two Pieces of Bread)
(Italy - France)
UA. Prods, Gianfranco Piccioli, Mauro Berardi. Dir, Sergio Citti. Sp, Citti, Giulio Pardizi; cam (Eastmancolor), Giuseppe Ruzzolini; edtr, Nino Baragli; art dir, Luciano Ricceri; mus, Alessandro Alessandroni.   105.
Vittorio Gassman, Philippe Noiret, Luigi Proietti.
03/28/79

Duelle
(Women Duelling)
(France)
GAU. Sunchild, Productions Jacques Roitfeld prodn. Dir, Jacques Rivette; sp, Rivette, Edouardo De Gregorio, Marilu Parolini; cam (Eastmancolor), William Lubtchansky; edtr, Nicole Lubtchansky, Cris Tullio-Altan; mus, Jean Wiener.   118.
Juliet Berto, Bulle Ogier, Jean Babilee, Hermine Karagheuz, Nicole Garcia, Claire Nadeau.
06/02/76

The Duellists
(Britain)
CII. Enigma prodn. Dir, Ridley Scott. Sp, Gerald Vaughan-Hughes; story, Joseph Conrad; cam, Frank Tidy; edtr, Pamela Power; art dir, Bryan Graves.   95.
Keith Carradine, Harvey Keitel, Cristina Raines, Edward Fox, Robert Stephens, John McEnery, Albert Finney, Diana Quick.
06/01/77

Du'er ikke alene
(You Are Not Alone)
(Denmark)
WCT. Steen Herdel Prodn. Dirs, Lasse Nielsen, Ernst Johansen. Story-sp Lasse Nielsen, Bent Petersen; cam (Eastmancolor), Henrik Herbert; mus, Sebastian (Knud Christensen); edtr, Hanne.   89.
Anders Agensoe, Peter Bjerg, Ove Sprogoe.
03/08/78

Dugun
(The Wedding)
(Turkey)
X. Erman Film Prodn, Istanbul. Wri-dir, Lutfi Akad; cam, Gani Turanh.   90.
Hulya Hocyigit, Ahmet Mekin, Kamuran Usluer.
08/02/78

Duios Anastasia Trecea
(Anastasia Passed By)
(Romania)
RMN. Rumaniafilm Prodn, Film Group One, Bucharest; dir, Alexandru Tatos. Sp, D R Popescu, based on his short story of same title; cam, Florin Mihailescu; sets, Andrei Both; mus, Lucian Metianu; edtr, Iolanda Mintulescu.   100.
Anda Onesa, Amza Pellea, Laszlo Tarr, Levente Biro, Christian Ghita, Razvan Onesa, Catalin Ciornei, Gheorghe Teasca, Daniel Petrescu, Stefan Kofalvy, Imola Gaspar, Dumitru Bordeianu, Ernest Kantor.
07/30/80

Dulscy
(A Non-Matrimonial Story)
(Poland)
POL. Pryzmat Film Unit prodn. Exec prod, Grzegorz Wozniak. Dir, Jan Rybkowski. Sp, Andrzej Jarecki, Jan Rybkowski, based on play by Gabriela Zapolska; cam, Zygmunt Samosiuk; mus, Piotr Figiel.   90.
Alina Janowska, Kazimierz Witkiewicz, Jerzy Matalowski, Maria Kowalik.
04/21/76

Dumb But Disciplined: SEE Bete Mais Discipline

The Dunce Class On Vacation: SEE Hababam Sinifi Tatilde

Dusman
(The Enemy)
(Turkey)
GUI. Guney Filmcilik Prodn. Dir, Zeki Okten. Sp, Yilmaz Guney; cam, Cetin Tunca; mus, Yavuz Top; edtr, Okten.   157.
Aytac Arman, Gungor Bayrak, Guven Sengil, Kamil Sonmez, Sevket Altug, Fahamet Atilla, Atiye Oklu, Ahmet Acar, Fehmi Yasar, Huseyin Kutman, Lutfu Engin.
03/19/80

Dvoboj Za Juznu Prugu
(Battle For The Railway)
(Yugoslavia)
YFR. Central Film Studio, Avala Film prodn. Dir, Zdravko Velimirovic. Sp, Purisa Dordevic, Velimirovic; cam (Eastmancolor), Steva Radovic; edtr, Miodrag Petrovic-Sarlo; mus, Zoran Hristic.   105.
Dragomir Bojanic-Gidra, Vojislav Miric, Nada Vojinovic, Neda Spasejevic.
08/16/78

Dvoynikat
(The Double)
(Bulgaria)
BGO. Bulgarian Film prodn, "Suvremenik" Film Group, Sofia; dir, Nikolai Volev. Sp, Mormarev Brothers; cam, Venko Kableshkov; art dir, Nikolai Surchadjiev; mus, Johann Sebastian Bach.   90.
Todor Kolev, Yordanka Kouzmanova, Lyuben Kalinov, Radosveta Vassileva, Pavel Poppandov.
07/30/80

Dym Bramborove Nate
(Smoke on the Potato Fields)
(Czechoslovakia)
X. Czech Film prodn, Prague, Barrandov Studios. Dir, Frantisek Vlacil. Sp, Vaclav Nyvlt, Vlacil; cam (Eastmancolor), Frantisek Uldrich; mus, Zdenek Liska.   95.
Rudolf Hrusinsky, Vera Galatikova, Alois Svehlik, Jana Ditetova, Vitezslav Jandak, Marie Logoidova, Josef Somr, Vaclav Lohnicky.
03/09/77

Dynasty
(Hong Kong)
CSH. Eastern Media prodn. Prod, Frank Wong. Dir, Mei Chung Chang. Cam (Technicolor), Zon Su Chang; 3-D filming supv, Mike Findlay. (MPAA rating: R).   94.
Bobby Ming, Pai Ying, Lin Ta Shing.
(English Dubbed soundtrack)
09/07/77

Dyrygent
(The Orchestra Conductor)
(Poland)
X. Film Polski-United X prodn. Dir, Andrzej Wajda; sp, Andrzej Kijowski; cam, Slawomir Idziak; snd, Piotr Zawadzki; edtr, Halina Prugar.   101.
John Gielgud, Krystyna Janda, Andrzej Seweryn.
09/10/80

Dzien Wisly
(The Day of the Vistula)
(Poland)
POL. Film Polski prodn. Profil Film Unit Warsaw. Dir, Tadeusz Kijanski. Sp, Ryszard Freiek; cam, Mathieu Przedpelski; mus, Waldemar Kazanecki; sets, Zenon Rozewica; prodn mgr, Tadeusz Karwanski.   75.
Henryk Talar, Ewa Borowik, Edmund Fetting, Jerzy Kamas, Emil Karewicz, Anna Milewska, Erwin Nowiaszek, Andrzej Preeigs, Mieczyslaw Voit.
10/01/80

E Atit De Aproape Fericirea
(Happiness Is So Near)
(Romania)
RMN. Rumaniafilm Prodn, Bucharest. Dir, Andrei-Catalin Baleanu. Sp, Constantin Stoicu; cams, Florin Paraschiv, Valentin Popescu; mus, Radu Goldis.   90.
Diana Lupescova, Albert Kitzi, Margareta Pogonatova, Constantin Diplan, Petre Gheorghiu, Alexandru Georgescu.
08/09/78

E Comincio Il Viaggio Nella Vertigini
(The Voyage Into the Whirlpool Has Begun)
(Italy)
ITG. Dir, Toni De Gregorio. Cam (Eastmancolor), Mario Vuipiani; mus, Eigsto Macchi. 115.
Ingrid Thulin, Sergio Fantoni, Gastone Moschin, Maria Vukotio, Franca Nut.
01/26/77

Eadweard Muybridge, Zoopraxographer
X. Thom Andersen prodn. Wri-dir-pho, Thom Andersen, with Fay Andersen, Morgan Fisher; edtr, Fisher; mus, Michael Cohen; narr, Dean Stockwell. 60.
(DOC) (16m)
09/22/76

Eagle: SEE Aguila

The Eagle and the Dove:
SEE L'Aigle Et La Colombe

The Eagle Has Landed
(Britain)
FWS. ITC Films (Lord Lew Grade)-Assoc. General Films-Weiner/Niven prodn. Dir, John Sturges. Prods, Jack Winer, David Niven Jr. Sp, Tom Mankiewicz, based on Jack Higgins novel; cam, Tony Richmond; aerial pho, Peter Allwork; prodn des, Peter Murton; art dir, Charles Bishop; asst dir, David Anderson; edtr, Irene Lamb. (MPAA rating: PG). 134.
Michael Caine, Donald Sutherland, Robert Duvall, Jenny Agutter, Donald Pleasence, Anthony Quayle, Jean Marsh, Sven Bertil Taube, John Standing, Judy Geeson, Treat Williams, Larry Hagman.
12/22/76

Eagle's Wing
(Britain)
RNK. Peter Shaw prodn. Exec prod, Peter Shaw. Prod, Ben Arbeid. Dir, Anthony Harvey. Sp, John Briley, based on an orig story by Michael Syson; cam, Billy Williams; edtr, Lesley Walker; mus, Marc Wilkinson; snd, Simon Kaye; prodn des, Herbert Westbrook; cos, Tim Hutchinson; prodn supv, Bruce Sharman; asst dirs, Jake Wright, Manuel Munoz. 104.
Martin Sheen, Sam Waterston, Harvey Keitel, Stephane Audran, Caroline Langrishe, John Castle, Jorge Luke, Jose Carlos Ruiz, Manuel Ojeda, Jorge Russek, Pedro Damieari, Farnesio De Bernal, Cecilia Camacho, Claudio Brook, Julio Lucena, Enrique Lucero.
08/01/79

Early Cranes
(USSR)
SOV. Kirghizfilm Studio Prodn, Frunze, Kirghizian Republic, Soviet Union, in co-prodn with Lenfilm, Leningrad. Dir, Bolotbek Shamshiev. Sp, Chinghiz Aitmatov, Shamshiev, based on a story by Aitmatov. 100.
Emil Boronchiev, Suimenkul Chikmorov, Gulsara Adjibekova, Hassan Abraimov, Akil Kulambaev.
06/25/80

The Earth and the Sky: SEE
La Tierra y el Cielo

The Earth Is Flat: SEE Jorden Er Flad

The Earthling
RDP. Filmways presentation of the Earthling Productions film. Prod, Elliot Schick. Dir, Peter Collinson; exec prod, Stephen Sharmat; sp, Lanny Cotler; prodn supv, John Weiley; cam (Panavision-color), Don McAlpine; prodn des, Bob Hilditch; edtr, Nick Beauman; asst dirs, Mark Egerton, Steve Andrews, Chris Williams; snd, Don Connolly; 2d unit dir, David Le Maistre. (MPAA rating: PG). 97.
William Holden, Ricky Schroder, Jack Thompson, Olivia Hamnett, Alwyn Kurts, Redmond Phillips, Willie Fennell, Ray Barrett, Pat Evison.
07/30/80

Eastern Territory: SEE
Anatoliki Periferia

Easy Road
(Greece)
ELG. Prod, Mikalis Lefakis for Greca Film and Andreas Thomopoulos. Dir, Thomopoulos. Sp, Thomopoulos; cam (Eastmancolor), Dimitris Vernikos; art dir, Maria Karayanopoulou; mus, George and Mikis Theodorakis, other songs and lyr, Thomopoulos. 110.
Paul Sideropoulous, Betty Levanon, Elen Manyiati, Vera Kruzka, Stavros Xenidis, Kostias Vrettos.
08/15/79

Eat My Dust
NW. Prod, Roger Corman. Wri-dir, Charles B Griffith. Cam (Metrocolor), Eric Saarinen; 2d unit cam, Peter Smokler; edtr, Tina Hirsch; mus, David Grisman; art dir, Peter Jamison; snd, Lee Alexander; asst dir, Nicole Scott; 2d-unit dir, Barbara Peeters; stunt coord, Ronald Clark Ross. (MPAA rating: PG). 89.
Ron Howard, Christopher Norris, Warren Kemmerling, Dave Madden, Robert Broyles, Evelyn Russel, Rance Howard, Jessica Potter, Charles Howerton, Kathy O'Dare, Brad David, Clint Howard.
04/28/76

Ecce Bombo
(Italy)
CID. Prod, Mario Gallo for Alphabeta Film and Filmalpha. Wri-dir, Nanni Moretti. Cam (Kodak), Giuseppe Pinori; art dir, Massimo Razzi; edtr, Enzo Meniconi; mus, Franco Piersanti. 100.
Nanni Moretti, Luisa Rossi, Fabio Tzaversa, Lina Sastri, Glauco Mari.
05/24/78

Ech Burdijn Domog
(Legend of the Oasis)
(Mongolia)
MGF. Dirs, Zhamyangiin Buntar, G Zigzidsuren. 88.
07/28/76

Echoes of a Summer
CAX. Sandy Howard/Richard Harris prodn. Prod, Robert L Joseph; exec prods, Howard, Harris. Dir, Don Taylor. Sp, Joseph; cam (Eastmancolor), John Coquillon; edtr, Michael F Anderson; mus, Terry James; song, "The Last Castle," Harris; art dir, Jack McAdams; snd, Richard Lightstone. (MPAA rating: PG). 99.
Richard Harris, Lois Nettleton, Geraldine Fitzgerald, William Windom, Brad Savage, Jodie Foster.
02/04/76

Eclair au Chocolat
(Chocolate Eclair)
(Canada)
FIM. Jean-Claude Lord film. Prods, Pierre David, Robert Menard for Les Prodns Mutuelles Ltd and Les Prods Videofilms Ltd. Dir, Jean-Claude Lord. Sp, Jean Salvy, Lord, based on Jean Santacroce novel; cam, Francois Portat; edtr, Lord; mus, Richard Gregoire; snd, Henri Blondeau; exec prod, Robert Menard. 105.
Lise Thouin, Jean Belzil-Gascon, Jean-Louis Roux, Colin Fox, Danielle Panneton, Aubert Pallascio, Olivier Fillion, Valerie Deltour.
02/21/79

Eclipse: SEE Grhana

Ecoute Voir. . .
(Look See. . .)
(France)
PSP. Dir, Hugo Santiago. Sp, Claude Ollier, Santiago; cam (Eastmancolor), Ricardo Aronovich; edtr, Alberto Yaccelini; prod, Maurice Bernart. 125.
Catherine Deneuve, Sami Frey, Florence Delay, Anne Parillaud, Didier Haudepin, Antoine Vitez.
10/25/78

Ecstatic Stigmatic
Prod, GSMC. Dir-edtr, Gordon Stevenson. Cam, Joanne Heey. 55.
Mary Kathryn Cervenka, Arto Lindsay, Johnny O'Kane, Brenda Bergman, Anita Paltrinieri.
(16m)
03/12/80

Edinstvennaja
(The Only One)
(USSR)
X. Lenfilm prodn, Leningrad. Dir, Iosif Heifitz. Sp, Heifitz, Pavel Nilin; cam, Heinrich Marandzhjan; mus, Nadeshda Simonian. 95.
Elena Proklova, Valery Zolothuhin, Ludmila Gladunko, Vladimir Vyssozki.
07/14/76

Editie Speciala
(Special Edition)
(Romania)
RMN. Dir, Mircea Daneliuc. Sp, Beno Merovici, Daneliuc; cam, Florin Mihailescu; mus, Lucian Metianu; sets, Filip Dumitru, Florin Gabrea. 103.
Stefan Irodache, Ioana Craciunescu, Costel Constantin, Mircea Albulescu, Paul Lavric, Mircea Daneliuc, Zaharia Volbea, Constantin Dinulescu, Dem Niculescu, Elena Bog, Dinu Ianculescu.
06/28/78

Eduardo the Healer
X. Prod-wris, Douglas G Sharon, Richard Cowan. Dir, Cowan. Cam, Robert Primes; edtr, Lee Rhoads; research, Sharon; mus, Centro Folklorico de Machu Picchu; Rafael Amaranto y son conjunto. 55.
(Spanish and English with English subtitles)
(DOC) (16m)
02/07/79

Educatore Autorizzato
(Authorized Instructor)
(Italy)
X. Prod, RAI Television, Channel 2. Dir-sp, Luciano Odorisio. from a book by Armando Rossini; cam (Eastmancolor), Massimo Sallusti; art dir, Mario Grazzini; edtr, Giancarlo Cersosimo; mus, Egisto Macchi. 120.
Gianfranco De Grassi.
06/11/80

Edvard Munch
(Sweden - Norway)
X. NRK-SR co-prodn. Wri-dir-narr, Peter Watkins. Cam, Odd Geir Saether; art dir, Grethe Hajer; cos, Ada Skolmen. 215.
Geir Westby, Gro Fraas, Johan Halsborg, Lotte Teig, Gro Jarto, Rachel Pedersen, Berit Rytter Hasle, Gunna Skjetne, Kare Stormark, Iselin Bast, Eli Ryg, Alf Kare Strindberg.
(English subtitles)
04/14/76

Een Vrouw Als Eva
(A Woman Like Eve)
(Netherlands)
X. Sigma Films B V prodn. Prod, Matthijs van Heyningen. Dir-wri, Nouchka van Brakel. Cam, Nurith Aviv; edtr, Ine Schenkkan; mus, Laurens van Rooyen; art dir, Inger Kolff; asst dir, Hans Kemna. 101.
Monique van de Ven, Maria Schneider, Marijke Merckens, Peter Faber.
In Dutch with English subtitles)
03/26/80

Een Vrouw Tussen Hond en Wolf
(A Woman Between Dog and Wolf)
(Belgium - France)
GAU. NIM, Productions De La Gueville, Gaumont prodn. Dir, Andre Delvaux. Sp, Ivo Michiels, Delvaux; cam (Eastmancolor), Charlie Van Damme; edtr, Nicole Berckmans; mus, Etienne Verschueren. 108.
Marie-Christine Barrault, Roger Van Hool, Rutger Hauer, Bert Andre, Rob Reymen, Senne Rouffaer.
05/16/79

Effects
X. The Image Works prodn. Prods, John Harrison, Pasquale Buba. Dir, Dusty Nelson. Sp, Nelson, from a novel by William H. Mooney; cam, Carl Augenstein; edtr, Buba; art dir, Ellen Hopkins; snd, Buba; spx, Tom Savini. 87.
John Harrison, Susan Chapek, Joseph Pilato, Bernard McKenna, Debra Gordon, Tom Savini, Chuck Hoyes, Blay Bahnsen.
09/19/79

Egy Erkolcsos Ejszaka
(A Very Moral Night)
(Hungary)
HU. Hungarofilm prodn, Dialog Studio, Budapest. Dir, Karoly Makk. Sp, Istvan Orkeny, Peter Bacso, based on the short story, "The House with the Red Light," by Sandor Hunyady; cam (Eastmancolor), Janos Toth. 103.
Iren Psota, Margit Makay, Gyoryg Cserhalmi, Gyorgyi Tarjan, Carla Romanelli.
05/10/78

Eierdiebe
(Petty Thieves)
(W Germany)
FDA. Albatros prodn, Munich. Dir, Michael Fengler. Sp, Burghard Schlicht, Fengler; cam, Juergen Juerges; edtr, Christa Reeh; mus, Juergen Knieper; art dir, Reinhard Donga; prodn mgr, Harry Baer. 84.
Marquard Bohm, Charlie Wierzejewski, Rolf Zacher, Gerhard Olschewski, Rita Scaturati, Gabi Klier, Adrian Hoven, Kurt Raab, Paul Lys.
05/11/77

The Eight Day: SEE Den attonde dagen

800 Heroes
(Peoples Republic of China)
X. Central Motion Picture Corp prodn. Exec prod, George F Chang. Prod, Mei Chang-ling. Dir, Ting Shan-shi. Sp, Ting Shan-shi; cam, Lin Wen-chin; military advisor, Wang Shi-hsu; mus, Huang Mou-shan. 126.
Koo Chuan-hsuing, Lin Chin-hsia, Chang Aicha, Chi Han, Chang Yi, Huang Cha-ta.
(Mandarin soundtrack)
11/10/76

Eight Kilos of Happiness: SEE Osam Kila Srece

80 Blocks From Tiffany's
X. Above Average prodn. Prod-dir, Gary Weis; from a story by Jon Bradshaw. Cam, Joan Churchill; edtr, Michael Goldman; snd, John Hampton. 62. (DOC) (16m)
03/26/80

80 Huszar
(80 Hussars)
(Hungary)
HU. Hungarofilm prodn, Objektiv Studio, Budapest. Dir-cam, Sandor Sara. Sp, Sara, Sandor Csoori; mus, Andras Szollosy. 137.
Jozsef Madaras, Gyorgy Cserhalmi, Gesa Polgar, Gabor Csikos, Jacint Junasz, Tibor Patassy, Zoltan Vadasz, Piotr Wysocki, Stefan Szmidt, Sandor Szabo.
05/24/78

Ein April Hat 30 Tage
(April Has 30 Days)
(E Germany)
DEE. DEFA Film Prodn, Babelsberg, GDR; dir, Gunther Scholz; sp, Carlos Cerda, Scholz; cam, Guenter Haubold; mus, Udo Zimmermann. 90.
Angelika Waller, Jurie Darie, Ronald Kubenz, Bert Brunn, Peter Slakakov.
07/30/80

Ein Irrer Duft Von Frischem Heu
(A Terrific Scent of Fresh Hay)
(E Germany)
DEE. DEFA Film Prodn, Berlin Group, Berlin. Dir, Roland Oehme. Sp, Rudi Stahl, Oehme; based on theatre play of same title by Stahl; cam, Juergen Lenz; sets, Dieter Adam; mus, Guenther Fischer; edtr, Helga Teichmann. 90.
Peter Reusse, Ursula Werner, Martin Hellberg, Jan Triska, Ursula Staack.
06/28/78

Ein Komischer Heiliger
(Some Kind of Saint)
(W Germany)
X. Co-prodn of Albatros Film, Munich and Popular Film, Berlin. Wri-dir, Klaus Lemke. Cam, Ruediger Meichsner, Erik Riechardt, Wolf Bachmann; edtr, Ines Regnier, Caya Piper; mus, Lothar Meid; "Follow Me," sung by Amanda Lear. 90.
Cleo Kretschmer, Wolfgang Fierek, Luitpold Roever, Horatius Haeberle, Peter Emmer, Arno Mathes.
06/06/79

Ein Maedchen Aus Zweiter Hand
(Second-Hand Girl)
(W Germany)
TRO. Wex-Film/Rina-Film (Munich) prodn. Dir, Alexander Ziebell. Sp, Hans Drawe; cam, Klaus Koenig. 90.
Susanne Uhlen, Beatrice Kessler, Kurt Wilhelm, Hans Quest, Herbert Thiede.
06/02/76

Ein Verdammt Gutes Leben
(A Hell of a Life)
(W Germany)
X. Sunset Mark prodn, Munich, in collaboration with Bayerischer Rundfunk, Munich. Sp-dir, Hans C Blumenberg. Cam, Bodo Kessler; edtr, Inge Gielow; snd, Pat Shea; prodn coord, Juergen Hellwig; tv edtr, Silvia Koller. 58.
(DOC) (16m)
03/29/78

Eine Frau Mit Verantwortung
(A Woman with Responsibilities)
(W Germany)
X. Eikon Film-ZDF prodn. Wri-dir, Ula Stockl. Cam, Mario Masini; edtr, Beate Levertow. 72.
Christina Scholz, Nikolaus Dutsch, Erwin Keusch, Philippe Nahoun.
(16m)
03/14/79

Einer Von Uns Beiden
(One or the Other)
(W Germany)
TRO. Wolfgang Petersen film, prod by Roxy-Film, Munich, Luggi Waldleitner. Dir, Wolfgang Petersen. Sp, Manfred Purzer, based on a thriller by Ky; cam, Charley Steinberger. 90.
Elke Sommer, Juergen Prochnow, Klaus Schwartzkopf, Klaus Theo Goertner, Otto Sander.
01/24/79

Ekdin Pratidin
(And Quiet Rolls the Day)
(India)
MSP. Wri-dir, Mrinal Sen from a story by Amalendu Chakraborty. Cam, K K Mahajan; edtr, G Naskar. 95.
Gita Sen, Mamata Shankar, Satya Banerjee, Srila Majundar.
02/06/80

El Anacoreta
(The Anchorite)
(Spain - France)
X. Incine and Hispano Fox Films co-prodn with Arcadie Prodns, presented by Alfredo Matas. Dir, Juan Estelrich; sp, Juan Estelrich, Rafael Azcona; cam (Eastmancolor), Alejandro Ulloa; edtr, Pedro del Rey; sets, Jacques Chambert. 106.
Fernando Fernan Gomez, Claude Dauphin, Charlo Soriano, Martine Audo, Jose Maria Mompin, Maribel Ayuso, Angel Alvarez, Ricardo Lillo.
01/12/77

El Apando
(The Heist)
(Mexico)
PEX. Conacite I prodn. Dir, Felipe Cazals. Sp, Jose Revueltas, Jose Agustin, Cazals, based on a novel by Revueltas; cam, Alex Philips Jr; edtr, Rafael Castanedo. 90.
Salvador Sanchez, Jose Carlos Ruiz, Delia Casanova, Manuel Ojeda, Maria Rojo.
08/25/76

El Asesino De Pedralbes
(The Pedralbes Murderer)
(Spain)
X. Figaro Films (Barcelona) prodn. Dir, Gonzalo Herralde. Exec prod, Pepon Coromina. Cam (Eastmancolor), Jaume Peracaula; edtr, Teresa Alcocer. 86.
Jose Luis Cerveto, Fernando Chamorro, Antonio Garcia, Rafael Gavilan, Jose Marti Gomez, Francisco Mas, Antonio Membrilla, Juan Merelo.
(DOC)
10/11/78

El Brigadista
(The Teacher)
(Cuba)
X. ICAIC prodn. Prod, Sergio San Pedro. Dir, Octavio Cortazar. Sp, Louis Rogelio Nogueras, Cortazar; cam, Pablo Martinez; mus, Sergio Vitier; edtr, Roberto Bravo; art dir, Carlos Arditi. 119.
Salvador Wood, Patricio Wood, Rene de la Cruz, Louis Alberto Ramirez, Luis Rielo, Mario Balmaseda.
03/15/78

El Cantor
(The Singer)
(E Germany)
FDD. German Democratic Republic Television Film, Berlin. Wri-dir, Dean Reed. Cam, Hans Heinrich; art dir, Heinz Roske; artistic advisor, Margit Schaumaeker; collaborator, Wolfgang Ebeling; mus, Karel Svoboda; edtr, Ruth Ebel. 90.
Dean Reed, Friederlike Aust, Gerry Wolf, Frank Bey, Thomas Wolf, George Rositsch, Isabel Oregana, Dimitrina Sawowa, Nikolai Dadon.
08/09/78

El Corazon del Bosque
(Heart of the Forest)
(Spain)
ARX. Dir, Manuel Gutierrez Aragon. Sp, Luis Megino, Aragon; cam (Eastmancolor), Teo Escamilla; edtr, Jose Salcedo. 105.
Norman Briski, Angela Molina, Luis Politti, Victor Valverde, Santiago Ramos.
03/14/79

El Crimen De Cuenca
(The Cuenca Crime)
(Spain)
X. Incine-Jet Films Prodn. Dir, Pilar Miro. Exec prod, Alfredo Matas. Sp, Salvador Maldonado, Miro, based on idea by Juan Antonio Porto; cam (Eastmancolor), Hans Burmann; edtr, Jose Luis Matesanz; sets, Fernando Sanez; mus, Anton Garcia Abril. 90.
Amparo Soler Leal, Hector Alterio, Fernando Rey, Daniel Dicenta, Jose Manuel Cervino, Mary Carrillo, Eduardo Calvo, Francisco Casares, Jose Vivo, Felix Rotaeta.
01/23/80

El Curso En Que Amamos A Kim Novak
(The Semester We Loved Kim Novak)
(Spain)
X. Togapor Prodns film. Dir, Juan Jose Porto. Sp, J J Porto, Carlos Puerto; cam (Eastmancolor), Miguel F Mila. 85.
Miguel Ayones, Miguel Arribas, Kity Manver, Cecilia Roth, Beatriz Elorrieta, Antonio Gamero, Roxanne Bach.
02/20/80

El Desencanto
(The Disenchantment)
(Spain)
X. Elias Querejeta prodn. Dir, Jaime Chavarri. Cam, Teodoro Escamilia, Juan Ruiz Anchia; edtr, Jose Salcedo Palomeque; snd, Bernardo Menz. 95.
Felicidad Blanch, Juan Luis Panero, Leopoldo Maria Panero, Mitzi Panero.
(B & W)
10/20/76

El Diputado
(The Congressman)
(Spain)
X. Figaro Films-Producciones Zeta-UFESA prodn. Dir, Eloy de la Iglesia. Sp, Gonzalo Goicochea, Eloy de la Iglesia; exec prod, J A Perez Giner; cam (Eastmancolor), Antonio Cuevas; edtr, Julio Pena; sets, Gumer. 111.
Jose Sacristan, Maria Luisa San Jose, Jose L Alonso, Angel Pardo, Agustin Gonzalez, J A Bardem, Queta Claver, Enrique Vivo.
02/07/79

El Elegido
(The Chosen One)
(Mexico)
PEX. Conacite II prodn. Wri-dir, Servando Gonzalez, based on a play by Carlos Solorzano. Cam (Eastmancolor), Angel Bilbatua. 105.
Katy Jurado, Manuel Ojeda, Hector Suarez, Rodrigo Puebla, Patricia Reyes Espindola, Jose Carlos Ruiz, Salvador Sanchez.
02/23/77

El Gordo de America
(America's Fat)
(Argentina)
AES. Prods, Nicolas Carreras, Louis O Repetto. Dir, Enrique Cahen Salaberry. Story, Jorge Porcel; sp, Oscar Viale; cam (Eastmancolor), Victor Hugo Caula; art dir, Oscar Piruzanto; mus, Buddy McCluskey; chor, Lia Jelin; edtr, Carlos Julio Piaggio. 80.
Jorge Porcel, Leonor Benedetto, Jorge Martinez, Javier Portales, Dorys Del Valle, Elizabeth Killian, Beto Gianola.
09/15/76

El Hombre De Los Hongos
(The Mushroom Eater)
(Mexico)
COX. Conacine, CCP prodn. Dir, Roberto Gavaldon. Sp, Emilio Carbillido, Tito Davison, Gavaldon, Sergio Galindo; cam (Eastmancolor), Raul Perez Cubero, Miguel Arana; mus, Raul Lavista. 100.
Isela Vega, Ofelia Medin, Adolfo Marsillach, Fernando Allende, Sandra Mozaro, Philip-Michael Thomas.
07/28/76

El Hombre De Moda
(Man of Fashion)
(Spain)
INS. Niebla films prodn. Dir, Fernando Mendez Leite. Sp, Leite, Manuel Marji. Cam, Porfirio Enriquez; edtr, Nieves Martin; snd, Julian Del Santo; mus, Luis Eduardo Aute. 113.

Xabier Elorriaga, Marilina Ross, Maite Blasco, Isabel Mestre, Alicia Sanchez, Carmen Maura, Francisco Merino.
10/29/80

El Hombre Que Supo Amar
(The Man Who Knew Love)
(Spain)
X. General Film Corp prodn. Dir, Miguel Picazo; prod, Jose Maria Carcasona; exec prod, Eduardo Bussalleu. Cam (Eastmancolor), Manuel Rojas; art dir, Horacio Rodriguez; mus, Antonio Perez Olea; edtr, Pablo G del Amo; sp, Santiago Moncada, based on book by Jose Cruset.   143.
Timothy Dalton, Antonio Ferrandis, Jonathan Burn, Jose Maria Prada, Alberto Mendoza, Queta Claver, Antonio Casas, Angela Molina, Jose Vivo, Pilar Bardem.
09/29/76

El Infierno Tan Temido
(So Feared a Hell)
(Argentina)
DPA. Prod, Pino Farina Producciones. Dir, Raul de la Torre; sp, Raul de la Torre, Oscar Vial, based on a story by Juan Carlos Onetti; exec prod, Kiko Tenebaum; cam (Eastmancolor), Juan Carlos Desanzo; edtr, Juan Carlos Macias; prodn des-cos, Graciela Galan; asst dir, Carlos Obes; mus, Astor Piazzolla.   113.
Alberto de Mendoza, Graciela Borges, Beba Bidart, Nora Cullen, Cacho Spindola, Enrique Almada, Arturo Garcia Buhr.
08/27/80

El Lugar Sin Limites
(The Place Without Limits)
(Mexico)
X. Conacite Dos prodn. Wri-dir, Arturo Ripstein. Story, Jose Donoso; cam (Eastmancolor Panoramic), Miguel Garzon; edtr, Francisco Chiu; mus, Joaquin Gutierrez Heras.   110.
Lucha Villa, Ana Martin, Gonzalo Vega, Julian Pastor, Carmen Salinas, Fernando Soler, Roberto Cobo.
10/04/78

El Ministro y Yo
(The Minister and Me)
(Mexico)
X. Rioma Films prodn. Prod, Jacques Gelmen. Dir, Miguel Delgado. Sp, Tito Davison, from story by Mario Mareno, Tito Davison; cam (Panavision-Eastmancolor), Jorge Stahl Jr, edtr, Gloria Schoemann; mus, Gustavo C Carreon.   100.
Mario (Cantinflas) Moreno, Lucia Mendez, Celia Castro, Angel Garasa, Hector Suarez.
08/04/76

El Monosabio
(The Wise Monkey)
(Spain)
X. El Iman (Madrid) prodn. Dir, Ray Rivas. Sp, Pedro Beltran, based on story by Rivas; cam (Eastmancolor), Fernando Arribas; mus, Jose Nieto; edtr, Jose Salcedo; sets, Adolfo Cofino. 88.
Jose Luis Lopez Vazquez, Curro Fajardo, Manuela Camacho, Antonita Linares, Chus Lampreave, Alberto Fernandez, Mercedes Barranco.
08/02/78

El Nido
(The Nest)
(Spain)
X. A-Punto E L S A prodn. Wri-dir, Jaime de Arminan; cam (Eastmancolor), Teo Escamilla; edtr, Jose Luis Matesanz; sets, Jean Claude Hoerner; snd, Bernardo Menz.   97.
Hector Alterio, Ana Torrent, Luis Politti, Agustin Gonzalez, Patricia Adrani, Maria Luisa Ponte, Ovidi Montllor, Mercedes Alonso, Luisa Rodrigo, Amparo Baro, Mauricio Calvo.
10/08/80

El Paso Wrecking Corp.
GAG. Prod, Sam Gage. Sp-dir, Joe Gage. Cam (Eastmancolor), Nick Elliott; mus, Al Steinman; snd, Harlan Archer, Glen Nathan. (Self-imposed X rating:)   94.
Fred Halsted, Richard Locke, Georgina Spelvin, Steve King, Jeanne Marie Marchaud, Robert Snowden, Aaron Taylor, Keith Anthoni, Ken Brown, Rob Carter, Clay Russell, Veronica Compton, Guillermo Ricardo, Lou Davis, Stan Braddock, Mike Morris, Jared Benson, Beth McDyer.
01/25/78

El Perro
(The Dog)
(Spain)
X. Deva Cinematografica prodn. Dir, Antonio Isasi. Sp, Juan Antonio Porto, Antonio Isasi, Alberto Vazquez Figueroa, based on novel, "Como Un Perro Rabioso," by Figueroa. Exec prod, Enrique Gutierrez. Cam (Eastmancolor), Juan Gelpi; sets, Jose Antonio Guerra; mus, Anton Garcia Abril; edtr, Carmen Frias; sfx, Antonio Bueno, Antonio Archilla.   155.
Jason Miller, Lea Massari, Marisa Paredes, Aldo Sambrell, Juan Antonio Bardem, Yolanda Farr, Francisco Carares, Eduardo Calvo, Manuel de Blas, Antonio Gamero, Luis Gaspar, Francisco Margallo, Vincent Cuesta, Miguel Angel Rellan, Jose Yepes, Rafael Albaicin, Antonio Mayans, Amparo Valle.
(English-dubbed soundtrack)
08/17/77

El Pez Que Fuma
(The Smoking Fish)
(Venezuela)
X. Gente de Cine prodn (Caracas). Dir, Roman Chalbaud. Sp, Jose Ignacio Cabrujas, Roman Chalbaud; edtr, Guillermo Carrera; cam (Eastmancolor), Cesar Bolivar. Distributed in USA by Columbia Pictures Spanish Division.   120.
Miguel Angel Landa, Orlando Urdaneta, Hilda Vera, Haydee Balza, Rafael Briceno, Arturo Calderon, Ignacio Navarro, Nelly Meruane, Herminia Valdez.
12/21/77

El Proceso De Burgos
(The Burgos Trial)
(Spain)
X. Cobra Films and Irrintzi Zinema prodn. Dir, Imanol Uribe. Cam (Eastmancolor), Javier Aguirresarobe; edtr, Julio Pena; mus, Hibai Rekondo; exec prod, Javier Vizcaino; prodn mgr, Mischa Muller.   134.
Josu Abrisketa, Itziar Aizpurua, Victor Arana, Julen Kalzada, Jose Antonio Karrera, Unai Dorronsoro, Jose Dorronsoro, Arantza Arruti, Eduardo Uriarte, Gregorio Lopez Irasuegi, Xabier Larena, Xabier Izko de la Iglesia, Jokin Gorostidi, Enrique Gesalaga, Jon Etxabe, Mario Onaindia.
(DOC)
10/03/79

El Qanas
(The Sniper)
(Iraq)
SCB. Iraqi Film Prodn. Wir-dir, Faisal Alyassiry. Cam, Abdul-Lateef Salin, Shakeeb Rasheed; mus, Talib El-Qaraghooli; edtr, Irena El-Adhadh; prodn, Ramadhan Katie Mozan; prodn mgr, Dhia El-Baiaty.   88.
Roge Assaf, Amal Aufaish, Sami Oaftan, Gazwah El-Khalidi, Sulaman El-Basha, Muhshin El-Azawi, Hassan Dahmesh, Oasim El-Mallak, Hani Hani, Nizar Qabbani.
04/09/80

El Recurso Del Metedo
(The Recourse to the Method)
(Mexico - Cuba - France)
X. Conacine-ICAIC-K.G Prodns-FR3 prodn. Dir, Miguel Littin. Sp, Littin, Jaime Augusto Shilley, Regis Debray from the book by Alejo Carpentier; cam (Eastmancolor), Ricardo Aronvich; edtr, Ramon Aupart; mus, Leo Brouver; art dir, Pedro Garcia Espinosa, Edith Verpirini.   190.
Nelson Villagra, Katy Jurado, Alain Cuny, Maria Adelina Vera, Salvador Sanchez, Reynaldo Miravalle, Gabriel Retes.
05/31/78

El Rey Del Joropo
(King Of The Joropo)
(Venezuela)
X. Balumba Films C A prodn. Prod, Edmundo Aray. Dir-wris, Carlos Rebolledo, Thaelman Urguelles, based on the book "Los Cuentos de Alfredo Alvardo, 'El Rey del Joropo' " by Edmundo Aray. Cam, Jose Antonio Ventura Jr; edtr, Justo Vega; mus, Leo Brouwer.   92.
Tito Aponte, Oscar Martinez, Alfredo Alvarado, Fausto Verdial, Rosario Val, Alfredo Carrasco.
(English soundtrack)
03/26/80

El Sakka Mat
(The Water Carrier Is Dead)
(Egypt - Tunisia)
X. Misr Int'l Films, Youssef Shahine & Co (Cairo) and SATPEC (Tunisia) prodn. Dir, Salah Abu Seif. Sp, Mohsen Zayed, based on novel by Youssef El Sebaei; cam, Mahmoud Sabo; art dir, Mokhtar Abdel Gawad; mus, Fouad El Zaheri.   90.

Farid Shawki, Ezzat El Alayli Shouikar, Amina Rizk, Tahia Karioka, Nahed Gabr Belkeiss, Cherif Salah El Din.
10/26/77

El Segundo Poder
(The Second Power)
(Spain)
X. Orfeo Films and C B Films prodn; dir, Jose Maria Forque. Sp, Forque, Hermogenes Sainz; cam (Eastmancolor), Alejandro Ulloa; mus, Adolfo Waitzman; sets, Rafael Richard; edtr, Mercedes Alonso. Based on novel by Segundo Serrano Poncela "El Hombre de la Cruz Verde." 110.
Jon Finch, Juliette Mills, Fernando Rey, Veronica Forque, Jose Maria Prada, Africa Pratt, Jose Vivo, Manuel de Blas.
03/16/77

El Super
(Cuba - USA)
MXM. Prods, Manuel Arce, Leon Ichaso. Dirs, L Ichaso, Orlando Jimenez-Leal. Sp, Arce, L Ichaso, based on the play by Ivan Acosta; cam, Orlando Jimenez-Leal; edtr, Gloria Pineyro; mus, Enrique Ubieta. 90.
Raymundo Hidalgo-Gato, Zully Montero, Reynaldo Medina, Efrain Lopez-Neri, Ann Margarita Martinez-Casado, Elizabeth Pena, Juan Granda.
03/28/79

El Tango Cuenta su Historia
(The Tango Tells Its Story)
(Argentina)
X. Aries Cinematografica Argentina prodn. Prod-dirs, Fernando Ayala, Hector Olivera. Sp, Julio Marbiz; cam (b&w/color), Victor Hugo Caula; edtr, Carlos Julio Piaggio. 82.
(DOC)
07/05/78

Elective Affinities: SEE Affinita Elettive

The Electric Horseman
COL. Ray Stark prodn. Prod, Ray Stark. Dir, Sydney Pollack; sp, Robert Garland from screen story by Paul Gaer, Garland, based on story by Shelly Burton; cam (Technicolor), Owen Roizman; prodn des, Stephen Grimes; edtr, Sheldon Kahn; mus, Dave Grusin; song sung by Willie Nelson; asst dir, M Michael Moore; art dir, J Dennis Washington; set decor, Mary Swanson; unit pa, Jack Hirshberg; sfx, Augie Lohman; snd edtr, Gordon Davidson. (MPAA rating: PG). 120.
Robert Redford, Jane Fonda, Valerie Perrine, Willie Nelson, John Saxon, Nicolas Coster, Allan Arbus, Wilford Brimley, Will Hare, Basil Hoffman, Timothy Scott, James B Sikking, James Kline, Frank Speiser, Quinn Redeker, Lois Areno, Sarah Harris, Tasha Zemrus, James Novak, Debra L Maxwell, Michelle Heyden, Robin Timm, Patricia Blair, Gary M Fox, Richard Perlmutter, Carol Eileen Montgomery, Theresa Ann Dent, Perry Sheehan Adair, Sarge Allen, Sylvie Strauss, Richard Knoll, Angelo Giouzelis.
12/05/79

Eleftherios Venizelos 1910-1927
(Greece)
X. Yannis Horn and Greek Film Centre prodn. Dir-wri, Panelis Voulgaris. Cam, George Arvanitis; mus, Loukianos Kelaedonis; sets-cos, Dionyssis Fotopoulos; edtr, Takis Yannopoulos. 150.
Menas Christides, Yannis Voglis, Dimitris Myrat, Manos Katrakis, Olga Karlatos, Anna Kalouta.
04/02/80

The Elephant God: SEE Joi Baba Felunath

The Elephant Man
(Britain)
PAR. Brooksfilms Prodn. Exec prod, Stuart Cornfeld. Prod, Jonathan Sanger. Dir, David Lynch. Sp, Christopher DeVore, Eric Bergren, Lynch, based on "The Elephant Man And Other Reminiscences" by Sir Frederick Treves and in part on "The Elephant Man: A Study In Human Dignity" by Ashley Montagu; cam (b&w processed by Rank Labs), Freddie Francis; edtr, Anne V Coates; mus, John Morris, with "Adagio For Strings" by Samuel Barber; prodn des, Stuart Craig; art dir, Bob Cartwright; set decor, Hugh Scaife; snd, Alan Splet, Lynch, Robin Gregory; asst dir, Anthony Waye. (MPAA rating: PG). 125.
Anthony Hopkins, John Hurt, Anne Bancroft, John Gielgud, Wendy Hiller, Freddie Jones, Michael Elphick, Hannah Gordon, Helen Ryan, John Standing, Dexter Fletcher, Lesley Dunlop, Phoebe Nicholls, Lydia Lisle.
(B & W)
10/01/80

Elephant Story: SEE Zo Monogatari

11 x 14
X. Prod-dir, James Benning. 81.
Serafina Bathrick, Paddy Whannel, Harvey Taylor, Barbara Frankel, Bette Gordon, Tim Welsh, Rick Goodwin, Ted Brady.
05/25/77

Elisa, Vida Mia
(Elisa, My Love)
(Spain)
X. Elias Querejeta prodn. Sp-dir, Carlos Saura. Cam (Eastmancolor), Teo Escamilla; edtr, Pablo G del Amo; sets, Antonio Belizon. 125.
Fernando Rey, Geraldine Chaplin, Isabel Mestres, Joaquin Hinojosa, Norman Briski, Francisco Guijar, Arancha and Jacobo Escamilla, Ana Torrent.
05/11/77

The Elixirs of the Devil: SEE Die Elixiere Des Teufels

Eliza Fraser
(Australia)
RDP. Hexagon prodn. Prod-dir, Tim Burstall. Sp, David Williamson; cam (Eastmancolor), Robin Copping, Dan Burstall; art dir, Leslie Binns; snd, Desmond Bone; mus, Bruce Smeaton; edtr, Edward McQueen-Mason; sfx, Graham Matherick. 130.
John Castle, Abigail, Gerard Kennedy, Arna-Maria Winchester, Noel Ferrier, Carole Skinner, Charles Tingwell, Vicki Bray, Susannah York, John Waters, Martin Harris, Trevor Howard, Leon Lissek, Graham Matherick, Dennis Miller, Bruce Spence, John Frawley, Gus Mercurio, Bill Hunter, Sean Scully, Serge Lazareff, Martin Phelan, John Cobley, Lindsay Rouchsey, George Mallaby, Ingrid Mason, Alan Finney, David Phillips.
12/29/76

Elve Vagy Halva
(Dead or Alive)
(Hungary)
HU. Mafilm Budapest Studio prodn. Dir, Tamas Renyi. Sp, Renyi, Peter Zimre; cam (Eastmancolor), Gabor Szabo; mus, Geza Berki. 83.
Lajos Balazsovits, Gyorgy Cserhalmi, Deszo Garas, Karoly Mecs, Geza Tordy, Zoltan Vadusz.
02/27/80

Elvis! Elvis!
(Sweden)
SVF. Bert Sundberg prodn for Moviemakers, the Swedish Film Institute, Sandrews, Stockholm. Dir, Kay Pollak. Sp, Maria Gripe, Pollak; cam (Eastmancolor), Mikhael Salomon, Torbjoern Andersson; mus, Ralph Lundsten; edtr, Lasse Lundberg. 101.
Lele Dorazio, Lena-Pia Bernhardsson, Fred Gunarsson, Elisaveta, Allan Edwall.
07/27/77

Embers: SEE Sholay

Embryo
CAX. Sandy Howard prodn, prods, Arnold H Orgolini, Anita Doohan; exec prod, Howard. Dir, Ralph Nelson. Sp, Doohan, Jack W Thomas, from a story by Thomas; cam (Deluxe Color), Fred Koenekamp; edtr, John Martinelli; mus, Gil Melle; art dir, Joe Alves; set decor, Phil Abramson; snd, Bud Alper; asst dir, Michael S Glick; stunt coord, Everett Creach. (MPAA rating: PG). 108.
Rock Hudson, Diane Ladd, Barbara Carrera, Roddy McDowall, Ann Schedeen, John Elerick, Jack Colvin, Vincent Bagetta, Joyce Spitz, Dick Winslowe, Lina Raymond, Dr Joyce Brothers.
05/26/76

Emden Geht Nach USA: Wir Koennen So Viel
(Emden Goes to the USA: We Can Do So Much)
(W Germany)
X. NDR/Westdeutsches Fernsehen/WDR prodn. Wri-dir, Klaus Wildenhahn. Cam (b&w), Gisela Tuchtenhagen; edtr, Beate Hugh; prodn mgr, Claus Trollmann. 60.
(DOC) (B & W) (16m)
09/15/76

Emily
(Britain)
X. Emily prodn, prod, Christopher Neame. Dir, Henry Herbert. Sp, Anthony Morris; cam, Jack Hildyard; mus, Rod McKuen; art dir, Jacquimine Charrott-Lodwidge; edtr, Keith Palmer; prodn mgr, Caroline Neame. 84.
Koo Stark, Sarah Brackett, Victor Spinetti, Jane Hayden, Constantin de Goguel, Ina Skriver, Richard Oldfield, David Auker, Jeremy Child, Jeannie Collings, Jack Haig, Pamela Cundell.
12/15/76

Emma Mae
POI. Bea-Bob Prouctions film. Prod-dir-wri, Jamaa Fanaka. Cam (Metrocolor), Stephen Posey; edtr, Robert Fitzgerald; mus, H B Barnum; art dir, Adel Mazen; cos, Stephanie A Bell, Beverly Ventriss, Marva Farmer; snd, Don Sanders; 2d unit dir-stunt coord, Alex Brown; asst dir, Henry Sanders. (MPAA rating: R). 100.
Jerri Hayes, Ernest Williams 2d, Charles David Brooks 3d, Eddie Allen, Robert Slaughter, Malik Carter, Teri Taylor, Leopoldo Mandeville, Gammy Burdett, Laetitia Burdett, Eddy Dyer, Synthia James, Jewell Williams.
12/29/76

Emmanuelle 2
(France)
PFC. Trinacra Films-Orphee Productions-Parafrance prodn. Dir, Francis Giacobetti. Sp, Giacobetti, Bob Elia from book by Emmanuelle Arsan; cam (Eastmancolor), Robert Fraisse; edtr, Marie Sophie Dubus; mus, Francis Lai. 90.
Sylvia Kristel, Umberto Orsini, Catherine Rivet, Frederic Lagache, Caroline Laurcence.
01/21/76

Emmenez-Moi Au Ritz
(Take Me to the Ritz)
(France)
HTR. Hamster Film, TF1, SFP prodn. Dir, Pierre Grimblat. Sp, Louis Martin, Claude Desailly, Frederic Dard, Grimblat; cam, Georges Leclerc; edtr, Jean-Raymond Cuguillere; mus, Claude Bolling. 100.
Maurice Ronet, Valerie Mairesse, Macha Meril, Tina Aumont, Marsha Grant, Henri Guybet, Paul Le Person.
10/12/77

The Emperor: SEE Kejsaren

Emperor Chien Lung And The Beauty
(Hong Kong)
SHF. Run Run Shaw Prodn. Prod, Mona Fong. Wri-dir, Li Han-hsiang. Cam, Lin Chiao; edtr, Chiang Hsing-lung; mus dir, Eddie Wang; martial arts instructor, Tang Chia, Huang Pei-Chi. 120.
Liu Ying, Hui Ying-hung, Pan Ping-chang, Li Kung, Liu Hui-Ling, Chiang Nan.
(Mandarin soundtrack - English subtitles)
04/02/80

Empire of the Ants
AIP. Prod-dir, Bert I Gordon; exec prod, Samuel Z Arkoff. Sp, Jack Turley, from a screen story by Gordon and a story by H G Wells; cam (Movielab Color), Reginald Morris; edtr, Michael Luciano; mus, Dana Kaproff; prodn des, Charles Rosen; set decor, Anthony C Montenaro; snd, Ryder Sound; cos-ward, Joanne Haas; asst dirs, David McGiffert, Mel Efros; stunt coord, Buddy Joe Hooker. (MPAA rating: PG). 89.
Joan Collins, Robert Lansing, John David Carson, Albert Salmi, Jacqueline Scott, Pamela Shoop, Robert Pine, Edward Power, Brooke Palance, Tom Fadden, Irene Tedrow, Harry Holcombe, Jack Kosslyn, Ilse Earl, Janie Gavin, Norman Franklin, Florence McGee.
07/06/77

The Empire Strikes Back
FOX. Prod, Gary Kurtz. Exec prod, George Lucas. Dir, Irvin Kershner. Sp, Leigh Brackett, Lawrence Kasdan, based on story by Lucas; cam (Rank Film Color/Deluxe Prints), Peter Suschitzy; edtr, Paul Hirsch; snd (Dolby Stereo), Peter Sutton; special visual effects, Brian Johnson, Richard Edlund; asso prods, Robert Watts, James Bloom; art dirs, Leslie Dilley, Harry Lange, Alan Tomkins; set decor, Michael Ford; make-up-special creature des, Stuart Freeborn; cos, John Mollo; des cnslt, Ralph McQuarrie; mus, John Williams. Prod supv, Bruce Sharman; studio 2nd-unit dirs, Harley Cokliss, John Barry; studio 2nd-unit cam, Chris Menges; location 2nd-unit dir, Peter MacDonald; location 2nd-unit cam, Geoff Glover; asst dirs, David Tomblin, Dominic Fulford, Bill Westley, Ola Solum; mechanical effects supv, Nick Allder; snd des, Ben Burtt. Effects pho, Dennis Muren; optical pho, Bruce Nicholson; art dir-visual effects, Joe Johnston; stop motion ani, Jon Berg, Phil Tippet; matte painting, Harrison Ellenshaw; model maker, Lorne Peterson; ani-rotoscope, Peter Kuran; visual effects edtr, Conrad Buff. (MPAA rating: PG). 124.
Mark Hamill, Harrison Ford, Carrie Fisher, David Prowse, Anthony Daniels, Peter Mayhew, Kenny Baker, Frank Oz, Billy Dee Williams, Alec Guinness, Jeremy Bulloch, John Hollis, Jack Purvis, Des Webb, Kathryn Mullen, Clive Revill, Kenneth Colley, Julian Glover, Michael Sheard; Michael Culver, John Dicks, Milton Johns, Mark Jones, Oliver Maguire, Robin Scobey, Bruce Boa, Christopher Malcom, Dennis Lawson, Richard Oldfield, John Morton, Ian Liston, John Ratzenberger, Jack McKenzie, Jerry Harte, Norman Chancer, Norwich Duff, Ray Hassett, Brigitte Kahn, Burnell Tucker.
05/14/80

En foraarsdag i helvede
(Springday in Hell)
(Denmark)
KID. Steen Herdel Film prodn. Conceived-dir, Joergen Leth. Cam team (27 cameras) coord, Dan Holmberg (Eastmancolor); snd recording coord, Ole Oersted; edtr, Lars Brydesen; mus, Gunner Moeller Pedersen. 110.
(DOC)
03/09/77

En kaerleks sommar
(A Summer Of Love)
(Sweden)
SVE. Nordisk Tonfilm (Ingemar Ejve) prodn. Dir, Mats Arehn. Wri, Jonas Cornell, based on novel by Ivan Klima; cam, Lars Bjoerne, Bertil Rosengren; mus, Terje Rypdal; exec prod, Peter Kropenin. 98.
Goesta Ekman Jr, Maria Andersson, Anita Ekstroem.
04/18/79

En och en
(One Plus One)
(Sweden)
SNA. Josephson Nykvist/Swedish Film Institute/AB Sandrews prodn. Story-sp, Erland Josephson. Dirs, Josephson, Sven Nykvist, Ingrid Thulin. Cam (Eastmancolor), Nykvist. Exec prod, Katinka Farago. 90.
Erland Josephson, Ingrid Thulin.
03/22/78

En rig mand
(A Rich Man)
(Denmark)
SFC. Statens Filmcentral/Denmark's Radio prodn. Wri-dir, Jon Bang Carlsen. Cam (Eastmancolor), Alexander Gruszynski. Mus, Ida Klemann, Torben Andersen. Prodn, Vibeke Windeloev. 67.
Hans and Cardy Smith.
(DOC) (16m)
02/21/79

En vandring i solen
(A Walk in the Sun)
(Sweden)
EUR. Swedish Film Institute/HB Three Leaf Clover prodn. Sp, Bibi Edlund based on Stig Claesson's novel. Dir, Hans Dahlberg. Cam (Eastmancolor), Roland Lundin, Bertil Rosengren; prodn des, Mona Forssen; edtr, Wic Kjellin; prodn planning, Bo Jonsson/Viking Film; in charge of prodn, Bengt Forslund; Greek locations supervisor, Francis Carabott. 96.
Goesta Ekman, Inger Lise Rypdal, Margaretha Krook, Sif Ruud, Irma Christensson, Kenneth Haigh.
01/10/79

The Enclosure: SEE In Kluis

Encore
(Hong Kong)
X. Prods, Philip Chan, Elaine Sung through Promotion Center. Dir, Clifford Choi. Sp, Choi, Philip Chan. Orig songs and mus, Danny Chan. 90.
Danny Chan, Leslie Cheung, Mary Yung, Winnie Yu, Paul Chung, Elizabeth Tam, Yang Kwan, Philip Chan.
(English subtitles)
10/29/80

The End
UA. Prod, Lawrence Gordon; exec prod, Hank Moonjean. Dir, Burt Reynolds; sp, Jerry Belson; cam (DeLuxe Color), Bobby Byrne; edtr, Donn Cambern; mus, Paul Williams; prodn des, Jan Scott; set decor, John Franco Jr; snd, Richard Portman, Jack Solomon; cosward, Norman Salling, Gene Deardorff, Violet Cane; asst dir, Kurt Baker; stunt coord, Hal Needham. (MPAA rating: R). 100.
Burt Reynolds, Dom DeLuise, Sally Field, Strother Martin, David Steinberg, Joanne Woodward, Norman Fell, Myrna Loy, Kristy McNichol, Pat O'Brien, Robby Benson, Carl Reiner, James Best, Jock Mahoney.
05/03/78

End Of Autumn: SEE Akibiori

End of Night: SEE Nishant

The End of the Rainbow:
SEE Das Ende Des Regenbogens

The End of the World in Our Usual Bed in a Night Full of Rain
WB. Liberty Film. Prod, Gil Shiva. Sp-dir, Lina Wertmuller. Exec prod, Harry Colombo; cam (Technicolor), Giuseppe Rotunno; edtr, Franco Fraticelli; art dir, Enrico Job; mus, G B Pergolesi, Roberto De Simone; asst dir, Gianni Arduini; cos des, Benito Persico; set des, Gianni Giovagnoni; prodn mgr, Jone Tuzi. (MPAA rating: R). 104.
Giancarlo Giannini, Candice Bergen, Michael Tucker, Mario Scarpetta, Lucio Amelio, Massimo Wertmuller, Anna Papa, Anne Byrne, Flora Carabella, Anita Paltrinieri, Giuliana Carnescecchi, Alice Colombo Oxman.
02/01/78

The Endless Trail: SEE Golapi Ekhon Trainey

The Enemy: SEE Dusman

The Enforcer
WB. Prod, Robert Daley. Dir, James Fargo. Sp, Stirling Silliphant, Dean Reisner; story, Gail Morgan Hickman, S W Schurr, based on characters created by Harry Julian Fink, R M Fink; cam (Technicolor), Charles W Short; edtrs, Ferris Webster, Joel Cox; mus, Jerry Fielding; art dir, Allen E Smith; set decor, Ira Bates; cos-ward, Glenn Wright; snd, Les Fresholtz, Bert Hallberg; asst dir, Joe Cavalier; stunt coord, Wayne Van Horn. (MPAA rating: R). 96.
Clint Eastwood, Harry Guardino, Bradford Dillman, John Mitchum, DeVeren Bookwalter, John Crawford, Tyne Daly.
12/22/76

Entanglement: SEE Tetetoria

Entire Days in the Trees:
SEE Des Journees Entieres Dans Les Arbres

Eqipaj
(The Crew)
(USSR)
SOV. Mosfilm Production, Moscow. Dir, Alexander Mitta; sp, Yuri Donsky, Valery Fried, Mitta in collab with Boris Urinowsky; cam (Eastmancolor), Valery Shuvalov. 150.
Georgy Jenov, Anatoly Vassiliel, Alexandra Yakovleva, Leonid Filatov, Irina Akulova.
06/18/80

Equus
UA. Prods, Lester Persky, Elliott Kastner. Dir, Sidney Lumet. Sp, Peter Shaffer, based on his play; cam (DeLuxe Color), Oswald Morris; edtr, John Victor-Smith; mus, Richard Rodney Bennett; prodn des, Tony Walton; art dir, Simon Holland; set decor, Gerry Holmes; snd, Richard Vorisek, Jimmy Sabat; cos-ward, Walton, Brenda Dabbs, Patti Unger; asst dir, David Tringham. (MPAA rating: R). 137.
Richard Burton, Peter Firth, Colin Blakely, Joan Plowright, Harry Andrews, Eileen Atkins, Jenny Agutter, John Wyman, Kate Reid.
10/19/77

Era E Lisi
(The Wind and the Oak)
(Yugoslavia)
YFR. Kosova Film-Televizija Pristina prodn. Dir, Besim Sahatciu. Sp, Perit Imamai from book by Sinana Hasanija; cam (Eastmancolor), Rudolf Sopi; mus, Rexho Mulioi. 110.
Abdurrahman Shala, Faruk Begolli, Hazir Myftari, Istref Begolli, Shani Pallaska, Quemaji Pallaska, Qemaji Ajdini, Xhevat Qorraj.
08/15/79

Eraserhead
X. American Film Institute-David Lynch prodn. Prod-dir-wri-edtr, Lynch. Cam, Fred Elms, Herbert Cardwell; mus, Fats Waller; art dir, Lynch; snd, Alan Splet. 100.
Jack Nance, Charlotte Stewart, Jeanne Bates, Allen Josephs, Judith Anna Roberts, Laurel Near, Jean Lange, V. Phipps-Wilson, Jack Fisk.
(B & W)
03/23/77

Eredita' Ferramonti
(The Inheritance)
(Italy)
TIT. Prod, Gianni Hecht Lucari for FLAG. dir, Mauro Bolognini; sp, Ugo Pirro-Sergio Bazzini; cam (Eastmancolor), Ennio Guarnieri; art dir, Luigi Scaccianoce; edtr, Nino Baragli; mus, Ennio Morricone. 121.
Anthony Quinn, Fabio Testi, Dominique Sanda, Luigi Proietti, Adriana Asti, Paolo Bonacelli.
06/09/76

Erika's Passions
(W Germany)
X. Ula Stockl Prodn (Munich) Germany. Wri-dir, Ula Stockl. Cam (b&w), Thomas Mauch; art dir, Hartmut Rathmayer, Daisy Boutique; snd, Martin Muller. 65.
Karen Baal, Vera Tschechowa.
(B & W)
11/08/78

Ernesto
(Italy)
X. Clesi Cinematografica-Jose Frade Prod - Albatros Produktion prodn. Dir, Salvatore Samperi. Sp, Barbara Alberti, Amadeo Paganini, Samperi; cam (Technicolor), Camillo Bazzoni; mus, Carmelo Bernaola. 98.
Martin Halm, Michele Placido, Virna Lisi.
03/07/79

Eroina
(Heroin)
(Italy)
X. Prods, Benedetto Conversi, Patrizia Tonon for Samar Film prodns. Wri-dir, Massimo Pirri; cam, Sergio Martinelli; mus, The Pretenders. 90.
Helmut Berger, Corinne Clery, Marzio C Honorato, Franco Citti.
10/15/80

The Erotic Adventures of Super Knight: SEE The Amorous Adventures Of Don Quixote & Sancho Panza

Erotic Stories: SEE Contos Eroticos

Es Herrscht Ruhe Im Land
(The Country Is Calm)
(W Germany)
FDA. FFAT-Film/ZDF/ORF co-prodn; producer, Christoph Holch. Dir, Peter Lilienthal. Sp, Lilienthal, Antonio Skarmeta; cam, Robby Mueller; edtr, Abel Alboim; mus, Angel Parra. 100.
Charles Vanel, Mario Pardo, Eduardo Duran, Zita Duarte, Henriqueta Maya, Luciano Noble, Miguel Franco, Uberlinda Skarmeta, Santiago Reyes, Carlos Silva.
06/30/76

Escapade: SEE Seitensprung

The Escape: SEE Die Flucht

Escape from Alcatraz
PAR. Prod-dir, Donald Siegel. Exec prod, Robert Daley. Sp, Richard Tuggle, based on the book by J Campbell Bruce; cam, Bruce Surtees; prodn des, Allen Smith; edtr, Ferris Webster; set decor, Edward J McDonald; snd, Bert Hallberg; asst dir, Luigi Alfano. (MPAA rating: PG). 112.
Clint Eastwood, Patrick McGoohan, Roberts Blossom, Jack Thibeau, Fred Ward, Paul Benjamin, Larry Hankin, Bruce M Fischer, Frank Ronzio.
06/20/79

Escape From the Dark
(The Littlest Horse Thief)
(Britain)
BV. Walt Disney Productions presentation. Prod, Ron Miller. Dir, Charles Jarrott. Sp, Rosemary Anne Sisson (based on story, Bert Kennedy, Sisson); cam (Technicolor), Paul Beeson; edtr, Richard Marden; art dir, Bob Laing; snd, Rusty Coppleman; asst dir, Allan James. (MPAA rating: G). 104.

Alastair Sim, Peter Barkworth, Maurice Colbourne, Susan Tebbs, Geraldine McEwan, Prunella Scales, Leslie Sands, Joe Gladwin, Chloe Franks, Andrew Harrison, Benjie Bolgar, Jeremy Bulloch.
06/16/76

Escape To Athena
(Britain)
AFC. Lew Grade presentation. Prods, Jack Wiener, David Niven Jr. Dir, George P Cosmatos. Sp, Richard S Lochte, Edward Anhalt, based on orig story by Lochte, Cosmatos. Cam, Gil Taylor; edtr, Ralph Kemplen; art dir, John Graysmark; mus, Lalo Schifrin; snd, Derek Ball; asst dir, Derek Cracknell. 125.
Roger Moore, Telly Savalas, David Niven, Claudia Cardinale, Richard Roundtree, Stefanie Powers, Sonny Bono, Elliott Gould, Anthony Valentine, Sigi Rauch, Michael Sheard, Richard Wren, Philip Locke, Steve Ubels, Elena Secota.
01/24/79

Esperando A Papa
(Waiting For Daddy)
(Spain)
X. Aspa P C and Penta Films prodn. Dir, Vicente Escriva; sp, Alvaro Lyon de Petre, Escriva; cam (Eastmancolor), Johnny Cabrera; mus, Julio Iglesias, Rafael Ferro; edtr, Soledad Lopez; exec prod, Vicente Escriva Jr; sets, Adolfo Lofino. 100.
Arturo Fernandez, Teresa Rabal, Maria Silva, Josele Roman, Mary Carmen Prendes, Angel Picazo, Javier.
07/30/80

Essakamat
(Death of the Water Carrier)
(Egypt - Tunisia)
X. MISR Int'l Film of Egypt and Societe Tunisienne de Cinematographie, Tunis. Wri-dir, Salah Abu Saif. Cam, Mahmud Sabu; mus, Fuad Az-Zahiri. 110.
Farid Shauqui, Ezzat al-Alayli, Shuyar, Amina Risq.
09/19/79

Esthappan
(India)
GLI. General Pictures (Kerala, India) prodn. Dir, Aravindam. Sp, Aravindam, Isaac Thomas Kottukapally, Kavalam; cam, Shaji; mus, Aravindam, Janardhan, Kottukapally. 93.
10/22/80

Et La Tendresse?. . .Bordel!
(Tenderness, My Fanny!)
(France)
GAU. Chloe Prodn - Foch Prodn co-prodn. Prod, Jean-Pierre Fougea; wri-dir, Patrick Schulmann; cam, Jacques Assuerus; edtr, Aline Freess; mus, Schulmann; snd, Pierre Lorrain; snd edtr, Michel Patient; make-up, Yatzu. 90.
Jean-Luc Bideau, Evelyne Dress, Bernard Girardeau, Anne-Marie Philipe, Regis Porte, Marie-Catherine Conti.
04/11/79

Et Vive La Liberte
(And Long Live Liberty)
(France)
GAU. Belstar Prodns prodn. Dir, Serge Korber. Sp, Albert Kantoff, Jacques Lanzmann, Korber; cam (Eastmancolor), Jean-Jacques Tarbes; edtr, Marie-Claire Korber. 90.
Les Charlots (3), Claude Pieplu, Georges Geret.
02/15/78

Ett anstaendigt liv
(A Decent Life)
(Sweden)
SVE. Stefan Jarl prodn. Wri-dir, Stefan Jarl. Cam (Eastmancolor, 16m blown up to 35m), Per Kaellberg, Staffan Lidqvist, Roland Lundin; edtrs, Anette Lykke-Lundberg, Jan Persson, Badis Andersson; mus, Ulf Dageby, Johannes Leyman, Nacksving, Kenta Gustafsson, Eva Blondin, Stoffe Svensson. 102. (DOC)
04/18/79

Eugenio
(Italy - France)
X. Co-prodn of Intercontinental Film Company (Rome) and Les Films Du Losange-Gaumont-Moonfleet (Paris). Prod, Achille Manzotti. Dir-wri, Luigi Comencini. Cam, Carlo Carlini; art dir-cos, Paoli Commencini. Edtr, Nino Baragli. Mus, Romano Checcacci. Asso prods, Margaret Menegoz, Simon Mizrahi. 105.
Saverio Marconi, Dalila Di Lazzaro, Bernard Blier, Francesco Bonelli, Carole Andre, Meme Perlini, Dina Sassoli, Gisela Sofio, Jose Luis De Villalonga, Alessandro Bruzzese.
11/19/80

The Europeans
(Britain)
L-P. Merchant-Ivory Prodns Ltd. Dir, James Ivory. Sp, Ruth Prawer Jhabvala; cam, Larry Pizer; edtr, Jeremiah Rusconi; mus, Richard Robbins. 90.
Lee Remick, Robin Ellis, Wesley Addy, Tim Choate, Lisa Eichhorn, Nancy New, Kristin Griffith, Tim Woodward.
05/16/79

Eutanasia Di Un Amore
(Break Up)
(Italy)
CNZ. Rizzoli Film picture. Prod, Mario Cecchi Gori for Capital Film, Koral Int'l. Dir, Enrico Maria Salerno. Sp, Arduino Maiuri, Massimo De Rita, from novel of same title by Giorgio Saviane; cam (Technospes), Marcello Gatti; mus, Daniele Patucchi; set des, Dante Ferretti; cos, Waine Finkelman; montage, Mario Morra.
Ornella Muti, Tony Musante, Monica Guerritore, Mario Scaccia, Elsa Trotter.
10/25/78

Even If You Are Mud, Still You Return To Dust: SEE Putik Ka Man. . .Sa Alabok Magbabalik

Evening Land: SEE Aftenlandet

Every Wednesday: SEE Minden Szerdan

Every Which Way But Loose
WB. Malpaso Co Film. Prod, Robert Daley. Dir, James Fargo. Sp, Jeremy Joe Kronsberg; cam, Rexford Metz; art dir, Elayne Ceder; edtr, Ferris Webster, Joel Cox; asso prod, Fritz Manes, Kronsberg; asst dir, Larry Powell; set decor, Robert De Vestel; stunt coord, Wayne Van Horn; snd, Bert Hallberg; sfx, Chuck Gaspar; cos, Glenn Wright. (MPAA rating: R). 119.
Clint Eastwood, Sondra Locke, Geoffrey Lewis, Beverly D'Angelo, Ruth Gordon.
12/20/78

Everyday Life in a Syrian Village: SEE Al Hayatt Al Yawmiyah Fi Qariah Suriyah

Everyone Dies in His Own Company: SEE Jeder Stirbt Fuer Sich Allein

Everyone For Himself In Life: SEE Sauve Qui Peut La Vie

The Evictor: SEE Der Umsetzer

The Evictors
AIP. Prod-dir, Charles B Pierce. Wris, Charles B Pierce, Garry Rusoff, Paul Fisk; cam (Movielab Color), Chuck Bryant; edtr, Shirak Khojayan; mus, Jaime Mendoza-Nava. (MPAA rating: PG). 92.
Michael Parks, Jessica Harper, Vic Morrow, Sue Ane Langdon, Dennis Fimple, Bill Thurman, Jimmy Clem, Harry Thomasson, Twyla Taylor, Glen Roberts.
04/18/79

The Evil
X. Rangoon prodn. Prod, Ed Carlin; exec prods, Paul A Joseph, Malcolm Levinthal. Dir, Gus Trikonis. Sp, Donald G Thompson; cam (Movie Lab Color), Mario Di Leo; edtr, Jack Kirshner; mus, Johnny Harris; art dir, Peter Jamison; snd, Bill Kaplan Jr; ward, Barbara Andrews, James Alvarez; asst dir, Scott Adam; stunts, Buddy Joe Hooker. (MPAA rating: R). 89.
Richard Crenna, Joanna Pettet, Andrew Prine, Cassie Yates, Lynne Moddy, Victor Buono, George O'Hanlon Jr, Mary Louise Weller, Robert Viharo, Milton Selzer, Galen Thompson.
03/29/78

The Evolution of Snuff
(Germany)
ATF. Richard R Rimmel prodn of Monopol Film, Munich. Based on an idea, with commentary by Carl Amery, Johanna Bardili. Dir, Karl Martine; pho, Richard R Rimmel; mus, Gerhard Heinz with themes from "Life Story" by E De Tissot; English dial-post prodn, Larry Dolgin. 89. (DOC)
03/30/77

Ex Und Hopp
(W Germany)
X. Lothar Lambert and Wolfram Zobus prodn. Wri-dir, Lothar Lambert, Wolfram Zobus. Cam, Zobus; edtr, Helga Schnurre. 60.
Lothar Lambert, Wolfgang Breiter, Tilman Hemp, Helga Schnurre, Inge Bongers, Dagmar Beiersdorf.
(B & W) (16m)
03/16/77

Executioners From Shaolin
(Hong Kong)
SHW. Prod, Rumme Shaw. Dir, Liu Chia-Ling. Sp, Yi Kuang; cam, Lo Yun-Cheng; edtr, Chiang Hsing-Lung; martial art instructor, Liu Chia-liang. 100.
Chen Kuan-Tai, Lo Lieh, Wang Yue, Lily Li, Cheng Kang Yeh, Tien Ching.
03/09/77

Exhibition 2
(France)
COH. Conceived-dir, Jean-Francois Davy. Cam (Eastmancolor), Roger Fellous; edtr, Claude Cohen. 80.
Sylvia Bourdon.
11/10/76

Exiled In A Central Avenue:
SEE *Exoristos Stin Kentriki Leoforo*

Exit. . .Nur Keine Panik
(Exit-But No Panic)
(Austria)
TER. Dir, Franz Novotny; sp, Gustav Ernst, Novotny; cam (Eastmancolor), Alfio Contini; edtr, Eliska Stibrova; mus, Otto M Zykan. 100.
Eddie Constantine, Hanno Poschl, Ulrich Neumann, Konrad Becker, Sabrina Thurm, Beatrice Frey, Peter Weibel.
08/20/80

Exit Sunset Boulevard
(W Germany)
CPZ. Bastia Cleve Film Prodn, Hamburg. Wri-dir-pho-edtr, Bastian Cleve. Asst and snd, Alf Olbrisch; asst and still-photos, Inga Di Mar-Wendnagel; prodn asst, Marlies Cleve. 94.
Elke Sommer.
(16m)
03/12/80

Exorcist II: The Heretic
WB. Richard Lederer prodn, prods, John Boorman, Lederer. Dir, Boorman. Wri, William Goodhart. Cam (Technicolor), William A Fraker; edtr, Tom Priestley; mus, Ennio Morricone; prodn des, Richard Macdonald; set decor, John Austin; snd, Walter Goss; asst dir, Phil Rawlins; art dir, Jack Collins; cos, Robert de Mora; special visual effects, Albert J Whitlock, Van der Veer Photo; sfx, Chuck Gaspar, Wayne Edgar, Jim Blount, Jeff Jarvis, Roy Kelly. (MPAA rating: R). 117.
Linda Blair, Richard Burton, Louise Fletcher, Max Von Sydow, Kitty Winn, Paul Henreid, James Earl Jones, Ned Beatty.
06/22/77

Exoristos Stin Kentriki Leoforo
(Exiled In A Central Avenue)
(Greece)
X. Nicos Zervos and George Emirzas prodn. Dir, Zervos; sp, Zervos, Costas Ferris; cam (b&w), Sakis Maniatis; mus, Zervos, Ferris; sets-cos, D Fininis; edtr, Ferris; snd, Panos Panoussopoulos. 90.
Costas Ferris, Marilli Tsopanelli.
11/14/79

The Experiment: SEE Ai Tejruba

Exploszia
(Explosion)
(Romania)
RMN. Dir, Mircea Dragan. Sp, Ioan Grigorescu; cam, Nicolae Margineanu; mus, Theodor Grigoriu; art dir, Constantine Simionescu. 103.
George Danica, Toma Caragiu, Radu Beligan, Jean Constantin, Dem Radulescu, George Mottoi, Florin Piersic, Colea Rautu, Draga Olteanu, Mircea Basta, Mircea Diaconu, Cezaro Dafinescu, Aurel Cioranu.
06/28/78

Expose Me Lovely
MAT. Capri Productions film. Prod-dir-sp, Armand Weston; cam, Harry Flecks; snd, Jack Justice; edtr, Weston; exec prod, Vahagn Hovannes. (Self-applied X rating). 96.
Jennifer Welles, Raf Kean, Eve Adams, Cary Lacy, Jody Maxwell.
03/03/76

Expropiacion
(Expropriation)
(Venezuela - Peru)
PXA. Exec prod, Juan Barandarian. Wri-pho-dir, Mario Robles. Cam, Carlos Pecheneda, Carlos Mendez, Walter Veliz; edtrs, Robles, Walter Veliz; mus, Arturo Ruiz del Pozo. 89.
Inhabitants of Oroya, Goylarisquisga, Paragsha.
07/14/76

The Expulsion from Paradise: SEE Die Vertreibung Aus Dem Paradies

Exterieur Nuit
(Exterior Night)
(France)
X. Films Noirs prodn. Dir-edtr, Jacques Bral; wris, Bral, Jean-Paul Leca, Julien Levi, from an orig idea by Noel Burch; cam, Pierre-William Glenn; mus, Karl-Heinz Schafer. 110.
Christine Boisson, Andre Dussolier, Gerard Lanvin, Jean-Pierre Sentier.
08/13/80

The Exterminator
AVE. Interstar prodn. Prod, Mark Buntzman; dir-sp, James Glickenhaus; cam, Bob Baldwin; edtr, Corky O'Hara; mus, Joe Renzetti; snd (Dolby stereo), Bill Daly; sfx, Tom Brumberger; asst dir, Jane Hershcopf. (MPAA rating: R). 101.
Christopher George, Samantha Eggar, Robert Ginty, Steve James, Tony Di Benedetto, Dick Boccelli, Patrick Farrelly, Michele Harrell, David Lipman, Cindy Wilks, Dennis Boutsikaris.
09/17/80

The Extras
(Hong Kong)
BNG. Film Force Prodn. Dir, Yim Ho. Sp, Yim Ho, Philip Chan, Ronny Yu; mus, Joseph Koo, James Wong; edtr, Wong Yee Shin; cam, Johnny Ko. 87.
James Yi Lui, Idi Chan, Ken Cheng, Tsang Kong.
12/27/78

Eyeball
(Gatti Rossi In Un Labirinto di Vetro)
(Italy)
BRE. Dir, Umberto Lenzi. Exec prod, Joseph Brenner. (MPAA rating: R). 91.
John Richardson, Martine Brochard, Ines Pellegrin, Silvia Solar, George Rigaud.
11/01/78

Eyes of Laura Mars
COL. Jon Peters Prodn. Prod, Jon Peters; exec prod, Jack H Harris. Dir, Irvin Kershner. Sp, John Carpenter, David Zelag Goodman, from a story by Carpenter; cam, Victor J Kemper; mus, Artie Kane; edtr, Michael Kahn; prodn des, Gene Callahan; cos des, Theoni V Aldredge; art dir, Robert Gundlach; asso prod, Laura Ziskin; set decor, John Godfrey; asst dirs, Louis A Stroller, Mel Howard; snd, Les Lazarowitz; theme words and mus, Karen Lawrence, John Desautels; gallery pho, Helmut Newton; Eyes of Laura Mars photographs, Rebecca Blake; stunt coord, Alex Stevens. (MPAA rating: R). 104.
Faye Dunaway, Tommy Lee Jones, Brad Dourif, Rene Auberjonois, Raul Julia, Frank Adonis, Lisa Taylor, Darlanne Fluegel, Rose Gregorio, Bill Boggs, Steve Marachuk.
06/02/78

The Eyes: SEE Dese Nise

F Comme Fairbanks
(F For Fairbanks)
(France)
GAU. Camera One-Gaumont-FR3 prodn. Dir, Maurice Dugowson. Sp, Jacques & Maurice Dugowson; cam (Eastmancolor), Andre Diot; edtr, Jean-Bernard Bonis; mus, Patrick Dewaere, Roland Vincent. 107.
Miou-Miou, Patrick Dewaere, Michael Piccoli, John Berry, Jean-Michel Folon.
05/05/76

Fabian
(W Germany)
UA. Regina Ziegler Filmproduktion prodn. Dir, Wolf Gremm. Sp, Gremm, Hans Borgalt from the book by Erich Kastner; cam, Jurgen Wagner; edtr, Sigrun Jager; mus, Charles Kalman.   116.
Hans-Peter Hallwachs, Herman Lause, Silvia Janisch, Mijanou Van Baarzel, Brigitte Mira, Ivan Desny.
10/29/80

Fabian Balint Talalkozasa Istennel
(Balint Fabian Meets God)
(Hungary)
HU. Dialog Studio prodn. Wri-dir, Zoltan Fabri from book by Jozsef Balazs. Cam (Eastmancolor), Gyorgy Illes; mus, Gyorgy Vukan.   113.
Gabor Koncz, Vera Venczel, Istvan Szabo, Gyorgy Szatmari, Jozsef Ivanyi, Matyas Lisztics.
07/23/80

The Fabulous Adventures of the Legendary Baron Munchausen: SEE Les Fabuleuses Adventures du

Lengendaire Baron de Munchausen

Face To Face
(Sweden)
PAR. Dino De Laurentiis presentaiton. A Cinematograph prodn. Wri-dir-prod, Ingmar Bergman. Cam (Eastmancolor), Sven Nykvist; edtr, Siv Lundgren; mus, Mozart's "Fantasia in E minor," played by Kabi Laretei; prodn des, Anne Hagegard; set decor, Peter Krupenin; snd, Owe Svensson. (MPAA rating: R).   136.
Liv Ullmann, Erland Josephson, Gunnar Bjornstrand, Aino Taube-Henrikson, Kari Sylwan, Siv Ruud, Sven Lindberg, Tore Segelcke, Ulf Johansson, Kristina Adolphson, Gosta Ekman, Kabi Laretei.
(English subtitles)
04/07/76

Face To The Sun: SEE Le Soleil en face

The Factory Outing: SEE Firmaskovturen

Fad, Jal
(Grandfather)
(Senegal)
X. Senegal Film prodn. Conceived-dir, Safi Faye. Cam, Patrick Fabry, Jean Monod, Papa Moctar Ndoye; edtr, Andree Davanture. 108. (DOC) (16m)
06/06/79

Fade To Black
AMC. Irwin Yablans, Sylvio Tabet prodn. Wri-dir, Vernon Zimmerman; exec prods, Irwin Yablans, Sylvio Tabet; prods, George Braunstein, Ron Hamady; cam, Alex Phillips Jr; asst dir, Ron Fury; edtr, Howard Kunin; set decor, Loma Lee Brookbank; sfx, James Wayne. (MPAA rating: R).   100.
Dennis Christopher, Linda Kerridge, Tim Thomerson, Morgan Paull, Hennen Chambers, Marya Small, Eve Brent Ashe, Bob Drew, Gwynne Gilford, John Steadman, Mickey Rourke, Melinda Fee, Jane K Wiley, Peter Horton, Norman Burton, James Luisi, Anita Converse, Marcie Barkin, Gilbert Lawrence Kahn.
10/15/80

Fagyongyok
(Mistletoes)
(Hungary)
HU. Hunnia Studio - Bela Balasz Studio prodn. Wri-dir, Judit Ember. Cam (b&w), Janos Illes; mus, Zsolt Dome.   91.
Jeno Sipos, Nora Sipos, Eleonora Lukasik, Mrs Lukasik.
(B & W)
08/22/79

Fah Larng Fon
(After The Rain)
(Thailand)
JIR. Prod, Jirawan Kampana Senyakorn. Wri-edtr-dir, Pisan Akaraseni. Story, Maj Gen Bunterng Kampana Senyakorn; cam, Boonseng Sitti; mus, Movala Vorakit; snd, Maitree Janjarasskul; art dir, Pisan Akaraseni; asst dir, Jaran.   120.
Vitoon Karuna, Ampha Pusit, Nawarat Yukthanan, Piathip Kumvongse, Dek Chai Apirat, Jamroon Huajun.
06/28/78

Fairy Dance: SEE Samodivsko Horo

The Faking of the President 1974
SPZ. Spencer Productions prodn. Prod-wri-dir, Jeanne and Alan Abel. Asso prod, Alan J Barinholtz. Color by TVC.   80.
Marshall Efron, Alan Barinholtz, Robert Staats, William Daprato, Richard Dixon.
05/19/76

The Fall: SEE A Queda

The Fall: SEE Der Sturz

Falling In Love Again
ITP. OTA prodn. Prod-dir, Steven Paul. Exec prod, Hank Paul. Sp, Steven Paul, Ted Allan, Susannah York; cam, Michael Mileham, Dick Bush, Wolfgang Suschitzky; edtrs, Bud Smith, Doug Jackson, Jacqueline Cambas; mus, Michael Legrand; songs--mus, Legrand, lyr, Sammy Cahn, Carol Connors, Dennis Lambert; co-prod, Patrick Wright; asso prods, Dan Murphy, Dorothy Koster-Paul. (MPAA rating: PG).   103.
Elliott Gould, Susannah York, Stuart Paul, Michelle Pfeiffer, Kaye Ballard, Robert Hackman, Steven Paul, Todd Helper, Herb Rudley, Marion McCargo, Bonnie Paul.
11/19/80

False Face
UIP. J J Prodns prodn. Prods, Joseph Weintraub, John Grissmer. Dir-sp, Grissmer, from an orig story, Weintraub; cam (Movielab Color), Edward Lachman Jr; edtr, Weintraub; prodn des, William DeSeta; snd, William Meredith, Emil Neroda; mus, Robert Cobert. (MPAA rating: R).   95.
Robert Lansing, Judith Chapman, Arlen Dean Snyder, David Scarroll, Sandy Martin, Bruce Atkins.
12/15/76

Fame
UA. Metro-Goldwyn-Mayer presentation. Prods, David De Silva, Alan Marshall. Dir, Alan Parker. Sp, Christopher Gore; cam (Metrocolor), Michael Seresin; mus, Michael Gore; prodn des, Geoffrey Kirkland; edtr, Gerry Hambling; chor, Louis Falco; asst dir, Robert F Colesberry; cos, Kristi Zea; snd edtr, Les Wiggins; art dir, Ed Wittstein; set decor, George DeTitta; songs-mus, Michael Gore, Dominic Bugatti, Frank Musker, Paul McCrane; lyrs, Dean Pitchford, Robert F Colesberry, Lesley Gore, Dominic Bugatti, Frank Musker, Dean Pitchford, Paul McCrane. (MPAA rating: R).   134.
Eddie Barth, Irene Cara, Lee Curreri, Laura Dean, Antonio Franceschi, Boyd Gaines, Albert Hague, Tresa Hughes, Steve Inwood, Paul McCrane, Anne Meara, Joanna Merlin, Barry Miller, Jim Moody, Gene Anthony Ray, Maureen Teefy.
04/30/80

Familien Gyldenkaal Spraenger Banken
(The Goldcabbage Family Breaks The Bank)
(Denmark)
PNR. Just Betzer prodn. Orig story-sp, Poul-Henrik Trampe. Dir, Gabriel Axel. Cam (Eastmancolor), Henning Kristiansen; mus, Bent Fabricius-Bjerre; edtr, Sven Methling; prodn mgrs, Erik Nissen, Peter Bach.   80.
Axel Stroebye, Kirsten Walther, Volmer-Soerensen.
12/29/76

Familien Gyldenkaal vinder valget
(The Goldcabbage Family Gets The Vote)
(Denmark)
PSD. Panorama (Just Betzer) prodn. Orig story-sp, Poul-Henrik Trampe. Dir, Bent Christensen. Cam, Jan Weincke; edtr, Finn Henriksen; mus, Ole Hoeyer; exec prod, Erik Nissen.   86.
Axel Stroebye, Kirsten Walther, Karen Lykkehus, Rolv Wesenlund.
10/26/77

The Family, Fine, Thanks: SEE La Familia, Bien, Gracias

The Family Honor
(Turkey)
AZZ. Dir, Orhan Aksoy. Sp, Aksoy, S Sendil, S Tekniker; cam (Eastmancolor), Huseyin Ozashin; mus, Melih Kibar.   90.
Munir Ozkul, Adile Nusit, Aysen Gruda.
01/26/77

Family Nest: SEE Gsaladi Tuzfezek

Family Plot
U. Dir, Alfred Hitchcock. Sp, Ernest Lehman, from novel, "The Rainbird Pattern," by Victor Canning; cam (Technicolor), Leonard J South; edtr, J Terry Williams; mus, John Williams; set decor, James W Payne; snd, James Alexander, Robert L Hoyt; asst dir, Howard G Kazanjian. (MPAA rating: PG).   120.
Karen Black, Bruce Dern, Barbara Harris, William Devane, Ed Lauter, Cathleen Nesbitt, Katherine Helmond, Warren J Kemmerling, Edith Atwater, William Prince, Nicholas Colasanto, Marge Redmond, John Lehne, Charles Tyner, Alexander Lockwood, Martin West.
03/24/76

Family Portrait: SEE Retrato De Familia

Fang and Claw: SEE La Griffe Et La Dent

Fantasm
(Australia)
FWS. TLN Film Productions prodn. Dir, Richard Franklin. Prod, Antony I Ginnane. Sp, Ross Dimsey, from an idea by Ginnane; exec prods, Leon Gorr, Ted Mulder; cam, Vincent Monton; edtr, Tony Patterson.   85.
John Bluthal, Dee Dee Levitt, Maria Arnold, Bill Margold, Gretchen Gayle, Rene Bond, Al Williams, Con Covert, Mara Lutra, Uschi Digart, Maria Welton, John Holmes, Mary Gavin, Gene Allan Poe, Robert Savage, Kirby Hall, Shayne, Sue Doloria, Al Ward, Clement St George, Serena.
08/04/76

Fantasm Comes Again
(Australia)
X. First Film Finance Picture for Australia Int'l Film Corp. Exec prods, Robert F Ward, Mark Josem; prod, Antony I Ginnane. Dir, Colin Eggleston; sp, Ross Dimsey; cam, Vincent Monton; edtr, Tony Patterson; art dir, Antony Brockliss; snd, Neil Rozensky; asst dir, Tom Jacobsen; snd edtr, Tony Patterson.   94.
Rick Cassidy, Mary Gacin, Con Covert, Bill Margold, Uschi Digart, Serena, Dee Dee Levitt, Rainbeaux Smith, Clive Hearne, John C Holmes, Angela Menzies-Willis, Tom Thumb, Liz Wolfe, Rosemarie Bern, Urias S Cambridge, Peter Kurzon, Lois Owens, Mike Stapp, Michael Barton, Suzy A Star, Amanda Smith, Herb Layen.
05/10/78

The Fantastic Balloon Trip: SEE Viaje Fantastico En Globo

Fantastica
(Canada - France)
GAU. E I Prodns (Paris), Les Prodns Du Verseau (Montreal). Wri-dir, Gilles Carle. Words-mus, Lewis Furey. Cam, Francois Protat; edtr, Hugues Darmois; chor, Larry Gradus; art dir, Jocelyn Joly.   104.
Carole Laure, Lewis Furey, Serge Reggiani, Claudine Auger, John Vernon, Denise Filiatrault, Claude Blanchard, Michel Labelle.
(MUSICAL)
05/14/80

Fantozzi Contro Tutti
(Fantozzi Against the World)
(Italy)
TIT. Prods, Bruno Altissimi, Claudio Saraceni for Maura Film Prodns. Dir, Paolo Villaggio, Neri Parenti. Sp, Leo Benvenuti, Piero De Bernardi, Villaggio, Parenti; cam (Technicolor), Claudio Cirillo; sets, Umberto Turco; edtr, Sergio Montanari; mus, Fred Bongusto.   97.
Paolo Villaggio, Milena Vukotic.
12/17/80

Far Away And Close: SEE Langt Borta Och Naera

The Far Road: SEE Toi Ippon no Michi

The Far Shore
(Canada)
NCN. Far Shore Inc prodn. Prods, Joyce Wieland, Judy Steed; exec prod, Pierre Lamy. Dir, Joyce Wieland. Sp, Brian Barney, from orig story, Wieland, cam (Kodacolor by Bellevue-PHE), Richard Leiterman; edtrs, George Appelby, Brian French; orig mus, Douglas Pringle; prodn des, Anne Pritchard; snd, Rod Haykin and Mel Lovell.   104.
Celine Lomez, Frank Moore, Lawrence Benedict, Sean McCann, Charlotte Blunt, Susan Petrie, Jean Carignan.
08/18/76

Faraway Tomorrow: SEE Toi Ashita

Farewell Scarlet
VF. Howard Winters prodn. Wris, Chuck Vincent, J Vidos, Winters; dir, Vincent. Cam, Stephen Todd; cos, Eddie Heath; art dir, F Maltese; edtr, Marc Ubell. (MPAA rating: X).   85.
J P Paradine, Terri Hall, Kim Pope, Doug Wood, Darby Lloyd Rains, Al Levitsky, Jennifer Jordan, Eric Edwards, Bob Stevens, Marlow Ferguson, Katia Mara, Dulce Mann, Chris Jordan.
02/04/76

The Farmer
COL. FAI Cinema-Milway prodn. Prod, Gary Conway; exec prod, Peter B Mills. Dir, David Berlatsky. Sp, George Fargo, Janice Colson-Dodge, Patrick Regan, John Carmody; cam (CFI Color), Irv Goodnoff; edtr, Richard Weber; mus, Hugo Montenegro; songs, Gene Clark, Jack Segal; art dir, Charlie Hughes; cos-ward, Vickie Sanchez, Marydith Chase, Angel Tompkins; snd, Bill Myers; stunt coord, Tom Huff. (MPAA rating: R).   97.
Gary Conway, Angel Tompkins, Michael Dante, George Memmoli, Timothy Scott, Jack Waltzer, Ken Renard, John Popwell.
03/02/77

Farodokument 1979
(Faro Document 1979)
(Sweden)
CGS. Wri-dir, Ingmar Bergman. Cam, Arne Carlsson; edtr, Sylvia Ingemarrson; mus, Svante Pettersson, Sigvard Hultdt, Dag & Lena, Ingmar Nordstorms, Strix Q.   103.
Inhabitants of Faro island.
(DOC)
11/05/80

The Fascist Jew: SEE L'Ebreo Fascista

Fast Break
COL. Stephen Friedman/Kings Road prodn. Exec prod, Jerry Frankel. Prod, Stephen Friedman. Dir, Jack Smight. Sp, Sandor Stern, based on a story by Marc Kaplan; cam, Charles Correll; edtr, Frank J Urioste; mus, David Shire, James di Pasquale; art dir, Norman Baron; snd, Lee Alexander; asst dir, Carl Olsen. (MPAA rating: PG).   197.
Gabriel Kaplan, Harold Sylvester, Mike Warren, Bernard King, Reb Brown, Mavis Washington, Bert Ramsen, Randee Heller, John Chappell, Rhonda Bates, K Callan, Richard Brestoff.
02/21/79

Fast Charlie. . .The Moonbeam Rider
U. Prods, Roger Corman, Saul Krugman. Dir, Steve Carver. Sp, Michael Gleason based on a story by Ed Spielman, Howard Friedlander; cam, William Birch; edtrs, Tony Redman, Eric Orner; mus, Stu Phillips; art dir, Bill Sandell, Michael Riva; set decor, Margie Fritz; snd, Glenn Williams; sfx, Roger George; asst dir, David McGiffert. (MPAA rating: PG).   99.
David Carradine, Brenda Vaccaro, L Q Jones, R G Armstrong, Terry Kiser, Jesse Vint, Noble Willingham, Whit Clay, Ralph James, Bill Hartman, Stephen Ferry.
05/30/79

Fast Company
(Canada)
X. Danton Films (Canada) presentation of a Quadrant Films prodn. Exec prod, David Perlmutter. Prods, Michael Lebowitz, Peter O'Brian, Courtney Smith. Dir, David Cronenberg; sp, Phil Savath, Smith, Cronenberg from original story by Alan Treen; cam, Mark Irwin; edtr, Ron Sanders; art dir, Carol Spier.   90.
William Smith, John Saxon, Claudia Jennings, Nicholas Campbell, Don Francks, Cedric Smith, Judy Foster, George Buza.
05/23/79

Fat Angels
(US - Spain)
X. Impala (Madrid) and Mambru Movies (New York) co-prodn. Dir, Manuel Summers; sp, M Summers, Chumy Chumez, Leon Tchaso, Joe Gonzales based on a story by M Summers; cam (Eastmancolor), Manuel Rojas; mus, Bob Dorough; show "A Night of Love," conceived-wri, Jose Raul Bernardo; direct snd, Neelon Crawford; sets, Ramiro Gomez; edtr, Gloria Pineyro; exec prod, Jose Vicuna. 92.
Farnham Scott, January Stevens, Jack Aaron, Amy Steel, Robert Reynolds, B Constance Barry, Peter Bogyo, Nina David, Sanford Seeger, Robert Caus.
(English Soundtrack)
10/29/80

Fatalnata Zapetaya
(The Fatal Comma)
(Bulgaria)
07/25/79
FBU. Bulgarian Film Prodn, Savremenik Unit, Sofia. Dir, Liliana Pencheva. Sp, Maxim Assenov; cam, Dimko Minev; art dir, Youlyana Boshkova; mus, Bozhidar Petkov. 90.
Tatyana Tsvetkova, Georgi Kadourin, Dimiter Marin, Nikolai Kolev, Katya Dineva, Yakim Mihov.

Father Master: SEE Padre Padrone

Father Serge: SEE Otietz Sergii

Fatso
FOX. Brooksfilms Ltd prodn. Prod, Stuart Cornfeld. Dir-wri, Anne Bancroft. Cam (DeLuxe Color), Brianne Murphy; edtr, Glenn Farr; mus, Joe Renzetti; prodn des, Peter Wooley; set decor, Linda DeScenna; cos, Patricia Norris; snd, Al Overton Jr; asst dir, Mark Johnson. (MPAA rating: PG). 94.
Dom Deluise, Anne Bancroft, Ron Carey, Candice Azzara, Michael Lombard, Sal Viscuso, Delia Salvi, Robert Costanzo, Estelle Reiner, Richard Karron.
01/30/80

Fatty Finn
(Australia)
HOY. Children's Film Corp prodn. Prod, Brian Rosen. Exec prod, John Sexton. Dir, Maurice Murphy. Sp, Bob Ellis, Chris McGill, from orig idea by Ellis; cam (Eastmancolor), John Seale; edtr, Bob Gibson; mus, Graham Bond, Rory O'Donohue. 91.
Ben Oxenbould, Bert Newton, Noni Hazelhurst, Gerard Kennedy, Greg Kelly, Lorraine Bayly, Henri Szeps, Frank Wilson, Peter Carroll, Ross Higgins.
07/23/80

The Fault: SEE A Culpa

Faux Pas De Deux
(W Germany)
Lothar Lambert prodn. Wri-dir-edtr, Lambert. Cam, Reza Dabui; mus, Jan Berger; snd, Shazi Dabui. 60.
Sylvia Heidemann, Uwe Sange, Claudia Barry, Beate Hasenau, Harry Jensen, Robert Cutts, Anita Sander, Bernd Lubowski, Wolfram Zobus, Hirosh.
10/20/76

Fear of Fear: SEE Angst Vor Der Angst

Fears: SEE Los Miedos

Fedora
(Germany - France)
RIA. Geria Film-Bavaria Studios, SFP prodn. Prod-dir, Billy Wilder. Sp, I A L Diamond, Wilder from book by Tom Tryon; cam (Eastmancolor), Gerry Fisher; edtr, Stefan Arsten; mus, Miklos Rosza. 110.
William Holden, Marthe Keller, Jose Ferrer, Hildegard Knef, Frances Sterhagen, Mario Adorf, Hans Jaray, Gottfried John, Michael York, Henry Fonda.
(English soundtrack)
08/23/78

Feedback
X. Feedback Co prodn. Prod-dir-wri, Bill Doukas. Cam (Movielab Color), Oliver Wood; mus, Jake Stern; edtr, Carol Hayward. 90.
Bill Doukas, Myriam Gibril, Denise Gordon, Taylor Mead, Louis Walden.
03/28/79

Feedback: SEE Obratinaya Sviaz

Feelings
KEX. Kemal Horulu prodn. Prod-dir, Horulu. Sp, Jack Parre; cam, Joe Mann; snd, Doug Angel; edtr, Horulu; mus, Selma Marks. (Self-imposed X rating). 93.
Lesllie Bovel, Jamie Gillis, Terri Hall, Ras Reen, Eva Henderson, Babby Astyr, Nancy Dare, Helen Madigan, Richard Bella, Edward B Davis, Lee Dupree.
08/17/77

Fehlschuss
(Misfire)
(W Germany - Austria)
X. Schoenbrunn-Film prodn, in collab with SFB and ORF Television (Berlin & Vienna). Dir, Rainer Boldt. Sp, Boldt, Alexander Steffen; cam, Xaver Schwarzenberger; mus, Alexander Steffen; edtr, Marie Homolkova; snd, Johannes Paiha, Peter Schwaba; art dirs, Roger von Moellendorff, Angelika Kroeber; cos, Barbara Bilabel, Reinhild Paul; tv coord mgrs, Jens-Peter Behrend, Wolfgang Ainberger. 120.
Wolfgang Ambros, Franz Buchrieser, Pola Kinski, Jan Kickert, Hannes Schuetz.
02/16/77

Fekete Gyemantok
(The Black Diamond)
(Hungary)
X. Budapest Studio prodn. Dir, Zoltan Varkonyi. Sp, Janos Erdody, Zoltan Varkonyi, based on novel by Mor Jokai; cam (Eastmancolor), Gyorgy Illes; mus, Smil Petrovics. 166.
Peter Huszti, Szilvia Sunyovszky, Peter Haumann, Sandor Szabo.
03/23/77

Felicite
(France)
GAU. Les Films 2001-Gaumont prodn. Wri-dir, Christine Pascal. Cam (Eastmancolor), Yves Lafaye; edtr, Thierry Derocles; mus, Antoine Duhamel. 96.
Christine Pascal, Dominique Laffin, Monique Chaumette, Paul Crauchet, Chil Marx, Judith Founry, Jean Champior.
05/23/79

Female Hamlet
(Turkey)
X. UGUR Film prodn. Dir, Metik Erksan. Adapted from Shakespeare's "Hamlet." 100.
Fatma Girik, Sevda Ferdag, Reha Yurdakul, Yuksei Gozen, Ahmet Sezerel, Orcun Sonat.
07/27/77

Femmes de Sade
VF. Alex deRenzy prodn. Prod-dir-sp, deRenzy. (Self-imposed X rating). 80.
Ken Turner, Joe Nassivera, Gail Lawrence, John Leslie, Monique Star, Mimi Morgan, Melba Bruce, Linda Wong, Kyoko Shoji, Leslie Bovee, Annette Haven, Sharon Thorpe.
05/05/76

Fen
(Sweetheart)
(Thailand)
HFT. Prod-dir, Lek Kitiparaporn. Exec prod, Chalie Amartyakul. Story-sp, Too Satabot; cam, Saravuth Vuthichai; mus, Prasert Choorakit; snd, Jaturong Studio. 105.
Pairoj Sangvoributr, Nawarat Yukthanan, Jamroon Nuatchim, Somkuan Kajangsart, Pong Ladda Pimolphan, Choosri Misomon.
04/25/79

Fernand
(France)
UGC. Films Arquebuse-C A A Maison de la Culture de la Seine Saint-Denis co-prodn. Prods, Rene Feret, Michelle Plaa. Dir, Feret. Wris, Feret, Christian Drillaud, Robert Guedigluian; cam, Gilberto Azevedo; snd, Alix Comte; art dir, Juan Carlos Conti; cos, Hilton McConnico; mus, Michel Coeuriot; edtr, Christiane Lack. 90.
Bernard Bloch, Jany Gastaldi, Yves Reynaud, Dominique Arden, Roland Amstutz.
04/09/80

Feste, Farina E. . .
(Festa, Flour and. . .)
(Italy)
X. RAI-Television Channel 2 film. Prod, Cooperativa Celimontana. Wri-dir, Nino Russo; cam, Massimo Lupi; art dir, Mimma Russo; edtrs, Mario Gargiulo, Marcello Malvestiti. 120.
Vittorio De Bisogno.
09/24/80

Feuer Um Mitternacht
(Red Midnight)
(W Germany)
TRO. Ehmck-Film prodn, Munich. Dir, Gustav Ehmck. Sp, Ehmck, Boy Lornsen, Hansch Schmid, Andrea Wagner; cam, Hubs Hagen; edtrs, K H Fugunt, Monika Gussner; mus, Gunter Hampel, Galaxie Dream Band; snd, Rainer Wiehr; sets, Margarete Fackelmann; art dir, Michael Fackelmann; prodn mgr, Martin Haeussler. 100.
Andreas Nutzhorn, Ina Trautmann, Joachim Dietman Mues, Carsta Loeck, Horst Gnekow, Nann Soederberg, Anke Joldrichsen, Joachim Richart, Heinz Joachim Klein, Gerhard Olschewski, Uwe Michael Wiebking, Annemie Winger, Joerg Zimmer.
03/29/78

Fever: SEE Fiebre

ffolkes
(Britain)
U. Elliott Kastner prodn. Exec prod, Moses Rothman. Dir, Andrew V McLaglen. Sp, Jack Davies, based on his novel, "Esther, Ruth & Jennifer," cam (Technicolor), Tony Imi; edtr, Alan Strachan; sfx, special sequences, John Richardson; art dir, Bert Davey; asst dir, Brian Cook; stunt supv, Eddie Stacey; set decor, Simon Wakefield; snd edtr, Alan Sones; mus-comp-cond, Michael J Lewis. (MPAA rating: PG). 99.
Roger Moore, James Mason, Anthony Perkins, Michael Parks, David Hedison, Jack Watson, George Baker, Jeremy Clyde, David Wood, Faith Brook, Lea Brodie, Anthony Pullen Shaw, Philip O'Brien, John Westbrook, Jennifer Hilary, John Lee, Brook Williams, Tim Bentinck, Saburo Kimura, Eiji Kusuhara, David Landbury, Alastair Llewellyn, Sean Arnold, Eric Mason, Thane Bettany, George Leach, Richard Graydon.
04/23/80

The Fiancee: SEE Die Verlobte

Fico D'India
(Prickly Pears)
(Italy)
TIT. Prod, Achille Manzotti for Intercontinental Film Co. Dir, Steno. Sp, Enrico Vanzina, Steno, Renato Pozzetto, Sandro Continenza, Raimondo Vianello. Cam, Carlo Carlini; art dir, Paola Comencini; edtr, Raimondo Crociani; mus, Giancarlo Chiaromello. 98.
Renato Pozzetto, Gloria Guida, Aldo Maccione.
11/19/80

Fiebre
(Fever)
(Venezuela)
X. PPCA CINE SA prodn; dir, Juan Santana. Sp, Salvador Garmendia, based on novel by Miguel Otero Silva; cam (16m blow up to 35m, Eastmancolor), Andres Agusti; edtrs, Olegario Barrera, Juan Santana; sets, Asdrubal Menendez; mus, Freddy Reina. 86.
Lucio Bueno, Asdrubal Melendez, Julio Mota, Freddy Galavis, Maria Adelina Vera, Chelo Rodriguez, Yolanda Celis, Olga Marin Irausqui.
10/13/76

The Fiendish Plot of Dr. Fu Manchu
UA. Zev Braun prodn. Prods, Zev Braun, Leland Nolan; exec prod, Hugh M Hefner; dir, Piers Haggard; sp, Jim Moloney, Rudy Dochtermann, based on characters from Sax Rohmer novels; cam (Technicolor), Jean Tournier; edtrs, Russell Lloyd, Claudine Bouche; mus, Marc Wilkinson; prodn des, Alex Trauner; cos des, John Bloomfield; snd, Daniel Brisseau; asso prod, Yannoulla Wakefield; asst dirs, Paul Feyder, Jerry Toomey. (MPAA rating: PG). 98.
Peter Sellers, Helen Mirren, David Tomlinson, Sid Caesar, Simon Williams, Steve Franken, Stratford Johns, John Le Mesurier.
08/13/80

15 Yok Yok
(Only 15)
(Thailand)
NKP. Prod-dir-edtr, Chana Krapayun. Story, Prai Maliwan; sp, Seeda Wichanupop; cam, Sophon Jaenpanit; mus, Seksan Sonimsart; theme song, "15 Yok Yok", mus-lyr, Seksan; sung by Suda Chuenban. 115.
Sorapong Chatri, Tasawan Seniwong, Suriya Chinaphan, Nawarat Yukthanan, Niroot Sirichanya.
02/15/78

The Fifth Commandment:
SEE Das Fuenfte Gebot

The Fifth Floor
FVI. Hickmar Productions film. Prod-dir, Howard Avedis. Exec prod, Marlene Schmidt. Sp, Meyer Dolinsky. Story, Avedis and Schmidt; cam, Dan Pearl; edtr, Stanford Allen; mus, Casablanca Record and Filmworks. (MPAA rating: R). 87.
Bo Hopkins, Dianne Hull, Patti D'Arbanville, Sharon Farrell, Mel Ferrer, Julie Adams, John David Carson, Patti Brooks, Robert Englund.
03/12/80

The 5th Musketeer
(Austria)
COL. Sascha Film-Ted Richmond prodn. Exec prod, Heinz Lazek; prod, Ted Richmond; dir, Ken Annakin; sp, David Ambrose, based upon novel by Alexandre Dumas and sp by George Bruce; cam, Jack Cardiff; edtr, Malcolm Cooke; mus, Riz Ortolani; snd, Simon Kaye; Jim Willis; prodn des, Elliot Scott; art dir, Theo Harisch; cos des, Tony Pueo; asst dir, David Anderson. (MPAA rating: PG.) 103.
Beau Bridges, Sylvia Kristel, Ursula Andress, Cornel Wilde, Ian McShane, Lloyd Bridges, Alan Hale Jr, Jose Ferrer, Helmut Dantine, Rex Harrison, Olivia De Havilland.
04/11/79

The Fifth Seal: SEE Az Otodik Pecset

Fifty-Fifty: SEE Halbe-Halbe

The 51 File: SEE Le Dossier 51

Fight For Freedom: SEE Ija Ominira

Fight For Your Life
MIS. Prods, William Mishkin, Robert A Endelson. Dir, Endelson. Sp, Straw Weisman; cam, Lloyd Freidus; edtr, Endleson; mus, Jeff Slevin. (MPAA rating: R). 89.
William Sanderson, Robert Judd, Catherine Peppers, Lela Small, Reginald Bythewood, Daniel Faraldo, Peter Yoshida, Bonni Martin, William Cargill, Richard A Rubin, David Dewlow, Ramon Saunders, Nick Mariano.
12/21/77

Fighting Mad
FOX. Santa Fe Prods film, prod, Roger Corman; co-prod, Evelyn Purcell. Wri-dir, Jonthan Demme. Cam (DeLuxe Color), Michael Watkins; addl pho, Bill Birch; edtr, Anthony Magro; mus, Bruce Langhorne; snd, Lovell Ellis; asst dir, David Osterhout; 2d unit dir, Evelyn Purcell; stunt coord, Allan Wyatt. (MPAA rating: R). 90.
Peter Fonda, Lynn Lowry, John Doucette, Philip Carey, Scott Glen, Kathleen Miller, Harry Northrup, Ted Markland, Gino Franco, Nobel Willingham.
04/28/76

Filip Cel Bun
(Filip The Good)
(Romania)
RMN. Rumaniafilm Prodn, Bucharest Group Three. Dir, Dan Pita. Sp, Constantin Stoiciu; cam, Florin Mihailescu. 92.
Mircea Diaconu, Vasile Nitulescu, Ica Matache, Lazar Vrabie, Ileana Popovici, Nunuta Hodos, Draga Olteanu, Georgi Dinica, George Mihaita.
06/14/78

Fill 'Er Up with Super: SEE Le Plein De Super

Filming "Othello"
X. Prods, Klaus Hellwig, Juergen Hellwig; dir, Orson Welles; cam, Gary Graver; mus, Francesco Lavagnino, Alberto Barbaris; edtr, Marty Roth. 90.
(B & W) (DOC)
06/28/78

Final Assignment
(Canada)
IOS. Financed by Canadian Film Development Corp, Famous Players Ltd, and CTV Television Network Ltd. Persephone Productions Ltd prodn. Prods, Lawrence Hertzog, Gail Thomson. Dir, Paul Almond. Sp, Marc Rosen; cam, John Coquillon; score, Peter Germyn; edtr, Debbie Karin; snd, Henri Blondeau; exec prods, James Shavick, Arnold Kopelson. 101.
Genevieve Bujold, Michael York, Burgess Meredith, Colleen Dewhurst, Alexandra Stewart, Richard Gabourie.
11/12/80

Final Chapter - Walking Tall
AIP. Bing Crosby Prods. Film; prod, Charles A Pratt. Dir, Jack Starrett. Sp, Howard B Kreitsek, Samuel A Peeples, based on a story by Krietsek; cam (Deluxe Color), Robert B Hauser; edtr, Houseley Stevenson; mus, Walter Scharf; art dir, Joe Altadonna; snd, John K Wilkinson, Robert Miller; cos-ward, Michael W Hoffman, Chris Zamiara; asst dir, Carl Olsen; stunt coord, Paul Nuckles. (MPAA rating: R). 112.
Bo Svenson, Margaret Blye, Forrest Tucker, Lurene Tuttle, Morgan Woodward, Libby Boone, Leif Garrett, Dawn Lyn, Bruce Glover, Taylor Lacher, Sandy McPeak, Logan Ramsey, Robert Phillips, Clay Tanner, David Adams, Vance Davis, H B Haggerty, John Malloy.
06/22/77

The Final Countdown
UA. Bryna Co prodn. Prod, Peter Vincent Douglas. Exec prod, Richard R St Johns. Dir, Don Taylor. Sp, David Ambrose & Gerry Davis, Thomas Hunter & Peter Powell; story, Hunter & Powell, Ambrose; cam (Technicolor), Victor J Kemper; 2d unit cam, David L Butler, Stan Lazan; mus, John Scott; edtr, Robert K Lambert; prodn des, Fernando Carrere; set dir, Dennis Peeples; snd, Bruce Bisenz, Robert J Litt, David J Kimball, Howard S Wollman; spec visual effects and storm sequence, Maurice Binder; 2d unit dirs, David Jones, Robert K Lambert; asst dir, Pat Kehoe. (MPAA rating: PG) 103.
Kirk Douglas, Martin Sheen, Katharine Ross, James Farentino, Ron O'Neal, Charles Durning, Victor Mohica, James C Lawrence, Soon-Teck Oh, Joe Lowry, Alvin Ing, Mark Thomas.
07/16/80

Final Cut
(Australia)
GUO. Wilgar prodn. Prod, Mike Williams; exec prod, Frank Gardiner; dir, Ross Dimsey. Sp, Jonathan Dawson, Dimsey, from an orig idea by Dawson; cam (Eastmancolor), Ron Johanson; edtr, Tony Patterson; mus wri-performed, Howard Davidson. 82.
Louis Brown, David Clendenning, Jennifer Cluff, Narelle Johnson, Carmen J McCall, Thaddeus Smith.
07/30/80

Fine Manners: SEE Les Belles Manieres

Fingers
BRU. Prod, George Barrie. Sp-dir, James Toback. Cam (Eastmancolor), Mike Chapman; edtr, Robert Lawrence; prodn des, Gene Rudolf; set decor, Fred Weiler; snd, Bill Varney, Lee Lasarowitz; cos-ward, Albert Wolsky; asst dir, Dan McCauley. (MPAA rating: R). 90.
Harvey Keitel, Tisa Farrow, Jim Brown, Michael V Gazzo, Marian Seldes, Carole Francis, Georgette Muir, Danny Aiello, Dominick Chianese, Anthony Siroco, Tanya Roberts, Ed Marinaro, Zack Norman, Murray Mosten, Jane Elder, Lenny Montana, Frank Pesche.
02/01/78

Firatin Cinleri
(The Bad Spirits Of The Euphrates)
(Turkey)
X. Korhan Film prodn, Istanbul. Dir, Korhan Yurtsever, Sp, Ihsan Yuce; cam, Salih Dikisci; mus, Cahit Barkay. 78.
Aytac Arman, Betul Ascioglu, Tugay Toksoz.
08/02/78

Fire In The Middle
X. Virgin Earth Inc. prodn. Wris-prods-dirs, William Word, Joan Kasich. Cam (CFI Color), Word, Kasich; edtrs, Word, Kashich, Brad Thompson; snd, Thompson, Kasich, Sue Burkland; mus, William Harkleroad; narr, Bob Barnett. 90.
(16m) (DOC)
05/31/78

Fire Sale
FOX. Prod, Marvin Worth. Dir, Alan Arkin. Sp, Robert Klane, based on his novel; cam (DeLuxe Color), Ralph Woolsey; edtr, Richard Halsey; mus, Dave Grusin; prodn des, James H Spencer; set decor, Dennis Peeples; snd, Don Bassman, Richard Wagner; cos-ward, Norman Burza, Lynn Bernay; asst dir, Tom Lofaro; 2d unit dir, Max Kleven. (MPAA rating: PG). 88.
Alan Arkin, Rob Reiner, Vincent Gardenia, Anjanette Comer, Kay Medford, Barbara Dana, Sid Caesar, Alex Rocco, Byron Stewart, Marvin Worth.
06/08/77

Firepower
(Britain)
AFD. Scimitar Films Prodn. Prod-dir, Michael Winner; sp, Gerald Wilson; cam (Technicolor), Robert Paynter, Dick Kratina; edtr, Arnold Crust; snd, Jim Willis, Newton Avrutis; prodn des, John Stoll, John Blezard, Robert Gundlach; asst dirs, Ted Moreley, Alex Hapsis, Francois Moullin; mus, Gato Barbieri. (MPAA rating: R.) 104.
Sophia Loren, James Coburn, O J Simpson, Eli Wallach, Anthony Franciosa, George Grizzard, Vincent Gardenia, Fred Stuthman, Richard Caldicot, Frank Singuineau, George Touliatos, Andrew Duncan, Hank Garrett, Billy Barty, Conrad Roberts, Victor Mature.
04/11/79

The Fire's Share: SEE La Part Du Feu

Firmaskovturen
(The Factory Outing)
(Denmark)
ASD. Klaus Pagh and Just Betzer prodn. Dir-edtr, John Hilbard. Sp, Hilbard, Ole Boje. Cam (Eastmancolor), Claus Loof, Alex Henningsen; mus, Ole Hoeyer; prodn mgr, Leif Jul. 84.
Joergen Ryg, Preben Kaas, Torben Jensen, Jesper Langberg, Lisbeth Dahl, Judy Gringer, Bjoern Puggaard-Mueller, Birgitte Federspiel, Kirste Norholt.
03/01/78

First Deadly Sin
FWS. Elliott Kastner presentation of an Artanis-Cinema 7 prodn. Exec prods, Frank Sinatra, Elliott Kastner. Prods, George Pappas, Mark Shanker. Dir, Brian Hutton. Sp, Mann Rubin; based on novel by Lawrence Sanders; cam, Jack Priestley; art dir, Woody Mackintosh; cos des, Gary Jones; edtr, Eric Albertson; asst dir, Joe Napolitano; set decor, Robert Drumheller; mus, Gordon Jenkins. (MPAA rating: R). 112.
Frank Sinatra, Faye Dunaway, David Dukes, George Coe, Brenda Vaccaro, Martin Gabel, Joe Spinell, Jeffrey De Munn, Anthony Zerbe, James Whitmore, Fred Fuster.
10/22/80

First Effort: SEE Opera Prima

The First Error Step
(Singapore)
07/25/79
GSB. Prod, Yap Chin Hock. Dir, Au-Yang Chong. Story-sp, Ma Sha; cam, Chin Hu; mus, Ma Hwa; sng, Chin Hon. 100.
Ma Sha, Yang Hui San, Chin Po.

First Family
WB. Indie-Prod Prodn. Prod, Daniel Melnick. Wri-dir, Buck Henry. Cam (Technicolor), Fred J Koenekamp; mus, John Philip Sousa, adapted and cond, Ralph Burns; edtrs, Stu Linder, Susan Martin; art dir, William Hiney; set decor, Rick Simpson; snd, Les Fresholtz, Tex Rudloff, Dick Alexander, Kevin F Cleary, Gerry Jost; sacrificial dance chor, Toni Basil; asso prods, Phil Rawlins, Leslie Hill; asst dir, Skip Beaudine. (MPAA rating: R). 104.
Gilda Radner, Bob Newhart, Madeline Kahn, Richard Benjamin, Bob Dishy, Harvey Korman, Austin Pendleton, Rip Torn, Fred Willard, Julius Harris, John Hancock, Maurice Sherbanee, Buck Henry, Shatsmi Sarumi Dance Troupe.
12/31/80

The First Great Train Robbery
(Great Britain)
UA. Dino De Laurentiis presentation. Prod, John Foreman. Dir, Michael Crichton. Sp, Crichton, based on his novel; Starling Prodns exec, Stanley Sopel; cam, Geoffrey Unsworth; mus, Jerry Goldsmith; edtr, David Bretherton; prodn des, Maurice Carter; cos, Anthony Mendleson; snd, Liam Saurin, Derek Ball; asst dir, Anthony Waye. 110.
Sean Connery, Donald Sutherland, Lesley-Anne Down, Alan Webb, Malcolm Terris, Robert Lang, Wayne Sleep, Michael Elphick, Pamela Salem, Gabrielle Lloyd, James Cossins, Peter Benson, Janine Duvitski.
01/17/79

First Love
PAR. Prods, Lawrence Turman, David Foster. Dir, Joan Darling. Sp, Jane Stanton Hitchcock, David Freeman, based on story, "Sentimental Education," by Harold Brodkey; cam (Metrocolor), Bobby Byrne; edtr, Frank Morriss; mus supv, Joel Sill; prodn des, Robert Luthardt; set decor-cos-ward, Donfeld; snd, David Dockendorf, Glenn Anderson; asst dir, Phil Rawlins. (MPAA rating: R). 91.

William Katt, Susan Dey, John Heard, Beverly D'Angelo, Robert Loggia, Tom Lacy, Swoozie Kurtz, June Barrett, Patrick O'Hara, Judy Kerr, Jenny Hill, Virginia Leith, Billy Beck.
11/02/77

First Love: SEE Moi Tinh Dau

The First Nudie Musical
PAR. Prod, Jack Reeves; exec prods, Stuart W Phelps, Peter S Brown. Dirs, Mark Haggard, Bruce Kimmel. Sp-mus-lyr, Kimmel; cam (DeLuxe Color), Douglas H Knapp; edtr, Allen Peluso; art dir, Tom Rassmussen; set decor, Timothy J Bloch; snd, Ted Gomillion, Art Names; asst dir, Edwin T Morgan. (MPAA rating: R). 97.
Stephen Nathan, Cindy Williams, Bruce Kimmel, Leslie Ackerman, Alan Abelew, Diana Canova, Alexandra Morgan, Frank Doubleday.
03/10/76

The First Polka: SEE Die Erste Polka

The First Time: SEE La Premiere Fois

First Voyage: SEE Premier Voyage

The First Waltz: SEE Der Erste Walzer

Fish Hawk
(Canada)
FKC. Dir, Donald Shebib. Sp, Blanche Hanalis from the book by Mitchell Jayne; cam, Rene Verzier; edtr, Ron Wisman. 97.
Will Sampson, Charlie Fields, Geoffrey Bowes, Mary Pirie, Don Francks, Chris Wiggins, Kay Hawtrey, Mavor Moore.
09/05/79

The Fish That Saved Pittsburgh
UA. Lorimar prodn. Prods, Gary Stromberg, David Dashev; dir, Gilbert Moses; sp, Jaison Starkes, Edmond Stevens, from story by Stromberg and Dashev; cam, Frank Stanley; edtr, Peter Zinner; art dir, Herbert Spencer Daverill; mus, Thom Bell; chor, Debra Allen; cos, Patricia Norris; snd, Bud (Henry) Maffett; asst dir, Jerry Grandey. (MPAA rating: PG.) 104.
Julius Erving, Jonathan Winters, Meadowlark Lemon, Jack Kehoe, Margaret Avery, James Bond III, Michael V Gazzo, Peter Isacksen, Nicholas Pryor, M Emmet Walsh, Stockard Channing, Julius J Carry III, Jerry Chambers, Jessie Lawrence Ferguson, Malek Abdul Mansour, Dwayne Mooney, Daryl Mooney, Brancombe Richmond, Flip Wilson.
11/07/79

F.I.S.T.
UA. Prod-dir, Norman Jewison; exec prod, Gene Corman. Sp, Joe Eszterhas, Sylvester Stallone, from a story by Eszterhas; cam (Technicolor), Laszlo Kovacs; edtrs, Tony Gibbs, Graeme Clifford; mus, Bill Conti; prodn des, Richard MacDonald; art dir, Angelo Graham; set decor, George Bob Nelson; snd, Chuck Wilborn; cos-ward; Anthea Sylbert, Tony Scarano, Thalia Phillips; asst dir, Andrew Stone. (MPAA rating: PG). 145.
Sylvester Stallone, Rod Steiger, Peter Boyle, Melinda Dillon, David Huffman, Tony Lo Bianco, Kevin Conway, Cassie Yates, Peter Donat, Henry Wilcoxon, John Lehne, Richard Herd, Elena Karam, Ken Kercheval, Tony Mockus, Brian Dennehy, James Karen.
04/19/78

Fist in the Pocket: SEE Die Faust in der Tasche

Fist of Fear Touch of Death
AQU. Aquarius Promotions Production. Prod, Terry Levene; dir, Matthew Mallinson; sp, Ron Harvey, based on orig story by Harvey and Mallinson; cam, John Hazard; score, Keith Mansfield; edtrs, Mallinson, Jeffrey Brown; snd, Jimmy Kwei; stunt coords, Ron Van Clief, Bill Louis. (MPAA rating: R). 90.
Fred Williamson, Ron Van Clief, Adolph Caesar, Aaron Banks, Bill Louis, Teruyuki Higa, Gail Turner, Richard Barathy, Hollywood Browde, Louis Neglia, Cydra Karlyn, Annett Bronson, Ron Harvey, John Flood.
(BRUCE LEE FILM CLIPS)
09/24/80

Five Days From Home
U. Prod-dir, George Peppard; exec prod, Robert S Bremson. Sp, William Moore; cam (CFI color), Harvey Genkins; edtr, Samuel E Beetley; mus, Bill Conti; song lyr, Norman Gimbel; snd, Jay Harding. (MPAA rating: PG). 108.
George Peppard, Neville Brand, Sherry Boucher, Victor Campos, Robert Donner, Ronnie Claire Edwards, Jessie Lee Fulton, William Larsen, Robert Magruder, Savannah Smith, Don Wyse, Ralph Story.
04/19/78

Five Evenings: SEE Pyat' Vecherov

Five Forks: SEE Cinco Tenedores

5% de Risque
(5% Risk)
(France - Belgium)
GAU. Unite 3/Framo Diffusion/Orion/Paradise Films (Brussels) co-prodn. Prod, Alain Dahan; dir, Jean Pourtale; sp, Pourtale, Jean Bany, Jean-Pierre Beaurenaud, Gilles Thibaut, based on novel by David Pearl; cam, Jean Penzer; edtrs, Caludine Merlin, Helene Muller; mus, Eric de Marsan; art dirs, Yves Bernard, Danka Semenowiecz; snd, Henri Morelle; stunts, Remy Julienne. 100.
Bruno Ganz, Jean-Pierre Cassel, Aurore Clement, Pierre Michael, Fernand Guiot, Chantal Akerman.
07/30/80

5+5
(Israel)
SHP. Roll Films Prodn. Prods, Yair Pradelsky, Israel Ringel. Dir, Shmuel Imberman. Sp, Avi Koren, Imberman, from play by Aharon Megged; exec prod, Asher Gat; cam, Nissim (Nitcho) Leon; edtr, Tova Neeman; cos, Sarah Wiener; mus, Benny Nagari; lyr, Avi Koren; chor, Yaakov Kalusky. 89.
Dalik Wollinitz, Menahem Eyni, Eli Gorenstein, Yoni Chen, Mai Seri, Avi Dor, Liron Nirgad, Gilat Ankori, Maya Rotschild, Shula Chen, Shlomit Rieger, Lilach Glicksman, Zaharira Harifai, Gideon Singer, Yaakov Bodo, Rachel Attas, Shmuel Wolf, Haim Polani, Moshe Timor, Yoel Libe.
04/02/80

The F.J. Holden
(Australia)
GUO. FJ Films prodn. Prod-dir, Michael Thornhill. Sp, Terry Larsen. Asso prods, Jenny Woods, Errol Sullivan; cam (Panavision), David Gribble; art dirs, Lissa Coote, Monte Fleguth; edtr, Max Lemon; mus, Jim Manzie. 105.
Paul Couzens, Eva Dickinson, Carl Stever, Gary Waddell, Colin Yarwood, Graham Rouse.
05/04/77

Flamin' Fire-Chief: SEE Brand-Boerge Rykker Ud

Flaming Hearts: SEE Flammende Herzen

Flamme Empor
(Torch High)
(W Germany)
X. Telefilm Saar Film Prodn. Wri-dir, Eberhard Schubert. Cam, Atze Glanert; mus, Gaby Mueller-Blattau. 98.
Mareike Carriere, Hans-Juergen Schatz, Michael Schories, Ulrich Gebauer.
06/06/79

Flammende Herzen
(Flaming Hearts)
(W Germany)
FDA. Enten-Prodn, Cologne, in collaboration with Das Kleine Fernsehspiel (ZDF), Wiesbaden-Mainz. Sp-dir,s, Walter Bockmayer, Rolf Buehrmann. Prodn mgr, Rolf Buehrmann; cam, Horst Knechtel, Peter Mertin; edtr-asst dir, Ila von Hasperg; snd, Gary Steel. 95.
Peter Kern, Barbara Valentin, Enzi Fuchs, Katja Rupe, Anneliese and Peter Geisler, Rolf Buehrmann, Armin Meyer, Ila von Hasperg, Evelyn Kuenneke, Bessie the Cow.
03/29/78

Flanagan
(Holland)
X. Sigma Films prodn, prod, Matthijs van Heyningen. Wri-dir, Adriaan Ditvoorst. Cam (Eastmancolor), Gust Verschueren; mus, Jurriaan Andriessen. 104.
Guido de Moor, Eric Schneider, Josee de Ruiter, Anne-Wil Blankers, Petra Laseur.
04/07/76

Flash Gordon
(Britain)
U. Dino De Laurentiis prodn. Exec prod, Bernard Williams. Prod, De Laurentiis. Dir, Mike Hodges. Sp, Lorenzo Semple Jr; adapt, Michael Allin from characters created by Alex Raymond; cam (Technicolor), Gil Taylor; edtr, Malcolm Cooke; prodn-cos-set des, Danilo Donati; mus, Howard Blake, Queen; supv art dir, Frank Van Der Veer; sfx supv, George Gibbs; 2d unit dir, William Kronick; snd, Ivan Sharrock, Gerry Humphreys, Robin O'Donoghue; asst dir, Brian Coook. (MPAA rating: PG).

Additional Special Effects unit Credits-Pho effects asst, Barry Nolan; sfx cnsltnt, Glen Robinson; art dir (models), Norman Dorme; sfx (models and skies), Richard Conway; coord of action and movement, Bill Hobbs; Zarkov brain-drain seq dir, Denis Postel; sfx edtr, Chris Kelly; illustrators, Mentor Huebner, Emanuela Alteri, Giovanna Lombardo; sculptors, Giulio Tomassy, Peter Voysey, Arthur Healey, Galliano Donati; asst art dirs, Giorgio Postiglione, Tony Reading, Steve Spence, Kent Court, Ted Clements, John Fenner; scenic artist, Ted Michell, addl pho, Harry Waxman; light cin (skies and clouds), Harry Oakes; skies and clouds artists, Count Ul De Rico, Tom Adams; sfx assts, Dave Watson, Pierre Tilley, Michael White; sfx (flying), Derek Botell; model makers, Martin Bower, Christine Overs, Bill Pearson, Don Sargent; optical effects, Van Der Veer Photo Effects, R/Greenberg Associates Inc; blue screen composites, Greg Van Der Veer; optical cin, Hugh Wade, Ray Monahan; matte paintings, Lou Lichtenfield, Bob Scifo. 110.
Sam J Jones, Melody Anderson, Topol, Max Von Sydow, Ornella Muti, Timothy Dalton, Brian Blessed, Peter Wyngarde, Mariangela Melato, John Osborne, Richard O'Brien, John Hallam, Philip Stone.
12/03/80

Fleisch
(Meat)
(W Germany)
X. Pentagramma Filmproduction. Wri-prod-dir, Rainer Erler; art dir, Paul Winslow; cam, Wolfgang Grasshoff; edtr, Hilwa Von Boro; mus, Eugen Thomass. 108.
Jutta Speidel, Wolf Roth, Herbert Herrmann, Charlotte Kerr, Bob Cuningham, Ted Altice, Ben Zeller, Christoph Lindert.
12/05/79

Flic ou Voyou
(Cop or Hood)
(France)
GAU. Gaumont Int'l Cerito Films co-prodn. Prod, Alain Poire. Dir, Georges Lautner. Sp, Jean Herman, based on novel, "L'Inspecteur De La Mer," Michel Grisolia; dial, Michel Audiard; cam (Eastmancolor), Henri Decae; snd, Alain Sempe; edtr, Michelle David; art dir, Tony Roman; mus, Philippe Sarde. 110.
Jean-Paul Belmondo, Georges Geret, Michel Galabru, Marie Laforet.
06/27/79

Fliers of the Open Skies:
SEE Letaci Velikog Neba

The Flight: SEE Die Flucht
Flight Level 450: SEE Flygniva 450
The Flock: SEE Suru

Floor Show
X. Wri-dir-cam, Richard Myers. 85.
11/08/78

Flores de Papel
(Paper Flowers)
(Mexico)
X. Comacine Uno prodn. Dir, Gabriel Retes. Sp, Ignacio Retes, Rosa del Caudillo, in adaptation of plays "The Invaders" and "Paper Flowers" by Egon Wolff; cam, Daniel Lopez; mus, Mario Lavista, Raul Lavista, Javier Mateos; edtr, Eugenio Rivera; art dir, Felida Medina. 98.
Ana Luisa Peluffo, Gabriel Retes, Tina Romero, Claudio Brook, Adriana Role, Ignacio Retes, Silva Mariscal.
03/15/78

Flourishing Times: SEE Blomstrande tider

Flunking Out: SEE Asignatura Pendiente

Flygniva 450
(Flight Level 450)
(Sweden)
EUR. Tax Productions-AB Europa Film-Swedish Film Institute prodn. Orig story-sp, Sandro Key-Aberg, Torbjoern Axelman. Dir, Axelman. Cam (Eastmancolor), Tony Forsberg, Lars Svanberg; edtr, Darek Hodar; exec prod, Bjoern Henricson; mus, Ralph Lundsten. 100.
Thomas Hellberg, Ann Zacharias, Ernst-Hugo Jaeregaard, Hakan Serner.
04/30/80

FM
U. Prod, Rand Holston; co-prod, Robert Larson. Dir, John A Alonzo; sp, Ezra Sacks; cam (Technicolor), David Myers; edtr, Jeff Gourson; prodn des, Lawrence G Paull; snd (Dolby), Bruce Bisenz; asst dir, Bert Gold; cos des, Kent Warner. (MPAA rating: PG). 104.
Michael Brandon, Eileen Brennan, Alex Karras, Cleavon Little, Martin Mull, Cassie Yates, Norman Lloyd, Jay Fenichel, James Keach, Joe Smith, Tom Tarpey, Linda Ronstadt, Jimmy Buffet.
05/03/78

Focal Point: SEE Le Point De Mire

The Fog
AVE. Prod, Debra Hill. Exec prod, Charles B Bloch; dir, John Carpenter. Sp, Carpenter, Hill; cam, Dean Cundey; edtrs, Tommy Wallace, Charles Bornstein; prodn des, Wallace; mus, Carpenter; snd, Craig Felburg; sfx, Dick Albain Jr; cos des, Bill Whittens, Stephen Loomis; art dir, Craig Stearns; asst dir, Larry Franco. (MPAA rating: R.) 91.
Adrienne Barbeau, Hal Holbrook, Janet Leigh, Jamie Lee Curtis, John Houseman, Tommy Atkins, Nancy Loomis, Charles Cyphers, Ty Mitchell.
01/16/80

Fogo Morto
(The Last Plantation)
(Brazil)
X. Miguel Borges Prod Cinematograficas prodn, Embrafilme, Rio de Janeiro. Dir, Marcos Farias. Sp, Farias, Salim Miguel, Engle Malheiros, based on the novel by Jose Lins do Rego; cam, Renato Neumann; mus, Quinteto Armorial, Pedro Santos; art dir, Raquel Sisson; edtrs, Miguel H Borges, Umberto Martins. 90.
Jofre Soares, Othon Bastos, Rafael de Carvalho, Angela Leal, Rodolfo Arena, Procopio Mariano, Fernando Peixoto, Mary Neubauer, Waldemar Solha.
07/14/76

Folies Bourgeoises
(The Twist)
(France)
UGP. Barnabe Productions, Gloria Films-CCC prodn. Dir, Claude Chabrol. Sp, Ennio De Concini, Maria Pafusto, Norman Enfield, Chabrol from the book by Licie Faure; cam (Eastmancolor), Jean Rabier; edtr, Monique Rossignol. 105.
Bruce Dern, Stephane Audran, Ann-Margret, Sydne Rome, Jean-Pierre Cassel, Curt Jurgens, Maria Schell, Charles Aznavour.
07/21/76

Follow The Star
(Hong Kong)
GHV. Golden Harvest prodn. Prod, Raymond Chow. Dir, John Y S Woo. Sp, John Y S Woo, T C Lau; cam, Franki Cheung; edtr, Chang Yiu Chung; mus, Frank Chan. 96.
Rowena Cortes, Roy Chiao, Fung Huk On, Lee Hoi Shen, Wong Ching, Chan Yu Shen, Chan Pa Sun.
(English subtitles)
03/01/78

Fontamara
(Italy)
SCI. Rai-Radiotelevisione Italiana-Erre Cinematographica prodn. Exec prod, Edmondo Ricci; dir, Carlo Lizzani; sp, Lizzani, Luciano De Caro; cam (Technospes), Mario Vulpiani; score, Roberto DeSimone. 134.
Michele Placido, Antonella Murgia, Ida di Benedetto, Imma Piro, Antonio Orlando, Diddi Savagnone, Marcello Monti, Enzo Monteduro, Lino Coletta, Liliana Gerace, Franco Javarone, Dino Sarti, Franco Ferri.
09/03/80

The Food of the Gods
AIP. Prod-wri-dir, Bert I Gordon; exec prod, Samuel Z Arkoff. Based on part of the novel by H G Wells. Cam (Movielab Color), Reginald Morris; edtr, Corky Ehlers; mus, Elliot Kaplan; art dir, Graeme Murray; set decor, John Stark; snd, George Mulholland; asst dir, Flora Gordon. (MPAA rating: PG). 88.
Marjoe Gortner, Pamela Franklin, Ralph Meeker, Ida Lupino, John Cypher, Belina Balaski, Tom Stovall, John McLiam.
06/09/76

Foolin' Around
COL. Prod, Arnold Kopelson. Dir, Richard T Heffron. Sp, Mike Kane, David Swift, based on a story by Swift; cam (Deluxe color), Philip Lathrop; edtr, Peter Zinner; mus, Charles Bernstein; prodn des, Fernando Carrere; set decor, Darrell Silvera; cos des, Joe Tompkins; snd, Michael Evje; asso prod, Deborah Castle; asst dir, Craig Huston. (MPAA rating: PG). 101.
Gary Busey, Annette O'Toole, John Calvin, Eddie Albert, Cloris Leachman, Tony Randall, Michael Talbott, Shirley Kane, W H Macy, Beth Bosacker, Roy Jenson, Gene Lebell.
04/23/80

Foolish Years: SEE Lude Godina

For Clemence: SEE Pour Clemence

For the Love of Benji
MLB. Wri-dir, Joe Camp. Exec prod, Camp. Prod, Ben Vaughn. Orig story, Vaughn and Camp. Cam (CFI Color), Don Reddy; mus, Fuel Box; edtr, Leon Seith; prodn des, Harland Wright; snd, Colin Charles; prodn mgr-first asst dir, Tony Alatis; Greek prodn mgr, Aspa Lambbrou; location mgrs, Mihalis Lambrinos; 2d asst dirs, Stavros kaplanidis, Freddy Vianellis, Mark Johnson; asso prods, A Z Smith, Ed Vanston; art dir-sfx, Jack Bennett. (MPAA rating: G). 85.
Patsy Garrett, Cynthia Smith, Allen Fiuzat, Ed Nelson, Art Vasil, Peter Bowles, Bridget Armstrong, Mihalis Lambrinos.
06/15/77

For Whom To Be Murdered
(Hong Kong)
BNG. Safety Walk Motion Picture Co prodn. Dir, Patrick Yuen. Sp, Raymond Wond, Raymond Lai; cam, Chung Chi Man. 102.
Tony Wong, Angie Chiu, Chan Wai Man, Lam Kin Ming, Raymond Wong, Lay Dan, Cheung Ying.
12/20/78

The Forbidden Room: SEE Anima Persa

Forbidden Zone
X. Carl Borack prodn. Prod-dir, Richard Elfman. Exec prod, Gene Cunningham. Sp, Richard Elfman, M Bright, Martin W Nicholson, Nick Jones; cam (b&w), Gregory Sandor; edtr-asso prod-asst dir, Martin W Nicholson; mus, Danny Elfman (Oingo-Boingo); prodn des, Marie-Pascale Elfman; art dir, David M Makler; set des, Ken Corrone. 76.
Herve Villechaize, Susan Tyrrell, Marie-Pascale Elfman, Viva.
(B & W)
03/26/80

Force 10 From Navarone
(Britain)
AIP. Guy Hamilton prodn, presented by Samuel Z Arkoff, Oliver A Unger. Prod, Unger. Dir, Hamilton. Sp, Robin Chapman, based on a screen story by Carl Foreman and novel by Alistair MacLean; cam, Chris Challis; mus, Ron Goodwin; prodn des, Geoffrey Drake; cos des, Emma Porteus; edtr, Ray Poulton; special effects, Rene Albouze; stunt coord, Eddie Stacey; asst dir, Bert Batt. (MPAA rating: G). 118.
Robert Shaw, Harrison Ford, Edward Fox, Barbara Bach, Franco Nero, Carl Weathers, Richard Kiel.
11/29/78

The Foreigner
APV. Prod-dir, Amos Poe. Sp, Poe, Eric Mitchell; cam (16m, b&w), Chirine El Khadem; edtrs, Michael Penland, Amos Poe, Johanna Heer; stills pho, Fernando Natalici; mus, Ivan Kral. 101.
Eric Mitchell, Patti Astor, Deborah Harry, Terens Severine, Anya Phillips, Duncan Hannah, David Forshtay, Klaus Mettig, Ana Marton, Pusante Byzantium, Chirine El Khadem.
(16m) (B & W)
01/18/78

Foretold By Fate: SEE Roy Likit

Forever Young, Forever Free
U. Film Trust-Milton Okun prodn, prod, Andre Pieterse; exec prod, Philo C Pieterse. Dir, Ashley Lazarus. Sp, Lazarus, from a story by Andre Pieterse; cam, Arthur J Ornitz; mus, Lee Holdridge; song, Rod McKuen, Holdridge; edtr, Lionel Selwyn; art dirs, Wendy Malan, Phil Rosenberg; cos, John Buckley, Joe Aulisi; snd, Trevor Pike, Richard Lomba; asst dir, Jannie Wienand. (MPAA rating: G). 87.
Jose Ferrer, Karen Valentine, Bess Finney, Muntu Ndebele, Norman Knox, Bingo Mbonjeni, Simon Sabela.
12/15/76

The Formula
MGM. Prod-wri, Steve Shagan from his novel. Dir, John G Avildsen. Cam (Metrocolor), James Crabe; edtrs, David Bretherton, Avildsen, John Carter; snd, Al Overton; art dir, Hans-Jurgen Keibach; prodn des, Herman A Blumenthal; asst dir, Dwight Williams; mus, Bill Conti. (MPAA rating: R). 117.
George C Scott, Marthe Keller, Marlon Brando, John Van Dreelen, Calvin Jung, John Gielgud, Beatrice Straight, Richard Lynch, Robin Clarke, Ike Eisenmann, Alan North, Ferdy Mayne, Gerry Murphy, David Byrd, Wolfgang Preiss, G D Spradlin.
12/10/80

Formynderne
(The Guardians)
(Norway)
NSK. Harald Ohrvik prodn. Dir, Nicole Mace; sp, Kirsten Bryhni, based on two novels by Amalie Skram; cam, Paul Rene Roestad; mus, Synne Skouen; edtr, Edith Toreg; art dir, Sven Wickman. 104.
Vibeke Lokkeberg, Helge Reiss, Odd Furoy.
10/29/90

The Fortress: SEE Az Erod

40 Anos Sin Sexo
(40 Years Without Sex)
(Spain)
X. Producciones Zeta S A prodn. Dir, Juan Bosch. Cam (Eastmancolor), Tomas Pladevall; sp, Juanjo Puigcorbe, Francisco Bellmunt and Enrique Josa; edtr, Emilio Rodriguez; mus, Maestro Soto; sets, Ramon Pou. 87.
Marta Angelat, Antonio Ceinos, Carlos Lucena, Alfredo Luchetti, Alicia Orozco, Maria Rubio, Taida Urruzola, Maria Rey.
02/21/79

Foul Play
PAR. Prods, Thomas L Miller, Edward K Milkis. Wri-dir, Colin Higgins. Cam (Movielab Color), David M Walsh; 2d unit cam, Rexford Metz; edtr, Pembroke J Herring; mus, Charles Fox; prodn des, Alfred Sweeney; set decor, Robert R Benton; snd, Jay Harding, Jeff Wexler; asst dir, Gary D Daigler; 2d unit dir, M James Arnett. (MPAA rating: PG). 116.
Goldie Hawn, Chevy Chase, Burgess Meredith, Rachel Roberts, Eugene Roche, Dudley Moore, Bruce Solomon, Marilyn Sokol, Brian Dennehy, Chuck McCann, Billy Barty, Don Calfa, Marc Lawrence, Cooper Huckabee, William Frankfather, Ion Teodorescu, Pat Ast, John Hancock, Queenie Smith, Hope Summers, Irene Tedrow, Cyril Magnin, Chuck Walsh.
07/12/78

Foul Play: SEE Przepraszam, Czy Tu Bija?

Four Days to Death: SEE Cetiri Dana Do Smrti

The Four Seasons: SEE Godisnja Doba

The Fox in the Chicken Coop
(Israel)
FFP. Hashualim Prodn. Prods, Itzhak Kol, Ephraim Kishon. Wri-dir, Ephraim Kishon. Cam, David Gurfinkel; mus, Nurit Hirsch; edtr, Hadassa Shani. 90.
Shai K Ophir, Shoshana Shani, Mosko Alkalay, Gideon Singer, Mordechai Ben-Zeev, Shlomo Vishinsky, Yoseph Bashi.
06/28/78

Foxbat
(Hong Kong)
BNG. Jimmy Ip-Bang Bang prodn. Dir, Leong Po-chih. Exec prod, May Lim. Sp, Les Roberts, from orig story by Philip Chan, Leong Po-chih; cam, Tony Hope; mus, Roy Budd. 90.
Henry Silva, Vonetta McGee, Rik Van Nutter, James Yi Liu, Philip Chan, Roy Chiao.
(English soundtrack)
12/21/77

Foxes
UA. Casablanca Record & Filmworks prodn. Prods, David Puttnam, Gerald Ayers. Dir, Adrian Lyne. Sp, Gerald Ayres; cam (Technicolor), Leon Bijou; orig mus comp-cond, Giorgio Moroder; art dir, Michael Levesque; edtr, Jim Coblentz; asst dir, Stuart Gross, sfx, Robert Horvatich. (MPAA rating: R).   106.
Jodie Foster, Scott Baio, Sally Kellerman, Randy Quaid, Lois Smith, Adam Faith, Cheri Currie, Marilyn Kagan, Kandice Stroh, Jon Sloan, Jill Barrie Bogart, Wayne Storm, Mary Margaret Lewis, Grant Wilson, Fredric Lehne, Robert Romanus, Roger Bowen, Buddy Foster, E Lamont Johnson, Mary Ellen O'Neill, Ben Frank, Kay A Toroborg, Scott Garrett, Laura Dern, Michael Taylor, Gino Baffa, Charles Shull, Tony Termini, Jeff Silverman, Mae Williams, R Scott Thomson, Ron Lombard, Steve Jones, Jon M Benson, Tom Pletts, Ken Novick, Angel.
02/27/80

Foxtrot
(Mexico - Switzerland)
NW. Conacine-Carvold film, prod, Gerald Green; exec prods, Maximiliano Vega Tato, Anuar Badin. Dir, Arturo Ripstein. Sp, Ripstein, Jose Emilio Pacheco, H A L Craig; cam (Technicolor), Alex Phillips Jr; edtr, Peter Zinner; mus, Pete Rugolo; title song, Jay Livingston, Ray Evans, Rugolo; art dir, Lucero Isaac; set decor, Jose Rodriguez Granada; snd, Manuel Topete; asst dirs, Luis Gaytan, Valerio Olivio, Claudio Isaac. (MPAA rating: R).   91.
Peter O'Toole, Charlotte Rampling, Max Von Sydow, Jorge Luke, Helena Rojo, Claudio Brook, Max Kerlow, Christa Walter, Mario Castillon, Anne Porterfield.
03/31/76

Fraiche
(Love and Cool Water)
(France)
GAU. Gaumont Int'l, Production 2000 prodn. Wri-dir, Jean-Pierre Blanc. Cam (Eastmancolor), Edmond Sechan; edtr, Catherine Michel; mus, Michel Bernhloc.   90.
Annie Girardot, Miou-Miou, Julien Clerc, Jean-Pierre Darras.
04/21/76

Frankenstein-Italian Style
(Italy)
EI. Prod, Filiberto Bandino. Dir, Armando Crispino. Exec prod, Carlo Capieri. Sp, Massimo Franciosa, Maria Luisa Montagnana; cam, Giuseppe Cipriani; edtr, Angela Cipriani; mus, Stelvio Cipriani; prodn des, Mario Molli.   97.
Aldo Maccione, Gianrico Tedeschi, Ninetto Davoli, Jenny Tamburi, Anna Mazzananio, Lorenza Guerrieri.
11/23/77

Fraternity Row
PAR. Prod-wri, Charles Gary Allison. Dir, Thomas J Tobin. Cam (CFI Color), Peter Gibbons; 2d-unit cam, Thomas W Joachim; edtr, 2d-unit dir, Eugene A Fournier; mus, Don McLean, Michael Corner, John Phillips Hutton, Matthew Roe; art dir, James Sbardellati; set decor, Greg Mellott; cos-ward, Beverly Ihnen, Richard A Davis; snd, William D Livingstone, Jay Harding, Bud Grinzbach, Dick Tyler; asst dirs, Richard N Graves, James M Davidson. (MPAA rating: PG).   101.
Peter Fox, Gregory Harrison, Scott Newman, Nancy Morgan, Wendy Phillips, Robert Emhardt, Robert Matthews, Bernard R. Kantor.
02/23/77

Freaky Friday
BV. Walt Disney prodn; prod, Ron Miller. Dir, Gary Nelson. Sp, Mary Rodgers, based on her book; cam (Technicolor), Charles F Wheeler; mus, Johnny Mandel; song, "I'd Like To Be You For A Day," Al Kasha, Joel Hirschhorn; edtr, Cotton Warburton; art dirs, John B Mansbridge, Jack Senter; set decor, Robert Benton; cos, Chuck Keehne, Emily Sundby; snd, Herb Taylor, Ron Ronconi; asst dir, Ronald R Grow. (MPAA rating: G).   95.
Barbara Harris, Jodie Foster, John Astin, Patsy Kelly, Dick Van Patten, Vicki Schreck, Sorrell Booke, Alan Oppenheimer, Ruth Buzzi, Kaye Ballard, Marc McClure, Marie Windsor, Sparky Marcus, Ceil Cabot, Brooke Mills, Karen Smith, Marvin Kaplan, Al Molinaro, Iris Adrian, Barbara Walden.
12/22/76

Free For All: SEE Piedra Libre

Freewheelin'
TUR. Turtle Releasing Organization. Prod-dir, Scott Dittrich. Exec prod, Daniel Rosenthal. Sp-edtr, George Van Noy; cam, Pat Darrin; mus, Stephen Freud; title song, Freud, Steve Cohn; snd, Janis Darrin. (MPAA rating: G).   80.
Stacy Peralta, Camille Darrin, Russ Howell, Ken Means, Tom Sims, Mike Weed, Paul Constantineau, Bobby Pierce, Stevie Monahan, Desiree Von Essen, Guy Grundy, Waldo Autrey.
11/17/76

Fremd Bin Ich Eigezogah
(I Came As A Stranger)
(Austria - W Germany)
X. Titus Leber Vienne-Clasart Munich prodn. Sp-dir-edtr, Titus Leber. Cam, Ditter Witich, Leber, Wittigo; mus, Franz Schubert.   70.
Axel Shanda, August Schnigg, Alicia Meyer-Stauffen, Ernst Dungl, Angenlika Berlage.
05/16/79

French Postcards
(W Germany - France)
PAR. Geria prodn. Prod, Gloria Katz. Dir, Willard Huyck; sp, Huyck, Katz; cam, Bruno Nuytten; edtr, Carol Littleton; mus, Lee Holdridge; art dir, Jean-Pierre Kohut-Svelko; cos des, Catherine Letherrier, Joan Mocine; set decor, Jacques Leguillon; snd, Bernard Bats; asst dir, Jean-Jacques Beineix. (MPAA rating: PG).   95.
Miles Chapin, Blanche Baker, David Marshall Grant, Valerie Quennessen, Debra Winger, Mandy Patinkin, Marie-France Pisier, Joan Rochefort, Lynn Carlin, George Coe, Christophe Bourseiller.
(English soundtrack)
09/12/79

Friday The 13th
PAR. Sean S Cunningham Film. Prod-dir, Cunningham. Sp, Victor Miller; cam, Barry Abrams; edtr, Bill Freda; mus, Harry Manfredini; art dir, Virginia Field; sfx-stunts, Tom Savini; asso prod, Stephen Miner. (MPAA rating: R).   95.
Betsy Palmer, Adrienne King, Harry Crosby, Laurie Bartram, Mark Nelson, Jeannine Taylor, Robbi Morgan, Kevin Bacon, Ari Lehman.
05/14/80

Friday the 13th...The Orphan
WNO. Gilman-Westergaard Enterprises and Cinema Investments Co, in asso with Trimmedia Southwest Associates II prodn. Wri-dir, John Ballard; cam, Beda F Patka; art dir, Sidney Ann MacKenzie; theme song, Janis Ian; mus, Ted Macero. (MPAA rating: R).   80.
Peggy Feury, Joanna Miles, Donn Whyte, Stanley Church, Eleanor Stewart, Afolabi Ajayi, Jane House, David Foreman, Mark Owens.
12/12/79

The Friend: SEE Arkadas

Frihetens murar
(The Walls Of Freedom)
(Sweden)
SVE. Swedish Film Institute (Exec prod, Joern Donner) - Three Leaf Clover HB prodn. Dir-edtr, Marianne Ahrne; wris, Marianne Ahrne, Renzo Casali; cam (Eastmancolor), Hans Welin, Solveig Warner.   100.
Renzo Casali, Marianne Stjernqvist, Annicka Kronberg, Christine Kronberg.
04/11/79

The Frisco Kid
WB. Mace Neufeld prodn. Prod, Neufeld. Exec prod, Howard W Koch Jr. Dir, Robert Aldrich. Sp, Michael Elias, Frank Shaw; cam, Robert B Hauser; edtrs, Maury Winetrobe, Irving Rosenblum, Jack Horger; mus, Frank DeVol; prodn des, Terence Marsh; set decor, Marvin March; snd, Jack Solomon; asst dir, Mel Dellar. (MPAA rating: PG).   122.
Gene Wilder, Harrison Ford, Ramon Bieri, Val Bisoglio, George Ralph DiCenzo, Leo Fuchs, Penny Peyser, William Smith, Jack Somack, Beege Barkett, Shay Duffin.
07/04/79

From Hell To Victory
(France - Italy - Spain)
X. New Film Prodn (Rome), Princess Films (Paris) and Jose Frade (Madrid) co-prodn. Dir, Hank Milestone. Sp, Umberto Lenzi, Jose Luis Martinez Molls, Gianfranco Clerici; cam (Eastmancolor), Jose Luis Alcaine; mus, Riz Ortolani; sets, Giuseppe Bassan, Rafael Ferry; edtr, Vicenzo Tomasi.   100.
George Peppard, George Hamilton, Horst Bucholz, Capucine, Sam Wanamaker, Jean Pierre

Cassel, Annie Duperey, Ray Lovelock, Angel Aranda, Antonio Mayans.
09/12/79

From Noon Till Three
UA. Prods, M J Frankovich, William Self. Wri- (from his novel)dir, Frank D Gilroy; cam (DeLuxe Color), Lucien Ballard; edtr, Maury Winetrobe; mus, Elmer Bernstein; song lyr, Alan and Marilyn Bergman; prodn des, Robert Clatworthy; art dir, Dick Lawrence; set decor, George Robert Nelson; snd, Arthur Piantadosi, Richard Tyler, Les Fresholtz, Al Overton; asst dir, Russ Saunders. (MPAA rating: PG). 98.
Charles Bronson, Jill Ireland, Douglas V Fowley, Stan Haze, Damon Douglas, Hector Morales, Bert Williams, William Lanteau, Betty Cole, Davis Roberts, Fred Franklyn, Sonny Jones, Hoke Howell, Howard Brunner, Donald (Red) Barry, Elmer Bernstein, Alan Bergman.
08/04/76

From The Abyss: SEE Desde El Abismo

From The Life Of The Marionettes
(W Germany)
ITC. Exec prods, Lord Grade, Martin Starger. Dir, Ingmar Bergman. Sp, Ingmar Bergman; cam, Sven Nykvist; edtr, Petra Voelffen; mus, Rols Wilhelm; prodn des, Rolf Zechetbauer; art dir, Herbert Strabel; cos, Charlotte Fleming; asst dirs, Trudy V Trotha, Johannes Kaetzler. (MPAA rating: R). 104.
Robert Atzorn, Christine Buchegger, Martin Benrath, Rita Russek, Lola Muethel, Walter Schmidinger, Heinz Bennent, Ruth Olafs, Karl Heinz Pelser, Gaby Dohm, Toni Berger.
(B & W - COLOR)
07/23/80

The Front
COL. Prod-dir, Martin Ritt; exec prod, Charles H Joffe. Sp, Walter Bernstein; cam (Metrocolor), Michael Chapman; edtr, Sidney Levin; mus, Dave Grusin; art dir, Charles Bailey; set decor, Robert Drumheller; snd, Jim Stewart, Tom Beckert, Walter Goss, James Sabat; asst dir, Peter Scoppa. (MPAA rating: PG). 94.
Woody Allen, Zero Mostel, Herschel Bernardi, Michael Murphy, Andrea Marcovicci, Remak Ramsay, Marvin Lichterman, Lloyd Gough, David Margulies, Joshua Shelley, Norman Rose, Charles Kimbrough, M Josef Sommer, Danny Aiello, Georgann Johnson, Scott McKay, David Clarke, I W Klein.
09/15/76

Frontiers of Darkness: SEE Die Schattengrenze

The Frozen Heart: SEE Das gefrorene Herz

The Fruit Is Ripe: SEE Griechische Feigen

Fuer Die Liebe Noch Zu Mager?
(Too Lean for Love?)
(E Germany)
DEE. Dir, Bernhard Stephan. Sp, Jochen Nestler, Manfred Freitag; cam, Hans-Juergen Kruse. 90.
Simone von Zglinicki, Ursula Staak, Christian Steyer, Karl Thiele, Norbert Christian, Carl-Hermann Risse, Uwe Kockisch, Fred Delmare.
05/11/77

Fukushu Suruwa Ware Ni Ari
(Vengeance Is Mine)
(Japan)
X. Shochiku Co prodn. Prod, Kazuo Inoue. Dir, Shohei Imamura. Sp, Masaru Baba, based on book by Ryuzo Saki; cam, Shinsaku Himeda; edtr, Keiichi Uraoka; mus, Shinichiro Ikebe. 128.
Ken Ogata, Rentaro Mikuni, Chocho Mikayo, Mitsuko Baisho, Mayumi Ogawa, Nijiko Kiyokawa.
(Japanese soundtrack - English subtitles)
03/26/80

Full Circle
(Britain - Canada)
X. Fester prodns Ltd film. Prods, Peter Fetterman, Alfred Pariser. Dir, Richard Longcraine. Sp, Dave Humphries; cam (Eastmancolor), Peter Hannan; mus, Colin Towns; edtr, Ron Wisman; art dir, Brian Morris; ward, Shuna Harwood; prodn supv, Hugh Harlow; cam operator, Terry Permane. 98.
Mia Farrow, Keir Dullea, Tom Conti, Jill Bennett, Robin Gammell, Cathleen Nesbitt, Anna Wing, Pauline Jameson, Peter Sallis, Sophie Ward, Samantha Gates.
09/28/77

Full Moon: SEE Pelnia

Fun Is Beautiful: SEE Un Sacco Bello

Fun With Dick And Jane
COL. Prod, Peter Bart, Max Palevsky. Dir, Ted Kotcheff. Sp, David Giler, Jerry Belson, Mordecai Richler; based on a story by Gerald Gaiser; cam (Metrocolor), Fred Koenekamp; edtr, Danford B Greene; mus, Ernest Gold, Lamont Dozier, Gene Page; prodn des, James G Hulsey; set decor, Jack Stevens; snd, Les Fresholtz, Dick Alexander, Vern Poore, Darin Knight; cos-ward, Donfeld, Lambert E Marks, Margo Baxley; asst dir, Charles Okun; stunt coord, Paul Baxley. (MPAA rating: PG). 95.
George Segal, Jane Fonda, Ed McMahon, Dick Gautier, Allan Miller, Hank Garcia, John Dehner, Mary Jackson, Walter Brooke, Sean Frye, James Jeter, Maxine Stuart, Fred Willard.
02/02/77

Funerailles A Bongo: Le Vieux Anai
(Funeral At Bongo: Old Anai)
(France)
X. Prod, by Les Films de l'Homme, Paris. Dirs, Jean Rouch, Germaine Dieterlen. Edtr, Daniele Tesier; snd, Moussa Hassidon, Ibralirna Guirido. 105.
(DOC)
09/19/79

Funny Note
(Japan)
NIK. Prods, Yoshihiro Yuuki, Takeo Nishiguchi. Dir, Kazunari Takeda. Story, Hiro Miyagawa; sp, Mei Kato, Yukio Yoshiwara; cam, Hidenobu Nimura; edtr, Fusako Matsumoto; mus, Masao Yagi; art dir, Heihachiro Watanabe; snd, Hideo Tatebe. 86.
Atsushi Watanabe, Masahiko Kimura, Nobuyo Ohashi, Mitsutoshi Nakata, Toru Nakai, Mitsuki Sejima.
12/14/77

Fuori Stagione
(Off Season)
(Italy)
X. Prods, Gianni Minervini, Antonio Avati for A M A Film prodns. Wri-dir, Luciano Manuzzi. Cam (Eastmancolor), Nino Celeste; art dir, Laura Ferri; edtr, Ugo De Rossi; mus, Amedeo Tommasi. 95.
Nicola Di Pinto, Saura Fabbri, Ciro Severi, Gigio Morra.
06/11/80

Further Adventures of the Wilderness Family - Part 2
PIE. Arthur Dubs prodn. Dir, Frank Zuniga. Sp, Arthur Dubs; cam, John Hora; mus, Douglas Lackey, Gene Kauer; lyr, Dennis Brockman; sngs perf, Barry Williams. (MPAA rating: G). 105.
Robert Logan, Susan D Shaw, Heather Rattray, Ham Larsen, George (Buck) Flower, Brian Cutler, Kurt Grayson.
10/25/78

The Fury
FOX. Prod, Frank Yablans; exec prod, Ron Preissman. Dir, Brian DePalma. Sp, John Farris, based on his novel; cam (DeLuxe Color), Richard H Kline; edtr, Paul Hirsch; mus, John Williams; prodn des, Bill Malley; art dir, Richard Lawrence; set decor, Audrey Blasdel-Goddard; snd, Richard Vorisek, Hal Etherington; cos-ward, Theoni V Aldredge, Seth Banks, Margo Baxley; asst dir, Donald E Heitzer; stunt coord, Mickey Gilbert; sfx, A D Flowers. (MPAA rating: R). 117.
Kirk Douglas, John Cassavetes, Carrie Snodgress, Charles Durning, Amy Irving, Fiona Lewis, Andrew Stevens, Carol Rossen, Rutanya Alda, Joyce Easton, William Finley, Jane Lambert, Dennis Franz, Michael O'Dwyer, Mickey Gilbert, Frank Yablans.
03/15/78

Fuses: SEE Zuendschnuere

Futureworld
AIP. Prods, Paul Lazarus III, James T Aubrey Jr; exec prod, Samuel Z Arkoff. Dir, Richard T Heffron. Sp, Mayo Simon; George Schenck; cam (Metrocolor), Howard Schwartz, Gene Polito; visual effects supv, Brent Sellstrom, 2d unit cam, Robert Jessup; edtr, James Mitchell; mus, Fred Karlin; art dir, Trevor Williams; set decors, Dennis Peeples, Marvin March; snd, Charlie Knight; asst dir, Robert Koster. (MPAA rating: PG). 107.
Peter Fonda, Blythe Danner, Arthur Hill, Yul Brynner, Jim Antonio, John Ryan, Stuart Margolin.
07/14/76

Ga pa vattnet om du kan
(Walk On Water If You Can)
(Sweden)
EUR. Swedish Film Institute/Audio Investment/HB Three Leaf Clover/AB Europa Film prodn. Dir, Stig Bjorkman. Wri, Sun Axelsson; cam (Eastmancolor), Petter Davidson; edtr, Margit Nordquist; mus, Berndt Eger; exec prod, Anna Lena Wibom. 95.
Lena Nyman, Tomas Ponten, Claire Wikholm, Norman Briski, Annifrid Lyngstad, Toni Valente.
09/12/79

Gable and Lombard
U. Prod, Harry Korshak. Dir, Sidney J Furie. Sp, Barry Sandler; cam (Technicolor), Jordan S Cronenweth; edtr, Argyle Nelson; mus, Michel Legrand; prodn des, Edward C Carfagno; set decor, Hal Gausman; snd, Robert L Hoyt, Don Sharpless; asst dir, James A Westman. (MPAA rating: R). 131.
James Brolin, Jill Clayburgh, Allen Garfield, Red Buttons, Melanie Mayron, Carol McGinnis, S John Launer, William Bryant, Joanne Linville, Noah Keen, Alice Backes, Morgan Brittany.
02/18/76

Gaijin-Caminos Da Liberdade
(Strangers-The Road To Liberty)
(Brazil)
EMZ. C P C, Embrafilme, Igreja, Mundial Do Brazil, Societa Brasilera De Cultura Japonesa prodn. Dir, Tizuka Yamasaki. Sp, Jorge Duran, Yamasaki; cam, Edgar Maura; mus, John Neschling. 105.
Kyoko Tsukamoto, Antonio Fagundes, Jiro Kawarasaki, Gianfrancesco Guarnieri.
05/14/80

Gal Young Un
X. Nunez Films prodn. Prod-dir, Victor Nunez; sp, Nunez based on a Marjorie Kinnan Rawlings short story; cam (TVC), Nunez, Greg Garner; score, Charles Engstrom, performed by Azalea Blossom String Band and Lohman-Crozier Trio; edtr, Nunez; snd, Pat Garner, Bob Dichter; set decor, Pat and Greg Garner. 105.
Dana Preu, David Peck, J Smith, Gene Densmore, Jennie Stringfellow, Tim McCormack, Casey Donovan, Mike Garlington, Marshal New, Bruce Cornwell, John Pieters, Gil Lazier, Tina Moore, Marc Glic, Kerry McKenney, Sarah Drylie, Randy Ser, Bernie Cook, Fred Wood, Sissy Wood, Mr and Mrs Lewis Ivey, J D Henry, Billie Henry, Susan Holzer, Brian Lietz, Gus Holzer, Ross Sturlin, Pat Garner.
11/07/79

Galaxina
CWN. Marimar Production. Prod, Marilyn J Tenser; asso prod, George E Mather; wri-dir, William Sachs; cam, Dean Cundy; prodn des, Tom Turlley; edtr, Larry Bock; supv spec photo effects, Chuck Colwell. (MPAA: R). 95.
Stephen Macht, Dorothy R Stratten, James David Hinton, Avery Schreiber, Ronald Knight, Lionel Smith, Tad Horino, Herp Kaplowitz, Nancy McCauley, Fred D Scott, George E Mather.
08/27/80

Gaman
(Going)
(India)
IGI Wri-dir, Muzaffar Ali. Cam (Eastmancolor), Nadeem Khan; edtr, Jethu Mundul; mus, Jaidev. 135.
Farooque Shaikh, Smita Patil, Gita Siddharth, Jabal Agha.
01/31/79

Game of Death
COL. Raymond Chow prodn. Prod, Raymond Chow. Dir, Robert Clouse. Sp, Jan Spears; cam, Godfrey A Godar; edtr, Alan Pattillo; mus, John Barry; snd, William Stevenson; prodn mgr, David Chan; sfx, Far East Effects; martial arts dir, Hung Kim Po; asst dir, Mike Gowans. (MPAA rating: R). 102.
Bruce Lee, Gig Young, Dean Jagger, Hugh O'Brian, Colleen Camp, Robert Wall, Mel Novak, Kareem Abdul-Jabbar, Chuck Norris, Danny Inosanto, Billy McGill, Hung Kim Po, Roy Chaio.
06/13/79

The Game of Solitaire: SEE *Le Jeu De Solitaire*

Game of the Apple: SEE *Uvadi Hra O Jablo*

Game Pass: SEE *Wildwechsel*

The Gamekeeper
(Britain)
X. ATV Network Ltd prodn. Dir-sp, Kenneth Loach; adapt, Barry Hines from his novel; cam, Chris Menges, Charles Stewart; edtr, Roger James; snd, Andrew Boulton, Peter Rann; art dirs, Martin Johnson, Graham Tew; cos, Maxine Henry. 84.
Phil Askham, Rita May, Andrew Grubb, Peter Steels, Michael Hinchcliffe, Philip Firth, Lee Hickin, Jackie Shinn, Paul Brian, Ted Beyer, Chick Barratt, Willoughby Gray, Mark Elwes.
09/24/80

Games of the XXI Olympiad Montreal 1976
(Canada)
NFC. Dir and conceived by Jean-Claude Labrecque with Jean Baudin, Marcel Carriere, Georges Dufaux. Cam, official crews; edtr, Werner Nold; mus, Andre Gagnon. 119. (DOC) *(English and French Versions in 16m and 35m with stereo sound for 35m version)*
06/08/77

Gamin
(Waif)
(Colombia)
X. Claude Antoine SND and Instituto Nacional de la Audiovisual and UNO Ltda prodn. Wri-dir, Ciro Duran. Cam, Luis Cuesta; edtrs, Ciro and Joyce Duran; mus, Francisco Zumaque. 104. (DOC) (16m)
10/03/79

Gangsterens laerling
(The Gangster's Apprentice)
(Denmark)
WBL. LEA/Anne Philipsen prodn. Dir, Esben Hoilund Carlsen. Sp, Lars Leergaard; cam, Dan Holmberg; edtr, Henrik Carlsen; mus, Aske Bentzon, Buki Yamaz; in charge of prodn, Lars Kolvig. 106.
Dick Kaysoe, Nina Louise Petersen, Peter Steen.
08/04/76

Garage Sale
X. Kyodi prodn; prod, Bruce Yonemoto, Norman Yonemoto. Dir-wri-edtr, Norman Yonemoto. Cam (Eastmancolor), Nick Ursin; mus, Sunset Blvd., The Dreaded Mr. Twister; title song, Gordon Skene; asst dir; Steven McGrew. (Self-imposed X rating). 92.
Michael Heesy, Tom White, Ruth Hagopian, Paul Mathews, Anastasia, Steven McGrew, Bruce Lovern, Bob Opel, L E Coulter, Loren Rhodes, Don Soker, Nick Ursin.
12/08/76

The Garden
(Israel)
X. Prod by Berkey Pathe Humphries (Israel) Ltd. Prods, Isaac Shani, Yosef Diamant. Dir, Victor Nord. Sp, Yosef Avissar; cam, Valerie Galperin; edtr, Zion Avrahamian; mus, Noham Sharif. 93.
Shai K Ophir, Melanie Griffith, Tuvia Tabi, Shoshanah Duer, Seadia Damari, Tsachi Noi.
06/01/77

The Garden of Stones: SEE *Baghe Sangui*

The Garden of Torture: SEE *Le Jardin Des Supplices*

Gas Pump Girls
CAN. Prod, David A Davies; exec prod, Davil Gil. Dir, Joel Bender; sp, Davies, Bender, Isaac Blech; cam (Movielab color), Nicholas Von Sternberg; mus, Leigh Crizoe. (MPAA rating: R). 90.
Kirsten Baker, Dennis Bowen, Huntz Hall, Sandy Johnson, Leslie King, Linda Lawrence, Rikki Marin, Joe E Ross, Mike Mazurski.
12/19/79

Gates of Heaven
X. Prod-dir, Errol Morris. Cam, Ned Burgess; supv edtr, Charles Laurence Silver; edtr, Morris; snd, Jay Miracle; prod mgr, George Csicsery. 82.
(DOC)
10/04/78

Gator
UA. Prods, Jules Levy, Arthur Gardner. Dir, Burt Reynolds. Sp, William Norton; cam (DeLuxe Color), William A Fraker; 2d unit cam, George Bouillet; edtr, Harold F Kress; mus, Charles Bernstein; songs, Jerry Reed, Bobby Goldsboro; art dir, Kirk Axtell; snd, Theodore Soderberg; William Randall; asst dir, Edward Teets; 2d unit dir, Hal Needham. (MPAA rating: PG). 115.
Burt Reynolds, Jack Weston, Lauren Hutton, Jerry Reed, Alice Ghostley, Dub Taylor, Mike Douglas, Burton Gilliam, William Engesser, John Steadman, Lori Futch, Stephanie Burchfield, Bob Yeager.
05/12/76

Gatti Rossi In Un Labirinto di Vetro: SEE Eyeball

The Gauntlet
WB. Prod, Robert Daley. Dir, Clint Eastwood. Sp, Michael Butler, Dennis Shryack; cam (DeLuxe Color), Rexford Metz; edtrs, Ferris Webster, Joel Cox; mus, Jerry Fielding; art dir, Allen E Smith; set decor, Ira Bates; snd, Les Fresholtz, Bert Hallberg; cos-ward, Glenn Wright; asst dir, Richard Hashimoto; stunt coord, Wayne Van Horn. (MPAA rating: R). 108.
Clint Eastwood, Sondra Locke, Pat Hingle, William Prince, Bill McKinney, Michael Cavanaugh, Carole Cook, Mara Corday, Douglas McGrath, Jeff Morris.
12/21/77

Gefundenes Fressen
(Scrounged Meals)
(W Germany)
X. Sentana Film Prodn, Munich. Dir, Michael Verhoeven. Sp, Elke Heidenriech, Bernd Schroeder, Verhoeven; cam, Heinz Hoelscher; edtr, Helga Borsche; mus, Stefan Melbinger; snd, Adolf Kredatus; art dirs, Heinz Eickmeyer, Katharina Litzinger. 95.
Heinz Ruehmann, Mario Adorf, Elisabeth Volkmann, Rene Deltgen, Karin Baal, Spomenca Petrovic.
04/27/77

Geheime Reichssache
(Top Secret--The History of German Resistance Against Hitler)
(W Germany)
X. Chronos Prodn, Berlin. Prod, Bengt von zur Muhlen. Dir, Jochen Bauer; wri, Karl-Heinz Janszen; res, Lola Braxton; English adapt, Esther and Albert Hemsing; asst dir, Manfred Helling; edtr, Evelyn Mundin; mus, Wolfgang De Gelmini; snd, Reiner Lorenz; optical work and effects, Studio Batoschek. 100.
(DOC) (B & W) *(English narr and subtitles)*
11/21/79

The Gendarme and the Creatures from Outer Space: SEE Le Gendarme et les Extra-Terrestres

Genese D'Un Repas
(Origins of a Meal)
(France)
X. Luc Moullet Prodns. Wri-dir, Luc Moullet. Cam (b&w), Richard Copans, Patrick Frederich. 117. (DOC) (B & W)
03/14/79

Genesis, Chapter X
(Ghana)
X. Ghana Film prodn. Dir, Thomas Ribero. Sp, Ato Janney. 96.
George Williams, Marilyn Meyer.
09/05/79

The Genius: SEE Un Genio, Due Compari, Un Pollo

Gente Fina E Otra Coisa
(The Rich Are Something Else)
(Brazil)
X. Prod, Pedro Carlos Rovai. Dir, Antonio Calmon. Cam (Eastmancolor), Roberto Pace; edtr, Silvio Renoldi. 99.
Marcia Rodrigues, Maria Dahl, Ney Sant'Anna, Nuno Maia.
11/23/77

German Spring: SEE Deutscher Fruehling

Germany In Autumn: SEE Deutschland Im Herbst

Germany, Pale Mother: SEE Deutschland Bleiche Mutter

Geschichten Aus Dem Wiener Wald
(Tales from the Vienna Woods)
(W Germany - Australia)
NCT. Co-prodn of MFG-Film, Munich-Arabella-Film, Vienna-Franz Seitz Film, Munich-Solaris-Film, Munich, and Bayerischer Rundfunk, Munich. Prod-dir, Maximilian Schell; sp, Christopher Hampton, Schell, based on folk play by Oedoen von Horvath with same title; cam, Klaus Koenig; sets, Ernst Wurzer; edtr, Dagmar Hirtz. 100.
Birgit Doll, Hanno Poeschl, Helmut Qualtinger, Jane Tilden, Adrienne Gessner, Goetz Kauffmann, Andre Heller, Norbert Schiller, Eric Pohlmann, Robert Meyer, Walter Schmiedinger, Elisabeth Epp, Lil Dagover, Vadim Glowna, Vera Borek, Gerry Kronberger, Maria Englstorfer.
11/21/79

Get Charlie Tully
(Britain)
TBS. Hal Thay, Steve Burn, Howard Smith (in assn with Checker Properties) presentation. Prod, E M Smedley Aston. Dir, Cliff Owen. Sp, John Warren, John Singer; cam, Ernest Steward; edtr, Bill Blunden; art dir, Geoffrey Tozer; snd, Kevin Sutton; score, Christopher Gunning; exec prods, Frank Launder, Sidney Gilliat. (MPAA rating: PG). 97.
Dick Emery, Darren Nesbitt, Ronald Fraser, Pat Coombs, William Franklyn, Cheryl Kennedy, Norman Bird, Roland Curram, Liza Goddard, Ambrosine Phillpotts, Brian Oulton, Steve Plytas, Louis Negin, Neil Wilson, Henry Gilbert, Antony Stamboulieh, Guido Adorni, Stefan Gryff, Louis Mansi, Frank Coda, Sheila Keith, Tucker Maguire, Phil Brown, Joan Ingram, Julie Crostwaite, Anna Gilcrist, Margaret Courtenay, Dinnie Powell, Larry Taylor.
07/28/76

Get Out Your Handkerchiefs
(France)
GCC. Les Films Ariane-CAPAC prodn. Dir-sp, Bertrand Blier. Cam (Eastmancolor), Jean Peuzer; edtr, Claudine Merlin; mus, Georges Delerue. 108.
Gerard Depardieu, Patrick Dewaere, Carole Laure, Riton, Michel Serrault, Eleonore Hirt, Sylvie Joly, Jean Rougerie.
01/11/78

Get Your Diploma First: SEE Passe Ton Bac D'Abord

The Getaway: SEE La Derobade

The Getting of Wisdom
(Australia)
RDP. Southern Cross prodn. Prod, Phillip Adams. Dir, Bruce Beresford. Sp, Eleanor Witcombe, from novel by Henry Handel Richardson; cam (Eastman-Panavision), Don McAlpine; snd, Desmond Bone, Gary Wilkins; asst dir, Michael Lake; prodn des, John Stoddart; edtr, William Anderson; cos des, Anna Senior; continuity, Moya Iceton; cam operator, Gale Tattersall; art dir, Richard Kent. 100.
Susannah Fowle, Barry Humphries, John Waters, Sheila Helpmann, Patricia Kennedy, Julia Blake, Dorothy Bradley, Kay Eklund, Max Fairchild, Jan Friedl, Diana Greentree, Maggie Kirkpatrick, Monica Maughan, Candy Raymond, Terence Donovan, Kerry Armstrong, Celia de Burgh, Kim Deacon, Alix Longman, Jo-Anne Moore, Amanda Ring, Hilary Ryan, Janet Shaw, Karen Sutton, Sigrid Thornton.
08/31/77

Getting Together
X. Total Impact prodn. Prods, Joey Asaro, David Secter. Wri-dir, Secter; cam, Marty Knopf; edtr, Jane Brodsky Altschuler; prodn des, Theodore S Hammer; art dir, Gerald Holbrook; mus, Tony Camillo; cos, Neil Cooper; prodn mgr, Avery Klauber; asso prod, Sam Kitt. 110.
Malcolm Groome, Kathleen Seward, Rhonda Hansome, Tony Collado, Charles Douglass,

Helga Kopperl.
11/24/76

Ghost Train: SEE *Spoegelsestoget*

Gibbi West Germany
(W Germany)
FDA. Bioskop Film Prodn, Munich, in collab with Westdeutscher Rundfunk (WDR). Wri-dir, Christel Buschmann. Cam, Frank Bruehne; songs, Paul Millns; edtr, Jane Sperr; sets, Winfried Hennig; prodn, Eberhard Junkersdorf; TV-prod, Wolf-Dietrich Bruecker. 90.
Joergen Pfennigwerth, Eva Maria Hagen, Eric Burdon, Rosalia de Kulessa, Angelika Kulessa, Martin Kippenberger, Soma Weissenseel, Hans Noever, Guenter Meissner, Claus-Dieter Ossenkoff, Martha Sievers.
05/28/80

Gilda Live
WB. Broadway Pictures Presentation. Dir, Mike Nichols. Prod, Lorne Michaels. Wris, Anne Beatts, Michaels, Marilyn Suzanne Miller, Don Novello, Michael O'Donoghue, Gilda Radner, Paul Shaffer, Rosie Shuster, Alan Zweibel; cam (Technicolor), Ted Churchill, James Contner, Alan Metzger, Peter Norman; mus prod, Howard Shore; chor, Patricia Birch; prodn des, Franne Lee, Akira Yoshimura; edtrs, Ellen Hivde, Lynzee Klingman, Muffie Meyer. (MPAA rating: R).   90.
Gilda Radner, Father Guido Sarducci (Don Novello), Diana Grasselli, Myriam Valle, Maria Vidal, Paul Shaffer, Bob Christianson, Nils Nichols, John Caruso, Howard Shore, G E Smith.
03/26/80

The Girl From Millelire Street: SEE *La Ragazza Di Via Millelire*

The Girl In The Yellow Pajamas: SEE *La Ragazza In Pigiama Giallo*

The Girl with Golden Hair: SEE *Chrissomaloussa*

The Girl With The Golden Panties: SEE *La Muchacha De Las Bragas De Oro*

The Girl With The Red Scarf: SEE *Selvi Boylum Al Yazmalim*

Girlfriends
WB. Cyclops Film. Prods, Claudia Weill, Jan Sanders. cam, Fred Murphy; edtr, Suzanne Pettit; mus, Michael Small; art dir, Patrizia von Brandenstein; snd, Ed Rothkowitz, Hanna Wajshonig, Emily Paine.   86.
Melanie Mayron, Eli Wallach, Anita Skinner, Bob Balaban, Christopher Guest,
05/10/78

Girls at Arms, Part 2: SEE *Piger i troejen, 2*

Girls at Sea: SEE *Piger til soes*

Girls For Sale
(Hong Kong)
SHW. Run Run Shaw prodn. Wri-dir, James Lu Chi.   100.
Ai Ti, Ling Tai, Frankie Wei, Shaw Yin-yin, James Lu Chi, Wei Lieh, Chen Yao-lin.
10/27/76

Giselle
(W Germany)
ITV. Unitel prodn. Exec prod, Fritz Buttenstedt; dir, Hugo Niebeling. Based on the ballet "Giselle" by Adolphe Adams, libretto by Vernoy de Saint-Georges, Theophile L Gautier, Jean Coralli; cam, Wolfgang Treu; edtr, Neibeling; set des, Georges Wakhevitch, Oliver Smith; cos, Peter Hall, Jeanne Renucci-Wakhevitch.   95.
Carla Fracci, Eric Bruhn, Bruce Marks, Toni Lander, Eleanor D'Antuono, Ted Kivitt.
(BALLET)
05/03/78

Give Me Back My Skin: SEE *Rendez-Moi Ma Peau*

Give Me Five: SEE *Qua La Mano*

Gizmo
NL. High Wire prodn. Prod-dir, Howard Smith. Exec prod, Francois de Menil. Narr-wris, Kathleen Cox, Nicholas Hollander, Clark Whelton; edtr, Terry Manning; mus prod, Dick Lavsky. (MPAA Rating: G).   79.
(COMPILATION)
07/27/77

The Glacier Fox
SRI. Sanrio film. Exec prod, Shintaro Tsuji. Prod, Hiromu Tsugawa. English version co-prod, Mark L Rosen; wri-dir, Koreyoshi Kurahara; English narr, by Walter Bloch; cam, Masao Tochizawa, Akira Shiizuka, Seizo Sengen, Tsuguzo Matsumae, Hideo Omura, Keisuke Tateishi, Yoshio Mamiya; edtrs, Kurahara, Akira Suzuki, Terry Anderson; snd, Kazumi Inamura; mus, Masuru Sato; asst dir, Junichi Mimura. Narr, Arthur Hill. (MPAA rating: G).   90. (*Dubbed English soundtrack*)
(DOC)
01/31/79

The Glass Cell: SEE *Die Glaeserne Zelle*

Gli Anni Struggenti
(The Burning Years)
(Italy)
FMG. Dir, Vittorio Sindoni. Sp, Nicola Badalucco, Sindoni, Mario Gallo; cam, Safai Teherani; edtr, Angelo Curi.   90.
Fabio Traversi, Laura Lenzi, Gabriele Ferzetti.
08/22/79

Gli Ultimi Tre Giorni
(The Last Three Days)
(Italy)
SCI. Enzo Porcelli, Antea Cooperativa, RAI prodn. Dir, Gianfranco Mingozzi. Cam, Safai Teherani; edtr, Sergio Nuti; mus, Nicola Piovani.   110.
Claudio Cassinelli, Lina Sastri, Franco Lotterio, Benedetto, Simonelli, Luigi Casellato, Mara Mariani.
08/31/77

Gloria
(France)
GAU. Prodn 2000. Wri-dir, Claude Autant-Lara from the book by Solange Bellegarde. Cam (Eastmancolor), Wladimir Ivanov; edtr, Robert/Monique Isnardon; mus, Bernard Gerard.   110.
Valerie Jeannet, Sophie Grimaldi, Nicole Maurey, Pierre Zimmer, Maurice Biraud, Jean Martinelli.
10/05/77

Gloria
COL. Wri-dir, John Cassavetes; cam, Fred Schuler; edtr, George C Villasenor; mus, Bill Conti; prod, Sam Shaw. (MPAA rating: PG).   123.
Gena Rowlands, John Adames, Buck Henry, Julie Carmen.
09/10/80

Gnezdo Na Vetru
(Nest in the Wind)
(USSR)
GOS. Tallinfilm Studio prodn, Tallin, Estonia, USSR. Dir, Olev Neuland. Sp, Isaak Fridbergas, Gregori Kanovichius; cam, Arvo Ikho; mus, Lepo Sumera.   95.
Rudolf Allabert, Nelli Taar, Evald Aavik, Tynu Kark, Anne Maayik.
07/23/80

Go For It
WOR. Wilt Chamberlain-Hal Jepsen presentation, prods, Paul Rapp, Richard Rosenthal; exec prod, Chamberlain. Dir, Rapp. Wri, Neil Rapp; cam (CFI Color), Rick Robertson, Pat Darren; edtr, John O'Connor; mus, Dennis Dragon. (MPAA rating: PG).   96.
(DOC)
07/28/76

Go On Mama: SEE *Vas Y Maman*

Go See Mother. . .Father Is Working: SEE *Va Voir Maman . . . Papa Travaille*

Go Tell the Spartans
AVE. Spartan Co prodn. Prod, Allan F Bodoh, Mitchell Cannold; exec prod, Michael Leone. Dir, Ted Post. Sp, Wendell Mayes, based on "Incident at Muc Wa" by Daniel Ford; cam (CFI Color), Harry Stradling, Jr; art dir, Jack Senter; edtr, Millie Moore; mus, Dick Halligan; asso prod, Jesse Corallo; cos, Ron Dawson; snd, Bill Randall. (MPAA rating: R).   114.
Burt Lancaster, Craig Wasson, Jonathan Goldsmith, Marc Singer, Joe Unger, Dennis Howard, David Clennon, Evan Kim.
06/14/78

God Bless Each Corner of This Room: SEE *Dios Bendiga Cada Rincon De Esta Casa*

God Told Me To
NW. Larco prodn. Wri-prod-dir, Larry Cohen. Mus, Frank Cordell. (MPAA rating: R). 87.
Tony Lo Bianco, Sandy Dennis, Sylvia Sidney, Sam Levene, Robert Drivas, Mike Kellin, Richard Lynch, Deborah Raffin.
12/01/76

God, Why Is There a Border In Love?: SEE Kamisama Naze Ai Ni Mo Kokkyo Ga Aru No

God Wills It So: SEE Dieu le veut

Godisnja Doba
(The Four Seasons)
(Yugoslavia)
ZAG. Zagreb Film prodn, Zagreb. Wri-dir, Petar Krelja. Cam, Ivica Rajkovic, Ante Verzotti; mus, Arsen Dedic. 85.
Slavko Stimac, Tatjana Ivko, Rajka Rusan, Marina Nemet, Sandra Langerholz, Boris Buzancic, Vanja Drach, Zvonko Torjaned, Lela Margetic.
09/05/79

The Godsend
CAN. Prod-dir, Gabrielle Beaumont; exec prods, Menahem Golan, Yoram Globus, Dennis Friedland. Sp, Olaf Pooley, based on the novel by Bernard Taylor; cam, Norman Warwick; edtr, Michael Ellis; mus, Roger Webb; art dir, Tony Curtis; snd, Aubrey Lewis; asso prod, Christopher Toyne; asst dir, Derek Whitehurst. (MPAA rating: R.) 90.
Cyd Hayman, Malcolm Stoddard, Angela Pleasence, Patrick Barr.
01/16/80

Godzilla vs. Megalon
(Japan)
CSH. Toho-Eizo film. (MPAA rating: G). 74.
06/16/76

Goin' Coconuts
OSM. Prod, John Cutts. Dir, Howard Morris. Sp, Raymond Harvey; cam (DeLuxe Color), Frank Phillips; edtr, Frank Bracht; snd, Herman Lewis; asst dir, Bob Huddleston. (MPAA rating: PG). 93.
Donny Osmond, Marie Osmond, Herbert Edelman, Kenneth Mars, Chrystin Sinclaire, Ted Cassidy, Marc Lawrence, Khigh Dhiegh, Harold Sakata, Charles Walker, Danny Wells, Jack Collins, Tommy Fujiwara.
10/11/78

Goin' Home
PTS. Wri-edtr-prod-dir, Chris Prentiss. Cam (DeLuxe Color), Prentiss, Christopher Sloan Nibley III; mus, Lee Holdridge; snd, Richard Portman, John Walker, Jan Brodin. (MPAA rating: G). 97.
Todd Christiansen, Bernard Triche, Kevin Oliver, Melvin Ruffin, Robert Dale Poole, Marion Forbes, Delia Bradford.
12/29/76

Goin' South
PAR. Prods, Harry Gittes, Harold Schneider. Dir, Jack Nicholson. Sp, John Herman Shaner, Al Ramus, Charles Shyer, Alan Mandel; cam, Nestor Almendros; edtrs, Richard Chew, John Fitzgerald Beck; snd, Arthur Rochester; asst dir, Michael Daves; prod des, Toby Carr Rafelson; cos, William Ware Theiss; mus, Van Dyke Parks, Perry Botkin Jr. (MPAA rating: PG). 101.
Jack Nicholson, Mary Steenburgen, Christopher Lloyd, John Belushi, Veronica Cartwright, Richard Bradford, Jeff Morris, Danny DeVito, Tracey Walter, Gerald H Reynolds, Luana Anders, George W Smith, Lucy Lee Flippin, Ed Begley Jr, Maureen Byrnes, B J Merholz, Britt Leach, Georgia Schmidt.
10/04/78

Going: SEE Gaman

Going for Broke: SEE Alt paa et braet

Going In Style
WB. Prods, Tony Bill, Fred T Gallo. Dir-wri, Martin Brest; exec prod, Leonard Gaines; cam, Billy Williams; edtrs, Robert Swink, C Timothy O'Meara; snd, James Sabat; prodn des, Stephen Hendrickson; art dirs, Gary Weist, Fred C Price; asst dir, Mike Rauch; mus, Michael Small. (MPAA rating: PG). 97.
George Burns, Art Carney, Lee Strasberg, Charles Hallahan, Pamela Payton Wright.
12/19/79

Going Steady: SEE Yotz'Im Kavua

Golapi Ekhon Trainey
(The Endless Trail)
(Bangladesh)
X. Prodn of Bangladesh Film Development Corp and Amjad Hossain Film Prodn. Wri-dir, Hossain, based on his book with same title. Cam, Rafiqul Bari Chowdhury; mus, Alauddin Ali; edtr, Enamul Huq; snd, Mustafe Kamal. 140.
Babita, Anwara, Roushan Jamil, Faruque, Rosy Samad, Anwar Hossain, A T M Shamsuzzaman, Abdullah Al-Mamun.
09/05/79

The Goldcabbage Family Breaks The Bank: SEE Familien Gyldenkaal Spraenger Banken

The Goldcabbage Family Gets The Vote: SEE Familien Gyldenkaal vinder valget

The Golden Lady
(Britain)
TGT. Jean Ubaud-Keith Cavele prodn. Exec prods, Jean Ubaud, Keith Cavele. Prod, Paul Cowan. Dir, Jose Larraz. Sp, Joshua Sinclair; cam, David Griffiths; mus, Georges Garvarentz; edtr, David Campling; art dir, Norris Spencer; cos, Sandy Moss; snd, Trevor Carliss; asst dir, Paul Fisher. 96.
Christina World, Suzanne Danielle, June Chadwick, Anika Pavel, Stephan Chase, Edward De Souza, David King, Patrick Newell, Richard Oldfield.
02/07/79

Golden Night: SEE Nuit D'Or

Golden Partners: SEE Ogon No Paatonaa

Golden Rendezvous
(Britain)
X. Film Trust-Milton Okun Prodns/Golden Rendezvous Prodns presentation. Exec prod, Murray Frank; prod, Andre Pieters. Dir, Ashley Lazarus. Sp, Stanley Price, based on the novel "The Golden Rendezvous," by Alistair MacLean; adaptation, John Gay; cam, Ken Higgins; edtr, Ralph Kemplen. 103.
Richard Harris, Ann Turkel, David Janssen, Burgess Meredith, John Vernon, Gordon Jackson, Keith Baxter, Dorothy Malone, John Carradine.
12/14/77

Golden Swan: SEE Hong Thong

Goldengirl
AVE. Backstage prodn. Prod, Danny O'Donovan. Exec prod, Elliot Kastner. Dir, Joseph Sargent. Sp, John Kohn, based on novel by Peter Lear; cam (Eastmancolor), Steven Larner; edtr, George Nicholson; snd, Don Sharpless; mus, Bill Conti; art dir, Syd Litwack; set decor, Gerald Adams; asst dir, Bill Martin. (MPAA rating: PG). 104.
Susan Anton, James Coburn, Curt Jurgens, Leslie Caron, Robert Culp, James A Watson Jr, Harry Guardino, Ward Costello, Michael Lerner, John Newcombe, Julianna Fjeld, Sheila DeWindt, Andrea Brown, Anette Tannander, Nicolas Coster.
06/20/79

Golem
(Poland)
POL. Film Polski prodn. Perspektywa Film Unit Warsaw. Dir, Piotr Szulkin. Sp, Szulkin, Tadeusz Sobolewski, based on and inspired by motifs in the legend and novel by Gustav Meyrink. Cam, Zygmunt Samosiuk; sets, Zbigniew Warpechowsi, Janusz Wlasow; prodn mgr, J Leszek Sobczyk. 92.
Marek Walczewski, Krystyna Janda, Joanna Zolkowska, Krzysztof Majchrzak, Mariusz Dmochowski, Wieslaw Drzewica, Henryk Bak, Wojciech Pszoniak, Jan Nowicki, Ryszard Pietruski, Andrzej Seweryn, Marian Opania, Boguslaw Sobczuk.
10/01/80

Golge
(W Germany)
Co-prod between Berlin Film & Television Academy (DFFB) and Sender Freies Berlin (SFB). Wri-dirs, Sema Poyraz, Sofoklis Adamidis; cam, Adamidis; snd, Nana Gravesen, Hanjo Breddermann; edtrs, Thomas Balkenhol, Eduard Genart; mus, Jo Liebau. 92.
Semru Uysal, Yuksel Topcugurler, Birgul Topcugurler, Fatos Alkan, Asil Basyildiz.
08/27/80

The Gong Show Movie
U. Prod, Budd Granoff. Dir, Chuck Barris. Sp, Barris, Robert Downey; cam (CFI color), Richard C Glouner; edtr, James Mitchell; snd, William Marky; art dir, Robert K Konoshita; asst dir, William H White; mus, Milton De Lugg. (MPAA rating: R). 89.
Chuck Barris, Robin Altman, Mabel King, Lillie Shelton, Jaye P Morgan, James B Douglas, Rip Taylor.
05/21/80

Good Evening, Irina: SEE Buna Seara, Irina

Good Evening to Everybody: SEE Magandang Gabi Sa Inyong Lahat

Good-For-Nothing: SEE Taugenichts

The Good Guys and the Bad Guys: SEE Le Bon Et Les Mechants

Good Guys Wear Black
AMC. Mar Vista Prodn. Dir, Ted Post. Prod, Allan F Bodoh; exec prod, Michael Leone. Sp, Bruce Cohn, Mark Medoff from story by Joseph Fraley; mus, Craig Safan. (MPAA rating: PG). 96.
Chuck Norris, Anne Archer, Lloyd Haynes, James Franciscus, Dana Andrews, Jim Backus.
06/28/78

Good Luck, Miss Wyckoff
BEG. Raymond Stross prodn. Prod, Raymond Stross. Asso prod, Robert Lecky. Dir, Marvin J Chomsky. Sp, Polly Platt, based on the novel by William Inge; cam (Metrocolor), Alex Phillips Jr; edtr, Rita Roland; mus, Ernest Gold; art dir, Jim Bissell; set decor, Roy Stennard; cos, Tom Rasmussen. (MPAA rating: R). 105.
Anne Heywood, Donald Pleasence, Robert Vaughn, Carolyn Jones, Dorothy Malone, Ronee Blakely, Dana Elcar, Doris Roberts, John Lafayette, Earl Holliman, Jocelyn Brando.
05/09/79

Good News: SEE Buone Notizie

Good Riddance: SEE Les Bons Debarras

The Good Thief: SEE Il Ladrone

Good-Bye Alicia: SEE Adios Alicia

Goodbye Emmanuelle
(France)
PFC. Trinacra Films-Parafrance prodn. Dir, Francois Leterrier. Sp, Leterrier, Monique Lange based on the characters of Emmanuelle Astier; cam (Eastmancolor), Jean Badal; edtr, Marie-Josephe Yoyotte; mus, Serge Gainsbourg. 95.
Sylvia Kristel, Umberto Orsini, Alexandra Stewart, Jean-Pierre Bouvier, Olga Georges Picot.
07/12/78

Goodbye, Flickmania
(Japan)
NIP. Kitty Films prodn. Prod, Hideto Isoda. Dir-sp, Masato Harada; cam, Genkichi Hasegawa; edtr, Ko Suzuki; mus, Ryudo Uzaki; art dir, Yuji Maruyama; snd, Senichi Beniya. 110.
Takuzo Kawatani, Naohiko Shigeta, Atsuko Asano, Renji Ishibashi, Hiromitsu Suzuki, Miyako Yamaguchi, Toby Kadoguchi, Yuji Kosugi.
(In Japanese with English subtitles)
12/19/79

The Goodbye Girl
WB. MGM/WB prodn. Prod, Ray Stark. Dir, Herbert Ross. Sp, Neil Simon; cam (Metroclor), David M Walsh; edtrs, Margaret Booth, John F Burnett; mus, Dave Grusin; song, David Gates; prodn des, Albert Brenner; set decor, Jerry Wunderlich; snd, Jerry Jost, William McCaughey, James Sabat (NY); cosward, Ann Roth, Seth Banks, Shirlee Strahm; asst dir, Jack Roe. (MPAA rating: PG). 110.
Richard Dreyfuss, Marsha Mason, Quinn Cummings, Paul Benedict, Barbara Rhoades, Theresa Merritt, Michael Shawn, Patricia Pearcy, Nicol Williamson.
11/16/77

Goodbye, Norma Jean
(Young Marilyn)
FWS. Mark Josem & Robert Ward presentation of Austamerican prodn. Prod-dir, Larry Buchanan. Sp, Lynn Hubert, Buchanan; exec prod, Amadeo Curcio; cam, Bob Sherry; mus, Joe Beck; theme song, "Norma Jean Wants to be a Movie Star," composed and sung by Johnny Cunningham. (MPAA rating: R). 95.
Misty Rowe, Terrence Locke, Patch Mackenzie, Preston Hanson, Marty Zagon, Andre Philippe, Ivey Bethune, Steve Brown, Adele Claire, Frank Curcio, Jean Sarah Frost, Stuart Lancaster, Lilyan McBride, Burr Middleton, Paula Mitchell, Garth Pillsbury.
01/28/76

Goodbye . . .See You Monday: SEE Au Revoir. . .A Lundi

Goodnight, Ladies and Gentlemen: SEE Signore E Signori, Buonanotte

Gori, Gori, Moja Zvezda
(Shine Brightly, My Star)
(USSR)
X. Mosfilm Studio prodn, Moscow. Dir, Alexander Mitta. Sp, Yuli Dunsky, Valery Fried, Mitta; cam, Yuri Sokol. 90.
Oleg Tabakov, Helena Proklova, Leonid Kuravlev, Yevgeni Leonov, Oleg Yefremov.
12/08/76

Gorp
AIP. Jeffery Konvitz prodn. Prods, Jeffrey Konvitz, Louis S Arkoff. Dir, Joseph Ruben. Sp, Konvitz, based on a story by Konvitz, Martin Zweiback; cam (Movielab), Michael Hugo; edtr, Bill Butler; asst dir, Chuck Russell. (MPAA rating: R). 90.
Michael Lembeck, Dennis Quaid, Philip Casnoff, Frank Drescher, David Huddleston, Robert Trebor, Lou Wagner, Richard Beauchamp, Julius Harris, Lisa Shure, Debi Richter, Rosana Arquette, Dale Robinette, Mark Deming.
05/07/80

Grabbes Letzter Sommer
(Grabbes Last Summer)
(W Germany)
X. Radio Bremen Prodn. Exec prod, Juergen Breest. Dir, Sohrab Shahid Saless. Sp, Thomas Valentin; cam, Rolf Romberg; sets, Guenther Naumann; cos, Ute Bergmann; edtr, Anna Koudelka; prodn mgr, Hans-Calixt Krug. 203.
Wilfried Grimpe, Renate Schroeter, Sonja Karzau, Marta Holler, Ulrich von Bock, Uwe Meister, Gabriele Fischer, Boris Guradze, Eberhard Fechner, Gunther Malzacher, Alexander Radzum, Heinz Rabe, Axel Ganz, Ruediger Schulzki, Kurt Ackermann, Jens Scholkmann, Norbert Kollakowsky, Frank Helmholz, Heinz Lieven.
(16m)
12/17/80

Gramma Ston Nazim Hikmet
(A Letter to Nazim Hikmet)
(Greece)
X. Positive EPE prodn. Wri-dir, Costas Aristopoulos. Commentator, Demetris Kamperides. 70.
10/27/76

The Grand Piano: SEE Royalut

Grand Theft Auto
NW. Prod, Jon Davison; exec prod, Roger Corman. Dir, Ron Howard; sp, Ranse Howard, Ron Howard; cam (Metrocolor), Gary Graver; 2d-unit cam, Jamie Anderson; edtr, Joe Dante; mus, Peter Ivers; art dir, Keith Michael; stunt coord, Allan Arkush; asst dir, Cal Naylor. (MPAA rating: PG). 89.
Ron Howard, Nancy Morgan, Marion Ross, Pete Isacksen, Barry Cahill, Hoke Howell, Lew Brown, Elizabeth Rogers, Ranse Howard, Don Steele, Paul Linke, Jim Ritz, Clint Howard.
06/15/77

Grandfather: SEE Fad, Jal

Grandma and the Eight Children in Town: SEE Mormor og de atte ungene i byen

The Grandmother: SEE La Nona

Grandpa Schulz: SEE Opa Schulz

The Grateful Dead
MNY. Exec prod, Ron Rakow. Prod, Eddie Washington; dir, Jerry Garcia. Edtr, Susan Crutcher; snd mix, Dan Healy (Burbank Studios); cam, Kevin Keating, Don Lenzer, Stephen Lighthill, Albert Maysles, David Myers, also Jonathan Else, Tom Hurwitz, Richard Panp, Robert Primes; ani, Gary Gutierrez; heavy water light show, Mary Anne Mayer, Joan Chase. (MPAA rating: PG).   131.
The Grateful Dead
(DOC)
06/08/77

Grauzone
(Zones)
(Switzerland)
CCZ. Nemo Film prodn. Wri-dir, Fredi M Murer. Cam (b&w), Hans Liechti; edtr, Rainer Trinkler; mus, Mario Beretta.   103.
Giovanni Fruh, Olga Piazza, Janet Huafler, Walo Luond.
(B & W)
08/22/79

Gray Lady Down
U. Mirisch Corp prodn. Prod, Walter Mirisch. Dir, David Greene. Sp, James Whittaker, Ronnie Cox, Dorian Harewood, Rosemary Forsyth, Hilly Hicks, Charles Cioffi. Howard Sackler, based upon the novel, "Event 1000" by David Lavallee; adaptation, Frank P Rosenberg; cam, Steven Larner; edtr, Robert Swink; mus, Jerry Fielding; prodn des, William Tuntke; set decor, John Dwyer; snd, John Kean, Kevin F Cleary; snd effects edtr, Peter Berkos; asst dir, Mack Bing; sfx, Curtis Dickson. (MPAA rating: PG).   111.
Charlton Heston, David Carradine, Stacy Keach, Ned Beatty, Stephen McHattie,
03/08/78

Grayeagle
AIP. Charles B Pierce film. Prod-dir-wri, Charles B Pierce. Prod, Tommy Clark; cam (Movielab Color)-edtr, Jim Roberson; mus, Jaime Mendoza-Nava; asst dir, Bud Davis; prodn mgr, Amy Roper; art dir, John Ball. (MPAA rating: PG).   104.
Ben Johnson, Iron Eyes Cody, Lana Wood, Jack Elam, Paul Fix, Alex Cord, Jacob Daniels, Jimmy Clem, Cindy Butler, Charles B Pierce, Blackie Wetzell.
12/28/77

Grease
PAR. Robert Stigwood, Allan Carr prodn. Dir, Randal Kleiser. Sp, Bronte Woodard; adapt, Allan Carr, based on orig mus by Jim Jacobs, Warren Casey; cam, Bill Butler; dances, musical sequences staged-chor, Patricia Birch; mus supv, Bill Oakes; edtr, John F Burnett; prodn des, Phillip Jefferies; cos, Albert Wolsky; set decor, James Berkey. (MPAA rating: PG).   110.
John Travolta, Olivia Newton-John, Stockard Channing, Jeff Conaway, Didi Conn, Jamie Donnelly, Dinah Manoff, Barry Pearl, Michael Tucci, Kelly Ward, Susan Buckner, Eddie Deezen, Lorenzo Lamas, Dennis C Stewart, Annette Charles, Dick Patterson, Fannie Flagg, Darrell Zwerling, Ellen Travolta, Eve Arden, Frankie Avalon, Joan Blondell, Edd Byrnes, Sid Caesar, Alice Ghostley, Dody Goodman, Sha Na Na.
(MUSICAL)
06/07/78

Greased Lightning
WB. Third World Cinema prodn, prod, Hannah Weinstein; exec prods, Richard Bell, J Lloyd Grant. Dir, Michael Schultz. Sp, Kenneth Vose, Lawrence DuKore, Melvin Van Peebles, Leon Capetanos; cam (Technicolor), George Bouillet; 2d unit cam, Richard Glouner; edtrs, Bob Wyman, Christopher Holmes, Randy Roberts; mus, Fred Karlin; song lyr, Bradford Craig, Norman Gimbel; art dir, Jack Senter; set decor, Jim Berkey; snd, Jim Cook, Wayne Hartman, Don Cahn, Willie Burton, Harland Riggs; cos-ward, Celia Bryant, Henry Salley; asst dirs, Terry Donnelly, Ken Swor; stunt coord, Ted Duncan. (MPAA rating: PG).   96.
Richard Pryor, Beau Bridges, Pam Grier, Cleavon Little, Vincent Gardenia, Richie Havens, Julian Bond, Earl Hindman, Minnie Gentry, Lucy Saroyan, Noble Willingham, Bruce Atkins, Steve Fifield, Bill Cobbs, Georgia Allen, Maynard Jackson, Danny Nelson, Cara Dunn, Alvin Huff, Willie McWhorter, Frederick Dennis Greene.
07/20/77

The Great American Bugs Bunny-Road Runner Chase
WB. Chuck Jones prodn. Prod-dir, Chuck Jones. Sp, Mike Maltese, Jones; prodn des, Maurice Noble; mus, Carl Stalling, Milt Franklyn; edtr, Treg Brown; graphics, Don Foster; "Bugs Bunny At Home" co-dir, Phil Monroe; prodn des, Ray Aragon; mus, Dean Elliott; edtr, Horta Editorial; voice, Mel Blanc. (MPAA rating: G).   97.
08/01/79
(ANI)

The Great Bank Hoax: SEE Shenanigans

The Great Day: SEE Una Giornata Speciale

The Great Document: SEE To Mega Docoumento

The Great Escape From Dien Bien Phu: SEE Haek Kai Narok Dien Bien Phu

The Great Gundown
SP. Prod, Paul Nobert; exec prod, John Leuthold. Dir, Paul Hunt. Sp, Steve Fisher; story, Robert Padilla, Hunt; cam (Technicolor), Ronald V Garcia; mus, Alan Caddy, Robert Fallon; edtr, Tony de Zarraga. (MPAA rating: PG).   95.
Robert Padilla, Malila St. Duval, Richard Rust, Steven Oliver, David Eastman, Stanley Adams, Rockne Tarkington, Michael Christian, Michael Green, Owen Orr.
08/10/77

The Great Indian Film Bazaar
(India)
KSH. Wri-dir, Sridhar Kshirsagar. Cam, S D Deodhar; edtr, Javed Sayyed.   150.
(DOC)
02/06/80

The Great Rock 'N' Roll Swindle
(Britain)
X. Kendon Film prodn in asso with Matrix Best and Virgin Records. Prods, Jeremy Thomas, Don Boyd. Dir-wri, Julian Temple. Cam (Kay Laboratories Ltd color), A Barker-Mills; edtrs, R Bedford, M D Maslin, G Swire; mus, The Sex Pistols; snd, John Lundsten, John Sanders, B R White, John Pierre Louvre; asst dirs, G White, Patrice Vanoni.   103.
Malcolm McLaren, Johnny Rotten, Sid Vicious, Steve Jones, Paul Cook, Ronnie Biggs, Liz Fraser, Jess Conrad, Mary Millington, Julian Holloway, James Aubrey, Johnny Shannon, Helen of Troy, Tenpole Tudor, Faye Hart, Alan Jones, Irene Handl.
03/05/80

The Great Rocky Mountain Jazz Party
X. Great Rocky Mountain Jazz Party prodn. Prods, Dick and Maddie Gibson. Dir-cam, Vilis Lapenieks. Edtrs, Rich and Bobby Meyer.   103.
Clark Terry, Zoot Sims, Phil Woods, Eubie Blake, Jon Faddis, Joe Venuti, Dick Hyman, Roger Kellaway, Ray Brown, Roland Hanna, Milt Hinton, Bob Wilder, Buddy DeFranco, Ruby Braff, Joe Newman, Ralph Sutton, Carl Fontana, Buddy Tate, Bill Watrous, Billy Butterfield, Budd Johnson, Pee Wee Erwin, Trummy Young.
(MUSICAL) (DOC)
04/26/78

The Great Santini
WBO. Bing Crosby Prods. Prod, Charles A Pratt. Wri-dir, Lewis John Carlino, based on novel by Pat Conroy; cam, Ralph Woolsey; edtr, Houseley Stevenson; snd, Lee Alexander; prodn des, Jack Poplin; asst dir, Edward Markley; set decor, Jeff Haley, Don Sullivan; aerial sequences, Clay Lacey; mus, Elmer Bernstein. (MPAA rating: PG).   115.
Robert Duvall, Blythe Danner, Michael O'Keefe, Lisa Jane Persky,

Julie Anne Haddock, Brian Andrews, Stan Shaw, Theresea Merritt, David Keith, Paul Mantee.
10/31/79

The Great Saturday: SEE Sao 5

The Great Scout & Cathouse Thursday
AIP. Jules Buck prodn. Prods, Buck and David Korda; exec prod, Samuel Z Arkoff. Dir, Don Taylor. Sp, Richard Shapiro; cam (Technicolor), Alex Phillips Jr; edtr, Sheldon Kahn; mus, John Cameron; prodn des, Jack Martin Smith; set decor, Enrique Esteves; snd, Ryder Sound Services, Manuel Topete; asst dir, Brad Aronson; stunt coord, Jerry Gatlin. (MPAA rating: PG). 102.
Lee Marvin, Oliver Reed, Robert Culp, Elizabeth Ashley, Strother Martin, Sylvia Miles, Kay Lenz, Howard Platt, Jac Zacha, Phaedra, Leticia Robles, Luz Maria Pena, Erika Carlson, C C Charity, Ana Verdugo.
06/16/76

The Great Smokey Roadblock
(The Last of the Cowboys)
DIM. Mar Vista, Ingo Preminger prodn. Wri-dir, John Leone. Cam, Ed Brown Sr; mus, Craig Safan; prod, Allan F Bodoh; exec prod, Michael Leone. (MPAA rating: PG). 100.
Henry Fonda, Eileen Brennan, Robert Englund, John Byner, Austin Pendelton, Susan Sarandon, Melanie Mayron, Marya Small, Leigh French, Dana House.
09/21/77

The Great Texas Dynamite Chase
(Canada)
NW. Yasny Talking Pictures II prodn. Prod, David Irving; exec prods, Marshall Backlar, Marshall Whitfield, Karen Whitfield. Dir, Michael Pressman. Sp, David Kirkpatrick, based on a story by Mark Rosin. Cam (Metrocolor), Jamie Anderson; edtr, Millie Moore; mus, Craig Safan; prodn des, Russel Smith; asst dir, Sean Daniel. (MPAA rating: R). 90.
Claudia Jennings, Jocelyn Jones, Johnny Crawford, Chris Pennock, Tara Strohmeier, Miles Watkins, Bart Braverman, Nancy Bleier, Buddy Kling.
08/18/76

Great Waves Purify the Sand: SEE Da Lang Tao Sha

The Greatest
COL. Prod, John Marshall. Dir, Tom Gries. Sp, Ring Lardner Jr, based on "The Greatest: My Own Story," Muhammad Ali, Herbert Muhammad, Richard Durham; cam (Metrocolor), Harry Stradling Jr; edtr, Byron Brandt; mus, Michael Masser; lyr, Linda Creed, Gerry Goffin; prodn des, Bob Smith; set decor, Solomon Brewer; snd, Bill Randall; cos-ward, Sandra Stewart, Eric Seelig; asst dir, Tom Shaw. (MPAA rating: PG). 101.
Muhammad Ali, Ernest Borgnine, John Marley, Lloyd Haynes, Robert Duvall, David Huddleston, Ben Johnson, James Earl Jones, Dina Merrill, Roger E Mosley, Paul Winfield, Annazette Chase, Mira Waters, Phillip MacAllister, Arthur Adams, Dorothy Meyer, Lucille Benson, Theodore R Wilson, Skip Homeier, Sally Gries.
05/25/77

The Greedy People: SEE Kilet Khon

The Greek Tycoon
U. Abkco Films prodn. Prods, Allen Klein, Ely Landau; exec prods, Mort Abrahams, Peter Howard, Les Landau; co-prods, Nico Mastorakis, Lawrence Myers. Dir, J Lee Thompson. Sp, Mort Fine from a story by Nico Mastorakis, Win Wells, Fine; cam (Technicolor), Tony Richmond; prodn des, Michael Stringer; edtr, Alan Strachan; mus, Stanley Myers; art dirs, Tony Readin, Gene Gurlitz, Mel Bourne; set decor, Vernon Dixon; snd, Robin Gregory; asst dir, Ariel Levy; asso prod, Eric Rattray. (MPAA rating: R). 106.
Anthony Quinn, Jacqueline Bisset, Raf Vallone, Edward Albert, James Franciscus, Camilla Sparv, Marilu Tolo, Charles Durning, Luciana Paluzzi, Robin Clarke, Kathryn Leigh Scott.
05/10/78

The Green Jacket: SEE La Giacca Verde

The Green Pastures: SEE Las Verdes Praderas

The Green Room: SEE La Chambre Verte

Grete Minde
(W Germany - Austria)
UA. Co-prodn between Solaris-Film, Peter Genee/Bernd Eichinger, Munich, and Zweites Deutsches Fernsehen (ZDF), Christoph Holch, Wiesbaden, in collab with Sascha-Film, Vienna. Wri-dir, Heidi Genee, based on Theodor Fontane's novel. Cam (Eastmancolor), Juergen Juerges; art dir, Hansjuergen Kiebach; mus, Niels Jannette Walen; cos, Ingrid Zore. 102.
Katerina Jacob, Siemen Ruehaak, Hannelore Elsner, Thilo Prueckner, Brigitte Grothum, Hilde Sessak, Martin Floerchinger, Kaethe Haack, Alexander May, W Wassmuth, K H Friedrich, Hans Christian Blech.
05/25/77

Grhana
(Eclipse)
(India)
HPP. Dir, T S Nagabharana. Sp, T S Ranga, Kodalli, Shivaram, Nagabharana; cam, S Ramachandra; edtr, J Stanley; mus, Vijaya Bhaskar. 125.
Anand Paricaran, Govind Rao, S N Rotti, B S Achar.
(B & W)
02/13/80

Griechische Feigen
(The Fruit Is Ripe)
(W Germany)
HBD. Lisa-Film, Munich, prodn. Dir, Siggi Goetz. Cam (Eastmancolor), Heinz Hoelscher; mus, Gerhard Heinz; prodn mgr, Erich Tomek. 90.
Betty Verges, Claus Richt, Olivia Pascal.
06/01/77

Griffin and Phoenix
FWS. ABC Circle Film in asso with Danny Thomas Prodns. Dir, Daryl Duke. Exec prod, Paul Junger Witt; prod, Tony Thomas. Sp, John Hill; cam, Richard C Glouner; mus, George Aliceson Tipton; title song wri-sung, Paul Williams. 94.
Peter Falk, Jill Clayburgh, George Chandler, John Harkins, Milton Parsons, Sally Kirkland, Russell Shannon, Irwin Charone, Caroline Yablans, John Lehne, Dorothy Tristan, Ben Hammer.
12/01/76

Grihapravesh
(The Housewarming)
(India)
PDI. Wri-dir, Basu Bhattacharya. Cam, Adeep Tandon; edtr, Om Prakash Takkar; mus, Kanu Roy; lyrs, Gular. 144.
Sanjeev Kumar, Sharmila Tagore, Sarika.
02/06/80

Grimaces
(Hungary)
HU. Dir-wris, Ferenc Kardos, Janos Rozsa. Cam, Sandor Sara; mus, Andras Szollosy. 77.
Istvan Geczy, Tundi Kassai, Rita Baranyai, Gabor Lontay.
10/22/80

Grizzly
FVI. Film Ventures Int'l and Edward L Montoro prodn. Prods, David Sheldon, Harvey Flaxman. Dir, William Girdler. Sp, Flaxman, Sheldon; mus, Robert O Ragland; color by Movie Lab; exec prod, Edward L Montoro. (MPAA rating: PG). 90.
Christopher George, Richard Jaeckel, Andrew Prine, Joan McCall, Joseph Dorsey, Maryann Hearn.
05/26/76

The Groper: SEE Le Trouble-Fesses

Gross Und Klein
(Big and Little)
(W Germany)
X. Regina Ziegler Film Production, in collab with the Schaubuehne am Halleschen Ufer, Berlin, and in co-prodn with Sender Freies Berlin (SFB). Dir, Peter Stein. Sp, Botho Strauss, adapt from his play; cam, Michael Ballhaus; sets, Fred Berndt; edtr, Clarissa Ambach. 240.
Edith Clever, Gunter Berger, Gerhard Bienert, Tina Engel, Johanna Hofer, Jutta Lampe, Hans Madin, Wilhelm Menne, Elke Petri, Udo Samel, Meray Uelgen, Hildegard Wensch.
07/02/80

Group Portrait with Lady:
SEE *Gruppenbild Mit Dame*

Growing Up Suddenly: SEE
Crecer De Golpe

Grozny Vek
(Ivan The Terrible)
(USSR)
SOV. Mosfilm prodn. Wri-dir, Vadim Derbeniov, Youri Grigorovitch, from Grigorovitch's ballet. Cam (Sovcolor), Vadim Derbeniov, Victor Pichtchalnikov; art dir, Valentin Vyrvytch, Youri Kokjaian. 100.
Youri Vladimirov, Natalia Bessmertnova, Boris Akimov, Bolshoi Ballet.
(BALLET)
11/16/77

Gruppenbild Mit Dame
(Group Portrait with Lady)
(W Germany - France)
UA. Les Artistes Asso prodn, Paris, in co-prodn with Stella Film/Cinema 77, Munich. Prod, Martin Hellstern. Dir, Aleksandar Petrovic. Sp, Petrovic, Heinrich Boell, based on Boell's novel; cam (Eastmancolor), Pierre William Glenn; art dirs, Reinhard Sigmund, Vlastimir Gavrik; snd, Gerhard Birkholz; asst dirs, Wigbert Wicker, Stevan Petrovic, Milan Dor; edtrs, Agape Dorstewitz, Marika Radvanyi; mus, Mozart and Schubert, Russian Folk Songs. 100.
Romy Schneider, Michel Galabru, Brad Dourif, Richard Muench, Fritz Lichtenhahn, Virus Zeplichal, Vadim Glowna, Milena Dravic, Ruediger Vogler, Rudolph Schuendler, Bata Zivojinovic, Gefion Helmke.
05/18/77

Grzeszny Zywot Franciszka Buly
(The Sinful Life of Franciszek Bula)
(Poland)
POL. Film Polski prodn, Silesia Film Unit, Warsaw. Wri-dir, Janusz Kidawa; cam, Zdzislaw Kaczmarek; sets, Jerzy Muller; mus, Zygmunt Zgraja; prodn mgr, Wanda Wojnarlliew. 106.
Andrzej Grabarczk, Jarek Antonik, Jerzy Cnota, Miroslaw Krawczyk, Adam Baumann, Henryk Stanek, Henryk Skolik, Tadeusz Cjrostek, Ginter Benkariek, Irena Moczygemba.
09/24/80

Gsaladi Tuzfezek
(Family Nest)
(Hungary)
HU. Bela Balasz Studio prodn. Wri-dir, Bela Tarr. Cam (b&w), Ferenc Pap, Barna Mihok; mus, Janos Brody. 115.
L Horvath, Laszlo Horvath, G Kun, Gabor Kun, Iren Racz.
(B & W)
02/28/79

The Guardian Angel: SEE
L'Ange Gardien

Guardian of the Wilderness
SSU. Prod, Charles E Sellier Jr. Dir, David O'Malley. Sp, Casey Conlon; based on story by Sellier. Cam, Henning Schellerup; mus comp-cond, Robert Summers; edtr, Sharron Miller; sfx, Doug Hubbard; art dir, Paul Staheli. (MPAA rating: G). 112.
Denver Pyle, John Dehner, Ken Berry, Cheryl Miller, Don Shanks, Cliff Osmond, Jack Kruschen, Prentiss Rowe, Brett Palmer, Melissa Jones, Ford Rainey.
03/02/77

The Guardians: SEE
Formynderne

The Guest at Steenkampskraal
(S Africa)
GST. Prod, Gerald Berman. Dir, Ross Devenish. Sp, Athol Fugard; cam, Rod Stewart; prodn des, Jeni Halliday; edtr, Lionel Selwyn; snd, Ian Ross. 105.
Athol Fugard, Marius Weyers, Gordon Vorster, Wilma Stockenstrom, James Borthwick, Emile Aucamp, Susan MacLennan, Trix Pienaar, Dan Poho.
03/09/77

Gui Xin Shi Jian
(Anxious to Return)
(China)
CFA. August First Film Studio prodn. Dir, Li Jun; sp, Li Keyi; cam, Yang Guangyang. 110.
Zhao Erkang, Siquin Gaowa, Ma Zhigang.
08/27/80

The Guignolo: SEE *Le Guignolo*

The Guinea Pig Couple: SEE
Le Couple Temoin

Gulliver's Travels
(Britain - Belgium)
EMI. Raymond Leblanc and Derek Horne prodn. Dir, Peter Hunt. Exec prod, Josef Shaftel. Sp-lyr, Don Black, based on the novel "Gulliver's Travels" by Jonathan Swift; cam (Eastmancolor), Alan Hume; prodn des, Michael Stringer; principal ani, Nic Broca, Marcel Colbrant, Vivian Miessen, Louis-Michel Carpentier, Jose Abel; backgrounds, Michel Leloup, Maddy Grogniet; cos, Anthony Mendelson; edtrs, Ron Pope, Robert Richardson. (MPAA rating: G). 80.
Richard Harris, Catherine Schell, Norman Shelley, Meredith Edwards.
With voices of: Michael Bates, Denis Bryer, Julian Glover, Stephen Jack, Bessie Love, Murray Melvin, Nancy Nevinson, Robert Rietty, Norman Shelley, Valdek Sheybal, Roger Snowden, Bernard Spear, Graham Stark.
(PART ANI)
08/03/77

The Gumball Rally
WB. First Artists prodn, prod-dir, Chuck Bail. Sp, Leon Capetanos, from a story by Bail, Capetanos; cam (Technicolor), Richard C Glouner; edtrs, Gordon Scott, Stuart H Pappe, Maury Winetrob; mus, Dominic Frontiere; art dir, Walter Simonds; set decor, Morrie Hoffman; snd, Arthur Piantadosi, Les Fresholtz, Michael Minkler, Bill Randall; asst dir, Frank Beetson; stunt coord, Eddy Donno. (MPAA rating: PG). 106.
Michael Sarrazin, Normann Burton, Gary Busey, John Durren, Susan Flannery, Harvey Jason, Steven Keats, Tim McIntire, Joanne Nail, J Pat O'Malley, Tricia O'Neil, Lazaro Perez, Nichols Pryor, Vaughn Taylor, Wally Taylor, Raul Julia.
07/28/76

The Gun: SEE *L'Arma*

Gunes Ne Zaman Dogacak
(When The Sun Rises)
(Turkey)
X. Orhun Filmcilik Prodn, Istanbul. Dir, Mehmet Kilinc. Sp, Tugan Guner; cam, Abdullah Gurek; mus, Tum Ata Grubu. 98.
Cuneyt Arkin, Oya Aydogan, Baki Tamer, Turgut Ozatay.
08/02/78

Gunesli Bataklik
(Sun Over The Swamp)
(Turkey)
X. Murat Film Prodn, Sureyya Duru, Istanbul. Dir, Sureyya Duru. Sp, Vedat Turkali; cam, Orhan Kapki; mus, Hursit Yenigun. 94.
Semra Ozdamar, Hakan Balamir, Aytac Arman, Cagaloglu, Ihsan Yuce.
08/16/78

Guns
(France)
SNX. Quasar prodn. Wri-dir, Robert Kramer; cam (Eastmancolor), Richard Kopans, Eric Pittard, Claude Michaud, Louis Bihi; edtrs, Valeria Sarmiento, Claudio Martinez; exec prod, Helene Vager. 95.
Patrick Bauchau, Juliet Berto, Peggy Frankston, Hermine Karagheuz, Beatrice Lord, Stephane Fey, Robert Kramer.
09/10/80

Gus
BV. Walt Disney prodn, prod, Ron Miller. Dir, Vincent McEveety. Sp, Arthur Alsberg, Don Nelson, from a story by Ted Key; cam (Technicolor), Frank Phillips; edtr, Robert Stafford; mus, Robert F Brunner; art dirs, John B Mansbridge, Al Roelofs; set decor, Frank R McKelvy; snd, Herb Taylor, Frank Regula; asst dir, Ronald R Grow; snd unit dir, Arthur J Vitarelli; stunt coord, Buddy Joe Hooker. (MPAA rating: G). 96.
Edward Asner, Don Knotts, Gary Grimes, Tim Conway, Liberty Williams, Dick Van Patten, Ronnie Schell, Bob Crane, Johnny Unitas, Dick Butkus, Harold Gould, Tom Bosley, Dick Enberg, George Putnam, Stu Nahan.
06/30/76

Gusanos De Seda
(Silk Worms)
(Spain)
X. Picasa prodn. Dir, Francisco Rodriguez. Exec prod, J A Cascales. Cam (Eastmancolor), Manuel Rojas; edtr, Eduardo Biurrun; sets, Jose Alguerol; sp, Ramon de Diego; mus, Emilio de Diego. 98.
Esperanza Roy, Antonio Ferrandis, Rafaela Aparicio, Alfredo Mayo, Agustin Gonzalez.
09/29/76

Guyana: Cult Of The Damned
(Mexico - Spain - Panama)
U. Prod-dir, Rene Cardona Jr. Sp, Carlos Valdemar, Cardona Jr; cam, Leopolda Villasenor; edtr, Earl Watson; mus, Nelson Riddle, Bob Summers, George S Price; snd, Simon Coke, Stephen Purvis, Dessy Markovsky; asst dir, Robert Schlosser. (MPAA rating: R). 90.
Stuart Whitman, Gene Barry, John Ireland, Joseph Cotton, Bradford Dillman, Jennifer Ashley, Yvonne De Carlo.
01/30/80

Gypsies Go To Heaven: SEE
Tabor Ollhodit Webo

Gziekolwiek Jestes, Panie Prezydencie
(Wherever You Are, Mr President)
(Poland)
X. Film Polski prodn, Warsaw, Film Unit "Tor." Dir, Andrzej Trzos-Rastawiecki. Sp, Wladislaw Terlecki, Trzos-Rastawiecki; cam (b&w), Zygmunt Samosiuk; sets, Zenon Rozewicz, Andrzej Kowalczyk; mus, Jerzy Maksymiuk; prodn mgr, Wielislawa Piotrowska. 90.
Henryk Czyz, Wanda Elbinska, Jozef Konieczny, Waldislaw Kozlow, Rudolof Golebiowski, Halina Labonarska, Andrzej Polkowski, Ryszard Sobolewski.
(B & W)
02/07/79

Ha Megjon Jozsef
(When Joseph Returns)
(Hungary)
HU. Budapest Studio prodn. Wri-dir, Zsolt Kezdi Kovacs. Cam (Eastmancolor), Janos Kende. 92.
Lili Monori, Eva Ruttkai, Gyogrgy Pogany, Gabor Koncz, Maria Ronyecz.
07/28/76

Hababam Sinifi Tatilde
(The Dunce Class On Vacation)
(Turkey)
X. Arzu Film Prodn, Istanbul. Dir, Ertem Egilmez. Sp, Sadik Sendil; cam, Erdogan Engin; mus, Melih Kibar. 100.
Munir Ozkul, Kemal Sunal, Sener Sen, Adile Nasit.
08/02/78

Habibeti-Ya Habba Atoot
(Sweet, Like Berries, My Love)
(Syria)
NCS. Nat'l Cinema Organization prodn, Syria. Wri-dir, Marwan Haddad, based on Ahmed Dawood's novel of same title. Cam, George Loutfi El Khoury, Mounir Gebawi; edtr, Marwan Akkowi; sets, Oussama Allash; prodn mgr, Amid Horani; drama consultant, Hassas Sami Joussef; rural milieu consultant, Nazih Abou Afash; asst dir, Zouheir Daioub; snd, Emil Saade. 105.
Abdul Hadi Sabbagh Nadin, Asad Fadda, Ahmed Addas, Joussef Hanna, Adnan Barakat, Housein Idilbi, Ingrid Jabbour, Nahed Halabi, Hassan Sami Joussef, Nazih Abou Afash, Adnan Habbal, Mohamed Horani, Jihad Saad, Mohamed Tarakji, Quamar Mortada, Hani Sadi, Yoland Asmar, Nabila Karam, Amal Hanna, Tewfiq Morad, Ibrahim Kurdie.
09/05/79

Hadashi No Gen
(Barefooted Gen)
(Japan)
GDA. Wri-dir, Tengo Yamada, from the book by Kenji Nakazawa. Cam (Eastmancolor), Shobun An; mus, Takeshi Shibuya. 107.
Rentaro Mikuni, Sachiko Hidari, Kenta Sato.
07/28/76

Haek Kai Narok Dien Bien Phu
(The Great Escape From Dien Bien Phu)
(Thailand)
HFT. Prod, Lek Kitiparaporn. Exec prod, Chari Amartyakul. Dir, Chumphorn Tepitak. Story, Sayoompoo Tosapon; sp, Pong Amart; cam, Saravuth Vuthichai; mus, Lek Kitiparaporn; edtr, Chari Amartyakul; art dir-prodn des, Urai Sirisombat; asst dir, Pao. 127.
Sombat Metanee, Nart Bhavanai, Yodchai Megsuan, Lak Apichat, Saard Piyampongsan, Tat Ekatat, So Asanachinda, Bu Vibulnan, Tarika Tarathit, Nawarat Yukthanan, Graham, Chat Jamrong, Chumphorn Tepitak.
11/23/77

Haervaerk
(Haroc)
(Denmark)
CTT. Lademann Film A/S prodn. Dir-edtr, Ole Roos. Sp, Klaus Rifbjerg, Ole Roos, based on Tom Kristensen novel; cam (Eastmancolor), Peter Roos; mus, Armstrong, Beiderbecke, etc; exec prod, Jacob Eriksen; cos, Ulla-Britt Soederlund; prod des, Bent Kielberg. 132.
Ole Ernst, Kirsten Peuliche, Jorgen Reenberg, Jesper Christensen, Ghita Noerby.
11/16/77

Haine
(Hate)
(France)
GAU. Radio-Cine/S Productions co-prodn. Wri-dir, Dominique Goult. Cam, Roland Dantigny; mus, Alain Jomy; edtr, Jean-Claude Bonfanti. 90.
Klaus Kinski, Maria Schneider, Patrice Melennes.
02/06/80

Hair
UA. Lester Persky-Michael Butler prodn. Dir, Milos Forman. Sp, Michael Weller, based on Gerome Ragni, James Rado and Galt MacDermot's musical play; cam, Miroslav Ondricek; chor, Twyla Tharp; mus, adapted and conducted by Galt MacDermot; lyr, Gerome Ragni, James Rado; cos, Ann Roth; prodn des, Stuart Wurtzel; edtr, Lynzee Klingman; 2d unit dir, Gerald Cotts; set decor, George De Titta; sfx, Al Griswold. (MPAA rating: PG). 118.
John Savage, Treat Williams, Beverly D'Angelo, Annie Golden, Dorsey Wright, Don Dacus, Cheryl Barnes, Richard Bright, Nicholas Ray, Charlotte Rae, Miles Chapin, Fern Tailer, Charles Deney, Herman Meckler, Agness Breen, Antonia Rey, George Manos, Linda Surh, Jane Brooke, Suki Love, Joe Acord, Michael Jeter, Janet York, Rahsaan Curry, Harry Gittleson, Donald Alsdurf, Steve Massicotte, Mario Nelson, Ben Woods.
03/14/79

Hajducka Vremena
(Daredevil's Time)
(Yugoslavia)
X. Jadran Film prodn, Zagreb. Dir, Vladimir Tadej. Sp, Branko Copic, Arsen Diklic, Vlastimir Radovanovic, Tadej; cam (Eastmancolor), Tomislav Pinter; art dir, Miomir Denic; mus, Zivan Cvitkovic. 92.
Boris Dvornik, Slavko Simic, Ruzica Sokic, Danilo Stojkovic, Nikola Simic, Mato Ergovic, Duro Utjesinovic, Olivera Markovic, Ivan Hajtl, Vesna Krajina, Dusko Bulajic, Zaim Muzaferija, Mile Rupcic, Aljosa Vuckovic.
03/02/77

Hajka
(Manhunt)
(Yugoslavia)
YFR. Centar FRZ SR Srbije prodn. Wri-dir, Zivojin Pavlovic. Cam (Eastmancolor), Jaksic Milorad. 93.
Rade Serbedzija, Pavle Vujisic, Boro Begovic, Ratislav Jovic, Zaim Musaferija.
08/17/77

Halbe-Halbe
(Fifty-Fifty)
(W Germany)
FDA. Prodn of DNS-Film Munich, in collaboration with Norddeutscher Rundfunk, Hamburg. Sp-dir, Uwe Brandner. Cam (b&w), Juergen Juerges; edtr, Helga Beyer; mus, J J Cale, Munich Factory, Peer Raben; prodn mgr, Denyse Noever. 105.
Hans Peter Hallwachs, Bernd Tauber, Agnes Duenneisen, Masch Gonska, Kai Fischer, Gerhard Olschewski, Nikolaus Dutsch, Alexandra Bogojevich, Beva McNeely, Joachim Regelien, Adrian Hoven, Ivan Desny, Alexander Allerson, Glenn Moray, Eva Schuckhardt.
(B & W)
03/29/78

Hallo, Baby
(Hello, Baby)
(Sweden)
SNA. Sandrews AB/Swedish Film Institute (Bengt Forslund) prodn. Dir, Johan Bergenstrahle. Story-sp, Maria-Louise de Geer Bergenstrahle; cam (Eastmancolor), Staffan Lamm; edtr, Lasse Hagstrom; mus, Julius Jacobsen, Richard Wagner; in charge of prodn, Jutta Ekman; prodn des, Birgitta Jonsson. 100.
Maria-Louise de Geer Bergenstrahle, Toivo Pawlo, Hakon Serner, Keve Hjelm.
03/10/76

Halloween
CFS. Falcon Int'l prodn. Prod, Debra Hill. Exec prod, Irwin Yablans. Dir, John Carpenter. Sp, Carpenter, Hill; cam, Dean Cundey; mus, Carpenter; edtrs, Tomy Wallace, Charles Burnstein; set decor, Craig Stearns; prodn des, Wallace; asst dir, Rick Wallace; snd, Tommy Causey. (MPAA rating: R). 93.
Donald Pleasence, Jamie Lee Curtis, Nancy Loomis, P J Soles, Charles Cyphers, Kyle Richards, Brian Andrews, John Michael Graham, Nancy Stephens.
10/25/78

Ham from the Ardennes:
SEE Jambon D'Ardenne

The Hamburg Syndrome:
SEE Die Hamburger Krankheit

Hamiskhak Ha'Amiti
(The Real Game)
(Israel)
X. Kayitz Films Prodn. Prod, David Tour. Asso prod, Amos Mokadi. Dir, Avi Cohen. Wri, Avi Cohen, Jonathan Aroch; cam, Danny Schneur; mus, Alona Tur-El; edtr, Anath Luberski; snd, Amnon Ben-Yaakov. 90.
Yossi Polack, Michal Bat-Adam, Gabi Amrani, David Ram, Izhak Haviss.
11/26/80

Hamlet
(Britain)
X. Royal College of Art prodn. Prod-dir, Celestino Coronado. Sp, Coronado (based on the play by William Shakespeare); cam, Robina Rose, Dick Perrin, A Humphreys; set des, Coronado, Anthony Meyer and students of the North London Polytechnic; cos, Mircea Marosin, Natasha Korniloff; mus, Carlos Miranda; edtrs, Richard Melling, Derek Wallbank. 65.
Anthony Meyer, David Meyer, Helen Mirren, Quentin Crisp, Barry Stanton, Vladek Sheybal.
12/01/76

Hanare Goze Orin
(Banished)
(Japan)
TOH. Prods, Kiyoshi Iwashita, Seikichi Izumi. Dir, Masahiro Shinoda. Based on novel by Tsutomu Minagami, adapt by Keiji Hasebe, Shinoda; cam, Kazuo Miyagawa; art dir, Kiyoshi Awazu; light, Takeharu Sano; mus, Toru Takemitsu; snd, Hideo Nishizaki. 109.
Shima Iwashita, Yoshhio Harada, Tomoko Naraoka, Taiji Tonoyama, Toru Abe, Jun Hamamura.
11/01/78

Hand of Death
(Hong Kong)
GHV. Wri-dir, Wu Yu-sheng. 95.
Tan Tao-Liang, James Tien, Chen Yuan-Lung, Chu Ching.
08/25/76

Handicapped Love: SEE
Behinderte Liebe

The Handyman: SEE Der
Gehulfe

Hang On, Doggy: SEE Teci,
Teci, Kuza Moj

Hangar 18
SSU. Prod, Charles E Sellier Jr. Dir, James L Conway; sp, Steven Thornley, based on a story by Tom Chapman, Conway. Cam (Technicolor), Paul Hipp; edtr, Michael Spence; sfx, Harry Woolman; optical effects supv, John Forrest. (MPAA rating: PG). 93.
Darren McGavin, Robert Vaughn, Gary Collins, James Hampton, Philip Abbott, Joseph Campanella, Pamela Bellwood, Tom Hallick, Steven Keats, William Schallert, Cliff Osmond, Andrew Bloch.
07/30/80

Hanover Street
(Britain)
COL. Lazarus/Hyams prodn. Prod, Paul N Lazarus III. Wri-dir, Peter Hyams. Cam, David Watkin; edtr, James Mitchell; prodn des, Philip Harrison; mus, John Barry; art dir, Malcolm Middleton, Robert Cartwright; snd, Robin Gregory; cos des, Joan Bridge; sfx, Martin Gutteridge. (MPAA rating: PG). 109.
Harrison Ford, Lesley-Anne Down, Christopher Plummer, Alec McCowen, Richard Masur, Michael Sacks, Patsy Kensit, Max Wall, Shane Rimmer.
05/16/79

The Happenings
(Hong Kong)
X. Raymond Chow Prodn. Prodn supv, Kitty Ip. Dir, Yim Ho. Sp, Shu Kei; Yim Ho; cam, Cheung Yiu Cho; edtr, Cheung Yiu Chung; theme songs wri, Stanley Pong, Ambrose Lo; sung by Patricia Chan; asst dirs, Shu Kei, Jobic Wong. 100.
Cheung, Kwok Keung, Lisa Yuen, Yim Chow Wah, Pejola Chu, Yim Chun Wah, Dick Keung.
(Cantonese soundtrack with English sub-titles)
05/07/80

Happiness Is So Near: SEE E
Atit De Aproape Fericirea

Happy Birthday, Gemini
UA. King Hitzig Prodn. Wri-dir, Richard Benner. Based on the play "Gemini" by Albert Innaurato. Prod, Rupert Hitzig. Exec prod, Alan King; cam, James B Kelly; edtr, Stephen Fanfara; mus, Rich Look, Cathy Chamberlain; prodn des, Ted Watkins. (MPAA rating: R). 107.
Madeleine Kahn, Rita Moreno, Robert Viharo, Alan Rosenberg, Sarah Holcomb, David Marshall Grant, Timothy Jenkins, David McIllwraith, Maura Swanson.
04/30/80
(B & W)

Happy Confusion: SEE Chuen
Chulamoon

Happy Day
(Greece)
X. Greek Film Centre prodn. Wri-dir, Pantelis Voulgaris, based on Andreas Fraguias novel, "Plague." Cam, George Panousopoulos; mus, Dionyssios Savopoulos; sets, Yannis Kalatzis. 101.
10/27/76

The Happy Hooker Goes Hollywood
CAN. Prods, Menahem Golan, Yoram Globus. Dir, Alan Roberts. Sp, Devi Goldenberg; cam, Stephen Gray; snd, Douglas Vaughan. (MPAA rating: R). 85.
Martine Beswicke, Adam West, Phil Silvers, Richard Deacon, Edie Adams, Chris Lemmon.
06/04/80

The Happy Hooker Goes To Washington
CAN. Movie Machine prodn; prod-dir, William A Levey. Exec prod, Alan C Marden; sp, Robert Kaufman; cam (Movielab Color), Robert Caramico; edtr, Lawrence Marinelli; snd, Richard Wagner; art dir, Robin Royce, B B Neel; cos, John David Ridge, Gail Viola; asst dir, John Patterson. (MPAA rating: R). 89.
Joey Heatherton, George Hamilton, Ray Walston, Jack Carter, Phil Foster, David White.
09/07/77

Happy New Year: SEE Buek

Harcmodor
(Strategy)
(Hungary)
HU. Mafilm-Dialog Studio prodn. Dir, Istvan Darday. Sp, Gyorgyi Szalai; cam (Eastmancolor), Lajos Koltai, Ferenc Papp. 164.
Ida Piri, Tivadar Kovacs, Kalman Feher, Janos Molnar, Janos Hegedus.
02/27/80

Hard Knocks
(Australia)
LYN. Andromeda Prodn. Prods, Don McLennan, Hilton Bonner; dir, Don McLennan; sp, McLennan, Bonner; cam, Zbigniew Friedrich; edtr, Friedrich; asst dir, Rod McNicol; snd, Lloyd Carrick; cos des, Julie Cutler, Penelope Hester. 85.
Tracey Mann, John Arnold, Bill Hunter, Max Cullen, Tony Barry,

Hilton Bonner, Kristy Grant.
10/08/80

Hardcore
COL. A-Team Prodn, prod, Buzz Feitshans. Wri-dir, Paul Schrader. Exec prod, John Milius. Cam, Michael Chapman; edtr, Tom Rolf; snd, Bud Maffett; prodn des, Paul Sylbert; art dir, Ed O'Donovan; asst dir, Richard Hashimoto; set decor, Bruce Weintraub; mus, Jack Nitzsche. (MPAA rating: R). 105.
George C Scott, Peter Boyle, Season Hubley, Dick Sargent, Leonard Gaines, David Nichols, Gary Rand Graham, Larry Block, Marc Alaimo, Leslie Ackerman, Charlotte McGinnis, Ilah Davis, Will Walker.
02/14/79

Hark to the Cock: SEE Chui Petela

Harlan County, U.S.A.
X. Cabin Creek Films prodn. Prod-dir, Barbara Kopple. Cam, Hart Perry, Kevin Keating, Phil Parmet, Flip McCarthy, Tom Hurwitz; edtrs, Nancy Baker, Mary Lampson, Lora Hays, Mirra Bank; snd, Kopple, Tim Colman, Josh Waletsky; mus, Merle Travis, David Morris, Nimrod Workman, Sarah Gunning, Hazel Dickens, Phyllis Boyens, Ms Raglin. (MPAA rating: PG). 103.
(DOC)
10/20/76

Harlequin
(Australia)
GUO. William Fayman's presentation of an Antony I Ginnane Prodn. Prod, Tony Ginnane. Exec prod, Bill Fayman. Dir, Simon Wincer. Asso prod, Jane Scott; sp, Everett De Roche; cam (Panavision-Eastmancolor), Gary Hansen; mus, Brian May; edtr, Adrian Carr; prodn des, Bernard Hides; sfx, Conrad Rothmann; asst dir, Mike McKeag; snd, Gary Wilkins. 96.
Robert Powell, Carmen Duncan, David Hemmings, Broderick Crawford, Gus Mercurio, Alan Cassell, Mark Spain, Sean Myers, Bevan Lee, Neville Teede, John Frawley, Mary Mackay, Alyson Best, Nita Pannell, Murray Ogden, Claus Schultz, Peter West, David Hough.
05/07/80

Haro
(Hue and Cry)
(France)
FLG. Cine Groupe 76-Audio-Spectacle Co-op prodn. Dir, Gilles Behat. Sp, Behat, Dominique Delpierre; cam (Fujicolor), Bernard Malaisy; edtr, Genevieve Vaury; mus, Jean-Michel Cayre. 100.
Jean-Claude Bouillon, Nathalie Courval, Laurent Malet, Valerie Maitresse.
03/01/78

Haroc: SEE Haervaerk

Harper Valley P.T.A.
APR. Exec prod, Phil Borack; prod, George Edwards. Dir, Richard Bennett. Sp, George Edwards, Barry Schneider, based on song "Harper Valley PTA", words and mus by Tom T Hall, sung by Jeannie C Riley; mus, Nelson Riddle; cam (DeLuxe), Willy Kurant; edtr, Michael Economu; art dir-cos, Tom Rasmussen; set decor, Bob Breen. (MPAA rating: PG). 93.
Barbara Eden, Ronny Cox, Nannette Fabray, Susan Swift, Louis Nye, Pat Paulsen, John Fiedler, Audrey Christie, DeVera Marcus, Irene Yah Ling Sun, Louise Foley, Clint Howard, Jan & Laura Teige, Pitt Hervert, Faye Dewitt, Molly Dodd, Ron Masak, Amzie Strickland, Brian Cook, Tobias Anderson, Bob Hastings, Arlene Stuart, J J Barry, Royce D Applegate, Whitey Hughes.
06/07/78

Harry and Walter Go to New York
COL. Prods, Don Devlin, Harry Gittes; exec prod, Tony Bill. Dir, Mark Rydell. Sp, John Byrum, Robert Kaufman, from a story by Devlin, Byrum; cam (Metrocolor), Laszlo Kovacs; edtrs, Fredric Steinkamp, David Bretherton, Don Guidice; mus, David Shire; lyr, Alan and Marilyn Bergman; prodn des, Harry Horner; art dir, Richard Berger; set decor, Ruby Levitt; snd, Arthur Piantadosi, Barry Thomas; asst dir, Jerry Ziesmer; spec asst, Joe Layton. (MPAA rating: PG). 120.
James Caan, Elliott Gould, Michael Caine, Diane Keaton, Charles Durning, Lesley Ann Warren, Val Avery, Jack Gilford, Dennis Dugan, Carol Kane, Kathryn Grody, David Proval, Michael Conrad, Burt Young, Bert Remsen.
06/16/76

Harukanaru Yama No Yobigoe
(A Distant Cry From Spring)
(Japan)
SKU. Prod, Kiyoshi Shimazu. Dir, Yoji Yamada. Sp, Yoji Yamada, Yoshitaka Asama; from a story by Yamada. Cam, Tetsuo Tekaba; art dir, Mitsuo Idegawa; mus, Masaru Sato. 124.
Ken Takakura, Chieko Baisho, Hidetaka Yoshioka, Mizuho Suzuki, Hajime Hana, Hideo Jimbo, Go Awazu.
05/28/80

Harvest: 3,000 Years
(Ethiopia)
X. Wri-prod-dir-edtr, Haile Gerima. Cam, Elliot Davis. 138.
Kasu Asfaw, Werke Abraha, Melaku Mekonnen, Adane Melaku, Gebru Kassa, Haregewen Tefferi, Nuguse Nailu.
(B & W) (16m)
04/07/76

Hasereth Festival Hayeladim
(The Children Song Festival - The Movie)
(Israel)
X. Classipop Prodn. Prods, Avshalom Rubin, Alex Barnea; exec prod, Tommy Lang; dir, Ilan Eldad; cam, Yehiel Neeman, Amnon Salomon, Danny Schneur, Yaakov Eisenman, Avi Daphna; edtr, Rachel Yagil; mus dir, Uri Kariv; cond, Itzhak Graziani. 84.
Mike Burstein, Igal Bashan, Rikki Gal, Dori Ben-Zeev, Ariel Zilber, Sexta, Ruchama, Dudu Zakkai, Jerry Heyman, Suzy Miller, Rachel Levin, Aharon Israeli, Jenny Blum, Ravith Berger, Limor Nachum, Israel Gurion, Ezra Dagan, Dorinne Caspi.
(DOC)
08/06/80

Hasta Que El Matrimonio Nos Separe
(Till Divorce Us Do Part)
(Spain)
X. Agata Films - Jose Luis Dibildos prodn. Dir, Pedro Lazaga. Sp, Jose Luis Dibildos, Antonio Mingote; cam (Eastmancolor), Manuel Rojas; edtr, Petra de Nieva; mus, Antonio Garcia Abril. 89.
Jose Sacristan, Maria Luisa San Jose, Roxanne Bach, Cristina Galbo, Juan Luis Galiardo, Mary Carrillo, Emilio Gutierrez Caba, Silvia Tortosa, Antonio Casas, Sandra Mozarovsky, Monica Randall.
03/23/77

Hate: SEE Haine

The Haunting of M
X. Prod-dir, Anna Thomas; sp, Thomas; cam, Gregory Nava; edtr, Michael Bockman, Trevor Black, Thomas; snd, Robert Yerington; asso prods, Gregory Nava, Robert Yerington. 98.
Sheelagh Gilbey, Nini Pitt, Evie Garratt, Alan Hay, Jo Scott Matthews, William Bryan, Peter Austin, Peter Stenson, Ernest Bale, Isolde Cazelet, Varvara Pepper.
11/28/79

Haunts
ICR. Prods, Herb Freed, Burt Weisbourd. Dir, Herb Freed. Sp, Anne Marisse, Freed; cam (Eastmancolor), Larry Secrist; asst dir, David McGiffert. (MPAA rating: PG). 98.
May Britt, Aldo Ray, Cameron Mitchell, William Gray Espy, Susan Nohr, Ben Hammer, E J Andre, Kendall Jackson.
07/20/77

Hauptlehrer Hofer
(Schoolmaster Hofer)
(W Germany)
X. FFAT-Film prodn, in collab with Westdeutsches Fernsehen (WDR), Cologne. Dir, Peter Lilienthal. Sp, Lilienthal, Herbert Broedl, Guenter Herburger, based on a story by Herburger; cam, Kurt Weber; edtr, Heidi Gene; mus, Robert Eliscu. 90.
Andre Watt, Sebastian Bleisch, Kim Parnass, Gerhard Sprunkel, Bernhard Jenn,

Reinhard Puetz, Tilo Prueckner, Eva Pampuch, Hanna von Rezzori, Pierre Pasquay.
02/09/77

Hauptmann Kreutzer
(Captain Kreutzer)
(W Germany)
X. Sunny Point, Multimedia and Bayerischer Rundfunk prodn. Dir-wri, Klaus Emmerich. Cam (Eastmancolor), Frank Bruehne; edtr, Thea Eymes; sets, Hans Gailling, Jurgen Karsch. 91.
Ruediger Vogler, Axel Wagner, Joerg Hube, Vitus Zeplichal, Kurt Weinzierl, Claus-Dieter Reents.
07/06/77

Hawk The Slayer
(Britain)
ITC. Chips Production presentation. Prod, Harry Robertson. Exec prod, Bernard J Kingham. Dir, Terry Marcel. Sp, Terry Marcel, Harry Robertson; cam, Paul Beeson; mus, Harry Robertson; edtr, Eric Boyd Perkins; art dir, Michael Pickwoad; stunts, Eddie Stacey; sfx, Effects Associates. 93.
Jack Palance, John Terry, Bernard Bresslaw, Ray Charleson, Peter O'Farrell, Morgan Sheppard, Cheryl Campbell, Annette Crosbie, Catriona MacColl, Shane Briant, Harry Andrews, Christopher Benjamin, Roy Kinnear, Ferdy Mayne, Graham Stark, Warren Clarke, Deelan Mulholland, Derrick O'Connor, Peter Benson.
12/24/80

Hawmps
MLB. Prod-dir, Joe Camp; co-prod, Ben Vaughn; exec prod, A Z Smith. Sp, William Bickley, Michael Warren, from story by Bickley, Warren, Camp; cam (CFI Color), Don Reddy; edtr, Leon Seith; mus, Euel Box; prodn des, Harland Wright; art decor, Ned Parsons; snd, Bruce Shearin; asst dir, Terry Donnelly; stunt coord, George Fisher. (MPAA rating: G). 126.
James Hampton, Christopher Connelly, Slim Pickins, Denver Pyle, Gene Conforti, Mimi Maynard, Jack Elam, Lee de Broux, Herb Vigran, Jesse Davis, Frank Inn.
05/26/76

Hayam Ha' Acharon
(The Last Sea)
(Israel)
X. Teudah Films & Lohamei HaGetaot House Prodn. Prods, Benny Shilo, Yehezkel Avneri. Dirs, Haim Guri, Jaquot Erlich, David Bergman. Cam, Emil Knebel; advisers, Yehuda Bauer, Gavriel Cohen; edtrs, Yoske Rabinovitz, Yehuda Hellman, Itzhak Sternberg, Uzi Harpaz; mus, Yossi Mar-Haim; mus advisers, Gil Aldema, Eliahu Hacohen. 100.
(DOC) (B & W)
05/07/80

Hazal
(Turkey)
UMU. Dir, Ali Ozgenturk. Sp, Onat Kutlar, Ozgenturk; cam (Eastmancolor), Muzaffer Turan; mus, Arif Sag. 90.
Turkan Soray, Talat Bulut, Meral Cetinkaya, Husedin Peyda, Keriman Ulusoy.
05/21/80

The Hazing
MRS. Robert Fridley/Dick Davis prodn. Prods, Douglas Curtis, Bruce Shelly. Dir, Curtis. Sp, Shelly, David Ketchum, based on an idea by Shelly; mus, Ian Freebairn-Smith. (MPAA rating: PG). 90.
Jeff East, Brad David, David Hayward, Charlie Martin Smith, Sandra Vacey, Kelly Moran, Jim Boelsen.
01/18/78

H.C. Andersen I Italien
(Denmark - Italy)
IDI. IDI prodn (Rome). Wris, Ulla Kampmann, Fernando Cavaterra. Dir, Cavaterra. Cam (blown-up 16m, color), Roberto Nappar, Gregers Nielsen, Tue Ruetzow; edtr, Riccardo Parmigiano; mus, Steven Schlacks, Lars Fjeldmose. 70.
Jesper Klein, Sune Schmidt, Jytte Abildstroem, Maude Berthelsen, Henrik Stangerup, Palle Schmidt.
(DOC)
04/18/79

He Is Heading To The Glory Again: SEE Ke Xana Pros Ti Doxa Trava

He Knows You're Alone
MGM. Lansbury/Beruh prodn. Prods, George Manasse, Robert Di Milia, Nan Pearlman; exec prods, Edgar Lansbury, Joseph Beruh; dir, Armand Mastroianni; sp, Scott Parker; cam (Metrocolor), Gerald Feil; edtr, George T Norris; mus, Alexander Peskanov, Mark Peskanov; art dir, Susan Kaufman; snd, Rolf Pardula; asst dir, Costa Mantis. (MPAA rating: R). 92.
Don Scardino, Caitlin O'Heaney, Elizabeth Kemp, Tom Rolfing, Lewis Arlt, Patsy Pease, James Rebhorn, Tom Hanks, Dana Barron, Joseph Leon, Paul Gleason, James Carroll.
08/27/80

He Never Gives Up
(Taipei)
07/25/79
CMT. Prod, Mei Chang-Ling. Dir, Lee Hsing. Exec prod, Koo Chen Fu. Story, Cheng Feng Shih; sp, Chang Yung Hsiang; cam, Chen Kuen Howe; lighting, Lin Den Huang; snd, Lee Ya Tong; mus, Tang Wong. 115.
Chin Han, Lin Feng-Chiao, Tsao Chien, Liu Meng Yian, Ou Di.

The Head: SEE Al Raas

The Head of Normande St. Onge: SEE La Tete De Normande St. Onge

Head On
(Canada)
X. Michael Grant film prodn. Prods, Michael Grant, Alan Simmonds. Dir, Grant. Sp, James Sanderson, Paul Illidge; cam, Anthony Richmond; prodn des, Antonin Dimitrov; mus, Peter Mann; edtr, Gary Oppenheimer; asst dirs, Mac Bradden, John Board. 98.
Sally Kellerman, Stephen Lack, John Huston, Lawrence Dane, John Peter Linton, Mina E Mina,

Hadley Kay, Robert Silverman, Maxwell Moffett.
10/01/80

Head Over Heels
UA. Triple Play prodn. Prods, Mark Metcalf, Amy Robinson, Griffin Dunne. Dir-wri, Joan Micklin Silver, based on the novel "Chilly Scenes of Winter" by Ann Beattie. Cam, Bobby Byrne; edtr, Cynthia Schneider; mus, Ken Lauber; prodn des, Peter Jamison; set decor, Linda Spheeris; cos des, Rosanna Norton; snd, Ron Curfman; asst dir, Lorin B Salob. (MPAA rating: PG). 97.
John Heard, Mary Beth Hurt, Peter Riegert, Kenneth McMillan, Gloria Grahame, Nora Heflin, Jerry Hardin, Tarah Nutter, Alex Johnson, Mark Metcalf, Angela Phillips, Griffin Dunne, Allan Joseph.
10/24/79

The Headless Ghost: SEE Pi Hua Kad

Heads or Tails: SEE Pile ou Face

Health
FOX. Lion's Gate Films prodn. Dir, Robert Altman; sp, Frank Barhydt, Paul Dooley, Altman; cam, Edmond Koons; snd, Bob Gravenor; edtr, Dennis M Hill. (MPAA rating: PG). 102.
Glenda Jackson, Carol Burnett, James Garner, Lauren Bacall, Dick Cavett, Paul Dooley, Henry Gibson.
08/27/89

The Hearse
CWN. Marimark prodn. Prods, Mark Tenser, Charles Russell; exec prod, Newton P Jacobs; dir, George Bowers; sp, Bill Bleich, from idea by Tenser; cam (Metrocolor), Mori Kawa; edtr, George Berndt; mus, Webster Lewis; art dir, Keith Michl; snd, Jan Brodin; asst dir, John Curran. (MPAA rating: PG). 95.
Trish Van Devere, Joseph Cotten, David Gautreaux, Donald Hotton, Med Flory, Perry Lang.
09/24/80

Heart Beat
WBO. Edward R Pressman prodn. Prods, Alan Greisman, Michael Shamberg; wri-dir, John Byrum; exec prods, Edward R Pressman, William Tepper; cam (Technicolor), Laszlo Kovacs; edtr, Eric Jenkins; mus, Jack Nitzsche; prodn des, Jack Fisk; cos, Patricia Norris; snd, Bill Kaplan; 2d unit dir, Gary Kibbe; asst dir, Bill Scott. (MPAA rating: R). 109.
Nick Nolte, Sissy Spacek, John Heard, Ray Sharkey, Anne Dusenberry, Margaret Fairchild, Tony Bill, Kent Williams, Stephen Davies, Jenny O'Hara, John Larroquette, Ray Vitte.
12/05/79

Heart of Glass: SEE Herz Aus Glas

Heart of the Forest: SEE El Corazon del Bosque

Heartbreak People: SEE Huadjai Ti Jom Din

Heartland
X. Wilderness Women's Prodns-Filmhaus prodn. Dir, Richard Pearce. Sp, Beth Ferris based on books and papers of Elinore Randall Stewart; cam, Fred Murphy; edtr, Bill Yahrus; mus, Charles Gross. 95.
Conchata Ferrell, Rip Torn, Barry Primus, Lilia Skala, Megan Folsom.
03/12/80

Heartland Reggae
(Canada)
X. Canada Offshore Cinema Ltd prodn. Prod-dir, J P Lewis. Sp, Lewis, John Sutton Smith; cam, Lewis, John Swabey, T Marsh; edtrs, Lewis, Randall Torno, John Mayes. 87.
Bob Marley and the Wailers, Peter Tosh, Jacob Miller and the Inner Circle Band, Althea and Donna, Dennis Brown, Little Jr Tucker, Judy Mowat, The I-Threes, U-Roy. (16m)
03/26/80

Hearts High: SEE Hjerter Er Trumf

Heave Up: SEE Hiev Up

Heaven and Hell: SEE Yompaban Cha

Heaven Can Wait
PAR. Sp-(with Elaine May)-prod-dir (with Buck Henry) Warren Beatty; exec prods, Howard W Koch Jr, Charles H Maguire. Based on the play by Harry Segall; cam (Movielab Color), William A Fraker; edtrs, Robert C Jones, Don Zimmerman; mus, Dave Grusin; prodn des, Paul Sylbert; art dir, Edwin O'-Donovan; set decor, George Gaines; snd, John K Wilkinson, Tommy Overton; cos-ward, Theadora Van Runkle, Richard Bruno, Mike Hoffman, Arlene Encell; asst dir, Koch. (MPAA rating: PG). 100.
Warren Beatty, Julie Christie, James Mason, Jack Warden, Charles Grodin, Dyan Cannon, Buck Henry, Vincent Gardenia, Joseph Maher, Dolph Sweet, R G Armstrong, John Randolph, William Sylvester, Keene Curtis, Hamilton Camp, Jeannie Linero, Arthur Malet, Stephanie Faracy.
06/28/78

Heaven's Gate
UA. Dir-wri, Michael Cimino. Prod, Joann Carelli. Exec in chg of prodn, Denis O'Dell, Charles Okum. Cam (Technicolor), Vilmos Zsigmond; edtrs, Tom Rolf, William Reynolds, Lisa Fruchtman, Gerald Greenburg; art dir, Tambi Larsen; mus, David Mansfield; cos, Allen Highfill; cho, Eleanor Fazan; prodn mgrs, Charles Okum, Bob Grand, Peter Price; asst dirs, Michael Grillo, Brian Cook; snd edtrs, Richard W Adams, Winston Ryder. (MPAA rating: R). 219.
Kris Kristofferson, Christopher Walken, John Hurt, Sam Waterston, Brad Dourif, Isabelle Huppert, Joseph Cotten, Jeff Bridges, Roseanne Vela, Ronnie Hawkins, Geoffrey Lewis.
11/26/80

Heavy Trouble: SEE Barra Pesada

Heinrich
(W Germany)
CII. Regina Ziegler Film prodn, Berlin, in collab with Westdeutscher Rundfunk (WDR), Cologne. Wri-dir, Helma Sanders-Brahms. Cam, Thomas Mauch; art dirs, Goetz Heymann, Guenter Naumann; cos, Barbara Baum; make-up, Barbara Naujok; prodn mgr, Michael Boehme. 135.
Heinrich Giskes, Grischa Huber, Hannelore Hoger, Lina Carstens, Siegfrit Steiner.
05/18/77

Heinrich Heine Revue
(W Germany)
PTP Peter Thomas Production, Duesseldorf. Dir, Guenter Fiedler. Based on Guenther Buech's Revue at the Kammerspiele Duesseldorf. Text, Heinrich Heine; cam, Juergen Schuermann; sets, Lioba Winterhalder; mus, Peter Jassens, Peter Frass-Wolfsburg; chor, Marlis Gruenberg; snd, Werner Vitalis; light and assistance, Hans Hoffmann. 90.
Katrin Schoenermark, Dagmar Soerensen, Ilona Wiedem, Georg Cadalbert, Klaus Jaegel, Manfred Repp, Michael Thiele. (16m)
09/10/80

The Heist: SEE El Apando

Hello, Baby: SEE Hallo, Baby

Hemat i natten
(Homeward in the Night)
(Sweden - Finland)
SVF. Finnkino (Helsinki)/Swedish Film Institute prodn. Wri-dir, Jon Lindstroem. Cam (Eastmancolor), Billie August; edtr, Irma Taina; mus, Heikki Valpola; exec prod, Joern Donner. 90.
Lasse Hjelt, Gunvor Sandkvist, Gunnel Fred, Rita Holst.
05/25/77

Hempas Bar
(Hempa's Bar)
(Sweden)
SVF. Bengt Forslund prodn. Dir, Lars G Thelestam. Story-sp, Bosse Andersson; cam (Eastmancolor), Joergen Persson; edtr, Sylvia Ingemarsson; mus, Bjoern Isfaelt and Elvis Presley; prodn des, Carl Johan de Geer; executive prod, Bo A Vibenius. 102.
Krister Hell, Jan Nielsen, Harriet Andersson, Carl-Axel Heiknert.
10/19/77

Her Family Jewels
(Britain)
MSY. Oscarina Films prodn. Dir, Martin Campbell. Mus, Mike Vickers, Chris Spierer, Michael Kaufman. (Self-imposed X rating). 86.
Nigil Evans, Elisabeth Aubrey, Edmond Searle, Colin Taylor, Megan Ross.
01/21/76

Herbie Goes Bananas
BV. Walt Disney prodn. Prod, Ron Miller. Dir, Vincent McEveety. Co-prods, Kevin Concoran, Don Tait. Sp, Tait, based on characters created by Gordon Buford; cam (Technicolor), Frank Phillips; edtr, Gordon D Brenner; mus, Frank De Vol; songs, De Vol; art dirs, John B Mansbridge, Rodger Maus; set decors, Norman Rockett, Roger M Shook; sfx, Art Cruickshank, Danny Lee; matte artist, Constantine Ganakes; 2d unit dir, Michael Dmytryk; asst dir, Win Phelps. (MPAA rating: G). 100.
Cloris Leachman, Charles Martin Smith, John Vernon, Stephan W Burns, Elyssa Davalos, Joaquin Garay III, Harvey Korman, Richard Jaeckel, Alex Rocco, Fritz Feld.
07/02/80

Herbie Goes to Monte Carlo
BV. Walt Disney prodn, prod, Ron Miller. Dir, Vincent McEveety. Sp, Arthur Alsberg, Don Nelson, based on characters created by Gordon Buford; cam (Technicolor), Leonard J South; mus, Frank De Vol; 2d unit dir, Arthur J Vitarelli; edtr, Cotton Warburton; art dirs, John B Mansbridge, Perry Ferguson; addl pho, Charles F Wheeler; asst dir, Paul "Tiny" Nichols; cos, Chuck Keehne, Emily Sundby; snd, Herb Taylor, Hal Etherington; sfx, Eustace Lycett, Art Cruickshank. (MPAA rating: G). 105.
Dean Jones, Don Knotts, Julie Sommars, Jacques Marin, Roy Kinnear, Bernard Fox, Eric Braeden, Xavier Saint Macary, Francoise Lalande, Alan Caillou, Laurie Main, Mike Kulcsar, Stanley Brock, Gerard Jugnot, Jean-Marie Proslier, Tom McCorrey, Lloyd Nelson, Jean-Jacques Moreau, Yveline Briere, Sebastian Floche, Madeleine Damien, Alain Janey, Raoul Delfosse, Ed Marcus.
06/22/77

Here Come The Tigers
AIP. Prods, Sean S Cunningham, Stephen Miner. Dir, Sean S Cunningham. Sp, Arch McCoy; cam (Movielab Color), Barry Abrams; mus, Harry Manfredini; edtr, Stephen Miner; art dir, Susan E Cunningham; asst prod, Cindy Veazey; asst dir, Nancy Hart; snd, Max Kalmanowicz. (MPAA rating: PG). 90.
Richard Lincoln, James Zvanut, Samantha Grey, Manny Lieberman, William Caldwell, Fred Lincoln, Xavier Rodrigo, Kathy Bell, Noel John Cunningham, Sean P Griffin, Max McClellan, Kevin Moore.
05/31/78

The Hereafter of Terror: SEE Mas Alla Del Terror

Here's Looking At You, Kid
BIM. Prod, Andrew McGuire, for the Burn Council of San Francisco General Hospital. Dir, William E Cohen; cam, Cohen, Paul Shain, Maggie Cole; edtr, Cohen; light, Barbara Dunn; snd, Jay Litvin, Andy Wiskes. 53.
Maggie Cole, Rob Cole, Andrew McGuire. (DOC)
10/08/80

Herfra min verden gaar
(The Wellsprings of My World)
(Denmark)
DAG. Kollektiv Film prodn. Wri-dir, Christian Braad Thomsen. Cam (Eastmancolor), Dirk Bruel; edtr, Grethe Moldrup; mus, anonymous Danish country musicians; in charge of prodn, Nina Crone. 80.
Anonymous citizens.
(DOC)
02/18/76

The Heritage: SEE Arven

The Heritage: SEE Orokseg

The Heritage: SEE Slaegten

Herkulesfurdoi Emlek
(A Strange Role)
(Hungary)
X. Hunnia Studio prodn. Dir, Pal Sandor. Sp, Zsuzsa Toth; cam (Eastmancolor), Elemer Ragalyi; mus, Zdenko Tamassy. 89.
Endre Holman, Erzsebet Kutvolgyi, Ildiko Pecsi, Sandor Szabo, Margit Dayka, Irma Patkos, Maria Lazar, Hedi Temessy, Dezso Garas, Carla Romanelli.
03/02/77

Hero At Large
MGM. Prod, Stephen Friedman. Dir, Martin Davidson. Sp, A J Carothers; cam (Metrocolor), David M Walsh; edtr, David Garfield; snd, Tommy Overton; prodn des, Albert Brenner; asst dir, Jack Roe; art dir, Norman Baron; mus, Patrick Williams. (MPAA rating: PG). 98.
John Ritter, Anne Archer, Bert Convy, Kevin McCarthy, Harry Bellaver, Anita Dangler, Jane Hallaren, Leonard Harris, Rick Podell.
02/06/80

Heroes
U. Prods, David Foster, Lawrence Turman. Dir, Jeremy Paul Kagan. Sp, James Carabatsos; cam (Technicolor), Frank Stanley; edtr, Patrick Kennedy; mus, Jack Nitzsche, Richard Hazard; prodn des, Charles Rosen; set decor, James Payne; snd, David S Ronne, Bill Varney; asst dir, Jon Anderson. (MPAA rating: PG). 113.
Henry Winkler, Sally Field, Harrison Ford, Val Avery, Olivia Cole, Hector Elias.
11/02/77

Heroes Are Not Wet Behind the Ears: SEE Les Heros N'Ont Pas Froid Aux Oreilles

Heroin: SEE Eroina

The Heroines of Evil: SEE Les Heroines du Mal

Herz Aus Glas
(Heart of Glass)
(W Germany)
CIG. Werner Herzog Film Produktion prodn. Wri-dir, Werner Herzog from a book by Herbert Achternbusch. Cam (Eastmancolor), Jorg Schmidt-Reitwein; edtr, Beate Mainka-Jellinghaus. 93.
Sepp Bierbichler, Clemens Scheitz, Stefan Guettler, Sonja Skiba.
12/01/76

Het Verloren Paradise
(Lost Paradise)
(Belgium)
ELN. Pierre Films Prodn. Prod, Jacqueline Pierreux. Dir, Harry Kumel. Sp, Harry Kumel, Kees Sengers; cam (Eastmancolor), Kenneth Hodges; edtr, Suzanna Rosberg; art dir, Pilippe Graff; mus, Roger Mores; snd, Henri Morelle; asst dirs, Dominique Janne, Maurice Noben. 95.
Willeke Van Ammelrooy, Hugo Van den Berghe, Hans De Waegeneer, Bert Andre, Gella Allaert, Stephen Windros, Blanka Heirman, Jos Kennis, Serge Henri Valcke, Nora Barten, Alfred Van Kuyck, Carlos Van Lanckere, Martha Woumans, Willy De Swaef, Raf Reymen, Gerda Lindekens, Nolle Versyp.
09/27/78

Heung
(Jealousy)
(Thailand)
TMK. Prod, Pratuang Trimek. Dir, Rangsri Tasanapayak. Story, Kwanmitr Nabangchang; sp, Panya Somsuan; cam, Tira Ekalat; edtr, Mahasak Tasanapayak; prodn des-art dir, Chuwit Opermpon. 120.
Sombat Metanee, Aranya Namwong, Sirikwan Nantasiri, Prachuab Lerkyamdi, Suwin Swangrat, Jaratsi Sayasirapin, Uma Ayathit.
08/10/77

Hey Mister I Am Your Wife: SEE Hoy Mister Ako Ang Misis Mo

Hidden in the Sunlight: SEE Ukryty W Sloncu

Hide And Seek
(Philippines)
X. MVN Cinema prodn. Prod, Manuel Nieto 3d. Dir, Joey Gosiengfiao. Sp, Toto Belano; cam, Edgardo Venarao; mus, Demet Velasquez. 106.
Christopher De Leon, Elizabeth Oropesa, Rosemarie Gill, Anthony Alonzo, Sandy Garcia, Laurice Guillen.
09/15/76

Hide In Plain Sight
UA. Metro-Goldwyn-Mayer film. Prods, Robert Christiansen, Rick Rosenberg. Dir, James Caan. Sp, Spencer Eastman, based on a book by Leslie Waller; cam (Metrocolor), Paul Lohmann; edtrs, Fredric Steinkamp, William Steinkamp; mus, Leonard Rosenman; prodn des, Pato Guzman; set decor, Mary Swanson; snd, Gene S Cantamessa; asst dir, David McGiffert. (MPAA rating: PG). 92.
James Caan, Jill Eikenberry, Robert Viharo, Joe Grifasi, Barbara Rae, Kenneth McMillian, Danny Aiello, Thomas Hill, Chuck Hicks, Andrew Gordon Fenwick, Heather Bicknell, David Margulies.
03/19/80

Hide 'n Seek: SEE Miskhak Makhbuim

The Hiding Place: SEE Das Versteck

Hidir
(Turkey)
X. Bizim Film Prodn, Cengiz Nacaroglu, Istanbul. Dir, Yavuz Figenli; sp, Ahmet Undag, Ihsan Yuce; cam, Rafet Siriner. 81.
Behcet Nacar, Menderes Samancilar, Gonul Eren, Kazim Kartal.
08/02/78

Hiev Up
(Heave Up)
(E Germany)
DEE. DEFA Film Prodn, in collaboration with GDR Television, Berlin. Wri-dir, Joachim Hasler. Cam, Peter Krause; sets, Georg Wratsch; mus, Gert Natschinski; edtr, Annelise Hinze-Sokolowa. 90.
Alfred Mueller, Regina Beyer, Juergen Heirich, Solveig Mueller, Dietmar Richter-Reineck, Madeleine Lierck, Fred Delmare, Renate Mallon, Ruediger Joswig, Erik S Klein, Ostara Koerner, Frank Strobel, Peter Friedrichson, Armin Muehlstaedt.
06/28/78

High Anxiety
FOX. Crossbow prodn. Prod-dir, Mel Brooks. Sp, Brooks, Ron Clark, Rudy DeLuca, Barry Levinson; cam (Deluxe Color), Paul Lohmann; edtr, John C Howard; prodn des, Peter Wooley; mus, John Morris; special visual effects, Albert J Whitlock; cos, Patricia Morris; prodn mgr, Ernest Wehmeyer; asst dir, Jonathan Sanger; set decor, Richard Kent, Anne MacCauley. (MPAA rating: PG). 94.
Mel Brooks, Madeline Kahn, Cloris Leachman, Harvey Korman, Ron Carey, Howard Morris, Dick Van Patten, Jack Riley, Charlie Callas, Ron Clark, Rudy DeLuca, Barry Levinson.
12/21/77

High-ballin'
AIP. Stanley Chase/Pando Co prodn. Prod, Jon Slan; exec prods, Stanley Chase, William Hayward. Dir, Peter Carter. Sp, Paul Edwards from a story by Richard Robinson and Stephen Schneck; cam (Movielab Color), Rene Verzier; art dir, Claude Bonniere; edtr, Eric Wrate; mus, Paul Hoffert; asst dir, Tony Thatcher; snd, Douglas Ganton; stunt coords, Gary Davis, Bud George Davis; sfx, Richard Helmer. (MPAA rating: PG). 100.
Peter Fonda, Jerry Reed, Helen Shaver, Chris Wiggins, David Ferry, Chris Langevin.
06/07/78

High Rolling
(Australia)
RDP. Hexagon prodns film. Prod, Tim Burstall. Dir, Igor Auzins. Sp, Forest Redlich; mus, Sherbet; cam, Dan Burstall; art dir, Leslie Binns; edtr, Edward Queen-Mason; stunts, Grant Page; asso prod, Alan Finney; prodn administrator, Robert Kirby. 89.
Joseph Bottoms, Grigor Taylor, Judy Davis, John Clayton, Wendy Hughes, Sandy McGregor, Simon Chilvers, Gus Mercurio, Robert Hewitt, Roger Ward, Peter Cummins.
07/06/77

High Street: SEE Rue Haute

High Velocity
MAN. Prod, Takashi Ohashi. Dir, Remi Kramer; exec prod, Joseph Wolf; asso prod, Michael J Parsons; sp, Kramer, Parsons; mus, Jerry Goldsmith.   106.
Ben Gazzara, Britt Ekland, Paul Winfield, Keenan Wynn, Alejandro Rey, Victoria Racimo.
09/28/77

The Hills Have Eyes
(London)
X. Blood Relations Co prodn. Prod, Peter Locke. Dir-sp, Wes Craven. Cam, Eric Sadrinen; edtr, Craven; art dir, Robert Burns; mus, Don Peake.   89.
Susan Lanier, Robert Houston, Virginia Vincent, Russ Grieve, Dee Wallace, Martin Speer, Brenda Marinoff, Flora, Stricker, James Whitworth, Cordy Clark, Janus Blythe, Michael Berryman, Lance Gordon, Arthur King, John Steadman.
12/20/78

Hinotori
(Japan)
TOH. Toho-Hinotori prodn. Exec prods, Kichi Ichikawa, Kunihiko Murai; dir, Kon Ichikawa; sp, Shuntaro Tanikawa; orig story, Osamu Tezuka; cam, Kiyoshi Hasegawa; sfx, Teruyoshi Nakano; ani, Tezuka Prodn; mus, Michel Legrand, Jun Fukamachi.   137.
Tomisabuuro Wakayama, Masao Kusakari, Kaoru Yumi, Reiko Ohara, Mieko Takamine, Tatsuya Nakadai.
10/22/80

Hirok Rajar Deshe
(The Kingdom of Diamonds)
(India)
X. GOVWB Prodn. Wri-dir-mus-lyr, Satyajit Ray. Cam, Soumendu Roy; edtr, Dulal Dutta; art dir, Ashoke Bose.   118.
Soumitra Chatterji, Utpal Dutt, Rabi Ghose, Tapen Chatterji, Samtosh Dutta.
12/17/80

Hirourzi
(Surgeons)
(Bulgaria)
BGO. BulgaroFilm prodn, Mladost Group, Sofia. Dir, Ivanka Grubcheva. Sp, Georgi Danailov; cam, Yatsek Todorov; art dir, Konstantin Roussakev; mus, Kiril Tsiboulka.   103.
Vassil Mihailov, Mihail Mihailov, Anton Radichev, Anghel Lambev, Iskra Radeva, Tsvetana Maneva, Stoycho Mazgalov, Lyudmilla Cheshmedjieva.
05/31/78

His Fight: SEE Sein Kampf

His Master's Eye: SEE L'Oeil du Maitre

Histoire D'Adrien
(Adrien's Story)
(France)
X. Dir, Jean-Pierre Denis. Sp, Denis, Francoise Dudognon; cam, Denis Gheerbrant; edtrs, Catherine Madilat, Patrick Genet, Danielle Lacoste.   90.
Bertrand Sautereau, Serge Dominique, Pierre Dienaide, Marcelle Dessalles, Marie Vergoat, Nadine Reynaud, J P Geneste.
(16m)
05/21/80

Historien om en Moder
(The Story of a Mother)
(Denmark)
SFK. Claus Weeke/The Danish Film Studio prodn. Prodn subsidized by Privatbanken (Copenhagen) and UNESCO (Paris). Dir, Claus Weeke. Sp, Paul Gegauff, Claus Weeke, based on Hans Christian Andersen story. Cam (Eastmancolor), Dirk Bruel; edtr, Lars Brydesen; mus, Mozart quotes; prodn mgr, Jacob Eriksen.   52.
Anna Karina, Daniel Duvall, Tove Maes, Bodil Udsen, Gustaf Hagstroem.
10/31/79

Hit Song: SEE Schlager

The Hitchhiker: SEE Stopar

Hitler, A Career: SEE Hitler, eine Karriere

Hitler, A Film From Germany
(W Germany - Britain - France)
X. TMS Film (Munich), WDR (Cologne), BBC (London), INA (Paris) prodn. Exec prod, Harry Nap; dir-sp, Hans-Jurgen Syberberg; pho, Dietrich Lohmann; edtr, Jutta Brandstaedter; snd, Heymo H Heyder; asst dir, Gerhard von Halem; prod mgr, Bernd Eichinger.   400.
Heinz Schubert, Harry Baer, Hellmuth Lange, Peter Moland, J Buzalsky, Andre Heller, Peter Kern, Rainer V Artenfels, Martin Sperr, Peter Luhr.
11/30/77

Hitler, eine Karriere
(Hitler, A Career)
(W Germany)
ITR. Interart, Munich, prodn. Dir, Joachim C Fest, Christian Herrendoerfer; Sp, Fest; research, Herrendoerfer, Dieter Kautzner, Lutz Becker, Werner Rieb; prodn mgr, Gerd Beham; sfx, Theo Nischwitz; snd, Willi Swadorf; edtr, Fritz Schwaiger; mus, Hans Posegga; prod, Werner Rieb.   150.
(DOC) (16m)
06/29/77

Hjerter Er Trumf
(Hearts High)
(Denmark)
LAD. Crone/Lars Brydesen prodn. Dir-edtr, Lars Brydesen. Sp, Brydesen, based on his orig story, and Jannick Storm, cam (Panavision/Eastmancolor), Mikael Salomon; mus, Hans Erik Philip; in charge of prodn, Christian Clausen.   115.
Lars Knutzon, Ann Mari Max Hansen, Ulla Gottlieb, Morten Grunwald, Bent Christensen, Klaus Pagh.
04/07/76

Hodina Pravdy
(The Hour Of Truth)
(Czechoslovakia)
CZS. Czechoslovensky Film Prodn, Studio Barrandov, Prague. Wri-dir, Vaclav Matejka, based on a radio play by Natasha Tanska; cam, Jaromir Sofr.   90.
Svatopluk Matyas, Ruzena Merunkova, Hana Maciuchova, Eliska Sirova, Jana Gyrova, Vladimir Brodsky, Jiri Pieskot, Rudolf Jelinek.
08/02/78

Hoer, var der ikke en, som Io?
(Did Somebody Laugh?)
(Denmark)
WCT. Dagmar (for SAM Films) prodn. Wri-dir, Henning Carlsen, based freely on novel by Eigil Jensen; cam (Eastmancolor), Henning Kristiansen; mus, Corelli, Smetana, Krystof Komeda; edtr, Henning Carlsen (with Christian Hartkopp); exec prod, Nina Crone.   100.
Jesper Christensen, Kirsten Olesen, Otto Brandenburg, Jessper Klein, Karl Stegger, Jens Okking.
09/20/78

Hog Wild
(Canada)
AVE. Filmplan International prodn. Exec prods, Pierre David, Victor Solnicki, Stephen Miller. Prod, Claude Heroux. Dir, Les Rose. Sp, Andrew Peter Marin based on an orig concept by Victor Solnicki, Stephen Miller; cam, Rene Verzier; art dir, Carol Spier; edtr, Dominique Boisvert; asst dir, John Fretz; snd, Don Cohen. (MPAA rating: PG).   97.
Michael Biehn, Patti D'Arbanville, Tony Rosato, Angelo Rizacos, Martin Doyle, Matt Craven, Matt Birman-Feldman, Claude Philippe, Thomas C Kovacs, Jacoba Knaapan, Michael Zelniker, Karen Stephen, Jack Blum, Stephanie Miller, Keith Knight, Mitch Martin, Robin McCulloch.
06/11/80

Hoito Rabu
(White Love)
(Japan)
TOH. Toho-Hori Pro co-prodn. Prods, Tsugunobu Hori, Hideo Sasai. Dir, Shusei Kotani. Sp, Toshiya Fujita, Tatsuo Kobayashi, based on work by Nichiko Nakagawa; cam, Kenji Hagiwara; snd, Noobumasa Fukushima; art dir, Mugen Sakaguchi; edtr, Osamu Inoue; asst dir, Yoshihisa Nakagawa.   110.
Momoe Yamaguchi, Tomokazu Miura, Kazuo Kitamura, Bunjaku Han, Yoshiki Kobayashi, Kaneko Iwasaki, Saeko Nagashima.
03/05/80

Holka Na Zabiti
(A Girl Fit To Be Killed)
(Czechoslovakia)
CZS. Barrandov Studio prodn. Dir, Juraj Herz. Sp, Josef Silhavy; cam (Eastmancolor), Andrej Baroa; mus, Bohuslav Ondracek. 97.
Dasa Veskrnova, Ilja Prachar, Vit Olmer, Josef Abrham, Karel Augusta, Zofie Vesela.
07/28/76

Hollywood Boulevard
NW. Prod, Jon Davison. Dir, Joe Dante, Allan Arkush. Sp, Patrick Hobby; cam (Metrocolor), Jamie Anderson; 2d unit cam, Eric Saarinen; edtrs, Amy Jones, Arkush, Dante; mus, Andrew Stein; art dir, Jack DeWolfe; snd, Bob Haddonfield; stunt coord, C D Smith. (MPAA rating: R). 83.
Candice Rialson, Mary Woronov, Rita George, Jeffrey Kramer, Dick Miller, Richard Doran, Tara Strohmeier, Paul Bartel, Jonathan Kaplan, George Wagner, John Kramer, W L Luckey, Charles B Griffith, Joe McBride, Milt Kahn, Todd McCarthy, Commander Cody and the Lost Planet Airmen.
04/28/76

The Hollywood Knights
COL. Polygram Pictures prodn. Prod, Richard Lederer. Exec prod, William Tennant. Dir, Floyd Mutrux. Sp, Mutrux, based on a story by Mutrux, Lederer, Tennant; cam (Metrocolor), William A Fraker; supv edtr, Danford B Greene; edtrs, Stan Allen, Scott Conrad; art dir, Lee Fischer; set decor, Bruce Kay; cos, Darryl Levine; snd Bill Randall; asst dir, Luigi Alfano. (MPAA rating: R). 91.
Fran Drescher, Leigh French, Randy Gornel, Gary Graham, Sandy Helberg, James Jeter, Stuart Pankin, P R Paul, Michelle Pfeiffer, Gailard Sartain, Richard Schaal, Robert Wuhl, Tony Danza.
05/21/80

Hollywood on Trial
X. Cinema Associates-October Films presentation. A James Gutman-David Helpern Jr prodn. Dir, Helpern. Prod, Gutman; asso prods, Frank Galvin, Juergen Hellwig; cam, Barry Abrams; wri, Arnie Reisman; edtr, Galvin. 105.
Walter Bernstein, Alvah Bessie, Lester Cole, Gary Cooper, Howard DaSilva, Walt Disney, Edward Dmytryk, Millard Lampell, Ring Lardner Jr, Sen Joseph McCarthy, Albert Maltz, Ben Margolis, Louis B Mayer, Adolph Menjou, Zero Mostel, Otto Preminger, Ronald Reagan, Martin Ritt, Gale Sondergaard, Robert Taylor, Leo Townsend, Dalton Trumbo.
(DOC) (16m)
06/09/76

Holocaust 2000
(Italy - Britain)
FIA. Prod by Edmondo Amati for Embassy Prodns (Rome) and Aston Film (London). Dir, Alberto De Martino. Sp, Sergio Donati, Aldo De Martino, Michael Robson; cam (Technicolor), Enrico Menczer; art dir, Umberto Betacca; edtr, Vincenzo Tumassi; mus, Ennio Morricone. 102.
Kirk Douglas, Agostina Belli, Simon Ward, Anthony Quayle, Virginia McKenna, Alexander Knox, Romolo Valli, Massimo Foschi.
01/11/78

The Holy Alliance: SEE A Santa Alianca

The Holy Year: SEE L'Annee Sainte

Homage To Chagall - The Colours Of Love
(Canada)
X. Prod-dir-wri, Harry Rasky. Cam, Kenneth W Gregg; edtr, Arla Saare; mus, Lou Applebaum; snd, Erik Hoppe; ani cam, Robert Mistysyn. Narr (English version), James Mason, Joseph Wiseman. 90.
(DOC)
05/18/77

Hombre del Puente
(Man on the Bridge)
(Mexico)
PEX. Conacine-STPC co-prodn. Dir, Rafael Baledon. Story-sp, Julio Alejandro; cam, Miguel Arana; edtr, Adolfo Rosas Priego; mus, Cesar Carrillon. 100.
Gregorio Casals, Diana Bracho, Rogelio Guerra, Jorge Russek, Wolf Rusinskys.
10/13/76

Home Movies
X. SLC Films prodn. Prods, Brian De Palma, Jack Temchin, Gil Adler. Dir, Brian De Palma. Sp, Robert Harders, Gloria Norris, Kim Ambler, Dana Edelman, Stephen Le May, Charles Loventhal, from story by De Palma; cam, James L Carter; edtr, Corky Ohara; art dir, Tom Surgal; Rachel Feldman; snd, Rick Wadell; mus, Pino Donaggio. 90.
Kirk Douglas, Nancy Allen, Keith Gordon, Gerrit Graham, Vincent Gardenia, Mary Davenport, Captain Haggerty, Bunny.
09/19/79

Homeland Fever: SEE Shigaon Shel Moledeth

Hometown USA
FVI. Baer/Camras prodn. Prod, Roger Camras, Jesse Vint. Dir, Max Baer. Story-sp, Jesse Vint; cam (CFI color); edtr, Frank Morris; mus coord, Marshall Leib. (MPAA rating: R). 93.
Gary Springer, David Wilson, Brian Kerwin, Pat Delaney, Julie Parsons.
07/04/79

Homeward in the Night: SEE Hemat i natten

Homicides: The Criminals, Part II
(Hong Kong)
SHW. Shaw Bros prodn. Dir, Keui Chih-hung, Hua Shan, Sun Chung. Wri, Yi Kuang, Szu Tu-an.
The Silent Killer- Cast: Han Kuo-tsai, Mai Meihua, Yang Tse-lin.
Mama-San- Cast: Rosie, Kang Kai, Mi Lan.
The Informer- Cast: Kang Kai, Han Kuo-tsai.
Nude in the Box- Cast: Lin Wei-tu, Wang Hsieh.
09/01/76

The Homosexual Century: SEE Race D'Ep

Honey: SEE La Miel

The Honey Flowers: SEE Les Fleurs Du Miel

Honeymoon: SEE Honning Maane

Honeymoon: SEE Taxidi Toy Melitos

The Honeymoon Trip: SEE Le Voyage De Noces

Honeysuckle Rose
WB. Prod, Gene Taft. Exec prod, Sydney Pollack. Dir, Jerry Schatzberg. Sp, Carol Sobieski, William D Wittliff, John Binder; cam (Technicolor), Robby Muller; edtrs, Aram Avakian, Norman Gay, Marc Laub, Evan Lottman; snd (Dolby Stereo), Arthur Rochester; prodn des, Joel Schiller; asst dir, David McGiffert; cos, Jo Ynocencio; mus, Willie Nelson, Richard Baskin. (MPAA rating: PG) 119.
Willie Nelson, Dyan Cannon, Amy Irving, Slim Pickens, Joey Floyd, Charles Levin, Priscilla Pointer, Mickey Rooney, Jr, Pepe Serna, Lane Smith, Diana Scarwid, Emmylou Harris, Rex Ludwick, Mickey Raphael.
07/16/80

Hong Kong Emmanuelle
(Hong Kong)
CIA. Dir, Man Hwa. 100.
Deborah, Li Tao Hung, Liu Tse Win, Liu Ah Yin, Jenifer Lau.
(Mandarin soundtrack)
04/06/77

The Hong Kong Tycoon
(Hong Kong)
DRO. Dir, Cecille Tang Shuen. 100.
Michael Lai, Tina Ti, Linda Liu, Leung Shing Po.
(English subtitles)
08/01/79

Hong Thong
(Golden Swan)
(Thailand)
NFT. Prod, Kiat lampungporn. Dir, Sakka Charuchinda. Story, Seni Busapaketr, Prae Choompoo; sp, Tanachai Chinotai; cam, Sompote Akarapin; edtr, Narong Charuchinda; mus, Uan Singyao. Title song, "Hong Thong," mus-lyr, Surapon Torawannit, sung by Chintana Kitiyapan. 125.
Pairoj Sangboriboot, Aranya Namwong, Leoh Yong Seow, Yodchai Megsuan, Pairoj Jaising, Liew Hoo Yu, Sayant Chantrawiboon, Lee Fang Feh, Fang Ye, Bu Vibulnan, William F Steven, Jr,

Jaruwan Panyopat, Orasa Pompatan, Kotai Lutaipracha.
09/14/77

Honjin Satsujin Jiken
(Death at an Old Mansion)
(Japan)
X. Takabayashi Yoichi prodn, Kyoto. Wri-dir, Yoichi Takabayashi, based on novel by Seishi Yokomizo. Cam, Fujio Morita; mus, Nobuhiko Obayashi; art dir, Yoshirobu Nishioka. 106.
Takahiro Tamura, Junko Takazawa, Akira Nitta, Akira Nakao.
07/14/76

Honning Maane
(Honeymoon)
(Denmark)
OBL. Honning Maane prodn. Orig story-dir, Bille August; cam (Eastmancolor), Dirk Bruel; prodn mgr, Vibeke Windeloew; asst dir, Birthe Frost; prodn des, Erling Joergensen; cos, Lissen Dirckinck-Holmfeld; mus, Fuzzy; edtr, Janus Billeskov Jansen. 99.
Claus Strandberg, Kirsten Olesen, Jens Okking, Grethe Holmer, Poul Bundgaard.
08/30/78

Honningmane
(In My Life)
(Denmark)
X. Konsortiet Honningmane (Copenhagen) prodn. Wri-dir, Bille August. Cam, Dirk Bruel; edtr, Janus Billeskov Jensen; art dir, Erling Jorgensen; mus, Fuzzy. 108.
Claus Stranberg, Kirsten Olesen, Jens Okking, Grethe Holmer, Poul Bundgaard.
11/05/80

Hooper
WB. Burt Reynolds-Lawrence Gordon prodn. Prod, Hank Moonjean; exec prod, Lawrence Gordon. Dir, Hal Needham. Sp, Thomas Rickman, Bill Kerby from a story by Walt Green and Walter S Herndon; cam (Metrocolor), Bobby Byrne; art dir, Hilyard Brown; edtr, Donn Cambern; mus, Bill Justis; snd, Jack Solomon; set decor, Ira Bates; cos supv, Norman Salling; stunt coord, Bobby Bass; asst dir, David Hamburger. (MPAA rating; PG).
Burt Reynolds, Jan-Michael Vincent, Sally Field, Brian Keith, John Marley, James Best, Adam West, Alfie West, Robert Klein.
07/26/78

Hope: SEE Umut

Hopla Paa Sengekanten
(Jumpin' at the Bedside)
(Denmark)
PAL. Dir, John Hilbard. Sp, Gritte Palsby, Hilbard. Cam (Eastmancolor), Jan Weincke; edtr, Hilbard; mus, Ole Hoeyer. 99.
Vivi Rau, Ole Soeltoft, Louise Frevert, Annebie Warburg, Ulla Jessen.
02/04/76

Hopscotch
AVE. Prods, Edie and Ely Landau. Exec prod, Otto Plaschkes. Dir, Ronald Neame. Sp, Brian Garfield, Bryan Forbes, based on Garfield novel; cam (Movielab Color), Arthur Ibbetson; edtr, Carl Kress; snd, Derek Ball, Oliver Moss; prodn des, William Creber; asst dirs, Patrick Clayton, William Hassell; mus, Ian Fraser. (MPAA rating: R). 104.
Walter Matthau, Glenda Jackson, Ned Beatty, Sam Waterston, Herbert Lom, David Matthau, George Baker, Ivor Roberts, Lucy Saroyan.
07/23/80

Hordubal
(Czechoslovakia)
CZS. Barrandov Production prodn. Dir, Jaroslav Balik. Sp, Vaclav Nyvit from the book by Karel Capek; cam, Viktor Svoboda; mus, Karel Mares. 92.
Anatoli Kuznezov, Luibuse Geptrova, Klara Pollertova, Sandor Oszter.
10/29/80

Horizonte Te Hapura
(Clear Horizons)
(Albania)
ALA. Albfilm prodn, Tirana. Dir-cam (b&w), Viktor Gjika. Sp, Dritero Agolli; art dir, Shyqyri Sako; mus, Limos Dizdari. 90.
Dhimiter Orgocka, Sander Prosi, Robert Ndrenika, Gaqo Spiro, Pandi Raidhi, Mirketa Cobani, Nikolin Xhoja.
(B & W)
01/24/79

The Hornet's Nest: SEE Le Guepier

Horse of Pride: SEE Le Cheval d'Orgeuil

Hoshizora No Marionette
(Puppets Under Starry Skies)
(Japan)
X. Tokyo Video Center prodn. Dir, Hojin Hashiura, Sp, Atuhsi Yamatoya, Hashiura from the book by Yushi Kita; cam (Eastmancolor), Yuji Pokumura; mus, Ryoichi Kuniyoshi. 99.
Yoichi Miura, Kazuhito Takei, Ako, Teizo Muta, Haruko Mabuchi, Mocko Ezawa.
08/23/78

Hospital of the Transfiguration: SEE Szpital Przemienienia

Hot Head: SEE Coup de Tete

Hot Lead and Cold Feet
BV. Walt Disney prodn. Prod, Ron Miller. Dir, Robert Butler. Sp, Joe McEveety, Arthur Alsberg, Don Nelson; cam (Technicolor), Frank Phillips; edtr Ray de Leuw; art dir, John B Mansbridge, Frank T Smith; cos des, Ron Talsky; snd, Gregory Valtierra; mus, Buddy Baker; sfx, Eustace Lycett, Art Cruickshank, Danny Lee, Hal Bigger, Billy Lee; stunt coord, Buddy Joe Hooker; asst dir, Paul "Tiny" Nicholas. (MPAA rating: G). 90.
Jim Dale, Karen Valentine, Don Knotts, Jack Elam, John Williams, Darren McGavin, Warren Vanders, Debbie Lytton, Michael Sharrett.
07/12/78

Hot Potato
WB. Weintraub-Heller prodn. Prods, Fred Weintraub, Paul Heller. Dir-wri, Oscar Williams. Cam (CFI color), Ronald Garcia; edtr, Peter Berger; mus, Christopher Trussell; art dir, Urai Sirisombat; snd, Ron Green; asst dir, Terry Marcel. (MPAA rating: PG). 87.
Jim Kelly, George Memmoli, Geoffrey Binney, Irene Tsu, Judith Brown, Sam Hiona, Ron Prince, Hardy Stockmann, Metta Rungrat, Supakorn Songsermvorakul.
04/07/76

Hot Potato: SEE La Patata Bollente

Hot Stuff
COL. Rastar-Mort Engelberg prodn. Exec prod, Paul Maslansky. Prod, Mort Engelberg. Dir, Dom DeLuise. Sp, Michael Kane, Donald E Westlake; mus, Patrick Williams. (MPAA rating: PG). 103.
Dom DeLuise, Jerry Reed, Suzanne Pleshette, Louis Avalof, Ossie Davis.
06/06/79

Hot Tomorrows
X. American Film Institute prodn. Prod-dir-wri-edtr, Martin Brest; cam-asso prod, Joacques Haitkin; chor, Lloyd Gordon; prodn mgr-line prod, Fredic Shore; snd, Mark Bovos. 73.
Ken Lerner, Ray Sharkey, Herve Villechaize, Victor Argo, George Memmoli, Donne Daniels, Dr Rose Marshall, Paul Schumacher.
05/03/78

H.O.T.S.
DEP. Great American Dream Machine Movie Co Prodn. Prods, W Terry Davis, Don Schain, Gerald Sindell. Exec prod, Davis. Dir, Gerald Sindell. Sp, Cheri Caffaro, Joan Buchanan; cam, Harvey Genkins; edtr, Barbara Pokras; mus, David Davis; snd, Art Names; asst dirs, Gerald Olson, Michael Healy. (MPAA rating: R). 95.
Susan Kiger, Lisa London, Pamela Jean Bryant, Kimberly Cameron, Mary Steelsmith, Angela Aamers, Lindsay Bloom, K C Winkler, Donald Petrie, Larry Gilman, David Gibbs, Danny Bonaduce, Ken Olfson, Dick Bakalyan, Louis Guss.
09/12/79

The Hound of the Baskervilles
(Britain)
HMD. Michael White and Andrew Braunsberg presentation. Prod, John Goldstone; exec prods, Michael White, Andrew Braunsberg. Dir, Paul Morrissey; sp, Peter Cook, Dudley Moore, Morrissey; cam, Dick Bush, John Wilcox; mus, Dudley Moore; edtrs, Richard Marden, Glenn Hyde; prodn des, Roy Smith; cos des, Charles Knode; asso prod, Tim Hampton. 84.
Peter Cook, Dudley Moore, Denholm Elliott, Joan Greenwood, Terry-Thomas, Max Wall,

Irene Handl, Kenneth Williams, Hugh Griffith, Dana Gillespie, Roy Kinnear, Prunella Scales, Penelope Keith, Spike Milligan.
11/08/78

The Hounds. . .Of Notre Dame
(Canada)
PCN. Fraser film prodn. Prod, Fil Fraser. Dir, Zale Dalen. Sp, Ken Mitchell; cam, Ron Orieux; art dir, Richard Hudolin; edtr, Tony Lower; mus, Maurice Marshall; asst dir, Joan Board. 95.
Thomas Peacocke, Frances Hyland, Barry Morse, David Ferry, Lawrence Reese, Lenore Zann, Phil Ridley, Dale Heiben, Paul Bougie, Rob MacLean, Bill Sorenson, Bill Morton.
10/22/80

The Hour of Mary and the Bird of Gold: SEE La Hora de Maria y el Pajaro de Oro

The Hour of the Wolf: SEE I Ora Tou Lykou

The Hour Of Truth: SEE Hodina Pravdy

House
(Japan)
TOH. Prod, Nobuhiko Obayashi, Norihiko Yamada. Dir, Obayashi. Sp, Chiho Katsura; cam, Yoshihisa Sakamoto; art dir, Kazuo Satsuya; edtr, Nobuo Ogawa; mus, Asei Kobayashi, Miki Yoshino; asst dir, Yasuhira Oguri. 87.
Kimiko Ikegami, Kumiko Oba, Ai Matsubara, Miki Jinbo, Mieko Sato, Miyako Masayo, Eriko Tanaka, Kiyohiko Ozaki, Saho Sasagawa, Haruko Wanibuchi.
09/21/77

The House By the Lake: SEE Death Weekend

The House By The Sea: SEE Huset ved Havet

House Calls
U. Prods, Alex Winitsky, Arlene Sellers. Exec prod, Jennings Lang. Dir, Howard Zieff. Sp, Max Shulman, Julius J Epstein, Alan Mandel, Charles Shyer, based on a story by Shulman, Epstein; cam (Technicolor), David M Walsh; edtr, Edward Warschilka; mus, Henry Mancini; prodn des, Henry Bumstead; set decor, Mickey S Michaels; snd, Don Sharpless, Robert L Hoyt; cos-ward, Burton Miller; asst dir, Gary Daigler. (MPAA rating: PG). 98.
Walter Matthau, Glenda Jackson, Art Carney, Richard Benjamin, Candice Azzara, Dick O'Neill, Thayer David.
03/15/78

House of The Lute
(Hong Kong)
X. Hung Way Films Prodn. Prod, Chan Hok-Yan. Dir, Lau Shing-hon. Sp, Lau Shing-hon; cam, Johnny Koo; art dir, David Chan; lute mus, John Thompson. 95.
(Cantonese soundtrack with English subtitles)
08/08/79

Houses In This Alley: SEE Maisons Dans Cette Ruelle

The Housewarming: SEE Grihapravesh

How Czar Peter the Great Married Off His Moor: SEE Skas Pro To, Kar Zar Petr Arapa Shenil

How To Beat The High Cost Of Living
AIP. Jerome M Zeitman/Robert Kaufman prodn. Prods, Jerome M Zeitman, Robert Kaufman. Exec prod, Samuel Z Arkoff. Dir, Robert Scheerer. Sp, Robert Kaufman, from a story by Leonora Thuna; cam (Movielab color), Jim Crabe; edtr, Bill Butler; prodn des, Larry Paull; set decor, Peg Cummings; asso prod, Robin Krause; asst dir, Irby Smith. (MPAA rating: PG). 110.
Susan Saint James, Jane Curtin, Jessica Lange, Richard Benjamin, Fred Willard, Eddie Albert, Dabney Coleman, Art Metrano, Ronnie Schell, Garrett Morris, Cathryn Damon, Sybil Danning, Al Checco, Carmen Zapata, Dru Wagner.
06/25/80

How to Lose a Wife and Find a Lover: SEE Come Perdere Una Moglie E Trovare Un'Amante

How Yukong Moved Mountains: SEE Comment Yukong Deplace Les Montagnes

Hoy Mister Ako Ang Misis Mo
(Hey Mister I Am Your Wife)
(Philippines)
X. JE prodn. Story-sp, Edgardo M Reyes; mus, Ernani Cuenco; cam, Fortunato Bernardo. Dir, Cesar Gallardo. 100.
Joseph Estrada, Elizabeth Oropesa, Paquito Diaz, Carlos Padilla Jr, Anita Linda, Quiel Segivia.
06/16/76

Huadjai Ti Jom Din
(Heartbreak People)
(Thailand)
SAH. Prod, Somsak Techaratanaprasert. Dir, Chao Mikunsoot. Story and sp, Torn Kosol; cam, Sanit Rujiratakul; mus, Chintanart Wacharasathien, Pisanu Srivonand; snd, Sngar Wacharasathien; prodn des, art dir, Anant Chantanakorn. 115.
Pisan Akaraseni, Pisamai Wilaisak, Yuwathida Pornprasert, Uthen Boonyong, Marasi Nabangchang.
04/25/79

Hue and Cry: SEE Haro

Hugasan Mo Ang Aking Kasalaman
(Wash Out My Faults)
(Philippines)
X. Jimmy L Pascual and Emperor Films Production presentation. Dir, Nilo Saez. Sp, Pablo S Gomez, Toto Bellano; cam, Ben Lobo, Rudy Dino; mus, George Canseco. 100.
Charito Solis, Eddie Garcia, Leila Hermosa, Ricky Belmonte.
06/23/76

Hugo the Hippo
(US - Hungary)
FOX. Brut Productions feature. Exec prod, George Barrie. Prod, Robert Halmi. Dir, Bill Feigenbaum. Sp, Tom Baum; prodn des, Graham Percy; mus-lyr, Robert Larimer; mus score, Burt Keyes. (MPAA rating: G). 78.
Voices: Robert Morley, Paul Lynde, Jesse Emmet, Lance Taylor Sr, Ronnie Cox, Len Maxwell, Percy Rodriguez, Burl Ives, Marie and Jimmy Osmond.
(ANI)
07/14/76

Hullabaloo Over Georgie And Bonnie's Pictures
(Britain)
CTY. Merchant/Ivory prodn in asso with London Weekend Television. Prod, Ismail Merchant. Dir, James Ivory. Sp, Ruth Prawer Jhabwala; cam, Walter Lassally; edtr, Humphrey Dixon; mus, Vic Flick; snd, Bob Bentley; art dir, Bansi Chandragupta. 82.
Peggy Ashcroft, Victor Bannerjee, Larry Pines, Aparna Sen, Saeed Jaffrey, Jane Booker, Shamsuddin, Alladdin Langa, Jenny Beavan.
(16m)
10/24/79

Human Bullet: SEE Nikudan

Human Experiments
X. Prods, Summer Brown, Gregory Goodell. Exec prod, Edwin Scott Brown. Dir, Goodell. Sp, Richard Rothstein; cam, Joao Fernandes. (MPAA rating: R). 82.
Linda Haynes, Geoffrey Lewis, Ellen Travolta, Aldo Ray, Jackie Coogan.
02/13/80

The Human Factor
(Britain)
UA. MGM film. Prod-dir, Otto Preminger; exec prod, Paul Crosfield; sp, Tom Stoppard, based on the novel by Graham Greene; cam, Mike Molloy; edtr, Richard Trevor; mus, Richard and Gary Logan; art dir, Ken Ryan; cos des, Hope Bryce; asso prods, Chris Dillinger, Val Robins; asst dir, Kip Gowans. (MPAA rating: R). 115.
Richard Attenborough, Joop Doderer, John Gielgud, Derek Jacobi, Robert Morley, Ann Todd, Richard Vernon, Nicol Williamson, Iman.
12/19/79

Humanoids From The Deep
NW. Roger Corman prodn. Prods, Martin B Cohen, Hunt Lowry. Dir, Barbara Peeters. Sp, Frederick James, based on story by Frank Arnold, Martin B Cohen; cam (Metrocolor), Daniele Lacambre; edtr, Mark Goldblatt; mus, James Horner; art dir, Michael Erler; humanoid des, Rob Bottin; snd, Mark Harris; asst dir-2d unit dir, James Sbadellari (MPAA rating: R). 80.
Doug McClure, Ann Turkel, Vic Morrow, Cindy Weintraub.
04/23/80

The Humpbacked Horse:
SEE Konek Gorbunok

Hungarian Rhapsody and Allegro Barbaro: SEE Magyar Rapszodia and Allegro Barbaro

The Hungarians: SEE Magyarok

Hunger: SEE Pasi

Hungerjahre
(Hunger Years)
(W Germany)
X. Jutta Brueckner Film Prodn, in co-prodn with Zweites Deutsches Fernsehen (ZDF), Mainz. Wri-dir, Jutta Brueckner. Cam (b&w), Joerg Jeshel, Rainer Maerz; mus, Johannes Schmoelling; edtr, Anneliese Krigar; tv prod, Sybille Rahn. 114.
Sylvia Ulrich, Britta Pohland, Claus Jurichs, Hilda Preuss, Ismail Mahdu, Heidi Joschko, Helga Lehner, Cordula Hubrich, Viola Recklies, Tobias Meister.
(B & W)
03/05/80

The Hunter
PAR. Rastar/Mort Engelberg prod. Prod, Mort Engelberg. Dir, Buzz Kulik. Sp, Ted Leighton, Peter Hyams, based on book by Christopher Keane and life of Ralph Thorson; cam (Metrocolor), Fred J Koenekamp; edtr, Robert Wolfe; mus, Michel Legrand; prodn des, Ron Hobbs; set des, Jim Tocci; set decor, George Ganes, Rick Simpson; snd, Al Overton Jr; asst dir, Richard Learman. (MPAA rating: PG). 117.
Steve McQueen, Eli Wallach, Kathryn Harrold, LeVar Burton, Ben Johnson, Richard Venture, Tracey Walter, Tom Rosales, Theodore Wilson, Ray Bickel, Bobby Bass, Karl Schueneman.
07/30/80

The Hunters: SEE I Kynighi

Hurricane
PAR. Dino De Laurentiis presentation of a Famous Films, N V prodn. Exec prod, Lorenzo Semple Jr. Prod, Dino De Laurentiis. Dir, Jan Troell. Sp, Lorenzo Semple Jr, based on the novel by Charles Nordhoff and James Norman Hall; cam (Technicolor, Todd-AO), Sven Nykvist, edtr, Sam O'Steen; prodn, cos, set des, Danilo Donati; mus, Nino Rota; 2d unit dir, Frank Clark; sfx, Glen Robinson, Aldo Puccini, Joe Day; asst dir, Jose Lopez Rodero. (MPAA rating: PG). 119.
Jason Robards, Mia Farrow, Max Von Sydow, Trevor Howard, Dayton Ka'ne, Timothy Bottoms, James Keach, Richard Sarcione, Ariirau Tekurarere, Willie Myers, Nick Rutgers, Nancy Hall Rutgers, Manu Tupou, Simplet Tefane, Piero Bushin, Noel Teparii, John Taea, Taeve Tetuamia.
04/04/79

Hurricane: SEE Bao Feng Chou Yu

Huset ved Havet
(The House By The Sea)
(Denmark)
X. Danish Film Studio-Skagen Kommune-Claus Weeke prodn. Wri-dir, Claus Weeke. Cam (Eastmancolor), Dirk Bruel; edtr, Lars Brydesen; mus, Hans Dal. 80.
Kurt Ravn, Lea Broegger, Lene Scharling, Dick Kaysoe, Claus Strandberg.
06/11/80

Hussy
(Britain)
WNO. Kendon Films prodn. Exec prod, Don Boyd. Prod, Jeremy Watt. Dir, Matthew Chapman. Sp, Chapman; cam, Keith Goddard; edtr, Bill Blunden; mus, George Fenton; snd, John Sanders; prodn des, Hazel Peiser; prodn mgr, Buzz Besgrove; asst dir, Gino Marotta. (MPAA rating: R). 95.
Helen Mirren, John Shea, Murray Salem, Paul Angelis, Jenny Runacre, Daniel Chasin, Patti Boulaye, Marika Rivera, Jill Melford, Sandy Ratcliff, Malcolm Reynolds, William Hootkins.
03/26/80

The Hussy: SEE La Drolesse

Hustler From Canton
(Hong Kong)
SHW. Prod, Run Run Shaw. Dir, Wang Feng. Sp, Szu Tu An; cam, Lin Chao, Huang Chieh; edtr, Chiang Hsing-lung; snd recording, Wang Yung-hua. 101.
Liu Lu-hua, Chang Ying, Hsia Ping, Mai Huamei, Chen Szu-chia, Tien Ching, Lin Wei-tu, Hua Lun, Ching Miao.
09/29/76

The Hypochondriac: SEE Il Malato Immaginario

Hypothesis of the Stolen Painting: SEE L'Hypothese du Tableau Vole

I Am a Delinquent: SEE Soy Un Delincuente

I Am Anna Magnani: SEE Io sono Anna Magnani

I Am Maria: SEE Jag ar Maria

I Am Pierre Riviere: SEE Je Suis Pierre Riviere

I Am What My Films Are:
SEE Was Ich Bin, Sind Meine Filme

I As In Icarus: SEE I Comme Icare

I Belong To Me: SEE Io Sono Mia

I Came As A Stranger: SEE Fremd Bin Ich Eigezogah

I Comme Icare
(I As In Icarus)
(France)
AMLF. V Films/SFP/Antenne 2 co-prodn. Prod-dir, Henri Verneuil. Sp, Verneuil, Didier Decoin; cam, Jean Louis Picavet; art dir, Jacques Saulnier; edtr, Henri Lanoe; mus, Ennio Morricone; snd, Serge Deraison, Jacques Maumont. 120.
Yves Montand, Michel Etcheverry, Roger Planchon, Jacques Denis.
01/23/80

I Dadathes
(The Nurses)
(Greece)
X. Andreas and Nicos Zapatinas prodn. Dir, Nicos Zapatinas. Sp, George Skourtis, based on his own play; cam (b&w), Lefteris Papadopoulos; sets-cos, Mikis Karapiperis, Tassos Diacomanolis; edtr, Takis Davlopoulos; snd, Argyris Lazaridis. 110.
Vaguelis Kazan, Thymios Karakatsanis, Nikitas Tsakiroglou.
10/31/79

I Giorni Cantati
(Swansong Days)
(Italy)
TIT. Co-op Lunga Gittata prodn. Dir, Paolo Pietrangeli. Sp, Giovanna Marini, Francesco Massaro, Paolo Pietrangeli; cam (Technicolor), Dario Di Palma; art dir, Elena Ricci Poccetto; edtr, Ruggero Mastroianni; songs by Ivan Della Mea, Pasquale Malinconico, Giovanna Marini, Paolo Pietrangeli. 110.
Roberto Benigni, Franco Bianchi, Ivan Della Mea, Francesco Guccini, Giovanna Marini, Mariangela Melato, Anna Nogara, Paolo Pietrangeli.
09/05/79

I Kynighi
(The Hunters)
(Greece)
AGI. Wri-dir, Theodor Angelopoulos. Cam (Eastmancolor), Georges Arvanitis; edtr, G Triandafillidis; mus, Loukianos Kilaidonis. 165.

I loevens tegn
(In the Sign of the Lion)
(Denmark)
DNS. Happy Film (Anders Sanderberg) prodn. Dir, Werner Hedmann. Sp-story, Hedmann, Edmondt Jensen, Sanderberg, based on idea by Peer Guldbrandsen. Cam (Eastmancolor), Rolf Roenne; prodn chief, Vibeke Windelov; edtr, May Soya; mus, Ole Hoeyer; cos, Keld Rex Holm. 90.
Ole Soeltoft, Sitter Horne-Rasmussen, Else Pedersen, Lizzi Varencke, Ib Mossin, William Kisum, Gina Janssen, Poul Bundgaard, Rent and Bie Warburg.
08/04/76

I Love You Me No Longer:
SEE Je T'Aime Moi Non Plus

I Love You, I Love You Not:
SEE Amo non Amo

I, Maureen
(Canada)
NCN. Jandu prodn in asso with P W S Assoc. Exec prods, Philip Speller, Duane Hanson. Prod, Duane Hanson. Dir, Janine Manatis. Sp, Janine Manatis based on a short story by Elizabeth Spencer; cam, Marc Champion; edtr, Kirk Jones; mus, Hagood Hardy; art dir, Nadia Salnick. 85.
Colleen Collins, Diane Bigelow, Donna Preece, Robert Crone, Michael Ironside, Brian Damude.
09/20/78

I Need You So Much, Love:
SEE Te Necesito Tanto, Amor

I Never Promised You A Rose Garden
NW. Imorh prodn. Prods, Terence F Deane, Daniel H Blatt, Michael Hausman. Exec prods, Roger Corman, Edgar J Sherick. Dir, Anthony Page. Sp, Lewis John Carlino, Gavin Lambert, based on Joanne Greenberg novel of same title; cam, Bruce Logan; score, Paul Chihara; des, Toby Rafelson; cos, Jane Ruhm; edtr, Garth Craven; snd, Art Names. (MPAA rating: R). 96.
Bibi Andersson, Kathleen Quinlan, Ben Piazza, Lorraine Gary, Darlene Craviotto, Reni Santoni, Susan Tyrrell, Signe Hasso, Norman Alden, Sylvia Sidney, Martine Bartlett, Robert Viharo, Jeff Conaway, Dick Herd, Sarah Cunningham, June C Ellis, Diane Varsi, Patricia Singer, Mary Carver, Barbara Steele, Cynthia Szigetti, Carol Androsky, Elizabeth Dartmoor, Cherry Davis, Lynne Stewart, Carol Worthington, Margo Burdichevsky, Gertrude Granor, Helen Verbit, Jan Burrell, Irene Roseen, Nancy Parsons, Leigh Curran, Donald Bishop, Samantha Harper, Dolores Quentin, Pamela Seaman.
07/20/77

I Ora Tou Lykou
(The Hour of the Wolf)
(Greece)
X. Panayotis Anguelopoulos prodn. Dir, Demetris Mavrikios; sp, George Mylonas; cam, Costas Papayannakis; mus, Sakis Tsilikis; edtr, Panos Anguelopoulos; snd, George Michaelides. 92.
Costas Messaris, Maria Tsopanaki.
(B & W)
1/21/79

I See This Land from Afar:
SEE Aus Der Ferne Sehe Ich Dieses Land

I Sent A Letter To My Love:
SEE Chere Inconnue

I Sing I Cry
(Taiwan)
CLZ. Chan Lin Kang Films prod. Dir-edtr, Sung Cheng Sheu; exec prod, Tsai Yu Wen; story-sp, Sung Hsiang Ju; cam, Liao Ching Sung; mus-snd, Wu Meg Lin; prodn supv, Shaw Che Wu. 100.
Hu Hwei Chung, Chang Ruo Chu.
12/12/79

I, Tintin: SEE Moi, Tintin

I Wanna Hold Your Hand
U. Prods, Tamara Asseyev, Alex Rose; exec prod, Steven Spielberg. Dir, Robert Zemeckis. Sp, Zemeckis, Bob Gale; cam (Technicolor), Donald M Morgan; art dir, Peter Jamison; edtr, Frank Morriss; special visual effects, Albert Whitlock; asso prod, Bob Gale; set decor, John Dwyer; asst dir, Newton Arnold; cos des, Roseanna Norton; sfx, Curtis Dickson; snd, Don Sharpless. (MPAA rating: PG). 104.
Nancy Allen, Bobby DiCicco, Marc McClure, Susan Kendall Newman, Theresa Saldana, Wendie Jo Sperber, Eddie Deezen, Christian Juttner, Will Jordan, Read Morgan, Claude Earl Jones, James Houghton, Michael Hewitson.
04/19/78

I Want To Be A Woman: SEE Cambio De Sexo

I Want To Live: SEE Ich Will Leben

I Will...I Will...For Now
FOX. Brut (George Barrie) prodn. Wri (with Albert E Lewin) and dir by Norman Panama. Cam (DeLuxe Color), John A Alonzo; edtr, Robert Lawrence; mus, John Cameron; prodn des, Fernando Carrere; set decor, Robert Signorelli; snd, Tex Rudloff, Verne Poore, Richard Alexander, Lawrence O Jost; asst dir, Daniel J McCauley. (MPAA rating: R). 107.
Elliott Gould, Diane Keaton, Paul Sorvino, Victoria Principal, Robert Alda, Madge Sinclair, Warren Berlinger, Candy Clark, Carmen Zapata, George Tyne.
02/11/76

Ice Castles
COL. Prod, John Kemeny. Exec prod, Rosilyn Heller. Dir, Donald Wrye. Sp, Wrye, Gary L Bain, based on a story by Bain; cam, Bill Butler; edtrs, Michael Kahn, Maury Winetrobe, Melvin Shapiro; mus, Marvin Hamlisch; prodn des, Joel Schiller; chor, Brian Foley; snd, Glen Anderson, Richard Raguse; asst dir, Jerry Grandey. (MPAA rating: PG).
Lynn-Holly Johnson, Robby Benson, Colleen Dewhurst, Tom Skerritt, Jennifer Warren, David Huffman, Diane Reilly.
12/20/78

Ich Bin Ein Antistar...
(I'm an Anti-Star)
(W Germany)
X. Rosa von Praunheim prodn, in collab with Westdeutscher Rundfunk (WDR), Cologne. Wri-dir-edtr, Rosa von Praunheim. Cam, Ed Lieber. 60.
Evelyn Kuenneke, Angele Durand, Nicolai Rhein, Christina, Dietmar Kracht.
04/27/77

Ich Will Leben
(I Want To Live)
(Austria)
X. Cine Mercury/Victoria Film, Vienna, prodn. Dir, Joerg A Eggers. Sp, Fritz Andraschko; cam, Walter Kindler. 99.
Heinz Bennent, Kathina Kaiser, Sonja Sutter, Alwy Becker, Signe Seidel, Claudia Buthenuth.
07/27/77

Ich Zwing Dich Zu Leben
(I'll Force You To Live)
(E Germany)
DEE. DEFA Film Prodn, "Babelsberg" Group. Wri-dir, Ralf Kirsten. Cam, Juergen Brauer; sets, Dieter Adam; mus, Siegfried Mattus; edtr, Ursula Zweig. 90.
Rolf Ludwig, Anne-Else Paetzold, Peter Welz, Horst Kotterba, Robert Pfeiffer, Eberhard Kirchberg, Dieter Bellmann, Erich Mirek, Elsa Grube-Deister.
06/28/78

Idealist
(Yugoslavia)
YFR. Viba Film prodn. Dir, Igor Pretnar. Sp, Vitomil Zupan, Pretnar from the book by Ivan Cankar; cam (Eastmancolor), Mile De Gleria; art dir, Mirko Lipuzic; edtr, Dusan Povh; mus, Bojan Adamic. 121.
Radko Polic, Milena Zupancic, Marjeta Gregorac, Bert Sotlar.
08/18/76

The Idolmaker
UA. Prods, Gene Kirkwood, Howard W Koch Jr. Dir, Taylor Hackford. Sp, Edward Di Lorenzo; cam (Technicolor), Adam Holender; mus-lyr, Jeff Barry; edtr, Neil Travis; art dir, David L Snyder; set decor, Barbara Kreiger; snd, Buzz Knudson, Don MacDougall, Bob Glass, Peter Hliddal; chor, Deney Terrio; asso prods, R J Louis, David Nichols; asst dir, Clifford C Coleman. (MPAA rating: PG). 107.
Ray Sharkey, Tovah Feldshuh, Peter Gallagher, Paul Land, Joe Pantoliano, Maureen McCormick, John Aprea, Richard Bright, Olympia Dukakis, Steven Apostlee Peck,

Leonard Gaines, Deney Terrio, Charles Guardino, Michael Mislove.
11/05/80

If Ever I See You Again
COL. Prod-dir-mus, Joe Brooks. Sp, Brooks, Martin Davidson. Cam (Technicolor), Adam Holender, Don Sweeney; edtr, Rick Shaine; art dir, Don Gilman; snd, Richard Dior, Roger Pietschman; asst dirs, Jim Maniolas, David Whorf. (MPAA rating: PG).   105.
Joe Brooks, Shelley Hack, Jimmy Breslin, Jerry Keller, Kenny Karen, George Plimpton, Michael Decker, Julie Ann Gordon, Danielle Brisebois, Branch Emerson, Shannon Bolin, Caroline Mignini, Joe Leon, Ed Kovins.
(MUSICAL)
05/17/78

If I Had a Girl: SEE Keby Som Mal Dievca

If It Were To Do Over Again: SEE Si C'Etait a Refaire

If Music Be the Food of Love: SEE Nedtur

If Pigs Had Wings: SEE Porci Con Le Ali

If Your Heart Can Feel: SEE Jesli Msz Serce Bijace

Ija Ominira
(Fight For Freedom)
(Nigeria)
FSH. Wri-dir, Ola Balogun from the book by Adebayo Faleti; mus, Duro Ladipe.   101.
Ade Folayan, Duro Ladipe, Oyin Adejobi, Jimoli Alu.
09/05/79

Ikarus
(E Germany)
DEE. DEFA Film Prodn, Gruppe Babelsberg. Dir, Heiner Carow. Sp, Klaus Schlesinger; cam, Juergen Brauer; mus, Peter Gotthardt; sets, Dieter Adam.   85.
Peter Welz, Karin Gregorek, Peter Aust, Hermann Beyer.
06/13/79

Il. . .Bel Paese
(Italy)
77. Prod, Fulvio Lucisano for Italian Intl Film. Dir, Luciano Salce. Sp, Castlelano and Pipolo; cam (Eastmancolor), Ennio Guarnieri; art dir, Ezio Altieri; mus, Gianni Boncompagni, Giorgio Farina, Paolo Ormi; edtr, Antonio Siciliano.   112.
Paolo Villaggio, Silvia Dionisio.
01/18/78

Il Cappotto Di Astrakan
(The Persian Lamb Coat)
(Italy)
CNZ. Prods, Franco Cristaldi, Nicola Carrara for Vides Prodn (Rome), Les Film Ariane (Paris). Dir, Marco Vicario; sp, Vicario, Sandro Parenzo; novel, Piero Chiari; cam (Eastmancolor), Ennio Guarnieri; edtr, Nino Baragli; mus, Bruno Nicolai.   100.
Johnny Dorelli, Andrea Ferreol, Carole Bouquet.
08/06/80

Il Casotto
(The Beach House)
(Italy)
MDU. Prod, Mauro Berardi. Dir, Sergio Citti. Sp, Citti, Vincenzo Cerami; cam, Tonino Delli Colli; mus, Gianni Mazza.   114.
Jodie Foster, Paolo Stoppa, Flora Mastroianni, Ugo Tognazzi, Mariangela Melato, Michele Placido, Luigi Proietti.
10/22/80

Il Corsaro Nero
(The Black Pirate)
(Italy)
CNZ. Rizzoli Film prodn. Dirs, Sergio Sollima, Alberto Silvestri. Cam (Eastmancolor), Alberto Spagnoli; art dir, Sergio Canevari; edtr, Alberto Gallitti; mus, Guido and Maurizio De Angelis.   121.
Kabir Bedi, Carole Andre, Mel Ferrer, Angelo Infante, Tony Renis, Dagmar Lassander, Sonja Jeanine.
01/19/77

Il Gabbiano
(The Sea Gull)
(Italy)
X. Lu Leone, Roberto Levi and Enzo Porcelli prodn for RAI-Radiotelevisione Italiana and Italtelevisionfilm; dir, Marco Bellocchio. Adapt from Anton Chekhov by Sandro Petraglia, Stefano Rulli, Lu Leone, Marco Bellocchio from the trans by Angelo Maria Ripellino. Cam (Eastmancolor), Tonino Nardi; edtr, Silvano Agosti; sets, Amedeo Fago; cos, Gabriella Pescucci; mus, Nicola Piovani. 125.
Laura Betti, Giulio Brogi, Pamela Villoresi, Remo Girone, Gisella Burinato, Antonio Piovanelli, Mattia Pinoli, Clara Colisimo, Remo Remotti, Gaetano Campisi.
09/28/77

Il Garofano Rosso
(The Red Carnation)
(Italy)
X. Filmcoop prodn. Dir, Luigi Faccini. Sp, Faccini, Paquito del Bosco, Piero Anchisi, based on novel by Elio Vittorini; cam (Cinecitta color), Arturo Zavattini; edtr, Luciano Benedetti; snd, Pasquale Rotolo; sets, Marco Dentici; mus, Banco di Mutuo Soccorso.   111.
Miguel Bose, Elsa Martinelli, Maria Monti, Marisa Mantovani, Giovanna di Bernardo, Denis Karvill, Alberto Gracco, Giuseppe Atanasio.
09/29/76

Il Gatto
(Italy)
UA. Rafran Cinematografica prodn. Prod, Sergio Leone. Dir, Luigi Comencini. Sp, Rodolfo Sonego, Augusto Caminito, Fulvio Marcolin; cam (Eastmancolor), Ennio Guarnieri; art dir, Dante Ferretti; edtr, Nino Baragli; mus, Ennio Morricone.   106.
Ugo Tognazzi, Mariangela Melato, Michel Galabrue, Dalila Di Lazzaro.
01/18/78

Il Ladrone
(The Good Thief)
(France - Italy)
ITI. Prod, Fulvio Lucisano for Daimo Cinematografica (Rome)-Italian International Film (Rome)-Carthago Film (Paris) with collab of RAI televison. Dir, Pasquale Festa Campanile. Sp, Festa Campanile, Renato Ghiotto, Ottavio Jemma, Stefano Ubezio, from a novel by Festa Campanile; cam (Technicolor), Giancarlo Ferrando; art dir, Enrico Fiorentini; edtr, Alberto Galletti; mus, Ennio Morricone. 98.
Enrico Montesano, Edwige French, Bernadette Lafont, Enzo Robutti.
04/02/80

Il Malato Immaginario
(The Hypochondriac)
(Italy)
CII. Prod, Piero La Mantia for Mars Film Produzione. Dir, Tonino Cervi. Sp, Cesare Frugoni, Tonino Cervi, Alberto Sordi, cam (Eastmancolor), Armando Nannuzzi; art dir, Piero Tosi; edtr, Nino Baragli; mus, Piero Piccioni.   110.
Alberto Sordi, Laura Antonelli, Marina Vlady, Giuliana De Sio, Bernard Blier, Stefano Satta Flores, Vittorio Ciprioli.
01/23/80

Il Mammasantissima
(Big Mamma)
(Italy)
PCI. Ciro Ippolito prodn for Orsa Maggiore Cinematografica. Dir, Alfonso Brescia; wris, Piero Regnoli, Ippolito, from story suggestion by Ippollito; cam, Silvio Fraschetti; edtr, Carlo Broglio; art dir, Romeo Costantini; mus, Eduardo Alfieri.   89.
Mario Merola, Malisa Longo, Ellio Zamuto, Biagio Pelligra.
04/11/79

Il Messia
(The Messiah)
(Italy)
X. Orizzonte 2000 prodn. Prod, Silvia d'Amico Bendico. Dir, Roberto Rossellini. Sp, Rossellini, Bendico; cam, Mario Montuori; edtrs, Yolanda Benvenuti, Laurent Quaglio; mus, Mario Nascimbene.   150.
Pier Maria Rossi, Mita Ungaro, Antonella Fasano, Tony Ucci, Flora Carabella, Carlos de Carvalho, Luis Suarez.
05/10/78

Il Mistero Di Oberwald
(The Mystery of Oberwald)
(Italy)
RTI. Rai Rete 2 prodn. Dir, Michelangelo Antonioni; sp, Antonioni, Tonino Guerra from "The Eagle Has Two Heads" by Jean Cocteau; cam, Luciano Tovoli; edtrs, Francesco Grandoni, Antonioni.   123.
Monica Vitti, Franco Branciaroli, Paolo Bonacelli, Elisabetta Pozzi, Luigi Diberti, Amad Saha Alan.
09/10/80

Il Piccolo Archimede
(The Little Archimedes)
(Italy)
X. RAI Italian Radio Television and TV2 prodn. Wri-dir, Gianni Amelio based on book by Aldous Huxley. Cam (Eastmancolor), Guido Bertoni, (16m blown up to 35m); sets, Ferdinando Ghelli; edtr, Giorgio Pozzi; mus, Roman Vlad. 83.
John Steiner, Laura Betti, Aldo Salvi, Shirley Corrigan, Mark Morganti, Graziano Giusti, Renato Moretti.
10/03/79

Il Prato
(The Meadow)
(Italy)
SCI. Prod, Giuliani De Negri for Filmtre and Rai2. Wri-dir, Paola and Vittorio Taviani. Cam (Eastmancolor), Franco Di Giacomo; edtr, Roberto Perpignani; mus, Ennio Morricone. 120.
Michele Placido, Saverio Marconi, Isabella Rossellini, Giulio Brogi.
09/05/79

Il Prefetto Di Ferro
(The Iron Prefect)
(Italy)
CNZ. Rizzoli Film-Gianni Hecht Lucari prodn. Dir, Pasquale Squittieri. Sp, Ugo Pirro, Arrigo Petacco from the book by Petacco; cam, Silvano Ippoliti; mus, Ennio Morricone. 120.
Giuliano Gemma, Claudia Cardinale.
11/16/77

Il Regno Di Napoli
(The Kingdom of Naples)
(W Germany - Italy)
X. Geissler Film Prodn, Munich, in collab with Zweites Deutsches Fernsehen, Wiesbaden, and PBC, Rome. Wri-dir, Werner Schroeter. Cam, Thomas Mauch; mus, M Tregadio; edtr, Ursula West, Schroeter. 125.
Romeo Giro, Antonio Orlando, Tiziana Ambretti, Maria Antonietta Riegel, Christina Donadio, Dino Mele, Renata Zamengo.
06/28/78

Il Ritorno Di Casanova
(The Return of Casanova)
(Italy)
X. RAI-Radiotelevisione Italiana presentation of RAI Channel 1. Prod, Monica Venturini for Filmes SpA, adapt, Paolo Battistuzzio. Dir, Pasquale Festa Campanile. Sp, Piero Chiara, based on a novel by Arthur Schnitzler; cam, Giuseppe Ruzzolini; mus, Riz Ortolani; edtr, Gian Maria Messeri. 124.
Giulio Bosetti, Mirella D'Angelo, Piero Vida, Grazia Maria Spina, Francesca Marciano, Pietro Tordi, Enzo Robutti, Bianca Toccafondi, Carlo Simoni, Ettore Carloni, Dino Emanuelli.
10/04/78

Il Visitatore
(The Visitor)
(Italy - US)
MAR. Ovidio Assonitis presents an International Picture Show Company release. Dir, Michael J Paradise (Giulio Paradisi). Story, Paradise, Assonitis; sp, Lou Comici, Robert Mundy; cam, Ennio Guarnieri; edtr, Robert Curi; art dir, Frank Venorio; mus comp-cond, Franco Mikalizzi; ani, Bozetto. 90.
Mel Ferrer, Glenn Ford, Lance Henriksen, John Huston, Joanne Nail, Sam Peckinpah, Shelly Winters, Paige Conner.
03/26/80

Il Y A Longtemps Que J't'aime
(It's A Long Time I've Loved You)
(France)
X. Films de la Tour presentation. Wri-dir, Jean-Charles Tacchella. Cam, George Lendi; edtr, Agnes Guillemot; mus, Gerard Anfosso. 93.
Jean Carmet, Marie Dubois, Alain Doutey.
09/05/79

Ileksen
(Australia - Papua)
X. Prod, Dennis O'Rourke. Dir, O'Rourke, Gary Kildea. Cam, O'Rourke; edtr, Peter Berry. 59.
(DOC) (16m)
03/28/79

I'll Force You To Live: SEE Ich Zwing Dich Zu Leben

I'll Love You Tomorrow: SEE Prong Nee Chan Ja Rak Koon

The Illegal: SEE Alambrista

Illuminations
(Australia)
MFM. Illumination Film Production prodn. Dir, Paul Cox; sp, Paul Cox; prod, Tibor Markus; mus, Norman Kaye, Alex Berry; cam, Wolfgang Beliharz. 70.
Tony Llewellyn-Jones, Gabi Trsek.
06/16/76

Illusion: SEE Iluzia

Il N'Y A Pas D'Oubli
(There Is No Forgetting)
(Canada)
NFC. Dirs, Rodrigo Gonzalez, Marilu Mallet, Jorge Fajardo. Editor, Pascale Laverriere, Mallet; cam, Martin Duckworth; mus, Alberto Sendra, Denis Larochelle. 100.
Enrique Sandoval, Lucia Barahona, Manuel Aranguiz.
(16m)
08/25/76

Ils Sont Fous Ces Sorciers
(These Sorcerers Are Mad)
(France)
AMLF. Lira Films prodn. Dir, Georges Lautner. Sp, Norbert Carbonneaux, Robert Kantof, Claude Mulot; cam (Eastmancolor), Henri Decae; edtr, Michele David. 90.
Jean Lefebvre, Henri Guybet, Renee St Cyr, Julien Guiomar, Catherine Lachens, Jean-Jacques Moreau.
08/02/78

Ils Sont Grands Ces Petits
(These Kids Are Grown-Ups)
(France)
UA. Cathala Films United Artists-FR3 co-prodn. Dir, Joel Santoni. Prod Norbert Saada. Sp, Daniel Boulanger, Jean-Claude Carriere, Joel Santoni, from an original scenario by Jean Jabely; cam (Eastmancolor), Walter Bal; art dir, Tony Roman; snd, Georges Prat and Luc Perini; edtr, Ava Zora. 95.
Catherine Deneuve, Claude Brasseur, Claude Pieplu. Jean Francois Balmer.
04/04/79

Ilse, Harem Keeper of The Oil Sheiks
CAM. Prod, William Brody. Dir, Don Edmonds. Sp, Langton Stafford; cam, Glenn Roland, Dean Cundey; edtr, Idi Yanamar; art dir, Mike Riva; snd, Al Ramirez. (MPAA rating: R). 93.
Dyanne Thorne, Michael Thayer, Wolfgang Roehm, Victor Alexander, Marlyn Joy, Tanya Boyd, Sharon Kelly, Dea Martenson, Elke Von, Bobby Woods, Su Ling, C D Lafluer, Ivan Roars, Haji Cat.
02/18/76

Iluzia
(Illusion)
(Bulgaria)
BGO. Bulgarofilm Prodn, Sofia. Dir, Lyudmil Staikov. Sp, Konstantin Pavlov; cam (Eastmancolor), Boris Yanakiev; art dir, Zahari Ivanov; mus, Goergi Genkov. 90.
Roussi Chanev, Lyuben Chatalov, Suzanna Kocurikova, Peter Slabakov.
07/23/80

Prijeki Sud
(Court Martial)
(Yugoslavia)
YFR. Adriafilm-Kinematografi-Zagreb Film-Morava Morava Film Prodn. Dir, Branko Ivanda. Sp, Zivko Jelicic, Ivanda; cam, Ivica Rajkovic; sets, Zeljko Senecic. 90.
Pero Kvrgic, Zarko Potocnjak, Vlatko Dulic, Krunoslav Valentic, Ljubo Kaper, Tanja Knezic, Sanja Vejnovic.
09/05/79

I'm an Anti-Star: SEE Ich Bin Ein Antistar. . .

I'm Expecting: SEE Jag Aer Med Barn

Im Feuer Bestanden
(Born of Fire)
(E Germany)
X. Prod-dir, Walter Heynowski, Gerhard Scheumann. Cam, Peter Hellmich; edtr, Trante Wischnewski. 75.
(Spanish Soundtrack) (DOC)
09/26/79

Im Herzen Des Hurrican
(In The Heart of the Hurricane)
(W Germany)
FDA. Hamburger Kino Kompanie Hark Bohm Film Production, Hamburg; prod, Natalia Bowakow, in co-prodn with Zweites Deutsches Fernsehen (ZDF), Mainz; Dir, Hark Bohm. Sp, Bohm, in collab with Gerhard Kelling; cam, Jaroslav Kucera; sets, Heidi and Tony Luedi; mus, Irmin Schmidt; edtr, Susanne Paschen. 103.
Uwe Bohm, Dschingis Bowakow, Brigitte Strohbauer, Jelka Bouvy, Verich von Bork, Marquand Bohm, Dieter Thomas, Hendrieke von Sydow.
04/02/80

Im Lauf Der Zeit
(In the Course of Time)
(W Germany)
FDA. Wim Wenders film prodn. Wri-dir, Wim Wenders; cam (b&w), Robbie Mueller; mus, Improved Sound Limited. 165.
Ruediger Vogeler, Hanns Zischler.
(B & W)
03/17/76

I'm Photogenic: SEE Sono Fotogenico

I'm Timid But I'm Treating It: SEE Je Suie Timide; Mais Je Me Soigne

Imi Hageneralit
(My Mother, The General)
(Israel)
X. Noah Films Presentation of a Golan-Globus Prodn. Prods, Menahem Golan, Yoram Globus. Exec prod, Dan Dimburt. Dir, Yoel Zilberg. Sp, Eli Tavor, Yoel Zilberg, based on the play by Eli Saghi; cam, David Gurfinkel; edtr, Irit Paz; art dir, Yossi Azmon; mus, Nurith Hirsch. 84.
Gideon Singer, Gilat Ankori, Uri Sali, Avi Pnini, Eyal Geffen, Makhram Khouri, Marlen Bejali, Haim Polani, Ariel Fourman.
06/20/79

Immacolata E Concetta: L'Altra Gelosia
(Immacolata and Concetta: The Other Jealousy)
(Italy)
TIT. Prod, Enzo Porcelli for ANTEA prodns. Dir, Salvatore Piscicelli. Sp, Carla Apuzzo, S Piscicelli. Cam (Eastmancolor), Emilio Bestetti; art dir, Giovanni Dionisi; edtr, Roberto Schiavone; mus, Remo Ugolinelli. 92.
Ida Di Benedetto, Marcella Michelangeli.
05/21/80

Imposters
X. Prod-dir, Mark Rappaport. Sp, Rappaport; cam, Fred Murphy; set des, Bob Edmonds. 110.
Charles Ludlam, Michael Burg, Ellen McElduff, Lina Todd, Peter Evans.
11/21/79

The Imprint of Giants: SEE L'Empreinte des Geants

In A Wild Moment: SEE Un Moment D'Egarement

In A Year of 13 Months: SEE In Einem Jahr Mit 13 Monden

In All Intimacy: SEE In Alle Stilte

In Alle Stilte
(In All Intimacy)
(Belgium)
PMB. Prod, Renaat Rombouts. Dir, Ralf Boumans; sp, Ralf Boumans, Ria Aerts; cam (Eastmancolor), Willem Baeckelmans; edtr, Henri Erismann; art dir, Philippe Graff; snd, Koen Pee; mus, Franz Schubert with arrangements by Pieter Verlinden. 93.
Mark Bober, Johan Leysen, Peggy De Landtsheer, Yvonne Mertens, Paula Sleyp, Nolle Verzijp, Beatrice Janssens, Netty Vangheei, Sien Eggers, Mieke Verheyden, Line Geysen, Blanca Heirman, Peter Strynckx, Lia Lee, Magda De Winter, Ludo Van Fraeyenhoven, Ronny Van de Loop, Ise Arnould.
05/03/78

In Einem Jahr Mit 13 Monden
(In A Year of 13 Months)
(W Germany)
FDA. Filmproduktion Im Filmverlag Der Autoren, Tango Film (Rainer Werner Fassbinder) prodn. Wri-dir, lensed (Eastmancolor) and edtr, Rainer Werner Fassbinder. 129.
Volker Spengler, Ingrid Caven, Gottfried John, Elisabeth Trissenaar, Eva Mattes.
03/07/79

In For Treatment: SEE Opname

In God We Trust
U. Howard West/George Shapiro prodn. Prods, West, Shapiro. Exec prod, Norman T Herman. Dir, Marty Feldman. Sp, Feldman, Chris Allen; cam (Technicolor), Charles Correll; edtr, David Blewitt; mus, John Morris; song, "Good For God" by Harry Nilsson; prodn des, Lawrence G Paull; set decor, Peg Cummings; cos des, Ruth Myers; snd, "Fast Eddie" Mahler; asso prod, Lauretta Feldman; asst dir, Stephen Barnett. (MPAA rating: PG). 97.
Marty Feldman, Peter Boyle, Louise Lasser, Richard Pryor, Andy Kaufman, Wilfrid Hyde-White, Severn Darden.
10/01/80

In Kluis
(The Enclosure)
(Belgium)
PRG. Visie-Filmproduction. Prod, Roland Verhavert. Sp-dir, Jan Gruyaert. Cam (Eastmancolor), Ben Tenniglo; mus, Koen De Bruyne; art dirs, Bob Van Reeth, Herman Jacobs; asst dir, Mary Hehuat; edtr, Gust Malfliet; snd, Joos Suetens. 100.
Bert Andre, Herman Jacobs, Mirjam Nuyten, Mary Hehuat.
02/01/78

In MacArthur Park
WWP. Wri-prod-dir-edtr, Bruce R Schwartz. Cam, John Sharaf; mus, Rocky Davis; co-edtr, Jerry Kutner; snd, Ken King; set decor, Judith Randall. 75.
Adam Silver, James Espinoza, Pete Homer Sr, Anna Shorter, Marcy Eudal, Doug Laffoon, Anita Noble.
(B & W)
04/06/77

In Memoriam
(Spain)
X. Emiliano Piedra prodn; dir, Enrique Braso. Sp, Juan Tebar, Jose Maria Carreno, Enrique Braso, based on story by Adolfo Bioy Casares; cam (Eastmancolor), Teo Escamilla; edtr, Guillermo Maldonado; sets, Eduardo Torre de la Fuente; mus, Luis Eduardo Aute. 95.
Geraldine Chaplin, Jose Luis Gomez, Eusebio Poncela, Jose Orjas, Eduardo Calvo.
09/21/77

In My Life: SEE Honningmane

In Nome Del Papa Re
(In The Name of the Pope King)
(Italy)
RIZ. Juppiter Generale Cinematografica (Italy). Prod, Franco Committeri. Sp-dir, Luigi Magni. Cam (Eastmancolor), Danilo Desideri; edtr, Ruggero Mastroianni; mus, Armando Trovaioli. 107.
Nino Manfredi, Damilo Mattei, Carmen Scarpitta, Giovanella Grifeo, Carlo Bagno, Salvo Randone.
03/22/78

In Praise of Older Women
(Canada)
AST. Astral Bellevue Pathe, R S L prodn. Exec prods, Stephen Roth, Harold Greenberg. Prods, Robert Lantos, Claude Heroux. Dir, George Kaczender. Sp, Paul Gottlieb from novel, "In Praise of Older Women" by Stephen Vizinczey; cam, Miklos Lente; mus, Tibor Polgar; edtrs, Kaczender, Peter Wintonick; art dir, Wolf Kroeger; cos, Olga Dimitrov. 105.
Tom Berenger, Karen Black, Susan Strasberg, Helen Shaver, Marilyn Lightstone, Alexandra Stewart, Marianne Mclsaac, Alberta Watson, Ian Tracey, Monique LePage.
09/20/78

In Search Of Historic Jesus
SSU. Prods, Charles E Sellier Jr, James L Conway. Dir, Henning Schellerup; wris, Marvin Wald, Jack Jacobs, based on the novel by Lee Roddy and Sellier Jr. Asso prod, Bill Cornford; cam (Technicolor), Paul Hipp; edtr, Kendall S Rase; mus, Bob Summers, the New London Orchestra; prodn des, Paul Staheli; sfx, John Cart; set decor, Randy Staheli; art dir, Doug Vandergrift. (MPAA rating: G). 91.
John Rubinstein, John Anderson, Nehemiah Persoff, Brad Crandall, Andrew Bloch, Morgan Brittany, Walter Brooke, Annette Charles, Royal Dano, Anthony De Longis, Lawrence Dobkin, Jeffrey Druce.
01/30/80

In Search Of Noah's Ark
SSU. Prod, Charles E Sellier Jr; dir, James L Conway. Exec prod, Raylan Jensen. Sp, Conway, Sellier from book by David Balsiger, Sellier; technical advisor-historian, Balsiger; cam, George Stapleford; prodn coord, Gerald Fleck; asst dir, David Oyster; art dir, Richard Sawyer; edtr, Randy Rennolds. (MPAA rating: G). 95.
Vern Adix
Narrated by: Brad Crandall.
(DOC)
02/09/77

In the Course of Time: SEE Im Lauf Der Zeit

In The Heart of the Hurricane: SEE Im Herzen Des Hurrican

In the Lost City of Sarzana: SEE Nella Citta' Perduta Di Sarzana

In the Mouth of the World: SEE Na Boca do Mundo

In the Name of the Fuhrer: SEE Au Nom du Fuhrer

In The Name of the Pope King: SEE In Nome Del Papa Re

In the Sign of the Lion: SEE I loevens tegn

The Incident: SEE Jiken

The Incorrigible Barbara: SEE Die Unverbesserliche Barbara

The Incredible Melting Man
AIP. Rosenberg-Gelfman prodn. Prod, Samuel W Gelfman; dir-sp, William Sachs. Cam, Willy Curtis; sfx, Rick Baker, Harry Woolman; make-up, Rick Baker; mus, Arlon Ober; art dir, Michael Levesque. (MPAA rating: R). 86.
Alex Rebar, Burr DeBenning, Myron Healey, Michael Alldredge, Ann Sweeny, Lisle Wilson, Rainbeaux Smith, Julie Drazen, Stuart Edmond Rodgers, Chris Whitney, Edwin Max, Dorothy Love, Janus Blythe, Jonathan Demme.
01/11/78

The Incredible Sarah
(Britain)
AVE. Readers Digest prodn. Prod, Helen M Strauss. Dir, Richard Fleischer. Sp, Ruth Wolff; cam (Technicolor), Christopher Challis; edtr, John Jympson; mus, Elmer Bernstein; prodn des, Elliot Scott; art dir, Norman Raynolds; set decor, Peter Howitt; snd, Brian Simmons; asst dir, Terry Marcel. (MPAA rating: PG). 105.
Glenda Jackson, Daniel Massey, Yvonne Mitchell, Douglas Wilmer, David Langton, Simon Williams, John Castle, Edward Judd, Rosemarie Dunham, Peter Sallis, Bridget Armstrong, Margaret Courtenay.
09/08/76

Independence
FOX. Production for US National Parks Service. Dir, John Huston. Prods, Joyce and Lloyd Ritter. Sp, the Ritters, Thomas McGrath; cam (Eastmancolor-Panavision), Owen Roizman; edtr, Eric Albertson; art dir, Stephen Grimes; cos, Ann Roth; mus, Jack Cortner; snd mixing, Christopher Newman; re-recording, Albert Gramahlia; 2d unit dir-pho, Lloyd Ritter; historical cnslnt, L H Butterfield. 28.
William Atherton, John Favorite, Pat Hingle, Ken Howard, Anne Jackson, Donald C Moore, Scott Mulherne, Patrick O'Neal, John Randolph, Joe Ritter, Paul Sparer, Tim Spratley, Donald Symington, James Tolkan, Eli Wallach, E G Marshall.
04/07/76

Independence Day
X. Independence Day Prodns prodn. Wri-dir, Bobby Roth. Cam, Elliot Davis; edtr, John Carnochan; mus, Mauro Bruno. 87.
Mel Rosier, Gammy Burdett, Michelle Davison, Henry Gayle Sanders, Charles Branklyn, Nikki Sanz.
(16m)
09/15/76

The Indians Are Still Far Away: SEE Les Indiens Sont Encore Loin

Inferno
(Italy)
FOX. Prod, Claudio Argento for Produzioni Intersound. Wri-dir, Dario Argento. Cam (Technicolor), Romano Albani; art dir, Giuseppe Bassan; edtr, Franco Fraticelli; mus, Keith Emerson. (MPAA rating: R). 107.
Irene Miracle, Leigh McCloskey, Eleonora Giorgi, Daria Nicolodi, Alida Valli.
04/02/80

Infra-Man
(Hong Kong)
BRE. Shaw Brothers prodn. Prod, Runme Shaw. Dir, Hua Shan. 92.
Li Hsiu-hsien, Wang Hsieh, Terry Liu, Lin Wen-wei.
03/31/76

The Inheritance: SEE Eredita' Ferramonti

The In-Laws
WB. Prod, Arthur Hiller, William Sackheim. Exec prod, Alan Arkin. Dir, Hiller. Sp, Andrew Bergman; cam, David M Walsh; edtr, Robert E Swink; mus, John Morris; prodn des, Pato Guzman; snd, Larry Jost; asst dir, Jack Rod. (MPAA rating: PG). 103.
Peter Falk, Alan Arkin, Richard Libertini, Nancy Dussault, Penny Peyser, Arlene Golonka, Michael Lembeck, Paul Lawrence Smith, Carmine Caridi, Ed Begley Jr, Sammy Smith, James Hong.
06/13/79

Insiang
(Philippines)
X. Mariposa prodn. Prod, Ruby Tiong Tan. Dir, Lino Brock. Sp, Mario O'Hara, Lamberto Antonio, from story by O'Hara. Edtr, Augusto Salvado; mus, Minda Azarcon; cam, Conrado Baltzar. 95.
Hilda Koronel, Mona Lisa, Ruel Vernal, Marlon Ramirez.
(Tagalog soundtrack)
05/24/78

Inside Jennifer Welles
EVT. Howard B. Howard prodn. Dir, Jennifer Welles. Based on "The Memoirs of Jennifer Welles," cam, James Hammermill. (Self-applied X rating). 107.
Jennifer Welles, James Chin, Ed Chin, Steve Mitchell, Richard Bolla, Cheri Baines, Ken Anderson, Peter Andrews, Pepe, Manny Duran, Marlane Willoughby, G G Palma, Teddy Ngai, David Innis, Mike DeMarco, Joji Tani, Moory Yank Park, David Shaker, Bobby Niles, Mike Dattore, Dave Ruby.
08/10/77

Inside Looking Out
(Australia)
X. Illumination Films prodn. Prod-dir, Paul Cox. Asst dir-prod, Bernard Eddy; asso prod, Tony Llewellyn-Jones; sp, Paul Cox, Susan Holly Jones; cam, Paul Cox, Peter Tammer, Bryan Gracey; art dir, Alan Stubenrauch; mus, Norman Kaye; edtrs, Paul Cox, Russell Hurley. 90.
Briony Behets, Tony Llewellyn-Jones, Danni Eddy, Juliet Bacskai, Norman Kaye, Elke Neidhart.
06/15/77

Inside Marilyn Chambers
MTL. (Self-imposed X rating). 78.
Marilyn Chambers, Jim Mitchell, Art Mitchell, Johnny Keyes, George S McDonald.
(DOC) (16m)
02/11/76

Inside Moves
AFD. Goodmark Prodn. Prods, Mark M Tanz, R W Goodwin. Dir, Richard Donner. Sp, Valerie Curtin, Barry Levinson, based on Todd Walton's novel; cam (Technicolor), Laszlo Kovacs; edtr, Frank Morriss; mus, John Barry; prodn des, Charles Rosen; set des, Boyd Willat; set decor, Dick Goddard; cos des, Ron Talsky; snd, Willie D Burton; asst dir-2d unit dir, Michael F Grillo. (MPAA rating: PG). 113.

John Savage, David Morse, Diana Scarwid, Amy Wright, Tony Burton, Bill Henderson, Steve Kahan, Jack O'Leary, Bert Remsen, Harold Russell, Pepe Serna, Harold Sylvester, Arnold Williams.
12/10/80

Inside Woman: SEE Kvindesind

Inspecteur La Bavure
(Inspector Blunder)
(France)
AMLF. Renn Productions-FR3 prodn. Prod, Claude Berri. Dir, Claude Zidi. Wri, Zidi, Jean Bouchaud; cam, Henri Decae; edtr, Nicole Saunier; snd, Bernard Aubouy; art dir, Jean-Baptiste Poirot; mus, Vladimir Cosma. 100.
Coluche, Gerard Depardieu, Dominique Lavanant, Julien Guiomar.
12/31/80

Inspection of the Scene of a Crime 1901: SEE Wizia Lokalna 1901

Inspector Blunder: SEE Inspecteur La Bavure

The Institution: SEE Die Anstalt

Interior Of A Convent: SEE Interno D'Un Convento

Interiors
UA. Jack Rollins - Charles H Joffe prodn. Prod, Charles H Joffe; exec prod, Robert Greenhut. Wri-dir, Woody Allen. Cam (Technicolor), Gordon Willis; edtr, Ralph Rosenblum; prodn des, Mel Bourne; cos des, Joel Schumacher; asst dir, Martin Berman. (MPAA rating: PG). 93.
Kristin Griffith, Marybeth Hurt, Richard Jordan, Diane Keaton, E G Marshall, Geraldine Page, Maureen Stapleton, Sam Waterston.
08/02/78

International Velvet
(Britain)
UA. MGM picture. Wri-prod-dir, Bryan Forbes. Adapted from the novel, "National Velvet," by Enid Bagnold; cam (Metrocolor), Tony Imi; aerial cam, Geoff Mulligan; USA race sequence cam, Edward R Brown; edtr, Timothy Gee; mus, Francis Lai; prodn des, Keith Wilson; set decor, Ian Whittaker; snd, Ken Barker, Gus Lloyd; cos-ward, John Furness, Dorothy Edwards; John Hilling; asst dir, Philip Shaw; stunt coord, Richard Graydon; USA racing sequences coord, Don Boyd. (MPAA rating: PG). 125.
Tatum O'Neal, Christopher Plummer, Anthony Hopkins, Nanette Newman, Peter Barkworth, Dinsdale Landen, Sarah Bullen, Jeffrey Byron, Richard Warwick, Daniel Abineri, Jason White, Martin Neil, Douglas Reith.
06/28/78

Interno D'Un Convento
(Interior Of A Convent)
(Italy)
PFC. Trust International Films prodn. Wri-dir, Walerian Borowczyk, loosely based on Stendhal's "Promenade in Rome." Cam (Eastmancolor), Luciano Tovoli; art dir, Luciano Spadoni; mus, Sergi Montori. 95.
Ligia Branice, Marina Pierro, Gabriella Giacobbe, Loredano Martinez, Marjo Maranzana.
08/02/78

Intoarcerea Lui Voda Lupusneanu
(The Return of the Banished)
(Romania)
X. Maison de Films Trois prodn. Wri-dir, Malvina Ursianu. Cam, Alexandru Intorsureanu, Gheorghe Fischer; edtr, Margareta Anescu; mus, Anatol Vieru. 148.
Georges Motoi, Silvia Popovici, Valeriu Paraschiv, Cornel Coman.
10/15/80

Invasion of the Body Snatchers
UA. Prod, Robert H Solo. Dir, Phillip Kaufman. Sp, W D Richter, based on the novel by Jack Finney; cam (Technicolor), Michael Chapman; edtr, Douglas Stewart; prodn des, Charles Rosen; mus, Denny Zeitlin; snd, Art Rochester; makeup effects, Thomas Burman, Edouard Henriques; sfx, Dell Rheaume, Russ Hessey; special sound effects, Ben Burtt; asst dir, Jim Bloom. (MPAA rating: PG). 115.
Donald Sutherland, Brooke Adams, Leonard Nimoy, Veronica Cartwright, Jeff Goldblum, Art Hindle, Lelia Goldoni, Kevin McCarthy.
12/20/78

Invasion of the Love Drones
X. Sensory Man prodn. Sp, Jerome Hamlin, with Dr. Conrad Baunz, Michael Gury, John Phillips; cam-edtr, Hamlin; snd, Sarah Nicholson. (Self-imposed X rating). 72.
Eric Edwards, Viveca Ash, Bree Anthony, Tony Blue, Sarah Nicholson, Jamie Gillis.
12/07/77

The Inventor: SEE Der Erfinder

The Investigator and the Woods: SEE Sledovateliat Y Gozato

Invisible Adversaries: SEE Unsichtbare Gegner

Io sono Anna Magnani
(I Am Anna Magnani)
(Belgium)
PFF. Chris Vermorcken/Pierre Film prodn. Dir, Chris Vermorcken. Exec prod, Jacqueline Pierreux. Spoken commentaries, Leonor Fini, Liliane Becker. Research and prodn assts, Louise Rocco, Agnes Rombaut. Mus, Willyl de Maesschalk. Edtr, Eva Houdova. 105.
(DOC) (COLOR & B & W)
11/05/80

Io Sono Mia
(I Belong To Me)
(Italy - Germany - Spain)
TIT. Clesi Cinematografica-Albatros Produktion-Munder Film prodn. Prod, Lu Leone for Spirale 76. Dir, Sofia Scandurra. Sp, Elena Ricci Poccetto, Giorgia Onofri, based on novel by Dacia Maraini; cam (Technospes Color), Nurith Aviv; edtr, Gabriella Cristiani; mus, Giovanna Marini. 99.
Stefania Sandrelli, Maria Schneider, Michele Placido.
03/15/78

Iphighenia
(Greece)
GKF. Wri-dir, Michael Cacoyannis, based on the ancient Greek tragedy of Euripides; cam (Eastmancolor), George Arvantis; edtrs, Cacoyannis, Takis Yannopoulos; mus, Mikis Theodrakis; art dir, Dionysis Photopoulos. 127.
Irene Papas, Costa Kazakos, Costa Carras, Tatiana Papamoskou, Christos Tsangas, Panos Michalopoulos.
05/25/77

Iracema
(Brazil)
CPM. Stop Film prodn. Dir, Jorge Brodansky. Sp, Orlando Sena, Brodansky; cam (Eastmancolor), Brodansky; edtr, Eva Grundmann. 90.
Edna De Cassia, Paolo Cesar Pereio.
05/19/76

The Irishman
(Australia)
GUO. Forest Home Film prodn. Prod, Anthony Buckley. Dir, Donald Crombie. Sp, Crombie from novel by Elizabeth O'Conner; cam (AGFA Color), Peter James; prodn des, Owen Williams; art dir, Graham Walker; asst dir, Mark Egerton; ward des, Judith Dorsman; edtr, Tim Wellburn; mus, Charles Marawood. 108.
Michael Craig, Simon Burke, Robin Nevin, Lou Brown, Tui Lorraine Bow, Andrew Maguire, Tony Barry, Marcella Burgoyne, Vincent Ball, Roberta Grant, Gerard Kennedy, Bryan Brown, Roger Ward, Babette Stevens.
05/10/78

The Iron Buffalo: SEE Ai Kwai Legg

The Iron Prefect: SEE Il Prefetto Di Ferro

Irreconcilable Memories: SEE Unversoehnliche Errinnerungen

Is This "Fate"?: SEE Von Wegen "Schicksal"

Isang Gabi Sa Buhay Ng Isang Babae
(One Night in Life with One Woman)
(Philippines)
SSH. Prod-dir, Gatt Maggay, Gene Generoso. Story and sp, A Makabuhay; cam, Carding Periodica; art dir, Ramon Gregorio; executive prods, Joe Jalbuena, Butch Gonzaga, Pio Cudilla; mus, Freddie Dandan.
Helen Morgan, Joseph Sytangco, Lito Legaspi, Anita Linda, Logan Clarke, Rebecca Gonzales, Lorli Villanueva, Babsy Paredes.
06/23/76

I Sao Untarai
(Dangerous Girl)
(Thailand)
NKP. Prod-dir, Chana Krapayun. Story, Thep Thaves; sp, Chana Krapayun; cam, Sophon Janpanich; edtr, Chana Krapayun; snd, Asvin Papiyon; prodn mgr, Mek Megsuan; cos, Pairoj Sarifian. 110.
Sorapong Chatri, Suriya Chinaphan, Tasawan Seniwong, Piyamatr Monjakul, Niroot Sirichanva, Tarika Tarathit, Lak Apichart, Singh Milintrasai, Vilaiwan Vattanapanich, Chindis Bunnag, Prapis Paphan, Choosri Misomon, Pipop Pupinyo.
01/19/77

Iskanja
(Search)
(Yugoslavia)
VIB. Viba Film, Ljubljana, Film prodn. Dir, Matjaz Klopcic. Sp, Marko Slodnjak; cam, Tomislav Pinter; sets, Niko Matul. 90.
Boris Cavazza, Boris Juh, Milena Zupancic, Tanja Poberznik, Iva Zupancic.
09/05/79

Iskindiria...Leh?
(Alexandria...Why?)
(Egypt - Algeria)
X. Misr Int'l Films prodn. Prod-dir, Youseff Chahine. Sp, Chahine, Mohsen Zayed; cam, Mohsen Nasr; mus, Fouad El Zaheri; edtr, Rashida Abdel Salam. 133.
Naglaa Fathi, Farid Shawki, Ezzat El Alayli, Gerry Sundquist, Mohsen Mohiedine.
03/21/79

The Island
U. Zanuck-Brown Prodn. Dir, Michael Ritchie. Prods, Richard D Zanuck, David Brown. Sp, Peter Benchley, from his novel; cam, Henri Decae; prodn des, Dale Hennesy; flm ed, Richard A Harris; mus, Ennio Moricone; special visual effects, Albert Whitlock; cos, Ann Roth; set decor, Robert de Vestel. (MPAA rating: R). 114.
Michael Caine, David Warner, Angela Punch McGregor, Frank Middlemass, Don Henderson, Dudley Sutton, Colin Jeavons, Zakes Mosae, Brad Sullivan, Jeffrey Frank.
06/04/80

The Island: SEE *La Isla*

The Island of Dr. Moreau
AIP. Skip Steloff/Sandy Howard/Major prodn. Prods, John Temple-Smith, Steloff; exec prod, Samuel Z Arkoff, Howard. Dir, Don Taylor. Sp, John Herman Shaner, Al Ramrus, from the novel by H G Wells; cam (Movielab Color), Gerry Fisher; 2d-unit cam, Ronnie Taylor; edtr, Marion Rothman; mus, Laurence Rosenthal; prodn des, Philip Jefferies; set decor, James Berkey; cos-ward, Richard LaMotte, Emma Porteus, Rita Woods; snd, David Hildyard; asst dir, Bob Bender. (MPAA rating: PG). 98.
Burt Lancaster, Michael York, Nigel Davenport, Barbara Carrera, Richard Basehart, Nick Cravat, The Great John L, Bob Ozman, Fumio Demura, Gary Baxley, John Gillespie, David Cass.
07/13/77

The Island of the Silver Herons: SEE *Ostrov Stribrnych Volavek*

Islands In The Stream
PAR. Prods, Peter Bart, Max Palevsky. Dir, Franklin J Schaffner. Sp, Denne Bart Petitclerc, based on the novel by Ernest Hemingway; cam (Metrocolor), Fred Koenekamp; edtr, Robert Swink; mus, Jerry Goldsmith; prodn des, William J Creber; set decor, Raphael Bretton; snd, John K Wilkinson, Darin Knight; asst dir, Kurt Neumann. (MPAA rating: PG). 105.
George C Scott, David Hemmings, Gilbert Roland, Susan Tyrrell, Richard Evans, Claire Bloom, Julius Harris, Hart Bochner, Brad Savage, Michael-James Wixted, Hildy Brooks, Jessica Rains, Walter Friedel, Charles Lampkin.
03/09/77

Ispravi Se, Delfina
(Stand Up Straight, Delphina)
(Yugoslavia)
YFR. Vardar Film-Koproducent Makedonia Film prodn. Wri-dir, Aleksander Durcinov. Cam (Eastmancolor), Kiro Bilbilovski; mus, Slave Dimitrov. 92.
Neda Aneric, Darko Dameski, Slobodan Dimitrijevic, Dime Ilijev.
08/17/77

Istoriya As: Klyachimol
(Asya's Happiness)
(USSR)
GOS. Mosfilm Prodn, Moscow. Dir, Andrei Mikhalkov-Konchalovsky. Sp, Yuri Klepikov; cam, G Rerberg; sets, M Romadin; mus, V Ovchinnikov. 90.
Iya Savina, nonprofessionals.
(B & W)
07/05/78

I Sua
(Lady Tiger)
(Thailand)
VFT. Prod, Virachai Chaiyayon. Wri-dir, Vinit Pakdivijit. Story, Saraboot; cam, Santat Srisampan; mus, King's Sound Studio; edtr, Vinit Vongsiri; prodn mgr-asst dir, Virachai Duangpatra. 110.
Vasana Chalakorn, Krung Srivilai, Sasima Singsiri, Runglawan Sripatimakul, Niroot Sirichanya, Krisana Amnuayporn, Siripong Issarangkul Na Ayuthaya, Salai Poomjai, Wipawadee Tiyakul, Chavalit Nutyam.
05/11/77

It All Adds Up: SEE *Kassen Stemmer*

It All Depends On Girls: SEE *Tout Depend des Filles*

It Can Only Get Worse: SEE *Der Durchdreher*

It Lives Again
WB. Prod-dir-wri, Larry Cohen. Cam (Technicolor), Fenton Hamilton; edtrs, Curt Burch, Louis Friedman, Carol O'Blath; asst dir, Reid Freeman; snd, Ken Scrivener; mus, Bernard Herrmann, with additional mus by Laurie Johnson. (MPAA rating: R). 91.
Frederic Forrest, Kathleen Lloyd, John P Ryan, John Marley, Andrew Duggan, Eddie Constantine, James Dixon.
05/10/78

It Shouldn't Happen To A Vet
(Britain)
EMI. Reader's Digest presentation of a David Susskind prodn. Exec prod, David Susskind. Prod, Margaret Matheson. Dir, Eric Till. Sp, Alan Plater, based on books by James Herriot; prodn exec, Ron Gilbert; asso prods, Cecil Ford, Roy Stevens; mus comp, Laurie Johnson; cam, Arthur Ibbetson; prodn des, Geoffrey Drake; edtr, Thom Noble; asst dir, Colin Brewer. 94.
John Alderton, Colin Blakely, Lisa Harrow, Bill Maynard, Paul Shelley, Richard Pearson, Rosemary Martin, Raymond Francis, John Barrett, Philip Stone, Clifford Kershaw, Kevin Moreton, Liz Smith, Leslie Sarony, Gwen Nelson, Juliet Cooke, Stacy Davies, Christine Hargreaves, May Warden, Richard Griffiths, Ian Hastings.
04/14/76

Itchy Fingers
(Hong Kong)
X. Advance Films Ltd and Golden Harvest Prodn-coprodn. Dir, Po Chi-leung. Sp, Richard Ng, Po Chi Leung, Wong Ching; cam, Cheung Yiu Jo; sfx, Arthur Lavis; edtr, Cheung Yiu Chung; mus; Frankie Chan, Ricky Fung. 94.
Richard Ng, Roy Chao, Cora Miao.
(English subtitles)
02/21/79

I Tembelides Tis Eforis Kiladas
(The Slothful Ones Of The Fertile Valley)
(Greece)
ALX. Wri-dir, Nicos Panayotopoulos from the book by Albert Cossery. Cam (Eastmancolor), Andreas Bellis; edtr, Yorgos Triantafylow; mus, Mahler. 115.

Olga Karlatos, Yorgos Dialegmenos, Dimitris Poulikakos, Nikitas Tsakirglouu, Vassilis Diamtopolous.
08/23/78

Itim
(The Rites of May)
(Phillipines)
X. Prod-dir, Mike de Leon. Sp, Doy del Mundo, Gil Quito; cam, Ely Cruz, Rody Lacap; edtr, Ike Jarlego Jr; mus, Max Jocson. 116.
Tommy Abuel, Charo Santos, Mario Montenegro, Moody Diaz, Mona Lisa, Susan Valdez.
03/21/79

It's A Funny, Funny World
(Israel)
NOA. Golan-Globus Prodn. Prods, Menahem Golan, Yoram Globus. Dir, Zvi Shissel. Sp, Boaz Davidson, Shissel; cam, Adam Greenberg, Amnon Salomon, edtr, Alain Jacubowicz; songs, comp-sung, Ariel Zilber. 90.
Boaz Davidson, Zvi Shissel, Izik Albalak, Ophelia Shtrall, Uri Gross.
07/19/78

It's A Long Time I've Loved You: SEE Il Y A Longtemps Que J't'aime

It's A World Full of Children: SEE Verden er fuld af boern

It's Me
(Holland)
X. Nico Crama prodn. Prod, Nico Crama. Dir-wri, Frans Zwartjes. Cam, Zwartjes, Mat van Hensbergen; mus, Lodewijk de Boer, Zwartjes; edtr, Wouter Snip; decor, Zwartjes, Trix, Zwartjes, Floor Peters. 68.
Willeke van Ammelrooy.
03/21/79

It's My Turn
COL. Rastar-Martin Elfand prodn. Prod, Martin Elfand. Dir, Claudia Weill. Exec prod, Jay Presson Allen. Sp, Eleanor Bergstein; cam (Metrocolor), Bill Butler; edtrs, Byron (Buzz) Brandt, Marjorie Fowler, James Coblenz; prodn des, Jack Delovia; mus, Patrick Williams; snd, Pat Somerset, Jeff Bushelman; cos, Ruth Myers; asst dir, David McGiffert. (MPAA rating: R). 91.
Jill Clayburgh, Michael Douglas, Charles Grodin, Beverly Garland, Steven Hill, Teresa Baxter, Joan Copeland, John Gabriel, Charles Kimbrough, Roger Robinson, Jennifer Salt, Daniel Stern.
10/22/80

It's Never Too Late: SEE Nunca Es Tarde

It's Not Me, It's Him: SEE C'est pas moi c'est lui

It's Not the Size That Counts
(Britain)
BRE. Betty E Box/Ralph Thomas prodn. Prod, Betty E Box. Exec prod, Larry Gordon. Dir, Ralph Thomas. Sp, Sid Colin, from a story by Harry Corbett; additional dialogue, Ian La Frenais; cam (Eastmancolor), Tony Imi; edtr, Ray Watts; mus, Tony Macaulay. (MPAA rating: R). 90.
Leigh Lawson, Elke Sommer, Denholm Elliott, Judy Geeson, Milo O'Shea, Vincent Price, Julie Ege, George Coulouris.
04/04/76

It's Showtime
UA. Weintraub-Heller prodn. Prods, Fred Weintraub, Paul Heller. Sp, Alan Myerson; mus, Artie Butler; edtrs, Alan Holzman, Peter E Berger. (MPAA rating: G). 86.
(COMPILATION)
04/07/76

It's The Rich Man's Fault That The Poor Man Is His Enemy: SEE Die Herren Machen Das Selber,

Dass Ihnen Der Arme Mann Feyndt Wird Ivan The Terrible: SEE Grozny Vek

I've Got You, You've Got Me, By The Hairs Of My Chinny Chin Chin: SEE Je Te Tiens Tu Me Tiens Par La Barbichette

Izbavitelj
(The Redeemer)
(Yugoslavia)
CFZ. Jadran Film, Zagreb, and Croatia Film, Zagreb, prodn. Dir, Krsto Papic. Sp, Ivo Bresan, Papic, based on novel by Alexander Greene; cam (Eastmancolor), Ivica Rajkovic; mus, Brane Zivkovic. 87.
Ivica Vidovic, Mirjana Majurec, Relja Basic, Fabijan Sovagovic, Ilija Ivezic.
03/09/77

Jabberwocky
(Britain)
C5. Michael White presentation, prod, Sandy Lieberson; exec prod, John Goldstone. Dir, Terry Gilliam. Sp, Terry Gilliam and Charles Alverson, based on poem by Lewis Carroll; cam (Technicolor), Terry Bedford; edtr, Michael Bradsell; art dir, Millie Burns; mus, De Wolfe; sfx, John F Brown, Effects Assos. (MPAA rating: PG). 100.
Michael Palin, Max Wall, Deborah Fallender, John Le Mesurier, Annette Badland, Warren Mitchell, Brenda Cowling, Harry H. Corbett, Rodney Bewes, Bernard Bresslaw, Alexandra Dane, Derek Francis, Peter Cellier, Frank Williams, Anthony Garrick, John Bird, Neil Innes, Paul Curran, Graham Crowden, Gordon Rollings, Glenn Williams, Bryan Pringle, Terry Jones, Brian Glover, John Gorman, Julian Hough, Dave Prowse, Harold Goodwin, Tony Sympson, Simon Williams, Jerrold Wells, Gordon Kaye.
04/06/77

Jack
(Sweden)
FXS. Europa Film/Stockholm Film prodn. Dir, Jan Halldoff. Sp, Ulf Lundell, Halldoff. Based on Lundell's novel. Cam (Eastmancolor), Hans Welin, Roland Sterner. Mus, Ulf Lundell & Nature. Prodn des, Anders Bareus. Edtr, Wic Kjellin. Exec prod, Bo Jonsson. Asst prod, Rune Hjelm. Prodn mgr, Anita Tesler. 108.
Goeran Stangertz, Kjell Bergquist, Oerjan Ramberg, Gunnel Fred, Tove Linde.
03/30/77

Jackson County Jail
NW. Prod, Jeff Begun; exec prod, Roger Corman. Dir, Michael Miller. Sp, Donald Stewart; cam, Bruce Logan; edtr, Caroline Ferriol; mus, Loren Newkirk; asso prod, Paul Gonsky; prodn mgr-asst dir, Richard Schor; snd, Bill Kaplan; art dir, Michael McCloskey; cos des, Caronelia McNamara; stunt coord, James Arnett. (MPAA rating: R). 89.
Yvette Mimieux, Tommy Lee Jones, Robert Carradine, Frederic Cook, Severn Darden, Howard Hesseman, John Lawlor, Mary Woronov, Britt Leach, Betty Thomas, Patrice Rohmer.
05/05/76

Jacob Two-Two Meets the Hooded Fang
(Canada)
GKN. Prod, Harry Gulkin. Exec prod, John Flaxman. Wri-dir, Theodore J Flicker, based on novel by Mordecai Richler. Cam, Francois Protat; edtr, Stan Cole; art dir, Seamus Flannery; mus comp and sung by Lewis Furey; cos, Francois Barbeau. 80.
Stephen Rosenberg, Alex Karras, Guy L'Ecuyer, Joy Coghill, Earl Pennington, Claude Gai, Marfa Richler, Thor Bishopric, Victor Desy.
03/14/79

Jacque A La Dama
(Check to the Queen)
(Spain)
X. Gregor Films S A, Duna Films P C, Cinema 2000 S A and Llama Films prodn. Dir, Francisco Rodriguez. Sp, Rodriguez, Montserrat Julio, Rene Palacios; cam (Eastmancolor), Andres Berenguer; sets, Jose Maria Alarcon; edtr, Eduardo Biurrun; mus, Harmony. 87.
Conchita Velasco, Ana Belen, Pedro Diez del Corral, Henry Gregor, Olvido Lorente, Eduardo MacGregor, Miguel Angel Rellan, Carmen Gran, Mary Leyva, Beatriz Elorrieta, Manuel Gijon.
10/04/78

Jag Aer Med Barn
(I'm Expecting)
(Switzerland)
SVE. Olle Helbom/Svensk Filmindustri prodn. Dir, Lasse Hallstroem; orig story, script, Lasse Hallstroem, Brasse Braennstroem, Olle Helbom; cam (Eastmancolor), Roland Ludin; edtr, Lasse Hallstroem; ani cartoon sequences, Per Ahlin; mus, Bengt Palmers. 103.
Magnus Haerenstam, Anki Liden, Mischa Gabay, Lis Niheim.
12/26/79

Jag ar Maria
(I Am Maria)
(Sweden)
SVF. Drakfilm AB/Swedish Film Institute/Three Leaf Clover HB Prodn. Sp-edtr-dir, Karsten Wedel. Based on novel by Hans-Eric Hellberg; co-sp, Goeran Setterberg; cam (Eastmancolor), Rune Ricsson; Micha Gavrjusjov; mus, Bengt Edquist, Boerje Sandquist; prodn des, Anders Barreus; exec prod, Hans Iveberg; prod mgrs, Lisbeth Wikner, Bengt Wendin. 90.
Lise Lotte Hjelm, Peter Lindgren, Frej Lindquist, Helena Brodin, Claire Wikholm.
05/28/80

Jaguar
(Phillipines)
ATP. Dir, Lino Brocka. Sp, Jose Lacaba, Richardo Lee; cam, Conrado Balthazar; edtr, Rene Tala; mus, Max Jocson. 90.
Phillip Salvador, Amy Austria, Menggie Cobarrubias, Anita Linda, Johnny Delgado, Tonio Gutierrez.
05/21/80

Jaguar Lives!
AIP. Prod, Derek Gibson. Exec prod, Sandy Howard. Dir, Ernest Pintoff. Sp, Yabo Yablonsky; cam, John Cabrera; edtr, Angelo Ross; mus, Robert O Ragland; art dir, Adolfo Cofino; cos des, Ron Talsky; snd, George Stephenson; asso prod, Quinn Donoghue; asst dir, Kuki Lopez Rodero. (MPAA rating: PG). 90.
Joe Lewis, Christopher Lee, Donald Pleasence, Barbara Bach, Capucine, Joseph Wiseman, Woody Strode, John Huston, Gabriel Melgar, Anthony De Longis, Sally Faulkner, Gail Grainger, Anthony Heaton.
09/05/79

Jakub
(Czechoslovakia)
X. Czech Film prodn, Prague, Barrandov Studios. Dir, Ota Koval. Sp, Katarina Slobodova; cam, Miroslav Ondricek; mus, Stepan Lucky. 90.
Filip Renc, Ladislav Mrkvicka, Vera Galatikova, Olga Karaskova.
03/16/77

Jamais Plus Toujours
(Never Again Always)
(France)
SNC. Les Films De L'Equinoxe-FR3 prodn. Wri-dir, Yannick Bellon. Cam (Eastmancolor), Georges Barsky; edtr, Janine See. 80.
Bulle Ogier, Loleh Bellon, Jean-Marc Bory.
04/07/76

J.A. Martin Photographe
(Canada)
NFC. Dir, Jean Beaudin. Sp, Bueadin, Marcel Sabourin; cam (Eastmancolor), Pierre Mignot; mus, Maurice Blackburn. 102.
Marcel Sabourin, Monique Mercure, Marthe Thierry, Jean Lapointe, Mariette Duval.
05/18/77

Jambon D'Ardenne
(Ham from the Ardennes)
(Belgium - France)
ELN. Lamy Films, Brussels - Reggane Films, Paris prodn. Dir, Benoit Lamy. Sp, Rudolph Pauli, Benoit Lamy; cam (Gevacolor), Michel Baudour; edtr, Susan Rosberg; mus, Pieter Verlinden; snd, Henri Morelle. 86.
Annie Girardot, Ann Petersen, Christian Barbier, Dominique Drouot, Nathalie Van de Walle, Alain Soriel, Bonbon, Michel Lechat, Serge Delvische, Marie-Louise Debouny, Andre Vercammen, Marie-Jeanne Megank.
05/04/77

Jane Austen In Manhattan
CTY. Merchant-Ivory prodn. Prod, Ismail Merchant. Dir, James Ivory. Sp, Ruth Prawer Jhabvala; cam, Ernest Vincze; mus, Richard Robbins; set, Michael Yeargan; cos, Jenny Beavan. 108.
Anne Baxter, Robert Powell, Sean Young, Kurt Johnson, Katrina Hodiak, Tim Choate, Nancy New, Chuck McCaughan, John Guerrasio, Michael Wager.
07/30/80

Jane Bleibt Jane
(Jane Is Jane Forever)
(W Germany)
X. Enten prodn. Prod, Rolf Buhrmann. Sp-dir, Walter Bockmayer, Buhrmann. Cam, Peter Martin; edtr, Inge Gielow; mus, David Bowie, Asha Putli, Mandingo, Stomu Yamshita; art dir, Norbert Schaub. 85.
Johanna Konig, Peter Chatel, Karl Blomer, Evelyn Hall, Hannelore Lubeck, Anita Riotte, Brigitte Gonsior.
04/26/78

Janiksen Vuosi
(The Year of the Hare)
(Finland)
X. Filminor prodn. Prod, Kullervo Kukkasjarvix. Dir, Risto Jarva. Sp, Arto Paasilinna, Risto Jarva, Kullervo Kukkasjarvi; cam, Antti Peippo, Erkki Peltomaa, Juha-Veli Akras; edtr, Risto Jarva, Matti Kuortti; mus, Markku Kopisto. 105.
Antti Ligja.
03/28/79

Jarha Fi Lhaite
(A Hole in the Wall)
(Morocco)
CMO. Farida Benlyazid-Kamar Film-Centre Cinematographique Morocain-Izza Gennini prodn. Wri-dir, Jillali Ferhati. Cam (Eastmancolor), Ahmed El Maanouni; edtr, Amelie Cabral; mus, Jil Jilala. 87.
Jillali Ferhati, Ahmed Ferhati, Bachir Skiredj, Ahmed Boudaoudi, Ghita Ben Abdeslam.
05/24/78

Jaroslaw Dabrowski
(Poland - USSR)
POL. Panorama-Mosfilm prodn. Dir, Bohdan Poreba. Sp, Yuri Nagiban; cam (Sovcolor), Wladimir Szelenkow, Jolanda Czen; art dir, Jerzy Skrzepinski, Siemier Uszakow. 143.
Zygmunt Malanowicz, Malgorzata Potocka, Aleksander Kaliagin, Wladimir Iwaszow.
07/28/76

Jaws 2
U. Prods, Richard D Zanuck, David Brown. Dir, Jeannot Szwarc. Sp, Carl Gottlieb, Howard Sackler, based on characters created by Peter Benchley; cam (Technicolor), Michael Butler; 2d unit cam, David Butler, Michael McGowan; underwater cam, Michael Dugan; live shark cam, Ron and Valerie Brown; edtr, Neil Travis; mus, John Williams; prodn des, Joe Alves; art dir, Gene Johnson, Stu Campbell; set decor, Philip Abramson; snd, Robert L Hoyt, Jim Alexander; cos-ward, Laurann Cordero, Gil Loe; asst dirs, Scott Maitland, Don Zepfel; 2d unit dir, Joe Alves; stunt coord, Ted Grossman. (MPAA rating: PG). 117.
Roy Scheider, Lorraine Gary, Murray Hamilton, Joseph Mascolo, Jeffrey Kramer, Collin Wilcox, Ann Dusenberry, Mark Gruner, Barry Coe, Susan French, Gary Springer, Donna Wilkes, Marc Gilpin, David Elliott, Gary Dubin, Gigi Vorgan, G Thomas Dunlop, Jerry M Baxter.
06/07/78

The Jazz Singer
AFD. Jerry Leider prodn. Prod, Jerry Leider. Dir, Richard Fleischer. Sp, Herbert Baker; adapt, Stephen H Foreman, based on Samson Raphaelson's play; cam (Deluxe color), Isidore Mankofsky; supv film edtr, Frank J Urioste; edtr, Maury Winetrobe; orig song score, Neil Diamond; incidental mus, Leonard Rosenman; prodn des, Harry Horner; art dir, Spencer Deverill; set des, Christopher Horner, Mark Poll; set decors, Ruby Levitt, Robert de Vestel; cos des, Albert Wolsky; snd (Dolby), T G Overton; asst dirs, James Turley, Robert M Webb; asso prod, Joel Morwood. (MPAA rating: PG). 115.
Neil Diamond, Laurence Olivier, Lucie Arnaz, Catlin Adams, Franklyn Ajaye, Paul Nicholas, Sully Boyar, Mike Kellin, James Booth, Luther Waters, Oren Waters, Rod Gist.
12/10/80

J.D.'s Revenge
AIP. Arthur Marks film, prod-dir, Marks. Sp, Jaison Starkes; cam (Movielab Color), Harry May; edtr, George Folsey Jr; mus, Robert Prince; song "I Will Never Let You Go," Prince, Joseph A Greene; snd, Ryder Sound Services; asst dir, Lee Rafner. (MPAA rating: R). 95.
Glynn Turman, Joan Pringle, Lou Gossett, Carl Crudup, James Louis Watkins, Alice Jubert, Stephanie Faulkner, Fred Pinkard, Fuddle Bagley, Jo Anne Meredith, David McKnight.
06/30/76

Je Suis Pierre Riviere
(I Am Pierre Riviere)
(France)
UAZ. Les Films De L'Ecluse prodn. Dir, Christine Lipinska. Sp, Lipinska, Regis Handron; cam (Eastmancolor), Jean Monsigny; edtr, Agnes Molinard. 80.
Jacques Spiesser, Michel Robin, Isabelle Huppert.
02/18/76

Je Suis Timide; Mais Je Me Soigne
(I'm Timid But I'm Treating It)
(France)
CCF. Albina Prodns prodn. Dir, Pierre Richard. Sp, Richard, Alain Godard, Jean-Jacques Annaud; cam (Eastmancolor), Claude Agostini; edtr, Pierre Gillette. 90.
Pierre Richard, Aldo Maccione, Mimi Coutelier, Robert Castel, Catherine Lachens, Jacques Francois.
09/06/78

Je T'Aime Moi Non Plus
(I Love You Me No Longer)
(France)
AMLF. President Films (Jacques-Eric Strauss)-Renn Productions (Claude Berri) prodn. Dir-wri, Serge Gainsbourg. Cam (Eastmancolor), Willy Kurant; edtr, Kenout Peltier; mus, Gainsbourg. 88.
Jane Birkin, Joe Dallesandro, Hugues Quester, Rene Kolldehoff, Jimmy Davis.
03/17/76

Je Te Tiens Tu Me Tiens Par La Barbichette
(I've Got You, You've Got Me, By The Hairs Of My Chinny Chin Chin)
(France)
SNC. Yanne Prodns/SNC/Tele-Hachette co-prodn. Prod-dir, Jean Yanne. Sp, Yanne and Gerard Sire; cam, Bernard Lutic; edtr, Anne-Marie Cotret; snd, Michel Vionnet; mus, Jacques Morali; art dir, Theo Meurisse; chor, Marylin Corwin. 100.
Mimi Coutelier, Micheline Presle, Georges Beller, Claude Brosset, Carlos, Jean-Pierre Cassel, Jean Desailly, Michel Duchaussoy, Jacques Francois, Jean Le Poulain, Jean Pierre Moulin, Marco Perrin, Francois Perrot, Daniel Prevost, Lawrence Riesner, Mort Shuman, Bernard Tiphaine, Jean Yanne, Les Clodettes, Ritchie Family, Village People.
06/27/79

Je Vais Craquer!
(The Rat Race)
(France)
CCF. Trinacra - FR3 co-prodn. Prod, Yves Rousset-Rouard. Dir, Francois Leterrier. Sp, Leterrier, Gerard Lauzier, from the "Rat Race" comic strip by Lauzier; cam, Jean-Francois Robin; art dir, Serge Douy; edtr, Marie-Josephe Yoyotte; mus, Jean-Pierre Sabar. 105.
Christian Clavier, Nathalie Baye, Maureen Kerwin, Anemone.
05/21/80

Jealousy: SEE Heung
Jealousy: SEE Rak Ri Sayar

Jeden Stribrny
(One Silver Piece)
(Czechoslovakia)
CZS. Dir, Jaroslav Balik. Sp, Zdenek Pluhar; cam (Eastmancolor), Jan Vanis; mus Karel Mares. 95.
Emil Horvath Jr, Anatoly Kuznetsov, Joszef Cierny, Olga Slabgova, Anna Javorkova.
08/04/76

Jeder Stirbt Fuer Sich Allein
(Everyone Dies in His Own Company)
(W Germany)
CTT. Lisa Film - Erste Filmproduktionsges - Constantin GmbH - and Terra Filmkunst GmbH. Dir, Alfred Vohrer. Sp, Miodrag Cubelic, Anton Czerwik; based on book by Hans Fallada; exec prod, Erich Tomek; cam, Heinz Hoelscher; edtr, Jutta Hering. 106.
Hildegard Knef, Carl Raddatz, Martin Hirthe, Gerd Boeckmann, Sylvia Manas, Peter Matic, Heinz Reincke, Beate Hasenau, Rudolf Fernau, Hans Korte, Brigitte Mira, Alexander Rdszun.
02/04/76

Jennifer
AIP. Steve Krantz prodn. Dir, Brice Mack. Sp, Kay Cousins Johnson, from story by Krantz; cam (CFI Color), Irv Goodnoff; edtr, Duane Hartzell; mus supv, Jerry Styne; title song, Porter Jordan. (MPAA rating: PG). 90.
Lisa Pelikan, Bert Convy, Nina Foch, Amy Johnston, John Gavin, Jeff Corey, Louise Hoven, Ray Underwood, Wesley Eure, Florida Friebus, Georganne La Piere.
05/24/78

The Jerk
U. Aspen Film Society, William E McEuen-David V Picker prodn. Prods, David V Picker, William E McEuen. Dir, Carl Reiner; sp, Steve Martin, Carl Gottlieb, Michael Elias, from a story by Martin, Gottlieb; cam (Technicolor), Victor J Kemper; edtr, Bud Molin; mus, Jack Elliott; prodn des, Jack T Collis; set des, Joe Hubbard; set decor, Richard Goddard; cos des, Theodora Van Runkle; snd, Charles M Wilborn; asso prod, Peter Macgregor-Scott; asst dir, Newton Arnold. (MPAA rating: R). 104.
Steve Martin, Bernadette Peters, Catlin Adams, Mabel King, Richard Ward, Dick Anthony Williams, Bill Macy, M Emmet Walsh, Dick O'Neill, Maurice Evans, Helena Carroll, Jackie Mason, Carl Reiner.
12/12/79

Jesli Msz Serce Bijace
(If Your Heart Can Feel)
(Poland)
POL. Film Polski prodn. Profil Film Unit Warsaw. Dir, Wojciech Fiwek. Sp, Fiwek, Konrad Frejdlich, based on Edmund de Amicis' "The Heart"; cam, Stefan Pindelski; sets, Tadeusz Myszorek; mus, Piotr Marczewski; prodn mgr, Wojciech Karmolinski. 91.
Wladyslaw Kowalski, Zofia Rysiowna, Alfred Struve, Boreslaw Smela, Adam Probosz.
10/01/80

Jesus
WB. Genesis Project prodn. Prod, John Heyman. Dirs, Peter Sykes, John Kirsh. Sp, Barnet Fishbein, based on the Gospel of Luke; asso prod, Richard Dalton; cos, Rochelle Zaltzman. 117.
Brian Deacon, Rivka Noiman, Yossef Shiloah, Niko Nitai, Gadi Rol, Itzhak Ne'eman, Shmuel Tal, Kobi Assaf, Michael Varshaviak, Mosko Alkalai, Nisim Gerama, Leonid Weinstein, Rafi Milo, David Goldberg, Eli Danker, Eli Cohen, Talia Shapira, Richard Peterson, Miki Mfir, Peter Frye, Alexander Scourby.
10/24/79

Jhor
(The Storm)
(India)
DPC. Wri-dir, Utpal Dutt. Cam, Dinen Gupta; edtr, H Mukhopadhya; mus, P Bhattacharya. 100.
Ujjal Sengupta, Indrami Mukhopadya, Sagarika Adhikari.
02/13/80

Jiken
(The Incident)
(Japan)
07/25/79
SKU. Prods, Yoshitaro Nomura, Akira Oda. Dir, Yoshitaro Nomura. Story, Shohei Oaka; sp, Kaneto Shindo; cam, Hakashi Karamata; mus, Yashushi Aktagawa; snd, Akagasko Yamamoto; edtr, Kasua Ota. 105.
Toshiyuki Nagashima, Keiko Matsuzaka, Shinobu Ohtake, Tsuneihiko Watase.

Jim, The World's Greatest
U. New Breed Prods film. Prod, Don Coscarelli; exec prods, D A Coscarelli, S T Coscarelli. Dir-wris, Don Coscarelli, Craig Mitchell. Cam (Technicolor), Rex Metz, Don Coscarelli, Mitchell; edtrs, J Terry Williams, Don Coscarelli, Mitchell; mus, Fred Myrow; songs, America, The Strawbs; art dirs, Phil Barber, Phil Neel, E G Culman, James Catti; snd, James Alexander, Robert Del Valle Jr, David Lloyd; asst dirs, Phil Bowles, Paul Pepperman, Richard Hashimoto. (MPAA rating: PG). 91.
Gregory Harrison, Robbie Wolcott, Rory Guy, Marla Pennington, Karen McLain, David Lloyd, Larry Gabriel, Tony Lucatorto, Ralph Richmond, Tim Simmons, Reggie Bannister, Larry Southwick, David Pollock, Larry Pollock, Shirley Coscarelli, Ernie Morrison, Charlotte Mitchell, George M Singer Jr, Walter Inman, Steve Goldman, Cyndie Coscarelli, Keith Mitchell, Mark Annerl, D A Coscarelli, J D Sarver, Richard Byers.
01/21/76

J-Men Forever
X. Prod, William Howard; wris, Phil Proctor, Peter Bergman. 80.
Phil Proctor, Peter Bergman.
(B & W)
02/13/80

Jo-Bachi
(Queen Bee)
(Japan)
TOH. Prods, Kazuo Baba, Osamu Tanaka. Dir, Kon Ichikawa. Sp, Masaya Hidaka, Chiho Katsura, Kon Ichikawa, based on novel by Yokomizo Seishi; cam, Kiyoshi Hasegawa; mus, Shinichi Tanabe; asst dir, Mune Matsubayashi; art dir, Iwao Akune. 140.
Koji Ishikawa, Keiko Kishi, Tatsuya Nakadai, Kie Nakae.
03/01/78

Joe Albany. . .A Jazz Life
X. Carole Langer Prodns. Prod-conceived-dir, Carole Langer. Cam, Jonathon Smith; edtr, Michael Schenkein. 60.
Joe Albany.
(DOC) (16m)
12/17/80

Joe and Maxi
(USA)
Maxi Cohen Prodn. Dir-snd, Joel Gold, Maxi Cohen. Cam, Joel Gold; edtrs, Pat Powell, Marion Kraft, Maxi Cohen. 78. (DOC) (16m)
06/21/78

Joe Panther
ACR. Prod, Stewart H Beveridge; exec prod, Leroy C Taylor. Dir, Paul Krasny. Sp, Dale Eunson, from the novel by Zachary Ball; cam (CFI Color), Robert L Morrison; 2d unit cam, Jordan Klein; edtrs, Mike Vejar, Millie Moore; mus, Fred Karlin; song, "The Time Has Come," by Norman Gimbel; snd, Howard Warren; 2d unit dir, Ricou Browning; stunt coord, Courtney Brown. (MPAA rating: G). 110.
Brian Keith, Ricardo Montalban, Alan Feinstein, Cliff Osmond, A Martinez, Ray Tracey, Robert W Hoffman, Gem Thorpe Osceola, Lois Red Elk, Monika Ramirez.
11/03/76

Joerg Ratgeb, Maler
(Joerg Ratgeb, Painter)
(E Germany)
DEE. Dir, Bernhard Stephan. Sp, Manfred Freitag, Jochen Nestler; cam, Otto Hanisch; edtr, Brigitte Krex; sets, Peter Wilde; mus, Andrzej Korzynski; snd, Bernd-Dieter Henning, Christfried Sobczyk, Guenter Witt; prodn mgr, Helmut Klein, Rolf Martius. 101.
Alois Svehlik, Margrit Tenner, Guenter Naumann, Olgierd Lukaszewicz, Malgorzata Braunek, Henry Huebchen, Rolf Hoppe, Marylu Poolman, Martin Trettau, Helga Goering, Hilmar Baumann, Thomas Neumann, Monika Hildebrand, Giso Weissbach, Werner Pauli, Guenter Rueger.
03/29/78

Johan
(France)
VLS. Wri-dir, Philippe Valois. 90.
(16m)
07/21/76

John Heartfield, Fotomonteur
(W Germany)
X. Cinegrafik, Hamburg, prodn. Dir, Helmut Herbst. Sp, Tom Fecht, Herbst, Eckhard Siepmann; cam, Axel Brandt; edtr, Heidi Breitel; snd, Wahed Askar; graphics, Robert Darroll; pho, Dernd Kuhnert; narr, C Caspari, Joerg Falkenstein. 63. (ANI - DOC)
04/27/77

Johnny Larsen
(Denmark)
PNR. Panorama (Just Betzer) prodn (with the State Film Institute). Based loosely on the novels of John Neghm. Dir, Morten Arnfred. Sp, Joergen Melgaard, Morten Arnfred; cam (Eastmancolor), Dirk Bruel; prodn des, Palle Nybo Arestrup; cos, Gitte Kolvig, Manon Rasmussen; edtr, Anders Refn; mus, Toots Thielemans, Kaspar Winding, Ole Arnfred; exec prod, Lars Kolvig; prodn mgr, Per Aaman. 105.
Allan Olsen, Frits Helmuth, Hanne Ribens, Berthe Quistgaard, Karl Stegger, Elsebeth Nielsen, Sven Hansson, Ole Meyer.
10/10/79

Johnny Unser
(Our Johnny)
(Austria)
ACV. Orig story-sp-dirs, Tone Fink, Robert Polak. Cam (Eastmancolor), Herbert Link; edtr, Robert Polak; mus, Dieter Kaufmann, Bela Koreni, Clockwork. 85.
Antonio Limacher, Hagnot Elischka.
(16m; available in 35m)
11/05/80

Johnny West
(W Germany)
X. Pete Welz prodn of Multimedia, Hamburg in co-prodn with Sunny Point Film, Berlin, Faust Film, Munich, and Terra Filmkunst, Berlin. Sp-dir, Roald Koller. Cam, Bahram Manocherie; sets-cos, Harold Waistnage; title song "Moving" composed by Winfried Lovett; sung by "The Manhattans". 129.
Rio Reiser, Kristina van Eyck, Jess Hahn, Karl Maslo, Rainer Westerfield, Birgit Bergen. The Groups: The Manhattans, Missus Beastly, The Platters.
03/29/78

Joi Baba Felunath
(The Elephant God)
(India)
RDB. R D B & Co Prodn. Wri-dir, Satyajit Ray; cam (Eastmancolor), Soumendu Roy; edtr, Dulal Dutt; mus, Ray. 112.
Soumitra Chatterjee, Utpal Dutta, Santosh Dutta, Sidhartha Chatterjee, Jit Bose, Haradhan Banerjee.
12/12/79

Jonas-Qui Aura 25 Ans En L'An 2000
(Jonas-Who Will Be 25 in the Year 2000)
(Switzerland - France)
GAU. Action Films-Citel Films-Societe Francaise Des Prodns-SSR prodn. Dir, Alain Tanner. Sp, John Berger, Tanner; cam (Eastmancolor), Renato Berta; edtr, Brigitte Sousselier; mus, Jean-Marie Senia. 110.
Jean-Luc Bideau, Myriam Boyer, Myriam Meziere, Rufus, Roger Jendly, Jacques Denis, Miou-Miou, Raymond Bussieres, Jonas.
08/25/76

Joni
WW. Prod, Frank R Hacobson. Exec prod, William F Brown. Dir-wri, James F Collier, based on the book by Joni Eareckson. Cam (Metrocolor), Frank Raymond; edtr, Duane Hartzell; mus, Ralph Carmichael; art dir, Bill Ross; snd, Dean Gilmore; asst dir, Stephen Lim. (MPAA rating: G).
Joni Eareckson, Bert Remsen, Katherine De Hetre, Cooper Huckabee, John Milford, Michael Mancini, Richard Lineback, Jay W MacIntosh, Louise Hoven, Cloyce Morrow, Sarah Rush, Jeff Austin, Cheryl Harvey, Ernie Hudson, Barbara Mallory, Jane Ralston, Betsy Jones-Moreland, Stephen Parr.
10/29/80

Jorden Er Flad
(The Earth Is Flat)
(Denmark)
DAG. Thorkild Kristensen/Henrik Stangerup/Danish State Film Institute (Stig Bjoerkman) prodn. Dir, Henrik Stangerup, based on Ludvig Holberg's stage comedy "Erasmus Montanus," Cam (Eastmancolor), Flemming Arnholm; asst dir, Luis Pellegrini; prodn des, Erik Boettzauw; mus, Jurij Moskvitin; edtr, Holde Loechen Trier; cos, Ulla-Britt Soederlund; Brazil prodn chores, Alter Films Ltda (Luis Fernando Goulart). 101.
Fausto Wolff, Wilson Grey, Lucia Mello Kohler, Abel Prazer, Paulo Fortes, Thelma Reston, Gloria Cristall, Fabio Camargo, Milton Luiz.
02/09/77

Joseph Andrews
(Britain)
PAR. Woodfall film, prod, Neil Hartley. Dir, Tony Richardson. Sp, Allan Scott, Chris Bryant, from a screen story by Richardson based on the novel by Henry Fielding; cam (Movielab Color), David Watkin: edtr, Thom Noble; mus, John Addison; songs, Bob Stewart, Jim Dale; prodn des, Michael Annals; art dir, Bill Brosie; set decor, Ian Whittaker; snd, Gerry Humphreys, Peter Handford; cos-ward, Annals, Jean Hunnisett, Arthur Davey, Patrick Wheatley: asst dir, Andrew Grieve, stunt coord, William Hobbs. (MPAA rating: R). 103.
Ann-Margret, Peter Firth, Michael Hordern, Beryl Reid, Jim Dale, Natalie Ogle, Peter Bull, Kenneth Cranham, Karen Dotrice, James Villiers.
03/16/77

Joshua
LOS. Po'boy prodn. Prod-dir, Larry Spangler. Story-sp, Fred Williamson. (MPAA rating: R). 80.
Fred Williamson, Isela Vega, Calvin Bartlett, Brenda Venus.
12/08/76

Journalist: SEE Novinar

Journey Among Women
(Australia)
GUO. Ko-An prodn. Prod, John Weiley. Dir, Tom Cowan. Sp, Weiley, Cowan, Dorothy Hewett; story, Cowan; cam (Eastmancolor), Cowan; mus, Roy Ritchie; snd, Leo Sullivan, Jef Doring; edtr, John Scott; sets, Sally Campbell; stunts, Heath Harris. 93.
Lillian Crombie, June Pritchard, Martin Phelan, Rose Lilley, Diane Fuller, Nell Campbell, Lisa Peers, Jude Kuring, Kay Self, Robyn Moase, Michelle Johnson, Kenneth Laird, Tim Elliot, Ralph Cotterell.
07/27/77

Journeys From Berlin 1971
X. Dir-edtr, Yvonne Rainer. Cam, Carl Teitelbaum, Michael Steinke, Wolfgang Senn, Jon Else, Shinichi Tajiri; snd, Larry Sider, Helene Kaplan, Dan Gillham, Christian Moldt. Financed by British Film Institute, Deutscher Akademischer Austauschdienst, New York State Council of the Arts, Center for Advanced Visual Studies M I T, Christophe de Menil, Beard's Fund Inc, Rockefeller Foundation. 125.
Annette Michelson, Ilona Halberstadt, Gabor Vernon, Chad Wollen, Amy Taubin, Vitto Acconci, Lena Hyun, Yvonne Rainer, Ruth Rainero, Leo Rainer, Cynthia Beatt, Antonio Skarmeta.
(16m)
02/06/80

Joy
MAT. Prod, Derek Davidson. Dir, Harley Mansfield. Sp, Davidson, Mansfield; cam, Keith McGovern; edtr, James F MacCrell; art dir, Pierre deLot; snd, Solomon Gemmorrah; mus, Martin Lewinter. (Self-imposed X Rating). 75.
Sharon Mitchell, Melinda Marlowe, Jack Teague, Richard Bolla, Gloria Leonard, Veri, Justine Fletcher, Ursula Brooke, Marco, Jay Pierce, Frank Kenwood, Jesse Wilson.
09/21/77

The Joy of Letting Go
SMB. Exec prod, Edwin Scott Brown. Prod, Summer Brown. Dir, John Gregory. Sp, Cynthia Holm; cam (Eastmancolor), Kurt Stem, Patrick Riley; edtr, David Peoples; mus, Bob Maser. (Self-imposed X rating). 86.
Dominique St Pierre, Leslie Hughes, James Kral, Pamela Strasser, Susie Sung Lee.
07/14/76

Joyride
AIP. Hal Landers-Bobby Roberts presentation; prod, Bruce John Curtis; co-prod, Eugene Mazzola; exec prod, Landers and Roberts. Dir, Joseph Ruben. Sp, Ruben, Peter Rainer; cam (DeLuxe Color), Stephen M Katz; edtr, Bill Butler; mus, Jimmie Haskell; songs, Electric Light Orchestra, Jeff Lynne, Barry Mann, Cynthia Weil; cos-ward, Cheryl Beasley; snd, Lee Alexander; stunt coord, Thomas Huff; asst dir, Chuck Russell. (MPAA rating: R). 92.
Desi Arnaz Jr, Robert Carradine, Melanie Griffith, Anne Lockhart, Tom Ligon, Cliff Lenz.
06/01/77

Juan Perez Jolote
(Mexico)
PEX. Conacine coprodn with Victor Fuentes. Dir-sp, Archibaldo Burns. Based on novel by Ricardo Pozas; cam, Eric Saarinen, Alexis Grivas, Armando Carillo; mus, recordings of orig Tzotzil mus, with addl mus, Richard Alderson; edtr, Rafael Castaneda, Bill Sagona; snd, Elias Martell. 95.
Candido Coeto and natives from the village.
03/09/77

Jubilee
(Britain)
CNG. Megalovision Film. Prods, Howard Malin, James Whaley. Dir, Derek Jarman. Cam, Peter Middleton; snd, John Hayes; supv edtr, Tom Priestley; edtr, Nick Barnard; des, Christopher Hobbs; continuity, Judy Futrille; asst dir, Guy Ford; prodn mgr, Mordechai Schreiber; mus, Suzi Pinns, Brian Eno, Adam and the Ants, Siouxsie and the Banshees, Chelsea, Wayne County and the Electric Chairs, Maneaters, and Amilcar. 103.
Jenny Runacre, Jordan, Little Nell, Linda Spurrier, Hermine Demoriane, Toyah Wilcox, Richard O'Brien, Adam Ant, Ian Charleson, Karl Johnson, Neil Kennedy, Orlando, Lindsay Kemp and troupe.
02/01/78

The Judge and the Assassin: SEE Le Juge Et L'Assassin

Judge Fayard Called the Sheriff: SEE Le Juge Fayard Dit Le Sheriff

The Judge's Friend: SEE Mijn Vriend

Judgment of an Assassin
(Hong Kong)
SHW. Prod, Run Run Shaw. Dir, Sun Chung. Sp, Yi Kuang; exec prod, Hsieh Chih; cam, Lan Nai-tsai; edtr, Chiang Hsing-lung; mus, Chen Yung Yu; snd, Wang Yung Hua; art dir, Chen Ching Shen; martial art instructors, Tang Chia, Huang Pei-chi. 103.
David Chiang, Tsung Hua, Ching Li, Chen Huimin, Ku Feng, Wang Lai, Frankie Wei Hung, Lui Hui-ling, Tan Ying, Ching Miao.
12/14/77

Judith Therpauve
(France)
GAU. Buffalo Films-Gaumont SA prodn. Dir, Patrice Chereau. Sp, Georges Conchon, Chereau; cam (Eastmancolor), Pierre Lhomme; edtr, Francoise Bonnot. 125.
Simone Signoret, Marcel Imhoff, Philippe Leotard, Robert Manuel, Francois Simon, Laszlo Szabo.
10/18/78

Jukyu-Sai No Chizu
(The Plan of His 19 Years)
(Japan)
GUN. Wri-dir, Mitsuo Yanagimachi from a book by Kenji Nakagami. Cam (Eastmancolor), Katsumi Sakakibara; edtr, Eiko Yoshida; art dir, Shunichi Hiraga; mus, Fumio Itabashi. 110.
Yuji Honma, Keizo Kanie, Hideko Okiyama, Hatsuo Yamaya, Chisako Hara.
05/21/80

Jula Treekul
(Jula Treekul River)
(Thailand)
AXT. Prod, Nanta Tansacha. Dir, Pornpoj Kanitkasen. Story, Panom Thien; sp, Thanachai Chinotai, Banjerd Thavee; cam, Sophon Jaenphanit; snd, Kasem Militachinda; mus, Prachin Songpao; art dir, Urai Srisombat; cos, Adjarn Soodsai Smitinan; asst dir, Apichat Pornpairoj. 105.
Sorapong Chatri, Nawarat Yukthanan, Piya Trakulrat, Vasana Sitthivej, Pisan Akaraseni, Manop Assawathep, Marasri Issrangkul, Na Ayudhya, Anchalee Chaisri.
05/07/80

Julefrokosten
(The Office Party)
(Denmark)
ASD. Klaus Pagh/Just Betzer prodn. Sp-dir, Finn Henriksen, based on Ole Boye's treatment of Simon Mikkelstrup's novel. Cam (Eastmancolor), Erik Wittrup-Willumsen, Clauf Loof; mus, Ole Hoyer; edtr, Finn Henriksen; in charge of prodn, Leif Jul. 65.
12/08/76

Jules Le Magnifique
(Jules the Magnificent)
(France - Canada)
NVR. Educfilm prodn; dir, Michel Moreau; cam, Michel Brault, Francois Gill; snd, Claude Beaugrand; edtr, Josee Lecours; narr, Jean-Jacques Blanchet with the participation of Jules Arbec. 84.
(DOC)
03/09/77

Jules Starts With Jules: SEE Julio comienza en Julio

Julia

FOX. Prod, Richard Roth; exec prod, Julian Derode. Dir, Fred Zinnemann. Sp, Alvin Sargent, based on story, "Pentimento," by Lillian Hellman; cam (DeLuxe Color), Douglas Slocombe; 2d unit cam, Paddy Carey, Guy Delattre; edtr, Walter Murch; mus, Georges Delerue; prodn des, Gene Gallahan, Willy Holt, Carmen Dillon; set decor, Pierre Charron, Tessa Davies; snd, Bill Rowe, Derek Ball; cosward, Anthea Sylbert, Joan Bridge, Annalisa Nasalli Rocca, John Apperson, Colette Baudot; asst dirs, Alain Bonnot, Anthony Waye. (MPAA rating: PG). 116.
Jane Fonda, Vanessa Redgrave, Jason Robards, Maximilian Schell, Hal Holbrook, Rosemary Murphy, Meryl Streep, Dora Doll, Elisabeth Mortensen, John Glover, Lisa Pelikan, Susan Jones, Cathleen Nesbitt, Maurice Denham, Gerard Buhr.
09/21/77

Julia: SEE *Der Lieberschuler*

Julie Pot De Colle
(Julie Glue Pot)
(France)
PDS. Les Films De L'Alma, SFP, FR3 prodn. Dir, Philippe De Broca. Sp, Jean-Claude Carriere; book, Peter De Polnay; cam (Eastmancolor), Rene Mathelin; edtr, Henri Lanoe; mus, Georges Delerue. 86.
Marlene Jobert, Jean-Claude Brialy, Alexandra Stewart, Alain David, Christian Alers, Philippe Rouleau.
04/20/77

Juliette et L'Air Du Temps
(Juliet and the Feel of the Times)
(France)
GMF. Wri-dir, Rene Gilson. Cam (Eastmancolor), Walter Bal; edtr, Chantal Elia-Gilson; mus, Bernard Gilson. 92.
Agnes Chateau, Jacques Zanetti, Evane Hanska, Mathieu Volta.
08/25/76

Julio comienza en Julio
(Jules Starts With Jules)
(Chile)
X. Alberto Celery-Silvio Ciaozzi-Nelson Fuentes prodn. Exec prod, Alberto Celery. Dir, Silvio Giaozzi. Cam, Nelson Fuentes; sp, Gustavo Frias; mus, Luis Advis. 115.
Elsa Alarcon, Jorge Alvarez, Luis Alarcon, Magdalena Aguirre, Rafael Benavente, Shlomit Beytelman, Jose Cabello, Maria Castiglione, Tennyson Ferrada, Ana Gonzalez, Delfina Guzman, Pedro Gaete, Alfonso Luco, Gloria Munchmeyer, Juan Cristobal Meza, Maria Elena Montero, Ana Maria Palma, Felipe Rabat, Aquiles Sepulvede, Fritz Stein, J M Salcedo, Lucy Salgado, Marion Soto, Nissim Sharim, Victor Sepulveda, Vincente Santamaria, Sergio Urrutia, Jaime Vadell, Jorge Yanez.
05/16/79

Jumpin' at the Bedside: SEE *Hopla Paa Sengekanten*

Jumping Ash
(Britain - Peoples Republic of China)
X. Bang Bang Films Co-Adpower Films prodn. Dirs, Po Chih Leon, Siu Fong Fong. Cam, Anthony Hope; edtr, Victor Costello; mus, Joseph and Michael Lai. 90.
Callan Leung, Siu Fong Fong, Chen Hsing.
09/15/76

Jun
(Japan)
KGS. Wri-dir, Hiroto Yokoyama from the book by So Kuramoto. Cam (Fujicolor), Akira Takada; edtr, Keiichi Uraoka; mus, Toshi Ichiyanagi. 90.
Jun Eto, Yoko Kizima, Koko Enami, Chiyoko Akaza.
05/16/79

Jungle Adventure Campa Campa: SEE *Djungelaeventyret Campa-Campa*

Junoon
(Obsession)
(India)
FVA. Dir-wri, Shyam Benegal. Cam (Eastmancolor), Govind Nihalni; edtr, Bhanudas; mus, Vanraj Bhatia. 144.
Shashi Kapoor, Nafisa Ali, Shabana Azmi, Jennifer Kendal.
01/31/79

Just a Gigolo
(W Germany)
X. Leguan Film presentation. Prod, Rolf Thiele. Dir, David Hemmings. Sp, Joshua Sinclair, Ennio de Concini; cam, Charly Steinberger; art dir, Peter Rothe; original mus, Gunther Fischer; cos des, Ingrid Zore; edtrs, Susan Jaeger, Fred Srp, Maxine Julius. 105.
David Bowie, Sydne Rome, Kim Novak, David Hemmings, Maria Schell, Curt Jurgens, Marlene Dietrich, Erika Pluhar, Rudolf Schundler, Hilde Weissner, Werner Pochath, Bela Erny, Friedhelm Lehmann, Rainer Hunold, Evelyn Kunneke, Karin Hardt, Gudrun Genest, Ursula Heyer, Christiane Maybach, Martin Hirthe, Rene Killdehoff, Gunter Meisner, Peter Schlesinger.
02/21/79

Just Crazy About Horses
FBK. Prod-sp, Tim Lovejoy, Joe Wemple. Dirs, Lovejoy, Wemple, Victor Kanefsky; cam, Peter Stein; additional photography, Cotter Watt, Ted Churchill, Mike Lerme; edtr, Samuel D Pollard; mus, Sam Waymon; narr, Tammy Grimes. (MPAA rating: PG). 105. (DOC)
12/27/78

Just Like At Home: SEE *Olyan Mint Otthon*

Just Out of Reach
(Australia)
X. Ross Matthews Prodn, made with the assistance of the Creative Development Branch of the Australian Film Commission. Prod, Ross Matthews. Dir, Linda Blagg; sp, Blagg; dir pho, Russell Boyd; cam (Eastmancolor), Nixon Binney; snd, Kevin Kearney; mus, Bill Motzig; edtr, Ted Otton; sfx, Bob McCarron; art dir, Grace Walker; prodn mgr, Barbara Gibbs. 62.
Lorna Lesley, Sam Neill, Martin Vaughan, Judi Farr, Ian Gilmour, Jackie Dalton, Lou Brown.
11/28/79

Just Tell Me What You Want
WB. Prods, Jay Presson Allen, Sidney Lumet. Exec prod, Burtt Harris. Dir, Sydney Lumet. Sp, Jay Presson Allen from her own novel; cam (Technicolor), Oswald Morris; edtr, John J Fitzstephens; snd, James J Sabat; prodn des, Tony Walton; asst dir, Alan Hopkins; art dir, John Jay Moore; mus, Charles Strouse. (MPAA rating: R). 112.
Ali MacGraw, Alan King, Myrna Loy, Keenan Wynn, Tony Roberts, Peter Weller, Sara Truslow, Judy Kaye, Dina Merrill, Joseph Maher.
02/06/80

Just the Beginning
(Korea)
YBK. Prod, Choi Chun Ji. Dir, Jung In Yup. Sp, Suh Yoon Sung; cam, Paing Jung Moon; edtr, Chang Kil Sang; mus, Jung Soung Jo; art dir, Cho Kyung Hwan; snd, Hang Yang Laboratories. 105.
Jin Yoo Young, Ha Myoung Jung, Kang Ju Hee, Doh Kum Bong, Han Se Hun.
12/14/77

Just You And Me, Kid
COL. Irving Fein/Jerome M Zeitman prodn. Prods, Fein, Zeitman. Dir, Leonard Stern. Sp, Oliver Hailey, Stern, from a story by Tom Lazarus; cam, David Walsh; edtr, John W Holmes; mus, Jack Elliott; prodn des, Ron Hobbs; art dir, Sig Tinglof; set decor, Rick Simpson; snd, Don Johnson; asst dir, Pat Kehoe. (MPAA rating: PG). 93.
George Burns, Brooke Shields, Burl Ives, Lorraine Gary, Nicolas Coster, Keye Luke, Carl Ballantine, Leon Ames, Ray Bolger, John Schuck, Andrea Howard, Christopher Knight, William Russ.
07/18/79

Juvenile Liaison
(Britain)
X. British Film Institute prodn. Dirs, Joan Churchill, Nicholas Broom. 101. (16m-DOC)
11/16/77

The JK Years - A Political Trajectory: SEE *Os Anos JK - Uma Trajetoria Politica*

Kaddu Beykat
(News from the Village)
(Senegal)
X. Safi prodn, Dakar. Wri-dir, Safi Faye. Cam, Patrick Fabry; edtr, Andree Davanture. 95.
Marguette Gueye, Assane Faye.
(B & W)
07/14/76

Kaerleken
(Love)
(Sweden)
SVF. AB Cinematograph/Europa Film/Swedish Film Institute prodn. Dir, Theodor Kallifatides; sp, Jeannette Donner, Kallifatides, based on Kallifatides novel. Cam (Eastmancolor), Bille August; edtr, Sylvia Ingemarsson; mus, Monica Dominique; exec prod, Katinka Farago. 71.
Per Ragnar, Lena Olin, Anna Godenius, Erik Tamm, Mathias Henrikson, Erland Josephson.
05/28/80

Kagemusha
(The Double)
(Japan)
TOH. Toho, Kurosawa Prodns prodn. Dir, Akira Kurosawa. Sp, Kurosawa, Masato Ide; cam (Eastmancolor), Kazuo Miyagawa, Asaichi Nakai; art dir, Yoshiro Muraki; mus, Shinichiro Ikebe. 179.
Tatsuya Nakadai, Tsutomu Yamazaki, Kenichi Hagiwara, Kota Yui, Hideji Otaki, Hideo Murata, Daisuke Ryu.
05/21/80

Kagirinaku Tomei Ni Chikai Buruu
(Almost Transparent Blue)
(Japan)
TOH. Kitty Film Corporation prodn. Prods, Hidenori Taga, Kei Ijisato. Wri-dir, Ryu Murakami, based on his book. Cam, Shuya Sekigawa; light, Kanji Akiyama; snd, Koichi Beniya; art dir, Hiroshi Wada; edtr, Hatoko Yamaji; mus, Masaru Hoshii; asst dir, Tomoya Yoshitomi. 103.
Kunihiko Mitamura, Mari Nakayama, Haruhiko Saito, Keiko Wakasa, Togo Igawa, Narumi Tokura, Yuri Takase, Goro Masaki.
04/23/80

Kaleidoskop: Valeska Gert, Nur zum Spass-nur zum Spiel
(Kaleidoscope: Valeska Gert, For Fun-For Play)
(W Germany)
X. Bioskop-Film Prodn. Prod-dir-wri, Volker Schlondorff; cam, Michael Ballhaus; edtr, Gisela Haller; mus, Friedrich Meyer. 41.
Valeska Gert, Pola Kinski.
(DOC) (16m)
04/11/79

Kaliwa't Kanan. . .Sakit Ng Katawan
(Left, Right, Sickness of the Body)
(Philippines)
X. H P S Film prodn. Story-sp, Ric M Torres; mus, D'Amarillo; cam, Alfonso Alvarez; Dir, F H Constantino. 106.
Eddie Rodriquez, Elizabeth Orepesa, Anna Gonzales.
06/23/76

Kalte Heimat
(Cold Homeland)
(W Germany)
X. Triangel Film, Cologne-Berlin, in co-prodn with Westdeutscher Rundfunk (WDR), Joachim Von Mengershausen. Dir, W Werner Schaefer. Sp, Peter Steinbach, Schaefer; cam (b&w), Gerard Vandenberg; mus, Juergen Knieper; cos, Uschi Welker; sets, Edwin Wengobowski, Norbert Scherer; snd, Rainer Wicker. 120.
Nikolaus Cohen, Dietlinde Turban, Barbara Adolph, Nikolas Lansky, Margit Carstensen, Rudolf Schindler, Brigitte Bottrich.
(B & W)
01/17/79

Kaltgestellt
(Put On Ice)
(W Germany)
X. ABS-Film/Von Vietinghoff Film prodn. Dir, Bernhard Sinkel. Sp, Sinkel, Alf Brustellin; cam, Dietrich Lohmann; sets, Winfried Hennig; edtr, Annette Dorn; mus, Charly Mariano, Jasper Van T'Hoft, Mike Thatcher. 100.
Helmut Griem, Angela Molina, Martin Benrath, Friedhelm Ptok, Hans-Guenther Martens, Meret Becker.
05/21/80

Kamisama Naze Ai Ni Mo Kokkyo Ga Aru No
(God, Why Is There a Border In Love?)
(Japan).
TOH. Toho Eiga prodn. Prod, Tsuneyasu Matsumoto, Kyoko Oshima, Michio Morioka. Dir, Yasuhiro Yoshimatsu; sp, Yoshimi Shinozaki, Yasuhiro Yoshimatsu, from orig story by Hiroshi Kusaka; cam, Kazutami Hara; art dir, Kazuo Takenaki; snd, Nobuyuki Tanaka; mus, Michkie Yoshino. 93.
Tomiyuki Kunihiro, Carole Lizon, Takenori Murano, Yoshitaka Tanba, Shohei Hino, Elvira Schalcher, Franz Sauer, Conrad Von Bork, Veronique Delbourg.
12/19/79

Kanal
(The Canal)
(Turkey)
UMU. Irmak Film prodn. Prod, Erden Kiral, Istanbul. Dir, Kiral. Sp, Ihsan Yuce; cam, Salih Dikisci; mus, Arif Erkin. 90.
Tank Akan, Meral Orhonsay, Tuncel Kurtiz, Kamuran Usluer.
09/05/79

Kanga Mussa
(Austria)
X. Sascha-Wien Film prodn, Vienna. Dirs, Goetz Hagmueller, Dietmar Graf. Sp, Hagmueller; cam, Graf; mus, Gheorghe Zamfir, orig mus, of Mali; edtr, Silvia Wallner; snd, Herbert Prasch. 95.
Cheick Gassama, Abdul Wares Asr, Mohammad Mohammadi.
05/18/77

The Kangaroo: SEE *A Kenguru*

Kansas City Trucking Co.
GAG. Prod, Sam Gage. Wri-dir, Joe Gage. Cam (Eastmancolor), Nick Elliot; mus, Al Steinman; snd, Glen Nathan. (Self-imposed X Rating). 67.
Jack Wrangler, Richard Locke, Steve Boyd, Dane Tremmell, Skip Sheppard, Duff Paxton, Bud Jaspar, Kurt Williams, Maria Reina.
11/10/76

Kapos Etsi
(Somewhat Like This)
(Greece)
X. Agamemnon Ditsas picture. Wri-dir, Agamemnon Ditsas. Cam, Vaguelis Nassopoulos; edtr, Popi Alkouli; mus, L Kelaedonis; snd, I Stavrou, K Kittou. 110.
An Antoniou, K Liacopoulos, A Dounias, I Avgoustidou, A Constantopoulou.
10/29/80

Kara Carsafli Gelin
(The Dark-Veiled Bride)
(Turkey)
X. Murat Film Prodn, Istanbul. Dir, Sureyya Duru. Sp, Vedat Turkali, based on short stories by Bekir Yildiz; cam, Ali Ugur. 90.
Hakan Balamir, Semra Ozdamar, Aytac Arman, Aliya Rona, Huseyin Peyda.
08/02/78

Kara Kafa
(Blinders)
(Turkey)
X. Korhan-Film prodn, Istanbul. Dir, Korhan Yurtsever. Sp, Yurtsever, Bulent Oran; cam, George Becker, Salin Dikisci; edtr, Yurtsever; sets, Kemal Yurt. 90.
Betul Ascioglu, Savas Yurttas, Cuneyt Kaymat, Oslem Guler, Macit Floroun, Markus Ueberhoff.
11/05/80

Karl May
(W Germany)
X. TMS Film Gessellschaft film. Wri-prod-dir, Hans Jurgen Syberberg. Cam, Dietrich Lohmann; edtr, Ingrid Brozat; mus, classical sources. 187.
Helmuth Kautner, Kathe Gold, Christina Soderbaum, Attila Horbiger, Heinz Moog.
03/31/76

Kasper in De Onderwereld
(Kasper in the Underworld)
(Belgium)
CII. Van de Velde Films prodn. Dir, Jef Van der Heyden. Sp, Hubert Lampo, based on his novel, Jef Van der Heyden; cam (Gevacolor), Fernand Tack, Theo Van der Sande; mus, Francois Glorieux; lighting, Claude Decibber, Jacques Borremans; snd, Frans Van der Laan, Haane Reichardt, Wim De Clercq; edtr, Jan Dop.   93.
Jos Houben, Lieve Berens, Rosemary Bergmans, Rik Bravenboer, Annelies Vaes, Charles Janssens, Gaston Vandermeulen, Loet Hanekroot, Hubert De Stobbeleer, Ann Petersen, Monica De Vos, Manu Verreth, Leo Haelterman, Anita Koninck, Max Schnur, Johan Van Lierde, Joris Collet, Bernard Verheyen, Bouk Martens, Piet Bergers.
02/07/79

Kassbach
(Austria)
X. Patzak Satel Film prodn. Dir, Peter Patzak. Sp, Patzak, Helmut Zenker from a book by Zenker; cam (Afgacolor), Dietrich Lohmann, Attila Szabo; edtr, Trude Gruber; Daniela Padalewski; mus, Peter Zwetkoff.   95.
Walter Kohut, Immy Schell, Maria Engelstorfer, Konrad Becker.
03/07/79

Kassen Stemmer
(It All Adds Up)
(Denmark)
Dir, Ebbe Langberg. Sp, Henning Bahs, Erik Balling, based on story by Sven Agard; cam (Eastmancolor), Claus Loof; edtr, Ole Askman; mus, George Quincy; in charge of prodn, Bo Christensen, Magnus Magnusson. 99.
Jess Ingerslev, Buster Larsen, Axel Stroebye, Holger Juul Hansen.
08/18/76

Katerina A Jeji Deti
(Catherine and Her Daughters)
(Czechoslovakia)
CZS. Barrandov Studio prodn. Dir, Vaclav Gajer. Sp, Gajer, Jiri Krenek from the book by Krenek; cam, Jan Curik; edtr, Zdenek Stehlik.   76.
Zora Rozsypalova, Drahomira Hofmanova, Jorga Kotrbova, Jana Vychodilova, Vaclav Sloup.
(B & W)
07/28/76

Keby Som Mal Dievca
(If I Had a Girl)
(Czechoslovakia)
CZS. Slovak Film prodn. Dir, Stefan Uher. Sp, Milan Ferko; cam (Eastmancolor), Stanislav Szomolanyi; mus, Stepan Konicek.   88.
Emilia Dosekova, Otakar Dadak, Brigita Hausnerova, Sona Kovacikova.
08/25/76

The Keeper
LIG. Prod, Donald Wilson. Wri-dir, Tom Drake, based on a story by David Curnick, Donald Wilson; cam, Doug McKay; mus, Eric Hoyt; snd, Zale Dalen; edtrs, Sally Paterson, George Johnson; art dir, Keith Pepper. 88.
Christopher Lee, Tell Schrieber, Sally Gray, Ross Vezarian, Ian Tracey, Jack & Leo Leavy, Bing Jensen.
05/26/76

Ke Ha See Dang
(The Red Mansion)
(Thailand)
AXT. Prod, Nanta Tansacha. Wri-dir, Prince Tipayachatr Chartchai. Exec prod, Orasee Chartchai; story, Princess Sawat Watanadom Pravit; cam, Prayong Mongkolmuang; mus, Prajin Songpao; snd dir, Pong Asvinikul. 120.
Nawarat Yukthanan, Aporn Tonnawannij, Toon Hiranyasap, Ampha Pusit, Projetr Ganpetr, Nantaporn Amphaparint, Malee Wetprasert, Sulaliwan Suwanatat, Choosri Misomon, Marasri Nabangchang.
11/05/80

Keiko
(Japan)
X. Les Prodns Yoshimura-Gagnon presentation. Prods, Yuri Yoshimura, Claude Gagnon. Dir-sp-edtr, Gagnon. Sp, Aiko Hanada; cam, Andre Pelletier; art dir, Toshio Hashimoto; mus, Jun Fukamachi.   120.
Junko Wakashiba, Akiko Kitamura, Takuma Ikeuchi, Toshio Hashimoto, Nobuo Nakanishi, Ryu Nakano.
(With French sub-titles)
09/12/79

Kejsaren
(The Emperor)
(Sweden)
SVF. Treklovern, Svenska Film Institutet prodn. Dir, Josta Hagelback. Sp, Hagelback, Sten Holmberg from the book by Brigitta Trotzig; cam (Eastmancolor), Sten Holmberg; edtr, Peter Falack; mus, Ragnar Grippe. 95.
Anders Aberg, Bo Lindstrom, Anna Lindroth, Rune Ek, Katarina Strandmark.
03/07/79

Ken Murray Shooting Stars
07/25/79
RYK. Exec prod, Bud Cole. Prod-dir, Ken Murray. Sp, Bette Lou Murray, Helen Rackin; cam, Ken Murray; edtrs, Ken Murray, Paul Vitella; mus, Richard LaSalle; asso prod, Steve Bushelman.   95.
(DOC)

Kenny & Co.
FOX. Wri-prod-dir-pho, (DeLuxe Color), edtr, Don Coscarelli; exec prods, D A Coscarelli, S T Coscarelli. Mus, Fred Myrow; art dir, S T Coscarelli; cos, Cyndie Coscarelli; snd, Paul Ratajczak, Michael J Rose, Don Booth; asst dir, Paul Pepperman. (MPAA rating: PG).   90.
Dan McCann, Mike Baldwin, Jeff Roth, Ralph Richmond, Reggie Bannister, Clay Foster, Ken Jones, Willy Masterson, David Newton, James E de Priest, S T Coscarelli, Terri Kalbus.
11/24/76

The Kentucky Fried Movie
UF. Kentucky Fried Theatre prodn; prod, Robert K Weiss; exec prod, Kim Jorgensen. Dir, John Landis. Sp, David Zucker, Jim Abrahams, Jerry Zuker; cam (DeLuxe Color), Stephen M Katz; mus coord, Igo Kantor; edtr, George Folsey Jr; art dir, Rich Harvel; cosward, Deborah Nadoolman, Joyce Unruh; snd, Bill Kaplan; asst dir, Peter Schindler. (MPAA rating: R).   90.
110 bits and cameos.
08/03/77

Keow
(Miss Keow)
(Thailand)
NFT. Prod, Kiat lampungporn. Dir-edtr, Piac Poster. Story-sp, Piac Poster, Boonyarak Nilawong; cam, Chome Bunnag; snd, Rewat Puthinan; mus, Saravuth Pachaiyo; orig song, "Pleng Rak Priac Ha" (When Love Calls You) by Vinai Pantarak, performed by Oriental Funk; continuity, Pichit Niyomsiri; asst dir, Boonyarak Nilawong.   112.
Rinda Katancharoen, Toon Hiranyasap, Srisalai Suchartboot, Kanchit Timkul, Marasri Issarangkul, Na Ayudha, Morakot Chanyadee.
04/23/80

Ket Elhatarozas
(A Quite Ordinary Life)
(Hungary)
X. Pro Vobis Film for ZDF. Dir-wri, Imre Gyongyossy, Barna Kabay. Cam (b&w), Gabor Szabo.   75.
(DOC & B & W)
11/22/78

Ke Xana Pros Ti Doxa Trava
(He Is Heading To The Glory Again)
(Greece)
X. Studio "S" and Greek Film Centre prodn. Wris, George Stampoulopoulos, Yannis Kakoulides. Dir, Stampoulopoulos. Cam, Sakis Maniatis; mus, Mimis Plessas; edtr, George Triantafyllou; snd, Thanassis Arvanitis, Nicos Achladis.   105.
Vera Krouska, Costas Arzoglou, Mimi Denissis, Yannis Floriniotes.
10/29/80

The Key Is In The Door: SEE *La Cle Sur La Porte*

The Key That Should Not Be Handed On: SEE *Klujch Bez Prava Peredachi*

The Key to Love: SEE *Koonche Rak*

Khao Yod
(Mark of the Chinese Temple)
(Thailand)
STH. Prod-dir-edtr, Suphan Pramphan. Story-sp, So Asanachinda; cam, Pansak Pramphan; mus-snd, Siam Pattanakong Co Ltd; art dir, Preecha Chuansathien; cos-make-up, Sukanya Buantiam.   130.
Pisamai Wilaisak, Paophan Pongnati, Sirikwan Nantasiri, Komapat Attaya, Anan Samasap, Metta Rungrath, Danai Dunyapan, Krai Kanchit, Tat Ekatat, Inthanon Tripet.
05/25/77

Khon Krang Detr
(Slum People In The Sun)
(Thailand)
SAH. Prod, Somsak Techaratanaprasert. Wri-dir, Kidd Suwannasorn. Cam, Pornitti Virayasiri; mus, Prat Suwannasorn; snd, Maitree Janjarasskul; prodn des, Somneuk Gohasuwan; cos, Suchada Takeesit.   130.
Ron Rittichai, Benjawan Boonyakart, Nopadoe Duangphorn, Sasithorn Pantoorat, Manat Putikiat.
06/27/79

The Kidnapping of the President
(Canada)
CWN. Sefel Pictures International prodn. Prods, George Mendeluk, John Ryan; exec prod, Joseph Sefel; dir, Mendeluk; sp, Richard Murphy; novel, Charles Templeton; cam (DeLuxe color), Mike Molloy; mus, Paul J Zaza; edtr, Michael McLaverty; art dir, Douglas Higgins; sfx, Peter Hutchinson, Richard Albain; asst dir, Gerry Arbeid. (MPAA rating: R).   113.
William Shatner, Hal Holbrook, Van Johnson, Ava Gardner, Miguel Fernandes, Cindy Girling, Michael J Reynolds, Elizabeth Shepherd, Gary Reineke, Maury Chaykin.
08/13/80

The Kids Are Alright
(Britain)
NW. Rock Films presentation. Prods, Bill Curbishley, Tony Klinger. Exec prod, Sydney Rose. Dir, Jeff Stein. Cam, Peter Nevard, Norman Wexler, Tony Richmond; edtr, Ed Rothkowitz; mus, Peter Townshend; mus dir, John Entwistle; prodn mgrs, Tim Van Rellim, Peter Price.   96.
Pete Townshend, Roger Daltrey, John Entwistle, Keith Moon (The Who).
(DOC)
05/23/79

Kihajolni Veszelyes
(Don't Lean Out The Window)
(Hungary)
HU. Hungarofilm prodn, Dialog Studio, Budapest. Dir, Janos Zsombolyai. Sp, Andras Simonffy; cam (Eastmancolor), Elemer Ragalyi; mus, Gabor Presser and Locomotiv GT Group.   81.
Nandor Tomanek, Gyula Bodrogi, Mari Kiss, Janos Szikora, Ferenc Bencze, Robert Koltai.
05/24/78

Kilas
(Killer)
(Portugal)
IPD. Film Forum prodn. Dir, Jose Fonseca e Costa; sp, Costa, Sergio Godinho, Tabajara Ruas; cam, Mario Barroso; edtr, Manuel Tomas.   125.
Mario Viegas, Lia Gama, Luis Lello, Milu, Paula Guedes, Duarte, Natalia Do Vale, Francisco Pestana.
(16m)
08/20/80

Kilas, O Mau Da Fita
(The Killers)
(Portugal)
X. Filmforum prodn, Lisbon. Dir, Jose Fonseca e Costa; sp, Jose Fonseca e Costa, Sergio Godinho, Tabajara Ruas; cam, Antonio H Escudeiro, Mario Barrosa; mus, Sergio Godinho.   25.
Mario Viegas, Lia Gama, Luis Lello, Milu, Paula Guedes, Francisco Pestana, Adelaide Ferreira.
10/15/80

Kilenc Honap
(Nine Months)
(Hungary)
HU. Hunnia Studio prodn, Budapest. Dir, Marta Meszaros. Sp, Gyula Hernadi, Ildiko Korodi, Marta Meszaros; cam (Eastmancolor), Janos Kende; mus, Gyorgy Kovacs.   93.
Lili Monori, Jan Nowicki, Djoko Rosie.
10/26/77

Kilet Khon
(The Greedy People)
(Thailand)
SFT. Prod, Chawinthorn Sibunruang. Story, Vimol Siri; sp, Sochirat Boonluang; cam, Sawaeng Diksayawantana; edtr-asst dir, Pote Siripan; mus, Montri Ong-iyam; snd, Pong Asavinitkul; dubbing, Siam Pattana Lab.   120.
Sombat Metanee, Pisamai Wilaisak, Somboon Sukinan, Pinyo Panui, Metta Rungrath, Katta Apaiwong, Hansa Jiriyapon, Promsin Sibunruang, Banchong Nilpet, Shoosri Misomon, Duangchai Hataikan, Chao Pongvilai, Sopha Sataporn, Nart Chaiyong, Siripen Bangyikang, Somchit Sapsamluay, Marasi Nabangchang.
06/15/77

Kill for the Truth: SEE Phai Kam Plerng

Kill Or Be Killed
FVI. Prod, Ben Vlok. Dir, Ivan Hall. Sp, C F Beyers-Boshoff. Cam (T V C), Mane Eotha; edtr, Brian Varaday; karate sequences staged by Norman Robinson. (MPAA rating: PG).   90.
James Ryan, Norman Combes, Charlotte Michelle, Danie DuPlessis.
05/21/80

Killer Clans
(Hong Kong)
SHW. Runme Shaw prodn. Dir, Chu Yuan. Sp, I Kuang; cam, Huang Chieh; snd, Wang Yung-hua; edtr, Chiang Hsing-lung; art dir, Chen Ching-shen; martial arts, Tang Chia, Yuan Hsiang-jen.   108.
Tsung Hua, Chen Ping, Wang Chung, Yueh Hua, Ku Feng.
04/07/76

Killer Fish
(Italy - Brazil)
AFC. Carlo Ponti/Filmar Do Brasil, Fawcett-Majors prodn. Prod, Alex Ponti; exec prods, Olivier Perroy, Turi Vasile, Enzo Barone. Dir, Anthony Dawson (Antonio Margheriti). Sp, Michael Rogers; cam, Alberto Spagnoli; edtr, Roberto Sterbini; mus, Guido, Maurizio De Angelis; art dir, Francesco Bronzi; cos, Adriana Berselli, Salvatore Russo; underwater sequences, Herbert V Theiss; asst dirs, Michel Salliouti, Giuseppe Pollini. (MPAA rating: PG).   101.
Lee Majors, Karen Black, James Franciscus, Margaux Hemingway, Marisa Berenson, Gary Collins, Roy Brocksmith, Dan Pastorini, Frank Pesce, Charlie Guardino, Anthony Steffen.
(English Soundtrack)
10/24/79

The Killer Inside Me
WB. Devi Prodn Systems film. Prod, Michael W Leighton; exec prod, Irving Cohen. Dir, Burt Kennedy. Sp, Edward Mann, Robert Chamblee, from novel by Jim Thompson; cam (Metrocolor), William A Fraker; mus, Tim McIntire, John Rubinstein; edtrs, Danford B Greene, Aaron Stell; snd, Hal Watkins, M Curtis Price, Aaron Rochin, Al Overton Jr; asst dir, Ray Marsh. (MPAA rating: R).   99.
Stacy Keach, Susan Tyrrell, Tisha Sterling, Keenan Wynn, Charles McGraw, John Dehner, Pepe Serna, Royal Dano, Julie Adams, John Carradine, Don Stroud.
10/20/76

Killer: SEE Kilas

The Killers: SEE Kilas, O Mau Da Fita

Killing Me Softly: SEE Mitgift

The Killing of a Chinese Bookie
FCS. Prod, Al Ruban. Wri-dir, John Cassavetes. Edtr, Tom Cornwell; mus, Bo Harwood; prodn des, Sam Shaw; snd, Harwood. (MPAA rating: R).   135.
Ben Gazzara, Timothy Agoglia Carey, Azizi Johari, Meade Roberts, Seymour Cassel, Alice Friedland, Donna Gordon, Robert Phillips, Morgan Woodward, Virginia Carrington, John Red Kullers, Al Ruban, Soto Joe Hugh.
02/18/76

Kindaichi Kosuke No Boken
(Kosuke Kindaichi's Adventure)
(Japan)
TOE. Kadokawa Prodn. Prod, Haruki Kadokawa. Dir, Nobuhiko Obayashi. Sp, Koichi Saito, Tomoaki Nakano, based on novel by Seishi Yokomizo; dial wri, Kohei Tsuka; ani, Makoto Wada; cam, Taisaku Kimura; lighting, Shinji Kojima; snd, Nobu Miyanaga; edtr, Shinya Inoue; asst dir, Nobuaki Inozaki; mus, Katsumi Kobayashi. 113.
Ikko Furuya, Kunie Tanaka, Hideko Yoshida, Jiro Sakagami, Miyuki Kumaya, Toshio Egi.
06/04/80

The King and the Mockingbird: SEE Le Roi et l'Oiseau

King For A Day: SEE Melech Leyom Echad

King Kong
PAR. Prod, Dino De Laurentiis; exec prods, Federico De Laurentiis, Christian Ferry. Dir, John Guillermin. Sp, Lorenzo Semple Jr, based on a script by James Creelman, Ruth Rose, from a concept of Merian C Cooper, Edgar Wallace; cam (Metrocolor), Richard H Kline; pho effects, Frank Van Der Veer, Barry Nolan, Harold E Wellman; edtr, Ralph E Winters; mus, John Barry; prodn des, Mario Chiari, Dale Hennesy; art dirs, Archie J Bacon, David A Constable, Robert Gundlach; set decor, John Franco Jr; cos-ward, Moss Mabry, Anthea Sylbert, Arny Lipin, Fern Weber; snd, Harry W Tetrick, William McCaughey, Jack Solomon, Aaron Rochin, Dan Wallin; asst dirs, David McGiffert, Kurt Neumann; 2d unit dir, William Kronick; stunt coord, Bill Couch. (MPAA rating: PG). 134.
Jeff Bridges, Charles Grodin, Jessica Lange, John Randolph, Rene Auberjonois, Julius Harris, Jack O'Halloran, Dennis Fimple, Ed Lauter, Jorge Moreno, Mario Gallo, John Agar, Keny Long, Rick Bakey.
12/15/76

King of the Gypsies
PAR. Dino De Laurentiis presentation. Prod, Federico De Laurentiis; exec prod, Dino De Laurentiis. Dir, Frank Pierson. Sp, Pierson, suggested by "King Of The Gypsies" by Peter Maas; cam (Technicolor), Sven Nykvist; prodn des, Gene Callahan; edtr, Paul Hirsch; mus, David Grisman; cos, Anna Hill Johnstone; asso prod, Anna Gross; set decor, Robert Drumheller, John Godfrey; art dir, Jay Moore; asst dir, J Alan Hopkins; snd, Dennis Maitland; chor, Julie Arenal. (MPAA rating: R). 112.
Sterling Hayden, Shelley Winters, Susan Sarandon, Judd Hirsch, Eric Roberts, Brooke Shields, Annette O'Toole, Annie Potts, Michael V Gazzo.
12/13/78

King Of The Joropo: SEE El Rey Del Joropo

The King Of The Street Cleaners: SEE Copculer Krali

The Kingdom of Diamonds: SEE Hirok Rajar Deshe

The Kingdom of Naples: SEE Il Regno Di Napoli

Kingdom Of The Spiders
DIM. Prods, Igo Kanter, Jeffrey M Sneller. Dir, John Cardos. Exec prod, Henry Fownes. Sp, Richard Robinson, Alan Caillou; cam (Eastmancolor), John Morrill; edtrs, Steve Zaillian, Igo Kantor; snd, Bill Kaplan, James Dehr; set decor, Rusty Rosene; asst dir, Larry Kostroff; sfx, Greg Auer. (MPAA rating: PG). 94.
William Shatner, Tiffany Bolling, Woody Strode, Lieux Dressler, Altovise Davis, David McLean, Natasha Ryan, Marcy Rafferty, Joe Ross, Adele Malis, Roy Engel.
11/16/77

Kiri-no-hata
(Sweet Revenge)
(Japan)
TOH. Prods, Takeo Hori, Hideo Sasai. Dir, Katsumi Nishikawa. Story, Seicho Matsumoto; sp, Kei Hattori; cam, Yonezo Maeda; edtr, Ko Suzuki; mus-snd, Nobumasa Fukushima; art dir, Teruyoshi Satani; asst dir, Tomozo Yamaguchi. 95.
Momoe Yamaguchi, Tomokazu Miura, Rentaro Mikuni, Akiko Koyama, Yusuke Natsu, Miyuki Kojima.
10/10/79

The Kirlian Witness
X. Jonathan Sarno prodn. Dir, Sarno. Sp, Sarno, Lamar Sanders, from a story by Sarno; cam (Technicolor), Joao Fernandes; edtrs, Len Dell' Amico, Edward Salier; asso edtr, Veronica Loza; mus, Harry Mandredini. (MPAA rating: PG). 91.
Nancy Snyder, Ted Laplat, Joel Colodner, Nancy Boykin, Lawrence Tierney, Maia Danziger.
11/22/78

Kisertet Lublon
(The Phantom on Horseback)
(Hungary)
X. Budapest Studio prodn. Dir, Robert Ban. Sp, Ban, Peter Molnar Gal, based on a novel by Kalman Mikszath; cam (Eastmancolor), Tamas Somlo; mus, Emil Petrovics. 111.
Gyorgy Czerhalmi, Iren Bordan, Dezso Garas, Laszlo Markus, Imre Raday, Reka Nagy, Agnes Banfalvi, Ferenc Kallai.
03/02/77

Kjaerleikens Ferjreiser
(A Commuter Kind of Love)
(Norway)
NOR. Wri-dir, Hans Otto Nicolaysen; book, Edvard Hoem; cam, Halvor Naess. 92.
Froydis Armand, Eilif Armand, Per Jansen, Karen Randers Person, Sigrid Huun, Sylvia Salvesen.
07/30/80

Kleine Frieren Auch Im Sommer
(Young Ones Are Even Cold In The Summer)
(Switzerland)
RIA. Cinov Producktion prodn. Dir, Peter Von Gunten. Sp, Von Gunten, Herbert Meier; cam (Eastmancolor), Fritz E Maeder; edtr, Alexander Rupp, Marianne Pfister. 100.
Verena Reichhardt, Lorenz Hugener, Esther Christinat, Heinz Sommer, Silvia Jost.
08/23/78

Klincz
(Clinch)
(Poland)
POL. Film Polski prodn, Kadr Unit, Warsaw. Dir, Piotr Andrejew. Sp, Filip Bajon, Andrejew; cam, Jacek Mieroslawski, Zbigniew Wichlacz; sets, Janusz Sosnowski. 96.
Tomasz Lengren, Boleslaw Smela, Janusz Sykutera, Janusz Tesarz, Wieslaw Golas, Agyei Johnson.
06/11/80

Klondike Fever
X. CFI Investments presentation. Prod, Gilbert W Taylor. Dir, Peter Carter. Sp, Charles E Israel, Martin Lager; cam, Bert Dunk; edtr, Stan Cole; mus, Hagood Hardy; prodn des, Seamus Flannery; sfx, John Thomas. (MPAA rating: PG). 60.
Jeff East, Rod Steiger, Angie Dickinson, Lorne Greene, Barry Morse, Michael Hogan, Merritt Sloper, Lisa Langlois, Sherry Lewis.
02/13/80

Klujch Bez Prava Peredachi
(The Key That Should Not Be Handed On)
(USSR)
X. Lenfilm prodn, Leningrad. Dir, Diana Assanova. Sp, Georgi Polonski; cam, Dimitri Dolin, Yuri Veksler; mus, E Krylatov. 95.
Elena Proklova, Alexei Petrenko, Ljubov Malinovskaia, L Fedosseeva-Schukshina, Ekaterina Vasilieva.
01/19/77

Kneeler Peak: SEE A Kiralylany Zsamolya

Kneuss
(Switzerland - Germany)
RXF. Cine Groupe Zurich and Sator Film Hamburg co-prodn. Dir, Gaudenz Meili. Sp, Beat Brechbuehl, Meili, based on novel by Brechbuehl; cam, Pio Corradi; mus, Tangerine Dream; snd, Stanislav Hromadnik; edtr, Edelgard Gielisch; art dir, Rica Mattmueller; tech dir, Werner Santschi. 96.
Ingold Wildenauer, Renate Schroeter, Harald Leipnitz, Mascha Gonska, Herlinde Latzko, Adolph Spalinger, Alex Freihart, Mario Hindermann, Ettore Cella, Hans Gaugler.
11/22/78

Knife in the Head: SEE Messer Im Kopf

The Knight: SEE Rycerz

Knockout
X. Turn of The Century Fights Inc prodn; prod, Bill Cayton. Dir, Jim Jacobs. Edtr, Steve Lott; narr, Kevin Kennedy. (MPAA rating: G). 104.
(COMPILATION)
03/16/77

Ko To Tamo Peva
(Who's That Singing Over There?)
(Yugoslavia)
YFR. Centar Film prodn. Dir, Slobodan Sijan; sp, Dusan Kovacevic; cam (Eastmancolor), Bozidar Nikolic; mus, Vojislav Kostic. 84.
Pavle Vujisic, Dragan Nikolic, Alekander Bercek, Neda Aneric, Slavko Stimac, Bora Stepanovic, Tasko Nacic.
08/27/80

Kobieta I Kobieta
(A Woman and a Woman)
(Poland)
POL. Film Polski prodn. Film Unit Warsaw. Wri-dirs, Ryszard Bugajski, Janusz Dymek. Cam, Janusz Kalicinski; mus, Wojciech Trzcinski; sets, Teresa Smus-Barska; prodn mgr, Michal Szczerbic. 102.
Halina Labonarska, Anna Romantowska, Witold Debicki, Stefan Szmidt, Stanislaw Jaroszynski, Jerzy Zelnik, Jerzy Kryszak, Andrzej Gloskowski.
10/01/80

Kloden rokker
(This Rockin' Globe)
(Denmark)
WCT. Ebbe Preisler/Film & Lyd prodn. Sp-dir, a collective headed by John Menzer. Cam (Eastmancolor), Morten Bruus Pedersen, Henrik Herbert, Dirk Bruel, Simon Plum, Freddy Torneberg, Andreas Fischer-Hansen, Bo Riemer, Dan Lausten, Jimmy Andreasen; edtr, Lars Brydesen; mus, Gnags, Culpepper, Lone Kellerman, Stig Moeller, Tania Maria Trio, The Jack Bruce Band, The Chieftains, Karsten Vogel & Birds of Beauty, Troels Trier, C V Joergensen, Skousen & Ingemann, Starfuckers. 88.
(MUSICAL) (DOC)
03/29/78

Kodiyettom
(The Ascent)
(India)
TVD. Chitralekha Film Cooperative prodn. Wri-dir, Adoor Gopalakrishnan; cam (b&w), Ravi Varma; edtr, M Moni. 130.
Gopi, Lalita Azeez, Kaviyoor Ponnamma, Adoor Bhavani, Vilasini Suseela.
(B & W)
01/31/79

Koncert Na Konci Leta
(Concert at the End of Summer)
(Czechoslovakia)
CZS. Czechoslovak Film Production, Studio Barrandov, Prague. Dir, Frantisek Vlacil. Sp, Zdenek Mahler; cam, Jiri Marak; sets, Jindrich Goetz; mus, Jaromil Burghauser, archives. 102.
Josef Vinklar, Jana Hlavackova, Svatopluk Benes, Vlasta Fabrianova, Frantisek Nemec, Bohus Zahorsky, Ondrej Pavelka, Ladislav Bambas, Ondrej Havelka.
06/11/80

Koncert Pre Pozostalych
(Concert for Mourners)
(Czechoslovakia)
X. Slovak Film prodn, Bratislava, Koliba Studios. Dir, Dusan Trancik. Sp, Trancik, Tibor Vichta; cam, Vincent Rosinec; mus, Karel Svobodov. 100.
Juraj Kukura, Barbara Brylska, Pavel Bobek, Sona Valentova, Marek Frackowiak, Kamila Magalova, Jana Paulova, Evelyna Steimarova.
03/09/77

Konek Gorbunok
(The Humpbacked Horse)
(USSR)
SOV. Soyuzmultfilm prodn. Wri-dir, Ivan Inanov-Vano from a book by Pyotr Yershov with A Volkov on script; cam (Sovcolor), M Fruyan; ani, L Milchin. 78.
(ANI)
07/28/76

Kontrakt
(Contract)
(Poland)
POL. Prf Unit prodn. Wri-dir, Krzysztof Zanussi. Cam, Tadeusz Wybult; mus, Wojciech Kilar. 100.
Leslie Caron, Maja Komorowska, Tadeusz Lomnicki, Magda Jaroszowna, Krzystof Kolberger, Beata Tyszkiewicz.
10/22/80

Koo Rak
(The Lovers)
(Thailand)
CHT. Prod-dir, Pornpoj Kanitkasen. Story-sp, Banjerd Tavee; cam, Sophon Jaenphanit; mus, Prachin Songpow; edtr, Pravit Lilawai; snd edtr, Montri Ongiam; prodn des, Prasobchai Kanitsen; cos, Rasaniwan Kanitsen. 120.
Pairoj Sangvoributr, Nawarat.
05/24/78

Koonche Rak
(The Key to Love)
(Thailand)
KKW. Prod, Opart Rangchaikul. Dir-edtr, Charthep Chantanimit. Story-sp, Spa & Co; cam, Pipat Payak; snd, Ram Inthra; mus, Jonrak Jankanna; asst dir, Lek Chantanimit; prod des-art dir, Rang Sant. 115.
Sorapong Chatri, Nantana Ngaokracharg, Suphan Titiang, Padee Jatrikat, Kitti Daskorn, Somsak Chaisongkram, Sokuan Krajangsart, Surachart Traipong, Marasi Issarangkul Na Ayudhya.
10/11/78

Koportos
(Hungary)
HU. Hunnia Studio ZDF Mainz prodn. Dir, Livia Gyarmathy. Sp, Gyarmathy, Joszef Balazs from the book by Balazs; cam (Eastmancolor), Ferenc Papp. 88.
Mihaly Rostas, Ferenc Bogdan, Rozalia Demeter, Lajos Szabo, Jiri Menzel.
02/27/80

Korpinpolska
(The Raven's Dance)
(Finland)
SFI. Suomi-Filmi Oy-SFI-Television Lulea prodn. Wri-dir, Markku Lehmuskallio. Cam (Fujicolor), Lehmuskallio, Bekka Martevo; edtr, Juho Gartz. 80.
Pertti Kalinainen, Paavo Katajsarri, Hilkka Matikainen.
03/26/80

Kosadate Gokko
(The Proper Way)
(Japan)
DFJ. Satsukisha-Haiyuza Eiga Hoso co-prodn. Prods, Enzaburo Honda, Seiji Matsuki, Daishiro Miura. Dir, Tadashi Imai. Sp, Naoyuki Suzuki, based on the book by Kyozo Miyoshi; cam, Kazumi Hara; light, Toshio Takashima; mus, Shinjiro Ikebe; snd, Shin Watae; art dirs, Yokoo Kiyoshi, Saburo Abe; edtr, Tatsuji Nakajo; asst dir, Masao Nagai. 118.
Go Kato, Komaki Kurihara, Yoshi Kato, Chio Ushiwara, Misako Watanabe, Iichiro Zaiitsu, Toyoji Fukuda.
05/07/80

Kosu Den
(Mali)
X. Dir, Sega Coulibaly.
12/26/79

Kosuke Kindaichi's Adventure: SEE Kindaichi Kosuke No Boken

Kramer Vs Kramer
COL. Stanley Jaffe prodn. Prod, Stanley R Jaffe. Wri-dir, Robert Benton. Based on a novel by Avery Corman. Cam, Nestor Almendros; edtr, Jerry Greenberg; mus, Henry Purcell (adapt by John Kander), Antonio Vivaldi (adapt by Herb Harris); prodn des, Paul Sylbert; cos, Ruth Morley; asso prod, Richard C Fischoff. (MPAA rating: PG). 105.
Dustin Hoffman, Meryl Streep, Jane Alexander, Justin Henry, Howard Duff, George Coe, Jobeth Williams, Bill Moor, Howland Chamberlain, Jack Ramage, Jess Osuna.
11/28/79

Kratko Sluntze
(A Ray of Sunlight)
(Bulgaria)
BGO. Bulgarian Film prodn, Sofia. Dir, Lyudmil Kirkov. Sp, Stanislav Stratiev, based on his own story; cam, Georgi Roussimov; mus, Boris Karadimchev; art dir, Assaya Poppova. 90.
Vihur Stoychev, Rossitsa Petrovna, Anton Gorchev, Pavel Poppandov, Nikola Todev, Georgi Kishkilov, Kiril Gospodinov.
02/07/79

Krawatten Fuer Olympia
(Ties for the Olympics)
(W Germany)
X. German Film & TV Academy (DFFB) prodn, Berlin. Dir, Stefan Lukschy. Sp, Lukschy, Hartmann Schmige; cam, Norbert Bunge; mus, Wilhelm Dieter Siebert; snd, Peter Lustig, Michael Gregor; edtr, Lukschy; art dir, Ursula Welter. 80.
Machael Beermann, Sylvia Dudek, Erika Fuhrmann, Ullrich Gressiker, Hansi Jochmann, Ute Koska, Kurt Pratsch-Kaufmann, Peter Schlesinger, Kurt Schmidtchen, Christian Sorge, Eric Vaessen.
(B & W) (16m)
05/18/77

Krc
(Cramp)
(Yugoslavia)
YFR. Viba Film prodn. Dir, Bozo Sprajc. Sp, Zeljko Kozinc; cam (Eastmancolor), Rado Likon; mus, Tomaz Pengov. 95.
Mateja Glazar, Boris Cavazza, Milena Zupanic, Ivo Ban, Stojan Colja, Janez Starina.
08/15/79

Krigernes Boern
(Children of the Warriors)
(Denmark)
PNR. (Just Betzer) prodn. Dir, Ernst Johansen. Sp, Hans Oversen; cam (Eastmancolor), Ernst Johansen, Peter Roos; edtr-asst dir, Lizzi Weischenfeldt; mus, Sebastian; prodn des, Palle Arestrup; exec prod, Lars Kolvig. 90.
Jannik Lesnaik, Soeren Hindborg, Lars Froehling, Susanne Storm, Charlotte Mortensen, Jeanette Hultberg, Ove Sprogoe, Pierre Lindstedt.
09/05/79

Kristoffers hus
(Kristoffer's House)
(Sweden)
SVE. Swedish Film Institute, HB Three Leaf Clover, AB Svensk Film prodn. Sp, Lars Lennart Forsberg, Vilgot Sjoman, Thommy Berggren, based on Johan Bargum's novel, "Darkroom"; Dir-edtr, Forsberg. Cam (Fujicolor) Lennart Carlsson, Lasse Karlsson; prodn des, Ulf Axen; exec prod for Swedish Film Institute, Mans Reutersvaerd; mus, Lars Dahlberg, Bjorn Isgaard. 96.
Thommy Berggren, Agneta Eckemyr, Mimi Pollack, Gunnel Brostroem, Boerje Ahlsted, Pia Garde, Linda Megner.
09/05/79

Kronprinsen
(Crown Prince)
(Norway)
X. EMI Prodn, Norway. Dir-sp, Pal Bang-Hansen, story, Bjorn Gunnar Olsen; cam, Bjorn Jegerstedt. 91.
Bjorn Sundquist, Reidun Nortvedt, Trini Lund, Bjorn Floberg.
07/09/80

Kru Ban Nok
(The Rural Teacher)
(Thailand)
DET. Prod, Kamol Kuntangwattana; exec prod, Boonlert Setthamongkol. Dir, Surasee Bhatham. Story, Kamnan Khonkhai; sp, Senyanupap Saengkawannij; cam-edtr, Niwat Sinlapasomsak; asst cam, Somwong Manivongse; mus, Phet Pingtong, Titsoh Lampreun; snd edtr, Porng Asavinikul; art dir, Krisanapong Nakathon; asst. dir, Issara Lookhong. 133.
Piya Trakulrat, Vasana Sitiwet, Somchart Prachatai; Nopadol Duangphorn, Kanya Mothong, Ton Tomol.
05/31/78

Kruta Lubost
(Cruel Love)
(Czechoslovakia)
CZS. Czechoslovak Film Prodn, Koliba Studios, Bratislava. Wri-dir, Martin Tapak. Cam, Vincent Rosinec; mus, Svetozar Stracina. 87.
Maria Macakova, Juraj Kukura, Magda Vasarypva, Jozef Majercik, Viliam Polonyi, Kveta Lukoskova, Beata Znakova, Maria Hajkova, Juraj Kovac, Zdenka Nereroya, Frantisek Desset.
06/21/78

Krylya
(Wings)
(USSR)
GOS. Mosfilm Prodn, Moscow. Dir, Larissa Shepitko. Sp, Valentin Yezhov, Natalia Ryantseva; cam, Igor Slabnevich; sets, Ivan Plastinkin; mus, Roman Ledenov. 90.
Maya Bulgakova, Zhanna Bulatova, Panteleimon Krymov, Leonid Djjatshkov, Sergei Nikonenko, Nikolai Grabbe.
(B & W)
07/05/78

Krystyna Et Sa Nuit
(Krystyna and Her Night)
(Belgium)
PRG. Spiralfilm prodn. Dir, Charles Conrad. Sp, Conrad, Gaston Desmedt; cam (Agfa-Gevaert), Conrad; edtr, Conrad; mus, Beethoven, Schubert, Berlioz. 80.
Marysia, Roger Van Hool, Bernard Marbaix, Beatrice Leymourre, Yves Collignon, Pierre Dumaine, Guy Lesire, Raymond Peira, Gisele Oudart, Menia Martinez, The Ballet de Wallonie company.
02/09/77

Kto Odchadza V Dazdi
(Who Leaves in the Rain)
(Czechoslovakia)
CZS. Koliba prodn. Dir, Martin Holly. Sp, Jan Jonas, Tibor Vichta, Holly; cam (Eastmancolor), Karol Krska; mus, Zdenek Liska. 92.
Gustav Valach, Emila Vasaryova, Steven Kvietik, Vilma Jamnicka.
08/18/76

Kuam Rak See Dam
(Love Is Blue)
(Thailand)
SAH. Thepsin Papiyon. Prod, Wacharee Atakaiwanwati. Dir, Panthep Atakaiwanwati. Story-sp, Thep Namkaeng; cam, Saman Hongtaksin; art dir, Wacharee Atakaiwanwati; mus, Thaweepong Maninin; edtr, Panthep Atakaiwanwati; cos, Ketr Siam; snd recording, Asvin Lab. 120.
Sombat Metanee, Pisamai Wilaisak, Sirikwan Nantasiri, Manop Assawathep, Vilaiwan Wattanapanit, Deth Duang, Marasi Issarangkul Na Ayudhya.
02/02/77

Kuldetes
(Portrait of a Champion)
(Hungary)
07/25/79
HU. Studio Objectiv prodn. Conceived and dir, Ferenc Kosa. Cam, Janos Gulyas, Ferenc Kaplar. 96.
(DOC) (16m)

Kummatty
(Bogeyman)
(India)
GLI. Dir, G Aravindan. Sp, K N Pannicker, Aravindan; cam, Shaji; edtr, Rameshan. 90.
Ramunni, Ashokan, Vilasini, Reema, Kothara Gopalkrishnan.
02/06/80

Kung-Fu
(Poland)
POL. Film Unit X prodn. Wri-dir, Janusz Kijowski; cam (Eastmancolor), Krysztof Wyszynski; edtr, Irena Choryinska; mus, Jacek Bednarek. 112.
Teresa Sawicka, Piotr Fronczewski, Daniel Olbrychski, Andrzej Sewerynm, Krzysztof Janczar.
09/03/80

Kung-Fu Wu-Su
(France)
GAU. Publistart-Gaumont-A2 prodn. Conceived-dir, Jean-Luc Magneron. Cam (Eastmancolor), Pierre Duponey. Jean-Noel Ferragut; edtr, Daniell Zetlaoei. 125.
(DOC)
10/12/77

Kutong Lupa
(Small Insect)
(Philippines)
X. Rootman prodn. Dirs, Fely Crisostomo, J Erastheo, C Navos. Cam, Ben Lobo; mus, Demet Velasquez; 101.
Nino Muhlach, Zaldy Zshomack, Nida Blanca, Celia Rodriquez, Johnny Delgado, Alicia Alonzo, Merle Tuason, Renato Robles, Joe Garcia, Rudy Manlapaz, Baby de Jesus.
09/22/76

Kvar
(Breakdown)
(Yugoslavia)
YFR. Film Danas prodn. Belgrade. Dir, Milos Radivojevic. Sp, Svetozar Vlajkovic, Radivojevic; cam, Aleksander Petkovic. 90.

Aleksandar Bercek, Neda Arneric, Milena Dravic, Ljuba Tadic, Dusko Janicijevic, Olga Spiridonovic, Danila Stojkovic, Irfan Mensur, Rada Zivkovic, Djordje Jelisic.
04/25/79

Kvindesind
(Inside Woman)
(Denmark)
OBL. Crone Film/Stig Bjoerkman in asso with The Danish Film Institute (Esben Hoilund Carlsen) prodn. Wri-dir, Stig Bjoerkman. Cam (Eastmancolor), Dirk Bruel; prodn des, Soeren Krag Soerensen; cos, Nico; edtr, Grete Moeldrup; mus, Anne Linnet, Ralph Lundsten, Eric Satie; exec prod, Nina Crone. 75.
Lotte Tarp, Peter Schroeder, George Bamford, Kim Magnusson, Ghita Noerby.
04/23/80

La Ballade Des Daltons
(The Ballad of the Daltons)
(France)
UA. Dargaud Prodns Films, Les Productions Rene Goscinny, Les Studios Idefix prodn. Wri-dir, Rene Goscinny, Morris; dir supv, Henri Gruel, Pierre Watrin; script adds, Pierre Tchernia. Cam (Eastmancolor), Claude Poinis; edtr, Gruel; mus, Claude Bolling. 82.
Voices by Daniel Ceccaldi, Pierre Trabaud, Jacques Balutin, Bernard Haller, Roger Carel, Jacques Fabbri, Jacques Deschamps, Jacques Morel.
(ANI)
09/27/78 Mimsy Farmer, Barry Primus, Ray Lovelock, Angela Goodwin.

La Banquiere
(The Woman Banker)
(France)
GAU. Partners/FR3 co-prodn, with the participation of the Societe Francaise de Production. Prod, Ariel Zeitoun; dir, Francis Girod; sp, Girod and Georges Conchon; cam, Bernard Zitzermann; mus, Ennio Morricone; art dir, Jean-Jacques Caziot; cos, Jacques Fonteray; edtr, Genevieve Winding; snd, Jean-Pierre Ruh. 125.
Romy Schneider, Jean-Louis Trintignant, Jean-Claude Brialy, Claude Brasseur, Daniel Mesguich, Marie-France Pisier.
09/03/80

La Barricade Du Point Du Jour
(The Barricade At Point Du Jour)
(France)
LUG. Les Films Du Point Du Jour prodn. Dir, Rene Richon. Sp, Richon, Yves Oppenheim; cam (Eastmancolor-Panavision), Ramon Suarez; edtr, Annie Baronnet; mus, Antoine Duhamel, Pascal Auberson. 110.
Anicee Alvina, Jean-Luc Bideau, Philippe Noiret, Claude Brosset, Laszlo Szabo, Julian Negulesco, Cecile Vassort, Eliane Boeri, Monique Chaumette.
03/08/78

La Batalla De Chile, II: El Golpe De Estado
(The Battle of Chile, II: The Coup d'Etat)
(Chile - Cuba)
X. Equipe Tercer Ano prodn, in collab with Chris Marker and the Cuban Film Institute ICAIC. Wri-dir, Patricio Guzman. Cam, Jorge Mueller; edtr, Pedro Chaskel; snd, Bernardo Menz. 90.
(DOC) (B & W)
07/14/76

La Battala de Chile - III
(The Battle Of Chile, Part III: The Power Of The People)
(Chile - Cuba)
UNF. Equipo Tercer Ano prodn, in collab with the Cuban Film Institute. Dir, Patricio Guzman; cam, Jorge Muller; edtr, Pedro Chaskel; snd, Bernardo Menz; asst dir, Jose Pino. 83. *(In Spanish with English subtitles and narration)* (DOC) (16m) (B & W)
05/07/80

La Brace Dei Biassoli
(The Biassoli Embers)
(Italy)
X. RAI-Television Channel 2 prodn. Dir, Giovanni Fago; sp, Fago, Mario Tobino; novel, Mario Tobino; cam, Sandro Messina; art dir, Emilio Voglino. 147.
Anna Maria Gherardi, Luigi Di Berti, Remo Girone, Gianni Garko, Giuseppe Anatrelli, Angelina Quinterno, Bruno Zanin, Gisella Burinato.
09/24/80

La Bulle
(The Bubble)
(Switzerland)
X. Serge Fradkoff prodn. Dir-wri, Raphael Rebibo. Cam (Eastmancolor), Maurice Fellous; edtr, Pierre Gillette; mus, Paul Misraki. 102.
Bernard Le Coq, Catherine Lachens, Francois Maistre, Fernand Berset, Roland Amstutz, Jacques Rispal, Pierre Nicole.
04/28/76

La Cage Aux Folles
(The Mad Cage)
(France - Italy)
UA. UA-France-Da Ma Produzione Sta prodn. Dir, Edouard Molinaro. Sp, Francis Veber, Molinaro, Marcello Danon, Jean Poiret from a play by Poiret; cam (Eastmancolor), Armando Mannuzzi; edtr, Robert and Monique Isnardon; mus, Ennio Morricone. 103.
Ugo Tognazzi, Michel Serrault, Michel Galabru, Claire Maurier, Reni Laurent, Bennie Luke.
11/01/78

La Cage Aux Folles II
(Italy - France)
UA. DaMa Produzione (Rome) UA (Paris) co-prodn. Prod, Marcello Danon. Dir, Edouard Molinaro. Wri, Danon, Jean Poiret, Francis Veber; cam (Technicolor), Armando Nannuzzi; cos, Ambra Danon; mus, Ennio Morricone; edtr, Robert Isnardon; makeup, Piero Antonio Mecacci; snd, Mario Dallimonti; art dir, Francesco Saverio Chianese. 100.
Ugo Tognazzi, Michel Serrault, Marcel Bozzuffi, Michel Galabru, Paola Borboni, Benny Luke, Giovanni Vettorazzo, Glauco Onorato, Roberto Bisacco.
12/31/80

La Campanada
(Leaving It All)
(Spain)
X. Jose Frade prodn. Dir, Jaime Camino. Sp, Roman Gubern, Camino; cam (Eastmancolor), Jose Luis Alcaine; edtr, Teresa Alcocer. 102.
Juan Luis Galiardo, Fiorella Faltoyano, Ovidi Montllor, Jose Maria Forn, Martin Galindo, Felix Moix, Luis Iriondo, Fermin Reixach, Jose Maria Loperena, Maria Asquerino.
04/16/80

La Carapate
(Out Of It)
(France)
GAU. Gaumont Int'l prodn. Dir, Gerard Oury. Sp, Oury, Daniele Thompson; cam (Eastmancolor), Edmond Sechan; edtr, Albert Jurgenson. 105.
Pierre Richard, Victor Lanoux, Raymond Bussieres, Jean-Pierre Darras, Yvonne Godeau, Claire Richard.
11/01/78

La Chambre Verte
(The Green Room)
(France)
UA. Les Films Du Carrosse-UA prodn. Dir, Francois Truffaut. Sp, Truffaut, Jean Gruault from two themes in stories by Henry James; cam (Eastmancolor), Nestor Almendros; edtr, Martine Barraque-Curie; mus, Maurice Jaubert. 94.
Francois Truffaut, Nathalie Baye, Jean Daste, Jean-Pierre Moulin, Jane Lobre, Patrick Maleon.
03/29/78

La Chanson De Roland
(The Song of Roland)
(France)
GAU. Z Prodns-FR3 prodn. Dir, Frank Cassenti. Sp, Michele Mercier, Thierry Joly, Cassenti; cam (Eastmancolor), Jean-Jacques Flori; edtr, Michele Mercier; mus, Antoine Duhamel; art dir, Renaud Sanson; cos, Galiane; prod, Jean-Serge Breton. 110
Klaus Kinski, Dominique Sanda, Alain Cluny, Pierre Clementi, Jean-Pierre Kalfon, Monique Mercure, Niels Arestrup, Serge Merlin, Laszlo Szabo.
10/11/78

La Citta' Delle Donne
(City of Women)
(Italy - France)
GAU. Prod, Renzo Rossellini for Opera Film-Gaumont S A. Dir, Federico Fellini. Sp, Fellini, Bernardino Zapponi, with collab of Brunello Rondi; cam (Eastman), Giuseppe Rotunno; art dir, Dante Ferretti; edtr, Ruggero Mastroianni; mus, Luis Bacalov; cos, Gabriella Pescucci. 140.
Marcello Mastroianni, Anna Prucnal, Bernice Stegers, Donatella Damiani, Iole Silvani, Ettore Manni.
04/09/80

La Ciudad Cremada
(The Burned City)
(Spain)
X. Leo Films - PC Teide prodn. Dir, Antoni Ribas. Sp, Miquel Sanz, Antoni Ribas; prods, Josep Maria Forn, Ferran Repiso; cam (Eastmancolor), Teo Minguell; mus, Manuel Valls Gorina; edtr, Ramon Quadreny; sets, Josep Masague, Jordi Berenguer. 157.
Xavier Elorriaga, Francesc Casares, Paul Garsaball, Montserrat Salvador, Jeannine Mestre, Angela Molina, Jose Luis Lopez Vazquez, Adolf Marsillach, Josep Vivo, Ovidi Montllor, Afredo Luccheti, Teresa Gimpera, Joan Manuel Serrat, Nuria Espert, Marta May, Ricard Palmerola, Patty Shepard, Mary Sampere, Ivan Tubau.
10/27/76

La Cle Sur La Porte
(The Key Is In The Door)
(France)
CCF. Cineproduction, SFP prodn. Dir, Yves Boisset. Sp, Andre Weinfeld, Boisset from book by Marie Cardinal; cam (Eastmancolor), Michel Carre; edtr, Albert Jurgenson; mus, Philippe Sarde. 102.
Annie Girardot, Patrick Dewaere, Stephane Jobert, Eleonore Klarwein, Barbara Steele, Malene Sveinbjornsson, Mathieu Schiffman.
12/13/78

La Communion Solennelle
(Solemn Communion)
(France)
PLF. Les Films Arquebeuse-FR3-INA-SFP prodn. Wri-dir, Rene Feret. Cam (Eastmancolor), Jean-Francois Robin; edtr, Vincent Pinel; art dir, Hilton McConnico; mus, Sergio Ortega. 105.
Claude-Emile Rosen, Claude Bouchery, Vincent Pinel, Yveline Ailhaud, Patrick Fierry, Jany Gastaldi, Marief Guittier, Roland Amstutz, Marcel Dalio, Andre Marcon, Philippe Leotard.
02/09/77

La Coquito
(Spain)
X. Impala-Pedro Maso P C (Madrid) prodn. Dir, Pedro Maso. Sp, Pedro Maso, Antonio Vich, based on novel by Joaquin Belda; cam (Eastmancolor), Alejandro Ulloa; mus, Gregorio Garcia Segura; sets, Ramiro Gomez; edtr, Alfonso Santacana. 105.
Ilyana Ross, Amparo Rivelles, Fernando Allende, Carlos Bracho, Juanito Navarro, Pancho Cordova, Rafael Navarro.
02/01/78

La Criatura
(The Creature)
(Spain)
X. Alborada P C-Guion P C prodn (Madrid). Dir, Eloy de la Iglesia. Sp, Enrique Barreiro; edtr, Julip Pena; cam (Eastmancolor), Raul Artigaut; mus, Victor Aute. 100.
Ana Belen, Juan Diego, Claudia Gravi, Ramon Reparaz, Manuel Pereiro, Barbara Lys, Francisco Melgares.
02/01/78

La Dentelliere
(The Lacemaker)
(France - Switzerland)
GAU. Citel Films - Action Films - FR3 - Janus Films prodn. Dir, Claude Goretta. Sp, Pascal Laine, Goretta from the book by Laine; cam (Eastmancolor), Jean Boffety; edtr, Joelle Van Effentere; mus, Pierre Jansen. 110.
Isabelle Huppert, Yves Beneyton, Florence Giorgetti, Anne-Marie Duringer, Michel De Re.
05/25/77

La Derniere Femme
(The Last Woman)
(France - Italy)
COL. Flaminia Produzioni Cinematografica-Productions Jacques Roitfeld prodn. Dir, Marco Ferreri. Sp, Rafael Azacona, Dante Matelli, Ferreri; cam (Technospes), Luciano Tovoli; edtr, Enzo Meniconi; mus, Philippe Sarde. 112.
Gerard Depardieu, Ornella Muti, Michel Piccoli, Zouzou, Renato Salvatori, Giuliana Calandra.
04/07/76

La Derobade
(The Getaway)
(France)
PDS. ATC 3000/Prodis co-prodn. Prod, Benjamin Simon. Dir, Daniel Duval; sp, Duval, Christopher Frank, Jeanne Cordelier, based on "The Life" by Cordelier; cam, Michel Cenet; snd, Michel Vionnet; art dir, Francois Chanut; edtr, Jean-Bernard Bonis; mus, Vladimir Kosma. 110.
Miou-Miou, Maria Schneider, Daniel Duval, Neil Arestrup.
12/12/79

La Discoteca Del Amor
(The Disco of Love)
(Argentina)
AES. Aries-Baires-Microfon Production. Prods, Fernando Ayala, Hector Olivera; dir-sp, Adolfo Aristarain; exec prod, Eva Harguindey de Cuesta; cam (Eastmancolor), Horacio Maira; edtr, Carlos Piaggio; snd, Daniel Castronouvo; sets, Oscar Piruzanto; asst dirs, Alejandro Pimentel, Armando Pronzato; cos, Katy Saavedra; mus, Emilio Kauderer. 93.
Cacho Castan, Monica Gonzaga, Ricardo Darin, Tito Mendoza, Marcos Woinsky, Tincho Zabala, Stella Maris Lanzani, Silvia Perez, Carlos del Burgo.
08/27/80

La Donna Della Domenica
(Sunday Woman)
(Italy - France)
FXE. Prods, Robert Infascelli, Marcello D'Amico for Primex and Fox Europa. Dir, Luigi Comencini. Sp, Age and Scarpelli, from the novel by Fruttero and Lucentini; cam (Eastmancolor), Luciano Tovoli; art dir, Mario Ambrosino; edtr, Antonio Siciliano; mus, Ennio Morricone. 110.
Marcello Mastroianni, Jacqueline Bisset, Jean Louis Trintignant, Aldo Reggiani, Pino Caruso.
01/28/76

La Drolesse
(The Hussy)
(France)
X. La Gueville Productions-Lola Films co-prodn. Prods, Daniele Delorme and Yves Robert. Wri-dir, Jacques Doillon. Script collab, Denis Ferraris; cam (Eastmancolor), Philippe Rousselot; art dir, Jean-Denis Robert; edtr, Laurent Quaglio; snd, Michel Kharat. 90.
Madeleine Desdevises, Claude Hebert.
05/09/79

La Empresa Perdona Un Momento de Locura
(The Management Forgives A Moment Of Madness).
(Venezuela)
X. Proa C A prodn. Dir-sp, Mauricio Walerstein. Cam, Hector Rios; mus, Alberto Slewynger; art dir, Tony Sanchez; edtr, Alberto Torija. 90.
Simon Dias, Eva Mondolfi, Rafael Briceno, Maria Escalona, Arturo Calderon, Rafael Gomez, Fausto Verdial.
05/30/79

La Escopeta Nacional
(The National Shotgun)
(Spain)
X. Incine prodn, presented by Alfredo Matas. Dir, Luis G Berlanga. Sp, Luis Berlanga, Rafael Azcona; cam (Eastmancolor), Carlos Suarez; sets, Rafael Palmero; edtr, Jose L Matesanz. 88.
Jose Sazatornil, Antonio Ferrandis, Jose Luis Lopez Vazques, Rafael Alonso, Luis Escobar, Agustin Gonzalez, Andres Mejuto, Conchita Montes, Monica Randall, Barbara Rey, Laly Soldevila, Amparo Soler Leal, Rossanna Yanni.
05/10/78

La Familia, Bien, Gracias
(The Family, Fine, Thanks)
(Spain)
X. Pedro Maso P C-Impala S A prodn. Dir, Pedro Maso. Sp, Maso, Rafael Azcona; cam (Eastmancolor), Alejandro Ulloa; mus, Juan Carlos Calderon; sets, Ramiro Gomez; edtr, Alfonso Santacana. 106.
Alberto Closas, Jose Luis Lopez Vazquez, Maria Jose Alfonso, Jaime Blanch, Francisco Benlloch, Lola Forner, Julita Martinez, Carlos Pinar, Julieta Serrano, Paco Valledares, Margot Cottens.
01/23/80

La Femme-Enfant
(The Child Woman)
(France)
GAU. Alma Films, GPFI, Gaumont prodn. Wri-dir, Raphaele Billetdoux. Cam (Eastmancolor), Alaine Derobe; edtr, Genevieve Winding; mus, Vladimir Cosma.   100.
Penelope Palmer, Klaus Kinski, Michel Robin, Helene Surgere.
05/28/80

La Femme Flic
(The Woman Cop)
(France)
AMLF. Sara Films/Antenne 2/Societe Nouvelle Cinevog co-prodn. Prod, Alain Sarde. Dir, Yves Boisset. Sp, Boisset, Claude Veillot; cam, Jacques Loiseleux; snd, Harald Maury, Jean Fontaine; edtr, Albert Jurgenson; mus, Philippe Sarde; art dirs, Maurice Sergent, Jimmy Vanstennkiste.   103.
Miou-Miou, Jean-Marc Thibault, Leny Escuder, Jean-Pierre Kalfon, Francois Simon.
01/23/80

La Femme Qui Pleure
(The Crying Woman)
(France)
AMLF. Dominique Laffin, Jacques Doillon, Haydee Politoff, Lola Doillon. Les Prodns De La Gueville-Lola Films-Renn Prodns prodn. Wri-dir, Jacques Doillon. Cam (Eastmancolor), Yves Lafaye; edtr, Isabelle Rathery.   90.
12/06/78

La Fete Sauvage
(The Savage Party)
(France)
X. Tele Hachette, Rafford prodn. Conceived-dir, Frederic Rossif. Commentary, Madeleine Chapsal; cam (Eastmancolor), Bernard Zitzerman; edtr, Dominique Casaneuve; mus, V Papaloussia.   90.
(DOC)
02/18/76

La Giacca Verde
(The Green Jacket)
(Italy)
X. Arturo La Pegna, CEP prodn. Dir, Franco Giraldi. Wris, Giraldi, Lucio Battistrada, Sandra Onofri, Cesare Garboli. Sets, Guido Josia; cam, Dario di Palma; mus, Luis Bacalov; edtr, Raimondo Crociani; cos, Danda Ortona.   120.
Jean Pierre Cassel, Renzo Montagnani, Senta Berger, Vittorio Senipoli.
08/29/79

La Griffe Et La Dent
(Fang and Claw)
(France)
CNE. Conceived-dir-cam, Gerard Vienne, Francois Bel. Snd, Michel Fano; edtr, Jacqueline Lecompte.
(DOC)
05/26/76

La Guerra De Papa
(Daddy's War)
(Spain)
X. Jose Frade prodn; dir, Antonio Mercero. Sp, Mercero, Horacio Valcarcel, based on novel by Miguel Delibes "El Principe Destronado." Cam (Eastmancolor), Manuel Rojas; edtr, Javier Moran; sets, Antonio Cortes; prodn supv, Jose Salcedo.   98.
Lolo Garcia, Teresa Gimpera, Hector Alterio, Rosario Garcia Ortega, Veronica Forque, Queta Claver, Agustin Navarro, Vicente Parra.
09/28/77

La Guerre des Policiers
(The Police War)
(France)
UGC. Stephan Film prodn. Prod, Vera Belmont. Dir, Robin Davis; sp, Jean-Marie Guillaume, Jacques Labib; adapt, Jean Patrick Manchette, Patrick Laurent, Guillaume, Labid, Davis; dial, Laurent, Manchette, Davis; cam (Eastmancolor), Ramon Saurez; edtr, Jose Pinheiro; snd, Pierre Befve, Jean-Paul Mugel; art dir, Joey Fare; mus, Jean Marie Senia.   102.
Claude Brasseur, Marlene Jobert, Claude Rich, Francois Perier.
12/05/79

La Gueule de l'autre
(The Other One's Mug)
(France)
AMLF. Films Gibe/Sara Films/Antenne 2 co-prodn. Dir, Pierre Tchernia. Wri, Jean Poiret. Cam, Rene Mathelin; mus, Claude Bolling; art dir, Willy Holt; edtr, Francoise Javet; snd, Jean-Philippe LeRoux.   90.
Michael Serrault, Jean Poiret, Andrea Parisy, Bernadette Lafont, Curt Jurgens.
02/13/80

La Hora de Maria y el Pajaro de Oro
(The Hour of Mary and the Bird of Gold)
(Argentina)
CTE. Neci prodn. Dir, Rodolfo Kuhn. Sp, Kuhn and Eduardo Gudino Kieffer; cam (Eastmancolor), Alberto Basail; mus, Oscar Lopez Ruiz; edtr, Alfredo Levinsky.   105.
Leonor Masno, Dora Baret, Jorge Rivera Lopez, Milagros de la Vega, Marta Albertini, Arturo Puig.
04/07/76

La Isla
(The Island)
(Argentina)
X. MBC Prodns Presentation. Dir, Alejandro Doria. Sp, Aida Bortnik; edtr, Miguel Perez; cam, Miguel Rodriguez; mus, Victor Pronchet.   106.
Selva Alaman, Hugo Arana, Aldo Barbero, Hector Bodonde, Luisina Brando, Alicia Bruzzo, Graciela Dufau, Luisa Vehil, Sandra Mihanovich, Lizardo Laphitz.
09/12/79

La Jument Vapeur
(The Steam Mare)
(France)
PLF. Stephane Films prodn. Sp-dir, Joyce Bunuel. Cam (Eastmancolor), Francois Portat; edtr, Jean-Bernard Bonis; mus, Jean-Marie Senia.   92.
Carole Laure, Pierre Santini, Liliane Roveyre.
04/05/78

La Legion Saute Sur Kolwezi
(Operation Leopard)
(France)
CCF. Bela Productions/SNC/FR3 co-prodn. Prod, Georges de Beauregard. Dir, Raoul Coutard. Sp, Andre G Brunelin, based on book by Pierre Sergent; cam, Georges Liron; edtr, Michael Lewin; snd, Michel Laurent; mus, Serge Franklin.   100.
Giuliano Gemma, Bruno Cremer, Laurent Malet, Jacques Perrin, Mimsy Farmer.
02/27/80

La Locandiera
(Italy)
CID. Prod, Giulio Scanni for DADA Film prodns and RAI Film. Dir, Paolo Cavara. Sp, Leo Benvenuti, Pietro De Bernardi, Lucia Demby, based on Carlo Goldoni play; cam (Eastmancolor), Mario Vulpiani; sets-cos, Giancarlo Bartolini Salimbeni; edtr, Angelo Curi; mus, Detto Mariano.   111.
Claudia Mori, Adriano Celentano, Paolo Villaggio, Gianni Cavina.
12/03/80

La Machine
(France)
LML. Diagonale prodn. Dir, Paul Vecchiali. Sp, Jean Michel Guillery, Jean-Christope Bouvet, Cecile Clairval, Vecchiali; cam (Eastmancolor), Georges Strouves; edtr, Francoise Merville, Frank Mathieu, Vecchiali; mus, Roland Vincent.   100.
Jean-Christophe Bouvet, Sonia Saviange, Monique Melinand, Philippe Chemin, Danielle Gain, Jean-Louis Cros, Gerard Blain, Helene Surgere.
09/14/77

La Mano Negra
(The Black Hand)
(Spain)
X. La Salamandra, Ogro Films, Incine co-prodn. Dir, Fernando Colomo; sp, Fernando Trueba, Fernando Colomo; cam (Eastmancolor), Angel Luis Fernandez; edtr, Miguel Angel Santamaria; mus, Jose Nieto; snd, Pierre Gamet; exec prod, Ramiro G Bermudez de Castro.   94.
Inigo Gurrea, Joaquin Hinojosa, Virginia Mataix, Carmen Maura, Mary Carrillo, Manuel Alexandre, Fabio Testi, Emilio Urdiales.
09/03/80

La Marge
(The Margin)
(France)
PF. Robert and Raymond Hakim prodn. Wri-dir, Walerian Borowczyk from the novel by Pieyre De Mandiargues; cam (Eastmancolor), Bernard Daillencourt; edtr, Louisette Hautecouer. 86.
Sylvia Kristel, Joe Dallesandro, Mireille Audibert, Denis Manuel, Andre Falcon, Louise Chevalier.
09/22/76

La Marquise D'O...
(France - Germany)
GAU. Les Films Du Losange-Janus-Film Produktion prodn. Wri-dir, Eric Rohmer, from book by Heinrich Von Kleist; cam (Eastmancolor), Nestor Almendros; edtr, Cecile Ducugis. (MPAA rating: PG). 102.
Edith Clever, Bruno Ganz, Peter Luhr, Edda Seippel, Otto Sander, Ruth Drexel.
05/19/76

La Mazzetta
(The Payoff)
(Italy)
UA. Filmauro Prodn. Prods, Luigi, Aurelio De Laurentiis. Dir, Sergio Corbucci. Sp, Dino Maiuri, Massimo De Rita, Luciano De Crescenzo, Elvio Porta, based on book by Attilio Veraldi; cam, Luigi Kuveiller; mus, Pino Daniele; set des, Giantito Burchiellaro. 120.
Nino Manfredi, Ugo Tognazzi, Paolo Stoppa, Marisa Laurito, Gennaro Di Napoli, Imma Piro, Marisa Merlini, Salvatore Borgese, Giovanni Borgese.
05/10/78

La Meilleure Facon De Marcher
(The Best Way To Get Along)
(France)
AMLF. Filmoblic prodn. Dir, Claude Miller. Sp, Luc Beraud, Miller; cam (Eastmancolor), Bruno Nytten; edtr, Jean-Bernard Bonis. 90.
Patrick Dewaere, Patrick Bouchitey, Christine Pascal, Claude Pieplu.
02/18/76

La Memoire Courte
(Short Memory)
(France)
UT. Unite Trois-Paradise Films prodn. Dir, Eduardo De Gregorio. Sp, Edgardo Cozarinsky, De Gregorio; cam (Eastmancolor), Willy Lubtchansky; mus, Eric Simon. 105.
Nathalie Baye, Philippe Leotard, Bulle Ogier, Xavier St Macary, Andrian Brine.
06/13/79

La Menace
(The Threat)
(France - Canada)
PFC. Prodn Du Daunou, Viaduc Prodn, Citeca, Canafox prodn. Dir, Alain Corneau. Sp, Daniel Boulanger, Corneau; cam (Eastmancolor), Pierre-William Glenn; edtr, Henri Lanoe; mus, Gerry Mulligan. 117.
Yves Montand, Marie Dubois, Carole Laure, Jean-Francois Balmer.
10/19/77

La Miel
(Honey)
(Spain)
X. Pedro Maso, PC Impala prodn. Dir, Pedro Maso. Sp, Pedro Maso, Rafael Azcona; cam (Eastmancolor), Hans Burmann; exec prod, Francisco Hueva; edtr, Alfonso Santana; sets, Ramiro Gomez. 102.
Jane Birkin, Jose Luis Lopez Vazquez, Jorge Sanz, Amelia de la Torre, Guillermo Marin, Agustin Gonzalez.
09/19/79

La Morte Al Lavoro
(Death At Work)
(Italy)
SCI. RAI-Napoli, Gaetano Stucci prodn. Dir, Gianni Amelio. Sp, Mimmo Rafele, Amelio from a story by Hanns H Ewers; cam (b&w from Video), Mario Selo; mus, Bernard Herrmann. 85.
Federico Pacifici, Clara Colosimo, Fautas Avelli, Eva Axen, Giovannella Grifeo.
(B & W)
08/23/78

La Muchacha De Las Bragas De Oro
(The Girl With The Golden Panties)
(Spain - Venezuela)
X. Morgana S A (Barcelona) Prozesa (Barcelona) and Proa Cinematografica C A (Caracas) co-prodn. Dir, Vicente Aranda. Exec prods, Jose Antonio Perez Giner, Carlos Duran; cam (Eastmancolor), Jose Luis Alcaine; sp, Vicente Aranda, Santiago San Miguel, Mauricio Wallerstein, based on novel by Juan Marse; edtr, Alberto Torija; mus, Manuel Camp; sets, Josep Rosell. 101.
Lautaro Murua, Victoria Abril, Isabel Mestres, Hilda Vera, Perla Vonasek, Pep Munne, Palmiro Aranda, Consuelo de Nieva.
05/07/80

La Mujer De La Tierra Caliente
(Woman From The Torrid Land)
(Spain - Italy)
X. Orfeo PSCA (Madrid) and I I F SRL (Rome) co-prodn. Dir, Jose Maria Forque. Exec prod, J M Forque. Sp, Hermogenes Sainz, Forque; cam (Eastmancolor), Alejandro Ulloa; edtr, Mercedes Alonso; mus (CAM), Carlo Savina; sets, Rafael Richart. 80.
Stuart Whitman, Laura Gemser, Pilar Velazquez, Enrique Alzucaray, Antonio Gamero, Francisco Algora, Javier Loyola.
07/26/78

La Nona
(The Grandmother)
(Argentina)
X. Aries Cinematografica Argentina S A prodn. Exec prods, Fernando Ayala, Luis Osvaldo Repetto. Dir, Hector Olivera. Sp, Roberto Cossa, Hector Olivera, based on Cossa's play of same name; cam (Eastmancolor), Victor Hugo Caula; sets, Oscar Piruzanto; mus, Oscar Cardozo Ocampo; edtr, Carlos Julio Piaggio. 74.
Pepe Soriano, Juan Carlos Altavista, Osvaldo Terranova, Graciela Alfano, Eva Franco, Guillermo Francisco, Nya Queseda.
05/23/79

La Nouba Des Femmes Du Mont Chenoua
(Nouba)
(Algeria)
ALG. Wri-dir, Assia Djebbar. Edtr, Nicole Schlemmer. 113.
(DOC) (16m)
09/19/79

La Nuit De Saint-Germain Des Pres
(The Night of Saint-Germain Des Pres)
(France)
FLG. Filmologies-Peri Prodns (Peter Riethof) - Oliane Prodns prodn. Dir, Bob Swaim. Sp, Swaim, Alain Petit, Robert Rea, Pierre Fabre; book, Leo Malet; cam (Eastmancolor), Yves Lafaye; edtr, Claudio Ventura; mus, Mort Shuman, Christian Gaubert; art dir, Hilton McConnico. 96.
Michel Galabru, Mort Shuman, Chantal Dupuy, Daniel Auteuil, Alain Mottet, Annick Alane, Gabriel Jabbour.
05/18/77

La Nuit Tous Les Chats Sont Gris
(At Night All Cats Are Gray)
(France)
PDS. Sam Films-FR3 prodn. Dir, Gerard Zingg. Sp, Zingg, Philippe Dumarcay; cam (Eastmancolor), Bruno Nuytten; edtr, Helene Viard; mus, Jean-Claude Vannier. 100.
Gerard Depardieu, Robert Stephens, Laura Betti, Charlotte Crow, Ann Zacharias, Virginie Thevenet, Simono.
11/16/77

La Odisea De Los Andes
(The Andes Odyssey)
(Mexico - Panama)
X. Concord Film Company, Inc prodn, (Panama). Dir, Alvaro J Covacevich. Sp, Mario Vargas Llosa; mus, Angel Parra; cam (Eastmancolor), Henry Weiss, Peter J Leading, Adrian Lopez Gomez, Arturo Hardy, George Amusset, Pedro Fuic, Vick Scaglione; edtr, Enrique Escalona. 98.
Fernando Parrado, Antonio Vizintin, Roberto Canessa, Gustavo Zerbino, Carlos Paez Jr, Carlos Paez Vilaro.
(DOC)
10/27/76

La Part Du Feu
(The Fire's Share)
(France)
PLF. Les Films De La tour/FR3/Films 66 prodn. Dir, Etienne Perrier. Sp, Perrier, Dominique Fabre; cam (Eastmancolor), Jean Charvein; edtr, Renee Lichtig; mus, Paul Misraki. 105.
Michel Piccoli, Claudia Cardinale, Jacques Perrin, Rufus, Roland Bertin, Gabriel Cattand, Veronique Silver.
01/11/78

La Patata Bollente
(Hot Potato)
(Italy)
CID. Prod, Achille Manzotti for Irrigazione Cinematografica. Dir, Steno. Sp, Giorgio Arlorio, Enrico Vanzina, Steno; cam (Telecolor), Emilio Loffredo; art dir, Mauro Passi; edtr, Raimondo Crociani; mus, Tato Savio. 105.
Renato Pozzeto, Edwige Fenech, Massimo Ranieri, Mario Scarpetta.
02/20/80

La Peticion
(The Request)
(Spain)
X. CIPI Cinematografica SA prodn. Dir, Pilar Miro. Exec prod, Miquel Echarri. Sp, Pilar Miro, Leo Anchoriz, based on story, "For a Night of Love," by Emile Zola; cam (Eastmancolor), Hans Burmann; sets, Santiago Ontanon; edtr, Pablo del Amo; mus, Roman Alix. 92.
Ana Belen, Emilio Gutierrez Caba, Frederic de Pascuale, Maria Luisa Ponte, Mairata O'Visiedo, Carman Maura.
08/25/76

La Petite Fille En Velours Bleu
(The Little Girl in Blue Velvet)
(France)
WBC. Orphee Arts-Columbia prodn. Dir, Alan Bridges. Sp, Christian Watton, Bridges; cam (Eastmancolor), Usama Rawi; mus, Georges Delerue. 110.
Michel Piccoli, Claudia Cardinale, Lara Wendel, Denholm Elliot, Marius Goring, Alexandra Stewart.
09/06/78

La Petite Sirene
(The Little Siren)
(France)
UGC. Apple Films/FR 3/J Roitfeld Prodns/Les Lyons/Stephan Films co-prodn. Prod-wri-dir, Roger Andrieux. Based on novel "Les Petites Sirenes", by Yves Dangerfield; cam, Robert Alazraki; mus, Alain Jomy; snd, Pierre Lorain; art dir, Jean-Baptiste Poirot; cos, Christian Gasc; edtr, Kenout Peltier. 104.
Laura Alexis, Philippe Leotard, Evelyne Dress, Marie Dubois.
08/20/80

La Portentosa Vida Del Padre Vincent
(The Prodigious Life of Father Vincent)
(Spain)
Ascle Films prodn. Exec prod, Antonio Alguero Garceran. Wri-dir, Carles Mira. Cam (Eastmancolor), Teo Escamilla; sets, Alejandro Soler; edtr, Pablo G del Amo. 82.
Albert Boadella, Ovidi Montllor, Angela Molina, Quico Carbonell, Rafa Miro, Cuca Avino, Fernando Mira, Toni Mira, Carmen Platero, Maria Rey, Paula Molina.
09/13/78

La Premiere Fois
(The First Time)
(France)
AMLF. Lira Films-Renn Prodns prodn. Wri-dir, Claude Berri. Cam (Eastmancolor), Jean-Cesar Chiabaut; edtr, Jacques Witta; mus, Rene Utreger. 85.
Alain Cohen, Charles Denner, Zorica Lozic, Delphine Levy, Claude Lubicki, Philippe Teboul, Jerome Loeb, Daniele Schneider.
12/01/76

La Provinciale
(The Provincial)
(France - Switzerland)
CIT. Phenix Productions-Gaumont-Fr3-S S R prodn. Dir, Claude Goretta. Prods, Yves Peyrot, Raymond Pousaz. Sp, Goretta, Jacques Kirsner, Rosine Rochette; adapt-dial, Goretta, Kirsner. Cam, Philippe Rousselot, Dominique Bringuier; mus, Arie Dzierlatka; edtrs, Joele Van Effenterre, Xavier Castano; art dir, Jacques Bufnoir; snd, Pierre Gamet, Bernard Chaumeil. 107.
Nathalie Baye, Angela Winkler, Bruno Ganz, Patrick Chesnais, Dominique Paturel, Pierre Vernier.
12/10/80

La Puente
(The Long Weekend)
(Spain)
X. Art 7 prodn, Madrid; prod, Jaime Fernandez-Cid. Dir, Juan A Bardem. Cam, Jose Luis Alcaine; mus, Jose Nieto; art dir, Eduardo Biurrum. 100.
Alfredo Landa, Paco Algora, Victoria Abril, Mabel Escano, Pilar Bardem.
08/10/77

La Querida
(The Mistress)
(Spain)
X. Equiluz Films prodn (Madrid). Dir, Fernando Fernan. Cam (Eastmancolor), Cecilio Paniagua; exec prods, Andres Vicente Gomez, Francisco Gordillo; mus, Manuel Alejandro, Jesus Gluck; sets, Enrique Alarcon; edtr, Rosa Salgado. 92.
Rocio Jurado, Fernando Fernan Gomez, Teresa Gimpera, Ricardo Merino.
05/26/76

La Question
(The Question)
(France)
PLF. Z Prodns (J S Breton)-Rush Films (C Guedj-Aufere)-Little Bear Prodn (B Tavernier) prodn. Dir, Laurent Heynemann. Sp, Heynemann, Claude Veillot; book, Henri Alleg; cam (Eastmancolor), Alain Levent; edtrs, Armand Psenny, Ariane Boeglin; mus, Antoine Duhamel. 112.
Jacques Denis, Nicole Garcia, Jean-Pierre Sentier, Francois Dyrek, Christian Rist, Francoise Thuries, Francois Lalande.
04/27/77

La Rabia
(Rage)
(Spain)
X. Producciones Teide film. Dir, Eugeni Anglada. Exec prod, Joseph Maria Forn. Sp, Anglada, Miguel Porter Moix, Miguel Hernan; cam (b&w), Tomas Pladavall, Anglada; mus, J Vidal; edtr, Anglada, M Glizancos. 98.
Marta May, Maria Asuncion Sancho, F Jarque Zurbano, Alfred Luchetti, Manuel Sanchez, Ramon Corominas, Carme Casanovas, Darius, Mariangels.
(16m) (B & W)
05/16/79

La Ragazza Di Via Millelire
(The Girl From Millelire Street)
(Italy)
RTI. RAI 2 TV prodn. Dir, Gianni Serra; sp, Tomaso Sherman, Serra; cam, Dario Di Palma; edtr, Maria Di Mauro; mus, Luis Bacalov. 119.
Oria Conforti, Maria Monti, Lisa Policaro, Lucia Sturiale, Ugo Campanile.
09/10/80

La Ragazza In Pigiama Giallo
(The Girl In The Yellow Pajamas)
(Italy - Spain)
MDU. Zodiak (Rome)-Picasa (Madrid) prodn. Prod, Giorgio Salvioni. Dir, Flavio Mogherini; sp, Mogherini and Rafael Sanchez Campoy; cam (Microstampa Color), Raul Arteguy; edtr, Adriano Tagliavia. 101.
Ray Milland, Dalila di Lazzaro, Michele Placido, Howard Ross, Ramiro Oliveros, Rod Mullinar, Mel Ferrer.
02/08/78

La Raison D'Etat
(State Reason)
(France - Italy)
SLG. Paris Cannes Prodn-Alpes Cinema-Mida Produzione Cinematographiche prodn. Dir, Andre Cayatte. Sp, Cayatte, Jean Curtelin, Jean-Marie Guillaume; cam (Eastmancolor), Armando Nannuzzi; edtr, Paul Cayatte; mus, Vladimir Cosma. 110.
Jean Yanne, Monica Vitti, Francois Perier, Michel Bouquet, Jean-Claude Bouillon.
05/24/78

La Sabina
(The Sabina)
(Spain - Switzerland)
X. El Iman (Madrid) and Svenska Filminstitutet (Stockholm) prodn. Prod-wri-dir, Jose Luis Borau; cam (Eastmancolor), Lars-Goran Bjorne; sets, Wolfgang Burmann; snd mixer, Lasse Summanen; edtr, Jose Salcedo; mus, Paco de Lucia. 105.
Carol Kane, Jon Finch, Harriet Andersson, Simon Ward, Angela Molina, Ovidi Montllor, Fernando Sanchez Polac, Francisco Sanchez.
(English soundtrack version available)
12/26/79

La Septieme Compagnie Au Clair Du Lune
(The Seventh Company Outdoors)
(France)
GAU. Prodns 2000-Gaumont Int'l prodn. Dir, Robert Lamoureux. Sp, Lamoureux, Jean-Marie Poire; cam (Eastmancolor), Marcel Grignon; edtr, Albert Jurgenson. 90.
Jean Lefebvre, Pierre Mondy, Henri Guybet, Patricia Karim, Andre Pousse.
12/28/77

La Spirale
(France)
LML. Films Moliere-Reggane Films-Seuil Audiovisuel prodn. Conceived-dir, Armand Matellart, Jacqueline Meppiel, Valerie Mayoux, aided by Chris Marker, Silvio Tendler, Pierre Flament. Addl cam (Eastmancolor), Ettienne Becker, Francois Catonne; mus, Jean-Claude Elyo; edtrs, Pierre Flament, Dona Ley. 145.
(DOC)
04/14/76

La Stanza Del Vescovo
(Bishop's Bedroom)
(Italy)
TIT. Prod, Giovanni Bertolucci for Merope. Dir, Dino Risi. Sp, Leo Benvenuti, Piero Di Bernardi, with collab of Piero Chiara, Dino Risi; cam (Technicolor), Franco Di Giacomo; art dir, Luigi Scaccianoce; edtr, Roberto Gallitti; mus, Armando Trovaioli. 118.
Ugo Tognazzi, Ornella Muti, Patrick Dewaere, Gabriella Giacobbe.
05/18/77

La Tercera Puerta
(The Third Door)
(Spain)
X. Ofelia Films prodn. Dir, Alvaro Forque. Exec prod, Carlos Escobedo. Sp, Alvaro Forque; cam (Eastmancolor), Alejandro Ulloa, Domingo Solano; edtr, Eduardo Biurrum; snd, Alberto Escobedo; sets, Luis Vazquez; mus, Carlos Vizziello. 92.
Yolanda Farr and her Music Hall ballet, Alfredo Amestoy, Jose Maria Montez, Andres Majuto, Enrique Mellado.
09/29/76

La Terrazza
(The Terrace)
(Italy)
UA. Prods, Pio Angeletti, Adriano De Micheli for Dean Film and Les Artistes Associes. Dir, Ettore Scola. Sp, Age-Scarpelli-Scola; cam (Technicolor), Pasqualino De Santis; art dir, Luciano Ricceri; edtr, Raimondo Crociani; mus, Armando Trovajoli. 158.
Ugo Tognazzi, Vittorio Gassman, Jean Louis Trintignant, Marcello Mastroianni, Stefania Sandrelli, Carla Gravina, Stefano Satta Flores, Serge Reggiani.
03/05/80

La Tete De Normande St. Onge
(The Head of Normande St. Onge)
(Canada)
X. Les Productions Carle/Lamy Ltd prodn. Dir, Gilles Carle. Sp, Carle, Ben Barzman; cam (Eastmancolor), Francois Protat, Michel Brault; edtrs, Carle, Avdei Chiriaeff; mus, Lewis Furey. 105.
Carole Laure, Reynald Bouchard, Raymond Cloutier.
05/19/76

La Tierra y el Cielo
(The Earth and the Sky)
(Cuba)
X. ICAIC prodn. Dir, Manuel Octavio Gomez. Cam, Livio Delgado; mus, Sergio Vitier; songs, Martha Jean Claude; edtr, Nelson Rodriguez. 87.
Samuel Claxton, Tito Junco, Martha Jean Claude.
03/15/78

La Tortue Sur Le Dos
(As A Turtle On Its Back)
(France)
WMF. Filmoblic Prodn, Paris. Prod, Hubert Niogret. Dir, Luc Beraud. Sp, Beraud, Claude Miller; cam, Bruno Nuytten; snd, Joele van Effenterre; edtr, Beraud. 110.
Bernadette Lafont, Jean-Francois Stevenin, Virginie Thevenet, Veronique Silver, Claude Miller, Marion Game, Valerie Quenessen, Veronique Dancigers, Jean Daste, Francois Lafarge, Etienne Chicot, Michel Blanc, Sandy Withelaw, Soare Bhime, Jo Perque, Florence Lafuma.
06/21/78

La Trastienda
(Back of the Store)
(Spain)
X. Jose Frade P C prodn. Dir, Jorge Grau. Script-sp, Grau, Alfonso Jimenez Romero; cam (Techniscope, Eastmancolor), Fernando Arribas; prodn chief, Jose Salcedo; edtr, Rosa Salgado. 100.
Maria Jose Cantudo, Frederick Stafford, Rosanna Schiaffino, Jose Suarez, Maruchi Fresno, Carmen de Lirio.
07/21/76

La Triple Mort Du Troisieme Personnage
(The Triple Death of The Third Personage)
(France - Belgium - Spain)
X. Babylone Films (Paris), 2000 Prodns Belgium (Brussels), Producciones Zeta SA (Barcelona) co-prodn. Wri-dir, Helvio Soto. Exec prod, Guy Jacobs; asso prods, J A Perez Giner, Ken Legaergeant; cam (Eastmancolor), Jose Luis Alcaine; edtr, Rodolfo Wedeles; mus, Juan Jose Mosalini; sets, Ramon Pou. 103.
Jose Sacristan, Brigitte Fossey, Andre Dussolier, Patricia Guzman, Rafael Anglada, Marcel Dossogne, Michel Lechat.
10/03/79

La Ultima Cena
(The Last Supper)
(Cuba)
TCF. Prodn by the Insituto Cubano Del Arte y Industria Cinematograficos. Prods, Santiago Llapur, Camilo Vives; dir, Tomas Gutierrez Alea; sp, Tomas Gonzalez, Maria Eugenia Haya and Alea; cam, Mario Garcia Joya; edtr, Nelson Rodriquez; mus, Leo Brouwer. 110.
Nelson Villagra, Silvano Rey, Luis Alberto Garcia, Jose Antonio Rodriguez, Samuel Claxton, Mario Balmaseda.
(*English subtitles*)
05/03/78

La Verdad Sobre El Caso Savolta
(The Truth On the Savolta Affair)
(Spain - France - Italy)
X. Domingo Pedret P C (Barcelona), Nef Diffusion (Paris), Filmalpha (Rome) co-prodn, dir, Antonio Drove. Exec prod, Andres Vicente Gomez; sp, Antonio Drove, Antonio Larreta based on novel by Eduardo Mendoza; cam (Eastmancolor), Gilberto Azevedo; mus, Egisto Macchi; sets, Louis Arguello; edtr, Guillermo Maldonad. 120.
Jose Luis Lopez Vazquez, Charles Denner, Ovidi Montllor, Omero Antonutti, Stefania Sandrelli, Ettore Manni, Alfred Pea, Rogelio Ibanez, Virginia Billetdoux, Pan Garsabell.
05/28/80

La Victoire En Chantant
(Black Victory)
(France)
AMLF. Reggane Films-SFP-FR3-Smart Film Produktions-Societe Ivorienne De Cinema prodn. Dir, Jean-Jacques Annaud. Sp, Georges Conchon, Annaud; cam (Eastmancolor), Claude Agostini, Edouardo Sera, Nanamoudou Magasouba; edtrs, Jean-Claude Huguet, Monique Laurent, Christine Greset; mus, Pierre Bachelet; prod, Arthur Cohn, Jacques Perrin, Giorgio Sylvagni. 100.
Jean Carmet, Jacques Dufilho, Catherine Rouvel, Jacques Spiesser, Dora Doll, Maurice Barrier, Claude Legros, Jacques Monnet, Peter Berling.
10/13/76

La Vida Cambia
(Life Changes)
(Mexico)
PEX. Conacine-STPC prodn. Dir-sp, Juan Manuel Torres. Cam, Gabriel Figueroa; mus, Gustavo Cesar Carreon; edtr, Alberto Valenzuela. 105.
Mercedes Carreno, Arturo Beristain, Martiza Olivares, Pancho Cordoba, Claudio Obregon, Gloria Mestre, Lola Beristain.
11/03/76

La Vie Devant Soi
(Life Before Him)
(France)
WBC. Lira Films prodn. Wri-dir, Moshe Mizrahi from book by Emile Ajar. Cam (Eastmancolor), Nestor Almendros; edtr, Sophie Coussein; mus, Philippe Sarde. 105.

Simone Signoret, Claude Dauphin, Samy Ben Youb, Gabriel Jabbour, Michal Bat Adam, Costa Gavras, Stella Anicette.
10/26/77

La Vie Parisienne
(The Parisian Life)
(France)
UCC. Belles Rives-SFP-Bavaria Atelier prodn. Dir, Christian-Jaque. Sp, Jaque, Jacques Emmanuel from the operetta by Meilhac and Halevy; cam (Eastmancolor), Michel Carre; edtrs, Michel Nezick, Christine Monge; mus, Jacques Offenbach; chor, Michel Ardan. 100.
Bernard Alane, Georges Aminel, Jacques Balutin, Evelyne Buyle, Jean-Pierre Darras, Martine Sarcey, Dany Saval.
01/18/78

La Vieja Memoria
(The Old Memory)
(Spain)
X. Profilmes SA prodn (Barcelona). Dir, Jaime Camino. Exec prods, Ricardo Munoz Suay, Jose Antonio Perez Giner. Cam (b&w), Jose Luis Claine, Teo Escamilla, Roberto Gomez, Tomas Pladevall, Francisco Sanchez, Magi Torruella; edtr, Teresa Alcocer. Interviews with Abad de Santillan, Federico Escofet, Raimundo Fernandez Cuesta, Jose Maria Gil Robles, Julian Gorkin, Eduardo de Guzman, Dolores Ibarruri, David Jato, Enrique Lister, Jaume Miratvilles, Federica Montseny, POUM group, Ricardo Sanz, Josep Tarradellas, Jose Luis de Villalonga. 165.
(DOC) (B & W)
10/04/78

La Viuda De Montiel
(The Widow Montiel)
(Mexico - Cuba - Venezuela - Columbia)
OMF. Universidada Veracruzana-Macuto Films-ICAIC-Macondo Films prodn. Dir, Miguel Littin. Sp, Jose Augustin, Littin from a story by Garcia Marquez; cam (Eastmancolor), Patricio Castilla; edtr, Nelson Rodriguez; mus, Leo Brower. 105.
Geraldine Chaplin, Nelson Villagra, Ernesto Gomez Cruz, Alejando Parodi, Katy Jurado.
03/05/80

La Zizanie
(The Spat)
(France)
AMLF. Films Christian Fechner prodn. Dir, Claude Zidi. Sp, Zidi, Michel Fabre, Pascal Jardin; cam (Eastmancolor), Claude Renoir; edtrs, Monique and Robert Isnardon; mus, Vladimir Cosma. 95.
Louis De Funes, Annie Girardot, Maurice Ritsch, Julien Guiomar.
04/05/78

Labyrintus
(Labyrinth)
(Hungary)
HU. Budapest Studio prodn. Wri-dir, Andras Kovacs. Cam, Janos Kende. 91.
Istvan Avar, Eva Ruttkai, Ferenc Kallai, Ilona Bencze.
(B & W)
08/25/76

The Lacemaker: SEE La Dentelliere

L'Acrobate
(The Acrobat)
(France)
AMLF. Ilios Films - Les Films Du Chef Lieu - Contrechamp prodn. Wri-dir, Jean-Daniel Pollet. Cam (Eastmancolor), Alain Levent; edtr, Nena Baratier. 98.
Claude Melki, Marion Game, Laurence Bru, Guy Marchand, Micheline Dax.
03/24/76

L'Adolescente
(The Adolescent)
(France - W Germany)
PFC. Carthago Films (Paris)-Janus Films and SWF (W Germany) coprodn. Prod, Philippe Dussart. Dir, Jeanne Moreau. Sp, Henriette Jelinek, Jeanne Moreau; cam (Eastmancolor), Pierre Gautard; edtrs, Albert Jurgenson, Colette Leloup; art dir, Noele Galland; snd, Dominique Dalmasso; mus, Philippe Sarde. 90.
Laetitia Chauveau, Simone Signoret, Edith Clever, Jacques Weber, Francis Huster, Roger Blin.
01/31/79

L'Adoption
(The Adoption)
(France)
LML. Reggane Film-Arthur Cohn Prodns-SFP-FR3 prodn. Dir, Marc Grunebaum. Sp, Grunebaum, Bernard Stora, Peter Krall, Magdeleine Dailloux; cam (Eastmancolor), Luciano Tovoli; edtr, Kenout Peltier; mus, Michel Portal. 93.
Geraldine Chaplin, Jacques Perrin, Patrick Norbert.
12/13/78

Ladroes de Cinema
(Sweet Thieves)
(Brazil)
EMZ. Fernando Campos film. Dir, Fernando Coni Campos; prod, Zakhia Elias, Morris G Israel, Noilton; wri, Fernando Coni Campos, Jorge Laclette; prodn mgr, Sergio Otero; set des, Dudu Continentino; cam (Eastmancolor)-edtr, Sergio Sanz. 105.
Milton Goncalves, Grande Otelo, Lutero Luiz, Wilson Grey, Ruth de Souza, Antonio Pitanga, Rodolpho Arena, Jesus Chediak, Lea Garcia, Celia Maracaja, Regina Linhares.
09/28/77

The Lady From Town: SEE Zonja Nga Qyteti

Lady Grey
MAV. Prod, Earl Owensby. Dir, Worth Keeter. Sp, Tom McIntyre; cam (DeLuxe), Darryl Cathcart; edtr, Jim Laudenslager; mus, Arthur Smith, Clay Smith; art dir, Sam Robbins; snd, John Dellinger, Emil Neroda; asst dir, William Olsen. 100.
Ginger Alden, David Allen Coe, Paul Ott, Herman Bloodsworth, Ed Grady, Paula Baldwin.
10/22/80

The Lady in Red
NW. Julie Corman prodn. Prod, Julie Corman. Co-prod, Steven Kovacs. Dir, Lewis Teague. Sp, John Sayles; cam, Daniel Lacambre; edtrs, Larry Bock, Ron Medico, Lewis Teague; prodn des, Jac McAnelly; art dir, Philip Thomas; set decor, Keith Hein; mus, James Horner; snd, Anthony Santa Croce; asst dir, Gerald T Olson; cos, Danny Morgan, Pat Tonnema; second unit dir, Pat Crowley. (MPAA rating: R). 93.
Pamela Sue Martin, Robert Conrad, Louise Fletcher, Robert Hogan, Laurie Heineman, Glenn Withrow, Rod Gist, Peter Hobbs, Christopher Lloyd, Dick Miller, Nancy Anne Parsons, Alan Vint.
08/01/79

Lady Oscar
(Japan - France)
TOH. Kitty Music Corp prodn. Dir, Jacques Demy; sp, Patricia Louisian Knop, Demy, from the comic strip "Rose of Versailles" by Ryoko Ikeda; cam (Eastmancolor), Jean Penzer; art dir, Bernard Evein; mus, Michel Legrand. 125.
Catriona Maccoll, Barry Stokes, Christina Bohm, Jonas Bergstrom,
(In English)
12/19/79

Lady Tiger: SEE I Sua

The Lady Vanishes
(Britain)
RNK. Hammer Film. Prod, Tom Sachs. Exec prods, Michael Carreras, Arlene Sellers, Alex Winitsky. Dir, Anthony Page. Sp, George Axelrod, based on novel by Ethel Lina White; cam, Douglas Slocombe; edtr, Russell Lloyd; mus, Richard Hartley; prodn des, Wilfred Shingleton; art dir, Bill Alexander, George von Kieseritzky; cos, Emma Porteous; asst dirs, Michael Dryhurst, Michael Mertineit. 99.
Elliott Gould, Cybill Shepherd, Angela Lansbury, Herbert Lom, Arthur Lowe, Ian Carmichael, Gerald Harper, Jean Anderson, Jenny Runacre, Vladek Sheybal, Madlena Nedeva, Wolf Kahler, Madge Ryan, Rosalind Knight, Jonathan Hackett, Barbara Markham, Hillevi, Gary McDermott, Jacki Harding.
05/16/79

Laemna mig inte ensam
(Leave Me Not Alone)
(Sweden)
SVF. Europa Film-RI Films-Swedish Film Institute prodn. Orig story-sp, Jan Halldoff, Rune Hjelm. Dir, Jan Halldoff. Cam (Eastmancolor), Sten Holmberg, Dan Myrman; edtr, Tomas Taeng; mus, Lennart Sjoeholm; exec prod, Rune Hjelm; prodn des, Mona Forsen. 92.
Lena Loefstroem, Anki Liden, Nicola Janic, Pelle Lindbergh, Gunvor Ponten, Nils Duebeck, Carl-Axel Heiknert.
06/04/80

L'Affaire Coffin
(The Coffin Affair)

(France - Canada)
MUT. Films Cine Scene and Les Productions Videofilms. Prod, Robert Menard. Dir, Jean-Claude Labrecque. Edtr, Andre Corriveau; cam, Pierre Mignot; mus, Anne Laubert; snd, Alain Corneau. 100.
August Schellenberg, Yvon Dufour, Micheline Lanctot, Jean-Marie Lemieux, Gabriel Arcand, Raymond Cloutier.
06/04/80

L'Affaire Suisse
(The Swiss Affair)

(Switzerland - France - Italy)
MNP. Peter Ammann-Saba Cinematografica-Cromix co-prodn. Dir, Peter Ammann. Sp, Fabio de Agostini, Bernard Bengloan, John L Huxley, Ammann; dialog, Huxley; cam (Eastmancolor), Aldo di Marcantonio; mus, Giancarlo Chairamello; exec prod, Bruno Paolinelli. 95.
Jean Sorel, Brigitte Fossey, Franco Fabrizi, Paul Muller, Colette Descombes, Guillaume Cheneviere, Michel Viala, Pierre Walker, Silvano Tranquilli, Guido Alberti.
12/20/78

L'Affiche Rouge
(The Red Poster)

(France)
INA. Dir, Frank Cassenti. Sp, Rene Richon, Cassenti; cam (Eastmancolor), Alix Conte; edtr, Bernadette Lombard. 90.
Roger Ibanez, Pierre Clementi, Anicee Alvina, Julian Neguelesco, Malka Ribowska, Jacques Rispal.
04/28/76

Lagerstrasse Auschwitz
(Auschwitz Street)

(W Germany)
X. Suedwestfunk TV Prodn, Baden-Baden; TV-prod, Klaus Simon. Wri-dir, Ebbo Demant. Cam, Juergen Bolz; edtr, Eva Maria Kramm; mus, Christobal Halffter; snd, Harald Lill, Manfred Schmidt. 60.
(DOC) (16m)
03/12/80

L'Aigle Et La Colombe
(The Eagle and the Dove)

(France)
X. Shangrilia prodn. Dir, Claude Bernard-Aubert. Sp, Bernard-Aubert, Michel Levine; cam (Eastmancolor), Claude Becognee; edtr, Gabriel Rongier; mus, Alain Goraguer. 100.
Lisbeth Hummel, Vania Vilers, Pierre Londiche, Colette Teissedre, Helen Surgere, Robert Bazil, Pierre Forget.
03/23/77

L'Aile et La Cuisse
(The Wing and the Thigh)

(France)
Films Christian Fechner prodn. Dir, Claude Zidi. Sp, Zidi, Michel Fabre; cam (Eastmancolor), Claude Renoir; edtrs, Monique and Robert Isnardon. 98.
Louis De Funes, Coluche, Julien Guiomar, Ann Zacharias, Claude Gensac, Marcel Dalio, Philippe Bouvard.
11/10/76

L'Albero Degli Zoccoli
(The Tree of Wooden Clogs)

(Italy)
IGR. GPC (Milan) prodn for RAI 1 and Italnoleggio. Wri-dir, Ermanno Olmi. Cam (Gevacolor), Olmi; art dir, Eurico Tovaglieri; edtr, Ermanno Olmi; mus, J S Bach, folk and choral. 175.
non-professionals from rural countryside of Bergamo.
05/24/78

L'Alpagueur
(The Predator)

(France)
AMLF. Cerito Films prodn. Dir, Philippe Labro. Sp, Labro, Jacques Lanzmann; cam (Eastmancolor), Jean Penzer; edtr, Jean Ravel; mus, Michel Colombier. 100.
Jean-Paul Belmondo, Bruno Cremer, Patrick Fierry, Jean Negroni, Jean-Pierre Jorris, Victor Garrivier.
03/31/76

Lam Ah Chun

(Hong Kong)
GHV. High Pitch prodn. Exec prod, Siao Fong Fong. Dir-sp, Rikkie Chan; songs, Siao Fong Fong. 94.
Siao Fong Fong, Yi Lui.
(Cantonese dialog with English subtitles)
07/26/78

L'Amant De Poche
(The Pocket Lover)

(France)
GAU. Progefi-SFP-Gaumont prodn. Dir, Bernard Queysanne. Sp, Pierre Pelegri, Queysanne from the book by Voldemar Lestienne; cam (Eastmancolor), Alain Levent; edtr, Agnes Molinard; mus, Laurent Petitgirard. 90.
Mimsy Farmer, Pascal Sellier, Andrea Ferreol, Serge Sauvion, Bernard Fresson, Madeleine Robinson, Stephane Jobert, Eva Ionesco.
02/15/78

Lamore

(Greece)
X. Ancora Film prodn. Wri-dir, Denetris Mavrikios; cam, Nicos Smaragdes; mus, Loukianos Kaleidonis; sets-cos, George Ziacas; edtr, Yanna Spyropoulou. 110.
Caterina Helmi, Anestis Vlahos.
(B & W)
11/28/79

L'Amour a la Bouche
(Mannequin)

(France)
BRE. Alain Vallier prodn. Wri, Alain van Damme. Dir, Van Damme, Alex Nubarr, Gerard Kikoine. Cam (Eastmancolor). (MPAA rating: R). 90.
Nadine Perles, Alain Schwartz, Elton Frame, Karin Mayer.
(Dubbed English soundtrack)
08/18/76

L'Amour En Fuite
(Love on the Run)

(France)
AMLF. Films du Carrosse prodn. Dir, Francois Truffaut. Sp, Truffaut, Pisier, Jean Aurel, Suzanne Schiffman; cam, Nestor Almendros; edtr, Martine Barraque-Curie; mus, Georges Delerue; set decor, Jean-Pierre Kohut-Svelko; title song sung by Alain Souchon. 94.
Jean-Pierre Leaud, Marie-France Pisier, Claude Jade, Dani, Dorothee, Rosy Varte, Julien Bertheau, Daniel Mesguich, Marie Henriau, Jean-Pierre Ducos, Pierre Dios, Alain Ollivier, Monique Dury, Emmanuel Clot, Christian Lentretien, Roland Thenot, Julien Dubois, Alexandre Janssen.
01/24/79

L'Amour En Herbe
(Budding Love)

(France)
Prodis. Sofracima prodn. Dir, Roger Andrieux. Sp, Andrieux, Jean-Marie Benard; cam (Eastmancolor), Ramon Suarez; edtr, Kenout Peltier; mus, Maxime Le Forestier. 100.
Pascal Meynier, Guilhaine Dubos, Bruno Raffaelli, Michel Galabru, Francoise Prevost, Alix Mahieux.
07/27/77

L'Amour En Question
(Love In Question)

(France)
SLN. Paris-Cannes-Prodn Alpes-Cinema prodn. Dir, Andre Cayatte. Sp, Jean Laborde, Cayatte; cam (Eastmancolor), Jean Badal; edtr, Paul Cayatte; mus, Olivier Dassault. 100.
Annie Girardot, Bibi Andersson, Michel Galabru, Michel Auclair, Georges Geret, Dominique Paturel.
11/01/78

L'Amour Viole
(Violated Love)

(France)
MMK. Les Films De L'Equinoxe-Les Films Du Dragon-MK2 Prodn prodn. Wri-dir, Yannick Bellon. Cam (Eastmancolor), Georges Barsky, Pierre William Glenn; edtr, Jeannine See; mus, Aram Sedefian. 110.
Nathalie Nell, Alain Foures, Michele Simmonet, Pierre Arditi, Daniel Auteuil, Bernard Granger, Alain Marcel, Tatiana Moukhine, Lucienne Hamon.
12/28/77

L'Anatra All'Arancia
(Duck in Orange Sauce)

(Italy)
CNZ. Prod, Mario Cecchi Gori for Capital Film. Dir, Luciano Salce; sp, Bernardino Zapponi; from comedy by William Douglas Home, Marc Gilbert Saugajon; cam (Eastmancolor), Franco Di Giacomo; art dir, Lorenzo Baraldi; edtr, Antonio Siciliano; mus, Armando Trovaioli. 105.
Monica Vitti, Ugo Tognazzi, Barbara Bouchet, John Richardson.
01/14/76

Land And Sons: SEE Land Og Synir

The Land Of Love: SEE Pendin Heng Kuam Rak

Land Og Synir
(Land And Sons)
(Iceland)
ISR. Jon Hermannsson prodn. Dir, Agust Gudmundsson; sp, Gudmundsson, based on a novel by Indridi G Thorsteinsson; cam, Sigurdur Sverrir Palsson; mus, Gunnar Raynir Sveinsson. 94.
Sigurdur Sigurjonsson, Jon Sigurdbjornsson, Gudny Ragnarsdottir, Jonas Tryggvason.
10/29/80

L'Ange et La Femme
(Angel and Woman)
(Canada)
CRL. Sp-dir, Gilles Carle. Cam (b&w), Francois Portat; mus, Lewis Furey. 90.
Carole Laure, Lewis Furey, Steve Lack.
02/01/78

L'Ange Gardien
(The Guardian Angel)
(Canada - France)
AMLF. Promedifilm (Marseille)-Les Films Prospec Inc (Montreal) co-prodn. Wri-dir, Jacques Fournier. Cam, Yves Pouffary; edtr, Frederic de Chateaubriant; mus, Marcel Napoleoni. 90.
Margaret Trudeau, Francis Lemaire, Andre Falcon, Jacqueline Jefford.
01/31/79

Langit, Lupa
(Pandemonium)
(Philippines)
EPP. Emperor Films prodn. Prod, Jimmy L Pascual. Dirs, Teddy Yip, Noli Villar. Cam, Ben Lobo; mus, Ernani Cueco. 100.
Susan Roces, Rosanna Ortiz, Loretta Marquez, Ronald Valdez; Bella Flores, Johnny Monteiro, Nancy de los Santos, Joseph Cavestany.
05/05/76

Langt Borta Och Naera
(Far Away And Close)
(Sweden)
FXS. Swedish Film Institute (Jorn Donner) prodn. Dir-edtr, Marianne Ahrne. Story-sp, Marianne Ahrne, Bertrand Hurault; cam (Eastmancolor), Hans Welin; prodn mgrs, Palle Sonesson, Peter Kropenin. 99.
Lilga Kowanka, Robert Farrant, Helge Skoog, Annicka Kronberg.
12/29/76

Languidi Baci, Perfide Carezze
(Languid Kisses, Wicked Caresses)
(Italy)
CID. Prod, Giulio Scanni and Filiberto Bandini for Staff Films. Dir, Alfredo Angeli. Sp, Bernardino Zapponi, Angeli; cam (Eastmancolor), Giuliano Giustini; art dir, Mario Molli; edtr, Luigia Magrini; mus, Ariston. 115.
Luigi Proietti, Giovanna Ralli, Cristiano Censi.
02/09/77

L'Animal
(The Animal)
(France)
AMLF. Cerito Films, Les Films Christina Fechner prodn. Dir, Claude Zidi. Sp, Zidi, Michel Audiard, Dominique Fabre; cam (Eastmancolor), Claude Renoir; edtr, Monique Isnardon; mus, Vladimir Cosma. 106.
Jean-Paul Belmondo, Raquel Welch, Dany Saval, Charles Gerard, Julien Guiomar, Aldo Maccioni.
10/19/77

L'Annee Sainte
(The Holy Year)
(France)
SNC. Dir, Jean Girault. Sp, Louis-Emile Galey, Jacques Vilfrid; cam (Eastmancolor), Guy Suzuki; edtr, Michel Lewin. 95.
Jean Gabin, Danielle Darrieux, Jean Claude Brialy.
05/05/76

Lantern Festival Adventure
(Taipei)
07/25/79
CMT. Prod, Hu Cheng Ting. Dir, Chang Pei Cheng. Exec prod, Ma Han Ying; story-sp, Szuma Ching Yuan; cam, Wang Chi Yang; lighting, Wu Chich; edtr, Li Chich; mus, Tony Wong; snd, Li Kuan U. 100.
Huang I-Lung, Liu Huan Kuo, Tang Chin, Chang Fu-Chine.

L'Anti Cristo: SEE The Tempter

Laong Dao
(Miss Laong Dao)
(Thailand)
VMB. Prod, Wanchai Termjitaree. Wri-dir, Pisan Akaraseni; based on orig story by Suphan Pramphan. Cam, Vichien Ruangwittayakul; snd, Union Lab (Hong Kong); songs, Tanongsap Pakdithiwa; prodn des, VC Promotion; asst dir, Kitti Akaraseni. 125.
Pisan Akaraseni, Nawarat Yukthanand, Rinda Katancharoen, Montri Jaenaksorn, Jamrak Chamnanpadit, Ratanaporn Indrakamhaeng, Marasri Issarangkul, Na Ayudhaya, Uthen Boonyong, Siriwat Kongkaketr, Singh Milintasai.
12/03/80

L'Apprenti Salaud
(The Apprentice Heel)
(France)
PDS. Elefilm-SFP prodn. Dir-wri, Michel Deville. Cam (Eastmancolor), Claude Lecomte; edtr, Raymond Guyot. 100.
Robert Lamoureux, Christine Lejoux, Claude Pieplu, Georges Wilson, Jean-Pierre Kalfon.
02/02/77

L'Argent De Poche
(Spending Money)
(France)
UA. Les Films Du Carrosse-UA prodn. Dir, Francois Truffaut. Sp, Truffaut, Suzanne Schiffmann; cam (Eastmancolor), Pierre-William Glenn; edtr, Yann Dedet; mus, Maurice Jaubert, song "Children Are Bored on Sunday" by Charles Trenet; art dir, J P Kohut-Svelko. 104.
Geory Desmouceaux, Philippe Goldman, Richard Golfier, Sylvie Grezel, Pascale Bruchon, Jean-Francois Stevenin, Chantal Mercier, Nicole Felix.
03/24/76

L'Argent Des Autres
(Other People's Money)
(France)
PLF. Fildebroc-FR3-SFP-Films De La Tour prodn. Dir, Christian De Chalonge. Sp, De Chalonge, Pierre Dumayet from a book by 105.
Jean-Louis Trintignant, Claude Brasseur, Michel Serrault, Catherine Deneuve, Francois Perrot, Juliet Berto, Umberto Orsini.
09/06/78

L'Arma
(The Gun)
(Italy)
CID. Prod, Maratea Film. Wri-dir, Pasquale Squittieri. Cam (Eastmancolor), Giulio Albonico; art dirs, Luciana Vedovelli, Renato Ventura; edtr, Pasquale Squittieri; mus, Tullio De Piscopo. 90.
Stefano Satta Flores, Claudia Cardinale, Benedetta Fantoli.
08/09/78

L'Arriviste
(The Thruster)
(Belgium - France)
ELN. Groupe Bleu Films (Brussels)-Z Prodns (Paris). Wri-dir, Samy Pavel. Cam (Eastmancolor-Kodachrome), Ramon Suarez; mus, Ennio Morricone, Klaus Schulz. 98.
Julian Negulesco, Anicee Alvina, Jacques Monod, Alice Sapritch, Lucien Charbonnier, Bruno Pradal, Gino Da Roncha, Anny Duperey, Michael Israel, Adinda Horst, Beatrice Roman.
02/09/77

Las Largas Vacaciones Del 36
(The Long Vacations of '36)
(Spain)
X. Jose Frade prodn. Dir, Jaime Camino. Sp, Camino, Manolo Gutierrez; cam (Eastmancolor), Fernando Arribas; edtr, Teresa Alcocer; mus, Javier Montsalvatge; sets, Jose Maria Espada. 106.
Conchita Velasco, Ismael Merlo, Angela Molina, Francisco Rabal, Charo Soriano, Vicente Parra, Jose Sacristan, Jose Vivo, Analia Gade.
04/21/76

Las Locas
(Crazy Women)
(Argentina)
X. Argentinian Film prodn. Dir, Enrique Carreras. Sp, Jose Dominiani, Carreras. 90.
Mercedes Carreras, Juan Jose Camer, Leonor Manso.
08/03/77

Las Palabras De Max
(What Max Said)
(Spain)
X. Elias Querejeta P C prodn. Prod, Elias Querejeta. Dir, Emilio Martinez Lazaro. Sp, Elias Querejeta, Emilio Martinez Lazaro; cam, Teo Escamilla; mus, Luis de Pablo; edtr, Pablo del Amor; art dir, Antonio Belizon. 97.
Ignacio Fernandez de Castro, Gracia Querejeta, Miriam Maeztu, Cecilia Villarean, Hector Alterio, Raul Sender, Maria de la Riva.
03/15/78

Las Poquianchis
(Mexico)
PEX. Conacine-Apha Centauri co-prodn. Dir, Felipe Cazales. Sp, Tomas Perez Turrent, Xavier Robles; story, Turrent; cam, Alex Phillips Jr; edtr, Rafael Castanedo. 115.
Diana Bracho, Jorge Martinez de Hoyos, Tina Romero, Salvador Sanchez, Pilar Pellicer, Leonor Llausas, Marlena Doria, Ana Ofelia Muguia, Gonzalo Vega.
02/09/77

Las Truchas
(Trout)
(Spain)
CTW. Prod, Luis Megino for Arandano S A. Dir, Luis Garcia Sanchez. Sp, Manuel Gutierrez Aragon, Garcia Sanchez, Luis Megino Grande; cam, Magi Torruella; mus, Victor Manuel; edtr, Eduardo Biurrun; art dir, Jose Antonio de la Guerra. 99.
Hector Alterio, Juan Amigo, Ofelia Angelica, Maria Carmen Arevalo, Maria Teresa Arteche, Norma Bacaicoa, Pedro Basanta, Mari Carrillo, Francisco Casares, Fernando Chinarro, Carla Cristi, Luis Ciges, Maria Luisa de la Cruz, Julian del Monte, Emilio de Diego, Juan Estelrich, Maria Elena Flores, Roberto Font, Veronica Forque, Irene Foster, Javier Gallifa, Antonio Gamero, Enrique Gregor, Yolanda Guardione, Manuel Garcia, Manuel Huete, Paloma Hurtado, Montserrat Julio, Irina Kouberskaya, Elisa Laguna, Conchita Leza, Veronica Llimera, Alejo Loren, Eduardo MacGregor, Federico Mendez, Amparo Merino, Lautaro Murua, Jesus Munarriz, Aramis Ney, Carlos Oller, Antonio Passy, Raul Pazos, Luis Politti, Quino Pueyo, Antonio Requena, Jose Maria Riera, Marichu Rosado, Juan Sala, Yelena Samarina, Kike San Francisco, Amparo Valle, Alfonso Vallejo, Juan J Valverde, Walter Vidarte, Maria and Susana Prados, Javier Romero, Federico Ruiz, J Carlos Sanchez, Cristina Torres.
03/15/78

Las Vegas Lady
CWN. Zappala/Slott prodn. Prods, Joseph Zappala, Gene Slott. Dir, Noel Nosseck. Sp, Walter Dallenbach; cam, Stephen Katz; edtr, Robert Gordon; mus, Alan Silverstri. (MPAA rating: PG). 87.
Stella Stevens, Stuart Whitman, George DiCenzo, Lynne Moody, Linda Scruggs, Joseph Della Sorte, Jesse White.
01/28/76

Las Verdes Praderas
(The Green Pastures)
(Spain)
X. Jose Luis Tafur P C prodn. Dir, Jose Luis Garci. Sp, Jose Maria Gonzalez Sinde, Jose Luis Garci; exec prod, Jose Maria Gonzalez Sinde; cam (Eastmancolor), Fernando Arribas; sets, Francisco Prosper; edtr, Miguel Gonzalez Sinde. 95.
Alfredo Landa, Maria Casanova, Carlos Larranga, Angel Picazo, Irene Gutierrez Caba, Pedro del Corral.
07/04/79

Laserblast
YAB. Charles Band prodn. Dir, Michael Rae. Sp, Franne Schact, Frank Ray Perilli; cam (Technicolor), Terry Bowen; edtr, Jodie Copelan; snd, Jerry Wolfe; ward, Jill Sheridan, Barbara Scott; sfx-make-up-props, Steve Neill; asst dir, Andy Gallerani. (MPAA rating: PG). 85.
Kim Milford, Cheryl Smith, Gianni Russo, Ron Masak, Dennis Burkley, Barry Cutler, Mike Bobenko, Eddie Deezen, Keenan Wynn, Roddy McDowall.
03/08/78

Laski Mezi Kapkami Deste
(Love Between the Raindrops)
(Czechoslovakia)
CZS. Barrandov Studio prodn. Dir, Karel Kachyna. Sp, Jan Otcenasek, Vladimir Kalina; cam (Eastmancolor), Jan Curik; mus, Lubos Fiser. 106.
Vladimir Mensik, Lukas Vaculik, Jan Hrusinski, Tereza Pokorna, Zlata Adamovska, Eva Jakoubova.
07/23/80

Lasse Og Geir
(Lasse and Geir)
(Norway)
ELN. Wri-dir, Svend Wam. Cam (Eastmancolor), Paul Rene Roestad; edtr, Fred Sassebo. 90.
Torgeir Schjerven, Lasse Tomte, Kjersti Dovigen.
08/25/76

L'Associe
(The Associate)
(France - Germany)
WBC. Magyar Prdctns/FR 3/Maran Film (Stuttgart) co-prodn. Dir, Rene Gainville. Wris, Gainville, Jean-Claude Carriere, from the novel "My Partner, Mister Davis" by Jenaro Prieto. Cam (Fujicolor), Etienne Szabo; snd, Harrik Maury; art dir, Sydney Bettex; mus, Mort Shuman; edtr, Raymonde Guyot. 94.
Michel Serrault, Claudine Auger, Catherine Alric, Judith Magre, Mathieu Carriere, Bernard Haller.
10/03/79

The Last Affair
X. Chelex Prodns. Wri-dir-prod-edtr, Henri Charbakshi. Exec prod, Alexander Boas. Pho, Robin Rutledge; mus, Sooren Alexander. (MPAA rating: R). 80.
Jack Wallace, Ron Dean, Del Close, Betty Thomas, Marigray Jobes, Debbie Dan, William Norris, Jack Hafferkamp.
10/20/76

The Last Battle: SEE Bou Posleden

The Last Campaign
X. Barbara Frank prodn. Conceived-dir, Barbara Frank. Cam, Joan Churchill, Robert Eberlein, Eli Hollander, James Joannides, Eric Saarinen; edtr, Jean-Claude Lubtchancsky; asso prod, Stephen Rohde. 85. (DOC)
09/20/78

The Last Challenge Of The Dragon
(Hong Kong)
CNW. Prods, Alex Gouw, Chow Hiap Hou. Dir, Steve Chan. Sp, Chan, Kung Ming; cam, Lee Man Kit; edtr, Hu Kie Chan; mus, Frankie Chan; action dir, Haung Peichi. (MPAA rating: R). 90.
Shi Chien, Ou Yang So Fei, Kuan Shan, Steve Chan, Chang Li, Chen Li Li, Anna Jones.
02/15/78

The Last Cry: SEE Der Letzte Schrei

The Last Dew Drop: SEE Nam Karng Yod Deo

Last Embrace
UA. Taylor/Wigutow prodn. Prods, Michael Taylor, Dan Wigutow. Dir, Jonathan Demme. Sp, David Shaber, based on novel "The Thirteenth Man" by Murray Teigh Bloom; cam, Tak Fujimoto; edtr, Barry Malkin; mus, Miklos Rosza; prodn des, Charles Rosen; cos des, Jane Greenwood; snd, Les Lazarowitz; asst dir, Michael Rauch. (MPAA rating: R). 103.
Roy Scheider, Janet Margolin, John Glover, Sam Levene, Charles Napier, Christopher Walken, Jacqueline Brooks, David Margulies, Andrew Duncan, Marcia Rodd.
05/02/79

Last Exit Before Roissy: SEE Derniere Sortie Avant Roissy

The Last Flight Of Noah's Ark
BV. Prod, Ron Miller. Dir, Charles Jarrot. Sp, Steven W Carabatsos, Sandy Glass, George Arthur Bloom, based on story by Ernest K Gann; cam (Technicolor), Charles F Wheeler; edtr, Gordon D Brenner; snd, Henry A Maffett; co-prod, Jan Williams; art dir, John B Mansbridge; prodn des, Preston Ames; sfx, Art Cruickshank, Eustace Lycett, Danny Lee; asst dir, Richard Learman; mus, Maurice Jarre. (MPAA rating: G). 97.

Elliott Gould, Genevieve Bujold, Ricky Schroder, Tammy Lauren, Vincent Gardenia, John Fujioka, Yuki Shimoda, John P Ryan, Dana Elcar.
06/11/80

The Last Hard Men
FOX. Belasco-Seltzer Thacher prodn, prod, Walter Seltzer, Russell Thacher; exec prod, William Belasco. Dir, Andrew V McLaglen. Sp, Guerdon Trueblood, from novel, "Gun Down," by Brian Garfield; cam (DeLuxe Color), Duke Callaghan; edtr, Fred Chulack; mus, Jerry Goldsmith; art dir, Edward Carfagno; set decor, Bob Signorelli; snd, Don Bassman, William Teague; asst dir, Jack Roe; stunt coord, Joe Canutt. (MPAA rating: R). 103.
Charlton Heston, James Coburn, Barbara Hershey, Jorge Rivero, Michael Parks, Larry Wilcox, Morgan Paull, Thalmus Rasulala, Bob Donner, John Quade, Christopher Mitchum.
04/21/76

Last Hurrah For Chivalry
(Hong Kong)
GHV. Raymond Chow presentation. Exec prod, Louis Sit. Wri-dir, John Y W Woo. Cam, Chang Yao Chua; fight sequences arranged by Feng Ke An; prodn mgr, Catherine Cheung. 100.
Wei Pai, Liu Sung Chen, Wei Chiu Hua, Liu Chiang.
10/15/80

The Last Kiss: SEE Le Dernier Baiser

Last Love: SEE Letze Liebe

The Last Married Couple In America
U. Prods, Edward S Feldman, John Herman Shaner. Exec prods, Gilbert and Joseph Cates. Dir, Gilbert Cates. Sp, John Herman Shaner; cam (Technicolor), Ralph Woolsey; edtr, Peter E Berger; snd, Don Sharpless; prod des, Gene Callahan; art dir, Peter Smith; asst dir, Thomas Lofaro. (MPAA rating: R). 103.
George Segal, Natalie Wood, Richard Benjamin, Arlene Golonka, Allan Arbus, Marilyn Sokol, Oliver Clark, Priscilla Barnes, Dom DeLuise, Valerie Harper, Bob Dishy, Mark Lonow, Sondra Currie, Robert Wahler, Catherine Hickland, Charlene Ryan.
02/06/80

The Last Melodrama: SEE Le Dernier Melodrame

The Last Metro: SEE Le Dernier Metro

The Last Mission Of Demolitions Man Cloud: SEE Posljednji Podvig Diverzanta Oblaka

The Last Of The Blue Devils
X. Prod, Last of the Blue Devils Film Co, John Kelly, Bruce Ricker, Edward Beyer. Dir, Ricker; wris, Ricker, John Arnoldy; cam, Arnie Johnson, Eric Menn, Bob Gardener; edtr, Thomas Henkel; snd, Rocky Rude, Wally Gaspar; exec prod, Mitchell Donian. 91.
Count Basie and his orchestra, Big Joe Turner, Jay McShann, Buddy Anderson, Ernie Williams, Eddie Durham, Speedy Huggins, Budd Johnson, Baby Lovett, Charles McPherson, Paul Quinichette, Gene Ramey, Herman Walder, Jimmy Forrest, Crook Goodwin, Curtis Foster, Paul Gunther, Joe Jones, Sonny Kenner, Jesse Price, Buster Smith, Richard Smith, Claude Williams, Milton Morris.
Also, film clips of Count Basie septet, Lester Young and the Charlie Parker-Dizzy Gillespie quintet.
(DOC)
11/14/79

The Last of the Cowboys: SEE The Great Smokey Roadblock

The Last Plantation: SEE Fogo Morto

The Last Remake of Beau Geste
U. Prod, William S Gilmore; exec prods, Howard West, George Shapiro. Dir, Marty Feldman. Sp, Feldman, Chris Allen, from a story by Feldman, Sam Bobrick; cam (Technicolor), Gerry Fisher; edtrs, Jim Clark, Arthur Schmidt; mus, John Morris; prodn des, Brian Eatwell; art dir, Les Dilley; set decor, Roger Christian; snd, Peter Sutton, Kevin L Cleary; cos-ward, May Routh, Ron Beck; asst dirs, Tom Joyner, Roberto Parra (Spain); stunt coord, Buddy Van Horn. (MPAA rating: PG). 84.
Ann-Margret, Marty Feldman, Michael York, Peter Ustinov, James Earl Jones, Trevor Howard, Henry Gibson, Terry-Thomas, Roy Kinnear, Spike Milligan, Avery Schreiber, Hugh Griffith, Irene Handl, Sinead Cusack, Philip Bollard, Nicholas Bridge, Michael McConkey, Bekki Bridge, Martin Snaric, Ed McMahon.
07/13/77

Last Rites
CAN. New Empire Features prodn. Dir, Domonic Paris. Prod, Kelly Van Horn. Sp, Ben Donnelly, Paris; cam (Deluxe), Paris; edtr, Elizabeth Lombardo; mus, Paul Jost, George Small. (MPAA rating: R). 88.
Patricia Lee Hammond, Gerlad Fielding, Victor Jorge, Michael Lally, Mimi Weddell.
03/26/80

The Last Romantic Lover: SEE Le Dernier Amant Romantique

The Last Sea: SEE Hayam Ha' Acharon

The Last Supper: SEE La Ultima Cena

The Last Survivor
(Italy)
AIP. United Producers film. Prod, Giorgio Carlo Rossi. Dir, Ruggero Deodato. Sp, Tito Cardi, Giafranco Clerici, Renzo Genta; cam (Movielab Color), uncredited; edtr, Danielle Alabiso; dubbing edtr, Nick Alexander; sfx, Paolo Ricci; asst dir, Stefano Rilla. (MPAA rating: R). 83.
Massimo Foschi, Me-Me Lai, Ivan Rassimov, Sheik Renal Shker, Judy Rosly, Suleiman, Sanshe.
(Dubbed English Soundtrack)
06/14/78

The Last Tasmanian
(Australia)
X. Artis prodn in association with the Australian Film Commission, Tasmanian Film Corp and Societe Francaise de Prodn. Prod-dir, Tom Haydon. Sp, Haydon, Rhys Jones; cam, Geoff Burton; mus, William Davies; edtr, Charles Rees; graphic des, Bernard Lodge; snd, Robert Wells, Mario Vinck, Edward Tise. Narr, Leo McKern. 105.
Dr Rhys Jones, Dr Jim Allen, D A Lowe (Premier of Tasmania), Dr Sir William Crowther, Andre Mary, Annette Mansell.
(DOC)
10/31/79

The Last Tempest
(Hong Kong)
SHW. Run Run Shaw prodn. Wri-dir, Li Hanhsiang. Cam, Lin Chao; art dir, Chen Chingshen; snd, Wang Yung-hua; edtr, Chiang Hsing-lung. 118.
Ti Lung, Lisa Lu, Liao Tien, Ivy Ling Po.
03/24/76

The Last Three Days: SEE Gli Ultimi Tre Giorni

The Last Tycoon
PAR. Prod, Sam Spiegel. Dir, Elia Kazan. Sp, Harold Pinter, based on the unfinished novel by F Scott Fitzgerald; cam (Technicolor), Victor Kemper; edtr, Richard Marks; mus, Maurice Jarre; prodn des, Gene Callahan; art dir, Jack Collis; sets, Bill Smith, Jerry Wunderlich; snd, Dick Vorisek, Larry Jost, cos-ward, Anna Hill Johnstone, Anthea Sylbert, Thalia Phillips, Richard Bruno; asst dir, Danny McCauley. (MPAA rating: PG). 122.
Robert DeNiro, Tony Curtis, Robert Mitchum, Jeanne Moreau, Jack Nicholson, Donald Pleasence, Ingrid Boulting, Ray Milland, Dana Andrews, Theresa Russell, Peter Strauss, Tige Andrews, Morgan Farley, John Carradine, Jeff Corey, Angelica Huston.
11/17/76

The Last Waltz
UA. Prod, Robbie Robertson; exec prod, Jonathan Taplin. Dir, Martin Scorsese. Cam (Deluxe Color), Michael Chapman, Laszlo Kovacs, Vilmos Zsigmond, David Myers, Bobby Byrne, Michael Watkins, Hiro Narita; edtrs, Yeu-Bun Yee, Jan Roblee; prodn des, Boris Leven; concert prod, Bill Graham; asso prod, Steven Prince; audio prodn, Rob Fraboni; concert mus prodn, John Simon; asst dirs, Jerry Grandey, James Quinn; set decor, Anthony Mondell. 115.

Bob Dylan, Joni Mitchell, Neil Diamond, Emmylou Harris, Neil Young, Van Morrison, Ron Wood, Muddy Waters, Eric Clapton, the Staples, Ringo Starr, Dr John, Ronnie Hawkins, Paul Butterfield, The Band.
(ROCK DOC)
04/12/78

The Last Wave
(Australia)
UA. Ayer Prodns Pty Ltd-South Australian Film Corp, Australian Film Commission prodn. Dir, Peter Weir. Sp, Tony Morphett, Petru Popescu, Weir; cam (Arlab), Russell Boyd; edtr, Max Lemon; mus, Charles Wain. 106.
Richard Chamberlain, Olivia Hamnett, Gulpilil, Frederick Parslow, Nandjiwarra Amagula.
11/16/77

The Last Winter: SEE Dimri I Fundit

The Last Woman: SEE La Derniere Femme

The Last Word
VF. Prods, Richard C Abramson, Michael C Varhol; exec prods, A J Leydton, John Berglas, Reiner Walch. Dir, Roy Boulting; sp, Michael Varhol, Greg Smith, L M Kit Carson, based on a story by Horatius Haeberle; cam, Jules Brenner; edtr, George Grenville; score, Carol Lees; prodn des, Jack Collis; snd, Bill Marky, Dick Portman; set decor, Dennis Peeples; sfx, Henry Millar. 105.
Richard Harris, Karen Black, Martin Landau, Dennis Christopher, Biff McGuire, Christopher Guest, Penelope Milford, Bonnie Bartlett, Jorge Cervera, Nathan Cook, Linda Dangcil, Alex Henteloff, Pat McNamara, Michael Pataki, Natasha Ryan, Charles Siebert, James Staley, Richard Venture.
11/21/79

The Last Years of Childhood: SEE Die Letzten Jahre Der Kindheit

The Late Blossom: SEE Le Soleil Se Leve En Retard

The Late Great Planet Earth
PIE. RCR prodn. Exec prod, Michael F Leone. Prods, Robert Amram, Alan Belkin. Wri-dir, Amram, based on the book by Hal Lindsey with C C Carlson; biblical sequences written and dir, Rolf Forsberg; mus, Dana Kaproff. Narrated by Orson Wells and Hal Lindsey. 90.
02/14/79

The Late Show
WB. Prod, Robert Altman. Wri-dir, Robert Benton. Cam (MGM color), Chuck Rosher; edtr, Lou Lombardo, Peter Appleton; mus, Kenn Wannberg; set decor, Bob Gould; snd, Sam Gemette. (MPAA rating: PG). 94.
Art Carney, Lily Tomlin, Bill Macy, Eugene Roche, Joanna Cassidy, John Considine, Ruth Nelson, John Davey, Howard Duff.
02/02/77

Late Show: SEE Nachtvorstellungen

The Latest on Robber Hotzenplotz: SEE Nues Vom Raeuber Hotzenplotz

Laura: les ombres de l'ete
(Laura: Shadows of Summer)
(France)
SNC. Alma Films-Cora co-prodn. Prod, Alain Terzian. Dir, David Hamilton. Sp, Joseph Morhaim, Andre Szots; cam, Bernard Daillencourt; mus, Patrick Juyet; edtr, J Van Effenterre; art-tech dir, Szots; snd, B Ortion. 90.
Maud Adams, Dawn Dunlap, James Mitchell.
01/23/80

L'Avare
(The Miser)
(France)
AMLF. Films Christian Fechner prodn. Prod, Christian Fechner. Dir, Jean Girault. Sp based on the play by Moliere; cam, Edmond Richard; snd, Paul Laine; edtr, Michael Lewin; mus, Jean Bizet; art dir, Sydney Bettex. 120.
Louis de Funes, Frank David, Claire Dupray, Herve Bellon, Michel Galabru, Claude Gensac.
03/26/80

The Lawyer: SEE Advokatka

Le Bar du Telephone
(The Telephone Bar)
(France)
AMLF. ATC 3000 prodn. Prod, Benjamin Simon; dir, Claude Barrois; sp, Claude Neron; cam, Bernard Lutic; mus, Vladimir Cosma; art dir, Didier Haudepin; edtr, Nicole Saunier; snd, Bernard Bats. 93.
Daniel Duval, Francois Perier, Georges Wilson, Julien Guiomar, Raymond Pellegrin, Valentine Monier, Christophe Lambert, Richard Anconina.
09/17/80

Le Beaujolais Nouveau Est Arrive...
(The New Beaujolais Wine Has Arrived)
(France)
CII. Camera One-Les Films De L'Alma prodn. Dir, Jean-Luc Voulfow. Sp, Marco Pico, Voulflow from book by Rene Fallet; cam (Eastmancolor), Jean-Paul Schwartz; edtr, Armand Psenny; mus, Carlo Rustichelli. 92.
Jean Carmet, Michel Galabru, Pierre Mondy, Rabah Loucif, Pascale Roberts, Kathy Mongadin.
04/26/78

Le Bon Et Les Mechants
(The Good Guys and the Bad Guys)
(France)
F13. Wri-dir-lensed, Claude Lelouch. Mus, Francis Lai; edtr, Georges Klotz. 125.
Jacques Dutronc, Marlene Jobert, Bruno Cremer, Jacques Villeret, Brigitte Fossey, Jean-Pierre Kalfon, Serge Reggiani.
(SEPIA)
02/04/76

Le Camion
(The Truck)
(France)
LML. Cinema 9-Auditel prodn. Wri-dir, Marguerite Duras. Cam (Eastmancolor), Bruno Nuytten. 80.
Marguerite Duras, Gerard Depardieu.
05/18/77

Le Cavaleur
(The Skirt Chaser)
(France)
X. Films Ariane-Mondex Film-FR3 prodn. Prods, Georges Danciger, Alexandre Mnouchkine. Dir, Philippe de Broca. Sp, Michel Audiard, Philippe de Broca; cam, Jean-Paul Schwatz; edtr, Henri Lanoe; mus, Georges Delerue. 104.
Jean Rochefort, Nicole Garcia, Catherine Alric, Catherine Leprince, Lila Kedrova, Danielle Darrieux, Jean Desailly, Carole Lixon.
01/24/79

Le Chemin Perdu
(The Lost Way)
(France - Switzerland - Belgium)
MK. Abilene Production/MK2 (Paris)/Saga Productions (Lausanne)/Cactus Film (Zurich)/F3 (Brussels) co-prodn. Wri-dir, Patricia Moraz; script collab, Serge Schoukine; cam, Sacha Vierny; edtr, Thierry Derocles; mus, Patrick Moraz; art dirs, Alain Nicolet, Pierre Gattoni. 107.
Charles Vanel, Delphine Seyrig, Magali Noel, Clarisse Barrere, Charles Dudoignon, Vania Vilers, Remo Girone, Christine Pascal.
08/27/80

Le Cheval d'Orgeuil
(Horse of Pride)
(France)
PLF. Bela prodn. Prod, Georges de Beauregard; dir, Claude Chabrol; sp, Chabrol, Daniel Boulanger, from book by Pierre-Jakez Helias; cam (Eastmancolor), Jean Rabier; mus, Pierre Jansen; cos, Magali Dray; art dir, Hilton McConnico; edtr, Monique Fardoulis. 120.
Jacques Dufilho, Bernadette Le Sache, Francois Cluzet, Paul Le Person, Pierre Le Rumeur, Michel Robin, Dominique Lavanant, and the voice of Georges Wilson.
09/17/80

Le Choix
(The Choice)
(Belgium - France)
BGA. Films du Belier (Brussels) - Peri Films (Paris) co-prodn. Dir, Jacques Faber. Sp, Faber, Nannina Zunnio; cam (Eastmancolor), Jean Rosenbaum, Robert Lezian; edtr, Patricia Canino; mus, Guy Boulanger; asst dir, Jean Goumain. 90.
Claude Jade, Gilles Kohler, Jacques Faber, Georges Lambert, Maurice Sevenant, Guy Pion, Suzy Falk, Eve Bonfanti, Pierre Laroche, Lucienne Troka, Michele Marcey.
01/28/76

Le Coeur a l'Envers
(My Heart is Upside-Down)
(France - Spain)
PDS. 5 Continents-JL Tafur (Madrid) co-prodn. Prod, Bernard Lenteric. Dir, Franck Apprederis. Sp, Odile Barsky, Apprederis, Gerard Brach; cam, Charlet Recors; snd, Bernard Ortion; mus, Jean Musy; art dir, Gerard Daoudal; edtr, Laurence Leinenger.   93.
Annie Girardot, Laurent Malet, Charles Denner, Stephane Audran.
11/05/80

Le Coeur Froid
(The Cold Heart)
(France)
LML. Les Prodns Heldes prodn. Dir, Henri Helman. Sp, Helman, Maurice Germain; book, G J Arnaud; cam (Eastmancolor), Jean-Francois Robin; edtr, Jose Pinheiro; mus, Guy Boulanger.   88.
Maud Rayer, Lauze, Janine, Maria Laborit, Michel Robin, Maurice Germain, Albert Medina, Andre Pousse.
05/04/77

Le Corps De Mon Ennemi
(The Body of My Enemy)
(France)
NOR. Cerito Films (Jean-Paul Belmondo) prodn. Dir, Henri Verneuil. Sp, Michel Audiard, Felecien Marceau, Verneuil from the book by Marceau; cam (Eastmancolor), Jean Penzer; edtr, Pierre Gillette; mus, Francis Lai. 120.
Jean-Paul Belmondo, Marie-France Pisier, Bernard Blier, Claude Brosset, Daniel Ivernel.
10/27/76

Le Coup du Parapluie
(The Umbrella Coup)
(France)
GAU. Gaumont International prodn. Prod, Alain Poire. Dir, Gerard Oury. Wri, Oury, Daniele Thompson; cam, Henri Decae; mus, Vladimir Cosma; edtr, Albert Jurgenson; art dir, Jean Andre; snd, Alain Sempe.   90.
Pierre Richard, Gerd Frobe, Valerie Maitresse, Christine Murillo.
11/05/80

Le Coup de Sirocco
(The Sirocco Blow)
(France)
GAU. Alma Films-Alexandre Films co-prodn. Prod, Serge Laski. Dir, Alexandre Arcady. Sp, Daniel Saint-Hamon, Jan Saint-Hamon, Arcady, from novel by Saint-Hamon; cam (Eastmancolor), Jean Francois Robin; snd, Guillaume Sciama; mus, Serge Franklin; edtr, Joelle Van Effenterre.   100.
Roger Hanin, Marthe Villalonga, Michel Auclair, Patrick Bruel, Lucien Layani.
05/02/79

Le Couple Temoin
(The Guinea Pig Couple)
(France)
PLF. Films Paris New York-INA-Artco Films prodn. Wri-dir, William Klein. Cam (Eastmancolor), Philippe Rousselot; mus, Michel Colombier; edtr, Valerie Mayoux; prod, Jeanne Klein.   90.
Andre Dussolier, Anemone, Zouc, Eddie Constantine, Georges Descrieres, Jacques Boudet.
04/06/77

Le Crabe-Tambour
(The Crab Drum)
(France)
AMLF. Bela-AMLF-Lira Films prodn. Dir, Pierre Schoendoerffer. Sp, J.F Chauvel, Schoendoerffer, from book by Schoendoerffer; cam, Raoul Coutard; edtr, Nguyen Long; mus, Philippe Sarde.   119.
Jean Rochefort, Claude Rich, Jacques Perrin, Jacques Dufilho, Odile Versois, Aurore Clement, Morgan-Jones.
11/16/77

Le Dernier Amant Romantique
(The Last Romantic Lover)
(France)
WBC. Film & Co-French Movie-PECF prodn. Dir, Just Jaeckin. Sp, Ennio De Concini, Jaeckin; cam (Eastmancolor), Robert Fraisse; edtr, Francoise Bonnot; mus, Pierre Bachelet. 100.
Dayle Haddon, Gerard Tybalt, Fernando Rey.
05/10/78

Le Dernier Baiser
(The Last Kiss)
(France - Belgium)
GAU. Belstar Prod, Showking prodn. Dir, Dolores Grassian. Sp, Grassian, Jean Reznikov, Jean Curtelin; cam (Eastmancolor), Alain Derobe; edtr, Francoise Bonnet. 100.
Annie Girardot, Maria Pacome, Bernard Fresson, Dagmar Meyniel.
06/15/77

Le Dernier Melodrame
(The Last Melodrama)
(France)
FR. Dir, Georges Franju. Sp, Bernard Dimey from an idea by Pierre Brasseur; cam (Eastmancolor), Marcel Fradetal; edtr, Fernand Manella.   80.
Michel Vitold, Edith Scob, Raymond Bussieres, Juliette Mills, Luis Masson.
(16m)
12/17/80

Le Dernier Metro
(The Last Metro)
(France)
GAU. Films du Carrosse/SEDIF/TFI/SFP co-prodn. Dir, Francois Truffaut; sp, Truffaut, Suzanne Schiffman, Jean-Claude Grumberg; cam (Fujicolor), Nestor Almendros; art dir, Jean-Pierre Kohut-Svelko; snd, Michel Laurent; mus, Georges Delerue; cos, Lisele Roos; edtrs, Martine Barraque, Marie-Aimee Debril, Jean-Francois Gire.   130.
Catherine Deneuve, Gerard Depardieu, Jean Poiret, Heinz Bennent, Andrea Ferreol, Paulette Dubost, Sabine Haudepin, Jean-Louis Richard, Maurice Risch.
09/17/80

Le Desert Des Tartares
(The Desert of the Tartars)
(France - Italy - Iran)
GAU. Reggane Films (Jacques Perrin)-Fildebroc (Michele De Broca)-FR3-Films De L'Astrophore-Corona Film-FIDCI (Iran) prodn. Dir, Valerio Zurlini. Sp, Andre Brunelin, Jean-Louis Bertucelli; book, Dino Buzzati; cam (Eastmancolor), Luciano Tovoli; edtr, Raimondo Crocianai; mus, Ennio Morricone. 140.
Vittorio Gassman, Giuliano Gemma, Helmut Griem, Philippe Noiret, Jacques Perrin, Francisco Rabal, Fernando Rey, Laurent Terzieff, Jean-Louis Trintignant, Max Von Sydow.
12/29/76

Le Diable Au Coeur
(The Devil in the Heart)
(France)
WBC. WB-Col-Dovidis-SND prodn. Dir, Bernard Queysanne. Sp, Pierre-Jean Remy, Queysanne; cam (Eastmancolor), Bernard Zitzermann; edtr, Andree Davanture.   95.
Jane Birkin, Jacques Speisser, Phillippe Lemaire, Emmanuelle Riva.
06/23/76

Le Diable Dans La Boite
(The Devil in the Box)
(France)
SNC. Cinemag - SFP - FR3 - Madeleine Films prodn. Dir, Pierre Lary. Sp, Lary, Huguette Debasieux, Jean-Claude Carriere; cam (Eastmancolor), Sacha Vierny; edtr, Michel Bienvenu; mus, Jean-Claude Dequeant.   100.
Jean Rochefort, Michel Lonsdale, Dominique Labourier, Micheline Presle, Bernard Haller.
05/04/77

Le Diable Probablement
(The Devil, Probably)
(France)
GAU. Sunchild-G M F prodn. Wri-dir, Robert Bresson. Cam (Eastmancolor), Pasqualino De Santis; edtr, Germaine Lany; mus, Philippe Sarde.   95.
Antoine Monnier, Tina Irissari, Henri De Maublanc, Laetitita Carcano, Regis Hanrion, Nicolas Deguy, Geoffroy Gaussen.
06/29/77

Le Divorcement
(France)
GAU. Les Films de L'Alma-SFP prodn. Dir, Pierre Barouh. Sp, Barouh, Marc Cadiot, from book by Cadiot; cam (Eastmancolor), Yves Lafaye; edtr, Alain Leamitre-Mory; mus, Barouh, Chris Rambault, Evelyne Dress. 115.
Michel Piccoli, Lea Massari, Jean-Claude Bouillon, Ann Lonnberg, Maurice Bacquet, Christine Murillo, Evelyne Dress.
08/22/79

Le Dossier 51
(The 51 File)
(France)
GAU. Elefilm-SFP-Maran Film prodn. Dir, Michel Deville. Sp, Gilles Perrault, Deville; cam (Eastmancolor), Claude Lecomte; edtr, Raymonde Guyot; mus, Jean Schwarz. 108.

Francois Marthouret, Claude Mercault, Philippe Rouleau, Nathalie Juvet, Roger Planchon, Francoise Lugagne.
05/31/78

Le Fond De L'Air Est Rouge
(The Base Of The Air Is Red)
(France)
IID. Conceived-sp-dir-edtr, Chris Marker, with help of Valerie Mayoux, Luce Marsant, Pierre Camus, Annie-Claire Mittelberger, Christine Aya, Patrick Sauvion, Jean-Roger Sahunet; mus, Luciano Berio. 240.
(DOC)
11/16/77

Le Gang
(France)
WBC. Adel Prodn (Alain Delon) prodn. Dir, Jacques Deray. Sp, Alphonse Boudard, Deray, J C Carriere, from the book by Roger Borniche; cam (Eastmancolor), Sylvano Ippoliti; edtr, Henri Lanoe. 100.
Alain Delon, Nicole Calfan, Laura Betti, Roland Bertin, Olivier Despax.
02/09/77

Le Gendarme et les Extra-Terrestres
(The Gendarme and the Creatures from Outer Space)
(France)
SNC. Prod, Gerard Beytout. Dir, Jean Giranet. Sp, Jacques Vilfrid, based on characters created by Richard Balducci; cam (Eastmancolor), Marcel Grignon, Didier Tarot; snd, Paul Laine; art dir, Sydney Bettex; mus, Raymond Lefevre; edtr, Michel Lewin. 92.
Louis de Funes, Michel Galabru, Maurice Risch, J P Rambal, Guy Grosso.
04/04/79

Le Grand Escogriffe
(The Big Operator)
(France)
GAU. Gaumont Int'l, Prodns 2000-Fildebrock-Da-Ma Prodns prodn. Dir, Claude Pinoteau. Sp, Michel Audiard, Pinoteau from the book by Rennie Airth; cam (Eastmancolor), Jean Collomb; edtr, Marie-Joseph Yoyotte. 100.
Yves Montand, Claude Brasseur, Agostina Belli, Adolfo Celli, Valentina Cortese, Aldo Maccione.
12/15/76

Le Grand Soir
(The Big Night)
(Switzerland)
IFS. Artcofilm prodn. Dir, Francis Reusser. Sp, Jacques Baynac; cam (Eastmancolor), Renato Berta; edtr, Edwige Ochenstein. 95.
Nils Arestrup, Jacqueline Parent.
08/25/76

Le Graphique De Boscop
(The Boscop Diagram)
(France)
CQD. Dir, Sotha, Georges Dumoulin. Sp, Sotha; cam (Eastmancolor), Jean-Cesar Chiabaut, Jean-Claude Bourgoin; edtr, Sotha, Dumoulin; mus, Sotha. 115.
12/29/76

Le Guepier
(The Hornet's Nest)
(France)
WBC. Filmel-PECF-PIC prodn. Dir, Roger Pigaut. Sp, Andre G Brunelin; cam (Eastmancolor), Daniel Vogel; edtr, Christian Gaudin; mus, Giancarlo Chiaramello. 90.
Claude Brasseur, Marthe Keller, Gabriele Ferzetti, John Steiner.
03/17/76

Le Guignolo
(The Guignolo)
(France)
GUD. Gaumont-Cerito Films prodn. Prod, Alain Poire. Dir, Georges Lautner. Sp, Jean Herman, Michel Audiard; cam, Henri Decae; mus, Philippe Sarde. 105.
Jean-Paul Belmondo, Michel Galabru, Georges Geret, Michel Beaune, Charles Gerard, Carla Romanelli, Mirella D'Angelo.
06/11/80

Le Jardin Des Supplices
(The Garden of Torture)
(France)
PFC. Stephen Films-Alexia Films prodn. Dir, Christian Gion. Sp, Pascal Laine from the book by Octave Mirbeau; cam (Eastmancolor), Lionel Legros; edtr, Anne-Marie Deshayes; mus, Jean-Pierre Doering. 90.
Roger Van Hool, Jacqueline Kerry, Toni Taffin, Ysabelle Lacamp.
10/20/76

Le Jeu De Solitaire
(The Game of Solitaire)
(France)
HTR. Wri-dir, Jean-Francois Adam. Cam (Eastmancolor), Andre Diot; edtr, Michele Gourot. 90.
Sami Frey, Alida Valli, Tanya Lopert, Romain Tagli.
06/16/76

Le Jouet
(The Toy)
(France)
AMLF. Renn Prodns-Fideline Films-Efve Films-Andrea Films prodn. Wri-dir, Francis Veber. Cam (Eastmancolor), Etienne Becker; edtr, Gerard Pollicand; mus, Vladimir Cosma. 92.
Pierre Richard, Michel Bouquet, Fabrice Greco, Suzy Dyson, Jacques Francois, Charles Gerard.
12/22/76

Le Jour De Gloire
(The Day of Glory)
(France)
PLF. Procinema-TFI-TeleCine-Films Produckction prodn. Dir, Jacques Besnard. Sp, Jacques-Henri Martin, Jacques Besnard, Richard Balducci, Alphonse Boudard; cam (Eastmancolor), Marcel Grignon; edtr, Gilbert Natot; mus, Darry Cowl. 90.
Jean Lefebvre, Pierre Tornade, Darry Cowl, Jacques Marin, Hans Verner.
12/29/76

Le Juge Et L'Assassin
(The Judge and the Assassin)
(France)
FEL. Lira Films (Raymond Danon) prodn. Dir, Bertrand Tavernier. Sp, Tavernier, Jean Aurenche, Pierre Bost; cam (Eastmancolor-Panavision), Pierre William Glenn; edtr, Armand Psenny; mus, Philippe Sarde. 125.
Philippe Noiret, Michel Galabru, Jean-Claude Brialy, Renee Faure, Isabelle Huppert, Cecile Vassort, Yves Robert.
03/03/76

Le Juge Fayard Dit Le Sheriff
(Judge Fayard Called the Sheriff)
(France)
CCF. Action Films-SFP-Filmedis prodn. Dir, Yves Boisset. Sp, Boisset, Claude Veillot; cam (Eastmancolor), Jacques Loiseleux; edtrs, Albert Jurgensson, Laurence Leininger; mus, Philippe Sarde. 110.
Patrick Dewaere, Aurore Clement, Philippe Leotard, Michel Auclair, Jean Bouise, Jean-Marc Thibault, Daniel Ivernel, Henri Garcin, Jacques Spiesser, Marcel Bozzuffi.
01/19/77

Le Lit. . .Ze Bawdy Bed
(Canada - France)
JOG. Prod, Paul Laffargue, a co-prodn of Impex Films and Productions Mutuelles. Dir, Jacques Lem from his own sp. Cam (Eastmancolor), Raymond Le Moigne; mus, Charles Dumont. 75.
Alice Sapritch, Michel Galabru, Jean Lefebvre, Anna Gael, Robert Castel, Henri Tisot, Claude Gensac, Patrick Topaloff, Denise Filiatrault, Claude Michaud.
01/14/76

Le Locataire
(The Tenant)
(France - US)
CII. Marianne Productions prodn. Prod, Andrew Braunsberg. Dir, Roman Polanski. Sp, Polanski, Gerard Brach; book, Roland Topor; cam (Eastmancolor), Sven Nykvist; edtr, Francoise Bonnet; mus, Philippe Sarde; art dir, Pierre Guffroy. (MPAA rating: R). 125.
Roman Polanski, Isabelle Adjani, Melvyn Douglas, Jo Van Fleet, Bernard Fresson, Lila Kedrova, Shelley Winters, Rufus, Claude Dauphin.
06/02/76

Le Mors Aux Dents
(The Bit Between the Teeth)
(France)
UCC. Sara Films/UGC co-prodn. Prod, Alain Sarde. Dir, Laurent Heynemann; sp, Heynemann, Claude Veillot, Pierre Fabre; cam (Fujicolor), Alain Levent; mus, Antoine Duhamel; edtr, Armand Psenny; art dir, Jean-Baptiste Poirot; snd, Michel Desrios.   99.
Jacques Dutronc, Michel Piccoli, Michel Galabru, Charles Gerard.
1/21/79

Le Mouton Noir
(The Black Sheep)
(France)
PFC. Sofracima/Golden International Prodn co-prodn. Dir, Jean-Pierre Moscardo. Sp, Moscardo and Jean-Claude Heberle; cam (Eastmancolor), Pierre Dupouey; snd, Raymond Adam; edr, Martine Barraque; mus, Georges Delerue.   98.
Jacques Dutronc, Helene Rolles, Arthur Wilkins, Tanya Lopert, Jean Desailly.
10/10/79

Le Musee du Louvre
(The Louvre Museum)
(Japan)
X. Fuji Telecasting Co prodn. Dir, Toshio Uruta. Sp, Shuntaro Tanikawa; cam (Fujicolor), Kozo Okazaki; mus, Toru Takemitsu. 119.
(DOC)
06/06/79

Le Nouveau Venu
(The Newcomer)
(Benin)
IIT. Dir, Richard De Meideros. Sp, De Meideros, Rene Ewagnion, Bouraima Lawani; cam (Eastmancolor), Maxime Lefevre, Lawani; edtr, Andree Davanture.   87.
Michel Djondo, Sikirou Ogoujobi, Ages Capo-Cichi, Sebastien De Souza.
08/22/79

Le Passe Simple
(The Simple Past)
(France)
GAU. Port Royal Film-Gaumont prodn. Victor Lanoux. Dir, Michel Drach. Sp, Drach, Pierre Uytterhoeven; book, Doninique St Alban; cam (Eastmancolor), Etienne Szabo; edtr, Francoise Bonnot.   96.
Marie-Josee Nat, Victor Lanoux, Anne Lonnbberg, Vania Vilers.
07/27/77

Le Pays Bleu
(The Blue Country)
(France)
GAU. Gaumont Int'l prodn. Wri-dir, Jean-Charles Tacchella. Cam (Eastmancolor), Edmond Sechan; edtr, Agnes Guillemot; mus, Gerard Anfosso.   77.
Brigitte Fossey, Jacques Serres, Ginette Garcin, Armand Meffre, Ginette Mathieu, Roger Crouzet, Albert Delpy.
02/23/77

Le Petit Marcel
(Little Marcel)
(France)
GAU. Gaumont--Productions De La Bueville prodn. Dir, Jacques Fansten. Sp, Fansten, Jean-Claude Grumber; cam (Eastmancolor), Jean Gonnet; edtr, Jean-Baptiste De Battista; mus, Gaeme Allwright.   105.
Jacques Speisser, Isabelle Huppert, Yves Robert, Pierre-Olivier Scotto, Anouk Ferjac, Jean Daste.
03/17/76

Le Pion
(The Pawn)
(France)
PON. Films 21 prodn. Wri-dir, Christian Gion. Cam (Eastmancolor), Lionel Legros.   90.
Henry Guybet, Claude Pieplu, Michel Galabru, Claude Jade.
11/22/78

Le Plein De Super
(Fill 'Er Up with Super)
(France)
UGC. La Gueville-Madeleine Films-CAPAC, Fideline Films-UGC prodn. Dir, Alain Cavalier. Sp, Cavalier, Patrick Bouchitey, Etienne Chicot, Bernard Crommbey, Xavier Saint-Marcary; cam (Eastmancolor), Jean-Francois Robin; edtr, Pierre Gillette.   97.
Patrick Bouchitey, Etienne Chicot, Bernard Crommbey, Xavier Saint-Macary.
04/07/76

Le Point De Mire
(Focal Point)
(France)
WBC. Columbia prodn. Dir, Jean-Claude Tramont. Sp, Gerard Brach, Tramont; cam (Eastmancolor), Henri Decae; edtr, Kenout Peltier; mus, Georges Delerue.   95.
Annie Girardot, Jacques Dutronc, Matthias Habich, Jean-Claude Brialy, Francoise Brion, Jean Bouise, Claude Dauphin, Michel Robin.
10/26/77

Le Pont De Singe
(The Monkey Bridge)
(France)
GAU. Conceived-dir, Andre Harris, Alain De Sedouy. Cam (Eastmancolor and b&w); Jimmy Glasberg; co-dir-edtr, Charles Nemes; mus, Jacques Delaporte.   131.
04/28/76

Le Pull-Over Rouge
(The Red Sweater)
(France)
GAU. Port Royal Films Gaumont co-prodn. Prod-wri-dir, Michel Drach; sp collab, Ariane Litaize, based on the book "The Red Sweater" by Gilles Perrault; cam (Panavision), Jean Boffety; snd, Bernard Ortion; edtr, Andre Gaultier; mus, Jean-Louis D'Onorio.   120.
Serge Avedikian, Michelle Marquais, Claire Deluca, Roland Bertin, Roland Blanche, Regis Porte, Robert Rimbaud.
12/12/79

Le Rebelle
(The Rebel)
(France)
LML. Roc/Pelican Films/Films Moliere/Auditrust/Telcipro co-prodn, with the participation of Antenne 2. Prod, Louis Duchesne. Dir, Gerard Blain. Wri, Blain, Andre Debaecque; cam (Eastmancolor), Emmanuel Machuel; edtr, Jean-Philippe Berger; snd, Alex Pront; mus, Catherine Lara.   105.
Patrick Norbert, Michel Subor, Isabelle Rosais, Jean-Jacques Aublanc, Francoise Michaud.
12/03/80

Le Risque De Vivre
(The Risk of Living)
(France)
RSS. Les Films Du Jeudi prodn. Dir, Gerald Calderon. Sp, Dominique Ludes, Cyril De Klem, Calderon; cam (Eastmancolor), Jean-Marie Baufle; mus, Georges Prost; commentary by Andre Langaney, spoken by Michel Lonsdale.   85.
(DOC)
05/28/80

Le Roi et l'Oiseau
(The King and the Mockingbird)
(France)
GAU. Paul Grimault Films/Gibe Films/Antenne 2 co-prodn. Dir, Paul Grimault. Wris, Grimault, Jacques Prevert; mus, Wojciech Kilar, songs, Prevert and Joseph Kosma; cam, Gerard Soirant; edtr, Grimault; set des, Grimault, Lionel Charpy, Roger Duclent; artistic collab, Pierre Prevert; sfx, Henri Gruel.   87.
Jean Martin, Pascal Mazzotti, Raymond Bussieres, Agnes Viala, Renaud Marx, Hubert Deschamps, Roger Blin, Philippe Derez, Albert Medina, Claude Pieplu.
(ANI)
04/23/80

Le Rose Di Danzica
(The Roses of Danzig)
(Italy)
X. RAI Italian Radio-Television prodn. Wri-dir, Alberto Bevilacqua. Cam (Eastmancolor), Giuseppe Aquari; mus, Luis Bacalov; sets, Mario Molli; edtr, Raimondo Crociani; exec prod, Filiberto Bandini.   110.
Franco Nero, Helmut Berger, Olga Karlatos, Macha Meril, Roberto Posse, Franco Javarone, Eleonora Vallone, Gianrico Tondinelli.
10/03/79

Le Soleil en face
(Face To The Sun)
(France)
UGC. Odyssey-FR 3 co-prodn. Prods, Humbert Balsan, Serge Marquand, Stephane Tchalgadjieff. Dir, Pierre Kast. Sp, Kast, Alain Aptekman; cam, Gerard de Battista; mus, Sergio Godinho; edtr, Nicole Berckmans.   95.
Jean-Pierre Cassel, Stephane Audran, Alexandra Stewart, Beatrice Bruno.
02/27/80

Le Soleil Se Leve En Retard
(The Late Blossom)
(Canada)
MUT. Pierre Lamy prodn, Montreal. Dir, Andre Brassard. Sp, Michel Tremblay; cam Alain Dostie; mus, Beau Dommage; edtr, Andre Corriveau. 111.
Rita Lafontaine, Denise Filiatrault, Huguette Oligny, Jean Mathieu, Claude Gai, Danielle Panneton, Yvon Descamps.
07/27/77

Le Sucre
(The Sugar)
(France)
GAU. Cineproduction SFP-Gaumont prodn. Dir, Jacques Rouffio. Sp, Georges Conchon, Rouffio; cam, Rene Mathelin; edtr, Genevieve Winding; mus, Philippe Sarde. 102.
Gerard Depardieu, Jean Carmet, Michel Piccoli, Nelly Borgeaud, Roger Hanin, Claude Pieplu.
11/08/78

Le Temoin
(The Witness)
(France - Italy)
CII. Belstar Prodns-M Films, PAC prodn. Dir, Jean-Pierre Mocky. Sp, Rodolfo Sonego, Augusto Caminito, Sergio Amidei, Mocky, Jacques Dreux from a book by Harrison Judd; cam (Eastmancolor), Sergio D'Offizi; edtr, Michel Lewin; prod, Jacques Dorfmann; mus, Piero Piccioni. 95.
Alberto Sordi, Philippe Noiret, Roland Dubillard, Giselle Preville, Paul Crauchet, Sandra Dobrigna, Consuelo Ferrara.
10/11/78

Le Temps De L'Avant
(The Time of Before)
(Canada)
NFC. Dir, Anne-Claire Poirier. Sp, Louise Carre, Marthe Blackburn, Poirier; cam, Michel Brault; edtr, Jacques Gagne; mus, Maurice Blackburn. 88.
Luce Guilbeault, Angele Arsenault, Jean Mathieu.
(16m)
05/19/76

Le Toubib
(The Medic)
(France)
CII. Adel Prodns/Antenne 2/Films 21 co-prodn. Prod, Alain Delon. Dir, Pierre Granier-Deferre; sp, Granier-Deferre, Pascal Jardin, based on the novel "Harmonie ou les horreurs de la guerre", by Jean Freustie; cam, Claude Renoir; art dir, Maurice Sergent; edtr, Jean Ravel; mus, Philippe Sarde; snd, Jean Labussiere. 90.
Alain Delon, Veronique Jannot, Bernard Giraudeau, Francine Berge.
12/12/79

Le Trouble-Fesses
(The Groper)
(France)
PDS. Daber-Films-SN Prodis-Films 21 prodn. Wri-dir, Raoul Foulon. Cam (Eastmancolor), Roland Dantigny; edtr, Boris Lewin. 90.
Maurice Risch, Anicee Alvina, Vittorio Caprioli, Bernadette Lafont, Michel Galabru.
10/13/76

Le Vieux Pays Pou Rimbaud Est Mort
(The Old Country Where Rimband Died)
(France - Canada)
CKI. Dir, Jean-Pierre Lefebvre. Sp, Mireille Amiel, Lefebvre; cam (Eastmancolor), Guy Dufaux; edtr, Marguerite Duparc; mus, Claude Fonfrede. 113.
Marcel Sabourin, Anouk Ferjac, Muriam Boyer, Roger Blin, Germaine Delbat, Francois Perrot, Mark Lesser.
05/25/77

Le Voyage Au Bout Du Monde
(Voyage to the End of the World)
(France)
GCC. Robert Amon-Les Films Du Requin-Cousteau-Marshall Flaum prodn. Conceived-dir, Jacques-Yves Cousteau, Philippe Cousteau. Cam (Eastmancolor), D Meyrand, Philippe Cousteau; edtr, Hedwige Bienvenu. 92.
(DOC)
12/08/76

Le Voyage De Noces
(The Honeymoon Trip)
(France)
FEL. Lira Films, UCC prodn. Wri-dir, Nadine Trintignant. Cam (Eastmancolor), Pierre William Glenn; edtr, Claudine Bouche; mus, Michel Legrand, Christian Chevalier. 88.
Jean-Louis Trintignant, Stefania Sandrelli, Francois Marthouret, Serge Marquand, Pascale Rivault.
05/05/76

Le Voyage en douce
(Travels On The Sly)
(France)
GAU. Prospectacle-Gaumont-Elefilm co-prodn. Prod, Maurice Bernart. Wri-dir, Michel Deville, with literary collab of Francois-Regis Bastide, Camille Bourniquel, Muriel Cerf, Jean Chalon, Pierrette Fleutiaux, Patrick Gainville, Yves Navarre, Jacques Perry, Maurice Pons, Beatrice Privat, Suzanne Prou, Frederic Rey, Dominique Rolin, Isaure de Saint-Pierre. Cam (Fujicolor), Claude Lecomte; snd, Henry Moline, Joel Beldent; edtr, Raymonde Guyot; art dir, Catherine Ardouin; mus, Brahams, Beethoven; addl mus, Quentin Damanne. 98.
Dominique Sanda, Geraldine Chaplin.
02/06/80

The Lead Brigade: SEE Olovna Brigada

Leadbelly
PAR. Prod, Marc Merson; exec prod, David Frost; Dir, Gordon Parks. Sp, Ernest Kinoy; cam (Eastmancolor), Bruce Surtees; edtr, Harry Howard; mus, Fred Karlin; prodn des, Robert Boyle; set decor, John Kuri; snd, Doc Wilkinson, Gene Cantamessa; asst dir, Reuben Watt; stunt coord, Harold Jones. (MPAA rating: PG). 126.
Roger E Mosley, Paul Benjamin, Madge Sinclair, Alan Manson, Albert P Hall, Art Evans, James E Brodhead, John Henry Faulk, Vivian Bonnell, Dana Manno, Timothy Pickard, Lynn Hamilton, Loretta Greene, Valerie Odell, Rozaa Jean.
03/03/76

The Leap from the Bridge:
SEE Der Sprung von der Bruecke

Leap Into the Void: SEE Salto Nel Vuoto

Leave It To God: SEE Oxala

Leave Me Alone: SEE Nechci Nic Slyset

Leave Me Not Alone: SEE Laemna mig inte ensam

Leaving It All: SEE La Campanada

Lebanon. . . Why?
(Lebanon)
X. Camera 9, Group 4 prodn. Prod-dir, Georges Chamchoum. Collaboration of Yuna Haikel, Gino Arigoni; cam, Vassilis Christomoglou; mus, Hussein Nazek; edtr, Marwan Akkawi. 100.
(DOC))English subtitles)
07/26/78

Leben Mit Uwe
(Life with Uwe)
(E Germany)
DEE. Dir, Lothar Warneke. Sp, Siegfried Pitschmann, Warneke; cam (Orwa-color), Claus Neumann. 90.
Eberhard Esche, Cox Habbema, Dieter Mann, Friedo Solter, Karin Gregorek, Carl Heinz Choynski, Rolf Hoppe, Micaela Kreissler, Ruth Kommerell.
05/11/77

L'Ebreo Fascista
(The Fascist Jew)
(Italy)
GAU. Prods, Enzo Boetani, Giuseppe Collura for Dionysio Cinematografica prodns. Dir, Franco Mole; sp, Piero Regnoli, Luigi Preti, based on Preti's book "A Jew During Fascism"; cam, Fausto Zuccoli; art dir, Vera Cozzolino; edtr, Luigi Russo; mus, Aldo Salvi. 96.
Ray Lovelock, Marine Brochard, Silvia Dionisio, Adalberto Rosseti, Jose Quaglio.
10/15/80

Left, Right, Sickness of the Body: SEE Kaliwa't Kanan...Sakit Ng Katawan

The Left-Handed Woman: SEE Die Linkshaendige Frau

Legacy Of Blood
KLF. Take One Film Group presentation. Prod-wri-dir-cam-edtr, Andy Milligan. 82.
Elaine Boies, Chris Broderick, Marilee Troncone, Jeannie Cusick, Pete Barcia, Louise Gallandra, Stanley Schwartz, Dale Hansen, Joe Downing, Julia Curry, Martin Reymert.
03/08/78

The Legacy
U. Arnold Kopelson presentation of a Turman-Foster prodn. Prod, David Foster. Dir, Richard Marquand. Exec prod, Arnold Kopelson. Sp, Jimmy Sangter, Patric Tilley, Paul Wheeler; story, Sangster; cam, Dick Bush, Alan Hume; edtr, Anne V Coates; mus, Michael J Lewis; prodn des, Disley Jones; sfx, Ian Wingrove. (MPAA rating: R). 100.
Katharine Ross, Sam Elliott, John Standing, Ian Hogg, Margaret Tyzack, Charles Gray, Lee Montague, Hildegarde Neil, Marianne Broome, Roger Daltrey.
10/03/79

Legato
(Hungary)
HU. Hungarofilm prodn, Budapest Studio, Budapest. Dir, Istvan Gaal. Sp, Gaal, Imre Szasz, based on a play by Imre Szasz; cam (Eastmancolor), Gyorgy Illes; mus, Andras Szollosy. 96.
Geza D Hegedus, Nora Kovacs, Klari Tolnay, Margit Dayka, Lujza Orosz, Sandor Szabo.
05/24/78

The Legend Of Julian Makabayan
(Philippines)
IAP. Prod, Romy Ching. Story-sp, Marina Feleo-Gonzales based on her story "Dahong Palay" (Ricefield Snake). Dir, Celso Ad Castillo. Cam, Romeo Vitug; mus, Lutgardo Labad; edtr, Abelardo Hulleza; art dir, Peter Perlas. 150.
Christopher de Leon, Celso Ad Castillo, Charo Santos, Eddie Garcia, Tony Santos, Johnny Delgado, Perla Bautista.
02/20/80

Legend Of The Fox
(Hong Kong)
SHF. Prod, Mona Fong. Dir, Chang Cheh. Sp, Chang Cheh, Erh Kuang; cam, Tsao Hui Chi; mus dir, Eddie Wang; fighting instructors, Lu Feng, Chiang Sheng, Kuo Chui. 100.
Chien Hsiao Hao, Chiang Sheng, Linda Chu, Kuo Chui, Lu Feng.
(Mandarin with English subtitles)
12/24/80

Legend of the Mountain
(Hong Kong)
KHU. Dir, King Hu. Sp, Ling Chung; cam, Henry Chen; mus, Ng Tai Kong; martial arts supv, Wu Mingtsai; cos-art des, King Hu; edtr, King Hu. 190.
Hsu Feng, Sylvia Chang, Shih Chun, Tung Lin, Tien Feng, Wu Ming-tsai, Rainbow Hsu, Chen Hui-lon, Sun Yueh, Wu Chia-hsiang.
(Mandarin soundtrack with English and French sub-titles)
04/25/79

Legend of the Oasis: SEE Ech Burdijn Domog

The Legend of Ubirajara: SEE A Lenda De Ubirajara

Leidenschaftliche Bluemchen
(Passion Flower Hotel)
(W Germany)
CXP. CCC-Film (Artur Brauner prodn). Dir, Andre Farwagi. Sp, Paul Nicolas, based on Rosalind Erskine's novel, "The Passion Flower Hotel"; cam, Richard Suzuki; mus, Francis Lai; original mus "See You Later Alligator," "Rock A Beatin' Boogie," "Shake Rattle And Roll" played by Bill Haley and his Comets; lyrics for "Debbie's Song," "My Baby Blue," "The First Kiss" by Andre Farwagi. 94.
Nastassja Kinski, Carolin Ohrner, Marion Kracht, Veronique Delbourg, Fabiana Udenio, Gerry Sundquist, Nigel Greaves, Sean Chapman, Stefano d'Amato.
(English soundtrack)
05/10/78

Lekcja Martwego Jezyka
(Lesson of a Dead Language)
(Poland)
POL. Film Polski Production, Zespoly Filmowe & Tor Film Units, Warsaw. Wri-dir, Janusz Majewski, based on Andrzej Kusniewicz's novel. Cam, Zygmunt Samosiuk; mus, Andrzej Kurylewicz; sets, Janusz Sosnowski; edtr, Elzbieta Kurkowska; prodn mgr, Tadeusz Drewno. 99.
Olgierd Lukaszewicz, Ewa Dalkowska, Malgorzata Pritulak, Gustaw Lutkiewicz, Juliusz Machulski, Irena Karel, Marek Kondrat, Piotr Pawlowski, Mieczyslaw Voit, Wlodzimierz Borunski, Zygmunt Malanowicz.
06/11/80

Lemon Popsicle
(Israel)
X. Noah Film prodn, Tel-Aviv; prods, Menahem Golan, Yoram Globus. Dir, Boaz Davidson. Sp, Davidson, Eli Tabor; cam (Eastmancolor), Adam Greenberg; edtr, Alain Jakubowicz; sets, Ariel Roshko, Alfred Gershoni; snd, Eli Yarkoni. 100.
Yiftach Katzur, Anat Atzmon, Jonathan Segal, Zachi Noy.
03/29/78

L'Empreinte des Geants
(The Imprint of Giants)
(France - W Germany)
SNC. Filmel/SNC/FR3/Rialto Film (Berlin) co-prodn. Prods, Eugene Lepicier, Gerard Beytout. Dir, Robert Enrico. Wris, Enrico, Francois Chevallier, from the novel, "La Marie-Marraine," by Hortense Dufour; cam, Didier Tarot; art dir, Jean-Claude Gallouin; edtr, Patricia Neny; mus, Karl Heinz Schafer. 140.
Mario Adorf, Zoe Chauveau, Patrick Chesnais, Andrea Ferreol, Raimund Harmstorf, Dominique Laffin, Philippe Leotard, Serge Reggiani, Anne Waizemsky.
04/23/80

Lena Rais
(W Germany)
X. Christian Rischert Film Prodn-Multimedia Munich-Zweites Deutsches Fernsehen (ZDF), Mainz. Dir, Christian Rischert. Sp, Manfred Grunert; cam, Gerard Vandenberg; mus, Eberhard Schoener; edtr, Annette Dorn; sets, Hans Gailing. 116.
Krista Stadler, Tito Prueckner, Nikolaus Paryla, Kai Fischer, Werner Asam, Manfred Lehmann, Rolf Schimpf, Tana Schanzara, Dan Van Husen.
03/26/80

L'Enfant De La Nuit
(Child of the Night)
(France - Italy)
SLN. Paris-Cannes Prodn-Alpes Film-A P K Cin prodn. Dir, Sergio Gobbi. Sp, Ugo Pirro, from the book by G J Arnaud; cam (Eastmancolor), Ennio Guarnieri; edtr, Ruggero Mastroianni; mus, Stelvio Cipriani. 102.
Agostina Bell, Stefano Satta Flores, Sergino, Jean Claude Bouilln.
11/22/78

L'Entourloupe
(The Swindle)
(France)
CCF. Cathala prodn. Prod, Norbert Saada. Dir, Gerard Pires. Sp, Jean Herman, Michel Audiard, based on novel "Nos Intentions Sont Pacifiques" by Francis Ryck. Mus, Django Reinhardt; cam (Fujicolor), Pierre William Glenn; edtr, Jacques Witta. Snd, Guy Rophe. 90.
Jean-Pierre Marielle, Jacques Dutronc, Gerard Lanvin, Anne Jousset.
07/23/80

Leo And Loree
UA. Prod, Jim Begg. Exec prod, Ron Howard. Dir, Jerry Paris. Sp, James Ritz; cam (CFI Color), Costa Petals; edtr, Ed Cotter; snd, Robbie Robinson; art dir, Linda Pearl; asst dir, Cheryl Downey; asso prod, James Ragan; mus, Lance Rubin. (MPAA rating: PG). 97.
Donny Most, Linda Purl, David Huffman, Jerry Paris, Shannon Farnon, Allan Rich, Susan Lawrence.
05/07/80

Leper: SEE Tredowata

Leptirov Oblak
(Butterfly Cloud)
(Yugoslavia)
X. Centar FRZ prodn, Belgrade. Dir, Zdravko Randic. Sp, Dragoljub Ivkov; cam, Miodrag Jaksic-Fandjo. 90.
Zoran Cvijanovic, Pavle Vujisic, Ruzica Sokic, Jelisaveta Sabljic, Vera Savic, Emilija Cerovic.
03/09/77

Les Ambassadeurs
(The Ambassadors)
(France - Tunisia)
FRM. SATPEC, OGEK, Unite 3 prodn. Wri-dir, Naceur Ktari. Cam (Eastmancolor), Jean-Jacques Rochut. 92.
04/28/76

Les Apprentis Sorciers
(The Apprentice Sorcerers)
(France)
BUI. Dir, Edgardo Cozarinsky. Sp, Cozarinsky, A Tauman; cam (Eastmancolor), Jean-Claude Riviere; edtr, Alberto Yaccelini; mus, Edgardo Canton. 91.
Zouzou, Peter Chatel, Marie-France Pisier, Christian Marquand, Dennis Hopper, Jean-Pierre Kalfon, Niels Arestrup, Pierre Clementi, Carlos Clarens.
02/09/77

Les Belles Manieres
(Fine Manners)
(France)
GAU. Diagonale prodn. Prod, Paul Vecchiali. Dir, Jean-Claude Guiguet. Sp, Guiguet and Gerard Frot-Coutaz; cam, Georges Strouve; edtrs, Vecchiali, Frank Mathieu; snd, Jean-Francois Chevalier; make-up, Ronaldo Abreu; cos, Nina Ricci. Mus extracts from Berlioz, Beethoven, Brukner, Mozart, and J Strauss. 90.
Helene Surgere, Emmanuel Lemoine, Martine Simonet.
05/16/79

Les Bons Debarras
(Good Riddance)
(Canada)
PRI. Dir, Francis Mankiewicz. Sp, Rejean Ducharme; cam (Eastmancolor), Michel Brault; edtr, Andre Corriveau. 109.
Charlotte Laurier, Marie Tifo, Germain Houde, Louise Marleau, Gilbert Sicotte.
03/05/80

Les Bronzes
(The Suntanned Ones)
(France)
CCF. Trinacra Films prodn. Dir, Patrice Leconte. Sp by cast and Leconte; cam (Eastmancolor), Jean-Francois Robin; mus, Serge Gainsbourg. 105.
12/06/78

Les Chemins de L'Exil, ou Les Dernieres Annees de Jean Jacques Rousseau
(The Roads of Exile)
(France)
X. TFI-SSR-Telecip-BBC-RTB-SRC-TV60 prodn. Dir, Claude Goretta. Sp, Georges Haldas, Goretta; cam, Philippe Rousselot; edtr, Joele van Effenterre; art dirs, Jacques Bufnoir, Enrique Sonois; cos, Jean-Yves Tavernier; snd, Daniel Ollivier, Pierre Gamet. 200.
Francois Simon, Dominque Labourier, Roland Bertin, Michel Berto, Gabriel Cattand, Martine Chevallier, Sylvain Clement, William Fox.
12/27/78

Les Chiens
(The Dogs)
(France)
GCC. A J Films-A M S Productions-Films de la Droutte (Paris)-Pacific Films (Tahiti) co-prodn. Prod, Laurent Mayniel. Dir, Alain Jessua. Sp, Andre Ruellan, Jessua, based on an original idea by Jessua; cam (Eastmancolor), Etienne Becker; edtr, Helene Plemmianikov; mus, Rene Koering; snd, Harald Maury; art dir, Jean-Louis Poveda; dog trainer, Andre Noel. 100.
Gerard Depardieu, Victor Lanoux, Nicole Calfan.
05/02/79

Les Conquistadores
(France)
PFC. IDTV-TV Productions prodn. Dir, Marco Pauly. Sp, Odile Barsky, Pauly; cam (Eastmancolor), Walter Bal; edtr, Monique Prim; mus, Joachim Kuhn, Daniel Humair, Michel Portal. 100.
Gerard Desarthe, Dominique Labourier, Yves Alonso, Fedor Atkine, Richard Boringer.
03/17/76

Les 12 Travaux D'Asterix
(The 12 Labors of Asterix)
(France)
PGS. Dargaud Films, Les Prodns Rene Goscinny, Studios Idefix prodn. Wri-dirs, Rene Goscinny, Albert Underzo. Ani dir, Pierre Watrin, artistic counsellors, Henri Gruel, Pierre Tcherina. 80.
(ANI)
11/17/76

Les Egouts du Paradis
(The Sewers of Paradise)
(France)
CFD. Alexia Films prodn. Prods, Jean-Pierre Rawson, Anne-Marie Toursky. Dir-sp, Jose Giovanni; dialog, Michel Audiard; based on novel by Albert Spaggiari; cam, Walter Bal; edtrs, Jacqueline Thiedot and Marie-Therese Boiche; snd, Jean-Francois Anger; mus, Jean-Pierre Doering; art dir, Georges Petitot. 115.
Francis Huster, Jean-Francois Balmer, Lila Kedrova, Clement Harari, Michel Subor.
04/25/79

Les Enfants de L'Oubli
(The Children of Oblivion)
(Belgium)
CAF. Joao Correa-Jules Brunin prodn. Dir, Joao Correa. Sp, Alain Verdier, Dominique Hanssens; cam, Jacques Duesberg, Jean-Paul Kesnier; edtrs, Bob Van Hammee, Luc Bourgeois, Maria Joao Tiago; mus, G Soccio. 90.
(DOC) (B & W) (16m)
02/21/79

Les Enfants Du Placard
(The Closet Children)
(France)
MK. GMF prodn. Wri-dir, Benoit Jacquot. Cam (Eastmancolor), Pierre Lhomme; edtr, Fanette Simonet. 105.
Brigitte Fossey, Lou Castel, Georges Marchal, Jean Sorel, Isabelle Weingarten.
05/18/77

Les Fabuleuses Adventures du Legendaire Baron de Munchausen
(The Fabulous Adventures of the Legendary Baron Munchausen)
(France)
X. Prod by Les Films Jean Image. Dir, Jean Image. Sp, Jean Image and France Image; dialog, France Image and Serge Nadaud; animation, Olivier Bonnet, Denis Boutin, Jean-Pierre Jacquet; mus, Michel Legrand; decors, Enrique Gonzalez; cam, Per Ofal Csongovai. 78.
(ANI)
05/23/79

Les Felines
(France)
KFF. Reda Productions film. Prod, Rene Levy-Balensi. Dir, Daniel Daert. Cam, Stanley Mills, Patrick Godaert; snd, Lecien Yvonnet; edtr, Ingrid Nicholson; mus, Yladimir Cosma; set, Andre Gillette; cos, Jean Parthei, Madam Georgette. (MPAA rating: X). 70.
Janine Reynaud, Nathalie Zeiger, Pauline Larrieu, Jacques Insermini, Georges Guerret.
03/17/76

Les Fleurs Du Miel
(The Honey Flowers)
(France)
GAU. Dimage-Contrechamps prodn. Wri-dir, Claude Faraldo. Cam (Eastmancolor-Panavision), Jean-Marc Ripert; edtrs, Anna Ruiz, Juliane Ruiz; mus, Jefferson Starship's "A Child is Coming." 96.
Brigitte Fossey, Gilles Segal, Claude Faraldo, Mireille Pame, Helene Henry, Marie Kerusore.
03/17/76

Les Fougeres Bleues
(The Blue Ferns)
(France)
UCC. Bela Prod-Corona Films-A2 prodn. Wri-dir, Francoise Sagan. Cam (Eastmancolor), Roland Dantigny; edtr, Chantal Delattre; mus, Frederic Bottom. 85.
Francoise Fabian, Jean-Marc Bory, Gilles Segal, Carolien Cellier, Francis Perrin.
06/15/77

Les Grands Moyens
(Short and Sweet)
(France)
FOX. CAPAC (Paul Claudon) prodn. Dir, Hubert Cornfield. Sp, Cornfield, Richard Caron; book, Charles Exbrayat; cam (Eastmancolor), Maurice Fellous; edtr, Georges Freedland; mus, Francois De Roubaix, song "Vendatta" by Cornfield. 84.
Helene Dieudonne, Yvette Maurech, Andree De Beaumont, Roger Carel, Catherine Rouvel, Fernand Sardou.
02/04/76

Les Heroines du Mal
(The Heroines of Evil)
(France)
X. Argos Films presentation of a Films du Jeudi prodn. Prod, Pierre Braunberger. Dir, Walerian Borowczyk. Sp, Borowczyk; cam (Fujicolor), Bernard Caillencourt; art dir, Jacques D'Ovidio; cos, Piet Bolscher; mus, Olivier Dassault, Philippe D'Aram. 109.
Marina Pierro, Francois Guetary, Jean-Claude Dreyfus, Gaelle Legrand, Assan Fall, Pascale Christophe, Gerard Ismael.
05/23/79

Les Heros N'Ont Pas Froid Aux Oreilles
(Heroes Are Not Wet Behind the Ears)
(France)
SNX. Atya Productions-Int'l Film Promotion, Terminus prodn. Dir, Charles Nemes. Sp, Gerard Jugnot, Nemes; cam (Eastmancolor), Etienne Faudet; edtr, Marie-Sophie Dubus; mus, Jacques Delaporte. 83.
Daniel Auteuil, Gerard Jugnot, Anne Jousset, Patricia Karim, Henri Guybet.
01/10/79

Les Indiens Sont Encore Loin
(The Indians Are Still Far Away)
(Switzerland - France)
FKZ. INA-Films 2001-Filmkollectiv prodn. Wri-dir, Patricia Moraz. Cam (Eastmancolor), Renato Berta; edtr, Thierry Derocles. 95.
Isabelle Huppert, Mathieu Carriere, Christine Pascal, Chil Boiscuille, Anton Diffring, Nicole Garcia.
09/14/77

Les Liens De Sang
(Blood Relatives)
(France - Canada)
SNC. Filmel-Cinevideo-Classic Films prodn. Dir, Claude Chabrol; sp, Chabrol, R Sydney from novel by Ed McBain; cam (Eastmancolor), Jean Rabier; edtr, Yves Langlois; mus, Paul Jensen. 100.
Donald Sutherland, Aude Landry, Lisa Langlos, Laurent Male, Micheline Lancta, Stephane Audran, Donald Pleasence, David Hemmings.
01/25/78

Les Lolos De Lola
(Lola's Lolos)
(France)
LML. Films Du Carrosse (F Truffaut) prodn. Wri-dir, Bernard Dubois. Cam (Eastmancolor), John Terry; edtr, Yann Dedet; mus, Jean-Claude Vannier. 83.
Jean-Pierre Leaud, Claudine Vannier, Zouzou, Yann Dedet, Julien Dubois, Serge Marquand, Lola Dolores, Claude Barrault, Bernard Menez.
01/28/76

Les Loulous
(The Wise Guys)
(France)
PFC. Stephen Films (Vera Belmont), Alexia Films prodn. Wri-dir, Patrick Cabouat from a book by Marc Casanova. Cam (Eastmancolor), Lionel Legros; edtr, Brigette Sousselier; mus, Elisabeth Wiener, Horacio Vaggione. 90.
Jean-Louis Robert, Charles Nelson, Balerie Mairesse, Francoise Pages.
03/30/77

Les Mal Partis
(The Bad Starters)
(France)
CCF. Greenwich Films (Serge Silberman) prodn. Wri-dir, Jean-Baptiste Rossi from his own book. Cam (Eastmancolor), Edmond Richard; edtr, Helene Plemiannikov; mus, Eric Demarsan. 114.
France Dougnac, Olivier Jallageas, Marie Dubois, Jean Gaven, Pascale Roberts, Bernard Verley, Marc Lesser.
02/11/76

Les Naufrages De L'Ile De La Tortue
(The Castaways of Turtle Island)
(France)
AMLF. Callipix prodn. Wri-dir, Jacques Rozier. Cam (Eastmancolor), Colin Mounier; edtr, Rozier, Francoise Thevenot; mus, Dorival Caymi, Nana Vasconellos. 140.
Pierre Richard, Maurice Risch, Jacques Villeret, Caroline Cartier.
09/01/76

Les Oeufs Brouilles
(The Scrambled Eggs)
(France)
WBC. Action Films (Yves Gasser) prodn. Dir, Joel Santoni. Sp, Jean Curtelin, Jean-Claude Carriere, Santoni; cam (Eastmancolor), Walter Bal; edtr, Thierry Derocles; mus, Vladimir Cosma. 95.
Jean Carmet, Jean-Claude Brialy, Anna Karina, Michel Lonsdale, Michel Aumont, Denise Bosc, Michel Peyrelson, Christian De Tiliere.
04/07/76

Les Passagers
(The Passengers)
(France)
WBC. Viaduc Prodns (Leo Fuchs)-Trianon Prodns-PIC prodn. Dir, Serge Leroy. Sp, Leroy, Christopher Frank from the novel by K R Dwyer; cam (Eastmancolor), Walter Wottitz, Jacques Assuerus; edtr, Francois Ceppi; mus, Claude Bolling. 102.
Jean-Louis Trintignant, Bernard Fresson, Mireille Darc, Richard Constantini, Adolfo Celi, Marco Perrin.
03/09/77

Les Petites Fugues
(Little Escapes)
(Switzerland - France)
CCZ. Cactus Film-MKA Diffusion Film Et Video Collectif, Filmkollektiv Zuerich-Television SSR Geneve-Television FR3 Paris-Les Films 2001 prodn. Dir, Yves Yersin. Sp, Yersin, Claude Muret; cam (Eastmancolor), Robert Alazraki; edtr, Yersin; mus, Leon Francioli. 140.
Michel Robin, Fabienne Barraud, Dore De Rosa, Fred Personne, Mista Prehac, Laurent Sandoz, Nicole Vatier, Leo Maillard.
05/23/79

Les Petits Calins
(The Little Wheedlers)
(France)
GAU. Gaumont Intl-Les Prodns De La Gueville prodns. Sp-dir, Jean-Marie Poire. Cam (Eastmancolor), Edmon Sechan; edtr, Marie-Josephe Yoyotte. 95.
Dominique Laffin, Caroline Cartier, Josiane Balasko, Roger Mirmont, Jacques Frantz, Patrick Cartie, Claire Maurier, Jean Bouise.
02/08/78

Les Rendez-Vous D'Anna
(The Meetings of Anna)
(Belgium - France - W Germany)
GAU. Helene Films (Paris)-Paradise Films (Brussels)-ZDF (Mainz) prodn. Wri-dir, Chantal Ackerman. Cam, Jean Penzer; edtr, Francine Sandberg. 127.
Aurore Clement, Helmut Griem, Magali Noel, Hanns Zieschler, Lea Massari, Jean-Pierre Cassel.
10/25/78

Les Ringards
(The Small Timers)
(France)
UCC. Les Films De L' Alma prodn. Dir, Robert Pouret. Sp, Jean Lacroix; cam (Eastmancolor), Guy Dourdan; mus, Francis Lai. 95.
Mireille Darc, Aldo Maccione, Charles Gerard, Julien Guiomar, Georges Wilson, Genevieve Fontanel.
10/11/78

Les Routes Du Sud
(The Roads of the South)
(France)
PFC. Trinacra Films-FR3-Profilmes prodn. Dir, Joseph Losey; sp, Jorge Semprun, Losey, Patricia Losey; cam (Eastmancolor), Gerry Fisher; edtr, Reginald Beck; art dir, Alexandre Trauner; prod, Yves Rousset-Rouard; mus, Michel Legrande. 97.
Yves Montand, Miou-Miou, Laurent Malet, France Lambiotte, Jose Luis Gomez, Jean Bouise, Maurice Benichou.
05/03/78

Les Servantes du Bon Dieu
(The Servants of the Good Lord)
(Canada)
PRI. Les Productions Prisma-SDICC-Radio-Quebec-OTEO prodn. Conceived and dir, Diane Letourneau. Cam, Jean-Charles Tremblay; edtr, Josee Beaudet. 90.
(DOC) (16m)
05/16/79

Les Soeurs Bronte
(The Bronte Sisters)
(France)
GAU. Action Films-Gaumont-FR3 prodn. Dir, Andre Techine. Sp, Techine, Pascal Bonitzer, Jean Gruault; cam, Bruno Nuytten; edtr, Claudine Merlin; art dir, Jean-Pierre Kohut-Svelco; mus, Philippe Sarde. 115.
Isabelle Adjani, Marie-France Pisier, Isabelle Huppert, Pascal Greggory, Patrick Magee, Helen Surgere, Roland Bertin.
05/16/79

Les Sous-Doues
(The Under-Gifted)
(France)
AMLF. Films 7 prodn. Prod-dir, Claude Zidi. Wris, Zidi, Didier Kaminka, Michel Fabre, cam (Fujicolor), Paul Bonis; mus, Bob Brault, snd, Jean-Louis Ughetto; edtr, Nicole Saunier. 92.
Maria Pacome, Hubert Deschamps, Tonie Marshall, Michel Galabru, Daniel Auteuil, Raymond Bussieres, Philippe Taccini, Catherine Erhardy.
07/02/80

Les Turlupins
(Rascals)
(France)
X. Gilbert de Goldschmidt prodn. Prod, Gilbert de Goldschmidt. Dir, Bernard Revon. Sp, Bernard Revon, Didier Bouquet-Nadaud in collab with Michel Zemer, Claude de Givray; cam (Fujicolor), Jacques Loiseleux, Gerard de Battista; edtr, Georges Klotz; mus, Roland Romanelli; snd, Bernard Rochut. 93.
Bernard Drieux, Thomas Chabrol, Pascale Rocard, Etienne Draber, Sebastien Drai-Dietrich, Pierre Vial, Brigitte Chamak.
(English subtitles)
03/05/80

Les Vautours
(The Vultures)
(France - Canada)
X. Prod with the financial assistance of the Canadian Film Dev Corp. Prod, Louise Ranger. Dir, Jean-Claude Labreque. Sp, Robert Gurik, asst, Jacques Jacob; cam (b&w), Alain Dostie; art dir, Normand Sarrazin; mus dir, Tony Roman; mus, Dominique Tremblay; snd, Serge Beauchemin. 91.
Gilbert Sicotte, Monique Mercure, Carmen Tremblay, Amulette Garneau, Denise Proulx, Jean Duceppe, Gilles Pelletier, Guy L'Ecuyer, Gabriel Arcand, Paule Baillargeon, Jacques Bilodeau, Raymond Cloutier, Robert Gravel, George Groulx, Rita Lafontaine, Robert Lebel, Nicole Leblanc, Gilbert Lepage, Claude Maher, Jean Mathieu, Anne-Marie Provencher, Philippe Robert, Yolande Roy, Jean-Pierre Saulnier.
(English subtitles) (B & W)
06/28/78

Lesson of a Dead Language: SEE Lekcja Martwego Jezyka

Let The Balloon Go
(Australia)
X. Film Australia prodn. Prod, Richard Mason. Dir, Oliver Howes. Sp, Richard Mason, Oliver Howes, Ivan Southall, from novel by Southall; addl dial, Cliff Green; cam, Dean Semler; mus, George Dreyfus; art dir, David Copping; snd, Don Connolly; asst dir, Elisabeth Knight; stunt coord, Grant Page; balloonist, Eddie Selmon. 92.
Robert Bettles, Jan Kingsbury, Ben Gabriel, Sally Whiteman, Matthew Wilson, Terry McQuillan, Bruce Spence, John Ewart, Kenneth Goodlet, Ray Barrett, Nigel Lovell, Babette Stephens, Brian Anderson, Charles Metcalfe, Phillip Ross, Scott Griffiths, Goff Vockler, Bob Lee.
05/05/76

Letaci Velikog Neba
(Fliers of the Open Skies)
(Yugoslavia)
YFR. Jadran Film-Croatia Film prodn. Dir, Marijan Arhanic. Sp, Milan Grgic; cam (Eastmancolor), Frano Vodopivec; mus, Alfi Kabiljo. 96.
Jasna Ivic, Ramiz Pasic, Boris Dvornik, Zvonko Lepetic, Milan Strljic.
08/17/77

L'Etat Sauvage
(The Savage State)
(France)
GAU. Films 66-Gaumont prodn. Dir, Francis Girod; sp, Georges Conchon, Girod from book by Conchon; cam (Eastmancolor), Pierre Lhomme; edtr, Genevieve Winding; mus, Pierre Jensen. 111.
Marie-Christine Barrault, Claude Brasseur, Michel Piccoli, Jacques Dutronc, Doura Mane, Baaron, Rudiger Vogler.
05/03/78

Let's Get Those English Girls: SEE A Nous Les Petites Anglaises

Let's Go, Barbara: SEE Vamonos, Barbara

Let's Leave the War in Peace: SEE Tengamos La Guerra En Paz

Letters from Marusia: SEE Actas De Marusia

Letze Liebe
(Last Love)
(W Germany)
TEF. Wri-dir, Ingemo Engstrom. Cam (Eastmancolor), Ingo Kratisch; edtr, Gerhard Theuring. 125.
Angela Winkler, Rudiger Vogler, Therese Affolter, Hildegarde Schmahl, Wolfgang Kinder, Geoffrey Layton.
08/22/79

L'Homme A tout Faire
(Canada)
X. Prod, Corporation Image Ltee, with financial participation of the Canadian Film Development Corporation and L'Institut Quebecois du cinema. Prod, Rene Malo; dir-sp, Micheline Lanctot. Cam, Andre Gagnon; art dir, Normand Sarazin; edtr, Annik de Bellefeuille; mus, Francois Lanctot. 99.
Jocelyn Berube, Andree Pelletier, Paul Dion, Gilles Renaud, Marcel Sabourin.
04/02/80

L'Homme En Colere
(The Angry Man)
(France - Canada)
UA. Films Ariane - F R 3 (Paris) - Cinevideo (Montreal) co-prodn. Prods, Alexandre Mnouchkine, Georges Dancigers, Denis Heroux; dir, Claude Pinoteau; Wri, Jean-Claude Carriere, Pinoteau; co-adaptor, Charles Israel; cam (Eastmancolor), Jean Boffety; edtr, Marie-Josee Yoyotte; art dir, Earl Preston; mus, Claude Bolling. 105.
Lino Ventura, Angie Dickinson, Laurent Malet, Hollis McLaren, Donald Pleasence, Chris Wiggins.
04/11/79

L'Homme Presse'
(Man In A Hurry)
(France)
AMLF. Lira Films-Adel prodns prodn. Dir, Edouard Molinaro. Sp, M Rheims, C Franck; book, Paul Monrand; cam (Eastmancolor), Jean Charvein; edtr, R Isnardon. 88.
Alain Delon, Mireille Darc, Michel Duchaussoy, Monica Guerritore.
08/31/77

L'Homme Qui Aimait Les Femmes
(The Man Who Loved Women)
(France)
UA. Les Films Du Carrosse-UA prodn. Dir, Francois Truffaut. Sp, Truffaut, Michel Fermaud, Suzanne Schiffman; cam (Eastmancolor), Nestor Almendros; edtr, Martine Barraque-Curie; mus, Maurice Jaubert. 119.
Charles Denner, Brigitte Fossey, Nelly Borgeaud, Genevieve Fontanel,

Nathalie Baye, Sabine Glaser, Valerie Bonnier, Leslie Caron, Nella Barbier.
04/27/77

L'Hotel De La Plage
(The Beach Hotel)
(France)
GAU. Prodn, 2000-Gaumont prodn. Sp-dir, Michel Lang. Cam (Eastmancolor), Daniel Gaudry; edtr, Helene Plemiannikov. 115.
Myriam Boyer, Daniel Ceccaldi, Martine Sarcey, Michele Grellier, Rosine Cadoret, Guy Marchand, Sophie Barjac, Blanche Ravalec.
02/08/78

L'Hypothese du Tableau Vole
(Hypothesis of the Stolen Painting)
(France)
INZ. Wri-dir, Raul Ruiz from an idea by Pierre Klossowski. Cam (b&w), Sacha Vierny, Maurice Pejimond; mus, Jose Arriagada. 67.
Jean Rougeul, Anne Debois, Chantal Palay, Alix Comte, Jean Narboni, Stephane Shandor.
(B & W)
03/07/79

Liar's Dice
X. Prods, Butros Makdissy, Ed Eubanks. Dir, Issam B Makdissy. Sp, Terry Eubanks-Makdissy; cam, Douglas Murray; edtr, Issam B Makdissy; mus, Coleman Burke, Gary Yamani; snd, David Bacon; light, Robert Shoup. 95.
Robert Ede, Terry Eubanks-Makdissy, Issam B Makdissy, Frank Triest, D G Buckles, Norma Small, Phran Gauci, Rafik Assad, Shirley James, Phil De Carla, Jerry La Rue, Judd Stelo, Jeannette Mignola, John Lovell.
05/07/80

Libertad Provisional
(Out On Parole)
(Spain)
X. Agata Films-Jose Luis Dibildos (Madrid) prodn. Dir, Roberto Bodegas. Story-sp, Juan Marse; mus, Patxi Andion; cam (Eastmancolor), Alejandro Ulloa; exec prods, Serafin Garcia Trueba, Antonio Martin; sets, Elisa Ruiz; edtr, Guillermo Maldonado. 98.
Concha Velasco, Patxi Andion, Montserrat Salvador, Francisco Jarque, Concha Bardem.
09/29/76

Licao de Amor
(Love Lesson)
(Brazil)
EMZ. Corisco Filmes Ltd. prodn. Prod, Luiz Carlos Barreto, Eduardo Escorel. Dir, Eduardo Escorel. Sp, Escorel, Eduardo Coutinho from the novel "Love Intransitive Verb" by Mario de Andrade; cam, Murillo Salles; edtr, Gilberto Santeiro; mus, Frances Hime. 75.
Lilian Lemmertz, Rogerio Froes, Irene Racache, Marcos Taquechel, Marie Claudia Costa, Magali Lemoine, Mariana Veloso, Marie Claude, William Wu, Deia Pereira.
05/10/78

Licne Stvari
(Personal Affairs)
(Yugoslavia)
YFR. Centar Film, Belgrade, Film prodn in collab with Belgrade Television. Wri-dir, Aleksandar Mandic. Cam, Radoslav Vladic; sets, Mandic; mus, Goran Bregovic. 85.
Maja Sabljic, Snezana Sabljic.
09/05/79

Lieb Vaterland, Magst Ruhig Sein
(Dear Fatherland, Be at Peace)
(W Germany)
CTT. Solaris Film prodn and Vaterland Productions. World rights, Bischoff & Co, Munich. Prod, Bernd Eichinger. Wri-dir, Roland Klick, based on novel of same name by Johannes Mario Simmel; cam, Jost Vacano; mus, Juergen Knieper; edtr, Sigrun Jaeger. 100.
Heinz Domez, Catherine Allegret, Guenter Pfitzmann, Dietrich Frauboes, Georg Mariaschka, Margot Werner, Eva Geib, Rolf Zacher, Gerd Kieslich, Rudolf Wessley, Gunter Berger, Guenther Notthoff, Uwe Gaudetz, John O'Connor, Joe Piech, Ulrich Radke.
04/07/76

Liebe Das Leben-Lebe Das Lieben
(Love Living, Live Loving)
(W Germany)
X. Lutz Eisholz Film prodn, Berlin. Wri-dir, Lutz Eisholz. Cam, Klaus Janschewski; snd, Christian Moldt; edtr, Hannelore Hoefer; pho, Helmut Roettgen. 90.
Brigitte Mira, Erhardt Dhein, Heidrun Kussin, Manfred Lehmann, Eleonore Tappert, Waltraut Habicht, Siegfried Unruh, Erwin Schaffner, Peter Jahns, Peter Heinrich, Bruno S.
03/09/77

Liebe Und Abenteuer
(Love and Adventure)
(W Germany)
X. Stelly-Film Prodn, Hamburg, in collab with Zweites Deutsches Fernsehen (ZDF), Wiesbaden-Mainz. Wri-dir, Gisela Stelly, Cam, David Slama; snd, Heiko von Sweiykowski; art dir, MAT-Peter Braun; edtr, Heidi Handorf; prodn mgr, Chris Sievernich. 88.
Brigitt Hoffmeister, Hub Martin, Harold Vogl, Leo Bardischewski.
01/17/79

Lieve Jongens
(Dear Boys)
(Netherlands)
X. Sigma Films prodn. Prod, Matthijs van Heijningen. Dir, Paul de Lussanet. Sp, Chiem van Houweninge, based on a novel by Gerard Reve; cam, Paul van de Bos; edtr, Hans van Dongen; mus, Laurens van Rooyen. 88.
Hugo Metsers, Hans Dagelet, Bill Van Dijk, Albert Mol.
05/28/80

Life and Love of Boy Zapanta: SEE Buhay At Pag-Ibig Ni Boy Zapanta

The Life And Times Of Rosie The Riveter
X. Prod-dir, Connie Field. Pho, Cathy Zheutin, Bonnie Friedman, Robert Handley, Emiko Omori. Edtrs, Lucy Massie Phenix and Field. 60.
Lola Weixel, Wanita Allen, Gladys Belcher, Lyn Childs, Margaret Wright.
(DOC) (B & W)
10/01/80

Life Before Him: SEE La Vie Devant Soi

Life Changes: SEE La Vida Cambia

The Life Guard: SEE Spasatel

Life of Brian
(Britain)
WBO. Prod, John Goldstone. Exec prods, George Harrison, Denis O'Brien. Dir, Terry Jones. Sp, Graham Chapman, John Cleese, Terry Gilliam, Eric Idle, Terry Jones, Michael Palin; des-ani, Terry Gilliam; cam, Peter Biziou; edtr, Julian Doyle; mus, Geoffrey Burgeon; art dir, Roger Christian; cos des, Hazel Pethig, Charles Knode; snd (Dolby Stereo), Garth Marshall; asso prod, Tim Hampton; asst dir, Jonathan Benson. (MPAA rating: R). 93.
Terry Jones, Graham Chapman, Michael Palin, John Cleese, Ken Colley, Gwen Taylor, Eric Idle, Sue Jones-Davis, Spike Milligan, George Harrison, Terry Gilliam.
08/22/79

The Life of Chikuzan: SEE Chikuzan Hitori Tabi

Life with Uwe: SEE Leben Mit Uwe

Lifeguard
PAR. Prod, Ron Silverman; exec prod, Ted Mann. Dir, Daniel Petrie. Sp, Ron Koslow; cam (CFI Color), Ralph Woolsey; edtr, Argyle Nelson Jr; mus, Dale Menten; songs, Menten, Paul Williams; snd, David Dockendorf, David Ronne, Glen Glenn Sound; asst dir, Richard Kobritz. (MPAA rating: PG). 96.
Sam Elliott, Anne Archer, Stephen Young, Parker Stevenson, Kathleen Quinlan, Steve Burns, Sharon Weber.
05/26/76

Ligabue
(Italy)
SCI. RAI-TV prodn. Dir, Salvatore Nocita. Sp, Cesare Zavattini, Arnaldo Bagnasco, based on a text by Zavattini; cam, Roberto Gerardi; mus, Armando Trovaioli. 126.
Flavio Bucci, Giuseppe Pambieri, Pamela Villoresi, Andrea Ferreol.
12/06/78

The Light on the Gallows: SEE Das Licht Auf Dem Galgen

Lightning Over Water
(Nick's Movie)
(W Germany - Sweden - US)
PIF. Road Movies, Viking Film prodn. Dir-conceived, Nick Ray, Wim Wenders. Cam (Movielab), Ed Lachman; edtr, Peter Przgodda; mus, Ronnee Blakley. 116.
Nicholas Ray, Wim Wenders, Ronee Blakley.
05/28/80

Like A Boomerang: SEE
Comme Un Boomerang

Lille Spejl
(Mirror, Mirror)
(Denmark)
PAL. Crone Film prodn. Co-prod-sp-dir, Edward Fleming. Cam (Eastmancolor), Claus Loof; exec prod, Nina Crone; edtrs, Fleming, Gert Fredholm, Grete Moeldrup; mus, Ole Hoeyer; prodn des, Peper Hoeimark; cos, Ulla-Britt Soederlund. 106.
Frits Helmuth, Bodil Kjer, Preben Kaas, Bent Reiner, Poul-Kristian, Ole Ernst, Jesper Klein.
03/01/78

Lille Virgil og Orla Froesnapper
(Little Virgil and Frogeater Orla)
(Denmark)
MTF. Metronome Film prodn, based on Ole Lund Kirkegaard's childrens' books. Wris, Hans Hansen, Gert Fredholm. Cam (Eastmancolor), Jeppe Jeppesen; edtr, Anker; prodn des-sfx, Peter Hoimark; cos, Jette Trmann; mus, Peter Bastian, Anders Koppel; lyr, Benny Andersen. 90.
Bror Bodtker-Naess, Christian Honore, Allan Olsen, Ktinka Bodtker-Naess, Karl Stegger, Elin Reimer, Jesper Klein, Claus Nissen, Gotha Andersen, Inger Hovmand, Peter Schroeder.
04/02/80

L'Image
AUD. Dir, Radley Metzger; prods, Marty Richards, Gill Champion; a Les Films Du Griffon - Catalyst co-prodn. Sp, Jake Barnes adapted from the novel by Jean de Berg; cam (Eastmancolor), Rene LeFevre; edtr, Film-Rite Inc; mus supv, George Craig; snd, Emil LeBrun; asst dir, Robert Renzulli. 89.
Mary Mendum, Carl Parker, Marilyn Roberts.
02/04/76

L'Imprecateur
(The Accuser)
(France)
PFC. Action Film-Citel Films prodn. Dir, Jean-Louis Bertuccelli. Sp, Rene-Victor Pilhes, Stephen Becker, Bertuccelli; book, Pilhes; cam (Eastmancolor), Andreas Winding; edtr, Francois Ceppi; art dir, Theo Meurisse; mus, Richard Rodney Bennett. 102.
Jean Yanne, Michel Piccoli, Jean-Pierre Marielle, Jean-Claude Brialy, Michel Lonsdale, Marlene Jobert, Robert Webber, Charles Cioffi, Anton Diffring.
09/14/77

Lin Tse-hsu
(The Opium War)
(Peoples Republic of China)
SIA. A Haiyen Film Studio (Shanghai) prodn. Dir, Chen Chun-li. 90.
Chao Tan, Kao Chen, Haiao Tien, Li Yung, Teng Nan, Lian Shan, Otto Williams, Gerald Tannenbaum, Chien Chien-li, Wen Hsi-ying, Ching Yin.
(English subtitles)
08/23/78

The Lincoln Conspiracy
SSU. Prods, Charles E Sellier Jr, Rayland D Jensen. Dir, James L Conway. Sp, Jonathan Cobbler; cam, Henning Schellerup; edtr, Martin Dreffke; art dir, William Cornford; mus, Bob Summers. (MPAA rating: G). 90.
Bradford Dillman, Robert Middleton, John Anderson, John Dehner, Whit Bissell, James Green.
10/12/77

Linea D'Ombra
(Shadow Line)
(Italy)
X. Prod, Antoniana Film prodns. Wri-dirs, Maurizio Targhetta, Gerardo Fontana; cam, Sergio Fontana; edtr, Emanuele Foglietti; mus, Manuel De Sica, Friedrich Handel. 90.
Giorgio Giacomini.
09/24/80

L'Ingorgo
(The Bottleneck)
(Italy - France - Spain - W Germany)
TIT. Prod, Silvio Clementelli for Clesi (Rome)-Greenwich Film (Paris)-Jose Frades (Madrid) and Albatross (Munich). Dir, Luigi Comencini. Sp, Comencini, Ruggero Maccari and Bernardino Zapponi. Cam (Eastmancolor), Ennio Guarnieri; art dir, Mario Chiari; edtr, Nino Baragli; mus, Fiorenzo Capri. 116.
Alberto Sordi, Orazio Orlando, Annie Girardot, Fernando Rey, Miou Miou, Gerard Depardieu, Ugo Tognazzi, Marcello Mastroianni, Gianni Cavina, Stefania Sandrelli, Harry Baer, Ciccio Ingrassia, Patrick Dewaere.
05/16/79

L'Innocente
(Italy)
RIZ. Rizzoli Film - Jacques Lietienne prodn. Dir, Luchino Visconti. Sp, Susi Ecchi D'Amico, Enrico Medioli, Visconti from book by Gabriele D'Annunzio; cam (Technicolor), Pasqualino De Santis; edtr, Ruggero Mastroianni; art dir, Mario Garbuglia; mus, Franco Mannino. 125.
Laura Antonelli, Giancarlo Giannini, Jennifer O'Neill, Marc Porel, Massimo Girotti, Didier Haudepin, Rina Morelli.
05/26/76

Linus Eller Tegelhusets Hemlighet
(Linus And The Mysterious Red Brick House)
(Sweden)
SVF. Svenska Filminstitutet, Trekovern prodn. Wri-dir, Vilgot Sjoman from his own book. Cam (Eastmancolor), Tony Forsberg, Roland Sterner; edtr, Carl-Olav Skeepstedt; mus, Bengt Ernyd. 113.
Harald Hamrell, Viveca Lindfors, Harriet Andersson, Pernilla Wallgren.
09/19/79

The Lion and the Rat: SEE
Ang Leon At Ang Daga

Lipstick
PAR. Dino De Laurentiis presentation, prod, Freddie Fields. Dir, Lamont Johnson. Sp, David Rayfiel; cam (Technicolor), Bill Butler, Willam A Fraker; edtr, Marion Rothman; mus, Michel Polnareff, Jimmie Haskell; prodn des, Robert Luthardt; set decor, Donfeld; snd, Richard Portman, Robert Post; asst dir, Mickey McCardle. (MPAA rating: R). 89.
Margaux Hemingway, Chris Sarandon, Perry King, Anne Bancroft, Robin Gammell, John Bennett Perry, Mariel Hemingway, Francesco, Bill Burns.
04/07/76

The Little Archimedes: SEE Il
Piccolo Archimede

The Little Convict
(Australia)
RDP. Prod-dir, Yoram Gross. Sp, John Palmer; ani dir, Paul McAdam; character des, Athol Henry, Paul McAdam. 80.
Rolf Harris.
(ANI)
04/23/80

Little Darlings
PAR. Prod, Stephen J Friedman. Dir, Ronald F Maxwell. Sp, Kimi Peck, Darlene Young; cam (Metrocolor), Fred Batka; edtr, Pembroke J Herring; snd, John Speak; prodn des, William Hiney; set decor, Charles Forian; asst dir, Michael Daves; mus, Charles Fox. (MPAA rating: R). 92.
Tatum O'Neal, Kristy McNichol, Armande Assante, Matt Dillon, Krista Errickson, Alexa Kenin, Abby Bluestone, Cynthia Nixon, Simone Schacter, Maggie Blye, Nicolas Coster, Mary Betten.
03/19/80

The Little Dragons
AUR. Eastwind prodn. Prods, Hannah Hempstead, Curtis Hanson. Exec prods, Tony Bill, Robert Bremson. Dir, Curtis Hanson. Sp, Harvey Applebaum, Louis G Atlee, Rudolph Borchert, Alan Ormsby; cam, Stephen Katz; mus, Ken Lauber; art dir, Spencer Quinn; snd, Trevor Black; asst dir, Rick Whiting. (MPAA rating: PG). 90.
Charles Lane, Ann Sothern, Chris Petersen, Pat Petersen, Sally Boyden, Rick Lenz, Sharon Weber, Joe Spinell, John Chandler, Clifford A Pellow, Stephen Young, Pat Johnson, Master Bong Soon Han, Donnie Williams,

Tony Bill, Brad Gorman.
07/23/80

Little Escapes: SEE Les Petites Fugues

The Little Girl in Blue Velvet: SEE La Petite Fille En Velours Bleu

The Little Girl Who Lives Down the Lane
(Canada)
RNK. Zev Braun prodn. Dir, Nicolas Gessner. Exec prods, Harold Greenberg, Alfred Pariser. Sp, Laird Koenig (based on his novel); cam (Panavision), Rene Verzier; edtr, Yves Langlois; asst dirs, Justine Bouchard-Heroux, Charles Braive. (MPAA rating: PG). 91.
Jodie Foster, Martin Sheen, Alexis Smith, Mort Shuman, Scott Jacoby, Dorothy Davis, Clesson Goodhue, Hubert Noel, Jacques Famery, Mary Morter, Judie Wildman.
03/16/77

Little Man: SEE Shraga Katan

Little Marcel: SEE Le Petit Marcel

The Little Mermaid: SEE Mala Morska Vila

The Little Mermaid: SEE Rousalochka

Little Miss Marker
U. Prod, Jennings Lang. Dir-wri, Walter Bernstein, based on a sory by Damon Runyon. Exec prod, Walter Matthau. Cam (Technicolor), Philip Lathrop; edtr, Eve Newman; snd, John Carter; prodn des, Edward C Carfagno; set decor, Hal Gausman; asst dir, Ronald J Martinez; cos, Ruth Morley; mus, Henry Mancini. (MPAA rating: PG). 103.
Walter Matthau, Julie Andrews, Tony Curtis, Bob Newhart, Sara Stimson, Lee Grant, Brian Dennehy, Kenneth McMillan, Andrew Rubin, Joshua Shelley, Nedra Volz, Jacquelyn Hyde.
03/19/80

Little Orphan Sammy
VF. T F P Sammy Co prodn. Prod, Michael Roberts. Dir, Arlo Schiffin; sp, Ron Wertheim; cam, Pierre Schwartz. (Self-applied X rating). 85.
Jennifer Welles, Rocky Millstone, Lin Flanagan, Andrea True, Jamie Gillis, Kim Pope, C J Laing, Sarah Nicholson, Helen Madigan, Nicki Hilton, Al Levitsky, Randy.
06/30/76

The Little Siren: SEE La Petite Sirene

The Little Town of Anara
(USSR)
SOV. Grouzia Film prodn. Wri-dir, Irakly Kvirikadze. Cam (Sovcolor), Youi Kikabidze; mus, T Bakourdaze. 90.
Revaz Essadze, Cecile Takaicvili, Ramaz Tchkhikvadze, Henriette Lejava.
08/23/78

The Little Valentino: SEE A Kis Valentino

Little Virgil and Frogeater Orla: SEE Lille Virgil og Orla Froesnapper

The Little Wheedlers: SEE Les Petits Calins

The Littlest Horse Thief: SEE Escape From the Dark

Living Legend
MAV. Prod, Earl Owensby. Dir, Worth Keeter. Sp, Tom McIntyre; cam (CFI Color), Darrell Cathcart; edtr, Richard Aldridge. (MPAA rating: PG). 92.
Earl Owensby, William T Hicks, Ginger Alden, Jerry Rushing, Greg Carswell, Toby Wallace, Kristina Reynolds.
07/23/80

Ljubav I Bijes
(Love And Rage)
(Yugoslavia)
YFR. Sutjeska Film prodn. Wri-dir, Bakir Tanovic, from story by Novak Simic. Cam (Eastmancolor), Danijal Sukalo; art dir, Kemai Hrustanovic; mus, Zoran Hristic. 92.
Viktor Starcic, Merima Isakovic, Adem Cejvan, Dragomir Bojanic-Gidra.
08/16/78

Ljubavni Zivot Budmira Trajkovica
(Beloved Love)
(Yugoslavia)
YFR. CFS Kosutnjak-Avala Film prodn. Dir, Dejan Karaklajic. Sp, Predrag Perisic, Milan Jelic; cam (Eastmancolor), Zivko Zalar; edtr, Vuksan Lukovac; mus, Milovoj Markovic. 88.
Milena Dravic, Ljubisa Samardzic, Mica Tomic, Predrag Bolpacic, Marina Nemet, Cvitjeta Mesic, Bata Zivojinovic.
08/17/77

Ljubica
(Violet)
(Yugoslavia)
YFR. Croatia Film prodn. Dir, Kreso Golik, Sp, Goran Massot; cam (Eastmancolor), Zivko Zaler; edtr, Katja Majer; mus, Antonio Vivaldi. 92.
Bozidarka Frait, Ivan Stancic, Relja Basic, Miodrag Krivokapic.
08/16/78

Local Color
X. Prod-dir-sp-edtr, Mark Rappaport. Cam (b&w), Fred Murphy. 116.
Jane Campbell, Bob Herron, Dolores Kenan, Michael Burg, Tom Bair, Barry de Jasu, Randy Danson, Temmie Brodkey. (B & W) (16m)
04/26/78

Location Hunting: SEE Reperages

L'Oeil du Maitre
(His Master's Eye)
(France)
GAU. Sabre Films prodn. Prod, Quentin Raspail. Dir, Stephane Kurc. Wris, Kurc, Pierre Geller; cam, Georges Campana; snd, Philippe Lemenuel; edtr, Monique Prim; mus, Pierre Jansen; art dir, Bruno Beauge. 95.
Patrick Chesnais, Olivier Granier, Dominique Laffin, Marina Vlady, Michel Aumont, Daniel Gelin, Jean-Claude Brialy.
04/23/80

Logan's Run
UA. MGM picture, prod, Saul David. Dir, Michael Anderson. Sp, David Zeelag Goodman, from the novel by William F Nolan, George Clayton Johnson; cam (Metrocolor), Ernest Laszlo; special visual effects, L B Abbott; addl visuals, Frank Van Der Veer; edtr, Bob Wyman; mus, Jerry Goldsmith; prodn des, Dale Hennesy; set decor, Robert De Vestel; snd, Jerry Jost, Harry W Tetrick, William McCaughey, Aaron Rochin; asst dir, David Silver; stunt coords, Glen Wilder, Bill Couch. (MPAA rating: PG). 118.
Michael York, Richard Jordan, Jenny Agutter, Roscoe Lee Browne, Farrah Fawcett-Majors, Michael Anderson Jr, Peter Ustinov, Randolph Roberts, Lara Lindsay, Gary Morgan, Michelle Stacy.
06/16/76

Lola's Lolos: SEE Les Lolos De Lola

The Lollipop Girls in Hard Candy
X. Hologram Prodns film. Prod-dir-edtr, Norm de Plume; exec prod, Ken Lambertini. Sp, Mark Thunderbuns, Ann Onymous; mus, The Luscious Lickers. (Self-applied X rating). 75.
Hal Walker, Brenda Ramm, Ken Scudder, Tyler Horne, Heather Grant, John Seemans, Eustis P Snickerton, Candy Collins, Barbara Brown, Sinthia Starr, Laura Raymond, Vicki Cunningham, Ginger Norwood, Sandra Reagan, John C Holmes.
10/20/76

L'Ombre Des Chateaux
(Shadow of the Castles)
(France)
PLF. Camera One prodn. Wri-dir, Daniel Duval. Cam (Eastmancolor), Pierre Lhomme; edtr, Jean-Bernard Bonis; mus, Maurice Wander; prod, Michel Seydoux. 95.
Philippe Leotard, Albert Dray, Zoe Chauveau, Dalio, Stephane Bouy.
12/01/76

Lone Wolf: SEE Birjuk

The Long Drive: SEE Cursa

The Long Good Friday
(Britain)
X. Calendar Prodn for Black Lion Films (Associated Communications Corp.) Prod, Barry Hanson. Dir, John MacKenzie. Sp, Barrie Keeffe; cam, Phil Meheux; edtr, Mike Taylor; mus, Francis Monkman; art dir, Vic Symonds; snd, David John; asst dir, Simon Hinkly. 105.
Bob Hoskins, Helen Mirren, Dave King, Brian Hall, Eddie Constantine, Stephen Davies, Derek Thompson, Bryan Marshall, P H Moriarty, Paul Freeman, Charles Cork, Paul Barber, Patti Love.
05/28/80

The Long Lament: SEE Der Lange Jammer

Long Live. . .: SEE Zendabad

Long Live Ghosts!: SEE At Ziji Duchove!

Long Live Hazana: SEE Arriba Hazana

Long Live Progress: SEE Awans

Long Live the Middle Class: SEE Viva La Clase Media

The Long Riders
UA. Prod, Tim Zinnemann. Dir, Walter Hill. Exec prods, James Keach, Stacy Keach. Sp, Bill Bryden, Steven Phillip Smith, Stacy Keach, James Keach; cam (Technicolor), Ric Waite; edtrs, David Holden, Freeman Davies; mus, Ry Cooder; prodn des, Jack T Collis; art dir, Peter Romero; set decor, Richard Goddard; cos supv, Tom Bronson; snd, James Webb, Chris McLaughlin; asst dir, Peter Gries. (MPAA rating: R). 100.
David Carradine, Keith Carradine, Robert Carradine, James Keach, Stacy Keach, Dennis Quaid, Randy Quaid, Kevin Brophy, Harry Carey Jr, Christopher Guest, Nicholas Guest, Shelby Leverington, Felice Orlandi, Pamela Reed, James Remar, Fran Ryan, Savannah Smith, Amy Stryker, James Whitmore Jr, John Bottoms, West Buchanan.
05/07/80

Long Shot
(Britain)
X. Mithras Films prodn. Prod-dir, Maurice Hatton. Sp, Hatton, Eoin McCann, and cast; cams, Michael Davis, Michael Dodds, Ivan Strasburg, Maurice Hatton, Teo Davis; edtr, Howard Sharp; mus, Terry Dougherty; snd, Diana Ruston, Eoin McCann, Peter Rann. 85.
Charles Gormley, Neville Smith, Ann Zelda, David Stone, Suzanne Danielle, Ron Taylor, Wim Wenders, Stephen Frears, Jim Haines, Maurice Bulbulian, William Forsyth, Richard Demarco, Alan Bennett, Sarah Boston, Mel Claman, Susannah York, Dennis Selinger, Sandy Lieberson, John Boorman.
11/29/78

The Long Vacation of Lotte H Eisner: SEE Die Langen Ferien Der Lotte H Eisner

The Long Vacations of '36: SEE Las Largas Vacaciones Del 36

Long Weekend
(Australia)
X. Dugong Films presentation. Prod, Richard Brennan. Dir, Colin Eggleston. Sp, Everett De Roche; mus, Michael Carlos; cam (Panavision-Eastmancolor), Vincent Monton; edtr, Brian Kavanagh; art dir, Larry Eastwood; cos, Kevin Reagan; snd, John Phillips; set decor, Tony Hunt. 100.
John Hargreaves, Briony Behets, Mike McEwen, Michael Aitkins, Roy Day, Sue Kiss von Soly.
05/10/78

The Long Weekend: SEE La Puente

The Longest Journey: SEE Najdolgiot Pat

Look Chao Phya
(Son Of Chao Phya)
(Thailand)
NTK. Prod-dir, Charint Nantanakorn. Story, Rapiporn; sp, Tavorn Suwan; cam, Pipat Payaka; mus, Narint Suvphapa; edtr, Palong Keowprasert; art dir, Charoen Radakom; asst dir, Nantavat; snd, Asvin Studio; mus, Paiboon Studio; snd mixing-color processing, Tokyo Laboratories and Toho Film Co. 120.
Sombat Metanee, Petchara Chaovarat, Suriya Chinaphan, Piyamatr Monjakul, Tat Ekatat, Pirumpon Yimlamai, Sopa Sopaporn, Ek Somchart, Taksin Jamporn, Prachuab Lerkyamdi.
11/30/77

Look See. . .: SEE Ecoute Voir. . .

Looking For Mr. Goodbar
PAR. Prod, Freddie Fields. Adapt-dir, Richard Brooks, based on the novel by Judith Rossner; cam (Metrocolor), William A Fraker; edtr, George Grenville; mus, Artie Kane; art dir, Edward Carfagno; set decor, Ruby Levitt; snd, Richard Portman, Curly Thirlwell, Robert W Glass Jr, Al Overton Jr; cos-ward, Jodie Lynn Tillen; asst dir, David Silver. (MPAA rating: R). 135.
Diane Keaton, Tuesday Weld, William Atherton, Richard Kiley, Richard Gere, Alan Feinstein, Tom Berenger, Priscilla Pointer, Laurie Prange, Joel Fabiani, Julius Harris, Richard Bright, LeVar Burton, Marilyn Coleman, Elizabeth Cheshire.
10/19/77

Looking Up
L-P. First American Films prodn. Prods, Linda Yellen, Karen Rosenberg. Dir, Yellen. Sp, Jonathan Platnick; cam (Movielab color), Arpad Makay, Lloyd Friedas; art dir, John Annus; edtr, John Carter; mus, Brad Fiedel. (MPAA rating: PG). 94.
Marilyn Chris, Dick Shawn, Doris Belack, Harry Goz, Jacqueline Brookes, Naomi Riseman, Will Hussing, Neva Small, George Reinholt, Gillian Goll, Ellen Sherman, Susan McKinley, Anthony Mannino, Paul Lieber, Paul Christopoulos, Lee Wilson, Estelle Harris, Izzy Singer, Barry Burns, Michael Vale, Andrew Smith, Jack Weissbluth, Barbara Andress, Ruth Franklin, Miguel Pinero, Dadi Pinero, Jacqueline Tuteur, June Berry, Sally DeMay, Edith Weissbluth, Jill Weissbluth, Sarah Phillips, Ted Butler, Frederica Minte, Joshua Freund, Ginger James, Gizella Mittleman.
03/16/77

Loose Ends
X. American Eagle - Fat Chance Inc prodn. Wri-dir-prods, David Burton Morris, Victoria Wozniak. Cam, Gregory M Cummins; mus, John Paul Hammond. 103.
Chris Mulkeuy, John Jenkins, Linda Jenkins. (B & W) (16m)
09/15/76

The Lord of the Rings
UA. Fantasy Films Saul Zaentz prodn. Dir, Ralph Bakshi. Sp, Chris Conkling, Peter S Beagle, based on stories of J R R Tolkien; cam, Timothy Galfas; edtr, Donald W Ernst; mus, Leonard Rosenman. (MPAA rating: PG). 131.
Voices of Christopher Guard, William Squire, Michael Scholes, John Hurt, Simon Chandler, Dominic Guard, Norman Bird, Michael Graham-Cox, Anthony Daniels, David Buck, Peter Woodthorpe, Fraser Kerr, Philip Stone, Michael Deacon, Andre Morell, Alan Tilvern, John Westbrook, Annette Crosbie.
(ANI)
11/08/78

L'Ordinateur Des Pompes Funebres
(The Undertaker Parlor Computer)
(France)
IMA. Lira Films-Prod Atlas Cinematografica prodn. Dir, Gerard Pires. Sp, Jean-Patrick Manchette, Pires from book by Walter Kempley; cam (Eastmancolor), Michael Serrezin; edtr, Jacques Witta. 95.
Jean-Louis Trintignant, Mireille Darc, Bernadette Lafont, Lea Massari, Bernard Fresson, Claude Pieplu.
04/21/76

L'Ordre Et La Securite Du Monde
(Order And Security Of The World)
(France)
CII. Dedalus-Seul Audio-visuel-FR3 prodn in asso with the American Sign Co. Dir, Claude D'Anna. Sp, D'Anna, Francoise Bonin; cam (Eastmancolor), Eddy Van Der Enden; edtr, Kenout Peltier; mus, Claude Nougaro, Maurice Vander; prods, Henry Lange, Francois Lesterlin. 105.
Bruno Cremer, Donald Pleasence, Laure Dechasnel, Dennis Hopper, Joseph Cotten, Gabriele Ferzetti, Michel Bouquet, Pierre Santini, Henri Serre.
07/26/78

L'Orfeo
(Orpheus)
(Germany - Switzerland)
X. Unitel Film Munich prodn. Wri-dir, Jean-Pierre Ponnelle, from the Claudio Monteverdi opera. Cond, Nikolaus Harnoncourt; cam (Eastmancolor), Wolfgang Treu; snd, H Muehle; cos, Pet Halmen; art dir, Claus Helmut Drese. 103.
Trudeliese Schmidt, Philippe Huttenlocher, Dietlinde Turban, Rachel Yakar, Glenys Linos, Hans Franzen, Werner Groeschel, Roland Hermann, Suzanne Calabro, Peter Keller, Francisco Araiza, Christian Boesch, Rudolf A Hartmann, Jozsef Dene.
(OPERA)
10/18/78

Los Adolescentes
(The Adolescents)
(Spain)
WBS. Impala prodn. Dir, Pedro Maso. Sp, Pedro Maso, Santiago Moncada; set, Gil Parrondo; cam (Eastmancolor), Jorge Herrero; edtr, Alfonso Santacana; mus, Juan Carlos Calderon. 93.
02/11/76

Los Albaniles
(The Bricklayers)
(Mexico)
X. Conacine S A and Marco Polo S A prodn. Dir, Jorge Fons. Sp, Vicente Lenero, Fons, Luis Carrion, based on story by Lenero; cam (Eastmancolor), Alex Phillips Jr; edtr, Eufemio Rivera; mus, Gustavo Cesar Carrion. 113.
Ignacio Lopez Tarso, Jaime Fernandez, David Silva, Katy Jurado, Jose Alonso, Salvador Sanchez, Jose Carlos Ruiz, Adalberto Martinez.
07/06/77

Los Dias Del Pasado
(Days of the Past)
(Spain)
X. Impala prodn. Dir, Mario Camus. Sp, Antonio Betancort, Mario Camus; cam (Eastmancolor), Hans Burmann; mus, Anton Garcia Abril; sets, Rafael Palmero; edtr, Javier Moran. 105.
Marisol, Antonio Gades, Gustavo Berges, Antonio Iranzo, Fernando Sanchez-Polack, Saturnino Cerra, Manuel Alexandre, Mario Pardo.
04/26/78

Los Gusanos
(The Worms)
(Cuba)
X. Danilo Bardisa prodn. Prod, Danilo Bardisa. Dir, Camilo Vila. Sp, Vila, Bardisa from play by Eduardo Corbe; cam, Ramon Saurez; edtrs, Stephen Sheppard, John Paul Jones; snd, Kert Vandermeulen; asst dir, Alan Martin. 95.
Orestes Matachena, Mario Pena, Raymundo Hidalgo-Gato, Clara Hernandez, Marco Santiago, Ruben Rebasa, Doris Castellanos, Reynaldo Medina, Angela Hayden.
(Spanish with English subtitles)
02/13/80

Los Miedos
(Fears)
(Argentina)
X. Isla Cinematographica prodn. Dir, Alejandro Doria; sp, Doria, Cernadas Lamadrid; cam, Miguel Rodriguez; score, Luis Maria Serra; edtr, Silvia Ripoll. 100.
Tita Merello, Soledad Silveyra, Miguel Angel Sola, Maria Leal, Sandra Mihanovich, Anibal Morixe, Littl Gonzalez.
09/10/80

Los Ojos Vendados
(Blindfolded Eyes)
(Spain)
X. Elias Querejeta prodn. Wri-dir, Carlos Saura; asso prods, Claude Pierson, Tony Moliere; edtr, Pablo G Del Amo; cam, Teo Escamilla; sets, Antonio Belizon. 109.
Geraldine Chaplin, Jose Luis Gomez, Xabier Elorriaga, Lolola Cardona, Andre Falcon, Carmen Maura.
05/31/78

Los Pajaros De Baden-Baden
(The Birds of Baden-Baden)
(Spain)
X. Impala and Arpa prodn. Dir, Mario Camus. Sp, Mario Camus, Manuel Marinero, based on novel by Ignacio Aldecoa; cam (Eastmancolor), Hans Burman; mus, Anton Garcia Abril; edtr, Javier Moran. 106.
Catherine Spaak, Frederic de Pasquale, Jose Luis Alonso, Carlos Larranaga, Andres Mejuto, Antonio Iranzo, Candida Losada, Alejandro de Enciso.
02/25/76

Los Restos Del Naufragio
(The Remains of the Shipwreck)
(Spain)
X. Icine-Televisa-Promociones Aura-Mon-Vel prodn. Exec prod, Jose Maria Pascual; prodn dir, Jose Maria Cunilles. Wri-dir, Ricardo Franco. Cam (Eastmancolor), Cecilio Paniagua; edtr, Guillermo Sanchez Maldonado; mus, David Thomas; sets, Joes Antonio de la Guerra. 98.
Fernando Fernan Gomez, Angela Molina, Ricardo Franco, Alfredo Mayo, Felicidad Blanc, Luis Ciges.
05/31/78

Los Sobrevivientes
(Survivors)
(Cuba)
X. ICAIC prodn. Dir, Thomas Gutierrez Alea. Sp, Antonio Benitez, Gutierrez Alea; cam, Mario Garcia Joya; mus, Leo Brouwer. 116.
Enrique Santisteban, Reinaldo Miravalles, German Pinelli, Ana Vinas, Vincente Revuelta; Carlos Ruiz de la Tejera, Leonor Borrero.
05/30/79

Los Tres Reyes Magos
(The Three Wise Men)
(Mexico)
COX. C F A Ruiz and Cinsa prodn. Dir-sp, Adolfo Torres Portillo. Mus, Jose Antonio Zavala; cam (Eastmancolor), Victor Pena, Francisco Mortera; ani dir, Fernando Ruiz; ani, Daniel Martinez, Ismael Linares, Moises Velazco, Rafael Escudero, Israel Vilchis, Rolando Ruccione, Carlos Rodriguez; dubbing, Carlos David Ortigosa. 90.
(ANI)
07/14/76

Lost and Found
COL. Prod-dir, Melvin Frank. Exec prod, Arnold Kopelson. Sp, Melvin Frank, Jack Rose; cam, Douglas Slocombe; edtr, Bill Butler; prodn des, Trevor Williams; set decor, Gerry Holmes; art dir, Ted Tester; snd, John Mitchell; mus, John Cameron; asst dir, Tony Lucibello. (MPAA rating: PG). 106.
George Segal, Glenda Jackson, Maureen Stapleton, Hollis McLaren, John Cunningham, Paul Sorvino, Kenneth Pogue, Janie Sell, Diana Barrington.
06/27/79

Lost And Found: SEE Oggetti Smarriti

The Lost Angel: SEE Der Verlorene Engel

Lost Paradise: SEE Het Verloren Paradise

The Lost Way: SEE Le Chemin Perdu

Louie
(Thailand)
NFT. Prod, Kiat lampungporn. Dir, Root Ronapop. Story, Seni Busapaketr; sp, Weeraprawat Wongpuapan; cam, Kawi Kiatnan; mus, Prasert Churaketr; snd, Pong Assavilakul; art dir, Prakob Yaisuri; asst dir, Chacheep Chantanimitr. 130.
Sombat Metanee, Sorapong Chatri, Uthen Boonyong, Aranya Namwong, Kanchit Kaunpracha, Adul Doonyarat, Saard Piyampongsan, Manop Assawathep, Duangchai Hataikan, Pipop Pupinyo, Krisana Amnuayporn, Poo Chindanoot, Sathit Kerdkampeng, Mayurachat Muenpasitiwet, Kitti Daskorn, Dam Daskorn, Bo Vibulnan.
03/16/77

Loulou
(France)
GAU. Gaumont-Action Films prodn. Dir, Maurice Pialat. Sp, Arlette Langmann, Pialat; cam (Eastmancolor), Pierre William Glenn, Jacques Loiseleux; edtr, Yann Dedet, Sophie Coussein. 110.
Isabelle Huppert, Gerard Depardieu, Guy Marchand, Humbert Balsan, Bernard Tronczyk, Christian Boucher.
05/28/80

The Louvre Museum: SEE Le Musee du Louvre

Love and Faith; Lady Ogin: SEE Oginsaga

Love: SEE Kaerleken

Love and Adventure: SEE Liebe Und Abenteuer

Love and Bullets
(Britain)
ITC. Lew Grade presentation. Prod, Pancho Kohner. Dir, Stuart Rosenberg. Sp, Wendell Mayes, John Melson; cam, Fred Koenekamp (US), Anthony Richmond (Switzerland); mus, Lalo Schifrin; prodn des, John De Cuir; edtr, Michael Anderson; snd, Gene Garvin, John Bramall; cos, Dorothy Jeakins; asst dir, Jack Aldworth. 95.
Charles Bronson, Rod Steiger, Jill Ireland, Strother Martin, Bradford Dillman, Henry Silva, Paul Koslo, Sam Chew, Michael Gazzo, Val Avery, Bill Gray, Andy Romano, Robin Clarke, Cliff Pellow, Lorraine Chase.
03/28/79

Love and Cool Water: SEE Fraiche

Love And Rage: SEE Ljubav I Bijes

Love And The Midnight Auto Supply
PRG. James Polakof film. Exec prod, Beverley Johnson. Prod-dir-wri, James Polakof; cam (Movielab Color), Lawrence Raimond; edtr, Irving Rosenblum; art dir, Perry Ferguson II; snd, Keith Wester; mus, Ed Bogas; stunt coord, Richard Butler. (MPAA rating: PG). 93.
Michael Parks, Linda Cristal, Scott Jacoby, Bill Adler, Colleen Camp, Monica Gayle, Sedena Spivey, George McCalister, John Ireland, Rory Calhoun, Rod Cameron, Burt Freed.
06/07/78

Love At First Bite
AIP. Melvin Simon prodn. Exec prods, George Hamilton, Robert Kaufman, Joel Freeman; dir, Stan Dragoti; wri, Robert Kaufman; cam (CFI), Edward Rosson; edtrs, Mort Fallick, Allan Jacobs; snd, Don Bassman; prodn des, Serge Krizman; asso prod, Harold L Vanarnum; chor, Alex Romero; mus, Charles Bernstein. (MPAA rating: PG.) 96.
George Hamilton, Susan Saint James, Richard Benjamin, Dick Shawn, Arte Johnson, Sherman Hemsley, Isabel Sanford.
04/11/79

Love At First Sight
(Canada)
AST. Quadrant Films prodn. Prod, Peter O'Brian. Exec prods, John Trent, David Perlmutter. Wri-dir, Rex Bromfield. Cam, Henri Fiks; edtr, Alan Collins; art dir, Tony Hall; snd, Douglas Ganton, Ronald Sanders, Paul Coombe; mus, Roy Payne. 85.
Mary Ann McDonald, Dan Aykroyd, Jane Mallett, George Murray, Barry Morse, Mignon Elkins, Les Carlson.
07/20/77

Love Between the Raindrops: SEE Laski Mezi Kapkami Deste

Love Follows Rain
(South Korea)
JWJ. Dir, Jin Woo Jung. Sp, Donghoon Yoo; cam (Eastmancolor), Jung Nin Suh;
01/26/77 mus, Sung Jo Chung. 100.
Hyung Tae Lee, Yung Ok Lee.

Love In A Taxi
X. Davey Company prodn. Prod-dir, Robert Sickinger; sp, Michael Kortchmar; cam, Joseph Mangine; art dir, Steven Vickers; edtr, Bill Freda; snd, Dale Whitman; mus, Susan Minsky. 90.
Diane Sommerfield, James H Jacobs, Earl Monroe, Malik Murray, Lisa Jane Persky, Lyle Kessler, Karen Grannum, Phil Rubinstein, Al Fann, Bill Moor, Hannibal Penney Jr, Tony Capra, Dorothy Leon.
09/17/80

Love In Question: SEE L'Amour En Question

Love Is Blue: SEE Kuam Rak See Dam

Love Lesson: SEE Licao de Amor

Love Living, Live Loving: SEE Liebe Das Leben-Lebe Das Lieben

The Love of a Little Girl: SEE Tirak Cong Norng Noo

Love Of Perdition: SEE Amor Der Perdicao

Love of the White Snake
(Hong Kong)
FOG. C H Wong, Exec Prod. Dir, Szu-Ma Ke. Cam, Chen Ching Chu; sp, Szu-Ma Ke; sfx, Tadashi Nishimoto. 98.
Lin Ching Hsia, Charles Chi, Chin Chih Min, Li Kun.
(English subtitles)
08/23/78

Love on the Run: SEE L'Amour En Fuite

Love Swindlers
(Hong Kong)
SHW. Run Run Shaw prodn. Wri-dir, Li Han-hsiang. Cam, Lin Chao; prodn mgr, Hsieh Chih; asst dirs, Hsia Tsu-hui, Ma Fei; edtr, Chiang Hsing-lung; art dir, Chen Ching-shen; makeup, Wu Hsu-ching; snd recording, Wang Yung-hua. 98.
Deadly Injections: Ku Feng, Wu Ming-tsai, Oyyang Sha-fei.
   Counterfiet: Shaw Yin-Yin, Dana, Chan Shen.
   Social Disease: Kang Kai, Hsia Ping, Wang Ping, Chaing Nan.
   Hire Purchase: Shirley Yu, Yueh Hua, Chen Ping, Tien Ching, Liu Lu-hua.
(English Subtitles)
10/20/76

Lover, Wife: SEE Mogliamante

The Lovers: SEE Koo Rak

The Lovers' Wind
(Iran)
X. Iran National Film Center prodn. Prod-dir, albert Lamorisse; re-edited by Mehrdad Azarmi; text, Roger Glachant; cam, Guy Tabary, Raymond Letouzey; edtrs, Denise de Casabianca, Claude Lamorisse; mus, Hosein Dehlavi. 74. (DOC)
04/11/79

The Loves And Times Of Scaramouche
(Italy - Yugoslavia)
AVE. Prod, Federico Aicardi. Dir, Enzo G Castellari. Sp, Tito Carpi, Castellari; cam (Telecolor), Giovanni Bergamini; edtr, Gianfranco Amicucci; mus, Dammico Bixio, Frizzi, Tempera; art dir, Enzo Bulgarelli; set decors, Riccardo Dominici, Tihomir Piletic; snd, Pietro Spadoni; asst dirs, Roberto Pariante, Vanja Aljinovic; stunt coord, Rocco Lero. (MPAA rating: PG). 91.
Michael Sarrazin, Ursula Andress, Aldo Maccione, Giancarlo Prete, Michael Forrest, Nico Il Grande, Romano Puppo, Massimo Vanni, Alex Togni, Damir Mejovsek, Lucia De Oliveira.
(Dubbed English soundtrack)
03/17/76

Loving Couples
FOX. Prod, Renee Valente; exec prod, David Susskind; dir, Jack Smight; sp, Martin Donovan; cam (Metrocolor), Philip Lathrop; edtrs, Grey Fox, Frank Urioste; snd, Lee Alexander; art dir, Jan Scott; asst dir, Carl Olsen; asso prod, Andrew Susskind; mus, Fred Karlin. (MPAA rating: PG). 97.
Shirley MacLaine, James Coburn, Susan Sarandon, Stephen Collins, Sally Kellerman, Nan Martin, Shelly Batt.
09/10/80

Loving Cousins
(Italy)
IIP. Carlo Ponti prodn. Dir, Sergio Martino. Sp, Martino, Sarro Scarosini, Fernando Poli; cam (Eastmancolor), Giancarlo Ferrando; edtr, Eugenio Alabiso; art dir, Franco Calabrese; mus, Claudio Narrone. (MPAA rating: R). 87.

Susan Player, Hugh Griffith, Claudio Nicastro, Riccardo Cucciola, Rosalba Neri, Alfredo Pea.
(Dubbed English soundtrack)
04/14/76

Lucie
(Norway)
NSK. Wri-dir, Jan Erik Duering, based on novel by Amalie Skram. Cam (Eastmancolor), Hans Nord; edtr, Bente Kaas; mus, Terje Rypdal; exec prod, Harld Ohrvik.   96.
Inger Lise Rypdal, Goesta Ekman, Kari Simonsen, Nils Sletta, Rut Tellefsen, Alf Nordvang.
09/19/79

The Lucky Star
(Canada)
X. Tele-Metropole International presentation of a Claude Leger Prodn. Exec prod, Andre Fleury. Prod, Claude Leger. Dir, Max Fischer. Cam, Frank Tidy; sp, Fischer, Jack Rosenthal from original idea by Roland Topor; mus, Art Philipps; edtr, Yves Langlois.   110.
Rod Steiger, Louise Fletcher, Lou Jacobi, Brett Marx, Helen Hughes, Yvon Dufour.
05/28/80

Luda Kuca
(A Mess In The House)
(Yugoslavia)
YFR. Jadran Film prodn. Dir, Ljubisa Ristic; sp, Nermina Ferizegovic, Nada Kokotovic, Lazar Stojanovic, Ristic; cam (Eastmancolor), Enes Midzic.   105.
Miodrag Krivokapic, Zvonimir Zoricic, Zdenka Hersak, Ratko Buljan, Janez Bormez, Stane Potisk, Petar Dobric, Jelica Lovric.
08/27/80

Lude Godina
(Foolish Years)
(Yugoslavia)
YFR. Zvezda Film prodn. Wri-dir, Zoran Calic. Cam (Eastmancolor), Milivoje Milivojevic; mus, Kornelije Kovac.   85.
Rialda Kadric, Vladimir Petrovic, Bata Zivojinovic, Ljubisa Samardzic.
08/16/78

Ludi Dani
(Crazy Days)
(Yugoslavia)
YFR. Jadran Film-Croatia Film prodn. Wri-dir, Nikola Babic. Cam (Eastmancolor), Andrija Pivcevic; mus, Branislav Zivkovic.   90.
Zvonko Lepetic, Ilija Ivezic, Spaso Papac, Perica Martinovic, Bozidar Bozan.
08/17/77

Lulekoqet Mbi Mure
(Red Poppies on the Wall)
(Albania)
ALA. Albfilm Prodn, Tirana. Dir, Dhimiter Anagnosti. Sp, Petraq Quafzezi, Anagnosti; cam (b&w), Pellumb Kallfa; art dir, Namik Prizreni; mus, Kujtim Laro.   100.
Timo Flloko, Agim Qirjaqi, Kadri Roshi, Alfred Kote, Liza Laska, Anastas Kristofori, Luan Qerimi, Enver Dauti, Strazimir Zaimi, Enea Zeku, Artur Huxholli.
(B & W)
01/24/79

Lulu
X. Prod-dir-cam-edtr, Ronald Chase. Sp, Frank Wedehind; mus, Alban Berg; co-edtrs, Jay Miracle, Todd Boekelheide, Bonnie Koehler; art dirs, Vance Martin, Donald Eastman.   94.
Paul Shenar, Elisa Leonelli, John Roberdeau, Norma Leistiko, Stephen Ashbrook, Warren Pierce, Michael Anderson, Thomas Roberdeau.
(OPERA)
05/24/78

Lulu
(France - Germany - Italy)
PFC. Television 13 (Munich)-Capitol Films, Medusa (Rome)-Elephant Prodn and Whodunit (Paris) co-prodn. Prod, Ralph Baum. Wri-des-dir, Walerian Borowczyk, based on "Earth Spirit" and "Pandora's Box" by Frank Wedekind. Cam (Fujicolor), Michael Steinke; snd, Wolfgang Kapst.   95.
Ann Bennent, Michele Placido, Jean-Jacques Delbo, Heinz Bennent, Hans Jurgen Schatz, Beate Kopp, Udo Kier.
07/23/80

Lumiere
(France)
GAU. Orphee Arts (Claire Duval) - FR3 prodn. Wri-dir, Jeanne Moreau. Cam (Eastmancolor), Richard Aronovitch; edtr, Albert Jurgenson; mus, Astor Piazzola.   95.
Jeanne Moreau, Francine Racette, Lucia Bose, Caroline Cartier, Marie Henriau, Monique Tarbes, Keith Carradine, Bruno Ganz, Francois Simon, Francis Huster, Niels Arestrup, Jacques Spiesser.
04/07/76

Luna
(Italy)
FOX. Prod, Fiction Film. Dir, Bernardo Bertolucci. Sp, Giuseppe and Clare Peploe; cam (Eastmancolor), Vittorio Storato; art dir, Gianni Silvestri, Maria Paola Maino; edtr, Gabriella Cristiani; mus excerpts from Giuseppe Verdi.   145.
Jill Clayburgh, Matthew Barry, Fred Gwynne, Veronica Lazar, Renato Salvatori, Tomas Milian.
09/05/79

L'Une Chante L'Antre Pas
(One Sings, The Other Does Not)
(France)
GAU. Cine Tamaris prodn. Wri-dir, Agnes Varda. Cam (Eastmancolor), Charlie Van Damme; edtr, Joelle Van Effenterre; mus, Francois Wertheimer.   120.
Valerie Mairesse, Therese Liotard, Robert Dadies, Ali Affi, Jean-Pierre Pellegrin, Francois Wertheimer.
02/16/77

Lyftet
(Sweden)
EUR. Europa Film/RI-Film prodn. Dir, Christer Dahl. Sp, Kennet Ahl; based on novel by Kennet Ahl (pseudonym for Christer Dahl and Lasse Storemstedt); cam (Eastmancolor), Lass Bjoerne; mus, Robert Cornford; edtrs, Kennet Ahl, Roger Sellberg.   118.
Anders Loennbro, Bodil Martensson, Roland Jansson, Karl-Erik Heiknert, Siv Eriks.
03/29/78

Ma Bhoomi
(Our Land)
(India)
PDI. Dir, Goutam Ghose. Sp, Kishan Chander, Partho Bannerji, Narasing Rao; cam, Kamal Naik; edtr, Raj Gopal.   150.
Siachand, Bhpal Reddy, Yadagini Kakarala.
(B & W)
02/06/80

Ma Cherie
(My Dearest)
(France - Belgium)
LML. Films Moliere-Challenge Prodns-Pierre Films (Brussels) co-prodn. Prod, Tony Moliere. Dir, Charlotte Dubreuil. Wris, Dubreuil, Judith Goldblath, Edouard Luntz; cam (Eastmancolor), Gilbert Duhalde; mus, Jean-Pierre Mas; sng, "Ma Cherie" wri and sung by Anne Sylvestre; edtr, Michele Maquet; snd, Alix Comte.   90.
Marie-Christine Barrault, Beatrice Bruno.
04/02/80

Ma'Agalim
(Circles)
(Israel)
X. Yehezkel Aloani Presentation. Prods, Yehezkel Aloani, Yaakov Kotzky. Wri-dir, Idith Schehori. Cam, Nurith Aviv; addl pho, Gad Danzig; edtr, Ludmilla Goliath.   84.
Galith Roitman, Hava Ortman, Noa Cohen-Raz, Rachel Schein.
07/09/80

Maaske Ku' Vi
(Could We Maybe)
(Denmark)
KID. Steen Herdel prodn. Dir, Morten Arnfred, based on idea by Lasse Nielsen. Cam (Eastmancolor), Arnfred, Morton Bruus; edtr, Janus Billeskov Jansen; mus, Sebastian (Knud Joergensen).   93.
Marianne Svendsen, Karl Wagner, Ole Ernst.
02/25/76

Mababangong Bangungot
(The Perfumed Nightmare)
(Philippines)
ZSP. Kidlat Tahimik prodn. Prod-dir-wri, Tahimik. Cam (8m), Tahimik, Harmut Lerch; edtr, Tahimik; mus, traditional (Filipino).   95.
Tahimik, Dolores Santamaria, Mang Fely, Georgette Baudry, Katrin Muller.
(16m)
12/10/80

Mackan
(Sweden)
SVE. Drakfilm (Hans Iveberg)-Swedish Film Institute-AB Svensk Film prodn. Sp-dir, Birgitta Svensson. Cam (Eastmancolor), Peter Davidson, Lasse Karlsson; mus, Jan Lindell with special arrangements by Christer Boustedt; edtr, Thomas Holewa; exec prod, Pelle Berglund.   106.
Maria Andersson, Kare Molder, Franciskan von Koch.
03/29/78

MacArthur

U. Zanuck/Brown prodn, prod, Frank McCarthy. Dir, Joseph Sargent. Sp, Hal Barwood, Matthew Robbins; cam (Technicolor), Mario Tosi; edtr, George Jay Nicholson; mus, Jerry Goldsmith; prodn des, John J Lloyd; set decor, Hal Gausman; snd, Don Sharpless, Robert L Hoyt; asst dir, Scott Maitland; stunt coord, Joe Canutt. (MPAA rating: PG). 128.
Gregory Peck, Ed Flanders, Dan O'Herlihy, Marj Dusay, Sandy Kenyon, Nicolas Coster, Dick O'Neill, Yuki Shimoda, John Fujioka.
06/29/77

The Mad Cage: SEE La Cage Aux Folles

Mad Dog
(Australia)
BEF. Motion Picture Company prodn. Prod, Jeremy Thomas. Dir-wri, Philippe Mora based on book, "Morgan the Bold Bushranger" by Margaret Carnegie; cam (Panavision), Mike Molloy; edtr, John Scott; mus, Patrick Flynn; art dir, Bob Hilditch; snd, Ken Hammond; asst dir, Michael Lake. (MPAA rating: R). 102.
Dennis Hopper, Jack Thompson, David Gulpilil, Frank Thring, Michael Pate, Wallas Eaton, Bill Hunter, John Hargreaves, Martin Harris, Robin Ramsay.
05/05/76

Mad Dog: SEE Wsciekly

Mad Max
(Australia)
RDP. Mad Max Pty Ltd prodn. Prod, Byron Kennedy. Dir, George Miller, Sp, George Miller, James McCausland, from story by Miller and Kennedy; cam (Todd-AO, Color), David Eggby; edtrs, Tony Paterson, Cliff Hayes; mus, Brian May; snd, Gary Wilkens; art dir, Jon Dowding; stunt coord, Grant Page. 90.
Mel Gibson, Joanne Samuel, Hugh Keays-Byrne, Steve Bisley, Roger Ward, Vince Gil, Tim Burns, Lulu Pinkus, Nick Lathouris, John Ley, Steve Millichamp, Sheila Florance, Max Fairchild, Steven Clark, George Novak.
05/16/79

Madam Kitty
(Italy - Germany - France)
TA. Coralta Cinematografica/Cinema Seven Film/Les Fox Europa co-prodn. Prods, Giulio Sbarigia, Ermanno Donati; exec prod, Carla Cipriani. Dir, Giovanni Tinto Brass. Sp, Ennio de Concini, Maria Pia Fusco, Tinto Brass; English dial, Louise Vincent; cam (Eastmancolor), Silvano Ippoliti; edtr, Tinto Brass; mus, Fiorenzo Carpi; songs, Carpi, Derry Hall; prodn des, Ken Adam; art dir, Enrico Fiorentini, Jan Schlubach; cos, Ugo Pericoli, Jost Jakob; asst dir, Peppe Scavuzzo. (MPAA rating: X). 110.
Helmut Berger, Ingrid Thulin, Therese Ann Savoy, Bekim Fehmiu, John Steiner, Stefano Satta Flores, Dan Van Husen, John Ireland, Alexandra Bogojevich, Rosemarie Lindt, Paola Senatore, Sara Sperati, Tina Aumont.
01/19/77

Madame Claude
(France)
WBC. Orphee Arts prodn. Dir, Just Jaeckin. Sp, Andre G Brunelin from the book "Allo" by Jacques Quoirez; cam (Eastmancolor), Robert Fraisse; edtr, Marie-Sophie Dubus; mus, Serge Gainsbourg. 110.
Francoise Fabian, Dayle Haddon, Murray Head, Maurice Ronet, Vibeke Knudsen, Klaus Kinski, Andre Falcon, Robert Webber, Jean Gaven, Francois Perrot.
05/18/77

Maden
(The Mine)
(Turkey)
X. Maden Film Prodn, Istanbul. Dir-sp, Yavuz Ozkan. Cam, Izzat Akay; mus, O Zulfu Livaneli. 95.
Cuneyt Arkim, Tarik Akan, Hale Soygazi, Meral Orhansoy.
08/02/78

Madness, The Whole Life Is Madness: SEE Wahnsinn, Das Ganze Leben Ist Wahnsinn

Mado
(France)
FBE. Dir, Claude Sautet. Sp, Claude Neron, Sautet; cam (Eastmancolor), Jean Boffety; edtr, Jacqueline Thiedot; mus, Philippe Sarde. 135.
Michel Piccoli, Ottavia Piccolo, Jacques Dutronc, Romy Schneider, Charles Denner, Julien Guiomar, Michel Arnaud, Bernard Fresson.
11/17/76

Maenak America
(The Pot)
(Thailand)
HFT. Prod-dir, Lek Kitipraporn; sp, Leo V Gordon; cam, Tom Lau; asst dir, Santa Pestonyi; edtr, Lek Kitipraporn. 95.
Lisa Farringer, Krung Srivilai, Peatip Kumvong, Malee Wetprasert, Sitao.
01/14/76

Maes
(May)
(Greece)
X. Synergatiki EPE prodn. Wri-dir, Tassos Psarras. Cam, Stavros Hassapis; mus, Loukianos Keleadonis. 100.
Vassilis Gopis, Aspassia Papathanassiou, Vaguelis Kazan.
10/27/76

The Mafu Cage
CLU. Dir, Karen Arthur. Sp, Don Chastain from French play by Eric Wesphal; cam, John Bailey; edtr, Carol Littleton; mus, Roger Kellaway. 102.
Lee Grant, Carol Kane, Will Geer, James Olson.
05/24/78

Magandang Gabi Sa Inyong Lahat
(Good Evening to Everybody)
(Philippines)
PMP. Nora Aunor and Tirso Cruz 3d prodn. Dir, Lupita A Concio. Story-sp, Orlando Nadres; cam, Joe Batac; mus, Ryan Cayabyab. 100.
Nora Aunor, Tirso Cruz 3d, Romy Mallari, Virginia Montes, Bebong Osorio.
06/23/76

Magic
FOX. Joseph E Levine presentation. Exec prod, C O Erickson. Prods, Joseph E Levine, Richard P Levine. Dir, Richard Attenborough. Sp, William Goldman, based on his novel of the same name; cam, Victor J Kemper; edtr, John Bloom; prodn des, Terence Marsh; mus, Jerry Goldsmith; art dir, Richard Lawrence; cos, Ruth Myers; snd, Larry Jost; asst dir, Arne Schmidt. (MPAA rating: R). 106.
Anthony Hopkins, Ann-Margret, Burgess Meredith, Ed Lauter, E J Andre, Jerry Houser.
11/01/78

The Magic of Lassie
ITP. Jack Wrather presentation. Prods, Bonita Granville Wrather, William Beaudine Jr. Dir, Don Chaffey. Sp, Jean Holloway, Robert M Sherman, Richard B Sherman; mus-lyrics, Sherman & Sherman; orchestrations, Irwin Kostal. (MPAA rating: G). 99.
James Stewart, Mickey Rooney, Pernell Roberts, Stephanie Zimbalist, Michael Sharrett, Alice Faye, Gene Vans, The Mike Curb Congregation, Lassie.
08/09/78

The Magic Blade
(Hong Kong)
X. Prod, Runme Shaw. Dir, Chu Yuan. Sp, Yi Kuang, Szu Tu An; cam, Huang Chieh; edtr, Chiang Hsing-lung; martial arts, Tang Chia, Huang Pei-Chi. 101.
Ti Lung, Lo Lieh, Ching Li.
08/04/76

The Magician of Lublin
(Israel - W Germany)
CAN. A Golan-Globus presentation of a N F Geria III Prodn. Prods, Menahem Golan, Yoram Globus. Exec prod, Harry N Blum. Dir, Golan. Written by Irving S White, Golan, based on novel by Isaac Bashevis Singer; cam, David Gurfinkel; edtr, Dov Henig; mus, Maurice Jarre; art dir, Yurgent Kibach. 115.
Alan Arkin, Louise Fletcher, Valerie Perrine, Shelley Winters, Maia Danziger, Linda Bernstein, Lou Jacobi, Shai K Ophir, Lachi Nov.
05/23/79

Magyar Rapszodia and Allegro Barbaro
(Hungarian Rhapsody and Allegro Barbaro)
(Hungary)
HU. Mafilm, Diolog Studio prodn. Dir, Miklos Jancso. Sp, Jancso, Gyula Hernadi; cam (Eastmancolor), Janos Kende. 175.
Gyorgy Cserhalmi, Lajos Balazsovits, Gabor Koncz, Bartalan Solti, Joszef Madaras,

Gyorgi Tarjan, Istvan Bujtor.
02/28/79

Magyarok
(The Hungarians)
(Hungary)
HU. Hungarofilm prodn, Dialog Studio, Budapest. Wri-dir, Zoltan Fabri, based on a novel by Jozsef Balazs. Cam (Eastmancolor), Gyorgy Illes; mus, Gyorgy Vukan.   110.
Gabor Koncz, Eva Pap, Bertalan Solti, Noemi Apor, Gellert Raksanyi, Erzsi Papai, Andras Muszte, Anna Muszte, Tibor Molnar, Istvan O Szabo, Zoltan Gera, Istvan Holl, Sandor Szabo, Janos Koltai.
05/24/78

The Maiden's War: SEE Der Madchenkrieg

The Main Actor: SEE Der Hauptdarsteller

The Main Event
WB. First Artists presentation of a Barwood (Jon Peters) Film prodn. Exec prods, Howard Rosenman, Renee Missel. Prods, Jon Peters, Barbra Streisand. Dir, Howard Zieff. Sp, Gail Parent, Andrew Smith; cam, Mario Tosi; edtr, Edward Warschilka; prodn des, Charles Rosen; asst dirs, Gary Daigler, Pat Kehoe; technical consultants, Hedgemon Lewis, Jose Torres; stunt coord, Denver Mattson; set decor, James Payne; mus supv, Gary Le Mel; publicist, Vic Heutschy; songs, "The Main Event," Paul Jabara, Bruce Roberts; "Fight," Jabara, Bob Esty; "Angry Eyes," Loggins & Messina; "The Body Shop," Michalski & Oosterveen (MPAA rating: PG).   112.
Barbra Streisand, Ryan O'Neal, Paul Sand, Whitman Mayo, Patti D'Arbanville, Chu Chu Malave, Richard Lawson, James Gregory, Richard Altman, Joe Amsler, Seth Banks, Lindsay Bloom, Earl Boen, Roger Bowen, Badja Medu Djola, Rory Calhoun, Sue Casey, Alvin Childress, Kristine De Bell, Al Denava.
06/20/79

Mais ou et Donc Ornicar
(France)
MAL. Mallia Films-Bertrand van Effenterre-Herbert de Zaltza prodn. Dir, Bertrand van Effenterre. Sp, Bertrand van Effenterre and Dominique Woldon; cam, Nurith Aviv, Jean-Louis Melun, Thierry Jault; snd, Pierre Gamet, Alain Lachassagne, Bernard Chaumeil, Patrice Noia; edtr, Joele van Effenterre; art dir, Max Berto; mus, Antoine Duhamel.   110.
Geraldine Chaplin, Brigitte Fossey, Jean-Francois Stevenin, Didier Flamand, Jean-Jacques Biraud.
03/14/79

Mais Qu'est-Ce Que J'Ai Fait Au Bon Dieu Pour Avoir Une Femme Qui Boit dans Les Cafes Avec Les Hommes!?
(What Did I Ever Do To The Good Lord To Deserve A Wife Who Drinks in Cafes with Men!?)
(France)
UA. Sofracima - UA co-prodn. Prods, Giselle Rebillon, Catherine Winter; dir, Jan Saint-Hamont; sp, Jan and Daniel Saint-Hamont, Alain Le Henry; tech adv, Christian Bricout; cam, Maurice Fellous; snd, Paul Laine; edtr, Michel Lewin; mus, Georges and Pierre-Marie Baux.   90.
Robert Castel, Antoinette Moya, Michel Boujenah.
09/17/80

Mais Qu'Est-Ce Qu'Elles Veulent?
(But What Do They Want?)
(France)
SNX. INA-Copra Films-SND prodn. Conceived-dir, Coline Serreau. Cam (Eastmancolor), Jean-Francoise Robin; edtrs, Sophie Tatischeff, Joelle Hache, Francoise Collin.   90.
(DOC)
03/08/78

Maisons Dans Cette Ruelle
(Houses In This Alley)
(Iran)
CTG. Dia Al Baytai prodn. Wri-dir, Kassem Hawl. Cam (Eastmancolor), Hatem Hussein; edtr, Ahmed Metwalli; mus, Abdel Amir Alsarraf.   90.
Saadie Al-Zyde, Nizar Assamourai, Suad Abdallah, Abdel Jabbar Kazem, Hana Mouhamed, Makki Badri.
08/16/78

Maitresse
(Mistress)
(France)
GAU. Les Films Du Losange - Gaumont prodn. Dir, Barbet Schroeder. Sp, Schroeder, Paul Voujargol; cam (Eastmancolor), Nestor Almendros; edtr, Denise De Casabianca; mus, Carlos D'Carlos D'Alessio.   112.
Gerard Depardieu, Bulle Ogier, Andre Rouyer, Nathalie Keryan, Tony Taffin, Holger Lowenadler.
02/11/76

Majd Holnap
(Maybe Tomorrow)
(Hungary)
HU. Mafilm Hunnia Studio. Dir, Judit Elek. Sp, Gyorgy Petho; cam (Eastmancolor), Elemer Ragalyi.   104.
Judit Meszleri, Andor Lukats, Istvan Szoke, Eszter Szakacs, Istvan Novak, Erszi Gaal.
02/27/80

Mala Morska Vila
(The Little Mermaid)
(Czechoslovakia)
X. Czech Film prodn, Prague, Barrandov Studios. Dir, Karel Kachyna. Sp, Ota Hofman; based on Hans Christian Andersen's fairy tale; cam (Eastmancolor), Jaroslav Kucera; mus, Zdenek Liska.   90.
Miroslava Safrankova, Petr Svojtka, Radovan Lukavsky, Libuse Safrankova, Milena Dvorska, Maria Rosulkova.
03/09/77

Maledetti Vi Amero'
(To Love the Damned)
(Italy)
FII. Prod, "Jean Vigo" Cooperative. Dir, Marco Tullio Giordana. Sp, Tullio Giordana, Vincenzo Caretti. Cam, Giuseppe Pinori; art dir-mus, Tullio Giordana; edtr, Sergio Nuti.   110.
Flavio Bucci, Biagio Pelligra, Pasquale Zito.
06/11/80

Malibu Beach
CWN. Marimark prodn. Prod, Marilyn J Tenser; exec prod, Newton P Jacobs. Dir, Robert J Rosenthal. Sp, Celia Susan Cotelo, Rosenthal; cam (DeLuxe), Jamie Anderson; edtr, Robert Barrere; snd, Don A Sanders; art dir, Fred Chriss; cos, Diana Daniels; stunt coord, Von Deming; asst dir, Gerald T Olson. (MPAA rating: R).   93.
Kim Lankford, James Daughton, Susan Player Jarreau, Stephen Oliver, Michael Luther, Flora Plumb, Roger Lawrence Pierce.
05/24/78

Maluala
(Cuba)
ICI. Dir, Sergio Giral. Sp, Jorge Sotolongo, Giral; cam, Raul Rodriguez; edtr, Roberto Bravo; mus, Sergio Vitier.   105.
Samuel Claxton, Miguel Navarro, Roberto Blanco, Miguel Guitierrez.
07/30/80

Mama Cumple 100 Anos
(Mom's 100 Years Old)
(Spain)
X. Elias Quereita prodn. Wri-dir, Carlos Saura. Cam (Eastmancolor), Teo Escamilla; edtr, Pablo G del Amo; sets, Antonio Belizon; exec prod, Primitivo Alvaro.   98.
Geraldine Chaplin, Amparo Munoz, Rafaela Aparicio, Fernando Fernan Gomez, Norman Brisky, Charo Soriano, Jose Vivo, Angeles Torres, Elisa Nandi, Rita Maiden, Monique Ciron.
10/03/79

Mama, Ich Lebe
(Mama, I'm Alive)
(E Germany - USSR)
X. DEFA-Film, Babelsberg Group, Film prodn, East Berlin, in collab with Lenfilm, Leningrad. Dir, Konrad Wolf. Sp, Wolfgang Kohlhaase; artistic advisors, Wolfgang Beck, Guenter Klein, Klaus Wischnewski, Dieter Wolf; cam, Werner Bergmann; art dir, Alfred Hirhscmeier: mus, Rainer Boehm; edtr, Evelyn Carow.   100.

Mamito
(France)
RSH. Caraibes Production. Prod, Anne Dolanec. Wri-dir, Christian Lara. Cam (Fuji-color), Jean-Claude Couty; mus, Emilhenco, Francisco Charles, Richard Cassin; edtr, Martine Rousseau-Carrere; snd, Pierre Befve. 90.
Lucrece Saintol, Greg Germain, Roger Tannous, Francisco Charles, Ibo Simon, Odette Laurent, Francois Maistre.
06/25/80

Mamma Dracula
(France - Belgium)
UGC. Valisa Films Productions-SND prodn. Prod-dir, Boris Szulzinger. Sp, Szulzinger, Pierre Sterckx, M H Wajnberg; English dial, Tony Hendra; cam, Willy Kurant; edtr, Claude Cohen; make-up, Pascale Kellen; cos, Mouchy Houblinne; mus, Roy Budd. 90.
Louise Fletcher, Maria Schneider, Marc-Henri Wajnberg, Alexander Wajnberg, Jimmy Shuman, Michel Israel, Jess Hahn.
(English Soundtrack)
12/03/80

Man Against Man: SEE Mann Gegen Mann

Man In A Hurry: SEE L'Homme Presse'

Man kan inte valtas
(Men Cannot Be Raped)
(Sweden)
X. Stockholm Film prodn. Sp-dir, Jorn Donner, based on Marta Tikkanen novel. Exec prods, Jorn and Jeanette Donner. Cam (Eastmancolor), Bille August; mus, Heiki Valpola; edtr, Irma Taina; prodn mgrs, Anssi Mantari, Jaako Talaskivi. 95.
Anna Godenius, Gosta Bredefeldt.
03/29/78

Man of Fashion: SEE El Hombre De Moda

Man of Marble: SEE Czlowiek Z Marmuru

Man on the Bridge: SEE Hombre del Puente

The Man to Kill: SEE Covjek Koga Treba Ubiti

The Man Who Fell To Earth
(Britain)
BLI. Michael Deeley and Barry Spikings presentation. Prods, Deeley, Spikings; exec prod, Si Litvinoff. Dir, Nicolas Roeg. Sp, Paul Mayersberg; novel, Walter Tevis; mus dir, John Phillips; cam (color-Panavision), Anthony Richmond; edtr, Graeme Clifford; asst dir, Kip Gowans; snd recordist, Robin Gregory. 140.
David Bowie, Rip Torn, Candy Clark, Buck Henry, Bernie Casey, Jackson D Kane, Rick Riccardo, Tony Mascia, Linda Hutton, Hilary Holland, Adrienne Larussa, Lilybell Crawford, Richard Breeding, Albert Nelson, Peter Prouse, Capt James Lovell, preacher & congregation of Presbyterian Church, Artesia, NM
03/24/76

The Man Who Knew Love: SEE El Hombre Que Supo Amar

The Man Who Loved Women: SEE L'Homme Qui Aimait Les Femmes

The Man Who Loves the Birds: SEE Chevelok Ukhodit Za Ptitsami

The Man Who Stole The Sun: SEE Taiyo o Nusunda Otoko

The Man With Bogart's Face
FOX. Melvin Simon Prodns presentation. Prod, Andrew J Fenady. Dir, Robert Day. Sp, Fenady based on his novel; cam (CFI) Richard C Glouner; edtr, Eddie Saeta; mus, George Duning; set des, Richard McKenzie; snd, James J Klinger; cos, Oscar Rodriguez, Jack Splangler, Voulee Giokaris; asst dir, David McGiffert. (MPAA rating: PG). 106.
Robert Sacchi, Franco Nero, Michelle Phillips, Olivia Hussey, Misty Rowe, Victor Buono, Herbert Lom, Dick Bakalyan, Sybil Danning, Gregg Palmer, Jay Robinson, George Raft, Yvonne de Carlo, Mike Mazurki, Henry Wilcoxon, Victor Sen Yung, Joe Theismann, Alshia Brevard, Buck Kartalian.
05/28/80

Man With The Axe: SEE Parasuram

The Man With The Red Carnation: SEE O Anthropos Me To Garyfallo

Man Without a Name: SEE Azonositas

The Man You Love to Hate
X. Prod by Film Profiles Inc in assoc with B B Corp, Fremantle Int'l, Killiam Shows, Norddeutscher Rundfunk. Prod-dir, Patrick Montgomery. Wri-res, Richard Koszarski. Edtr, William Loeffler; mus, comp-cond, Herbert Deutsch. Narr Edward Binns. 90.
(DOC)
08/15/79

The Management Forgives A Moment Of Madness: SEE La Empresa Perdona Un Momento de Locura

Manaos
(Italy - Mexico - Spain)
X. Federico G Aicardi (Rome). Producciones Elmes S A (Mexico) and Izaro Films S A (Madrid) co-prodn. Wri-dir, Alberto Vazquez Figueroa, based on his novel of the same name. Exec prod, Carlos Vasallo; cam (Eastmancolor), Alejandro Ulloa; edtr, Sigfrido Garcia; mus, Fabio Frizzi; sets, Kliomenes Stomatiades. 94.
Fabio Testi, Agostina Belli, Jorge Rivero, Andres Garcia, Florinda Bolkan, Alberto de Mendoza, Alfredo Mayo, Milton Rodrigues, Jorge Luke, Carlos East.
02/13/80

Mandagarna med Fanny
(Mondays with Fanny)
(Sweden)
SVS. Sp-edtr-mus score-dir, Lars Lennart Forsberg, based on novel by Per Gunnar Evander. Cam (Eastmancolor), Lars Bjoerne; exec prod, Bengt Forslund. 99.
Tommy Johnson, Maria Selbing, Agneta Ekmanner.
05/25/77

Manesgazda
(The Stud Farm)
(Hungary)
HU. Objectiv, Dialog Studios. Wri-dir, Andras Kovacs from a book by Istvan Gaal. Cam (Eastmancolor), Lajos Koltai. 100.
Joszef Madaras, Ferenc Fabian, Sandor Horvath, Karoly Sinka, Ferenc Baks.
02/28/79

Manganinnie
(Australia)
GUO. Tasmanian Film Corp prodn. Prod, Gilda Baracchi. Exec prods, Gil Brealey, Malcolm Smith. Dir, John Honey. Sp, Ken Kelso; cam (Eastmancolor), Gary Hansen; edtr, Mike Woolveridge. 91.
Mawuyul Yathalawuy, Anna Ralph, Phillip Hinton, Elaine Mangan, Buruminy Dhamarrandji, Reg Evans, Jonathan Elliott, Timothy Latham.
07/16/80

The Mango Tree
(Australia)
GUO. Pisces prodn. Prod, Michael Pate; asso prod, Michael Lake. Dir, Kevin Dobson. Sp, Michael Pate, based on Ronald McKie novel; cam, Brian Probyn; mus, Marc Wilkinson; edtr, John Scott; snd, Barry Brown; art dir, Leslie Binns. 105.
Geraldine Fitzgerald, Robert Helpmann, Christopher Pate, Gerald Kennedy, Gloria Dawn, Carol Burns, Barry Pierce, Diane Craig, Ben Gabriel, Gerry Duggan, Jonathan Atherton, Tony Bonner.
12/21/77

Manha Submersa
(Morning Mist)
(Portugal)
X. Lauro Antonio prodn. Portuguese Institute of Cinema, Lisbon. Wri-dir, Lauro Antonio, based on a novel by Vergilio Ferreira; cam, Elso Roque; edtr, Antonio; mus, Verdi, Gregorian Chant. 127.

Eunice Munoz, Vergilio Ferreira, Canto e Castro, Jacinto Ramos, Carlos Wallenstein, Joaquim Manuel Dias.
10/15/80

Manhattan
UA. Jack Rollins-Charles H Joffe prodn. Exec prod, Robert Greenhut. Prod, Charles H Joffe. Dir, Woody Allen. Sp, Allen, Marshall Brickman; cam, Gordon Willis; prodn des, Mel Bourne; cos, Albert Wolsky; film edtr, Susan E Morse; mus, George Gershwin, performed by the New York Philharmonic, conducted by Zubin Mehta and the Buffalo Philharmonic, conducted by Michael Tilson Thomas; mus, adapted and arranged by Tom Pierson; asst dir, Frederic B Blankfein; set decor, Robert Drumheller; unit publicist, Scott MacDonough. (MPAA rating: R). 96.
Woody Allen, Diane Keaton, Michael Murphy, Mariel Hemingway, Meryl Streep, Anne Byrne, Karen Ludwig, Michael O'Donahue, Victor Truro, Tisa Farrow, Helen Hanft, Bella Abzug, Gary Weiss, Kenny Vance, Charles Levin, Karen Allen, David Rasche, Damion Sheller, Wallace Shawn, Mark Linn Baker, Frances Conroy, Bill Anthony, John Doumanian, Ray Serra.
(B & W)
04/25/79

Manhunt: SEE Hajka

Mani Di Velluto
(Velvet Hands)
(Italy)
CNZ. Prod, Mario Cecchi Gori for Capital Film. Wri-dirs, Castellano and Pipolo. Cam (Eastmancolor), Alfio Contini; art dir, Bruno Amalfitano; edtr, Antonio Siciliano; mus, Nando De Luca. 102.
Adriano Celentano, Eleanora Giorgi, John Sharp, Olga Karlatos.
02/20/80

The Manitou
AVE. Herman Weist/Melvin Simon presentation. Prod-dir, William Girdler. Exec prod, Melvin G Gordy. Sp, Girdler, Jon Cedar, Tom Pope, based on novel by Graham Masterton; cam (CFI Color), Michel Hugo; edtr, Bub Asman; mus, Lalo Schifrin; conceptual des-2d unit dir, Nikita Knatz; prodn des, Walter Scott Herndon; asso prods, Cedar, Gilles A DeTurenne; asst dir, Bob Bender; set decor, Cheryal Kearney; cos, Michael Faeth, Agnes Lyon; snd, Glenn Anderson. (MPAA rating: PG). 104.
Tony Curtis, Michael Ansara, Susan Strasberg, Stella Stevens, Jon Cedar, Ann Southern, Burgess Meredith, Paul Mantee.
03/01/78

Mann Gegen Mann
(Man Against Man)
(E Germany)
DEE. Berlin Gruppe prodn. Wri-dir, Kurt Maetzig from book by Kurt Biesalski. Cam (Orwocolor), Erich Gusko; edtr, Ursula Rudzki; mus, Gerhard Wholgemuth. 98.
Regimantas Adomaitis, Klaus-Peter Thiele, Karin Schroeder, Michael Gwisdek.
07/28/76

Mannen Pa Taget
(Sweden)
SVE. Swedish Film Institute/AB Svensk Film prodn. Sp-dir, Bo Widerberg, based on Maj Sjoewall and Max Wahloo's novel. Cam (Eastmancolor), Odd Geiger Saether, Per Kallberg, Lars Ake Palen, Hans Welin; exec prod, Per Berglund; in charge of prodn, Suzanne Branner, Stefan Jarl; mus, Bjoern Jason Lindh; edtrs, Bo Widerberg, Sylvia Ingemarsson. 112.
Carl-Gustaf Lindstedt, Sven Wollter, Hakan Serner, Thomas Hellberg.
10/27/76

Mannequin: SEE L'Amour a la Bouche

Manoa
(Venezuela - Germany)
X. Helkon Films-Xanadu Films and Bayerischer Rundfunk co-prodn. Dir, Solveig Hoogesteijn. Sp, Hoogesteijn; cam, Hector Rios; edtrs, Giuliano Ferioni, Bruno Bianchini; mus, Victor Cuica. 102.
Victor Cuica, Diego Silva, Azdrubal Melendez, Hector Duvauchelle, Emilia Rojas, Julio Mota, Kiki Mendive.
05/28/80

Manoeuvre
X. Zipporah Films prodn. Doc on the US Army. Prod-dir, Frederick Wiseman; cam, John Davey; edtr, Wiseman. 115.
(DOC) (B & W)
12/05/79

Manthan
(Churning)
(India)
X. Gujarat Milk Co-op Marketing Federation Ltd prodn. Dir, Shyam Benegal. Sp, Vijay Tendulkar; cam, Govind Nihalani; mus, Vanraj Bhatia; edtr, Bhanudas Diwkar. 130.
Girish Karnad, Smita Patil, Naseeruddin Shah, Kulbhushan, Amrish Puri.
01/26/77

Many Times: SEE Muzhki Vremena

Mar De Rosas
(Sea of Roses)
(Brazil)
EMZ. Embrafilme prodn. Prod, Mario Volcoff; dir-sp, Ana Carolina; cam, Lauro Escorel; edtr, Vera Freire; mus, Paulo Herculano; asst dir, Paulo Adario. 90.
Norma Benguel, Hugo Carvana, Cristina Pereira, Otavio Augusto, Ary Fontoura, Miriam Muniz.
09/24/80

Marathon Man
PAR. Prods, Robert Evans, Sidney Beckerman. Dir, John Schlesinger. Sp, William Goldman, based on his novel; cam (Metrocolor), Conrad Hall; edtr, Jim Clark; mus, Michael Small; prodn des, Richard MacDonald; art dir, Jack De Shields; set decor, George Gaines; snd, John K Wilkinson, David Ronne; asst dirs, Howard W Koch Jr, Burtt Harris; 2d unit dir-stunt coord, Everett Creach. (MPAA rating: R). 125.
Dustin Hoffman, Laurence Olivier, Roy Scheider, William DeVane, Marthe Keller, Fritz Weaver, Richard Bright, Marc Lawrence, Allen Joseph, Tito Goya, Ben Dova, Lou Gilbert, Jacques Marin, James Wing Woo, Nicole Deslauriers, Lotta Andor-Palfi.
09/29/76

The March On Paris, 1914
HWK. Prod-dir-wri, Walter Gutman. Cam, Gutman, Mike Cuchar; edtrs, Gutman, Shirley Clarke; mus, Jessie Holladay Duane. 75.
Wulf Brandes, Jessie Holladay Duane, Barrows Mussey.
(16m)
04/26/78

March or Die
(Britain)
COL. ITC Entertainment (Lord Lew Grade)-Associated General Films prodn. Prod, Dick Richards, Jerry Bruckheimer. Dir, Richards. Sp, David Zelag Goodman; story, Goodman, Richards; cam (Technicolor), John Alcott; mus, com-cond, Maurice Jarre; edtr, O Nicholas Brown; prodn des, Gil Parrondo; asst dirs, Jose Lopez Rodero, Andre Delacroix, Larry Franco, Mustapha Laghaz; supv snd edtr, William Stevenson; art dir, Jose Maria Tapiador; set decor, Julian Mateos; sfx, Robert MacDonald; stunt coords, Glenn Wilder, Chuck Hayward, Juan Majan. (MPAA rating: PG). 106.
Gene Hackman, Terence Hill, Max von Sydow, Catherine Deneuve, Ian Holm, Rufus, Jack O'Halloran, Marcel Bozzuffi, Andre Penvern, Paul Sherman, Vernon Dobtcheff, Marne Maitland, Gigi Bonds, Wolf Kahler, Mathias Hell, Jean Champion, Walter Gotell, Paul Antrim, Catherine Willmer, Arnold Diamond, Maurice Arden, Albert Woods, Liliane Rovere, Elisabeth Mortensen, Leila Shenna, Francois Valorbe, Villena, Guy Deghy, Jean Rougerie, Guy Mairesse, Eve Brenner, Guy Marly, Margaret Modlin.
08/03/77

Marcia Trionfale
(Victory March)
(Italy - France - W Germany)
CNZ. Prod, Silvio Clementelli for Clesi Cinematografica, Renn Production (Paris), and Lisa Film (Munich). Dir, Marco Bellocchio. Sp, Marco Bellocchio, Sergio Bazzini; cam (Technicolor), Franco Di Giacomo; art dir, Amedeo Fago; edtr, Sergio Montanari; mus, Nicola Piovani. 118.
Franco Nero, Miou Miou, Michele Placido, Patrick Dewaere.
04/07/76

Marco Polo
(Hong Kong)
X. Shaws prodn; Dir, Chang Cheh. Sp, I Kuang, Chang Cheh; cam, Kung Mu To; edtr, Kuo Ting-hung; mus, Chen Yung-yu. 106. Alexander Fu Sheng, Chi Kuan-chun, Shih Szu, Richard Harrison.
02/04/76

The Margin: SEE La Marge

Maria D'Oro und Bello Blue
(Once Upon A Time)
(Italy - Germany)
GGC. Italo-German co-prodn. Prod-dir, Rolf Kauka. Art dir, Louis Gaviolo; tech dir, Paul Piffarerio; mus, Peter Thomas; prodn supv, Robert Gaviolo. (Movielab color). (MPAA rating: G). 83.
(ANI)
05/05/76

Marian
(Spain)
X. Iruna P C and Cinema 2000 prodn. Dir, Luis Cortes. Sp, Juan Antonio Porto, Luis Cortes; cam (Eastmancolor), Jose Luis Alcaine; edtr, Guillermo Maldonado; sets, Jose Antonio de la Guerra. 87.
Isabel Mestres, Javier Escriva, Javier Elorriaga, Maria Asquerino, Hector Alterio, Lina Canalejas, Susana Prados, Alberto Belmonte.
03/14/79

Maria's Hours: SEE As Horas De Maria

Marie-Anne
(Canada)
X. Motion Picture Corp of Alberta presentation. Prod, Fil Fraser. Dir, R Martin Walters. Sp, Marjorie Morgan, adapt, George Salverson; cam, Reginald Morris; edtr, Stanley Frazen; mus, Maurice Marshall; art dir, Phillip Silver; asso prod, Bill Davidson. 91.
John Juliani, Andree Pelletier, Tantoo Martin, Paul Jolicoeur, David Schurmann, Patrick Hughes.
09/20/78

Marie-Poupee
(Marie-The Doll)
(France)
PFC. Coquelicot Films, PHPG prodn. Wri-dir, Joel Seria. Cam (Eastmancolor), Marcel Combes; edtr, Etienette Muse; mus, Philippe Sarde. 120.
Jeanne Goupil, Andre Dussolier, Bernard Fresson, Andrea Ferreol, Francois Perrot, Marie Mergey.
09/15/76

Marigolds in August
(S Africa)
X. Serpent (Southern) Prodns/R-M Prodns prodn. Dir, Ross Devenish. Sp, Athol Fugard; cam, Michael Davis; edtr, Lionel Selwyn. 87.
Winston Ntshona, John Kani, Athol Fugard.
(In English)
03/12/80

Mark of the Chinese Temple: SEE Khao Yod

The Marksman: SEE Skytten

Marmeladupporet
(The Marmalade Revolution)
(Sweden)
SVF. Josephson & Nykvist HB-SFI-Svensk Filmindustri prodn. Dirs, Erland Josephson, Sven Nykist. Sp, Josephson; cam (Eastmancolor), Nykvist; edtr, Sylvia Ingemarrsson; mus, Antoine Forqueray. 91.
Erland Josephson, Bibi Andersson, Marie Goranzon, Jan Malmsjo, Kristina Adolphson, Susanna Hellberg.
03/12/80

The Marriage: SEE O Casamento

The Marriage of Maria Braun: SEE Die Ehe der Maria Braun

Marriage, Tel Aviv Style: SEE Nissuim Nosach Tel Avi

Married for the First Time: SEE Vpervye Zamuzhem

Martin
LBR. Laurel Group presentation. Prod, Richard Rubinstein. Wri-dir, George A Romero. Cam, Michael Gornick; edtr, Romero; mus, Donald Rubinstein; snd, Tony Buba; sfx-make-up, Tom Savini. (MPAA rating: R). 95.
John Amplas, Lincoln Maazel, Christine Forrest, Elayne Nadeau, Tom Savini, Sarah Venable, Fran Middleton, Al Levitsky.
01/10/79

Martin Et Lea
(France)
MK. Les Productions De La Gueville prodn. Dir, Alain Cavalier. Sp, Cavalier, Isabelle Ho, Xavier Saint-Macary; cam (Eastmancolor), Jean-Francois Robin; edtr, Joelle Hache. 92.
Isabelle Ho, Xavier Saint Macary, Richard Bohringer, Cecile La Bailly, Louis Navarre, Pham Q'Tri, Zina Delouange, Francois Berlean.
12/27/78

Mas Alla Del Terror
(The Hereafter of Terror)
(Spain)
X. Cinevision Production (Madrid). Dir, Tomas Aznar; sp, Aznar, Miguel Lizondo, Alfredo Casado; cam (Eastmancolor), Julio Bragado; edtr, Maruja Soriano; sets, Gumersindo Andres; exec prod, Alfredo Casado. 80.
Francisco Sanchez Grajera, Raquel Ramirez, Emilio Siegrist, Antonio Jabalera, Alexia Loreto, David Forrest.
09/17/80

Masoch
(Italy)
DIF. Difilm S r L-Tierre SAS (Rome) prodn. Dir-sp, Franco Brogi Taviani; cam (Eastmancolor), Angelo Bevilacqua; score, Gianfranco Plenizio; prods, Taviani, Giancarlo di Fonzo, Tonino Paoletti. 109.
Paolo Malco, Francesca DeSapio, Fabrizio Bentivoglio, Inga Alexandrova, Dario Mazzoli, Remo Remotti, Valeria D'Obici, Stefano Calanchi, Franca Lumachi, Claudio Sorrentino, Stefano Stefanelli, Farris Fabio.
09/10/80

Massacre At Central High
BRI. Evan Co prodn; prod, Harold Sobel. Wri-dir, Renee Daalder. Mus, Tony Leonetti; cam, Bert Van Munster. (MPAA rating: R). 85.
Derrel Maury, Andrew Stevens, Kimberly Beck, Bob Carradine, Rainbeaux Smith.
11/17/76

Mater Amatisima
(Mother, Dearly Beloved)
(Spain)
X. Imatco S A prodn. Wri-dir, J A Salgot, based on story by Bigas Luna. Exec prod, Ricardo Munoz-Suay; cam, Jaime Peracaula; prod, J Cuxart Guardia; edtr, Anastasi Rinos; sets, Carlos Riart; mus, Vangelis. 93.
Julito de la Cruz, Victoria Abril, Consuelo Tura, Jaime Sorribas, Carmen Contreras, Carlos Lucena.
06/11/80

Maternale
(Mother and Daughter)
(Italy)
X. Rai-Radiotelevisione Italiana, Cooperative AATA and Pantheon I prodn. Sp-dir, Giovanna Gagliardo; cam, Giuseppe Lanci; art dir, Maria-Palo Maino; mus, Stelvio Cipriani; edtr, Roberto Perpignani; snd, Gianni Sardo; artistic collab, Giorgio Barattolo. 95.
Carla Gravina, Anna Maria Gherardi, Marino Mase, Francesca Muzio, Benedetta Fantoli, Francesco, Lajos Balaszovits, Umberto Silva.
(English subtitles)
04/19/78

Matilda
AIP. Albert S Ruddy Prodn. Prod, Albert Ruddy; exec prod, Richard R St Johns. Dir, Daniel Mann. Sp, Ruddy, Timothy Galfas based on the book by Paul Gallico; cam (Movielab Color), Jack Woolf; prodn des, Boris Leven; edtr, Allan A Jacobs; cos, Jack Martell. Donna Roberts Orme; asso prod. Paul Sapounakis; sfx, Jerry Endler. (MPAA Rating G). 105.
Elliott Gould, Robert Mitchum, Harry Guardino, Clive Revill, Karen Carlson, Roy Clark, Lionel Stander, Art Metrano, Larry Pennell, Roberta Collins.
06/21/78

Matriarhat
(Matriarchy)
(Bulgaria)
BGO. BulgaroFilm prodn, Savremennik Group, Sofia. Dir, Lyudmil Kirkov. Sp, Georgi Mishev; cam, Georgi Roussinov; art dir, Bogoya Sapoundjiev, Assya Popova; mus, Boris Karadimchev. 90.

Katya Paskaleva, Nevena Kokanova, Emilia Radeva, Katia Tchoukova, Georgi Georgiev-Getz, Georgi Roussev.
05/31/78

Matsuri No Junbi
(Preparation For The Festival)
(Japan)
X. Japan Art Theatre Guild, Soeisha Ltd prodn. Exec prod, Eiga Dojinsha. Dir, Kazuo Kuroki. Sp, Takehiro Nakajima; cam, Tatsuo Suzuki; art dirs, Takeo Kimura, Yuji Maruyama; mus, Teizo Matsumura. 116.
Jun Eto, Keiko Takeshita, Yoshio Harada.
(English Subtitles)
10/11/78

Max Havelaar
(Holland - Indonesia)
FXN. PT Mondial Motion Pictures (Jakarta) and Fons Rademakers Productie (Amsterdam) co-prodn. Prods, Fons Rademakers, Hiswara Darmaputera. Dir, Rademakers. Sp, Gerard Soeteman, based on book by Multatuli; cam (Eastmancolor ECN 2 and Panavision), Jan de Bont; sets, Frank Raven; cos, Elly Claus; edtr, Pieter Bergema. 170.
Peter Faber, Sacha Bulthuis, Herry Iantho, Menny Zulaini, Rina Melati, Elang Mohamad Adenan Soesilaningrat, Maruli Sitompul, Rutger Hauer.
10/06/76

May I Have the Floor: SEE Proshu Slova

May: SEE Maes

Mayakovsky Smejotsja
(Mayakovsky Laughs)
(USSR)
X. Mosfilm prodn. Dirs, Sergei Yutkevich, Anatoly Karanovich; sp, Yutkevich; cam, Y Neuman; mus, Yuri Dashkovich. 85.
Yuri Chernov, Iya Savvina, Nikolai Grinko, Leonid Bronevoy.
06/16/76

Maybe Tomorrow: SEE Majd Holnap

McVicar
(Britain)
X. Curbishley-Baird prodn for The Who Film and Polytel. Exec prods, David Gideon Thompson, Jackie Curbishley. Prods, Roy Baird, Bill Curbishley, Roger Daltrey. Dir, Tom Clegg. Sp, John McVicar, Clegg; cam, Vernon Layton; mus, Jeff Wayne; edtr, Peter Boyle; art dir, Brian Ackland-Snow; snd, David Crozier; asso prod, John Peverall; prodn mgr, Ray Corbett; asst dir, Barry Langley. 111.
Roger Daltrey, Adam Faith, Cheryl Campbell, Steven Berkoff, Brian Hall, Jeremy Blake, Leonard Gregory, Peter Jonfield, Tony Haygarth, Ralph Watson, Georgina Hale, Malcolm Tierney, Billy Murray, Ricky Parkinson, Ian Hendry.
04/30/80

Me and Charly: SEE Mig og Charly

Me Vang Nha
(When Mother Is Out)
(Viet Nam)
VIE. Wri-dir, Khanh Du; book, Neguyen Thi. Cam, Ngoc Lan. 80.
Van Dung, Hong Phuong, Ngoc Thu.
(B & W)
07/30/80

The Meadow: SEE Il Prato

Mean Dog Blues
AIP. Bing Crosby Prodns film. Prods, Charles A Pratt, George Lefferts. Dir, Mel Stuart. Sp, Lefferts; cam (DeLuxe Color), Robert B Hauser; edtr, Houseley Stevenson; art dir, J S Poplin; snd, Dwight Mobley; mus, Fred Karlin; set decor, Don Sullivan; cos, Bill Milton, Chris Zamiara; stunt coord, Bill Couch; asst dir, Kenneth Swor. (MPAA rating: R). 108.
Gregg Henry, Kay Lenz, George Kennedy, Scatman Crothers, Tina Louise, Felton Perry, Gregory Sierra, James Wainwright, William Windom, John Daniels.
02/22/78

Meat: SEE Fleisch

Meatballs
(Canada)
PAR. Ivan Reitman prodn. Prod, Dan Goldberg. Dir, Ivan Reitman. Sp, Len Blum, Don Goldberg, Janis Allen, Harold Ramis; mus, Elmer Bernstein; edtr, Debra Karen; art dir, David Charles; cam, Don Wilder; songs, Norman Gimbel, Elmer Bernstein. (MPAA rating: PG). 92.
Bill Murray, Harvey Atkin, Kate Lynch, Russ Banham, Kristine DeBell, Sarah Torgov, Jack Blum, Keith Knight, Cindy Girling, Todd Hoffman, Margot Pinwidic, Matt Cravenn, Norma Dell'Agnese, Chris Makepeace, Michael Kirby, Greg Swangon, Ron Barry, Paul Boyle, Vince Guerriero, James McLarty, Heather Preece, Ruth Rennie, Alison Diver, Valerie Fersht, Allan Levson, Patrick Hynes, Hadley Kay, Bill Kishonti, Peter Hume.
06/27/79

Mecava
(Snowstorm)
(Yugoslavia)
YFR. Jadran Film-Croatia Film prodn. Wri-dir, Antun Vrdoljak. Cam (Eastmancolor), Tomaslav Pinter; mus, Pero Gotovac. 88.
Slododan Perovic, Milka Podrug-Kokotovic, Vera Zima, Vinko Kralkevic.
08/17/77

Med Strahom In Dolznostjo
(Between Fear and Duty)
(Yugoslavia)
YFR. Viba Film prodn. Dir-wri, Voljko Duletic; from a book by Karla Grabeljska; cam (Eastmancolor), Jure Pervanje; art dir, Miko Matul. 89.
Boris Juh, Marjeta Gregac, Angela Hlebce, Ivan Jezernik, Demeter Bitence.
08/18/76

The Medal: SEE Signum Laudis

The Medic: SEE Le Toubib

The Medusa Raft: SEE Splav Meduze

The Medusa Touch
(Britain)
ELN. ITC Entertainment prodn. Prods, Lew Grade, Arnon Milchan, Elliot Kastner. Dir, Jack Gold. Sp, John Briley, Jack Gold, from novel by Peter Van Greenaway; cam (Technicolor, Panavision), Arthur Ibbetson; edtr, Anne V Coate; art dir, Peter Mullins. 110.
Richard Burton, Lino Ventura, Lee Remick, Harry Andrews, Marie-Christine Barrault, Michael Hordern, Gordon Jackson, Derek Jacobi, Michael Byrne, Jeremy Brett, Robert Lang.
02/08/78

The Meetings of Anna: SEE Les Rendez-Vous D'Anna

Meetings With Remarkable Men
(Britain)
LBR. Remar Productions (Stuart Lyons) prodn. Dir, Peter Brook. Sp, Jeanne Salzmann, Brook from the book by G I Gurdjieff; cam (Eastmancolor), Gilbert Taylor; edtr, John Jympson; mus, Thomas De Hartman, Laurence Rosenthan. 110.
Dragan Maksimovic, Terence Stamp, Athol Fugard, Gerry Sundquist, Donald Sumpter, Tom Fleming.
03/14/79

The Megalomaniac: SEE Rai Saneh Ha

Melancholy Baby
(France - Belgium - Switzerland)
UGC. Dimage/Luna Films/Cine Vog Films/SSR-RTSI co-prodn. Prod, Michele Dimitri. Dir, Clarisse Gabus. Sp, Gabus, Daniel Jouanisson, Andre Puig; cam, Charlie Van Damme; snd, Auguste Galli; mus, Serge Gainsbourg; art dir, Denis Martin-Sisteron; edtrs, Luciano Berini, Genevieve Letellier, Catherine Brasier-Snopko. 100.
Jane Birkin, Jean-Louis Trintignant, Jean-Luc Bideau.
10/31/79

Melech Leyom Echad
(King For A Day)
(Israel)
X. Nachshon Films presentation. Prods, Isaac Shani, Naotali Alter. Dir, Assaf Dayan; sp, Dayan, Alter; cam, Ilan Rosenberg; edtr, Reuven Kornfeld; cos, Sara Wiener; mus, Alter; lyr, Dayan; snd, Yaakov Goldstein. 85.
Gabi Amrani, Carolyn Langford, Hanan Goldblatt, Eyal Geffen, Irith Mohar, Uri Alter, Yohanan Raviv, Danny Segev, Rivka Michaeli, Yosef Shiloach, Miriam Fuchs.
08/06/80

Melodrama?
(Greece)
X. Christos Mangos prodn. Wri-dir, Nikos Panayotopoulos; cam, Stavros Hassapis; edtr, Andreas Andreadakis. 93.
Lefteris Voyatzis, Maria Xenoudaki, Kostas Kokakis, Aliki Georgouli,

Melodrame
(France)
X. Fanny Berchaux prodn. Wri-dir, Jean-Louis Jorge. Cam, Ramon Suarez; edtrs, Anne Brotons, Jorge.   86.
Martine Simonet, Vicente Criado, Maud Molyneux, Benoit Ferreux.
(B & W)
05/19/76

Melvin And Howard
U. Linson-Phillips-Demme prodn. Prods, Art Linson, Don Phillips; dir, Jonathan Demme; sp, Bo Goldman; cam (Technicolor), Tak Fujimoto; edtr, Craig McKay; mus, Bruce Langhorne; prodn des, Toby Rafelson; art dir, Richard Sawyer; set decor, Bob Gould; snd, David Ronne; asso prod, Terry Nelson; asst dir, Don Heitzer; 2d unit dir, Evelyn Purcell. (MPAA rating: R).   93.
Paul Le Mat, Jason Robards, Mary Steenburgen, Jack Kehoe, Michael J Pollard, Pamela Reed, Dabney Coleman, John Glover, Charles Napier, Elizabeth Cheshire, Melvin E Dummar, Gloria Grahame, Susan Peretz, Danny Dark, Martine Beswicke, Charlene Holt, Melissa Williams, Rick Lenz, Joseph Ragno.
09/10/80

Memorias de Leticia Valle
(Memoirs of Leticia Valle)
(Spain)
X. Prod-dir, Miguel Angel Rivas. Sp, Marigel Alonso, Alberto Porlan, Miguel Angel Rivas based on Rosa Chacel novel of same name; cam (Eastmancolor), Carlos Suarez; edtr, Eduardo Biurrun; mus, Alberto Bourbon; exec prod, Manuel F Manchon.   105.
Ramiro Oliveros, Jeannine Mestre, Fernando Rey, Hector Alterio, Emma Suarez, Queta Claver, Francisco Casares, Helga Line, Irina Kuberskaya, Maria Elena Flores, Esperanza Roy.
09/26/79

The Memory of Justice
(W Germany - US)
CII. Max Palevski-Hamilton Fish prodn in association with Polytel Int. (Hamburg). Conceived-dir, Marcel Ophuls. Cam (Eastmancolor), Michael Davis; edtr, Inge Behrens. (MPAA rating: PG).   278.
(DOC)
06/09/76

Men Cannot Be Raped: SEE Man kan inte valtas

Men of Bronze
X. Men of Bronze Inc presentation. Res-prod-dir, William Miles. Exec prod, Paul Killiam. Cam-edtr, Richard W Adams; snd, Dale Whitman.   60. (DOC)
09/28/77

Men or Not Men: SEE Uomini E No

Menschenfrauen
(Woman Rhymes With Human)
(Austria)
TPF. Valie Export-Top Film prodn. Sp & structural assistance, Peter Weibel. Co-sp-dir, Valie Export. Cam (Eastmancolor), Wolfgang Dickmann, Karl Kases; edtrs, Tina Frese, Friedl Mayer.   116.
Renee Felden, Maria Martina, Susanne Widl, Christiane von Aster, Klaus Wildbolz.
11/05/80

The Message
(Britain)
TIY. Filmco Int'l prodn, prod-dir, Moustapha Akkad. Sp, H A L Craig; cam (Eastmancolor), Jack Hildyard; edtr, John Bloom; art dir, Norman Dorme, Abdel Mouneim Chukri; mus, Maurice Jarre; snd, Chris Greenham; asst dirs, Gus Agosti, Carlos Gil, Abdessamad Dinia.   179.
Anthony Quinn, Irene Papas, Michael Ansara, Johnny Sekka, Michael Forest, Damien Thomas, Garrick Hagon, Ronald Chenery, Michael Godfrey, Peter Madden, Habib Ageli, George Camiller, Neville Jason, Martin Benson, Robert Brown, Wolfe Morris, Bruno Barnabe, John Humphry, John Bennett, Donald Burton, Andre Morell, Rosalie Crutchley, Ewen Solon, Elaine Ives Cameron, Nicholas Amer, Gerard Hely, Hassan Joundi, Earl Cameron, Ronald Leigh-Hunt, Leonard Trolley, Wahshi, Mohammad Al Gaddary.
08/18/76

Message From Space
(Japan)
UA. Toei Co Ltd-Tohokushinsha Film Co Ltd prodn. Prod, Banjiro Uemura, Yoshinori Watanabe, Tan Takaiwa. Dir, Kinji Fukasaku. Sp, Hiroo Matsuda; cam, Toro Nakajima; created by Shotaro Ishimori, Masahiro Noda, Hiroo Matsuda, Kinji Fukasaku; mus, Ken-Ichiro Morioka, perf, Columbia Symphony Orchestra (Japan); sfx tech unit-sci-fi supv, Masahiro Noda; space-flying objects, Shotaro Ishimori; special pho effects, Minoru Nakano; art dir, Tetsuzo Osawa; dir-pho, sfx sequences, Nobaru Takanashi; dir, entire sfx, Nobuo Yajim. (MPAA rating: PG).   105.
Vic Morrow, Sonny Chiba, Philip Casnoff, Peggy Lee Brennan, Sue Shiomi, Tetsuro Tamba, Mikio Narita, Makoto Sato, Hiroyuki Sanada, Isamu Shimuzu, Masazumi Okabe, Noburo Mitani, Hideyo Amamoto, Junkichi Orimoto, Harumi Sone.
(English-dubbed soundtrack)
11/01/78

Messer Im Kopf
(Knife in the Head)
(W Germany)
FDA. Bioskop Film Hallelujah Film prodn. Dir, Reinhard Hauff. Sp, Peter Schneider; cam (Eastmancolor), Frank Bruhne; edtr, Peter Przygodda; mus, Irmin Schmidt.   108.
Bruno Ganz, Angela Winkler, Hans Christian Blech, Heinz Honig, Hans Brenner, Udo Samel, Eike Gallwitz.
10/25/78

The Messiah: SEE Il Messia

Messidor
(France - Switzerland)
GAU. Citel Film-SSR Geneva-Action Films-Gaumont co-prodn. Wri-dir, Alain Tanner. Cam (Eastmancolor), Renato Berta; mus, Arie Dzierlatka; edtr, Brigitte Sousselier; snd, Pierre Gamet; prodn mgr, Bernard Lorain.   120.
Clementine Amouroux, Catherine Retore.
02/28/79

Metamorphoses
SRI. Prods, Terry Ogisu, Hiro Tsugawa; exec prod, Shintaro Tsuji. Wri-prod-dir, Takashi, based on material from Ovid's "Metamorphoses". Cam (Technicolor), Bill Millar; anim edtr, Barbara Ottinger; mus coord, Bob Randles; snd effects, Sound Arts; scene planner, Ruth Tompson. (MPAA rating: PG).   89.
Sequence dirs, Jerry Eisenberg, Richard Huebner, Sadao Miyamoto, Amby Paliwoda, Ray Patterson, Manny Perez, George Singer, Stan Walsh; prodn des, Paul Julian, Ray Aragon, Kuni Fukai, Rebecca Ortega Mills, Akira Uno; anim, Edwin Aardal, John Ahern, Mikiharu Akabori, Robert Carlson, Brad Case, Marija Dail, Edward DeMattia, Joan Drake, Edgar Friedman, Edwardo Fuentes, Morris Gollub, Fred Grable, Masami Hata, Fred Hellmich, Ernesto Lopez, Daniel Noonan, Ken O'Brian, Jack Ozark, William Pratt, Thomas Ray, Virgil Ross, Glenn Schmitz, Martha Swanson, Reuben Timmins, James Walker, John Walker, Shigeru Yamamoto, Rudolfo Zamora; layout, Nino Carbe, Oscar Dufaux, Don Morgan, Lew Ott, Mike Ploog, Jose Rivera, Ed Verraux; background, Yukio Abe, Ron Dias, Alison Julian, Phil Lewis, Eric Semones, Gloria Wood.
(ANI)
05/17/78

Meteor
AIP. Prod, Arnold Orgolini, Theodore Parvin. Exec prods, Sandy Howard, Gabriel Katzka. Dir, Ronald Neame. Sp, Stanley Mann, Edmund H North, based on a story by North; cam, Paul Lohmann; edtr, Carl Kress; prodn des, Edward Carfagno; art dir, David Constable; set decor, Barbara Krieger; mus, Laurence Rosenthal; snd, Jack Solomon; sfx, Glen Robinson, Robert Steaples; asst dir, Daniel J McCauley. (MPAA rating: PG).   103.
Sean Connery, Natalie Wood, Karl Malden, Brian Keith, Martin Landau, Trevor Howard, Richard Dysart, Henry Fonda, Joseph Campanella.
10/17/79

Mi Hija Hildegart
(My Daughter Hildegart)
(Spain)
X. Camara P C and Jet Films prodn. Exec prods, Luis Sanz, Alfredo Matas. Dir, Fernando Fernan Gomez; sp, Rafael Azcona, Fernando Fernan Gomez, based on book "Aurora de Sangre" by Eduardo de Guzman; Cecilio Paniagua; cam (Eastmancolor), Cecilio Paniagua; mus, Luis Eduardo Aute.   110.
Amparo Soler Leal, Carmen Roldan, Manuel Galiana, Carlos Velat, Pedro Diez del Corral, Jose Maria Mompin, Ricardo Tundidor, Maribel Auyso, Luisa Rodrigo, Guillermo Marin.

Mi Primer Pecado
(My First Sin)
(Spain)
X. Kalender Films Int'l and Paraguas Films prodn. Dir, Manuel Summers. Sp, Luis Murillo, Summers; cam (Eastmancolor), Luis Cuadrado; edtr, Pablo G del Amo; mus, Carlos Vizzielo. 103.
Francisco M Summers, Beatriz Galbo, Mary Paz Pondal, Jose Rodriquez, Manuel Rodriquez, Jose Luis Bresso, Rafael Conesa.
05/25/77

Michael Kohlhaas
(W Germany)
X. Prod, Horst Film GmbH & Co. KG, Berlin-Munich for Westdeutsches Werbefernsehen. Dir-wri, Wolf Vollmar. Cam, Wolfgang Hannemann; mus, Peter Sandloff. 95.
Rolf Boysen, Alfred Schieske, Wilhelm Borchert, Wolfgang Buettner, Irene Marhold, Kaspar Brueninghaus, Hans Elwenspoek, Alexander Allerson.
06/13/79

Middle Age Crazy
(Canada)
FOX. Tormont Film Prodn. Prods, Robert Cooper, Ronald Cohen, John Eckert. Dir, John Trent; exec prods, Sid and Marty Krofft. Sp, Carl Kleinschmidt; cam, Reginald Morris; edtr, John Kelly; art dir, Karen Bromley; snd, David Lee; mus, Matthew McCauley. 89.
Bruce Dern, Ann-Margret, Graham Jarvis, Eric Christmas, Helen Hughes, Geoffrey Bowes, Deborah Wakeham, Michael Kane.
05/28/80

Middle Age Spread
(New Zealand)
ENZ. Endeavour Prodns. Prod, John Barnett. Dir, John Reid. Sp, Keith Aberdein from play by Roger Hall; cam, Alun Bollinger; snd, Craig McLeod; edtr, Michael Horton; mus, Stephen McCurdy. 94.
Grant Tilly, Dorothy McKegg, Peter Sumner, Bridget Armstrong, Donna Akersten, Bevan Wilson.
07/18/79

The Middleman: SEE
Dahana-Aranja

Midnight Desires
AMX. Prod, Warren Evans. Wri-dir, Amanda Barton. Cam, David Measless; edtr, Joseph Masolini. (Self-applied X rating). 74.
Karen Regis, Jaimie Gillis, C J Laing, Eric Edwards, Ursula Pasarell, Linda Lovemore, Ray Jeffries.
04/21/76

Midnight Express
(Britain)
COL. Casablanca Filmworks prodn. Prod, David Puttnam, Alan Marshall; exec prod, Peter Guber. Dir, Alan Parker. Sp, Oliver Stone, based on the book by William Hayes with William Hoffer; cam (Eastmancolor), Michael Seresin; edtr, Gerry Hambling; mus, Giorgio Moroder; prodn des, Geoffrey Kirkland; art dir, Evan Hercules; snd, Clive Winter; cosward, Milena Canonero, Bobby Lavender; asst dir, Ray Corbett. 120.
Brad Davis, Randy Quaid, John Hurt, Bo Hopkins, Paul Smith, Mike Kellin, Norbert Wiesser, Irene Miracle.
05/24/78

Midnight Madness
BV. Prod, Ron Miller. Dirs, David Wechter, Michael Nankin. Sp, Wechter, Nankin; cam (Technicolor), Frank Phillips; mus, Julius Wechter; edtrs, Norman R Palmer, Jack Sekely; art dirs, John R Mansbridge, Richard Lawrence; snd, Herb Taylor; set dirs, R Chris Westlund, Roger M Shook; sfx, Danny Lee. (MPAA rating: PG). 110.
David Naughton, Debra Clinger, Eddie Deezen, Brad Wilkin, Maggie Roswell, Stephen Furst, Irene Tedrow, Michael J Fox, Joel P Kenney, Alan Solomon.
02/06/80

Midway
U. Prod, Walter Mirisch. Dir, Jack Smight. Sp, Donald S Sanford; cam (Technicolor), Harry Stradling Jr; edtrs, Robert Swink, Frank J Urioste; mus, John Williams; art dir, Walter Tyler; set decor, John Dwyer; snd, Robert Martin, Leonard Peterson; asst dir, Jerome Siegel. (MPAA rating: PG). 132.
Charlton Heston, Henry Fonda, James Coburn, Glenn Ford, Hal Holbrook, Toshiro Mifune, Robert Mitchum, Cliff Robertson, Robert Wagner, Robert Webber, Ed Nelson, James Shigeta, Christina Kokubo, Monte Markham, Biff McGuire, Kevin Dobson, Christopher George, Glenn Corbett, Gregory Walcott, Edward Albert.
06/16/76

Mig og Charly
(Me and Charly)
(Denmark)
WCT. Steen Herdel prodn. Sp-dir-cam (Eastmancolor), Henning Kristiansen, Morten Arnfred, based on Ben Rasmussen's novel "The White Hands". Prod mgr, Lars Kolvig; edtr, Anders Refn; mus, Kasper Winding, song-lyr, C V Jorgensen. 98.
Kim Eduard Jensen, Allan Olsen, Ghita Noerby, Helle Nielsen, Jens Okking.
03/29/78

The Mighty Peking Man
(Hong Kong)
SHW. Prod, Vee King Shaw, Chua Lam. Dir, Ho Meng-hua. Cam, Tsao Hui-chi, Wu Chohua; snd, Wang Yung-hua. 100.
Li Hsiu-hsien, Evelyne Kraft, Hsiao Yao, Ku Feng, Lin Wei-tu, Hsu Shao-chiang, Wu Hangsheng, Chen Ping.
(Cantonese soundtrack; English subtitles)
08/31/77

Mijn Vriend
(The Judge's Friend)
(Holland - Belgium)
ELN. Fons Rademakers (Amsterdam)-Cinemagna (Brussels) prodn. Prod, Jos Van der Linden. Dir, Fons Rademakers, Sp, Gerard Soeteman; cam (Eastmancolor), Theo Van de Sande; mus, Georges Delerue; prodn des, Philippe Graff; snd, Frank Struys; asst dir, Lili Rademakers. 128.
Peter Faber, Andre Van Den Huevel, Magda Cnudde, Dirk De Batist, Pleuni Touw, Florence Jamin, Kees Ter Bruggen, Camilia Blereau, Paul Cammermans, Frans Vercammen, Idwig Stephane, Frank Aendenboom, Dirk Celis, Herbert Flack, Herman Coessens, Germaine Pascal, Frank Bravenboer, Piet Marchie, Alexis Sachnovsky.
04/18/79

Mike Test: SEE Proba De Microfon

Mikey and Nicky
PAR. Prod, Michael Hausman; exec prod, Bud Austin. Wri-dir, Elaine May. Cam (Movielab Color), Victor J Kemper, Lucien Ballard, Jerry File, Jack Cooperman; edtr, John Carter; mus, John Stauss; prodn des, Paul Sylbert; set decor, John P Austin; snd, Richard Vorisek, Christopher Newman, Larry Jost; asst dir, Peter Scoppa. (MPAA rating: R). 119.
Peter Falk, John Cassavetes, Ned Beatty, Rose Arrick, Carol Grace, William Hickey, Sanford Meisner, Joyce Van Patten, M Emmet Walsh.
12/22/76

Milano Odia: La Polizia non puo'Sparare
(Almost Human)
(Italy)
BRE. Dania prodn. Prod, Luciano Martino; dir, Umberto Lenzi; cam, (Eastmancolor); edtr, Eugenio Alabiso; mus, Ennio Morricone. (MPAA rating: R). 92.
Tomas Milian, Henry Silva, Anita Strindberg, Raymond Lovelock, Laura Belli, Guido Alberti.
07/30/80

Milano Odia: La Polizia non puo'Sparare: SEE Almost Human

Milionario e Ze Rico na Estrada da Vida
(Milionario and Ze Rico in The Highway of Life)
(Brazil)
EMZ. Villafilmes Producoes Cinematograficas prodn. Prod, Dora Suerner Vilals Boas, Luiz Carlos Villas Boas. Dir, Nelson Pereira dos Santos. Sp, Chico de Assis; mus dir, Dooby Ghizzy; cam (Eastmancolor), Francisco Botelho; snd, Juarez Dagoberto; edtr, Carlos Alberto Camuyrano. 100.
Milionario, Jose Rico, Nadia Lippi, Silvia Leblon, Raimundo Silva, Turibio Ruiz, Jose Raimundo.
11/26/80

Milk War in Bavaria: SEE Die Farbe des Himmels

Millionaire In Trouble
(Israel)
SHP. Roll Film prodn. Prod, Israel Ringel, Yair Pradelsky. Wri-dir, Yoel Silberg. Cam, Nisim (Nitcho) Leon; prodn des, Kuli Sander; edtr, Tova Neeman; mus, Dox Selzer; lyr, Uriel Ofek. 85.

Yehuda Barkan, Yaakov Bodo, Edna Flidel, Gideon Singer, Hannah Laslow, Uriela White, Mandy Rice-Davies.
07/19/78

Mimi: SEE Un Dramma Borghese

Mimino
(USSR)
X. Mosfilm prodn, Moscow. Dir, Georgi Daneliya. Sp, Revaz Gabriadze, Victoria Tokareva, Daneliya; cam, Anatoli Petritsky. 90.
Vakhtang Kikabidze, Frunzik Mkrtchyan, Yelena Proklova, Yevgeny Leonov.
08/03/77

Min aelskade
(My Beloved)
(Sweden)
SVE. AB Svensk Film/Cinematograph AB (Ingmar Bergman, exec prod) Swedish Film Institute with the 3 Leaf Clover Assocs prodn. Film Institute prod, Mans Reuytersvaerd. Wri-dir, Kjell Grede. Cam (Eastmancolor), Tony Forsberg (with 16m additions by Lasse Karlsson); edtr, Lasse Hagstroem, prodn des, Anna Asp; cos, Inger Pehrsson. 108.
Bjoern Skagestad, Lena Nyman, Agneta Ekmanner, Keve Hjelm.
04/25/79

The Mina Cycle: SEE Dayereh Cycle

Mina droemmars stad
(City of My Dreams)
(Sweden)
SVE. Exec prods, Olle Helbom, Olle Nordemar. Dial-sp-dir, Ingvar Skogsberg, based on novel by Per Anders Fogelstroem. Narration spoken by Fogelstroem. Cam (Eastmancolor), John Olsson; prodn des, P A Lundgren; cos des, Inger Pehrsson; edtr, Jan Persson; mus, Bjoern Isfaelt, using quotes from traditional and classical mus,; prodn mgr, Johan Clason. 160.
Eddie Axberg, Britt-Louise Tillbom, Mona Seilitz.
11/24/76

Mina, Viento De Libertad
(Mina, Wind of Freedom)
(Mexico - Cuba)
X. Conacite Uno (Mexico) and El Icaic (Cuba) prodn; dir, Antonio Eceiza; sp, Tomas Perez Turrent, Eceiza and Jesus Diaz; cam (Eastmancolor), Jorge Stahl Jr; mus, Leo Brouwer. 113.
Jose Alonso, Pedro Armendariz Jr, Hector Bonillo, Sergio Corrieri, Fernando Balzaretti, Rosaura Revueltas, Eslinda Nunez.
09/28/77

Mind Your Back, Professor: SEE Pas paa ryggen, professor

Minden Szerdan
(Every Wednesday)
(Hungary)
HU. Dir, Livia Gyarmathy. Sp, Guyka Marosi, Gyarmathy; cam (Eastmancolor), Ferenc Papp. 90.
Janos Ban, Miklos Markovics, Judit Mezlery, Tiber Szilagi.
07/23/80

The Mine: SEE Maden

Mineiro Cabaret: SEE Cabaret Mineiro

The Minister and Me: SEE El Ministro y Yo

The Miracle Tree: SEE Drevo Jelania

Miracles of the Gods: SEE Botschaft Der Goeter

Miris Poljs Kog Cveca
(The Smell of Wild Flowers)
(Yugoslavia)
YFR. Centar Film prodn. Dir, Srdjan Karanovic. Sp, Karanovic, Rajko Grlic; cam (Eastmancolor), Zivko Zalar; edtr, Branka Ceperac; mus, Zoran Simjanovic. 99.
Ljuba Tadic, Aleksander Bercek, Olga Spirironovic, Sonja Divac, Mrgud Radovanic, Branko Cvejic.
05/31/78

Miris Zemlje
(The Scent Of Earth)
(Yugoslavia)
YFR. Central Film Studio-Avala Film-Zespoly Filmowe Profil prodn. Wri-dir, Dragovan Jovanovic. Cam (Eastmancolor), Waclaw Dybowski; mus, Szeslaw Nieman. 86.
Kazimierz Borowiec, Neda Spasojevic, Ana Krasojevic, Ferdinand Wojcik, Crazyna Szapolawska.
08/16/78

The Mirror: SEE Zerkalo

The Mirror Crack'd
(Britain)
AFD. EMI Films presentation. Prod, John Brabourne, Richard Goodwin. Dir, Guy Hamilton. Sp, Jonathan Hales, Barry Sandler, from the novel, "The Mirror Crack'd From Side To Side," by Agatha Christie; cam (Technicolor), Christopher Challis; mus, John Cameron; edtr, Richard Marden; prodn des, Michael Stringer; art dir, John Roberts; snd, Bill Rowe, John Richards, John Mitchell; asst dir, Derek Cracknell. (MPAA rating: PG). 105.
Angela Lansbury, Geraldine Chaplin, Tony Curtis, Edward Fox, Rock Hudson, Kim Novak, Elizabeth Taylor, Marella Oppenheim, Wendy Morgan, Margaret Courtenay, Charles Gray, Maureen Bennett, Carolyn Pickles, Eric Dodson, Charles Lloyd Pack, Anthony Steel, Dinah Sheridan, Oriana Grieve, Kenneth Fortescue, Hildegarde Neil, Allan Cuthbertson, George Silver, John Bennett, Nigel Stock.
12/17/80

Mirror, Mirror: SEE Lille Spejl

Mis Dias con Veronica
(My Days With Veronica)
(Argentina)
DPA. Prod, Tilt Producciones Cinematograficas. Dir, Nestor Lescovich. Sp, Jorge Martinez; cam (Eastmancolor), Miguel Rodriguez; edtr, Julio Di Risio; snd, Abelardo Kushnir; mus, Luis Maria Serra. 85.
Dora Baret, Oscar Cruz, Susu Pecoraro, Hector Bidonde, Chela Ruiz.
04/23/80

The Miser: SEE L'Avare

Misfire: SEE Bomsalva

Misfire: SEE Fehlschuss

Miskhak Makhbuim
(Hide 'n Seek)
(Israel)
X. Jeff Justin-Dan Wolman Production. Wridir, Dan Wolman. Cam, Ilan Rosenberg; edtr, Shoshana Wolman; mus, Amnon Wolman; art dir, Ruth Dar. 90.
Gila Almagor, Doron Tavori, Chaim Hadaya, Efrat Lavie, Binyamin Armon, Rachel Shor.
06/25/80

Miss Keow: SEE Keow

Miss Laong Dao: SEE Laong Dao

Miss Salak Jitr: SEE Salak Jitr

The Missing Link
(France - Belgium)
SND. Pils Films - S N D co-prodn. Prods, Picha, Jenny Gerard, Michel Gast. Dsgn-dir, Picha. Sp, Tony Hendra, from a story by Picha, Pierre Bartier, Jean Collette; songs, Leo Sayer; mus arr, Roy Budd; edtr, Claude Cohen; snd track, Roy Baker; recorded in Dolby stereo; art dirs, Jean Lemens, Claude Lambert, Jean-Jacques Maquaire. 95.
Voices of Ron Venable, John Graham, Bob Kaliban, Christopher Guest, Clark Warren, Mark Smith.
(English-language track) (ANI)
05/14/80

The Missouri Breaks
UA. Prods, Elliott Kastner, Robert M Sherman. Dir, Arthur Penn. Sp, Thomas McGuane; cam (DeLuxe Color), Michael Butler; 2d unit cam, Rex Metx; edtrs, Jerry Greenberg, Stephen Rotter, Dede Allen; mus, John Williams; prodn des, Albert Brenner; art dir, Stephen Berger; set decor, Marvin March; snd, Richard Vorisek, Jack Solomon, Dennis Maitland; asst dir, Malcolm Harding; 2d unit dir, Michael Moore. (MPAA rating: PG). 126.
Marlon Brando, Jack Nicholson, Kathleen Lloyd, Randy Quaid, Frederick Forrest, Harry Dean Stanton, John McLiam, John Ryan, Sam Gilman, Steve Franken, Richard Bradford, James Greene, Luana Anders, Danny Goldman, Hunter Von Leer.
05/19/76

Mrs. Abad, I Am Bing: SEE Mrs. Teresa Abad Ako Po Si Bing

Mrs. Dery, Where Are You?:
SEE Deryne, Hol Van?

Mrs. Teresa Abad Ako Po Si Bing
(Mrs. Abad, I Am Bing)
(Philippines)
NVP. Dir, Danila Cabreira. Story-sp, Toto Belano; cam, Rodolfo Dino; mus, Willie Cruz. 103.
Charito Solia, Christopher de Leon, Tony Santos Jr, Johnny Delgado, Anita Linda.
06/23/76

Mr. Billion
FOX. Pantheon Pictures/Kaplan-Friedman prodn, prods, Steven Bach, Ken Friedman; exec prod, Gabriel Katzka. Dir, Jonathan Kaplan. Sp, Friedman, Kaplan; cam (DeLuxe Color), Matthew F Leonetti; edtr, O Nicholas Brown; mus, Dave Grusin; art dir, Richard Berger; set decor (USA), Sam Jones, (Italy) Joe Chavalier; cos/ward, Seth Banks, Stephanie Colin, Bill Jobe, Mal Pape; snd, Richard Portman, Richard Birnbaum (USA), Darren Knight (Italy); 2d-unit dir, Nate Long; aerial sequences, Jim Garvin; stunt coord, Walter Scott; asst dir, Peter Bogart (USA), Victor Tourjansky (Italy). (MPAA rating: PG). 91.
Terence Hill, Valerie Perrine, Jackie Gleason, Slim Pickens, William Redfield, Chill Wills, Dick Miller, R G Armstrong, Dave Cass, Sam Laws, John Ray McGhee, Kate Heflin, Leo Rossi, Bob Minor, Frances Heflin, Ralph Chesse.
03/02/77

Mr. Klein
(France)
FEL. Raymond Danon, Alain Delon, Jean-Pierre Labrande, Robert Kupferberg prodn. Dir, Joseph Losey. Sp, Franco Solinas; cam (Eastmancolor), Gerry Fisher; edtr, Henri Lanoe; art dir, Alexander Trauner; mus, Egisto Macchi, Pierre Porte. 122.
Alain Delon, Jeanne Moreau, Suzanne Flon, Michel Lonsdale, Juliet Berto, Jean Bouise, Francine Berge.
06/02/76

Mr. Mike's Mondo Video
NL. Prod-dir, Michael O'Donoghue. Exec prod, Lorne Michaels. Wri, O'Donoghue, Mitchell Glazer, Emily Prager, Dirk Wittenborn; cam (Video), Barry Rebo; edtrs, Bob Tischler, Alan Miller; prodn des, Eugene Lee, Franne Lee. (MPAA rating: R). 60.
Dan Aykroyd, Jane Curtin, Carrie Fisher, Teri Garr, Joan Hackett, Deborah Harry, Margot Kidder, Bill Murray, Gilda Radner, Sid Vicious.
10/03/79

Mr. Patman
(Canada)
FCD. Prods, Bill Marshall, Alexander MacDonald. Dir, John Guillermin; exec prod, Henk Van der Kolk; sp, Thomas Hedley. Cam, John Coquillon; edtrs, Max Benedict, Vince Hatherly; prodn des, Trevor Williams; snd, Brian Simmons; mus, Paul Hoffert. 105.
James Coburn, Kate Nelligan, Fionnuala Flanagan, Les Carlson, Candy Kane, Michael Kirby, Alan McRae, Jan Rubes, Hugh Webster, Lyn Griffin, Tabitha Herrington, Lois Maxwell.
05/28/80

Mistletoes: SEE Fagyongyok

The Mistress: SEE La Querida

Mistress: SEE Maitresse

Mitgift
(Killing Me Softly)
(W Germany)
EXB. Sentana Film prodn. Prod, Volker Messerschmidt. Wri-dir, Michael Verhoeven. Cam, Igor Luther. 90.
Senta Berger, Mario Adorf, Ron Ely, Helmut Qualtinger, Heidi Stroh.
05/26/76

Mlady Muz A Bila Velryba
(The Young Man and Moby Dick)
(Czechoslovakia)
CZS. Barrandov Studio prodn. Dir, Jaromil Jires. Sp, Maria Rudlovcakova, Jires from the story by Vladimir Paral; cam (Eastmancolor), Emil Sirotek; mus, Ladislav Staidl. 92.
Eduard Cupak, Ivan Vyskocil, Jana Brejchova, Zlata Adamovska.
09/05/79

Mo Hoozue Wa Tsukanai
(No More Easy Going)
(Japan)
X. Angle-ATG prodn. Prods, Takashi Arima, Hidehiro Kudo; dir, Yoichi Higashi; sp, Higashi, Tatsuo Kobayashi; cam, Koichi Kawakami; snd, Yukio Kubota; score, Michi Tanaka. 113.
Kaori Momoi, Eiji Okuda, Leo Morimoto, Sakura Kamo, Akemi Negishi, Juzo Itami.
09/10/80

The Moelleby Affair: SEE Affaeren I Moelleby

Moemoea
(The Dream)
(Tahiti)
HIT. Wri-dir, Dominique Arnaud. Cam, Jean-Claude Boshel; edtr, Eugene Haoa; mus, Tokiri. 85.
Richmond Terorohauepa.
(16m)
05/14/80

Mogliamante
(Lover, Wife)
(Italy)
PIC. Vides prodn. Prod, Franco Cristaldi. Dir, Marco Vicario. Sp, Rodolfo Sonego; cam (Technicolor), Ennio Guarnieri; edtr, Nino Baragli; mus, Armando Trovajoli; art dir, Mario Garbuglia. 104.
Laura Antonelli, Marcello Mastroianni, Leonard Mann, Olga Karlatos, Annie Belle, Gastone Moschin.
11/16/77

Moi, Fleur Bleue
(Stop Calling Me Baby)
(France)
CII. Axe Films-Victorine Studios-Prodns Yanne prodn. Dir, Eric Le Hung. Sp, Philippe Bourgoin, Le Hung; cam, Marcel Combes; edtr, Christiane Lack; mus, Francois D'Aime. 98.
Jodie Foster, Jean Yanne, Sydne Rome, Bernard Giraudeau, Lila Kedrova.
11/16/77

Moi Laskoviy I Niejnie Zver
(A Hunting Accident)
(USSR)
SOV. Mosfilm prodn. Dir-wri, Emil Lotianu from a story by Anton Chekhov. Cam (Sovcolor), A Petritzki; mus, Yevgueni Doga. 107.
Galina Belaieva, Oleg Yankovski, Kirill Lavrov, Svetlana Toma, Grigori Grigouiou.
05/24/78

Moi Tinh Dau
(First Love)
(Vietnam)
X. A Vietnamese Film Prodn. Dir, Nguyen Hai Ninh. Cam, Nguyen Guang Tuan. 90.
Tra Giang, Nhu Quynh, Hong Lien.
(B & W)
08/09/78

Moi, Tintin
(I, Tintin)
(Belgium - France)
ELN. Pierre Films and Rova (Brussels), Belvision (Paris) prodn. Dirs, Andre Roanne, Gerard Valet. Sp, Roanne and Valet; cam (Eastmancolor-Belvision), Jos Marissen; for ani, Andre Goeffers, Walter Vanden Enden for live action; edtr, Michele Marquet; mus, Alain Pierre; commentary, Gerard Valet, Jose Fostier, Jean-Paul Andret, Anne Rieter, with extracts of newsreels and films. (MPAA rating: G). 87.
11/24/76

Moja Wojna - Moja Milosc
(My War - My Love)
(Poland)
X. Film Polski prodn, "Iluzion" group, prodn mgr, Zbigniew Breitkopf. Dir, Janusz Nasfeter. Sp, Teresa and Janusz Nasfeter; cam, Witold Sobocinski; mus, Piotr Figiel; art dir, Halina Dobrowolska. 90.
Piotry Lysak, Grazyna Michalska, Ryszard Barycz.
06/02/76

Moliere
(France)
UA. Films 13-Films Du Soleil et la Nuit-Antenne 2-RAI prodn. Wri-dir, Ariane Mnouchkine. Cam (Eastmancolor), Bernard Zitzerman; edtrs, Francoise Javet, Georges Klotz; art dir, Guy-Claude Francois; mus, Rene Clemencile. 255.
Philippe Caubere, Marie-France Audollent, Jonathon Sutton, Frederic Ladonne, Odile Cointepas, Armand Delcampe, Jean Daste, Francoise Jamet, Jean-Claude Penchenat.
05/31/78

The Moment: SEE Clipa The Moment: SEE Oejeblikket

Moment: SEE Tren

Moment By Moment
U. Robert Stigwood prodn. Exec prod, Kevin McCormick. Prod, Stigwood. Wri-dir, Jane Wagner. Cam, Phillip Lathrop; edtr, John F Burnett; prodn des, Harry Horner; mus, Lee Holdridge; cos des, Albert Wolsky; snd, Charles M Wilborn; asst dir, Michael Grillo. (MPAA rating: R).   105.
Lily Tomlin, John Travolta, Andra Akers, Bert Kramer, Shelley R Bonus, Debra Feuer, James Luisi.
12/20/78

Moments
(Israel - France)
X. Rosa Prodns-Mica Films-Bein Hashurot prodn. Wri-dir, Michal Bat-Adam. Cam (Eastmancolor), Yves Lafaye; mus, Hubert Rostaign.   90.
Michal Bat-Adam, Brigitte Catillon, Assaf Dayan, Avi Pnini.
05/16/79

Mom's 100 Years Old: SEE Mama Cumple 100 Anos

Mon and Ino: SEE Ani Imouto

Mon Coeur Est Rouge
(My Heart Is Red)
(France)
LML. Go-Films prodn. Wri-dir, Michele Rosier. Cam (Eastmancolor), Bruno Nuytten; edtr, Suzanne Baron; mus, Keith Jarrett.   105.
Francoise Lebrun, Ghedalia Tazartes, Jean Ipousteguy, Hermine Karagheuz.
03/09/77

Mon Oncle d'Amerique
(My American Uncle)
(France)
FGG. Philippe Dussart/Andrea Films/T F 1 co-prodn. Prod, Philippe Dussart. Dir, Alain Resnais. Wri, Jean Gruault, inspired by the writings of Henri Laborit. Cam, Sacha Vierny. Mus, Arie Dzierlatka. Snd, Jean-Pierre Ruh, Jacques Maumont. Art dir, Jacques Saulnier. Cos, Catherine Leterrier. Edtr, Albert Jurgenson.   125.
Gerard Depardieu, Nicole Garcia, Roger Pierre, Marie Dubois, Nelly Bourgeaud, Henri Laborit.
05/21/80

Mon Premier Amour
(My First Love)
(France)
GAU. 7 Films-Gaumont-FR3 prodn. Wri-dir, Elie Chouraqui, from the book by Jack Alain Leger. Cam (Eastmancolor), Bernard Zitzermann; edtr, Marie-Josephe Yoyotte.   100.
Anouk Aimee, Richard Berry, Gabriele Ferzetti, Jacques Villeret, Nathalie Baye.
09/27/78

Monarch
(W Germany)
X. Prod, Regina Ziegler. Dir-wri-pho-snd-edtrs, Fluetsch & Stelzer.   80.
(DOC)
03/05/80

Mondays with Fanny: SEE Mandagarna med Fanny

Money Movers
(Australia)
RDP. South Australian Film Corp prodn. Prod, Matt Carroll. Dir, Bruce Beresford. Sp, Beresford, from novel by Devon Minchin; cam, Don McAlpine; edtr, William Anderson; stunt coord, Alf Joint; art dir, David Copping; tech adv, Devon Minchin; snd, Don Connolly; prodn mgr, Pat Clayton; asst dirs, Mark Egerton, Mark Turnbull, Scott Hicks; wardrobe, Anna Senior; sfx, Ian Jamieson.   94.
Terence Donovan, Ed Devereaux, Tony Bonner, Lucky Grills, Alan Cassell, Frank Wilson, Candy Raymond, Bryan Brown, Charles "Bud" Tingwell, Gary Files, Hu Price, Ray Marshall, Jeanie Drynan, Terry Camilleri, Ted Hodgeman, James Elliott, Max Fairchild, Rick Hart, Robert Essex, Alan Penney, Tom Farley, Stuart Littlemore, Jo-Anne Moore, Mimi Mattin, Brian Harrison, Kathy Dior.
10/18/78

The Monkey Bridge: SEE Le Pont De Singe

The Monkey Hustle
AIP. Prod-dir, Arthur Marks. Sp, Charles Johnson; story, Odie Hawkins; cam (Movielab), Jack L Richards; edtr, Art Seid; mus, Jack Conrad; snd, William Pellak; ward, Llandys Williams. (MPAA rating: PG).   90.
Yaphet Kotto, Rudy Ray Moore, Rosalind Cash, Randy Brooks, Debbi Morgan, Thomas Carter, Donn Harper, Lynn Caridine, Patricia McCaskill, Lynn Harris, Fuddle Bagley, Frank Rice, Carl Crudup, Duchyll Smith, Kirk Calloway.
12/29/76

Monsieur Albert
(France)
GAU. Screen-France Regions-FR3-Films Ariane prodn. Wri-dir, Jacques Renard. Cam (Eastmancolor), Ghislain Cloquet; edtr, Genevieve Letellier.   100.
Philippe Noiret, Dominique Labourier, Patrick Chesnais, Suzanne Flon, Fabrice Pluciennek, Catherine Lachens, Monique Chaumette.
04/07/76

Monsieur Papa
(France)
GAU. Euro France-Gaumont Int'l prodn. Dir, Philippe Monnier. Sp, Jean-Marie Poire, Monnier; book, Patrick Cauvin; cam (Eastmancolor), Edmond Sechan; edtr, Marie-Josephe Yoyotte; mus, Mort Shuman.   90.
Claude Brasseur, Nicholas Reboul, Nathalie Baye, Catherine Lachens.
09/14/77

Moods Of Love
(Hong Kong)
SHW. Runme Shaw prodn. Wri-dir, Li Han-hsiang. Cam, Lin Chao; art dir, Chen Ching-sen; edtr, Chiang Hsing-lung; mus dir, Wu Hsu-ching.   100.
Chiang Nan, Yueh Hua, Shirley Yu, Shaw Yin Yin, Hu Chin, Chen Ping, Tanny.
02/02/77

Mool-Dori Village
(Korea)
07/25/79
HAP. Prod, Kwak Jung Hwan. Dirs, Lee Doo Yong, Zee Doo Yong. Story-sp, Yu Dong Fun; cam-lighting-sfx, Song Ung Cha; mus, Choi Yon Dong; snd, Han So Jong of Hanang Studio (Seoul).   100.
Kim Young-Ran, Han So Ryong, Hyung Kil Soo, Kim Jung Ah.

Moon In Taurus
(Switzerland)
STW. Alive Film Productions GmbH Zurich prodn. Prod-wri-dir, Steff Gruber; cam, Andy Humphreys; snd, Jim Hawkins; edtrs, Gruber, Beni Mueller, Daniel Koch; mus, "Cordoba" from "Iberia" by Isaac Albeniz, played by Ruedi Burkhalter; mus advice, Paul Fischli; asst cam, Billy Sherrill.   100.
Wanda Linn Wester, Jack Wright, Bonnie T, Steff Gruber.
09/10/80

Moon Over The Alley
(Britain)
BFI. Dir, Joseph Despins. Sp, William Dumaresq; cam, Peter Hannan; edtr, Despins; mus, Galt MacDermot; lyrs, Dumaresq; snd, Conrad Weyns; prodn mgr, Geoffrey Evans; asst dir, Ian Sellar.   107.
Doris Fishwick, Peter Farrell, Erna May, John Gay, Sean Caffrey, Sharon Forester, Patrick Murray, Lesley Roach, Basil Clarke, Bill Williams, Vari Sylvester, Joan Geary, Norman Mitchell, Leroy Hyde, Miguel Sergides, Debbie Evans.
(B & W) (16m)
10/01/80

Moonlight Serenade: SEE Serenata A La Luz De La Luna

Moonraker
(Britain)
UA. Albert R Broccoli prodn. Dir, Lewis Gilbert. Exec prod, Michael G Wilson. Sp, Christopher Wood, based on Ian Fleming novel; cam, Jean Tournier; mus, John Barry, Hal David; prodn des, Ken Adam; edtr, John Glen; visual effects supv, Derek Meddings; prodn mgrs, (France) Jean-Pierre Spiri-Mercanton, (U K) Terence Churcher; second unit dirs, Ernie Day, John Glan; asst dir, Michael Cheyko; art dirs, Max Douy, Charles Bishop; set decor, Peter Howitt; snd mixer, Daniel Brisseau; sfx, John Evans, John Richardson; pub, Steve Swan, Gilles Durieux; title song sung by Shirley Bassey. (MPAA rating: PG).   126.
Roger Moore, Lois Chiles, Michael Lonsdale, Richard Kiel, Corinne Clery, Bernard Lee, Geoffrey Keen, Desmond Llewelyn, Lois Maxwell, Emily Bolton, Toshiro Suga, Blanche Ravalec,

Jean-Pierre Castaldi, Leila Shenna, Walter Gotell, Arthur Howard, Irka Bochenko, Michael Marshall, Douglas Lambert, Alfie Bass, Anne Lonnberg, Brian Keith, George Birt, Kim Fortune, Chris Dillinger, Georges Beller, Johnny Traber, Lizzie Warville, Chichinou Kaeppler, Francoise Gayat, Catherine Serre, Christina Hui, Nicaise Jean-Louis, Beatrice Libert.
06/27/79

Moonshine County Express
NW. Ed Carlin prodn; dir, Gus Trikonis. Sp, Hubert Smith, Daniel Ansley; cam (Movielab Color), Gary Graver; edtr, Gene Ruggiero; mus, Fred Werner; asst dirs, Nicole Scott, Jack Bohrer; art dir, Peter Jamison; snd, Bill Kapland Jr; stunt coord, Bill Burton. (MPAA rating: PG).   95.
John Saxon, Susan Howard, William Conrad, Morgan Woodward, Claudia Jennings, Jeff Corey, Dub Taylor, Maureen McCormick, Fred Foresman.
06/08/77

The Moravian Land: SEE O Moravske Zemi

Mords Pas On T'Aime
(Don't Bite, We Love You)
(France)
GCC. UNC-FR3 prodn. Dir, Yves Allegret. Sp, Francois Boyer, Allegret; cam (Eastmancolor), Jean Boffety; edtr, Jacques Gaillard; mus, Pierre Jansen. 97.
Bernard Fresson, Catherine Allegret, Jean-Pierre Darras, Yves Coudray, Sylviane Bressy, Micheline Presle.
05/05/76

More American Graffiti
U. Lucasfilm Ltd prodn. Prod, Howard Kazanjian. Exec prod, George Lucas. Dir, B W L Norton. Sp, Norton, based on characters created by Lucas, Gloria Katz, Willard Huyck; cam (Technicolor), Caleb Deschanel; edtr, Tina Hirsch; art dir, Ray Storey; snd (Dolby Stereo), David McMillan; cos des, Agnes Rodgers; set decor, Doug Van Koss; asst dir, Thomas Lofaro.   111.
Candy Clark, Bo Hopkins, Ron Howard, Paul Le Mat, Mackenzie Phillips, Charles Martin Smith, Cindy Williams, Anna Bjorn, Richard Bradford, John Brent, Scott Glenn, James Houghton, John Lansing, Ken Place, Mary Kay Place, Will Seltzer, Ralph Wilcox.
07/25/79

The More It Goes, The Less It Goes: SEE Plus Ca Va, Moins Ca Va

Moritz, Lieber Moritz
(Moritz, Dear Moritz)
(W Germany)
FDA. Prodn of the Hamburger Kino Kompanie/Hark Bohm Film prodns. Sp-dir, Hark Bohm. Cam (Eastmancolor), Wolfgang Treu; edtr, Jane Sperr; sets, Hans Zillmann; mus, Klaus Doldinger; snd, Peter Kellerhals; animal trainer, Natalia Bowakow.   96.
Michael Kebschull, Myra Mladeck, Walter Klosterfelde, Elvira Thom, Kerstin Wehlmann, Uwe Enkelmann, Dschingis Bowakow, Armand Hacaturyan, Nico Lafrentz, Richard Schuhmacher, Wolf-Dietrich Berg, Eva Fiebig, Uwe Dallmeier, Christa Siems, Grete Mosheim.
03/29/78

Mormor og de atte ungene i byen
(Grandma and the Eight Children in Town)
(Norway)
X. Vampyrfilm-Norsk Film prodn. Prods, Hans Lindgren, Gunnar Svensrud. Wri-dir, Espen Thorstenson, from novels by Anne-Cath Vestly. Cam, Halvor Naess; edtrs, Leif Erisboe, Thorstenson; art dir, Sven Wickman. 96.
Anne-Cath Vestly, Eli Ryg, Jon Eikemo, Nils Sletta, Kari Simonsen, Grim Snorre Langen.
11/19/80

Morning Mist: SEE Manha Submersa

The Morning Star
(Mongolia)
X. Mongolian Film Prodn. Dir, Zhemyangiin Buntar.   90.
Sh Davaasamba, J Suhuyag, Ts Damagindorj, J Delgerjargal.
(B & W)
07/02/80

Mort D'Un Pourri
(Death Of A Corrupt Man)
(France)
CII. Adel Prodn (Alain Delon) prodn. Dir, Georges Lautner. Sp, Michel Audiard, Delon, from book by Raf Vallet; cam (Eastmancolor), Henri Decae; edtr, Michelle David; mus, Philippe Sarde, Stan Getz.   120.
Alain Delon, Ornella Muti, Stephane Audran, Maurice Ronet, Mireille Darc, Klaus Kinski, Daniel Ceccaldi, Julien Guiomar, Michel Aumont.
12/21/77

Morte Di Un Operatore
(Death of a Cameraman)
(Italy)
07/25/79
RTI. Ager Cinematografica, RAI prodn. Wri-dir, Faliero Rosati. Cam, Angelo Bevilacqua. 65.
Daniele Griggio, Remo Remotti.
(16m)

Mosch
(W Germany)
X. Westdeutscher Rundfunk film prodn, Cologne. Dir, Tankred Dorst. Sp, Dorst, Ursula Ehler; cam, Juergen Juerges; mus, Peer Raben; sets, Guenther Naumann; edtr, Liesgret Schmitt-Klink; TV prodn mgr, Hartwig Schmidt.   105.
Marius Mueller-Westernhagen, Valter Taub, Katharina Thalbach, Ulrich Wildgruber, Rosel Zech, Sonja Karzau, Rudolf Voss, Ernst Konarek, Franz-Adolph Rampelmann, Maria-Luise Marjan, Horst Laube.
(B & W)
10/29/80

Moscow Does Not Believe In Tears: SEE Moskwa Sljesam Nje Jerit

Moses
(Britain - Italy)
ITC. ITC-RAI co-prodn, prod, Vincenzo Labella. Dir, Gianfranco de Bosio. Sp, Anthony Burgess, Vittorio Bonicelli, Gianfranco de Bosio; cam (Technicolor), Marcello Gatti; edtrs, Gerry Hambling, Peter Boita, John Guthridge, Alberto Gallitti, Freddie Wilson; mus, Ennio Morricone; addl mus, songs and dances, Dov Seltzer; snd, Luciano Welisch; set des, Pierluigi Basile; cos, Enrico Sabbatini; sfx, Mario Bava; asst dir, Francesco Cinieri. (MPAA rating: PG).   140.
Burt Lancaster, Anthony Quayle, Ingrid Thulin, Irene Papas, Mariangela Melato, William Lancaster, Laurent Terzieff, Aharon Ipale, Marina Berti, Mario Ferrari, Yousef Shiloah, Shmuel Rodensky.
02/25/76

Moskwa Sljesam Nje Jerit
(Moscow Does Not Believe In Tears)
(USSR)
MSF. Dir, Vladimir Menshov. Sp, Valentin Tschernych; cam (Sovcolor), Igor Slabnjewitsch; edtr, Jelene Mischajova.   145.
Vera Alentova, Alexei Batalov, Irina Murawjova, Raissa Rjasanova, Juri Wassiliev.
03/05/80

Motel Hell
UA. Camp Hill prodn. Exec prod, Herb Jaffe. Prod-wris, Steven-Charles Jaffe, Robert Jaffe. Dir, Kevin Connor. Cam, Thomas Del Ruth; edtr, Bernard Gribble; mus, Lance Rubin; art dir, Joseph M Altadonna; asst dir, Jack Barry; sfx, Adams R Calvert. (MPAA rating: R).   106.
Rory Calhoun, Paul Linke, Nancy Parsons, Nina Axelrod, Wolfman Jack, Elaine Joyce, Dick Curtis, Monique St Pierre, Rosanne Katon, E Hampton Beagle, Michael Melvin.
10/22/80

The Moth: SEE Cma

Mother and Daughter: SEE Maternale

Mother Kuster's Trip to Heaven: SEE Mutter Kusters Fahrt Zum Himmel

Mother, Dearly Beloved: SEE Mater Amatisima

Mother, Jugs & Speed
FOX. Prods, Peter Yates, Tom Mankiewicz; exec prod, Joseph R Barbera. Dir, Yates. Sp, Mankiewicz, from story by Stephen Manes, Mankiewicz; cam (DeLuxe Color), Ralph Woolsey; edtr, Frank P Keller; prodn des, Walter Scott Herndon; set decor, Cheryl Kearney; snd, Theodore Soderberg, Gene Cantamessa; asst dir, Arthur Levinson. (MPAA rating: PG). 95.

Raquel Welch, Bill Cosby, Harvey Keitel, Allen Garfield, Larry Hagman, L Q Jones, Bruce Davison, Dick Butkus, Milt Kamen, Barra Grant, Allan Warnick, Valerie Curtin, Ric Carrott, Severn Darden, Bill Henderson, Mike McManus, Toni Basil, Edwin Mills, Erica Hagen, Arnold Williams, Charles Knapp, Linda Geray.
05/19/76

Mother's Day
UF. Michael Kravitz, Charles Kaufman prodn. Dir, Kaufman; sp, Kaufman, Warren D Leight; cam, Joe Mangine; asso prods, Lloyd Kaufman, Michael Heriz; mus, Phil Gallo, Clem Vicari. 98.
Nancy Hendrickson, Deborah Luce, Tiana Pierce, Holden McGuire, Billy Ray McQuade, Rose Ross, Kevin Loew, Karl Sandys, Ed Battle, Stanley Knapp, Marsella Davidson, Robert Carnegie, Scott Lucas, Bobby Collins.
09/24/80

Mount Hakkoda
(Japan)
TOH. Prod, Shinobu Hashimoto, Toho. Dir, Shiro Moriya. Sp, Shinobu Hashimoto; story, Jiro Nitta; mus, Yasushi Akutagawa; cam Daisaku Kimura. 170.
Shogo Shimada, Hideji Ohtaki, Ken Takakura, Tetsuro Tanba, Takuya Fujioka, Gin Maeda, Kinya Kitaohji, Rentaro Mikuni, Yuzo Kayama, Keiji Kobayashi, Shigeru Kohyama, Kensaku Morita, Ken Ogata, Komaki Kurihara, Mariko Kaga, Kumiko Akiyoshi.
07/27/77

Mountain Family Robinson
PIE. Arthur R Dubs prodn. Exec prod, Fred R Krug. Wri-prod, Arthur R Dubs. Dir, John Cotter. Cam (CFI), James Roberson; mus, Robert O Ragland; lyrs, Carol Connors, songs performed by Dann Rogers. (MPAA rating: G). 100.
Robert F Logan, Susan Damante Shaw, William Bryant, Heather Rattray, Ham Larsen, George (Buck) Flower.
10/24/79

The Mountain Men
COL. Martin Ransohoff Prodn. Prods, Martin Shafer, Andrew Scheinman; exec prod, Richard R St Johns. Dir, Richard Lang. Sp, Fraser Clarke Heston; cam (Metrocolor), Michel Hugo; 2d unit cam, Herb Pearl; mus, Michel Legrand; edtr, Eva Ruggiero; prodn des, Bill Kenney; set decor, Rick T Gentz; snd, Glenn Anderson, Les Fresholtz; 2d unit dir, Joe Canutt; asso prod, Cathleen Summers. (MPAA rating: R). 102.
Charlton Heston, Brian Keith, Victoria Racimo, Stephen Macht, John Glover, Seymour Cassel, David Ackroyd, Cal Bellini, Bill Lucking, Ken Ruta, Victor Jory.
07/23/80

Mountain Pass: SEE Passe Montagne

Mourir a Tue-Tete
(A Scream from Silence)
(Canada)
NFC. Office Nat'l Du Film Du Canada prodn. Dir, Anne Claire Poirier. Sp, Marthe Blackburn, Poirier; cam, Michel Brault; edtr, Andre Corriveau; mus, Maurice Blackburn. 95.
Julie Vincent, Germain Houde, Paul Savoie, Monique Miller, Micheline Lanctot.
06/06/79

The Mouse And His Child
X. deFaria-Lockhart-Sanrio prodn, in asso with Murakami-Wolf Prods. Exec prods, Warren Lockhart, Shintaro Tsuji; prod, Walt deFaria; dirs, Fred Wolf, Charles Swenson; sp, Carol Mon Pere, from novel by Russell Hoban; mus, Roger Kellaway; lyr, Gene Lees; edtr, Rich Harrison; ani cam (Deluxe Color), Wally Bullock; ani, Murakami-Wolf Prods; ani, Fred Wolf, Charles Swenson, Dave Brain, Vince Davis, Gary Mooney, Mike Sanger, Lu Guarnier, Willie Lye, Bob Zamboni, Brad Case, Irv Anderson, Duane Crowther. (MPAA Rating: G). 83.
Voices: Peter Ustinov, Cloris Leachman, Sally Kellerman, Andy Devine, Neville Brand, Alan Barzman, Marcy Swenson, Bob Holt, Joan Gerber, Mel Leven.
(ANI)
06/29/77

Mouth to Mouth
(Australia)
X. Vega Film Prodns presentation. Prods, Jon Sainken, John Duigan. Dir-sp, John Duigan; art dir, Tracy Watt; cam (Eastmancolor), Tom Cowan; snd, Lloyd Carrick; mus, Roy Ritchie; edtr, Tony Paterson. 93.
Kim Krejus, Sonia Peat, Ian Gilmour, Sergio Frazzetto, Walter Pym, Michael Carman.
05/10/78

Movie Movie
WB. Stanley Donen prodn. Prod-dir, Stanley Donen. Sp, Larry Gelbart, Sheldon Keller; exec prod, Martin Starger; cam, "Dynamite Hands," Charles Rosher Jr; cam, "Baxter's Beauties of 1933," Bruce Surtees; art dir, Jack Fisk; edtr, George Hively; mus, Ralph Burns; chor, "Baxter's," Michael Kidd; cos, Patty Norris; sngs, lyr, Larry Gelbart, Sheldon Keller; mus, Ralph Burns, Buster Davis; asst dir, Joanthan Sanger; set des, Chris Horner; set decor, Jerry Wunderlich. (MPAA rating: PG). 105.
George C Scott, Barbara Harris, Barry Bostwick, Trish Van Devere, Red Buttons, Eli Wallach, Rebecca York, Art Carney, Maidie Norman, Jocelyn Brando, Charles Lane, Barney Martin, Dick Winslow, John Hudkinds, Robert Herron, Sebastian Brook, Jerry Von Hoeltke, Paula Jones, John Henry, Harry Hamlin, Ann Reinking, Michael Kidd, Kathleen Beller, Clay Hodges, George P Wilbur, Peter T Stader, James Lennon, Denver R Mattson, James Nickerson, Harvey G Parry, Wally Rose.
11/15/78

Moving Violation
FOX. Santa Fe Prods film, prod, Julie Corman; exec prod, Roger Corman. Dir, Charles S Dubin. Sp, David R Osterhout, William Norton, from a story by Osterhout; cam (DeLuxe Color), Charles Correll; edtrs, Richard Sprague, Howard Terrill; mus, Don Peake; art dir, Sherman Loudermilk; snd, Darin Knight; 2d unit dir, Barbara Peeters (MPAA rating: PG). 91.
Stephen McHattie, Kay Lenz, Eddie Albert, Lonny Chapman, Will Geer, Jack Murdock, John S Ragin, Dennis Redfield, Michael Ross Verona, Francis de Sales, Dick Miller.
07/28/76

Mozart - Aufzeichnungen Einer Jugend
(Mozart - A Childhood Chronicle)
(W Germany)
X. Artfilm Pitt Koch prodn, in collab with Bayerischer Rundfunk and Kuratorium junger deutscher Film. Wri-dir, Klaus Kirschner. Cam, Pitt Koch; scenes-cos, Adler; mus dramaturgy, Franz Beyer; dramaturgy, Helmut Dotterweich; asst dir, Birgitt Straach. 224.
Pavlos Bekiaris, Diego Crovetti, Santiago Ziesmer, Marianne Lowitz, Ingeborg Schroeder, Nina Palmers, Elisabeth Bronfen, Dietlind Huebner, Karl-Maria Schley.
(B & W)
07/14/76

Mrigayaa
(The Royal Hunt)
(India)
SHS. K Rajeswara Rao prodn. Dir, Mrinal Sen. Sp, Sen, Mohit Chattopadhyaya Aryn Kaul from story by Charan Panigrahi; cam (Eastmancolor), K K Mahajan; edtr, Gangadhar Naskar; mus, Salil Chaudhury. 112.
Mittun Chakraborty, Mamata Shankar, Robert Wright, Sadhu Meher.
01/26/77

The Mucker: SEE Os Mucker

Mue Peun Khia
(The Reluctant Gunfighter)
(Thailand)
SAT. Prod, Oijay Walaipan. Dir, Anumat Bunnag. Exec prod, Chanarong Damraskul. Story-sp, Gan Roongkan; cam, Sawaeng Ditsayawanna; mus, Prasert Churaketr; titles, Jack Siam. 120.
Sombat Metanee, Naiyana Chivanand, Piyamatr Monjakul, Sayant Chatawiboon, Prachuab Lerkyamdi, Dam Daskorn, Pipop Pupinyo, Tawan, Marasi, Chaopetr Chaiyanetr.
01/19/77

Mueda
(Mozambique)
X. Prod Mozambique Film Organization. Dir, Ruy Guerra, asst by Jose Pedro Pimenta; sp, Calisto Dos Lagos. 90.
Filipe Gunoguacala, Romao Canapoquele, Balthasar Nohilema.
(B & W)
06/18/80

Muenchhausen
(The Adventures of Baron Muenchhausen)
(W Germany)
ATF. Ufa Prodn, Berlin, restored by the Friedrich-Wilhelm-Murnau Foundation. Dir, Josef von Baky. Sp, Erich Kaestner (under pseudonym Berthold Buerger); cam, Werner Krien; sfx, Konstantin Irmen-Tschet; art dir, Emil Hasler, Otto Guelstorff; mus, Georg Haentzschel; prod, Eberhard Schmidt. 100.
Hans Albers, Brigitte Horney, Wilhelm Bendow, Michael Bohnen, Hans Brausewetter, Marina von Ditmar, Andrews Engelmann, Kaethe Haack, Herman Speelmanns, Walter Lieck, Ferdinand Marian, Leo Slezak, Gustav Waldau, Ilse Werner.
(MADE IN 1934)
06/21/78

Muerte Al Amanecer
(Death at Dawn)
(Peru - Venezuela)
PII. Dir, Francisco Jose Lombardi. Sp, Guillermo Thordike, Lombardi; cam (Eastmancolor), Ramon Carthy; edtr, Pili Flores-Guera; mus, Arturo Pinto. 113.
Gustavo Rodriguez, William Moreno, Sylvia Galvez, Jorge Rodriguez Paz, Hugo Soriano, Alberto Arese.
08/31/77

The Muppet Movie
AFD. ITC Entertainment film; Jim Henson prodn. Exec prod, Martin Starger. Prod, Jim Henson. Co-prod, David Lazer. Dir, James Frawley. Sp, Jerry Juhl, Jack Burns; cam (CFI Color), Isidore Mankofsky; edtr, Chris Greenbury; prodn des, Joel Schiller; mus, Paul Williams; art dir, Les Gobruegge; snd (Dolby), Charles Lewis; cos (Muppets), Calista Hendrickson; cos des, Gwen Capetanos; asst dir, Ron Wright. (MPAA rating: G) 98.
Jim Henson, Frank Oz, Jerry Nelson, Richard Hunt, Dave Goelz, Charles Durning, Austin Pendleton, Scott Walker, Edgar Bergen, Milton Berle, Mel Brooks, James Coburn, Dom De Luise, Elliott Gould, Bob Hope, Madeline Kahn, Carol Kane, Cloris Leachman, Steve Martin, Richard Pryor, Telly Savalas, Orson Welles, Paul Williams.
05/30/79

Murder by Death
COL. Prod, Ray Stark. Dir, Robert Moore. Sp, Neil Simon; cam (Metrocolor), David M Walsh; edtrs, Margaret Booth, John F Burnett; mus, Dave Grusin; prodn des, Stephen Grimes; art dir, Harry Kemm; set decor, Marvin March; snd, Tex Rudloff, Jerry Jost; asst dir, Fred T Gallo. (MPAA rating: PG). 94.
Eileen Brennan, Truman Capote, James Coco, Peter Falk, Alec Guinness, Elsa Lanchester, David Niven, Peter Sellers, Maggie Smith, Nancy Walker, Estelle Winwood, James Cromwell, Richard Narita, Myron.
06/23/76

Murder By Decree
(Britain)
AVE. Ambassador Films prodn, prod in cooperation with Canadian Film Development Corp and Famous Players Ltd. Exec prod, Len Herberman. Co-prods, Rene Dupont, Bob Clark. Dir, Clark. Sp, John Hopkins; cam (Metrocolor), Reg Morris; edtr, Stan Cole; prodn des, Harry Pottle; cos des, Judy Moorcroft; snd, John Mitchell; asst dir, Ariel Levy. (MPAA rating: PG). 120.
Christopher Plummer, James Mason, Donald Sutherland, Genevieve Bujold, David Hemmings, Susan Clark, Anthony Quayle, John Gielgud, Frank Finlay.
01/24/79

The Mushroom Eater: SEE El Hombre De Los Hongos

The Music Machine
(Britain)
NFL. Norfolk Int'l Pictures presentation. Exec prod, James Kenelm Clarke. Prod, Brian Smedley-Aston. Dir, Ian Sharp. Sp, Kenelm Clarke; cam, Phil Meheux; edtrs, Alan Patillo, Smedley-Aston; art dir, Roger King; snd, Mickey Hickey; mus comp-perf by the Music Machine, with guest singer Patti Boulaye; asst dir, Vic Priggs. 90.
Gerry Sundquist, Patti Boulaye, Clarke Peters, David Easter, Mandy Perryment, Billy McColl, Chrissy Wickham, Ray Burdis, Frances Lowe, Garry Shail, Mickey Feast.
06/20/79

Mustang Country
U. Wri-prod-dir, John Champion. Cam (Technicolor), J Barry Herron; edtr, Douglas Robertson; mus, Lee Holdridge; song, "Follow Your Restless Dreams," by Joe Henry, Holdridge; set decor, Peter Young; snd, Rodney Haykin; asst dir, Frank Arrigo. (MPAA rating: G). 79.
Joel McCrea, Robert Fuller, Patrick Wayne, Nika Mina.
03/24/76

Mustang: The House That Joe Built
X. RG Productions II prodn, prod-dir-pho, Robert Guralnick. Exec prod, William Walker; asso prod, Sean Daniel; edtr, Irving Lerner; mus, Carmine Coppola, plus seven hit songs from TK Productions; snd, Curt Hahn, David Macmillan. 85.
(DOC)
04/14/76

The Mute: SEE Der Stumme

Mutter Kusters Fahrt Zum Himmel
(Mother Kuster's Trip to Heaven)
(W Germany)
TGO. Dir-story-sp, Rainer Werner Fassbinder. Edtr, Eymesz; sets, Kurt Raab. 105.
Margit Carstensen, Brigitte Mira, Ingrid Caven, and Karl Bohn.
05/12/76

Muzhki Vremena
(Many Times)
(Bulgaria)
BGO. BulgaroFilm prodn, Hemus Group, Sofia. Dir, Eduard Zahariev. Sp, Nikolai Haitov; cam (Eastmancolor), Radoslav Spassov; art dir, Anghel Ahbrahnov; mus, Kiril Donchev. 100.
Grigor Vachkov, Marianna Dimitrova, Nikola Todev, Trayan Yankov, Georgi Georgiev, Velko Kunev, Teofil Badelov.
05/31/78

My American Uncle: SEE Mon Oncle d'Amerique

My Asylum: SEE Chiedo Asilo

My Beloved: SEE Min aelskade

My Bodyguard
FOX. Prod, Don Devlin; exec prod, Melvin Simon; dir, Tony Bill; sp, Alan Ornsby; cam (Deluxe color), Michael D Margulies; edtr, Stu Linder; snd, Nat Boxer, Ray Cymoszinski; prod des, Jackson de Govia; asst dir, Michael Daves; asso prod, Phillip Goldfarb; mus, Dave Grusin. (MPAA rating: PG). 97.
Chris Makepeace, Adam Baldwin, Matt Dillon, Ruth Gordon, Martin Mull, Paul Quandt, Hank Salas, Joan Cusack, Craig Richard Nelson, John Houseman, Kathryn Grody, Dean R Miller, Tim Reyna, Richard Bradley, Denise Baske.
06/18/80

My Brilliant Career
(Australia)
NSW. New South Wales Corp.-GUO prodn. Dir, Gil Armstrong. Sp, Eleanor Witcombe from the book by Miles Franklin; cam (Eastmancolor, Panavision), Don McAlpine; edtr, Nick Beauman; mus, Nathan Waks. 98.
Judy Davis, Sam Neill, Wendy Hughes, Robert Grubb, Pat Kennedy, Max Cullen.
05/23/79

My Daughter Hildegart: SEE Mi Hija Hildegart

My Days With Veronica: SEE Mis Dias con Veronica

My Dear Friend: SEE Phuen Rak

My Dearest: SEE Ma Cherie

My Fabulous Girlfriends: SEE Stupende Le Mie Amiche

My Father's Happy Years: SEE Apam Nehany Boldog Eve

My First Love: SEE Mon Premier Amour

My First Sin: SEE Mi Primer Pecado

My Heart Is Red: SEE Mon Coeur Est Rouge

My Heart is Upside-Down: SEE Le Coeur a l'Envers

My Love Has Been Burning: SEE Waga Koi Wa Moenu

My Mother, The General: SEE Imi Hageneralit

My War - My Love: SEE Moja Wojna - Moja Milosc

My Way Home
(Britain)
X. BFI prodn. Dir-wri, Bill Douglas. 78. (B & W)
11/15/78

Mysteries
(Holland)
CVG. Sigma Film (Amsterdam). Prods, Matthijs Van Heyningen, Yannick Bernard. Dir, Paul De Lussanet. Sp, De Lussanet, from novel by Knut Hamsun; cam, Robby Muller; mus, Laurens Van Rooyen; edtr, Jane Sperr. 100.
Rutger Hauer, Sylvia Kristel, David Rappaport, Rita Tushingham, Andrea Ferreol, Kees Brusse, Liesbeth List, Fons Rademakers, Adrian Brine, Peter Faber.
02/07/79

The Mysterious House of Dr. C.
Jo Anna and Ted Kneeland's prodn. Prod-dir, Ted Kneeland. Story-sp, freely adapted and expanded from "Coppelia" ballet by the Kneelands. Chor, Jo Anna Kneeland (Dame Alicia Markova, artistic consultant). Pho, Cecillo Paniagua; mus, Leo Delibes conducted by Adrian Sardo with Liceo Opera Orchestra; ani, Estudios Filman; backgrounds, Joe Maria Gimeno. 88.
Walter Slezak, Claudia Corday, Caj Selling, Eileen Elliott, Terry-Thomas.
11/03/76

The Mysterious Monsters
SSU. David L Wolper prodn. Prods, Charles E Sellier Jr, Robert Guenette; exec prod, Raylan Jenson. Wri-dir, Guenette. Cam, David Myers, Eric Daarstadt, Tony Coggans; edtrs, Earle Herdan, Robert Lambert; mus, Rudy Raksin; snd, Martin Bolger, Pierre Adidge, Joseph Dunton. (MPAA rating; G). 86.
Peter Graves, Peter Hurkos, William Stenberg, Sidney Walter, Jerilou Whelchel.
08/04/76

The Mystery of Oberwald: SEE Il Mistero Di Oberwald

Na Boca do Mundo
(In the Mouth of the World)
(Brazil)
X. Lente Films-Embrafilme (Brazilian Nat'l Film Industry) - Antonio Pitanga prodn. Prods, Morris Israel, Zakhia Elias, Noilton, Cezar Antonio Elias. Dir, Antonio Pitanga. Sp, Leopold Serran, from the book by Carlos Diegues and Antonio Pitanga; cam, Fernando Duarte; scenic des, Regis Monteiro; edtr, Sergio Sanz; asst dir, Jorge Fernando Duran Parra; mus, Jorge Ben; title song sung by Caetano Veloso. 108.
Norma Bengell, Antonio Pitanga, Sibele Rubia, Angelito Mello, Milton Goncalves.
02/07/79

Na Samote U Lesa
(Seclusion Near a Forest)
(Czechoslovakia)
CZS. Barrandov Film Studio prodn. Dir, Jiri Menzel. Sp, Zdenek Sverak, Ladislav Smoljak; cam (Eastmancolor), Jaromir Sofr; mus, Jiri Sust. 92.
Josef Kemr, Zdenek Sverak, Dana Kolarova, Ladislav Smoljak, Jan Trska.
07/28/76

Na Wlasna Prosbe
(At Your Own Request)
(Poland)
PTV. Poltel (Polish Television) prodn. Wridirs, Ewa and Czeslaw Petelski, based on novel "No Problem" by Janina Wieczerska. 60.
09/24/80

Nachtvorstellungen
(Late Show)
(W Germany)
X. Lothar Lambert Prodn, West Berlin. Wri-prod-dir-edtr, Lothar Lambert. Cam, Reza Dabui. With excerpts taken from an incompleted film by Harry Puhlmann. 89.
Cihan Anasai, Dagmar Beiersdorf, Beate Hasenau, Sylvia Heidemann, Mustafa Iskandarani, Lothar Lambert, Dorothea Moritz, Ethel Reschke, Erika Wilde.
(16m)
06/28/78

Nacionalna Klasa Do 785 CM3
(National Class)
(Yugoslavia)
YFR. Centar Film Prodn, Belgrade. Wri-dir, Goran Markovic. Cam, Zivko Zalar; sets, Miodrag Miric; mus, Zoran Simjanovic. 90.
Dragan Nikolic, Bogdan Diklic, Gorica Popovic, Danilo Stojkovic, Olivera Markovic, Aleksandar Bercek.
04/18/79

Naeste Stop Paradis
(Next Stop Paradise)
(Denmark)
OBL. Obel Film prodn (with the Danish Film Institute/Erik Crone). Original story wri-dir, Jon Bang Carlsen. Cam, Alexander Gruszynski; edtrs, Kasper Schyberg, Anders Refn; prodn mgr, Michael Christensen; mus, Gunnar Moller Pedersen. 95.
Karen Lykkehus, Preben Lerdorff Rye, Suzet Kempf, Ole Larsen, Jessie Rindom, Peter Boesen.
11/26/80

Nahla
(Algeria)
RTA. Dir, Farouk Beloufa. Sp, Rachid Boudjedra, Beloufa; cam (Eastmancolor), Alell Yahiaoui; edtr, Moufida Tlatli; mus, Ziad Rahbani. 180.
Yasmine Khlat, Lina Tebbara, Nabila Zitouni, Youcef Saiah, Roger Assaf, Ahmed Zine, Fayek Hamissi.
09/05/79

Najdolgiot Pat
(The Longest Journey)
(Yugoslavia)
YFR. Vardar Film-Makedonia Film prodn. Dir, Branko Gapo. Sp, Petre Andreevski; cam (Eastmancolor), Kiro Bibilovski; mus, Tomislav Zografski. 110.
Risto Siskov, Darko Dameski, Petre Temelkovski, Dusko Janicijevic.
08/25/76

Nam Karng Yod Deo
(The Last Dew Drop)
(Thailand)
AXT. Prod, Nanta Tansacha. Wri-dir, Suchart Vuthivichai. Original mus score, Seksan Somimsart; cam, Choochart Tohprathip; snd, Prasert and Paeh of King Sound Studio; dubbing, Jaturong Studio; art dir-prodn des, Suthee Piboravudh; publicity, Suriya Rajitwattana; cos, Charin Choochitr; make-up, Sam. 103.
Nit Alissa, Suradej Srichoomsin, Krit Wongyai, Sanok Suchima, Somkid Bukoontot.
12/06/78

The Name Was S N: SEE Se Llamaba S N

Namida o Shishi no Tategami
(Tears On The Lion's Mane)
(Japan)
SKU. Masahiro Shinoda film. Dir, Masahiro Shinoda; sp, Shuji Tereayama, Ichiro Mizunuma, Masahiro Shinoda; cam, Maso Kosugi; mus, Toru Takemitsu. 91.
Takashi Fujiki, Komi Nambara, Kyoko Kishida, Mariko Kaga, So Yamamura.
(MADE IN 1962)
10/29/80

Naomi
(Japan)
TOE. Prod, Toei Central Film. Dir, Yoichi Takabayashi. Sp, Takabayashi, based on "Chijin No Ai," by Junichiro Tanizaki; cam, Sotaro Takamura; snd, Toshiya Ban; light, Kazuo Yamada; art dir, Hitoshi Nojiri; edtr, Osamu Tanaka. 100.
Yuki Mizuhara, Makoto Saito, Akihiro Mitsuda, Takashi Tanaka, Tsutomu Kuroda, Eiji Tsuyama, Ai Mori.
07/02/80

Nasa Lupa Ang Langit At Impiyerno
(Between Heaven and Hell)
(Philippines)
GDW. Prods, Cherry L Ong, Jose C Paredes. Wri-dir, Emmanuel H Borlaza from story by Allan Rabaya, Manalo Hombrebueno, Ben Abarquez Villaluz. Cam, Felipe Santiago; mus, Danny Holmsen. 101.
Vic Vargas, Maureen Ava Vieira, Gloria Romero, Chanda Romero, Geraldine, Rafael Roco Jr, Dante Vernona, Ernie Garcia, Pancho Pelagio, Butz Aquino, Lilian Laing, Sandy Garcia.
05/05/76

Nasty Habits
(Britain)
BRU. Bowden Prodns Ltd film. Prod, Robert Enders; exec prod, George Barrie. Dir, Michael Lindsay-Hogg. Sp, Enders, adapted from Muriel Spark's "The Abbess of Crewe," cam (Technicolor-Panavision), Douglas Slocombe; art dir, Robert Jones; mus, John Cameron; edtr, Peter Tanner; asst dir, Ariel Levy; asso prod, Gordon L T Scott. (MPAA rating: PG). 98.
Glenda Jackson, Melina Mercouri, Geraldine Page, Sandy Dennis, Anne Jackson, Anne Meara, Edith Evans, Jerry Stiller, Rip Torn, Eli Wallach, Suzanne Stone, Peter Bromilow, Shane Rimmer, Harry Ditson, Chris Muncke, Oliver Maguire, Alick Hayes, Bill Reimbold, Anthony Forrest, Mike Douglas, Bill Jorgensen, Jessica Savitch, Howard K Smith.
10/27/76

Nasvidenje V. Naslednji Vojni
(See You In The Next War)
(Yugoslavia)
YFR. Viba Film, Vesna Film prodn. Wri-dir, Zivojin Pavlovic; book, Vitomil Zupan; cam (Eastmancolor), Tomoslav Pinter; mus, Bojan Adamic. 113.
Metod Pevec, Hans Christian Blech, Milan Puzic, Boris Juh, Tanja Poberznik, Ruth Gassman.
08/13/80

National Class: SEE Nacionalna Klasa Do 785 CM3

National Lampoon's Animal House
U. Prods, Matty Simmons, Ivan Reitman. Dir, John Landis. Sp, Harold Ramis, Douglas Kenney, Chris Miller; cam (Technicolor), Charles Correll; edtr, George Folsey Jr; mus, Elmer Bernstein; art dir, John J Lloyd; set decor, Hal Gausman; snd, Bill Varney, Howard Wollman, Alan Holly, William B Kaplan; cos-ward, Deborah Nadoolman, Dan Chichester, Gene Deardorff; asst dir, Cliff Coleman; 2d unit dir and stunt coord, Gary R McLarty. (MPAA rating: R). 109.
John Belushi, Tom Matheson, John Vernon, Verna Bloom, Thomas Hulce, Cesare Danova, Mary Louise Weller, Stephen Furst, James Daughton, Bruce McGill, Mark Metcalf, DeWayne Jessie, Karen Allen, James Widdoes, Martha Smith, Sarah Holcomb, Lisa Baur, Kevin Bacon, Peter Riegert, Douglas Kenney, Christian Miller, Joshua Daniel, Bruce Bonnheim, Donald Sutherland.
06/28/78

The National Shotgun: SEE La Escopeta Nacional

Natural Enemies
C5. John E Quill prodn. Wri-dir-edtr, Jeff Kanew, based on a novel by Julius Horwitz; cam, Richard E Brooks; asso prods, Harry Daley, Robert Burke; mus, Don Ellis; art dir, Hank Aldrich; asst dir, Sol Fol. (MPAA rating: R). 100.
Hal Holbrook, Louise Fletcher, Peter Armstrong, Beth Berridge, Steve Austin, Jim Pappas, Ellen Barber, John Bartholomew, Charles Randall, Jose Ferrer, Lisa Carroll, June Berry, Alisha Fontaine, Pat Mauceri, Michele O'Brien, Claire Reilly, Viveca Lindfors, Frank Bongiorno, Harry Daley, Patricia Elliott, Robert Perry.
10/31/79

Ne Bolit Golowa U Djatla
(Woodpeckers Don't Get Headaches)
(USSR)
X. Lenfilm, Leningrad, prodn. Dir, Dinari Asanova. Sp, Yuri Klepikove; cam, Dimitri Dolinin; set des, Vladimir Svetosarov; mus, Yevgeni Krylatov; snd, Boris Andrejev. 79.
Sasha Shesljaev, Lena Zyplakova, Sasha Bogdanov, Ira Oboliskaja, Denis Koslov, Andrei Nikitin, Julja Schischkina, Jekatherina Vassileva.
09/08/76

Ne Fillim Te Veres
(At the Beginning of Summer)
(Albania)
ALA. Albfilm prodn, Tirana. Dir, Gezim Erebara. Sp, Peci Dado; cam, Faruk Basha; art dir, Astrit Tota; mus, Kujtim Laro. 105.
Astrit Cerma, Sander Prosi, Demir Hyskja, Agim Shuke, Albert Verria, Elida Cangonji, Ndrek Luca.
01/24/79

Ne Naginji Se Van
(Don't Lean Out the Window)
(Yugoslavia)
YFR. Jadran Film-Croatia Film prodn. Dir, Bogdan Zizic. Sp, Zizic, Kruno Quien; cam (Eastmancolor), Branko Blazina; mus, Ozren Depolo. 92.
Ivo Gregurevic, Fabjian Sovgovic, Mira Banjac, Jadranaka Stilin, Zdenko Jelcic.
08/17/77

Ne Pleure Pas
(Don't Cry)
(France)
GAU. Gaumont-TFI-SFP prodn. Dir, Jacques Ertaud. Sp, Ertaud, Guy Lagorce from the book by Lagorce. 105.
Sylvain Joubert, Charles Vanel, Xavier Labouze, Christine Laruent, Marc Chapiteau, Andre Falcon.
04/05/78

Ne Si Otivai
(Don't Go Away)
(Bulgaria)
X. Bulgarian Film prodn. Dir, Ludmil Kirkov. Sp, Georgi Mishev; cam, Georgi Roussinov; art dir, Bogoya Sapoundjiev; mus, Boris Karadimchev. 90.
Philip Trifonov, Nevena Kokonova, Sashka Bratanova, Elena Mirchovska.
11/17/76

Nea
(France)
FBE. Multimedia-Les Films La Boetie prodn. Dir, Nelly Kaplan. Sp, Kaplan, Jean Chapot; book, Emmanuelle Arsan; cam (Eastmancolor), Andreas Winding; edtr, Helen Plemiannikov. 95.
Ann Zacharias, Sami Frey, Micheline Presle, Francoise Brion.
09/01/76

Nechci Nic Slyset
(Leave Me Alone)
(Czechoslovakia)
CZS. A Czechoslovak Film prodn, Studio Barrandov, Prague. Wri-dir, Ota Koval. 90.
Vladimir Brodsky, Jana Brejchova.
02/28/79

Nedelni Matchove
(Sunday Games)
(Bulgaria)
BGO. Dir, Todor Andrejkov. Sp, Anton Kafeztchiev, Andrejkov; cam, Ivan Tzonev, Stojan Zlatchkine; edtr, Tzvetana Jankova-Tomova. 92.
(B & W)
08/25/76

Nedtur
(If Music Be the Food of Love)
(Norway)
X. Norsk Film prodn. Prod, Harald Ohrvik. Wri-dir, Hans Lindgren. Cam, Halvor Naess; edtr, Ola Solum; mus, Christian Reim; art dir, Ingeborg Kvamme. 91.
Nils Sletta, Sigrid Huun, Froydis Armand, Helge Jordal.
11/19/80

Neem Annapurna
(Bitter Morsel)
(India)
CUI. Dir, Buddhadeb Das Gupta. Sp, Kamal Kumar Majumdar, Das Gupta; cam, Kamal Nayekleditor, G Naskar. 95.
Manidipa Ray, Sunil Mukhopadhyaya, Jayita Sarkar, Manojit Lahiri.
(B & W)
02/20/80

Nella Citta' Perduta Di Sarzana
(In the Lost City of Sarzana)
(Italy)
X. RAI-Television Channel 2 prodn. Dir, Luigi Faccini; sp, Luigi Faccini, Piero Anchisi; cam, Nevio Sivini; mus, Vittorio, Gianni Nocenzi. 100.
Franco Graziosi, Riccardo Cucciolla, Bruno Corazzari, Bruno Cattaneo,

Ernesto Colli, Roberto Posse, Ezio Marano, Marisa Mantovani, Claudio Gora.
10/08/80

Nene
(Italy)
COL. Prod, Giovanni Bertolucci for San Francisco Film. Dir, Salvatore Samperi. Sp, Alessandro Parenzo, Samperi; cam (Technicolor), Pasqualino Di Santis; art dir, Ezio Altieri; edtr, Sergio Montanari; mus, Francesco Guccini. 108.
Leonora Fani, Tino Schirinzi, Paola Senatore, Sven Valsecchi, Rita Savagnone.
12/14/77

Neskolko Interwju Po Litschnym Woprosam
(Some Interviews on Personal Questions)
(USSR)
GOS. Grusiafilm Studios prodn, Tbilisi (Georgia); Dir, Lana Gogoberidze. 90.
Sofiko Chiaureli.
02/28/79

The Nest: SEE El Nido

Nest in the Wind: SEE Gnezdo Na Vetru

Nest of Vipers: SEE Ritratto di Borghesia in Nero

Nestbruch
(Nest Break)
(Switzerland)
RIA. Kuert-Riesen/Filmkollektiv Zurich AG prodn. Dir, Beat Kuert. Prod, Barbara Eva Riesen. Sp, Michael Maassen, Kuert; mus, Cornelius Wernle, Collettivo Teatrale Operaio, Wolfgang Amadeus Mozart; cam, Hansueli Schenkel, Bernhard Lehner; edtr, Kuert; snd, Florian Eidenbenz, Hanspeter Fischer; art dir, Hans Gloor, Charles Moser; light, Hans Meier, Markus Fischer; cos, Marion Steiner; exec prod, Rolf Schmid. 93.
Anna-Marie Blanc, Therese Affolter, Michael Maassen, Hans Madin, Jost Osswald, Collettivo Teatrale Operaio.
12/31/80

The Net: SEE Das Netz

Netepichnaja Istoria
(An Untypical Story)
(USSR)
GOS. Mosfilm Prodn, Moscow. Dir, Grigori Chukhrai. Sp, Chukhrai, V Merejko; cam, P Sokal, M Demurov; mus, M Ziv. 95.
Nona Mirdjukova, Valentina Telichkina, Vadim Spirdonov, Andrei Nikonaev.
07/26/78

Network
UA. MGM picture. Prod, Howard Gottfried. Dir, Sidney Lumet. Sp, Paddy Chayefsky; cam (Metrocolor), Owen Roizman; edtr, Alan Heim; mus, Elliot Lawrence; prodn des, Philip Rosenberg; set decor, Edward Stewart; snd, Richard Vorisek, James Sabat; asst dir, Jay Allan Hopkins. (MPAA rating: R). 121.
Faye Dunaway, William Holden, Peter Finch, Robert Duvall, Wesley Addy, Ned Beatty, Arthur Burghardt, Bill Burrows, Kathy Cronkite, Darryl Hickman, Roy Poole, William Prince, Beatrice Straight, Marlene Warfield, Lee Richardson.
10/13/76

Neung Toh Jet
(The Dirty Seven)
(Thailand)
SAH. Prod, Somsak Techaratanaprasert. Wridir, So Asanachinda. Cam, Vichian Virachote; mus-snd, King's Sound Studio; prodn mgr, Sanga Attawilokitr. 130.
Krung Srivilai, Sorapong Chatri, Aranya Namwong, Tarika Tarathit, Sayant Chantawiboon, Lak Apichat, Dam Daskorn, Gecha Pianwitti, Adul Doonyarat, Siripong Issarangkul, Na Ayuthaaya, Niroot Sirichanya, Taksin Jampon, Lawadee Patapong.
04/27/77

Never Again Always: SEE Jamais Plus Toujours

The New Beaujolais Wine Has Arrived: SEE Le Beaujolais Nouveau Est Arrive...

New Fist of Fury
(Hong Kong)
LWM. Hsu Li Wa prodn. Dir, Lo Wei. Sp, P'An Lei, Lo Wei; cam, Chen Jung Shu, Chen Chaou Yung; martial arts dir, Ho Ying Kit. 120.
Nora Miao, Chang King, Chan Sing, Jacky Chan, Lo Wei.
06/23/76

New Generation
(France)
SLN. French Lollipop prodn. Prod-wri-dir, Jean-Pierre Lowf Legoff. Mus conception, Robert Bonnaire, Iser, Jean-Pierre Lowf Legoff, Dominique Rousseau; cam, Serge Halsdorf; snd, Gerard Barra; edtr, Pauline Leroy; choreography, Amadeo.
Jeff Manzetti, Eric Rawson, Lollie Serres, Wilson Lambert, Serge Malik, Caroline Tabourin, Jean-Luc Autret, Nathalie Boutigny, Jackie Sardou, Henri-Jacques Huet.
(MUSICAL)
02/07/79

The New Toy: SEE Nyt legetoej

New York, New York
UA. Prods, Irwin Winkler, Robert Chartoff. Dir, Martin Scorsese. Sp, Earl Mac Rauch, Mardik Martin; cam (DeLuxe Color), Laszlo Kovacs; edtrs, Irving Lerner, Marcia Lucas; mus supv, Ralph Burns; songs, John Kander, Fred Ebb; prodn des, Boris Leven; snd, Lawrence Jost; asst dir, Melvin D Dellar; cos, Theadora Van Runkle; asso prod, Gene Kirkwood. (MPAA rating: PG). 153.
Liza Minnelli, Robert De Niro, Lionel Stander, Barry Primus, Mary Kay Place, Georgie Auld, George Memmoli.
06/22/77

The Newcomer: SEE Le Nouveau Venu

News from the Village: SEE Kaddu Beykat

Newsfront
(Australia)
RDP. Palm Beach Pictures Prodn. Prod, David Elfick. Dir, Phillip Noyce. Sp, Noyce, based on a concept by Elfick; cam (Panavision-Color/b&w), Vince Monton; snd, Tim Lloyd; prodn des, Lissa Coote; art dir, Larry Eastwood; graphic des, Lee Whitmore; sfx, Kim Hilder; edtr, John Scott; mus, William Motzing. 110.
Bill Hunter, Gerard Kennedy, Angela Punch, Wendy Hughes, Chris Hayward, John Ewart, Don Crosby, John Dease, John Clayton, Bryan Brown, Tony Barry, Drew Forsythe, Lorna Leslie.
(Color-B & W)
05/10/78

The Next Man
AA. Artists Entertainment Complex (Martin Bregman) prodn. Dir, Richard C Sarafian. Sp, Mort Fine, Alan Trustman, David M Wolf, Richard C Sarafian, based on a story by Bregman and Trustman; cam (Technicolor), Michael Chapman; prodn des, Gene Callahan; cos, Anna Hill Johnstone; edtrs, Aram Avakian, Robert Lovett; mus, Michael Kamen; set decor, Robert Drumheller. (MPAA rating: R). 108.
Sean Connery, Cornelia Sharpe, Albert Paulsen, Adolfo Celi, Marco St John, Ted Beniades, Charles Cioffi, Salem Ludwig, Tom Klunis, Roger Omar Serbagi, Armand Dahan, Charles Randall, Ian Collier, Michael Storm, Maurice Copeland, George Pravda, Alex Jawdokimov, James Bulleit, Jaime Sanchez, Stephen D Newman, Holland Taylor, Peggy Feury, Patrick Bedford, Toru Nagai, Ryokei Kanokogi, Camill Yarbrough, plus Martin Bregman, Richard C Sarafian in non-speaking roles.
11/03/76

Next Stop Paradise: SEE Naeste Stop Paradis

Next Stop, Greenwich Village
FOX. Wri-prod-(with Tony Ray)-dir, Paul Mazursky. Cam (DeLuxe Color), Arthur Ornitz; edtr, Richard Halsey; mus, Bill Conti; prodn des, Phil Rosenberg; set decor, Ed Stewart; snd, Dennis Maitland; asst dir, Terry Donnelly. (MPAA rating: R). 111.
Lenny Baker, Shelley Winters, Ellen Greene, Lois Smith, Christopher Walken, Dori Brenner, Antonio Fargas, Lou Jacobi, Mike Kellin, Michael Egan, Denise Galik, John C Becher, John Ford Noonan, Helen Hanft, Rashel Novikoff, Joe Madden, Joe Spinnel, Rochelle Oliver, Gui Adrisano, Carole Manferdini, Jeff Goldblum, Rutanya Alda.
02/04/76

Nezabybaemaya Osen
(The Unforgettable Autumn)
(USSR - Mongolia)
GOS. Mongolian Film prodn. Dir, Haltariyn Damdin. 100.
(B & W)
07/27/77

Nezha Nao Hai
(Nezha Defeats the Dragon)
(Peoples Republic of China)
SHA. Dirs, Wang Shucken, Yang Dingxlan, Jingda. Sp, Wang Wang; cam, Duang Hsiaohsian, Tchiang Youyi, Jing Tchetchen. 61.
(ANI)
05/28/80

The Nice Neighbor: SEE A Kedves Somszed

Nicht Alles Was Fliegt, Ist Ein Vogel
(Not Everything That Flies Is a Bird)
(W Germany)
X. Francis J Stockman prodn. Prod, Stockman. Dir-wri, Borislav Sajtinac. Animator, Branco Ilic; mus, sfx, Rolf Adrian. 80.
(ANI)
03/21/79

Nickelodeon
COL. Prods, Irwin Winkler, Robert Chartoff. Dir, Peter Bogdanovich. Sp, W D Richter, Bogdanovich; cam (Metrocolor), Laszlo Kovacs; edtr, William Carruth; mus, Richard Hazard; art dir, Richard Berger; set decor, Darrell Silvera; snd, Arthur Piantadosi, Les Fresholtz, Michael Minkler, Barry Thomas; cosward, Theadora Van Runkle, Norman Salling, Sandra Berke; asst dir, Jack Sanders; stunt coord, Hal Needham. (MPAA rating: PG). 121.
Ryan O'Neal, Burt Reynolds, Tatum O'Neal, Brian Keith, Stella Stevens, John Ritter, Jane Hitchcock.
12/22/76

Nick's Movie: SEE Lightning Over Water

Niedzielne Dzieci
(Sunday Children)
(Poland)
POL. Film Polski prodn, Warsaw, "X" film unit. Wri-dir, Agnieszka Holland. Cam, Jacek Stachlewski; prodn mgr, Zygmunt Krol. 80.
Zofia Graziewicz, Ryszard Kotys, Krystayna Wachelko-Zaleska.
05/18/77

The Night Before Christmas: SEE Questo Si Che E' Amore

Night Creature
DIM. Lee Madden Associates prodn. Prod, Ross Hagen. Dir, Lee Madden. Sp, Hubert Smith, based on a story by Lee Madden, Smith. Exec prod, Madden; cam (CFI Color), Pemylot Cheydon; edtr, Martin Draffke; mus, Jim Helms; asso prod, Suzanne Jesse. (MPAA rating: PG). 83.
Donald Pleasence, Nancy Kwan, Ross Hagen, Lesly Fine, Jennifer Rhodes.
10/03/79

Night Games
AVE. Pan Pacific prodn. Prods, Andre Morgan, Roger Lewis. Exec prod, Raymond Chow. Dir, Roger Vadim. Sp, Anton Diether, Clarke Reynolds, based on a story by Diether and Barth Jules Sussman; cam (Technicolor), Dennis Lewiston; edtr, Peter Hunt; mus, John Barry; prodn des, Robert Laing; art dir, Frank Israel; snd, Danny Daniel; sfx, Gene Grigg; asst dir, Denys Grenier de Ferre. (MPAA rating: R). 100.
Cindy Pickett, Joanna Cassidy, Barry Primus, Paul Jenkins, Gene Davis, Juliet Fabriga, Clem Parsons.
01/30/80

The Night of Saint-Germain Des Pres: SEE La Nuit De Saint-Germain Des Pres

Night Of The Juggler
COL. Prod, Jay Weston. Exec prod, Arnold Kopelson. Dir, Robert Butler. Sp, Bill Norton, Sr, Rick Natkin, from novel by William P McGivern. Cam (Technicolor), Victor J Kemper; edtr, Argyle Nelson; snd, Dennis Maitland, Sr; prodn des, Stuart Wurtzel; stunt coord, Chris Howell; asst dirs, Mike Haley, Ron Walsh, Mel Howard; asso prod, Stephen F Kesten; mus, Artie Kane. (MPAA rating: R). 100.
James Brolin, Cliff Gorman, Richard Castellano, Abby Bluestone, Dan Hedaya, Julie Carmen.
05/14/80

The Night The Prowler
(Australia)
NSW. Chariot Films (Anthony Buckley) prodn. Dir, Jim Sharman. Sp, Patrick White, based on his short story; cam, David Sanderson; mus, Cameron Alan. 90.
Ruth Cracknell, John Frawley, Kerry Walker, John Derum, Maggie Kirkpatrick, Terry Camilleri.
11/15/78

The Night with Chandler: SEE Die Nacht Mit Chandler

Night-Flowers
LFA. Willow Prodn Co Ltd presentation. Prod, Sally Faile. Dir-edtr, Luis San Andres. Sp, Gabriel Walsh; cam, Larry Pizer; mus, Harry Manfredini. 92.
Jose Perez, Sabra Jones, Gabriel Walsh.
09/05/79

Nighthawks
(Britain)
X. Four Corner Films Prodn. Prods, Ron Peck, Paul Hallam. Dir, Peck. Sp, Peck, Hallam; cam (b&w), Joanna Davis; snd, Diana Ruston; edtrs, Richard Taylor, Mary Pat Leece; mus, David Graham Ellis; lyr, Stuart Craig Turton. 113.
Ken Robertson, Tony Westrope, Rachel Nicholas James, Maureen Dolan, Stuart Craig Turton, Clive Peters, Robert Merrick, Frank Dilbert, Peter Radmall.
(16m) (B & W)
11/29/78

Nightmare in Blood
PFE. Xeromega prodn. Wri-prods, John Stanley, Kenn Davis. Dir, Stanley. Cam (Techniscope), Charles Rudnick; edtr, Alfred Katzman; snd, Robert Gravenor, John Brumbaugh; asst dir, Julie Staheli. (MPAA rating: R). 90.
Kerwin Mathews, Jerry Walter, Dan Caldwell, Barrie Youngfellow, John J Cochran, Ray K Goman, Hy Pyke, Irving Israel, Drew Eshelman, Morgan Upton, Justin Bishop, Stan Ritchie, Charles Murphy, Yvonne Young, Mike Hitchcock, Erika Stanley.
07/26/78

Nightmares: SEE Cauchmars

Nightmares: SEE Zmory

Nightwing
COL. Martin Ransohoff prodn. Prod, Ransohoff. Exec prod, Richard St Johns. Dir, Arthur Hiller. Sp, Steve Shagan, Bud Shrake, Martin Cruz Smith, based on novel by Smith; cam, Charles Rosher; edtr, John C Howard; mus, Henry Mancini; prodn des, James Vance; set decor, Richard Kent; snd, Larry Jost; special visual effects, Carlo Rambaldi; asst dir, Gary Daigler. (MPAA rating: PG). 103.
Nick Mancuso, David Warner, Kathryn Harrold, Stephen Macht, Strother Martin, George Clutesi, Ben Piazza, Donald Hotten, Charles Hallahan, Judith Novgrod, Alice Hirson.
07/04/79

Nije Nego
(Tit For Tat)
(Yugoslavia)
YFR. Central Film Studio-Avala Films prodn. Dir, Mica Miloscevic. Sp, Ljuba Radicevic, Miloscevic; cam (Eastmancolor), Predrag Popovic; mus, Korenlje Kovac. 92.
Bata Zivojinovic, Marko Taodrovic, Ruzica Sokic, Nikola Simic.
08/16/78

Nijinsky
(Britain)
PAR. Hera prodn. Dir, Herbert Ross. Prods, Nora Kaye, Stanley O'Toole. Sp, Hugh Wheeler, based on "Nijinsky" by Romola Nijinsky and "The Diary of Vaslav Nijinsky." Exec prod, Harry Saltzman; cam (Metrocolor), Douglas Slocombe; film edtr, William Reynolds; asso prod, Howard Jeffrey; mus adapt-cond, John Lanchbery; prodn des, John Blezard; cos des, Alan Barrett. (MPAA rating: R). 125.
Alan Bates, George De La Pena, Leslie Browne, Alan Badel, Carla Fracci, Colin Blakely, Ronald Pickup, Ronald Lacey, Janet Suzman, Sian Phillips.
03/12/80

Nikudan
(Human Bullet)
(Japan)
ATG. Dir, Kihachi Okamoto. Sp, Kihachi Okamoto; cam, Hiroshi Murai. 109.
Minoru Terada, Naoko Otani, Chishu Ryu, Tanie Kitabayashi, Yunosuke Ito.
(B & W)
11/26/80

Nine Months: SEE Kilenc Honap

9/30/55
U. Prod, Jerry Weintraub. Wri-dir, James Bridges. Cam (Technicolor), Gordon Willis; edtr, Jeff Gourson; mus, Leonard Rosenman; art dir, Robert Luthardt; set decor, Sharon Thomas; snd, Larry Jost, Christopher Newman, Kevin F Cleary; cos-ward, Kent Warner, Patricia Zinn, Mina Mittleman; asst dirs, Fred Gallo, Cliff Bole; stunt coord, R A Rondell. (MPAA rating: PG). 101.
Richard Thomas, Susan Tyrrell, Deborah Benson, Lisa Blount, Thomas Hulce, Dennis Quaid, Mary Kai Clark, Dennis Christopher, Collin Wilcox, Ben Fuhrman, Ouida White, Bryan Scott, Glen Irby, Mike Farris, Tom Bonner.
08/31/77

Nine To Five
FOX. IPC Films prodn. Prod, Bruce Gilbert. Dir, Colin Higgins. Sp, Higgins and Patricia Resnick, based on Resnick's story; cam (Deluxe), Reynaldo Villalobos; edtr, Pembroke J Herring; prodn des, Dean Mitzner; mus, Charles Fox; snd, Nicholas Eliopoulos; cos, Ann Roth; art dir, Jack Gammon Taylor Jr; set decor, Anne McCulley; sfx, Chuck Gaspar, Matt Sweeney; ani, Mishkin, Hellmuch, Virgien & Friends; asst dir, Gary Daigler. (MPAA rating: PG). 110.
Jane Fonda, Lily Tomlin, Dolly Parton, Dabney Coleman, Sterling Hayden, Elizabeth Wilson, Henry Jones, Lawrence Pressman, Marian Mercer, Ren Woods, Norma Donaldson, Roxanna Bonilla-Giannini, Peggy Pope.
12/17/80

1941
U. A-Team prodn. Prod, Buzz Feitshans. Dir, Steven Spielberg; exec prod, John Milius; sp, Robert Zemeckis, Bob Gale from a story by Zemeckis, Gale, Milius; cam, William A Fraker; edtr, Michael Kahn; mus, John Williams; prodn des, Dean Edward Mitzner; snd, Gene S Cantamessa; sfx, A D Flowers; min supv, Gregory Jein; cos, Deborah Nadoolman; art dir, William F O'Brien; matte paintings, Matthew Yuricich; visual effects supv, Larry Robinson; prodn illustrator, George Jensen; set decor, John Austin; stunt coord, Terry Leonard; add'l pho, Frank Stanley; chor, Paul De Rolf; optical cnslt, L B Abbott; optical effects, Van Der Veer Photo Effects; asst dirs, Jerry Ziesmer, Steve Perry. (MPAA rating: PG). 118.
Dan Aykroyd, Ned Beatty, John Belushi, Lorraine Gary, Murray Hamilton, Christopher Lee, Tim Matheson, Toshiro Mifune, Warren Oates, Robert Stack, Treat Williams, Nancy Allen, Eddie Deezen, Bobby DiCicco, Dianne Kay, John Candy, Frank McRae, Perry Lang, Slim Pickens, Wendie Jo Sperber, Lionel Stander, Ignatius Wolfington, Joseph P Flaherty.
12/19/79

1900
(Italy)
PAR. Prod, Alberto Grimaldi for PEA. Dir, Bernardo Bertolucci; sp, Bertolucci, Franco Arcalli, Giuseppe Bertolucci; cam (Technicolor), Vittorio Storaro; art dir, Ezio Frigerio; edtr, Franco Arcalli; mus, Ennio Morricone. (MPAA rating: R). 320.
Burt Lancaster, Sterling Hayden, Robert De Niro, Dominique Sanda, Gerard Depardieu, Donald Sutherland, Stefania Sandrelli, Laura Betti, Alida Valli.
06/02/76

The Ninth Configuration
WB. Prod, William Peter Blatty. Exec prod, William Paul. Dir, Blatty, who wrote sp from his novel. Cam, Gerry Fisher; edtr, T Battle Davis, Peter Lee Thompson. Mus, Roberto Silvi, Barry DeVorzon; prodn des, Bill Malley, J Dennis Washington; set decor, Sydney Ann Kee; snd, Marvin Walowitz, Andrew Londn; asst dir-asso prod, Tom Shaw. (MPAA rating: R). 105.
Stacy Keach, Scott Wilson, Jason Miller, Ed Flanders, Neville Brand, George DiCenzo, Moses Gunn, Robert Loggia, Joe Spinell, Alejandro Rey, Tom Atkins, Steve Sandor, Richard Lynch.
02/06/80

The Ninth Heart
(Czechoslovakia)
CEK. Dir, Juraj Herz. Sp, Herz; story, Josef Hanzlik; cam, Jiri Machane; des, Vladimir Labsky. mus, Petr Hapka. 90.
Ondrej Pavelka, Julie Juristova, Anna Malova, Frantisek Filipovsky, Josef Kemr, Juraj Kukura, Premyal Koci, Ruzena Rudnicka, Josef Somr.
10/22/80

Nippon No Don-Yabohen
(The Don of Japan-Big Schemes)
(Japan)
TOE. Prod, Koji Shundo, Goro Kusakabe, Norimichi Matsudaira, Mitsuru Taoka. Dir, Sadao Nakajima. Cam, Toshio Matsuda; sp, Koji Takada; cos, Jun Ashida; mus, Toshiro Mayuzumi. 141.
Saburi Shin, Toshiro Mifune, Kyoko Kishida, Hiroki Matsukata, Bunta Sugawara.
01/18/78

Nishant
(End of Night)
(India)
BLZ. Blaze Enterprises prodn. Dir, Shyam Benegal. Sp, Vijay Tendulkar, Pandit Stya Dev Dubey; cam (Eastmancolor), Govind Nihalani; mus, Vanraj Bhatia. 145.
Girish Karnad, Shabana Azmi, Naseeruddin Shah, Pandit Stya Dev Dubey.
05/26/76

Nissuim Nosach Tel Avi
(Marriage, Tel Aviv Style)
(Israel)
NOA. Menahem Golan-Yoram Globus Prod. Wri-dir, Yoel Zilberg, based on Moliere's "L'Avare"; cam, David Gurfinkel; mus, Yannis Petritsis; edtr, Irith Raz. 90.
Tuvia Zafir, Yossef Shiloah, Menahem Eyni, Shosh Marciano, Miri Aloni, Gilath Ankori, Sassi Kesheth
12/26/79

Nje Udhetimi I Veshtire
(A Difficult Transport)
(Albania)
ALA. Albanian Film Prodn, Studio New Albania, Tirana. Dir, P Llanaj, Xhezair Dafa. Sp, P Llanaj, B Hexha, H Rama; cam, J Kandsci, J Kenemi; sets, A Basha; mus, Sh Kosha. 90.
Demir Hyskja, Pandi Siku, Sotirog, Cili.
(B & W)
06/13/79

No Deposit, No Return
BV. Walt Disney Productions presentation prod, Ron Miller; co-prod, Joe L McEveety. Dir, Norman Tokar. Sp, Arthur Alsberg, Don Nelson; story, McEveety; cam (Technicolor), Frank Phillips; mus, Buddy Baker; art dirs, John B Mansbridge, Jack Senter; edtr, Cotton Warburton; snd, Herb Taylor, Frank Regula. (MPAA rating: G). 112.
David Niven, Darren McGavin, Don Knotts, Herschel Bernardi, Barbara Feldon, Kim Richards, Brad Savage, John Williams, Charlie Martin Smith, Vic Tayback, Bob Hastings.
01/28/76

No Longer Alone
WW. Prod, Frank R Jacobson. Exec prod, William F Brown. Dir, Nicholas Webster. Sp, Lawrence Holben, based on Joan Winmill Brown's autobiography; cam, Michael Reed; edtr, J Michael Hooser; prod des, John Lageu; cos, Klara Kerpin; mus, Tedd Smith; asst dir, Ed Harper; snd, Michael Strong. (MPAA rating: PG). 99.
Belinda Carroll, Roland Culver, James Fox, Wilfrid Hyde-White, Simon Williams, Helen Cherry, Samantha Gates, Karen Dines, Gordon Devol, Reginald Marsh, John Alkin, Mary Kerridge, Robert Rietty, Helen Cotterill, John Clive, Vivienne Burgess.
10/04/78

No Man's Daughter: SEE
Arvacska

No Maps on my Taps
X. GTN prodn. Prod-dir, George T Nierenberg; cam, Robert Achs, Phil Parmet, Robert Elfstrom, Vic Losic, Ted Churchill, George T Nierenberg, Paul Goldsmith; mus dir, Lionel Hampton; mus arr, Dick Vance; edtr, Paul Barnes; snd, Larry Loewinger, Nigel Nobel, Mike Scott Goldbaum, Peter Hliddal, Chat Gunter. 58.
Sandman Sims, Bunny Briggs, Chuck Green, Lionel Hampton, John Bubbles.
(DOC) (16m)
03/21/79

No More Easy Going: SEE Mo
Hoozue Wa Tsukanai

No Nukes
WB. MUSE (Musicians for a Safe Environment) presentation. Prods, Julian Schlossberg, Danny Goldberg. Dirs, Schlossberg, Goldberg, Anthony Potenza. Tech dir, Mark Pines; doc footage dir, Potenza; cin, Haskell Wexler; snd mixers, Mark Berger, Richard Beggs; creative coord, David Silver. (MPAA rating: PG)   103.
Jackson Browne, Crosby, Stills & Nash, Doobie Bros, John Hall, Graham Nash, Bonnie Raitt, Gil Scott-Heron, Carly Simon, Bruce Springsteen, James Taylor, Jesse Colin Young.
(DOC)
07/16/80

No Trespassing: SEE Pe Aici Nu Se Trece

No Way Back
ATF. Po' Boy Prods film. Wri-prod-dir, Fred Williamson; exec prod, Jeff Williamson. Cam (CFI Color), Robert Hopkins; edtr, James E Nownes; snd, Oliver Moss; asst dir, Phillip Browning. (MPAA rating: R).   91.
Fred Williamson, Charles Woolf, Tracy Reed, Virginia Gregg, Stack Pierce, Argy Allen, Paula Sills.
06/16/76

Noche De Curas
(Priest's Night)
(Spain)
X. Loxos Film prodn. Dir, Carlos Morales Mengotti. Cam (Eastmancolor), Augusto Fernandez Balbuena; edtr, Gloria Carrion. 75.
(DOC)
07/19/78

Nochi Nad Chili
(A Night Over Chile)
(USSR - Chile)
X. Mosfilm, Moscow, prodn. Dirs, Sebastian Alarcon, Alexander Kosarev.   90.
Grigori Grigoriu, Gyuli Chokhonelidze, Mircha Voiniscescu-Sotsky, Victor Voinichescu-Sotsky, Nina Krechetnikova, Maria Sagaidak.
08/03/77

Nocturnal Uproar: SEE Tapage Nocturne

Nomugi Pass: SEE Ah! Nomugi Toge

Non Contate Su Di Noi
(Don't Count On Us)
(Italy)
VSI.   90.
Francesca Ferrari, Maurizio Rota, Sergio Nuti, Francesco Scalco. Manfredi Marzano-Istlan Film prodn. Dir, Sergio Nuti. Sp, Francesca Ferrari, Nuti, Gianloreto Carbone; cam, Renato Tufari; mus, Maurizio Rota.
08/23/78

Nordsee Ist Mordsee
(North Sea Is Dead Sea)
(W Germany)
X. Hark Bohm Film Prodn, Hamburger Kino Kompanie. Wri-dir, Hark Bohm. Cam, Wolfgang Treu; edtr, Heidi Genee; art dir, Jochen Wolfart; mus, Udo Lindenberg.   85.
Uwe Enkelmann, Dschingis Bowakow, Marquard Bohm, Herma Koehn, Katja Bowakow, Guenter Lohmann, Corinna Schmidt, Ingrid Boje, Gerhard Stoehr, Rolf Becker.
06/16/76

Norma Rae
FOX. Martin Ritt/Rose and Asseyev prodn. Prod by Tamara Asseyev, Alex Rose. Dir, Martin Ritt. Sp, Irving Ravetch, Harriet Frank Jr; cam (Deluxe Color), John A Alonzo; prodn dsgn, Walter Scott Herndon; mus, David Shire; edtr, Sidney Levin; art dir, Tracy Bousman; set decor, Gregory Garrison; snd, Bruce Bisenz; asst dir, James Nicholson. (MPAA rating: PG)   113.
Sally Field, Beau Bridges, Ron Leibman, Pat Hingle, Barbara Baxley, Gail Strickland, Morgan Paull.
02/28/79

Norman. . .Is That You?
UA. MGM picture. Prod-dir, George Schlatter. Sp, Ron Clark, Sam Bobrick, Schlatter, based on the play by Clark, Bobrick; cam (Metrocolor), Gayne Rescher; edtr, George Folsey Jr; mus, William Goldstein; lyr, Ron Miller; art dir, Stephen M Berger; set decor, Fred R Price; snd, Tom Ancell, William McCaughey, Bill Hawley, Hal Belcher; asst dirs, William J Hole Jr, Tom Foulkes. (MPAA rating: PG). 91.
Redd Foxx, Pearl Bailey, Dennis Dugan, Michael Warren, Tamara Dobson, Vernee Watson, Jayne Meadows, George Furth, Barbara Sharma, Sergio Aragones, Sosimo Hernandez, Wayland Flowers, Allan Drake.
09/29/76

Normannerne
(The Normans)
(Denmark)
WBL. Crone Film prodn. Wri-dirs, Poul Gernes, Per Kirkeby. Cam (Eastmancolor), Teit Joergensen; edtr, May Soya; mus, Henning Christiansen; sfx, Peter Hoejmark; in charge of prodn, Nina Crone, Joergen Hinsch.   88.
Henning Jensen, Lisabeth Dahl.
04/07/76

Norng Mia
(The Sister-in-Law)
(Thailand)
SAH. Wri-prod-dir, Prince Chatri Chalerm Yukol. Story, Prince Anusorn Yukol; cam, Prince Chatri Chalerm; mus, Keow Achariyakul, Sanga Arampi, Preecha Metrai and Prachamitr; snd, Kasem Militachinda. 110.
Sorapong Chatri, Viyda Umarin, Lalana Sulawan, Choosri Misomon, Adul Green, Chinadit Bunnag.
05/24/78

Noroit
(Northwest Wind)
(France)
X. Sunchild, Paris, prodn. Stephen Tschalgadjieff, prod. Dir, Jacques Rivette. Sp, Eduardo de Gregorio, Maria Ludovica Parolini; cam, William Lubschansky; edtr, Nicole Lubschansky.   142.
Bernadette Lafont, Geraldine Chaplin, Kika Markham, Anne-Marie Reynaud, Georges Gatecloud, Anne Bedou, Marie-Christine Moureau-Maynard, Babette Lamy, Elisabeth Medveczky.
09/21/77

The Norseman
AIP. Charles B Pierce/Fawcett-Majors Prodn. Wri-prod-dir, Charles B Pierce. Cam (Movielab color), Robert Bethard; mus, Jaime Mendoza-Nava; edtrs, Stephen Dunn, Shirak Kojayan, Aladar Klein, Sarah Legor, Robert Bell; asso prod, Tom Moore; asst dir, Dave Woody; snd, Ken King; cos, Bonney Langfitt; set des, John Ball, Henry Peterson. (MPAA rating: PG).   90.
Lee Majors, Cornel Wilde, Mel Ferrer, Jack Elam, Chris Connelly, Kathleen Freeman, Danny Miller, Seaman Glass, Jimmy Clem, Susie Coelho, Jerry Daniels, Deacon Jones.
07/05/78

The North Avenue Irregulars
BV. Walt Disney Prodn. Prods, Ron Miller, Tom Leetch. Dir, Bruce Bilson. Sp, Don Tait, from book by Rev Albert Fay Hill; cam (Technicolor), Leonard J South; mus, Robert F Brunner; songs, Al Kasha, Joel Hirschhorn; edtr, Gordon D Brenner; art dirs, John B Mansbridge, Jack T Collis; asso prod, Kevin Corcoran; set decor, Norman Rockett; sfx, Eustance Lycett, Art Cruickshank, Danny Lee; stunt coord, Eddy Donno; titles, Art Stevens, Joe Hale; asst dir, Christopher Seiter; cos, Chuck Keehne, Emily Sundby; snd, Bub Maffett. (MPAA rating: G).   99.
Edward Herrmann, Barbara Harris, Susan Clark, Karen Valentine, Michael Constantine, Cloris Leachman, Patsy Kelly, Douglas V Fowley, Virginia Capers, Steve Franken, Dena Dietrich, Dick Fuchs, Herb Voland, Alan Hale, Melora Hardin, Bobby Rolofson, Frank Campanella, Ivor Francis, Louisa Mortiz, Marjorie Bennett, Ruth Buzzi.
01/17/79

North China Commune
(Canada)
NFC. Prod, Tom Daly. Exec prods, Arthur Hammond, Barrie Howells. Dirs, Tony Ianzelo, Boyce Richardson. Narr, Donald Sutherland; res-wri, Boyce Richardson; cam, Tony Ianzelo, John Dyer; edtr, Ginny Stikeman; snd edtrs, Margaret Wong, Jacqueline Newell. 80.
(DOC)
03/12/80

North Dallas Forty
PAR. Frank Yablans prodn. Prod, Frank Yablans. Exec prod, Jack B Bernstein. Dir, Ted Kotcheff. Sp, Yablans, Kotcheff, Peter Gent, based upon the novel by Gent; cam (Metrocolor), Paul Lohmann; edtr, Jay Kamen; prodn des, Alfred Sweeney; mus, John Scott; cos des, Dorothy Jeakins; set decor, Art Parker; snd, Larry Jost; asst dir, Victor Hsu. 119.
Nick Nolte, Mac Davis, Charles Durning, Dayle Haddon, Bo Svenson, Steve Forrest, G D Spradlin, Dabney Coleman, Savannah Smith, Marshall Colt, Guich Koock, John Matuszak.
07/25/79

North Sea Is Dead Sea: SEE
Nordsee Ist Mordsee

Northern Lights
CMY. Prod-dir-wri-edtr, John Hanson, Rob Nilsson. Cam (b&w), Judy Irola; mus, David Ozzie Ahlers; art dir, Richard Brown; prod des, Marianne Astrom-DeFina; snd edtr, Susan Slanhoff. 90.
Robert Behling, Susan Lynch, Joe Spano, Marianne Astrom-DeFina, Ray Ness, Helen Ness, Thorbjorn Rue, Nick Eldridge, Jon Ness, Gary Hanisch, Melvin Rodvold, Adelaide Thornveit, Mabel Rue, Krist Toresen.
(B & W)
11/15/78

Northwest Wind: SEE Noroit

Nosferatu; Phantom Der Nacht
(Nosferatu, The Vampire)
(France - Germany)
GAU. Werner Herzog Filmproduktion-Gaumont co-prodn. Prod-sp-dir, Werner Herzog. Cam, Jorg Schmidt-Reitwein; edtr, Beate Mainka-Jellinghaus; mus, Popol Vuh, Florian Fricke; make-up, Reiko Kruk; snd, Harald Maury; sfx, Cornelius Siegel; art dir, Henning Von Gierke. 106.
Klaus Kinski, Isabelle Adjani, Bruno Ganz, Jacques Dufilho, Roland Topor, Walter Ladengast.
(German soundtrack)
01/24/79

Not Everything That Flies Is A Bird: SEE Nicht Alles Was Fliegt, Ist Ein Vogel

Not For Children: SEE
Barnfoerbjudet

Nothing Personal
AIP. Prod, David M Perlmutter. Dir, George Bloomfield. Exec prods, Alan Hamel, Jay Bernstein, Norman Hirschfield; Sp, Robert Kaufman; cam (Movielab Color), Laszlo George, Arthur Ibbetson; edtr, George Appelby; art dir, Mary Kerr; set decors, Mark Freeborn, Anthony Greco; cos, Lynda Kemp; snd, Chris Large; asst dir, R Martin Walter. (MPAA rating: PG). 97.
Donald Sutherland, Suzanne Somers, Lawrence Dane, Roscoe Lee Browne, Dabney Coleman, Saul Rubinek, Catherine O'Hara, Maury Chakin, Kate Lynch, Hugh Webster, Sean McCann.
03/12/80

Nouba: SEE La Nouba Des Femmes Du Mont Chenoua

Nous Etions Un Seul Homme
(We Were One Man)
(France)
X. Philippe Vallois prodn. Wri-dir-edtr, Vallois. Cam (Eastmancolor), Francois About; snd, Alain Villeval; score, Jean Jacques Ruhlmann. 90.
Serge Avedikian, Piotr Stanislas, Catherine Albin.
12/24/80

Nous Irons Tous Au Paradis
(We Will All Go To Heaven)
(France)
GAU. Prodns De La Gueville-Gaumont Int'l prodn. Dir, Yves Robert. Sp, Jean-Loup Dabadie, Robert; cam (Eastmancolor), Rene Mathelin; edtr, Pierre Gilette; mus, Valdimir Cosma. 110.
Jean Rochefort, Claude Brasseur, Guy Bedos, Victor Lanoux, Daniele Delorme, Daniel Gelin, Gaby Sylvia.
11/23/77

Nous Maigrirons Ensemble
(We'll Grow Thin Together)
(France)
SLN. Alpes Cinema/Le Goff Prodn co-prodn. Prods, Jean-Pierre Le Moine, Sybil Le Goff. Wri-dir, Michel Vocoret. Cam, Georges Barsky; snd, Georges Barra; edtr, Claudio Ventura; mus, Pierre Perret. 100.
Peter Ustinov, Bernadette Lafont, Catherine Alric, Sylvie Joly.
09/05/79

Nous Sommes Des Juifs Arabes En Israel
(We Are Arab Jews In Israel)
(Switzerland)
LML. Niddam prodn. Conceived-prod-dir-cam, Igaal Niddam. Asst-artistic collab, Monique Nizard-Florack; edtr, Laurent Ulher; mus, Moshe, Habalo. 120.
(DOC) (16m)
11/23/77

November 1828
(Indonesia)
07/25/79
X. Prod, Nyoohansiang. Wri-dir, Teguh Karya. Cam, Tantra Suryadi; mus, Frankie Raden; snd, S Parman; edtr, Tantra Suryadi; prodn des, Benni Benhari. 135.
Slamet Rahardjo, Jenny Rachman, Maruli Sitompul, El Manik, Rahmat Hidayat, Sumarti Rendra.

Novinar
(Journalist)
(Yugoslavia)
YFR. Jadran Film-Croatia Film-Radna Filma prodn. Wri-dir, Fadil Hadzic. Cam (Eastmancolor), Tomislav Pinter; mus, Alfi Kabilgo. 105.
Rade Serbedjija, Fabijan Sovagovic, Mladen Budiscak, Milena Zupancic, Vera Zima, Tonko Lonza.
08/29/79

Now or Never
(W Germany)
X. Lothar Lambert Film prodn. Prod-wri-dir-cam-edtr, Lambert, in collab with Uwe Sange. Dedicated to the memory of Sylvia Heidemann. 81.
Sylvia Heidemann, Tally Brown, Ronald Perry, Dagmar Beiersdorf, Pat Evans, Exuma, Erskine Philip, Maryse Richter, Rufus Harper, Lothar Lambert.
(16m) (B & W)
08/15/79

The Nude Bomb
U. Jennings Lang prodn. Prod, Lang. Dir, Clive Donner. Sp, Arne Sultan, Bill Dana, Leonard B Stern based on characters created by Mel Brooks and Buck Henry; cam (Technicolor), Harry L Wolf; edtrs, Walter Hannemann, Phil Tucker; mus, Lalo Schifrin; prodn des, William Tuntke; set decor, Marc E Meyer Jr, snd, Lowell Harris; cos, Burton Miller; asst dir, Don Zepfel. (MPAA rating: PG). 94.
Don Adams, Sylvia Kristel, Rhonda Fleming, Dana Elcar, Pamela Hensley, Andrea Howard, Norman Lloyd, Bill Dana, Gary Imhoff, Sarah Rush, Vittorio Gassman, Walter Brooke, Thomas Hill, Ceil Cabot, Joey Forman.
05/07/80

Nues Vom Raeuber Hotzenplotz
(The Latest on Robber Hotzenplotz)
(W Germany)
TRO. Gustav Ehmck Film Prodn, Munich. Dir, Gustav Ehmck. Sp, Karl U Nastvogel, Andy Hoetzel; cam, Hubs Hagen. 90.
Peter Kern, Muckenstruntz and Bamschabl, Barbara Valentin, Wal Davis, Hans Richter, Karl U Nastvogel, Carsta Loeck.
05/23/79

Nuit D'Or
(Golden Night)
(France)
UGC. UGC-SFP-Eurofrance Films-FR3-Maran Film prodn. Dir, Serge Moati. Sp, Moati, Francoise Verny; cam (Eastmancolor), Andre Neau; edtr, Jacqueline Tarrit; mus, Pierre Jansen. 87.
Bernard Blier, Klaus Kinski, Marie Dubois, Jean-Luc Bideau, Charles Vanel, Anny Duperey, Valerie Pascale, Maurice Ronet, Elisabeth Flickenschildt.
12/15/76

Nunca Es Tarde
(It's Never Too Late)
(Spain)
X. Incine and Impala prodn. Dir, Jaime de Arminan; exec prod, Francisco Hueva. Sp-dialogs, Jaime de Arminan, Juan Carlos Eguillor, based on idea by Concha Gregori; cam (Eastmancolor), Teo Escamilla; mus, Jose Nieto; edtr, Jose Luis Matesanz. 98.
Jose Luis Gomez, Angela Molina, Madeleine Christie, Maria Silva, Maite Blasco, Eduardo Calvo, Chus Lampreave, Julia Trujillo, Josefina del Cid, Julia Lorente.
10/26/77

Nunzio
U. Prod, Jennings Lang. Dir, Paul Williams. sp, James Andronica. Cam, Ed Brown; edtr, Johanna Demetrakas; snd, Les Lazarowitz; prodn des, Mel Bourne; mus, Lalo Schifrin; cos, Ann Roth; set decor, George De Titta; asst dir, J Allan Hopkins. (MPAA rating: R). 86.
David Proval, James Andronica, Morgana King, Tovah Feldshuh, Vincent Russo, Maria Smith, Jamie Alba, Joe Spinell, Theresa Saldana, Glenn Scarpelli, Joseph Sullivan.
04/26/78

The Nurses: SEE I Dadathes

Nutcracker Fantasy
SRI. Prods, Walt deFaria, Mark L Rosen, Arthur Tomioka. Exec prod, Shintaro Tsuji. Dir, Takeo Nakamura. Sp adaptation, Thomas Joachim, Eugene Fournier; story, Shintaro Tsuji, based on "The Nutcracker and the Mouseking," E T A Hoffman; cam, Fumio Otani, Aguri Sugita, Ryoji Takamori; light, Toshikiyo Nakatani; edtrs, Jack Woods, Nobuo Ogawa, Takeo Nakamura; mus, Peter Ilyich Tchaikovsky, adapted and arr, Akihito Wakatsuki, Kentaro Haneda; set des, Mayasa Kaburagi, Hiroshi Yamashita; dial sup, Jack Woods. (MPAA rating: G). 82.
Voices: Michele Lee, Melissa Gilbert, Lurene Tuttle, Christopher Lee, Jo Anne Worley, Ken Sansom, Dick Van Patten, Roddy McDowall, Mitchel Gardner, Jack Angel, Gene Moss, Eva Gabor, Joan Gerber, Maxine Fisher, Robin Haffner.
(ANI) (MUS)
08/08/79

Nyt legetoej
(The New Toy)
(Denmark)
CDK. Anne Philipsen prodn. Wri-dir, Peter D Ringgaard. Cam (Eastmancolor), Peter Davidson; edtr, Grete Moeldrup; prodn des, Palle Nybo Arestrup; mus, (arranged by) Niels Harrit, Michael Hove, Henrik Hove. 107.
Ann-Mari Max Hansen, Joern Leslie Fauerschou, Henning Jensen, Holger Juul Hansen.
05/18/77

O Anthropos Me To Garyfallo
(The Man With The Red Carnation)
(Greece)
X. Arma Films prodn. Wri-dir, Nicos Tzemas. Cam, Nicos Kavoukides; mus, Mikis Theodorakis; sets and cos, Ersi Dryni, Tassos Zografos; edtr, Petros Lycas; snd, George Nicalaedes. 120.
Manos Katrakis, Alecos Alexandrakis, Costas Kazacos, Anguelos Antonopoulos, Peter Fyssoun, Vaguelis Kazan, Emilia Ipsilanti, Mirca Papaconstantinou, Phoebus Guicopoulos.
12/24/80

O Asymvivastos
(An Uncompromising Man)
(Greece)
X. Michael-Lefakis, Greka Fil and Andreas Thomopoulos prodn. Wri-dir, Andreas Thomopoulos. Cam (b&w), Demetris Vernicos; mus, George Theodorakis; sets-cos, Chris Protin; edtr, George Triantafyllou; snd, Yannis Dermitzakis. 105.
Pavlos Sidiropoulos, Vera Krouska, Betty Livanou, Costas Vrettos.
10/31/79

O Caso Claudia
(The Claudia Case)
(Brazil)
X. Artenova Films Ltds prodn. Dir, Miguel Borges. Sp, Valerio Meinel, Jose Louzeiro, Miguel Borges, Alvaro Pacheco; cam, Renato Neumann; mus, Remo Usai. 110.
Katia D'Angelo, Carlos Eduardo Dollabela, Roberto Bonfim, Nuno Leal Maia, Jonas Bloch, Luiz Armando Queiroz, Claudio Correare Castro.
(Portuguese Soundtrack)
10/17/79

O Coronel e O Lobisomem
(The Colonel and the Werewolf)
(Brazil)
X. Alcino Diniz Filmes Lda and Embrafilme prodn. Dir-sp, Alcino Diniz. dialogs, Jose Candido de Carvalho, based on his novel; cam, Antonio Goncalves; edtr, Giuseppe Baldacconi; exec dir, Maria Santo Cristo; mus, Helvius Vilela, Marco Versiani. 118.
Mauricio do Valle, Nogueira Maria Claudia, Cleo Simoes, Jofre Soares, Nildo Parente, Selma Egrei, Louise Cardoso, Izabel Ribeiro, Lutherio Luiz, Fernando Reski, Tonico Pereira, Wilson Grey, Otavio Augusto, Oscar Polidoro.
05/30/79

O Megalexandros
(Alexander The Great)
(Greece - Italy)
RTI. RAI Rete 2-ZDF-Anghelopulos Productions prodn. Wri-dir, Theodoros Anghelopulos; cam, Ghiorgos Arvanitis; mus, Christodulos Halaris. 230.
Omero Antonutti, Eva Kotmanid, Grigoris Evanghelatos, Norma Mozzato.
09/17/80

O Moravske Zemi
(The Moravian Land)
(Czechoslovakia)
CZS. Czechoslovak Film Prodn, Barrandov Studio, Prague. Dir, Antonin Kachlik. Sp, Josef Vaculik, Kachlik, based on a story, "Slogan on the Gates," by Fanek Jilik; cam, Josef Illik. 100.
Radoslav Brzobohaty, Jana Vyslouzilova, Karel Kabicek, Bohus Pastorek, Karel Kolousek, Helena Ruzickova.
08/16/78

O Passado E O Presente
(The Past and the Present)
(Portugal)
X. Manoel de Oliveira Film prodn, Oporto. Wri-dir, Manoel de Oliveira, adapted from a play by Vincente Sanches; cam, Acacio de Almeida; mus, Mendelssohn; edtr, Oliveira. 120.
Maria de Saisset, Manuela de Freitas, Barbara Maria, Alberto Inacio, Pedro Pinheiro.
10/15/80

Objasnenie W Lubwi
(Confession of Love)
(USSR)
GOS. Lenfilm prodn, Leningrad. Dir, Ilya Averbach. Sp, Yevgeni Gabrilovich. 120.
Yuri Bogatirojov, Eva Shikulska.
02/07/79

Obratinaya Sviaz
(Feedback)
(USSR)
X. Lenfilm prodn. Dir, Victor Tregoubovitch. Sp, Aleksandr Gelman; cam, Eduard Rozovsky; snd, N Levitina; mus, A Rybnikov. 93.
Oleg Yankovsky, Mikhail Oulianov, Kirill Lavrov, Liudmila Gourtchenko, Natalya Gundareva, Igor Vladimirov.
09/06/78

Obsession
COL. Prods, George Litto, Harry N Blum; exec prod, Robert S Bremson. Dir, Brian De Palma. Sp, Paul Schrader, from a story by De Palma, Schrader; cam (Technicolor), Vilmos Zsigmond; edtr, Paul Hirsch; mus, Bernard Herrmann; art dir, Jack Senter; set decor, Jerry Wunderlich; snd, David Ronne; asst dirs, William Pool, Bob Bender. (MPAA rating: PG). 98.
Cliff Robertson, Genevieve Bujold, John Lithgow, Sylvia Kuumba Williams, Wanda Blackman.
07/07/76

Obsession: SEE Junoon

Ocalic Miasto
(Save the City)
(Poland - USSR)
X. Film Polski & Mosfilm co-prodn, Warsaw and Moscow. Wri-dir, Jan Lomnicki, based on novel by Andrzej Szczypiorski. Cam, Jerzy Goscik, Ewa Strzalka; art dir, Halina Dobrowolska, Jaroslaw Switoniak; mus, Piotr Hertel. 100.

Teresa Budzisz-Krzyzanowska, Jan Krzyzanowski, Jacek Maskiewicz, Aleksander Bielawski, Nina Maslova, Kiryl Arbuzov, Sergei Polezhayev, Oleg Makshantsev, Herbert Siewers, Zbigniew Krynski, Jerzy Sagan.
08/03/77

Ocana, Retrat Intermitent
(Ocana, An Intermittent Portrait)
(Spain)
X. Teide-Prozesa prodn (Barcelona). Prod, Jose Maria Forn. Wri-dir, Ventura Pons. Cam (Eastmancolor), Lucho Poirot; edtrs, Emlio Rodriguez, Valeria Sarmiento.   80.
Jose Perez Ocana and friends.
05/24/78

O Casamento
(The Marriage)
(Brazil)
VPF. Wri-dir, Arnaldo Jabor, from book by Nelson Rodrigues. Cam (Eastmancolor), Dib Lutfi; edtr, Rafael Valverde.   111.
Adriana Prieto, Paulo Porto.
05/19/76

Occupation In 26 Pictures:
SEE Okupacija U 26 Slika

The Octagon
AMC. Prod, Joel Freeman; exec prods, Michael Leone, Alan Belkin; dir, Eric Karson; sp, Leigh Chapman; story, Paul Aaron, Chapman; cam (CFI Color), Michel Hugo; mus, Dick Halligan; edtr, Dann Cahn; prodn des, James Schoppe; set dir, Jim Hassinger; snd, Glen Anderson; karate fight chor, Chuck Norris, Aaron Norris; stunt coord, Aaron Norris; asst dir, Skip Surguine. (MPAA rating: R).   103.
Chuck Norris, Karen Carlson, Lee Van Cleef, Art Hindle, Carol Bagdasarian, Kim Lankford, Tadashi Yamashita, Kurt Grayson, Yuki Shimoda, Larry D Mann, John Fujioka, Jack Carter.
08/13/80

The Odd Angry Shot
(Australia)
RDP. Samson Productions Film. Prods, Tom Jeffrey, Sue Milliken. Dir, Jeffrey. Cam, Don McAlpine; prodn des, Bernard Hides; edtr, Brian Kavanagh; mus, Michael Carlos; snd, Don Connolly; asst dir, Mark Egerton; sfx, Brett Nolen; fight coordinator, Buddy Joe Hooker; stunts, Grant Page.   90.
Graham Kennedy, John Hargreaves, John Jarratt, Bryan Brown, Graeme Blundell, Richard Moir, Ian Gilmour, John Allen, Brandon Burke, Graham Rouse, Tony Barry, Max Cullen, John Fitzgerald, Johnny Garfield, Ray Meagher, Frankie J Holden, Roger Newcombe, Brian Evis, Rose Ricketts, Chuck McKinney, Freddie Paris, Joy Westmore, Brian Wenzel, Sharon Higgins, Sarah Lee, Brian Anderson.
04/25/79

The Odd Job
(Britain)
COL. Tavlorda Ltd prodn; exec prods, Tony Stratton Smith, Steve O'Rourke; prods, Mark Forstater, Graham Chapman. Dir, Peter Medak. Sp, Bernard McKenna, Graham Chapman; cam, Ken Hodges; prodn des, Tony Curtis; edtr, Barrie Vince; mus, Howard Blake; cos des, Shuna Harwood; snd, Claude Hitchcock; prodn mgr, John Wilcox; asst dir, Stephen P Christian.   86.
Graham Chapman, David Jason, Diana Quick, Simon Willliams, Edward Hardwicke, Bill Paterson, Michael Elphick, Stewart Harwood, Carolyn Seymour, Joe Melia, George Innes.
11/01/78

Ode To Billy Joe
WB. Prod (with Roger Camras) and dir, Max Baer. Sp, Herman Raucher, based on the song by Bobbie Gentry; cam (Technicolor), Michel Hugo; 2d unit cam, Robert Jessup, Lyn Lockwood; edtr, Frank E Morriss; mus, Michel Legrand; new song lyr, Alan and Marilyn Bergman; art dir, Philip Jefferies; set decor, Harry Gordon; snd, Richard Portman, Darin Knight; asst dir, Anthony Brand; stunt coord, Beau Gibson. (MPAA rating: PG).   105.
Robby Benson, Glynnis O'Connor, Joan Hotchkis, Sandy McPeak, James Best, Terence Goodman, Becky Bowen, Simpson Hemphill, Ed Shelnut, Eddie Talr, Rebecca Jernigan, Pat Purcell, Jim Westerfield, Jack Capelle.
06/09/76

Odyssey
ASX. Gerard Damiano film. Wri-prod-dir, Gerard Damiano. (Self-imposed X Rating). 86.
Richard Bolla, Nancy Dare, Sandy Long, Michael Gaunt, Celia Dargent, Gloria Leonard, Samantha Fox, Linda Maidstone, Sue Bright, Leonie Mars, Paul Hues, Philip Marlowe, Valerie Adami, Susan McBain, C J Laing, Gil Perkins, Wade Nichols, Bobby Astyr, Vanessa Del Rio, Pepe, Terri Hall, Eva Henderson, Sharon Mitchell, Ellyn Grant, Tony Mansfield.
02/16/77

Oejeblikket
(The Moment)
(Denmark)
PNR. Just Betzer prodn. Wri-dir, Astrid Henning-Jensen; cam (Eastmancolor), Lasse Bjoerne; prodn des, Palle Arestrup; edtrs, Grete Moeldrup, Astrid Henning-Jensen; mus, "Greensleeves" & Lars Henning Jensen. 90.
Ann-Mari Max Hansen, Soeren Spanning, Kathrine Helmuth, Torbjorn Rafn, Lisbeth Movin, Helle Merete Soerensen.
10/15/80

Of Death and Deads: SEE Des Morts

Off Season: SEE Fuori Stagione

Off the Edge
X. Pentacle Films presentation; prod-dir, Michael Firth. Cam (Eastmancolor), Geoff Cocks, Tony Lilleby, Jeff Stevens, Firth; edtr, Michael Economou; mus, Richard Clements. (MPAA rating: PG).   77.
(SEMI - DOC)
03/16/77

Off the Wall
X. Prod-edtr, James Gregory. Wri-dir, Rick King. Addl dial, Marly Swick, Harvey Waldman; asst dir, George Reinhardt; cam, Chris Beaver, Jon Else, Judy Irving; snd, Lisa Jackson, Kris Samuelson; continuity, Vicky Golden; mix, Andy Wiskes.   83.
Harvey Waldman, Gary Schnell, John French, Katy Roberts, Judy Feil, Pat Crowley.
(B & W)
04/06/77

The Office Party: SEE
Julefrokosten

Oficio De Tinieblas
(Mexico)
X. Conacito Dos presentation. Dir-sp, Archibaldo Burns, based on a novel by Rosario Castellanos. Cam, Miguel Garzon; mus, Manuel Enriquez.   96.
Enrique Lizalde, Julissa, Manuel Ojeda, Monica Miguel, Lilia Prado.
10/29/80

Oggetti Smarriti
(Lost And Found)
(Italy)
FOX. Fiction Cinematografica prodn. Wri-dir, Giuseppe Bertolucci. Cam, Renato Tafuri; art dir, Paolo Biagetti.   94.
Mariangela Melato, Bruno Ganz, Renato Salvatori, Laura Morante, Maria Luisa Santella.
05/14/80

Oginsaga
(Love and Faith; Lady Ogin)
(Japan)
TOH. Prod, Tsuneyasu Matsumoto, Kyoko Oshima, Muneo Shimojo. Dir, Kei Kumai. Sp, Yoshitaka Yorita, based on a story by Toko Kon; cam, Kozo Okazaki; mus, Akira Ikufube; art dir, Takeo Kimura; edtr, Tatsuji Nakashizu.   150.
Takashi Shimura, Ryoko Nakano, Toshiro Mifune, Daijiro Harada, Atsuo Nakamura, Kichiemon Nakamura, Eji Okada, Akira Nishimura.
04/18/79

Ogon No Paatonaa
(Golden Partners)
(Japan)
TOH. Prod, Yorihiko Yamada. Dir, Kiyoshi Nishimura; sp, Hiroshi Nagano; based on Ryotaro Nishimura's "Hasshinnin was Shisha" (The Sender Was Dead); cam, Yashushi Ichihara; underwater cam, Masao Nakamura; art, Kazuo Takenaka; snd, Toshiya Ban; lighting, Toshi Takashima.   98.
Tomokazu Miura, Tatsuya Fuji, Misako Konno, Ruji Tonoyama, Shinsuke Ashida, Kai Sato, Noboru Nakamura, Kazuo Yoshiyaki.
12/26/79

Ogro
(Italy - France - Spain)
VDE. Vides (Rome)-Sabre Films (Madrid)-Action Films (Paris) co-prodn. Prods, Franco Cristaldi, Nicola Carraro. Dir, Gillo Pontecorvo. Sp, Pontecorvo, Ugo Pirro, Giorgio Arlorio; cam (Eastmancolor), Marcello Gatti; mus, Ennio Morricone; edtr, Mario Morra. 115.
Gian Maria Volonte, Eusebio Poncela, Angela Molina, Saverio Marconi, Jose Sacristan, Feodor Atkin, George Stacquet, Isabel Garcia.
09/19/79

Oh Heavenly Dog
FOX. Mulberry Square Prodn. Prod-dir, Joe Camp. Sp, Rod Browning, Camp; cam (DeLuxe Color), Don Reddy; mus, Evel Box; songs, Elton John, Gary Osborne, Paul McCartney; edtr, Leon Seith; prodn des, Garrett Lewis; art dir, George Richardson; snd, Colin Charles, Don Bassman, Pat Egan, Chris Carpenter; asst dir, Derek Cracknell; dog trainers, Frank Inn, Juanita Inn. (MPAA rating: PG) 103.
Chevy Chase, Benji, Jane Seymour, Omar Sharif, Robert Morley, Alan Sues, Donnelly Rhodes, Stuart Germain, John Stride, Barbara Leigh-Hunt, Margaret Courtenay, Frank Williams, Albin Pahernik, Susan Kellerman, Lorenzo Music, Marguerite Corriveau.
07/16/80

Oh, God!
WB. Prod, Jerry Weintraub. Dir, Carl Reiner. Sp, Larry Gelbart, based on the novel by Avery Corman; cam (Technicolor), Victor Kemper; edtr, Bud Molin; mus, Jack Elliott; art dir, Jack Senter; set decor, Stuart Reiss; snd, Jim Cook, Wayne Artman, Don Cahn, Richard Wagner; cos-ward, Michael J Harte, Nancy McArdle; asst dir, Bob Birnbaum. (MPAA rating: PB). 97.
George Burns, John Denver, Teri Garr, Donald Pleasence, Ralph Bellamy, William Daniels, Barnard Hughes, Paul Sorvino, Barry Sullivan, Jeff Corey, George Furth, Titos Vandis, David Ogden Stiers, Dinah Shore, Carl Reiner.
10/05/77

Oh, God! Book II
WB. Prod-dir, Gilbert Cates. Sp, Josh Greenfeld, Hal Goldman, Fred S Fox, Seaman Jacobs, Melissa Miller from a story by Greenfeld; cam, (Technicolor), Ralph Woolsey; edtr, Peter E Berger; mus, Charles Fox; prodn des, Preston Ames; set decor, Chris Westlund; snd, Don Sharpless; asst dir, Tom Lofaro. (MPAA rating: PG). 94.
George Burns, Suzanne Pleshette, David Birney, Louanne, John Louie, Howard Duff, Hans Conried, Conrad Janis, Anthony Holland, Wilfrid Hyde-White, Hugh Downs, Joyce Brothers, Marian Mercer, Bebe Drake Massey, Mari Gorman, Vernon Weddle, Alma Beltran.
10/01/80

Oily Maniac
(Hong Kong)
SHW. Run Run Shaw prodn. Dir, Ho Menghua. Sp, Chua Lam; cam, Tsao Hui-chi; art dir, Chen Ching-shen; martial arts instructor, Yuan Hsiang-jen. 90.
Li Hsiu-hsien, Chen Ping, Lily Li, Angela Yu Chien, Ku Feng, Frankie Wei, Hua Lun, Wang Hsieh.
10/20/76

Ojciec Krolowej
(The Queen's Father)
(Poland)
POL. Film Polski prodn. Kadr Film Unit, Warsaw. Dir, Wojciech Solarz. Sp, Jerzy Stefan Stawinski; cam, Stefan Matyjaskiewica; sets, Boleslaw Kamykowski; mus, Maciej Malecki; prodn mgrs, Urszula Orczykowska, Zygmunt Wojcik. 110.
Jan Englert, Dorota Pomykala, Ignacy Machowski, Anna Seniuk, Mariusz Dmochowski, Ludwik Benoit, Emund Fetting, Wienczyslaw Glinski.
10/01/80

Ok Ketten
(The Two Of Them)
(Hungary)
HU. Studio Dialog prodn. Dir, Marta Meszaros. Sp, Ildiko Korody, Joszef Balasz, Geza Beremenyi; cam (Eastmancolor), Janos Kende; mus, Gyorgy Kovacs. 94.
Marina Vlady, Lili Monori, Miklos Tolnay, Jan Nowicki, Zsuzsa Czinocky.
11/16/77

Oktoberi Vasarnap
(A Sunday in October)
(Hungary - W Germany)
HU. MafilmDialog Studio ZDF (Mainz) prodn. Wri-dir, Andras Kovacs. Cam (b&w), Istvan Lugossy. 99.
Ferenc Bacs, Tibor Tancos, Laszlo Pataky, Laszlo Peredy, Marianne Moor.
(B & W)
02/27/80

Okupacija U 26 Slika
(Occupation In 26 Pictures)
(Yugoslavia)
YFR. Jadran Film-Croatia Film prodn. Dir, Lordan Zafronovic. Sp, Mirko Kovac, Zafronovic; cam (Eastmancolor), Karpo Acimovic-Godina; edtr, Josip Premenar; mus, Alfi Kabilho. 116.
Frano Lasic, Boris Kralj, Milvan Strljic, Stevo Zigon, Zvonko Pepetic, Tatjana Roberznik, Gordana Pavlov.
08/09/78

Old Boyfriends
AVE. Edward R Pressman prodn. Prod, Edward R Pressman, Michele Rappaport. Exec prod, Paul Schrader. Dir, Joan Tewkesbury. Written by Paul Schrader, Leonard Schrader; cam, William A Fraker; film edtr, Bill Reynolds; art dir, Peter Jamison; asst dir, Tony Bishop; snd, Bill Kaplan; cos, Tony Faso, Suzanne Grace. (MPAA rating: R). 103.
Talia Shire, Richard Jordan, Keith Carradine, John Belushi, John Houseman, Buck Henry, Nina Jordan, Gerritt Graham, P J Soles, Bethel Leslie, Joan Hotchkis, William Bassett.
03/21/79

The Old Comedy: SEE *Staromodnaia Komedia*

The Old Country Where Rimband Died: SEE *Le Vieux Pays Pou Rimbaud Est Mort*

The Old House
(Korea)
TCK. Prod, Kim Tai Soo. Dir, Cho Moon Jin. Sp, Kim So Dong; cam, Yang Young Kil; edtr, Yoo Jae Won; mus, Choi Chang Kwon; art dir, Ro In Taik; snd, Yoo Chang Kuk. 95.
Han In Soo, Yoon Mi Ra, Han Un Jin, Choi Nam Hyon.
12/14/77

The Old Memory: SEE *La Vieja Memoria*

Olimpiada 40
(Olympics 40)
(Poland)
POL. X Production Unit prodn. Dir, Andrej Kotkowski; sp, Michal Kamar, Kotkowski; cam (Eastmancolor), Witold Adamek; mus, Andrej Korynski. 103.
Mariusz Benoit, Jerzy Bonisak, Tadeusz Galia, Krystof Jancsar, Rysiard Kotys, Wojiech Psioniak.
07/30/80

Oliver's Story
PAR. Prod, David V Picker. Dir, John Korty. Sp, Erich Segal, Korty, based on Segal's novel; cam, Arthur Ornitz; edtr, Stuart H Pappe; mus, Frances Lai, Lee Holdridge; art dir, Robert Gundlach; set decor, Phil Smith; snd, Jack C Jacobsen; asst dir, Mel Howard. (MPAA rating: PG). 92.
Ryan O'Neal, Candice Bergen, Nicola Pagett, Edward Binns, Benson Fong, Charles Haid, Kenneth McMillan, Ray Milland, Josef Sommer, Sully Boyar, Swoosie Kurtz, Meg Mundy.
12/20/78

Olly, Olly, Oxen Free
SRI. A Rico Lion Prodn. Prod-dir Richard A Colla; exec prod, Don Henderson. Sp, Eugene Poinc, based on story by Maria L de Ossio, Poinc and R Colla; cam (Metrocolor), Gayne Rescher; edtr, Lee Burch; prodn des, Peter Wooley; mus, Bob Alcivar. (MPAA rating: G). 83.
Katharine Hepburn, Kevin McKenzie, Dennis Dimster, Peter Kilman.
08/16/78

Olovna Brigada
(The Lead Brigade)
(Yugoslavia)
YFR. Vardar Film-Makedonia Film prodn. Dir, Kiril Cenevski; sp, Cenevski; cam (Eastmancolor), Miso Samoilovski; mus, Ilija Pejovski. 100.
Miralem Zupcevic, Darko Dameski, Milja Vujanovic, Aco Janovski, Pavle Vujisic.
08/13/80

Olsen Banden Ser Roedt
(The Olsen Gang Sees Red)
(Denmark)
NOR. Dir, Erik Balling. Sp, Henning Bahs, Balling. Cam, (Eastmancolor), Henning Kristiansen; edtr, Ole Steen Nielsen; prodn des-sfx, Henning Bahs, Peter Hoejmark; in charge of prodn, Jacob Eriksen; prodn supv, Bo Christensen; mus, Bent Fabricius Bjerre, Frederik Kuhlau. 105.
Ove Sprogoe, Poul Bundgaard, Morten Grunwald, Jess Holtsoe, Kirsten Walther.
10/13/76

Olsen-Banden deruda'
(The Olsen Gang Outta Sight)
(Denmark)
NOR. Dir, Erik Balling. Orig story-sp, Henning Bahs, Balling; cam (Eastmancolor), Claus Loof; edtr, Ole Steen Nielsen; mus, Bent Fabricius-Bjerre; exec prod, Bo Christensen; prodn des-sfx, Bahs. 100.
Ove Sprogoe, Morten Grunwald, Poul Bundgaard, Kirsten Walther, Claus Ryskjaer, Ove Verner Hansen, Paul Hagen.
10/19/77

Olsen-Banden gaar i krig
(The Olsen Gang Goes To War)
(Denmark)
NOR. Dir, Erik Balling. Original story and script, Henning Bahs, Balling; prodn des-sfx, Bahs; cam (Eastmancolor), Jeppe Jeppesen; mus, Bent Fabricius-Bjerre; edtr, Ole Steen Nielsen. 95.
Ove Sprogoe, Morten Grunwald, Poul Bundgaard, Kirsten Walther.
11/22/78

Olsen Banden overgiver sig aldrig
(The Olsen Gang Never Surrenders)
(Denmark)
NOR. Nordisk Film Kompagni prod. Orig story-sp, Henning Bahs, Erik Balling; dir, Erik Balling; prodn des-sfx, Henning Bahs; cam (Eastmancolor), Claus Loof; prodn mgr, Bo Christensen, Christian Clausen, Lene Christiansen; edtr, Finn Henriksen; mus, Bent Fabricius-Bjerre. 119.
Ove Sprogoe, Morten Grunwald, Poul Bundgaard, Kirsten Walther, Bjoern Watt-Boolsen, Peter Steen, Axel Stroebye.
12/26/79

Oltre Il Bene E Il Male
(Beyond Good and Evil)
(Italy - France - W Germany)
UA. Clesi Cinematografica SPA, Lotar Films, UA (Paris), Artemis GmbH prodn. Prod, Robert Gordon Edwards. Dir, Lilliana Cavani. Sp, Cavani, Franco Arcalli, Italo Moscati; cam, Armando Nanuzzi; art dir, Lorenzo Mongiardino; mus, Daniele Paris. 127.
Dominique Sanda, Erland Josephson, Robert Powell, Virna Lisi, Philippe Leroy, Elisa Cegani, Michael Degen, Umberto Orsini.
(English soundtrack)
10/12/77

Olyan Mint Otthon
(Just Like At Home)
(Hungary)
HU. Hungarofilm prodn, Dialog Studio, Budapest. Wri-dir, Marta Meszaros. Cam (Eastmancolor), Lajos Koltai. 95.
Anna Karina, Zsuzsa Czinkoczy, Jan Nowicki.
05/24/78

Olympics 40: SEE Olimpiada 40

O, Madda
(Thailand)
NKP. Prod-dir-edtr, Chana Krapayun. Exec prod, Kamolvan Visetprapa. Story, See Fa; Sp, Seeda Wisanupok; mus, Seksan Sonimsat; cam, Sophon Jaenphanit; snd, Asvin Pictures; cos, Nee Shop; asst dir, Surachai Komonnimee; theme song, "O, Madda," orig mus-lyr, Seksan Sonimsat; sung by Suvalli Pakaphan. 120.
Pisamai Wilaisak, Sorapong Chatri, Yodchai Megsuan, Nawarat Yukthanan, Niroot Sirichanya, Choosri Misomon, Vilaiwan Wattanapanit, Tarika Taratit, Mayurachat Muenpasitiwet, Dekchai Sirasak, Kunoo Suwanasang, Komapat Attaya.
05/18/77

Omar Gatlato
(Algeria)
ONC. Wri-dir, Allouache Merzak. Cam (Eastmancolor), Smail Lakhdar Hamina; edtr, Moufida Tlatli; mus, Malek Ahmed. 90.
Boualem Benani, Farida Guenaneche, Aziz Degga, Abdelkader Chaou, Rbah Bouchial.
05/18/77

The Omen
FOX. Prod, Harvey Bernhard; exec prod, Mace Neufeld. Dir, Richard Donner. Sp, David Seltzer; cam (DeLuxe Color), Gilbert Taylor; edtr, Stuart Baird; mus, Jerry Goldsmith; art dir, Carmen Dillon; snd, Gordon Everett; asst dir, David Tomblin. (MPAA rating: R). 111.
Gregory Peck, Lee Remick, David Warner, Billie Whitelaw, Leo McKern, Harvey Stevens, Patrick Troughton, Martin Benson, Anthony Nicholls, Holly Palance, John Stride, Robert MacLeod, Sheila Raynor.
06/09/76

The Ominous House: SEE Suria Dighal Bari

The Omniscient: SEE Sarvasakshi

On A Vole la Cuisse de Jupiter
(Somebody's Stolen the Thigh of Jupiter)
(France)
CCF. Ariane Films/Mondex Films/FR3 co-prodn. Prods, Alexandre Mnouchkine, Georges Dancigers, Robert Amon. Dir, Philippe de Broca. Wris, De Broca, Muchel Audiard, based on the personage of Commissioner Tanquerelle created by Jean-Paul Rouland and Claude Olivier; cam (Eastmancolor), Jean-Paul Schwartz; snd, Jean Labussiere; mus, Georges Hatzinassios; art dirs, Eric Moulard, Mikes Karapiperis; edtr, Henri Lanoe. 102.
Annie Giradot, Philippe Noiret, Francis Perrin, Catherine Alric, Marc Dudicourt.
02/27/80

On Aura Tout Vu
(We've Seen Everything)
(France)
GAU. Dir, Georges Lautner. Sp, Francis Veber; cam (Eastmancolor), Maurice Fellous; edtr, Michele David. 96.
Pierre Richard, Miou-Miou, Jean-Pierre Marielle, Renee Saint-Cyr.
07/21/76

On Company Business
X. Howard Dratch, Allan Francovich, Isla Negra/Blanca Films Prodn, San Francisco. Wri-dir, Allan Francovich. Res, Howard Dratch, Francovich, Kathleen Weaver; cam, Kevin Keating; edtrs, Veronica Selver, Alice Erber; edtng asst, Deborah Hoffman; snd, Peter Van Dyke. 180.
(DOC) (16m)
03/12/80

On Efface Tout!
(We Forget Everything!)
(France)
IFS. Les Films Du Sioux prodn. Dir, Pascal Vidal. Sp, Pierre Philippe; cam (Eastmancolor), Jacques Boumendil; edtr, Arnaud Peit. 110.
Yves Beneyton, Christine Pascal, Christine Murillo, Bruno Cremer, Bernard Fresson, Micheline Presle, J M Thibault, Gerard Lartigau, Guy Trjan.
08/23/78

On Peut Le Dire Sans Se Facher
(One Can Say It Without Getting Angry)
(France)
FLG. Oliane Prodns-Gerland Prodns-Filmologies prodn. Dir, Roger Coggio. Sp, Coggio, Elisabeth Huppert, Bernard Landry; cam (Eastmancolor), Etienne Becker; edtr, Denise De Casablanca; mus, Michel Legrand. 91.
Roger Coggio, Elisabeth Huppert, Madeleine Robinson, Louisa Colpeyn, Jole Silvani, Andriana Innocenti.
01/18/78

On the Fertile Land: SEE Bereketli Topraklar Uzerinde

On the Island: SEE Auf Der Insel

On the Move: SEE Die Abfahrer

On The Move: SEE Utkozben

On the Nickel
LOR. Rose's Park prodn. Prod-dir-wri, Ralph Waite. Cam (TVC Labs color), Ric Waite; edtr, Wendy Greene Bricmont; mus, Fredric Myrow; cos, Patrick Norris; snd, Don Matthews; asso prod, William Bushnell; asst dir, Ralph Ferrin. (MPAA rating: R).   96.
Donald Moffat, Ralph Waite, Hal Williams, Penelope Allen, Jack Kehoe.
03/26/80

On the Sideline: SEE Szepek Es Bolondok

On the Tip of the Tongue: SEE Du Bout Des Levres

On the Tracks of the Missing: SEE Po Diryata Na Bezsledno Izcheznalite

On The Yard
MWE. Midwest Film Prodn. Prod, Joan Micklin Silver. Dir, Raphael D Silver. Sp, Malcolm Braly; mus, Charles Grois.
John Heard, Tom Waites, Mike Kellin, Richard Bright, Joe Grifasi, Lane Smith, Richard Hayes, Hector Troy, Richard Jamieson, Thomas Toner, Ron Faber, David Clennon, Don Blakely, JC Quinn, Dominic Chianese, Eddie Jones, Ben Slack, James Remar, Dave McCalley, Ludwick Villani.
11/15/78

Once in Paris
X. Frank D Gilroy prodn. Co-prods, Manny Fuchs, Gerard Croce. Presented by Mitch Leigh and the McLaughlins. Dir-sp, Gilroy; cam (color-TVC Labs), Claude Saunier; edtr, Robert Q Lovett; mus, Mitch Leigh; snd, Daniel Brisseau, David B Cohn; asst dir, Francois X Moullin.   100.
Wayne Rogers, Gayle Hunnicutt, Jack Lenoir, Phillippe March, Clement Harari, Tanya Lopert, Marthe Mercadier, Yves Massard, Sady Rebbot, Matt Carney, Doris Roberts, Max Fournel, Gerard Croce Victoria Ville, Frank Peyrinaud, Jean Jacques Charriere, Sylviane Charlet, Pierre Dupray, Patrick Aubree, Stephane Delcher, Jean Jacques Rousselet, Jacques Bouanich, Henri Attal, Beatrice Chatelier, Marta Andras, Chouky Sergent, Manny Fuchs, Andre Fetet, Caroline Carliez, Edgar Croce, Nicole Teboul, Michael Teboul.
11/08/78

Once Upon A Time: SEE Maria D'Oro und Bello Blue

Once Upon a Time: SEE Ondanondu Kaladalli

Once Upon Andrea: SEE Tous A Poil Et Qu'on En Finisse!

Ondanondu Kaladalli
(Once Upon a Time)
(India)
LKN. Dir, Girish Karnad. Sp, Karnad, Krishan Basrur; cam (Eastmancolor), Apurba Kishore Bir; edtr, P Bhaktavatsalam; mus, Bhaskar Chandvarkar.   160
Shankar Nag, Sundar Krishna Urs, Akshata Rao, Sushilendra Joshi, Sundar Rajan, V Ramamurthy.
01/31/79

The One And Only
PAR. First Artists prodn. Prods, Steve Gordon, David V Picker; exec prod, Robert Halmi. Dir, Carl Reiner. Sp, Gordon; cam (Movielab Color), Victor J Kemper; edtr, Bud Molin; mus, Patrick Williams; new song, Alan and Marilyn Bergman; prodn des, Edward Carfagno; set decor, Ruby Levitt; snd, John K Wilkinson, Bud Alper; asst dir, Bob Birnbaum. (MPAA rating: PG).   98.
Henry Winkler, Kim Darby, Gene Saks, William Daniels, Polly Holliday, Harold Gould, Herve Villechaize, Dick Lane, Bill Baldwin, Dennis James, Anthony Battaglia, Ed Begley Jr, Brandon Cruz, Charles Frank.
01/25/78

One Can Say It Without Getting Angry: SEE On Peut Le Dire Sans Se Facher

The 141 Days: SEE De 141 Dage

One Man
(Canada)
NFC. Dir, Robin Spry. Sp, Spry, Peter Pearson, Peter Madden; cam (Eastmancolor), Douglas Keifer; edtr, John Kramer; mus, Ben Low.   88.
Len Cariou, Alicia Brady, Marion Galbraith, Colin Angus Campbell, August Schellenberg.
05/25/77

One Man's Loss...: SEE Den enes doed...

One Night in Life with One Woman: SEE Isang Gabi Sa Buhay Ng Isang Babae

One Night Stand
(France)
FBE. ONS Co prodn. Dir, Pierre Rissient. Sp, Rissient with collab of Kenneth White; cam (Eastmancolor), Alain Derobe; edtr, Bob Wade.   102.
Richard Jordan, Ting Pei, Tien Ni, Mei Fang, Tsang Kong, Ken Wayne, Marie Daems.
(English soundtrack)
08/25/76

One of a Kind
HI. Prod-dir-pho-edtr, Troy Benny. Exec prod, Mike Merino. Sp, Michelangelo Gianini; snd, Jack Maisel. (Self-imposed X rating).   88.
Leslie Bovee, Bob Migleano, Joey Severa, Sharon Thorpe, Laura Vereneti, Annette Haven.
05/26/76

One On One
WB. Prod, Martin Hornstein. Dir, Lamont Johnson. Sp, Robby Benson, Jerry Segal; cam (Technicolor), Donald M Morgan; mus, Charles Fox; songs, Fox, Paul Williams; edtr, Robbe Roberts; art dir, Sherman Loudermilk; set decor-cos-ward, Donfeld; snd, Jim Cook, Don Johnson; asst dirs, Chico Day, Anthony Brand, Gene De Ruelle. (MPAA rating: PG).   98.
Robby Benson, Annette O'Toole, G D Spradlin, Gail Strickland, Melanie Griffith, James G Richardson, Hector Morales, Cory Faucher, Doug Sullivan, Lamont Johnson.
06/15/77

One or the Other: SEE Einer Von Uns Beiden

One People: SEE Wan Pipel

One Plus One: SEE En och en

1+1=3
(W Germany)
X. Genee & Von Furstenberg FilmProduktionsges MBH and Heidi Genee Filmproduktion prodn. Dir, Heidi Genee; sp, Genee, Helga Kraus; cam, Gernot Roll; score, Andreas Kobner; edtr, Helga Beyer; set des, Peter Grenz; cos, Beyer; asst dir, Robert Busch.   120.
Adelheid Arndt, Dominik Graf, Christoph Quest, Helga Storck, Dietrich Leiding, Charlotte Witthauer, Kelle Riedl, Helga Krauss, Hark Bohm, Ina and Daniel Genee, Greta Kelwing, Karin Kussauer.
11/07/79

One Silver Piece: SEE Jeden Stribrny

One Sings, The Other Does Not: SEE L'Une Chante L'Antre Pas

One Trick Pony
WB. Prods, Michael Yannen, Michael Hausman. Dir, Robert M Young. Sp-mus, Paul Simon; cam (Technicolor), Dick Bush; edtrs, Edward Beyer, Barry Malkin, David Ray; prodn des, David Mitchell; art dir, Woods Macintosh; set decor, Justin Scoppa; cos, Hilary Rosenfeld; snd (Dolby), Chris Newman, Larry Jost; asst dir, Michael Hausman. (MPAA rating: R).   98.
Paul Simon, Blair Brown, Rip Torn, Joan Hackett, Allen Goorwitz, Mare Winningham, Michael Pearlman, Lou Reed, Steve Gadd, Eric Gale, Tony Levin, Richard Tee, Harry Shearer, The B-52's, Lovin Spoonful, Sam and Dave, Tiny Tim.
10/01/80

122 Rue De Provence
(One Two Two)
(France)
WBC. Orphee Arts prodn. Dir, Christian Gion. Sp, Albert Kantoff, Christian Watton; cam (Eastmancolor), Robert Fraisse; edtr, Natalie Lafaurie; mus, Ennio Morricone.   98.
Nicole Calfan, Francis Huster, Jacques Francois, Henri Guybet,

1 2 3 Duan Mahaphai
(1 2 3 Monster Express)
(Thailand)
NPP. Prod, Narong Poomin. Dirs, Prinya Lilason, Vinai Poomin, Narong Poomin. Story, Narong Poomin; sp, Rom Bunnag, Narong Poomin; cam, Pisan Prasingh; edtr, Manat Topayat; snd, Maitree Janjarasskul; mus, Seksan Sonimsat; art dir-prodn des, Ulai Sirisombat. Theme song, "Muan Kerd Mai" (A New Lease on Life), mus-lyr, Seksan Sonimsat, sung by Setha Sirichaya and Anyarat Suthat Na Ayudhaya. 125.
Krung Srivilai, Sorapong Chatri, Patravadi Sritrairatana, Piyamatr Monjakul, Naiyana Chivanand, Nawarat Yukthanan, Niroot Sirichaya, Lak Apichat, Setta Sirichaya, Anyarat Suthat Na Ayudhaya, Banchong Nilpet, Sulaliwan Suwanatat, Bu Vibulnan, Ratanaporn Noi, Somchai Samipak, Pinyo Panui, Ratanaporn Indrakamhaeng, Muang Apollo, Tawin Jaengsawang, Somboon Sukinan, Kitti Daskorn.
06/22/77

1 2 3 Monster Express: SEE
1 2 3 Duan Mahaphai

One Two Two: SEE *122 Rue De Provence*

One Way Boogie Woogie
X. All technical credits by James Benning. 60.
04/26/78

The Onion Field
AVE. Black Marble Prodn. Sp, Joseph Wambaugh from his book. Prod, Walter Coblenz. Dir, Harold Becker. Mus, Eumir Deodato; prodn des, Brian Eatwell; edtr, John W Wheeler; cam, Charles Rosher; asst dir, Tom Mack; snd edtr, Keith Stafford; set decor, Dick Goddard; set des, Joe Hubbard; technical advisors courtroom, Phillip Halpin, Dino Fulgoni; technical advisor police procedure, Richard Falk. 122.
John Savage, James Woods, Franklyn Seales, Ted Danson, Ronny Cox, David Huffman, Christopher Lloyd, Diane Hull, Priscilla Pointer, Beege Barkett, Richard Herd, Le Tari, Richard Venture, Lee Weaver, Phillip R Allen, Pat Corley, K Callan, Sandy McPeak, Lillian Randolph, Ned Wilson, Jack Rader, Raleigh Bond, Brad English, Stanley Grover, Michael Pataki.
05/23/79

Only 15: SEE *15 Yok Yok*

Only Once In A Lifetime
MVT. Sierra Madre Motion Picture Co-Moctezuma Esparza Prods prodn. Prods, Moctezuma Esparza, and Alejandro Grattan. Wri-dir, Grattan. Cam, Turner Browne; mus, Robert O Ragland; edtr, Esperanza Vasquez. 97.
Miguel Robelo, Estrellita Lopez, Sheree North, Claudio Brook.
09/26/79

Anicee Alvina, Catherine Alric, Sophie Deschamps, Nicole Seguin.
05/10/78

The Only One: SEE *Edinstvennaja*

Only Sixteen, Part 2: SEE *Rak Otaroot*

Only Their Clothes Are Old: SEE *Velhos Sao Os Trapos*

Opa Schulz
(Grandpa Schulz)
(W Germany)
X. Erika Runge Film prodn, in collab with Suedwestfunk, Baden-Baden. Wri-dir, Erika Runge; cam, Ulrich Burtin; edtr, Helga Scharf; mus, Neils Frederick Hoffmann; snd, Wilhelm Dusil; art dir, Johannes Otta; prodn mgr, Hans-Bolko Marcard. 85.
Erhard Dhein, Waltraud Zuehlke, Rene Diehne, Johanna Galonska, Ernst Blenke, Dieter Riedel, Angela Briesen, Elsbeth Krebs, Erna Bahlsen, Heinz Herrmann, Dietrich Luedemann.
(16m)
05/18/77

Opening Night
FCS. Prod, Al Ruban. Dir-sp, John Cassavetes. Exec prod, Sam Shaw; cam (Metrocolor), Ruban; edtr, Tom Cornwell; asso prod, Michael Lally; art dir, Brian Ryman; cos des, Alexandra Corwin-Hankin; snd, Bo Harwood; mus comp, Harwood; mus arr-cond, Booker T Jones; prodn mgr, Foster H Phinney, Ed Ledding. 144.
Gena Rowlands, Ben Gazzara, John Cassavetes, Joan Blondell, Paul Stewart, Zohra Lampert, Laura Johnson, John Tuell, Ray Powers, John Finnegan, Louise Fitch, Fred Draper, Katherine Cassavetes, Lady Rowlands.
12/28/77

The Opening Of Misty Beethoven
CAY. Prod, L Sultana. Dir, Henry Paris (Radley Metzger). Sp, Jake Barnes; cam, Robert Rochester; edtr, Bonnie Karrin; mus, George Craig; snd, Joe Masefield; art dir, Anton Stone. (Self-applied X rating). 87.
Contance Mooney, Jamie Gillis, Jacqueline Beudant, Terri Hall, Gloria Leonard, Casey Donovan, Ras Kean.
04/07/76

Opera Prima
(First Effort)
(Spain - France)
X. La Salamandra (Madrid) and Les Films Moliere (Paris) co-prodn. Dir, Fernando Trueba. Prod, Fernando Colomo. Sp, Fernando Trueba, Oscar Ladoire; cam (Eastmancolor), A Luis Fernandez; mus, Fernando Ember; edtr, M A Santamaria. 92.
Oscar Ladoire, Paula Molina, Antonio Resines, Luis Gonzalez Regueral, Kitty Manver, Marisa Paredes.
06/25/80

Operasjon Cobra
(Operation Cobra)
(Norway)
NSK. Based on Anders Bodelsen's novel. Wri-dir, Ola Solum. Cam (Eastmancolor), Hans Nord. 82.
Roy Bjoernstad, Nils Ole Oftebro, Wencke Medboe.
10/24/79

Operation Black Panther: SEE *Yeh Nuat Sua*

Operation Cobra: SEE *Operasjon Cobra*

Operation Daybreak
(Seven Men At Daybreak)
WB. Howard Schuster Inc-American Allied Pictures prodn, prod, Carter De Haven. Dir, Lewis Gilbert. Sp, Ronald Harwood (based on the novel "Seven Men at Daybreak") by Alan Burgess); cam (Technicolor), Henri Decae; edtr, Thelma Connell; mus, David Hentschell; asso prod, Stanley O'Toole; art dirs, William McCrow, Bob Kulic; sfx, Roy Whybrow; 2d unit dir, Ernest Day; snd, Doub Turner. (MPAA rating: PG). 118.
Timothy Bottoms, Karel Curda, Joss Ackland, Nicola Pagett, Anthony Andrews, Anton Diffring, Diana Coupland, Ronald Radd, Kim Fortune, Pavla Matejovska, Carl Duering, Gyril Shaps, Ray Smith.
03/03/76

Operation Leopard: SEE *La Legion Saute Sur Kolwezi*

Operation Stadium: SEE *Akcija Stadion*

Operation Thunderbolt
(Israel)
X. Golan-Globus film of a G S Films Prodn. Prods, Menahem Golan, Yoram Globus. Dir, Golan. Sp, Clark Reynolds; cam, Adam Greenberg; mus, Dov Seltzer; edtr, Dov Henig. (MPAA rating: PG). 120.
Yehoram Gaon, Assaf Dayan, Ori Levy, Arik Lavi, Klaus Kinsky, Sybil Danning, Oded Teomi, Hi Kelos, Henry Czerniak, Gila Almagor, Rachel Marcus, Reuben Bar Yotam, Shoshik Shani, Shaike Ophir, Shlomo Vishinsky, Shmuel Rodenski, Ben Yosef.
02/16/77

The Opium War: SEE *Lin Tse-hsu*

Opname
(In For Treatment)
(Holland)
X. Het Werkeatre prodn. Prod-sp, the Het Werkeatre. Dirs, Erik van Zuylen, Marja Kok. Cam, Robby Muller; edtr, Hans van Dongen. 99.
Helmert Woundenberg, Frank Groothof, Joop Admiraal.
(English subtitles)
03/05/80

Orca

PAR. Dino De Laurentiis presentation, prod, Luciano Vincenzoni. Dir, Michael Anderson. Sp, Vincenzoni, Sergio Donati; cam (Technicolor), Ted Moore; underwater cam, Vittorio Dragonetti; edtrs, Ralph E Winters, John Bloom, Marion Rothman; mus, Ennio Morricone; song lyr, Carol Connors; prodn des, Mario Garbuglia; art dir, Boris Juraga, Ferdinando Giovannoni; set decors, Armando Scarano, John Godfrey; snd, Trevor Pyke, John Bramall; cos-ward, Jost Jakob, Philippe Pickford; asst dir, Brian Cook; 2d unit and underwater dir, Folco Quilici; stunt coords, Romano Puppo, Emilio Messina. (MPAA rating: PG). 92.
Richard Harris, Charlotte Rampling, Will Sampson, Bo Derek, Keenan Wynn, Robert Carradine, Scott Walker, Peter Hooten, Wayne Heffley, Vincent Gentile, Don (Red) Barry.
07/13/77

The Orchestra Conductor: SEE Dyrygent

Orchestra Rehearsal: SEE Prova D'Orchestra

Order And Security Of The World: SEE L'Ordre Et La Securite Du Monde

Order: SEE Ordnung

Ordinary People

PAR. Wildwood Enterprises prodn. Prod, Ronald L Schwary; dir, Robert Redford; sp, Alvin Sargent, based on novel by Judith Guest; cam (Technicolor), John Bailey; edtr, Jeff Kanew; mus adapt, Marvin Hamlisch; art dirs, Phillip Bennett, J Michael Riva; set decors, Jerry Wunderlich, William Fosser; cos des, Bernie Pollack; snd, Charles Wilborn; asst dir, Steven H Perry. (MPAA rating: R). 123.
Donald Sutherland, Mary Tyler Moore, Judd Hirsch, Timothy Hutton, M Emmet Walsh, Elizabeth McGovern, Dinah Manoff, Fredric Lehne, James B Sikking, Basil Hoffman, Quinn Redeker, Mariclare Costello, Meg Mundy, Elizabeth Hubbard, Adam Baldwin, Richard Whiting.
09/17/80

Ordnung

(Order)
(W Germany)
CIG. Marten Taege Film Prodn, Wiesbaden, in collab with Zweites Deutsches Fernsehen (ZDF), Mainz; Dir, Sohrab Shahid Saless. Sp, Saless, Dieter Reifarth, Bert Schmidt; cam, Ramin Molai, mus, Rolf Bauer; edtr, Yvonne Koelsch. 96.
Heinz Lieven, Dorothea Moritz, Ingrid Domann, Peter Schuetz, Dagmar Hessenland, Dieter Schaad.
(B & W)
05/07/80

Oriental Playgirls

(Hong Kong)
X. Prod, Run Run Shaw. Director James Lu Chi. Sp, James Lu Chi. 102.
Ai Ti, Shaw Yin-yin, Frankie Wei, Hu Feng, James Lu Chi.
03/17/76

Origins of a Meal: SEE Genese D'Un Repas

Oro Rojo

(Red Gold)
(Spain - Mexico)
X. Izaro Films (Madrid), Esme Producciones (Mexico) prodn. Wri-dir, Alberto Vazquez Figueroa. Cam (Eastmancolor), Jose Luis Alcaine; edtr, Enrique Alarcon; exec prod, J Estelrich; sets, R G Salgado; mus, Carmelo Bernaola. 95.
Jose Sacristan, Isela Vega, Hugo Stiglitz, Patricia Adriani, Jorge Luque, Alfredo Mayo, Monica Randall.
09/20/78

Orokseg

(The Heritage)
(Hungary - France)
GAU. Mafilm, Hunnia Studio, Gaumont prodn. Dir, Marta Meszaros. Sp, Ildiko Korody, Meszaros; cam (Eastmancolor), Elemer Ragalyi; edtr, Kovacs Gyorgy. 100.
Isabelle Huppert, Lili Monori, Jan Nowicki, Zita Perzel, Sandor Szabo.
05/21/80

Orphans: SEE Podranki

Orpheus: SEE L'Orfeo

The Ortlieb Women: SEE Die Ortliebschen Frauen

Os Anos JK - Uma Trajetoria Politica

(The JK Years - A Political Trajectory)
(Brazil)
EMZ. Terra Filmes prodn. Features newsreels, documents and interviews. Dir, Silvio Tendler; cam, Lucio Kodato; edtr, Francisco Sergeio Moreira; research, Francisco Quental, Antonio Paulo Ferraz; text, Claudio Bojunga; narr, Othon Bastos; mus, Caique Botkay; snd, Christiano Maciel; asst dir-edtr, Francisco Sergio Moreira; asst research, Olga d'Arc Pimentel, Silvia Bregman. 110.
(DOC)
09/10/80

Os Mucker

(The Mucker)
(Brazil - W Germany)
X. Stopfilm Ltd prodn. Prods-dirs, Wolf Gauer, Jorge Bodanzky. Sp, Gauer; cam, Bodanzky; edtr, Renato Volpato. 106.
Marlise Saueressig, Jose Lewgoy, Paulo Cesar Pereio, Ricardo Hoepper.
(English subtitles)
03/05/80

Os Pastores da Noite

(Otalia da Bahia)
(France - Brazil)
CII. Orphee Arts Fr3-CIC Brazil prodn. Prod, Claire Duval. Dir, Marcel Camus. Sp-dial, Jorge Amado, Camus, based on novel by Amado; cam (Eastmancolor), Andre Domage; mus, Antonio Carlos, Jocafi; edtr, Andree Feix. 121.
Mira Fonseca, Zeni Pereira, Maria Viana, Antonio Pitanga, Paco Sanches, Massu, Jofre Soares, Emmanuel Cavalcanti, Maria do Rosario, Djalma Correa, Josephine Helene, Licidio Lopes, Grande Otelo, Mirinha do Portao, Joao dos Prazeres, Riachao, Telma.
08/31/77

Osam Kila Srece

(Eight Kilos of Happiness)
(Yugoslavia)
YFR. Radna Organizacija Film Cetedesetprva - Avala Film - Televizija Beograd prodn. Wri-dir, Purisa Dordevic; cam (Eastmancolor), Zika Milic; mus, Vojkan Simic. 70.
Milena Dravic, Dragan Maksimovic, Maja Lalevic, Predrag Kristovic.
08/13/80

Oscar, Kina y El Laser

(Oscar, Kina and the Laser)
(Spain)
X. Signo P C prodn. Exec prod, Salvador Porqueras. Dir, Jose Maria Blanco. Sp, Blanco, Salvador Porqueras, based on story by Carmen Kurtz; cam (Eastmancolor), Juan Gelpi; mus, Castro Dario; edtr, Ramon Cuadreny; sfx, Juan Palleja. 92.
Jose Manuel Alonso, Manuel Alberto, Carlos Castellanos, Monica Garcia, Dora Santacreu, Jose Ballester, Cesar Ojinaga.
03/14/79

Osenny Maraphon

(Autumn Marathon)
(USSR)
GOS. Lenfilm Prodn, Leningrad. Dir, Georgi Danelia. 90.
09/12/79

Osinda

(The Doom)
(Romania)
X. Romaniafilm prodn, Bucharest. Dir, Sergiu Nicolaescu. Sp, A Salamanian, Nicolaescu; cam, Alexandru David; mus, Tiberiu Olah; art dir, Constantin Simionescu; cos, Oltea Ionescu, Hortensia Georgescu; edtr, Margareta Anescu. 120.
Amza Pellea, Ernest Maftei, Sergiu Nicolaescu, Gheorghe Dinica, Ioana Pavelescu, Emerich Schaeffer, Mihai Mereuta, Aimee Iacobescu, Elena Dacian.
07/27/77

Ossudeni Doushi

(Doomed Souls)
(Bulgaria)
X. BulgaroFilm prodn. Wri-dir, Vulo Radev, based on novel of same name by Dimiter Dimov. Cam, Hristo Totev; art dir, Konstantin Djidrov; mus, Mitko Shterev. 150.
Edith Soloy, Jan Englerd, Roussi Chanev, Vulcho Kamarashev, Marianna Dimitrova,

Roumen Kostadinov, Svetoplug Matias, Sylvia Ranghelova, Roman Gramadski.
01/14/76

Ostrov Stribrnych Volavek
(The Island of the Silver Herons)
(Czechoslovakia - E Germany)
X. Czechoslovak, Barrandov Studios, Prague, co-prodn with East Germany, DEFA Berlin. Dir, Jaromil Jires. Sp, Vera Kolabova; cam, Jan Curik; mus, Lubos Fiser. 90.
Milan Vavrusa, Petr Vorisek, Erwin Geschonneck, Heide Marie Wenzelova, Guenter Naumann, Vladimir Dlouhy.
03/09/77

Osvajanje Slobode
(Winning of Freedom)
(Yugoslavia)
YFR. Avala Film, Belgrade, prodn. Dir, Zdravko Sotra. Sp, Gordon Michic; cam, Dragoljub Mancic; sets, Bora Njezic; mus, Vojkan Borisavljevic. 90.
Radko Polic, Ivo Gregurevic, Radox Bajic, Gordana Kosanovic, Milan Puzic, Milivoj Tomic.
09/05/79

Ot Nishto-Neshto
(Something Out Of Nothing)
(Bulgaria)
BGO. Bulgarofilm Production, Hemus Film Group, Sofia. Dir, Nikola Roudarov. Sp, Nikolai Nikiforov; cam, Georgi Georgiev; sets, Vladimir Lekarski; mus, Boris Karadimchev. 90.
Anetta Sotirova, Stefan Danailov, Assen Angelov.
06/11/80

Otalia da Bahia: SEE Os Pastores da Noite

The Other Letter: SEE To Allo Gramma

The Other One's Mug: SEE La Gueule de l'autre

Other People's Money: SEE L'Argent Des Autres

The Other Side of Midnight
FOX. Prod, Frank Yablans; exec prod, Howard W Koch Jr. Dir, Charles Jarrott. Sp, Herman Raucher, Daniel Taradash, based on the novel by Sidney Sheldon; cam (DeLuxe Color), Fred J Koenekamp; 2d unit cam, Robert Huke; serial sequences, Tallmantz Aviation; edtrs, Donn Cambern, Harold F Kress; mus, Michel Legrand; prodn des, John De Cuir; set decors, Raphael Bretton, Tony Mondell; snd, Theodore Soderberg, Larry Jost; cos-ward, Irene Sharaff; asst dir, Fred Brost; 2d unit dir, Donn Cambern. (MPAA rating: R). 165.
Marie-France Pisier, John Beck, Susan Sarandon, Raf Vallone, Clu Gulager, Christian Marquand, Michael Lerner, Sorrell Booke, Antony Ponzini, Louis Zorich, Charles Cioffi.
06/08/77

The Other Side of the Mountain - Part 2
U. Filmways prodn. Prod, Edward S Feldman. Dir, Larry Peerce. Sp, Douglas Day Stewart; cam (Technicolor), Ric Waite; edtrs, Eve Newman, Walter Hannemann; art dir, William Campbell; mus, Lee Holdridge; set decor, John Dwyer; snd, Don Sharpless, Robert L Hoyt; snd effects edtr, Gordon Ecker Jr; sfx, Art Brewer. (MPAA rating: PG). 105.
Marilyn Hassett, Timothy Bottoms, Nan Martin, Belinda J Montgomery, Gretchen Corbett, William Bryant, James A Bottoms, June Dayton, Curtis Credel, Carol Tru Foster, Charles Frank, George Petrie, Ross Durfee, Jackie Russell, Gerri Nelson, Tom Jordan, Harry Moses, Myron Healey, Rev Bee Landis, Steve Conte, Craig Chudy, David Yanez, Marlina Vega.
02/08/78

The Other Smile: SEE Das Andere Laecheln

Otietz Sergii
(Father Serge)
(USSR)
SOV. Mosfilm prodn. Wri-dir, Igor Talankin from the book by Leo Tolstoy. Cam (Sovcolor), Guerogui Rerberg; edtr, M Verevnikov; mus, A Chnitke. 95.
Serge Bondarchuk, Irina Skopeseva, Y Bourbov, A Demidova, T Korotkova.
10/25/78

Ottokar Der Weltverbesserer
(Ottokar, The World Reformer)
(E Germany)
DEE. DEFA Film Prodn, Group Roter Kreis. Dir, Hans Kratzert. Sp, Gudrun Duebener; cam, Wolfgang Braumann; sets, Joachim Otto; mus, Guenther Fischer. 85.
Lars Herrmann, Steffen Bannischka, Steffen Endert, Guenter Junghans, Micaela Kriessler, Kurt Boewe, Wolfgang Winkler, Walfriede Schmitt, Fred Artur Geppert, Simone von Zglinicki, Karin Gregorek, Dieter Wien, Marianne Wuenscher.
06/28/78

Our Johnny: SEE Johnny Unser

Our Land: SEE Ma Bhoomi

Our Winning Season
AIP. Prod, Joe Roth; exec prod, Samuel Z Arkoff; exec in charge of prodn, Louis S Arkoff. Dir, Joseph Ruben. Sp, Nick Niciphor; cam (Movielab Color), Stephen Katz; edtr, Bill Butler; mus, Charles Fox; art dir, Angelo Graham; snd, Larry Jost; cos, Jimmy George; stunt coord, Mickey Gilbert; asst dir, Ed Markley. (MPAA rating: PG). 92.
Scott Jacoby, Deborah Benson, Dennis Quaid, Randy Herman, Joe Penny, Jan Smithers, P J Soles, Robert Wahler, Wendy Rastatter, Damon Douglas, Joanna Cassidy.
05/17/78

Out Of It: SEE La Carapate

Out of the Blue
RBS. Dir, Dennis Hopper. Sp, Leonard Yakir, Gary Jules Jouvenat; cam, Marc Champion; edtr, Doris Dyck; mus, Tom Lavin; exec prod, Paul Lewis. 94.
Linda Manz, Sharon Farrell, Dennis Hopper, Raymond Burr, Don Gordon.
05/28/80

Out Of Whack: SEE Rien ne va plus

Out On Parole: SEE Libertad Provisional

Outlaw Blues
WB. Prod, Steve Tisch; exec prods, Fred Weintraub, Paul Heller. Dir, Richard T Heffron. Sp, B W L Norton; cam (Technicolor), Jules Brenner; 2d unit cam, Jim Etheridge; edtrs, Danford B Greene, Scott Conrad; mus, Charles Bernstein, Bruce Langhorne; songs, John Oates, Harlan Sanders, R C O'Leary, Lee Clayton, Hoyt Axton; art dir, Jack Marty; snd, Richard Portman, Michael Evje; cos-ward, Rosanna Norton, Pam Scrape; asst dir, Dennis Jones; stunt coord, Carey Loftin. (MPAA rating: PG). 100.
Peter Fonda, Susan Saint James, John Crawford, James Callahan, Michael Lerner, Steve Fromholz, Richard Lockmiller, Matt Clark, Jan Rita Cobler, Jeffrey Friedman, Gene Rader, Curtis Harris, Jerry Greene, Dave Helfert, James N Harrel.
07/06/77

The Outlaw Josey Wales
WB. Prod, Robert Daley. Dir, Clint Eastwood. Sp, Phil Kaufman, Sonia Chernus, based on the book "Gone To Texas," by Forrest Carter; cam (DeLuxe Color), Bruce Surtees; edtr, Ferris Webster; mus, Jerry Fielding; prodn des, Tambi Larsen; set decor, Chuck Pierce; snd, Tex Rudloff, Bert Hallberg; asst dir, Jim Fargo; stunt coord, Walter Scott. (MPAA rating: PG). 135.
Clint Eastwood, Chief Dan George, Sondra Locke, Bill McKinney, John Vernon, Paula Trueman, Sam Bottoms, Geraldine Keams, Woodrow Parfrey, Joyce Jameson, Sheb Wooley, Royal Dano, Matt Clarke, John Verros, Will Sampson, William O'Connell, John Quade.
06/30/76

Outlaw Morality: SEE Die Moral Der Banditen

Outrageous
(Canada)
FCD. In cooperation with the Canadian Film Development Corp. Prods, William Marshall, Hendrick J Van der Kolk; asso prod, Peter O'Brian. Wri-dir, Richard Benner, based on a story from "Butterfly Ward" by Margaret Gibson. Cam (Eastmancolor), James B Kelly; mus, Paul Hoffert; orig lyr, Brenda Hoffert; art dir, Karen Bromley; set dresser, Bruce Calnan; edtr, George Appleby. 100.
Craig Russell, Hollis McLaren, Richert Easley, Allen Moyle, David McIlwraith, Gerry Salzberg, Andree Pelletier, Helen Shaver, Martha Gibson, Helen Hughes, Jonah Royston, Richard Moffatt,

David Woito, Rusty Ryan, Jackie Loren, Michael Daniels, Michel.
06/01/77

Outside Chance
X. Miller, Begun TV, Roger Corman prodn. Dir, Michael Miller. Sp, Ralph Gaby Wilson, Miller; cam, Willy Kurant; mus, Murphy Dunne, Lou Levy. 94.
Yvette Mimieux.
09/20/78

The Outsider
PAR. Cinematic Arts B V Prodn. Dir, Tony Luraschi; sp, Luraschi, based on the novel, "The Heritage Of Michael Flaherty" by Colin Leinster; cam, Ricardo Aronovitch; edtr, Catherine Kelber; prodn supv, Philippe Modave; art dir, Franco Fumagalli; cos, Judy Dolan; mus, Ken Thorne; asst dirs, Barry Blackmore, Bernard Farrel. 128.
Craig Wasson, Sterling Hayden, Patricia Quinn, Niall O'Brien, T P McKenna, Niall Tobin, Frank Grimes, Elizabeth Begley, Bosco Hogan, Ray Macanally, Jimmy Devlin, Joe Dowling, Aiden Grennell.
12/05/79

The Outsider: SEE Berlinger

Outsiders: SEE Ceddo

Over the Edge
WBO. George Litto prodn. Prod, George Litto. Dir, Jonathan Kaplan. Sp, Charlie Hass, Tim Hunter; cam, Andrew Davis; edtr, Robert Barere; mus, Sol Kaplan; prodn des, Jim Newport; set decor, A C Montenaro; snd, William Kaplan; sfx, Richard Johnson; asst dir, Ed Ledding. (MPAA rating: PG). 95.
Michael Kramer, Pamela Ludwig, Matt Dillon, Vincent Spano, Tom Fergus, Harry Northup, Andy Romano, Ellen Geer, Richard Jamison, Julia Pomeroy, Tiger Thompson.
05/23/79

Over-Under, Sideways-Down
X. Steve Wax/CineManifest prodn. Dir, Eugene Corr, Wax, Peter Gessner. Sp, Corr, Gessner; cam, Stephen Lighthill; edtrs, David Schickele, Corr; mus, Ozzie Ahlers. 86.
Robert Viharo, Sharon Goldman, Roy Andrews, Robert A Behling, Michael Cavanaugh, Lonnie Ford, Fran Furey, Esteban Oropreza, Larry Patterson.
11/16/77

Oxala
(Leave It To God)
(Portugal)
VO. Wri-dir, Antonio Pedro Vasconcelos; cam, Joao Rocha; edtr, Antoine Bonfanti. 145.
Manuel Baeta Neves, Marta Reynolds, Laura Soveral, Judith Magre, Rue Furtado, Karen Blangueron, Lia Gama, Teresa Madruga, Adelaide Joao.
09/10/80

Oz
(Australia)
BEF. Count Features Inc prodn in asso with Australian Film Commission and BEF Film Distributors. Wri-dir, Chris Lofven. Prods, Lofven, Lyne Helms; asso prod, Jane Scott. Mus, Ross Wilson; cam (Eastmancolor), Dan Burstall; edtr, Les Luxford. 100.
Joy Dunstan, Graham Matters, Bruce Spence, Michael Carmen, Gary Waddell, Robin Ramsay, Paula Maxwell, Ned Kelly.
08/11/76

Pablo
(Cuba)
X. Cuban Film Institute (ICAIC) prodn. Dir, Victor Casaus. Sp, Victor Casaus, Mario Crespo; cam, Raul Rodriguez; mus, Silvio Rodriguez; edtr, Roberto Bravo. 95.
(DOC)
10/04/78

Pacific High
X. Prod, Roy Edward Disney. Dir, Michael Ahnemann. Cam (Metrocolor), Stephen H Burum; edtrs, Thomas Stanford, Michael Ahnemann; snd, Peter Pilafian; mus, Robert F Brunner. (MPAA rating: R; revised to PG). 90.
02/13/80

Paciorki Jednego Rozanca
(The Beads of One Rosary)
(Poland)
POL. Kadr Unit prodn. Wri-dir, Kazimierz Kutz from book by A Siekierski. Cam (Eastmancolor), Wieslaw Zdort; mus, Wojiech Kilar. 116.
Augustyn Halotta, Marta Straszna, Ewa Wisniewska, Fransiczek Pieczka, Jan Bogdol, Jerzy Rzepka.
07/30/80

The Pack
WB. Prod, Fred Weintraub, Paul Heller. Dir-wri, Robert Clouse, based on the novel by Dave Fisher. Cam (Technicolor), Ralph Woolsey; 2d unit cam, Jim Glennon; edtr, Peter E Berger; mus, Lee Holdridge; snd, Les Fresholtz, Dick Alexander, David E Campbell, Darin Knight; cos-ward, Lynn Bernay; asst dir, Tommy Lofaro. (MPAA rating: PG). 99.
Joe Don Baker, Hope Alexander-Willis, Richard B Shull, R G Armstrong, Ned Wertimer, Bibi Besch, Delos V Smith Jr, Richard O'Brien, Sherry Miles, Paul Willson, Eric Knight, Steve Lytle, Rob Narke, Peggy Price, Steve Butts.
08/24/77

Paco L'infaillible
(Paco The Infallible)
(France - Spain)
X. Filmoblic/Lotus Films/Bloody Mary/Tanagra/Record Film prodn. Prods, Hubert Niogret, Luis Mendes. Dir, Didier Haudepin. Sp, Haudepin, Nadie Feuz; dial, Haudepin, Jose M Forque, based on the novel by Andras Naszlo; cam (Fujicolor), Gilberto Azevedo; edtr, Alberto Yaccelini; mus, Serge Perathoner; set decor, Wolfgang Burman; ward, Antonio Munoz; snd, Jaime Velasco, Alix Comte; asst dirs, Philippe Leriche, Gerardo Herrero Perez. 90.
Alfredo Landa, Patrick Dewaere, Christine Pascal, Jean Bouise.
(English subtitles)
03/12/80

Padre Padrone
(Father Master)
(Italy)
RTS. Prod, Giuliani De Negri for RAI and Cinema S.r.l. Wri-dir, Paolo and Vittorio Taviani, based on book by Gavino Ledda. Cam (Eastmancolor), Mario Masini; art dir, Giovanni Sbarra; edtr, Roberto Perpignani; mus, Egisto Macchi. 114.
Omero Antonutti, Saverio Marioni, Marcella Michelangeli, Fabrizio Forte.
05/25/77

Pae Kao
(The Scar)
(Thailand)
CHZ. Prod, Thomchant Thanyachart. Dir, Cherd Songsri. Story, Mai Muang Derm; sp, Rapeeporn, Thom Thatree; mus, Samarn Karnchanapalin, Sanga Arampee, Chalie Intravichit, Cholmoo Chalanukroh; cam, Kavee Kiattinan, Suthat Bureepakdee, Somchai Leelanuruk; art dirs, Urai Sirisombat, Sathorn Srichan; edtr, Rom Ramnee. 105.
Sorapong Chatri, Nantana Ngaokrachang, So Asanachinda, Suwin Swangrat, Sirinthip Siriwan, Suphan Buranaphim, Kitti Daskorn, Setta Sirachaiya, Chalit Fuangarom.
01/25/78

Pafnucio Santo
(Mexico)
X. Conacine prodn. Prod-wri-dir, Rafael Corkidi. Cam, Corkidi; edtr, Angel Camacho; snd, Roberto Munoz, Guillermo Carrasco; art dir, Tedeo Maus; cos, Tere Corkidi; prodn mgr, Luis Urquidi. 98.
Pablo Corkidi, Maria de la Luz Zendejas, Jorge Humberto Robles, Gina Morett, Susana Kamini, Piya, Don Juan Barron, Jose Luis Urquietta, Sebastian.
10/05/77

Pais Portatil
(Portable Country)
(Venezuela)
X. Ficciones C A prodn. Wris-dirs, Ivan Feo, Antonio Lierandi, based on novel by Adriano Gonzalez Leon. Cam (Eastmancolor), Hector Rios; sets, Tony Sanchez, Lesbia Hernandez, Alvaro Rodriguez, Miguel Corzo; mus, Chuchito Sanoja; edtrs, Alberto Torija, Antonio Llerandi. 103.
Alejandra Pinedo, Hector Duvachelle, Ivan Feo, Eliseo Perera, Silvia Santelices,

Eduardo Gil, Ibsen Martinez.
10/10/79

Palac
(The Palace)
(Poland)
POL. Film Polski prodn, Perspektywa Film Unit, Warsaw. Dir, Tadeusz Junak; sp, Wieslawa Mysiliwskiego, based on a novel by W Mysliwski; cam, Ryszard Lenczewski; mus, Leszek Orlewicz; sets, Elzbieta Karwanska, Jerzy Michalak, Tadeusz Cielewica, Stefan Burzynski; prodn mgr, Halina Kawecka. 95.
Janusz Michalowski, Danuta Kisiel, Wiktor Sadecki, Halina Gryglaszewska, Elzbieta Karkoszka, Teresa Budzisz-Kezyzanowska, Zdzislaw Kozien, Roman Stankiewicz, Stanislaw Frackowiak, Stefan Szmidt.
10/15/80

Palermo-Wolfsburg
(W Germany)
X. Thomas Mauch Film Prodn. Wri-dir, Werner Schroeter. Dial asst, Giuseppe Fava; cam, Thomas Mauch; snd, Heiko von Swieykowski; sets-cos, Alberte Barsaq, Magdalena Montezuma, Roberto Lagana; edtr, Schroeter. 180.
Nicola Zarbo, Calogero Arancio, Padre Pace, Cavaliere Comparato, Brigitte Tilg, Gisela Hahn, Antonio Orlando, Ida de Benedetto, Magdalena Montezuma, Otto Sander, Johannes Wacker, Ula Stoeckl, Tamara Kafka, Harry Baer, Ines Zamurovic.
02/13/80

Palm Beach
(Australia)
X. Albie Thoms prodn. Prod-dir-sp, Albie Thoms. Cam, Oscar Scherl; location snd, Michael Moore; prodn mgr, Bob Hill; asst dir, Jan Chapman; edtr, Thoms; helicopter cam, Keith Lamber, Terry Lee; mus, Terry Hannigan. 88.
Nat Young, Ken Brown, Amanda Berry, Bryan Brown, Julie McGregor, John Flaus, Bronwyn Stevens-Jones, David Lourie, Peter Wright, John Clayton, Lyn Collingwood, Adrian Rawlins, P J Jones, Mick Eyre, Jim Roberts, Cathy Power, Mick Winter, Tony Hardwick, David Elfick.
05/23/79

The Pals: SEE Drugarcine

Panagulis Zei
(Panagoulis Lives)
(Italy)
X. RAI-Television Channel 2 film. Prod, Cine 2000 Prodns. Dir, Giuseppe Ferrara; sp, Ferrara, Piergiovanni Anchisi, Riccardo Iacona, Gianfrancesco Ramacci, with collab of Tanassis Valtinos; cam, Silvio Fraschetti; mus, Dimitri Nicolau. 100.
Stathis Giallelis, Pupella Maggio, Victor Cavallo, Adalberto Maria Merli, Cristiano Censi, Luigi Montini, Marcella Michelangeli.
10/15/80

Pandemonium: SEE Langit, Lupa

Panel Story
(Prefab Story)
(Czechoslovakia)
CZS. Czechoslovak Film Production, Studio Barrandov, Prague. Dir, Vera Chytilova. Sp, Eva Kacirkova. 90.
Lukas Bech, Eva Kacirkova, J Kode.
06/11/80

Panische Zeiten
(Panic Times)
(W Germany)
FDA. Udo Lindenberg Production in collab with Amazonas Film, Roba Music, Regina Ziegler Film Production. Dir, Udo Lindenberg, in collab with Peter Fratzscher. Sp, Lindenberg, Kalle Freynik; idea, Horst Koenigstein, Kalle Freynik, Lindenberg; cam, Bernd Heinl; mus, Udo Lindenberg; edtr, Helga Borsche; sets, Toni Luedi; prodn mgr, Michael Wiedemann. 101.
Udo Lindenberg, Leata Galloway, Walter Kohut, Vera Tschechova, Felix Scholtz, Klaus Kauroff, Otto Wanz, Hark Bohm, Beate Jensen, Eddie Constantine, Rudolf Beiswanger, Peter Ahrweiler, Fritz Rau, Heinz Domez, Werner Boehm, Willi Hermann, Renate Schubert, Egon Mueller, Juergen Baumgarten, Karl Dall, Ingeborg Thomsen, Werner Veigel.
06/11/80

Panny Z Wilka
(The Young Ladies of Wilko)
(Poland-France)
07/25/79
POL. Ensemble X-Pierson Prodns prodn. Dir, Andrzej Wajda. Sp, Zbigniew Kaminski from the book by Jaroslav Iwaszkiewicz; cam (Eastmancolor), Edward Klosinski; edtr, Halina Prugar; mus, Karol Szymanowski. 118.
Daniel Olbrychski, Anna Seniuk, Christine Pascal, Maja Komorowska, Stanislawa Celinska, Krystyna Zachwatowicz.

Pantelei
(Bulgaria)
BGO. BulgaroFilm Prodn, Sredets Group, Sofia. Dir, Georgi Stoyanov. Sp, Vassil Akyov; cam, Radoslav Spassov; art dir, Georgi Todorov; mus, Bozhidar Petkov. 100.
Pavel Poppandov, Dobrinka Stankova, Velko Kunev, Nikoa Anastassov, Nikolai Nikolaev.
05/31/78

Paper Flowers: SEE Flores de Papel

Paradies
(Paradise)
(W Germany)
X. Alligator Film F-T Aeckerle prodn in collab with Zelimir Zilnik and Andrej Popovic. Wri-dir, Zilnik. Cam, Popovic; mus, Pedja Vranesevic, Sparifankal; snd, Horst Schoenberger; edtr, Elisabeth Orlov. 90.
Giesela Siebauer, Michael Stralek, Natasa Stanojevic, Barbara K Siegfried Broesecke, Dan van Husen, Gernot Boesser, Akki Ahrens, Johannes Zeh, Ameli Olbricht.
07/14/76

Paradise Alley
U. Force Ten prodn. Prods, John F Roach, Ronald A Suppa; exec prod, Edward Pressman. Wri-dir, Sylvester Stallone. Cam (Technicolor), Laszlo Kovacs; prodn des, John W Corso; edtr, Eve Newman; mus, Bill Conti; art dir, Deborah Beaudet; set decor, Jerry Adams; costumers, Sandra Berke, Lambert Marks; snd, Charles Wilborn; wrestling chor, Terry Funk; asso prod, Arthur Chobanian; asst dir, Cliff Coleman; unit prodn mgr, Michael S Glick. (MPAA rating: PG). 107.
Sylvester Stallone, Kevin Conway, Anne Archer, Joe Spinell, Armand Assante, Lee Canalito, Aimee Eccles, Terry Funk, Joyce Ingalls, Frank McRae, Tom Waits.
09/13/78

Paradise Square: SEE
Paradistorg

Paradiso
(France)
ZPF. Wri-dir, Christain Bricout. Cam (Eastmancolor), Philippe Rousselet. 90.
Didier Sauvegrain, Gerard Darrieu, Annie Savarin, Bernadette Le Sache, Brigitte Rouan, Poussine Mercanton.
09/07/77

Paradistorg
(Paradise Square)
(Sweden)
SVF. Cinematograph AB (Ingmar Bergman)/Swedish Film Institue/Svensk Film AB prodn. Dir, Gunnel Lindblom. Sp, Ulla Isaksson, Gunnel Lindblom, based on Ulla Isaksson's novel "Paradistorg." Asst dir, Ulla Ledin. Cam (Eastmancolor), Tony Forsberg. Prodn des, Anna Asp. Cos, Inger Pehrsson. Edtr, Siv Lundgren. Mus, Georg Riedel. Prodn mgr, Katinka Farago, Johan Clason. 112.
Birgitta Valberg, Sif Ruud, Agneta Ekmanner, Margretha Bystroem, Per Myrberg, Goeran Stangertz, Holger Lowenadler.
03/30/77

Paraguelia
(Greece)
X. Pavlos Tassios-Greca Film-M Lefakis-Greek Film Centre prodn. Wri-dir, Pavlos Tassios. Cam, Sakis Maniatis, Costas Papayannakis; mus, Kyriavos Sfetsas; edtr, Yannis Tsitsopoulos. 95.
Antonis Antoniou, Katerina Gogou, Sophia Roubou, Nikitas Tsakirooglou, Olia Lazaridou, Antonis Kaftzoglou, Vicki Vanita.
10/29/80

Parallels
(Canada)
CRX. Group 3 films prodn. Prod, Jack Wynters; dir, Mark Schoenberg; sp, Schoenberg, Jaron Summers; cam, Douglas Cole; art dir, Drew Borland; mus, Don Archbold; edtr, Marke Slipp; snd, Don Paches. 92.
David Fox, Judith Mabey, Gerard Lepage, Kyra Harper, David Ferry, Walter Kaasa, Howard Dallin, Jennifer Riach, Stephen Walsh.
10/15/80

Parashat Winchell
(The Winchell Affair)
(Israel)
X. KN Films prodn. Prod, Yaakov Kozky. Wri-dir, Avraham Heffner. Cam, Daniel Schneur; edtr, David Tor; art dir, Yael Heffner; mus, Naomi Shemer. 91.
Tal Nativ, Etty Zevko, Oded Kotler, Dov Feigin, Tova Firon, Nathan Meisler, Shimon Finkel, Nava Sh'an.
10/03/79

Parasuram
(Man with the Axe)
(India)
PDI. Dir, Mrinal Sen. Sp, Sen Mohit; cam (Eastmancolor), Ranjit Roy; edtr, Gangadhar Mashkar; mus, B V Karanth. 99.
Arum Mukherjee, Bisvas Chakraborty, Nirmal Ghosh, Sreela Majumdar.
01/31/79

Parceiros De Aventura
(Partners of Adventure)
(Brazil)
EMZ. A F Sampaio Prod Art prodn. Wri-dir, Jose Arujo De Madeiros; book, Joao Falicio; cam (Eastmancolor), Madeiros; edtr, Raphael Valverde; mus, Paulo Moura. 90.
Vinicios, Paula Moura, Ana Madelena, Paulo, Catalina Bonak, Reginaldo Faria, Luiz Armando Quieroz.
08/20/80

The Parisian Life: SEE La Vie Parisienne

Parranda
(Binge)
(Spain)
X. Lotuc Films (Madrid) prodn, dir, Gonzalo Suarez. Cam (Eastmancolor), Carlos Suarez; edtr, Antonio Gimeno; sets, Eduardo Torre de la Fuente; sp, Eduardo Blancoamor, Gonzalo Suarez, based on Blancoamer's book, "A Esmorga." 86.
Jose Louis Gomez, Jose Sacristan, Antonio Ferrandis, Fernando Fernan Gomez, Charo Lopez, Queta Claver, Isabel Mestre, Marilina Ross.
03/23/77

Part 2, Sounder
GMA. Radnitz-Mattel prodn in asso with ABC, prod, Terry Nelson; exec prod, Robert B Radnitz. Dir, William Graham. Sp, Lonne Elder III, based on novel by William H Armstrong; cam (Movielab Color), Urs B Furrer; edtr, Sid Levin; mus, Taj Mahal; prodn des, Walter Scott Herndon; set decor, Cheryal Kearney; snd, John Wilkinson, Jack Finlay, Fred Faust; asst dir, Art Levinson. (MPAA rating: G). 98.
Harold Sylvester, Ebony Wright, Taj Mahal, Annazette Chase, Darryl Young, Erica Young, Ronald Bolden, Barbara Chaney, Kuumba, Ted Airhart, Walter Breaux, Harry Franklin Sr.
10/13/76

Partners
(Canada)
AST. Clearwater Films presentation. Prods, Chalmers Adams, Dan Owen. Dir, Owen. Sp, Norman Snider, Owen; cam, Marc Champion; mus, Murray McLauchlan; edtr, George Appleby; snd, James McCarthy. 96.
Denholm Elliott, Hollis McLaren, Michael Margotta, Lee Broker, Judith Gault, Robert Silverman, Irena Mayeska.
10/06/76

Partners of Adventure: SEE Parceiros De Aventura

Parts The Clonus Horror
G1. Myrl A Schreibman prodn. Prods, Schreibman, Robert S Fiveson; exec prod-dir, Fiveson; sp adapt, Schreibman, Fiveson; cam, Max Beaufort; edtr, Bob Gordon; mus, Hod David Schudson; art dir, Steve Nelson; cos, Dorinda Rice Wood; snd, Ken Robinson; asso prod, Peter R J Deyell; asst dirs, Michael Lee, Paul Berkowitz. (MPAA rating: R.) 90.
Tim Donnelly, Dick Sargent, Peter Graves, Paulette Breen, David Hooks, Keenan Wynn, James Mantell, Zale Kessler, Frank Ashmore, Lurene Tuttle, Boyd Holister.
11/14/79

Pas Koji Je Voleo Vozove
(The Dog That Liked Trains)
(Yugoslavia)
YFR. Centar Film prodn, Belgrade. Dir, Goran Paskaljevic. Sp, Gordan Mihic; cam (Eastmancolor), Aleksandar Petkovic; edtr, Olga Skirgin; sets, Dragoljub Ivkov; mus, Zoran Hristic. 89.
Svetlana Bojokvic, Irfan Mensur, Bafa Zivojinovic, Dusan Jancijevic, Bata Stojkovic, Pavle Vujisic, Gordana Pavlov, Ljiljana Jovanovic.
02/22/78

Pas paa ryggen, professor
(Mind Your Back, Professor)
(Denmark)
PNR. Wri-dir, Jens Okking, based on novel by Orea Johansen. Cam (Eastmancolor), Mikael Salomon; edtr, Lizzi Weischenfeldt; mus, Steen Holkenow. 92.
Ulf Pilgaard, Lisbeth Lundquist.
08/31/77

Pascual Duarte
(Spain)
X. Elias Querejeta prodn. Dir, Ricardo Franco. Sp, Emilio Martinez Lazaro, Querejeta, Franco, based on novel "La Familia de Pascual Duarte" by Camilo Jose Cela; cam, Luis Cuadrado; edtr, Antonio del Amo; mus, Luis de Pablo; direct snd, Bernard Menz; cos, Maiki Marin. 98.
Jose Luis Gomez, Diana Perez de Guzman, Hector Alterio, Paca Djea, Eduardo Calvo, Joaquin Hinojosa, Maribel Ferrero.
05/19/76

Pasi
(Hunger)
(India)
X. Prod, G Lalitha for Sunitha Cine Arts Madras 86. Orig story-sp-dir, Durai. Cam, V Ranga; edtr, M Vellachami; mus, Shanker-Ganesh. 165.
Delhi Ganesh, Vijayan, Surulirajan, Narayanan, Shoba, Tambaram Lalitha, Sathya, S N Parvathy, Jayabharathi, Pravenna.
04/23/80

Pasja
(Passion)
(Poland)
POL. Film Polski Prodn, Warsaw. Dir, Stanislaw Rozewicz. Sp, Andrzej Kijowski, Edward Zebrowski; cam, Jerzy Wojcik; mus, Piotr Mosy. 120.
Piotr Garlicki, Zbigniew Zapasiewicz, Boguslav Smela, Wojciech Alaborski, Henryk Machalica, Mieczyslaw Hryniewicz, Stanis- law Ignar.
08/02/78

Pasqualino Settebelleze
(Seven Beauties)
(Italy)
MDU. Prods, Lina Wertmuller, Giancarlo Giannini, Arrigo Colombo. Wri-dir, Lina Wertmuller. Cam (Eastmancolor), Tonino Delli Colli; art dir, Enrico Job; edtr, Franco Fraticelli; mus, Enzo Jannacci. 115.
Giancarlo Giannini, Fernando Rey, Shirley Stoler, Elena Fiore, Piero Di Iorio.
01/14/76

The Passage
(Britain)
UA. Hemdale and United Artists Theatre Circuit Inc presentation of The General Film Co Ltd prodn. Prod, John Quested in asso with Maurice Binder and Lester Goldsmith. Exec prods, John Daly and Derek Dawson; asso prod, Geoffrey Helman. Dir, J Lee Thompson. Sp, Bruce Nicolaysen, based on his book "Perilous Passage"; cam, Mike Reed; score, Michael J Lewis; snd, Norman Bolland; edtr, Alan Strachan; (MPAA rating: R). 99.
Anthony Quinn, James Mason, Malcolm McDowell, Patricia Neal, Kay Lenz, Christopher Lee, Michael Lonsdale, Marcell Bozzuffi, Paul Clemons, Rose Alba, Neville Jason, Robert Rhys, James Broadbent, Peter Arne, Frederick Jaeger, Terence York, Terence Maidment.
02/28/79

Passe Montagne
(Mountain Pass)
(France)
PIF. Les Films Du Losange prodn. Dir, Jean-Francois Stevenin. Sp, Stevenin, Babou Rappeneau, Stephanie Granel, Michel Delahaye; cam (Eastmancolor), Lionel Legros, Jean Yves Escoffier; edtr, Yann Dedet; mus, Philippe Sarde. 110.
Jacques Villeret, Jean-Francois Stevenin, Texandre Barberat, Yves Lemoign, Andre Riva.
07/26/78

Passe Ton Bac D'Abord
(Get Your Diploma First)
(France)
AMLF. Livardois Films/Renn Prodns/FR 3/INA co-prodn. Wri-dir, Maurice Pialat. Cam (color), Pierre-William Glenn, Jean-Paul Janssen; snd, Pierre Gamet, Michel Laurent; edtrs, Arlette Langmann, Sophie Coussein, Martine Giordano. 90.

Sabine Haudepin, Philippe Marlaud, Valerie Chassigneux, Annick Alane, Michel Caron.
10/03/79

The Passengers: SEE Les Passagers

Passing Through
CLK. Larry Clark prodn. Dir, Larry Clark. Sp, Ted Lange, Clark; cam, Roderick Young, George Geddis; edtr, Clark; mus, Pan African People's Arkestra. 105.
Nathaniel Taylor, Clarence Muse, Pamela Jones.
(16m)
08/31/77

Passion: SEE Pasja

Passion Flower Hotel: SEE Leidenschaftliche Bluemchen

The Passover Plot
(US - Israel)
ATF. Prod, Wolf Schmidt. Exec prod, Menahem Golan. Dir, Michael Campus. Sp, Millard Cohan, Patricia Knop, from the book by Hugh J Schonfield; cam (DeLuxe Color), Adam Greenberg; edtr, Dov Hoenig; mus, Alex North; art dir, Kuli Sander; cos des, Mary Wills; snd, Cyril Collick. (MPAA rating: PG). 108.
Harry Andrews, Hugh Griffith, Zalman King, Donald Pleasence, Scott Wilson, Dan Ades, Michael Baseleon, Lewis van Bergen, William Burns, Daniel Hedaya, Helena Kallianiotes, Kevin O'Connor, Robert Walker, William Watson.
11/03/76

The Past and the Present: SEE O Passado E O Presente

Pastorale
(USSR)
GOS. A Gruzia-Film Prodn. Wri-dir, Otar Yoseliani. 90.
(B & W)
06/28/78

Paths of War: SEE Shtigje Te Luftes

Patrick
(Australia)
FWS. Australian International Film Corp prodn. Prods, Antony I Ginnane, Richard Franklin. Exec prod, Bill Fayman. Dir, Richard Franklin. Sp, Everett De Roche; cam (Agfacolor), Don McAlpine; art dir, Leslie Binns; sfx, Conrad Rothman; asst dirs, Tom Burstall, James Parker; snd, Paul Clarke; ward, Kevin Regan; edtr, Edward Queen-Mason; mus, Brian May. 110.
Susan Penhaligon, Robert Helpmann, Rod Mullinar, Bruce Barry, Julia Blake, Helen Heminway, Maria Mercedes, Frank Wilson, Peter Culpan, Marilyn Rodgers, Peggy Nichols, Carole-Ann Aylett, Walter Pym.
07/26/78

The Patriot: SEE Die Patriotin

The Patriot Game - A Decade Long Battle for The North of Ireland
(France)
X. Prodn Iskra Films, Paris. Dir, Arthur Mac Caig; cam, MacCaig, Theo Robichet; edtr, MacCaig, Dominique Greussay; commentary voice, Winnie Marshall. 93.
(DOC) (B & W) (16m)
06/18/80

Patty
TW. Robert L Roberts prodn. Prod-dir, Roberts; sp, Joyce Richards, Roberts; cam, Henry Smalwitz; snd, Jeff King; score, Al Goodman, Sammy Lowe. (Self-applied X rating). 90.
Sarah Nicholson, Turk Turpin, Lenny Montana, Frank Sciocia, Rene Granville, Howard Don Smolen, Jamie Gillis.
02/18/76

Paul, Lisa And Caroline
BED. Prod-dir, Peter Balakoff. Exec prod, Alberto Fasana. Sp, Peter & Belinda Balakoff; cam, Roy Snowden; snd, John Clarke; edtr, Balakoff; art dir, Pierre Bardot; prodn mgr, Jean LeGrand. (Self-imposed X Rating). 90.
Gena Lee, Tovia Borodyn, Diane Miller, Margaret Monroe, William Margold, John Boland, Ann Webster, Tomy, Jana Knox, Karla Garrett, Hillary Scott, Charles Gabriels, Jacques Girard, Richard Aaron, Robert Monday.
02/16/77

Pavilion VI
(Yugoslavia)
X. Centre Film (Belgrade) prodn. Dir, Lucian Pintilie. Sp, Pintilie; cam, Milorad Jaksic. 92.
Slobodan Perovic, Zoran Radmilovic, Slavko Simic, Pavle Vujisic, Ljuba Tadic, Stevo Zigon, Drago Cuma.
10/31/79

The Pawn: SEE Le Pion

The Payoff: SEE La Mazzetta

Pe Aici Nu Se Trece
(No Trespassing)
(Romania)
RMN. Rumaniafilm Prodn. Group Five, Bucharest. Dir, Doru Nastase. Sp, Titus Popovici; cam (Color-Cinemascope), Aurel Kostrakiewicz; mus, Tiberiu Olah; sets, Guta Stirbu. 150.
Silviu Stanculescu, Vlad Radescu, Ana Szeles, Vladimir Gaitan, George Motoi, Mihai Mereuta, Victor Mavrodineanu, Eugenia Bosinceanu, Cornel Coman, Sorin Kepa, Stefan Velniciuc, Ovidiu Moldovan, Ilarion Ciobanu.
06/21/78

The Peaks of Zelengore: SEE Vrhovi Zelengore

The Pedralbes Murderer: SEE El Asesino De Pedralbes

Pedro Paramo
(Mexico)
X. Conacine prodn; dir-wri, Jose Bolanos, based on story by Juan Rulfo; cam (Eastmancolor), Jorge Stahl Jr; mus, Ennio Morricone; sets, Pedro Miret; edtr, Carlos Savage; snd, Manuel Topete; cos, Guillermo Barclay. 173.
Manuel Ojeda, Vanetia Vianello, Bruno Rey, Fernando Soler, Abelardo San Miguel, Narciso Busquets, Patricia Reyes Spindola, Blanca Guerra, Marta Verduzco, Ofelia Murgia, Roberto Cobo, Elena Bercovich, Socorro Avelar.
09/28/77

Peking Duck Soup: SEE Chinois, Encore un Effort Pour Etre Revolutionaires

Pele
(France - Mexico)
TVA. Video World Panama prodn. Dir, Francois Reichenbach. Sp-cam (Eastmancolor), Reichbach, Jacqueline Lefevre; edtrs, Georges Klotz, Francoise Orsoni; mus, Arantes Do Nascimento. 85.
(DOC)
05/25/77

Pelnia
(Full Moon)
(Poland)
POL. Film Polski Production, Warsaw. Wri-dir, Andrzej Kondratiuk; cam, Witold Leszczynski; edtr, Kryzsztof Osieki; mus, Wlodzimierz Nahomy. 100.
Tomasz Zaliwski, Anna Seniuk, Iga Cembrzynska, Tadeusz Fijewski.
06/11/80

Pelvis
(Toga Party)
FKY. Lew Mishkin prodn. Prod, Mishkin. Dir, R T Megginson. Sp, Straw Weisman; story, Weisman, Megginson; cam (Guffanti Film Labs), Lloyd Freidus; edtr, Megginson; snd, Mark Solwasser; art dir, John Lawless. (MPAA rating: R). 84.
Luther "Bud" Whaney, Mary Mitchell, Cindy Tree, Billy Padgett, Bobby Astyr, Jai Oscar St John, Chris Thomas, Carole Baxter, Mike DeMarco, Patricia John, Rick Endelson, the Amazing Dorian
03/09/77

Pendin Heng Kuam Rak
(The Land Of Love)
(Thailand)
NTK. Prod-dir, Charin Nantanakorn. Story, Saengpetr Senabodin; sp, Khun Prasai; cam, Pipak Payaka; asst cam, Virat Dakasa; mus, Chalie Intravijit, Smarn Kanjanaparint, Bang Laeh; snd, Kasem Militachinda; prodn des, Charoen Rakdakrom; asst dir, Nantawat. 130.
Jarunee Sooksawat, Rawin Buralak, Sor Asanachinda, Kanchai Gemangkang, Lak Apichat, Promsin Siburnruang, Prachuab Lerkyamdi, Jirasak Issarangkul, Na Ayudhya, Tuam Toranong.
11/26/80

Penitentiary
GRO. Prod-dir-wri, Jamaa Fanaka; cam, Marty Ollstein; edtr, Besty Blankett; mus, Frankie Gaye; art dir, Adel Mazen. (MPAA rating: R).   99.
Leon Issac Kennedy, Thommy Pollard, Hazel Spears, Badja Djola, Gloria Delaney, Chuck Mitchell, Wilbur (Hi-Fi) White.
12/26/79

The Pentecost Outing: SEE Der Pfingstausflug

Pentimento
(Netherlands)
X. Prod-dir-wri-cam-edtr, Fran Zwartjes. 72.
Aimee, Marianne, Monique, Toebosch, Helen Hedy.
(English subtitles)
03/26/80

People of the Wind
CAL. Elizabeth E Rogers prodn. Prods, Anthony Howarth, David Koff. Dir, Anthony Howarth. Sp, David Koff; narr, James Mason; cam (Deluxe Color, Todd-AO stereo mix), Mike Dodds; edtr, Carolyn Hicks; mus, G T Moore and Shusha. (MPAA rating: G). 127. (DOC)
10/27/76

The People That Time Forgot
AIP. Samuel Z Arkoff presentation of a Max J Rosenberg prodn; prod, John Dark. Dir, Kevin Connor. Sp, Patrick Tilley, based on novel by Edgar Rice Burroughs; cam (Movielab Color), Alan Hume; edtrs, John Ireland, Barry Peters; mus, John Scott; prodn des, Maurice Carter; art dirs, Bery Davey, Fernando Gonzalez; asst dir, Bryan Coates; snd, George Stephenson; sfx, John Richardson, Ian Wingrove; cos, Brenda Dabbs. (MPAA rating: PG).   90.
Patrick Wayne, Doug McClure, Sarah Douglas, Dana Gillespie, Thorley Walters, Shane Rimmer, Tony Britton, John Hallam, Dave Prowse, Gaylord Reid, Kiran Shah, Richard Parmentier, Jimmy Ray, Tony McHale.
06/22/77

Per Jom Phen
(Per, Jom and Phen)
(Thailand)
SAH. Prod, Somsak Techaratanaprasert. Dir, Somgpong Tribupa. Story-sp, Laem Bandit; cam, Saravuth Vudhichai; asst cam, Suwan Julavutr; snd, Maitree Janjarasskul; mus, Buan Savatcho; art dir, Chuwit Permpohem; continuity, Khun Pao.   125.
Thep Thienchai, Long Kaomonkadee, Buan Savatcho, Supansa Nuangpirom, Suda Puavilai, Choosri Misomon, Sitao, Poonsawat Timakorn, Sompong Pongmitr, Jantree Sarikavutr, Thep Po Ngarm, Jin Po Ngarm.
10/29/80

Perceval Le Gallois
(France)
GAU. Les Films DuLosange, FR3, ARD, RAI, Gaumont prodn. Prod, Margaret Menegoz. Wri-dir, Eric Rohmer from the book by Chretien De Troyes. Cam (Eastmancolor), Nestor Almendros; edtr, Cecile Ducugis; mus, Guy Robert; art dir, J Pierre Kohut-Svelk; prod, Margaret Menegoz; cos, Jacques Schmidt.   140.
Fabrice Luchini, Andre Dussolier, Ariel Dussolier Dombas, Marc Eyraud, Marie Christine Barrault, Clementine Amouroux.
09/13/78

The Perfumed Nightmare: SEE Mababangong Bangungot

Periplanissis
(Wandering)
(Greece)
X. Creativity Films Hellas prodn. Wri-dir, Christoforos Christofis. Cam (b&w), Andreas Bellis; mus, Eleni Karaendrou; sets-cos, Christoforos Christofis, Georgette Themeli; edtr, Depie-Danae Maroulakou; snd, Panss Panoussopoluos.   95.
10/31/79

Pero No Vas A Cambiar Nunca Margarita?
(But Aren't You Ever Going To Change, Margarita?)
(Spain)
X. Paraguas Films S A prodn. Wri-dir, Chumy Chumez. Exec prod, Antonio Cuevas; cam (Eastmancolor), Carlos Suarez; edtr, Pablo G del Amo; sets, Wolfgang Burman; mus, Carlos A Vizziello.   87.
Silvia Aguilar, Antonio Garisa, Fernando Rubio, Josefina Calatayud, Francisco Vidal.
11/22/78

Perro de Alambre
(Wire Dog)
Spain - Venezuela)
X. Fernandez-Cid/Poleo-Urdaneta prodn. Dir, Manuel Cano. Sp, Cano, C A Montaner; color, Hans Burman.   120.
11/19/80

The Persian Lamb Coat: SEE Il Cappotto Di Astrakan

Personal Affairs: SEE Licne Stvari

Personel
(The Staff)
(Poland)
POL. Tor Unit prodn, made at the Documentary Film Studio, Warsaw. Wri-dir, Kryzsztof Kieslowski. Cam, Witold Stok; prodn mgr, Zbigniew Stanek; snd-mus score, Michal Zarnecki; edtr, Lidia Zonn; scenes from "Aida," soloists of the Warsaw Opera.
Irena Lorentowicz, Wzodzimierz Borunski, Michal Tarkowski, Andrzej Siedlecki, Tomasz Lengren, Tomasz Zygadko, Janusz Skalski.
(16m)
04/21/76

Peruvaziambalan
(A Dead End)
(India)
BMM. Wri-dir, P Padmarajan. Cam, Kannan Narayan. Edtr, Ravi; mus, M G Radhakishman.   120.
Gopi Ashok, Lalita, Aziz, Jose Prakash, Adoor Bhavani.
(B & W)
02/13/80

Perverse Tales: SEE Contes Pervers

Pete's Dragon
BV. Walt Disney prodn. Prods, Ron Miller, Jerome Courtland. Dir, Don Chaffey. Sp, Malcolm Marmorstein, based on story by Seton I Miller, S S Field; cam (Technicolor), Frank Phillips; sngs, mus and lyr, Al Kasha, Joel Hirschhorn; mus supv, arr-cond, Irwin Kostal; chor, Onna White; "Elliott" created by Ken Anderson; ani dir, Don Bluth; ani art dir, Ken Anderson; layout, Joe Hale; effects ani, Dorse A Lanpher; art dirs, John B Mansbridge, Jack Martin Smith; edtr, Gordon D Brenner; set decor, Lucien M Hafley; sfx, Eustace Lycett, Art Cruickshank, Danny Lee. (MPAA rating: G).   134.
Helen Reddy, Jim Dale, Mickey Rooney, Red Buttons, Shelley Winters, Sean Marshall, Jean Kean, Jim Backus, Charles Tyner, Gary Morgan, Jeff Conway, Cal Bartlett, Charlie Callas.
(LIVE - ANI)
11/09/77

Petey Wheatstraw
TSU. Prod, Theodore Toney; exec prod, Burt Steiger. Wri-dir, Cliff Roquemore; cam (Pacific Film Lab Color), Nickolas Von Sternberg; edtrs, Cecelia Hall, Jack Tucker; asst dir, Ayanna DuLaney. (MPAA rating: R). 93.
Rudy Ray Moore, Jimmy Lynch, Leroy & Skillet, Eboni Wryte, Wildman Steve, G Tito Shaw, Lady Reed, Doc Watson.
05/03/78

Petrijin Venac
(Petrija's Wreath)
(Yugoslavia)
YFR. Centar Film prodn. Dir-sp, Srdan Karanovic; book, Dragoslav Mihakilovic; art dir, Miodrag Miric; mus, Zoran Simjanovic. 97.
Mirjana Karanovic, Dragan Maksimovic, Marko Nicolic, Pavle Vujisic.
08/13/80

Petschki-Lawotschki
(Travelling Companions)
(USSR)
X. Gorky Studios prodn, Moscow. Wri-dir, Vassili Shukshin. Cam (b&w), Anatoli Sabolozki; mus, Pavel Chekalov.   100.
Vassili Shukshin, Lidia Fedossejeva, Vsevolod Sanajev.
12/08/76

Petty Thieves: SEE Eierdiebe

Petualang Cinta
(The Playboy)
(Indonesia)
SAI. Prod-dir, Turino Junaidy. Wri, David R Manan; cam, Sutardjo; edtr, Alex Hassan; mus, T Junaidy; snd-light, Kemal; prodn des, Winarto; asst dir, M Yusof. 110.
Robby Sugara, Paula Romokoy, Nenny Triana, Mansursia, Rendra Karno.
04/25/79

Phai Kam Plerng
(Kill for the Truth)
(Thailand)
CFZ. Prod, Phonpimol Poopilomlart. Dir, Kom Akadaet. Story, Sak Suriya; sp, So Asanachinda; cam, Manoo Wanayop; mus, Hong Kong Lab; art dir, Uan Poster; snd recording, King Sound Studio; lighting, Kom Akadaet; prodn mgr, Chao Ampooknan. 120.
Sombat Metanee, Aranya Namwong, Yodchai Megsuan, Naiyana Chivanand, Mayurachat Muenpasitiwet, Kanchit Kaunpracha, Dam Daskorn, Sayant Chantawiboon, Kom Akadaet, Pipop Pupinyo, Chumphorn Tepitak.
02/23/77

Phantasm
AVE. Prod by D A Coscarelli. Wri-dir, Don Coscarelli. Co-prod, Paul Pepperman. Cam (Technicolor), Coscarelli; edtr, Coscarelli; snd, Michael Gross; prodn des, S Tyer; art dir, David Gavin Brown; visual cnsltnt, Roberto Quezeda; mus, Fred Myrow, Malcolm Seagrave; sfx, Pepperman. (MPAA rating: R). 90.
Michael Baldwin, Bill Thornbury, Reggie Bannister, Kathy Lester, Angus Scrimm.
03/07/79

Phantom Love: SEE Ai No Borei

The Phantom on Horseback: SEE Kisertet Lublon

Phobia
(Canada - US)
SPB. Dir, John Huston; sp, Ronald Shusett, Gary Sherman, Lew Lehman, James Sangster, Peter Bellwood; cam, Reginald Morris; edtr, Stan Cole; mus, Andre Gagnon. (MPAA rating: R). 94.
Paul Michael Glaser, John Colicos, Susan Hogan, Alexandra Stewart, Robert O'Ree, David Bolt, David Eisner, Lisa Langlois.
09/10/80

Phooying
(A Woman)
(Thailand)
AXT. Prod, Nanta Tansacha. Wri-dir, Tipayachatr Chartchai. Cam, Wanlop Srisamarng; asst cam, Sanit Rujiratikul; snd-mus dir, Jaratphong Janjarasskul; art dir, Patanachat Rakpipat; cos, Pimpham Buranaphim. 96.
Nawarat Yukthanan, Sorapong Chatri, Aporn Tonnawannij, Chakris Hanvichai, Needa Suksawat, Tanipha Gantatum, Tirawan Ruapiyakul, Metta Ruapiyakul.
07/09/80

Phooying Yay Chai Daeng
(The Village Head At the Border)
(Thailand)
CBT. Prod, Charoen Poolvoralaks. Dir-edtr, Chutima Suwanarat. Sp, Neenart Chamchongyuth; cam, Chalerm Vutboroot; mus, Chonati Tantong; sfx, Prayoon Ming; snd recording, Chutima Studios. 135.
Krung Srivilai, Sorapong Chatri, Yodchai Megsuan, Tasawan Seniwong, Naiyana Chivanand, Duangchai Hataikan, Manop Assawathep, Asvin Ratanapracha, Metta Rungrath, Wittaya Supdamrong, Sermpan Sutinetr, Somchai Samipak, Suwin Swangrat.
07/06/77

Photo Souvenir
(France)
FR. Dir, Edmond Sechan. Sp, Jean-Claude Carriere, Sechan; cam, Guy Delattre; mus, Georges Delerue. 90.
Jean-Claude Carriere, Vania Vilers, Daniele Ayme, Ginette Mathieu, Bernard Lecoq.
02/01/78

Phuen Rak
(My Dear Friend)
(Thailand)
NFT. Prod, Kiat lampungporn. Dir, Sakka Charuchinda. Story, See Fa; sp, Supa Tewakul; cam, Somphat Akaraphan; light, Poonsawat Dimakorn; mus, Prasert Churaketr; snd, Kasem Mirintachinda; art dir, Suphot Charuchinda; make-up, Pochana Charuchinda; prodn mgr, Chaiwat Tawiwongsangthorn; asst dir, Nukoon Silapakan. 120.
Sombat Metanee, Tasawan Seniwong, Dana Myers, Pohatai Pookanasutr, Pat Patamajit, Sulaliwan Suwanatat, Komapat Attaya, Chuangyod Kolakit.
03/09/77

Pi Hua Kad
(The Headless Ghost)
(Thailand)
SRS. Prod, Sathit Klongvesa. Dir, Vichit Usahajitr. Story, Thawee Wisanukorn; sp, Songpet Senibodin; cam, Sophon Jaenphanit; mus-snd, Klongvesa. 100.
Sorapong Chatri, Vasana Sittivej, Lor Tok, Setta Sirachaiya, Ruangnapha Kromkom, Promain Sibunruang.
04/09/80

Picassos aeventyr
(The Adventures of Picasso)
(Sweden)
SVE. AB Svenska Ord/AB Svensk Filmindustri prodn. Original story-script, Hans Alfredson, Tage Danielsson with additional ideas by Goesta Ekman. Dir, Tage Danielsson. Cam (Eastmancolor), Tony Forsberg, Roland Sterner; prodn des, Hans Alfredson, Per Ahlin, Stig Boquist; exec prod, Staffan Hedquist; edtr, Jan Persson; mus, Gunnar Svensson with quotes from Eric Satie, Puccini, etc. 110.
Goesta Ekman, Hans Alfredson, Margretha Krook, Birgitta Andersson, Bernard Cribbins, Wilfrid Brambell.
06/21/78

The Picture Show Man
(Australia)
RDP. Limelight Prodn picture, prod, Joan Long. Dir, John Power. Sp, Joan Long; cam (Panavision-Eastmancolor), Geoff Burton; edtr, Nick Beauman; art dir, David Copping; cos, Judy Dorsman; mus, Peter Best; snd, Ken Hammond; first asst dir, Mark Egerton. 99.
Rod Taylor, John Meillon, John Ewart, Harold Hopkins, Patrick Cargill, Yelena Zigon, Garry McDonald, Sally Conabere, Judy Morris, Jeannie Drynan.
04/13/77

Piedra Libre
(Free For All)
(Argentina)
MBC. Dir, Leopoldo Torre Nilsson. Sp, Nilsson, Rodolfo Mortola, Beatriz Guido, based on a story by Miss Guido; cam (Eastmancolor), Anibal Di Salvo; art dir, Miguel Angel Lumaldo; mus dir, Roberto Lar; edtr, Gerardo Rinaldi. 97.
Marilina Ross, Juan Jose Camero, Luisina Brando, Mecha Ortiz, Enrique Alonso, Adriana Parets, Francisco de Paula, Flora Steinberg, Jorge Petraglia.
05/05/76

Piger i troejen, 2
(Girls at Arms, Part 2)
(Denmark)
DNS. Merry Film prodn. Orig story, Henrik Sandberg, Peer Guldbrandsen. Sp-dir, Finn Henriksen. Cam (Eastmancolor), Erik Wittrup Willumsen; mus, Ole Hoeyer; edtr, Lizzie Weischenfeldt; in charge of prodn, Palle Schnedler Soerensen. 98.
Dirch Passer, Klaus Pagh, Berrit Kvorning.
10/27/76

Piger til soes
(Girls at Sea)
(Denmark)
MRR. Merry Film (Henrik Sandberg) prodn. Wri-dir, Finn Henriksen. Cam (Eastmancolor), Erik Wittrup Willumsen. Prodn mgr, Lars Kolvig; edtr, Jens Groenborg; mus, Ole Hoeyer and the Danish Navy Tanibour Corps. 104.
Marianne Toensberg, Helle Merete Soerensen, Ulla Jessen, Soeren Stroemberg, Ole Soeltoft.
09/28/77

Pile ou Face
(Heads or Tails)
(France)
GCC. FDR/Antenne 2 co-prodn. Prod, Georges Cravenne; dir, Robert Enrico; sp, Enrico, Marcel Jullian, Michel Audiard, based on the novel, "Baroni" by Alfred Harris; cam (Eastmancolor), Didier Tarot; edtr, Patricia Neny; snd, Alain Lachassagne, Jean Neny; art dir, Jean-Claude Gallouin; mus, Lino Leonardi. 105.
Philippe Noiret, Michel Serrault, Dorothee, Andre Falcon.
09/10/80

Pilgrim, Farewell
X. Post Mills Productions Inc prodn. Wri-dir, Michael Roemer; cam, Franz Rath; edtr, Terry Lewis; prod, Stanley Plotnick. 102.
Elizabeth Huddle, Christopher Lloyd, Laurie Prange, Lesley Paxton, Shelley Wyant, Elizabeth Franz, Robert Brown.
09/17/80

The Pink Panther Strikes Again
(Britain)
UA. Prod-dir, Blake Edwards. Sp, Frank Waldman, Edwards; ani and titles, Richard Williams Studio; cam (Eastmancolor), Harry Waxman; edtr, Alan Jones; mus, Henry Mancini; lyrics, Don Black; prodn des, Peter Mullins; art dir, John Siddall; snd, Gerry Humphries, Peter Sutton; ward, Bridget Sellers, Tiny Nicholls; (MPAA rating: PG). 103.
Peter Sellers, Herbert Lom, Colin Blakely, Leonard Rossiter, Lesley-Anne Down, Burt Kwouk, Andre Maranne, Marne Maitland, Richard Vernon, Michael Robbins, Briony McRoberts, Dick Crockett, Byron Kane.
12/15/76

Pink Zone: SEE Zona Roja

The Pioneers
(Taiwan)
CMT. Dir, Richard Y Chen. Wris, Chang Yung-Hsiang, Chang Yi. Cam (Eastmancolor, Cinemascope), Lin Wen-Chin; mus, Oun Ching-Shi. 102.
Wang Tao, Hsu Feng, John Philip Law, Shih Chun, Tien Yeh, Lin Yueh-yun.
11/05/80

Pipe Dreams
AVE. Prod-dir-wri, Stephen Vernoa. Exec prod, Barry Hankerson. Cam (CFI Color), Steve Larner; edtr, Robert L Estrin; mus, Dominick Frontiere; songs, Michael Masser, Jerry Goffin, Tony Camillo, Ivory Joe Hunter, Rev. James Cleveland, Jerry Spikes, Mildred Spikes, Clyde Otis, Vin Corso, Barry Mann, Cynthia Weil, Bobby Arvon; cos des, Glenda Ganis; snd, Tex Rudloff, Verne Poore, Arthur Piantadosi, Mike Minkler, Stanley Paul Gordon; asst dir, Jerry Lee Ballew. (MPAA rating: PG). 87.
Gladys Knight, Barry Hankerson, Bruce French, Sherry Bain, Mike Tippit, Altovise Davis, Sylvia Hayes, Frank McRae, Carol Ita White, Bobbi Shaw, Arnold Johnson, Robert Corso, Sally Kirkland, Redmond Gleeson.
11/03/76

Piranha
NW. Exec prods, Roger Corman, Jeff Schechtman; prod, Jon Davison. Dir, Joe Dante. Sp, John Sayles, based on a story by Richard Robinson, Sayles; cam (Metrocolor), Jamie Anderson; edtrs, Mark Goldblatt, Dante; art dirs, Bill and Kerry Mellin; mus, Pino Donaggio; sfx, Jon Berg; stunt coord, Conrad Palmisano; 2d unit dir, Dick Lowry. (MPAA rating: R). 92.
Bradford Dillman, Heather Menzies, Kevin McCarthy, Keenan Wynn, Dick Miller, Barbara Steel.
08/09/78

The Place Without Limits:
SEE *El Lugar Sin Limites*

The Plan of His 19 Years:
SEE *Jukyu-Sai No Chizu*

Platanov
(USSR)
MSF. Mosfilm, Moscow, prodn. Dir, Nikita Mikhalkov. Sp, based on Anton Chekhov's play of same name; cam, Pavel Lebeshev; mus, A Artemjev. 100.
A Kaljagin, Helene Solovej.
01/19/77

The Playboy: SEE *Petualang Cinta*

Players
PAR. Robert Evans prodn. Exec prod, Arnold Schulman. Prod, Robert Evans. Dir, Anthony Harvey. Sp, Arnold Schulman; cam (Metrocolor), James Crabe; edtr, Randy Roberts; prodn des, Richard Sylbert; mus, Jerry Goldsmith; set decor, Robert Gould; cos des, Richard Bruno, Calvin Klein; second unit dir, Rimas Vainorious; snd, Rene Borisewitz; asst dir, Jack Sanders. (MPAA rating: PG). 120.
Ali MacGraw, Dean-Paul Martin, Maximilian Schell, Pancho Gonzalez, Steven Guttenberg, Melissa Prophet.
06/13/79

Pleasantville
X. Visions-KCET-Pleasantville Prodns prodn. Wri-dirs, Kenneth Locker, Vicki Polon. Cam (TVC-Chemtone Color), Walter Lassally; edtr, Jill Godmilow; mus, Michael Riesman. 85.
Gale Sondergaard, Suzanne Weber, Michael Del Viscovo Jr, John Bottoms, Robert Hitt, Marcia Jean Kurtz.
(16m)
08/25/76

Pleasure At Her Majesty's
(Britain)
X. Amnesty Int'l and Roger Graef prodn. Dir, Graef. Cam, Charles Stewart, Ernest Vinzce; edtr, Thomas Schwalm; snd, Iain Bruce. 100.
Alan Bennett, John Bird, Eleanor Bron, Tim Brooke-Taylor, Graham Chapman, John Cleese, Carol Cleveland, Peter Cook, John Fortune, Graeme Garden, Terry Gilliam, Barry Humphries, Neil Inness, Des Jones, Terry Jones, Jonathan Lynn, Jonathan Miller, Bill Oddie, Michael Palin. Narr: Dudley Moore.
(DOC)
11/24/76

Plern
(Dr Plern)
(Thailand)
AXT. Prod, Nanta Tansacha. Wri-dir, Prince Tipayachatr Chartchai. Exec prod, Orasri Chartchai. Cam, Sanit Rujiratrakul; mus, Prasit Payomyong; snd, Maitree Janjarasskul; edtr, Sngar Janjarasskul; prodn des, M R Rapipat Patanachatr; cos, Poon Pansomboon; make-up and hairstyle, Kiat Syarm; asst dir, Tiow Karna. 110.
Choompoonuj Yukthanan, Nawarat Yukthanan, Pisan Akarasenji, Aporn Tonnawanij, Mathurot Ratana, Needa Suksawat, Acharee Chaisiri, Cherd Tansacha, Dekying Orachaiya.
05/30/79

The Plumber
(Australia)
X. South Australian Film Corp/Australian Film Commission/TCN prodn. Prod, Matt Carroll. Dir-sp, Peter Weir. Cam (Colorfilm color), David Sanderson; edtr, G Tunney-Smith; mus, Gerry Tolland; art dirs, Ken James, Herbert Pinter; snd, Rod Pascoe. 76.
Judy Morris, Robert Coleby, Ivar Kants, Candy Raymond, Henri Szeps.
(16m)
03/26/80

Plurielles
(Plurals)
(France)
X. Films Arquebuse-Maison de la Culture de la Seine Saint-Denis co-prodn. Prods, Michelle Plaa, Rene Fere. Wri-dir, Jean-Patrick Lebel. Cam (b&w), Jean Monsigny; edtr, Christine Lack; snd, Rene Levert and Auguste Galli. Theatre extracts from the play, "Jacotte or The Pleasures of Daily Life," by Jacques Kramer. 90.
Christine Murillo, Jacques Denis, Monique Melinand, Jenny Cleve, Michel Amphoux, Judith Comets, Guillaume Lebel.
(B & W) (16m)
03/14/79

Plus Ca Va, Moins Ca Va
(The More It Goes, The Less It Goes)
(France)
PFC. Films & Co prodn. Wri-dir, Michel Vianey. Cam (Eastmancolor), Georges Barsky; edtr, Marie-Sophie Dubus; mus, Mort Shuman. 95.
Jean Carmet, Jean-Pierre Marielle, Louis Jourdan, Henri Garcin, Nadiusba, Caroline Cartier, Mort Shuman.
08/31/77

Plutonium
(W Germany)
X. Pentagramma film prodn. GmbH & Co prodn in cooperation with the ZDF (Second German Television). Wri-prod-dir, Rainer Erler. Cam, Wolfgang Grasshoff; edtr, Hilma von Boro; mus, Eugen Thomass; scientific consultant, Karl Kompa. 90.
Charlotte Kerr, Wolf Roth, Werner Rundshagen, Bob Cunningham, Lester C Muller.
08/15/79

Po Diryata Na Bezsledno Izcheznalite
(On the Tracks of the Missing)
(Bulgaria)
FBU. Bulgarian Film Prodn, Hemus Unit, Sofia. Dir, Margarit Nikolov. Sp, Nikolai Hristozov; cam, Ivan Samardjiev; art dir, Zahari Savov; mus, Kiril Donchev. 200.

Naoum Shopov, Boris Loukanov, Assen Milanov, Lyubomir Mladenov, Dimiter Hadjiyanev, Isaac Fintsi, Lyubomir Buchvarov.

Po Mai Tidet
(The Widower)
(Thailand)
NFT. Prod, Kiat lampungporn. Dir, Sakka Charuchinda. Story, Kanok Rekka; sp, Settawit; cam, Sompote Akarapan; edtr, Narong Charuchinda; mus, Prasert Chulaketr; snd, Pong Asavinikul, Kasem Militachinda; art dir, Supote Charuchinda. 115.
Pairoj Sangvoributr, Lalana Sulawan, Setta Sirachaiya, Kamol Ngarmphinit, Chuangyod Kolakit, Poompat Tamsekat, Poonthep Tamsekat.
01/25/78

Pochti Lyubovna Istorya
(Almost A Love Story)
(Bulgaria)
BGO. Bulgarofilm Production, Suvrremenik Film Group, Sofia. Dir, Eduard Zahariev. Sp, Zahariev, Georgi Danailov, Georgi Mishev; cam, Georgi Nikolov; sets, Peter Goranov; mus, Mitko Sterev. 90.
Marianna Dimitrova, Yavor Spassov, Grigor Vachkov.
06/11/80

The Pocket Lover: SEE
L'Amant De Poche

Podranki
(Orphans)
(USSR)
SOV. Mosfilm prodn. Wri-dir, Nikolay Goubenko. Cam (Sovcolor), Alexander Kniajinsky, mus, from Vivaldi, Marcello, Corelli. 92.
Y Boudraitis, A Tcherstvov, A Kaliaguine, E Bourkov.
05/18/77

Poet and Muse: SEE Runoilija
Ja Muusa

Poitin
(Ireland)
X. Cinegael prodn. Prod, dir, edtr, Bob Quinn. Sp, Colm Bairead; cam, Seamus Deasy; art dir, Frankie MacDonncha. 65.
Cyril Cusack, Niall Toibin, Donal McCann, Mairead Ni Conghaile, MacDara O Fatharta, Sean O Coisdealbha.
03/21/79

Pokfoci
(Spider Football)
(Hungary)
X. Objektiv Studio prodn. Dir, Janos Rozsa. Sp, Istvan Kardos; cam (Eastmancolor), Elemer Ragalyi; mus, Janos Brody. 87.
Jozsef Madaras, Judit Halasz, Adam Rajhona, Hedi Temessy, Robert Koltai, Jozsef Mentes, Peter Balazs, Ildiko Peczi.
03/02/77

Pokoj Z Widkiem Na Morze
(A Room With A View On The Sea)
(Poland)
POL. Dir, Janusz Zaorski. Sp, Maciej Karpinski, Zaorski; cam (Eastmancolor), Edward Klossinski; mus, Adam Stawinski. 94.
Marek Bargielowski, Piotr Franczewski, Gustav Holoubek.
08/23/78

Pokriv
(A Roof)
(Bulgaria)
BGO. Hemus Group, Prodn Sofia. Dir, Ivan Andonov. Sp, Kuncho Atanassov; cam, Victor Chichov; art dir, Juliana Boshkova; mus, Georgi Genkov. 93.
Peter Slabakov, Pepa Nikolova, Katya Paskaleva, Velko Kunev, Maria Stazlova, Nadia Todorova.
05/31/78

Polare
(Buddies)
(Sweden)
FXE. Europa Film/Stockholm Film prodn. Dir, Janne Halldoff. Story-sp, Lars Molin, Halldoff; cam (Eastmancolor), Hans Welin; prodn chief, Bo Jonsson; edtr, Wic Kjellin; mus, Lalla Hansson. 94.
Goeran Stangertz, Anki Liden, Thomas Hellberg, Ted Astroem, Bonzo Jonsson.
04/07/76

Polenta
(Switzerland)
EOS. Dir, Maya Simon; sp, Jean-Marc Lovay; cam (Eastmancolor), Maurice Giraud; edtr, Marc Blavet. 133.
Bruno Ganz, Jean-Marc Stehle, Aude Eggimann, Marina Golovine, Guy Touraille, Jean-Marc Lovay.
08/20/80

Police Python 357
(France)
FBE. Albina Productions (Albina Du Boisrouvray)-TIT Film Produktion prodn. Dir, Alain Corneau. Sp, Corneau, Daniel Boulanger; cam (Eastmancolor), Etienne Becker; edtr, Marie-Joseph Yoyotte; mus, Georges Delerue. 125.
Yves Montand, Simone Signoret, Francois Perier, Stefania Sandrelli, Mathieu Carriere.
04/07/76

The Police War: SEE La Guerre
des Policiers

Poloh
(Disturbance)
(USSR)
GOS. Gruzia Film Studios, Georgia, prodn. Dir, Lana Gogoberidze. Sp, Gogoberidze, Zaura Arsenaschvili; cam, Lomer Ashvlediani; mus, M Gabunia. 85.
Nadjda Haradze, Sofico Chiaurelli.
01/19/77

The Pom Pom Girls
CWN. Prod-dir, Joseph Ruben; exec prod, Marilyn J Tenser. Sp, Ruben, from story by Ruben and Robert Rosenthal; cam (DeLuxe Color), Stephen M. Katz; edtr, George Bowers; mus, Michael Lloyd; snd, Alex Van De Kar; asst dir, Cal Naylor. (MPAA rating: R). 90.
Robert Carradine, Jennifer Ashley, Lisa Reeves, Michael Mullins, Bill Adler, James Gammon.
09/15/76

Poo Lom
(A Girl Named Poo Lom)
(Thailand)
MHT. Prod, Chokchai Mahasombat. Dir, Choomphorn Tepitak. Exec prod, Gluamart Soibiri. Story-sp, Lom Maniya; cam, Pi Tak; mus, Siam Pattana; edtr, Choomphorn Tepitak; prodn mgr, Phoom Phorn. 120.
Sombat Metanee, Nawarat Yukthanan, Kanchit Kaunpracha, Chaopetr Chaiyanetr, Tarika Tarathit, Jirasak Pinsuwan, Chaiyant Chantawiboon, Oma Ayathit, Simeuk, Long Kaomoankalu, Mom Luang Kamon Pramoj, Manop Assawathep, Marasi.
01/19/77

Poodle: SEE Caniche

Poor Lucas: SEE Bedniyat
Louka

Popeye
PAR. Paramount Pictures and Walt Disney Prodns presentation of a Robert Evans prodn. Exec prod, C O Erickson. Dir, Robert Altman. Sp, Jules Feiffer; cam, Giuseppe Rotunno; mus-lyrs, Harry Nilsson; prodn des, Wolf Kroeger; edtng supv, Tony Lombardo; cos, Scott Bushnell; based on E C Segar's "Popeye" characters; chor, Sharon Kinney, Hovey Burgess, Lou Wills; snd, Robert Gravenor; edtrs, John W Holmes, David Simmons; set decor, Jack Stephens. (MPAA rating: PG). 114.
Robin Williams, Shelley Duval, Ray Walston, Paul Dooley, Paul L Smith, Richard Libertini, Donald Moffat, MacIntyre Dixon, Roberta Maxwell, Donovan Scott, Allan Nicholls, Wesley Ivan Hurt.
12/10/80

The Popovich Brothers of South Chicago
X. Ethel Raim, Martin Koenig and Jill Godmillow prodn for the Balkan Arts Center. Dir, Jill Godmillow. Cam, Tom Hurwitz; snd, Chat Gunter. 60.
(DOC)
04/12/78

Porci Con Le Ali
(If Pigs Had Wings)
(Italy)
X. Eidoscrope-Uschi Film prodn. Dir, Paolo Pietrangeli. Exec prod, Mario Orsini. Sp, Paolo Pietrangeli, Giuseppe Milani, based on novel by Rocco and Antonia (Marco Lombardo-Radice, Lidia Ravera); cam (Technicolor), Dario di Palma; mus, Giovanna Marini. 102.

Christiana Mancinelli, Franco Bianchi, Lou Castel, Anna Nogara, Susanna Javicoli.
07/13/77

Porn Flakes
RFP. RFD prodn. Dir, Chuck Vincent. Sp, Vincent, Christopher Covino; cam (Eastmancolor), Pierre Schwartz; edtr, Mark Ubell; snd, Sonny Heiser. (Self-imposed X Rating). 81.
C J Laing, Jeffrey Hurst, Jennifer Jordan, Brenda Basse, Lynn Bishop, Jaymie Bloom, John Christopher, Michael Datorre, Erica Eaton, Marlow Ferguson, Cecelia Gardner, Misty Grey, Lance Knight, Wade Nichols, David Savage, Annie Sprinkle, Tracy West, Marlene Willoughby.
03/23/77

Porridge
(Britain)
ITC. Witzend prod presented by Jack Gill for Black Lion Films. Prod, Allan McKeown, Ian La Frenais. Dir, Dick Clement. Sp, Dick Clement, Ian La Frenais; cam, Bob Huke; edtr, Alan Jones; snd, Clive Winter; art dir, Tim Gleeson; asst dir, Richard Hoult. 95.
Ronnie Barker, Richard Beckinsale, Fulton Mackay, Brian Wilde, Peter Vaughan, Julian Holloway, Geoffrey Bayldon, Christopher Godwin, Barrie Rutter, Daniel Peacock.
07/25/79

Portable Country: SEE Pais Portatil

The Porter: SEE Baara

Portrait In The Rain: SEE Portret S Dojdem

Portrait of a Champion: SEE Kuldetes

Portrait of a Female Drunkard: SEE Bildnis Einer Trinkerin

Portrait Of A 60% Perfect Man
(France)
JAN. Action Film prodn. Interview by Michel Ciment. Dir, Annie Tresgot. Cam, Gary Graver; edtr, Francois Ceppi. 58.
Billy Wilder, Jack Lemmon, Walter Matthau, Michel Ciment.
(In English) (DOC) (16m)
05/28/80

Portrait of Teresa: SEE Retrato De Teresa

Portret S Dojdem
(Portrait In The Rain)
(USSR)
GOS. Mosfilm Prodn, Moscow. Dir, Grigori Egiazarov. Sp. Alexander Volodin; cam, Valeri Shuvalov; sets, Anatoli Kusnezov; mus, Alexei Mashukov. 90.
Galina Polskich, Igor Ledogorov, Alexei Petrenko, Valentina Talysina.
07/12/78

Poseban Tretman
(Special Treatment)
(Yugoslavia)
YFR. Centar Film, Dan Tana Prodns prodn. Dir, Goran Paskaljevic. Sp, Paskaljevic, Dusan Kovacevic, Filip David; cam (Eastmancolor), Aleksander Petkovic. 94.
Ljuba Tadic, Milena Dravic, Dusica Zegarac, Danilo Stojkovic, Petar Kralj, Milan Srdoc, Radmilla Zivkovic.
05/14/80

Posljednji Podvig Diverzanta Oblaka
(The Last Mission Of Demolitions Man Cloud)
(Yugoslavia)
YFR. Jadran Film-Croatia Film prodn. Wri-dir, Vatroslav Mimica. Cam (Eastmancolor), Bozidar Nikolic; mus, Marijan Makar. 113.
Pavle Vuisic, Slavica Jukic, Predrag Manojilovic, Ivica Pajer.
08/09/78

Posowi Mnja W Dal Swjet Luju
(Call Me From Afar)
(USSR)
GOS. Mosfilm Prodn, Moscow. Dirs, Stanislav Lyubshin, German Lavrov. Sp, Vassili Shukshin; cam, Yuri Ardeev; mus, Yuri Butcko. 90.
Lidia Fedosseva-Shukshina, Stanislav Lyubshin, Mihail Uilanov, Ivan Ryjov.
07/05/78

Postav Dom, Zasad Strca
(Build A House, Plant A Tree)
(Czechoslovakia)
CZS. Bratislava prodn. Dir, Juraj Jakubisko. Sp, Nikulas Kovac, Lydia Ragatova; cam (Eastmancolor), Stanislav Dorsic, Vladimir Hollos; mus, Petr Hapka. 90.
Josef Matus, Jana Siniakova, Ondrej Pavelka, Virsitzender Simiak.
03/05/80

The Pot: SEE Maenak America

Potato Fritz
(W Germany)
JUG. Schamoni-Eucent prodn. Dir, Peter Schamoni. Sp, Paul Hengge; cam, Wolf Wirth; edtr, Peter Schamoni; action dir, Bob Simmons; art dir, Jose Maria Tapiador; asst dir, Pepe Lopez Rodero; settings, Ludwig M H Wiedemann; mus, Udo Jergens, Anton Dvorak. 96.
Hardy Kruger, Stephen Boyd, Anthony Diffring, Arthur Brauss, Friedrich von Ledebur, Christiane Goett, Malachy McCourt, Diana Koerner, David Hess, Peter Schamoni, Paul Breitner, Rainer Basedow, Helmut Brasch.
05/26/76

Poto and Cabengo
(USA - W Germany)
ZDF. J P Gorin, ZDF prodn. Conceived-dir, Jean-Pierre Gorin. Cam, Les Blank; edtr, Greg Durbin. 75.
(DOC)
12/12/79

Pour Clemence
(For Clemence)
(France)
RIG. Dir, Charles Belmont. Sp, Belmont, Marielle Issartel; cam (Eastmancolor), Philippe Rousselot; mus, Michel Portal, Jean Schwarz. 100.
Jean Curbelier, Eva Darlan, Jean Deschamps, Jacques Lalande, Mario Gonzales.
08/31/77

Pourquoi Pas
(Why Not)
(France)
SNX. Dismage, SND prodn. Wri-dir, Coline Serreau. Cam, Jean-Francois Robin; edtr, Sophie Tatischeff; mus, Jean-Pierre Mas. 93.
Sami Frey, Mario Gonzalez, Christine Murillo, Michel Aumont, Nicole Jamet, Mathe Souverbie.
12/14/77

Povra tak Otpisanih
(The Written-Off Return)
(Yugoslavia)
YFR. CFS Kasutnjak-Avala Film-TV Beograd prodn. Dir, Aleksander Dordevic. Sp, Dragan Markovic; cam (Eastmancolor), Dorde Nikolic; mus, Milivoj Markovic. 90.
Pavle Vujisic, Dragan Nikolic, Voja Brajovic, Aleksander Bercek.
08/17/77

Povratak
(The Return)
(Yugoslavia)
YFR. Jadran Film-Slavica Film-Croatia Film, FRZ prodn. Dir and wri, Antun Vrdoljak. Cam (Eastmancolor), Tomislav Pinter; mus, Miljenko Prohaska. 95.
Boris Dwornik, Fabijan Sovagovic, Boris Buzanic, Milena Dravic.
08/15/79

The Power of Men Is the Patience of Women: SEE Die Macht Der Maenner Ist Die Geduld Der Frauen

Power Play
(Canada - Britain)
X. Robert Cooper presentation of Canada United Kingdom prodn, prod by Magnum Int'l Inc and Cowry Ltd. Co-prod, David Hemmings; exec prods, Robert Cooper, Ronald I Cohen; prod, Christopher Dalton; asso prod, John M Eckert. Wri-dir, Martyn Burke. Edtr, John Victor-Smith; cam, Ousama Rawi. 109.
Peter O'Toole, David Hemmings, Donald Pleasence, Barry Morse, Jon Granik, Marcella Saint-Amant, George Touliatos, Chuck Shamata, Gary Reineke, Harvey Atkin, August Schellenberg, Eli Rill, Dick Cavett.
08/30/78

Poznajete Li Pavla Plesa
(Do You Know Pavla Plesa)
(Yugoslavia)
YFR. Telefilm/Belgrade prodn. Wri, Juga Grizelja. Dirs, Jovan Acin, Miljenko Dereta, Dejan Durkovic, Milan Secerovic; cam (Eastmancolor), Milan Spasic; mus, Djordje Karaklajic. 90.
Adem Cejvan, Milan Striljic, Ruzica Sokic, Zika Milenkovic, Neda Arneric.
08/25/76

Pratyusha
(Before Dan)
(India)
SWI. Dir, V N Jatla. Sp, Siva Reddy; cam, R S Agarwal; edtr, Ravishankar Patnaik. 100.
Kadambini, Gangaram.
(B & W)
02/27/80

Praznovanje Pomladi
(The Call Of Spring)
(Yugoslavia)
YFR. Viba Film prodn. Dir, France Stiglic. Sp, Francek Rudolf; cam (Eastmancolor), Rudi Vavpotic; art dir, Niko Matul; mus, Alojz Srebotnjak. 94.
Zonve Agrez, Relja Basic, Zvone Hribar, Angela Hlebec, Andrej Kurent.
08/16/78

The Precarious Bank Teller:
SEE *Rag. Arturo De Fanti, Bancario-Precario*

The Predator: SEE *L'Alpagueur*

Prefab Story: SEE *Panel Story*

Premier Voyage
(First Voyage)
(France)
PLF. Fildebroc/Oliane Productions/Antenne 2 co-prodn. Prods, Michelle de Broca, Marie-Laure Reyre; dir, Nadine Trintignant; wris, Trintignant, Henriette Jelinek; Cam (Eastmancolor), William Lubtchansky; mus, George Delerue; edtr, Carol Marquand; snd, Pierre Gamet. 90.
Marie Trintignant, Vincent Trintignant, Patrick Chesnais, Lucienne Hamon, Richard Berry, Phillippe Rouleau.
07/02/80

Preparation For The Festival: SEE *Matsuri No Junbi*

Pressure
(Britain)
British Film Institute. Prod, Robert Buckler. Dir, Horace Ove. Sp, Ove, Samuel Selvon; cam, Mike Davis; snd, Chris Wangler; edtr, Alan J Cumner-Price; continuity, Genise Michelle; illustrations, Una Howe; graphic presentation, Darell Pockett, Haydon Young. 120.
Herbert Norville, Oscar James, Frank Singuineau, Lucita Lijertwood, Sheila Scott-Wilkinson, Ed Deveraux, T-Bone Wilson, Ramjohn Holder, Norman Beaton, John Landry, Archie Pool, Whitty Vialva Forde, Marlene Davis.
12/01/76

Presuda
(The Verdict)
(Yugoslavia)
YFR. Vardar Film-Koproducent Makedonia Film prodn. Dir, Trajce Popov. Sp, Jovo Kamberski; cam (Eastmancolor), Miso Samoilovski; mus, Tomislav Zografski. 100.
Zarko Radic, Petar Arsovski, Blagoja Corevski, Doko Lukarovski, Janez Verhovec, Illija Milcin.
08/17/77

Pretty Baby
PAR. Prod-dir, Louis Malle. Sp, Polly Platt, based on a story by Platt, Malle from material in "Storyville", by Al Rose; cam (Metrocolor), special pho, Maureen Lambray; edtrs, Suzanne Baron, Suzanne Fenn; mus supv, Jerry Wexler; piano solos, Bob Greene; prodn des, Trevor Williams; set decor, Jim Berkey; snd, Richard Vorisek, Don Johnson; cos-ward, Mina Mittelman; asst dirs, John M Poer, Don Heitzer. (MPAA rating: R). 109.
Keith Carradine, Susan Sarandon, Brooke Shields, Frances Faye, Antonio Fargas, Gerrit Graham, Mae Mercer, Diana Scarwid, Barbara Steele, Matthew Anton, Seret Scott, Cheryl Markowitz, Susan Manskey, Laura Zimmerman, Miz Mary, Don Hood.
04/05/78

Pretty Good For A Human:
SEE *Aika Hyva Ihmiseksi*

Pri Nikogo
(With Nobody)
(Bulgaria)
X. BulgaroFilm prodn. Dir, Ivanka Grubcheva. Sp, Georgi Danailov; cam Yatsek Todorov; art dir, Konstantin Roussakov; mus, Symeon Pironkov. 90.
Aleko Kochev, Annie Bakalova, Stoycho Mazgalov, Giocco Rossich, Peter Petrov, Anghel Lambrev.
01/14/76

The Price for Survival: SEE *Der Preis Fuers Ueberleben*

Prickly Pears: SEE *Fico D'India*

Priest's Night: SEE *Noche De Curas*

Primo Amore
(Italy)
UA. Prods, Pio Angeletti, Adriani de Micheli for Dean Films. Dir, Dino Risi. Sp, Ruggero Maccari; cam (Technicolor), Tonino delli Colli; art dir, Luciano Ricceri; edtr, Alberto Gallitti; mus, Riz Ortolani. 112.
Ugo Tognazzi, Ornella Muti, Caterina Boratto, Mario del Monaco.
01/10/79

Prin Cenusa Imperiului
(Through the Ashes of the Empire)
(Romania)
RMN. Film House No. 3 prodn. Dir, Andrei Baier. Sp, Zaharia Stancu from his novel; cam (Eastmancolor), Dinu Tanase; mus, Radu Serban. 105.
Gheorghe Dinica, Gabriel Osecuis, Cornel Coman, Irina Petrescu.
07/28/76

The Prince and the Pauper
FOX. An Alexander Salkind presentation. Prod, Pierre Spengler; exec prod, Ilya Salkind. Dir, Richard Fleischer. Final sp, George Macdonald Frazer, from orig sp, Berta Dominguez D and Pierre Spengler, based on novel "The Prince and the Pauper" by Mark Twain; cam (Technicolor), Jack Cardiff; edtr, Ernest Walter; mus, Maurice Jarre; cos, Judy Moorcroft, Ulla Britt Soderland; snd, Roy Charman; prodn des, Tony Pratt; fight arr, B H Barry; asst dir, Nigel Wooll. 121.
Oliver Reed, Raquel Welch, Mark Lester, Ernest Borgnine, George C Scott, Rex Harrison, David Hemmings, Charlton Heston, Harry Andrews, Murray Melvin, Sybil Danning, Felicity Dean, Lalla Ward, Julian Orchard, Graham Stark.
06/15/77

Princess Chang Ping
(Hong Kong)
X. Golden Phoenix prodn. Dir, Wu Yu-sheng. Prodn mgr, Louis Sit; cam, Chang Yao-chu; mus dir, Joseph Koo; edtr, Chang Yao-chung; cos, Chu Sheng-hsi. 100.
Lung Kim Sung, Lui Shuet Sih, Lang Chih Pai, Yen Suet Fun.
03/10/76

The Prisoner Of Zenda
U. Walter Mirisch prodn. Prod, Walter Mirisch. Dir, Richard Quine. Sp, Dick Clement, Ian La Frenais, based on the novel by Anthony Hope, as dramatized by Edward Rose; cam (Technicolor), Arthur Ibbetson; edtr, Byron "Buzz" Brandt; mus, Henry Mancini; prodn des, John J Lloyd; special visual effects, Albert Witlock; cos, Susan Yelland; set decor, Joe Chevalier, Marc Meyer; art dir, Herwig Libowitzky; snd, Brian Marshall, Lowell Harris; asso prod, Peter MacGregor-Scott; asst dirs, Ted Morley, Victor Tourjansky, David Menteer. (MPAA rating: PG). 108.
Peter Sellers, Lynne Frederick, Lionel Jeffries, Elke Sommer, Gregory Sierra, Jeremy Kemp, Catherine Schell, Simon Williams, Stuart Wilson, Norman Rossington, John Laurie, Graham Stark, Michael Balfour, Arthur Howard, Ian Abercrombie, Michael Segal.
05/23/79

Prisoneros Desaparecidos
(Sweden - Cuba)
X. Svenska Filminstitutet and Instituto Cubano del Arte y la Industria Cinematografica co-prodn. (Swedish title "De Forsvunna".) Dir, Sergio Castilla. Sp, Sergio, Patricio Castilla; exec prod, Sergio Castilla; cam (Eastmancolor), Patricio Castilla; mus, Juanito Rodriguez, Chembo; sets, Betty Fischman; prod, Humberto Fernandez; edtr, Roberto Bravo. 84.

Nelson Villagra, Lenardo Perucci, Elisabeth Menz, Hugo Medina.
(Spanish Soundtrack)
09/26/79

Prisonniers de Mao
(Prisoners of Mao)
(France)
CCF. Stephan-Films prodn. Sp based on "Prisoner of Mao" by Jean Pasqualini in collab with Rudolph Chelminski. Dir, Vera Belmont. Cam, Jean-Marie Esteve, Pierre Boffety, Daniel Bernard, Wang Sheng; snd, Pierre Befve, Dominique Hennequin; art dir, Ku Ching Tien; edtr, Anne-Marie Deshayes; Annick Breuil, Elizabeth Graine; historical advisor, Jean Pasqualini. 110.
Liu Tsung Hui, Hung Liu, Chang Feng, Hu Pao Hsiang, Ching Yung Hsiang, Meng Yuan, Lee Ying, Wang Yu, Pao Jo Wang.
03/14/79

Private Benjamin
WB. Meyers-Shyler-Miller prodn. Exec prod, Goldie Hawn; wri-prod, Nancy Meyers, Charles Shyer, Harvey Miller; dir, Howard Zeiff; cam (Technicolor), David M Walsh; prodn des, Robert Boyle; edtr, Sheldon Kahn; mus, Bill Conti; asst dir, Jerry Sobul; snd, Martin Bolger; art dir, Jeff Howard; set decor, Arthur J Parker; sfx, Robert Peterson. (MPAA rating: R). 109.
Goldie Hawn, Eileen Brennan, Armand Assante, Robert Webber, Sam Wanamaker, Barbara Barrie, Mary Kay Place, Harry Dean Stanton, Albert Brooks.
10/08/80

Private Collections: SEE Collections Privees

The Private Eyes
(Hong Kong)
GHV. Wri-dir, Michael Hui. Cam, Chang Yao-Chu; recording, Chow Shao-Lung; edtr, Chang Yao-Chung; mus, Samuel Hui and The Lotus; action chor, Hung Chin-Pao; asst dir, Yip Seng. 100.
Michael Hui, Samuel Hui, Ricky Hui, Shek Kin, Richard Ng, Agee Chui, Lo Wai Chi, Chu Mu, Ko Hung.
(English Subtitles)
01/26/77

The Private Eyes
NW. Tristar Pictures Prodn. Prods, Lang Elliott, Wanda Dell. Dir, Lang Elliott. Sp, Tim Conway, John Myhers; cam, Jacques Haitkin; edtr, Fabien Tordjmann; art dir, Vincent Peranio; mus, Peter Matz. (MPAA rating: PG). 91.
Tim Conway, Don Knotts, Trisha Noble, Bernard Fox, Grace Zabriskie, Irwin Keyes, Susie Mandel, Stan Ross, John Fujioka, Fred Stuthman, Mary Nell Santacroce.
11/26/80

The Private Files of J. Edgar Hoover
AIP. Larco prodn. Prod-dir-sp, Larry Cohen. Cam (Movielab Color), Paul Glickman; edtr, Christopher Lebenzon; asso prods, Arthur Mandelberg, Peter Sabiston; snd, Robert Geraldini, Jane Landis; asst dir, Reid Freeman; set des, Cathy Davis; set decor, Carolyn Loewenstein; cos, Lewis Friedman; tech adv, John M Crewdson; mus, Miklos Rozsa. (MPAA rating: PG). 112.
Broderick Crawford, Jose Ferrer, Michael Parks, Ronee Blakley, Rip Torn, Celeste Holm, Michael Sacks, Dan Dailey, Raymond St Jacques, Andrew Duggan, John Marley, Howard Da Silva, June Havoc, James Wainwright, Lloyd Nolan, Ellen Barber, Lloyd Gough, Brad Dexter, Jennifer Lee, George Plimpton, Jack Cassidy.
01/11/78

Private Vices, Public Virtue: SEE Vizi Privati, Pubbliche Virtu

The Prize Fighter
NW. Prods, Lang Elliott, Wanda Dell. Dir, Michael Preece; sp, Tim Conway, John Myhers; cam, Jacques Haitkin; edtr, Fabien Tordjmann; snd, Richard Goodman; asst dir, Pat Kehoe; cos, Jane Jones; art dir, Vincent Peranio; mus, Peter Matz. (MPAA rating: PG). 99.
Tim Conway, Don Knotts, David Wayne, Robin Clarke, Cisse Cameron, Mary Ellen O'Neill, Michael LaGuardia, George Nutting, Irwin Keyes, John Myhers, Alfred E Covington, Dan Fitzgerald.
12/05/79

Prkosna Delta
(Defiant Delta)
(Yugoslavia)
YFR. Sutjeska Film prodn. Wri-dir, Vesna Ljubic; cam (Eastmancolor), Dragan Resner; mus, Vangelius Papatanisu. 90.
Glorica Popovic, Ante Vican, Ivica Klenenc, Jadranka Matkovic, Spaso Papac.
08/13/80

Proba De Microfon
(Mike Test)
(Romania)
RMN. Three prodn. Wri-dir, Mircea Daneliuc; cam, Ion Marinescu; edtr, Maria Neagu; mus, Maja Stepanenco. 108.
Mircea Daneliuc, Tora Vasilescu, Gina Patrichi, Geta Grapa, Gheorghe Negoescu, Maria Junghieta.
07/30/80

Proceedings: SEE Diadicassia

The Prodigious Life of Father Vincent: SEE La Portentosa Vida Del Padre Vincent

Profondo Rosso
(Deep Red)
(Italy)
MAH. Seda Spettacoli (Salvatore Argento) prodn. Exec prod, Claudio Argento. Dir, Dario Argento. Sp, Giuseppe Bassan from story and treatment by Dario Argento, Bernardo Zapponi; cam, Luigi Kuveiller; cos, Elena Mannini; mus, Giorgio Gaslini. (MPAA rating: R). 98.
David Hemmings, Daria Nicolodi, Gabriele Lavia, Clara Calamai, Macha Meril, Glauco Mauri, Eros Pagni, Giuliana Calandra.
(English soundtrack)
06/23/76

Prom Night
AVE. Simcom Prodn. Prod, Peter Simpson. Dir, Paul Lynch. Sp, William Gray; story, Robert Gunza Jr; cam (Medallion), Robert New; edtr, Brian Ravok; mus, Carl Zittrer, Paul Zaza; art dir, Reuben Freed; snd, Brian Day; asst dir, Steve Wright. (MPAA rating: R). 91.
Leslie Nielsen, Jamie Lee Curtis, Casey Stevens, Eddie Benton, Antoinette Bower, Michael Tough, Robert Silverman, Pita Oliver, David Mucci, Jeff Wincott, Marybeth Rubins, Joy Thompson, Brock Simpson, Debbie Greenfield, Tammy Bourne, Dean Bosacki, Leslie Scott, Karen Forbes, Joyce Kite.
07/23/80

The Promise
U. Gilbert Cates Film. Prods, Fred Weintraub, Paul Heller. Dir, Gilbert Cates. Sp, Garry Michael White, based on story by Weintraub and Heller; exec prod, Tully Friedman; cam, Ralph Woolsey; edtr, Peter E Berger; art dir, William Sandell; set decor, Jeff Haley; snd, Michael Evje; mus, David Shire; title song, lyr, Marilyn and Alan Bergman; mus, David Shire; sfx, Greg Auer. (MPAA rating: PG). 97.
Kathleen Quinlan, Stephen Collins, Beatrice Straight, Laurence Luckinbill, William Prince, Michael O'Hare, Bibi Besch, Robin Gammell, Katherine DeHetre, Paul Ryan, Tom O'Neill, Kirchy Prescott, John Allen Vick, Dan Leegant, Jerry Walter, Bob Hirschfeld, Alan Newman, Carey Loftin, Max Balchowsky, Mickey Gilbert.
02/21/79

Promises In The Dark
WBO. Prod, Jerome Hellman; exec prod, Sheldon Schrager. Dir, Hellman. Sp, Loring Mandel; cam, Adam Holender; edtr, Bob Wyman; mus, Leonard Rosenman; prodn des, Walter Scott Herndon; cos des, Ann Roth; snd, Darin Knight; asst dir, Kim Kurumada. (MPAA rating: PG). 115.
Marsha Mason, Ned Beatty, Susan Clark, Michael Brandon, Kathleen Beller, Paul Clemens, Donald Moffat, Philip Sterling, Bonnie Bartlett, James Noble.
10/31/79

Prong Nee Chan Ja Rak Koon
(I'll Love You Tomorrow)
(Thailand)
SFT. Prod, Dao Noi Sibunruang. Dir-edtr, Promsin Sibunruang. Story, Suwanee Sukhontha; sp, Sojirat Sibunruang; cam, Sawaeng Disayawan; snd, Maitree Janjarasskul; mus, Okawee Sathakovit, Samarn Kanchanapalin; art dir, Prakob Yaisiri; cos, Outlook Tailoring, Sukanya Boutique. 130.
Sombat Metanee, Jarunee Suksawat, Jatuporn Puapirom, Ampha Pusit, Lord Enzo, Yordsoi Komarachoon, Choosri Misomon, Rungnapha Kromkrom.
05/21/80

Proof of the Wild: SEE Yasei No Shomei

The Proper Way: SEE Kosadate Gokko

Prophecy
PAR. Prod, Robert L Rosen. Dir, John Frankenheimer. Sp, David Seltzer; cam, Harry Stradling Jr; edtr, Tom Rolf; snd (Dolby), Gene Cantamesa; prodn des, William Craig Smith; set decor, George Gaines; special make-up and artifacts, Thomas R Burman; sfx, Robert Dawson; asst dir, Andy Stone; mus, Leonard Rosenman. (MPAA rating: PG). 102.
Talia Shire, Robert Foxworth, Armand Assante, Richard Dysart, Victoria Racimo, George Clutesi, Tom McFadden.
06/13/79

Proshu Slova
(May I Have the Floor)
(USSR)
SOV. Lenfilm prodn. Wri-dir, Gleb Panfilov. Cam (Sovcolor), Alexander Antipenko; mus, Cadim Bigergan. 136.
Inna Churikova, Nikolei Gutenko, Leonid Bronevoi, Vasili Shukshin.
07/28/76

Prostitute
(Britain)
X. Kestrel Films prodn. Prod-dir-sp, Tony Garnett. Cam, Charles Stewart; edtr, Bill Shapter; art dir, Martin Johnson; cos, Monica Howe; mus, The Gangsters; snd, Malcolm Hirst; asst dir, Raymond Day. 96.
Eleanor Forsythe, Kate Crutchley, Kim Lockett, Nancy Samuels, Richard Mangan, Ann Whitaker, Paul Arlington, Carol Palmer, Brigid Mackay, Colin Hindley, Count Prince Miller, Howard Dickenson, Paul Moriarty, Mary Waterhouse.
06/04/80

Prostitution
(France)
EF. Contrechamp-Felix Films prodn. Conceived-dir, Jean-Francois Davy. Cam (Eastmancolor), Roger Fellous; edtr, Christel Micha; mus, Alan Reeves. 105.
(DOC)
06/16/76

The Proud Twins
(Hong Kong)
SHW. Prod, Run Run Shaw. Dir, Chu Yuan. Sp, Chin Yu, based on novel by Ku Lung; cam, Hung Chieh; mus, Eddie Wang; martial arts instructors, Tang Chia, Huang Pei-chi. 100.
Alexander Fu Sheng, Wang Yung, Wen Hsueh Erh, Ou Yang Pei San, Wu Wei Ku, Meng Chiu, Ai Fei, Liu Hui Ling.
08/22/79

Prova D'Orchestra
(Orchestra Rehearsal)
(Italy - France - W Germany)
GAU. RAI Channel I presentation, prod, Daimo Cinematografica (Rome) and Albatross Prodns (Munich). Wri-dir, Federico Fellini with script collab by Brunello Rondi. Cam (Eastmancolor), Giuseppe Rotunno; art dir, Dante Ferretti; edtr, Ruggero Mastroianni; mus, Nino Rota. 70.
Balduin Baas.
03/07/79

Providence
(France)
CCF. Action Films-SFP prodn. Dir, Alain Resnais. Sp, David Mercer; cam (Eastmancolor-Panavision), Ricardo Aronovitch; art dir, Jacques Saulnier; edtr, Albert Jurgenson; mus, Miklos Rosza; prods, Klaus Hellwig, Yves Gasser, Yves Peyrot. 110.
Dirk Bogarde, Ellen Burstyn, John Gielgud, David Warner, Elaine Stritch, Cyril Luckham, Denis Lawson, Kathryn Leigh-Scott.
(English soundtrack)
01/12/77

Provincial Actors: SEE Aktorzy Prowincjonalni

The Provincial: SEE La Provinciale

Prune Des Bois
(The Wolf-cubs of Niquoluna)
(Belgium)
CDB. Violette and Jacques Vercruysen prodn. Dir, Marcel Lobet. Sp, Kathleen de Bethune, Marielle Paternostre; adapt, Lobet; cam (Eastmancolor), Michel Baudour; mus, Pierre Perret; prodn des, Viviane Fleming; snd, Henri Morelle; edtr, Anne Christophe. 81.
Christian Marin, Arlette Biernaux, Bonbon Lamy, Alexandre von Sivers, Michel Castel, Julie Dubart, Quentin Staes, Alexandre Chikowsky, Maud Noerdinger, Emmanuelle Taymans, Isabelle Bourgeois.
02/06/80

Przed Odlotem
(Break Away)
(Poland)
POL. Film Polski prodn, Silesia Film Unit, Warsaw. Dir, Krzysztof Rogulski; sp, Ryszard Sadaj; cam, Jacek Prosinski; sets, Tadeusz Kosarewicz; mus, Elzbieta Sikora; prodn mgr, Michal Zablocki. 96.
Mariusz Benoit, Grazyna Szapolowska, Jerzy Kryszak, Igor Przegrodzki, Henryk Boukolowski, Jozef Fryzlewic, Ewa Dec, Mieczyslaw Milecki, Marek Siudym, Marcin Tronski, Stanislaw Michalski, Teresa Sawicka, Eugeniusz Kujawski, Alfred Freudenheim, Ewa Zietek.
10/15/80

Przepraszam, Czy Tu Bija?
(Foul Play)
(Poland)
POL. Film Polski Prodn, Warsaw, Silesia Unit. Wri-dir, Marek Piwowski. Cam, Witold Stok; mus, Piotr Figiel; art dirs, Bogdan Soelle, Bozyslawa Chmielewska. 90.
Jerzy Kulej, Jan Szczepanski, Zdzislaw Rychter, Ryszard Faron, Alfred Freudenheim, Wlodzimierz Stepinski, Bogdan Kowalczyk, Jerzy Gorecki, Zbigniew Buczkowski, Jan Himilsbach, Wiktoria Litwin.
06/01/77

P.S.
(E Germany)
DEE. DEFA Film Production, East Berlin. Dir, Roland Graef. Sp, Helga Schuetz; cam, Claus Neumann. 90.
Andrzej Pieczynski, Jutta Wachowiak, Sigrid Roehl-Reintsch, Franziska Troegner, Dieter Franke.
06/11/80

The Psychic: SEE Sette Note in Mero

The Psychotronic Man
IHA. Spelson Prodns and Jack M Sell Associates prodn. Prod, Peter Spelson. Dir, Jack M Sell. Sp, Spelson, Sell, based on Spelson's orig story; cam (Astro Color Labs), Sell; score, Tommy Irons; art dir, Fred Becht; snd, Bob Bennett, Diane Haglund, Karl Navarette; sfx, Bob Vanni; edtr, Bill Reese. (MPAA rating: PG). 90.
Peter Spelson, Christopher Carbis, Curt Colbert, Robin Newton, Paul Marvel, Jeff Caliendo, Lindsey Novak, Irwin Lewin, Corney Morgan, Bob McDonald.
05/07/80

Pumping Iron
C5. George Butler and Jerome Gary prodn. Dirs, Butler, Robert Fiore. Conceived by Butler, based on Charles Gaines and Butler's book of same title; cam, Robert Fiore; snd, Harry Lapham; cnsltnt, Peter Davis, Gaines; edtrs, Larry Silk, Geof Bartz; title song-mus, Michael Small; film titles, Martin S Moskof. (MPAA rating: PG). 85.
Arnold Schwarzenegger, Louis Ferrigno, Matty and Victoria Ferrigno, Mike Katz, Franco Columbu, Ed Corney, Ken Waller, Serge Nubret, Robin Robinson, Marianne Claire.
(DOC)
01/19/77

Punk in London
(W Germany)
X. HFF Munich prodn. Dir-wri, Wolfgang Buld. Cam, Helge Weindler, Willy Brunner; mus, The Stranglers, X-Ray Spex, The Lurkers, Anonymous Chaos, Subway Sect, The Adverts, Kill Joys, Wayne County and The Electric Chairs, Chelsea, The Jam, Boom Town Rats, Rough Trade, Jolt, The Clash.   111.
(DOC) (16m)
03/28/79

The Punk Rock Movie
(Britain)
CTB. Punk Rock Films presentation. Prod, Peter Clifton & Notting Hill Studios. Dir-cam, Don Letts; asso prods, Andrew Czezdwski, Franz Schneider, Serafim Karalexis; edtr, John Hackney; photos, Nurry & Sheila Rock. (MPAA rating: R).   86.
Johnny Rotten & The Sex Pistols, The Clash, The Slits, Siouxsie & The Banshees, X-Ray Spex, Slaughter & The Dogs, Generation X, Subway Sect, Shane, Wayne County, Eater, Johnny Thunders & The Heartbreakers.
(DOC)
06/21/78

Puppe Kaputt
(Dolly Kaputt)
(W Germany)
X. Dagmar Beiersdorf Film prodn, Berlin. Prod-wir-dir, Beiersdorf. Cam, Reza Dabui; edtr, Lothar Lambert.   80.
Georgia Maeker, Lothar Lambert, Sylvia Heidemann, Cullen Maiden, Heidi Nielsen, Peter Schiff, Hansi Jochmann, Bernd Lubowski, Marion Michael.
(16m)
10/12/77

Puppets Under Starry Skies: SEE Hoshizora No Marionette

Pure S
(Australia)
AIT. Prod, Bob Weis. Dir, Bert Deling. Sp, Deling and cast members; cam, Tom Cowan; edtr, John Scott; mus, Red Symons, Martin Armiger.   77.
Gary Waddell, John Laurie, Ann Heatherington, Carol Porter, Helen Garner, Phil Motherwell, Max Gillies.
05/26/76

Purity Of Heart: SEE Die Reinheit Des Herzens

The Purple Taxi: SEE Un Taxi Mauve

Pursuit In The Steppe
(USSR)
SOV. Kazakhfilm Studio Production, Alma-Ata, Kazakhstan Republic, Soviet Union. Dir, Abdulla Karsakbaev. Sp, Anatoly Stephanov.   100.
06/25/80

Put On Ice: SEE Kaltgestellt

Putik Ka Man. . .Sa Alabok Magbabalik
(Even If You Are Mud, Still You Return To Dust)
(Philippines)
X. Emperor Films Int'l prodn. Prod, Jimmy Pascual. Dir, Jun Raquiza. Sp, Joe Sibal, Jun Raquiza; cam, Lucky Guillermo; edtr, Vic Ramos.   106.
Gloria Diaz, Tommy Abuel.
09/29/76

Pyat' Vecherov
(Five Evenings)
(USSR)
GOS. Mosfilm prodn, Moscow; Dir, Nikita Mikhalkov. Sp based on   100.
02/28/79

Qua La Mano
(Give Me Five)
(Italy)
TIT. Prods, Luigi, Aurelio De Laurentis for Filmauro prodn. Dir, Pasquale Festa Campanile; sp, Enrico Oldoini, Ottavio Jemma; cam (Eastmancolor), Giancarlo Ferrando; art dirs, Enrico Fiorentini, Enrico Tovaieri; edtr, Alberto Galletti; mus, Detto Mariano.   120.
Adriano Celentano, Renzo Montagnani, Enrico Montesano, Philippe Leroy.
08/13/80

Quadrophenia
(Britain)
X. Curbishley-Baird prodn for The Who Films Ltd. Prods, Roy Baird, Bill Curbishley. Exec prods, The Who. Dir, Franc Roddam. Sp, Dave Humphries, Martin Stellman, Franc Roddam, based on the album, "Quadrophenia," by Pete Townshend; cam, Brian Tufano; edtr, Mike Taylor; mus dirs, John Entwistle, Pete Townshend; snd, Chris Wranger; des, Simon Holland; chor, Gillian Gregory; asst dir, Ray Corbett.   120.
Phil Daniels, Mark Wingett, Philip Davis, Leslie Ash, Garry Cooper, Toyah Wilcox, Sting (Gordon Sumner), Trevor Laird, Kate Williams, Michael Elphick, Kim Neve, Raymond Winstone, Gary Shail.
05/02/79

Quatermass Conclusion
(Britain)
X. Euston Films Prodn. Prod, Ted Childs. Dir, Piers Haggard. Cam, Ian Wilson. Sp, Nigel Kneale; edtr, Keith Palmer. Mus, Marc Wilkinson, Nick Rowley.   105.
John Mills, Simon MacCorkindale, Barbara Kellerman, Margaret Tyzack, Brewster Mason.
02/13/80

Que Es El Otono?
(What's Autumn?)
(Argentina)
MBC. Dir, David Jose Kohon. Sp, Kohon, Mario Diament; cam (Eastmancolor), Alberto Basail; mus, Astor Piazzolla; art dir, Miguel Lumaldo; edtr, Armando Blanco; asst dir, Jorge Mobaied.   115.
Alfredo Alcon, Dora Baret, Aldo Barbero, Alberto Argibay, Fernanda Mistral, Javier Portales, Flora Steinberg, Alicia Zanca.
06/01/77

Que Viva Mexico
(USA - USSR)
SOV. Upton Sinclair & Assocs prodn. Wri-dir, Sergei Eisenstein. Cam, (b&w), Edward Tisse; edtr, Grigori Alexandrov.   90.
(B & W) (ORIGINALLY MADE 1930)
09/05/79

Queen Bee: SEE Jo-Bachi

The Queen's Father: SEE Ojciec Krolowej

Quelle Strane Occasioni
(Strange Events)
(Italy)
CNZ. Prod, Rizzoli Films. Three episodes: dir, first-unidentified, 2d-Luigi Magni, third-Luigi Comencini. Sp, Rodolfo Sonego, Leo Benvenuti, Piero De Bernardi; cam (Eastmancolor), Aldo Tonti, Armando Nannuzzi, Claudio Aragona; art dirs, Lucia Mirisola, Fiorenzo Senese, Osvaldo Desideri; edtrs, Ruggero Mastroianni, Franco Fraticelli, Nino Baragh; mus, Piero Piccione.   114.
Paolo Villaggio, Valeria Morricone, Nino Manfredi, Olga Carlatos, Giovanna Steffan, Alberto Sordi, Stefania Sandrelli.
03/09/77

Queridas Amigas
(Dear Friends)
(Argentina)
PMA. Prod, Juan Jose Luciano. Dir, Carlos Orgambide. Sp, Miguel Stocki, Orgambie; based on story by Elena Antoniette, Orgambide; cam (Eastmancolor), Juan Carlos Lenardi; mus, Victor Proncet.   90.
Luisina Brando, Graciela Dufau, Dora Baret, Rodolfo Ranni, Carlos Estrada, Marcela Lopez Rey, Hector Pellegrini.
07/09/80

Queridisimos Verdugos
(Dearest Executioners)
(Spain)
X. Turner Films prodn. Sp-dir, Basilio Martin Patino. Prodn mgr, Jose Maria Gonzalez Sinde; cam (Eastmancolor), Alfredo Fernandez Mayo; edtr, Eduardo Biurrum; mus, Antonio Gamero.   101.
(DOC)
05/04/77

Queridos Companeros
(Dear Comrades)
(Chile - Venezuela)
X. Cinematografica Proa C A and Grupo Renta-cine C A prodn. Dir, Pablo de la Barra. Sp, De la Barra, Ione Borg; cam, Wellinta Dinis; mus, Jesus Sanoja Jr; edtr, Giuliano Ferrioli; art dir, Sergio Zapata.   90.
Marcelo Romo, Hugo Medina, Andrea Bacay, Eduardo Duran, Paz Irarazabal.
03/22/78

Qu'est Ce Que Tu Veux Julie?
(What Do You Want Julie?)
(France)
GAU. Films De La Perussiere Prodns prodn. Wri-dir, Charlotte Dubreuil. Cam (Eastmancolor), Gilbert Duhalde: edtr, Monique Prim; mus, Janez Matcic. 100.
Arlette Bonnard, Jean-Claude Jay, Noelle Fremont, Helene Sautreau, Alain Grusteau.
03/23/77

The Question: SEE La Question

Questo Si Che E' Amore
(The Night Before Christmas)
(Italy)
COL. Creative Films Century-Roma. Prod, Ovidio Assonitis. Dir, Filippo Ottoni. Sp, Francesco Vanorio; cam (Technicolor), Mario Vulpiani; edtr, Angelo Curi; mus, Steve Powder; title song, Stefano Torossi. 99.
Christopher George, Gay Hamilton, Sven Valsecchi, Mauro Curi.
03/01/78

Quien Puede Matar A Un Nino?
(Who Can Kill A Child?)
(Spain)
MSV. Penta Films, S L (Madrid) prodn. Dir, Narciso Ibanez Serrador. Sp, Luis Penafiel Maria Luisa Arias, Marisa Porcel. (Narciso Ibanez Serrador), based on novel, "The Game," by J J Plans, cam (Eastmancolor), Jose Luis Alcaine; sets, Ramiro Gomez; mus, Waldo de los Rios; edtrs, Juan Serra, Antonio Ramirez. 110.
Lewis Fiander, Prunella Ransome, Antonio Iranzo, Miguel Narros,
05/05/76

Quiet Is The Night: SEE Wsrod Nocnej Ciszy

Quintet
FOX. Robert Altman prodn. Prod-dir, Altman. Sp, Frank Barhydt, Altman, Patricia Resnick, based on story by Altman, Lionel Chetwynd, Resnick; cam (Deluxe Color), Jean Boffety; exec prod, Tommy Thompson; mus, compcond, Tom Pierson; prodn des, Leon Ericksen; art dir, Wolf Kroeger; edtr, Dennis M Hill; asst dir, Tommy Thompson; cos, Scott Bushnell; mus performed by the London Symphony; snd, Robert Gravenor; snd effects, David Horton; sfx, Tom Fisher, John Thomas. (MPAA rating: R). 100.
Paul Newman, Vittorio Gassman, Fernando Rey, Bibi Anderson, Brigitte Fossey, Nina Van Pallandt, David Langton, Tom Hill, Monique Mercure, Craig Richard Nelson, Maruska Stankova, Anne Gerety, Michael Maillot, Max Fleck, Francoise Berd.
02/07/79

Raba Lubvi
(Slave of Love)
(Russia)
C5. Sovexport prodn. Dir, Nikita Mikhalkov. Sp, Friedrich Gorenstein, Andrei Mikhalkov-Konchalovsky; cam, Pavel Lebeshev; set des, A Adabashyan, A Samulekin; snd, V Bobrovsky; mus, Eduard Artemiev. 94.
Elena Solovey, Rodion Nakhapetov, Alexander Kaliagin, Oleg Basilashivili, Konstantin Grigoryev.
(English subtitles)
06/14/78

The Rabbi and the Shikse
(Israel)
X. Rolls Films Int'l prodn, Yair Pradelsky, Israel Ringel. Dir-sp, Yoel Silberg. Cam, Nissim Leon; mus, Dov Selttzer, lyr, Amos Ettinger, Mike Burstyn. 90.
Mike Burstyn, Mandy Rice Davies, Zeev Berlinsky, Tuvia Tishler, Zvi Lahat, Itamar Gurevich, Shlomo Rozmarin, Daliah Gur, Yoseph Bashi, Ronit Port.
06/30/76

The Rabbit Case: SEE Causa Kralik

Rabbit Test
AVE. Laugh or Die prodn in ass'n with Mel Simon prodns. Prod, Edgar Rosenberg. Dir, Joan Rivers. Sp, Rivers, Jay Redack; cam (CFI Color), Lucien Ballard; edtr, Stanford C Allen; mus, Mike Post, Pete Carpenter; art dir, Robert Kinoshita; asst dir, Joseph M Ellis. (MPAA rating: PG). 84.
Billy Crystal, Joan Prather, Alex Rocco, Doris Roberts.
02/22/78

Rabid
NW. Cinema Entertainment Enterprises Ltd prodn. Prod, John Dunning. Wri-dir, David Cronenberg. Exec prods, Andre Link, Ivan Reitman; edtr, Jean Lafleur; cam, Rene Verzier; art dir, Claude Marchand. (MPAA rating: G). 91.
Marilyn Chambers, Frank Moore, Joe Silver, Howard Ryshpan, Patricia Gage, Susan Roman, J Roger Periard, Gary McKeehan.
06/29/77

Race D'Ep
(The Homosexual Century)
(France)
X. Little Sisters prodn. Dir, Lionel Soukaz. Sp, Soukaz, Guy Hocqenghen; cam, Jerome De Missolz, Soukaz; edtr, Soukaz. 95.
Elizar Von Efenterre, Copi, Remy Germain.
(COLOR & B & W) (16m)
03/05/80

Race For Your Life, Charlie Brown
PAR. Prods, Lee Mendelson, Bill Melendez. Dir, Melendez; co-dir, Phil Roman. Sp, Charles M Schulz, based on his "Peanuts" characters; edtrs, Chuck McCann, Roger Donley; cam (Metrocolor), Dickson/Vasu; mus, Ed Bogas; ani, Don Lusk, Bob Matz, Hank Smith, Rod Scribner, Ken O'Brien, Al Pabian, Joe Roman, Jeff Hall, Sam Jaimes, Bob Bachman, George Singer, Bill Littlejohn, Bob Carlson, Patricia Joy, Terry Lennon, Larry Leichliter; snd, Producers' Sound Service, Coast Recorders. (MPAA rating: G). 75.
Voices: Duncan Watson, Greg Felton, Stuart Brotman, Gail Davis, Liam Martin, Kirk Jue, Jordan Warren, Jimmy Ahrens, Melanie Kohn, Tom Muller, Bill Melendez, Fred Van Amburg.
(ANI)
06/29/77

Race, The Spirit Of Franco: SEE Raza, El Espiritu De Franco

Radio On
(Britain - W Germany)
X. British Film Institute and Road Movies Film Produktion GmbH co-prodn in asso with the National Film Finance Corp. Exec prods, Renee Gundelach, Peter Sainsbury. Prod, Keith Griffiths. Dir, Christopher Petit; asso prod, Wim Wenders; sp, Petit, Heidi Adolph; cam, Martin Schafer; edtr, Anthony Sloman; snd, Martin Muller; art dir, Susannah Buxton; prodn supv, Patsy Nightingale; mus, David Bowie, Sting, Kraftwerk, Eddie Cochran, Wreckless Eric and various Stiff Records artists. 101.
David Beames, Lisa Kreuzer, Sandy Ratcliff, Andrew Byatt, Sue Jones-Davies, Sting, Sabina Michael, Katja Kersten, Paul Hollywood.
(B & W)
09/12/79

Rag. Arturo De Fanti, Bancario-Precario
(The Precarious Bank Teller)
(Italy)
PCI. Dir, Luciano Salce. Sp, Salce, Augusto Caminito, Ottavio Alessi; cam (Technicolor), Sergio Rubini; art dir, Elio Micheli; edtr, Antonio Siciliano; mus, Piero Piccioni. 94.
Paolo Villaggio, Catherine Spaak, Annamaria Rizzoli, Enrica Bonaccorti.
04/23/80

Ragazzo di Borgata
(Slum Boy)
(Italy)
X. Registi Pubblicitari Associati prodn. Dir, Giulio Paradisi. Sp, Alfredo Giannetti, Lucio Battistrada, Giulio Paradisi; cam, Giuliano Giustini; mus, Carlo Savina, Nino Rota. 106.
Giacomo Piperno, Stefano Arquilla, Ennio Panosetti, Rita Tushingham.
06/16/76

Rage: SEE La Rabia

Raggedy Ann & Andy

FOX. Prod, Richard Horner. Dir, Richard Williams. Sp, Patricia Thackray, Max Wilk, based on characters created by Johnny Gruelle; cam (DeLuxe Color), Al Rezek; edtrs, Harry Chang, Lee Kent, Kenneth Maxwell Seligman; mus, Joe Raposo; prodn des, Corny Cole; asst dir, Fred Berner; sequence dir, Gerald Potterton. (MPAA rating: G). 84.
Voices of: Didi Conn, Mark Baker, Fred Stuthman, Niki Flacks, George S Irving, Arnold Stang, Joe Silver, Alan Sues, Marty Brill, Paul Dooley, Mason Adams, Allen Swift, Hetty Galen, Sheldon Harnick, Ardyth Kaiser, Margery Gray, Lynne Stuart.
(ANI)
03/16/77

Raging Bull

UA. Chartoff-Winkler prodn. Prods, Irwin Winkler, Robert Chartoff in asso with Peter Savage. Dir, Martin Scorsese. Sp, Paul Schrader, Mardik Martin, from the book "Raging Bull" by Jake La Motta with Joseph Carter and Savage; cam (b&w and color prints by Technicolor), Michael Chapman; edtr, Thelma Schoonmaker; mus from prerecorded classical and pop sources; prodn des-visual cnslt, Gene Rudolf; art dirs, Alan Manser, Kirk Axtell, (LA); Sheldon Haber, (NY); set decor, Fred Weiler, Phil Abramson; snd, Les Lazarowitz, Michael Evje, Donald Q Mitchell, Bill Nicholson, David J Kimball; asso prod, Hal W Polaire; stunt coord, Jim Nickerson; boxing tech advisor, Al Silvai; tech advisor, Frank Topham; asst dirs, Allan Wertheim, Jerry Grandey. (MPAA rating: R). 119.
Robert DeNiro, Cathy Moriarty, Joe Pesci, Frank Vincent, Nicholas Colosanto, Theresa Saldana, Frank Adonis, Mario Gallo, Frank Topham, Johnny Barnes, Floyd Anderson, Kevin Mahon, Ed Gregory, Louis Raftis, Johnny Turner.
11/12/80

Rai Saneh Ha
(The Megalomaniac)
(Thailand)
NKP. Prod, Wannapha Krapayun. Dir, Chana Krapayun. Story, Woh Vinitchaikul; sp, Pratin Puangsamri; cam, Thavee Kiatinan; mus, Seksan Sominsart; snd, Kasem Militachinda. 115.
Pisamai Wilaisak, Sorapong Chatri, Nipaporn Nongnuj, Tarika Tidatit, Niroot Sirichanya, Hansa Jariyaporn, Choosri Misomon, Sompop Benjatikul.
07/11/79

Raices De Sangre
(Roots of Blood)
(Mexico)
AZT. Conacine prodn. Dir-story-sp, Jesus Salvador Trevino; cam (Eastmancolor), Rosalio Solano; edtr, Joaquin Ceballos; mus, Sergio Guerrero; snd, Sigfrido Garcia. 100.
Richard Yniquez, Ernesto Gomez Cruz, Malena Doria, Pepe Serna, Adriana Rojo, Roxana Bonila-Gianini.
06/20/79

Raining in the Mountain
(Hong Kong)
Lo and Hu Co-Prodn Ltd film. Dir, King Hu. Prods, Lo Kai-muk, Wu Sau-Yee, Ling Chung. Sp, King Hu; cam, Henry Chen; edtr, King Hu; mus, Ng Tai King. 125.
Hsu Feng, Sun Yuek, Shik Chun.
07/18/79

Raise Ravens: SEE Cria Cuervos

Raise The Titanic

AFD. Prod, William Frye; exec prod, Martin Starger; dir, Jerry Jameson; sp, Adam Kennedy; adapt, Eric Hughes; novel, Clive Cussler; cam (DeLuxe Color), Matthew F Leonetti, Rex Metz (2d unit), Jack Cooperman (underwater inserts), Bob Steadman (model unit), Arthur Wooster (Malta sequences); mus, John Barry; edtrs, J Terry Williams, Robert F Shugrue; prodn des, John F DeCuir; art dir, John F DeCuir Jr; set decors, Mickey S Michaels, Raphael Breton (Washington, D C), Ian Whittaker (Europe); snd, Dean Gilmore, John Mitchell (Europe), John K Wilkinson, Robert W Glass Jr, Robert Thirlwell; 2d unit dir, Mickey Moore; model-mech effects supv, (Europe) John Richardson; model unit dir, (Europe) Ricou Browning; sfx supv, Alex Weldon; asst dir, Jim Westman. (MPAA rating: PG). 112.
Jason Robards, Richard Jordan, David Selby, Anne Archer, Alec Guinness, J D Cannon, Bo Brundin, M Emmet Walsh.
08/06/80

Rak Kam Lok
(September Love)
(Thailand)
BGK. Prod-dir, P Chalong. Story-sp, So Asanachinda; cam, Visit Saengtavee; mus, Prachin Songpao; edtr, Dachanee; snd edtr, Maitree Janjarasskul; prodn des, Sumol Pakdivijit. 100.
Krung Srivilai, Vitoon Karuna, Nawarat Yukthanan, Lalana Sulawan, Piathip Kumvongse, Somchai Samipak, Carol Green, Michael Theros, William R Barbridge, Federico Coburn, Eddie Coburn.
05/24/78

Rak Otaroot
(Only Sixteen, Part 2)
(Thailand)
NFT. Prod, Kiat Iampungporn. Dir, Piac Poster. Story-asst dir, Boonrak Nilwong; sp, Nantawat; cam, Chon Bunnag; asst cam, Yong Namyen; edtr, Palong Kaewprasert; mus, Pairath Theptiam; prodn des-art dir, Saman Choopsuwan; snd, Pramuan Lab. 125.
Lairoj Sangboriboot, Lalana Sulawan, Jirasak Issarangkul, Na Ayudhaya, Pochanee Indramanon, Jaroowan Banjamatr, Somchit Sapsamluay, Somkuan Kajangsart, Siripong Issarangkul, Na Ayudhaya, Boonsong Tanakorn, Niran Imson, Pisit Chaempreecha, Nootsara Saengrat.
07/06/77

Rak Ri Sayar
(Jealousy)
(Thailand)
GPP. G P Film Promotions. Prod, Opas Rangchaikul. Dir, Patravadee Sritrairat. Story-sp, Thavorn Suwan; cam, Chome Bunnag; lighting, Patrick Govain; mus, Menrat Srikanond; snd, Kasem Militachinda; art dir, Vorachon Yuchinda. 120.
Tatima Sangkapitak, Chalit Fuang-arome, Duangjai Hataikan, Kamthorn Suwanpiyasiri, Jakarat Virasant, Juree Osiree.
06/20/79

Rallarblod
(Blood of the Railroad Workers)
(Norway)
NSK. Wri-dir, Erik Solbakken. Cam (Eastmancolor), Bjorn Jegerstedt; edtr, Edith Toreg; mus, Gunnar Germeten. 112.
Nils Olle Oftebro, Ragnhild Hilt, Svein Tindberg, Katja Medboe, Espen Skjonberg.
08/22/79

Ran & Ran
(Run & Run)
(Japan)
FUJ. Prod, Hisao Masuda. Dir, Junzen Nemoto. Cam, Kitsuru Kuroyanagi; snd, Takashi Miyamoto; edtr, Koichi Atami; mus dir, Eikichi Yazawa. 98.
06/11/80

Raoni
(France - Belgium)
SBD. Conceived-dir, Jean-Pierre Dutilleux. Cam (Eastmancolor-Scope), Carlos Saldanha; mus Egberto Gismonti. 82.
(DOC)
03/08/78

Rapture: SEE *Arrebato*

Rascals: SEE *Les Turlupins*

Rasskaz O Neisvestnom Celoveke
(Story of an Unknown Man)
(USSR)
SOV. Mosfilm prodn. Wri-dir, Vitautas Zalakjavicjus from a story by Anton Chekhov; cam (Sovcolor), A Kuznetcov; mus, A Firtic. 99.
E Simonova, A Kajdanovski, G Taratorkin.
09/17/80

The Rat Race: SEE *Je Vais Craquer!*

Ratataplan
(Italy)
CNZ. Prods, Franco Cristaldi, Nicola Carraro for Vides Prodns. Wri-dir, Maurizio Nichetti; cam (Eastmancolor), Mario Battistoni; art dir, Maria Pia Angelini; edtr, Giancarlo Rossi; mus, Detto Mariano. 90.
Maurizio Nichetti, Angela Finocchiaro, Edy Angelillo, Lidia Biondi, Roland Topor.
09/05/79

The Rattlesnake: SEE *Cascabel*

Ravagers

COL. Prod, John W Hyde. Exec prod, Saul David. Dir, Richard Compton. Sp, Donald S Sanford, based on novel, "Path to Savagery," by Robert Edmond Alter; cam (Metrocolor), Vincent Saizis; edtr, Maury Winetrobe; snd, Garry Cunningham; prodn des, Ronald E Hobbs; cos, Ron Talsky; asst dir, Pat Kehoe; Fred Karlin. 91.
Richard Harris, Ann Turkel, Art Carney, Ernest Borgnine, Anthony James, Woody Strode, Alana Hamilton, Seymour Cassel.
05/30/79

The Raven's Dance: SEE Korpinpolska

Raw Deal
(Australia)
GUO. Homestead Films prodn. Prods, Russell Hagg, Patrick Edgeworth. Dir, Russell Hagg. Sp, Patrick Edgeworth; cam, Vincent Monton; mus, Ron Edgeworth; asso prod, Jenny Henry; art dir, John Dowding; ward, Clare Griffin; theme song recorded by Margaret Roadnight. 90.
Gerard Kennedy, Gus Mercurio, Rod Mullinar, Christopher Pate, Hu Pryce, John Cousins, Michael Carmen, Norman Yemm, Patrick Edgeworth.
02/09/77

Raza, El Espiritu De Franco
(Race, The Spirit Of Franco)
(Spain)
X. Septiembre Prodns film. Dir, Gonzalo Herralde. Inverviews prepared by Herralde. Roman Gubern; edtr, Emilio Rodriguez; cam (Eastmancolor), Tomas Pladevall. Pilar Franco, Alfred Mayo, plus extracts of film, "The Spirit of a Race." 80.
(DOC)
11/23/77

Razza Selvaggia
(Savage Breed)
(Italy)
TIT. Prod, Luigi Borghese for Cinematografica Alex prodn. Dir, Pasquale Squitieri; sp, Squitieri, De Concini; cam, Giulio Albonico; art dir, Marco Canevari; edtr, Mauro Bonanni; mus, Tullio De Piscopo. 95.
Saverio Marconi, Stefano Madia.
10/15/80

The Real Game: SEE Hamiskhak Ha'Amiti

Real Life
PAR. Prod, Penelope Spheeris. Dir, Albert Brooks. Exec prods, Norman Epstein, Jonathan Kovler. Sp, Brooks, Monica Johnson, Harry Shearer; cam, Eric Saarinen; edtr, David Finfer; mus, Mort Lindsey; art dir, Linda Spheeris, Linda Marder. (MPAA rating: R). 99.
Charles Grodin, Frances Lee McCain, J A Preston, Matthew Tobin, Albert Brooks, Lisa Urette, Robert Stirrat, David Spielberg, Jennings Lang, Norman Bartold.
03/07/79

The Rebel: SEE Le Rebelle

The Rebel Intruders
(Hong Kong)
SHF. Prod, Runme Shaw. Dir, Chang Cheh. Exec prod, Mona Fong; sp, Yi Huang, Chang Cheh; cam, Hui Chi Tsao; art dir, Johnson Tsao; mus, Eddie Wang; martial art instructors, Kuo Chue, Chiang Sheng, Lu Feng. 95.
Kuo Chue, Chiang Sheng, Lo Meng, Lu Peng, Sun Chien, Wang Li, Chu Hsiang Yun, Yang Hsiung, Yu Tai Ping, Tan Chen Tu.
10/29/80

Recollections: SEE Rekolekcje

The Recourse to the Method: SEE El Recurso Del Metedo

Red Blossoms in the Tian Mountains
(China)
X. Sian Film Studio Prodn, Sian. Dir, Tsu Wei. Sp, Ou Lin. 100.
01/10/79

The Red Carnation: SEE Il Garofano Rosso

Red Gold: SEE Oro Rojo

The Red Mansion: SEE Ke Ha See Dang

Red Midnight: SEE Feuer Um Mitternacht

Red Poppies on the Wall: SEE Lulekoqet Mbi Mure

The Red Poster: SEE L'Affiche Rouge

Red Seedlings: SEE Chuvanna Vithukal

The Red Stocking: SEE Der Rote Strumpf

The Red Sweater: SEE Le Pull-Over Rouge

The Redeemer: SEE Izbavitelj

Reflections: SEE Tukerkepek

Reflections: SEE Zrcadleni

Reggae Sunsplash
(W Germany - Jamaica)
X. Aresenal Filmtheatre, Filmvertreibs Stephen Paul KG prodn. Dir, Stefan Paul. Cam, Hans Schalk, Rainer Heinzelmann, Peter Rees; edtr, Hildegard Schroder; snd, Roland Engele, Amel Thomae. 107.
Bob Marley, Peter Tosh, The Third World Band, Burning Spear.
(MUSIC DOC)
10/01/80

Reifezeit
(Time of Maturity)
(W Germany)
X. Provobis prodn of O E Kress. Prodn mgr, Juergen Mohrbutter. Dir, Sohrab Shahid-Saless. Sp, Saless, Helga Houzer; cam (b&w), Ramin R Molai; snd, Guenther Kortvich, Karl Heinz Reiber, Max Gallinsky; edtr, Christel Orthman. 107.
Eva Manhardt, Mike Hennig, Eva Lissa, Charles-Hans Vogt, Heinz Lieven, Lothar Koester.
(B & W)
04/21/76

Reina Zanahoria
(The Carrot Queen)
(Spain)
X. Labarone Films prodn. Sp-dir, Gonzalo Suarez. Exec prods, Oscar Kidelan, Leonardo Echegaray; cam (Eastmancolor), Carlos Suarez; mus, Luis de Pablo; edtr, Antonio Gimeno; sets, Alberto Corazon. 90.
Jose Sacristan, Marilina Ross, Fernando Fernan Gomez, Diana Polakov, Fernando Hilbeck.
01/25/78

Rejs
(The Cruise)
(Poland)
X. Tor unit prodn. Dir, Marek Piwowski. Sp, Janusz Glowacki, Marek Piwowski, with coop of Andrzej Barszczynski, Jerzy Karaszkiewicz; cam, Marek Nowicki; mus, Wojciech Kilar; set des, Wieszaw Aniadecki; cos, Tadeusz Urbanowicz. 65.
Stanislaw Tym, Jolanta Lothe, Wanda Stanislawska-Lote, Andrzej Dobosz, Feridun Erol, Jan Himilsbach, Zdzislaw Maklakiewicz.
(B & W)
03/05/80

Rekolekcje
(Recollections)
(Poland)
X. Polish Corp for Film Prodn PROFIL Unit. Wri-dir, Witold Leszczynski. Cam (Eastmancolor), Maciej Kijowski; mus, Helmut Nadolski; sets, Bogdan Kobierski; edtr, Zofia Dworank. 80.
Ryszard Cieslak, Wojciech Pszoniak, Ewa Pokas, Hanna Skarzanka, Andrzej Precigs, Gabriela Kownacka, Zdzislaw Maklakiewicz, Zdzislaw Wardejn.
10/04/78

The Reluctant Gunfighter: SEE Mue Peun Khia

The Remains of the Shipwreck: SEE Los Restos Del Naufragio

Rembrandt - 1669
(Netherlands)
X. Jos Stelling Film Produkties film. Prod-dir, Jos Stelling. Sp, Stelling, Wil Hildebrand, Chlem van Houweninge; cam, Ernest Bresser; edtrs, Jan Overweg, Floris Hazemeijer, Marcel Bayer, Ate de Jong; mus, Laurens van Rooyen. 114.

Frans Stelling, Ton de Koff, Aya Fil, Lucie Singeling, Hanneke van der Velden.
05/10/78

Remember My Name
COL. Lion's Gate Films prodn. Prod, Robert Altman. Wri-dir, Alan Rudolph; exec in chg of prodn Tommy Thompson; cam (DeLuxe Color), Tak Fujimoto; edtr, Thomas Walls, William A Sawyer; snd, Bob Gravenor, Chris McLaughlin; mus, Alberta Hunter; cos, J Allen Highfill; asst dir, Thompson; snd, Dolby Snd Systems. (MPAA rating: R). 95.
Geraldine Chaplin, Anthony Perkins, Moses Gunn, Berry Berenson, Jeff Goldblum, Timothy Thomerson, Alfre Woodard.
10/11/78

Renaldo & Clara
CIR. Lombard Street Films prodn; supervised by Jack Baran, Mel Howard. Sp-dir, Bob Dylan. Cam, David Myers, Paul Goldsmith, Howard Alk, Michael Levine; edtrs, Dylan, Alk; snd, Gary Bourgeois, L A Johnson; snd edtrs, Bruce Nyznik, Peter Thillaye; mixers, Arthur Piantadosi, Les Fresholtz, Michael Minkler; blow-up, Osvaldo Zornizer. (MPAA rating: R). 232.
Bob Dylan, Sara Dylan, Joan Baez, Ronnie Hawkins, Ronee Blakely, Jack Elliott, Harry Dean Stanton, Bob Neuwirth, Helena Kalloaniotes, Allen Ginsberg, David Blue, Roger McGuinn, Sam Shepard, Arlo Guthre, Roberta Flack.
02/01/78

Rend mig i traditionerne
(Traditions, My Behind)
(Denmark)
OBL. Gunnar Obel (with Edward Fleming and The State Film Institute) prodn. Based on Leif Panduro's novel. Wri-dir, Edward Fleming. Cam (Eastmancolor), Jan Wincke; edtr, Maj Soya; mus, Ole Hoyer and (title tune) Kim Larsen. 90.
Henrik Kofoed, Karin Wedel, Bodil Kjer, Axel Stroeby, Olaf Ussing, Masja Dessau, Jan Gustavsen, Niels Hinrichsen.
10/03/79

Rendez-Moi Ma Peau
(Give Me Back My Skin)
(France)
CCF. Chloe Production-Parano Films co-prodn. Prod, Jean-Pierre Fougeau. Wri-dir, Patrick Schulmann. Cam, Jacques Assuerus, Andre Zarra. Snd, Alix Comte. Edtr, Aline Asseo; art dir, Marc Heyden. Sfx, Bertrand Bellouin. 110.
Bee Michelin, Erik Colin, Chantal Neuwirth, Jean-Luc Bideau, Alain Flick.
11/19/80

Rene La Canne
(Rene the Cane)
(France)
AMLF. President Films (Jacques-Eric Strauss)-Rizzoli Films prodn. Dir, Francis Girod. Sp, Girod, Jacques Rouffio from the book by Roger Borniche; cam (Eastmancolor), Aldo Tonti; edtr, Eva Zora; mus, Ennio Morricone. 100.
Gerard Depardieu, Michel Piccoli, Sylvia Kristel.
03/09/77

Renuncia Por Motivos de Salud
(Resigned for Reasons of Health)
(Mexico)
PEX. Conacine-STPC co-prodn. Dir, Rafael Baledon. Story-sp, Fernanda Villela, Josefina Vicens; cam, Miguel Arana; edtr, Adolfo Rosas Priego. 95.
Ignacio Lopez Tarso, Carmen Montejo, Silvia Mariscal, Aaron Hernan, Adriana Roel, Juan Antonio Edwards.
10/20/76

Reperages
(Location Hunting)
(Switzerland - France)
GAU. Citel Films-Action Films-GAU-SSR prodn. Wri-dir, Michel Soutter. Cam (Eastmancolor), Renato Berta; edtr, Albert Jurgenson; mus, Arie Dzierlatka. 100.
Jean-Louis Trintignant, Delphine Seyrig, Lea Massari, Valerie Mairesse, Roger Jendly.
11/16/77

Repmanad
(The Call-Up)
(Sweden)
EUR. Bo Jonsson-Viking Film with RiFilm and Europa Film prodn. Story by Lasse Aberg. Written by Aberg and Bo Jonsson. Dir, Aberg. Cam (Eastmancolor), Hanno-Heinz Fuchs; edtr, Sylvia Ingemarsson; mus, Janne Schaffer; prodn des, Rolf Larsson. 84.
Lasse Aberg, Janne Carlsson, Lena-Maria Gardenaes-Lawton.
05/09/79

The Request: SEE *La Peticion*

Requiem for a Revolutionary: SEE *Voros Rekviem*

Requiem for a Village
(Britain)
X. British Film Institute Prodn Board film. Prod, Michael Raeburn. Dir-wri-edtr, David Gladwell. Cam, Bruce Parsons; addl pho, Walter Lassally; asst cam, Gordon Steinforth; location snd, Michael Pharey; dubbing mixer, Doug Turner; asst dir, Neil Thomson; mus comp-cond, David Fanshawe. 68.
Vic Smith and the villagers of Witnesham and Metfield in Suffolk.
(DOC) (16m)
11/10/76

The Rescuers
BV. Walt Disney prodn, prod, Wolfgang Reitherman; exec prod, Ron Miller. Dirs, Reitherman, John Lounsbery, Art Stevens. Story, Larry Clemmons, Ken Anderson, Vance Gerry, David Michener, Burny Mattinson, Frank Thomas, Fred Lucky, Ted Berman, Dick Sebast, suggested by "The Rescuers" and "Miss Bianca" by Margery Sharp; mus, Artie Butler; songs, Carol Connors, Ayn Robbins, Sammy Fain, Robert Crawford; edtrs, James Melton, Jim Koford; art dir, Don Griffith; color styling, Al Dempster; snd, Herb Taylor; asst dirs, Jeff Patch, Richard Rich. Directing animators, Ollie Johnston, Frank Thomas, Milt Kahl, Don Bluth; character ani, John Pomeroy, Andy Gaskill, Art Stevens, Chuck Harvey, Bob McCrea, Cliff Nordberg, Gary Goldman, Dale Baer, Ron Clements, Bill Hajee, Glen Keane; layout, Joe Hale, Tom Lay, Guy Deel, Sylvia Roemer; background painting, Jim Coleman, Ann Guenther, Daniela Bielecka; titles, Melvin Shaw, Eric Larson, Burny Mattinson; effects ani, Jack Buckley, Dorse A Lanpher, Ted Kierscey, James L George, Dick Lucas; key asst ani, Stan Green, Chuck Williams, Walt Stanchfield, Dale Oliver, Harry Hester, Dave Suding, Leroy Cross. (MPAA rating: G). 76.
Voices: Bob Newhart, Eva Gabor, Geraldine Page, Joe Flynn, Jeanette Nolan, Pat Buttram, Jim Jordan, John McIntire, Michelle Stacy, Bernard Fox, Larry Clemmons, James Macdonald, George Lindsey, Bill McMillan, Dub Taylor, John Fiedler.
(ANI)
06/15/77

Resigned for Reasons of Health: SEE *Renuncia Por Motivos de Salud*

The Restless Corpse: SEE *Chitegu Chinte*

Resurrection
U. Prods, Renee Missel, Howard Rosenman; dir, Daniel Petrie; sp, Lewis John Carlino; cam (Technicolor), Mario Tosi; spec visual seq, Tony Silver, Richard Greenberg, Robert Greenberg; mus, Maurice Jarre; edtr, Rita Roland; prodn des, Paul Sylbert; art dir, Edwin O'Donovan; set decor, Bruce Weintraub; snd, John Kean, Richard Portman; asst dir, Craig Huston. (MPAA rating: PG). 103.
Ellen Burstyn, Sam Shepard, Richard Farnsworth, Roberts Blossom, Clifford David, Pamela Payton-Wright, Jeffrey DeMunn, Eva Le Gallienne, Lois Smith, Madeleine Thornton-Sherwood, Richard Hamilton, Carlin Glynn, Lane Smith, Penelope Allen, Ebbe Roe Smith.
09/10/80

Resurrection of the Golden Wolf: SEE *Yomegaeru Kinro*

Retour a la Bien-Aimee
(Return To The Beloved)
(France)
PDS. ATC 3000-F R 3-Prodis co-prodn. Prod, Benjamin Simon. Dir, Jean-Francois Adam. Sp, Adam, Georges Perec, Jean-Claude Carriere, Benoit Jacquot; cam, Pierre Lhomme; snd, Pierre Lenoir; mus, Antoine Duhamel; edtr, Eric Pluet; art dirs, Yves Bernard, Nicole Bertrand; cos, Christian Gasc. 98.
Isabelle Huppert, Jacques Dutronc, Bruno Ganz.
05/30/79

Retour a Marseille
(Return to Marseilles)
(France)
GAU. Action Films-FR3-Filmproduktion Janus prodn. Wri-dir, Rene Allio; cam (Eastmancolor), Renato Berta; mus, Lucien Bertolina, Georges Boeuf. 117.
Raf Vallone, Andrea Ferreol, Jean Maurel, Paul Allio, Rene Fontanarava, Danielle Durand.
08/20/80

Retour En Force
(Return in Bond)
(France)
GAU. Gaumont Int'l/FR3 co-prodn. Prod, Alain Poire. Dir, Jean-Marie Poire. Wris, Poire, Josiane Balasko; cam, Yves Lafaye; edtr, Marie-Joseph Yoyotte; art dir, Gerard Viard; snd, Pierre Lenoir; mus, William Sheller. 100.
Victor Lanoux, Bernadette Lafont, Pierre Mondy.
03/26/80

Retrato De Familia
(Family Portrait)
(Spain)
X. Sabre Films prodn. Dir, Antonio Jimenez Rico. Exec prod, Jose Samano. Sp, Jose Samano, Antonio Jimenez Rico, based on novel "My Idyllic Son Sisi" by Miguel Delibes; sets, Rafael Palmero; cos, Javier Artimano; cam (Eastmancolor), Jose Luis Alcaine; edtr, Rosa G Salgado; mus, Carmelo Bernaola. 99.
Antonio Ferrandis, Amparo Soler Leal, Monica Randall, Miguel Bose, Gabriel Llopart, Encarna Paso, Alberto Fernandez, Josefina Diaz, Carmen Cuesta, Jose Luis Alexandre, Carmen Lozano, Mirta Miller.
09/29/76

Retrato De Teresa
(Portrait of Teresa)
(Cuba)
IDP. Prod, IDP. Dir, Pastor Vega. Sp, Ambrosio Fornet, Vega; cam, Livio Delgado; edtr, Mirita Lores; mus, Carlos Farinas. 103.
Daysy Grandados, Adolfo Llaurado, Alina Sanchez, Raul Pomares.
09/05/79

The Return: SEE *Povratak*

Return From Witch Mountain
BV. Walt Disney prodns. Prods, Ron Miller, Jerome Courtland. Dir, John Hough. Sp, Malcolm Marmorstein, based on characters created by Alexander Key; cam (Technicolor), Frank Phllips; edtr, Bob Bring; mus, Lalo Schifrin; art dir, John B Mansbridge, Jack Senter; set decor, Frank R McKelvy; snd, Herb Taylor, Ron Ronconi; cos, Chuck Keehne, Emily Sundby; asst dir, Michael Dmytryk; sfx, Eustace Lycett, Art Cruickshank, Danny Lee. (MPAA rating: G). 93.
Bette Davis, Christopher Lee, Kim Richards, Ike Eisenmann, Jack Soo, Anthony James, Dick Bakalyan, Ward Costello, Christian Juttner, Poindexter, Brad Savage, Jeffrey Jacquet.
03/15/78

Return in Bond: SEE *Retour En Force*

The Return of a Man Called Horse
UA. Sandy Howard/Richard Harris prodn. Prod, Terry Morse Jr. Dir, Irvin Kershner. Exec prods, Sandy Howard, Richard Harris. Sp, Jack De Witt, based upon a character by Dorothy M Johnson; cam (Panavision-DeLuxe Color), Owen Roizman; mus, Laurence Rosenthal; 2d unit dir, Michael D Moore; prodn des, Stewart Campbell; cos, Dick La Motte; edtr, Michael Kahn; stunt coord, Mickey Gilbert; sfx, Joe Zomar, Federico Farfan; snd, Bill Daniels; set decor, Ernesto Carrasco; unit publicist, Blanche Sands. (MPAA rating: PG). 125.
Richard Harris, Gale Sondergaard, Geoffrey Lewis, Bill Lucking, Jorge Luke, Claudio Brook, Enrique Lucero, Jorge Russek, Ana De Sade, Pedro Damien, Humberto Lopez-Pineda, Patricia Reyes, Regino Herrera, Rigoberto Rico, Alberto Marsical.
07/28/76

The Return of Casanova:
SEE *Il Ritorno Di Casanova*

The Return of the Banished:
SEE *Intoarcerea Lui Voda Lupusneanu*

Return Of The Secaucus Seven
X. Salsipuedes prodn. Prods, Jeffrey Nelson, William Aydelott. Dir-wri-edtr, John Sayles. Cam (DuArt Film Labs color), Austin de Besche; mus, K Mason Darling. 110.
Mark Arnott, Gordon Clapp, Maggie Cousineau, Brian Johnson, Adam LeFevre, Bruce MacDonald, Jean Passanante, Maggie Renzi, John Sayles, David Strathairn, Karen Trott. (16m)
03/26/80

Return to Marseilles: SEE *Retour a Marseille*

Return To The Beloved: SEE *Retour a la Bien-Aimee*

The Revelation: SEE
Alpenbaringen

Revenge
(Italy)
TIT. Liberty prodn. Wri-dir, Lina Wertmuller. Cam (Eastmancolor), Tonino Delli Colli; prodn supv, Enrico Job; edtr, Franco Fraticelli; mus, Dangio and Nando De Luca. 112.
Sophia Loren, Marcello Mastroianni, Giancarlo Giannini, Turi Ferro.
02/07/79

Revenge of the Cheerleaders
MNR. Cheerful Film, by Richard Lerner and Nathaniel Dorsky. Dir, Lerner. Sp, Ted Greenwald, Ace Bandage, Dorsky; cam, Dorsky; edtrs, Richard S Brummer, Joseph Ancore, Jr; mus, John Sterling; chor, Xavier Chatman. (MPAA rating: R). 88.
Jerii Woods, Rainbeaux Smith, Helen Lang, Patrice Rohmer, Susie Elene, Eddra Gale, William Bramley, Norman Thomas Marshall, Regina Gleason, Carl Ballantine, Fred Gray, Carrie Dietrich, Sheri Myers, Lillian McBride, Bert Conroy, Gary Walberg, Mike Steele, David Hasselhoff, David Robinson, Patrick Wright, Ivanna Moore.
07/14/76

Revenge of the Pink Panther
UA. Prod-dir, Blake Edwards; exec prod, Tony Adams; sp, Frank Waldman, Ron Clark, Edwards, based on an Edwards story; cam (Technicolor), Ernie Day; edtr, Alan Jones; mus, Henry Mancini; prodn des, Peter Mullins; art dir, John Siddall; snd, Roy Charman; cos-ward, Tiny Nichols; asst dir, Terry Marcel; 2d unit dir, Anthony Squire; stunt coords, Joe Dunne, Dick Crockett. (MPAA rating: PG). 98.
Peter Sellers, Herbert Lom, Dyan Cannon, Robert Webber, Burk Kwouk, Paul Stewart, Robert Loggia, Graham Stark, Sue Lloyd, Tony Beckley, Valerie Leon.
07/19/78

Revolt of the Thralls: SEE *Traellenes oproer*

Rheingold
(W Germany)
CIG. Visual Filmproduktion, Munich. Prod, Elke Haltaufderheide. Sp-dir, Niklaus Schilling. Cam (Eastmancolor), Ernst Wild; edtr, Thomas Nikel; sets, Gretel Zeppel; mus, Eberhard Schoener; snd, Rolf Maas. 91.
Ruediger Kirschstein, Gunther Malzacher, Elke Haltaufderheide, Alice Treff, Reinfried Keilich, Alfred Baarovy, Petra Maria Gruehn, Franz Zimmermann, Ulrike Quien.
02/22/78

Riasztoloves
(Warning Shot)
(Hungary)
X. Dialog Studio prodn. Wri-dir, Peter Bacso. Cam (Eastmancolor), Janos Zsombolyai. 96.

Agoston Simon, Erzsebet Kutvolghi, Istvan Iglodi, Peter Andorai, Teri Foldi.
03/09/77

The Rich Are Something Else: SEE Gente Fina E Otra Coisa

Rich Kids
UA. Lion's Gate Film. A Robert Altman and George W George presentation. Prods, George and Michael Hausman. Exec prod, Altman. Dir, Robert M Young. Sp, Judith Ross. Cam, Ralf D Bode; edtr, Edward Beyer; art dir, David Mitchell; mus score, Craig Doerge; songs, Doerge, Allan Nichols. MPAA rating: PG.   96.
Trini Alvarado, Jeremy Levy, Kathryn Walker, John Lithgow, Terry Kiser, David Selby, Roberta Maxwell, Paul Dooley, Diane Stilwell, Dianne Kirksey, Irene Worth.
08/15/79

Richard's Things
(Britain)
SOE. Dir, Anthony Harvey; sp, Frederic Raphael from his book; cam, Freddie Young; edtr, Lesley Walker; mus, Georges Delerue. 104.
Liv Ullmann, Amanda Redman, Tom Piggott-Smith, Elizabeth Spriggs, Michael Maloney, Mark Eden.
09/10/80

The Riddle of the Sands
(Britain)
RNK. Prod, Drummond Challis. Dir, Tony Maylam. Sp, Tony Maylam, John Bailey based on novel of same title by Erskine Childers; cam, Christopher Challis; edtr, Peter Hollywood; mus, Howard Blake; art dir, Terry Pritchard; snd, Rene Borisewitz; 2d unit cam, Arthur Wooster, asst dir, Neill Vine-Miller. 102.
Michael York, Jenny Agutter, Simon MacCorkindale, Alan Badel, Jurgen Andersen, Olga Lowe, Hans Meyer, Michael Sheard, Wolf Kahler, Ronald Markham.
05/02/79

Rien ne va plus
(Out Of Whack)
(France)
GAU. Renn Production/Partners Production co-prodn. Prod, Ariel Zeitoun. Dir, Jean-Michel Ribes; sp, Ribes, Philippe Khorsand, Laurent Heynemann; mus, Michel Rivard; cam (Fujicolor), Bernard Zitzermann; edtr, Jacques Witta; snd, Jean-Louis Ughetto; art dir, Jacques Bufnoir.   92.
Jacques Villeret, Eva Darlan, Roland Blanche, Philippe Khorsand, Tonie Marshall, Evelyne Bouix, Micheline Presle, Jacques Francois, Judith Magre, Daniel Prevost, Michel Blanc, Henri Cremieux.
01/16/80

Right Out Of History - The Making Of Judy Chicago's Dinner Party
Pl. Prod, Thom Tyson; dir, Johanna Demetrakas; cam, Baird Bryant; edtrs, Demetrakas, Nina Toumanoff; mus, Catherine MacDonald; snd, Tyson, Demetrakas.   75. (DOC) (16m)
09/03/80

Rio Negro
(Black River)
(Cuba)
X. Cuban Film prodn, Havana. Dir, Manuel Perez. Sp, Perez, Victor Casaus.   200.
Sergio Corrieri, Nelson Villagra.
08/03/77

Rising Damp
(Britain)
ITC. Cinema Arts Int'l Prodn for Black Lion Films; prod, Roy Skeggs. Exec prod, Brian Lawrence. Dir, Joe McGrath. Sp, Eric Chappell; cam, Frank Watts; mus, David Lindup; edtr, Peter Weatherley; snd, Alan Kane; asst dir, Roger Simons.   96.
Leonard Rossiter, Frances de la Tour, Don Warrington, Christopher Strauli, Denholm Elliott, Carrie Jones, Glynn Edwards, John Cater, Derek Griffiths.
03/12/80

Rising Sun
(Hong Kong)
X. Edwin Kong prodn. Wri-edtr-mus, Kong. 100.
(DOC) (B & W)
04/09/80

The Risk of Living: SEE Le Risque De Vivre

The Rites of May: SEE Itim

Ritratto di Borghesia in Nero
(Nest of Vipers)
(Italy)
PAR. Mars Film prodn. Prod, Piero La Mantia. Dir, Tonino Cervi. Sp, Tonino Cervi, Cesare Frugoni, Geoffredo Parise, based on short story, "The Piano Teacher", by Roger Peyrefitte; cam, Armando Nannuzzi; edtr, Nino Baragli; mus, Vincenzo Tempera. (MPAA rating: R).   105.
Ornella Muti, Senta Berger, Christian Borromeo, Capucine, Giuliana Calandra, Stefano Patrizi, Giancarlo Sbragia, Paolo Bonacelli, Mattia Sbragia, Maria Monti, Eros Pagni, Antonia Cancellieri, Suxanne Creese Bates, Raffaele Di Mario, Giancarlo Marinaangeli, Giovanni Caenazzo.
09/05/79

Rituals
(Canada)
DD. Prod, Lawrence Dane. Dir, Peter Carter; sp, Ian Sutherland; cam (Bellevue Pathe Color), Rene Verzier; art dir, Karen Bromley; asst dir, John Eckert.   94.
Hal Holbrook, Lawrence Dane, Robin Gammell, Ken James, Gary Reineke.
04/26/78

The Ritz
WB. Prod, Denis O'Dell. Dir, Richard Lester. Sp, Terrence McNally, based on his play; cam (Technicolor), Paul Wilson; edtr, John Bloom; mus, Ken Thorne; prodn des, Phillip Harrison; snd, Gerry Humphreys, Roy Charman; asst dir, Dusty Symonds. (MPAA rating: R). 90.
Jack Weston, Rita Moreno, Jerry Stiller, Kaye Ballard, F Murray Abraham, Paul B Price, Treat Williams, John Everson, Christopher Brown, Dave King, Bessie Love, George Coulouris, Ben Aris, Peter Butterworth, Ronnie Brody, John Ratzenberger, Hal Gallili, Chris Harris, Leon Greene, Freddie Earle, Tony De Santis, Hugh Fraser, Samantha Weyson, Richard Holmes, Bart Allison.
08/11/76

The River
(Iraq)
X. Prod by General Establishment for Film and Stage, Baghdad. Wri-dir, Faisal Yasini. Cam, Nuhad Ali; mus, Faiq Hanna.   100. Sami Kaftan, Kaid al Numani, Karim Awad.
09/19/79

The River Niger
CAX. Prods, Sidney Beckerman, Isaac L Jones. Dir, Krishna Shah. Sp, Joseph A Walker, from his own play; cam (Movielab color), Michael Margulies; edtr, Irving Lerner; mus, War; prodn des, Seymour Klate; snd, Dean Buddah Hodges; stunt coord, Marvin Walters; asst dir, Tony Brand. (MPAA rating: R).   105.
Cicely Tyson, James Earl Jones, Lou Gossett, Glynn Turman, Roger E Mosley, Jonelle Allen, Hilda Haynes, Theodore Wilson, Charles Weldon, Ralph Wilcox, Shirley-Joe Finney.
03/31/76

Roadie
UA. Alive Enterprises/Vivant prodn. Prod, Carolyn Pfeiffer. Dir, Alan Rudolph. Exec prod, Zalman King. Sp, Big Boy Medlin, Michael Ventura, based on story by Medlin, Ventura, King, Rudolph; cam (Technicolor), David Myers; co-edtr, Tom Walls; supv edtr, Carol Littleton; mus, Craig Hundley; prodn des, Paul Peters; set decor, Richard Friedman; cos, Jered Edd Grenn, Gail Bixby; snd (Dolby), Richard Goodman; asso prod, John E Pommer; asst dir, Ed Ledding. (MPAA rating: PG).   105.
Meat Loaf, Kaki Hunter, Art Carney, Gailard Sartain, Don Cornelius, Rhonda Bates, Joe Spano, Richard Marion, Sonny Davis, Alice Cooper, Blondie (Deborah Harry, Chris Stein, Clem Burke, Jimmy Destri, Nigel Harrison, Frank Infante), Roy Orbison, Hank Williams Jr, Merle Kilgore, Ramblin' Jack Elliot, Ray Benson, Sheryl Cooper, Alvin Crow.
06/11/80

The Roads of Exile: SEE Les Chemins de L'Exil, ou Les Dernieres Annees de Jean Jacques Rouss

The Roads of the South: SEE
Les Routes Du Sud

Robber Jurko: SEE Zbojnik
Jurko

Robert Et Robert
(France)
AMLF. Films 13 prodn. Wri-dir, Claude Lelouch. Cam (Eastmancolor), Jacques Lefrancois; edtr, Sophie Bhaud; mus, Francis Lai, J C Nachon. 105.
Charles Denner, Jacques Villeret, Jean-Claude Brialy, Macha Meril, Regine.
06/28/78

Roberte
(France)
WMF. Filmoblic prodn. Dir, Pierre Zucca; sp, Pierre Klossowski, Zucca from a book by Klossowski; cam (Eastmancolor), Paul Bonis; edtr, Nicole Lubtchansky; mus, Eric Demarsan. 100.
Denise Morin Sinclaire, Pierre Klossowski, Martin Loeb, Barbet Schroeder, Juliet Berto, Jean-Francois Stevenin, Frederic Mitterand.
08/23/78

Robin And Marian
COL. Ray Stark-Richard Shepherd prodn, prod, Denis O'Dell; exec prod, Shepherd. Dir, Richard Lester. Sp, James Goldman; cam (Technicolor), David Watkin; 2d unit cam, Paul Wilson; edtr, John Victor Smith; mus, John Barry; prodn des, Michael Stringer; art dir, Gil Perondo; snd, Roy Charman, Gerry Humphreys; asst dir, Jose Lopez Rodero. (MPAA rating: PG). 106.
Sean Connery, Audrey Hepburn, Robert Shaw, Richard Harris, Nicol Williamson, Denholm Elliott, Kenneth Haigh, Ronnie Barker, Ian Holm.
03/10/76

Rock 'n' Roll
(Italy)
MDN. Cinemaster Production. Prod, Galliano Juso. Wri-dir, Vittorio De Sisti. Cam (Eastmancolor), Giovanni Ciarlo; mus, Little Richard, Bill Haley, B C Corporation and the Darts. 97.
Rudolfo Banchelli, Rosaria Biccica, Macha Meril, Carlo Monni.
01/10/79

Rock 'n' Roll High School
NW. Exec prod, Roger Corman. Prod, Michael Finnell. Dir, Allan Arkush. Sp, Richard Whitley, Russ Dvonch, Joseph McBride, based on a story by Arkush, Joe Dante; cam, Dean Cundey; edtr, Larry Bock, Gail Werbin, art dir, Marie Kordus; set decor, Linda Pearl; snd, Michael Moore; mus, The Ramones; asst dir, Gerald T Olson. (MPAA rating: PG). 93.
P J Soles, Vincent Van Patten, Clint Howard, Dey Young, Mary Woronov, Paul Bartel, Loren Lester, Daniel Davies, Alix Elias, Don Steele, Lynn Farrell.
04/25/79

Rock 'n' Roll Wolf
(Romania - Russia - France)
X. Rumanian, Soviet & French Coprodn, Group Three, Bucharest. Dir, Elisabeta Bostan. Sp, Vasilica Istrate; cam, Ion Marinescu, Konstantin Petricenco; mus, Temistocle Popa, Gerald Bourgeois. 90.
Ludmila Gurcenco, Florian Pittis, Mihail Boiarski, George Mihaita, Violeta Andrei, Oleg Popov, Saveli Kremerov, Valentin Manohin, Paula Radulescu, Vasile Mentzel, Vera Ivleva, Liliana Petrescu, Evgheni Ghercikov, Marina Poliak, Natalia Kracikovskaia, Lulu Mihaiescu, Matei Opris, Timur Asaliev, Adtian Cristea, Petia Dektiarev.
06/14/78

Rockers
X. Prod, Patrick Hulsey. Wri-dir, Theodoros Bafaloukos. Cam, Peter Sova; snd, Nigel Noble; edtr, Susan Steinberg; assoc prod, Avrom Robin; art dir, Lilly Kilvert; cos des, Eugenie Bafaloukos; asst dir, Walter Rearick. 100.
Leroy Wallace, Richard Hall, Monica Craig, Marjorie Norman, Jacob Miller, Gregory Isaacs, Winston Rodney, Frank Dowding, Robert Shakespeare, Manley Buchanan, Lester Bullocks, The Mighty Diamonds, Ashley Harris, Leroy Smart, Peter Honiball, L Lindo, Trevor Douglas, Herman Davis, Raymond Hall, Junior Wilby, Errol Brown, Robert Van Campbell, Berris Simpson, Theophilus Beckford, Phylip Richards.
10/18/78

Rockinghorse: SEE Susetz

Rockshow
MRX. Prod, MPL Communications. Cam, Jack Priestley; edtr, Robin Clark; snd mix, Chris Thomas, Paul McCartney. (MPAA rating: PG). 105.
Paul McCartney, Linda McCartney, Jimmy McCulloch, Joe English, Denny Laine.
(MUSICAL DOC)
12/10/80

Rocky
UA. Prods, Irwin Winkler, Robert Chartoff; exec prod, Gene Kirkwood. Dir, John G Avildsen. Sp, Stallone; cam (DeLuxe Color), James Crabe; edtrs, Richard Halsey, Scott Conrad; mus, Bill Conti; songs, Conti, Frank Stallone Jr; prodn des, Bill Cassidy; art dir, James H Spencer; set decor, Raymond Molyneaux; snd, Ray Alba, Burt Schoenfeld, B Eugene Ashbrook; cos-ward, Joanne Hutchinson, Robert Cambel; asst dir, Fred Gallo. (MPAA rating: PG). 119.
Sylvester Stallone, Talia Shire, Burt Young, Carl Weathers, Burgess Meredith, Thayer David, Joe Spinell, Joe Frazier, Judi Letizia.
11/10/76

Rocky II
UA. Irwin Winkler and Robert Chartoff prodn. Wri-dir, Sylvester Stallone. Cam (Panavision-Technicolor), Bill Butler; mus, Bill Conti; edtr, Danford B Greene; art dir, Richard Berger; asst dir, Jerry Zeismer; fight sequence edtrs, James D Mitchell, Christopher V Holmes; snd effects edtr, Frank Warner; "Street Scat," "Two Kinds of Love," words and mus, Frank Stallone; set decor, Ed Baer; boxing tech advisor, Al Silvani. (MPAA rating: PG). 119.
Sylvester Stallone, Talia Shire, Burt Young, Carl Weathers, Burgess Meredith, Tony Burton, Joe Spinell, Leonard Gaines, Sylvia Meals, Frank McRae, Al Silvani, John Pleshette, Stu Nahan, Bill Baldwin, Jerry Ziesmer, Paul J Micale.
06/13/79

Roger Corman: Hollywood's "Wild Angel"
X. Christian Blackwood Prodn, in collab with Michael Blackwood. 58.
(DOC) (16m)
06/28/78

The Role: SEE Bhumika

Roller Boogie
UA. Irwin Yablans prodn. Exec prod, Irwin Yablans; prod, Bruce Cohn Curtis. Dir, Mark L Lester; sp, Barry Schneider, from an orig story by Yablans; cam (Technicolor), Dean Cundey; supv edtr, Howard Kunin; edtrs, Byron (Buzz) Brandt, Ediberto Cruz, Edward Salier; mus, Bob Esty; mus numbers staged, David Winters; art dir, Keith Michl; snd (Dolby), Anthony Santa Croce; asst dir, Dan Allingham. (MPAA rating: PG). 103.
Linda Blair, Jim Bray, Beverly Garland, Roger Perry, Jimmy Van Patten, Kimberly Beck, Rick Sciacca, Sean McClory, Mark Goddard, Albert Insinnia, Stoney Jackson, M G Kelly, Chris Nelson.
12/12/79

Rollercoaster
U. Prod, Jennings Lang. Dir, James Goldstone. Sp, Richard Levinson, William Link, from a story by Sanford Sheldon, Levinson, Link, suggested by a Tommy Cook story; cam (Technicolor), David M Walsh; addl pho, William Birch; edtrs, Edward A Biery, Richard Sprague; mus, Lalo Schifrin; prodn des, Henry Bumstead; set decor, James W Payne; snd, Jim Alexander, Edwin J Somers; cos-ward, Burton Miller; asst dir, L Andrew Stone; stunt coord, John Daheim. (MPAA rating: PG). 119.
George Segal, Richard Widmark, Timothy Bottoms, Henry Fonda, Harry Guardino, Susan Strasberg, Helen Hunt, Dorothy Tristan, Harry Davis, Stephen Pearlman, Dennis Spiegel, Michael Bell, Monica Lewis.
04/27/77

Rolling Thunder
AIP. Lawrence Gordon prodn. Prod, Norman T Herman; exec prod, Gordon. Dir, John Flynn. Sp, Paul Schrader, Heywood Gould; cam (Deluxe Color), Jordon Cronenweth; edtr, Frank P Keller; snd, Don Johnson; art dir, Steve Berger; mus, Barry DeVorzon; asst dir, Joseph Lenzi; sfx, Richard Helmer. (MPAA rating: R). 99.

William Devane, Tommy Lee Jones, Linda Haynes, Lisa Richards, Dabney Coleman, James Beat, Cassie Yates, Lawrason Driscoll, Jordan Gerler, Luke Askew.
10/05/77

Roma A Mano Armata
(Rome: Armed to the Teeth)
(Italy)
MDU. Prod, Luciano Martino of Dania in co-prod with Medusa. Dir, Umberto Lenzi. Sp, Dardano Sacchetti; cam (Eastmancolor), Federico Zanni; art dir, Giorgio Bertolini; edtr, Daniele Alabiso; mus, Franco Micalizzi. 105.
Maurizio Merli, Tomas Milian, Arthur Kennedy, Maria Rosaria Omaggio.
04/14/76

Romance During Office Hours: SEE Sluzhebni Roman

Rome: Armed to the Teeth: SEE Roma A Mano Armata

Roots of Blood: SEE Raices De Sangre

The Rose
FOX. Marvin Worth/Aaron Russo prodn. Prod, Worth, Russo. Dir, Mark Rydell. Exec prod, Tony Ray. Sp, Bill Kerby, Bo Goldman, based on a story by Kerby; cam, Vilmos Zsigmond; edtr, Robert L Wolfe; prodn des, Richard MacDonald; cos des, Theoni V Aldredge; mus arr, Paul A Rothchild; chor, Toni Basil; art dir, Jim Schoppe; snd (Dolby Stereo), Jim Webb, Chris McLaughlin; asst dir, Larry Franco. (MPAA rating: R). 134.
Bette Midler, Alan Bates, Frederic Forrest, Harry Dean Stanton, Barry Primus, David Keith, Sandra McCabe, Will Hare, Rudy Bond, Don Calfa, James Keane, Michael Greer, Doris Roberts, Sandy Ward.
10/10/79

Roseland
CSH. Merchant-Ivory prod. Prod, Ismail Merchant Dir, James Ivory. Sp, Ruth Prawere Jhabvala; cam, Ernest Vincze; edtrs, Humphrey Dixon, Richard Schmiechen; snd, Cabell Smith; mus, Michael Gibson; chor, Patricia Birch; cos, Dianne Finn Chapman. 103.
Teresa Wright, Lou Jacobi, Don de Natale, Louise Kirtland, Geraldine Chaplin, Helen Gallagher, Joan Copeland, Christopher Walken, Conrad Janis, Lilia Skala, David Thomas, Edward Kogan, Madeline Lee, Stan Rubin.
10/05/77

The Roses of Danzig: SEE Le Rose Di Danzica

Rose-Tinted Dreams: SEE Ruzove Sny

Rosszemberek
(The Bad Guys)
(Hungary)
HU. Mafilm Hunnia Studio prodn. Dir, Gyorgy Szomjas. Sp, Peter Dobai, Szomjas; cam (Eastmancolor), Mihaly Halasz; mus, Ferenc Sebo. 93.
Djoko Rosic, Janos Derzsi, Gyorgy Dorner, Mari Kiss, Miklos Benedek.
02/28/79

Rough Cut
(Britain)
PAR. Siegel Film. Prod, David Merrick; dir, Donald Siegel; sp, Francis Burns based on Derek Lambert's "Touch The Lion's Paw"; cam (Movielab), Freddie Young; edtr, Doug Stewart; prodn des, Ted Haworth; mus, Nelson Riddle adapt from mus of Duke Ellington; art dir, Tim Hutchinson; set dec, Peter James; snd, John Mitchell; asst dir, David Tringham. (MPAA rating: PG). 112.
Burt Reynolds, Lesley-Anne Down, David Niven, Timothy West, Patrick Magee, Al Matthews, Susan Littler, Joss Ackland, Isobel Dean, Wolf Kabler, Andrew Ray.
06/18/80

Rough Diamond: SEE Diamante Bruto

Round Trip: SEE Aller Retour

Rousalochka
(The Little Mermaid)
(USSR)
SOV. Gorki Studios prodn. Dir, V Bychkov. Sp, V Vitkovitch from the story by Hans Christian Andersen; cam (Sovcolor), Emil Vageschain; mus, Evgueni Krylatov. 80.
Vika Novikova, Valentin Nikulin, Galina Artemova, Y Senkevitch, G Volchek.
07/28/76

Roveh Huliot
(The Wooden Gun)
(Israel)
X. Prods, Eitan Even, Richard Sanders, John Hardy. Wri-dir, Ilan Moshenson; cam, Gadi Danzig; prodn des, Eytan Levy. 91.
Judith Sole, Leo Yung, Ophelia Strahl, Louis Rosenberg, Michael Kfir, Eric Rosen.
03/21/79

Roy Likit
(Foretold By Fate)
(Thailand)
NFT. Jirabanterng Films prodn. Prod, Jirawan Kampana Senyakorn. Dir, Supravat Patamasoot. Story, Tomayanti; sp, Busaba Dao Rueang; cam, Morojon; mus, Pim Patiphan Poontamajitr; snd edtr, Maitree Janjaraskul; art dir, Waroj; cos, Jirawan Kampana Senyakorn; make-up, Kiat Syarm. 105.
Pisamai Wilaisak, Suphansa Nuangpirom, Ampha Pusith, Metta Rungrath, Kamthorn Suwanpiyasiri, Chamroon Nuatjim, Sutijitr Viradejkamhaeng, Pojetr Granpetr, Suchart Kongcharoen, Bu Vibulnan.
09/26/79

The Royal Hunt: SEE Mrigayaa

Royal Vacation: SEE Vacances Royales

Royalut
(The Grand Piano)
(Bulgaria)
07/25/79
FBU. Bulgarian Film Prodn, Sredets Unit, Sofia. Dir, Borislav Pounchev. Sp, Nikola Roussev; cam, Georgi Mateyev; art dir, Peter Goranov; mus, Simeon Pronkov. 90.
Georgi Kaloyanchev, Ivan Grigorev, Georgi Partsalev, Naoum Shopov, Konstantin Kotsev, Velko Kunev, Madeleine Cholakova.

The Rubber Gun
(Canada)
FAW. St. Lawrence Film Prod. prodn. Dir, Allan Moyle. Sp, Steve Lack; cam, Frank Vitale, Jim Lawrence; edtr, John Laing; mus, Lewis Furey. 86.
Steve Lack, Pierre Robert, Peter Brawley, Alain Moyle, Pam Holmes.
08/31/77

Ruby
DIM. Steve Krantz prodn. Exec prod, Krantz. Prod, George Edwards. Dir, Curtis Harrington. Sp, Edwards, Barry Schneider; cam, William Mendenhall; edtr, Bill McGee; mus, Don Ellis. (MPAA rating: R). 84.
Piper Laurie, Stuart Whitman, Roger Davis, Janit Baldwin, Crystin Sinclaire, Paul Kent, Len Lesser, Jack Perkin, Edward Donno, Sal Vecchio, Fred Kohler.
05/18/77

Rude Boy
(Britain)
X. Michael White presentation of a Buzzy Enterprises prodn. Prods-dirs, Jack Hazan, David Mingay. Sp, Mingay, Ray Gange, Hazan; cam, Hazan; edtrs, Mingay, Peter Goddard; mus, Joe Strummer, Mick Jones; snd, Greg Bailey, Bob Edwards, Garth Marshall; prodn services, Solus Enterprises; asst dir, Goddard. (MPAA rating: R). 133.
Ray Gange, The Clash (Joe Strummer, Mick Jones, Paul Simonon, Nicky Headon), John Green, Barry Baker, Terry McQuade, Caroline Coon, Elizabeth Young, Sarah Hall, Colin Bucksey, Colin Richards, Lizard Brown, Hicky Etienne, Inch Gordon, Lee Parker, Kenny Joseph, Jimmy Pursey.
02/27/80

Rue du Pied-De-Grue
(Street of the Crane's Foot)
(France - Belgium)
CII. Werlaine and Co/Little Bear/F3SA co-prod. Prod, Francois Grand-Jouan. Exec prod, Jean-Serge Breton. Wri-dir, Grand-Jouan; cnsltng wris, Philippe Dumarcay, Giorgio Bontempi; cam, Jean-Francois Robin; edtrs, Grand-Jouan, Francine Sandberg, Jacques Arhex; snd, Alix Comte; mus, Andre Gerget. 100.
Philippe Noiret, Pascale Audret, Jacques Dufilho, Jean Daste, Guiliana De Sio.
12/19/79

Rue Haute
(High Street)
(Belgium - France)
CVG. Alain Guilleaume, Pierre Drouot (Brussels) - Filmel (Paris) prodn. Dir, Andre Ernotte. Sp, Ernotte, Elliot Tiber; cam, Walther Vanden Ende; edtr, Susana Rossberg; mus, Mort Shuman; prodn des, Elliot Tiber; set decor, Philippe Graff; snd, Jean-Marie Buchet, Henri Morelle; asst dir, Susana Rossberg; cos, Yan Tax.   95.
Annie Cordy, Mort Shuman, Bert Struys, Guy Verda, Elliot Tiber, Anne Marisse, Nadia Gary, Louise Rocco, Raymond Peira, Martine Willequet, Suzy Falk, Michel de Warzee, Pierre Fox, Henny Alma, Esther Christinat, Lucien Charbonnier, Simone Durieu.
04/28/76

Run After Me Until I Catch You: SEE Cours Apres Moi Que Je T'Attrape

Run & Run: SEE Ran & Ran

Run For The Roses
KDK. Pan-American Films prodn. Prod, Mario Crespo Jr, Wolf Schmidt; exec prod, Arnold Pessin. Dir, Henry Levin. Sp, Joseph G Prieto, Mimi Avins; cam (Metrocolor), Raul Dominguez; mus, Raul Lavista; edtr, Alfredo Rosas Priego; stunt coord, Tom Sutton; snd, Paco Guerrero; asso prod, Richard A Rivers. (MPAA rating: PG).   93.
Vera Miles, Stuart Whitman, Sam Groom, Panchito Gomez, Theodore Wilson, Lisa Eilbacher.
11/15/78

The Runner Stumbles
FOX. Stanley Kramer Prodn. Exec prod, Melvin Simon; prod-dir, Stanley Kramer; wri, Milan Stitt, based on his Broadway play; cam (CFI), Laszlo Kovacs, ASC; snd, James H Pilcher; prodn des, Al Sweeney Jr; edtr, Pembroke J Herring; mus, Ernest Gold; asst dir, Craig Huston. (MPAA rating: PG.)   99.
Dick Van Dyke, Kathleen Quinlan, Maureen Stapleton, Ray Bolger, Tammy Grimes, Beau Bridges, Allen Nause, John Procaccino, Billy J Jacoby, Sister Marguerite Morrissey, Zoaunne LeRoy, Don Riley, Ted D'Arms, Kendall Kay Munsey, Casey Kramer, Jim Doyle, Katherine Kramer, Bill Dore, Jock Dove, Larry Buck.
04/11/79

Running
(Canada)
U. Robert Cooper-Ronald Cohen prodn. Exec Prod, Michael Douglas. Prods, Robert Cooper, Ronald Cohen; line prod, John Eckert. Wri-dir, Steven Stern. Cam, Lazlo George; mus, Andre Gagnon; edtr, Kurt Hirschler.   102.
Michael Douglas, Susan Anspach, Larry Dane, Charles Shamata, Eugene Levy.
06/06/79

Running Fence
MA. A film by David Maysles, Charlotte Zwerin, Albert Maysles. Asso edtr, Kate Hirson; asst edtr, Donald Klocek; filming teams, Albert and David Maysles; cam, Robert Elfstrom, Donald Lenzer, Stephen Lighthill, Richard Pearce; snd, Petur Hliddal, Larry Johnson, David Mac Millan, Nelson Stoll; location prod, Stanley Hirson; location prodn mgr, Mike Giovingo; mus arr-cond, Jim Dickinson; singer, Jill Lancaster; snd mixer, Lee Dichter.   57.
(DOC)
01/25/78

Runoilija Ja Muusa
(Poet and Muse)
(Finland)
FLY. Dir, Jaakko Pakkasvirta. Sp, Titta Karakorpi, Pakkasvirta.   102.
Esko Salminen, Elina Salo, Katja Salminen.
09/05/79

The Rural Teacher: SEE Kru Ban Nok

Rust Never Sleeps
07/25/79
IHA. Prod, L A Johnson. Exec prod, Elliot Rabinowitz. Dir, Bernard Shakey; cam (Deluxe Color), Paul Goldsmith, Jon Else, Robby Greenberg, Hiro Narita, Richard Pearce, Daniel Pearl; edtr, Bernard Shakey; snd (Dolby Stereo), David Briggs, Tim Mulligan. (MPAA rating: PG).   103.
Neil Young, Billy Talbot, Ralph Molina, Frank "Pancho" Sampedro.

Ruzove Sny
(Rose-Tinted Dreams)
(Czechoslovakia)
X. Slovak Film prodn, Bratislava, Koliba Studios. Wri-dir, Dusan Hanak. Cam, Dodo Simoncic; mus, Petr Hapka.   85.
Juraj Nvota, Iva Bittova, Josef Hlinomaz, Marie Motlova, Arpad Rigo, Hana Slivkova, Sally Salingova, Ludovit Kroner, Vaclav Babka.
03/09/77

Rycerz
(The Knight)
(Poland)
POL. Film Polski prodn, Profil Film Unit, Warsaw. Wri-dir, Lech J Majewski; cam, Czeslaw Swirta; sets, Jerzy Szeski; mus, Zdzislaw Szostak; prodn mgr, Jerzy Nitecki.   85.
Piotr Skarga, Daniel Olbrychski, Katarzyna Kozak, Czeclaw Meissner, Andrzej Hudziak, Stanislaw Holly, Irena Jun.
10/15/80

S Lyubov I Nezhnost
(With Love and Tenderness)
(Bulgaria)
BGO. Bulgarofilm Prodn, Meadost Creative Group, Sofia. Dir, Rangel Vulchanov. Sp, Valeri Petrov; cam, Dimko Minov; art dir, Maria Ivanova; mus, Kiril Donchev.   100.
Alexander Dyakov, Tsvetana Eneva, Gergana Gerassimova, Yossif Surchadjiev, Theodor Youroukov.
05/10/78

Saan Ka Papunta
(Where Are You Going)
(Philippines)
X. Silver Films prodn. Prod, Armando Silverio; asso prods, Domingo Silverio, Eddie Silverio. Dir, Armando Silverio, Eduard Palmas. Story-sp, Eduardo Palmos; cam, Higino J Fallorna; mus, George Canseco.   96.
Boots Anson Roa, Arnold Mendoza, Lorli Villanueva, Lito Arzures, Ramon D'Salva, Mario Escudero, Tita Villa.
03/03/76

The Sabina: SEE La Sabina

Sabine Wulff
(E Germany)
DEE. DEFA Film prodn. Berlin Group. E Berlin. Wri-dir, Erwin Stranka, based on a novel by Heinz Kruschel. Cam, Peter Brand; mus, Karl Heinz Sasse; dramatic advisor, Anne Pfeuffer.   91.
Karen Duewel, Manfred Ernst, Juergen Heinrich, Hans-Joachim Frank, Lars Jung, Jutta Wachowiak.
10/01/80

Sadan Er Jeg Ogsaa
(That's Me, Too)
(Denmark)
ASD. Focus Film prodn. Wri-dir, Lise Roos. Cam (Eastmancolor) Jan Weincke; prodn des, Finn Karlsson; edtr, Edith Toreg; exec prod, Erik Overbye.   90.
Stine Sylverstersen, Preben Kaas, Avi Sagild, Inger Stender, Annelise Gabold.
05/07/80

Sado
(Third Base)
(Japan)
X. Gentosha, ATG prodn. Dir, Yoichi Higashi. Sp, Shuji Terayama, based on novel "September Town" by Haka Kenjo; cam, Koichi Kawakami; mus, Michi Tanaka; art dir, Ikuro Ayabe.   102.
Toshiyuki Nagashima, Chiyoko Shimagura.
(English Subtitles)
10/11/78

Saellskapsresan
(The Charter Trip)
(Sweden)
EUR. Viking Film/Europa Film/RiFilm prodn. Dir, Lasse Aberg. Story-sp, Aberg, Bo Jonsson; tech dir, Peter Hald; prodn mgrs, Christer Abrahamsen, Gisela Bergquist; cam (Eastmancolor), Joergen Persson; prodn des, Bo Lindgren; cos, Denise Gruenstein; mus, Bengt Palmers; edtr, Sylvia Ingemarsson. 104.
Lasse Aberg, Lottie Ejebrandt, Magnus Haerenstam, Roland Jansson, Kim Anderzon, Sven Melander, Weiron Holmberg, German Perez, Jon Skolmen, Ted Astroem.
09/03/80

Saen Saeb
(Saen Saeb Canal)
(Thailand)
SAH. Prod, Nitra Kasiwat. Dir-edtr, Pairat Kasiwat. Story, Pai Muangderm; sp-prodn dsgn, Tosapon Nakphorn; cam, Sophon Melintasai; snd and color processing, Tokyo Laboratories; mus, Seksan Sominsart; cos-makeup, Niran Sangkaroj; prodn mgr, Karom Sangborivutr. 120.
Pairoj Sangborivutr, Yuwathida Phonprasert, Nirachara Rachakul.
09/06/78

Sai Thip
(Thailand)
SAY. Wri-prod-dir, Uthai Wongwaisayawan. Based on a story by Pochana Kiatchinda; cam, Athee Wong; mus, Panthip Virayaphanit, Asvinikul; prodn des-cos, Kanokorm Kanakornkhan; asst dir, Gan Boonchoo. 125.
Nantana Ngaokrachang, Patompong Singha, Sidemi Aoki, Piathip Kumvong, Sompop Benjatikul, Suphan Buranaphim, Wallaya Chindanoot, Prachon Chindanoot.
07/18/79

Saiehaieh Bolan de Bad
(Tall Shadows of the Wind)
(Iran)
X. Farmanara prodn. Dir, Bahman Farmanara. Sp, Houshang Golshiri, Farmanara from the book by Golshiri; mus, Ahmad Pejamn. 104.
Faramarz Gharibian, Said Nikpour, Hossein Kasbian, Atash Khaeyer.
05/16/79

The Sailor Who Fell From Grace With The Sea
(Britain)
AVE. Martin Poll-Lewis John Carlino prodn. Prod, Martin Poll. Wri-dir, Lewis John Carlino, based on book by Yukio Mishima. Cam (Eastmancolor), Douglas Slocombe; edtr, Anthony Gibbs; mus, John Mandel; art dir, Brian Ackland-Snow; prodn des, Ted Haworth; snd, David Hildyard. (MPAA rating: R). 104.
Sarah Miles, Kris Kristofferson, Jonathan Kahn, Margo Cunningham, Earl Rhodes, Paul Tropea, Gary Lock, Stephen Black, Peter Clapham, Jennifer Tolman.
04/14/76

The Sailor's Return
(Britain)
OSP. Euston Films Prodn made by Ariel Prodns Ltd in asso with NFFC. OProd, Otto Plaschkes; exec prod, Verity Lambert. Dir, Jack Gold. Sp, James Saunders, based on the novel by David Garnett; mus, Carl Davis. 112.
Tom Bell, Shope Shodeinde, Mick Ford, Paola Dionisotti, George Costigan, Clive Swift, Ray Smith, Ivor Roberts, Bernard Hill, Anthony Langdon.
06/21/78

St. Ives
WB. Prods, Pancho Kohner, Stanley Canter. Dir, J Lee Thompson. Sp, Barry Beckerman, from the novel, "The Procane Chronicle," by Oliver Bleeck; cam (Technicolor), Lucien Ballard; edtr, Michael F Anderson; mus, Lalo Schifrin; prodn des, Philip M Jefferies; set decor, Robert De Vestel; snd, Harlan Riggs, Arthur Piantadosi; asst dir, Ronald L Schwary; stunt coord, Max Kleven. (MPAA rating: PG). 93.
Charles Bronson, John Houseman, Jacqueline Bisset, Maximilian Schell, Harry Guardino, Harris Yulin, Dana Elcar, Michael Lerner, Dick O'Neill, Elisha Cook, Val Bisoglio, Burr De Benning, Daniel J Travanti.
07/21/76

Saint Jack
NW. Playboy-Shoals Creek-Copa de Oro Picture. Exec prods, Hugh M Hefner, Edward L Rissien. Prod, Roger Corman. Dir, Peter Bogdanovich. Sp, Howard Sackler, Paul Theroux, Bogdanovich, based on novel by Theroux. Cam, Robby Muller; edtr, William Carruth; snd, Jean-Pierre Ruh; art dir, David Ng. (MPAA rating: R). 112.
Ben Gazzara, Denholm Elliott, James Villiers, Joss Ackland, Rodney Bewes, Mark Kingston, Lisa Lu, Monika Subramaniam, Judy Lim, George Lazenby, Peter Bogdanovich, Joseph Noel, Ong Kian Bee, Tan Yan Meng.
05/02/79

Sakada
(The Tenants)
(Philippines)
X. Sagisag Films (Oscar Miranda) prodn. Dir, Behn Cervantes. Sp, Oscar Miranda, based on his "Apoy Sa Langit"; cam, Edmund Cupcupin; edtr, Edgardo Vinarao; mus, Lucio D San Pedro. 102.
Robert Arevalo, Hilda Koronel, Pancho Magalona, Rafael Roco Jr, Gloria Romero, Rosa Rosal, Joseph Sytangco, Alicia Alonzo.
04/07/76

Salad-Days: SEE Zielone Lata

Salak Jitr
(Miss Salak Jitr)
(Thailand)
X. Kiattisak Film Prodns. Prod, Kanchana Metanee. Dir, Sombat Metanee. Story, Vuth Piyamatr; sp, Pan Kam; cam, Niyom Srisuphan; snd, Pong Asvinikul; mus, Piac; prodn mgr, Niyom Panpreecha. 110.
Sombat Metanee, Jarunee Suksawat, So Asanachinda, Supranee Jitiang, Marasri Nabangchang, Manop Assawathep.
06/13/79

Salangit Mesra
(Sky-High Love)
(Indonesia)
SAI. Prod-wri-dir, Turino Junaidy. Co-wri, Mutingo Busye; cam, Sutardjo; snd-light, Kemal; edtr, Alex Hassan; mus, Benjamin; prodn des, Winarto; asst dir, M Yusof. 110.
Benjamin, Amalia, Ade Irawan, Bambang Irawan, Bambang Siswando, Chandra Devi.
04/25/79

Sale Reveur
(Dirty Dreamer)
(France)
GAU. Les Prodns De La Gueville-FR3 prodn. Dir, Jean-Marie Perier. Sp, Pascal Jardin, Lucien Elia, Perier; cam (Eastmancolor), Yves Lafaye; edtr, Nicole Saulnier; mus, Jacques Dutronc. 90.
Jacques Dutronc, Lea Massari, Maurice Benichou, Greg Germain, Nathalie Perier, Jacques Dichamp.
04/05/78

Salsa
FAA. Jerry Masucci prodn. Dirs, Masucci, Leon Gast. Narr wri, Masucci, Gast; edtr, Jeff Cahn. (MPAA rating: G). 80.
Ray Barretto, Willie Colon, Larry Harlow, Johnny Pacheco, Roberta Roena, Bobby Valentin, Celia Cruz, Bobby Cruz, Jose "Cheo" Feliciano, Ricardo Ray, Mongo Santamaria, Billy Cobham, Manu Dibango, Geraldo Rivera.
(DOC)
04/07/76

Salto Nel Vuoto
(Leap Into the Void)
(France - Italy)
CNZ. Prods, Silvio and Annamaria Clementelli for Clesi Cinematografica (Rome) and M K 2 prodns (Paris). Dir, Marco Bellocchio. Sp, Bellocchio, Piero Natoli, Vincenzo Cerami; cam (Eastmancolor), Beppe Lanci; art dirs, Andrea Crisanti, Amedeo Fago; edtr, Roberto Perpignani; mus, Nicola Piovani. 120.
Michel Piccoli, Anouk Aimee, Michele Placido, Gisella Burinato.
03/26/80

Salut I Forca Al Canut
(Catalan Cuckold)
(Spain)
X. Prozesa prodn. Dir, Francesc Bellmunt. Sp, M Sanz, J Puigcorbe, F Bellmunt; cam (Eastmancolor), Tomas Pladevall; edtr, Anastasi Rinos; mus, Josep Maria Duran; sets, Francesc Candini; exec prod, J A Perez Giner. 94.
Juanjo Puigcorbe, Alicia Orozco, Isabel Mestres, Pepon Coromina, Joan Borras, Carme Molina, Anna Lizaran, Josep Maria Loperena.
(Versions in Catalan and Castilian)
02/27/80

Salvo D'Acquisto
(Italy)
CNZ. Dir, Romolo Guerrieri. Sp, Giussepi Berto, Mino Roli, Nino Ducci; cam (Technicolor), Aldo Giordani. 97.
Massimo Ranieri, Lina Polito, Enrico Maria Salerno, Massimo Serato.
07/28/76

Samba Da Criacao do Mundo
(Samba of the Creation of the World)
(Brazil)
X. Circofilm Beija-Flori Livio Bruni prodn. Dir, Vera Figueiredo. Snd edtr, Walter Goulart; snd and film technicians, Victor Rasposeiro, Jorge Saldanha, Mario de Silva, Antonio Cesar, Helio Vicente, Jose Sette, Didi Guper. 90.
(DOC)
02/21/79

Same Time, Next Year
U. Walter Mirisch-Robert Mulligan Prodn. Prods, Walter Mirisch, Morton Gottlieb. Dir, Robert Mulligan. Sp, Bernard Slade based on his play; cam, Robert Surtees; mus, Marvin Hamlisch; prodn des, Henry Bumstead; edtr, Sheldon Kahn; cos des, Theadora Van Runkle; set decor, Hal Guasman; snd, Gene Cantamesa; montage sequences, Charles Braverman, Ken Rudolph; make-up, William Tuttle; sfx, Tim Moran; asst dir, Donald Roberts. (MPAA rating: PG). 119.
Ellen Burstyn, Alan Alda, Ivan Bonar.
11/22/78

Sammy Stops The World
SPV. Ed Rood Sr prodn. Prod, Mark Travis, Del Jack. Exec prods, Saul Barnett, Hillard Elkins. Dir, Mel Shapiro. Book, mus and lyr by Leslie Bricusse, Anthony Newley; chor, Billy Wilson; cam (DeLuxe Color), David Myers; edtr, William H Yahraus; snd, Thomas W Morse; asso prod, Robert Becker; asst dir, Jonathan Haze; set des-cos, Santo Loquasto; light, Pat Collins. 105.
Sammy Davis Jr, Dennis Daniels, Donna Lowe, Marian Mercer.
(MUSICAL)
12/27/78

Samodivsko Horo
(Fairy Dance)
(Bulgaria)
X. Bulgarian Film prodn. Dir, Ivan Andonov. Sp, Georgi Michev; cam, Radoslav Spassov; mus, Simeon Pironkov. 90.
Pavel Popandov, Mariana Dimitrova, Peter Slabakov, Katia Choukova, Yordanka Kouzmanova, Leda Tasseva.
11/17/76

Samuel Fuller & The Big Red One
(Holland)
X. Prods, Thijs Ockersen, Tom Burghard. Dir-wri, Ockersen. Cam, Hans den Bezemer and Steve Posey; snd, Bert Steeman and Travor Black; edtr, Ot Louw; prodn in U S A, Paula Reiskin. Narrator, Aldo Ray. 72.
Samuel Fuller, Lee Marvin, Mark Hamill, Kelly Ward, Robert Carradine, Bobby Dicicco.
(DOC) (16m)
05/16/79

San Babila: 20 H.
(San Babila: 8P.M.)
(Italy)
X. Carlo Lizzani prodn. Dir, Lizzani. 100. Agostina Belli, plus nonprofessionals.
08/10/77

San Gottardo
(Switzerland)
FKZ. Filmkollectiv Zurich AG prodn. Dir, Villi Herman. Sp, Herman, Eve Martin; cam, Renato Berta, Hans Sturm; edtr, Elisabeth Waelchli, Rainer Trinkler. 90.
Hans-Dieter Zeidler, Maurice Aufari, Dimitri, Roger Jendly.
(16m)
08/31/77

Sandstone
HDS. Prod-dirs, Jonathan Dana, Bunny Peters Dana. Cam, Patrick Darrin, Robert Primes; edtr, Darrin with the Danas; mus, Dennis Dragon, Darryl Dragon; snd, Peter Pilafian, Richard Waddell. (MPAA rating: X). 75. (DOC)
02/23/77

Santa Esperanza
(USSR)
MSF. Dir, Sebastian Alarcon. Sp, Alarcon, Vladimir Amlinski; cam, Vadim Allissov; art dir, Irina Chreter; mus, Gabriel Casto, Ramiro Soriano, Adrian Chamorro. 94.
Borislav Brondoukov, Pavel Kadotchinikov, Evgueni Leonov-Gladychev.
10/29/80

Santi Veena
(Santi and Veena)
(Thailand)
HFT. Prod, Lek Kitiparaporn. Dir, San Pestonji. Sp, Maroot, Vijit Koonabut; cam-edtr, San Pestonji; art dir, Anan Avasri; cos, Kanokporn; mus, Seksan. 110.
Nart Bhavanai, Naiyana Chivanand, Sompop Benjatikul, Yod Konkit, Marasi Issarangkul Na Ayudhya, Punpan Rangkuan, Sathien Hamcharoen, Unruen, Pia Pestonji, Klochai Boonhitanon, Sawat Saengrabin.
12/29/76

Sao 5
(The Great Saturday)
(Thailand)
BGK. Prod-dir, Vinit Pakdivijit; Exec prod, Ulaiwan Pakdivijit. Story-sp, Dares; mus, Pramual Lab; cam, Santad Srisampan; edtr, Vinit Pakdivijit; light, Vichit Sangtavee. 110.
Krung Srivilai, Sorapong Chatri, Niroot Sirichanya, Singha Suriyong, Pairoj Jaising, Tasawan Seniwong, Duangchai Hataikan, Sasima Singsiri, Piyamatr Monyakul, Mayurachat Muenpasitiwet.
09/22/76

Sao Jomken
(The Tomboy)
(Thailand)
SUW. Prod, Kingh Tawinkeow. Wri-dir, Daeng Seni. Story, Naruemitr; cam, Jamrong Makanan; mus, Kong; snd, Manop Janjarasskul; title song, "Sao Jomken," mus-lyrs, Jonglak Chantana. 110.
Nawarat Yukthanan, Sorapong Chatri, Choomporn Tepitak, Sompop Banjatikul, Duantem Saritoon, Somboon Sukinai, Toh, Jirawat Chaluwijit, Poom Patanayoot, Tisukon Yukthanan, Kim Bangurah, Saner Comarachoon.
08/31/77

Sao Thang Tam
(The August Star)
(Viet Nam)
X. Vietnamese Film prodn, Hanoi. Dir, Tran Dac. Sp, Cong Vu, Tran Dac; cam, Do Manh Hung. 160.
Vu Trank Tu, Duc Hoan, Tran Phuong.
(B & W)
07/27/77

Saraba Eiga No Tomo Yo
(So Long, Movie Friend)
(Japan)
NIP. Kitty Films prodn. Prod, Hideto Isoda; wri-dir, Masato Harada; cam, Masakichi Hasegawa; edtr, Ko Suzuki; mus, Ryudo Uzaki; art dir, Yuji Maruyama; snd, Senichi Beniya.
Naohiko Shigeta, Takuzo Kawatani, Atsuko Asano, Renji Ishibashi, Hiromitsu Suzuki, Miyako Yamaguchi, Toby Kadoguchi, Yuji Kosugi.
11/07/79

Sartre Par Lui-Meme
(Sarte by Himself)
(France)
MK. INA prodn. Conceived-dir, Alexander Astruc, Michel Contat. Cam (Eastmancolor), Renato Perini. 190.
(DOC)
12/15/76

Sarvasakshi
(The Omniscient)
(India)
GIR. Wri-dir, Ramdas Phutane. Cam, Sharad Navle; mus, Bhaskar Chandawarkar. 135.
Smita Patil, Jayram Hardikar, Anjali Paigankar, Vijay Joshi.
(B & W)
02/20/80

Sasquatch
NA. John Fabian prodn. Exec prod, Ronald B Olson. Dir, Ed Ragozzini. Sp, Edward H Hawkins, based on story by Ronald B Olson; cam (DeLuxe), John Fabian, Bill Farmer; edtrs, Fabian, Farmer; snd, Steve Winitzky. (MPAA rating: G). 102.
George Lauris, Steve Boergadine, Jim Bradford, Ken Kenzle, William Emmons, Joe Morello.
01/18/78

Satansbraten
(Satan's Brew)
(W Germany)
FDA. Albatross Prodn prod, Trio-Film. Prod, Michael Fengler. Wri-dir, Rainer Werner Fassbinder. Cam, Michael Ballhaus; set des, Kurt Raab, Ulrike Bode; mus, Peer Raben; edtr, Thea Eymesz, Gabi Eichel. 100.
Kurt Raab, Helen Vita, Margit Carstensen, Volker Spengler, Ingrid Caven, Marquard Bohm, Ulli Lommel, Y Sa Lo, Katherina Buchhammer.
11/24/76

Saturday Night Fever
PAR. Prod, Robert Stigwood; exec prod, Kevin McCormick. Dir, John Badham. Sp, Norman Wexler, based on a story by Nik Cohn; cam (Movielab Color), Ralph D Bode; edtr, David Rawlins; mus, Barry, Robin and Maurice Gibb, David Shire; prodn des, Charles Bailey; set decor, George Detitta; snd, John K Wilkinson, Robert W Glass Jr, John T Reitz, Les Lazarowitz; cos-ward, Patrizia Von Brandenstein, Jennifer Nichols; asst dir, Allan Wertheim; stunt coord, Paul Nuckles. (MPAA rating: R).   119.
John Travolta, Karen Lynn Gorney, Barry Miller, Joseph Cali, Paul Pape, Bruce Ornstein, Donna Pescow, Val Bisoglio, Julie Bovasso, Martin Shaker, Nina Hansen, Lisa Peluso, Sam J Coppola, Denny Dillon, Bert Michaels, Donald Gantry, Monte Rock III.
12/14/77

Saturn 3
AFC. Presented by Lord Lew Grade and Elliott Kastner. Prod-dir, Stanley Donen. Exec prod, Martin Starger. Sp, Martin Amis, from story by John Barry; cam, Billy Williams; mus, Elmer Bernstein; edtr, Richard Marden; prodn des, Stuart Craig; art dir, Norman Dorme; sfx, Colin Chilvers; mus perf by Royal Philharmonic Orchestra with orchestrations by Christopher Palmer. (MPAA rating: R). 88.
Farrah Fawcett, Kirk Douglas, Harvey Keitel, Douglas Lambert, Ed Bishop, Christopher Muncke.
02/20/80

Sauve Qui Peut La Vie
(Everyone For Himself In Life)
(Switzerland - France)
MK. Sara Films-Sonimage-Saga-MK2 prodn. Dir, Jean-Luc Godard. Sp, Godard, Jean-Claude Carriere, Anne-Marie Mieville. Cam (Eastmancolor), Renato Berta, William Lubtchansky; mus, Gabriel Yared.   88.
Isabelle Huppert, Jacques Dutronc, Nathalie Baye.
05/28/80

Savage Breed: SEE Razza Selvaggia

The Savage Party: SEE La Fete Sauvage

The Savage State: SEE L'Etat Sauvage

Save the City: SEE Ocalic Miasto

The Saviour
(Hong Kong)
X. Pearl City Films prodn by Teddy Robin. Prod, Teddy Robin; dir, Ronny Yu; story, Ronny Yu; sp, Alfred Chow; cam, Tony Hope; mus, Teddy Robin.   87.
Pak Wing-Ying, Danny Ng, Gigi Wong, Nick Cox.
(Cantonese dialog with English sub-titles)
08/13/80

Savithri
(The Wife)
(India)
PHZ. Dir, T D Ranga. Sp, Ram Sha, Ranga; cam, Barun Mukherjee; edtr, J Stanley; mus, Gunasingh.   102.
H G Somashekara, Anil Thakker, Vasant Kumar, Ashwini.
02/13/80

Saxofone
(Italy)
CID. Irrigazione Cinematografica prodn. Dir, Renato Pozzetto. Prod, Achille Manzotti; sp, Enzo Jannacci, Renato Pozzetto, Cochi Ponzoni, Giuseppe Viola; cam (Eastmancolor), Roberto Seveso; edtr, Sergio Montanari; mus, Enzo Jannacci.   100.
Renato Pozzetto, Mariangelo Melato, Teo Teocoli, Cochi Ponzoni, Massimi Baldo, Felice Andreassi.
11/22/78

Sayat Nova
(USSR)
GOS. Armenian, Georgian, and Azerbaijan Prodn, Soviet Union. Dir, Sergei Paradjanov. 90.
06/21/78

Scandal: SEE Shuban

Scandalo
(Submission)
(Italy)
BRE. Silvio Clementelli prodn. Dir, Salvatore Samperi. Sp, Ottavio Jemma, Salvatore Samperi; cam (Technicolor), Vittorio Storaro; art dir, Ezio Altieri; edtr, Sergio Montanari; cos, Gitt Magrini; mus, Riz Ortolani. (MPAA rating: R).   107.
Lisa Gastoni, Franco Nero, Raymond Pellegrin, Andrea Ferreol, Claudia Marsani.
(Dubbed English soundtrack)
07/20/77

The Scar: SEE Blizna

The Scar: SEE Pae Kao

Scavenger Hunt
FOX. Melvin Simon prodn. Prod, Steven A Vail; co-prod, Paul Maslansky; exec prod, Simon. Dir, Michael Schultz; sp, Vail, Henry Harper from a story by Vail; adapt, John Thompson, Gerry Woolery; cam, Ken Lamkin; edtr, Christopher Holmes; art dir, Richard Berger; mus, Billy Goldenberg; set decor, Ed Baer; snd, Don Johnson; stunt coord, Jon Parker Ward; sfx, Phil Cory, Ray Svedin; asst dirs, Daniel J McCauley, Benjamin Rosenberg. (MPAA rating: PG).   116.
Richard Benjamin, James Coco, Scatman Crothers, Cloris Leachman, Cleavon Little, Roddy McDowall, Robert Morley, Richard Mulligan, Tony Randall, Dirk Benedict, Willie Aames, Stephanie Faracy, Richard Masur, Avery Schreiber, Stuart Pankin, Maureen Teefy, Hal Landon Jr, Vincent Price.
12/26/79

Scenes from the Class Struggle in Portugal
X. New York Cinema Company presentation. Prods, Barbara and David Stone. Dirs, Robert Kramer, Philip Spinelli.   89.
(DOC)
12/21/77

Scenes of Fire: SEE Brandstellen

The Scenic Route
X. Wri-dir-prod, Mark Rappaport. Cam, Fred Murphy; art dir, Lilly Kilvert; snd, Samantha Heilwell; edtr, Mark Rappaport.   76.
Randy Danson, Marilyn Jones, Kevin Wade.
06/07/78

The Scent Of Earth: SEE Miris Zemlje

Schatten Der Engel
(Shadows of Angels)
(Switzerland - W Germany)
ARZ. Albatros-Artcofilm prodn. Dir, Daniel Schmid. Sp, Schmid, Rainer Werner Fassbinder, based on Fassbinder play; cam (Eastmancolor), Renato Berta; edtr, Ila Von Hasperg.   105.
Ingrid Caven, Rainer Werner Fassbinder, Klaus Lowitsch, Annemarie Duringer, Adrian Hoven, Jean-Claude Dreyfus.
05/26/76

Schilten
(Sweden)
X. Beat Kuert and Barbara Risen Film Prodn, in co-prodn with the Film Kollektiv Zurich. Dir, Beat Kuert. Sp, Kuert, Michael Maassen, based on Hermann Burger's novel of the same name; cam, Hansueli Schenkel; mus, Cornelius Wernle.   90.
Michael Maassen, Gudrun Geir, Norbert Schwientek, Kaarina Schenk, Rudolf Ruf, Peter Schweiger, Ferdinand Mattmann.
02/27/80

Schizoid
CAN. Golan-Globus Prodn. Prods, Menahem Golan, Yoram Globus. Wri-dir, David Paulsen. Cam (TVC Color), Norman Leigh; mus, Craig Hundley; edtrs, Robert Fitzgerald, Dick Brummer; art dir, Kathy Curtis Cahill; snd, Kenard King; asso prod, Christopher Pearce; asst dir, Caren Singer. (MPAA rating: R). 91.
Klaus Kinski, Mariana Hill, Craig Wasson, Donna Wilkes, Richard Herd, Joe Regalbuto, Christopher Lloyd, Flo Gerrish, Kiva Lawrence, Claude Duvernoy, Cindy Dolan.
10/22/80

Schlager
(Hit Song)
(Israel)
X. AKA Films Prodn. Prod, Yaakov Kozky. Wri-dir, Assaf Dayan. Cam, Danny Schneur; edtr, Tal Shuval; sets, Yaron Turel; mus, Zvika Pik; lyr, Assaf Dayan.   94.
HaGashash HaHiver, Shayke Levi, Ofra Haza, Shula Revach, Menahem Zilberman.
07/11/79

Schluchtenflitzer
(Whizzer)
(W Germany)
CIG. Monika Neuchtern Film Prodn, Munich. Wri-dir, Ruediger Neuchtern. Cam, Juergen Juerges; mus, Joerg Evers; edtr, Manja Rock; snd, Kurt Huettl. 112.
Hans Kollmannsberger, Hans Brenner, Ruth Drexel, Eva Mattes, Renard Hatzke, Verena Disch, Anette Juenger, Rudolf Plommer, Anton Teintinger, Peter Scharrer.
05/23/79

Schneegloeckchen Bluehn In September
(Snowdrops Bloom in September)
(W Germany)
X. Basis-Film prodn, Berlin. Dir, Christian Ziewer. Sp, Ziewer, Klaus Wiese; cam, Kurt Weber; snd, Hayo von Zuendt; edtr, Stephanie Wilke; mus and song-texts, Lokomotive Kreuzberg. 108.
Claus Eberth, Wolfgang Liere.
07/07/76

Schoolmaster Hofer: SEE
Hauptlehrer Hofer

Schwarz Und Weiss Wie Tage Und Naechte
(Black and White Like Days and Nights)
(W Germany)
X. Monaco-Film and Radiant-Film co-prodn with ORF and WDR, Cologne. Georg Althammer, prod; Gunther Witte, WDT-TV prod. Dir, Wolfgang Petersen. Sp, Karl-Heinz Willschrei, Jochen Wedegaertner, Petersen; cam, Joerg-Michael Baldenius; art dir, O Jochen Schmidt; mus, Klaus Doldinger; edtr, Johannes Nickel; prodn mgr, Michael Bittins. 103.
Bruno Ganz, Gila von Weitershauen, Rene Deltgen, Ljubo Tadic, Joachim Wichmann, Annemarie Wendl, Alexis von Hagemeister, Alexander Hegarth, Gudrun Vaupel, Markus Helis, Elke Schuessler, Eberhard Stanjek.
09/20/78

Schwestern, Oder Die Balance Des Gluecks
(Sisters, or The Balance of Happiness)
(W Germany)
FDA. Bioskop Film Production, Munich. Prod Eberhard Junkersdorff, in collab with Westdeutscher Rundfunk (WDR), Cologne, Gunther Witte, tv-edtr-in-chief. Dir, Margarete von Trotta. Sp, Trotta, with additions by Luisa Francia, Martje Grohmann, Jutta Lampe; cam, Franz Fath; edtr, Annette Dorn; snd, Vladimir Vizner, Stanislav Litera; mus, Konstantin Wecker; sets, Winfried Hennig; cos, Ingrid Zore; light, Jockel Stellmacher; asst dir, Helenka Hummel. 92.
Jutta Lampe, Gudrun Gabriel, Jessica Frueh, Konstantin Wecker, Rainer Delventhal, Agnes Fink, Heinz Bennent, Fritz Lichtenhahn, Guenther Schuetz, Ilse Bahrs, Barbara Sauerbaum, Marie-Helene Diekmann, Liselotte Arnold, Editha Horn,
Ellen Esser, Heinrich Marmann, Edith Garten, Kathie Thomsen, Volker Schwab, Dionysos Kawathas.
10/10/79

Scorchy
AIP. Hickmar Prods film. Prod-wri-dir, Hikmet Avedis. Exec prod, Marlene Schmidt. Cam (Alpha Cine Color), Laszlo Pal; edtr, Michael Luciano; mus, Igo Kantor; snd, Kenneth Hansen; asst dir, Bruce Wilson. (MPAA rating: R). 99.
Connie Stevens, Cesare Danova, William Smith, Normann Burton, John David Chandler, Joyce Jameson, Greg Evigan, Nick Dimitri, Nate Long, Ingrid Cedergren, Ellen Thurston, Ray Sebastian, Mike Esky, Gene White, Marlene Schmidt.
10/06/76

Scorpion Woods: SEE
Alakdang Gubat

Scott Joplin
U. Motown prodn; prod, Stan Hough; exec prod, Rob Cohen. Dir, Jeremy Paul Kagan. Sp, Christopher Knopf; cam (Technicolor), David M Walsh; edtr, Patrick Kennedy; mus, Scott Joplin, arranged and performed by Richard Hyman, also "Hang Over Blues" by Harold Johnson; art dir, William H Hiney; set decor, James W Payne; cos, Bernard Johnson; snd, David Ronne, Robert L Hoyt; asst dir, Jon C Andersen. (MPAA rating: PG). 96.
Billy Dee Williams, Clifton Davis, Margaret Avery, Eubie Blake, Godfrey Cambridge, Seymour Cassel, DeWayne Jessie, Mabel King, Taj Mahal, Spo-De-Odee, Art Carney, David Healy, Samuel Fuller, Leon Charles, Fred Pinkard, Delos W Smith Jr, Marcus Grapes, Denise Gordy, Rita Ross, The Commodores, David Hubbard.
02/09/77

The Scrambled Eggs: SEE
Les Oeufs Brouilles

Screams Of A Winter Night
DIM. Full Moon prodn. Prods, Richard H Wadsack, James L Wilson. Dir, James L Wilson. Exec prod, S Mark Lovell. Sp, Richard H Wadsack; cam (PSI Color), Robert E Rogers; edtrs, Gary Ganote, Craig Mayes; mus, Don Zimmers; set - cos des, Mar'Sue Wilson. (MPAA rating: PG). 91.
Matt Borel, Gil Glascow, Patrick Byers, Mary Agen Cox, Robin Bradley, Ray Gaspard, Beverly Allen, Brandy Barrett, Charles Rucker, Jan Norton.
10/03/79

Screen Tests: SEE Zdjecia
Probne

Scrounged Meals: SEE
Gefundenes Fressen

Scum
(Britain)
X. Boyd's Co prodn. Exec prods, Don Boyd, Michael Relph. Prods Davina Belling, Clive Parsons. Dir, Alan Clarke. Sp, Roy Minton; cam, Phil Meheux; edtr, Mike Bradsell; snd, David John; art dir, Mike Porter; asso prod, Martin Campbell; asst dir, Raymond Day. 96.
Ray Winstone, Mick Ford, John Judd, Phil Daniels, John Blundell, Ray Burdis, Julian Firth, Alrick Riley, John Fowler, Nigel Humphreys, Philip Jackson, Peter Howell, Jo Kendall, John Grillo, Alan Igpon.
08/15/79

Se Llamaba S N
(The Name Was S N)
(Venezuela)
X. Tiuna Films prodn. Prod, Roberto Bataille. Dir-wir, Luis Correa; based on novel by Jose Vicente Abreu; cam (Eastmancolor), Mariano Volpi; edtr, Alejandro Sandeman. 85.
Asdrubal Melendez, Jose Torres, Maria Gracia Bianchi, Pedro Marthan and Ricardo Blanco.
09/28/77

The Sea Gull: SEE *Il Gabbiano*

The Sea Gypsies
WB. Raffill prodn; prod, Joseph C Raffill; exec prod, Peter R Simpson. Sp-dir, Stewart Raffill. Cam (CFI Color), Thomas McHugh; edtrs, Dan Greer, R Hansel Brown, Art Stafford; mus, Fred Steiner; asso prod-2d unit dir, Gerard Alcan; prodn supv-asst dir, Hal Schwartz; animal supv, Hubert Wells; animal trainers, Wells, Lloyd Beebe, Cheryl Shawver, George Toth, Gwen Johnson, Marinho Correia, Mickey Bailey, Helena Walsh, Sonny Allen; snd, Craig Felburg. (MPAA rating: G). 101.
Robert Logan, Mikki Jamison-Olsen, Heather Rattray, Cjon Damitri Patterson, Shannon Saylor.
04/05/78

Sea of Roses: SEE Mar De
Rosas

The Sea Wolves
(Britain)
UA. Lorimar presentation. Prod, Euan Lloyd. Dir, Andrew V McLaglen. Exec prod, Chris Chrisafis; sp, Reginald Rose (based on James Leasor's novel "The Boarding Party"); cam, Tony Imi; edtr, John Glen; mus, Roy Budd; prodn des, Syd Cain; art dir, Maurice Cain; asso prod, Harold Buck; asst dir, Bert Batt. (MPAA rating: PG). 120.
Gregory Peck, Roger Moore, David Niven, Trevor Howard, Barbara Kellermann, Patrick MacNee, Patrick Allen, Bernard Archard, Martin Benson, Faith Brook, Allan Cuthbertson, Kenneth Griffith, Donald Houston, Glyn Houston, Percy Herbert, Patrick Holt, Wolf Kahler, Terence Longdon, Michael Medwin, John Standing, Graham Stark, Jack Watson, Moray Watson, Brook Williams, Mark Zuber, George Mikell, Morgan Sheppard, Edward Dentith, Clifford Earl, Robert Hoffmann, Dan Van Husen.
07/09/80

Seabo
X. Prod, Earl Owensby. Dir-edtr, Jimmy Huston. Sp, Tom McIntyre; cam, Darrell Cathcart; mus, David Allan Coe, Clay Smith, Arthur Smith. 88.
Earl Owensby, David Alan Coe, Don Barry, Ed Parker, Leonard Dixon, Sunset Carson, Holly Conover, Rod Sachanrnoski, Ron Lampkin.
12/07/77

The Sealed Soil
(Iran)
X. Nabili Films prodn. Prod-dir-sp-edtr, Marva Nabili. Cam (16m), Barbod Taheri. 90.
Flora Shabaviz and the villagers of Noo-Asquar Village.
(16m)
05/10/78

Search: SEE Iskanja

The Search for Solutions
X. Playback Associates prodn. Prod, James C Crimmins. Dir, Michael Jackson; co-prods, Jackson, Kathy Mendoza; nar, Stacy Keach; cam, Mike Jackson; edtrs, Ken Werner, Kris Liem, Kathryn Barnier, Arnold Briedman; sp, Jim Crimmins, Brad Darrach, L L Larison Cudmore, Gerald Jonas; mus, Pat Metheny, Lyle Mayers; perf, Janet Forman, Ken Werner. 180. (DOC)
12/19/79

Sebastian
(Britain)
DSC. Megalovision (Howard Malin, James Whaley) prodn. Wri-dirs, Paul Humfress, Derek Jarman. Cam (Eastmancolor), Peter Middleton; edtr, Humfress; mus, Brian Eno, Andrew Wilson. 85.
Leonardo Treviglio, Barney James, Neil Kennedy, Richard Warwick, Donald Dunham, Ken Hicks.
(In Latin with English subtitles)
08/25/76

Seclusion Near a Forest: SEE Na Samote U Lesa

The Second Awakening of Krista Klages: SEE Das Zweite Erwachen Der Christa Klages

The Second Power: SEE El Segundo Poder

The Second Shift: SEE Det Andre Skiftet

Second Wind
(Canada)
AMB. Olympic Films Inc prodn. Prod, James Margellos; exec prod, Les Weinstein. Dir, Donald Shebib. Sp, Hal Ackerman; cam, Reginald Morris; edtr, Shebib; mus, Hagood Hardy; snd, Russel Heise; asst dirs, John Eckert, Michael Zenon. 92.
James Naughton, Lindsay Wagner, Kenneth Pogue, Tedde Moore, Tom Harvey, Louis Del Grande, Gerard Parkes, Jonathan Welsh, Cec Linder, Alan Levson.
04/14/76

Second-Hand Girl: SEE Ein Maedchen Aus Zweiter Hand

Second-Hand Hearts
LOR. Caribou prodn of a Northstar International picture. Prod, James William Guercio; dir, Hal Ashby; sp, Charles Eastman; cam (Technicolor), Haskell Wexler; edtr, Amy Holden Jones; mus, Willis Alan Ramsey; art dir, Richard Carter; prodn des, Peter Wooley; asst dir, David Hamburger; asso prod-unit prod mgr, Charles Mulvchill. (MPAA rating: PG). 98.
Robert Blake, Barbara Harris, Sondra Blake, Bert Remsen, Shirley Stoler, Collin Boone, Amber Rose Gold.
09/10/80

The Secret
(Hong Kong)
X. Unique Films Prodn. Dir, Ann Hui; prod, Lo K M, S Y Wu; sp, Joyce Chan; cam, C M Chung; edtr, C F Yu; mus comp, Violet Lam. 100.
Sylvia Chiang, Chiu Ah Chi, Tsui Siu Keung, Man Chi Leung, Li Hai Suk.
(Cantonese soundtrack; English subtitles)
11/07/79

The Secret Life of Plants
PAR. Infinite Enterprises Film. Exec prods, Burt Kleiner, Paul Kantor. Prod, Michael Braun. Dir, Walon Green. Sp, Peter Tompkins, Green, Braun, based on the book "The Secret Life Of Plants" by Tompkins and Christopher Bird; cam (Metrocolor), Bob Bailin, Ghislain Cloquet, Mike Hoover, Ed Janss, Robin Lehman, Ian Masters, David Myers, Daniel Pearl, Robert Primes, Peter Smolker, Louis Schwartzberg; natural history cinematography, Ken Middleham; mus, Stevie Wonder; edtrs, Christopher Lebenzon, Robert Lambert, Masters; snd (Dolby), Jeff Wexler, Michael Vionnet, Jan Ross, David Ronnee, Bob Leighton, Larry Johnson; art dir, John Told; cos, Jeanne Blackburn, Barbara Whitaker; narr, Tompkins, Elizabeth Vreeland, Ruby Crystal. (MPAA rating: G). 98. (DOC)
12/13/78

The Secret of Nikola Tesla: SEE Tajna Nikole Tesle

The Secret Policeman's Ball
(Britain)
X. Document Films prodn for Amnesty International. Prods, Roger Graef, Thomas Schwalm. Dir, Roger Graef. Documentary of a live show presented in aid of Amnesty International; dir, John Cleese; cam, Ernest Vincze, Clive Tickner, Pascoe MacFarlane; edtr, Thomas Schwalm; snd, Judy Freeman, Simon Hayter. 91.
John Cleese, Peter Cook, Clive James, Eleanor Bron, Pete Townshend, Rowan Atkinson, Michael Palin, Beetles and Buckman, John Williams, Ken Campbell, Sylvester McCoy, Billy Connolly, Terry Jones, Tom Robinson.
(DOC)
12/05/79

The Secret Rivals
(Hong Kong)
X. Seasonal Films Corp prodn, prod, Ng See-yuen. Dir, Ng See-yuen. Sp, Tung Lu, Ng See-yuen; cam, Chang Chee; mus, Chow Fu-liang; martial arts, Li Ming-wen, Chang Chuan. 90.
Liu Chung-liang, Wang Tao.
07/07/76

Secrets
LOS. Prod, John Hanson. Dir, Philip Saville. Sp, Rosemary Davies from a story by Saville; cam, Nic Knowland, Harry Hart; edtr, Tony Woollard; mus, Mike Gibbs. (MPAA rating: R). 92.
Jacqueline Bisset, Per Oscarsson, Shirley Knight Hopkins, Robert Powell, Tarka Kings, Martin C Thurley, Stephen Martin.
11/01/78

The Seduction of Joe Tynan
U. Martin Bregman prodn. Prod, Bregman. Exec prod, Louis A Stroller. Dir, Jerry Schatzberg. Sp, Alan Alda; cam, Adam Holender; edtr, Evan Lottman; art dir, David Chapman; set decor, Alan Hicks; mus, Bill Conti; snd, Jim Sabat; asst dir, Ralph Singleton. (MPAA rating: R). 107.
Alan Alda, Barbara Harris, Meryl Streep, Rip Torn, Melvyn Douglas, Charles Kimbrough, Blanche Baker, Adam Ross, Carrie Nye, Chris Arnold, Maurice Copeland, Robert Christian.
08/15/79

See You In The Next War: SEE Nasvidenje V. Naslednji Vojni

Seems Like Old Times
COL. Ray Stark Prodn. Prod, Ray Stark. Dir, Jay Sandrich. Exec prod, Roger M Rothstein. Sp, Neil Simon; cam (Metrocolor), David M Walsh; edtr, Michael A Stevenson; prodn des, Gene Calahan; mus, Marvin Hamlisch; art dir, Pete Smith; set decor, Lee Poll; cos, Betsy Cox; asst dir, Jack Aldworth. (MPAA rating: PG). 102.
Goldie Hawn, Chevy Chase, Charles Grodin, Robert Guillaume, Harold Gould, George Grizzard, Yvonne Wilder, T K Carter, Judd Omen, Marc Alaimo.
11/26/80

Seetha Kalyanam
(Sita's Wedding)
(India)
X. Chitrakalpana Films Prodn of Ananda Lakshmi Art Movies. Prod, P Ananda Rao. Dir, Bapu. Sp, Mullapudi Venkata Ramana; cam, K S Prasad; sfx, Ravee Nagaich; mus, K V Mahadevan; songs, Arudra, C Narayana Reddy; art dir, K Nageswara Rao. 110.
Ravi Kumar, Jaya Prada, Satyanarayana, Gummadi, Jamuna, Mukkamala.
11/29/78

Sein Kampf
(His Fight)
(W Germany)
X. Lothar Lambert and Wolfram Zobus prodn, Berlin. Wri-dirs, Lambert and Zobus. Cam, Zobus; edtr, Helga Schnurre. 85.
Lothar Lambert, Christine Oberlander, Tilman Hemp, Gabriele Reuleaux,

Dietmar Kracht, Dean Zoghby.
(B & W) (16m)
01/19/77

Seisheun No Satsujinsha
(The Youth Killer)
(Japan)
ATG. Imamura Prodns, Soeisha, prodn. Dir, Kazuhiko Hasegawa. Sp, Tsutomu Tamura; story, Kenji Nakagami; cam (Eastmancolor), Tatsuo Suzuki; edtr, Sachiko Yamaji; mus, Godaigo. 110.
Yutaka Mizutani, Mioko Barada, Ryohei Uchida, Etsuko Ichihara.
05/18/77

Seitensprung
(Escapade)
(E Germany)
DEE. DEFA Film Prodns, Group Babelsberg, East Berlin. Dir, Evelyn Schmidt. Sp, Regina Weicker, Schmidt; cam, Juergen Kruse; sets, Georg Wratsch; mus, Peter Rabenalt; edtr, Helga Emmrich. 89.
Renate Geissler, Uwe Zerbe, Annette Voss, Tobias Zander, Renate Reinicke, Karin Beewers, Ursula Braun, Angela Brunner, Johanna Clas.
03/05/80

Seitseman Valjesta
(Seven Brothers)
(Finland)
X. Nelimarkka/Seeck prodn. Prod-dirs, Riitta Nelimarkka, Jaakko Seeck. Sp-adapt, Nelimarkka from novel by Aleksis Kivi; cam (Eastmancolor), Seeck; edtrs, Kaija Ahopelto, Pipsa Valavaara; mus, Pekka Jalkanen; watercolor backgrounds, Nelimarkka; cut-out ani, Seeck; snd mix, Pauli Vellnonen; voice dir, Kari Franck; narr, Esko Salminen. 80. (ANI)
11/19/80

The Sell Out
(Britain)
VDI. Hemdale prodn, prod, Josef Shaftel. Dir, Peter Collinson. Sp, Murray Smith, Judson Kinberg, based on a story by Smith; cam, Arthur Ibbetson; mus, Mick Green, Colin Frichter. (MPAA rating: PG). 88.
Richard Widmark, Oliver Reed, Gayle Hunnicut, Sam Wanamaker, Vladek Sheybal, Ori Levy, Assaf Dayan, Shmuel Rodensky, Peter Frye.
05/26/76

Selvi Boylum Al Yazmalim
(The Girl With The Red Scarf)
(Turkey)
X. Yesilcam Filmcilik Prodn, Istanbul. Dir, Atif Yilmaz. Sp, Ali Habib Ozgenturk, based on book by Gengiz Aytmatov; cam, Cetin Tunca; mus, Cahit Berkay. 90.
Turkan Soray, Kadir Inanir, Ahmet Mekin, Hulya Tuglu.
08/02/78

The Semester We Loved Kim Novak: SEE El Curso En Que Amamos A Kim Novak

Semi-Tough
UA. Prod, David Merrick. Dir, Michael Ritchie. Sp, Walter Bernstein, based on the novel by Dan Jenkins; cam (DeLuxe Color), Charles Rosher Jr; edtr, Richard A Harris; mus, Jerry Fielding; prodn des, Walter Scott Herndon; set decor, Cheryal Kearney; snd, Richard Portman, Barry Thomas; cos-ward, Theoni V Aldredge, Richard Bruno, Norman Salling, Darryl Levine; asst dir, Ken Swor; stunt coord, Hal Needham. (MPAA rating: R). 107.
Burt Reynolds, Kris Kristofferson, Jill Clayburgh, Robert Preston, Bert Convy, Roger E Mosley, Lotte Lenya, Richard Masur, Carl Weathers, Brian Dennehy, Mary Jo Catlett.
11/09/77

Semmelweis
(Italy - Switzerland)
X. RAI-Television Channel 1 (Italy) and RTSI-Television (Switzerland) film. Prods, Gaspare Palumbo, Giuseppe Tortorella for Milano Cinema prodns. Dir, Gianfranco Bettettini. Sp, Bettettini, Aldo Grasso; cam, Lamberto Caimi; art dir, Paolo Bregni; edtrs, Gaspare Palumbo, Jolanda Adamo; mus, Gino Negri. 100.
Giulio Brogi, Alain Cuny, Pier Paolo Capponi, Tino Carraro, Umberto Ceriani.
10/15/80

Sengoku Yaro
(Warring Clans)
(Japan)
TOH. Dir, Kihachi Okamoto. Sp, Takeshi Sano, Kihachi Okamoto, Shinichi Sekizawa; cam (b&w), Uzuru Aizawa; mus, Masaru Sato. 97.
Yuzo Kayama, Ichiro Nakatani, Makoto Sato, Yuriko Hoshi.
12/03/80

The Sensitive Lion: SEE Sing Sam Oy

Sentados Al Borde De La Manana Con Los Pies Colgando
(Sitting on the Edge of Tomorrow with the Feet Hanging)
(Spain)
X. Incine-Impala S A-Ofelia S A prodn. Prod, Carlos Escobedo. Dir, Antonio Jose Betancor. Sp, Javier Moro; mus, Carlos Vizziello; sets, Christian Boyer; edtr, Eduardo Biurrun; cam (Eastmancolor), Hans Burman. 98.
Miguel Bose, Beatriz Elorrieta, Bettina Bose, Esther Farre, Concha Gregori, Josema Yuste, Fernando Conde, Millan Salcedo, Quique Sanfrancisco, Saturno Cerra, Fernando Colomo, Luis Ciges, Alberto de Mendoza, Carlos Otero, Fojo, Eva Lesmes, Manuel Ayuso, Francisco Betancor.
02/07/79

Sentence of Death: SEE Wyrok Smierci

Sentimentalnyi Roman
(A Sentimental Story)
(USSR)
X. Lenfilm prodn, Leningrad. Wri-dir, Igor Maslennikov, based on novel by Vera Panova. Cam, D Meshi; mus, Victor Dareshevich. 90.
Elena Proklova, Elena Koreneva, Nikolai Denisov, Stanislav Lubshin, Ludmila Gurchenko.
01/12/77

The Sentinel
U. Wri-prod (with Jeffrey Konvitz)-dir, Michael Winner. Based on the novel by Konvitz; cam (Technicolor), Dick Kratina; special visual effects, Albert Whitlock; edtrs, Bernard Gribble, Terence Rawlings; mus, Gil Melle; prodn des, Philip Rosenberg; set decor, Ed Stewart; snd, Hugh Train, Les Lazarowitz; cos-ward, Peggy Farrell; asst dir, Charles Okun. (MPAA rating: R). 91.
Chris Sarandon, Cristina Raines, Martin Balsam, John Carradine, Jose Ferrer, Ava Gardner, Arthur Kennedy, Burgess Meredith, Sylvia Miles, Deborah Raffin, Eli Wallach, Christopher Walken, Jerry Orbach, Beverly D'Angelo, Hank Garrett, Robert Gerringer, Nana Tucker, Tom Berenger, William Hickey, Gary Allen, Tresa Hughes, Kate Harrington, Jane Hoffman, Elaine Shore, Sam Gray, Reid Shelton, Fred Stuthman, Lucie Lancaster, Anthony Holland, Jeff Goldblum, Zane Lasky, Mady Heflin, Diane Stilwell, Ron McLarty.
02/16/77

September Love: SEE Rak Kam Lok

Septemberweizen
(September Wheat)
(W Germany)
X. Teldok Film, Freiburg, prodn in collab ZDF (Second Channel), Mainz; wri-dir-edtr, Peter Krieg; asst dir-snd, Heidi Knott; mus, Rolf Riehm. 90.
(DOC) (16m)
08/06/80

Serail
(France)
FCO. Filmoblic - Openfilm prodn. Dir, Eduardo De Gregorio. Sp, Michael Graham, De Gregorio; cam (Eastmancolor-Panavision), Ricardo Aronovitch; edtr, Alberto Yaccelini; mus, Michel Portal. 90.
Leslie Caron, Bulle Ogier, Marie-France Pisier, Corin Redgrave.
05/26/76

Serenata A La Luz De La Luna
(Moonlight Serenade)
(Spain)
X. Imatge Comunicacions, Producciones Cinematograficas Teide film. Dirs, Josep A. Salgot Carles Jover. Sp, Jover, Salgot, Albert Cruells, Jaume Sorribas; cam (Eastmancolor), Pedro Aznar; mus, Joan Pineda, Albert Moraleda; edtr, Emilio Rodriguez; exec prod, Josep Maria Forn. 81.
Jaume Sorribas, Isabel Mestres, Rosa Morata, Hector Alterio, Felix Rotaeta, Pep Corominas,

Carlota Marquina, Rosete Espinet, Carme Contreras, Fatima Sangareau.
09/12/79

Sgt Buntung: SEE Sib Tamruat Toh Buntung

Sgt Pepper's Lonely Hearts Club Band
U. Prod, Robert Stigwood; exec prod, Dee Anthony. Dir, Michael Schultz. Sp, Henry Edwards; cam (Technicolor), Owen Roizman; edtr, Christopher Holmes; mus, John Lennon, Paul McCartney, George Harrison; prodn des, Brian Eatwell; set decor, Marvin March; snd, Arthur Piantadosi, Les Fresholtz, Michael Minkler, Charles M Wilborn; cos-ward, May Routh, Jennifer Parsons, Anthony Faso; asst dir, L Andrew Stone. (MPAA rating: PG). 111.
Peter Frampton, Barry Gibb, Robin Gibb, Maurice Gibb, Frankie Howerd, Paul Nicholas, Donald Pleasence, Sandy Farina, Dianne Seinberg, Steve Martin, Aerosmith, Alice Cooper, Billy Preston, Stargard, Earth Wind & Fire, George Burns.
07/19/78

Sergeant Steiner: SEE Breakthrough

Serial
PAR. Sidney Beckerman Prodn. Prod, Sidney Beckerman. Dir, Bill Persky. Sp, Rich Eustis, Michael Elias, based on the novel by Cyra McFadden; Cam (Movielab Color), Rexford Metz; edtr, John W Wheeler; snd, Jack Solomon; art dir, Bill Sandell; set decors, Bob Gould, Paul Dal Porto; mus, Lalo Schifrin; asst dir, Jerry Sobul. (MPAA rating: R). 91.
Martin Mull, Tuesday Weld, Jennifer McAlister, Sam Chew Jr, Sally Kellerman, Anthony Battaglia, Nita Talbot, Bill Macy, Pamela Bellwood, Barbara Rhoades, Ann Weldon, Peter Bonerz, Jon Fong, Christopher Lee, Patch Mackenzie, Stacey Helkin, Tom Smothers, Clark Brandon, Clyde Ventura.
03/26/80

Serie Noire
(Thriller Story)
(France)
GAU. Gaumont-Prospectacle co-prodn. Prod, Maurice Bernart. Dir, Alain Corneau. Sp, Corneau, Georges Perec, based on the novel "A Hell Of A Woman," by Jim Thompson; cam, (Fujicolor, Panavision), Pierre-William Glenn; edtr, Thierry Derocles; snd, Michel Desrois. 110.
Patrick Dewaere, Myriam Boyer, Marie Trintignant, Bernard Blier, Andreas Katsulas.
05/02/79

The Serious Game: SEE Den allvarsamme Leken

The Serpent's Egg
(Germany - USA)
UA. Rialto Film (Berlin)-Dino de Laurentiis Corp (Los Angeles) prodn. Orig story-sp-dir, Ingmar Bergman. Cam (Eastmancolor), Sven Nykvist; prodn des, Rolf Zehetbauer; cos, Charlotte Flemming; mus, Rolf Wilhelm; exec prod, Horst Wendtlandt; edtr, Petra von Oelffen. 120.
Liv Ullmann, David Carradine, Gert Frobe, Heinz Bennent, James Whitmore.
11/02/77

Servante Et Maitresse
(Servant and Mistress)
(France)
FCM. Madeleine Films (Gilbert De Goldschmidt), SFP-Shanrila Prodns prodn. Dir, Bruno Gantillon. Sp, Dominique Fabre, Frantz-Andre Burguet; cam (Eastmancolor), Etienne Szabo; edtr, Georges Klotz; mus, Jean-Marie Benjamin. 90.
Victor Lanoux, Andrea Ferreol, Evelyne Buyle, Gabriel Cattand, David Pontremoli, Jean Rougerie.
02/23/77

The Servants
(Hong Kong)
BNG. Prod, Jimmy Ip. Dirs, Ronny Yu, Philip Chan. Cam, Henry Chan; edtr, Wong Yee Shun; mus, Joseph Koo; lyr, James Wong; sp, Joyce Chan, Philip Chan, William Ho, Ronny Yu. 90.
Chu Kong, Hu Terry (Hu Yan Mou), Chan Wai Man, Philip Chan, Melvin Wong, Lam Wai Kei.
(English subtitles)
08/01/79

The Servants of the Good Lord: SEE Les Servantes du Bon Dieu

Servus Bayern!
(Bye-Bye Bavaria)
(W Germany)
FDA. Herbert Achternbusch Prodn Buchendorf. Wri-dir, Herbert Achternbusch. Cam (Eastmancolor), Joerg Schmidt-Reitwein; snd, Peter van Anft; edtr, Cristl Layrer; prodn mgr, Walter Saxer. 84.
Annamiri Bierbichler, Herbert Achternbusch, Sepp Bierbichler, Heinz Braun, Barbara Gass, Karolina Herbig, Gunter Freyse, Gerda Achternbusch.
06/28/78

Sesuatau Yang Indah
(Something Beautiful)
(Indonesia)
IAA. Prods, Wim Umboh, R M Hudiono. Dir, edtr, W Umboh. Sp, Arifin C Noer; cam, Lukmanhakim Nain; mus, Idris Sardi; snd, Suparman Sidik; art dir, Paula Roemokoy. 95.
Roy Marten, Christine Hakim, Fadly, Marini.
12/14/77

Sette Note in Mero
(The Psychic)
(Italy)
G 1. Brandon Chase presentation. Prod, Cinecompany. Dir, Lucio Fulci. Cam (Deluxe Color), Sergio Salvati. (MPAA rating: R). 89.
Jennifer O'Neill, Gabriele Ferzetti, Marc Porel, Gianni Garko, Evelyn Stewart, Jenny Tamburi, Fabrizio Jovine, Riccardo Parisio Perrotti, Vito Passeri, Luigi Diberti.
(Dubbed English Soundtrack)
05/16/79

Seven
AIP. Melvin Simon prodn. Prod-dir, Andy Sidaris. Exec prod, Melvin Simon. Sp, William Driskill, Robert Baird, from a story by Sidaris; set des, Sal Grasso; sfx, Joe Lombardi. (MPAA rating: R). 100.
William Smith, Barbara Leigh, Guich Koock, Art Metrano, Martin Kove, Richard Le Pore, Christopher Joy, Susan Kiger, Robert Relyea, Little Egypt, Lenny Montana, Reggie Nalder.
10/03/79

Seven Beauties: SEE Pasqualino Settebelleze

Seven Brothers: SEE Seitseman Valjesta

7 Dias de Enero
(7 Days in January)
(Spain)
X. Goya Films and Les Films des Deux Mondes prodn. Dir, Juan Antonio Bardem. Exec prod, Serafin Garcia Trueba. Sp, Bardem, Gregorio Moron; cam (Eastmancolor), Leopoldo Villasenor; mus, Nicolas Peyrac; edtr, Guillermo Maldonado; sets, Antonio de Miguel. 130.
Manuel Egea Martinez, Fernando Sanchez Pollack, Virginia Gonzalez Mataix, Madeleine Robinson, Jack Francois, Alberto Alonso Lopez.
05/02/79

Seven Freckles: SEE Sieben Sommerprossen

Seven Men At Daybreak: SEE Operation Daybreak

Seven Nights in Japan
(Britain - France)
EMI. EMI-Paramount prodn. Prod-dir, Lewis Gilbert. Sp, Christopher Wood; cam (Technicolor) Henri Decae; edtr, John Glen; prodn des, John Stoll; mus, David Hentschel; snd, Daniel Brisseau; asst dir, Brian Cook. 104.
Michael York, Hidemi Aoki, Charles Gray, Ann Lonnberg, Eleonore Hirt, James Villiers, Yolande Donlan, Peter Jones, Lionel Murton.
09/22/76

Seven Per-Cent Solution
(Britain)
U. Prod-dir, Herbert Ross. Exec prods, Arlene Sellers, Alex Winitsky. Sp, Nicholas Meyer, based on his novel; cam (Technicolor), Oswald Morris; 2d unit cam, Alex Thomson; edtrs, William Reynolds, Chris Barnes; mus, John Addison; song, Stephen Sondheim; prodn des, Ken Adam; art dir, Peter Lamont; set decor, Peter James; snd, Gordon McCallum, Cyril Swern; asst dir, Scott Wodehouse; 2d unit dir, Howard Jeffrey. (MPAA rating: PG). 113.
Alan Arkin, Vanessa Redgrave, Robert Duvall, Nicol Williamson, Laurence Olivier, Joel Gray, Samantha Eggar, Charles Gray, Jeremy Kemp, Georgia Brown, Regine.
10/06/76

Seven-Man Army
(Hong Kong)
SHW. Dir, Chang Cheh. Sp, I Kuang, Chang Cheh; cam, Kung Mu To; edtr, Kuo Ting-hung; martial art, Hsieh Hsing, Chen Hsin-yi; mus, Chen Yung-yu. 100.
David Chiang, Ti Lung, Chen Kuan-tai, Alexander Fu Sheng.
04/28/76

The Seventh Company Outdoors: SEE La Septieme Compagnie Au Clair Du Lune

The Sewers of Paradise: SEE Les Egouts du Paradis

Sex O'Clock U.S.A.
(France)
FCM. Yang Film (Eric Rochat)-France Opera Films prodn. Conceived-dir, Francois Reichenbach. Cam (Eastmancolor), Jean Collomb; edtr, Delfine Dephos; mus, Mort Schuman, Claude Gaubert. 90.
(DOC) (English soundtrack)
08/04/76

Sextette
CWN. Briggs and Sullivan presentation. Prods, Daniel Briggs, Robert Sullivan; exec prod, Warner G Toub. Dir, Ken Hughes. Sp, Herbert Baker, based on the play by Mae West; cam (Metrocolor), James Crabe; mus, Artie Butler; edtr, Argyle Nelson; art dir, James F Clayton; set decor, Reg Allen; asso prod, Harry Weiss; chor, Marc Breaux; prodn mgr-asst dir, Gene Marum; mus coord, Michael Arciaga; mus, Gene Cantamessa. (MPAA rating: PG). 91.
Mae West, Timothy Dalton, Dom DeLuise, Tony Curtis, Ringo Starr, George Hamilton, Alice Cooper, Keith Allison, Rona Barrett, Van McCoy, Keith Moon, Regis Philbin, Walter Pidgeon, George Raft.
03/08/78

Sey Seyeti
(A Man, Some Women)
(Senegal)
X. Ben Diogaye prodn. Wri-dir-cam, Ben Diogaye Beye; edtr, Andree Daventure. 77.
El Abaye Seck, Dienaba Niang, Fatim Diagne.
08/20/80

Shades of Silk
(Canada)
X. Alexandra Brouwer, Mary Stephen, John Cressey, Isabel Beers. John and Mary Prodns prodn. Dir, Mary Stephen; sp, Stephen, Ann Martin; cam, John Cressy; edtr, Stephen Martin; mus, Alain Leroux. 65.
12/12/79

Shadow Line: SEE Linea D'Ombra

Shadow Of A Flying Bird: SEE Stin Letajiciho Ptacka

Shadow of the Castles: SEE L'Ombre Des Chateaux

Shadows Of A Hot Summer: SEE Stiny Horkeho Leta

Shadows of Angels: SEE Schatten Der Engel

The Shaggy D.A.
BV. Walt Disney prodn; prod, Bill Anderson; exec prod, Ron Miller. Dir, Robert Stevenson. Sp, Don Tait, suggested by "The Hound Of Florence" by Felix Salten; cam (Technicolor), Frank Phillips; mus, Buddy Baker; title song, Shane Tatum, Richard McKinley; edtrs, Bob Bring, Norman Palmer; art dirs, John B Mansbridge, Perry Ferguson; set decor, Robert Benton; cos, Chuck Keehne, Emily Sundby; 2d unit dir, Arthur J Vitarelli; asst dir, Christopher Seiter. (MPAA rating: G). 91.
Dean Jones, Tim Conway, Suzanne Pleshette, Keenan Wynn, Jo Anne Worley, Dick Van Patten, Shane Sinutko, Vic Tayback, John Myhers, Dick Bakalyan, Warren Berlinger, Ronnie Schell, Jonathan Daly, John Fiedler, Hans Conreid, George Kirby.
12/15/76

The Shah of Iran
(Britain)
X. Prod, Dean Maksor; dir, Walter Ellaby; narr, Orson Welles; prod in cooperation with the Iranian Ministry of Culture and Arts. 60.
(DOC) (16m)
01/16/80

Shadow of the Hawk
(Canada)
COL. Prod, John Kemeny; exec prod, Henry Gellis. Dir, George McCowan. Sp, Norman Thaddeus Vane, Herbert J Wright, from a story by Peter Jensen, Lynette Cahill, Vane; cam (Eastmancolor), John Holbrook, Reginald Morris; edtr, O Nicholas Brown; mus, Robert McMullin; art dir, Keith Pepper; set decor, Peter Young; snd, Bill O'Neill, George Mulholland; asst dirs, Roland L Schwary, Jim Scott; stunt coord, Buddy Joe Hooker. (MPAA rating: PG). 92.
Jan-Michael Vincent, Marilyn Hassett, Chief Dan George, Pia Shandel, Marianne Jones.
07/14/76

Shaolin Abbot
(Hong Kong)
SHW. Shaw Bros prodn. Prod, Run Run Shaw. Dir, Ho Meng-hua; exec prod, Mona Fong; sp, Yi Kuang; cam, Yu Chi; art dir, Chen Chinsam; edtr, Chiang Hsing-lung; mus, Chen Yung-yu. 95.
David Chiang, Lo Lieh, Lily Li, Hsu Shaochiang, Ku Kuan-chung, Sze Wei, Pan Pinchang, Yu Yung, Tang Yin-charn, Wu Hangsheng.
11/21/79

Shaolin Avengers
(Hong Kong)
SHW. Dir, Chang Cheh. Sp, Yi Kuang, Chang Cheh; edtr, Kuo Ting-hung; cam, Kung Mu-to; martial arts, Hsieh Hsing, Chen Hsin-yi; mus dir, Chen Yung-yu. 99.
Alexander Fu Sheng, Chi Kuan-chun, Tang Yen-tsan, Ma Chih-chin.
07/21/76

Shaolin Rescuers
(Hong Kong)
07/25/79
SHW. Prod, Run Run Shaw. Dir, Chang Cheh. Exec prod, Mona Fong. Sp, Chang Cheh, Yi Kuang, Chei Nai-bin; cam, Tsao Hui-chi; edtrs, Chiang Hsing-lung, Li Yen-kai; art dir, Johnson Tsao; mus, Cheng Yung-yu; martial art instructors, Tai Chi-hsien, Lu Fung, Chiang Sheng. 100.
Lo Meng, Kuo Chue, Sun Chien, Chiang Sheng, Lu Feng, Pai Piao, Ku Kuan-chung, Yang Huan, Tsao Tao-hua.

The Shape of Things to Come
(Canada)
FVI. CFI Investments presentation. Prod, William Davidson; exec prod, Harry Alan Towers. Dir, George McCowan; sp, Martin Lager. (MPAA rating: PG). 95.
Jack Palance, Carol Lynley, John Ireland, Barry Morse, Nicholas Campbell, Eddie Benton, Greg Swanson, Marc Parr.
12/19/79

Shatranj Ke Khilari
(The Chess Player)
(India)
X. Devki Chitra prodn. Prod, Suresh Jindai. Dir, Satyajit Ray. Sp, Satyajit Ray, based on a story by Munshi Premchand; dialogue, Satyajit Ray, Shama Zaidi, Javed Siddiqui; edtr, Dulal Dutta; cam, Soumendu Roy; art dir, Banshi Chandragupta; mus, Satyajit Ray; cos, Shama Zaidi; chor, Birju Maharaj; anim, Ram Mohan; snd, Narinder Singh; mus, Samir Majumdar. 130.
Richard Attenborough, Amjad Khan, Sanjeev Kumar, Saeed Jaffrey, Shabana Azmi, Farida Jalal.
12/14/77

Shenanigans
(The Great Bank Hoax)
X. Prod, Joseph Jacoby, Ralph Rosenbaum. Wri-dir, Jacoby. Cam (Movielab), Walter Lassally; edtr, Rosenbaum; mus, Arthur B Rubinstein. (MPAA rating: PG). 93.
Burgess Meredith, Richard Basehart, Ned Beatty, Charlene Dallas, Paul Sand,

Michael Murphy, Constance Forslund, Arthur Godfrey.
09/21/77

Shigaon Shel Moledeth
(Homeland Fever)
(Israel)
X. United Studios Prodn; prod, Itzhak Kol; wri-dir, Yoram Levy; edtr, Nissim Mussak; narration, Dan Almagor, Yossi Banai; narrator, Banai; mus, Yoav Kutner, Nir Hakhlili. 90.
(DOC) (B & W)
05/21/80

The Shillingbury Blowers
(Britain)
X. Inner Circle Films prodn. Prod, Greg Smith. Dir, Val Guest. Sp, Francis Essex; cam, Frank Watts; edtr, Bill Lenny; mus, Ed Welch; art dir, Albert Witherick; snd, Laurie Clarkson; asst dir, Vic Priggs. 82.
Trevor Howard, Robin Nedwell, Diane Keen, Jack Douglas, Sam Kydd, Eric Francis, Joe Black, Tony Simpson, John LeMesurier.
03/26/80

Shine Brightly, My Star: SEE Gori, Gori, Moja Zvezda

The Shining
WB. Prod-dir, Stanley Kubrick, in asso with The Producers Circle Co. Exec prod, Jan Harlan. Sp, Kubrick, Diane Johnson, based on the novel by Stephen King; cam, John Alcott; edtr, Ray Lovejoy; snd, Ivan Sharrock, Richard Daniel; prodn des, Roy Walker; art dir, Les Tomkins; asst dir, Brian Cook; make-up, Tom Smith; cos, Milena Canonero; mus, Bela Bartok. (MPAA rating: R). 146.
Jack Nicholson, Shelley Duvall, Danny Lloyd, Scatman Crothers, Barry Nelson, Philip Stone, Joe Turkel, Anne Jackson, Tony Burton.
05/28/80

Shiwjot Takoj Paren
(There Was A Lad)
(USSR)
GOS. Gorky Studios Prodn, Moscow. Wri-dir, Vassili Shukshin, based on his own short stories. Cam (b&w), Valeri Ginsburg; mus, Pavel Chekalov; sets, A Vagichev; snd, V Vhlobynin. 101.
Leonid Kuravlev, Lidia Alexandrova, Larissa Burkova, Boris Kalakin, Bella Achmadulina, Rodion Nachapetov, N Sazonova, R Grigoryeva, A Suyeva, J Teterin.
(B & W)
07/05/78

Shock Waves
BRE. Zopix prodn. Prod, Reuben Trane; dir, Ken Wiederhorn; sp, John Harrison, Wiederhorn; cam (TVC color), Trane; edtr, Norman Gay; mus, Richard Einhorn; prodn mgr, Jessica Sack; make-up, Alan Ormsby. (MPAA rating: PG). 84.
Peter Cushing, Brooke Adams, John Carradine, Fred Buch, Jack Davidson, Luke Halprin, D J Sidney, Don Stout.
10/08/80

Shogun Assassin
(Japan)
NW. Toho Company-Katsu prodn. Exec prod, Peter Shanaberg. Orig version prod by Shintaro Katsu, Hisaharu Matsubara. American version prod by David Weisman. Orig version dir, Kenji Misumi. American version dir, Robert Houston. Sp, Robert Houston, David Weisman, Kazuo Koike, based on an orig story by Koike, Goseki Kojima; cam (Metrocolor), Chriski Makiura; orig edtr, Toskio Taniguchi; American edtr, Lee Percy; mus, W Michael Lewis, Mark Lindsay; snd (Dolby), Tsuchitaro Hayaski; asso prods, Larry Franciose, Michael Maiello, Albert Ellis Jr, Joseph Ellis. (MPAA rating: R). 86.
Tomisaburo Wakayama, Masahiro Tomikawa, Kayo Matsuo, Minoru Ohi, Shoji Kobayashi, Shin Kishida.
Voices by- Lamont Johnson, Marshal Efron, Sandra Bernhard, Vic Davis, Lennie Weinrib, Lainie Cook, Sam Weisman, Mark Lindsay, Robert Houston, David Weisman, Gibran Evans.
11/19/80

Sholay
(Embers)
(India)
X. Sippy Films/United Prods picture; prod, G P Sippy. Dir, Ramesh Sippy. Sp, Salim-Javed; cam, S M Anwar. 192.
Sanjeev Kumar, Dharmendra, Amitabh Bachan, Hema Malini, Amzad Khan.
02/09/77

Shoot
(Canada)
AVE. Melniker-Ben Efraim-Getty Pictures Corp-Essex Enterprises film, prod, Harve Sharman; exec prod, Dick Berg. Dir, Harvey Hart. Sp, Dick Berg, from the novel by Douglas Fairbairn; cam (Technicolor), Zale Magder; edtrs, Ron Wisman, Peter Shatalow; mus, Doug Riley; art dir, Earl Preston, snd, Paul Coombe, Karl Scherer; asst dir, Tim Rowse. (MPAA rating: R). 92.
Cliff Robertson, Ernest Borgnine, Henry Silva, James Blendick, Larry Reynolds, Les Carlson, Helen Shaver, Gloria Carlin Chetwynd, Kate Reid, Alan McRae, Ed MacNamara, Peter Langley, Helena Hart.
06/02/76

The Shootist
PAR. Dino De Laurentiis presentation, prods, Mike Frankovich, William Self. Dir, Don Siegel. Sp, Miles Hood Swarthout, Scott Hale, based on novel by Glendon Swarthout; cam (Technicolor), Bruce Surtees; edtr, Douglas Stewart; mus, Elmer Bernstein; prodn des, Robert Boyle; set decor, Arthur Parker; snd, Arthur Piantadosi, Les Fresholtz, Michael Minkler, Alfred J Overton; asst dir, Joe Cavalier. (MPAA rating: PG.) 99.
John Wayne, Lauren Bacall, Ron Howard, Bill McKinney, James Stewart, Richard Boone, Hugh O'Brian, Harry Morgan, John Carradine, Sheree North, Richard Lenz, Scatman Crothers, Gregg Palmer, Alfred Dennis, Dick Winslow, Melody Thomas, Kathleen O'Malley.
07/28/76

Short and Sweet: SEE Les Grands Moyens

Short Eyes
FGU. Harris-Fox prodn. Prod, Lewis Harris; exec prod, Marvin Stuart. Dir, Robert M Young. Sp, Miguel Pinero (based on his play). cam, Peter Sova; asso prods, Walker Stuart, Martin Hirsh; edtr, Edward Beyer; mus scorcomp, Curtis Mayfield; prodn mgr, Doro Bachrach; asst dir, Robert Colesberry; cos des, Paul Martino; prodn des, Joe Babas. (MPAA rating: R). 104.
Bruce Davison, Jose Perez, Nathan George, Don Blakely, Shawn Elliott, Tito Goya, Joe Carberry, Kenny Steward, Bob Maroff, Keith Davis, Miguel Pinero, Willie Hernandez, Tony De Benedetto, Bob O'Connell, Mark Margolis, Richard Matamoros, Curtis Mayfield.
10/05/77

Short Memory: SEE La Memoire Courte

The Shout
(Britain)
RNK. Recorded Picture Company prodn. Dir, Jerzy Skolimovksy. Sp, Michael Austin, Skolimovsky from a story by Robert Graves; cam, Mike Molloy; edtr, Barrie Vince; art dir, Simon Holland; mus, Rupert Hine, Anthony Banks, Michael Rutherford; prod, Jeremy Thomas. 87.
Alan Bates, Susannah York, John Hurt, Robert Stephens, Tim Curry, Julian Hough, Carol Drinkwater, Nick Stringer, John Rees, Susan Woolridge.
05/24/78

Shout At The Devil
(Britain)
X. Michael Klinger's prodn of a Peter Hunt film; prod, Klinger; asso prods, Stanley Sopel, Robert Sterne. Dir, Hunt. Sp, Wilbur Smith, Stanley Price, Alistair Reid; novel, Smith; cam (Technicolor-Panavision), Mike Reed; 2d unit cam, Alan Hume; prodn des, Sid Cain; asst dir, Frank Ernst; 2d unit dir, John Glen; art dirs, Ernie Archer, Bob Laing; sfx, Derek Meddings; edtr, Michael Duthie; mus, Maurice Jarre; titles designed by Maurice Binder. (MPAA rating: PG). 147.
Lee Marvin, Roger Moore, Barbara Parkins, Ian Holm, Rene Kolldehoff, Horst Janson, Karl Michael Vogler, Gernot Endemann, Maurice Denham, Jean Kent, Heather Wright, Bernard Horsfall, Robert Lang, Peter Copley, Murray Melvin, Geoff Davidson, Gerard Paquis, George Coulouris, Renu Setna.
04/14/76

Showboat 1988
X. Living Legend prodn. Prod-dir-cam-edtr, Richard Schmidt. A film created by Henry Bean, Bill Farley, Nick Kazan, Joe DiVincenzo, Richard Richardson. Sp, Bean, Farley, Kazan, Schmidt. 94.
Ed Nylund, Skip Covington, Carolyn Zaremba, Richard A Richardson, Willy Walker.
04/26/78

Shraga Katan
(Little Man)
(Israel)
X. Erez Films prodn. Prod, Baruch Ellah. Exec prod, Mirha Sharpstein. Dir, Zeev Revach. Sp, Hillel Mittelpunkt, Zeev Revach; cam, Gad Danzig; edtr, Zion Avramian; mus, Shem-tov Levi; prod des, Sara Vinner; snd, Itamar Ben Yaakov. 90.
Zeev Revach, Niza Shaul, Zahi Noy, Yossi Karmon, Izhak Hizkia, Hille Mittelpunkt, Rafael Klatchtkin, Liora Tikozky, Lia Dulitzkaya, Ilan Dar.
09/27/78

Shtigje Te Luftes
(Paths of War)
(Albania)
ALA. Albanian Film Prodn, Tirana. Dir, Piro Milkani. Sp, Safet Kurti, Skender Plasari; cam, Faruk Basha; sets, M Fushekati; mus, Kujtim Laro. 90.
Timo Flloko, Robert Ndrenika, Perike Gjezi, Sander Prosi, Pandi Raidhi, Ndrek Luca, Albert Verria, Liza Laska.
(B & W)
06/13/79

Shtourets V Ouhoto
(Cricket in the Ear)
(Bulgaria)
X. Bulgarian Film prodn. Dir, Georgi Stoyanov. Sp, Nicolas Roussev; cam, Ivailo Trentchev; art dir, Helena Dimyakova; mus, Kiril Dontchev. 100.
Pavel Popandov, Stefan Mavrodiev.
11/17/76

Shuban
(Scandal)
(Japan)
EMQ. Shochiku prodn. Prod, Takashi Koide; dir, Akira Kurosawa; sp, Kurosawa, Ryuzo Kikushima; cam, Toshio Ubakata; mus, Fumio Hayasaka. 105.
Toshiro Mifune, Yoshiko Yamaguchi, Takashi Shimura.
(Japanese with English subtitles) (MADE IN 1950) (B & W)
08/20/80

Shunkin Sho
(A Portrait of Shunkin)
(Japan)
TOH. Hori Kikaku prodn. Exec prods, Takeo Hori, Hideo Sasai. Dir, Katsumi Nishikawa. Sp, Teinosuke Kinugasa, Nishikawa; orig story, Junichiro Tanizaki; cam, Kenji Hagiwara; mus, Masaru Sato. 97.
Momoe Yamaguchi, Tomokazu Miura, Takeya Nakamura, Masahiko Tsugawa, Nobuo Nakamura.
05/25/77

Si C'Etait a Refaire
(If It Were To Do Over Again)
(France)
UA. Les Films 13 prodn. Wri-dir, Claude Lelouch. Cam (Eastmancolor), Jacques Lefrancois; edtr, Georges Klotz; mus, Francis Lai. 100.
Catherine Deneuve, Anouk Aimee, Charles Denner, Francis Huster, Niels Arestrup, Colette Baudot, Manuella Papatakis.
11/10/76

Siawase No Cakusoku Hankeci
(A Yellow Handkerchief Of Happiness)
(Japan)
X. Shochiku Film Prodn, Japan. Dir, Yoji Yamada. Sp, Yamada, Yoshitaka Asama; cam, Tecuo Takaba; music, Masaru Sato. 90.
Ken Takakura, Chieko Baisho, Tecuya Takeda, Kaori Mamoio, Kiyoshi Acumi.
08/09/78

Sib Tamruat Toh Buntung
(Sgt Buntung)
(Thailand)
AMQ. Prod, Kittipong Wetpooyant. Wri-dir, Pote Siriphan, based on the novel by Sangphet Senibaddin; cam, Niyom Srisuwan; snd, Sanan Aroonrat; mus, Montri Ong-iam; art dir, Narong Patpreow. 125.
Piya Trakulrat, Jarunee Suksawat, Suwin Swangrat, Poom Patanayuth, Tosapon Srisai, Uap Tomchat.
06/20/79

Siberiade
(USSR)
SOV. Mosfilm prodn. Dir, Andrei Mikhalkov-Konchalovsky. Sp, Valentin Ejov, Mikhalkov-Konchalovsky; cam (Sovcolor), Levan Paatashvili; edtr, Valentina Koulaguine; mus, Edouard Artemiev. 210.
Vladimir Smailov, Vitale Solomina, Nathalia Andreitchenko, Erqueni Petrov, Mikhail Knonov, Nikita Mikhalkov, Ludmila Gourtchenko, Sergei Shakourov.
(70m)
06/06/79

Sidewinder 1
AVE. Ibex Films prodn; prod, Elmo Williams. Dir, Earl Bellamy. Sp, Nancy Voyles Crawford, Thomas McMahon; cam (DeLuxe Color), Dennis Dalzell; mus, Mundell Lowe; art dirs, Tracy Bousman, Liz Bousman; set decor, Ray Paul; cos-ward, Bernadene Mann; snd, Al Overton; asst dir, Danny McCauley; stunt coord, Gary Davis. (MPAA rating: PG). 96.
Marjoe Gortner, Michael Parks, Susan Howard, Alex Cord, Charlotte Rae, Barry Livingston, Bill Vint, Byron Morrow.
07/27/77

Sieben Sommerprossen
(Seven Freckles)
(E Germany)
DEE. DEFA Film Prodn, Johannisthal Group, Berlin. Dir, Herrmann Zschoche. Sp, Christa Kozik; cam, Guenter Jaeuthe; sets, Harry Leupold; mus, Guenter Erdmann; edtr, Rita Hiller. 90.
Kareen Schroeter, Harald Rathmann, Christa Loeser, Evelyn Opocynski, Jan Bereska, Barbara Dittus, Hilmar Baumann, Janine Beilfuss, Carola Spindler, Sabine Schmich, Michael Boettcher, Rene Rudolph.
06/28/78

Signore E Signori, Buonanotte
(Goodnight, Ladies and Gentlemen)
(Italy)
TIT. Prod, Franco Committeri for 15 Maggio Cooperativa. Wri-dirs, Age, Scarpelli, Leo Benvenuti, Luigi Comencini, Piero De Bernardi, Nanni Loy, Ruggero Maccari, Luigi Magni, Mario Monicelli, Ugo Pirro, Ettore Scola. Cam (Eastmancolor), Claudio Ragona; art dir, Lucia Mirisola; Lorenzo Baraldi, Luciano Spadoni; edtr, Amedeo Salfa; mus, Lucio Dalla, Antonello Venditti, Giuseppe Mazzuca, Nicola Samale. 119.
Senta Berger, Adolfo Celi, Vittorio Gassman, Nino Manfredi, Marcello Mastroianni, Ugo Tognazzi, Paolo Villaggio.
01/19/77

Signum Laudis
(The Medal)
(Czechoslovakia)
CZS. Barrandov Studio, Slovak Film Studio prodn. Dir, Martin Holly; sp, Valdimir Kalina, Jiri Krizan; cam (Eastmancolor), Frantisek Uldrich; mus, Zdenek Liska. 85.
Vlado Muller, Ilja Prachar, Jan Skopecek, Jiri Zahajsky, Jiri Kodet, Josef Blaha.
07/30/80

Silence... On Tourne
(Silence...We're Shooting)
(France)
FLG. Gerland Productions prodn. Dir, Roger Coggio. Sp, Coggio, Elisabeth Huppert; cam (Eastmancolor), Etienne Szabo; edtr, Chantal Piquet. 90.
Elisabeth Huppert, Roger Coggio, Paul Mercey, Francoise Thuries, Yvan Marco.
05/05/76

The Silent Cry
(Britain - W Germany - France)
X. Stephen Dwoskin (Britain), ZDF (West Germany), and INA (France) prodn. Prod-dir-cam-edtr, Stephen Dwoskin. Sp, Dwoskin, Bobby Gill; mus, Benedict Mason, Dwoskin, Roger Ollerhead; snd, Ollerhead. 96.
Bobby Gill, Ernst Brightmoer, Harry Waistnage, Mary Rose.
11/30/77

Silent Movie
FOX. Prod, Michael Hertzberg. Dir, Mel Brooks. Sp, Brooks, Ron Clark, Rudy DeLuca, Barry Levinson, from a story by Clark; cam (DeLuxe Color), Paul Lohmann; edtrs, John C Howard, Stanford C Allen; mus, John Morris; prodn des, Al Brenner; asst dir, Ed Teets; 2d unit dir-stunt coord, Max Kleven. (MPAA rating: PG). 86.
Mel Brooks, Marty Feldman, Dom DeLuise, Bernadette Peters, Sid Caesar, Harold Gould, Ron Carey, Carol Arthur, Liam Dunn, Fritz Feld, Chuck McCann, Valerie Curtin, Yvonne Wilder, Arnold Soboloff, Patrick Campbell, Harry Ritz, Charlie Callas, Henny Youngman, Eddie Ryder, Al Hopson, Rudy DeLuca, Barry Levinson, Howard Hesseman, Lee Delano, Jack Riley, Inga Nielsen, Sivi Aberg, Erica Hagen, Robert Lussier.
06/23/76

The Silent Nephew: SEE Un Neveu Silencieux

The Silent Partner
(Canada)
EM. Mario Kassar and Andrew Vajna presentation. Exec prod, Garth H Drabinsky. Prod, Joel B Michaels, Stephen Young. Dir, Daryl Duke. Sp, Curtis Hanson, based on Anders Bodelson novel, "Think of a Number"; cam, Billy Williams; prodn des, Trevor Williams; orig mus, Oscar Peterson. (MPAA rating: R). 103.
Susannah York, Christopher Plummer, Elliott Gould, Celine Lomez, Michael Kirby, Ken Pogue, John Candy, Gail Dahms, Michael Donaghue, Jack Duffy, Nancy Simmonds, Nuala Fitzgerald, Guy Sanvido, Aino Pirskanen, Michele Rosen, Ben Williams, Sandy Crawley, Jan Campbell, Jimmy Davidson, Eve Norman, John Kerr, Sue Lumsden, Candace O'Connor, Stephen Levy.
04/04/79

Silent Scream
AMC. Jim and Ken Wheat prodn. Exec prods, Joan and Denny Harris. Dir, Denny Harris. Sp, Ken and Jim Wheat; cam (MGM Color), Michael D Murphy, David Shore; edtr, Edward Salier; snd, Larry Goga; prodn des, Christopher Henry; sfx, Steve Karkus; mus, Roger Kellaway. (MPAA rating: R). 87.
Rebecca Balding, Cameron Mitchell, Avery Schreiber, Barbara Steele, Steve Doubet, Brad Reardon, John Widelock, Juli Andelman, Yvonne de Carlo.
01/30/80

The Silent Witness
IIP. Screenpro Films prodn. Prod-dir, David W Wolfe. Exec prods, Adam J Otterbein, Peter M Rinaldi. Sp, Ian Wilson, Henry Lincoln, David W Rolfe; cam, Bahram Monocheri; edtr, Peter Hollywood; snd, Wally Plummer. (MPAA rating: PG). 55.
(DOC)
09/27/78

Silk Worms: SEE Gusanos De Seda

Silna Voda
(Strong Water)
(Bulgaria)
X. BulgaroFilm prodn. Dir, Ivan Terziev. Sp, Boyan Papazov, based on motifs from Gencho Stoyev's novel "A Bad Day"; cam, Plamen Vagenshtine; art dir, Boyanka Ahryanova. 90.
Ivan Grigorov, Kiril Kovadarkov, Philip Trifonov, Velko Kunev, Meglena Popova, Marianna Dimitrova.
06/16/76

Silver Bears
COL. Prod, Alex Winitsky, Arlene Sellers. Dir, Ivan Passer. Sp, Peter Stone, based on novel by Paul E Erdman; cam (Technicolor), Anthony Richmond; edtr, Bernard Gribble; mus, Claude Bolling; art dir, Edward Marshall; snd, Roy Charman, asst dir, Mike Gowans. (MPAA rating: PG). 113.
Michael Caine, Cybill Shepherd, Louis Jourdan, Stephane Audran, Tom Smothers, David Warner, Martin Balsam, Jay Leno, Tony Mascia, Charles Gray, Joss Ackland, Jeremy Clyde.
11/23/77

Silver Dream Racer
(Britain)
RNK. David Wickes prodn. Prod, Rene Dupont. Dir, David Wickes. Sp, Wickes; cam, Paul Beeson; edtr, Peter Hollywood; mus, Essex; mus dir, John Cameron; art dir, Malcolm Middleton; snd, John Mitchell; cos, Judy Moorcroft; asst dir, Ken Baker. 111.
David Essex, Beau Bridges, Cristina Raines, Clarke Peters, Harry H Corbett, Diane Keen, Lee Montague, Sheila White, David Baxt, Ed Bishop, Nick Brimble, Stephen Hoye, T P McKenna, Richard Parmentier, Patrick Ryecart.
04/02/80

Silver Streak
FOX. Miller-Milkis-Colin Higgins prodn. Exec prods, Martin Ransohoff, Frank Yablans. Prod, Thomas L Miller, Edward K Milkis. Dir, Arthur Hiller. Sp, Colin Higgins; cam (DeLuxe Color), David M Walsh; film edtr, David Bretherton; prodn des, Alfred Sweeney; set decorator, Marvin March; snd, Hal Etherington, Don Mitchell; sfx, Fred Cramer; stunt coord, Mickey Gilbert; asst dir, Jack Roe; mus, comp-cond, Henry Mancini. (MPAA rating: PG). 113.
Gene Wilder, Jill Clayburgh, Richard Pryor, Patrick McGoohan, Ned Beatty, Clifton James, Ray Walston, Stefan Gierasch, Len Birman, Valerie Curtin, Richard Kiel, Lucille Benson, Scatman Crothers, Fred Willard, Delos V. Smith.
12/01/76

Simon
WBO. Prod, Martin Bregman. Wri-dir, Marshall Brickman. Exec prod, Louis A Stroller. Cam (Technicolor), Adam Holender; edtr, Nina Feinberg; snd, Steve Scanlon; prodn des, Stuart Wurtzel; asst dir, Michael Rauch; cos, Santo Loquasto; mus, Stanley Silverman. (MPAA rating: PG). 97.
Alan Arkin, Austin Pendleton, Judy Graubart, William Finley, Jayant, Wallace Shawn, Max Wright, Fred Gwynne, Madeline Khan, Adolph Green.
02/27/80

Simone Barbes ou la Vertu
(Simone Barbes, or Virtue)
(France)
MK. Diagonale prodn. Prod-edtr, Paul Vecchiali. Wri-dir, Marie-Claude Treilhou. Cam (Fujicolor), Jean-Yves Escoffier; snd, Yves Zlotnicka; art dir, Benedict Beauge. 77.
Ingrid Bourgoin, Martine Simonet, Michel Delahaye.
05/07/80

The Simple Past: SEE Le Passe Simple

Sinbad And The Eye Of The Tiger
COL. Charles H Schneer Prodn; prods, Schneer, Ray Harryhausen. Dir, Sam Wanamaker. Sp, Beverley Cross; story, Cross, Harryhausen; cam (Metrocolor), Ted Moore; mus, Roy Budd; edtr, Roy Watts; prodn des, Geoffrey Drake; art dir, Fernando Gonzales, Fred Carter; cos-ward, Cynthia Tingey; snd, George Stephenson; asst dir, Miguel A Gil Jr; special visual effects, Harryhausen. (MPAA rating: G). 112.
Patrick Wayne, Taryn Power, Margaret Whiting, Jane Seymour, Patrick Troughton, Kurt Christian, Nadim Sawaiha, Damien Thomas, Bruno Barnabe, Bernard Kay, Salami Coker, David Sterne.
05/25/77

Sindoor
(Nepal)
X. Nepal Film Production. Wri-dir, Prakash Thapa. 90.
Beenakshi, Biswa Basnet, Prakash Thapa.
06/18/80

The Sinful Life of Franciszek Bula: SEE Grzeszny Zywot Franciszka Buly

Sing Sam Oy
(The Sensitive Lion)
(Thailand)
DKF. Prod, Banchong Kanyaman. Wri-dir, Dokdin Kanyaman. Exec prod, Siriman Kanyaman; cam-edtr, Manat Tokoyat; mus, Dang Studio; snd recording, Kasem Milintachinda. 125.
Sombat Metanee, Mayura Tanabut, Dokdin Kanyaman, Suriya Chinaphan, Lak Apichat, Chomchai Chartvilai, Tarika Taratit, Daodai, Suthisat Somchart, Choomphorn Tepitak, Prachuab Lerkyamdi.
04/06/77

The Singer: SEE El Cantor

The Singer and The Dancer
(Australia)
COL. Gillian Armstrong film. Prod-dir, Armstrong. Sp, John Pleffer, Gill Armstrong; cam, Russell Boyd; prodn mgr, Errol Sullivan; art dir, Sue Armstrong; snd, Laurie Fitzgerald; edtr, Nick Beauman; mus, Robert Murphy. 54.
Ruth Cracknell, Elizabeth Crosby, Jude Kuring, Russell Kiefel, Gerry Duggan, Jane Buckland, Kate Sheil.
04/27/77

Singing During the Occupation: SEE Chantons Sous L'Occupation

Sir Henry At Rawlinson End
(Britain)
X. Charisma Films prodn. Exec prod, Martin Wesson. Prod, Tony Stratton Smith. Dir, Steve Roberts. Sp, Vivian Stanshall, Roberts; cam, Martin Bell; edtr, Chris Rose; mus, Stanshall; art dir, Jim Acheson; snd, Keith Desmond; asso prod, Peter R Smith; asst dir, Raymond Day. 72.

Trevor Howard, Patrick Magee, Denise Coffey, J G Devlin, Harry Fowler, Sheila Reid, Vivian Stanshall, Suzanne Danielle, Daniel Gerroll, Ben Aris, Liz Smith, Jeremy Child, Susan Porrett.
(B & W)
07/16/80

Siripala and Ranmenika
(Sri Lanka)
CMJ. Dir, Amarnath Jayatilaka. Sp, Dhasrmasiri Gamage; cam, Donald Karunaratine; edtr, M P Rupasena. 100.
Ravindra Randeniya, Malini Fonseka, Joe Abeywickrama, Robin Fernando.
(B & W)
01/26/77

Sirius
(Czechoslovakia)
X. Czech prodn. Dirs, Frantisek Vlacil, Michael Vavrusa, Jana Hlavackova. 53.
07/14/76

The Sirocco Blow: SEE Le Coup de Sirocco

The Sister-in-Law: SEE Norng Mia

Sisters, or The Balance of Happiness: SEE Schwestern, Oder Die Balance Des Gluecks

Sita's Wedding: SEE Seetha Kalyanam

Sitting Ducks
X. Sunny Side Up prodn. Prod, Meira Attia Dor. Dir-sp, Henry Jaglom; cam (Metrocolor), Paul Glickman; mus, Richard Romanus; snd, Jeffrey Hayes; asst dir, Jan Foster. (MPAA rating: R). 90.
Michael Emil, Zack Norman, Patrice Townsend, Irene Forrest, Richard Romanus, Henry Jaglom.
1/21/79

Sitting on the Edge of Tomorrow with the Feet Hanging: SEE Sentados Al Borde De La Manana Con Los Pies Colgando

Six Bears and a Clown
(Czechoslovakia)
X. Dir, Oldrich Lipsky. Sp-story, Milos Macourek, Lipsky; cam, Vladimir Novotny; mus, Vlastimil Hala. 82.
Lubomir Lipsky, Jifi Sovak, Jan Libieek, Milos Kopecky, Franticsek Filipovsky.
07/14/76

Sixth And Main
NTC. Wri-prod-dir, Christopher Cain; exec prod, Jerry Rogers. Cam (CFI Color), Hilyard John Brown; edtr, Ken Johnson; mus, Bob Summers; lyr, Penny Askey; snd, John Wilkinson, John Reitz, Gordon Day, Robbie Robinson, Glen Glenn Sound; cos-ward, Gwen Capetanos, Bianca Dorso; asst dir, Cal Roberts; stunt coord, Sandy Gimpel. 103.
Leslie Nielsen, Roddy McDowall, Beverly Garland, Leo Penn, Joe Maross, Bard Stevens, Sharon Tomas.
08/31/77

Skal vi danse foerst
(Do We Start Off With A Dance)
(Denmark)
CDK. Kosmorama prodn. Story-sp, Marie Louise Lauridsen, Katai Forbert-Petersen, Annette Olsen; dir, Annette Olsen; cam (Eastmancolor), Dan Laustsen; edtr, Janus Billeskov Jansen; prodn des, Soeren Skjaer; exec prod, Katherine Nyholm. 96.
Lene Gurtler, Kirsten Rolffes, Frits Helmuth, Karen Berg, Benny Dahl, Erick Wedersoe.
12/26/79

Skas Pro To, Kar Zar Petr Arapa Shenil
(How Czar Peter the Great Married Off His Moor)
(USSR)
X. Mosfilm prodn, Moscow. Dir, Alexander Mitta. Sp, Yuli Dunsky, Valeri Frid, Mitta; cam, Valeri Shuvalov. 90.
Vladimir Visozskij, Aleksei Petrenko.
12/08/76

Skateboard
U. Blum Group prodn. Prods, Harry N Blum, Richard A Wolf. Dir, George Gage. Sp, Richard A Wolf, George Gage, based on a story by Wolf; cam, Ross Kelsay; edtr, Robert Angus; snd, Galen Handy, Roger Heman; cos des, Elizabeth Gage. (MPAA rating: G). 97.
Allen Garfield, Kathleen Lloyd, Leif Garrett, Richard Van Der Wyk, Tony Alva, Steve Monahan, David Hyde, Ellen Oneal, Pam Kenneally, Anthony Carbone.
03/22/78

Skatetown, U.S.A.
COL. Rastar prodn. Prods, William A Levey, Lorin Dreyfuss. Exec prod, Peter E Strauss. Dir, William A Levey. Sp, Nick Castle, based on story by William A Levey, Lorin Dreyfuss, Castle; cam, Donald M Morgan; edtr, Gene Fowler Jr; set decor, George Gaines; art dir, Larry Weimer; mus, Miles Goodman; chor, Bob Banas; stunt coord, Hank Hooker; snd, Al Overton, Jr; cos, Betsy Heimann, Bob Labansat; asst dir, Victor Hsu. (MPAA rating: PG). 98.
Scott Baio, Flip Wilson, Ron Palillo, Ruth Buzzi, Dave Mason, Greg Bradford, Maureen McCormick, Patrick Swayze, Billy Barty, Kelly Lang, David Landsberg, Lenny Bari, Murray Langston, Bill Kirkchenbauer, Denny Johnstone, Vic Dunlop, Gary Mule Deer.
10/24/79

Skazany
(Condemned)
(Poland)
POL. Kadr Film Unit prodn. Exec prod, Wilhelm Hollender. Dir-wri, Andrzej Trzos-Rastawiecki. Cam, Zygmunt Samosiuk; mus, Johann Sebastian Bach.
Wojciech Pszoniak, Zdzislaw Kozien.
04/14/76

Skin Deep
(New Zealand)
X. Phase Three Films (John Maynard) prodn. Dir, Geoff Steven. Sp, Piers Davies, Roger Horrocks, Steven; cam (Gevacolor), Leon Narby; snd, Graham Morris. 103.
Jim Macfarlane, Ken Blackburn, Alan Jervis, Grant Tilly, Bill Johnson, Arthur Wright, Kevin J Wilson, Glenis Leverstam, Deryn Cooper, Wendy Macfarlane, Bob Harvey.
10/04/78

The Skip Tracer
(Canada)
X. Highlights prodn presentation, prod, Laara Dalen. Dir, Zale Dalen. Financed by Canadian Film Development Corp and private financing. Cam, Ron Oreiux; snd, Richard Patton; prodn asst, Paul Tucker. 93.
08/24/77

The Skirt Chaser: SEE Le Cavaleur

Sky-High Love: SEE Salangit Mesra

The Sky Is Clearing
(Mongolia)
GOS. Mongolian Film prodn. Dir, R Dorzhpalam. Sp, S Dashchdoorov. 90.
Zh Selengesuren, A Ochirbat, B Tsetsebalzhid.
09/05/79

Sky Riders
(US - Greece)
FOX. Sandy Howard prodn. Prod, Terry Morse Jr; exec prod, Howard. Dir, Douglas Hickox. Sp, Jack DeWitt, Stanley Mann, Garry Michael White; cam (DeLuxe Color), Ousama Rawi; aerial cam, Greg MacGillivray, Jim Freeman; edtr, Malcolm Cooke; mus, Lalo Schifrin; art dir, Terry Ackland-Snow; set decor, Ian Whittaker; snd, Don Bassman, Thanassis Arvanitis; asst dir, Ted Sturgis; asst for aerial unit, Peter Bennett. (MPAA rating: PG). 91.
James Coburn, Susannah York, Robert Culp, Charles Aznavour, Werner Pochath, Zou Zou, Kenneth Griffith, Harry Andrews, John Beck, Ernie Orsatti, Steven Keats, Henry Brown, Cherie Latimer, Barbara Trentham, Simon Harrison, Stephanie Matthews, Anthony Antypas, Telis Zottos.
03/24/76

Skytten
(The Marksman)
(Denmark)
WCT. Steen Herdel prodn. Dir, Tom Hedegaard. Story-sp, Anders Bodelsen; cam (Eastmancolor), Mikael Salomon; prodn mgr, Helge Sten Knudsen. 87.
Peter Sten, Pia Maria Wohlert, Jens Okking, Ebbe Langberg, Per Pallesen.
03/01/78

Sladkaia Jentchina
(Sweet Woman)
(USSR)
X. Lenfilm prodn, Leningrad. Dir, Vladimir Fetin. Sp, Iren Velenbovskaia; cam, V Kovsel; mus, Soloviev-Sedoi. 90.
Natalia Gundoreva, Svetlana Karpinskaia, Oleg Jankovski, Peter Valiaminov, Rima Markova.
02/09/77

Slaegten
(The Heritage)
(Denmark)
PNR. Just Betzer, A/S Panorama prodn. Sp, Anders Refn, Fleming Quist Moeller, based on Gustav Wild novel. Dir, Anders Refn. Cam (Eastmancolor-Panavision), Mikael Salomon; art dir, Helge Refn; mus, Kasper Winding; edtrs, Anders Refn, Kasper Schyberg; prodn mgr, Lars Kolvig; cos, Gitte Kolvig. 117.
Jens Okking, Helle Hertz, Bodil Udsen, Poul Reichhardt, Stefan Ekman.
01/10/79

Slap Shot
U. Prods, Robert J Wunsch, Stephen Friedman. Dir, George Roy Hill. Sp, Nancy Dowd; cam (Technicolor), Victor Kemper; edtr, Dede Allen; mus supv, Elmer Bernstein; art dir, Henry Bumstead; set decor, James Payne; cos, Tom Bronson; snd, Don Sharpless; asst dirs, James Westman, Tom Joyner; stunt coord-tech advisor, Ned Dowd. (MPAA rating: R). 123.
Paul Newman, Strother Martin, Michael Ontkean, Jennifer Warren, Lindsay Crouse, Jerry Houser, Andrew Duncan, Jeff Carlson, Steve Carlson, David Hanson Yvon Barrette, Allan Nicholls, Brad Sullivan, Stephen Mendillo, Yvan Ponton, Matthew Cowles, Kathryn Walker, Melinda Dillon, M Emmet Walsh, Swoosie Kurtz, Paul D'Amato, Ned Dowd, Nancy Dowd.
03/02/77

Slave of Love: SEE Raba Lubvi

Slavers
(W Germany)
X. Jurgen Goslar prodn of Lord film, Munich. Dir, Jurgen Goslar. Sp, Henry Morrison, Nathaniel Kohn, Marcia MacDonald; cam (Eastmancolor), Igor Luther; edtr, Fred Srp; mus, Eberhard Schoener; cos, Siegbert Kammerer; art dirs, John Rosearne, Peter Roehrig; sfx, Richard Richtsfeld, Helmut Klee. 102.
Trevor Howard, Ron Ely, Britt Ekland, Jurgen Goslar, Ray Milland, Don Jack Rousseau, Helen Morgan, Ken Gampu, Cameron Mitchell, Larry Taylor, Brian O'Shaughnessy, Art Brauss, Eric Schumann, Vera Jesse, Rinaldo Talamonti.
05/25/77

Sledovateliat Y Gozato
(The Investigator and the Woods)
(Bulgaria)
X. BulgaroFilm prodn. Wri-dir, Ranghel Vulchanov. Cam, Victor Chichov; mus, Kiril Donchev. 90.
Sonia Bozhkova, Lyubomir Bucharov, Alexander Pritoup.
06/16/76

The Sleeping Car: SEE Vagon Li

Sleeping Dogs
(New Zealand)
X. Aardvark Film. Prod-dir, Roger Donaldson. Sp, Ian Mune, Arthur Baysting, based on the novel "Smith's Dream" by Karl Stead; cam, Michael Sarasin; edtr, Ian John; snd, Craig McLeod; mus, Murray Grindlay, David Calder, Mathew Brown; sfx, Geoff Murphy. 107.
Sam Neill, Bernard Kearns, Nevan Rowe, Ian Mune, Ian Watkin, Don Selwyn, Tommy Tinirau, Bill Johnson, Roger Oakley, Clyde Scott, Dorothy McKegg, Tony Groser, Davina Whitehouse, Bill Juliff, Donna Akersten, Warren Oates.
10/19/77

The Slipper And The Rose
(Britain)
CII. Paradine Co-Productions Ltd presentation. Prod, Stuart Lyons; exec prod, David Frost; prodn coords, Naim Attalah, John Asprey. Dir, Bryan Forbes. Sp, Forbes, Richard M Sherman, Robert B Sherman; mus-lyr, Richard M Sherman, Robert B Sherman; mus arr-cond, Angela Morely; chor, Marc Breaux; cam (Technicolor-Panavision), Tony Imi; prodn des, Raymond Simm; cos, Julie Harris; edtr, Timothy Gee; asst dir, Jack Causey; mus edtr, Bob Hathaway. (MPAA rating: G). 146.
Richard Chamberlain, Gemma Craven, Annette Crosbie, Edith Evans, Christopher Gable, Michael Hordern, Margaret Lockwood, Kenneth More, Julian Orchard, Lally Bowers, Sherrie Hewson, Rosalind Ayres, John Turner, Keith Skinner, Polly Williams, Norman Bird, Roy Barraclough, Elizabeth Mansfield, Peter Graves, Gerald Sim, Geoffrey Bayldon, Valentine Dyall, Tim Barrett, Vivienne McKee, Andre Morell, Myrtle Reed, Ludmilla Nova, Peter Leeming, Marianne Broome, Tessa Dahl, Lea Dreghorn, Eva Reuber-Staier, Ann Rutherford, Suzette St Claire, Jenny Lee Wright, Patrick Jordan, Rocky Taylor, Paul Schmitzburger.
04/14/76

Slnchev Udar
(Sunstroke)
(Bulgaria)
BGO. Bulgarian Film Prodn, Sofia. Wri-dirs, Christo Piskov, Irena Aktasheva, based on Georgi Dzhagarov's story "This Little Earth." Cam, Leonik Kalashnikov; mus, Kiril Donchev; art dirs, Assen Milev, Borislav Borisov. 120.
Armen Djigarhanian, Itzhak Fintsi, Nikolai Binev, Rashko Mladenov, Katya Paskaleva, Bella Tsoneva, Ivan Kondov, Nevena Kokonova, Konstantin Kotsev.
08/09/78

The Slothful Ones Of The Fertile Valley: SEE I Tembelides Tis Eforis Kiladas

Slovo Dlia Zaschity
(The Defense Takes the Floor)
(USSR)
MSF. Mosfilm, Moscow, prodn. Dir, Vadim Abdraschitov. Sp, A Minadze; cam, A Zabolotckii; mus, V Martynov. 90.
Olge Jankovskii, Stanislav Ljubshin, Victor Schulgin, Elana Kebul.
01/19/77

Slow Dancing in the Big City
UA. Prods, Michael Levee, John G Avildsen. Dir-edtr, Avildsen. Sp, Barra Grant; cam, Ralf Bode; mus, Bill Conti; art dir, Henry Shrady; set decor, Charlie Truhan; cos des, Ruth Morley; chor, Robert North; roof solo chor by Anne Ditchburn; asso prod, George Manasse; asst dir, Dwight Williams; snd, Dennis Maitland. (MPAA rating: PG). 101.
Paul Sorvino, Anne Ditchburn, Nicolas Coster, Anita Dangler, Hector Jaime Mercado, Thaao Penghlis, Linda Selman, G Adam Gifford, Tara Mitton, Dick Carballo, Jack Ramage, Daniel Faraldo.
11/08/78

Slow Motion: SEE Usporeno Kretanje

Slum Boy: SEE Ragazzo di Borgata

Slum People In The Sun: SEE Khon Krang Detr

Slumber Party '57
CAN. Movie Machine Inc/Athena Film Co prodn, prod, John Ireland Jr; exec prod, William A Levey. Dir, Levey. Sp, Frank Farmer; story, Levey; cam (Movielab Color), Robert Caramico; edtr, Bill Casper; mus, Miles Goodman; set des, Ed Bash; cos, Francis Dennis; snd, Richard Wagner; asst dir, Ralph Burris. (MPAA rating: R). 89.
Noelle North, Bridget Hollman, Debra Winger, Mary Ann Appleseth, Rainbeaux Smith, Janet Wood, R L Armstrong, Rafael Campos, Larry Gelman, Will Hutchins, Joyce Jillson, Victor Rogers, Joe E Ross, Bill Thurman.
02/09/77

Sluzhebni Roman
(Romance During Office Hours)
(USSR)
GOS. Mosfilm Prodn, Moscow. Dir, Eldar Ryazanov. Sp, Emil Braginsky, based on his play; cam, Vladimir Nakhabtsev; sets, Alexander Borisov; mus, Andrei Petrov. 150.

Andrei Miagkov, Alicia Freindikh, Svetlana Nemolyaeva, Oleg Basilashvili, Lia Akhedzhakova, Lyudmila Ivanova.
07/19/78

Smak Wody
(The Taste of Water)
(Poland)
POL. Film Polski prodn, Profil Film Unit, Warsaw. Wri-dir, Leszek Wosiewicz; cam, Wladyslaw Nagy; sets, Andrzej Kowalczyk; mus, Leszek Orlewicz; prodn mgr, Jerzy Szebesta. 74.
Magda Teresa Wojcik, Zdizislaw Kozien, Jadwiga Hanska, Eugeniusz Kojawski, Edwin Petrykant, Emilia Krakowska, Halina Buyno-Loza, Daria Trafankowska, Andrzej Kozak, Wiktor Grotowicz.
10/15/80

Small Insect: SEE Kutong Lupa

The Small Timers: SEE Les Ringards

The Small World: SEE Die Kleine Welt

The Smell of Wild Flowers: SEE Miris Polis Kog Cveca

Smertens Boern
(Children of Agony)
(Denmark)
FCT. Kollektiv Film prodn. Prod-wri-dir, Christian Braad Thomsen. Prodn mgr, Nina Crone; cam (Eastmancolor and b&w), Dirk Bruel; edtr, Grete Moeldrup; mus, Gunnar Moeller Pedersen. 97.
Tania Fox, Nicolai Bruel.
10/26/77

Smile Hello: SEE Yim Sawasdi

Smile Orange
(Jamaica)
X. Knuts Prods Ltd film. Prod, Edward Knight; exec prod, Milton L Verley. Dir, Trevor D Rhone. Sp, Rhone, David Ogden, from Rhone's play; cam, David McDonald; edtr, Mike Gilligan; mus, Melba Liston, Rhone; asst dir, Yvonne Jones-Brewster. (MPAA rating: PG). 86.
Carl Bradshaw, Glenn Morrison, Stanley Irons, Vaughn Crosskill.
03/31/76

Smoke on the Potato Fields: SEE Dym Bramborove Nate

Smokey And The Bandit
U. Prod, Mort Engelberg; exec prod, Robert L Levy. Dir, Hal Needham. Sp, James Lee Barrett, Charles Shyer, Alan Mandel; story, Needham, Levy; cam (Technicolor), Bobby Byrne; 2d unit cam, George Bouillet, Bob Jessup; edtrs, Walter Hanneman, Angelo Ross; mus, Bill Justis, Jerry Reed, Dick Feller; art dir, Mark Mansbridge; set decor, Tony Montenaro; snd, John Speak, Ray West; asst dir, David Hamburger; 2d unit dir, Alan Gibbs. (MPAA rating: PG). 96.
Burt Reynolds, Sally Field, Jerry Reed, Jackie Gleason, Mike Henry, Paul Williams, Pat McCormick.
05/18/77

Smokey And The Bandit II
U. Rastar/Mort Engelberg Prodn. Prod, Hank Moonjean; dir, Hal Needham; sp, Jerry Belson, Brock Yates; story, Michael Kane, based on characters created by Needham, Robert L Levy; cam (Technicolor), Michael Butler; mus supv, Snuff Garrett; edtrs, Donn Cambern, William Gordean; prodn des, Henry Bumstead; art dir, Bernie Cutler; set decor, Richard De Cinces; snd, Jack Solomon, Donald O Mitchell, Bill Nicholson, Rick Kline; stunt coord, Richard Ziker; asst dir, David Hamburger. (MPAA rating: PG). 101.
Burt Reynolds, Jackie Gleason, Jerry Reed, Dom DeLuise, Sally Field, Paul Williams, Pat McCormick, David Huddleston, Mike Henry, John Anderson, Brenda Lee, The Statler Brothers, Don Williams, Terry Bradshaw, "Mean Joe" Greene, Joe Klecko, Mel Tillis.
08/20/80

The Smoking Fish: SEE El Pez Que Fuma

Smyateniye Chuvstv
(Confused Feelings)
(USSR)
X. M Gorki Central Studios prodn. Dir, Pavel Arsenov. Sp, Alexander Volodin; cam, Mijail Yakovich. 79.
Elena Proklova, Serguei Nagorni, Ia Savina, Alexander Kaliaguin, Inna Maguer, Arina Aleinikova.
10/04/78

Snaha
(The Daughter-In-Law)
(Bulgaria)
X. Bulgarian Film prodn. Dir, Vassil Mirtchev. Sp, Slav G Karaslavov, based on the novel by Georgi Karaslavov; cam, Tsvetan Chobanski; art dir, Milko Marinov; mus, Kiril Chibolka. 90.
Stefan Getsov, Emilia Radeva, Debromir Manev, Violetta Ghindeva, Anton Karastoyanov, Svoboda Mollerova.
12/01/76

Snails in the Head: SEE Un Escargot Dans la Tete

The Snake Prince
(Hong Kong)
SHW. Rumme Shaw prodn. Dir, Lo Chen. Sp, Yi Kuang; cam, Kuang Han-le; edtr, Chiang Hsing-lung; makeup, Wu Hsu-ching; snd, Wang Yung-hua; mus, Wang Fu-ling. 96.
Ti Lung, Lin Chen-chi, Wang Yu, Wu Hang-sheng, Wang Ching-ho, Ling Wei-tu, Fanny Helen Ko.
09/22/76

Snap-Shot
(Australia)
FWS. Australian Int'l Film Corp prodn. Prod, Anthony I Ginnane. Exec prod, William Fayman. Dir, Simon Wincer. Sp, Chris and Everett de Roche; cam (Eastmancolor), Vincent Monton; art dirs, Jon Dowding, Jill Eden; snd, Paul Clark; edtng, Phil Reid; mus, Brian May; sfx, Chris Murray; fire stunts, Grant Page. 92.
Chantal Contouri, Sigrid Thornton, Robert Bruning, Hugh Keays-Byrne, Vincent Gil, Denise Drysdale, Jacqui Gordon, Peter Stratford, Lulu Pinkus, Stewart Faichney, Julia Blake, Jon Sidney, Christine Amor, Chris Milne, Peter Flemingham, Bob Brown.
01/17/79

The Sniper: SEE El Qanas

Snovi, Zivot, Smrt Filipa Filipovic
(Dreams, Life, the Death of Filip Filipovic)
(Yugoslavia)
YFR. CFS Kosutnjak - Oour Avala Film - Televizija Beograd prodn. Dir, Milos Radivojevic; sp, Slobodan Stojanvic, Milovan Vitezovic, Alesander Popovic, Novica Savic, Misa Stanislavjevic, Radivojevic; cam (Eastmancolor), Bozidar Nikolic; mus, Kornelije Kovac. 100.
Aleksander Bercek, Milena Dravic, Bata Zivojinovic, Drago Cuma, Predrag Ejdus.
08/13/80

Snowdrops Bloom in September: SEE Schneegloeckchen Bluehn In September

Snowstorm: SEE Mecava

Snuff
(Argentina - US)
MNR. 82.
02/25/76

So Feared a Hell: SEE El Infierno Tan Temido

So Long, Movie Friend: SEE Saraba Eiga No Tomo Yo

So Weit Das Auge Reicht
(As Far As The Eye Sees)
(W Germany)
CCZ. Prokino-Films Du Losange-Cactus Film-Swiss TV-DRS prodn. Wri-dir, Erwin Keusch; cam, Dietrich Lohmann; edtr, Bettina Lewertoff. 137.
Bernd Tauber, Aurore Clement, Jurgen Prochnow, Antonia Reininghaus, Hans-Michael Rehberg.
08/20/80

Sobstvennoie Minienie
(A Personal Opinion)
(USSR)
SOV. Mosfilm prodn. Dir, Youli Kavrassik. Sp, Valentin Tchernykh; cam (Sovcolor), Anatoli Kouznetsov; mus, Boris Tchaikovski. 105.
11/16/77

Sodom and Gomorrah
MTL. Prod-dirs, James and Artie Mitchell. Sp, Bill Boyer, Artie Mitchell; cam, Jon Fontana, snd prodn, Alex Benton; prodn des, Richard Mezzavilla; edtrs, Fontana and E E Mitchell; set construction, Charlie Benton; mus, Mike Bloomfield, Barry Goldberg. (Self-imposed X rating). 90.
Sean Brancato, Deborah Brast, Jacquie Brody, Gina Fornelli, Giovanina, Thom Glardon, Johnnie Keyes, Yank Levine, George S McDonald, Tyler Reynolds, Ken Turner, Mark Us, Raffles.
03/03/76

Soemaend paa sengekanten
(Bedside Sailors)
(Denmark)
PAL. Wri-dir, John Hilbard. Cam (Eastmancolor), Jan Weincke; in charge of prodn, Lars Kolvig; edtrs, Hilbard, Peer Rievers, Marit Jensen; mus, Ole Hoeyer. 93.
Anne Bie Warburg, Ole Soeltoft, Soeren Stroemberg, Annie Birgit Garde.
10/20/76

Sola
(Alone)
(Argentina)
X. Raul de la Torre prodn, wri-dir, de la Torre. Cam (Eastmancolor), Ricardo Younis; edtrs, Oscar Souto, Sergio Zottola; snd, Anibal Libenson, Nerio Barberis; sets, Saulo Benavente; mus, Jorge Calandreli. 97.
Graciela Borges, Mabel Manzotti, Marta Bianchi, Luis Brandoni, Lautaro Murua, Adrian Ghio, Hector Pellegrini.
09/29/76

Soldados
(Soldiers)
(Spain)
X. Antonio Gregori P C prodn. Dir, Alfonso Ungria. Sp, Ungria, Antonio Gregori, based on Max Aub novel "Las Buenas Intenciones"; cam (Eastmancolor), Jose Luis Alcaine; edtr, Javier Moran; sets, Antonio Cortes. 124.
Marilina Ross, Ovidi Monllo, Francisco Algora, Claudia Gravy, Jose Calvo, Julieta Serrano, Lautaro Murua, Jose Maria Munoz.
01/17/79

Soldaty Svobody
(Soldiers of Freedom)
(USSR)
MSF. Mosfilm, Moscow, film prodn, in collab with Bulgaria, Hungary, German Democratic Republic, Poland, Romania, and Czechoslovakia. Dir, Yuri Ozerov. 30.
07/27/77

Soldier Of Orange
(Netherlands)
ITP. Rob Houwer Prodn. Dir, Paul Verhoeven. Sp, Gerard Soeteman, Kees Holierhoek, Verhoeven, based on a novel by Erik Hazelhoff Roelfzema; cam, Jost Vacano, Peter De Bont; mus, Rogier Van Otterloo; edtr, Jane Speer. 165.
Rutger Hauer, Jeroen Krabbe, Peter Faber, Derek De Lint, Eddy Habbema, Lex Van Delden, Edward Fox, Belinda Meuldijk, Susan Penhaligon, Andrea Domburh.
(English subtitles)
01/17/79

Soldiers: SEE Soldados

Soldiers Never Cry
Romania)
RMN. Romaniafilm prodn, Film Group One, Bucharest; Dir, Dinu Cocea. Sp, Mihai Opris, Vasile Chirita; cam, Marian Stanciu; sets, Mara Cuculas; mus, Stefan Zorzor; edtr, Magda Ghise Ghincioiu. 108.
02/28/79

Soldiers of Freedom: SEE Soldaty Svobody

Soledade
(Brazil)
EMZ. Thiago Productions, Embrafilme prodn. Dir, Paulo Thiago. Sp, Ivan Cavalcanti, Thiago from book by Jose Americo Almeida; cam (Eastmancolor), Fernando Durante; edtr, Gustavo Dahl. 81.
Rejane Madeiros, Ney Sant'Anna, Nelson Xavier, Jofre Soares, Emmanuel Cavalcanti.
07/28/76

Soleil Des Hyenes
(Sun of the Hyenes)
(Tunisia - Holland)
X. Newin prodns (Ridha Behi), Stichting Fugitive Cinema, and Zegert Huisman, Holland, Film prodn. Wri-dir, Ridha Behi. Cam (Eastmancolor), Theo van de Sande; mus, Nicola Piovani; edtr, Ton De Graaf; art dir, Jean-Robert Marquis. 100.
Larbi Doghmi, Mahmoud Morsi, Habachi, Ahmed Snoussi, Helene Catzaras.
05/25/77

Solemn Communion: SEE La Communion Solennelle

Solo
(New Zealand - Australia)
X. Hannay-Williams prodn. Prod, Tony Williams, David Hannay. Dir, Tony Williams. Sp, Williams, Martyn Sanderson; cam, John Blick. 97.
Martyn Sanderson, Lisa Peers, Jock Spence, Vincent Gil, Perry Armstrong, Frances Edmund, Davina Whitehouse, Maxwell Fernie, Gillian Hope, Veronica Lawrence, Val Murphy.
03/08/78

Solo Sunny
(E Germany)
DEF. DEFA Film Prodn, Group Babelsberg, East Berlin. Dirs, Konrad Wolf, Wolfgang Kohlhaase. Sp, Kohlhasse; cam, Eberhard Geick; edtr, Evelyn Carow; sets, Alfred Hirschmeier; mus, Guenter Fiescher. 102.
Renate Kroessner, Alexander Lang, Dieter Montag, Klaus Brasch, Heide Kipp.
03/05/80

Solos En La Madrugada
(Alone At Daybreak)
(Spain)
X. Jose Luis Tafur prodn. Dir, Jose Luis Garci; sp, J M Gonzalez Sinde, J L Garci; cam (Technicolor), Manuel Rojas; mus, Jesus Gluck; sets, Ramiro Gomez; edtr, Miguel Gonzalez Sinde. 103.
Jose Sacristan, Fiorella Faltoyano, Emma Cohen, Maria Casanova, Claudio Rodriguez.
04/26/78

Some Interviews on Personal Questions: SEE Neskolko Interwju Po Litschnym Woprosam

Some Kind of Saint: SEE Ein Komischer Heiliger

Somebody Killed Her Husband
COL. Martin Poll prodn, in asso with Melvin Simon. Dir, Lamont Johnson. Sp, Reginald Rose; cam (Panavision-color), Andrew Laszlo; edtr, Barry Malkin; mus comp-adapt, Alex North; sng, "Love Keeps Getting Stronger Every Day," mus, Neil Sedaka, lyr, Howard Greenfield, sung by Sedaka; prodn des, Ted Haworth; art dir, David Chapman; set decor, Leslie Bloom; asst dir, Alex Hapsas; unit publicist, Ann Guerin. (MPAA rating: PG). 96.
Farrah Fawcett-Majors, Jeff Bridges, John Wood, Tammy Grimes, John Glover, Patricia Elliott, Mary McCarty, Laurence Guittard, Vincent Robert Santa Lucia, Beeson Carroll, Eddie Lawrence, Arthur Rhytis, Jean-Pierre Stewart, Terri DuHaime, Sands Hall, Joseph Culliton, Dave Johnson, Melissa Ferris, Jeremiah Sullivan, Sloan Shelton, Mary Alan Hokanson, John Corcoran, Mark Haber.
09/27/78

Somebody's Stolen the Thigh of Jupiter: SEE On A Vole la Cuisse de Jupiter

Something Beautiful: SEE Sesuatau Yang Indah

Something Out Of Nothing: SEE Ot Nishto-Neshto

Something Short of Paradise
AIP. James C Gutman/David Halpern Jr prodn. Prods, Gutman, Lester Berman. Dir, Helpern. Exec prods, Michael Ingber, Herbert Swartz. Sp, Fred Barron; cam, Walter Lassally; edtr, Frank Bracht; mus, Mark Snow; art dir, William De Seta; asst dir, Michael Kravitz. (MPAA rating: PG). 91.
Susan Sarandon, David Steinberg, Jean-Pierre Aumont, Marilyn Sokol, Joe Grifasi, Robert Hitt.
09/26/79

Something's Rotten
(Canada)
DEB. Hazelton Motion Pictures Inc presentation. Prod, David F Eustace, Nancy E Stewart. Dir, F Harvey Frost. Sp, Norman Fox; cam, Brian R R Hebb; mus, John Kuipers; snd, Peter Shewchuk; edtr, Brian Ravok. 90.
Charlotte Blunt, Geoffrey Bowes, Trudy Weiss, Christopher Barry, Cec Linder, Jean-Peter Linton.
05/16/79

Somewhat Like This: SEE Kapos Etsi

Somewhere In Time
U. Rastar/Stephen Deutsch prodn. Prod, Deutsch; dir, Jeannot Szwarc; sp, Richard Matheson, from his novel "Bid Time Return"; cam (Technicolor), Isidore Mankofsky; mus, John Barry, "Rhapsody On A Theme Of Paganini" by Rachmaninoff; edtr, Jeff Gourson; prodn des, Seymour Klate; set decor, Mary Ann Biddle; snd, Charles L King III, Roger Heman, Earl M Madery, Rex A Slinkard; asst dir, Burt Bluestein. (MPAA rating: PG). 103.
Christopher Reeve, Jane Seymour, Christopher Plummer, Teresa Wright, Bill Erwin, George Voskovec, Susan French, John Alvin, Eddra Gale, Sean Hayden, Richard Matheson.
09/24/80

Sommergaeste
(Summer Guests)
(W Germany)
CTT. Regina Ziegler Film Production, World rights, Exportfilm Bishoff & Co, Munich. In collab with ensemble of Schaubuehne am Halleschen Ufer, Berlin. Dir, Peter Stein. Sp, Botho Strauss, adapted from Maxim Gorki; cam, Michael Ballhaus; edtr, Siegrun Jaeger; sets, Karl-Ernst Herrmann; cos, Susanne Raschig; mus, Peter Fischer. 120.
Wolf Redl, Edith Clever, Ilse Ritter, Michael Koenig, Jutta Lampe, Otto Sander, Elke Petri, Werner Rehm, Sabiner Andreas, Ruediger Hacker, Guenther Lampe, Gerd Wameling, Otto Maechtlinger, Eberhard Feik, Katharina Tueschen.
02/11/76

Son Of Chao Phya: SEE Look Chao Phya

Sonambulos
(Spain)
X. Profilmes SA prodn. Wri-dir, Manuel Gutierrez Aragon; exec prod, Jose A Perez Giner. Cam (Eastmancolor), Teo Escamilla; sets, Miguel Narros; edtr, Jose Salcedo; mus, Jose Nieto. 93.
Ana Belen, Norman Brisky, Maria Rosa Salgado, Javier Delgado, Lola Gaos, Richard Franco, Felix Rotaeta, Jose Manuel Cervino, Eduardo MacGregor, Jose Luis Borau, Miguel Narros, Fernando Chinarro, Laly Soldevila, Jose Luis Gomez.
10/11/78

Sonata Nad Ozerom
(Sonata Over the Lake)
(USSR)
X. Latvian Film Studio, Riga, prodn. Dir, Gunar Tcelinski, Varis Brasla. Sp, R Ezer; based on his novel, "The Well"; cam, Gvido Skulte; mus, Imant Kalnynsh; art dir, Andris Merkmanis. 90.
Gunar Tcelinski, Astida Kairisha, Lilita Ozolina, Gird Ikovlev, Lidia Fraimane.
01/19/77

The Song of Roland: SEE La Chanson De Roland

Song of the Canary
X. "Song of the Canary" prodn. Prod-dirs, Josh Hanig, David Davis; cam, John Else, Michael Anderson; mus, Doug McKechnie, Si Kahn; edtrs, Davis, Hanig, Stephen Stept. 58.
(DOC) (16m)
03/28/79

The Song Remains The Same
(Britain)
WB. Prod, Swan Song Inc; exec prod, Peter Grant. Dirs, Peter Clifton, Joe Massot. Cam, Ernie Day; edtr, Peter Clifton; snd, Jimmy Page; sfx, Shelly of Camera Effects; makeup effects, Colin Arthur. (MPAA rating: PG). 136.
Led Zeppelin (John Bonham, John Paul Jones, Jimmy Page, Robert Plant), Peter Grant, Richard Cole, Derek Skilton, Colin Rigdon.
(DOC)
10/20/76

Sonntagskinder
(Sunday Children)
(W Germany)
HBD. Sentana Film Prodn, Munich, Michael Verhoeven. Dir, Michael Verhoeven. Sp, Gerlind Reinshagen, Verhoeven; cam, Gero Erhardt; edtr, Dagmar Hirtz. 103.
Nora Barner, Erika Pluhar, Gerd Seid, Pola Kinski, Mario Fischel, Elisabeth Schwarz, Rudolf Wessely, Ruth Maria Kubitschek, Carolin Orner, Christoph Quest, Pierre Franckh, Maria Hartmann, Friedrich von Thun, Hartmut Becker, Santiago Ziesmer, Dieter Prochnow.
(B & W)
05/21/80

Sono Fotogenico
(I'm Photogenic)
(Italy - France)
UA. Prods, Pio Angeletti, Adriano De Micheli for Dear Film (Rome) and Film Marceau Cocinor (Paris). Dir, Dino Risi. Cam (Eastmancolor), Tonino Delli Colli; art dir, Ezio Altieri; edtr, Alberto Galliti; mus, Manuel De Sica. 118.
Renato Pozzeto, Edwige Fenech.
05/28/80

Sono Stato Un Agente Cia
(Covert Action)
(Italy)
CAP. Prod, Gibi Milesi for Mires Cinematografico. Dir, Romolo Guerrieri. Sp, Vittorio Schiraldi, Mino Roti, Nico Ducci; cam (Technicolor), Erico Menczer; art dir, Eugenio Leverani; edtr, Antonio Siciliano; mus, Stelvio Cipriani. 100.
David Janssen, Corinne Clery, Maurizio Merli, Arthur Kennedy, Philippe Leroy.
08/23/78

Sons For The Return Home
(New Zealand)
X. New Zealand Film Commission presentation. Exec prod, Don Blakeney. Dir, Paul Maunder. Sp, Maunder, from novel by Albert Wendt; cam, Alun Bollinger; mus, Malcolm Smith; snd, Don Reynolds. 115.
Uelese Petaia, Fiona Lindsay, Mira Walker, Lani Tupu, Alan Jervis, Anne Flannery.
10/31/79

Sonya and the Madman
(Egypt)
X. Hossam Eddin Mostafa prodn, Cairo. Prod-dir, Hossam El Dine Mostafa. Sp, Mahmoud Dyab, based on Dostoievsky's "Crime and Punishment". 90.
Naglaa Fat-Hi, Mahmoud Yassin, Nour El Sherif.
08/03/77

Sophia: SEE Zofia

Sorcerer
UPR. Dir-prod, William Friedkin. Sp, Walon Green, from novel "The Wages Of Fear" by Georges Arnaud; cam (Technicolor), John M Stephens, Dick Bush; edtr, Bud Smith; mus, Tangerine Dream, with addl mus by Charlie Parker, Keith Jarrett; prodn des, John Box; art dir, Roy Walker; set decor, Bob Laing; cos-ward, Anthony Powell; snd, Buzz Knudsen, Bob Glass, Dick Tyler, Jean-Louis Ducarme; stunt coord, Bud Ekins; asst dir, Newton Arnold. (MPAA rating: PG). 121.
Roy Scheider, Bruno Cremer, Francisco Rabal, Amidou, Ramon Bieri, Peter Capell, Karl John, Frederick Ledebur, Chico Martinez.
06/29/77

The Sorrows of Young Werther: SEE Die Leiden Des Jungen Werther

Soulsister
(Soul Sister)
(W Germany)
Dietmar Buchmann Production, Berlin, in collab with Zweites Deutsches Fernsehen (ZDF), Wiesbaden-Mainz. Wri-dir, Dietmar Buchmann. 90.
Tatjana Blacher, Holmes McHenry, Eberhard Feik, Edith Elsholtz, Dieter Stolz.
09/03/80

Sourdough
FSI. Exec prods, George E Lukens Jr, Robert B Pendleton. Dir, Martin J Spinelli. Sp, Lewis N Turner, Spinelli, from a story by Rod Perry; cam (Eastmancolor), Perry; edtr, George Folsey Jr; mus, Jerrold Immel; narr, Gene Evans. 94.
Gil Perry.
03/02/77

Soy Un Delincuente
(I Am a Delinquent)
(Venezuela)
PYO. Dir, Clemente De La Cerda. Sp, Luis Correa; book, Ramon Brizuela; cam (Eastmancolor), Jose Jimenez; edtr, Alcides Longa; mus, Miguel Angel Fuster. 116.
Orlando Zarramera, Maria Escalona, Maria Garcia Bianchi, Carlos Carrero.
09/07/77

Space Coast
X. Prods, Ross McElwee, Michel Negroponte. All tech credits by McElwee and Negroponte. 90.
(DOC)
05/23/79

Space Cruiser Yamato
(Japan)
EPI. Prod-dir-sp, Yoshinobu Nishizaki. Character des, Leiji Matsumoto; chief ani, Noboru Ishiguro; mus, Hiroshi Miyagawa. 107.
(ANI)
12/21/77

The Space Movie
(Britain)
X. Virgin Films Ltd prodn. Prods, Richard Branson, Simon Draper. Dir-wri, Tony Palmer. Mus, Mike Oldfield; edtrs, Graham Bunn, John Beech. 78. (DOC)
03/05/80

Sparkle
WB. Robert Stigwood Organization prodn, prod, Howard Rosenman; exec prods, Beryl Vertue, Peter Brown. Dir, Sam O'Steen. Sp, Joel Schumacher, from a story by Schumacher, Rosenman; cam (Technicolor), Bruce Surtees; edtr, Gordon Scott; mus, Curtis Mayfield; art dir, Peter Wooley; set decor, Cheryal Kearney; snd, Tom Overton; asst dir, Ken Swor. (MPAA rating: PG). 98.
Philip M Thomas, Irene Cara, Lonette McKee, Dwan Smith, Mary Alice, Dorian Harewood, Tony King, Beatrice Winde, Paul Lambert.
04/07/76

Spasatel
(The Life Guard)
(USSR)
SOV. Mosfilm prodn. Wri-dir, Sergei Soloviov; cam (Sovcolor), Pavel Lebsev; edtr, A Abramova; mus, Isaak Svarc. 101.
Tatiana Drubic, Vasili Miscenko, Sergei Sakurov, Olga Beljavskaya, Vjaselav Konenko, Alejsandr Kajdonovski.
09/10/80

The Spat: SEE La Zizanie

Special Delivery
AIP. Bing Crosby Prods film, prod, Richard Berg; exec prod, Charles A Pratt. Dir, Paul Wendkos. Sp, Don Gazzaniga; cam (DeLuxe Color), Harry Stradling Jr; edtr, Houseley Stevenson; mus, Lalo Schifrin; art dir, Jack Poplin; set decor, Don Sullivan; snd, David Dockendorf; stunt coord, Carey Loftin. (MPAA rating: PG). 98.
Bo Svenson, Cybill Shepherd, Tom Atkins, Sorrell Booke, Gerrit Graham, Michael C Gwynne, Jeff Goldblum, Robert Ito, Lynnette Mettey, Richard Drout Miller, John Quade, Vic Tayback, Edward Winter, Kim Richards.
07/07/76

Special Edition: SEE Editie Speciala

Special Education: SEE Specijalno Vaspitanje

Special Treatment: SEE Poseban Tretman

Specijalno Vaspitanje
(Special Education)
(Yugoslavia)
YFR. Centar Filmski Radni, Zajednica SR Srbije, Belgrade, film prodn. Dir, Goran Markovic. Sp, Markovic, Miroslav Simic; cam, Zivko Zalar; mus, Zoran, Simjanovic; art dir, Miljen Kljakovic; cos, Nada Perovic. 90.
Slavko Stimac, Bekim Fehmiu, Ljubisa Samardzic, Aleksandar Bercek, Cvijeta Mesic, Jovan Janicejevic, Slobodan Aligrudic.
05/25/77

Speed Fever
(Italy)
TIT. Alessandro Fracassi prodn for Racing Pictures. Dir, Mario Morra, Oscar Orefici. Sp, Pietro Rizzo; cam (Technicolor), Ottavio Fabbri; mus, Guido and Maurizio De Angelis. 105.
Niki Lauda, James Hunt, Mario Andretti, Emerson Fittipaldi, Carlos Reutemann.
09/20/78

Spending Money: SEE L'Argent De Poche

Spermula
(France)
PPFC. Film and Co prodn. Wri-dir, Charles Matton. Cam (Eastmancolor), Jean-Jacques Flori; edtrs, Isabelle Rathery, Sarah Matton; art dir, Matton; prod, Bernard Lenteric. 105.
Dayle Haddon, Udo Kier, Georges Geret, Ginette Leclerc, Jocelyne Boisseau, Francois Dunoyer, Isabelle Mercanton.
06/23/76

Spetters
(Holland)
TUS. VSE Prodn. Dir, Paul Verhoeven. Prod, Joop Van Den Ende. Wri, Gerard Soeteman; cam (Eastmancolor), Jost Vacano; edtr, Ineke Schenkkan; mus, Ton Scherpenzeel & KAJAK; snd, Wim Wolf & Dieter Schwartz; art dir, Dick Schillemans; unit pa, Gysbert Versluys. 115.
Hans van Tongeren, Renee Soutendijk, Toon Agterberg, Maarten Spanjer, Marianne Boyer, Hugo Metsers, Kitty Courbois, Rutger Hauer, Jeroen Krabbe.
04/02/80

Spider Football: SEE Pokfoci

Spirala
(Spiral)
(Poland)
POL. TOR prodn. Wri-dir, Krzysztof Zanussi. Cam (Eastmancolor), Edward Klosinski; mus, Wojiech Kilar. 90.
Jan Nowicki, Maja Komorowska, Aleksander Bardini.
05/31/78

Spirit of the Wind
RVD. Raven Pictures-Doyon Ltd prodn. Dir, Ralph Liddle. Sp, Liddle, John Logue; cam, Logue; edtr, Mark Goldblatt; mus, composed by and with original songs sung by Buffy Sainte-Marie. 98.
Pius Savage, Chief Dan George, Slim Pickens, George Clutesi.
05/23/79

Splav Meduze
(The Medusa Raft)
(Yugoslavia)
YFR. Viba Film-Televizija Beograd prodn. Dir-pho (Eastmancolor)-edtr, Karpo Godina. 93.
Olga Kacjan, Vladilava Jevic, Boris Komnenic, Erol Kadic, Franco Lasic, Radmila Zilkovic, Petar Kralj.
08/13/80

Spodelena Lyubov
(With Shared Love)
(Bulgaria - USSR)
X. Bulgarian and Soviet Film Co-prodn. Sofia and Moscow Sredets Film Unit, Sofia. Dir, Sergei Mikaelian. Sp, Rustam Ibrahimbekov, Katya Goumnerova, Mikaelien; cam, Leonid Kalashnikov; art dir, Yuri Fomenko; mus, Kiril Tsiboulka. 90.
Velko Kunev, Simeon Morozov, Rossitsa Petrova, Veronica Isotova, Georgi Roussev, Bogomil Simeonov.
07/18/79

Spoegelsestoget
(Ghost Train)
(Denmark)
DNS. Saga A/S prodn. Dir, Bent Christensen. Sp, Leif Panduro, Bent Christensen, based on Paul Sarauw adaptation of Arnold Ridley's play; cam (Eastmancolor), Henning Kristiansen; prodn des, Sven Wickman; cos, Ulla-Britt Soederlund, others; mus, Soeren Christensen; edtr, Anker; in charge of prodn. Erik Nissen/Gerd, Erik Overbye. 85.
Dirch Passer, Preben Kaas, Axel Stroebye, Lisbeth Dahl.
08/25/76

Spoiled Children: SEE Des Enfants Gates

Sport, Sport, Sport
(USSR)
GOS. Mosfilm Prodn, Moscow. Dir, Elem Klimov. Sp, H Klimov; cam, B Brozhovsky, O Zguridi; sets, N Serebryakov, A Speshneva; mus, A Shnitke. 90.
G Svetlani, L Novozhilova, B Andreev, V Lyakhov, V Brumel, H Klimov, Nikita Mikhalkov, Larissa Shepitko.
(DOC)
07/05/78

Spotkanie Na Atlantyku
(Chance Meeting on the Ocean)
(Poland)
POL. Film Polski prodn, Kadr Film Unit, Warsaw. Dir, Jerzy Kawalerowicz; sp, Boleslaw Michalek, Kawalerowicz; cam, Jerzy Lukaszewicz; mus, Piotr Figiel; prodn mgrs, Urszula Orczykowska, Zygmunt Wojcik. 110.
Teresa Budzisz-Krzyzanowska, Malgorzata Niemirska, Ignacy Gogolewski, Marek Walczewski, Feliks Parnell, Waclaw Ulewicz, Marek Lewandowski, Gustaw Lutkiewicz, Jerzy Braszka.
09/24/80

Springday in Hell: SEE En foraarsdag i helvede

The Spy Who Loved Me
(Britain)
UA. Albert R Broccoli prodn. Dir, Lewis Gilbert. Sp, Christopher Wood, Richard Maibaum, based on the Ian Fleming character; cam, Claude Renoir; mus, Marvin Hamlisch; theme, "Nobody Does It Better," mus, Hamlisch, lyr, Carole Bayer Sager, sung by Carly Simon; prodn des, Ken Adam; edtr, John Glen; art dir, Peter Lamont; snd, Gordon Everett; 2d unit dirs, Ernest Day, John Glen; special visual effects, Derek Meddings; special optical effects, Alan Maley; sfx (studio), John Evans. (MPAA rating: PG). 125.
Roger Moore, Barbara Bach, Curt Jurgens, Richard Kiel, Caroline Munro, Walter Gotell, Geoffrey Keen, Bernard Lee, George Baker, Michael Billington, Olga Bisera, Desmond Llewellyn, Edward De Souza, Vernon Dobtcheff, Valerie Leon, Lois Maxwell, Sydney Tafler, Nadim Sawalha, Sue Vanner, Eva Rueber-Staier, Robert Brown, Marilyn Galsworthy, Milton Reid, Cyril Shaps.
(JAMES BOND SERIES)
07/06/77

The Squeeze
(Britain)
WB. Prod, Stanley O'Toole. Dir, Michael Apted. Sp, Leon Griffiths (based on David Craig novel, "Whose Little Girl Are You?"); cam (Technicolor), Dennis Lewiston; edtr, John Shirley; mus, David Hentschel; art dir, William McCrow; snd, Cyril Swern. 106.
Stacy Keach, Freddie Starr, Edward Fox, Stephen Boyd, David Hemmings, Carol White, Alan Ford, Roy Marsden, Stuart Harwood, Hilary Gasson, Alison Portes, Keith Miles, Lee Strand, Lucinda Duckett, Lucita Lijertwood.
03/02/77

The Squeeze
(Italy)
MAV. Dritte Centama GmbH prodn. Prod, Turi Vasile; exec prod, Raymond R Homer. Dir, Anthony M Dawson (Antonio Margheriti); sp, Simon O'Neil, Marc Princi, Paul Costello; cam (Technicolor), Sergio D'Offizi; edtr, Robert Sterbini; mus, Paolo Vasile; art dir, Francesco Bronzi, Hans Zillman; cos des, Adrianna Berselli; snd, Miro Branoti; asst dir, Ignazio Dolce. (MPAA rating: R). 100.
Lee Van Cleef, Karen Black, Edward Albert, Lionel Stander, Robert Alda, Angelo Infanti, Antonella Murgia, Peter Carsten.
(English soundtrack)
07/30/80

Squeeze
(New Zealand)
X. Trilogic Film Productions (Auckland, N Zealand). Prod-dir, Richard Turner. Sp, Turner; cam, Ian Paul; edtr, Jamie Selkirk; score, Toy Love; mus, The Features, Streetplayer, Hagan & Young. 82.
Robert Shannon, Paul Eadv, Donna Akersten, Peter Heperi, David Herkt, Fay Flegg, Lynn Robson, Dinah Russell, Eileen Swann, Bruce Weston, Don Farr, Sandy Gauntlett, Martyn Sanderson, Ian Westbury, Arthur Wright.
12/03/80

Squirm
AIP. Prod, George Manasse; exec prods, Edgar Lansbury, Joseph Beruh. Wri-dir, Jeff Lieberman. Cam (Movielab Color), Joseph Mangine; edtr, Brian Smedley-Aston; mus, Robert Prince; art dir, Henry Shrady; snd, Al Gramaglia, George Goen; asst dir, Mark Hindenberg. (MPAA rating: R). 93.
John Scardino, Patricia Pearcy, R A Dow, Jean Sullivan, Peter MacLean, Fran Higgins, William Newman, Barbara Quinn, Carl Dagenhart.
08/11/76

Sredi Ludei
(Among People)
(USSR)
GOS. Kirghizfilm Prodn, Kirghizia. Dirs, Bolotbek Shamshiev, Artyk Suyundukov. Sp, Talip Ibraimov, Shamshiev; cam, Manas Musayev; sets, Mikhail Scheglov; mus, Rumil Vildanov. 90.
Sabira Kumushalieva, Mir Nurmakhanov, Ayturgan Temirova, Orozbek Kutmanaliev, Baidyla Kaltayev.
(B & W)
09/12/79

S.T.A.B.
(Hong Kong - Thailand)
GHV. Paragon Films prodn. Exec prod, Raymond Chow. Prod-dir, Chalong Pakdivijit. English-language version prod, Leonard K C Ho. Sp, Andre Morgan; English dialog, Voicetrax; mus, Noel Quinlan; post-prodn facilities, Golden Studios. 100.
Greg Morris, Sombat Metanee, Krung Srivilai, Tham Thuy Hang, Anoma Palalak, Krisana Amnueyporn, Darm Daskorn, Dolna Sopir.
(English soundtrack)
08/25/76

The Staff: SEE Personel

The Stain: SEE Daag

Stalker
(USSR - W Germany)
X. Mosfilm Prodn, Moscow, in co-prodn with Zweites Deutsches Fernsehen (ZDF), Wiesbaden-Mainz. Wri-dir-sets, Andrei Tarkovsky, based on motifs in book, "Picnic on the Road," by the Strugatsky Brothers. Cam, Alexander Knayzhinsky; mus, Eduard Artemev; asst dir, Larissa Tarkovsky. 140.
Alexander Kaidanovsky, Anatoly Solonitsyn, Nikolai Grinko, Alisa Freindlich.
09/19/79

Stand Up Straight, Delphina: SEE Ispravi Se, Delfina

Stand Up Virgin Soldiers
(Britain)
WB. Prod, Greg Smith. Dir, Norman Cohen. Sp, Leslie Thomas, based on his novel "Stand Up Virgin Soldiers"; cam (Technicolor), Ken Hodges; edtr, Geoffrey Foot; mus, Ed Welch; prodn des, Harry Pottle; snd, Dennis Whitlock; asst dirs, Bill Westley, Chris Carreras, Roy Stevens. 91.
Robin Askwith, Nigel Davenport, George Layton, John Le Mesurier, Warren Mitchell, Robin Nedwell, Edward Woodward, Irene Handl, Fiesta Mei Ling, Pamela Stephenson, Lynda Bellingham, David Auker, Robert Booth, Peter Bourke, Leo Dolan, Brian Godfrey, Paul Rattee, Patrick Newell, Miriam Margoyles.
04/20/77

Starcrash
NW. Prods, Nat and Patrick Wachsberger. Dir, Lewis Coates (Luigi Cozzi). Sp, Coates, Wachsberger; cam (Metrocolor), Paul Beeson, Roberto D'Ettore; edtr, Sergio Montanari; Dolby consultant, Don Digirolamo; mus, John Barry; prodn des, Aurelio Crugnolla; sfx dirs, Armando Valcuda, Germano Natali; electronic visual effects supv, Ron Hays. (MPAA rating: PG). 92.
Marjoe Gortner, Caroline Munro, Christopher Plummer, David Hasselhoff, Robert Tessier, Joe Spinnell, Nadia Cassini, Judd Hamilton, Hamilton Camp.
03/28/79

Stardust Memories
UA. Prod, Robert Greenhut. Wri-dir, Woody Allen. Exec prods, Jack Rollins, Charles H Joffe. Cam, Gordon Willis; edtr, Susan E Morse; snd, James Sabat; prodn des, Santo Loquasto; asst dir, Frederic B Blankfein; art dir, Michael Molly; various songs-mus credited. (MPAA rating: PG). 89.
Woody Allen, Charlotte Rampling, Marie-Christine Barrault, Jessica Harper, John Rothman, Amy Wright, Helen Hanft, Daniel Stern, Tony Roberts, Anne Desalvo.
(B & W)
10/01/80

Starhops
FFU. Grodnik/Sharpe prodn of a Roseworld film. Prods, John B Kelley, Robert D Krintzman; exec prods, Daniel Grodnik, Robert Sharpe. Dir, Barbara Peters. Sp, Dallas Meredith; cam (CFI Color), Eric Saarinen; edtr, Steve Zaillian; snd, Mike C Moore; cos-ward, Elan. (MPAA rating: R). 82.
Dorothy Buhrman, Sterling Frazier, Jillian Kenser, Peter Paul Iapis, Anthony Mannino, Paul Ryan, Al Hobson, Dick Miller.
03/22/78

Staromodnaia Komedia
(The Old Comedy)
(USSR)
SOV. Mosfilm prodn. Dir, E Savelieva, Tatyana Berezantseva. Sp, A Abrouzov, V Jelenzniakov from the play by Abrouzov; cam (Sovcolor), B Kotcherov; edtr, L Boulgakova; mus, M Tariverdiev. 100.
Alissa Freyndikh, Igor Validimirov.
08/22/79

Stars in the Hair, Tears in the Eyes: SEE Zvezdi V Kossite, Salzi V Ochiete

Starship Invasions
(Canada)
WB. Hal Roach Studios presentation. Prods, Norman Glick, Ed Hunt, Ken Gord. Exec prods, Earl A Glick, Norman Glick. Wri-dir, Ed Hunt. Cam, Mark Irwin; edtr, Millie Moore, Ruth Hope; snd, Tony Van Den Akker; mus, Gil Melle; sfx, Warren Keillor; art dir, Karen Bromley; asst dir, Gary Flanagan. (MPAA rating: PG). 89.
Robert Vaughn, Christopher Lee, Daniel Pilon, Tiiu Leek, Helen Shaver, Henry Ramer, Victoria Johnson, Doreen Lipson.
10/19/77

Starting Over
PAR. James L Brooks prodn. Prods, Alan J Pakula, Brooks. Dir, Pakula. Sp, Brooks, based on the novel by Dan Wakefield; cam, Sven Nykvist; edtr, Marion Rothman; prodn des, George Jenkins; cos des, John Boxer; mus, Marvin Hamlisch; snd, James Sabat; asst dir, Alex Hapsas. (MPAA rating: R). 106.
Burt Reynolds, Jill Clayburgh, Candice Bergen, Charles Durning, Frances Sternhagen, Austin Pendleton, Mary Kay Place, MacIntyre Dixon, Jay Sanders, Richard Whiting, Sturgis Warner.
10/03/79

Star Trek
PAR. Prod, Gene Roddenberry. Dir, Robert Wise; sp, Harold Livingston, based on a story by Alan Dean Foster; cam (Metrocolor), Richard H Kline; edtr, Todd Ramsay; prodn des, Harold Michelson; mus, Jerry Goldsmith; cos des, Robert Fletcher; special pho effects, Douglas Trumbull, John Dykstra; art dir, Michelson, Leon Harris; make-up, Fred Phillips. (MPAA rating: G). 132.
William Shatner, Leonard Nimoy, DeForest Kelly, James Doohan, George Takei, Majel Barrett, Walter Koening, Nichelle Nichols, Persis Khambatta, Stephen Collins, Mark Lenard, Billy Van Zandt, Grace Lee Whitney, David Gautreaux, Howard Itzkowitz, Marcy Lafferty, Terrence O'Connor, Michael Rougas.
12/12/79

Star Wars
FOX. Prod, Gary Kurtz. Wri-dir, George Lucas; cam (Technicolor; prints by Deluxe), Gilbert Taylor; 2d unit cam, Carroll Ballard, Rick Clemente, Robert Dalva, Tak Fujimoto; edtrs, Paul Hirsch, Marcia Lucas, Richard Chew; mus, John Williams; prodn des, John Barry; art dirs, Norman Reynolds, Leslie Dilley; set decor, Roger Christian; snd (Dolby), Don McDougal, Bob Minkler, Ray West, Mike Minkler, Les Fresholtz, Richard Portman, Derek Ball, Stephen Katz; cos-ward, John Mollo, Ron Beck; stunt coord, Peter Diamond.
Additional Prodn Credits-Special pho effects supv, John Dykstra; special prodn-mechanical effects supv, John Stears; prodn supv, Robert Watts; prodn illustration, Ralph McQuarrie; special dial-snd effects, Ben Burtt; snd edtrs, Sam Shaw, Robert R Rutledge, Gordon Davidson, Gene Corso.
Miniature And Optical Effects Credits-First cam, Richard Edlund; composite optical pho, Robert Blalack (Praxis); optical pho, Paul Roth; ani-rotoscope des, Adam Beckett; stop-motion ani, Jon Berg, Philip Tippet. (MPAA rating: PG). 121.
Mark Hamill, Harrison Ford, Carrie Fisher, Peter Cushing, Alec Guinness, Anthony Daniels, Kenny Baker, Peter Mayhew, David Prowse, Phil Brown, Shelagh Fraser, Jack Purvis, Alex McCrindle, Eddie Byrne, Don Henderson, Richard LeParmentier, Leslie Schofield, Drewe Henley, Dennis Lawson, Garrick Hagon, Jack Klaff, William Hootkins, Angus McInnis, Jeremy Sinden, Graham Ashley.
05/25/77

State Reason: SEE La Raison D'Etat

Stay As You Are: SEE Cosi Come Sei

Stay Hungry
UA. Prods, Harold Schneider, Bob Rafelson. Dir, Rafelson. Sp, Charles Gaines, Rafelson, based on Gaines' novel; cam (DeLuxe Color), Victor Kemper; edtr, John F Link II; mus, Bruce Langhorne, Byron Berline; prodn des, Toby Carr Rafelson; set decor, Bob Gould; snd, Richard Portman, Barry Thomas; asst dir, Michael Haley. (MPAA rating: R). 102.
Jeff Bridges, Sally Field, Arnold Schwarzenegger, R G Armstrong, Robert Englund, Helena Kallianiotes, Robert E Mosley, Woodrow Parfrey, Scatman Crothers, Kathleen Miller, Fannie Flagg, Joanna Cassidy, Richard Gilliland, Ed Begley Jr, John David Carson, Joe Spinell, Cliff Pellow, Dennis Fimple, Mayf Nutter.
04/28/76

The Steam Mare: SEE La Jument Vapeur

Steel
WNO. Peter S Davis/William N Panzer prodn. Prods, Davis, Panzer. Dir, Steven Carver. Exec prod, Lee Majors. Sp, Leigh Chapman; cam (Movielab), Roger Shearman; edtr, David Blewitt; prodn des, Ward & Preston; mus, Michael Colombier; set decor, Lloyd Linean; sfx, Roger George; stunt coord, James Arnett; cos, Doris Lynch, Sydney Gilbert; snd, William Griffith; asst dirs, Tom Connors, Richard Hashimoto. (MPAA rating: PG). 99.
Lee Majors, Jennifer O'Neill, Art Carney, George Kennedy, Harris Yulin, Redmond Cleason, Terry Kiser, Richard Lynch, Ben Marley, Roger Mosley, Albert Salmi, Robert Tessier, Hunter Von Leer, R G Armstrong, Joseph DeNicola.
08/06/80

The Steppe
(USSR)
X. Mosfilm prodn. Wri-dir, Sergei Bondarchuk. Cam, Leonid Kalashnikov; mus, V Ovtchinikov; snd, Y Michailov. 113.
Oleg Kuznetzov, Ivan Lapidov, Georgy Burkov, Stanislav Liubshin, Serge Bondartchouk.
08/30/78

Sternsteinhof
(The Sternstein Manor)
(W Germany)
X. Roxy-Film prodn. Dir, Hans W Geissendoerfer. Sp, Geissendoerfer, Hermann Weigel, based on novel with same name by Ludwig Anzengruber; cam, Frank Bruehne; mus, Eugen Thomas; snd, Peter Beil. 125.
Katja Rupe, Tilo Prueckner, Peter Kern, Agnes Fink, Elfriede Kuzmany, Irm Hermann, Ulrike Luderer, Gustl Bayrhammer.
07/14/76

Stevie
(Britain)
FAS. Bowden Prodn. Prod-dir, Robert Enders. Sp, Hugh Whitemore, based on his play and the works of Stevie Smith; cam (Technicolor), Freddie Young; mus, Patrick Young; edtr, Peter Tanner; art dir, Bob Jones; asst dir, Ken Baker; snd, Claude Hitchcock. 102.
Glenda Jackson, Mona Washbourne, Alec McCowen, Trevor Howard.
09/06/78

Stici Pre Svitanja
(Arrive Before Breakfast)
(Yugoslavia)
YFR. Neoplanata prodn. Dir, Aleksander Dordevic. Sp, Vlasta Radovanovic, from the books by Paasko Romac and Stanka Veselinov; cam (Eastmancolor), Dusan Ninkov; mus, Mladen and Predrag Vranesevic. 94.
Bata Zivojinovic, Ljubisa Samardzic, Stevan Gardinovacki, Pater Carsten.
08/09/78

The Stick Up
(Britain)
TDB. Elliott Kastner, Danny O'Donovan presentation. Prod, George Pappas. Wri-dir, Jeffrey Bloom. Cam, Michael Reed; mus, Michael J Lewis; snd, Ron Butcher; asst dir, Frank Ernst; ward, Mike Jarvis. 101.
David Soul, Pamela McMyler, Johnny Wade, Tony Melody, Norman Jones, Glynn Edwards, Robert Longden, Pat Durkin, Alan Tilern, Cyd Child, Michael Balfour.
05/24/78

Stilleben
(Still Life)
(Switzerland)
FPZ. Cinemonde Zurich prodn. Wri-dir, Elisabeth Gujer. Cam, Rob Gnant, Werner Zuber; edtr, Uli Meier; snd, Hans Toni Aschwanden. 70.
Margrit Winter, Hans Heinz Moser, Elmar Schulte, Maja Stolle, Peter Oehme, Wolfram Berger, Ernst Baechi, Rodi Nater, Heinz Trudel, Robert Boner, Hedy Knorr, Lo de Fleury, Bouallala Riad, Johann Schaad.
(B & W)
10/24/79

Stin Letajiciho Ptacka
(Shadow Of A Flying Bird)
(Czechoslovakia)
CZS. Czechoslovak Film Prodn, Barradov Studios, Prague. Dir, Jaroslav Balik. Sp, Jan Otcenasek. 90.
06/21/78

Stiny Horkeho Leta
(Shadows Of A Hot Summer)
(Czechoslovakia)
CZS. Czechoslovak, Studio Barrandov, Film Prodn, Prague. Dir, Frantisek Vlacil. Sp, Jiri Krizan; cam, Ivan Slapeta; mus, Zdenek Liska. 90.
Juraj Kukura, Marta Vancurova, Gustav Valach, Karel Chromik, Zdenek Kutil, Jiri Bartoska, Augustin Kuban, Gustav Opocensky.
08/02/78

Stir
(Australia)
HOY. Smiley Films prodn. Prod, Richard Brennan. Dir, Stephen Wallace. Sp, Bob Jewson; cam (Eastmancolor), Geoffrey Burton; edtr, Henry Dangar; mus, Cameron Allan; sfx, Chris Murray. 100.
Bryan Brown, Max Phipps, Dennis Miller, Michael Gow, Phil Motherwell, Gary Waddell, Ray Marshall, Ted Robshaw, James Marsh, Paul Sonkkila, Keith Gallasch, Robert Noble, Syd Heylen, Peter Kowitz, Robert "Tex" Morton
Tony Wager, Les Newcombe, Morris Saidi, Dave Taylor, Margaret Throsby, Chris Smith, Ian Gray, Peter Barton, James Cameron, Greg Smith, Dennis Hunt.
07/16/80

Stir Crazy
COL. Hannah Weinstein prodn. Prod, Hannah Weinstein. Dir, Sidney Poitier. Exec prod, Melville Tucker. Sp, Bruce Jay friedman; cam (Metrocolor), Fred Schuler; edtr, Harry Keller; prodn des, Alfred Sweeney; mus, Tom Scott; snd, Glen Anderson; set decor, Arthur Jeph Parker; asst dir, Daniel J McCauley. (MPAA rating: R). 111.
Gene Wilder, Richard Pryor, Georg Sanford Brown, Jobeth Williams, Miguelangel Suarez, Craig T Nelson, Barry Corbin, Charles Weldon, Nicolas Coster, Joel Brooks, Jonathan Banks, Erland Van Lidth De Jeude, Lewis Van Bergen, Lee Purcell.
12/03/80

Stone Cold Dead
(Canada)
DIM. KoZak Prodns presentation. Exec Prod, Peter Wilson. Prods, George Mendeluk, John Ryan. Dir, Mendeluk. Sp, Mendeluk, based on novel "The Sin Sniper" by Hugh Garner; cam, Dennis Miller; edtr, Martin Pepler; art dir, Ted Watkins; set decor, Jac Bradette. 97.
Richard Crenna, Paul Williams, Linda Sorenson, Belinda J Montgomery, Charles Shamata, Alberta Watson, Monique Mercure, Andree Cousineau, Frank Moore, George Chuvalo, George Touliatos, Dennis Strong, Jennifer Dale.
02/27/80

Stony Island
WNO. Prods, Andrew Davis, Tamar Hoffs. Dir, Andrew Davis; wris, Andrew Davis, Tamar Hoffs; cam, Tak Fujimoto; edtr, Dov Hoenig; mus, David Matthews, perf, Stony Island Band; supv, Gene Barge. (MPAA rating: PG). 97.
Richard Davis, Edward Stoney Robinson, George Englund, Gene Barge, Ronnie Barron, Tennyson Stephens, Larry Ball, Windy Barnes, Rae Dawn Chong, Donnell Hagen, Criss Johnson, Kenneth Brass, Edwin William, Steele L Seals, Susanna Hoffs, Nathan Davis, Tom Mula, Carmi Simon, Dennis Franz.
11/15/78

Stop Calling Me Baby: SEE
Moi, Fleur Bleue

Stop It!: SEE At Dere Tor!

Stopar
(The Hitchhiker)
(Czechoslovakia)
CZS. Czechoslovak Film prodn, Gottwaldov Film Studio. Wri-dir, Petr Tucek. Cam, Jiri Kolin; mus, Ferdinand Havlik. 90.
Josef Vinklar, Ivanka Devata, Julie Juristava, Oldrich Navratil.
02/28/79

Stories From A Flying Trunk
(Britain)
EMI. John Brabourne-Richard Goodwin prodn. Prods, John Brabourne, Richard Goodwin. Devised - dir, Christine Edzard; sp, Edzard, from three stories by Hans Christian Andersen: "The Kitchen", "The Little Match Girl", "Little Ida"; cam, Robin Browne, Brian West; edtrs, Rex Pyke, M J Knatchbull; mus, Gioacchino Rossini; mus arr, John Dalby, cond, Philip Gammon; snd, Edgar Vetter, Hugh Strain; prodn mgr, Jim Brennan; ballet settings, Irene Groudinsky; effects pho, Ken Worringham. 88.
Murray Melvin, Ann Firbank, Tasneem Maqsood, John Tordoff, John Dalby, Johanna Sonnex, Gerd Larsen, Patricia Napier, Graham Fletcher, Lesley Collier, Dancers of the Royal Ballet, London.
11/21/79

The Storm: SEE Jhor

Storm Boy
(Australia)
SAF. Prod, Matt Carroll. Dir, Henri Safran. Sp, Sonia Borg from novel by Colin Thiele; cam-snd, Ken Hammond; prodn des, David Copping; tech advisor, Grant Page; edtr, G Turney-Smith; continuity, Moya Iceton; pelican trainer, Gordon Noble; mus, Michael Carlos. 88.
Greg Rowe, Peter Cummins, David Gulpilil, Judy Dick, Tony Allison, Michael Moody, Graham Dow, Frank Foster-Brown, Eric Mack, Michael Caulfield, Paul Smith, Hedley Cullen, schoolchildren from the Port Elliot Primary School.
12/29/76

Stormtroopers: SEE
Sturmtruppen

Stormy Wine: SEE Bourlive
Vino

The Story of a Good Guy:
SEE *Bushkhugin Ulger*

The Story of a Mother: SEE
Historien om en Moder

Story of an Unknown Man:
SEE *Rasskaz O Neisvestnom Celoveke*

The Story of Chinese Gods
(Peoples Republic of China)
X. Prod, Chang Ying. Dir, Tang Chow Lup. Story cnslt, Chan Kong; chief admn ani, Chang Che Fai; mus, Wong Koy Shin; snd effects, Chang Wah. 90.
(ANI)
05/19/76

The Story Of Susan
(Hong Kong)
GHV. Dir, Chen Chi-wah. Sp-cam, Chen Chi-wah. 100.
Yu Yang, Shaw Yin Yin, Yang Chuen, Tanny.
(English soundtrack)
05/11/77

The Story of the Dragon
(Hong Kong)
CON. Golden Sun Films prodn. Exec prod, Li Pao-tang. Prod, Wu Yu Yun. Dirs, Chen Wah, Chang Chee. Sp, Ching Hsin-I; cam Chang Chi; fighting instructor, Huang Lung; mus, Chou Fuliang. 100.
Ho Tsung-tao, Fuang Chia-ta, Chang Hui, Huang Cheng-min, Wu Yen, Su Shen, Robert Karvek, Roy Horan.
(Cantonese soundtrack)
10/27/76

Straight Time
WB. First Artists-Sweetwall film. Prod, Stanley Beck, Tim Zinnemann; exec prod, Howard B Pine. Dir, Ulu Grosbard. Sp, Alvin Sargent, Edward Bunker, Jeffrey Boam, based on Bunker's novel, "No Beast So Fierce"; cam (Technicolor), Owen Roizman; edtrs, Sam O'Steen, Randy Roberts; mus, David Shire; song lyr, Norma Helms; prodn des, Stephen Grimes; art dir, Dick Lawrence; set decor, Marvin March; snd, Richard Portman, Jim Webb; cos-ward, Bernie Pollack; asst dir, Jack Roe; stunt coords, Everett Creach, Dick Ziker. (MPAA rating: R). 114.
Dustin Hoffman, Theresa Russell, Gary Busey, Harry Dean Stanton, M Emmet Walsh, Rita Taggart, Kathy Bates, Sandy Baron, Jacob Busey, Edward Bunker, James Ray, Stuart I Berton, Barry Cahill, Corey Rand, Fran Ryan.
03/22/78

Strange Events: SEE Quelle Strane Occasioni

Strange Letters: SEE Tschushije Pissma

Strange People: SEE Strannye Ljudi

Strange Shadows In An Empty Room
(Italy)
AIP. Prod, Edmondo Amati. Dir, Martin Herbert (Alberto de Martino). Sp, Vincent Mann, Frank Clark; cam (Eastmancolor), Anthony Ford; edtr, Vincent P Thomas; mus, Armando Trovajoli; art dir, Michel Proulx; cos, Louise Jobin. (MPAA rating: R). 99.
Stuart Whitman, John Saxon, Martin Landau, Tisa Farrow, Carole Laure, Gayle Hunnicutt.
02/16/77

Stranger's Melody: SEE Dendang Perantau

Strangers-The Road To Liberty: SEE Gaijin-Caminos Da Liberdade

Strannaya Zhenshina
(A Strange Woman)
(USSR)
GOS. Mosfilm Prodn, Moscow. Dir, Yuli Raizman. Sp, Yevgeni Gabrilovich, Raizman. 180.
Irina Kupechenko.
09/12/79

Strannye Ljudi
(Strange People)
(USSR)
X. Gorky Studios prodn, Moscow. Wri-dir, Vassili Shukshin, based on his stories "Strange People," "A Thousand Pardons, M'am," and "Thoughts." Cam, Valeri Ginsburg; mus, Karen Khachaturyan; art dir, I Bakhmetiev. 100.
Sergei Nikonenko, Yevgeni Yevstignejev, Y Lebedev, Vsevolod Sanajev.
(B & W)
12/01/76

Strategy: SEE Harcmodor

Strauberg Ist Da
(Strauberg Is Here)
(W Germany)
X. Galle Film prodn, Munich, in collaboration with Suedwestfunk, Baden-Baden. Sp-dir, Mischa Galle. Cam, Dieter Matzka; edtr, Dieter Matzka, Beate Schlegel; mus, Stefan Melbinger; snd, Rolf Schwarze, Vladimir Vizner; prodn mgrs, Demetrio Mathiopoulos, Dieter Matzka. 120.
Michel Piccoli, Theodor Kotulla, Bernadette Lafont, Udo Heiland, Karl-Heinz Heitmann, Joerg Richter.
(B & W)
03/29/78

Strawberry, Lemon and Mint: SEE De Fresa, Limon Y Menta

Street of the Crane's Foot: SEE Rue du Pied-De-Grue

Street People
(US - Italy)
AIP. Aetos Produzioni Cinematografiche prodn, prods, Manolo Bolognini, Luigi Borghese. Dir, Maurizio Lucidi. Sp, Ernest Tidyman, Gianfranco Bucceri, Niccola Badalucco, Randall Kleiser, Roberto Leoni, Maurizio Lucidi, from a story by Bucceri and Leoni; cam (Movielab Color), Aiace Parolin; edtr, Renzo Lucidi; mus, Luis Enriquez; art dir, Gastone Carsetti; set decor, Luigi Urbani; asst dirs, Mauro Sacripanti, Franco Fantasia; stunt coord, Remo DeAngelis; car scenes dir, William Garroni. (MPAA rating: R). 92.
Roger Moore, Stacy Keach, Ivo Garrani, Ettore Manni, Ennio Balbo, Fausto Tozzi, Pietro Martellanz, Romano Puppo.
(Dubbed English soundtrack)
09/29/76

Stroemer
(Cop)
(Denmark)
CTT. Crone (Nina Crone) prodn. Dir, Anders Refn. Story, Refn; sp, Refn, Anders Bodelsen, Peter Ronild, Claus Rohweder, Thomas Winding; cam (Panavision/Eastmancolor) Mikael Salomon; edtr, Kasper Schyberg; mus, Kasper Winding; in charge of prodn, Lars Kolvig. 102.
Jens Okking, Dick Kaysoe, Lotte Hermann, Bodil Kjer.
11/17/76

Strong Ferdinand: SEE Der Starke Ferdinand

Strong Water: SEE Silna Voda

Stronger Than The Sun
(Britain)
X. BBC prodn. Prod, Margaret Matheson. Dir, Michael Apted. Sp, Stephan Poliakoff; cam, Elmer Cossey; edtr, David Martin; mus, Howard Blake; cos, Amy Roberts. 101.
Francesca Annis, Tom Bell.
(16m)
03/12/80

The Strongest Karate
(Japan)
SKU. Sankyo Production Ltd, prod, Yasuhiko Kawano; exec prod, Ikki Kajiwara; tech adv, Mas Ohyama. Dir, Takashi Nomura, Shuji Goto. Sp, Moshimi Shinozaki; cam, Kimiaki Kimura; snd, Tetsuo Segawa; edtr, Takao Shirae; mus, Keisuke Hidaka; narr, Harry J Quini. With cooperation of Int'l Karate Organization Kyokushin Kaikan. 90. (DOC)
05/12/76

Stroszek
(W Germany)
NY. Werner Herzog Filmprodn/Skellig Edition. Prod-dir-sp, Werner Herzog. Cam, Thomas Mauch; asst dir, Ed Lachmann; snd, Maymo Henry Heyder, Peter van Anft; edtr, Beate Mainka-Jellinghaus; mus, Chet Atkins, Sonny Terry. 108.
Bruno S, Eva Mattes, Clemens Scheitz, Wilhelm von Homburg, Burkhard Driest, Pitt Bedewitz, Clayton Szlapinski, Ely Rodriguez, Alfred Edel, Scott McKain, Ralph Wade.
07/20/77

Stuckey's Last Stand
RYK. Summer Camp Company prodn. Prod-dir-wri, Lawrence G Goldfarb. Exec prod, Erich Von Forbes. Cam, Arthur J Fitzsimmons; mus, Carson Whitsett; Dixieland mus, the St Louis Ragtimers; art dir, Julia Norris; edtrs, Arthur J Fitzsimmons, Ethan Edwards; asst dir, Peg Berry. (MPAA rating: PG). 92.
Whit Reichert, Ray Anzalone, Will Shaw, Tom Murray, Richard Cosentino, Marilyn Terschluse, Jeanne L Austin, John Zimmerman, Dan Dierdorf, Pat Ball.
05/07/80

The Stud
(Britain)
WKR. Prod, Ronald S Kass; exec in charge of prodn, Oscar S Lerman; exec prods, George A Walker, Edward D Simons. Dir, Quentin Masters. Sp, Jackie Collins; cam, Peter Hannan; art dir, Michael Bastow; edtr, David Camplin; mus, Sammy Cahn, Biddu; ward, Penny Rose; snd, Stan Phillips; asst dir, Vincent Winter. 90.
Joan Collins, Oliver Tobias, Emma Jacobs, Sue Lloyd, Walter Gotell, Mark Burns, Nathalie Ogle, Felicity Buirski, Doug Fisher, Tony Allyn, Peter Lukas, Constantin De Goguel, Guy Ward, Minah Bird, Hilda Fenemore, Bernard Stone, Hugh Morton, Howard Nelson, Sarah Lawson, Leonard Trolley, Jeremy Child,

Franc De Rosa, Shango Baku, Tania Rogers, Michael Barrington, Rynagh O'Grady, Edmond Warwick, Robert Tayman, Giorgio Bosso.
03/29/78

The Stud Farm: SEE
Manesgazda

Stunde Null
(Zero Hour)
(W Germany)
X. Edgar Reitz Film prodn/Solaris/Westdeutsches Fernsehen (WDR), Exec prods, Joachim von Mengershausen, Cologne. Dir, Edgar Reitz. Sp, Peter Steinbeck, Reitz; cam, Gernot Roll; edtr, Ingrid Boszat; mus, Nicos Mamangakis; snd, Vladimir Vizner.   108.
Kai Taschner, Anette Juenger, Herbert Weissbach, Klaus Dierig, Guenter Schiemann, Erika Wackernagel, Torsten Henties, Erich Kleiber, Bernd Linzel.
(B & W)
04/27/77

The Stunt Man
FOX. Melvin Simon prodn. Prod, Richard Rush. Exec prod, Melvin Simon. Sp, Lawrence B Marcus, adaptation, Richard Rush, based on novel by Paul Brodeur; cam (Metrocolor), Mario Tosi; edtrs, Jack Hofstra, Caroline Ferriol; mus, Dominic Frontiere; art dir, James Schoppe; set decor, Richard Spero; cos des, Rosanna Norton; snd, Jim Tanenbaum; asso prod, Paul Lewis; asst dir, Frank Beetson. (MPAA rating: R).   129.
Peter O'Toole, Steve Railsback, Barbara Hershey, Allen Goorwitz, Alex Rocco, Sharon Farrell, Adam Roarke, Philip Bruns, Chuck Bail.
06/11/80

Stunts
NL. Prods, Raymond Lofaro, William Panzer, in asso with Mark Fleischman Ltd; exec prods, Peter S Davis, Robert Shaye. Dir, Mark L Lester. Michael Harpster; cam, Bruce Logan; addl pho, Daniel Pearl; special unit pho, Bob Bailin; edtr, Corky Ehlers; mus, Michael Kamen; Sp, Dennis Johnson, Barney Cohen, from a story by Lofaro, Shaye, stunt coord; Paul Nuckles; asst dir, Carl Olson. (MPAA rating: PG).   90.
Robert Forster, Fiona Lewis, Joanna Cassidy, Darrell Fetty, Bruce Glover, Jim Luisi, Richard Lynch, Candice Rialson, Malachi Throne, Ray Sharkey.
06/08/77

Stupende Le Mie Amiche
(My Fabulous Girlfriends)
(Italy)
X. Prods, Clara Gallini, Sergio Martinat, Domenico Vizzari, Alessandro Scalco, Luisa Corsini. Wri-dir, Alessandro Scalco; cam, Maurizio Calvesi; edtr, Enzo Meniconi; mus, Gioele and Elvio Boeri.   95.
Luigi Fioravante, Maurizio Lembo, Orazio Marino, Claudio Moscatelli, Ferdinando Moscatelli, Sergio Moscatelli, Toni Zaza.
10/08/80

The Stupid Boyfriend: SEE
Ang Boyfriend Kung Badoy

Stupid Life: SEE Chiwit Batsop

Sturmtruppen
(Stormtroopers)
(Italy)
CID. Prod, Achille Manzotti for Irrigazione Cinematografica. Dir, Salvatore Samperi. Sp, Renato Pozzetto, Cochi Ponzoni; cam (Technicolor), Giuseppe Rotunno; art dir, Uberto Bertacca; edtr, Sergio Montanari; mus, Enzo Janacci.   99.
Renato Pozzetto, Lino Toffolo, Cochi Ponzoni, Teo Teocoli, Felice Anbreasi, Massimo Boldi, Corinne Clery.
01/26/77

Submission: SEE Scandalo

Such A Lovely Town: SEE Un Si Joli Village

Suckalo
X. Wri-prod-dir-cin, Ron Taylor.   150.
11/17/76

Sudbine
(Destinies)
(Yugoslavia)
YFR. Dunav Film prodn. Wri-dir, Predrag Golubovic. Cam (Eastmancolor), Bert Sotlar, Faruk Begoli, Miroljub Leso, Mirceta Vukcic. Milivoje Milivojevic.   70.
08/16/78

The Sudden Loneliness of Konrad Steiner: SEE Die Ploetzliche Einsamkeit Des Konrad Steiner

Sufferloh
(W Germany)
TEG. Distelfilm Berlin Stenzel & Co Prodnn, with Werbedistel, Holzkirchen. Dir, Hans-Christof Stenzel; sp, Stenzel, Karl Guenther Hufnagel; cam, Paco Joan; edtr, Rosemarie Stenzel-Quast.   84.
Michael Langenbeck, Sandro Hauth, Martina Winkelbach, Susanne Baer, Herbert Berent, H C Artmann, Uli Kasten.
10/31/79

The Sugar: SEE Le Sucre

Sugar, Honey and Pepper: SEE Zucchero, Miele E Peperoncino

Suite California, Stops and Passes
X. Prod-wri-dir, Robert Nelson; snd-technical asst, Diane and Steve Nelson; mus, Mike Henderson, Chuck Wiley, Hobert Nelson, Gil Turner, Steve Nelson; cam, Robert Nelson.   90.
Pete Maccan, Diane Nelson, Mike Henderson, Mertis Schecaloff, Robert Nelson.
04/11/79

Summer Camp
BOR. Borson prodn. Exec prods, Seymour Borde, Dan Sonney. Prod, Mark Borde. Dir, Chuck Vincent. Sp, Avrumie Schnitzer, based on a story by Mark Borde, Schnitzer; cam, Ken Gibb; edtr, Mark Ubell; mus, Sparky Sugarman; snd, Trevor Black; chor, Dino Joseph Giannetta. (MPAA rating: R).   85.
Michael Abrams, Jake Barnes, Bud Bogart, Louise Carmona, Verkina Flower, Brenda Fogarty, Barbara Gold, Shelly Hart, Walt Hill, Ray Holland, Peter Lovett, Debra Marx, John C McLaughlin, Matt Michaels, George Mills, Collene O'Neil, Dustin Pacino Jr, Harry Reardon, Alexis Schreiner, Valdesta, Ralph Von Albertson, Robert Wald, Bonnie Werchan.
06/06/79

Summer Guests: SEE
Sommergaeste

Summer of Secrets
(Australia)
GUO. Secret Picture Prods film. Prod, Michael Thornhill. Dir, Jim Sharman; cam, Russell Boyd; sp, John Aitken; art dir, Jane Norris; snd, Ken Hammond; asst dir, Errol Sullivan; mus, Cameron Allen.   100.
Arthur Dignam, Rufus Collins, Nell Campbell, Andrew Sharp, Kate Fitzpatrick.
12/29/76

Summerfield
(Australia)
GUO. Clare Beach Film. Prod, Pat Lovell. Dir, Ken Hannam. Sp, Cliff Green from own story; cam (Panaflex-Eastmancolor), Mike Molloy; asst dir, Mark Egerton; snd, Ken Hammond, Gary Wilkins; mus, Bruce Smeaton; art dir, Grace Walker; edtr, Sarah Bennet.   95.
Nick Tate, John Walters, Elizabeth Alexander, Michelle Jarman, Charles Tingwell, Geraldine Turner, Max Cullen, Sheila Florance, Isabel Harley, Joy Westmore, Adrian Wright, Barry Donnelly, David Smeed, Max Fairchild.
09/07/77

Summer's Children
(Canada)
X. Prods, Julius Kohanyi, Don Haig. Dir, Kohanyi; sp, Jim Osborne; cam, Joe Seckeresh; wardrobe, Elinor Galbraith; edtr, M C Manne. 95.
Tom Hauff, Paully Jardine, Don Francks, Kate Lynch, Patricia Collins, Ken James.
05/16/79

Sun of the Hyenes: SEE Soleil Des Hyenes

Sun Over The Swamp: SEE
Gunesli Bataklik

Sunburn
PAR. John Daly, Gerald Green prodn. Exec prods, Jay Bernstein, John Quested, in assoc with Philip A Waxman. Dir, Richard C Sarafian. Sp, John Daly, Stephen Oliver, James Booth based on book, "The Bind," by Stanley Ellin; cam (Technicolor), Alex Phillips Jr; mus-comp-arr, John Cameron; prodn des, Ted Tester; edtr, Geoff Foot; asst dir, Steve Barnett; underwater sequences, Ramon Bravo; snd edtr, Vernon Messenger; art dir, Augustin Ituarte; set decor, Dick Purdy; sfx, Laurencio Cordero, Jesus Duran. (MPAA rating: PG). 99.

Farrah Fawcett, Charles Grodin, Art Carney, Joan Collins, William Daniels, John Hillerman, Eleanor Parker, Keenan Wynn, Robin Clarke, Joan Goodfellow, Jack Kruschen, Alejandro Rey, Jorge Luke, Seymour Cassel, Joanna Lehmann, Alex Sharpe, Bob Orrison, Deloy White, Christa Walters, Youigi Rogi, Miguel Burciaga, Steven Wilensky, George Belanger, Dick Subley, Ken Smith, Enrique Kahn, Delores Devine.
08/08/79

Sunday Children: SEE Niedzielne Dzieci

Sunday Children: SEE Sonntagskinder

Sunday Games: SEE Nedelni Matchove

Sunday Lovers
(France - Italy)
PDS. Viaduc Productions (Paris) Medusa Distribuzione (Rome) co-prodn. Prod, Leo Fuchs. Dir, Edouard Molinarao, Bryan Forbes, Dino Risi and Gene Wilder. Sp, Francis Veber, Leslie Bricusse, Age & Scarpelli and Wilder. French segment: Cam, C Lecomte; snd, D Brisseau; edtr, P Shaw. Italian segment: Cam, T Delli Colli; snd, V Massi; edtr, A Gallitti. American segment: Cam, J Hirschfeld; snd, P Mitchell; edtr, C Greenbury. Mus for entire film, Manuel de Sica. 125.

France: Lino Ventura, Robert Webber, Catherine Salviat.
England: Roger Moore, Denholm Elliott, Lynn Redgrave, Priscilla Barnes.
Italy: Ugo Tognazzi, Rossana Podesta, Sylva Koscina, Beba Loncar.
America: Gene Wilder, Kathleen Quinlan, Dianne Crittenden.
12/17/80

Sunday Parents: SEE Vasarnapi Szulok

Sunday Woman: SEE La Donna Della Domenica

Sunnyside
AIP. Robert Schaffel prodn. Prod, Robert L Schaffel. Dir, Timothy Galfas. Sp, Timothy Galfas, Jeff King, from story by Jeff King, Robert L Schaffel; cam (Movielab color), Gary Graver; edtr, Herbert H Dow; supv edtrs, Eric Albertson, Alan Douglas, Harold Wheeler; asst dir, Ramiro Jaloma. (MPAA rating: R). 100.

Joey Travolta, John Lansing, Stacey Pickren, Andrew Rubin, Michael Tucci, Talia Balsam, Chris Mulkey, Joan Darling, Richard Beauchamp, Heshimu Cumbuka, Jonathan Gries, E Lamont Johnson.
06/06/79

Sunstroke: SEE Slnchev Udar

The Suntanned Ones: SEE Les Bronzes

Super Van
EMR. Indie prodn, Sal A Capra, Sandy Cohen. Exec prod, Nolan Russell Bradford. Dir, Lamar Card. Sp, Neva Friedenn, Robert Easter, based on story by John Arnoldy; cam, Irv Goodnoff; snd, Doniel Prodns; edtr, Steve Butler; stunt coord, Von Deeming; sfx, Harry Woolman; mus, Andy DeMartino, Mark Gibbons, Bob Stone. (MPPA rating: PG). 91.

Mark Schneider, Katie Saylor, Morgan Woodward, Len Lesser, Skip Riley, Bruce Kimball, Tom Kindle, Ralph Seeley, Richard Sobek.
04/13/77

Superman
WB. Alexander and Ilya Salkind prodn. Prod, Pierre Spengler. Dir, Richard Donner. Sp, Mario Puzo, David Newman, Leslie Newman, Robert Benton; story, Puzo; based on characters created by Jerry Siegel, Joel Shuster; exec prod, Ilya Salkind; mus, John Williams; edtr, Stuart Baird; cam, Geofrey Unsworth; prodn des, John Barry; additional script material, Norman Enfield; creative supv & dir-sfx, Colin Chilvers; creative supv & dir of optical visual effects, Roy Field; creative supv and dir of mattes and composite, Les Bowie; creative dir of process photography, Denys Coop; model sets dir and created by Derek Meddings. (MPAA rating: PG). 143.

Marlon Brando, Gene Hackman, Christopher Reeve, Ned Beatty, Jackie Cooper, Glenn Ford, Trevor Howard, Margot Kidder, Jack O'Halloran, Valerie Perrine, Maria Schell, Terence Stamp, Phyllis Baxter, Susannah York, Jeff East, Marc McClure, Sarah Douglas, Harry Andrews, Lee Quigley, Aaron Smolinski.
12/13/78

Superman II
WB. Alexander Salkind presentation. International Film Prodn/Alexander and Ilya Salkind prodn. Exec prod, Ilya Salkind. Prod, Pierre Spengler. Dir, Richard Lester. Sp, Mario Puzo, David Newman, Leslie Newman; story, Puzo, based on characters created by Jerry Siegel, Joe Shuster; crea cnsltnt, Tom Mankiewicz; cam (Technicolor), Geoffrey Unsworth, Robert Paynter; edtr, John Victor-Smith; mus, Ken Thorne from orig material composed by John Williams; prodn desgn, John Barry, Peter Murton; supv art dir, Maurice Fowler; sfx dir, Colin Chilvers; 2d-unit dirs, David Tomblin, Robert Lynn; snd mixer, Roy Charman; cos, Yvonne Blake, Susan Yelland; prodn mgr, Vincent Winter; asst dir, Dusty Symonds; make-up, Stuart Freeborn.

Additional Special Effects Unit Credits-Supv of optical, visual effects, Roy Field; addl flying sequences, dir, miniature effects, Derek Meddings; flying unit sfx dir, Zoran Perisic; flying unit dir of pho, Denys Coop; dir, of minature pho, Paul Wilson; optical and sfx edtr, Peter Watson; zoptic operator, David Speed; flying effects, Bob Harman; optical printers, Dick Dimbleby, David Docwra; matte artists, Ivor Beddoes, Doug Ferris; 60aerial cam seq, Wesscam; Wesscam pho, Ronald Goodman; matte cam opers, Peter Harman, Peter Hammond; NY process stills, Cervin Robinson; special lighting effects, The Lightflex System; astronautical cnsltnt, Harry Lange. 127.

Gene Hackman, Christopher Reeve, Ned Beatty, Jackie Cooper, Sarah Douglas, Margot Kidder, Jack O'Halloran, Valerie Perrine, Susannah York, Clifton James, E G Marshall, Marc McClure, Terence Stamp.
12/03/80

Supersonic Man
(Spain)
X. Almena Films S A prodn. Dir, Juan Piquer. Sp, Sebastian Moi, Juan Piquer; cam (Eastmancolor-Supercolor and Dinavision), Juan Marine; edtr, Pedro del Rey; sfx-sets, Emilio Ruiz, Francisco Prosper; optical effects, Jack Elkubi, Miguel Villa; mus, Gino Peguri, Juan Luis Izaguirre, Carlos Attias. 85.

Michael Coby, Cameron Mitchell, Richard Yesteran, Diana Polakov, Jose Maria Caffarel, Frank Brana, Javier de Campos, Tito Garcia, Quique Camoiras, Luis Barboo, Angel Ter.
08/29/79

The Supply Column Soldier: SEE Voinikat Ot Oboza

The Supreme Kid
(Canada)
CPX. Seventh Wave Films prodn. Wri-dir, Peter Bryant. Cam (Eastmancolor), Tony Westman; edtrs, Homer Powell, Sally Paterson; mus, Howie Vickers. 90.

Frank Moore, Jim Henshaw, Don Granberry, Helen Shaver, Gordon Robertson.
08/04/76

Surgeons: SEE Hirourzi

Suria Dighal Bari
(The Ominous House)
(Bangladesh)
BND. Wri-dir, Massiouddin Shaker, Shiekh Niamat Ali from a book by Abu Ishak; cam, Answar Hosen, Alaouddin Ali. 130. Dolly Anwar, Flora, Keramat Mulla, Sajib, Roushan Jami.
(B & W)
07/30/80

Surprise Sock: SEE *Chaussette Surprise*

Suru
(The Flock)
(Turkey)
GUI. Dir, Zeki Okten. Sp, Yilmaz Gueney. 129.
04/25/79

Survival Run
FVI. Spiegel-Bergman prodn. Prod, Lance Hool. Dir, Larry Spiegel. Exec prods, Ruben Broido, Mel Bergman. Sp, Spiegel, G M Cahill, based on a story by Cahill and Fredric Shore; cam (Deluxe Color), Alex Phillips Jr; mus, Gary William Friedman; edtr, Chris Greenbury. (MPAA rating: R). 90.
Peter Graves, Ray Milland, Vincent Van Patten, Pedro Armendariz Jr, Alan Conrad, Anthony Charnota, Gonzalo Vega, Cosie Costa, Randi Meryl, Marianne Sauvage, Robby Weaver, Danny Ades, Susan Pratt O'Hanlon.
03/05/80

Survivors: SEE *Los Sobrevivientes*

Sus Anos Dorados
(Their Golden Years)
(Spain)
X. Prod-dir-wri, Emilio Martinez Lazaro; exec prod, Jesus Martinez Leon; cam (Eastmancolor), Porfirio Enriquez; mus, Suburbano; edtr, Nieves Martin; direct snd, Julian del Santo, Miguel Angel Rospir; sets, Matoya del Real. 98.
Jose Pedro Carrion, Patricia Adriani, Marisa Paredes, Louis Politti, Pep Munne, Mirela Ros.
11/05/80

Susetz
(Rockinghorse)
(Israel)
SUS. Dir, Yaki Yosha. Sp, Yosha, Yoram Kaniuk from book by Kaniuk; cam, Ilan Rosenberg; edtr, Yosha. 85.
Schmuel Kraus, Gedalia Besses, Arik Lavi, Jozi Katz, Miriam Bernstein-Cohen.
08/23/78

Suspiria
(Italy)
PCI. Prod, Claudio Argento for Salvatore Argento and Seda Spettacoli. Dirs, Stefania Casini, Dario Argento. Sp, Argento, Daria Nicolodi; cam (Technicolor), Luciano Tovoli; art dir, Giuseppe Bassan; edtr, Franco Fraticelli; mus, The Gobelins and Dario Argento. (MPAA rating: R). 97.
Jessica Harper, Stefania Casini, Joan Bennett, Alida Valli.
03/09/77

Sutedelan
(Desiderium)
(Iran)
HSM. Prod, Ali Abbasi for Payam Film Organization. Wri-dir, Ali Hatami. Cam (Eastmancolor), Houshang Baharloo; art dir, Ali Hatami; edtr, Moosa Afshar; mus, Persian folk mus, NIRT archives. 109.
Behrooz Vosughi, Jamshid Mashayekhi, Shohre Aghdashloo.
12/14/77

Suzanne
(Canada)
AMB. RSL prodn. Prod, Robert Lantos; exec prod, Stephen J Roth; dir, Robin Spry; sp, Spry, Ronald Sutherland, based on novel "Snow Lark", by Sutherland; cam, Miklos Lente; art dir, Vianney Gauthier; cos des, Louise Jobin; edtr, Fima Noveck; mus, Francois Cousineau; theme, Luc Plamondon, Cousineau. 114.
Jennifer Dale, Winston Rekert, Gabriel Arcand, Ken Pogue, Michelle Rossignol, Marianne McIsaac, Michael Ironside, Gina Dick, Pierre Curzi, Gordon Thompson, Helen Hughes, Adam Chase.
09/17/80

Sven Klangs Kvintett
(The Sven Klang Quintet)
(Sweden)
SVF. Swedish Film Institute/Europa Film/Stockholm Film/Swedish Radio-TV 2/Folkets Husfoereningars Riksorganisation/Music Theatre Group October prodn. Script based on their play, Henric Holmberg, Ninne Olsson. Dir, Stellan Olsson. Cam, Kent Persson; mus, jazz standards, Christer Boustedt, Jan Lindell; edtr, Roger Sellberg; exec prod for Swedish Film Institute, Per Berglund; prodn mgr, Hans Iveberg. 109.
(B & W)
12/29/76

Sverige at Svenskarna
(Sweden For The Swedes)
(Sweden)
EUP. Mats Helge Olsson Filmproduktion/Per Oscarsson prodn. Orig story-sp- dir, Per Oscarsson; cam (Eastmancolor), Jiri Tirl; exec prods, Robert Ekman, Ake Brandhild, Dan Krantz; prodn des, Per Oscarsson, Dick Ljunggren, Jiri Kotlar; edtrs, Per Oscarsson, Henrik Ahlen; mus, Carl-Axel Dominique. 113.
Per Oscarsson, Ernst Gunther, Sonya Hedenbratt, Allan Edwall, Monica Zetterlund, Lena Nyman, Bjoern Skifs, Martin Ljung.
09/17/80

Svetozar Markovic
(Yugoslavia)
YFR. CFS Kosutnjak-Oour Avala Film - Televizija Beograd - Televizija Novi Sad prodn. Dir, Eduard Galic; sp, Momcilo Milankov, Milan Secerovic; cam (Eastmancolor), Aleksander Petkovic; mus, Zoran Hristic. 109.
Lazar Hristovski, Petar Kralj, Ljuba Tadic, Gojko Santic, Milan Strljic, Branislav Lecic.
08/13/80

Swami
(India)
JCI. Prod, Jaya Chakravarthy. Dir-sp, Basu Chatterjee. Cam, K K Mahajan; edtr, Mayekar; mus, Rajesh Roshan; art dir, Bansi Chander Gupta; snd, Narender Singh. 110.
Shanaha Azmi, Girish Karnad.
12/14/77

Swansong Days: SEE *I Giorni Cantati*

Swap: SEE *Trampa*

Swap Meet
DIM. Prod, Steve Krantz. Dir, Brice Mack. Sp, Steve Krantz; mus, Hemlock; art dir, Donald Harris; snd, Bill Nelson; asst dir, Thomas M Hammel. (MPAA rating: R). 84.
Ruth Cox, Debi Richter, Danny Goldman, Cheryl Rixon, Jonathan Gries, Dan Spector, Loren Lester.
09/19/79

The Swarm
WB. Prod-dir, Irwin Allen. Sp, Stirling Silliphant, based on a novel by Arthur Herzog; cam (Technicolor), Fred J Koenekamp; sfx, L B Abbott; edtr, Harold F Kress; mus, Jerry Goldsmith; prodn des, Stan Jolley; set decor, Stuart Reiss; snd, Arthur Piantadosi, Les Fresholtz, Michael Minkler, Herman Lewis; cosward, Paul Zastupnevich; asst dir, Mike Salamunovich; stunt coord, Paul Stader. (MPAA rating: PG). 116.
Michael Caine, Katharine Ross, Richard Widmark, Richard Chamberlain, Olivia De Havilland, Ben Johnson, Lee Grant, Jose Ferrer, Patty Duke Astin, Slim Pickens, Bradford Dillman, Fred MacMurray, Henry Fonda, Cameron Mitchell, Christian Juttner, Morgan Paull, Alejandro Rey, Don (Red) Barry.
07/19/78

Swashbuckler
U. Prod, Jennings Lang; exec prod, Elliott Kastner. Dir, James Goldstone. Sp, Jeffrey Bloom; story, Paul Wheeler; cam (Technicolor), Philip Lathrop; edtr, Edward A Biery; mus, John Addison; prodn des, John Lloyd; set decor, Hal Gausman; snd, Don Johnson, Robert Hoyt; asst dir, Peter Bogart; stunt coords, Buddy Van Horn, Victor Paul. (MPAA rating: PG). 101.
Robert Shaw, James Earl Jones, Peter Boyle, Genevieve Bujold, Beau Bridges, Geoffrey Holder, Avery Schreiber, Tom Clancy, Anjelica Huston, Bernard Behrens, Dorothy Tristan, Mark Baker, Kip Niven.
07/28/76

Sweden For The Swedes: SEE *Sverige at Svenskarna*

Swedish Minx
(Sweden)
CAM. Swedish Filmprod prodn. Prod, Inge Ivarson. Dir, Mac Ahlberg. (Self-imposed X rating). 99.

Harry Reems, Maria Lynn, Bie Warburg, Brigette Maier.
(Dubbed English soundtrack)
07/06/77

Sweeney
(Britain)
EMI. Euston Films prodn, prod, Ted Childs; exec prods, Lloyd Shirley, George Taylor. Dir, David Wickes. Sp, Ranald Graham (based on a television series created by Ian Kennedy Martin); cam (Technicolor), Dusty Miller; edtr, Chris Burt; mus, Denis King; prodn mgr, Laurie Greenwood; art dir, Bill Alexander. 97.
John Thaw, Dennis Waterman, Barry Foster, Ian Bannen, Colin Welland, Diane Keen, Michael Coles, Joe Melia, Brian Glover, Lynda Bellingham, Morris Perry, Paul Angelis, Nick Brimble, John Alkin, Bernard Kay, Anthony Scott, Anthony Brown.
01/19/77

Sweeney 2
(Britain)
EMI. Euston Films prodn. Prod, Ted Childs. Exec prod, Lloyd Shirley, George Taylor; dir, Tom Clegg; sp, Troy Kennedy Martin; cam (Technicolor), Dusty Miller; mus, Tony Hatch; art dir, Bill Alexander; edtr, Chris Burt; snd, Derek Rye; asst dir, Bill Westley. 108.
John Thaw, Dennis Waterman, Denholm Elliott, Georgina Hale, Nigel Hawthorne, Lewis Fiander, James Warrior, John Flanagan, David Casey, Derrick O'Connor, John Alkin, Michal Jackson, Ken Hutchison, Brian Gwaspari, John Lyons, Brian Hall, Matthew Scurfield, Anna Gael, Lynn Dearth, Fiona Mollison, Sarah Atkinson, George Mikell, Marc Zuber, Leon Lissek, Stefan Gryff, Diana Weston, Anna Nygh, George Innes, Roddy McMillan.
05/03/78

The Sweet Creek County War
KYI. Imagery Films prodn. Exec prods, Ray Cardi, Marie Cardi. Prods, Ken Byrnes, J Frank James. Wri-dir, James; cam, Gregory von Berblinger; edtr, Ronald Sinclair; prodn des, Allen H Jones; mus, Richard Bowden; cos des, Peggy Sjulstad; snd, Kenneth Isley; asst dir, John Hockridge. (MPAA rating: PG). 99.
Richard Egan, Albert Salmi, Nita Talbot, Slim Pickens, Robert J Wilke, Joe Orton, Ray Cardi, Tom Jackman.
01/24/79

Sweet, Like Berries, My Love: SEE Habibeti-Ya Habba Atoot

Sweet Punkin'
X. Prod, Robert Michaels. Dir, Robert Norman. Cam, Norman Roberts; edtr, Anna Riva; snd, Mike Shadow; mus, Harold Hindgrind, Slim Pickins. (Self-imposed X rating). 80.
Cast; C J Laing, Tony Perez, John C Holmes, Jeff Hurst, Eric Edwards, Crystal Sync, Jennifer Jordan, Tootsie Robusto, Dance Warren, Tony Dee, Marlene Willoughby, Sarah Silver, Brandy Wine, Jerry Fuzzie, David Christ, Slim Pickins.
04/07/76

Sweet Revenge: SEE Kiri-no-hata

Sweet Thieves: SEE Ladroes de Cinema

Sweet William
(Britain)
X. Kendon Films prodn. Exec prod, Don Boyd. Prod, Jeremy Watt. Dir, Claude Whatham. Sp, Beryl Bainbridge, from her novel; cam, Les Young; edtr, Peter Coulson; prodn des, Eileen Diss; snd, Simon Okin; asst dir, Gino Marotta. (MPAA rating: R). 92.
Sam Waterson, Jenny Agutter, Anna Massey, Geraldine James, Daphne Oxenford, Rachel Bell, David Wood, Tim Pigott-Smith, Emma Bakhle, Sara Clee.
04/02/80

Sweet Woman: SEE Sladkaia Jentchina

Sweetheart: SEE Fen

The Swimming Pool: SEE Basseinut

The Swindle: SEE L'Entourloupe

The Swiss Affair: SEE L'Affaire Suisse

The Swissmakers: SEE Die Schweizermacher

The Sword: SEE A Kard

The System
(Hong Kong)
X. Trinity Asia Ltd prodn. Dir-prod, Peter Yung. Sp, Peter Yung, Lee Sien; cam, Peter Yung, Tom Lau; art dirs, Oliver Wong, David Chan; edtr, Wong Yee Shuen; mus, Lam. 100.
Pak Ying, Shek Kin, Chiao Chiao, Erwin Panos, Peter Brent, Mike Lovatt.
(Cantonese soundtrack with English sub-titles)
05/07/80

Szabadits Meg A Gonosztol
(Deliver Us from Evil)
(Hungary)
HU. Mafilm Hunnia Studio prodn. Dir, Pal Sandor. Sp, Zsuzsa Toth from the play by Ivan Mandy; cam (Eastmancolor), Elemer Ragalyi; mus, Gabor Presser. 94.
Iren Opsota, Erzebet Kutvolgyi, Andras Kern, Deszo Andorai, Otto Stetner.
02/28/79

Szansa
(Chance)
(Poland)
POL. Film Polski Production X Film Unit, Warsaw. Wri-dir, Feliks Falk; cam, Edward Klosinski; mus, Jan Kanty Pawluslziewicz; sets, Teresa Smus-Barska. 94.
Krzysztof Zaleski, Jerzy Stuhr, Elzbieta Kokoszka, Ewa Kolasinska, Slawa Kwasniewska, Iwona Biernacka, Andrzej Buszewicz, Jerzy Nowak.
06/11/80

Szepek Es Bolondok
(On the Sideline)
(Hungary)
X. Hunnia Studio prodn. Dir-sp, Peter Szasz. Cam (Eastmancolor), Lajos Koltai; mus, Gabor Presser, Gyorgy Vukan. 105.
Ferenc Kallai, Gyula Bodrogi, Tamas Andor, Judit Meszlery, Nora Tabori.
03/02/77

Szpital Przemienienia
(Hospital of the Transfiguration)
(Poland)
POL. Film Polski prodn, Warsaw; Dir, Edward Zebrowski. Sp, Zebrowski, Michal Komar; cam, Witold Sobocinski. 90.
Gustav Holoubek, Zbigniew Zapasiewicz.
02/28/79

Ta Kourelia Tragoudoun Akoma
(The Thrushes Are Still Singing)
(Greece)
X. N Nicolaides prodn. Wri-dir, Nicolaides; cam, Stavros Hasapis; sets-cos, Marie Louise Vartholomeou; edtr, Andreas Adreadakis; snd, Marinos Athanassopoulos. 125.
Alkis Panayotides, Rita Bensousan, Constantine Tzoumas, Christos Valavanides, Olia Lazaridou.
(B & W)
1/28/79

Taboo: SEE Tabu

Tabor Ollhodit Webo
(Gypsies Go To Heaven)
(USSR)
SOV. Mosfilm prodn. Dir, Emile Lotianu. Sp, Lotianu from a story by Maxim Gorki; cam (Sovcolor), Serge Vronski; mus, Evgueni Doga. 102.
Grigory Grigoriou, Svetlana Toma.
12/01/76

Tabu
(Taboo)
(Sweden)
SVF. Swedish Film Institute with Swedish Television/Stockholm Film/Europa Film/Vilgot Sjoman AB prodn. Wri-dir, Vilgot Sjoman. Cam (Eastmancolor), Lars Bjoerne; prodn des, Hakon Alexandersson; edtrs, Wic Kjellin, Tomas Taeng. 110.
Kjell Berquist, Licka Sjoman, Viveca Lindfors, Halvar Bjoerk, Gunnar Bjornstrand.
02/23/77

Tachi and Her Fathers
(China)
X. Omei Film Studio and Changhun Film Studio co-prodn, China. Dir, Wang Chiayi. Sp, Kao Ying; cam, Wang Chun-chuan, Chang Hui; mus, Lei Chen-pang, Ya Hsin; art dir, Li Chun-chieh. 110.
Chen Hsueh-chieh, Liu Lien-chih, Chu Tannan, Niu Chien, Hsuan Haichih, Chou Shu,

Hsu Shih, Hamailo, Wang Chun-ying, Yu Chung-lien, Jung Jo-pei.
06/13/79

Tagebuch
(The Diary)
(W Germany)
X. Rudolf Thome prodn. Wri-dir, Rudolf Thome, based freely on Goethe's "The Elective Affinities." Cam (b&w), Martin Schaefer; snd, Christoph Buchwald; edtr, Clarissa Ambach. 146.
Rudolf Thome, Angelika Kettelhack, Cynthia Beatt, Holger Henze.
(B & W)
04/21/76

Tagebuch Eines Liebenden
(Diary of a Lover)
(W Germany)
X. Provobis, O A Kress, prodn (Hamburg) in collab with Westdeutscher Rundfunk (WDR), Cologne, prodn mgr, Wolf-Dietrich Bruecker. Dir, Sohrab Shahid Saless. Sp, Saless, Helga Houzer; cam, Manzur Yazdi; mus, Rolf Bauer; snd, Gunther Kortwich, Max Galinsky; noises, Karl Heinz Reiber; edtr, Christel Orthmann. 90.
Klaus Salge, Eva Manhardt, Edith Hildebrandt, Ingebord Ziemendorff, Ursula Alexa, Dorothea Moritz, Gerhard Wollner.
01/19/77

The Tailor From Ulm: SEE
Der Schneider Von Ulm

Taiyo o Nusunda Otoko
(The Man Who Stole The Sun)
(Japan)
X. Kitty Films prodn. Dir, Kazuhiko Hasegawa; sp, Leonard Schrader, Kazuhiko Hasegawa; cam, Tatsuo Suzuki; mus, Takayuki Inoue. 130.
Kenji Sawada, Bunta Sugawara, Kimiko Ikegami, Yonusuke Ito.
10/29/80

Tajna Nikole Tesle
(The Secret of Nikola Tesla)
(Yugoslavia)
YFR. Zagreb Film-Kinematografi prodn. Dir, Krsto Papic; sp, Ivo Bresan, Ivan Kusan, Papic; cam (Eastmancolor), Ivica Rajkovic; art dir, Veljko Despotovic; mus, Andelko Klobucar. 120.
Petar Bozovic, Orson Welles, Strother Martin, Dennis Patrick, Oja Kodar, Boris Buzancic, Charles Millot, Ana Karic.
(In English)
08/13/80

Take All Of Me
(Italy)
G1. Prod, Mario Cotone. Dir, Luigi Cozzi. Sp, Cozzi, Michele Delle Aie, Daniele Del Giudice, Sonia Molteni; cam (Technicolor), Roberto Piazzoli; mus, Stelvio Cipriani. 90.
Richard Johnson, Pamela Vincent, Maria Antonietta Beluzzi.
03/08/78

Take Down
BV. American Film Consortium prodn of a Kieth Merrill Film. Exec prod, David B Johnston. Prod-dir, Kieth Merrill. Sp, Merrill, Eric Hendershot, based on a story idea by Hendershot; cam (DeLuxe color), Reed Smoot; edtr, Richard Fetterman; mus, Merrill B Jenson; art dir, Douglas G Johnson; tech advisory, Eric Hendershot; snd, Robert E Sheridan; mus score performed by The Nat'l Symphony, London. (MPAA rating: PG). 107.
Edward Herrmann, Kathleen Lloyd, Lorenzo Lamas, Maureen McCormick, Nick Beauvy, Stephen Furst, Kevin Hooks, Vincent Roberts, Darryl Peterson, "T" Oney Smith, Salvador Feliciano, Boyd Silversmith, Scott Burgi, Lynn Baird, Ron Bartholomew, Kip Otanez, Larry Miller, Gary Petersen, Oscar Roland, Hyde Clayton, Prentiss Rowe, Elizabeth Grand, Christy Neal, Bob Kawa.
01/24/79

Take It To The Limit
VF. Peter Starr Film. Prod-dir, Peter Starr. Exec prod, Leroy Lefkowitz. Wris, Charles Michael Lorre, Starr; cam (Deluxe Color), Michael Chevalier, Jeremy Lepard, Mark Zavad; edtr, John Bryant; ani, Jon Wokuluk; snd, Todd-AO, Bob Glass, William Knudson, Don MacDougall; orig sngs by Foreigner, Jean Luc Ponty, Arlo Guthrie, John McEuen, Tangerine Dream, Starwood. (MPAA rating: PG). 95.
Barry Sheene, Russ Collins, Steve Baker, Scott Autrey, Mike Hailwood, Kenny Roberts.
(DOC)
03/26/80

Take Me to the Ritz: SEE
Emmenez-Moi Au Ritz

Take One
RRX. Wakefield Poole prodn. Prod-dir, Poole. Cam-edtr, Edd Dundas, Poole; snd, Charles Oringer; mus, Tommy Tally. (Self-imposed X rating). 98.
Jeff Addison, Phillip Borden, Tony Franco, Sal Guange, Richard Locke, Bill O'Connell, Dick Ogden, Guillermo Ricardo.
08/17/77

The Takeoff: SEE *Bzlet*

The Taking of Christina
UNI. Prod, Jason Russell. Dir-wri, Armand Weston. Mus score, Jack Malken; performed by David Webster. (Self-applied X rating). 90.
Al Levitsky, Eric Edwards, Bree Anthony, Jack Thompson, Terri Hall, C J Lange, Chris Jordan, Daniel Fitzgerald, Jim Gordon, Sol Weiner, Leila, Frank Simmons.
03/17/76

Tales from the Vienna Woods: SEE *Geschichten Aus Dem Wiener Wald*

Talisman
(Bulgaria)
BGO. BulgaroFilm prodn, Hemus Group, Sofia. Sofia. Dir, Rashko Ouzounov. Sp, Pravda Kirova; cam, Tsvetan Chobanski; art dir, Milko Marinov; mus, Alexander Yossifov. 89.
Daniella Boyanova, Lilyana Yovanovich, Emilia Radeva, Lyubomir Kirilov.
05/31/78

Tall Shadows of the Wind: SEE *Saiehaieh Bolan de Bad*

Tally Brown, N.Y.
(W Germany)
X. Rosa von Praunheim prodn. Dir, Rosa von Praunheim, with the assistance of Mike Shephard. Cam, Juliana Wang, Ed Lieber, Michael Oblowicz, von Praunheim; other assistance, Reno Sweeney's, Hans Dudelheim, Anja Philipps. 110.
Tally Brown, Taylor Mead, Holly Woodlawn, Divine, Ching, Elisabeth and Robert Kashy, Edward Caton.
(DOC) (16m)
04/18/79

Talpuk Alatt Futyul A Szel
(The Wind Blows Under Your Feet)
(Hungary)
X. Studio Hunnia (Budapest) prodn. Dir, Gyorgy Szomjas. Sp, Peter Zimre, Szomjas; cam (Eastmancolor), Elemer Ragalyi; mus, Ferenc Sebo. 90.
Djoko Rosic, Istvan Bujtor, Vladen Holec, Iren Bordan.
09/26/76

Tanasse Scatiu
(Romania)
X. Dir, Dan Pita; sp, Mihnea Gheorghiu; cam (Eastmancolor), Nicolae Margineanu; cos, Lidia Luludis; mus, Adrian Enescu; edtr, Cristina Jonescu. 125.
Victor Rebengiuc, Eliza Petrachescu, Vasile Nitulescu, Cataline Pintilx.
09/28/77

Tanczacy Jastrzab
(The Dancing Hawk)
(Poland)
POL. Film Polski Prodn, Profil Unit, Warsaw. Wri-dir, Grzegorz Krolikiewicz; based on the novel by Julian Kawalec. Cam, Zbigniew Rybczynski. 100.
Franciszek Trzeciak, Beata Wedrychowicz, Beata Tyskiewicz.
06/21/78

Tang Sua Phan
(The Tiger's Way)
(Thailand)
STC. Prod, Visant Santisucha. Dir, Chumphorn Tepitak. Exec prod, Amporn Limpipholpaibul. Story, Panom Tien; sp, Tawan Suwan; cam, Anant Nontachai; edtr, Toi Chaleuk; prodn des-art dir, Prakob Yaisiri; mus, Maitree Janjarasskul; snd recording, Siam Pattana Lab. 120.
Krung Srivilai, Nart Bhavanai, Sorapong Chatri, Naiyana Chivanand, Piyamatr Monjakul, Lak Apichat, Dam Daskorn.
08/10/77

Tango Durch Deutschland
(Tango Through Germany)
(W Germany)
X. Lutz Mommartz Film prodn, in collab with ZDF (Second Channel), "Das kleine Fernsehspiel." 90.

Eddie Constantine, Maya Farber-Jansen.
10/29/80

The Tango Tells Its Story:
SEE El Tango Cuenta su Historia

Tango Through Germany:
SEE Tango Durch Deutschland

The Tanner Steel Mill: SEE
Die Tannerhuette

Tapage Nocturne
(Nocturnal Uproar)
(France)
GAU. Axe Films-French Prodn co-prodn. Prod, Pierre Sayag. Wri-dir, Catherine Breillat. Cam, Jacques Boumendil; snd, Alain Curvelier; edtrs, Annie Charrier, Claudio Ventura; art dir, Dominique Anthony; mus, Serge Gainsbourg, performed by Bijou. 95.
Dominique Laffin, Marie-Helene Breillat, Bertrand Bonvoisin, Joe Dallessandro.
10/31/79

Target: Harry
ABX. Corman Company prodn. Prod, Gene Corman. Dir, Henry Neill (Roger Corman). Sp, Bob Barbash; cam, Patrice Pouget; edtr, Monte Hellman; mus, Les Baxter. (MPAA rating: R). 81.
Vic Morrow, Suzanne Pleshette, Victor Buono, Cesar Romero, Stanley Holloway, Charlotte Rampling, Michael Ansara, Anna Capri.
(MADE IN 1968)
03/26/80

The Taste of Water: SEE
Smak Wody

Tattooed Tears
(London)
X. Documentary funded by Corporation for Public Broadcasting and National Endowment for the Arts. Prod-dir, Nick Broomfield, Joan Churchill. Cam-edtr-snd, Broomfield, Churchill. 85. (DOC)
12/13/78

Taugenichts
(Good-For-Nothing)
(W Germany)
FDA. ABS/Solaris-Film prodn, Munich. Dir, Bernhard Sinkel. Sp, Alf Brustellin, Sinkel, based on Joseph Freiherr von Eichendorff's novel, "Memoirs of a Good-for-Nothing"; cam, Dietrich Lohmann; edtr, Dagmar Hirtz; sets, Nicos Perakis; cos, Barbara Matthee; mus, Hans Werner Henze; snd, Ed Parente. 91.
Jacques Breuer, Eva-Maria Meineke, Sybil Schreiber, Mareike Carriere, Matthias Habich, Wolfgang Reichman, Peter Berling, Pizi Adam, Jiri Kritnar, Maria Grazia de Giorgi.
03/29/78

Taut Bamispar
(Wrong Number)
(Israel)
X. Erez Films presentation of a Baruch Ellah and Zeev Revach Prodn. Prod, Baruch Ellah. Dir, Zeev Revach; sp, Revach, Shay K Ophir; cam, Amnon Salomon; art dir, Arieh Halleh; edtr, Tal Shuval; mus, Yoel Sher. 90.
Zeev Revach, Shay K Ophir, Shula Revach, Ophelia Strahl, Gideon Singer, Menashe Warshawsky, Miriam Fuchs.
12/19/79

Tauwetter
(Thaw)
(Switzerland - W Germany)
X. Prodn of Limbo Film, Zurich, and Condor Film, Zurich, in coprodn with Solaris, Munich. Wri-dir, Markus Imhoof; Cam, Gerald Vandenberg; mus, Bruno Spoerri; sets, Dani Bodmer; edtr, Marianne Jaeggi. 90.
12/07/77

Taxi Driver
COL. Bill/Phillips prodn, prods, Michael and Julia Phillips. Dir, Martin Scorsese. Sp, Paul Schrader; cam (Metrocolor), Michael Chapman; 2d unit cam, Michael Zingale; edtrs, Marcia Lucas, Tom Rolf, Melvin Shapiro; mus, Bernard Herrmann; art dir, Charles Rosen; set decor, Herbert Mulligan; snd, Tex Rudolff, Dick Alexander, Vern Poore, Les Lazarowitz, Roger Peitschman; asst dir, Peter Scoppa. (MPAA rating: R). 113.
Robert De Niro, Cybill Shepherd, Peter Boyle, Albert Brooks, Leonard Harris, Harvey Keitel, Jodie Foster, Murray Moston, Richard Higgs, Vig Argo, Steven Prince, Martin Scorsese.
02/04/76

Taxidi Toy Melitos
(Honeymoon)
(Greece)
X. George Panoussopoulos-Movie Makers and Betty Livanou picture. Wri-dir, George Panoussopoulos; cam, Andreas Bellis; mus, Manos Hatzidakis; sets - cos, Thanassis Papayannacos, Yannis Kalaitzis; edtrs, Yanna Spyropoulou, Panos Panoussopoulos. 112.
Stavros Xenides, Aleca Paizi, Betty Livanou, Guely Mavropoulou, Marica Nezer, Koulis Stoliguas, Malena Anoussaki.
(B & W)
11/28/79

Te Necesito Tanto, Amor
(I Need You So Much, Love)
(Argentina)
PDP. Emilio Spitz prodn. Dir, Julio Saraceni. Cam (Eastmancolor), Ricardo Younis; mus, Tito Ribero; set des, Carlos T Dowling. 85.
Elio Roca, Elizabeth Killian, Rosanna Falasca, Carlos Scazziotta, Rodolfo Ranni, Jorge Barreiro.
03/24/76

The Teacher: SEE El Brigadista

Tears On The Lion's Mane:
SEE Namida o Shishi no Tategami

Teci, Teci, Kuza Moj
(Hang On, Doggy)
(Yugoslavia)
YFR. Viba Film, Ljubljana, prodn. Dir, Jan Kavcic. Sp, Vitan Mal; cam, Mile de Gleria; art dir, Niko Matul; cos, Zvonka Makuc; edtr, Dusan Povh; prodn mgr, Ivan Mazgon. 95.
Matjaz Grunden, Nino de Gleria, Mitja Tavcar, Andrej Djordjevic, Jure Zargi, Nina Zidannic, Polona Rajster, Natasa Roje, Vesena Jevnikar.
12/15/76

Telefon
UA. MGM picture, prod, James B Harris. Dir, Don Siegel. Sp, Peter Hyams, Stirling Silliphant, based on the novel by Walter Wager; cam (Metrocolor), Michael Butler; edtr, Douglas Stewart; mus, Lalo Schifrin; prodn des, Ted Haworth; art dir, William F O'Brien; set decor, Robert Benton; snd, Alfred J Overton, William McCaughey, Aaron Rochin, Michael J Kohut; cos-ward, Jane Robinson, Luster Bayless, Edna Taylor; asst dirs, David Hamburger, Luigi Alfano; stunt coord, Paul Baxley. (MPAA rating: PG). 103.
Charles Bronson, Lee Remick, Donald Pleasence, Tyne Daly, Alan Badel, Patrick Magee, Sheree North, Frank Marth, Helen Page Camp, Roy Jenson, Jacqueline Scott, Ed Bakey, John Mitchum, Iggie Wolfington.
12/14/77

The Telephone Bar: SEE Le
Bar du Telephone

Telephone Public
(France)
GAU. Prospectacle prodn. Prods, Maurice Bernart, Claudia Ossaro. Dir, Jean-Marie Perier. Cam (Eastmancolor-Cinemascope), Lionel Legros, Alain Masseron; edtr, Thierry Derocles; snd, Harald Maury, Laurent Pele, recorded in Dolby stero. 100.
The Telephone rock group (Jean-Louis Aubert, Corine Marienneau, Richard Kolinka, Louis Bertignac).
(DOC)
07/16/80

Tell Him I Love Him: SEE
Dites Lui Que Je L'Aime

Tell Me A Riddle
FWS. Godmother prodn. Prods, Mindy Affrime, Rachel Lyon, Susan O'Connell. Exec prod, Michael Rosenberg. Dir, Lee Grant. Sp, Joyce Eliason, Alev Lytle; based on Tillie Olsen novella; cam (CFI Color), Fred Murphy; edtr, Suzanne Pettit; snd, David McMillan; prodn mgr, Tony Wade; prodn des, Patrizia Von Brandenstein; asst dir, Peter Schindler; mus, Sheldon Shkolnik. (MPAA rating: PG). 90.
Melvyn Douglas, Lila Kedrova, Brooke Adams, Lili Valenty, Dolores Dorn, Bob Elross, Jon Harris, Zalman King, Winifred Mann, Peter Owens, Deborah Sussel.
12/10/80

Temne Slunce
(Dark Sun)
(Czechoslovakia)
CZS. Barrandov Studio prodn. Dir, Otakar Vavra; sp, Jiri Sotala, Vavra from book by Karel Capek; cam (Eastmancolor), Miroslav Ondricek; mus, Martin Kratochvili; art dir, Karel Lior. 135.
Radoslav Hrzobohaty, Jiri Tomas, Rudolf Hrusinsky, Magda Vasaryova, Gunther Naumann, Vladimir Sneral.
07/30/80

The Tempest
(Britain)
X. Boyd's Co prodn. Exec prod, Don Boyd. Prod, Guy Ford, Mordecai Schreiber. Dir, Derek Jarman. Asso prod, Sarah Radclyffe. Sp, Jarman, from Shakespeare's play; cam, Peter Middleton; edtr, Leslie Walker; des, Yolanda Sonnaband; mus, Wavemaker; asst dir, Anthony Annis. 96.
Heathcote Williams, Karl Johnson, Jack Birkett, Toyah Wilcox, David Meyer, Peter Bull, Richard Warwick, Ken Campbell, Neil Cunningham, Christopher Biggins, Peter Turner, Claire Davenport, Elizabeth Welch.
09/12/79

Temps Morts
(Dead Times)
(France)
X. Les Films Du Sabre-Centre Georges Pompidou prodn. Conceived-dir-pho, Claude Godard; edtr, C Tronquet. 76.
(DOC) (16m)
09/17/80

Temptations
VBX. Prod, Louis F Antonero. Dir, Dexter Egale. Sp, John T Hansen; cam, Valentine Murana; (Self-applied X rating). 80.
Jennifer Welles, Jake Teague, Marlena Willoughby, John Leslie Dupre, Roger Caine, Hope Stockton, Vanessa Del Rio, Davio Innis, Alexandria.
06/16/76

The Tempter
(L'Anti Cristo)
(Italy)
AVE. Prod, Edmondo Amati. Dir, Alberto de Martino. Sp, Martino, Vincenzo Mannino, Gianfranco Clerici; cam, Aristide Massaccesi; edtr, Vincenzo Tomassi; art dir, Umberto Bertacca; mus, Ennio Morricone. (MPAA rating: R). 96.
Carla Gravina, Mel Ferrer, Arthur Kennedy, George Coulouris, Alida Valli, Anita Strindberg, Mario Scaccia, Umberto Orsini.
11/01/78

10
WBO. Geoffrey prodn. Prods, Blake Edwards, Tony Adams. Dir-Wri, Blake Edwards. Cam (Technicolor, Panavision), Frank Stanley; edtr, Ralph E Winters; mus, Henry Mancini; prodn des, Rodger Maus; set decor, Reg Allen, Jack Stevens; cos des, Pat Edwards; snd, Bruce Bisenz; asst dir, Mickey McCardle. 122.
Dudley Moore, Julie Andrews, Bo Derek, Robert Webber, Dee Wallace, Sam Jones, Brian Dennehy, Max Showalter, Rad Daly, Nedra Volz, James Noble, Virginia Kiser, John Hawker, Deborah Rush, Don Calfa, Walter George Alton, Annette Martin, Lorry Goldman.
09/26/79

10% Nadeja
(Ten Percent of Hope)
(Czechoslovakia)
CZS. Slovak Film prodn. Dir, Jozef Zachar. Sp, Stefan Sokel; cam (Eastmancolor), Vladimir Ondrus; mus, Tibor Andrasovan. 86.
Bronislav Krizan, Bozidara Turzonovova, Jan Triska, Radoslav Brzobohat.
01/26/77

The Tenant: SEE *Le Locataire*

The Tenants: SEE *Sakada*

Tenda Dos Milagres
(The Tent of Miracles)
(Brazil)
X. Regina Films prodn. Dir, Nelson Pereira dos Santos. Exec prod, Ney Sant'Anna. Sp, Nelson Pereira dos Santos, based on novel by Jorge Amado; cam (Eastmancolor), Helio Silva; edtrs, Raimundo Higino, Severino Dada; sets, Tizuca Yamasaki; cos, Yurika Yamasaki; mus theme, Gilberto Gil. 148.
Juarez Paraiso, Jards Macale, Hugo Carvana, Sonia Dias, Anecy Rocha, Wilson Jorge Mello, Geraldo Freire, Laurence R Wilson, Severino Dada.
07/13/77

Tender Cop: SEE *Tendre Poulet*

Tender Cousins: SEE *Tendres Cousines*

Tenderness, My Fanny!: SEE *Et La Tendresse?. . .Bordel!*

Tendre Poulet
(Tender Cop)
(France)
GCC. Les Films Ariane-Mondex Films prodn. Dir, Philippe De Broca. Sp, De Broca, Michel Audiard, from book by Jean-Paul Rouland, Claude Olivier; cam (Eastmancolor), Jean-Paul Schwartz; edtr, Francoise Javet; mus, Georges Delerue. 105.
Annie Girardot, Philippe Noiret, Catherine Alric, Hubert Deschamps, Paulette Dubost, Roger Dumas, Simone Renant, Georges Wilson, Raymond Gerome.
12/21/77

Tendres Cousines
(Tender Cousins)
(France)
AMLF. Stephan Films/Filmedis co-prodn. Dir, David Hamilton. Sp, Pascal Laine, Josiane Leveque, Claude D'Anna; cam, Bernard Daillencourt; snd, Pierre Befve; art dir, Aric Simon; edtr, Jean-Bernard Bonis. 90.
Anja Shute, Thierry Teveni, Macha Meril, Catherine Rouvel, Pierre Vernier, Jean Rougerie.
12/03/80

Tengamos La Guerra En Paz
(Let's Leave the War in Peace)
(Spain)
X. Impala-Vega Film S L prodn. Dir, Eugenio Martin. Sp, Antonio Fos, Martin; cam (Eastmancolor), Manuel Rojas; edtr, Alfredo Santacana; mus, Antonio Garcia Abril; sets, Wolfgang Burman. 89.
Francisco Cecilio, Fedra Lorente, Veronica Miriel, Mari Carrillo, Eduardo Calvo, Queta Claver, Jose Maria Caffarel, Aurora Redondo.
08/24/77

The Tent of Miracles: SEE *Tenda Dos Milagres*

Tentacles
(Italy)
FOX. Ovidio Assonitis presentation. Prod, E F Doria. Dir, Oliver Hellman, (Ovidio Assonitis). Sp, Jerome Max, Tito Carpi, Steve Carabatsos, Sonia Molteni; cam (Technicolor), Roberto D'Ettorre; mus, S W Cipriani; art dir, M Spring; underwater sequences dir-coord, Nestore Ungaro; edtr, A J Curi; cos, N Hercules; snd, G Lawrence; asst dir, Peter Shepherd. (MPAA rating: PG). 102.
John Huston, Shelley Winters, Bo Hopkins, Henry Fonda, Delia Boccardo, Cesare Danova, Alan Boyd, Claude Akins, Sherry Buchanan, Franco Diogene, Marc Fiorini, Helena Makela.
(English soundtrack)
06/15/77

The Terrace: SEE *La Terrazza*

Terror
(Denmark)
CTT. Lademann Film A/S prodn. Dir, Gert Fredholm. Sp, Hans Hansen, based on novel by Torben Nielsen. Cam (Eastmancolor), Morten Arnfred. Edtr, Anders Refn. Mus, Palle Mikkelborg. Prodn mgr, Lars Kolvig. 101.
Bo Loevetand, Johnny Olsen, Ole Meyer, Jess Ingerslev, Poul Reichhardt, Ole Ernst, Ulf Pilgaard, Holger Juul Hansen.
03/16/77

Terror
(Britain)
CWN. Prods, Les Young, Richard Crafter. Dir, Norman J Warren; sp, David McGillivray, from a story by Young and Moira Young; cam, Les Young; edtr, Jim Elderton; mus, Ivor Slaney; art dir, Hayden Pearce; snd, Simon Okin; asst dir, Bryan Hirst. (MPAA rating: R). 86.
John Nolan, Carolyn Courage, James Aubrey, Sarah Keller, Tricia Walsh, Glynis Barber, Michael Craze, Rosie Collins, L E Mack.
12/19/79

Terror of Cavite: SEE *Bergado*

Terror Train
(Canada)
FOX. Astral Bellevue Pathe Prodn in asso with Sandy Howard Prods Corp, Daniel Grodnik. Exec prod, Lamar Card. Prod, Harold Greenberg. Dir, Roger Spottiswoode. Sp, Y T Drake; cam (DeLuxe Color), John Alcott; addl pho, Rene Verzier, Al Smith, Peter Beninson; edtr, Anne Henderson; mus, John Mills-Cockell; prodn des, Glenn Bydwell; art dir, Guy Comtois; snd, Bo Harwood, Dave Appleby, Dino Pigat; asst dir, Ray Sager. (MPAA rating: R). 97.
Ben Johnson, Jamie Lee Curtis, Hart Bochner, David Copperfield, Derek MacKinnon, Sandee Currie, Timothy Webber, Anthony Sherwood, Howard Busgang, Steve Michaels, Greg Swanson, D D Winters, Joy Boushel, Victor Knight.
10/01/80

Tess
(France - Britain)
AMLF. Renn Productions (Paris) Burrill Productions (London) co-prodn. Prod, Claude Berri; dir, Roman Polanski; sp, Polanski, Gerard Brach, John Brownjohn, based on the novel "Tess of the D'Urbervilles," by Thomas Hardy; cam, Geoffrey Unsworth, Ghislain Cloquet; prodn des, Anthony Powell; mus, Philippe Sarde; edtr, Alastair McIntyre; art dir, Jack Stephens; exec prod, Pierre Grunstein; co-prod, Timothy Burrill; asso prod, Jean-Pierre Rassam. (MPAA rating: PG.) 180.
Nastassia Kinski, Leigh Lawson, Peter Firth, John Collin, David Markham, Rosemary Martin, Richard Pearson, Carolyn Pickles, Pascale de Boysson.
11/07/79

Test Pilot Pirx
(Poland)
X. prodn of the Polish Corporation for Film. Prod, Zespoly Filmowe and Tallinnfilm. Dir, Marek Piestrak. Sp, Piestrak, based on book of same title by Stanislaw Lem; cam, Janusz Pawlowski; mus, Arvo Part; set decor, Jerry Sniezawski, Wiktor Zilko. 104.
Sergei Desnitsky, Boleslaw Abart, Vladimir Ivashov, Aleksander Kajdanowski, Zbigniew Lesien.
08/15/79

Tetetoria
(Entanglement)
(Hungary)
X. Hunnia Studio prodn. Wri-dir, Gyula Maar. Cam (Eastmancolor), Lajos Koltai; mus, Gyorgy Selmeczi, Tomas Cseh. 103.
Mari Torcsik, Lenke Loren, Stefan Kvietik, Peter Fried, Jozef Kroner, Tomas Major.
03/02/77

Thampu
(The Circus Tent)
(India)
PDI. Wri-dir, G Aravindan. Cam (b&w), Shaji; edtr, Ramesh; mus, M G Radakrishnan. 130.
Gopi, Venu, Sheeraman, Jalaja, artists of the Great Chitra Circus.
(B & W)
01/31/79

Thank God It's Friday
COL. Prod, Rob Cohen; exec prod, Neil Bogart. Dir, Robert Klane. Sp, Barry Armyan Bernstein; cam (Metrocolor), James Crabe; aerial pho, Frank Holgate; edtr, Richard Halsey; prodn des, Tom H John; set decor, Jeff Haley; snd, Arthur Piantadosi, Les Fresholtz, Michael Minkler, Al Overton Jr; cos-ward, Betsy Jones, Michael Kaplan, Jack Angel, Kathy O'Rear, Paula Cain; asst dir, Charles Ziarko; 2d unit dir, Jim Gavin; stunt coord, Phil Adams. (MPAA rating: PG). 89.
Donna Summer, Valerie Landsburg, Terri Nunn. Chick Vennera, Ray Vitte, Mark Lonow, Andrea Howard, Jeff Goldblum, Robin Menken, Debra Winger, John Freidrich, Paul Jabara, Marya Small, Chuck Sacci, Hilary Beane, DeWayne Jessie, The Commodores.
05/17/78

That Brief Summer: SEE Den Korte Sommer

That House In The Outskirts: SEE Aquella Casa En Las Afueras

That Long Night: SEE Aquella Larga Noche

That Obscure Object of Desire: SEE Cet Obscure Objet Du Desir

That Sinking Feeling
(Scotland)
X. Minor Miracle Film Cooperative prodn in asso with the Glasgow Youth Theater. Prod-dir, Bill Forsyth; sp, Forsyth; cam, Michael Coulter; edtr, John Gow; des, Adrienne Atkinson; snd, Alec Brown; mus, Colin Tully. 80.
Robert Buchanan, John Hughes, Billy Greenlees, Douglas Sannachan, Alan Love, Danny Benson, Eddie Burt, Tom Mannion.
09/19/79

That Summer
(Britain)
COL. Prod, Davina Belling, Clive Parsons. Dir, Harley Cokliss. Sp, Janey Preger, based on a story by Tony Attard; cam, David Watkin; edtr, Michael Bradsell; art dir, Tim Hutchinson; snd, Peter Sutton, Archie Ludski; orig mus, Ray Russell; asst dir, Selwyn Roberts. 94.
Ray Winstone, Tony London, Emily Moore, Julie Shipley, Jon Morrison, Andrew Byatt, Ewan Stewart, David Daker, Jo Rowbottom, John Judd, John Junkin, Stephanie Cole, Nick Donnelly.
07/04/79

That's Entertainment, Part 2
UA. MGM picture, prods, Saul Chaplin, Daniel Melnick. New sequences directed by Gene Kelly. Narr wri, Leonard Gershe; cam (Metrocolor), George Folsey; edtrs, Bud Friedgen, David Blewitt, David Bretherton, Peter C Johnson; mus supv, Nelson Riddle; spec lyr, Howard Deitz, Saul Chaplin; prodn des, John De Cuir; snd, Hal Watkins, Aaron Rochin, Bill Edmondson; asst dir, William R Poole. (MPAA rating: G). 133.
05/05/76

That's Life: SEE C'Est La Vie!

That's Me, Too: SEE Sadan Er Jeg Ogsaa

That's The Way The Cookie Crumbles: SEE Zivi Bili Pa Vidjeli

Thaw: SEE Tauwetter

Theatre Girls
(Britain)
X. Nat'l Film School of London prodn. Dir, edtr, Kimona Longinotto, Claire Pollack; cam (b&w), Longinotto. 82.
(DOC) (B & W) (16m)
03/21/79

Their Golden Years: SEE Sus Anos Dorados

Theo Gegen Den Rest Der Welt
(Theo Against the Rest of the World)
(W Germany)
CIG. Altura-film, Munich, Popular-Film, Hans H Kaden, Stuttgart, Trio-Film, Duisburg; in co-prodn with Westdeutscher Rundfunk (WDR), Cologne. Dir, Peter F Bringmann. Sp, Matthias Seelig; cam, Helge Weindler; edtr, Annette Dorn; sets, Goetz Heymann; mus, Lothar Meid; prodn mgr, Michael Wiedemann; exec prod, Alena Rimbach. 106.
Marius Mueller-Westerhagen, Guido Gagliardi, Claudia Demarmels, Carlheinz Heitmann, Peter Berling, Eolo Capritti, Ricardo Parisio Perotti, Marquard Bohm.
06/04/80

There Goes The Bride
(Britain)
VGD. Cooney-Schute prodn. Prods, Ray Cooney, Martin Schute. Dir, Terence Marcel. Sp, Cooney, Marcel, from play by Cooney, John Chapman; cam (Rank Film Lab), James Devis; edtr, Alan Jones; mus, Harry Robinson; prodn des, Peter Mullin; art dir, John Siddal; chor, Gillian Gregory. (MPAA rating: PG). 88.
Tom Smothers, Twiggy, Martin Balsam, Sylvia Syms, Michael Whitney, Geoffrey Sumner, Graham Stark, Hermione Baddeley, Toria Fuller, Margot Moser, John Terry, Jim Backus, Phil Silvers,

There Is No Forgetting: SEE Il N'Y A Pas D'Oubli

There Was A Lad: SEE Shiwjot Takoj Paren

These Kids Are Grown-Ups: SEE Ils Sont Grands Ces Petits

These Sorcerers Are Mad: SEE Ils Sont Fous Ces Sorciers

They Are Their Own Gifts
X. Rhodes-Murphy Venture prodn. Dir and conceived by Lucille Rhodes, Margaret Murphy. Cam (Eastmancolor), Babete Mangolte; edtr, Susan Fanshel, Rhodes, Murphy; mus, Susanna Nason. 52.
(DOC) (16m)
03/14/79

They Came From Within
(Canada)
AIP. DAL-Reitman prodn. Prod, Ivan Reitman. Wri-dir, David Cronenberg. Exec prods, John Dunning, Andre Link, Alfred Pariser. Cam, Robert Saad; make-up-sfx, Joe Blasco; prodn mgr, Don Carmody; edtr, Patrick Dodd; mus supv, Ivan Reitman. (MPAA rating: R). 88.
Paul Hampton, Joe Silver, Lynn Lowry, Alan Migicovsky, Susan Petrie, Barbara Steele, Ronald Mlodzik.
03/24/76

They Went That-A-Way & That-A-Way
ITP. Exec prod, Lloyd N Adams Jr. Prod, Lang Elliott. Dirs, Edward Montagne, Stuart E McGowan. Sp, Tim Conway; cam, Jacques Haitkin; edtr, Fabien Tordjmann; art dir, Joseph M Altadonna; set decor, Don Daniel, Mark Shavin, mus, Michael Leonard; asso prods, Eric Weston, Wanda Dell. (MPAA rating: PG). 95.
Tim Conway, Chuck McCann, Richard Kiel, Dub Taylor, Reni Santoni, Lenny Montana, Ben Jones, Timothy Blake, Hank Worden.
12/06/78

Thieves
PAR. Brut Prodn, prod, George Barrie. Dir, John Berry. Sp, Herb Gardner, based on his play; cam (Technicolor), Arthur J Ornitz, Andrew Lazlo; edtr, Craig McKay; mus, Jule Styne, Mike Miller, Shel Silverstein; prodn des, John Robert Lloyd; art dir, Robert Gundlach; set decor, George DeTitta; snd, Dick Vorisek, Jack C Jacobsen, James A Perdue; asst dir, Burt Bluestein; cos-ward, Albert Wolsky, Max Solomon, Beverly Cycon. (MPAA rating: PG). 103.
Marlo Thomas, Charles Grodin, Irwin Corey, Hector Elizondo, Mercedes McCambridge, John McMartin, Gary Merrill, Ann Wedgeworth, Larry Scott, Bob Fosse, Norman Matlock.
02/16/77

The Thin Line
(Israel)
ISM. G U Y Film Productions Ltd prodn. Prod, Avi Kleinberger, Gideon Amir. Dir, Michal Bat-Adam; sp, Bat-Adam; cam, Nurith Aviv; set des, Gaby Klasmer; snd, Dany Natovich. 93.
Gila Almagor, Alex Peleg, Liat Panski.
12/03/80

Third Base: SEE Sado

The Third Door: SEE La Tercera Puerta

The Third Generation: SEE Die Dritte Generation

The Third Walker
(Canada)
X. Melvin Simon-Quadrant Films-Wychwood prodn. Prod-dir, Teri McLuhan. Co-prod, Brian Winston. Sp, Robert Thom from orig story by Teri McLuhan; cam, Robert Fiore; mus, Paul Hoffert; edtr, Ulla Ryghe; art dir, William McCrow; prodn cnslt, Patrick Watson; wardrobe, Julie Ganton. 83.
Colleen Dewhurst, William Shatner, Frank Moore, Monique Mercure, Tony Meyer, David Meyer, Andree Pelletier, Simon Rankin, Andrew Rankin, Darren DiFonzo, Diane LeBlanc, Marshall McLuhan.
09/20/78

Third World, Prisoner in the Street
(France)
MDN. Island International and Mediane Films prodn. Wri-dir, Jerome Laperrousaz; cam, Etienne Fauduet; edtrs, Roselyne Petit, Noun Serra; mus, Third World. 80.
The Third-World musicians (Michael Cooper, Stephen Coore, Bunny Rugs, Richard Daley, Irwin Jarret, William Stewart).
(English Soundtrack) (DOC)
08/13/80

Thirst
(Australia)
GUO. F G Film Prods film, made in assoc with the New South Wales Film Corp. Exec prod, William Fayman; prod, Antony I Ginnane. Dir, Rod Hardy; sp, John Pinkney; cam (Panavision-Eastmancolor), Vincent Monton; art dir, Jon Dowding, Jill Eden; asst dir, Tom Burstall; snd, Stuart Beatty; ward, Leo Reyes; mus, Brian May; edtr, Phil Reid; sfx, Conrad Rothman; stunts, Grant Page. 98.
Chantal Contouri, David Hemmings, Henry Silva, Max Phipps, Shirley Cameron, Rod Mullinar, Robert Thompson, Walter Pym, Rosie Sturgess, Lula Pinkus, Amanda Muggleton.
12/26/79

The 39 Steps
(Britain)
RNK. Prod, Greg Smith. Dir, Don Sharp; exec prod, James Kenelm-Clarke; sp, Michael Robson (based on the novel by John Buchan); cam, John Coquillion; edtr, Eric Boyd-Perkins; snd, Peter Sutton; prodn des, Harry Pottle; mus, Ed Welch; asst dir, Barry Langley; asso prod, Frank Bevis. 102.
Robert Powell, David Warner, Eric Porter, Karen Dotrice, John Mills, George Baker, Ronald Pickup, Donald Pickering, Timothy West, Miles Anderson, Andrew Keir, Robert Flemyng, William Squire, Paul McDowell, David Collings, John Normington, John Welsh, Edward De Souza, Tony Steedman, John Grieve, Andrew Downie, Donald Bissett, Derek Anders, Oliver Maguire, Joan Henley, Prentis Hancock, Leo Dolan, James Garbutt, Artro Morris, Robert Gillespie, Raymond Young, Paul Jerricho, Michael Bilton.
11/29/78

This Age Without Pity: SEE Cet Age Sans Pitie

This Is Love, Isn't It: SEE Was Heisst'n Hier Liebe

This Rockin' Globe: SEE Kloden rokker

Those Lips Those Eyes
UA. Herb Jaffe prodn. Dir, Michael Pressman; prods, Steven-Charles Jaffe, Michael Pressman; exec prod, Herb Jaffe; sp, David Shaber; cam (Technicolor), Bobby Byrne; orig mus comp-cond, Michael Small; mus staging-chor, Dan Siretta; edtr, Millie Moore; prodn des, Walter Scott Herndon; set decor, Cloudia. (MPAA rating: R). 107.
Frank Langella, Glynnis O'Connor, Thomas Hulce, George Morfogen, Jerry Stiller, Rose Arrick, Herbert Berghof, Kevin McCarthy, William Robertson, Joseph Maher, Marshall Colt.
08/13/80

Those Wonderful Men with a Crank: SEE Bajecni Muzi S Klikou

The Threat: SEE La Menace

Three Card Monte
(Canada)
SGY. Regenthall Films prodn. Dir, Les Rose. Sp, Richard Gabourie; cam, Henry Fiks; edtr, Ron Wisman; mus, Jim Caverhill, Paul Zaza; snd, Peter Burgess, Paul Coombe. 91.
Richard Gabourie, Chris Langevin, Lynne Cavanagh, Valerie Waburton, John Rutter, Tony Sheer, Sean McCann.
09/20/78

Three Men to Destroy: SEE Trois Hommes a Abattre

Three Tigers Against Three Tigers: SEE Tri Tigre Contro Tri Tigre

Three Warriors
FYF. Saul Zaentz prodn. Prods, Zaentz, Sy Gomberg. Dir, Kieth Merrill. Sp, Gomberg; cam, Bruce Surtees. 109.
McKee "Kiko" Red Wing, Charles White Eagle, Randy Quaid, Lois Red Elk.
11/09/77

The Three Wise Men: SEE Los Tres Reyes Magos

Three Women
FOX. Wri-prod-dir, Robert Altman, based on his dream. Cam (DeLuxe Color), Chuck Rosher; edtr, Dennis Hill; mus, Gerald Busby; art dir, James D Vance; snd, Richard Portman, Jim Webb, Chris McLaughlin; asst dir, Tommy Thompson. (MPAA rating: PG). 122.
Shelley Duvall, Sissy Spacek, Janice Rule, Robert Fortier, Ruth Nelson, John Cromwell, Sierra Pecheur, Craig Richard Nelson, Maysie Hoy, Belita Moreno, Leslie Ann Hudson, Patricia Ann Hudson, Beverly Ross, John Davey.
04/13/77

Threshold of Spring
(China)
X. Peking Film Prodn. Wri-dir, Hsie Tie-li, based on the novel by Jou Shih. Cam, Li-Wung-hu. 90.
Sun Tao-lin, Hsieh Fang.
06/06/79

Thriller Story: SEE Serie Noire

Through the Ashes of the Empire: SEE Prin Cenusa Imperiului

Through the Looking Glass
MAT. Mastermind prodn. Prod-dir, Jonas Middleton. Sp, Ronald Wertheim; cam, Harry Flecks; edtrs, Maurizio Zaubmann, James Macreading; snd, Rolf Pardula; prodn des, Tyrone Browne; mus, Arlon Ober. (Self imposed X Rating). 91.
Catharine Burgess, Douglas Wood, Jamie Gillis, Laura Nicholson, Marie Taylor, Al Letivsky, Terri Hall, Jeffrey Hurst, Ultramax, Kim Pope, Eve Every, Jacob Pomerantz, Susan Swanson.
09/15/76

The Thrushes Are Still Singing: SEE Ta Kourelia Tragoudoun Akoma

The Thruster: SEE L'Arriviste

Thunder And Ligntning
FOX. Roger Corman prodn. Dir, Corey Allen. Sp, William Hjortsberg; cam (DeLuxe Color), James Pergola; edtr, Anthony Redman; mus, Andy Stein; asst dir, Phil Goldfarb; 2nd unit dir, Lewis Teague; stunt coord, Joie Chitwood Jr; snd, Ed Wright; cos, Dyke Davis; sfx, J B Jones. (MPAA rating: PG). 93.
David Carradine, Kate Jackson, Roger C Carmel, Sterling Holloway, Ed Barth, Ron Feinberg, George Murdock, Pat Cranshaw, Charles Napier, Hope Pomerance, Malcom Jones, Charles Willeford, Christopher Raynolds, Claude Jones, Emilio Rivera.
06/29/77

Thundercrack
THB. Prods, John Thomas, Charles Thomas. Dir-pho (b&w)-edtr, Curt McDowell. Sp, Kuchar; mus, Mark Ellinger. 150.
Marion Eaton, George Kuchar, Melinda McDowell, Mookie Blodgett, Moira Benson, Rick Johnson, Ken Scudder, Maggie Pyle.
(B & W)
04/07/76

Thursdays Never Again
(USSR)
GOS. Mosfilm Prodn, Moscow. Dir, Anatoli Efros. 100.
07/05/78

Tic-Tac-Toe: SEE Tres En Raya

Ti-Cul Tougas
(Canada)
NUI. ACPAV prodn. Wri-dir, Jean-Guy Noel. Cam, Francois Beachemin; edtr, Marthe de la Chevrotiere; mus, Georges Langford; art dir, Fernand Durand; cos, Mickie Hamilton; asst dir, Francois Labonte. 83.
Claude Maher, Micheline Lanctot, Gilbert Sicotte, Suzanne Garceau.
(French soundtrack-English subtitles)
05/18/77

Tidal Wave and West Wind: SEE Daluyong At Habagat

Tiempos De Constitucion
(Times of the Constitution)
(Spain)
X. Prod-dir-wri, Rafael Gordon. Cam (Eastmancolor), Miguel Angel Martin; mus, Fernando Brunet, Luis Fernandez Soria; edtr, Jesus Valdizan. 101.
Veronica Forque, Hector Alterio, Francisco Algora, Jose Bodalo, Victoria Hernan, David Thompson, Jose Calvo, Yelena Samarina, Alfonso del Real, Kiti Manver, Carmen Vazquez Vigo.
10/18/78

Tieng Goi, Phiatruoc
(The Call of the Front)
(Viet Nam)
VIE. Dir, Long Van. Sp; Phu Thang; cam, Nghien Phu My. 82.
Huy Cong, Doan Dung, Dang Viet Bao, Nguyen Dang Khoa.
(B & W)
09/05/79

Tiergarten
(W Germany)
X. Prod-wri-dir-pho-edtr, Lothar Lambert, with addl poetry, Dagmar Beiersdorf and archive music. 80.
Steven Adamczewski, Dagmar Beiersdorf, Erich Foertsch, Marion Herschel, Mustafa Iskandarani, Alfredo Julian, J W Kurth, Dorthea Moritz, Erika Rabau, Uwe Sange, Ulrike Schirm, Roland Stoos, Beate Hasenau.
(16m)
03/05/80

Ties for the Olympics: SEE Krawatten Fuer Olympia

Tigar
(The Tiger)
(Yugoslavia)
YFR. Central Film Studio-Avala Film prodn. Dir, Milan Jelic. Sp, Gordan Milic; cam (Eastmancolor), Predrag Popovic; edtr, Lana Vukobratovic; mus, Vojislav Kostic. 90.
Ljubisa Samardzic, Slavko Simac, Vera Cukic, Bata Zivojinovic, Pavle Vujisic.
08/16/78

Tiger and Crane Fists
(Hong Kong)
FFF. Wong Cheuk-hon-Luk Pak-sang-Wang Feng prodn. Dir, Jimmy Wang Yu; sp, Yi Kwan; edtr, Mak Tzu-shan; cam, Chuang Yin-chien; light, Tsao Hsiao-pin; martial arts chor, Lau Ka-wing, Jen Shih-kuan; mus, Wong Mao-shan. 90.
Jimmy Wang Yu, Lau Ka-wing.
09/22/76

The Tiger's Way: SEE Tang Sua Phan

Tiina
(Finland - Estonia)
X. Prod-wri-pho-dir-edtr-set decor, Edmund J Martin. Based on August Kitzberg's play, "Libahunt"; mus, comp-cond, Taavo Virkhaus; cos, Juta Virkmaa; folk art counsellors, Juta and Rain Virkmaa. 120.
Valli Martin, Oudi Kalm, Tarvo Kass, Heinz Riivald, Velli Kerjan, Alma Ambre, Aleksander Soosaar, Ferdinand Tammann, Kiti Kati Sirkel.
(English subtitles)
09/14/77

Till Divorce Us Do Part: SEE Hasta Que El Matrimonio Nos Separe

Tilt
WB. Melvin Simon prodn. Exec prod, Ron Joy; prod-dir, Rudy Durand; sp, Durand, Donald Cammell, based on story by Durand; cam (Technicolor), Richard Kline; edtrs, Bob Wyman, Don Guidice; prodn des, Ned Parsons; mus, Lee Holdridge; snd, Dean Salmon; asst dir, Pat Kehoe. (MPAA rating: PG.) 111.
Brooke Shields, Ken Marshall, Charles Durning, John Crawford, Harvey Lewis, Robert Brian Berger, Geoffrey Lewis, Gregory Walcott, Helen Boll.
04/11/79

Tim
(Australia)
X. Pisces Prodn of a Michael Pate film. Prod-dir-sp, Michael Pate from novel by Colleen McCullough; cam, Paul Onorato; edtr, David Stiven; art dir, John Carroll; snd, Bob Cogger, Les McKenzie; asst dir, Michael Midlam. 108.
Piper Laurie, Mel Gibson, Alwyn Kurts, Pat Evison, Peter Gwynne, Deborah Kennedy, David Foster, Margo Lee, James Condon, Michael Caulfield, Brenda Senders, Brian Barrie, Kevin Leslie, Louise Pago, Arthur Faynes, Geoff Usher, Sheila McGuire-Taylor, Alan Penny, Catherine Bray, Doris Goddard.
05/23/79

Time After Time
(Britain)
WBO. Herb Jaffe prodn. Prod, Jaffe. Dir, Nicholas Meyer. Sp, Meyer, based on a story by Karl Alexander, Steve Hayes; cam, Paul Lohmann; edtr, Donn Cambern; mus, Miklos Rozsa; prodn des, Edward C Carfagno; snd, Jerry Jost; stunt coord, Everett Creach; sfx, Larry Fuentes, Jim Blount; asst dir, Michael Daves. 112.
Malcolm McDowell, David Warner, Mary Steenburgen, Charles Cioffi, Andonia Katsaros, Patti D'Arbanville, Geraldine Baron.
09/05/79

The Time of Before: SEE Le Temps De L'Avant

Time of Maturity: SEE Reifezeit

Times of the Constitution: SEE Tiempos De Constitucion

Times Square
AFD. Butterfly Valley NV/RSO Films Ltd prodn. Prods, Robert Stigwood, Jacob Brackman; exec prods, Kevin McCormick, John Nicolella; dir, Alan Moyle; sp, Jacob Brackman, based on a story by Alan Moyle, Leanne Unger; cam (DeLuxe color), James A Contner; edtr, Tom Priestley; prodn des, Stuart Wurtzel; set decor, Leslie Bloom; cos, Robert de Mora; snd, Les Lazarowitz; asst dir, Alan Hopkins; 2d unit dirs, Edward Bianchi, John Nicolella. (MPAA rating: R). 111.
Tim Curry, Trini Alvarado, Robin Johnson, Peter Coffield, Herbert Berghof, David Margulies, Anna Maria Horsford.
09/10/80

The Tin Drum: SEE Die Blechtrommel

Tirak Cong Norng Noo
(The Love of a Little Girl)
(Thailand)
SAH. S P Prodns film. Prod, Chartchapong Suphan. Wri-dir, Rungsiri Lim-aksorn. Based on an idea by Wan Voravudhi. Cam, Sophon Jaenphanit; mus, Prachin Songpao; snd, Johnny Wong's Cinelab Syarm; art dir, Rungsiri Lim-aksorn; asst dir, Rayat Plaikeow. Theme song, "Rak Rong Tang" (Love Lost Its Way), mus-arr, Prachin Songpao, lyrs, Chalie Intravijit. 120.
Vitoon Karuna, Kanang Damrongkat, Piathip Kumvong, Pinyo Tongchua, Wan Voravudhi, Anyarat Suthat Na Ayudhya, Pete Tongchua, Sutichit Viradejkamhaeng, Soomjin Tamatat, Malee Wetprasert.
08/15/79

Tiro Al Aire
(Unpredictable Guy)
(Argentina)
MXF. Prod by Rey Films. Prod, Toto Rey. Dir-sp, Mario Sabato. Cam (Eastmancolor), Leonardo Rodriguez Solis. Sets, Marchegiani-Olivo; cos, Marta de Serpi; mus, Victor Proncet. 104.
Hector Alterio, Adrian Ferrario, Graciela Duffau, Graciela Alfano, Aldo Barbero, Hector Bidonde, Julio de Grazia, Diana Ingro, Enrique Pinti, Rodolfo Ranni, Elena Sedova, Fernando Siro, Luis Tasca, Marcos Zucker, Paula Dominguez, Antonio Gasalla.
11/05/80

Tit For Tat: SEE Nije Nego

Title Shot
(Canada)
AMB. Regenthall Film Presentation of a Title Shot prodn. Prod, Rob Iveson. Exec prod, Richard Gabourie. Dir, Les Rose. Sp, John Saxton from an orig story by Gabourie; cam, Henry Fiks; edtr, Ronald Sanders; art dir, Karen Bromley; mus, Paul James Zaza. Prod in coop with the Canadian Film Development Corp. 96.
Tony Curtis, Richard Gabourie, Susan Hogan, Allan Royal, Robert Delbert, Natsuko Ohama, Jack Duffy, Sean McCann, Taborah Johnson, Robert O'Ree, Dennis Strong.
09/26/79

To Allo Gramma
(The Other Letter)
(Greece)
X. Lambros Liaropoulos and Greek Film Centre prodn. Wri-dir, Lambros Liaropoulos. Cam, Stavros Hassapis; edtr, Andreas Andreakis. 75.
10/27/76

To an Unknown God: SEE A Un Dios Desconocido

To Be Afraid and Make Others Afraid: SEE Angst Haben Und Angst Machen

To Each His Hell: SEE A Chacun Son Enfer

To Forget Venice: SEE Dimenticare Venezia

To Kill This Love: SEE Trzeba Zabic Te Milosc

To Live A Long Life
(USSR)
SOV. Armenfilm Studio Prodn, Erevan, Armenian Republic, Soviet Union. Dir, Frunze Dovlatyan. Sp, Shagen Tatikyan, Dovlatyan; cam, Albert Yavuryan; mus, Martyn Vertazaryan. 95.
Armen Dzhigarkhanyan, Violetta Gevorkyan, Ovanes Vanyan.
06/25/80

To Love the Damned: SEE Maledetti Vi Amero'

To Mega Docoumento
(The Great Document)
(Greece)
X. George Filis and Katia Tsamati's prodn. Wri, Katia Tsamati; dir-edtr, George Filis. 120.
(DOC) (B & W)
10/31/79

To The Devil A Daughter
(Britain - W Germany)
EMI. Hammer-Terra co-prodn, prod, Roy Skeggs. Dir, Peter Sykes. Sp, Chris Wicking (based on novel by Dennis Wheatley); cam (Technicolor), David Watkin; art dir, Don Picton; sfx, Les Bowie; edtr, John Trumper; snd, Dennis Whitlock; asst dir, Barry Langley. 92.
Richard Widmark, Christopher Lee, Honor Blackman, Denholm Elliot, Michael Goodliffe, Nastassja Kinski, Eva-Maria Meineke, Anthony Valentine, Derek Francis, Isabella Telezynska, Constantin de Goguel, Anna Bentinck.
03/10/76

To The Last Drop: SEE Ate a ultima gota

To Woody Allen, From Europe With Love
(Belgium)
X. Iblis Film, BRT prodn. Conceived and dir, Andre Delvaux. Cam, Michael Badour, Walther Van Den Ende; edtrs, John Reznikov, Annette Wauthoz; mus, Egisto Macchi. 40.
(In English) (DOC)
12/17/80

Tobi
(Spain)
X. Blau Films prodn (Madrid). Exec prod, Antonio Martin. Dir, Antonio Mercero. Sp, Horacio Valcarcel, Antonio Mercero; cam (Eastmancolor), Manuel Rojas; sets, Wolfgang Burmann; edtr, Javier Moran. 91.
Lolo Garcia, Maria Casanova, Antonio Ferrandis, Francisco Vidal, Silvia Tortosa, Jose Ruiz Lifante, Andres Mejuto, Walter Vidarte, Joaquin Prats, Manuel Martin Ferrand, Norma Aleandro.
01/17/79

Tod Ode Freiheit
(Death Or Freedom)
(W Germany)
CII. Regina Ziegler Film prodn, Berlin, in collaboration with Paramount Films, Germany. Sp-dir, Wolf Gremm. Cam, Jost Vacano; edtr, Siegrun Jaeger; sets, Goetz Heymann, Juergen Henze; cos, Ingrid Zore; snd, Gunther Kortwich. 90.
Peter Sattmann, Erika Pluhar, Wolfgang Schumacher, Harold Leipnitz, Christine Boehm, Mario Adorf, Gert Frobe, Dieter Schidor, Guido de Angelis, George Meyer-Goll, Seidenschwan, Stefan Ostertag, Volker Bogdan.
03/29/78

Today Is For The Championship
X. Prod-dir, Dan Weisburd. Exec prod, Daniel Miller. Cam (Foto-Kem color), Peter Smokler; edtr, James Oliver; snd, Robert Eber; mus, Buddy Collette. (MPAA rating: PG). 110.
(DOC)
07/23/80

Todesmagazin order Wie werde ich ein Blumentopf?
(Death Magazine or How To Become a Flowerpot)
(W Germany)
FWG. Rosa Von Praunheim Prodn. Wri-dir-prod-cam, Von Praunheim. 73. (DOC)
12/05/79

Todo Modo
(Italy)
NUI. Cinevera S P A prodn. Prod, Daniele Senatore. Dir, Elio Petri. Sp, Petri, Berto Pelosso; cam (Eastmancolor), Luigi Kuweiller; edtr, Ruggio Mastroianni; mus, Ennio Morricone. 112.
Gian Maria Volonte, Marcello Mastroianni, Mariangela Melato, Michel Piccoli.
(Italian with English subtitles)
03/26/80

Toga Party: SEE Pelvis

Together: SEE Amo Non Amo

Toi Ashita
(Faraway Tomorrow)
(Japan)
TOH. Prod, Osamu Tanaka. Dir, Tatsumi Kamishiro. Sp, To Baba, based on novel by A J Cronin; cam, Kazumi Hara; art dir, Yukio Higuchi; snd, Noboru Kamikura; light, Shinji Kojima; mus, Kawachi Kuni; edtr, Michiko Ikeda; asst dir, Ippei Imamura. 95.
Tomokazu Miura, Ayumi Ishida, Junko Miyashita, Tomisaburo Wakayama, Taiji Tomoyama.
04/23/80

Toi Ippon no Michi
(The Far Road)
(Japan)
X. Prod-dir, Sachiko Hidari. Sp, Ken Miyamoto; cam, Junichi Segawa; art dir, Shigeichi Ikuno; mus, Minoru Miki. 115.
Hisashi Igawa, Sachiko Hidari, Yoshie Shimo, Kenji Isomura, Kyozo Nagatsuka, Masaaki Maeda, Kazuko Imai.
(English subtitles)
02/22/78

Tom Horn
WB. First Artists picture. Prod, Fred Weintraub. Exec prod, Steve McQueen. Dir, William Wiard. Sp, Thomas McGuane, Bud Shrake, based on "Life of Tom Horn, Government Scout and Interpreter" by Horn; cam (Technicolor), John Alonzo; edtr, George Grenville; snd, Jerry Jost, Joe Kite; art dir, Ron Hobbs; asst dir, Cliff Coleman; cos, Luster Bayless; set decor, Rick Simpson; mus, Ernest Gold. (MPAA rating: R). 98.
Steve McQueen, Richard Farnsworth, Linda Evans, Billy Green Bush, Slim Pickens.
04/02/80

Tomas - et barn, duu ikke kan naa
(Tomas - A Child You Cannot Reach)
(Denmark)
HTM. HTM production with the Danish Film Institute (Erik Crone). Wri-dir, Mads Egmont Christensen, Lone Hertz. Cam (Eastmancolor/Widescreen), Billie August, Alexander Gruszynski; edtr, Janus Billeskov Jansen; exec prod-prodn mgr, Tivi Magnusson. 100.
Lone Hertz, Tomas Stroebye.
(DOC)
12/03/80

The Tomboy: SEE Sao Jomken

Tomorrow Never Comes
(Britain - Canada)
RNK. Prods, Julian Melzack, Michael Klinger. Dir, Peter Collinson. Sp, David Pursall, Jack Seddon, Sydney Banks; cam (Eastmancolor), Francois Protat; edtr, John Shirley; art dir, Michael Proulx; set dresser, Norman Sarrazin; asso prods, Denis Heroux, Bob Sterne; stunt dir, Jerome Tiberghien; asst dirs, Peter Price, Avde Chiriaeff, Michele St Arnaud. 107.
Oliver Reed, Susan George, Raymond Burr, John Ireland, Stephen McHattie, Donald Pleasence, Paul Koslo, Cec Linder, Richard Donat, Dolores Etienne, Sammy Snyder, Jane Eastwood, Mario Di Iorio, Stephen Mendel, Walter Massey, Earl Pennington, Jack Fisher, John Osborne.
03/01/78

Tomorrow's Children: SEE Demain les Momes

Too Lean for Love?: SEE Fuer Die Liebe Noch Zu Mager?

The Toolbox Murders
CAW. Tony Didio prodn. Dir, Dennis Donnelly. Sp, Robert Easter, Ann N Kindberg; cam, Gary Graver; edtr, Skip Lusk; asso prods, Kenneth A Yates, Jack Kindberg; snd, Robert Dietz; mus, George Deaton. (MPAA rating: R). 93.
Cameron Mitchell, Pamelyn Ferdin, Wesley Eure, Nicholas Beauvy, Aneta Coraut, Tim Donnelly.
11/08/78

Top Dog: SEE Wodzirej

Top Hat: SEE Chapeau Claque

Top Secret–The History of German Resistance Against Hitler: SEE Geheime Reichssache

Toplo
(Warmth)
(Bulgaria)
BGO. Dir, Vladimir Yanchev. 90.
Grigor Vachkov, Stefan Danailov, Todor Kolev.
02/28/79

Torch High: SEE Flamme Empor

Total Vereist
(Totally Frozen)
(W Germany)
X. DNS-Film Production, Munich in collab with Bayerischer Rundfunk, Munich; exec prod, OLGA-Film Munich. Dir, Hans Noever. Sp, Noever, Ursula Jeshel; cam, Jacques Steyn; snd, Olof Griepenkerl, Peter Kellerhals; sets, Georg von Kieseritzky; edtr, Christine Leyrer; prodn mgr, Elvira Senft. 80.
Rio Reiser, Adam Alexander Kaz, Juergen von Alten, Renate Reiche, Silvia Janisch, Ginka Steinwachs, Ursula Wachnowski, Kurt Raab, Hanns Zischler, Margie Subee, Albert Heins, Dominic Raacke.
12/24/80

Touch And Go
(Australia)
GUO. Mutiny Pictures prodn. Prod, John Pellatt. Exec prods, Peter Maxwell, Peter Yeldham. Dir, Maxwell. Sp, Yeldham (from an orig story by Maxwell and Yeldham); prodn mgr, Michael McKeag; cam (Eastmancolor), John McLean; edtrs, Sara Bennett, Paul Maxwell. 92.
Wendy Hughes, Chantal Contouri, Carmen Duncan, Jeanie Drynan, Liddy Clark, Christine Amor, Jon English, John Bluthal, Brian Blain, Vince Martin, Barbara Stephens, Pamela Norman, Cynthia Cooper, Beryl Cheers.
07/16/80

Touched By Love
COL. Prod, Michael Viner. Dir, Gus Trikonis. Exec prod, Peter E Strauss. Sp, Hesper Anderson, based on book "To Elvis With Love" by Lena Canada; cam (Metrocolor), Richard H Kline; edtr, Fred Chulack; mus, John Barry; art dir, Claudio Guzman; set decor, Ray Molyneaux; cos des, Moss Mabry; snd, David Ronne; asst dir, Bert Gold. (MPAA rating: PG). 95.
Deborah Raffin, Diane Lane, Michael Learned, John Amos, Cristina Raines, Mary Wickes, Clu Gulager, Twyla Volkins, Clive Shalom.
04/23/80

Touchy: SEE A Flor Da Pele

The Tourist Trap
CPQ. Charles Band prodn. Exec prod, Charles Band. Prod J Larry Carroll. Dir, David Schmoeller. Sp, Schmoeller, Carroll; cam (Metrocolor), Nicholas Von Sternberg; mus, Pino Donaggio; edtr, Ted Nicolaou; snd mixer, Courtney Goodin; special snd effects, Joel Goldsmith; sfx, Rich Helmer; art dir, Robert Burns; set decor, Amanda Flick; asst dirs, Ron Underwood, David Wyler. (MPAA rating: PG). 85.
Chuck Connors, Jon Van Ness, Jocelyn Jones, Robin Sherwood, Tanya Roberts, Keith McDermott, Dawn Jeffory.
03/21/79

Tous A Poil Et Qu'on En Finisse!
(Once Upon Andrea)
(France)
X. Les Films Oniris prodn. Wri-prod-dir, Henri Glaeser. Cam (Eastmancolor), Claude Lecomte; edtr, Nicole Berckmans. 95.
Odette Laurent, Jacques Zolty, Jean-March Dupuich, Marie Christine Descouard.
(English subtitles)
04/07/76

Tous Vedettes
(All Stars)
(France)
GAU. Gaumont International Prodns/Marcel Dassault co-prodn. Prod, Alain Poire. Wri-dir, Michel Lang. Mus, Mort Shuman; sngs, Shuman, Lang, Claude Lemesle; cam, (Eastmancolor), Daniel Gaudry; edtr, Helene Plemiannikov; snd, Alain Sempe; art dir, Bernard Evein; cos, Annie Perier. 120.
Leslie Caron, Remi Laurent, Kitty Kortes-Lynch, Jerome Foulon, Francoise Pinaud, Claude Swieca, Daniel Ceccaldi, Robert Webber.
02/06/80

Tout Depend des Filles
(It All Depends On Girls)
(France)
SNC. Bela Productions/SNC/Credo/FR3 co-prodn. Prod, Georges de Beauregard. Wri-dir, Pierre Fabre. Cam (Eastmancolor), Alain Masseron; snd, Raymond Saint-Martin; mus, Michel Bernholc; art dir, Daniel O'Nillon; edtr, Jean-Claude Bonfanti. 94.
Jean-Luc Bideau, Jean-Pierre Sentier, Christine Murillo, Tonie Marshall, Michel Galabru, Michelene Presle.
06/25/80

Towing
UIP. Sibling Prodns. Prod, Frederick A Smith; exec prods, Alan Gelband, Bob Greenberg. Dir-wri, Maura Smith. Cam, Hal Schullman; mus, Martin Rubinstein; edtr, Bernard F Caputo; snd, Art Ziemke, Kurt Kreutz. (MPAA rating: PG). 85.
Jennifer Ashley, Sue Lyon, Bobby DiCicco, Joe Mantegna, J J Johnston, Audry Neenan, Steve Kampman, Don DePollo, Nan Mason, Mike Nusbaum, Susanne Smith, Jake Stockwell, Lee Stein, Sandy Halpin, Bob Wallace.
05/24/78

Town Bloody Hall
PNB. Pennebaker Inc prodn. Prod, D A Pennebaker. Dirs, Pennebaker, Chris Hegedus. Cam, Pennebaker, Jim Desmond; edtr, Hagedus; asso prod, Shirley Broughton. 88.
Norman Mailer, Germaine Greer, Diana Trilling, Jacqueline Ceballos, Jill Johnston.
03/19/80

The Town That Dreaded Sundown
AIP. Prod-dir, Charles B Pierce. Sp, Earl E Smith; cam (Movielab Color), Jim Roberson; edtr, Tom Boutross; mus, Jaime Mendoza-Nava; art dir, Myrl Teeter, Grant Sinclair; cos, Bonnie Langfliff, Karen Jones; stunt coord, Bud Davis. (MPAA rating: R). 90.
Ben Johnson, Andrew Prine, Dawn Wells, Jimmy Clem, Charles B Pierce, Cindy Butler, Earl E Smith, Christine Ellsworth, Mike Hackworth, Jim Citty, Robert Aquino, Misty West, Rick Hildreth, Steve Lyons, Bud Davis.
01/26/77

The Toy: SEE Le Jouet

Trackdown
UA. Essaness Pictures prodn. Prod, Bernard Schwartz. Dir, Richard T Heffron. Sp, Paul Edwards, from story by Ivan Nagy; cam (DeLuxe Color), Gene Polito; edtr, Anthony De Marco; mus, Charles Bernstein; art dir, Vincent M Cresciman; set decor, Robert Bradfield; snd, John Vincent; asst dir, Dennis Jones; stunt coord, Eddy Donno. (MPAA rating: R). 98.
Jim Mitchum, Karen Lamm, Anne Archer, Erik Estrada, Cathy Lee Crosby, Vince Cannon, John Kerry.
03/31/76

Tracks
CMR. Howard Zucker, Irving Cohen, Ted Shapiro prodn. Wri-dir, Henry Jaglom. Cam, Paul Glickman; exec prod, Bert Schneider; edtr, George Folsey Jr. 90.
Dennis Hopper, Taryn Power, Dean Stockwell, Topo Swope, Michael Emil, Zack Norman, Alfred Ryder.
05/19/76

Traditions, My Behind: SEE
Rend mig i traditionerne

Traellenes oproer
(Revolt of the Thralls)
(Denmark)
X. Traellenes Boern (Ebbe Preisler) prodn. Based on Sven Wernstroem's novels. Exec prod, Ebbe Preisler. Artist/animator, Jannik Hastrup; mus, Benny Holst, Anders Koppel, Peter Bastian; edtr, Jon Bille Brahe. 90.
Voices, Berthe Quistgaard, Otto Brandenburg, Ove Sprogoe, Poul Thomsen, Birgit Bruel, Jesper Klein.
(ANI)
10/17/79

Tragedy of Love
(Singapore)
07/25/79
SHF. Prod, Runme Shaw. Wri-dir, Chen Hung Lieh. Cam, Chen Kuan Ho; mus, Lua Ming Toh; snd, Tien Loo; exec prod, Mona Fong. 110.
Liu Shang Chien, Chow Tan Wei.

Train in the Snow: SEE Vlak U Snijegu

Trampa
(Swap)
(Hungary)
BGO. Bulgarofilm prodn, Sofia. Dir, Georgi Dyulgerov. Sp, Vladimir Ganev, Dyulgerov, based on Ivailo Petrov's story "Three Meetings"; cam, Radoslav Spassov. 100.
Iliya Dobrev, Margarita Pehlivanova, Maria Karel, Jeanna Marcheva, Vulcho Kamarashev, Tanya Shahova, Petya Doubarova.
02/28/79

Transit
(Israel)
X. Transit Film Prodn. Prod, Yaakov Goldwasser. Dir, Daniel Wachsmann. Sp, Daniel Horowitz, Wachsmann; cam, Illan Rosenberg; edtrs, Asher Tlalim, Levy Zini; mus score, Schlomo Gronich; snd, Danny Natowitz; art dir, Danny Verete. 87.
Gedalia Besser, Yitzhak (Picho) Ben-Zur, Liora Rivlin, Yair Elazar, Amnon Meskin, Gideon Singer.
02/20/80

The Trap
(Syria)
X. Syrian Film Production, Damascus. Dir, Wadi Yossef; sp, Ali Ogla Ursan. 90.
Samar Sami, Osama Khuluki, Addulhadi Sabbag.
06/18/80

Travelling Companion: SEE
Companero De Viaje

Travelling Companions: SEE
Petschki-Lawotschki

Travels On The Sly: SEE Le
Voyage en douce

Travels with Anita
(Italy)
UA. PEA prodn. Dir, Mario Monicelli. Sp, Leo Benvenuti, Piero De Bernardi, Tullio Pinelli, Paul Zimmermann and Mario Monicelli; cam (Eastmancolor), Tonino Delli Colli; edtr, Ruggero Mastroianni; art dir, Lorenzo Baraldi; mus, Ennio Morricone. 125.
Goldie Hawn, Giancarlo Giannini, Claudine Auger, Aurore Clement, Renzo Montagnani.
02/14/79

Treasure of Matecumbe
BV. Walt Disney prodn, prod, Bill Anderson; exec prod, Ron Miller. Dir, Vincent McEveety. Sp, Don Tait, from the novel, "A Journey To Matecumbe" by Robert Lewis Taylor; cam (Technicolor), Frank Phillips; edtr, Cotton Warburton; mus, Buddy Baker; prodn des, Robert Clatworthy; art dir, John B Mansbridge; set decor, Frank R McKelvy; snd, Herb Taylor, Frank C Regula; asst dir, Paul Nichols. (MPAA rating: G). 117.
Robert Foxworth, Joan Hackett, Peter Ustinov, Vic Morrow, Johnny Doran, Billy Attmore, Jane Wyatt, Robert DoQui, Mills Watson, Val De Vargas, Virginia Vincent, Don Knight, Dub Taylor, Dick Van Patten.
07/07/76

Tredowata
(Leper)
(Poland)
POL. Dir, Jerzy Hoffman. Based on novel by Helena Miniszkowna; cam, Stanislaw Loth; mus, Wojciech Kilar; art dir, Jerzy Szeski; prodn mgr, Wilhelm Hollender. 100.
Elizbieta Starostecka, Leszek Teleszynski, Czeslaw Wollejko, Mariusz Dmochowski, Anna Dymna.
02/02/77

The Tree of Wooden Clogs:
SEE L'Albero Degli Zoccoli

Tren
(Moment)
(Yugoslavia)
YFR. Avala Film prodn. Dir, Stole Jankovic. Sp, Jankovic, Antonije Isakovic from the book by Isakovic; cam (Eastmancolor), Bozidar Miletic. 97.
Velimir-Bata Zivojinovic, Pavle Vujistic, Radko Polic, Svjetlana Knezevic, Dragan Nikolic.
09/05/79

Trener
(The Coach)
(Yugoslavia)
YFR. Central Film Studio-Avala Film prodn. Wri-dir, Purisa Dordevic. Cam (Eastmancolor), Zika Milic; edtr, Mira Mitic; mus, Milomir. 90.
Tansije Uzonovic, Ljuba Tadic, Peter Karsten, Drago Cuma, Dorde Nenadovic, Dijana Sporcic.
08/16/78

Tres En Raya
(Tic-Tac-Toe)
(Spain)
X. Enrique Belloch-Togaport P.C. prodn. Wri-dir, Francisco Roma. Cam (Eastmancolor), Miguel Mila; mus, Pedro Luis Domingo; edtr, Jose Luis Pelaez; sets, Carlos Marco. 90.
Pep Munne, Mireia Ros, Inaki Miramon, Hector Alterio, Irene Gutierrez, Caba, Gemma Cuervo, Miguel Arribas, Mayrata O'Wisiedo, Antonio Gamero, Carmen Belloch.
09/12/79

The Trespassers
(Australia)
FWS. Vega Film Productions prodn. Prod-dir-wri, John Duigan; exec prod, Richard Brennan. Cam, Vince Monton; mus, Bruce Smeaton. 93.
John Derum, Judy Morris, Briony Behets, Hugh Keys-Byrne, Peter Carmody, Max Gilles, John Frawley, Syd Conabere, Chris Haywood, John Orcsik, Ross Thompson, John Bowman.
06/09/76

Tri Tigre Contro Tri Tigre
(Three Tigers Against Three Tigers)
(Italy)
ITI. Prod, Primex and Italian Int'l. Dirs, Sergio Corbucci, Steno (Stefano Vanzina). Sp, Renato Pozzetto, Aurelio Ponzoni, Sergio Corbucci, Mario Amendola, Enrico Vanzina, Giacomo Guerrini, Franco Castellano, Giuseppe Moccia (Pipolo); cam (Technicolor), Marcello Gatti, Emilio Loffredo; edtr, Amedeo Salfa; mus, Guido and Maurizio de Angelis; art dirs, Mario Ambrosino, Andrea Crisanti. 113.
Renato Pozzetto, Aurelio Ponzoni, Dalila di Lazzaro, Enrico Montesano, Paolo Villaggio.
11/23/77

The Trials of Alger Hiss
X. History on Film presentation. Prod-dir, John Lowenthal. Cam, Steven L Alexander, Adam Giffard, Vic Losick, Mark Obenhaus, Edward Gray, William G Markle; edtr, Marion Kraft; snd, Richard Brick, Robert Funk, Francis Daniel, Ronald S Yoshida. 166.
(DOC) (16m)
03/12/80

Tribute
(Canada)
FOX. Prods, Joel B Michaels, Garth B Drabinsky. Dir, Bob Clark. Exec prods, Lawrence Turman, David Foster, Richard S Bright. Sp, Bernard Slade, based on his stage play; cam (Medallion Film Laboratories), Reginald H Morris; edtr, Richard Halsey, snd, David Lee; prodn des, Trevor Williams; art dir, Reuben Freed; asst dir, Ken Goch; asso prod, Hannah Hempstead; mus, Ken Wannberg, Barry Manilow, Jack Feldman, Bruce Sussman, Jack Lemmon, Alan Jay Lerner. (MPAA rating: PG). 123.
Jack Lemmon, Robby Benson, Lee Remick, Kim Cattrall, Colleen Dewhurst, John Marley, Gale Garnett.
12/03/80

Trilogie des Wiedersehens
(Trilogy of Wiedersehens)
(W Germany)
X. Regina Ziegler Film Prodn, West Berlin. Dir, Peter Stein. Sp, Botho Strauss based on his drama; cam, Michael Ballhaus; sets, Karl-Ernst Herrmann; edtr, Clarissa Ambach; snd, Peter Kellerhals. 128.
Lipgart Schwartz, Peter Fritz, Otto Maechtlinger, Gerd Wameling, Elke Petri, Ben Becker, Werner Rehm, Edith Clever, Tina Engel, Roland Schaefer, Sabine Andreas, Otto Sander, Hans Madin, Christine Oesterlein, Paul Burian, Guenter Mayer.
05/23/79

Trip to the Centre of the Earth: SEE Viaje Al Centro De La Tierra

The Triple Death of the Third Character: SEE La Triple Mort Du Troisieme Personnage

Trocadero Bleu Citron
(Trocadero Blue and Yellow)
(France)
WBC. Madeleine Films, SFP, Films De Gueville prodn. Wri-dir, Michael Schock. Cam (Eastmancolor), Bernard Laug; edtr, Georges Klotz; mus, Alec Costadinos. 90.
Anny Duperey, Lionel Melet, Berangere De Lagatineau, Henri Garcin.
09/27/78

Trofej
(Trophy)
(Yugoslavia)
YFR. Neoplanta Film prodn. Dir, Karolj Vicek. Sp, Ferenc Deak, Vicek; cam (Eastmancolor), Dusan Ninkov; mus, Mladen and Pedrag Vranjesevic. 93.
Stole Arandelovic, Slobodan Dimitrijevic, Eva Ras, Jagoda Kaloper, Tanja Boskovic, Vojislav Miric, Mica Tomic, Velemir Zivotic.
08/15/79

Trois Hommes a Abattre
(Three Men to Destroy)
(France)
UGC. Adel Productions-Antenne 2 co-prodn. Prod, Alain Delon. Dir, Jacques Deray. Sp, Deray, Christopher Frank, based on a novel by Jean Patrick Manchette. Cam, Jean Tournier. Snd, Kean Labussiere. Mus, Claude Bolling; art dir, Jacques Brizzio. Edtr, I Garcia de Herreros; prodn mgr, Henri Jaquillard. 90.
Alain Delon, Dalila DiLazzaro, Pierre Dux, Michel Auclair, Simone Renant.
11/12/80

Trophy: SEE Trofej

Trout: SEE Las Truchas

The Truck: SEE Le Camion

The True Life Of Dracula:
SEE Vlad Tepes

The Trumpeter: SEE A Trombitas

Trust: SEE Doverie

The Truth On the Savolta Affair: SEE La Verdad Sobre El Caso Savolta

Tryptych
(USSR)
SOV. Uzbekfilm Studio Production, Tashkent, Uzbekistan Republic, Soviet Union. Wri-dir, Ali Khamraev; cam, Yuri Kilmenko. 100.
Gula Khamrayova.
06/18/80

Trzeba Zabic Te Milosc
(To Kill This Love)
(Poland)
POL. Film Polski prodn, Warsaw. Dir, Janusz Morgenstern. Sp, Janusz Glowacki. 90.
Jadwiga Jankowska-Cieslak, Alicja Jachiewicz, Barbara Wrzesinska, Andrzej Malec, Wladyslaw Kowalski.
06/01/77

Tschushije Pissma
(Strange Letters)
(USSR)
X. Lenfilm, Leningrad, Film prodn. Dir, Ilja Averbach. Sp, Natalija Rjasanzeva; cam, Dmitri Dolinin; mus, Oleg Karawaitchuk. 90.
Irinia Kuptschenko, Svetlana Smirnova, Sergei Kovolenkov, Sinaida Scharko, Oleg Jankovski, Ivan Bortnik, Natascha Skvorzova.
03/09/77

Tsekloput
(Cyclops)
(Bulgaria)
X. Bulgarian Film prodn. Wri-des-dir, Christo Christov. Cam, Vanets Dimitrov; mus, Kiril Chiboulka. 100.

Michail Moutafov, Penka Citselkova, Nevena Kokanova, Penko Penkov.
11/10/76

Tsenu Smerti Sprosi u Miortvykh
(The Dead Pay the Price for Death)
(USSR)
X. Tallin Film prodn. Dir, Kalio Kiisk. Wri, Mati Unt; sets, Tynu Virve; cam, Juri Sillart. 75.
Juozas Kisielus, Gediminas Girdvainis, Kabjn Kommissarov, Maria Klens Kaya, Elle Kul.
08/29/79

Tu Me Enloqueces
(You Make Me Crazy)
(Argentina)
PDP. Ansa prodn, prods, Sandro and Oscar Anderle. Dir, Sandro. Sp, Sandro, Jorge Falcon; cam (Eastmancolor), Anibal Gonzalez Paz; art dir, Carlos T Dowling; mus-dir, Jorge Leone; edtr, Carlos Lavillotti; songs by Sandro and Anderle. 90.
Sandro, Susana Gimenez, Marcelo Jose, Hector Pellegrini, Luis Tasca, Raimundo Soto, Julio Lopez.
09/22/76

Tukerkepek
(Reflections)
(Hungary)
HU. Hunnia Studio prodn. Dir, Reszo Szoreny. Cam (Eastmancolor), Peter Jankura. 90.
Jana Plichtova, Erika Bodnar.
02/09/77

Tunnel Warfare: SEE Di Dao Chan

Tunnelvision
WW. Int'l Harmony/Woodpecker Music Inc film. Prod, Joe Roth; exec prod, Neil Israel. Dirs, Brad Swirnoff, Israel. Sp, Israel, Michael Mislove; cam, Don Knight; edtrs, Roger Parker, Dayle Mustain; mus, Dennis Lambert, Brian Potter; art dir, C D Taylor; snd, Jan Broden; asst dir, Edward Markley. (MPAA rating: R). 75.
Phil Proctor, Howard Hesseman, Ernie Anderson, Edwina Anderson.
04/07/76

The Turning Point
FOX. Prod, Herbert Ross, Arthur Laurents; exec prod, Nora Kaye. Dir, Ross. Sp, Laurents; cam (DeLuxe Color), Robert Surtees; edtr, William Reynolds; mus, John Lanchbery; prodn des, Albert Brenner; set decor, Marvin March; snd, Ted Soderberg, Jerry Jost; cos-ward, Albert Wolsky, Tony Faso, Jennifer Parsons; asst dir, Jack Roe. (MPAA rating: PG). 119.
Anne Bancroft, Shirley MacLaine, Mikhail Baryshnikov, Leslie Browne, Tom Skerritt, Martha Scott, Antoinette Sibley, Alexandra Danilova, Starr Danias, Marshall Thompson, James Mitchell, Scott Douglas, Daniel Levans, Jurgen Schneider, Anthony Zerbe, Phillip Saunders, Lisa Lucas.
10/19/77

Tusk
(France)
X. Yang Film-Films 21 prodn. Prod, Rochat. Exec prods, Eric Rochat, Sylvio Tabet, Jean-Jacques Fourgeaud. Dir, Alexandro Jodorowsky. Sp, Nick Niciphor, Jeffrey O'Kelly, Jodorowsky, based on novel, "Poo Lorn Of The Elephants," by Reginald Campbell. Cam (Technicolor), Jean-Jacques Flori; mus orig theme, Jean-Claude Petit; addl mus, Guy Skornik; edtr, Jean-Philippe Berger; art dir, Philip King; snd, Raymond Adam; 2d unit dir, Peter Ferguson; asst dirs, Francois Mimet, Serge Menard, Eric Rochat Jr, Vijay Talwar, Jimmy Kacy. 119.
Cyrielle Clair, Anton Diffring, Serge Merlin, Christopher Mitchum, Michael Peyrelon, Sukumar Anhana, B Chandrasherkhra, Oriole Henry, Andy Jenny, Krake, Tusk the Elephant.
(English soundtrack)
03/26/80

Twee Vrouwen
(Twice a Woman)
(Holland)
AEF. William Howerd/MGS prodn. Prods, William Howerd, Anne Lordon. Dir, George Sluizer. Sp, George Sluizer, Jurrien Rood, based on the novel, "Twee Vrouwen," by Harry Mulisch; cam, Mat van Hensbergen; mus, Willem Breuker; snd, Pjotr van Dijk; art dir, Michel Bodt; cutting, Leo de Boer; asst dir, Jurrien Rood. 113.
Bibi Andersson, Anthony Perkins, Sandra Dumas, Tilly Perin Bouwmeester, Kitty Courbeois, Astrid Weyman, Georg Frenkel Frank, Charles Gormley, Adrian Brine, Arnold Gelderman.
(English Soundtrack)
05/16/79

The 12 Labors of Asterix: SEE Les 12 Travaux D'Asterix

Twelve Months
(Japan)
X. Japanese Film Production. Dir, Yasuhiro Yamaguchi. Sp, Kimio Yabuki. 90. (ANI)
06/25/80

25 Years - Impressions
(Britain)
EMI. Film by Peter Morley. Prod-dir, Morley. Cam (Technicolor), Tony Coggans, Eric Van Haren Norman, Mike Delaney, Harvey Harrison. Edtr, Jeff Harvey; snd, Colin Charles, Bernard Child, Clive Winter, Laurie Clarkson; asst cam, Mike Shackleton, Paul Hennessey, Tony Browning, John Coe; dubbing, Trevor Pyke; titles, Alison Inglis. 77. (DOC)
02/23/77

22nd June, 1897
(India)
NJI. Wris-dirs, Nachiket, Jayoo Patwardhan. Cam, Navroze Contractor; edtr, Madhu Sinha; mus, Anand Modak. 120.
Prabhakar Patankar, Ravindra Mankani, Udayan Dixit, Rod Gilbert.
02/13/80

2076 Olympiad
X. Aragon prodn Company film. Prod, wri-dir, James R Martin. Cam, Mannuel Whitaker; art dir, Suzanne M Steiner; mus, Lawrence J Ponzak; ani-graphics, Paul Fierlinger, Pavel Voisicy. (MPAA rating: X). 90.
Jerry Zafer, Sandy Martin, Dean Bennett, Joel Camphausen, Joann Secunda, Alan Kirk, Sigrid Heath, Meredith Rile, J R Martin, Robert Boxco, Gene Shay, Gladys Williams, John LaMotta.
06/22/77

Twice a Woman: SEE Twee Vrouwen

Twilight's Last Gleaming
(US - W Germany)
AA. Lorimar(USA)-Bavaria (Munich) presentation of a Geria prodn; prod, Merv Adelson. Exec prod, Helmut Jedele. Dir, Robert Aldrich. Sp, Ronald M Cohen, Edward Huebsch, based on the novel, "Viper Three," by Walter Wager, cam (Technicolor), Robert Hauser; edtng supv, Michael Luciano; mus, Jerry Goldsmith; prodn des, Rolf Zehetbauer; art dir, Werner Achmann; snd, John Wilkinson, James Willis; cos-ward, Tom Dawson; asst dir, Wolfgang Glattes. (MPAA rating: R). 146.
Burt Lancaster, Richard Widmark, Charles Durning, Melvyn Douglas, Paul Winfield, Burt Young, Joseph Cotten, Roscoe Lee Browne, Gerald S O'Loughlin, Richard Jaeckel, William Marshall, Charles Aidman, Leif Erickson, Charles McGraw, Morgan Paull, Simon Scott, William Smith, Bill Walker.
02/02/77

The Twist: SEE Folies Bourgeoises

Two Champions of Shaolin
(Hong Kong)
SHF. Prod, Run Run Shaw. Exec prod, Mona Fong. Dir, Chang Cheh. Story-sp, Chang Cheh, I Kuang; cam, Tsao Hui Chi; art dir, Johnson Tsao; mus-snd, Eddie Wang; edtrs, Chiang Hsing Lung, Li Ying Hoi; martial art instrs, Lu Feng, Chiang Sheng, Kuo Che. 79.
Lo Meng, Chiang Sheng, Sun Chien, Wang Li, Wen Hsueh Erh, Lu Feng, Chien Hsiao Hao, Yang Ching Ching, Yu Tai Ping, Kuan Tsung, Liang Yao Wen.
07/02/80

Two Days for Life: SEE Zwei Tage Fuers Leben

Two Lions in the Sun: SEE Deux Lions Au Soleil

Two-Minute Warning
U. Filmways (Edward S Feldman) prodn. Dir, Larry Peerce. Sp, Edward Hume, based on the novel by George La Fountaine; cam (Technicolor), Gerald Hirschfeld; edtrs, Eve Newman, Walter Hannemann; mus, Charles Fox; art dir, Herman A Blumenthal; set decor, John M Dwyer; snd, Jim Alexander, Robert L Hoyt; asst dir, Ken Swor; stunt coord, Glen Wilder; football coord, Tom Fears. (MPAA rating: R).   115.
Charlton Heston, John Cassavetes, Martin Balsam, Beau Bridges, Marilyn Hassett, David Janssen, Jack Klugman, Gena Rowlands, Walter Pidgeon, Brock Peters, David Groh, Mitchell Ryan, Joe Kapp, Jon Korkes, Juli Bridges, Brooke Mills, Pamela Bellwood, Andy Sidaris, Fred Hice, Jack Brodsky, Arnold Carr, Christine Nelson, Holly Irving, Allan Miller, Glen Wilder, David Cass, Warren Miller, Howard Cossell, Frank Gifford, Dick Enberg, Merv Griffin.
11/03/76

The Two Of Them: SEE Ok Ketten

Two Pieces of Bread: SEE Due Pezzi di Pane

Two Solitudes
(Canada)
CFS. Two Solitudes Film Corp prodn. Dir-sp, Lionel Chetwynd, from the book by Hugh McLennan. Cam, Rene Verzier; edtr Ralph Brunjes; mus, Maurice Jarre.   116.
Jean-Pierre Aumont, Stacy Keach, Gloria Carlin, Christopher Wiggins, Claude Jutra, Raymond Cloutier, Jean-Louis Roux.
08/23/78

Two Super Cops: SEE Deux Super Flics

Udhetim Ne Pranvere
(A Journey into Spring)
(Albania)
ALA. Albfilm Prodn, Tirana. Dir, Qerim Mata. Sp, Gjergj Zheji; cam, Pellumb Kallfa; art dir, Kleo Nini.   80.
Minella Borova, Liliana Kondakci, Nikolin Xhoja.
01/10/79

Ugly, Dirty and Bad: SEE Brutti, Sporchi E Cattivi

Ukryty W Sloncu
(Hidden in the Sunlight)
(Poland)
POL. Film Polski prodn, Iluzion Film Unit, Warsaw. Dir, Jerzy Trojan; sp, Ireneusz Iredynski, based on his own book; cam, Wieslaw Zdort; mus, Zbigniew Namyslawski; sets, Tadeusz Kusarewicz, Barbara Komosinska; prodn mgr, Zbigniew Tolioczko.   91.
Jan Englert, Gabriela Kownacka, Ewa Dalkowska, Eugen-iusz Priwiezencew, Teresa Sawicka, Dorota Pomykala, Kazimierz Kaczor, Mieczyslaw Voit.
10/15/80

The Umbrella Coup: SEE Le Coup du Parapluie

Umut
(Hope)
(Turkey)
X. Guney Film, Abudrrahman Heshine, Prodn, Istanbul. Dir, Yilmaz Guney. Sp, Guney, Serif Goren; cam, Kaya Ererez, mus, Arif Erkin; edtr, Celal Kose.   105.
Yilmaz Guney, Gulsen Alniacik, Tuncel Kurtiz, Osman Alyanak, Sema Engin, Sevgi Tatli, Kursat Alniacik, Hicret Gursen, Nizam Erguder, Enver Donmez, Lutti Engin, Kemal Tatli, Almet Koc.
08/02/78

Un Anno Di Scuola
(A Year of School)
(Italy)
SCI. SET, RAI prodn. Dir, Franco Giraldi. Sp, Lucio Guzzinati, Giraldi, Lucille Laks; book, M Stuparich; cam Dario Di Palma; edtr, Gabriella Cristiani; mus, Luis Bacalov.   110.
Laura Lenzi, Stefano Patrizi, Mario D'Arrigo, Giovanni Visentin, Margherita Guzzinati.
08/31/77

Un Autre Homme, Une Autre Chance
(Another Man, Another Chance)
(France - USA)
UA. UA-Films 13-Ariane Film prodn. Prods, Alexandre Mnouchkine, Georges Dancigers. Wri-dir, Claude Lelouch. Cam (Eastmancolor), Jacques Lefrancois; edtr, Georges Klotz; mus, Francis Lai; art dirs, Eric Moulard, Robert Clatworthy.   132.
James Caan, Genevieve Bujold, Francis Huster, Susan Tyrrell, Jennifer Warren.
10/12/77

Un Borghese Piccolo Piccolo
(An Average Man)
(Italy)
CNZ. Prods, Luigi and Aurelio De Laurentiis for Auro Cinematografica. Dir, Mario Monicelli. Sp, Sergio Amidei, Mario Monicelli, based on Vincenzo Cerami novel; cam (Eastmancolor), Mario Vulpiani; art dir, Lorenzo Baraldi; edtr, Ruggero Mastroianni; mus, Giancarlo Chiaramello.   128.
Alberto Sordi, Shelley Winters, Romolo Valli, Vincenzo Crociti, Renzo Carboni.
05/25/77

Un Cuore Semplice
(A Simple Heart)
(Italy)
X. Cooperative Nashira prodn. Dir, Giorgio Ferrara; Sp, Cesare Zavattini, based on a Gustave Flaubert story; cam (Eastmancolor), Arturo Zavattini; edtr, Roberto Perpignani; mus, Franco Mannino.   94.
Adriana Asti, Joe Dallessandro, Alida Valli, Tina Aumont.
10/25/78

Un Dramma Borghese
(Mimi)
(Italy)
VF. Prods, Gianni Minervini, Antonio Avati for AMA Film and UTI Prodns. Dir, Florestano Vancini. Sp, Lucio Battistrada, Florestano Vancini, based on novel by Guido Morselli; cam (Eastmancolor), Alfio Contini; edtr, Nino Baragli; mus, Riz Ortolani.   110.
Franco Nero, Dalila Di Lazzaro, Lara Wendel.
09/12/79

Un Elephant Ca Trompe Enormement
(An Elephant Can Be Extremely Deceptive)
(France)
GAU. Gaumont Int'l-Les Prodns De La Gueville prodn. Dir, Yves Robert. Sp, Jean-Loup Dabadie, Robert; cam (Eastmancolor), Rene Mathelin; edtr, Gerard Pollicand; mus, Vladimir Cosma.   100.
Jean Rochefort, Claude Brasseur, Guy Bedos, Victor Lanoux, Daniele Delorme, Annie Duperey, Martine Sarcey, Marthe Villalonga.
10/06/76

Un Enfant Dans La Foule
(A Child in the Crowd)
(France)
SNC. Cinepol, SFP, Telepresse Films France, Renn Productions prodn. Dir, Gerard Blain. Sp, Blain, Michel Perez; cam (Eastmancolor), Emmanuel Machuel; edtr, Marie-Aimee Debril; mus, Jean Schwarz.   85.
Cesar Chauveau, Annie Kovacs, Claire Treille, Jean Bertal, Gabrielle Sassoum.
06/02/76

Un Escargot Dans la Tete
(Snails in the Head)
(France)
GAU. Link prodn. Prods, Maurice Molina, Andre de Blanzy. Wri-dir, Jean-Etienne Siry. Cam (Eastmancolor), Francois About. Edtr, Antoinette Perraud. Snd, Jean-Luc Rault Cheynet. Art dirs, Kim Doan, Patrice Mercier. 90.
Florence Giorgetti, Renaud Verley, Jeanne Allard, Jean-Claude Bouillon, Charles Dubois, Marcel Gassouk.
11/19/80

Un Genio, Due Compari, Un Pollo
(The Genius)
(Italy - France - Germany)
TIT. Prods, Fulvio Morsella, Claudio Mancini for Rafran Cinematografica (Rome) - AMLF (Paris) - Rialto (Berlin). Dir, Damiano Damiani. Sp, Ernesto Gastaldi, Damiani, Morsella; cam (Technicolor), Giuseppe Ruzzolini; art dirs, Francesco Bronzi, Carlo Simi; edtr, Nino Baragli; mus, Ennio Morricone.   126.
Terence Hill, Miou-Miou, Robert Charlebois, Patrick McGoohan, Klaus Kinski.
01/28/76

Un Hombre Llamado Flor De Otono
(A Man Called Autumn Flower)
(Spain)
X. Jose Frade prodn. Dir, Pedro Olea. Sp, Pedro Olea, Rafael Azcona, based on story by Jose Maria Rodriquez Mendez; cam (Eastmancolor Panoramic), Fernando Arribas; edtr, Jose Antonio Rojo; sets, Antonio Cortes; mus, Carmelo Bernaola. 102.
Jose Sacristan, Paco Algora, Carmen Carbonell, Roberto Camardiel, Antonio Corencia, Jose Franco, Felix Dafauca, Carlos Pineiro, Paco Espana, Mimi Munoz.
10/04/78

Un Homme en fuite
(A Man on the Run)
(Switzerland - France)
CIT. Video Programs Geneva-SSR Geneva-Action Films SA Paris co-prodn. Dir, Simon Edelstein. Wri, Edelstein in collab with Anita Peyrot, Xavier Torre, Gy de Belleval. Cam, Hans Liechti; edtr, Martine Barraque; mus, Pierre Jansen; exec prod, Claude Richardet. 91.
Roger Jendly, Malene Sveinbjornsson, Florence Giorgetti, Jaroslav Vizner, Maurice Aufair.
06/11/80

Un Mauvais Fils
(A Bad Son)
(France)
PFC. Sara Films-Antenne 2-SFP co-prodn. Prod, Alain Sarde. Dir, Claude Sautet. Wris, Sautet, Daniel Biasini, Jean-Paul Torok. Cam, Jean Boffety; mus, Philippe Sarde; edtr, Jacqueline Thiedot; art dir, Dominique Andre; snd, Pierre Lenoir. 110.
Patrick Dewaere, Yves Robert, Brigitte Fossey, Jacques Dufilho, Claire Maurier.
11/19/80

Un Moment D'Egarement
(In A Wild Moment)
(France)
AMLF. Renn Prodns (Claude Berri), SFP prodn. Wri-dir, Claude Berri. Cam (Eastmancolor), Andre Neau; edtr, Jacques Witta; mus, Michel Stelio. 85.
Jean-Pierre Marielle, Victor Lanoux, Christine Dejoux, Agnes Soral, Martine Sarcey.
12/21/77

Un Neveu Silencieux
(The Silent Nephew)
(France)
X. Prod-dir, Robert Enrico. Sp, Paul Savatier, with adaptation and dialog by Savatier and Enrico. 97.
Joel Dupuis, Sylvain Seyrig, Coralie Seyrig, Andrew Falcon, Aline Bertrand, Jean Bouise, Lucienne Hamon, Renee Faure.
11/08/78

Un Oursin Dans La Poche
(A Sea Urchin In The Pocket)
(France)
AMLF. AMLF-Renn Prodns-Antinea-FR3-SFP-Les Films Du Chef Lieu prodn. Dir, Pascal Thomas. Sp, Thomas, Jacques Lourcelles; cam (Eastmancolor), Colin Mounier; mus, Vladimir Cosma. 90.
Darry Cowl, Maurice Risch, Bernard Menez, Rene Lefevre, Brigitte Gruel, Michel Duchaussoy, Daniel Ceccaldi.
12/28/77

Un Papillon Sur L'Epaule
(A Butterfly on the Shoulder)
(France)
GAU. Action Films-Gaumont, Citel Films prodn. Dir, Jacques Deray. Sp, Jean-Claude Carriere, Tonino Guerra from book by Jean Gearon, "The Velvet Well"; cam (Eastmancolor), Jean Boffety, Jean Charvein; edtr, Henri Lanoe. 95.
Lino Ventura, Claudine Auger, Paul Crauchet, Jean Bouise, Nicole Garcia, Laura Betti, Xavier Depraz.
05/10/78

Un Sacco Bello
(Fun Is Beautiful)
(Italy)
MDU. Prod, Romano Cardarelli for Rafran Prodns. Dir, Carlo Verdone. Sp, Leo Benvenuti, Piero De Bernardi, Verdone; cam (Eastmancolor), Ennio Guarnieri; art dir, Carlo Simi; edtr, Eugenio Alabiso; mus, Ennio Morricone. 99.
Carlo Verdone, Veronica Miriel, Mario Brega, Renato Scarpa.
03/26/80

Un Second Souffle
(A Second Wind)
(France)
GAU. Cinepole-Film Produktion Janus-TFI prodn. Dir, Gerard Blain. Sp, Blain, Michel Perez; cam (Eastmancolor), Emmanuel Machuel; edtr, Jean-Phillippe Berger; mus, Jean-Pierre Stora. 101.
Robert Stack, Anicee Alvina, Sophie Desmarets, Marieke Carriere, Frederic Meisner.
08/30/78

Un Si Joli Village
(Such A Lovely Town)
(France)
PLF. Planfilm-Films de la Tour-Jacques Roitfield-Films de la Drouette co-prodn. Sp, Andre G Brunelin, Etienne Perier, based on the novel "The Lesser Evil," by Jean Laborde. Dir, Etienne Perier. Cam, Jean Charvein; snd, Michel Desrois; mus, Paul Misraki; art dir, Jean-Jacques Caziot; prodn mgr, Roland Thenot; asst dir, Olivier Gerard. 116.
Victor Lanoux, Jean Carmet, Valerie Mairesse, Michel Robin, Jacques Richard, Gerard Jugnot, Francis Lemaire.
03/28/79

Un Taxi Mauve
(The Purple Taxi)
(France - Italy - Ireland)
PFC. Sofracima (Giselle Rebillon, Catherine Winter) - Rizzoli Film-TFI prodn in asso with National Film Studios of Ireland-Sphinx Films, Pete Rawley, Hugo Lodrini prodn. Dir, Yves Boisset. Sp, Michel Deon, Boisset from Deon's book; cam (Eastmancolor), Tonino Delli Colli; edtr, Albert Jurgensen; mus, Philippe Sarde. 120.
Charlotte Rampling, Philippe Noiret, Agostina Belli, Peter Ustinov, Fred Astaire, Edward Albert Jr, Mairin O'Sullivan, Jack Watson.
(English soundtrack)
05/25/77

Un Type Comme Moi Ne Devrait Jamais Mourir
(A Guy Like Me Should Never Die)
(France)
PLF. Film & Co (Bernard Lenteric) prodn. Wri-dir, Michel Vianey. Cam (Eastmancolor), Georges Barsky; edtr, Agnes Guillemot; mus, Mort Shuman. 105.
Jean-Michel Folon, Francine Racette, Bernard Fresson, Mort Shuman, Henri Garcin, Sabine Glaser, Bernadette Lafont.
09/01/76

Una Giornata Speciale
(The Great Day)
(A Special Day)
(Italy - Canada)
C5. Prod, Champion Cinematografica (Italy) and Canafox Films Inc (Canada). Dir, Ettore Scola. Sp, Ruggero Maccari, Scola, with collab, Maurizio Costanzo; cam (Technicolor), Pasqualino De Santis; art dir, Luciano Ricceri; edtr, Raimondo Crociani; mus, Armando Trovaioli. 105.
Sophia Loren, Marcello Mastroianni, John Vernon, Francoise Berd.
05/18/77

Una Mujer, Un Hombre, Une Ciudad
(Woman, Man, City)
(Cuba)
X. Cuban Film Prodn. Dir, Manuel Octavio Gomez. Sp, Gomez, Antonio Benites Rojo; cam, Pablo Martinez; mus, Sergio Vitier. 100.
Idalia Anreus, Mario Balmaseda, Raul Pomarez, Omar Valdes, Alden Knight, Raquel Gonzalez.
08/02/78

Una Settimana Come Un'altra
(Week In, Week Out)
(Italy)
X. Arsnova Co-op prodn. Dir, Daniele Costantini. Sp, Costantini, Sergio Marconi, Domenico Calandruccio; cam (Eastmancolor), Antonio Maccoppi. 90.
Leonardo Treviglio, Marcella Michelangeli, Nicoletta, Amadio, Donato Sanniti, Roberto Tortorella.
08/16/78

Una Spirale Di Nebbia
(A Spiral of Mist)
(Italy - France)
SFO. Prod, Danilo Marciani, Arcangelo Picchi for ATA CINETV (Rome), Messapia Film, Serena 75; co-prodn with La Fiduciaire Prodns des Films (Fides) Paris, Intercontinental Prodns Paris. Dir, Eriprando Visconti. Sp, Visconti, Luciano Lucignani, Flavio Mauri, Lisa Morpurjo, from book by Michele Prisco; cam (Technicolor), Blasco Giurato; edtr, Franco Arcalli; mus, Ivan Vandor. 106.
Marina Berti, Martine Brochard, Flavio Bucci, Carole Chauvet, Duilio del Prete, Corrado Gaipa, Eleanora Giorgi, Claude Jade, Marc Porel, Stefano Satta Flores.
10/12/77

Uncle Joe Shannon
UA. Robert Chartoff-Irwin Winkler prodn. Exec prod, Gene Kirkwood. Prods, Irwin Winkler, Robert Chartoff. Dir, Joseph C Hanwright. Sp, Young; cam, Bill Butler; edtr, Don Zimmerman; mus, Bill Conti; prodn des, Bill Kenney; cos des, Bobbie Mannix; snd, Michael Evje; exec in chg of prodn, Hal W Polaire; asst dir, Brian E Frankish. (MPAA rating: PG). 108.
Burt Young, Doug McKeon, Madge Sinclair, Jason Bernard, Bert Remsen, Allan Rich.
11/29/78

Under Lock And Key: SEE Unter Verschluss

The Under-Gifted: SEE Les Sous-Doues

Underground
NY. Film by Emile De Antonio, Mary Lampson, and Haskell Wexler. Prodn staff; Tucker Ashworth, Larry Bensky, John Douglas, Jane Franklin, Robert Friedman, Alan Jacobs, Eleanore Kennedy, Sandy Levinson, Claude Marks, Antoinette O'Connor, P Michael Sullivan, Hart Perry, George Pillsbury, Ellen Ray, Steven H Scheuer, Paul Sequera, Stanley Sheinbaum, Carol Stein, Mitch Tuchman, Marc N Weiss, Myrna Zimmerman. (MPAA rating: M). 88.
Billy Ayers, Kathy Bouldin, Bernardine Dohrn, Jeff Jones, Cathy Wilkerson, Emile De Antonio, Mary Lampson, Haskell Wexler.
(DOC) (16m)
05/12/76

Underground and Emigrants
(W Germany)
X. Rosa von Praunheim prodn, in collab with the Berliner Festwochen and Sender Freies Berlin. Dir-narr, Rosa von Praunheim. Cam, Edvard Lieber, Lloyd Williams, Scott Sorenson, Praunheim; asst, Alice Carey. 90.
Greta Keller, Ron Mullen, William Burroughs, Fred Neumann, Charles Ludlam, Tony Carrol, Mario Montez, Mary Boylen, Brenda Bergman, Bobby, Harvey Firestein, Taylor Mead, Cindy Doll, Slugger Anne, Alice Carey, Chinese Theatre Group, Nelly Vivas, Bob Wilson, Al Carmines, Elsie Bordon, Cherry Vanilla, Brenda Mitchell, Leslie Edgar, Stewart Sherman, Yvonne Rainer, The Family, Danny Partridge, Tom Eyen, Lil Picard, Diana Vreeland, Wolfgang Nepmeyer, Etmar Kline, Belle Star, Lee Breuer, John Vaccaro, Lutze, Paul Venase, Gabi Larifari, Telly Brown, Alexis de Largo, Harvey Tavel, Minette, Jackie Curtis, Holly Woodlawn, Ellen Stewart, Fernando Arrabal, Grete Mosheim, David Woodberry, Lee Gilliot, Stephen Holt, Cyril Cyprian, Craig Hoke, Jessica James, Shusaku Arakawa, Lawrence Weiner, Steve Friedman, Jack Smith, Divine, Andy Warhol, Rosa von Praunheim.
(DOC) (16m)
09/29/76

Underground U.S.A.
X. New Cinema Prodn. Prod-dir-wri, Eric Mitchell. Cam, Tom DiCillo; edtr, J P Roland-Levy; mus, James White & the Blacks, Lounge Lizards, Walter Stedding; snd, Jim Jarmusch, co-prod, Erdner Rauschalle; asst dir, Becky Johnston. 85.
Patti Astor, Eric Mitchell, Rene Ricard, Tom Wright, Jackie Curtis, Cookie Mueller, Taylor Mead, Duncan Smith, Steve Mass, Terry Toye, John Lurie.
(16m)
06/25/80

The Undertaker Parlor Computer: SEE L'Ordinateur Des Pompes Funebres

Une Femme A Sa Fenetre
(A Woman at Her Window)
(France)
SNC. Albina Prodns-Rizzoli Film-Cinema 77 prodn. Dir, Pierre Granier-Deferre. Sp, Jorge Semprun, Granier-Deferre from book by Pierre Drieu La Rochelle; cam (Eastmancolor), Aldo Tonti; edtr, Jean Ravel; prod, Albina De Boisrouvray. 110.
Romy Schneider, Philippe Noiret, Victor Lanoux, Umberto Orsini, Delia Boccardo, Gastone Moschin, Carl Mohner.
10/27/76

Une Femme Fidele
(A Faithful Woman)
(France)
ALP. Les Films Ege-Francos Films-Paradoxe Films prodn. Dir, Roger Vadim. Sp, Daniel Boulanger, Vadim; cam (Eastmancolor), Claude Renoir; edtr, Victoria Mercanton; mus, Mort Shuman, Pierre Porte. 92.
Sylvia Kristel, Jon Finch, Nathalie Delon.
09/15/76

Une Femme, Un Jour
(A Woman, One Day)
(France)
PLF. Les Films Du Guepart-Filmoblic prodn. Dir, Leonard Keigel. Sp, Keigel, Simone Bach; cam (Eastmancolor), Ricardo Aronovitch. 90.
Melane Brevan, Caroline Cellier, Jean-Luc Bideau, Henri Garcin, Gilles Bony.
02/02/77

Une Fille Cousue De Fil Blanc
(A Strait-Laced Girl)
(France)
PFC. Trinacra Films prodn. Dir-wri, Michel Lang; book, Claire Gallois. Cam (Eastmancolor), Daniel Gaudry; edtr, Helene Plemianikov; mus, Oliver Dassault, Christian Gaubert. 105.
Aude Landry, France Dougnac, Serge Regiani, Maria Mauban, Marie Daems, Bruno Pradal, Umberto Orsini, May Marquet, Claire Ackilli.
01/12/77

Une Fille Unique
(An Unusual Girl)
(France)
NHN. Wri-dir, Philippe Nahoun. Cam (b&w), Thomas Mauch; edtr, Olivier Froux. 102.
Sophie Chemineau, Bruno Labraska, Philippe Nahoun, Josianne Balaska, Serge Maggiani, Adee Salicetti, Irene Moreau.
(B & W)
05/19/76

Une Histoire Simple
(A Simple Story)
(France)
AMLF. Renn Prodns-Sara Films-FR3-Rialto Film-SFP prodn. Dir, Claude Sautet. Sp, Sautet, Jean-Loup Dabadie; cam (Eastmancolor), Jean Boffety; edtr, Jacquelin Thiedot; mus, Philippe Sarde. 107.
Romy Schneider, Bruno Cremer, Claude Brasseur, Arlette Bonnard, Sophie Daumier, Eva Darlan, Francine Berge, Roger Pigaut, Madeline Robinson.
11/15/78

Une Page D'Amour
(A Page Of Love)
(Belgium - France)
PRG. Metafilm (Brussels)-Cinopsis (Paris) prodn. Dir, Maurice Rabinowicz. Sp, Yvette Michelems, Maurice Rabinowicz; cam (Gevacolor), Jean-Jacques Mathy; edtr, Jean-Claude Bonfanti; mus, Marc Herouet; sets, Stephane Collas; snd, Francis Bonfanti. 92.
Geraldine Chaplin, Sami Frey, Quentin Milo, Guy Pion, Monetta Loza, Eve Bonfanti, Marcel Dalio, Denise Volny, Bella Szafran, Severyn Lipszyc, Zelman Koletsknikov, Niusia Gold, Veronique Peynet, Jan Decleir, Adrian Brine, Pierre Dumaine, Roland Mahauden, Chantal Lempereur, Arie Yass, Ramon Berry.
12/28/77

Une Sale Histoire
(A Dirty Story)
(France)
FDL. Dir, Jean Eustache. Sp, Jean-Noel Picq; cam (35m Eastmancolor), Dominique Le Rigoleur, cam (16m Color), Pierre Lhomme; edtr, Chantale Colomer. 50.
First Story: Michel Lonsdale, Jean Douchet, Jadques Burloux, Douchka;
Second Story: Jean Noel Picq, Elisabeth Lanchener, Annette Wademant.
(16m/35m)
11/16/77

Une Semaine De Vacances
(A Week's Vacation)
(France)
PAR. Sara Films, Little Bear, A2 prodn. Dir, Bertrand Tavernier. Sp, Tavernier, Colo Tavernier, Marie-Francoise Hans. Cam (Eastmancolor), Pierre William Glenn; edtrs, Armand Psenny, Sophie Cornu; mus, Pierre Papadiamandis. 102.
Nathalie Baye, Gerard Lanvin, Michel Galabru, Philippe Noiret, Philippe Leotard, Flore Fitzgerald, Jean Daste, Marie-Louise Ebeli.
05/21/80

The Unforgettable Autumn:
SEE Nezabybaemaya Osen

The Unidentified Flying Oddball
(Britain)
BV. Walt Disney prodn. Prod, Ron Miller. Dir, Russ Mayberry. Sp, Don Tait based on Mark Twain's "A Connecticut Yankee in King Arthur's Court". Cam, Paul Beeson; art dir, Albert Witherick; edtr, Peter Boita; special pho effects, Cliff Culley; mus comp-cond, Ron Goodwin. 93.
Dennis Dugan, Jim Dale, Ron Moody, Kenneth Moore, John LeMesurier, Rodney Bewes, Sheila White, Robert Beatty, Cyril Shaps, Kevin Brennan, Ewen Solon, Pat Roach, Reg Lye.
07/18/79

Union City
KNS. Prod, Graham Belin; dir, Mark Riechert; sp, Reichert; story, Cornell Woolrich; cam, Ed Lachman; edtng supv, Eric Albertson; edtrs, Lana Tokel, J Michaels; mus, Chris Stein; art dir, George Stavrinos; snd, Luke Yersin. (MPAA rating: PG). 87.
Dennis Lipscomb, Deborah Harry, Irina Maleeva, Everett McGill, Sam McMurray, Terina Lewis, Pat Benatar, Tony Azito, Paul Andor, Taylor Mead, Cynthia Crisp, Charles Rydell.
09/10/80

Unordnung Und Fruehes Leid
(Disorder and Early Torment)
(W Germany)
JUG. Franz Seitz prodn, Seitz-Film, Munich. Wri-dir, Franz Seitz, based on story by Thomas Mann. Cam, Wolfgang Treu; mus, Hans Pfitzner, Rolf Wilhelm, Friedrich Meyer; art dir, Michael Girschek; cos, Ina Stein; edtr, Adolph Schlyssleder. 85.
Martin Held, Ruth Leuwerik, Sabine von Maydell, Frederic Meissner, Sophie Seitz, Markus Sieburg, Christian Kohlund, Eva Vaitl, Hans Kraus, Michael Schwarzmaier, Christine Buchegger, C P Corzilius.
02/09/77

Unpredictable Guy: SEE Tiro Al Aire

Unsichtbare Gegner
(Invisible Adversaries)
(Austria)
X. Prod-dir, Valie Export. Sp, Peter Weibel; cam, Wolfgang Simon; edtr, Juno Sylva Englander; mus, Hartl-Kalchauser. 112.
Susann Widl, Peter Weibel.
05/10/78

Unter Verschluss
(Under Lock And Key)
(W Germany)
X. Artus-Film Prodn, Munich, Dr. Harald Mueller. Wri-dir, Wilma Kottusch. Cam, Gerard Vandenberg, Jochen Rademacher; snd, Klaus Eckelt; mus, Edgar Froese; cos, Franziska Liphart; sets, Gerd B Fleischer. 90.
Lisa Kreuzer, Juergen Prochnow, Rudolf Schuendler, Edith Schulze-Westrum, Isolde Barth, Dieter Schidor, Michaela May, Vera Tschechova, Thomas Astan, Kurt Raab.
02/20/80

Until Death Do Us Part: SEE Bis Dass Der Tod Euch Scheidet

Unversoehnliche Errinnerungen
(Irreconcilable Memories)
(W Germany)
BSG. Journal-Film Klaus G Volkenborn prodn in collab with Zweites Deutsches Fernsehen (ZDF) Mainz. Dirs, Klaus G Volkenborn, Johann Feindt, Karl Siebig; tv prods, Eckhart Stein, Annegret Even; mus, Andi Brauer. 92.
(DOC) (16m)
02/20/80

Uomini E No
(Men or Not Men)
(Italy)
ITG. Ager Cinematografica - RAI Rete 2 prodn. Dir, Valentino Orsini; sp, Faliero Rosati, Giuliana De Negri, Orsini; book, Elio Vittorini; cam, Franco De Giacomo; edtr, Roberto Perpigini; mus, Ennio Morricone. 102.
Flavio Bucci, Ivana Monti, Massimo Foschi, Renato Scarpa.
09/10/80

Up
RHM. Russ Meyer prodn. Prod-dir-edtr, Meyer, Sp, B Callum; cam, Meyer; art dir, Michele Levesque; snd, Dan Holland, Richard Anderson, Fred Owens; mus, William Loose, Paul Ruhland. (Self-imposed X rating). 80.
Robert McLane, Edward Schaaf, Mary Gavin, Elaine Collins, Su Ling, Janet Wood, Linda Sue Ragsdale, Harry, Monte Bane, Raven De La Croix, Larry Dean, Marianne Marks, Bob Schott, Foxy Lae, Fred Owens, Wilburn Kluck, Ray Reinhardt, Francesca "Kitten" Natividad.
10/27/76

Up from the Depths
(Philippines)
NW. Exec prod, Jack Atienza. Prod, Cirio H Santiago. Dir, Charles B Griffith. Sp, Alfred Sweeney; cam (Metrocolor), Rick Remington; edtr, G V Bass; mus, Russell O'Malley; asst dirs, Jill Griffith, Manny Norman. 75.
Sam Bottoms, Susanne Reed, Virgil Frye, Kedric Wolfe, Charles Howerton, Denise Hayes, Charles Doherty, Helen McNelly.
06/27/79

Up In Smoke
(Cheech and Chong's Up In Smoke)
PAR. Lou Adler prodn. Prods, Lou Adler, Lou Lombardo. Dir, Adler. Sp, Tommy Chong, Cheech Marin; cam (Metrocolor), Gene Polito; supv edtr, Lou Lombardo; edtr, Scott Conrad; art dir, Leon Ericksen; asst dir, Mike Moder; snd, Pat Mitchell; ward, Ernie Misko. (MPAA rating: R). 86.
Cheech Marin, Tommy Chong, Stacy Keach, Edie Adams, Tom Skerritt, Zane Buzby, Anne Wharton, Louisa Moritz, June Fairchild.
09/13/78

Up The Academy
WB. Marvin Worth/Danton Rissner Prodn. Prods, Worth, Rissner. Dir, Robert Downey. Exec prod, Bernie Brillstein. Sp, Tom Patchett, Jay Tarses; cam (Technicolor), Harry Stradling; edtr, Bud Molin; mus, Jody Taylor Worth; prodn des, Peter Wooley; set decor, Mary Swanson; snd, Marty Bolger; asst dir, James J Quinn. (MPAA rating: R). 96.
Ron Liebman, Wendell Brown, Tom Citera, J Hutchinson, Ralph Macchio, Harry Teinowitz, Tom Poston, Ian Wolfe, Stacy Nelkin, Barbara Bach, Leonard Frey, Antonio Vargas.
06/11/80

Up Wind: SEE Aufwind

The Uprising: SEE Der Aufstand

The Uranium Conspiracy
(Israel)
NOA. Golan-Globus-Dunamis prodn. Prod, Francesco Corti, Menahem Golan. Dir, Menahem Golan. Sp, David Paulsen based on story by Y Ben Porath. Cam, Adam Greenberg; edtr, Dov Henig. 105.
Siegfried Rauch, Oded Kotler, Gianni Rizzo, Rolf Eden, Herbert Fux, Jay Koller.
08/30/78

Urban Cowboy
PAR. Prods, Robert Evans, Irving Azoff. Dir, James Bridges. Exec prod, C O Erickson. Sp, James Bridges, Aaron Latham, based on Latham's story; cam (Movielab Color), Ray Villalobos; edtr, Dave Rawlins; snd, Willie Burton; prodn des, Stephen Grimes; art dir, Stewart Campbell; chor, Patsy Swayze; asst dir, Kim Kuramada; mus, Ralph Burns. (MPAA rating: PG). 135.
John Travolta, Debra Winger, Scott Glenn, Madolyn Smith, Barry Corbin, Brooke Alderson, Cooper Huckabee, James Gammon, Mickey Gilley, Johnny Lee, Bonnie Raitt, Charlie Daniels Band.
06/04/80

Urgia
(Calamity)
(Romania)
RMN. Rumaniafilm Prodn, Bucharest. Dirs, Josif Demlan, Andrei Blaier. Sp, FI N Nastase; cam, Gheorghe Voicu; mus, Adrian Enesca; sets, Stefan Antonescu. 90.
Gheorghe Cozorici, Luiza Orosz, Nicolae Praida, Dana Dogaru, Ica Matache, Costel Consantinescu, Jean Sandulescu, Dan Condurache, Mihai Cafrita, Gelu Birau, Ion Musca.
08/02/78

Urodziny Mlodego Warszawiaka
(The Birthday)
(Poland)
POL. Film Polski prodn. Iluzion Film Unit Warsaw. Dirs, Ewa and Czeslaw Petelski. Sp, Jerzy Stefan Stawinski, based on his own novel; cam, Jacek Stachlewski; mus, Jerzy Maksymiuk; sets, Andrzej Borecki; prodn mgrs, Zbigniew Brejtkopf, Wieslaw Grzelczak. 105.
Piotr Lysak, Andrzej Lapicki, Jolanta Grusznic, Gabriela Kownacka, Hanna Skarzanka, Kazimierz Kaczor, Roman Frankl, Tomasz Zaliwski, Arkadiusz Bazak, Krzysztof Chamiee, Henryk Kluba, Witold Prykosz.
10/01/80

Us Two: SEE A Nous Deux

Used Cars
COL. Prod, Bob Gale. Dir, Robert Zemeckis. Exec prods, Steven Spielberg, John Milius. Sp, Zemeckis, Gale; cam, (Metrocolor), Donald M Morgan; edtr, Michael Kahn; mus, Patrick Williams; prodn des, Peter M Jamison; set decor, Linda Spheeris; snd, Ronald G Cogswell; 2d unit dir-stunt coord, Terry J Leonard; asst dir, Richard Luke Rothschild. (MPAA rating: R) 113.
Kurt Russell, Jack Warden, Gerrit Graham, Frank McRae, Deborah Harmon, Joseph P Flaherty, David L Lander, Michael McKean, Michael Talbott, Harry Northup, Alfonso Arau, Al Lewis, Woodrow Parfrey, Andrew Duncan, Dub Taylor, Claude Earl Jones, Dan Barrows, Cheryl Rixon.
07/02/80

Usijanje
(Burning)
(Yugoslavia)
YFR. Centar Film prodn. Dir, Bosko Draskovic. Sp, Draskovic, Mirko Kovac; cam (Eastmancolor), Predrag Popovic; mus, Arhivska. 93.
Dragan Maksomovic, Rade Serbedzija, Gordana Kosanovic, Ivo Gregurovic, Marko Todorovic, Fabijan Sovagovic.
08/15/79

Usporeno Kretanje
(Slow Motion)
(Yugoslavia)
YFR. Jadran Film, Zagreb, Croatia Film, Zagreb, and Radna Zajednica Filma Prodn. Dir, Vanca Kljakovic. Sp, Tomislav Sabljak; cam, Drago Novak; sets, Zeljko Senecic; mus, Alfi Kabiljo. 90.
Vlatko Dulic, Ivica Vidovic, Mia Oremovic, Kostadinka Velkovska, Vanja Drach, Relja Basic, Boris Buzancic.
09/05/79

Utamaro's World
(Japan)
NIP. Taiyosha prodn. Exec prod, Katsumi Furukawa; prod, Kinshiro Kuzui. Dir, Akio Jissoji. Sp, Jissoji, Masaru Takesue; cam, Masao Nakabori; edtr, Keiichi Uraoka, mus, Ryohei Hirose. 120.
Shin Kishida, Shingo Yamashiro, Isao Bito, Mikio Narita, Ryo Tamura, Minori Terada, Ryohei Uchida, Eiji Okada, Kazuyo Mita, Rie Nakagawa, Kyoko Kishida, Tokuko Watanabe, Mako Midori, Mikijiro Hira.
05/25/77

Utkozben
(On The Move)
(Hungary)
HU. Mafilm, Dialog Studio prodn. Dir, Marta Meszaros. Sp, Meszaros, Jan Nowicki, Marek Piwowski; cam (Eastmancolor), Tamas Andor; mus, Zygmunt Konieczny. 104.
Delphine Seyrig, Jan Nowici, Djoko Rosic, Beata Tyszkiewiz.
02/27/80

Utopia
(France)
X. Utopia Prods and FR3 prodn. Wri-dir, Iradj Azimi. Cam (Eastmancolor), Etienne Becker; mus, Henri Raschle, Patrice Holiner; edtr, Anita Fernandez; prodn dir, Marcel Mossotti. 92.
Laurent Terzieff, Dominique Sanda, Jean Daste, Gerard Blain, Anne Marie Descotte, Catherine Gauvreu.
10/04/78

Uvadi Hra O Jablo
(Game of the Apple)
(Czechoslovakia)
X. Czech Film prodn, Barrandov Studios, Prague. Dir, Ver Chytilova. Sp, Chytilova, Kristina Vlachova; cam, Frantisek Vlacek; art dir, Vladimir Labsky; mus, Miroslav Korinek. 90.
Dagmar Blachova, Jiri Menzel, Evelyna Steimarova.
04/13/77

Va Voir Maman . . . Papa Travaille
(Go See Mother. . .Father Is Working)
(France)
GAU. Action Films-Gaumont prodn. Dir, Francois Leterrier. Sp, Daniele Thompson, Francoise Dorin, Leterrier from book by Dorin; cam (Eastmancolor), Jean Penzer; edtr, Marie-Josephe Yoyotte; mus, Georges Delerue. 95.
Marlene Jobert, Philippe Leotard, Micheline Presle, Macha Meril, Catherine Rich, Sylvia Joly, Vladimir Andres, Albina Du Boisrouvray, Daniel Duval.
03/15/78

Vacances Royales
(Royal Vacation)
(France)
FFP. Dir, Gabriel Auer. Sp, Auer, Carlos Andreu; cam (Eastmancolor), Robert Alazraki; edtr, Joelle Hache; mus, Francois Tusques, Andreu. 86.
Agnes Chateau, Didier Sauvegrain, Francisco Curto, Emilio Sanchez Ortiz.
05/14/80

Vacanze In Val Trebbia
(Vacations in Val Trebbia)
(Italy)
X. Prod, Enzo Porcelli for Antea-Odissya Prodns. Wri-dir, Marco Bellocchio; cam, Luigi Verga; art dir, Gianluigi Olmi; edtr, Anna Napoli; mus, Nicola Piovani. 50.
Piergiorgio Bellocchio, Gisella Burinato, Marco Bellocchio, Gianni Schicchi, Beppe Ciavatta.
10/08/80

Vagon Li
(The Sleeping Car)
(Yugoslavia)
YFR. Danas Film prodn. Wri-dir, Dragoslav Ilic. Cam (Eastmancolor), Bozidar Miletic; mus, Vojislav Simic. 76.
Vladimir Oopovic, Bozidarka Freajt.
08/25/76

Valentino
(Britain)
UA. Robert Chartoff, Irwin Winkler prodn. Dir, Ken Russell. Sp, Russell, John Byrum; cam, Peter Suschitsky; edtr, Stuart Baird; art dir, Philip Harrison; chor, Gillian Gregory. (MPAA rating: R). 132.
Rudolf Nureyev, Leslie Caron, Michelle Phillips, Carol Kane, Felicity Kendal, Seymour Cassel, Huntz Hall, Alfred Marks, David De Keyser.
09/21/77

Vamonos, Barbara
(Let's Go, Barbara)
(Spain)
X. Incine SA, Jet Films prodn, presented by Alfredo Matas. Dirs, Cecilia Bartolome, Concha Romero, Sara de Azcarate; cam (Eastmancolor), Jose Luis Alcaine; edtr, Jose Luis Matesanz; mus, Carlos Laporta. 98.
Amparo Soler Leal, Cristina Alvarez, Ivan Tubau, Julieta Serrano, Jose Ruiz Lifante, Josefina Tapias.
10/11/78

Van Nuys Blvd.
CWN. Marimark prodn. Exec prod, Newton P Jacobs. Prod, Marilyn J Tenser. Wri-dir, William Sachs. Cam (Deluxe Color), Joseph Mangine; edtr, George Bowers; mus, Ron Wright, Ken Mansfield; snd, Don A Sanders, Ove H Schested; art dir, Kenneth H Hergenroeder; cos, Diana Daniels. (MPAA rating: R). 93.
Bill Adler, Cynthia Wood, Dennis Bowen, Melissa Prophet, David Hayward, Tara Strohmeier, Dana Gladstone, DiAnn Monaco, Don Sawyer, Jim Kester, Minnie E Lindsey.
05/16/79

Vanessa
(W Germany)
ICR. Lisa-Film prodn. Exec prod, Erich Tomek. Dir, Hubert Frank. Sp, Joos De Ridder; cam, Franz X Lederle; edtrs, Evan Zeyn, Mimi Wekmann; art dir, Klaus Haase; cosward, Ursula Eggert. (MPAA rating: X). 91.
Olivia Pascal, Anton Diffring, Gunther Clemens, Uschi Zech, Eva Eden, Henry Heller, Eva Louise, Astrid Bohner, Giesela Krauss, Peter M Kruger, Tom Garven.
(English-dubbed sndtrack)
05/04/77

Vas Y Maman
(Go On Mama)
(France)
AMLF. Renn Prodns, Les Films Montfort, SFP, Les Films 21 prodn. Dir, Nicole De Buron. Sp, De Buron, Pierre Sisser, Mathilde Pean; cam (Eastmancolor), Etienne Becker; edtr, Jacques Vitta; mus, Marie-Paule Belle. 95.
Annie Girardot, Pierre Mondy, Eleonore Klarwein, Richard Constantini, Henri Garcin, Nicole Calfan.
08/30/78

Vasarnapi Szulok
(Sunday Parents)
(Hungary)
HU. Mafilm-Objektiv Studio prodn. Dir, Janos Rosza. Sp, Istvan Kardos; cam (Eastmancolor), Levente Szorenyo; mus, Elemer Ragalyi; mus, Levente Szorenyi. 100.
Julianna Nyako, Melinda Szakacs, Julianna Balogh, Andrea Blizik, Erszi Pasztor, Agi Kakasi, Sergei Elistratov.
02/27/80

Vdovstvo Karoline Zasler
(The Widowhood of Karolina Zasler)
(Yugoslavia)
YFR. Viba Film, Ljubljana, prodn. Dir, Matjaz Klopcic. Sp, Tone Partljic; cam (Eastmancolor), Tomislav Pinter; art dir, Niko Matul; cos, Alenka Bartl; edtr, Darinka Persin; prodn mgr, Bosko Klobucar. 105.
Milena Zupancic, Polde Bibic, Marjeta Gregorac, Boris Cavazza, Dare Ulaga, Radko Polic, Zlatko Sugman, Milena Muhic.
12/29/76

Velhos Sao Os Trapos
(Only Their Clothes Are Old)
(Portugal)
X. Monique Rutler, Filmforum prodn, Libson. Wri-dir, Monique Rutler; cam, Mario de Carvalho. 83.
Joao Guedes, Luis Santos, Luisa Neto.
10/15/80

Velvet Hands: SEE Mani Di Velluto

Venezia, Ultima Serata Di Carnevale
(Venice: Last Night of Carnival)
(Italy)
RTI. Third Channel of RAI-TV prodn. Dir, Carlo Tuzil; cam, Nino Celeste; edtr, Carlo Valerio. 50.
(DOC)
09/17/80

Vengeance Is Mine: SEE Fukushu Suruwa Ware Ni Ari

Venice: Last Night of Carnival: SEE Venezia, Ultima Serata Di Carnevale

Vera Romeyke Ist Nicht Tragbar
(Vera Romeyke Is Not Acceptable)
(W Germany)
X. Basis-Film prodn, Berlin. Dir, Max Willutzki. Sp, Willutzki, Renke Korn; cam, Dietrich Lohmann; mus, Wilhelm Dieter Siebert. 102.
Rita Engelmann, Dieter Eppler, Ina Halley, Gerd Burckhard, Herbert Chwoika, Renate Koehler, Angelika Milster.
07/14/76

Vera's Training: SEE Angi Vera

Verden er fuld af boern
(It's A World Full of Children)
(Denmark)
PNR. Just Betzer prodn. State Film Institute prodn cnslts, Sven Methling, Frits Raben. Wris, Aase Schmidt, Henrik Herbert. Dir, Aase Schmidt. Cam (Eastmancolor), Henrik Herbert; prodn des, Palle Arestrup; edtr, Lizzi Weischenfeldt; mus, Henning Christiansen; main title lyr, Niels Lund. 99.
Karen-Lise Mynster, Jasper Christensen, Kurt Ravn, Lane Lind, Per Pallesen, Solbjoerg Hoejfeldt.
02/13/80

The Verdict: SEE Presuda

Veri Az Ordog A Feleseget
(The Devil Is Beating His Wife)
(Hungary)
HU. Studio Hunnia prodn. Dir, Ferenc Andras. Sp, Andras, Geza Beremenyi; cam (Eastmancolor), Akos Kertesz, Lajos Koltai. 103.
Imre Sarlai, Lajos Szabo, Erszi Pasztor, Zoltan Biro, Maria Fesus, Ildiko Pecsi, Anatol Konstantin, Zsuzsa Szakacs.
11/16/77

Verlorenes Leben
(A Lost Life)
(W Germany)
FDA. Ottokar Runze Film prodn. Prod-dir, Ottokar Runze. Sp, Peter Hirche; cam (b&w), Michael Epp; mus, Hans Martin Majewski; edtr, Marlies Dux. 91.
Gerhard Olschewski, Marius Mueller-Westernhagen, Gert Haucke, Richard Beek, Willmut Borell, Juergen Feindt, Henning Schlueter, Peter Schulze-Rohr, Uwe Dallmeier, Katrin Schaake, Wolfgang Spier, Heinz Schubert.
(B & W)
04/14/76

Veronicas Svededug
(Veronica's Veil)
(Denmark)
SFK. Jytte Rex prodn/Statens Filmcentral and Kollektiv Film release. Sp-prod-dir-cam-snd, Jytte Rex, (8m blown up to 16m). Economics advisor, Nina Crone. 90.
Helle Ryslinge, Elli Rex, Clemens Hildebrandt, Inge Eriksen.
(16m)
11/30/77

Viaje Al Centro De La Tierra
(Trip to the Centre of the Earth)
(Spain)
X. Almena Films prodn. Dir, Juan Piquer. Sp, Piquer, Carlos Puerto, based on novel by Jules Verne; cam (Eastmancolor), Andres Berenguer; mus, Juan Jose Garcia Caffi; edtr, Maruja Soriano; sets, Emilio Ruiz; sfx, Francisco Prosper and E Ruiz; cos, Gumersindo Andres. 90.
Kenneth More, Pep Munne, Ivonne Sentis, Frank Brana, Jack Taylor, Lone Fleming, Jose Maria Caffarel, Emiliano Redondo.
(English soundtrack available.)
09/28/77

Viaje Fantastico En Globo
(The Fantastic Balloon Trip)
(Mexico)
COX. Conacine S A and Avant Films prodn. Dir, Rene Cardona Jr. Story-sp, Antonio Orellana, Mario Marzac, Rene Cardona Jr, based on Jules Verne novel, "Five Weeks in a Balloon"; cam (Eastmancolor), Daniel Lopez; mus, J A Zavala; edtr, Victor Pena. 86.
Hugo Stiglitz, Jeff Cooper, Carmen Vicarte, Carlos East, Zamorita.
07/14/76

Vice Squad: SEE Brigade Mondaine

Vicious Circle: SEE Cardena Perpetua

Victor Frankenstein
(Sweden - Ireland)
FAW. Aspekt Film AB prodn. Prod in asso with The National Film Society of Ireland. Sp, Yvonne and Calvin Floyd, based on Mary Shelley's novel. Dir, Calvin Floyd. Cam (Eastmancolor), Tony Forsberg and (Irish location sequences) John Wilcox; prodn mgrs, Henry Cagarp, Don Geraghty; edtr, Susanna Linnman; mus, Gerard Victory; cos, Kersti Gustafsson. 92.
Leon Vitali, Per Oscarsson.
(English soundtrack)
05/25/77

Victoria
(Sweden - W Germany)
X. Widerberg-Corona Film prodn. Wri-dir, Bo Widerberg, from the novel by Knut Hamsun. Cam (Eastmancolor), Hanno H Fuchs; mus, Verdi. 107.
Michaela Jolin, Stephan Schwartz, Pia Skagermark, Erik Eriksson.
06/06/79

Victory
(Peoples Republic of China)
X. Prods, Mei Chang-ling, Huang Tso-han. Dir, Liu Cha-chan. Mus, Liu Cha-chan, Hang-Mao-shan; cam, Lin Tsen-tin; sp, Teng Yu-kun; edtr, Wang Chin-chen. 87.
Lin Yi-yuan, Hsu Hsiao-huy, Ikeda, Chang Ming Chu, Lin Yi-kuan.
03/17/76

Victory March: SEE Marcia Trionfale

Vigilante Force
UA. Prod, Gene Corman. Wri-dir, George Armitage. Cam (DeLuxe Color), William Cronjager; edtr, Morton Tubor; mus, Gerald Fried; art dir, Jack Fisk; snd, Darin Knight; asst dir, Don Heitzer; stunt coord, Joe Buddy Hooker. (MPAA rating: PG). 89.
Kris Kristofferson, Jan-Michael Vincent, Victoria Principal, Bernadette Peters, Brad Dexter, Judson Pratt, David Doyle, Antony Carbone, Andrew Stevens, Shelly Novack, Paul X Gleason, John Steadman, Lilyan McBride, James Lydon.
04/14/76

Villa Zone
(Bulgaria)
X. BulgaroFilm prodn. Dir, Eduard Zahariev. Sp, Georgi Mishev; cam, Radoslav Spassov; art dir, Nikolai Surchadjiev; mus, Kiril Donchev. 95.
Katya Paskaleva, Itskhac Fintsi, Naoum Shopov, Evstati Stratev, Ivan Yanchev, Stefka Berova, Anton Karastoyanov, Nevena Symeonova.
01/14/76

The Village Head At the Border: SEE Phooying Yay Chai Daeng

Village Of The Eight Tombs: SEE Yatsu Hakamura

The Villain
COL. Rastar-Mort Engelberg prodn. Prod, Engleberg. Exec prod, Paul Maslansky. Dir, Hal Needham. Sp, Robert G Kane; cam, Bobby Byrne; edtr, Walter Hannemann; art dir, Carl Anderson; mus, Bill Justis; snd, John V Speak; stunt coord, Gary Combs; asst dir, David Shamroy Hamburger. (MPAA rating: PG). 93.
Kirk Douglas, Ann-Margret, Arnold Schwarzenegger, Paul Lynde, Foster Brooks, Ruth Buzzi, Jack Elam, Strother Martin, Robert Tessier, Mel Tellis, Laura Lizer Sommers.
07/18/79

Vinterboern
(Winterborn)
(Denmark)
PNR. Panorama (Just Betzer) prodn in economic collab with Danish Film Institute (Frits Raben). Based on novel by Dea Trie Moerch. Wri-dir, Astrid Henning-Jensen. Edtrs, Henning-Jensen, Grete Moeldrup; cam (Eastmancolor), Lars Bjoerne; mus, Hans Erik Phillip. 90.
Ann-Mari Max Hansen, Helle Hertz, Lone Keller, Lea Risum Broegger.
09/20/78

Violanta
(Switzerland)
X. Condor Film (Zurich) and Artcofilm (Geneva) prodn; presented by Jordan Bojilov, Daniel Carrillo, Eric Franck and Peter Christian Fueter. Prod, Peter Christian, Jordan Bojilov. Dir, Daniel Schmid; sp, Wolf Wondratschek, Daniel Schmid from the novel "Die Richterin" by C F Meyer. Cam (Eastmancolor), Renato Berta; mus, Peer Raben; edtr, Ila Von Hasperg. 97.
Maria Schneider, Lucia Bose, Lou Castel, Ingrid Caven, Francois Simon, Raul Gimenez, Marilu Marini, Anne-Marie Blanc, Luciano Simeoni, Gerard Depardieu.
(English dubbed soundtrack)
09/28/77

Violated Love: SEE L'Amour Viole

The Violation of Claudia
LST. Prod-dir-edtr, William B Lustig. Sp, Sally McKinley, Travis Webb; cam (Technicolor), Rob Lindsay; mus, Michael Karp. (Self-imposed X Rating). 67.
Sharon Mitchell, Jamie Gillis, Don Peterson, Waldo Short, Crystal Sync, Victor Hines, Gandi Sanders, Cheri Baines, Jack Jeffries, Justine Fletcher, Long Jeanie Silvers, Guido D'Alisa, Andrew Bellina.
06/15/77

Violet: SEE Ljubica

Violette et Francois
(France)
GAU. President Films (Jacques-Eric Strauss), FR3 prodn. Dir, Jacques Rouffio. Sp, Jean-Loup Dabadie; cam (Eastmancolor), Andreas Winding; edtr, Genevieve Winding; mus, Philippe Sarde. 98.
Isabelle Adjani, Jacques Dutronc, Serge Reggiani, Lea Massari, Sophie Daumier, Francoise Arnoul, Catherine Lachens.
03/30/77

Violette Noziere
(France)
GAU. Filmel-FR3-Cine Video prodn. Dir, Claude Chabrol. Sp, Odile Barski from book by Jean-Marie Fitere; cam (Eastmancolor), Jean Rabier; edtr, Yves Langlois. 122.
Isabelle Huppert, Stephane Audran, Jean Carmet, Jean-Francois Garreaud.
05/24/78

The Virgin Witch
(Britain)
BRE. Prod, Ralph Solomons. Dir, Ray Austin. Sp, Klaus Vogel; Ann Michelle, Patricia Haines, Vicki Michelle, Keith Buckley, James Chase, Neal Hallett. cam, Gerald Moss; edtr, Philip Barknel; mus, Ted Dicks, snd, Derek Ball; asst dir, Garth Haines.(MPAA rating: R). 90.
06/21/78

Virilita
(Virility)
(Italy)
COI. Carlo Ponti prodn. Dir, Paolo Cavara. Sp, Gian Paolo Callegari; cam, Claudio Cirillo; mus, Daniele Patucchi. (MPAA rating: R). 87.
Turi Ferro, Agostina Belli, Marc Porel, Anna Bonaiuto, Mario Carrara, Geraldine Hooper, Giuseppe Lo Presti, Tuccio Musumeci, Maria Tolu.
02/18/76

Virus
(Japan)
TOH. Haruki Kadokawa Films presentation. Prod, Kadokawa. Dir, Kinji Fukasaku. Sp, Koji Takada, Gregory Knapp. Fukasaku, based on novel by Sakyo Komatsu; cam, Daisaku Kimura; miniature cnslt, Gregory Jein; mus, Teo Macero; theme song, Janis Ian. 155.
Sonny Chiba, Chuck Connors, Stephanie Faulkner, Glenn Ford, Stuart Gillard, Olivia Hussey, George Kennedy, Masao Kusakari, Cecil Linder, Isao Natsuki, Ken Ogata, Edward J Olmos, Henry Silva, Bo Svenson, Yumi Takigawa, Robert Vaughn.
(English soundtrack)
05/28/80

The Visitor: SEE Il Visitatore

Viva Italia
(Italy)
C5. Dean Films prodn. Prods, Pio Angeletti, Adriano De Micheli. Dirs, Marie Monicelli, Dino Risi, Ettore Scola. Sp, Age, Scarpelli, Ruggero Maccari, Bernardino Zapponi; cam (Technispes Color), Tonino Delli Colli; edtr, Alberto Gallitti; mus, Armando Trovajoli; set des, Luciano Ricceri. 90.
Vittorio Gassman, Ornella Muti, Alberto Sordi, Ugo Tognazzi, Orietta Berti, Luigi Diberti, Eros Pagni, Fiona Florence, Emilia Fabi, Yorgo Voyagis.
(English subtitles)
07/12/78

Viva Knievel!
WB. Sherrill C Corwin prodn; prod, Stan Hough. Exec prod, Corwin. Dir, Gordon Douglas. Sp, Antonio Santillan, Norman Katkov; cam (Technicolor), Fred Jackman; edtr, Harold Kress; mus, Charles Bernstein; snd, Herman Lewis; stunt coord, Gary Davis; asst dir, Malcolm Harding. (MPAA rating: PG). 104.
Evel Knievel, Gene Kelly, Marjoe Gortner, Lauren Hutton, Leslie Nielsen, Red Buttons, Cameron Mitchell, Eric Olson, Frank Gifford, Albert Salmi.
06/08/77

Viva La Clase Media
(Long Live the Middle Class)
(Spain)
X. Garci-Sinde Acuarius Films prodn. Dir, Jose Maria Garcias Sinde. Sp, Jose Luis Garci, Jose Maria Garcia Sinde; cam (Eastmancolor), Hans Burman; edtr, Miguel Gonzalez Sinde; exec prod, Jose Luis Garci. 99.
Emilio Gutierrez Caba, Enriqueta Caballeira, Maria Casanova, Irene Gutierrez Caba, Jose Luis Garci, Raul Fraile, Maria Vico, Charo Soriano, Javier Beringola.
05/07/80

Vizi Privati, Pubbliche Virtu
(Private Vices, Public Virtue)
(Italy - Yugoslavia)
FIA. Filmes-Jadran Film prodn. Dir, Miklos Jancso. Sp, Giovanna Gagliardo; cam (Eastmancolor), Tomislav Pinter; edtr, Roberto Perpignani; mus, Francesco De Masi; art dir, Maria Paola Maino. 104.
Lajos Balazsovits, Pamela Villoresi, Franco Branciaroli, Therese Ann Savoy, Laura Betti, Ivica Pajer.
05/26/76

Vlad Tepes
(The True Life Of Dracula)
(Romania)
RMN. Romaniafilm Prodn, Bucharest. Dir, Doru Nastase. Sp, Mircea Mohor; cam, Aurel Kostrakiewicz; mus, Tiberiu Olah; sets, Guta Stirbu; edtr, Adina Georgescu Obrocea. 100.
Stefan Sileanu, Ernest Maftei, Emanoil Petrut, Alexandra Repan, George Constantin, Teofil Vilcu, Constantin Codrescu, Constantin Barbulescu, Vasile Cosman, Ion Marinescu, Kovacs Gyorgy, Vadasz Zoltan, Petre Gheorghiu-Dolj, Mihai Paladescu.
05/30/79

Vlak U Snijegu
(Train in the Snow)
(Yugoslavia)
YFR. Croatia film prodn. Wri-dir, Mate Relja. Cam (Eastmancolor), Ivici Rajkovic; mus, Arsen Dedic. 83.
Stavko Stimic, Edo Perocevic, Ratko Buljan.
08/18/76

Voices
UA. Metro-Goldwyn-Mayer picture, prod, Joe Wizan. Dir, Robert Markowitz. Sp, John Herzfeld; cam, (Metrocolor), Alan Metzger; edtr, Danford B Green; snd, Les Lazarowitz, Gustave E Mortensen; art dir, Richard Bianchi; asst dir, Michael Rauch; set decor, Fred Weiler; asso prod, Betty Gumm; mus, Jimmy Webb. (MPAA rating: PG). 106.
Michael Ontkean, Amy Irving, Alex Rocco, Barry Miller, Herbert Berghof, Viveca Lindfors.
02/21/79

Voinikat Ot Oboza
(The Supply Column Soldier)
(Bulgaria - USSR)
X. Bulgaro-Soviet co-prodn. Dir, Igor Dobrolubov. Sp, Slavtcho Doudov, Athanas Tsenev, Alexei Leontiev; cam, Grigori Massalski, Tsancho Tsanchev; mus, Yan Frenckel. 90.
Anatoli Kuznetsov, Vladimir Bassov, Stefan Danailov, Svetlana Toma.
11/17/76

Volunteer Jam
RGR. Roger Grod Prodns Inc and Good Vibes Prodns Inc film. Exec prods, Grod and Joseph E Sullivan; dir, Stanley Dorfman. 143.
The Charlie Daniels Band, The Marshall Tucker Band, Richard Betts, Chuck Leavell from the Allman Brother's Band, Jimmy Hall from Wet Willie, Dru Lombar of Grinderswitch, Roni Stoneman, Mylon Lefevre, Paul Hornsby.
(ROCK DOC)
01/12/77

Von Wegen "Schicksal"
(Is This "Fate"?)
(W Germany)
X. Literarisches Colloquium, Deutsche Film- und Fernsehakademie and Second German Televison (ZDF) co-prodn, Berlin. Dir, Helga Reidemeister; sp, Irene Rakowitz, Reidemeister; cam, Axel Brandt. 110. (DOC) (B & W) (16m)
09/17/80

Voros Rekviem
(Requiem for a Revolutionary)
(Hungary)
HU. Hunnia Studio prodn. Dir, Ferenc Grunwalsky. Sp, Guyula Hernadi; cam, Elemer Ragalyi. 102.
Peter Andorai, Miklos Lantay, Laszlo Szacsvay, Adam Rajhona, Istvan Molnar.
(B & W)
08/25/76

Voshojdenie
(The Ascent)
(USSR)
X. Mosfilm prodn, Moscow. Dir, Larissa Shepitko. Sp, Yuri Klepikov, Shepitko; cam, V Chuhnov; mus, A Shnitke. 105.
Boris Plotnikov, Vladimir Gostjuhin, Sergei Jakovlev, Anatoli Solonitzin, Ludmila Poliakova.
(B & W)
01/12/77

Vota A Gundisalvo
(Vote For Gundisalvo)
(Spain)
X. Agata Films-Jose Luis Dibidos prodn. Dir, Pedro Lazaga. Sp, Jose Luis Dibidos, Antonio Mingote; cam (Eastmancolor), Manuel Rojas; edtr, Petra de Nieva; mus, Antonio Garcia Abril. 90.
Antonio Ferrandis, Emilio Gutierrez Caba, Laly Soldevila, Tina Sainz, Yolanda Rios, Ivonne Sentis, Silvia Tortosa, Rafael Hernandez, Manuel Alexandre, Jose Ruiz Lifante.
03/01/78

Vous n'Aurez Pas L'Alsace et La Lorraine
(You Won't Have Alsace-Lorraine)
(France)
AMLF. Les Films Du Triangle-World Prodn prodn. Wri-dir, Michel Coluche. Cam (Eaastmancolor), Claude Agostini; edtr, Armand Psenny; art dir, Max Douy. 95.
Michel Coluche, Anemone Gerard, Michel Blanc, Martin Lamotte.
11/02/77

The Voyage Into the Whirlpool Has Begun: SEE E Comincio Il Viaggio Nella Vertigini

The Voyage of Emperor Chien Lung
(Hong Kong)
SHW. Sir Run Run Shaw prodn. Prod, Mona Fong. Wri-dir, Li Han-hsiang. Cam, Lin Chao; art dir, Chen Ching-shen; edtr, Chiang Hsinglung; martial arts instructors, Tang Chia, Huang Pei-chi. 100.
Liu Yung, Chiang Nan, Li Kun, Chow Shen, Hui Ying-hung, Wu Hang-sheng, Lun Chiachun, Ho Li-jen.
(Cantonese/Mandarin soundtrack; English subtitles)
10/25/78

Voyage of the Damned
(Britain)
AVE. Associated General Films prodn, prod, Robert Fryer. Dir, Stuart Rosenberg. Sp, Steve Shagan, David Butler; based on book by Gordon Thomas, Max Morgan-Witts; cam, Billy Williams; edtr, Tom Priestley; mus, Lalo Schifrin; prodn des, Wilfred Shingleton; art dir, Jack Stephens; snd, Derek Ball, cos-ward, Phyllis Dalton, Betty Adamson, John Billing; asst dir, David Tringham. (MPAA rating: PG). 155.
Faye Dunaway, Max Von Sydow, Oskar Werner, Malcolm McDowell, Orson Welles, James Mason, Lee Grant, Ben Gazzara, Katharine Ross, Luther Adler, Paul Koslo, Michael Constantine, Nehemiah Persoff, Jose Ferrer, Fernando Rey, Lynne Frederick, Maria Schell, Helmut Griem, Victor Spinetti, Julie Harris, Janet Suzman, Wendy Hiller, Sam Wanamaker, Denholm Elliott.
12/01/76

Voyage to the End of the World: SEE Le Voyage Au Bout Du Monde

Vpervye Zamuzhem
(Married for the First Time)
(USSR)
SOV. Lenfilm prodn. Dir, Iosif Heifits; sp, Pavel Nilin, Heifits; mus, O Karavaychuk. 92.
Yevgenie Glushenkova, Nikolai Volkov, Valentina Telichkin, Svetlana Smirnov, Igor Starygin.
07/30/80

Vrhovi Zelengore
(The Peaks of Zelengore)
(Yugoslavia)
YFR. Film Ski Studio Titograd'Centar FRZ Belgrade-Zeta Film-Jadran Film Zagreb. Dir, Zdravko Velimorovic. Sp, Mladen Oljaca, Djurica Labovic, Velimorovic; cam (Eastmancolor), Nenad Jovacic; mus, Zoran Hristic. 105.
Sergei Bondarchuk, Bata Zivojinovic, Josephine Chaplin, Alain Nouri, Voja Miric.
08/18/76

Vsichko e Lyubov
(All Is Love)
(Bulgaria)
BGO. Bulgarofilm Production, Hemus Film Group, Sofia. Dir, Borislav Sharaliev. Sp, Boyan Papazov, cam, Stefan Trifonov; sets, Georgi Ivanov; mus, Vesselin Nikolov. 90.
Ivan Ivanov, Janina Kasheva, Maria Stefanova, Vulcho Kamarashev, Yordan Spirov.
06/11/80

The Vultures: SEE *Les Vautours*

W.C. Fields And Me
U. Prod, Jay Weston. Dir, Arthur Hiller. Sp, Bob Merrill. Based on the book by Carlotta Monti and Cy Rice; cam (Technicolor), David M Walsh; edtr, John C Howard; mus, Henry Mancini; prodn des, Robert Boyle; set decor, Arthur Jeph Parker; snd, Robert L Hoyt, John Kean; asst dir, Frederic Brost. (MPAA rating: PG). 111.
Rod Steiger, Valerie Perrine, John Marley, Jack Cassidy, Bernadette Peters, Dana Elcar, Paul Stewart, Billy Barty, Allan Arbus, Milt Kamen, Louis Zohric, Andrew Parks.
03/31/76

Waga Koi Wa Moenu
(My Love Has Been Burning)
(Japan)
NY. Shochiku prodn. Prods, Hisao Itoya, Kiyoshi Shimazu. Dir, Kenji Mizoguchi. Sp, Yoshikata Yoda, Kaneto Shindo, based on story by Kogo Noda; cam (b&w), Kohei Sugiyama, Tomotaro Nashiki; mus, Senji Ito; snd, Taro Takahashi, Takeo Kawakita; art dirs, Hiroshi Mizutani, Dai Arakama, Jun'ichi Osumi; historical research, Sunao Kai. 84.
Kinuyo Tanaka, Ichiro Sugai, Mitsuko Mito, Eitaro Ozawa, Kuniko Miyake, Koreya Senda, Eijiro Tono.
(B & W)
01/10/79

Wahnsinn, Das Ganze Leben Ist Wahnsinn
(Madness, The Whole Life Is Madness)
(W Germany)
X. C & H Film prodn, Berlin in collab with Zweites Deutsches Fernsehen (ZDF), Wiesbaden-Mainz; dir, Petra Haffter; sp, Haffter, Richard Claus; cam, Claus. 90.
Germaine Riedinger, Ronni Ranner, Andrea Schurig, Ludwig Kaschke, Ellen Esser.
09/03/80

Wai Tok Kra
(An Old Woman)
(Thailand)
NKP. Prod-dir-edtr, Chana Krapayun. Storysp, Siri Madda; cam, Thavee Kiatinan; snd and dubbing, Kasem Militachinda; mus, Nopadol Busapaketr; cos, Khun Too. 126.
Suan Prakkard, Sorapong Chatri, Tarika Taratit, Choosri Misomon, Sompop Benjatikul, Kumalee Komarakoon Nanakorn, Somjin Tamatat, Vivian Suksom.
10/25/78

Waif: SEE *Gamin*

Waiting For Daddy: SEE *Esperando A Papa*

Waiting For Fidel
(Canada)
OPC. National Film Board of Canada prodn. Prods, Tom Daly, Michael Rubbo. Dir-edtr-wri-narr, Rubbo. Cam, Douglas Kiefer. 57.
(DOC)
02/04/76

Walk On Water If You Can: SEE *Ga pa vattnet om du kan*

Walk Proud
U. Prod, Lawrence Turman. Dir, Robert Collins. Sp, Evan Hunter; cam (Technicolor), Bobby Byrne; edtr, Douglas Stewart; snd, Jim Alexander; art dir, William L Campbell; asst dir, Ronald J Martinez; mus, Robby Benson. (MPAA rating: PG). 102.
Robby Benson, Sarah Holcomb, Henry Darrow, Pepa Serna, Trinidad Silva, Ji-Tu Cumbuka, Lawrence Pressman, Domingo Ambriz, Brad Sullivan, Irene De Bari, Gary Cervantes, Eloy Phil Casados, Tony Alvarenga, Daniel Faraldo, Panchito Gomez, Joe D Jacobs.
05/16/79

Walking Upright: SEE *Der Aufrechte Gang*

The Wall: SEE *Deewar*

The Wall: SEE *Zidul*

The Walls: SEE *Al Aswar*

The Walls Of Freedom: SEE *Frihetens murar*

Wan Pipel
(One People)
(Surinam)
AEF. Scorpio Films prodn. Prods, Wim Verstappen, Pim de la Parra. Dir, Pim de la Parra. Sp, Pim de la Parra, Rudi F Korss; cam (Eastmancolor), Marc Felperlaan; edtr, Jutta Brandstaedter. 110.
Borger Breeveld, Diana Gangaram Panday, Willeke van Ammelrooy.
10/13/76

Wanda Nevada
UA. Exec prod, William Hayward. Prod, Neal Dobrofsky, Dennis Hackin. Dir, Peter Fonda. Sp, Dennis Hackin; cam, Michael Butler; edtr, Scott Conrad; mus, Ken Lauber; asso prods, Hilary Holden, Thomas Perry; art dir, Lynda Paradise; asst-dir, Ric Rondell. 105.
Peter Fonda, Brooke Shields, Fiona Lewis, Luke Askew, Ted Markland, Severn Darden, Paul Fix, Henry Fonda, Larry Golden, John Denos, Bert Williams.
05/30/79

The Wanderers
WBO. Martin Ransohoff prodn. Prod, Ransohoff. Exec prod, Richard R St Johns. Dir, Philip Kaufman. Sp, Rose Kaufman, Philip Kaufman, based on the novel by Richard Price; cam, Michael Chapman; edtrs, Ronald Roose, Stuart H Pappe; cos des, Robert de Mora; art dir, Jay Moore; snd, Nat Boxer; asst dir, Alan Hopkins. (MPAA rating: R). 113.
Ken Wahl, John Friedrich, Karen Allen, Toni Kalem, Alan Rosenberg, Jim Youngs, Tony Ganios, Linda Manz, William Andrews, Erland Van Lidth de Jeude, Val Avery, Dolph Sweet, Michael Wright.
07/11/79

Wandering: SEE *Periplanissis*

Wandering Soul: SEE *Ashwathama*

The War At Home
X. Catalyst Film Prodn, in collab with the Wisconsin Educational Television Network. Prod-dirs, Glenn Silber, Barry Alexander Brown; asso prod-wri, Elizabeth Duncan; cam, Rick March, Bob Lerner; edtr, Chuck France; dir of film res, Jon Aleckson; res, Ken Weiss, Bob Newton. 100.
(DOC) (16m) (B & W)
12/05/79

Warlords of Atlantis
(Britain)
COL. EMI Films presentation. Prod, John Dark. Dir, Kevin Connor. Sp, Brian Hayles; cam, Alan Hume; edtr, Bill Blunden; art dir, Jack Maxsted; prodn des, Elliot Scott; mus, Mike Vickers; snd, George Stephenson, Ken Barker; monster sequences, Roger Dicken; sfx supv, John Richardson. 96.
Doug McClure, Peter Gilmore, Shane Rimmer, Lea Brodie, Michael Gothard, Hal Galili, John Ratzenberger, Derry Power, Donald Bisset, Ashley Knight, Robert Brown, Cyd Charisse, Daniel Massey.
07/26/78

Warmth: SEE *Toplo*

Warning Shot: SEE *Riasztoloves*

Warring Clans: SEE *Sengoku Yaro*

The Warrior Within
CVT. Prod, Robert Plone. Exec prod, Manuel Ortiz Braschi. Dir, Burt Rashby. Sp, Karen Iase Golightly; cam, Lowell McFarland; edtr, Arthur Ginsburg; snd, Orlando Cordero; mus, Robert Lee; asst dir, Mike Sobie. (MPAA rating: G). 80.
(DOC)
06/29/77

The Warriors
PAR. Lawrence Gordon prodn. Exec prod, Frank Marshall. Prod, Lawrence Gordon. Dir, Walter Hill. Sp, David Shaber, Hill, based on novel by Sol Yurick; cam, Andrew Laszlo; edtr, David Holden; art dirs, Don Swanagan, Bob Wightman; mus, Barry DeVorzon; cos des, Bobbie Mannix; set decor, Fred Weiler; snd, Jack Jacobsen, Al Mian; stunt coordinator, Craig Baxley; asst dir, David Sosna. (MPAA rating: R). 90.
Michael Beck, James Remar, Thomas Waites, Dorsey Wright, Brian Tyler, David Harris, Tom McKitterick, Marcelino Sanchez, Terry Michos, Deborah Van Valkenburgh, David Patrick Kelly, Roger Hill.
02/14/79

Warui Yatsura
(Bad Sorts)
(Japan)
SKU. Prod, Kotaro Nomuramm, Koki Nomura. Sp, Masato Ide, based on a book by Seicho Matsumoto; dir, Kotaru Nomura; cam, Noboru Kawamata; art dir, Kohei Morita; mus, Satoshi Akutagawa; snd, Tadahiko Yamamoto; edtr, Kazuo Ota; asst dir, Toshinori Oryo. 129.
Takao Kataoka, Keiko Matsuzaka, Meiko Kaji, Mariko Fuji, Junko Miyashita, Ai Kanzaki, Makoto Fujita, Ken Ogata.
07/30/80

Was Heisst'n Hier Liebe
(This Is Love, Isn't It)
(W Germany)
FDA. Project Film Prodn in Filmverlag der Autoren, a DENKmal-Film. Dirs-wris-cam-edtrs, Walter Harrich, Claus Strigel, Bertram Verhaag. Based on a play with the same title by Holger Franke, Helma Fehrmann, Juergen Fluegge, with the cooperation of Guenter Brombacher and Alfred Cybulska; mus, Heiner Goebbels. 133.
Helma Fehrmann, Guenter Brombacher, Ulli Radhoefer, Holger Franke, Alfred Cybulska, Juergen Fluegge, the "Rote Gruetze" ensemble.
05/23/79

Was Ich Bin, Sind Meine Filme
(I Am What My Films Are)
(W Germany)
FWG. Nanuk-Film prodn, Munich. A Werner Herzog portrait. Dirs, Christian Weisenborn, Erwin Keusch. Cam, Rene Perraudin, Martin Schaefer; interviewer, Laurens Straub. 93.
(DOC) (16m)
01/24/79

Was Oshidajet Grashdanka Nikanorova
(Comrade Nikanorova Awaits You)
(USSR)
GOS. Mosfilm Prodn, Moscow; Dir, Leonid Marjagin. 90.
Natalya Gundareva.
02/28/79

Was Soll'n Wir Denn Machen Ohne Den Tod?
(What Should We Do Without Death?)
(W Germany)
X. Oh Muvie prodn, Berlin, in collab with Zweites Deutsches Fernsehen, Wiesbaden-Mainz. Dir, Elfi Mikesch. 105.
Anke-Rixa Hansen, Barbara Gold, Brigitte, Christa Weisenseel, Christian Sievers, Edith London, Elfi Mikesch, Gabi, Gysel, Joscha, Kaethe, Katharina Rosa, Liebchen, Los Seitz, Maria, Maya Farber-Jansen, Petra, Renate Merck, Soma, Traute, Ursula Weck, Uschi Gerhard Jensen, Steve Adamschevski.
(DOC) (16m)
09/17/80

Wasch Syn I Brat
(Your Son and Brother)
(USSR)
X. Gorky Studios prodn, Moscow. Wri-dir, Vassili Shukshin, based on his stories "Stefan," "Snake Venom," and "Ignat Returned Home." Cam, Valeri Ginsburg; mus, Pavel Chekalov; art dir, A Vagichev. 100.
A Vanin, A Filippova, M Grachova, Leonid Kuravljov, L Reutov, V Stschachov.
(B & W)
12/01/76

Wash Out My Faults: SEE Hugasan Mo Ang Aking Kasalaman

Watch Out for the Eyes: SEE Attention Les Yeux

The Watcher In The Woods
(Britain)
BV. Walt Disney prodn. Prod, Ron Miller. Dir, John Hough. Sp, Brian Clemens, Harry Spalding, Rosemary Anne Sisson, based on Florence Engel Randall's novel, "A Watcher In The Woods;" cam (Technicolor), Alan Hume; co-prod, Tom Leetch; mus comp-cond, Stanley Myers; edtr, Geoffrey Foot; prodn des, Elliott Scott; art dir, Alan Cassie; set decor, Ian Whittaker; snd edtr, Jim Shields; asst dir, Richard Hoult; sfx, John Richardson. (MPAA rating: PG). 100.
Bette Davis, Carroll Baker, David McCallum, Lynn-Holly Johnson, Kyle Richards, Ian Bannen, Richard Pasco, Frances Cuka, Benedict Taylor, Eleanor Summerfield, Georgina Hale, Katherine Levy.
04/23/80

The Water Babies
(Britain)
PHI. Productions Associates (U K) of an Ariadne Films prodn. Prod, Peter Shaw. Dir, Lionel Jeffries. Sp, Michael Robson, based on Charles Kingsley's novel; cam, Ted Scaife; edtr, Peter Weatherly; art dir, Herbert Westbrook; cos, Phyllis Dalton; snd, Cyril Collick; in charge of U K prodn, Ben Arbeid; prodn supv, Bruce Sharman; songs, Phil Coulter, Bill Martin; animation, Miroslaw Kijowicz (Film Polski), J Stokes and Cuthbert Cartoons; asst dir, Ray Frift. 93.
James Mason, Billy Whitelaw, Bernard Cribbins, Joan Greenwood, David Tomlinson, Paul Luty, Tommy Pender, Samantha Gates.
04/25/79

The Water Carrier Is Dead: SEE El Sakka Mat

Watership Down
(Britain)
AVE. Nepenthe Prodns Ltd picture. Prod-dir-wri, Martin Rosen (from Richard Adams novel); ani dir, Tony Guy; ani supv, Philip Duncan; edtr, Terry Rawlings; mus, Angela Morley, Malcolm Williamson. (MPAA rating: PG). 92.
John Hurt, Richard Briers, Michael Graham-Cox, John Bennett, Simon Cadell, Roy Kinnear, Richard O'Callaghan, Terence Rigby, Ralph Richardson, Denholm Elliott, Zero Mostel, Mary Maddox, Hannah Gordon, Lyn Farleigh, Harry Andrews, Nigel Hawthorne, Clifton Jones, Michael Hordern, Joss Ackland.
(ANI)
10/18/78

The Watts Monster
DIM. Prod, Charles Walker; exec prod, Manfred Bernhard. Dir. William Crain. Sp, Larry Le Bron; cam, Tak Fujimoto; mus, Johnny Pate. (MPAA rating: R). 90.
Bernie Casey, Rosalind Cash, Marie O'Henry.
10/24/79

The Way of the Wind
RCR. Film by Charles Tobias. Cam (CFI Color), Tobias; edtr, Pieter S Hubbard; mus, John Bilezikjian; (MPAA rating: G). 104.
(DOC)
12/22/76

We Are Arab Jews In Israel: SEE Nous Sommes Des Juifs Arabes En Israel

We Are The Guinea Pigs
PLL. Prod, Ralph Klein. Dir, John Harvey. Cam, Tom Hurwitz; edtrs, Joan Harvey, Trudy Bagdon; snd, Albee Gordon. 90.
(DOC) (16m)
05/07/80

We Forget Everything!: SEE On Efface Tout!

We Were One Man: SEE Nous Etions Un Seul Homme

We Will All Go To Heaven: SEE Nous Irons Tous Au Paradis

The Wedding: SEE Dugun The Wedding of Zien
(Kuwait)
X. Prod-dir-wri, Khaled Siddik, based on Altayeb Saleh's novel. Cam, Towsik Amir, Siddik; edtr, Mohyee A Jawad; snd, M Breima; prodn des, Ebrahim Ebid; mus, Siddik and Souleiman Jamil. 110.
Ali Mahdi, Tahiya Saroug, Ibrahim Salahi.
07/05/78

Week In, Week Out: SEE Una Settimana Come Un'altra

Weekend of Shadows
(Australia)
RDP. Samson-South Australia Film Corp prodn. Prods, Tom Jeffrey, Matt Carroll. Dir, Tom Jeffrey. Sp, Peter Yeldham, from a novel by Hugh Atkinson; cam (Eastmancolor), Richard Wallace; edtr, Rod Adamson; mus, Charles Marawood; snd, Ken Hammond; art dir, Christopher Webster. 94.
John Waters, Melissa Jaffer, Wyn Roberts, Barbara West, Graham Rouse, Graeme Blundell, Bill Hunter, Keith Lee, Les Foxcroft, Kit Taylor, Mark Gaweda.
05/10/78

Welcome: SEE Dobro Poshalovat

Welcome To Blood City
(Britain - Canada)
EMI. EMI/Len Herberman prodn. Prod, Marilyn Stonehouse. Dir, Peter Sasdy. Sp, Stephen Schneck, Michael Winder; cam, Reginald Morris CSC; edtr, Keith Palmer; art dir, Tony Hall; mus, Roy Budd; snd, Ronald Barrow. 96.
Jack Palance, Keir Dullea, Samantha Eggar, Barry Morse, Hollis McLaren, Chris Wiggins, Henry Ramer, Allan Royale, John Evans.
10/26/77

Welcome to Britain
(Britain)
X. British Film Institute Prodn Board prodn. Dir-edtr, Ben Lewin. Cam, Roger Deakins; snd, Edward Tise; prodn asst, Iris Hintlian; edtng asst, Anne Webber; asst dir, Karin Altmann. 72.
(DOC) (16m)
11/10/76

Welcome To LA
UA. Prod, Robert Altman. Wri-dir, Alan Rudolph. Cam (DeLuxe Color), Dave Myers; edtrs, William A Sawyer, Tom Walls; mussongs, Richard Baskin; snd, Richard Portman, Jim Webb, Chris McLaughlin; asst dir, Tommy Thompson. (MPAA rating: R). 103.
Keith Carradine, Sally Kellerman, Geraldine Chaplin, Harvey Keitel, Lauren Hutton, Viveca Lindfors, Sissy Spacek, Denver Pyle, John Considine, Richard Baskin, Allan Nicholls, Cedric Scott, Mike Kaplan, Diahann Abbott.
12/01/76

Welcome To My Nightmare
(Britain)
PRO. Dabill prodn, prod-dir-chor, David Winters. Co-prod, Joe Gannon; exec prod, William B Silberkleit. Cam (Eastmancolor), Larry Pizer; light, Gannon; edtr, Stuart Baird; mussongs, Alice Cooper, Dick Wagner, Bob Ezrin; snd, Garth Marsha, Terry Rawlings; asst dir, Emma Gowing. (MPAA rating: PG). 85.
Alice Cooper.
(DOC)
01/21/76

We'll Grow Thin Together: SEE Nous Maigrirons Ensemble

The Wellsprings of My World: SEE Herfra min verden gaar

We're Going To Eat You
(Hong Kong)
SEH. Prod, Ng See Yuen. Dir, Tsui Hark. Prodn mgr, Richard Cheung; martial arts chor, Yuen Kwei, Chien Yue-Sheng. 92.
Tsui Siu-Chang, Cheung Mu-Lian, Han Kuo-Tsai, Kao Shiung, Mel Wong.
(Cantonese or Mandarin soundtrack available with English sub-titles)
05/07/80

We've Seen Everything: SEE On Aura Tout Vu

What Did I Ever Do To The Good Lord To Deserve A Wife Who Drinks in Cafes with Men!?: SEE Mais Qu'est-Ce Que J'Ai Fait Au Bon Dieu Pour Avoir Une Femme Qui

What Do You Want Julie?: SEE Qu'est Ce Que Tu Veux Julie?

What Max Said: SEE Las Palabras De Max

What Should We Do Without Death?: SEE Was Soll'n Wir Denn Machen Ohne Den Tod?

Whatever You Can Spare: SEE Daj Sto Das

What's Autumn?: SEE Que Es El Otono?

When A Stranger Calls
COL. Melvin Simon prodn. Prods, Doug Chapin, Steve Feke. Exec prods, Melvin Simon, Barry Krost. Dir, Fred Walton. Sp, Feke, Walton; cam, Don Peterman; edtr, Sam Vitale; mus, Dana Kaproff; prodn des, Elayne Barbara Ceder; snd, Martin Bolger; asst dir, Ed Ledding. (MPAA rating: R). 97.
Carol Kane, Charles Durning, Colleen Dewhurst, Tony Beckley, Rachel Roberts, Rutanya Alda, Carmen Argenziano, Ron O'Neal, Steven Anderson.
09/05/79

When Joseph Returns: SEE Ha Megjon Jozsef

When Mother Is Out: SEE Me Vang Nha

When Svante Disappeared: SEE Da Svante forsvandt

When the Poppies Bloom Again: SEE Dokter Pulder Zaait Papavers

When The Sun Rises: SEE Gunes Ne Zaman Dogacak

When Time Ran Out
WB. Irwin Allen Prodn. Prod, Irwin Allen. Dir, James Goldstone. Sp, Carl Foreman, Stirling Silliphant based on the novel "The Day The World Ended" by Gordon Thomas, Max Morgan Witts. Cam (Technicolor), Fred J Koenekamp; edtr, Edward Biery, Freeman A Davies; prodn des, Philip M Jeffries; mus, Lalo Schifrin; special pho effects, L B Abbott; art dir, Russell C Menzer; cos, Paul Zastupnevich; set decor, Stuart Reiss; asst dir, L Andrew Stone. (MPAA rating: PG). 121.
Paul Newman, Jacqueline Bisset, William Holden, Edward Albert, Red Buttons, Barbara Carrera, Valentina Cortesa, Veronica Hamel, Alex Karras, Burgess Meredith, Ernest Borgnine, James Franciscus, John Considine, Sheila Allen, Pat Morita.
04/02/80

When You Comin' Back, Red Ryder?
COL. Melvin Simon prodn. Exec prod, Melvin Simon. Prod, Marjoe Gortner. Co-prod, Paul Maslansky. Dir, Milton Katselas. Sp, Mark Medoff, based on his play of the same title; cam, Jules Brenner; edtr, Richard Chew; mus, Jack Nitzsche; prodn des, Ted Haworth; cos des, Joe J Thompkins; snd, Don Johnson; asst dir, David Whorf. (MPAA rating: R). 118.
Candy Clark, Marjoe Gortner, Stephanie Faracy, Lee Grant, Hal Linden, Peter Firth, Pat Hingle, Bill McKinney, Audra Lindley.
02/07/79

Where Are You Going on Holiday?: SEE Dove Vai In Vacanza?

Where Are You Going: SEE Saan Ka Papunta

Where The Buffalo Roam
U. Prod-dir, Art Linson. Sp, John Kaye; cam (Technicolor), Tak Fujimoto; edtr, Christopher Greenbury; mus, Neil Young; prodn des, Richard Sawyer; set decor, Barbara Krieger; cos supv, Eddie Marks, Gilda Texter; snd, Peter Hliddal; asst dir, Gene Law. (MPAA rating: R). 96.
Peter Boyle, Bill Murray, Bruno Kirby, Rebe Auberjonois, R G Armstrong, Danny Goldman, Rafael Campos, Leonard Frey, Leonard Gaines, De Wayne Jessie, Mark Metcalf, Jon Matthews, Joseph Ragno.
04/02/80

Wherever You Are, Mr President: SEE Gziekolwiek Jestes, Panie Prezydencie

Which Way Is Up?
U. Prod, Steve Krantz. Dir, Michael Schultz. Sp, Carl Gottlieb, Cecil Brown, based on the film script, "The Seduction Of Mimi" by Lina Wertmuller; cam (Technicolor), John A Alonzo; edtr, Danford B Greene; mus, Paul Riser, Mark Davis; prodn des, Lawrence G Paull; set decor, John M Dwyer; snd, Willie D Burton, Robert L Hoyt; asst dir, Scott Maitland; stunt coord, Allen Oliney. (MPAA rating: R). 94.
Richard Pryor, Lonette McKee, Margaret Avery, Morgan Woodward, Marilyn Coleman, Bebe Drake-Hooks, Gloria Edwards, Ernesto Hernandez, Diane Rodrigues, Danny Valdez, Dewayne Jessie, Morgan Roberts, Dolph Sweet, Luis Valdez, Pat Ast.
11/02/77

Whispering Death
(W Germany - S Africa)
CRC. Lord & Eichberg Film, Munich. Dir, Juergen Goslar. Sp, Juergen Goslar, Scot Finch, based on the novel by Daniel Carney; cam, Wolfgang Treu; edtr, Richard Meyer; mus, Erich Ferstl; exec prod, Barrie Saint-Clair; prodn mgr, Dieter Nobbe. 97.
Christopher Lee, James Faulkner, Trevor Howard, Horst Frank, Sybil Danning, Sascha Hehn, Sam Williams, Erik Schumann.
04/21/76

White Bim With Black Ear: SEE Beli Bim-Chornoye Ukho

The White Buffalo
UA. Dino De Laurentiis presentation, prod, Pancho Kohner. Dir, J Lee Thompson. Sp, Richard Sale, based on his novel; cam (DeLuxe Color), Paul Lohmann; edtr, Michael F Anderson; mus, John Barry; prodn des, Tambi Larsen; set decor, James Berkey; snd, William McCaughey, Lyle J Burbridge, Michael J Kohut, Harlan Riggs; ward-cos, Eric Seelig, Dennis Fill; asst dir, Jack Aldworth; stunt coord, Ben Dobbins. (MPAA rating: PG). 97.
Charles Bronson, Jack Warden, Will Sampson, Kim Novak, Clint Walker, Stuart Whitman, Slim Pickens, John Carradine, Cara Williams, Shay Duffin, Douglas V Fowley, Cliff Pellow, Ed Lauter.
09/21/77

White Grass: SEE Belle Trave

White Love: SEE Hoito Rabu

White Rock
(Britain)
EMI. Shueisha Publishing Co presentation of a Worldmark Prodns-Samuelson Int'l Film. Prod, Michael Samuelson. Asso prod, Drummond Challis. Wri-dir, Tony Maylam. Cam (Fujicolor-Panavision-Technicolor), Arthur Wooster; snd, Colin Charles, Clive Winter, Peter Debois; edtr, Gordon Swire; mus, Rick Wakeman; prodn mgr, Terry Gould. 76.
James Coburn.
(DOC)
02/02/77

The White Ship: SEE Belyi Parohod

Whitey: SEE De Witte Van Sichem

Whizzer: SEE Schluchtenflitzer

Who Are The DeBolts? (And Where Did They Get 19 Kids?)
PYR. Exec prods, Shintaro Tsuji, Warren Lockhart. Prod, Dan McCann. Dir, John Korty. Sp, Joseph P Blank from his book, "19 Steps Up The Mountain"; cam, Jon Else; edtr, David Webb Peoples; mus, Ed Bogas; narr, Sidney Walker; snd, David McMillan, Kristine Samuelson, Kent Gibson. 72. (DOC)
10/12/77

Who Can Kill A Child?: SEE Quien Puede Matar A Un Nino?

Who Has Seen The Wind?
(Canada)
AST. Souris River Films prodn. Exec prod, Pierre Lamy. Dir, Allan King. Sp, Patricia Watson from the novel by W O Mitchell; cam, Richard Leiterman; art dir, Anne Pritchard; edtr, Arla Saare; mus, Eldon Rathburn; snd, John Kelly; asst dir, Patricia Watson. 100.
Brian Painchaud, Douglas Junor, Gordon Pinsent, Chapelle Jaffe, Jose Ferrer, Charmion King, David Gardner, Patricia Hamilton, Helen Shaver, Tom Hauff, Gerard Parkes, Nan Stewart.
11/16/77

Who Is Killing The Great Chefs of Europe?
(US - W Germany)
WB. Lorimar presentation of Aldrich Co-Lorimar prodn. Exec prods, Merv Adelson, Lee Rich. Prod, William Aldrich. Dir, Ted Kotcheff. Sp, Peter Stone, based on the Nan and Ivan Lyons' novel, "Someone is Killing the Great Chefs of Europe;" cam, John Alcott; in asso with Geria Prodns-Bavaria Films (Munich); asst dir, Wolfgang Gattes; art dir, Werner Achmann; cos, Judy Moorcroft; mus, Henry Mancini. (MPAA rating: PG). 112.
George Segal, Jacqueline Bisset, Robert Morley, Jean-Pierre Cassel, Philippe Noiret, Jean Rochefort, Luigi Proietti, Stefano Satta Flores, Madge Ryan, Frank Windsor, Peter Sallis, Tim Barlow, John LeMesurier, Joss Ackland, Jean Gaven, Daniel Emilfork, Jacques Marin, Jacques Balutin, Jean Paredes, Kenneth Fortescue.
09/20/78

Who Leaves in the Rain: SEE Kto Odchadza V Dazdi

Who'll Stop The Rain?
UA. UA-Herb Jaffe-Gabriel Katzka prodn. Dir, Karel Reisz. Sp, Judith Roscoe, Robert Stone from the book by Stone; cam, Richard H Kline; edtr, John Bloom; mus, Laurence Rosenthal. 125.
Nick Nolte, Tuesday Weld, Michael Moriarty, Anthony Zerbe, Richard Masur, Ray Sharkey, Gail Strickland, Charles Haid, David Opatoshu.
05/24/78

Wholly Moses!
COL. Prod, Freddie Fields; exec prod, David Begelman; dir, Gary Weis; sp, Guy Thomas; cam (Metrocolor Panavision), Frank Stanley; edtr, Sidney Levin; mus, Patrick Williams; prodn des, Dale Hennesy; set des, Diane Wager; set decor, Robert De Vestel; cos des, Guy Verhille; snd, John Speak; asst dir, L Andrew Stone. (MPAA rating: PG). 109.
Dudley Moore, Laraine Newman, James Coco, Paul Sand, Jack Gilford, Dom DeLuise, John Houseman, Madeline Kahn, David L Lander, Richard Pryor, John Ritter.
06/18/80

Who's That Singing Over There?: SEE Ko To Tamo Peva

Why Not: SEE Pourquoi Pas

Why Shoot the Teacher
(Canada)
AMB. Fraser Films and Lancer Telprodns presentation, prod, Lawrence Hertzog; exec prod, Fil Fraser. Dir, Silvio Narizzano. Sp, James Defelice, based on book, "Why Shoot The Teacher," by Max Braithwaite; cam, Marc Champion; art dir, Karen Bromley; mus, Ricky Hyslop; edtrs, Bruce Nyznik, Ian McBride, Peter Thillaye. 96.
Bud Cort, Samantha Eggar, Chris Wiggins, Gary Reineke, John Friesen, Michael J Reynolds.
07/13/77

Why Would I Lie?
UA. MGM release. Prod, Pancho Kohner; exec prods, Rich Irvine, James L Stewart; dir, Larry Peerce. Sp, Peter Stone, based on novel, "The Fabricator", by Hollis Hodges; cam (Metrocolor), Gerald Hirschfeld; edtr, John C Howard; snd, Bud Alper; art dir, James Schoppe; asst dir, Steve Barnett; mus, Charles Fox. (MPAA rating: PG)). 105.
Treat Williams, Lisa Eichhorn, Gabriel Swann, Valerie Curtin, Anne Byrne, Susan Heldfond, Jocelyn Brando, Nicolas Coster, Severn Darden, Sonny Davis.
08/06/80

The Widow Montiel: SEE La Viuda De Montiel

The Widower: SEE Po Mai Tidet

The Widowhood of Karolina Zasler: SEE Vdovstvo Karoline Zasler

Widow's Nest
(USA - Spain)
NVA. Sp-prod-dir, Tony Navarro. Cam, John Cabrera; edtr, Juan Serra; mus, Francis Lai; song lyric, Paul Taylor; art dir, Jose A De La Guerra; set decor, Edda Dorini; snd, Ivan Sharrock, Eduardo Fernandez; cos-ward, Tony Pueo, Luis Lopez, Adela Velasco; asst dir, Kuki Lopez Rodero. 119.
Patricia Neal, Valentina Cortese, Susan Oliver, Yvonne Mitchell, Jadwiga Baranska, Jerzy Zelnik, Lila Kedrova, Angel del Pozo, Helen Horton, Jorge Lago.
12/14/77

The Wife: SEE Savithri

The Wild Duck: SEE Die Wildente

The Wild Geese
(Britain)
RNK. Euan Lloyd prodn. Dir, Andrew V McLaglen. Sp, Reginald Rose, based on book by Daniel Carney; cam (Panavision-Color), Jack Hildyard; edtr, John Glen; mus, Roy Budd; snd, Gordon Everett; asst dir, Derek Cracknell; asso prod, Chris Chrisafis. 132.
Richard Burton, Roger Moore, Richard Harris, Hardy Kruger, Stewart Granger, Jack Watson, Winston Ntshona, John Kani, Kenneth Griffith, Frank Finlay, Barry Foster, Jeff Corey, Ronald Fraser, Ian Yule, Brook Williams, Percy Herbert, Patrick Allen, Glyn Baker, Rosalind Lloyd, Jane Hylton, David Ladd, Paul Spurrier.
05/24/78

Wild Horse Hank
(Canada)
X. Film Consortium of Canada prodn. Exec prods, Jerry Leider, Dan Wilson; prods, Bill Marshall, Henk Van Der Kolk. Dir, Eric Till. Sp, James Lee Barrett from novel, "The Wild Horse Killers," by Mel Ellis; mus, Paul and Brenda Hoffert; cam, Richard Leiterman; edtr, George Appelby. 94.
Linda Blair, Michael Wincott, Al Waxman, Pace Bradford.
05/23/79

Wild Hunting of King Stakh: SEE Dikaia Okhota Korolia Stakha

Wildwechsel
(Game Pass)
(W Germany)
CIG. Interel prodn, in collab with Sender Freies Berlin. Dir, Rainer Werner Fassbinder. Sp, Franz Xaver Kroetz, based on his play of same name; cam, Dietrich Lohmann; art dir, Kurt Raab; mus, Peer Raben. 100.
Eva Mattes, Harry Baer, Ruth Drexel, Joerg von Liebenfels, R W Brem, Hanna Schygulla, Kurt Raab, Karl Scheydt, Klaus-Micheal Loewitsch, Marquard Bohm.
06/02/76

The Willi Busch Report: SEE Der Willi Busch Report

Willi Und Die Kameraden
(Willie and the Comrades)
(W Germany)
X. Regina Ziegler Film Prodn, West Berlin, in collab with Second German Television (ZDF), Wiesbaden, Christoph Holch. Wri-dir, Helmut Kopetzky. Cam, David Slama; sets, Juergen Henze; make-up, cos, Barbara Naujok, Cornelia Leitner; snd, Heiko von Swieykowski; edtr, Susanne Busse-Lahaye; mus, Rio Raiser. 78.
Thomas Vahl, Dorothea Moritz, Horst Pinnow, Peter Schiff, Arnfried Lerche, Heinz Hoenig, Jako Benz, Silvia Bommert.
05/23/79

Willie & Phil
FOX. Prods, Paul Mazursky, Tony Ray; wri-dir, Mazursky; cam (DeLuxe Color), Sven Nykvist; mus, Claude Bolling; addl mus from "Jules Et Jim" by Georges Delerue; edtr, Donn Cambern; prodn des, Pato Guzman; set decors, Ed Stewart, Ernie Bishop; snd, Dennis Maitland, Arthur Piantadosi, Les Fresholtz, Michael Minkler; asso prod-asst dir, Terry Donnelly. (MPAA rating: R). 116.
Michael Ontkean, Margot Kidder, Ray Sharkey, Jan Miner, Tom Brennan, Julie Bovasso, Louis Guss, Kathleen Maguire, Kaki Hunter, Kristine DeBell, Alison Cass Shurpin, Christine Varnai, Laurence Fishburne III, Walter N Lowery, Jerry Hall, Helen Hanft, Hubert J Edwards, Natalie Wood.
08/13/80

Willie and the Chinese Cat: SEE Also Es War So. . .

Willie and the Comrades: SEE Willi Und Die Kameraden

The Winchell Affair: SEE Parashat Winchell

The Wind and the Oak: SEE Era E Lisi

The Wind Blows Under Your Feet: SEE Talpuk Alatt Futyul A Szel

Windows
UA. Michael Lobell prodn. Prod, Michael Lobell. Dir, Gordon Willis. Sp, Barry Siegel; cam (Technicolor), Willis; mus, Ennio Morricone; edtr, Barry Malkin; prodn des, Melvin Bourne; art dir, Richard Fuhrman; snd, Christopher Newman; set decor, Les Bloom; asst dir, Robert Colesberry. (MPAA rating: R). 96.
Talia Shire, Joseph Cortese, Elizabeth Ashley, Kay Medford, Michael Gorrin, Russell Horton, Michael Lipton.
01/23/80

Windwalker
PIE. Windwalker Prods film. Prods, Arthur R Dubs, Thomas E Ballard. Dir, Kieth Merrill. Sp, Ray Goldrup, from novel by Blaine M Yorgason; cam (CFI Color), Reed Smoot; mus, Merrill Jensen; prodn des, Thomas Pratt; edtrs, Stephen J Johnson, Janice Hampton, Peter L McCrea. (MPAA rating: PG). 108.
Trevor Howard, Nick Ramus, James Remar, Serene Hedin, Dusty Iron Wing McCrea, Silvana Gallardo, Billy Drago, Rudy Diaz, Harold Goss-Coyote, Roy J Cohoe, Jason Stevens, Roberta Deherrera, Wamni-OmniSka-Romideau.
(Cheyenne and Crow Indian languages-English subtitles and narration)
12/10/80

The Wing and the Thigh: SEE L'Aile et La Cuisse

Wings: SEE Krylya

Winifried Wagner Und Die Geschichte Des Hauses Wahnfried 1914-1975
(The Confessions of Winifred Wagner)
(W Germany)
CIG. Film by Hans Juergen Syberberg. Cam, Dietrich Lohmann. 300.
Winifred Wagner.
(DOC) (B & W) (16m)
06/02/76

Winning of Freedom: SEE Osvajanje Slobode

Winter Kills
AVE. Leonard J Goldberg-Robert Sterling prodn. Exec prods, Leonard J Goldberg, Robert Sterling. Prod, Fred Caruso. Wri-dir, William Richert, based on novel of same title by Richard Condon; cam, Vilmos Zsigmond; edtr, David Bretherton; mus, Maurice Jarre; cos, Robert De Mora; prodn des, Robert Boyle,; art dir, Norman Newberry; snd, Chris Newman. (MPAA rating: R). 97.
Jeff Bridges, John Huston, Anthony Perkins, Sterling Hayden, Eli Wallach, Dorothy Malone, Tomas Milian, Belinda Bauer, Ralph Meeker, Toshiro Mifune, Richard Boone.
05/16/79

Winter Trip in the Olympic Stadium: SEE Winterreisen Im Olympiastadion

Winterborn: SEE Vinterboern

Winterhawk
HOW. Charles B Pierce Film Production Inc film. Prod-dir, Pierce. Sp, Pierce, narr wri, Earl E Smith; cam (Technicolor), Jim Roberson; edtr, Tom Boutrouss; mus, Lee Holdridge; art dir, Charles Hughes; snd, Dick Damon; stunt coord, Bud Davis. (MPAA rating: PG). 98.
Leif Erickson, Woody Strode, Denver Pyle, L Q Jones, Michael Dante, Elisha Cook Jr, Seaman Glass, Dennis Fimple, Arthur Hunnicutt, Dawn Wells, Chuck Pierce Jr,

Jimmy Clem, Sacheen Littlefeather, Ace Powell.
01/28/76

Winterreisen Im Olympiastadion
(Winter Trip in the Olympic Stadium)
(W Germany)
X. Klaus Michael Grueber film prodn in collab with Spender Freies Berlin (SFB), West Berlin, based on a Schaubuehne am Halleschen Ufer legit prodn in the Berlin Olympic Stadium. Text fragments, Friedrich Hoederlin's "Hyperion, or The Hermit in Greece;" artistic advisor, Bernard Pautrat, Ellen Hammer; Images, Antonio Recalcati; cam, Wolfgang Knigge. 70.
Armin Baumert, Andreas Eisenschenk, Thomas Foelsch, Wolfram Goetz, Hans-Peter Jaeggi, Heiko Neumann, Hans-Joachim Schulze, Martin Szafranski, Rainer Stender, Tina Engel, Eberhard Feik, Guenter Lampe, Felix Prader, Werber Rehm, Paul Burian, Gerd David, Ruediger Hacker, Jan Kauenhowen, Michael Koenig, Wolf Redl, Sabine Andreas, Grischa Huber, Christine Oesterlein, Otto Maechtlinger, Ruth Walz, Libgart Schwarz, Willem Menne.
02/13/80

Winterspelt
(W Germany)
X. Ullstein AV, Berlin, prodn in collaboration with Sender Freies Berlin and Hessischer Rundfunk, Frankfurt. Sp-dir, Eberhard Fechner, based on novel of same name by Alfred Andersch. Cam, Rudolf Korosi, Kurt Weber; edtr, Barbara Grimm; mus, Gyorgy Ligeti; snd, Jochen Schwarzat, Pete Kellerhals; sets, Hans-Huergen Kiebach; cos, Elisabeth Schewer; prodn mgr, Dieter Graber. 108.
Ulrich von Dobschuetz, Katherina Thalbach, Hans-Christian Blech, Henning Schlueter, George Roubicek, Frederick Jaeger, Claus Theo Gaertner, Andreas von Studnitz, Ulrich Radke.
03/29/78

Wire Dog: SEE Perro de Alambre

Wise Blood
(USA - W Germany)
NL. Ithaca-Anthea prodn. Dir, John Huston. Sp, Benedict Fitzgerald, based on Flannery O'Connor story; cam, Gerald Fisher. 108.
Brad Dourif, Ned Beatty, Harry Dean Stanton, Daniel Shor, Amy Wright, Mary Nell Santacroce, John Huston.
06/06/79

The Wise Guys: SEE Les Loulous

The Wise Monkey: SEE El Monosabio

With Babies And Banners: Story of the Women's Emergency Brigade
X. Prods, Anne Bohlen, Lyn Goldfarb, Lorraine Gray. Dir, Gray; cam, Ting Barrow, Max Reid, Gray; edtrs, Mary Lampson, Melanie Maholick; snd, Samantha Heilweill, Carol Polakoff, Bohlen. 45.
(DOC) (16m)
04/11/79

With Clean Hands: SEE Cu Minile Curate

With Lots Of Love: SEE Con Mucho Carino

With Love and Tenderness: SEE S Lyubov I Nezhnost

With Nobody: SEE Pri Nikogo

With Shared Love: SEE Spodelena Lyubov

Without Anaesthetic: SEE Bez Znieczulenia

Without Love: SEE Bez Milosci

Without Warning
FWS. Prod-dir, Greydon Clark; exec prods, Skip Steloff, Paul Kimatian; sp, Lyn Freeman, Daniel Grodnik, Ben Nett, Steve Mathis; cam, (Movielab color), Dean Cundy; edtr, Curtis Burch; snd, Bob Dietz; asst dir, Caren Singer; asso prods, Burch, Milton Spencer; mus, Dan Wyman. (MPAA rating: R). 89.
Jack Palance, Martin Landau, Tarah Nutter, Christopher S Nelson, Cameron Mitchell, Neville Brand, Sue Ane Langdon, Larry Storch, Ralph Meeker, Lynn Theel, David Caruso, Darby Hinton.
09/24/80

The Witness: SEE Le Temoin

The Wiz
U. Motown Prodn. Exec prod, Ken Harper. Prod, Rob Cohen. Dir, Sidney Lumet. Sp, Joel Schumacher, based on play, "The Wiz," book by William F Brown, and book, "The Wonderful Wizard of Oz," by L Frank Baum; edtr, Dede Allen; cam (Technicolor), Oswald Morris; special visual effects, Albert Whitlock; prod des-cos, Tony Walton; sngs, Charlie Smalls; mus adapt-supv, Quincy Jones. (MPAA rating: G). 133.
Diana Ross, Michael Jackson, Nipsey Russell, Lena Horne, Richard Pryor, Ted Ross, Mabel King.
(MUS)
10/04/78

The Wizard Of Waukesha
X. Stray Cat prodn. Prod, Catherine Orentreich. Dirs, Orentreich, Susan Brockman; cam, Mark Obenhaus, Don Lenzer, Ed Gray; edtr, Brockman; snd, Ron Yoshida, Danny Michel, Franklin Haber. 59.
Les Paul.
(DOC) (16m)
03/12/80

Wizards
FOX. Wri-prod-dir, Ralph Bakshi. Cam (DeLuxe Color), Ted C Bemiller; edtr, Donald W Ernst; mus, Andrew Belling; layout, John Sparey; sequence ani, Irven Spence. (MPAA rating: PG). 80.
Voices: Bob Holt, Jesse Wells, Richard Romanus, David Proval, James Connell, Steve Gravers, Barbara Sloane, Angelo Grisanti, Hyman Wien, Christopher Tayback, Mark Hamil, Peter Hobbs, Tina Bowman.
(ANI)
02/02/77

Wizia Lokalna 1901
(Inspection of the Scene of a Crime 1901)
(Poland)
POL. Film Polski prodn, Tor Film Unit, Warsaw. Wri-dir, Filip Bajon; cam, Jerzy Zielinski; mus, Zdzislaw Szostak; sets, Andrzej Kawalczk. 98.
Tadeusz Lomnicki, Daniel Olbryschski, Jerzy Stuhr, Henryk Bista, Wieslaw Drzewicz, Zdzislaw Wardejn, Zygmunt Bielawski, Jerzy Trela, Stanislaw Igar, Mieczyslaw Voit, Stanislaw Michalski, Janusz Michalski.
09/24/80

The Wobblies
X. Funded by Nat'l Endowment for the Humanities, The Film Fund, The Joint Foundation for Support and the United Auto Workers. Dirs, Stewart Bird, Deborah Shaffer; cam, Sandi Sissel, Judy Irola, Peter Gessner, Bonnie Friedman; snd, Dixie Beckham, Joe De Francesco, Shaffer; research, Perce Rafferty, Erika Gottfried, Peter Smallman; edtrs, Gessner, Marilyn Frauenglass; snd edtr, Joan Morris. 88.
(DOC)
10/24/79

Wodzirej
(Top Dog)
(Poland)
POL. Zespoly Filmowe X prodn. Wri-dir, Feliks Falk. Cam (Eastmancolor), Edward Klosinski; mus, Jan Kanty-Pawluskiewicz. 115.
Jerzy Sthur, Slawa Kwasniewska, Wiktor Sadecki, Michal Tarkowski, Ewa Kolasinska.
10/25/78

The Wolf-cubs of Niquoluna: SEE Prune Des Bois

Wolz: Leben Und Verklaerung Eines Deutschen Anarchisten
(Wolz: Life and Illusion of a German Anarchist)
(E Germany)
X. DEFA prodn. Dir, Guenter Reisch. Sp, Guenther Ruecker; cam, Juergen Brauer. 95.
Regimontas Adomaitis, Heidemarie Wenzel, Stanislaw Ljubschin, Joerg-Detlef Panknin, Peter Hoelzel.
06/02/76

The Woman Across The Way: SEE Die Frau Gegenuber

The Woman Banker: SEE La Banquiere

The Woman Cop: SEE La Femme Flic

Woman From The Torrid Land: SEE La Mujer De La Tierra Caliente

Woman, Man, City: SEE Una Mujer, Un Hombre, Une Ciudad

Woman Rhymes With Human: SEE Menschenfrauen

Womanlight: SEE Clair de Femme

Women Duelling: SEE Duelle

Won Ton Ton, The Dog Who Saved Hollywood
PAR. Prods, David V Picker, Arnold Schulman, Michael Winner. Dir, Winner. Sp, Schulman, Cy Howard; cam (Technicolor), Richard H Kline; edtr, Bernard Gribble; mus, Neal Hefty; art dir, Ward Preston; set decor, Ned Parsons; snd, Hugh Strain, Bob Post; asst dir, Charles Okun; dog trainer, Karl Miller. (MPAA rating: PG). 92.
Bruce Dern, Madeline Kahn, Art Carney, Phil Silvers, Teri Garr, Ron Leibman, Augustus Von Schumacher.
05/05/76

The Wonderful Years: SEE Die Wunderbaren Jahre

The Wooden Gun: SEE Roveh Huliot

Woodpeckers Don't Get Headaches: SEE Ne Bolit Golowa U Djatla

Word Is Out
X. Mariposa Film Group prodn. Prod, Peter Adair. Dir, Mariposa Film Group (Peter Adair, Nancy Adair, Veronica Selver, Andrew Brown, Robert Epstein, Lucy Massie Phenix). Cam-snd-interviews-edtrs, Lucy Massie Phenix, Robert Epstein, Andrew Brown, Veronica Selver, Nancy Adair, Peter Adair; technical services, Fantasy Films, Ferco Inc., Monaco Labs; women's mus performed by Trish Nugent; men's mus performed by Buena Vista. 135.
(DOC)
03/08/78

The World Is Full of Married Men
(Britain)
NRP. Married Men Prodn. Exec prod, Adrienne Fancey. Prod, Malcolm Fancey, Oscar Lerman. Dir, Robert Young. Sp, Jackie Collins (with additional dialog by Terry Howard), based on her novel; cam, Ray Parslow; edtr, David Campling; mus, Frank Musker, Dominic Bugatti; art dir, Tony Curtis; snd, Claude Hitchcock, Trevor Pyke; asst dir, David Anderson; mus, Hot Gossip, title song sung by Mick Jackson, Bonnie Tyler, and various disco tracks. 107.
Anthony Franciosa, Carroll Baker, Sherrie Cronn, Paul Nicholas, Gareth Hunt, Georgina Hale, Anthony Steele, John Nolan, Jean Gilpin, Moira Downie, Alison Elliott, Eva Louise.
06/06/79

The World's Greatest Lover
FOX. Sp-prod-dir, Gene Wilder; co-prod-prodn des, Terence Marsh; co-prod-supv edtr, Chris Greenbury; cam (DeLuxe Color), Gerald Hirschfeld; edtr, Anthony A Pellegrino; mus, John Morris; song, Wilder; art dir, Steve Sardanis; sets, Craig Edgar, John Franco Jr; snd, Theodore Soderberg, Jack Solomon; cos-ward, Ruth Myers, Ed Wynigear, Phyllis Garr, Darryl Athons, Carolina Ewart; asst dir, Mel Dellar; stunt coord, Mickey Gilbert. (MPAA rating: PG). 89.
Gene Wilder, Carol Kane, Dom DeLuise.
11/16/77

The Worms: SEE Los Gusanos

Woyzeck
(W Germany)
GAU. Werner Herzog-Munich-ZDF prodn. Wri-dir, Werner Herzog from the play by Georg Buchner. Cam (Eastmancolor), Jorg Schmidt-Reitwein; edtr, Beate Mahka-Jellinghaus. 82.
Klaus Kinski, Eve Mattes, Wolfgang Reichman, Willy Semmerlbrogge, Josef Bierbichler, Paul Burian.
05/16/79

The Written-Off Return: SEE Povra tak Otpisanih

Wrong Number: SEE Taut Bamispar

Wsciekly
(Mad Dog)
(Poland)
POL. Film Polski prodn. Iluzion Film Unit Warsaw. Wri-dir, Roman Zaluski based on motifs in a story by Jerzy Romuald Milicz. Cam, Janusz Pawlowski; sets, Jerzy Sniezawski; mus, Jerzy Matula; prodn mgr, Tadeusz Urbanowicz. 102.
Bronislaw Cieslak, Barbara Brylska, Liliana Glabczynska, Halina Gryglaszewska, Ewa Kania, Tadeusz Borowski, Zbigniew Buczkowski, Andrzej Chrzanowski.
10/15/80

Wsrod Nocnej Ciszy
(Quiet Is The Night)
(Poland)
POL. A Film Polski Prodn, Film Unit "X," Warsaw. Dir, Tadeusz Chmielewski. Sp, based on novel by Ladislav Fuks, "Inspector Heumann"; cam, Jerzy Sawicki; mus, Jerzy Matuszkiewicz; sets, Teresa Smus-Barska. 128.
Tomasz Zaliwski, Piotr Lysak, Antonina Barczewska, Halina Kowalska, Zygmunt Maciejewski, Czeslaw Lipowska, Tadeusz Teodorczyk.
05/30/79

Wyrok Smierci
(Sentence of Death)
(Poland)
POL. Film Polski prodn, Silesia Film Unit, Warsaw. Dir, Witold Orzechowski; sp, Jerzego Gieraltowskiego, based on a story by Jerzy Gieraltowski, cam, Kazimierz Konrad; sets, Adam Kopczynski; prodn mgr, Ryszard Jasionowski. 105.
Wojciech Wysocki, Jerzy Bonczak, Doris Kunstmann, Stanislaw Igar, Slawomira Lozinska, Piotr Dejmek, Leon Niemczyk, Holger Mahlich, Erich Thiede, Klaus-Peter Thiele.
10/15/80

Xanadu
U. Prod, Lawrence Gordon; exec prod, Lee Kramer; dir, Robert Greenwald; sp, Richard Christian Danus, Marc Reid Rubel; cam (Technicolor), Victor J Kemper; edtr, Dennis Virkler; snd (Dolby Stereo), Robert Gravenor; co-prod, Joel Silver; prodn des, John W Corso; cos, Bobbie Mannix; chors, Kenny Ortega, Jerry Trent; asst dir, Dan Kolsrud; ani, Don Bluth; vis effects, Richard Greenberg; mus, Barry DeVorzon; songs, Jeff Lynne, John Farrar, perf, Olivia Newton-John, Electric Light Orch. (MPAA rating: PG). 93.
Olivia Newton-John, Gene Kelly, Michael Beck, James Sloyan, Dimitra Arliss, Katie Hanley, Fred McCarren, Ren Woods.
(MUSICAL)
08/13/80

Xica Da Silva
(Brazil)
EMZ. Jarbas Barbosa-Distrifilmes-Embrafilme prodn. Dir, Carlos Diegues. Sp, Diegues, Joao Felicio Dos Santos; cam (Eastmancolor), Jose Madeiros; edtr, Mair Tavares; mus, Roberto Menescal, Jorge Ben. 117.
Zeze Motta, Walmor Chagas, Altair Lima, Elke Maravilha.
12/01/76

...Y Al Tercer Ano Resucito
(. . .And the Third Year, He Resuscitated)
(Spain)
X. Cinco Films prodn. Dir, Rafael Gil. Sp, F Vizcaino Casas, based on his own novel; cam (Eastmancolor), Jose F Aguayo; mus, Gregorio Garcia Segura; edtr, Jose Luis Matasanz. 88.
Mary Begona, Jose Badalo, Francisco Cecilio, Florinda Chico, Tip and Coll, Antonio Garisa, Isabel Luque, Fernando Sancho, Juan Luis Galiardo, Jose Sancho, Jose Nieto, Adrian Ortega, Juan Santamaria.
05/07/80

Yanks
U. Prods, Joseph Janni, Lester Persky. Dir, John Schlesinger. Sp, Colin Welland, Walter Bernstein; cam (Technicolor), Dick Bush; edtr, Jim Clar; snd, Simon Kaye; prodn des, Brian Morris; art dir, Milly Burns; cos, Shirley Russell; asso prod, Teddy Joseph; asst dir, Simon Relph; mus, Richard Rodney Bennett. (MPAA rating: R). 141.
Richard Gere, Lisa Eichhorn, Vanessa Redgrave, William Devane, Chick Vennera, Wendy Morgan, Rachel Roberts, Tony Melody, Martin Smith, Philip Whileman, Derek Thompson, Simon Harrison.
09/19/79

Yasei No Shomei
(Proof of the Wild)
(Japan)
NIP. Kadokawa Publishing Co prodn. Exec prod, Haruki Kadokawa. Prods, Jun Sakagami, Masaya Endoh, Fumio Matsuda, Simon Tse. Dir, Junya Satoh. Sp, Koji Takada, based on book by Seiichi Morimuma; cam, Masahisa Himeda; edtr, Jun Nabeshima; mus, Kuji Ono; art dir, Horoshi Tokuda; light, Hideo Kumagai. 143.
Ken Takakura, Ryoko Nakano, Horoko Yakushimaru, Isao Natsuki, Rentaro Mikuni, Hajime Hana.
11/15/78

Yashaga Ike
(Demon Pond)
(Japan)
SKU. Prods, Kanji Nakagawa, Shigemi Sugisaki, Yukio Tomizawa. Dir, Masahiro Shinoda. Sp, Haruhiko Minura, Takeshi Tamura, based on a story by Kyoka Izumi; cam, Masao Kosugi, Noritaka Sakamoto; edtrs, Zen Ikeda, Sachiko Yamachi; mus, Isao Tomita. 124.
Tamasaburo Bando, Go Kato, Tsutomi Yamazaki, Koji Nanbara.
(English subtitles)
03/26/80

Yatsu Hakamura
(Village Of The Eight Tombs)
(Japan)
SKU. Prods, Yoshitaro Nomura, Shigemi Sugisaki, Akira Oda. Dir, Yoshitaro Nomura. Sp, Shinobu Hashimoto, based on Seishi Yokomizo novel; cam, Akira Kawamata; mus, Yashushi Akutagawa. 151.
Kenichi Hagiwara, Kiyoshi Atsumi, Mayumi Ogawa.
12/14/77

Yawmun Akher
(Another Day)
(Iraq)
IRQ. Dir, Sahib Haddad. Sp, Sabah Attwan, Mohammed Shoukry Jamil; cam, Majid Kamil. 90.
Khalil Shawki, Nahida Al Raman, Shaidha Salim, Talib Al Forati.
02/20/80

The Year of the Hare: SEE Janiksen Vuosi

Yeh Nuat Sua
(Operation Black Panther)
(Thailand)
MEH. Prod, Kanchana Metanee. Dir, Sombat Metanee. Story-sp, Ta Tait; cam, Niyom Srisuwan; edtr-asst dir, Pao Viramitr; mus, Chalie Intravijit; snd, Piac Tamahon; prodn mgr, Siri Pentaradet; cos, Nuanjit. 120.
Sombat Metanee, Aranya Namwong, Ratanaporn Indrakamhaeng, Rujira Issarangkul Na Ayudhya, Kamthorn Suwanpiyasiri, Manop Assawathep, Tarika Tarathit, Moi Fa, Choosri Misomon, Pipop Pupinyo.
06/08/77

The Yellow Flower: SEE Dao Ruang

The Yellow Star: SEE Der Gelbe Stern

Yesterday
(Canada)
CPX. Dal Prodns film. Dir, Larry Kent. Prods, John Dunning, Andre Link. Sp, Bill Lamond, John Dunning, from an orig idea of Dunning; asst dir, Don Buchsbaum; art dir, Roy Forge Smith; cam, Richard Ciupka; snd, Patrick Rousseau; edtr, Debra Karen. 97.
Claire Pimpare, Vince Van Patten, Eddie Albert, Nicholas Campbell, Daniel Gadouas, Jacques Godin, Gerald Parkes.
04/16/80

Yesterday's Hero
(Britain)
EMI. Cinema Seven prodn. Exec prod, Elliott Kastner; prods, Oscar S Lerman, Ken Regan. Dir, Neil Leifer; sp, Jackie Collins; cam, Brian West; edtr, Anthony Gibbs; sngs, Bugatti and Musker; mus dir, Stanley Myers; prodn des, Keith Wilson; asso prod, Denis Holt; tech adv (soccer), Frank McLintock. 95.
Ian McShane, Suzanne Somers, Adam Faith, Paul Nicholas, Sam Kydd, Glynis Barber, Trevor Thomas, Sandy Ratcliffe, Alan Lake, Matthew Long, John Motsom, Paul Medford.
11/28/79

Yesterday's Tomorrow: SEE Zwischengleis

Yeti
(Italy)
SFO. Prod, Nicolo Pomilia and Wolfranco Coccia for Stefano Film. Dir, Frank Kramer. Sp, Mario Di Nardo, Kramer; cam (Technicolor), Sandro Mancori; art dir, Claudio De Santis; sfx, Ermanno Biamonte; mus, Santa Maria Romitelli. 105.
Mimmo Crau, Phoenix Grant, Jim Sullivan, John Stacey, Eddie Faye, Tony Kendall.
01/18/78

Yim Sawasdi
(Smile Hello)
(Thailand)
CHT. Prod-dir-edtr, Pornpoj Kanitkasen. Exec prod, Rachiniwan Kanitkasen. Story, Banjered Tawee; sp, Tanachai Chinothai; cam, Sophon Jaenphanit; mus, Prachin Songpow; prodn des, Urai Srisombat; art dir, Prasobchai Kanitkasen; snd, Montri Ong-iam. 110.
Pairoj Sangborivutr, Nawarat Yukthanan, Setta Sirachaiya, M L Rujira Issarangkul, Na Ayudhya, Supravat Patamasoot, Juree Osiree.
11/29/78

Yod Manoot Computer
(The Computer Superman)
(Thailand)
CHY. Prod, Somphote Saengduangchai. Dir, Santa Pestonji. Story, Ratiporn; sp, Karn Boonchu; Santa Pestonji; cam, Tirapong; mus, Mandarin Lab. (Hong Kong). 120.
Yodchai Megsuan, Duangchiwan Komonsen, Poh Teng, Thep Tianchai, Krong Kangkengdang, Jamroon, Choosri Misomon.
05/11/77

Yomegaeru Kinro
(Resurrection of the Golden Wolf)
(Japan)
TOE. Kadokawa Prodn. Exec prod, Haruki Kadokawa. Prods, Michiru Kurosawa, Gosukei Ito, Tatsuro Shigaki. Dir, Toru Murakawa. Sp, Shuichi Nagahara, based on novel by Haruhiko Oyabu; cam, Seizo Sengen; mus, Casey Rankin. 131.
Yusaku Matsuda, Jun Fubuki, Kei Ito, Mikio Marita, Shinichi Chiba, Joji Shin, Asao Koike.
01/23/80

Yompaban Cha
(Heaven and Hell)
(Thailand)
ASV. Conceived-story, Prince Bhanubhandu Yugala. Sp-dir, Niramitr. Exec prod, Mom Prim Yugala; cam, Anant Inroah; edtr, Prom Rungrangsri; mus, Chalie Intravijit, Sanga Arampi; snd, Kasem Militachinda. 135.
Krung Srivilai, Aranya Namwong, Manop Assawathep, Choosri Misomon, Chinadit Bunnag, Pairoj Jaising, Anant Samasap, Sayant Chantrawiboon, Orsa Issarangkul Na Ayudhya.
02/01/78

Yotz'lm Kavua
(Going Steady)
(Israel - W Germany)
NOA. Golan-Globus Prodn. Prods, Sam Weintberg, Menahem Golan, Yoram Globus. Dir, Boaz Davidson. Sp, Davidson, Eli Tavor; cam, Adam Greenberg; edtr, Alain Jacubowicz; art dir, Eytan Levi.   100.
Yiftach Katzur, Jonathan Segal, Zachi Noy, Yvonne Michaeli, Daphna Armoni, Rachel Steiner.
05/30/79

You Are Not Alone: SEE Du'er ikke alene

You Better Watch Out
X. Edward R Pressman presentation. Prod, Burt Kleiner, Pete Kameron. Asso prod, Michael Levine. Dir-wri, Lewis Jackson. Edtrs, Corky O'Hara, Linda Leeds; cam, Ricardo Aronovich; cos, Dierdre Williams; prodn des, Lorenzo Jodie Harris.   100.
Brandon Maggart, Dianne Hull, Scott McKay, Joe Jamrog, Peter Friedman, Ray Barry, Bobby Lesser, Sam Gray, Ellen McElduff, Patty Richardson.
12/03/80

You Light Up My Life
COL. Prod-dir-wri-mus, Joseph Brooks. Cam (Metrocolor), Eric Saarinen; edtr, Lynzee Klingman; art dir-set des, Tom Rasmussen; snd, Richard Vorisek, Rick Dior, Art Names, Trans Audio Inc.; cos-ward, John Patton, Nancy Chadwick; asst dir, Ed Morgan. (MPAA rating: PG).   90.
Didi Conn, Joe Silver, Michael Zaslow, Stephan Nathan, Melanie Mayron, Amy Letterman, Marty Zagon.
08/10/77

You Make Me Crazy: SEE Tu Me Enloqueces

You Won't Have Alsace-Lorraine: SEE Vous n'Aurez Pas L'Alsace et La Lorraine

The Young Cycle Girls
PPY. Prod-dir, Peter Perry. Exec prod, Sue Perry. Sp, John Arnoldy; cam, Ron Garcia; edtr, Marco Perri. (MPAA rating: R).   80.
Loraine Ferris, Daphne Lawrence, Deborah Marcus, Lonnie Pense, Kevin O'Neill, Bee Lechat, Billy Bullet.
01/24/79

The Young Ladies of Wilko: SEE Panny Z Wilka

Young Lady Chatterley
POI. Alan Roberts/David Winters prodn for Young L C Ltd; exec prod, William B Silberkleit. Prods, Roberts, Winters. Sp, Steve Michaels; cam (Metrocolor), Bob Brownell; mus, Don Bagley, adapted from the works of Claude Debussy; songs, "Lonely Rider" by Russell Thomas Bennett, Ray Martin, and "My Reverie" by Michaels; edtr, Soly Bina; art dir, Gale Peterson; cos, Lennie Barin; snd, Paul Moro; asst dir, Danny Biederman. (Self-applied X Rating).   100.
Harlee McBride, Peter Ratray, William Beckley, Ann Michelle, Joi Staton, Mary Forbes, Patrick Wright.
05/18/77

The Young Man and Moby Dick: SEE Mlady Muz A Bila Velryba

Young Marilyn: SEE Goodbye, Norma Jean

The Young Master
(Hong Kong)
GHV. Leonard Ho prodn. Dir, Jackie Chan. Sp, Lau Tin-Chee, Tung Lu, Tang Kin-Sang; action chors, Chan, Feng Ke-An; mus, Frankie Chan; cam, Chen Ching-Chueh.   120.
Jackie Chan, Yuan Biao, Wei Pai, Whong In Sik, Lily Li, Shek Kin, Feng Ke-An, Li Hai-Sheng, Tien Feng, Feng Feng.
(Cantonese dialogue, English subtitles)
02/27/80

The Young Monk: SEE Der Junge Moench

Young Ones Are Even Cold In The Summer: SEE Kleine Frieren Auch Im Sommer

Youngblood
AIP. Aion prodn. Prods, Nick Grillo, Alan Riche. Dir, Noel Nosseck. Sp, Paul Carter Harrison; cam (CFI Color), Robbie Greenberg; edtr, Frank Morriss; mus, WAR; art dir, James Dultz; snd, Jan Schulti; ward, Adrianne Levesque; asst dir, Bill Kerr; stunt coord, Eddie Smith. (MPAA rating: R).   90.
Lawrence-Hilton Jacobs, Bryan O'Dell, Ren Woods, Tony Allen, Vince Cannon, Art Evans, Jeff Hollis, Dave Pendleton, Ron Trice, Sheila Wills, Ann Weldon.
05/10/78

Your Smiling Face
(Taiwan)
TYW. Prod, Chou Lin Kang. Dir-edtr, Larry C H Tu. Exec prod, Shao Chi-Wu; story-sp, Sung Hsiang-lu; cam, Yu Chi Len; art dir, Chang Chi Ping; prodn consultants, Xi Fong Lu, Tang Chi.   100.
Hu Hui Chung, Chang Hua Chu, Jao Sao Thong.
09/19/79

Your Son and Brother: SEE Wasch Syn I Brat

You're Out Of Your Mind, Maggie: SEE Du aer inte klok, Madicken

The Youth Killer: SEE Seisheun No Satsujinsha

Youthquake
WW. Prod-dir, Max B Miller. Exec prod, Carl A Albert. Asso prod, Marvin Young; cam (Eastmancolor), Bob Grant; edtr, Max B Miller; snd, Danny Wallin. (MPAA rating: PG).   90.
(DOC)
05/25/77

You've Been Had. . .You Turkey!: SEE Achalta Ota

Yukinojo Henge
(Yukinojo's Revenge)
(Japan)
PIF. Nagata prodn. Dir, Kon Ichikawa. Sp, Natto Wada; cam (Eastmancolor), Setsuo Koba; mus, Yasushi Akutgawa.   110.
Kasuo Hasegawa, Fujiko Yamamato, Ayako Wakao, Raizo Ichikawa, Shintaro Katsu.
08/02/78

Zamach Stanu
(Coup d'Etat)
(Poland)
POL. Film Polski prodn, Profil Film Unit, Warsaw. Dir, Ryszard Filipski; sp, Ryszard Gontarz; cam, Jacek Stachiewski; mus, Piotr Marczewski; sets, Czeslaw Siekiera.   176.
Ryszard Filipski, Jerzy Sagan, Gabriel Nehrebecki, Lech Bijald, Wlodzimierz Wiszniowski, Jerzy Ziotnicki, Zygmunt Malanowicz, Jozef Pieracki, Arkadiusz Bazak, Jozef Fryzlewicz, Henryk Boukolowski, Wlodzimierz Borunski, Henryk Machalica, Andrezej Krasicki, Czeslaw Wollejko, Kazimierz Wichniarz, Tomasz Zaliwski, Tadeusz Janczar, Jozef Nowak.
09/24/80

Zanim Nadejdzie Dzien
(Before the Day Breaks)
(Poland)
POL. Film Polski prodn, Warsaw, "Zespoly Filmowe" Profil unit. Dir, Ryszard Rydzewski. Sp, Ewa Przybylska, Rydzewski; cam, Waclaw Dybowski; mus, Maciej Malecki; art dir, Wieslaw Sniadecki; prodn mgr, Edward Klosowicz.   91.
Anna Nehrebecka, Krzysztof Janczar, Maria Klejdysz, Zdzislaw Kozien, Waclaw Ulewicz, Ewa Lejczak, Roman Mosior.
06/01/77

Zbojnik Jurko
(Robber Jurko)
(Czechoslovakia)
X. Slovak Film prodn, Bratislava, Koliba Studios for animation. Idea-sp-ani-dir, Viktor Kubal.   85.
(ANI)
03/09/77

Zdjecia Probne
(Screen Tests)
(Poland)
X. Film Polski prodn, Warsaw, Cinema Group and X units. Dirs, Agnieszka Holland, Pawel Kedzierski, Jerzy Domaradzki. Sp, Holland, Kedzierski, Domaradzki, Feliks Falk; cam, Jacek Zygadla; art dir, Zbieniew Tolloczko. 90.
Daria Trafankowska, Andrzej Pieczynski, Miroslawa Marcheluk, Urszula Modrzynska, Wieslawa Kwasniewska, Zbigniew Bielski, Aleksander Maciejewski.
05/25/77

Zemaljski Dani Teku
(The Days Are Passing)
(Yugoslavia)
YFR. Center Film prodn, Belgrade, and Belgrade Television. Wri-dir, Goran Paskaljevic. Cam, Milan Spasic; sets, Dragoljub Ivkov; mus, Zoran Simijanovic. 85.
Dimitrije Vujovic, Obren Helcer, Sarlota Pesic, Mila Keca.
09/05/79

Zendabad
(Long Live. . .)
(Iran)
IR. Wri-dir, Khosrow Sinai; cam, Fereidun Kavanlu. 100.
Soroyya Kasemi, Mehdi Hashemi, Gholanreza Tabataba, Ema il Mohammadi, Ahmad Kashani.
(B & W)
07/30/80

Zerkalo
(The Mirror)
(USSR)
X. Mosfilm prodn, Moscow. Wri-dir, Andrei Tarkovsky. Cam, Georgi Rerberg. 90.
Margareta Terehova.
(COLOR & B & W)
02/02/77

Zero Hour: SEE Stunde Null

Zidul
(The Wall)
(Romania)
RMN. Rumaniafilm Prodn, Group Three, Bucharest. Dir, Constantin Vaeni. Sp, Dumitru Carabat, Costache Ciubotaru; cam (b&w), Iosif Demian; mus, Cornelia Tautu; sets, Vittorio Holtier. 95.
Gabriel Oseciuc, Gheorghe Dinica, Victor Rebengiuc, Cornelia Pavlovici, Mitica Popescu, Nicolae Radu, George Mihaita, Constantin Vaeni, Theo Partisch.
(B & W)
06/14/78

Zielone Lata
(Salad-Days)
(Poland)
POL. Film Polski prodn, Silesia Film Unit, Warsaw. Dir, Stanislaw Jedryka; sp, Jerzy Przezdziecki, based on his own book; cam, Jacek Korcelli; sets, Boleslaw Kamykowski; mus, Andrzej Korzynski; prod mgr, Jerzy Owoc. 102.
Tomasz Jarosinski, Jacek Bryniarski, Agnieszka Konopczynska, Malgorzata Pritulak, Krzysztof Kiersznowski, Anna Chodakowska, Zygmunt Hobot, Irena Laskowska.
10/15/80

Zivi Bili Pa Vidjeli
(That's The Way The Cookie Crumbles)
(Yugoslavia)
YFR. Zagreb Film prodn. Wris-dirs, Bruno Gamulin, Milivoj Puhlovski. Cam (Eastmancolor), Zivko Zalar; mus, Bulldozer Rock Group. 100.
Sanja Vejnovic, Boris Buzanic, Ana Karic, Zarko Potocnjak, Danko Ljustina.
08/15/79

Zmierc Prezydenta
(Death of the President)
(Poland)
POL. Film Group Kadr. Dir, Jerzy Kawalerowicz. Sp, Boleslaw Michalek, Kawalerowicz; cam, Witold Sobocinski, Jerzy Lukaszewicz; edtr, Wieslawa Otocka; sets, Wojciech Krysztofiak, Adam Nowakowski; mus, Adam Walacinski. 144.
Zdzislaw Mrozewski, Marek Walczewski, Czeslaw Byszewski, Jerzy Duszynski, Zbigniew Krynski, Tomasz Zaliwski, Erwin Kohkund, Hans-Gerd Kuebel, Henryk Bista, Edmund Fetting, Kazimierz Iwor, Julian Jabszynski, Wlodzimierz Saar, Jerzy Sagan, Roman Sikora, Janusz Sykutera, Marek Dowmunt, Lucjan Dytrych, Marian Godlewski, Andrzej Krasicki, Leszek Kubanek, Marian Nosek, Tadeusz Sabara, Josef Zbirog, Antoni Lewek, Marek Prazanowski, Jacek Reknitz, Mieczyslaw Szargan.
02/22/78

Zmory
(Nightmares)
(Poland)
POL. Film Polski Prodn, Warsaw, Tor Unit. Dir, Wojciech Marczewski. Sp, Pawel Jajny, Marczewski, based on a novel by Emil Zegadlowicz; cam, Wieslaw Zdort; edtr, Irena Chorynska; mus, Zigmunt Konieczny. 111.
Thomasz Hudziec, Piotr Lysak, Hanna Skarzanka, Maria Chwalibog, Teresa Marczewski, Bronislaw Pawlik, Janusz Michalowski.
05/30/79

Zo Monogatari
(Elephant Story)
(Japan)
THW. Kurahara Production. Gen supv, Koreyoshi Kurahara. Dirs, Koretsugu Kurahara, Seido Hino. Narr script, Jinichi Mimura; cam, Yoshio Mamiya, Masao Tochizawa, Sadanori Shibata; edtr, Akira Suzuki; mus, Makato Kawaguchi; theme song, Ryudo Uzaki; lyr, Yoko Aki; narr, Eiji Okada. 112.
(DOC)
06/11/80

Zofia
(Sophia)
(Poland)
POL. Film Polski prodn, Warsaw, Kadr unit. Wri-dir, Ryszard Czekala. Cam, Czeslaw Swirta; mus, Czeslaw Niemen; art dir, Roman Wolyniec; prodn mgr, Zbigniew Tolloczko. 95.
Ryszarda Hanin, Zdzislaw Mrozewski, Alicja Jachiewicz, Sefan Szmidt, Halina Buyno-Loza, Andrzej Gazdeczka, Zdzislaw Makakiewica, Jozef Pieracki.
06/08/77

Zombie
(Italy)
GRO. Variety Film prodn. Prod, Ugo Tucci, Fabrizio de Angelis; dir, Lucio Fulci. Sp-story, Elisa Briganti; cam (Technicolor), Sergio Salvati; edtr, Vincenzo Tomassi; mus, Fabio Frizzi, Giorgio Tucci; sfx-makeup supv, Gianneto de Rossi. (Self-imposed X Rating). 91.
Tisa Farrow, Ian McCulloch, Richard Johnson, Al Cliver, Annetta Gay, Olga Karlatos, Stefania D'Amario.
07/30/80

Zona Roja
(Pink Zone)
(Mexico)
PEX. Conacine prodn. Wri-dir, Emilio Fernandez. Cam, Daniel Lopez; edtr, Jorge Bustos; mus, Manuel Esperon. 100.
Fanny Cano, Armando Silvestre, Tito Junco, Venetia Vianello, Mecho Carreno, Lina Michel.
06/23/76

Zones: SEE Grauzone

Zongora A Levegoben
(A Piano in Mid-Air)
(Hungary)
X. Budapest Studio prodn. Dir-wri, Peter Bacso. Cam (Eastmancolor), Janos Zsombolyai; mus, Gyorgy Vukan. 93.
Juraj Durdiak, Lajos Oze, Nandor Tomanek, Ferenc Kallai, Ildiko Pesci, Eva Ujvari, Tamas Major, Eva Spanyik.
03/02/77

Zonja Nga Qyteti
(The Lady From Town)
(Albania)
ALA. Albfilm prodn, Tirana. Dir, Piro Milkani. Sp, Ruzhdi Pulaha, based on Pulaha's play with the same name; cam, Lionel Konomi; art dir, Arben Basha; mus, Agim Krajka. 105.
Violeta Manushi, Rajmonda Bulku, Stavri Shkurti, Pandi Raidhi, Yilka Mujo, Petraq Kita.
01/24/79

Zrcadleni
(Reflections)
(Czechoslovakia)
CZS. Czechoslovak Film Prodn, Barrandov Studios, Prague. Dir, Jaroslav Balik. Sp, Vladimir Kalina, Balik. 90.
Stanislaw Zaczyk, Eva Sitteova.
08/02/78

Zucchero, Miele E Peperoncino
(Sugar, Honey and Pepper)
(Italy)
MDU. Prod, Luciano Martino for Dania Film prodns. Dir, Sergio Martino. Sp, Castellano, Pipolo; cam (Eastmancolor), Giancarlo Ferrando; art dir, Adriana Bellone; edtr, Eugenio Alabiso; mus, Detto Mariani.   113.
Lino Banfi, Edwige Fenech, Pippo Franco, Dagmar Lassander, Renato Pozzetto, Patrizia Garganese.
12/03/80

Zuendschnuere
(Fuses)
(W Germany)
X. Reinhard Hauff Film prodn, Munich, in collab with Westdeutscher Rundfunk (WDR), Cologne. Exec prod, Wolf-Dietrich Bruecker. Dir, Reinhard Hauff. Sp, Burkhard Driest, based on novel with same name by Franz Josef Degenhardt; cam, Frank Bruehne; art dir, Wolfgang Schuenke; mus, Franz Josef Degenhardt,   105.
Michael Olbrich, Bettina Porsch, Thomas Visser, Kurt Funk, Tilli Breidenbach, Erich Kleiber, Hans Beerhenke, Katrin Tuerks, Tana Schanzara, Heinz Wildhagen, Guenter Zulla, Renate Becker, Hans Meier, Hermann Guenther, Hilde Wensch, Christine Wodetzky.
(B & W)
05/11/77

Zulu Dawn
(Britain)
WBO. Lamitas presentation of a Samarkand prodn. Prod, Nate Kohn; exec prod, Barrie Saint Claire; co-prod, James Faulkner. Dir, Douglas Hickox. Original story and scenario, Cy Enfield; sp, Enfield, Anthony Storey; mus, Elmer Bernstein; asst dir, John O'Connor; cam (Technicolor), Ousama Rawi; snd mixer, Robin Gregory; edtr, Malcolm Cook; prodn des, John Rosewarne; art dir, Peter Williams; action sequences and stunt coord, Bob Simmons; 2d unit dir, David Tomblin.   117.
Burt Lancaster, Peter O'Toole, Simon Ward, John Mills, Nigel Davenport, Michael Jayston, Ronald Lacey, Denholm Elliott, Freddie Jones, Christopher Cazenove, Ronald Pickup, Donald Pickering, Anna Calder-Marshall, James Faulkner, Peter Vaughn, Graham Armitage, Bob Hoskins, Dai Bradley, Paul Copley, Christ Chittell, Nicholas Clay, Patrick Mynhardt, Brian O'Shaughnessy, Simon Sabela, Midge Carter, Phil Daniels, Raymond Davies, Ken Gampu.
05/23/79

Zvezdi V Kossite, Salzi V Ochiete
(Stars in the Hair, Tears in the Eyes)
(Bulgaria)
BGO. BulgaroFilm prodn, Hemus Group, Sofia. Dir, Ivan Nichev. Sp, Anghel Wagenstein; cam, Tsvetan Chobanski; art dir, Anghel Ahryanov; mus, Kiril Tsiboulka.   100.
Katya Paskaleva, Peter Slabakov, Tatyana Lolova, Nikolai Binev, Ivan Dervishev, Leda Taseva, Antony Ghenov, Ivan Tsvetarski, Nikolai Nachkov.
05/31/78

Zwei Tage Fuers Leben
(Two Days for Life)
(W Germany)
X. German Film and Television Academy Berlin (DFFB) prodn, in collab with Norddeutscher Rundfunk (NDR), Hamburg. Wri-dir-edtr, Rainer Boldt. Cam, Helmut Wietz, Rene Perradin.   60.
Wolfgang Wiehe, Andrea Klinge, Renate Koehler, Rene Reincke.
02/02/77

Zwischengleis
(Yesterday's Tomorrow)
(W Germany)
WBC. Artus Film/Bayerischer Rundfunkt tv prodn. Sp, Dorothee Dhan; cam, Igor Luther; mus, Eugen Illin; prod, Dr Harold Mueller; dir, Wolfgang Staudte.   106.
Mel Ferrer, Pola Kinski, Martin Luettge, Hannelore Schroth, Volker Kraeft.
10/11/78

OSCARS

1927/28

BEST PICTURE:
WINGS, PAR.
THE LAST COMMAND, PAR.
THE RACKET, Caddo, PAR.
SEVENTH HEAVEN, FOX.
THE WAY OF ALL FLESH, PAR.

ACTOR:
EMIL JANNINGS, The Last Command.
EMIL JANNINGS, The Way Of All Flesh.
RICHARD BARTHELMESS, *The Noose*, FN.
RICHARD BARTHELMESS, *The Patent Leather Kid*, FN.
CHARLES CHAPLIN, *The Circus*, Chaplin, UA.

ACTRESS:
JANET GAYNOR, Seventh Heaven.
JANET GAYNOR, Street Angel, FOX.
JANET GAYNOR, Sunrise, FOX.
LOUISE DRESSER, *A Ship Comes In*, Pathe-RKO.
GLORIA SWANSON, *Sadie Thompson*, UA.

DIRECTING:
FRANK BORZAGE, Seventh Heaven.
HERBERT BRENON, *Sorrell And Son*, UA.
KING VIDOR, *The Crowd*, MGM.
(COMEDY Direction)
LEWIS MILESTONE, Two Arabian Knights, UA.
CHARLES CHAPLIN, *The Circus*.
TED WILDE, *Speedy*, PAR.

WRITING:
(Adaptation)
SEVENTH HEAVEN. Benjamin Glazer.
GLORIOUS BETSY, WB. Anthony Coldeway.
THE JAZZ SINGER, WB. Alfred Cohn.
(Original Story)
UNDERWORLD, PAR. Ben Hecht.
THE LAST COMMAND, PAR. Lajos Biro.
THE PATENT LEATHER KID. Rupert Hughes.
(Title Writing)
THE FAIR CO-ED, MGM. Joseph Farnham.
LAUGH, CLOWN, LAUGH, MGM. Joseph Farnham.
TELLING THE WORLD, MGM. Joseph Farnham.
THE PRIVATE LIFE OF HELEN OF TROY, FN. Gerald Duffy.
OH KAY!, FN. George Marion, Jr.
(Award discontinued after this year.)

CINEMATOGRAPHY:
SUNRISE. Charles Rosher and Karl Struss.
DEVIL DANCER, UA. George Barnes.
DRUMS OF LOVE, UA. Karl Struss.
MAGIC FLAME, UA. George Barnes.
MY BEST GIRL, Pickford, UA. Charles Rosher.
SADIE THOMPSON. George Barnes.
THE TEMPEST, UA. Charles Rosher.

ART DIRECTION - SET DECORATION:
THE DOVE, UA. William Cameron Menzies.
THE TEMPEST. William Cameron Menzies.
SEVENTH HEAVEN. Harry Oliver.
SUNRISE. Rochus Gliese.

HONORARY AND OTHER:
(Other)
WB for producing The Jazz Singer, the pioneer outstanding talking picture, which has revolutionized the industry.
CHARLES CHAPLIN for versatility and genius in writing, acting, directing and producing The Circus.

ARTISTIC QUALITY OF PRODUCTION:
SUNRISE.
CHANG, PAR.
THE CROWD.
(Award discontinued after this year.)

ENGINEERING EFFECTS:
WINGS. Roy Pomeroy.
THE JAZZ SINGER. Nugent Slaughter.
THE PRIVATE LIFE OF HELEN OF TROY. Ralph Hammeras.
(Award discontinued after this year.)

1928/29

BEST PICTURE:
BROADWAY MELODY, MGM.
ALIBI, Feature Prod., UA.
HOLLYWOOD REVUE, MGM.
IN OLD ARIZONA, FOX.
THE PATRIOT, PAR.

ACTOR:
WARNER BAXTER, In Old Arizona.
GEORGE BANCROFT, *Thunderbolt*, PAR.
CHESTER MORRIS, *Alibi*.
PAUL MUNI, *The Valiant*, FOX.
LEWIS STONE, *The Patriot*.

ACTRESS:
MARY PICKFORD, Coquette, Pickford, UA.
RUTH CHATTERTON, *Madame X*, MGM.
BETTY COMPSON, *The Barker*, FN.
JEANNE EAGELS, *The Letter*, PAR.
BESSIE LOVE, *Broadway Melody*.

DIRECTING:
FRANK LLOYD, The Divine Lady, FN.
LIONEL BARRYMORE, *Madame X*.
HARRY BEAUMONT, *Broadway Melody*.
IRVING CUMMINGS, *In Old Arizona*.
FRANK LLOYD, *Weary River*, FN.
FRANK LLOYD, *Drag*, FN.
ERNST LUBITSCH, *The Patriot*.

WRITING:
(Achievement)
THE PATRIOT. Hans Kraly.
IN OLD ARIZONA. Tom Barry.
THE LEATHERNECK, Pathe, Elliott Clawson.
OUR DANCING DAUGHTERS, MGM. Josephine Lovett.
THE VALIANT. Tom Barry.
WONDER OF WOMEN, MGM. Bess Meredyth.

CINEMATOGRAPHY:
WHITE SHADOWS IN THE SOUTH SEAS, MGM. Clyde De Vinna.
THE DIVINE LADY. John Seitz.
FOUR DEVILS, FOX. Ernest Palmer.
IN OLD ARIZONA. Arthur Edeson.
OUR DANCING DAUGHTERS. George Barnes.
STREET ANGEL, FOX. Ernest Palmer.

ART DIRECTION - SET DECORATION:
THE BRIDGE OF SAN LUIS REY, MGM. Cedric Gibbons.
DYNAMITE, Pathe. Mitchell Leisen.
HOLLYWOOD REVUE. Cedric Gibbons.
THE IRON MASK, UA. William Cameron Menzies.
THE PATRIOT. Hans Dreier.
STREET ANGEL. Harry Oliver.

1929/30

BEST PICTURE:
ALL QUIET ON THE WESTERN FRONT, U.
THE BIG HOUSE, MGM.
DISRAELI, WB.
THE DIVORCEE, MGM.
THE LOVE PARADE, PAR.

ACTOR:
GEORGE ARLISS, Disraeli.
GEORGE ARLISS, *The Green Goddess*, WB.
WALLACE BEERY, *The Big House*.
MAURICE CHEVALIER, *The Love Parade*.
MAURICE CHEVALIER, *The Big Pond*, PAR.
RONALD COLMAN, *Bulldog Drummond*, Goldwyn, UA.
RONALD COLMAN, *Condemned*, Goldwyn, UA.
LAWRENCE TIBBETT, *The Rogue Song*, MGM.

ACTRESS:
NORMA SHEARER, The Divorcee.
NANCY CARROLL, *The Devil's Holiday*, PAR.
RUTH CHATTERTON, *Sarah And Son*, PAR.
GRETA GARBO, *Anna Christie*, MGM.
GRETA GARBO, *Romance*, MGM.
NORMA SHEARER, *Their Own Desire*, MGM.
GLORIA SWANSON, *The Trespasser*, Kennedy, UA.

DIRECTING:
LEWIS MILESTONE, All Quiet On The Western Front.
CLARENCE BROWN, *Anna Christie*.
CLARENCE BROWN, *Romance*.
ROBERT LEONARD, *The Divorcee*.
ERNST LUBITSCH, *The Love Parade*.
KING VIDOR, *Hallelujah*, MGM.

WRITING:
(Achievement)
THE BIG HOUSE. Frances Marion.
ALL QUIET ON THE WESTERN FRONT. George Abbott, Maxwell Anderson and Dell Andrews.
DISRAELI. Julian Josephson.
THE DIVORCEE. John Meehan.
STREET OF CHANCE, PAR. Howard Estabrook.
(Award discontinued after this year.)

CINEMATOGRAPHY:
WITH BYRD AT THE SOUTH POLE, PAR. Joseph T. Rucker and Willard Van Der Veer.
ALL QUIET ON THE WESTERN FRONT. Arthur Edeson.
ANNA CHRISTIE. William Daniels.
HELL'S ANGELS, UA. Gaetano Gaudio and Harry Perry.
THE LOVE PARADE. Victor Milner.

ART DIRECTION - SET DECORATION:
KING OF JAZZ, U. Herman Rosse.
BULLDOG DRUMMOND. William Cameron Menzies.
THE LOVE PARADE. Hans Dreier.
SALLY, FN. Jack Okey.
THE VAGABOND KING, PAR. Hans Dreier.

SOUND:
THE BIG HOUSE. Douglas Shearer.
THE CASE OF SERGEANT GRISCHA, RKO. John Tribby.
THE LOVE PARADE. Franklin Hansen.
RAFFLES, Goldwyn, UA. Oscar Lagerstrom.
SONG OF THE FLAME, FN. George Groves.

1930/31

BEST PICTURE:
CIMARRON, RKO.
EAST LYNNE, FOX.
THE FRONT PAGE, Caddo, UA.
SKIPPY, PAR.
TRADER HORN, MGM.

ACTOR:
LIONEL BARRYMORE, A Free Soul, MGM.
JACKIE COOPER, *Skippy*.
RICHARD DIX, *Cimarron*.
FREDRIC MARCH, *The Royal Family of Broadway*, PAR.
ADOLPHE MENJOU, *The Front Page*.

ACTRESS:
MARIE DRESSLER, Min And Bill, MGM.
MARLENE DIETRICH, *Morocco*, PAR.
IRENE DUNNE, *Cimarron*.
ANN HARDING, *Holiday*, RKO Pathe.
NORMA SHEARER, *A Free Soul*.

DIRECTING:
NORMAN TAUROG, Skippy.
CLARENCE BROWN, *A Free Soul*.
LEWIS MILESTONE, *The Front Page*.
WESLEY RUGGLES, *Cimarron*.
JOSEF VON STERNBERG, *Morocco*.

WRITING:
(Adaptation)
CIMARRON. Howard Estabrook.
THE CRIMINAL CODE, COL. Seton Miller and Fred Niblo, Jr.
HOLIDAY. Horace Jackson.
THE LITTLE CAESAR, WB. Francis Faragoh and Robert N. Lee.
SKIPPY. Joseph Mankiewicz and Sam Mintz.
(Original Story)
THE DAWN PATROL, WB.-FN. John Monk Saunders.
DOORWAY TO HELL, WB.-FN. Rowland Brown.
LAUGHTER, PAR. Harry d'Abbadie d'Arrast, Douglas Doty and Donald Ogden Stewart.
THE PUBLIC ENEMY, WB.-FN. John Bright and Kubec Glasmon.
SMART MONEY, WB.-FN. Lucien Hubbard and Joseph Jackson.

CINEMATOGRAPHY:
TABU, PAR. Floyd Crosby.
CIMARRON. Edward Cronjager.
MOROCCO. Lee Garmes.
THE RIGHT TO LOVE, PAR. Charles Lang.
SVENGALI, WB-FN. Barney "Chick" McGill.

ART DIRECTION - SET DECORATION:
CIMARRON. Max Ree.
JUST IMAGINE, FOX. Stephen Goosson and Ralph Hammeras.
MOROCCO. Hans Dreier.
SVENGALI. Anton Grot.
WHOOPEE, Goldwyn, UA. Richard Day.

SOUND:
PAR STUDIO SOUND DEPARTMENT.
MGM STUDIO SOUND DEPARTMENT.
RKO STUDIO SOUND DEPARTMENT.
SAMUEL GOLDWYN SOUND DEPARTMENT.

SCIENTIFIC OR TECHNICAL:
(Class I)
ELECTRICAL RESEARCH PRODUCTS, INC., RCA-PHOTOPHONE, INC., and RKO PICTURES, INC., for noise reduction recording equipment.
DuPONT FILM MANUFACTURING CORP. and EASTMAN KODAK CO. for super-sensitive panchromatic film.
(Class II)
FOX FILM CORP. for effective use of synchro-projection composite photography.
(Class III)
ELECTRICAL RESEARCH PRODUCTS, INC., for moving coil microphone transmitters.
RKO PICTURES, INC., for reflex type microphone concentrators.
RCA-PHOTOPHONE, INC., for ribbon microphone transmitters.

1931/32

BEST PICTURE:
GRAND HOTEL, MGM.
ARROWSMITH, Goldwyn, UA.
BAD GIRL, FOX.
THE CHAMP, MGM.
FIVE STAR FINAL, FN.
ONE HOUR WITH YOU, PAR.
SHANGHAI EXPRESS, PAR.
SMILING LIEUTENANT, PAR.

ACTOR:
WALLACE BEERY, The Champ.
FREDRIC MARCH, Dr. Jekyll And Mr. Hyde, PAR.
ALFRED LUNT, *The Guardsman,* MGM.

ACTRESS:
HELEN HAYES, The Sin Of Madelon Claudet, MGM.
MARIE DRESSLER, *Emma,* MGM.
LYNN FONTANNE, *The Guardsman.*

DIRECTING:
FRANK BORZAGE, Bad Girl.
KING VIDOR, *The Champ.*
JOSEF VON STERNBERG, *Shanghai Express.*

WRITING:
(Adaptation)
BAD GIRL. Edwin Burke.
ARROWSMITH. Sidney Howard.
DR. JEKYLL AND MR. HYDE. Percy Heath and Samuel Hoffenstein.
(Original Story)
THE CHAMP. Frances Marion.
LADY AND GENT, PAR. Grover Jones and William Slavens McNutt.
STAR WITNESS. Lucien Hubbard.
WHAT PRICE HOLLYWOOD, RKO. Adela Rogers St. John.

CINEMATOGRAPHY:
SHANGHAI EXPRESS. Lee Garmes.
ARROWSMITH. Ray June.
DR. JEKYLL AND MR. HYDE. Karl Struss.

ART DIRECTION - SET DECORATION:
TRANSATLANTIC, FOX. Gordon Wiles.
A NOUS LA LIBERTE, (French). Lazare Meerson.
ARROWSMITH. Richard Day.

SOUND:
PAR STUDIO SOUND DEPARTMENT.

SHORT FILMS:
(Cartoons)
FLOWERS AND TREES, Walt Disney, UA.
MICKEY'S ORPHANS, Walt Disney, COL.
IT'S GOT ME AGAIN, Leon Schlesinger, WB.
(Comedy)
THE MUSIC BOX, Hal Roach, MGM. (Laurel & Hardy)
THE LOUD MOUTH, Mack Sennett. EDU.
STOUT HEARTS AND WILLING HANDS, RKO. (Masquers Comedies)
(Novelty)
WRESTLING SWORDFISH, Mack Sennett, EDU. (Cannibals of The Deep)
SCREEN SOUVENIRS, PAR.
SWING HIGH, MGM. (Sport Champion)

HONORARY AND OTHER:
(Other)
WALT DISNEY for the creation of Mickey Mouse.

SCIENTIFIC OR TECHNICAL:
(Class II)
TECHNICOLOR MOTION PICTURE CORP. for their color cartoon process.
(Class III)
EASTMAN KODAK CO. for the Type II-B Sensitometer.

1932/33

BEST PICTURE:
CAVALCADE, FOX.
A FAREWELL TO ARMS, PAR.
FORTY-SECOND STREET, WB.
I AM A FUGITIVE FROM A CHAIN GANG, WB.
LADY FOR A DAY, COL.
LITTLE WOMEN, RKO.
THE PRIVATE LIFE OF HENRY VIII, London Films, UA (British).
SHE DONE HIM WRONG, PAR.
SMILIN' THRU, MGM.
STATE FAIR, FOX.

ACTOR:
CHARLES LAUGHTON, The Private Life Of Henry VIII.
LESLIE HOWARD, *Berkeley Square,* FOX.
PAUL MUNI, *I Am A Fugitive From A Chain Gang.*

ACTRESS:
KATHARINE HEPBURN, Morning Glory, RKO.
MAY ROBSON, *Lady For A Day.*
DIANA WYNYARD, *Cavalcade.*

DIRECTING:
FRANK LLOYD, Cavalcade.
FRANK CAPRA, *Lady For A Day.*
GEORGE CUKOR, *Little Women.*

WRITING:
(Adaptation)
LITTLE WOMEN. Victor Heerman and Sarah Y. Mason.
LADY FOR A DAY. Robert Riskin.
STATE FAIR. Paul Green and Sonya Levien.
(Original Story)
ONE WAY PASSAGE, WB. Robert Lord.
THE PRIZEFIGHTER AND THE LADY, MGM. Frances Marion.
RASPUTIN AND THE EMPRESS, MGM. Charles MacArthur.

CINEMATOGRAPHY:
A FAREWELL TO ARMS. Charles Bryant Lang, Jr.
REUNION IN VIENNA, MGM. George J. Folsey, Jr.
SIGN OF THE CROSS, PAR. Karl Struss.

ART DIRECTION - SET DECORATION:
CAVALCADE. William S. Darling.
A FAREWELL TO ARMS. Hans Dreier and Roland Anderson.
WHEN LADIES MEET, MGM. Cedric Gibbons.

SOUND:
A FAREWELL TO ARMS. Harold C. Lewis.
FORTY-SECOND STREET. Nathan Levinson.
GOLDDIGGERS of 1933. Nathan Levinson.
I AM A FUGITIVE FROM A CHAIN GANG. Nathan Levinson.

SHORT FILMS:
(Cartoons)
THE THREE LITTLE PIGS, Walt Disney, UA.
BUILDING A BUILDING, Walt Disney, UA.
THE MERRY OLD SOUL, Walter Lantz, U.
(Comedy)
SO THIS IS HARRIS, RKO. (Special)
MISTER MUGG, U. (Comedies)
PREFERRED LIST, RKO. (Headliner Series #5)
(Novelty)
KRAKATOA, EDU. (Three-reel Special)
MENU, Pete Smith, MGM. (Oddities)
THE SEA, EDU. (Battle For Life)

SCIENTIFIC OR TECHNICAL:
(Class II)
ELECTRICAL RESEARCH PRODUCTS, INC., for their wide range recording and reproducing system.
RCA-VICTOR CO., INC., for their high-fidelity recording and reproducing system.
(Class III)
FOX FILM CORP., FRED JACKMAN and WB PICTURES, INC., and SIDNEY SANDERS of RKO Studios, Inc., for their development and effective use of the translucent cellulose screen in composite photography.

ASSISTANT DIRECTOR:
CHARLES BARTON, PAR.
SCOTT BEAL, U.
CHARLES DORIAN, MGM.
FRED FOX, UA.
GORDON HOLLINGSHEAD, WB.
DEWEY STARKEY, RKO.
WILLIAM TUMMEL, FOX.
(Multiple award given this year only.)

1934

BEST PICTURE:
IT HAPPENED ONE NIGHT, COL.
THE BARRETTS OF WIMPOLE STREET, MGM.
CLEOPATRA, PAR.
FLIRTATION WALK, FN.
THE GAY DIVORCEE, RKO.
HERE COMES THE NAVY, WB.
THE HOUSE OF ROTHSCHILD, 20th Cent., UA.
IMITATION OF LIFE, U.
ONE NIGHT OF LOVE, COL.
THE THIN MAN, MGM.
VIVA VILLA, MGM.
THE WHITE PARADE, FOX.

ACTOR:
CLARK GABLE, It Happened One Night.
FRANK MORGAN, *Affairs Of Cellini*, FOX, UA.
WILLIAM POWELL, *The Thin Man*.

ACTRESS:
CLAUDETTE COLBERT, It Happened One Night.
GRACE MOORE, *One Night Of Love*.
NORMA SHEARER, *The Barretts Of Wimpole Street*.

DIRECTING:
FRANK CAPRA, It Happened One Night.
VICTOR SCHERTZINGER, *One Night Of Love*.
W. S. VAN DYKE, *The Thin Man*.

WRITING:
(Adaptation)
IT HAPPENED ONE NIGHT. Robert Riskin.
THE THIN MAN. Frances Goodrich and Albert Hackett.
VIVA VILLA. Ben Hecht.
(Original Story)
MANHATTAN MELODRAMA, MGM. Arthur Caesar.
HIDE-OUT, MGM. Mauri Grashin.
THE RICHEST GIRL IN THE WORLD, RKO. Norman Krasna.

CINEMATOGRAPHY:
CLEOPATRA. Victor Milner.
THE AFFAIRS OF CELLINI. Charles Rosher.
OPERATION 13, MGM. George Folsey.

ART DIRECTION - SET DECORATION:
THE MERRY WIDOW, MGM. Cedric Gibbons and Frederic Hope.
AFFAIRS OF CELLINI. Richard Day.
THE GAY DIVORCEE. Van Nest Polglase and Carroll Clark.

FILM EDITING:
ESKIMO, MGM. Conrad Nervig.
CLEOPATRA. Anne Bauchens.
ONE NIGHT OF LOVE. Gene Milford.

MUSIC - SCORING:
(Best Score)
ONE NIGHT OF LOVE. Louis Silvers, Head. Thematic music by Victor Schertzinger and Gus Kahn.
THE GAY DIVORCEE, RKO Music Dept. Max Steiner, Head. Score by Kenneth Webb and Samuel Hoffenstein.
THE LOST PATROL, RKO Music Dept. Max Steiner, Head. Score by Max Steiner.

MUSIC - BEST SONG:

THE CONTINENTAL, *The Gay Divorcee*, RKO. Music, Con Conrad. Lyrics, Herb Magidson.
CARIOCA, *Flying Down To Rio*, RKO. Music, Vincent Youmans. Lyrics, Edward Eliscu and Gus Kahn.
LOVE IN BLOOM, *She Loves Me Not*, PAR. Music, Ralph Rainger. Lyrics, Leo Robin.

SOUND:

ONE NIGHT OF LOVE. Paul Neal.
AFFAIRS OF CELLINI. Thomas T. Moulton.
CLEOPATRA. Franklin Hansen.
FLIRTATION WALK. Nathan Levinson.
THE GAY DIVORCEE. Carl Dreher.
IMITATION OF LIFE. Gilbert Kurland.
VIVA VILLA. Douglas Shearer.

SHORT FILMS:

(Cartoons)
THE TORTOISE AND THE HARE, Walt Disney.
HOLIDAY LAND, Charles Mintz, COL.
JOLLY LITTLE ELVES, U.
(Comedy)
LA CUCARACHA, RKO. (Special)
MEN IN BLACK, COL. (Broadway Comedies)
WHAT, NO MEN!, WB. (Broadway Brevities)
(Novelty)
CITY OF WAX, EDU. (Battle For Life)
BOSOM FRIENDS, EDU. (Treasure Chest)
STRIKES AND SPARES, MGM. (Oddities)

HONORARY AND OTHER:

(Other)
SHIRLEY TEMPLE, in grateful recognition of her outstanding contribution to screen entertainment during the year 1934.

SCIENTIFIC OR TECHNICAL:

(Class II)
ELECTRICAL RESEARCH PRODUCTS, INC., for their development of the vertical cut disc method of recording sound for motion pictures (hill and dale recording).
(Class III)
COL PICTURES CORP. for their application of the vertical cut disc method (hill and dale recording) to actual studio production, with their recording of the sound on the picture "One Night of Love".
BELL AND HOWELL CO. for their development of the Bell and Howell fully automatic sound and picture printer.

ASSISTANT DIRECTOR:

JOHN WATERS, Viva Villa.
SCOTT BEAL, *Imitation Of Life.*
CULLEN TATE, *Cleopatra.*

1935

BEST PICTURE:

MUTINY ON THE BOUNTY, MGM.
ALICE ADAMS, RKO.
BROADWAY MELODY OF 1936, MGM.
CAPTAIN BLOOD, WB.-Cosmopolitan.
DAVID COPPERFIELD, MGM.
THE INFORMER, RKO.
LES MISERABLES, 20th Cent., UA.
LIVES OF A BENGAL LANCER, PAR.
A MIDSUMMER NIGHT'S DREAM, WB.
NAUGHTY MARIETTA, MGM.
RUGGLES OF RED GAP, PAR.
TOP HAT, RKO,

ACTOR:

VICTOR McLAGLEN, The Informer.
CLARK GABLE, *Mutiny On The Bounty.*
CHARLES LAUGHTON, *Mutiny On The Bounty.*
FRANCHOT TONE, *Mutiny On The Bounty.*

ACTRESS:

BETTE DAVIS, Dangerous, WB.
ELISABETH BERGNER, *Escape Me Never*, British & Dominions, UA. (British)
CLAUDETTE COLBERT, *Private Worlds*, PAR.
KATHARINE HEPBURN, *Alice Adams.*
MIRIAM HOPKINS, *Becky Sharp*, Pioneer, RKO.
MERLE OBERON, *The Dark Angel*, Goldwyn, UA.

DIRECTING:

JOHN FORD, The Informer.
HENRY HATHAWAY, *Lives Of A Bengal Lancer.*
FRANK LLOYD, *Mutiny On The Bounty.*

WRITING:

(Original Story)
THE SCOUNDREL, PAR. Ben Hecht and Charles MacArthur.
BROADWAY MELODY OF 1936. Moss Hart.
THE GAY DECEPTION, Lasky, FOX. Don Hartman and Stephen Avery.
(Screenplay)
THE INFORMER. Dudley Nichols.
LIVES OF A BENGAL LANCER. Achmed Abdullah, John L. Balderston, Grover Jones, William Slavens McNutt and Waldemar Young.
MUTINY ON THE BOUNTY. Jules Furthman, Talbot Jennings and Carey Wilson.

CINEMATOGRAPHY:

A MIDSUMMER NIGHT'S DREAM. Hal Mohr.
BARBARY COAST, Goldwyn, UA. Ray June.
THE CRUSADES, PAR. Victor Milner.
LES MISERABLES. Gregg Toland.

ART DIRECTION - SET DECORATON:

THE DARK ANGEL. Richard Day.
LIVES OF A BENGAL LANCER. Hans Dreier and Roland Anderson.
TOP HAT. Carroll Clark and Van Nest Polglase.

FILM EDITING:

A MIDSUMMER NIGHT'S DREAM. Ralph Dawson.
DAVID COPPERFIELD. Robert J. Kern.
THE INFORMER. George Hively.
LES MISERABLES. Barbara McLean.
LIVES OF A BENGAL LANCER. Ellsworth Hoagland.
MUTINY ON THE BOUNTY. Margaret Booth.

MUSIC - SCORING:
(Best Score)

THE INFORMER, RKO Music Dept. Max Steiner, Head. Score by Max Steiner.
MUTINY ON THE BOUNTY, MGM Music Dept. Nat W. Finston, Head. Score by Herbert Stothart.
PETER IBBETSON, PAR Music Dept. Irvin Talbot, Head. Score by Ernst Toch.

MUSIC - BEST SONG:

LULLABY OF BROADWAY, Gold Diggers of 1935, WB. Music, Harry Warren. Lyrics, Al Dubin.
CHEEK TO CHEEK, *Top Hat*. Music and Lyrics by Irving Berlin.
LOVELY TO LOOK AT, *Roberta*, RKO. Music, Jerome Kern. Lyrics, Dorothy Fields and Jimmy McHugh.

SOUND:

NAUGHTY MARIETTA. Douglas Shearer.
THE BRIDE OF FRANKENSTEIN, U. Gilbert Kurland.
CAPTAIN BLOOD. Nathan Levinson.
THE DARK ANGEL. Goldwyn Sound Department. Thomas T. Moulton.
I DREAM TOO MUCH, RKO. Carl Dreher.
LIVES OF A BENGAL LANCER. Franklin Hansen.
LOVE ME FOREVER, COL. John Livadary.
ONE THOUSAND DOLLARS A MINUTE, REP. Republic Sound Department.
THANKS A MILLION, FOX. E. H. Hansen.

SHORT FILMS:
(Cartoons)

THREE ORPHAN KITTENS, Walt Disney, UA.
THE CALICO DRAGON, Harman-Ising, MGM.
WHO KILLED COCK ROBIN?, Walt Disney, UA.
(Comedy)
HOW TO SLEEP, MGM. (Miniature)
OH, MY NERVES, COL. (Broadway Comedies)
TIT FOR TAT, Hal Roach, MGM. (Laurel & Hardy)
(Novelty)
WINGS OVER MT. EVEREST, EDU. (Special)
AUDIOSCOPIKS, MGM. (Special)
CAMERA THRILLS, U. (Special)

HONORARY AND OTHER:
(Other)

DAVID WARK GRIFFITH, for his distinguished creative achievements as director and producer and his invaluable initiative and lasting contributions to the progress of the motion picture arts.

SCIENTIFIC OR TECHNICAL:
(Class II)

AGFA ANSCO CORP. for their development of the Agfa infra-red film.
EASTMAN KODAK CO. for their development of the Eastman Pola-Screen.
(Class III)
MGM STUDIO for the development of anti-directional negative and positive development by means of jet turbulation, and the application of the method to all negative and print processing of the entire product of a major producing company.
WILLIAM A. MUELLER of WB-FN Studio Sound Department for his method of dubbing, in which the level of the dialogue automatically controls the level of the accompanying music and sound effects.
MOLE-RICHARDSON CO. for their development of the "Solar-spot" spot lamps.
DOUGLAS SHEARER and MGM STUDIO SOUND DEPARTMENT for their automatic control system for cameras and sound recording machines and auxiliary stage equipment.
ELECTRICAL RESEARCH PRODUCTS, INC., for their study and development of equipment to analyze and measure flutter resulting from the travel of the film through the mechanisms used in the recording and reproduction of sound.
PARAMOUNT PRODUCTIONS, INC., for the design and construction of the PARAMOUNT transparency air turbine developing machine.
NATHAN LEVINSON, Director of Sound Recording for WB.-FN Studio, for the method of intercutting variable density and variable area sound tracks to secure an increase in the effective volume range of sound recorded for motion pictures.

ASSISTANT DIRECTOR:

CLEM BEAUCHAMP, Lives Of A Bengal Lancer.
PAUL WING, Lives Of A Bengal Lancer.
ERIC STACEY, *Les Miserables*.
JOSEPH NEWMAN, *David Copperfield*.

DANCE DIRECTION:

DAVE GOULD, "I've Got A Feeling You're Fooling" number, Broadway Melody Of 1936. "Straw Hat" number, Folies Bergere, 20th Cent, UA.
BUSBY BERKELEY, "Lullaby Of Broadway" number, and "The Words Are In My Heart" number, *Gold Diggers Of 1935*, WB.
BOBBY CONNOLLY, "Latin From Manhattan" number, *Go Into Your Dance*, WB. "Playboy From Paree" number, *Broadway Hostess*, WB.
SAMMY LEE, "Lovely Lady" number, and "Too Good To Be True" number, *King Of Burlesque*, FOX.
HERMES PAN for "Piccolino" number, and "Top Hat" number, *Top Hat*.
LEROY PRINZ, "Elephant Number -- It's The Animal In Me", *Big Broadcast Of 1936*, PAR. "Viennese Waltz" number, *All The King's Horses*, PAR.
B. ZEMACH, "Hall Of Kings" number, *She*, RKO.

1936

BEST PICTURE:

THE GREAT ZIEGFELD, MGM.
ANTHONY ADVERSE, WB.
DODSWORTH, Goldwyn, UA.
LIBELED LADY, MGM.
MR. DEEDS GOES TO TOWN, COL.
ROMEO AND JULIET, MGM.
SAN FRANCISCO, MGM.
THE STORY OF LOUIS PASTEUR, WB.
A TALE OF TWO CITIES, MGM.
THREE SMART GIRLS, U.

ACTOR:

PAUL MUNI, The Story Of Louis Pasteur.
GARY COOPER, *Mr. Deeds Goes To Town*.
WALTER HOUSTON, *Dodsworth*.
WILLIAM POWELL, *My Man Godfrey*, U.
SPENCER TRACY, *San Francisco*.

ACTRESS:

LUISE RAINER, The Great Ziegfeld.
IRENE DUNNE, *Theodora Goes Wild*, COL.
GLADYS GEORGE, *Valiant Is The Word For Carrie*, PAR.
CAROLE LOMBARD, *My Man Godfrey*.
NORMA SHEARER, *Romeo And Juliet*.

SUPPORTING ACTOR:

WALTER BRENNAN, Come And Get It, Goldwyn, UA.
MISCHA AUER, *My Man Godfrey*.
STUART ERWIN, *Pigskin Parade*, FOX.
BASIL RATHBONE, *Romeo And Juliet*.
AKIM TAMIROFF, *The General Died At Dawn*, PAR.

SUPPORTING ACTRESS:
GALE SONDERGAARD, Anthony Adverse.
BEULAH BONDI, *The Gorgeous Hussy*, MGM.
ALICE BRADY, *My Man Godfrey.*
BONITA GRANVILLE, *These Three*, Goldwyn, UA.
MARIA OUSPENSKAYA, *Dodsworth.*

DIRECTING:
FRANK CAPRA, Mr. Deeds Goes To Town.
GREGORY LACAVA, *My Man Godfrey.*
ROBERT Z. LEONARD, *The Great Ziegfeld.*
W. S. VAN DYKE, *San Francisco.*
WILLIAM WYLER, *Dodsworth.*

WRITING:
(Original Story)
THE STORY OF LOUIS PASTEUR. Pierre Collings and Sheridan Gibney.
FURY, MGM. Norman Krasna.
THE GREAT ZIEGFELD. William Anthony McGuire.
SAN FRANCISCO. Robert Hopkins.
THREE SMART GIRLS. Adele Commandini.

(Screenplay)
THE STORY OF LOUIS PASTEUR. Pierre Collings and Sheridan Gibney.
AFTER THE THIN MAN, MGM. Frances Goodrich and Albert Hackett.
DODSWORTH. Sidney Howard.
MR. DEEDS GOES TO TOWN. Robert Riskin.
MY MAN GODFREY. Eric Hatch and Morris Ryskind.

CINEMATOGRAPHY:
ANTHONY ADVERSE. Gaetano Gaudio.
THE GENERAL DIED AT DAWN, PAR. Victor Milner.
THE GORGEOUS HUSSEY. George Folsey.

ART DIRECTION - SET DECORATION:
DODSWORTH. Richard Day.
ANTHONY ADVERSE. Anton Grot.
THE GREAT ZIEGFELD. Cedric Gibbons, Eddie Imazu and Edwin B. Willis.
LLOYDS OF LONDON, FOX. William S. Darling.
THE MAGNIFICENT BRUTE, U. Albert S. D'Agostino and Jack Otterson.
ROMEO AND JULIET. Cedric Gibbons, Frederic Hope and Edwin B. Willis.
WINTERSET, RKO. Perry Ferguson.

FILM EDITING:
ANTHONY ADVERSE. Ralph Dawson.
COME AND GET IT. Edward Curtiss.
THE GREAT ZIEGFELD. William S. Gray.
LLOYDS OF LONDON. Barbara McLean.
A TALE OF TWO CITIES. Conrad A. Nervig.
THEODORA GOES WILD. Otto Meyer.

MUSIC - SCORING:
(Best Score)
ANTHONY ADVERSE, WB Music Dept. Leo Forbstein, Head. Score by Erich Wolfgang Korngold.
THE CHARGE OF THE LIGHT BRIGADE, WB Music Dept. Leo Forbstein, Head. Score by Max Steiner.
THE GARDEN OF ALLAH, Selznick Int'l Pictures Music Dept. Max Steiner, Head. Score by Max Steiner.
THE GENERAL DIED AT DAWN, PAR Music Dept. Boris Morros, Head. Score by Werner Janssen.
WINTERSET, RKO Music Dept. Nathaniel Shilkret, Head. Score by Nathaniel Shilkret.

MUSIC - BEST SONG:
THE WAY YOU LOOK TONIGHT, Swing Time, RKO. Music, Jerome Kern. Lyrics, Dorothy Fields.
DID I REMEMBER, *Suzy*, MGM. Music, Walter Donaldson. Lyrics, Harold Adamson.
I'VE GOT YOU UNDER MY SKIN, *Born To Dance*, MGM. Music and Lyrics by Cole Porter.
A MELODY FROM THE SKY, *Trail of The Lonesome Pine*, PAR. Music, Louis Alter. Lyrics, Sidney Mitchell.
PENNIES FROM HEAVEN, *Pennies From Heaven*, COL. Music, Arthur Johnston. Lyrics, Johnny Burke.
WHEN DID YOU LEAVE HEAVEN, *Sing Baby Sing*, FOX. Music, Richard A. Whiting. Lyrics, Walter Bullock.

SOUND:
SAN FRANCISCO. Douglas Shearer.
BANJO ON MY KNEE, FOX. E. H. Hansen.
THE CHARGE OF THE LIGHT BRIGADE. Nathan Levinson.
DODSWORTH. Oscar Lagerstrom.
GENERAL SPANKY, Roach, MGM. Elmer A. Raguse.
MR. DEEDS GOES TO TOWN. John Livadary.
THE TEXAS RANGERS, PAR. Franklin Hansen.
THAT GIRL FROM PARIS, RKO. J. O. Aalberg.
THREE SMART GIRLS. Homer G. Tasker.

SHORT FILMS:
(Cartoons)
COUNTRY COUSIN, Walt Disney, UA.
OLD MILL POND, Harman-Ising, MGM.
SINBAD THE SAILOR, PAR.

(One-reel)
BORED OF EDUCATION, Hal Roach, MGM. (Our Gang)
MOSCOW MOODS, PAR. (Headliners)
WANTED, A MASTER, Pete Smith, MGM (Pete Smith Specialties)

(Two-reel)
THE PUBLIC PAYS, MGM. (Crime Doesn't Pay)
DOUBLE OR NOTHING, WB. (Broadway Brevities)
DUMMY ACHE, RKO. (Edgar Kennedy Comedies)

(Color)
GIVE ME LIBERTY, WB. (Broadway Brevities)
LA FIESTA DE SANTA BARBARA, MGM. (Musical Revues)
POPULAR SCIENCE J-6-2, PAR.

HONORARY AND OTHER:
(Other)
MARCH OF TIME for its significance to motion pictures and for having revolutionized one of the most important branches of the industry - the newsreel.
W. HOWARD GREENE and HAROLD ROSSON for the color cinematography of the Selznick Int'l Production, The Garden Of Allah.

SCIENTIFIC OR TECHNICAL:
(Class I)
DOUGLAS SHEARER and the MGM STUDIO SOUND DEPARTMENT for the development of a practical two-way horn system and a biased Class A push-pull recording system.

(Class II)
E. C. WENTE and the BELL TELEPHONE LABORATORIES for their multi-cellular high-frequency horn and receiver.
RCA MANUFACTURING CO., INC., for their rotary stabilizer sound head.

(Class III)
RCA MANUFACTURING CO., INC., for their development of a method of recording and printing sound records utilizing a restricted spectrum (known as ultra-violet light recording).
ELECTRICAL RESEARCH PRODUCTS, INC., for the ERPI "Type Q" portable recording channel.
RCA MANUFACTURING CO., INC., for furnishing a practical design and specifications for a non-slip printer.

UA STUDIO CORP. for the development of a practical, efficient and quiet wind machine.

ASSISTANT DIRECTOR:
JACK SULLIVAN, The Charge Of The Light Brigade.
CLEM BEAUCHAMP, *Last Of The Mohicans,* Reliance, UA.
WILLIAM CANNON, *Anthony Adverse.*
JOSEPH NEWMAN, *San Francisco.*
ERIC G. STACEY, *Garden Of Allah.*

DANCE DIRECTION:
SEYMOUR FELIX, "A Pretty Girl Is Like A Melody", number The Great Ziegfeld.
BUSBY BERKELEY, "Love And War" number, *Gold Diggers Of 1937,* WB.
BOBBY CONNOLLY, "1000 Love Songs" number, *Cain And Mabel,* WB.
DAVE GOULD, "Swingin' The Jinx" number, *Born To Dance.*
JACK HASKELL, "Skating Ensemble" number, *One In A Million,* FOX.
RUSSELL LEWIS, "The Finale" number, *Dancing Pirate,* RKO.
HERMES PAN, "Bo Jangles" number, *Swing Time.*

1937

BEST PICTURE:
THE LIFE OF EMILE ZOLA, WB.
THE AWFUL TRUTH, COL.
CAPTAINS COURAGEOUS, MGM.
DEAD END, Goldwyn, UA.
THE GOOD EARTH, MGM.
IN OLD CHICAGO, FOX.
LOST HORIZON, COL.
100 MEN AND A GIRL, U.
STAGE DOOR, RKO.
A STAR IS BORN, Selznick Int'l, UA.

ACTOR:
SPENCER TRACY, Captains Courageous.
CHARLES BOYER, *Conquest,* MGM.
FREDRIC MARCH, *A Star Is Born.*
ROBERT MONTGOMERY, *Night Must Fall,* MGM.
PAUL MUNI, *The Life Of Emile Zola.*

ACTRESS:
LUISE RAINER, The Good Earth.
IRENE DUNNE, *The Awful Truth.*
GRETA GARBO, *Camille,* MGM.
JANET GAYNOR, *A Star Is Born.*
BARBARA STANWYCK, *Stella Dallas,* Goldwyn, UA.

SUPPORTING ACTOR:
JOSEPH SCHILDKRAUT, The Life Of Emile Zola.
RALPH BELLAMY, *The Awful Truth.*
THOMAS MITCHELL, *Hurricane,* Goldwyn, UA.
H. B. WARNER, *Lost Horizon.*
ROLAND YOUNG, *Topper,* Roach, MGM.

SUPPORTING ACTRESS:
ALICE BRADY, In Old Chicago.
ANDREA LEEDS, *Stage Door.*
ANNE SHIRLEY, *Stella Dallas.*
CLAIRE TREVOR, *Dead End.*
DAME MAY WHITTY, *Night Must Fall.*

DIRECTING:
LEO McCAREY, The Awful Truth.
WILLIAM DIETERLE, *The Life Of Emile Zola.*
SIDNEY FRANKLIN, *The Good Earth.*
GREGORY LACAVA, *Stage Door.*
WILLIAM WELLMAN, *A Star Is Born.*

WRITING:
(Original Story)
A STAR IS BORN. William A. Wellman and Robert Carson.
BLACK LEGION, WB. Robert Lord.
IN OLD CHICAGO. Niven Busch.
THE LIFE OF EMILE ZOLA. Heinz Herald and Geza Herczeg.
100 MEN AND A GIRL. Hans Kraly.
(Screenplay)
THE LIFE OF EMILE ZOLA. Heinz Herald, Geza Herczeg and Norman Reilly Raine.
THE AWFUL TRUTH. Vina Delmar.
CAPTAINS COURAGEOUS. Marc Connolly, John Lee Mahin and Dale Van Every.
STAGE DOOR. Morris Ryskind and Anthony Veiller.
A STAR IS BORN. Alan Campbell, Robert Carson and Dorothy Parker.

CINEMATOGRAPHY:
THE GOOD EARTH. Karl Freund.
DEAD END. Gregg Toland.
WINGS OVER HONOLULU. U. Joseph Valentine.

ART DIRECTION - SET DECORATION:
LOST HORIZON. Stephen Goosson.
CONQUEST. Cedric Gibbons and William Horning.
A DAMSEL IN DISTRESS, RKO. Carroll Clark.
DEAD END. Richard Day.
EVERY DAY'S A HOLIDAY, Major Prods., PAR. Wiard Ihnen.
THE LIFE OF EMILE ZOLA. Anton Grot.
MANHATTAN MERRY-GO-ROUND, REP. John Victor Mackay.
THE PRISONER OF ZENDA, Selznick, UA. Lyle Wheeler.
SOULS AT SEA, PAR. Hans Dreier and Roland Anderson.
VOGUES OF 1938, Wanger. UA. Alexander Toluboff.
WEE WILLIE WINKIE, FOX. William S. Darling and David Hall.
YOU'RE A SWEETHEART, U. Jack Otterson.

FILM EDITING:
LOST HORIZON. Gene Havlick and Gene Milford.
THE AWFUL TRUTH. Al Clark.
CAPTAINS COURAGEOUS. Elmo Vernon.
THE GOOD EARTH. Basil Wrangell.
100 MEN AND A GIRL. Bernard W. Burton.

MUSIC - SCORING:
(Best Score)
100 MEN AND A GIRL, U Music Dept. Charles Previn, Head. No composer credit.
HURRICANE, Samuel Goldwyn Music Dept. Alfred Newman, Head. Score by Alfred Newman.
IN OLD CHICAGO, FOX Music Dept. Louis Silvers, Head. No composer credit.
THE LIFE OF EMILE ZOLA, WB. Music Dept. Leo Forbstein, Head. Score by Max Steiner.
LOST HORIZON, COL Music Dept. Morris Stoloff, Head. Score by Dimitri Tiomkin.
MAKE A WISH, Principal Productions. Dr. Hugo Riesenfeld, Musical Director. Score by Dr. Hugo Riesenfeld.
MAYTIME, MGM Music Dept. Nat W. Finston, Head. Score by Herbert Stothart.
PORTIA ON TRIAL, REP Music Dept. Alberto Colombo, Head. Score by Alberto Colombo.
THE PRISONER OF ZENDA, Selznick Int'l Pictures Music Dept. Alfred Newman, Musical Director. Score by Alfred Newman.

QUALITY STREET, RKO Music Dept. Roy Webb, Musical Director. Score by Roy Webb.
SNOW WHITE AND THE SEVEN DWARFS, Walt Disney Music Dept. Leigh Harline, Head. Score by Frank Churchill, Leigh Harline and Paul J. Smith.
SOMETHING TO SING ABOUT, GN Music Dept. C. Bakaleinikoff, Musical Director. Score by Victor Schertzinger.
SOULS AT SEA, PAR Music Dept. Boris Morros, Head. Score by W. Franke Harling and Milan Roder.
WAY OUT WEST, Hal Roach Music Dept. Marvin Hatley, Head. Score by Marvin Hatley.
(through 1937, this was a Music Achievement Award and presented to department head
instead of to the composer).

MUSIC - BEST SONG:

SWEET LEILANI, Waikiki Wedding, PAR. Music and Lyrics by Harry Owens.
REMEMBER ME, *Mr. Dodd Takes The Air*, WB. Music, Harry Warren. Lyrics, Al Dubin.
THAT OLD FEELING, *Vogues Of 1938*. Music, Sammy Fain. Lyrics, Lew Brown.
THEY CAN'T TAKE THAT AWAY FROM ME, *Shall We Dance*, RKO. Music, George Gershwin. Lyrics, Ira Gershwin.
WHISPERS IN THE DARK, *Artists and Models*, PAR. Music, Frederick Hollander. Lyrics, Leo Robin.

SOUND:

THE HURRICANE. Thomas Moulton.
THE GIRL SAID NO, GN. A. E. Kaye.
HITTING A NEW HIGH, RKO. John Aalberg.
IN OLD CHICAGO. E. H. Hansen.
THE LIFE OF EMILE ZOLA. Nathan Levinson.
LOST HORIZON. John Livadary.
MAYTIME, MGM. Douglas Shearer.
100 MEN AND A GIRL. Homer Tasker.
TOPPER. Elmer Raguse.
WELLS FARGO, PAR. L. L. Ryder.

SHORT FILMS:

(Cartoons)
THE OLD MILL, Walt Disney, RKO.
EDUCATED FISH, PAR.
THE LITTLE MATCH GIRL, Charles Mintz, COL.
(One-reel)
PRIVATE LIFE OF THE GANNETS, EDU.
A NIGHT AT THE MOVIES, MGM. (Robert Benchley)
ROMANCE OF RADIUM, Pete Smith, MGM. (Pete Smith Specialties)
(Two-reels)
TORTURE MONEY, MGM. (Crime Doesn't Pay)
DEEP SOUTH, RKO. (Radio Musical Comedies)
SHOULD WIVES WORK, RKO. (Leon Errol Comedies)
(Color)
PENNY WISDOM, Pete Smith, MGM. (Pete Smith Specialties)
THE MAN WITHOUT A COUNTRY, WB. (Broadway Brevities)
POPULAR SCIENCE J-7-1, PAR.

HONORARY AND OTHER:

(Irving G. Thalberg Memorial Award)
Darryl F. Zanuck
(Other)
MACK SENNETT, "for his lasting contribution to the comedy technique of the screen, the basic principles of which are as important today as when they were first put into practice, the Academy presents a Special Award to that master of fun, discoverer of stars, sympathetic, kindly, understanding comedy genius - Mack Sennett."
EDGAR BERGEN for his outstanding comedy creation, Charlie McCarthy.
THE MUSEUM OF MODERN ART FILM LIBRARY for its significant work in collecting films dating from 1895 to the present and for the first time making available to the public the means of studying the historical and aesthetic development of the motion picture as one of the major arts.
W. HOWARD GREENE for the color photography of A Star Is Born. (This Award was recommended by a committee of leading cinematographers after viewing all the color pictures made during the year.)

SCIENTIFIC OR TECHNICAL:

(Class I)
AGFA ANSCO CORP. for Agfa Supreme and Agfa Ultra Speed pan motion picture negatives.
(Class II)
WALT DISNEY PRODS., LTD., for the design and application to production of the Multi-Plane Camera.
EASTMAN KODAK CO. for two fine-grain duplicating film stocks.
FARCIOT EDOUART and PARAMOUNT PICTURES, INC., for the development of the PARAMOUNT dual screen transparency camera setup.
DOUGLAS SHEARER and the MGM STUDIO SOUND DEPARTMENT for a method of varying the scanning width of variable density sound tracks (squeeze tracks) for the purpose of obtaining an increased amount of noise reduction.
(Class III)
JOHN ARNOLD and the MGM STUDIO CAMERA DEPARTMENT for their improvement of the semi-automatic follow focus device and its application to all of the cameras used by the MGM Studio.
JOHN LIVADARY, Director of Sound Recording for Columbia Pictures Corp. for the application of the bi-planar light valve to motion picture sound recording.
THOMAS T. MOULTON and the UNITED ARTISTS STUDIO SOUND DEPARTMENT for the application to motion picture sound recording of volume indicators which have peak reading response and linear decibel scales.
RCA MANUFACTURING CO., INC., for the introduction of the modulated high-frequency method of determining optimum photographic processing conditions for variable width sound tracks.
JOSEPH E. ROBBINS and PARAMOUNT PICTURES, INC., for an exceptional application of acoustic principles to the sound proofing of gasoline generators and water pumps.
DOUGLAS SHEARER and the MGM STUDIO SOUND DEPARTMENT for the design of the film drive mechanism as incorporated in the ERPI 1010 reproducer.

ASSISTANT DIRECTOR:

ROBERT WEBB, In Old Chicago.
C. C. COLEMAN, JR., *Lost Horizon*.
RUSS SAUNDERS, *The Life Of Emile Zola*.
ERIC STACEY, *A Star Is Born*.
HAL WALKER, *Souls At Sea*.
(Award discontinued after this year.)

DANCE DIRECTION:

HERMES PAN, "Fun House" number, Damsel In Distress.
BUSBY BERKELEY, "The Finale" number, *Varsity Show*, WB.
BOBBY CONNOLLY, "Too Marvelous For Words" number, *Ready, Willing And Able*, WB.
DAVE GOULD, "All God's Children Got Rhythm" number, *A Day At The Races*, MGM.
SAMMY LEE, "Swing Is Here To Stay" number, *Ali Baba Goes To Town*, FOX.
HARRY LOSEE, "Prince Igor Suite" number, *Thin Ice*, FOX.
LEROY PRINZ, "Luau" number, *Waikiki Wedding*.
(Award discontinued after this year).

1938

BEST PICTURE:
YOU CAN'T TAKE IT WITH YOU, COL.
THE ADVENTURES OF ROBIN HOOD, WB.
ALEXANDER'S RAGTIME BAND, FOX.
BOYS TOWN, MGM.
THE CITADEL, MGM (British).
FOUR DAUGHTERS, WB.-FN.
GRAND ILLUSION, R.A.O., World Pictures (French).
JEZEBEL, WB.
PYGMALION, MGM. (British)
TEST PILOT, MGM.

ACTOR:
SPENCER TRACY, Boys Town.
CHARLES BOYER, *Algiers*, Wanger, UA.
JAMES CAGNEY, *Angels With Dirty Faces*, WB.
ROBERT DONAT, *The Citadel.*
LESLIE HOWARD, *Pygmalion.*

ACTRESS:
BETTE DAVIS, Jezebel.
FAY BAINTER, *White Banners*, WB.
WENDY HILLER, *Pygmalion.*
NORMA SHEARER, *Marie Antoinette*, MGM.
MARGARET SULLAVAN, *Three Comrades*, MGM.

SUPPORTING ACTOR:
WALTER BRENNAN, Kentucky, FOX.
JOHN GARFIELD, *Four Daughters.*
GENE LOCKHART, *Algiers.*
ROBERT MORLEY, *Marie Antoinette.*
BASIL RATHBONE, *If I Were King*, PAR.

SUPPORTING ACTRESS:
FAY BAINTER, Jezebel.
BEULAH BONDI, *Of Human Hearts*, MGM.
BILLIE BURKE, *Merrily We Live*, Roach, MGM.
SPRING BYINGTON, *You Can't Take It With You.*
MILIZA KORJUS, *The Great Waltz*, MGM.

DIRECTING:
FRANK CAPRA, You Can't Take It With You.
MICHAEL CURTIZ, *Angels With Dirty Faces.*
MICHAEL CURTIZ, *Four Daughters.*
NORMAN TAUROG, *Boys Town.*
KING VIDOR, *The Citadel.*

WRITING:
(Adaptation)
PYGMALION. Ian Dalrymple, Cecil Lewis and W. P. Lipscomb.
(Original Story)
BOYS TOWN. Eleanore Griffin and Dore Schary.
ALEXANDER'S RAGTIME BAND, FOX. Irving Berlin.
ANGELS WITH DIRTY FACES. Rowland Brown.
BLOCKADE, Wanger, UA. John Howard Lawson.
MAD ABOUT MUSIC, U. Marcella Burke and Frederick Kohner.
TEST PILOT. Frank Wead.
(Screenplay)
PYGMALION. George Bernard Shaw.
BOYS TOWN. John Meehan and Dore Schary.
THE CITADEL. Ian Dalrymple, Elizabeth Hill and Frank Wead.
FOUR DAUGHTERS. Lenore Coffee and Julius J. Epstein.
YOU CAN'T TAKE IT WITH YOU. Robert Riskin.

CINEMATOGRAPHY:
THE GREAT WALTZ. Joseph Ruttenberg.
ALGIERS. James Wong Howe.
ARMY GIRL, REP. Ernest Miller and Harry Wild.
THE BUCCANEER, PAR. Victor Milner.
JEZEBEL. Ernest Haller.
MAD ABOUT MUSIC. Joseph Valentine.
MERRILY WE LIVE. Norbert Brodine.
SUEZ, FOX. Peverell Marley.
VIVACIOUS LADY, RKO. Robert de Grasse.
YOU CAN'T TAKE IT WWTH YOU. Joseph Walker.
THE YOUNG IN HEART, Selznick, UA. Leon Shamroy.

ART DIRECTION - SET DECORATION:
ADVENTURES OF ROBIN HOOD. Carl J. Weyl.
ADVENTURES OF TOM SAWYER, Selznick, UA. Lyle Wheeler.
ALEXANDER'S RAGTIME BAND. Bernard Herzbrun and Boris Leven.
ALGIERS. Alexander Toluboff.
CAREFREE, RKO. Van Nest Polglase.
HOLIDAY, COL. Stephen Goosson and Lionel Banks.
IF I WERE KING. Hans Dreier and John Goodman.
MAD ABOUT MUSIC. Jack Otterson.
MARIE ANTOINETTE. Cedric Gibbons.
MERRILY WE LIVE. Charles D. Hall.

FILM EDITING:
THE ADVENTURES OF ROBIN HOOD. Ralph Dawson.
ALEXANDER'S RAGTIME BAND. Barbara McLean.
THE GREAT WALTZ. Tom Held.
TEST PILOT. Tom Held.
YOU CAN'T TAKE IT WITH YOU. Gene Havlick.

MUSIC - SCORING:
(Best Score)
ALEXANDER'S RAGTIME BAND. Alfred Newman.
CAREFREE, Victor Baravalle.
GIRLS SCHOOL, COL. Morris Stoloff and Gregory Stone.
GOLDWYN FOLLIES, Goldwyn, UA. Alfred Newman.
JEZEBEL. Max Steiner.
MAD ABOUT MUSIC. Charles Previn and Frank Skinner.
STORM OVER BENGAL, REP. Cy Feuer.
SWEETHEARTS, MGM. Herbert Stothart.
THERE GOES MY HEART, Hal Roach, UA. Marvin Hatley.
TROPIC HOLIDAY, PAR. Boris Morros.
THE YOUNG IN HEART. Franz Waxman.
(Original Score)
THE ADVENTURES OF ROBIN HOOD. Erich Wolfgang Korngold.
ARMY GIRL. Victor Young.
BLOCKADE. Werner Janssen.
BLOCKHEADS, Hal Roach, UA. Marvin Hatley.
BREAKING THE ICE, RKO. Victor Young.
THE COWBOY AND THE LADY, Goldwyn, UA. Alfred Newman.
IF I WERE KING. Richard Hageman.
MARIE ANTOINETTE. Herbert Stothart.
PACIFIC LINER, RKO. Russell Bennett.
SUEZ. Louis Silvers.
THE YOUNG IN HEART. Franz Waxman.

MUSIC - BEST SONG:
THANKS FOR THE MEMORY, Big Broadcast Of 1938, PAR. Music, Ralph Rainger. Lyrics, Leo Robin.
ALWAYS AND ALWAYS, *Mannequin*, MGM. Music, Edward Ward. Lyrics, Chet Forrest and Bob Wright.
CHANGE PARTNERS AND DANCE WITH ME, *Carefree*. Music and Lyrics by Irving Berlin.
COWBOY AND THE LADY, *The Cowboy And The Lady.* Music, Lionel Newman. Lyrics, Arthur Quenzer.
DUST, *Under Western Stars*, REP. Music and Lyrics by Johnny Marvin.
JEEPERS CREEPERS, *Going Places*, WB. Music, Harry Warren. Lyrics, Johnny Mercer.
MERRILY WE LIVE, *Merrily We Live.* Music, Phil Craig. Lyrics, Arthur

Quenzer.
A MIST OVER THE MOON, *The Lady Objects,* COL. Music, Ben Oakland. Lyrics, Oscar Hammerstein II.
MY OWN, *That Certain Age,* U. Music, Jimmy McHugh. Lyrics, Harold Adamson.
NOW IT CAN BE TOLD, *Alexander's Ragtime Band.* Music and Lyrics by Irving Berlin.

SOUND:
THE COWBOY AND THE LADY. Thomas Moulton.
ARMY GIRL. Charles Lootens.
FOUR DAUGHTERS. Nathan Levinson.
IF I WERE KING. L. L. Ryder.
MERRILY WE LIVE. Elmer Raguse.
SWEETHEARTS. Douglas Shearer.
SUEZ. Edmund Hansen.
THAT CERTAIN AGE, U. Bernard B. Brown.
VIVACIOUS LADY. James Wilkinson.
YOU CAN'T TAKE IT WITH YOU. John Livadary.

SHORT FILMS:
(Cartoons)
FERDINAND THE BULL, Walt Disney, RKO.
BRAVE LITTLE TAILOR, Walt Disney, RKO.
MOTHER GOOSE GOES HOLLYWOOD, Walt Disney, RKO.
GOOD SCOUTS, Walt Disney, RKO.
HUNKY AND SPUNKY, PAR.
(One-reel)
THAT MOTHERS MIGHT LIVE, MGM (Miniature)
THE GREAT HEART, MGM. (Miniature)
TIMBER TOPPERS, FOX. (Ed Thorgensen-Sports)
(Two-reel)
DECLARATION OF INDEPENDENCE, WB. (Historical Featurette)
SWINGTIME IN THE MOVIES, WB. (Broadway Brevities)
THEY'RE ALWAYS CAUGHT, MGM. (Crime Doesn't Pay)

HONORARY AND OTHER:
(Irving G. Thalberg Memorial Award)
Hal B. Wallis
(Other)
DEANNA DURBIN and MICKEY ROONEY for their significant contribution in bringing to the screen the spirit and personification of youth, and as juvenile players setting a high standard of ability and achievement.
HARRY M. WARNER in recognition of patriotic service in the production of historical short subjects presenting significant episodes in the early struggle of the American people for liberty.
WALT DISNEY, Snow White And The Seven Dwarfs, recognized as a significant screen innovation which has charmed millions and pioneered a great new entertainment field for the motion picture cartoon.
OLIVER MARSH and ALLEN DAVEY for the color cinematography of the MGM production, Sweethearts. (plaques)
For outstanding achievement in creating Special Photographic and Sound Effects in the PAR production, Spawn Of The North. Special Effects by GORDON JENNINGS, assisted by JAN DOMELA, DEV JENNINGS, IRMIN ROBERTS and ART SMITH. Transparencies by FARCIOT EDOUART, assisted by LOYAL GRIGGS. Sound Effects by LOREN RYDER, assisted by HARRY MILLS, LOUIS H. MESENKOP and WALTER OBERST.
J. ARTHUR BALL for his outstanding contributions to the advancement of color in Motion Picture Photography.

SCIENTIFIC OR TECHNICAL:
(Class III)
JOHN AALBERG and the RKO STUDIO SOUND DEPARTMENT for the application of compression to variable area recording in motion picture production.
BYRON HASKIN and the SPECIAL EFFECTS DEPARTMENT of WB STUDIO for pioneering the development and for the first practical application to motion picture production of the triple head background projector.

1939

BEST PICTURE:
GONE WITH THE WIND, Selznick, MGM.
DARK VICTORY, WB.
GOODBYE, MR. CHIPS, MGM (British).
LOVE AFFAIR, RKO.
MR. SMITH GOES TO WASHINGTON, COL.
NINOTCHKA, MGM.
OF MICE AND MEN, Roach, UA.
STAGECOACH, Wanger, UA.
WIZARD OF OZ, MGM.
WUTHERING HEIGHTS, Goldwyn, UA.

ACTOR:
ROBERT DONAT, Goodbye, Mr. Chips.
CLARK GABLE, *Gone With The Wind.*
LAURENCE OLIVIER, *Wuthering Heights.*
MICKEY ROONEY, *Babes In Arms,* MGM.
JAMES STEWART, *Mr. Smith Goes To Washington.*

ACTRESS:
VIVIEN LEIGH, Gone With The Wind.
BETTE DAVIS, *Dark Victory.*
IRENE DUNNE, *Love Affair.*
GRETA GARBO, *Ninotchka.*
GREER GARSON, *Goodbye, Mr. Chips.*

SUPPORTING ACTOR:
THOMAS MITCHELL, Stagecoach.
BRIAN AHERNE, *Juarez,* WB.
HARRY CAREY, *Mr. Smith Goes To Washington.*
BRIAN DONLEVY, *Beau Geste,* PAR.
CLAUDE RAINS, *Mr. Smith Goes To Washington.*

SUPPORTING ACTRESS:
HATTIE McDANIEL, Gone With The Wind.
OLIVIA DE HAVILLAND, *Gone With The Wind.*
GERALDINE FITZGERALD, *Wuthering Heights.*
EDNA MAY OLIVER, *Drums Along The Mohawk,* FOX.
MARIA OUSPENSKAYA, *Love Affair.*

DIRECTING:
VICTOR FLEMING, Gone With The Wind.
FRANK CAPRA, *Mr. Smith Goes To Washington.*
JOHN FORD, *Stagecoach.*
SAM WOOD, *Goodbye, Mr. Chips.*
WILLIAM WYLER, *Wuthering Heights.*

WRITING:
(Original Story)
MR. SMITH GOES TO WASHINGTON. Lewis R. Foster.
BACHELOR MOTHER, RKO. Felix Jackson.
LOVE AFFAIR. Mildred Cram and Leo McCarey.
NINOTCHKA. Melchior Lengyel.
YOUNG MR. LINCOLN, FOX. Lamar Trotti.
(Screenplay)
GONE WITH THE WIND. Sidney Howard.
GOODBYE, MR. CHIPS. Eric Maschwitz, R.C. Sherriff and Claudine West.
MR. SMITH GOES TO WASHINGTON. Sidney Buchman.
NINOTCHKA. Charles Brackett, Walter Reisch and Billy Wilder.
WUTHERING HEIGHTS. Ben Hecht and Charles MacArthur.

CINEMATOGRAPHY:
(Black-and-White)
WUTHERING HEIGHTS. Gregg Toland.
STAGECOACH. Bert Glennon.
(Color)
GONE WITH THE WIND. Ernest Haller and Ray Rennahan.
THE PRIVATE LIVES OF ELIZABETH AND ESSEX, WB. Sol Polito and W. Howard Greene.

ART DIRECTION - SET DECORATION:
GONE WITH THE WIND. Lyle Wheeler.
BEAU GESTE. Hans Dreier and Robert Odell.
CAPTAIN FURY, Roach, UA. Charles D. Hall.
FIRST LOVE, U. Jack Otterson and Martin Obzina.
LOVE AFFAIR. Van Nest Polglase and Al Herman.
MAN OF CONQUEST, REP. John Victor Mackay.
MR. SMITH GOES TO WASHINGTON. Lionel Banks.
THE PRIVATE LIVES OF ELIZABETH AND ESSEX. Anton Grot.
THE RAINS CAME, FOX. William Darling and George Dudley.
STAGECOACH. Alexander Toluboff.
THE WIZARD OF OZ. Cedric Gibbons and William A. Horning.
WUTHERING HEIGHTS. James Basevi.

FILM EDITING:
GONE WITH THE WIND. Hal C. Kern and James E. Newcom.
GOODBYE, MR. CHIPS. Charles Frend.
MR. SMITH GOES TO WASHINGTON. Gene Havlick and Al Clark.
THE RAINS CAME. Barbara McLean.
STAGECOACH. Otho Lovering and Dorothy Spencer.

MUSIC - SCORING:
(Best Score)
STAGECOACH. Richard Hageman, Frank Harling, John Leipold and Leo Shuken.
BABES IN ARMS. Roger Edens and George E. Stoll.
FIRST LOVE. Charles Previn.
THE GREAT VICTOR HERBERT, PAR. Phil Boutelje and Arthur Lange.
THE HUNCHBACK OF NOTRE DAME, RKO. Alfred Newman.
INTERMEZZO, Selznick, UA. Lou Forbes.
MR. SMITH GOES TO WASHINGTON. Dimitri Tiomkin.
OF MICE AND MEN, Roach, UA. Aaron Copland.
THE PRIVATE LIVES OF ELIZABETH AND ESSEX. Erich Wolfgang Korngold.
SHE MARRIED A COP, REP. Cy Feuer.
SWANEE RIVER, FOX. Louis Silvers.
THEY SHALL HAVE MUSIC, Goldwyn, UA. Alfred Newman.
WAY DOWN SOUTH, Lesser, RKO. Victor Young.
(Original Score)
THE WIZARD OF OZ. Herbert Stothart.
DARK VICTORY. Max Steiner.
ETERNALLY YOURS, Walter Wanger, UA. Werner Janssen.
GOLDEN BOY, COL. Victor Young.
GONE WITH THE WIND. Max Steiner.
GULLIVER'S TRAVELS, PAR. Victor Young.
THE MAN IN THE IRON MASK, Small, UA. Lud Gluskin and Lucien Moraweck.
MAN OF CONQUEST. Victor Young.
NURSE EDITH CAVELL, RKO. Anthony Collins.
OF MICE AND MEN. Aaron Copland.
THE RAINS CAME. Alfred Newman.
WUTHERING HEIGHTS. Alfred Newman.

MUSIC - BEST SONG:
OVER THE RAINBOW, The Wizard Of Oz. Music, Harold Arlen. Lyrics, E. Y. Harburg.
FAITHFUL FOREVER from *Gulliver's Travels.* Music, Ralph Rainger. Lyrics, Leo Robin.
I POURED MY HEART INTO A SONG, *Second Fiddle,* FOX. Music and Lyrics by Irving Berlin.
WISHING, *Love Affair.* Music and Lyrics by Buddy de Sylva.

SOUND:
WHEN TOMORROW COMES, U. Bernard B. Brown.
BALALAIKA, MGM. Douglas Shearer.
GONE WITH THE WIND. Thomas T. Moulton.
GOODBYE, MR. CHIPS. A. W. Watkins.
THE GREAT VICTOR HERBERT. Loren Ryder.
THE HUNCHBACK OF NOTRE DAME. John Aalberg.
MAN OF CONQUEST. C. L. Lootens.
MR. SMITH GOES TO WASHINGTON. John Livadary.
OF MICE AND MEN. Elmer Raguse.
THE PRIVATE LIVES OF ELIZABETH AND ESSEX. Nathan Levinson.
THE RAINS CAME. E. H. Hansen.

SHORT FILMS:
(Cartoons)
THE UGLY DUCKLING, Walt Disney, RKO.
DETOURING AMERICA, WB.
PEACE ON EARTH, MGM.
THE POINTER, Walt Disney, RKO.
(One-reel)
BUSY LITTLE BEARS, PAR. (Paragraphics)
INFORMATION PLEASE, RKO.
PROPHET WITHOUT HONOR, MGM. (Miniature)
SWORD FISHING, WB. (Vitaphone Varieties)
(Two-reel)
SONS OF LIBERTY, WB. (Historical Featurette)
DRUNK DRIVING, MGM. (Crime Doesn't Pay)
FIVE TIMES FIVE, RKO. (Special)

SPECIAL EFFECTS:
THE RAINS CAME. E. H. Hansen and Fred Sersen.
GONE WITH THE WIND. John R. Cosgrove, Fred Albin and Arthur Johns.
ONLY ANGELS HAVE WINGS, COL. Roy Davidson and Edwin C. Hahn.
PRIVATE LIVES OF ELIZABETH AND ESSEX. Byron Haskin and Nathan Levinson.
TOPPER TAKES A TRIP, Roach, UA. Roy Seawright.
UNION PACIFIC, PAR. Farciot Edouart, Gordon Jennings and Loren Ryder.
THE WIZARD OF OZ. A. Arnold Gillespie and Douglas Shearer.

HONORARY AND OTHER:
(Irving G. Thalberg Memorial Award)
David O. Selznick
(Other)
DOUGLAS FAIRBANKS (Commemorative Award) - recognizing the unique and outstanding contribution of Douglas Fairbanks, first President of the Academy, to the international development of the motion picture.
MOTION PICTURE RELIEF FUND - acknowledging the outstanding services to the industry during the past year of the Motion Picture Relief Fund and its progressive leadership. Presented to JEAN HERSHOLT, President; RALPH MORGAN, Chairman of the Executive Committee; RALPH BLOCK, First Vice-President; CONRAD NAGEL. (plaques)
JUDY GARLAND for her outstanding performance as a screen juvenile during the past year.
WILLIAM CAMERON MENZIES for outstanding achievement in the use of color for the enhancement of dramatic mood in the production of Gone With The Wind.
TECHNICOLOR COMPANY for its contributions in successfully bringing three-color feature production to the screen.

SCIENTIFIC OR TECHNICAL:
(Class III)
GEORGE ANDERSON of WB Studio for an improved positive head for sun arcs.
JOHN ARNOLD of MGM Studio for the MGM mobile camera crane.
THOMAS T. MOULTON, FRED ALBIN and the **SOUND DEPARTMENT** of the **SAMUEL GOLDWYN STUDIO** for the origination and applica-

tion of the Delta db test to sound recording in motion pictures.
FARCIOT EDOUART, JOSEPH E. ROBBINS, WILLIAM RUDOLPH and PARAMOUNT PICTURES, INC., for the design and construction of a quiet portable treadmill.
EMERY HUSE and RALPH B. ATKINSON of Eastman Kodak Co. for their specifications for chemical analysis of photographic developers and fixing baths.
HAROLD NYE of WB Studio for a miniature incandescent spot lamp.
A. J. TONDREAU of WB Studio for the design and manufacture of an improved sound track printer.
Multiple Award for important contributions in cooperative development of new improved Process Projection Equipment:
F. R. ABBOTT, HALLER BELT, ALAN COOK and BAUSCH & LOMB OPTICAL CO. for faster projection lenses.
MITCHELL CAMERA CO. for a new type process projection head.
MOLE-RICHARDSON CO. for a new type automatically controlled projection arc lamp.
CHARLES HANDLEY, DAVID JOY and NATIONAL CARBON CO. for improved and more stable high intensity carbons.
WINTON HOCH and TECHNICOLOR MOTION PICTURE CORP. for an auxiliary optical system.
DON MUSGRAVE and SELZNICK INTERNATIONAL PICTURES, INC., for pioneering in the use of coordinated equipment in the production, Gone With The Wind.

1940

BEST PICTURE:

REBECCA, Selznick Int'l, UA.
ALL THIS, AND HEAVEN TOO, WB.
FOREIGN CORRESPONDENT, Wanger, UA.
THE GRAPES OF WRATH, FOX.
THE GREAT DICTATOR, Chaplin, UA.
KITTY FOYLE, RKO.
THE LETTER, WB.
THE LONG VOYAGE HOME, Argosy-Wanger, UA.
OUR TOWN, Lesser, UA.
THE PHILADELPHIA STORY, MGM.

ACTOR:

JAMES STEWART, The Philadelphia Story.
CHARLES CHAPLIN, *The Great Dictator.*
HENRY FONDA, *The Grapes Of Wrath.*
RAYMOND MASSEY, *Abe Lincoln In Illinois*, RKO.
LAURENCE OLIVIER, *Rebecca.*

ACTRESS:

GINGER ROGERS, Kitty Foyle.
BETTE DAVIS, *The Letter.*
JOAN FONTAINE, *Rebecca.*
KATHARINE HEPBURN, *The Philadelphia Story.*
MARTHA SCOTT, *Our Town.*

SUPPORTING ACTOR:

WALTER BRENNAN, The Westerner.
ALBERT BASSERMANN, *Foreign Correspondent.*
WILLIAM GARGAN, *They Knew What They Wanted.*
JACK OAKIE, *The Great Dictator.*
JAMES STEPHENSON, *The Letter.*

SUPPORTING ACTRESS:

JANE DARWELL, The Grapes Of Wrath.
JUDITH ANDERSON, *Rebecca.*
RUTH HUSSEY, *The Philadelphia Story.*
BARBARA O'NEIL, *All This, And Heaven Too.*
MARJORIE RAMBEAU, *Primrose Path*, RKO.

DIRECTING:

JOHN FORD, The Grapes Of Wrath.
GEORGE CUKOR, *The Philadelphia Story.*
ALFRED HITCHCOCK, *Rebecca.*
SAM WOOD, *Kitty Foyle.*
WILLIAM WYLER, *The Letter.*

WRITING:

(Original Story)

ARISE, MY LOVE, PAR. Benjamin Glazer and John S. Toldy.
COMRADE X, MGM. Walter Reisch.
EDISON THE MAN, MGM. Hugo Butler and Dore Schary.
MY FAVORITE WIFE, RKO. Leo McCarey, Bella Spewack & Samuel Spewack.
THE WESTERNER. Stuart N. Lake.

(Original Screenplay)

THE GREAT McGINTY, PAR. Preston Sturges.
ANGELS OVER BROADWAY, COL. Ben Hecht.
DR. EHRLICH'S MAGIC BULLET, WB. Norman Burnside, Heinz Herald and John Huston.
FOREIGN CORRESPONDENT. Charles Bennett and Joan Harrison.
THE GREAT DICTATOR. Charles Chaplin.

(Screenplay)

THE PHILADELPHIA STORY. Donald Ogden Stewart.
THE GRAPES OF WRATH. Nunnally Johnson.
KITTY FOYLE. Dalton Trumbo.
THE LONG VOYAGE HOME. Dudley Nichols.
REBECCA. Robert E. Sherwood and Joan Harrison.

CINEMATOGRAPHY:

(Black-and-White)

REBECCA. George Barnes.
ABE LINCOLN IN ILLINOIS. James Wong Howe.
ALL THIS, AND HEAVEN TOO. Ernest Haller.
ARISE, MY LOVE. Charles B. Lang, Jr.
BOOM TOWN, MGM. Harold Rosson.
FOREIGN CORRESPONDENT. Rudolph Mate.
THE LETTER. Gaetano Gaudio.
THE LONG VOYAGE HOME. Gregg Toland.
SPRING PARADE, U. Joseph Valentine.
WATERLOO BRIDGE, MGM. Joseph Ruttenberg.

(Color)

THIEF OF BAGDAD, Korda, UA (British). George Perinal.
BITTER SWEET, MGM. Oliver T. Marsh and Allen Davey.
THE BLUE BIRD, FOX. Arthur Miller and Ray Rennahan.
DOWN ARGENTINE WAY, FOX. Leon Shamroy and Ray Rennahan.
NORTH WEST MOUNTED POLICE, PAR. Victor Milner and W. Howard Greene.
NORTHWEST PASSAGE, MGM. Sidney Wagner and William V. Skall.

ART DIRECTION - SET DECORATION:
(Black-and-White)

PRIDE AND PREJUDICE, MGM. Cedric Gibbons and Paul Groesse.
ARISE, MY LOVE. Hans Dreier and Robert Usher.
ARIZONA, COL. Lionel Banks and Robert Peterson.
THE BOYS FROM SYRACUSE, U. John Otterson.
DARK COMMAND, REP. John Victor Mackay.
FOREIGN CORRESPONDENT. Alexander Golitzen.
LILLIAN RUSSELL, FOX. Richard Day and Joseph C. Wright.
MY FAVORITE WIFE. Van Nest Polglase and Mark-Lee Kirk.
MY SON, MY SON, Small, UA. John DuCasse Schulze.
OUR TOWN. Lewis J. Rachmil.
REBECCA. Lyle Wheeler.
SEA HAWK, WB. Anton Grot.
THE WESTERNER. James Basevi.

(Color)

THIEF OF BAGDAD. Vincent Korda.
BITTER SWEET. Cedric Gibbons and John S. Detlie.
DOWN ARGENTINE WAY. Richard Day and Joseph C. Wright.
NORTH WEST MOUNTED POLICE. Hans Dreier and Roland Anderson.

FILM EDITING:

NORTH WEST MOUNTED POLICE. Anne Bauchens.
THE GRAPES OF WRATH. Robert E. Simpson.
THE LETTER. Warren Low.
THE LONG VOYAGE HOME. Sherman Todd.
REBECCA. Hal C. Kern.

MUSIC - SCORING:
(Best Score)

TIN PAN ALLEY, FOX. Alfred Newman.
ARISE, MY LOVE. Victor Young.
HIT PARADE OF 1941, REP. Cy Feuer.
IRENE, Imperadio, RKO. Anthony Collins.
OUR TOWN. Sol Lesser. Aaron Copland.
THE SEA HAWK. Erich Wolfgang Korngold.
SECOND CHORUS, PAR. Artie Shaw.
SPRING PARADE. Charles Previn.
STRIKE UP THE BAND, MGM. Georgie Stoll and Roger Edens.

(Original Score)

PINOCCHIO, Disney, RKO. Leigh Harline, Paul J. Smith and Ned Washington.
ARIZONA. Victor Young.
THE DARK COMMAND. Victor Young.
THE FIGHT FOR LIFE, U.S. Government-COL. Louis Gruenberg.
THE GREAT DICTATOR. Meredith Willson.
THE HOUSE OF SEVEN GABLES, U. Frank Skinner.
THE HOWARDS OF VIRGINIA, COL. Richard Hageman.
THE LETTER. Max Steiner.
THE LONG VOYAGE HOME. Richard Hageman.
THE MARK OF ZORRO, FOX. Alfred Newman.
MY FAVORITE WIFE. Roy Webb.
NORTH WEST MOUNTED POLICE. Victor Young.
ONE MILLION B. C., Hal Roach, UA. Werner Heymann.
OUR TOWN. Aaron Copland.
REBECCA. Franz Waxman.
THE THIEF OF BAGDAD. Miklos Rozsa.
WATERLOO BRIDGE. Herbert Stothart.

MUSIC - BEST SONG:

WHEN YOU WISH UPON A STAR, Pinocchio. Music, Leigh Harline. Lyrics, Ned Washington.
DOWN ARGENTINE WAY, *Down Argentine Way*. Music, Harry Warren. Lyrics, Mack Gordon.
I'D KNOW YOU ANYWHERE, *You'll Find Out*, RKO. Music, Jimmy McHugh. Lyrics, Johnny Mercer.
IT'S A BLUE WORLD, *Music In My Heart*, COL. Music and Lyrics by Chet Forrest and Bob Wright.
LOVE OF MY LIFE, *Second Chorus*. Music, Artie Shaw. Lyrics, Johnny Mercer.
ONLY FOREVER, *Rhythm On The River*, PAR. Music, James Monaco. Lyrics, John Burke.
OUR LOVE AFFAIR, *Strike Up The Band*. Music and Lyrics by Roger Edens and Georgie Stoll.
WALTZING IN THE CLOUDS, *Spring Parade*. Music, Robert Stolz. Lyrics, Gus Kahn.
WHO AM I?, *Hit Parade Of 1941*. Music, Jule Styne. Lyrics, Walter Bullock.

SOUND:

STRIKE UP THE BAND. Douglas Shearer.
BEHIND THE NEWS, REP. Charles Lootens.
CAPTAIN CAUTION, Roach, UA. Elmer Raguse.
THE GRAPES OF WRATH. E. H. Hansen.
THE HOWARDS OF VIRGINIA. Jack Whitney, General Service.
KITTY FOYLE. John Aalberg.
NORTH WEST MOUNTED POLICE. Loren Ryder.
OUR TOWN. Thomas Moulton.
THE SEA HAWK. Nathan Levinson.
SPRING PARADE. Bernard B. Brown.
TOO MANY HUSBANDS, COL. John Livadary.

SHORT FILMS:
(Cartoons)

MILKY WAY, MGM. (Rudolph Ising Series)
PUSS GETS THE BOOT, MGM. (Cat and Mouse Series)
A WILD HARE, Leon Schlesinger, WB.

(One-reel)

QUICKER 'N A WINK, Pete Smith, MGM.
LONDON CAN TAKE IT, WB. (Vitaphone Varieties)
MORE ABOUT NOSTRADAMUS, MGM.
SIEGE, RKO. (Reelism)

(Two-reel)

TEDDY, THE ROUGH RIDER, WB. (Historical Featurette)
EYES OF THE NAVY, MGM. (Crime Doesn't Pay)
SERVICE WITH THE COLORS, WB. (National Defense Series)

SPECIAL EFFECTS:

THE THIEF OF BAGDAD. Photographic: Lawrence Butler. Sound: Jack Whitney.
THE BLUE BIRD. Photographic: Fred Sersen. Sound: E. H. Hansen.
BOOM TOWN. Photographic: A. Arnold Gillespie. Sound: Douglas Shearer.
THE BOYS FROM SYRACUSE. Photographic: John P. Fulton. Sound: Bernard B. Brown and Joseph Lapis.
DR. CYCLOPS, PAR. Photographic: Farciot Edouart and Gordon Jennings. Sound: No credit listed.
FOREIGN CORRESPONDENT. Photographic: Paul Eagler. Sound: Thomas T. Moulton.
THE INVISIBLE MAN RETURNS, U. Photographic: John P. Fulton. Sound: Bernard B. Brown and Willim Hedgecock.
THE LONG VOYAGE HOME. Photographic: R. T. Layton and R. O. Binger. Sound: Thomas T. Moulton.
ONE MILLION B. C. Photographic: Roy Seawright. Sound: Elmer Raguse.
REBECCA. Photographic: Jack Cosgrove. Sound: Arthur Johns.
THE SEA HAWK. Photographic: Byron Haskin. Sound: Nathan Levinson.
SWISS FAMILY ROBINSON, RKO. Photographic: Vernon L. Walker. Sound. John O. Aalberg.
TYPHOON, PAR. Photographic: Farciot Edouart and Gordon Jennings. Sound: Loren Ryder.
WOMEN IN WAR, REP. Photographic: Howard J. Lydecker, William Bradford and Ellis J. Thackery. Sound: Herbert Norsch.

HONORARY AND OTHER:
(Other)

BOB HOPE, in recognition of his unselfish services to the Motion Picture Industry.
COLONEL NATHAN LEVINSON for his outstanding service to the industry and the Army during the past nine years, which has made

possible the present efficient mobilization of the motion picture industry facilities for the production of Army Training Films.

SCIENTIFIC OR TECHNICAL:
(Class I)
20TH CENTURY-FOX FILM CORP. for the design and construction of the 20th Century Silenced Camera, developed by **DANIEL CLARK, GROVER LAUBE, CHARLES MILLER** and **ROBERT W. STEVENS.**
(Class III)
WB STUDIO ART DEPARTMENT and **ANTON GROT** for the design and perfection of the WB water ripple and wave illusion machine.

1941

BEST PICTURE:
HOW GREEN WAS MY VALLEY, FOX.
BLOSSOMS IN THE DUST, MGM.
CITIZEN KANE, Mercury, RKO.
HERE COMES MR. JORDAN, COL.
HOLD BACK THE DAWN, PAR.
THE LITTLE FOXES, Goldwyn, RKO.
THE MALTESE FALCON, WB.
ONE FOOT IN HEAVEN, WB.
SERGEANT YORK, WB.
SUSPICION, RKO.

ACTOR:
GARY COOPER, Sergeant York.
CARY GRANT, *Penny Serenade,* COL.
WALTER HUSTON, *All That Money Can Buy,* RKO.
ROBERT MONTGOMERY, *Here Comes Mr. Jordan.*
ORSON WELLES, *Citizen Kane.*

ACTRESS:
JOAN FONTAINE, Suspicion.
BETTE DAVIS, *The Little Foxes.*
OLIVIA DE HAVILLAND, *Hold Back The Dawn.*
GREER GARSON, *Blossoms In The Dust.*
BARBARA STANWYCK, *Ball Of Fire,* Goldwyn, RKO.

SUPPORTING ACTOR:
DONALD CRISP, How Green Was My Valley.
WALTER BRENNAN, *Sergeant York.*
CHARLES COBURN, *The Devil And Miss Jones,* RKO.
JAMES GLEASON, *Here Comes Mr. Jordan.*
SYDNEY GREENSTREET, *The Maltese Falcon,* WB.

SUPPORTING ACTRESS:
MARY ASTOR, The Great Lie, WB.
SARA ALLGOOD, *How Green Was My Valley.*
PATRICIA COLLINGE, *The Little Foxes.*
TERESA WRIGHT, *The Little Foxes.*
MARGARET WYCHERLY, *Sergeant York.*

DIRECTING:
JOHN FORD, How Green Was My Valley.
ALEXANDER HALL, *Here Comes Mr. Jordan.*
HOWARD HAWKS, *Sergeant York.*
ORSON WELLES, *Citizen Kane.*
WILLIAM WYLER, *The Little Foxes.*

WRITING:
(Original Story)
HERE COMES MR. JORDAN. Harry Segall.
BALL OF FIRE. Thomas Monroe and Billy Wilder.
THE LADY EVE, PAR. Monckton Hoffe.
MEET JOHN DOE, WB. Richard Connell and Robert Presnell.
NIGHT TRAIN, FOX. Gordon Wellesley.
(Original Screenplay)
CITIZEN KANE. Herman J. Mankiewicz and Orson Welles.
THE DEVIL AND MISS JONES. Norman Krasna.
SERGEANT YORK. Harry Chandlee, Abem Finkel, John Huston and Howard Koch.
TALL, DARK AND HANDSOME, FOX. Karl Tunberg and Darrell Ware.
TOM, DICK AND HARRY, RKO. Paul Jarrico.
(Screenplay)
HERE COMES MR. JORDAN. Sidney Buchman and Seton I. Miller.
HOLD BACK THE DAWN. Charles Brackett and Billy Wilder.
HOW GREEN WAS MY VALLEY. Philip Dunne.
THE LITTLE FOXES. Lillian Hellman.
THE MALTESE FALCON. John Huston.

CINEMATOGRAPHY:
(Black-and-White)
HOW GREEN WAS MY VALLEY. Arthur Miller.
THE CHOCOLATE SOLDIER, MGM. Karl Freund.
CITIZEN KANE. Gregg Toland.
DR. JEKYLL AND MR. HYDE, MGM. Joseph Ruttenberg.
HERE COMES MR. JORDAN. Joseph Walker.
HOLD BACK THE DAWN. Leo Tover.
SERGEANT YORK. Sol Polito.
SUN VALLEY SERENADE, FOX. Edward Cronjager.
SUNDOWN, Wanger, UA. Charles Lang.
THAT HAMILTON WOMAN, Korda, UA. Rudolph Mate.
(Color)
BLOOD AND SAND, FOX. Ernest Palmer and Ray Rennahan.
ALOMA OF THE SOUTH SEAS, PAR. Wilfred M. Cline, Karl Struss and William Snyder.
BILLY THE KID, MGM. William V. Skall and Leonard Smith.
BLOSSOMS IN THE DUST. Karl Freund and W. Howard Greene.
DIVE BOMBER, WB. Bert Glennon.
LOUISIANA PURCHASE, PAR. Harry Hallenberger and Ray Rennahan.

ART DIRECTION - SET DECORATION:
(Black-and-White)
HOW GREEN WAS MY VALLEY. Richard Day and Nathan Juran. Interior Decoration: Thomas Little.
CITIZEN KANE. Perry Ferguson and Van Nest Polglase. Interior Decoration: Al Fields and Darrell Silvera.
FLAME OF NEW ORLEANS, U. Martin Obzina and Jack Otterson. Interior Decoration: Russell A. Gausman.
HOLD BACK THE DAWN. Hans Dreier and Robert Usher. Interior Decoration: Sam Comer.
LADIES IN RETIREMENT, COL. Lionel Banks. Interior Decoration: George Montgomery.
THE LITTLE FOXES. Stephen Goosson. Interior Decoration: Howard Bristol.
SERGEANT YORK. John Hughes. Interior Decoration: Fred MacLean.
SON OF MONTE CRISTO, Small, UA. John DuCasse Schulze. Interior Decoration: Edward G. Boyle.
SUNDOWN. Alexander Golitzen. Interior Decoration: Richard Irvine.
THAT HAMILTON WOMAN. Vincent Korda. Interior Decoration: Julia Heron.
WHEN LADIES MEET, MGM. Cedric Gibbons and Randall Duell. Interior Decoration: Edwin B. Willis.
(Color)
BLOSSOMS IN THE DUST. Cedric Gibbons and Urie McCleary. Interior Decoration: Edwin B. Willis.
BLOOD AND SAND. Richard Day and Joseph C. Wright. Interior Decoration: Thomas Little.
LOUISIANA PURCHASE. Raoul Pene du Bois. Interior Decoration: Ste-

phen A. Seymour.

FILM EDITING:
SERGEANT YORK. William Holmes.
CITIZEN KANE. Robert Wise.
DR. JEKYLL AND MR. HYDE. Harold F. Kress.
HOW GREEN WAS MY VALLEY. James B. Clark.
THE LITTLE FOXES. Daniel Mandell.

MUSIC - SCORING:
(Scoring of a Dramatic Picture)
ALL THAT MONEY CAN BUY. Bernard Herrmann.
BACK STREET, U. Frank Skinner.
BALL OF FIRE. Alfred Newman.
CHEERS OF MISS BISHOP, Rowland, UA. Edward Ward.
CITIZEN KANE. Bernard Herrmann.
DR. JEKYLL AND MR. HYDE. Franz Waxman.
HOLD BACK THE DAWN. Victor Young.
HOW GREEN WAS MY VALLEY. Alfred Newman.
KING OF THE ZOMBIES, MNG. Edward Kay.
LADIES IN RETIREMENT. Morris Stoloff and Ernst Toch.
THE LITTLE FOXES. Meredith Willson.
LYDIA, Korda, UA. Miklos Rozsa.
MERCY ISLAND, REP. Cy Feuer and Walter Scharf.
SERGEANT YORK. Max Steiner.
SO ENDS OUR NIGHT, Loew-Lewin, UA. Louis Gruenberg.
SUNDOWN. Miklos Rozsa.
SUSPICION. Franz Waxman.
TANKS A MILLION, Roach, UA. Edward Ward.
THAT UNCERTAIN FEELING, Lubitsch, UA. Werner Heymann.
THIS WOMAN IS MINE, U. Richard Hageman.

(Scoring of a Musical Picture)
DUMBO, Disney, RKO. Frank Churchill and Oliver Wallace.
ALL AMERICAN CO-ED, Roach, UA. Edward Ward.
BIRTH OF THE BLUES, PAR. Robert Emmett Dolan.
BUCK PRIVATES, U. Charles Previn.
THE CHOCOLATE SOLDIER. Herbert Stothart and Bronislau Kaper.
ICE-CAPADES, REP. Cy Feuer.
THE STRAWBERRY BLONDE, WB. Heinz Roemheld.
SUN VALLEY SERENADE. Emil Newman.
SUNNY, RKO. Anthony Collins.
YOU'LL NEVER GET RICH, COL. Morris Stoloff.

MUSIC - BEST SONG:
THE LAST TIME I SAW PARIS, Lady Be Good, MGM. Music, Jerome Kern. Lyrics, Oscar Hammerstein II.
BABY MINE, *Dumbo*. Music, Frank Churchill. Lyrics, Ned Washington.
BE HONEST WITH ME, *Ridin' On A Rainbow*, REP. Music and Lyrics by Gene Autry and Fred Rose.
BLUES IN THE NIGHT, *Blues In The Night*, WB. Music, Harold Arlen. Lyrics, Johnny Mercer.
BOOGIE WOOGIE BUGLE BOY OF COMPANY B, *Buck Privates*. Hugh Prince. Lyrics, Don Raye.
CHATTANOOGA CHOO CHOO, *Sun Valley Serenade*. Music, Harry Warren. Lyrics, Mack Gordon.
DOLORES, *Las Vegas Nights*, PAR. Music, Lou Alter. Lyrics, Frank Loesser.
OUT OF THE SILENCE, *All American Co-Ed*. Music and Lyrics by Lloyd B. Norlind.
SINCE I KISSED MY BABY GOODBYE, *You'll Never Get Rich*. Music and Lyrics by Cole Porter.

SOUND:
THAT HAMILTON WOMAN. Jack Whitney, General Service.
APPOINTMENT FOR LOVE, U. Bernard B. Brown.
BALL OF FIRE. Thomas Moulton.
THE CHOCOLATE SOLDIER. Douglas Shearer.
CITIZEN KANE. John Aalberg.
THE DEVIL PAYS OFF, REP, Charles Lootens.
HOW GREEN WAS MY VALLEY. E. H. Hansen.
THE MEN IN HER LIFE, COL. John Livadary.
SERGEANT YORK. Nathan Levinson.
SKYLARK, PAR. Loren Ryder.
TOPPER RETURNS, Roach, UA. Elmer Raguse.

SHORT FILMS:
(Cartoons)
LEND A PAW, Walt Disney, RKO.
BOOGIE WOOGIE BUGLE BOY OF COMPANY B, Walter Lantz, U.
HIAWATHA'S RABBIT HUNT, Leon Schlesinger, WB.
HOW WAR CAME, COL. (Raymond Gram Swing Series)
THE NIGHT BEFORE CHRISTMAS, MGM. (Tom and Jerry Series)
RHAPSODY IN RIVETS, Leon Schlesinger, WB.
THE ROOKIE BEAR, MGM. (Bear Series)
RHYTHM IN THE RANKS, PAR. (George Pal Puppetoon Series)
SUPERMAN NO. 1, PAR.
TRUANT OFFICER DONALD, Walt Disney, RKO.

(One-reel)
OF PUPS AND PUZZLES, MGM. (Passing Parade Series)
ARMY CHAMPIONS, Pete Smith, MGM. (Pete Smith Specialties)
BEAUTY AND THE BEACH, PAR. (Headliner Series)
DOWN ON THE FARM, PAR. (Speaking of Animals)
FORTY BOYS AND A SONG, WB. (Melody Master Series)
KINGS OF THE TURF, WB. (Color Parade Series)
SAGEBRUSH AND SILVER, FOX. (Magic Carpet Series)

(Two-reel)
MAIN STREET ON THE MARCH, MGM. (Two-reel Special)
ALIVE IN THE DEEP, Woodard Productions, Inc.
FORBIDDEN PASSAGE, MGM. (Crime Doesn't Pay)
THE GAY PARISIAN, WB. (Miniature Featurette Series)
THE TANKS ARE COMING, WB. (National Defense Series)

DOCUMENTARY:
CHURCHILL'S ISLAND, NFC, UA.
ADVENTURES IN THE BRONX, Film Assocs.
BOMBER, U.S. Office for Emergency Management Film Unit.
CHRISTMAS UNDER FIRE, British Ministry of Information, WB.
LETTER FROM HOME, British Ministry of Information.
LIFE OF A THOROUGHBRED, FOX.
NORWAY IN REVOLT, MOT, RKO.
SOLDIERS OF THE SKY, FOX.
WAR CLOUDS IN THE PACIFIC, NFC.

SPECIAL EFFECTS:
I WANTED WINGS, PAR. Photographic: Farciot Edouart and Gordon Jennings. Sound: Louis Mesenkop.
ALOMA OF THE SOUTH SEAS. Photographic: Farciot Edouart and Gordon Jennings. Sound: Louis Mesenkop.
FLIGHT COMMAND, MGM. Photographic: A. Arnold Gillespie. Sound: Douglas Shearer.
THE INVISIBLE WOMAN, U. Photographic: John Fulton. Sound: John Hall.
THE SEA WOLF, WB. Photographic: Byron Haskin. Sound: Nathan Levinson.
THAT HAMILTON WOMAN. Photographic: Lawrence Butler. Sound: William H. Wilmarth.
TOPPER RETURNS. Photographic: Roy Seawright. Sound: Elmer Raguse.
A YANK IN THE R.A.F., FOX. Photographic: Fred Sersen. Sound: E. H. Hansen.

HONORARY AND OTHER:
(Irving G. Thalberg Memorial Award)

Walt Disney

(Other)

REY SCOTT for his extraordinary achievement in producing Kukan, the film record of China's struggle, including its photography with a 16mm camera under the most difficult and dangerous conditions.
THE BRITISH MINISTRY OF INFORMATION for its vivid and dramatic presentation of the heroism of the RAF in the documentary film, Target For Tonight.
LEOPOLD STOKOWSKI and his associates for their unique achievement in the creation of a new form of visualized music in Walt Disney's production Fantasia, thereby widening the scope of the motion picture as entertainment and as an art form.
WALT DISNEY, WILLIAM GARITY, JOHN N. A. HAWKINS and the RCA MANUFACTURING COMPANY, for their outstanding contribution to the advancement of the use of sound in motion pictures through the production of Fantasia.

SCIENTIFIC OR TECHNICAL:
(Class II)

ELECTRICAL RESEARCH PRODUCTS DIVISION OF WESTERN ELECTRIC CO., INC., for the development of the precision integrating sphere densitometer.
RCA MANUFACTURING CO. for the design and development of the MI-3043 Uni-directional microphone.

(Class III)

RAY WILKINSON and the PARAMOUNT STUDIO LABORATORY for pioneering in the use of and for the first practical application to release printing of fine grain positive stock.
CHARLES LOOTENS and the REPUBLIC STUDIO SOUND DEPARTMENT for pioneering the use of and for the first practical application to motion picture production of CLASS B push-pull variable area recording.
WILBUR SILVERTOOTH and the PARAMOUNT STUDIO ENGINEERING DEPARTMENT for the design and computation of a relay condenser system applicable to transparency process projection, delivering considerably more usable light.
PARAMOUNT PICTURES, INC., and 20TH CENTURY-FOX FILM CORP. for the development and first practical application to motion picture production of an automatic scene slating device.
DOUGLAS SHEARER and the MGM STUDIO SOUND DEPARTMENT, and to LOREN RYDER and the PARAMOUNT STUDIO SOUND DEPARTMENT for pioneering the development of fine grain emulsions for variable density original sound recording in studio production.

1942

BEST PICTURE:

MRS. MINIVER, MGM.
THE INVADERS, Ortus, COL (British).
KINGS ROW, WB.
THE MAGNIFICENT AMBERSONS, Mercury, RKO.
THE PIED PIPER, FOX.
THE PRIDE OF THE YANKEES, Goldwyn, RKO.
RANDOM HARVEST, MGM.
THE TALK OF THE TOWN, COL.
WAKE ISLAND, PAR.
YANKEE DOODLE DANDY, WB.

ACTOR:

JAMES CAGNEY, Yankee Doodle Dandy.
RONALD COLMAN, Random Harvest.
GARY COOPER, The Pride Of The Yankees.
WALTER PIDGEON, Mrs. Miniver.
MONTY WOOLLEY, The Pied Piper.

ACTRESS:

GREER GARSON, Mrs. Miniver.
BETTE DAVIS, Now, Voyager, WB.
KATHARINE HEPBURN, Woman Of the Year, MGM.
ROSALIND RUSSELL, My Sister Eileen, COL.
TERESA WRIGHT, The Pride Of The Yankees.

SUPPORTING ACTOR:

VAN HEFLIN, Johnny Eager, MGM.
WILLIAM BENDIX, Wake Island, PAR.
WALTER HUSTON, Yankee Doodle Dandy.
FRANK MORGAN, Tortilla Flat, MGM.
HENRY TRAVERS, Mrs. Miniver.

SUPPORTING ACTRESS:

TERESA WRIGHT, Mrs. Miniver.
GLADYS COOPER, Now, Voyager.
AGNES MOOREHEAD, The Magnificent Ambersons.
SUSAN PETERS, Random Harvest.
DAME MAY WHITTY, Mrs. Miniver.

DIRECTING:

WILLIAM WYLER, Mrs. Miniver.
MICHAEL CURTIZ, Yankee Doodle Dandy.
JOHN FARROW, Wake Island.
MERVYN LEROY, Random Harvest.
SAM WOOD, Kings Row.

WRITING:
(Original Story)

THE INVADERS, Ortus, COL (British). Emeric Pressburger.
HOLIDAY INN, PAR. Irving Berlin.
THE PRIDE OF THE YANKEES. Paul Gallico.
THE TALK OF THE TOWN. Sidney Harmon.
YANKEE DOODLE DANDY. Robert Buckner.

(Original Screenplay)

WOMAN OF THE YEAR. Michael Kanin & Ring Lardner, Jr.
ONE OF OUR AIRCRAFT IS MISSING, Powell, UA (British). Michael Powell and Emeric Pressburger.
THE ROAD TO MOROCCO, PAR. Frank Butler and Don Hartman.
WAKE ISLAND. W. R. Burnett and Frank Butler.
THE WAR AGAINST MRS. HADLEY, MGM. George Oppenheimer.

(Screenplay)

MRS. MINIVER. George Froeschel, James Hilton, Claudine West and Arthur Wimperis.
THE INVADERS. Rodney Ackland and Emeric Pressburger.
THE PRIDE OF THE YANKEES. Herman J. Mankiewicz and Jo Swerling.
RANDOM HARVEST. George Froeschel, Claudine West and Arthur Wimperis.
THE TALK OF THE TOWN. Sidney Buchman and Irwin Shaw.

CINEMATOGRAPHY:
(Black-and-White)
MRS. MINIVER. Joseph Ruttenberg.
KINGS ROW. James Wong Howe.
THE MAGNIFICENT AMBERSONS. Stanley Cortez.
MOONTIDE, FOX. Charles Clarke.
THE PIED PIPER. Edward Cronjager.
THE PRIDE OF THE YANKEES. Rudolph Mate.
TAKE A LETTER, DARLING, PAR. John Mescall.
THE TALK OF THE TOWN. Ted Tetzlaff.
TEN GENTLEMEN FROM WEST POINT, FOX. Leon Shamroy.
THIS ABOVE ALL, FOX. Arthur Miller.

(Color)
THE BLACK SWAN, FOX. Leon Shamroy.
ARABIAN NIGHTS, Wanger, U. Milton Krasner, William V. Skall and W. Howard Greene.
CAPTAINS OF THE CLOUDS, WB. Sol Polito.
JUNGLE BOOK, Korda, UA. W. Howard Greene.
REAP THE WILD WIND, PAR. Victor Milner and William V. Skall.
TO THE SHORES OF TRIPOLI, FOX. Edward Cronjager and William V. Skall.

ART DIRECTION - SET DECORATION:
(Black-and-White)
THIS ABOVE ALL. Richard Day and Joseph Wright. Interior Decoration: Thomas Little.
GEORGE WASHINGTON SLEPT HERE, WB. Max Parker and Mark-Lee Kirk. Interior Decoration: Casey Roberts.
THE MAGNIFICENT AMBERSONS. Albert S. D'Agostino. Interior Decoraton: Al Fields and Darrell Silvera.
THE PRIDE OF THE YANKEES. Perry Ferguson. Interior Decoration: Howard Bristol.
RANDOM HARVEST. Cedric Gibbons and Randall Duell. Interior Decoration: Edwin B. Willis and Jack Moore.
THE SHANGHAI GESTURE, Arnold, UA. Boris Leven. Interior Decoration: Boris Leven.
SILVER QUEEN, Sherman, UA. Ralph Berger. Interior Decoration: Emile Kuri.
THE SPOILERS, U. John B. Goodman and Jack Otterson. Interior Decoration: Russell A. Gausman and Edward R. Robinson.
TAKE A LETTER, DARLING. Hans Dreier and Roland Anderson. Interior Decoration: Sam Comer.
THE TALK OF THE TOWN. Lionel Banks and Rudolph Sternad. Interior Decoration: Fay Babcock.

(Color)
MY GAL SAL, FOX. Richard Day and Joseph Wright. Interior Decoration: Thomas Little.
ARABIAN NIGHTS. Alexander Golitzen and Jack Otterson. Interior Decoration: Russell A. Gausman and Ira S. Webb.
CAPTAINS OF THE CLOUDS. Ted Smith. Interior Decoration: Casey Roberts.
JUNGLE BOOK. Vincent Korda. Interior Decoration: Julia Heron.
REAP THE WILD WIND. Hans Dreier and Roland Anderson. Interior Decoration: George Sawley.

FILM EDITING:
THE PRIDE OF THE YANKEES. Daniel Mandell.
MRS. MINIVER. Harold F. Kress.
THE TALK OF THE TOWN. Otto Meyer.
THIS ABOVE ALL. Walter Thompson.
YANKEE DOODLE DANDY. George Amy.

MUSIC - SCORING:
(Scoring of a Dramatic or Comedy Picture)
NOW, VOYAGER. Max Steiner.
ARABIAN NIGHTS. Frank Skinner.
BAMBI, Disney, RKO. Frank Churchill and Edward Plumb.
THE BLACK SWAN. Alfred Newman.
THE CORSICAN BROTHERS, Small, UA. Dimitri Tiomkin.
FLYING TIGERS, REP. Victor Young.
THE GOLD RUSH, Chaplin, UA. Max Terr.
I MARRIED A WITCH, Cinema Guild, UA. Roy Webb.
JOAN OF PARIS, RKO. Roy Webb.
JUNGLE BOOK. Miklos Rozsa.
KLONDIKE FURY, MNG. Edward Kay.
THE PRIDE OF THE YANKEES. Leigh Harline.
RANDOM HARVEST. Herbert Stothart.
THE SHANGHAI GESTURE. Richard Hageman.
SILVER QUEEN. Victor Young.
TAKE A LETTER, DARLING. Victor Young.
THE TALK OF THE TOWN. Frederick Hollander and Morris Stoloff.
TO BE OR NOT TO BE, Lubitsch, UA. Werner Heymann.

(Scoring of a Musical Picture)
YANKEE DOODLE DANDY. Ray Heindorf and Heinz Roemheld.
FLYING WITH MUSIC, Roach, UA. Edward Ward.
FOR ME AND MY GAL, MGM. Roger Edens and Georgie Stoll.
HOLIDAY INN. Robert Emmett Dolan.
IT STARTED WITH EVE, U. Charles Previn and Hans Salter.
JOHNNY DOUGHBOY, REP. Walter Scharf.
MY GAL SAL. Alfred Newman.
YOU WERE NEVER LOVELIER, COL. Leigh Harline.

MUSIC - BEST SONG:
WHITE CHRISTMAS, Holiday Inn. Music and Lyrics by Irving Berlin.
ALWAYS IN MY HEART, *Always In My Heart*, WB. Music, Ernesto Lecuona. Lyrics, Kim Gannon.
DEARLY BELOVED, *You Were Never Lovelier*. Music, Jerome Kern. Lyrics, Johnny Mercer.
HOW ABOUT YOU? from *Babes On Broadway*, MGM. Music, Burton Lane. Lyrics, Ralph Freed.
IT SEEMS I HEARD THAT SONG BEFORE, *Youth On Parade*, REP. Music, Jule Styne. Lyrics, Sammy Cahn.
I'VE GOT A GAL IN KALAMAZOO, *Orchestra Wives*, FOX. Music, Harry Warren. Lyrics, Mack Gordon.
LOVE IS A SONG, *Bambi*. Music, Frank Churchill. Lyrics, Larry Morey.
PENNIES FOR PEPPINO, *Flying With Music*. Music, Edward Ward. Lyrics, Chet Forrest and Bob Wright.
PIG FOOT PETE, *Hellzapoppin*, U. Music, Gene de Paul. Lyrics, Don Raye.
THERE'S A BREEZE ON LAKE LOUISE, *The Mayor Of 44th Street*, RKO. Music, Harry Revel. Lyrics, Mort Greene.

SOUND:
YANKEE DOODLE DANDY. Nathan Levinson.
ARABIAN NIGHTS. Bernard Brown.
BAMBI. Sam Slyfield.
FLYING TIGERS. Daniel Bloomberg.
FRIENDLY ENEMIES, Small, UA. Jack Whitney, Sound Service, Inc.
THE GOLD RUSH. James Fields, RCA Sound.
MRS. MINIVER. Douglas Shearer.
ONCE UPON A HONEYMOON, RKO. Steve Dunn.
THE PRIDE OF THE YANKEES. Thomas Moulton.
ROAD TO MOROCCO. Loren Ryder.
THIS ABOVE ALL. E. H. Hansen.
YOU WERE NEVER LOVELIER. John Livadary.

SHORT FILMS:

(Cartoons)

DER FUEHRER'S FACE, Walt Disney, RKO.
ALL OUT FOR V, FOX.
THE BLITZ WOLF, MGM.
JUKE BOX JAMBOREE, Walt Lantz, U.
PIGS IN A POLKA, Leon Schlesinger, WB.
TULIPS SHALL GROW, PAR. (George Pal Puppetoon)

(One-reel)

SPEAKING OF ANIMALS AND THEIR FAMILIES. PAR. (Speaking Of Animals)
DESERT WONDERLAND, FOX. (Magic Carpet Series)
MARINES IN THE MAKING, MGM. (Pete Smith Specialties)
UNITED STATES MARINE BAND, WB. (Melody Master Bands)

(Two-reel)

BEYOND THE LINE OF DUTY, WB. (Broadway Brevities)
DON'T TALK, MGM. (Two-reel Special)
PRIVATE SMITH OF THE U.S.A., RKO. (This Is America Series)

DOCUMENTARY:

BATTLE OF MIDWAY, U.S. Navy, FOX.
KOKODA FRONT LINE, Australian News Information Bureau.
MOSCOW STRIKES BACK, ARK (Russian).
PRELUDE TO WAR, U.S. Army Special Services.
A SHIP IS BORN, U.S. Merchant Marine, WB.
AFRICA, PRELUDE TO VICTORY, MOT, FOX.
COMBAT REPORT, U.S. Army Signal Corps.
CONQUER BY THE CLOCK, Office of War Information, RKO. Frederic Ullman, Jr.
THE GRAIN THAT BUILT A HEMISPHERE, Coordinator's Office, Motion Picture Society for the Americas. DNY.
HENRY BROWNE, FARMER, U.S. Department of Agriculture, REP.
HIGH OVER THE BORDERS, NFC.
HIGH STAKES IN THE EAST, Netherlands Information Bureau.
INSIDE FIGHTING CHINA, NFC.
IT'S EVERYBODY'S WAR, Office of War Information, FOX.
LISTEN TO BRITAIN, British Ministry of Informaton.
LITTLE BELGIUM, Belgian Ministry of Information.
LITTLE ISLES OF FREEDOM, WB. Victor Stoloff and Edgar Loew.
MR. BLABBERMOUTH, Office of War Information, MGM.
MR. GARDENIA JONES, Office of War Information, MGM.
NEW SPIRIT, U.S. Treasury Department. DNY.
THE PRICE OF VICTORY, Office of War Information, PAR. Pine-Thomas.
TWENTY-ONE MILES, British Ministry of Information.
WE REFUSE TO DIE, Office of War Information, PAR. William C. Thomas.
WHITE EAGLE, Cocanen Films.
WINNING YOUR WINGS, U.S. Army Air Force, WB.

SPECIAL EFFECTS:

REAP THE WILD WIND. Photographic: Farciot Edouart, Gordon Jennings and William L. Pereira. Sound: Louis Mesenkop.
THE BLACK SWAN. Photographic: Fred Sersen. Sound: Roger Heman and George Leverett.
DESPERATE JOURNEY, WB. Photographic: Byron Haskin. Sound: Nathan Levinson.
FLYING TIGERS. Photographic: Howard Lydecker. Sound: Daniel J. Bloomberg.
INVISIBLE AGENT, U. Photographic: John Fulton. Sound: Bernard B. Brown.
JUNGLE BOOK. Photographic: Lawrence Butler. Sound: William H. Wilmarth.
MRS. MINIVER. Photographic: A. Arnold Gillespie and Warren Newcombe. Sound: Douglas Shearer.
THE NAVY COMES THROUGH, RKO. Photographic: Vernon L. Walker. Sound: James G. Stewart.
ONE OF OUR AIRCRAFT IS MISSING. Photographic: Ronald Neame. Sound: C. C. Stevens.
PRIDE OF THE YANKEES. Photographic: Jack Cosgrove and Ray Binger. Sound: Thomas T. Moulton.

HONORARY AND OTHER:

(Irving G. Thalberg Memorial Award)

Sidney Franklin

(Other)

CHARLES BOYER for his progressive cultural achievement in establishing the French Research Foundation in Los Angeles as a source of reference for the Hollywood Motion Picture Industry.
NOEL COWARD for his outstanding production achievement in In Which We Serve.
MGM STUDIO for its achievement in representing the American Way of Life in the production of the Andy Hardy series of films.

SCIENTIFIC OR TECHNICAL:

(Class II)

CARROLL CLARK, F. THOMAS THOMPSON and the **RKO STUDIO ART** and **MINIATURE DEPARTMENTS** for the design and construction of a moving cloud and horizon machine.
DANIEL B. CLARK and the **20TH CENTURY-FOX FILM CORP.** for the development of a lens calibration system and the application of this system to exposure control in cinematography.

(Class III)

ROBERT HENDERSON and the **PARAMOUNT STUDIO ENGINEERING** and **TRANSPARENCY DEPARTMENTS** for the design and construction of adjustable light bridges and screen frames for transparency process photography.
DANIEL J. BLOOMBERG and the **REPUBLIC STUDIO SOUND DEPARTMENT** for the design and application to motion picture production of a device for marking action negative for pre-selection purposes.

1943

BEST PICTURE:

CASABLANCA, WB.
FOR WHOM THE BELL TOLLS, PAR.
HEAVEN CAN WAIT, FOX.
THE HUMAN COMEDY, MGM.
IN WHICH WE SERVE, Two Cities, UA (British).
MADAME CURIE, MGM.
THE MORE THE MERRIER, COL.
THE OX-BOW INCIDENT, FOX.
THE SONG OF BERNADETTE, FOX.
WATCH ON THE RHINE, WB.

ACTOR:

PAUL LUKAS, Watch On The Rhine.
HUMPHREY BOGART, *Casablanca.*
GARY COOPER, *For Whom The Bell Tolls.*
WALTER PIDGEON, *Madame Curie.*
MICKEY ROONEY, *The Human Comedy.*

ACTRESS:

JENNIFER JONES, The Song Of Bernadette.
JEAN ARTHUR, *The More The Merrier.*
INGRID BERGMAN, *For Whom The Bell Tolls.*
JOAN FONTAINE, *The Constant Nymph,* WB.
GREER GARSON, *Madame Curie.*

SUPPORTING ACTOR:

CHARLES COBURN, The More The Merrier.
CHARLES BICKFORD, *The Song Of Bernadette.*
J. CARROL NAISH, *Sahara,* COL.
CLAUDE RAINS, *Casablanca.*
AKIM TAMIROFF, *For Whom The Bell Tolls.*

SUPPORTING ACTRESS:
KATINA PAXINOU, For Whom The Bell Tolls.
GLADYS COOPER, *The Song Of Bernadette.*
PAULETTE GODDARD, *So Proudly We Hail*, PAR.
ANNE REVERE, *The Song Of Bernadette.*
LUCILE WATSON, *Watch On The Rhine.*

DIRECTING:
MICHAEL CURTIZ, Casablanca.
CLARENCE BROWN, *The Human Comedy.*
HENRY KING, *The Song Of Bernadette.*
ERNST LUBITSCH, *Heaven Can Wait.*
GEORGE STEVENS, *The More The Merrier.*

WRITING:
(Original Story)
ACTION IN THE NORTH ATLANTIC, WB. Guy Gilpatric.
THE HUMAN COMEDY. William Saroyan.
DESTINATION TOKYO, WB. Steve Fisher.
THE MORE THE MERRIER. Frank Ross and Robert Russell.
SHADOW OF A DOUBT, U. Gordon McDonell.

(Original Screenplay)
PRINCESS O'ROURKE, WB. Norman Krasna.
AIR FORCE, WB. Dudley Nichols.
IN WHICH WE SERVE. Noel Coward.
THE NORTH STAR, Goldwyn, RKO. Lillian Hellman.
SO PROUDLY WE HAIL. Allan Scott.

(Screenplay)
CASABLANCA. Julius J. Epstein, Philip G. Epstein and Howard Koch.
HOLY MATRIMONY, FOX. Nunnally Johnson.
THE MORE THE MERRIER. Richard Flournoy, Lewis R. Foster, Frank Ross and Robert Russell.
THE SONG OF BERNADETTE. George Seaton.
WATCH ON THE RHINE. Dashiell Hammett.

CINEMATOGRAPHY:
(Black-and-White)
THE SONG OF BERNADETTE. Arthur Miller.
AIR FORCE. James Wong Howe, Elmer Dyer and Charles Marshall.
CASABLANCA. Arthur Edeson.
CORVETTE K-225, U. Tony Gaudio.
FIVE GRAVES TO CAIRO, PAR. John Seitz.
THE HUMAN COMEDY. Harry Stradling.
MADAME CURIE. Joseph Ruttenberg.
THE NORTH STAR. James Wong Howe.
SAHARA. Rudolph Mate.
SO PROUDLY WE HAIL. Charles Lang.

(Color)
PHANTOM OF THE OPERA, U. Hal Mohr and W. Howard Greene.
FOR WHOM THE BELL TOLLS. Ray Rennahan.
HEAVEN CAN WAIT. Edward Cronjager.
HELLO, FRISCO, HELLO, FOX. Charles G. Clarke and Allen Davey.
LASSIE COME HOME, MGM. Leonard Smith.
THOUSANDS CHEER, MGM. George Folsey.

ART DIRECTION - SET DECORATION:
(Black-and-White)
THE SONG OF BERNADETTE. James Basevi and William Darling. Interior Decoration: Thomas Little.
FIVE GRAVES TO CAIRO. Hans Dreier and Ernst Fegte. Interior Decoration: Bertram Granger.
FLIGHT FOR FREEDOM, RKO. Albert S. D'Agostino and Carroll Clark. Interior Decoration: Darrell Silvera and Harley Miller.
MADAME CURIE. Cedric Gibbons and Paul Groesse. Interior Decoration: Edwin B. Willis and Hugh Hunt.
MISSION TO MOSCOW, WB. Carl Weyl. Interior Decoration: George J. Hopkins.
THE NORTH STAR. Perry Ferguson. Interior Decoration: Howard Bristol.

(Color)
PHANTOM OF THE OPERA. Alexander Golitzen and John B. Goodman. Interior Decoration: Russell A. Gausman and Ira S. Webb.
FOR WHOM THE BELL TOLLS. Hans Dreier and Haldane Douglas. Interior Decoration: Bertram Granger.
THE GANG'S ALL HERE, FOX. James Basevi and Joseph C. Wright. Interior Decoration: Thomas Little.
THIS IS THE ARMY, WB. John Hughes and Lt. John Koenig. Interior Decoration: George J. Hopkins.
THOUSANDS CHEER. Cedric Gibbons and Daniel Cathcart. Interior Decoration: Edwin B. Willis and Jacques Mersereau.

FILM EDITING:
AIR FORCE. George Amy.
CASABLANCA. Owen Marks.
FIVE GRAVES TO CAIRO. Doane Harrison.
FOR WHOM THE BELL TOLLS. Sherman Todd and John Link.
THE SONG OF BERNADETTE. Barbara McLean.

MUSIC - SCORING:
(Scoring of a Dramatic or Comedy Picture)
THE SONG OF BERNADETTE. Alfred Newman.
THE AMAZING MRS. HOLLIDAY, U. Hans J. Salter and Frank Skinner.
CASABLANCA. Max Steiner.
THE COMMANDOS STRIKE AT DAWN, COL. Louis Gruenberg and Morris Stoloff.
THE FALLEN SPARROW, RKO. C Bakaleinikoff and Roy Webb.
FOR WHOM THE BELL TOLLS. Victor Young.
HANGMEN ALSO DIE, Arnold, UA. Hanns Eisler.
HI DIDDLE DIDDLE, Stone, UA. Phil Boutelje.
IN OLD OKLAHOMA, REP. Walter Scharf.
JOHNNY COME LATELY, Cagney, UA. Leigh Harline.
THE KANSAN, Sherman, UA. Gerard Carbonara.
LADY OF BURLESQUE, Stromberg, UA. Arthur Lange.
MADAME CURIE. Herbert Stothart.
THE MOON AND SIXPENCE, Loew-Lewin, UA. Dimitri Tiomkin.
THE NORTH STAR. Aaron Copland.
VICTORY THROUGH AIR POWER, Disney, UA. Edward H. Plumb, Paul J. Smith and Oliver G. Wallace.

(Scoring of a Musical Picture)
THIS IS THE ARMY. Ray Heindorf.
CONEY ISLAND, FOX. Alfred Newman.
HIT PARADE OF 1943, REP. Walter Scharf.
THE PHANTOM OF THE OPERA. Edward Ward.
SALUDOS AMIGOS, Disney, RKO. Edward H. Plumb, Paul J. Smith and Charles Wolcott.
THE SKY'S THE LIMIT, RKO. Leigh Harline.
SOMETHING TO SHOUT ABOUT, COL. Morris Stoloff.
STAGE DOOR CANTEEN, Lesser, UA. Frederic E. Rich.
STAR SPANGLED RHYTHM, PAR. Robert Emmett Dolan.
THOUSANDS CHEER. Herbert Stothart.

MUSIC - BEST SONG:
YOU'LL NEVER KNOW, Hello, Frisco, Hello. Music, Harry Warren. Lyrics, Mack Gordon.
BLACK MAGIC, *Star Spangled Rhythm.* Music, Harold Arlen. Lyrics, Johnny Mercer.
CHANGE OF HEART, *Hit Parade Of 1943.* Music, Jule Styne. Lyrics, Harold Adamson.
HAPPINESS IS A THING CALLED JOE, *Cabin In The Sky,* MGM. Music, Harold Arlen. Lyrics, E. Y. Harburg.
MY SHINING HOUR, *The Sky's The Limit.* Music, Harold Arlen. Lyrics, Johnny Mercer.
SALUDOS AMIGOS, *Saludos Amigos.* Music, Charles Wolcott. Lyrics, Ned Washington.
SAY A PRAYER FOR THE BOYS OVER THERE, *Her's To Hold,* U. Music, Jimmy McHugh. Lyrics, Herb Magidson.
THEY'RE EITHER TOO YOUNG OR TOO OLD, *Thank Your Lucky Stars,* WB. Music, Arthur Schwartz. Lyrics, Frank Loesser.
WE MUSTN'T SAY GOOD BYE, *Stage Door Canteen.* Music, James Monaco. Lyrics, Al Dubin.
YOU'D BE SO NICE TO COME HOME TO, *Something To Shout About.* Music and Lyrics by Cole Porter.

SOUND:

THIS LAND IS MINE, RKO. Stephen Dunn.
HANGMEN ALSO DIE. Jack Whitney, Sound Service, Inc.
IN OLD OKLAHOMA. Daniel J. Bloomberg.
MADAME CURIE. Douglas Shearer.
THE NORTH STAR. Thomas Moulton.
THE PHANTOM OF THE OPERA. Bernard B. Brown.
RIDING HIGH, PAR. Loren L. Ryder.
SAHARA. John Livadary.
SALUDOS AMIGOS. C. O. Slyfield.
SO THIS IS WASHINGTON, Votion, RKO. J. L. Fields, RCA Sound.
THE SONG OF BERNADETTE. E. H. Hansen.
THIS IS THE ARMY. Nathan Levinson.

SHORT FILMS:

(Cartoons)

YANKEE DOODLE MOUSE, MGM. Frederick Quimby, Prod.
THE DIZZY ACROBAT, Walter Lantz, U. Walter Lantz, Prod.
THE FIVE HUNDRED HATS OF BARTHOLOMEW CUBBINS, PAR. (George Pal Puppetoon)
GREETINGS, BAIT, WB. Leon Schlesinger, Prod.
IMAGINATION, COL. Dave Fleischer, Prod.
REASON AND EMOTION, Walt Disney, RKO. Walt Disney, Prod.

(One-reel)

AMPHIBIOUS FIGHTERS, PAR. Grantland Rice, Prod.
CAVALCADE OF THE DANCE WITH VELOZ AND YOLANDA, WB. (Melody Master Bands) Gordon Hollingshead, Prod.
CHAMPIONS CARRY ON, FOX. (Sports Reviews) Edmund Reek, Prod.
HOLLYWOOD IN UNIFORM, COL. (Screen Snapshots #1, Series 22) Ralph Staub, Prod.
SEEING HANDS, MGM. (Pete Smith Specialty)

(Two-reel)

HEAVENLY MUSIC, MGM. Jerry Bresler and Sam Coslow, Prods.
LETTER TO A HERO, RKO. (This Is America) Fred Ullman, Prod.
MARDI GRAS, PAR. (Musical Parade) Walter MacEwen, Prod.
WOMEN AT WAR, WB. (Technicolor Special) Gordon Hollingshead, Prod.

DOCUMENTARY:

(Short Subjects)

DECEMBER 7TH, U.S. Navy, Field Photographic Branch, Office of Strategic Services.
CHILDREN OF MARS, This is America Series, RKO.
PLAN FOR DESTRUCTION, MGM.
SWEDES IN AMERICA, Office of War Information, Overseas Motion Picture Bureau.
TO THE PEOPLE OF THE UNITED STATES, U.S. Public Health Service, Walter Wanger Prods.
TOMORROW WE FLY, U.S. Navy, Bureau of Aeronautics.
YOUTH IN CRISIS, MOT, FOX.

(Features)

DESERT VICTORY, British Ministry of Information.
BATTLE OF RUSSIA, Special Service Division of the War Department.
BAPTISM OF FIRE, U.S. Army, Fighting Men Series.
REPORT FROM THE ALEUTIANS, U.S. Army Pictorial Service, Combat Film Series.
WAR DEPARTMENT REPORT, Field Photographic Branch, Office of Strategic Services.

SPECIAL EFFECTS:

CRASH DIVE, FOX. Photographic: Fred Sersen. Sound: Roger Heman.
AIR FORCE. Photographic: Hans Koenekamp and Rex Wimpy. Sound: Nathan Levinson.
BOMBARDIER, RKO. Photographic: Vernon L. Walker. Sound: James G. Stewart and Roy Granville.
THE NORTH STAR. Photographic: Clarence Slifer and R. O. Binger. Sound: Thomas T. Moulton.
SO PROUDLY WE HAIL. Photographic: Farciot Edouart and Gordon Jennings. Sound: George Dutton.
STAND BY FOR ACTION, MGM. Photographic: A. Arnold Gillespie and Donald Jahraus. Sound: Michael Steinore.

HONORARY AND OTHER:

(Irving G. Thalberg Memorial Award)

Hal B. Wallis

(Other)

GEORGE PAL for the development of novel methods and techniques in the production of short subjects known as Puppetoons. (plaque)

SCIENTIFIC OR TECHNICAL:

(Class II)

FARCIOT EDOUART, EARLE MORGAN, BARTON THOMPSON and the **PARAMOUNT STUDIO ENGINEERING** and **TRANSPARENCY DEPARTMENTS** for the development and practical application to motion picture production of a method of duplicating and enlarging natural color photographs, transferring the image emulsions to glass plates and projecting these slides by especially designed stereopticon equipment.
PHOTO PRODUCTS DEPARTMENT, E. I. duPONT de NEMOURS AND CO., INC., for the development of fine-grain motion picture films.

(Class III)

DANIEL J. BLOOMBERG and the **REPUBLIC STUDIO SOUND DEPARTMENT** for the design and development of an inexpensive method of converting Moviolas to Class B push-pull reproduction.
CHARLES GALLOWAY CLARKE and the **20TH CENTURY-FOX STUDIO CAMERA DEPARTMENT** for the development and practical application of a device for composing artificial clouds into motion picture scenes during production photography.
FARCIOT EDOUART and the **PARAMOUNT STUDIO TRANSPARENCY DEPARTMENT** for an automatic electric transparency cueing timer.
WILLARD H. TURNER and the **RKO STUDIO SOUND DEPARTMENT** for the design and construction of the phono-cue starter.

1944

BEST PICTURE:

GOING MY WAY, PAR.
DOUBLE INDEMNITY, PAR.
GASLIGHT, MGM.
SINCE YOU WENT AWAY, Selznick Int'l, UA.
WILSON, FOX.

ACTOR:

BING CROSBY, Going My Way.
CHARLES BOYER, *Gaslight*.
BARRY FITZGERALD, *Going My Way*.
CARY GRANT, *None But The Lonely Heart*, RKO.
ALEXANDER KNOX, *Wilson*.

ACTRESS:

INGRID BERGMAN, Gaslight.
CLAUDETTE COLBERT, *Since You Went Away*.
BETTE DAVIS, *Mr. Skeffington*, WB.
GREER GARSON, *Mrs. Parkington*, MGM.
BARBARA STANWYCK, *Double Indemnity*.

SUPPORTING ACTOR:

BARRY FITZGERALD, Going My Way.
HUME CRONYN, *The Seventh Cross*, MGM.
CLAUDE RAINS, *Mr. Skeffington*.
CLIFTON WEBB, *Laura*, FOX.
MONTY WOOLLEY, *Since You Went Away*.

SUPPORTING ACTRESS:
ETHEL BARRYMORE, None But The Lonely Heart.
JENNIFER JONES, *Since You Went Away.*
ANGELA LANSBURY, *Gaslight.*
ALINE MacMAHON, *Dragon Seed*, MGM.
AGNES MOOREHEAD, *Mrs. Parkington.*

DIRECTING:
LEO McCAREY, Going My Way.
ALFRED HITCHCOCK, *Lifeboat*, FOX.
HENRY KING, *Wilson.*
OTTO PREMINGER, *Laura.*
BILLY WILDER, *Double Indemnity.*

WRITING:
(Original Story)
GOING MY WAY. Leo McCarey.
A GUY NAMED JOE, MGM. David Boehm and Chandler Sprague.
LIFEBOAT. John Steinbeck.
NONE SHALL ESCAPE, COL. Alfred Neumann and Joseph Than.
THE SULLIVANS, FOX. Edward Doherty and Jules Schermer.

(Original Screenplay)
WILSON. Lamar Trotti.
HAIL THE CONQUERING HERO, PAR. Preston Sturges.
THE MIRACLE OF MORGAN'S CREEK, PAR. Preston Sturges.
TWO GIRLS AND A SAILOR, MGM. Richard Connell and Gladys Lehman.
WING AND A PRAYER, FOX. Jerome Cady.

(Screenplay)
GOING MY WAY. Frank Butler and Frank Cavett.
DOUBLE INDEMNITY. Raymond Chandler and Billy Wilder.
GASLIGHT. John L. Balderston, Walter Reisch and John Van Druten.
LAURA. Jay Dratler, Samuel Hoffenstein and Betty Reinhardt.
MEET ME IN ST. LOUIS, MGM. Irving Brecher and Fred F. Finkelhoffe.

CINEMATOGRAPHY:
(Black-and-White)
LAURA. Joseph LaShelle.
DOUBLE INDEMNITY. John Seitz.
DRAGON SEED. Sidney Wagner.
GASLIGHT. Joseph Ruttenberg.
GOING MY WAY. Lionel Lindon.
LIFEBOAT. Glen MacWilliams.
SINCE YOU WENT AWAY. Stanley Cortez and Lee Garmes.
THIRTY SECONDS OVER TOKYO, MGM. Robert Surtees and Harold Rosson.
THE UNINVITED, PAR. Charles Lang.
THE WHITE CLIFFS OF DOVER, MGM. George Folsey.

(Color)
WILSON. Leon Shamroy.
COVER GIRL, COL. Rudy Mate and Allen M. Davey.
HOME IN INDIANA, FOX. Edward Cronjager.
KISMET, MGM. Charles Rosher.
LADY IN THE DARK, PAR. Ray Rennahan.
MEET ME IN ST. LOUIS. George Folsey.

ART DIRECTION - SET DECORATION:
(Black-and-White)
GASLIGHT. Cedric Gibbons and William Ferrari. Interior Decoration: Edwin B. Willis and Paul Huldschinsky.
ADDRESS UNKNOWN, COL. Lionel Banks and Walter Holscher. Interior Decoration: Joseph Kish.
THE ADVENTURES OF MARK TWAIN, WB. John J. Hughes. Interior Decoration: Fred MacLean.
CASANOVA BROWN, Int'l, RKO. Perry Ferguson. Interior Decoration: Julia Heron.
LAURA. Lyle Wheeler and Leland Fuller. Interior Decoration: Thomas Little.
NO TIME FOR LOVE, PAR. Hans Dreier and Robert Usher. Interior Decoration: Sam Comer.
SINCE YOU WENT AWAY. Mark-Lee Kirk. Interior Decoration: Victor A. Gangelin.
STEP LIVELY, RKO. Albert S. D'Agostino and Carroll Clark. Interior Decoration: Darrell Silvera and Claude Carpenter.

(Color)
WILSON. Wiard Ihnen. Interior Decoration: Thomas Little.
THE CLIMAX, U. John B. Goodman and Alexander Golitzen. Interior Decoration: Russell A. Gausman and Ira S. Webb.
COVER GIRL. Lionel Banks and Cary Odell. Interior Decoration: Fay Babcock.
THE DESERT SONG, WB. Charles Novi. Interior Decoration: Jack McConaghy.
KISMET. Cedric Gibbons and Daniel B. Cathcart. Interior Decoration: Edwin B. Willis and Richard Pefferle.
LADY IN THE DARK. Hans Dreier and Raoul Pene du Bois. Interior Decoration: Ray Moyer.
THE PRINCESS AND THE PIRATE, Goldwyn, RKO. Ernst Fegte. Interior Decoration: Howard Bristol.

FILM EDITING:
WILSON. Barbara McLean.
GOING MY WAY. Leroy Stone.
JANIE, WB. Owen Marks.
NONE BUT THE LONELY HEART. Roland Gross.
SINCE YOU WENT AWAY. Hal C. Kern and James E. Newcom.

MUSIC - SCORING:
(Scoring of a Dramatic or Comedy Picture)
SINCE YOU WENT AWAY. Max Steiner.
ADDRESS UNKNOWN, COL. Morris Stoloff and Ernst Toch.
THE ADVENTURES OF MARK TWAIN. Max Steiner.
THE BRIDGE OF SAN LUIS REY, Bogeaus, UA. Dimitri Tiomkin.
CASANOVA BROWN. Arthur Lange.
CHRISTMAS HOLIDAY, U. H. J. Salter.
DOUBLE INDEMNITY. Miklos Rozsa.
THE FIGHTING SEABEES, REP. Walter Scharf and Roy Webb.
THE HAIRY APE, Levey, UA. Michel Michelet and Edward Paul.
IT HAPPENED TOMORROW, Arnold, UA. Robert Stolz.
JACK LONDON, Bronston, UA. Frederic E. Rich.
KISMET. Herbert Stothart.
NONE BUT THE LONELY HEART. C. Bakaleinikoff and Hanns Eisler.
THE PRINCESS AND THE PIRATE. David Rose.
SUMMER STORM, Angelus, UA. Karl Hajos.
THREE RUSSIAN GIRLS, R & F Prods., UA. Franke Harling.
UP IN MABEL'S ROOM, Small, UA. Edward Paul.
VOICE IN THE WIND, Ripley-Monter, UA. Michel Michelet.
WILSON. Alfred Newman.
WOMAN OF THE TOWN, Sherman, UA. Miklos Rozsa.

(Scoring of a Musical Picture)
COVER GIRL. Carmen Dragon and Morris Stoloff.
BRAZIL, REP. Walter Scharf.
HIGHER AND HIGHER, RKO. C. Bakaleinikoff.
HOLLYWOOD CANTEEN, WB. Ray Heindorf.
IRISH EYES ARE SMILING, FOX. Alfred Newman.
KNICKERBOCKER HOLIDAY, RCA, UA. Werner R. Heymann and Kurt Weill.
LADY IN THE DARK. Robert Emmett Dolan.
LADY LET'S DANCE, MNG. Edward Kay.
MEET ME IN ST. LOUIS. Georgie Stoll.
THE MERRY MONAHANS, U, H. J. Salter.
MINSTREL MAN, PRC. Leo Erdody and Ferdie Grofe.
SENSATIONS OF 1945, Stone, UA. Mahlon Merrick.
SONG OF THE OPEN ROAD, Rogers, UA. Charles Previn.
UP IN ARMS, Avalon, RKO. Louis Forbes and Ray Heindorf.

MUSIC - BEST SONG:
SWINGING ON A STAR, Going My Way. Music, James Van Heusen. Lyrics, Johnny Burke.
I COULDN'T SLEEP A WINK LAST NIGHT, *Higher And Higher.* Music, Jimmy McHugh. Lyrics, Harold Adamson.

I'LL WALK ALONE, *Follow The Boys,* U. Music, Jule Styne. Lyrics, Sammy Cahn.
I'M MAKING BELIEVE, *Sweet And Lowdown,* FOX. Music, James V. Monaco. Lyrics, Mack Gordon.
LONG AGO AND FAR AWAY, *Cover Girl.* Music, Jerome Kern. Lyrics, Ira Gershwin.
NOW I KNOW, *Up In Arms.* Music, Harold Arlen. Lyrics, Ted Koehler.
REMEMBER ME TO CAROLINA, *Minstrel Man.* Music, Harry Revel. Lyrics, Paul Webster.
RIO DE JANEIRO, *Brazil.* Music, Ary Barroso. Lyrics, Ned Washington.
SILVER SHADOWS AND GOLDEN DREAMS, *Lady Let's Dance.* Music, Lew Pollack. Lyrics, Charles Newman.
SWEET DREAMS SWEETHEART, *Hollywood Canteen.* Music, M. K. Jerome. Lyrics, Ted Koehler.
TOO MUCH IN LOVE, *Song Of The Open Road.* Music, Walter Kent. Lyrics, Kim Gannon.
THE TROLLEY SONG, *Meet Me In St. Louis.* Music and Lyrics by Ralph Blane and Hugh Martin.

SOUND:

WILSON. E. H. Hansen.
BRAZIL. Daniel J. Bloomberg.
CASANOVA BROWN. Thomas T. Moulton, Goldwyn Sound Department.
COVER GIRL. John Livadary.
DOUBLE INDEMNITY. Loren Ryder.
HIS BUTLER'S SISTER, U. Bernard B. Brown.
HOLLYWOOD CANTEEN. Nathan Levinson.
IT HAPPENED TOMORROW, Arnold, UA. Jack Whitney, Sound Service, Inc.
KISMET. Douglas Shearer.
MUSIC IN MANHATTAN, RKO. Stephen Dunn.
VOICE IN THE WIND. W. M. Dalgleish, RCA Sound.

SHORT FILMS:

(Cartoons)
MOUSE TROUBLE, MGM. Frederick C. Quimby, Prod.
AND TO THINK I SAW IT ON MULBERRY STREET, PAR. (George Pal Puppetoon)
THE DOG, CAT AND CANARY, COL. (Screen Gems)
FISH FRY, U. Walter Lantz, Prod.
HOW TO PLAY FOOTBALL, Walt Disney, RKO. Walt Disney, Prod.
MY BOY, JOHNNY, FOX. Paul Terry, Prod.
SWOONER CROONER, WB.
(One-reel)
WHO'S WHO IN ANIMAL LAND, PAR. (Speaking of Animals) Jerry Fairbanks, Prod.
BLUE GRASS GENTLEMEN, FOX. (Sports Review) Edmund Reek, Prod.
JAMMIN' THE BLUES, WB. (Melody Master Bands) Gordon Hollingshead, Prod.
MOVIE PESTS, MGM. (Pete Smith Specialty)
50TH ANNIVERSARY OF MOTION PICTURES, COL. (Screen Snapshots #9, Series 23) Ralph Staub, Prod.
(Two-reel)
I WON'T PLAY, WB. (Featurette) Gordon Hollingshead, Prod.
BOMBALERA, PAR. (Muscial Parade) Louis Harris, Prod.
MAIN STREET TODAY, MGM. (Two-reel Special) Jerry Bresler, Prod.

DOCUMENTARY:

(Short Subjects)
WITH THE MARINES AT TARAWA, U.S. Marine Corps.
ARTURO TOSCANINI, Motion Picture Bureau, Overseas Branch, Office of War Information.
NEW AMERICANS, This is America Series, RKO.
(Features)
THE FIGHTING LADY, FOX and U.S. Navy.
RESISTING ENEMY INTERROGATION, U.S. Army Air Force.

SPECIAL EFFECTS:

THIRTY SECONDS OVER TOKYO. Photographic: A. Arnold Gillespie, Donald Jahraus and Warren Newcombe. Sound: Douglas Shearer.
THE ADVENTURES OF MARK TWAIN. Photographic: Paul Detlefsen and John Crouse. Sound: Nathan Levinson.
DAYS OF GLORY, RKO. Photographic: Vernon L. Walker. Sound: James G. Stewart and Roy Granville.
SECRET COMMAND, COL. Photographic: David Allen, Ray Cory and Robert Wright. Sound: Russell Malmgren and Harry Kusnick.
SINCE YOU WENT AWAY. Photographic: John R. Cosgrove. Sound: Arthur Johns.
THE STORY OF DR. WASSELL, PAR. Photographic: Farciot Edouart and Gordon Jennings. Sound: George Dutton.
WILSON. Photographic: Fred Sersen. Sound: Roger Heman.

HONORARY AND OTHER:

(Irving G. Thalberg Memorial Award)
Darryl F. Zanuck
(Other)
MARGARET O'BRIEN, outstanding child actress of 1944.
BOB HOPE, for his many services to the Academy, a Life Membership in the Academy of Motion Picture Arts and Sciences.

SCIENTIFIC OR TECHNICAL:

(Class II Plaque)
STEPHEN DUNN and the **RKO STUDIO SOUND DEPARTMENT** and **RADIO CORPORATION OF AMERICA** for the design and development of the electronic compressor-limiter.
(Class III)
LINWOOD DUNN, CECIL LOVE and **ACME TOOL MANUFACTURING CO.** for the design and construction of the Acme-Dunn Optical Printer.
GROVER LAUBE and the **20TH CENTURY-FOX STUDIO CAMERA DEPARTMENT** for the development of a continuous loop projection device.
WESTERN ELECTRIC CO. for the design and construction of the 1126A Limiting Amplifier for variable density sound recording.
RUSSELL BROWN, RAY HINSDALE and **JOSEPH E. ROBBINS** for the development and production use of the Paramount floating hydraulic boat rocker.
GORDON JENNINGS for the design and construction of the Paramount nodal point tripod.
RADIO CORPORATION OF AMERICA and the **RKO STUDIO SOUND DEPARTMENT** for the design and construction of the RKO reverberation chamber.
DANIEL J. BLOOMBERG and the **REPUBLIC STUDIO SOUND DEPARTMENT** for the design and development of a multi-interlock selector switch.
BERNARD B. BROWN and **JOHN P. LIVADARY** for the design and engineering of a separate soloist and chorus recording room.
PAUL ZEFF, S. J. TWINING and **GEORGE SEID** of the Columbia Studio Laboratory for the formula and application to production of a simplified variable area sound negative developer.
PAUL LERPAE for the design and construction of the Paramount traveling matte projection and photographing device.

1945

BEST PICTURE:

THE LOST WEEKEND, PAR.
ANCHORS AWEIGH, MGM.
THE BELLS OF ST. MARY'S, Rainbow, RKO.
MILDRED PIERCE, WB.
SPELLBOUND, Selznick Int'l, UA.

ACTOR:
RAY MILLAND, The Lost Weekend.
BING CROSBY, *The Bells Of St. Mary's.*
GENE KELLY, *Anchors Aweigh.*
GREGORY PECK, *The Keys Of The Kingdom,* FOX.
CORNEL WILDE, *A Song To Remember,* COL.

ACTRESS:
JOAN CRAWFORD, Mildred Pierce.
INGRID BERGMAN, *The Bells Of St. Mary's.*
GREER GARSON, *The Valley Of Decision,* MGM.
JENNIFER JONES, *Love Letters,* Wallis, PAR.
GENE TIERNEY, *Leave Her To Heaven,* FOX.

SUPPORTING ACTOR:
JAMES DUNN, A Tree Grows In Brooklyn, FOX.
MICHAEL CHEKHOV, *Spellbound.*
JOHN DALL, *The Corn Is Green,* WB.
ROBERT MITCHUM, *G. I. Joe,* Cowan, UA.
J. CARROL NAISH, *A Medal For Benny,* PAR.

SUPPORTING ACTRESS:
ANNE REVERE, National Velvet, MGM.
EVE ARDEN, *Mildred Pierce.*
ANN BLYTH, *Mildred Pierce.*
ANGELA LANSBURY, *The Picture Of Dorian Gray,* MGM.
JOAN LORRING, *The Corn Is Green.*

DIRECTING:
BILLY WILDER, The Lost Weekend.
CLARENCE BROWN, *National Velvet.*
ALFRED HITCHCOCK, *Spellbound.*
LEO McCAREY, *The Bells Of St. Mary's.*
JEAN RENOIR, *The Southerner,* Loew-Hakim, UA.

WRITING:
(Original Story)
THE HOUSE ON 92ND STREET, FOX. Charles G. Booth.
THE AFFAIRS OF SUSAN, Wallis, PAR. Laszlo Gorog and Thomas Monroe.
A MEDAL FOR BENNY. John Steinbeck and Jack Wagner.
OBJECTIVE-BURMA, WB. Alvah Bessie.
A SONG TO REMEMBER. Ernst Marischka.
(Original Screenplay)
MARIE-LOUISE, PRA (Swiss). Richard Schweizer.
DILLINGER, MNG. Philip Yordan.
MUSIC FOR MILLIONS, MGM. Myles Connolly.
SALTY O'ROURKE, PAR. Milton Holmes.
WHAT NEXT, CORPORAL HARGROVE?, MGM. Harry Kurnitz.
(Screenplay)
THE LOST WEEKEND. Charles Brackett and Billy Wilder.
G. I. JOE. Leopold Atlas, Guy Endore and Philip Stevenson.
MILDRED PIERCE. Ranald MacDougall.
PRIDE OF THE MARINES, WB. Albert Maltz.
A TREE GROWS IN BROOKLYN. Frank Davis and Tess Slesinger.

CINEMATOGRAPHY:
(Black-and-White)
THE PICTURE OF DORIAN GRAY. Harry Stradling.
THE KEYS OF THE KINGDOM. Arthur Miller.
THE LOST WEEKEND. John F. Seitz.
MILDRED PIERCE. Ernest Haller.
SPELLBOUND. George Barnes.
(Color)
LEAVE HER TO HEAVEN. Leon Shamroy.
ANCHORS AWEIGH. Robert Planck and Charles Boyle.
NATIONAL VELVET. Leonard Smith.
A SONG TO REMEMBER. Tony Gaudio and Allen M. Davey.
THE SPANISH MAIN, RKO. George Barnes.

ART DIRECTION - SET DECORATION:
(Black-and-White)
BLOOD ON THE SUN, Cagney, UA. Wiard Ihnen. Interior Decoration: A. Roland Fields.
EXPERIMENT PERILOUS, RKO. Albert S. D'Agostino and Jack Okey. Interior Decoration: Darrell Silvera and Claude Carpenter.
THE KEYS OF THE KINGDOM. James Basevi and William Darling. Interior Decoration: Thomas Little and Frank E. Hughes.
LOVE LETTERS, Hal Wallis, PAR. Hans Dreier and Roland Anderson. Interior Decoration: Sam Comer and Ray Moyer.
THE PICTURE OF DORIAN GRAY. Cedric Gibbons and Hans Peters. Interior Decoration: Edwin B. Willis, John Bonar and Hugh Hunt.
(Color)
FRENCHMAN'S CREEK, PAR. Hans Dreier and Ernst Fegte. Interior Decoration: Sam Comer.
LEAVE HER TO HEAVEN. Lyle Wheeler and Maurice Ransford. Interior Decoration: Thomas Little.
NATIONAL VELVET. Cedric Gibbons and Urie McCleary. Interior Decoration: Edwin B. Willis and Mildred Griffiths.
SAN ANTONIO, WB. Ted Smith. Interior Decoration: Jack McConaghy.
A THOUSAND AND ONE NIGHTS, COL. Stephen Goosson and Rudolph Sternad. Interior Decoration: Frank Tuttle.

FILM EDITING:
NATIONAL VELVET. Robert J. Kern.
THE BELLS OF ST. MARY'S. Harry Marker.
THE LOST WEEKEND. Doane Harrison.
OBJECTIVE-BURMA. George Amy.
A SONG TO REMEMBER. Charles Nelson.

MUSIC - SCORING:
(Scoring of a Dramatic or Comedy Picture)
SPELLBOUND. Miklos Rozsa.
THE BELLS OF ST. MARY'S. Robert Emmett Dolan.
BREWSTER'S MILLIONS, Small, UA. Lou Forbes.
CAPTAIN KIDD, Bogeaus, UA. Werner Janssen.
ENCHANTED COTTAGE, RKO. Roy Webb.
FLAME OF THE BARBARY COAST, REP. Dale Butts and Morton Scott.
G. I. HONEYMOON, MNG. Edward J. Kay.
G. I. Joe. Louis Applebaum and Ann Ronell.
GUEST IN THE HOUSE, Guest in The House, Inc., UA. Werner Janssen.
GUEST WIFE, Greentree Prods., UA. Daniele Amfitheatrof.
THE KEYS OF THE KINGDOM. Alfred Newman.
THE LOST WEEKEND. Miklos Rozsa.
LOVE LETTERS. Victor Young.
MAN WHO WALKED ALONE, PRC. Karl Hajos.
OBJECTIVE-BURMA. Franz Waxman.
PARIS-UNDERGROUND, Bennett, UA. Alexander Tansman.
A SONG TO REMEMBER. Miklos Rozsa and Morris Stoloff.
THE SOUTHERNER. Werner Janssen.
THIS LOVE OF OURS, U. H. J. Salter.
VALLEY OF DECISION. Herbert Stothart.
WOMAN IN THE WINDOW, Int'l, RKO. Hugo Friedhofer and Arthur Lange.
(Scoring of a Musical Picture)
ANCHORS AWEIGH. Georgie Stoll.
BELLE OF THE YUKON, Int'l, RKO. Arthur Lange.
CAN'T HELP SINGING, U. Jerome Kern and H. J. Salter.
HITCHHIKE TO HAPPINESS, REP. Morton Scott.
INCENDIARY BLONDE, PAR. Robert Emmett Dolan.
RHAPSODY IN BLUE, WB. Ray Heindorf and Max Steiner.
STATE FAIR, FOX. Charles Henderson and Alfred Newman.
SUNBONNET SUE, MNG. Edward J. Kay.
THE THREE CABALLEROS, Disney-RKO. Edward Plumb, Paul J. Smith and Charles Wolcott.
TONIGHT AND EVERY NIGHT, COL. Marlin Skiles and Morris Stoloff.
WHY GIRLS LEAVE HOME, PRC. Walter Greene.
WONDER MAN, Beverly, RKO. Lou Forbes and Ray Heindorf.

MUSIC - BEST SONG:

IT MIGHT AS WELL BE SPRING, State Fair. Music, Richard Rodgers. Lyrics, Oscar Hammerstein II.
ACCENTUATE THE POSITIVE, *Here Come The Waves,* PAR. Music, Harold Arlen. Lyrics, Johnny Mercer.
ANYWHERE, *Tonight And Every Night.* Music, Jule Styne. Lyrics, Sammy Cahn.
AREN'T YOU GLAD YOU'RE YOU, *The Bells Of St. Mary's.* Music, James Van Heusen. Lyrics, Johnny Burke.
THE CAT AND THE CANARY, *Why Girls Leave Home.* Music, Jay Livingston. Lyrics, Ray Evans.
ENDLESSLY, *Earl Carroll Vanities,* REP. Music, Walter Kent. Lyrics, Kim Gannon.
I FALL IN LOVE TOO EASILY, *Anchors Aweigh.* Music, Jule Styne. Lyrics, Sammy Cahn.
I'LL BUY THAT DREAM, *Sing Your Way Home,* RKO. Music, Allie Wrubel. Lyrics, Herb Magidson.
LINDA, *G. I. Joe.* Music and Lyrics by Ann Ronell.
LOVE LETTERS, *Love Letters.* Music, Victor Young. Lyrics, Edward Heyman.
MORE AND MORE, *Can't Help Singing,* U. Music, Jerome Kern. Lyrics, E. Y. Harburg.
SLEIGHRIDE IN JULY, *Belle Of The Yukon.* Music, James Van Heusen. Lyrics, Johnny Burke.
SO IN LOVE, *Wonder Man.* Music, David Rose. Lyrics, Leo Robin.
SOME SUNDAY MORNING, *San Antonio.* Music, Ray Heindorf and M. K. Jerome. Lyrics, Ted Koehler.

SOUND:

THE BELLS OF ST. MARY'S. Stephen Dunn.
THE FLAME OF THE BARBARY COAST. Daniel J. Bloomberg.
LADY ON A TRAIN, U. Bernard B. Brown.
LEAVE HER TO HEAVEN. Thomas T. Moulton.
RHAPSODY IN BLUE, WB. Nathan Levinson.
A SONG TO REMEMBER. John Livadary.
THE SOUTHERNER. Jack Whitney, General Service.
THEY WERE EXPENDABLE, MGM. Douglas Shearer.
THE THREE CABALLEROS. C. O. Slyfield.
THREE IS A FAMILY, Master Productions, UA. W. V. Wolfe, RCA Sound.
THE UNSEEN, PAR. Loren L. Ryder.
WONDER MAN. Gordon Sawyer.

SHORT FILMS:
(Cartoons)

QUIET PLEASE, MGM. (Tom & Jerry Series) Frederick Quimby, Prod.
DONALD'S CRIME, Walt Disney, RKO. (Donald Duck) Walt Disney, Prod.
JASPER AND THE BEANSTALK, PAR. (Pal Puppetoon-Jasper Series) George Pal, Prod.
LIFE WITH FEATHERS, WB. (Merrie Melodies) Eddie Selzer, Prod.
MIGHTY MOUSE IN GYPSY LIFE, FOX. (Terrytoon) Paul Terry, Prod.
POET AND PEASANT, U. (Lantz Technicolor Cartune) Walter Lantz, Prod.
RIPPLING ROMANCE, COL. (Color Rhapsodies)

(One-reel)

STAIRWAY TO LIGHT, MGM. (John Nesbitt Passing Parade) Herbert Moulton, Prod.
ALONG THE RAINBOW TRAIL, FOX. (Movietone Adventure) Edmund Reek, Prod.
SCREEN SNAPSHOTS 25TH ANNIVERSARY, COL. (Screen Snapshots) Ralph Staub, Prod.
STORY OF A DOG, WB. (Vitaphone Varieties) Gordon Hollingshead, Prod.
WHITE RHAPSODY, PAR. (Sportlights) Grantland Rice, Prod.
YOUR NATIONAL GALLERY, U. (Variety Views) Joseph O'Brien and Thomas Mead, Prods.

(Two-reel)

STAR IN THE NIGHT, WB. (Broadway Brevities) Gordon Hollingshead, Prod.
A GUN IN HIS HAND, MGM. (Crime Does Not Pay) Chester Franklin, Prod.
THE JURY GOES ROUND 'N' ROUND, COL. (All Star Comedies) Jules White, Prod.
THE LITTLE WITCH, PAR. (Musical Parade) George Templeton, Prod.

DOCUMENTARY:
(Short Subjects)

HITLER LIVES?, WB.
LIBRARY OF CONGRESS, Overseas Motion Picture Bureau, Office of War Information.
TO THE SHORES OF IWO JIMA, U.S. Marine Corps.

(Features)

THE TRUE GLORY, Governments of Great Britain and USA.
THE LAST BOMB, U.S. Army Air Force.

SPECIAL EFFECTS:

WONDER MAN. Photographic: John Fulton. Sound: A. W. Johns.
CAPTAIN EDDIE, FOX. Photographic: Fred Sersen and Sol Halprin. Sound: Roger Heman and Harry Leonard.
SPELLBOUND. Photographic: Jack Cosgrove. Sound: No credits listed.
THEY WERE EXPENDABLE. Photographic: A. Arnold Gillespie, Donald Jahraus and R. A. MacDonald. Sound: Michael Steinore.
A THOUSAND AND ONE NIGHTS. Photographic: L. W. Butler. Sound: Ray Bomba.

HONORARY AND OTHER:
(Other)

WALTER WANGER for his six years service as President of the Academy of Motion Picture Arts and Sciences.
PEGGY ANN GARNER, outstanding child actress of 1945.
THE HOUSE I LIVE IN, tolerance short subject; produced by Frank Ross and Mervyn LeRoy; directed by Mervyn LeRoy; screenplay by Albert Maltz; song "The House I Live In," music by Earl Robinson, lyrics by Lewis Allen; starring Frank Sinatra; released by RKO.
REPUBLIC STUDIO, DANIEL J. BLOOMBERG and the REPUBLIC SOUND DEPARTMENT for the building of an outstanding musical scoring auditorium which provides optimum recording conditions and combines all elements of acoustic and engineering design.

SCIENTIFIC OR TECHNICAL:
(Class III)

LOREN L. RYDER, CHARLES R. DAILY and the **PARAMOUNT STUDIO SOUND DEPARTMENT** for the design, construction and use of the first dial controlled step-by-step sound channel line-up and test circuit.
MICHAEL S. LESHING, BENJAMIN C. ROBINSON, ARTHUR B. CHATELAIN and ROBERT C. STEVENS of 20th Century-Fox Studio and JOHN G. CAPSTAFF of Eastman Kodak Co. for the 20th Century-Fox film processing machine.

1946

BEST PICTURE:

THE BEST YEARS OF OUR LIVES, Goldwyn, RKO.
HENRY V, Rank-Two Cities, UA (British).
IT'S A WONDERFUL LIFE, Liberty, RKO.
THE RAZOR'S EDGE, FOX.
THE YEARLING, MGM.

ACTOR:

FREDRIC MARCH, *The Best Years Of Our Lives.*
LAURENCE OLIVIER, *Henry V.*
LARRY PARKS, *The Jolson Story,* COL.
GREGORY PECK, *The Yearling.*
JAMES STEWART, *It's A Wonderful Life.*

ACTRESS:
OLIVIA DE HAVILLAND, To Each His Own, PAR.
CELIA JOHNSON, *Brief Encounter*, Rank, UI. (British)
JENNIFER JONES, *Duel In The Sun*, SZI.
ROSALIND RUSSELL, *Sister Kenny*, RKO.
JANE WYMAN, *The Yearling*.

SUPPORTING ACTOR:
HAROLD RUSSELL, The Best Years Of Our Lives.
CHARLES COBURN, *The Green Years*, MGM.
WILLIAM DEMAREST, *The Jolson Story*.
CLAUDE RAINS, *Notorious*, RKO.
CLIFTON WEBB, *The Razor's Edge*.

SUPPORTING ACTRESS:
ANNE BAXTER, The Razor's Edge.
ETHEL BARRYMORE, *The Spiral Staircase*, RKO.
LILLIAN GISH, *Duel In The Sun*.
FLORA ROBSON, *Saratoga Trunk*, WB.
GALE SONDERGAARD, *Anna And The King Of Siam*, FOX.

DIRECTING:
WILLIAM WYLER, The Best Years Of Our Lives.
CLARENCE BROWN, *The Yearling*.
FRANK CAPRA, *It's A Wonderful Life*.
DAVID LEAN, *Brief Encounter*.
ROBERT SIODMAK, *The Killers*, Hellinger, U.

WRITING:
(Original Story)
VACATION FROM MARRIAGE, London Films, MGM (British). Clemence Dane.
THE DARK MIRROR, UI. Vladimir Pozner.
THE STRANGE LOVE OF MARTHA IVERS, Wallis, PAR. Jack Patrick.
THE STRANGER, Int'l, RKO. Victor Trivas.
TO EACH HIS OWN, PAR. Charles Brackett.
(Original Screenplay)
THE SEVENTH VEIL, Rank, U (British). Muriel Box and Sydney Box.
THE BLUE DAHLIA, PAR. Raymond Chandler.
CHILDREN OF PARADISE, Pathe-Cinema, Tricolore (French). Jacques Prevert.
NOTORIOUS. Ben Hecht.
THE ROAD TO UTOPIA, PAR. Norman Panama and Melvin Frank.
(Screenplay)
THE BEST YEARS OF OUR LIVES. Robert E. Sherwood.
ANNA AND THE KING OF SIAM. Sally Benson and Talbot Jennings.
BRIEF ENCOUNTER. Anthony Havelock-Allan, David Lean and Ronald Neame.
THE KILLERS. Anthony Veiller.
OPEN CITY, MNV (Italian). Sergio Amidei and F. Fellini.

CINEMATOGRAPHY:
(Black-and-White)
ANNA AND THE KING OF SIAM. Arthur Miller.
THE GREEN YEARS, MGM. George Folsey.
(Color)
THE YEARLING. Charles Rosher, Leonard Smith and Arthur Arling.
THE JOLSON STORY. Joseph Walker.

ART DIRECTION - SET DECORATION:
(Black-and-White)
ANNA AND THE KING OF SIAM. Lyle Wheeler and William Darling. Interior Decoration: Thomas Little and Frank E. Hughes.
KITTY, PAR. Hans Dreier and Walter Tyler. Interior Decoration: Sam Comer and Ray Moyer.
THE RAZOR'S EDGE. Richard Day and Nathan Juran. Interior Decoration: Thomas Little and Paul S. FOX.
(Color)
THE YEARLING. Cedric Gibbons and Paul Groesse. Interior Decoration: Edwin B. Willis.
CAESAR AND CLEOPATRA, Rank, UA (British). John Bryan. Interior Decoration: No credits listed.
HENRY V. Paul Sheriff and Carmen Dillon. Interior Decoration: No credits listed.

FILM EDITING:
THE BEST YEARS OF OUR LIVES. Daniel Mandell.
IT'S A WONDERFUL LIFE. William Hornbeck.
THE JOLSON STORY. William Lyon.
THE KILLERS. Arthur Hilton.
THE YEARLING. Harold Kress.

MUSIC - SCORING:
(Scoring of a Dramatic or Comedy Picture)
THE BEST YEARS OF OUR LIVES. Hugo Friedhofer.
ANNA AND THE KING OF SIAM. Bernard Herrmann.
HENRY V. William Walton.
HUMORESQUE, WB. Franz Waxman.
THE KILLERS. Miklos Rozsa.
(Scoring of a Musical Picture)
THE JOLSON STORY, COL. Morris Stoloff.
BLUE SKIES, PAR. Robert Emmett Dolan.
CENTENNIAL SUMMER, FOX. Alfred Newman.
THE HARVEY GIRLS, MGM. Lennie Hayton.
NIGHT AND DAY, WB. Ray Heindorf and Max Steiner.

MUSIC - BEST SONG:
ON THE ATCHISON, TOPEKA AND SANTA FE, Harvey Girls. Music, Harry Warren. Lyrics, Johnny Mercer.
ALL THROUGH THE DAY, *Centennial Summer*. Music, Jerome Kern. Lyrics, Oscar Hammerstein II.
I CAN'T BEGIN TO TELL YOU, *The Dolly Sisters*, FOX. Music, James Monaco. Lyrics, Mack Gordon.
OLE BUTTERMILK SKY, *Canyon Passage*, Wanger, U. Music, Hoagy Carmichael. Lyrics, Jack Brooks.
YOU KEEP COMING BACK LIKE A SONG, *Blue Skies*. Music and Lyrics by Irving Berlin.

SOUND:
THE JOLSON STORY. John Livadary.
THE BEST YEARS OF OUR LIVES. Gordon Sawyer.
IT'S A WONDERFUL LIFE. John Aalberg.

SHORT FILMS:
(Cartoons)
THE CAT CONCERTO, MGM. (Tom & Jerry) Frederick Quimby, Prod.
CHOPIN'S MUSICAL MOMENTS, U. (Musical Miniatures) Walter Lantz, Prod.
JOHN HENRY AND THE INKY POO, PAR. (Puppetoon) George Pal, Prod.
SQUATTER'S RIGHTS, Disney-RKO. (Mickey Mouse) Walt Disney, Prod.
WALKY TALKY HAWKY, WB. (Merrie Melodies) Edward Selzer, Prod.
(One-reel)
FACING YOUR DANGER, WB. (Sports Parade) Gordon Hollingshead, Prod.
DIVE-HI CHAMPS, PAR. (Sportlights) Jack Eaton, Prod.
GOLDEN HORSES, FOX. (Movietone Sports Review) Edmund Reek, Prod.
SMART AS A FOX, WB. (Varieties) Gordon Hollingshead, Prod.
SURE CURES, MGM. (Pete Smith Specialty) Pete Smith, Prod.
(Two-reel)
A BOY AND HIS DOG, WB. (Featurettes) Gordon Hollingshead, Prod.
COLLEGE QUEEN, PAR. (Musical Parade) George Templeton, Prod.
HISS AND YELL, COL. (All Star Comedies) Jules White, Prod.
THE LUCKIEST GUY IN THE WORLD, MGM. (Two-reel Special) Jerry Bresler, Prod.

DOCUMENTARY:
(Short Subjects)

SEEDS OF DESTINY, U.S. War Department.
ATOMIC POWER, FOX.
LIFE AT THE ZOO, ARK.
PARAMOUNT NEWS ISSUE #37, PAR.
TRAFFIC WITH THE DEVIL, MGM.

SPECIAL EFFECTS:

BLITHE SPIRIT, Rank UA (British). Visual: Thomas Howard. Audible: No credit.
A STOLEN LIFE, WB. Visual: William McGann. Audible: Nathan Levinson.

HONORARY AND OTHER:
(Irving G. Thalberg Memorial Award)

Samuel Goldwyn

(Other)

LAURENCE OLIVIER for his outstanding achievement as actor, producer and director in bringing Henry V to the screen. (statuette)
HAROLD RUSSELL for bringing hope and courage to his fellow veterans through his appearance in The Best Years Of Our Lives.
ERNST LUBITSCH for his distinguished contributions to the art of the motion picture.
CLAUDE JARMAN, JR., outstanding child actor of 1946.

SCIENTIFIC OR TECHNICAL:
(Class III)

HARLAN L. BAUMBACH and the PARAMOUNT WEST COAST LABORATORY for an improved method for the quantitative determination of hydroquinone and metol in photographic developing baths.
HERBERT E. BRITT for the development and application of formulas and equipment for producing cloud and smoke effects.
BURTON F. MILLER and the WB STUDIO SOUND and ELECTRICAL DEPARTMENTS for the design and construction of a motion picture arc lighting generator filter.
CARL FAULKNER of the 20th Century-Fox Studio Sound Department for the reversed bias method, including a double bias method for light valve and galvonometer density recording.
MOLE-RICHARDSON CO. for the Type 450 super high intensity carbon arc lamp.
ARTHUR F. BLINN, ROBERT O. COOK, C. O. SLYFIELD and the WALT DISNEY STUDIO SOUND DEPARTMENT for the design and development of an audio finder and track viewer for checking and locating noise in sound tracks.
BURTON F. MILLER and the WB STUDIO SOUND DEPARTMENT for the design and application of an equalizer to eliminate relative spectral energy distortion in electronic compressors.
MARTY MARTIN and HAL ADKINS of the RKO Studio Miniature Department for the design and construction of equipment providing visual bullet effects.
HAROLD NYE and the WB STUDIO ELECTRICAL DEPARTMENT for the development of the electronically controlled fire and gaslight effect.

1947

BEST PICTURE:

GENTLEMAN'S AGREEMENT, FOX.
THE BISHOP'S WIFE, Goldwyn, RKO.
CROSSFIRE, RKO.
GREAT EXPECTATIONS, Rank-Cineguild, U (British).
MIRACLE ON 34TH STREET, FOX.

ACTOR:

RONALD COLMAN, A Double Life, Kanin, U.
JOHN GARFIELD, *Body And Soul*, Enterprise, UA.
GREGORY PECK, *Gentleman's Agreement*.
WILLIAM POWELL, *Life With Father*, WB.
MICHAEL REDGRAVE, *Mourning Becomes Electra*, RKO.

ACTRESS:

LORETTA YOUNG, The Farmer's Daughter, RKO.
JOAN CRAWFORD, *Possessed*, WB.
SUSAN HAYWARD, *Smash Up - The Story Of A Woman*, Wanger, U.
DOROTHY McGUIRE, *Gentleman's Agreement*.
ROSALIND RUSSELL, *Mourning Becomes Electra*.

SUPPORTING ACTOR:

EDMUND GWENN, Miracle On 34th Street.
CHARLES BICKFORD, *The Farmer's Daughter*.
THOMAS GOMEZ, *Ride The Pink Horse*, U.
ROBERT RYAN, *Crossfire*.
RICHARD WIDMARK, *Kiss Of Death*, FOX.

SUPPORTING ACTRESS:

CELESTE HOLM, Gentleman's Agreement.
ETHEL BARRYMORE, *The Paradine Case*, SRO.
GLORIA GRAHAME, *Crossfire*.
MARJORIE MAIN, *The Egg And I*, U.
ANNE REVERE, *Gentleman's Agreement*.

DIRECTING:

ELIA KAZAN, Gentleman's Agreement.
GEORGE CUKOR, *A Double Life*.
EDWARD DMYTRYK, *Crossfire*.
HENRY KOSTER, *The Bishop's Wife*.
DAVID LEAN, *Great Expectations*.

WRITING:
(Original Story)

MIRACLE ON 34TH STREET. Valentine Davies.
A CAGE OF NIGHTINGALES, GAU-LOP (French). Georges Chaperot and Rene Wheeler.
IT HAPPENED ON FIFTH AVENUE, Roy Del Ruth, AA. Herbert Clyde Lewis and Frederick Stephani.
KISS OF DEATH. Eleazar Lipsky.
SMASH-UP - THE STORY OF A WOMAN. Dorothy Parker and Frank Cavett.

(Original Screenplay)

THE BACHELOR AND THE BOBBY-SOXER, RKO. Sidney Sheldon.
BODY AND SOUL. Abraham Polonsky.
A DOUBLE LIFE. Ruth Gordon & Garson Kanin.
MONSIEUR VERDOUX, Chaplin, UA. Charles Chaplin.
SHOE-SHINE, LOP (Italian). Sergio Amidei, Adolfo Franci, C. G. Viola and Cesare Zavattini.

(Screenplay)

MIRACLE ON 34TH STREET. George Seaton.
BOOMERANG!, FOX. Richard Murphy.
CROSSFIRE. John Paxton.
GENTLEMAN'S AGREEMENT. Moss Hart.
GREAT EXPECTATIONS. David Lean, Ronald Neame and Anthony Havelock-Allan.

CINEMATOGRAPHY:
(Black-and-White)

GREAT EXPECTATIONS. Guy Green.
THE GHOST AND MRS. MUIR, FOX. Charles Lang, Jr.
GREEN DOLPHIN STREET, MGM. George Folsey.

(Color)

BLACK NARCISSUS. Rank-Archers, U (British). Jack Cardiff.
LIFE WITH FATHER. Peverell Marley and William V. Skall.
MOTHER WORE TIGHTS, FOX. Harry Jackson.

ART DIRECTION - SET DECORATION:
(Black-and-White)

GREAT EXPECTATIONS. John Bryan. Set Decoration: Wilfred Shingleton.
THE FOXES OF HARROW, FOX. Lyle Wheeler and Maurice Ransford. Set Decoration: Thomas Little and Paul S. Fox.

(Color)

BLACK NARCISSUS. Alfred Junge. Set Decoration: Alfred Junge.
LIFE WITH FATHER. Robert M. Haas. Set Decoration: George James Hopkins.

FILM EDITING:
BODY AND SOUL. Francis Lyon and Robert Parrish.
THE BISHOP'S WIFE. Monica Collingwood.
GENTLEMAN'S AGREEMENT. Harmon Jones.
GREEN DOLPHIN STREET. George White.
ODD MAN OUT, Rank-Two Cities, U (British). Fergus McDonnell.

MUSIC - SCORING:
(Scoring of a Dramatic or Comedy Picture)

A DOUBLE LIFE. Miklos Rozsa.
THE BISHOP'S WIFE. Hugo Friedhofer.
CAPTAIN FROM CASTILE, FOX. Alfred Newman.
FOREVER AMBER, FOX. David Raksin.
LIFE WITH FATHER. Max Steiner.

(Scoring of a Musical Picture)

MOTHER WORE TIGHTS. Alfred Newman.
FIESTA, MGM. Johnny Green.
MY WILD IRISH ROSE, WB. Ray Heindorf and Max Steiner.
ROAD TO RIO, Hope-Crosby, PAR. Robert Emmett Dolan.
SONG OF THE SOUTH, Disney, RKO. Daniele Amfitheatrof, Paul J. Smith and Charles Wolcott.

MUSIC - BEST SONG:
ZIP-A-DEE-DOO-DAH, Song Of The South. Music, Allie Wrubel. Lyrics, Ray Gilbert.
A GAL IN CALICO, *The Time, Place And The Girl*, WB. Music, Arthur Schwartz. Lyrics, Leo Robin.
I WISH I DIDN'T LOVE YOU SO, *The Perils Of Pauline*, PAR. Music and Lyrics by Frank Loesser.
PASS THAT PEACE PIPE, *Good News*, MGM. Music and Lyrics by Ralph Blane, Hugh Martin and Roger Edens.
YOU DO, *Mother Wore Tights*. Music, Josef Myrow. Lyrics, Mack Gordon.

SOUND:
THE BISHOP'S WIFE. Goldwyn Sound Department.
GREEN DOLPHIN STREET. MGM Sound Department.
T-MEN, Reliance Pictures, EAG, Sound Services. Inc.

SHORT FILMS:
(Cartoons)

TWEETIE PIE, WB. (Merrie Melodies) Edward Selzer, Prod.
CHIP AN' DALE, Walt Disney, RKO. (Donald Duck) Walt Disney, Prod.
DR. JEKYLL AND MR. MOUSE, MGM. (Tom & Jerry) Frederick Quimby, Prod.
PLUTO'S BLUE NOTE, Walt Disney, RKO. (Pluto) Walt Disney, Prod.
TUBBY THE TUBA, PAR. (George Pal Puppetoon) George Pal, Prod.

(One-reel)

GOODBYE MISS TURLOCK, MGM. (John Nesbitt Passing Parade) Herbert Moulton, Prod.
BROOKLYN, U.S.A., U. (Variety Series) Thomas Mead, Prod.
MOON ROCKETS, PAR. (Popular Science) Jerry Fairbanks, Prod.
NOW YOU SEE IT, MGM. Pete Smith, Prod.
SO YOU WANT TO BE IN PICTURES, WB. (Joe McDoakes) Gordon Hollingshead, Prod.

(Two-reel)

CLIMBING THE MATTERHORN, MNG. (Color) Irving Allen, Prod.
CHAMPAGNE FOR TWO, PAR, (Musical Parade Featurette) Harry Grey, Prod.
FIGHT OF THE WILD STALLIONS, U. (Special) Thomas Mead, Prod.
GIVE US THE EARTH, MGM. (Special) Herbert Morgan, Prod.
A VOICE IS BORN, COL. (Muscial Featurette) Ben Blake, Prod.

DOCUMENTARY:
(Short Subjects)

FIRST STEPS, United Nations Division of Films and Visual Education.
PASSPORT TO NOWHERE, RKO (This Is America Series). Frederic Ullman, Jr., Prod.
SCHOOL IN THE MAILBOX, Australian News and Information Bureau.

(Features)

DESIGN FOR DEATH, RKO. Sid Rogell, Ex Prod; Theron Warth and Richard O. Fleischer, Prods.
JOURNEY INTO MEDICINE, U.S. Dept. of State, Office of Information and Educational Exhange.
THE WORLD IS RICH, British Information Services. Paul Rotha, Prod.

SPECIAL EFFECTS:
GREEN DOLPHIN STREET. Visual: A. Arnold Gillespie and Warren Newcombe. Audible: Douglas Shearer and Michael Steinore.
UNCONQUERED, PAR. Visual: Farciot Edouart, Devereux Jennings, Gordon Jennings, Wallace Kelley and Paul Lerpae. Audible: George Dutton.

HONORARY AND OTHER:
(Other)

JAMES BASKETTE for his able and heart-warming characterization of Uncle Remus, friend and story teller to the children of the world.
BILL AND COO, in which artistry and patience blended in a novel and entertaining use of the medium of motion pictures.
SHOE-SHINE - the high quality of this motion picture, brought to eloquent life in a country scarred by war, is proof to the world that the creative spirit can triumph over adversity.
COLONEL WILLIAM N. SELIG, ALBERT E. SMITH, THOMAS ARMAT and GEORGE K. SPOOR (one of) the small group of pioneers whose belief in a new medium, and whose contributions to its development, blazed the trail along which the motion picture has progressed, in their lifetime, from obscurity to world-wide acclaim.

SCIENTIFIC OR TECHNICAL:
(Class II Plaque)

C. C. DAVIS and **ELECTRICAL RESEARCH PRODUCTS, DIVISION OF WESTERN ELECTRIC CO.**, for the development and application of an improved film drive filter mechanism.
C. R. DAILY and the **PAR STUDIO FILM LABORATORY, STILL and ENGINEERING DEPARTMENTS** for the development and first practical application to motion picture and still photography of a method of increasing film speed as first suggested to the industry by E. I. duPont de Nemours & Co.

(Class III)

NATHAN LEVINSON and the **WB STUDIO SOUND DEPARTMENT** for the design and construction of a constant-speed sound editing machine.
FARCIOT EDOUART, C. R. DAILY, HAL CORL, H. G. CARTWRIGHT and the **PARAMOUNT STUDIO TRANSPARENCY and ENGINEERING DEPARTMENTS** for the first application of a special anti-solarizing glass to high intensity background and spot arc projectors.
FRED PONEDEL of WB Studio for pioneering the fabrication and practical application to motion picture color photography of large translucent photographic backgrounds.
KURT SINGER and the **RCA-VICTOR DIVISION** of the **RADIO CORPORATION OF AMERICA** for the design and development of a continuously variable band elimination filter.
JAMES GIBBONS of WB Studio for the development and production of large dyed plastic filters for motion picture photography.

1948

BEST PICTURE:
HAMLET, Rank-Two Cities, U (British).
JOHNNY BELINDA, WB.
THE RED SHOES, Rank-Archers, EAG. (British)
THE SNAKE PIT, FOX.
TREASURE OF SIERRA MADRE, WB.

ACTOR:
LAURENCE OLIVIER, Hamlet.
LEW AYRES, *Johnny Belinda.*
MONTGOMERY CLIFT, *The Search,* Praesens Films, MGM. (Swiss)
DAN DAILEY, *When My Baby Smiles At Me,* FOX.
CLIFTON WEBB, *Sitting Pretty,* FOX.

ACTRESS:
JANE WYMAN, Johnny Belinda.
INGRID BERGMAN, *Joan Of Arc,* Sierra, RKO.
OLIVIA DE HAVILLAND, *The Snake Pit.*
IRENE DUNNE, *I Remember Mama,* RKO.
BARBARA STANWYCK, *Sorry, Wrong Number,* Wallis, PAR.

SUPPORTING ACTOR:
WALTER HUSTON, Treasure Of Sierra Madre.
CHARLES BICKFORD, *Johnny Belinda.*
JOSE FERRER, *Joan Of Arc.*
OSCAR HOMOLKA, *I Remember Mama.*
CECIL KELLAWAY, *The Luck Of The Irish,* FOX.

SUPPORTING ACTRESS:
CLAIRE TREVOR, Key Largo, WB.
BARBARA BEL GEDDES, *I Remember Mama.*
ELLEN CORBY, *I Remember Mama.*
AGNES MOOREHEAD, *Johnny Belinda.*
JEAN SIMMONS, *Hamlet.*

DIRECTING:
JOHN HUSTON, Treasure Of Sierra Madre.
ANATOLE LITVAK, *The Snake Pit.*
JEAN NEGULESCO, *Johnny Belinda.*
LAURENCE OLIVIER, *Hamlet.*
FRED ZINNEMANN, *The Search.*

WRITING:
(Motion Picture Story)
THE SEARCH. Richard Schweizer and David Wechsler.
THE LOUISIANA STORY, Robert Flaherty, LOP. Frances Flaherty and Robert Flaherty.
THE NAKED CITY, Hellinger, U. Malvin Wald.
RED RIVER, Monterey Productions, UA. Borden Chase.
THE RED SHOES. Emeric Pressburger.
(Screenplay)
TREASURE OF SIERRA MADRE. John Huston.
A FOREIGN AFFAIR, PAR. Charles Brackett, Billy Wilder and Richard L. Breen.
JOHNNY BELINDA. Irmgard Von Cube and Allen Vincent.
THE SEARCH. Richard Schweizer and David Wechsler.
THE SNAKE PIT. Frank Partos and Millen Brand.

CINEMATOGRAPHY:
(Black-and-White)
THE NAKED CITY. William Daniels.
A FOREIGN AFFAIR. Charles B. Lang, Jr.
I REMEMBER MAMA. Nicholas Musuraca.
JOHNNY BELINDA. Ted McCord.
PORTRAIT OF JENNIE, SRO. Joseph August.
(Color)
JOAN OF ARC. Joseph Valentine, William V. Skall and Winton Hoch.
GREEN GRASS OF WYOMING, FOX. Charles G. Clarke.
THE LOVES OF CARMEN, Beckworth Corp, COL. William Snyder.
THE THREE MUSKETEERS, MGM. Robert Planck.

COSTUME DESIGN:
(Black-and-White)
HAMLET. Roger K. Furse.
B. F.'S DAUGHTER, MGM. Irene.
(Color)
JOAN OF ARC. Dorothy Jeakins and Karinska.
THE EMPEROR WALTZ, PAR. Edith Head and Gile Steele.

ART DIRECTION - SET DECORATION:
(Black-and-White)
HAMLET. Roger K. Furse. Set Decoration: Carmen Dillon.
JOHNNY BELINDA. Robert Haas. Set Decoration: William Wallace.
(Color)
THE RED SHOES. Hein Heckroth. Set Decoration: Arthur Lawson.
JOAN OF ARC. Richard Day. Set Decoration: Edwin Casey Roberts and Joseph Kish.

FILM EDITING:
THE NAKED CITY. Paul Weatherwax.
JOAN OF ARC. Frank Sullivan.
JOHNNY BELINDA. David Weisbart.
RED RIVER. Christian Nyby.
THE RED SHOES. Reginald Mills.

MUSIC - SCORING:
(Scoring of a Dramatic or Comedy Picture)
THE RED SHOES. Brian Easdale.
HAMLET. William Walton.
JOAN OF ARC. Hugo Friedhofer.
JOHNNY BELINDA. Max Steiner.
THE SNAKE PIT. Alfred Newman.
(Scoring of a Musical Picture)
EASTER PARADE, MGM. Johnny Green and Roger Edens.
THE EMPEROR WALTZ. Victor Young.
THE PIRATE, MGM. Lennie Hayton.
ROMANCE OF THE HIGH SEAS, Curtiz, WB. Ray Heindorf.
WHEN MY BABY SMILES AT ME. Alfred Newman.

MUSIC - BEST SONG:
BUTTONS AND BOWS, The Paleface, PAR. Music and Lyrics by Jay Livingston and Ray Evans.
FOR EVERY MAN THERE'S A WOMAN, *Casbah,* Marston Pictures, UI. Music, Harold Arlen. Lyrics, Leo Robin.
IT'S MAGIC, *Romance On The High Seas.* Music, Jule Styne. Lyrics, Sammy Cahn.
THIS IS THE MOMENT, *That Lady In Ermine,* FOX. Music, Frederick Hollander. Lyrics, Leo Robin.
THE WOODY WOODPECKER SONG, *Wet Blanket Policy,* Walter Lantz, UA (Cartoon). Music and Lyrics by Ramey Idriss and George Tibbles.

SOUND:
THE SNAKE PIT. FOX Sound Department.
JOHNNY BELINDA. WB Sound Department.
MOONRISE, Marshall Grant Prods., REP. REP Sound Department.

SHORT FILMS:
(Cartoons)
THE LITTLE ORPHAN, MGM. (Tom & Jerry) Fred Quimby, Prod.
MICKEY AND THE SEAL, Walt Disney, RKO. (Pluto) Walt Disney, Prod.
MOUSE WRECKERS, WB. (Looney Tunes) Edward Selzer, Prod.
ROBIN HOODLUM, United Productions Of America, COL. (Fox & Crow)
TEA FOR TWO HUNDRED, Walt Disney, RKO. (Donald Duck) Walt Disney, Prod.
(One-reel)
SYMPHONY OF A CITY, FOX. (Movietone Specialty) Edmund H. Reek, Prod.
ANNIE WAS A WONDER, MGM. (John Nesbitt Passing Parade) Herbert Moulton, Prod.
CINDERELLA HORSE, WB. (Sports Parade) Gordon Hollingshead, Prod.
SO YOU WANT TO BE ON THE RADIO, WB. (Joe McDoakes) Gordon Hollingshead, Prod.
YOU CAN'T WIN, MGM. (Pete Smith Specialty) Pete Smith, Prod.
(Two-reel)
SEAL ISLAND, Walt Disney, RKO. (True Life Adventure Series) Walt Disney, Prod.
CALGARY STAMPEDE, WB. (Technicolor Special) Gordon Hollingshead, Prod.
GOING TO BLAZES, MGM. (Special) Herbert Morgan, Prod.
SAMBA-MANIA, PAR. (Musical Parade) Harry Grey, Prod.
SNOW CAPERS, UI. (Special Series) Thomas Mead, Prod.

DOCUMENTARY:
(Short Subjects)
TOWARD INDEPENDENCE, U.S. Army.
HEART TO HEART, Fact Film Organization. Herbert Morgan, Prod.
OPERATION VITTLES, U.S. Army Air Force.
(Features)
THE SECRET LAND, U.S. Navy, MGM. O.O. Dull, Prod.
THE QUIET ONE, MAB. Janice Loeb, Prod.

SPECIAL EFFECTS:
PORTRAIT OF JENNIE. Visual: Paul Eagler, J. McMillan Johnson, Russell Shearman and Clarence Slifer. Audible: Charles Freeman and James G. Stewart.
DEEP WATERS, FOX. Visual: Ralph Hammeras, Fred Sersen and Edward Snyder. Audible: Roger Heman.

HONORARY AND OTHER:
(Irving G. Thalberg Memorial Award)
Jerry Wald
(Other)
MONSIEUR VINCENT (French) - voted by the Academy Board of Governors as the most outstanding foreign language film released in the United States during 1948.
IVAN JANDL, for the outstanding juvenile performance of 1948, The Search.
SID GRAUMAN, master showman, who raised the standard of exhibition of motion pictures.
ADOLPH ZUKOR, a man who has been called the father of the feature film in America, for his services to the industry over a period of forty years.
WALTER WANGER for distinguished service to the industry in adding to its moral stature in the world community by his production of the picture Joan Of Arc.

SCIENTIFIC OR TECHNICAL:
(Class II)
VICTOR CACCIALANZA, MAURICE AYERS and the PARAMOUNT STUDIO SET CONSTRUCTION DEPARTMENT for the development and application of "Paralite," a new lightweight plaster process for set construction.
NICK KALTEN, LOUIS J. WITTI and the 20TH CENTURY-FOX STUDIO MECHANICAL EFFECTS DEPARTMENT for a process of preserving and flame-proofing foliage.
(Class III)
MARTY MARTIN, JACK LANNON, RUSSELL SHEARMAN and the RKO STUDIO SPECIAL EFFECTS DEPARTMENT for the development of a new method of simulating falling snow on motion picture sets.
A. J. MORAN and the WB STUDIO ELECTRICAL DEPARTMENT for a method of remote control for shutters on motion picture arc lighting equipment.

1949

BEST PICTURE:
ALL THE KING'S MEN, Rossen, COL.
BATTLEGROUND, MGM.
THE HEIRESS, PAR.
A LETTER TO THREE WIVES, FOX.
TWELVE O'CLOCK HIGH, FOX.

ACTOR:
BRODERICK CRAWFORD, All The King's Men.
KIRK DOUGLAS, *Champion*, Screen Plays Corp., UA.
GREGORY PECK, *Twelve O'Clock High*.
RICHARD TODD, *The Hasty Heart*, WB.
JOHN WAYNE, *Sands Of Iwo Jima*, REP.

ACTRESS:
OLIVIA DE HAVILLAND, The Heiress.
JEANNE CRAIN, *Pinky*, FOX.
SUSAN HAYWARD, *My Foolish Heart*, Goldwyn, RKO.
DEBORAH KERR, *Edward, My Son*, MGM.
LORETTA YOUNG, *Come To The Stable*, FOX.

SUPPORTING ACTOR:
DEAN JAGGER, Twelve O'Clock High.
JOHN IRELAND, *All The King's Men*.
ARTHUR KENNEDY, *Champion*.
RALPH RICHARDSON, *The Heiress*.
JAMES WHITMORE, *Battleground*.

SUPPORTING ACTRESS:
MERCEDES McCAMBRIDGE, All The King's Men.
ETHEL BARRYMORE, *Pinky*.
CELESTE HOLM, *Come To The Stable*.
ELSA LANCHESTER, *Come To The Stable*.
ETHEL WATERS, *Pinky*.

DIRECTING:
JOSEPH L. MANKIEWICZ, A Letter To Three Wives.
CAROL REED, *The Fallen Idol*, London Films, SRO (British).
ROBERT ROSSEN, *All The King's Men*.
WILLIAM A. WELLMAN, *Battleground*.
WILLIAM WYLER, *The Heiress*.

WRITING:
(Motion Picture Story)
THE STRATTON STORY, MGM. Douglas Morrow.
COME TO THE STABLE. Clare Boothe Luce.
IT HAPPENS EVERY SPRING, FOX. Shirley W. Smith and Valentine Davies.
SANDS OF IWO JIMA. Harry Brown.
WHITE HEAT. Virginia Kellogg.

(Screenplay)
A LETTER TO THREE WIVES. Joseph L. Mankiewicz.
ALL THE KING'S MEN. Robert Rossen.
THE BICYCLE THIEF, De Sica, MAB (Italian). Cesare Zavattini.
CHAMPION. Carl Foreman.
THE FALLEN IDOL. Graham Greene.

(Story and Screenplay)
BATTLEGROUND. Robert Pirosh.
JOLSON SINGS AGAIN, COL. Sidney Buchman.
PAISAN, Roberto Rossellini, MAB (Italian). Alfred Hayes, Federico Fellini, Sergio Amidei, Marcello Pagliero and Roberto Rossellini.
PASSPORT TO PIMLICO, Rank-Ealing, EAG (British). T.E.B. Clarke.
THE QUIET ONE, Film Documents, MAB. Helen Levitt, Janice Loeb and Sidney Meyers.

CINEMATOGRAPHY:
(Black-and-White)
BATTLEGROUND. Paul C. Vogel.
CHAMPION. Frank Planer.
COME TO THE STABLE. Joseph LaShelle.
THE HEIRESS. Leo Tover.
PRINCE OF FOXES, FOX. Leon Shamroy.

(Color)
SHE WORE A YELLOW RIBBON, Argosy, RKO. Winton Hoch.
THE BARKLEYS OF BROADWAY, MGM. Harry Stradling.
JOLSON SINGS AGAIN. William Snyder.
LITTLE WOMEN, MGM. Robert Planck and Charles Schoenbaum.
SAND, FOX. Charles G. Clarke.

COSTUME DESIGN:
(Black-and-White)
THE HEIRESS. Edith Head and Gile Steele.
PRINCE OF FOXES. Vittorio Nino Novarese.

(Color)
ADVENTURES OF DON JUAN, WB. Leah Rhodes, Travilla and Marjorie Best.
MOTHER IS A FRESHMAN, FOX. Kay Nelson.

ART DIRECTION - SET DECORATION:
(Black-and-White)
THE HEIRESS. John Meehan and Harry Horner. Set Decoration: Emile Kuri.
COME TO THE STABLE. Lyle Wheeler and Joseph C. Wright. Set Decoration: Thomas Little and Paul S. FOX.
MADAME BOVARY, MGM. Cedric Gibbons and Jack Martin Smith. Set Decoration: Edwin B. Willis and Richard A. Pefferle.

(Color)
LITTLE WOMEN. Cedric Gibbons and Paul Groesse. Set Decoration: Edwin B. Willis and Jack D. Moore.
ADVENTURES OF DON JUAN. Edward Carrere. Set Decoration: Lyle Reifsnider.
SARABAND, Rank-Ealing, EAG (British). Jim Morahan, William Kellner and Michael Relph. Set Decoration: No credits listed.

FILM EDITING:
CHAMPION. Harry Gerstad.
ALL THE KING'S MEN. Robert Parrish and Al Clark.
BATTLEGROUND. John Dunning.
SANDS OF IWO JIMA. Richard L. Van Enger.
THE WINDOW, RKO. Frederic Knudtson.

MUSIC - SCORING:
(Scoring of a Dramatic or Comedy Picture)
THE HEIRESS. Aaron Copland.
BEYOND THE FOREST, WB. Max Steiner.
CHAMPION. Dimitri Tiomkin.

(Scoring of a Musical Picture)
ON THE TOWN, MGM. Roger Edens and Lennie Hayton.
JOLSON SINGS AGAIN. Morris Stoloff and George Duning.
LOOK FOR THE SILVER LINING, WB. Ray Heindorf.

MUSIC - BEST SONG:
BABY, IT'S COLD OUTSIDE, Neptune's Daughter, MGM. Music and Lyrics by Frank Loesser.
IT'S A GREAT FEELING, *It's A Great Feeling*, WB. Music, Jule Styne. Lyrics, Sammy Cahn.
LAVENDER BLUE, *So Dear To My Heart*, Disney-RKO. Music, Eliot Daniel. Lyrics, Larry Morey.
MY FOOLISH HEART, *My Foolish Heart*, Goldwyn-RKO. Music, Victor Young. Lyrics, Ned Washington.
THROUGH A LONG AND SLEEPLESS NIGHT, *Come To The Stable*. Music, Alfred Newman. Lyrics, Mack Gordon.

SOUND:
TWELVE O'CLOCK HIGH. FOX Sound Department.
ONCE MORE, MY DARLING, Neptune Films, U. U Sound Department.
SANDS OF IWO JIMA. REP Sound Department.

SHORT FILMS:
(Cartoons)
FOR SCENT-IMENTAL REASONS, WB. (Looney Tunes) Edward Selzer, Prod.
HATCH UP YOUR TROUBLES, MGM. (Tom & Jerry) Fred Quimby, Prod.
MAGIC FLUKE, United Productions Of America, COL. (Fox & Crow) Stephen Bosustow, Prod.
TOY TINKERS, Walt Disney, RKO. Walt Disney, Prod.

(One-reel)
AQUATIC HOUSE-PARTY, PAR. (Grantland Rice Sportlights) Jack Eaton, Prod.
ROLLER DERBY GIRL, PAR. (Pacemaker) Justin Herman, Prod.
SO YOU THINK YOU'RE NOT GUILTY, WB. (Joe McDoakes) Gordon Hollingshead, Prod.
SPILLS AND CHILLS, WB. (Black-and-White Sports Review) Walton C. Ament, Prod.
WATER TRIX, MGM. (Pete Smith Specialty) Pete Smith, Prod.

(Two-reel)
VAN GOGH, Canton-Weiner. Gaston Diehl and Robert Haessens, Prods.
BOY AND THE EAGLE, RKO. William Lasky, Prod.
CHASE OF DEATH, Irving Allen Productions. (Color Series) Irving Allen, Prod.
THE GRASS IS ALWAYS GREENER, WB. (Black-and-White) Gordon Hollingshead, Prod.
SNOW CARNIVAL, WB. (Technicolor) Gordon Hollingshead, Prod.

DOCUMENTARY:
(Short Subjects)
A CHANCE TO LIVE, MOT, FOX. Richard de Rochemont, Prod.
SO MUCH FOR SO LITTLE, WB. Cartoons, Inc. Edward Selzer, Prod.
1848, A.F. Films, Inc. French Cinema General Cooperative, Prod.
THE RISING TIDE, NFC. St. Francis-Xavier University (Nova Scotia), Prod.

(Features)
DAYBREAK IN UDI, British Information Services. Crown Film Unit, Prod.
KENJI COMES HOME, A Protestant Film Commission Prod. Paul F. Heard, Prod.

SPECIAL EFFECTS:
MIGHTY JOE YOUNG, ARKO, RKO.
TULSA, Walter Wanger Pictures, EAG.

HONORARY AND OTHER:
(Other)
THE BICYCLE THIEF - voted by the Academy Board of Governors as the most outstanding foreign language film released in the United States during 1949.
BOBBY DRISCOLL, as the outstanding juvenile actor of 1949.
FRED ASTAIRE for his unique artistry and his contributions to the technique of musical pictures.
CECIL B. DEMILLE, distinguished motion picture pioneer, for 37 years of brilliant showmanship.
JEAN HERSHOLT, for distinguished service to the motion picture industry.

SCIENTIFIC OR TECHNICAL:
(Class I)
EASTMAN KODAK CO. for the development and introduction of an improved safety base motion picture film.
(Class III)
LOREN L. RYDER, BRUCE H. DENNEY, ROBERT CARR and the PARAMOUNT STUDIO SOUND DEPARTMENT for the development and application of the supersonic playback and public address system.
M. B. PAUL for the first successful large-area seamless translucent backgrounds.
HERBERT BRITT for the development and application of formulas and equipment producing artificial snow and ice for dressing motion picture sets.
ANDRE COUTANT and JACQUES MATHOT for the design of the Eclair Camerette.
CHARLES R. DAILY, STEVE CSILLAG and the PARAMOUNT STUDIO ENGINEERING, EDITORIAL and MUSIC DEPARTMENTS for a new precision method of computing variable tempo-click tracks.
INTERNATIONAL PROJECTOR CORP. for a simplified and self-adjusting take-up device for projection machines.
ALEXANDER VELCOFF for the application to production of the infrared photographic evaluator.

1950

BEST PICTURE:
ALL ABOUT EVE, FOX.
BORN YESTERDAY, COL.
FATHER OF THE BRIDE, MGM.
KING SOLOMON'S MINES, MGM.
SUNSET BOULEVARD, PAR.

ACTOR:
JOSE FERRER, Cyrano De Bergerac, Stanley Kramer, UA.
LOUIS CALHERN, The Magnificent Yankee, MGM.
WILLIAM HOLDEN, Sunset Boulevard.
JAMES STEWART, Harvey, U.
SPENCER TRACY, Father Of The Bride.

ACTRESS:
JUDY HOLLIDAY, Born Yesterday.
ANNE BAXTER, All About Eve.
BETTE DAVIS, All About Eve.
ELEANOR PARKER, Caged, WB.
GLORIA SWANSON, Sunset Boulevard.

SUPPORTING ACTOR:
GEORGE SANDERS, All About Eve.
JEFF CHANDLER, Broken Arrow, FOX.
EDMUND GWENN, Mister 880, FOX.
SAM JAFFE, The Asphalt Jungle, MGM.
ERICH VON STROHEIM, Sunset Boulevard.

SUPPORTING ACTRESS:
JOSEPHINE HULL, Harvey.
HOPE EMERSON, Caged.
CELESTE HOLM, All About Eve.
NANCY OLSON, Sunset Boulevard.
THELMA RITTER, All About Eve.

DIRECTING:
JOSEPH L. MANKIEWICZ, All About Eve.
GEORGE CUKOR, Born Yesterday.
JOHN HUSTON, The Asphalt Jungle.
CAROL REED, The Third Man, Selznick-London Films, SRO (British).
BILLY WILDER, Sunset Boulevard.

WRITING:
(Motion Picture Story)
PANIC IN THE STREETS, FOX. Edna Anhalt and Edward Anhalt.
BITTER RICE, LUX (Italian). Giuseppe De Santis and Carlo Lizzani.
THE GUNFIGHTER, FOX. William Bowers and Andre de Toth.
MYSTERY STREET, MGM. Leonard Spigelgass.
WHEN WILLIE COMES MARCHING HOME, FOX. Sy Gomberg.
(Screenplay)
ALL ABOUT EVE. Joseph L. Mankiewicz.
THE ASPHALT JUNGLE. Ben Maddow and John Huston.
BORN YESTERDAY. Albert Mannheimer.
BROKEN ARROW. Michael Blankfort.
FATHER OF THE BRIDE. Frances Goodrich and Albert Hackett.
(Story and Screenplay)
SUNSET BOULEVARD. Charles Brackett, Billy Wilder and D. M. Marshman, Jr.
ADAM'S RIB, MGM. Ruth Gordon and Garson Kanin.
CAGED. Virginia Kellogg and Bernard C. Schoenfeld.
THE MEN, Kramer, UA. Carl Foreman.
NO WAY OUT, FOX. Joseph L. Mankiewicz and Lesser Samuels.

CINEMATOGRAPHY:
(Black-and-White)
THE THIRD MAN. Robert Krasker.
ALL ABOUT EVE. Milton Krasner.
THE ASPHALT JUNGLE. Harold Rosson.
THE FURIES, Wallis, PAR. Victor Milner.
SUNSET BOULEVARD. John F. Seitz.
(Color)
KING SOLOMON'S MINES. Robert Surtees.
ANNIE GET YOUR GUN, MGM. Charles Rosher.
BROKEN ARROW. Ernest Palmer.
THE FLAME AND THE ARROW, Norma-F.R., WB. Ernest Haller.
SAMSON AND DELILAH, DeMille, PAR. George Barnes.

COSTUME DESIGN:
(Black-and-White)
ALL ABOUT EVE. Edith Head and Charles LeMaire.
BORN YESTERDAY. Jean Louis.
THE MAGNIFICENT YANKEE. Walter Plunkett.
(Color)
SAMSON AND DELILAH. Edith Head, Dorothy Jeakins Elois Jenssen, Gile Steele and Gwen Wakeling.
THE BLACK ROSE, FOX. Michael Whittaker.
THAT FORSYTE WOMAN, MGM. Walter Plunkett and Valles.

ART DIRECTION - SET DECORATION:
(Black-and-White)

SUNSET BOULEVARD. Hans Dreier and John Meehan. Set Decoration: Sam Comer and Ray Moyer.
ALL ABOUT EVE. Lyle Wheeler and George Davis. Set Decoration: Thomas Little and Walter M. Scott.
THE RED DANUBE, MGM. Cedric Gibbons and Hans Peters. Set Decoration: Edwin B. Willis and Hugh Hunt.

(Color)

SAMSON AND DELILAH. Hans Dreier and Walter Tyler. Set Decoration: Sam Comer and Ray Moyer.
ANNIE GET YOUR GUN. Cedric Gibbons and Paul Groesse. Set Decoration: Edwin B. Willis and Richard A. Pefferle.
DESTINATION MOON, George Pal, ELC. Ernst Fegte. Set Decoration: George Sawley.

FILM EDITING:
KING SOLOMON'S MINES. Ralph E. Winters and Conrad A. Nervig.
ALL ABOUT EVE. Barbara McLean.
ANNIE GET YOUR GUN. James E. Newcom.
SUNSET BOULEVARD. Arthur Schmidt and Doane Harrison.
THE THIRD MAN. Oswald Hafenrichter.

MUSIC - SCORING:
(Scoring of a Musical Picture)

SUNSET BOULEVARD. Franz Waxman.
ALL ABOUT EVE. Alfred Newman.
THE FLAME AND THE ARROW. Max Steiner.
NO SAD SONGS FOR ME, COL. George Duning.
SAMSON AND DELILAH. Victor Young.

(Scoring of a Dramatic or Comedy Picture)

ANNIE GET YOUR GUN. Adolph Deutsch and Roger Edens.
CINDERELLA, Disney, RKO. Oliver Wallace and Paul J. Smith.
I'LL GET BY, FOX. Lionel Newman.
THREE LITTLE WORDS, MGM. Andre Previn.
THE WEST POINT STORY, WB. Ray Heindorf.

MUSIC - BEST SONG:
MONA LISA, *Captain Carey, USA,* PAR. Music and Lyrics by Ray Evans and Jay Livingston.
BE MY LOVE, *The Toast Of New Orleans,* MGM. Music, Nicholas Brodszky. Lyrics, Sammy Cahn.
BIBBIDY-BOBBIDI-BOO, *Cinderella.* Music and Lyrics by Mack David, Al Hoffman and Jerry Livingston.
MULE TRAIN, *Singing Guns,* Polomar Pictures, REP. Music and Lyrics by Fred Glickman, Hy Heath and Johnny Lange.
WILHELMINA, *Wabash Avenue,* FOX. Music, Josef Myrow. Lyrics, Mack Gordon.

SOUND:
ALL ABOUT EVE. FOX Sound Department.
CINDERELLA. Disney Sound Department.
LOUISA, U. U Sound Department.
OUR VERY OWN, Goldwyn, RKO. Goldwyn Sound Department.
TRIO, Rank-Sydney Box, PAR (British).

SHORT FILMS:
(Cartoons)

GERALD MCBOING-BOING, United Productions Of America, COL. (Jolly Frolics Series) Stephen Bosustow, Ex Prod.
JERRY'S COUSIN, MGM. (Tom & Jerry) Fred Quimby, Prod.
TROUBLE INDEMNITY, United Productions Of America, COL. (Mr. Magoo Series) Stephen Bosustow, Ex Prod.

(One-reel)

GRANDAD OF RACES, WB. (Sports Parade) Gordon Hollingshead, Prod.
BLAZE BUSTERS, WB. (Vitaphone Novelties) Robert Youngson, Prod.
WRONG WAY BUTCH, MGM. Pete Smith, Prod.

(Two-reel)

IN BEAVER VALLEY, Walt Disney, RKO. (True-Life Adventure) Walt Disney, Prod.
GRANDMA MOSES, Falcon Films, Inc., A.F. Films. Falcon Films, Inc., Prod.
MY COUNTRY 'TIS OF THEE, WB. (Featurette Series) Gordon Hollingshead, Prod.

DOCUMENTARY:
(Short Subjects)

WHY KOREA?, FOX Movietone. Edmund Reek, Prod.
THE FIGHT: SCIENCE AGAINST CANCER, NFC in cooperation with the Medical Film Institute of the Association of American Medical Colleges.
THE STAIRS, Film Documents, Inc.

(Features)

THE TITAN: STORY OF MICHELANGELO, Michelangelo Co., Classics Pictures, Inc. Robert Snyder, Prod.
WITH THESE HANDS, Promotional Films Co., Inc. Jack Arnold and Lee Goodman, Prods.

SPECIAL EFFECTS:
DESTINATION MOON.
SAMSON AND DELILAH.

HONORARY AND OTHER:
(Irving G. Thalberg Memorial Award)

Darryl F. Zanuck

(Other)

GEORGE MURPHY for his services in interpreting the film industry to the country at large.
LOUIS B. MAYER for distinguished service to the motion picture industry.
THE WALLS OF MALAPAGA (Franco-Italian) - voted by the Board of Governors as the most outstanding foreign language film released in the United States in 1950.

SCIENTIFIC OR TECHNICAL:
(Class II)

JAMES B. GORDON and the **20TH CENTURY-FOX STUDIO CAMERA DEPARTMENT** for the design and development of a multiple image film viewer.
JOHN PAUL LIVADARY, FLOYD CAMPBELL, L. W. RUSSELL and the **COLUMBIA STUDIO SOUND DEPARTMENT** for the development of a multi-track magnetic re-recording system.
LOREN L. RYDER and the **PARAMOUNT STUDIO SOUND DEPARTMENT** for the first studio-wide application of magnetic sound recording to motion picture production.

1951

BEST PICTURE:
AN AMERICAN IN PARIS, MGM. Arthur Freed, Prod.
DECISION BEFORE DAWN, FOX. Anatole Litvak & Frank McCarthy, Prods.
A PLACE IN THE SUN, PAR. George Stevens, Prod.
QUO VADIS, MGM. Sam Zimbalist, Prod.
A STREETCAR NAMED DESIRE, Charles K. Feldman Group Prods., WB. Charles K. Feldman, Prod.

ACTOR:
HUMPHREY BOGART, *The African Queen,* Horizon, UA.
MARLON BRANDO, *A Streetcar Named Desire.*
MONTGOMERY CLIFT, *A Place In The Sun.*
ARTHUR KENNEDY, *Bright Victory,* U.
FREDRIC MARCH, *Death Of A Salesman,* Stanley Kramer, COL.

ACTRESS:
VIVIEN LEIGH, *A Streetcar Named Desire.*
KATHARINE HEPBURN, *The African Queen.*
ELEANOR PARKER, *Detective Story,* PAR.
SHELLEY WINTERS, *A Place In The Sun.*
JANE WYMAN, *The Blue Veil,* Wald-Krasna, RKO.

SUPPORTING ACTOR:
KARL MALDEN, *A Streetcar Named Desire.*
LEO GENN, *Quo Vadis.*
KEVIN McCARTHY, *Death Of A Salesman.*
PETER USTINOV, *Quo Vadis.*
GIG YOUNG, *Come Fill The Cup,* WB.

SUPPORTING ACTRESS:
KIM HUNTER, *A Streetcar Named Desire.*
JOAN BLONDELL, *The Blue Veil.*
MILDRED DUNNOCK, *Death Of A Salesman.*
LEE GRANT, *Detective Story.*
THELMA RITTER, *The Mating Season,* PAR.

DIRECTING:
GEORGE STEVENS, *A Place In The Sun.*
JOHN HUSTON, *The African Queen.*
ELIA KAZAN, *A Streetcar Named Desire.*
VINCENTE MINNELLI, *An American In Paris.*
WILLIAM WYLER, *Detective Story.*

WRITING:
(Motion Picture Story)
SEVEN DAYS TO NOON, Boulting Bros., MKD (British). Paul Dehn and James Bernard.
BULLFIGHTER AND THE LADY, REP. Budd Boetticher and Ray Nazarro.
THE FROGMEN, FOX. Oscar Millard.
HERE COMES THE GROOM, PAR. Robert Riskin and Liam O'Brien.
TERESA, MGM. Alfred Hayes and Stewart Stern.
(Screenplay)
A PLACE IN THE SUN. Michael Wilson and Harry Brown.
THE AFRICAN QUEEN. James Agee and John Huston.
DETECTIVE STORY. Philip Yordan and Robert Wyler.
LA RONDE, Sacha Gordine, CME (French). Jacques Natanson and Max Ophuls.
A STREETCAR NAMED DESIRE. Tennessee Williams.
(Story and Screenplay)
AN AMERICAN IN PARIS. Alan Jay Lerner.
THE BIG CARNIVAL, PAR. Billy Wilder, Lesser Samuels and Walter Newman.
DAVID AND BATHSHEBA, FOX. Philip Dunne.
GO FOR BROKE!, MGM. Robert Pirosh.
THE WELL, Popkin, UA. Clarence Greene and Russell Rouse.

CINEMATOGRAPHY:
(Black-and-White)
A PLACE IN THE SUN. William C. Mellor.
DEATH OF A SALESMAN. Franz Planer.
THE FROGMEN. Norbert Brodine.
STRANGERS ON A TRAIN, WB. Robert Burks.
A STREETCAR NAMED DESIRE. Harry Stradling.
(Color)
AN AMERICAN IN PARIS. Alfred Gilks; Ballet photographed by John Alton.
DAVID AND BATHSHEBA. Leon Shamroy.
QUO VADIS. Robert Surtees and William V. Skall.
SHOW BOAT, MGM. Charles Rosher.
WHEN WORLDS COLLIDE, PAR. John F. Seitz and W. Howard Greene.

COSTUME DESIGN:
(Black-and-White)
A PLACE IN THE SUN. Edith Head.
KIND LADY, MGM. Walter Plunkett and Gile Steele.
THE MODEL AND THE MARRIAGE BROKER, FOX. Charles LeMaire and Renie.
THE MUDLARK, FOX. Edward Stevenson and Margaret Furse.
A STREETCAR NAMED DESIRE. Lucinda Ballard.
(Color)
AN AMERICAN IN PARIS. Orry-Kelly, Walter Plunkett and Irene Sharaff.
DAVID AND BATHSHEBA. Charles LeMaire and Edward Stevenson.
THE GREAT CARUSO, MGM. Helen Rose and Gile Steele.
QUO VADIS. Herschel McCoy.
TALES OF HOFFMANN, Powell-Pressburger, LOP (British). Hein Heckroth.

ART DIRECTION - SET DECORATION:
(Black-and-White)
A STREETCAR NAMED DESIRE. Richard Day. Set Decoration: George James Hopkins.
FOURTEEN HOURS, FOX. Lyle Wheeler and Leland Fuller. Set Decoration: Thomas Little and Fred J. Rode.
HOUSE ON TELEGRAPH HILL, FOX. Lyle Wheeler and John DeCrui. Set Decoration: Thomas Little and Paul S. Fox.
LA RONDE. D'Eaubonne. Set Decoration: No credits listed.
TOO YOUNG TO KISS, MGM. Cedric Gibbons and Paul Groesse. Set Decoration: Edwin B. Willis and Jack D. Moore.
(Color)
AN AMERICAN IN PARIS. Cedric Gibbons and Preston Ames. Set Decoration: Edwin B. Willis and Keogh Gleason.
DAVID AND BATHSHEBA. Lyle Wheeler and George Davis. Set Decoration: Thomas Little and Paul S. Fox.
ON THE RIVIERA, FOX. Lyle Wheeler and Leland Fuller. Musical Settings: Joseph C. Wright. Set Decoration: Thomas Little and Walter M. Scott.
QUO VADIS. William A. Horning, Cedric Gibbons and Edward Carfagno. Set Decoration: Hugh Hunt.
TALES OF HOFFMANN. Hein Heckroth. Set Decoration: No credits listed.

FILM EDITING:
A PLACE IN THE SUN. William Hornbeck.
AN AMERICAN IN PARIS. Adrienne Fazan.
DECISION BEFORE DAWN. Dorothy Spencer.
QUO VADIS. Ralph E. Winters.
THE WELL. Chester Schaeffer.

MUSIC - SCORING:
(Scoring of a Dramatic or Comedy Picture)
A PLACE IN THE SUN. Franz Waxman.
DAVID AND BATHSHEBA. Alfred Newman.
DEATH OF A SALESMAN. Alex North.
QUO VADIS. Miklos Rozsa.
A STREETCAR NAMED DESIRE. Alex North.
(Scoring of a Musical Picture)
AN AMERICAN IN PARIS. Johnny Green and Saul Chaplin.
ALICE IN WONDERLAND, Disney, RKO. Oliver Wallace.
THE GREAT CARUSO. Peter Herman Adler and Johnny Green.
ON THE RIVIERA. Alfred Newman.
SHOW BOAT. Adolph Deutsch and Conrad Salinger.

MUSIC - BEST SONG:
IN THE COOL, COOL, COOL OF THE EVENING, *Here Comes The Groom.* Music, Hoagy Carmichael. Lyrics, Johnny Mercer.
A KISS TO BUILD A DREAM ON, *The Strip,* MGM. Music and Lyrics by Bert Kalmar, Harry Ruby and Oscar Hammerstein II.
NEVER, *Golden Girl,* FOX. Music, Lionel Newman. Lyrics, Eliot Daniel.
TOO LATE NOW, *Royal Wedding,* MGM. Music, Burton Lane. Lyrics, Alan Jay Lerner.

WONDER WHY, *Rich, Young And Pretty,* MGM. Music, Nicholas Brodszky. Lyrics, Sammy Cahn.

SOUND:
THE GREAT CARUSO. Douglas Shearer, Sound Director.
BRIGHT VICTORY. Leslie I. Carey, Sound Director.
I WANT YOU, Samuel Goldwyn Prods., Inc., RKO. Gordon Sawyer, Sound Director.
A STREETCAR NAMED DESIRE. Col. Nathan Levinson, Sound Director.
TWO TICKETS TO BROADWAY, RKO. John O. Aalberg, Sound Director.

SHORT FILMS:
(Cartoons)
TWO MOUSEKETEERS, MGM. (Tom & Jerry) Fred Quimby, Prod.
LAMBERT, THE SHEEPISH LION, Walt Disney, RKO. (Special) Walt Disney, Prod.
ROOTY TOOT TOOT, United Productions Of America, COL. (Jolly Frolics) Stephen Bosustow, Ex Prod.
(One-reel)
WORLD OF KIDS, WB. (Vitaphone Novelties) Robert Youngson, Prod.
RIDIN' THE RAILS, PAR. (Sportlights) Jack Eaton, Prod.
THE STORY OF TIME, A Signal Films Production by Robert G. Leffingwell, Cornell Film Co (British).
(Two-reel)
NATURE'S HALF ACRE, Walt Disney, RKO. (True-Life Adventure) Walt Disney, Prod.
BALZAC, Les Films Du Compass, A.F. Films, Inc. (French). Les Films Du Compass, Prod.
DANGER UNDER THE SEA, UI. Tom Mead, Prod.

DOCUMENTARY:
(Short Subjects)
BENJY, Made by Fred Zinnemann with the cooperation of PAR for the Los Angeles Orthopaedic Hospital.
ONE WHO CAME BACK, Owen Crump, Prod. (Film sponsored by the Disabled American Veterans, in cooperation with the United States Department of Defense and the Association of Motion Picture Prods.)
THE SEEING EYE, WB. Gordon Hollingshead, Prod.
(Features)
KON-TIKI, An Artfilm Prod., RKO (Norwegian). Olle Nordemar, Prod.
I WAS A COMMUNIST FOR THE F.B.I., WB. Bryan Foy, Prod.

SPECIAL EFFECTS:
WHEN WORLDS COLLIDE.

HONORARY AND OTHER:
(Irving G. Thalberg Memorial Award)
Arthur Freed
(Other)
GENE KELLY in appreciation of his versatility as an actor, singer, director and dancer, and specifically for his brilliant achievements in the art of choreography on film.
RASHOMON (Japanese) - voted by the Board of Governors as the most outstanding foreign language film released in the United States during 1951.

SCIENTIFIC OR TECHNICAL:
(Class II)
GORDON JENNINGS, S. L. STANCLIFFE and the Paramount STUDIO SPECIAL PHOTOGRAPHIC and ENGINEERING DEPARTMENTS for the design, construction and application of a servo-operated recording and repeating device.
OLIN L. DUPY of MGM Studio for the design, construction and application of a motion picture reproducing system.
RADIO CORPORATION OF AMERICA, VICTOR DIVISION, for pioneering direct positive recording with anticipatory noise reduction.
(Class III)
RICHARD M. HAFF, FRANK P. HERRNFELD, GARLAND C. MISENER and the ANSCO FILM DIVISION OF GENERAL ANILINE AND FILM CORP. for the development of the Ansco color scene tester.
FRED PONEDEL, RALPH AYRES and GEORGE BROWN of WB Studio for an air-driven water motor to provide flow, wake and white water for marine sequences in motion pictures.
GLEN ROBINSON and the MGM STUDIO CONSTRUCTION DEPARTMENT for the development of a new music wire and cable cutter.
JACK GAYLORD and the MGM STUDIO CONSTRUCTION DEPARTMENT for the development of balsa falling snow.
CARLOS RIVAS of MGM Studio for the development of an automatic magnetic film splicer.

1952

BEST PICTURE:
THE GREATEST SHOW ON EARTH, Cecil B. DeMille, PAR. Cecil B. DeMille, Prod.
HIGH NOON, Stanley Kramer Prods., UA. Stanley Kramer, Prod.
IVANHOE, MGM. Pandro S. Berman, Prod.
MOULIN ROUGE, Romulus Films, UA.
THE QUIET MAN, Argosy Pictures Corp., REP. John Ford and Merian C. Cooper, Prods.

ACTOR:
GARY COOPER, High Noon.
MARLON BRANDO, *Viva Zapata!,* FOX.
KIRK DOUGLAS, *The Bad And The Beautiful,* MGM.
JOSE FERRER, *Moulin Rouge.*
ALEC GUINNESS, *The Lavender Hill Mob,* J. Arthur Rank Presentation-Ealing Studios, U. (British)

ACTRESS:
SHIRLEY BOOTH, Come Back, Little Sheba, Hal Wallis, PAR.
JOAN CRAWFORD, *Sudden Fear,* Joseph Kaufman Prods., RKO.
BETTE DAVIS, *The Star,* Bert E. Friedlob, FOX.
JULIE HARRIS, *The Member Of The Wedding,* Stanley Kramer, COL.
SUSAN HAYWARD, *With A Song In My Heart,* FOX.

SUPPORTING ACTOR:
ANTHONY QUINN, Viva Zapata!
RICHARD BURTON, *My Cousin Rachel,* FOX.
ARTHUR HUNNICUTT, *The Big Sky,* Winchester, RKO.
VICTOR McLAGLEN, *The Quiet Man.*
JACK PALANCE, *Sudden Fear.*

SUPPORTING ACTRESS:
GLORIA GRAHAME, The Bad And The Beautiful.
JEAN HAGEN, *Singin' In The Rain,* MGM.
COLETTE MARCHAND, *Moulin Rouge.*
TERRY MOORE, *Come Back, Little Sheba.*
THELMA RITTER, *With A Song In My Heart.*

DIRECTING:
JOHN FORD, The Quiet Man.
CECIL B. DEMILLE, *The Greatest Show On Earth.*
JOHN HUSTON, *Moulin Rouge.*
JOSEPH L. MANKIEWICZ, *Five Fingers,* FOX.
FRED ZINNEMANN, *High Noon.*

WRITING:
(Motion Picture Story)
THE GREATEST SHOW ON EARTH. Frederic M. Frank, Theodore St. John and Frank Cavett.
MY SON JOHN, Rainbow, PAR. Leo McCarey.
THE NARROW MARGIN, RKO. Martin Goldsmith and Jack Leonard.

THE PRIDE OF ST. LOUIS, FOX. Guy Trosper.
THE SNIPER, Kramer, COL. Edna Anhalt and Edward Anhalt.

(Screenplay)

THE BAD AND THE BEAUTIFUL. Charles Schnee.
FIVE FINGERS. Michael Wilson.
HIGH NOON. Carl Foreman.
THE MAN IN THE WHITE SUIT, Rank-Ealing, U (British). Roger Mac-Dougall, John Dighton and Alexander Mackendrick.
THE QUIET MAN. Frank S. Nugent.

(Story and Screenplay)

THE LAVENDER HILL MOB. T.E.B. Clarke.
THE ATOMIC CITY, PAR. Sydney Boehm.
BREAKING THE SOUND BARRIER, London Films, UA (British). Terence Rattigan.
PAT AND MIKE, MGM. Ruth Gordon and Garson Kanin.
VIVA ZAPATA! John Steinbeck.

CINEMATOGRAPHY:

(Black-and-White)

THE BAD AND THE BEAUTIFUL. Robert Surtees.
THE BIG SKY. Russell Harlan.
MY COUSIN RACHEL. Joseph LaShelle.
NAVAJO, Bartlett-Foster, LIP. Virgil E. Miller.
SUDDEN FEAR. Charles B. Lang, Jr.

(Color)

THE QUIET MAN. Winton C. Hoch and Archie Stout.
HANS CHRISTIAN ANDERSEN, Goldwyn, RKO. Harry Stradling.
IVANHOE. F. A. Young.
MILLION DOLLAR MERMAID, MGM. George J. Folsey.
THE SNOWS OF KILIMANJARO, FOX. Leon Shamroy.

COSTUME DESIGN:

(Black-and-White)

THE BAD AND THE BEAUTIFUL. Helen Rose.
AFFAIR IN TRINIDAD, Beckworth, COL. Jean Louis.
CARRIE, PAR. Edith Head.
MY COUSIN RACHEL. Charles LeMaire and Dorothy Jeakins.
SUDDEN FEAR. Sheila O'Brien.

(Color)

MOULIN ROUGE. Marcel Vertes.
THE GREATEST SHOW ON EARTH. Edith Head, Dorothy Jeakins and Miles White.
HANS CHRISTIAN ANDERSEN. Clave, Mary Wills and Madame Karinska.
THE MERRY WIDOW, MGM. Helen Rose and Gile Steele.
WITH A SONG IN MY HEART. Charles LeMaire.

ART DIRECTION - SET DECORATION:

(Black-and-White)

THE BAD AND THE BEAUTIFUL. Cedric Gibbons and Edward Carfagno. Set Decoration: Edwin B. Willis and Keogh Gleason.
CARRIE. Hal Pereira and Roland Anderson. Set Decoration: Emile Kuri.
MY COUSIN RACHEL. Lyle Wheeler and John DeCuir. Set Decoration: Walter M. Scott.
RASHO-MON, Daiei, RKO (Japanese). Matsuyama. Set Decoration: H. Motsumoto.
VIVA ZAPATA! Lyle Wheeler and Leland Fuller. Set Decoration: Thomas Little and Claude Carpenter.

(Color)

MOULIN ROUGE. Paul Sheriff. Set Decoration: Marcel Vertes.
HANS CHRISTIAN ANDERSEN. Richard Day and Clave. Set Decoration: Howard Bristol.
THE MERRY WIDOW. Cedric Gibbons and Paul Groesse. Set Decoration: Edwin B. Willis and Arthur Krams.
THE QUIET MAN. Frank Hotaling. Set Decoration: John McCarthy, Jr. and Charles Thompson.
THE SNOWS OF KILIMANJARO. Lyle Wheeler and John DeCuir. Set Decoration: Thomas Little and Paul S. Fox.

FILM EDITING:

HIGH NOON. Elmo Williams and Harry Gerstad.
COME BACK, LITTLE SHEBA. Warren Low.
FLAT TOP, MNG. William Austin.
THE GREATEST SHOW ON EARTH. Anne Bauchens.
MOULIN ROUGE. Ralph Kemplen.

MUSIC - SCORING:

(Scoring of a Dramatic or Comedy Picture)

HIGH NOON. Dimitri Tiomkin.
IVANHOE. Miklos Rozsa.
MIRACLE OF FATIMA, WB. Max Steiner.
THE THIEF, Fran Prods., UA. Herschel Burke Gilbert.
VIVA ZAPATA! Alex North.

(Scoring of a Musical Picture)

WITH A SONG IN MY HEART. Alfred Newman.
HANS CHRISTIAN ANDERSEN. Walter Scharf.
THE JAZZ SINGER, WB. Ray Heindorf and Max Steiner.
THE MEDIUM, Transfilm-Lopert (Italian). Gian-Carlo Menotti.
SINGIN' IN THE RAIN. Lennie Hayton.

MUSIC - BEST SONG:

HIGH NOON (DO NOT FORSAKE ME, OH MY DARLIN'), High Noon. Music, Dimitri Tiomkin. Lyrics, Ned Washington.
AM I IN LOVE, *Son Of Paleface*, PAR. Music and Lyrics by Jack Brooks.
BECAUSE YOU'RE MINE, *Because You're Mine*, MGM. Music, Nicholas Brodszky. Lyrics, Sammy Cahn.
THUMBELINA, *Hans Christian Andersen*. Music and Lyrics by Frank Loesser.
ZING A LITTLE ZONG, *Just For You*, PAR. Music, Harry Warren. Lyrics, Leo Robin.

SOUND:

BREAKING THE SOUND BARRIER. London Film Sound Department.
HANS CHRISTIAN ANDERSEN. Goldwyn Sound Department. Gordon Sawyer, Sound Director.
THE PROMOTER, Rank, Ronald Neame, UI (British). Pinewood Studios Sound Department.
THE QUIET MAN. REP Sound Department. Daniel J. Bloomberg, Sound Director.
WITH A SONG IN MY HEART. FOX Sound Department. Thomas T. Moulton, Sound Director.

SHORT FILMS:

(Cartoons)

JOHANN MOUSE, MGM. (Tom & Jerry) Fred Quimby, Prod.
LITTLE JOHNNY JET, MGM. (MGM Series) Fred Quimby, Prod.
MADELINE, UPA, COL. (Jolly Frolics) Stephen Bosustow, Ex Prod.
PINK AND BLUE BLUES, UPA, COL. (Mister Magoo) Stephen Bosustow, Ex Prod.
ROMANCE OF TRANSPORTATION, NFC (Canadian). Tom Daly, Prod.

(One-reel)

LIGHT IN THE WINDOW, Art Films Prods., FOX. (Art Series) Boris Vermont, Prod.
ATHLETES OF THE SADDLE, PAR. (Sportlights Series) Jack Eaton, Prod.
DESERT KILLER, WB. (Sports Parade) Gordon Hollingshead, Prod.
NEIGHBOURS, NFC (Canadian). Norman McLaren, Prod.
ROYAL SCOTLAND, Crown Film Unit, British Information Services (British).

(Two-reel)

WATER BIRDS, Walt Disney, RKO. (True-Life Adventure) Walt Disney, Prod.
BRIDGE OF TIME, A London Film Prod., British Information Services (British).
DEVIL TAKE US, A Theatre Of Life Prod. (Theatre Of Life Series) Herbert Morgan, Prod.
THAR SHE BLOWS!, WB. (Technicolor Special) Gordon Hollingshead, Prod.

DOCUMENTARY:
(Short Subjects)

NEIGHBOURS, NFC, MAK (Canadian). Norman McLaren, Prod.
DEVIL TAKE US, Theatre of Life Prod. Herbert Morgan, Prod.
THE GARDEN SPIDER (EPEIRA DIADEMA), Cristallo Films, IFE. (Italian). Alberto Ancilotto, Prod.
MAN ALIVE!, Made by United Productions of America for the American Cancer Society. Stephen Bosustow, Ex Prod.

(Features)

THE SEA AROUND US, RKO. Irwin Allen, Prod.
THE HOAXTERS, MGM. Dore Schary, Prod.
NAVAJO, Hall Bartlett, Prod.

SPECIAL EFFECTS:
PLYMOUTH ADVENTURE, MGM.

HONORARY AND OTHER:
(Irving G. Thalberg Memorial Award)

Cecil B. DeMille

(Other)

GEORGE ALFRED MITCHELL for the design and development of the camera which bears his name and for his continued and dominant presence in the field of cinematography.
JOSEPH M. SCHENCK for long and distinguished service to the motion picture industry.
MERIAN C. COOPER for his many innovations and contributions to the art of motion pictures.
HAROLD LLOYD, master comedian and good citizen.
BOB HOPE for his contribution to the laughter of the world, his service to the motion picture industry, and his devotion to the American premise.
FORBIDDEN GAMES (French) - Best Foreign Language Film first released in the United States during 1952.

SCIENTIFIC OR TECHNICAL:
(Class I)

EASTMAN KODAK CO. for the introduction of Eastman color negative and Eastman color print film.
ANSCO DIVISION, GENERAL ANILINE AND FILM CORP., for the introduction of Ansco color negative and Ansco color print film.

(Class II)

TECHNICOLOR MOTION PICTURE CORP. for an improved method of color motion picture photography under incandescent light.

(Class III)

PROJECTION, STILL PHOTOGRAPHIC and DEVELOPMENT ENGINEERING DEPARTMENTS of MGM STUDIO for an improved method of projecting photographic backgrounds.
JOHN G. FRAYNE and R. R. SCOVILLE and WESTREX CORP. for a method of measuring distortion in sound reproduction.
PHOTO RESEARCH CORP. for creating the Spectra color temperature meter.
GUSTAV JIROUCH for the design of the Robot automatic film splicer.
CARLOS RIVAS of MGM Studio for the development of a sound reproducer for magnetic film.

1953

BEST PICTURE:
FROM HERE TO ETERNITY, COL. Buddy Adler, Prod.
JULIUS CAESAR, MGM. John Houseman, Prod.
THE ROBE, FOX. Frank Ross, Prod.
ROMAN HOLIDAY, PAR. William Wyler, Prod.
SHANE, PAR. George Stevens, Prod.

ACTOR:
WILLIAM HOLDEN, Stalag 17, PAR.
MARLON BRANDO, *Julius Caesar.*
RICHARD BURTON, *The Robe.*
MONTGOMERY CLIFT, *From Here To Eternity.*
BURT LANCASTER, *From Here To Eternity.*

ACTRESS:
AUDREY HEPBURN, Roman Holiday.
LESLIE CARON, *Lili,* MGM.
AVA GARDNER, *Mogambo,* MGM.
DEBORAH KERR, *From Here To Eternity.*
MAGGIE McNAMARA, *The Moon Is Blue,* Preminger-Herbert, UA.

SUPPORTING ACTOR:
FRANK SINATRA, From Here To Eternity.
EDDIE ALBERT, *Roman Holiday.*
BRANDON DE WILDE, *Shane.*
JACK PALANCE, *Shane.*
ROBERT STRAUSS, *Stalag 17.*

SUPPORTING ACTRESS:
DONNA REED, From Here To Eternity.
GRACE KELLY, *Mogambo.*
GERALDINE PAGE, *Hondo.*
MARJORIE RAMBEAU, *Torch Song,* MGM.
THELMA RITTER, *Pickup On South Street,* FOX.

DIRECTING:
FRED ZINNEMANN, From Here To Eternity.
GEORGE STEVENS, *Shane.*
CHARLES WALTERS, *Lili.*
BILLY WILDER, *Stalag 17.*
WILLIAM WYLER, *Roman Holiday.*

WRITING:
(Motion Picture Story)

ROMAN HOLIDAY. Ian McLellan Hunter.
ABOVE AND BEYOND, MGM. Beirne Lay, Jr.
THE CAPTAIN'S PARADISE, London Films, Lopert-UA (British). Alec Coppel.
LITTLE FUGITIVE, Little Fugitive Prod. Co., BYN. Ray Ashley, Morris Engel and Ruth Orkin.

(Screenplay)

FROM HERE TO ETERNITY. Daniel Taradash.
THE CRUEL SEA, Rank-Ealing, UI (British). Eric Ambler.
LILI. Helen Deutsch.
ROMAN HOLIDAY. Ian McLellan Hunter and John Dighton.
SHANE. A. B. Guthrie, Jr.

(Story and Screenplay)

TITANIC, FOX. Charles Brackett, Walter Reisch and Richard Breen.
THE BAND WAGON, MGM. Betty Comden and Adolph Green.
THE DESERT RATS, FOX. Richard Murphy.
THE NAKED SPUR, MGM. Sam Rolfe and Harold Jack Bloom.
TAKE THE HIGH GROUND, MGM. Millard Kaufman.

CINEMATOGRAPHY:
(Black-and-White)

FROM HERE TO ETERNITY. Burnett Guffey.
THE FOUR POSTER, Kramer, COL. Hal Mohr.
JULIUS CAESAR. Joseph Ruttenberg.
MARTIN LUTHER, DRH. Joseph C. Brun.
ROMAN HOLIDAY. Franz Planer and Henry Alekan.

(Color)

SHANE. Loyal Griggs.
ALL THE BROTHERS WERE VALIANT, MGM. George Folsey.
BENEATH THE TWELVE-MILE REEF, FOX. Edward Cronjager.
LILI. Robert Planck.
THE ROBE. Leon Shamroy.

COSTUME DESIGN:
(Black-and-White)
ROMAN HOLIDAY. Edith Head.
THE ACTRESS, MGM. Walter Plunkett.
DREAM WIFE, MGM. Helen Rose and Herschel McCoy.
FROM HERE TO ETERNITY. Jean Louis.
THE PRESIDENT'S LADY, FOX. Charles LeMaire and Renie.
(Color)
THE ROBE. Charles LeMaire and Emile Santiago.
THE BAND WAGON. Mary Ann Nyberg.
CALL ME MADAM, FOX. Irene Sharaff.
HOW TO MARRY A MILLIONAIRE, FOX. Charles LeMaire and Travilla.
YOUNG BESS, MGM. Walter Plunkett.

ART DIRECTION - SET DECORATION:
(Black-and-White)
JULIUS CAESAR. Cedric Gibbons and Edward Carfagno. Set Decoration: Edwin B. Willis and Hugh Hunt.
MARTIN LUTHER. Fritz Maurischat and Paul Markwitz. Set Decoration: No credits listed.
THE PRESIDENT'S LADY. Lyle Wheeler and Leland Fuller. Set Decoration: Paul S. Fox.
ROMAN HOLIDAY. Hal Pereira and Walter Tyler. Set Decoration: No credits listed.
TITANIC. Lyle Wheeler and Maurice Ransford. Set Decoration: Stuart Reiss.
(Color)
THE ROBE. Lyle Wheeler and George W. Davis. Set Decoration: Walter M. Scott and Paul S. Fox.
KNIGHTS OF THE ROUND TABLE, MGM. Alfred Junge and Hans Peters. Set Decoration: John Jarvis.
LILI. Cedric Gibbons and Paul Groesse. Set Decoration: Edwin B. Willis and Arthur Krams.
THE STORY OF THREE LOVES, MGM. Cedric Gibbons, Preston Ames, Edward Carfagno and Gabriel Scognamillo. Set Decoration: Edwin B. Willis, Keogh Gleason, Arthur Krams and Jack D. Moore.
YOUNG BESS. Cedric Gibbons and Urie McCleary. Set Decoration: Edwin B. Willis and Jack D. Moore.

FILM EDITING:
FROM HERE TO ETERNITY. William Lyon.
CRAZYLEGS, Bartlett, REP. Irvine (Cotton) Warburton.
THE MOON IS BLUE. Otto Ludwig.
ROMAN HOLIDAY. Robert Swink.
WAR OF THE WORLDS, PAR. Everett Douglas.

MUSIC - SCORING:
(Scoring of a Dramatic or Comedy Picture)
LILI. Bronislau Kaper.
ABOVE AND BEYOND. Hugo Friedhofer.
FROM HERE TO ETERNITY. Morris Stoloff and George Duning.
JULIUS CAESAR. Miklos Rozsa.
THIS IS CINERAMA, CRC. Louis Forbes.
(Scoring of a Musical Picture)
CALL ME MADAM. Alfred Newman.
THE BAND WAGON. Adolph Deutsch.
CALAMITY JANE, WB. Ray Heindorf.
5,000 FINGERS OF DR. T., Kramer-COL. Frederick Hollander and Morris Stoloff.
KISS ME KATE, MGM. Andre Previn and Saul Chaplin.

MUSIC - BEST SONG:
SECRET LOVE, Calamity Jane. Music, Sammy Fain. Lyrics, Paul Francis Webster.
THE MOON IS BLUE, *The Moon Is Blue*. Music, Herschel Burke Gilbert. Lyrics, Sylvia Fine.
MY FLAMING HEART, *Small Town Girl*, MGM. Music, Nicholas Brodszky. Lyrics, Leo Robin.
SADIE THOMPSON'S SONG (BLUE PACIFIC BLUES), *Miss Sadie Thompson*, Beckworth, COL. Music, Lester Lee. Lyrics, Ned Washington.
THAT'S AMORE, *The Caddy*, York Pictures, PAR. Music, Harry Warren. Lyrics, Jack Brooks.

SOUND:
FROM HERE TO ETERNITY. COL Sound Department. John P. Livadary, Sound Director.
CALAMITY JANE. WB Sound Department. William A. Mueller, Sound Director.
KNIGHTS OF THE ROUND TABLE, MGM. A. W. Watkins, Sound Director.
THE MISSISSIPPI GAMBLER, U. U Sound Department. Leslie I. Carey, Sound Director.
THE WAR OF THE WORLDS. PAR Sound Department. Loren L. Ryder, Sound Director.

SHORT FILMS:
(Cartoons)
TOOT, WHISTLE, PLUNK AND BOOM, Walt Disney, BV. (Special Music Series) Walt Disney, Prod.
CHRISTOPHER CRUMPET, UPA, COL. (Jolly Frolics) Stephen Bosustow, Prod.
FROM A TO Z-Z-Z-Z, WB. (Looney Tunes) Edward Selzer, Prod.
RUGGED BEAR, Walt Disney, RKO. (Donald Duck) Walt Disney, Prod.
THE TELL TALE HEART, UPA, COL. (UPA Cartoon Special) Stephen Bosustow, Prod.
(One-reel)
THE MERRY WIVES OF WINDSOR OVERTURE, MGM. (Overture Series) Johnny Green, Prod.
CHRIST AMONG THE PRIMITIVES, IFE (Italian). Vincenzo Lucci-Chiarissi, Prod.
HERRING HUNT, (NFC), RKO (Canadian). (Canada Carries On Series)
JOY OF LIVING, Art Film Prods., FOX. (Art Film Series) Boris Vermont, Prod.
WEE WATER WONDERS, PAR. (Grantland Rice Sportlights Series) Jack Eaton, Prod.
(Two-reel)
BEAR COUNTRY, Walt Disney, RKO. (True-Life Adventure) Walt Disney, Prod.
BEN AND ME, Walt Disney, BV. (Cartoon Special Series) Walt Disney, Prod.
RETURN TO GLENNASCAUL, Dublin Gate Theatre Prod., MAK.
VESUVIUS EXPRESS, FOX. (CinemaScope Shorts Series) Otto Lang, Prod.
WINTER PARADISE, WB. (Technicolor Special) Cedric Francis, Prod.

DOCUMENTARY:
(Short Subjects)
THE ALASKAN ESKIMO, Walt Disney Prods., RKO. Walt Disney, Prod.
THE LIVING CITY, Encyclopaedia Britannica Films, Inc. John Barnes, Prod.
OPERATION BLUE JAY, U.S. Army Signal Corps.
THEY PLANTED A STONE, World Wide Pictures, British Information Services (British). James Carr, Prod.
THE WORD, FOX. John Healy and John Adams, Prods.
(Features)
THE LIVING DESERT, Walt Disney Prods., BV. Walt Disney, Prod.
THE CONQUEST OF EVEREST, Countryman Films, Ltd. & Group 3 Ltd., UA (British) John Taylor, Leon Clore and Grahame Tharp, Prods.
A QUEEN IS CROWNED, J. Arthur Rank Organization, Ltd., UI (British). Castleton Knight, Prod.

SPECIAL EFFECTS:
THE WAR OF THE WORLDS.

HONORARY AND OTHER:

(Irving G. Thalberg Memorial Award)

George Stevens

(Other)

PETE SMITH for his witty and pungent observations on the American scene in his series of Pete Smith Specialties.
20TH CENTURY-FOX FILM CORPORATION in recognition of their imagination, showmanship and foresight in introducing the revolutionary process known as CinemaScope.
JOSEPH I. BREEN for his conscientious, open-minded and dignified management of the Motion Picture Production Code.
BELL AND HOWELL COMPANY for their pioneering and basic achievements in the advancement of the motion picture industry.

SCIENTIFIC OR TECHNICAL:

(Class I)

PROFESSOR HENRI CHRETIEN and EARL SPONABLE, SOL HALPRIN, LORIN GRIGNON, HERBERT BRAGG and CARL FAULKNER of 20th Century Fox Studios for creating, developing and engineering the equipment, processes and techniques known as CinemaScope.
FRED WALLER for designing and developing the multiple photographic and projection systems which culminated in Cinerama.

(Class II)

REEVES SOUNDCRAFT CORP. for their development of a process of applying stripes of magnetic oxide to motion picture film for sound recording and reproduction.

(Class III)

WESTREX CORP. for the design and construction of a new film editing machine.

1954

BEST PICTURE:

ON THE WATERFRONT, Horizon-American Corp., COL. Sam Spiegel, Prod.
THE CAINE MUTINY, A Stanley Kramer Prod., COL. Stanley Kramer, Prod.
THE COUNTRY GIRL, Perlberg-Seaton, PAR. William Perlberg, Prod.
SEVEN BRIDES FOR SEVEN BROTHERS, MGM. Jack Cummings, Prod.
THREE COINS IN THE FOUNTAIN, FOX. Sol C. Siegel, Prod.

ACTOR:

MARLON BRANDO, On The Waterfront.
HUMPHREY BOGART, The Caine Mutiny.
BING CROSBY, The Country Girl.
JAMES MASON, A Star Is Born, Transcona, WB.
DAN O'HERLIHY, Adventures Of Robinson Crusoe, Dancigers-Ehrlich, UA.

ACTRESS:

GRACE KELLY, The Country Girl.
DOROTHY DANDRIDGE, Carmen Jones, Otto Preminger, FOX.
JUDY GARLAND, A Star Is Born.
AUDREY HEPBURN, Sabrina, PAR.
JANE WYMAN, The Magnificent Obsession, U.

SUPPORTING ACTOR:

EDMOND O'BRIEN, The Barefoot Contessa, Figaro, UA.
LEE J. COBB, On The Waterfront.
KARL MALDEN, On The Waterfront.
ROD STEIGER, On The Waterfront.
TOM TULLY, The Caine Mutiny.

SUPPORTING ACTRESS:

EVA MARIE SAINT, On The Waterfront.
NINA FOCH, Executive Suite, MGM.
KATY JURADO, Broken Lance, FOX.
JAN STERLING, The High And The Mighty, Wayne-Fellows, WB.
CLAIRE TREVOR, The High And The Mighty.

DIRECTING:

ELIA KAZAN, On The Waterfront.
ALFRED HITCHCOCK, Rear Window, Patron, Inc., PAR.
GEORGE SEATON, The Country Girl.
WILLIAM WELLMAN, The High And The Mighty.
BILLY WILDER, Sabrina.

WRITING:

(Motion Picture Story)

BROKEN LANCE. Philip Yordan.
BREAD, LOVE AND DREAMS, Titanus, IFE (Italian). Ettore Margadonna.
FORBIDDEN GAMES, Silver Films, TIM. (French). Francois Boyer.
NIGHT PEOPLE, FOX. Jed Harris and Tom Reed.
THERE'S NO BUSINESS LIKE SHOW BUSINESS, FOX. Lamar Trotti.

(Screenplay)

THE COUNTRY GIRL. George Seaton.
THE CAINE MUTINY. Stanley Roberts.
REAR WINDOW. John Michael Hayes.
SABRINA. Billy Wilder, Samuel Taylor and Ernest Lehman.
SEVEN BRIDES FOR SEVEN BROTHERS. Albert Hackett, Frances Goodrich and Dorothy Kingsley.

(Story and Screenplay)

ON THE WATERFRONT. Budd Schulberg.
THE BAREFOOT CONTESSA. Joseph Mankiewicz.
GENEVIEVE, A J. Arthur Rank Presentation-Sirius Prods., Ltd., UI (British). William Rose.
THE GLENN MILLER STORY, U. Valentine Davies and Oscar Brodney.
KNOCK ON WOOD, Dena Prods., PAR. Norman Panama and Melvin Frank.

CINEMATOGRAPHY:

(Black-and-White)

ON THE WATERFRONT. Boris Kaufman.
THE COUNTRY GIRL. John F. Warren.
EXECUTIVE SUITE. George Folsey.
ROGUE COP, MGM. John Seitz.
SABRINA. Charles Lang, Jr.

(Color)

THREE COINS IN THE FOUNTAIN. Milton Krasner.
THE EGYPTIAN, FOX. Leon Shamroy.
REAR WINDOW. Robert Burks.
SEVEN BRIDES FOR SEVEN BROTHERS. George Folsey.
THE SILVER CHALICE, A Victor Saville Prod., WB. William V. Skall.

COSTUME DESIGN:

(Black-and-White)

SABRINA. Edith Head.
THE EARRINGS OF MADAME DE. . ., Franco-London Prods., Arlan Pictures (French). Georges Annenkov and Rosine Delamare.
EXECUTIVE SUITE. Helen Rose.
INDISCRETION OF AN AMERICAN WIFE, A Vittorio DeSica Prod., COL. Christian Dior.
IT SHOULD HAPPEN TO YOU, COL. Jean Louis.

(Color)

GATE OF HELL, A Daiei Prod., EDH (Japanese). Sanzo Wada.
BRIGADOON, MGM. Irene Sharaff.
DESIREE, FOX. Charles LeMaire and Rene Hubert.
A STAR IS BORN. Jean Louis, Mary Ann Nyberg and Irene Sharaff.
THERE'S NO BUSINESS LIKE SHOW BUSINESS. Charles LeMaire, Travilla and Miles White.

ART DIRECTION - SET DECORATION:
(Black-and-White)

ON THE WATERFRONT. Richard Day. Set Decoration: No credits listed.
THE COUNTRY GIRL. Hal Pereira and Roland Anderson. Set Decoration: Sam Comer and Grace Gregory.
EXECUTIVE SUITE. Cedric Gibbons and Edward Carfagno. Set Decoration: Edwin B. Willis and Emile Kuri.
LE PLAISIR, Stera Film-CCFC Prod., MAK (French). Max Ophuls. Set Decoration: No credits listed.
SABRINA. Hal Pereira and Walter Tyler. Set Decoration: Sam Comer and Ray Moyer.

(Color)

20,000 LEAGUES UNDER THE SEA, Walt Disney Prods., BV. John Meehan. Set Decoration: Emile Kuri.
BRIGADOON. Cedric Gibbons and Preston Ames. Set Decoration: Edwin B. Willis and Keogh Gleason.
DESIREE. Lyle Wheeler and Leland Fuller. Set Decoration: Walter M. Scott and Paul S. Fox.
RED GARTERS, PAR. Hal Pereira and Roland Anderson. Set Decoration: Sam Comer and Ray Moyer.
A STAR IS BORN. Malcolm Bert, Gene Allen and Irene Sharaff. Set Decoration: George James Hopkins.

FILM EDITING:
ON THE WATERFRONT. Gene Milford.
THE CAINE MUTINY. William A. Lyon and Henry Batista.
THE HIGH AND THE MIGHTY. Ralph Dawson.
SEVEN BRIDES FOR SEVEN BROTHERS. Ralph E. Winters.
20,000 LEAGUES UNDER THE SEA. Elmo Williams.

MUSIC - SCORING:
(Scoring of a Dramatic or Comedy Picture)

THE HIGH AND THE MIGHTY. Dimitri Tiomkin.
THE CAINE MUTINY. Max Steiner.
GENEVIEVE. Muir Mathieson.
ON THE WATERFRONT. Leonard Bernstein.
THE SILVER CHALICE. Franz Waxman.

(Scoring of a Musical Picture)

SEVEN BRIDES FOR SEVEN BROTHERS. Adolph Deutsch and Saul Chaplin.
CARMEN JONES. Herschel Burke Gilbert.
THE GLENN MILLER STORY. Joseph Gershenson and Henry Mancini.
A STAR IS BORN. Ray Heindorf.
THERE'S NO BUSINESS LIKE SHOW BUSINESS. Alfred Newman and Lionel Newman.

MUSIC - BEST SONG:
THREE COINS IN THE FOUNTAIN, Three Coins In The Fountain. Music, Jule Styne. Lyrics, Sammy Cahn.
COUNT YOUR BLESSINGS INSTEAD OF SHEEP, *White Christmas*, PAR. Music and Lyrics, Irving Berlin.
THE HIGH AND THE MIGHTY, *The High And The Mighty*. Music, Dimitri Tiomkin. Lyrics, Ned Washington.
HOLD MY HAND, *Susan Slept Here*, RKO. Music and Lyrics by Jack Lawrence and Richard Myers.
THE MAN THAT GOT AWAY, *A Star Is Born*. Music, Harold Arlen. Lyrics, Ira Gershwin.

SOUND:
THE GLENN MILLER STORY. Leslie I. Carey, Sound Director.
BRIGADOON. Wesley C. Miller, Sound Director.
THE CAINE MUTINY. John P. Livadary, Sound Director.
REAR WINDOW. Loren L. Ryder, Sound Director.
SUSAN SLEPT HERE. John O. Aalberg, Sound Director.

SHORT FILMS:
(Cartoons)

WHEN MAGOO FLEW, UPA, COL. Stephen Bosustow, Prod.
CRAZY MIXED UP PUP, Walter Lantz Prods., U. Walter Lantz, Prod.
PIGS IS PIGS, Walt Disney Prods., RKO. Walt Disney, Prod.
SANDY CLAWS, WB. Cartoons, Inc. Edward Selzer, Prod.
TOUCHE, PUSSY CAT, MGM. Fred Quimby, Prod.

(One-reel)

THIS MECHANICAL AGE, WB. Robert Youngson, Prod.
THE FIRST PIANO QUARTETTE, FOX. Otto Lang, Prod.
THE STRAUSS FANTASY, MGM. Johnny Green, Prod.

(Two-reel)

A TIME OUT OF WAR, Carnival Prods., Denis and Terry Sanders, Prods.
BEAUTY AND THE BULL, WB. Cedric Francis, Prod.
JET CARRIER, FOX. Otto Lang, Prod.
SIAM, Walt Disney Prods., BV. Walt Disney, Prod.

DOCUMENTARY:
(Short Subjects)

THURSDAY'S CHILDREN, British Information Services (British). World Wide Pictures and Morse Films, Prods.
JET CARRIER, FOX. Otto Lang, Prod.
REMBRANDT: A SELF-PORTRAIT, DCA. Morrie Roizman, Prod.

(Features)

THE VANISHING PRAIRIE, Walt Disney Prods., BV. Walt Disney, Prod.
THE STRATFORD ADVENTURE, NFC, CON. (Canadian). Guy Glover, Prod.

SPECIAL EFFECTS:
20,000 LEAGUES UNDER THE SEA.
HELL AND HIGH WATER, FOX.
THEM!, WB.

HONORARY AND OTHER:
(Other)

BAUSCH & LOMB OPTICAL COMPANY for their contributions to the advancement of the motion picture industry.
KEMP R. NIVER for the development of the Renovare Process which has made possible the restoration of the Library of Congress Paper Film Collection.
GRETA GARBO for her unforgettable screen performances.
DANNY KAYE for his unique talents, his service to the Academy, the motion picture industry, and the American people.
JON WHITELEY for his outstanding juvenile performance in The Little Kidnappers.
VINCENT WINTER for his outstanding juvenile performance in The Little Kidnappers.
GATE OF HELL - Best Foreign Language Film first released in the United States during 1954.

SCIENTIFIC OR TECHNICAL:
(Class I)

PARAMOUNT PICTURES, INC., LOREN L. RYDER, JOHN R. BISHOP and all the members of the technical and engineering staff for developing a method of producing and exhibiting motion pictures known as VistaVision.

(Class III)

DAVID S. HORSLEY and the UI STUDIO SPECIAL PHOTOGRAPHIC DEPARTMENT for a portable remote control device for process projectors.
KARL FREUND and FRANK CRANDELL of Photo Research Corp. for the design and development of a direct reading brightness meter.
WESLEY C. MILLER, J. W. STAFFORD, K. M. FRIERSON and the MGM STUDIO SOUND DEPARTMENT for an electronic sound printing comparison device.
JOHN P. LIVADARY, LLOYD RUSSELL and the COLUMBIA STUDIO SOUND DEPARTMENT for an improved limiting amplifier as applied

to sound level comparison devices.
ROLAND MILLER and **MAX GOEPPINGER** of Magnascope Corp. for the design and development of a cathode ray magnetic sound track viewer.
CARLOS RIVAS, G. M. SPRAGUE and the **MGM STUDIO SOUND DEPARTMENT** for the design of a magnetic sound editing machine.
FRED WILSON of the Samuel Goldwyn Studio Sound Department for the design of a variable multiple-band equalizer.
P. C. YOUNG of the MGM Studio Projection Department for the practical application of a variable focal length attachment to motion picture projector lenses.
FRED KNOTH and **ORIEN ERNEST** of the UI Studio Technical Department for the development of a hand portable, electric, dry oil-fog machine.

1955

BEST PICTURE:

MARTY, Hecht & Lancaster's Steven Prods., UA. Harold Hecht, Prod.
LOVE IS A MANY-SPLENDORED THING, FOX. Buddy Adler, Prod.
MISTER ROBERTS, An Orange Prod., WB. Leland Hayward, Prod.
PICNIC, COL. Fred Kohlmar, Prod.
THE ROSE TATTOO, Hal Wallis, PAR. Hal B. Wallis, Prod.

ACTOR:

ERNEST BORGNINE, Marty.
JAMES CAGNEY, *Love Me Or Leave Me*, MGM.
JAMES DEAN, *East Of Eden*, WB.
FRANK SINATRA, *The Man With The Golden Arm*, Preminger, UA.
SPENCER TRACY, *Bad Day At Black Rock*, MGM.

ACTRESS:

ANNA MAGNANI, The Rose Tattoo.
SUSAN HAYWARD, *I'll Cry Tomorrow*, MGM.
KATHARINE HEPBURN, *Summertime*, Ilya Lopert-David Lean, UA. (Anglo-American)
JENNIFER JONES, *Love Is A Many-Splendored Thing*.
ELEANOR PARKER, *Interrupted Melody*, MGM.

SUPPORTING ACTOR:

JACK LEMMON, Mister Roberts.
ARTHUR KENNEDY, *Trial*, MGM.
JOE MANTELL, *Marty*.
SAL MINEO, *Rebel Without A Cause*, WB.
ARTHUR O'CONNELL, *Picnic*.

SUPPORTING ACTRESS:

JO VAN FLEET, East Of Eden.
BETSY BLAIR, *Marty*.
PEGGY LEE, *Pete Kelly's Blues*, A Mark VII Ltd. Prod., WB.
MARISA PAVAN *The Rose Tattoo*.
NATALIE WOOD, *Rebel Without A Cause*.

DIRECTING:

DELBERT MANN, Marty.
ELIA KAZAN, *East Of Eden*.
DAVID LEAN, *Summertime*.
JOSHUA LOGAN, *Picnic*.
JOHN STURGES, *Bad Day At Black Rock*.

WRITING:

(Motion Picture Story)

LOVE ME OR LEAVE ME. Daniel Fuchs.
THE PRIVATE WAR OF MAJOR BENSON, U. Joe Connelly and Bob Mosher.
REBEL WITHOUT A CAUSE. Nicholas Ray.
THE SHEEP HAS 5 LEGS, Raoul Ploquin, UMP (French). Jean Marsan, Henry Troyat, Jacques Perret, Henri Verneuil and Raoul Ploquin.
STRATEGIC AIR COMMAND, PAR. Beirne Lay, Jr.

(Best Screenplay)

MARTY. Paddy Chayefsky.
BAD DAY AT BLACK ROCK. Millard Kaufman.
BLACKBOARD JUNGLE, MGM. Richard Brooks.
EAST OF EDEN. Paul Osborn.
LOVE ME OR LEAVE ME. Daniel Fuchs and Isobel Lennart.

(Story and Screenplay)

INTERRUPTED MELODY, MGM. William Ludwig and Sonya Levien.
THE COURT-MARTIAL OF BILLY MITCHELL, A United States Pictures Prod., WB. Milton Sperling and Emmet Lavery.
IT'S ALWAYS FAIR WEATHER, MGM. Betty Comden and Adolph Green.
MR. HULOT'S HOLIDAY, Fred Orain Prod., GBD. (French). Jacques Tati and Henri Marquet.
THE SEVEN LITTLE FOYS, Hope Enterprises, Inc. and Scribe Prods. Melville Shavelson and Jack Rose.

CINEMATOGRAPHY:

(Black-and-White)

THE ROSE TATTOO. James Wong Howe.
BLACKBOARD JUNGLE. Russell Harlan.
I'LL CRY TOMORROW. Arthur E. Arling.
MARTY. Joseph LaShelle.
QUEEN BEE, COL. Charles Lang.

(Color)

TO CATCH A THIEF, PAR. Robert Burks.
GUYS AND DOLLS, Samuel Goldwyn Prods., Inc. MGM. Harry Stradling.
LOVE IS A MANY-SPLENDORED THING. Leon Shamroy.
A MAN CALLED PETER, FOX. Harold Lipstein.
OKLAHOMA!, Rodgers & Hammerstein Pictures, Inc., MNA. Robert Surtees.

COSTUME DESIGN:

(Black-and-White)

I'LL CRY TOMORROW. Helen Rose.
THE PICKWICK PAPERS, Renown Prod., KGY (British). Beatrice Dawson.
QUEEN BEE. Jean Louis.
THE ROSE TATTOO. Edith Head.
UGETSU, Daiei Motion Picture Co., EDH (Japanese). Tadaoto Kainoscho.

(Color)

LOVE IS A MANY-SPLENDORED THING. Charles LeMaire.
GUYS AND DOLLS. Irene Sharaff.
INTERRUPTED MELODY. Helen Rose.
TO CATCH A THIEF. Edith Head.
THE VIRGIN QUEEN, FOX. Charles LeMaire and Mary Wills.

ART DIRECTION - SET DECORATION:

(Black-and-White)

THE ROSE TATTOO. Hal Pereira and Tambi Larsen. Set Decoration: Sam Comer and Arthur Krams.
BLACKBOARD JUNGLE. Cedric Gibbons and Randall Duell. Set Decoration: Edwin B. Willis and Henry Grace.
I'LL CRY TOMORROW. Cedric Gibbons and Malcolm Brown. Set Decoration: Edwin B. Willis and Hugh B. Hunt.
THE MAN WITH THE GOLDEN ARM. Joseph C. Wright. Set Decoration: Darrell Silvera.
MARTY. Edward S. Haworth and Walter Simonds. Set Decoration: Robert Priestley.

(Color)

PICNIC. William Flannery and Jo Mielziner. Set Decoration: Robert Priestley.
DADDY LONG LEGS, FOX. Lyle Wheeler and John DeCuir. Set Decoration: Walter M. Scott and Paul S. Fox.
GUYS AND DOLLS. Oliver Smith and Joseph C. Wright. Set Decoration: Howard Bristol.
LOVE IS A MANY-SPLENDORED THING. Lyle Wheeler and George W. Davis. Set Decoration: Walter M. Scott and Jack Stubbs.

TO CATCH A THIEF. Hal Pereira and Joseph McMillan Johnson. Set Decoration: Sam Comer and Arthur Krams.

FILM EDITING:
PICNIC. Charles Nelson and William A. Lyon.
BLACKBOARD JUNGLE. Ferris Webster.
THE BRIDGES AT TOKO-RI, Perlberg-Seaton, PAR. Alma Macrorie.
OKLAHOMA! Gene Ruggiero and George Boemler.
THE ROSE TATTOO. Warren Low.

MUSIC - SCORING:
(Scoring of a Dramatic or Comedy Picture)
LOVE IS A MANY-SPLENDORED THING. Alfred Newman.
BATTLE CRY, WB. Max Steiner.
THE MAN WITH THE GOLDEN ARM. Elmer Bernstein.
PICNIC. George Duning.
THE ROSE TATTOO. Alex North.
(Scoring of a Musical Picture)
OKLAHOMA! Robert Russell Bennett, Jay Blackton and Adolph Deutsch.
DADDY LONG LEGS. Alfred Newman.
GUYS AND DOLLS. Jay Blackton and Cyril J. Mockridge.
IT'S ALWAYS FAIR WEATHER, MGM. Andre Previn.
LOVE ME OR LEAVE ME. Percy Faith and George Stoll.

MUSIC - BEST SONG:
LOVE IS A MANY-SPLENDORED THING, Love Is A Many-Splendored Thing. Music, Sammy Fain. Lyrics, Paul Francis Webster.
I'LL NEVER STOP LOVING YOU, *Love Me Or Leave Me.* Music, Nicholas Brodszky. Lyrics, Sammy Cahn.
SOMETHING'S GOTTA GIVE, *Daddy Long Legs.* Music and Lyrics by Johnny Mercer.
(LOVE IS) THE TENDER TRAP, *The Tender Trap,* MGM. Music, James Van Heusen. Lyrics, Sammy Cahn.
UNCHAINED MELODY, *Unchained,* Hall Bartlett Prods., Inc., WB. Music, Alex North. Lyrics, Hy Zaret.

SOUND:
OKLAHOMA!, Todd-AO Sound Department, Fred Hynes, Sound Director.
LOVE IS A MANY-SPLENDORED THING, FOX Studio Sound Department. Carl W. Faulkner, Sound Director.
LOVE ME OR LEAVE ME, MGM Studio Sound Department. Wesley C. Miller, Sound Director.
MISTER ROBERTS, WB. Studio Sound Department. William A. Mueller, Sound Director.
NOT AS A STRANGER, Radio Corp of America Sound Department. Watson Jones, Sound Director.

SHORT FILMS:
(Cartoons)
SPEEDY GONZALES, WB. Cartoons, Inc. Edward Selzer, Prod.
GOOD WILL TO MEN, MGM. Fred Quimby, William Hanna and Joseph Barbera, Prods.
THE LEGEND OF ROCK-A-BYE-POINT, Walter Lantz Prods., UI. Walter Lantz, Prod.
NO HUNTING, Walt Disney Prods., RKO. Walt Disney, Prod.
(One-reel)
SURVIVAL CITY, FOX. Edmund Reek, Prod.
GADGETS GALORE, WB. Robert Youngson, Prod.
3RD AVE. EL, Carson Davidson Prods., Ardee Films. Carson Davidson, Prod.
THREE KISSES, PAR. Justin Herman, Prod.
(Two-reel)
THE FACE OF LINCOLN, University Of Southern California Presentation, Cavalcade Pictures, Inc. Wilbur T. Blume, Prod.
THE BATTLE OF GETTYSBURG, MGM. Dore Schary, Prod.
ON THE TWELFTH DAY. . ., Go Pictures, Inc., George Brest & Assocs. George K. Arthur, Prod.
SWITZERLAND, Walt Disney Prods., BV. Walt Disney, Prod.

24 HOUR ALERT, WB. Cedric Francis, Prod.

DOCUMENTARY:
(Short Subjects)
MEN AGAINST THE ARCTIC, Walt Disney Prods., BV. Walt Disney, Prod.
THE BATTLE OF GETTYSBURG, MGM. Dore Schary, Prod.
THE FACE OF LINCOLN, University of Southern California Presentation, CVC. Wilbur T. Blume, Prod.
(Features)
HELEN KELLER IN HER STORY, Nancy Hamilton Presentation. Nancy Hamilton, Prod.
HEARTBREAK RIDGE, Rene Risacher Prod., Tudor Pictures (French). Rene Risacher, Prod.

SPECIAL EFFECTS:
THE BRIDGES AT TOKO-RI.
THE DAM BUSTERS, ABR. (British).
THE RAINS OF RANCHIPUR, FOX.

HONORARY AND OTHER:
(Other)
SAMURAI, The Legend of Musashi (Japanese) - Best Foreign Language Film first released in the United States during 1955.

SCIENTIFIC OR TECHNICAL:
(Class I)
NATIONAL CARBON CO. for the development and production of a high efficiency yellow flame carbon for motion picture color photography.
(Class II)
EASTMAN KODAK CO. for Eastman Tri-X panchromatic negative film.
FARCIOT EDOUART, HAL CORL and the **PARAMOUNT STUDIO TRANSPARENCY DEPARTMENT** for the engineering and development of a double-frame, triple-head background projector.
(Class III)
20TH CENTURY-FOX STUDIO and **BAUSCH & LOMB CO.** for the new combination lenses for CinemaScope photography.
WALTER JOLLEY, MAURICE LARSON and **R. H. SPIES** of 20th Century-Fox Studio for a spraying process which creates simulated metallic surfaces.
STEVE KRILANOVICH for an improved camera dolly incorporating multi-directional steering.
DAVE ANDERSON of 20th Century-Fox Studio for an improved spotlight capable of maintaining a fixed circle of light at constant intensity over varied distances.
LOREN L. RYDER, CHARLES WEST, HENRY FRACKER and **PARAMOUNT STUDIO** for a projection film index to establish proper framing for various aspect ratios.
FARCIOT EDOUART, HAL CORL and the **PARAMOUNT STUDIO TRANSPARENCY DEPARTMENT** for an improved dual stereopticon background projector.

1956

BEST PICTURE:
AROUND THE WORLD IN 80 DAYS, The Michael Todd Co., Inc., UA. Michael Todd, Prod.
FRIENDLY PERSUASION, AA. William Wyler, Prod.
GIANT, Giant Prod., WB. George Stevens & Henry Ginsberg, Prods.
THE KING AND I, FOX. Charles Brackett, Prod.
THE TEN COMMANDMENTS, Motion Picture Assocs., Inc., PAR. Cecil B. DeMille, Prod.

ACTOR:
YUL BRYNNER, The King And I.
JAMES DEAN, *Giant.*
KIRK DOUGLAS, *Lust For Life,* MGM.
ROCK HUDSON, *Giant.*
SIR LAURENCE OLIVIER, *Richard III,* Laurence Olivier Prod., Lopert Films Dist. Corp. (British)

ACTRESS:
INGRID BERGMAN, Anastasia, FOX.
CARROLL BAKER, *Baby Doll,* A Newtown Prod., WB.
KATHARINE HEPBURN, *The Rainmaker,* Hal Wallis Prods., PAR.
NANCY KELLY, *The Bad Seed,* WB.
DEBORAH KERR, *The King And I.*

SUPPORTING ACTOR:
ANTHONY QUINN, Lust For Life.
DON MURRAY, *Bus Stop,* FOX.
ANTHONY PERKINS, *Friendly Persuasion.*
MICKEY ROONEY, *The Bold And The Brave,* Filmakers Releasing Org., RKO.
ROBERT STACK, *Written On The Wind,* U.

SUPPORTING ACTRESS:
DOROTHY MALONE, Written On The Wind.
MILDRED DUNNOCK, *Baby Doll.*
EILEEN HECKART, *The Bad Seed.*
MERCEDES McCAMBRIDGE, *Giant.*
PATTY McCORMACK, *The Bad Seed.*

DIRECTING:
GEORGE STEVENS, Giant.
MICHAEL ANDERSON, *Around The World In 80 Days.*
WALTER LANG, *The King And I.*
KING VIDOR, *War And Peace,* A Ponti-DeLaurentiis Prod., PAR (Italo-American).
WILLIAM WYLER, *Friendly Persuasion.*

WRITING:
(Motion Picture Story)
THE BRAVE ONE, King Bros. Prods., Inc., RKO. Dalton Trumbo aka Robert Rich.
THE EDDY DUCHIN STORY, COL. Leo Katcher.
HIGH SOCIETY, AA. Edward Bernds and Elwood Ullman. (Withdrawn from final ballot)
THE PROUD AND THE BEAUTIFUL, La Compagnie Industrielle Commerciale Cinematographique, KGY (French). Jean Paul Sartre.
UMBERTO D., Rizzoli-De Sica-Amato Prod., HD (Italian). Cesare Zavattini.
(Best Screenplay adapted)
AROUND THE WORLD IN 80 DAYS. James Poe, John Farrow and S. J. Perelman.
BABY DOLL. Tennessee Williams.
GIANT. Fred Guiol and Ivan Moffat.
LUST FOR LIFE. Norman Corwin.
FRIENDLY PERSUASION. (Writer ineligible for nomination under Academy By-Laws.)
(Best Screenplay original)
THE RED BALLOON, Films Montsouris, LOP. (French). Albert Lamorisse.
THE BOLD AND THE BRAVE. Robert Lewin.
JULIE, Arwin Prods., MGM. Andrew L. Stone.
LA STRADA, Ponti-De Laurentiis Prod., TL. (Italian). Federico Fellini and Tullio Pinelli.
THE LADY KILLERS, Ealing Studios Ltd., CON. (British). William Rose.

CINEMATOGRAPHY:
(Black-and-White)
SOMEBODY UP THERE LIKES ME, MGM. Joseph Ruttenberg.
BABY DOLL. Boris Kaufman.
THE BAD SEED. Hal Rosson.
THE HARDER THEY FALL, COL. Burnett Guffey.
STAGECOACH TO FURY, Regal Films, Inc. Prod., FOX. Walter Strenge.
(Color)
AROUND THE WORLD IN 80 DAYS. Lionel Lindon.
THE EDDY DUCHIN STORY. Harry Stradling.
THE KING AND I. Leon Shamroy.
THE TEN COMMANDMENTS. Loyal Griggs.
WAR AND PEACE. Jack Cardiff.

COSTUME DESIGN:
(Black-and-White)
THE SOLID GOLD CADILLAC, COL. Jean Louis.
THE MAGNIFICENT SEVEN, A Toho Prod., KGY (Japanese). Kohei Ezaki.
THE POWER AND THE PRIZE, MGM. Helen Rose.
THE PROUD AND THE PROFANE, The Perlberg-Seaton Prod., PAR. Edith Head.
TEENAGE REBEL, FOX. Charles LeMaire and Mary Wills.
(Color)
THE KING AND I. Irene Sharaff.
AROUND THE WORLD IN 80 DAYS. Miles White.
GIANT. Moss Mabry and Marjorie Best.
THE TEN COMMANDMENTS. Edith Head, Ralph Jester, John Jensen, Dorothy Jeakins and Arnold Friberg.
WAR AND PEACE. Marie De Matteis.

ART DIRECTION - SET DECORATION:
(Black-and-White)
SOMEBODY UP THERE LIKES ME. Cedric Gibbons and Malcolm F. Brown. Set Decoration: Edwin B. Willis and F. Keogh Gleason.
THE MAGNIFICENT SEVEN, A Toho Prod., KGY (Japanese). Takashi Matsuyama. Set Decoration: No credits listed.
THE PROUD AND THE PROFANE. Hal Pereira and A. Earl Hedrick. Set Decoration: Samuel M. Comer and Frank R. McKelvy.
THE SOLID GOLD CADILLAC. Ross Bellah. Set Decoration: William R. Kiernan and Louis Diage.
TEENAGE REBEL. Lyle R. Wheeler and Jack Martin Smith. Set Decoration: Walter M. Scott and Stuart A. Reiss.
(Color)
THE KING AND I. Lyle R. Wheeler and John DeCuir. Set Decoration: Walter M. Scott and Paul S. Fox.
AROUND THE WORLD IN 80 DAYS. James W. Sullivan and Ken Adams. Set Decoration: Ross J. Dowd.
GIANT. Boris Leven. Set Decoration: Ralph S. Hurst.
LUST FOR LIFE. Cedric Gibbons, Hans Peters and Preston Ames. Set Decoration: Edwin B. Willis and F. Keogh Gleason.
THE TEN COMMANDMENTS. Hal Pereira, Walter H. Tyler and Albert Nozaki. Set Decoration: Sam M. Comer and Ray Moyer.

FILM EDITING:
AROUND THE WORLD IN 80 DAYS. Gene Ruggiero and Paul Weatherwax.
THE BRAVE ONE. Merrill G. White.
GIANT. William Hornbeck, Philip W. Anderson and Fred Bohanan.
SOMEBODY UP THERE LIKES ME. Albert Akst.
THE TEN COMMANDMENTS. Anne Bauchens.

FOREIGN LANGUAGE FILM:
LA STRADA. Dino De Laurentiis and Carlo Ponti, Prods.
THE CAPTAIN OF KOPENICK, Real-Film (Germany). Gyula Trebitsch and Walter Koppel, Prods.
GERVAISE, Agnes Delahaie Productions Cinematographiques & Silver Film (France). Annie Dorfmann, Prod.
HARP OF BURMA, Nikkatsu Corp (Japan). Masayuki Takagi, Prod.
QIVITOQ, A/S Nordisk Films Kompagni (Denmark). O. Dalsgaard-

Olsen, Prod.

MUSIC - SCORING:
(Scoring of a Dramatic or Comedy Picture)
AROUND THE WORLD IN 80 DAYS. Victor Young.
ANASTASIA. Alfred Newman.
BETWEEN HEAVEN AND HELL, FOX. Hugo Friedhofer.
GIANT. Dimitri Tiomkin.
THE RAINMAKER. Alex North.
(Scoring of a Musical Picture)
THE KING AND I. Alfred Newman and Ken Darby.
THE BEST THINGS IN LIFE ARE FREE, FOX. Lionel Newman.
THE EDDY DUCHIN STORY. Morris Stoloff and George Duning.
HIGH SOCIETY. Johnny Green and Saul Chaplin.
MEET ME IN LAS VEGAS, MGM. George Stoll and Johnny Green.

MUSIC - BEST SONG:
WHATEVER WILL BE, WILL BE (QUE SERA, SERA), The Man Who Knew Too Much, Filwite Prods., Inc., PAR. Music and Lyrics by Jay Livingston and Ray Evans.
FRIENDLY PERSUASION (THEE I LOVE), *Friendly Persuasion*. Music, Dimitri Tiomkin. Lyrics, Paul Francis Webster.
JULIE, *Julie*. Music, Leith Stevens. Lyrics, Tom Adair.
TRUE LOVE, *High Society*. Music and Lyrics by Cole Porter.
WRITTEN ON THE WIND, *Written On The Wind*. Music, Victor Young. Lyrics, Sammy Cahn.

SOUND:
THE KING AND I, FOX Studio Sound Department. Carl Faulkner, Sound Director.
THE BRAVE ONE. John Myers, Sound Director.
THE EDDY DUCHIN STORY, COL Studio Sound Department. John Livadary, Sound Director.
FRIENDLY PERSUASION. Westrex Sound Services, Inc., Gordon R. Glennan, Sound Director; and Samuel Goldwyn Studio Sound Department. Gordon Sawyer, Sound Director.
THE TEN COMMANDMENTS, PAR Studio Sound Department. Loren L. Ryder, Sound Director.

SHORT FILMS:
(Cartoons)
MISTER MAGOO'S PUDDLE JUMPER, UPA Pictures, COL. Stephen Bosustow, Prod.
GERALD MCBOING-BOING ON PLANET MOO, UPA Pictures, COL. Stephen Bosustow, Prod.
THE JAYWALKER, UPA Pictures, COL. Stephen Bosustow, Prod.
(One-reel)
CRASHING THE WATER BARRIER, WB. Konstantin Kalser, Prod.
I NEVER FORGET A FACE, WB. Robert Youngson, Prod.
TIME STOOD STILL, WB. Cedric Francis, Prod.
(Two-reel)
THE BESPOKE OVERCOAT, George K. Arthur. Romulus Films, Prod.
COW DOG, Walt Disney Prods., BV. Larry Lansburgh, Prod.
THE DARK WAVE, FOX. John Healy, Prod.
SAMOA, Walt Disney Prods., BV. Walt Disney, Prod.

DOCUMENTARY:
(Short Subjects)
THE TRUE STORY OF THE CIVIL WAR, Camera Eye Pictures, Inc. Louis Clyde Stoumen, Prod.
A CITY DECIDES, Charles Guggenheim & Assocs., Inc. Prod.
THE DARK WAVE, FOX. John Healy, Prod.
THE HOUSE WITHOUT A NAME, U. Valentine Davies, Prod.
MAN IN SPACE, Walt Disney Prods., BV. Ward Kimball, Prod.
(Features)
THE SILENT WORLD, A Filmad-F.S.J.Y.C. Prod., COL (French). Jacques-Yves Cousteau, Prod.
THE NAKED EYE, Camera Eye Pictures, Inc. Louis Clyde Stoumen, Prod.
WHERE MOUNTAINS FLOAT, BRA. (Danish). The Government Film Committee of Denmark, Prod.

SPECIAL EFFECTS:
THE TEN COMMANDMENTS. John Fulton.
FORBIDDEN PLANET, MGM. A. Arnold Gillespie, Irving Ries and Wesley C. Miller.

HONORARY AND OTHER:
(Irving G. Thalberg Memorial Award)
Buddy Adler
(Jean Hersholt Humanitarian Award)
Y. Frank Freeman
(Other)
EDDIE CANTOR for distinguished service to the film industry.

SCIENTIFIC OR TECHNICAL:
(Class III)
RICHARD H. RANGER of Rangertone, Inc., for the development of a synchronous recording and reproducing system for quarter-inch magnetic tape.
TED HIRSCH, CARL HAUGE and **EDWARD REICHARD** of Consolidated Film Industries for an automatic scene counter for laboratory projection rooms.
THE TECHNICAL DEPARTMENTS of PAR PICTURES CORP. for the engineering and development of the Paramount light-weight horizontal-movement VistaVision camera.
ROY C. STEWART AND SONS of Stewart-Trans Lux Corp., **DR. C. R. DAILY** and the **TRANSPARENCY DEPARTMENT** of PARAMOUNT PICTURES CORP. for the engineering and development of the Hi-Trans and Para-HiTrans rear projection screens.
THE CONSTRUCTION DEPARTMENT of MGM STUDIO for a new hand-portable fog machine.
DANIEL J. BLOOMBERG, JOHN POND, WILLIAM WADE and the **ENGINEERING** and **CAMERA DEPARTMENTS** of REPUBLIC STUDIO for the Naturama adaptation to the Mitchell camera.

1957

BEST PICTURE:
THE BRIDGE ON THE RIVER KWAI, A Horizon Picture, COL. Sam Spiegel, Prod.
PEYTON PLACE, Jerry Wald Prods., Inc., FOX. Jerry Wald, Prod.
SAYONARA, William Goetz, Prod., WB. William Goetz, Prod.
12 ANGRY MEN, Orion-Nova Prod., UA. Henry Fonda & Reginald Rose, Prods.
WITNESS FOR THE PROSECUTION, Edward Small-Arthur Hornblow Prod., UA. Arthur Hornblow, Jr., Prod.

ACTOR:
ALEC GUINNESS, The Bridge On The River Kwai.
MARLON BRANDO, *Sayonara*.
ANTHONY FRANCIOSA, *A Hatful Of Rain*, FOX.
CHARLES LAUGHTON, *Witness For The Prosecution*.
ANTHONY QUINN, *Wild Is The Wind*, A Hal Wallis Prod., PAR.

ACTRESS:
JOANNE WOODWARD, The Three Faces Of Eve, FOX.
DEBORAH KERR, *Heaven Knows, Mr. Allison*, FOX.
ANNA MAGNANI, *Wild Is The Wind*.
ELIZABETH TAYLOR, *Raintree County*, MGM.
LANA TURNER, *Peyton Place*.

SUPPORTING ACTOR:
RED BUTTONS, Sayonara.
VITTORIO DE SICA, *A Farewell To Arms,* The Selznick Co., Inc., FOX.
SESSUE HAYAKAWA, *The Bridge On The River Kwai.*
ARTHUR KENNEDY, *Peyton Place.*
RUSS TAMBLYN, *Peyton Place.*

SUPPORTING ACTRESS:
MIYOSHI UMEKI, Sayonara.
CAROLYN JONES, *The Bachelor Party,* Norma Prod., UA.
ELSA LANCHESTER, *Witness For The Prosecution.*
HOPE LANGE, *Peyton Place.*
DIANE VARSI, *Peyton Place.*

DIRECTING:
DAVID LEAN, The Bridge On The River Kwai.
JOSHUA LOGAN, *Sayonara.*
SIDNEY LUMET, *12 Angry Men.*
MARK ROBSON, *Peyton Place.*
BILLY WILDER, *Witness For The Prosecution.*

WRITING:
(Best Story and Screenplay written directly for the screen)
DESIGNING WOMAN, MGM. George Wells.
FUNNY FACE, PAR. Leonard Gershe.
MAN OF A THOUSAND FACES. U. Story by Ralph Wheelright. Screenplay by R. Wright Campbell, Ivan Goff and Ben Roberts.
THE TIN STAR, The Perlberg-Seaton Prod., PAR. Story by Barney Slater and Joel Kane. Screenplay by Dudley Nichols.
VITELLONI, Peg Films/Cite Films, API (Italian). Story by Federico Fellini, Ennio Flaiano and Tullio Pinelli. Screenplay by Federico Fellini and Ennio Flaiano.

(Best Screenplay based on material from another medium)
THE BRIDGE ON THE RIVER KWAI. Pierre Boulle.
HEAVEN KNOWS, MR. ALLISON. John Lee Mahin and John Huston.
PEYTON PLACE. John Michael Hayes.
SAYONARA. Paul Osborn.
12 ANGRY MEN. Reginald Rose.

CINEMATOGRAPHY:
THE BRIDGE ON THE RIVER KWAI. Jack Hildyard.
AN AFFAIR TO REMEMBER. Jerry Wald Prods., Inc., FOX. Milton Krasner.
FUNNY FACE, PAR. Ray June.
PEYTON PLACE. William Mellor.
SAYONARA. Ellsworth Fredericks.

COSTUME DESIGN:
LES GIRLS, Sol C. Siegel Prods., Inc., MGM. Orry-Kelly.
AN AFFAIR TO REMEMBER. Charles LeMaire.
FUNNY FACE. Edith Head and Hubert de Givenchy.
PAL JOEY, Essex-George Sidney Prod., COL. Jean Louis.
RAINTREE COUNTY. Walter Plunkett.

ART DIRECTION - SET DECORATION:
SAYONARA. Ted Haworth. Set Decoration: Robert Priestley.
FUNNY FACE. Hal Pereira and George W. Davis. Set Decoration: Sam Comer and Ray Moyer.
LES GIRLS. William A. Horning and Gene Allen. Set Decoration: Edwin B. Willis and Richard Pefferle.
PAL JOEY. Walter Holscher. Set Decoration: William Kiernan and Louis Diage.
RAINTREE COUNTY. William A. Horning and Urie McCleary. Set Decoration: Edwin B. Willis and Hugh Hunt.

FILM EDITING:
THE BRIDGE ON THE RIVER KWAI. Peter Taylor.
GUNFIGHT AT THE O.K. CORRAL, A Hal Wallis Prod., PAR. Warren Low.
PAL JOEY. Viola Lawrence and Jerome Thoms.
SAYONARA. Arthur P. Schmidt and Philip W. Anderson.
WITNESS FOR THE PROSECUTION. Daniel Mandell.

FOREIGN LANUAGE FILM:
THE NIGHTS OF CABIRIA, Dino De Laurentiis Production (Italy).
THE DEVIL CAME AT NIGHT, Gloria Film (Germany).
GATES OF PARIS, Filmsonor S.A. Production (France).
MOTHER INDIA, Mehboob Productions (India).
NINE LIVES, Nordsjofilm (Norway).

MUSIC - SCORING:
THE BRIDGE ON THE RIVER KWAI, (Dramatic or Comedy). Malcolm Arnold.
AN AFFAIR TO REMEMBER, (Dramatic or Comedy). Hugo Friedhofer.
BOY ON A DOLPHIN, (Dramatic or Comedy), FOX. Hugo Friedhofer.
PERRI, (Dramatic or Comedy), Walt Disney Prods., BV. Paul Smith.
RAINTREE COUNTY, (Dramatic or Comedy). Johnny Green.

MUSIC - BEST SONG:
ALL THE WAY, The Joker Is Wild A.M.B.L. Prod., PAR. Music, James Van Heusen. Lyrics, Sammy Cahn.
AN AFFAIR TO REMEMBER, *An Affair To Remember.* Music, Harry Warren. Lyrics, Harold Adamson and Leo McCarey.
APRIL LOVE, *April Love,* FOX. Music, Sammy Fain. Lyrics, Paul Francis Webster.
TAMMY, *Tammy And The Bachelor,* U. Music and Lyrics by Ray Evans and Jay Livingston.
WILD IS THE WIND, *Wild Is The Wind.* Music, Dimitri Tiomkin. Lyrics, Ned Washington.

SOUND:
SAYONARA, WB Studio Sound Department. George Groves, Sound Director.
GUNFIGHT AT THE O.K. CORRAL, PAR Studio Sound Department. George Dutton, Sound Director.
LES GIRLS, MGM Studio Sound Department. Dr. Wesley C. Miller, Sound Director.
PAL JOEY, COL Studio Sound Department. John P. Livadary, Sound Director.
WITNESS FOR THE PROSECUTION, Samuel Goldwyn Studio Sound Department. Gordon Sawyer, Sound Director.

SHORT FILMS:
(Cartoons)
BIRDS ANONYMOUS, WB. Edward Selzer, Prod.
ONE DROOPY KNIGHT, MGM. William Hanna and Joseph Barbera, Prods.
TABASCO ROAD, WB. Edward Selzer, Prod.
TREES AND JAMAICA DADDY, UPA Pictures, COL. Stephen Bosustow, Prod.
THE TRUTH ABOUT MOTHER GOOSE, Walt Disney Prods., BV. Walt Disney, Prod.

(Live Action Subjects)
THE WETBACK HOUND, Walt Disney Prods., BV. Larry Lansburgh, Prod.
A CHAIRY TALE, NFC, KGY. Norman McLaren, Prod.
CITY OF GOLD, NFC, KGY. Tom Daly, Prod.
FOOTHOLD ON ANTARCTICA, World Wide Pictures, SCH. James Carr, Prod.
PORTUGAL, Walt Disney Prods., BV. Ben Sharpsteen, Prod.

DOCUMENTARY:
(Features)
ALBERT SCHWEITZER, Hill and Anderson Prod., DRH. Jerome Hill, Prod.
ON THE BOWERY, Lionel Rogosin Prods., FRP. Lionel Rogosin, Prod.
TORERO!, PBP, COL (Mexican). Manuel Barbachano Ponce, Prod.

SPECIAL EFFECTS:
THE ENEMY BELOW, FOX. Audible: Walter Rossi.
THE SPIRIT OF ST. LOUIS, Leland Hayward-Billy Wilder, WB. Visual: Louis Lichtenfield.

HONORARY AND OTHER:
(Jean Hersholt Humanitarian Award)
Samuel Goldwyn
(Other)
CHARLES BRACKETT for outstanding service to the Academy.
B. B. KAHANE for distinguished service to the motion picture industry.
GILBERT M. (Broncho Billy) ANDERSON, motion picture pioneer, for his contributions to the development of motion pictures as entertainment.
THE SOCIETY OF MOTION PICTURE AND TELEVISION ENGINEERS for their contributions to the advancement of the motion picture industry.

SCIENTIFIC OR TECHNICAL:
(Class I)
TODD-AO CORP. and WESTREX CORP. for developing a method of producing and exhibiting wide-film motion pictures known as the Todd-AO System.
MOTION PICTURE RESEARCH COUNCIL for the design and development of a high efficiency projection screen for drive-in theatres.
(Class II)
SOCIETE D'OPTIQUE ET DE MECANIQUE DE HAUTE PRECISION for the development of a high speed vari-focal photographic lens.
HARLAN L. BAUMBACH, LORAND WARGO, HOWARD M. LITTLE and the UNICORN ENGINEERING CORP. for the development of an automatic printer light selector.
(Class III)
CHARLES E. SUTTER, WILLIAM B. SMITH, PARAMOUNT PICTURES CORP. and GENERAL CABLE CORP. for the engineering and application to studio use of aluminum lightweight electrical cable and connectors.

1958

BEST PICTURE:
GIGI, Arthur Freed Prods., Inc., MGM. Arthur Freed, Prod.
AUNTIE MAME, WB.
CAT ON A HOT TIN ROOF, Avon Prods., Inc. MGM, Lawrence Weingarten, Prod.
THE DEFIANT ONES, Stanley Kramer, UA. Stanley Kramer, Prod.
SEPARATE TABLES, Clifton Prods., Inc., UA. Harold Hecht, Prod.

ACTOR:
DAVID NIVEN, Separate Tables.
TONY CURTIS, The Defiant Ones.
PAUL NEWMAN, Cat On A Hot Tin Roof.
SIDNEY POITIER, The Defiant Ones.
SPENCER TRACY, The Old Man And The Sea, Leland Hayward, WB.

ACTRESS:
SUSAN HAYWARD, I Want To Live!, Figaro, Inc., UA.
DEBORAH KERR, Separate Tables.
SHIRLEY MACLAINE, Some Came Running, Sol C. Siegel Prods., Inc., MGM.
ROSALIND RUSSELL, Auntie Mame.
ELIZABETH TAYLOR, Cat On A Hot Tin Roof.

SUPPORTING ACTOR:
BURL IVES, The Big Country, Anthony-Worldwide Prods., UA.
THEODORE BIKEL, The Defiant Ones.
LEE J. COBB, The Brothers Karamazov, Avon Prods., Inc., MGM.
ARTHUR KENNEDY, Some Came Running.
GIG YOUNG, Teacher's Pet, Perlberg-Seaton, PAR.

SUPPORTING ACTRESS:
WENDY HILLER, Separate Tables.
PEGGY CASS, Auntie Mame.
MARTHA HYER, Some Came Running.
MAUREEN STAPLETON, Lonelyhearts, Schary Prods., Inc., UA.
CARA WILLIAMS, The Defiant Ones.

DIRECTING:
VINCENTE MINNELLI, Gigi.
RICHARD BROOKS, Cat On A Hot Tin Roof.
STANLEY KRAMER, The Defiant Ones.
MARK ROBSON, The Inn Of The Sixth Happiness, FOX.
ROBERT WISE, I Want To Live!

WRITING:
(Best Story and Screenplay written directly for the screen)
THE DEFIANT ONES. Nathan E. Douglas and Harold Jacob Smith.
THE GODDESS, Carnegie Prods., Inc., COL. Paddy Chayefsky.
HOUSEBOAT, PAR and Scribe, PAR. Melville Shavelson and Jack Rose.
THE SHEEPMAN, MGM. Story by James Edward Grant. Screenplay by William Bowers and James Edward Grant.
TEACHER'S PET. Fay and Michael Kanin.
(Best Screenplay based on material from another medium)
GIGI. Alan Jay Lerner.
CAT ON A HOT TIN ROOF. Richard Brooks and James Poe.
THE HORSE'S MOUTH, Knightsbridge, UA (British). Alec Guinness.
I WANT TO LIVE! Nelson Gidding and Don Mankiewicz.
SEPARATE TABLES. Terence Rattigan and John Gay.

CINEMATOGRAPHY:
(Black-and-White)
THE DEFIANT ONES. Sam Leavitt.
DESIRE UNDER THE ELMS, Don Hartman, PAR. Daniel L. Fapp.
I WANT TO LIVE! Lionel Lindon.
SEPARATE TABLES. Charles Lang, Jr.
THE YOUNG LIONS, FOX. Joe MacDonald.
(Color)
GIGI. Joseph Ruttenberg.
AUNTIE MAME. Harry Stradling, Sr.
CAT ON A HOT TIN ROOF. William Daniels.
THE OLD MAN AND THE SEA. James Wong Howe.
SOUTH PACIFIC, South Pacific Enterprises, Inc., MNA. Leon Shamroy.

COSTUME DESIGN:

GIGI. Cecil Beaton.
BELL, BOOK AND CANDLE, Phoenix Prods., Inc., COL. Jean Louis.
THE BUCCANEER, Cecil B. DeMille, PAR. Ralph Jester, Edith Head and John Jensen.
A CERTAIN SMILE, FOX. Charles LeMaire and Mary Wills.
SOME CAME RUNNING. Walter Plunkett.

ART DIRECTION - SET DECORATION:

GIGI. William A. Horning and Preston Ames. Set Decoration: Henry Grace and Keogh Gleason.
AUNTIE MAME. Malcolm Bert. Set Decoration: George James Hopkins.
BELL, BOOK AND CANDLE. Cary Odell. Set Decoration: Louis Diage.
A CERTAIN SMILE. Lyle R. Wheeler and John DeCuir. Set Decoration: Walter M. Scott and Paul S. Fox.
VERTIGO, Alfred J. Hitchcock Prods., Inc., PAR. Hal Pereira and Henry Bumstead. Set Decoration: Sam Comer and Frank McKelvy.

FILM EDITING:

GIGI. Adrienne Fazan.
AUNTIE MAME. William Ziegler.
COWBOY, Phoenix Pictures, COL. William A. Lyon and Al Clark.
THE DEFIANT ONES. Frederic Knudtson.
I WANT TO LIVE! William Hornbeck.

FOREIGN LANGUAGE FILM:

MY UNCLE, Specta-Gray-Alter Films in association with Films del Centaure (France).
ARMS AND THE MAN, H. R. Sokal-P. Goldbaum Production, Bavaria Filmkunst A.G. (Germany).
LA VENGANZA, Guion Producciones Cinematograficas (Spain).
THE ROAD A YEAR LONG, Jadran Film (Yugoslavia).
THE USUAL UNIDENTIFIED THIEVES, Lux-Vides-Cinecitta (Italy).

MUSIC - SCORING:

(Scoring of a Dramatic or Comedy Picture)
THE OLD MAN AND THE SEA. Dimitri Tiomkin.
THE BIG COUNTRY. Jerome Moross.
SEPARATE TABLES. David Raksin.
WHITE WILDERNESS, Walt Disney Prods., BV. Oliver Wallace.
THE YOUNG LIONS, FOX. Hugo Friedhofer.

(Scoring of a Musical Picture)
GIGI. Andre Previn.
THE BOLSHOI BALLET, A Rank Organization Presentation-Harmony Film, RNK (British). Yuri Faier and G. Rozhdestvensky.
DAMN YANKEES, WB. Ray Heindorf.
MARDI GRAS, Jerry Wald Prods., Inc., FOX. Lionel Newman.
SOUTH PACIFIC. Alfred Newman and Ken Darby.

MUSIC - BEST SONG:

GIGI, Gigi. Music, Frederick Loewe. Lyrics, Alan Jay Lerner.
ALMOST IN YOUR ARMS (Love Song from "Houseboat"), Houseboat, PAR and Scribe, PAR. Music and Lyrics by Jay Livingston and Ray Evans.
A CERTAIN SMILE, A Certain Smile. Music, Sammy Fain. Lyrics, Paul Francis Webster.
TO LOVE AND BE LOVED, Some Came Running. Music, James Van Heusen. Lyrics, Sammy Cahn.
A VERY PRECIOUS LOVE, Marjorie Morningstar, Beachwold Pictures, WB. Music, Sammy Fain. Lyrics, Paul Francis Webster.

SOUND:

SOUTH PACIFIC, Todd-AO Sound Department. Fred Hynes, Sound Director.
I WANT TO LIVE!, Samuel Goldwyn Studio Sound Department. Gordon E. Sawyer. Sound Director.
A TIME TO LOVE AND A TIME TO DIE, U Studio Sound Department. Leslie I. Carey, Sound Director.
VERTIGO, PAR Studio Sound Department. George Dutton, Sound Director.
THE YOUNG LIONS, FOX Studio Sound Department. Carl Faulkner, Sound Director.

SHORT FILMS:

(Cartoons)
KNIGHTY KNIGHT BUGS, WB. John W. Burton, Prod.
PAUL BUNYAN, Walt Disney Prods., BV Film Distribution Co., Inc. Walt Disney, Prod.
SIDNEY'S FAMILY TREE, Terrytoons, FOX. William M. Weiss, Prod.

(Live Action Subjects)
GRAND CANYON, Walt Disney Prods., BV. Walt Disney, Prod.
JOURNEY INTO SPRING, British Transport Films, SCH. Ian Ferguson, Prod.
THE KISS, Cohay Prods., CON. John Patrick Hayes, Prod.
SNOWS OF AORANGI, New Zealand Screen Board, George Brest Associates.
T IS FOR TUMBLEWEED, CON. James A Lebenthal, Prod.

DOCUMENTARY:

(Short Subjects)
AMA GIRLS, Walt Disney Prods., BV. Inc. Ben Sharpsteen, Prod.
EMPLOYEES ONLY, Hughes Aircraft Co. Kenneth G. Brown, Prod.
JOURNEY INTO SPRING, British Transport Films, SCH. Ian Ferguson, Prod.
THE LIVING STONE, NFC. Tom Daly, Prod.
OVERTURE, United Nations Film Service. Thorold Dickinson, Prod.

(Features)
WHITE WILDERNESS, Walt Disney Prods., BV. Ben Sharpsteen, Prod.
ANTARCTIC CROSSING, World Wide Pictures, SCH. James Carr, Prod.
THE HIDDEN WORLD, Small World Co. Robert Snyder, Prod.
PSYCHIATRIC NURSING, Dynamic Films, Inc. Nathan Zucker, Prod.

SPECIAL EFFECTS:

tom thumb, Galaxy Pictures, MGM. Visual: Tom Howard.
TORPEDO RUN, MGM. Visual: A. Arnold Gillespie. Audible: Harold Humbrock.

HONORARY AND OTHER:

(Irving G. Thalberg Memorial Award)
Jack L. Warner
(Other)
MAURICE CHEVALIER for his contributions to the world of entertainment for more than half a century.

SCIENTIFIC OR TECHNICAL:

(Class II)
DON W. PRIDEAUX, LEROY G. LEIGHTON and the LAMP DIVISION of GENERAL ELECTRIC CO. for the development and production of an improved 10 kilowatt lamp for motion picture set lighting.
PANAVISION, INC., for the design and development of the Auto Panatar anamorphic photographic lens for 35mm CinemaScope photography.

(Class III)
WILLY BORBERG of the General Precision Laboratory, Inc., for the development of a high speed intermittent movement for 35mm motion picture theatre projection equipment.
FRED PONEDEL, GEORGE BROWN and CONRAD BOYE of the WB Special Effects Department for the design and fabrication of a new rapid fire marble gun.

1959

BEST PICTURE:
BEN-HUR, MGM. Sam Zimbalist, Prod.
ANATOMY OF A MURDER, Otto Preminger, COL. Otto Preminger, Prod.
THE DIARY OF ANNE FRANK, FOX. George Stevens, Prod.
THE NUN'S STORY, WB. Henry Blanke, Prod.
ROOM AT THE TOP, Romulus Films, Ltd., Continental Distr., Inc., (British). John & James Woolf, Prods.

ACTOR:
CHARLTON HESTON, Ben-Hur.
LAURENCE HARVEY, *Room At The Top.*
JACK LEMMON, *Some Like It Hot,* Ashton Prods. & The Mirisch Co., UA.
PAUL MUNI, *The Last Angry Man,* Fred Kohlmar Prods., COL.
JAMES STEWART, *Anatomy Of A Murder.*

ACTRESS:
SIMONE SIGNORET, Room At The Top.
DORIS DAY, *Pillow Talk,* Arwin Prods., Inc., U.
AUDREY HEPBURN, *The Nun's Story.*
KATHARINE HEPBURN, *Suddenly, Last Summer,* Horizon Prod., COL.
ELIZABETH TAYLOR, *Suddenly, Last Summer.*

SUPPORTING ACTOR:
HUGH GRIFFITH, Ben-Hur.
ARTHUR O'CONNELL, *Anatomy Of A Murder.*
GEORGE C. SCOTT, *Anatomy Of A Murder.*
ROBERT VAUGHN, *The Young Philadelphians,* WB.
ED WYNN, *The Diary Of Anne Frank.*

SUPPORTING ACTRESS:
SHELLEY WINTERS, The Diary Of Anne Frank.
HERMIONE BADDELEY, *Room At The Top.*
SUSAN KOHNER, *Imitation Of Life,* U.
JUANITA MOORE, *Imitation Of Life.*
THELMA RITTER, *Pillow Talk.*

DIRECTING:
WILLIAM WYLER, Ben-Hur.
JACK CLAYTON, *Room At The Top.*
GEORGE STEVENS, *The Diary Of Anne Frank.*
BILLY WILDER, *Some Like It Hot.*
FRED ZINNEMANN, *The Nun's Story.*

WRITING:
(Best Story and Screenplay written directly for the screen)
PILLOW TALK. Story by Russell Rouse and Clarence Greene. Screenplay by Stanley Shapiro and Maurice Richlin.
THE 400 BLOWS, Les Films du Carrosse & SEDIF, ZEN (French). Francois Truffaut and Marcel Moussy.
NORTH BY NORTHWEST, MGM. Ernest Lehman.
OPERATION PETTICOAT, Granart Co., U. Story by Paul King and Joseph Stone. Screenplay by Stanley Shapiro and Maurice Richlin.
WILD STRAWBERRIES, Svensk Filmindustri, JAN (Swedish). Ingmar Bergman.
(Best Screenplay based on material from another medium)
ROOM AT THE TOP. Neil Paterson.
ANATOMY OF A MURDER. Wendell Mayes.
BEN-HUR. Karl Tunberg.
THE NUN'S STORY. Robert Anderson.
SOME LIKE IT HOT. Billy Wilder and I.A.L. Diamond.

CINEMATOGRAPHY:
(Black-and-White)
THE DIARY OF ANNE FRANK. William C. Mellor.
ANATOMY OF A MURDER. Sam Leavitt.
CAREER, Hal Wallis Prods., PAR. Joseph LaShelle.
SOME LIKE IT HOT. Charles Lang, Jr.
THE YOUNG PHILADELPHIANS. Harry Stradling, Sr.
(Color)
BEN-HUR. Robert L. Surtees.
THE BIG FISHERMAN, Rowland V. Lee Prods., BV. Lee Garmes.
THE FIVE PENNIES, Dena Prod., PAR. Daniel L. Fapp.
THE NUN'S STORY. Franz Planer.
PORGY AND BESS, Samuel Goldwyn Prods., COL. Leon Shamroy.

COSTUME DESIGN:
(Black-and-White)
SOME LIKE IT HOT. Orry-Kelly.
CAREER. Edith Head.
THE DIARY OF ANNE FRANK. Charles LeMaire and Mary Wills.
THE GAZEBO, Avon Prod., MGM. Helen Rose.
THE YOUNG PHILADELPHIANS. Howard Shoup.
(Color)
BEN-HUR. Elizabeth Haffenden.
THE BEST OF EVERYTHING, Co of Artists, Inc., FOX. Adele Palmer.
THE BIG FISHERMAN. Renie.
THE FIVE PENNIES. Edith Head.
PORGY AND BESS. Irene Sharaff.

ART DIRECTION - SET DECORATION:
(Black-and-White)
THE DIARY OF ANNE FRANK. Lyle R. Wheeler and George W. Davis. Set Decoration: Walter M. Scott and Stuart A. Reiss.
CAREER. Hal Pereira and Walter Tyler. Set Decoration: Sam Comer and Arthur Krams.
THE LAST ANGRY MAN. Carl Anderson. Set Decoration: William Kiernan.
SOME LIKE IT HOT. Ted Haworth. Set Decoration: Edward G. Boyle.
SUDDENLY, LAST SUMMER. Oliver Messel and William Kellner. Set Decoration: Scot Slimon.
(Color)
BEN-HUR. William A. Horning and Edward Carfagno. Set Decoration: Hugh Hunt.
THE BIG FISHERMAN. John DeCuir. Set Decoration: Julia Heron.
JOURNEY TO THE CENTER OF THE EARTH, Joseph M. Schenck Enterprises, Inc. & Cooga Mooga Film Prods., Inc., FOX. Lyle R. Wheeler, Franz Bachelin and Herman A. Blumenthal. Set Decoration: Walter M. Scott and Joseph Kish.
NORTH BY NORTHWEST. William A. Horning, Robert Boyle and Merrill Pye. Set Decoration: Henry Grace and Frank McKelvy.
PILLOW TALK. Richard H. Riedel. Set Decoration: Russell A. Gausman and Ruby R. Levitt.

FILM EDITING:
BEN-HUR. Ralph E. Winters and John D. Dunning.
ANATOMY OF A MURDER. Louis R. Loeffler.
NORTH BY NORTHWEST. George Tomasini.
THE NUN'S STORY. Walter Thompson.
ON THE BEACH, Lomitas Prods., UA. Frederic Knudtson.

FOREIGN LANGUAGE FILM:
BLACK ORPHEUS, Dispatfilm & Gemma Cinematografica (France).
THE BRIDGE, Fono Film (Germany).
THE GREAT WAR, Dino De Laurentiis Cinematografica (Italy).
PAW, Laterna Film (Denmark).
THE VILLAGE ON THE RIVER, N. V. Nationale Filmproductie Maatschappij (The Netherlands).

MUSIC - SCORING:
(Scoring of a Dramatic or Comedy Picture)
BEN-HUR. Miklos Rozsa.
THE DIARY OF ANNE FRANK. Alfred Newman.
THE NUN'S STORY. Franz Waxman.
ON THE BEACH. Ernest Gold.
PILLOW TALK. Frank DeVol.

(Scoring of a Musical Picture)
PORGY AND BESS. Andre Previn and Ken Darby.
THE FIVE PENNIES. Leith Stevens.
LI'L ABNER, Panama and Frank, PAR. Nelson Riddle and Joseph J. Lilley.
SAY ONE FOR ME, Bing Crosby Prods., FOX. Lionel Newman.
SLEEPING BEAUTY, Walt Disney Prods., BV. George Bruns.

MUSIC - BEST SONG:
HIGH HOPES, A Hole In The Head, Sincap Prods., UA. Music, James Van Heusen. Lyrics, Sammy Cahn.
THE BEST OF EVERYTHING, *The Best Of Everything*. Music, Alfred Newman. Lyrics, Sammy Cahn.
THE FIVE PENNIES, *The Five Pennies*. Music and Lyrics by Sylvia Fine.
THE HANGING TREE, *The Hanging Tree*, Baroda Prods., Inc., WB. Music, Jerry Livingston. Lyrics, Mack David.
STRANGE ARE THE WAYS OF LOVE from *The Young Land*, C. V. Whitney Pictures, Inc., COL. Music, Dimitri Tiomkin. Lyrics, Ned Washington.

SOUND:
BEN-HUR, MGM Studio Sound Department. Franklin E. Milton, Sound Director.
JOURNEY TO THE CENTER OF THE EARTH, FOX Studio Sound Department. Carl Faulkner, Sound Director.
LIBEL!, MGM London Sound Department (British). A. W. Watkins, Sound Director.
THE NUN'S STORY, WB Studio Sound Department. George R. Groves, Sound Director.
PORGY AND BESS, Samuel Goldwyn Studio Sound Department. Gordon E. Sawyer, Sound Director; and Todd-AO Sound Department. Fred Hynes, Sound Director.

SHORT FILMS:
(Cartoons)
MOONBIRD, Storyboard, Inc., EDH, John Hubley, Prod.
MEXICALI SHMOES, WB. John W. Burton, Prod.
NOAH'S ARK, Walt Disney Prods., BV. Walt Disney, Prod.
THE VIOLINIST, Pintoff Prods., Inc., KGY. Ernest Pintoff, Prod.

(Live Action Subjects)
THE GOLDEN FISH, Les Requins Associes, COL (French). Jacques-Yves Cousteau, Prod.
BETWEEN THE TIDES, British Transport Films, SCH (British). Ian Ferguson, Prod.
MYSTERIES OF THE DEEP, Walt Disney Prods., BV. Walt Disney, Prod.
THE RUNNING, JUMPING AND STANDING-STILL FILM, Lion Int'l Films Ltd., KGU (British). Peter Sellers, Prod.
SKYSCRAPER, BYN. Shirley Clarke, Willard Van Dyke and Irving Jacoby, Prods.

DOCUMENTARY:
(Short Subjects)
GLASS, Netherlands Government, George K. Arthur-Go Pictures, Inc. (The Netherlands) Bert Haanstra, Prod.
DONALD IN MATHMAGIC LAND, Walt Disney Prods., BV. Walt Disney, Prod.
FROM GENERATION TO GENERATION, Cullen Assocs., Maternity Center Assoc. Edward F. Cullen, Prod.

(Features)
SERENGETI SHALL NOT DIE, Okapia-Film Prod., Transocean Film (German). Bernhard Grzimek, Prod.
THE RACE FOR SPACE, Wolper, Inc. David L. Wolper, Prod.

SPECIAL EFFECTS:
BEN-HUR. Visual: A. Arnold Gillespie and Robert MacDonald. Audible: Milo Lory.
JOURNEY TO THE CENTER OF THE EARTH. Visual: L. B. Abbott and James B. Gordon. Audible: Carl Faulkner.

HONORARY AND OTHER:
(Jean Hersholt Humanitarian Award)
Bob Hope

(Other)
LEE DE FOREST for his pioneering inventions which brought sound to the motion picture.
BUSTER KEATON for his unique talents which brought immortal comedies to the screen.

SCIENTIFIC OR TECHNICAL:
(Class II)
DOUGLAS G. SHEARER of MGM, Inc., and **ROBERT E. GOTTSCHALK** and **JOHN R. MOORE** of Panavision, Inc., for the development of a system of producing and exhibiting wide-film motion pictures known as Camera 65.
WADSWORTH E. POHL, WILLIAM EVANS, WERNER HOPF, S. E. HOWSE, THOMAS P. DIXON, STANFORD RESEARCH INSTITUTE and **TECHNICOLOR CORP.** for the design and development of the Technicolor electronic printing timer.
WADSWORTH E. POHL, JACK ALFORD, HENRY IMUS, JOSEPH SCHMIT, PAUL FASSNACHT, AL LOFQUIST and **TECHNICOLOR CORP.** for the development and practical application of equipment for wet printing.
DR. HOWARD S. COLEMAN, DR. A. FRANCIS TURNER, HAROLD H. SCHROEDER, JAMES R. BENFORD and **HAROLD E. ROSENBERGER** of the Bausch & Lomb Optical Co. for the design and development of the Balcold projection mirror.
ROBERT P. GUTTERMAN of General Kinetics, Inc., and the **LIPSNER-SMITH CORP.** for the design and development of the CF-2 Ultrasonic Film Cleaner.

(Class III)
UB IWERKS of Walt Disney Prods. for the design of an improved optical printer for special effects and matte shots.
E. L. STONES, GLEN ROBINSON, WINFIELD HUBBARD and **LUTHER NEWMAN** of the MGM Studio Construction Department for the design of a multiple cable remote controlled winch.

1960

BEST PICTURE:
THE APARTMENT, The Mirisch Co., Inc., UA. Billy Wilder, Prod.
THE ALAMO, Batjac Prod., UA. John Wayne, Prod.
ELMER GANTRY, Burt Lancaster-Richard Brooks Prod., UA. Bernard Smith, Prod.
SONS AND LOVERS, Co of Artists, Inc., FOX. Jerry Wald, Prod.
THE SUNDOWNERS, WB. Fred Zinnemann, Prod.

ACTOR:
BURT LANCASTER, Elmer Gantry.
TREVOR HOWARD, *Sons And Lovers.*
JACK LEMMON, *The Apartment.*
LAURENCE OLIVIER, *The Entertainer,* Woodfall Prod., Continental Dist., Inc. (British)
SPENCER TRACY, *Inherit The Wind,* Stanley Kramer, UA.

ACTRESS:
ELIZABETH TAYLOR, Butterfield 8, Afton-Linebrook Prod., MGM.
GREER GARSON, *Sunrise At Campobello,* Schary Prod., WB.
DEBORAH KERR, *The Sundowners.*
SHIRLEY MACLAINE, *The Apartment.*
MELINA MERCOURI, *Never On Sunday,* Melinafilm Prod., LOP. (Greek)

SUPPORTING ACTOR:
PETER USTINOV, Spartacus, Bryna Prods., Inc., UI.
PETER FALK, *Murder, Inc.*, FOX.
JACK KRUSCHEN, *The Apartment*.
SAL MINEO, *Exodus*, Carlyle-Alpina S.A. Prod., UA.
CHILL WILLS, *The Alamo*.

SUPPORTING ACTRESS:
SHIRLEY JONES, Elmer Gantry.
GLYNIS JOHNS, *The Sundowners*.
SHIRLEY KNIGHT, *The Dark At The Top Of The Stairs*, WB.
JANET LEIGH, *Psycho*, Alfred J. Hitchcock Prods., PAR.
MARY URE, *Sons And Lovers*.

DIRECTING:
BILLY WILDER, The Apartment.
JACK CARDIFF, *Sons And Lovers*.
JULES DASSIN, *Never On Sunday*.
ALFRED HITCHCOCK, *Psycho*.
FRED ZINNEMANN, *The Sundowners*.

WRITING:
(Best Story and Screenplay written directly for the screen)
THE APARTMENT. Billy Wilder and I.A.L. Diamond.
THE ANGRY SILENCE, Beaver Films Ltd Prod., Joseph Harris-Sig Shore (British). Story by Richard Gregson and Michael Craig. Screenplay by Bryan Forbes.
THE FACTS OF LIFE, Panama & Frank Prod., UA. Norman Panama and Melvin Frank.
HIROSHIMA, MON AMOUR, Argos Films-Como Films-Daiei Pictures, Ltd.-Pathe Overseas Prod., ZEN. (French-Japanese). Marguerite Duras.
NEVER ON SUNDAY. Jules Dassin.

(Best Screenplay based on material from another medium)
ELMER GANTRY. Richard Brooks.
INHERIT THE WIND. Nathan E. Douglas and Harold Jacob Smith.
SONS AND LOVERS. Gavin Lambert and T.E.B. Clarke.
THE SUNDOWNERS. Isobel Lennart.
TUNES OF GLORY, H. M. Films Ltd Prod., LOP. (British). James Kennaway.

CINEMATOGRAPHY:
(Black-and-White)
SONS AND LOVERS. Freddie Francis.
THE APARTMENT. Joseph LaShelle.
THE FACTS OF LIFE. Charles B. Lang, Jr.
INHERIT THE WIND. Ernest Laszlo.
PSYCHO. John L. Russell.
(Color)
SPARTACUS. Russell Metty.
THE ALAMO. William H. Clothier.
BUTTERFIELD 8. Joseph Ruttenberg and Charles Harten.
EXODUS. Sam Leavitt.
PEPE, G. S.-Posa Films International Prod., COL. Joe MacDonald.

COSTUME DESIGN:
(Black-and-White)
THE FACTS OF LIFE. Edith Head and Edward Stevenson.
NEVER ON SUNDAY. Denny Vachlioti.
THE RISE AND FALL OF LEGS DIAMOND, United States Prod., WB. Howard Shoup.
SEVEN THIEVES, FOX. Bill Thomas.
THE VIRGIN SPRING, Svensk Filmindustri Prod., JAN. (Swedish). Marik Vos.
(Color)
SPARTACUS. Valles and Bill Thomas.
CAN-CAN, Suffolk-Cummings Prods., FOX. Irene Sharaff.
MIDNIGHT LACE, Ross Hunter-Arwin Prod., U. Irene.
PEPE. Edith Head.
SUNRISE AT CAMPOBELLO. Marjorie Best.

ART DIRECTION - SET DECORATION:
(Black-and-White)
THE APARTMENT. Alexander Trauner. Set Decoration: Edward G. Boyle.
THE FACTS OF LIFE. Joseph McMillan Johnson and Kenneth A. Reid. Set Decoration: Ross Dowd.
PSYCHO. Joseph Hurley and Robert Clatworthy. Set Decoration: George Milo.
SONS AND LOVERS. Tom Morahan. Set Decoration: Lionel Couch.
VISIT TO A SMALL PLANET, Hall Wallis Prods., PAR. Hal Pereira and Walter Tyler. Set Decoration: Sam Comer and Arthur Krams.
(Color)
SPARTACUS. Alexander Golitzen and Eric Orbom. Set Decoration: Russell A. Gausman and Julia Heron.
CIMARRON, MGM. George W. Davis and Addison Hehr. Set Decoration: Henry Grace, Hugh Hunt and Otto Siegel.
IT STARTED IN NAPLES, PAR and Capri Prod., PAR. Hal Pereira and Roland Anderson. Set Decoration: Sam Comer and Arrigo Breschi.
PEPE. Ted Haworth. Set Decoration: William Kiernan.
SUNRISE AT CAMPOBELLO. Edward Carrere. Set Decoration: George James Hopkins.

FILM EDITING:
THE APARTMENT. Daniel Mandell.
THE ALAMO. Stuart Gilmore.
INHERIT THE WIND. Frederic Knudtson.
PEPE. Viola Lawrence and Al Clark.
SPARTACUS. Robert Lawrence.

FOREIGN LANGUAGE FILM:
THE VIRGIN SPRING.
KAPO, Vides-Zebrafilm-Cineriz (Italy).
LA VERITE, Han Productions (France).
MACARIO, Clasa Films Mundiales, S.A. (Mexico).
THE NINTH CIRCLE, Jadran Film Production (Yugoslavia).

MUSIC - SCORING:
(Scoring of a Dramatic or Comedy Picture)
EXODUS. Ernest Gold.
THE ALAMO. Dimitri Tiomkin.
ELMER GANTRY. Andre Previn.
THE MAGNIFICENT SEVEN, Mirisch-Alpha Prod., UA. Elmer Bernstein.
SPARTACUS. Alex North.
(Scoring of a Musical Picture)
SONG WITHOUT END (The Story Of Franz Liszt), Goetz-Vidor Pictures Prod., COL. Morris Stoloff and Harry Sukman.
BELLS ARE RINGING, Arthur Freed Prod., MGM. Andre Previn.
CAN-CAN. Nelson Riddle.
LET'S MAKE LOVE, Co of Artists, Inc., FOX. Lionel Newman and Earle H. Hagen.
PEPE. Johnny Green.

MUSIC - BEST SONG:
NEVER ON SUNDAY, *Never On Sunday*. Music and Lyrics by Manos Hadjidakis.
THE FACTS OF LIFE, *The Facts Of Life*. Music and Lyrics by Johnny Mercer.
FARAWAY PART OF TOWN, *Pepe*. Music, Andre Previn. Lyrics, Dory Langdon.
THE GREEN LEAVES OF SUMMER, *The Alamo*. Music, Dimitri Tiomkin. Lyrics, Paul Francis Webster.
THE SECOND TIME AROUND, *High Time*, Bing Crosby Prods., FOX. Music, James Van Heusen. Lyrics, Sammy Cahn.

SOUND:

THE ALAMO, Samuel Goldwyn Studio Sound Department, Gordon E. Sawyer, Sound Director; and Todd-AO Sound Department, Fred Hynes, Sound Director.
THE APARTMENT, Samuel Goldwyn Studio Sound Department. Gordon E. Sawyer, Sound Director.
CIMARRON, MGM Studio Sound Department. Franklin E. Milton, Sound Director.
PEPE, COL Studio Sound Department. Charles Rice, Sound Director.
SUNRISE AT CAMPOBELLO, WB. Studio Sound Department. George R. Groves, Sound Director.

SHORT FILMS:

(Cartoons)

MUNRO, Rembrandt Films, FRP. William L. Snyder, Prod.
GOLIATH II, Walt Disney Prods., BV. Walt Disney, Prod.
HIGH NOTE, WB.
MOUSE AND GARDEN, WB.
A PLACE IN THE SUN, George K. Arthur-Go Pictures, Inc. (Czechoslovakian). Frantisek Vystrecil, Prod.

(Live Action Subjects)

DAY OF THE PAINTER, Little Movies, KGU. Ezra R. Baker, Prod.
THE CREATION OF WOMAN, Trident Films, Inc., SWD. (Indian). Charles F. Schwep and Ismail Merchant, Prods.
ISLANDS OF THE SEA, Walt Disney Prods., BV. Walt Disney, Prod.
A SPORT IS BORN, PAR. Leslie Winik, Prod.

DOCUMENTARY:

(Short Subjects)

GIUSEPPINA, James Hill Prod., SCH (British). James Hill, Prod.
BEYOND SILENCE, United States Information Agency.
A CITY CALLED COPENHAGEN, Statens Filmcentral, Danish Government Film Office (Danish).
GEORGE GROSZ' INTERREGNUM, Educational Communications Corp. Charles and Altina Carey, Prods.
UNIVERSE, NFC, SCH (Canadian). Colin Low, Prod.

(Features)

THE HORSE WITH THE FLYING TAIL, Walt Disney Prods., BV. Larry Lansburgh, Prod.
REBEL IN PARADISE, Tiare Co. Robert D. Fraser, Prod.

SPECIAL EFFECTS:

THE TIME MACHINE, Galaxy Films Prod., MGM. Visual: Gene Warren and Tim Baar.
THE LAST VOYAGE, Andrew and Virginia Stone Prod., MGM. Visual: A. J. Lohman.

HONORARY AND OTHER:

(Jean Hersholt Humanitarian Award)

Sol Lesser

(Other)

GARY COOPER for his many memorable screen performances and the international recognition he, as an individual, has gained for the motion picture industry.
STAN LAUREL for his creative pioneering in the field of cinema comedy.
HAYLEY MILLS for Pollyanna, the most outstanding juvenile performance during 1960.

SCIENTIFIC OR TECHNICAL:

(Class II)

AMPEX PROFESSIONAL PRODUCTS CO. for the production of a well-engineered multi-purpose sound system combining high standards of quality with convenience of control, dependable operation and simplified emergency provisions.

(Class III)

ARTHUR HOLCOMB, PETRO VLAHOS and COLUMBIA STUDIO CAMERA DEPARTMENT for a camera flicker indicating device.

ANTHONY PAGLIA and the 20TH CENTURY-FOX STUDIO MECHANICAL EFFECTS DEPARTMENT for the design and construction of a miniature flak gun and ammunition.
CARL HAUGE, ROBERT GRUBEL and EDWARD REICHARD of Consolidated Film Industries for the development of an automatic developer replenisher system.

1961

BEST PICTURE:

WEST SIDE STORY, Mirisch Pictures, Inc. and B and P Enterprises, Inc., UA. Robert Wise, Prod.
FANNY, Mansfield Prod., WB. Joshua Logan, Prod.
THE GUNS OF NAVARONE, Carl Foreman Prod., COL. Carl Foreman, Prod.
THE HUSTLER, Robert Rossen Prod., FOX. Robert Rossen, Prod.
JUDGMENT AT NUREMBERG, Stanley Kramer Prod., UA. Stanley Kramer, Prod.

ACTOR:

MAXIMILIAN SCHELL, Judgment At Nuremberg.
CHARLES BOYER, *Fanny.*
PAUL NEWMAN, *The Hustler.*
SPENCER TRACY, *Judgment At Nuremberg.*
STUART WHITMAN, *The Mark,* Raymond Stross-Sidney Buchman Prod., Continental Dist., Inc. (British)

ACTRESS:

SOPHIA LOREN, Two Women, Champion-Les Films Marceau-Cocinor and Societe Generale De Cinematographie Prod., EBP. (Italo-French)
AUDREY HEPBURN, *Breakfast At Tiffany's,* Jurow-Shepherd Prod., PAR.
PIPER LAURIE, *The Hustler.*
GERALDINE PAGE, *Summer And Smoke,* Hal Wallis Prod., PAR.
NATALIE WOOD, *Splendor In The Grass,* NBI Prod., WB.

SUPPORTING ACTOR:

GEORGE CHAKIRIS, West Side Story.
MONTGOMERY CLIFT, *Judgment At Nuremberg.*
PETER FALK, *Pocketful Of Miracles,* Franton Prod., UA.
JACKIE GLEASON, *The Hustler.*
GEORGE C. SCOTT, *The Hustler.*

SUPPORTING ACTRESS:

RITA MORENO, West Side Story.
FAY BAINTER, *The Children's Hour,* Mirisch-Worldwide Prod., UA.
JUDY GARLAND, *Judgment At Nuremberg.*
LOTTE LENYA, *The Roman Spring Of Mrs. Stone,* Seven Arts Presentation, WB.
UNA MERKEL, *Summer And Smoke.*

DIRECTING:

JEROME ROBBINS, West Side Story.
ROBERT WISE, West Side Story.
FEDERICO FELLINI, *La Dolce Vita,* Riama Film Prod., ASR. (Italian).
STANLEY KRAMER, *Judgment At Nuremberg.*
ROBERT ROSSEN, *The Hustler.*
J. LEE THOMPSON, *The Guns Of Navarone.*

WRITING:

(Best Story and Screenplay written directly for the screen)

SPLENDOR IN THE GRASS. William Inge.
BALLAD OF A SOLDIER, Mosfilm Studio Prod., KYM. (Russian). Valentin Yoshov and Grigori Chukhrai.
GENERAL DELLA ROVERE, Zebra & S.N.E. Gaumont Prod., CON. (Italian). Sergio Amidei, Diego Fabbri and Indro Montanelli.

LA DOLCE VITA. Federico Fellini, Tullio Pinelli, Ennio Flaiano and Brunello Rondi.
LOVER COME BACK, U-The 7 Pictures Corp., Nob Hill Prods., Inc., Arwin Prods., Inc., UI. Stanley Shapiro and Paul Henning.

(Best Screenplay based on material from another medium)
JUDGMENT AT NUREMBERG. Abby Mann.
BREAKFAST AT TIFFANY'S. George Axelrod.
THE GUNS OF NAVARONE. Carl Foreman.
THE HUSTLER. Sidney Carroll and Robert Rossen.
WEST SIDE STORY. Ernest Lehman.

CINEMATOGRAPHY:
(Black-and-White)
THE HUSTLER. Eugen Shuftan.
THE ABSENT MINDED PROFESSOR, Walt Disney Prods., BV. Edward Colman.
THE CHILDREN'S HOUR. Franz F. Planer.
JUDGMENT AT NUREMBERG. Ernest Laszlo.
ONE, TWO, THREE, Mirisch Co, Inc. in association with Pyramid Prods., A. G., UA. Daniel L. Fapp.

(Color)
WEST SIDE STORY. Daniel L. Fapp.
FANNY. Jack Cardiff.
FLOWER DRUM SONG, U-Ross Hunter Prod. in association with Joseph Fields, U. Russell Metty.
A MAJORITY OF ONE, WB. Harry Stradling, Sr.
ONE-EYED JACKS, Pennebaker Prod., PAR. Charles Lang, Jr.

COSTUME DESIGN:
(Black-and-White)
LA DOLCE VITA. Piero Gherardi.
THE CHILDREN'S HOUR. Dorothy Jeakins.
CLAUDELLE INGLISH, WB. Howard Shoup.
JUDGMENT AT NUREMBERG. Jean Louis.
YOJIMBO, TOH. & Kurosawa Prod., Toho Co, Ltd. (Japanese). Yoshiro Muraki.

(Color)
WEST SIDE STORY. Irene Sharaff.
BABES IN TOYLAND, Walt Disney Prods., BV. Bill Thomas.
BACK STREET, U-Ross Hunter Prods., Inc.-Carrollton, Inc., U. Jean Louis.
FLOWER DRUM SONG. Irene Sharaff.
POCKETFUL OF MIRACLES. Edith Head and Walter Plunkett.

ART DIRECTION - SET DECORATION:
(Black-and-White)
THE HUSTLER. Harry Horner. Set Decoration: Gene Callahan.
THE ABSENT MINDED PROFESSOR. Carroll Clark. Set Decoration: Emile Kuri and Hal Gausman.
THE CHILDREN'S HOUR. Fernando Carrere. Set Decoration: Edward G. Boyle.
JUDGMENT AT NUREMBERG. Rudolph Sternad. Set Decoration: George Milo.
LA DOLCE VITA. Piero Gherardi.

(Color)
WEST SIDE STORY. Boris Leven. Set Decoration: Victor A. Gangelin.
BREAKFAST AT TIFFANY'S. Hal Pereira and Roland Anderson. Set Decoration: Sam Comer and Ray Moyer.
EL CID, Samuel Bronston Prod., in association with Dear Film Prod., AA. Veniero Colasanti and John Moore.
FLOWER DRUM SONG. Alexander Golitzen and Joseph Wright. Set Decoration: Howard Bristol.
SUMMER AND SMOKE. Hal Pereira and Walter Tyler. Set Decoration: Sam Comer and Arthur Krams.

FILM EDITING:
WEST SIDE STORY. Thomas Stanford.
FANNY. William H. Reynolds.
THE GUNS OF NAVARONE. Alan Osbiston.
JUDGMENT AT NUREMBERG. Frederic Knudtson.
THE PARENT TRAP, Walt Disney Prods., BV. Philip W. Anderson.

FOREIGN LANGUAGE FILM:
THROUGH A GLASS DARKLY, A. B. Svensk Filmindustri (Sweden).
HARRY AND THE BUTLER, Bent Christensen Production (Denmark).
IMMORTAL LOVE, Shochiku Co., Ltd. (Japan).
THE IMPORTANT MAN, Peliculas Rodriguez, S.A. (Mexico).
PLACIDO, Jet Films (Spain).

MUSIC - SCORING:
(Scoring of a Dramatic or Comedy Picture)
BREAKFAST AT TIFFANY'S. Henry Mancini.
EL CID. Miklos Rozsa.
FANNY. Morris Stoloff and Harry Sukman.
THE GUNS OF NAVARONE. Dimitri Tiomkin.
SUMMER AND SMOKE. Elmer Bernstein.

(Scoring of a Musical Picture)
WEST SIDE STORY. Saul Chaplin, Johnny Green, Sid Ramin and Irwin Kostal.
BABES IN TOYLAND. George Bruns.
FLOWER DRUM SONG. Alfred Newman and Ken Darby.
KHOVANSHCHINA, Mosfilm Studios, ARK (Russian). Dimitri Shostakovich.
PARIS BLUES, Pennebaker, Inc., UA. Duke Ellington.

MUSIC - BEST SONG:
MOON RIVER, Breakfast At Tiffany's. Music, Henry Mancini. Lyrics, Johnny Mercer.
BACHELOR IN PARADISE, *Bachelor In Paradise,* Ted Richmond Prod., MGM. Music, Henry Mancini. Lyrics, Mack David.
LOVE THEME FROM EL CID (The Falcon And The Dove), *El Cid.* Music, Miklos Rozsa. Lyrics, Paul Francis Webster.
POCKETFUL OF MIRACLES. *Pocketful Of Miracles.* Music, James Van Heusen. Lyrics, Sammy Cahn.
TOWN WITHOUT PITY, *Town Without Pity,* Mirisch Co in association with Gloria Films, UA. Music, Dimitri Tiomkin. Lyrics, Ned Washington.

SOUND:
WEST SIDE STORY, Todd-AO Sound Department, Fred Hynes, Sound Director; and Samuel Goldwyn Studio Sound Department, Gordon E. Sawyer, Sound Director.
THE CHILDREN'S HOUR, Samuel Goldwyn Studio Sound Department. Gordon E. Sawyer, Sound Director.
FLOWER DRUM SONG, Revue Studio Sound Department. Waldon O. Watson, Sound Director.
THE GUNS OF NAVARONE, Shepperton Studio Sound Department. John Cox, Sound Director.
THE PARENT TRAP, Walt Disney Studio Sound Department. Robert O. Cook, Sound Director.

SHORT FILMS:
(Cartoons)
ERSATZ (The Substitute), Zagreb Film, HLI.
AQUAMANIA, Walt Disney Prods., BV. Walt Disney, Prod.
BEEP PREPARED, WB. Chuck Jones, Prod.
NELLY'S FOLLY, WB. Chuck Jones, Prod.
PIED PIPER OF GUADALUPE, WB. Friz Freleng, Prod.

(Live Action Subjects)
SEAWARDS THE GREAT SHIPS, Templar Film Studios, SCH.
BALLON VOLE (Play Ball!), Cine-Documents, KGY.
THE FACE OF JESUS, Dr. John D. Jennings, Harry Stern, Inc. Dr. John D. Jennings, Prod.
ROOFTOPS OF NEW YORK, McCarty-Rush Prod. in association with

Robert Gaffney, COL.
VERY NICE, VERY NICE, NFC, KGY.

DOCUMENTARY:
(Short Subjects)

PROJECT HOPE, MacManus, John & Adams, Inc., Ex-Cell-O Corp. A Klaeger Film Production. Frank P. Bibas, Prod.
BREAKING THE LANGUAGE BARRIER, United States Air Force.
CRADLE OF GENIUS, Plough Prods., An Irving M. Lesser Film Presentation (Irish). Jim O'Connor and Tom Hayes, Prods.
KAHL, Dido-Film-GmbH., AEG-Filmdienst (German).
L'UOMO IN GRIGIO (The Man In Gray), (Italian). Benedetto Benedetti, Prod.

(Features)

LE CIEL ET LA BOUE (Sky Above And Mud Beneath), Ardennes Films and Michael Arthur Film Prods., RNK. (French). Arthur Cohn and Rene Lafuite, Prods.
LA GRANDE OLIMPIADE (Olympic Games 1960), dell Istituto Nazionale Luce, Comitato Organizzatore Del Giochi Della XVII Olimpiade. CNZ (Italian).

SPECIAL EFFECTS:

THE GUNS OF NAVARONE. Visual: Bill Warrington. Audible: Vivian C. Greenham.
THE ABSENT MINDED PROFESSOR. Visual: Robert A. Mattey and Eustace Lycett.

HONORARY AND OTHER:
(Irving G. Thalberg Memorial Award)

Stanley Kramer

(Jean Hersholt Humanitarian Award)

George Seaton

(Other)

WILLIAM L. HENDRICKS for his outstanding patriotic service in the conception, writing and production of the Marine Corps film, A Force In Readiness, which has brought honor to the Academy and the motion picture industry.
FRED L. METZLER for his dedication and outstanding service to the Academy of Motion Picture Arts and Sciences.
JEROME ROBBINS for his brilliant achievements in the art of choreography on film.

SCIENTIFIC OR TECHNICAL:
(Class II)

SYLVANIA ELECTRIC PRODUCTS, INC., for the development of a hand held high-power photographic lighting unit known as the Sun Gun Professional.
JAMES DALE, S. WILSON, H. E. RICE, JOHN RUDE, LAURIE ATKIN, WADSWORTH E. POHL, H. PEASGOOD and **TECHNICOLOR CORP.** for a process of automatic selective printing.
20TH CENTURY-FOX RESEARCH DEPARTMENT, under the direction of **E. I. SPONABLE** and **HERBERT E. BRAGG,** and **DELUXE LABORATORIES, INC.,** with the assistance of **F. D. LESLIE, R. D. WHITMORE, A. A. ALDEN, ENDEL POOL** and **JAMES B. GORDON** for a system of decompressing and recomposing CinemaScope pictures for conventional aspect ratios.

(Class III)

HURLETRON, INC., ELECTRIC EYE EQUIPMENT DIVISION, for an automatic light changing system for motion picture printers.
WADSWORTH E. POHL and **TECHNICOLOR CORP.** for an integrated sound and picture transfer process.

1962

BEST PICTURE:

LAWRENCE OF ARABIA, Horizon Pictures (G.B.), Ltd.-Sam Spiegel-David Lean Prod., COL. Sam Spiegel, Prod.
THE LONGEST DAY, Darryl F. Zanuck Prod., FOX. Darryl F. Zanuck, Prod.
Meredith Willson's THE MUSIC MAN, WB. Morton Da Costa, Prod.
MUTINY ON THE BOUNTY, Arcola Prod., MGM. Aaron Rosenberg, Prod.
TO KILL A MOCKINGBIRD, U-Pakula-Mulligan-Brentwood Prod., U. Alan J. Pakula, Prod.

ACTOR:

GREGORY PECK, To Kill A Mockingbird.
BURT LANCASTER, *Bird Man Of Alcatraz*, Harold Hecht Prod., UA.
JACK LEMMON, *Days Of Wine And Roses*, Martin Manulis-Jalem Prod., WB.
MARCELLO MASTROIANNI, *Divorce - Italian Style*, Lux-Vides-Galatea Film Prod., EBP.
PETER O'TOOLE, *Lawrence Of Arabia*.

ACTRESS:

ANNE BANCROFT, The Miracle Worker, Playfilms Prod., UA.
BETTE DAVIS, *What Ever Happened To Baby Jane?*, Seven Arts-Associates & Aldrich Co. Prod., WB.
KATHARINE HEPBURN, *Long Day's Journey Into Night*, Ely Landau Prods., EBP.
GERALDINE PAGE, *Sweet Bird Of Youth*, Roxbury Prod., MGM.
LEE REMICK, *Days Of Wine And Roses*.

SUPPORTING ACTOR:

ED BEGLEY, Sweet Bird Of Youth.
VICTOR BUONO, *What Ever Happened To Baby Jane?*
TELLY SAVALAS, *Bird Man Of Alcatraz.*
OMAR SHARIF, *Lawrence Of Arabia.*
TERENCE STAMP, *Billy Budd,* Harvest Prods., AA.

SUPPORTING ACTRESS:

PATTY DUKE, The Miracle Worker.
MARY BADHAM, *To Kill A Mockingbird.*
SHIRLEY KNIGHT, *Sweet Bird Of Youth.*
ANGELA LANSBURY, *The Manchurian Candidate,* M. C. Prod., UA.
THELMA RITTER, *Bird Man Of Alcatraz.*

DIRECTING:

DAVID LEAN, Lawrence Of Arabia.
PIETRO GERMI, *Divorce - Italian Style.*
ROBERT MULLIGAN, *To Kill A Mockingbird.*
ARTHUR PENN, *The Miracle Worker.*
FRANK PERRY, *David And Lisa,* Heller-Perry Prods., CON.

WRITING:
(Best Story and Screenplay written directly for the screen)

DIVORCE - ITALIAN STYLE. Ennio de Concini, Alfredo Giannetti and Pietro Germi.
FREUD, U-John Huston Prod., U. Story by Charles Kaufman. Screenplay by Charles Kaufman and Wolfgang Reinhardt.
LAST YEAR AT MARIENBAD, Preceitel-Terra Film Prod., ASR. Alain Robbe-Grillet.
THAT TOUCH OF MINK, U-Granley-Arwin-Nob Hill Prod., U. Stanley Shapiro and Nate Monaster.
THROUGH A GLASS DARKLY. Ingmar Bergman.

(Best Screenplay based on material from another medium)

TO KILL A MOCKINGBIRD. Horton Foote.
DAVID AND LISA. Eleanor Perry.
LAWRENCE OF ARABIA. Robert Bolt.
LOLITA, Seven Arts Prods., MGM. Vladimir Nabokov.
THE MIRACLE WORKER. William Gibson.

CINEMATOGRAPHY:

(Black-and-White)

THE LONGEST DAY. Jean Bourgoin and Walter Wottitz.
BIRD MAN OF ALCATRAZ. Burnett Guffey.
TO KILL A MOCKINGBIRD. Russell Harlan.
TWO FOR THE SEESAW, Mirisch-Argyle-Talbot Prod. in association with Seven Arts Prods., UA. Ted McCord.
WHAT EVER HAPPENED TO BABY JANE? Ernest Haller.

(Color)

LAWRENCE OF ARABIA. Fred A. Young.
GYPSY, WB. Harry Stradling, Sr.
HATARI!, Malabar Prods., PAR. Russell Harlan.
MUTINY ON THE BOUNTY, Arcola Prod., MGM. Robert L. Surtees.
THE WONDERFUL WORLD OF THE BROTHERS GRIMM, MGM & CRC. Paul C. Vogel.

COSTUME DESIGN:

(Black-and-White)

WHAT EVER HAPPENED TO BABY JANE? Norma Koch.
DAYS OF WINE AND ROSES. Don Feld.
THE MAN WHO SHOT LIBERTY VALANCE, John Ford Prod., PAR. Edith Head.
THE MIRACLE WORKER. Ruth Morley.
PHAEDRA, Jules Dassin-Melinafilm Prod., LOP. Denny Vachlioti.

(Color)

THE WONDERFUL WORLD OF THE BROTHERS GRIMM. Mary Wills.
BON VOYAGE, Walt Disney Prod., BV. Bill Thomas.
GYPSY. Orry-Kelly.
Meredith Willson's THE MUSIC MAN. Dorothy Jeakins.
MY GEISHA, Sachiko Prod., PAR. Edith Head.

ART DIRECTION - SET DECORATION:

(Black-and-White)

TO KILL A MOCKINGBIRD. Alexander Golitzen and Henry Bumstead. Set Decoration: Oliver Emert.
DAYS OF WINE AND ROSES. Joseph Wright. Set Decoration: George James Hopkins.
THE LONGEST DAY. Ted Haworth, Leon Barsacq and Vincent Korda. Set Decoration: Gabriel Bechir.
PERIOD OF ADJUSTMENT, Marten Prod., MGM. George W. Davis and Edward Carfagno. Set Decoration: Henry Grace and Dick Pefferle.
THE PIGEON THAT TOOK ROME, Llenroc Prods., PAR. Hal Pereira and Roland Anderson. Set Decoration: Sam Comer and Frank R. McKelvy.

(Color)

LAWRENCE OF ARABIA. John Box and John Stoll. Set Decoration: Dario Simoni.
Meredith Willson's THE MUSIC MAN. Paul Groesse. Set Decoration: George James Hopkins.
MUTINY ON THE BOUNTY. George W. Davis and J. McMillan Johnson. Set Decoration: Henry Grace and Hugh Hunt.
THAT TOUCH OF MINK. Alexander Golitzen and Robert Clatworthy. Set Decoration: George Milo.
THE WONDERFUL WORLD OF THE BROTHERS GRIMM. George W. Davis and Edward Carfagno. Set Decoration: Henry Grace and Dick Pefferle.

FILM EDITING:

LAWRENCE OF ARABIA. Anne Coates.
THE LONGEST DAY. Samuel E. Beetley.
THE MANCHURIAN CANDIDATE. Ferris Webster.
Meredith Willson's THE MUSIC MAN. William Ziegler.
MUTINY ON THE BOUNTY. John McSweeney, Jr.

FOREIGN LANGUAGE FILM:

SUNDAYS AND CYBELE, Terra-Fides-Orsay-Trocadero Films (France.)
ELECTRA, A Michael Cacoyannis Production (Greece).
THE FOUR DAYS OF NAPLES, Titanus-Metro (Italy).
KEEPER OF PROMISES (The Given Word), Cinedistri (Brazil).
TLAYUCAN, Producciones Matouk, S.A. (Mexico).

MUSIC - SCORING:

(Music Score-substantially original)

LAWRENCE OF ARABIA. Maurice Jarre.
FREUD. Jerry Goldsmith.
MUTINY ON THE BOUNTY. Bronislau Kaper.
TARAS BULBA, Harold Hecht Prod., UA. Franz Waxman.
TO KILL A MOCKINGBIRD. Elmer Bernstein.

(Scoring of Music-adaptation or treatment)

Meredith Willson's THE MUSIC MAN. Ray Heindorf.
Billy Rose's JUMBO, Euterpe-Arwin Prod., MGM. George Stoll.
GIGOT, Seven Arts Prods., FOX. Michel Magne.
GYPSY. Frank Perkins.
THE WONDERFUL WORLD OF THE BROTHERS GRIMM. Leigh Harline.

MUSIC - BEST SONG:

DAYS OF WINE AND ROSES, Days Of Wine And Roses. Music, Henry Mancini. Lyrics, Johnny Mercer.
LOVE SONG FROM MUTINY ON THE BOUNTY (Follow Me), Mutiny On The Bounty. Music, Bronislau Kaper. Lyrics, Paul Francis Webster.
SONG FROM TWO FOR THE SEESAW (Second Chance), Two For The Seesaw. Music, Andre Previn. Lyrics, Dory Langdon.
TENDER IS THE NIGHT, Tender Is The Night, FOX. Music, Sammy Fain. Lyrics, Paul Francis Webster.
WALK ON THE WILD SIDE, Walk On The Wild Side, Famous Artists Prods., COL. Music, Elmer Bernstein. Lyrics, Mack David.

SOUND:

LAWRENCE OF ARABIA, Shepperton Studio Sound Department. John Cox, Sound Director.
BON VOYAGE, Walt Disney Studio Sound Department. Robert O. Cook, Sound Director.
Meredith Willson's THE MUSIC MAN. WB Studio Sound Department. George R. Groves, Sound Director.
THAT TOUCH OF MINK, U Studio Sound Department. Waldon O. Watson, Sound Director.
WHAT EVER HAPPENED TO BABY JANE?, Glen Glenn Sound Department. Joseph Kelly, Sound Director.

SHORT FILMS:

(Cartoons)

THE HOLE, Storyboard Inc., BRA. John and Faith Hubley, Prods.
ICARUS MONTGOLFIER WRIGHT, Format Films, UA. Jules Engel, Prod.
NOW HEAR THIS, WB.
SELF DEFENSE---FOR COWARDS, Rembrandt Films, FRP. William L. Snyder, Prod.
SYMPOSIUM ON POPULAR SONGS, Walt Disney Prods., BV. Walt Disney, Prod.

(Live Action Subjects)

HEUREUX ANNIVERSAIRE (Happy Anniversary), CAPAC Prods., ATL. Pierre Etaix and J. C. Carriere, Prods.
BIG CITY BLUES, MFR. Martina and Charles Huguenot van der Linden, Prods.
THE CADILLAC, United Prods Releasing Org. Robert Clouse, Prod.
THE CLIFF DWELLERS (formerly titled One Plus One), Group II Film Prods., SCH. Hayward Anderson, Prod.
PAN, MFR. Herman van der horst, Prod.

DOCUMENTARY:
(Short Subjects)

DYLAN THOMAS, TWW Ltd., JAN (Welsh). Jack Howells, Prod.
THE JOHN GLENN STORY, Department of the Navy, WB. William L. Hendricks, Prod.
THE ROAD TO THE WALL, CBS Films, Inc., Department of Defense. Robert Saudek, Prod.

(Features)

BLACK FOX, Image Prods., Inc., Heritage Films, Inc. Louis Clyde Stoumen, Prod.
ALVORADA (Brazil's Changing Face), MW Filmproduktion (German). Hugo Niebeling, Prod.

SPECIAL EFFECTS:
THE LONGEST DAY. Visual: Robert MacDonald. Audible: Jacques Maumont.
MUTINY ON THE BOUNTY. Visual: A. Arnold Gillespie. Audible: Milo Lory.

HONORARY AND OTHER:
(Jean Hersholt Humanitarian Award)

Steve Broidy

SCIENTIFIC OR TECHNICAL:
(Class II)

RALPH CHAPMAN for the design and development of an advanced motion picture camera crane.
ALBERT S. PRATT, JAMES L. WASSELL and HANS C. WOHLRAB of the Professional Division, Bell & Howell Co., for the design and development of a new and improved automatic motion picture additive color printer.
NORTH AMERICAN PHILIPS CO., INC., for the design and engineering of the Norelco Universal 70/35mm motion picture projector.
CHARLES E. SUTTER, WILLIAM BRYSON SMITH and LOUIS C. KENNELL of Paramount Pictures Corp. for the engineering and application to motion picture production of a new system of electric power distribution.

(Class III)

ELECTRO-VOICE, INC., for a highly directional dynamic line microphone.
LOUIS G. MACKENZIE for a selective sound effects repeater.

1963

BEST PICTURE:
TOM JONES, Woodfall Prod., UA-Lopert Pictures. Tony Richardson, Prod.
AMERICA AMERICA, Athena Enterprises Prod., WB. Elia Kazan, Prod.
CLEOPATRA, FOX Ltd.-MCL Films S.A.-WALWA Films S.A. Prod., FOX. Walter Wanger, Prod.
HOW THE WEST WAS WON, MGM & CRC. Bernard Smith, Prod.
LILIES OF THE FIELD, Rainbow Prod., UA. Ralph Nelson, Prod.

ACTOR:
SIDNEY POITIER, Lilies Of The Field.
ALBERT FINNEY, Tom Jones.
RICHARD HARRIS, This Sporting Life, Julian Wintle-Leslie Parkyn Prod., WRS-CON.
REX HARRISON, Cleopatra.
PAUL NEWMAN, Hud, Salem-Dover Prod., PAR.

ACTRESS:
PATRICIA NEAL, Hud.
LESLIE CARON, The L-Shaped Room, Romulus Prods., Ltd., COL.
SHIRLEY MACLAINE, Irma La Douce, Mirisch-Phalanx Prod., UA.
RACHEL ROBERTS, This Sporting Life.
NATALIE WOOD, Love With The Proper Stranger, Boardwalk-Rona Prod., PAR.

SUPPORTING ACTOR:
MELVYN DOUGLAS, Hud.
NICK ADAMS, Twilight Of Honor, Perlberg-Seaton Prod., MGM.
BOBBY DARIN, Captain Newman, M.D., U-Brentwood-Reynard Prod., U.
HUGH GRIFFITH, Tom Jones.
JOHN HUSTON, The Cardinal, Gamma Prod., COL.

SUPPORTING ACTRESS:
MARGARET RUTHERFORD, The V.I.P.s, MGM.
DIANE CILENTO, Tom Jones.
DAME EDITH EVANS, Tom Jones.
JOYCE REDMAN, Tom Jones.
LILIA SKALA, Lilies Of The Field.

DIRECTING:
TONY RICHARDSON, Tom Jones.
FEDERICO FELLINI, Federico Fellini's 8 1/2, Cineriz Prod., EBP.
ELIA KAZAN, America America.
OTTO PREMINGER, The Cardinal.
MARTIN RITT, Hud.

WRITING:
(Best Story and Screenplay written directly for the screen)

HOW THE WEST WAS WON. James R. Webb.
AMERICA AMERICA. Elia Kazan.
FEDERICO FELLINI'S 8 1/2. Federico Fellini, Ennio Flaiano, Tullio Pinelli and Brunello Rondi.
THE FOUR DAYS OF NAPLES, Titanus Prod., MGM. Story by Pasquale Feste Campanile, Massimo Franciosa, Nanni Loy and Vasco Pratolini. Screenplay by Carlo Bernari, Pasquale Festa Campanile, Massimo Franciosa and Nanni Loy.
LOVE WITH THE PROPER STRANGER. Arnold Schulman.

(Best Screenplay based on material from another medium)

TOM JONES. John Osborne.
CAPTAIN NEWMAN, M.D. Richard L. Breen, Phoebe and Henry Ephron.
HUD. Irving Ravetch and Harriet Frank, Jr.
LILIES OF THE FIELD. James Poe.
SUNDAYS AND CYBELE, Terra-Fides-Orsay-Films Trocadero Prods., COL. Serge Bourguignon and Antoine Tudal.

CINEMATOGRAPHY:
(Black-and-White)

HUD. James Wong Howe.
THE BALCONY, Walter Reade-Sterling-Allen-Hodgdon Prod., George Folsey.
THE CARETAKERS, Hall Bartlett Prod., UA. Lucien Ballard.
LILIES OF THE FIELD. Ernest Haller.
LOVE WITH THE PROPER STRANGER. Milton Krasner.

(Color)

CLEOPATRA. Leon Shamroy.
THE CARDINAL. Leon Shamroy.
HOW THE WEST WAS WON. William H. Daniels, Milton Krasner, Charles Lang, Jr. and Joseph LaShelle.
IRMA LA DOUCE. Joseph LaShelle.
IT'S A MAD, MAD, MAD, MAD WORLD, Casey Prod., UA. Ernest Laszlo.

COSTUME DESIGN:
(Black-and-White)

FEDERICO FELLINI'S 8 1/2. Piero Gherardi.
LOVE WITH THE PROPER STRANGER. Edith Head.
THE STRIPPER, Jerry Wald Prods., FOX. Travilla.
TOYS IN THE ATTIC, Mirisch-Claude Prod., UA. Bill Thomas.
WIVES AND LOVERS, Hal Wallis Prod., PAR. Edith Head.

(Color)

CLEOPATRA. Irene Sharaff, Vittorio Nino Novarese and Renie.
THE CARDINAL. Donald Brooks.
HOW THE WEST WAS WON. Walter Plunkett.
THE LEOPARD, Titanus Prod., FOX. Piero Tosi.
A NEW KIND OF LOVE, Llenroc Prods., PAR. Edith Head.

ART DIRECTION - SET DECORATION:
(Black-and-White)

AMERICA AMERICA. Gene Callahan.
FEDERICO FELLINI'S 8 1/2. Piero Gherardi.
HUD. Hal Pereira and Tambi Larsen. Set Decoration: Sam Comer and Robert Benton.
LOVE WITH THE PROPER STRANGER. Hal Pereira and Roland Anderson. Set Decoration: Sam Comer and Grace Gregory.
TWILIGHT OF HONOR. George W. Davis and Paul Groesse. Set Decoration: Henry Grace and Hugh Hunt.

(Color)

CLEOPATRA. John DeCuir, Jack Martin Smith, Hilyard Brown, Herman Blumenthal, Elven Webb, Maurice Pelling and Boris Juraga. Set Decoration: Walter M. Scott, Paul S. Fox and Ray Moyer.
THE CARDINAL. Lyle Wheeler. Set Decoration: Gene Callahan.
COME BLOW YOUR HORN, Essex-Tandem Enterprises Prod., PAR. Hal Pereira and Roland Anderson. Set Decoration: Sam Comer and James Payne.
HOW THE WEST WAS WON. George W. Davis, William Ferrari and Addison Hehr. Set Decoration: Henry Grace, Don Greenwood, Jr. and Jack Mills.
TOM JONES. Ralph Brinton, Ted Marshall and Jocelyn Herbert. Set Decoration: Josie MacAvin.

FILM EDITING:
HOW THE WEST WAS WON. Harold F. Kress.
THE CARDINAL. Louis R. Loeffler.
CLEOPATRA. Dorothy Spencer.
THE GREAT ESCAPE, Mirisch-Alpha Picture Prod., UA. Ferris Webster.
IT'S A MAD, MAD, MAD, MAD WORLD. Frederic Knudtson, Robert C. Jones and Gene Fowler, Jr.

FOREIGN LANGUAGE FILM:
FEDERICO FELLINI'S 8 1/2.
KNIFE IN THE WATER, A Kamera Unit of Film Polski Production (Poland).
LOS TARANTOS, Tecisa-Films R.B. (Spain).
THE RED LANTERNS, Th. Damaskinos & V. Michaelides A.E. (Greece).
TWIN SISTERS OF KYOTO, Shochiku Co., Ltd. (Japan).

MUSIC - SCORING:
(Music Score-substantially original)

TOM JONES. John Addison.
CLEOPATRA. Alex North.
55 DAYS AT PEKING, Samuel Bronston Prod., AA. Dimitri Tiomkin.
HOW THE WEST WAS WON. Alfred Newman and Ken Darby.
IT'S A MAD, MAD, MAD, MAD WORLD. Ernest Gold.

(Scoring of Music-adaptation or treatment)

IRMA LA DOUCE. Andre Previn.
BYE BYE BIRDIE, Kohlmar-Sidney Prod., COL. John Green.
A NEW KIND OF LOVE. Leith Stevens.
SUNDAYS AND CYBELE. Maurice Jarre.
THE SWORD IN THE STONE, Walt Disney Prods., BV. George Bruns.

MUSIC - BEST SONG:
CALL ME IRRESPONSIBLE, Papa's Delicate Condition, Amro Prods., PAR. Music, James Van Heusen. Lyrics, Sammy Cahn.
CHARADE, *Charade,* U-Stanley Donen Prod., U. Music, Henry Mancini. Lyrics, Johnny Mercer.
IT'S A MAD, MAD, MAD, MAD WORLD, *It's A Mad, Mad, Mad, Mad World.* Music, Ernest Gold. Lyrics, Mack David.
MORE, *Mondo Cane,* Cineriz Prod., TIM. Music, Riz Ortolani and Nino Oliviero. Lyrics, Norman Newell.
SO LITTLE TIME, *55 Days At Peking.* Music, Dimitri Tiomkin. Lyrics, Paul Francis Webster.

SOUND:
HOW THE WEST WAS WON, MGM Studio Sound Department. Franklin E. Milton, Sound Director.
BYE BYE BIRDIE, COL Studio Sound Department. Charles Rice, Sound Director.
CAPTAIN NEWMAN, M.D., U Studio Sound Department. Waldon O. Watson, Sound Director.
CLEOPATRA, FOX Studio Sound Department, James P. Corcoran, Sound Director; and Todd-AO Sound Department, Fred Hynes, Sound Director.
IT'S A MAD, MAD, MAD, MAD WORLD, Samuel Goldwyn Studio Sound Department. Gordon E. Sawyer, Sound Director.

SHORT FILMS:
(Cartoons)

THE CRITIC, Pintoff-Crossbow Prods., COL. Ernest Pintoff, Prod.
AUTOMANIA 2000, Halas and Batchelor Prod., PC. John Halas, Prod.
THE GAME (Igra), Zagreb Film, RBF. Dusan Vukotic, Prod.
MY FINANCIAL CAREER, NFC, WSC Distributing. Colin Low and Tom Daly, Prods.
PIANISSIMO, Cinema 16. Carmen D'Avino, Prod.

(Live Action Subjects)

AN OCCURRENCE AT OWL CREEK BRIDGE, Films Du Centaure-Filmartic, Cappagariff-Janus Films. Paul de Roubaix and Marcel Ichac, Prods.
THE CONCERT, James A. King Corp., George K. Arthur-Go Pictures. Ezra Baker, Prod.
HOME-MADE CAR, BP (North America) Ltd., SCH. James Hill, Prod.
SIX-SIDED TRIANGLE, Milesian Film Prod. Ltd., LIO. Christopher Miles, Prod.
THAT'S ME, Stuart Prods., PC. Walker Stuart, Prod.

DOCUMENTARY:
(Short Subjects)

CHAGALL, Auerbach Film Enterprises, Ltd.-Flag Films. Simon Schiffrin, Prod.
THE FIVE CITIES OF JUNE, United States Information Agency. George Stevens, Jr., Prod.
THE SPIRIT OF AMERICA, Spotlite News. Algernon G. Walker, Prod.
THIRTY MILLION LETTERS, British Transport Films. Edgar Anstey, Prod.
TO LIVE AGAIN, Wilding Inc. Mel London, Prod.

(Features)

ROBERT FROST: A LOVER'S QUARREL WITH THE WORLD, WGBH Educational Foundation. Robert Hughes, Prod.
LE MAILLON ET LA CHAINE (The Link And The Chain), Films Du Centaure-Filmartic. Paul de Roubaix, Prod.
THE YANKS ARE COMING, David L. Wolper Prods., Marshall Flaum, Prod.

VISUAL EFFECTS:
CLEOPATRA. Emil Kosa, Jr.
THE BIRDS, Alfred J. Hitchcock Prod., U. Ub Iwerks.

SOUND EFFECTS:
IT'S A MAD, MAD, MAD, MAD WORLD. Walter G. Elliott.
A GATHERING OF EAGLES, U. Robert L. Bratton.

HONORARY AND OTHER:
(Irving G. Thalberg Memorial Award)
Sam Spiegel

SCIENTIFIC OR TECHNICAL:
(Class III)
DOUGLAS G. SHEARER and A. ARNOLD GILLESPIE of MGM Studios for the engineering of an improved Background Process Projection System.

1964

BEST PICTURE:

MY FAIR LADY, WB. Jack L. Warner, Prod.
BECKET, Hal Wallis Prod., PAR. Hal B. Wallis, Prod.
DR. STRANGELOVE OR: HOW I LEARNED TO STOP WORRYING AND LOVE THE BOMB, Hawk Films, Ltd. Prod., COL. Stanley Kubrick, Prod.
MARY POPPINS, Walt Disney Prods. BV. Walt Disney and Bill Walsh, Prods.
ZORBA THE GREEK, Rochley, Ltd. Prod., Int'l Classics. Michael Cacoyannis, Prod.

ACTOR:

REX HARRISON, My Fair Lady.
RICHARD BURTON, *Becket.*
PETER O'TOOLE, *Becket.*
ANTHONY QUINN, *Zorba The Greek.*
PETER SELLERS, *Dr. Strangelove Or: How I Learned To Stop Worrying And Love The Bomb.*

ACTRESS:

JULIE ANDREWS, Mary Poppins.
ANNE BANCROFT, *The Pumpkin Eater,* Romulus Films, Ltd. Prod., RYI.
SOPHIA LOREN, *Marriage Italian Style,* Champion-Concordia Prod., EBP.
DEBBIE REYNOLDS, *The Unsinkable Molly Brown,* Marten Prod., MGM.
KIM STANLEY, *Seance On A Wet Afternoon,* Richard Attenborough-Bryan Forbes Prod., ART.

SUPPORTING ACTOR:

PETER USTINOV, Topkapi, Filmways Prod., UA.
JOHN GIELGUD, *Becket.*
STANLEY HOLLOWAY, *My Fair Lady.*
EDMOND O'BRIEN, *Seven Days In May,* Joel Prods., PAR.
LEE TRACY, *The Best Man,* Millar-Turman Prod., UA.

SUPPORTING ACTRESS:

LILA KEDROVA, Zorba The Greek.
GLADYS COOPER, *My Fair Lady.*
DAME EDITH EVANS, *The Chalk Garden,* Quota Rentals, Ltd.-Ross Hunter Prod., U.
GRAYSON HALL, *The Night Of The Iguana,* Seven Arts Prod., MGM.
AGNES MOOREHEAD, *Hush. . .Hush, Sweet Charlotte,* Associates & Aldrich Co. Prod., FOX.

DIRECTING:

GEORGE CUKOR, My Fair Lady.
MICHAEL CACOYANNIS, *Zorba The Greek.*
PETER GLENVILLE, *Becket.*
STANLEY KUBRICK, *Dr. Stangelove Or: How I Learned To Stop Worrying And Love The Bomb.*
ROBERT STEVENSON, *Mary Poppins.*

WRITING:
(Best Story and Screenplay written directly for the screen)
FATHER GOOSE, U-Granox Prod., U. Story by S. H. Barnett. Screenplay by Peter Stone and Frank Tarloff.
A HARD DAY'S NIGHT, Walter Shenson Prod., UA. Alun Owen.
ONE POTATO, TWO POTATO, Bawalco Picture Prod., C5. Story by Orville H. Hampton. Screenplay by Raphael Hayes and Orville H. Hampton.
THE ORGANIZER, Lux-Vides-Mediterranee Cinema Prod., WRC. Age, Scarpelli and Mario Monicelli.
THAT MAN FROM RIO, Ariane-Les Artistes Prod., LOP. Jean-Paul Rappeneau, Ariane Mnouchkine, Daniel Boulanger and Philippe De Broca.
(Best Screenplay based on material from another medium)
BECKET. Edward Anhalt.
DR. STRANGELOVE OR: HOW I LEARNED TO STOP WORRYING AND LOVE THE BOMB. Stanley Kubrick, Peter George and Terry Southern.
MARY POPPINS. Bill Walsh and Don DaGradi.
MY FAIR LADY. Alan Jay Lerner.
ZORBA THE GREEK. Michael Cacoyannis.

CINEMATOGRAPHY:
(Black-and-White)
ZORBA THE GREEK. Walter Lassally.
THE AMERICANIZATION OF EMILY, Martin Ransohoff Prod., MGM. Philip H. Lathrop.
FATE IS THE HUNTER, Arcola Pictures Prod., FOX. Milton Krasner.
HUSH. . .HUSH, SWEET CHARLOTTE. Joseph Biroc.
THE NIGHT OF THE IGUANA. Gabriel Figueroa.
(Color)
MY FAIR LADY. Harry Stradling.
BECKET. Geoffrey Unsworth.
CHEYENNE AUTUMN, John Ford-Bernard Smith Prod., WB. William H. Clothier.
MARY POPPINS. Edward Colman.
THE UNSINKABLE MOLLY BROWN. Daniel L. Fapp.

COSTUME DESIGN:
(Black-and-White)
THE NIGHT OF THE IGUANA. Dorothy Jeakins.
A HOUSE IS NOT A HOME, Clarence Greene-Russell Rouse Prod., EBP. Edith Head.
HUSH. . .HUSH, SWEET CHARLOTTE. Norma Koch.
KISSES FOR MY PRESIDENT, Pearlayne Prod., WB. Howard Shoup.
THE VISIT, Cinecitta-Dear Film-Les Films du Siecle-P.E.C.S. Prod., FOX. Rene Hubert.
(Color)
MY FAIR LADY. Cecil Beaton.
BECKET. Margaret Furse.
MARY POPPINS. Tony Walton.
THE UNSINKABLE MOLLY BROWN. Morton Haack.
WHAT A WAY TO GO, Apjac-Orchard Prod., FOX. Edith Head and Moss Mabry.

ART DIRECTION - SET DECORATION:
(Black-and-White)
ZORBA THE GREEK. Vassilis Fotopoulos.
THE AMERICANIZATION OF EMILY. George W. Davis, Hans Peters and Elliot Scott. Set Decoration: Henry Grace and Robert R. Benton.
HUSH. . .HUSH, SWEET CHARLOTTE. William Glasgow. Set Decoration: Raphael Bretton.
THE NIGHT OF THE IGUANA. Stephen Grimes.
SEVEN DAYS IN MAY. Cary Odell. Set Decoration: Edward G. Boyle.
(Color)
MY FAIR LADY. Gene Allen and Cecil Beaton. Set Decoration: George James Hopkins.
BECKET. John Bryan and Maurice Carter. Set Decoration: Patrick

McLoughlin and Robert Cartwright.
MARY POPPINS. Carroll Clark and William H. Tuntke. Set Decoration: Emile Kuri and Hal Gausman.
THE UNSINKABLE MOLLY BROWN. George W. Davis and Preston Ames. Set Decoration: Henry Grace and Hugh Hunt.
WHAT A WAY TO GO. Jack Martin Smith and Ted Haworth. Set Decoration: Walter M. Scott and Stuart A. Reiss.

FILM EDITING:
MARY POPPINS. Cotton Warburton.
BECKET. Anne Coates.
FATHER GOOSE. Ted J. Kent.
HUSH. . .HUSH, SWEET CHARLOTTE. Michael Luciano.
MY FAIR LADY. William Ziegler.

FOREIGN LANGUAGE FILM:
YESTERDAY, TODAY AND TOMORROW, A Champion-Concordia Production (Italy).
RAVEN'S END, AB Europa Film (Sweden).
SALLAH, A Sallah Film Ltd. Production (Israel).
THE UMBRELLAS OF CHERBOURG, A Parc-Madeleine-Beta Films Production (France).
WOMAN IN THE DUNES, A Teshigahara Production (Japan).

MUSIC - SCORING:
(Music Score—substantially original)
MARY POPPINS. Richard M. Sherman and Robert B. Sherman.
THE FALL OF THE ROMAN EMPIRE, Bronston-Roma Prod., PAR. Dimitri Tiomkin.
HUSH. . .HUSH, SWEET CHARLOTTE. Frank DeVol.
THE PINK PANTHER, Mirisch-G-E Prod., UA. Henry Mancini.
(Scoring of Music-adaptation or treatment)
MY FAIR LADY. Andre Previn.
A HARD DAY'S NIGHT. George Martin.
MARY POPPINS. Irwin Kostal.
ROBIN AND THE 7 HOODS, P-C Prod., WB. Nelson Riddle.
THE UNSINKABLE MOLLY BROWN. Robert Armbruster, Leo Arnaud, Jack Elliott, Jack Hayes, Calvin Jackson and Leo Shuken.

MUSIC - BEST SONG:
CHIM CHIM CHER-EE, Mary Poppins. Music and Lyrics by Richard M. Sherman & Robert B. Sherman.
DEAR HEART, *Dear Heart*, W.B.-Out-Of-Towners Prod., WB. Music, Henry Mancini. Lyrics, Jay Livingston and Ray Evans.
HUSH. . .HUSH, SWEET CHARLOTTE, *Hush. . .Hush, Sweet Charlotte*. Music, Frank DeVol. Lyrics, Mack David.
MY KIND OF TOWN, *Robin And The 7 Hoods*. Music, James Van Heusen. Lyrics, Sammy Cahn.
WHERE LOVE HAS GONE, *Where Love Has Gone*, PAR-Embassy Pictures Prod., PAR. Music, James Van Heusen. Lyrics, Sammy Cahn.

SOUND:
MY FAIR LADY, WB. Studio Sound Department. George R. Groves, Sound Director.
BECKET, Shepperton Studio Sound Department. John Cox, Sound Director.
FATHER GOOSE, U Studio Sound Department. Waldon O. Watson, Sound Director.
MARY POPPINS, Walt Disney Studio Sound Department, Robert O. Cook, Sound Director.
THE UNSINKABLE MOLLY BROWN, MGM Studio Sound Department. Franklin E. Milton, Sound Director.

SHORT FILMS:
(Cartoons)
THE PINK PHINK, Mirisch-Geoffrey Prods., UA. David H. DePatie and Friz Freleng, Prods.
CHRISTMAS CRACKER, NFC, FA.
HOW TO AVOID FRIENDSHIP, RBF. William L. Snyder, Prod.
NUDNIK #2, RBF. William L. Snyder, Prod.
(Live Action Subjects)
CASALS CONDUCTS: 1964, Thalia Films, BEC. Edward Schreiber, Prod.
HELP! MY SNOWMAN'S BURNING DOWN, Carson Davidson Prods., PC. Carson Davidson, Prod.
THE LEGEND OF JIMMY BLUE EYES, Robert Clouse Associates, Topaz Film Corp. Robert Clouse, Prod.

DOCUMENTARY:
(Short Subjects)
NINE FROM LITTLE ROCK, United States Information Agency, Guggenheim Productions.
BREAKING THE HABIT, American Cancer Society, Modern Talking Picture Service. Henry Jacobs and John Korty, Prods.
CHILDREN WITHOUT, National Education Association, Guggenheim Productions.
KENOJUAK, NFC.
140 DAYS UNDER THE WORLD, New Zealand National Film Unit, RNK (New Zealand). Geoffrey Scott and Oxley Hughan, Prods.
(Features)
Jacques-Yves Cousteau's WORLD WITHOUT SUN, Filmad-Les Requins Associes-Orsay-CEIAP, COL. Jacques-Yves Cousteau, Prod.
THE FINEST HOURS, Le Vien Films, Ltd., COL. Jack Le Vien, Prod.
FOUR DAYS IN NOVEMBER, David L. Wolper Prods., UA. Mel Stuart, Prod.
THE HUMAN DUTCH, Haanstra Filmproductie. Bert Haanstra, Prod.
OVER THERE, 1914-18, Zodiac Prods., PC. Jean Aurel, Prod.

VISUAL EFFECTS:
MARY POPPINS. Peter Ellenshaw, Hamilton Luske and Eustace Lycett.
7 FACES OF DR. LAO, Galaxy-Scarus Prod., MGM. Jim Danforth.

SOUND EFFECTS:
GOLDFINGER, Eon Prod., UA. Norman Wanstall.
THE LIVELY SET, U. Robert L. Bratton.

HONORARY AND OTHER:
(Other)
WILLIAM TUTTLE for his outstanding make-up achievement for 7 Faces Of Dr. Lao.

SCIENTIFIC OR TECHNICAL:
(Class I)
PETRO VLAHOS, WADSWORTH E. POHL and UB IWERKS for the conception and perfection of techniques for Color Traveling Matte Composite Cinematography.
(Class II)
SIDNEY P. SOLOW, EDWARD H. REICHARD, CARL W. HAUGE and JOB SANDERSON of Consolidated Film Industries for the design and development of a versatile Automatic 35mm Composite Color Printer.
PIERRE ANGENIEUX for the development of a ten-to-one Zoom Lens for cinematography.
(Class III)
MILTON FORMAN, RICHARD B. GLICKMAN and DANIEL J. PEARLMAN of ColorTran Industries for advancements in the design and application to motion picture photography of lighting units using quartz iodine lamps.
STEWART FILMSCREEN CORPORATION for a seamless translucent Blue Screen for Traveling Matte Color Cinematography.

ANTHONY PAGLIA and the 20TH CENTURY-FOX STUDIO MECHANICAL EFFECTS DEPARTMENT for an improved method of producing Explosion Flash Effects for motion pictures.
EDWARD H. REICHARD and CARL W. HAUGE of Consolidated Film Industries for the design of a Proximity Cue Detector and its application to motion picture printers.
EDWARD H. REICHARD, LEONARD L. SOKOLOW and CARL W. HAUGE of Consolidated Film Industries for the design and application to motion picture laboratory practice of a Stroboscopic Scene Tester for color and black-and-white film.
NELSON TYLER for the design and construction of an improved Helicopter Camera System.

1965

BEST PICTURE:

THE SOUND OF MUSIC, Argyle Enterprises Prod., FOX. Robert Wise, Prod.
DARLING, Anglo-Amalgamated, Ltd. Prod., Embassy. Joseph Janni, Prod.
DOCTOR ZHIVAGO, Sostar S.A.-MGM British Studios, Ltd. Prod., MGM. Carlo Ponti, Prod.
SHIP OF FOOLS, COL. Stanley Kramer, Prod.
A THOUSAND CLOWNS, Harrell Prod., UA. Fred Coe, Prod.

ACTOR:

LEE MARVIN, Cat Ballou, Harold Hecht Prod., COL.
RICHARD BURTON, *The Spy Who Came In From The Cold*, Salem Films, Ltd. Prod., PAR.
LAURENCE OLIVIER, *Othello*, B.H.E. Prod., WB.
ROD STEIGER, *The Pawnbroker*, Ely Landau Prod., AIP.
OSKAR WERNER. *Ship Of Fools.*

ACTRESS:

JULIE CHRISTIE, Darling.
JULIE ANDREWS, *The Sound Of Music.*
SAMANTHA EGGAR, *The Collector,* The Collector Co, COL.
ELIZABETH HARTMAN, *A Patch Of Blue*, Pandro S. Berman-Guy Green Prod., MGM.
SIMONE SIGNORET, *Ship Of Fools.*

SUPPORTING ACTOR:

MARTIN BALSAM, A Thousand Clowns.
IAN BANNEN, *The Flight Of The Phoenix*, Associates & Aldrich Co Prod., FOX.
TOM COURTENAY, *Doctor Zhivago.*
MICHAEL DUNN, *Ship Of Fools.*
FRANK FINLAY, *Othello.*

SUPPORTING ACTRESS:

SHELLEY WINTERS, A Patch Of Blue.
RUTH GORDON, *Inside Daisy Clover*, Park Place Prod., WB.
JOYCE REDMAN, *Othello.*
MAGGIE SMITH, *Othello.*
PEGGY WOOD, *The Sound Of Music.*

DIRECTING:

ROBERT WISE, The Sound Of Music.
DAVID LEAN, *Doctor Zhivago.*
JOHN SCHLESINGER, *Darling.*
HIROSHI TESHIGAHARA, *Woman In The Dunes*, Teshigahara Prod., PC.
WILLIAM WYLER, *The Collector.*

WRITING:

(Best Story and Screenplay written directly for the screen)

DARLING. Frederic Raphael.
CASANOVA '70, C.C. Champion-Les Films Concordia Prod., EBP. Age, Scarpelli, Mario Monicelli, Tonino Guerra, Giorgio Salvioni and Suso Cecchi D'Amico.
THOSE MAGNIFICENT MEN IN THEIR FLYING MACHINES, FOX, Ltd. Prod., FOX. Jack Davies and Ken Annakin.
THE TRAIN, Les Prods. Artistes Associes, UA. Franklin Coen and Frank Davis.
THE UMBRELLAS OF CHERBOURG, Parc-Madeleine Films Prod., American Int'l. Jacques Demy.

(Best Screenplay based on material from another medium)

DOCTOR ZHIVAGO. Robert Bolt.
CAT BALLOU. Walter Newman and Frank R. Pierson.
THE COLLECTOR. Stanley Mann and John Kohn.
SHIP OF FOOLS. Abby Mann.
A THOUSAND CLOWNS. Herb Gardner.

CINEMATOGRAPHY:

(Black-and-White)

SHIP OF FOOLS. Ernest Laszlo.
IN HARM'S WAY, Sigma Prods., PAR. Loyal Griggs.
KING RAT, Coleytown Prod., COL. Burnett Guffey.
MORITURI, Arcola-Colony Prod., FOX. Conrad Hall.
A PATCH OF BLUE. Robert Burks.

(Color)

DOCTOR ZHIVAGO. Freddie Young.
THE AGONY AND THE ECSTASY, Int'l Classics Prod., FOX. Leon Shamroy.
THE GREAT RACE, Patricia-Jalem-Reynard Prod., WB. Russell Harlan.
THE GREATEST STORY EVER TOLD, George Stevens Prod., UA. William C. Mellor & Loyal Griggs.
THE SOUND OF MUSIC. Ted McCord.

COSTUME DESIGN:

(Black-and-White)

DARLING. Julie Harris.
MORITURI. Moss Mabry.
A RAGE TO LIVE, Mirisch Corp. of Delaware-Araho Prod., UA. Howard Shoup.
SHIP OF FOOLS. Bill Thomas and Jean Louis.
THE SLENDER THREAD, PAR. Edith Head.

(Color)

DOCTOR ZHIVAGO. Phyllis Dalton.
THE AGONY AND THE ECSTASY. Vittorio Nino Novarese.
THE GREATEST STORY EVER TOLD. Vittorio Nino Novarese and Marjorie Best.
INSIDE DAISY CLOVER. Edith Head and Bill Thomas.
THE SOUND OF MUSIC. Dorothy Jeakins.

ART DIRECTION - SET DECORATION:

(Black-and-White)

SHIP OF FOOLS. Robert Clatworthy. Set Decoration: Joseph Kish.
KING RAT. Robert Emmet Smith. Set Decoration: Frank Tuttle.
A PATCH OF BLUE. George W. Davis and Urie McCleary. Set Decoration: Henry Grace and Charles S. Thompson.
THE SLENDER THREAD. Hal Pereira and Jack Poplin. Set Decoration: Robert Benton and Joseph Kish.
THE SPY WHO CAME IN FROM THE COLD. Hal Pereira, Tambi Larsen and Edward Marshall. Set Decoration: Josie MacAvin.

(Color)

DOCTOR ZHIVAGO. John Box and Terry Marsh. Set Decoration: Dario Simoni.
THE AGONY AND THE ECSTASY. John DeCuir and and Jack Martin Smith. Set Decoration: Dario Simoni.
THE GREATEST STORY EVER TOLD. Richard Day, William Creber and

David Hall. Set Decoration: Ray Moyer, Fred MacLean and Norman Rockett.
INSIDE DAISY CLOVER. Robert Clatworthy. Set Decoration: George James Hopkins.
THE SOUND OF MUSIC. Boris Leven. Set Decoration: Walter M. Scott and Ruby Levitt.

FILM EDITING:
THE SOUND OF MUSIC. William Reynolds.
CAT BALLOU. Charles Nelson.
DOCTOR ZHIVAGO. Norman Savage.
THE FLIGHT OF THE PHOENIX. Michael Luciano.
THE GREAT RACE. Ralph E. Winters.

FOREIGN LANGUAGE FILM:
THE SHOP ON MAIN STREET, A Ceskoslovensky Film Production (Czechoslovakia).
BLOOD ON THE LAND, Th. Damaskinos & V. Michaelides, A.E.-Finos Film (Greece).
DEAR JOHN, A.B. Sandrew-Ateljeerna (Sweden).
KWAIDAN, A Toho Co, Ltd. Production (Japan).
MARRIAGE ITALIAN STYLE, A Champion-Concordia Production (Italy).

MUSIC - SCORING:
(Music Score-substantially original)
DOCTOR ZHIVAGO. Maurice Jarre.
THE AGONY AND THE ECSTASY. Alex North.
THE GREATEST STORY EVERY TOLD. Alfred Newman.
A PATCH OF BLUE. Jerry Goldsmith.
THE UMBRELLAS OF CHERBOURG. Michel Legrand and Jacques Demy.
(Scoring of Music-adaptation or treatment)
THE SOUND OF MUSIC. Irwin Kostal.
CAT BALLOU. DeVol.
THE PLEASURE SEEKERS, FOX. Lionel Newman and Alexander Courage.
A THOUSAND CLOWNS. Don Walker.
THE UMBRELLAS OF CHERBOURG. Michel Legrand.

MUSIC - BEST SONG:
THE SHADOW OF YOUR SMILE, The Sandpiper, Filmways-Venice Prod., MGM. Music, Johnny Mandel. Lyrics, Paul Francis Webster.
THE BALLAD OF CAT BALLOU, *Cat Ballou*. Music, Jerry Livingston. Lyrics, Mack David.
I WILL WAIT FOR YOU, *The Umbrellas Of Cherbourg*. Music, Michel Legrand. Lyrics, Jacques Demy.
THE SWEETHEART TREE, *The Great Race*. Music, Henry Mancini. Lyrics, Johnny Mercer.
WHAT'S NEW PUSSYCAT?, *What's New Pussycat?*, Famous Artists-Famartists Prod., UA. Music, Burt Bacharach. Lyrics, Hal David.

SOUND:
THE SOUND OF MUSIC, FOX Studio Sound Department, James P. Corcoran, Sound Director; and Todd-AO Sound Department, Fred Hynes, Sound Director.
THE AGONY AND THE ECSTASY, FOX Studio Sound Department. James P. Corcoran, Sound Director.
DOCTOR ZHIVAGO, MGM British Studio Sound Department, A. W. Watkins, Sound Director; and MGM Studio Sound Department. Franklin E. Milton, Sound Director.
THE GREAT RACE, WB. Studio Sound Department. George R. Groves, Sound Director.
SHENANDOAH, U Studio Sound Department. Waldon O. Watson, Sound Director.

SHORT FILMS:
(Cartoons)
THE DOT AND THE LINE, MGM. Chuck Jones and Les Goldman, Prods.
CLAY OR THE ORIGIN OF SPECIES, Harvard University, PC. Eliot Noyes, Jr., Prod.
THE THIEVING MAGPIE (La Gazza Ladra), Giulio Gianini-Emanuele Luzzati, AA. Emanuele Luzzati, Prod.
(Live Action Subjects)
THE CHICKEN (Le Poulet), Renn Prods., PC. Claude Berri, Prod.
FORTRESS OF PEACE, Lothar Wolff Prods. for Farner-Looser Films, CRC. Lothar Wolff, Prod.
SKATERDATER, Byway Prods., UA. Marshal Backlar and Noel Black, Prods.
SNOW, British Transport Films in association with Geoffrey Jones (Films) Ltd., MAN. Edgar Anstey, Prod.
TIME PIECE, Muppets, Inc., PC. Jim Henson, Prod.

DOCUMENTARY:
(Short Subjects)
TO BE ALIVE!, Johnson Wax. Francis Thompson, Inc., Prod.
MURAL ON OUR STREET, Henry Street Settlement, PC. Kirk Smallman, Prod.
OUVERTURE, Mafilm Prods., Hungarofilm-Pathe Contemporary Films.
POINT OF VIEW, Vision Associates Prod., National Tuberculosis Assoc.
YEATS COUNTRY, Aengus Films Ltd. for the Dept. of External Affairs of Ireland. Patrick Carey and Joe Mendoza, Prods.
(Features)
THE ELEANOR ROOSEVELT STORY, Sidney Glazier Prod., AIP. Sidney Glazier, Prod.
THE BATTLE OF THE BULGE. . .THE BRAVE RIFLES, Mascott Prods. Laurence E. Mascott, Prod.
THE FORTH ROAD BRIDGE, Random Film Prods., Ltd., Shell-Mex and B.P. Film Library. Peter Mills, Prod.
LET MY PEOPLE GO, Wolper Prods. Marshall Flaum, Prod.
TO DIE IN MADRID, Ancinex Prods., ALT. Frederic Rossif, Prod.

VISUAL EFFECTS:
THUNDERBALL, Broccoli-Saltzman-McClory Prod., UA. John Stears.
THE GREATEST STORY EVERY TOLD. J. McMillan Johnson.

SOUND EFFECTS:
THE GREAT RACE. Tregoweth Brown.
VON RYAN'S EXPRESS, P-R Prods., FOX. Walter A. Rossi.

HONORARY AND OTHER:
(Irving G. Thalberg Memorial Award)
William Wyler
(Jean Hersholt Humanitarian Award)
Edmond L. DePatie
(Other)
BOB HOPE for unique and distinguished service to our industry and the Academy.

SCIENTIFIC OR TECHNICAL:
(Class II)
ARTHUR J. HATCH of The Strong Electric Corp, subsidiary of General Precision Equipment Corp, for the design and development of an Air Blown Carbon Arc Projection Lamp.
STEFAN KUDELSKI for the design and development of the Nagra portable 1/4' tape recording system for motion picture sound recording.

1966

BEST PICTURE:

A MAN FOR ALL SEASONS, Highland Films, Ltd. Prod., COL. Fred Zinnemann, Prod.
ALFIE, Sheldrake Films, Ltd. Prod., PAR. Lewis Gilbert, Prod.
THE RUSSIANS ARE COMING, THE RUSSIANS ARE COMING, Mirisch Corp. of Delaware Prod., U.A. Norman Jewison, Prod.
THE SAND PEBBLES, Argyle-Solar Prod., FOX. Robert Wise, Prod.
WHO'S AFRAID OF VIRGINIA WOOLF?, Chenault Prod., WB. Ernest Lehman, Prod.

ACTOR:

PAUL SCOFIELD, A Man For All Seasons.
ALAN ARKIN, *The Russians Are Coming, The Russians Are Coming.*
RICHARD BURTON, *Who's Afraid Of Virginia Woolf?*
MICHAEL CAINE, *Alfie.*
STEVE MC QUEEN, *The Sand Pebbles.*

ACTRESS:

ELIZABETH TAYLOR, Who's Afraid Of Virginia Woolf?
ANOUK AIMEE, *A Man And A Woman*, Les Films 13 Prod., AA.
IDA KAMINSKA, *The Shop On Main Street*, Ceskoslovensky Film Co Prod., PRM.
LYNN REDGRAVE, *Georgy Girl*, Everglades Prods., Ltd., COL.
VANESSA REDGRAVE, *Morgan!*, Quintra Films, Ltd. Prod., C5.

SUPPORTING ACTOR:

WALTER MATTHAU, The Fortune Cookie, Phalanx-Jalem-Mirisch Corp. of Delaware Prod., UA.
MAKO, *The Sand Pebbles.*
JAMES MASON, *Georgy Girl.*
GEORGE SEGAL, *Who's Afraid Of Virginia Woolf?*
ROBERT SHAW, *A Man For All Seasons.*

SUPPORTING ACTRESS:

SANDY DENNIS, Who's Afraid Of Virginia Woolf?
WENDY HILLER, *A Man For All Seasons.*
JOCELYNE LAGARDE, *Hawaii*, Mirisch Corp. of Delaware Prod., UA.
VIVIEN MERCHANT, *Alfie.*
GERALDINE PAGE, *You're A Big Boy Now*, Seven Arts.

DIRECTING:

FRED ZINNEMANN, A Man For All Seasons.
MICHELANGELO ANTONIONI, *Blow-Up*, Carlo Ponti Prod., PRE.
RICHARD BROOKS, *The Professionals*, Pax Enterprises Prod., COL.
CLAUDE LELOUCH, *A Man And A Woman.*
MIKE NICHOLS, *Who's Afraid Of Virginia Woolf?*

WRITING:

(Best Story and Screenplay written directly for the screen)

A MAN AND A WOMAN. Story by Claude Lelouch. Screenplay by Pierre Uytterhoeven and Claude Lelouch.
BLOW-UP. Story by Michelangelo Antonioni. Screenplay by Michelangelo Antonioni, Tonino Guerra and Edward Bond.
THE FORTUNE COOKIE. Billy Wilder and I.A.L. Diamond.
KHARTOUM, Julian Blaustein Prod., UA. Robert Ardrey.
THE NAKED PREY, Theodora Prod., PAR. Clint Johnston and Don Peters.

(Best Screenplay based on material from antoher medium)

A MAN FOR ALL SEASONS. Robert Bolt.
ALFIE. Bill Naughton.
THE PROFESSIONALS. Richard Brooks.
THE RUSSIANS ARE COMING, THE RUSSIANS ARE COMING. William Rose.
WHO'S AFRAID OF VIRGINIA WOOLF? Ernest Lehman.

CINEMATOGRAPHY:

(Black-and-White)

WHO'S AFRAID OF VIRGINIA WOOLF? Haskell Wexler.
THE FORTUNE COOKIE. Joseph LaShelle.
GEORGY GIRL. Ken Higgins.
IS PARIS BURNING?, Transcontinental Films-Marianne Prod., PAR. Marcel Grignon.
SECONDS, The Seconds Co, PAR. James Wong Howe.

(Color)

A MAN FOR ALL SEASONS. Ted Moore.
FANTASTIC VOYAGE, FOX. Ernest Laszlo.
HAWAII. Russell Harlan.
THE PROFESSIONALS. Conrad Hall.
THE SAND PEBBLES. Joseph MacDonald.

COSTUME DESIGN:

(Black-and-White)

WHO'S AFRAID OF VIRGINIA WOOLF?. Irene Sharaff.
THE GOSPEL ACCORDING TO ST. MATTHEW, Arco-Lux Cie Cinematografique de France Prod., WRC. Danilo Donati.
MANDRAGOLA, Europix-Consolidated. Danilo Donati.
MISTER BUDDWING, DDD-Cherokee Prod., MGM. Helen Rose.
MORGAN! Jocelyn Rickards.

(Color)

A MAN FOR ALL SEASONS. Elizabeth Haffenden and Joan Bridge.
GAMBIT, U. Jean Louis.
HAWAII. Dorothy Jeakins.
JULIET OF THE SPIRITS, RIZ. S.P.A. Prod., Rizzoli Films. Piero Gherardi.
THE OSCAR, Greene-Rouse Prod., EBP. Edith Head.

ART DIRECTION - SET DECORATION:

(Black-and-White)

WHO'S AFRAID OF VIRGINIA WOOLF? Richard Sylbert. Set Decoration: George James Hopkins.
THE FORTUNE COOKIE. Robert Luthardt. Set Decoration: Edward G. Boyle.
THE GOSPEL ACCORDING TO ST. MATTHEW. Luigi Scaccianoce.
IS PARIS BURNING? Willy Holt. Set Decoration: Marc Frederix and Pierre Guffroy.
MISTER BUDDWING. George W. Davis and Paul Groesse. Set Decoration: Henry Grace and Hugh Hunt.

(Color)

FANTASTIC VOYAGE. Jack Martin Smith and Dale Hennesy. Set Decoration: Walter M. Scott and Stuart A. Reiss.
GAMBIT. Alexander Golitzen and George C. Webb. Set Decoration: John McCarthy and John Austin.
JULIET OF THE SPIRITS. Piero Gherardi.
THE OSCAR. Hal Pereira and Arthur Lonergan. Set Decoration: Robert Benton and James Payne.
THE SAND PEBBLES. Boris Leven. Set Decoration: Walter M. Scott, John Sturtevant and William Kiernan.

FILM EDITING:

GRAND PRIX, Douglas-Lewis-John Frankenheimer-Cherokee Prod., MGM. Fredric Steinkamp, Henry Berman, Stewart Linder and Frank Santillo.
FANTASTIC VOYAGE. William B. Murphy.
THE RUSSIANS ARE COMING, THE RUSSIANS ARE COMING. Hal Ashby and J. Terry Williams.
THE SAND PEBBLES. William Reynolds.
WHO'S AFRAID OF VIRGINIA WOOLF? Sam O'Steen.

FOREIGN LANGUAGE FILM:

A MAN AND A WOMAN.
THE BATTLE OF ALGIERS, Igor Film-Casbah Film Production (Italy).
LOVES OF A BLONDE, Barrandov Film Production (Czechoslovakia).
PHARAOH, Kadr Film Unit Production (Poland).
THREE, Avala Film Production (Yugoslavia).

MUSIC - SCORING:
(Original Music Score)

BORN FREE, Open Road Films, Ltd.-Atlas Films, Ltd. Prod., COL. John Barry.
THE BIBLE, Thalia-A.G. Prod., FOX. Toshiro Mayuzumi.
HAWAII. Elmer Bernstein.
THE SAND PEBBLES. Jerry Goldsmith.
WHO'S AFRAID OF VIRGINIA WOOLF? Alex North.

(Scoring of Music-adaptation or treatment)
A FUNNY THING HAPPENED ON THE WAY TO THE FORUM, Melvin Frank Prod., UA. Ken Thorne.
THE GOSPEL ACCORDING TO ST. MATTHEW. Luis Enrique Bacalov.
RETURN OF THE SEVEN, Mirisch Prods., UA. Elmer Bernstein.
THE SINGING NUN, MGM. Harry Sukman.
STOP THE WORLD--I WANT TO GET OFF, WB. Prods., Ltd., WB. Al Ham.

MUSIC - BEST SONG:
BORN FREE, Born Free. Music, John Barry. Lyrics, Don Black.
ALFIE, Alfie. Music, Burt Bacharach. Lyrics, Hal David.
GEORGY GIRL, Georgy Girl. Music, Tom Springfield. Lyrics, Jim Dale.
MY WISHING DOLL, Hawaii. Music, Elmer Bernstein. Lyrics, Mack David.
A TIME FOR LOVE, An American Dream, WB. Music, Johnny Mandel. Lyrics, Paul Francis Webster.

SOUND:
GRAND PRIX, MGM Studio Sound Department. Franklin E. Milton, Sound Director.
GAMBIT, U Studio Sound Department. Waldon O. Watson, Sound Director.
HAWAII, Samuel Goldwyn Studio Sound Department. Gordon E. Sawyer, Sound Director.
THE SAND PEBBLES, FOX Studio Sound Deparment. James P. Corcoran, Sound Director.
WHO'S AFRAID OF VIRGINIA WOOLF?, WB. Studio Sound Department. George R. Groves, Sound Director.

SHORT FILMS:
(Cartoons)
HERB ALPERT AND THE TIJUANA BRASS DOUBLE FEATURE, Hubley Studio, PAR. John and Faith Hubley, Prods.
THE DRAG, NFC, FA. Wolf Koenig and Robert Verrall, Prods.
THE PINK BLUEPRINT, Mirisch-Geoffrey-DePatie-Freleng, UA. David H. DePatie and Friz Freleng, Prods.

(Live Action Subjects)
WILD WINGS, British Transport Films, MAN. Edgar Anstey, Prod.
TURKEY THE BRIDGE, Samaritan Prods., SCH. Derek Williams, Prod.
THE WINNING STRAIN, Winik Films, PAR. Leslie Winik, Prod.

DOCUMENTARY:
(Short Subjects)
A YEAR TOWARD TOMORROW, Sun Dial Films, Inc. Prod. for Office of Economic Opportunity. Edmond A. Levy, Prod.
ADOLESCENCE, M.K. Prods. Marin Karmitz and Vladimir Forgency, Prods.
COWBOY, United States Information Agency. Michael Ahnemann and Gary Schlosser, Prods.
THE ODDS AGAINST, Vision Associates Prod. for The American Foundation Institute of Corrections. Lee R. Bobker and Helen Kristt Radin, Prods.
SAINT MATTHEW PASSION, Mafilm Studio, HU.

(Features)
THE WAR GAME, BBC Prod. for the British Film Institute, PC. Peter Watkins, Prod.
THE FACE OF GENIUS, WBZ-TV, Group W, Boston. Alfred R. Kelman, Prod.
HELICOPTER CANADA, Centennial Commission, NFC. Peter Jones and Tom Daly, Prods.
LE VOLCAN INTERDIT (The Forbidden Volcano), Cine Documents Tazieff, ATO. Haroun Tazieff, Prod.
THE REALLY BIG FAMILY, David L. Wolper Prod. Alex Grasshoff, Prod.

VISUAL EFFECTS:
FANTASTIC VOYAGE. Art Cruickshank.
HAWAII. Linwood G. Dunn.

SOUND EFFECTS:
GRAND PRIX. Gordon Daniel.
FANTASTIC VOYAGE. Walter Rossi.

HONORARY AND OTHER:
(Irving G. Thalberg Memorial Award)
Robert Wise
(Jean Hersholt Humanitarian Award)
George Bagnall
(Other)
Y. FRANK FREEMAN for unusual and outstanding service to the Academy during his thirty years in Hollywood.
YAKIMA CANUTT for achievements as a stunt man and for developing safety devices to protect stunt men everywhere.

SCIENTIFIC OR TECHNICAL:
(Class II)
MITCHELL CAMERA CORPORATION for the design and development of the Mitchell Mark II 35mm Portable Motion Picture Reflex Camera.
ARNOLD & RICHTER KG for the design and development of the Arriflex 35mm Portable Motion Picture Reflex Camera.
(Class III)
PANAVISION INCORPORATED for the design of the Panatron Power Inverter and its application to motion picture camera operation.
CARROLL KNUDSON for the production of a Composers Manual for Motion Picture Music Synchronization.
RUBY RAKSIN for the production of a Composers Manual for Motion Picture Music Synchronization.

1967

BEST PICTURE:
IN THE HEAT OF THE NIGHT, Mirisch Corp. Prod., UA. Walter Mirisch, Prod.
BONNIE AND CLYDE, Tatira-Hiller Prod., WB.-Seven Arts. Warren Beatty, Prod.
DOCTOR DOLITTLE, Apjac Prods., FOX. Arthur P. Jacobs, Prod.
THE GRADUATE, Mike Nichols-Lawrence Turman Prod., EBP. Lawrence Turman, Prod.
GUESS WHO'S COMING TO DINNER, COL. Stanley Kramer, Prod.

ACTOR:
ROD STEIGER, In The Heat Of The Night.
WARREN BEATTY, Bonnie And Clyde.
DUSTIN HOFFMAN in The Graduate.
PAUL NEWMAN, Cool Hand Luke, Jalem Prod., WBS.
SPENCER TRACY, Guess Who's Coming To Dinner.

ACTRESS:
KATHARINE HEPBURN, Guess Who's Coming To Dinner.
ANNE BANCROFT, The Graduate.
FAYE DUNAWAY, Bonnie And Clyde.
DAME EDITH EVANS, The Whisperers, Seven Pines Prods., Ltd., UA.
AUDREY HEPBURN, Wait Until Dark, WBS.

SUPPORTING ACTOR:
GEORGE KENNEDY, Cool Hand Luke.
JOHN CASSAVETES, *The Dirty Dozen*, MKH Prods., Ltd., MGM.
GENE HACKMAN, *Bonnie And Clyde*.
CECIL KELLAWAY, *Guess Who's Coming To Dinner*.
MICHAEL J. POLLARD, *Bonnie And Clyde*.

SUPPORTING ACTRESS:
ESTELLE PARSONS, Bonnie And Clyde.
CAROL CHANNING, *Thoroughly Modern Millie*, Ross Hunter-U Prod., U.
MILDRED NATWICK, *Barefoot In The Park*, Hal Wallis Prod., PAR.
BEAH RICHARDS, *Guess Who's Coming To Dinner*.
KATHARINE ROSS, *The Graduate*.

DIRECTING:
MIKE NICHOLS, The Graduate.
RICHARD BROOKS, *In Cold Blood*, Pax Enterprises Prod., COL.
NORMAN JEWISON, *In The Heat Of The Night*.
STANLEY KRAMER, *Guess Who's Coming To Dinner*.
ARTHUR PENN, *Bonnie And Clyde*.

WRITING:
(Best Story and Screenplay written directly for the screen)
GUESS WHO'S COMING TO DINNER. William Rose.
BONNIE AND CLYDE. David Newman and Robert Benton.
DIVORCE AMERICAN STYLE, Tandem Prods. for NGP, COL. Story by Robert Kaufman. Screenplay by Norman Lear.
LA GUERRE EST FINIE, Sofracima and Europa-Film Prod., BRA. Jorge Semprun.
TWO FOR THE ROAD, Stanley Donen Films Prod., FOX. Frederic Raphael.

(Best Screenplay based on material from another medium)
IN THE HEAT OF THE NIGHT. Stirling Silliphant.
COOL HAND LUKE. Donn Pearce and Frank R. Pierson.
THE GRADUATE. Calder Willingham and Buck Henry.
IN COLD BLOOD. Richard Brooks.
ULYSSES, Walter Reade, Jr.-Joseph Strick Prod., WRC. Joseph Strick and Fred Haines.

CINEMATOGRAPHY:
BONNIE AND CLYDE. Burnett Guffey.
CAMELOT, WBS. Richard H. Kline.
DOCTOR DOLITTLE. Robert Surtees.
THE GRADUATE. Robert Surtees.
IN COLD BLOOD. Conrad Hall.

COSTUME DESIGN:
CAMELOT. John Truscott.
BONNIE AND CLYDE. Theadora Van Runkle.
THE HAPPIEST MILLIONAIRE, Walt Disney Prods., BV. Bill Thomas.
THE TAMING OF THE SHREW, Royal Films Int'l-Films Artistici Internazionali S.r.L. Prod., COL. Irene Sharaff and Danilo Donati.
THOROUGHLY MODERN MILLIE. Jean Louis.

ART DIRECTION - SET DECORATION:
CAMELOT. John Truscott and Edward Carrere. Set Decoration: John W. Brown.
DOCTOR DOLITTLE. Mario Chiari, Jack Martin Smith and Ed Graves. Set Decoration: Walter M. Scott and Stuart A. Reiss.
GUESS WHO'S COMING TO DINNER. Robert Clatworthy. Set Decoration: Frank Tuttle.
THE TAMING OF THE SHREW. Renzo Mongiardino, John DeCuir, Elven Webb and Giuseppe Mariani. Set Decoration: Dario Simoni and Luigi Gervasi.
THOROUGHLY MODERN MILLIE. Alexander Golitzen and George C. Webb. Set Decoration: Howard Bristol.

FILM EDITING:
IN THE HEAT OF THE NIGHT. Hal Ashby.
BEACH RED, Theodora Prods., UA. Frank P. Keller.
THE DIRTY DOZEN. Michael Luciano.
DOCTOR DOLITTLE. Samuel E. Beetley and Marjorie Fowler.
GUESS WHO'S COMING TO DINNER. Robert C. Jones.

FOREIGN LANGUAGE FILM:
CLOSELY WATCHED TRAINS, Barrandov Film Studio Production (Czechoslovakia).
EL AMOR BRUJO, Films R.B., S.A. Production (Spain).
I EVEN MET HAPPY GYPSIES, Avala Film Production (Yugoslavia).
LIVE FOR LIFE, Les Films Ariane-Les Productions Artistes Associes-Vides Films Production (France).
PORTRAIT OF CHIEKO, Shochiku Co., Ltd. Production (Japan).

MUSIC - SCORING:
(Original Music Score)
THOROUGHLY MODERN MILLIE. Elmer Bernstein.
COOL HAND LUKE. Lalo Schifrin.
DOCTOR DOLITTLE. Leslie Bricusse.
FAR FROM THE MADDING CROWD, Appia Films, Ltd. Prod., MGM. Richard Rodney Bennett.
IN COLD BLOOD. Quincy Jones.

(Scoring of Music-adaptation or treatment)
CAMELOT. Alfred Newman and Ken Darby.
DOCTOR DOLITTLE. Lionel Newman and Alexander Courage.
GUESS WHO'S COMING TO DINNER. DeVol.
THOROUGHLY MODERN MILLIE. Andre Previn and Joseph Gershenson.
VALLEY OF THE DOLLS, Red Lion Prods., FOX. John Williams.

MUSIC - BEST SONG:
TALK TO THE ANIMALS, Doctor Dolittle. Music and lyrics by Leslie Bricusse.
THE BARE NECESSITIES, *The Jungle Book*, Walt Disney Prods., BV. Music and Lyrics by Terry Gilkyson.
THE EYES OF LOVE, *Banning*, U. Music, Quincy Jones. Lyrics, Bob Russell.
THE LOOK OF LOVE, *Casino Royale*, Famous Artists Prods., Ltd., COL. Music, Burt Bacharach. Lyrics, Hal David.
THOROUGHLY MODERN MILLIE, *Thoroughly Modern Millie*. Music and lyrics by James Van Heusen and Sammy Cahn.

SOUND:
IN THE HEAT OF THE NIGHT, Samuel Goldwyn Studio Sound Department.
CAMELOT, WBS Sound Department.
THE DIRTY DOZEN, MGM Studio Sound Department.
DOCTOR DOLITTLE, FOX Studio Sound Department.
THOROUGLY MODERN MILLIE, U Studio Sound Department.

SHORT FILMS:
(Cartoons)
THE BOX, Murakami-Wolf Films, BRA. Fred Wolf, Prod.
HYPOTHESE BETA, Films Orzeaux, PC. Jean-Charles Meunier, Prod.
WHAT ON EARTH!, NFC, COL. Robert Verrall and Wolf Koenig, Prods.

(Live Action Subjects)
A PLACE TO STAND, T.D.F. Prod. for the Ontario Department of Economics and Development, COL. Christopher Chapman, Prod.
PADDLE TO THE SEA, NFC, FA. Julian Biggs, Prod.
SKY OVER HOLLAND, John Ferno Prod. for The Netherlands, SEN. John Ferno, Prod.
STOP, LOOK AND LISTEN, MGM. Len Janson and Chuck Menville, Prods.

DOCUMENTARY:
(Short Subjects)
THE REDWOODS, King Screen Prods. Mark Harris and Trevor Greenwood, Prods.
MONUMENT TO THE DREAM, Guggenheim Prods. Charles E. Guggenheim, Prod.
A PLACE TO STAND, T.D.F. Prod. for The Ontario Dept. of Economics and Development. Christopher Chapman, Prod.
SEE YOU AT THE PILLAR, ABP. Robert Fitchett, Prod.
WHILE I RUN THIS RACE, Sun Dial Films for VISTA, An Economic Opportunity Program. Carl V. Ragsdale, Prod.

(Features)
THE ANDERSON PLATOON, French Broadcasting System. Pierre Schoendoerffer, Prod.
FESTIVAL, Patchke Prods. Murray Lerner, Prod.
HARVEST, United States Information Agency. Carroll Ballard, Prod.
A KING'S STORY, Jack Le Vien Prod. Jack Le Vien, Prod.
A TIME FOR BURNING, Quest Prods. for Lutheran Film Associates. William C. Jersey, Prod.

VISUAL EFFECTS:
DOCTOR DOLITTLE. L. B. Abbott.
TOBRUK, Gibraltar Prods.-Corman Co-U Prod., U. Howard A. Anderson, Jr. and Albert Whitlock.

SOUND EFFECTS:
THE DIRTY DOZEN. John Poyner.
IN THE HEAT OF THE NIGHT. James A. Richard.

HONORARY AND OTHER:
(Irving G. Thalberg Memorial Award)
Alfred Hitchcock
(Jean Hersholt Humanitarian Award)
Gregory Peck
(Other)
ARTHUR FREED for distinguished service to the Academy and the production of six top-rated Awards telecasts.

SCIENTIFIC OR TECHNICAL:
(Class III)
ELECTRO-OPTICAL DIVISION of the KOLLMORGEN CORPORATION for the design and development of a series of Motion Picture Projection Lenses.
PANAVISION INCORPORATED for a Variable Speed Motor for Motion Picture Cameras.
FRED R. WILSON of the SAMUEL GOLDWYN STUDIO SOUND DEPARTMENT for an Audio Level Clamper.
WALDON O. WATSON and the UNIVERSAL CITY STUDIO SOUND DEPARTMENT for new concepts in the design of a Music Scoring Stage.

1968

BEST PICTURE:
OLIVER!, Romulus Films, COL, John Woolf, Prod.
The Franco Zeffirelli Prodn of ROMEO & JULIET, B.H.E. Film-Verona Prod.-Dino De Laurentiis Cinematografica Prod., PAR. Anthony Havelock-Allan and John Brabourne, Prods.
FUNNY GIRL, Rastar Prods., COL. Ray Stark, Prod.
THE LION IN WINTER, Haworth Prods., AVE. Martin Poll, Prod.
RACHEL, RACHEL, Kayos Prod., WB.-Seven Arts. Paul Newman, Prod.

ACTOR:
CLIFF ROBERTSON, Charly, American Broadcasting Companies-Selmur Pictures Prod., CRC.
ALAN ARKIN, The Heart Is A Lonely Hunter, WBS.
ALAN BATES, The Fixer, John Frankenheimer-Edward Lewis Prods., MGM.
RON MOODY, Oliver!
PETER O'TOOLE, The Lion In Winter.

ACTRESS:
KATHARINE HEPBURN, The Lion In Winter.
BARBRA STREISAND, Funny Girl.
PATRICIA NEAL, The Subject Was Roses, MGM.
VANESSA REDGRAVE, Isadora, Robert and Raymond Hakim-U, Ltd. Prod., U.
JOANNE WOODWARD, Rachel, Rachel.

SUPPORTING ACTOR:
JACK ALBERTSON, The Subject Was Roses.
SEYMOUR CASSEL, Faces, John Cassavetes Prod., WRC.
DANIEL MASSEY, Star!, Robert Wise Prod., FOX.
JACK WILD, Oliver!
GENE WILDER, The Prods, Sidney Glazier Prod., AVE.

SUPPORTING ACTRESS:
RUTH GORDON, Rosemary's Baby, William Castle Enterprises Prod., PAR.
LYNN CARLIN, Faces.
SONDRA LOCKE, The Heart Is A Lonely Hunter.
KAY MEDFORD, Funny Girl.
ESTELLE PARSONS, Rachel, Rachel.

DIRECTING:
CAROL REED, Oliver!
ANTHONY HARVEY, The Lion In Winter.
STANLEY KUBRICK, 2001: A Space Odyssey, Polaris Prod., MGM.
GILLO PONTECORVO, The Battle Of Algiers, Igor-Casbah Film Prod., AA.
FRANCO ZEFFIRELLI, The Franco Zeffirelli prodn of ROMEO & JULIET.

WRITING:
(Best Story and Screenplay written directly for the screen)
THE PRODUCERS. Mel Brooks.
THE BATTLE OF ALGIERS. Franco Solinas and Gillo Pontecorvo.
FACES. John Cassavetes.
HOT MILLIONS, Mildred Freed Alberg Prod., MGM. Ira Wallach and Peter Ustinov.
2001: A SPACE ODYSSEY. Stanley Kubrick and Arthur C. Clarke.

(Best Screenplay based on material from another medium)
THE LION IN WINTER. James Goldman.
THE ODD COUPLE, Howard W. Koch Prod., PAR. Neil Simon.
OLIVER! Vernon Harris.
RACHEL, RACHEL. Stewart Stern.
ROSEMARY'S BABY. Roman Polanski.

CINEMATOGRAPHY:
The Franco Zeffirelli prodn of ROMEO & JULIET. Pasqualino De Santis.
FUNNY GIRL. Harry Stradling.
ICE STATION ZEBRA, Filmways Prod., MGM. Daniel L. Fapp.
OLIVER! Oswald Morris.
STAR! Ernest Laszlo.

COSTUME DESIGN:

The Franco Zeffirelli prodn of ROMEO & JULIET. Danilo Donati.
THE LION IN WINTER. Margaret Furse.
OLIVER! Phyllis Dalton.
PLANET OF THE APES, APJAC Prods., FOX. Morton Haack.
STAR! Donald Brooks.

ART DIRECTION - SET DECORATION:

OLIVER! John Box and Terence Marsh. Set Decoration: Vernon Dixon and Ken Muggleston.
THE SHOES OF THE FISHERMAN, George Englund Prod., MGM. George W. Davis and Edward Carfagno.
STAR! Boris Leven. Set Decoration: Walter M. Scott and Howard Bristol.
2001: A SPACE ODYSSEY. Tony Masters, Harry Lange and Ernie Archer.
WAR AND PEACE, Mosfilm Prod., WRC. Mikhail Bogdanov and Gennady Myasnikov. Set Decoration: G. Koshelev and V. Uvarov.

FILM EDITING:

BULLITT, Solar Prod., WBS. Frank P. Keller.
FUNNY GIRL. Robert Swink, Maury Winetrobe and William Sands.
THE ODD COUPLE. Frank Bracht.
OLIVER!. Ralph Kemplen.
WILD IN THE STREETS, AIP. Fred Feitshans and Eve Newman.

FOREIGN LANGUAGE FILM:

WAR AND PEACE.
THE BOYS OF PAUL STREET, Bohgros Films-Mafilm Studio I Production (Hungary).
THE FIREMEN'S BALL, Barrandov Film Studio Production (Czechoslovakia).
THE GIRL WITH THE PISTOL, Documento Film Production (Italy).
STOLEN KISSES, Les Films du Carrosse-Les Productions Artistes Associes Production (France).

MUSIC - SCORING:

(Best Original Score for a Motion Picture-not a musical)
THE LION IN WINTER. John Barry.
THE FOX, Raymond Stross-Motion Pictures Int'l Prod., CLR. Lalo Schifrin.
PLANET OF THE APES. Jerry Goldsmith.
THE SHOES OF THE FISHERMAN. Alex North.
THE THOMAS CROWN AFFAIR, Mirisch-Simkoe-Solar Prod., UA. Michel Legrand.

(Best Score of a Musical Picture—original or adaptation)
OLIVER! Adapted by John Green.
FINIAN'S RAINBOW, WBS. Adapted by Ray Heindorf.
FUNNY GIRL. Adapted by Walter Scharf.
STAR! Adapted by Lennie Hayton.
THE YOUNG GIRLS OF ROCHEFORT, Mag Bodard-Gilbert de Goldschmidt-Parc Film-Madeleine Films Prod., WBS. Michel Legrand and Jacques Demy.

MUSIC - BEST SONG:

THE WINDMILLS OF YOUR MIND, The Thomas Crown Affair. Music, Michel Legrand. Lyrics, Alan and Marilyn Bergman.
CHITTY CHITTY BANG BANG, *Chitty Chitty Bang Bang*, Warfield Prods., UA. Music and lyrics by Richard M. Sherman and Robert B. Sherman.
FOR LOVE OF IVY, *For Love Of Ivy*, American Broadcasting Companies-Palomar Pictures Int'l Prod., CRC. Music, Quincy Jones. Lyrics, Bob Russell.
FUNNY GIRL, *Funny Girl*. Music, Jule Styne. Lyrics, Bob Merrill.
STAR! *Star!* Music, Jimmy Van Heusen. Lyrics, Sammy Cahn.

SOUND:

OLIVER! Shepperton Studio Sound Department.
BULLITT, WBS.-Seven Arts Studio Sound Department.
FINIAN'S RAINBOW, WBS.-Seven Arts Studio Sound Department.
FUNNY GIRL, COL Studio Sound Department.
STAR! FOX Studio Sound Department.

SHORT FILMS:

(Cartoons)
WINNIE THE POOH AND THE BLUSTERY DAY, Walt Disney Prods., BV. Walt Disney, Prod.
THE HOUSE THAT JACK BUILT, COL. Wolf Koenig and Jim MacKay, Prods.
THE MAGIC PEAR TREE, Murakami-Wolf Prods., BCP. Jimmy Murakami, Prod.
WINDY DAY, Hubley Studios, PAR. John and Faith Hubley, Prods.

(Live Action Subjects)
ROBERT KENNEDY REMEMBERED, Guggenheim Prods., NGP. Charles Guggenheim, Prod.
THE DOVE, Coe-Davis, SCH. George Coe, Sidney Davis and Anthony Lover, Prods.
DUO, NFC, COL.
PRELUDE, Prelude Co, EX. John Astin, Prod.

DOCUMENTARY:

(Short Subjects)
WHY MAN CREATES, Saul Bass & Associates. Saul Bass, Prod.
THE HOUSE THAT ANANDA BUILT, Films Division, Government of India. Fali Bilimoria, Prod.
THE REVOLVING DOOR, Vision Associates for the American Foundation Institute of Corrections. Lee R. Bobker, Prod.
A SPACE TO GROW, Office of Economic Opportunity for Project Upward Bound. Thomas P. Kelly, Jr., Prod.
A WAY OUT OF THE WILDERNESS, John Sutherland Prods. Dan E. Weisburd, Prod.

(Features)
JOURNEY INTO SELF, Western Behavioral Sciences Institute. Bill McGaw, Prod.
A FEW NOTES ON OUR FOOD PROBLEM, United States Information Agency. James Blue, Prod.
THE LEGENDARY CHAMPIONS, Turn Of The Century Fights. William Cayton, Prod.
OTHER VOICES, DHS Films. David H. Sawyer, Prod.
YOUNG AMERICANS, The Young Americans Prod. Robert Cohn and Alex Grasshoff, Prods. (Declared ineligible May 7, 1969 because first released during 1967.)

VISUAL EFFECTS:

2001: A SPACE ODYSSEY. Stanley Kubrick.
ICE STATION ZEBRA. Hal Millar and J. McMillan Johnson.

HONORARY AND OTHER:

(Jean Hersholt Humanitarian Award)

Martha Raye

(Other)

JOHN CHAMBERS for his outstanding make-up achievement for Planet Of The Apes.
ONNA WHITE for her outstanding choreography achievement for Oliver!.

SCIENTIFIC OR TECHNICAL:

(Class I)
PHILIP V. PALMQUIST of MINNESOTA MINING AND MANUFACTURING CO., DR. HERBERT MEYER of the MOTION PICTURE AND TELEVISION RESEARCH CENTER, and CHARLES D. STAFFELL of the RANK ORGANISATION for the development of a successful embodiment of the reflex background projection system for composite cinematography.
EASTMAN KODAK COMPANY for the development and introduction

of a color reversal intermediate film for motion pictures.
(Class II)
DONALD W. NORWOOD for the design and development of the Norwood Photographic Exposure Meters.
EASTMAN KODAK COMPANY and PRODUCERS SERVICE COMPANY for the development of a new high-speed step-optical reduction printer.
EDMUND M. DiGIULIO, NIELS G. PETERSEN and NORMAN S. HUGHES of the CINEMA PRODUCT DEVELOPMENT COMPANY for the design and application of a conversion which makes available the reflex viewing system for motion picture cameras.
OPTICAL COATING LABORATORIES, INC., for the development of an improved anti-reflection coating for photographic and projection lens systems.
EASTMAN KODAK COMPANY for the introduction of a new high speed motion picture color negative film.
PANAVISION INCORPORATED for the conception, design and introduction of a 65mm hand-held motion picture camera.
TODD-AO COMPANY and the MITCHELL CAMERA COMPANY for the design and engineering of the Todd-AO hand-held motion picture camera.
(Class III)
CARL W. HAUGE and EDWARD H. REICHARD of CONSOLIDATED FILM INDUSTRIES and E. MICHAEL MEAHL and ROY J. RIDENOUR of RAMTRONICS for engineering an automatic exposure control for printing-machine lamps.
EASTMAN KODAK COMPANY for a new direct positive film and CONSOLIDATED FILM INDUSTRIES for the application of this film to the making of post-production work prints.

1969

BEST PICTURE:

MIDNIGHT COWBOY, Jerome Hellman-John Schlesinger Production. UA. Jerome Hellman, Prod.
ANNE OF THE THOUSAND DAYS, Hal B. Wallis-U Pictures, Ltd. Production, U. Hal B. Wallis, Prod.
BUTCH CASSIDY AND THE SUNDANCE KID, George Roy Hill-Paul Monash Prod., FOX. John Foreman, Prod.
HELLO, DOLLY!, Chenault Production, FOX. Ernest Lehman, Prod.
Z, Reggane Films-O.N.C.I.C. Production, Cinema V. Jacques Perrin and Hamed Rachedi, Prods.

ACTOR:

JOHN WAYNE, True Grit, Hal Wallis Prod., PAR.
RICHARD BURTON, Anne Of The Thousand Days.
DUSTIN HOFFMAN, Midnight Cowboy.
PETER O'TOOLE, Goodbye, Mr. Chips, APJAC Prod., MGM.
JON VOIGHT, Midnight Cowboy.

ACTRESS:

MAGGIE SMITH, The Prime Of Miss Jean Brodie, FOX Prods, Ltd., FOX.
GENEVIEVE BUJOLD, Anne Of The Thousand Days.
JANE FONDA, They Shoot Horses, Don't They?, Chartoff-Winkler-Pollack Prod., ABC Pictures Presentation, CRC.
LIZA MINNELLI, The Sterile Cuckoo, Boardwalk Prods., PAR.
JEAN SIMMONS, The Happy Ending, Pax Films Prod., UA.

SUPPORTING ACTOR:

GIG YOUNG, They Shoot Horses, Don't They?
RUPERT CROSSE, The Reivers, Irving Ravetch-Arthur Kramer-Solar Prods., Cinema Center Films Presentation, NGP.
ELLIOTT GOULD, Bob & Carol & Ted & Alice, Frankovich Prods., COL.
JACK NICHOLSON, Easy Rider, Pando-Raybert Prods., COL.
ANTHONY QUAYLE, Anne Of The Thousand Days.

SUPPORTING ACTRESS:

GOLDIE HAWN, Cactus Flower, Frankovich Prods., COL.
CATHERINE BURNS, Last Summer, Frank Perry-Alsid Prod., AA.
DYAN CANNON, Bob & Carol & Ted & Alice.
SYLVIA MILES, Midnight Cowboy.
SUSANNAH YORK, They Shoot Horses, Don't They?

DIRECTING:

JOHN SCHLESINGER, Midnight Cowboy.
COSTA-GAVRAS, Z.
GEORGE ROY HILL, Butch Cassidy And The Sundance Kid.
ARTHUR PENN, Alice's Restaurant, Florin Prod., UA.
SYDNEY POLLACK, They Shoot Horses, Don't They?

WRITING:

(Best Story and Screenplay based on material not previously published or produced)
BUTCH CASSIDY AND THE SUNDANCE KID. Willaim Goldman.
BOB & CAROL & TED & ALICE. Paul Mazursky and Larry Tucker.
THE DAMNED, Pegaso-Praesidens Film Prod., WB. Story by Nicola Badalucco. Screenplay by Nicola Badalucco, Enrico Medioli and Luchino Visconti.
EASY RIDER. Peter Fonda, Dennis Hopper and Terry Southern.
THE WILD BUNCH, Phil Feldman Prod., WB. Story by Walon Green and Roy N. Sickner. Screenplay by Walon Green and Sam Peckinpah.
(Best Screenplay based on material from another medium)
MIDNIGHT COWBOY. Waldo Salt.
ANNE OF THE THOUSAND DAYS. John Hale and Bridget Boland. Adaptation by Richard Sokolove.
GOODBYE, COLUMBUS, Willow Tree Prods., PAR. Arnold Schulman.
THEY SHOOT HORSES, DON'T THEY? James Poe and Robert E. Thompson.
Z. Jorge Semprun and Costa-Gavras.

CINEMATOGRAPHY:

BUTCH CASSIDY AND THE SUNDANCE KID. Conrad Hall.
ANNE OF THE THOUSAND DAYS. Arthur Ibbetson.
BOB & CAROL & TED & ALICE. Charles B. Lang.
HELLO, DOLLY! Harry Stradling.
MAROONED, Frankovich-Sturges Prod., COL. Daniel Fapp.

COSTUME DESIGN:

ANNE OF THE THOUSAND DAYS. Margaret Furse.
GAILY, GAILY, Mirisch-Cartier Prod., UA. Ray Aghayan.
HELLO, DOLLY! Irene Sharaff.
SWEET CHARITY, U. Edith Head.
THEY SHOOT HORSES, DON'T THEY? Donfeld.

ART DIRECTION - SET DECORATION:

HELLO, DOLLY! John DeCuir, Jack Martin Smith and Herman Blumenthal. Set Decoration: Walter M. Scott, George Hopkins and Raphael Bretton.
ANNE OF THE THOUSAND DAYS. Maurice Carter and Lionel Couch. Set Decoration: Patrick McLoughlin.
GAILY, GAILY. Robert Boyle and George B. Chan. Set Decoration: Edward Boyle and Carl Biddiscombe.
SWEET CHARITY. Alexander Golitzen and George C. Webb. Set Decoration: Jack D. Moore.
THEY SHOOT HORSES, DON'T THEY? Harry Horner. Set Decoration: Frank McKelvey.

FILM EDITING:

Z. Francoise Bonnot.
HELLO, DOLLY! William Reynolds.
MIDNIGHT COWBOY. Hugh A. Robertson.
THE SECRET OF SANTA VITTORIA, Stanley Kramer Co Prod., UA. William Lyon and Earle Herdan.
THEY SHOOT HORSES, DON'T THEY? Fredric Steinkamo.

FOREIGN LANGUAGE FILM:
Z.
ADALEN '31, AB Svensk Filmindustri Production (Sweden).
THE BATTLE OF NERETVA, United Film Prods-Igor Film-Eichberg Film-Commonwealth United Production (Yugoslavia).
THE BROTHERS KARAMAZOV, Mosfilm Production (U.S.S.R.)
MY NIGHT WITH MAUD, Films du Losange-F.F.P.-Films du Carrosse-Films des Deux Mondes- Films de la Pleiade-Gueville-Renn-Simar Films Production (France).

MUSIC - SCORING:
(Best Original Score for a Motion Picture-not a musical)
BUTCH CASSIDY AND THE SUNDANCE KID. Burt Bacharach.
ANNE OF THE THOUSAND DAYS. Georges Delerue.
THE REIVERS. John Williams.
THE SECRET OF SANTA VITTORIA. Ernest Gold.
THE WILD BUNCH. Jerry Fielding.
(Best Score of a Musical Picture-original or adaptation)
HELLO, DOLLY! Adapted by Lennie Hayton and Lionel Newman.
GOODBYE, MR. CHIPS. Musics and lyric by Leslie Bricusse. Adapted by John Williams.
PAINT YOUR WAGON, Alan Jay Lerner Prod., PAR. Adapted by Nelson Riddle.
SWEET CHARITY. Adapted by Cy Coleman.
THEY SHOOT HORSES, DON'T THEY? Adapted by John Green and Albert Woodbury.

MUSIC - BEST SONG:
RAINDROPS KEEP FALLIN' ON MY HEAD, *Butch Cassidy And The Sundance Kid.* **Music, Burt Bacharach. Lyrics, Hal David.**
COME SATURDAY MORNING, *The Sterile Cuckoo.* Music, Fred Karlin. Lyrics, Dory Previn.
JEAN, *The Prime Of Miss Jean Brodie.* Music and lyrics by Rod McKuen.
TRUE GRIT, *True Grit.* Music, Elmer Bernstein. Lyrics, Don Black. Lyrics, Don Black.
WHAT ARE YOU DOING THE REST OF YOUR LIFE, *The Happy Ending.* Music, Michel Legrand. Lyrics, Alan and Marilyn Bergman.

SOUND:
HELLO DOLLY! Jack Solomon and Murray Spivack.
ANNE OF THE THOUSAND DAYS. John Aldred.
BUTCH CASSIDY AND THE SUNDANCE KID. Willaim Edmundson and David Dockendorf.
GAILY, GAILY. Robert Martin and Clem Portman.
MAROONED. Les Fresholtz and Arthur Piantadosi.

SHORT FILMS:
(Cartoons)
IT'S TOUGH TO BE A BIRD, Walt Disney Prods., BV. Ward Kimball, Prod.
OF MEN AND DEMONS, Hubley Studios, PAR. John and Faith Hubley, Prods.
WALKING, NFC, COL. Ryan Larkin, Prod.
(Live Action Subjects)
THE MAGIC MACHINES, Fly-By-Night Prods., MAN. Joan Keller Stern, Prod.
BLAKE, NFC, VAU. Doug Jackson, Prod.
PEOPLE SOUP, Pangloss Prods., COL. Marc Merson, Prod.

DOCUMENTARY:
(Short Subjects)
CZECHOSLOVAKIA 1968, Sanders-Fresco Film Makers for United States Information Agency. Denis Sanders and Robert M. Tresco, Prods.
AN IMPRESSION OF JOHN STEINBECK: WRITER, Donald Wrye Prods. for United States Information Agency. Donald Wrye, Prod.
JENNY IS A GOOD THING, A.C.I. Prod. for Project Head Start. Joan Horvath, Prod.
LEO BEUERMAN, Centron Prod. Arthur H. Wolf and Russell A. Mosser, Prods.
THE MAGIC MACHINES, Fly-By-Night Prods. Joan Keller Stern, Prod.
(Features)
ARTHUR RUBINSTEIN - THE LOVE OF LIFE, Midem Prod. Bernard Chevry, Prod.
BEFORE THE MOUNTAIN WAS MOVED, Robert K. Sharpe Prods. for The Office of Economic Opportunity. Robert K. Sharpe, Prod.
IN THE YEAR OF THE PIG, Emile de Antonio Prod. Emile de Antonio, Prod.
THE OLYMPICS IN MEXICO, Film Section of the Organizing Committee for the XIX Olympic Games.
THE WOLF MEN, MGM Documentary. Irwin Rosten, Prod.

VISUAL EFFECTS:
MAROONED. Robbie Robertson.
KRAKATOA, EAST OF JAVA, American Broadcasting Companies-CRC Prod., Cinerama. Eugene Lourie and Alex Weldon.

HONORARY AND OTHER:
(Jean Hersholt Humanitarian Award)
George Jessel
(Other)
CARY GRANT for his unique mastery of the art of screen acting with the respect and affection of his colleagues.

SCIENTIFIC OR TECHNICAL:
(Class II)
HAZELTINE CORPORATION for the design and development of the Hazeltine Color Film Analyzer.
FOUAD SAID for the design and introduction of the Cinemobile series of equipment trucks for location motion picture production.
JUAN DE LA CIERVA and DYNASCIENCES CORPORATION for the design and development of the Dynalens optical image motion compensator.
(Class III)
OTTO POPELKA of Magna-Tech Electronics Co., Inc., for the development of an Electronically Controlled Looping System.
FENTON HAMILTON of MGM Studios for the concept and engineering of a mobile battery power unit for location lighting.
PANAVISION INCORPORATED for the design and development of the Panaspeed Motion Picture Camera Motor.
ROBERT M. FLYNN and RUSSELL HESSY of Universal City Studios, Inc. for a machine-gun modification for motion picture photography.

1970

BEST PICTURE:
PATTON, FOX. Frank McCarthy, Prod.
AIRPORT, Ross Hunter-U Prod., U. Ross Hunter, Prod.
FIVE EASY PIECES, BBS Prods., COL. Bob Rafelson and Richard Wechsler, Prod.
LOVE STORY, The Love Story Co Prod., PAR. Howard G. Minsky, Prod.
M*A*S*H, Aspen Prods., FOX. Ingo Preminger, Prod.

ACTOR:
GEORGE C. SCOTT, Patton.
MELVYN DOUGLAS, *I Never Sang For My Father,* Jamel Prods., COL.
JAMES EARL JONES, *The Great White Hope,* Lawrence Turman Films Prod., FOX.
JACK NICHOLSON, *Five Easy Pieces.*
RYAN O'NEAL, *Love Story.*

ACTRESS:
GLENDA JACKSON, Women In Love, Larry Kramer-Martin Rosen Prod., UA.
JANE ALEXANDER, *The Great White Hope.*
ALI MacGRAW, *Love Story.*
SARAH MILES, *Ryan's Daughter,* Faraway Prods, MGM.
CARRIE SNODGRESS, *Diary Of A Mad Housewife,* Frank Perry Films Prod., U.

SUPPORTING ACTOR:
JOHN MILLS, Ryan's Daughter.
RICHARD CASTELLANO, *Lovers And Other Strangers,* ABC Pictures Prod., CRC.
CHIEF DAN GEORGE, *Little Big Man,* Hiller Prods., Ltd.-Stockbridge Prods., Cinema Center Films Presentation, NGP.
GENE HACKMAN, *I Never Sang For My Father.*
JOHN MARLEY, *Love Story.*

SUPPORTING ACTRESS:
HELEN HAYES, Airport.
KAREN BLACK, *Five Easy Pieces.*
LEE GRANT, *The Landlord,* A Mirisch-Cartier II Prod., UA.
SALLY KELLERMAN, *M*A*S*H.*
MAUREEN STAPLETON, *Airport.*

DIRECTING:
FRANKLIN J. SCHAFFNER, Patton.
ROBERT ALTMAN, *M*A*S*H.*
FEDERICO FELLINI, *Fellini Satyricon,* Alberto Grimaldi Prod., UA.
ARTHUR HILLER, *Love Story.*
KEN RUSSELL, *Women In Love.*

WRITING:
(Best Story and Screenplay based on factual material or material not previously published or produced)
PATTON. Francis Ford Coppola and Edmund H. North.
FIVE EASY PIECES. Story by Bob Rafelson and Adrien Joyce. Screenplay by Adrien Joyce.
JOE, Cannon Group Prod., Cannon Releasing. Norman Wexler.
LOVE STORY. Erich Segal.
MY NIGHT AT MAUD'S, Films du Losange-Carrosse-Renn-Deux Mondes-La Gueville-Simar-La Pleiade-F.F.P. Prod., PC. Eric Rohmer.
(Best Screenplay based on material from another medium)
M*A*S*H. Ring Lardner, Jr.
AIRPORT. George Seaton.
I NEVER SANG FOR MY FATHER. Robert Anderson.
LOVERS AND OTHER STRANGERS. Renee Taylor, Joseph Bologna and David Zelag Goodman.
WOMEN IN LOVE. Larry Kramer.

CINEMATOGRAPHY:
RYAN'S DAUGHTER. Freddie Young.
AIRPORT. Ernest Laszlo.
PATTON. Fred Koenekamp.
TORA! TORA! TORA!, FOX. Charles F. Wheeler, Osami Furuya, Sinsaku Himeda & Masamichi Satoh.
WOMEN IN LOVE. Billy Williams.

COSTUME DESIGN:
CROMWELL, Irving Allen, Ltd. Prod., COL. Nino Novarese.
AIRPORT. Edith Head.
DARLING LILI, Geoffrey Prods., PAR. Donald Brooks and Jack Bear.
THE HAWAIIANS, Mirisch Prods., UA. Bill Thomas.
SCROOGE, Waterbury Films, Ltd. Prod., Cinema Center Films Presentation, NGP. Margaret Furse.

ART DIRECTION - SET DECORATION:
PATTON. Urie McCleary and Gil Parrondo. Set Decoration: Antonio Mateos and Pierre-Louis Thevenet.
AIRPORT. Alexander Golitzen and E. Preston Ames. Set Decoration: Jack D. Moore and Mickey S. Michaels.
THE MOLLY MAGUIRES, Tamm Prods., PAR. Tambi Larsen. Set Decoration: Darrell Silvera.
SCROOGE. Terry Marsh and Bob Cartwright. Set Decoration: Pamela Cornell.
TORA! TORA! TORA! Jack Martin Smith, Yoshiro Muraki, Richard Day and Taizoh Kawashima. Set Decoration: Walter M. Scott, Norman Rockett and Carl Biddiscombe.

FILM EDITING:
PATTON. Hugh S. Fowler.
AIRPORT. Stuart Gilmore.
M*A*S*H. Danford B. Greene.
TORA! TORA! TORA! James E. Newcom, Pembroke J. Herring and Inoue Chikaya.
WOODSTOCK, Wadleigh-Maurice, Ltd. Prod., WB. Thelma Schoonmaker.

FOREIGN LANGUAGE FILM:
INVESTIGATION OF A CITIZEN ABOVE SUSPICION, Vera Films Prod. (Italy).
FIRST LOVE, Alfa Prods.-Seitz Film Prod. (Switzerland).
HOA-BINH, Madeleine-Parc-La Gueville-C.A.P.A.C. Prod. (France).
PAIX SUR LES CHAMPS, Philippe Collette-E.G.C. Prod. (Belgium).
TRISTANA, Forbes Films, Ltd.-United Cineworld-Epoca Films- Talia Film-Les Films Corona-Selenia Cinematografica Prod. (Spain).

MUSIC - SCORING:
(Best Original Score)
LOVE STORY. Francis Lai.
AIRPORT. Alfred Newman.
CROMWELL. Frank Cordell.
PATTON. Jerry Goldsmith.
SUNFLOWER, Sostar Prod., AVE. Henry Mancini.
(Best Original Song Score)
LET IT BE, Beatles-Apple Prod., UA. Music and lyrics by The Beatles.
THE BABY MAKER, Robert Wise Prod., NGP. Music, Fred Karlin. Lyrics, Tylwyth Kymry.
A BOY NAMED CHARLIE BROWN, Lee Mendelson-Melendez Features Prod., Cinema Center Films Presentation, NGP. Music by Rod McKuen and John Scott Trotter. Lyrics by Rod McKuen, Bill Melendez and Al Shean. Adapted by Vince Guaraldi.
DARLING LILI. Music, Henry Mancini. Lyrics, Johnny Mercer.
SCROOGE. Music and lyrics by Leslie Bricusse. Adapted, Ian Fraser and Herbert W. Spencer.

MUSIC - BEST SONG:
FOR ALL WE KNOW, Lovers And Other Strangers. Music, Fred Karlin. Lyrics, Robb Royer and James Griffin aka Robb Wilson and Arthur James.
PIECES OF DREAMS, *Pieces Of Dreams,* RFB Enterprises Prod., UA. Music, Michel Legrand. Lyrics, Alan and Marilyn Bergman.
THANK YOU VERY MUCH, *Scrooge.* Music and lyrics by Leslie Bricusse.
TILL LOVE TOUCHES YOUR LIFE, *Madron,* Edric-Isracine-Zev Braun Prods., 4SX. Music, Riz Ortolani. Lyrics, Arthur Hamilton.
WHISTLING AWAY THE DARK, *Darling Lili.* Music, Henri Mancini. Lyrics, Johnny Mercer.

SOUND:
PATTON. Douglas Williams and Don Bassman.
AIRPORT. Ronald Pierce and David Moriarty.
RYAN'S DAUGHTER. Gordon K. McCallum and John Bramall.
TORA! TORA! TORA! Murray Spivack and Herman Lewis.
WOODSTOCK. Dan Wallin and Larry Johnson.

SHORT FILMS:
(Cartoons)

IS IT ALWAYS RIGHT TO BE RIGHT?, Stephen Bosustow Prods., SCH. Nick Bosustow, Prod.
THE FURTHER ADVENTURES OF UNCLE SAM: PART TWO, The Haboush Co, GOL. Robert Mitchell and Dale Case, Prods.
THE SHEPHERD, Cameron Guess and Associates, BRA. Cameron Guess, Prod.

(Live Action Subjects)

THE RESURRECTION OF BRONCHO BILLY, University of Southern California, Dept. of Cinema, U. John Longenecker, Prod.
SHUT UP. . .I'M CRYING, Robert Siegler Prods., SCH. Robert Siegler, Prod.
STICKY MY FINGERS. . .FLEET MY FEET, The American Film Institute, SCH. John Hancock, Prod.

DOCUMENTARY:
(Short Subjects)

INTERVIEWS WITH MY LAI VETERANS, Laser Film Corp. Joseph Strick, Prod.
THE GIFTS, Richter-McBride Prods. for the Water Quality Office of the Environmental Protection Agency. Robert McBride, Prod.
A LONG WAY FROM NOWHERE, Robert Aller Prods. Bob Aller, Prod.
OISIN, An Aengus Film. Vivien and Patrick Carey, Prods.
TIME IS RUNNING OUT, Gesellschaft fur bildende Filme. Horst Dallmayr and Robert Menegoz, Prods.

(Features)

WOODSTOCK. Bob Maurice, Prod.
CHARIOTS OF THE GODS, Terra-Filmkunst GmbH. Dr. Harald Reinl, Prod.
JACK JOHNSON, The Big Fights. Jim Jacobs, Prod.
KING: A FILMED RECORD. . .MONTGOMERY TO MEMPHIS. CUE. Ely Landau, Prod.
SAY GOODBYE, A Wolper Prod. David H. Vowell., Prod.

VISUAL EFFECTS:

TORA! TORA! TORA! A. D. Flowers and L. B. Abbott.
PATTON. Alex Weldon.

HONORARY AND OTHER:

(Irving G. Thalberg Memorial Award)

Ingmar Bergman

(Jean Hersholt Humanitarian Award)

Frank Sinatra

(Other)

LILLIAN GISH for superlative artistry and for distinguished contribution to the progress of motion pictures.
ORSON WELLES for superlative artistry and versatility in the creation of motion pictures.

SCIENTIFIC OR TECHNICAL:

(Class II)

LEONARD SOKOLOW and **EDWARD H. REICHARD** of Consolidated Film Industries for the concept and engineering of the Color Proofing Printer for motion pictures.

(Class III)

SYLVANIA ELECTRIC PRODUCTS INC. for the development and introduction of a series of compact tungsten halogen lamps for motion picture production.
B. J. LOSMANDY for the concept, design and application of microminiature solid state amplifier modules used in motion picture recording equipment.
EASTMAN KODAK COMPANY and **PHOTO ELECTRONICS CORPORATION** for the design and engineering of an improved video color analyzer for motion picture laboratories.
ELECTRO SOUND INCORPORATED for the design and introduction of the Series 8000 Sound System for motion picture theatres.

1971

BEST PICTURE:

THE FRENCH CONNECTION, A Philip D'Antoni Prod. in association with Schine-Moore Prods., FOX. Philip D'Antoni, Prod.
A CLOCKWORK ORANGE, A Hawks Films, Ltd. Prod., WB. Stanley Kubrick, Prod.
FIDDLER ON THE ROOF, Mirisch-Cartier Prods., UA. Norman Jewison, Prod.
THE LAST PICTURE SHOW, BBS Prods., COL. Stephen J. Friedman, Prod.
NICHOLAS AND ALEXANDRA, A Horizon Pictures Prod., COL. Sam Spiegel, Prod.

ACTOR:

GENE HACKMAN, The French Connection.
PETER FINCH, *Sunday Bloody Sunday*, A Joseph Janni Prod., UA.
WALTER MATTHAU, *Kotch*, A Kotch Company Prod., ABC Pictures Presentation, CRC.
GEORGE C. SCOTT, *The Hospital*, A Howard Gottfried-Paddy Chayefsky Prod. in association with Arthur Hiller, UA.
TOPOL, *Fiddler On The Roof*, A Mirisch-Cartier Prods., UA.

ACTRESS:

JANE FONDA, Klute, A Gus Prod., WB.
JULIE CHRISTIE, *McCabe & Mrs. Miller*, A Robert Altman-David Foster Prod., WB.
GLENDA JACKSON, *Sunday Bloody Sunday*.
VANESSA REDGRAVE, *Mary, Queen Of Scots*, A Hal Wallis-U Pictures, Ltd. Prod., U.
JANET SUZMAN, *Nicholas And Alexandra*.

SUPPORTING ACTOR:

BEN JOHNSON, The Last Picture Show.
JEFF BRIDGES, *The Last Picture Show*.
LEONARD FREY, *Fiddler On The Roof*.
RICHARD JAECKEL, *Sometimes A Great Notion*, A U-Newman-Foreman Co Prod., U.
ROY SCHEIDER, *The French Connection*.

SUPPORTING ACTRESS:

CLORIS LEACHMAN, The Last Picture Show.
ELLEN BURSTYN, *The Last Picture Show*.
BARBARA HARRIS, *Who Is Harry Kellerman, And Why Is He Saying Those Terrible Things About Me?*, A Who Is Harry Kellerman Co Prod., Cinema Center Films Presentation, NGP.
MARGARET LEIGHTON, *The Go-Between*, A World Film Services, Ltd. Prod., COL.
ANN-MARGRET, *Carnal Knowledge*, Icarus Prods., AVE.

DIRECTING:

WILLIAM FRIEDKIN, The French Connection.
PETER BOGDANOVICH, *The Last Picture Show*.
NORMAN JEWISON, *Fiddler On The Roof*.
STANLEY KUBRICK, *A Clockwork Orange*.
JOHN SCHLESINGER, *Sunday Bloody Sunday*.

WRITING:

(Best Story and Screenplay based on factual material or material not previously published or produced)

THE HOSPITAL. Paddy Chayefsky.
INVESTIGATION OF A CITIZEN ABOVE SUSPICION, A Vera Films, S.P.A. Prod., COL. Elio Petri and Ugo Pirro.
KLUTE. Andy and Dave Lewis.
SUMMER OF '42, A Robert Mulligan-Richard Alan Roth Prod., WB. Herman Raucher.
SUNDAY BLOODY SUNDAY. Penelope Gilliatt.

(Best Screenplay based on material from another

medium)
THE FRENCH CONNECTION. Ernest Tidyman.
A CLOCKWORK ORANGE. Stanley Kubrick.
THE CONFORMIST, Mars Film Produzione, S.P.A.-Marianne prods., PAR. Bernardo Bertolucci.
THE GARDEN OF THE FINZI-CONTINIS, A Gianni Hecht Lucari-Arthur Cohn Prod., C5. Ugo Pirro and Vittorio Bonicelli.
THE LAST PICTURE SHOW. Larry McMurtry and Peter Bogdanovich.

CINEMATOGRAPHY:
FIDDLER ON THE ROOF. Oswald Morris.
THE FRENCH CONNECTION. Owen Roizman.
THE LAST PICTURE SHOW. Robert Surtees.
NICHOLAS AND ALEXANDRA. Freddie Young.
SUMMER OF '42. Robert Surtees.

COSTUME DESIGN:
NICHOLAS AND ALEXANDRA. Yvonne Blake and Antonio Castillo.
BEDKNOBS AND BROOMSTICKS, Walt Disney Prods., BV. Bill Thomas.
DEATH IN VENICE, An Alfa Cinematografica-P.E.C.F. Prod., WB. Piero Tosi.
MARY, QUEEN OF SCOTS. Margaret Furse.
WHAT'S THE MATTER WITH HELEN?, A Filmways-Raymax Prod., UA. Morton Haack.

ART DIRECTION - SET DECORATION:
NICHOLAS AND ALEXANDRA. John Box, Ernest Archer, Jack Maxsted and Gil Parrondo. Set Decoration: Vernon Dixon.
THE ANDROMEDA STRAIN, A U-Robert Wise Prod., U. Boris Leven and William Tuntke. Set Decoration: Ruby Levitt.
BEDKNOBS AND BROOMSTICKS. John B. Mansbridge and Peter Ellenshaw. Set Decoration: Emile Kuri and Hal Gausman.
FIDDLER ON THE ROOF. Robert Boyle and Michael Stringer. Set Decoration: Peter Lamont.
MARY, QUEEN OF SCOTS. Terence Marsh and Robert Cartwright. Set Decorations: Peter Howitt.

FILM EDITING:
THE FRENCH CONNECTION. Jerry Greenberg.
THE ANDROMEDA STRAIN. Stuart Gilmore and John W. Holmes.
A CLOCKWORK ORANGE. Bill Butler.
KOTCH. Ralph E. Winters.
SUMMER OF '42. Folmar Blangsted.

FOREIGN LANGUAGE FILM:
THE GARDEN OF THE FINZI-CONTINIS.
DODES'KA-DEN, A Toho Co, Ltd.-Yonki no Kai Prod. (Japan).
THE EMIGRANTS, A Svensk Filmindustri Prod. (Sweden).
THE POLICEMAN, An Ephi-Israeli Motion Picture Studios Prod. (Israel)
TCHAIKOVSKY, A Dimitri Tiomkin-Mosfilm Studios Prod. (U.S.S.R.)

MUSIC - SCORING:
(Best Original Dramatic Score)
SUMMER OF '42. Michel Legrand.
MARY, QUEEN OF SCOTS. John Barry.
NICHOLAS AND ALEXANDRA. Richard Rodney Bennett.
SHAFT, Shaft Prods., Ltd., MGM. Isaac Hayes.
STRAW DOGS, A Talent Associates, Ltd.-Amerbroco Films, Ltd. Prod., ABC Pictures Presentation, CRC. Jerry Fielding.

(Best Scoring-Adaptation and Original Song Score)
FIDDLER ON THE ROOF. Adapted by John Williams.
BEDKNOBS AND BROOMSTICKS. Song Score by Richard M. Sherman and Robert B. Sherman. Adapted by Irwin Kostal.
THE BOY FRIEND, A Russflix, Ltd. Prod., MGM. Adapted by Peter Maxwell Davies and Peter Greenwell.
TCHAIKOVSKY. Adapted by Dimitri Tiomkin.
WILLY WONKA AND THE CHOCOLATE FACTORY, A Wolper Pictures, Ltd. Prod., PAR. Song Score by Leslie Bricusse and Anthony Newley. Adapted by Walter Scharf.

MUSIC - BEST SONG:
THEME FROM SHAFT, Shaft. Music and lyrics by Isaac Hayes.
THE AGE OF NOT BELIEVING, *Bedknobs And Broomsticks*. Music and lyrics by Richard M. Sherman and Robert B. Sherman.
ALL HIS CHILDREN, *Sometimes A Great Notion*. Music, Henry Mancini. Lyrics, Alan and Marilyn Bergman.
BLESS THE BEASTS & CHILDREN, *Bless The Beasts & Children*, COL. Music and lyrics by Barry DeVorzon and Perry Botkin, Jr.
LIFE IS WHAT YOU MAKE IT, *Kotch*. Music, Marvin Hamlisch. Lyrics, Johnny Mercer.

SOUND:
FIDDLER ON THE ROOF. Gordon K. McCallum and David Hildyard.
DIAMONDS ARE FOREVER, An Albert R. Broccoli-Harry Saltzman Prod., UA. Gordon K. McCallum, John Mitchell and Alfred J. Overton.
THE FRENCH CONNECTION. Theodore Soderberg and Christopher Newman.
KOTCH. Richard Portman and Jack Solomon.
MARY, QUEEN OF SCOTS. Bob Jones and John Aldred.

SHORT FILMS:
(Animated)
THE CRUNCH BIRD, Maxwell-Petok-Petrovich Prods., RGY. Ted Petok, Prod.
EVOLUTION, NFC, COL. Michael Mills, Prod.
THE SELFISH GIANT, Potterton Prods., Pyramid Films. Peter Sander and Murray Shostak, Prods.

(Live Action)
SENTINELS OF SILENCE, Producciones Concord, PAR. Manuel Arango and Robert Amram, Prods.
GOOD MORNING, E/G Films, BOR. Denny Evans and Ken Greenwald, Prods.
THE REHEARSAL, A Cinema Verona Prod., SCH. Stephen F. Verona, Prod.

DOCUMENTARY:
(Short Subjects)
SENTINELS OF SILENCE, Producciones Concord, PAR. Manuel Arango and Robert Amram, Prods.
ADVENTURES IN PERCEPTION, Han van Gelder Filmproduktie for Netherlands Information Service. Han van Gelder, Prod.
ART IS. . ., Henry Strauss Associates for Sears Roebuck Foundation. Julian Krainin and DeWitt L. Sage, Jr., Prods.
THE NUMBERS START WITH THE RIVER, A WH Picture for United States Information Agency. Donald Wrye, Prod.
SOMEBODY WAITING, Snider Prods. for University of California Medical Film Library. Hal Riney, Dick Snider and Sherwood Omens, Prods.

(Features)
THE HELLSTROM CHRONICLE, David L. Wolper Prods. C5. Walon Green, Prod.
ALASKA WILDERNESS LAKE, Alan Landsburg Prods. Alan Landsburg, Prod.
ON ANY SUNDAY, Bruce Brown Films-Solar Prods., C5. Bruce Brown, Prod.
THE RA EXPEDITIONS, Swedish Broadcasting Co, INT. Lennart Ehrenborg and Thor Heyerdahl, Prods.
THE SORROW AND THE PITY, Television Rencontre-Norddeutscher Rundfunk-Television Swiss Romande, C5. Marcel Ophuls, Prod.

VISUAL EFFECTS:
BEDKNOBS AND BROOMSTICKS. Alan Maley, Eustace Lycett and Danny Lee.
WHEN DINOSAURS RULED THE EARTH, A Hammer Film Prod., WB. Jim Danforth and Roger Dicken.

HONORARY AND OTHER:
(Other)
CHARLES CHAPLIN for the incalculable effect he has had in making motion pictures the art form of this century.

SCIENTIFIC OR TECHNICAL:
(Class II)
JOHN N. WILKINSON of Optical Radiation Corp for the development and engineering of a system of xenon arc lamphouses for motion picture projection.
(Class III)
THOMAS JEFFERSON HUTCHINSON, JAMES R. ROCHESTER and FENTON HAMILTON for the development and introduction of the Sunbrute system of xenon arc lamps for location lighting in motion picture production.
PHOTO RESEARCH, a Division of Kollmorgen Corp, for the development and introduction of the film-lens balanced Three Color Meter.
ROBERT D. AUGUSTE and CINEMA PRODUCTS CO. for the development and introduction of a new crystal controlled lightweight motor for the 35mm motion picture Arriflex camera.
PRODUCERS SERVICE CORPORATION and CONSOLIDATED FILM INDUSTRIES; and CINEMA RESEARCH CORPORATION and RESEARCH PRODUCTS, INC. for the engineering and implementation of fully automated blow-up motion picture printing systems.
CINEMA PRODUCTS CO. for a control motor to actuate zoom lenses on motion picture cameras.

1972

BEST PICTURE:
THE GODFATHER, An Albert S. Ruddy Production, PAR. Albert S. Ruddy, Prod.
CABARET, An ABC Pictures Production, AA. Cy Feuer, Prod.
DELIVERANCE, WB. John Boorman, Prod.
THE EMIGRANTS, A Svensk Filmindustri Production, WB. Bengt Forslund, Prod.
SOUNDER, Radnitz/Mattel Productions, FOX. Robert B. Radnitz, Prod.

ACTOR:
MARLON BRANDO, The Godfather.
MICHAEL CAINE, *Sleuth*, A Palomar Pictures Int'l Production, FOX.
LAURENCE OLIVIER, *Sleuth*.
PETER O'TOOLE, *The Ruling Class*, A Keep Films, Ltd. Production, AVE.
PAUL WINFIELD, *Sounder*.

ACTRESS:
LIZA MINNELLI, Cabaret.
DIANA ROSS, *Lady Sings The Blues*, A Motown-Weston-Furie Production, PAR.
MAGGIE SMITH, *Travels With My Aunt*, Robert Fryer Productions, MGM.
CICELY TYSON, *Sounder*.
LIV ULLMANN, *The Emigrants*.

SUPPORTING ACTOR:
JOEL GREY, Cabaret.
EDDIE ALBERT, *The Heartbreak Kid*, A Palomar Pictures Int'l Production, FOX.
JAMES CAAN, *The Godfather*.
ROBERT DUVALL, *The Godfather*.
AL PACINO, *The Godfather*.

SUPPORTING ACTRESS:
EILEEN HECKART, Butterflies Are Free, Frankovich Productions, COL.
JEANNIE BERLIN, *The Heartbreak Kid*.
GERALDINE PAGE, *Pete 'N' Tillie*, A U-Martin Ritt-Julius J. Epstein Production, U.
SUSAN TYRRELL, *Fat City*, Rastar Productions, COL.
SHELLEY WINTERS, *The Poseidon Adventure*, An Irwin Allen Production, FOX.

DIRECTING:
BOB FOSSE, Cabaret.
JOHN BOORMAN, *Deliverance*.
FRANCIS FORD COPPOLA, *The Godfather*.
JOSEPH L. MANKIEWICZ, *Sleuth*.
JAN TROELL, *The Emigrants*.

WRITING:
(Best Story and Screenplay based on factual material or material not previously published or produced)
THE CANDIDATE, A Redford-Ritchie Prod., WB. Jeremy Larner.
THE DISCREET CHARM OF THE BOURGEOISIE, A Serge Silberman Prod., FOX. Luis Bunuel in collaboration with Jean-Claude Carriere.
LADY SINGS THE BLUES. Terence McCloy, Chris Clark and Suzanne de Passe.
MURMUR OF THE HEART, A Nouvelles Editions De Films-Marianne Productions-Vides Cinematografica-Franz Seitz Filmproduktion, CON. Louis Malle.
YOUNG WINSTON, An Open Road Films, Ltd. Prod., COL. Carl Foreman.

(Best Screenplay based on material from another medium)
THE GODFATHER. Mario Puzo and Francis Ford Coppola.
CABARET. Jay Allen.
THE EMIGRANTS. Jan Troell and Bengt Forslund.
PETE N' TILLIE. Julius J. Epstein.
SOUNDER. Lonne Elder, III.

CINEMATOGRAPHY:
CABARET. Geoffrey Unsworth.
BUTTERFLIES ARE FREE. Charles B. Lang.
THE POSEIDON ADVENTURE. Harold E. Stine.
1776, A Jack L. Warner Production, COL. Harry Stradling, Jr.
TRAVELS WITH MY AUNT. Douglas Slocombe.

COSTUME DESIGN:
TRAVELS WITH MY AUNT. Anthony Powell.
THE GODFATHER. Anna Hill Johnstone.
LADY SINGS THE BLUES. Bob Mackie, Ray Aghayan and Norma Koch.
THE POSEIDON ADVENTURE. Paul Zastupnevich.
YOUNG WINSTON. Anthony Mendleson.

ART DIRECTION - SET DECORATION:
CABARET. Rolf Zehetbauer and Jurgen Kiebach. Set Decoration: Herbert Strabel.
LADY SINGS THE BLUES. Carl Anderson. Set Decoration: Reg Allen.
THE POSEIDON ADVENTURE. William Creber. Set Decoration: Raphael Bretton.
TRAVELS WITH MY AUNT. John Box, Gil Parrondo and Robert W. Laing.
YOUNG WINSTON. Don Ashton, Geoffrey Drake, John Graysmark and William Hutchinson. Set Decoration: Peter James.

FILM EDITING:
CABARET. David Bretherton.
DELIVERANCE. Tom Priestley.
THE GODFATHER. William Reynolds and Peter Zinner.
THE HOT ROCK, A Landers-Roberts Production, FOX. Frank P. Keller and Fred W. Berger.
THE POSEIDON ADVENTURE. Harold F. Kress.

FOREIGN LANGUAGE FILM:
THE DISCREET CHARM OF THE BOURGEOISIE.
THE DAWNS HERE ARE QUIET, A Gorky Film Studios Prod. (U.S.S.R.)
I LOVE YOU ROSA, A Noah Films Ltd. Prod. (Israel).
MY DEAREST SENORITA, An El Iman Prod. (Spain).
THE NEW LAND, A Svensk Filmindustri Prod. (Sweden).

MUSIC - SCORING:
(Best Original Dramatic Score)
LIMELIGHT, A Charles Chaplin Prod., COL. Charles Chaplin, Raymond Rasch and Larry Russell.
IMAGES, A Hemdale Group, Ltd.-Lion's Gate Films Prod., COL. John Williams.
NAPOLEON AND SAMANTHA, A Walt Disney Prods., BV. Buddy Baker.
THE POSEIDON ADVENTURE. John Williams.
SLEUTH. John Addison.
(Best Scoring-Adaptation and Original Song Score)
CABARET. Adapted by Ralph Burns.
LADY SINGS THE BLUES. Adapted by Gil Askey.
MAN OF LA MANCHA, A PEA Produzioni Europee Associate Prod., UA. Adapted by Laurence Rosenthal.

MUSIC - BEST SONG:
THE MORNING AFTER, The Poseidon Adventure. Music and lyrics by Al Kasha and Joel Hirschhorn.
BEN, *Ben,* BCP Productions, CRC. Music, Walter Scharf. Lyrics, Don Black.
COME FOLLOW, FOLLOW ME, *The Little Ark,* Robert Radnitz Productions, Ltd., Cinema Center Films Presentation, NGP. Music, Fred Karlin. Lyrics, Marsha Karlin.
MARMALADE, MOLASSES & HONEY, *The Life And Times Of Judge Roy Bean,* A First Artists Production Co, Ltd. Production, NGP. Music, Maurice Jarre. Lyrics, Marilyn and Alan Bergman.
STRANGE ARE THE WAYS OF LOVE, *The Stepmother,* Magic Eye of Hollywood Productions, Crown Int'l. Music, Sammy Fain. Lyrics, Paul Francis Webster.

SOUND:
CABARET. Robert Knudson and David Hildyard.
BUTTERFLIES ARE FREE. Arthur Piantadosi and Charles Knight.
THE CANDIDATE. Richard Portman and Gene Cantamessa.
THE GODFATHER. Bud Grenzbach, Richard Portman and Christopher Newman.
THE POSEIDON ADVENTURE. Theodore Soderberg and Herman Lewis.

SHORT FILMS:
(Animated)
A CHRISTMAS CAROL, A Richard Williams Production, American Broadcasting Co Film Serivces. Richard Williams, Prod.
KAMA SUTRA RIDES AGAIN, Bob Godfrey Films, Ltd., LIO. Bob Godfrey, Prod.
TUP TUP, A Zagreb Film-Corona Cinematografica Production, MAN. Nedeljko Dragic, Prod.
(Live Action)
NORMAN ROCKWELL'S WORLD. . .AN AMERICAN DREAM, A Concepts Unlimited Production, COL. Richard Barclay, Prod.
FROG STORY, Gidron Productions, SCH. Ron Satlof and Ray Gideon, Prods.
SOLO, Pyramid Films, UA. David Adams, Prod.

DOCUMENTARY:
(Short Subjects)
THIS TINY WORLD, A Charles Huguenot van der Linden Production. Charles and Martina Huguenot van der Linden, Prods.
HUNDERTWASSER'S RAINY DAY, An Argos Films-Peter Schamoni Film Prod. Peter Schamoni, Prod.
K-Z, A Nexus Film Production. Giorgio Treves, Prod.
SELLING OUT, A Unit Productions Film. Tadeusz Jaworski, Prod.
THE TIDE OF TRAFFIC, A BP-Greenpark Production. Humphrey Swingler, Prod.
(Features)
MARJOE, A Cinema X Production, C5. Howard Smith and Sarah Kernochan, Prods.
APE AND SUPER-APE, A Bert Haanstra Film Production, Netherlands Ministry of Culture, Recreation and Social Welfare. Bert Haanstra, Prod.
MALCOLM X, A Marvin Worth Production, WB. Marvin Worth and Arnold Perl, Prods.
MANSON, Robert Hendrickson and Laurence Merrick, Prods.
THE SILENT REVOLUTION, A Leonaris Film Production. Eckehard Munck, Prod.

HONORARY AND OTHER:
(Jean Hersholt Humanitarian Award)
Rosalind Russell
(Special Achievement)
L.B. ABBOTT and A.D. FLOWERS for Visual Effects for The Poseidon Adventure.
(Other)
CHARLES S. BOREN, Leader for 38 years of the industry's enlightened labor relations and architect of its policy of non-discrimination. With the respect and affection of all who work in films.
EDWARD G. ROBINSON, who achieved greatness as a player, a patron of the arts and a dedicated citizen. . .in sum, a Renaissance man. From his friends in the industry he loves.

SCIENTIFIC OR TECHNICAL:
(Class II)
JOSEPH E. BLUTH for research and development in the field of electronic photography and transfer of video tape to motion picture film.
EDWARD H. REICHARD and HOWARD T. LA ZARE of Consolidated Film Industries, and EDWARD EFRON of IBM for the engineering of a computerized light valve monitoring system for motion picture printing.
PANAVISION INCORPORATED for the development and engineering of the Panaflex motion picture camera.
(Class III)
PHOTO RESEARCH, a Division of Kollmorgen Corp, and PSC TECHNOLOGY INC., Acme Products Division, for the Spectra Film Gate Photometer for motion picture printers.
CARTER EQUIPMENT COMPANY, INC. and RAMTRONICS for the RAMtronics light-valve photometer for motion picture printers.
DAVID DEGENKOLB, HARRY LARSON, MANFRED MICHELSON and FRED SCOBEY of DeLuxe General Inc for the development of a computerized motion picture printer and process control system.
JIRO MUKAI and RYUSHO HIROSE of Canon, Inc. and WILTON R. HOLM of the AMPTP Motion Picture and Television Research Center for development of the Canon Macro Zoom Lens for motion picture photography.
PHILIP V. PALMQUIST and LEONARD L. OLSON of the 3M Co, and FRANK P. CLARK of the AMPTP Motion Picture and Television Research Center for development of the Nextel simulated blood for motion picture color photography.
E. H. GEISSLER and G. M. BERGGREN of Wil-Kin Inc. for engineering of the Ultra-Vision Motion Picture Theater Projection System.

1973

BEST PICTURE:
THE STING, A U-Bill/Phillips-George Roy Hill Film Prod., Zanuck/Brown Presentation, U. Tony Bill, Michael and Julia Phillips, Prods.
AMERICAN GRAFFITI, A U-Lucasfilm, Ltd.-Coppola Co Prod., U. Francis Ford Coppola, Prod. Gary Kurtz, Co-Prod.
CRIES AND WHISPERS, A Svenska Filminstitutet-Cinematograph AB Prod., NW. Ingmar Bergman, Prod.
THE EXORCIST, Hoya Prods., WB. William Peter Blatty, Prod.
A TOUCH OF CLASS, Brut Prods., AVE. Melvin Frank, Prod.

ACTOR:
JACK LEMMON, Save The Tiger, Filmways-Jalem-Cirandinha Prods., PAR.
MARLON BRANDO, *Last Tango In Paris*, A PEA Produzioni Europee Associate S.A.S.-Les Productions Artistes Associes S.A. Prod., UA.
JACK NICHOLSON, *The Last Detail*, An Acrobat Films Prod., COL.
AL PACINO, *Serpico*.
ROBERT REDFORD, *The Sting*.

ACTRESS:
GLENDA JACKSON, A Touch Of Class.
ELLEN BURSTYN, *The Exorcist*.
MARSHA MASON, *Cinderella Liberty*, A Sanford Prod., FOX.
BARBRA STREISAND, *The Way We Were*, Rastar Prods., COL.
JOANNE WOODWARD, *Summer Wishes, Winter Dreams*, A Rastar Pictures Prod., COL.

SUPPORTING ACTOR:
JOHN HOUSEMAN, The Paper Chase, Thompson-Paul Productions, FOX.
VINCENT GARDENIA, *Bang The Drum Slowly*, A Rosenfield Production, PAR.
JACK GILFORD, *Save The Tiger*.
JASON MILLER, *The Exorcist*.
RANDY QUAID, *The Last Detail*.

SUPPORTING ACTRESS:
TATUM O'NEAL, Paper Moon, A Directors Co Prod., PAR.
LINDA BLAIR, *The Exorcist*.
CANDY CLARK, *American Graffiti*.
MADELINE KAHN, *Paper Moon*.
SYLVIA SIDNEY, *Summer Wishes, Winter Dreams*.

DIRECTING:
GEORGE ROY HILL, The Sting.
INGMAR BERGMAN, *Cries And Whispers*.
BERNARDO BERTOLUCCI, *Last Tango In Paris*.
WILLIAM FRIEDKIN, *The Exorcist*.
GEORGE LUCAS, *American Graffiti*.

WRITING:
(Best Story and Screenplay based on factual material or material not previously published or produced)
THE STING. David S. Ward.
AMERICAN GRAFFITI. George Lucas, Gloria Katz and Willard Huyck.
CRIES AND WHISPERS. Ingmar Bergman.
SAVE THE TIGER. Steve Shagan.
A TOUCH OF CLASS. Melvin Frank and Jack Rose.

(Best Screenplay based on material from another medium)
THE EXORCIST. William Peter Blatty.
THE LAST DETAIL. Robert Towne.
THE PAPER CHASE. James Bridges.
PAPER MOON. Alvin Sargent.
SERPICO, A Produzioni De Laurentiis Int'l Manufacturing Co S.p.A. Prod., PAR. Waldo Salt and Norman Wexler.

CINEMATOGRAPHY:
CRIES AND WHISPERS. Sven Nykvist.
THE EXORCIST. Owen Roizman.
JONATHAN LIVINGSTON SEAGULL, A JLS Ltd Partnership Prod., PAR. Jack Couffer.
THE STING. Robert Surtees.
THE WAY WE WERE. Harry Stradling, Jr.

COSTUME DESIGN:
THE STING. Edith Head.
CRIES AND WHISPERS. Marik Vos.
LUDWIG, A Mega Film S.p.A. Prod., MGM. Piero Tosi.
TOM SAWYER, An Arthur P. Jacobs Prod., Reader's Digest Presentation, UA. Donfeld.
THE WAY WE WERE. Dorothy Jeakins and Moss Mabry.

ART DIRECTION - SET DECORATION:
THE STING. Henry Bumstead. Set Decoration: James Payne.
BROTHER SUN SISTER MOON, Euro Int'l Films-Vic Film (Prods.), Ltd., PAR. Lorenzo Mongiardino and Gianni Quaranta. Set Decoration: Carmelo Patrono.
THE EXORCIST. Bill Malley. Set Decoration: Jerry Wunderlich.
TOM SAWYER. Philip Jefferies. Set Decoration: Robert de Vestel.
THE WAY WE WERE. Stephen Grimes. Set Decoration: William Kiernan.

FILM EDITING:
THE STING. William Reynolds.
AMERICAN GRAFFITI. Verna Fields and Marcia Lucas.
THE DAY OF THE JACKAL, Warwick Film Prods., Ltd.-U Prods., France S.A., U. Ralph Kemplen.
THE EXORCIST. Jordan Leondopoulos, Bud Smith, Evan Lottman and Norman Gay.
JONATHAN LIVINGSTON SEAGULL. Frank P. Keller and James Galloway.

FOREIGN LANGUAGE FILM:
DAY FOR NIGHT, A Les Films Du Carrosse-P.E.C.F. (Paris)-P.I.C. (Rome) Prod. (France).
THE HOUSE ON CHELOUCHE STREET, A Noah Films Prod. (Israel).
L'INVITATION, A Groupe 5 Geneve-Television Suisse Romande-Citel Films-Planfilm (Paris) Prod. (Switzerland).
THE PEDESTRIAN, An ALFA Glarus-MFG-Seitz-Zev Braun Prod. (Federal Republic of West Germany).
TURKISH DELIGHT, A Rob Houwer Film Prod. (The Netherlands).

MUSIC - SCORING:
(Best Original Dramatic Score)
THE WAY WE WERE. Marvin Hamlisch.
CINDERELLA LIBERTY. John Williams.
THE DAY OF THE DOLPHIN, Icarus Prods., AVE. Georges Delerue.
PAPILLON, A Corona-General Production Co Prod., AA. Jerry Goldsmith.
A TOUCH OF CLASS. John Cameron.

(Best Scoring-Original Song Score and/or Adaptation)
THE STING. Adapted by Marvin Hamlisch.
JESUS CHRIST SUPERSTAR, A U-Norman Jewison-Robert Stigwood Prod., U. Adapted by Andre Previn, Herbert Spencer and Andrew Lloyd Webber.
TOM SAWYER. Song Score by Richard M. Sherman and Robert B. Sherman. Adapted by John Williams.

MUSIC - BEST SONG:
THE WAY WE WERE, *The Way We Were*. Music, Marvin Hamlisch. Lyrics, Alan and Marilyn Bergman.
ALL THAT LOVE WENT TO WASTE, *A Touch Of Class*. Music, George Barrie. Lyrics, Sammy Cahn.
LIVE AND LET DIE, *Live And Let Die*, Eon Prods., UA. Music and lyrics by Paul and Linda McCartney.
LOVE, *Robin Hood*, Walt Disney Prods., BV. Music, George Bruns.

Lyrics, Floyd Huddleston.
NICE TO BE AROUND, *Cinderella Liberty*. Music, John Williams. Lyrics, Paul Williams.

SOUND:
THE EXORCIST. Robert Knudson and Chris Newman.
THE DAY OF THE DOLPHIN. Richard Portman and Lawrence O. Jost.
THE PAPER CHASE. Donald O. Mitchell and Lawrence O. Jost.
PAPER MOON. Richard Portman and Les Fresholtz.
THE STING. Ronald K. Pierce and Robert Bertrand.

SHORT FILMS:
(Animated)
FRANK FILM, A Frank Mouris Production. Frank Mouris, Prod.
THE LEGEND OF JOHN HENRY, A Stephen Bosustow-Pyramid Films Prod. Nick Bosustow and David Adams, Prods.
PULCINELLA, A Luzzati-Gianini Prod. Emanuele Luzzati and Guilio Gianini, Prods.
(Live Action)
THE BOLERO, An Allan Miller Production. Allan Miller and William Fertik, Prods.
CLOCKMAKER, James Street Prods. Ltd. Richard Gayer, Prod.
LIFE TIMES NINE, Insight Prods. Pen Densham and John Watson, Prods.

DOCUMENTARY:
(Short Subjects)
PRINCETON: A SEARCH FOR ANSWERS, Krainin-Sage Prods. Julian Krainin and DeWitt L. Sage, Jr., Prods.
BACKGROUND, D'Avino and Fucci-Stone Prods. Carmen D'Avino, Prod.
CHILDREN AT WORK, (Paisti Ag Obair), Gael-Linn Films. Louis Marcus, Prod.
CHRISTO'S VALLEY CURTAIN, A Maysles Films Prod. Albert and David Maysles, Prods.
FOUR STONES FOR KANEMITSU, A Tamarind Prod. (Prod credit in controversy)
(Features)
THE GREAT AMERICAN COWBOY, Kieth Merrill Associates-Rodeo Film Prods. Kieth Merrill, Prod.
ALWAYS A NEW BEGINNING, Goodell Motion Pictures. John D. Goodell, Prod.
BATTLE OF BERLIN, Chronos Film. Bengt von zur Muehlen, Prod.
JOURNEY TO THE OUTER LIMITS, The National Geographic Society and Wolper Prods. Alex Grasshoff, Prod.
WALLS OF FIRE, Mentor Prods. Gertrude Ross Marks and Edmund F. Penney, Prods.

HONORARY AND OTHER:
(Irving G. Thalberg Memorial Award)
Lawrence Weingarten
(Jean Hersholt Humanitarian Award)
Lew Wasserman
(Other)
HENRI LANGLOIS for his devotion to the art of film, his massive contributions in preserving its past and his unswerving faith in its future.
GROUCHO MARX in recognition of his brilliant creativity and for the unequalled achievements of the Marx Brothers in the art of motion picture comedy.

SCIENTIFIC OR TECHNICAL:
(Class II)
JOACHIM GERB and ERICH KASTNER of The Arnold and Richter Co for the development and engineering of the Arriflex 35BL motion-picture camera.
MAGNA-TECH ELECTRONIC CO., INC. for the engineering and development of a high-speed re-recording system for motion-picture production.
WILLIAM W. VALLIANT of PSC Technology Inc., **HOWARD F. OTT** of Eastman Kodak Co, and **GERRY DIEBOLD** of The Richmark Camera Service Inc. for the development of a liquid-gate system for motion-picture printers.
HAROLD A. SCHEIB, CLIFFORD H. ELLIS and ROGER W. BANKS of Research Products Inc for the concept and engineering of the Model 2101 optical printer for motion-picture optical effects.
(Class III)
ROSCO LABORATORIES, INC. for the technical advances and the development of a complete system of light-control materials for motion-picture photography.
RICHARD H. VETTER of the Todd-AO Corp for the design of an improved anamorphic focusing system for motion-picture photography.

1974

BEST PICTURE:
THE GODFATHER PART II, A Coppola Co Production, PAR. Francis Ford Coppola, Prod. Gray Frederickson and Fred Roos, Co-Prods.
CHINATOWN, A Robert Evans Production, PAR. Robert Evans, Prod.
THE CONVERSATION, A Directors Co Production, PAR. Francis Ford Coppola, Prod. Fred Roos, Co-Prod.
LENNY, A Marvin Worth Production, UA. Marvin Worth, Prod.
THE TOWERING INFERNO, An Irwin Allen Production, FOX/WB. Irwin Allen, Prod.

ACTOR:
ART CARNEY, Harry And Tonto, FOX.
ALBERT FINNEY, *Murder On The Orient Express*, A G.W. Films, Ltd. Production, PAR.
DUSTIN HOFFMAN, *Lenny*.
JACK NICHOLSON, *Chinatown*.
AL PACINO, *The Godfather Part II*.

ACTRESS:
ELLEN BURSTYN, Alice Doesn't Live Here Anymore, WB.
DIAHANN CARROLL, *Claudine*, Third World Cinema Productions in association with Joyce Selznick and Tina Pine, FOX.
FAYE DUNAWAY, *Chinatown*.
VALERIE PERRINE, *Lenny*.
GENA ROWLANDS, *A Woman Under The Influence*, A Faces Int'l Films Production.

SUPPORTING ACTOR:
ROBERT DE NIRO, The Godfather Part II.
FRED ASTAIRE, *The Towering Inferno*.
JEFF BRIDGES, *Thunderbolt And Lightfoot*, A Malpaso Co Film Production, UA.
MICHAEL V. GAZZO, *The Godfather Part II*.
LEE STRASBERG, *The Godfather Part II*.

SUPPORTING ACTRESS:
INGRID BERGMAN, Murder On The Orient Express.
VALENTINA CORTESE, *Day For Night*, A Les Films Du Carrosse and P.E.C.F., Paris; P.I.C., Rome Prod., WB.
MADELINE KAHN, *Blazing Saddles*, WB.
DIANE LADD, *Alice Doesn't Live Here Anymore*.
TALIA SHIRE, *The Godfather Part II*.

DIRECTING:
FRANCIS FORD COPPOLA, The Godfather Part II.
JOHN CASSAVETES, *A Woman Under The Influence*.
BOB FOSSE, *Lenny*.
ROMAN POLANSKI, *Chinatown*.
FRANCOIS TRUFFAUT, *Day For Night*.

WRITING:
(Best Original Screenplay)

CHINATOWN. Robert Towne.
ALICE DOESN'T LIVE HERE ANYMORE. Robert Getchell.
THE CONVERSATION. Francis Ford Coppola.
DAY FOR NIGHT. Francois Truffaut, Jean-Louis Richard, and Suanne Schiffman.
HARRY AND TONTO. Paul Mazursky and Josh Greenfeld.

(Best Screenplay adapted from other medium)

THE GODFATHER PART II. Screenplay by Francis Ford Coppola and Mario Puzo.
THE APPRENTICESHIP OF DUDDY KRAVITZ, An Int'l Cinemedia Centre, Ltd. Prod., PAR. Screenplay by Mordecai Richler. Adaptation by Lionel Chetwynd.
LENNY. Screenplay by Julian Barry.
MURDER ON THE ORIENT EXPRESS. Screenplay by Paul Dehn.
YOUNG FRANKENSTEIN, A Gruskoff/Venture Films-Crossbow Prods.-Jouer, Ltd. Production, FOX. Screenplay by Gene Wilder and Mel Brooks.

CINEMATOGRAPHY:

THE TOWERING INFERNO. Fred Koenekamp & Joseph Biroc.
CHINATOWN. John A. Alonzo.
EARTHQUAKE, A U-Mark Robson-Filmakers Group Prod., U. Philip Lathrop.
LENNY. Bruce Surtees.
MURDER ON THE ORIENT EXPRESS, A G.W. Films, Ltd. Prod., PAR. Geoffrey Unsworth.

COSTUME DESIGN:

THE GREAT GATSBY, A David Merrick Prod., PAR. Theoni V. Aldredge.
CHINATOWN, A Robert Evans Prod., PAR. Anthea Sylbert.
DAISY MILLER, A Directors Co Prod., PAR. John Furness.
THE GODFATHER PART II, A Coppola Co Prod., PAR. Theadora Van Runkle.
MURDER ON THE ORIENT EXPRESS, A G.W. Films, Ltd. Prod., PAR. Tony Walton.

ART DIRECTION - SET DECORATION:

THE GODFATHER PART II. Dean Tavoularis and Angelo Graham. Set Decoration: George R. Nelson.
CHINATOWN. Richard Sylbert and W. Stewart Campbell. Set Decoration: Ruby Levitt.
EARTHQUAKE, A U-Mark Robson-Filmakers Group Prod., U. Alexander Golitzen and E. Preston Ames. Set Decoration: Frank McKelvy.
THE ISLAND AT THE TOP OF THE WORLD, Walt Disney Prods., BV. Peter Ellenshaw, John B. Mansbridge, Walter Tyler and Al Roelofs. Set Decoration: Hal Gausman.
THE TOWERING INFERNO, An Irwin Allen Prod., FOX/WB. William Creber and Ward Preston. Set Decoration: Raphael Bretton.

FILM EDITING:

THE TOWERING INFERNO. Harold F. Kress and Carl Kress.
BLAZING SADDLES, WB. John C. Howard and Danford Greene.
CHINATOWN. Sam O'Steen.
EARTHQUAKE. Dorothy Spencer.
THE LONGEST YARD, An Albert S. Ruddy Prod., PAR. Michael Luciano.

FOREIGN LANGUAGE FILM:

AMARCORD, An F.C. (Rome)-P.E.C.F. (Paris) Prod. (Italy).
CATSPLAY, A Hunnia Studio Prod. (Hungary).
THE DELUGE, A Film Polski Prod. (Poland).
LACOMBE, LUCIEN, An NEF-UPF (Paris)-Vides Film (Rome)-Hallelujah Film (Munich) Prod. (France).
THE TRUCE, A Tamames-Zemborain Prod. (Argentina).

MUSIC - SCORING:
(Best Original Dramatic Score)

THE GODFATHER PART II. Nino Rota and Carmine Coppola.
CHINATOWN. Jerry Goldsmith.
MURDER ON THE ORIENT EXPRESS. Richard Rodney Bennett.
SHANKS, William Castle Prods., PAR. Alex North.
THE TOWERING INFERNO. John Williams.

(Best Scoring-Original Song Score and/or Adaptation)

THE GREAT GATSBY, A David Merrick Prod., PAR. Adapted by Nelson Riddle.
THE LITTLE PRINCE, A Stanley Donen Enterprises, Ltd. Prod., PAR. Song Score by Alan Jay Lerner and Frederick Loewe. Adapted by Angela Morley and Douglas Gamley.
PHANTOM OF THE PARADISE, Harbor Prods., FOX. Song score by Paul Williams. Adapted by Paul Williams and George Aliceson Tipton.

MUSIC - BEST SONG:

WE MAY NEVER LOVE LIKE THIS AGAIN, The Towering Inferno. Music and lyrics by Al Kasha and Joel Hirschhorn.
BENJI'S THEME (I FEEL LOVE), *Benji*, Mulberry Square. Music, Euel Box. Lyrics, Betty Box.
BLAZING SADDLES, *Blazing Saddles*. Music, John Morris. Lyrics, Mel Brooks.
LITTLE PRINCE, *The Little Prince*. Music, Frederick Loewe. Lyrics, Alan Jay Lerner.
WHEREVER LOVE TAKES ME, *Gold*, Avton Film Productions, Ltd. AA. Music, Elmer Bernstein. Lyrics, Don Black.

SOUND:

EARTHQUAKE. Ronald Pierce and Melvin Metcalfe, Sr.
CHINATOWN. Bud Grenzbach and Larry Jost.
THE CONVERSATION, A Directors Co Production, PAR. Walter Murch and Arthur Rochester.
THE TOWERING INFERNO. Theodore Soderberg and Herman Lewis.
YOUNG FRANKENSTEIN, A Gruskoff/Venture Films-Crossbow Prods.-Jouer, Ltd. Production, FOX. Richard Portman and Gene Cantamessa.

SHORT FILMS:
(Animated)

CLOSED MONDAYS, Lighthouse Productions. Will Vinton and Bob Gardiner, Prods.
THE FAMILY THAT DWELT APART, NFC. Yvon Mallette and Robert Verrall, Prods.
HUNGER, NFC. Peter Foldes and Rene Jodoin, Prods.
VOYAGE TO NEXT, The Hubley Studio. Faith and John Hubley, Prods.
WINNIE THE POOH AND TIGGER TOO, Walt Disney Productions. Wolfgang Reitherman, Prod.

(Live Action)

ONE-EYED MEN ARE KINGS, C.A.P.A.C. Productions (Paris). Paul Claudon and Edmond Sechan, Prods.
CLIMB, Dewitt Jones Productions. Dewitt Jones, Prod.
THE CONCERT, The Black And White Colour Film Co, Ltd. Julian and Claude Chagrin, Prods.
PLANET OCEAN, Graphic Films. George V. Casey, Prod.
THE VIOLIN, A Sincinkin, Ltd. Production. Andrew Welsh and George Pastic, Prods.

DOCUMENTARY:
(Short Subjects)

DON'T, R. A. Films. Robin Lehman, Prod.
CITY OUT OF WILDERNESS, Francis Thompson Inc. Francis Thompson, Prod.
EXPLORATORIUM, A Jon Boorstin Prod. Jon Boorstin, Prod.
JOHN MUIR'S HIGH SIERRA, Dewitt Jones Prods. Dewitt Jones and Lesley Foster, Prods.
NAKED YOGA, A Filmshop Prod. Ronald S. Kass and Mervyn Lloyd, Prods.

(Features)

HEARTS AND MINDS, A Touchstone-Audjeff-BBS Prod., Howard Zucker/Henry Jaglom-Rainbow Pictures Presentation. Peter Davis and Bert Schneider, Prods.
ANTONIA: A PORTRAIT OF THE WOMAN, Rocky Mountain Prods. Judy Collins and Jill Godmilow, Prods.
THE CHALLENGE...A TRIBUTE TO MODERN ART, A World View Prod. Herbert Kline, Prod.
THE 81ST BLOW, A Film by Ghetto Fighters House. Jacquot Ehrlich, David Bergman and Haim Gouri, Prods.
THE WILD AND THE BRAVE, E.S.J. Prods. in association with Tomorrow Entertainment Inc. & Jones/Howard Ltd. Natalie R. Jones and Eugene S. Jones, Prods.

HONORARY AND OTHER:

(Jean Hersholt Humanitarian Award)

Arthur B. Krim

(Special Achievement)

FRANK BRENDEL, GLEN ROBINSON and **ALBERT WHITLOCK** for Visual Effects, Earthquake.

(Other)

HOWARD HAWKS - A master American filmmaker whose creative efforts hold a distinguished place in world cinema.
JEAN RENOIR - a genius who, with grace, responsibility and enviable devotion through silent film, sound film, feature, documentary and television, has won the world's admiration.

SCIENTIFIC OR TECHNICAL:

(Class II)

JOSEPH D. KELLY of Glen Glenn Sound for the design of new audio control consoles which have advanced the state of the art of sound recording and rerecording for motion picture production.
THE BURBANK STUDIOS Sound Department for the design of new audio control consoles engineered and constructed by the Quad-Eight Sound Corp.
SAMUEL GOLDWYN STUDIOS Sound Department for the design of a new audio control console engineered and constructed by the Quad-Eight Sound Corp.
QUAD-EIGHT SOUND CORPORATION for the engineering and construction of new audio control consoles designed by The Burbank Studios Sound Department and by the Samuel Goldwyn Studios Sound Department.
WALDON O. WATSON, RICHARD J. STUMPF, ROBERT J. LEONARD and the **UNIVERSAL CITY STUDIOS** Sound Department for the development and engineering of the Sensurround System for motion picture presentation.

(Class III)

ELEMACK COMPANY, Rome, Italy, for the design and development of their Spyder camera dolly.
LOUIS AMI of the Universal City Studios for the design and construction of a reciprocating camera platform used when photographing special visual effects for motion pictures.

1975

BEST PICTURE:

ONE FLEW OVER THE CUCKOO'S NEST, A Fantasy Films Production, UA. Saul Zaentz and Michael Douglas, Prods.
BARRY LYNDON, A Hawk Films, Ltd. Production, WB. Stanley Kubrick Prod.
DOG DAY AFTERNOON, WB. Martin Bregman and Martin Elfand, Prods.
JAWS, A U-Zanuck/Brown Production, U. Richard D. Zanuck and David Brown, Prods.
NASHVILLE, An ABC Entertainment-Jerry Weintraub-Robert Altman Production, PAR. Robert Altman, Prod.

ACTOR:

JACK NICHOLSON, One Flew Over The Cuckoo's Nest.
WALTER MATTHAU, *The Sunshine Boys*, A Ray Stark Production, MGM.
AL PACINO, *Dog Day Afternoon*.
MAXIMILIAN SCHELL, *The Man In The Glass Booth*, An Ely Landau Organization Production, AFT.
JAMES WHITMORE, *Give 'em Hell, Harry!*, A Theatrovision Production, AVE.

ACTRESS:

LOUISE FLETCHER, One Flew Over The Cuckoo's Nest.
ISABELLE ADJANI, *The Story Of Adele H.*, A Les Films du Carrosse-Les Productions Artistes Associes Production, NW.
ANN-MARGRET, *Tommy*, A Robert Stigwood Organisation, Ltd. Production, COL.
GLENDA JACKSON, *Hedda*, A Royal Shakespeare-Brut Productions-George Barrie/Robert Enders Film Production, Brut Productions.
CAROL KANE, *Hester Street*, Midwest Film Productions.

SUPPORTING ACTOR:

GEORGE BURNS, The Sunshine Boys.
BRAD DOURIF, *One Flew Over The Cuckoo's Nest.*
BURGESS MEREDITH, *The Day Of The Locust*, A Jerome Hellman Production, PAR.
CHRIS SARANDON, *Dog Day Afternoon.*
JACK WARDEN, *Shampoo*, Rubeeker Productions, COL.

SUPPORTING ACTRESS:

LEE GRANT, Shampoo.
RONEE BLAKELY, *Nashville.*
SYLVIA MILES, *Farewell, My Lovely*, An Elliott Kastner-ITC Production, AVE.
LILY TOMLIN, *Nashville,*
BRENDA VACCARO in Jacqueline Susann's *Once Is Not Enough*, A Howard W. Koch Production, PAR.

DIRECTING:

MILOS FORMAN, One Flew Over The Cuckoo's Nest.
ROBERT ALTMAN, *Nashville.*
FEDERICO FELLINI, *Amarcord,* An F.C. Productions-P.E.C.F. Production, NW.
STANLEY KUBRICK, *Barry Lyndon.*
SIDNEY LUMET, *Dog Day Afternoon.*

WRITING:

(Best Original Screenplay)

DOG DAY AFTERNOON. Frank Pierson.
AMARCORD. Federico Fellini and Tonino Guerra.
AND NOW MY LOVE, A Rizzoli Film-Les Films 13 Production, AVE. Claude Lelouch and Pierre Uytterhoeven.
LIES MY FATHER TOLD ME, Pentimento Productions, Ltd.-Pentacle VIII Productions, Ltd., COL. Ted Allan.
SHAMPOO. Robert Towne and Warren Beatty.

(Best Screenplay adapted from other material)

ONE FLEW OVER THE CUCKOO'S NEST. Screenplay by Lawrence Hauben and Bo Goldman.
BARRY LYNDON. Screenplay by Stanley Kubrick.
THE MAN WHO WOULD BE KING, An AA-COL Pictures Production, AA. Screenplay by John Huston and Gladys Hill.
SCENT OF A WOMAN, A Dean Film Production, FOX. Screenplay by Ruggero Maccari and Dino Risi.
THE SUNSHINE BOYS. Screenplay by Neil Simon.

CINEMATOGRAPHY:

BARRY LYNDON. John Alcott.
THE DAY OF THE LOCUST. Conrad Hall.
FUNNY LADY, A Rastar Pictures Production, COL. James Wong Howe.
THE HINDENBURG, A Robert Wise-Filmakers Group-U Production, U. Robert Surtees.

ONE FLEW OVER THE CUCKOO'S NEST. Haskell Wexler and Bill Butler.

COSTUME DESIGN:
BARRY LYNDON. Ulla-Britt Soderlund and Milena Canonero.
THE FOUR MUSKETEERS, A Film Trust S.A. Production, FOX. Yvonne Blake and Ron Talsky.
FUNNY LADY, A Rastar Pictures Production, COL. Ray Aghayan and Bob Mackie.
THE MAGIC FLUTE, A Sveriges Radio A.B. Production, Surrogate Releasing. Henny Noremark and Karin Erskine.
THE MAN WHO WOULD BE KING. Edith Head.

ART DIRECTION - SET DECORATION:
BARRY LYNDON. Ken Adam and Roy Walker. Set Decoration: Vernon Dixon.
THE HINDENBURG. Edward Carfagno. Set Decoration: Frank McKelvy.
THE MAN WHO WOULD BE KING. Alexander Trauner and Tony Inglis. Set Decoration: Peter James.
SHAMPOO. Richard Sylbert and W. Stewart Campbell. Set Decoration: George Gaines.
THE SUNSHINE BOYS. Albert Brenner. Set Decoration: Marvin March.

FILM EDITING:
JAWS. Verna Fields.
DOG DAY AFTERNOON. Dede Allen.
THE MAN WHO WOULD BE KING. Russell Lloyd.
ONE FLEW OVER THE CUCKOO'S NEST. Richard Chew, Lynzee Klingman and Sheldon Kahn.
THREE DAYS OF THE CONDOR, A Dino De Laurentiis Production, PAR. Frederic Steinkamp and Don Guidice.

FOREIGN LANGUAGE FILM:
DERSU UZALA, A Mosfilms Studios Production (U.S.S.R.).
LAND OF PROMISE, A Film Polski Production (Poland).
LETTERS FROM MARUSIA, A Conacine Production (Mexico).
SANDAKAN NO. 8, A Toho-Haiyuza Production (Japan).
SCENT OF A WOMAN. (Italy).

MUSIC - SCORING:
(Best Original Score)
JAWS. John Williams.
BIRDS DO IT, BEES DO IT, A Wolper Pictures Production, COL. Gerald Fried.
BITE THE BULLET, A Pax Enterprises Production, COL. Alex North.
ONE FLEW OVER THE CUCKOO'S NEST. Jack Nitzsche.
THE WIND AND THE LION, A Herb Jaffe Production, MGM. Jerry Goldsmith.
(Best Scoring-Original Song Score and/or Adaptation)
BARRY LYNDON. Adapted by Leonard Rosenman.
FUNNY LADY. Adapted by Peter Matz.
TOMMY. Adapted by Peter Townshend.

MUSIC - BEST SONG:
I'M EASY, Nashville. Music and lyrics by Keith Carradine.
HOW LUCKY CAN YOU GET, *Funny Lady.* Music and lyrics by Fred Ebb and John Kander.
NOW THAT WE'RE IN LOVE, *Whiffs*, Brut Productions, FOX. Music, George Barrie. Lyrics, Sammy Cahn.
RICHARD'S WINDOW, *The Other Side Of The Mountain,* A Filmways-Larry Peerce-U Production, U. Music, Charles Fox. Lyrics, Norman Gimbel.
THEME FROM MAHOGANY (DO YOU KNOW WHERE YOU'RE GOING TO), *Mahogany,* A Jobete Film Production, PAR. Music, Michael Masser. Lyrics, Gerry Goffin.

SOUND:
JAWS. Robert L. Hoyt, Roger Heman, Earl Madery and John Carter.
BITE THE BULLET. Arthur Piantadosi, Les Fresholtz, Richard Tyler and Al Overton, Jr.
FUNNY LADY. Richard Portman, Don MacDougall, Curly Thirlwell and Jack Solomon.
THE HINDENBERG. Leonard Peterson, John A. Bolger, Jr., John Mack and Don K. Sharpless.
THE WIND AND THE LION. Harry W. Tetrick, Aaron Rochin, William McCaughey and Roy Charman.

SHORT FILMS:
(Animated)
GREAT, Grantstern Ltd. and British Lion Films Ltd. Bob Godfrey, Prod.
KICK ME, Robert Swarthe Productions. Robert Swarthe Prod.
MONSIEUR POINTU, NFC. Rene Jodoin, Bernard Longpre and Andre Leduc, Prods.
SISYPHUS, Hungarofilms. Marcell Jankovics, Prod.
(Live Action)
ANGEL AND BIG JOE, Bert Salzman Productions. Bert Salzman, Prod.
CONQUEST OF LIGHT, Louis Marcus Films Ltd. Louis Marcus, Prod.
DAWN FLIGHT, Lawrence M. Lansburgh Productions. Lawrence M. Lansburgh and Brian Lansburgh, Prods.
A DAY IN THE LIFE OF BONNIE CONSOLO, Barr Films. Barry Spinello, Prod.
DOUBLETALK, Beattie Productions. Alan Beattie, Prod.

DOCUMENTARY:
(Short Subjects)
THE END OF THE GAME, Opus Films Ltd. Claire Wilbur and Robin Lehman, Prods.
ARTHUR AND LILLIE, Department of Communication, Stanford University. Jon Else, Steven Kovacs and Kristine Samuelson, Prods.
MILLIONS OF YEARS AHEAD OF MAN, BASF. Manfred Baier, Prod.
PROBES IN SPACE, Graphic Films. George V. Casey, Prod.
WHISTLING SMITH, NFC. Barrie Howells and Michael Scott, Prods.
(Features)
THE MAN WHO SKIED DOWN EVEREST, A Crawley Films Presentation. F.R. Crawley, James Hager and Dale Hartleben, Prods.
THE CALIFORNIA REICH, Yasny Talking Pictures. Walter F. Parkes and Keith F. Critchlow, Prods.
FIGHTING FOR OUR LIVES, A Farm Worker Film. Glen Pearcy, Prod.
THE INCREDIBLE MACHINE, The National Geographic Society and Wolper Prods. Irwin Rosten, Prod.
THE OTHER HALF OF THE SKY: A CHINA MEMOIR, MacLaine Productions. Shirley MacLaine, Prod.

HONORARY AND OTHER:
(Irving G. Thalberg Memorial Award)
Mervyn LeRoy
(Jean Hersholt Humanitarian Award)
Jules C. Stein
(Special Achievement)
PETER BERKOS for Sound Effects, The Hindenburg.
ALBERT WHITLOCK and GLEN ROBINSON for Visual Effects, The Hindenburg.
(Other)
MARY PICKFORD in recognition of her unique contributions to the film industry and the development of film as an artistic medium.

SCIENTIFIC OR TECHNICAL:
(Class II)
CHADWELL O'CONNOR of the O'Connor Engineering Laboratories for the concept and engineering of a fluid-damped camerahead for motion-picture photography.
WILLIAM F. MINER of Universal City Studios, Inc. and the WESTING-

HOUSE ELECTRIC CORPORATION for the development and engineering of a solid-state, 500 kilowatt, direct-current static rectifier for motion-picture lighting.
(Class III)
LAWRENCE W. BUTLER and ROGER BANKS for the concept of applying low inertia and stepping electric motors to film transport systems and optical printers for motion-picture production.
DAVID J. DEGENKOLB and FRED SCOBEY of Deluxe General Inc and JOHN C. DOLAN and RICHARD DUBOIS of the Akwaklame Co for the development of a technique for silver recovery from photographic wash-waters by ion exchange.
JOSEPH WESTHEIMER for the development of a device to obtain shadowed titles on motion-picture films.
CARTER EQUIPMENT CO., INC. and RAMTRONICS for the engineering and manufacture of a computerized tape punching system for programming laboratory printing machines.
THE HOLLYWOOD FILM COMPANY for the engineering and manufacture of a computerized tape punching system for programming laboratory printing machines.
BELL & HOWELL for the engineering and manufacture of a computerized tape punching system for programming laboratory printing machines.
FREDRIK SCHLYTER for the engineering and manufacture of a computerized tape punching system for programming laboratory printing machines.

1976

BEST PICTURE:
ROCKY, A Robert Chartoff-Irwin Winkler Production, UA. Irwin Winkler and Robert Chartoff, Prods.
ALL THE PRESIDENT'S MEN, A Wildwood Enterprises Production, WB. Walter Coblenz, Prod.
BOUND FOR GLORY, The Bound For Glory Co Production, UA. Robert F. Blumofe and Harold Leventhal, Prods.
NETWORK, A Howard Gottfried/Paddy Chayefsky Production, MGM/UA. Howard Gottfried, Prod.
TAXI DRIVER, A Bill/Phillips Production of a Martin Scorsese Film, COL. Michael Phillips and Julia Phillips, Prods.

ACTOR:
PETER FINCH, Network.
ROBERT DE NIRO, Taxi Driver.
GIANCARLO GIANNINI, Seven Beauties, A Medusa Distribuzione Production, C5.
WILLIAM HOLDEN, Network.
SYLVESTER STALLONE, Rocky.

ACTRESS:
FAYE DUNAWAY, Network.
MARIE-CHRISTINE BARRAULT, Cousin, Cousine, Les Films Pomereu-Gaumont Production, NTH.
TALIA SHIRE, Rocky.
SISSY SPACEK, Carrie, A Redbank Films Production, UA.
LIV ULLMANN, Face To Face, A Cinematograph A.B. Production, PAR.

SUPPORTING ACTOR:
JASON ROBARDS, All The President's Men.
NED BEATTY, Network.
BURGESS MEREDITH, Rocky.
LAURENCE OLIVIER, Marathon Man, A Robert Evans-Sidney Beckerman Production, PAR.
BURT YOUNG, Rocky.

SUPPORTING ACTRESS:
BEATRICE STRAIGHT, Network.
JANE ALEXANDER, All The President's Men.
JODIE FOSTER, Taxi Driver.
LEE GRANT, Voyage Of The Damned, An ITC Entertainment Production, AVE.
PIPER LAURIE, Carrie.

DIRECTING:
JOHN G. AVILDSEN, Rocky.
INGMAR BERGMAN, Face To Face.
SIDNEY LUMET, Network.
ALAN J. PAKULA, All The President's Men.
LINA WERTMULLER, Seven Beauties.

WRITING:
(Best Screenplay written directly for the screen)
NETWORK. Story and Screenplay by Paddy Chayefsky.
COUSIN, COUSINE. Story and Screenplay by Jean-Charles Tacchella. Adaptation by Daniele Thompson.
THE FRONT, COL Pictures. Story and Screenplay by Walter Bernstein.
ROCKY. Story and Screenplay by Sylvester Stallone.
SEVEN BEAUTIES. Story and Screenplay by Lina Wertmuller.
(Best Screenplay based on material from another medium)
ALL THE PRESIDENT'S MEN. Screenplay by William Goldman.
BOUND FOR GLORY. Screenplay by Robert Getchell.
FELLINI'S CASANOVA, A P.E.A.-Produzioni Europee Associate S.p.A. Production, U. Screenplay by Federico Fellini and Bernadino Zapponi.
THE SEVEN-PER-CENT SOLUTION, A Herbert Ross Film/Winitsky-Sellers Production, A U Release. Screenplay by Nicholas Meyer.
VOYAGE OF THE DAMNED. Screenplay by Steve Shagan and David Butler.

CINEMATOGRAPHY:
BOUND FOR GLORY. Haskell Wexler.
KING KONG, A Dino De Laurentiis Production, PAR. Richard H. Kline.
LOGAN'S RUN, A Saul David Production, MGM. Ernest Laszlo.
NETWORK. Owen Roizman.
A STAR IS BORN, A Barwood/Jon Peters Production, First Artists Presentation, WB. Robert Surtees.

COSTUME DESIGN:
FELLINI'S CASANOVA. Danilo Donati.
BOUND FOR GLORY. William Theiss.
THE INCREDIBLE SARAH, A Helen M. Strauss-Reader's Digest Films, Ltd. Production, BOR. Anthony Mendleson.
THE PASSOVER PLOT, Coast Industries-Golan-Globus Productions, Ltd., ATF. Mary Wills.
THE SEVEN-PER-CENT SOLUTION. Alan Barrett.

ART DIRECTION - SET DECORATION:
ALL THE PRESIDENT'S MEN. George Jenkins. Set Decoration: George Gaines.
THE INCREDIBLE SARAH. Elliot Scott and Norman Reynolds.
THE LAST TYCOON, A Sam Spiegel-Elia Kazan Film Production, PAR. Gene Callahan and Jack Collis. Set Decoration: Jerry Wunderlich.
LOGAN'S RUN. Dale Hennesy. Set Decoration: Robert de Vestel.
THE SHOOTIST, A Frankovich/Self Production, Dino De Laurentiis Presentation, PAR. Robert F. Boyle. Set Decoration: Arthur Jeph Parker.

FILM EDITING:
ROCKY. Richard Halsey and Scott Conrad.
ALL THE PRESIDENT'S MEN. Robert L. Wolfe.
BOUND FOR GLORY. Robert Jones and Pembroke J. Herring.
NETWORK. Alan Heim.
TWO-MINUTE WARNING, A Filmways/Larry Peerce-Edward S. Feldman Film Production, U. Eve Newman and Walter Hannemann.

FOREIGN LANGUAGE FILM:

BLACK AND WHITE IN COLOR, An Arthur Cohn Production/Societe Ivoirienne De Cinema (Ivory Coast).
COUSIN, COUSINE. (France).
JACOB, THE LIAR, A VEB/DEFA Production (German Democratic Republic).
NIGHTS AND DAYS, A Polish Corp for Film-"KADR" Film Unit Production (Poland).
SEVEN BEAUTIES. (Italy).

MUSIC - SCORING:

(Best Original Score)
THE OMEN, FOX Productions, Ltd., FOX, Jerry Goldsmith.
OBSESSION, George Litto Productions, COL. Bernard Herrmann.
THE OUTLAW JOSEY WALES, A Malpaso Co Production, WB. Jerry Fielding.
TAXI DRIVER. Bernard Herrmann.
VOYAGE OF THE DAMNED. Lalo Schifrin.

(Best Original Song Score and Its Adaptation or Best Adaptation Score)
BOUND FOR GLORY. Adapted by Leonard Rosenman.
BUGSY MALONE, A Goodtimes Enterprises, Ltd. Production, PAR. Song score and Its Adaptation by Paul Williams.
A STAR IS BORN. Adapted by Roger Kellaway.

MUSIC - BEST SONG:

EVERGREEN (Love Theme From A STAR IS BORN), A Star Is Born. Music, Barbra Streisand. Lyrics, Paul Williams.
AVE SATANI, *The Omen*. Music and lyrics by Jerry Goldsmith.
COME TO ME, *The Pink Panther Strikes Again*, Amjo Productions, Ltd., UA. Music, Henri Mancini. Lyrics, Don Black.
GONNA FLY NOW, *ROCKY*. Music, Bill Conti. Lyrics, Carol Connors and Ayn Robbins.
A WORLD THAT NEVER WAS, *Half A House*, Lenro Productions, First American Films. Music, Sammy Fain. Lyrics, Paul Francis Webster.

SOUND:

ALL THE PRESIDENT'S MEN. Arthur Piantadosi, Les Fresholtz, Dick Alexander and Jim Webb.
KING KONG. Harry Warren Tetrick, William McCaughey, Aaron Rochin and Jack Solomon.
ROCKY. Harry Warren Tetrick, William McCaughey, Lyle Burbridge and Bud Alper.
SILVER STREAK, A Frank Yablans Presentations Production, FOX. Donald Mitchell, Douglas Williams, Richard Tyler and Hal Etherington.
A STAR IS BORN. Robert Knudson, Dan Wallin, Robert Glass and Tom Overton.

SHORT FILMS:

(Animated)
LEISURE, A Film Australia Production. Suzanne Baker, Prod.
DEDALO, A Cineteam Realizzazioni Production. Manfredo Manfredi, Prod.
THE STREET, NFC. Caroline Leaf and Guy Glover, Prods.

(Live Action)
IN THE REGION OF ICE, An American Film Institute Production. Andre Guttfreund and Peter Werner, Prods.
KUDZU, A Short Production. Marjorie Anne Short, Prod.
THE MORNING SPIDER, The Black and White Colour Film Co. Julian Chagrin and Claude Chagrin, Prods.
NIGHTLIFE, Opus Films, Ltd. Claire Wilbur and Robin Lehman, Prods.
NUMBER ONE, Number One Productions. Dyan Cannon and Vince Cannon, Prods.

DOCUMENTARY:

(Short Subjects)
NUMBER OUR DAYS, Community Television of Southern California. Lynne Littman, Prod.
AMERICAN SHOESHINE, Titan Films. Sparky Greene, Prod.
BLACKWOOD, NFC. Tony Ianzelo and Andy Thompson, Prods.
THE END OF THE ROAD, Pelican Films. John Armstrong, Prod.
UNIVERSE, Graphic Films Corp. for NASA. Lester Novros, Prod.

(Features)
HARLAN COUNTY, U.S.A., Cabin Creek Films. Barbara Kopple, Prod.
HOLLYWOOD ON TRIAL, October Films/Cinema Associates Production. James Gutman and David Helpern, Jr., Prods.
OFF THE EDGE, Pentacle Films. Michael Firth, Prod.
PEOPLE OF THE WIND, Elizabeth E. Rogers Productions. Anthony Howarth and David Koff, Prods.
VOLCANO: An Inquiry Into The Life And Death Of Malcolm Lowry, NFC. Donald Brittain and Robert Duncan, Prods.

HONORARY AND OTHER:

(Irving G. Thalberg Memorial Award)
Pandro S. Berman

(Special Achievement)
CARLO RAMBALDI, GLEN ROBINSON and FRANK VAN DER VEER for Visual Effects, King Kong.
L.B. ABBOTT, GLEN ROBINSON and MATTHEW YURICICH for Visual Effects, Logan's Run.

SCIENTIFIC OR TECHNICAL:

(Class II)
CONSOLIDATED FILM INDUSTRIES and the **BARNEBEY-CHENEY COMPANY** for the development of a system for the recovery of film-cleaning solvent vapors in a motion-picture laboratory.
WILLIAM L. GRAHAM, MANFRED G. MICHELSON, GEOFFREY F. NORMAN and **SIEGFRIED SEIBERT** of Technicolor for the development and engineering of a Continuous, High-Speed, Color Motion-Picture Printing System.

(Class III)
FRED BARTSCHER of the Kollmorgen Corp and **GLENN BERGGREN** of the Schneider Corp for the design and development of a single-lens magnifier for motion-picture projection lenses.
PANAVISION INCORPORATED for the design and development of super-speed lenses for motion-picture photography.
HIROSHI SUZUKAWA of Canon and **WILTON R. HOLM** of AMPTP MotionPicture and Television Research Center for the design and development of super-speed lenses for motion-picture photography.
CARL ZEISS COMPANY for the design and development of super-speed lenses for motion-picture photography.
PHOTO RESEARCH DIVISION of the **KOLLMORGEN CORPORATION** for the engineering and manufacture of the spectra TriColor Meter.

1977

BEST PICTURE:

ANNIE HALL, Jack Rollins-Charles H. Joffe Productions, UA. Charles H. Joffe, Prod.
THE GOODBYE GIRL, A Ray Stark Production, MGM/WB. Ray Stark, Prod.
JULIA, FOX. Richard Roth, Prod.
STAR WARS, A Lucasfilm Ltd. Prodn., FOX. Gary Kurtz, Prod.
THE TURNING POINT, Hera Productions, FOX. Herbert Ross and Arthur Laurents, Prods.

ACTOR:
RICHARD DREYFUSS, The Goodbye Girl.
WOODY ALLEN, *Annie Hall*.
RICHARD BURTON, *Equus*, A Winkast Co, Ltd./P.B., Ltd. Production, UA.
MARCELLO MASTROIANNI, *A Special Day*, A Canafox Films Production, C5.
JOHN TRAVOLTA, *Saturday Night Fever*, A Robert Stigwood Production, PAR.

ACTRESS:
DIANE KEATON, Annie Hall.
ANNE BANCROFT, *The Turning Point*.
JANE FONDA, *Julia*.
SHIRLEY MACLAINE, *The Turning Point*.
MARSHA MASON, *The Goodbye Girl*.

SUPPORTING ACTOR:
JASON ROBARDS, Julia.
MIKHAIL BARYSHNIKOV, *The Turning Point*.
PETER FIRTH, *Equus*.
ALEC GUINNESS, *Star Wars*.
MAXIMILIAN SCHELL, *Julia*.

SUPPORTING ACTRESS:
VANESSA REDGRAVE, Julia.
LESLIE BROWNE, *The Turning Point*.
QUINN CUMMINGS, *The Goodbye Girl*.
MELINDA DILLON, *Close Encounters Of The Third Kind*, A Julia Phillips/Michael Phillips-Steven Spielberg Film Prodn., COL.
TUESDAY WELD, *Looking For Mr. Goodbar*, A Freddie Fields Production, PAR.

DIRECTING:
WOODY ALLEN, Annie Hall.
GEORGE LUCAS, *Star Wars*.
HERBET ROSS, *The Turning Point*.
STEVEN SPIELBERG, *Close Encounters Of The Third Kind*.
FRED ZINNEMANN, *Julia*.

WRITING:
(Best Screenplay written directly for the screen)
ANNIE HALL. Story and screenplay by Woody Allen and Marshall Brickman.
THE GOODBYE GIRL. Story and screenplay by Neil Simon.
THE LATE SHOW, A Lion's Gate Film Production, WB. Story and screenplay by Robert Benton.
STAR WARS. Story and screenplay by George Lucas.
THE TURNING POINT. Story and screenplay by Arthur Laurents.

(Best Screenplay based on material from another medium)
JULIA. Screenplay by Alvin Sargent.
EQUUS. Screenplay by Peter Shaffer.
I NEVER PROMISED YOU A ROSE GARDEN, A Scherick/Blatt Production, NW. Screenplay by Gavin Lambert and Lewis John Carlino.
OH, GOD!, WB. Screenplay by Larry Gelbart.
THAT OBSCURE OBJECT OF DESIRE, A Greenwich-Les Films Galaxie-Incine Compania Industrial, S.A. Production, First Artists. Screenplay by Luis Bunuel and Jean-Claude Carriere.

CINEMATOGRAPHY:
CLOSE ENCOUNTERS OF THE THIRD KIND. Vilmos Zsigmond.
ISLANDS IN THE STREAM, A Peter Bart/Max Palevsky Production, PAR. Fred J. Koenekamp.
JULIA. Douglas Slocombe.
LOOKING FOR MR. GOODBAR. William A. Fraker.
THE TURNING POINT. Robert Surtees.

COSTUME DESIGN:
STAR WARS, A Lucasfilm Ltd. Prodn, FOX. John Mollo.
AIRPORT '77. Edith Head and Burton Miller.
JULIA. Anthea Sylbert.
A LITTLE NIGHT MUSIC, A Sascha-Wien Film Production in association with Elliott Kastner, NW. Florence Klotz.
THE OTHER SIDE OF MIDNIGHT, A Frank Yablans Presentations Production, FOX. Irene Sharaff.

ART DIRECTION - SET DECORATION:
STAR WARS. John Barry, Norman Reynolds and Leslie Dilley. Set Decoration: Roger Christian.
AIRPORT '77. George C. Webb. Set Decoration: Mickey S. Michaels.
CLOSE ENCOUNTERS OF THE THIRD KIND. Joe Alves and Dan Lomino. Set Decoration: Phil Abramson.
THE SPY WHO LOVED ME, Eon Productions, UA. Ken Adam and Peter Lamont. Set Decoration: Hugh Scaife.
SET TURNING POINT. Albert Brenner. Set Decoration: Marvin March.

FILM EDITING:
STAR WARS. Paul Hirsch, Marcia Lucas and Richard Chew.
CLOSE ENCOUNTERS OF THE THIRD KIND. Michael Kahn.
JULIA. Walter Murch.
SMOKEY AND THE BANDIT, A U/Rastar Production, U. Walter Hannemann and Angelo Ross.
THE TURNING POINT. William Reynolds.

FOREIGN LANGUAGE FILM:
MADAME ROSA, A Lira Films Production (France).
IPHIGENIA, A Greek Film Centre Production (Greece).
OPERATION THUNDERBOLT, A Golan-Globus Production (Israel).
A SPECIAL DAY, A Canafox Films Production (Italy).
THAT OBSCURE OBJECT OF DESIRE. (Spain).

MUSIC - SCORING:
(Best Original Score)
STAR WARS. John Williams.
CLOSE ENCOUNTERS OF THE THIRD KIND. John Williams.
JULIA. Georges Delerue.
MOHAMMAD-MESSENGER OF GOD, A Filmco Int'l Production, Irwin Yablans Co. Maurice Jarre.
THE SPY WHO LOVED ME. Marvin Hamlisch.

(Best Original Song Score and Its Adaptation or Best Adaptation Score)
A LITTLE NIGHT MUSIC. Adapted by Jonathan Tunick.
PETE'S DRAGON, Walt Disney Productions, BV. Song Score by Al Kasha and Joel Hirschhorn. Adapted by Irwin Kostal.
THE SLIPPER AND THE ROSE - THE STORY OF CINDERELLA, Paradine Co-Productions, Ltd., U. Song Score by Richard M. Sherman and Robert B. Sherman. Adapted by Angela Morley.

MUSIC - BEST SONG:
YOU LIGHT UP MY LIFE, You Light Up My Life, The Session Co Production, COL. Music and lyrics by Joseph Brooks.
CANDLE ON THE WATER, *Pete's Dragon*. Music and lyrics by Al Kasha and Joel Hirschhorn.
NOBODY DOES IT BETTER, *The Spy Who Loved Me*. Music, Marvin Hamlisch. Lyrics, Carole Bayer Sager.
THE SLIPPER AND THE ROSE WALTZ (He Danced With Me/She Danced With Me), *The Slipper And The Rose - The Story Of Cinderella*. Music and lyrics, Richard M. Sherman and Robert B. Sherman.
SOMEONE'S WAITING FOR YOU, *The Rescuers*, Walt Disney Productions, BV. Music, Sammy Fain. Lyrics, Carol Connors and Ayn Robbins.

SOUND:

STAR WARS. Don MacDougall, Ray West, Bob Minkler and Derek Ball.
CLOSE ENCOUNTERS OF THE THIRD KIND. Robert Knudson, Robert J. Glass, Don MacDougall and Gene S. Cantamessa.
THE DEEP, A Casablanca Filmworks Production, COL. Walter Goss, Dick Alexander, Tom Beckert and Robin Gregory.
SORCERER, A William Friedkin Film Production, PAR-U. Robert Knudson, Robert J. Glass, Richard Tyler and Jean-Louis Ducarme.
THE TURNING POINT. Theodore Soderberg, Paul Wells, Douglas O. Williams and Jerry Jost.

SHORT FILMS:
(Animated)

SAND CASTLE, NFC. Co Hoedeman, Prod.
THE BEAD GAME, NFC. Ishu Patel, Prod.
THE DOONESBURY SPECIAL, The Hubley Studio. John and Faith Hubley and Gary Trudeau, Prods.
JIMMY THE C, A Motionpicker Production. Jimmy Picker, Robert Grossman and Craig Whittaker, Prods.

(Live Action)

I'LL FIND A WAY, NFC. Beverly Shaffer and Yuki Yoshida, Prods.
THE ABSENT-MINDED WAITER, The Aspen Film Society. William E. McEuen, Prod.
FLOATING FREE, A Trans World Int'l Production. Jerry Butts, Prod.
NOTES ON THE POPULAR ARTS, Saul Bass Films. Saul Bass, Prod.
SPACEBORNE, A Lawrence Hall of Science Production for the Regents of the University of California with the cooperation of NASA. Philip Dauber, Prod.

DOCUMENTARY:
(Short Subjects)

GRAVITY IS MY ENEMY, A John Joseph Production. John Joseph and Jan Stussy, Prods.
AGUEDA MARTINEZ: OUR PEOPLE, OUR COUNTRY, A Moctesuma Esparza Production. Moctesuma Esparza, Prod.
FIRST EDITION, D. L. Sage Productions. Helen Whitney and DeWitt L. Sage, Jr., Prods.
OF TIME, TOMBS AND TREASURE, A Charlie/Papa Production. James R. Messenger and Paul N. Raimondi, Prods.
THE SHETLAND EXPERIENCE, Balfour Films. Douglas Gordon, Prod.

DOCUMENTARY:
(Features)

WHO ARE THE DEBOLTS? AND WHERE DID THEY GET NINETEEN KIDS?, Korty Films and Charles M. Schulz Creative Associates in association with Sanrio Films. John Korty, Dan McCann and Warren L. Lockhart, Prods.
THE CHILDREN OF THEATRE STREET, Mack-Vaganova Co. Robert Dornhelm and Earle Mack, Prods.
HIGH GRASS CIRCUS, NFC. Bill Brind, Torben Schioler and Tony Ianzelo, Prods.
HOMAGE TO CHAGALL--THE COLOURS OF LOVE, A CBC Production. Harry Rasky, Prod.
UNION MAIDS, A Klein, Reichert, Mogulescu Production. James Klein, Julia Reichert and Miles Mogulescu, Prods.

SPECIAL VISUAL EFFECTS:

STAR WARS. John Stears, John Dykstra, Richard Edlund, Grant McCune andRobert Blalack.
CLOSE ENCOUNTERS OF THE THIRD KIND. Roy Arbogast, Douglas Trumbull, Matthew Yuricich, Gregory Jein and Richard Yuricich.

HONORARY AND OTHER:
(Irving G. Thalberg Memorial Award)

Walter Mirisch

(Jean Hersholt Humanitarian Award)

Charlton Heston

(Special Achievement)

BENJAMIN BURTT, JR. for the creation of the alien, creature and robot voices featured in "Star Wars".
Sound Effects Editing: FRANK E. WARNER for "Close Encounters Of The Third Kind".

(Other)

MARGARET BOOTH for her exceptional contribution to the art of film editing in the motion picture industry.
GORDON E. SAWYER in appreciation for outstanding service and dedication in upholding the high standards of the Academy of Motion Picture Arts and Sciences.
SIDNEY PAUL SOLOW in appreciation for outstanding service and dedication in upholding the high standards of the Academy of Motion Picture Arts and Sciences.

SCIENTIFIC OR TECHNICAL:
(Class I)

GARRETT BROWN and the CINEMA PRODUCTS CORP. engineering staff under the supervision of JOHN JURGENS, for the invention and development of Steadicam.

(Class II)

JOSEPH D. KELLY, EMORY M. COHEN, BARRY K. HENLEY, HAMMOND H. HOLT and JOHN AGALSOFF of Glen Glenn Sound for the concept and development of a Post-production Audio Processing System for Motion Picture Films.
PANAVISION INC., for the concept and engineering of the improvements incorporated in the Panaflex Motion Picture Camera.
N. PAUL KENWORTHY JR. and WILLIAM R. LATADY, for the invention and development of the Kenworthy Snorkel Camera System for motion picture photography.
JOHN C. DYKSTRA, for the development of a facility uniquely oriented toward visual effects photography, and to ALVAH J. MILLER and JERRY JEFFRESS, for the engineering of the Electronic Motion Control System used in concert for multiple exposure visual effects motion picture photography.
EASTMAN KODAK COMPANY, for the development and introduction of a new duplicating film for motion pictures.
STEFAN KUDELSKI of Nagra Magentic Recorders Inc., for the engineering of the improvements incorporated in the Nagra 4.2L sound recorder for motion picture production.

(Class III)

ERNST NETTMANN of the Astrovision Division of Continental Camera Systems Inc., for the engineering of its Periscope Aerial Camera System.
EECO (Electronic Engineering Co of California), for developing a method for interlocking non-sprocketed film and tape media used in motion picture production.
DR. BERNHARD KUHL and WERNER BLOCK of OSRAM, GmbH, for the development of the HMI high-efficiency discharge lamp for motion picture lighting.
PANAVISION INC., for the design of Panalite, a camera-mounted controllable light for motion picture photography.
PANAVISION INC., for the engineering of the Panahead gearhead for motion picture cameras. (Panavision rejected the three awards because its Panaflex camera was voted a Class Two instead of a Class One award.)
PICLEAR INC., for originating and developing an attachment to motion picture projectors to improve screen image quality.

1978

BEST PICTURE:

THE DEER HUNTER, An EMI Films/Michael Cimino Film Prod., U. Barry Spikings, Michael Deeley, Michael Cimino and John Peverall, Prods.

COMING HOME. A Jerome Hellman Enterprises Prods, UA. Jerome Hellman, Prod.
HEAVEN CAN WAIT. Dogwood Productions, PAR. Warren Beatty, Prod.
MIDNIGHT EXPRESS, A Casablanca-Filmworks Prod., COL. Alan Marshall and David Puttnam, Prods.
AN UNMARRIED WOMAN, A FOX Prod., FOX. Paul Mazursky and Tony Ray, Prods.

ACTOR:
JON VOIGHT, Coming Home.
WARREN BEATTY, *Heaven Can Wait.*
GARY BUSEY, *The Buddy Holly Story,* An Innovisions-ECA Prod., COL.
ROBERT DE NIRO, *The Deer Hunter.*
LAURENCE OLIVIER, *The Boys From Brazil,* An ITC Entertainment Prod., FOX.

ACTRESS:
JANE FONDA, Coming Home.
INGRID BERGMAN, *Autumn Sonata,* A Personafilm GmbH Prod., Sir Lew Grade-Martin Starger-ITC Entertainment Presentation, NW.
ELLEN BURSTYN, *Same Time, Next Year,* A Walter Mirisch-Robert Mulligan Prod., Mirisch Corporation/U Pictures Presentation, U.
JILL CLAYBURGH, *An Unmarried Woman.*
GERALDINE PAGE, *Interiors,* A Jack Rollins-Charles H Joffe Prod., UA.

SUPPORTING ACTOR:
CHRISTOPHER WALKEN, The Deer Hunter.
BRUCE DERN, *Coming Home.*
RICHARD FARNSWORTH, *Comes a Horseman,* A Robert Chartoff-Irwin Winkler Prod., UA.
JOHN HURT, *Midnight Express.*
JACK WARDEN, *Heaven Can Wait.*

SUPPORTING ACTRESS:
MAGGIE SMITH, California Suite, A Ray Stark Prod., COL.
DYAN CANNON, *Heaven Can Wait.*
PENELOPE MILFORD, *Coming Home.*
MAUREEN STAPLETON, *Interiors.*
MERYL STREEP, *The Deer Hunter.*

DIRECTING:
MICHAEL CIMINO, The Deer Hunter.
WOODY ALLEN, *Interiors.*
HAL ASHBY, *Coming Home.*
WARREN BEATTY, *Heaven Can Wait.*
BUCK HENRY, *Heaven Can Wait.*
ALAN PARKER, *Midnight Express.*

WRITING:
(Best Screenplay Written Directly For The Screen)
COMING HOME. Story by Nancy Dowd. Screenplay by Waldo Salt and Robert C Jones.
AUTUMN SONATA. Story and screenplay by Ingmar Bergman.
THE DEER HUNTER. Story by Michael Cimino, Deric Washburn, Louis Garfinkle and Quinn K Redeker. Screenplay by Deric Washburn.
INTERIORS. Story and screenplay by Woody Allen.
AN UNMARRIED WOMAN. Story and screenplay by Paul Mazursky.
(Best Screenplay Based On Material From Another Medium)
MIDNIGHT EXPRESS. Screenplay by Oliver Stone.
BLOODBROTHERS, A WB Prod., WB. Screenplay by Walter Newman.
CALIFORNIA SUITE. Screenplay by Neil Simon.
HEAVEN CAN WAIT. Screenplay by Elaine May and Warren Beatty.
SAME TIME, NEXT YEAR. Screenplay by Bernard Slade.

CINEMATOGRAPHY:
DAYS OF HEAVEN, An OP Prod., PAR. Nestor Almendros.
THE DEER HUNTER. Vilmos Zsigmond.
HEAVEN CAN WAIT. William A Fraker.
SAME TIME, NEXT YEAR. Robert Surtees.
THE WIZ, A Motown/U Pictures Prod., U. Oswald Morris.

COSTUME DESIGN:
DEATH ON THE NILE, A John Brabourne-Richard Goodwin Prod., PAR. Anthony Powell.
CARAVANS, An Ibex Films-F.I.D.C.I. Prod., U. Renie Conley.
DAYS OF HEAVEN. Patricia Norris.
THE SWARM, A WB Prod., WB. Paul Zastupnevich.
THE WIZ. Tony Walton.

ART DIRECTION - SET DECORATION:
HEAVEN CAN WAIT. Paul Sylbert and Edwin O'Donovan. Set Decoration: George Gaines.
THE BRINK'S JOB, A William Friedkin Film/U Prod., Dino De Laurentiis Presentation, U. Dean Tavoularis and Angelo Graham. Set Decoration: George R Nelson and Bruce Kay.
CALIFORNIA SUITE. Albert Brenner. Set Decoration: Marvin March.
INTERIORS. Mel Bourne. Set Decoration: Daniel Robert.
THE WIZ. Tony Walton and Philip Rosenberg. Set Decoration: Edward Stewart and Robert Drumheller.

FILM EDITING:
THE DEER HUNTER. Peter Zinner.
THE BOYS FROM BRAZIL. Robert E Swink.
COMING HOME. Don Zimmerman.
MIDNIGHT EXPRESS. Gerry Hambling.
SUPERMAN, A Dovemead Ltd Prod., Alexander Salkind Presentation, WB. Stuart Baird.

FOREIGN LANGUAGE FILM:
GET OUT YOUR HANDKERCHIEFS, A Les Films Ariane - C.A.P.A.C. Prod. (France).
THE GLASS CELL, A Roxy Film Prod. (German Federal Republic).
HUNGARIANS, A Dialog Studio Prod. (Hungary).
VIVA ITALIA!, A Dean Film Prod. (Italy).
WHITE BIM BLACK EAR, A Central Studio of Films for Children and Youth Prod. (U.S.S.R.).

MUSIC - SCORING:
(Best Original Score)
MIDNIGHT EXPRESS. Giorgio Moroder.
THE BOYS FROM BRAZIL. Jerry Goldsmith.
DAYS OF HEAVEN. Ennio Morricone.
HEAVEN CAN WAIT. Dave Grusin.
SUPERMAN. John Williams.
(Best Adaptation Score)
THE BUDDY HOLLY STORY. Adaptation score by Joe Renzetti.
PRETTY BABY, A Louis Malle Film Prod., PAR. Adaptation score by Jerry Wexler.
THE WIZ. Adaptation score by Quincy Jones.

MUSIC - BEST SONG:
LAST DANCE, Thank God It's Friday, A Casablanca-Motown Prod., COL. Music and lyrics by Paul Jabara.
HOPELESSLY DEVOTED TO YOU, *Grease,* A Robert Stigwood/Allan Carr Prod., PAR. Music and lyrics by John Farrar.
THE LAST TIME I FELT LIKE THIS, *Same Time, Next Year.* Music by Marvin Hamlisch. Lyrics by Alan and Marilyn Bergman.
READY TO TAKE A CHANCE AGAIN, *Foul Play,* A Miller-Milkis/Colin Higgins Picture Prod., PAR. Music by Charles Fox. Lyrics by Norman Gimbel.
WHEN YOU'RE LOVED, *The Magic of Lassie,* Lassie Prods., The Int'l Picture Show Co. Music and lyrics by Richard M Sherman and Robert B Sherman.

SOUND:

THE DEER HUNTER. Richard Portman, William McCaughey, Aaron Rochin and Darrin Knight.
THE BUDDY HOLLY STORY. Tex Rudloff, Joel Fein, Curly Thirlwell and Willie Burton.
DAYS OF HEAVEN. John K Wilkinson, Robert W Glass, Jr, John T Reitz and Barry Thomas.
HOOPER, A WB Prod., WB. Robert Knudson, Robert J Glass, Don MacDougall and Jack Solomon.
SUPERMAN. Gordon K McCallum, Graham Hartstone, Nicolas Le Messurier and Roy Charman.

SHORT FILMS:
(Animated)

SPECIAL DELIVERY, National Film Board of Canada. Eunice Macaulay and John Weldon, Prods.
OH MY DARLING, Nico Crama Prods. Nico Crama, Prod.
RIP VAN WINKLE, A Will Vinton/Billy Budd Film, Will Vinton Prod. Will Vinton, Prod.

(Live Action)

TEENAGE FATHER, New Visions Inc. for the Children's Home Society of California. Taylor Hackford, Prod.
A DIFFERENT APPROACH, A Jim Belcher/Brookfield Prod. Jim Belcher and Fern Field, Prods.
MANDY'S GRANDMOTHER, Illumination Films. Andrew Sugerman, Prod.
STRANGE FRUIT, The America Film Institute. Seth Pinsker, Prod.

DOCUMENTARY:
(Short Subjects)

THE FLIGHT OF THE GOSSAMER CONDOR, A Shedd Prod. Jacqueline Phillips Shedd, Ben Shedd, Prods.
THE DIVIDED TRAIL: A Native American Odyssey, A Jerry Aronson Prod. Jerry Aronson, Prod.
AN ENCOUNTER WITH FACES, Films Division, Government of India. K K Kapil, Prod.
GOODNIGHT MISS ANN, An August Cinquegrana Films Prod. August Cinquegrana, Prod.
SQUIRES OF SAN QUENTIN, The J Gary Mitchell Film Co. J Gary Mitchell, Prod.

(Features)

SCARED STRAIGHT!, A Golden West Television Prod. Arnold Shapiro, Prod.
THE LOVERS' WIND, Ministry of Culture & Arts of Iran. Albert Lamorisse, Prod.
MYSTERIOUS CASTLES OF CLAY, A Survival Anglia Ltd Prod. Alan Root, Prod.
RAONI, A Franco-Brazilian Prod. Jean-Pierre Dutilleux, Barry Williams and Michel Gast, Prods.
WITH BABIES AND BANNERS: STORY OF THE WOMEN'S EMERGENCY BRIGADE, A Women's Labor History Film Project Prod. Anne Bohlen, Lyn Goldfarb and Lorraine Gray, Prods.

HONORARY AND OTHER AWARDS:
(Jean Hersholt Humanitarian Award):

Leo Jaffe.

(Special Achievement Awards):

Visual Effects: LES BOWIE, COLIN CHILVERS, DENYS COOP, ROY FELD, DEREK MEDDINGS and ZORAN PERISIC, Superman.
(Other)
WALTER LANTZ for bringing joy and laughter to every part of the world through his unique animated motion pictures.
THE MUSEUM OF MODERN ART, DEPARTMENT OF FILM for the contribution it has made to the public's perception of movies as an art form.
LAURENCE OLIVIER for the full body of his work, for the unique achievements of his entire career and his lifetime of contribution to the art of film.
KING VIDOR for his incomparable achievements as a cinematic creator and innovator.

(Medals Of Commendation)
LINWOOD G DUNN, LOREN L RYDER and WALDON O WATSON in appreciation for outstanding service and dedication in upholding the high standards of the Academy of Motion Picture Arts and Sciences.

SCIENTIFIC OR TECHNICAL
(Academy Award of Merit)

EASTMAN KODAK COMPANY, for the research and development of a Duplicating Color Film for Motion Pictures.
STEFAN KUDELSKI of Nagra Magnetic Recorders, Inc., for the continuing research, design and development of the Nagra Production Sound Recorder for Motion Pictures.
PANAVISION, INC., and its engineering staff under the direction of ROBERT E GOTTSCHALK, for the concept, design and continuous development of the Panaflex Motion Picture Camera System.

(Scientific and Engineering Award)
RAY M DOLBY, IOAN R ALLEN, DAVID P ROBINSON, STEPHEN M KATZ and PHILIP S J BOOLE of Dolby Laboratories, Inc., for the development and implementation of an improved Sound Recording and Reproducing System for Motion Picture Prod. and Exhibition.

(Technical Achievement Award)
KARL MACHER and GLENN M BERGGREN of Isco Optische Werke for the development and introduction of the Cinelux-ULTRA Lens for 35mm Motion Picture Projection.
DAVID J DEGENKOLB, ARTHUR L FORD and FRED J SCOBEY of DeLuxe General, Inc., for the development of a method to Recycle Motion Picture Laboratory Photographic Wash Waters by Ion Exchange.
KIICHI SEKIGUCHI of CINE-FI International for the development of the CINE-FI Auto Radio Sound System for Drive-in Theaters.
LEONARD CHAPMAN of Leonard Equipment Co., for the design and manufacture of a small, mobile, motion picture camera platform known as the Chapman Hustler Dolly.
JAMES L FISHER of J L Fisher, Inc., for the design and manufacture of a small, mobile, motion picture camera platform known as the Fisher Model Ten Dolly.
ROBERT STINDT of Production Grip Equipment Co., for the design and manufacture of a small, mobile, motion picture camera platform known as the Stindt Dolly.

1979

BEST PICTURE:

KRAMER VS. KRAMER, Stanley Jaffe Productions, Col. Stanley R Jaffe Prod.
ALL THAT JAZZ, A Columbia/Twentieth Century-Fox Production, Fox. Robert Alan Aurthur, Prod.
APOCALYPSE NOW, An Omni Zoetrope Production, UA. Francis Coppola, Prod. Fred Roos, Gray Frederickson and Tom Sternberg, Co-Prods.
BREAKING AWAY, Fox. Peter Yates, Prod.
NORMA RAE, Fox. Tamara Asseyev and Alex Rose, Prods.

ACTOR:

DUSTIN HOFFMAN, Kramer vs. Kramer.
JACK LEMMON, *The China Syndrome,* A Michael Douglas/IPC Films Production, Col.
AL PACINO, *. . .And Justice For All,* A Malton Films Limited Production, Col.
ROY SCHEIDER, *All That Jazz.*
PETER SELLERS, *Being There,* A Lorimar Film-Und Fernsehproduktion GmbH Production, UA.

ACTRESS:
SALLY FIELD, Norma Rae.
JILL CLAYBURGH, *Starting Over,* An Alan J Pakula/James L Brooks Production, Par.
JANE FONDA, *China Syndrome.*
MARSHA MASON, *Chapter Two,* A Ray Stark Production, Col.
BETTE MIDLER, *The Rose,* Fox.

SUPPORTING ACTOR:
MELVYN DOUGLAS, Being There.
ROBERT DUVALL, *Apocalypse Now.*
FREDERIC FORREST, *The Rose.*
JUSTIN HENRY, *Kramer vs. Kramer.*
MICKEY ROONEY, *The Black Stallion,* An Omni Zoetrope Production, UA.

SUPPORTING ACTRESS:
MERYL STREEP, Kramer vs. Kramer.
JANE ALEXANDER, *Kramer vs. Kramer.*
BARBARA BARRIE, *Breaking Away.*
CANDICE BERGEN, *Starting Over.*
MARIEL HEMINGWAY, *Manhattan,* A Jack Rollins-Charles H Joffe Production, UA.

DIRECTING:
ROBERT BENTON, Kramer vs. Kramer.
BOB FOSSE, *All That Jazz.*
FRANCIS COPPOLA, *Apocalypse Now.*
PETER YATES, *Breaking Away.*
EDOUARD MOLINARO, *La Cage Aux Folles,* A Les Productions Artistes Associes Da Ma Produzione SPA Production, UA.

WRITING:
(Best Screenplay Written Directly For The Screen)
BREAKING AWAY. Story and screenplay by Steve Tesich.
ALL THAT JAZZ. Story and screenplay by Robert Alan Aurthur and Bob Fosse.
. . .AND JUSTICE FOR ALL. Story and screenplay by Valerie Curtin and Barry Levinson.
THE CHINA SYNDROME. Story and screenplay by Mike Gray, T S Cook and James Bridges.
MANHATTAN. Story and screenplay by Woody Allen and Marshall Brickman.

(Best Screenplay Based On Material From Another Medium)
KRAMER VS. KRAMER. Screenplay by Robert Benton.
APOCALYPSE NOW. Screenplay by John Milius and Francis Coppola.
LA CAGE AUX FOLLES. Screenplay and adaptation by Francis Veber, Edouard Molinaro, Marcello Danon and Jean Poiret.
A LITTLE ROMANCE, A Pan Arts Associates Production, Orion Pictures Company. Screenplay by Allan Burns.
NORMA RAE. Screenplay by Irving Ravetch and Harriet Frank, Jr.

CINEMATOGRAPHY:
APOCALYPSE NOW. Vittorio Storaro.
ALL THAT JAZZ. Giuseppe Rotunno.
THE BLACK HOLE, Walt Disney Productions, Frank Phillips.
KRAMER VS. KRAMER. Nestor Almendros.
1941, An A-Team/Steven Spielberg Film Production, Universal-Columbia Presentation, U. William A Fraker.

COSTUME DESIGN:
ALL THAT JAZZ. FOX. Albert Wolsky.
AGATHA, A Sweetwall Production in association with Casablanca Filmworks, First Artists Presentation. WB. Shirley Russell.
BUTCH AND SUNDANCE: THE EARLY DAYS. FOX. William Ware Theiss.
THE EUROPEANS, Merchant Ivory Productins, Levitt-Pickman. Judy Moorcroft.
LA CAGE AUX FOLLES, UA Piero Tosi and Ambra Danon.

ART DIRECTION - SET DECORATION:
ALL THAT JAZZ. Philip Rosenberg and Tony Walton. Set Decoration: Edward Stewart and Gary Brink.
ALIEN. Michael Seymour, Les Dilley and Roger Christian. Set Decoration: Ian Whittaker.
APOCALYPSE NOW. Dean Tavoularis and Angelo Graham. Set Decoration: George R Nelson.
THE CHINA SYNDROME. George Jenkins. Set Decoration: Arthur Jeph Parker.
STAR TREK - THE MOTION PICTURE, A Century Associates Production, PAR. Harold Michelson, Joe Jennings, Leon Harris and John Vallone. Set Decoration: Linda DeScenna.

FILM EDITING:
ALL THAT JAZZ. Alan Heim.
APOCALYPSE NOW. Richard Marks, Walter Murch, Gerald B Greenberg and Lisa Fruchtman.
THE BLACK STALLION. Robert Dalva.
KRAMER VS. KRAMER. Jerry Greenberg.
THE ROSE. Robert L Wolfe and C Timothy O'Meara.

FOREIGN LANGUAGE FILM:
THE TIN DRUM, A Franz Seitz Film/Bioskop Film/Artemis Film/ Hallelujah Film/ GGB 14.KG/Argos Films Production (Federal Republic of Germany).
THE MAIDS OF WILKO, A Polish Corporation for Film Production (Poland).
MAMA TURNS A HUNDRED, Elias Querejeta P C Production (Spain).
A SIMPLE STORY, A Renn Productions/Sara Films/F R 3/Rialto Films Production, Quartet Films (France).
TO FORGET VENICE, A Rizzoli Film/Action Film Production, Quartet Films (Italy).

MUSIC - SCORING:
(Best Original Score)
A LITTLE ROMANCE. WB. Georges Delerue.
THE AMITYVILLE HORROR, An American International/Professional Films Production. AIP. Lalo Schifrin.
THE CHAMP. MGM Dave Grusin.
STAR TREK - THE MOTION PICTURE. Jerry Goldsmith.
10, Geoffrey Productions, Orion Pictures Company. WB. Henry Mancini.

(Best Original Song Score and Its Adaptation or Best Adaptation Score)
ALL THAT JAZZ. Adaptation Score by Ralph Burns.
BREAKING AWAY. Adaptation Score by Patrick Williams.
THE MUPPET MOVIE, A Jim Henson Production. Lord Grade/Martin Starger Presentation. AFD. Original Song Score by Paul Williams and Kenny Ascher. Adapted by Paul Williams.

MUSIC - BEST SONG:
IT GOES LIKE IT GOES, Norma Rae. Music by David Shire. Lyric by Norman Gimbel.
THE RAINBOW CONNECTION, *The Muppet Movie.* Music and lyric by Paul Williams and Kenny Ascher.
IT'S EASY TO SAY, *10.* Music by Henry Mancini. Lyric by Robert Wells.
THROUGH THE EYES OF LOVE, *Ice Castles,* An International Cinemedia Center Production, Col. Music by Marvin Hamlisch. Lyric by Carole Bayer Sager.
I'LL NEVER SAY "GOODBYE", *The Promise,* A Fred Weintraub-Paul Heller Present/Universal Production, U. Music by David Shire. Lyric by Alan and Marilyn Bergman.

SOUND:
APOCALYPSE NOW. Walter Murch, Mark Berger, Richard Beggs and Nat Boxer.
THE ELECTRIC HORSEMAN. Arthur Piantadosi, Les Fresholtz, Michael Minkler and Al Overton.

METEOR, Meteor Productions, AIP. William McCaughey, Aaron Rochin, Michael J Kohut and Jack Solomon.
1941. Robert Knudson, Robert J Glass, Don MacDougall and Gene S Cantamessa.
THE ROSE. Theodore Soderberg, Douglas Williams, Paul Wells and Jim Webb.

SHORT FILMS:
(Animated)
EVERY CHILD, National Film Board of Canada. Derek Lamb, Prod.
DREAM DOLL, Bob Godfrey Films/Zagreb Films/Halas and Batchelor, Filmwright. Bob Godfrey and Zlatko Grgic, Prods.
IT'S SO NICE TO HAVE A WOLF AROUND THE HOUSE, AR&T Productions for Learning Corporation of America. Paul Fierlinger, Prod.
(Live Action)
BOARD AND CARE, Ron Ellis Films. Sarah Pillsbury and Ron Ellis, Prods.
BRAVERY IN THE FIELD, National Film Board of Canada. Roman Kroitor and Stefan Wodoslawsky, Prods.
OH BROTHER, MY BROTHER, Ross Lowell Productions, Pyramid Films, Inc. Carol and Ross Lowell, Prods.
THE SOLAR FILM, Wildwood Enterprises Inc. Saul Bass and Michael Britton, Prods.
SOLLY'S DINER, Mathias/Zukerman/Hankin Productions. Harry Mathias, Jay Zukerman and Larry Hankin, Prods.

DOCUMENTARY:
(Short Subjects)
PAUL ROBESON: TRIBUTE TO AN ARTIST, Janus Films, Inc. Saul J Turell, Prod.
DAE, Vardar Film/Skopje. Risto Teofilovski, Prod.
KORYO CELADON, Charlie/Papa Productions, Inc. Donald A Connolly and James R Messenger, Prods.
NAILS, National Film Board of Canada. Phillip Borsos, Prod.
REMEMBER ME, Dick Young Productions, Ltd. Dick Young, Prod.
(Features)
BEST BOY, Only Child Motion Pictures, Inc. Ira Wohl, Prod.
GENERATION ON THE WIND, More Than One Medium. David A Vassar, Prod.
GOING THE DISTANCE, National Film Board of Canada. Paul Cowan and Jacques Bobet, Prods.
THE KILLING GROUND, ABC News Closeup Unit. Steve Singer and Tom Priestley, Prods.
THE WAR AT HOME, Catalyst Films/Madison Film Production Co. Glenn Silber and Barry Alexander Brown, Prods.

VISUAL EFFECTS:
ALIEN. H R Giger, Carlo Rambaldi, Brian Johnson, Nick Allder and Denys Ayling.
THE BLACK HOLE. Peter Ellenshaw, Art Cruickshank, Eustace Lycett, Danny Lee, Harrison Ellenshaw and Joe Hale.
MOONRAKER, Eon Productions Ltd, UA. Derek Meddings, Paul Wilson and John Evans.
1941. William A Fraker, A D Flowers and Gregory Jein.
STAR TREK - THE MOTION PICTURE. Douglas Trumbull, John Dykstra, Richard Yuricich, Robert Swarthe, Dave Stewart and Grant McCune.

HONORARY AND OTHER:
(Irving G. Thalberg Memorial Award)
RAY STARK.
(Jean Hersholt Humanitarian Award)
ROBERT BENJAMIN.

SPECIAL ACHIEVEMENT AWARD:
(Sound Editing)
ALAN SPLET, The Black Stallion.
(Other)
HAL ELIAS for his dedication and distinguished service to the Academy of Motion Picture Arts and Sciences.
ALEC GUINNESS for advancing the art of screen acting through a host of memorable and distinguished performances.
(Medals Of Commendation)
JOHN O AALBERG, CHARLES G CLARKE and **JOHN G FRAYNE** in appreciation for outstanding service and dedication in upholding the high standards of the Academy of Motion Picture Arts and Sciences.

SCIENTIFIC OR TECHNICAL AWARDS:
(Academy Award of Merit)
Mark Serrurier for the progressive development of the Moviola from the 1924 invention of his father, Iwan Serrurier, to the present Series 20 sophisticated film editing equipment.
(Scientific and Engineering Award)
Neiman-Tillar Associates for the creative development, and to Mini-Micro Systems, Inc., for the design and engineering of an Automated Computer Controlled Editing Sound System (ACCESS) for motion picture post-production.
(Technical Achievement Award)
Michael V Chewey, Walter G Eggers and Allen Hecht of M-G-M Laboratories for the development of a Computer-controlled Paper Tape Programmer System and its applications in the motion picture laboratory.
Irwin Young, Paul Kaufman and Fredrik Schlyter of Du Art Film Laboratories, Inc., for the development of a Computer-controlled Paper Tape Programmer System and its applications in the motion picture laboratory.
James S Stanfield and Paul W Trester for the development and manufacture or a device for the repair or protection of sprocket holes in motion picture film.
Zoran Perisic of Courier Films, Limited, for the Zoptic Special Optical Effects Device for motion picture photography.
A D Flowers and Logan R Frazee for the development of a device to control flight patterns of miniature airplanes during motion picture photography.
The Photo Research Division of Kollmorgen Corp. for the development of the Spectra Series II Cine Special Exposure Meter for motion picture photography.
Bruce Lyon and John Lamb for the development of a Video Animation System for testing motion picture animation sequences.
Ross Lowell of Lowel-Light Manufacturing, Inc., for the development of compact lighting equipment for motion picture photography.

ALL-TIME FILM RENTAL CHAMPS

This compilation represents film rentals received by distribution companies from the U.S.–Canada market through Dec. 31, 1980. It should not be confused with total box-office ticket sales grosses.

Due to widely differing deals and methods of reporting revenues, no accurate summary of worldwide revenues is possible.

In the following list, the film title is followed by the name of the director; the producer or production company; the distribution company; the year of release, the total revenues to date.

Because of ties there are actually 101 films listed.

100 ALL TIME FILM RENTAL CHAMPS

TITLE / DIRECTOR-PRODUCER-DISTRIBUTOR	TOTAL RENTALS
Star Wars (G. Lucas; G. Kurtz; Fox; 1977)	$175,685,000
Jaws (S. Spielberg; Zanuck/Brown; U; 1975)	133,435,000
The Empire Strikes Back (I. Kershner; G. Lucas/G. Kurtz; Fox; 1980)	120,000,000
Grease (R. Kleiser; R. Stigwood/A. Carr; Par; 1978)	96,300,000
The Exorcist (W. Friedkin; W. P. Blatty; WB; 1973)	88,500,000
The Godfather (F. Coppola; A. Ruddy; Par; 1972)	86,275,000
Superman (R. Donner; P. Spengler; WB; 1978)	82,500,000
The Sound of Music (R. Wise; Fox; 1965)	79,748,000
The Sting (G. R. Hill; T. Bill/M. & J. Phillips; U; 1973)	78,963,000
Close Encounters of the Third Kind (S. Spielberg; J. & M. Phillips; Col; 1977)	77,000,000
Gone With The Wind (V. Fleming; D. Selznick; MGM/UA; 1939)	76,700,000
Saturday Night Fever (J. Badham; R. Stigwood; Par; 1977)	74,100,000
National Lampoon Animal House (J. Landis; M. Simmons/I. Reitman; U; 1978)	74,000,000
Smokey and The Bandit (H. Needham; M. Engelberg; U; 1977)	61,055,000
Kramer Vs. Kramer (R. Benton; S. Jaffe; Col; 1979)	60,528,000
One Flew Over The Cuckoo's Nest (M. Forman; S. Zaentz/M. Douglas; UA; 1975)	59,000,000
Star Trek (R. Wise; G. Roddenberry; Par; 1979)	56,000,000
American Graffiti (G. Lucas; F. Coppola; U; 1973)	55,886,000
Jaws II (J. Szwarc; Zanuck/Brown; U; 1978)	55,608,000
Rocky (J. Avildsen; Chartoff/Winkler; UA; 1976)	54,000,000
Every Which Way But Loose (J. Fargo; R. Daley; WB; 1978)	51,800,000
Love Story (A. Hiller; H. Minsky; Par; 1970)	50,000,000
Towering Inferno (J. Guillermin; I. Allen; Fox/WB; 1975)	50,000,000
Heaven Can Wait (W. Beatty; Par; 1978)	49,400,000
The Graduate (M. Nichols; L. Turman; AVE; 1968)	49,078,000
Doctor Zhivago (D. Lean; C. Ponti; MGM/UA; 1965)	46,550,000
Butch Cassidy and the Sundance Kid (G. R. Hill; J. Foreman; Fox; 1969)	46,039,000
Airport (G. Seaton; R. Hunter; U; 1970)	45,300,000
Blazing Saddles (M. Brooks; M. Hertzberg; WB; 1974)	45,200,000
Mary Poppins (R. Stevenson; W. Disney; BV; 1964)	45,000,000
Rocky II (S. Stallone; UA; 1979)	43,049,274
The Ten Commandments (C. B. DeMille; Par; 1956)	43,000,000
The Jerk (C. Reiner; D. V. Picker/W. E. McEuen; U; 1979)	43,000,000
The Poseidon Adventure (R. Neame; I. Allen; Fox; 1972)	42,000,000
Goodbye Girl (H. Ross; R. Stark; MGM/WB; 1977)	41,700,000
Fiddler on the Roof (N. Jewison; UA; 1971)	40,498,669
Alien (R. Scott; G. Carroll/D. Giler/W. Hill; Fox; 1979)	39,847,000
Young Frankenstein (M. Brooks; M. Gruskoff; Fox; 1975)	38,823,000
Airplane (J. Abrahams/D. Zucker/J. Zucker; H. W. Koch/J. Davison; Par; 1980)	38,000,000
Smokey and The Bandit II (H. Needham; H. Moonjean; U; 1980)	37,600,000
A Star Is Born (F. Pierson; J. Peters; WB; 1976)	37,100,000
King Kong (J. Guillermin; D. DeLaurentiis; Par; 1976)	36,915,000
Apocalypse Now (F. Coppola; UA; 1979)	36,846,471
M*A*S*H (R. Altman; I. Preminger; Fox; 1970)	36,720,000
Ben-Hur (W. Wyler; S. Zimbalist; MGM; 1959)	36,650,000
Earthquake (M. Robson; U; 1974)	36,250,000
Coal Miner's Daughter (M. Apted; B. Larson; U; 1980)	36,000,000
Amityville Horror (S. Rosenberg; R. Saland/E. Geisinger; FWS/AIP; 1979)	35,000,000
Hooper (H. Needham; B. Reynolds/L. Gordon; WB; 1978)	34,900,000
Moonraker (L. Gilbert; A. Broccoli; UA; 1979)	33,934,074
Private Benjamin (H. Zieff; N. Meyers/C. Shya/H. Miller; WB; 1980)	33,500,000
Billy Jack (T. Frank; M. Solti; WB; 1971)	32,500,000
The Muppet Movie (J. Frawley; J. Henson; AFD; 1979)	32,000,000
Oh, God! (C. Reiner; J. Weintraub; WB; 1977)	31,440,000
The Deep (P. Yates; P. Guber; Col; 1977)	31,300,000
The Blues Brothers (J. Landis; R. K. Weiss; U; 1980)	31,000,000
The Electric Horseman (S. Pollack; Col; 1979)	30,917,000
The Godfather Part II (F. Coppola; Coppola/Fredrickson/Roos; Par; 1974)	30,673,000
The Deer Hunter (M. Cimino; B. Spikings/M. Deeley/M. Cimino; U; 1978)	30,425,000
The Shining (S. Kubrick; WB; 1980)	30,200,000
Silver Streak (A. Hiller; E. K. Milkis/T. L. Miller; Fox; 1976)	30,018,000
All The President's Men (A. Pakula; W. Coblenz; WB; 1976)	30,000,000
California Suite (H. Ross; R. Stark; Col; 1978)	29,200,000
The Omen (R. Donner; H. Bernhard; Fox; 1976)	28,544,000
Thunderball (T. Young; Eon; UA; 1965)	28,530,000
The Blue Lagoon (R. Kleiser; Col; 1980)	28,456,000
Up In Smoke (L. Adler; Adler/Lombardo; Par; 1978)	28,300,000
Patton (F. Schaffner; F. McCarthy; Fox; 1970)	28,100,000
What's Up Doc? (P. Bogdanovich; WB; 1972)	28,000,000
Foul Play (C. Higgins; Miller/Milkis; Par; 1978)	27,500,000
The Jungle Book (W. Reitherman; W. Disney; BV; 1967)	27,300,000
Snow White (animated; W. Disney; RKO/BV; 1937)	26,750,000
Funny Girl (W. Wyler; R. Stark; Col; 1968)	26,325,000

TITLE / DIRECTOR-PRODUCER-DISTRIBUTOR	TOTAL RENTALS
The French Connection (W. Friedkin; P. D'Antoni/Schine-Moore; Fox; 1971)	26,315,000
Main Event (H. Zieff; J. Peters/B. Streisand; WB; 1979)	26,300,000
The China Syndrome (J. Bridges; M. Douglas; Col; 1979)	26,073,700
Cleopatra (J. Mankiewicz; W. Wanger; Fox; 1963)	26,000,000
Airport 1975 (J. Smight; W. Frye; U; 1974)	25,805,000
Guess Who's Coming To Dinner? (S. Kramer; Col; 1968)	25,500,000
The Way We Were (S. Pollack; R. Stark; Col; 1973)	25,000,000
Revenge of the Pink Panther (B. Edwards; UA; 1978)	25,000,000
10 (B. Edwards; B. Edwards/T. Adams; Orion; 1979)	25,000,000
Black Hole (G. Nelson; R. Miller; BV; 1979)	25,000,000
The Lady and the Tramp (animated; W. Disney; BV; 1955)	24,900,000
The Bad News Bears (M. Ritchie; S. Jaffe; Par; 1976)	24,888,000
2001: A Space Odyssey (S. Kubrick; MGM/UA; 1968)	24,100,000
Trial of Billy Jack (F. Laughlin; J. Cramer; T-L/WB; 1974)	24,000,000
The Enforcer (J. Fargo; R. Daley; WB; 1976)	24,000,000
In Search of Noah's Ark (J. L. Conway; C. E. Sellier Jr.; SSU; 1977)	23,770,000
1941 (S. Spielberg; B. Feitshans; U; 1979)	23,400,000
The Love Bug (R. Stevenson; W. Walsh; BV; 1969)	23,150,000
Around the World in 80 Days (M. Anderson; M. Todd; UA; 1956)	23,120,000
The Longest Yard (R. Aldrich; A. Ruddy; Par; 1974)	23,017,000
Goldfinger (G. Hamilton; Eon; UA; 1964)	22,860,000
Semi-Tough (M. Ritchie; D. Merrick; UA; 1977)	22,807,962
101 Dalmatians (animated; W. Disney; BV; 1961)	22,750,000
Bonnie and Clyde (A. Penn; W. Beatty; WB; 1967)	22,700,000
Urban Cowboy (J. Bridges; R. Evans/I. Azoff; Par; 1980)	22,700,000
Deliverance (J. Boorman; WB; 1972)	
Papillon (F. Schaffner; R. Dorfmann; AA; 1973)	22,500,000
Dog Day Afternoon (S. Lumet; M. Bregman/M. Elfand; WB; 1975)	22,500,000

FESTIVALS, MARKETS and CONVENTIONS 1981

NOTE: Festivals listed in boldface type have in the past been approved by the International Federation of Film Producers Associations.

Some dates are tentative.

DATE	EVENT	LOCATION
Jan. 3-17	New Delhi	India
Jan. 12-18	U.S. Film Fest (Park City, Utah)	U.S.
Jan. 14-18	Avoriaz (fantastic)	France
Jan. 14-19	Manila	Philippines
Jan. 15-18	Helsinki (Nordic)	Finland
Jan. 15-25	Brussels	Belgium
Jan. 16-29	Minneapolis (Minn.)	U.S.
Jan. 18-21	INTV (Indie Tv Stations) (Los Angeles)	U.S.
Jan. 19-23	Berlin (consumer films)	W. Germany
Jan. 23-29	MIDEM (Cannes)	France
Jan. 28-Feb. 1	Goteborg	Sweden
Jan. 31	Golden Globe Awards (Los Angeles)	U.S.
January	Miami	U.S.
January	Ghent	Belgium
January	Berlin (agriculture)	W. Germany
Feb. 2-4	Hemisfilm (San Antonio)	U.S.
Feb. 4-6	Texas Cable Tv Assn. (San Antonio)	U.S.
Feb. 4-8	Tampere (shorts)	Finland
Feb. 5-8	Quebec Int'l Super 8 (Montreal)	Canada
Feb. 6-8	SMPTE (San Francisco)	U.S.
Feb. 7-15	Monte Carlo Tv Fest	Monaco
Feb. 9-12	Sho West (Reno)	U.S.
Feb. 13-15	Ann Arbor 8m (Michigan)	U.S.
Feb. 13-24	**Berlin**	W. Germany
February	Belgrade	Yugoslavia
March 6-8	Florida Independent Film & Video (Tampa)	U.S.
March 13-18	NATPE (New York)	U.S.
March 14-28	Clarence Gardens (childrens)	Australia
March 15-18	Int'l Tape Assn. (Hollywood, Fla.)	U.S.
March 19-25	San Remo (auteur)	Italy
March 21-31	American Film Market (Los Angeles)	U.S.
March 22-29	INPUT (Venice)	Italy
March 27-April 5	USA Film Fest (Dallas)	U.S.
March 29-April 5	Berlin (radio/tv/Prix Futura)	W. Germany
March 30	Academy Awards (Los Angeles)	U.S.
March	Cartagena	Colombia
March	Lille (shorts/documentaries)	France
March	Philadelphia (visual anthropology)	U.S.
March	Vid 81 (London)	England
April 1-18	FILMEX (Los Angeles)	U.S.
April 3-7	Zaragoza (agrarian)	Spain
April 9-24	Hong Kong	Hong Kong
April 11-15	NARM (Hollywood, Fla.)	U.S.
April 12-15	NAB (Las Vegas)	U.S.
April 14-23	MIFED (Milan)	Italy
April 23-May 7	Denver	U.S.
April 24-30	MIP-TV (Cannes)	France
April 24-30	Santa Fe, N.M.	U.S.
April	Ljubljana (Balkan)	Yugoslavia
April	Saint Vincent (sports)	Italy
May 2-9	Montreux (tv)	Switzerland
May 3-9	Trento (mountain)	Italy
May 4-7	Show-A-Rama (Kansas City)	U.S.
May 5-10	Oberhausen (shorts)	W. Germany
May 7-8	Chicago (industrial)	U.S.
May 13-15	London (int'l video)	England
May 14-17	Amsterdam (Clio Awards)	Netherlands
May 14-29	Cannes (tentative)	France
May 17-23	Amsterdam (Christian tv)	Netherlands
May 18-22	Ostrava-Paruba (environmental)	Czechoslovakia
May 25-29	Galway (Golden Harp tv)	Ireland
May 25-June 2	Ljubljana (tv)	Yugoslavia
May 29-June 3	National Cable Tv Assn. (Los Angeles)	U.S.
June 1-6	American (New York)	U.S.
June 2-7	Cracow (shorts)	Poland
June 5-20	Melbourne	Australia
June 5-21	Sydney	Australia
June 8-12	New York (U.S. Clio Awards)	U.S.
June 9-12	Brighton (industrial)	England
June 9-14	Annecy (animation)	France
June 12-19	Tarbes (tourist)	France
June 13-28	Greenwich	England
June 15-19	Munich (Prix Jeunesse Seminar)	W. Germany
June 16-25	Varna (health and Red Cross)	Bulgaria

DATE	EVENT	LOCATION
June 17-25	Prague (Golden Prague tv)	Czechoslovakia
June	Chicago (dance)	U.S.
June	Verona (Greek films)	Italy
June	Cannes (advertising)	France
July 1-5	San Rafael (Marin County)	U.S.
July 7-21	**Moscow**	U.S.S.R
July 11-17	Festival of Arts (Grahamstown)	South Africa
July 22-26	Int'l Children Film & Video (Orlando, Fla.)	U.S.
July 25-Aug. 2	Salerno (children)	Italy
July 26-30	IAAM (Miami Beach)	U.S.
July 26-Aug. 2	Pula (Yugoslavian films)	Yugoslavia
July 31-Aug. 9	Locarno	Switzerland
July	Oxford	England
July	Gijon (children)	Spain
July	Trieste (sci-fi)	Italy
July	La Rochelle	France
Aug. 16-19	Edinburgh	Scotland
Aug. 20-30	**Montreal**	Canada
August	Odense (fairytale)	Denmark
August	Robert Flaherty Seminar (N.Y.)	U.S.
Sept. 2-19	Venice	Italy
Sept. 9-21	Rome (Prix Italia-tv)	Italy
Sept. 10-19	Toronto	Canada
Sept. 24-Oct. 4	Banff (tv)	Canada
Sept. 25-Oct. 11	**New York**	U.S.
Sept. 28-30	CATEL/EXPO (cable tv) (Las Vegas)	U.S.
September	San Sebastian	Spain
September	Thessaloniki	Greece
September	Cattolica (mystery)	Italy
September	Intercom 81 (Chicago)	U.S.
September	Adelaide	Australia
September	Huesca (shorts)	Spain
Oct. 3-10	Sitges (fantastic)	Spain
Oct. 5-10	Mannheim	W. Germany
Oct. 9-13	VIDCOM (Cannes)	France
Oct. 12-16	MIFED-TV (Milan)	Italy
Oct. 16-19	MIFED (East-West)	Italy
Oct. 16-21	Nice (childhood)	France
Oct. 17-24	Varna (animation)	Bulgaria
Oct. 19-24	MIFED (Indian Summer)	Italy
Oct. 22-Nov. 1	San Diego	U.S.
Oct. 28-Nov. 1	Hof Film Days	W. Germany
October	San Francisco	U.S.
October	Cork	Ireland
October	Arnhem	Netherlands
October	Nyon (documentaries)	Switzerland
October	Las Vegas	U.S.
October	Tokyo (shorts)	Japan
October	Sorrento (Egyptian films)	Italy
October	Tokyo (cultural)	Japan
October	Strasbourg (human rights)	France
October	Huy (amateur)	Belgium
October	Valladolid	Spain
Nov. 2-8	Yorkton, Sask. (Canadian)	Canada
Nov. 3-15	Viennale 81 (Vienna)	Austria
Nov. 4-6	New York (film and tv)	U.S.
Nov. 8-13	NATO (Las Vegas)	U.S.
Nov. 14-23	Neo-Youth Film (Bombay)	India
Nov. 16-21	Katowice (scientific)	Poland
November	London	England
November	Chicago	U.S.
November	Montreal (16m)	Canada
November	Neuilly (sci-fi)	France
November	Espinho (animation)	Portugal
November	Leipzig (documentaries/shorts)	E. Germany
November	Rome (nature/man/environment)	Italy
November	SMPTE (New York)	U.S.
Dec. 2-4	Western Cable Show (Anaheim, Calif.)	U.S.
Dec. 2-10	Florence (social documentaries)	Italy
Dec. 8-14	Huelva (Ibero-Americano)	Spain
December	Bilbao (documentaries)	Spain
December	Tokyo (video)	Japan

TV CREDITS

Jan. 1, 1976–Dec. 31, 1980

NOTE: Letters after the dates of reviews indicate the type of TV show:
- F   Foreign
- S   Syndicated
- C   Cable
- PI Prix Italia competitors

A BARBED WIT: THE CINEMA OF BILLY WILDER
(Witz Mit Widerhaken)
Supplier: Zweites Deutsches Fernsehen (ZDF), Wiesbaden
Dir-wri-narr: Hans C. Blumenberg.
45 Mins, Tues, 10 pm.
ZDF, Second Channel, from Wiesbaden, West Germany
08/11/76F

A BIG COUNTRY
Supplier: Australian Broadcasting Commission
Exec Prod: John Sparkes;
Prods: David Flatman, Geoff Barnes, John Mabey, Ron Iddon, David Leonard, Peter Lipscomb, Max Donnellan;
Reporters: Bob Plasto, Ian McNamara, Mabey, Iddon, Ron Drynan, Paul Williams, David Flatman.
30 Mins, Thurs, 8:25 pm.
ABC TV, Channel 2, Sydney, Australia
08/01/79F

A CHAPTER IN ITSELF (Ein Kapitel Fuer Sich)
Prod-Supplier: Ullstein AV & Zweites Deutsches Fernsehen (ZDF)
240 Mins, in 3 Parts
ZDF, Second Channel, from Wiesbaden-Mainz, West Germany
01/16/80F

A CHOICE OF CHAMPIONS: QUEST FOR THE GOLD
Supplier: Conrad Film Associates (Syndicast Services)
Prod-Dir-Wri: Derek Conrad.
30 Mins, Thurs, 7:30 pm.
WCBS-TV New York
06/11/80S

A CHRISTMAS FOR BOOMER
With Lawrie Driscoll, Margie Impert, Jonathan Ward, Gillian Grant, Larry Linville, Joyce Van Patten, Sheree North, Al Molinaro, Marty Gold, Jane Greer, Harriet Nelson, Boomer
Supplier: A C Lyles Prods & Paramount TV
Prod: Lyles;
Dir: William Asher;
Wris: Gerry Day & Bethel Leslie, Dan Balluck & Jim Rogers.
60 Mins, Thurs (6), 8 pm.
NBC-TV
12/12/79

A CHRISTMAS WITHOUT SNOW
With Michael Learned, John Houseman, Ramon Bieri, James Cromwell, Valerie Curtin, David Knell, Calvin Levels, Ruth Nelson, Beah Richards, William Swetland, Joy Carlin, Anne Lawder, Barbara Tarbuck, Ed Bogas, Daisietta Kim, Matthew Hautau.
Supplier: Korty Films & Frank Kongsberg Prodns
Exec Prod: Konigsberg;
Prods: John Korty, Whitney Green;
Dir: Korty;
Wris: Korty, Richard Beban, Judith Nielsen.
120 Min, Tues (9), 9 pm.
CBS-TV
12/10/80

A CIRCLE OF CHILDREN
With Jane Alexander, Rachel Roberts, David Ogden Stiers, Nan Martin, Mathew Laborteaux, others
Supplier: Edgar J Scherick Prods & 20th-Fox TV
Prods: Edgar J Scherick, Daniel H Blatt;
Prod: Steven Gethers;
Dir: Don Taylor;
Wri: Gethers (from the novel by Mary McCracken).
120 Mins, Thurs (10), 9 pm.
CBS-TV
03/16/77

A CONVERSATION WITH ROBERT MOSES
(WNET Reports)
with Robert Sam Anson
Prod: Alan Goldberg;
Dir: Mick Colgan.
60 Mins, Tues (5), 10 pm.
WNET-TV New York
04/13/77

A COSMIC CHRISTMAS
Supplier: Nelvana Prods, Viacom
Exec Prod: Jeffrey Kirsch;
Prods: Michael Hirsh, Patrick Loubert;
Dir: Clive Smith;
Wris: Ida Nelson Fruet, Martin Lavut, Laura Paull, Ken Sobol.
30 Mins, Wed (7), 7:30 pm.
WNBC-TV N Y
12/14/77S

A DAY WITH PRESIDENT CARTER
With John Chancellor
Supplier: NBC News
Exec Prod: Gordon Manning;
Prod-Dir: Ray Lockhart.
60 Mins, Thurs (14), 9 pm.
NBC-TV
04/20/77

A DEATH IN CANAAN
(CBS Wednesday Night Movies)
With Stefanie Powers, Paul Clemens, Tom Atkins, Jacqueline Brookes, Brian Dennehy, Conchata Farrell, Charles Haid, Floyd Levine, Kenneth McMillan, Gavan O'Herlihy, Yuki Shimoda, James Sutorius, William Bronder, Sally Kemp, Mary Jackson, Lane Smith, others
Supplier: Chris-Rose Prods & Warner Bros TV
Prods: Robert W Christiansen, Rick Rosenberg;
Dir: Tony Richardson;
Wris: Thomas Thompson, Spencer Eastman, based on book by Joan Barthel.
150 Mins, Wed (1), 9 pm.
CBS-TV
03/08/78

A DEATH IN THE FAMILY
With Dave Moore, Dr George Gerbner, Rose Goldsen, Tracy Weston, Donn O'Brien, others
Prod-Wri: James Hayden;
Dir: Dave Andre.
60 Mins, Sun (3), 9 pm.
WCCO-TV, Minneapolis
12/13/78

A DOG'S LIFE
(NBC Comedy Theatre)
With Charles Martin Smith, Barney Martin, Beej Johnson, Sherry Lynn, Hamilton Camp, Michael Huddleston, Cliff Norton
Supplier: TAT Communications
Prod: Charlie Hauck;
Dir: Peter Bonerz;
Wris: Hauck, Arthur Julian.
30 Mins, Fri (15), 8:30 pm.
NBC-TV
06/20/79

A DOONESBURY SPECIAL
With voices of Barbara Harris, Jack Gilford, Will Jordan, William Sloane Coffin, Richard Cox, Charles Levin, others
Supplier: John & Faith Hubley Films, with Universal Press Syndicate
Prod-Dirs: Hubleys, Gary Trudeau;
Wri: Trudeau.
30Mins, Sun (27), 9:30 pm.
NBC-TV
11/30/77

A DREAM IN A DIFFERENT KEY
(Shiki-Utopiano)
With Sachiyo Nakao
Supplier: NHK (Japan)
Prod: Takeshi Kobayashi;
Dir-Wri: Shoichiro Sasaki.
100Mins.
(RAI Prizewinner, Drama)
10/08/80PI

A E S HUDSON STREET
With Gregory Sierra, Stefan Gierasch, Rosana Soto, Allan Miller, Susan Peretz, Ralph Manza, Ray Stewart, Bill Cort, Jack Dodson, Julienne Wells, Margaret Avery, John Davis, Jack Grapes
Supplier: Triseme Corp
Exec Prod: Danny Arnold;
Prod-Wri: Roland Kibbee;
Dir: Noam Pitlik.
30 Mins, Thurs, 9:30 pm.
ABC-TV
03/29/78

A FUNNY THING HAPPENED ON THE WAY TO THE WHITE HOUSE
With Steve Allen, Bob & Ray, Norm Crosby, Nipsey Russell, Jayne Meadows
60 Mins, Fri, 9 pm.
Home Box Office
11/05/80PC

A GIFT TO LAST
With Gordon Pinsent, Gerard Parkes, Janet Amos, Ruth Springford, Alan Scarfe, Mark Polley, Kate Parr
Exec Prod: Robert Allen;
Prod: Herb Rolland;
Dir: Sheldon Larry;
Wri: Pinsent.
60 Mins, Sun, 7 pm.
CBC-TV, from Toronto, Canada
03/01/78F

A LETTER FROM COLLEEN
With Colleen McCullough, Maureen White, Bill Tapp, June Tapp
Supplier: Australian Broadcasting Commission
Exec Prod: John Sparkes;
Dir: Bob Connolly.
50 Mins, Thurs, 8:20 pm.
ABC (Australia) TV, Channel 2, Sydney
02/13/80F

A LUCILLE BALL SPECIAL
With Vivian Vance, Gale Gordon, Mary Wickes, Steve Allen, Ed McMahon, Mary Jane Croft, Joey Forman, James E Brodhead, Stack Pierce, John William Young, Lillian Carter
Supplier: Lucille Ball Prods
Exec Prod: Ball;
Prod: Gary Morton;
Dir: Marc Daniels;
Wris: Madelyn Davis & Bob Carroll Jr.
60 Mins, Mon (21), 8:30 pm.
CBS-TV
11/30/77

A LUCILLE BALL SPECIAL (LUCY COMES TO NBC)
With Bob Hope, Johnny Carson, Jack Klugman, Gene Kelly, Gary Coleman, Donald O'Connor, Gloria DeHaven, Gale Gordon, Sidney Miller, Scotty Plummer, Robert Alda, Ruta Lee, Gary Imhoff, Doris Singleton, Ivery Wheeler, Micki McKenzie, Takayo Doran, Louis DaPron Dancers
Suppliers: Lucille Ball Prods.
Exec Prod: Ball;
Prod: Hal Kanter;
Dir: Jack Donohue;
Wris: Kanter, Bob O'Brien, Paul Pumpian.
90 Mins, Fri, (8), 8:30 pm.
NBC-TV
02/13/80

A MAN CALLED SLOANE
With Robert Conrad, Dan O'Herlihy, Ji-Tu Cumbuka, Roddy McDowall, Christine DeLisle, Diane Stilwell, Christian Marlowe, Heather Hewitt
Supplier: Woodruff Prods & QM Prods
Exec Prod: Philip Saltzman;
Prod: Gerald Sanford;
Dir: Alan J Levi;
Wri: Peter Allan Fields.
60 Mins, Sat, 10 pm.
NBC-TV
09/26/79

A MATTER OF POLICY
With Mort Crim
Prods: Scott Craig, Jim Hatfield;
Dir: Craig;
Wris: Craig, Hatfield, Molly Bedell.
120 Mins, Sun & Mon (26-27), 10 pm.
WBBM-TV Chicago
03/29/78

A MIDSUMMER NIGHT'S DREAM
With The Free Theatre of Germantown Theatre Guild
Supplier: Capital Cities Television Prod
Exec Prod: Charles Keller;
Prod: Dan Lounsbery;
Dir: Leonard Valenta (staged by Katharine Minehart);
Wri: William Shakespeare.
60 Mins, Sun (27), 5 pm.
WPVI-TV Philadelphia
Fidelity Bank
04/06/77S

A NEW KIND OF FAMILY
With Eileen Brennan, Gwynne Gilford, David Hollander, Lauri Hendler, Rob Lowe, Connie Ann Hearn, Chuck McCann, George Reynolds, Luis Avalos, Ken Lerner, O J, Jenna McMahon
Supplier: Gordon-Eisner Prods
Exec Prods: Jane Eisner, Margie Gordon;
Prod: Nick Arnold, Jenna McMahon, Dick Clair;
Dir: James Burrows;
Wri: Roy Kammerman.
30 Mins Sun, 7:30 pm.
ABC-TV
09/19/79

A PERMANENT CONDITION
With Tony Franciosa, narrator
Prod-Dir: Sandra Weir;
Wri: Bonnie Rerisberg.
30 Mins, Wed, 7 pm.
WMAQ-TV Chicago
10/03/79

A PINK CHRISTMAS
Supplier: DePatie-Freleng Enterprises, United Artists TV
Prods: David H DePatie, Friz Freleng;
Animation Dir: Bill Perez;
Wri: Jack Kaplan.
30 Mins, Thurs (7), 8:30 pm.
ABC-TV
Parker Bros (Humphrey Browning MacDougall)
12/20/78

A PLACE IN THE WORLD
With John Gregg, John Gaden, Nick Tate, Paul Mason, Kerry Francis
Supplier: Australian Broadcasting Commission
Exec Prod: Eric Tayler;
Dirs: Michael Carlson, Chris Thomson, Carl Schultz, Tayler;
Wri: Michael Cove.
60 Mins, Sun, 8:30 pm.
ABC TV, Channel 2 Sydney, Australia
09/05/79F

A RACE WITH DEATH
With Gary Axelson, reporter
Prod: Kathy Cunningham;
Dir: Paul Fine.
30 Mins, Sat, 7:30 pm.
WJLA-TV Washington
08/02/78

A RATHER REASSURING PROGRAM
(What's Happened to Our Moral Fiber?)
With Ned Sherrin
Supplier: ATV
Prod-Dir: John Sheppard;
Wris: Caryl Brahms, Ian Davidson, Neil Shand, N F Simpson, Keith Waterhouse, Willis Hall.
30 Mins, Sat, 10:30 pm.
ATV, from Birmingham, England
08/10/77F

A ROOF OVER MY HEAD
(First, Find Your House)
With Brian Rix, Lynda Baron, Francis Matthews, Gail Harrison
Supplier: BBC
Prod: Douglas Argent;
Wri: Barry Took.
30 Mins, Wed, 8:30 pm.
BBC, from London, England
09/07/77F

A RUMOR OF WAR
With Brad Davis, Keith Carradine, Michael O'Keefe, Richard Bradford, Brian Dennehy, John Friedrich, Perry Lang, Christopher Mitchum, Steve Forrest, Stacy Keach, Dan Shor, Lane Smith, Nicholas Woodeson, Gail Youngs, Phillip Allen, Michael Cavanaugh, Bobby Ellerbee, David Elliott, Larry Fishburne, Redmond Gleeson, Edward Grover, Gavan O'Herlihy, Christopher Allport, others
Supplier: Stonehenge Prods - Charles Fries Prods
Exec Prods: Fries, Dick Berg;
Prod: David Manson;
Dir: Richard T. Heffron;
Wri: John Sacret Young, based on Philip Caputo book.
240 Mins, Wed-Thurs (24-25) 9 pm.
CBS-TV
10/01/80

A SALUTE TO AMERICAN IMAGINATION
With Paul Newman, Joanne Woodward, Madeline Kahn, Telly Savalas, Henry Ford, Edward Asner, Neil Armstrong, Martin Balsam, Ronee Blakley, Dr Joyce Brothers, Sid Caesar, Imogene Coca, Ray Charles, Rita Coolidge, Fritz Feld, Henry Fonda, Aretha Franklin, Lee Grant, Kevin Hagan, Wolfman Jack, Kris Kristofferson, Johnny Mathis, Ethel Merman, Arthur Miller, Redd, Hedwig and Crossley, John Ritter, Martin Sheen, Neil Simon, Marianna Tcherkassky, Tennessee Williams
Supplier: Bob Banner Associates
Exec Prod: Banner;
Prod: Stephen Pouliot;
Dir: Don Mischer;
Wri: Rod Warren.
120 Mins, Thurs (5), 8 pm.
CBS TV
Ford Motor Co (Kenyon & Eckhardt)
10/11/78

A SELECTION VISION
With Tina Freeman, Martin Shambra, Johnny Donnels
Prod-Dir-Wri: Madeleine Butler.
30 Mins, Fri, 8 pm.
WYES-TV New Orleans
10/03/79

A SHINING SEASON
With Timothy Bottoms, Allyn Ann McLerie, Connie Forslund, Ed Begley Jr., Rip Torn, Mason Adams, Ellen Geer, Arthur Rosenberg, Steve Shaw, Tamar Howard, Michael Sharrett, Bill Dowson, Jerry Riopelle, Rodney Plomp, others
Supplier: Green-Epstein Prods., T/M Prods. & Columbia Pictures TV
Exec Prods: Jim Green, Allen Epstein;
Prod: Harry Thomason;
Dir: Stuart Margolin;
Wri: William Harrison, based on William S. Buchanan's book.
120 Mins, Wed, (26), 9 pm.
CBS-TV
General Motors (N.W. Ayer)
01/02/80

A SPECIAL EVENING WITH CAROL BURNETT
With Carol Burnett, Vicki Lawrence, Tim Conway, Ernest Flatt Dancers
Exec Prod: Joe Hamilton;
Prod: Ed Simmons;
Dir: Dave Powers.
120 Mins, Wed (29), 8 pm.
CBS-TV
04/05/78

A SPECIAL KENNY ROGERS
With Ray Charles, Oak Ridge Boys, Dottie West
Supplier: Kenny Rogers Prods
Exec Prod: Ken Kragen;
Prods: Stan Harris, Rocco Urbisci;
Dir: Harris;
Wris: Rick Kellard, Bob Comfort, Cort Casady, Urbisci.
60 Mins, Thurs (12), 9 pm.
CBS-TV
04/18/79

A SPECIAL OLIVIA NEWTON-JOHN
With Elliott Gould, others
Supplier: Katz, Gallin, Cleary Prods
Exec Prods: Ray Katz, Sandy Gallin, Danny Cleary;
Prod: Joe Layton;
Dir: Norman Campbell;
Wris: Gerry Gardner, Dee Caruso, Fred Smoot.
60 Mins, Wed (17), 10 pm.
ABC-TV
Life & Health Insurance Cos in America (Grey)
11/24/76

A STATE DINNER FOR QUEEN ELIZABETH II
With Robert MacNeil, Frank Gillard, Jean Marsh, Julia Child
Supplier: WETA-TV Washington
Exec Prod: Wally Westfeldt;
Prod: Martin Clancy;
Dir: James Silman.
270 Mins, Wed (7), 8 pm.
PBS
07/14/76

A TIME THERE WAS
(A Profile of Benjamin Britten)
With Peter Pears, Leonard Bernstein, Frank Bridge, Paul Rotha, Joan Cross, Rudolf Bing, Julian Bream
Supplier: London Weekend TV (U.K.)
Prod-Dir: Tony Palmer (Ladbroke Films);
Mus: Benjamin Britten.
101 Mins.
(Winner of Prix Italia, Music)
10/01/80PI

A TOAST TO MELBA
With Robyn Nevin, Roslyn Dunbar, Donald McDonald, Mervyn Drake Gottlieb, Tim Eliot, Anna Volska, Michael Aitkens, Henri Szeps, Jane Harders, Shane Tapper
Supplier: Australian Broadcasting Commission
Exec Prod-Dir: Alan Burke;
Wri: Jack Hibberd.
70 Mins, Sun, 8:30 pm.
ABC (Australia) TV, Channel 2, Sydney
08/13/80F

A TRIAL FOR RAPE
(Un Processo Per Stupro)
Supplier: RAI (Italy)
Prog Mkrs: Maia Grazia Belmonti, Anna Carini, Rony Daopoulos, Paola De Martiis, Annabella Miscuglio, Loredana Rotondo.
65 Mins.
(Prix Italia winner, documentary)
10/03/79PI

A TRIBUTE TO CHET ATKINS FROM HIS FRIENDS
With Roy Acuff, Bobby Bare, Foster Brooks, "Jethro" Burns, Archie Campbell, Floyd Cramer, Charlie Daniels Band, Danny Davis, Jimmy Dean, Don Everly, Don Gibson, Tom T Hall, Earl Klugh, George Lindsey, Roger Miller, Minnie Pearl, Charley Pride, Boots Randolph, Dale Robertson, Lonnie Shorr, Jim Stafford, Statler Brothers, Ray Stevens, Porter Wagoner, Don Sheffield Orch.
Supplier: Jim Owens Prods & Multimedia Program Prods.
Exec Prods: Owens, Steven A Womack;
Prod: Owens;
Dir: Alan Angus;
Wri: Terry Calvin, Angus.
120 Min, Fri, (26), 8 pm.
WPIX-TV New York
12/24/80

A TRIBUTE TO HANK WILLIAMS: THE MAN & HIS MUSIC
With Jim Owen, Hank Williams Jr., Teresa Brewer, Johnny Cash, Waylon Jennings, Kris Kristofferson, Brenda Lee, Faron Young, Bill Walker Orch, Roy Acuff, Little Jimmy Dickens, Minnie Pearl, Dan Helms, Jerry Rivers, Rufus Thomas, Jeff Owens, Doug Clements, Adrian Marshall, Gary Gentry, Henry Arnold, Dan Cox, Nan Gurley, Ed Masters, Dennis Allen, Jerry Seabolt, Cindy Leake, Randy Moore, Laney Smallwood-Hicks
Supplier: Jim Owens Enterprises (Multimedia Program Prods)
Exec Prod: Richard C. Thrall;
Prod: Jim Owens;
Dir: Allan Angus;
Wris: Billy & Pat Galvin.
120 Mins, Wed, (28) 8 pm.
WPIX-TV New York
06/11/80S

A TRIBUTE TO 'MR TELEVISION' MILTON BERLE
With Lucille Ball, Joey Bishop, George Carlin, Johnny Carson, Angie Dickinson, Kirk Douglas, Bob Hope, Gabriel Kaplan, Gene Kelly, Donny & Marie Osmond, Gregory Peck, Carl Reiner, Don Rickles, Frank Sinatra, Marlo Thomas, Flip Wilson, Kermit the Frog
Supplier: The Jerry Frank Co
Exec Prod: Frank;
Prods: Frank, Bill Carruthers;
Dir: Carruthers;
Wri: Marty Farrell.
60 Mins, Sun (26), 9 pm.
NBC-TV
03/29/78

A WOMAN CALLED MOSES - PART ONE
(NBC Monday Night At The Movies)
With Cicely Tyson, Will Geer, Robert Hooks, James Wainwright, Jason Bernard, Dick Anthony Williams, Hari Rhodes, Clifford David, Judyann Elder, John Getz, Mae Mercer, James Sikking, Charles Weldon
Supplier: I K E Prods and Henry Jaffe Enterprises
Prods: Ike Jones, Michael Jaffe;
Dir: Paul Wendkos;
Wri: Lonnie Elder III, from Marcy Heidish's novel.
120 Mins, Mon (11), 9 pm.
NBC-TV
12/13/78

A WOMAN IS. . .IN A NEW WORLD
Exec Prod: Mary Catherine Kilday;
Dir: Louise Tiranoff;
Wri: Leslie Bravman Jacobson.
30 Mins, Tues (9), 7:30 pm.
WRC-TV Washington
03/24/76

A WOMAN IS. . .WITH BESS MYERSON
With Bess Myerson
Exec Prod: Philip Burton;
Prod: Fern McBride.
30 Mins, Fri (26), 7:30 pm.
WCBS-TV New York
12/01/76

A YEAR AT THE TOP
With Greg Evigan, Paul Shaffer, Gabe Dell, Priscilla Morrill, Nedra Volz, Mickey Rooney, Pricilla Lopez
Supplier: TAT Communications, with Don Kirshner Prods
Exec Prod: Norman Lear;
Prod: Darryl Hickman;
Dirs: Alan Rakfin, Marlena Laird;
Wri: Sandy Veith.
60 Mins, Fri (5), 8 pm.
CBS-TV
08/10/77

ABC NEWS CLOSEUP: PORTRAITS
With John Lindsay, Clive Barnes, Peter Jennings, Steve Bell
Prod: Pamela Hill;
Dirs: Hill, Richard Gerdau, Gardner Compton;
Wris: Hill, Eileen Russell.
90 Mins, Thurs, (17), 10 pm.
ABC-TV
06/23/76

ABC'S SILVER ANNIVERSARY CELEBRATION
With Barry Manilow, Alan King, Henry Winkler, The Captain & Tennille, Fred McMurray, Cheryl Ladd, Kate Jackson, Jaclyn Smith, Marlo Thomas, John Wayne, Gabe Kaplan, Howard Cosell, Frank Gifford, Jim McKay, Keith Jackson, Penny Marshall, Cindy Williams, Hal Linden, Harry Reasoner, Barbara Walters, Robert Young, Vince Edwards, Hal Holbrook, Brenda Vaccaro, Robert Blake, Julie Andrews, John Travolta, Billy Dee Williams, Edward Asner, Lawrence Welk, The Lennon Sisters, Annette Funicello, others
Supplier: ABC-Dick Clark Prods
Exec Prod: Clark;
Prod: Bill Lee;
Dir: Perry Rosemond;
Wris: Lee, Stuart Bloomberg, Phil Hahn.
240 Mins, Sun (5), 7 pm.
ABC-TV
02/08/78

ACE
(NBC Comedy Theatre)
With Bob Dishy, Rae Allen, Barbara Brownell, Ruth Manning, Dick Van Patten, Liam Dunn, Frank Campanella, Erica Hagen, Harvey Solen
Supplier: Larry White Prods. & Columbia Pictures TV
Prod: White;
Dir: Gary Nelson;
Wri: Jerry Davis.
30 Mins, Mon (26), 8 pm.
NBC-TV
08/04/76

ACT OF LOVE
(NBC Wednesday Night At The Movies)
With Ron Howard, Robert Foxworth, Mickey Rourke, David Spielberg, Jacqueline Brookes, Sondra West, Gail Youngs, Mary Kay Place, Peter Michael Goetz, Peter Hobbs, others
Supplier: Cypress Point Prods & Paramount TV
Exec Prod: Gerald L. Abrams;
Supv Prod: Erv Zavada;
Prod: Bruce J. Sallan;
Dir: Jud Taylor;
Wri: Michael De Guzman from Paige Mitchell novel.
120 Mins, Wed (24) 9 pm.
NBC-TV
10/01/80

ADA
(For The Record)
With Anne Anglin, Janet Amos, Kate Reid, Jayne Eastwood, Kay Hawtrey, Sabena Maydell
Prod: Ralph Thomas;
Dir: Claude Jutra;
Wir: Jutra (from story by Margaret Gibson).
60 Mins, Sun, 9 pm.
CBC-TV, from Toronto, Canada
02/16/77F

ADVENTURE WORLD: FROM THE OCEAN TO THE SKY
Supplier: Dillon/Hillary Prods
Exec Prod: Michael Gill;
Dir: Mike Dillon.
50 Mins, Sun, 7 pm.
Television One, New Zealand
10/03/79F

THE ADVENTURE WORLD OF SIR EDMUND HILLARY
With Edmund Hillary, Michael Gill, Graeme Dingle, Jim Wilson, Murray Jones, Peter Hillary
Prod: Warwick Brock;
Dir: Roger Donaldson.
35 Mins, Fri, 9:40 pm.
TV-1, from Wellington, New Zealand
08/17/77F

AEROMEDS
With John Bennett Perry, Lauren Tewes, Carl Anderson, Elinor Donahue, Jan LaPrade, Sherry Lynne Hummer, Sanford Gibbons
Supplier: Bruce Lansbury Prods & Columbia Pictures TV
Exec Prod: Lansbury;
Prod-Dir: Leonard Katzman;
Wri: Laurence Heath.
30 Mins, Mon (17), 7:30 pm
WNBC-TV New York
01/19/77S

THE AFRICAN QUEEN
With Warren Oates, Mariette Hartley, Johnny Sekka, Clarence Thomas, Tyrone Jackson, Albert Paulsen, Wolf Roth, Frank Schuller
Supplier: Mark Carliner Prods & Viacom
Exec Prod: Carliner;
Prod: Leonard B Kaufman;
Dir: Richard Sarafian;
Wri: Irving Gaynor Neiman, based on C S Forester's novel.
60 Mins, Fri (18), 8 pm.
CBS-TV
03/23/77

AGAINST THE WIND
With Mary Larkin, Jon English, Gerard Kennedy, Kerry McGuire, Warwick Sims, Frank Gallagher, Lyn Rainbow, Frederick Parslow, Hu Price, Frank Thring, Wallas Eaton
Supplier: Pegasus Prods
Exec Prods-Wris: Ian Jones, Bronwyn Binns;
Prod: Henry Crawford;
Dir: Simon Wincer.
60 Mins, Tues (12), 8:30 pm.
7 Network, Melbourne, Australia
09/27/78F

THE AGE OF UNCERTAINTY
(The Prophets and Promise of Classical Capitalism)
With John Kenneth Galbraith, others
Supplier: BBC-TV
Exec Prod: Adrian Malone;
Prod: Dick Gilling;
Wri: Galbraith.
55 Mins, Mon (10), 10 pm.
BBC-2, Britain
01/19/77F

AGENT ORANGE: THE HUMAN HARVEST
With Bill Kurtis
Prods: Brian Boyer, Rose Economou.
60 Mins, Wed (28), 10:30 pm.
WBBM-TV Chicago
04/11/79

AGENT ORANGE - VIETNAM'S DEADLY FOG
With Bill Kurtis
Prods: Rose Economou, Brian Boyer;
Dir: Phil Ruskin;
Wri: Kurtis.
60 Mins, Thurs (23), 10:30 pm.
WBBM-TV Chicago
03/29/78

AIR MAIL SPECIAL
With John Johnson, Ellen Fleysher
Exec Prod: Jim Lutton;
Wri-Prod: Clay Cole;
Dir: Paulette Douglas.
30 Mins, Sat (4) 7:30 pm.
WABC-TV New York
10/08/80

AKTION ABENDSONNE
(Operation Sunset)
With Erneest Stankovski, Monika Jetter, Aenne Bruck, Aenne Nau, Heinrich Gertstetter, Rudolf Schuendler, Gertrud Sorge, Rainer Luxem, Henry Keilmann, Franz-Josef Steffens, Heidi Kabel
Supplier: ZDF (Zweites Deutsches Fernsehen)
Exec Prod: Heinz Ungureit;
Dir-Wri: Diethard Klante.
90 Mins, Mon, 9:20 pm.
ZDF, from Second Channel, Wiesbaden-Mainz, West Germany
08/01/79F

THE ALAN HAMEL SHOW
Exec Prod: Arthur Weinthal;
Prod: Craig Tennis.
60 Mins, weekdays, 2 pm.
CTV, from Vancouver, Canada
05/25/77F

THE ALAN HAMEL SHOW
Exec Prods: W C Elliott, Arthur Weinthal;
Prod: Craig Tennis;
Dir: Robert Wilson.
60 Mins, weekdays, 2 pm.
CTV, from Vancouver, Canada
12/28/77F

ALAN KING'S THANKSGIVING SPECIAL: WHAT DO WE HAVE TO BE THANKFUL FOR?
With Angie Dickinson, McLean Stevenson, Dick Van Patten, Logan Ramsey
Supplier: King-Hitzig Prods
Exec Prod: King;
Prods: Rupert Hitzig, Neal Marshall;
Dir: Bill Davis;
Wris: Jeffrey Barron, Howard Albrecht, Sol Weinstein, David Castro, Richard Marcus, Harry Crane, King.
60 Mins, Tues, (25) 10 pm.
NBC-TV
12/03/80

ALCATRAZ: THE WHOLE SHOCKING STORY
With Michael Beck, Telly Savalas, Ronny Cox, Art Carney, James MacArthur, John Amos, Alex Karras, Charles Aidman, Richard Lynch, John Amos, Ed Lauter
Exec Prod: Mark E. Massari;
Prod: James Brown;
Dir: Paul Krasny;
Wri: Ernest Tidyman.
240 Mins, Wed, (5) 9 pm. Thurs, (6) 8 pm.
NBC-TV
11/12/80

ALEX & THE DOBERMAN GANG
With Jack Stauffer, Lane Binkley, Taurean Blacque, Bill Lucking, Jerry Orbach, Martha Smith
Supplier: Bennett-Katleman Prods & Columbia Pictures TV
Supv Prod-Wris: James D. Parriott, Richard Chapman;
Prod: Ralph Sariego;
Dir: Byron Chudnow.
60 Mins, Fri, (11) 9 pm.
NBC-TV
04/16/80

ALICE
With Linda Lavin, Alfred Lutter, Vic Tayback, Beth Howland, Polly Holliday, Dennis Dugan, Arthur Space
Supplier: Warner Bros. TV
Exec Prod: David Susskind;
Prod: Bruce Johnson;
Dir: Paul Bogart;
Wri: Robert Getchell.
30 Mins, Tues (31), 9:30 pm.
CBS-TV
09/08/76

ALICE
With Linda Lavin, Vic Tayback, Polly Holliday, Beth Howland, Philip McKeon, Denny Miller
Supplier: Warner Bros TV & D'Angelo/Bullock/Allen Prods
Exec Prods: William P D'Angelo, Harvey Bullock, R S Allen
Prod: Bruce Johnson;
Dir: Jim Drake;
Wri: Martin Donovan.
30 Mins, Wed, 9:30 pm.
CBS-TV
10/06/76

ALL ABOARD AMERICA
With Robert Lansing, Joe Julian (narrator)
Supplier: 1776 Prods. & Avon Prods.
Prods: Ralph Weisinger, Ron Van Nostrand;
Dir: Weisinger;
Wri: Jerry Alden.
30 Mins, Sat (24), 2:30 pm.
WCBS-TV New York
07/28/76

THE ALL-AMERICAN COLLEGE COMEDY SHOW
(CBS Late Movie)
With Jaye P Morgan, Princeton U Triangle Club, Northwestern U Waa-Mu Show, Indiana U Laugh Tracks, U of Pennsylvania Mask & Wig Club
Exec Prod-Dir: Mike Gargiulo;
85 Mins, Fri (14), 11:30 pm.
CBS-TV
12/19/79

ALL-AMERICAN PIE
With Joe Namath (host)
Supplier: Kukoff-Harris Partnership Prods
Exec Prod-Dir-Wris: Bernie Kukoff, Jeff Harris;
Supv Prod: Caryn Sneider.
60 Mins, Sun, (17) 8 pm.
ABC-TV
08/27/80

ALL-STAR ANYTHING GOES
With Bill Boggs, Chuck Healy
Supplier: Bob Banner Associates & Robert Stigwood Organization
Exec Prods: Banner, Beryl Vertue;
Prod: Sam Riddle;
Dir: Louis Horwitz.
30 Mins, Sat (17), 7:30 pm.
WCBS-TV New York
09/21/77S

ALL-STAR FAMILY FEUD SPECIAL
With Richard Dawson, host
Supplier: Goodson-Todman Prods
Prod: Howard Felsher;
Dir: Paul Alter.
60 Mins, Mon (8), 8 pm.
ABC-TV
05/17/78

THE ALL-STAR GONG SHOW SPECIAL
With Tony Randall, Rosey Grier, Aretha Franklin, Ray Charles, Ben Vereen, Senator Alan Cranston, UCLA Marching Band, Arte Johnson, Jamie Farr, Jaye P Morgan, Chuck Barris
Supplier: Chuck Barris Prods
Exec Prod: Chuck Barris;
Prod: Gene Banks;
Dir: John Dorsey.
60 Mins, Tues, 8 pm.
NBC-TV
05/04/77

ALL THE GREEN YEAR
With Darius Perkins, Greg Stroud, Carl Hansen, Alan Hopgood, Monica Maughan, May Hewlett, Tom Farley, Patricia Kennedy, Larry Held, Jan Friedl, Jennifer Mellett, Pepe Trevor, Sally Cooper, Jamie Adamson, Juliana Cronin, Alwyn Kurts, Basil Clarke
Supplier: Australian Broadcasting Commission
Exec Prod: Oscar Whitbread;
Dir: Douglas Sharp;
Wri: Cliff Green.
25 Mins, Mon, 5:30 pm.
ABC (Australia) TV, Channel 2, Sydney
11/12/80F

ALL STAR SECRETS
With Bob Eubanks (host), Nipsey Russell, Abbe Lane, Jamie Farr, Lynn Redgrave, Billy Crystal
Supplier: Hill-Eubanks Group & 20th-Fox TV
Prod: Walt Case;
Dir: Bill Caruthers.
30 Mins, Mon-Fri, 10:30 am.
NBC-TV
01/17/79

ALL'S FAIR
With Richard Crenna, Bernadette Peters, Salome Jens, J A Preston
Supplier: T A T Communications
Exec Prod: Rod Parker;
Prods: Bob Schiller, Bob Weiskopf;
Dir: Hal Cooper;
Wris: Weiskopf, Schiller, Parker.
30 Mins, Mon, 9:30 pm.
CBS-TV
09/22/76

ALMOST ANYTHING GOES
With Charlie Jones, Lynn Shackelford, Regis Philbin, Sam Riddle
Supplier: Bob Banner Associates & Robert Stigwood Organization
Exec Prods: Banner, Beryl Vertue;
Prods: Riddle, Kip Walton;
Dir: Walton;
Wri: Rowby Goren.
60 Mins, Sat, 8 pm.
ABC-TV
01/28/76

ALMOST HEAVEN
With Robert Hays, Jay Leno, Laurie Heineman, Richard Roat, Eva Gabor, Ellen Regan, Anne Schedeen, Larry Gelman
Supplier: Gloria Hickey Prods & Paramount TV
Exec Prod-Wri: Dale McRaven;
Prods: David Pollock & Elias Davis;
Dir: Bill Persky.
30 Mins, Thurs (28), 9:30 pm.
ABC-TV
01/10/79

ALTON OCHSNER AT EIGHTY
With James A Keyser (narrator)
Prods: Robert Grevemberg, Keyser;
Wri: Keyser.
30 Mins, Thurs (4), 9:30 pm.
WYES-TV New Orleans
01/10/79

ALVIN PURPLE
With Graeme Blundell, Chris Haywood, Jacki Weaver, John Ewart, Leonard Teale, Suzanne Church, Jane Haaders, Kate Ferguson, Noeline Brown, Judy Lynn, Judy Morris, Belinda Giblin, Briony Behets, Anna Russell, others
Supplier: Australian Broadcasting Commission
Exec Prod: Maurice Murphy;
Dir: Ted Robinson;
Wri: Alan Hopgood.
30 Mins, Fri, 9:15 pm.
ABC (Australia) TV
09/01/76F

THE AMAZING SPIDER-MAN
With Nicholas Hammond, Robert F Simon, Chip Fields, Michael Pataki, JoAnna Cameron, Robert Alda, Randy Powell, Lawrence Casey, Simon Scott, Sid Clute, Steven Anderson, Anne Bloom, Herbert S Braha, Emil Farkas, Wil Albert, Dick Kyker
Supplier: Charles Fries Prods, Dan Goodman Prods
Exec Prods: Fries, Goodman;
Prods: Robert Janes, Ron Satlof;
Dir: Satlof;
Wri: Janes.
60 Mins, Wed, 8 pm.
CBS-TV
04/12/78

THE AMBASSADORS
(Play of the Month)
With Paul Scofield, Lee Remick, Delphine Seyrig, Gayle Hunnicutt, Don Fellows, David Huffman, others
Supplier: BBC-TV
Prod: Cedric Messina;
Dir: James Cellan Jones;
Wri: Denis Constanduros.
95 Mins, Sun (13), 8:15 pm.
BBC-1, Britain
03/23/77F

AMBUSH AT IROQUOIS POINT
With R H Thomson, Ken Pogue, Diana Barrington, Stephen Markle, Sean McCann
Exec Prod: Lister Sinclair;
Prod: Beverley Roberts;
Dir: Ralph Thomas.
60 Mins, Wed, 9:30 pm.
CBC, from Toronto, Canada
03/14/79F

AMERICA ALIVE
With Jack Linkletter, Bruce Jenner, Janet Langhart, Pat Mitchell, David Horowitz, Virginia Graham, David Sheehan, Dick Orkin & Bert Berdis, Dr William H Masters & Virginia E Johnson, Chevy Chase
Supplier: Fraser-Greengrass Prods
Exec Prod: Woody Fraser;
Prods: Marty Berman, Bob Raser, Joan Auritt, Raysa Bonow;
Dirs: Don King, Bob Loudin;
Wri: Bob Blum.
60 Mins, Mon-Fri, 12 noon.
NBC-TV
07/26/78

AMERICA ENTERTAINS VICE PREMIER TENG HSIAO-PING
With Dick Cavett (host), Broadway Company of "Eubie", Rudolf Serkin, Harlem Globetrotters, John Denver, Joffrey Ballet, National Children's Choir
Supplier: WETA-TV Washington DC
Prod: George Stevens Jr;
Dir: Don Mischer.
105 Mins, Mon (29), 9 pm.
PBS
01/31/79

AMERICA SALUTES RICHARD RODGERS: THE SOUND OF HIS MUSIC
With Gene Kelly, Henry Winkler, Diahann Carroll, Vic Damone, Sammy Davis Jr, Sandy Duncan, Lena Horne, Cloris Leachman, Peggy Lee, John Wayne
Supplier: 20th Century Fox-Talent Associates and Smith-Hemion Prods
Prods: Gary Smith, Dwight Hemion;
Dir: Hemion;
Wris: Buz Kohan, Ted Strauss.
120 Mins, Thurs (9), 9 pm.
CBS-TV
Anheuser-Busch (D'Arcy, MacManus & Masius)
12/15/76

AMERICA: 2100
With Karen Valentine, Jon Cutler, Mark King, voice of Sid Caesar
Supplier: Paramount TV & Arim Prods
Exec Prods: Austin & Irma Kalish;
Supv Prod: Don Silverman;
Prod: Gary Menteer;
Dir: Joel Zwick;
Wris: Mark Rothman, Lowell Ganz.
30 Mins, Tues (24), 8:30 pm.
ABC-TV
08/01/79

THE AMERICAN GIRLS
With Priscilla Barnes, Debra Clinger, David Spielberg, Ross Martin, William Prince, Dana Andrews, Edward Bell, Michael Twain, Ion Teodorescu, Zitto Kazann, others
Supplier: Bennett-Katleman Prods & Columbia Pictures TV
Exec Prods: Harve Bennett, Harris Katleman;
Prod-Wri: Simon Muntner;
Dir: Rod Holcomb.
60 Mins, Sat, 9 pm.
CBS-TV
09/27/78

AMERICAN LIFE STYLE
With E.G. Marshall (host)
Supplier: Comco Prods.
Prod-dir: Ann Zane Shanks.
30 Mins, Tues, 8 pm.
WOR-TV New York
USF&G Cos. (Vansandt, Dugdale)
03/24/76

THE AMERICAN MOVIE AWARDS
With David Frost, Dudley Moore, Angie Dickinson
Supplier: David Paradine TV Prodns., Jack Haley Jr. Prodns.
Exec Prod: Frost;
Prod: Haley;
Dir: Marty Pasetta;
Wris: Stanley Ralph Ross, Tony Thomas, Haley.
120 Mins, Mon, (11), 9 pm.
NBC-TV
02/20/80

THE AMERICAN NEWSREEL OF CRIME
With Jimmy Breslin
Supplier: RKO General Prods
Prod: Al Korn;
Dir: Don Horan;
Wri: David Askling.
60 Mins, Fri (29), 10 pm.
WOR-TV New York
11/03/76

THE AMERICAN SHORT STORY
Supplier: Learning in Focus, South Carolina Television Network
Exec Prod: Robert Geller.
90 Mins, Tues, 8 pm.
PBS
04/06/77

AMERICA'S TOP TEN
With Casey Kasem (host), The Pink Floyd, The Brothers Johnson, Air Supply, Deborah Harry
Supplier: Scotti Brothers & Syd Vinnedge TV (Gold Key Media)
Exec Prods: Vinnedge, Tony Scotti;
Prod: Greg Sills;
Dir: Bill Rainbolt.
30 Mins, Wed, 7:30 pm.
WCBS-TV New York
05/14/80S

AMORE IN ITALIA
(Love In Italy)
Supplier: RAI-TV
Luigi Comencini, wth Fabio Pellarin and Italo Moscati.
45 Mins, Sat, (23), 10 pm.
RAI-TV 1, from Rome, Italy
01/10/79F

AN ALL-STAR TRIBUTE TO JOHN WAYNE
With John Wayne, Frank Sinatra, Charles Bronson, John Byner, Glen Campbell, Sammy Davis Jr, Angie Dickinson, Monty Hall, Bob Hope, Ron Howard, Dick Martin, Lee Marvin, Maureen O'Hara, Dan Rowan, James Stewart, Claire Trevor, Henry Winkler
Supplier: Paul Keyes Prods
Prod: Keyes;
Dir: Dick McDonough;
Wris: Keyes, Marc London.
60 Mins, Fri (26), 8 pm.
ABC-TV
Sears, Roebuck
12/01/76

AN ENGLISHMAN'S CASTLE
With Kenneth More, Anthony Bate, Isla Blair, others
Supplier: BBC-TV
Prod: Innes Bloyd;
Dir: Paul Ciapessoni;
Wri: Philip Mackie.
50 Mins, Mon 9 pm.
BBC-2, from London, England
06/28/78F

THE ANDROS TARGETS
With James Sutorius, Pamela Reed, Roy Poole, Alan Mixon, Ted Beniades, F Murray Abraham, Josef Sommer, Leon Janney, Dixie Carter, Kipp Osborne, Kate Kelly
Supplier: CBS-TV
Exec Prod: Bob Sweeney;
Prod: Edward H Feldman;
Dir: Sweeney;
Wri: Frank Cucci, based on works by Nicholas Gage.
60 Mins, Mon, 10 pm.
CBS-TV
02/02/77

ANDY
With Andy Williams, Wayland Flowers, Osmond Brothers, Donny & Marie Osmond, George Wyle orch
Supplier: Pierre Cossette Co (Grey Prods)
Exec Prod: Cossette;
Prod-dir: Robert Scheerer;
Wris: Jeremy Stevens, Tom Moore
30 Mins, Wed, 7:30 pm.
WNBC-TV New York
P & G (Grey Advertising)
09/22/76S

ANGIE
With Donna Pescow, Robert Hays, Tammy Lauren, Sharon Spelman, Debralee Scott, Diane Robin, Doris Roberts, Joseph Perry
Supplier: Miller-Milkis Prods, Henderson Prods & Paramount TV
Exec Prods: Bob Ellison, Dale McRaven, Thomas L Miller, Edward K Milkis;
Prods: Alan Eisenstock & Larry Mintz, Bruce Johnson;
Dir: Howard Storm;
Wris: Eisenstock & Mintz.
30 Mins, Thurs, 8:30 pm.
ABC-TV
02/14/79

THE ANGRY TAXPAYER
With Walter Cronkite
Supplier: CBS News
Exec Prod: Russ Bensley;
Prod: George Murray;
Dirs: Bill Linden, Ken Sable;
Wri: Charles West.
60 Mins, Thurs (15), 8 pm.
CBS-TV
06/21/78

ANIMALS ANIMALS ANIMALS
With Hal Linden, Lynn Kellogg, Roger Caras
Supplier: ABC News Public Affairs
Exec Prod: Lester Cooper;
Prod: Peter Weinberg;
Dir-wri: Cooper.
25 Mins, Sun, 11:30 am.
ABC-TV
09/15/76

ANIMALYMPICS
With voices of Gilda Radner, Billy Crystal, Harry Shearer, Michael Fremer
Supplier: Lisberger Studios
Prods: Steven Lisberger, Donald Kushner;
Dir: Lisberger;
Wris: Lisberger, Fremer.
30 Mins, Fri, (1), 8 pm.
NBC-TV
02/06/80

ANNA KARENINA
With Nicola Pagett, Eric Porter, Stuart Wilson, Caroline Langrishe, Robert Swann, David Harries, others
Supplier: BBC-TV
Exec Prod: Ken Riddington;
Prod: Donald Wilson;
Dir: Basil Coleman;
Wri: Wilson.
50 Mins, Sun (25), 8:10 pm.
BBC-2, from London, England
09/28/77F

ANNE HUTCHINSON: RHODE ISLAND'S FIRST INDEPENDENT WOMAN
With the Rhode Island Feminist Theatre
Prod-Adaptor: Ada McAlister;
Dir: Brandon French.
90 Mins, Sat, 4:30 pm.
WSBE-TV Providence
02/15/78

ANNE MURRAY: NUMBER ONE WITH A BULLET
With Anne Murray, Mike Douglas, Jim Stafford, Phil Esposito
Prod: Alan Thicke;
Dir: J Edward Shaw;
Wris: Thicke, Ben Gordon, Lorne Frohman.
60 Mins, Mon, 9 pm.
CBC-TV, from Toronto, Canada
Ford Motor Co of Canada
10/26/77F

ANNIE FLYNN
With Barrie Youngfellow, Carol Potter, Harvey Lewis, Louis Guss, Charles Frank, Jack Fletcher, Lisa Loring, Josh Grenrock, Renee Lippin
Supplier: Uncle Toby Prods & Columbia Pictures TV
Prods-Wris: Coleman Mitchell, Geoffrey Neigher;
Dir: Robert Moore.
30 Mins, Sat (21), 8:30 pm.
CBS-TV
01/25/78

ANN-MARGRET...RHINESTONE COWGIRL
With Ann-Margret, Bob Hope, Perry Como, Minnie Pearl, Chet Atkins
Supplier: Smith-Hemion Prods & Roger Smith Video Prods
Exec Prods: Roger Smith, Allan Carr;
Prods: Gary Smith, Dwight Hemion;
Dir: Hemion;
Wri: Buz Kohan.
60 Mins, Tues (26), 9 pm.
NBC-TV
05/11/77

ANOTHER DAY
With David Groh, Joan Hackett, Hope Summers, Lisa Lindgren, Al Eisenmann, Dean Lawrence
Supplier: The Komack Co
Exec Prod: James Komack;
Prod: Paul Mason;
Dirs: Komack, Gary Shimokawa;
Wri: Carl Kleinschmitt.
30 Mins, Sat, 9 pm.
CBS-TV
04/12/78

APOLLO
With George Kirby (host), Cab Calloway, Harold Melvin and the Blue Notes with Sharon Paige, "Bubbling Brown Sugar" cast, Stephanie Mills, Willie Tyler & Lest, Mighty Clouds Of Joy
Supplier: Perin Film Enterprises, Group W Prods.
Exec Prods: David Salzman, Richard Perin, Bobby Schiffman;
Prods: Fred Dukes, William Easley;
Dir: Stan Lathan.
90 Mins, Sat (8), 11 pm.
WNEW-TV New York
05/12/76S

APPLE PIE
With Rue McClanahan, Dabney Coleman, Jack Gilford, Gaitlin O'Heaney, Derrel Maury, James Cromwell, Laurence Haddon, Richard Stahl
Supplier: TAT Communications
Prod-Wri: Charlie Hauck;
Dir: Peter Bonerz.
30 Mins, Sat, 8:30 pm.
ABC-TV
09/27/78

ARA'S SPORTS WORLD
With Ara Parseghian
Supplier: Viacom Enterprises
Exec Prod: Jack Jones;
Prod: Herb Golden Organization (Jeff Pill, Russ Lunday, Phil Harmon);
Dir-wri: Golden.
30 Mins, Sat (2), 7 pm.
WOR--TV New York
10/06/76S

ARCADE
With Garth Meade, Coral Kelly, Bill Charlton, Maggie Stuart, Lorrae Desmond, Peggy Toppano, Anne Semler, Joy Miller, Danny Adcock, Aileen Britton, Syd Heylen, Lucy Taylor, Raymond Nock, Sinan Leong, Christine Harri, Mike Dorsey, Olga Tamara, Patrick Ward, others
Supplier: Channel TEN 10 in Sydney for the 10 Network
Exec Prod: Peter Benardos;
Dirs: Mike Murphy, Howard Scrivener, Tony Nielsen;
Wris: David Sale, Johnny Whyte, Lynn Foster, Ross Napier, Derek Strahan.
30 Mins, 7 pm. weekdays
Channel TEN 10 Sydney, Australia
02/06/80F

ARCHIE
With Dennis Bowen, Audrey Landers, Hilary Thompson, Mark Winkworth, Derrel Maury, Jim Boelsen, Susan Blu, Michelle Stacy, Byron Webster, Jane Lambert, Gordon Jump, Amzie Strickland, Whit Bissell, Tifni Twitchell, Bill Mumy, Paul Gordon, Mae Marmy, Nick Uhrig's Archie Show Music Group
Supplier: Komack Co
Exec Prod: James Komack;
Prods: Perry Cross, Eric Cohen, George Yanok;
Dir: Robert Scheerer;
Wris: Cohen, Yanok, Beverly Bloomberg, Peter Gallay, Mickey Rose, Neil Rosen & George Tricker.
60 Mins, Sun (19), 7 pm.
ABC-TV
12/22/76

ARE YOU A MISSING HEIR?
With Hal Linden (host), Brooke Bundy, Michael Williams, Constance McCashen, Toni Kalem, Joanna Kerns, Vanessa Brown, others
Supplier: Alan Landsburg Prods
Exec Prod: Landsburg;
Prod-Dir: Robert Scheerer;
Wri: Noreen Stone.
60 Mins, Thurs, (8), 10 pm.
ABC-TV
06/14/78

ARENA
With John Meillon, Ray Barrett, Vincent Ball, Julie Hamilton, Chelsea Brown, Brian Blain, Patrick Amer, Max Osbiston, David Nettheim, Max Meldrum, others
Supplier: Australian Broadcasting Commission
Dir: Eric Tayler;
Wri: Michael Craig.
50 Mins, Mon (12), 8 pm.
ABC (Australia) TV
01/28/76F

AROUND HERE
Prod: Kevin Meagher.
30 Mins, 7:30 pm.
KIRO-TV, Seattle
05/03/78

ARSON: FIRE FOR HIRE
(ABC News Closeup)
With Brit Hume, Michael Connor
Supplier: ABC News
Exec Prod: Pamela Hill;
Sr Prod: Dick Richter;
Prod-Dir: Richard Gerdau;
Wris: Gerdau, Hume.
60 Mins, Thurs (3), 10 pm.
ABC-TV
08/09/78

ARTHUR C. CLARKE'S MYSTERIOUS WORLD
With Clarke
Supplier: Yorkshire TV
Exec Prod: John Fairley;
Prods: John Fanshawe; Simon Welfare;
Dirs: Charles Flynn, Peter Jones, Michael Weigall
30 Mins, Tues, 8:30 pm.
ITV Network, England
09/10/80F

ARTHUR FIEDLER WITH THE BOSTON POPS FROM CARNEGIE HALL
(Monsanto Night)
With Lena Horne, Richard Morse, Rasa Allen, Barnette Ricci Dancers
Supplier: York Enterprises
Prod: Jack Sobel;
Dir: Clark Jones;
Wris: Ed Haas, Sobel.
60 Mins, Sat (25), 7 pm.
WNBC-TV New York
Monsanto (Vitt Media)
12/29/76

THE ARTS IN NEW ORLEANS
Dir: David Frentz.
30 Mins
WYES-TV New Orleans
06/08/77

ASIAN INSIGHT SERIES
Supplier: Film Australia
Dir: Arch Nicholson;
Wri-Prod: John Temple.
60 Mins, Sat, 8 pm.
ABC-TV, Australia
03/09/77F

ASPEN (Part I)
(NBC Saturday Night At the Movies)
With Sam Elliott, Perry King, Gene Barry, Martine Beswick, Roger Davis, Lee deBroux, George DiCenzo, Anthony Franciosa, Jessica Harper, Doug Heyes, Bo Hopkins, John Houseman, John McIntire, Michelle Phillips, William Prince, Debi Richter
Supplier: Universal TV & Roy Huggins/Public Arts Prods
Exec Prod: Michael B Klein;
Prod: Jo Swerling Jr;
Dir: Douglas Heyes;
Wri: Heyes, based on Bert Hirschfeld's novel and Bart Spicer's "The Adversary" novel
120 Mins, Sat, 9 pm.
NBC-TV
11/09/77

THE ASPHALT COWBOY
With Max Baer, Robin Dearden, Lory Walsh, Lori Lowe, James Luisi, Noah Beery, James Sloyan, Jennifer Holmes, Michael Mullins, Cal Bellini, Richard Denning, Russ Marin, Ben Frommer.
Supplier: Michael Fisher Prodns & Universal TV
Exec Prod-Wri: Fisher;
Prod: Mike Vejar;
Dir: Cliff Bole.
60 Mins, Sun (7), 10 pm.
NBC-TV
12/10/80

THE ASSASSINATION OF PRESIDENT KENNEDY: WHAT DO WE KNOW NOW THAT WE DIDN'T KNOW THEN
With Bob Sherman (narrator)
Supplier: Witness Prods & Syndicast Services
Exec Prods: Mark Hollo, David Osterlund;
Prod: Anthony Summers;
Wri: Michael Cockerell.
90 Mins, Sat (13), 6:30 pm.
WOR-TV New York
05/17/78

THE ASSOCIATES
With Wilfrid Hyde-White, Martin Short, Alley Mills, Joe Regalbuto, Shelley Smith, Tim Thomerson, John Getz, Madelyn Cates, Sandra McCabe
Supplier: John Charles Walters Prods & Paramount TV
Exec Prods: James L Brooks, Stan Daniels, Ed Weinberger;
Prod-Wri: Michael Leeson;
Dir: James Burrows.
30 Mins, Sun, 8:30 pm.
ABC-TV
09/26/79

AUDIENCE
With Rex Brigham & Lovice Weller, Gesa Sklaroff, Ginnine Cocuzza, Harry Harris
Exec Prod-Dir: Richard Crew;
Wris: Various.
30 Mins, Sun, 8 pm.
WHYY-TV Philadelphia
02/09/77

AVERY SCHREIBER'S TIME SLOT
Supplier: Columbia Pictures TV
Prod: Alan Sloan;
Dir: Steve Katten;
Wri: E Jack Kaplan.
30 Mins, Sat (18), 7:30 pm.
WABC-TV New York

01/22/78S

THE AWAKENING LAND
(Big Event)
With Elizabeth Montgomery, Hal Holbrook, Jane Seymour, Steven Keats, Devon Ericson, Tony Mockus, Louis Latham, Derin Altay, Michelle Stacy, William H Macy, Jeanette Nolan, Charles Ross, Dorrie Kavanaugh, Bert Remsen, Sean Prye, Johnny Timko, Pia Romans, Theresa Landreth, Joan Tompkins, Katy Kurtzman, Dennis Dimster, Tracy Kleronomos, Barney McFadden
Supplier: Harry Bernsen-Tom Kuhn-Boris Sagal Prods, & Warner Bros TV
Exec Prods: Bernsen, Kuhn;
Prod: Robert L. Relyea;
Dir: Sagal;
Wris: James Lee Barrett, Liam O'Brien (based on Conrad Richter trilogy).
120 Mins, Sun-Tue (19-21).
NBC-TV

02/22/78

AYCLIFFE
Supplier: Thames TV
Prod-Dir: Michael Whyte.
90 Mins, Tues, 10:30 pm.
Thames TV, from London, England

12/14/77F

BAA BAA BLACK SHEEP
With Robert Conrad, Dana Elcar, James Whitmore Jr, Dirk Blocker, Robert Ginty, John Larroquette, W K Stratton, Simon Oakland, others
Supplier: Universal TV
Exec Prod-wri: Stephen J. Cannell.
Prod: Phil DeGuere;
Dir: Russ Mayberry.
120 Mins, Tues, 8 pm.
NBC-TV

09/29/76

BABY, I'M BACK
With Demond Wilson, Denise Nicholas, Helen Martin, Kim Fields, Tony Holmes, Ed Hall, Nick La Tour, Bill Cobbs, Fuddle Bagley
Supplier: Charles Fries Prods, Lila Garrett Prods
Exec Prod: Fries;
Prod: Garrett;
Wris: Garrett, Mort Lachman;
Dir: Bill Persky.
30 Mins, Sat (22), 9:30 pm.
CBS-TV

10/26/77

BABY, I'M BACK
With Demond Wilson, Denise Nicholas, Kim Fields, Tony Holmes, Helen Martin, Ed Hall, Allan Rich, Jack Fletcher, Timmie Rogers, Nick LaTour, Bella Bruck, Pat Ast, Pat Cranshaw
Supplier: Lila Garrett Prods, Dewil Prods, Charles Fries Prods
Exec Prod: Fries;
Prod: Garrett;
Dir: Dick Harwood;
Wris: April Kelly, George Geiger.
30 Mins, Mon, 8:30 pm.
CBS-TV

02/08/78

BACKSTAIRS AT THE WHITE HOUSE - PART 1
(NBC Monday Night At The Movies)
With Olivia Cole, Leslie Uggams, Louis Gossett Jr, Robert Hooks, Leslie Nielsen, Hari Rhodes, Bill Overton, Helena Carroll, David Downing, Cloris Leachman, Paul Winfield, Julie Harris, Victor Buono, Robert Vaughn, Kim Hunter, Claire Bloom, Celeste Holm, George Kennedy, Ed Flanders, Lee Grant, Larry Gates, Jan Sterling, Eileen Heckart, John Anderson, Harry Morgan, Estelle Parsons, Barbara Barrie, Andrew Duggan, Kevin Hooks, Tania Johnson, Murphy Robinson, Gary Borden, Dana Wynter, John Randolph, others
Supplier: Ed Friendly Prods
Exec Prod: Friendly;
Prods: Friendly, Michael O'Herlihy;
Dir: O'Herlihy;
Wris: Gwen Bagni & Paul Dubov, based on novel by Lillian Rogers Parks & Frances Spatz Leighton.
160 Min, Mon (29), 8 pm.
NBC-TV

02/07/79

BAD BOYS
With Alan & Susan Raymond
Supplier: WNET TV Laboratory
Exec Prod: David Loxton;
Prods-Dirs-Wris: Raymonds.
120 Mins, Sun (29), 10 pm.
WNET New York

11/01/78

B.A.D. CATS
With Asher Brauner, Steve Hanks, Michelle Pfeiffer, La Wanda Page, Jimmie Walker, Vic Morrow, Charles Cioffi, Michael V. Gazzo, James Hampton, George Murdock, Nehemiah Persoff, Tom Simcox
Supplier: Aaron Spelling Prods.
Exec Prods: Spelling, Douglas S. Cramer;
Supv Prod: E. Duke Vincent;
Prod: Everett Chambers;
Dir: Bernard L. Kowalski;
Wri: Al Martinez.
90 Mins, Fri, 8 pm.
ABC-TV

01/16/80

THE BAD NEWS BEARS
With Jack Warden, J Brennan Smith, Tricia Cast, Billy Jacoby, Corey Feldman, Sparky Marcus, Meeno Peluce, Shane Butterworth, Christoff St John, Catherine Hicks, Philip R Allen, Richard Roat
Supplier: Frog Prods, Huk Inc & Paramount TV
Exec Prods-Wris: Arthur Silver, Bob Brunner;
Prods: John Boni, Norman Stiles, Jeffrey Ganz;
Dir: Bruce Bilson.
30 Mins, Sat, 8 pm.
CBS-TV

03/28/79

BAILEY'S BIRD
(Touchdown)
With Hu Pryce, Mark Lee, Samit Buranakol, Vincent Ball, Mick Parer
Supplier: John McCallum Prods
Exec Prod: John McCallum;
Dir: Peter Maxwell;
Wris: J Benn Darrow, Gregory Bond.
30 Mins.
Seven Network (previewed at Supreme Film, Sydney, Australia)

04/19/78F

BALL FOUR
With Jim Bouton, Jack Somack, David-James Carroll, Ben Davidson, Bill McCutcheon, Lenny Schultz, Marco St. John, Jaime Tirelli, Sam Wright, others
Supplier: CBS-TV
Prod: Don Segall;
Dir: Jay Sandrich;
Wris: Bouton, Seagall, Greg Antonacci, Jay Sommers.
30 Mins, Wed, 8:30 pm.
CBS-TV

09/29/76

BANANA BENDER
With John Hargreaves, Lyndell Rowe, Maurice Fields, Martin Phelan, Geoff Parry, Tony Barry
Supplier: Australian Broadcasting Commission
Dir: John Walker;
Wri: John May.
50 Mins, Sun, 8:30 pm.
ABC TV, Channel 2, Sydney, Australia

12/05/79F

THE BANANA CO
With John Reilly, Ted Gehring, Ron Masak, Sam Chew Jr, Eddie Quillan, Gaylord Sartain, Robert Brown, Gino Silva, John Orchard
Supplier: O'Connor-Becker Prods
Exec Prods: Carroll O'Connor, Terry Becker;
Prod: Ron Rubin;
Dir: Bruce Bilson;
Wri: David John Tracy.
30 Mins, Thurs (25), 9:30 pm.
CBS-TV

08/31/77

BARBARA MANDRELL & THE MANDRELL SISTERS
With Louise & Irlene Mandrell, Dolly Parton, John Schneider, Krofft Puppets, Georgi Irene
Supplier: Krofft Entertainment
Exec Prods: Sid & Marty Krofft;
Prod: Ernest Chambers;
Dir: Bob Henry;
Wris: Al Gordon, Peter Gallay, Cort Casady, Tom Moore, Jeremy Stevens, Sam Greenbaum, Lisa Medway, Chambers, Phil Hahn.
60 Mins, Tues, (18) 10 pm.
NBC-TV
11/26/80

THE BARBARA WALTERS SPECIAL
With Barbra Streisand, Jon Peters, Jimmy Carter, Rosalynn Carter
Prod: Lucy Jarvis;
Dir: John J. Desmond.
60 Mins, Tues (14), 10 pm.
ABC-TV
General Electric (BBDO)
12/22/76

THE BARRY MANILOW SPECIAL
With Penny Marshall, Lady Flash
Supplier: Kamakazi Music Corp & Steve Binder Prods
Exec Prod: Miles Lourie;
Prod-Dir: Binder;
Wris: Allan Thicke, Don Clark, Susan Clark, Ronny Pearlman, Bruce Vilanich, Manilow, Binder.
60 Mins, Wed (2), 10 pm.
ABC-TV
Kraft (JWT)
03/09/77

BARRY'S PEOPLE: A GALLERY OF PORTRAITS
With Barry Bernson, others
Prod-Wri: Bernson;
Dir: Alan Kartun.
30 Mins, Wed, 6:30 pm.
WMAQ-TV Chicago
06/20/79

BARYSHNIKOV ON BROADWAY
With Mikhail Baryshnikov, Liza Minnelli, Nell Carter, "A Chorus Line" cast
Supplier: Jodat/Smith-Hemion Prods
Exec Prod: Herman Krawitz;
Prods: Gary Smith, Dwight Hemion;
Dir: Hemion;
Wri: Fred Ebb
60 Mins. Thurs, (24) 9 pm.
ABC-TV
IBM (Doyle Dane Bernbach).
04/30/80

THE BASTARD - PART 1
(Operation Prime Time)
With Andrew Stevens, Tom Bosley, Kim Cattrall, Buddy Ebsen, Lorne Greene, Olivia Hussey, Cameron Mitchell, Harry Morgan, Patricia Neal, Eleanor Parker, Donald Pleasence, William Shatner, Barry Sullivan, Noah Beery, Peter Bonerz, John Colicos, William Daniels, James Gregory, Herb Jefferson Jr, Mark Neely, Keenan Wynn, Charles Haid, Jim Antonio, John DeLancie, James Whitmore Jr, Russell Johnson, Ike Eisenmann, Robert Burke, Elizabeth Shepherd, George Chandler, Beege Barkette, Raymond Burr (narrator)
Supplier: John Wilder Prods & Universal TV (MCA-TV)
Exec Prod: Wilder;
Prod: Joe Byrne;
Dir: Lee H Katzin;
Wri: Guerdon Trueblood, from John Jakes' novel.
120 Mins, Mon (22), 8 pm.
WPIX-TV New York
05/24/78

BATTLE OF THE GENERATIONS
(See: Not Until Today; But Mother!; Paul Williams Show; Starting Fresh)
07/04/79

BATTLES: THE MURDER THAT WOULDN'T DIE
(Sunday Big Event)
With William Conrad, Lane Caudell, Robin Mattson, Marj Dusay, Tommy Aguilar, Jimmy Borges, Roger Bowen, Sharon Acker, Edward Binns, Jose Ferrer, John Hillerman, Mike Kellin, Ben Piazza, Don Porter, Ken Tobey
Supplier: Glen A Larson Prods. & Universal TV
Exec Prod: Larson;
Prod: Ben Kadish;
Dir: Ron Satlof;
Wris: Larson, Michael Sloan.
120 Mins, Sun, (9) 9 pm.
NBC-TV
03/12/80

BATTLESTAR GALACTICA
(ABC Sunday Night Movie)
With Richard Hatch, Dirk Benedict, Lorne Greene, Herb Jefferson Jr, Maren Jensen, John Colicos, Laurette Spang, Jane Seymour, others
Supplier: Glen Larson Prods, Universal TV
Exec Prod-Wri: Larson;
Supv Prod: Leslie Stevens;
Prod: John Dykstra;
Dir: Richard A Colla.
180 Mins, Sun (17), 8 pm.
ABC-TV
09/20/78

THE BAXTERS
With Harriet Rogers, Frank Dolan, Muriel Dolan, Scott Evans
Supplier: BBI Productions
Exec Prod: Lew Barlow;
Prod: Hubert Jessup;
Dir: Alex Frisbee;
Wri: Rachel Singer.
30 Mins, Sat (5), 7 pm.
WCVB-TV Boston
03/16/77S

THE BAXTERS
With Anita Gillette, Larry Keith, Terri Lynn Wood, Derin Altay, Chris Petersen, and, for WPIX, Carol McKillop
Supplier: TAT Communications, BBI Inc
Exec Prod: Norman Lear and, for WPIX, Kathleen S Maynard;
Prod: Fern Field;
Dir: John Bowab and, for WPIX, Peter Pontillo;
Wris: Jon Surgal, Carmen Finestra.
30 Mins, Sun, 10 pm.
WPIX-TV New York
10/10/79S

B.B. BEEGLE SHOW
With Joyce De Witt, Arte Johnson, voices of Michael Bell, Norm Grohman, Marilyn Schreffler
Supplier: Hanna-Barbera Prods., CTV Television Network & British Columbia TV (Y & R Program Services)
Exec Prods: Joseph Barbera, Arthur Weinthal, W.C. Elliott;
Prods: Stan Jacobson, John Joachims;
Dir: Jacobson;
Wri: Dick Robbins, Duane Poole.
30 Mins, Tues, (22), 8 pm.
WNEW-TV New York
01/30/80S

THE BEACH GIRLS
With Ava Lazar, Kim O'Brien, Rita Wilson, Don Calfa, Frankie Avalon
Supplier: Hanna-Barbera Prods (Lexington Broadcast Services)
Exec Prod: Joseph H Barbera;
Prod: Walt de Faria;
Dir: Stan Cherry;
Wri: Marian C Freeman.
30 Mins, Tues (27), 7:30 pm.
WNBC-TV New York
Procter & Gamble (Grey)
01/11/78S

BEACH PATROL
(ABC Monday Night Movie Double Feature)
With Robin Strand, Jonathan Frakes, Christine DeLisle, Richard Hill, Michael Gregory, Michael V Gazzo, Panchito Gomez, Mimi Maynard, Princess O'Mahoney, Lillian Adams, Bella Bruck, Paul Burke
Supplier: Spelling-Goldberg Prods
Exec Prods: Aaron Spelling & Leonard Goldberg;
Supv Prods-Wris: Ronald Austin, James D Buchanan;
Prod: Phil Fehrle;
Dir: Bob Kelljan.
90 Mins, Mon (30), 8 pm.
ABC-TV
05/09/79

THE BEACHCOMBERS
With Bruno Gerussi, Robert Clothier, Rae Brown
Exec Prod: Hugh Beard;
Prod: Ken Juvenhill;
Dir: Rene Bonniere;
Wri: Tony Robinson.
30 Mins, Sun, 7 pm.
CBC-TV, from Vancouver, Canada
10/19/77F

BEANE'S OF BOSTON
With John Hillerman, Charlotte Rae, Alan Sues, George O'Hanlon Jr, Larry Bishop, Lorna Patterson, Tom Poston, Morgan Farley, Don Bexley, Dana House
Supplier: Henderson Prods & Paramount TV
Exec Prods: Garry K Marshall, Tony Marshall;
Prods-Wris: Sheldon Bull, David Croft, Bill Idelson, Jeremy Lloyd;
Dir: Jerry Paris.
30 Mins, Sat (5), 8:30 pm.
CBS-TV

05/16/79

BEAT THE CLOCK
With Monty Hall(host), Jack Narz (announcer)
Supplier: Goodson-Todman Prods
Exec Prod: Frank Wayne;
Prod-Dir: Paul Alter.
30 Mins, Mon-Fri, 10 am.
CBS-TV

09/26/79

THE BEATLES FOREVER
With Diahann Carroll, Ray Charles, Anthony Dowell, Anthony Newley, Bernadette Peters, Tony Randall, Mel Tillis, Paul Williams
Supplier: ATV
Prod: Syd Vinnedge;
Dir: Jon Scoffield;
Wris: Sheldon Keller, Richard Albrecht, Casey Keller.
60 Mins, Thurs (24), 10 pm.
NBC-TV
Sentry Insurance Co (Grey)

11/30/77

BEAUTY & THE BEAST
(Hallmark Hall Of Fame)
With George C. Scott, Trish Van Devere, Virginia McKenna, Bernard Lee, Michael Harbour, William Relton, Patricia Quinn
Supplier: Palm Prods
Exec Prod: Thomas Johnston;
Prod: Hank Moonjean;
Dir: Fielder Cook;
Wri: Sherman Yellen.
90 Mins, Fri (3), 8:30 pm.
NBC-TV
Hallmark Cards (Foote, Cone & Belding)

12/08/76

BEAVERBROOK; THE LIFE & TIMES OF MAX AITKEN
With John Colicos, Neil Munro, Brian Petchey, Rebecca West, A J P Taylor, Chapelle Jaffe, Gerard Parks, others
Prod-dir: John McGreevy;
Wris: McGreevy, V M Rakoff
90 Mins, Tue, 9 pm.
CBC Canada

09/08/76F

BECAUSE HE'S MY FRIEND
With Karen Black, Keir Dullea, Jack Thompson, Tom Oliver, Barbara Stephens, Don Reid, Warwick Poulsen, June Salter, Tony Wager, Michael Long, Tom McCarthy, Ray Meagher, Kevin Howard, Barry Donnelly, Alan Faulkner, Ian Dyson, Hugh Logan, Will Barker
Supplier: Australian Broadcasting Commission & Trans-Atlantic Enterprises
Exec Prods: Robert Kline, Preston Fischer, James Davern;
Prod: Geoffrey Daniels;
Dir: Ralph Nelson;
Wri: Peter Schreck.
90 Mins, Sun, 7:40 pm.
ABC (Australia) TV, from Channel 2, Sydney

06/21/78F

BECOMING JEANNE...A SEARCH FOR SEXUAL IDENTITY
With Frank Field, Lynn Redgrave
Prod-Wri: Madeline Amgott;
Dir: Jay Miller.
30 Mins Thurs (22), 10:30 pm.
WNBC-TV New York

06/28/78

BEDFELLOWS
With Carol Burns, Robin Ramsay, John Walters
Supplier: Australian Broadcasting Commission and AAV-Australian Prods Pty Ltd
Author: Barry Oakley;
Exec Prod: Alan Burke (for ABC);
Prod: Jill Robb (for AAV);
Dir: Julian Pringle.
70 Mins, Sun, (10) 8:30 pm.
ABC (Australia) TV, Channel 2, Sydney

08/20/80F

BEDTIME STORIES
With Al Lohman, Roger Barkley (hosts)
Supplier: Heater/Quigley Prods & Filmways TV
Exec Prod: Robert Noah;
Prod: Jay Redack;
Dir: Bob Loudin;
Wris: Redack, Stuart Alan, Stan Drebin, Bob Lovka, Brian Pollack, Harry Friedman, Deedee Fay, Isabel Williams.
30 Mins, Mon-Fri, 11 pm.
WNEW-TV New York

06/27/79S

BEGGAR ARTS IN A CORPORATE TOWN
With Dale Connelly, others
Wri-Prod: Jeff Strate
Exec Prod: Don Knox;
Dir: Tom Adair;
Edtr: Alan Moorman.
30 Mins, Mon, (23) 7:30 pm.
KTCA-TV St. Paul

07/02/80

BELAFONTE SINGS
With Harry Belafonte, Falumi Prince, Catherine McKinnon, Winnipeg Symphony
Exec Prod: Rob Webb;
Prods: Dale Nelson, Michael Steele.
60 Mins, Sun, 8 pm.
CTV, from Winnipeg, Canada
IBM

02/22/78F

BEN VEREEN - HIS ROOTS
(Sentry Collection)
With Lou Gossett, Debbie Allen, Cheryl Ladd, Jeffrey Jackay, Ron Field Dancers
Supplier: Smith-Hemion Prods & Turtle IV Prods
Exec Prod: Jerrold H Kushnick;
Prods: Gary Smith, Dwight Hemion;
Dir: Hemion;
Wris: Michael Kagan, Ken & Mitzie Welch.
60 Mins, Thurs (2), 10 pm.
ABC-TV
Sentry Insurance (Grey)

03/08/78

BENDER
With Harry Guardino, Nicolas Coster, Joseph Burke, Susan Damante Shaw, Ben Piazza, Stephen Elliott, Will Hare, Robert Phalen, Sean Thomas Roche, Chad Roche, Nancy Bleier
Supplier: O'Connor-Becker Prods
Exec Prods: Carroll O'Connor, Terry Becker;
Prod-Wri: Sy Gomberg;
Dir: Ray Danton.
60 Mins, Wed (12), 10 pm.
CBS-TV

09/19/79

BENNY & BARNEY: LAS VEGAS UNDERCOVER
(NBC Movie of the Week)
With Terry Kiser, Timothy Thomerson, Jack Colvin, Hugh O'Brian, Dick Gautier, Pat Harrington, Michael Pataki, Don Marshall, Jane Seymour, Jack Cassidy, Ted Cassidy, Rodney Dangerfield, Marty Allen, George Gobel, Bobby Troup
Supplier: Glen Larson Prods & Universal TV
Prod-Wri: Larson;
Dir: Ronald Satlof.
90 Mins, Wed (19), 9:30 pm.
NBC-TV

01/26/77

BENSON
With Robert Guillaume, James Noble, Inga Swenson, Caroline McWilliams, Missy Gold, David Hedison, Norman Bartold
Supplier: Witt Thomas Harris Prods
Exec Prods: Paul Junger Witt, Tony Thomas;
Prod: Don Richetta;
Dir: Jay Sandrich;
Wri: Susan Harris.
30 Mins, Thurs, 8:30 pm.
ABC-TV

09/19/79

THE BERENSTAIN BEARS' CHRISTMAS TREE
With voices of Ron McLarity, Gabriela Glatzer, Jonathan Lewis, Pat Lysinger
Supplier: Cates Bros Co & Perpetual Motion Pictures Inc
Exec Prods: Joseph & Gilbert Cates;
Prod: Buzz Potamkin;
Dir: Mordicai Gerstein;
Wris: Stan & Jan Berenstain.
30 Mins, Mon (3), 8 pm.
NBC-TV
Kellogg's (Leo Burnett)

12/12/79

THE BERGIN AND McHUGH EXPEDITION
With Tom Bergin, Paddy McHugh and Aborigines Nugget and Frankie; John Gaden, narrator
Supplier: Australian Broadcasting Commission
Exec Prod: John Sparkes;
Prod: Bob Connolly.
55 Mins, Wed, 8:30 pm.
ABC (Australia) TV
05/31/78F

BERNICE BOBS HER HAIR
With Shelley Duvall, Veronica Cartwright, Bud Cort, others
Prod: Paul R Gurian;
Dir-Wri: Joan Micklin Silver.
45 Mins
PBS
04/06/77

BERT D'ANGELO-SUPERSTAR
With Paul Sorvino, Robert Pine, Dennis Patrick, Wynn Irwin, Francine York, Ed Vasgerian, Leigh McCloskey, Lisa Lyon, Robert A. Gehling, George Dzundza, Anne Helm, Shelly Novack
Supplier: Quinn Martin Prod.
Exec prod: Martin;
Prod: Mort Fine;
Dir: David Friedkin;
Wri: Larry Alexander.
60 Mins, Sat, 10 pm.
ABC-TV
02/25/76

THE BEST OF FAMILIES
With Guy Boyd, William Carden, Frederick Coffin, Alice Drummond, George Ede, Jill Eikenberry, Peter Evans, Clarence Felder, Pauline Flanagan, Victor Garber, Sean Griffin, George Hearn, William Hurt, Suzanne Lederer, Kate McGregor-Stewart, Julia McKenzie, Milo O'Shea, Lisa Pelikan, William Prince, Josef Sommer, Sigourney Weaver; narrator, John Houseman
Supplier: CTW
Exec Prod: Ethel Winant;
Prod: Gareth Davis;
Dir: Glenn Jordan (Premiere);
Wri: Loring Mandel (Premiere).
120 Mins, Thurs (27), 9 pm.
WNET-TV New York
11/02/77S

THE BEST PLACE IN THE WORLD
(Maailman Paras Paikka)
Supplier: YLE (Finnish Broadcasting Co) and Polish TV
Prod-Dir-Wri: Jarmo Jaaskelainen.
39 Mins.
(Puglia Region winner, documentary)
10/03/79PI

BETHUNE
With Donald Sutherland, Kate Nelligan, David Gardner
Exec Prod: Robert Allen;
Prod: Robert Sherrin;
Dir: Eric Till;
Wri: Thomas Rickman.
90 Mins, Sun, 9 pm.
CBC-TV, from Toronto, Canada
10/05/77F

THE BETTE MIDLER SHOW
With The Harlettes (Sharon Redd, Ula Hedwig, Charlotte Crossley)
Supplier: Aaron Russo Prods.
Prod: Russo;
Dir: Tom Trbovich;
Wri: Bruce Vilanche, Jerry Blatt.
135 Mins, Sat (19), 9 pm.
HBO
06/23/76PC

THE BETTE MIDLER SPECIAL
With Dustin Hoffman, Emmett Kelly, Harlettes
Supplier: Divine TV, with Smith-Hemion Prods
Exec Prod: Aaron Russo;
Prods: Gary Smith, Dwight Hemion;
Dir: Hemion;
Wris: Buz Kohan, Jerry Blatt, Tom Eyen, Pat McCormick, Rod Warren.
60 Mins, Wed (7), 10 pm.
NBC-TV
12/14/77

BETTER LATE THAN NEVER
(NBC Movie Of The Week)
With Harold Gould, Tyne Daly, Strother Martin, Harry Morgan, Victor Buono, Lou Jacobi, Donald Pleasence, Jeanette Nolan, Larry Storch, Paula Trueman, Marjorie Bennett
Supplier: Ten Four Prods
Exec Prods: Greg Strangis, William Hogan;
Prod: Peter Katz;
Dir: Richard Crenna;
Wris: Strangis, John Carpenter.
120 Mins, Wed (17), 9 pm.
NBC-TV
10/24/79

THE BETTER SEX
With Sarah Purcell, Bill Anderson (hosts)
Supplier: Goodson-Todman Prods
Exec Prod: Ira Skutch;
Prod: Robert Sherman;
Dir: Paul Alter.
30 Mins, Mon-Fri, noon
ABC-TV
07/27/77

BETTY WHITE SHOW
With John Hillerman, Georgia Engel, Alex Henteloff, Barney Phillip, Carla Borelli, Charles Cyphers
Supplier: MTM Prods
Exec Prods: Ed Weinberger, Stan Daniels;
Prod: Bob Ellison;
Dir: Bill Persky;
Wri: David Lloyd.
30 Mins, Mon, 9 pm.
CBS-TV
09/14/77

BETWEEN THE LINES
With Adam Arkin, Squire Fridell, Sandy Helberg, Susan Krebs, Nancy Lane, Charley Lang, Kristoffer Tabori, Gene Conforti, Peggy Pope, Howard Honig
Supplier: Time-Life TV
Exec Prod: Philip Mandelker;
Supv Prod: Freyda Rothstein;
Prods: Patricia Nardo, Russ Petranto;
Dir: Charlotte Brown;
Wri: Fred Barron.
30 Mins, Mon, (7) 8:30 pm.
ABC-TV
07/16/80

BETWEEN THE WARS
With Eric Sevareid
Supplier: Mobil Oil & Alan Landsburg Prods
Exec Prod: Landsburg;
Prod-Wri: Anthony Potter;
30 Mins, Wed, 7:30 pm.
WNEW-TV New York
04/12/78S

BEULAH LAND
With Lesley Ann Warren, Michael Sarrazin, Meredith Baxter-Birney, Eddie Albert, Hope Lange, Dorian Harewood, Paul Rudd, Paul Shenar, Martha Scott, Allyn Ann McLerie, Jenny Agutter, Don Johnson
Supplier: David Gerber Prods & Columbia Pictures TV
Exec Prod: Gerber;
Prod: Christopher Morgan;
Dirs: Virgil Vogel, Harry Falk;
Wri: Jacques Meunier, based on Lonnie Coleman novels
360 Mins, Tues (7) 8-10 pm.; Wed-Thurs (8-9) 9-11 pm.
NBC-TV
10/15/80

BEVERLY & FRIENDS
With Beverly Sills, Steve Edwards (co-hosts), Burt Lancaster, Martha Reeves, Charles Nelson Reilly, Joan Rivers, Lily Tomlin, Mike Wallace, Barbara Walters, Dr Ronald Lawrence, Dr David Fischer
Supplier: Company III Prods & CBS-TV O&O Stations
Prod: Carolyn Raskin;
Dir: Mark Waren;
Wri: Ken Harris.
90 Mins, Wed (6), 4:30 pm.
WCBS-TV New York
12/20/78S

BEYOND WESTWORLD
With Jim McMullan, James Wainwright, Judith Chapman, William Jordan, Stewart Moss, Dennis Holahan, Morgan Paull, Alex Kubik, John Kirby, Mo Lauren
Supplier: Lou Shaw Prods. & MGM-TV
Exec Prod-Wri: Shaw;
Prod: John Meredyth Lucas;
Dir: Ted Post.
60 Mins, Wed, 8 pm.
CBS-TV
03/12/80

BIG CITY BOYS
With Austin Pendleton, Chris Barnes, Laurie Heineman, David Yanez, Francesca Bill
Supplier: Silliphant-Konigsberg Co & Warner Bros TV
Exec Prod: Frank Konigsberg;
Prods: Bruce Paltrow, Stephanie Sills;
Dir: Bill Persky;
Wri: Bob De Laurentis.
30 Mins, Tues, (11), 8:30 pm.
CBS-TV
04/19/78

BIG CITY COMEDY
With John Candy, Tino Insana, Tim Kazurinsky, Don Lamont, Audrie J. Neenan, Patti Oatman, Billy Crystal, Martin Mull, McLean Stevenson, Margaret Trudeau, Fred Willard
Supplier: Big City Comedy Prods & CTV Television Network (Osmond TV)
Exec Prod: Toby Martin;
Prod: Carolyn Raskin;
Dir: Mark Warren;
Wris: Jim Fisher, Jim Staahl.
30 Mins, Sat, 7:30 pm.
WNBC-TV New York
10/01/80S

BIG HAWAII
With Cliff Potts, John Dehner, Lucia Stralser, Bill Lucking, Elizabeth Smith, Remi Abellira, Josie Oser, Don Johnson, Peter Marshall, Kimo Kahoano, Bill Edwards, Hank Challacombe, Jackie Bean, Kathy Paulo, Rap Reiplinger
Supplier: Finnegan Associates, Filmways
Exec Prod: Perry Lafferty;
Prod: William Wood;
Dir: Lawrence F. Doheny;
Wris: Tim Maschler, Don Belisario.
60 Mins, Wed, 10 pm.
NBC-TV
09/28/77

THE BIG PARTY
With Ethel Merman, Marvin Hamlisch, Hal Linden, Joanne Woodward, Lauren Bacall, Leonard Nimoy, Dick Cavett, Blood, Sweat & Tears, Muhammed Ali, Ken Norton, Bob Elliot & Ray Goulding, others
Exec Prod: Alvin Cooperman;
Prod: John Gilroy;
Dir: Clark Jones;
Wris: Harvey Jacobs, Brian McConnachie
90 Mins, Sun (26), 9:30 pm.
NBC-TV New York
09/29/76

BIG SHAMUS, LITTLE SHAMUS
With Brian Dennehy, Doug McKeon, George Wyner, Kathryn Leigh Scott, Cynthia Sikes, Amanda McBroom, Jared Martin, Jack Carter, Louise Latham, Ty Henderson
Supplier: Lorimar Prods
Exec Prods: Lee Rich, Sam H Rolfe;
Prod: Fred Freiberger;
Dir: Leslie H Martinson;
Wris: Dick Robbins, Don Heckman.
60 Mins, Sat, 9 pm.
CBS-TV
10/03/79

THE BIG TALK SHOW
With Gary Coleman, Steve Allen (hosts), Alexander Godunov, Steve Martin, Peggy Fleming, Loni Anderson, Cynthia Gregory, Graham Chapman, Mimi Kennedy, Charlie Hill, Owen Sullivan, Adolfo Quinones & Shabba-Doo, Gallagher, Mummenshanz, Dionne Warwick, Jim Bray, Dancing Waters, Jerry Dye, Greg Lewis, Jimmy Martinez, David Winters Dancers
Suppliers: Nick Vanoff Presents
Prods: Vanoff, William O. Harbach;
Dir: Walter C. Miller;
Wri: Gary Belkin, Bill Dana, Jim Fisher, Jim Staahl, Frank Peppiatt,
Barry Adelman, Barry Silver, Allen.
120 Mins, Tues, (4) 9 pm.
NBC-TV
03/12/80

BIG TOYS
With Diane Cilento, John Gaden, Max Cullen
Supplier: Australian Broadcasting Commission
Exec Prod: Alan Burke;
Dir: Chris Thomson;
Wri: Patrick White.
70 Mins, Sun, 8:30 pm.
ABC (Australia) Channel 2, Sydney
09/03/80F

BILL BRAND
With Jack Shepherd, Karen Silver, Cherie Lunghi, others
Supplier: Thames-TV
Exec Prod: Stella Richman;
Prod: Stuart Burge;
Dir: Michael Lindsay-Hogg;
Wri: Trevor Griffiths.
60 Mins, Mon, 9 pm.
ITV Network, London
06/23/76F

BILL MOYERS' JOURNAL
(Reflections on a Revolution)
Supplier: WNET-TV New York
Exec prod: Charles Rose;
Prod: Martin Clancy.
60 Mins, Sun, 10 pm.
PBS
03/03/76

BILL MOYERS' JOURNAL
(Politics and the Evening News)
With Bill Leonard, Roone Arledge, others
Exec Prod: Joan Konner;
Exec Edtr: Moyers.
60 Min, Fri, (19), 9 pm.
PBS (WNET New York)
12/24/80

BILL MOYERS' JOURNAL: SPECIAL REPORT
Supplier: WNET New York, Corp for Public Broadcasting
Exec Prod: Joan Konner;
Dir: Jack Sameth.
60 Mins, Mon (13), 9 pm.
PBS
11/15/78

THE BILL OF MY DREAMS
With Jan Hacha, Danielle Gagnon
Prod: Judy Girard;
Wri-dir: Rick Sands.
30 Mins, Fri, 7:30 pm.
WBNG-TV Binghamton, N.Y.
05/26/76

BILLION DOLLAR BUBBLE
With James Woods, Sam Wanamaker, Bill Hootkins, Christopher Guest, Shane Rimmer, Lionel Murton
Supplier: BBC-TV, Time-Life TV
Prod-Wri: Tom Clarke;
Dir: Brian Gibson.
60 Mins, Thurs (8), 10 pm.
NBC-TV
06/14/78

BILLION DOLLAR THREAT
(ABC Sunday Night Movie)
With Dale Robinette, Ralph Bellamy, Keenan Wynn, Parick Macnee, Robert Tessier, Beth & Karen Specht, Stephen Keep, William Bryant, Harold Sakata, Ronnie Carol, others
Supplier: David Gerber Prods & Columbia Pictures TV
Exec Prod: Gerber;
Prod: Jay Daniel;
Dir: Barry Shear;
Wri: Jimmy Sangster.
120 Mins, Sun (15), 9 pm.
ABC-TV
04/18/79

BILLY
With Steve Guttenberg, James Gallery, Peggy Pope, Paula Trueman, Michael Alaimo, Bruce Talkington, Don Adams, Peggy Lee Brennan, Janice Kent, Ron Vernan, Nataraj Watkins
Supplier: John Rich Prods & 20th-Fox TV
Prod-Dir: Rich;
Wris: Dick Clement & Ian LaFrenais.
30 Mins, Mon 8 pm.
CBS-TV
02/21/79

BING. . .A 50th ANNIVERSARY GALA
With Bing Crosby, Bob Hope, Paul Anka, Pearl Bailey, Joe Bushkin, Rosemary Clooney, Kathryn Crosby, Harry Crosby, Mary Frances Crosby, Nathaniel Crosby, Sandy Duncan, The Mills Brothers, Donald O'Connor, Martha Raye, Debbie Reynolds, Anson Williams, Bette Midler
Supplier: Konigsberg Co
Exec Prod: Frank Konigsberg;
Prod-Dir: Marty Pasetta;
Wri: Buz Kohan.
90 Mins, Sun (20), 9 pm.
CBS-TV
Kraft Foods (JWT)
03/23/77

BING CROSBY: HIS LIFE & LEGEND
With William Holden (narrator)
Supplier: The Konigsberg Co
Exec Prod: Franklin Konigsberg;
Prod-Dir-Wri: Marshall Flaum.
120 Mins, Thurs (25), 9 pm.
ABC-TV
05/31/78

BING CROSBY'S MERRIE OLDE CHRISTMAS
With Bing, Kathryn, Mary Frances, Harry & Nathaniel Crosby, David Bowie, Twiggy, Ron Moody, Stanley Baxter, Trinity Boys Choir
Exec Prod: Frank Konigsberg;
Prods: Gary Smith, Dwight Hemion;
Dir: Hemion;
Wri: Buz Kohan.
60 Mins, Wed (30), 9 pm.
CBS-TV
12/07/77

THE BIONIC WOMAN
With Lindsay Wagner, Richard Anderson, Martin E. Brooks, Dennis Patrick, Martha Scott, Richard Lenz, Roger Davis, Lee Majors, Ford Rainey, Dee Timberlake
Supplier: Harve Bennett Prods. & Universal TV
Exec Prod: Bennett;
Prod-Wri: Kenneth Johnson;
Dir: Alan Crosland.
60 Mins, Wed, 8 pm.
ABC-TV
01/21/76

THE BIRTH OF TELEVISION
With Leslie Mitchell (host), Gracie Fields, Arthur Askey, Dinah Sheridan, others
Prod: Bruce Norman;
Dir: Laurie John;
Wri: Bruce Norman.
90 Mins, Mon (1), 9:25 pm.
BBC-1, Britain
11/10/76F

BIZARRE
With Richard Dawson (host), Toby Hoffman, Melissa Steinberg, Eric Taslitz, Dennis Johnson, Nathan Jung, Brad Sanders, Tanya L Boyd, Nancy Steen, Anne Randall Stewart, George Allen, Tom Harmon, others
Supplier: Blye-Einstein Prods & E M Associates
Prods: Allan Blye, Bob Einstein;
Dir: Bill Carruthers;
Wris: Blye, Einstein, Mike Marmer, Jack Handey, Tom DeLisle, Susan Elliot, Ralph Harris,
Tom Sheroman, Dennis Snee.
30 Mins, Tues (20), 10:30 pm.
ABC-TV
04/04/79

BJ & THE BEAR
(Wednesday Night At The Movies)
With Gregg Evigan, Penny Peyser, Claude Akins, Mills Watson, Julius Harris
Supplier: Glen A Larson Prods & Universal TV
Exec Prod: Larson;
Prods: Christopher Crowe, John Peyser;
Dir: Bruce Bilson;
Wris: Larson, Crowe.
120 Mins, Wed (4), 9 pm.
NBC-TV
10/11/78

BJ & THE BEAR
With Greg Evigan, Claude Akins, JoAnne Harris, Mills Watson, Randi Oakes, Susan Buckner, Michael Champion, William Bryant, James Griffith, Bill Williams, Sunshine Parker, Sam
Supplier: Glen A Larson Prods & Universal TV
Exec Prods: Larson, Michael Sloan;
Prods: Joe Boston, Lester William Berke;
Dir: Christian I Nyby II;
Wris: Kenneth Realman, Sloan.
90 Mins, Sat, 8 pm.
NBC-TV
02/14/79

THE BLACK AND WHITE MINSTREL SHOW
With Dai Francis, Ted Darling, Les Rawlings, Bob Hunter, Dorothy Ogden, Gaye Collins
Supplier: BBC-TV
Prod: Brian Whitehouse.
45 Mins, Fri, 7:45 pm.
BBC-1, from London, England
07/05/78F

BLACK BEAUTY
With Martin Milner, Ike Eisenmann, Cameron Mitchell, Diane Ladd, others
Supplier: Universal TV
Exec Prod: Peter S Fischer;
Prod: Ben Bishop;
Dir: Daniel Haller;
Wri: Fischer, from the book by Anna Sewell.
60 Mins, Tues, 8 pm.
NBC-TV
02/08/78

BLACK FILMMAKERS HALL OF FAME
With James Earl Jones, Cicely Tyson, LeVar Burton, Roscoe Lee Lawrence, Peters, Bee Freeman, Bernard Johnson, Lou Gossett, Denise Nicholas
Supplier: KQED San Francisco
Exec Prod: Christopher Lukas;
Prods: Carol Munday Lawrence;
Dir: Robert N Zagone.
90 Mins, Sat (9), 9 pm.
PBS
04/13/77

BLACK PERSPECTIVE ON THE NEWS
With David Duke, Ku Klux Klan grand wizard; Frank Collin, national American Nazi Party co-ordinator; Lawrence Reddick, Harvard historian; Dr Charles King, head of the Urban Crisis Center, Atlanta; Reginald Bryant, moderator
Exec Prod: Richard Crew;
Prods: Reginald Bryant, Acel Moore;
Dir: Russell Kneeland.
60 Mins, Fri (30), 9 pm.
WHYY-TV Philadelphia
10/05/77

BLACK SHEEP SQUADRON
With Robert Conrad, Simon Oakland, Dana Elcar, W K Stratton, Robert Ginty, Dirk Blocker, John Larroquette, Larry Manetti, Jeff MacKay, Red West, Scott Hylands, Soon-Teck Oh, J Kenneth Campbell, Katherine Cannon, Lloyd Keno, James Saito
Supplier: Stephen J Cannell Prods & Universal TV
Exec Prod: Cannell;
Supv Prods: Philip DeGuere, Alex Beaton;
Prods: Donald Bellisario, Chuck Bowman;
Dir: Lawrence Doheny;
Wri: Bellisario.
60 Mins, Wed, 9 pm.
NBC-TV
12/21/77

BLADE ON THE FEATHER
With Donald Pleasence, Denholm Elliott, Kika Markham, Tom Conti, Phoebe Nicholls
Supplier: London Weekend TV & Pennies From Heaven Ltd
Exec Prod: Tony Wharmby;
Prod: Kenith Trodd;
Dir: Richard Loncraine;
Wri: Dennis Potter.
87 Mins, Sun (19) 10 pm.
ITV Network, Britain
11/05/80F

BLANSKY'S BEAUTIES
With Nancy Walker, Roz Kelly, Caren Kaye, Johnny Desmond, Eddie Mekka, Scot Baio, Lynda Goodfriend, George Pentecost, Taafe O'Connell, Rhoda Bates, Bond Gideon, Gerri Reddick, Shirley Kirkes, Antoinette Yuskis, Jill Owens, Elaine Bolton
Supplier: Miller-Milkis Prods, Henderson Prod Co, Paramount TV
Exec Prods: Garry Marshall, Thomas L Miller, Edward K Milkis;
Prods: Bruce Johnson, Tony Marshall, Nick Abdo;
Dir: Marshall;
Wri: Warren S Murray.
30 Mins, Sat, 8 pm.
ABC-TV
02/16/77

BLEACHER BUMS
With Joe Mantegna, Richard Fire, Michael Saad, Roberta Custer, Dennis Franz, Carolyn Purdy-Gordon, Ian Williams, Willie Daniels, Keith Szarabajka
Prod: Patterson Denny;
Dirs: Denny, Stuart Gordon.
60 Mins, Sat (13), 8 pm.
WTTW Chicago for PBS
10/24/79

BLIND AMBITION - PART ONE
With Martin Sheen, Theresa Russell, Michael Callan, William Daniels, Ed Flanders, Clifford David, Christopher Guest, Graham Jarvis, Gerald S O'Loughlin, Alan Oppenheimer, Lawrence Pressman, John Randolph, Peter Mark Richman, William Windom, Rip Torn
Supplier: Time-Life TV
Exec Prod: David Susskind;
Prods: George Schaefer, Renee Valente;
Dir: Schaefer;
Wri: Stanley R Greenberg, from books by John and Maureen Dean.
120 Mins, Sun (20), 8 pm.
CBS-TV
05/23/79

BLOCKBUSTERS
With Bill Cullen (host)
Supplier: Goodson-Todman Prods
Exec Prod-Dir: Ira Skutch;
Prod: Robert Sherman.
30 Mins, Mon-Fri, 10:30 am.
NBC-TV
11/05/80

BLOOD SWEAT AND TEARS
(Superspecial)
With Blood Sweat and Tears & David Clayton-Thomas,Chaka Khan, Flo & Eddie, Chuck Berry, Carl Perkins, Bo Diddley, Cubby Checker
Prod-Dir: Stan Jacobson.
60 Mins, Sun, 8 pm.
CBC-TV, from Toronto, Canada
04/13/77F

BLOODY KIDS
With Derrick O'Connor, Gary Holton, Richard Thomas, Peter Clark, Gwyneth Strong, Caroline Embling, Jack Douglas
Supplier: ATV (Black Lion Films)
Prod: Barry Hanson;
Dir: Stephen Frears;
Wri: Stephen Poliakoff.
90 Mins, Sun, 9:30 pm.
ITV Network, Britain
04/16/80F

BLUEY
(The First Bloody Day)
With Lucky Grills, John Diedrich, Gerda Nicholson, Victoria Quilter, Max Bruch, Lew Luton, Richard Meikle, Keith Eden, Briony Behets
Supplier: Crawford Productions
Dir: Graeme Arthur;
Wris: Ian Jones, Jock Blair.
90 Mins, 7:30 pm.
Seven Network, from Melbourne, Australia
08/18/76F

BOB BROTHERS
With Robbie McGregor, Sigrid Thornton, Ian Gilmour, Harold Baigent, John Wood, Maggie Millar, Carillo Gatner, others; George Mallaby, narrator
Supplier: Australian Broadcasting Commission
Prod: Oscar Whitbread;
Wri: Cliff Green;
Narr: George Mallaby.
55 Mins, Sat, 9:10 pm.
ABC (Australia), Channel 2 Sydney
02/06/80F

BOB HOPE ON THE ROAD TO CHINA
With Mikhail Baryshnikov, Crystal Gayle, Big Bird, Shields & Yarnell, Peaches & Herb, Dolores Hope, others
Supplier: Hope Enterprises, with James Lipton Prods
Exec Prods: Linda Hope, Lipton;
Prod-Dir: Bob Wynn;
Wris: Gig Henry, Robert L Mills, Lipton.
180 Mins, Sun (16), 8 pm.
NBC-TV
09/19/79

BOB HOPE – ON THE ROAD WITH BING
With Bing Crosby
Supplier: Hope Enterprises & NBC
Exec Prod: Hope;
Prod-Dir: Howard W Koch;
Wris: Norm Sullivan, Charles Lee, Gig Henry, Robert Mills.
120 Mins, Fri, 8 pm.
NBC-TV
11/02/77

BOB HOPE'S ALL-STAR COMEDY TRIBUTE TO VAUDEVILLE
With Lucille Ball, Bernadette Peters, Vivian Reed, Jack Albertson, Captain & Tennille, Jimmie Walker, Les Brown band, Sid Gould, Vonda Barra, Chaz Chase, Isobel McCloskey, Jack Baker Dancers
Supplier: Hope Enterprises
Exec Prod: Hope;
Prod: Sheldon Keller;
Dir: Dick McDonough;
Wris: Charles Lee & Gig Henry, Jeffrey Barron, Katherine Green, Howard Albrecht & Sol Weinstein, Keller.
90 Mins, Fri (25), 8:30 pm.
NBC-TV
Texaco (Benton & Bowles)
03/30/77

BOB HOPE'S WORLD OF COMEDY
With Lucille Ball, Norman Lear, Don Rickles, Neil Simon, Big Bird
Supplier: Hope Enterprises
Exec Prod: Hope;
Prod-dir: Jack Haley Jr;
Wris: Charles Lee, Gig Henry, Jeffrey Barron, Katherine Green, Haley.
120 Mins, Fri (29), 8 pm.
NBC-TV
Texaco (Benton & Bowles)
11/03/76

THE BODY HUMAN: THE FACTS FOR BOYS
With Ken Howard (host)
Supplier: Tomorrow Entertainment/Medcom Co
Exec Prod: Thomas W. Moore;
Prods: Alfred R. Kelman, Dr. Robert E. Fuisz;
Dir: Kelman;
Wri: Fuisz.
30 Mins, Thurs, (6) 4pm.
CBS-TV
11/12/80

THE BODY HUMAN: THE RED RIVER
With Alexander Scourby (narrator)
Supplier: Tomorrow Entertainment-Medcom Co
Exec Prod: Thomas W Moore;
Prod: Alfred R Kelman;
Dir: Robert Elfstrom;
Wri: Dr Robert E Fuisz.
60 Mins, Mon (6), 8 pm.
CBS-TV
03/15/78

THE BODY IN QUESTION
With Jonathan Miller, others
Supplier: BBC-TV
Exec Prod: Karl Sabbagh;
Prod: Patrick Uden;
Dirs: Jonathan Crane, Fisher Dilke;
Wri: Miller.
50 Mins, Mon (6), 9:30 pm.
BBC-2, Britain
11/15/78F

THE BOLSHOI BALLET: ROMEO & JULIET
With Mary Tyler Moore (hostess), Natalja Bessmertnova, Michail Lavrovsky, Bolshoi troupe
Supplier: USSR State Committee for Radio & TV, in association wth Teleglob AG and BBC
Exec Prod: Lothar Bock;
Am Prod: Alvin Cooperman;
Dir: John Vernon;
Comp: Sergei Prokofiev.
120 Mins, Sun (27), 8 pm.
CBS-TV
GE (BBDO)
06/30/76

BOLWIESER
With Kurt Raab, Elisabeth Trissenaar, Bernhard Helfrich, Karl-Heinz von Hassel, Volker Spengler, Gustl Bayrhammer, Udo Kier, Armin Meier, Peter Kern, Gerhard Zwerenz
Supplier: Zweites Deutsches Fernsehen (ZDF), Wiesbaden-Mainz, West Germany
Dir-Wri: Rainer Werner Fassbinder.
200 Mins, (2 parts), 8:15 & 10:15 pm.
ZDF, Channel 2, Berlin, West Germany
08/24/77F

BON APPETIT!
Prod-Wri: Patricia Gormin;
Dir: Gary Furlow.
30 Mins, Thurs, 8 pm.
WVUE-TV New Orleans
12/13/78

BONKERS
With Hudson Bros, Bob Monkhouse, Paul Williams
Supplier: ITC Entertainment
Exec Prod: Tom Battista;
Prod: Jack Burns;
Dir: Peter Harris;
Wris: Elias Davis, David Pollock.
30 Mins, Fri, 7:30 pm.
WCBS New York
09/27/78S

BOOMERANG SPRING SPECIAL
With Marni Nixon, Lee Olson, Kathy Tolan, Nick LeFeuvre Puppets, Tacoma Performing Dance Co
Prod: Barbara Groce;
Dir: Ken Schwedop;
Wri: Nancy Schwedop.
30 Mins, Tues
KOMO-TV Seattle
04/13/77

BOSOM BUDDIES
With Peter Scolari, Tom Hanks, Donna Dixon, Telma Hopkins, Holland Taylor, Wendie Jo Sperber, Edie Adams Supplier: Miller-Milkis-Boyett Prods & Paramount TV
Exec Prods: Thomas L Miller, Edward K Milkis, Robert L Boyett;
Prod-Wri: Chris Thompson;
Dir: Joel Zwick.
30 Mins, Thurs, 8:30 pm.
ABC-TV
12/03/80

BOSTON & KILBRIDE
With Tom Selleck, James Whitmore Jr, Don Ameche, Jaime Lyn Bauer, William Daniels, Kathryn Leigh Scott, June Whitley Taylor, Lane Bradbury, Elizabeth Halliday, Michael Brick, Marlena Amey
Supplier: Stephen J Cannell Prods & Universal TV
Supv Prod: Alex Beaton;
Prod: J Rickley Dumm;
Dir: Lou Antonio.
60 Mins, Sat (3), 10 pm.
CBS-TV
03/07/79

THE BRADY BUNCH HOUR
With Florence Henderson, Robert Reed, Maureen McCormick, Barry Williams, Geri Reischl, Chris Knight, Susan Olsen, Mike Lookinland, Lee Majors, Farrah Fawcett-Majors, Rip Taylor, Kaptain Kool & the Kongs, Ann B Davis, Krofftette Dancers & Water Follies
Supplier: Sid & Marty Krofft TV Prods & Paramount TV
Exec Prods: Sid & Marty Krofft;
Prod: Lee Miller;
Dir: Jack Regas;
Wris: Carl Kleinschmitt, Ronny Graham, Bruce Vilanch, Steve Bluestein, Mike Kagan.
60 Mins, Sun, 7 pm.
ABC-TV
01/26/77

THE BRADY BUNCH VARIETY HOUR
With Florence Henderson, Robert Reed, Barry Williams, Maureen McCormick, Chris Knight, Geri Reischl, Mike Lookinland, Susan Olson, Ann B. Davis, Tony Randall, Donny & Marie Osmond
Supplier: Sid & Marty Krofft Prods & Paramount TV
Prods: Lee Miller, Jerry McPhie;
Dir: Art Fisher;
Wris: Carl Kleinschmitt, Ronnie Graham, Terry Hart, Steve Bluestein.
60 Mins, Sun (28), 7 pm.
ABC-TV
12/01/76

BRAVO TWO
With Bruce Fairbairn, David Gilliam, James Hampton, Cooper Huckabee
Supplier: Lorimar Prods
Exec Prods: Lee Rich, Philip Capice;
Prods: Robert Stambler, Guerdon Trueblood;
Dir: Ernest Pintoff;
Wris: Leo Gordon, Trueblood.
30 Mins, Fri, 10:30 pm.
CBS-TV
03/30/77

BREAK THE BANK
With Tom Kennedy (host), Lynda Carter, Jo Ann Pflug, Jan Murray, Liz Torres, Dick Gautier, Alice Ghostley, Marjoe Gortner, Abe Vigoda, Robert Hegyes
Supplier: Barry-Enright Prods.
Dir: Richard S. Kline.
30 Mins, Mon-Fri, 2:30 pm.
ABC-TV
04/21/76

BREAK THE BANK
With Jack Barry
Supplier: Barry & Enright Prods.
Prod: Dan Enright;
Dir: Richard Kline.
30 Mins, Sat, 6 pm.
WNEW-TV New York
09/22/76S

BREAKING AWAY
With Shaun Cassidy, Jackie Earle Haley, Tom Wiggin, Thom Bray, Vincent Gardenia, Barbara Barrie, John Ashton, Steve Doubet, Shelby Brammer, Wendi Wimmer, Coleen Riley, others
Supplier: 20th-Fox TV
Exec Prod: Peter Yates;
Prod: Herbert B Leonard;
Wri: Steve Tesich.
Dir: Joseph Ruben;
60 Mins, Sat, 8 pm.
ABC-TV
12/03/80

BRENDA STARR
With Jill St. John, Jed Allen, Sorrell Booke, Tami Cooper, Victor Buono, Joel Fabiani, Barbara Luna, Marcia Strassman, Torin Thatcher, Art Roberts, Roy Applegate
Supplier: David L. Wolper Productions
Exec Prod: Paul Mason;
Prod: Bob Larson;
Dir: Mel Stuart;
Wri: George Kirgo.
90 Mins, Sat (8), 8 pm.
ABC-TV
05/12/76

BRENDA STARR
With Sherry Jackson, Shelley Berman, Barbara Minkus-Barron, Jonathan Segal, others
Supplier: Jll Prods (Syndicast Services)
Exec Prod: Jerry Harrison;
Prods: Joe Siegman, Harrison;
Dir: Lawrence Dobkin;
Wris: Howard Berk, Lou Shaw (based on Dale Messick comic strip).
30 Mins Thurs (25), 7:30 pm.
WNBC-TV New York
Colgate-Palmolive
01/31/79S

BROADWAY EXTRA
With Stewart Klein, Wendy Sherman, others
Exec Prod: Art Stark;
Prod: Mike Luisl;
Dir: Norman Ross.
30 Mins, Sun, 11 pm.
WNEW-TV New York
06/28/78

BROKEN PROMISES: THE NEXT INDIAN WAR
Prod-Dir-Wri: Mike Kirk.
30 Mins, Fri, 10 pm.
KCTS-TV Seattle
02/15/78

BROTHERS & SISTERS
With Chris Lemmon, Jon Cutler, Randy Brooks, Amy Johnston, Larry Anderson, Mary Crosby, LaWanda Page, Roy Teicher, Susan Cotton, Fay Hauser
Supplier: Paramount TV, Frog Prods & Huk Inc
Supv Prods: Bob Brunner, Arthur Silver;
Prod: Nick Abdo;
Dir: Lowell Ganz;
Wris: Brian Levant, Ron Leavitt.
30 Mins, Sun (21), 8:12 pm.
NBC-TV
01/24/79

BRUCE FORSYTH AND THE GENERATION GAME
With Bruce Forsyth, Anthea Redfern
Supplier: BBC
Exec Prod: Robin Nash;
Prod: Alan Boyd.
55 Min, Sat, 6:30 pm.
BBC 1, England
11/16/77F

BUCK ROGERS IN THE 25TH CENTURY
With Gil Gerard, Erin Gray, Tim O'Connor, David Groh, Roddy McDowall, Brianne Leary, Macdonald Carey, Karen Carlson, Michael Mullins, Buster Crabbe, Jack Palance, Felix Silla, Mel Blanc, Robert Dowdell, Sheila DeWindt, Don Marshall, William Conrad (narrator)
Supplier: Glen A Larson Prods, Bruce Lansbury Prods & Universal TV
Exec Prod: Larson;
Supv Prod: Lansbury;
Prods: John Gaynor, David J O'Connell;
Dir: Michael Caffey;
Wris: Steve Greenberg, Aubrey Solomon, Cory Applebaum.
120 Mins, Thurs (27), 8 pm.
NBC-TV
10/03/79

BUCKS COUNTY, U S A
With Robert L Green
Exec Prod: Robert L Woodruff;
Dir: Judy Vogelsang.
60 Mins, Fri, 8 pm.
WCAU-TV Philadelphia
10/05/77

THE BUFFALO SOLDIERS
With Stan Shaw, John Beck, Richard Lawson, Hilly Hicks, Ralph Wilcox, Angel Tompkins, L Q Jones, Don Knight
Supplier: Media Productions Inc and MGM-TV
Exec Prods: Jim Byrnes, Douglas Netter;
Prod: Les Sheldon;
Dir: Vincent McEveety;
Wri: Byrnes.
60 Mins, Sat (26), 10 pm.
NBC-TV

05/30/79

THE BUREAU
(NBC Comedy Theatre)
With Henry Gibson, Richard Gilliland, Barbara Rhoades, Beeson Carroll, Dick Yarmy, John Lawlor, Arnold Stang, Stanley Brock, Pearl Shear, Phil Leeds
Supplier: Jozak Co.
Exec Prod: Gerald I. Isenberg;
Prod: Gerald W. Abrams;
Dir: Hy Averback;
Wris: Charles Sailor, Eric Kaldor
30 Mins, Mon (26), 8:30 pm.
NBC-TV

08/04/76

BURN THE BUTTERFLIES
With Ray Barrett, Monica Maughan, Frederick Parslow, Gerard Maguire, George Mallaby, Alan Hopgood, John Bowman, Rowena Wallace, Kit Taylor, Helmut Bakaitis, Kristy Child, John Wood
Supplier: Australian Broadcasting Commission
Dir: Oscar Whitbread;
Wri: Cliff Green.
74 Mins, Sun, 8:30 pm.
ABC TV, Channel 2, Sydney, Australia

10/17/79F

BURTON CUMMINGS
(Superspecial)
With Burton Cummings, The Manhattan Transfer, Randy Bachman
Prod-Dir: Rob Iscove;
Wri: Les Pouliot.
60 Mins, Mon, 9 pm.
CBC-TV, from Toronto, Canada

10/19/77F

BURTON CUMMINGS: PORTAGE AND MAIN
With Cummings, The Guess Who, The Devrons, MacLean & MacLean,, Bobby Hull, Don Percy, Rick Moranus
Supplier: CBC
Prod-Dir: Stan Jacobson.
60 Mins, Sun, 8 pm.
CBC-TV, Canada

11/21/79F

THE BUSINESS OF NEWSPAPERS
With Hughes Rudd, reporter
Supplier: CBS News
Exec Prod: Perry Wolff;
Prod-Dir-Wri: Irina Posner.
60 Mins, Fri (14), 10 pm.
CBS-TV

07/19/78

THE BUSTERS
With Bo Hopkins, Brian Kerwin, Slim Pickens, Devon Ericson, Buck Taylor, Chris Robinson, Lance LeGault, Susan Howard
Supplier: MTM Prods
Exec Prod: Stu Erwin;
Prod-Wri: Jim Byrnes;
Dir: Vincent McEveety.
60 Mins, Sun (28), 10 pm.
CBS-TV

05/31/78

BUSTING LOOSE
With Adam Arkin, Jack Kruschen, Pat Carroll, Barbara Rhoades, Danny Goldman, Stephen Nathan, Greg Antonacci, Paul Sylvan, Paul B Price, Ralph Wilcox, others
Supplier: Paramount TV
Exec Prod-Wris: Mark Rothman, Lowell Ganz;
Prod: Lawrence Kasha;
Dir: Bill Persky.
Wris: Rothman, Ganz.
30 Mins, Mon (17), 8:30 pm.
CBS-TV

01/19/77

BUT MOTHER!
(BATTLE OF THE GENERATIONS)
With Dena Dietrich, Amy Johnston, Allan Rich, James Callahan, Harry Gold, Gloria LeRoy, Philip Bruns, Robert Alda
Supplier: TAT Communications
Prod-Wris: Bob Weiskopf, Bob Schiller;
Dir: Jack Shea.
120 Min, Wed (27), 9 pm.
NBC-TV

07/04/79

BY HOOK OR CROOK
Supplier: WVUE-TV
Prod-Wri-Narr: Patricia Gormin;
Dir: Robert Weaver;
30 Mins, Thurs, 7:30 pm.
WVUE-TV New Orleans

04/02/80

THE CAKE MAN
With Brian Syron, Justine Saunders, Neil Fitzpatrick, Graham Rouse, Hugh Keays-Byrne, Teddy Phillips
Supplier: Australian Broadcasting Commission
Exec Prod: Lynn Bayonas;
Dir: Doug Sharp;
Wri: Robert J Merritt.
60 Mins, Sun,8:30 pm.
ABC, Australia

10/26/77F

CAL STOLL SHOW
With Cal Stoll, Rod Trongard
Prod-Dir: Steve Hammergren.
30 Mins, Sun, 11 am.
KSTP-TV St Paul

11/16/77

CALIFORNIA FEVER
With Jimmy McNichol, Marc McClure, Michele Tobin, Lorenzo Lamas, Rex Smith, Michael McGuire, Ronnie Schell, Bryan Gordan, Larry D Mann, Andy Romano, Eric Laneuville, Mark Lonow
Supplier: Lou-Step Prods & Warner Bros TV
Dir: Claudio Guzman;
Wri: Stephen Kandel.
60 Mins, Tues, 8 pm.
CBS-TV

10/03/79

CALLING DR STORM M D
(Comedy Time)
With Larry Linville, Sharon Spelman, Bruce Gordon, Richard Libertini, James Sikking, Marian Mercer, Mary Louise Weller, P J Soles, Robert Hogan
Supplier: Silliphant-Konigsberg Co & Warner Bros TV
Exec Prod: Sterling Silliphant;
Prod: Frank Konigsberg;
Dir: James Burrows;
Wris: Lawrence J Cohen & Fred Freeman.
30 Mins, Thurs (25), 8:30 pm.
NBC-TV

09/07/77

CALLOWAY'S CLIMB
With Patrick O'Neal, Mariette Hartley, Mike Hoover, Tony Jefferson, Rick Ridgeway
Supplier: Robert Halmi Prods & Hughes Television Network
Prod: Halmi;
Dir: Paul Stanley;
Wri: Mort Fine (from a Peter Sandburg short story).
60 Mins, Mon (28), 9 pm.
WPIX-TV New York
Liberty Mutual Insurance Co

09/06/78S

CALYPSO'S SEARCH FOR THE BRITANNIC
With Jacques-Yves Cousteau
Supplier: KCET-TV Los Angeles
Exec Prods: Cousteau & Philippe Cousteau
Prod: Andrew Solt;
Wri-Nar: Theodore Strauss
60 Mins, Tues (22), 8 pm.
PBS

11/30/77

CAMBODIA-YEAR ONE
With John Pilger, reporter
Supplier: ATV
Prod-Dir: David Munro.
52 Mins, Wed, (10) 9 pm.
ITV Network, Britain
09/24/80F
Prod-Wri-Narr: Stan Atkinson. 30 Min, Wed, 9:30 pm. KCRA-TV Sacramento

12/17/80

CAMOUFLAGE
With Tom Campbell (host)
Supplier: Chuck Barris Prods (Firestone Program Syndication)
Prods: Michael Metzger, Steve Friedman;
Dir: John Dorsey.
30 Mins, Wed, 7:30 pm.
WCBS-TV New York

02/13/80S

CAN YOU HEAR THE LAUGHTER? THE STORY OF FREDDIE PRINZE
With Ira Angustain, Kevin Hooks, Randee Heller, Julie Carmen, Ken Sylk, Devon Erickson, Stephen Elliott, James Callahan, Michael Binder
Supplier: Roger Gimbel Prods/-EMI-TV
Exec Prods: Gimbel, Tony Converse;
Prod: Peter S Greenberg;
Dir: Burt Brinckerhoff;
Wri: Dalene Young.
120 Mins Tues (11), 9 pm.
CBS-TV
09/19/79

CANADA AFTER DARK
With Paul Soles
Exec Prod: Alex Frame;
Prod: Robert Ennis.
60 Mins, weekdays, 11:45 pm.
CBC-TV, from Toronto, Canada
11/01/78F

CANADA JAM
With Funzone, Ozard Mountain Daredevils, Doobie Brothers, Atlanta Rhythm Section, Village People, Dave Mason, Wha-Koo, Prism, Kansas, Commodores, Triumph; Ritchie York, Veronique Beliveau, hosts
Exec Prod: John Barnett;
Prod: Sanford Feldman;
Dir: Jorn Winther.
120 Mins, Mon, 8 pm.
Global TV, from Toronto, Canada
02/21/79F

CANADIAN EXPRESS
With Ryan's Fancy
Prod-Dir: Jack Kellum.
60 Mins, Thurs, 9 pm.
CBC, from Toronto, Canada
11/01/78F

CAN'T IT BE ANYONE ELSE?
Supplier: ABC-TV (U.S.)
Prod: Bill Couturie;
Dir-Wri: Dennis Lofgren;
Co-Wri: Michael Chandler.
49 Mins.
(City of Trento Prizewinner, Documentary)
10/08/80PI

CAPTAIN AMERICA
With Reb Brown, Len Birman, Heather Menzies, Lance LeGault, Frank Marth, Robin Mattson, Joseph Ruskin, Steve Forrest, James Ingersoll, others
Supplier: Universal TV
Exec Prod: Allan Balter;
Dir: Rod Holcomb;
Wri: Don Ingalls.
120 Mins, Fri (19), 8 pm.
CBS-TV
01/24/79

CAPTAIN & TENNILLE
With Daryl Dragon, Toni Tennille, Penny Marshall, Ron Palillo, Lawrence-Hilton Jacobs, Roz Kelly, Jackie Gleason
Supplier: Moonlight & Magnolias, Bob Henry Prods
Exec Prod: Alan Bernard;
Prod: Bob Henry;
Dir: Tony Charmoli;
Wris: John Boni, Norman Stiles, Stephen Spears, Thad Mumford, Tom Dunsmuir, Ed Hider, Ruth Merithew, Walter Stone.
60 Mins, Mon, 8 pm.
ABC-TV
09/22/76

THE CAPTAIN & TENNILLE SPECIAL
With Daryl Dragon, Toni Tennille, Art Carney, Roy Clark, Bob Thompson Dancers
Supplier: Moonlight & Magnolia Inc & Bob Henry Prods
Exec Prod: Alan Bernard;
Prod-dir: Henry;
Wris: John Boni, Norman Stiles, Stephen Spears, Henry.
60 Mins, Tues (17), 8:30 pm.
ABC-TV
08/25/76

THE CAPTAINS & THE KINGS
(Best Sellers)
With Richard Jordan, Ray Bolger, Neville Brand, John Carradine, Katherine Crawford, Peter Donat, Charles Durning, Celeste Holm, Harvey Jason, Joe Kapp, Vic Morrow, Barbara Parkins, Joanna Pettet, Ann Sothern, Beverly D'Angelo, Johnny Doran, Sean McClory, William Gordon, Linda Kelsey, Martin Kove, Woody Skaggs
Supplier: Roy Huggins/Public Arts & Universal TV
Exec Prod: Huggins;
Prod: Jo Swerling Jr;
Dir-wri: Douglas Heyes;
120 Mins, Thurs (30), 9 pm.
NBC-TV
10/06/76

CAPTAINS COURAGEOUS
With Karl Malden, Jonathan Kahn, Johnny Doran, Neville Brand, Fred Gwynne, Charles Dierkop, Jeff Corey, Fritz Weaver, Ricardo Montalban, Stan Haze
Supplier: Norman Rosemont Prods
Prod: Rosemont;
Dir: Harvey Hart;
Wri: John Gay, based on Rudyard Kipling's novel.
120 Mins, Sun (4), 7 pm.
ABC-TV
AT&T (N W Ayer)
12/07/77

CARD SHARKS
With Jim Perry (host)
Supplier: Goodson-Todman Prods
Exec Prod: Chester Feldman;
Prod: Jonathan M Goodson;
Dir: Marc Breslow.
30 Mins, Mon-Fri, 10 am.
NBC-TV
04/26/78

CAROL BURNETT & CO
With Tim Conway, Vicki Lawrence, Kenneth Mars, Craig Richard Nelson, Cheryl Ladd, Don Crichton Dancers
Supplier: Joe Hamilton Prods
Prod: Hamilton;
Dir: Roger Beatty;
Wris: Kenny Solms, Beatty, Ann Elder, Bob Arnott, Conway, Arnie Kogen.
60 Mins, Sat, 8 pm.
ABC-TV
08/22/79

CARTAS DE MAMA
(Letters From Mother)
With Susana Mara, Julio Nunez, Guillermo Gentile, Luisa Rodrigo, Felix Defauce, Mercedes Borque
Supplier: Radiotelevision Espanola
Dir: Miguel Picazo;
Wri: Jacobo Langsner, adapted from Julio Cortazar story.
60 Mins, Sun, 10:15 pm.
TVE from Madrid, Spain
06/27/79F

CARTER COUNTRY
With Victor French, Kene Holliday, Richard Paul, Vernee Watson, Barbara Cason, Guich Koock, Harvey Vernon
Supplier: TOY Prods
Exec Prods: Bud Yorkin, Bernie Orenstein, Saul Turteltaub;
Prods-Wris: Phil Doran, Douglas Arango;
Dir: Yorkin.
30 Mins, Thurs, 9:30 pm.
ABC-TV
09/21/77

THE CASTAWAYS
(The Boy Chief of Tonga)
With David Mahon, Tu'i Nuia Tuita, Taniela Manu, Eva Ve'ehala
Prod: Edwin Morrisby;
Dir: Bruce Morrison;
Wris: Morrisby, Morrison.
55 Mins, Sun, 8:30 pm.
South Pacific TV, Auckland, N Z
09/13/78F

THE CASTAWAYS OF GILLIGAN'S ISLAND
With Bob Denver, Alan Hale Jr, Jim Backus, Natalie Schafer, Judith Baldwin, Russell Johnson, Dawn Wells, Tom Bosley, Marcia Wallace, Mokihana, Ronnie Scribner, Rod Browning, Joan Roberts, Peter McLean, Lanna Saunders
Supplier: Redwood Prods
Exec Prod: Sherwood Schwartz;
Prod: Lloyd J Schwartz;
Dir: Earl Bellamy;
Wris: Sherwood, Elroy & Al Schwartz.
90 Mins, Thurs (3), 8:30 pm.
NBC-TV
05/09/79

CASUALTY
Supplier: BBC
Prod-Dir: Tim King.
44 Mins.
(Winner of Prix Italia, Documentary)
10/04/78PI

CAT ON A HOT TIN ROOF
(A Tribute To American Theatre)
With Laurence Olivier, Natalie Wood, Robert Wagner, Maureen Stapleton, Jack Hedley, Mary Peach
Supplier: Granada TV
Prods: Derek Granger, Olivier;
Dir: Robert Moore;
Wri: Tennessee Williams.
120 Mins, Mon (6), 9 pm.
NBC-TV
12/08/76

CATASTROPHE: AIRSHIPS
With Glenn Ford
Supplier: ITC Entertainment
Exec Prod: Charles Denton;
Prod: Brian Lewis;
Dirs: Lewis, Franc Roddam;
Wri: Warren Trabent
30 Mins, Fri (28), 7:30 pm.
WABC-TV New York
02/02/77S

CATCH A RAINBOW
With Nancy Aronie, Elaine Bromka, Peter Kovner, Doncharles Manning, Jody Scalise, Alli Singer
Supplier: BBI Prods
Exec Prod: Linda Janower;
Dirs: William Lowell, Bob Loudin;
Adapt: Ingrid Furlong.
30 Mins, Tues, 7:30 pm.
WCVB-TV Boston
11/09/77

CATCH A RISING STAR
With Tom Curtis
Prods: Holly Fine, Kathy Cunningham;
Dir: Fine.
30 Mins, Tue, 7:30 pm.
WMAL-TV Washington
04/13/77

CATSPLAY
With Helen Burns, Doris Petrie, Francis Hyland, Moya Fenwick, Jan Rubes
Exec Prod: Robert Allen;
Prod: Beverley Roberts;
Dir: Stephen Katz;
Wri: Timothy Findlay, from the play by Istvan Orkeny.
90 Mins, Wed, 8:30 pm.
CBC-TV, from Toronto, Canada
04/05/78F

CBS NEWS SUNDAY MORNING
With Charles Kuralt, Richard Threlkeld, Jeff Greenfield, Blair Sabol, Heywood Hale Broun, Bernard Redmont, Bernard Kalb, Ray Brady, Ray Gandolf, Morton Dean, Len Tucker
Exec Prod: Robert Northshield;
Prods: Bud Lamoreaux, Elliot Bernstein, Martin Clancy, Sid Feders, Alan Harper, James Houtrides;
Dir: Ken Sable;
Wri: Mel Lavine.
90 Mins, Sun, 9 am.
CBS-TV
01/31/79

CBS: ON THE AIR: PART 1
With Mary Tyler Moore, Walter Cronkite (hosts), Telly Savalas, Jean Stapleton, Alfred Hitchcock, Bob Keeshan, Alan Johnson Dancers
Supplier: CBS Entertainment
Exec Prod: Alexander H Cohen;
Prod: Lee Miller;
Dir: Clark Jones;
Wri: Hildy Parks.
120 Mins, Sun (26), 9 pm.
CBS-TV
03/29/78

CBS SALUTES LUCY - THE FIRST 25 YEARS
With Lucille Ball, Desi Arnaz Sr, Milton Berle, Carol Burnett, Richard Burton, Johnny Carson, Sammy Davis Jr, Gale Gordon, Bob Hope, Danny Kaye, Dean Martin, James Stewart, Danny Thomas, Vivian Vance, Dick Van Dyke, John Wayne, William S. Paley
Supplier: Lucille Ball Prods
Prods: Gary Morton, Sheldon Keller;
Wri: Keller.
120 Mins, Sun (28), 8 pm.
CBS-TV
12/01/76

CELEBRITY CHALLENGE OF THE SEXES
With McLean Stevenson, Barbara Rhoades, Tom Brookshier, Billy Crystal, Gavin MacLeod, Erin Moran, Mackenzie Phillips, Jim Tunney
Supplier: CBS Sports, Trans World International
Exec Prod: Howard Katz;
Prod: Mel Ferber;
Dir: Bernie Hoffman;
Wris: Howard Albrecht, Sol Weinstein.
30 Mins, Tues, 8 pm.
CBS-TV
02/15/78

CELLAR GEORGE
With Steve Sneed, Charles Canada, Jamar Jenkins, Sara Jackson, Yvonne Jackson, James Judy, Frank Valdez, Phoebe Thayer, Glenda Despar, Douglas Barnet
Exec Prod: John Coney;
Prods: Lee Olson, Olivia Dorsey;
Wri: Aki Llorens.
90 Mins, Sun, 10 pm.
KCTS-TV Seattle
01/23/80

CENTENNIAL - PART ONE
(The Big Event)
With Raymond Burr, Barbara Carrera, Richard Chamberlain, Robert Conrad, Richard Crenna, Chad Everett, David Janssen, Alex Karras, Brian Keith, Sally Kellerman, Donald Pleasence, Lynn Redgrave, Dennis Weaver, Michael Ansara, Henry Darrow, Ray Tracey, Robert Walden, Clint Walker, Yolanda Aquayo, Annette Charles, Ivan Naranjo, Duane Loken, David Yanez, James A Michener
Supplier: John Wilder Prods & Universal TV
Exec Prod-Wri: Wilder;
Prod: Howard Alston;
Dir: Virgil W Vogel.
180 Mins, Sun (1), 8:24 pm.
NBC-TV
10/04/78

CERTAIN PRACTICES
(For The Record)
With Richard Monette, Alan Scarfe, David Gardner, Susan Hogan
Exec Prod: Sam Levene;
Prod: Bill Gough;
Dir: Martin Lavut;
Wri: Ian Sutherland.
60 Mins, Sun, 9 pm.
CBC, from Toronto, Canada
03/21/79F

CHAIN REACTION
With Bill Cullen (host), Patty Duke Astin, Joyce Bulifant, Nipsey Russel;, Fred Grandy
Supplier: Bob Stewart Prods.
Exec Prod: Bob Stewart;
Prod: Sande Stewart;
Dir: Mike Gargiulo.
30 Mins, Mon-Fri, noon
NBC-TV
01/23/80

THE CHAMPIONS
Prods: Donald Brittain, Janet Leissner;
Dir-Wri: Brittain.
120 Mins, Sun-Mon, 10 pm.
CBC-TV, from Toronto, Canada
02/22/78F

THE CHANNEL 2 ROAD SHOW
With John Stossel, Carol Martin (hosts)
Supplier: WCBS-TV New York, KNXT Los Angeles
Prods-Dirs: Don King, Joel Tatter.
30 Mins, Fri (15), 7:30 pm.
WCBS-TV New York
06/20/79

CHARLESTON
(NBC Monday Night At The Movies)
With Delta Burke, Lynne Moody, Patricia Pearcy, Jordan Clarke, Richard Lawson, Martha Scott, Mandy Patinkin, Lucille Benson
Supplier: Robert Stigwood Org
Prod: Beryl Vertue;
Dir: Karen Arthur;
Wri: Nancy Lynn Schwartz.
120 Mins, Mon (15), 9 pm.
NBC-TV
01/17/79

CHARLIE'S ANGELS
(ABC Sunday Movie Double Feature)
With Kate Jackson, Farrah Fawcett-Majors, Jaclyn Smith, David Doyle, David Ogden Stiers, Diana Muldaur, John Lehne, Bo Hopkins, Tommy Lee Jones, Grant Owens, Ken Sansom
Supplier: Spelling-Goldberg Prods.
Exec Prods: Aaron Spelling, Leonard Goldberg;
Prods-wris: Ivan Goff, Ben Roberts;
Dir: John Llewellyn Moxey.
90 Mins, Sun (21), 9 pm.
ABC-TV
03/24/76

CHARLIE'S ANGELS
With Kate Jackson, Farrah Fawcett-Majors, Jaclyn Smith, David Doyle, Don Gordon, Mayf Nutter, Kurt Grayson, John Dennis Johnston, Jenny O'Hara, Ric Mancini, voice of John Forsythe
Supplier: Spelling-Goldberg Prods
Exec Prods: Aaron Spelling, Leonard Goldberg;
Prod: Rick Husky;
Dir: Richard Lang;
Wri: Edward J. Lakso.
60 Mins, Wed, 10 pm.
ABC-TV
09/29/76

CHARO
With Mike Connors, David Michaels, Frank DeVol, Beatrice Colen, Ray Stewart, Philip Tanzini
Supplier: Ilson/Chambers Prods. & Baeza Inc.
Exec Prods: Saul Ilson, Ernest Chambers;
Prods: Bob Booker, George Foster;
Dir: Jack Regas;
Wris: Booker, Foster, Jeffrey Baron, Rubin Carson, Bruce Vilanich, Sybil Adelman.
30 Mins, Mon (24), 8 pm.
ABC-TV
06/02/76

THE CHEAP DETECTIVE
With Flip Wilson, Murray Hamilton, Paula Kelly, Richard Beauchamp, Michael Keenan, John Quade, Franklin Ajaye
Supplier: Rastar TV & Columbia Pictures TV
Exec Prods: Bob Sweeney, Edward H. Feldman, Larry Rosen;
Dir: Feldman;
Wri: Richard M. Powell
30 Mins, Tues, (3) 10:30 pm.
NBC-TV
06/11/80

THE CHEAP SHOW
With Dick Martin, host: Bob Newhart, Anthony Newley
Supplier: 20th Century-Fox TV
Exec Prods: Chris Bearde, Robert D Wood;
Prods: Terry Kyne, Kathe Connolly;
Dir: Kyne;
Wris: Bearde, David M Hackel, Steve Kahn.
30 Mins, Wed, 7:30 pm.
WCBS-TV New York
09/27/78S

CHER...SPECIAL
With Dolly Parton, Rod Stewart
Supplier: Isis Prods
Exec Prods: Raymond Katz, Sandy Gallin;
Prod-Dir: Art Fisher;
Wris: Buz Kohan, Patricia Resnick, Cher, Rod Warren.
60 Mins, Mon (3), 9 pm.
ABC-TV
04/12/78

THE CHERYL LADD SPECIAL
With the Mission Mountain Wood Band, Waylon Jennings, Ben Vereen, Melanie Griffith, Don Correia, Dorothy Konrad, Ron Field Dancers
Supplier: Smith-Hemion Prods & Ladd Prods
Exec Prods: Gary Smith, Dwight Hemion, David Ladd;
Prod: Ron Field;
Dir: Hemion;
Wris: Rod Warren, Larry Grossman, Richard Riddle.
60 Mins, Mon (9), 9 pm.
ABC-TV
Lever Bros (Lever Media); J B Williams (Parkson Agency)
04/18/79

CHILD ABUSE: A CRY FOR HELP
With Carol Jenkins, John Hambrick
Supplier: WNBC-TV Public Affairs Dept
Exec Prod: David Ochoa;
Prod: Beverly Schanzer;
Dir: Jack Simcox
60 Mins, Fri, (25) 10 pm.
WNBC-TV New York
07/30/80S

CHILDREN OF FIRE MOUNTAIN
With Peter Vere-Jones, Paul Airey, Rachel Weston, Martyn Sanderson, Terence Cooper, Waric Slyfield, Marion Parry. others
Supplier: South Pacific Television
Exec Prod: John McRae;
Dir: Peter Sharp;
Wri: Roger Simpson.
30 Mins, Sun, 7 pm.
South Pacific TV, Auckland, N Z
10/24/79F

CHINA: THE NEW REVOLUTION
With Angela Hill
Prods-Wris: Jim Boyer, Hill;
Dirs: Lee Huffman, Steve Wegmann.
30 Mins, Wed (22), 7 pm.
WWL-TV New Orleans
08/29/79

CHIPS
With Larry Wilcox, Erik Estrada, Robert Pine, Paul Mantee, Thomas Huff, Michael Christian, Brodie Greer, Lew Saunders, Brooke Bundy, Hoke Howell, Philip Simms
Supplier: Rosner TV, MGM-TV
Prod: Rick Rosner;
Dir: Paul Krasny;
Wri: Paul Playdon.
60 Mins, Thurs, 8 pm.
NBC-TV
09/21/77

THE CHISHOLMS - PART 1
With Robert Preston, Rosemary Harris, Ben Murphy, Brian Kerwin, Jimmy Van Patten, Stacey Nelkin, Susan Swift, Charles Frank, Anthony Zerbe, Glynnis O'Connor, Doug Kershaw
Supplier: Alan Landsburg Prods
Exec Prods: Landsburg, David Dortort;
Prod: Paul Freeman;
Dir: Mel Stuart;
Wri: Evan Hunter.
120 Mins, Thurs (29), 8 pm.
CBS-TV
04/04/79

THE CHISHOLMS
With Robert Preston, Rosemary Harris, Ben Murphy, James Van Patten, Brett Cullen, Delta Burke, Susan Swift, Victoria Racimo, Reid Smith, Mitchell Ryan, Devon Ericson, Guich Koock, Les Lannom, Nick Ramus, Tom Steckshulte, Chief Eugene Standingbear
Supplier: Alan Landsburg Prods
Exec Prod: Landsburg;
Prod: Paul Freeman;
Dir: Mel Stuart;
Wri: Paul Savage, Corey Blechman
120 Mins, Sat, (19), 8 pm.
CBS-TV
01/23/80

CHOOSING SUICIDE
With Richard Ellison (narr), Jo Roman
Supplier: LRE/Video Team Prods
Prod-Wri: Ellison.
60 Mins, Mon, (16) 8 pm.
PBS
06/18/80

THE CHRISTIANS
Supplier: Granada Television
Exec Prod: Norman Swallow;
Prod: Michael Murphy;
Wri: Bamber Gascoigne.
60 Mins, Tues (Aug 2 & 9), 10:30 pm.
ITV, Britain
08/17/77F

CHRISTINA - MUSIC FOR A WINTER QUEEN
(Christina - En Drottning Begav Sig Till Rom)
With Andrew Dalton, Lars Leishem, Torbjorn Lillieqvist, Tuvalisa Rangstrom, Catarina Davidsson, Gudrun Mesch, Ann-Christine Wickberg, Predrag Novovic, Ulf Gadd
Supplier: Swedish Television TV1
Prod-Dir: Inger Aby;
Wri: Alf Henrikson;
Mus Adap: Arnold Ostman.
53 Mins.
(Prix Italia winner, music)
10/03/79PI

CHRISTINA'S WORLD
With Julie Harris, narrator
Supplier: Hardtimes Movie Co.
Dir-wri: Sonja Gilligan.
60 Mins, Tues (13), 10 pm.
WNET-TV
04/21/76S

CHRISTMAS LACE
With Guylaine Croteau, Germaine Lemyre, Monique Mercure, Marcel Sabourin, Michel Cote, narrated by Genevieve Bujold
Prods-Wris: George Mendeluk, Linda Sorenson;
Dir: Mendeluk.
30 Mins, Thurs, 9 pm.
CTV, from Toronto, Canada
12/20/78F

CHRISTMAS LILIES OF THE FIELD
(The Big Event)
With Billy Dee Williams, Maria Schell, Fay Hauser, Judith Piquet, Hanna Hertelendy, Lisa Mann, Donna Johnson, Jean Jenkins, Sam DiBello, Fred Hart, Adolfo Flores, Danny Zapien, Tommy Arnell, Oliver Nguyen, Julie Delgado, Michael Witt, Bob Hastings, Regina Simons
Supplier: Rainbow Prods & Osmond TV
Exec Prod-Dir: Ralph Nelson;
Prods: Jack N Reddish, Toby Martin;
Wris: John McGreevey, Nelson.
120 Mins, Sun (16), 8 pm.
NBC-TV
12/19/79

THE CHRISTMAS RACCOONS
With Rich Little, Rita Coolidge, Rupert Holmes, Michael Magee, Fred Little, Carl Banas, Bobby Dermer, Len Carlson, Tammy Bourne, Hadley Kay
Supplier: Time Buying Services Inc.
Exec Prod: Sheldon Wiseman;
Prod: Kevin Gillis;
Dirs: Gillis, Paul Schibley;
30 Min, Wed (3), 7:30 pm.
WCBS-TV New York
12/17/80S

CHUCK BARRIS RAH RAH SHOW
With Barris (host), The Spinners, Fred Travalena, Johnny Paycheck, Yvonne Elliman, George Carlin, Samantha Sang, England Dan & John Ford Coley, Jaye P. Morgan & Originals, Tony Van Doren, Michael Sherman, Hilary Carlip, Dr Flame-o, Gallagher, Kevin Parker, Milt Delugg orch
Supplier: Chuck Barris Prods
Exec Prod: Barris;
Prod: Gene Banks;
Dir: John Dorsey.
60 Mins, Tues, 8 pm.
NBC-TV
03/08/78

CHURCHILL & THE GENERALS
With Timothy West, Joseph Cotten, Arthur Hill, Alexander Knox, Ian Richardson, Eric Porter, Patrick Magee, Richard Dysart, Patrick Allen, Lyndon Brook, others
Supplier: BBC, Le Vien International
Exec Prod: Jack Le Vien;
Prod: Alan Shallcross;
Dir: Alan Gibson;
Wri: Ian Curteis.
165 Mins, Sun (23), 8:05 pm.
BBC-2, Britain
10/03/79F

CINDERELLA AT THE PALACE
With Gene Kelly (host), Paul Anka, Ann-Margret, Sammy Davis Jr, Tom Jones, Frank Sinatra, Andy Williams, Marlene Ricci, Merv Griffin, Jimmie Walker, Don Knotts, Rip Taylor, Elaine Joyce, Jackie Gayle
Supplier: Tom McDermott Prods, Smith-Hemion Prods
Exec Prods: Gary Smith, Dwight Hemion, McDermott;
Prod-Dir: Bob Henry;
Wris: Harry Crane, Norm Liebman, Marty Farrell.
120 Mins, Thurs (2), 9 pm.
CBS-TV
P&G (Benton & Bowles)
11/08/78

CINDY
(ABC Friday Night Movie)
Charlaine Woodard, Clifton Davis, Scoey Mitchill, Mae Mercer, Nell-Ruth Carter Alaina Reed, Cleavant Derricks, W Benson Terry, Noble Willingham, John Hancock
Supplier: John Charles Walters Prods & Paramount TV
Prods-Wris: James L Brooks, Stan Daniels, David Davis, Ed Weinberger;
Dir: William H Graham.
120 Mins, Fri (24), 9 pm.
ABC-TV
03/29/78

CIRCUS
With Leslie Nielsen, Cal Dodd, Sherisse Laurence
Exec Prod: Arthur Weinthal;
Prods: Jorn Winther, Bill Hartley;
Wri: Hartley.
60 Mins, Sun, 8 pm.
CTV, from Toronto, Canada
08/09/78F

CIRCUS
With Cal Dodd, Sherisse Laurence
Exec Prods: Arthur Weinthal, Ed Richardson;
Prod: Bill Hartley;
Dir: Jack Sampson;
Wri: Hartley.
30 Mins, Fri, 7:30 pm.
CTV, from Toronto, Canada
10/25/78F

THE CITY
With Robert Forster, Don Johnson, Ward Costello, Jimmy Dean, Mark Hamill, Susan Sullivan, Felton Perry, Leslie Ackerman, Paul Cavonis, Paul Fix, Joby Baker
Supplier: Quinn Martin Prods
Exec Prod: Martin;
Prod-Wri: John Wilder;
Dir: Harvey Hart.
90 Mins, Wed (12), 9:30 pm.
NBC-TV
01/19/77

THE CITY IS OURS
Prod: Jean Walkinshaw;
Exec Prod: John Coney.
30 Mins, Sun, 10 pm.
KCTS-TV Seattle
02/13/80

CITY KIDS
With Jerry Nutter
Supplier: KPIX
Exec Prod: Galen Daily;
Prod-Dir: Marion Whigham.
30 Mins, Sat, 1 pm.
KPIX San Francisco
09/27/78

CITY OF ANGELS
With Wayne Rogers, Elaine Joyce, Diane Ladd, Meredith Baxter Birney, Lawrence Luckinbill, Lloyd Nolan, others
Supplier: Roy Huggins-Public Arts, in association wth Universal TV
Exec Prod: Jo Swerling Jr.;
Dir: Don Medford;
Wri: Stephen J. Cannell.
60 Mins, Tues, 10 pm.
NBC-TV
02/11/76

CITY OF ANGELS (PART I) ANGELS' DEFENSE (PART II)
Supplier: ATV Network
Prod-Dir: John Ingram.
60 Mins, Tues (5), 10:30 pm; 60 Mins, Wed (6), 10:40 pm.
ITV, London, England
07/20/77F

CLAPPER'S
With Jennifer Perito, Leah Ayres, Larry Breeding, Starr Danias, Byron Webster, Nita Talbott, Cosie Costa, Rick Warner, Morgan Farley
Supplier: Pheebo Prods & Columbia Pictures TV
Prod-Wri: Patricia Nardo;
Dir: Hal Cooper.
30 Mins, Wed (28),8 pm.
NBC-TV
07/05/78

CLEVER JACK, PART ONE
With Lucie Arnaz (host), The First All Children's Theatre
Supplier: Fish Communications, The Corp for Entertainment & Learning and Meredith Broadcasting
Exec Prods: Sandy Fisher, Charles Grinker;
Prod: Fisher;
Dirs: Meridee Stein, Merrily Mossman;
Wris: Ian Elliott, Stein.
30 Mins, Fri (7), 7:30 pm.
WCBS-TV New York
12/12/79S

CLIFFHANGERS
(See: Stop Susan Williams; The Secret Empire; The Curse of Dracula).
03/07/79

THE CLONE MASTER
(NBC Movie Of The Week)
With Art Hindle, Robyn Douglas, Ralph Bellamy, John Van Dreelen, Mario Roccuzzo, Ed Lauter
Supplier: Mel Ferber Prods, Paramount TV
Exec Prod: Ferber;
Prod-Wri: John D F Black;
Dir: Don Medford.
120 Mins, Thurs (14), 8 pm.
NBC
09/20/78

CLOUDS OF GLORY
(William and Dorothy)
With David Warner, Felicity Kendal, others
Supplier: Granada TV
Prod: Norman Swallow;
Dir: Ken Russell;
Wris: Melvyn Bragg, Russell.
60 Mins, Sun (9), 9:30 pm.
LWT, from London, England
07/26/78F

CLOWNS
(Superspecial)
With Brian Mackay, Barbara Barskey, Judy Marshak, Marek Norman
Prod-Dir: Rob Iscove;
Wris: Jeri Craden, Peter Mann, Iscove.
60 Mins, Mon, 9 pm.
CBC-TV, from Toronto, Canada
11/01/78F

CODE NAME: DIAMOND HEAD
With Roy Thinnes, France Nuyen, Zulu, Ward Costello, Don Knight, Ian McShane, Eric Braeden, Dennis Patrick, Alex Henteloff, Frank Michael Liu, Harry Endo
Supplier: QM Prods
Exec Prod: Quinn Martin;
Prod-Wri: Paul King;
Dir: Jeannot Szwarc.
90 Mins, Tues (3), 9:30 pm.
NBC-TV
05/11/77

CODE R
With James Houghton, Martin Kove, Tom Simcox, Susanne Reed, Ben Davidson, Robbie Rundle, W T Zacha, others
Supplier: Warner Bros TV
Prod: Edwin Self;
Dir: Andrew V McLaglen;
Wri: Self.
60 Mins, Fri (21), 8 pm.
CBS-TV
01/26/77

CO-ED FEVER
With David Keith, Alexa Kenin, Christopher S Nelson, Cathryn O'Neil, Michael Pasternak, Tacey Phillips, Jane Rose, Heather Thomas, Jillian Kesner, Hamilton Camp
Supplier: Martin Ransohoff Prods
Exec Prod: Ransohoff;
Prod: Frank Shaw;
Dir: Marc Daniels;
Wris: Michael Elias, Shaw.
30 Mins, Sun (4), 10:30 pm.
CBS-TV
02/07/79

COLD COMFORT
With Steve Bisley, Lynette Curran, May Howlett, Tim Hughes, Rob Baxter, Rob Thomas, Jill McKay, Chris Lewis, Frank Garfield
Supplier: Australian Broadcasting Commission
Exec Prod: Sandra Levy;
Dir: Chris Thomson;
Wri: Laura Jones.
50 Mins, Wed, (13) 8:30 pm.
ABC (Australia) TV, Channel 2, Sydney
08/20/80F

THE COLLECTION
(Laurence Olivier Presents)
With Alan Bates, Malcolm McDowell, Helen Mirren, Laurence Olivier, others
Supplier: Granada TV
Prods: Derek Granger, Olivier;
Dir: Michael Apted;
Wri: Harold Pinter.
60 Mins, Sun (5), 9:05 pm.
ITV Network, Britain
12/22/76F

COLLEGE SPORTS INC - BIG MONEY ON CAMPUS
(NBC Reports)
With Edwin Newman
Supplier: NBC News
Exec Prod: Stuart Schulberg;
Prods: Jeff Walsh, Marion Lear Swaybill, Bill Turque;
Wris: Schulberg, Walsh, Turque.
60 Mins, Sun (29), 10 pm.
NBC-TV
05/02/79

COLORADO C I
With John Elerick, Marshall Colt, L Q Jones, Laurette Spang, Christine Belford, David Hedison, Bill Lucking, Chris DeLisle, Van Williams, Randy Powell, Lou Frizzell, John Karlen, Joan Roberts, George Wallace, Anne H Bradley
Supplier: Woodruff Prods & QM Prods
Exec Prod: Philip Saltzman;
Prod: Christopher Morgan;
Dir: Virgil W Vogel;
Wri: Robert W Lenski.
60 Mins, Fri (26), 10 pm.
CBS-TV
05/31/78

COLORS OF GRAY
With Studs Terkel narrator, others
Prod-dir: Scott Craig;
Wri: Joe Sander.
60 Mins, Sun (27), 9 pm.
WBBM-TV Chicago
06/30/76

THE COLUMBIA: VOICES OF THE RIVER
Prod: Jean Walkinshaw.
30 Mins, Tues (15), 9 pm.
KCTS-TV Seattle
08/23/78

COMEBACK
With James Whitmore (host)
Supplier: Maramy Prods & American International TV
Exec Prod: Lawrence Jacobson;
Prod: Richard Arlett;
Dir-Wri: Paul C Morgan.
30 Mins, Sat, 3:30 pm.
WCBS-TV New York
09/26/79S

COMEDY IN AMERICA REPORT
With George Hamilton, Ray Charles, Ray Stevens, Conrad Bain, Redd Foxx, Marilyn Michaels, the International Children's Choir, Susan Astor, Susan Batson, Nancy Bleier, Steve Bluestein, Robert Miller Driscoll, Marie Halton, Dulcie Jordan, Helene Lucas, Danny Mora, Karen Philipp, Charlie Robinson, Natasha Ryan, Pamela Serpe, Joe Warfield, Don Knotts, Art Metrano, Roger Bowen
Supplier: DRB/Bilskip Prods.
Prods: Scoey Mitchill, Donald R Boyle;
Dirs: Coby Ruskin, Sterling Johnson;
Wris: Larry Arnstein & David Hurwitz, Richard Blasucci & Douglas Stackler, Larry Mintz & Alan Eisenstock, Paul Pumpian & Harvey Weitzman, Tracy Morgan, Mitchill, Boyle
60 Mins, Fri (9), 10 pm.
NBC-TV
04/14/76

THE COMEDY SHOP
With Norm Crosby (host), Jackie Vernon, Billy Fellows, Jackie Kahane, Fred Smoot, Bobby Kosser, Annette Funicello, Rip Taylor, Jill St John
Supplier: Siroco Prods (JWT Syndication)
Exec Prod: Paul Roth;
Prod: Joe Seigman, Perry Rosemond;
Dir: Rosemond;
Wri: David Panich.
30 Mins, Sun, 3 pm.
WNBC-TV New York
09/13/78S

COMPLETELY OFF THE WALL
With John Ritter, Wendy Cutter, Tony DeLia, Susan Elliot, Rod Gist, Andy Goldberg, Dee Marcus, Nancy Steen and Paul Willson
Supplier: Right Time Prods-Thursday's Child Prods
Exec Prod: Devera Marcus;
Prod: George Van Noy;
Dir: Jim Drake.
30 Mins, Fri (7), 11:30 pm.
ABC-TV
09/12/79

THE CONFESSIONS OF RONALD BIGGS
With Ronald Biggs, Charmian Biggs, Colin McKenzie, Ian McColl, Jack Slipper, Mike Biggs; Don Barkham, narrator
Supplier: Grundy Organization
Prod-Dir: Barry Sloane.
75 Mins.
0-10 Network (previewed), Sydney, Australia
04/19/78F

CONGRESSIONAL OUTLOOK
With Pat Tyler (host)
Supplier: WCET-TV Cincinnati
Prods: Gene Walz, Bob Gilbert.
30 Mins, Fri, 10 pm.
PBS
10/11/78

CONNECTIONS
With Warner Troyer; narration by Jon Granik
Exec Prod: Richard Nielsen;
Prods: William Macadam, Martyn Burke.
90 Mins, Sun-Mon, 9:30 pm.
CBC-TV, from Toronto, Canada
06/22/77F

CONNECTIONS - THE SECOND SERIES
Exec Prod: Richard Nielsen;
Prods: William Macadam, Martyn Burke.
210 Mins, Mon, Tues, Wed 10 pm.
CBC, from Toronto, Canada
04/04/79F

THE CONTENDER
With Marc Singer, Moses Gunn, Katherine Cannon, Louise Latham, Alan Stack, Tina Andrews, Don Gordon, Art Lund, Gregory Walcott, William Watson, Clifton Tompkins, John Dayey, Art Aragon, Jack Griffin, Walt Davis, Albert Myles, Damon Douglas, Rick Hall, Nocona Aranda, Alfonso Tafoya, Nico DeSilva
Suppliers: Universal Television
Exec Prod: Jon Epstein;
Prod: Robert Dozier;
Dirs: Harry Falk, Lou Antonio;
Wris: Dozier, Robert Hamilton, Herman Groves
90 Mins, Thurs, (3) 10 pm.
CBS-TV
04/09/80

CONVERSATION
With Ron Kistler, Lucian Bicci
Prod: Robert D. Clark.
30 Mins, Tues, 6 pm.
CBOT, Ottawa, Canada
06/09/76F

COP SHOP
With Peter Adams, Tomy Bonner, Paula Duncan, Joanna Lockwood, George Mallaby, JoAnne Moore, Terry Norris, Terry Ross, Greg Ross, Peter Sumner, Rowena Wallace, Patrick Ward
Supplier: Crawford Productions
Exec Prod: Hector Crawford;
Dirs: Marie Trevor, Graham Foreman, Phil East, Terry Stapleton, Ian Crawford;
Wris: Terry Stapleton, Kate Thompson, James Hood, Bill Freeman, Peter Kinlock, Everett de Roche.
60 Mins, Mon, 8:30 pm.
Channel 7, Sydney, Australia
12/28/77F

THE CORAL JUNGLE
With Leonard Nimoy, host
Supplier: Group W Prods
Exec Prod: Jack Reilly;
Prod: Richard Perin;
Dir: Ben Cropp;
Wri: Richard Schickel.
60 Mins, Sat, 4 pm.
WABC-TV New York
09/08/76S

CORALIE LANSDOWNE SAYS NO
With Wendy Hughes, David Waters, Brian Blain, Robert Coleby, Elaine Mangan, Marylou Stewart, Basil Clarke
Supplier: Australian Broadcasting Commission
Exec Prod: Alan Burke;
Dir: Michael Carson;
Wri: Alexander Buzo.
95 Mins, Sun, 8:30 pm.
ABC (Australia) TV, Channel 2
07/30/80F

COS
With Bill Cosby, Cindy Williams, Charlie Callas, Rod Hull & Emu, Bruce Jenner, Chicago, Lynda Carter, Gabriel Kaplan, Jeff Altman, Willie Bobo, Mauricio Jarrin, Buzzy Linhart, Marion Ramsey, Tim Thomerson
Supplier: Jemmin Prod
Prod: Chris Bearde;
Dir: Jeff Margolis;
Wris: Jeremy Stevens, Tom Moore, Rick Kellard, Bob Comfort, Sandra Harmon, China Clark, Kevin Hartigan, David Garber, Stuart Bloomberg, Gina Goldman, Nita Schroeder, John Donley, Nance McCormick.
60 Mins, Sun, 7 pm.
ABC-TV
09/22/76

COSMOS
With Carl Sagan (host)
Supplier: KCET, Carl Sagan Prod, BBC-TV, Polytel International
Exec Prod-Dir: Adrian Malone;
Sr Prods: Geoffrey Haines-Stiles, David Kennard;
Prods: Gregory Andorfer, Rob McCain;
Sequence Dirs: Kennard, Haines-Stiles, McCain, David Oyster, Tom Weidlinger, Richard Wells;
Wris: Sagan, Ann Druyan, Dr. Steven Soter.
60 Mins, Sun (28) 8 pm.
PBS, from KCET Los Angeles
10/01/80

COTTAGE TO LET
(Saving It For Albie)
With Penelope Keith, Colin Welland, William Gaunt
Supplier: ATV
Prod-Dir: John Cooper;
Crea-Wri: Richard Harris.
60 Mins, Tues, 9 pm.
ITV, from London, England
09/21/77F

COTTON CANDY
With Charles Martin Smith, Clint Howard, Leslie King, Kevin Lee Miller, Manuel Padilla Jr, Dino Scofield, Mark Wheeler, Alvy Moore, Joan Crosby, Rance Howard
Supplier: Major H Prods
Exec Prod-Dir: Ron Howard;
Prods: John Thomas Lennox, Rance Howard;
Wris: Ron & Clint Howard.
120 Mins, Thurs (26), 8 pm.
NBC-TV
11/01/78

THE COURT-MARTIAL OF GEORGE ARMSTRONG CUSTER
(Hallmark Hall of Fame)
With Brian Keith, Ken Howard, Stephen Elliott, James Olson, Blythe Danner, J D Cannon, Nicolas Coster, William Daniels, Richard Dysart, Biff McGuire, Susan Sullivan, Anthony Zerbe, Dehl Berti, James Blendick, John Cunningham, Duncan Gamble, Rick Goldman, John Horn, Laurence Hugo, Christopher Pennock, Lane Smith
Supplier: Norman Rosemont Prods & Warner Bros TV
Prod: Rosemont;
Dir: Glenn Jordan;
Wri: John Gay, based on Douglas C Jones novel.
120 Mins, Thurs (1), 9 pm.
NBC-TV
Hallmark Cards (Foote, Cone & Belding)
12/07/77

COVER STORY: ADOPTION IN AMERICA
With Rick Smith, Lynn Povich, George Will, others
Exec Prod: Alvin H Perlmutter;
Sr Prod: Imre Horvath.
60 Mins, Wed, 9 pm.
PBS, (from WNET New York)
12/03/80

CPO SHARKEY
With Don Rickles, Elizabeth Allen, Harrison Page, Peter Isacksen, Dennis Kort, Jeff Hollis, Tom Ruben, Jeffrey Kramer, David Landsberg, James Callahan
Supplier: R & R Prods
Prod-wri: Aaron Ruben;
Dir: Peter Baldwin.
30 Mins, Wed, 8 pm.
NBC-TV
12/08/76

CREAM IN MY COFFEE
With Peggy Ashcroft, Lionel Jeffries, Martin Shaw, Peter Chelsom, Shelagh McLeod, Faith Brook.
Supplier: London Weekend TV & Pennies From Heaven Ltd
Exec Prod: Tony Wharmby;
Prod: Kenith Trodd;
Dir: Gavin Millar;
Wri: Dennis Potter.
87 Min, Sun, 10 pm.
ITV Network-Britain
12/10/80F

CREGGAN
Supplier: Thames TV (U.K.)
Prods-Wris: Michael Whyte, Mary Holland;
Dir: Michael Whyte.
52 Mins.
(Winner of Prix Italia, Documentary)
10/01/80PI

THE CREZZ
With Joss Ackland, Hugh Burden, Elspet Gray, others
Supplier: Thames TV, London
Prod: Paul Knight;
Dir: John Glenister;
Wri: Clive Exton.
60 Mins, Thurs, 8 pm.
ITV Network, Britain
09/29/76F

CRIME AND PUNISHMENT
(Masterpiece Theatre)
With John Hurt, Frank Middlemass, Sian Phillips, Beatrix Lehmann
Supplier: BBC-TV, Time-Life TV
Prod: Jonathan Powell;
Dir: Michael Darlow;
Wri: Jack Pulman, from Dostoevsky's novel.
60 Mins, Sun, 9 pm.
PBS
10/01/80

CRIMES OF PASSION
With Brian Blessed, Isobel Black, John Phillips, Anthony Newlands, Daniel Moynihan, Bernard Heton, Nancie Jackson
Supplier: ITC
Prod: Cecil Clarke, Robert D. Cardona;
Dir: Valerie Hanson;
Wri: Ted Willis.
60 Mins, Wed (3), 9 pm.
WPIX-TV New York
03/10/76S

CRISIS AT SUN VALLEY
With Dale Robinette, Taylor Lacher, Bo Hopkins, Tracy Brooks Swope, Paul Brinegar, Jason Johnson, John McIntire, Ken Swofford, Susan Adams, Julie Parsons
Supplier: Columbia Pictures TV & Barry Weitz Prods
Exec Prod: Weitz;
Prod: Robert Stambler;
Dir: Paul Stanley;
Wris: Carl Gottlieb, Alvin Boretz.
120 Mins, Wed (29), 9 pm.
NBC
04/05/78

THE CRITICAL LIST
With Lloyd Bridges, Melinda Dillon, Buddy Ebsen, Barbara Parkins, Robert Wagner, Ken Howard, Pat Harrington, Richard Basehart, Louis Gossett Jr, Linwood McCarthy, James Whitmore Jr, Robert Hogan, Scott Marlowe, Felton Perry, John Larch, Jim Antonio, Joanne Linville, Ben Piazza, Brad David, Will Hare, Noble Willingham, Regis J Cordic, others
Supplier: MTM Enterprises
Exec Prod: Jerry McNeely;
Dir: Lou Antonio;
Wri: McNeely, based on Marshall Goldberg's novels.
240 Mins, Mon-Tues (11-12), 9 pm.
NBC-TV
09/20/78

CROSSBAR
With John Ireland, Kate Reid, Brent Carver, Kim Cattrall
Exec Prod: Stanley Colbert;
Prod: Brian Walker;
Dir: John Trent;
Wri: Keith Leckie, from a story by Bill Boyle.
90 Mins, Sat, 9:30 pm.
CBC-TV, from Toronto, Canada
Ford Of Canada
10/17/79F

CRYSTAL GAYLE SPECIAL
With Judy Collins, B B King, Statler Bros, Doug Henning, Peter Gennaro Dancers
Supplier: Southpaw Prods & Sullivan Prods
Exec Prods: Bill Gatzimos, Robert H Precht;
Prod: Precht;
Dirs: Francesco Scavullo, Russ Petranto;
Wris: Martin Ragaway, Donald K Epstein.
60 Mins, Wed (12), 10 pm.
CBS-TV
12/19/79

CTV REPORTS
With Peter Trueman, Bruce Phillps, Barbara Amiel, Michael Maclear
Exec Prod: Michael Maclear;
Prods: Andrew Cochrane, Don McQueen;
Dir: Edward Mercel.
60 Mins, Sun, 10 pm.
CTV, from Toronto, Canada
10/26/77F

CUBA: THE CASTRO GENERATION
(ABC News Closeup)
With Howard K Smith
Prod-Dir-Wri: Arthur Holch.
60 Mins, Fri (4), 10 pm.
ABC-TV
03/09/77

CURIOUS CASE OF UNCLE TOM'S CABIN
With Rex Ellis, Tom Brennan III, Amy Levy, Stephen Rabousky
Exec Prod: Art Garland;
Prod-Dir: Don Calderwood;
Wri: Stephen Hirsch.
30 Mins, Thurs, 7:30 pm.
WRGB-TV Schenectady, New York
12/28/77

THE CURSE OF DRACULA - (Chapter 6) (CLIFFHANGERS)
With Michael Nouri, Carol Baxter, Stephen Johnson, Bever-Leigh Banfield, Antoinette Stella, Mark Montgomery
Supplier: Universal TV
Exec Prod-Dir-Wri: Kenneth Johnson;
Prod: Richard Milton
60 Min, Tues, 8 pm.
NBC-TV
03/07/79

CUSTARD PIE
With Peter Kastner, Kate Lynch, Nancy Dolman, Derek McGrath, Robert Joy
Prod: Perry Rosemond;
Dir: Ray Arsenault;
Wri: Ken Ross.
30 Min, Tues, 7:30 pm.
CBC-TV, from Toronto, Canada
10/26/77F

DAFFY DUCK'S EASTER SHOW
With Daffy Duck, Sylvester the Cat, Foghorn Leghorn, Prissy the Hen, Speedy Gonzalez
Supplier: Warner Bros. Television
Exec Prod: Hal Geer;
Prods: David DePatie, Friz Freleng;
Dir: Freleng;
Wris: Freleng, John Dunn, Tony Benedict.
30 Mins, Tues, (1) 8 pm.
NBC-TV
04/09/80

DAFFY DUCK'S THANKS-FOR-GIVING SPECIAL
With voices by Mel Blanc
Supplier: Chuck Jones Enterprises & Warner Bros TV
Exec Prod: Hal Geer;
Prod-Dir: Chuck Jones;
Wris: Jones, Mike Maltese, Warren Foster.
30 Mins, Thurs, (20) 8 pm.
NBC-TV
11/26/80

THE DAIN CURSE - PART 1
With James Coburn, Jason Miller, Jean Simmons, Paul Stewart, Beatrice Straight, Nancy Addison, Tom Bower, David Canary, Martin Cassidy, Clarence Felder, Paul Harding, Malachy McCourt, Hattie Winston, Ellis Rabb, Hector Elizondo, others
Supplier: Martin Poll Prods
Prods: Poll, William C Gerrity;
Dir: E W Swackhamer;
Wri: Robert Lenski (from Dashiell Hammett novel).
120 Mins, Mon (22), 9 pm.
CBS-TV
05/24/78

DALLAS
With Barbara Bel Geddes, Jim Davis, Patrick Duffy, Larry Hagman, Victoria Principal, Charlene Tilton, Linda Gray, Steve Kanaly, Ken Kercheval, Tina Louise, David Wayne, Donna Bullock
Supplier: Lorimar Prods
Exec Prods: Lee Rich, Philip Capice;
Prod: Leonard Katzman;
Dir: Robert Day;
Wri: David Jacobs.
60 Mins, Sun, 10 pm.
CBS-TV
04/05/78

DAMIEN
With Terence Knapp
Supplier: Hawaii Public Television
Prod-Dir: Nino Martin:
Wri: Aldyth Morris.
90 Mins, Tues, 8 pm.
PBS
02/01/78

DANGER IN PARADISE
(NBC Movie of the Week)
With Cliff Potts, John Dehner, Ina Balin, Bill Lucking, Jean Marie Hon, Richard McKenzie, Harry Moses, Michael Mullins, Lucia Strasler, Moe Keale, Elizabeth Smith Anthony Charnota, Richard Venture, David Clennon, Peter Brandon, Sandra Will, Denny Miller
Supplier: Finnegan & Associates, Filmways
Exec Prod: Perry Lafferty;
Prod: William Finnegan;
Dir: Marvin J Chomsky;
Wri: William Wood.
120 Mins, Thurs (12), 9 pm.
NBC-TV
05/18/77

DANGER U X B
With Anthony Andrews, Marice Roeves, Deborah Watling
Supplier: Thames International
Dir: Ferdinand Fairfax;
Prod: John Hawkesworth.
60 Mins, Mon, 9 pm.
Thames-TV, from London, England
02/07/79F

DANIEL FOSTER MD
With Daniel Foster
Supplier: KERA-TV Dallas
Prod: Pat Alexander;
Dir: George Zimmermann.
30 Mins, Wed, 7 pm.
WNET-TV New York
11/16/77

THE DARK SECRET OF HARVEST HOME
(Big Event)
With Bette Davis, David Ackroyd, Rosanna Arquette, Rene Auberjonois, John Calvin, Norman Lloyd, Linda Marsh, Joanna Miles, Michael O'Keefe, Richard Venture, Laurie Prange, Lena Raymond, Tracey Gold, Stephen Joyce, Michael Durell, Martin Shakar, Grayce Grant; voice of Donald Pleasence
Supplier: Universal TV
Prod: Jack Laird;
Dir: Leo Penn;
Wris: Jack Guss, Charles E Israel, (based on Tom Tryon novel).
300 Mins, Mon (23), 9 pm; Tues (24), 8 pm.
NBC-TV
02/01/78

DARK SECRETS
With Linda Mintz, David Stone
Prod-Dir: Julian Craggs.
60 Mins, Mon (14)
WYES-TV New Orleans
03/23/77S

THE DARK SIDE OF INNOCENCE
(NBC Double Feature Night At The Movies)
With Joanna Pettet, Anne Archer, John Anderson, Lawrence Casey, Kim Hunter, Claudette Nevins, Robert Sampson, James Houghton, Ethellin Block, Denise Nickerson, Dennis Bowen, Kristopher Marquis, Tiger Williams, Shane Butterworth, Gail Strickland, Doreen Lang, Peggy Walton
Supplier: Warner Bros. TV
Exec Prod-dir: Jerry Thorpe;
Prod: Philip Mandelker;
Wri: Barbara Turner.
90 Mins, Thurs (20), 9:30 pm.
NBC-TV
05/26/76

DAUGHTERS
(Comedy Time)
With Michael Constantine, Julie Bovasso, Robin Groves, Judy Landers, Olivia Barash, Doug Rowe, Ted Wass
Supplier: Witt-Thomas-Harris Prods
Exec Prods: Paul Junger Witt, Tony Thomas;
Prod-Wri: Susan Harris;
Dir: Bob Claver.
30 Mins, Wed (20), 9:30 pm.
NBC-TV
07/27/77

THE DAVE PATTERSON SHOW
Exec Prod: John Pike;
Dir: Lou Gattozzi.
60 Mins, weekdays, 9 am.
WKYC-TV Cleveland
09/12/79

DAVID CASSIDY - MAN UNDERCOVER
With Simon Oakland, Wendy Rastatter, Ray Vitte, Joe Santos, Brian Kerwin, Alan Vint, Brad Rearden, Joseph Hacker, Christina Hart, Elissa Leeds, Michael A Salcido, Jo DeWinter
Supplier: David Gerber Prods, Columbia Pictures TV
Exec Prod: Gerber;
Prods: Mark Rodgers, Mel Swope;
Dir: Bernard McEveety;
Wri: Sean Baine.
60 Mins Thurs, 10 pm.
NBC TV
11/08/78

DAVID HOROWITZ: CONSUMER BUYLINE
Supplier: Burt Rosen Co
Prod: Lloyd Thaxton.
30 Mins, Sat (14), 6 pm.
WNBC-TV New York
01/18/78S

DAVID NIVEN'S WORLD
With David Niven (host)
Supplier: Survival Anglia (JWT Syndication)
Exec Producer: John Fairley;
Prod-Dir: Peter Taylor;
Wri: Jim DeKay
30 Mins, Wed (4), 5:30 pm.
WABC-TV New York
Miles Labs (JWT)
02/11/76S

THE DAVID SOUL & FRIENDS SPECIAL
With England Dan & John Ford Coley, Donna Summer, Ron Moody, Lynne Marta, Dick Clark
Supplier: Dick Clark Teleshows
Exec Prod: Clark;
Prod: Robert Arthur;
Dirs: Perry Rosemond, Steve Turner;
Wris: Phil Hahn, Arthur.
60 Mins, Thurs (18), 8 pm.
ABC-TV
Dr Pepper; Pentel of America (Y & R)
08/24/77

THE DAVID STEINBERG SHOW
With Bill Saluga
Exec Prod: Arthur Weinthal;
Prod-dir: Perry Rosemond;
Wris: Ziggy Steinbeg, Fernell Silver, Bill Saluga.
30 Mins, Fri, 7:30 pm.
CTV, from Toronto, Canada
11/03/76F

THE DAY MY GRANDDAD DIED
With Jan Rubes, John Horton, Joan Karasevitch, August Schellenberg
Dir: Rene Bonniere;
Wri: Michael John Nimchuk.
60 Mins, Sun, 9 pm.
CBC-TV, from Toronto, Canada
02/09/77F

DAYS OF LIBERTY
Supplier: Tele-Tactics Inc
Prod-dir: Barry Drucker;
Wri: Lawrence Schoen.
60 Mins, Sat, (11), 8 pm.
WABC-TV New York
Burger King (JWT)
12/15/76

DAYTIME STAR
With John Gabriel, Pamela Lincoln, Susan Lucci, Ilene Kristen, Leslie Ann Ray, Joyce Brothers, Michael Levin, Nicholas Benedict, John Aniston, Andrea McArdle, Sandy Gabriel
Supplier: Maramay Prods (American International TV)
Exec Prod: Larry Jacobson;
Prods: Ed Pierce, Don Epstein;
Dir: Elliot Lawrence.
60 Mins, Fri, 10 am.
WABC-TV New York
01/31/79S

THE DEADLIEST SEASON
With Michael Moriarty, Kevin Conway, Sully Boyar, Jill Eikenberry, Walter McGinn, Andrew Duggan, Meryl Streep, Patrick O'Neal, Paul D'Amato
Supplier: Titus Prods
Exec Prod: Herbert Brodkin;
Prod: Robert Berger;
Dir: Robert Markowitz;
Wri: Ernest Kinoy.
120 Mins, Wed (16), 9 pm.
CBS-TV
Xerox (Needham, Harper & Steers)
03/23/77

THE DEADLY GAME
(NBC Saturday Movie)
With David Birney, Burt Young, Allen Garfield, Tom Atkins, Lane Bradbury, Christine Jones, Will Kuluva, Walter McGinn, Mario Roccuzzo, Sydney Lassick, Anthony Charnota, Carl Lee, Richard C. Adams, Paulette Breen
Supplier: Emmet G. Lavery Jr. Prods. & Paramount TV
Prod: Lavery;
Dir-wri: Robert Collins, based on Peter Maas book.
120 Mins, Sat (24), 9 pm.
NBC-TV
04/28/76

DEAN MARTIN CELEBRITY ROAST
With Don Rickles, Orson Welles, Bob Hope, John Wayne, Muhammad Ali, Joe Namath, Rich Little, Tony Orlando, Joey Bishop, Paul Lynde, Angie Dickinson, Sens. Hubert H. Humphrey and Barry Goldwater, Ruth Buzzi, James Stewart, Gene Kelly, Foster Brooks, Howard Cosell, Charlie Callas, Nipsey Russell, Gabe Kaplan, Dan Rowan & Dick Martin, Georgia Engel
Prod-Dir: Greg Garrison;
Wris: Harry Crane, Billy Daley, Howard Albrecht, Sol Weinstein, Milt Rosen, Larry Markes, Terry Hart, Jeffrey Barron, Stan Burns, Mike Marmer.
120 Mins, Fri, 9 pm.
NBC-TV
03/03/76

DEAN MARTIN'S RED HOT SCANDALS OF 1926
With Jonathan Winters, Dom DeLuise, Hermione Baddeley, Abe Vigoda, Georgia Engel, Chalene Ryan, The Golddiggers
Supplier: Sasha Prods & Greg Garrison Prods
Exec Prod: Garrison;
Prod: Lee Hale;
Dirs: Garrison, Robert Sidney;
Wris: Mike Marmer, Stan Burns.
60 Mins, Mon (8), 10 pm.
NBC-TV
11/17/76

DEAR DETECTIVE
With Brenda Vaccaro, Arlen Dean Snyder, Ron Silver, Michael MacRae, John Dennis Johnston, Jack Ging, Leslie Woods, Jet Yardum, Constance Forslund, R G Armstrong, Steven McNally, Corinne Conley, M Emmet Walsh, others
Supplier: Kibbee & Hargrove Prods and Viacom
Prods-Wris: Dean Hargrove, Roland Kibbee;
Dir: Hargrove.
120 Mins, Wed (28), 9 pm.
CBS-TV
04/04/79

DEATH OF A PRINCESS
(World)
With Paul Freeman, Zia Mohyeddin, Judy Parfitt, Paul Copley, Salah Jaheen, Suzanne Abou Taleb, Mohammed Tewfik
Supplier: WGBH-TV Boston, ATV & Telepictures Corp.
Exec Prod: David Fanning;
Prods: Martin McKeand, Anthony Thomas;
Dir: Thomas;
Wris: Thomas, Fanning.
120 Mins, Mon, (12) 8 pm.
WNET-TV New York (PBS)
05/14/80

DEATH TRAP
With Vincent Price (host)
Supplier: Oxford Scientific Films & Swan Prods (Juno Films Ltd)
Dir-Wris: Hugh Falkus, Bill Travers, James Hill.
60 Mins, Thurs (28), 8 pm.
NBC-TV
05/04/77

THE DEFECTION OF SIMAS KUDIRKA
With Alan Arkin, Richard Jordan, Donald Pleasence, George Dzundza, John McMartin, Shirley Knight, Marvin Silbersher, Peter Evans, Ted Shackleford, Barton Heyman, Jack Blessing, Nicholas Guest, Matthew Arkin, Salem Ludwig
Supplier: Jozak & Paramount TV
Exec Prods: Gerald I Eisenbeg, Gerald W Abrams;
Prod: Richard Briggs;
Dir: David Lowell Rich;
Wri: Bruce Feldman.
120 Mins, Mon (23), 9 pm.
CBS-TV
United Technologies (Visualscope) & Allstate Insurance (Leo Burnett)
02/01/78

DELTA HOUSE
With John Vernon, Stephen Furst, Bruce McGill, Jamie Widdoes, Josh Mostel, Peter Fox, Gary Cookson, Brian Patrick Clarke, Priscilla Lauris, Richard Seer, Susanna Dalton, Wendy Goldman, Lee Wilkof, others
Supplier: Matty Simmons-Ivan Reitman Prods & Universal TV
Exec Prods: Simmons, Reitman;
Prod: Edward J Montagne;
Dir: Alan Myerson;
Wris: Harold Ramis, Douglas Kenney, Chris Miller.
30 Mins, Thurs (18), 8:30 pm.
ABC-TV
01/24/79

DELVECCHIO
With Judd Hirsch, Charles Haid, Michael Conrad, Mario Gallo, James J Sloyan, Henry Brown, Bruce Kirby, George Memmoli, Tony Burton, Frank Doubleday, Connie Sawyer
Supplier: Crescendo Prods & Universal TV
Exec Prod: William Sackheim;
Prods: Steven Bochco, Michael Rhodes;
Dir: Jerry London;
Wri: Joseph Polizzi.
60 Mins, Thurs (9), 9 pm.
CBS-TV
09/15/76

DENISE
With Jack Hynes (narr)
Supplier: BBI Communications
Exec Prod: Philip Scribner Balboni
Prod: Mishka Harnden;
Wri: Jean P. Boucualt, Harnden.
60 Mins, Fri, (25) 9 pm.
07/30/80S

DENNY'S SHO
With Denny Doherty
Prod-Dir: Jack O'Neill;
Wri: Elaine Linds.
30 Mins, Thurs, 9 pm.
CBC-TV, from Halifax
08/09/78F

THE DEPARTMENT
With Peter Sumner, John Ewart, Phillip Ross, Grant Dodwell, Russell Newman, Barbara Stephens, Tony Blackett, Richard Moir, Brian Young, Howard Vernon
Supplier: Australian Broadcasting Commission
Exec Prod: Alan Burke;
Dir: Brian Bell;
Wri: David Williamson.
65 Mins, Sun, 8:30 pm.
ABC (Australia) TV, Channel 2, Sydney
08/06/80F

DEPARTMENTAL
With Ray Barrett, Martin Vaughan, Gary Day, Rod Williams
Supplier: Australian Broadcasting Commission
Exec Prod: Alan Burke;
Dir: Keith Wilkes;
Wri: Mervyn Rutherford.
70 Mins, Sun, 8:30 pm.
ABC (Australia) Channel 2, Sydney
09/03/80F

THE DEPTFORD TRILOGY
With Eric House, Eric Peterson, Ruth Springford, Chris Wiggins, Zoe Caldwell, Barry Morse, Henry Ramer, Clare Coulter, Douglas Rain
Exec Prod: John Douglas;
Prod-Dir: Ron Hartmann;
Wri: Adapted by Hartmann from Robertson Davies' novels "Fifth Business," "The Manticore," "World of Wonders."
120 Mins, Mon, 9:05 pm.
CBC, Toronto, Canada
04/02/80F

DER GEIST DER MIRABELLE
(The Spirit Of Mirabelle)
With Wolfgang Buettner, Johanna Hofer, Wolfgang Kieling, Monica Bleibtreu, Hans Michael Rehberg, others
Supplier: Zweites Deutsches Fernsehen (ZDF), Wiesbaden-Mainz
Eberhard Pieper;
Wri: Pieper, adapted from Siegfried Lenz's story.
100 Mins, Sun (24), 8 pm.
ZDF-TV, from Wiesbaden-Mainz, West Germany
01/10/79F

DETECTIVE SCHOOL
With Randolph Mantooth, LaWanda Page, Jo Ann Harris, Douglas V Fowley, Pat Proft, Taylor Negron, James Gregory, Ivor Francis
Supplier: Kukoff-Harris Partnership
Exec Prods-Dirs-Wris: Bernie Kukoff, Jeff Harris.
Prod: Hank Bradford.
30 Mins, Tues, 8:30 pm.
ABC-TV
08/08/79

THE DEVIL AND DANIEL MOUSE
With the voices of Chris Wiggins, Jim Henshaw, Annabelle Kershaw, Martin Lavut, John Sebastian
Exec Prod: Jeffrey Kirsch;
Prod: Martin Hirsh;
Dir: Clive Smith;
Wri: Ken Sobol.
30 Mins, Sun, 7:30 pm.
CBC, from Toronto, Canada
10/18/78S

THE DEVIL'S CROWN
With Brian Cox, Michael Byrne, Jane Lapotaire, John Duttine
Supplier: BBC-TV
Prod: Richard Beynon;
Wris: Ken Taylor, Jack Russell.
55 Mins, Sun, 10:20 pm.
BBC-2, from London, England
07/05/78F

DIAHANN CARROLL SHOW
With Telly Savalas, Jon Lucien, Sammy Davis Jr, Carl Jablonski Dancers
Supplier: Su Mo Prods
Exec Prods: Robert DeLeon, Max Youngstein;
Prod: Ray Aghayan;
Dir: Mark Warren;
Wris: Jeremy Stevens, Tom Moore.
60 Mins, Sat, 10 pm.
CBS-TV
08/18/76

DIARY OF THE CANNES FILM FESTIVAL
With Rex Reed
Supplier; ITC
Prod: Billy Baxter;
Dir: Iain Johnstone.
60 Mins, Fri, July 18
ATV, From England
07/23/80F

DICK CAVETT SHOW
With Sophia Loren, Marcello Mastroianni
Supplier: Daphne Productions and WNET New York
Exec Prod: Joan Konner;
Prod: Christopher Porterfield;
Dir: Gordon Rigsby.
30 Mins, Mon-Fri, 11 pm.
PBS
10/12/77

DICK CLARK'S LIVE WEDNESDAY
With Clark (host), Kristy & Jimmy McNichol, Rick Nelson, Diana Ross, L A Rams Cheerleaders, Dar Robinson, Johnny Yune, Tiny Tim, Doc Severinsen, Paul Williams, Erik Estrada
Supplier: Dick Clark Co
Exec Prod: Clark;
Prod: Bill Lee;
Dir: John Moffitt.
60 Mins, Wed, 8 pm.
NBC-TV
09/27/78

THE DICK CURTIS PARTY
With Dick Curtis, host; Leslie Gore, Colleen Sharp, Marsha Richardson, Gaylord Marshall, Tiffany Gildred, Mark Franklin & Co
Prod-wri: Curtis;
Dir: Tom Johnson.
60 Mins, Fri, 9 pm.
WFAA-TV Dallas
08/18/76

DICKENS OF LONDON
With Roy Dotrice, Diana Coupland, others
Supplier: Yorkshire Television
Exec Prod: David Cunliffe;
Prod-dir: Marc Miller;
Wri: Wolf Mankowitz.
60 Mins, Tues, 9 pm.
ITV Network, Britain
10/06/76F

DID YOU HEAR ABOUT JOSH & KELLY?
With Dennis Dugan, Jane Daly, Jimmie Samuels, Denise Galik, Dawson Mays, Cliff Norton, Arthur Julian
Supplier: Hal Cooper-Rod Parker-Elmar Prods
Exec Prods: Cooper, Parker;
Dir: Cooper;
Wri: Parker.
30 Mins, Mon (13) 8 pm.
CBS-TV
10/22/80

DIE ROTE LEINWAND
(The Red Screen)
Supplier: Westdeutsches Fernsehen, Sender Freies Berlin
Prod: Westdeutsches Fernsehen, Sender Freies Berlin;
Dir-narr: Peter B. Schumann;
7 Hours (in 4 parts)
WDR, Third Program, from Cologne, West Germany
06/09/76F

DIFFERENT AS NIGHT AND DAY
With Greg & Bryant Gumbel
Prod-Dir: Sandra Weir;
Wirs: Mike Downey, Brian Hewitt.
60 Mins, Fri (5) 9 pm.
WMAQ-TV Chicago
09/17/80

DIFF'RENT STROKES
With Conrad Bain, Gary Coleman, Todd Bridges, Dana Plato, Charlotte Rae
Supplier: Tandem Prods
Exec Prod: Budd Grossman;
Prods: Howard Leeds, Herbert Kenwith;
Dir: Kenwith;
Wri: Ben Starr.
30 Mins, Fri, 8 pm.
NBC-TV
11/08/78

DINAH & HER NEW BEST FRIENDS
With Dinah Shore (host), Jean Stapleton, Carol Burnett, Diana Canova, Bruce Kimmel, Gary Mule Deer, Mike Neun, Leland Palmer, Michael Preminger
Supplier: Tullahoma Prods.
Exec Prod: Henry Jaffe;
Prod: Carolyn Raskin;
Dir: Jeff Margolis;
Wris: Don Hinkley & Peter Galley, Mort Scharfman, George Tricker & Neil Rosen, Bob Arnott.
60 Mins, Sat, 10 pm.
CBS-TV
06/09/76

THE DIONNE QUINTUPLETS
With Pierre Berton
Exec Prods: Paul Wright, Peter Kadadodis;
Prod-Dir: Donald Britain;
Wri: Berton.
90 Mins, Sun, 9:30 pm.
CBC, from Toronto, Canada
12/06/78F

DIRECTION '78: MORALITY OF TELEVISION
With Robert Mulholland, Daniel Schorr, Martin Agronsky, Virginia Carter, Harlan Ellison
Supplier: WYES-TV New Orleans
Prod-Dir: David Frentz.
60 Mins, Sun (10), 2 pm.
PBS
09/13/78

THE DISAPPEARANCE OF AIMEE
(Hallmark Hall of Fame)
With Faye Dunaway, Bette Davis, James J. Sloyan, James Woods, John Lehne, Lelia Goldoni, Severn Darden, William Jordan, Sandy Ward, Barry Brown
Supplier: Tomorrow Entertainment
Exec Prod: Thomas W. Moore;
Prod: Paul Leaf;
Dir: Anthony Harvey;
Wri: John McGreevey.
120 Mins, Wed (17), 8 pm.
NBC-TV
Hallmark (Foote Cone & Belding)
11/24/76

DISCO BEAVER FROM OUTER SPACE
With Alica Playten, Pete Elbling, Rodger Bumpass, Lee Wilkof, Peter Simmons, Sarah Durkee, Lynn Redgrave, Jamie Widdoes
Supplier: National Lampoon
Exec Prod: Matty Simmons;
Prod: Tony Hendra;
Dir: Joshua White;
Wris: Elbling, Jeff Greenfield, Ted Mann, Harvey Shearer, John Weidman.
60 Mins, Fri (23), 10 pm.
HBO
02/21/79PC

DISCO MAGIC
With Evelyn "Champagne" King (host), Jimmy "Bo" Horne
Supplier: Marcus-Wohl Prods (Alfred Haber)
Exec Prod: Steve Marcus, Arnie Wohl.
30 Mins, Tues (12), 7:30 pm.
WCBS-TV New York
09/20/78S

DISRAELI
With Ian McShane, Mary Peach, Rosemary Leach, John Carlisle, others
Supplier: ITC Entertainment
Dir: Claude Whatham;
Prod: Cecil Clarke;
Wri: David Butler.
45 Mins, Tues, 8:45 pm.
ATV, from England
11/01/78F

DO YA KNOW WHERE JIMMY CARTER LIVES?
With Denis Touhy, reporter
Supplier: BBC TV, London
Prod: Patricia Meehan;
Wri: Touhy.
50 Mins, Sun (22), 4:05 pm.
BBC-1, Britain
02/01/78F

DO YOU REMEMBER VIETNAM?
With John Pilger, narrator
Supplier: ITC
Prod-Dir: David Munro.
60 Mins, Tues, 9 pm.
ATV, from England
10/18/78F

DOCTOR FRANKEN
(Sunday Big Event)
With Robert Vaughn, Robert Perault, David Selby, Teri Garr, Josef Sommer, Cynthia Harris
Supplier: Titus Prods. & Janus Prods.
Exec Prod: Herbert Brodkin;
Prod: Robert Berger;
Dir: Marvin J. Chomsky, Jeff Lieberman;
Wri: Lee Thomas.
120 Mins, Sun, (13), 9 pm.
NBC-TV
01/23/80

DR NORMAN BETHUNE
With Gerald Tannenbaum
120 Mins, Sun, 2 pm.
CBC, from Toronto, Canada
05/09/79F

DR. SCORPION
(ABC Friday Night Movie)
With Nick Mancuso, Christine Lahti, Richard T Herd, Sandra Kerns, Roscoe Lee Browne, Bill Lucking, Granville Van Dusen, Philip Sterling, Lincoln Kilpatrick, Denny Miller, Joseph Ruskin, James Murtaugh, James Hong, Eric Server
Supplier: Stephen J Cannell Prods & Universal TV
Exec Prod-Wri: Cannell;
Prod: Alex Beaton;
Dir: Richard Lang.
120 Mins, Fri (24), 9 pm.
ABC-TV
03/01/78

DR. SEUSS' PONTOFFEL POCK, WHERE ARE YOU?
With voices of Wayne Morton, Ken Lundie, Hal Smith, Don Messick, Sue Allen, Joe Raposo
Supplier: De Patie-Freleng Prods
Exec Prods: David H. Depatie, Friz Freleng;
Prod-Wri: Ted Geisel;
Dir: Gerald Baldwin.
30 Mins, Fri, (2) 8:30 pm.
ABC-TV
05/07/80

DR STRANGE
With Peter Hooten, Jessica Walter, Eddie Benton, Clyde Kusatsu, John Mills, David Hooks, June Barrett, Philip Sterling, Diana Webster, Blake Marion, Bob Delegall, Larry Anderson, Michael Clark, Lady Rowlands
Supplier: Universal TV
Exec Prod-Dir-Wri: Philip DeGuere.
Prod: Alex Beaton.
120 Mins, Wed (6), 8 pm.
CBS-TV
09/13/78

DOCTOR WHO
With Tom Baker, Elisabeth Sladen, Michael Kilgarriff, Nicholas Courtney, Edward Burnham
Supplier: BBC-TV, Time-Life TV
Prod: Barry Letts;
Dir: Christopher Barry;
Wri: Terrance Dicks.
30 Mins, Sat, 6:30 pm.
WOR-TV New York
10/25/78S

DOCTORS' PRIVATE LIVES
With Ed Nelson, John Gavin, Randolph Powell, Phil Levien, Gwen Humble, Eddie Benton, Laraine Stephens, Tracy Reed, Natalie Schafer, William Smithers
Supplier: David Gerber Prods & Columbia Pictures TV
Exec Prod: Gerber;
Prod: Matthew Rapf;
Dir: Marc Daniels;
Wri: James Henerson.
60 Mins, Thurs, 10 pm.
ABC-TV
04/11/79

DOG & CAT
With Lou Antonio, Kim Basinger, Matt Clark, Joh Cypher, Veronica Hamel, Gene Conforti, Gilbert Green, Ben Jeffrey
Supplier: Largo Prods
Exec Prod: Lawrence Gordon;
Prod: Robert Singer;
Dir: Michael Preece;
Wri: Larry Alexander.
60 Mins, Sat, 10 pm.
ABC-TV
03/09/77

DOIN' TIME
Exec Prod: William Cosmas;
Prods: Holly Fine, Paul Fine;
Wris: Marianna Spicer, Ed Turney.
60 Mins, Thurs, 9 pm.
WJLA-TV, Washington
11/12/80

THE $1.98 BEAUTY SHOW
With Rip Taylor (host), Suzy Chaffee, Erik Estrada, Joyce Haber
Supplier: Chuck Barris Prods
Exec Prod: Barris;
Prod: Gene Banks;
Dir: John Dorsey.
30 Mins, Tues, 7:30 pm.
WNBC-TV New York
09/06/78S

DOLLY
With Dolly Parton, The Hues Corporation
Supplier: Show Biz Inc
Prods: Bill Graham, Reg Dunlap;
Dir: Bill Turner;
Wris: Graham, Paul Elliott.
30 Mins, Sat, 11 pm.
WNEW-TV New York
09/15/76S

DOLLY & CAROL IN NASHVILLE
With Carol Burnett, Dolly Parton, B C M Choir, Joe Layton Dancers
Supplier: Jocar Prods
Exec Prod: Joe Hamilton;
Prods: Ken & Mitzie Welch, Layton;
Dir: Roger Beatty;
Wris: The Welches, Beatty.
60 Mins, Wed (14), 10 pm.
CBS-TV
02/21/79

DON GIOVANNI
With Benjamin Luxon, Stafford Dean, Horianna Branisteanu, Leo Goeke, Rachel Yakar, John Rawnsley, Elizabeth Gale, Pierre Thad Glyndebourne Chorus, London Philharmonic conducted by Bernard Haitink
Supplier: Southern-TV
Prod: David Heather.
190 Mins, Wed, 9:30 pm.
ITV Network, from England
09/27/78F

DON HO SHOW
Supplier: Bob Banner Associates
Exec Prod: Banner;
Prod: Brad Lachman;
Dir: Jack Regas;
Wris: George Atkins, Jay Burton.
30 Mins, Mon-Fri, noon.
ABC-TV
11/10/76

DON KIRSHNER PRESENTS NEW STARS
With Frankie Avalon (host), Tony Orlando, Kirshner, Lisa Hartman, Buzby & Berkeley, Marion Ramsey
Supplier: Don Kirshner Prods. & Viacom Enterprises
Exec Prod: Kirshner;
Prod-Dir: Bob Wynn;
Wri: Bob O'Brien.
30 Mins, Tues (3), 7:30 pm.
WNBC-TV New York
02/11/76S

THE DONNA FARGO SHOW
With Tom Biener, Tammy Wynette
Supplier: Osmond Television Prods & Metromedia Producers Corp
Exec Prod: Osmond Bros;
Prod: Biener;
Dir: Rick Bennewitz;
Wris: George Geiger, David Brown.
30 Mins, Sat, 11 pm.
WNEW-TV New York
10/04/78S

DONNY AND MARIE
With Donny and Marie Osmond, Lee Majors, The Osmond Brothers, The Ice Vanities, Farah Fawcett-Majors, Paul Lynde
Supplier: Osmond Prods. & Sid and Marty Krofft Prods.
Exec Prod: Raymond Katz;
Prods: Sid and Marty Krofft;
Dir: Art Fisher;
Wris: William Larkin, Gary Ferrier, Aubrey Todman, Walter Dalton, Shelley Zellman.
60 Mins, Tues, 9 pm.
ABC-TV
01/28/76

DON'T ASK US
With Brian Hannan, Julie McGregor, Liddy Clark, David Whitford, Doug Scroope, David Hough
Prod-Dir: Austin Steele.
30 Mins, Wed, 9 pm.
ATN7 Sydney, Australia
06/27/79F

DON'T FORGET-JE ME SOUVIENS
(For The Record)
With Len Cariou, Lousie Marleau, Gilles Renaud, Peter Jobin
Exec Prod: Sam Levene;
Prod: Gary Plaxton;
Dir: Robin Spry;
Wri: Carmel Dumas.
60 Mins, Sun, 9 pm.
CBC, from Toronto, Canada
03/07/79F

THE DOOLEY BROTHERS
With Garrett M Brown, Robert Peirce, John Myhers, Shelly Long, Dub Taylor, Pete Schrum, Rusty Lee, Grizzly Green
Supplier: Arnold Margolin Prods & The Bud Austin Co
Prod-Wri: Margolin;
Dir: Don Weis.
30 Mins, Tues (31), 8 pm.
CBS-TV
08/08/79

DOROTHEA MERZ
With Sabine Sinjen, Dieter Wernecke, Fritz Rasp
Supplier: Westdeutsches Fernsehen (WDR), Cologne
Prod: Westdeutsches Fernsehen (WDR), Cologne;
Dirs: Peter Beauvais, Ursula Ehler;
Wri: Tankred Dorst.
170 Mins, Sun, 8:15 pm.
WDR, from Cologne, West Germany
06/09/76F

DOROTHY
With Dorothy Loudon, Linda Manz, Elissa Leeds, Susan Brecht, Michele Greene, Russell Nype, Priscilla Morrill, Kenneth Gilman
Supplier: The Konigsberg Co, David Carroll Communications & Warner Bros TV
Exec Prods: Bob Carroll Jr, Madelyn Davis, Frank Konigsberg;
CoProd: Jerry Madden;
Dir: John Rich;
Wris: Rick Hawkins, Liz Sage.
30 Mins, Wed, 8 pm.
CBS-TV
08/15/79

DOROTHY FULDHEIM AT HOME
With Fred Griffith
Prods: Bill Baker, Jane Temple Hughes;
Dir: Mike Bachman.
30 Mins, Sat, 10 pm.
WEWS-TV Cleveland
07/14/76

THE DOROTHY HAMILL SPECIAL
With Gene Kelly, Jim McKay, Carrie Weber
Supplier: Smith-Hemion Prods
Exec Prod: Jerry Weintraub;
Prods: Gary Smith, Dwight Hemion;
Dir: Hemion;
Wri: Alan Kohan.
60 Mins, Wed (17), 8 pm.
ABC-TV
Metropolitan Life (Y&R), Bristol-Myers (Boclaro)
11/24/76

DOUBLE DARE
With Alex Trebek, host
Supplier: Goodson-Todman Prods
Exec Prod: Jay Wolpert;
Prod: Jonathan Goodson;
Dir: Marc Breslow.
30 Mins, Mon-Fri, 11 am.
CBS-TV
12/22/76

DOWN HOME
With Robert Hooks, Madge Sinclair, Beah Richards, Lincoln Kilpatrick, Kevin Hooks, Eric Hooks, Beverly Hope Atkinson, Sonny Jim Gaines, Anne Seymour, Edward Binns, Norma Connolly, Tia Rance, Dena Crowder, Woodrow Parfrey, William Watson, Paul Koslo, Timothy Scott
Supplier: MTM Prods
Prod: Phil Barry;
Dir: Fielder Cook;
Wri: Melvin Van Peebles.
60 Mins, Wed (16), 8 pm.
CBS-TV
08/23/78

DREAMSPEAKER
With Ian Tracey, George Clutesi, Jacques Hubert, others
Prod: Ralph L Thomas;
Dir: Claude Jutra;
Wri: Cam Hubert.
90 Mins, Sun, 9:30 pm.
CBC, from Vancouver Canada
02/02/77F

THE DRIFTING REED
(Ashibune)
With Fukuko Sayo, Hiroki Iwase, Takahiro Tammura, Mariko Fuji
Supplier: NKH (Japan Broadcasting Corp)
Prod: Shigenori Waki;
Dir: Masaaki Tamura;
Wri: Tsutomu Minakami;
Comp: Teizo Matsumura.
35 Mins.
(RAI winner, music)
10/03/79PI

DRYING UP THE STREETS
With Don Francks, Len Cariou, Jayne Eastwood, August Schellenberg, Calvin Butler, Sarah Torgov, Jacques Hubert, Warren Davis
Exec Prod: Ralph Thomas;
Dir: Robin Spry;
Wri: B A Cameron.
90 Mins, Wed, 9:30 pm.
CBC-TV, from Toronto, Canada
03/07/79F

THE DUKE
With Robert Conrad, Larry Manetti, Red West, Patricia Conwell, Michael Baseleon, Joey Green, Peter Haskell, Frederick Herrick, Daphne Maxwell, Percy Rodrigues, Ed O'Bradovich
Supplier: Stephen J Cannell Prods & Universal TV
Exec Prod-Wri: Cannell;
Supv Prod: Alex Beaton;
Prods: Don Carlos Dunaway, J Rickley Dumm;
Dir: Lawrence Doheny.
120 Mins Thurs (5), 9:30 pm.
NBC-TV
04/11/79

DUKES OF DIXIELAND & FRIENDS
With N.O. Pops Orch
Prod-Dir: John Beyer.
73 1/2 Mins, Wed, 9:10 pm.
WYES-TV New Orleans (for PBS)
03/19/80

THE DUKES OF HAZZARD
With Tom Wopat, John Schneider, Catherine Bach, Denver Pyle, James Best, Sorrell Booke, Waylon Jennings, Ben Jones, Sonny Schroyer, Tisch Raye, Ernie Brown
Supplier: Paul R Picard Prods, Piggy Prods & Warner Bros TV
Exec Prods: Picard, Philip Mandelker;
Supv Prod: Joseph Gantman;
Prods: Gy Waldron, Bill Kelley;
Dir: Rod Amateau;
Wri: Waldron.
60 Mins, Fri, 9 pm.
CBS-TV
01/31/79

DUMMY
With Geraldine James
Supplier: ATV Network
Prod-Dir: Franc Roddam;
Wri: Hugh Whitemore.
90 Mins, Wed, 8:30 pm.
ITV, from Birmingham, England
11/16/77F

THE DUMPLINGS
With James Coco, Geraldine Brooks, George S. Irving, George Furth, Marcia Rodd, Jane Connell, Mort Marshall
Supplier: T.A.T. Communications & NRW Prods.
Prod-Wris: Don Nicholl, Michael Ross, Bernie West;
Dir: Paul Bogart.
30 Mins, Wed, 9:30 pm.
NBC-TV
02/04/76

THE DUPONT-COLUMBIA AWARDS
With Charlayne Hunter Gault, host
Supplier: WNET-TV New York
Prod: Gail Macandrew;
Dir: Jon Merdin.
120 Mins, Tues (14), 9:30 pm.
PBS
02/22/78

DYING
Exec Prod: Michael Ambrosino;
Prod-dir: Michael Roemer.
97 Mins, Thurs, 9 pm.
WGBH-TV Boston
05/12/76

DYNASTY
(NBC Saturday Night At The Movies)
With Sarah Miles, Stacy Keach, Harris Yulin, Harrison Ford, Amy Irving, Granville Van Dusen, Charles Weldon, Gerrit Graham, Stanley Clay, Tony Swartz, John Carter, others
Supplier: David Paradine TV Prods. & Marjay Prods.
Exec Prod: David Frost;
Prod: Buck Houghton;
Dir: Lee Philips;
Wri: Sidney Carroll, from James A. Michener's story.
120 Mins, Sat (13), 9 pm.
NBC-TV
03/17/76

THE EAGLE OF THE NINTH
(Frontier Fort)
Anthony Higgins, Bernard Gallagher, Matthew Long, Laura Graham, others
Supplier: BBC
Prod: Phari MacLaren;
Dir: Michael Simpson;
Wri: Bill Craig.
30 Mins, Sun, 5:45 pm.
BBC, Scotland
09/21/77F

EAST OF THE CITY...WEST OF THE SEA
Exec Prod: Dan Sitarski;
Prod: Colin Hill;
Dir: Robert Lopez.
30 Mins Tues (21), 7:30 pm.
WCAU-TV Philadelphia
11/22/78

THE EASTER BUNNY IS COMIN' TO TOWN
With voices of Fred Astaire, Skip Hinnant, Robert McFadden, Allen Swift, Ron Marshall, Jill Choder, Raymond Owens, Meg Sargent, James Spies, Karen Dahle, Michael McGovern,
Supplier: Rankin Bass Prods
Prod-Dirs: Arthur Rankin Jr, Jules Bass;
Wri: Romeo Muller.
60 Mins, Wed (6), 8 pm.
ABC-TV
04/13/77

EASTER FEVER
With voices of Garrett Morris, Maurice Lamoch, others
Suppliers: Nelvana Prods (Viacom)
Exec Prods: Robert Foster, Ted Kernaghan, Nigel Martin;
Prods: Patrick Loubert, Michael Hirsch;
Dirs: Gian Celestri, Greg Duffell;
Wri: Larry Mollin.
30 Mins, Wed, (26) 7:30 pm.
WNBC-TV New York
04/02/80S

EASY DOES IT - STARRING FRANKIE AVALON
With Andy Griffith, Annette Funicello, Vic Glazer, The War Babies, Tim Reed
Supplier: Dick Clark Teleshows
Exec Prod: Clark;
Prods: Bill Lee, Bob Arthur;
Dir: John Moffitt;
Wris: John Boni, Norman Stiles, Thad Mumford, Barry Adelman, Barry Silver.
30 Mins, Wed, 8:30 pm.
CBS-TV
09/01/76

EBONY, IVORY & JADE
With Bert Convy, Debbie Allen, Martha Smith, Claude Akins, David Brenner, Frankie Valli, Donald Moffat, Nina Foch, Clifford David, Nicolas Coster, Lucille Benson, Ji-Tu Cumbuka, Ted Shackelford, Quinn Redecker, Ray Guth
Supplier: Frankel Films
Exec Prod: Ernie Frankel;
Prod: Jimmy Sangster;
Dir: John L Moxey;
Wris: Annie Scott, D D Cooper, Sangster.
90 Mins, Fri (3), 9:30 pm.
CBS-TV
08/08/79

ECHOES BRIGHT AND CLEAR: A DISCOVERY OF AMERICAN MUSIC
With Benny Goodman (host narrator)
Prod: Herbert Seltz;
Dir: Mickey Klein.
60 Mins, Wed (16), 8 pm.
PBS
J.C. Penney Co (underwriter)
06/23/76

ED KELLY AND THE FIGHTING 47TH
With Walter Jacobson, narrator
Prod-Dir: Scott Craig;
Wri: Michael Flannery.
60 Mins, Sun (17), 7 pm.
WBBM-TV Chicago
06/27/79

EDDIE CAPRA MYSTERIES: NIGHTMARE AT PENDRAGON'S CASTLE
(NBC Movie Of The Week)
With Vincent Baggetta, Wendy Phillips, Ken Swofford, Michael Horton, Seven Ann McDonald, John Considine, George Hamilton, Robert Hogan, Janet Margolin, Lois Nettleton, Gerald S O'Loughlin, Stella Stevens, Robert Vaughn, Robert Walker, Michael Conrad, Ivor Francis, Titos Vandis, Jeff David, Lynne Topping, Louis Guss
Supplier: Universal TV
Prod-Wri: Peter S Fischer.
Dir: James Frawley.
120 Mins, Fri (8), 9 pm.
NBC-TV
09/13/78

EDWARD AND MRS SIMPSON
With Edward Fox, Cynthia Harris, Marius Goring, Cherie Lunghi, others
Supplier: Thames TV International
Prod: Andrew Brown;
Dir: Waris Hussein.
60 Mins, Wed, 9 pm.
Thames-TV, from London, England
11/22/78F

EIGHT IS ENOUGH
With Dick Van Patten, Diana Hyland, Mark Hamill, Susan Richardson, Lauri Walters, Lani O'Grady, Kimberly Beck, Connie Newton, Chris English, Adam Rich, Michael Thoma, Virginia Vincent, Lucy Saroyan, Charles Aidman
Supplier: Lorimar Prods
Exec Prod: Lee Rich;
Prod: Hal Sitowitz;
Dir: E W Swackhamer;
Wri: William Blinn, based on book by Thomas W Braden.
60 Mins, Tues (15), 8:30 pm.
ABC-TV
03/23/77

EIN ALTES MODELL
(An Old Model)
With Erwin Geschonneck
Supplier: DDR-TV, East Berlin
Dir: Ulrich Thein;
Wri: Joachim Nowotny.
70 Mins, Sun, 9 pm.
DDR-TV, from East Berlin, East Germany
09/06/78F

EISCHIED - PART 1
With Joe Don Baker, Alan Oppenheimer, Alan Fudge, Eddie Egan, Suzanne Lederer, Vincent Bufano, Waldo, Karen Valentine, James Stephens, Raymond Burr, Laraine Stephens, Tom Ewell, Vincent Baggetta, Ellen Travolta, Joe Cirillo, Sheila DeWindt, Ben Frank, Jonathan Goldsmith, Roger Robinson
Supplier: David Gerber Prods & Columbia Pictures TV
Exec Prod: Gerber;
Supv Prod: Matthew Rapf;
Prod: Jay Daniel;
Dir: Bob Kelljan;
Wri: Mark Rodgers.
120 Mins, Fri (21), 9 pm.
NBC-TV
09/26/79

EKSILEEN AKJAMM: WELCOME HOME
With Malcolm Poindexter
Exec Prod: Susan Horowitz;
Prod-Dir: Hal Yates;
Wri-Narr: Poindexter.
60 Mins, Tues, 8 pm.
KYW-TV Philadelphia
07/06/77

EL CABALLERO DE LA MANO EN EL PECHO
(El Greco in Toledo)
With Jose Maria Rodero, Nuria Torray, Jose Maria Prada, Tomas Blanco, Manual Gallardo, Candida Losada, Miguel Angel
Supplier: Spanish Television
Dir-Wri: Juan Guerrero Zamora.
120 Mins, Sun, 10:15 pm.
TVE, Spain
03/09/77F

EL DERECHO DE ASILO
(Political Asylum)
With Jabier Elorriaga, Susana Mara, Agustin Gonzalez, Jose Maria Caffarel, Luis Ciges, Jose Ruiz Lifante, Felix Herranz, Jose Riesgo
Supplier: Spanish Radiotelevision
Dir: Pascual Cervera;
Wri: Story by Alejo Carpentier adapted by Solly Wolodarsky.
55 Mins, Sun, 11 pm.
TVE, Channel 1, Madrid, Spain
10/03/79F

ELEANOR & FRANKLIN
(ABC Theatre)
With Jane Alexander, Edward Herrmann, Rosemary Murphy, Pamela Franklin, David Huffman, Mackenzie Phillips, Lilia Skala, Ed Flanders, others
Supplier: Talent Associates
Exec Prod: David Susskind;
Prods: Harry R. Sherman, Audrey Maas;
Dir: Daniel Petrie;
Wri: James Costigan.
200 Min, Sun (10), 9 pm, & Mon (11), 9 pm.
ABC-TV
01/14/76

ELEANOR & FRANKLIN: THE WHITE HOUSE YEARS
With Jane Alexander, Edward Herrmann, Priscilla Pointer, Walter McGinn, Rosemary Murphy, Blair Brown, David Healy, Toni Darnay, others
Supplier: Talent Associates
Exec Prod: David Susskind;
Prod: Harry R Sherman;
Dir: Daniel Petrie;
Wri: James Costigan.
180 Mins, Sun (13), 8 pm.
ABC-TV
IBM (Conahay & Lyon)
03/16/77

ELECTRIC FUZZ
With the Bob Elnicky Puppets (Bob Elnicky, Olga Felemacher, Craig Marin and Roman Paska, puppeteers)
Supplier: WRC-TV
Exec Prod: J Clifford Curley;
Wri-Prod: Bary Hurd;
Dir: Ray Williams.
30 Mins, Fri (7), 7:30 pm.
WRC-TV Washington
12/26/79

ELECTRONICLE
With Michael Boyle, Robert Schulman, Steve Isaacs, Charles Bailey, John Finnegan, others
Prod: Georgianna Day;
Exec Prod: Jim Russell;
Dir: Chuck Waggoner.
30 Mins, Tues, 7:30 pm.
KTCA-TV St Paul-Minneapolis
05/14/80

ELEGIES ON THE DEATHS OF THREE SPANISH POETS
(Elegien auf Tod dreir spanischer Dichter)
With Christobal Halffter
Supplier: ZDF (West Germany)
Prod: Adalbert Wellnitz (Allegro films, Calsart);
Dir-Wri: Christopher Nupen;
Mus: Halfter.
40 Mins.
(RAI Prizewinner, Music)
10/08/80PI

THE EMIGRANTS
With Michael Craig, Sheila Reid, Brian Deacon, Penne Hackforth-Jones, Leslie Manville, Simon Gipps-Kent, Joe Ritchie, Gordon McDougall, Alister Smart, Lyn James, Peter Gwynne, Graham Rouse, Joan Bruce, Drew Forsythe, Tina Bursill, Willie Fennell
Supplier: Australian Broadcasting Commission
Prods: Frank Hatherly (BBC), Eric Tayler (ABC);
Dirs: David Giles, Tayler;
Wris: Brian Phelan, Charles Stamp, Peter Kenna, Keith Dewhurst.
ABC (Australia)
06/08/77F

EMMET OTTER'S JUG-BAND CHRISTMAS
With Jim Henson Muppets (voices of Frank Oz, Jerry Nelson, Richard Hunt, Dave Goetz, Henson, Marilyn Sokol)
Supplier: Henson Associates
Exec Prod: David Lazer
Prod-Dir: Henson
Wri: Jerry Juhl, based on Russell & Lillian Hoban's book
60 Min, Mon, (15), 8 pm.
ABC-TV
12/24/80

THE EMPEROR OF ATLANTIS
Supplier: ARD (Westdeutscher Rundfunk)
Prod: WDR/Clasart;
Dir: John Goldschmidt.
57 Mins.
(RAI Prizewinner, Music-Dance)
10/11/78PI

END OF THE LINE
Supplier: WVUE
Prod-Wri: Patricia Gormin;
Dir: Robert Weaver.
30 Mins, Thurs, 8 pm.
WVUE New Orleans
06/14/78

THE END OF THE LINE
With Warner Saunders
Prod-Dir: Scott Craig;
Wri: Clarence Page.
60 Mins Thurs (29), 9 pm.
WBBM-TV Chicago

04/11/79

ENDANGERED SPECIES
Supplier: WVUE-TV
Prod-Wri-Narr: Patricia Gormin;
Dir: Gary Furlow.
30 Mins, Fri.
WVUE-TV New Orleans

11/12/80

ENOS
With Sonny Shroyer, Samuel E. Wright, John Dehner, John Milford, Michelle Pfeiffer, Anthony James, Bill Vint, Catherine Bach
Supplier: Gy Waldron Prods & Warner Bros TV
Exec Prod-Wri: Waldron;
Supv Prod-Dir: Rod Amateau.
60 Mins, Wed, 8 pm.
CBS-TV

11/19/80

THE ENTERTAINER
(Mobil Showcase)
With Jack Lemmon, Ray Bolger, Sada Thompson, Tyne Daly, Michael Cristofer, Annette O'Toole, Mitch Ryan, Allyn Ann McLerie
Supplier: Robert Stigwood Org & Persky-Bright Prods.
Prods: Beryl Vertue, Marvin Hamlisch;
Dir: Donald Wrye;
Wri: Elliott Baker (based on John Osborne drama).
120 Mins, Wed (10), 9 pm.
NBC-TV
Mobil (Doyle Dane Bernbach)

03/17/76

ENTERTAINMENT '76
With Art Carney, Lee Grant, Diahann Carroll, Tony Bennett, Karen Black, Robert Blake, Ken Bookstein, Sammy Cahn, Frank Capra, Norm Crosby, Sandy Duncan, Henry Fonda, Frank Gorshin, Janet Leigh, William Lewis, Ethel Merman, Clive Revill, Rosalind Russell, Ricky Segall, Brenda Vaccaro, Sarah Vaughan, Ben Vereen
Supplier: Rothman-Wohl Productions
Prods: Bernard Rothman, Jack Wohl;
Dir: Sid Smith;
Wris: Alex Barris, Rothman, Wohl.
120 Mins, Sat (12), 10 pm.
NBC-TV
Procter & Gamble (Leo Burnett)

06/16/76

ERIC HOFFER: THE CROWDED LIFE
With Hoffer, Richard Basehart
Supplier: WPBT Miami
Exec Prod-Dir: Shep Morgan;
Prod-Wri: Jeanne Wolf.
90 Mins, Tues, (17), 8 pm.
PBS

01/18/78

ESSERE ATTORE
(To Be An Actor)
With Jean-Louis Barrault, Vittorio Gassman, Giancarlo Giannini, Sir John Gielgud, Dustin Hoffman, Ottavia Piccolo, Lee Strasberg, Giorgio Strehler, Liv Ullmann, Romolo Valli, others
Supplier: RAI-TV
Prod-Wris: Corrado Augias, Marco Guarnaschelli;
Dir: Guarnaschelli.
Five Parts, 60 Mins each.
RAI-TV, Ch.2, from Rome, Italy

02/11/76F

EVANS & NOVAK
With Rowland Evans, Robert Novak, Aryeh Neier, George V Higgins, James M LaRossa
Supplier: RKO General
Exec Prod: Al Korn;
Prod: Gordon Hyatt;
Dir: Ross Cibella.
60 Mins, Sat (9), 10:30 pm.
WOR-TV New York

07/13/77S

EVENING IN BYZANTIUM - PART ONE
(Operation Prime Time)
With Glenn Ford, Eddie Albert, Vince Edwards, Patrick Macnee, Gregory Sierra, Harry Guardino, Simon Oakland, Michael Cole, Gloria DeHaven, Marcel Hillaire, Len Birman, George Lazenby, Erin Gray, Shirley Jones, Cynthia Ford, George Skaff, Byron Morrow
Supplier: GLP Prods & Universal TV (MCA-TV)
Exec Prod: Glen A Larson;
Prod: Michael Sloan;
Prod: Robert F O'Neill;
Dir: Jerry London;
Wris: Larson, Sloan, from Irwin Shaw's novel.
120 Mins, Mon (14), 8 pm.
WPIX-TV New York

08/16/78S

THE EVENING SHOW
With Steve Fox, Jan Yanehiro, Erik Smith, others
Exec Prod: Bill Hillier;
Prod: Bob Zagone;
Dir: Dominic Bonavolonta.
30 Mins, M-F, 7:30 pm.
KPIX San Francisco

08/25/76

EVERY PERSON IS GUILTY
(For The Record)
With Ken Pogue, Gerard Parker, Lynne Griffin, R H Thomson
Exec Prod: Sam Levene;
Prod: Vivienne Leebosh;
Dir: Paul Almond;
Wri: Ralph Thomas.
60 Mins, Sun, 9 pm.
CBC, from Toronto, Canada

04/11/79F

EVERYBODY RIDES THE CAROUSEL
(Mobil Showcase)
With Cicely Tyson, Lou Jacobi, Jack Gilford, Alvin Epstein, Deedee Bridgewater, Juanita Moore, Jane Hoffman, Lawrence Pressman, John Randolph, Meryl Streep
Prods: John & Faith Hubley;
Dir: John Hubley.
90 Mins, Fri (10), 8 pm.
CBS-TV
Mobil (Doyle Dane Bernbach)

09/15/76

EVERYDAY
With Stephanie Edwards, John Bennett Perry, Anne Bloom, Tom Chapin, Robert Corff, Judy Gibson, Murray Langston, Ron Howard, Donny Most, Jesse Potter, Brianne Leary
Supplier: Group W Prods
Exec Prod: David Salzman;
Prod: Viva Knight;
Dir: Lou Horvitz;
Wris: George Tricker, Neil Rosen, Don Seagall, Cynthia Santillo, Allyn Warner.
60 Mins, Mon-Fri, 9 am.
WCBS-TV New York

10/04/78S

EVERYWOMAN
Prod-Wri-Narr: Shirley Robson.
30 Mins, Sat (30), 7:30 pm.
WTOP-TV

05/04/77S

EXECUTIVE SUITE
With Mitchell Ryan, Stephen Elliott, Sharon Acker, Leigh McCloskey, Richard Cox, Gwyda DonHowe, Paul Lambert, Byron Morrow, Trisha Noble, Wendy Phillips, Joan Prather, Madlyn Rhue, Percy Rodrigues, William Smithers, Maxine Stuart, Brenda Sykes, Carl Weintraub, others
Supplier: OStanley Rubin-Arena Prods with MGM-TV
Exec Prods: Norman Felton, Stanley Rubin;
Prod: Don Brinkley;
Dirs: Joseph Hardy, Charles S Dubin;
Wris: Henry Slesar, Barbara Avedon, Barbara Corday.
60 Mins, Mon, 10 pm.
CBS--TV

09/22/76

EYE ON. . .A SLICE OF NIGHT
Exec Prod: Geoffrey Haines-Stiles;
Prod: Erna Akuginow;
Dir: Don Matticks.
30 Mins, Fri (25), 7:30 pm.
WCAU-TV Philadelphia

06/30/76

EYE ON. . .WARNINGS FROM INSIDE
Exec Prod: Geoffrey Haines-Stiles;
Prods: Dan Sitarski, Ena Akuginow;
Dir: Don Matticks.
30 Mins, Tues (19), 10:30 pm.
WCAU-TV Philadelphia

04/27/77

EYE ON...WEAPONS OF PEACE
With Mercedes McCambridge
Exec Prod: Geoffrey Haines-Stiles;
Prod: Erna Akuginow;
Dirs: Don Matticks, George Jason;
Wris: Haines-Stiles, Akuginow.
60 Mins, Tues (18), 7 pm.
WCAU-TV Philadelphia
10/26/77

F. LEE BAILEY AND THE LAW
With Jim Harriott
Prod: Harriott.
30 Mins, Mon (8), 7 pm.
KCPQ Tacoma
03/17/76

F.D.R. THE LAST YEAR
With Jason Robards, Eileen Heckart, Edward Binns, Augusta Dabney, Larry Gates, Michael Gross, Kim Hunter, James Karen, Mike Kellin, Jan Miner, Nehemiah Persoff, Ted Ross, Sylvia Sidney, Kathryn Walker, Laurinda Barrett, Olympia Dukasis, Andrew Duncan, Richard Hamilton, Tom Harvey, Mandel Kramer, Cec Linder, Avon Long, Terrence O'Quinn, Wensley Pithey, Ken Pogue, George R. Robertson, Norman Rose, Sloane Shelton, Kenneth Welsh, Murray Westgate, Wally Bondarenko, Jay Garner, Elan Ross Gibson, Robert Hitt, Edward J. Moore, Michael Reynolds, Ed Zang
Supplier: Titus Prods & Tamara Prods
Exec Prod: Herbert Brodkin;
Prod: Robert Berger;
Dir: Anthony Page;
Wri: Stanley R. Greenberg, based on Jim Bishop book.
180 Mins, Thurs, (15), 8 pm.
NBC-TV
05/21/80

FACE THE MUSIC
With Ron Ely (host), Lisa Donovan, Tommy Oliver Orch., Dave Williams
Supplier: Sandy Frank Prods. (Sandy Frank TV Distributors)
Exec Prods: David Levy, Bruno Zirato;
Prods: Ray Horl, Peggy Touchstone;
Dir: Lou Tedesco.
30 Mins, Mon-Fri, 7 pm.
WOR-TV New York
03/12/80S

FACE TO FACE/RACE TO RACE
With Charles H King Jr
Prod: Ellen Cooper;
Dir: Stuart Pollock.
60 Mins, Sat (26), 7 pm.
KDKA-TV Pittsburgh
03/09/77S

THE FACTS OF LIFE
With Charlotte Rae, John Lawlor, Jenny O'Hara, Lisa Whelchel, Felice Schachter, Julie Piekarski, Kim Fields, Julie Ann Haddock, Molly Ringwald, Mindy Cohn, Pam Huntington, Donald May
Supplier: TAT Communications
Prod-Wri: Jerry Mayer;
Dir: Jim Drake.
30 Mins, Fri, 8:30 pm.
NBC-TV
09/05/79

THE FALL AND RISE OF REGINALD PERRIN
With Leonard Rossiter, Pauline Yates, John Barron, others
Supplier: BBC-TV
Prod: John Howard Davies;
Wri: David Nobbs.
30 Mins, Wed, 9:25 pm.
BBC-1, Britain
09/29/76F

FAME
(Hallmark Hall of Fame)
With Richard Benjamin, Jose Ferrer, Raf Vallone, Robert Alda, Oliver Clark, Shera Danese, Linda Hunt, Joe Bennett, Nipsey Russell, Richard Libertini, Tom Poston
Supplier: Cates Bros
Exec Prods: Gilbert & Joseph Cates;
Prods: Marc Daniels, Patricia Rickey;
Dir: Daniels;
Wri: Arthur Miller.
60 Mins, Thurs (30), 10 pm.
NBC-TV
Hallmark Cards (Foote, Cone & Belding)
12/06/78

FAMILY
With Sada Thompson, James Broderick, Elayne Heilveil, Gary Frank, Kristy McNichol, John Rubinstein
Supplier: Icarus Prods. & Spelling-Goldberg Prods.
Exec Prods: Mike Nichols, Aaron Spelling, Leonard Goldberg;
Dir: Mark Rydell;
Wri: Jay Presson Allen.
60 Mins, Tues (9), 10 pm.
ABC-TV
03/17/76

FAMILY FEUD
With Richard Dawson (host)
Supplier: Goodson-Todman Prods.
Prod: Howard Felsher;
Dir: Paul Alter.
30 Mins, Mon-Fri, 1:30 pm.
ABC-TV
07/21/76

FAMILY FEUD
With Richard Dawson
Supplier: Goodson-Todman Prods
Prod: Howard Felsher;
Dir: Paul Alter.
30 Mins, Wed, 7:30 pm.
WNBC-TV
09/28/77S

THE FAMILY
With Scott Osborne (narrator)
Prod: Osborne.
30 Mins, Fri (31), 7:30 pm.
WMAQ-TV Chicago
04/05/78

THE FANTASTIC FUNNIES
With Loni Anderson, Howard Hesseman, Keene Curtis, Patricia Patts, Charles Schulz, Mort Walker, Hank Ketcham, Johnnie Hart, Brad Andersn, Morrie Turner, Mell Lazarus, Russell Myers, Dik Browne, Cathy Guisewite, Dean Young, John Raymond, John Cullen Murphy
Supplier: Lee Mendelson Prods
Prods: Mendelson, Karen Crommie;
Dir-Wri: Mendelson.
60 Mins, Thurs, (15) 8 pm.
CBS-TV
05/21/80

THE FANTASTIC JOURNEY
With Jared Martin, Carl Franklin, Ike Eisenmann, Scott Thomas, Susan Howard, Leif Erickson, Ian McShane, Don Knight, Gary Collins, Mary Ann Mobley, Jason Evers, Karen Somerville, Scott Brady, Jack Stauffer, Byron Chung, Tom McCorry
Supplier: Bruce Lansbury Prods & Columbia Pictures TV
Exec Prod: Bruce Lansbury;
Prod: Leonard Katzman;
Dir: Andrew V McLaglen;
Wris: Merwin Gerard, Michael Michaelian, Kathryn Michaelian Powers.
90 Mins, Thurs, 8 pm.
NBC-TV
02/09/77

FANTASY ISLAND
With Ricardo Montalban, Herve Villechaize, Diana Canova, Ann Dowd, Georgia Engel, John Saxon, Bert Convy
Supplier: Spelling-Goldberg & Columbia Pictures TV
Exec Prods: Aaron Spelling, Leonard Goldberg;
Prod: Michael Fisher;
Dir: Don Weis;
Wris: Michael Fisher, Steve Fisher.
60 Mins, Sat, 10 pm.
ABC-TV
02/15/78

FAREWELL TO MANZANAR
With Yuki Shimoda, Nobu McCarthy, Akemi Kikumura, Clyde Kasatu, Mako, Pat Morita, James Saito, Dori Takeshita, Greta Chi (narrator)
Supplier: Korty Films & Universal TV
Exec Prod: George J. Santoro
Prod-Dir: John Korty;
Wris: Jeanne Wakatsuki Houston, James D. Houston, Korty.
130 Mins, Thurs(11), 9 pm.
NBC-TV
03/17/76

FARNHAM & BYRNE
With John Farnham, Debbie Byrne
Supplier: Australian Broadcasting Commission
Exec Prod: Ric Birch;
Dirs: Vas Kontis, Grant Rule, Steve Wood
50 Mins, Tues, 7:30 pm.
ABC (Australia), Channel 2, Sydney
08/27/80F

FATHER O FATHER
With Iggie Wolfington, Dennis Dugan, Barbara Sharma, Spo-De-Odee, Kathleen Freeman, Richard Stahl, Helen Page Camp, Sandra Vacey, Ray Vitte, Maria O'Brien
Supplier: Fours Company Prods.
Exec Prod: Jerry Weintraub;
Prods: Rich Eustis, Al Rogers, Ron Clark;
Dirs: Peter Bonerz, Lee Bernhardi;
Wris: Eustis, Rogers, Jim Mulligan.
60 Mins, Sat (26), 9 pm.
ABC-TV
06/30/76

FEATHER & FATHER
With Stefanie Powers, Harold Gould, Frank Delfino, Joan Shawlee, William Windom, Alan McRae, Edward Winter, Andrew A Rubin, Dick O'Neill, Lewis Charles, Monte Landis, William H. Bassett, Robert Caspar, Diane Shalet
Supplier: Larry White Prods & Columbia Pictures TV
Exec Prod: White;
Prods: Bill Driskill, Robert Mintz;
Dir: Seymour Robbie;
Wri: Harold Livingston.
60 Mins, Mon (6), 8 pm.
ABC-TV
12/08/76

THE FEATHER & FATHER GANG
With Stefanie Powers, Harold Gould, Frank Delfino, Joan Shawlee, Gene Barry, Bruce Glover, Jeff Donnell, Joseph Stern, Edward Winter, Ray Danton, Monte Landis, Lewis Charles, Linda Foster, Eddie Firestone
Supplier: Larry White Prods & Columbia Pictures TV
Exec Prod: White;
Prods: Bill Driskill, Robert Mintz;
Dir: Ernie Pintoff;
Wri: Calvin Clements Jr.
60 Mins, Mon, 10 pm.
ABC-TV
03/09/77

FEATHERSTONE'S NEST
With Ken Berry, Virginia Capers, Susan Swift, Phil Leeds, Dana Hill, Fred Morsell, Kate Zentall, Anita Jodelsohn, Rhonda Foxx
Supplier: Danny Thomas Prods.
Exec Prods: Thomas, Ronald Jacobs;
Prod-Wri: Michael Norell;
Dir: James R. Drake.
30 Mins, Wed, (30), 8 pm.
CBS-TV
02/06/80

FELLINI: WIZARDS, CLOWNS & HONEST LIARS
With John Huddy
Supplier: Juliet Prods, Wizard Inc
Exec Prods: Huddy, Joan Gherman;
Prod-Dir: Roger Ailes;
Wri: Huddy.
60 Mins, Sat (3), 9 pm.
WNEW-TV
09/07/77S

FERNWOOD 2-NIGHT
With Martin Mull, Fred Willard, Frank De Vol, Bruce Mahler, Felix Fisher, others
Supplier: TAT Communications
Prod: Alan Thicke;
Dirs: Jim Drake, Louis J Horwitz;
Wris: Tom Moore, Jeremy Stevens, Thicke.
30 Mins, Mon-Fri, 11 pm.
WNEW-TV New York
07/13/77S

FESTERING FOREFATHERS AND RUNNING SONS
(Peep Show)
With Codco Revue Troupe from Newfoundland
Exec Prod: George Bloomfield;
Prod: Deborah Peaker;
Dir: Alan Erlich.
30 Mins, Thurs, 10:30 pm.
CBC-TV, from Toronto, Canada
02/18/76F

FEUERWASSER
(Firewater)
With Hans-Helmut Dickow, Helmut Dickow, Helmut Qualtinger
Supplier: ZDF-TV
Dir: Wolfgang Staudte;
Wri: Ulrich Becher.
90 Mins, Mon, 9:30 pm.
ADF (2d Channel), from Wiesbaden-Mainz, West Germany
08/09/78F

51ST STATE
With Crane Davis, Lynn Sherr, Lisa Feiner, others
Exec Prod: Gordon Hyatt;
Wri: Feiner.
30 Mins, Thurs, 8:30 pm.
WNET-TV New York
01/14/76

THE FIGHTING NIGHTINGALES
With Adrienne Barbeau, Kenneth Mars, Livia Genise, Erica Yohn, Stephanie Faracy, Jerry Houser, Rod McCary, Randy Stumpf, George Whiteman, Jonathan Banks, Frank Whiteman, Lawrence Rosenberg, Kim Kahana
Supplier: 20th-Fox TV
Prods-Wris: Barry Sand, Alan Uger;
Dir: George Tyne.
30 Mins, Mon (16), 9:30 pm.
CBS-TV
01/25/78

FIRE AND ICE
With John Lindsay
Prods-Wris-Dirs (on location): Don Dunwell, Dan Helfgott;
Dir (studio): Richard Crew.
60 Mins, Mon, 8 pm.
WHYY-TV Philadelphia, for EEN and PPTN
03/16/77

THE FIRST FIFTY YEARS
(The Big Event)
With Orson Welles, Jack Albertson, Milton Berle, David Brinkley, Johnny Carson, John Chancellor, Angie Dickinson, Joe Garagiola, Bob Hope, Gene Kelly, Jerry Lewis, Dean Martin, Don Meredith, Gregory Peck, Freddie Prinze, George C. Scott, others
Exec Prod: Greg Garrison;
Prods: Lee Hale, Chet Hagan;
Wris: Abby Mann, Jess Oppenheimer, Mike Marmer, Bill Angelos, Orson Welles.
270 Mins, Sun (21), 7 pm.
NBC-TV
11/24/76

FIRST YOU CRY
With Mary Tyler Moore, Anthony Perkins, Richard Crenna, Jennifer Warren, Richard Dysart, Don Johnson, Florence Eldridge, Patricia Barry, Antoinette Bower, James A Watson Jr
Supplier: MTM Prods
Prod: Philip Barry;
Dir: George Schaefer;
Wri: Carmen Culver, from Betty Rollin's book.
120 Mins, Wed (8), 9 pm.
CBS-TV
11/15/78

FISH
With Abe Vigoda, Florence Stanley, Barry Gordon, John Cassisi, Denise Miller, Todd Bridges, Lenny Bari, Sarah Natoli, Joe George, Walter Matthews
Supplier: Minus Corp
Exec Prod: Danny Arnold;
Prod: Steve Pritzker;
Dir: Lee Bernhardi;
Wris: Barbara Corday, Barbara Avedon, Richard Baer.
30 Mins, Sat, 8:30 pm.
ABC-TV
02/09/77

FIT TO PRINT
With Henry Beckman, Catherine O'Hara, Martin Short, Jack Duffy, Helen Hughes
Prod: Bill Lynn;
Dir: Norman Campbell;
Wris: Lynn, Jack Duffy.
30 Mins, Tues, 9:30 pm.
CBC-TV, from Toronto, Canada
07/13/77F

THE FITZPATRICKS
With Bert Kramer, Mariclare Costello, Clark Brandon, James Vincent McNichol, Michele Tobin, Sean Marshall, Derek Wells, Helen Hunt
Supplier: Warner Bros TV
Prod: Philip Mandelker;
Dir: Gene Reynolds;
Wri: John Sacret Young.
60 Mins, Mon (5), 9 pm.
CBS-TV
09/07/77

FIVE VIEWS OF THE AMERICAN DREAM
With Fahey Flynn, others
Prod: Lawrence Pont;
Dir: Nancy Callaway.
60 Min, Fri (26), 8 pm.
WLS-TV Chicago
12/31/80

FLAMINGO ROAD
(NBC Monday Night At The Movies)
With John Beck, Woody Brown, Howard Duff, Morgan Fairchild, Mark Harmon, Kevin McCarthy, Cristina Raines, Barbara Rush, Stella Stevens, Mason Adams, Norman Alden, Diane Kay, Melba Moore
Supplier: MF Prods & Lorimar Prods
Exec Prods: Michael Filerman, Lee Rich;
Prod: Edward H. Feldman;
Dir: Gus Trikonis;
Wri: Rita Lakin, based on Robert Wilder novel.
120 Mins, Mon, (12) 9 pm.
NBC-TV
05/21/80

FLATBUSH
With Joseph Cali, Adrian Zmed, Vincent Bufano, Randy Stumpf, Sandy Helberg, Antony Ponzini, Helen Verbit, Donna Ponterotto, Jack Murdock, James Cromwell, Olivia Barash
Supplier: Lorimar Film-Und Fernsehproduktion, GmbH
Exec Prods: Philip Capice, Gary Adelson;
Prod: Norman S Powell;
Dir: William Asher;
Wri: Dennis Palumbo.
30 Mins, Mon, 8:30 pm.
CBS-TV
02/21/79

FLIGHT TO HOLOCAUST
With Patrick Wayne, Christopher Mitchum, Fawne Harriman, Desi Arnaz Jr, Sid Caesar, Rory Calhoun, Greg Morris, Lloyd Nolan, Paul Williams, Robert Patten, Anne Schedeen, Kathrine Baumann, Argentina Brunetti
Supplier: First Artists Prods & Aycee Prods
Prod: A C Lyles;
Dir: Bernard L Kowalski;
Wris: Robert Heverly, Anthony Lawrence.
120 Mins, Sun (27), 8 pm.
NBC-TV
03/30/77

FLO
With Polly Holliday, Geoffrey Lewis, Jim B. Baker, Sudie Bond, Joyce Bulifant, Leo Burmester, Lucy Lee Flippin, Stephen Keep, James Cromwell, Buck Flower, Gordon Hurst
Supplier: Warner Bros. TV
Exec Prod: Jim Mulligan;
Supv Prods: Ron Landry, George Geiger, Tom Biener;
Dir: Marc Daniels;
Wris: Dick Clair & Jenna McMahon.
30 Mins, Mon, 9:30 pm.
CBS-TV
03/26/80

FLOWERS FROM HORSEBACK
With Lynne Joiner
Supplier: Group W TV Station Group
Prod-dir: Tom Fleming;
Wri: Joiner.
60 Mins.
Group W. Stations
06/16/76S

FLYING HIGH
With Kathryn Witt, Pat Klous, Connie Sellecca, Howard Platt, Marcia Wallace, Jim Hutton, David Hayward, Martin Speer, Lynn Marie Johnston, Richard Hack, Casey Biggs, Lilyan Chauvin, Carmen Zapata, Karen Rushmore, Brion James, Steve Shaw, Louis Zito, Val Bisoglio
Supplier: Mark Carliner Prods
Prod: Carliner;
Dir: Peter H Hunt;
Wris: Marty Cohan, Dawn Aldredge.
120 Mins, Mon (28), 9 pm.
CBS-TV
09/06/78

FLYING HIGH
With Kathryn Witt, Connie Sellecca, Pat Klous, Howard Platt, George Gobel, James Gregory, Rosey Grier, Stubby Kaye, Michael Parks, Severn Darden, Wynn Irwin, Bibi Osterwald, Edith Head
Supplier: Mark Carliner Prods
Exec Prod: Carliner;
Prod: Robert Van Scoyk;
Dir: Nicholas Sgarro;
Wris: Joyce Armor, Judie Neer.
60 Mins, Fri, 10 pm.
CBS-TV
10/04/78

FOCUS ON: HOLLYWOOD NOW
With David Sheehan, Clint Eastwood, Burt Reynolds, John Travolta, Susan Harris, Sada Thompson, Penny Marshall, Hal Holbrook, O J Simpson
Supplier: Sheehan Enterprises & DID Prods (TV Reps Intl)
Exec Prod: Susan Haymer;
Prod-Wri: Sheehan;
Dir: Bob E Frye.
30 Mins, Thurs (9), 7:30 pm.
WCBS-TV New York
03/15/78

FOR RICHER FOR POORER
With David Abbott, Rod Arrants, Richard Backus, Laurinda Barrett, Patricia Barry, Charles Bateman, Cynthia Bostick, Robert Skip Burton, Patricia Englund, Breon Gorman, Tom Happer, Julia MacKenzie, Christine Jones, Stephen Joyce, David Knapp, Lynne MacLaren, Darlene Parks, Roy Poole, Flora Plumb, Albert Stratton
Supplier: Procter & Gamble Prods
Exec Prod: Paul Rauch;
Dirs: Jack Hofsiss, Barnet Kellman;
Wris: Harding Lemay, Tom King.
30 Mins, Tues (6), 1 pm.
NBC-TV
12/14/77

FOR YOU...BLACK WOMAN
With Alice Travis, host
Supplier: Gerber/Carter Communications
Prods: Fred Dukes, Felicidad;
Dir: Dukes.
30 Mins, Sun (6), 2:30 pm.
WABC-TV New York
Nicholas Laboratories
08/09/78

FOREVER FERNWOOD
With Greg Mullavey, Debralee Scott, Graham Jarvis, Claudia Lamb, Dody Goodman, Mary Kay Place, William Bogert, Dabney Coleman, Marian Mercer, Shelley Fabares, Norman Parker, Judy Kahan, Richard Hatch, Robert Stoneman, Rona Barrett, Tab Hunter, others
Supplier: TAT Communications
prods: Eugenie Ross-Leming, Brad Buckner;
Dir: Jim Drake;
Wris: Jerry Adelman, Peggy Goldman, Karen Jones, Mara Lideks, Mitch Markowitz.
30 Mins, Mon-Fri, 11 pm.
KTTV Los Angeles
10/05/77S

FORTUNATA Y JACINTA
With Ana Belen, Maribel Martin, Mario Pardo, Francois Eric Gendron, Manuel Alexandre, Paco Algora, Mary Carrillo, Fernando Fernan Gomez, Charo Lopez, Julio Nunez, Maria Luisa Ponte, Bera Riaza, Paco Rabal, Cristina Torres, Jean Marc Thibault, Manolo Zarzo, Margarita Garcia Ortega, Luis Ciges, Paco Marso, Mayte Blasco, Alejandro Enciso, Mirta Miller, Virginia Mataix, Jose Yepes, Candida Losada, Antonio Passy, Mercedes Borque, Mimi Munoz, Gabriel Llopart, Paul Mercey
Supplier: Radiotelevision Espanola
Exec Prod: Salvador Augustin;
Prods: RTVE, Thelvetia (Geneva) and Telefrance (Paris)
60 Mins
RTE, Madrid, Spain
05/14/80F

THE FOSTERS
With Norman Beaton, Isabelle Lucas, Carmen Munro, Lenny Henry, Sharon Rosita, Lawrie Mark, Joseph Charles
Supplier: London Weekend TV
Prod-dir: Stuart Allen;
Wri: Jon Watkins.
30 Mins, Fri, 7:30 pm.
ITV Network, Britain
05/05/76F

THE FOUNDATION
With Lynette Davies, William Gaunt, Fulton Mackay, Geoffrey Whitehead, John Barron, others
Supplier: ATV
Prod: John Cooper;
Wri: Richard Gregson.
60 Mins, Fri, 9 pm.
LWT, from London, England
07/26/78F

THE FOUR FEATHERS
(Bell System Family Theatre)
With Beau Bridges, Robert Powell, Simon Ward, Jane Seymour, Harry Andrews, David Robb, Richard Beale, Robin Bailey, John Hallam, Julian Barnes, Mary Maude, Frank Gatliff, Robert Flemyng, Robert James, Alexander Bird, Jonathan Scott-Taylor, Pauline Yates, Neil Hallet
Supplier: Norman Rosemont Prod, Trident Films Ltd
Prod: Rosemont;
Dir:
Wri: Gerald DiPego (from novel by A E W Mason).
120 Mins, Sun (1), 9 pm.
NBC-TV
AT&T (N W Ayer)
01/11/78

THE 416TH
With Richard Lewis, Raymond St Jacques, John Larroquette, Richard Dimitri, Donald Petrie, Bo Kaprall, Joan Hotchkis, Louise Hoven, Susan Lanier
Supplier: Rick Bernstein Enterprises & Warner Bros TV
Exec Prod: Bernstein;
Prods: Peter H Engel, Eric Cohen;
Dir: Buddy Tyne;
Wri: Cohen.
30 Mins, Sat (25), 8:30 pm.
CBS-TV
08/29/79

THE FOUR OF US
With Barbara Feldon, Heather MacRae, Vicky Dawson, Kathy Jo Kelly, Will McMillan, K Callan, Lawrence Keith, Marcia Jean Kurtz, Sam Schacht, Sudie Bond, Peter Maloney, Herb Davis, Robert Phalen
Supplier: Titus-Defenders Prods (Herb Brodkin & Reginald Rose)
Exec Prod: Brodkin;
Prod: Robert Berger;
Dir: James Cellan Jones;
Wri: Rose.
60 Mins, Mon (18), 8 pm.
ABC-TV
07/27/77

FOX AND LEONARD GO TO THE MOVIES
With Sonny Fox, Bob Leonard
Exec Prod: Don Davidson;
Prod: Fox;
Dir: Bob Fitzpatrick;
Wris: Fox, Leonard.
60 Mins, Fri (Dec 30), 8 pm.
WPHL-TV Philadelphia
01/11/78S

FRANKIE & ANNETTE: THE SECOND TIME AROUND
With Frankie Avalon, Annette Funicello, Taurean Blacque, Doug Rowe, Marki Post, Helaine Lembeck, Louis Welch, Lucia Stralser, Don Porter, Herb Edelman, Mark L Taylor
Supplier: Dick Clark Co
Exec Prod: Clark;
Prods-Wris: Don Nelson, Arthur Alsberg;
Dir: Bob LaHendro.
60 Mins, Sa (18), 9 pm.
NBC-TV
11/22/78

FREE COUNTRY
With Rob Reiner, Judy Kahan, Fred McCarren, Renee Lippin, Larry Hankin
Supplier: Reiner/Mishkin Co, with Columbia Pictures TV
Exec Prods-Wris: Reiner, Phil Mishkin;
Prod: Gareth Davies;
Dir: Hal Cooper.
30 Mins, Sat (24), 8 pm.
ABC-TV
06/28/78

FREEBIE & THE BEAN
With Hector Elizondo, Tom Mason, William Daniels, Katherine Justice, Lori Lethin, Donald May, Mel Stewart, William Bronder, Peter Brocco, Louis Guss, Ben Hammer, Amzie Strickland.
Supplier: Warner Bros TV
Exec Prod: Philip Saltzman;
Prods: Robert Sherman, Norman Jolley;
Dir: Lawrence Dobkin;
Wri: Dick Nelson.
60 Min, Sat, 9 pm.
CBS-TV
12/10/80

FREEDOM ROAD - PART ONE
With Muhammad Ali, Kris Kristofferson, Ron O'Neal, Edward Hermann, Barbara-O Jones, Sonny Jim Gaines, Joel Fluellen, Bill Mackey, Earl D A Smith, Ossie Davis (narrator)
Supplier: Zev Braun Prods & Worldvision Enterprises
Prod: Braun;
Dir: Jan Kadar;
Wri: David Zelag Goodman, from Howard Fast's novel.
120 Mins, Mon (29), 9 pm.
NBC-TV
10/31/79

FREEMAN
With Stu Gilliam, Beverly Sanders, Linden Chiles, Jimmy Baio, Melinda Dillon
Supplier: Kukoff-Harris Prods. & Harry Stoones Inc.
Prods: Bernie Kukoff, Jeff Harris;
Dir: Hal Cooper;
Wris: Kukoff, Harris, Paul Mooney.
30 Mins, Sat (19), 8:30 pm.
ABC-TV
06/23/76

FRIDAYS
With Mark Blankfield, Maryedith Burrell, Melanie Chartoff, Barry David, Darrow Igus, Brandis Kemp, Bruce Mahler, Michael Richards, John Roarke, Kenny Loggins
Supplier: Moffitt-Lee Prods
Prods: John Moffitt, Bill Lee.
Dir: Moffitt
70 Mins, Fri, 11:30 pm.
ABC-TV
04/16/80

FRIEND OF THE FAMILY
With Andonia Katsaros, Graham Rouse, Martin Harris, Mervyn Drake, Les Foxcroft
Supplier: Australian Broadcasting Commission
Prod: Eric Taylor;
Dir: Peter Fisk;
Wri: Steve J. Spears
30 Mins, Mon, 10:30 pm.
ABC (Australia) TV, Channel 2, Sydney
10/15/80F

FRIENDLY FIRE
(ABC Theatre)
With Carol Burnett, Ned Beatty, Sam Waterston, Dennis Erdman, Timothy Hutton, Fanny Spies, Sherry Hursey, Michael Flanagan, Hilly Hicks, William Jordan, Vernon Weddle, Jack Rader, Robert Wahler, David Keth, Bernard Behrens
Supplier: Marble Arch Prods
Exec Prod: Martin Starger;
Prods: Philip Barry, Fay Kanin;
Dir: Harry May;
Wri: Kanin.
180 Mins, Sun (22), 8 pm.
ABC-TV
04/25/79

FRIENDS
With Harry Chapin (host), Bill Cosby, Peter Sellers, Henry Winkler
Supplier: Syd Vinnedge Prods.
Exec Prod: Vinnedge;
Prod: Joe Byrne;
Dir: Nick Webster;
Wri: Dyann Rivkin.
90 Mins, Fri (12), 1 am.
NBC-TV
03/17/76

FRIENDS
With Michael Tucci, Darrell Fetty, Dori Brenner, Susan Buckner, Brian Cutler, Larry Cedar, Diane Lander, Rae Dawn Chong, Stephen Mond, George Wyner
Supplier: Music-Pritzker Prods & Universal TV
Prods-Wris: Lorenzo Music, Steve Pritzker;
Dir: Hy Averback.
30 Mins, Sat (19), 8:30 pm.
CBS-TV
08/23/78

FRIENDS
With Charles Aiken, Jill Whelan, Jarrod Johnson, Andy Romano, Karen Morrow, Alicia Fleer, Dennis Redfield, Roger Robinson, Janet MacLachlan, Patty McCormack, Tania Johnson
Supplier: Aaron Spelling Prods
Exec Prods: Spelling, Douglas S Cramer;
Prods: Bo Kaprall & Bob Sand and Cindy Dunne
Dir: Arnold Laven;
Wri: Liz Coe.
60 Mins, Sun, 7 pm.
ABC-TV
03/28/79

FRIENDS & FEELINGS
(Pushcart Players Present)
With Jason Alexander, Rona Birnbaum, Darrell Casey, Sarah Cloud, Dan Drew, Ruth Fost, Christine Jennings, David Saybrook, Ernie Semento
Supplier: Cybele/Pushcart Prods & WCBS-TV
Prod-Dir: Bob Bielecki;
Wris: Fost, Gretchen Johnson, Carole Wechter.
30 Mins, Thurs (31), 7:30 pm.
WCBS-TV New York
09/06/78

FROM HERE TO ETERNITY
(NBC Monday Night At The Movies)
With William Devane, Roy Thinnes, Barbara Hershey, David Spielberg, Rocky Echevarria, Lacey Neuhaus, John Calvin, Will Sampson, Kim Basinger, Don Johnson, Salome Jens, Priscilla Pointer, Richard Roat, Gary Swanson, Claude Jones
Supplier: Bennett-Katleman Prods & Columbia Pictures TV
Exec Prods: Harve Bennett, Harris Katleman;
Supv Prod: Lionel E. Siegel;
Prod: Carl Pingitore;
Dir: Ron Satlof;
Wris: Rudy Day, Tony Palmer, Harold Gast (based on James Jones novel)
120 Mins, Mon, (10) 9 pm.
NBC-TV
03/19/80

FROM HERE TO ETERNITY - PART ONE
(NBC Novels For Television)
With Natalie Wood, William Devane, Steve Railsback, Roy Thinnes, Joe Pantoliano, Kim Basinger, Rick Hurst, Andrew Robinson, Salome Jens, Andy Griffith, others
Supplier: Bennett-Katleman Prods & Columbia Pictures TV
Exec Prods: Harve Bennett, Harris Katleman;
Prod-Dir: Buzz Kulik;
Wri: Don McGuire.
120 Mins, Wed (14), 9 pm.
NBC-TV
02/21/79

FRONT PAGE CHALLENGE
With Fred Davis, Gordon Sinclair, Betty Kennedy, Pierre Berton
Prod-Dir: Ray McConnell;
Wri: Chuck Weir.
30 Mins, Mon, 8:30 pm.
CBC-TV, from Toronto, Canada
10/26/77F

FRONT PAGE FEENEY
With Don Knotts, Jed Allan, Susan Tolsky, Jennie Blackton, Denny Evans, Edward Andrews, Victoria Ann Berry, Karen Knotts, Duncan McLeod, Byron Webster, Danny Dayton, Joe Baker, Al Checco, Boris Vanoff
Supplier: Yongstreet Entertainment Corp
Exec Prod: Nick Vanoff;
Prod: John Aylesworth;
Dir: Howard Morris;
Wris: Frank Peppiatt, Aylesworth, Jack Burns.
30 Mins, Mon (29), 7:30 pm.
WCBS-TV New York
08/31/77S

FROSTY'S WINTER WONDERLAND
With Andy Griffith (narrator) and voices of Shelley Winters, Dennis Day, Paul Frees, Shelley Hines, Eric Stern, Manfred Olca, Barbara Jo Ewing, Wee Winter Singers
Supplier: Rankin-Bass Prods
Prods-dirs: Arthur Rankin Jr, Jules Bass;
Wri: Romeo Muller.
30 Mins, Thurs (2), 8 pm.
ABC-TV
Parker Bros (Humphrey Browning MacDougall)
12/08/76

THE FUN FACTORY
With Bobby Van (host), Betty Thomas, Debbi Harmon, Rhonda Bates, Doug Steckler, Dick Blasucci, Marty Barris, Buddy Douglas
Supplier: Ed Fishman-Randall Freer Prods. & Columbia Pictures TV
Exec Prods: Ed Fishman, Freer;
Prod: David Fishman;
Dir: Walter C. Miller;
Wris: Mort Green, Don Ross, Bruce Taylor, Josef Anderson, Ed Torray.
30 Mins, Mon-Fri, noon
NBC-TV
06/16/76

FUNNY BUSINESS
With Walter Matthau (host)
Supplier: Heyday Prods & Universal TV
Exec Prod: Leonard B Stern;
Prod-Dir-Wri: Richard Schickel.
120 Mins, Wed (26), 8 pm.
CBS-TV
08/02/78

THE FUNNY WORLD OF FRED & BUNNI
With Fred Travalena, Sandy Duncan, Pat Harrington, Vicki Lawrence, Kathy Lee Johnson, Rob Iscove Dancers
Supplier: Hanna-Barbera Prods & Yongestreet Entertainment Corp
Exec Prod: Joe Barbera;
Prods: John Aylesworth, Frank Peppiatt;
Dir: Bill Davis;
Wris: Aylesworth, Peppiatt, Barry Adelman, Barry Silver, Harrington, James Burr-Johnson.
60 Mins, Wed (30), 8 pm.
CBS-TV
09/06/78

FUTURE COP
With Ernest Borgnine, Michael Shannon, John Amos, John Larch, Herbert Nelson, Ronnie Clair Edwards, James Lusi, Stephan Pearlman, James Daughton
Supplier: Paramount TV
Exec Prod: Gary Damsker;
Prod: Anthony Wilson;
Dir: Jud Taylor;
Wri: Wilson.
90 Mins, Sat (1), 8 pm.
ABC-TV
05/05/76

FUTURE COP
With Ernest Borgnine, Michael Shannon, John Amos, Michael V Gazzo, Rod McCary, Mwako Cumbuka, Steve Gravers, Irene Tsu, Herbert Nelson
Supplier: The Culzean Corp, Tovern Prods & Paramount TV
Exec Prods: Anthony Wilson, Gary Damsker;
Prod: Everett Chambers;
Dir: Robert Douglas;
Wri: Mann Rubin.
60 Mins, Sat, 8 pm.
ABC-TV
03/09/77

FYI: NUCLEAR POWER BY CHOICE OR BY CHANCE
With Sarah Wye, Dr Andrew Kadak, Dr Joseph Turnage, Sister Arlene Violet, Sam Sealy, Dr Peter Franchot
Prod: Gary Dreispul;
Dir: Jay Mullan.
60Mins, Tues, 8 pm.
WJAR-TV Providence
12/28/77

GAIL
With Sally Cooper, Terry Gill, Nanette Wallace, Jackie Kerin, Alma Joseph, others
Supplier: Australian Broadcasting Commission
Dir: John Gauci;
Wri: Keith Thompson.
50 Mins, Sun, 8:30 pm.
ABC TV, Ch 2, Sydney Australia
11/07/79F

GALACTICA 1980-PART 1
With Kent McCord, Barry Van Dyke, Robyn Douglass, Lorne Greene, Richard Lynch, Robbie Rist, Robert Reed, Pamela Susan Shoop, Sharon Acker, Fred Holliday, Richard Eastham
Supplier: Glen A. Larson Prods. & Universal TV
Exec Prod-Wri: Larson;
Supv Prod: David J. O'Connell;
Prod: Gary B. Winter;
Dir: Sidney Hayers.
60 Mins, Sun, (27), 7 pm.
ABC-TV
01/30/80

GAMES PEOPLE PLAY
With Bryant Gumbel, Cyndy Garvey, Johnny Bench, Mike Adamle, Donna de Verona, Arte Johnson, Ian Wooldridge, Reggie Jackson, Gil Gerard, Greg Evigan, Jay Randolph, Al McGuire
Supplier: Ohlmeyer Prods & Trans World Int'l
Exec Prod: Don Ohlmeyer;
Prod: Howard Katz;
Dir: Jim Cross;
Wris: Norman Bleichman, Ohlmeyer, Katz.
90 Mins, Thurs, 8 pm.
NBC-TV
08/27/80

GANGSTERS
With Ahmed Khalil, Elizabeth Cassidy, Paul Antrim, others
Supplier: BBC
Prod: David Rose;
Dir: Alastair Reid;
Wri: Phillip Martin.
50 Mins Thurs, 9:55 pm.
BBC-1, Britain
09/29/76F

THE GARRY MCDONALD SHOW
With Garry McDonald, Ric Hutton, Ron Blanchard, Jude Kuring, Colleen Hewett, Jenny Lee, others
Supplier: Australian Broadcasting Commission
Prod-Dir: John Eastway;
Wris: Peter Thorburn, Angela Webber, Paul Leadon, David Poltorak, Morris Gleitzman, Tim Gooding, John A Scott, Steve J Spears, Rob George, Bill Harding.
30 Mins, Thurs, 8:30 pm.
ABC (Australia), Channel 2 Sydney
08/03/77F

GATHER YOUR DREAMS
With Kerry McGregor, Jenny Ludlam, Gerry Duggan, Bridget Armstrong, Charlie Strachan, Grant Bridger, Patrick Whyte, Terence Cooper, others
Supplier: South Pacific TV
Exec Prod: John McRae;
Prod: Roger LeMeasurier;
Dir: Tom Parkinson;
Wri: Roger Simpson.
25 Mins, Sun, 7 pm Dec 17.
South Pacific Television, TV2 New Zealand
01/10/79F

THE GATHERING
(ABC Theatre)
With Edward Asner, Maureen Stapleton, Rebecca Balding, Sarah Cunningham, Bruce Davison, Veronica Hamel, Gregory Harrison, James Karen, Lawrence Pressman, John Randolph, Gail Strickland, Eward Winter, Stephanie Zimbalist
Supplier: Hanna-Barbera Prods
Prod: Harry R Sherman;
Wri: James Poe.
Dir: Randal Kleiser;
120 Mins, Sun (4), 9 pm.
ABC-TV
12/07/77

THE GEEKS
With Judy Morris, John Stanton, Lynette Curran, Rod Mullinar.
Supplier: Australian Broadcasting Commission
Exec Prod: Lynn Bayonas;
Prod-Dir: Julian Pringle;
Wri: Colin Free.
60 Mins, (Thurs) 8:55 pm.
ABC (Australia) TV, from Sydney Channel 2
04/05/78F

GEMINI MAN
With Ben Murphy, Katherine Crawford, Richard Dysart, Dana Elcar, Paul Shenar, Quinn Redeker, Greg Walcott, others
Supplier: Universal TV, Harve Bennett Prods.
Exec Prod: Harve Bennett;
Prod-wri: Leslie Stevens;
Dir: Alan Levi.
120 Mins, Mon (10), 8 pm.
NBC-TV
05/19/76

GEMINI MAN
With Ben Murphy, William Sylvester, Katherine Crawford, Alan Oppenheimer, Andrew Prine, Jim Stafford, Gil Serna
Supplier: Universal TV
Exec Prod: Harve Bennett;
Prods: Frank Telford, Robert F. O'Neill;
Dir: Alan J Levi;
Wri: Telford.
60 Mins, Thurs, 7:30 pm.
NBC--TV
09/29/76

GENERAL ELECTRIC'S ALL-STAR ANNIVERSARY
With John Wayne (host), Lucille Ball, Albert Brooks, Henry Fonda, Alex Haley, Pat Hingle, Bob Hope, Cheryl Ladd, Michael Landon, Penny Marshall, Donny & Marie Osmond, Charley Pride, John Ritter, Sha Na Na, Red Skelton, Suzanne Somers, James Stewart, Elizabeth Taylor, Leslie Uggams, Jimmie Walker, James Whitmore, Cindy Williams, Henry Winkler
Supplier: Paul W Keyes Prods
Prod: Keyes;
Dir: Dick McDonough;
Wris: Keyes, Bob Howard, Jeffrey Barron, Monty Aidem.
120 Mins, Fri (29), 9 pm.
ABC-TV
10/04/78

GENERATION
With Richard Goldsmith, Deedee Besas (co-hosts)
Exec Prod: Miskit Airth;
New Generation Prods & WABC-TV
Prod: Goldsmith;
Dir: Arnie Nocks.
30 Mins, Wed, 7:30 pm.
WABC-TV New York
05/09/79S

GENESIS, JUBA AND OTHER JEWELS: A SONGFEST OF BLACK AMERICA
Exec Prod: Peggy Cooper;
Prod: Mike Malone;
Dir: Gardner Compton.
60 Mins, Sun (4), 8 pm.
WTOP-TV Washington
04/21/76

GEORGE AND MILDRED
With Yootha Joyce, Brian Murphy, Norman Eshley, Sheila Fearn
Supplier: Thames-TV
Prod: Peter Frazer-Jones;
Wris: Johnnie Mortimer, Brian Cooke.
30 Mins, Mon, 8 pm.
Thames-TV, from London, England
09/29/76F

THE GEORGE BURNS ONE MAN SHOW
With George Burns, Bob Hope, Ann-Margret, The Captain & Tennille, Gladys Knight & The Pips
Exec Prod: Irving Fein;
Prod-Dir: Stan Harris;
Wris: Elon Packard, Fred S Fox, Seaman Jacobs.
60 Mins, Wed (23), 10 pm.
CBS-TV
11/30/77

THE GEORGE BURNS SPECIAL
With George Burns, Walter Matthau, The Osmond Brothers, Johnny Carson, Madeline Kahn, Chita Rivera
Supplier: GBF Prods
Exec Prod: Irving Fein;
Prods: Bernard Rothman, Jack Wohl;
Dir: Bill Hobin;
Wris: Fred S Fox Jr, Seaman Jacobs, Elon Packard.
60 Mins, Weds (1), 10 pm.
CBS-TV
12/08/76

GEORGE HALAS, AN AMERICAN LEGEND
With Hugh Hill (narrator), George Halas
Prod-Wri: Hill;
Dir: John Kochan.
60 Mins, Sat (26), 6 pm.
WLS-TV Chicago
02/16/77S

GERALD R FORD: PRESIDENTIAL DECISIONS
With Ford, John Chancellor
Supplier: NBC News
Exec Prod: Gordon Manning;
Prod: Kenneth Donoghue;
Dir: Marvin Einhorn.
60 Mins, Wed (26), 10 pm.
NBC-TV
05/03/78

GETTING MARRIED
(Wide World Of Entertainment)
With Cloris Leachman (narr)
Supplier: Supplier: Braverman Picture Corp.
Prod-dir: Charles Braverman;
Wri: Marc B. Ray.
90 Mins, Mon (14), 11:30 pm.
ABC-TV
06/16/76

GETTING THERE
With George S. Irving, Brett Somers, Jane Connell, Cathryn Damon, Norman Fell, Todd Susman, Dub Taylor, Tim Thomerson, Diane Venora, Kelly Mohre, Steven Mond, Kristi Jill Wood
Suppliers: Lila Garrett Prods. & Metromedia Producers Corp.
Exec Prod: Garrett;
Dir: John Astin;
Wris: Garrett, Sandy Krinski.
30 Mins, tues, (12), 8 pm.
CBS-TV
02/20/80

GEZORNINPLATZ
With Bill Daily, Johnny Brown, Vicki Lawrence, Jim Backus, Barbara Sharma, Gene Conforti, Don Galloway, Murray Langton, Art Metrano, Ken Olfson, Susan Silo, Kenneth Mars, others
Supplier: Filmways & Rothman/Wohl Prods
Exec Prod: Perry Lafferty;
Prods: Bernie Rothman, Jack Wohl;
Dir: Art Fisher
Wris: Bob Arnott, Coslough Johnson, Rothman, Wohl.
30 Mins, Tues (18), 7:30 pm.
WNBC-TV New York
General Foods (Benton & Bowles)
01/26/77S

GHOST OF A CHANCE
With Shelley Long, Barry Van Dyke, Steven Keats, Gretchen Wyler, Archie Hahn, Roslyn Kind, John O'Leary
Supplier: Arim Prods & Paramount TV
Exec Prod-Wris: Austin and Irma Kalish;
Prod: Gene Marcione;
Dir: Nick Havinga.
30 Mins, Mon, (7) 8 pm.
ABC-TV
07/16/80

GIBBSVILLE
With John Savage, Gig Young, Biff McGuire, Peggy McCay, Bert Remsen, Frank Campanella, Walter Pidgeon, Jane Wyatt, Diana Scarwid
Supplier: David Gerber Prods & Columbia TV
Exec Prod: Gerber;
Prod: John Furia Jr;
Dir: Harry Harris;
Wri: Jerry Ludwig.
60 Mins, Thurs, 10 pm.
NBC-TV
11/17/76

GIDEON'S TRUMPET
(Hallmark Hall of Fame)
With Henry Fonda, Jose Ferrer, John Houseman, Fay Wray, Sam Jaffe, Dean Jagger, Nicholas Pryor, William Prince, Lane Smith, Richard McKenzie, Dolph Sweet, Ford Rainey
Supplier: Worldvision Enterprises
Exec Prod: Houseman;
Prod-Wri: David W. Rintels (from the book by Anthony Lewis)
Dir: Robert Collins
120Mins, Wed, 9 pm.
CBS-TV
05/07/80

GINGER
With Ginger Rogers
Supplier: Seven Network
Exec Prod: Julian Gover.
60 Mins, Fri, 7:30 pm.
HSV-7 Melbourne, Australia
06/30/76F

THE GIRL, THE GOLD WATCH & EVERYTHING (Operation Prime Time)
With Robert Hays, Pam Dawber, Jill Ireland, Maurice Evans, Ed Nelson, Zohra Lampert, Macdonald Carey, Burton Gilliam, Larry Hankin, Peter Brown, John O'Leary
Supplier: Fellows-Keegan Co & Paramount TV
Exec Prods: Arthur Fellows, Terry Keegan;
Prod: Myrl A. Schreibman;
Dir: William Wiard;
Wri: George Zateslo, adapted from John D. MacDonald novel.
120 Mins, Fri, (13) 8 pm.
WPIX-TV New York
06/18/80S

GIRLS RUNNING THE CHINHSI RIVER ON RAFTS
Supplier: Peking Television
Dirs & Cameramen: Chu Ching-Ho, Chang Mao-Hsi.
26 Mins
MIP-TV, Cannes
05/18/77

GLENVIEW HIGH
With Grigor Taylor, Elaine Lee, Bill Kerr, Ken James, Brandon Burke, Rebecca Gilling, Camilla Rountree and guests
Supplier: Reg Grundy Productions Pty Ltd
Prod: Ron McLean
Dirs: Max Parnell, Bill Hughes;
Wris: Ron McLean, Tony Morphett, Derek Strachan, Bob Caswell.
60 Mins, Fri, 7:30 pm.
Channel 7 Network, Australia
10/26/77F

GLI OCCHI DEL DRAGO
(The Eyes Of The Dragon)
With Mario Adorf, Stefania Casini, Ugo Maria Morosi
Supplier: RAI
Dir: Piero Schivazappa;
Wri: Lucio Battistrada.
3 1 hour segments, Sept 25, Oct 2 & 9, 8:40 pm.
RAI-TV, Rome, Italy
10/12/77F

GLIDE TIME
With Ginette McDonald, Ken Blackburn, Peter Vere Jones, Grant Tilly, Ross Jolly, Jamie Higgins, Ian Watkin
Prod: Murray Reece;
Wris: Michael Anthony Noonan, Reece, (based on stage play by Roger Hall).
60 Mins, Sun, 8 pm.
TV-1 Wellington, N Z
09/06/78F

THE GLITTERING PRIZES
With Tom Conti, Eric Porter, Angela Down, Barbara Kellerman, Mark Wing-Davey, Leonard Sachs, David Robb, Anna Carteret, Clive Merrison, Anna Cunningham, Renee Goddard, others
Supplier: BBC-TV
Prod: Mark Shivas;
Dirs: Waris Hussein, Robert Knights;
Wri: Frederic Raphael.
80 Mins, Wed, 10:15 pm.
BBC-2, Britain
02/11/76F

GLOBAL PAPER: THE FIGHT FOR FOOD - PART ONE
With Julian Bond (host)
Supplier: WQED-TV Pittsburgh & American Universities Field Staff, for PBS
Exec Prod: Alvin H Perlmutter;
Prod-Dir: Robert Bendick;
Wri: Louis Solomon.
60 Mins, Sun (12), 8 pm.
WNET New York
11/15/78

THE GLORY OF THEIR TIMES
Exec Prod: Cappy Petrash;
Prod-Dir-Wri: Bud Greenspan.
60 Mins, Thurs (17), 9 pm.
PBS
03/23/77

GO TELL IT...BEN HOOKS REPORTS
With Ben Hooks
Supplier: Post-Newsweek Stations/WDIV Detroit
Exec Prod: Edmund S Dorsey;
Prod: Ronald Johnson;
Dir: Mike Strong.
30 Mins, Sat (6), 8 pm.
WNEW-TV New York
10/10/79S

THE GOD BOY
With Jamie Higgins, Ivan Beavis, Maria Craig, Graeme Tetley, Judy Douglass
Prod-dir: Murray Reece.
85 Mins, Sun 9 pm.
TV-1, from Wellington, New Zealand
04/14/76F

GOIN' HOME
With Ed McMahon, Roy Clark
Supplier: Marathon Entertainment
Exec Prod: Alan Lubell;
Prods: Paul Block, Anthony Eaton;
Dir: Phil Olsmen.
30 Mins, Thurs (5), 7:30 pm.
WNBC-TV New York
Alpo (Weightman Advertising)
01/11/78S

GOING HOME
With Terry Donovan, Rowena Wallace, Jennifer Cluff, Bill Hunter, Vincent Ball, Mark Clark, Tom Oliver, Jennifer West, Peter Gwynne, Kerry McGuire, Tom Farley, Moya O'Sullivan
Supplier: Australian Broadcasting Commission
Dir: Frank Arnold;
Wri: Colin Free.
55 Min, Thurs, 9 pm.
ABC (Australia) TV
05/25/77F

GOING UP EASY...COMING DOWN HARD
With Warner Saunders, others
Prod-Dir: Scott Craig;
Wri: Hank DeZutter.
30 Mins, Sat (11), 8:30 pm.
WBBM-TV Chicago
03/15/78

THE GOLDEN EELS
(Zlati Uhori)
With Martin Mikulas, Vladimir Mensik, Rudolf Hrusinsky, Slavka Stepankova-Hozova
Supplier: Czechoslovak TV
Dir-Wri: Karel Kachyna, based on book, "How I Met The Fishes," by Ota Pavel.
83 Mins.
(Prix Italia winner, drama)
10/03/79PI

GOLDEN SOAK
With Ray Barrett, Christiane Kruger, Elizabeth Alexander, Heinz Schimmelpfennig, Gunther Ungeheuer, Ruth Cracknell, others
Supplier: Australian Broadcasting Commission, in association with Portman Prods Ltd and Westdeutsches Werbefernsehen GmbH
Exec Prods: James Gatward, Geoffrey Daniels;
Prod: Ray Alchin, Gatward;
Dir: Henri Safran;
Wri: Peter Yeldham.
53 Mins, Tues, 8:30 pm.
ABC TV, Channel 2, Sydney, Australia
04/11/79F

GOLDIE
With Goldie Hawn, George Burns, Harlem Globetrotters, John Ritter, Shaun Cassidy, Patricia Birch Dancers
Supplier: George Schlatter Prods & Rutledge Prods
Prod: Schlatter;
Dir: Don Mischer;
Wris: Digby Wolfe, Schlatter, Earl Brown.
60 Mins, Wed (1), 8 pm.
CBS-TV
03/08/78

THE GONG SHOW
With Chuck Barris (host), Anson Williams, Phyllis Diller, Jamie Farr
Supplier: Chuck Barris-Chris Bearde Prods.
Prod: Barris;
Dir: Terry Kyne.
25 Mins, Mon-Fri, 12:30 pm.
NBC-TV
06/16/76

THE GONG SHOW
With Gary Owens (host), Phyllis Diller, Rex Reed, Elke Sommer
Supplier: Chuck Barris-Chris Bearde Prods (Firestone Syndication)
Prod: Barris;
Dir: John Dorsey.
30 Mins, Fri, 7:30 pm.
WABC-TV New York
09/29/76S

GOOD HEAVENS
With Carl Reiner, Peter Bonerz, Bert Convy, Kristina Holland, Brenda Vaccaro, Jack Riley, Joe Bernard, Ian Wolfe
Supplier: Columbia Pictures TV
Prod: Mel Swope;
Dir: Reiner;
Wri: Bernard Slade.
30 Mins, Sun (29), 10:25 pm.
ABC-TV
03/03/76

THE GOOD LIFE
With Richard Briers, Felicity Kendal, Penelope Keith, Paul Eddington
Supplier: BBC
Prod-dir: John Howard Davies;
Wris: John Esmonde, Bob Larby.
30 Min, Fri, 8:30 pm.
BBC-1, Britain
10/06/76F

GOOD MORNIN', BLUES
With narrator B B King
Supplier: Mississippi Authority for Educational Television
Exec Prod-Dir: Walt Lowe;
Prod: Rob Cooper.
60 Mins.
WMAA-TV Jackson, Miss
03/29/78

GOOD OL' BOYS
(NBC Comedy Theatre)
With Jerry Reed, Lane Caudell, Linda Thompson, Mo Malone, Mel Stewart, Dennis Harrison, Byron Warner
Supplier: Filmways TV
Exec Prod: Perry Lafferty;
Prods: William Finnegan, Ted Bergman;
Dir: Harry Falk;
Wri: Bergman.
30 Mins, Thurs (7), 8:30 pm.
NBC-TV
06/13/79

GOOD TIME GIRLS
With Annie Potts, Lorna Patterson, Georgia Engel, Francine Tacker, Marcia Lewis, Merwin Goldsmith, Peter Scolari, Adrian Zmed, Russ Thacker, Sparky Marcus, Alan McRae, Jack Blessing, Jennifer George
Supplier; Miller-Milkis-Boyett Prods. & Paramount TV
Exec Prods: Thomas L. Miller, Edward K. Milkis, Robert L. Boyett, Leonora Thuna;
Dir: Joel Zwick;
Wris: Sheldon Bull, E.J. Purdum, Leonard Ripps.
30 Mins, Tues, 8:30 pm.
ABC-TV
01/30/80

GOOD TIME HARRY
With Ted Bessell, Eugene Roche, Marcia Strassman, Jesse Wells, Richard Karron, Barry Gordon, Dan Hedaya, Ruth Manning, Steve Peterman, Jay Gerber, Phil Leeds, Julia Jennings
Supplier: Rollins-Joffe-Bessell Prods & Universal TV
Exec Prods: Charles Joffe, Larry Brezner;
Supv Prod-Wri: Steve Gordon;
Prod: Gareth Davies;
Dir: Jeff Chambers
60 Mins, Sat, (19) 10 pm.
NBC-TV
07/23/80

GOOD TIMES ROCK & ROLL
With Dick Liberatore, others
Exec Prod: Liberatore;
Dir: Pat Murray.
30 Mins, Sun, 10 pm.
WUAB-TV Cleveland
04/21/76

THE GOODIES
With Bill Oddie, Tim Brooke-Taylor, Graeme Garden
Supplier: BBC Television
Prod: Jim Franklin;
Wris: Oddie, Brooke-Taylor, Garden.
30 Mins, Tues, 8 pm.
Eastern Educational Network (WNET-TV)
08/11/76

THE GOODIES
With Tim Brooke-Taylor, Graeme Garden, Bill Oddie, others
Supplier: BBC
Prod: Jim Franklin;
Wris: Brooke-Taylor, Garden, Oddie.
30 Mins, Tues, 9:10 pm.
BBC-2, Britain
09/29/76F

THE GOVERNOR
With Corin Redgrave, Grant Tilly, George Henare, Tamahina Timarau, Judy Cleine, Anne Flannery, others
Supplier: Television One
Prod-Dir: Tony Isaac;
Wri: Keith Aberdein.
90 Mins, Sun, 8:30 pm.
TV-1, Wellington, New Zealand
10/19/77F

GRAMMY AWARDS
With Andy Williams, others
Supplier: Pierre Cossette Prod.
Exec Prod: Cossette;
Prod-Dir: Marty Pasetta.
105 Mins, Sat (28), 10 pm.
CBS-TV
03/03/76

GRAND SLAM
With Tom Kennedy (host)
Supplier: Ralph Andrews Prods
Exec Prod: Andrews;
Prod: George Vosburgh;
Dir: Dick McDonough.
30 Mins, Mon-Fri, noon.
NBC-TV
10/13/76

GRANDPA GOES TO WASHINGTON
With Jack Albertson, Larry Linville, Sue Anne Langdon, Michele Tobin, Sparky Marcus, Madge Sinclair, Nicholas Coster, William Daniels, Sandra Kerns, Rue McClanahan, James McEachin, Roger Bowen, Parley Baer, William Bogert, Fredd Wayne, Richard Eastham
Supplier: Paramount TV
Exec Prod: Richard P Rosetti;
Prod: Robert Stambler;
Dir: Richard Crenna;
Wris: Rosetti, Noel Baldwin, Lane Slate.
60 Mins, Thurs (7), 9 pm.
NBC-TV
09/13/78

GRAPEVINE
With Maggie Pinhorn, Iain Watkinson
Supplier: BBC
Prod: Mike Bolland;
Dir: Marilyn Wheatcrot.
30 Mins, Mon, 7:45 pm.
BBC, from London, England
08/03/77F

THE GRASS IS ALWAYS GREENER OVER THE SEPTIC TANK
With Carol Burnett, Charles Grodin, Alex Rocco, Linda Gray, Robert Sampson, Vicki Belmonte, Craig Richard Nelson, Annrae Walterhouse, Eric Stolz, David Hollander, Pat Wilson, Edwina Gough, Frank Reilly, Morgan Upton
Supplier: Joe Hamilton Prods
Supv Prods: Roger Beaty, Tom Egan;
Prod: Hamilton;
Dir: Robert Day;
Wris: Dick Clair & Jenna McMahon, from Erma Bombeck's book.
120 Mins, Wed (25), 9 pm.
CBS-TV
11/01/78

THE GREAT AMERICAN MUSIC CELEBRATION
With Lorne Greene, Dionne Warwick, Harve Presnell, The Four King Cousins, Brian Davies, Dale Verdugo, Rich Page, UCLA Marching Band, Southern California Mormon Choir
Supplier: Show Prods. & LenJen Prods. (Program Syndication Services & 20th-Fox TV)
Exec Prod: George Paris;
Prod-dir: Buddy Bregman;
Wri: John Bradford.
60 mins, Sun (27), 9 pm.
WNEW-TV New York
General Mills (Dancer-Fitzgerald-Sample)
06/30/76S

THE GREAT DETECTIVE
With Douglas Campbell
Exec Prod: Robert Allen;
Prod: Peter Wildblood;
Dir: Herb Rolland;
Wri: David Helwig.
60 Mins, Wed, 8:30 pm.
CBC-TV, from Toronto, Canada
02/21/79F

THE GREAT METRIC MYSTERY
With Alan Sues
Exec Prod: Inez Gottlieb;
Prod-Wri: Ted Field;
Dir: Don Matticks.
30 Mins, Tues (22), 7:30 pm.
WCAU-TV Philadelphia
12/14/77

THE GREAT WALLENDAS
(NBC Movie Of the Week)
With Lloyd Bridges, Britt Ekland, Taina Elg, Cathy Rigby, John van Dreelen, Michael McGuire, Ben Fuhrman, William Sadler, Bruce Ornstein, Stephen Parr, Travis Hudson, Isa Thomas, Casey Biggs, Lucinda Bridges
Supplier: Daniel Wilson Prods
Exec Prod: Wilson;
Prod: Linda Marmelstein;
Dir: Larry Elikann;
Wri: Jan Hartman.
120 Mins, Sun (12), 7 pm.
NBC-TV
02/15/78

THE GREATER CLEVELAND TV TEST SHOW
With David Patterson, Wilma Smith
Prod-Dir: Joseph Horning;
Dir: Bill Weidemann.
60 Mins, Thurs, 7 pm.
WEWS-TV Cleveland
09/27/78

GREATEST SPORTS LEGENDS
With Tom Seaver, Ted Williams
Supplier: Sport Legends Inc Prods-Marathon Entertainment
Exec Prod: Bert Rotfeld;
Dir: Mort Kasman.
30 Mins, Sun, 1 pm.
WOR-TV New York
04/05/78S

GRUPPENBILD MIT HAIFISCH
(Group Portrait With Shark)
With Hans C. Blumenberg, narrator
Supplier: Westdeutsches Fernsehen, Cologne
Prod: Westdeutsches Fernsehen, Cologne;
Dir-wri: Blumenberg.
45 Mins, Thurs, 9 pm.
WDR, from Cologne, West Germany
04/07/76F

GUESS WHO'S PREGNANT?
Prod-Wris: Elayne Goldstein, Michael Hirsh.
60 Mins, Fri (3), 10 pm.
PBS via WTTW-TV Chicago
06/15/77

THE GUINNESS GAME
With Bob Hilton (host)
Supplier: David Paradine TV Prods, Hill-Eubanks Group (20th-Fox TV & Ogilvy & Mather)
Exec Prod: Marvin Minoff;
Prods: Walt Case, Michael Hill;
Dir: George Paul;
Wris: Bill Mitchell, Peter Berlin.
30 Mins, Mon (12), 7:30 pm.
WNBC-TV New York
General Foods (Ogilvy & Mather)
02/21/79S

THE GUINNESS GAME
With Don Galloway (host)
Supplier: David Paradine TV, Hill-Eubanks Group & 20th-Fox TV (Ogilvy & Mather)
Exec Prod: Marvin Minoff;
Prods: Michael Hill, Walt Case;
Dir: George Paul.
30 Mins, Sat, 7:30 pm.
WNBC-TV New York
09/26/79S

GUN CONTROL
With Lucian Bicci, Lowell Green, others
Prod: Robert D Clark.
30 Mins, Sat, 7 pm.
CBOT Ottawa, Canada
03/23/77F

GUNTHER GEBEL-WILLIAMS: LORD OF THE RING
With Tony Curtis (host), Siegfried & Roy, Ray Berwick, Sigrid, Tina & Buffy Gebel-Williams
Supplier: Ringling Bros and Barnum & Bailey Circus
Exec Prods: Irvin & Kenneth Feld;
Prods: John Moffitt, Robert Arthur;
Dir: Moffitt;
Wri: Arthur.
60 Mins, Fri (25), 8 pm.
CBS-TV
11/30/77

GUYANA TRAGEDY: THE STORY OF JIM JONES
With Powers Boothe, Ned Beatty, Irene Cara, Veronica Cartright, Rosalind Cash, Brad Dourif, Meg Foster, Michael C. Gwynne, Albert Hall, Linda Haynes, Diane Ladd, Ron O'Neal, Randy Quaid, Diana Scarwid, Madge Sinclair, Brenda Vaccaro, LeVar Burton, Colleen Dewhurst, Clifton James, Ed Lauter, James Earl Jones, Dimitra Arliss, Benji Wilhoite
Supplier: The Konigsberg Co.
Exec Prod: Frank Konigsberg;
Prods: Ernest Tidyman, Sam Manners;
Dir: William A. Graham;
Wri: Tidyman.
240 Mins, (two parts), Tues-Wed, (15-16) 9 pm.
CBS-TV
04/23/80

GYPSY IN MY SOUL
With Shirley MacLaine, Lucille Ball, others
Exec Prod: William O. Harbach;
Prods: Cy Coleman, Fred Ebb;
Dir: Tony Charmoli.
60 Mins, Tues (20), 10 pm.
CBS-TV
Kraft Foods (JWT)
01/28/76

THE GYPSY WARRIORS
With James Whitmore Jr, Tom Selleck, Joseph Ruskin, Lina Raymond, Michael Lane, Ted Gehring, Albert Paulsen, Kenneth Tigar, William Wheatly, Hubert Noel, Kathryn Leigh Scott, Lester Fletcher, Linda Pierson
Supplier: Stephen J Cannell Prods & Universal TV
Exec Prod: Cannell;
Prod: Alex Beaton;
Dir: Lou Antonio;
Wris: Cannell, Philip DeGuere.
60 Mins, Fri (12), 10 pm.
CBS-TV
05/17/78

HAGEN
With Chad Everett, Arthur Hill, Stephanie Zimbalist, Paul Pape, Carmen Zapata, Wendy Phillips, Lee DeBroux, Robert Shields, Aldine King, Paul Larson, Stefanie Kramer, Ray Stricklyn
Supplier: Frank Glicksman Prods., Chad Everett Prods. & 20th-Fox TV
Exec Prod: Glicksman;
Prod: Jack B. Sowards;
Dir: Vincent Sherman;
Wri: Charles Larson.
60 Mins, Sat, 10 pm.
CBS-TV
03/05/80

HAILEY'S GIFT
With Barry Morse, Kate Parr
Prod: Robert Vale;
Dir: Bruce Pitman;
Wri: Chris Wardrope.
30 Mins, Sun, 7:30 pm.
CBC-TV, from Toronto, Canada
10/12/77F

THE HAL LINDEN SPECIAL
With Linda Lavin, Bonnie Franklin, Cathryn Damon, Joe Layton Dancers
Supplier: INJA Inc & Welch-Layton-Welch Prods
Exec Prods: Jerry Levy, Paul Tush;
Prods: Layton, Ken & Mitzie Welch;
Dirs: Kip Walton, Layton;
Wris: Stan Hart, Jules Tasca, Mitzie Welch.
60 Mins, Wed (11), 10 pm.
ABC-TV
Kentucky Fried Chicken (Y&R)
04/18/79

HALLOWEEN IS GRINCH NIGHT
(Dr Seuss Presents)
With voices of Hans Conried, Hal Smith, Gary Shapiro, Irene Tedrow, Jack DeLeon, Henry Gibson
Supplier: Dr Seuss & A S Geisel Prods & DePatie-Freleng Enterprises
Exec Prods: David H DePatie, Friz Freleng;
Prod: Ted Geisel;
Dir: Gerald Baldwin;
Wri: Dr Seuss (Geisel).
30 Mins, Sat, 8 pm.
ABC-TV
Parker Bros (Humphrey, Browning & MacDougal)
11/09/77

HANDWORK IN HOLLYWOOD
With Hans C. Blumenberg, narrator
Supplier: Westdeutsches Fernsehen, Cologne;
Prod: Westdeutsches Fernsehen, Cologne;
Dir-wri: Blumenberg.
45 Mins, Wed (10), 9:35 pm.
WDR, Third Program, from Cologne, West Germany
03/24/76F

HANGING IN
With Bill Macy, Barbara Rhoades, Dennis Burkley, Nedra Volz, Darian Mathias, Billy Beck
Supplier: TAT Communications
Prod: Sy Rosen;
Dir: Alan Rafkin;
Wris: Charlie Hauck, Arthur Julian, Bill Davenport.
30 Mins, Wed, 8:30 pm.
CBS-TV
08/15/79

THE HANNA BARBERA HAPPY HOUR
With Honey and Sis, Charo, Anson Williams, Gavin MacLeod, Leif Garrett, Yogi Bear
Supplier: Hanna-Barbera Prods
Exec Prod: Joseph Barbera;
Prods: Joe Layton, Ken Welch, Mitzie Welch;
Dirs: Layton, Jim Washburn;
Wri: Stan Hart.
60 Mins, Thurs, 8 pm.
NBC-TV
04/19/78

HANSEL AND GRETEL
With Adelaide Nelson, Patricia Lee Bates, Philip Kraus, Jenny Klein, James Rensink, Catherine Caccavallo, others
Prod: Richard Carter;
Dirs: Robert Gay, Carter.
60 Mins, Tues, 8 pm.
WTTW-TV Chicago
02/22/78

HAPPY BIRTHDAY, BEULAH WITCH
With Burr Tillstrom, Fran Allison, Kuklapolitan Players
Supplier: Lexington Broadcast Services
Prod: Nick Aronson;
Dir: James Tanker;
Wris: Tillstrom, Allison.
30 Mins, Fri, 6:30 pm.
WMAQ-TV, Chicago
11/05/80

HAPPY BIRTHDAY, BOB
With Lynn Anderson, Pearl Bailey, Lucille Ball, George Burns, Charo, Bert Convy, Kathryn Crosby, Mac Davis, Sammy Davis Jr, Redd Foxx, Elliott Gould, Dolores Hope, K C & Sunshine Band, Alan King, Dorothy Lamour, Carol Lawrence Fred MacMurray, Jim Henson's Muppets with Frank Oz, Tony Orlando, Donny & Marie Osmond, Charles Nelson Reilly, Telly Savalas, George C Scott, Shields & Yarnell, David Soul, Elizabeth Taylor, Danny Thomas, Fred Travalena, John Wayne, Les Brown orch, Carl Jablonski Dancers, Bob Hope
Supplier: James Lipton Prods & Rafshoon Communications
Exec Prods: Lipton, Gerald Rafshoon;
Prods: Bob Wynn, John Hamlin;
Dir: Wynn;
Wris: Lipton, Bob Arnott.
180 Mins, Mon (29), 8 pm.
NBC-TV
05/31/78

HARD TIME
With Aaron Brown
Prod: Roger Bergson;
Exec Prod: Don LaCombe.
30 Mins, Tues, 10:30 pm.
KING-TV Seattle
05/07/80

HARD TIMES
(Great Performances)
With Patrick Allen, Timothy West, Alan Dobie, Jacqueline Tong, Michelle Dibnah, Rosalie Crutchley, Barbara Ewing, others
Supplier: Granada TV, WNET N Y
Prod: Peter Eckersley;
Dir: John Irvin;
Wri: Arthur Hopcraft, from novel by Charles Dickens.
60 Mins, Wed (11), 9 pm.
PBS
05/18/77

THE HARD WAY
With Patrick McGoohan, Lee Van Cleef, Edna O'Brien, Donal McCann, Ronan Wilmot, Kevin Flood, Derek Lord.
Supplier: ATV (Skyring Ltd.)
Exec Prod: John Boorman;
Prod-Dir: Michael Dryhurst.
87 Mins, Wed, (20), 8 pm.
ITV Network, Britain
02/27/80F

HARDY BOYS MYSTERIES
(Hardy Boys & Nancy Drew Mysteries)
With Shaun Cassidy, Parker Stevenson, Lisa Eilbacher, Edmond Gilbert, Edith Atwater, Roger Davis, Simon Scott, Richard Kiel, Jim Antonio, John Kerry, George Murdock, Lew Brown, Dick Ryal, Reggie Nalder, Bonnie Ebsen
Supplier: Universal TV & Glen Larson Prods
Exec Prod-Dir-Wri: Glen A. Larson;
Prods: Joyce Heft Brotman, Arlene Sidaris.
60 Mins, Sun, 7 pm.
ABC-TV
02/02/77

HARRIS & COMPANY
With Bernie Casey, David Hubbard, Renee Brown, Lia Jackson, Dain Turner, Eddie Singleton, Stu Gilliam, C Tillery Banks, Louis Walden, James Luisi, Rory Calhoun, Bibi Besch, Isabel Cooley
Supplier: Universal TV
Exec Prod: Stanley G Robertson;
Prod: Arnold F Turner;
Dir: Tom Blank;
Wri: Lee Reynolds.
60 Mins, Thurs, 8 pm.
NBC-TV
03/21/79

HART TO HART
(ABC Saturday Night Movie)
With Robert Wagner, Stefanie Powers, Lionel Stander, Roddy McDowall, Jill St John, Eugene Roche, Clifton James, Michael Lerner, Stella Stevens, Lee Bryant, James Noble, Mimi Maynard, David Landsberg, Paul Napier, Paul Tuerpe, Art Kassul, Tara Buckman, Lina Raymond
Supplier: Rona II & Spelling-Goldberg Prods
Prods: Aaron Spelling, Leonard Goldberg;
Dir: Tom Mankiewicz;
Wris: Sidney Sheldon, Mankiewicz.
120 Mins, Sat (25), 9 pm.
ABC-TV
08/29/79

HARVEY KORMAN SHOW
With Susan Lawrence, Milton Selzer, Barry Van Dyke, Penelope Windust, Dino Natali, Don Sparks, Bart Braverman, Alma Beltran
Supplier: Chrisma Prods
Exec Prod-Wri: Hal Dresner;
Prod: Don Van Atta;
Dir: Alan Myerson.
30 Mins, Thurs (19), 9:30 pm.
ABC-TV
05/25/77

HARVEY KORMAN SHOW
With Christine Lahti, Barry Van Dyke, Milton Selzer, Marian Mercer, Harry Gold, Peggy Rea
Supplier: Chrisma Prods
Exec Prod: Hal Dresner;
Prod: Don Van Atta;
Dir: Alan Myerson;
Wris: Michael Kagan, Harry Cauley.
30 Mins, Tues (31), 9:30 pm.
ABC-TV
02/08/78

HAS ANYBODY HERE SEEN CANADA?
Narrated by Michael Kane
Exec Prod: Arthur Hammond;
Prods: Kirwan Cox, Mike McKennirey;
Dir: John Kramer;
Wri: Donald Brittain.
90 Mins, Tues, 9:30 pm.
CBC, from Toronto, Canada
05/09/79F

HAZARD'S PEOPLE
With John Houseman, Jesse Welles, John Elerick, Roger Hill, Stefan Gierasch, Michael Tolan, Hope Lange, Doreen Lang, Cliff Emmich, Richard Herd, James Whitmore Jr., Joseph Burke, Red Colbin
Supplier: Roy Huggins Public Arts & Universal TV
Exec Prod: Jo Swerling Jr.;
Prod: Huggins;
Dir: Jeannot Szwarc;
Wri: Heywood Gould.
60 Mins, Fri (9), 10 pm.
CBS-TV
04/14/76

HEADLINERS WITH DAVID FROST
With Richard Helms, Bee Gees, John Travolta, Kelly Garrett, Liz Smith
Supplier: David Paradine TV Prods
Exec Prod: Frost
Prod: John Gilroy;
Dir: Bruce Gowers.
60 Mins, Wed, 9 pm.
NBC-TV
06/07/78

HEE HAW HONEYS
With Kathie Epstein, Catherine Hickland, Muffi Durham, Kenny Price, John Tuell, Joe Higgins, Jackie Kahane, Bob McClurg, Roy Clark, Billy Carter
Supplier: Yongestreet Prods (Lexington Broadcast Services)
Exec Prods: Frank Peppiatt & John Aylesworth;
Prod: Sam Lovullo;
Wris: Peppiatt, Aylesworth, Barry Adelman, Barry Silver.
30 Mins, Wed (28), 7:30 pm.
WNBC-TV New York
Procter & Gamble (Grey)
01/11/78S

HEE HAW HONEYS
With Lulu Roman, Kenny Price, Gailard Sartain, Kathie Lee Johnson, Misty Rowe, Sammi Smith
Supplier: Yongestreet Prods (Lexington Broadcast Services)
Exec Prod: Sam Lovullo;
Dir: Bob Boatman;
Wris: Barry Adelman, Barry Silver, Jeanine Burnier, Don Sherman.
30 Mins, Sat, 5 pm.
WNBC-TV New York
10/04/78S

HEE HAW 10TH ANNIVERSARY SHOW
With Roy Clark, Buck Owens, Minnie Pearl, Chet Atkins, Tennessee Ernie Ford, Larry Gatlin, Crystal Gayle, Tom T Hall, Loretta Lynn, Barbara Mandrell, Ronnie Milsap, Charley Pride, Kenny Rogers, Roy Rogers, Dale Evans, Mel Tillis, Conway Twitty, Tammy Wynette, and show regulars
Supplier: Yongestreet Entertainment Corp
Exec Prods: Frank Peppiatt, John Aylesworth;
Prod: Sam Lovullo;
Dir: Bill Davis;
Wris: Peppiatt, Aylesworth.
120 Mins, Sun (22), 8 pm.
NBC-TV
10/25/78

HELLO, LARRY
With McLean Stevenson, Joanna Gleason, Kim Richards, Donna Wilkes, George Memmoli, Joe Medalis
Supplier: T A T Communications
Exec Prods: Dick Bensfield, Perry Grant;
Prod: George Tibbles;
Dir: Doug Rogers;
Wris: Bensfield, Grant.
30 Mins, Fri, 9:30 pm.
NBC-TV
01/31/79

HELTER SKELTER
With George DiCenzo, Steve Railsback, Nancy Wolfe, Marilyn Burns, Christina Hart, Cathey Paine, Alan Oppenheimer, Rudy Ramos, Sondra Blake, George Garro, Vic Werber, Howard Caine, Jason Ronard, Skip Homeier, others
Supplier: Lorimar Prods.
Exec Prods: Lee Rich, Philip Capice;
Prod-dir: Tom Gries;
Wri: JP Miller, from the book by Vincent Bugliosi wth Curt Gentry.
240 Mins Thurs & Fri (1-2), 9-11 pm.
CBS-TV
04/07/76

THE HENDERSON MONSTER
With Jason Miller, Christine Lahti, Stephen Collins, David Spielberg, Nehemiah Persoff, Larry Gates, Josef Sommer, Peter Evans, Kenneth Kimmins, Mark Hulcher, Andrew Early, Glenn Crone, Lalla Rolfe, David Kilgore, Cherie Scheer, Deborah Nunamaker, Anne Goodwin, Steve Boschen, Carl Lester, Beatrice Bush
Supplier: Titus Prods
Exec Prod: Herbert Brodkin;
Prod: Robert Berger;
Dir: Waris Hussein;
Wri: Ernest Kinoy.
120 Mins, Tues, (27) 9 pm.
CBS-TV
06/11/80

HENRY KISSINGER: ON THE RECORD
With David Brinkley
Supplier: NBC News
Exec Prod: Stuart Schulberg;
Prods: Thomas Tomizawa, William Cosmas;
Dirs: Schulberg, Tomizawa, Tony Reidl.
90 Mins, Fri (13), 9:30 pm.
NBC-TV
01/18/78

HERE COMES THE SUN
Prod-Wri: Wendall Anschutz
30 Mins, Fri, 9:30 pm.
KCMO-TV Kansas City
05/11/77S

HERE'S BOOMER
With Johnny (dog), Dee Wallace, Guy Boyd, Fran Bennett, Natasha Ryan, Betty Baird
Supplier: A.C. Lyles Prods., Daniel Wilson Prods, & Paramount TV
Exec Prods: Lyles, Wilson;
Prod: Fran Sears;
Dir: Larry Elikann;
Wris: Carolyn Handler Miller, Daryl Warner
30 Mins, Fri, 8 pm.
NBC-TV
03/19/80

HERE'S TO YOU, MR. ROBINSON
Supplier: Melbourne Film-Makers Cooperative
Prods-dirs: Peter Tammer, Gary Patterson.
50 Mins.
Melbourne, Australia
07/14/76F

THE HERITAGE OF IRELAND
With Douglas Gageby, voices of Hilton Edwards, Denis Brennan, Derek Lord, Niall Toibin
Supplier: Louis Marcus Films
Prod-Dir: Marcus;
Wri: Gageby.
50 Mins, Mon, 7:55 pm.
Radio Telefis Eireann, Dublin, Ireland
12/06/78F

HESS
With Wolf Kahler, John Stride, David Robb, others
Supplier: Scottish Television
Rex Firkin;
Dir: Tina Wakerell;
Wri: Ian Curteis.
60 Mins, Sat, 10 pm.
ITV, Britain
11/15/78F

HEWITT'S JUST DIFFERENT
(ABC Afterschool Special)
With Perry Lang, Moosie Drier, Peter Brandon, Gloria Strook, Peggy McCay, Russell Johnson, Christopher Maleki, Doney Oatman, Jarrod Johnson, Tom Gulager, Stack Pierce, Mike Luther
Supplier: Danny Wilson Prods
Exec Prod: Wilson;
Prod: Fran Sears;
Dir: Larry Elikann;
Wri: Jan Hartman.
60 Mins, Wed (12), 4:30 pm.
ABC-TV
10/19/77

HI SUMMER
With Leslie Crowther, Anna Dawson, Pearly Gates, Derek Griffiths, others
Supplier: London Weekend Television
Prods: Bruce Gowers, Dougie Squires;
Dirs: Bruce Gowers, Paul Smith;
Wri: Erick Davidson.
45 Mins, Sun, 7:15 pm.
ITV, from London, England
08/31/77F

HICKEY VS ANYBODY
With Jack Weston, Malcolm Atterbury, Liberty Williams, Beverly Sanders, Jack Gilford, Alan Manson, Jessamine Milner
Supplier: Alan Alda-Marc Merson Helix Prods
Prod: Merson;
Dir-wri: Alda.
30 Mins, Sun (19), 10 pm.
NBC-TV
09/22/76

HIGH HOPES
With Bruce Gray, Marianne McIsaac, Doris Petrie, Nuala FitzGerald, Barbara Kyle, Colin Fox, Jan Muszinski, Gordon Thomson, Jayne Eastwood, Gina Dick, Norma Reis, Michael Tait, Debra Turnbull
Supplier: Y&R Prods & DCA Prods (Y&R Ventures for The Serial Network)
Exec Prod: Dick Cox;
Prods: Robert M Driscoll, Karen Hazzard;
Dir: Bruce M Minnix;
Wris: Winnifred Wolfe, Mort Forer.
30 Mins, Mon-Fri, 10:30 am.
WNEW-TV New York
04/05/78S

HIGHCLIFFE MANOR
With Shelley Fabares, Stephen McHattie, Eugenie Ross-Leming, Audrey Landers, Gerald Gordon, Christian Marlowe, Jenny O'Hara, David Byrd, Luis Avalos, Ernie Hudson, Harold Sakata
Supplier: TAT Prods
Supv Prod: Alan Horn;
Prods-Wris: Ross-Leming, Brad Buckner;
Dir: Nick Havinga.
30 Mins, Thurs, 8:30 pm.
NBC-TV
04/18/79

HIGHLIGHTS OF RINGLING BROS AND BARNUM & BAILEY CIRCUS
With Dick Van Dyke, host; Charly Bamann, Flying Gaonas, Michu, King Charles Troupe, Elvin Bale, Jewell New, Woodcock Family, Kondovi, Slavovi, Romanovi, Paniotovi, Kehaiovi, Oblocki, Wozniaks, Michu, Maria Augustin, Harold Ronk
Supplier: Ringling Bros & Barnum & Bailey Prods
Exec Prods: Irving Feld, Kenneth Feld;
Prod-Dir: John Moffitt;
Wri: Ken Shapiro.
60 Mins, Wed, (8), 8 pm.
NBC-TV
Borden (Conahey & Lyons Inc)
03/15/78

HIGHLIGHTS OF THE RUSSIAN DANCE FESTIVAL
With Orson Welles (host), Georgian State Dance Company, Ukrainian Dance Company, Piatnitsky Folk Choir & Dancers, Natalia & Oleg Kiriushkin, Komuzisty Chamber Ensemble, Mengo Ensemble of the Northern Nations, Artists from the Tadzhik Republic
Supplier: United Euram in association with Gosconcert, Moscow, USSR (Worldvision)
Prod-Dir: Mike Gargiulo;
Art Dir: Igor Moiseyev;
Commentary Wri: Chuck Horner.
60 Mins, Thurs (7), 8 pm.
NBC-TV
07/13/77

HIP HIP PARADE
With Kermit the Frog (Jim Henson), Fozzie Bear (Frank Oz)
Supplier: Educational Broadcasting Corp
Exec Prod: Edward Hann;
Prod: Isabella Dane;
Dir: David Heeley.
30 Mins, Wed (22), 8:30 pm.
WNET New York
11/29/78

HITACHI SOUTHERN CROSS CUP SERIES 1979
Supplier: Australian Broadcasting Commission
Exec Prod: James Allan;
Dir: Peter Lipscombe;
Wri-Narr: Gordon Bray.
55 Mins, Fri, 7:30 pm.
ABC (Australia) TV, Channel 2, Sydney
02/20/80F

HIZZONNER
With David Huddleston, Diana Muldaur, Mickey Deems, Kathy Cronkite, Will Seltzer, Gina Hecht, Don Galloway, Sid Gould, Elizabeth Kerr, Don Wyatt, Dale Malone, Allan Louw
Supplier: The Huddleston Co.
Exec Prod: Huddleston;
Prod-Wri: Sheldon Keller;
Dir: Joan Darling.
30 Mins, Thurs, 8 pm.
NBC-TV
05/16/79

THE HOBBIT
With voices of Orson Bean, Richard Boone, Hans Conreid, John Huston, Otto Preminger, Cyril Ritchard, Theodore, Paul Frees, John Stephenson, Don Messick, Jack DeLeon
Supplier: Rankin-Bass Prods
Prod-Dirs: Arthur Rankin Jr, Jules Bass;
Wri: Romeo Muller, from novel by J R R Tolkien.
90 Mins, Sun (27), 8 pm.
NBC-TV
Xerox Corp (Needham, Harper & Steers)
11/30/77

HOLIDAY WITH BILL PEACH
With Bill Peach, Janet Kingsbury, Jeff Watson, Peter Wilkinson
Supplier: Australian Broadcasting Commission
Exec Prod: Bruce Buchanan;
Dir: David Telfer.
30 Mins, Wed, 7:30 pm.
ABC TV, Channel 2, Sydney, Australia
04/11/79F

HOLLOW IMAGE
(ABC Theatre)
With Saundra Sharp, Dick Anthony Williams, Robert Hooks, Morgan Freeman, Hattie Winston, Anna Maria Horsford, Samuel E Wright, Minnie Gentry
Supplier: Titus Prods
Exec Prod: Herb Brodkin;
Supv Prod: Buzz Berger;
Prods: Thomas DeWolfe, Stephen Rotter;
Dir: Marvin J Chomsky;
Wri: Lee Hunkins.
120 Mins, Sun (24), 9 pm.
ABC-TV
06/27/79

HOLLYWOOD
With James Mason
Supplier: Thames Television-D.L. Taffner Ltd
Exec Prod: Mike Wooller;
Wris-Dirs: Kevin Brownlow, David Gill.
60 Mins, Mon, 8 pm.
WOR-TV New York
04/30/80S

HOLLYWOOD DREAM-MAKER
With Robert Stevenson
Prod: James Wilson.
50 Mins, Sat.
BBC-TV, from Glasgow, Scotland
09/29/76F

HOLLYWOOD HIGH
With Annie Potts, Roberta Wallach, Darrin O'Conner, John Guerrasio, Beverly Sanders, Dick O'Neill, Will MacKenzie, Janet Wood
Supplier: The Jozak Co & Paramount TV
Exec Prods: Gerald I Isenberg, Gerald W Abrams;
Prods: Elias Davis & David Pollock;
Dir: Burt Brinckerhoff;
Wris: Pollock, Davis (first); Lloyd Garver (2d).
60 Mins, Thurs, 8 pm.
NBC-TV
08/03/77

HOLLYWOOD OUT-TAKES
With Marilyn Beck, Jenny Agutter, David Carradine, Blake Edwards, Bob Evans, William Holden, Bob Hope, Alan Pakula, Jon Peters, Michael Phillips, Talia Shire, Sylvester Stallone, Burt Young
Supplier: Frederick-Miner-Saunder Prods
Exec Prod-Dir: Dick Schneider;
Prod: Herman Saunders;
Wris: Bill Richmond, Gene Perret.
60 Mins, Sun (27), 10 pm.
NBC-TV
03/30/77

HOLMES & YOYO
With Richard B. Shull, John Schuck, Bruce Kirby, Andrea Howard, Allan Miller, Larry Hovis, G Wood, Madison Arnold, Sarah Janes Miller, Ralph Manza
Supplier: Heyday Prods & Universal TV
Exec Prod: Leonard B. Stern;
Prod-dir: Jackie Cooper;
Wris: Jack Sher, Lee Hewitt, Stern.
30 Mins, Sat, 8 pm.
ABC-TV
09/29/76

HOLOCAUST - PART ONE
(The Big Event)
With Fritz Weaver, Rosemary Harris, Joseph Bottoms, James Woods, Meryl Streep, Michael Moriarty, George Rose, David Warner, Tom Bell, Tovah Feldshuh, Sam Wanamaker, Marius Goring, Deborah Norton, Robert Stephens, Blanche Baker, Ian Holm, Anthony Haygarth
Supplier: Titus Prods
Exec Prod: Herbert Brodkin;
Prod: Robert Berger;
Dir: Marvin J Chomsky;
Wri: Gerald Green.
180 Mins, Sun (16), 8 pm.
NBC-TV
04/19/78

HOMAGE TO CHAGALL--THE COLORS OF LOVE
With James Mason, Joseph Wiseman
Prod-Dir-Wri: Harry Rasky.
90 Mins, Wed, 9:30 pm.
CBC-TV, from Toronto, Canada
04/13/77F

HOME SWEET HOME
With John Bluthal, Arianthe Galani, Christopher Bell, Carmen Tanti, Miles Buchanan, Maria Rose Cerizzi, Edmunde Pegge, Sandra Lee Paterson, Ray Barrett, Chelsea Brown, Brian Wenzal, David Goddard, Peter Whitford, Gerry Duggan, Terry Bader, Doug Scroope
Supplier: Australian Broadcasting Commission
Exec Prod: John O'Grady;
Prod: Michael Mills;
Wris: Vince Powell, David Dominic, Charles Stamp, Hugh Stuckey;
Dirs: Michael Mills, Geoff Portman, David Goldie.
30 Mins, Mon, 7:30 pm.
ABC (Australia) TV, Channel 2, Sydney
10/15/80F

THE HOMECOMING
With Hagood Hardy, Veronica Tennant, Frank Augustyn, Toller Cranston, Shirley Eikhard
Prod-wri: Ray McConnell;
Dir: Ron Cantor;
60 Mins, Fri, 9 pm.
CBC-TV, from Toronto, Canada
05/05/76F

HONEST AL'S A-OK USED CAR & TRAILER RENTAL TIGERS
With Herb Edelman, Danny Bonaduce, Zoey Wilson, Kyra Stempel, D White, Marc Jason, J R Miller
Supplier: Daniel Wilson Prods (Program Syndication Services)
Exec Prod: D Wilson;
Prod: Fran Sears;
Dir: Jeff Bleckner;
Wri: Lee Kalcheim.
30 Mins, Fri, 7:30 pm.
WABC-TV New York
02/08/78S

THE HONEYMOONERS CHRISTMAS SPECIAL
With Jackie Gleason, Art Carney, Audrey Meadows, Jane Kean, Gale Gordon, Johnny Olsen
Supplier: Peekskill Enterprises
Exec Prod: Jack Philbin;
Prod: Ed Waglin;
Dir: Gleason;
Wris: Walter Stone, Robert Hilliard.
60 Mins, Mon (28), 8 pm.
ABC-TV
12/07/77

THE HONEYMOONERS - THE SECOND HONEYMOON
With Jackie Gleason, Audrey Meadows, Art Carney, Jane Kean, Templeton Fox
Supplier: Peekskill Productions
Exec Prod: Jack Philbin;
Prod: Ed Waglin;
Dir: Gleason;
Wri: Walter Stone.
60 Mins, Mon (2), 8 pm.
ABC-TV
02/04/76

HORIZON
(The Case of The Ancient Astronauts)
Supplier: BBC
Prod-Wri: Graham Massey.
90 Mins, Fri, 9 pm.
BBC 2, from England
12/14/77F

HORN OF PLENTY
With Patricia Gormin
Prod-Wri: Gormin;
Dir: Robert Weaver.
30 Mins, Mon (29), 6:30 pm.
WVUE-TV New Orleans
02/14/79

HOSPITAL
(Casualty)
Supplier: BBC
Prod: Tim King.
45 Mins, Wed, 9 pm.
BBC, England
11/16/77F

HOT CITY
With Linda Clifford, Sylvers, Fyre
Supplier: Viacom Enterprises
Exec Prod: Ed Warren;
Prod-Dir: Kip Walton.
60 Mins, Mon, 8 pm & Fri, Midnight.
KTTV Los Angeles
08/16/78S

HOT HERO SANDWICH
With L Michael Craig, Vicky Dawson, Denny Dillon, Matt McCoy, Nan-Lynn Nelson, Paul O'Keefe, Jarett SmithWrick, Andrew Duncan, Frankie Russell Faison, Saundra McClain, Claudette Sutherland, Adam Ross, Thomas Cottle
Supplier: NBC
Exec Prods: Bruce & Carole Hart;
Prod: Howard Malley;
Dir: Tom Trbovich;
Wris: The Harts, David Axelrod, Joseph Bailey, Andy Breckman,
Northern Calloway, Richard Camp, Sherry Cohen, Marianne Meyer.
60 Mins, Sat, 12 noon.
NBC-TV
11/14/79

HOT POPS
With The Raes, Bee Gees, Village People, Stonebolt, Ironhorse, Blondie, Fred Latroumille
Supplier: Canadian Recording Industry Assn & Nielson-Ferns
Prod: Ken Gibson;
Dir: Michael Watt.
30 Mins, Mon (26), 7 pm, Thurs (29), 11:45 pm.
CBC-TV, from Toronto, Canada
04/11/79F

HOT SEAT
With Jim Peck (host)
Supplier: Heatter-Quigley Prods.
Exec Prod: Robert Noah;
Prod: Bob Synes;
Dir: Jerome Shaw .
30 Mins, Mon-Fri, Noon
ABC-TV
07/21/76

HOT STUFF: THE RESTAURANTS OF NEW ORLEANS
With Julian Craggs (narr)
Supplier: WYES-TV
Prod-Wri: John Beyer.
60 Mins,
WYES-TV, New Orleans
08/27/80

HOUSE CALLS
With Wayne Rogers, Lynn Redgrave, David Wayne, Ray Buktenica, Candice Azzara, Vincent Howard, Vivi Janiss, Margaret Nesbitt, Aneta Corsaut, Sharon DeBord, Diane Lander, DiAnn Monaco, Deedy Peters
Supplier: Universal TV, Alex Winitsky & Arlene Sellers Prods
Exec Prod: Jerry Davis;
Prod: Sheldon Keller;
Dir: Alex March;
Wris: Max Shulman, Julius J Epstein.
30 Mins, Mon, 9:30 pm.
CBS-TV
12/19/79

THE HOUSE THAT HALF-JACK BUILT
With Tim Rail, Aidan Mc Nulty, Mark Neely, Patrick Collins, Carol Lawrence, Karlene Crockett, Don Dunlap, Roberta Jean Williams, Kevin Dudley
Supplier: Half-Jack Inc.-Scholastic Prods.
Prod: Dennis Johnson;
Dir: Stephen Gyllenhaal;
Wris: Paul Elliott, Fred Freiberger.
60 Mins, Thurs, (3), 4 pm.
CBS-TV
01/16/80

HOW THE BEATLES CHANGED THE WORLD
With David Frost (narrator), Richie Havens, Melissa Manchester, Melanie, David Clayton-Thomas with Blood, Sweat & Tears, Frankie Valli
Supplier: Greengrass Enterprises
Exec Prods: Charles Andrews, Ken Greengrass;
Prod-Wri: Andrews;
Dir: Jean-Christophe Averty.
60 Mins, Tues (22), 4 pm.
NBC-TV
11/30/77

HOW THE WEST WAS WON
(ABC Sunday Movie)
With James Arness, Eva Marie Saint, Bruce Boxleitner, Kathryn Holcomb, William Kirby Cullen, Vicki Schreck, Anthony Zerbe, Don Murray, Brit Lind, Royal Dano, John Dehner, Richard Angarola, David Huddleston, John Lisbon Wood, Sander Johnson, Herman Poppe, Howard McGillin, Med Flory, Todd Lookinland, Roy Jenson, Robert Padilla, John Pickard, Peggy Rea, Eddie Firestone, Dan Ferrone, William Conrad (narrator)
Supplier: Albert S Ruddy Prods & MGM-TV
Exec Prod: John Mantley;
Prods: Jeffrey Hayden, John G Stephens;
Dirs: Burt Kennedy, Daniel Mann;
Wris: Jim Byrnes, William Kelley, Mantley, Earl W Wallace, Ron Bishop.
120 Mins, Sun (6), 9 pm.
ABC-TV
02/09/77

HOW THE WEST WAS WON
With James Arness, Fionnula Flanagan, Bruce Boxleitner, Kathryn Holcomb, William Kirby Cullen, Vicki Schreck, Lloyd Bridges, Horst Buchholz, Elyssa Davalos, Mel Ferrer, Brian Keith, Christopher Lee, Cameron Mitchell, Ricardo Montalban, Trisha Noble, John Reilly, Morgan Woodward, William Conrad (narrator), others
Supplier: John Mantley Prods & MGM-TV
Exec Prod: Mantley;
Prod: John G. Stephens;
Dirs: Vincent & Bernard McEveety;
Wris: Colley Cibber, Calvin Clements, William Kelley, Mantley, Katharyn Michaelian Powers, Earl W Wallace.
180 Mins, Sun (12), 8 pm.
ABC-TV
02/15/78

HOW TO SURVIVE THE '70S & MAYBE EVEN BUMP INTO HAPPINESS
With Mary Tyler Moore, Harvey Korman, John Ritter, Dick Van Dyke, Bill Bixby, Catlin Adams, Candice Azzara, Eddie Barth, Allen Case, Gene Conforti, Sam Denoff, Michael Durrell, Arny Freeman, Christopher Guest, Steve Landesberg, Alan Oppenheimer, Henry Polic II, Beverly Sanders, Tony Stevens Dancers
Supplier: MTM Prods
Prod-Dir: Bill Persky;
Wris: Persky, Phil Hahn, April Kelly, Wayne Kline, Tom Sawyer, Sam Bobrick.
60 Mins, Wed (22), 10 pm.
CBS-TV
03/01/78

HOW WARS BEGIN
With A J P Taylor
Supplier: BBC
Prod: Edward Mizoeff.
30 Mins, Sun (11), 11:15 pm.
BBC, from London, England
08/03/77F

HOW WE GOT THE VOTE
With Jean Stapleton, narrator
Supplier: Gould Entertainment
Exec Prod: Ray Hubbard;
Prod-Dir: Charles Horich;
Wri: Nancy Gager.
60 Mins, Sun (15), 10 pm.
WTOP-TV Washington
02/18/76S

HULLO!
(Central State Puppet Theatre of Soviet Union)
Supplier: Granada International
Exec Prod: Norman Swallow;
Prod-Dir: John Sheppard.
50 Mins, Tues (10), 9 pm.
ITV (Granada), from Manchester, England
01/18/78F

HUNCHBACK OF NOTRE DAME
With Kenneth Haigh, Warren Clarke, Michelle Newell, Christopher Gable, David Rintoul, Richard Morant, Henrietta Baynes, others
Supplier: BBC
Prod: Cedric Messina;
Dir: Alan Cooke;
Wri: Robert Muller.
120 Mins, Mon (18), 9 pm.
NBC-TV
07/27/77

HUNTER
With James Franciscus, Linda Evans, Ralph Bellamy, Edward Mulhare, Lee Jones-DeBroux, Paul Mantee, Del Monroe, Maxine Stuart, Joe Renteria
Supplier: Lorimar Prods
Exec Prods: Lee Rich, Philip Capice;
Prod: Christopher Morgan;
Dir: Gerald Meyer;
Wri: Seth Freeman.
60 Mins, Fri, 10 pm.
CBS-TV
02/23/77

HUNTER'S GOLD
With Andrew Hawthorn, Terence Cooper, Ken Blackburn, Ilona Rodgers, others
Prod: John McRae;
Wri: Roger Simpson.
25 Mins, Sun, 7 pm.
TV-2, from Auckland, New Zealand
10/27/76F

HUNTER'S MOON
With Cliff De Young, Alex Cord, Robert Do Qui, Leif Erickson, Ty Hardin, Dan O'Herlihy, Lynn Benesch, John Erickson, Roy Jenson, Michael Le Clair, John Quade, Logan Ramsey, Morgan Stevens, Martha Nix
Supplier: Aurora Enterprises Prods & 20th-Fox TV
Exec Prod-Wri: David Dortort;
Dir: Ken Annakin.
60 Mins, Sat (1), 10 pm.
CBS-TV
12/05/79

HUSBANDS & WIVES
With Alex Rocco, Cynthia Harris, Ed Barth, Suzanne Zenor, Mark Lonow, Randee Heller, Ron Rifkin, Linda Miller. Charles Siebert, Claudette Nevins
Supplier: 20th-Fox TV
Exec Prods: Hal Dresner, Edgar Rosenberg;
Prod: Don Van Atta;
Dir: Bill Persky;
Wris: Dresner, Joan Rivers.
60 Mins, Mon (18), 10 pm.
CBS-TV
07/27/77

HUSBANDS, WIVES AND LOVERS
With Jesse Welles, Ron Rifkin, Mark Lonow, Randee Heller, Eddie Barth, Lynne Marie Stewart, Charles Siebert, Claudette Nevins, Cynthia Harris, Stephen Pearlman, Colby Chester
Supplier: 20th-Fox TV
Exec Prod: Hal Dresner;
Prod: Don Van Atta;
Dir: Marc Daniels;
Wri: Harry Cauley.
60 Mins, Fri, 10 pm.
CBS-TV
01/22/78

I CAN!
(The Winners)
With Debbie Phillips, Bob Purvey, Connie Hunter, Dick Gjonola, Jim Kester, George Cooper, Gwen Van Dam, Mary Matthews
Supplier: Guenette-Asselin Prods
Exec Prod: Robert Guenette;
Prod: Diane & Paul Asselin;
Dir: Paul Asselin;
Wri: Hindi Brooks.
30 Mins, Thurs (13), 4 pm.
CBS-TV
Kenner (Sive); General Mills (Dancer-Fitzgerald-Sample)
10/19/77

I, CLAUDIUS
(A Touch of Murder)
With Derek Jacobi, Brian Blessed, Christopher Guard, Sian Phillips, John Paul, Frances White, George Baker, Ian Ogilvy, others
Supplier: BBC-TV
Prod: Martin Lisemore;
Dir: Herbert Wise;
Wri: Jack Pulman.
100 Mins, Mon (20), 9 pm.
BBC-2, Britain
09/29/76F

ICH WILL DOUCH NUR, DASS IHR MICH LIEBT
(I Only Want That You Love Me)
With Vitus Zeplichal, Elke Aberle, Alexander Allerson, Erni Mangold, Johanna Hofer
Supplier: Westdeutsches Fernsehen
Prod: Peter Maethesheimer;
Dir-wri: Rainer Werner Fassbinder.
100 Mins, Tues, 9 pm.
WDR, Cologne, West Germany
04/14/76F

IF IT WASN'T FOR YOU
(Superspecial)
With Carroll Baker, Conway Twitty, Gordie Tapp, Roxanne Goldade
Prod: Ken Gibson;
Dir: Maurice Abraham.
60 Mins, Sun, 8 pm.
CBC-TV, from Toronto, Canada
Kraft
11/15/78F

IF ONLY MY PIANO COULD SING
(Superspecial)
With Andre Gagnon, Karen Kain, Suzanne Stevens, Famous People Players, Jean Carignan
Prod-Dir: Bernard Picard;
Wris: Picard, Chuck Weir.
60 Mins, Mon, 9 pm.
CBC-TV, from Toronto, Canada
03/01/78F

IF TONIGHT WE FALL IN LOVE
With Claude Leveille
Prod: Serge Doyon;
Dir: Gary Vlaxton.
60 Mins, Mon, 9 pm.
CBC-TV, Canada
10/05/77F

IF YOU LOVED ME. . .
With Nancy Lynn Berkman, Yale Summers, Tommy Manns, Margaret O'Hara, Margaret Travolta
Supplier: Operation Cork
Prod-Dir-Wri: Gerald Rogers.
54 Mins, Sat (9), 6 pm.
WMAQ-TV Chicago
09/27/78S

IKE
With Robert Duvall, Lee Remick, Dana Andrews, J D Cannon, Paul Gleason, Laurence Luckinbill, Darren McGavin, Ian Richardson, Richard T Herd, Stephen Roberts, Wensley Pithey, William Schallert, Vernon Dobtcheff, Maurice Marsac
Supplier: ABC Circle Films
Exec Prod-Wri: Melville Shavelson;
Prod: Bill McCutchen;
Dirs: Boris Sagal, Shavelson.
360 Mins, Thurs (3), Fri (4) and Sun (6), 9-11 pm.
ABC-TV
05/09/79

IL FURTO DELLA GIOCONDA
(The Theft Of The Mona Lisa)
With Enzo Cerusico, Bruno Cirino, Michele Mirabella, Emilio Cigoli, Paolo Carlini, Elisabetta Carta, Renzo Palmer, Philippe Leroy, others
Supplier: RAI-TV
Prod: RTR;
Dir: Renato Castellani;
Wri: Giorgio Bertolini.
80 Mins, Wed, 8:40 pm.
RAI-TV 2, from Rome, Italy
02/22/78F

THE ILLUSION OF POSSIBILITY
(Die Illusion der Moeglichkeit)
With Tilly Lauenstein, Kaethe Haack, Hilde Wensch, Ilse Trautschold
Supplier: Zweites Deutsches Fernsehen (ZDF), Wiesbaden
Dir: Claudia Holldack.
75 Mins,Thurs, 10 pm.
ZDF (Second Channel), Wiesbaden, West Germany
08/18/76F

I'M A BIG GIRL NOW
With Diana Canova, Danny Thomas, Sheree North, Michael Durrell, Rori King, Terry Kiser
Supplier: Witt/Thomas/Harris Prods
Exec Prods: Paul Junger Witt, Tony Thomas;
Prod: Don Richetta;
Dir: Noam Pitlik;
Wri: Susan Harris.
30 Mins, Fri, 8:30 pm.
ABC-TV
11/05/80

I'M A FOOL
With Ron Howard, Santiago Gonzalez, Amy Irving, others
Prod: Dann McCann;
Dir: Noel Black;
Wri: Ron Cowen.
36 Mins
PBS
04/06/77

THE IMAGE MAKERS
With Richard Gilbert, narrator
Supplier: National Film Board of Canada
Dir: Albert Kish;
Wris: Marjorie Morton, Kish;
Prod: Adam Symansky
87 Mins, Sun, 9 pm.
CBC-TV, from Winnipeg, Canada
02/27/80F

IMAGES OF INDIANS
With Will Sampson, others
Exec Prod: Robert Hagopian;
Prods-Wris-Dirs: Hagopian, Phil Lucas
30 Mins, Thurs, (10) 9:30 pm.
KCTS-TV Seattle
07/16/80

IMUS, PLUS
With Don Imus
Supplier: Translor Films (Colbert TV Sales)
Exec Prods: Henri Bollinger, Robert Yamin;
Prod: Hal Parets.
90 Mins, Sat, 11:30 pm.
WNEW-TV New York
07/05/78S

IN BROAD DAYLIGHT
Prod-Wri: Patricia Gormin;
Dir: Robert Weaver.
30 Mins, Sat, 7 pm.
WVUE-TV New Orleans
11/08/78

IN CHARACTER
With Vincent Dowling, host; Robert Elliott, Sally Mertz, Robert Black
Prod: Dowling;
Dir: Jack Tucker.
30 Mins, Tues.
WVIZ-TV Cleveland
07/28/76

IN FOR TREATMENT (Opname)
With Helmert Woudenberg, Frank Groothof, Marja Kok, Hans Man In't Veld
Supplier: NOS (Holland)
Prod: Henk Poncin (Vara-TV);
Dirs: Erick van Zuylen, Marja Kok;
Wris: Members of Werkteater.
95 Mins.
(Winner of Prix Italia, Drama)
10/01/80PI

IN HER MAJESTY'S SERVICE
Supplier: BBC
Prod: Frances Whitaker;
John Burrowes.
20 Mins, Thurs, 7:40 pm.
BBC, London, England
07/20/77F

IN PURSUIT OF LIBERTY
With Charles Frankel, host
Exec Prod: Don Dixon;
Dir: Jack Sameth;
Wri: Frankel.
60 Mins, Thurs (8), 9 pm.
WNET-TV New York
09/14/77S

IN SEARCH OF. . .
With Leonard Nimoy
Supplier: Alan Landsburg Prods
Exec Prod: Landsburg;
Prod: Bob Long.
30 Mins, Mon, 7:30 pm.
WNBC-TV New York
09/22/76S

IN THE BEGINNING
With McLean Stevenson, Priscilla Lopez, Jack Dodson, Priscilla Morrill, Olivia Barash, Bobby Ellerbee, Bill Hunt, John Moskoff, David Pendleton, John Widlock
Supplier: TAT Communications
Exec Prod: Norman Steinbeg;
Prods: Jack Shea, Jim Mulligan;
Dirs: Shea, Doug Rogers;
Wris: Mulligan, Steinberg.
30 Mins, Wed, 8:30 pm.
CBS-TV
09/27/78

INAUGURAL EVE GALA PERFORMANCE
With Hank Aaron, Donnie Ray Albert, Jack Albertson, Muhammad Ali, Alvin Ailey American Dance Theatre, Dan Aykroyd, Warren Beatty, Leonard Bernstein & National Symphony Orchestra, Chevy Chase, Clamma Dale, Bette Davis, James Dickey, Mignon Dunn, Redd Foxx, Elton John, Loretta Lynn, Shirley MacLaine, Elaine May, Paul Newman, Mike Nichols, Freddie Prinze, Florence Quiver, Linda Ronstadt, Robert Shaw, Beverly Sills, Paul Simon, Jean Stapleton, John Wayne, Joanne Woodward
Supplier: James Lipton Prods & Time-Life TV
Exec Prod: Lipton;
Prod: Bob Wynn;
Dir: Marty Pasetta;
Wris: Lipton, Herb Sargent, Chase, Prinze.
210 Mins, Wed (19), 9 pm.
CBS-TV
01/26/77

THE INCREDIBLE HULK
With Bill Bixby, Susan Sullivan, Jack Colvin, Lou Ferrigno, Susan Batson, Charles Siebert, Mario Gallo, Eric Server, Eric Deon, Jake Mitchell, Lara Parker, William Larsen, Olivia Barash, George Brenlin, June Whitley, Terence Locke
Supplier: Universal
Prod-Dir-Wri: Kenneth Johnson.
120 Mins, Fri, 8 pm.
CBS-TV
11/09/77

THE INCREDIBLE HULK
With Bill Bixby, Lou Ferrigno, Jack Colvin, Martin Kove, Fran Myers, Al Ruscio, John Witherspoon, Paul Henry Itkin, Tony Brubaker
Supplier: Universal TV
Exec Prod-Wri: Kenneth Johnson;
Prods: James D Parriott, Chuck Bowman;
Dir: Kenneth Gilbert.
60 Mins, Fri, 9 pm.
CBS-TV
01/22/78

THE INCREDIBLE JOURNEY OF DR MEG LAUREL
(CBS Tuesday Night Movies)
With Lindsay Wagner, Jane Wyman, Andrew Duggan, Gary Lockwood, Brock Peters, John Reilly, Charles Tyner, James Woods, Dorothy McGuire, Woodrow Parfrey, Peggy Walton, Kathi Soucie, Tracey Gold, Cherilyn Parsons, Ronald Peterson
Supplier: Columbia Pictures TV
Exec Prod: Ron Samuels;
Prod: Paul Radin;
Dir: Guy Green;
Wris: Michael Berk, Douglas Schwartz, Joseph Fineman.
180 Mins Tues (2), 8 pm.
CBS-TV
01/10/79

THE INHERITANCE
With Dave Moore, others
Prod-Wri: Mike Sullivan.
60 Mins, Wed 9 pm.
WCCO-TV Minneapolis
03/14/79

INSEL DER ROSEN (ISLE OF ROSES)
With Christine Wodetzky, Sigfrit Steiner, Guenther Lamprecht, Jan Kollwitz
Supplier: Sueddeutscher Rundfunk, Stuttgart
Prod: Sueddeutscher Rundfunk, Stuttgart;
Wri: Slawomir Mrozek (translated by Christa Vogel);
Dir: Franz Peter Wirth.
120 Mins, Tues, 9 pm.
First Channel, from Stuttgart, West Germany
05/12/76F

INSIDE PUBLIC TELEVISION
With Charles Kuralt
Exec Prod: Perry Wolff;
Prod-dir-wri: Paul W. Greenberg.
60 Mins, Tues (20), 10 pm.
CBS-TV
04/28/76

INSIDE TELEVISION
With Mike Shapiro, Paul Harvey, Tracy Rowlett, Bill Hooks, Michael Brown
Prod-Dir: Tom Johnson;
Wris: Shapiro, Johnson.
60 Mins, Mon, 7 pm.
WFAA-TV Dallas
05/09/79

INSIDE THE CUCKOO'S NEST
Supplier: KQED San Francisco
Exec Prod: Zev Putterman;
Prods: Martin Fink, Paul Kaufman;
Dir: Robert N Zagone.
90 Mins, Mon (5), 9 pm.
PBS
09/07/77

INSIDE YESTERDAY
(Target: USA)
With Mike Wallace, George Crile
Supplier: CBS News
Exec Prod-Dir-Wri: John Sharnik.
30 Mins, Tues (21), 10:30 pm.
CBS-TV
08/29/79

INSTITUTE FOR REVENGE
(NBC Monday Night At The Movies)
With Sam Groom, Lane Binkley, TJ McCavitt, Robert Coote, Lauren Hutton, Murray Salem, Leslie Nielsen, Ray Walston, George Hamilton, Robert Emhardt, James Karen
Supplier: Bill Driskill & Otto Salamon Prods, Columbia Pictures TV
Exec Prods: Salamon, Driskill;
Prods: Driskill, Bert Gold;
Dir: Ken Annakin;
Wri: Driskill.
90 Mins, Mon (22), 9:30 pm.
NBC-TV
01/24/79

THE INSURANCE MAN FROM INGERSOLL
With Michael Magee, Charlotte Blunt, Warren Davis, Mavor Moore, David Gardner, Franz Russell, George Sperdakos
Exec Prods: Stephen Patrick, Ralph Thomas;
Dir: Peter Pearson;
Wris: Norman Hartley, Pearson
60 Mins, Sun, 9 pm.
CBC-TV, from Toronto, Canada
02/11/76F

INTUITION
With Alex Trebek (host), Jamie Farr, Lyle Waggoner, Charlie Brill
Supplier: Alan Sloan Inc (Syndicast Services)
Exec Prod: Sloan;
Prod: Bill Armstrong;
Dir: Jeff Goldstein;
Wris: Elaine Trebek, Paula Levenback, Scott Sternberg.
30 Mins, Thurs (4), 7:30 pm.
WNBC-TV
Colgate Palmolive (Ted Bates, D'Arcy MacManus & Masius)
01/10/79S

THE INVASION OF JOHNSON COUNTY
(NBC Saturday Night At The Movies)
With Bill Bixby, Bo Hopkins, John Hillerman, Billy Green Bush, Lee deBroux, M. Emmet Walsh, Mills Watson, Alan Fudge, Luke Askew, Robert Donner, Ed Winter, Stephen Elliott
Supplier: Roy Huggins/Public Arts & Universal TV
Exec Prod: Jo Swerling Jr.;
Prod: Huggins;
Dir: Jerry Jameson;
Wri: Nicholas E. Baehr.
120 Mins, Sat (31), 9 pm.
NBC-TV
08/04/76

THE INVENTORS
With Stuart Wagstaff, Diana Fisher, Ross Quinlivan, Prof. Neville Quarry
Supplier: Australian Broadcasting Commission
Exec Prod: Lloyd Capps;
Dir: Bruce Bromhead.
30 Mins, Wed, 8 pm.
ABC (Australia) TV, Channel 2, Sydney
07/09/80F

THE IRISH ROVERS COMEDY HOUSE
With Will Millar, George Millar, Joe Millar, Jimmy Ferguson, Wilcil McDowell, Carmel Quinn, Tommy Makem, Liam Clancey, Jimmy Kennedy
Prod-Dir: Ken Gibson;
Wris: Will Millar, Kennedy.
60 Mins, Sun (12) 8 pm.
CBC-TV (Toronto), Canada
10/22/80F

IS BOURBON ON THE ROCKS?
Prods: Julian Craggs, Aggie Isacks;
Dir: Craggs.
30 Mins, Mon (28), 8:30 pm.
WYES-TV New Orleans
05/30/79

ISHI, THE LAST OF HIS TRIBE
(NBC Wednesday Night At The Movies)
With Dennis Weaver, Eloy Phil Casados, Devon Erickson, Joaquin Martinez, Geno Silva, Joseph Running Fox, Lois Red Elk, Arlene Nofchissey Williams, Michael Medina, Patricia Ganem, Gregory Norman Cruz, Eddie Marquez, Dennis Dimster, Wayne Heffley
Supplier: Edward & Mildred Lewis Prods & International Producers Services
Exec Prods: Edward & Mildred Lewis;
Prod: James F Sommers;
Dir: Robert Ellis Miller;
Wris: Dalton & Christopher Trumbo, based on Theodora Kroeber's book.
120 Mins, Wed (20), 9 pm.
NBC-TV
12/27/78

THE ISLANDER
With James Best, Mary Anderson Stelby
Supplier: Mississippi ETV Network
Prod-Dir: Ron Harris.
30 Mins, Mon, 8 pm.
WMAA-TV Jackson, MS
12/28/77

IT'S A LIVING
With Susan Sullivan, Marian Mercer, Gail Edwards, Barrie Youngfellow, Wendy Schaal, Ann Jillian, Paul Kreppel, Bert Remsen
Supplier: Witt/Thomas Prods
Prods: Paul Junger Witt, Tony Thomas;
Dir: John Tracy;
Wri: Stu Silver.
30 Mins, Thurs, 9:30 pm.
ABC-TV
11/05/80

IT'S ANYBODY'S GUESS
With Monty Hall, Jay Stewart
Supplier: Stefan Hatos-Monty Hall Prods
Exec Prod: Stu Billett;
Prod: Steve Feke;
Dir: Joe Behar.
30 Mins, Mon-Fri, 11:30 am.
NBC-TV
06/22/77

IT'S TOUGH TO MAKE IT IN THIS LEAGUE
With Walt Garrison (narrator)
Supplier: Gateway Productions Inc
Exec Prods: Paul Galan, Dick Hubert;
Prod: Joe Gallagher;
Dir: Galan;
Wri: Zimmerman.
60 Mins, Sat (28), 8 pm.
ABC-TV
U. S. Tobacco
09/01/76

IT'S YOUR BUSINESS
With Karna Small, moderator
Supplier: US Chamber of Commerce
Exec Prod: Robert L Adams;
Prods: Bob Mead, Anne Morrissy Merick;
Dir: Charles Stopek.
30 Mins, Sun (9), 12:30 pm.
WJLA-TV Washington
09/19/79

IVAN THE TERRIBLE
With Lou Jacobi, Maria Karnilova, Phil Leeds, Despo, Christopher Hewett, Matthew Barry, Alan Cauldwell, Caroline Kava, Manuel Martinez, Nana Tucker
Supplier: King-Hitzig Productions
Exec Prod: Alan King;
Prod: Rupert Hitzig;
Dir: Peter H Hunt;
Wris: Mike Barrie, Jim Mulholland.
30 Mins, Sat, 8:30 pm.
CBS-TV
08/25/76

I'VE GOT A SECRET
With Bill Cullen (emcee), Richard Dawson, Elaine Joyce, Henry Morgan, Pat Collins, Norman Paris Quartet, Buddy Rich
Supplier: Goodson-Todman Telecasts
Exec Prod: Gil Fates;
Prod: Chester Feldman;
Dir: Lloyd Gross.
30 Mins, Tues, 8 pm.
CBS-TV
06/30/76

JACK FROST
With voices of Buddy Hackett, Robert Morse, Paul Frees, Larry Storch, Dave Garroway, Debra Clinger, Don Messick, Dee Stratton, Sonny Melendez
Supplier: Rankin-Bass Prods
Prods-Dirs: Arthur Rankin Jr, Jules Bass;
Wri: Romeo Muller.
60 Mins, Thurs (13), 8 pm.
NBC-TV
12/19/79

JACK WINTER'S DREAM
With Patric Carey, Bernard Kearns, Michael McGrath, Martyn Sanderson, Bill Juliff, Norbert Heuser, Fiona Lindsay, Anthony Groser; narrator, Mervyn Thompson
Supplier: National Film Unit
Dir: David Sims;
Wri: James K. Baxter.
50 Mins, Sun, 9:55 pm.
Televison New Zealand
06/11/80F

JACKIE & DARLENE
(ABC Saturday Comedy Special)
With Sarina C Grant, Anna L Pagan, Lou Frizzel, Nathaniel Taylor Jr, Richard Beauchamp, Jeff Hollis, Dick DeCoit, Gerald Evans
Supplier: Andomar Prods
Exec Prod-Wri: Aaron Ruben;
Prod: Gene Marcione;
Dir: Russ Petranto.
30 Mins, Sat (8), 8:30 pm.
ABC-TV

07/12/78

THE JACKSONS
With Jacksons (Michael, Jackie, Tito, Marlon, Randy, Latoya, Maureen and Janet), Sonny Bono, Jim Samuels, Marty Cohen
Exec Prods: Joe Jackson, Richard Arons;
Prods: Bill Davis, Arnie Kogen, Ray Jessel;
Dir: Davis;
Wris: Kogen, Jessel, Winston Moss, April Kelly, Tom Chapman.
30 Mins, Wed, 8 pm.
CBS-TV

06/23/76

THE JACKSONS
With Michael, Marion, Tito, Jackie & Randy Jackson, The Jackson Sisters (LaToya, Rebie & Janet), Redd Foxx
Supplier: Jackson TV Prods
Exec Prods: Joe Jackson, Richard Arons;
Prods: Bill Davis, Jim Mulligan, Bonnie Burns;
Dir: Davis;
Wris: Mulligan, James W Tisdale, Wayne Kline, Biff Manard, David H Smilow.
30 Mins, Wed, 8:30 pm.
CBS-TV

02/02/77

JAMES AT 15
(NBC Monday Night At The Movies)
With Lance Kerwin, Linden Chiles, Lynn Carlin, Melissa Sue Anderson, Kim Richards, Kate Jackson, Vincent Van Patten, Dierdre Berthrong, Marc McClure, Anne Seymour, Dennis Rucker
Supplier: 20th-Fox TV
Exec Prods: Martin Manulis, Joseph Hardy;
Prod: Manulis;
Dir: Hardy;
Wri: Dan Wakefield.
120 Mins, Mon (5), 9 pm.
NBC-TV

09/07/77

JAMES AT 15
With Lance Kerwin, Linden Chiles, Lynn Carlin, Kim Richards, Deirdre Berthrong, Susan Myers, David Hubbard, Lisa Pelikan, J A Preston, Lee Chamberlin, Lillian Lehman, Marian McCargo, Elliott Reid
Supplier: Martin Manulis Prods & MGM-TV
Exec Prods: Manulis, Joseph Hardy;
Prod: Ernest Losso;
Dir: Hardy;
Wri: Dan Wakefield.
60 Mins, Thurs, 9 pm.
NBC-TV

11/02/77

JANUARY MAGAZINE
With Sylvia Chase
Exec Prod: Joel Heller;
Prods: Mary Drayne, Don Blauvelt.
60 Mins, Tues (18), 10 am.
CBS-TV

01/26/77

JESSE JACKSON AND THE POSSIBLE DREAM
Wri-Prod: Mickey Wellman;
Dir: Glenn Dieterich.
30 Mins, Sat.
WWL-TV New Orleans

11/08/78

JESSE OWENS RETURNS TO BERLIN (The Olympians)
With Jesse Owens
Suppliers: Cappy Prods., 20th-Fox TV
Exec Prod: Cappy Petrash;
Prod-Dir-Wri: Bud Greenspan.
60 Mins, Sun, 9 pm.
WNEW-TV New York

04/02/80S

JESUS OF NAZARETH—PART 1
With Robert Powell, Anne Bancroft, Valentina Cortese, James Farentino, James Earl Jones, Ian McShane, Donald Pleasence, Christopher Plummer, Fernando Rey, Ralph Richardson, Peter Ustinov, Michael York, Olivia Hussey, Cyril Cusack, Ian Holm, Yorgo Voyagis, others
Supplier: ITC-RAI
Exec Prod: Bernard J Kingham;
Prod: Vincenzo Labella;
Dir: Franco Zeffirelli;
Wris: Anthony Burgess, Suso Cecchi d'Amico, Zeffirelli.
192 Mins, Sun (3), 8 pm.
NBC-TV

04/06/77

JIGSAW JOHN
With Jack Warden, Alan Feinstein, Pippa Scott, Robert Reed, Anjanette Comer, Bo Hopkins, Brock Peters, Rudi Gernreich, Cynthia Sikes
Supplier: MGM-TV
Prods: Ronald Austin, James David Buchanan;
Dir: Harry Falk;
Wri: Arthur Rowe.
60 Mins, Mon, 10 pm.
NBC-TV

02/04/76

JIM NABORS SHOW
With Susan Ford, Fred Werner Orch, Carol Burnett, Burt Reynolds, Betty White, Mavis Nabors
Supplier: NTR Prods (Syndicast Services)
Exec Prods: Carolyn Raskin, Larry Thompson;
Prods: Ken Harris, Charles Colarusso;
Dir: Barry Glazer;
Wris: Harris, Colarusso, Cort Casady, Brian Pollack, Milt Larsen.
60 Mins, Mon-Fri, 9 pm.
WCBS-TV New York

01/11/78S

JOAN SUTHERLAND: A LIFE ON THE MOVE
With Joan Sutherland, Richard Bonynge
Supplier: Australian Broadcasting Commission
Prod: Brian Adams.
80 Mins, Sun, 8:30 pm.
ABC TV, Channel 2 Sydney, Australia

08/22/79F

JOE & VALERIE
With Paul Regina, Char Fontane, Bill Beyers, David Elliott, Donna Ponterotto, Pat Benson, Robert Costanzo, John Michael Graham, Don Diamond
Supplier: Hope Enterprises
Exec Prod: Linda Hope;
Prod-Wri: Bernie Kahn;
Dir: Bill Persky.
30 Mins, Mon, 8:30 pm.
NBC-TV

05/03/78

JOE'S WORLD
Sid Clute, Frank Coppola With Ramon Bieri, K Callan, Christopher Knight, Melissa Sherman, Michael Sharrett, Ari Zeltzer, Missy Francis, Russ Banham, Larry Gelman, Joan Shawlee,
Supplier: TAT Communications
Exec Prods: Mel Tolkin & Larry Rhine;
Prod-Dir: Herbert Kenwith;
Wris: Rhine & Tolkin, Burt & Adele Styler.
60 Mins, Fri, (28), 10 pm.
NBC-TV

01/02/80

JOEY & REDHAWK
With Chris Petersen, Guillermo San Juan, Bert Kramer, Hersha Parady, Bob Hastings, Stephen Furst, Lucille Benson, Danny Bonaduce, Ronald Joseph Godines, Joshua Gallegos, Monika Ramirez, Lois Red Elk, Frank Sotonoma Salsedo, Scott Durnavich, Eric Stoltz
Supplier: Daniel Wilson Prods
Exec Prod: Wilson;
Prod: Fran Sears;
Dir: Larry Elikann;
Wri: Art Wallace.
150 Mins, Mon-Fri (4-8), 4 pm.
CBS-TV

12/06/78

JOHN ADAMS: LAWYER
(The Adams Chronicle)
With George Grizzard, John Tillinger, John Houseman, W.B. Brydon, Addison Powell, Kathryn Walker, Nancy Marchand, Curt Dawson, James Noble, Pirie MacDonald, Michael Tolan (narrator)
Supplier: WNET-TV
Exec Prod: Jac Venza;
Prods: Paul Bogart, Venza;
Dir: Bogart;
Wri: Sherman Yellen
60 Mins, Tues, 9 pm.
PBS

01/28/76

JOHN DAVIDSON SHOW
With George Burns, Tanya Tucker, Jimmie Walker, Pete Barbutti, Lenny Stack orch, Mac Davis
Supplier: Hidden Hills Prods & Dick Clark Teleshows
Exec Prods: Alan Bernard, Clark;
Prod: Bill Lee;
Dir: Barry Glazer;
Wris: Phil Hahn, Iris Rainer, Barry Adelman, Barry Silver.
60 Mins, Mon, 8 pm.
NBC-TV
06/02/76

JOHN DENVER & FRIEND
With Frank Sinatra, Count Basie, Harry James Orch, Tommy Dorsey Orch conducted by Murray McEachern, Nelson Riddle Orch, The World Famous Blue Grass Salad
Supplier: John-Jer Prods.
Exec Prod: Jerry Weintraub;
Prod: George Schlatter;
Dir: Bill Davis;
Wris: Digby Wolfe, Schlatter.
60 Mins, Mon (29), 9 pm.
ABC-TV
Timex (Grey Advertising)
04/07/76

JOHN DENVER IN AUSTRALIA
With Robby Benson, Debby Boone, John Newcombe, Susan Saint James, Lee Marvin
Supplier: John-Jer Prods & The 7 Network (Sydney)
Exec Prod: Jerry Weintraub;
Prods: Al Rogers, Bill Davis;
Dir: Davis;
Wris: Phil Hahn, George Geiger, Rogers, April Kelly, Larry Murray.
90 Mins, Thurs (16), 8:30 pm.
ABC-TV
02/22/78

JOHN DENVER'S ROCKY MOUNTAIN REUNION
With John Denver (host)
Supplier: Stouffer Enterprises & John-Jer Prods
Exec Prod: Jerry Weintraub;
Prod-Dir: Mark J Stouffer;
Wri: John P. Gilligan.
60 Mins, Sun, (29), 7 pm.
ABC-TV
GE (BBDO)
05/09/79

JOHN KOMEN WITH...
With John Biggs
30 Mins, Wed, 8:30 pm.
KCPQ Tacoma, Washington
01/19/77

THE JOHN SULLIVAN STORY
With Andrew McFarlane, Vera Plevnik, Frank Gallacher, Olivia Hammett, Carol Burns
Supplier: Crawford Prods Ltd, with Channel 9 Network and Australian Film Commission
Prod: Hector Crawford;
Dir: David Stevens;
Wris: Brian Wright, Tony Morphett.
120 Mins, Sun, 8:30 pm.
Channel 9 Network, from Sydney Australia
08/22/79F

JOHNNY CASH & FRIENDS
With Roy Clark, Tanya Tucker, June Carter, Steve Martin, Jim Varney, Howard Mann, Baptist-Catholic-Methodist Choir
Supplier: Joseph Cates Co
Prod: Cates;
Dir: Walter C Miller.
60 Mins, Sun, 8 pm.
CBS-TV
09/01/76

JOHNNY CASH CHRISTMAS SPECIAL
With Roy Clark, June Carter Cash, Carter Family, Jerry Lee Lewis, Roy Orbison, Carl Perkins, Statler Bros, The Tennessee Three
Supplier: Cates Bros Co
Exec Prods: Joseph Cates, Marty Klein;
Prod: Chet Hagan;
Dir: Walter C Miller;
Wris: Hagan, Frank Slocum.
60 Mins, Wed (30), 10 pm.
CBS-TV
Polaroid (Doyle Dane Bernbach)
12/14/77

JOKER! JOKER! JOKER!
With Jack Barry, host
Supplier: Barry-Enright Prods. (Colbert TV Sales)
Exec Prod: Ron Greenberg;
Dir: Richard S. Kline.
30 Mins, Sun, 5 pm.
WOR-TV New York
01/30/80S

JOKES
With Noni Hazelhurst, Robyn Moase, Chris Haywood, Terry Bader
Supplier: Australian Broadcasting Commission
Prods-Dirs: Martin Coombes, Geoffrey Nottage;
Wris: Geoffrey Atherden, John Alsop, Coombes, Robert Eagle, Andrew Knight, Paul Leadon, Robert Moore, Nottage, David Poltorak, John Scott, Angela Weber, Bill McDonough.
30 Mins, Tues, 8 pm.
ABC-TV, from Sydney, Australia
02/21/79F

THE JORDAN CHANCE
(CBS Tuesday Night Movies)
With Raymond Burr, Ted Shackelford, James Canning, Jeannie Fitzsimmons, Stella Stevens, George DiCenzo, John McIntire, Peter Haskell, Maria-Elena Cordero, Gerald McRaney, others
Supplier: Roy Huggins Prods, with R B Prods & Universal TV
Exec Prod: Huggins;
Prod: Jo Swerling Jr;
Dir: Jules Irving;
Wri: Stephen J Cannell.
120 Mins, Tues (12), 9 pm.
CBS-TV
12/20/78

JOSHUA'S WORLD
With Richard Crenna, Tonya Crowe, Randy Gray, Mary Alice, Carl Franklin, Chez Lister, LaShana Dendy, Carol Vogel, Carolyn Coates, Alexandra Pauley, Hunter Von Leer, Bobby Rolofson
Supplier: Lorimar Prods
Exec Prods: Lee Rich, Earl Hamner, Michael Filerman;
Prod: Claylene Jones;
Dir: Peter Levin;
Wri: Hamner, based on Mary Dutton's "Thorpe" novel
60 Mins, Thurs, (21) 8 pm.
CBS-TV
08/27/80

JOURNAL
With Charles Zewe
Exec Prod: Karin Giger;
Prod: Zewe;
Dir: David Frentz.
30 Mins, 6:30 pm weekdays.
WYES-TV New Orleans
01/24/79

JOURNEY INTO INDIA
With Keith Adam
Prod-Wri-Narr: Adam;
Dir: Lloyd Capp.
30 Mins, Tues, 8 pm.
ABC, Australia
02/15/78F

JOURNEY INTO THE HIMALAYAS
With Keith Adam
Supplier: Australian Broadcasting Commission
Exec Prods: Chris McCullough, Bill Steller;
Prod-Dir: Stafford Garner.
30 Mins, Wed 8 pm.
ABC (Australia) TV, Channel 2, Sydney
10/08/80F

THE JOYCE DAVIDSON SHOW
Exec Prod: Gerard Rochon;
Prod-Dir: Sandra Faire.
30 Mins, Weekdays, 1:30 pm.
CFTO-TV Toronto, Canada
06/01/77F

JOYCE DAVIDSON SHOW
Prod: Cliff Tomlinson;
Dir: Bernard Russell.
30 Mins, weekdays, 1:30 pm.
CTV, from Toronto, Canada
12/28/77F

JOYS
With Bob Hope, Don Adams, Jack Albertson, Marty Allen, Steve Allen, Desi Arnaz, Billy Barty, Rona Barrett, Milton Berle, Foster Brooks, Les Brown, George Burns, Red Buttons, Pat Buttram, John Byner, Sid Caesar, Sammy Cahn, Glen Campbell, Jack Carter, Charo, Jerry Colonna, Mike Connors, Scatman Crothers, Bill Dana, Angie Dickinson, Phyllis Diller, Jamie Farr, George Gobel, Jim Hutton, David Janssen, Alan King, George Kirby, Don Knotts, Fred MacMurray, Dean Martin, Groucho Marx, Jan Murray, Wayne Newton, Vincent Price, Freddie Prinze, Don Rickles, Harry Ritz, Telly Savalas, Phil Silvers, Larry Storch, Abe Vigoda, Jimmie Walker, Flip Wilson
Supplier: Bob Hope Enterprises
Exec prod: Hope;
Prod: Hal Kanter;
Dir: Dick McDonough;
Wris: Ben Starr, Charles Lee, Gig Henry, Paul Pumpian, Harvey Weitzman, Ruth Batchelor, Jeffrey Barron.
90 Mins, Fri (5), 8:30 pm.
NBC-TV
Texaco (Benton & Bowles)
03/10/76

JUBILEE
(Bell System Family Theatre)
With Bing Crosby, Liza Minnelli, Roy Clark, Eydie Gorme & Steve Lawrence, Joel Grey, Marvin Hamlisch, Ben Vereen
Supplier: Henry Jaffe Enterprises & Smith-Hemion Prods.
Exec Prod: Jaffe;
Prods: Gary Smith, Dwight Hemion;
Dir: Hemion;
Wris: Buz Kohan, Marty Farrell.
90 Mins, Fri (26), 8:30 pm.
NBC-TV
AT&T (N.W. Ayer)
04/07/76

JUBILEE! A RIGHT ROYAL CELEBRATION
With Anthony Carthew (reporter), Prince Charles, others
Supplier: Thames International
Prod: Tony Millett;
Wri: Anthony Carthew.
56 Mins, Fri (16), 9 pm.
ITV Network, Britain
12/28/77F

JUDGE HORTON AND THE SCOTTSBORO BOYS
With Arthur Hill, Lewis J. Stadlen, Ken Kercheval, Vera Miles
Supplier: Tomorrow Entertainment
Prod: Paul Leaf;
Dir: Fielder Cook;
Wri: John McGreevey.
120 Mins, Thurs (22), 9 pm.
NBC-TV
04/28/76

JUKE-BOX
With Twiggy (host), Ace, Kiki Dee, Cliff Richard, Sailor
Supplier: American International TV
Exec Prods: Roy Nevans, Malcolm J Gold, Mike Mansfield;
Dir: Mansfield;
Wri: Hilary Tipping.
30 Mins, Fri, Midnight.
WPIX-TV New York
10/04/78S

JULIE
With Julie Amato, Patrick Rose, R G Brown
Prod: Bill Hartley;
Dir: Ron Meraska;
Wris: Hartley, Cliff Jones, Lorne Frohman.
30 Mins, Tues, 9:30 pm.
CTV, from Toronto, Canada
10/27/76F

JULIE ANDREWS' INVITATION TO THE DANCE WITH RUDOLF NUREYEV
(CBS Festival of Lively Arts For Young People)
With Ann Reinking, Eva Evdokimova, Peggy Lyman, Sandman Sims, Green Grass Cloggers, Rob Iscove Dancers
Supplier: Rothman-Wohl Prods
Prods: Jack Wohl, Bernard Rothman;
Dir: Tony Charmoli;
Wri: Buz Kohan.
60 Mins, Sun, (30) 5 pm.
CBS-TV
12/03/80

JULIE ANDREWS: ONE STEP INTO SPRING
With Leslie Uggams, Leo Sayer, Jim Henson's Muppets, Alan King, Paddy Stone Dancers
Supplier: Bob Banner Associates & Artista, A G
Exec Prod: Banner;
Prod: Stephen Pouliot;
Dir: Jeff Margolis;
Wri: Kenny Solms.
60 Mins, Thurs (9), 8 pm.
CBS-TV
Sears Roebuck (Foote, Cone & Belding)
03/15/78

JULIE ANTHONY ON THE GOLD COAST
With Julie Anthony, Robin Nedwell, Geoffrey Davis, Glen Shorrock, Wayne Bartholomew
Prod: Dick Foster;
Wri: Robin Heeps.
60 Mins, Wed, 7:30 pm.
Channel ATN7 Sydney, Australia
04/11/79F

JULIE ANTHONY'S FIRST SPECIAL
With Noel Ferrier, Stuart Wagstaff, Garry McDonald, Karen Mahoney, Tommy Tycho Orch
Supplier: Seven Network
Prod: Dick Foster;
Dir: Russell Boyd;
Wri: Trevor Farrant.
60 Mins, Wed, 7:30 pm.
Channel 7, Sydney, Australia
08/02/78F

THE JUNO AWARDS
With David Steinberg
Prod: Paddy Sampson.
90 Mins, Wed, 9:30 pm.
CBC-TV, from Toronto, Canada
03/23/77F

THE JUNO AWARDS
With David Steinberg
Exec Prod: Paddy Sampson;
Prod: Jack Budgell.
84 Mins, Wed (29), 8:30 pm.
CBC-TV, from Toronto, Canada
04/05/78F

JUST A LITTLE INCONVENIENCE
(Big Event)
With James Stacy, Lee Majors, Barbara Hershey, Charles Ciofffi, Jim Davis, Lane Bradbury, Bob Hastings, Frank Parker
Supplier: Fawcett-Majors Prods, Universal TV
Exec Prod: Majors;
Prod: Allan Balter;
Dir: Theodore J Flicker;
Wris: Balter, Flicker.
120 Mins, Sun (2), 9 pm.
NBC-TV
10/05/77

JUST AN OLD SWEET SONG
(G E Theater)
With Cicely Tyson, Robert Hooks, Beah Richards, Lincoln Kilpatrick, Minnie Gentry, Edward Binns, Sonny Jim Gaines, Mary Alice, Tia Rance, Kevin Hooks, Erick Hooks
Supplier: MTM Enterprises
Prod: Philip Barry;
Dir: Robert Ellis Miller;
Wri: Melvin Van Peebles.
90 Mins, Tues (14), 8:30 pm.
CBS-TV
General Electric (BBDO)
09/22/76

JUST FOR LAUGHS
With Milton Berle, Martha Raye, Connie Stevens, Red Buttons, Lloyd Nolan, Will Geer, Robert Guillaume, Rose Marie, Marcia Wallace, Tom Dreesen, Skip Stephenson, Alison Arngrim, Jackie Mason
Supplier: George Schlatter Prods
Exec Prod: Schlatter;
Prod: Hal Kanter;
Dirs: Dick McDonough, Dennis Steinmetz;
Wris: Kanter, Milt Rosen, Bob O'Brien, Lorne Frohman, Ben Gordon.
60 Mins, Tues (7), 8 pm.
NBC-TV
02/15/78

THE KALLIKAKS
With David Huddleston, Edie McClurg, Bonnie Ebsen, Pat Petersen, Peter Palmer
Supplier: Neila Productions-NBC-TV
Exec Prod: Stanley Ralph Ross;
Prod: George Yanok;
Dir: Dennis Steinmetz;
Wris; Ross, Roger Price.
30 Mins, Wed, 9:30 pm.
NBC-TV
08/10/77

KATE LOVES A MYSTERY
With Kate Mulgrew, Henry Jones, Lili Haydn, Don Stroud, Dee Wallace, John Aprea, Tom Stenschulte, Ted Danson, Howard Witt, Robert Feero, Deborah Shelton, Charles Thomas Murphy
Supplier: Universal TV
Exec Prod: Bill Driskill;
Supv Prod: Jim McAdams;
Prods: Merwin Gerard, Stuart Cohen;
Dir: Don Medford;
Wri: Larry Hertzog.
60 Mins, Thurs, 10 pm.
NBC-TV
10/24/79

KAZ
With Ron Leibman, Patrick O'Neal, Floyd Levine, Linda Carlson, Mark Withers, Gloria LeRoy, Edith Atwater, George Wyner, Nicholas Pryor, Eric Kilpatrick, Allan Rich
Supplier: Lorimar Prods
Exec Prods: Lee Rich, Marc Merson;
Prod: Peter Katz;
Dir: Russ Mayberry;
Wri: Sam H Rolfe.
60 Mins, Sun, 10 pm.
CBS-TV
09/13/78

THE KEANE BROTHERS
With Tom & John Keane, Tash the Wonder Dog, Jimmy Caesar, Anita Mann Dancers, Alan Copeland Orch, Burt Reynolds
Supplier: Pierre Cossette Prods
Exec Prod: Cossette;
Prod: Buz Kohan;
Dir: Tony Charmoli;
Wris: Bob Arnott, Aubrey Tadman, Garry Ferrier, Kohan.
30 Mins, Fri, 8 pm.
CBS-TV
08/17/77

KEEFER
With William Conrad, Michael O'Hare, Cathy Lee Crosby, Kate Woodville, Brioni Farrell, Marcel Hillaire, Bill Fletcher, Ian Abercrombie, Jack L Ging, Jeremy Kemp, Richard Sanders, others
Supplier: David Gerber Prods & Columbia Pictures TV
Exec Prods: Gerber, Bill Driskill;
Prod: James H Brown;
Dir: Barry Shear;
Wris: Driskill, Simon Muntner.
90 Mins, Thurs, (16), 9:30 pm.
ABC-TV
01/22/78

KEEPER OF THE WILD
With Denny Miller, James Reynolds, Pamela Shoop
Supplier: Elbekay Prods, 20th-Fox TV & Colgate-Palmolive
Prod-Wri: Leonard B. Kaufman;
Dir: Dick Moder.
30 Mins, Thurs (19), 7:30 pm.
WNBC-TV New York
Colgate-Palmolive
01/25/78S

KEEPING IN TOUCH
(Super Special)
With Anne Murray, The Spinners, Pat Paulsen
Prods: Alan Thicke, J Edward Shaw;
Dir: Shaw;
Wris: Thicke, Ian Anderson, Bill Langstroth.
60 Mins, Sun, 7:30 pm.
CBC-TV, from Toronto, Canada
12/29/76F

THE KELLY MONTEITH SHOW
With Freddie Prinze, Nellie Bellflower, Henry Corden
Supplier: CBS-TV
Exec Prod: Robert Tamplin;
Prod: Ed Simmons;
Dir: Dave Powers;
Wris: Gene Perret, Bill Richmond, Rick Hawkins, Liz Sage, Monteith.
30 Mins, Wed, 8:30 pm.
CBS-TV
06/23/76

KENNY ROGERS & THE AMERICAN COWBOY
With Mac Davis, Charlie Daniels Band, Rex Allen (announcer)
Supplier: Kenny Rogers Prods
Prod: Ken Kragen;
Dir: Stan Harris, Kieth Merrill.
60 Mins, Wed (28), 10 pm.
CBS-TV
Polaroid (Doyle Dane Bernbach); Shasta (Botsford Ketchum)
12/05/79

KICKS
With Jeff Kutash & The Dancin' Machine, First Choice, The Sylvers, Robert Guillaume, The Flying Escavelles
Supplier: Kip Walton Prods & Filmways Enterprises
Exec Prod: Jamie Kellner;
Prod-Dir: Walton.
60 Mins, Sat, 7 pm.
WNEW-TV New York
05/09/79S

KIDS ARE PEOPLE, TOO
With Bob McAllister
Supplier: ABC-TV
Prod-Dir: Lawrence Einhorn.
90 Mins, Sun, 10 am.
ABC-TV
09/20/78

KIDSWORLD
With David Parkes, Janet Wu, McLean Stevenson, others
Supplier: Behrens Co (Videotape Associates of Florida)
Dirs-wris: Betsy & Bob Behrens;
30 Mins, Sat (2), 6 pm.
WNBC-TV New York
10/06/76S

THE KILLER WHALE HUNTERS
Prod-narr: Emory Bundy.
30 Mins, Thurs, 7 pm.
KING-TV Seattle
07/07/76

THE KILLER WHO WOULDN'T DIE
(ABC Sunday Movie)
With Mike Connors, Gregoire Aslan, Mariette Hartley, Patrick O'Neal, Clu Gulager, James Shigeta, Robert Colbert, Robert Hooks, Samantha Eggar, Lucille Benson, Phillip Ahn, Kwan Hi Lim, Leslie Howard Fong Jr., Christopher L. Gardner, Tony Becker
Supplier: Paramount TV
Prods: Ivan Goff, Ben Roberts;
Dir: William Hale;
Wri: Cliff Gould
120 Mins, Sun (4), 9 pm.
ABC-TV
04/07/76

KING - PART ONE
(The Big Event)
With Paul Winfield, Cicely Tyson, Tony Bennett, Roscoe Lee Browne, Lonny Chapman, Ossie Davis, Cliff DeYoung, Al Freeman Jr, Clu Gulager, Steven Hill, William Jordan, Warren Kemmerling, Lincoln Kilpatrick, Kenneth McMillan, Howard Rollins, David Spielberg, Dolph Sweet, Dick Anthony Williams, Art Evans, Frances Foster, Charles Robinson, Roger Robinson, Ernie Banks, Yolanda King, others
Supplier: Abby Mann Prods & Filmways
Exec Prod: Edward S Feldman;
Prod: Paul Maslansky;
Dir-Wri: Mann.
120 Mins, Sun (12), 9 pm.
NBC-TV
02/15/78

KING OF KENSINGTON
With Al Waxman, Fiona Reid, Helene Winston
Prods-wris: Jack Humphrey, Lewis Del Grade;
Dir: Gary Plaxton.
30 Mins, Tues, 8:30 pm.
CBC-TV, from Toronto, Canada
10/27/76F

KING OF KENSINGTON
With Al Waxman, Fiona Reid, Helen Winston
Exec Prods: Jack Humphrey, Louis Del Grande;
Dir: Gary Plaxton;
Wri: Anna Sandor.
30 Mins, Sun, 8 pm.
CBC-TV, from Toronto, Canada
10/19/77F

KING OF THE ROAD
With Roger Miller, Larry Haines, Marian Mercer, Lee Crawford, R G Brown, Ric Carrot
Supplier: T A T Communications & Management Three Prods
Exec Prods: Norman Lear, Jerry Weintraub;
Prod-Wri: Rod Parker;
Dir: Hal Cooper.
60 Mins, Wed, (10), 8 pm.
CBS-TV
05/24/78

KINGSTON: CONFIDENTIAL
With Raymond Burr, Art Hindle, Pamela Hensley, Mariette Hartley, Robert Sampson, Michael McGuire, Curtis Credel, John Launer, Joseph Miksak
Supplier: Groverton Prods, R B Prods & Universal TV
Exec Prod: David Victor;
Prods: Joe L Cramer, James R Hirsch;
Dir: Christian I Nyby;
Wri: Richard Fielder.
60 Mins, Wed, 10 pm.
NBC-TV
03/30/77

KINGSTON: THE POWER PLAY
(NBC Wednesday Night At The Movies)
With Raymond Burr, James Canning, Pamela Hensley, Lenka Peterson, Bradford Dillman, Biff McGuire, Robert Sampson, Milt Kogan, Dina Merrill, Martin Kove
Supplier: Groverton Prods, R B Prods & Universal TV
Exec Prod: David Victor;
Prod: David J O'Connell;
Dir: Robert Day;
Wri: Dick Nelson.
120 Mins, Wed (15), 9 pm.
NBC-TV
09/22/76

KINGSWOOD COUNTRY
With Ross Higgins, Judi Farr, Peter Fisher, Laurel McGowan, Lex Marinos
Supplier: RS Productions Pty. Ltd.
Prod-Wris: Gary Reilly, Tony Sattler;
Dir: Kevin Burston.
30 Mins, Wed, 7:30 pm.
Channel ATN 7, Sydney, Australia
02/27/80F

KIRBY'S COMPANY
With Ken Blackburn, Willie Fennell, Ted Ogden, Vince Martin, Peter de Salis, Tom Burlinson, Margaret Nelson, Margaret Cruikshank, Louis Howitt, Olivia Brown, others
Supplier: Australian Broadcasting Commission
Prod: John Martin;
Dirs: Frank Arnold, Rob Stewart, Sue Willis, Jim Roberts, Chris Thompson, David Cahill;
Wris: John Martin, David Boutland, Charles Stamp, Margaret Kelly, Don Catchlove, Judith Bell.
50 Mins, Mon, 8:30 pm.
ABC Australia
10/12/77F

KISS ME, KILL ME
With Stella Stevens, Claude Akins, Pat O'Brien, Robert Vaughn, Michael Anderson Jr., Dabney Coleman, Bruce Boxleitner, Alan Fudge, Bruce Glover, Morgan Paull, Tisha Sterling, Charles Weldon
Supplier: Columbia Pictures TV
Exec Prod: Stanley Kallis;
Dir: Michael O'Herlihy;
Wri: Robert E. Thompson.
90 Mins, Sat (8), 9:30 pm.
ABC-TV
05/12/76

KISSINGER IN RETROSPECT
With Martin Agronsky, Stanley Karnow
Supplier: WETA-TV Washington
Prod: Wally Westfeldt;
Wri: Stanley Karnow.
90 Mins, Tues (11), 8 pm.
PBS
01/19/77S

KNOCKOUT
With Arte Johnson (host)
Supplier: Ralph Edwards Prods
Prod: Bruce Belland;
Dir: Arthur Forrest.
30 Mins, Mon-Fri, 11:30 am.
NBC-TV
10/12/77

KNOTS LANDING
With James Houghton, Kim Lankford, Michele Lee, Constance McCashin, Don Murray, John Pleshette, Ted Shackelford, Joan Van Ark, Karen Allen, Patrick Duffy, Claudia Lonow, Pat Petersen, Justin Dana, Steve Shaw
Supplier: Roundelay Prods. & Lorimar Prods.
Exec Prod: Lee Rich;
Prod-Wri: David Jacobs;
Dir: Peter Levin.
60 Mins, Thurs, 10 pm.
CBS-TV
01/02/80

KOMEDY TONITE
With Cleavon Little, Paula Kelly, Marilyn Coleman, Marion Ramsey, Shon Vaughn, Charles Valentino, Pau Lynde, Lawrence-Hilton Jacobs, Danielle Spencer, Todd Bridges
Supplier: Katz-Gallin Prods
Exec Prods: Raymond Katz, Sandy Gallin;
Prods: Lawrence Kasha, Mark Warren;
Dir: Warren;
Wris: Matt Robinson, Tony Peyser, J Stanford Parker, Bob Hackett.
60 Mins, Tues (9), 8 pm.
NBC-TV
05/31/78

KRAFT 75TH ANNIVERSARY SPECIAL
With Bob Hope, Leslie Uggams, Bob Crosby, Hal Peary, Edgar Bergen, Milton Berle, Alan King, Donna McKechnie, Roy Clark
Supplier: Smith-Hemion Prods
Prods: Gary Smith, Dwight Hemion;
Dir: Hemion;
Wris: Buz Kohan, Marty Farrell, Jerry Perzigian, Don Siegel.
90 Mins, Tues, 9:30 pm.
CBS-TV
Kraft (JWT)
02/15/78

KROFFT COMEDY HOUR
(ABC Comedy Special)
With Pat Harrison, Robin Tyler, Redd Foxx, Sha Na Na, Kaptain Kool & Kongs, Sheryl Lee Ralph, Deborah Malone, John-Anthony Bailey, Bill Henderson, Bart Braverman, David Levy, Gene Conforti, Dan Barton, John J Fox, Krofftette Dancers
Supplier: Sid & Marty Krofft TV Prods
Exec Prods: Sid & Marty Krofft;
Prod: Bonny Dore;
Prods: William Bickley, Michael Warren;
Dirs: Jack Regas, Alan Myerson, Howard Storm;
Wris: Michael Kagan, Harrison, Tyler, Bickley, Warren, Dick Robbins, Duane Poole.
60 Mins, Sat (29), 8 pm.
ABC-TV
08/02/78

LA BOHEME
With Angela Punch, Andrew Macfarlane, Kirrily Nolan, John Hargreaves, Matthew O'Sullivan, Mervyn Drake, Walter Sullivan, Gino Zancanaro, John Faassen; the voices of Marilyn Richardson, Beverly Bergen, Jonathan Summers, Neil Warren-Smith, Ronald Maconaghie, Roger Howell
Supplier: Australian Broadcasting Commission
Exec Prod: Anthony Hughes;
Prod-Dir: Brian Bell;
Cond: Robert Rosen.
116 Mins, Wed(14), 8 pm.
ABC (Australia) TV
02/04/76F

LA GATTA
(The She-Cat)
With Catherine Spaak, Orso Maria Guerrini, Mario Valdemarin, Nino Castelnuovo, Silvana Pamphili
Supplier: RAI-TV
Dir: Leandro Castellani;
Wris: Castellani, Paolo Levi.
55 Mins, Wed, 8:40 pm.
RAI-TV 2, from Rome, Italy
11/15/78F

LA GIOCONDA ESTA TRISTE
(The Mona Lisa Is Sad)
With Alfredo Goda, Walter Vidarte, Alfredo Castizo, William Layton, Louis Rio, Rafael Vaquero, Aurora Pastor
Supplier: Spanish Television
Dir: Antonio Mercero
Wris: Jose Luis Garci, Mercero.
45 Mins, Wed, 9:30 pm.
TVE, Spain
03/09/77F

LA HORA DE MASSIEL
(The Massiel Hour)
With Massiel, Ignacio Lopez Tarso, Marachi Vargas, Andres Pajares, Johnny Mathis, Luis Eduardo Aute and Trebol
Supplier: TVE
Dir: Fernando Garcia de la Vega.
55 Mins, Wed, 10:30 pm.
TVE from Spain
01/28/76F

LACY & THE MISSISSIPPI QUEEN
With Kathleen Lloyd, Debra Feuer, Jack Elam, Edward Andrews, Matt Clark, Les Lannom, Christopher Lloyd, James Keach, Sandy Ward, Cliff Pellow
Supplier: Lawrence Gordon Prods & Paramount TV
Exec Prod: Gordon;
Supv Prod: Robert Singer;
Prod: Lew Gallo;
Dir: Robert Butler;
Wris: Kathy Donnell, Madeline DiMaggio Wagner.
90 Mins, Wed (17), 8 pm.
NBC-TV
05/24/78

LADIES' MAN
With Lawrence Pressman, Karen Morrow, Natasha Ryan, Simone Griffeth, Allison Argo, Betty Kennedy, Louise Sorel
Supplier: Herbert B. Leonard Prods & 20th-Fox TV
Exec Prod: Leonard;
Supv Prod: Michael Loman;
Prod: Lee Miller;
Dir: H. Wesley Kenney;
Wris: David Wiltse, Loman.
30 Mins, Mon, 8:30 pm.
CBS-TV
11/05/80

LADY LAW
With Jessica Savitch
Exec Prod: Susan Horowitz;
Prod: Cliff Abromats;
Wri-rep: Savitch.
60 Mins, Tues (14), 8 pm.
KYW-TV Philadelphia
09/29/76

LAKME
With Joan Sutherland, Huguette Tourangau, Clifford Grant, John Pringle, Henri Wilden, Isobel Buchanan, Graeme Ewer, Jennifer Bermingham, Rosina Raisbeck, chorus of the Australian Opera and the Australian Elizabethan Theatre Trust Sydney orchestra conducted by Richard Bonynge Music: Leo Delibes Libretto: Edmond Gondinet, Philippe Gille
Supplier: Australian Broadcasting Commission
Exec Prods: Anthony Hughes, Noel Clark;
Stage Dir: Norman Ayrton;
TV Dir: John Charles.
150 Mins, Sun, 8:30 pm.
ABC (Australia) TV
11/03/76F

LAND OF HOPE
With Marian Winters, Michael Lombard, Philip Fisher, Richard Leiberman, Roy Poole, Carol Williard, Maria Tucci, Roberta Wallach, Anthony C. Cannon, Robin Pearson Rose, Robert Singa, others
Supplier: CBS-TV
Exec Prod: Herbert Brodkin;
Prod: Robert Berger;
Dir: George Schaefer;
Wri: Rose Leiman Goldemberg.
60 Mins, Thurs (13), 9 pm.
CBS-TV
06/02/76

LAND OF HYPE & GLORY
(NBC Reports)
With Edwin Newman
Supplier: NBC News
Prod: Karen Lerner;
Dir: Tom Priestly;
Wri: Newman.
60 Mins, Tues (10), 10 pm.
NBC-TV
01/18/78

LANIGAN'S RABBI
(NBC Thursday Night At The Movies)
With Art Carney, Stuart Margolin, Janis Paige, Janet Margolin, Robert Reed, Andrew Robinson, David Sheiner, Jim Antonio, Lorraine Gary, Barbara Carney, Robert Doyle, William Wheatley, Steffen Zacharias
Supplier: Heyday Prods. & Universal TV
Exec Prod: Leonard B. Stern;
Prods: Robert C. Thompson, Rod Paul;
Dir: Lou Antonio;
Wris: Don M. Mankiewicz, Gordon Cotler, from Harry Kemelman's novel.
120 Mins, Thurs (17), 9 pm.
NBC-TV
06/23/76

LANIGAN'S RABBI
(NBC Sunday Mystery Movie)
With Art Carney, Bruce Solomon, Janis Paige, Janet Margolin, Rita Moreno, Andrea Howard, Donna Theodore, Peter Marshall, Brendan Burns, Brian Dennehy, Robert Doyle, Barbara Carney, Milt Kamen, Reva Rose, John Wyler
Supplier: Heyday Prods & Universal TV
Exec Prod-Dir: Leonard B Stern;
Supv Prod-Wris: Don M Mankiewicz, Gordon Cotler;
Prod: David J O'Connell.
90 Mins, Sun (30), 9:30 pm.
NBC-TV
02/02/77

LAS VEGAS GAMBIT
With Wink Martindale (host)
Supplier: Heatter-Quigley Prods & Filmways
Prod: Robert Noah;
Dir: Jerome Shaw.
30 Mins, Mon-Fri, 10 am.
NBC-TV
11/05/80

LASSIE: THE NEW BEGINNING - PART ONE
With John Reilly, Lee Bryant, Gene Evans, Sally Boyden, Shane Sinutko, Jeff Harlan, David Wayne, Jeanette Nolan, John McIntire, Charles Tyner, Jim Antonio, Logan Ramsey, Gwen Van Dam
Supplier: Wrather Corp - Lassie Prods
Exec Prod: Tom McDermott;
Prods: Jack Miller, William Beaudine Jr;
Dir: Don Chaffey;
Wri: Miller.
60 Mins, Sun (17), 7 pm.
ABC-TV
09/20/78

LAST CHANCE
(Comedy Time)
With Sorrell Booke, Will Mackenzie, Steve Guttenberg, Albert Insinnia, J Andrew Kenney, Alvin Kupperman, Jaison Walker, Lauren Frost, Debi Richter, Burton Gilliam
Supplier: Lorimar Prods
Exec Prods: Lee Rich, Philip Capice;
Prod: Lew Gallo;
Dir: Robert Moore;
Wri: Hal Dresner.
30 Mins, Fri (21), 8 pm.
NBC-TV
04/26/78

THE LAST DETAIL
With Robert F. Lyons, Charles P. Robinson, Lonny Chapman, Cindy Williams, Val Bisoglio, David Proval, Richard Gilliland, Ted Lange
Supplier: Acrobat Films & Columbia Pictures TV
Prod: Gerald Ayres;
Dir: Jackie Cooper;
Wri: Bill Kerby.
30 Mins, Sun (20), 9 pm.
ABC-TV
06/23/76

THE LAST HURRAH
(Hallmark Hall of Fame)
With Carroll O'Connor, Patrick O'Neal, Patrick Wayne, Mariette Hartley, Robert Brown, John Anderson, Kitty Winn, Dana Andrews, Burgess Meredith, Leslie Ackerman, Jack Carter, Tom Clancy, Brendan Dillon, Arthur Franz, Alan Hamel, Stewart Moss, Paul Picerni, Mel Stewart, Katherine Bard, Bill Quinn, Sandy Kenyon, James Sikking, Art Batanides, William Benedict
Supplier: O'Connor-Becker Prods, Columbia Pictures TV
Exec Prod: Terry Becker;
Prods: Mike Wise, Franklin R Levy;
Dir: Vincent Sherman;
Wri: O'Connor (adapted from Edwin O'Connor's novel).
120 Mins, Wed (16), 8 pm.
NBC-TV
11/30/77

THE LAST OUTLAW
With John Jarratt, Elaine Cusick, Jacki Kerin, Debra Lawrance, Gerard Kennedy, Paul Mason, John Stone, Les Dayman, David Bradshaw, John Murphy, Stephen Millichamp, John Ley, Lewis Fitzgerald, Stephen Bisley, Peter Hehir, Ric Herbert, Celia de Burgh, Tim Eliott
Supplier: The Seven Network & Pegasus Prods
Wris & Exec Prods: Ian Jones, Bronwyn Binns;
Prod: Roger le Mesurier
Dirs: Kevin Dobson, George Miller.
120 Mins, Tues, 8:30 pm.
Seven Network, from Sydney, Australia
11/05/80F

THE LAST RESORT
With Larry Breeding, Stephanie Faracy, Zane Lasky, Walter Olkewicz, Ray Underwood, John Fujioka, Robert Costanzo, Dorothy Konrad, Scott Mulhern, Taylor Negron
Supplier: MTM Enterprises Prods
Prod-Wri: Gary David Goldberg;
Dir: Asaad Kelada.
30 Mins,Wed (19), 8 pm.
CBS-TV
09/26/79

THE LAST TENANT
With Tony LoBianco, Lee Strasberg, Christine Lahti, Julie Bovasso, Danny Aiello, Jeffrey De Munn, Anne DeSalvo, Victor Arnold, Joanna Merlin, Ruth Jaraslow, Antonia Rey, Evan Michael Turz
Supplier: Titus Prods
Exec Prod: Herbert Brodkin;
Prod: Robert Berger;
Dir: Jud Taylor;
Wri: George Rubino.
120 Mins, Sun (25), 9 pm.
ABC-TV
06/28/78

THE LATE SUMMER, EARLY FALL BERT CONVY SHOW
With Henry Polic II, Sallie Janes, Marty Barris, Donna Ponterotto, Lenny Schultz, Dee Dee Wood Dancers
Supplier: 3J Co
Exec Prod: Howard Hinderstein;
Prods: Sam Bobrick, Sam Denoff;
Dir: Bill Hobin;
Wris: Jim Mulligan, Jay Grossman, Bobrick, Denoff.
30 Mins, Wed, 8 pm.
CBS-TV
09/01/76

THE LATHE OF HEAVEN
With Bruce Davison, Kevin Conway, Margaret Avery, Peyton Parks, Miki Flacks, Vandi Clark, Bernadette Whitehead, Jo Livingston, Jane Roberts, Tom Matts, Frank Miller, Joye Nash, Gena Sleete, Ben McKinley III, R.A. Mihailoff
Supplier: TV Laboratory at WNET New York in association with Taurus-Film
Prod-Dirs: David R. Loxton, Fred Barzyk;
Wris: Roger Swaybill, Diane English, based on book by Ursula K. LeGuin.
120 Min, Wed, (9), 9 pm.
PBS
01/16/80

LAUGH-IN
With Bette Davis, Sen Barry Goldwater, Ralph Nader, Kareem Abdul Jabbar, Rich Little, Nancy Bleiweiss, Ed Bluestone, Kim Braden, Claire Faulconbridge, Wayland Flowers & Madame, June Gable, Jim Giovanni, Ben Powers, Bill Rafferty, Michael Sklar, Lenny Schultz, Antoinette (Toad) Atell, Robin Williams, April Tatro
Supplier: George Schlatter Prods
Prod: Schlatter;
Dir: Don Mischer;
Wris: Digby Wolfe, Monty Aidem, Trevor Farrant, Ernie Glucksman, Bryan Gordon, Sonny Gordon, Mort Greene, Argus Hamilton 3d, Michael HKagan, Wayne Kline, Emily Levine, Merrill Markoe, Tom Parew, Kendis Rochlen, Mitchell Walters, Harriett Weiss.
60 Mins, Mon (5), 8 pm.
NBC-TV
09/07/77

LAVERNE & SHIRLEY
With Penny Marshall, Cindy Williams, Hery Winkler, Eddie Mekka, Mary Treen, Mr. & Mrs. Richard Stahl, Lyman Ward, David L. Lander
Supplier: Miller-Milkis Prods., Henderson Prods., & Paramount TV
Exec Prods: Garry K. Marshall, Thomas L. Miller, Edward K. Milkis;
Prods: Tony Marshall, Lowell Ganz, Mark Rothman;
Dir: Garry Marshall;
Wri: Bob Brunner.
30 Mins, Tues, 8:30 pm.
ABC-TV
02/04/76

LAW OF THE LAND
(NBC Thursday Night At The Movies)
With Jim Davis, Don Johnson, Cal Bellini, Charlie Martin Smith, Nicholas Hammond, Darleen Carr, Andrew Prine, Moses Gunn, Glenn Corbett, Jim McMullan, Dana Elcar, Ward Costello, Barbara Parkins, Paul Stevens, Regis J. Cordic, Patti Jerome, Barney Phillips
Supplier: QM Prods.
Exec Prod: Quinn Martin;;
Prod: John Wilder;
Dir: Virgil W. Vogel;
Wris: Wilder, Sam Rolfe.
120 Mins, Thurs (29), 9 pm.
NBC-TV
05/05/76

THE LAZARUS SYNDROME
With Louis Gossett Jr, Ronald Hunter, E G Marshall, Sheila Frazier, Lara Parker, Peggy Walton Walker, Rene Enriques, Phillip Sterling, Peggy McCay, Arthur Rosenberg
Supplier: Blinn-Thorpe Prods & Viacom
Prods: William Blinn, Jerry Thorpe;
Dir: Thorpe;
Wri: Blinn.
90 Mins, Tues (4), 9:30 pm.
ABC-TV
09/05/79

LE CLUB
With Susan Roman, Robert Lalonde, Victor Desy, Edward Atienza, Andree Cousineau, Gail Dahms
Exec Prod-Wri: Jack Humphrey;
Prod: Joseph Partington;
Dir: David Main.
30 Mins, Sun, 9 pm.
CBC, from Toronto, Canada
12/06/78F

LE MANI SPORCHE
(Dirty Hands)
With Marcello Mastroianni, Giovanni Visentin, Anna Maria Gherardi, Giuliana De Sio, Omero Antonutti, Massimo Foschi, Pietro Biondi, Giorgio Trestini, Bruno Pagni
Supplier: RAI-TV
Dir: Elio Petri;
Adaptation, translation of Jean Paul Sartre's'Les Mains Sales': Elio Petri.
230 Mins, (3-parts), Sun, 8:40 pm.
RAI-TV 1, from Rome, Italy
11/29/78F

THE LEGEND OF JIMMY GOVERNOR
With Fred Schepisi, Tom Keneally, Tommy Lewis, Ray Barrett
Supplier: Australian Broadcasting Commission
Exec Prod: John Sparkes;
Prod: Geoff Barnes.
30 Mins, Mon, 8 pm.
ABC (Australia) TV Channel 2, Sydney
05/10/78F

THE LEGEND OF THE GOLDEN GUN
(The Big Event)
With Jeffrey Osterhage, Carl Franklin, Robert Davi, Keir Dullea, Michele Carey, John McLiam, Elissa Leeds, R G Armstrong, Hal Holbrook, William Bryant, Rex Holman
Supplier: Bennett-Katleman Prods & Columbia Pictures TV
Exec Prods: Harve Bennett, Harris Katleman;
Supv Prod-Wri: James D Parriott;
Prod: B W Sandifur;
Dir: Alan J Levi.
120 Mins, Tues (10), 9 pm.
NBC-TV
04/18/79

LEGS
With Caren Kaye, Marcia Lewis, Scott Baio, Lynda Goodfriend, Dawson Mays, Laurie Mahaffey, Tammy Lauren, Dave Ketchum, Marv Dennis, Ed Cree, Fred Fox Jr, Shirley Kirkes, Elaine Bolton, Sayra Hummel, Ceil Cabot, Dale Phillips, Alan Kent
Supplier: Henderson Production Co & Paramount TV
Exec Prods: Garry K Marshall, Tony Marshall;
Prod-Dir: Alan Rafkin;
Wris: Walter Kempley, Marty Nadler.
60 Mins, Fri (19), 8 pm.
NBC-TV
05/24/78

THE LEIF GARRETT SPECIAL
With Leif Garrett, Pink Lady, Marie Osmond, Brooke Shields, Flip Wilson, Bob Hope
Supplier: Scotti Bros-Syd Vinnedge Prods
Prod-Dir: Bob Henry;
Wris: Rod Warren, Stephan Spears.
60 Mins, Fri, (18), 8 pm.
CBS-TV
05/23/79

LEONARD BERNSTEIN REFLECTIONS
With Leonard Bernstein, others
Supplier: U S International Communication Agency
Prod-Dir: Peter Rosen.
55 Min, Fri (25), 8:05 pm.
BBC-2, Britain
09/13/78F

LEOPARD OF THE WILD
With David Niven (Narrator)
Supplier: Survival Anglia Ltd & World Wildlife Fund
Exec Prod: Aubrey Buxton;
Prod-Wri: Colin Willock.
60 Mins, Thurs (1), 8 pm.
NBC-TV
American Gas Assn, Northwestern Mutual Life (J Walter Thompson)
03/07/79

LET'S HEAR IT FOR THE PATIENTS
With Bill Kurtis, narrator
Exec Prod-dir: Scott Craig;
Prod-wri: Jim Hatfield.
60 Mins, Wed, 9 pm.
WBBM-TV Chicago
03/31/76

THE LET'S SAVE CANADA HOUR
With Don Harron, Yvon Deschamps, Jean-Guy Moreau, Mary Traynor, Al Waxman, Harvey Atkens
Prods: Wayne Grigsby, Gary Plaxton;
Dir: Plaxton.
60 Mins, Sun, 10 pm.
CBC-TV, from Toronto, Canada
04/27/77F

THE LIAR'S CLUB
With Bill Armstrong, Larry Hovis, Burt Reynolds, Norman Fell, Betty White
Supplier: Ralph Andrews Prods (20th Fox-TV)
Prod: Andrews.
30 Mins, Mon-Fri, 7:30 pm.
WOR-TV New York
09/22/76S

THE LIBRARY OF CONGRESS
With Huw Wheldon, Daniel Boorstin, Henry Kissinger, others
Supplier: BBC, PBS
Exec Prod: Humphrey Burton;
Prod-Dir: Ann Turner;
Wri: Wheldon.
90 Mins, Sun (21), 8:05 pm.
BBC-2, Britain
01/31/79F

THE LIFE & TIMES OF EDDIE ROBERTS (L.A.T.E.R)
With Renny Temple, Udana Power, Allison Balson, Stephen Parr, Annie O'Donnell, Loyita Chapel, Allen Case, Maria O'Brien, Daryl Roach, Wendy Schaal, Lenora Nemetz, John Crawford
Supplier: Marestone Inc & Columbia Pictures TV
Exec Prods-Wris: Ann & Ellis Marcus;
Prod: Leonard Friedlander;
Dir: Jim Drake.
30 Mins, Mon-Fri, 11 pm.
WNEW-TV New York
01/16/80S

THE LIFE & TIMES OF GRIZZLY ADAMS
With Dan Haggerty, Denver Pyle, Hank Kendrick, Lucky Hayes, Kristen Curry
Supplier: Schick Sunn Classic Prods
Exec Prod: Charles E Sellier Jr;
Prod: Art Stolnitz;
Dir: James L Conway;
Wri: Arthur Heinemann.
60 Mins, Wed, 8 pm.
NBC-TV
02/16/77

LIFE GOES TO THE MOVIES
(The Big Event)
With Shirley MacLaine, Henry Fonda, Liza Minnelli
Supplier: 20th Century-Fox TV & Time-Life TV
Exec Prod: Jack Haley Jr;
Prods: Mel Stuart, Richard Schickel, Malcolm Leo;
Dir: Stuart;
Wri: Schickel.
180 Mins, Sun (31), 8 pm.
NBC-TV
11/03/76

LIFELINE
With Jackson Beck (narrator)
Supplier: Tomorrow Entertainment-Medcom Co
Exec Prods: Thomas W Moore, Robert E Fuisz, MD;
Prod-Dir: Alfred R Kelman;
Wri: Fuisz.
60 Mins, Thurs (7), 10 pm.
NBC-TV
Xerox (Needham, Harper & Steers)
09/13/78

LIFESTYLES WITH BEVERLY SILLS
With Melba Moore, Tammy Grimes, Phyllis Diller
Exec Prod: Larry Johnson;
Prod: Edith Luray;
Dir: Paul Freeman.
60 Mins, Sat, 5 pm.
WNBC-TV New York
10/20/76

LIL' ABNER IN DOGPATCH TODAY
With Susan Tolsky, Don Potter, Debra Feuer, Stephan Burns, Louis Nye, Rhonda Bates, Kaye Ballard, Polly Bergen, The Graduates, Deborah Zon, Diki Lerner, Ben Davidson, Charlene Ryan, Leonard Feiner
Supplier: George Schlatter Prods
Prod: Schlatter;
Dir: Jack Regas;
Wris: Norman Panama, Jim Staahl, Tino Insana, Jim Fisher, Digby Wolfe.
60 Mins Thurs (9), 8 pm.
NBC-TV
11/15/78

LILLIE
With Francesca Annis, Anton Rodgers, Denis Lill, Peter Egan, others
Supplier: Richard Price Television Associates
Prod: Jack Williams;
Dirs: Christopher Hodson, John Gorrie;
Wri: David Butler.
60 Mins, Sun, 8:15 pm.
London Weekend TV, Britain
11/15/78F

LINDA IN WONDERLAND
With Linda Lavin, Lynn Redgrave, Anthony Newley, Ron Leibman
Supplier: Big Deal Inc & Smith-Hemion Prods
Exec Prods: Gary Smith, Dwight Hemion;
Prods: Ken & Mitzie Welch;
Dir: Hemion;
Wris: Mitzie Welch, Tom Whedon.
60 Mins, Thurs, (27), 10 pm.
CBS-TV
12/03/80

LINDA YU IN CHINA
Prod: Don Varyu;
Wri-Dir: Linda Yu.
60 Mins, Tues, (19) 7 pm.
WMAQ-TV, Chicago
09/17/80

THE LINDBERGH KIDNAPPING CASE
(NBC Thursday Night At the Movies)
With Cliff DeYoung, Anthony Hopkins, Joseph Cotten, Walter Pidgeon, Denise Alexander, Sian Barbara Allen, Martin Balsam, Peter Donat, John Fink, Dean Jagger, Laurence Luckinbill, Frank Marth, Tony Roberts, Robert Sampson, David Spielberg, Joseph Stern, Kate Woodville, Keenan Wynn, others
Supplier: David Gerber Prods. & Columbia Pictures TV
Exec Prod: Gerber;
Prod-Dir: Buzz Kulik;
Wri: JP Miller.
180 Mins, Thurs (26), 8 pm.
NBC-TV
03/03/76

THE LION, THE WITCH & THE WARDROBE - PART 1
With the voices of Dick Vosborough, Rachel Warren, Victor Spinetti, Don Parker, Liz Proud, Stephen Thorne, Beth Porter, Susan Sokol, Reg Williams, Simon Adams
Supplier: Children's TV Workshop wth Bill Melendez Prods
Exec Prod: David Connell;
Prod: Steve Melendez;
Dir: Bill Melendez;
Wris: Bill Melendez, Connell, from C S Lewis book.
60 Mins, Sun (1), 8 pm.
CBS-TV
Kraft (JWT)
04/04/79

THE LISA HARTMAN SHOW
With Lisa Hartman, Ricci Martin, Andy Kaufman, The Muglestons, Duck's Breath, Karyn Turner & Hard Knocks, Bill Kirchenbauer, The "Hot Stuff" Singers, The Street Dancers
Supplier: George Schlatter Prods
Exec Prod: Schlatter;
Prods: Rod Warren, David Winters;
Dir: Tim Kiley;
Wri: Warren.
60 Mins, Sat(30), 8 pm.
ABC-TV
07/04/79

LISTEN TO AMERICA
With Gabe Pressman, Harry Chapin
Exec Prod: Mark Monsky;
Prod: John Parsons;
Dir: Norman Ross;
Wri: Pressman.
30 Mins, Mon (1), 8 pm.
WNEW-TV New York
11/03/76

THE LITTLE DRUMMER BOY BOOK II
With Greer Garson (narrator), voices of Zero Mostel, David Jay, Robert McFadden, Ray Owens, Allen Swift
Supplier: Rankin-Bass Prods
Prods-dirs: Arthur Rankin Jr, Jules Bass;
Wri: Julian P. Gardner.
30 Mins, Mon (13), 8 pm.
NBC-TV
American Gas Assn (JWT)
12/29/76

THE LITTLE RASCALS CHRISTMAS SPECIAL
With voices of Philip Tanzini, Jimmy Gatherum, Al Jocko Fann, Randi Kiger, Robbi Kiger, Jack Somack, Darla Hood Granson, Matthew "Stymie" Beard, Naomi Lewis, Frank Nelson, Hal Smith, Cliff Norton, Mel Levin, Ike Eisenmann
Supplier: King World Prods, RLR Associates & Murakami Wolf Swenson
Exec Prods: Robert L Rosen, Robert A King;
Prods: Romeo Muller, Fred Wolf;
Dirs: Wolf, Chuck Swenson;
Wri: Muller.
30 Mins, Mon (3), 8:30 pm.
NBC-TV
12/12/79

LITTLE VIC
With Joey Green, Jack Collins, Med Flory, Doney Oatman
Supplier: Daniel Wilson Prods, ABC-TV o&o's
Exec Prod: Daniel Wilson;
Prod: Linda Marmelstein;
Dir: Harvey Herman;
Wri: Art Wallace.
30 Mins, Wed, 7:30 pm.
WABC-TV New York
03/02/77S

LITTLE WOMEN
With Jessica Harper, Ann Dusenberry, Susan Walden, Dorothy McGuire, William Schallert, Richard Gilliland, Virginia Gregg, David Ackroyd, Mildred Natwick, Cliff Potts, Robert Young, Eve Plumb
Supplier: Universal TV
Exec Prod: David Victor;
Prod: Richard Collins;
Dir: Leo Penn;
Wri: Suzanne Clauser.
60 Mins, Thurs, 8 pm.
NBC-TV
02/14/79

THE LITTLEST HOBO
With Monte Markham, Kate Lynch
Exec Prods: Ed Richardson, Seymour Berns;
Prod: Simon Christopher Dew;
Dir: Allan Eastman;
Wri: Paul Cooper.
30 Mins, Thurs, 7:30 pm.
CTV, from Toronto, Canada
10/24/79F

LIVE AT THE AGORA
With Southside Johnny & the Ashbury Jukes
Supplier: Agora Theatre
Exec Prod: Henry LoConti;
Prods: Denny Martin, Shirley Fredericks and Judy Jurisich, WJKW-TV; John Gorman and Dan Garfunkel, WMMS-FM.
60 Mins, Sat (22), 11:30 pm.
WJKW-TV, WMMS-FM Cleveland
11/01/78

LIVE FROM LINCOLN CENTER
With Andre Previn and the New York Philharmonic, Van Cliburn
Supplier: WNET-TV New York
Prod: John Goberman;
Dir: Kirk Browning.
120 Mins, Fri (30), 8:30 pm.
PBS
02/04/76

LIVE FROM STUDIO 8H
With N.Y. Philharmonic, Zubin Mehta, Leontyne Price, Itzhak Perlman, Martin Bookspan
Prods: Judith DePaul, Alvin Cooperman;
Dir: Rodney Greenberg;
Wri: Francis Robinson.
90 Mins, Wed, (9), 9:30 pm.
NBC-TV
01/16/80

LIVE FROM THE MARDI GRAS, IT'S SATURDAY NIGHT ON SUNDAY
(Big Event)
With Buck Henry, Randy Newman, Henry Winkler, Penny Marshall, Cindy Williams, Eric Idle, Not Ready for Primetime Players, others
Prod: Lorne Michaels;
Dir: Dave Wilson;
Wris: Anne Beatts, Jim Downey, Al Franken, Tom Davis, Michaels, Marilyn Suzanne Miller, Michael O'Donoghue, Tom Schiller, Rosie Shuster, Alan Zweigel, Danny Aykroyd, John Belushi
90 Mins, Sun (20), 9:30 pm.
NBC-TV
02/23/77

LIVE IT UP
With Jack McGaw, Mary Lou Finlay, Alan Edmonds
Exec Prod: Donald Cameron;
Prod: McGaw;
Dir: Ron Carlysle.
30 Mins, Thurs, 9 pm.
CTV, from Toronto, Canada
11/01/78F

THE LIVES WE LIVE
With Joyce Spector, Linda Tarry, Nancy Tigue
Supplier: WCBS-TV
Exec Prod: Hilary Schacter;
Prod: Joanne Roberts;
Dir: Michael Albanese
30 Mins, Mon-Fri, Noon
WCBS-TV New York
11/05/80

LIZA'S PIONEER DIARY
(Visions)
With Ayn Ruymen, Dennis Redfield, Katherine Helmond, Andrea Akers
Supplier: Nell Cox Films
Exec Prod: Barbara Schultz;
Prods: Nell Cox, Eileen Sopannen;
Dir-wri: Cox.
90 Mins, Thurs (18), 9 pm.
PBS
11/24/76

LOCUSTS AND WILD HONEY
With Frank Gallacher, Beverley Blankenship, Tim Robertson, Jan Norris, Sarah Norris, Gerard Kennedy
Exec Prod: Oscar Whitbread;
Dir: Douglas Sharp;
Wri: Everett de Roche.
50 Mins, Sun, 8:30 pm.
ABC (Australia) TV, Ch. 2, Sydney
04/30/80F

LOGAN'S RUN
With Gregory Harrison, Heather Menzies, Donald Moffat, Randy Powell, Lina Raymond, Keene Curtis, Wright King, E J Andre, Morgan Woodward, Ted Markland, Kimberly La Page
Supplier: Goff-Roberts-Steiner Prods & MGM-TV
Exec Prods: Ivan Goff, Ben Roberts;
Prod: Leonard Katzman;
Dir: Robert Day;
Wris: William F Nolan, Saul David, Katzman.
90 Mins, Fri (16), 9:30 pm.
CBS-TV
09/21/77

THE LONG DAYS OF SUMMER
(ABC Friday Night Movie Double Feature)
With Dean Jones, Joan Hackett, Ronnie Scribner, Louanne, Donald Moffat, David Baron, Michael McGuire, Lee deBroux, Baruch Lumet, Stephen Roberts, Leigh French, John Karlen
Supplier: Dan Curtis Associates
Exec Prod-Dir: Curtis;
Prods: Joseph Stern, Lee Hutson;
Wri: Hutson.
90 Mins, Fri, (23) 8 pm.
ABC-TV

05/28/80

LOOK AT ME
With Phil Donahuue, others
Prods: Jane Kaplan, Wendy Roth.
30 Mins, various times and dates
WTTW-TV Chicago for PBS

05/14/80

LOOK WHAT THEY'VE DONE WITH MY SONG
With Damita Jo Freeman, Dale Gonyea, Howard Itzkowitz, Marsha Myers, Joe Restivo, Karen Rushmore, Shelley Werk, Ty Whitney, Norman Fell
Supplier: Ernest Chambers Prods. (Lexington Broadcast Services)
Exec Prod: Chambers;
Prods: Jack Watson, James Ritz;
Dir: Joshua White;
Wris: Ritz, Ian Bernard, Bob Silberg, Dick Rossner.
30 Mins, Fri, (11), 7:30 pm.
WNBC-TV New York

01/16/80S

LOOK WHAT'S HAPPENED TO ROSEMARY'S BABY
With Stephen McHattie, Patty Duke Astin, Broderick Crawford, Ruth Gordon, Lloyd Haynes, David Huffman, Tina Louise, George Maharis, Ray Milland, Donna Mills
Supplier: Culzean Corp & Paramount TV
Prod-wri: Anthony Wilson;
Dir: Sam O'Steen.
120 Mins, Fri (29), 9 pm.
ABC-TV

11/10/76

LOOSE CHANGE - PART I
(Big Event)
With Cristina Raines, Laurie Heineman, Season Hubley, Stephen Macht, Ben Masters,, Michael Tolan, June Lockhart, Theodore Bikel, David Wayne, Guy Boyd, Gregg Henry, John Getz, Peggy McKay, Kate Reid
Supplier: Universal TV
Exec Prod: Jules Irving;
Prod: Michael Rhodes;
Dir: Irving;
Wris: Corinne Jacker, Charles E Israel, Jennifer Miller (based on book by Sara Davidson).
120 Mins, Sun (26), 9 pm.
NBC-TV

03/01/78

LORENZO & HENRIETTA MUSIC SHOW
With Mary Tyler Moore, Dave Willock, Erik Darling, Bob Gibson
Supplier: MTM Enterprises & Metromedia Producers Corp
Exec Prods: Lorenzo Music, Lewis Arquette;
Prod: Albert J Simon;
Dir: Bob Lally;
Wris: L Music, John Gibbons, Sandy Helberg, Richard Philip Lewis, Ira Miller, Dennis Reagan, Arquette.
60 Mins, Mon-Fri, 11:30 pm.
WNEW-TV New York

09/15/76S

LOS SEISES
With Andahazy Ballet Borealis, Ron Magers
Prods: Steve Hammergren, John Degan;
Dir: Hammergren.
30 Mins, Sun (11), 4:30 pm.
KSTP-TV St. Paul-Minneapolis

04/14/76

LOSS OF INNOCENCE
With John Fitzgerald, Ronald Falk, Monica Maughan, Carol Burns, Alwyn Kurts, Carol Raye, Jacqueline Kott, Louise Howitt, Paul Bertram, Enid Lorimer, Michele Fawdon, David Franklin, Jacqui Dalton, David Waters, Edward Howell, Julieanne Newbould
Prod: Eric Tayler;
Dirs: Tayler, Michael Carson;
Wri: John May.
60 Mins, Thurs, 8:55 pm.
ABC, Australia, from Sydney

03/01/78F

LOST AND FOUND - THE STORY OF COOK'S ANCHOR
With David Lean
Supplier: South Pacific TV & Faraway Prods
Prods: George Andrews, Wayne Tourell;
Dir: Lean.
40 Mins, Sun, 8 pm.
South Pacific TV-TV2 Auckland, New Zealand

05/09/79F

LOU GRANT
With Edward Asner, Robert Walden, Rebecca Balding, Mason Adams, Jack Bannon, Daryl Anderson, Nancy Marchand, Peter Hobbs, James Whitmore Jr, Gordon Jump, Michael Bond, Rachel Bard
Supplier: MTM Enterprises
Exec Prods: James L Brooks, Allan Burns, Gene Reynolds;
Prod-Dir: Reynolds;
Wri: Leon Tokatyan.
60 Mins, Tues, 10 pm.
CBS-TV

09/28/77

LOVE AND MR SMITH
(Superspecial)
With Grant Smith, Barbara Law, Tommy Banks
Prod: Paddy Sampson;
Dir: Bob Gibbons;
Wri: Paul Perlove.
60 Mins, Sun, 8 pm.
CBC, from Toronto, Canada

03/07/79F

LOVE AT FIRST SIGHT
With Philip Levien, Susan Bigelow, Deborah Baltzell, Angela Aames, Robert Rockwell, Peggy McCay, Pat Cooper
Supplier: Century Towers Prods, Nick's Bar & Grill Prods & Filmways
Exec Prod-Wri: Nick Arnold;
Prod: Peter Locke;
Dir: Bill Persky.
30 Mins, Mon (13) 8:30 pm.
CBS-TV

10/22/80

THE LOVE BOAT
With Gavin MacLeod, Bernie Kopell, Fred Grandy, Ted Lange, Lauren Tewes, Bonnie Franklin, Robert Symonds, Meredith Baxter-Birney, Shelly Novack, Suzanne Somers, Brenda Sykes, Jimmie Walker
Supplier: Aaron Spelling Prods
Exec Prods: Spelling, Douglas S Cramer;
Prods: Gordon & Lynne Farr, Henry Colman;
Dirs: Stuart Margolin, Richard Kinon, Alan Rafkin;
Wris: Michael Norell, Jay Grossman, Judy Skelton, Paula A Roth.
60 Mins, Sat, 10 pm.
ABC-TV

09/28/77

THE LOVE EXPERTS
With Bill Cullen (host), Geoff Edwards, Elaine Joyce, Jack Carter, Rhonda Bates
Supplier: Bob Stewart Prods (Viacom)
Prod: Stewart;
Dir: Bruce Burmester.
30 Mins, Mon, 11 pm.
WOR-TV New York

10/11/78S

LOVE IS NOT ENOUGH
(NBC Monday Night At The Movies)
With Bernie Casey, Stuart K Robinson, Renee Brown, Lia Jackson, Eddie Singleton, Dain G Turner, Stu Gilliam, James Luisi, James Canning, Bill Duke, Lois Walden, Sherman Miller, Mel Carter, Carol Tillery Banks
Supplier: Universal TV
Exec Prod: Stanley G Robertson;
Dir: Ivan Dixon;
Wri: Arthur Ross.
120 Mins, Mon (12), 9 pm.
NBC-TV

06/14/78

LOVE ON THE NOSE
With Saul Rubineck, Marilyn Lightstone, Al Waxman, Joe Silver, Paul Soles
Exec Prod: Stan Colbert;
Prod: Eoin Sprott;
Dir: George Bloomfield;
Wri: John Smith (Ted Allan).
90 Mins, Sat, 9:30 pm.
CBC, from Toronto, Canada

10/18/78F

LOVE, NATALIE
With Judy Kahan, Christopher Allport, Corey Feldman, Kimberly Woodward, Kenneth Tigar, Jean DeBaer, Becky Michelle, Darian Mathias
Supplier: MTM Productions
Exec Prod: Kahan;
Prod: Patricia Rickey;
Dir: Peter Bonerz;
Wri: Kahan, Merrill Markoe
30 Mins, Fri, (11) 8:30 pm.
NBC-TV
07/16/80

THE LOVEBIRDS
With Louis Welch, Lorna Patterson, Ellen Regan, Eugene Levy
Supplier: Hayoudo Prods & Paramount TV
Exec Prods-Wris: Mark Rothman, Lowell Ganz;
Dir: Peter Baldwin.
30 Mins, Wed (18), 8 pm.
CBS-TV
07/25/79

LOVERS & FRIENDS
With Ron Randell, Nancy Marchand, Rod Arrants, Margaret Barker, Patricia Estrin, Patricia Englund, John Heffernan, Bob Purvey, Richard Backus, Flora Plumb, David Abbott, Vicky Dawson, Stephen Joyce, Diane Harper, Karen Phillipp, Christine Jones, David Knapp, Susan Foster
Supplier: Procter & Gamble Prods.
Exec Prod: Paul Rauch;
Dir: Peter Levin;
Wris: Harding Lemay, Tom King.
30 Mins., Mon.-Fri., 12:30 pm.
NBC-TV
P&G (Young & Rubicam)
01/12/77

LOVES ME, LOVES ME NOT
With Susan Dey, Kenneth Gilman, Art Metrano, Udana Power, Ivor Francis
Supplier: Witt-Thomas-Harris Prods & 20th-Fox TV
Prods: Paul Junger Witt, Tony Thomas;
Dir: Jay Sandrich;
Wri: Susan Harris.
30 Mins, Sun (20), 10:30 pm.
CBS-TV
03/23/77

LUCAN
With Kevin Brophy, Stephanie Zimbalist, Paul Hecht, George Sperdakos, Helen Lockwood, Brian Dennehy, Guy Remsen, Michael Keenan, A J Bakunas
Supplier: MGM-TV & Barry Lowen Prods
Exec Prod: Barry Lowen;
Prod: Harold Gast;
Dir: Peter H Hunt;
Wris: Michael Zagor, Camille Marchetta, Rick Edelstein.
60 Mins, Mon (12), 8 pm.
ABC-TV
09/14/77

LUCINDA BRAYFORD
With Wendy Hughes, Sam Neil, Carol Burns, Barry Quin, Edmund Pegge, George Dixon, Lise Rodgers, David Page, Roy Edmunds, Myra de Groot, Kirk Alexander, Michael Duffield, Marie Redshaw, Virginia Rooksby, Stephen Oldfield, Lloyd Cunnington, Penelope Stewart
Supplier: Australian Broadcasting Commission
Exec Prod: Oscar Whitbread;
Dir: John Gauci;
Wri: Cliff Green.
60 Mins, Sun, 8:30 pm.
ABC (Australia) TV, Channel 2, Sydney
07/02/80F

LUKE'S KINGDOM
(The King's Gentlemen)
With Oliver Tobias, James Condon, Gerard Maguire, Elizabeth Crosby, Bettina Kenter, Helen Morse, John Krummel
Supplier: Trident TV and National Nine Network, Australia
Exec Prod: Tony Essex;
Dir: Peter Hammond;
Wri: John Dorsman.
60 Mins, Wed, 7:30 pm.
GTV-9, Melbourne, Australia
04/14/76F

LYNDA CARTER'S SPECIAL
With Kenny Rogers, Leo Sayer, Richard Rizzo, Lester Wilson Dancers
Supplier: Lyn-Ron Prods.
Exec Prod: Ron Samuels;
Prod-Wri: Saul Ilson;
Dir: Stan Harris.
60 Mins, Sat, (12), 8 pm.
CBS-TV
01/16/80

THE MAC DAVIS CHRISTMAS SPECIAL...WHEN I GROW UP
With Richard Thomas, Raquel Welch, Beverly Hills Youth Orch, William B Lee & Valley Master Chorale, Lennie Browning, Tony Dickson, Brian Eissler, Andy Holmes, Christopher Maleki, William Miron, P Pruett, Kenia Hernandez, Lia Jackson, Estelle Herzberg, Carlyn Jue, Deborah Kaplan, Ingrid Konupek, Andrea Leon, Tami Weigand, Sherrie Wills, Terri Lynn Wood
Supplier: Cauchemar Prods
Exec Prods: Gary Smith, Dwight Hemion;
Prods: Mike Post, Steve Binder;
Dir: Binder;
Wris: Buz Kohan, Alan Thicke.
60 Mins, Wed (15), 10 pm.
NBC-TV
12/22/76

MAC DAVIS SHOW
With Dean Martin, Tina Turner, Anson Williams, Shields & Yarnell, Strutt, Ron Silver
Supplier: Cauchemar Prods.
Exec Prods: Gary Smith, Dwight Hemion;
Prods: Mike Post, Steve Binder;
Dir: Binder;
Wris: Danny Simon, Thad Mumford, Neil Israel, Mike Mislove, Leonard Ripps & Neil Rosen,
George Tricker.
60 Mins, Thurs, 8 pm.
NBC-TV
03/24/76

THE MACAHANS
(ABC Monday Movie)
With James Arness, Eva Marie Saint, Richard Kiley, Bruce Boxleitner, Kathryn Holcomb, William Kirby Cullen, Vicki Schreck, Gene Evans, John Crawford, Vic Mohica, Frank Ferguson, Ann Doran
Supplier: Albert S. Ruddy Prods. & MGM-TV
Exec Prod: John Mantley;
Prod-Wri: Jim Byrnes;
Dir: Bernard McEveety.
150 Mins, Mon (19), 8:30 pm.
ABC-TV
01/21/76

THE MACKENZIE AFFAIR
With James Cosmo, Roddy McMillan, Ann Hasson, Derek Anders, Martin Cochrane, Arthur Boland, others
Prod: John McRae;
Dir: Joan Craft;
Wri: Alistair Bill, from novel by James McNeish.
50 Mins, Wed, 8 pm.
TV-2, from Auckland, New Zealand
09/21/77F

THE MACKENZIES OF PARADISE COVE
With Clu Gulager, Lory Walsh, Shawn Stevens, Sean Marshall, Randi Kiger, Keith Mitchell, Barry Van Dyke, Moe Keale, Leinaala Heine, Sean Tyler Hall, Scott Kingston, Barbara Bingham
Supplier: Blinn-Thorpe Prods & Viacom
Prods: William Blinn, Jerry Thorpe;
Dir: Thorpe;
Wris: J Miyoko Hensley, Steven Hensley.
60 Mins, Tues (27), 8:30 pm.
ABC-TV
04/04/79

MACMILLAN'S MAYERLING
Supplier: London Weekend Television
Prod-Dir-Wri: Derek Bailey.
117 Mins.
(Winner of Premio Italia, Music Dance)
10/04/78PI

MAD AS HELL - THE TAXPAYERS' REVOLT
With David Brinkley
Supplier: NBC News
Exec Prod: Stuart Schulberg;
Prods: Ken Donoghue, Gene Farinet, Ray Lockhart;
Dir: Tony Verdi.
60 Mins, Fri (16), 8 pm.
NBC-TV
06/21/78

THE MADHOUSE BRIGADE
With Carlos Carrasco, J J Lewis, Alexander Marshall, Frank Nastasi, Joe Piscopo, Dan Resin, Karen Rushmore, Nola Fairbanks, Bob Kaliban, Mary McMillan, "Rocket" Ryan
Supplier: Cockamanie Prods (MG Films)
Exec Prod: Jim Larkin;
Prods: Dale Deidel, Marshall;
Dir: Deidel;
Wris: Marshall, Larkin, Ryan, Lewis, Piscopo.
30 Mins, Fri, 11:30 pm.
WPIX-TV New York
10/04/78S

MAGIC
With Shari Lewis, Mark Wilson, The Great Tomsoni & Co, Flip, The Amazing Randi, Karen Kain, Frank Augustyn, Billy Van
Exec Prod: Bryn Matthews;
Prod: Bill Hartley;
Dir: John Thomson;
Wris: Hatley, Cliff Jones, Shari Lewis.
60 Mins, Tues, 7 pm.
CTV, from Toronto, Canada
04/11/79F

MAGIC AT THE ROXY
With Peter Graves (host), Richard Ross, David Copperfield, Carl Ballantine, Shimada, Dorian, The Amazing Randi
Supplier: Show Prods., Laurel Tape & Film
Exec Prods: Philip Burrell, Richard Rubinstein, George Romero;
Prod-dir: Michael Gargiulo;
Wri: Betty Cornfeld.
60 Mins, Wed (26), 8 pm.
WPIX-TV New York
06/02/76S

THE MAGIC BALLOON
With Jeff A Lee, Joey Van, Nancy Witt, Barney Simpson, Mardia Luttrell, others
Dir: Vernon Nobles.
30 Mins, Wed, 4 pm.
WXYZ-TV Detroit
11/29/78

THE MAGIC OF MUSIC
With Doug Adair, narrator; Cleveland Orchestra, high schools' chorus
Prod-Wri-Cin: Dennis Goulden;
Dir: John Oven.
60 Mins, Mon (11), 8 pm.
WKYC-TV Cleveland
07/20/77

MAGNUM, P.I.
With Tom Selleck, John Hillerman, Roger E Mosley, Larry Manetti, Pamela Susan Shoop, W K Stratton, Allen Williams, Clyde Kusatsu, Robert Loggia, Fritz Weaver, Dorit Stevens, Yuliis Ruval, Jeff MacKay, Judge Reinhold, Murray Salem, Eugenia Wright, Mel Carter
Supplier: Belisarius Prods, Glen A Larson Prods & Universal TV
Exec prods-wris: Donald P Bellisario, Larson.
Prod: J Rickley Dumm;
Dir: Roger Young.
120 Min, Thurs (11), 8 pm.
CBS-TV
12/17/80

MAGTIME
Prod-Dirs: Ron Ciro, Gary Gibson.
60 Mins, Mon, 7 pm.
KCTS Seattle
01/14/76

MAGTIME
With Dianne Roberts, Buddy Song, Rajeeve Gupta, Michael B. McClellan orchestra, others
Prods-dirs: Ron Ciro, Gary Gibson.
Mon (8), 11 pm.
KCTS Seattle
03/24/76

MAKIN' IT
With David Naughton, Greg Antonacci, Denise Miller, Ellen Travolta, Rebecca Balding, Ralph Seymour, Gary Prendergast, Lou Antonio, Jennifer Perrito, Wendy Hoffman, Diane Robin, Leslie Winston
Supplier: Miller-Milkis Prods, Henderson Prods, The Stigwood Group & Paramount TV
Exec Prods: Thomas L Miller, Edward K Milkis, Lowell Ganz, Mark Rothman;
Prods: David W Duclon, Deborah Leschin, Jeff Ganz;
Dir: Lowell Ganz;
Wris: Lowell Ganz, Rothman.
30 Mins, Thurs (1), 8:30 pm.
ABC-TV
02/07/79

MAKING TELEVISION DANCE
With Twyla Tharp, Mikhail Baryshinkov, Tow Rawe, Jennifer Way, Shelley Washington, Christine Ucida, Snuffy Jenkins, Pappy Sherrill, The Hired Hands, Don Mischer
Supplier: TV Lab of WNET, Tharp Dance Foundation
Prods: David Loxton, Rhoda Grauer;
Dir: Don Mischer.
60 Mins, Wed (5), 8 pm.
WNET New York
10/12/77S

MALLORY: CIRCUMSTANTIAL EVIDENCE
(NBC Sunday Mystery Movie)
With Raymond Burr, Robert Loggia, Roger Robinson, Mark Hamill, A Martinez, Peter Mark Richman, Vic Mohica, Eugene Roche, Allan Rich, Philip Sterling, Stanley Kamel, Joyce Easton, Bill Lucking, Cliff Emmich
Supplier: Crescendo Prods., R.B. Prods & Universal TV
Prod: William Sackheim;
Dir: Boris Sagal;
Wris: Joel Oliansky, Joseph Polizzi.
120 Mins, Sun (8), 9 pm.
NBC-TV
02/11/76

MAN AND WOMAN
With Gaie Houston, narrator
Supplier: Yorkshire TV
Exec Prod: Peter Scroggs;
Prod-Dir: Graham Watts.
30 Mins, Thurs (14), 11:15 pm.
ITV, England
07/27/77F

MAN FROM ATLANTIS
With Patrick Duffy, Belinda J Montgomery, Dean Santoro, Art Lund, Victor Buono, Lawrence Pressman, Mark Jenkins, Allen Case, Joshua Bryant, Steve Franken, Virginia Gregg
Supplier: Solow Prod Co
Exec Prod: Herbert F Solow;
Prod: Robert H Justman;
Dir: Lee H Katzin;
Wri: Mayo Simon.
120 Mins, Fri (4), 9 pm.
NBC-TV
03/09/77

MAN FROM ATLANTIS
With Patrick Duffy, Belinda Montgomery, Alan Fudge, Victor Buono, Robert Lussier, James E Brodhead, Richard Laurence Williams, J Victor Lopez, Jean Marie Hon, Anson Downes
Supplier: Solow Prod Co
Exec Prod: Herbert F Solow;
Prod: Herman Miller;
Dir: Virgil Vogel;
Wri: Tom Greene.
60 Mins, Thurs, 9 pm.
NBC-TV
09/28/77

THE MAN IN THE SANTA CLAUS SUIT
(The Big Event)
With Fred Astaire, Gary Burghoff, John Byner, Bert Convy, Tara Buckman, Brooke Bundy, Eddie Barth, Ron Feinberg, Nanette Fabray, Harold Gould, Danny Wells, David Greener, Ray Vitte
Supplier: Dick Clark Cinema Programs
Exec Prods: Dick Clark, Al Schwartz;
Prod: Lee Miller;
Dir: Corey Allen;
Wris: George Kirgo, Leonard Gershe.
120 Mins, Sun (23), 8 pm.
NBC-TV
12/26/79

THE MAN INSIDE
With James Franciscus, Stefanie Powers, Jacques Godin, Len Birman, Donald Davis
Exec Prod: John Ross;
Prod: Wilton Schiller;
Dir: Gerald Mayer;
Wri: Tony Sheer.
120 Mins, Sat, 8:30 pm.
CBC-TV, from Toronto, Canada
07/06/77F

THE MAN WHO LOVED BEARS
With Henry Fonda, Marty Stouffer
Supplier: Marty Stouffer Prods
Prod-Dir: Stouffer;
Wri: John Savage.
60 Mins, Sun (17), 7 pm.
ABC-TV
06/20/79

MANDRAKE
(NBC Wednesday Night At The Movies)
With Anthony Herrera, Simone Griffeth, Ji-Tu Cumbuka, Hank Brandt, Gretchen Corbett, Peter Haskell, Robert Reed, James Hong, David Hooks, David Hollander, Donna Benz, Harry Blackstone Jr
Supplier: Universal TV
Prod-Wri: Rick Husky;
Dir: Harry Falk.
120 Mins, Wed (24), 8 pm.
NBC-TV
01/31/79

THE MANHATTAN TRANSFER: A SOUNDSTAGE SPECIAL
With The Manhattan Transfer
Exec Prod: Thea Flaum;
Prod: Ken Ehrlich;
Dir: Dick Carter.
60 Min, Tues, (6), 10 pm.
WTTW-TV Chicago
12/24/80

MAN'S GREATEST SPORTS
(Dribble)
With Joseph Hacker, Julius J. Carry 3d, Edward Edwards, Larry Anderson, Dan Frazer, Dee Wallace, Vernee Watson, Basil Hoffman, Amy Stryker
Supplier: Linda Bloodworth Prods, Green-Epstein Prods & Columbia Pictures TV
Exec Prod: Jim Green, Allen Epstein;
Prod-Wri: Bloodworth;
Dir: Charles S. Dubin.
90 Mins, Thurs, (21) 9:30 pm.
NBC-TV
08/27/80

MAN'S GREATEST SPORTS
(The Further Adventures of Wally Brown)
With Clinton Derricks-Carroll, Peter Scolari, Ron Masak, Arlene Golonka, Marvin Braverman, Gilbert Gottfried, Sally Hightower, Peter Wise, Bobby Ellerbee, Richard Karron
Supplier: Haywood Prods & Paramount TV
Exec Prods: Mark Rothman, Lowell Ganz;
Prod: John Chulay;
Dir: Ganz;
Wri: Mark Mandel.
90 Mins, Thurs, (21) 9:30 pm.
NBC-TV
08/27/80

MAN'S GREATEST SPORTS
(The Single Life)
With Barrie Youngfellow, Fred McCarren, Joyce Reehling, Celia Weston, Paul Regina
Supplier: Paramount TV
Exec Prod: Bob Ellison;
Prod: Steve Pritzker;
Dir: Bill Persky;
Wris: Laura Levine, Persky
90 Mins, Thurs, (21) 9:30 pm.
NBC-TV
08/27/80

MARCIA HINES MUSIC
With Marcia Hines, John Waters, Doug Ashdown, Kevin Johnson, Janice Slater, Trevor White, Jon English, Ross Ryan, Johnnie Farnham, Linda George
Supplier: Australian Broadcasting Commission
Exec Prod: Ric Burch;
Dirs: Paul Drane, Tony Nielsen;
Wri: Ken Sterling.
45 Mins, Sat 7:30 pm.
ABC (Australia) TV, from Channel 2, Sydney
03/29/78F

MARCIA'S MUSIC
With Marcia Hines, Johnny Farnham, Glenn Shorrock, Mona Lisa, Terry Young, Doug Ashdown, Doug Parkinson, Don Burrows & George Golla, Brenda Kristen, Graham Matters, Graeme Connors, Anne Kirkpatrick, Gillian Eastoe, Jon English, Darryl Cotton, Robin Moase, Kim Durant & Alison MacCallum
Supplier: Australian Broadcasting Commission
Exec Prod: Ric Burch;
Dirs: Robert Guillemot, Vas Kontis.
45 Mins, Fri, 8:15 pm.
ABC TV, from Ch2, Sydney, Australia
07/11/79F

MARIA
(Here to Stay)
With Diane D'Aquila, Jean Gascon, Alfie Scopp, Robert Silverman, Janet Amos
Prod: Stephen Patrick;
Dir: Allan King;
Wri: Rick Salutin.
60 Mins, Sun, 9 pm.
CBC-TV, from Toronto, Canada
04/13/77F

MARIE
With Marie Osmond, Ellen Travolta, Telma Hopkins, Zan Charisse, Tony Ramirez, Stephen Shortridge, Bruce Kirby, Cliff Pellow, Jeannetta Arnette, Barry Cutler
Supplier: Osmond TV
Exec Prods-Wris: Norman Paul, Joe Bonaduce;
Prod: Dennis Johnson;
Dir: Richard Crenna.
30 Mins, Sat (1), 8:30 pm.
ABC-TV
12/05/79

MARIE
With Marie Osmond, Gavin MacLeod, Jeff Conaway, Howard Itzkowitz
Supplier: Osmond Entertainment
Exec Prods: Alan & Merill Osmond, Jerry McPhie;
Prods: Neal Israel, Pat Proft;
Dir: Jeff Margolis;
Wris: Bob Arnott, Bryan Blackburn, Earl Brown, Chris Cluess, Jim Fisher, Joyce Gittlin, Gina Goldman, Chris Hart, Stu Kreissman, Jeff Richman, Jim Staahl.
60 Min, Fri, 8 pm.
NBC-TV
12/17/80

MARIE CURIE
With Jane Lapotaire, Nigel Hawthorne, Marion Mathie, Robin Halstead, Denis Carey, others
Supplier: BBC
Prod: Peter Goodchild;
Dir: John Glenister;
Wri: Elaine Morgan.
55 Mins, Tues, 9 pm.
BBC, from London, England
08/31/77F

MARIJUANA: THE GRASS IS GETTING GREENER
(Channel 7 Special Report)
With Roger Grimsby
Exec Prod: Alan L Cohen;
Prod-Wri: Gene Marciona.
30 Mins, Mon (11), 7:30 pm.
WABC-TV, New York
04/20/77

THE MARILYN McCOO & BILLY DAVIS JR SHOW
With Marilyn McCoo, Billy Davis Jr, Jay Leno, Lewis Arquette, Tim Reid
Exec Prod: Dick Broder;
Prod-Wris: Ann Elder, Ed Sharlach;
Dir: Gerren Keith.
30 Mins, Wed (15), 8:30 pm.
CBS-TV
06/22/77

MARK RUSSELL COMEDY SHOW
Supplier: WNED-TV Buffalo
Prod: Wiley Hance;
Dir: Tedd Tramalom.
30 Mins, Mon, 8:30 pm.
PBS via WNED-TV Buffalo
03/14/79

MARK TWAIN'S AMERICA
With Walker Edmiston (host), David Huffman, Michael Callan, Adam Arkin, Rosemary DeCamp, James Griffith, John Myhers
Supplier: Schick Sunn Classic Prods
Exec Prod: Charles E Sellier Jr;
Prod: James L Conway;
Dir: Henning Schellerup;
Wri: Brian Russell.
60 Mins Thurs (11), 8 pm.
NBC-TV
01/17/79

MARQUE
With Peter Wherrett
Supplier: Australian Broadcasting Commission
Dir: Andrew Lloyd James.
30 Mins, Thurs, 7:30 pm.
ABC TV, Channel 2, Sydney, Australia
04/11/79F

MARRIED: THE FIRST YEAR
With Legh McCloskey, Cindy Grover, Claudette Nevins, K Callan, Stanley Grover, Gigi Vorgan, Stefanie Kramer, Gary Epp, Stephen Manley, Jennifer McAllister, Christine Belford, Joshua Bryant, Constance McCashin, Casey Biggs, Martha Scott, Henry Wilcoxon, Pitt Herbert, Peter Levien, Tracy Justrich, Matthew Tobin
Supplier: Lorimar Prods
Exec Prods: Lee Rich, Philip Capice;
Prod-Wri: David Jacobs;
Dir: Robert Michael Lewis.
60 Mins, Wed, 8 pm.
CBS-TV
03/07/79

MARTINELLI: OUTSIDE MAN
With Ron Leibman, Woody Strode, Janet Margolin, Nicholas Colasanto, Al Ruscio, Pepper Martin, Robert Donner, Ray Vitte, William Wintersole, Nicholas Pryor, Jack Thibeau
Supplier: MTM Enterprises
Exec Prod-Wri: Paul Magistretti;
Prod: William F Phillips;
Dir: Russ Mayberrry.
60 Mins, Fri (8), 10 pm.
CBS-TV
04/13/77

MARY
With Mary Tyler Moore, James Hampton, Swoosie Kurtz, David Letterman, Michael Keaton, Judy Kahan, Dick Shawn, others
Supplier: MTM Prods
Prods: Tom Patchett, Jay Tarses;
Dir: Rob Iscove;
Wris: Arnie Kogen, David Axelrod, Jeffrey Barron & Valri Bromfield, Stan Burns, Carol Gary, Patricia Jones, Merrill Markoe, Gary Markowtz, Pat Proft, Donald Reiker.
60 Mins, Sun, 8:20 pm.
CBS-TV
09/27/78

MARY AND MICHAEL
With Mary Bellows, Michael Ayoub, Luba Goy, Harvey Atkins
Prod: Gayle Gibson Sedawie;
Wri: N A Wood.
30 Mins, Sat, 9:30 pm.
Global TV, from Toronto, Canada
10/19/77F

MARY HARTMAN, MARY HARTMAN
With Louise Lasser, Greg Mullavey, Dody Goodman, Phil Burns, Victor Kilian, Mary Kay Place, Graham Jarvis, Debralee Scott, Claudia Lamb
Supplier: Tandem-Filmways
Exec Prod: Norman Lear;
Dirs: Joan Darling, Jim Drake;
Wris: Gail Parent, Ann Marcus, Jerry Adelman, Daniel Gregory Browne.
30 Mins, Mon-Fri, 11 pm.
WNEW-TV New York
01/14/76

MARY TYLER MOORE HOUR
With Mary Tyler Moore, Michael Keaton, Michael Lombard, Ron Rifkin, Joyce Van Patten, Lucille Ball, Mike Douglas, Florence Halop, Wayne Dvorak
Supplier: MTM Prods
Prod: Perry Lafferty;
Dir: Robert Scheerer;
Wris: Arnie Kogen, David Axelrod, Stan Burns, Peter Gallay, Carol Gary, Gary Jacobs, Coslough Johnson, Patricia Jones, Donald Reiker, Pat Proft, Aubrey Tadman, Garry Ferrier.
60 Mins, Sun, 10 pm.
CBS-TV
03/07/79

MARY WHITE
(ABC Theatre)
With Kathleen Beller, Ed Flanders, Fionnuala Flanagan, Tim Matheson, Donald Moffatt, Diana Douglas
Supplier: Radnitz-Mattel Prods
Prod: Robert B Radnitz;
Dir: Jud Taylor;
Wri: Caryl Ledner.
120 Mins, (18), 9 pm.
ABC-TV
IBM
11/23/77

MARY'S INCREDIBLE DREAM
With Mary Tyler Moore, Ben Vereen, Doug Kershaw, Arthur Fiedler, Manhattan Transfer, others
Supplier: MTM Enterprises
Prod-Wri: Jack Good;
Dir: Gene McAvoy, Jaime Rogers.
60 Mins, Thurs (22), 10 pm.
CBS-TV
01/28/76

MASTER OF THE WORLD
(Famous Classic Tales)
With voices of John Ewart, Tim Eliott, Matthew O'Sullivan, Ron Haddrick, Judy Morris
Supplier: Air Programs International
Prod: Walter J. Hucker;
Dir: Leif Gram;
Wri: John Palmer.
60 Mins, Sat (23), 1 pm.
CBS-TV
Kenner Toys (Sive Associates)
10/27/76

MATT AND JENNY
With Neil Dainard, Derrick Jones, Megan Follows, Duncan Regehr
Exec Prod: Ralph C Ellis;
Prod-Wri: William Davidson;
Dir: Joseph Scanlan.
30 Mins, Sun, 7 pm.
Global TV, from Toronto, Canada
10/24/79F

MAYFLOWER: THE PILGRIMS' ADVENTURE
With Anthony Hopkins, Richard Crenna, Jenny Agutter, Michael Beck, David Dukes, Trish Van Devere, John Heffernan, Paul Sparer, Frank Hamilton, W B Brydon, William Converse-Roberts, Nicholas Surovy, Guy Sorel, Karen Sunde, George Taylor, Martha Sinnard Wright
Supplier: Syzygy Prods
Exec Prod: Linda Yellen;
Dir: George Schaefer;
Wri: James Lee Barrett.
120 Mins, Wed (21), 9 pm.
CBS-TV
Amway (Stevens Inc); DuPont (BBDO Int'l)
11/28/79

THE MAYOR OF CASTERBRIDGE
With Alan Bates, Anne Stallybrass, Janet Maw, Avis Bunnage, Jack Galloway, others
Supplier: BBC
Prod: Jonathan Powell;
Dir: David Giles;
Wri: Dennis Potter (from novel by Thomas Hardy).
50 Mins, Sun, 8:05 pm.
BBC-1, Britain
02/08/78F

THE McLEAN STEVENSON SHOW
With Barbara Stuart, Madge West, Ayn Ruymen, Steve Nevil, David Hollander, Jason Whitney, Jerry Hauser, Janus Blyth, Suzanne Wishner
Supplier: McLean Stevenson Enterprises & Monty Hall Enterprises
Exec Prod: Hall;
Prods: Arnold Margolin, Don Van Atta;
Dir: Alan Myerson;
Wri: Lloyd Garvey.
30 Mins, Wed, 8:30 pm.
NBC-TV
12/08/76

McNAMARA'S BAND
With John Byner, Bruce Kirby, Sid Haig, Joe Pantoliano, Steve Doubet, Geoffrey Lewis, Janice Heiden, Albert Salmi
Supplier: Colomby-Byner Enterprises, Kukoff-Harris Prods & Boiney Stoones Inc
Exec Prods-Wris: Jeff Harris, Bernie Kukoff;
Prods: E Darrell Hallenback, Harry Colomby;
Dir: Bill Bixby.
60 Mins, Mon (5), 8 pm.
ABC-TV
12/14/77

McNAUGHTON'S DAUGHTER
(NBC Thursday Night At The Movies)
With Susan Clark, Ricardo Montalban, James Callahan, John Elerick, Vera Miles, Ralph Bellamy, Louise Latham, others
Supplier: Universal TV, & Groverton Prods.
Exec Prod: David Victor;
Prod: David J. O'Connell;
Dir: Jerry London;
Wri: Ken Trevey
120 Mins, Thurs (4), 9 pm.
NBC-TV
03/10/76

McNAUGHTON'S DAUGHTER
With Susan Clark, Ricardo Montalban, John Elerick, James Callahan, Monte Markham, Gene Raymond, Michael Richardson, Anjanette Comer, Maria Elena Cordero, Byron Morrow, Marla Adams
Supplier: Groverton Prods. & Universal TV
Exec Prod: David Victor;
Prod: Harold Gast;
Dir: Daniel Haller;
Wri: Stephen Kandel.
60 Mins, Wed, 10 pm.
NBC-TV
03/31/76

ME AND MAXX
With Joe Satos, Melissa Michaelsen, Jenny Sullivan, Jim Weston
Supplier: James Komack Co.
Exec Prod-Wri: Komack;
Prods: Don Van Atta, Stan Cutler, George Tricker, Neil Rosen;
Dir: Herbert Kenwith
30 Mins, Sat, 9:30 pm.
NBC-TV
03/26/80

ME AND MR. THORNE
With Johnny Farnham, Gordon Chater, Beverley Phillips, Wallas Eaton, Chuck Faulkner
Supplier: Crawford Productions, Melbourne
Exec Prod: Ian Crawford
Prod: Henry Crawford;
Dir: Paul Eddey;
Wri: Terry Stapleton.
60 Mins.
Melbourne, Australia
09/29/76F

MEDICINE IN AMERICA: LIFE, DEATH & DOLLARS
(NBC Reports)
With Tom Snyder, Jane Pauley, Edwin Newman, Betty Rollin, Carl Stern
Supplier: NBC News
Exec Prod: Daniel P. O'Connor;
Sr Prod: Earl Ubell;
Prods: Adrienne Cowles, Darold Murray, Bill Turque;
Dirs: Joel Banow, Murray;
Wris: Cowles, Murray, Janet Pearce, Rollin, Karen Rutledge, Michael B. Silver, Snyder, Stern, Turque, Ubell, Jean Sprain Wilson.
180 Mins, Tues (3), 8 pm.
NBC-TV
01/11/78

THE MEDICINE SHOW
With Ken Lefoli, host
Supplier: Canadian Broadcasting Corp.
Exec Prod: Andrew Cochran;
Prods: Duncan McEwen, Dave Hodgekinson;
Wri: Lefoli.
28 Mins, Thurs, (17), 9:30 pm.
CBC-TV, from Winnipeg, Canada
02/27/80F

MEL AND SUSAN TOGETHER
With Mel Tillis, Susan Anton, Donny & Marie Osmond, Billy Carter
Supplier: Osmond TV Prods
Exec Prods: Merrill & Alan Osmond;
Prods: Jerry McPhie, Toby Martin;
Dir: Jack Regas;
Wris: Michael Kagan, Sonny Gordon, Carmen Finestra, Arthur Sellars.
30 Mins, Sat (22), 8 pm.
ABC-TV
04/26/78

MELODY'S MALADY
With Heather Schulz, David Wisniewski
Prod-Wri: Mark Young;
Dir: Kim Thomas.
30 Mins, Fri (29), 7:30 pm.
WJLA-TV Washington
01/10/79

THE MEXICANS
Supplier: ATV
Prod-Dir: David Munro.
53 Mins, Wed, (4) 9 pm.
ITV Network, Britain
06/25/80F

MICHOUD: THE OUTER SPACE CONNECTION
Exec Prod: Don Wilburn;
Prod-Wri: Patricia Gormin;
Dir: Robert Weaver.
30 Mins, Sat.
WVUE-TV New Orleans
04/11/79

MILITARY WIVES
Prod-Reporter: Mike Kirk.
30 Mins, Tues, 10 pm.
KCTS-TV Seattle
11/05/80

MILLION DOLLAR PLAYOFFS
With Richie Hayes, Carl Kraft
Supplier: Marvin H Sugarman Prods
Prod: Lou Tyrrell;
Dir: Bob Bielecki;
Wri: Leah Jay.
30 Mins, Fri, 5:30 pm.
WOR-TV New York
08/09/78

THE MILLIONAIRE
(CBS Tuesday Night Movies)
With Robert Quarry, Martin Balsam, Edward Albert, Bill, Mark & Brett Hudson, Pat Crowley, Pamela Toll, Allan Rich, John Ireland, Ralph Bellamy, Jane Wyatt, William Demarest, Talia Balsam, Michael Minor, Milt Kogan, Sally Kemp, Patricia Hindy
Supplier: Don Fedderson Prods
Prod: Fedderson;
Dir: Don Weis;
Wri: John McGreevey.
120 Mins, Tues (19), 9 pm.
CBS-TV
12/27/78

MINDREADERS
With Dick Martin (host)
Supplier: Goodson-Todman Prods
Exec Prod: Ira Skutch;
Dir: Ira Skutch;
Prod: Mimi O'Brien.
30 Mins, Mon-Fri, noon.
NBC-TV
08/29/79

MINSTREL MAN
With Glynn Turman, Ted Ross, Stanley Clay, Sandra Sharp, Art Evans, Gene Bell, Earl Billings, Anthony Amos, Amechi Uzodinma, Arthur Rooks, Carol Sutton, Wilber Swartz, Robert Earle, Don Lutenbacher, Billy Holiday, Robert L Harper
Supplier: First Artist
Exec Prods: Roger Gimbel, Edward L Rissien;
Prods: Mitchell Brower, Robert Lovenheim;
Dir: William A Graham;
Wris: Richard Shapiro, Esther Mayesh Shapiro.
120 Mins, Wed (2), 9 pm.
CBS-TV
03/09/77

THE MISADVENTURES OF SHERIFF LOBO
With Claude Akins, Mills Watson, Brian Kerwin, Christopher George, Caren Kaye, Booth Colman, Greg Evigan, Leann Hunley
Supplier: Glen Larson Prods and Universal TV
Exec Prod: Larson;
Supv Prod: Bill D'Angelo;
Prod: Joe Boston;
Dir: Dick Harwood;
Wris: Larson, Chris Bunch, Allan Cole.
60 Mins, Tues, 8 pm.
NBC-TV
09/26/79

MISMATCH
With Jane Harders, Stephen O'Rourke, Michael Aitkens, Margo Lee, John Bluthal, Michael Caulfield, Jennifer Claire, others
Supplier: Australian Broadcasting Commission
Exec Prod: Oscar Whitbread;
Dir: Ken Hannam;
Wri: Barry Donnelly.
70 Mins, Sun, 8:30 pm.
ABC Ch 2, Sydney Australia
11/07/79F

MISS WINSLOW & SON
With Darleen Carr, Roscoe Lee Browne, Elliott Reid, Sarah Marshall, William Bogert, Hope Clarke, Pamela Dunlap, Joe Rassulo, Ellen Sherman, Benjamin Margolis
Supplier: T T C Prods
Exec Prods: Ted Bergmann, Don Taffner;
Supv Prod-Wri: Alan J Levitt;
Co-Prod: Mimi Seawell;
Dir: George Tyne.
30 Mins, Wed, 8:30 pm.
CBS-TV
04/04/79

MRS COLUMBO
(NBC Monday Night At The Movies)
With Kate Mulgrew, Henry Jones, Lili Haydn, Robert Culp, Edie Adams, Bob Dishy, Rene Auberjonois, Priscilla Pointer, Allan Rich, Frederic Forrest, Barney Martin, Christopher Allport, Herb Armstrong
Supplier: Gambit Prods & Universal TV
Exec Prod-Wri: Richard Alan Simmons;
Prod: James McAdams;
Dir: Boris Sagal.
120 Mins, Mon (26), 9 pm.
NBC-TV
02/21/79

MR & MRS DRACULA
With Dick Shawn, Carol Lawrence, Barry Gordon, Anthony Battaglia, Gail Mayron, Rick Aviles, Johnny Haymer, Robert Ellerbee, Ken Olfson, Susan Garia, Vicki Belmonte, Dick Wieand, Robert Ackerman
Supplier: ABC Circle Films
Exec Prod-Wri: Robert Klane;
Prod: Stanton Korey;
Dir: Doug Rogers.
30 Mins, Fri, (5) 8:30 pm.
ABC-TV
09/10/80

MR. ROONEY GOES TO DINNER
With Andrew Rooney
Supplier: CBS News
Prod-dir-wri: Andrew Rooney.
60 Mins, Tues, (20), 8 pm.
CBS-TV
04/28/76

MR T & TINA
With Pat Morita, Susan Blanchard, Pat Suzuki, Ted Lange, Miriam Byrd-Nethery, Jerry Hatsuo Fujikawa, June Angela, Gene Profanato, Muriel Weldon
Supplier: The Komack Co
Exec Prod: James Komack;
Prods: Bob Carroll Jr, Madelyn Davis, Gary Shimokawa;
Dir: James Sheldon;
Wris: Carroll, Davis.
30 Mins, Sat, 8:30 pm.
ABC-TV
09/29/76

MITZI...ROARIN' IN THE 20'S
With Mitzi Gaynor, Carl Reiner, Linda Hopkins, Ken Berry
Supplier: Green Isle Enterprises
Exec Prod: Jack Bean;
Prod: Harry Waterson:
Dir-chor: Tony Charmoli;
Wri: Jerry Mayer.
60 Mins, Sun (14), 9 pm.
CBS-TV
Kraft (JWT)
03/17/76

THE MONEYCHANGERS
With Kirk Douglas, Timothy Bottoms, Susan Flannery, Anne Baxter, Percy Rodriguez, Ralph Bellamy, Joan Collins, Robert Loggia, Jean Peters, Patrick O'Neal, Lorne Greene, Helen Hayes
Supplier: Ross Hunter Prods-Paramount TV-NBC-TV
Prods: Hunter, Jacque Mapes;
Dir: Boris Sagal;
Wris: Dean Riesner, Stanford Whitmore.
120 Mins, Sat (4), 9 pm.
NBC-TV
12/08/76

THE MORECAMBE & WISE SHOW
With Eric Morecambe, Ernie Wise, Terru Wogan, others
Supplier: Thames TV
Prod-Dir: Michael Mills;
Wri: Eddie Braben.
30 Mins, Wed, 8:30 pm.
ITV Network, England
09/10/80F

MORK & MINDY
With Robin Williams, Pam Dawber, Elizabeth Kerr, Conrad Janis, Jeffrey Jacquet, Geoffrey Lewis, Dick Yarmy, Michael Prince, Jeff Harlan, Woody Eney, Hank Jones, Leslie Vallen, Henry Winkler, Penny Marshall
Supplier: Henderson Prods, Miller-Milkis Prods & Paramount TV
Exec Prods: Garry K Marshall, Tony Marshall;
Prods: Dale McRaven, Bruce Johnson;
Dir: Howard Storm;
Wri: McRaven.
60 Mins, Thurs (14), 8 pm.
ABC-TV
09/20/78

MORNING
With Bob Schieffer, Dan Rather, Ray Brady, Ray Gandolf, others
Supplier: CBS News
Exec Prod: Robert Northshield;
Prods: Mark Harrington, Christie Basham, David Miller, Jennifer Siebens;
Dir: Eric Shapiro;
Wris: Frank Teltsch, Gandolf.
60 Mins, Mon-Fri, 7 am.
CBS-TV
01/31/79

THE MORNING SHOW
With Ann Fraser, Ross McGowan
Supplier: KPIX
Exec Prod: Galen Daily;
Prod: Ann Miller;
Dir: Marion Whigham.
60 Mins, Mon-Fri, 9:30 am.
KPIX San Francisco
09/27/78

MORTIMER'S PATCH
With Terence Cooper, Don Selwyn, Sean Duffy, Derek Hardwick, Ken Blackburn
Supplier: Television New Zealand
Prod: Tom Finlayson;
Dir: Chris Bailey;
Wri: Keith Aberdein.
52 Mins, Tues, 9 pm.
TV-1 Network, N.Z.
09/03/80F

MOST WANTED
(ABC Sunday Movie Double Feature)
With Robert Stack, Leslie Charleson, Shelly Novack, Tom Selleck, Marj Dusay, Jack Kehoe, Sheree North, Roger Perry, Percy Rodrigues, Fred Sadoff, Kitty Winn
Supplier: Quinn Martin Prods.
Exec Prod: Martin;
Prod: John Wilder;
Dir: Walter Grauman;
Wri: Laurence Heath.
90 Mins, Sun (21), 10:30 pm.
ABC-TV
03/31/76

MOST WANTED
With Robert Stack, Shelly Novack, Jo Ann Harris, Harris Yulin, Allan Miller, Roy Poole, Ward Costello, Robert Mandan, Laurette Spang, Jerry Ayers, Carl Weathers, Burke Byrnes
Supplier: QM Prods
Exec Prod: Quinn Martin;
Prod: Harold Gast;
Dir: Don Medford;
Wri: Guerdon Trueblood.
60 Mins, Sat, 10 pm.
ABC-TV
10/20/76

MOTHER & ME, MD
(NBC Comedy Theater)
With Rue McClanahan, Leah Ayres, Kenneth Gilman, Rick Podell, Howard Witt, Jack Riley, Parris Buckner, Beverly Kushido, Arny Freeman, David Fresco
Supplier: MTM Prods
Exec Prod-Dir: Michael Zinberg;
Prods: Jennie Blackton, Joan Desberg Greenberg, Charles Raymond;
Wris: Blackton, Greenberg.
30 Mins, Thurs (14), 8:30 pm.
NBC-TV
06/20/79

MOTHER, JUGGS AND SPEED
With Ray Vitte, Joanne Nail, Joe Penny, Rod McCary, Harvey Lembeck, Barbara Minkus-Barron, Jan Shutan, Shay Duffin, Charlotte Stewart, Marcus Smythe
Supplier: Bruce Geller Unit Prods, Hanna-Barbera Prods & 20th-Fox TV
Exec Prods: Geller, Joseph Barbera;
Prod: Geller;
Dir: John Rich;
Wri: Tom Mankiewicz.
30 Mins, Thurs (17), 9:30 pm.
ABC-TV
08/23/78

MOVIOLA
(The Scarlet O'Hara War)
With Tony Curtis, Bill Macy, Harold Gould, Sharon Gless, George Furth, Edward Winter, Barrie Youngfellow, Carrie Nye, Clive Revill, Gwen Humble, Morgan Brittany, Patricia Smith, James Ray, William Bogart, Joey Forman, Jane Kean
06/04/80

MOVIOLA
(The Silent Lovers)
With Kristina Wayborn, Barry Bostwick, Brian Keith, Howard Gould, John Rubinstein, James Olson, Barney Martin, Audra Lindley, Cecelia Hart, Joseph Hacker, Mackenzie Phillips, Hank Garrett, Terrance McNally, Thaao Penghlis
06/04/80

MOVIOLA
(This Year's Blondie)
With Lloyd Bridges, Constance Forslund, Norman Fell, Vic Tayback, Michael Lerner, John Marley, Richard Seer, Lee Wallace, William Frankfather, Philip Sterling, Sondra Blake, Barney Martin, Michael Strong, Peter Maloney, Stephen Keep, Fred Sadoff
Supplier: David L. Wolper-Stan Margulies Prods & Warner Bros TV
Exec Prod: Wolper;
Prod: Margulies;
Dir: John Erman;
Wris: James Lee, Willian Hanley, based on Garson Kanin book
360 Mins, Sun-Tues, (May 19-21) 9 pm.
NBC-TV
06/04/80

MOWGLI'S BROTHERS
(The Jungle Books)
With voices of Roddy McDowall, June Foray
Supplier: Chuck Jones
Prod-dir-adapt: Chuck Jones.
30 Mins, Wed (11), 8:30 pm.
CBS-TV
02/18/76

MOYNIHAN
(The Going Rate)
With Ian Mune, Stratford Johns, Sheila Hammond, Louise Pajo, Walt Brown, Ken Blackburn, Ken Goodlet
Supplier: ABC
Exec Prod: Eric Price;
Dirs: Brian Bell, John Croyston, Peter Muxlow;
Wris: Jane Galletly, Earle Spence.
50 Mins, Fri, 8:30 pm.
ABC, from Melbourne, Australia
03/24/76F

MOYNIHAN
With Ian Mune, Walt Brown, Julia Blake, Bill Johnson, Louise Pajo, Ken Blackburn, Don Selwyn, Terence Finnigan, Johnny Johnstone, Patrick Smyth, others
Supplier: Australian Broadcasting Commission
Prods: New Zealand Television One and ABC;
Exec Prod: Douglas Drury.
50 Mins, Thurs, 8:55 pm.
ABC (Australia) TV
03/16/77F

MOZART IN SEATTLE
With Milton Katims, Henryk Szeryng, Seattle Symphony Orchestra
Prod-dir: Robert Hagopian;
60 Mins, Wed (14), 10 pm.
KCTS-TV Seattle
05/05/76

MULLIGAN'S STEW
With Elinor Donahue, Lawrence Pressman, Lory Kochheim, Johnny Doran, Suzanne Crough, Julie Anne Haddock, Chris Ciampa, K C Martel, Sunshine Lee, Matthew Laborteaux, Donegan Smith
Supplier: Christiana Prod & Paramount TV
Prod: Joanna Lee;
Dir: Holly Morse;
Wris: Nancy Sackett, Lee.
60 Mins, Tues, 9 pm.
NBC-TV
11/02/77

MULTI-COLORED SWAP SHOP
With Noel Edmonds, others
Prod: Crispin Evans.
180 Mins, Sat, 9:30 am.
BBC-1, from London, England
04/11/79F

THE MUPPET SHOW
With Jim Henson's Muppets, Rita Moreno
Supplier: ITC Entertainment & Henson Associates
Exec Prod: Henson;
Prod: Jack Burns;
Dir: Jerry Juhl;
Wris: Henson, Burns, Juhl.
30 Mins, Mon, 7:30 pm.
WCBS-TV New York
09/22/76S

MURDER IN MUSIC CITY
(Big Event)
With Sonny Bono, Lee Purcell, Claude Akins, Belinda Montgomery, Morgan Fairchild, Lucille Benson, Michael MacRae, Harry Bellaver
Supplier: Frankel Films-Gank Inc
Exec Prod: Ernie Frankel;
Prod: Jimmy Sangster;
Dir: Leo Penn;
Wris: Sangster, Frankel.
120 Mins Tues (16), 9 pm.
NBC-TV
01/24/79

MUSIC
With Murry Sidlin
Supplier: WETA-TV Washington
Exec Prod: Ruth Leon;
Dir: Clark Santee.
30 Mins, Sat (8), 7:30 pm.
PBS
10/12/77

MUSIC HALL AMERICA
With Ray Stevens (host), Kenny Rogers, Chet Atkins, Lonnie Shorr, Bo Donaldson & the Heywoods, Dean Rutherford, The Even Dozen
Supplier: Viacom Enterprises & Opryland Prods
Exec Prods: Roy Smith, Henry Gillespie;
Prod: Lee Miller;
Dir: Lee Bernhardi;
Wris: Wally Dalton, Mike Kagen.
60 Mins, Sun, 8 pm.
WPIX-TV New York
09/29/76S

MUSICAL COMEDY TONIGHT
With Carol Burnett, Richard Chamberlain, John Davidson, Agnes de Mille, Sandy Duncan, Rock Hudson, Ethel Merman, Bernadette Peters, Bobby Van
Supplier: Dena Pictures, KCET Los Angeles
Exec Prod: Sylvia Fine Kaye;
Prod: Eric Lieber;
Dir: Stan Harris;
Arr-Cond: Peter Matz.
90 Mins, Mon (1), 9 pm.
WNET New York
10/03/79

MUTINY ON THE WESTERN FRONT
Supplier: Mingara Films
Prod: Brian Morris;
Wri-Dir: Dick Dennison.
94 Mins Tues, 7:30 pm.
Ch 7 Network, from Sydney, Australia
08/15/79F

MY BUDDY
With Redd Foxx, Pamela Mason, Basil Hoffman, Irwin C Watson, Slappy White, Iron Jaw Wilson, others
Supplier: Redd Foxx Prods
Exec Prod-Wri: Foxx;
Prod: Norman Hopps;
Dir: Gerren Keith.
30 Mins, Tues (3), 10:30 pm.
ABC-TV
07/11/79

MY NAME IS JANE
With Jane Harvey, Billy Taylor Quintet, others
Supplier: NBC-TV Stations
Prod-dir: Sid Smith;
Wri: Lan Okun.
30 Mins, Sat(31), 7 pm.
WNBC-TV New York
08/04/76

MY WASHINGTON, MY WORLD: MEXICO CHALLENGES UNCLE SAM
With Carl Rowan
Exec Prod: Rowan;
Prod-Dir: Greg Reid.
60 Mins, Sun, 8 pm.
WDVM-TV Washington
07/25/79

THE MYSTERY OF THE ANDREA DORIA
With Donald Madden, narrator
Supplier: Blue Gander Inc.
Prods: Elga Andersen, Peter Gimbel;
Wri: Gimbel.
60 Mins, Wed (24), 8 pm.
CBS-TV
Xerox (Needham, Harper & Steers)
04/07/76

NADIA - FROM ROMANIA WITH LOVE
With Nadia Comaneci, Flip Wilson, Olympia, Theodora Ungureanu, Romanian Rhapsody Folk Dancers
Supplier: Clerow Prods, Radioteleviziunea Romana
Exec Prods: Monte Kay, Dick Foster;
Prod-wri: Tom Egan;
Dirs: Foster, Sterling Johnson.
60 Mins, Tues, (23), 8 pm.
CBS-TV
Sperry Remington (DKG Inc)
12/01/76

NANCY DREW MYSTERIES
(Hardy Boys & Nancy Drew Mysteries)
With Pamela Sue Martin, George O'Hanlon Jr, Jean Rasey, William Schallert, Monte Markham, Robert Karnes, Arthur Peterson, Skip Ward, Joe Penny
Supplier: Glen Larson Prods & Universal TV
Exec Prod-Wri: Glen A Larson
Prods: Arlene Sidaris, Joyce Heft Brotman;
Dir: E W Swackhamer.
60 Mins, Sun, 7 pm.
ABC-TV
02/09/77

THE NANCY WALKER SHOW
With Nancy Walker, William Daniels, Ken Olfson, Beverly Archer, Jack Dodson, Pamela Bellwood
Supplier: T A T Communications
Exec Prod: Norman Lear;
Prod-wri: Rod Parker;
Dir: Hal Cooper.
30 Mins, Thurs, 9:30 pm.
ABC-TV
10/06/76

NASHVILLE 99
With Claude Akins, Jerry Reed, Lucille Benson, Ned Beatty, Belinda Montgomery, Don Johnson, Mel Tillis, Dianne Sherrill, T Tommy Cuterer, Jackie Wright, O B McClinton
Supplier: Frankel Prods & 20th-Fox TV
Exec Prod: Ernie Frankel;
Dir: Don McDougall;
Wri: Jimmy Sangster.
60 Mins, Fri, 9 pm.
CBS-TV
04/06/77

NATALIE COLE SPECIAL
With Earth, Wind & Fire, Johnny Mathis, Stephen Bishop, Linda Williams, Nelson Riddle orch
Supplier: Dick Clark Teleshows & R A Y Prods
Exec Prods: Kevin Hunter, Clark;
Prod-Wri: Robert Arthur;
Dir: Tim Kiley.
60 Mins, Thurs (27), 10 pm.
CBS-TV
Toyota (Dancer Fitzgerald Sample)
05/03/78

NATIONAL COLLEGIATE CHEERLEADING CHAMPIONSHIPS
With Cheryl Ladd, George Burns, Phyllis George, Bruce Jenner, Gene Kelly, Lou Rawls
Supplier: Interpublic Television
Prods: Brad Marks, Lee Mendelson;
Dir: Walter Miller;
Wris: Marks, Mendelson, Fred Fox, Seaman Jacobs.
90 Mins, Mon (24), 8 pm.
CBS-TV
05/03/78

THE NATIONAL DISASTER SURVIVAL TEST
With Tom Snyder, Shana Alexander, John Amos, Kate Jackson, Wally Shirra
Supplier: Warren V Bush-Guenette/Asselin Productions
Exec Prod: Bush;
Prods: Robert Guenette, Paul Asselin;
Dir: Don Horan;
Wri: Guenette.
90 Mins, Sun (1), 8 pm.
NBC-TV
05/04/77

NATIONAL KIDS' QUIZ
With Michael Landon
Exec Prod: Sonny Fox;
Prods: Jane Norman, Jack Kuney;
Dir: Kuney.
60 Mins, Sat 12 noon.
NBC-TV
02/01/78

NATIONWIDE
With Clive Hale, Richard Carleton, Paul Murphy, Paul Griffiths, Andrew Olle, Bill Nicol, Mark Colvin
Supplier: Australian Broadcasting Commission
Exec Prod: John Penlington.
40 Mins, Mon to Thurs, 9:30 pm.
ABC TV from Sydney, Australia
02/28/79F

NBC MAGAZINE WITH DAVID BRINKLEY
With Betsy Aaron, Douglas Kiker, Jack Perkins, Garrick Utley
Supplier: NBC News
Exec Prod: Paul Friedman;
Supv Prod: Wallace Westfeldt;
Sr Prod: Daniel Sullivan;
Dir: George Paul.
60 Mins, Fri, 10 pm.
NBC-TV
10/01/80

NBC REPORTS-HENRY KISSINGER: AN INTERVIEW WTH DAVID FROST
Supplier: NBC News
Prod: Thomas Tomizawa;
Dir: Gerald Polikoff.
60 Mins, Thurs (11), 10 pm.
NBC-TV
10/17/79

NBC: THE FIRST 50 YEARS – A CLOSER LOOK
(The Big Event)
With Orson Welles (narrator), George Burns, Burt Reynolds, Don Rickles, Dan Haggerty, Chevy Chase
Supplier: NBC, Greg Garrison Prods
Exec Prod-Dir: Garrison;
Prod: Lee Hale;
Wri: Jess Oppenheimer, Bill Angelos, Bill Box, Welles.
150 Mins, Sun (23), 8:30 pm.
NBC-TV
10/26/77

NEIGHBORS
Prods: Don Knox, Valerie Gentile;
Wri: Gentile.
60 Mins, Sat (6), 8 pm.
WTTW-TV Chicago
11/17/76

THE NEIGHBORS
With Regis Philbin, Jane Nelson
Supplier: Carruthers Co. & Warner Bros. TV
Exec Prod: Bill Carruthers;
Prod: Joel Stein;
Dir: John Dorsey;
Wris: Brian Joseph, Jan McCormack, Bill Mitchell, Ray Reese.
30 Mins, Mon-Fri, 2:30 pm.
ABC-TV
01/14/76

THE NEIL DIAMOND SPECIAL
Suppliers: Smith-Hemion, Arch Angel Prods
Prods: Gary Smith, Dwight Hemion;
Dir: Hemion;
Wri: Buz Kohan.
60 Mins, Mon (21), 9 pm.
NBC-TV
02/23/77

NEIL DIAMOND SPECIAL: I'M GLAD YOU'RE HERE WITH ME TONIGHT
With Alan Lindgren & Diamond's band, Marilyn & Alan Bergman
Supplier: Arch Angel Prods & Art Fisher Prods
Exec Prod: Jerry Weintraub;
Prod-Dir: Fisher;
Wri: Rod Warren.
60 Mins, Thurs (17), 10 pm.
NBC-TV
11/23/77

NELLIE McCLUNG
With Kate Reid, David Gardner, Ruth Springford, Gerard Parkes
Exec Prod: Robert Allen;
Prod: Herb Rolland;
Dir: George Bloomfield;
Wri: Susanne Grosman.
60 Mins, Sun, 9 pm.
CBC-TV, Toronto, Canada
04/05/78F

NEVER SAY NEVER
With George Kennedy, Anne Schedeen, Irene Tedrow, Rick Podell, Bruce Kimmel, Danny Wells, Jan Jorden, Rochelle Richelien, Maidie Norman
Supplier: Four R Prods & Warner Bros TV
Exec Prod: Leonard A Rosenberg;
Prods: Lee Miller, Elliot Shoenman;
Dir: Charles S Dubin;
Wri: Shoenman.
30 Mins, Wed (11), 8 pm.
CBS-TV
07/25/79

NEW ADVENTURES OF ROBIN HOOD
With Barry Andrews, Briony McRoberts, Michael Culver, Barry Stanton
Supplier: Trident Films Ltd
Prod: Robert D Cardona;
Dir: Peter Duffell;
Wri: Terry Nation.
30 Mins, Tues (19), 7:30 pm.
WCBS-TV New York
04/27/77S

THE NEW AVENGERS
(The Eagle's Nest)
With Patrick Macnee, Joanna Lumley, Gareth Hunt, Peter Cushing, others
Supplier: IDTV-TV
Prods: Brian Clemens, Albert Fennell;
Dir: Desmond Davis;
Wri: Brian Clemens.
60 Mins, Tues, 8 pm.
Thames TV, London, England
10/27/76F

THE NEW AVENGERS
With Patrick Macnee, Joanna Lumley, Gareth Hunt, Terry Wood
Supplier: Thames TV
Prods: Albert Fennell, Brian Clemens;
Dir: Ray Austin;
Wri: Clemens.
60 Mins, Thurs, 8 pm.
ITV, from England
11/30/77F

THE NEW DAUGHTERS OF JOSHUA CABE
(ABC Saturday Night Movie)
With John McIntire, Jeanette Nolan, Liberty Williams, Renne Jarrett, Lezlie Dalton, Jack Elam, John Dehner, Geoffrey Lewis, Sean McClory, Joel Fabiani, Ford Rainey, Larry Hovis, James Lydon
Supplier: Spelling-Goldberg Prods.
Exec Prods: Aaron Spelling, Leonard Goldberg;
Prod-wri: Paul Savage.
Dir: Bruce Bilson.
90 Mins, Sat (29), 8:30 pm.
ABC-TV
06/02/76

NEW ENGLAND ALCOHOL AWARENESS TEST
With Vince Gibbens, John Sweeney, Sarah Wye
Prod-Dir: Gary Dreispul.
60 Mins, Thurs, 8 pm.
WJAR-TV Providence
11/09/77

NEW HOWDY DOODY SHOW
With Bob Smith, Lew Anderson, others
Supplier: Nicholson-Muir Productions
Prod: E Roger Muir;
Dir: Nick Nicholson;
Wris: Willie Gilbert, Lydia Wilen, Nicholson.
30 Mins, Mon-Fri, 3:30 pm.
WNEW-TV New York
09/15/76S

THE NEW LORENZO MUSIC SHOW
(ABC Comedy Special)
With Lorenzo & Henrietta Music, David Odgen Stiers, Jack Eagle, Steve Anderson, Roz Kelly, Lewis Arquette, Bandini Bros.
Supplier: MTM Enterprises
Exec Prod: L Music;
Prod: Carl Gottlieb;
Dir: Tony Mordente;
Wris: L Music, Gottlieb, James Brooks, Jerry Davis, Allan Burns.
30 Mins, Tues (10), 9 pm.
ABC-TV
08/18/76

THE NEW LOVE BOAT
With Gavin MacLeod, Bernie Kopell, Fred Grandy, Ted Lange, Lauren Tewes, Stella Stevens, Pat Harrington Jr, Phil Silvers, Audra Lindley, Georgia Engel, Gary Frank, Melanie Mayron
Supplier: Aaron Spelling Prod
Exec Prods: Spelling, Douglas S Cramer;
Prod: Henry Colman;
Dir: Richard Kinon
Wris: Brad Buckner, Rick Hawkins, Liz Sage, Michael Norell.
90 Mins, Thurs (5), 8:30 pm.
ABC-TV
05/18/77

THE NEW MAVERICK
(ABC Sunday Night Movie)
With James Garner, Charles Frank, Jack Kelly, Susan Blanchard, Eugene Roche, Susan Sullivan, George Loros, Woodrow Parfey, Gary Allen, Helen Page Camp, Jack Garner, Graham Jarvis
Supplier: Warner Bros TV
Exec Prod: Meta Rosenberg;
Prod: Robert Foster;
Dir: Hy Averback;
Wri: Juanita Bartlett.
120 Mins, Sun (3), 9 pm.
ABC-TV
09/06/78

NEW MICKEY MOUSE CLUB
Supplier: Walt Disney Prods
Exec Prod: Ron Miller;
Prods: Ed Ropolo, Michael Wuergler.
30 Mins, Mon-Fri, 4 pm.
WNEW-TV New York
01/26/77S

NEW VOICES, NEW VISIONS
With Martha Coolidge, Jill Godmilow, Karen Arthur
Prod: Madeleine Butler, Andrea Roane;
Dir: David Frentz.
30 Mins, 9:30 pm.
WYES-TV, New Orleans
08/31/77S

NEWPORT JAZZ '79
With Buddy Rich, Dave Brubeck, Gerry Mulligan, Phil Woods, Joe Williams, Herbie Mann, Ramsay Lewis, Anita O'Day
Supplier: Visiondisc Connecticut Corp.
Exec Prods: Charles & Vivian Arden.
90 Mins, Sun, (23), 7:30 pm.
Showtime via Manhattan Teleprompter Cable, N.Y.
01/02/80PC

NEWSBAG
With Avi Adler, Meredith Schor, Courtney Heath, Heather Simpkins, Melissa Marquez
Exec Prod: Jill Krasner;
Prod: Juliann Martinez;
Dir: Lou Iacoviello.
30 Mins, Sat, 7:30 am.
WWTTG-TV Washington
04/26/78

NEWSCENTER 5
With Ron Hunter, Tim Weigel, Jim Tilmon, others
Exec Prod: Paul Beavers;
Prod: Marty Ryan;
Dir: Dean Rowe.
30 Mins, Mon-Fri, 10 pm.
WMAQ-TV Chicago
06/30/76

NEWSCENTER 5
With Ron Hunter, Tim Weigel, Jim Tilmon, Royal Kennedy & Rich Newberg, Jorie Lueloff, Dr. Barry Kaufman, Ron Powers, Barry Bernson, Andy Shaw, Chuck Neff, others
Exec Prod: Alvin Snyder;
Prod: Dick Goldbeg;
Dir: Dean Rowe.
90 Mins, Mon-Fri, 4:30 pm.
WMAQ-TV Chicago
11/03/76

THE NEXT STEP BEYOND
With John Newland (host), Laraine Stephens, Craig Littler, Angus Duncan, Bryan Scott, Dee Carroll, Martin Rudy, William Wintersole
Supplier: Factor-Newland Prods (Worldvision Enterprises)
Exec Prod: Collier Young;
Prod: Alan Jay Factor;
Dir: Newland;
Wri: Merwin Gerard.
30 Mins, Thurs (5), 7:30 pm.
WABC-TV New York
Procter & Gamble (Benton & Bowles)
01/11/78S

THE NEXT STEP BEYOND
With John Newland (host), Louis Van Bergen, Alan Frost, Karin Mani, Paul Hampton
Supplier: Factor-Newland Prods (Worldvision)
Exec Prod: Collier Young;
Prod: Alan Jay Factor;
Dir: Newland;
Wri: Merwin Gerard.
30 Mins, Sat, 6 pm.
WCBS-TV New York
Procter & Gamble
09/27/78S

NICK & THE DOBERMANS
With Michael Nouri, Robert Davi, Judith Chapman, Charles Knox Robinson, John Cunningham, Dave Cass, Louis Guss, Vivian Bonnell, Hector Morales
Supplier: Bennett-Katleman Prods & Columbia Pictures TV
Exec Prods: Harve Bennett, Harris Katleman;
Prod-Wris: James D. Parriott, Richard Chapman;
Dir: Bernard L. Kowalski.
60 Mins, Fri, (25) 9 pm.
NBC-TV
04/30/80

NIGHT FLIGHT
With Trevor Howard, Bo Svenson, Celine Lomez, Ted Follows, others
Supplier: Marlow Pictures & The Singer Co
Exec Prod: Lawrence F Mihlon;
Prods: Susan A Lewis, Howard Ryshpan;
Dir: Desmond David;
Wri: Alvin Goodman, from Antoine de Saint Exupery novel.
30 Mins, Fri (26), 7:30 pm.
WCBS-TV, New York
Singer (Y&R Special Markets Division)
01/31/79S

NIGHT NURSE
With Kate Fitzpatrick, Davina Whitehouse, Kay Taylor, Gary Day
Supplier: Grundy Organization
Dir: Igor Auzins;
Wri: Ron McLean.
90 Mins.
Seven Network (previewed), Sydney, Australia
04/19/78F

THE NIGHT RIDER
(ABC Friday Night Movie Double Feature)
With David Selby, Percy Rodrigues, Kim Cattrall, George Grizzard, Anthony Herrera, Anna Lee, Pernell Roberts, Michael Sharrett, Harris Yulin, Hugh Gillin, Hildy Brooks, Curt Lowens, Van Williams, Claude Woolman, Sydney Penny
Supplier: Stephen J Cannell Prods & Universal TV
Exec Prods: Cannell, Alex Beaon;
Supv Prod: William E Phillips;
Prod: J Rickley Dumm;
Dir: Hy Averback;
Wri: Cannell.
90 Mins, Fri (11), 9:30 pm.
ABC-TV
05/23/79

1990
With Edward Woodward, Barbara Kellermann, Robert Lang, Donald Gee, others
Supplier: BBC-TV
Prod: Prudence Fitzgerald;
Dir: Alan Gibson;
Wri: Wilfred Greatorex.
55 Mins, Sun (18), 8:10 pm.
BBC-2, from London, England
09/28/77F

THE 1976 JEFFERSON AWARDS
With Charles Nelson Reilly, Joey Bishop, Truman Capote, others
Exec Prod: Scott Craig;
Prod: Jim Coursen;
Dir: Phil Ruskin.
90 Mins, Mon (18), 9 pm.
WBBM-TV Chicago
10/27/76

1968
With Harry Reasoner
Supplier: CBS News
Exec Prod: Perry Wolff;
Prod: Shareen Blair Brysac.
120 Mins, Fri (25), 9 pm.
CBS-TV
08/30/78

1968: A CRACK IN TIME
With Frank Reynolds, Cliff Robertson
Supplier: ABC News
Exec Prod: Jeff Gralnick;
Prod: Bruce Cohn;
Dir: Joel Tator;
Wris: Cohn, Reynolds.
60 Mins, Sun (11), 8 pm.
ABC-TV
06/14/78

90 MINUTES LIVE
With Peter Gzowski
Exec Prod: Alex Frame.
90 Mins, Mon thru Fri, 11:35 pm.
CBC-TV, from Toronto, Canada
12/29/76F

THE NIXON INTERVIEWS
With David Frost, Richard Nixon
Supplier: Paradine Prods, RAI (Italy), TFI (France), Ch 9 (Australia), Polygram (Germany) Dist: Syndicast Services
Exec Prod: Frost;
Prods: John Birt, Frost;
Dir: Jorn Winther.
90 Mins, Wed (4), 8:30 pm.
WNEW-TV New York
05/11/77S

NO HOLDS BARRED
With Kelly Monteith (host)
Supplier: Alan Landsburg Prods
Exec Prod: Landsburg;
Prod: Herbert Danska;
Dir: Arthur Forrest;
Wris: Hank Bradford, Monteith.
60 Mins, Fri, 11:30 pm.
CBS-TV
09/17/80

NO MAN'S LAND
With John Gielgud, Ralph Richardson, Terrence Rigby, Michael Kitchen
Supplier: Granada-TV
Exec Prod: Derek Granger;
Dir: Julian Ames;
Wri: Harold Pinter.
100 Mins, Wed, 10:30 pm.
Granada-TV, from England
10/18/78F

NO PLACE TO HIDE
Prod-Wri: Patricia Gormin;
Dir: Gary Furlow.
30 Mins, Thurs (29), 8 pm.
WVUE New Orleans
07/05/78

NO ROOM TO RUN
With Richard Benjamin, Paula Prentiss, Barry Sulivan, Noel Ferrier, Ray Barrett, Anne Haddy, Cul Cullen, Phillip Hinton, Stuart Finch, Matthew O'Sullivan, Ann Grey, Sandra McGregor, Colin Taylor, Brian Wright, Brian Hinselwood, Roger Ward, Joy Hruby, Max Aspin, Rick Gardiner
Supplier: Australian Broadcasting Commission & Trans-Atlantic Enterprises
Exec Prods: Robert Kline, James Davern;
Prod: Joseph Gantman;
Dir: Robert Michael Lewis;
Wri: George Kirgo.
97 Mins, Wed, 8:30 pm.
ABC (Australia) TV
05/25/77F

NO WAY TO TREAT A RIVER
With John Rawlins, narrator
Prod: Randy Covington;
Wri: Wanda Bryant.
30 Mins, Mon 7 pm.
WAVE-TV Louisville
11/22/78

NOBODY EVER ASKED ME
With Dave Moore, Doug Moore (hosts), Skip Loescher, Don Shelby, Al Austin, Karen Boros, Pat Miles, Mike Walcher, others
Exec Prod: James Rupp;
Prods: Mike Sullivan, Peter Maroney, Nancy Mate;
Dir: Dave Higgins;
Wri: Sullivan.
180 Mins, Wed, 7 pm.
WCCO-TV Minneapolis-St Paul
10/03/79

THE NORMAN CONQUESTS
(Table Manners)
With Tom Conti, Penelope Keith, Richard Briers, Penelope Wilton, Fiona Walker, David Troughton
Supplier: Thames TV, London
Prods: Verity Lambert, David Susskind;
Dir: Herbert Wise;
Wri: Alan Ayckbourn.
120 Mins, Wed, 8 pm.
ITV Network, Britain
10/12/77F

NOT UNTIL TODAY (HOME AGAIN)
(BATTLE OF THE GENERATIONS)
With Darren McGavin, Dick Sargent, Raleigh Bond, Michael Horton, Peter Jurasik, Alexandra Stoddart, David Cohn
Supplier: MTM Prods
Exec Prods: David Lloyd, Michael Zinberg;
Prod: Charles Raymond;
Dir: Zinberg;
Wri: Lloyd.
120 Min, Wed (27), 9 pm.
NBC-TV
07/04/79

NOW
With Linda Ellerbee, Jack Perkins
Supplier: NBC News
Exec Prod: Stuart Schulberg;
Prod: William Cosmas;
Dir: Sidney A Vassall;
Wris: Ellerbee, Perkins.
60 Mins, Thurs (30), 8 pm.
NBC-TV
07/06/77

NOW!
With Dale Harimoto, Tom Fitzsimmons, Burt Wolf, Barrett Nolan, Mariann Aalda, Susan Silver
Exec Prod: David Ochoa;
Prod: Leni-Joy Zimmerman;
Dirs: Marcia Kuyper Schneider, Enid Roth, Jack Sumroy.
30 Mins, Mon (30), 7:30 pm.
WNBC-TV New York
08/08/79

NUCLEAR NIGHTMARES
With Peter Ustinov, narr
Exec Prod: Thomas Johnston;
Prod: Peter Batty;
Wri: Nigel Calder.
90 Mins, Wed (1) 8 pm.
WNET New York
10/08/80

NUMBER 96
With Eddie Barth, Charles Bloom, Jill Choder, William Brian Curran, Randee Heller, Sherry Hursey, Christine Jones, Barney Martin, Howard McGillin, Greg Mullavey, James Murtaugh, Maria O'Brien, Betsy Palmer, John Reilly, Todd Susman, Hilary Thompson, Ellen Travolta, Rosina Widdowson-Reynolds
Supplier: Paramount TV
Exec Prod: Bob Ellison;
Supv Prod: Allan Manings;
Prod: Mitch Gamson;
Dir: Robert Scheerer;
Wri: David Lloyd.
60 Min, Wed (10), 10 pm.
NBC-TV
12/17/80

NO. 10 TORONTO STREET
(The Canadian Establishment)
With Patrick Watson
Exec Prod: Cameron Graham;
Prod-Dir: Michael Gerard.
60 Mins, Sun, 9 pm.
CBC-TV, From Toronto, Canada
10/08/80F

OAK PARK: ALL AMERICAN
Prod-dir: Jim McPharlin;
30 Mins, Thurs (16), 8:30 pm.
WLS-TV, Chicago
12/22/76

OCEAN FLIGHT
With U. of Washington Chorale & Symphony Orchestra, others
Exec Prod: Richard J. Meyer;
Prod-Dir: John Coney.
40 Mins, Sat, 10:30 pm.
KCTS-TV Seattle
10/01/80

OF SAINTS & CIRCUSES
Supplier: WVUE-TV
Prod-Wri: Patricia Gormin;
Dir: Gary Furlow.
30 Mins, Wed (30), 6:30 pm.
WVUE-TV New Orleans
09/06/78

OFF HOLLYWOOD
With Chase Newhart, Glenn Daniels, Susan Elliot, Cyndi James-Reese, Dizzy Llowell, Lorna Patterson
Supplier: Pierre Cossette Prods
Exec Prod: Cossette;
Prod: Mario Beguiristain;
Dir: Sterling Johnson;
Wris: David Garber, Kevin Hartigan, Beguiristain, David Curry, Vic Dunlop, Christopher Durang, Marty Farrell, Peter Krikes, Steve Meerson, Newhart, Frank Pendergast.
90 Mins, Sat (14), 11:30 pm.
NBC-TV
01/18/78

OFF THE WALL
With Todd Susman, Barbara Deutsch, Sandy Helberg, Sean Roche, Frank O'Brien, Harry Gold, Dana House, Hal Williams
Supplier: Barton Prods & Universal TV
Exec Prod: Franklin Barton;
Prods-Wris: Neil Rosen, George Tricker;
Dir: Bob LaHendro.
30 Mins, Sat (7), 8 pm.
NBC-TV
05/18/77

OLD FRIENDS. . .NEW FRIENDS
With Fred Rogers, Lee Strasberg, Susan Strasberg, Shelley Winters
Supplier: Family Communications
Prod-Dir: Arthur Barron.
30 Mins, Fri, (1) 9:30 pm.
WNET-TV N.Y.
08/13/80

THE OLDEST LIVING GRADUATE
With Henry Fonda, George Grizzard, Cloris Leachman, Penelope Milford, John Lithgow, Harry Dean Stanton, David Ogden Stiers, Timothy Hutton, Allyn Ann McLerie
Supplier: Gideon Prods
Exec Prod: David Rintels;
Prod: Gareth Davies;
Dir: Jack Hofsiss;
Wri: Preston Jones.
120 Mins, Mon, (7) 9 pm.
NBC-TV
04/09/80

THE OLYMPIC CHAMPIONS AND CHALLENGERS
With Telly Savalas
Supplier: Lee Mendelson Film Prods.
Exec Prod: A.G. Atwater Jr.;
Prods: Mendelson, Gary Kaney;
Dirs: Mendelson, Chuck Barbee;
Wri: Mendelson.
60 Mins, Sat (17), 8 pm.
ABC-TV
Wrigley (Arthur Meyerhoff Assoc.)
04/21/76

OMNIBUS (GE Theatre)
With Hal Holbrook (host), Sandy Duncan, Edith Head, Gene Kelly, Lorretta Lynn, Bob Mackie, Peter Martins, Luciano Pavarotti, Lewis J. Stadlen, Meryl Streep, Lynn Swann, Twyla Tharp, The National Theatre of the Deaf
Supplier: Marble Arch Prods
Exec Prod: Martin Starger;
Prod: Bob Shanks;
Dir: Don Mischer;
Wris: Leonard Harris, Frank Rich, Shanks.
60 Mins, Sun, (15) 8 pm.
ABC-TV
GE (BBDO)
06/18/80

ON CAMERA
(ABC New Closeup)
With Howard K Smith, Peter Jennings, Sandy Hill
Prods: William Peters, Aram Boyajian, Ene Riisna.
60 Mins, Thurs (21), 10 pm.
ABC-TV
07/27/77

ON LOCATION
With David Steinberg
Supplier: Home Box Office
Exec Prod: Brad Schreiber;
Prod: John Gilroy;
Dir: Marty Callner.
60 Mins, Sat (20), 10 pm.
HBO
03/24/76PC

ON OUR OWN
With Bess Armstrong, Lynnie Greene, Gretchen Wyler, Dixie Carter, Dan Resin, John Christopher Jones, John Getz, James Dupont, Terry Ellisor
Supplier: Time-Life TV
Exec Prod: David Susskind;
Prod: Sam Denoff;
Dir: James Burrows;
Wri: Bob Randall.
30 Mins, Sun, 8:30 pm.
CBS-TV
10/12/77

ON THE RECORD
With Sheila Rabb Weidenfeld, host
Exec Prod: Weidenfeld;
Dir: George Light.
30 Mins, Sat, 7 pm.
WRC-TV Washington
10/19/77

ON THE ROAD WITH CHARLES KURALT
Supplier: CBS News
Exec Prod: Leslie Midgley;
Prods: Kuralt, Bernard Birnbaum.
60 Mins, Fri (24), 10 pm.
CBS-TV
12/29/76

ON THE TUNICA TRAIL
Prod-Wri: Madeleine Butler;
Dir: David Frentz.
60 Mins, Tues (11), 8 pm.
WYES-TV New Orleans
07/12/78

ON TRIAL
With Ina Balin, Hank Brandt, James Callahan, Clifford David, June Dayton, Bill Furnell, Peggy McCay, Terri Nunn, Sean Roche, Margaret Willock
Supplier: Alan Sloan Inc (Syndicast Services)
Exec Prod: Sloan;
Prod: Robert Justman;
Dir: Joseph L. Scanlan;
Wri: Anthony Lawrence.
30 Mins, Mon, (30), 7:30 pm.
WABC-TV, New York
02/08/78S

ON YOUR SIDE WITH JOHN STOSSEL
Exec Prod: Morton Silverstein;
Prod: Elisabeth Lawrence;
Dir: Ormond West;
Wri: Stossel.
30 Mins, Thurs (1), 7:30 pm.
WCBS-TV New York
02/07/79

ONCE A PRIEST. . .
With Bill Kurtis (narrator)
Prod-Dir: Scott Craig;
Wris: Linda Olin, Craig.
60 Mins, Thurs (24), 9 pm.
WBBM-TV Chicago
03/30/77

ONCE AN EAGLE
(Best Sellers)
With Sam Elliott, Cliff Potts, Darleen Carr, Amy Irving, Glenn Ford, Clu Gulager, Lynda Day George, Robert Hogan, Gary Grimes
Supplier: Universal TV, wth NBC-TV
Exec Dir: William Sackheim;
Prod-wri: Peter Fischer;
Dir: E W Swackhamer.
120 Mins, Thurs (2), 9 pm.
NBC-TV
12/08/76

ONCE UPON A BROTHERS GRIMM
With Dean Jones, Paul Sand, Ruth Buzzi, Teri Garr, Arte Johnson, Cleavon Little, Clive Revill, Chita Rivera, Mia Bendixsen, Sorrell Booke, Corinne Conley, Gordon Connell, Don Correia, Todd Lookinland, Edie McClurg, John McCook, Gary Morgan, Ken Olfson, Maria Pogge, Susan Silo, Dan Tobin, Joe Giamalva
Supplier: Rothman-Wohl Prods
Prods: Bernard Rothman, Jack Wohl;
Dir: Norman Campbell;
Wri: Jean Holloway.
120 Mins, Wed (23), 8 pm.
CBS-TV
Procter & Gamble (Benton & Bowles)
11/30/77

ONCE UPON A TREE
Prod-Wri-Dir: Tyler Johnson.
30 Mins, Fri, 8 pm.
KING-TV Seattle
01/18/78

ONE CANADIAN
With John Diefenbaker; Douglas Rain, narrator-interviewer
Prod: Cameron Graham;
Wri-dir: Munroe Scott.
30 Mins, Wed, 8:30 pm.
CBC, from Ottawa, Canada
10/27/76F

ONE DAY MILLER
With Tony Llewellyn-Jones, Penne Hackforth-Jones, Lucky Grills, Maggie Blinco, Michael Aitkens, Geraldine Turner, Paul Mason, Carmen Duncan
Supplier: Australian Broadcasting Commission
Exec Prod: Bruce Best;
Dirs: Michael Jenkins, David Goldie;
Wri: Geoffrey Atherden.
30 Mins, Fri, 8:15 pm.
ABC TV, Channel 2 Sydney, Australia
08/22/79F

THE $128,000 QUESTION
With Mike Darow
Supplier: Cinelar Associates (Viacom)
Exec Prod: Steve Carlin;
Prod: Willie Stein;
Dir: Dick Schneider.
30 Mins, Sat, 5:30 pm.
WNEW-TV New York
09/22/76S

ONE IN A MILLION
With Shirley Hemphill, Richard Paul, Carl Ballantine, Dorothy Fielding, Ralph Wilcox, Keene Curtis, Ann Weldon, Billy Wallace, Mel Stewart, William Jackson
Supplier: TOY Prods. & Columbia Pictures TV
Prods: Saul Turtletaub & Bernie Orenstein;
Dir: Peter Baldwin;
Wris: Alan Livingston, Turtletaub, Orenstein.
30 Mins, Tues, (8), 8:30 pm.
ABC-TV
01/16/80

ONE NIGHT A YEAR
With Frank Gibbuena, narrator
Prods: Hal Pontious, Frank Gilbuena;
Dir: Bob Fitzpatrick.
30 Mins, Mon (29), 7:30 pm.
WPHL-TV Philadelphia
Rustler Steak Houses
03/31/76

OPENING NIGHT
With George Baker, Noel Trevarthen, Celia West, Sheila Hammond, Alex Trousdell, Ian Watkin, others
Supplier: South Pacific Television
Exec Prod: John McRae;
Dir: Brian McDuffie;
Wri: Dean Parker (from a novel by Ngaio Marsh).
90 Mins, Sat, 9 pm.
TV-2 Auckland, New Zealand
08/16/78F

OPENING SOON AT A THEATRE NEAR YOU
With Gene Siskel, Roger Ebert
Prod: Thea Flaum;
Dir: Patterson Denny.
30 Mins, Wed (2), 9 pm.
WTTW-TV Chicago
03/23/77S

OPERATING ROOM
With Barbara Babcock, Bruce Bauer, Oliver Clark, David Spielberg, James Sutorius, Janice Kent, Barbara Bosson, Cyb & Tricia Barnstable, Patricia Conklin, Ronne Troup, Barbara Perry
Supplier: MTM Enterprises Prods
Exec Prods-Wris: Steven Bochco, Bruce Paltrow;
Prod: Mark Tinker;
Dir: Paltrow.
60 Mins, Thurs (4), 10 pm.
NBC-TV
10/10/79

OPERATION PETTICOAT
With John Astin, Richard Gilliland, Yvonne Wilder, Melinda Naud, Jamie Lee Curtis, Dorrie Thomson, Bond Gideon, Richard Brestoff, Christopher J Brown, Jesse Dizon, Wayne Long, Richard Marion, Michael Mazes, Jack Murdock, Peter Schuck, Raymond Singer, Jim Varney, Kraig Cassity
Supplier: Heyday Prods, Universal TV
Exec Prod: Leonard Stern;
Prods: David O'Connell, Si Rose;
Dir: John Astin;
Wri: Rose.
30 Mins, Sat, 8:30 pm.
ABC-TV
09/21/77

OPERATION PETTICOAT
With Randolph Mantooth, Robert Hogan, JoAnn Pflug, Warren Berlinger, Hilary Thompson, Richard Brestoff, James Varney, Fred Kareman, Don Sparks, Scott McGinnis, Melinda Naud
Supplier: Boiney Stoones Inc-Kukoff-Harris Prods & Universal TV
Exec Prods-Wris: Jeff Harris, Bernie Kukoff;
Prod: Michael Rhodes;
Dir: Holly Morse.
30 Mins, Mon 8:30 pm.
ABC-TV
09/27/78

OPERATION: RUNAWAY
With Robert Reed, Karen Machon, Michael Biehn, Ruth Cox, Christina Hart, Terri Nunn, James Olson, Felton Perry, Richard Stanley, Tom Troupe
Supplier: Quinn Martin Prods
Exec Prod-Wri: William Robert Yates;
Prod: Mark Rodgers;
Dir: William Wiard.
120 Mins, Thurs, 9 pm.
NBC-TV
05/10/78

THE ORACLE
With John Gregg, Pamela Gibbons, Julie Hamilton, Don Pascoe, Hugh Keays-Byrne, Geraldine Turner, Murray Rose, Ralph Cotterill, Robyn Nevin, Tina Bursill, Ruth Cracknell, others
Supplier: Australian Broadcasting Commission
Exec Prod: Alan Burke;
Dirs: Michael Carson, Julian Pringle, Burke, Chris Thomson, Sandra Levy;
Wris: Laura Jones, Michael Cove, Tony Morphett, Colin Free, Burke, Barry Donnelly.
50 Mins, Mon, 8:30 pm.
ABC (Australia) TV

03/21/79F

THE OREGON TRAIL
(NBC Saturday Night At The Movies)
With Rod Taylor, Blair Brown, David Huddleston, Douglas V. Fowley, Andrew Stevens, Tony Becker, Gina Marie Smika, G.D. Spradlin, Linda Purl, George Keymas, Robert Karnes
Supplier: Universal TV
Prod-Wri: Michael Gleason;
Dir: Boris Sagal.
120 Mins, Sat (10), 9 pm.
NBC-TV

01/14/76

THE OREGON TRAIL
With Rod Taylor, Darleen Carr, Charles Napier, Andrew Stevens, Tony Becker, Gina Marie Smika, William Windom, John Vernon, Ken Swofford, A Wilford Brimley
Supplier: Universal TV
Exec Prod: Michael Gleason;
Prod: Carl Vitale;
Dirs: Burt Brinckerhoff, Herb Wallerstein;
Wris: Gleason, Eugene Price.
120 Mins, Wed (21), 8 pm.
NBC-TV

09/28/77

ORPHAN TRAIN
(DuPont Cavalcade)
With Jill Eikenberry, Kevin Dobson, Linda Manz, Graham Fletcher-Cook, Melissa Michaelsen, Glenn Close, Morgan Farley, Severn Darden, Charlie Fields, Peter Neuman, John Femia, Sarah Ingliss, Andreas Manske, Scott Rogers, Justine Johnston
Supplier: EMI-TV Programs
Exec Prods: Roger Gimbel, Marian Rees, Tony Converse;
Prod: Dorothea G Petrie;
Dir: William A Graham;
Wri: Millard Lampell, from Petrie's story.
180 Mins, Sat (22), 8 pm.
CBS-TV
DuPont (BBDO)

12/26/79

THE OSMOND FAMILY SHOW
With Donny & Marie Osmond, The Osmond Brothers (Alan, Jay, Merrill & Wayne), Jimmy Osmond, Roy Clark, David Copperfield, US Ski Team, Ice Angels, Lassie, Virl, Tom, Aaron, Jared and Mother & Father Osmond
Supplier: Osmond Prods
Exec Prods: Osmond Bros;
Prods: Alan Osmond & Phil Hahn;
Dir: Walter C Miller;
Wris: Hahn, Stuart Gillard, Earl Brown, Steven Adams, Bruce Kirschbaum.
60 Mins, Sun 7 pm.
ABC-TV

01/31/79

OUR BROTHERS' KEEPER
With Laurence Luckinbill, Camilla Hawk, Mike Nussbaum, James O'Reilly, Jill Shellabarger, Marge Kotlisky, Brian Van Den Broucke, Caryn Burkhart, Gary Goren, Marie Brady, Frank Howard, Gail Farnsworth
Prod-Dir-Wri: Gerald T Rogers
60 Min, Sun (21), 3 pm.
WTTW-TV Chicago

12/31/80S

OUT
With Tom Bell, Brian Croucher, Lynn Farleigh, Norman Rodway, others
Supplier: Thames-TV
Exec Prod: Johnny Goodman;
Prod: Barry Hanson;
Dir: Jim Goddard;
Wri: Trevor Preston.
55 Mins, Mon, 9 pm.
ITV Network, from England

09/27/78F

OUT OF THE BLUE
With Jimmy Brogan, Dixie Carter, Tammy Lauren, Hannah Dean, Clark Brandon, Olivia Barash, Jason & Shane Keller, Eileen Heckart, Robin Williams, Basil Hoffman
Supplier: Miller-Milkis-Boyett Prods & Paramount TV
Exec Prods: Austin & Irma Kalish;
Supv Prods: Thomas L Miller, Edward K Milkis, Robet L Boyett;
Prods: William Bickley & Michael Warren;
Dirs: Peter Baldwin, Jeff Chambers;
Wri: Barry Kemp.
60 Mins, Sun, (9), 7 pm.
ABC-TV

09/12/79

OVER EASY
With Hugh Downs (host)
Supplier: KQED San Francisco
Exec Prod: Richard R. Rector;
Prod: Jules Power;
Dir: James Crum;
Wri: Christopher Lukas.
30 Mins, Mon, Tues (13-14), 8 pm.
PBS

09/15/76

OVER EASY
With Hugh Downs
Supplier: KQED San Francisco, for PBS
Exec Prod: Richard R Rector;
Prods: Jules Power, Christopher Lukas;
Dirs: Haig Mackey, Paul Blake, Vincent Casalaina;
Wris: Steve Yafa, Jennifer Arps.
30 Mins, Mon-Fri, 6:30 pm.
PBS

11/16/77

OWNER OCCUPIED
With Robert Hardy, Hannah Gordon, Richard Murdoch
Supplier: Thames TV
Prod-Dir: Robert Reed;
Wri: Robert Banks Stewart.
30 Mins, Mon, 8 pm.
Thames TV, from London, England

08/10/77F

PACIFIC SONG CONTEST
With Peter Sinclair
Prod: Ken Sudell;
Dir: Michael Kemp.
51 Mins, Thurs, 8 pm.
TV-1, New Zealand

10/25/78F

PADRI E FIGLI
(Fathers and Children)
With Federica Taddei, Claudia Aloisi
Supplier: RAI-TV
Prod: RAI-TV;
Dir: Vito Minore.
45 Mins, Wed, 9:35 pm.
Rete Uno, from Rome, Italy

01/22/78F

THE PALACE
With Jack Jones, Diahann Carroll, Ben Vereen, Charles Aznavour, Pat Paulsen, Mary Macgregor, Michel Legrand, Hamilton Philharmonic Orchestra
Supplier: Wilks-Close Prods (Gold Key Entertainment)
Prods: Wendell Wilks, David Close;
Dir: Stanley Dorfman.
60 Mins, Sun, 7 pm.
WPIX-TV New York

10/10/79S

PALESTINE
Supplier: Thames TV
Exec Prod: Mike Wooller;
Prod: Richard Broad.
90 Mins, Tues, 10:30 pm.
Thames TV, from London, England

07/26/78F

PALMERSTOWN, USA
With Jonelle Allen, Beeson Carroll, Bill Duke, Janice St. John, Michael J. Fox, Star-Shemah Bobatoon, Jermain H. Johnson, Brian G. Wilson, Iris Korn, Arthur Malet, Claudia McNeil, Davis Roberts, John Hancock, Ted Gehring, Royce D. Applegate
Supplier: Haley-TAT Communications
Exec Prods: Norman Lear, Alex Haley;
Prod-Wri: Ronald Rubin;
Dir: Peter Levin
120 Mins, Thurs, (20) 8 pm.
CBS-TV

03/26/80

PANACHE
With Rene Auberjonois, David Healy, Charles Frank, Charles Seibert, Joseph Ruskin, others
Supplier: Warner Bros. TV
Exec Prod: E. Duke Vincent;
Prod: Robert E. Relyea;
Dir: Gary Nelson;
Wri: Vincent.
90 Mins, Sat. (15), 8 pm.
ABC-TV
05/19/76

THE PAPER CHASE
With John Houseman, James Stephens, Tom Fitzsimmons, Katharine Dunfee, Robert Ginty, James Keane, Jonathan Segal, Deka Beaudine, Peter Fitzsimmons, Marilu Henner, Lewis Charles, Kurt Krueger, Charles Seaverns, Channing Clarkson, Nelson Welch, Jed Cooper, Betty Harford
Supplier: 20th Century-Fox TV
Prod: Robert C Thompson;
Dir: Joe Hardy;
Wri: James Bridges.
60 Mins, Sat (9), 8 pm.
CBS-TV
09/13/78

PARENTHOOD: A LEARNING EXPERIENCE
Prod: Mary Ellen Amos;
Dir: David Frentz.
30 Mins, Sun, 4 pm.
WYES-TV New Orleans
11/29/78

PARIS
With James Earl Jones, Lee Chamberlin, Hank Garrett, Cecelia Hart, Jake Mitchell, Frank Ramirez, Michael Warren, Vic Morrow, Barbara Babcock, Frank Marth, Candy Ann Brown, Kiel Martin, Joe Spano, Eugene Peterson, Maidie Norman
Supplier: MTM Enterprises Prods
Exec Prod-Wri: Steven Bochco;
Prod: Gregory Hoblit;
Dir: Jackie Cooper.
60 Mins, Sat, 10 pm.
CBS-TV
10/03/79

PARIS-LINE
(Standing Room Only)
With Line Renaud
Supplier: Home Box Office
Exec Prod: Michael Fuchs;
Prods: Marty Callner, Neal Marshall;
Dir: Callner.
80 Mins, Sun (27), 8 pm.
HBO
11/30/77PC

PARKINSON IN AUSTRALIA
With Michael Parkinson
Supplier: Australian Broadcasting Commission
Exec Prod: Lloyd Capps;
Dir: Jacqui Culliton.
60 Mins, Sat, 7:30 pm.
ABC, Channel ABN2, Sydney, Australia
05/09/79F

PASS THE BUCK
With Bill Cullen (host)
Supplier: Bob Stewart Prods
Exec Prod: Bob Stewart;
Prod: Sande Stewart;
Dir: Mike Gargiulo.
30 Mins, Mon-Fri, 10am.
CBS-TV
04/05/78

PASSWORD PLUS
With Allen Ludden (host), Elizabeth Montgomery, Robert Foxworth
Supplier: Goodson-Todman Prods & The Password Co
Exec Prod: Howard Felsher;
Prod: Robert Sherman;
Dir: Paul Alter.
30 Mins, Mon-Fri, 12:30 pm.
NBC-TV
01/17/79

PAT BOONE & FAMILY
With Shirley, Cherry, Lindy, Laury & Debby Boone, Parker Stevenson, Perry Lang, Greg Lewis, Fran Ryan, Dick Van Patten, Don Rickles, The Unknown Comic, George Burns
Supplier: Management 3-Cooga Mooga Prods
Exec Prod: Jerry Weintraub;
Prods: Bernard Rothman, Jack Wohl;
Dir: Perry Rosemond;
Wris: Burt & Adele Styler, Tom Sawyer, Joe Neustein, Rothman, Wohl.
60 Mins, Sat (8), 8 pm.
ABC-TV
04/12/78

PATENT PENDING
(American Documents)
With William Shatner, narrator
Supplier: Gould Entertainment
Exec Prod: Ray Hubbard;
Prod: Charles Wintner;
Wri: Mark Olshaker.
60 Mins, Fri, 8 pm.
WTOP-TV Washington
03/24/76

PATHS OF REBELLION: NEW YORK IN THE REVOLUTION
With Bill Shustik
Prod-dir-wri: Dan Chaykin.
30 Mins, Sun (7), 7 pm.
WNET-TV New York
03/10/76

PATHS TO THE FUTURE
With Derek Jacobi, Margaret Mead, Bernard Dixon
Supplier: Paths To The Future Partnership
Prod-Dir: Alan Lindsay;
Wri: Arthur Baysting.
51 Mins, Sun, 8:30 pm.
South Pacific Television - TV-2, New Zealand
10/25/78F

PATROL BOAT
With Andrew McFarlane, Robert Coleby, Danny Adcock, Tim Burns, Rob Baxter, Dennis Linehan, Nick Magasic, Phillip Parnell, others
Supplier: Australian Broadcasting Commission
Exec Prod: Ray Alchin;
Dirs: Frank Arnold, Rob Stewart, Brian McDuffie, Russ Webb;
Wris: James Davern, Barry Donnelly, Peter Schreck, Ted Roberts, Robert Caswell, Tony Morphett.
50 Mins, Thurs, 7:30 pm.
ABC TV, from Channel 2, Sydney, Australia
07/11/79F

THE PATSY GALLANT SHOW
Exec Prod: Ed Richardson;
Prod: Clif Tomlinson.
30 Mins, Thurs, 7:30 pm.
CTV, from Toronto, Canada
10/18/78F

PATTY HEARST: ON THE WITNESS STAND
With Susan Hawkins, Lary Lewman, Robert Bornarth, Dan Dabrowski
Prod: Tim McDonald;
Dir: Bill Dobbs.
60 Mins, Sun (11), 11 pm.
WTTG-TV Washington
Britches of Georgetowne
04/21/76

PAUL ANKA
(Standing Room Only)
With Jack Ackerman, Odia Coates
Supplier: Pasetta Productions
Exec Prod: Michael Fuchs;
Prod-Dir: Marty Pasetta;
Mus Dir: John Harris.
90 Mins, Sun (10), 9 pm.
Home Box Office
07/13/77PC

PAUL ANKA. . .MUSIC MY WAY
With Natalie Cole, Dr Buzzard's Original Savannah Band, St Paul's Baptist Church Choir, The Anka Family, Alan Johnson Dancers
Supplier: Pasetta Prods
Prod-Dir: Marty Pasetta;
Wri: Buz Kohan
60 Mins, Mon (25), 10 pm.
ABC-TV
Dr Pepper (Y&R); Kodak (JWT)
05/11/77

THE PAUL HOGAN SHOW
With John (Strop) Cornell, Marcia Hines, Daryl Braithwaite, Delvene Delaney, Steve Dodd
Supplier: GTV-9 Melbourne
Prods: Hogan, Cornell;
Dir: Peter Faiman;
Wris: Bill Harding, Hogan, Cornell.
60 Mins, Sun, 7:30 pm.
GTV-9 Melbourne, Australia
06/01/77F

PAUL JACOBS & THE NUCLEAR GANG
(Non Fiction Television)
With Jacobs, Saul Landau
Supplier: Independent Documentary Fund
Prod: Jack Willis;
Dirs-Wris: Willis, Landau.
60 Mins, Sun (25), 8 pm.
WNET New York
02/21/79

PAUL LYNDE COMEDY HOUR
With Cloris Leachman, Tony Randall, K C & The Sunshine Band, R G Brown, others
Supplier: Hoysyl Productions
Exec Prods: Ray Katz, Sandy Gallin;
Prods: Rich Eustis, Al Rogers;
Dir: Sid Smith;
Wris: Chet Dowling, Sandy Krinski, April Kelly, George Geiger, David Letterman, Jim Mulligan.
60 Mins, Sat (23), 8 pm.
ABC-TV
04/27/77

THE PAUL SIMON SPECIAL
With Simon, Chevy Chase, the Jesse Dixon Singers, Art Garfunkel, Charles Grodin, Lily Tomlin
Supplier: Above Average-Peregrine Prods
Prod: Lorne Michaels;
Dir: Dave Wilson;
Wris: Michaels, Simon, Chase, Grodin, Tomlin, Al Franken & Tom Davis, Alan Zweibel.
60 Mins, Thurs (8), 9 pm.
NBC-TV
12/14/77

PAUL WILLIAMS SHOW
(BATTLE OF THE GENERATIONS)
With Rick Podell, Amanda McBroom, Rex Riley, Dana Hill, Sandra Kerns, Earl Boen.
Supplier: First Artists TV Prods
Exec Prod: Dennis M Bond;
Prod: Peter H Engel;
Dir: Dennis Steinmetz;
Wri: Bruce Kane.
120 Min, Wed (27), 9 pm.
NBC-TV
07/04/79

PAULE PAULAENDER
With Manfred Reiss, Angelika Kulessa, Manfred Knoth, Katharina Tueschen
Supplier: Westdeutsches Fernsehen, Cologne
Prods: BioskoFilm/WDR. Wolf-Dietrich Bruecker;
Dir: Reinhard Hauff (from book by Burkhard Driest).
90 Mins (color), Tues, 9 pm.
WDR, Cologne, West Germany
05/05/76F

PEACH'S AUSTRALIAN CITIES
With Bill Peach
Supplier: Australian Broadcasting Commission
Exec Prod: Chris McCullough;
Dirs: Stafford Garner, Bill Steller, Richard Walker;
Wri: Peach.
30 Mins, Wed, 7:30 pm.
ABC (Australia) TV, Channel 2, Sydney
02/27/80F

PEANUTS TO THE PRESIDENCY: THE JIMMY CARTER CAMPAIGN
With Joseph Campanella (narrator)
Supplier: Braverman Picture Corp (Program Syndication Services)
Prod-Dir: Chuck Braverman;
Wri: Kandy Stroud.
90 Mins, Sat (18), 7 pm.
WNEW-TV New York
03/29/78S

PEEPING TIMES
With Alan Oppenheimer, David Letterman (hosts), Charles Murphy, James Cromwell, Sharon Spelman, Bill Fiore, Lew Horn, Richard Stahl, Pat Cronin, Richard Libertini, Johnie Dexter, J David Hall, J J Barry, Valerie Curtin, Ron Carey, Philip Bruns, Murphy Dunne, Jerry Ziman, Ketty Lester, Gordon Connell, Harvey Solin, Peggy Pope, Michael Fairman, Mel Brooks, others
Supplier: De Luca-Levinson Prods & Paradine TV Prods
Exec Prods: David Frost, Marvin Minoff;
Prods-Dirs: Barry Levinson, Rudy DeLuca;
Wris: Levinson, DeLuca, Bill Richmond, Gene Perret, Robert Illes, James Stein, Christopher Guest.
60 Mins, Wed (25), 9 pm.
NBC-TV
02/01/78

PENNIES FROM HEAVEN
With Bob Hoskins, Gemma Craven, Kenneth Colley, Cheryl Campbell, others
Supplier: BBC-TV
Prod: Kenith Trodd;
Dir: Piers Haggard;
Wri: Dennis Potter.
75 Mins, Thurs, (8), 10 pm.
WNET-TV New York
02/14/79

PEOPLE
With Lily Tomlin
Supplier: Time-Life TV
Exec Prod: Jane Wagner;
Prods: David Loxton, Fred Barzyk;
Wri: Wagner.
90 Mins, Sat (28), 11:30 pm.
NBC-TV
09/01/76

PEOPLE
With Phyllis George
Supplier: Time-Life TV
Exec Prod: David Susskind;
Prod: Charlotte Schiff Jones;
Dir: Merrill M Mazuer;
Wris: Sue Berman, Richard Camp, Clay Cole, Susan Seeger Cavrell, Marjorie Rosen.
30 Mins, Mon, 9:10 pm.
CBS-TV
09/20/78

THE PEOPLE-BRIAN PRIESTMAN
With Brian Priestman, Bob Martin
Prods: Bob Martin, Dick Connor;
Wri: Dick Connor.
30 Mins, Thurs, 7:30 pm.
KOA-TV Denver
10/27/76

PEOPLE COVER STORY: ANN-MARGRET
With Roger Smith
Supplier: Time-Life TV
Exec Prod: Peter Hansen;
Prod-Dir-Wri: Rift Fournier.
30 Mins, Wed(11), 7:30 pm.
WABC-TV New York
02/18/76S

THE PEOPLE VS INEZ GARCIA
With Silvano Gallardo, Robert Loggia, Marc Jacobs, Robert Haswell, Jearado Carmona, Barbara Oliver, Judith Weston, others
Supplier: KQED San Francisco
Exec Prod: Zev Putterman;
Prod-Dirs: Rena Down, Christoper Lukas;
Wri: Down.
90 Mins, Wed (25), 10 pm.
PBS
06/01/77

PEOPLE'S CHOICE AWARDS
With Jack Albertson, Army Archerd, Carol Burnett, Henry Fonda, Bob Hope, Mary Tyler Moore, Telly Savalas, John Wayne, Morris Albert, Ann-Margret, Beatrice Arthur, Karen Black, Robert Blake, James Brolin, Raymond Burr, Glen Campbell, Tony Curtis, John Denver, Wayland Flowers, Henry Gibson, Earl Holliman, Gabe Kaplan, Sally Kellerman, Ted Knight, Robert Mitchum, Paul Newman, Valerie Perrine, Diana Ross, Roy Scheider, Neil Sedaka, Barbra Streisand, Robert Wagner, Dennis Weaver, Henry Winkler, Natalie Wood
Supplier: Bob Stivers Prod.
Exec Prod: Bob Stivers;
Prod: Bob Finkel;
Dir: Walter Miller.
135 Mins, Thurs, 9-11:15 pm.
CBS-TV
Procter & Gamble (Wells, Rich, Greene)
02/25/76

PEOPLEPLACE
With Barbara Stenson, John Sandifer, others
Prod-wri: Jack Norman.
60 Mins, Thurs (4), 7 pm.
KOMO-TV Seattle
12/01/76

THE PEOPLE'S FORCE
(Ch 7 Special Report)
With Roger Grimsby
Prod-wri: Gene Marciona.
30 Mins, Wed (15), 7:30 pm.
WABC-TV
09/29/76

PERRY COMO'S CHRISTMAS IN AUSTRIA
With Sid Caesar, Senta Berger, Karl Schranz, Vienna Boys Choir, Salzburg Marionette Theatre, Vienna Waltz Champions, Stierwascher Dancers, Maria Deubl-Kaindl
Supplier: Roncom Prods, Bob Banner Associates, ORF
Exec Prod: Banner;
Prod-dir-wri: Stephen Pouliot.
60 Mins, Mon (13), 10 pm.
NBC-TV
GTE (Doyle Dane Bernbach)
12/22/76

PETE!
With Phil Harris, narr
Supplier: WYES-TV
Prod-Dir-Wri: John Beyer.
60 Mins, Sun, 8 pm.
WYES-TV New Orleans
08/27/80

PETER ALLEN IN CONCERT
Supplier: Australian Broadcasting Commission
Exec Prod: Lloyd Capes;
Dir: Tony Nielsen.
50 Mins, Sun, 7:40 pm.
ABC Australia
10/12/77F

PETER AND THE WOLF
With Bob McGrath
Exec Prod: Susan Horowitz;
Prod: Anita Klever;
Dir: Jim Schmidt.
30 Mins, Fri (29), 8 pm.
KYW-TV Philadelphia, for Group W
01/10/79S

PETER LUNDY & THE MEDICINE HAT STALLION
With Leif Garrett, Mitchell Ryan, Bibi Besch, Milo O'Shea, Ann Doran, John Anderson, John Quade, Ned Romero, Charles Tyner, Brad Reardon, James Lydon, Bill Hicks
Supplier: NBC & Ed Friendly Prods
Prod: Friendly;
Dir: Michael O'Herlihy;
Wri: Jack Turley, based on Marguerite Henry novel.
120 Mins, Sun, 7 pm.
NBC-TV
11/09/77

PETER MARSHALL VARIETY SHOW
With Chapter 5, Wayne Rogers, Arte Johnson, The Manhattans, Jim Stafford, Alice Ghostley, Rod Gist & Denny Evans, Alan Copeland orch
Supplier: Group W Prods & Marshall-Lewellen Prods
Exec Prod: David Salzman;
Prods: Rocco Urbisci, Neal Marshall;
Dir: Jeff Margolis;
Wris: George Tricker, Ed Scharlach.
90 Mins, Sat, 8:30 pm.
WNEW-TV New York
09/15/76S

PHILADELPHIA: ART PAST - ART PROLOGUE
With Richard J Boyle
Exec Prod: Geoffrey Haines-Stiles;
Prod: Erna Akuginow;
Dirs: George Jason, Don Matticks;
Wris: Haines-Stiles, Akuginow, Boyle.
90 Mins, Tues (26), 7:30 pm.
WCAU-TV Philadelphia
Mrs Paul's Kitchens Inc
12/27/78

PHILBY, BURGESS & MACLEAN
With Anthony Bate, Michael Culver, Derek Jacobi, Arthur Lowe, Peter Vaughan, others
Supplier: Granada TV
Exec Prod: Jeremy Wallington;
Dir: Gordon Flemyng;
Wri: Ian Curteis.
90 Mins, Tues (31), 8:30 pm.
ITV Network, Britain
06/08/77F

PHILLIE PHANATIC'S CHRISTMAS - A DREAM COME TRUE
With David Raymond, Bob Temple, Jerry Wheeler, Ballet des Jeunes
Exec Prod: Jay Garfinkel;
Dirs: Neil Bobrick, Jack Smith, Hal Yates;
Wri: Liz Matt.
60 Mins, Wed (19), 8 pm.
KYW-TV Philadelphia
12/26/79

THE PHOENIX TEAM
With Don Francks, Elizabeth Shepherd, Noel Harrison
Exec Prod: Stanley Colbert;
Prod: Lawrence Mirkin;
Dir: Bob Lyons;
Wri: John Saxton.
60 Mins, Sun, 9 pm.
CBC, Toronto, Canada
04/02/80F

THE PHOENIX TEAM
With Don Francks, Elizabeth Shepherd, Mavor Moore, others
Exec Prod: Stanley Colbert;
Prod: Lawrence Mirkin;
Dir: Douglas Williams;
Wri: John Kent Harrison.
60 Mins, Tues, 10 pm.
CBC-TV, from Toronto, Canada
10/15/80F

PHYL & MIKHY
With Rick Lohman, Murphy Cross, Larry Haines, Rae Allen, Michael Pataki, Jack Dodson
Supplier: Elmar Prods
Exec Prods: Rod Parker, Hal Cooper;
Dir: Cooper;
Wri: Tom Reeder.
30 Mins, Mon, 8:30 pm.
CBS-TV
05/28/80

PIG IN A POKE
With Paul Mason, Justine Saunders, Julie Dawson, Samantha Cox, Maree D'Arcy, Jill Howard, Elizabeth Chance, Vicki Battese, George Platras, Arianthe Galani, Tessa Mallos, Phillipa Baker, Carol Burns, Brian Syron, John Hargreaves, Reg Gillam, Gordon Glenwright, Neil Fitzpatric, Holly Brown, Eve Sunners, Athol Compton, Max Osbiston, Muriel Hopkins, David Goddard, Keith Lee
Supplier: Australian Broadcasting Commission
Exec Prod-Dir: Brian Bell;
Wris: Margaret Kelly, John Dingwall.
75 Mins, Sun, 8:35 pm.
ABC (Australia), Channel 2, Sydney
08/03/77F

PINE CANYON IS BURNING
(NBC Double Feature Movie of the Week)
With Kent McCord, Shane Sinutko, Megan McCord, Diana Muldaur, Andrew Duggan, Brit Lind, Dick Bakalyan, Doreen Lang, Curtis Credel
Supplier: Universal TV
Exec Prod-Wri: Robert A Cinader;
Prods: Gino Grimaldi, Hannah Shearer;
Dir: Christian Nyby 3d.
90 Mins, Wed (18), 8 pm.
NBC-TV
05/25/77

PINK LADY
With Jeff Altman, Mie Nemoto, Kei Masuda, Blondie, Bert Parks, Sherman Hemsley, Cheri Eichen, Anna Mathias, Jim Varney
Supplier: Krofft Entertainment
Exec Prod: Albert Tenzer;
Prods: Sid & Marty Krofft;
Dir: Art Fisher;
Wris: Mark Evanier, Rowby Goren, Lorne Frohman, Jim Brochu, Paul Pumpian, Stephen Spears, Biff Manard.
60 Mins, Sat, (1), 10 pm.
NBC-TV
03/05/80

PIPER'S PETS
(Comedy Theater)
With Don Knotts, Peter Isacksen, Maggie Roswell, Jacque Lyn Colton, Sosimo Hernandez, Dorothy Konrad, Sarina Grant, Herb Voland
Supplier: Andomar Prods
Exec Prod: Aaron Ruben;
Prod: Gene Marcione;
Wris: Aaron & Andy Ruben, Michael Brown.
30 Mins, Thurs (31), 8:30 pm.
NBC-TV
06/06/79

PLAY FOR TODAY
(Bar Mitzvah Boy)
With Jeremy Steyn, Adrienne Posta, Maria Charles, Bernard Spear, Jonathan Lynn, Cyril Shaps, Jack Lynn, others
Supplier: BBC
Prod: Graeme McDonald;
Dir: Michael Tuchner;
Wri: Jack Rosenthal.
75 Mins, Tues, 9:35 pm.
BBC-1, Britain
09/29/76F

PLAY FOR TODAY
(Stronger than the Sun)
With Francesca Annis, Tom Bell, Clive Merrison, John Proctor, Gerald James
Supplier: BBC-1
Prod: Margaret Matheson;
Dir: Michael Apted;
Wri: Stephen Proliakoff.
95 Mins, Tues (18), 9:25 pm.
BBC, from England
10/26/77F

PLAY OF THE WEEK
(Abel's Will)
With Daniel Massey, Elizabeth Spriggs, Sharon Duce, Dominic Guard, Atlanta White, others
Supplier: BBC-2
Prod: Innes Lloyd;
Dir: Stephen Frears;
Wri: Christopher Hampton.
80 Mins, Wed, 9 pm.
BBC, England
10/26/77F

PLAY THE PERCENTAGES
With Geoff Edwards (host)
Supplier: Barry & Enright Prods. (Colbert TV Sales)
Prod: Ron Greenberg;
Dir: Richard S. Kline.
30 Mins, Mon-Fri, 7:30 pm.
WOR-TV New York
01/16/80S

PLAYERS TO THE GALLERY
With Kate Fitzpatrick, Peter Sumner, Richard Moir, Neil Fitzpatrick, Brian Young, Trevor Kent, Don Pascoe, Philip Hinton, Howard Vernon, Jennifer Claire, Camilla Rountree, Ian Mune, Tessa Mallos, Elizabeth Kirkby
Supplier: Australian Broadcasting Commissiion
Exec Prod: Eric Tayler;
Dir: Brian Bell;
Wri: Roger Simpson.
60 Mins, Sun, 8:30 pm.
ABC (Australia) TV, Channel 2, Sydney
04/23/80F

PLAYING FOR TIME
With Vanessa Redgrave, Jane Alexander, Melanie Mayron, Marisa Berenson, Viveca Lindfors, Shirley Knight, Verna Bloom, Maud Adams, Lenore Harris
Supplier: Syzgy Prods
Exec Prod: Linda Yellen;
Dir: Daniel Mann;
Wri: Arthur Miller, from Fania Fenelon's autobiography.
180 Mins, Tues (30) 8 pm.
CBS-TV
10/08/80

PLEASE STAND BY
With Richard Schaal, Elinor Donahue, Stephen Michael Schwartz, Darian Mathias, Bryan Scott, Marcie Barkin, Danny Mora, Gary Oakes, Doris Hess, Eddie Rayden
Supplier: Bob Banner Associates (Viacom Enterprises)
Exec Prods: Banner, Ed Warren;
Prods: William Bickley, Michael Warren;
Dir: Howard Storm;
Wri: Brian Levant.
30 Mins, Fri (8), 7:30 pm.
WNBC-TV New York
09/13/78S

PLEASURE COVE
(NBC Wednesday Night At The Movies)
With Constance Forslund, Melody Anderson, Jerry Lacy, James Murtaugh, Ernest Harada, Joan Hackett, Harry Guardino, Shelley Fabares, David Hasslehoff, Ron Masak, Barbara Luna, Tanya Roberts, Rhonda Bates, Tom Jones, David Ankrum, Wes Parker, Sandy Champion, Diane Lander, Harry Basch, Earl Boen, Les Brown Band
Supplier: Lou Shaw Prods & David Gerber Co
Exec Prod-Wri: Shaw;
Prod: Mel Swope;
Dir: Bruce Bilson.
120 Mins, Wed (3), 9 pm.
NBC-TV
01/10/79

THE PLEASURE OF YOUR COMPANY
(Superspecial)
With Karen Kain, Frank Augustyn, Douglas Campbell, Jeff Hyslop, Maureen Forrester
Prod-Dir: Norman Campbell;
Wris: Norman and Elaine Campbell.
60 Mins, Sun, 8 pm.
CBC, from Toronto, Canada
04/11/79F

PM NORTHWEST
With Paul Ryan, others
Prods: Patrick Scott, Jack Norman;
Dir: Tom Cohen.
30 Mins, 7 pm.
KOMO-TV Seattle
09/27/78

POLITICS OF POISON
With Michael Learned
Exec Prod: Matthew Shapiro;
Prod-Dir-Wri: John David Rabinovitch.
60 Mins, Wed (25), 8 pm.
KRON-TV San Francisco
05/09/79

THE POOR OLD WOMAN
With David Ravenswood, Bruce Kerr, John Frawley, Charles Tingwell, Paul Karo, Tim Robertson, Michael Duffield, John Murphy, Hu Pryce, Danny Spooner, Liz Johnston
Supplier: Australian Broadcasting Commission
Prod-Wri: John Nicholson;
Dir: Maurice Lockie.
45 Mins, Mon, 10:20 pm.
ABC, from Melbourne, Australia
06/15/77F

POPI
With Hector Elizondo, Edith Diaz, Anthony Perez, Dennis Vasquez, Lou Criscuolo, Pippa Scott, Frank Lugo, Ken Sansom
Supplier: ITP Prods. & Allied Artists
Exec Prod: Herbert B. Leonard;
Prod: Don Van Atta;
Dir: Hy Averback
Wris: Dick Bensfield, Perry Grant.
30 Mins, Tues, 8:30 pm.
CBS-TV
01/28/76

THE POSSESSED
(NBC Sunday Movie)
With James Farentino, Joan Hackett, others
Supplier: Warner Bros TV
Exec Prod: Jerry Thorpe;
Prod: Philip Mandelker;
Dir: Thorpe;
Wri: John Sacret Young.
90 Mins, Sun (1), 9:30 pm.
NBC-TV
05/04/77

POWER TO THE PEOPLE
Prod-Wri-Narr: Patricia Gormin;
Dir: Robert Weaver.
30 Mins, Sat, 7 pm.
WVUE-TV New Orleans
05/07/80

THE POWER WITHIN
(ABC Friday Night Movie Double Feature)
With Art Hindle, Edward Binns, Joe Rassulo, Eric Braeden, David Hedison, Susan Howard, Richard Sargent, Karen Lamm, John Dennis
Supplier: Aaron Spelling Prods
Exec Prods: Spelling, Douglas S Cramer;
Prod: Alan S Godfrey;
Dir: John L Moxey;
Wri: Edward J Lakso.
90 Mins, Fri (11), 8 pm.
ABC-TV
05/23/79

POWER WITHOUT GLORY
(Heads I Win, Tails You Lose: A Remedy Against Sin)
With Martin Vaughn, Rosalind Spiers, Terry Donovan, George Mallaby, Michael Pate, Irene Inescort, Heather Canning, Sean Scully, John Wood
Supplier: Australian Broadcasting Commission
Exec Prod: Oscar Whitbread;
Dirs; David Zweck, Keith Wilkes, Douglas Sharp, John Gauci;
Wris: Cliff Green, Howard Griffiths, Sonia Borg, Tom Heggarty, Roger Simpson.
50 Mins, Mon, 8:30 pm.
ABC (all Australian capital cities)
06/16/76F

THE PRACTICE
With Danny Thomas, David Spielberg, Dena Dietrich, Didi Conn, Shelley Fabares, Allen Price, Damon Raskin, J. Pat O'Malley, Dean Santoro
Supplier: Danny Thomas Prods. & MGM-TV
Exec Prod: Paul Junger Witt;
Prod-Wri: Steve Gordon;
Dir: Lee Philips.
30Mins, Fri, 8:30 pm.
NBC-TV
02/04/76

PREMIERE
(A Hymn From Jim)
With Harry H Corbett, George Innes, Christopher Guard, Heather Wright
Prod: Graham Benson;
Dir: Colin Bucksey;
Wri: Richard O'Brien.
30 Mins, Thurs (22), 9 pm.
BBC-2, from London, England
09/28/77F

PREMIERE
(Pit Strike)
With Brewster Mason, Jennie Linden
Supplier: BBC-TV
Prod: Graham Benson;
Dir: Roger Bamford;
Wri: Alan Sillitoe.
30 Mins, Thurs (22), 9 pm.
BBC-2, from London, England
09/28/77F

THE PRESENT
(The Newcomers)
With Bruno Gerussi, Martha Henry
Exec Prod: Gordon Hinch;
Prods: Richard Nielson, Pat Ferns;
Dir: Rene Bonniere;
Wri: Douglas Bowie.
60 Mins, Sun, 7 pm.
CBC, from Toronto, Canada
Imperial Oil
04/11/79F

PRESENTING SUSAN ANTON
With Joyce DeWitt, Big Bird, Martin Mull, Jack Fletcher, Jack Knight, Terry McGovern, Dick Wilson, Water Painter Dancers, others
Supplier: Ernest Chambers Prods & LuWalla Inc
Exec Prod: Jack Stein;
Prod: Chambers;
Dir: Jeff Margolis;
Wris: Rick Kellard & Bob Comfort, Lane Sarasohn & Carol Hatfield, Allyn Warner, Fred Fox Jr, Terry Hart, Chambers.
60 Mins, Thurs (26), 10 pm.
NBC-TV
05/02/79

THE PRESIDENTS: 80 YEARS ON CAMERA
(Part One-The Public President: Wit & Warmth in the White House)
With James Garner (host)
Supplier: The Corp. for Entertainment & Learning, Post-Newsweek Stations & Scripps-Howard Broadcasting (Gould Enterainment Corp.)
Exec Prods-Wris-Dirs: Mert Koplin, Charles Grinker;
Prod: Robert L. Garthwaite.
60 Mins, Thurs, 9 pm.
WPIX-TV New York
05/07/80S

PRIDE, POISE AND POTENTIAL
With Barry Tompkins, Oakland Raiders, San Francisco 49ers
Supplier: KRON-TV News
Prod: Richard Scott;
Dir: Ken Cyzs;
Wri: Tompkins.
60 Mins, Thurs (7) 8 pm.
KRON-TV San Francisco
09/13/78

THE PRIMARY ENGLISH CLASS
(ABC Monday Comedy Special)
With Valerie Curtin, Murphy Dunne, Harvey Jason, Maria O'Brien, Joe Bennett, Bob Holt, Suesie Elene, Freeman King, Lupe Ontiveros, Kaiser Chu
Supplier: Joe Hamilton Prods
Exec Prod: Hamilton;
Dirs: Roger Beatty, Tim Conway;
Wris: Arnie Kogan, Beatty.
30 Mins, Mon (15), 8 pm.
ABC-TV
08/24/77

THE PRIME OF MISS JEAN BRODIE
With Geraldine McEwan, Robert Urquhart, John Castle, others
Supplier: Scottish Television, 20th Century-Fox TV
Exec Prod: Beryl Vertue;
Prod: Richard Bates;
Dir: Tina Wakerell, others
Wri: Jay Presson Allen, others
60 Mins, Sun, 10:15 pm.
ITV Network, Britain
02/15/78F

PRIME TIME
With Paricia Gormin, narrator
Prod-Wri: Gormin;
Dir: Robert Weaver.
30 Mins, Sat.
WVUE-TV New Orleans
05/09/79

PRIME TIME SUNDAY
With Tom Snyder, Jack Perkins, Chris Wallace
Supplier: NBC News
Exec Prod: Paul Friedman;
Prods: Clare-Crawford Mason, Christine Huneke, Craig Leake, Bill Brown;
Dir: George Paul.
60 Mins, Sun, 10 pm.
NBC-TV
06/27/79

THE PRINCE OF CENTRAL PARK
With T J Hargrave, Lisa Richards, Ruth Gordon, Marc Vahanian, Eda Reiss Merin, Carol Gustafson, Estelle Omens, Jo Flores Chase
Supplier: Lorimar Prods
Exec Prod: Philip Capice;
Prod-Dir: Harvey Hart;
Wri: Jeb Rosebrook, based on Evan Rhodes novel.
90 Mins, Fri (17), 8 pm.
CBS-TV
06/22/77

PRISON
With Tom Mangold
Supplier: BBC
Prod-Dir: John Penycate.
30 Mins, Thurs (11), 8:30 pm.
BBC, from London, England
08/24/77F

PRISONER: CELL BLOCK H
With Peita Toppano, Val Lehman, Margaret Laurence, Carol Burns, Kerry Armstrong, Colette Mann, Elspeth Ballantyne, Fiona Spence, Patsy King, Barry Quin, Richard Moir, others
Supplier: Grundy Organization (Firestone Program Syndication)
Exec Prod-Wri: Reg Watson;
Prod: Ian Bradley;
Dir: Graeme Arthur.
50 Mins, Mon, (21), 11:10 pm.
WPIX-TV New York
01/30/80S

PROFESSIONAL FOUL
(Great Performance)
With Peter Barkworth, John Shrapnel, Stephen Rea, Richard O'Callaghan, Shane Rimmer, Bernard Hill, Billy Hamon, David de Keyser
Supplier: BBC-TV and WNET-TV
Exec Prod: Jac Venza;
Prod: Mark Shivas;
Dir: Michael Lindsay-Hogg;
Wri: Tom Stoppard.
90 Mins, Wed (26), 9 pm.
WNET-TV New York
04/26/78

PROJECT U F O
With William Jordan, Caskey Swaim, Aldine King, Anne Schedeen, Frances Reid, John Findlater, Len Wayland, Linwood McCarthy, Hoke Howell, Tim Donnelly, William Wellman Jr, Jim B Smith
Supplier: Mark VII Ltd & Worldvision
Exec Prod: Jack Webb;
Prod: William T Coleman;
Dir: Richard Quine;
Wri: Harold Jack Bloom.
60 Mins, Sun, 8 pm.
NBC-TV
02/22/78

THE PROMISE OF LOVE
(CBS Tuesday Night Movies)
With Valerie Bertinelli, Shelley Long, Jameson Parker, Andy Romano, Joanna Miles, David James Carroll, Lauri Hendler, Virginia Kiser, Craig T. Nelson, Karlene Crockett, Dey Young
Supplier: Pierre Cossette Prods
Exec Prod: Cossette;
Prod: Jay Benson;
Dir: Don Taylor;
Wri: Harry & Renee Longstreet, Carol Saraceno.
120 Mins, Tues, (11) 9 pm.
CBS-TV
11/19/80

PSYCHIC PHENOMENA: EXPLORING THE UNKNOWN
(Big Event)
With Burt Lancaster, Alan Neuman
Supplier: Alan Neuman Prods
Prod-Dir-Wri: Neuman.
90 Mins, Sun, 9:30 pm.
NBC-TV
11/02/77

THE PUBLIC PRESIDENT: WIT & WARMTH IN THE WHITE HOUSE
(The Presidents: 76 Years On Camera)
With James Garner (narrator)
Supplier: Post-Newsweek Stations, Scripps-Howard Broadcasting
Exec Prods-Wris-Dirs: Mert Koplin & Charles Grinker.
60 Mins, Sun (25), 9 pm.
WNEW-TV New York
04/28/76S

PUZZLE
With James Franciscus, Sir Robert Helpmann, Wendy Hughes, Peter Gwynne, Gerard Kennedy, Kerry McGuire, Ivar Kants, Max Meldrum, Shane Porteous, Tony Barry, Kenneth Goodlet, Sheila Kennelly, Richard Gilbert, Alan Russel, Terry Jowett, Charlesa Pointon, Peter Armstrong, Bill Buckle, Gordon Piper, Carolyn Davies
Supplier: Australian Broadcasting Commission & Trans-Atlantic Enterprises
Exec Prods: Robert Kline, Preston Fischer;
Prod-Wri: Herbert J Wright;
Dir: Gordon Hessler.
90 Mins Tues, 8 pm.
Channel 2, from Sydney, Australia
12/20/78F

QUARK
With Richard Benjamin, Timothy Thomerson, Douglas V Fowley, Tricia & Cibbie Barnett, Conrad Janis, Misty Rowe, Alan Caillou, Bobby Porter
Supplier: David Gerber Prods & Columbia Pictures TV
Exec Prods: Gerber, Mace Neufeld;
Prod-Wri: Buck Henry;
Dir: Peter H Hunt.
30 Mins, Sat, 8:30 pm.
NBC-TV
05/25/77

QUARK
With Richard Benjamin, Tim Thomerson, Richard Kelton, Tricia Barnstable, Cyb Barnstable, Bobby Porter, Conrad Janis, Alan Caillou, Henry Silva, Hans Conreid
Supplier: David Gerber Prods & Columbia Pictures TV
Exec Prods: Gerber, Mace Neufeld;
Prod: Bruce Johnson;
Dir: Hy Averback;
Wris: Steve Zacharias, Bruce Kane, Jonathan Kaufer.
60 Mins, Fri (24), 8 pm.
NBC-TV
03/01/78

QUARTERLY REPORT
With David Halton
Exec Prod: Ray Hazzan;
Prod: Dick Bocking.
150 Mins, Sun, 8:30 pm.
CBC-TV, from Toronto, Canada
10/26/77F

QUEST
With Tim Matheson, Kurt Russell, Brian Keith, Keenan Wynn, Will Hutchins, Neville Brand, Cameron Mitchell, Irene Yah-Ling Sun, others
Supplier: David Gerber Prod. & Columbia Pictures TV
Exec Prod: David Gerber;
Prod: Christopher Morgan;
Dir: Lee H. Katzin;
Wri: Tracy Keenan Wynn.
120 Mins, Thurs (13), 9 pm.
NBC-TV
05/19/76

QUEST
With Kurt Russell, Tim Matheson, Richard Egan, Susan Dey, others
Supplier: Columbia Pictures TV
Exec Prod: David Gerber;
Prods: Mark Rodgers, James H Brown;
Dir: Barry Shear;
Wri: Rodgers.
90 Mins, Wed (29), 9:30 pm.
NBC-TV
09/29/76

QUINCY, M E
(NBC Sunday Mystery Movie)
With Jack Klugman, Garry Walberg, Lynnette Mettey, John S. Ragin, Robert Ito, Joseph Roman, Val Bisoglio, Harry Rhodes, Denny Miller, Henry Darrow, Rick Podell, George Uyner, Woodrow Parfrey, Martha Smith
Supplier: Glen A. Larson Prods & Universal TV
Exec Prod: Larson;
Prod: Lou Shaw;
Dir: E W Swackhamer;
Wris: Larson, Shaw.
90 Mins, Sun, 9:30 pm.
NBC-TV
10/06/76

RACCONTARE LA CITTA
(Speaking of the City)
Supplier: RAI-TV, Rome
Prods: Giulio Macchi, Franco Donato, Carla Ghelli, Anna Giolitti;
Dirs: Giancarlo Ravasio, Gianfranco Mingozzi, Marcello Ugolini, Carlo Alberto Pinelli, Ghelli, Donato.
60 Mins, Wed, 9:45 pm.
RAI-TV, Rome, Italy
10/19/77F

THE RACERS
With Curt Gowdy (host)
Supplier: Maramy Prods (American International TV)
Exec Prod: Lawrence Jacobson;
Dir: Doug Mole;
Wri: Jay Davidson.
30 Mins, Sat, 2:30 pm.
WABC-TV New York
05/09/79S

RACHEL
With Barbara Ewing, Grant Tilly, Martyn Sanderson, Dorothy McKegg, Deborah Doole, John Bach, Bill Stalker
Supplier: Television One
Prod: John Anderson;
Dir: Peter Muxlow;
Wri: Keith Aberdein.
51 Mins, Tues, 8:30 pm.
TV-1, Wellington, N Z
10/25/78F

THE RAES
With Cherril & Robbie Rae
Prod: Ken Gibson;
Dirs: Mike Watt, Patsy McDonald.
60 Mins, Fri, 9 pm.
CBC-TV from Vancouver, Canada
08/09/78F

RAFFERTY
With Patrick McGoohan, Millie Slavin, John Getz, Sam Wanamaker, Herb Edelman, Andra Akers
Supplier: Warner Bros TV
Exec Prod-Dir: Jerry Thorpe;
Prod-Wri: James Lee.
60 Mins, Mon, 10 pm.
CBS-TV
09/07/77

THE RAG BUSINESS
(ABC Saturday Comedy Special)
With Conchata Ferrell, Dick O'Neill, Sudie Bond, Sarina Grant, Susan Lawrence, Jeannie Linero, Fred McCarran, Anna L Pagan, Peggy Pope
Supplier: Andomar Prods
Exec Prod: Aaron Ruben;
Prod: Gene Marcione;
Dir: Russ Petranto;
Wris: Ronald Wolfe, Ronald Chesney.
30 Mins, Sat (1), 8:30 pm.
ABC-TV
07/05/78

RAGGEDY ANN & ANDY: THE GREAT SANTA CLAUS CAPER
With voices of June Foray, Daws Butler, Les Tremayne
Supplier: Chuck Jones Enterprises & Bobbs-Merrill
Prod-Dir-Wri: Jones.
30 Mins, Thurs (30), 8:30 pm.
CBS-TV
12/06/78

RAID ON ENTEBBE
(The Big Event)
With Charles Bronson, Peter Finch, Martin Balsam, Yaphet Kotto, Jack Warden, Horst Bucholz, John Saxon, Sylvia Sidney, Tige Andrews, Eddie Constantine, Warren Kemmerling, Robert Loggia, David Opatoshu, Stephen Macht, Allan Arbus, Mariclare Costello, James Woods, Lou Gilbert, Alex Colon, Harvey Lembeck, Peter Brocco, Aharon Ipale, others
Supplier: Edgar J Scherick Associates & 20th-Fox TV
Exec Prods: Scherick, Daniel H Blatt;
Dir: Irvin Kershner;
Wri: Barry Beckerman.
180 Mins, Sun (9), 8:25 pm.
NBC-TV
01/12/77

RAIN ON THE ROOF
With Cheryl Campbell, Malcolm Stoddard, Ewan Stewart, Michael Culver, Madeline Hinde
Supplier: London Weekend TV & Pennies From Heaven Ltd
Exec Prod: Tony Wharmby;
Prod: Kenith Trodd;
Dir: Alan Bridges;
Wri: Dennis Potter.
87 Mins, Sun, 10 pm.
ITV Network, Britain
11/05/80F

RALPH NADER: FOR THE PEOPLE
With Michael Jacobson, Gus Speth, Ron Brownstein
77 Mins, Sat, 7:30 pm. Showtime
10/08/80PC

RAYMOND CHANDLER: MURDER WAS HIS BUSINESS
With Henry Ramer, Bud Knapp
Exec Prod: Howard Engel;
Prod-Wri: Patrick Hynan;
Dir: Bill Howell.
90 Mins, Sat, 9:05 pm.
CBC, Toronto, Canada
04/02/80F

RAZZMATAZZ
With Barry Bostwick (host)
Supplier: CBS News & Scholastic Magazines Inc
Exec Prod-Wri: Joel Heller;
Prod-Dir: Vern Diamond.
60 Mins, Sat (16), 1 pm.
CBS-TV
04/20/77

RAZZMATAZZ
With Barry Bostwick (host)
Supplier: CBS News
Exec Prod: Joel Heller;
Prod-Dir: Vern Diamond.
30 Mins, Sat, 1:30 pm.
CBS-TV
Kenner (Sive Associates)
11/09/77

REAL LIFE!
With Huell Howser
Supplier: WCBS-TV
Exec Prod: Jim Dauphinee;
Prods: Sheila Bowe, Steven Schwartz.
30 Mins, Tues, 7:30 pm.
WCBS-TV New York
11/21/79

REAL PEOPLE
With Fred Willard, John Barbour, Sara Purcell, Bill Rafferty, Skip Stephenson, Jimmy Breslin, Mark Russell
Supplier: George Schlatter Prods
Prod: Schlatter;
Dir: Merrill Mazuer;
Wris: Digby Wolfe, Barbour, David Panich, Gene Farmer.
60 Mins, Wed, 8 pm.
NBC-TV
04/25/79

REDD FOX
With LaWanda Page, L A Cast of "The Wiz", others
Supplier: Blye-Einstein Prods, Redd Foxx Prods
Exec Prod: Foxx;
Prods: Allan Blye, Bob Einstein;
Dir: Donald Davis;
Wris: Pat Proft, Lenny Ripps, Andrew Johnson, Levi Taylor, Stuart Birnbaum, Matt Neuman, Joe Shulkin, Henry Wallace, Foxx.
60 Mins, Thurs, 10 pm.
ABC-TV
09/21/77

REFLECTIONS IN A MIRROR?
Supplier: BBC
Prod: John Miller.
(Part I: ABC in Kansas City); 50 Mins, Fri (15), 8:10 pm. (Part II: Television and Politics); 90 Mins, Sat (16), 8:40 pm.
BBC, from London, England
07/27/77F

REFLECTIONS OF CHINA
Exec Prod: Paul Steinle;
Prod: Phil Sturholm;
Wri-Narr: Jean Enersen.
30 Mins, Sat (9), 7:30 pm.
KING-TV Seattle
09/19/79

REMEMBER JACK BUCHANAN
With Christopher Gable, others
Prod: Brian Izzard;
Wris: Sid Colin, Michael Marshall.
60 Mins
Scottish TV, Glasgow
09/24/80F

RENDEZVOUS HOTEL
With Bill Daily, Jeff Redford, Teddy Wilson, Bobbie Mitchell, Talya Ferro, Carole Cook, Severn Darden, Kathryn Witt, Nellie Bellflower, Emory Bass, Dolph Sweet, Ed Winter, Bruce French, Sean Garrison, Jeff Donnell, Jane Abbott, Jack O'Leary, Diane Lander
Supplier: Mark Carliner Prods
Exec Prods: Austin & Irma Kalish;
Prod: Carliner;
Dir: Peter Hunt;
Wris: Kalishes, Clayton Baxter.
105 Mins, Wed (11), 9 pm.
CBS-TV
07/25/79

THE RENE SIMARD SHOW
With Gloria Loring
Exec Prod: Ken Gibson;
Prod: Alan Thicke;
Dir: Michael Watt;
Wris: Jack Newman, Richard Ozounian, Jan Nablo, Bill Muss.
30 Mins, Tues, 8:30 pm.
CBC-TV, from Vancouver, Canada
General Foods
10/19/77F

REPORT FROM GALLIPOLI
With Barry Eaton, Michael Craig, Martin Vaughan, Ken Goodlet, Brian Anderson, Brian Adams, Noel Trevarthen, Douglas Luke, Harold Hopkins, Brian Wenzel, Peter Gwynne, Olivia Brown, Shane Porteous, John Ewart, Martin Harris, Vincent Ball, Peter Collingwood, Ivar Kants, Ben Gabriel, John Allen
Supplier: Australian Broadcasting Commission
Prod: John Martin;
Dir: James Roberts.
60 Mins, Mon, 8:30 pm.
ABC (Australia) TV
04/13/77F

REPORT FROM JAPAN: THE BILLION DOLLAR DEBATE
With Maureen Bunyan
Prod: Gerald Grossman;
Wri: Bunyan.
30 Mins, Sun (29), 9 pm.
WDVM-TV Washington
05/02/79

RESCUE FROM GILLIGAN'S ISLAND - PART ONE
(NBC Saturday Specials)
With Bob Denver, Alan Hale, Jim Backus, Natalie Schafer, Judith Baldwin, Russell Johnson, Dawn Wells, Vincent Schiavelli, Art LaFleur
Supplier: Redwood Prods & Sherwood Schwartz Prods
Exec Prod: Sherwood Schwartz;
Prod: Lloyd Schwartz;
Dir: Leslie H Martinson;
Wris: Sherwood, Elroy & Al Schwartz, David Harmon.
60 Mins, Sat (14), 9 pm.
NBC-TV
10/18/78

THE RESTLESS YEARS
With Sonny Blake, Nick Hedstrom, Julieanne Newbould, Deborah Coulls, Graham Thorburn, June Salter, Stanley Walsh, Redmond Phillips, Barbara Wyndon, Brian Wenzel, Queenie Ashton, Lynette Curran, Jacqueline Kott, Jessica Noad, Tiny Grenville, Malcolm Thompson, Brendan Lunney, Elizabeth Crosby, John Meillon Jr
Supplier: Reg Grundy Prods
Exec Prod: Reg Watson;
Dir: Peter Bernardos;
Wris: Watson, Peter Rawling, Mike Murphy.
60 Mins, Wed, Thurs, 7:30 pm.
Channel TEN 10, Sydney, Australia
12/21/77F

THE RETURN OF CAPTAIN NEMO
With Jose Ferrer, Burr deBenning, Tom Hallick, Burgess Meredith, Warren Stevens, Med Flory
Supplier: Warner Bros TV-Irwin Allen Prods
Prod: Allen;
Dir: Alex March;
Wris: Preston Wood, Norman Katkov.
60 Mins, Wed, 8 pm.
CBS-TV
03/15/78

THE RETURN OF THE SAINT
With Ian Ogilvy, Joss Ackland, Kathryn Leigh Scott, Moira Redmond, others
Supplier: ITC
Prod: Anthony Spinner;
Dir: Peter Sasdy;
Wri: John Kruse.
60 Mins, Sun, 7:15 pm.
ATV, from England
10/11/78F

REVIVAL
With Alex Pollock, narrator; Four Tops, Mary Gutzi & Friendship, others
Supplier: WXYZ-TV
Exec Prods: Jeanne Findlater, Cliff Curley;
Prods: Harvey Kurek Ovshinsky, Bill Pace.
30 Mins, Sat
WXYZ-TV Detroit
09/07/77S

REWARD
(ABC Friday Night Movie Double Feature)
With Michael Parks, Richard Jaeckel, Louis Giambalvo, Malachy McCourt, Annie McEnroe, Andrew Robinson, Calvin Jung, Bridget Hanley, Lance LeGault, David Clennon, James A. Watson Jr., Martin Cassidy
Supplier: Jerry Adler Prods, Esprit Enterprises & Lorimar Prods
Exec Prod: Lee Rich;
Prod: Adler;
Dir: E.W. Swackhamer;
Wri: Jason Miller.
90 Mins, Fri, (23) 9:30 pm.
ABC-TV
05/28/80

THE RHINEMANN EXCHANGE PART 1
(NBC Best Sellers)
With Stephen Collins, Lauren Hutton, Claude Akins, Len Birman, Vince Edwards, Gene Evans, Larry Hagman, John Huston, Jeremy Kemp, Werner Klemperer, Roddy McDowall, Trisha Noble, William Prince, John Van Dreelen, Isela Vega, Thayer David, Charles Siebert, John Hoyt, Jose Ferrer
Supplier: Universal TV
Exec Prod: George Eckstein;
Prod-Wri: Richard Collins;
Dir: Burt Kennedy.
120 Mins, Thurs (10), 9 pm.
NBC-TV
03/16/77

RICH LITTLE SHOW
With Susan Saint James, John Davidson, Glenn Ford, Charlotte Rae, Julie McWhirter, Spo-De-Odee, R. G. Brown
Supplier: Dudley Enterprises
Exec Prod: Jerry Goldstein;
Prods: Rich Eustis, Al Rogers;
Dir: Lee Bernhardi;
Wris: Arnie Kogen, Ray Jessel, Don Hinckley, Jim Mulligan, Peter Gallay, April Kelly, Dave O'Malley, Tom Chapman, Mort Scharfman, Barry Levinson, Rudy Deluca, Eustis, Rogers.
60 Mins, Mon, 8 pm.
NBC-TV
02/04/76

RICH LITTLE'S CHRISTMAS CAROL
Supplier: Tel Pro Communications
Prods: Norman Sedawie, Gayle Sedawie;
Dir: Trevor Evans;
Mus: Saul Ilson.
60 Mins, Sun, 8 pm.
CBC-TV, from Toronto, Canada
Kraft Foods
12/27/78F

RICH LITTLE'S WASHINGTON FOLLIES
With Suzanne Somers, Dick Van Patten, Robert Guillaume, Tom Bosley, Kevin Carlisle Dancers
Supplier: Dudley Enterprises & Saul Ilson Prods
Exec Prod: Jerry Goldstein;
Prod: Ilson;
Dir: Stan Harris;
Wris: Hal Goldman, Jeffrey Barron, Wayne Kline, Kevin Hartigan, David Garber, Ilson.
60 Mins, Sat (13), 8 pm.
ABC-TV
05/17/78

RICH MAN, POOR MAN
With Peter Strauss, Nick Nolte, Susan Blakely, Edward Asner, Dick Butkus, Michael Evans, Gloria Grahame, Dorothy McGuire, Robert Reed
Supplier: ABC, in association wth Harve Bennett Productions and U-TV
Exec Prod: Bennett;
Prod: Jon Epstein;
Dir: David Greene;
Wri: Dean Reisner.
120 Mins, Sun (1), 9 pm.
ABC-TV
02/04/76

RICH MAN, POOR MAN - BOOK II
With Peter Strauss, Susan Blakely, Gregg Henry, James Carrol Jordon, Ray Milland, Van Johnson, Kay Lenz, William Smith, Tim McIntire, Susan Sullivan, Dick Sargent, Herbert Jefferson Jr, Dimitra Arliss, Nick Nolte
Supplier: Universal TV
Exec Prod: Michael Gleason;
Prod: Jon Epstein;
Dir: Lou Antonio;
Wri: Millard Lampell.
120 Mins, Tues, 9 pm.
ABC-TV
09/29/76

THE RICHARD PRYOR SHOW
With Paula Kelly, The O'Jays, others
Supplier: Burt Sugarman Prods & Richard Pryor Enterprises
Exec Prod: Sugarman;
Prods: Rocco Urbisci, John Moffitt;
Dir: Moffitt;
Wris: David Banks, Jeffrey Barron, Booker Bradshaw, Paul Mooney, Arthur Sellers, Jeremy Stevens, Tom Moore, Urbisci, Pryor.
60 Mins, Tues, 8 pm.
NBC-TV
09/21/77

RICHIE BROCKELMAN: MISSING 24 HOURS
(NBC Movie Of The Week)
With Dennis Dugan, Suzanne Pleshette, Norman Fell, Helen Page Camp, Barbara Bosson, Lloyd Bochner, Sharon Gless, William Windom
Supplier: Universal TV
Exec Prods-Wris: Stephen J. Cannell, Steve Bochco;
Prod: William F. Phillips;
Dir: Hy Averback.
90 Mins, Wed (27), 8:30 pm.
NBC-TV
11/03/76

RICHIE BROCKELMAN, PRIVATE EYE
With Dennis Dugan, Robert Hogan, Barbara Bosson, David Spielberg, John Randolph, Jerry Douglas, Tasha Martell, Regis J Cordic, Rosanna Huffman, Earl Boen, James Karen, William Mims, Anthony Charnota
Supplier: Stephen J Cannell Prods, Bunky Prods & Universal TV
Exec Prods: Cannell, Steven Bochco;
Prod: Peter S Fischer;
Dir: Arnold Laven;
Wri: Michael Kozoll.
60 Mins, Fri, 9 pm.
NBC-TV
01/22/78

RIDE ON STRANGER
With Liddy Clark, Noni Hazlehurst, Warwick Sims, Peter Carroll, John Bluthal, Barbara Wyndon, Henri Szeps, Michael Aitkens, Margo Lee, Ron Graham, Moya O'Sullivan, Bunney Brooke, Neol Trevarthen, Lorna Leslie, Walter Pym
Supplier: Australian Broadcasting Commission
Exec Prod: Alan Burke;
Dir: Carl Schultz;
Wri: Peter Yeldham.
60 Mins, Sun, 8:30 pm.
ABC TV, Channel 2, Sydney, Australia
08/01/79F

RIDING FOR THE PONY EXPRESS
With John Hammond, Harry Crosby, Victor French, Susan Myers, Richard Lineback, Glenn Withrow, Byron Morrow, Philip Baker Hall, Alex Kubik, Del Hinkley, Jerry Stites
Supplier: O'Connor-Becker Prods
Exec Prod-Prod: Terry Becker;
Dir: Don Chaffey;
Wri: James Menzies.
60 Mins, Wed, (3) 8 pm.
CBS-TV
09/10/80

RIDING HIGH
(Comedy Time)
With Charles Frank, Allan Miller, Wendy Phillips, Lonny Chapman, Don Calfa, Allen Case, Pat Cranshaw, Bill Hart, Pearl Shear, Jim Varney
Supplier: MGM-TV
Prod: Marc Merson;
Dir: Lee Phillips;
Wri: Larry Gelbart.
30 Mins, Thurs (25), 8 pm.
NBC-TV
08/31/77

RIEL
With Raymond Cloutier, Roger Blay, Christopher Plummer, Don Harron, William Shatner, Arthur Hill, Leslie Nielsen, Gary Reinecke, Barry Morse, August Schellenberg, Marcel Sabourin, Paxton Whitehead, Lloyd Bochner, Jean-Louis Roux, Claude Jutra
Exec Prod: Stan Colbert;
Prod: John Treat;
Dir: George Bloomfield;
Wri: Roy Moore.
180 Mins, Sun & Tues, 8:30 pm.
CBC, from Toronto, Canada
General Motors
05/09/79F

THE RIMSHOTS
With Andrea Martin, Saul Rubinek, Catherine O'Hara, Dave Thomas
Prod: Perry Rosemond;
Dir: George Bloomfield;
Wris: Lorne Frohman, Ben Gordon.
30 Mins, Tues, 7:30 pm.
CBC-TV, from Toronto, Canada
02/22/78F

RINGO
With Ringo Starr, John Ritter, Art Carney, Angie Dickinson, George Harrison, Mike Douglas, Vincent Price, Jaime Rogers Dancers
Supplier: DIR Broadcasting Prods, Montico Corp
Exec Prods: Robert Meyrowitz, Peter Kauff, Alan Steinberg;
Prod: Ken Ehrlich;
Dir: Jeff Margolis;
Wris: Neil Israel, Pat Proft.
60 Mins, Wed (26), 9 pm.
NBC-TV
05/03/78

RIPPING YARNS
(Tomkinson's Schooldays)
With Michael Palin, Terry Jones, Gwen Waford, Ian Ogilvie
Supplier: BBC Television
Prod-Dir: Terry Hughes;
Wris: Palin, Jones.
30 Mins, Sun, 10 pm.
WNET New York
11/14/79

RISKO
With Gabriel Dell, Joel Fabiani, Laraine Stephens, John Durren, others
Supplier: Larry White Productions-Columbia TV
Exec Prod: Larry White;
Prod: Bob Stambler;
Dir: Bernie Kowalski;
Wris: Adrian Spies, Bill Driskill.
60 Mins, Sun (9), 10 pm.
CBS-TV
05/12/76

RITA MORENO SHOW
With Victor Buono, Louis Nye, Kathy Bendett, Bert Rosario, Kit McDonough, Paul P Price, Billy Sands, Shirley Mitchell, Ron Vernan
Supplier: Hayoudo Prods & Paramount TV
Exec Prods-Wris: Mark Rothman, Lowell Ganz;
Dir: Tony Mordente.
30 Mins, Tues (2), 9 pm.
CBS-TV
05/10/78

ROACH
With Rhozier (Roach) Brown
Exec Prod: Stan Rudick;
Prod: Tim McDonald;
Dir: Bill Dobbs
30 Mins, Sat (24), 7:30 pm.
WTTG Washington, D.C.
01/28/76

THE ROAD FROM ELTHAM
With Bob Hope, others
Supplier: Thames Television
Prods: Charles Thompson, Terence Dixon
Dir: Dixon.
65 Mins, Mon (29), 10:15 pm.
ITV Network, Britain
06/07/78F

ROADRUNNER
With Trevor Thomas, Nadia Cattouse, Barry Reckord, Janet Bartley, Ram John Holder, Rudolph Walker, Neville Philips
Supplier: Thames Television
Exec Prod: Verity Lambert;
Prod-Dir: Barry Hanson;
Wri: Michael Abbensetts.
50 Mins, Tues, 9 pm.
ITV, London, England
08/03/77F

ROALD DAHL'S TALES OF THE UNEXPECTED
With Jack Weston, Gladys Spencer, Don Fellows
Supplier: Survival Anglia Ltd
Exec Prod: Sir John Woolf;
Prod: John Rosenberg;
Dir: Michael Tuchner;
Wri: Dahl.
30 Mins, Sat, 11:30 pm.
WNEW-TV New York
10/10/79S

ROBERT REDFORD ON THE OUTLAW TRAIL
Supplier: London Weekend Television
Prod: Richard Drewett;
Dir: Alan Ravenscroft.
60 Mins, Sat, 7 pm.
LWT, from England
10/04/78F

ROBIN WILLIAMS: OFF THE WALL
(On Location)
Supplier: Home Box Office
Exec Prod: Michael Fuchs;
Prod-Dir: Marty Callner.
60 Mins.
11/01/78PC

THE ROCK POOL
With Ed Deveraux, Lyn James, Bunney Brooke
Supplier: Australian Broadcasting Commission
Dir: Chris Thomson;
Wri: Colin Free.
60 Mins, Sun, 8:30 pm.
ABC TV, Channel 2, Sydney, Australia
11/21/79F

THE ROCK RAINBOW
With Ellen Greene, Susan Bigelow, Louisa Flaningam, John V Shea, John Aprea, Scott Porter, Kenneth Tigar, Jeff David, Robert Alda, Monte Landis
Supplier: Marstar Prods & TTC Prods
Exec Prod: Martin Starger
Prods: Alan Sacks, Robert Scheerer;
Dir: Scheerer;
Wri: Diana Gould.
60 Mins, Sat (15), 10 pm.
ABC-TV
07/19/78

ROGER & HARRY
(ABC Monday Night Movie Double Feature)
With John Davidson, Barry Primus, Carole Mallory, Anne Randall Stewart, Richard Lynch, Susan Sullivan, Tito Vandis, Biff McGuire, Harris Yulin, Alan McRae, Henry Sutton
Supplier: Bruce Lansbury Prods & Columbia Pictures TV
Exec Prod: Lansbury;
Prod: Anthony Spinner;
Dir: Jack Starrett;
Wri: Alvin Sapinsley.
90 Mins, Mon (2), 9:30 pm.
ABC-TV
05/11/77

ROGUE MALE
With Peter O'Toole, John Standing, Alastair Sim, Cyd Hayman, Harold Pinter, others
Supplier: BBC & 20th-Fox
Prod: Mark Shivas;
Dir: Clive Donner;
Wri: Frederic Raphael.
100 Mins, Wed 9 pm.
BBC-2, Britain
10/06/76F

ROLF HARRIS SHOW
Prod: Paul Kimberley.
CTV Network, from Vancouver, Canada
03/24/76F

ROLL OF THUNDER, HEAR MY CRY
With Claudia McNeil, Janet MacLachlan, Robert Christian, Larry Scott, Roy Poole, Rockne Tarkington, Lark Ruffin, Tony Ross, Rodney King Adams, Eric Dunaway, John Cullum, Morgan Freeman, Charles Briggs, Lisa Whittington, Colia Lafayette, Mark Keith, Lou Walker
Supplier: Tomorrow Entertainment
Exec Prod: Thomas W Moore;
Prod: Jean Anne Moore;
Dir: Jack Smight;
Wri: Arthur Heinemann, from Mildred D Taylor novels.
180 Mins, Fri (8 pm), Sat (8 pm), Sun (7 pm), June 2-4.
ABC-TV
06/07/78

ROLLERGIRLS
With Terry Kiser, Rhonda Bates, Candy Ann Brown, Joanna Cassidy, Marcy Hanson, Marilyn Tokuda, James Murtaugh, Jed Allan, Clark Burckhalter
Supplier: The James Komack Co
Exec Prod: Komack;
Prods: Stan Cutler, George Tricker, Neil Rosen;
Dir: Burt Brinckerhoff;
Wris: Tricker, Rosen.
30 Mins, Mon, 8 pm.
NBC-TV
05/03/78

ROMEO AND JULIET
With Celia Johnson, John Gielgud, Michael Hordern, Patrick Ryecart, Rebecca Saire, Joseph O'Conor, Anthony Andrews, Laurence Naismith, others
Supplier: BBC-TV & Time-Life TV
Prod: Cedric Messina;
Dir: Alvin Rakoff.
175 Mins, Sun (3), 8:10 pm.
BBC2-TV, Britain
12/13/78F

ROMIE-O AND JULIE-8
With the voices of Greg Swanson, Donna-Ann Cavin, Max Ferguson, Suzette Couture, Nick Nichols, Bill Osler
Exec Prod: Gordon Arnold;
Prods: Patrick Noubert, Michael Hirsh;
Dir: Clive Smith;
Wris: Ken Sobol, Elaine Pope.
30 Mins, Sun, 8 pm.
CBC, from Toronto, Canada
04/04/79S

ROOTS
With Edward Asner, O J Simpson, Ralph Waite, Maya Angelou, Ji-Tu Cumbuka, Moses Gunn, Thalmus Rasulala, Harry Rhodes, William Watson, Ren Woods, LeVar Burton, Cicely Tyson, others
Supplier: David L Wolper Prods
Exec Prod: Wolper;
Prod: Stan Margulies;
Dir: David Greene;
Wris: William Blinn, Ernest Kinoy, from book by Alex Haley.
120 Mins, Sun (23), 9 pm.
ABC-TV
01/26/77

ROOTS: THE NEXT GENERATIONS - PART 1
(ABC Novel For Television)
With Georg Stanford Brown, Olivia de Havilland, Henry Fonda, Paul Koslo, Avon Long, Lynne Moody, Greg Morris, Marc Singer, Richard Thomas, Fay Hauser, Brian Mitchell, Debbi Morgan, Kathleen Doyle, Ja'net Dubois, Lou Frizzell, Don Keefer, Cynthia Sye, Royce Wallace, others
Supplier: David L Wolper Prods & Warner Bros TV
Exec Prod: Wolper;
Prod: Stan Margulies;
Dir: John Erman;
Wri: Ernest Kinoy, based on Alex Haley books.
120 Mins, Sun (18), 8 pm.
ABC-TV
02/21/79

THE ROPERS
With Norman Fell, Audra Lindley, Jeffrey Tambor, Patricia McCormack, Evan Cohen
Supplier: NRW Company-T T C Prods
Exec Prods: Don Nicholl, Michael Ross, Bernie West;
Prod: George Sunga;
Dir: Dave Powers;
Wris: Johnnie Mortimer, Brian Cooke.
30 Mins, Tues (13), 9:30 pm.
ABC-TV
03/21/79

ROSETTI & RYAN
(NBC World Premiere Movie)
With Tony Roberts, Squire Fridell, Jane Elliot, Bill Dana, Patty Duke Astin, Susan Anspach, Al Molinaro, William Marshall
Supplier: Heyday Prods, Universal TV
Exec Prod: Leonard B Stern;
Prod: Jerry Davis;
Dir: John Astin;
Wris: Sam Rolfe, Don M Mankiewicz, Gordon Cotler.
120 Mins, Mon (23), 9 pm.
NBC-TV
05/25/77

ROSETTI & RYAN
With Tony Roberts, Squire Fridell, Jane Elliot, Julie Cobb, Robert Hogan, Dana Baker, Margaret Impert, John Fink, Dick O'Neill, Randi Oakes, Penny Santon, Ruth Manning, John Wyler, Lew Brown
Supplier: Heyday Prods & Universal TV
Exec Prod: Leonard B Stern;
Prod: Jerry Davis;
Dir: Alex March;
Wris: Richard Bluel, Pat Fielder.
60 Mins, Thurs, 10 pm.
NBC-TV
09/28/77

ROUGH JUSTICE
(Mutual Consent)
With Clive Francis, Wendy Allnutt, Leon Sinden, Joy Harington, Don Fellows, others
Supplier: BBC-TV
Prod: Morris Barry;
Dir: David Askey;
Wri: Ian Curteis.
50 Mins, Fri, 9:25 pm.
BBC, London, England
08/17/77F

ROYCE
With Robert Forster, Marybeth Hurt, Moosie Drier, Terry Lynn Wood
Supplier: MTM Enterprises
Exec Prod: Jim Byrnes;
Prod: William T Phillips;
Dir: Andrew V McLaglen;
Wri: Byrnes.
60 Mins, Fri (21), 8 pm.
CBS-TV
05/26/76

RUBENS, PAINTER AND DIPLOMAT
With John Leysen, Ingrid De Vos, Nele Van den Dreissche, Dora Van der Groen, Tine Balder, Henk Van Ulsen, Hugo Van den Berghe, Domien De Gruyter, Ann Petersen
Prod: Jan Van Raemdonck;
Dir: Roland Verhavert;
Wri: Hugo Claus.
Five 52 minute segments
BRT, Brussels, Belgium
10/19/77F

RUBY AND OSWALD
With Michael Lerner, Fredric Forrest, Doris Roberts, Lou Frizzell, Bruce French, Sandy McPeak, Lanna Saunders, Sandy Ward, James E. Brodhead, Brian Dennehy, Gwynne Gilford, Gordon Jump, Eric Kilpatrick, Walter Mathews, Michael Pataki, Al Ruscio, Jodean Russo, Richard Sanders, Vickery Turner, others
Supplier: Alan Landsburg Prods
Exec Prod: Landsburg;
Prod: Paul Freeman;
Dir: Mel Stuart;
Wris: John McGreevey, Michael McGreevey.
180Mins, Wed (8), 8 pm.
CBS-TV
02/15/78

RUDOLPH'S SHINY NEW YEAR
With Red Skelton (narrator), voices of Frank Gorshin, Morey Amsterdam, Hal Peary, Paul Frees, Billie Richards, Don Messick, Iris Rainer
Supplier: Rankin-Bass Prods
Prods-Dir: Arthur Rankin Jr, Jules Bass;
Wri: Romeo Muller.
60 Mins, Fri (10), 8 pm.
ABC-TV
Parker Bros (Humphrey Browning MacDougall)
12/15/76

RUMPELSTILTSKIN
With Sal Biagini, Rose Mary Tichenor, Allen Koob, Mary Lee Harris, Lynne Goldman, Don Campora
Prod-Dir: Julian Craggs.
75 Mins, Sun 7 pm.
WYES-TV New Orleans
03/29/78

RUN FROM THE MORNING
With Michael Aitkens, Carol Burns, Rod Mullinar, Barbara Stephens, Charles Tingwell, Margo Lee, Bill Kerr, Vincent Gil, Louise Pajo, Ray Barrett, Don Pascoe, Walter Sullivan, others
Supplier: Australian Broadcasting Commission
Exec Prod: Eric Tayler;
Dir: Carl Schultz;
Wri: Peter Yeldham.
30 Mins, Tues, 8 pm.
Channel 2, from Sydney, Australia
09/27/78F

RYAN'S FANCY
With Denis Ryan, Dermot O'Reilly, Fergus O'Byrne, others
Prod-Dir: Jack Kellum.
30 Mins, Fri, 7:30 pm.
CBC, Canada
01/19/77F

THE SACKETTS
With Glenn Ford, Sam Elliott, Tom Selleck, Jeff Osterhage, Gilbert Roland, Mercedes McCambridge, Marcy Hanson, John Vernon, Ana Alicia, Ben Johnson, Wendy Rastatter, Frank Ramirez, Buck Taylor, Gene Evans, Jack Elam, James Gammon, Paul Koslo, Henry Capps, Ramon Chavez
Supplier: Media Prods Inc, wth Shalako Prods
Exec Prods: Douglas Netter, Jim Byrnes;
Prod: Netter;
Dir: Robert Totten;
Wri: Byrnes, based on novels by Louis L'Amour.
240 Mins, Tues-Wed (15-16), 9 pm.
NBC-TV
05/23/79

SALOME
With Nuria Espert, Enric Majo, Conchita Bardem, Enrique Casamitjana, Felipe Pena, Galo Soler, Jose Torrents, others
Supplier: Spanish Television
Dir: Sergio Schaaf;
Wri: Terenci Moix adaptation of the Oscar Wilde play.
60 Mins
TVE, Spain
06/15/77F

SALVAGE
(ABC Movie Special)
With Andy Griffith, Joel Higgins, Trish Stewart, J Jay Saunders, Raleigh Bond, Jacqueline Scott, Peter Brown, Lee De Broux, Richard Eastham, Richard Jaeckel
Supplier: Bennett-Katleman Prods & Columbia Pictures TV
Exec Prods: Harve Bennett, Harris Katleman;
Prod: Norman S Powell, Mike Lloyd Ross;
Dir: Lee Philips;
Wri: Ross.
120 Mins, Sat (20), 9 pm.
ABC-TV
01/24/79

SAM
With Sam (a dog), Mark Harmon, Gary Crosby, Edward Winter, Kristin Nelson, James S Smith, William Boyett, others
Supplier: Mark VII Ltd
Exec Prods: Jack Webb, Paul Donnelly;
Prod: James Doherty;
Dir: Webb;
Wri: John Randolph, Don Noble.
30 Mins, Tues (24), 8 pm.
CBS-TV
06/01/77

SAM
With Mark Harmon, Len Wayland, Virginia Gregg, John Bertwick, Kevin Hearst, Buck Young, Janear Hines, John Milton, Bob Navarro, Viola Harris, John C Colton, Kristi Jill Wood
Supplier: Mark VII Ltd
Exec Prod: Jack Webb;
Prod: Leonard B Kaufman;
Dir: Robert Leeds;
Wri: Robert I Holt.
30 Mins, Tues (14), 8 pm.
CBS-TV
01/22/78

SAMURAI
(ABC Monday Night Movie Double Feature)
With Joe Penny, Dana Elcar, Beulah Quo, James Shigeta, Charles Cioffi, Geoffrey Lewis, Norman Alden, Morgan Brittany, Ralph Manza, Shane Sinutko, Michael Pataki, James McEachin, Randolph Roberts
Supplier: Danny Thomas Prods & Universal TV
Exec Prods: Thomas, Ron Jacobs & Fernando Lamas;
Prod: Allan Balter;
Dir: Lee H Katzin;
Wri: Jerry Ludwig.
90 Mins, Mon (30), 9:30 pm.
ABC-TV
05/09/79

THE SAN PEDRO BEACH BUMS
With Christopher Murney, Stuart Pankin, John Mark Robinson, Christopher DeRose, Darryl McCullough, Louise Hoven, Susan Mullen, Lisa Reeves, Christoff St John, Nancy Morgan, Kate Jackson, Jaclyn Smith, Cheryl Ladd, Herb Edelman, Jenny Sherman
Supplier: Aaron Spelling Prods
Exec Prods: Spelling, Douglas S Cramer;
Prod: Earl Barret;
Dir: Allen Baron;
Wri: Simon Muntner.
60 Mins, Mon, 8 pm.
ABC-TV
09/21/77

SAN PEDRO BUMS
(ABC Friday Night Movie Double Feature)
With Christopher Murney, Jeffry Druce, John Mark Robinson, Stuart Pankin, Darryl McCullough, Bill Lucking, others
Supplier: Aaron Spelling Prod
Exec Prods: Spelling, Douglas S Cramer;
Prod-Wri: E Duke Vincent;
Dir: Barry Shear.
90 Mins, Fri (13), 8 pm.
ABC-TV
05/18/77

SANCTUARY OF FEAR
(NBC Monday Night At The Movies)
With Barnard Hughes, Kay Lenz, Michael McGuire, George Hearn, Robert Schenkkan, David Rasche, Fred Gwynne, Elizabeth Wilson, Peter Maloney, Saul Rubineck, Jeffrey DeMunn, Donald Symington, Maureen Silliman, Alice Drummond
Supplier: Marble Arch Prods
Exec Prod: Martin Starger;
Supv Prods-Wris: Don M Mankiewicz, Gordon Cotler;
Prod: Philip Barry;
Dir: John L Moxey.
120 Mins, Mon (23), 9 pm.
NBC-TV
05/02/79

THE SANDBAGGERS
With Roy Marsden, Ray Lonnen, David Glyder, Diane Keane, others
Supplier: Trident Anglia
Exec Prod: David Gunliffe;
Prod-Dir: Michael Ferguson.
60 Mins, Mon, 9 pm.
Yorkshire-TV, Britain
11/15/78F

SANDOKAN
With Kabir Bedi, Philippe Leroy, Carole Andre, Adolfo Celi, Hans Caninenbeg, others
Supplier: RAI-ORTF-Bavaria Film
Prod: Elio Scardamaglia for Titanus Distribuzione S.p.A.
Dir: Sergio Sollima.
Wris: A. Lucatelli, G. Mangione, A. Silvestri, M. Scarpelli, S. Sollima.
60 Mins, Sun, 8:30 pm.
RAI-TV, First Ch., from Rome, Italy
02/04/76F

SANFORD
With Redd Foxx, Dennis Burkley, Marguerite Ray, Nathaniel Taylor, Suzanne Stone, Cathy Cooper, Percy Rodrigues, Davis Roberts
Supplier: Tandem Prods
Exec Prod: Mort Lachman;
Prods: Sy Rosen, Mel Tolkin, Larry Rhine;
Dir: Jim Drake;
Wris: Rosen, Ted Bergman.
60 Mins, Sat, (15) 9 pm.
NBC-TV
03/19/80

SANFORD ARMS
With Theodore Wilson, LaWanda Page, Tina Andrews, Whitman Mayo, John Earl, Don Bexley, Bebe Drake-Hooks, Norma Miller
Supplier: TOY Prods
Exec Prods: Bud Yorkin, Saul Turteltaub, Bernie Orenstein;
Prod: Woody King;
Dir: Russ Petranto;
Wris: Turteltaub, Orenstein.
30 Mins, Fri, 8 pm.
NBC-TV
09/21/77

SARA
With Brenda Vaccaro, Bert Kramer, Mariclare Costello, Albert Stratton, Louise Latham, William McKinney, Michael Leclair, William Phipps, William Wintersole, Jerry Hardin, Patricia Ganem, Kraig Metzinger, Sylvia Soares, Debbie Lytton
Supplier: Universal TV
Exec Prod: George Eckstein;
Prod: Richard Collins;
Dir: Jud Taylor;
Wri: Michael Gleason, from Marian Cockrell's novel
60 Mins, Fri, 8 pm.
CBS-TV
02/18/76

SATURDAY NIGHT LIVE
With Elliott Gould (guest host), Denny Dillon, Gilbert Gottfried, Gail Matthius, Joe Piscopo, Ann Risley, Charles Rocket, Kid Creole & The Coconuts
Supplier: NBC Entertainment
Prod: Jean Doumanian;
Dir: Dave Wilson;
Wris: Larry Arnstein & David Hurwitz, Barry Blaustein, Billy Brown & Mel Green, Ferris Butler, John DeBellis, Leslie Fuller, Sean Kelly, Mitchell Kriegman, Doug McGrath, Pamela Norris, Terrence Sweeney.
90 Mins, Sat, 11:30 pm.
NBC-TV
11/19/80

SATURDAY, SUNDAY, MONDAY
With Anne Jackson, Eli Wallach, Jean Gascon, Saul Rubinek, Susan Fletcher, Pam Hyatt, Paul Soles, Ed McNamara
Prod: Henry Tarvainen;
Dir: George Bloomfield;
Wri: Eduardo DeFillipo.
90 Mins, Wed, 9 pm.
CBC-TV, from Toronto, Canada
12/29/76F

SATURDAY'S HEROES
(Ha'way The Lads)
With John Bowler, others
Supplier: Thames Television
Exec Prod: Jolyon Wimhurst;
Prod-Dir: Frank Cvitanovich;
60 Mins, Wed, 9 pm.
ITV Network, Britain
10/27/76F

SCAPINO
With Jim Dale, Joel Grey (host)
Supplier: Post-Newsweek Prods
Prods: Ray Hubbard, Richard Pack;
Dir: Michael Redington.
90 Mins, Sun (12), 7 pm.
WTOP-TV, Washington, D C
12/15/76

SCARED STRAIGHT! ANOTHER STORY
With Cliff DeYoung, Stan Shaw, Terri Nunn, Randy Brooks, Tony Burton, Nathan Cook, Linden Chiles, Don Fullilove, Eric Laneuville, Bill Sanderson, John Hammond, Michael Fairman, S. John Launer, Bebe Drake-Massey, Jean Demter Barton, Al White
Supplier: Golden West TV
Exec Prod: John T. Reynolds;
Prod: Arnold Shapiro;
Dir: Richard Michaels;
Wri: T.S. Cook.
120 Mins, Thurs, (6) 8 pm.
CBS-TV
11/12/80

THE SCARLET LETTER
With Meg Foster, John Heard, Kevin Conway, Danielle Hoebeke, Jessica Ruth Olin, Elisa Erali, Josef Sommer, Penny Allen, George Martin, C K Alexander
Supplier: WGBH-TV Boston
Exec Prod: Herbert Hirschman;
Prod-Dir: Rick Hauser;
Wris: Allan Knee, Alvin Sapinsley, from Nathaniel Hawthorne's novel
240 Mins, Mon-Thurs (2-5), 9 pm.
PBS
04/11/79

SCHOOL PLAY
With Denholm Elliott, Jeremy Kemp, Tim Pigott-Smith, Jenny Agutter, John Normington, Michael Kitchen, Richard Warwick, Jeremy Clyde, Richard Morant.
Supplier: BBC-TV
Prod: Richard Broke;
Dir: James Cellan Jones;
Wri: Frederic Raphael.
80 Mins, Wed (7), 9:35 pm.
BBC2, England
11/14/79F

SCHOOL'S OUT 'FOREVER'
With Melissa Forsythe (narrator)
Prod-Wri: Randy Covington.
60 Mins, Tues, 8 pm.
WAVE-TV Louisville
07/12/78

SCOTCH AND WRY
With Rikki Fulton, Claire Nielson, David Hayman, John Bett, Margo Cunningham, Barbara Dickson & Her Band
Supplier: BBC Scotland
Prod: Gordon Menzies;
Wris: John Byrne, Robert Sykes Andrews, Chris Miller, Tom Magee-Englefield, Rikki Fulton, Maggie Allen.
30 Mins, Sat 10:30 pm.
BBC TV Scotland
10/18/78F

SCOTT FREE
With Michael Brandon, Susan Saint James, Robert Loggia, Ken Swofford, Michael Lerner, Dehl Berti, others
Supplier: U-TV & Cherokee Prods
Exec Prods: Stephen Cannell, Meta Rosenberg;
Prod: Alex Beaton;
Dir: William Wiard;
Wri: Cannell.
90 Mins, Wed (13), 8:30 pm.
NBC-TV
10/20/76

SEATTLE TONIGHT-TONITE
With Ross McGowan, others
Prod: John Tyers.
30 Mins, Mon to Fri, 7 pm.
KING-TV Seattle
10/27/76

SEATTLE TONIGHT TONITE
With Dick Klinger, others
Prod: Ron Lorentzen;
Dir: Mike Beck.
30 Mins, 7 pm.
KING-TV Seattle
03/01/78

SECOND ANNUAL COMEDY AWARDS
With Alan King, Steve Allen, Sid Caesar, Imogene Coca, Professor Irwin Corey, Bill Dana, Bob Hope, Howard Morris, Louis Nye, Tom Poston, Carl Reiner, Bobby Van, Ben Vereen, James Whitmore
Supplier: King-Hitzig Productions
Exec Prods: Alan King, Rupert Hitzig, Herb Sargent;
Prod: Rita Scott;
Dir: John Moffitt;
Wris: Harry Crane, George Bloom, Mike Barrie, Jim Mulholland, Bill Dana, King.
90 Mins, Sat (10), 10 pm.
ABC-TV
04/14/76

THE SECOND BARRY MANILOW SPECIAL
With Ray Charles, Adrienne Anderson
Supplier: Kamikazi Music Corp & Ernest Chambers Prods
Exec Prod: Miles J Lourie;
Prods-Wris: Chambers, Manilow;
Dir: George Schaefer.
60 Mins, Fri (24), 8 pm.
ABC-TV
Dr. Pepper (Y & R)
03/01/78

SECOND CHANCE
With Jim Peck (host), Joe Seiter
Supplier: Carruthers Co & Warner Bros TV
Exec Prod: Bill Carruthers;
Prod: Joel Stein;
Dir: Chris Darley;
Wris: Jan McCormack, Bill Mitchell, Ray Reese.
30 Mins, Mon-Fri, Noon
ABC-TV
03/16/77

SECOND CITY
With Andrea Martin, John Candy, Joe Flaherty, Eugene Levy, Catherine O'Hara, Dave Thomas, Harold Ramis
Exec Prods: Bernard Sablins, Andrew Alexander;
Prod: Milad Bessada;
Dir: George Bloomfield;
Wris: The entire cast.
30 Mins, Mon, 9 pm.
Global TV, from Toronto, Canada
10/19/77F

SECOND CITY TV
With John Candy, Joe Flaherty, Eugene Levy, Andrea Martin, Catherine O'Hara, Harold Ramis, Dave Thomas
Supplier: Rhodes Prods
Exec Prods: Andrew Alexander, Jack E Rhodes, Bernard Sahlins;
Dirs: George Bloomfield, Milad Bessada;
Wris: Brian Doyle-Murray, Sheldon Patinkin.
60 Mins, Sat (27), 7 pm.
KHJ-TV Los Angeles
08/31/77S

SECOND HOUSE
(A Common Tongue)
With Melvyn Bragg (host), Edwin Newman, Norman Podhoretz, Tom Wolfe, Smokey Robinson
Supplier: BBC-TV
Prod-Wri: Tony Cash.
60 Mins, Sat (10), 9 pm.
BBC-2, Britain
01/28/76F

SECOND RATE INTERSTATE
Narrated by Dan Cullen
Prod-Wri: Randy Covington.
30 Mins, Mon, 7 pm.
WAVE-TV Louisville
03/14/79

THE SECOND TIME AROUND
With Ed Winter, Mariette Hartley, Simone Griffeth, Jim Staahl, Brad Savage, Mary Jo Catlett, Harry Sutton, Mary Betten
Supplier: Jerry Tokofsky Prods & 20th-Fox TV
Exec Prod: Tokofsky;
Prod-Wri: Elliot Shoenman;
Dir: Robert Drivas.
30 Mins, Tues (24), 10:30 pm.
ABC-TV
08/01/79

SECRET ARMY
(Second Chance)
With Bernard Hepton, Jan Francis, Christopher Neame, Angela Richards, Paul Copley, others
Supplier: BBC
Prod: Gerard Glaister;
Dir: Paul Annett;
Wri: James Andrew Hall.
55 Mins, Wed, 8:05 pm.
BBC-1, from London, England
10/19/77F

THE SECRET EMPIRE - (Chapter 3) (CLIFFHANGERS)
With Geoffrey Scott, Carlene Watkins, Tiger Williams, Pamela Brull, Diane Markoff
Supplier: Universal TV
Exec Prod-Dir-Wri: Kenneth Johnson;
Prod: Richard Milton
60 Min, Tues, 8 pm.
NBC-TV
03/07/79

THE SECRET HOSPITAL
Supplier: Yorkshire TV (U K)
Exec Prods: John Fairley, Michael Deakin;
Prod-Dir: John Willis.
102 Mins.
(Screened in competition at Prix Italia)
10/03/79PI

THE SECRET LIFE OF JOHN CHAPMAN
(GE Theatre)
With Ralph Waite, Susan Anspach, Brad Davis, Elayne Heilveil, Pat Hingle, Maury Cooper, Gardner Hayes, Bill Tredwell, Curtis Jackson, others
Supplier: The Jozak Co
Exec Prod: Gerald I Isenberg;
Prod: Gerald W Abrams;
Dir: David Lowell Rich;
Wri: Albert Ruben, from John R Coleman book.
90 Mins, Mon (27), 9:30 pm.
CBS-TV
General Electric (JWT)
12/29/76

SECRETS OF MIDLAND HEIGHTS
With Bibi Besch, Jordan Christopher, Robert Hogan, Mark Pinter, Lorenzo Lamas, Doran Clark, Linda Grovenor, Linda Hamilton, Jim Youngs, Daniel Zippi, Stephen Manley, Melora Hardin, Martha Scott.
Supplier: Roundelay-MF Prodns & Lorimar Prodns
Exec Prods: Lee Rich, Michael Filerman, David Jacobs;
Prod: Joseph B Wallenstein;
Dir: Robert Lewis;
Wri: Jacobs.
60 Mins, Sat, 10 pm.
CBS-TV
12/10/80

SEER WAS HERE
With Saul Rubinek
Exec Prod: Ralph Thomas;
Prod: Anne Frank;
Dir: Claude Jutra;
Wri: Don Bailey.
60 Mins, Sun, 9 pm.
CBC, from Toronto, Canada
12/13/78F

SELF TO SELF
With Alexandra Self (host)
Supplier: Self To Self Interviews
Prod: Self;
Dir: Arnie Nocks.
30 Mins, Thurs (27), 10 am.
WNEW-TV New York
08/23/78S

THE SELKIRK ILLUSION
With Mary Robin Roth, Tom Straffey, Dennis Cushing, Armande Auger, Buzz Fawcett, Tom Joyal, Bill Herbert, Pat Auger, Steve Doyle, Dan Gabriel, others
Prod-Dir: Len De Panicis.
Wri: Jean Torkelson.
60 Mins, Mon (13), 7 pm.
KMSP-TV Minneapolis-St Paul
09/29/76

SEMI-TOUGH
With Bruce McGill, David Hasselhoff, Markie Post, Hugh Gillin, Mary Jo Catlett, Jim McKrell, Joe Bennett, Ed Peck, Bubba Smith, Freeman King, Carlos Brown
Supplier: Universal TV
Exec Prod: David Merrick;
Supv Prod: Jerry Davis;
Dir: Richard Benjamin;
Wris: Wally Dalton & Shelley Zellman, Reinhold Weege.
30 Mins, Thurs, 9:30 pm.
ABC-TV
06/04/80

SEMI-TOUGH
With Josh Taylor, Mary Louise Weller, Douglas Barr, Hugh Gillin, Dennis Holahan, Sandy Helberg, Sandy Kenyon, Pamela Bryant, Ed Peck, Bubba Smith, Paul Wilson, Freeman King, Pieter Jan Van Niel, Don Boyt, Arthur Kasarjian, Francine Cornfield
Supplier: Universal TV
Exec Prod: David Merrick;
Prod: Bud Wiser;
Dir: Bill Persky;
Wris: Jim Fritzell & Everett Greenbaum.
30 Mins, Sun, (6), 10:30 pm.
ABC-TV
01/16/80

MIND OVER MEDICINE
With Dave Moore, Norman Cousins, D. Norman Shealy, others
Prod-Wri: James Hayden;
Edtr: Mark Falstad.
60 Mins, Mon, (23) 9 pm.
WCCO-TV, Minneapolis
07/02/80

THE SENTIMENTAL BLOKE
With Graeme Blundell, Jimmy Hannan, Geraldine Turner, Nancye Hayes, Jon Finlayson, Joy Westmore, David Ravenswood, Anne Phelan
Supplier: Australian Broadcasting Commission
Exec Prod: Michael Shrimpton;
Dir: Alan Burke;
Wri: Adapted by Alan Burke for musical by Albert Arlen (music), Nancy Brown and Lloyd Thomson (book and lyrics).
90 Mins, Wed (8), 8:30 pm.
ABC, from Melbourne, Australia
07/14/76F

SEPARATION
With Emile Genest, Paul Hecht, Alexandra Stewart, Robert Rivard, Monique LePage, Sabine Maydelle, Barry Morse
Exec Prod: Gerard Rochon;
Prod: Rochon, Chris Dalton;
Dir: George McGowan;
Wri: Sandy Stern, from the novel by Richard Rohmer.
120 Mins, Wed, 9 pm.
CFTO-TV, Toronto, Canada
04/05/78F

SGT T K YU
With Johnny Yune, John Lehne, Martin Brill, Floyd Levine, Steve Eastin, Monica Gayle, Harold Gould, John Colicos, Tim Thomerson, Char Fontane, Barbara Sammeth, Mike Mazurki, Bruce Glover
Supplier: Hanna-Barbera Prods
Exec Prod: Joseph Barbera;
Prod: Terry Morse Jr;
Dir: Paul Stanley;
Wri: Gordon Dawson.
60 Mins, Thurs (19), 10 pm.
NBC-TV
04/25/79

SERPICO
With David Birney, Tom Atkins, Billy Green Bush, Harry Davis, Gary Baker, Barra Grant, others
Supplier: Emmet Lavery Jr Prods - Paramount TV
Exec Prod: Lavery;
Prod: Don Ingalls;
Dir: Reza Badiyi;
Wri: Robert Dellinger.
60 Mins, Fri, 10 pm.
NBC-TV
09/29/76

7:30 LIVE
With Frank Getlein, Chris Curle
Exec Prod: Adam Valone;
Dir: Ed Moore.
30 Mins, Weekdays, 7:30 pm.
WMAL-TV Washington
10/13/76

7:30 MAGAZINE
With Bill O'Reilly, host
Supplier: WCBS-TV
Exec Prod: Jim Dauphinee;
Prods: Shiela Bowe, Mark Smith, Marc Wallace.
30 Mins, Wed, 7:30
WCBS-TV New York
09/17/80

SEVENTH AVENUE
(Best Sellers)
With Steven Keats, Dori Brenner, Kristoffer Tabori, Jane Seymour, Anne Archer, Ray Milland, Alan King, Richard Dimitri, John Pleshette, William Windom, Herschel Bernardi, Jack Gilford, Eli Wallach, Ellen Greene, Leora Dana, Robert Symonds
Supplier: Universal TV
Exec Prod: Franklin Barton
Prod-Dir: Richard Irving
Wri: Laurence Heath
120 Mins, Thurs, 9 pm.
NBC-TV
02/16/77

THE SEVENTH SENSE
With Jim Peck, host; Elroy Schwartz
Supplier: Filmways TV Prods (Rhodes Prods)
Exec Prod: Perry Lafferty;
Prod: Schwartz;
Dir: Tom Trbovich.
30 Mins, Sun (27), 9 pm.
WNEW-TV New York
08/30/78S

79 PARK AVENUE
With Lesley Ann Warren, Marc Singer, David Dukes, Michael Constantine, Albert Salmi, Jack Weston, Barbara Barrie, Polly Bergen, John Saxon, Raymond Burr, Lloyd Haynes, Peter Marshall, Jane Marla Robbins, Sandy Helberg, Matthew Laborteaux, Margaret Fairchild
Supplier: Universal TV, Harold Robbins International Co
Exec Prod: George Eckstein;
Prod-Dir: Paul Wendkos;
Wris: Richard DeRoy (Part I), Jack Guss (Part II), Lionel Siegel (Part III).
120 Mins, Sun (16), 9 pm (Part I)
NBC-TV
10/19/77

SEX NEXT DOOR
With Frank Greif, Roger Forbes, Seth Fulcher
Prod-Host: Greif.
30 Mins, Mon, 7:30 pm.
KOMO-TV Seattle
04/07/76

THE SEX ROLE DEBATE
With Tom Ellis
Exec Prod: Alan L Cohen;
Prod: Gene Marciona.
30 Mins, Thurs, 10 pm.
WABC-TV New York
08/18/76

SHA NA NA
With Rita Moreno, Pamela Myers
Supplier: Pierre Cossette Prods (Lexington Syndication Service)
Exec Prod: Cossette;
Prod-Wris: Bernard Rothman, Jack Wohl;
Dir: Tom Trbovich.
30 Mins, Tues (11), 7:30 pm.
WABC-TV New York
Procter & Gamble (Gray)
01/19/77S

SHA NA NA
With Bernadette Peters, Avery Schreiber, Kenneth Mars, Phil Roth, Jane Dulo, Pam Myers
Supplier: Pierre Cossette Co (Lexington Broadcast Services)
Exec Prod: Cossette;
Prods: Bernard Rothman, Jack Wohl;
Dir: Walter Miller;
Wris: Bob Arnott, Aubrey Tadman, Garry Ferrier, Rothman, Wohl.
30 Mins, Tues, 7:30 pm.
WNBC-TV New York
Procter & Gamble (Grey Advtg)
09/28/77S

SHARK KILL
(NBC Double Feature Night At the Movies)
With Richard Yniguez, Phillip Clark, Jennifer Warren, Elizabeth Gill, Victor Campos, David Huddleston, Carmen Zapata, Jimmie B. Smith, Roxanna Bonilla-Giannini, Richard Foronjy
Supplier: D'Antoni-Weitz TV Prods.
Exec Prods: Philip D'Antoni, Barry Weitz;
Prod: Weitz;
Dir: William A. Graham;
Wri: Sandor Stern.
90 Mins, Thurs (20), 8 pm.
NBC-TV
05/26/76

S.H.E.
(CBS Saturday Night Movies)
With Omar Sharif, Cornelia Sharpe, Robert Lansing, William Traylor, Isabella Rye, Tom Christopher, Anita Ekberg, Fabio Testi, Mario Colli, Claudio Ruffini, Geoffrey Copplestone
Supplier: Martin Bregman Prods.
Prod: Bregman;
Dir: Robert Lewis;
Wri: Richard Maibaum.
120 Mins, Sat, (23), 9 pm.
CBS-TV
02/27/80

SHEILA
With Dori Brenner, Milton Berle, Barbara Trentham, George Wyner, Larry Breeding, Phillip R Allen
Supplier: Paramount TV
Exec Prod: Gail Parent;
Prod: Martin Cohan;
Dir: Peter Bonerz;
Wris: Parent, Kenny Solms, Andrew Smith.
30 Mins, Mon (29), 9:30 pm.
CBS-TV
09/07/77

SHE'LL BE SWEET
With Tony Lo Bianco, Sally Kellerman, Anne Semler, Rod Mullinar, Kevin Leslie, Jacqueline Kott, Ken Fraser, Vincent Gil, Kenneth Laird, Peter Collingwood, Gareth Wilding-Forbes, Peter Snook, Revelly Jones, Aileen Britton, David Bracks, Kay Yates, Richard Gilbert, Alex Macintosh
Supplier: Australian Broadcasting Commission, Trans-Atlantic Enterprises
Exec Prods: Robert Kline, Preston Fischer, James Davern;
Prod: Geoffrey Daniels;
Dir: Gene Levitt;
Wri: Colin Free.
990 Mins, Sun, 8:30 pm.
ABC (Australia)
01/24/79F

SHIELDS & YARNELL
With Robert Shields, Lorene Yarnell, Ted Zeigler, Joanna Cassidy, Joe Baker, Fayard Nicholas
Supplier: Steve Binder Prods, Get the Hook Prods & Yongestreet Entertainment Corp
Exec Prod-Dir: Binder;
Prods: Frank Peppiatt, John Aylesworth;
Wris: Barry Adelman, Aylesworth, Peppiatt, Don Sandburg, Barry Silver, Shields.
30 Mins, Mon, 8:30 pm.
CBS-TV
06/15/77

SHIELDS & YARNELL
With Robert Shields, Lorene Yarnell, Gaillard Sartain, Bob Gardiner
Supplier: Steve Binder Prods, Get The Hook Prods, Yongestreet Entertainment
Exec Prod-Dir: Binder;
Prods: Frank Peppiatt, John Aylesworth;
Wris: Jim Millaway, Sartain, Peppiatt, Aylesworth, Shields.
30 Mins, Tues, 8:30 pm.
CBS-TV
02/08/78

SHIMMERING LIGHT
With Beau Bridges, Lloyd Bridges, Victoria Shaw, John Meillon, Ingrid Mason, Wendy Playfair, Mark Hembrow, Tim Simpson, Nicholas Frazer, Bobby Bettles, Mark Edwards, Patrick Ward
Supplier: Australian Broadcasting Commission & Trans-Atlantic Enterprises
Exec Prod: Robert Kline, Preston Fischer;
Prod: Frank Arnold;
Dir: Don Chaffey;
Wris: George Kirgo, Paul Savage.
80 Mins, Tues, 8 pm.
Channel 2, from Sydney, Australia
12/20/78F

SHIPSHAPE
With Deborah Ryan, Andrew Bloch, Lorenzo Lamas, Demetre Phillips, Gary Veney, Earl Boen, Shell Kepler, Ted Hartley, Kristin Larkin
Supplier: James Komack Co
Exec Prod: Komack;
Prods: Al Gordon & Jack Mendelsohn;
Dirs: Komack, Gary Shimokawa;
Wris: George Tricker & Neil Rosen, Stan Cutler, Gary Belkin.
30 Mins, Tues (1), 8 pm.
CBS-TV
08/09/78

SHIRIN'S HOCHZEIT
(Shirin's Wedding)
With Ayten Erten, Juergen Prochnow
Supplier: Westdeutsches Fernesehen, Cologne;
Prod: Westdeutsches Fernsehen, Cologne;
Dir-Wri: Helma Sanders.
120 Mins, Sat, (28), 8:15 pm.
WDR, from Cologne, West Germany
03/10/76F

SHIRLEY
With Shirley Jones, Patrick Wayne, Peter Barton, Rosanna Arquette, Bret Shryer, Tracey Gold, John McIntire, Ann Doran, Cindy Eilbacher, Pat Corley, Louis Guss, Greenleaf & Horn, Jack Knight
Supplier: Ten Four Prods & Universal TV
Exec Prods: Greg Strangis, William Hogan;
Prods: Bob Birnbaum, Gwen Bagni, Paul Dubov;
Dir: Stan Lathan;
Wris: Strangis, Bagni, Dubov.
60 Mins, Fri, 8 pm.
NBC-TV
P&G
10/31/79

SHIRLEY MacLAINE..."EVERY LITTLE MOVEMENT"
With Kurt Thomas, Dean Martin, Alan Johnson Dancers
Supplier: MacLaine Enterprises & Smith-Hemion Prods
Prods: Gary Smith, Dwight Hemion;
Dir: Hemion;
Wri: Buz Kohan.
60 Mins, Thurs, (22) 10 pm.
CBS-TV
Sentry Insurance (Grey Advtg)
05/28/80

SHOGUN-PART ONE
(NBC Monday Night At The Movies)
With Richard Chamberlain, Toshiro Mifune, Yoko Shimada, Frankie Sakai, Alan Badel, Michael Hordern, Damien Thomas, John Rhys-Davies, Vladek Sheybal, George Innes, Leon Lissek, Yuki Meguro, Nobuo Kanedo, Edward Peel, Eric Richard, Stewart MacKenzie, Orson Wells (narr)
Supplier: Paramount TV
Exec Prod: James Clavell;
Prod: Eric Bercovici;
Dir: Jerry London;
Wri: Bercovici, adapted from Clavell's novel.
180 Mins, Mon, (15) 8 pm.
NBC-TV
09/17/80

SHOOT FOR THE STARS
With Geoff Edwards (host), Anne Meara, Soupy Sales, Bob Clayton
Supplier: Bob Stewart Prods
Exec Prod: Stewart;
Prod: Bruce Burmester;
Dir: Mike Gargiulo.
30 Mins, Mon-Fri, 11:30 am.
NBC-TV
01/12/77

THE SHOOTING OF BIG MAN: ANATOMY OF A CRIMINAL CASE
(ABC News Closeup)
With Tim O'Brien
Supplier: ABC News, Evidence Films
Exec Prod: Pamela Hill;
Prods: Tom Bywaters, Eric F Saltzman;
Wris: Bywaters, Saltzman, Christopher Isham, O'Brien, Richard Richter.
120 Mins, Fri (8), 9 pm.
ABC-TV
06/13/79

SHOWDOWN OF THE DREAM TEAMS
With Gary Owens (host), Phyllis Diller, Marty Allen, Della Reese, Barbara Rhoades, Joe Morgan, William Christopher, Johnny Rutherford, Cathy Rigby, Tommy John, Lyle Waggoner, Bill Daily, Jay Stewart
Supplier: Alan P. Sloan Inc (Syndicast)
Exec Prod: Sloan;
Prod: George Vosburgh;
Dir: Arthur Forrest;
Wri: E Jack Kaplan.
30 Mins, Wed, 7:30 pm.
WABC-TV New York
Warner Lambert
02/08/78S

SIDE BY SIDE
With Stubby Kaye, Barbara Luna, Janie Sell, Luis Avalos, Keith Charles, Peggy Pope, Don Scardino, Diane Stilwell
Supplier: CBS-TV
Prod: Darryl Hickman;
Dir: H. Wesley Kenney;
Wri: Robert Kimmel Smith.
30 Mins, Tues (27), 9:30 pm.
CBS-TV
08/04/76

SIEGFRIED & ROY, SUPERSTARS OF MAGIC
With Lido de Paris Revue, Eddie Albert, Loni Anderson, Lola Falana
Supplier: Ringling Bros. and Barnum & Bailey Circus Prods.
Exec Prods: Irvin & Kenneth Feld;
Prods: Frank Brill, Art Fisher;
Dir: Fisher;
Wris: Mort Scharfman, Harvey Weitzman.
60 Mins, Fri, (1) 10 pm.
NBC-TV
02/06/80

SIGHT & SOUND
Supplier: WNBC-TV Public Affairs Dept
Exec Prod: Albert Waller;
Prod: Marc Brugnoni.
30 Mins, Sat, 7 pm.
WNBC-TV New York
10/06/76

SIGNS OF SILENCE
With Father Robert Jordon
Prod: Art Garland.
15 Mins, Sun, 7:30 am.
WRGB-TV Schenectady, N Y
04/13/77S

THE SILENT CRY
With Michelle Fawdon, Edmund Pegge, Anne Haddy, Annette Andre, Robert Alexander, Jennifer Claire, Ken Lawrence, Samantha Cox, Peter Blakeman, Gabrielle Schornegg, Lisa Isaaca, Len Kaserman, Kevin Manser, Nicholas Lidstone
Supplier: Australian Broadcasting Commission
Prod: Sandra Levy;
Dir: Michael Carson;
Wri: Marion Ord
50 Mins, Wed, 8:30 pm.
ABC (Australia) TV, Channel 2, Sydney
09/24/80F

SILLS & BURNETT AT THE MET
(Sentry Collection)
With Carol Burnett, Beverly Sills, Ernest Flatt Dancers, Paul Newley
Supplier: Jocar Prods
Prod: Joe Hamilton;
Dir: Dave Powers;
Wris: Ken & Mitzie Welch, Gail Parent & Kenny Solms.
60 Mins, Thurs (25), 10 pm.
CBS-TV
Sentry Ins (Grey)
12/01/76

SIMON TOWNSEND'S WONDER WORLD
With Simon Townsend, Jonathan Coleman, Hugh Piper, Sandra Mauger, Angela Catterns
Supplier: Townsend Entertainments Pty Ltd
Prod: Harvey Shore;
Wris: Cathie Maloney, Patricia Silverman.
30 Mins, weekdays, 4 pm.
Channel TEN10, Sydney, Australia
09/24/80F

SINATRA & FRIENDS
With Frank Sinatra, Tony Bennett, Natalie Cole, John Denver, Loretta Lynn, Dean Martin, Robert Merrill, Leslie Uggams, Nelson Riddle orch
Supplier: Paul W Keyes Prods
Prod: Keyes;
Dir: Bill Davis;
Wris: Keyes, Marc London.
60 Mins, Thurs (21), 10 pm.
ABC-TV
Sears (Foote, Cone & Belding)
04/27/77

SING COUNTRY
With Carl Perkins, Vernon Oxford, Dottie West, Kenny Rogers, Joe Eley & Band, Charlie McCoy
Supplier: BBC Television
Prod: Douglas Hespe;
Dir: Rick Gardner.
40 Mins, Tues, 9 pm.
BBC-2, from London, England
07/12/78F

SIROTA'S COURT
With Michael Constantine, Cynthia Harris, Kathleen Miller, Ted Ross, Fred Willard, Owen Bush, Victor Buono, Philip M. Thomas, Mickey Fox, Andrew Johnson
Supplier: Peter Engel Prods & Universal TV
Prods: Harvey Miller, Peter H. Engel;
Dir: Mel Ferber;
Wri: Jack Winter.
30 Mins, Wed, 9 pm.
NBC-TV
12/08/76

SITCOM: THE ADVENTURES OF GARRY MARSHALL
With Gary Marshall, others
Supplier: Television City Prods
Exec Prod: Nick DeMartino;
Prods: Megan Williams, Wendy Apple;
Dir: Apple.
30 Mins, Wed (3), 10:30 pm.
PBS
10/10/79

THE SIX O'CLOCK FOLLIES
With A.C. Weary, Larry Fishburne, Philip Charles MacKenzie, Randall Carver, Jody Baker, David Hubbard, George Kee Cheung, Aarika Wells, Phil Hartman, James B. Douglas, Howard Witt
Supplier: P.S. 235 Prods., Ella Prods & Warner Bros. TV
Prod-Wris: Norman Steinberg, Marvin Kupfer;
Dir: Robert Sweeney.
60 Mins, Thurs, (24) 9 pm.
NBC-TV
04/30/80

SKAG
With Karl Malden, Piper Laurie, Craig Wasson, George Voskovec, Kathryn Holcomb, Peter Gallagher, Leslie Ackerman, Powers Boothe, M. Emmet Walsh, Tom Atkins, Charles Hallahan, Juanin Clay, Gwen Humble, Bert Freed
Suppliers: Abby Mann Prods. & Milcar Prods, & Lorimar Prods.
Exec Prods: Mann, Lee Rich;
Supv Prod: Douglas Benton;
Prod: Brad Dexter;
Dir: Frank Perry;
Wri: Mann.
180 Mins, Sun, (6), 8 PM.
NBC-TV
01/16/80

SKYWARD
With Bette Davis, Howard Hesseman, Suzy Gilstrap, Ben Marley, Clu Gulager, Marion Ross, Lisa Whelchel
Supplier: Major H-Anson Prods
Exec Prods: Ron Howard, Anson Williams;
Prod: John Kuri;
Dir: Howard;
Wri: Nancy Sackett.
120 Mins, Thurs, (20) 9 pm.
NBC-TV
General Electric (BBDO)
11/26/80

SKYWAYS
With Bruce Barry, Bartholomew John, Ken James, Deborah Coulls, Judy Morris, Brian James, Tony Bonner, Tina Bursill, Carmen Dunca, Bill Stalker, Kris McQuade, Joanne Samuel, Irene Inescourt, Ronald Falk, Charles Tingwell, Beverley Blankenship
Supplier: Crawford Productions Ltd
Exec Prods: Ian Crawford, Jock Blair;
Prod: Graham Moore;
Dirs: Crawford, David Charles;
Wris: Terry Stapleton, Edward Roche.
50 Mins, Mon & Thurs, 9:30 pm.
Channel 7 Network, Sydney, Melbourne, Adelaide, Australia
08/01/79F

SNAVELY
(ABC Saturday Comedy Special)
With Harvey Korman, Betty White, Frank LaLoggia, Ivor Francis, Deborah Zon, Jack Dodson, George Pentecost
Supplier: Strathmore Prods, with Viacom Enterprises
Prods-Wris: Roland Kibbee, Dean Hargrove;
Dir: Hal Cooper.
30 Mins, Sat (24), 8:30 pm.
ABC-TV
06/28/78

SNEAK PREVIEWS
With Roger Ebert, Gene Siskel
Prod: Thea Flaum;
Dir: Patterson Denny.
30 Mins Thurs (16), 8 pm.
WTTW Chicago for PBS
10/25/78

SNEAK PREVIEWS/TAKE 2
With Gene Siskel, Roger Ebert
Exec Prod: Thea Flaum;
Prod: Ray Solley;
Dir: Rudi Goldman.
30 Mins, Thurs (1), 9 pm.
WTTW-TV (Chicago) for PBS
11/14/79

SO THE STORY GOES
With Austin Willis
Prod: Nancy McLean;
Dir: Barry McLean;
Wri: William Whitehead.
30 Mins, Sat, 8:30 pm.
CHCH-TV, from Toronto, Canada
10/26/77F

SOAP
With Jimmy Baio, Diana Canova, Billy Crystal, Cathryn Damon, Robert Guillaume, Katherine Helmond, Robert Mandan, Arthur Peterson, Jennifer Salt, Robert Urich, Ted Wass, others
Supplier: Witt-Thomas-Harris Prods
Exec Prod: Paul Junger Witt, Tony Thomas;
Prod: Susan Harris;
Dir: Jay Sandrich;
Wri: Harris.
30 Mins, Tues, 9:30 pm.
ABC-TV
09/21/77

THE SOAP FACTORY
With Paul Harriss (host)
Supplier: DMB Prods (Brookville Marketing Corp)
Exec Prod: David Bergman;
Prod: Andrew Baddish;
Dir: Joe Lo-re.
30 Mins, Sat, noon.
WPIX-TV New York
07/12/78S

SOLO 1
(The Runaway)
With Paul Cronnin, Keith Eden, Aileen Britton, Gregory Stroud, Peter Cummins, Fay McFeeter
Supplier: Crawford Productions
Exec Prod: Henry Crawford;
Dir: David Stevens;
Wris: Tom Heggarty, Vince Moran.
30 Mins, Fri, 7 pm.
HSV-7 Melbourne, Australia
06/30/76F

SOMALIA: THE SILENT TRAGEDY
Prod-Wri: J.C. Hayward;
Pho: Mike Murphy;
Tech Adv: Terry Fox;
Edtr: Bill Moore.
30 Mins, Sunday, (3) 8 pm.
WDVM-TV, Washington
08/20/80

SOME THINGS MY FRIENDS WROTE
With Danny Millrood, host
Exec Prod: Inez Gottlieb;
Prod: Ted Field;
Dir: Judith Ayers Vogelsang.
30 Mins, Fri (17), 7:30 pm.
WCAU-TV Philadelphia
12/22/76

SOMEDAY SOON
With John Vernon, George Waight, Deborah Kipp, others
Prod: Ralph L Thomas;
Dir: Don Haldane;
Wris: Rudy Wiebe, Barry Pearson.
60 Mins, Sun, 9 pm.
CBC-TV Canada
01/19/77F

SOMETHING FOR JOEY
With Geraldine Page, Gerald S O'Loughlin, Marc Singer, Jeff Lynas, Linda Kelsey, Brian Farrell, Kathleen Beller, Steven Guttenberg, Paul Picerni, Stephen Parr, David Hooks, Kevin McKenzie
Supplier: MTM Enterprises
Prod-Wri: Jerry McNeely;
Dir: Lou Antonio.
110 Mins, Wed (6), 9 pm.
CBS-TV
IBM (Conahay & Lyon)
04/13/77

SON-RISE: A MIRACLE OF LOVE
(NBC Theater)
With James Farentino, Kathryn Harrold, Stephen Elliott, Henry Olek, Carrie Sherman, Erica Yohn, Michael & Casey Adams, Shelby Balik, Missy Francis, others
Supplier: Rothman-Wohl Prods, Filmways TV
Exec Prods: Bernard Rothman, Jack Wohl;
Prod: Richard M Rosenbloom;
Dir: Glenn Jordan;
Wris: Stephen Kandel, Barry Neil Kaufman, Suzi Lyte Kaufman, based on B Kaufman's book.
120 Mins, Mon (14), 9 pm.
NBC-TV
P&G (Benton & Bowles)
05/23/79

THE SONG OF LEONARD COHEN
(Spectrum)
Prod-Wri: Harry Rasky.
90 Mins, Wed, 9:30 pm.
CBC-TV, Toronto, Canada
11/12/80F

SONG OF MYSELF
(The American Parade)
With Rip Torn, Ron Faber, Brad Davis, David Hooks, Betty Henritze, Thomas Hulce, Leonardo Cimono, John Cain
Supplier: CBS News
Exec Prod: Joel Heller;
Prod-dir: Robert Markowitz;
Wri: Jan Hartman.
60 Mins, Tues (9), 10 pm.
CBS-TV
Eaton (JWT)
03/17/76

THE SONNY & CHER SHOW
With Cher, Sonny Bono, Billy Van, Gaylord Sartain, others
Supplier: Apis Prods. and Yongestreet Entertainment
Prod: Nick Vanoff;
Dir: Tim Kiley;
Wris: Phil Hahn, Bob Arnott, Jeannine Burnier, Coslough Johnson, Iris Rainer, Stuart Gillard.
60 Mins, Sun, 8 pm.
CBS-TV
02/04/76

SORORITY '62
With Marcy Hanson, Marya Small, Suzanne Wishner, Karen Smith-Bercovici, Fabian Forte, Dick Clark, Joey Bishop, Marj Dusay, Jonathan Torp
Supplier: Dick Clark Teleshows, Jerry Frank Co (Lexington Broadcast Services)
Exec Prods: Clark, Frank;
Prods-Wris: Gerry Gardner, Dee Caruso;
Dir: Tony Csiki.
30 Mins Tues (10), 7:30 pm.
WABC-TV New York
General Foods (Grey)
01/18/78S

THE SORROWS OF GIN
(Great Performances)
With Mara Hobel, Sigourney Weaver, Edward Herrmann, Eileen Heckart, Rachel Roberts, Marcella Lowry, Charlotte Moore, John Harkins, Baxter Harris, William Prince, Sally-Jane Heit
Supplier: WNET-TV New York
Exec Prod: Jac Venza;
Prods: Ann Blumenthal, Peter Weinberg;
Dir: Jack Hofsiss;
Wri: Wendy Wasserstein, from John Cheever's short story.
60 Mins, Wed (24), 9 pm.
PBS
10/31/79

THE SOUND OF LAUGHTER
(Young at Heart)
with Stratford Johns, Richard Pearson
Supplier: ATV
Prod-Dir: Les Chatfield;
Wri: Ronnie Taylor.
30 Mins, Thurs, 7 pm.
ITV, from London, England
08/17/77F

THE SOUNDS OF SCOTLAND
With Rod Stewart, Gallagher & Lyle, Lonnie Donegan, Alex Welsh Band, Stuart Gillies, Sunshine (5), Kimberley Clarke, Brian Fahey & Scottish Radio Orchestra
Prod: David Mallet.
45 Mins, Sat.
BBC-TV, from Glasgow, Scotland
08/25/76F

SOUNDSTAGE
With Leo Sayer
Prod: Ken Erlich;
Dir: Dick Carter.
60 Mins, Tues, 8 pm.
WTTW-TV Chicago for PBS
11/01/78

SOUNDSTAGE–FIDDLERS THREE
With Doug Kershaw, Jean-Luc Ponty, Itzhak Perlman
Prods: William Heitz, Charles Mitchell, Jane Kaplan.
60 Mins, Sun, 11 pm.
WTTW Chicago
03/16/77

SPACE FORCE
(Comedy Time)
With Fred Willard, Jim Boyd, Hilly Hicks, William Phipps, Larry Block, Maureen Mooney, Joe Medalis, Richard Paul, Zito Kazann, Billy Braver
Supplier: Columbia Pictures TV
Prods-Wris: John Boni, Norman Stiles;
Dir: Peter Baldwin.
30 Mins, Fri (28), 8 pm.
NBC-TV
05/03/78

SPACESHIPS OF THE MIND
With Nigel Calder, Prof Gerard O'Neill, others
Supplier: BBC Television
Prod: Dick Gilling.
50 Mins, Wed, 7:35 pm.
BBC-2, from London, England
07/12/78F

SPARROW
With Randy Herman, Don Gordon, Beverly Sanders, Karen Sedgely, Tom Quinn, Jack Wallace, Lenny Bakr, Dori Brenner
Supplier: L & B Prods
Exec Prod: Herbert B Leonard;
Prod: Walter Bernstein;
Dir: Stuart Hagmann;
Wri: Larry Cohen.
60 Mins, Wed (12), 10 pm.
CBS-TV
01/19/77

SPARROW
With Randy Herman, Gerald S O'Loughlin, Cathy Hicks, Lillian Gish, Jonelle Allen, Kurt Knudson, Dolph Sweet, Dick Anthony Williams, Lou Gilbert
Supplier: L & B Prods
Exec Prod: Herbert B Leonard;
Prods: Walter Bernstein, Sam Manners;
Dir: Jack Sold;
Wri: Bernstein.
60 Mins, Fri (11), 10 pm.
CBS-TV
08/16/78

SPARTACADE '79
With Win Elliot, Andrea Kirby, Suzy Chaffee, Paul Hornung, Leroy Walker, Barry Tompkins, Michael O'Hara, Jerry Quarry, Kathy Sullivan, Marty Sullivan
Supplier: Syndicast Services, LBA Associates, Pyramid Ent
Exec Prod: Lothar Bock;
Prods: Robert Wussler, Andy Kindle.
120 Mins, Sun, 8:30 pm.
WNEW-TV N Y
07/25/79

SPEAK UP AMERICA
With Marjoe Gortner, Felicia Jeter
Supplier: George Schlatter Prods
Exec Prod: Schlatter;
Prods: Bob Wynn, John Barbour;
Dir: Dave Caldwell;
Wris: Barbour, Schlatter, David Panish, Gene Farmer, Bill Dana.
60 Mins, Tues, 8 pm.
NBC-TV
05/07/80

SPEAK UP AMERICA
With Marjoe Gortner, Jayne Kennedy, Rhonda Bates, Magic Johnson, Sergio Aragones
Supplier: George Schlatter Prods
Exec Prods: Schlatter, Bob Wynn;
Prods: Lloyd Thaxton, Andy Friendly;
Dir: Dave Caldwell;
Wris: Schlatter, Bill Dana, John Barbour, Bill Paskay
60 Mins, Fri, 9 pm.
NBC-TV
08/06/80

SPEARHEAD
With Michael Billington, Jacqueline Tong, Roy Holder, others
Supplier: Southern TV
Prod-Dir: James Ormerod.
60 Mins, Tues, 7:30 pm.
Southern TV, England
08/16/78F

SPECIAL EDITION
With Barbara Feldon
Supplier: Columbia Pictures TV
Prod: Alan Sloan;
Dir: Steve Katten;
Wri: Ron Raley.
30 Mins, Sat, 7:30 pm.
WABC-TV
09/21/77S

SPENCER'S PILOTS
With Christopher Stone, Todd Susman, Gene Evans, Margaret Impert, Britt Leach, Bill Bixby, Linda Kelsey, Erik Estrada, Gerald Hiken, Steven P. Trevor, Bill Heywood, Earl Hickman
Supplier: CBS-TV & Sweeney-Finnegan Prods.
Exec Prods: Bob Sweeney, Bill Finnegan;
Prod: Larry Rosen;;
Dir: Sweeney;
Wri: Alvin Sapinsley.
60 Mins, Fri (9), 9 pm.
CBS-TV
04/14/76

SPENCER'S PILOTS
With Christopher Stone, Todd Susman, Gene Evans, Margaret Impert, Britt Leach, Sam Groom, John McLiam, Michael McGuire, Eldon Quick
Supplier: CBS-TV
Exec Prods: Bob Sweeney, Edward H. Feldman;
Prod: Larry Rosen;
Dir: Bill Bixby;
Wris: Karl & Terence Tunberg.
60 Mins, Fri, 8 pm.
CBS-TV
09/22/76

SPIDERMAN
With Nicholas Hammond, Thayer David, David White, Michael Pataki, Hilly Hicks, Lisa Eilbacher, Dick Balduzzi, Jeff Donnell, Robert Hastings, Barry Cutler
Supplier: Charles Fries Prods, Dan Goodman Prods
Exec Prods; Fries, Goodman;
Prod: Edward J Montagne
Dir: E W Swackhamer
Wri: Alvin Boretz.
90 Mins, Wed (14), 8 pm.
CBS-TV
09/21/77

SPIRIT IN LANDSCAPE
(Images of Canada)
Exec Prod: Vincet Tovell;
Prod-Dir: Carol Myers;
Wri: Barbara Moon.
60 Mins, Wed, 9 pm.
CBC-TV, from Toronto, Canada
11/03/76F

THE SPONGERS
Supplier: BBC
Prod: Tony Garnett;
Dir: Roland Joffe.
91 Mins.
(Winner of Prix Italia, Drama)
10/04/78PI

SPORTSWORLD
With Dick Enberg, Mike Adamle, Fred Thompson, Charlie Jones, Nancy Thies, Sam Nover
Supplier: NBC Sports
Exec Prod: Don Ohlmeyer;
Prod: Don Ellis.
90 Mins, Sun, 2:30 pm.
NBC-TV
01/25/78

STAR CHART
With Terry David Mulligan (host), Ray, Goodman & Brown; David Bowie, Cano, Janis Ian, GQ, Billy Preston & Syreeta; Earth, Wind & Fire
Supplier: Doug Hutton Video & Canadian Broadcasting Corp. (Fremantle Corp.)
Exec Prod: Hutton;
Prod: Ken Gibson;
Dir: Michael Watt.
30 Mins, Sat, 8 pm.
WNEW-TV New York

05/07/80S

THE STAR SHOW
With Jimmie Walker (host), Jeffrey Altman, Adele Blue, Murray Langston, David Letterman, Jay Leno, Mike Neun, The Village Idiots
Supplier: Group W Prods & Lexington Broadcast Services
Exec Prod: David S Salzman;
Prod: Craig Tennis;
Dir: Tom Trbovich;
Wris: Neil Rosen, George Tricker.
60 Mins, Sun (5), 9 pm.
WNEW-TV New York
Revlon (Grey Advtg)

06/08/77S

THE STARLAND VOCAL BAND SHOW
With Bill Danoff, Taffy Danoff, Margot Chapman, Jon Carroll, Mark Russell, Dave Letterman, Jeff Altman, Phil Proctor, Peter Bergman
Supplier: Star-Jer Prods
Exec Prod: Jerry Weintraub;
Prod: Al Rogers;
Dir: Rick Bennewitz;
Wris: April Kelly, George Geiger, Letterman, Proctor, Bergman.
30 Mins, Sun (31), 8:30 pm.
CBS-TV

08/03/77

STARS ON ICE
With Alex Trebek
Exec Prods: Arthur Weinthal, Gerard Rochon;
Prod: Ed Richardson;
Dir: Michael Steele.
30 Mins, Tues, 7:30 pm.
CTV, Canada

11/17/76F

THE STARS SALUTE AMERICA'S GREATEST MOVIES
(The American Film Institute 10th Anniversary Gala)
Supplier: AFI & Pasetta Prods
Exec Prod: George Stevens Jr;
Prod-Dir: Marty Passetta;
Wris: Larry McMurtry, Rod Warren.
90 Mins, Wed (21), 9:30 pm.
CBS-TV

11/23/77

STARSTRUCK
With Beeson Carroll, Lynne Lipton, Guy Raymond, Meegan King, Tania Myren, Elvia Allman, Kevin Brando, Robin Strand, Sarah Kennedy, Joe Silver, Roy Brocksmith, Herb Kaplowitz, Dick Durock, Mousie Garner, Robert Short, Buddy Douglas, J C Wells, Chris Walas, Cynthia Latham
Supplier: Herbert B Leonard Prods
Exec Prod: Leonard;
Dir: Al Viola;
Wri: Arthur Kopit.
30 Mins, Sat (9), 8:30 pm.
CBS-TV

06/13/79

STARTING FRESH
(BATTLE OF THE GENERATIONS)
With Lynette Mettey, Kimberly Beck, Michael MacRae, Ike Eisenmann, Susan Duvall, Janie Sell, Jeffrey Byron, Rob Browning
Supplier: Danny Thomas Prods
Exec Prods: Thomas, Ron Jacobs;
Prods: Leonora Thuna, Pamela Chais;
Dir: Bob Claver;
Wri: Chais.
120 Min, Wed (27), 9 pm.
NBC-TV

07/04/79

STATE FAIR AMERICA
With Lynn Anderson, Roy Clark, Steven Ford, Kansas, Gabriel Kaplan, Alan King, Robert Klein, Hal Linden, Mary McGregor, Marilyn McCoo & Billy Davis Jr, Mel Tillis, Jimmy Walker, Jimmy & Buck Trent
Supplier: Rothman-Wohl Prods
Exec Prods: Bernard Rothman, Jack Wohl;
Prod: Eric Lieber;
Dir: Jeff Margolis;
Wris: Aubrey Tadman, Garry Ferrier.
120 Mins, Sat (10), 8 pm.
CBS-TV
Procter & Gamble (Leo Burnett)

09/14/77

STEPPING OUT
With Gary Gibson, Joan Houston
Exec Prod: John Coney;
Prod: Gibson, Houston;
Dir: Lee Olson.
30 Mins, Thurs, 7:30 pm.
KCTS-TV Seattle

02/14/79

STEVE ALLEN COMEDY HOUR
With Lucille Ball, Steve Martin, George Kennedy, Steve Landesberg, Louis Nye, Joe Baker, Bill Saluga, Barry Diamond, Catherine O'Hara, Suzanne Buhrer, Tom Leopold, Bunny Summers, Greg Travis, Terry Gibbs Orch
Supplier: Meadowlane Enterprises
Exec Prod: William H Harbach, Frank Peppiatt;
Prod: Rocco Urbisci;
Dir: Bob Bowker;
Wris: Allen, Jay Burton, Rod Gist, Robert Illes, Phil Kellard, Sheldon Keller, Leopold, Tom Moore, O'Hara, Bob Shaw, James Stein, Jeremy Stevens.
60 Mins, Sat (18) 10 pm.
NBC-TV

10/22/80

STEVE ALLEN'S LAUGH BACK
With Eydie Gorme, Pat Harrington Jr, Tom Poston, Jayne Meadows
Supplier: IPS Prods - Hughes TV
Prod: Jerry Harrison.
90 Mins, Mon, 8 pm.
WOR-TV New York

10/27/76S

STEVE & EYDIE CELEBRATE IRVING BERLIN
(The Big Event)
With Steve Lawrence, Eydie Gorme, Oscar Peterson, Leslie Browne, Carol Burnett, Sammy Davis Jr, Rob Iscove Dancers
Supplier: Stage 2 Prods & Smith-Hemion Prods
Exec Prods: Lawrence, Gary Smith;
Prods: Smith, Dwight Hemion;
Dir: Hemion;
Wris: Harry Crane, David Axelrod.
90 Mins, Tues (22), 9:30 pm.
NBC-TV

08/30/78

STEVE MARTIN: A WILD AND CRAZY GUY
With Steve Martin, Milton Berle, George Burns, Johnny Cash, Bob Hope, Strother Martin
Supplier: William E McEuen Prods, Cates Bros Co & Aspen Film Society
Exec Prod: McEuen;
Prod: Joe Cates;
Dir: Gary Weis;
Wris: Martin, Michael Elias, Alan Metter, Jack Handey.
60 Mins, Wed (22), 10 pm.
NBC-TV

11/29/78

STICKING TOGETHER
(ABC Friday Night Movie Special Double Feature)
With Clu Gulager, Sean Roche, Lory Walsh, Sean Marshall, Randi Kiger, Keith Mitchell, Richard Venture, Gwen Arner, Deborah White, Talia Balsam, Moe Keale, Santos Morales, Sean Tyler Hall, Leinaala Heina, Don Pomes, Harry Chang
Supplier: Blinn-Thorpe Prods & Viacom
Prods: William Blinn, Jerry Thorpe;
Dir: Thorpe;
Wri: Blinn.
90 Mins, Fri (14), 8 pm.
ABC-TV

04/19/78

THE STINGIEST MAN IN TOWN
With voices of Walter Matthau, Tom Bosley, Theodore Bikel, Robert Morse, Dennis Day, Paul Frees, Sonny Melendrez, Debra Clinger, Robert Rolofson, Steffani Calli, Eric Hines, Dee Stratton, Darlene Conley, Shelby Flint, Diana Lee, Charles Matthau
Supplier: Rankin-Bass Prods
Prods-Dirs: Arthur Rankin Jr, Jules Bass;
Wri: Romeo Muller, based on Charles Dickens' "A Christmas Carol".
60 Mins, Sat (23), 8 pm.
NBC-TV
Alcoa (Creamer)

12/27/78

STOCKARD CHANNING IN JUST FRIENDS
With Gerrit Graham, Mimi Kennedy, Lou Criscuolo, Sydney Goldsmith, Albert Insinnia, Lawrence Pressman
Supplier: Little Bear Prods
Exec Prod: David Debin;
Supv Prod: Peter Locke;
Prod: Al Rogers;
Dirs: Robert Drivas, Rick Bennewitz;
Wris: Nick Arnold, Eric Cohen.
30 Mins, Sun, 9:30 pm.
CBS-TV
03/07/79

STOCKARD CHANNING SHOW
With Jack Somack, Max Showalter, Sydney Goldsmith, Ron Silver, Leonard Stone, Diane Civita
Supplier: Little Bear Prods.
Exec Prod-Wri: Aaron Ruben;
Prod: George Yanok;
Dir: Jeff Bleckner.
30 Mins, Mon, 8:30 pm.
CBS-TV
03/26/80

STONE
(ABC Sunday Night Movie)
With Dennis Weaver, Pat Hingle, Roy Thinnes, Joby Baker, Joey Forman, Kim Hamilton, Vic Morrow, Tom Pedi, David Spielberg, Mel Stewart, Steve Allen, Mariette Hartley, William Bronder, Nancy McKeon, Tara Buckman, Philip Pine, Colby Chester, others
Supplier: Stephen J Cannell Prods, Gerry Prods & Universal TV
Exec Prod-Wri: Cannell;
Prods: J Rickley Dumm, Don Carlos Dunaway;
Dir: Corey Allen.
120 Mins, Sun (26), 9 pm.
ABC-TV
08/29/79

STONE
With Dennis Weaver, Pat Hingle, Robby Weaver, Robert Hogan, Sharon Acker, Paul Lambert, Priscilla Pointer, Granvile van Dusen, Shannon Terhune
Supplier: Stephen J. Cannell Prods., Gerry Prods. & Universal TV
Exec Prod: Cannell;
Supv Prod: Alex Beaton
Prods: J. Rickley Dumm, Don Carlos Dunaway;
Dir: Winrich Kolbe;
Wri: Dunaway.
60 Mins, Mon, 9 pm.
ABC-TV
01/16/80

STONESTREET
(NBC Movie of the Week)
With Barbara Eden, Joseph Mascolo, Joan Hackett, Richard Basehart, Louise Latham, Elaine Giftos, James Ingersoll, Val Avery, Sally Kirkland, Gene Conforti, Robert Burton, LaWanda Page, Ryan MacDonald
Supplier: Universal TV
Prod-Wri: Leslie Stevens;
Dir: Ross Mayberry.
90 Mins, Sun (16), 9:35 pm.
NBC-TV
01/19/77

STOP, LOOK AND LISTEN
With Barry Bernson, others
Prod-Wri: Barry Bernson;
Dir: Dean Rowe.
30 Min, Thurs (25), 6 pm.
WMAQ-TV Chicago
12/31/80

STOP SUSAN WILLIAMS - (Chapter 2) (CLIFFHANGERS)
With Susan Anton, Ray Walston, Michael Swan, John Hancock, Santos Morales, H B Haggerty
Supplier: Universal TV
Exec Prod-Dir-Wri: Kenneth Johnson;
Prod: Richard Milton
60 Min, Tues, 8 pm.
NBC-TV
03/07/79

STOP THE PRESSES
With John Rubinstein, Bryan Gordon, James Gregory, Allan Rich, Kit McDonough, Basil Hoffmar, Leonard Barr, Sharon Farrell
Supplier: Mark Carliner Prods & Viacom
Exec Prod: Carliner;
Prod-Wris: Don Reo & Allan Katz;
Dir: Joan Darling.
30 Mins, Fri (15), 10:30 pm.
CBS-TV
07/20/77

THE STORYTELLER
(NBC Monday Movie)
With Martin Balsam, Patty Duke Astin, Doris Roberts, Rose Gregorio, James Daly, David Spielberg, Dick Anthony Williams, Milt Kogan, Susan Adams, Ivan Bonair
Supplier: Fairmount-Foxcroft Prods & Universal TV
Prod-Wris: Richard Levinson, William Link;
Dir: Robert Markowitz.
120 Mins, Mon (5), 9 pm.
NBC-TV
12/14/77

STRANDED
With Kevin Dobson, Lara Parker, Marie Windsor, Devon Ericson, Jimmy McNichol, Rex Everhart, Erin Blunt, Lal Baum, James Cromwell, John Fujioka
Exec Prod: David Victor;
Prod: Howie Horwitz;
Dir: Earl Bellamy;
Wri: Anthony Lawrence.
60 Mins, Wed (26), 8 pm.
CBS-TV
06/02/76

STRANGERS: THE STORY OF A MOTHER & DAUGHTER
With Bette Davis, Gena Rowlands, Ford Rainey, Donald Moffat, Whit Bissell, Royal Dano, Kate Riehl, others
Supplier: Chris-Rose Productions
Prods: Robert W Christiansen, Rick Rosenberg;
Dir: Milton Katselas;
Wri: Michael de Guzman.
120 Mins, Sun (13), 9 pm.
CBS-TV
05/23/79

STREET KILLING
With Andy Griffith, Bradford Dillman, Harry Guardino, Robert Loggia, Ben Hammer, Don Gordon, Adam Wade, Anna Berger, Debbie White, Sandy Faison, Gigi Semone
Supplier: ABC Circle Films
Exec Prod: Everett Chambers;
Prod: Richard Rosenbloom;
Dir: Harvey Hart;
Wri: Bill Driskell.
90 Mins, Sun (12), 9 pm.
ABC-TV
09/15/76

STREET OF DREAMS
Exec Prod: Don Wilburn;
Prod-Wri-Narr: Patricia Gormin.
30 Mins, Thurs, 8:30 pm.
WVUE-TV New Orleans
06/13/79

STRUCK BY LIGHTNING
With Jack Elam, Jeffrey Kramer, Millie Slavin, Bill Erwin, Jeff Cotler, Richard Stahl
Supplier: Fellows-Keegan Co, Paramount TV
Exec Prods: Arthur Fellows, Terry Keegan;
Prod: John Thomas Lenox;
Dir: Joel Zwick;
Wris: Fred Freeman, Lawrence J Cohen.
30 Mins, Wed (19), 8:30 pm.
CBS-TV
09/26/79

STUDIO A STARTIME
With Kenneth McKellar, Janet Brown, Rita Morris, Fyfe Robertson
Supplier: Scottish Television
Prod: David Bell;
Dir: Clarke Tait.
60 Mins, Fri, 8 pm.
Scottish TV, from Glasgow, Scotland
02/25/76F

STUDIO SEE
Supplier: South Carolina ETV
Prod: Jayne Adair.
30 Mins, Thurs, 7 pm.
PBS
03/30/77

STUMPERS
With Allen Ludden (host), Dick Gautier, Robert Reed
Supplier: Lin Bolen Prods
Exec Prod: Bolen;
Prod: Walt Case;
Dir: Jeff Goldstein.
30 Mins, Mon-Fri, 11:30 am.
NBC-TV
10/13/76

STUNTS UNLIMITED
(ABC Friday Night Movie)
With Chip Mayer, Susanna Dalton, Sam J. Jones, Glenn Corbett, Linda Grovenor, Alejandro Rey, Stefan Gierasch, Victor Mohica, Lina Raymond
Supplier: Lawrence Gordon Prods. & Paramount TV
Exec Prod: Gordon;
Prod: Lionel E. Siegel;
Dir: Hal Needham;
Wri: Laurence Heath.
90 Mins, Fri, (4), 9:30 pm.
ABC-TV
01/23/80

SUDDENLY AN EAGLE
With Lee J. Cobb, Kenneth Griffith
Supplier: ABC News
Exec Prod: Av Westin;
Prod-Dir: William Peters;
Wris: Peters, Griffith.
60 Mins, Wed (7), 8 pm.
ABC-TV
Travelers Insurance (Ammirati, Puris & Avrutick)
01/14/76

SUGAR TIME
With Barbi Benton, Marianne Black, Didi Carr, Wynn Irwin, Mark Winkworth, Terry Kiser, Charles Fleischer
Supplier: James Komack Co
Exec Prod: Komack;
Prods: Hank Bradford, Martin Cohan;
Dir: Bill Hobin;
Wri: Bradford.
30 Mins, Sat, 8:30 pm.
ABC-TV
08/24/77

THE SULLIVANS
With Paul Cronin, Lorraine Bayly, Andrew McFarlane, Steven Tandy, Richard Morgan, Susan Hannaford, Michael Caton, Maggie Dence, Vivean Gray, Fred Parslow, Charmion Jacka, Peter Hehir, Vikki Hammond, Reg Gorman, Noni Hazlehurst, Norman Yemm, Denzil Howson, Leon Lissek, Marcella Burgoyne, Ingrid Mason, John Bowman
Supplier: Crawford Productions
Exec Prods: Ian Jones, Ian Crawford;
Prod: Henry Crawford;
Dirs: Simon Wincer, Rod Hardy, John Barningham.
30 Mins, Mon thru Fri, 8 pm.
GTV-9 Melbourne, Australia
11/17/76F

THE SULLIVANS
With Paul Cronin, Lorraine Bayly, Michael Caton, Maggie Dence, Vivean Gray, Frederick Parslow, Vikki Hammond, Reg Gorman, Norman Yemm, Leon Lissek, Marcella Burgoyne, Ingrid Mason, others
Supplier: Crawford Prods
30 Mins, Mon-Fri, 8 pm.
Channel 9, Sydney, Australia
12/01/76F

SUMTHIN' GOOD
With Patti Austin, Kole & Parham, Mal Z Lawrence, Kelly Garrett, The Lockers
Supplier: BBS Prods (Program Syndications Services)
Exec Prods: Seymour Seitz, Hal Blake;
Prod-Dir: Fred L Dukes;
Wri: Felicidad.
60 Mins, Sat (23), 9 pm.
WNEW-TV New York
07/27/77S

THE SUNDAY DRAMA
(A Good Human Story)
With Kenneth Haigh, Michael Elphick, Warren Clarke, others
Supplier: Granada TV
Prod: Julian Amyes;
Dir: Gordon Flyming;
Wri: David Nathan.
60 Mins, Sun, 10 pm.
Granada, from Manchester, England
07/27/77F

THE SUNDAY GAMES
With Bruce Jenner, O.J. Simpson, Joe Namath, Bryant Gumbel, Dionne Warwick, Fernando Lamas, Dick Butkus, Arte Johnson, Donna de Varona, Charlie Jones, Mike Adamle, Sally Struthers, Nancy Thies, Christopher Lee
Supplier: Don Ohlmeyer Prods-Trans World Int'l
Exec Prod: Ohlmeyer;
Prod: Howard Katz;
Dir: Jim Cross;
Wri: Norman Bleichman.
120 Mins, Sun, (27) 9 pm.
NBC-TV
04/30/80

SUNSHINE AND SHADOWS
With Jack Thompson, narrator
Supplier: Australian Broadcasting Commission
Dir: Brian Adams;
Wri: David Stratton.
90 Mins.
ABC, from Melbourne, Australia
08/18/76F

THE SUNSHINE BOYS
With Red Buttons, Lionel Stander, Michael Durrell, Bobbie Mitchell, Sarina Grant, George Wyner, Barra Grant, Danny Mora, Bella Bruck, Philip Tanzani, Tony Sherman, Ann Cooper
Supplier: Rastar Prods & MGM-TV
Exec Prod: Michael Levee;
Prod: Sam Denoff;
Dir: Robert Moore;
Wri: Neil Simon.
60 Mins, Thurs (9), 8 pm.
NBC-TV
06/15/77

SUPERKID
(Superspecial)
With Rene Simard, Diahann Carroll, Sandy Duncan
Exec Prod: Rin Lilly;
Prod: Bill Lynn;
Dir: Buddy Bregman;
Wris: Stan Shabinsky, Lynn, Tasso Lakas, Bregman.
60 Mins, Sun, 7:30 pm.
CBC-TV, from Toronto, Canada
10/27/76F

SUPERMAN AND THE BRIDE
Supplier: Thames TV
Exec Prod: Ian Martin;
Prod Team: Alan Horrox, Douglas Lowndes, Julian McCreadie, John Roe, Gillian Skirrow.
45 Mins, Thurs, 10:30 pm.
ITV, England
10/26/77F

SUPERSONIC
With Andy Bown, Cliff Richard, Pilot, Bay City Rollers, Chris Farlowe, Albert Hammond
Supplier: Fremantle Corp.
Prod-dir: Mike Mansfield.
30 Mins, Sat, 5:30 pm.
WPIX-TV New York
06/23/76S

SUPER-STARS ON STAGE AT THE OHIO STATE FAIR
With Cheryl Tiegs, Dan Rowan (hosts), Pat & Debby Boone, Bob Hope, Donny & Marie Osmond, Osmond Brothers, Jimmy Osmond, Charley Pride, Eddie Rabbitt, Kenny Rogers, Sha Na Na, Tavares, Dottie West
Supplier: Osmond TV Prods
Exec Prods: Osmond Bros, Toby Martin;
Prod-Dir: Walter C Miller;
Wri: Rod Warren.
60 Mins, Mon (23), 8 pm.
ABC-TV
11/01/78

SUPERTRAIN
With Steve Lawrence, Char Fontane, Don Stroud, Keenan Wynn, Deborah Benson, Ron Masak, Don Meredith, Vicki Lawrence, George Hamilton, Stella Stevens, Fred Williamson, Edward Andrews, Patrick Collins, Harrison Page, Robert Alda, Nita Talbot, Aarika Wells, William Nuckols, Michael Delano, Charlie Brill, John Karlen, Frank R Christi
Supplier: Dan Curtis Enterprises & NBC-TV
Exec Prod-Dir: Curtis;
Prod: Anthony Spinner;
Wri: Earl W Wallace.
120 Mins, Wed, 8 pm.
NBC-TV
02/14/79

THE SWEENEY
(Golden Boy)
With John Thaw, Dennis Waterman, Dudley Sutton, Andy Morton, John Nolan, others
Supplier: Thames Television
Exec Prods: Lloyd Shirley, George Taylor;
Prod: Ted Childs;
Dir: Tom Clegg;
Wri: Martin Hall.
60 Mins, Wed, 9 pm.
ITV, London, England
08/03/77F

SWEEPSTAKES
With Edd Byrnes, Katherine Helmond, Bill Daily, Priscilla Barnes, Kim Richards, Adam Arkin, Abe Vigoda, Elaine Joyce, Greg Mullavey, Foster Brooks, Paul Benedict, Audrey Christie, Erin Moran, Grover the dog
Supplier: Miller-Milkis Prods & Paramount TV
Exec Prod: Robert Dozier;
Prods: John Furia, Ben Kadish;
Dir: Philip Leacock;
Wri: Herman Groves.
60 Mins, Fri, 10 pm.
NBC-TV
01/31/79

SWEET LAND OF LIBERTY - THE MOSCOW-PULLMAN GAY COMMUNITY
With Mike Kirk, others
30 Mins, Tues (14), 8:30 pm.
KCTS Seattle
10/06/76

SWORD OF JUSTICE
(The Big Event)
With Dack Rambo, Bert Rosario, Alex Courtney, Larry Hagman, J D Cannon, Christina Ferrare, June Lockhart, Jack Kelly, Nehemiah Persoff, H M Winant, Milton Selzer, Lorenzo Lamas, Legh Christian, Michael Baseleon, John Myhers, Victor Holchak, Melinda Naud, Colby Chester, William Mims, Roy Jenson, Dennis Buckley
Supplier: Glen Larson Prods & Universal TV
Exec Prod: Larson;
Prod: Michael Sloan;
Prod: Joe Boston;
Dir: Daniel Haller;
Wris: Larson, Michael Gleason.
120 Mins, Sun (10), 8 pm.
NBC-TV
09/13/78

SYDNEY-HOBART YACHT RACE
With Tim Eliot, Narrator
Supplier: Australian Broadcasting Commission
Prod-Dir: James Allan;
Wri: Martyn Goddard.
60 Mins, Wed, 8:30 pm.
ABC, Australia
02/15/78F

SYMPHONIC SOUL
With Diahann Carroll, Francois Clemmons, Horatio Miller, James Frazier, Festival Symphony Orchestra, Zion Baptist Church Choirs
Exec Prod: Norman Marcus;
Prod: Joan Reisner Auritt;
Dir: Clark Santee.
60 Mins, Mon (12), 9 pm.
PBS from WHYY-TV, Philadelphia
04/21/76

SZYSZNYK
With Ned Beatty, Olivia Cole, Susan Lanier, Leonard Barr, Jarrod Johnson, Barry Miller, Scott Colomby, Thomas Carter
Supplier: Four's Company Prods
Exec Prod: Jerry Weintraub;
Prod: Rich Eustis;
Dir: Peter Bonerz;
Wris: Jim Mulligan, Ron Landry.
30 Mins, Mon (1), 8:30 pm.
CBS-TV
08/03/77

SZYSZNYK
With Ned Beatty, Olivia Cole, Leonard Barr, Jarrod Johnson, Barry Miller, Scott Colomby, Thomas Carter, Reggie Jackson, Eric Laneuvillie
Supplier: Four's Co
Exec Prod: Jerry Weintraub;
Prods: Rich Eustis, Michael Elias;
Dir: James Burrows;
Wris: Alan Rosen, Fred Rubin.
30 Mins, Wed, 8:30 pm.
CBS-TV
12/14/77

TABATHA
With Liberty Williams, Bruce Kimmel, Barbara Cason, Cindi Haynie, Archie Hahn, Barbara Rhoades, Arnold Soboloff, Maria O'Brien, Dave Carlile, John-Anthony Bailey
Supplier: Ashmont Prods. & Columbia Pictures TV
Prod-dir: William Asher;
Wri: Ed Jurist.
30 Mins, Sat (24), 8 pm.
ABC-TV
04/28/76

TABITHA
With Lisa Hartman, Robert Urich, Mel Stewart, David Ankrum, Karen Morrow, Peter Palmer, Robert Clarke, Chuck Gradi
Supplier: Columbia Pictures TV
Exec Prod-Wri: Jerry Mayer;
Prod: Bob Stambler;
Dir: Charles Dubin.
60 Mins, Sat, 8:30 pm.
ABC-TV
09/14/77

TABLOID
With Carl Gottlieb, Miranda Dunne, Jason Laskay
Supplier: M A Hooper Prods, with Metromedia
Prod: Mary Ann Hooper;
Dir: Don David.
30 Mins, Mon (18), 11:30
WNEW-TV New York
07/27/77S

TAGGART'S TREASURE
With Don Reid, David Gumpilil, Rowena Wallace, Michael Duffield
Supplier: Hanna-Barbera Prods & Australian Broadcast Commission
Exec Prod: Joseph R Barbera;
Prod: Oscar Whitehead;
Dir: Burt Topper;
Wris: Clint Free, Topper.
30 Mins, Wed (5), 7:30 pm.
WABC-TV New York
01/12/77S

TAIL GUNNER JOE
With Peter Boyle, Burgess Meredith, Patricia Neal, John Forsythe, Heather Menzies, Ned Beatty, Charles Cioffi, others
Supplier: Universal TV
Prod: George Eckstein;
Dir: Jud Taylor;
Wri: Lane Slate.
180 Mins, Sun (6), 8 pm.
NBC-TV
02/09/77

TAKE FIVE WITH STILLER & MEARA
With Jerry Stiller, Anne Meara
Supplier: J Walter Thompson
Exec Prod: John H P Davis;
Prod: William T Watts;
Dir: Ivan Cury;
Wris: Paul Dooley, Frank Jacobs, Bill Weeden, David Finkle.
5 Mins, Mon-Fri, 4:55 pm.
WNBC-TV New York
10/12/77S

TAKE ME HOME
With Fred Griffith
Prods-dirs-wris: Peter & Carol Griesinger.
30 Mins, Mon, 8:30 pm.
WEWS-TV Cleveland
09/29/76

TAKE ME UP TO THE BALL GAME
With the voices of Phil Silvers, Bobby Dermer, Derek McGrath, Don Ferguson, Paul Soles, Anna Bourque, Maurice LaMarche, Melleny Brown
Exec Prods: Robert Foster, Ted Kernaghan, Nigel Martin;
Prods: Patrick Loubert, Michael Hirsh;
Dir: Ken Stephenson;
Wri: Ken Sobol.
30 Mins, Sun, 7:30 pm.
CBC-TV, from Toronto, Canada
10/15/80F

TAKE MY ADVICE
With Kelly Lange (host), Sammy & Altovise Davis Jr., Carroll & Nancy O'Connor
Supplier: Burt Sugarman Prods. & Armand Grant DGS Prods.
Exec Prod: Sugarman;
Prod: Mark Massari;
Dir: Hank Behar;
Wris: Ann Elder, Stan Dreben.
30 Mins, Mon-Fri, 12:30 pm.
NBC-TV
01/14/76

TAKE THIRTY
With Paul Soles, Hanna Gartner
Exec Prod: Ain Soodor;
Prod: Margaret Slaight.
30 Mins, weekdays, 3 pm.
CBC, from Toronto, Canada
12/28/77F

TALES OF THE UNEXPECTED
(The Last Chapter)
With William Conrad (narrator), Roy Thinnes, Ned Beatty, Lincoln Kilpatrick, R G Armstrong, Don Calfa, Ramon Bieri, Tim O'Connor, Neva Patterson, others
Supplier: QM Prods
Exec Prod: Quinn Martin;
Prod-Wri: John Wilder;
Dir: Richard Lang.
60 Mins, Wed, 10 pm.
NBC-TV
02/09/77

TANDARRA
(Tandarra and Shadow of the Past)
With Gerard Kennedy, Gus Mercurio, Penne Hackforth-Jones, Bruce Kerr, George Mallaby, David Ravenswood, Norman Yemm, Anne Pendlebury
Supplier: Homestead Films
Prods: Patrick Edgeworth, Russell Hagg;
Dirs: Russell Hagg, Simon Wincer;
Wri: Patrick Edgeworth.
60 Mins, Mon, 7:30 pm, Melbourne, Tues, Sydney & Adelaide; Thurs, Brisbane
Seven Network, Australia
02/18/76F

THE TAR SANDS
With Kenneth Welsh, Ken Pogue, Mayor Moore
Prod: Ralph Thomas;
Dir: Peter Pearson;
Wris: Thomas, Pearson, Peter Rowe, based on Larry Pratt book.
60 Mins, Mon, 9 pm.
CBC-TV, from Toronto, Canada
10/05/77F

TARGET
(Hunting Party)
With Patrick Mower, Philip Madoc, Brendan Price, Vivian Heilbron, Lee Montague
Supplier: BBC
Prod: Philip Hinchcliffe;
Dir: Chris Menaul;
Wri: David Agnew.
50 Mins, Fri, 9:25 pm.
BBC-1, from London, England
10/19/77F

TARHEELS IN THE NORTHWEST
Wri-Prod: Jean Walkinshaw;
Exec Prod: John Coney.
30 Mins, Mon, 8:30 pm.
KCTS Seattle
07/25/79

TATTLETALES
With Bert Convy, Dick & Dolly Martin, Bob & Ginnie Newhart, Anthony Newley & Dareth Rich
Supplier: Goodson-Todman
Prods: Mark Goodson, Bill Todman;
Dir: Paul Alter.
30 Mins, Sat, 7:30 pm.
WCBS-TV
09/28/77S

TAUSEND LIEDER OHNE TON
(A Thousand Songs Without Tone)
With Eva Mattes, Michael Tregor
Supplier: Zweites Deutsches Fernsehen (ZDF)
Prod: Zweites Deutsches Fernsehen;
Dir: Claudia Holldack;
Wri: Christiane Hoellger.
90 Mins, Thurs, 10 pm.
ZDF, from Wiesbaden-Mainz, West Germany
03/16/77F

TAXI
(Hallmark Hall Of Fame)
With Martin Sheen, Eva Marie Saint
Supplier: Glen-Warren Prods
Exec Prod: Stan Parlan;
Prod-Dir: Joseph Hardy;
Wri: Lanford Wilson.
60 Mins, Thurs (2), 10 pm.
NBC-TV
Hallmark Cards (Foote, Cone & Belding)
02/08/78

TAXI
With Judd Hirsch, Jeff Conaway, Danny De Vito, Marilu Henner, Tony Danza, Randall Carver, Andy Kaufman, Talia Balsam
Supplier: John Charles Walters Prods, Paramount TV
Prods-Wris: James Brooks, Stan Daniels, David Davis, Ed Weinberger;
Dir: James Burrows.
30 Mins, Tues, 9:30 pm.
ABC-TV
09/20/78

THE TED KNIGHT MUSICAL COMEDY VARIETY SPECIAL SPECIAL
With Ted Knight, Edward Asner, Rue McClanahan, Ethel Merman, Phil Silvers, Loretta Swit, Fred MacMurray
Supplier: Kono Prods
Exec Prod: Ned Shankman;
Prod: Bob Finkel;
Dir: Sid Smith;
Wris: Herbert Baker, Mike Harmer, Stan Burns.
60 Mins, Tues (30), 8 pm.
CBS-TV
12/08/76

TED KNIGHT SHOW
With Barbara Rhoades, Greg Antonacci, Adam Arkin, Emory Bass, Lorna Thayer, Nancy New, Iris Adrian, Colleen Minahan, Cissy Colpitts, Susan Walden, Orville Sherman
Supplier: Hayoudo Prods & Paramount TV
Exec Prods: Mark Rothman, Lowell Ganz, Ned Shankman;
Prod: John Thomas Lenox;
Dir: James Burrows;
Wris: Rothman, Ganz.
30 Mins, Wed, 8:30 pm.
CBS-TV
11/02/77

TED KNIGHT SHOW
With Ted Knight, Normann Burton, Thomas Leopold, Iris Adrian, Ciccy Colpitts, Fawne Harriman, Ellen Regan, Tanya Boyd, Janice Kent, Debbie Harmon, Claude Stroud, Charles Hallahan, Crystin Sinclaire
Supplier: Kono Prods Paramount TV
Exec Prods: Mark Rothman, Lowell Ganz, Ned Shankman;
Prods: Martin Cohan, David Duclon;
Wri: Barry Rubinowitz;
Dir: Joel Zwick.
30 Mins, Sat (8), 8:30 pm.
CBS-TV
04/12/78

TEDDY
(CBS Reports)
With Roger Mudd
Supplier: CBS News
Exec Prod: Howard Stringer;
Prod-Dir: Andrew Lack;
Wri: Mudd.
60 Mins, Sun (4), 10 pm.
CBS-TV
11/07/79

TELETONE NEWS
With Fred Foy, Fred Collins, Mel Allen
Exec Prod: Al Ittleson;
Prod: Rudy Bednar;
Wri: Joe Cook.
30 Mins, Fri (26) 7:30 pm.
WABC-TV New York
10/01/80

TELFORD'S CHANGE
With Peter Barkworth, Hannah Gordon, others
Supplier: BBC Enterprises
Prod: Mark Shivas;
Dir: Barry Davis;
Wri: Brian Clark.
75 Mins, Sun, 7:15 pm.
BBC-1, from London
02/28/79F

TELL ME MY NAME
(GE Theatre)
With Arthur Hill, Barbara Barrie, Barnard Hughes, Glenn Zachar, Douglas McKeon, Deborah Turnbull, Murray Westgate, Dawn Grenehalgh, Valerie Mahaffey
Supplier: Reid-Cowan Prods, Talent Associates, Time-Life TV
Exec Prods: David Susskind, Frederick Brogger;
Prod: Donald W Reid;
Dir: Delbert Mann;
Wri: Joanna Lee, from Mary Carter book.
90 Mins, Tues (20), 9:30 pm.
CBS-TV
GE (BBDO)
12/28/77

TELL ME ON A SUNDAY
With Marti Webb, London Philharmonic Orchestra
Supplier: BBC-TV & Metromedia
Prod: Herbert Chappell;
Wri: Andrew Lloyd Webber
45 Mins, Sun, 9:25 pm.
BBC1, Britain
04/02/80F

TELLY...WHO LOVES YA, BABY?
With Telly Savalas, Diahann Carroll, Barbara Eden, Cloris Leachman
Supplier: Allwym Pictures Corp. & Aries Films
Prod: Howard W. Koch;
Dir: Marty Pasetta;
Wri: Buz Kohan.
60 Mins, Wed (18), 10 pm.
CBS-TV
Kraft Foods (JWT)
03/03/76

THE TEN THOUSAND DAY WAR
With Richard Basehart
Exec Prod: Michael Maclear;
Prod: Ian McLeod;
Wri: Peter Arnett.
60 Mins, Wed, 9 pm.
CBC-TV Toronto, Canada
11/05/80F

TENSPEED AND BROWN SHOE
With Ben Vereen, Jeff Goldblum, Robyn Douglass, Robert Webber, Jayne Meadows, Richard Romanus, John Harkins, Simone Griffeth, Larry Manetti, A.C. Weary, Luke Andreas
Supplier: Stephen J. Cannell Prods.
Exec Prod-Wri: Cannell;
Prod: Alex Beaton;
Dir: E.L. Swackhamer.
120 Mins, Sun, 8 pm.
ABC-TV
01/30/80

THE TENTH LEVEL
With William Shatner, Lynn Carlin, Ossie Davis, Viveca Lindfors, Estelle Parsons, Roy Poole, Mike Kellin, Richard McKenzie, Fred J. Scollay, Stephen Macht, Lindsay Crouse, Charles White, Robert Burr, Tom Quinn, Damon Evans, others
Supplier: CBS-TV
Exec Prod: Robert Markell;
Prod: Anthony Masucci;
Dir: Charles S. Dubin;
Wri: George Bellak.
120 Mins, Thurs (26), 9 pm.
CBS-TV
09/01/76

TERROR INTERNATIONAL
With Tom Mangold, reporter
Supplier: BBC-TV, London
Exec Prod: Frank Smith;
Prod: John Penycate.
90 Mins, Mon, 8:10 pm.
BBC-1, Britain
02/08/78F

TERRORISM - THE WORLD AT BAY
With James Hoge, Marciarose Shestack
Supplier: WHYY-TV Philadelphia
Exec Prod: Jim Karayn;
Prod: Don Fouser;
Dir: Alvin R Mifelow.
120 Mins, Tues (21), 9 pm.
PBS
03/29/78

TESTIMONY OF TWO MEN
(Operation Primetime)
With Tom Bosley (narrator), David Birney, Barbara Parkins, Steve Forrest, Ralph Bellamy, Theodor Bikel, Tom Bosley, J D Cannon, Dan Dailey, Leonard Frey, David Huffman, Randolph Mantooth, Ray Milland, Cameron Mitchell, Kathleen Nolan, Margaret O'Brien, Laurie Prange, Linda Purl, William Shatner, Inga Swenson, others
Supplier: MCA-TV
Prod: Jack Laird;
Dirs: Larry Yust, Leo Penn;
Wris: William Hanley, James M Miller, Jennifer Miller, from novel by Taylor Caldwell.
360 Mins, Sat (7 & 14), 9 pm. and Mon (9), 8 pm.
KCOP-TV Los Angeles
Bristol-Myers (Boclaro), General Foods (Benton & Bowles)
05/18/77S

THANKS A MILLION
With Susan Elliott, Peter Hallenberg, Morris Engle, Sujay Johnson, Michele Valeri
Exec Prod: Bill Cosmas;
Prod-Wri: Mark Young;
Dir: Mike Albro.
30 Mins, Thurs (22), 7:30 pm.
WJLA-TV Washington
11/28/79

THAT MARITIME FEELIN'
With Marg Osburne
Exec Prod: Jack O'Neil.
30 Mins, Fri, 7:30 pm.
CBC-TV, from Halifax, Canada
06/08/77F

THAT THING ON ABC
With Denny Evans, Shelley Long, Judy Carter, Andrea Martin, Mandy Patinkin, Will Porter, Paul Tracey, Marsha Warfield, Deborah Zon, Cheryl Ladd, John Ritter, Bill Bixby, Henny Youngman, John Cameron Swayze
Supplier: Kukoff-Harris Boiney Stoones Prods
Exec Prods: Bernie Kukoff, Jeff Harris;
Dir: Tim Kiley;
Wris: Ray Taylor, Valri Bromfield, Allyn Warner, Tom Moore, Kukoff, Harris.
60 Mins, Wed (4), 8 pm.
ABC-TV
01/11/78

THAT WAS THE YEAR THAT WAS
With Blythe Danner, Buck Henry, Robert Klein, Brenda Vaccaro, Art Buchwald, James Coco, William Daniels, Charles Durning, Jules Feiffer, Ruth Gordon, Tammy Grimes, George Irving, Melba Moore, Edwin Newman, Estelle Parsons, Rex Reed, Cyril Ritchard, Gloria Steinem
Supplier: Rush-Wilson Prods
Exec Prods: Irv Wilson, Herman Rush, Burt Shevelove;
Prod: Frank Badami;
Dir: Don Mischer;
Wris: Buchwald, Feiffer, Henry, Steinem, Mike Barrie, Jim Mulholland, Anthony Geiss, Herb Hartig, Harvey Jacobs, Tom Meehan, Jane Richmond, Lynn Roth, Jonathan Reynolds.
90 Mins, Sun (26), 9:30 pm.
NBC-TV New York
12/29/76

THAT'S HOLLYWOOD
With Anthony Franciosa (host)
Supplier: Grinberg-Lyon Prods (20th-Fox TV)
Exec Prod: Sherman Grinberg;
Prod-dir-wri: John Vincent.
30 Mins, Fri (17), 7:30 pm.
WABC-TV New York
09/22/76S

THAT'S HOLLYWOOD
With Tom Bosley, narrator
Supplier: 20th Century Fox-TV
Exec Prod: Jack Haley Jr;
Prod: Lawrence Einhorn;
Wris: Eytan Keller, Stu Bernstein.
30 Mins, Wed (14), 7:30 pm.
WABC-TV
09/21/77S

THAT'S INCREDIBLE
With John Davidson, Fran Tarkenton, Cathy Lee Crosby (hosts)
Supplier: Alan Landsburg Prods.
Exec Prods: Landsburg, Merrill Grant;
Supv Prod: Woody Franser;
Prod: David Yarnell;
Dir: Arthur Forrest;
Wri: Landsburg.
60 Mins, Mon, 8 pm.
ABC-TV
03/12/80

THERE'S ALWAYS ROOM
With Maureen Stapleton, Conrad Janis, Debbie Zipp, Barry Nelson, Royce D Applegate, Woody Chambliss, Leland Palmer
Supplier: Chris-Rose Prods & Paramount TV
Exec Prods: Robert W Christiansen, Rick Rosenberg;
Prod-Wri: Michael Leeson,
Dir: Robert Moore.
30 Mins, Sun (24), 8:30 pm.
CBS-TV
04/27/77

THEY SAID IT WITH MUSIC: YANKEE DOODLE TO RAGTIME
With Bernadette Peters, Tony Randall, Jason Robards, Jean Stapleton, Flip Wilson, Ladd Anderson, Robert Babb, Teddy Buskner, Tammi Bula, Michael Dess, Avril M Chown, Paul De Korte, Art Evans, Donna Fein, Guy Finley, Kathy Gale, Tammy Glenn, Leeyan Granger, Bessie Griffin, Jimmy Griffin, Helen Judson, Marty Kaniger, Kathleen Kernohan, Bill Lee, Jay Meyer, Thurl Ravenscroft, Vi Redd
Exec Prod: Goddard Lieberson;
Prod-Dir: Bob Henry;
Wris: Lieberson, Max Wilk.
120 Mins, Mon (4), 9 pm.
CBS-TV
07/06/77

13 QUEENS BLVD
With Eileen Brennan, Jerry Van Dyke, Marcia Rodd, Helen Page Camp, Louise Williams, Stanley Brock
Supplier: TOY Prods
Prods: Bud Yorkin, Bernie Orenstein & Saul Turteltaub;
Dir: Kim Friedman;
Wris: Linda Marsh, Margie Peters.
30 Mins, Tues (20), 9:30 pm.
ABC-TV
03/28/79

30TH ANNUAL EMMY AWARDS
With Alan Alda (emcee), Pamela Myers, Ernest Flatt Dancers
Supplier: CBS Entertainment
Prod: Alexander H Cohen;
Dir: Clark Jones;
Wri: Hildy Parks.
210 Mins, Sun (17), 8:30 pm.
CBS-TV
09/20/78

30TH ANNUAL TONY AWARDS
With Eddie Albert, Richard Burton, Jane Fonda, Diana Rigg, George C. Scott, Trish Van Devere, Jerry Orbach, Vivian Reed, Clifton Davis, Michele Lee, Hal Linden, Leslie Uggams, others
Supplier: Bentwood TV Corp.
Prod: Alexander H. Cohen.
Dir: Clark Jones;
Wri: Hildy Parks.
150 Mins, Sun (18)
ABC-TV
04/21/76

30 MINUTES
With Jim Harriott, Wayne Shannon, others
30 Mins, Sun, 6:30 pm.
KIRO-TV Seattle
03/16/77S

30 MINUTES
With Hank Baughman, host; Vicki Rogal, Linda Goldstein
Prod: Ruth Lando;
Dir: John Cochran.
30 Mins, Sat, 6:30 pm.
WIIC-TV Pittsburgh
03/29/78

30 MINUTES
With Betsy Aaron, Christopher Glenn
Supplier: CBS News
Exec Prod: Joel Heller;
Dir: Vern Diamond.
30 Mins, Sat, 1:30 pm.
CBS-TV
09/20/78

32D ANNUAL EMMY AWARDS
With Dick Clark, Steve Allen (hosts)
Supplier: NBC-TV
Exec Prod: Ken Ehrlich;
Dir: Walter C. Miller;
Wris: Rod Warren; Ehrlich.
180 Mins, Sun, (7) 9 pm.
NBC-TV
09/10/80

THIS WAS AMERICA
With William Shatner, narr
Supplier: BBI Communications
Exec Prod: Lew Barlow;
Prod-Dir: Steve Schlow;
Wris: Martin W. Sandler, Schlow.
30 Mins, Mon (1) 7:30 pm.
WNBC-TV New York
09/03/80S

THIS WAS BURLESQUE
(Standing Room Only)
With Ann Corio, Jerry Lester, Lee Meredith, Maxie Furman, Josip Elic, Steve Mills, Charlie Naples, Mike Cooper, Luna, Phoenix Flame, Jennifer Fox
Prod: Michael Brandman;
Dir: Marty Callner.
105 Mins, Sun (16), 9 pm.
HBO
04/20/77PC

THOSE AMAZING ANIMALS
With Burgess Meredith, Jim Stafford, Priscilla Presley
Supplier: Alan Landsburg Prods
Exec Prods: Landsburg, Woody Fraser, Merrill Grant;
Prod-Wri: Draper Lewis;
Dirs: Martin Morris, Mary Hardwick.
60 Mins, Sun, (24) 8 pm.
ABC-TV
08/27/80

THREE ARTISTS IN THE NORTHWEST
Roberta Byrd Barr, narrator
Prod-wri: Jean Walkinshaw.
30 Mins, Fri (1), 7:30 pm.
KCTS Seattle
10/27/76

3 GIRLS 3
With Debbie Allen, Ellen Foley, Mimi Kennedy, Bob Hope, Carol Burnett, Florence Henderson, Zsa Zsa Gabor, Larry Kert, Alan Johnson Dancers, Oliver Clark, Kenny Solms
Supplier: 3 Girls 3 Prods
Exec Prods: Gary Smith & Dwight Hemion;
Prods: Solms & Gail Parent;
Dir: Tony Mordente;
Wris: Solms, Parent, Ed Scharlach, Ann Elder, Sam Greenbaum, Tony Peyser.
60 Mins, Wed (30), 9 pm.
NBC-TV
04/06/77

THREE PIECE SUITE
With Diana Rigg, Peter Barkworth, Barry Norman, Don Henderson, Ken Watson, Jennifer Croxton, others
Supplier: BBC-TV
Prod-Dir: Michael Mills;
Wris: Richard Waring, Roy Clarke, Keith Waterhouse, Willis Hall.
30 Mins, Tues, 9 pm.
BBC-2, Britain
03/16/77F

THREE TIMES DALEY
With Don Adams, Liam Dunn, Jerry House, Bibi Besch
Supplier: Universal TV
Prod-wri: John Rappaport.
30 Mins, Tues (3), 9:30 pm.
CBS-TV
08/11/76

3-2-1
With Liz Moses, Leon Grant, Ginny Ortiz, Nan-Lynn Nelson, Marcellino Sanchez, Kelly Pease
Exec Prod: Kathy Mendoza;
Exec Dir: Keith Mielke;
Dir: Bob Bowker;
Wri: Boyce Rensberger.
30 Mins, Mon-Fri, 5 pm. or various
PBS
01/23/80

THREE'S A CROWD
With Kay Hawtrey, Ita D'Arcy, Alan Royce
Prods-wris: Jack Humphrey, Lois Del Grande;
Dir: Gary Plaxton.
30 Mins, Tues 7:30 pm.
CBC-TV, from Toronto, Canada
10/27/76F

THREE'S A CROWD
with Jim Peck, host
Supplier: Chuck Barris Prods
Exec Prod: Barris;
Prod-Wri: Mike Metzger;
Dir: John Dorsey.
30 Mins, Fri (21), 7:30 pm.
WCBS-TV New York
09/26/79S

THREE'S COMPANY
With John Ritter, Joyce DeWitt, Suzanne Somers, Audra Lindley, Norman Fell, Kit McDonough
Supplier: NRW Co & TTC Prods
Exec Prods: Ted Bergmann, Don Taffner;
Prods: Don Nicholl, Michael Ross, Bernie West;
Dir: Bill Hobin;
Wris: Nicholl, Ross, West, based on Thames TV "Man About the House," by Johnnie Mortimer &
Brian Cooke.
30 Mins, Tues (15), 9:30 pm.
ABC-TV
03/23/77

THURSDAY'S CHILD
Supplier: WVUE-TV
Prod-Wri: Patricia Gormin;
Dir: Gary Furlow.
30 Mins, Wed, 6:30 pm.
WVUE-TV New Orleans
08/09/78

TIC TAC DOUGH
With Wink Martindale (host)
Supplier: Barry-Enright Prods
Exec Prods: Jack Barry, Dan Enright;
Prod: Ron Greenberg;
Dir: Richard Kline.
30 Mins, Mon-Fri, 10 am.
CBS-TV
07/05/78

THE TICHBORNE AFFAIR
With Hugh Keays-Byrne, Aileen Britton, Neil Fitzpatrick, Kevin Miles, Ken Goodlet, Sandra McGregor, Peter Whitford, Peter Gwynne, Tim Eliot, Melissa Jaffer, John Gaden, Keith Lee
Supplier: Australian Broadcasting Commission
Prod: Charles Russell;
Dir: Carl Schultz;
Wris: Brian Faull, James Workman.
75 Mins, Thurs, 8:55 pm.
ABC (Australia) TV
02/16/77F

TICKLED PINK
With Peter Sumner, Cornelia Frances, Noel Ferrier, Judi Farr, Max Gillies, Dawn Lake, John Meillon, Bunney Brooke, Jill Perryman, Martin Harris, Barry Lovett, Barry Otto, Penne Hackforth-Jones, Tony Llewellyn-Jones, others
Supplier: Australian Broadcasting Commission
Exec Prod: Bruce Best;
Dirs: Carl Schultz, David Goldie, Michael Jenkins, Best;
Wris: Colin Hawke, Martin MacAdoo, Michael Aitkens, John Sweetensen, Peter Thorburn, Charles Stamp, Geoffrey Atherden.
30 Mins, Thurs, 8:30 pm.
ABC, Channel 2, Sydney, Australia
11/01/78F

TIGER, TIGER
With Richard Widmark, narrator
Supplier: Survival Anglia Ltd
Exec Prod: Aubrey Buxton;
Wri: Colin Willock.
60 Mins, Thurs (28), 8 pm.
CBS-TV
Kraft Foods (JWT)
05/11/77

TIM CONWAY SHOW
With Carol Burnett, Don Knotts, Craig Richard Nelson, Village People
Supplier: Dummy Prods
Exec Prod: Phil Weltman;
Prod: Joe Hamilton;
Dir: Roger Beatty;
Wris: Conway, Beatty.
60 Mins, Mon (15), 8 pm.
CBS-TV
01/17/79

THE TIM CONWAY SHOW
With Tim Conway, Maggie Roswell, Jack Riley, Eric Boardman, Miriam Flynn, Dick Orkin, Bert Berdis, Michele Lee, The Don Crichton Dancers
Suppliers: Dummy Prods
Exec Prod: Joe Hamilton;
Prods: Bill Richmond, Gene Perret;
Dir: Roger Beatty;
Wris: Richmond, Perret, Beatty, Garry Ferrier, Aubrey Tadman, George Atkins, Jack Handley, Berdis, Orkin, Boardman, Flynn, Conway.
60 Mins, Sat, (22) 8 pm.
CBS-TV
03/26/80

TIME EXPRESS
With Vincent Price, Coral Browne, James Reynolds, William Edward Phipps, Woodrow Parfrey, Jerry Stiller, Anne Meara, James MacArthur, Pamela Toll, Michael Conrad, Bob Delegall, Jan Clayton, Alan Sues, Del Monroe, Doris Dowling, John DeLancie, Richard Angarola
Supplier: Warner Bros TV
Exec Prods: Ivan Goff, Ben Roberts;
Prod: Leonard B Kaufman;
Dir: Arnold Laven;
Wri; Gerald Sanford.
60 Mins Thurs, 8 pm.
CBS-TV
05/02/79

TIME TRAVELERS
With Sam Groom, Tom Hallick, Richard Basehart, Trish Stewart, Francine York, Booth Colman
Supplier: Irwin Allen-20th Century-Fox-TV
Prod: Irwin Allen;
Dir: Alex Singer;
Wri: Jackson Gillis.
90 Mins, Fri, 9 pm.
ABC-TV
03/24/76

TIMELAPSE
With Robert Coleby, John Meillon, Vincent Ball, Karry Francis, Kate Sheil, Anne Charleston
Supplier: Australian Broadcasting Commission
Exec Prod: Eric Tayler;
Dirs: Carl Schultz, Julian Pringle, Frank Arnold, Russ Webb;
Wris: Colin Free, John May, Robert Caswell.
60 Mins, Wed, 8:30 pm.
ABC (Australia) TV, Channel 2, Sydney
03/19/80F

THE TIMELESS LAND
With Michael Craig, Nicola Pagett, Angela Punch McGregor, Ray Barrett, Peter Collingwood, Charles Yunupingu, Chris Haywood, Peter Cousens, Brian Hinselwood, Anna Volska, Noel Trevarthen, Robin Stewart, John Frawley, Patrick Dickson, Max Cullen, Brian Blain, Trevor Kent, Ralph Cotterill, Kirrily Nolan, John Hamblin, Tony Wager, others
Supplier: Australian Broadcasting Commission
Exec Prod: Ray Alchin;
Dirs: Rob Stewart, Michael Carson;
Wri: Peter Yeldham.
50 Mins, 7:30 pm. Thurs
ABC (Australia) TV, Channel 2, Sydney
09/17/80F

TINKER, TAILOR, SOLDIER, SPY
With Alec Guinness, Alexander Knox, Beryl Reid, Ian Richardson, Michael Aldridge, Michael Jayston, Anthony Bate, Hywel Bennett, Ian Bannen, others
Supplier: BBC, Paramount TV
Prod: Jonathan Powell;
Dir: John Irvin;
Wri: Arthur Hopcraft.
50 Mins, Mon, 9 pm.
BBC-2, Britain
10/03/79F

TINY TOWN
With Carrie Cochran
Exec Prod-Dir: Scott Craig;
Prod-Wri: Molly Bedell.
30 Mins, Sat, 9:30 pm.
WBBM-TV, Chicago
11/05/80

TIS THE SEASON TO BE OLLIE
With Burr Tillstrom, Fran Allison & Friends
Prod: Nick Aronson;
Dir: James Tanker;
Wri-Crea: Burr Tillstrom;
30 Mins, Fri (14), 7 pm.
WMAQ-TV Chicago
12/19/79S

TO AMERICA
(CBS Wednesday Night Movie)
With Alan Arkin, Jean-Ivan & Violette Dorin, Andrzej & Alec Bozek
Supplier: Krainin-Sage Prods.
Prod-wri: DeWitt L. Sage Jr.;
Dirs: Sage, Julian Krainin.
105 Mins, Wed (4), 9 pm.
CBS-TV
08/11/76

TO SAY THE LEAST
With Tom Kennedy (host), Rita Moreno, Lee Meriwether, Jamie Farr, Robert Fuller
Supplier: Heatter-Quigley Prods & Filmways
Prod: Robert Noah;
Dir: Jerome Shaw.
30 Mins, Mon-Fri, noon
NBC-TV
10/12/77

TO TELL THE TRUTH
With Robin Ward (host), Soupy Sales, Lynn Redgrave, Jay Johnson, Peggy Cass
Supplier: Goodson-Todman Prods (Viacom)
Exec Prod: Gil Fates;
Prod; Mimi O'Brien;
Dir: Lloyd Gross.
30 Mins, Mon-Fri, 10:30 am.
WABC-TV New York
09/17/80S

TOLLER
With Toller Cranston
Prods-dirs: Pen Densham, John Watson;
60 Mins, Sat, 7 pm.
CTV, from Toronto, Canada
Noranda Mines
11/17/76F

TOM & DICK SMOTHERS BROTHERS SPECIAL 1
With Tom Smothers, Dick Smothers, Martin Mull, Pat Paulsen, Fred Willard, Nicolette Larson, Tom Waits, The Flying Karamazov Brothers
Supplier: Dulcimer Co.
Exec Prods: Tom Smothers, Dick Smothers;
Prod-Dir: Art Fisher;
Wris: Mason Williams, John Barrett, Bob Gardiner, Don Novello, Carl Gottlieb
60 Mins, Sat (1) 10 pm.
NBC-TV
11/05/80

TOM & JOANN
With Elizabeth Ashley, Joel Fabiani, Jennifer Cooke, Colin McKenna, David Ackroyd, Bibi Besch, Tim Okon, Marie McCann, Brenda Donohue, Louis DelGrande
Supplier: Time-Life TV
Exec Prod: David Susskind;
Prods: Frederick Brogger, Diana Kerew;
Dir: Delbert Mann;
Wri: Loring Mandel.
60 Mins, Wed (5), 9 pm.
CBS-TV
07/12/78

TOM SNYDER'S CELEBRITY SPOTLIGHT
With Barry Manilow, Gary Coleman, Clint Eastwood, Bo Derek
Supplier: NBC
Prod: Andrew Friendly;
Dir: George Paul.
60 Mins, Mon, (21) 10 pm.
NBC-TV
01/30/80

TONY RANDALL SHOW
With Tony Randall, Barney Martin, Allyn Ann McLerie, Devon Scott, Brad Savage, Rachel Roberts, Melendy Britt
Supplier: MTM Enterprises
Prods-wris: Tom Patchett, Jay Tarses;
Dir: Jay Sandrich.
60 Mins, Thurs, (23), 9 pm.
ABC-TV
09/29/76

TOO CLOSE FOR COMFORT
With Ted Knight, Nancy Dussault, Deborah Van Valkenburgh, Lydia Cornell, Fern Fitzgerald, Jeff Maxwell, Mike Nomad, Kristin Kelly, Jamie Mizada
Supplier: Don-El Prods
Exec Prod: Arne Sultan;
Supv Prod: Earl Barret;
Prod: Jerry McPhie;
Dir: Will Mackenzie;
Wris: Sultan & Barret, Brian Cooke, based on Cooke's "Keep It In the Family" for Thames TV
30 Mins, Tues, 9:30 pm.
ABC-TV
11/19/80

THE TOP OF THE HILL
(Operation Prime Time)
With Wayne Roger, Elke Sommer, Adrienne Barbeau, Sonny Bono, Peter Brown, J.D. Cannon, Macdonald Carey, Mel Ferrer, Gary Lockwood, Carmen Mathews, Richard O'Brien, Paula Prentiss, Denise DuBarry, Rae Dawn Chong, Allisson Carroll, Chuck Hicks
Supplier: Fellows-Keegan Co., & Paramount TV
Exec Prods: Arthur Fellows, Terry Keegan;
Prod: John Cutts;
Dir: Walter Grauman;
Wri: Eric Bercovici, from story by Irwin Shaw.
240 Mins, Tues, (29), Part One, 8-10 pm., Tues, (5), Part Two, 8-10 pm.
KCOP-TV Los Angeles
02/13/80S

TORQUE
With Peter Wherrett
Suupplier: Australian Broadcasting Commission
Exec Prod: Brian Adams;
Dirs: Andrew Lloyd James, Brian Nicholls.
30 Mins, Wed, 7:30 pm.
ABC (Australia) TV, Channel 2, Sydney
07/16/80F

TRANSFORMATIONS: 3 LOUISIANA ARTISTS
Supplier: WYES-TV
Prod: Madeleine Butler;
Dir: David Frentz.
30 Mins, Tues (12), 6:30 pm.
WYES-TV New Orleans
09/27/78

TRAPPER JOHN, MD
With Pernell Roberts, Gregory Harrison, Mary McCarty, Charles Siebert, Christopher Norris, Brian Mitchell, Jack Gilford, Barbara Stuart, Jessica Walter, Roddy McDowall, Stephen Pearlman, Ned Wilson, Joe Spano, Mariko Tse
Supplier: Frank Glicksman Prods, Don Brinkley Prods & 20th-Fox TV
Prod: Glicksman;
Dir: Jackie Cooper;
Wri: Brinkley.
60 Mins, Sun, 10 pm.
CBS-TV
09/26/79

TRIAL BY MARRIAGE
With Jacki Weaver, Peter Sumner, Terry Bader, Bill Kerr, Maggie Dence, Carole Skinner
Supplier: Australian Broadcasting Commission
Exec Prod: John O'Grady;
Dirs: David Goldie, Geoff Portman;
Wri: Michael Aitkens.
30 Mins, Mon, 7:30 pm.
ABC (Australia) Channel 2, Sydney
09/03/80F

THE TRIALS AND TRIUMPHS OF FREDERICK DOUGLASS
With Rep Ronald Dellums
Exec Prod: Dewey Hughes;
Prod: Sandra Butler;
Wri: Charlene Porter.
60 Mins, Thurs (14), 8 pm.
WRC-TV Washington
04/20/77

THE TRUCKIES
With Michael Aitkens, Colleen Hewett, John Wood, John Ewart, Lois Ramsay, Michael Carman, Frank Wilson, Tom Oliver, Tommy Dysart, Peter Cummins, Sue Jones, John Arnold, Rosie Sturgess, Bruce Spence, Vic Gordon, Graeme Blundell, Sandra McGregor, Sigrid Thornton, Helen Heminway, Jackie Keren, Wendy Gilmore, Monica Maughan, Gordon Glenwright, Kerry Dwyer, Denise Drusdale, Brian Hannan, Gerard Kennedy, Hamish Hughes, Maurie Fields
Supplier: Australian Broadcasting Commission
Exec Prod: Oscar Whitbread;
Dirs: John Gauci, Douglas Sharp, Michael Ludbrook, David Zweck, Whitbread;
Wris: Keith Thompson, Phil Freedman, Everett de Roche, Aitkens, Wood, Howard Griffiths.
55 Mins, Mon, 8:30 pm.
ABC TV, from Sydney, Australia
08/09/78F

TRUE GRIT
(ABC Friday Night Movie)
With Warren Oates, Lisa Pelikan, Jeff Osterhage, Lee Meriwether, James Stephens, Lee H Montgomery, Ramon Bieri, Redmond Gleason, Lee DeBroux, Jack Fletcher, Parley Baer, Fred Cook, Richard McKenzie
Supplier: Paramount TV
Prod-Wri: Sandor Stern;
Dir: Richard T Heffron.
120 Mins, Fri (19), 9 pm.
ABC-TV
05/31/78

TRUMAN AT POTSDAM
(Hallmark Hall Of Fame)
With Ed Flanders, John Houseman, Jose Ferrer, Alexander Knox, others
Supplier: Talent Assoc's. Clarion Prods.
Prod: David Susskind;
Dir: George Schaefer;
Wri: Sidney Carroll.
90 Mins, Thurs (8), 8 pm.
NBC-TV
Hallmark (F C & B)
04/14/76

TURNABOUT
With Gerri Lange
Supplier: KQED San Francisco
Exec Prod: Martha Glessing;
Prod: Roxanne Russell;
Dir: Louise Lo.
30 Mins, Fri, 10 pm.
PBS
TURNABOUT A
02/15/78

TURNABOUT
With Gerri Lange, Felicia Lowe
Supplier: KQED San Francisco
Exec Prod: Martha Glessing;
Prod: Roxanne Russell;
Dir: Louise Lu.
30 Mins, week of Oct 1, various times.
PBS
10/04/78S

TURNABOUT
With John Schuck, Sharon Gless, Richard Stahl, Bobbi Jordan, Bruce Kirby, James Sikking, Dena Dietrich
Supplier: Universal TV
Exec Prod: Sam Denoff;
Prods: Michael Rhodes, Arnold Kane;
Dir: Richard Crenna;
Wri: Steven Bochco.
30 Mins, Fri, 9 pm.
NBC-TV
01/31/79

TV CRITICS CIRCLE AWARDS
With Beverly Sills, Steve Lawrence, others
Supplier: Talent Associates
Exec Prod: David Susskind;
Prods: Gary Smith, Dwight Hemion;
Dir: Hemion;
Wris: Marty Farrell, Pat Proft, Leonard Ripps.
120 Mins, Mon (11), 9 pm.
CBS-TV
04/13/77

TV FOLLIES
With Noni Hazlehurst, Robyn Moase, David Atkins, Max Cullen, Gus Mercurio, Arthur Dignam, Kathy Lloyd, Normie Rowe, Jane Harders, Debbie Byrne, Geraldine Turner, Julie McGregor, Terry Bader, Freddie Paris, Brenda Kristen, Norman Erskine, others
Supplier: Australian Broadcasting Commission
Prod: Ric Birch;
Dirs: Eric Black, Mike Jenkins, Johnny Walker.
60 Mins, Sat, 7:30 pm.
ABC, from Sydney, Australia
06/13/79F

TV ON TRIAL
With Richard Reeves, host
Supplier: WPBT Miami
Exec Prod: Shep Morgan;
Prod: Don Fouser.
120 Mins, Tues (23), 9 pm.
PBS
05/31/78

TV: THE FABULOUS '50'S
With Red Skelton, Lucille Ball, David Janssen, Michael Landon, Mary Martin, Dinah Shore
Supplier: Henry Jaffe Enterprises & 20th Century Fox
Exec Prod: Henry Jaffe;
Prods-Wris: David Lawrence, Draper Lewis;
Dir: Jonathan Lucas.
90 Mins, Sun, 8 pm.
NBC
03/08/78

THE TVTV SHOW
With Howard Hessman, Mary Frann, Carl Gottlieb, Mina Kolb, Gary Goodrow, Annie Poth, Mike Darnell
Supplier: TVTV Productions Co
Prod: Michael Shamberg;
Dir: Alan Myerson;
Wris: Mary Kay Brown, Peter Elbling, Brian McConnachie, Billy Murray, Shamberg.
90 Mins, Sat (30), Midnight
NBC-TV
05/04/77

'TWAS THE NIGHT BEFORE CHRISTMAS
With Paul Lynde, Anne Meara, Foster Brooks, Martha Raye, Alice Ghostley, Howard Morris, George Gobel, Anson Williams, Susan Page, Tiffany Ann Francis, Rachel Jacobs, Sparky Marcus, Tommy Krebs
Supplier: Hoysyl Prods & Welch-Layton-Welch Prods
Exec Prods: Raymond Katz, Sandy Gallin;
Prods: Joe Layton, Ken Welch, Mitzi Welch;
Dir: Tim Kiley;
Wris: Dick Clair, Jenna McMahon.
120 Mins, Wed (7), 8 pm.
ABC-TV
12/14/77

THE 20TH ANNIVERSARY SPECIAL
With Bert Newton, Graham Kennedy, Eric Pearce, Michael Schielberger, Tony Ward, Tommy Hanlon Jr, Noel Ferrier
Prods: Peter Fairman, Bob Phillips, John Crilly;
Wri: Pat Tennison.
190 Mins, Wed, 8:30 pm.
GTV-9 Melbourne, Australia
10/06/76F

28TH ANNUAL EMMY AWARDS
With Mary Tyler Moore, John Denver
Prod: Norman Rosemont;
Dir: John Moffitt;
Wri: Marty Farrell.
159 Mins, Mon (17), 9 pm.
ABC-TV
05/19/76

25 YEARS OF DISNEY - PART ONE
With Ron Howard, Suzanne Somers, others
Supplier: Walt Disney Prods
Exec Prod: Ernest Chambers;
Prod: Rocco Urbisci;
Dir: Art Fisher;
Wris: Hal Kanter, Rick Kellard & Bob Comfort, Dennis Landa, Tom Adair, Urbisci, Chambers.
240 Mins, Wed (13) & Sun (17), 8 pm.
NBC-TV
09/20/78

TWENTY GOOD YEARS
With Anne Pendlebury, Harold Hopkins, Julia Blake, Jonathan Hardy, Leila Hayes, John Murphy, Michael Carmen, Anne Charleston
Supplier: Australian Broadcasting Commission
Exec Prod: Keith Wilkes;
Dirs: Norman Johnson, David Zweck, Robin Wischusen, Margaret Greenwell;
Wris: Sandy Ringer, Judith Colquhoun, Alan McCoy, Brian Wright, Richard Lane, Oriel Gray, Sheila Sibley, Alan Hopgood.
50 Mins, Tues, 8:30 pm.
ABC (Australia)
05/09/79F

21 HOURS AT MUNICH
(ABC Sunday Night Movie)
With William Holden, Shirley Knight, Franco Nero, Anthony Quayle, Noel Willman, Georg Marischka, Paul Smith, Martin Gilat, Richard Basehart
Supplier: Filmways & Moonlight Prods
Exec Prod: Edward S. Feldman;
Prods: Frank von Zerneck, Robert Greenwald;
Dir: William A. Graham;
Wris: Edward Hume, Howard Fast.
120 Mins, Sun (7), 9 pm.
ABC-TV
11/10/76

UNITED STATES   TV CREDITS

20 SHADES OF PINK
(GE Theatre)
With Eli Wallach, Anne Jackson, Edward Binns, Keenan Wynn, Jane Mallett, Jodi Farber, Miles McNamara, Joey Davidson, others
Exec Prod: Robert Markell;
Prod: Anthony Masucci;
Dir: Paul Stanley;
Wris: Gwen Bagni, Paul Dubov.
120 Mins Fri (12), 9 pm.
CBS-TV
General Electric (BBDO)
03/17/76

20/20
With Harold Hayes, Robert Hughes, David Marash, Sander Vanocur, Sylvia Chase, Geraldo Rivera
Supplier: ABC News
Exec Prod: Bob Shanks;
Wris: Brock Brower, Edward Tivnan;
Dir: Jorn Winter.
60 Mins, Tues, 10 pm.
ABC-TV
06/14/78

TWIN DETECTIVES
(ABC Saturday Night Movie)
With Jim Hager, Jon Hager, Lillian Gish, others
Supplier: Charles Fries Productions-Worldvision
Exec Prod: Charles Fries;
Prod: Everett Chambers;
Dir: Robert Day;
Wri: Robert Specht.
90 Mins, Sat (1), 9:30 pm.
ABC-TV
05/05/76

TWO BROTHERS
(Visions)
With Judd Hirsch, David Spielberg, Sarah Cunningham, Diane Shallet, Stephen Elliot, Tom Rosqui, others
Supplier: KCET-TV Los Angeles
Prod: Barbara Schultz;
Dir: Burt Brinckerhoff;
Wri: Conrad Bromberg.
85 Mins, Thurs (21), 9 pm.
PBS
10/27/76

THE TWO-FIVE
(ABC Friday Night Movie Special Double Feature)
With Don Johnson, Joe Bennett, Michael Durrell, George Murdock, John Crawford, Carlene Watkins, Richard O'Brien, Sandy McPeak, Jacques Aubuchon, Henry Olek, Walter Matthews, Curtis Credel, Maurice Downs, Tara Buckman, Marty Zagon
Supplier: Universal TV
Exec Prod: R A Cinader;
Prods: Gian R Grimaldi, Hannah L Shearer;
Dir: Bruce Kessler;
Wris: Cinader, Joseph Polizzi.
90 Mins Fri (14), 9:30 pm.
ABC-TV
04/19/78

THE TWO-FIVE
With Don Johnson, Joe Bennett, Michael Durrell, George Murdock, John Crawford, Shelley Berman, Curtis Credel, Richard Herd, Stephen Johnson
Supplier: Universal TV
Exec Prod-Wri: R A Cinader;
Prods: Gian R Grimaldi, Hannah Shearer;
Dir: Jules Irving.
60 Mins, Sun (7), 8 pm.
ABC-TV
01/10/79

240-ROBERT
With John Bennett Perry, Mark Harmon, Joanna Cassidy, Lew Saunders, JoeAl Nicassio, Mac Wilkins, Michael Toland, Burt Marshall, Pamelyn Ferdin, Karen Lamm, Christian Zika, Janice Lynde, Chip Lucia, Irene Tedrow, Marie Earle, Sandie Newton, Susan McDonald, Bob Hoy, Yale Summers
Supplier: Rosner TV & Filmways TV Prods
Exec Prod: Rick Rosner;
Prod: Richard M Rosenbloom;
Dir: Paul Krasny;
Wri: John Furia Jr.
90 Mins, Tues (28), 8:30 pm.
ABC-TV
09/05/79

TYLER
With R H Thomson, Sharon Smits, Robert McClure, Murray Westgate, Sean McCann, Kay Hawtrey
Exec Prod-Dir: Ralph Thomas;
Prod: David Pears;
Wri: Roy MacGregor.
90 Mins, Sat, 9:30 pm.
CBC-TV, from Toronto, Canada
09/27/78F

THE ULTIMATE IMPOSTER
With Joseph Hacker, Keith Andes, Macon McCalman, Erin Gray, Tracy Brooks Swope, Rosalind Chao, John Van Dreelen, Bobby Riggs, Robert Phillips, Normann Burton
Supplier: Universal TV
Exec Prod-Wri: Lionel E Siegel;
Dir: Paul Stanley.
120 Mins, Sat, (12), 9 pm.
CBS-TV
05/16/79

UN MITO LLAMADO ELECTRA
(A Myth Called Electra)
With Nuria Torray, Paquita Rico, Andres Resino, Manuel Gallardo, Marisa Lahoz, Montserrat Blanch, Paca Quintero, Antonio Zori
Supplier: Spanish Radiotelevision
Prod: Angel Masso;
Dir-Wri: Juan Guerrero Zamora.
60 Mins, Thurs, 8:30 pm.
RTVE, from Madrid, Spain
03/14/79F

UNCLE TIM WANTS YOU
With Tim Conway, Bernadette Peters, Jonathan Winters, Bob Holt, Chuck Blore, Brad Trumbull, The Marquis Chimps, George Foster Dancers
Supplier: Noway Prods
Prod: Joe Hamilton;
Dir: Dave Powers;
Wris: Bill Richmond, Gene Perret, Roger Beatty, Conway, Winters
60 Mins, Sat (17), 8 pm.
CBS-TV
09/21/77

UNCLE TOM'S CABIN (1926)
Raymond Massey, narrator; Sterling Smith, host
WGNO-TV New Orleans
07/07/76

THE UNCOMMON COLD
Prod-Wri: Tyler Johnson.
30 Mins, Thurs, 7:30 pm.
KING-TV Seattle
02/09/77

UNDER MONUMENT PROTECTION
Supplier: Hessischer Rundfunk, Frankfurt
Prod: Hessischer Rundfunk, Frankfurt;
Dir-wri-narr: Eberhard Fechner.
90 Mins, Sun, 3:25 pm.
HR, First Program, from Frankfurt, West Germany
04/14/76F

THE UNEXPLAINED
With Leonard Nimoy (host)
Supplier: Wolper Prods. (Columbia Pictures TV)
Prod-Wri: Robert Guenette
Dir: Don Horan
30 Mins, Fri (13), 7:30 pm.
WNBC-TV New York
02/18/76S

THE UNFINISHED CHILD
With Patricia Neal, narrator
Supplier: ABC-TV o&o's, Lirol Prods.
Prods-wris: Bill Stewart, Fred Rhinestein.
30 Mins, Mon (7), 7:30 pm.
WABC-TV New York
06/16/76S

UNITED STATES
With Beau Bridges, Helen Shaver, Rossie Harris, Justin Dana
Supplier: O.T.P. Ltd
Exec Prod-Wri: Larry Gelbart;
Prod: Gary Markowitz;
Dir: Nick Havinga.
30 Mins, Tues, 10:30 pm.
NBC-TV
03/19/80

UNIVERSE
With Walter Cronkite, Charles Osgood, Terry Drinkwater
Supplier: CBS News
Exec prod: Ron Bonn;
Prods: David Turecamo, Jonathan Ward, David Browning, Barbara Moss, Roger Field;
Dir: Joel Banow;
Wri: Bonn.
30 Mins, Wed (27), 8 pm.
CBS-TV
07/04/79

THE UNKNOWN WAR
With Burt Lancaster (narrator)
Supplier: Air Time International
Exec Prod: Isaac Kleinerman;
Prod: Fred Weiner;
Dir: Roman Karmen;
Wris: Weiner, Karmen, John Lord, Rod McKuen.
60 Mins, Sat, 7 pm.
WOR-TV New York
10/11/78S

UP FROM THE CRADLE OF JAZZ
With Neville Brothers, Lastie Family
Supplier: WYES-TV
Prod: Jason Berry, Jonathan Foose;
Dir: David Frentz;
Wri: Berry.
60 Mins, 6 pm.
WYES-TV, New Orleans
10/22/80

UPTOWN-A TRIBUTE TO THE APOLLO THEATRE
With Natalie Cole, Lou Rawls, Ben Vereen, Flip Wilson, Bunny Briggs, Cab Calloway, Billy Eckstine, Gladys Knights & Pips, Might Clouds of Joy, Nipsey Russell, Doc Severinsen, Sandman Sims, Temptations, Sarah Vaughan, Jack Albertson, Lester Wilson Dancers
Supplier: Smith-Hemion Prods & Hope Enterprises
Prods: Gary Smith, Dwight Hemion;
Dir: Hemion;
Wris: Harry Crane, Marty Farrell.
120 Mins, Fri, (30) 9 pm.
NBC-TV
06/04/80

US MAGAZINE LOOKS AT THE '70S
With David Letterman (host)
Supplier: Crossover Programming co.
Prod: Charles Braverman;
Dir: Marshall Harvey;
Wri: Peter Travers.
60 Mins, Sun, (27), 8 pm.
Showtime Entertainment
01/30/80PC

VALDY: FOLKSINGER DELUXE
(Superspecials)
With Valdy, Homemade Theatre, The Hometown Band
Prod-Dir: David Acomba;
Wris: Acomba, others.
60 Mins, Sun, 7:30 pm.
CBC-TV, from Toronto, Canada
02/09/77F

VALENTINE'S SECOND CHANCE
(ABC Short Story Special)
With Ken Berry, Greg Morris, Elizabeth Baur, Sean Marshall, Ham Larson, Max Showalter, Burke Byrnes
Supplier: ABC Circle Films
Exec Prod: Allen Ducovny;
Prod: William Beaudine Jr;
Dir: Hollingsworth Morse;
Wri: Alvin Boretz.
30 Mins, Sat (29), Noon
ABC-TV
Mego Corp (Ted Bates), Nabisco (William Esty)
02/09/77

VAN DYKE & COMPANY
With Dick Van Dyke, Chevy Chase, Flip Wilson, Andy Kaufman, Katee McClure, Dinah Shore, George Foreman, others
Supplier: Catspaw Prods-Blye-Einstein Prods
Exec Prod: Byron Paul;
Prods: Allan Blye, Bob Einstein;
Dir: John Moffitt;
Wris: Blye, Einstein, Van Dyke, George Burditt, Paul Wayne, Mickey Ross, Ken Finkelman, Aubrey Tadman, Gary Ferrier, Pat Proft, Lennie Rips, Don Novello, Mitch Markowitz
60 Mins, Mon, (20), 10 pm.
NBC-TV
09/22/76

VARIETY '77 - THE YEAR IN ENTERTAINMENT
With Alan King, Sada Thompson, Telly Savalas, Dionne Warwick, Valerie Perrine (hosts); Steve Martin, Andy Kaufman, Judd Hirsch, Anita Gillette, Rose Royce, Peter Frampton, Barry Manilow, Kenny Rogers, Sex Pistols, others
Supplier: Ernest Chambers Prods
Prod: Chambers;
CoProds: Marshall Flaum, Rudy Tellez;
Dir: Stan Harris;
Wris: John Box, Chambers.
90 Mins, Mon (9), 8 pm.
CBS-TV
01/11/78

VEGA$
(ABC Movie Special)
With Robert Urich, Will Sampson, Chick Vennera, Michael Lerner, Elissa Leeds, Red Buttons, June Allyson, Edd Byrnes, Scatman Crothers, Jack Kelly, Greg Morris, Tony Curtis, Phyllis Davis, Colby Chester, Judy Landers, John Quade, Jason Wingreen, Ned Glass, Bart Braverman, Diane Parkinson, Katherine Hickland
Supplier: Aaron Spelling Prods
Exec Prods: Spelling, Douglas S Cramer;
Prod: E Duke Vincent;
Dir: Richard Lang;
Wri: Michael Mann.
90 Mins, Tues (25), 9:30 pm.
ABC-TV
05/03/78

VEGA$
With Robert Urich, Tony Curtis, Bart Braverman, Phyllis Davis, Judy Landers, Naomi Stevens, Christine Ferrare, John Ericson, Richard Roat, Will Sampson, Dane Clark, Abe Vigoda, Morey Amsterdam, Vic Tayback
Supplier: Aaron Spelling Prods
Exec Prods: Spelling, Douglas S Cramer;
Prod: Alan S Godfrey;
Dir: Harry Falk;
Wri: Burton Armus.
60 Mins, Wed, 10 pm.
ABC-TV
09/27/78

VERNA: U S O GIRL
(Great Performances)
With Sissy Spacek, Sally Kellerman, Howard da Silva, William Hurt
Supplier: WNET New York
Prods: Jac Venza, Ronald F. Maxwell;
Dir: Maxwell;
Wri: Albert Innaurato, from Paul Gallico short story.
90 Mins, Wed (25), 9 pm.
PBS
02/01/78

VERY LIKE A WHALE
With Alan Bates, Gemma Jones, Ann Bell, Leslie Sands, Myra Frances, Anne Stallybrass, Christopher Benjamin, Anna Cropper, Ian Hogg
Supplier: ATV (Black Lion Films)
Exec Prod: Barry Hanson;
Prod: Jacky Stoller;
Dir: Alan Bridges.
83 Mins, Wed, (13), 8 pm.
ITV Network, England
02/27/80F

VERY SPECIAL PEOPLE
(Man Alive)
With Roy Bonisteel, Famous People Players
Exec Prod: Leo Rampen;
Prod: Louis Lore.
30 Mins, Mon, 10:30 pm.
CBC-TV, from Toronto, Canada
12/08/76F

VIETNAM: PICKING UP THE PIECES
(Visa)
Supplier: Downtown Community TV Center and TV Laboratory at WNET-TV
Exec Prod: David Loxton;
Prods-Wris: Jon Alpert and Keiko Tsuno.
60 Mins, Tues (11), 9 pm.
WNET-TV New York
04/19/78

VIKINGS
With Colin Blakely, Jeremy Kemp, John Bennett, Daniel Massey
Supplier BBC-TV & KTCA-TV
Prods: Ray Sutcliffe, David Collison;
Wri-Narr: Magnus Magnusson.
KTCA-TV St Paul-Minneapolis
10/08/80

VIOLENCE IN AMERICA
With Ed Newman, Linda Ellerbee, Floyd Kalber, Carl Stokes, others
Exec Prod: Stuart Schulberg;
Prods: William Cosmas, Adrienne Cowles;
Dirs: Darold Murray, Ivan Cury;
Wris: William A Bales, Cowles, Les Dennis, Mike Gavin, Alan Mohan, Newman, Marion Lear Swaybill, Bill Turque, Jean Sprain Wilson.
180 Mins, Wed (5), 8 pm.
NBC-TV
01/12/77

VIVA VALDEZ
With Carmen Zapata, Rodolfo Hoyos, James Victor, Nelson D. Cuevas, Lisa Mordente, Claudio Martinez, Jorge Cervera Jr.
Supplier: Rothman/Wohl Prods., Stan Jacobson Prods. & Columbia Pictures TV
Exec Prods: Jacobson, Bernard Rothman, Jack Wohl;
Prods: Phil Mishkin, Alan Rafkin;
Dir: Rafkin;
Wri: Earl Barret.
30 Mins, Mon, 8 pm.
ABC-TV
06/02/76

THE VOICE
(Die Stimme)
With Christian Brueckner
Supplier: Sender Freies Berlin (SFB)
Dir: Wolfgang Tumler.
45 Mins, Sun, 10:25 pm.
SFB (First Channel) Berlin, West Germany
09/01/76F

VOICE OF THE FUGITIVE
(Adventures in History)
With George Ashley, Taborah Johnson, Arleigh Peterson, Dennis Picaud, Chris Wiggins, Ruth Springford
Dir: Rene Bonierre;
Wri: John Kent Harrison.
30 Mins, Sun, 9 pm.
CBC, from Toronto, Canada
05/09/79F

THE VOICES OF AFRICA
With Roger Grimsby
Exec Prod: Ron Tindiglia;
Prod: Daryl Griffin;
Wri: Grimsby.
60 Mins, Sat (9), 7 pm.
WABC-TV New York
10/13/76

VOLCANO
With Richard Burton, narrator
Exec Prod: James de B. Domville;
Prods: Donald Brittain, R.A. Duncan
Dir-wris: Brittain, John Kramer;
Mus: Alain Clavier.
90 Mins, Wed, 9:30 pm.
CBS-TV, from Toronto
04/14/76

VOTER APATHY: THE LAST MAJOR SHACKLE
Prod-reporter: Bruce Johnson;
60 Mins, Sun (21), 4 pm.
WDVM-TV Washington DC
11/07/79

WAKE OF '38
Exec Prod: Ray Fass;
Prod-Wri: Fred Muhly;
Dir: Ray Terchiak.
60 Mins, Tues, 9 pm.
WSBE-TV Providence
11/22/78

WAR BRIDES
With Layne Coleman, Sonja Smits, Sharry Flett, Geoffrey Bowes, Wendy Clewson, Elizabeth Richardson, Timothy Webber, Ken Pogue
Prod: Bill Gough;
Dir: Martin Lavut;
Wri: Grahame Woods.
120 Mins, Sat, 9 pm.
CBC-TV, from Toronto, Canada
10/08/80F

WARNER WOLF SHOW
Exec Prod: Wolf;
Prod: Carmine Cincotta;
Dir: Joseph Terry.
30 Mins, Tues, 7:30 pm.
WCBS-TV New York
09/17/80

WASHINGTON: BEHIND CLOSED DOORS
With Cliff Robertson, Jason Robards, Stefanie Powers, Robert Vaughn, Lois Nettleton, Barry Nelson, Harold Gould, Tony Bill, Andy Griffith, John Houseman
Supplier: Stanley Kallis, Daivd W Rintels, Eric Bercovici, with Paramount TV
Exec Prod: Kallis;
Prod: Norman Powell;
Dir: Gary Nelson;
Wris: Rintels, Bercovici; based on "The Company", by John Ehrlichman.
150 Mins, Tues (6), 8:30 pm.
ABC-TV
09/07/77

THE WATER MARGIN
With Atsuo Nakamura, Kei Sato, Hajime Hana, Sanae Tsuchida, Yoshiyo Matsuo
Supplier: BBC
Dir: Toshio Masuda.
45 Mins, Tues, 9:40 pm.
BBC-2, Britain
09/29/76F

WATER UNDER THE BRIDGE
With Robyn Nevin, David Cameron, Judy Davis, Jaci Weaver, Chris Milne, Jan Hamilton, Linden Wilkinson, Rod Mullinar, Rowena Wallace, Peter Whitford, John Howard, Ralph Cotterill, Peita Toppano, Sean Scully, Briony Behets, Graeme Blundell, Tommy Dysart, Arthur Dignam, Geraldine Morrow, others
Exec Prod: John McRae;
Dir: Igor Auzins;
Wris: Eleanor Witcombe, Michael Jenkins.
120 Mins, Wed, 8:30 pm.
Channel 10, Sydney, Australia
10/08/80F

THE WAVERLY WONDERS
With Joe Namath, Charles Bloom, Kim Lankford, Ben Piazza, Joshua Grenrock, Tierre Turner, James Staley, Conrad Bain, Hope Alexander-Willis
Supplier: Lorimar Prods
Exec Prods: Lee Rich, Marc Merson;
Prods: Steve Zacharias, Bruce Kane;
Dir: Dick Martin;
Wris: Ben Wilcox, Thad Mumford.
30 Mins, Fri, 8 pm.
NBC-TV
09/27/78

WAYNE & SHUSTER
With Johnny Wayne, Frank Shuster, Carol Robinson, others
Exec Prod: Leonard J Starmer;
Prods: Wayne, Shuster;
Dir: Trevor Evans;
Wris: Wayne, Shuster, Dave Mayerovitch, Bob Sandler.
60 Mins, Sun, 8 pm.
CBC, from Toronto, Canada
03/16/77F

WE INTERRUPT THIS WEEK
With Ned Sherrin, Nora Ephron, Jeff Greenfield, Marshall Brickman, Pat Buchanan, Richard Reeves, Jimmy Breslin
Supplier: The Film Writers Co
Prod: John Gilroy;
Dir: David Heeley.
30 Mins, Sat, 9 pm.
WNET-TV New York
11/09/77S

WE INTERRUPT THIS WEEK
With Ned Sherrin (host), Marshall Brickman, Carrie Nye, Richard Reeves, Barbara Howar, Robert Newman, Robin MacNeil
Supplier: WNET-TV New York, for PBS
Exec Prod: Tom Slevin;
Prod: John Gilroy;
Dir: David Heeley;
Wris: Sherrin, Tony Geiss.
30 Mins, Fri, 9 pm.
WNET-TV
10/11/78

WEATHER REPORT '80: THE ALMOST, NOT QUITE, SURE THING
With Fritz Weaver (narrator)
Supplier: Playback Associates (George Back & Associates, Richard Perin)
Exec Prod: James C. Crimmins;
Prod: Webster F. Golinkin;
Wris: Rockwell Stensrud, Crimmins.
60 Mins, Wed, (16), 8 pm.
WPIX New York
01/23/80S

W. E. B.
With Pamela Bellwood, Alex Cord, Lee Wilkof, Howard Witt, Richard Basehart, Andrew Prine, Zalman King, John Collcos, Tisch Raye, Peter Coffield
Supplier: Lin Bolen Prods, 20th-Fox TV
Exec Prod: Bolen;
Prod: Chris Morgan;
Dir: Harvey Hart;
Wri: David Karp.
60 Mins, Wed (13), 10 pm.
NBC
09/20/78

WEEKDAY FEVER
With Tim Byrd, Nanci Glass, others
Exec Prod: John Pike;
Dirs: Stuart Pollock Stuart Calcotte.
60 Mins, Mon-Fri, 4 pm.
WKYC-TV Cleveland
11/08/78

WEEKEND
With Linda Ellerbee, Lloyd Dobyns
Exec Prod: Reuven Frank;
Prods: Sy Pearlman, Craig Leake, Vernon Hixson.
60 Mins, Sun (10), 10 pm.
NBC-TV
09/13/78

WE'RE NO HEROES
Prod: Jan Skrentny.
30 Mins, Thurs (9), 8 pm.
WMAL-TV Washington
12/22/76

WESTSIDE MEDICAL
With James Sloyan, Linda Carlson, Ernest Thompson, Season Hubley, Alice Nunn, Reed Diamond, Jane Wilk, Darrell Larson, Pat Ast, Larry Pleet, MD
Supplier: Marstar Prods
Exec Prod: Martin Starger;
Prod: Alan A Armer;
Dir: Ralph Senensky;
Wri: Worley Thorne.
60 Mins, Tues (15), 10 pm.
ABC-TV
03/23/77

WE'VE GOT EACH OTHER
With Oliver Clark, Beverly Archer, Joan Van Ark, Ren Woods, Martin Kove, Tom Poston, Anitra Ford
Supplier: MTM Prods
Exec Prod-Wris: Tom Patchett & Jay Tarses;
Prod: Jack Burns;
Dir: James Burrows.
30 Mins, Sat, 8:30 pm.
CBS-TV
10/05/77

WHAT A YEAR - 1978
With Melissa Sue Anderson, Shirley Hemphill, Fred Berry, Mark Brown, Rae Dawn Chong, David Cooper, Peter Horton, Helen Lockwood, Michael Misita, Donovan Scott, Lois Young
Supplier: Bob Banner Associates, with Golden West TV (Syndicast Services)
Exec Prod: Banner;
Prod: Sam Riddle;
Dir Arthur Forrest;
Wris: Bill Larkin, Martin Ragaway, Joe Shulkin.
30 Mins, Thurs, (4), 7:30 pm.
KNBC-TV Los Angeles
Colgate Palmolive
01/10/79S

WHAT DO YOU WANT TO BE...WHEN YOU GROW OLD?
With Lorne Greene (narrator)
Supplier: DCA Prod (Y&R Ventures)
Exec Prod: Dick Cox;
Prod-dir-wri: William Peters.
30 Mins, Sat (18), 6 pm.
WCBS-TV New York
Roerig (Young & Rubicam)
09/22/76S

WHAT REALLY HAPPENED TO THE CLASS OF '65?
With Annette O'Toole, Priscilla Pointer, Denny Miller, Charles Frank, Tim Matheson, Valerie Armstrong, Tony Bill
Supplier: Pan Arts Prods & Universal TV
Exec Prod: Richard Irving;
Dir: Harry Falk;
Wri: Ann Beckett.
60 Mins, Thurs, 10 pm.
NBC-TV
12/14/77

WHATEVER TURNS YOU ON
With Ruth Buzzi, Trooper, Les Lyle, Marc Baillon, Jonathan Gebert, Rodney Helal, Christine McGlade, Elizabeth Mitchell, Kevin Schenk, Kevin Sommers
Exec Prod: Bryn Matthews;
Prod: Roger Price;
Dir: Geoffrey Darby;
Wris: Price, Darby.
60 Mins, Sat, 10:30 am.
CTV, from Ottawa, Canada
05/09/79F

WHAT'S HAPPENED TO CAMBODIA
(CBS Reports)
With Ed Bradley, Peter Collins
Supplier: CBS News
Exec Prod: Leslie Midgley;
Prods: Ernest Leiser, Phyllis Bosworth, Brian Ellis.
60 Mins, Wed (7), 8 pm.
CBS-TV
06/14/78

WHAT'S HAPPENING
With Ernest Thomas, Haywood Nelson, Fred Berry, Mabel King, Danielle Spencer, others
Supplier: TOY Productions
Prods: Saul Turtletaub, Bernie Orenstein;
Dir: Dennis Steinmetz;
Wri: Alan Eisenstock, Larry Mintz.
30 Mins, Thurs, 8:30 pm.
ABC-TV
08/11/76

WHAT'S UP, AMERICA?
With Chuck Braverman
Supplier: Braverman Pictures Corp & Showtime
60 Mins.
11/01/78PC

WHEELS - PART ONE
With Rock Hudson, Lee Remick, Blair Brown, John Beck, Ralph Bellamy, Scott Brady, John Durren, Marj Dusay, Lisa Eilbacher, Anthony Franciosa, James Carroll Jordan, Adele Mara, Howard McGillin, Tim O'Connor, Gerald S O'Loughlin, Allan Rich, David Spielberg, Harold Sylvester, Jessica Walter, Fred Williamson, Raymond Bieri, James Booth, Anthony Costello, John Crawford, Marilyn Devin, Sheila deWindt, Danna Hansen, Randy Kirby, Carole Mallory, Stewart Moss, James Ray, Debi Richter, Dave Shelley, Ellen Travolta, Al C White
Supplier: Universal
Exec Prod: Roy Huggins;
Prod: Robert O'Neill;
Dir: Jerry London;
Wris: Millard Lampell, Hank Searls, Robert Hamilton, Nancy Lynn Schwartz.
120 Mins, Sun (7), 9 pm.
NBC-TV
05/10/78

WHEN EVERY DAY WAS THE FOURTH OF JULY
(Big Event)
With Dean Jones, Louise Sorel, Chris Petersen, Katy Kurtzman, Harris Yulin, Geoffrey Lewis, Scott Brady, Ronnie Claire Edwards, Ben Plazza, Henry Wilcoxon, Eric Shea, Michael Pataki, Woodrow Palfrey, Moosie Drier, Michael Durrell, Bruce French
Supplier: Dan Curtis Prods
Prod-Dir: Curtis;
Wri: Lee Hutson.
120 Mins, Sun (12), 9 pm.
NBC-TV
03/15/78

WHEN HAVOC STRUCK
(Camille Was No Lady)
With Glenn Ford, narrator
Supplier: ITC Entertainment
Exec Prod: Martin MacKeand;
Dir: David C Rea;
Wri: John Wynne Jones.
30 Mins Wed (11), 7:30 pm.
WNEW-TV New York
Mobil (Doyle Dane Bernbach)
01/18/78S

WHEN THE WHISTLE BLOWS
With Dolph Sweet, Doug Barr, Susan Buckner, Philip Brown, Tim Rossovich, Sue Ane Langdon, Alice Hirson, Gary Allen, Nobel Willingham, Jeffrey Jacquet, Billy Jacoby, Dennis Rucker, Walter Scott, Morgan Hart, Dennis Howard, Doris Belack
Supplier: Daydream Prods
Exec Prods: Leonard Goldberg, Jerry Weintraub;
Prods: Carroll Newman, Gerald Sanford
Dir: Michael Preece;
Wris: Sanford, Rick Mittleman, Wally Dalton, Shelley Zellman.
60 Mins, Fri, 8 pm.
ABC-TV

03/19/80

WHERE YOUR MONEY GOES
With Lou Sette
Prod: Jay Seaton;
Dir: John Oven.
30 Mins, Tues, 7:30 pm.
WKYC-TV Cleveland

10/12/77

WHETHER YOU LIKE IT OR NOT, JULY 4, 1976 IS COMING
With Marciarose, Richard Maloney, Mike Douglas, The Gallery, The Committee of Correspondence, the U. of Pennsylvania Glee Club
Exec Prod: Norman Marcus;
Prods: Don Dunwell, Dick Crew;
Dir: Crew.
90 Mins, Mon (12), 7:30 pm.
WHYY-TV Philadelphia

04/21/76

WHEW!
With Tom Kennedy (host)
Supplier: Bud Austin Co
Exec Prods: Austin, Burt Sugarman;
Prod: Jay Wolpert;
Dir: William Carruthers;
Wris: Wolpert, Gary Jonke, Lee Goldstein.
25 Mins, Mon-Fri, 10:30 am.
CBS-TV

05/02/79

THE WHITE SHADOW
With Ken Howard, Jason Bernard, Joan Pringle, Thomas Carter, Kevin Hooks, Eric Kilpatrick, Bryan Stewart, Timothy Van Patten, Ken Michelman, Ira Angustain, Robin Rose, Jerry Fogel, Marilyn Coleman, Jonathan Ian, Gerry Black, Al Stellone, John Davis, Bethel Leslie
Supplier: MTM Enterprises
Exec Prod-Wri: Bruce Paltrow;
Prod: Mark C Tinker;
Dir: Jackie Cooper.
60 Mins, Mon, 8 pm.
CBS-TV

11/29/78

WHO DO YOU THINK YOU ARE?
With Barbara Stephens, Tony Llewellyn-Jones, Stephen O'Rourke
Supplier: Australian Broadcasting Commission
Dirs: Brian Bell, Ted Robinson;
Wri: John O'Grady.
30 Mins, Tues, 8:30 pm.
ABC (Australia) TV

10/27/76F

WHODUNNIT?
With Ed McMahon, Jack Klugman, Dolph Sweet, others
Supplier: Marble Arch Prods
Exec Prod: Martin Starger;
Supv Prod: Bill Carruthers;
Prod: Doris Quinlan;
Dirs: Don Wallace, Carruthers;
Wris: Jeremy Lloyd, Lance Percival.
30 Mins, Thurs, 8 pm.
NBC-TV

04/18/79

WHO'S MINDING THE ZOO?
With Werner Klemperer, Nancy Dolman
Exec Prods: Bob Sweeney, Edward Feldman;
Prod: Larry Rosen;
Dir: Frank Andreoli;
Wris: Everett Greenbaum, Jim Fritzell.
30 Mins Tues, 8:30 pm.
CBC, from Toronto, Canada

04/11/79F

WHO'S ON CALL?
With Forbesy Russell, Matt Landers, Frank Corsentino, Jim McKrell, David Rupprecht, Fran Ryan, Melissa Steinberg
Supplier: Uncle Toby Prods & Columbia Pictures TV
Prods: Geoffrey Neigher, Coleman Mitchell;
Dir: Tony Mordente;
Wri: Laura Levine.
30 Mins, Sun (16), 10:30 pm.
ABC-TV

12/19/79

WHO'S WATCHING THE KIDS
With Caren Kaye, Larry Breeding, Scott Baio, Marcia Lewis, Lynda Goodfriend, Jim Belushi, Tammy Lauren, Lorrie Mahaffey, Elaine Bolton, Shirley Kirkes
Supplier: Henderson Prods & Paramount TV
Exec Prods: Garry Marshall, Tony Marshall, Don Silverman;
Prods: Marty Nadler, Gary Menteer;
Dir: John Lennox;
Wris: Howard Albrecht, Sol Weinstein.
30 Mins, Fri, 8:30 pm.
NBC-TV

09/27/78

WHO'S WHO
With Dan Rather, Barbara Howar, Charles Kuralt (reporters), Leopold Stokowski, Richard Burton, others
Supplier: CBS News
Exec Prod: Don Hewitt;
Prods: Grace Diekhaus (senior), Paul Loewenwarter, Sheila Nevins
Dir: Arthur Bloom.
60 Mins., Tues. (4), 8 pm.
CBS-TV

01/12/77

WHY DIDN'T THEY ASK EVANS?
With Francesca Annis, Eric Porter, Leigh Lawson, James Warwick, Madeline Smith, Connie Booth, Robert Longden, Joan Hickson, Doris Hare, John Gielgud, Bernard Miles
Suppliers: London Weekend TV
Exec Prod: Tony Wharmby;
Prod: Jack Williams;
Dirs: John Davies, Wharmby.
210 Mins, Sun, (30) 7:45 pm.
ITV Network, Britain

04/09/80F

WHY DO I FEEL THIS WAY?
With Dr Timothy Johnson, Karen MacDonald, Lee Nelson, Hamilton Benz
Exec Prod: Steve Schlow;
Prod-Dir: G Hayden Brown;
Wri: Doris Kriegshaber.
60 Mins, Tues, (30), 10 pm.
WCVB-TV Boston

02/14/79

WHY MEN RAPE?
With Frank Shoosey, Jeffrey Rovins, Sgt. Harry O'Reiley, Marie-Helene LeClerc, Lorenne Clark, Roy McMurtry, Patrick Watson
Supplier: National Film Board of Canada & CBC
Dir: Douglas Jackson;
Prod: Wolf Koenig.
57 Mins, Sun, (6), 10 pm.
CBC-TV, from Winnipeg, Canada

02/27/80F

WILD & WOOLLY
(ABC Monday Night Movie)
With Chris DeLisle, Susan Bigelow, Elyssa Davalos, Doug McClure, David Doyle, Ross Martin, Charles Siebert, Sherry Bain, Vic Morrow, Paul Burke, Jessica Walter, Kenneth Tobey, Robert J. Wilkie, Med Florey, Mark Withers, Eugene Butler, Wayne Grace
Supplier: Aaron Spelling Prods
Exec Prods: Spelling, Douglas S Cramer;
Prod-Wri: Earl W Wallace;
Dir: Philip Leacock.
120 Mins, Mon (20), 9 pm.
ABC-TV

02/22/78

WILD TIMES - PART 1
(The Golden Circle)
With Sam Elliott, Ben Johnson, Bruce Boxleitner, Penny Peyser, Timothy Scott, Cameron Mitchell, Gene Evans, Harry Carey Jr., Leif Erickson, L.Q. Jones, Pat Hingle, Dennis Hopper, Trish Stewart, Geno Silva, Marianne Marks
Supplier: Rattlesnake Prods. & Metromedia Producers Corp.
Exec Prod: Douglas Netter;
Supv Prod: Jim Byrnes;
Prod: Les Sheldon;
Dir: Richard Compton;
Wri: Don Balluck, based on Brian Garfield's novel.
120 Mins, Thurs, (24), 8 pm.
WNEW-TV New York

01/30/80S

THE WILD WILD WEST REVISITED
With Robert Conrad, Ross Martin, Paul Williams, Harry Morgan, Rene Auberjonois, Jo Ann Harris, Trisha Noble, Jeff MacKay, Susan Blu, Pavla Ustinov, Robert Shields & Lorene Yarnell, Wilford A Brimley, Ted Hartley, Jacquelyn Hyde, Alberto Morin, Jeff Redford, Skip Homeier
Supplier: CBS Entertainment
Exec Prod: Jay Bernstein;
Prod: Robert L Jacks;
Dir: Burt Kennedy;
Wri: William Bowers.
120 Mins, Wed (9), 8 pm.
CBS-TV
05/16/79

WILDER & WILDER
With Greg Mullavey, Meredith MacRae, T K Carter, Lonnie Shorr, Louis Criscuolo, Susan Lanier, Warren Burton, Vaughn Armstrong
Supplier: Mark Carliner Prods & Viacom Enterprises
Exec Prod: Carliner;
Prods-Wris: Austin & Irma Kalish;
Dir: Peter H Hunt.
30 Mins, Sat (26), 8:30 pm.
CBS-TV
08/30/78

WILDLIFE ON ONE
(Garden Jungle)
With David Attenborough, narrator
Supplier: BBC
Prods: Densey Clyne, Jim Frazier.
5 Mins, Tues, 8:35 pm.
BBC, from Bristol, England
08/31/77F

THE WILDS OF TEN THOUSAND ISLANDS
With Chris Robinson, Julie Gregg, Mary Ellen McKeon, Charles Aiken, Rachel Roberts, John Kauffman, Monica Gayle, John Ashton
Supplier: Lorimar Prods
Exec Prods: Lee Rich, Philip Capice;
Prod: Andy White;
Dir: Charles Dubin;
Wris: White, Paul West.
60 Mins, Fri (24), 8 pm.
CBS-TV
03/01/78

WILL SHAKESPEARE
With Tim Curry, Ian McShane, John McEnery, Andre Morell, Nicholas Clay, Ron Cook
Supplier: ATV-ITC
Prod: Cecil Clarke;
Wri: John Mortimer.
60 Mins, Tues, 9 pm.
ITV Network, Britain
07/05/78F

WILLIE NELSON AT LAKE TAHOE
Supplier: Charles Braverman Pictures Corp, Showtime
Prod-Dir: Braverman.
85 Mins, Sun (11), 9 pm.
Teleprompter Manhattan
02/14/79PC

WILMA
With Cicely Tyson, Shirley Jo Finney, Joe Seneca, Jason Bernard, Charles Blackwell, Drury Cox, Pauletta Rashelle Pearson, Andrea Frierson, Denzel Washington, Rejane Magliore, Larry B Scott, Piper Carter
Supplier: Cappy Prods
Exec Prod: Cappy Petrash Greenspan;
Prod-Dir-Wri: Bud Greenspan.
120 Mins, Mon (19), 9 pm.
NBC-TV
Procter & Gamble (Benton & Bowles)
12/28/77

WINDOWS, DOORS & KEYHOLES
With Telly Savalas, Lindsay Wagner, John Schuck, Bill Dana, Hamilton Camp, Peter Palmer, Pat Cronin, Esther Sunderland, Lyman Ward, Candy Ann Brown, Ceil Cabot, Robert Doyle, MacIntyre Dixon, Dee Dee Rescher, Linda Redford, Joy Garrett, Hilary Beane, Trisha Hart, Mickey Deems
Supplier: Heyday Prods & Universal TV
Exec Prod-Dir: Leonard B Stern;
Prod: Arne Sultan;
Wris: Sultan, Earl Barret, Dana, Stern.
60 Mins, Tues (16), 10 pm.
NBC-TV
05/24/78

WINFIELD MASTERS SNOOKER
With Ray Reardon, Doug Mountjoy, Pierre Mans, John Spencer, Dennis Taylor, Rex Williams, Eddie Charlton, Ian Anderson, Ted Lowe
Supplier: Australian Broadcasting Commission
Exec Prod: James Allan;
Dir: Brian Harvey.
30 Mins
ABC (Australia) TV, Sydney
07/09/80F

WINNER TAKE ALL
With Michael Murphy, Joanna Pettet, Clive Revill, Mark Gordon, David Huddleston, Signe Hasso, John Fiedler, Martine Beswick, James Hong, Alain Patrick, Dorothy Meyer, Loni Anderson, James McCallion
Supplier: QM Prods
Exec Prod: Quinn Martin;
Prod: John Wilder;
Dir: Robert Day;
Wri: Cliff Gould.
60 Mins, Fri (1), 10 pm.
CBS-TV
04/06/77

WINNERS AND LOSERS
(Shining With The Shiner)
With Ivan Beavis, Ian Mune, Harold Kissin, others
Supplier: Aardvark-Mune Prods./TV-1
Dirs: Roger Donaldson, Mune.
30 Mins, Mon, 8:30 pm.
TV-1, from Wellington, New Zealand
04/14/76F

THE WINNINGS OF FRANKIE WALLS
(For The Record)
With Al Waxman, Chapelle Jaffe, Samantha Langevin, Doug McGrath
Exec Prod: Sam Levene;
Prod: Bill Gough;
Dir: Martin Lavut;
Wri: Bob Forsyth.
60 Mins, Sun, 9 pm.
CBC, Toronto, Canada
04/02/80F

WITH JEANNE PARR
Prod: Dolores Danska.
30 Min, Mon-Fri, 9:30 am.
WCBS-TV New York
09/22/76

WITH NO DIRECTION HOME
With Dina Merrill, Nicolas Coster, John Getz, Elizabeth Lawrence
Prod-Wri: Dinitia Smith;
Dir: Gene Lasko.
60 Mins, Tues (14), 8 pm.
WNBC-TV New York
06/22/77

WITHIN THESE WALLS
With Patricia Gormin
Exec Prod: Don Wilburn;
Wri-Prod: Gormin;
Dir: Robert Weaver.
30 Mins, Thurs, 8 pm.
WVUE-TV New Orleans
03/14/79

WKRP IN CINCINNATI
With Gary Sandy, Gordon Jump, Loni Anderson, Richard Sanders, Tim Reid, Frank Bonner, Jan Smithers, Howard Hesseman, Sylvia Sidney
Supplier: MTM Prods
Prod-Wri: Hugh Wilson;
Dir: Jay Sandrich.
30 Mins, Mon, 8:30 pm.
CBS-TV
09/20/78

THE WOLFMAN JACK SHOW
With Wolfman Jack, Gladys Knight and the Pips, Danny Wells, Murray Langston, Peter Cullen
Supplier: Howl Prods, CBC
Dirs: Mark Warren, Don Davis;
Wris: Mart Scharfman, Brad Hammond.
30 Mins, Sat, 1 pm.
WPIX-TV New York
10/05/77S

WOMAN IN THE HOUSE
With Neil Fitzpatrick, Penne Hackforth-Jones, Wendy Hughes, Anne Semmler, Julie Hamilton, Vicki Bateese, Brian Hinselwood, Ray Meagher, others
Supplier: Australian Broadcasting Commission
Exec Prod: Lynn Bayonas;
Dir: Chris Thomson;
Wri: Luis Bayonas.
Thurs, 9 pm.
ABC from Sydney, Australia
09/06/78F

WOMAN OF THE YEAR
With Joseph Bologna, Renee Taylor, Dick O'Neill, Anthony Holland, Dick Bakalyan, Chuck Bergansky, Hugh Downs, others
Supplier: MGM-TV
Exec Prod-dir: Jud Taylor;
Prod: Hugh Benson;
Wris: Bologna, Taylor, Bernard M. Kahn.
120 Mins, Wed (28), 8 pm.
CBS-TV

08/04/76

WOMEN IN WHITE - PART 1
With Susan Flannery, Kathryn Harrold, Howard McGillin, Sheree North, David Ackroyd, Stuart Whitman, Robert Culp, Caroline Smith, Patty Duke Astin, Maggie Cooper, Laraine Stephens, Stewart Moss, Gerald S O'Loughlin, Gerald McRaney
Supplier: Groverton Prods & Universal TV
Exec Prod: David Victor;
Prod: Robert F O'Neill;
Dir: Jerry London;
Wri: Robert Malcolm Young, from Frank G Slaughter's novel.
120 Mins, Thurs (8), 9 pm.
NBC-TV

02/14/79

THE WOMEN'S ROOM
(ABC Theatre)
With Lee Remick, Colleen Dewhurst, Patty Duke Astin, Kathryn Harrold, Tovah Feldshuh, Tyne Daly, Lisa Pelikan, Heidi Vaughn, Mare Winningham, Ted Danson, Gregory Harrison, Jenny O'Hara, Christopher Pennock, Al Corley
Supplier; Philip Mandelker Prods & Warner Bros TV
Exec Prod: Mandelker;
Prods: Kip Gowans, Anna Cottle;
Dir: Glenn Jordan;
Wri: Carol Sobieski.
180 Mins, Sun, (14) 8 pm.
ABC-TV

09/17/80

WORDS FOR TENDERNESS AND WILL
(Superspecial)
With Pauline Julien
Prods: Serge Doyon, Guy Latraverse;
Dirs: Laurent Larouche, Jacques Menthe.
60 Mins, Mon, 9 pm.
CBC, from Toronto, Canada

11/29/78F

WORKING STIFFS
With Jim Belushi, Michael Keaton, Neil Thompson, Kate Zentall, Michael Conrad
Supplier: Frog Prods, Huk Inc & Paramount TV
Exec Prods: Bob Brunner, Arthur Silver;
Supv Prod-Wri: Marc Sotkin;
Prod: Harry Colomby;
Dir: Penny Marshall.
30 Mins, Sat (15), 8 pm.
CBS-TV

09/19/79

WORLD IN ACTION
(A Calculated Risk)
With Anatole Scharansky, Vladimir Slepak, Alexander Lerner, others
Supplier: Granada TV
30 Mins, Mon (14), 8:30 pm.
ITV Network, Britain

06/23/76F

WORLD OF DARKNESS
With Granville van Dusen, Beatrice Straight, Tovah Feldshuh, Gary Merrill, James Austin
Supplier: Talent Associates
Exec Prod: David Susskind;
Prod: Diana Kerew;
Dir: Jerry London;
Wri: Art Wallace.
60 Mins, Sun (17), 10 pm.
CBS-TV

04/20/77

THE WORLD OF WIZARDS
With The Amazing Randi
Prod-Dirs: Pen Densham, John Watson.
60 Mins, Sat, 8 pm.
CBC-TV, from Toronto, Canada
General Foods

10/19/77F

WORLD PRESS IN MOSCOW
With Paul E. Zinner, Andrew Stern
Supplier: KQED-TV San Francisco
Prods: Andrew Stern, Donna Woolf.
30 Mins, Sun (8), 6:30 pm.
PBS

02/11/76

WORLD WAR II: G.I. DIARY
With Lloyd Bridges (narrator)
Supplier: Time-Life TV
Exec Prod: Arthur Holch;
Prod: Anne Chamers;
Wri: Bill Brown.
30 Mins, Tues, 7:30 pm.
WCBS-TV, New York

09/27/78S

WORLDWIDE
(Russia Through A Looking Glass)
With Frank Gillard, reporter
Supplier: BBC-TV
Prod: Maryse Addison;
Wri: Frank Gillard.
10120 Mins, Thurs (9), 9:25 pm.
BBC-2, Britain

09/29/76F

WPIX EDITORIAL REPORT: THE CONCORDE, BIRD OF PREY OR BIRD OF PARADISE?
Prod-wri: Richard N. Hughes.
60 Mins, Sun (18), 7:30 pm.
WPIX-TV New York

04/21/76

WRAP-UP
With Dan Milham, Andrea Roane, hosts
Exec Prod; Sharon Litwin;
Dir: David Frentz.
60 Mins, Thurs
WYES-TV New Orleans

11/09/77

THE XYY MAN
(The Big Bang)
With Stephen Yardley, Brian Croucher, Johnny Shannon, Fiona Curzon, others
Supplier: Granada TV
Prod: Richard Everett;
Dir: Ken Grieve;
Wri: Tim Aspinall.
60 Mins, Mon (11), 9 pm.
ITV, from London, England

07/27/77F

YABBA DABBA DOO! THE HAPPY WORLD OF HANNA-BARBERA
With Gene Kelly, Cloris Leachman, Jonathan Winters, Lorne Greene
Supplier: Hanna-Barbera Prods
Exec Prods: Joseph Barbera & William Hanna;
Prod-Dir-Wri: Marshall Flaum.
120 Mins, Thurs (24), 8 pm.
CBS-TV

11/30/77

YANKEE COME BACK
With Belva Davis
Supplier: KPIX San Francisco, for Group W
Exec Prod: Pat Polillo;
Prod-Wri: Susan Anderson.
60 Mins, Sun, 10 pm.
KPIX San Francisco

11/02/77

YANKS GO HOME
With Alan MacNaughton, Bruce Boa, Stuart Damon, Richard Oldfield, Norman Bird, Meg Johnson, Catherine Neilson, others
Supplier: Granada TV
Prod-dir: Eric Prytherch;
Wri: Michael Carter.
30 Mins, Mon, 8 pm.
ITV Network, Britain

12/01/76F

THE YEAGERS
With Andy Griffith, David Ackroyd, James Whitmore Jr., Kevin Brophy, Molly Cheek, Deborah Shelton, Jimmy Mair, Rob Olivi, Gregg Henry, Peter Hobbs, Craig T. Nelson, Richard McKenzie, John Quade, Guy Boyd, Wayne Heffley
Supplier: Witt-Thomas Prods & Warner Bros TV
Exec Prods: Paul Junger Witt, Tony Thomas;
Prod: Robert A. Papazian;
Dir: Winrich Kolbe;
Wri: Joel Steiger.
60 Mins, Sun, (1) 7-8 pm.
ABC-TV

06/04/80

THE YEAR (SO FAR) IN REVIEW
With Denis Arndt, Megan Dean, Marnie Mosiman, Jeff Steitzer, Bob Wright, Al Wallace
Exec Prod: Don LaCombe;
Wri-Dir: Greg Palmer.
30 Mins, Wed (18), 7:30 pm.
KING-TV Seattle

07/25/79

YEAR ZERO - THE SILENT DEATH OF CAMBODIA
With John Pilger
Supplier: ATV
Prod-Dir: David I Munro;
Wri: Pilger.
52 Mins, Tues (30), 9 pm.
ATV Network, Great Britain
11/07/79F

YIPE! DON'T BE AFRAID
With Stan Freberg, Mark Ritts Puppets
Exec Prod: Inez Gottlieb;
Prod-Wri: Ted Field;
Dir: Don Matticks.
30 Mins, Sat (2), 7:30 pm.
WCAU-TV Philadelphia
12/13/78

YORK
With Charles Canada, others
Dir: Nate Long.
30 Mins, Sun, 5:30 pm.
KOMO-TV Seattle
06/09/76

YOU!
With Jerry Stiller & Anne Meara, hosts
Supplier: WABC-TV New York
Exec Prod: Miskit Airth;
Prod: Mort Fleischner;
Wris: Fleischner, Raymond J Bouley.
60 Mins, Sat, 7 pm.
WABC-TV
05/10/78

YOU
With Ellie Dylan, Marie Torre
Supplier: WABC-TV New York
Exec Prod: Miskit Airth;
Prods: Torre, Ann Petrie.
30 Mins, Sat, 7 pm.
WABC-TV New York
10/04/78S

YOU BET YOUR LIFE
With Buddy Hackett, Ron Husmann
Supplier: Hill-Eubanks Group (MCA-TV)
Exec Prods: Michael Hill, Bob Eubanks;
Prods: Earl Durham, Bill Paolantionio;
Dir: Chris Darley.
30 Mins, Mon-Fri 12:30 pm.
WPIX-TV New York
09/17/80S

YOU CAN'T GO HOME AGAIN
With Lee Grant, Chris Sarandon, Hurd Hatfield, Tammy Grimes, Christopher Murney, Roland Winters, Paul Sparer, Malachy McCourt
Supplier: CBS Entertainment
Exec Prod: Bob Markell;
Dir: Ralph Nelson;
Wri: Ian McLellan Hunter, based on the Thomas Wolfe novel.
120 Mins, Wed (25), 9 pm.
CBS-TV
05/02/79

YOU CAN'T TAKE IT WITH YOU
With Jean Stapleton, Art Carney, Barry Bostwick, Blythe Danner, Marla Gibbs, Howard Hesseman, Polly Holliday, Beth Howland, Robert Mandan, Kenneth Mars, Harry Morgan, Mildred Natwick, Tim Reid, Eugene Roche, Paul Sand, Joyce Van Patten, Alan Oppenheimer
Supplier: Warner Bros TV
Exec Prod-Dir: Paul Bogart;
Prod: Lindsay Law;
Wris: George S Kaufman, Moss Hart.
120 Mins, Wed (16), 9 pm.
CBS-TV
05/23/79

YOU HAD TO BE THERE
With Avery Schreiber, Pat Paulsen, Will Jordan, Susan Lanier, Barton Heyman, Addison Powell, Chuck Blore, Bob Gale
Exec Prod: Norman Marcus;
Prod-dir: Doug Bailey;
Wri: Charles Hauck.
30 Mins, Tues (8), 7:30 pm.
WHYY-TV Philadelphia
06/23/76

YOUNG DAN'L BOONE
With Rick Moses, Devon Erickson, Ji-Tu Cumbuka, John Joseph Thomas, Eloy Phil Casados, Len Birman, Jeremy Brett, Joe Dorsey, Robert F Shaw, Jimmy Sangster
Supplier: Frankel Films Inc -- 20th-Fox TV
Exec Prod: Ernie Frankel;
Prod: Sangster;
Dir: Earl Bellamy;
Wri: David P Harmon.
60 Mins, Mon, 8 pm.
CBS-TV
09/14/77

THE YOUNG DOCTORS
With Alfred Sandor, Michael Beecher, Joanna Moore-Smith, Delvene Delaney, John Walton, John Dommett, Peita Toppano, Ugle Dave Gray, Cornelia Frances, Mark Holden, Beryl Cheers, others
Supplier: Reg Grundy Prods
30 Mins, Mon-Fri, 7:30 pm.
Channel 9, Sydney, Australia
12/01/76F

YOUNG MAVERICK
With Charles Frank, Susan Blanchard, John Dehner, James Garner, Denny Miller, Dick O'Neill, Warren Berlinger, Burton Gilliam, Morgan Woodward, Joanne Nail, Dave Cass
Supplier: Warner Bros TV
Exec Prod: Robert Van Scoyk;
Supv Prod: Andy White;
Prod: Chuck Bowman;
Dir: Bernard McEveety;
Wri: David E Peckinpah.
60 Mins, Wed, 8 pm.
CBS-TV
12/05/79

YOUNG PIONEERS
(ABC Monday Movie)
With Roger Kern, Linda Purl, Robert Hays, Shelley Juttner, Robert Donner, Frank Marth, Brendan Dillon, Charles Tyner, Jonathan Kidd, Arnold Soboloff, Bernice Smith, Britt Leach, Dennis Fimple
Supplier: ABC Circle Films
Exec Prod: Ed Friendly;
Dir: Michael O'Herlihy;
Wri: Blanche Hanalis (based on Rose Wilder Lane novel).
120 Mins, Mon (1), 8 pm.
ABC-TV
03/03/76

THE YOUNG PIONEERS
With Linda Purl, Roger Kern, Robert Hays, Robert Donner, Mare Winningham, Michelle Stacy, Jeff Cotler, David Huddleston, A Martinez, W K Stratton, Cynthia Avila, Geno Silva, Guillermo San Juan, Britt Leach
Supplier: Lorimar Prods & Amanda Prods
Exec Prods: Lee Rich, Earl Hamner;
Prod: Robert L Jacks;
Dir: Harry Harris;
Wris: Robert Pirosh, Kathryn Michaelian Powers.
120 Mins, Sun (2), 7 pm.
ABC-TV
04/05/78

YOUNG RAMSAY
With John Hargreaves, Barbara Llewellyn, Serge Lazareff
Supplier: Crawford Prods
Exec Prod: Ian Crawford;
Prod: Henry Crawford;
Dir: Graeme Arthur;
Wri: John Graham.
60 Mins, Sun, 6:30 pm.
Seven Web, from Sydney, Australia
12/14/77F

YOUR CHILDREN, MY CHILDREN (A PARENT'S GUIDE TO DRUGS)
With Bob McGrath
Exec Prod: J. Clifford Curley;
Wri-Prod: Shirley Robson;
Dir: George Light.
60 Mins, Fri, (12) 10 pm.
WRC-TV, Washington D.C.
09/24/80

YOUR TURN: LETTERS TO CBS NEWS
With Sharron Lovejoy
Supplier: CBS News
Exec Prod: Joel Heller;
Prod: Anne Chambers;
Dir: Vern Diamond.
30 Mins, Sun (5), 10:30 am.
CBS-TV
02/15/78

YOU'RE NEVER TOO OLD
With Lisa Hartman, Robb Weller, Ann Ryerson, Jay Johnson, Dr Hook, Honey Bears, others
Exec Prod: John W Coleman;
Prod: Scott Sternberg;
Dir: Howard Shapiro;
Wris: Steve Kahn, Dick Wolfsie, Sternberg.
60 Mins, Sat, 9 pm.
WLS-TV Chicago
10/03/79

Z CARS
With James Ellis, Douglas Fielding, Joseph Brady, others
Supplier: BBC Television
Prod: Ron Craddock;
Dir: Terence Williams.
50 Mins, Wed, 8:10 pm.
BBC-1, from London, England
07/26/78F

ZWEI HIMMLISCHE TOECHTER
(Two Heavenly Daughters) (The Gimmicks)
With Ingrid Steeger, Iris Berben, Klaus Dahlen, Herta Worell, Winni Riva, Heinz Schubert, Dieter Hildebrandt, Wichart von Roell, Peer Augustinski, Wolfgang Mascher, Werner Schulze Erdel, Monica Teuber, Monika Sorice
Dir: Michael Pfleghar.
90 Mins, Sat, 8:15 pm.
First German TV Net, Cologne, West Germany
02/22/78F

EMMYS

1948

MOST OUTSTANDING TELEVISION PERSONALITY

SHIRLEY DINSDALE and her puppet Judy Splintes (KTLA)
RITA LeROY (KTLA)
PATRICIA MORRISON
MIKE STOKEY (KTLA)
BILL WELSH (KTLA)

MOST POPULAR TELEVISION PROGRAM

PANTOMIME QUIZ TIME (Mike Stokey) (KTLA)
ARMCHAIR DETECTIVE (KTLA)
DON LEE MUSIC HALL (KTSL)
FELIX DE COLA SHOW (KTLA)
JUDY SPLINTERS (KTLA)
MABEL'S FABLES (KTLA)
MASKED SPOONER (KTSL)
TREASURE OF LITERATURE (KFI-TV)
TUESDAY VARIETIES (KTLA)
WHAT'S THE NAME OF THAT SONG (KTSL)

BEST FILM MADE FOR TELEVISION

THE NECKLACE Marshall Grant-Realm Productions (Your Show Time Series)
CHRISTOPHER COLUMBUS Emerson Film Corp.
HOLLYWOOD BREVITIES Tele-features
IT COULD HAPPEN TO YOU Vallee Video
TELL TALE HEART Telepak
TIME SIGNAL Centaur Productions

STATION AWARD

KTLA For outstanding overall achievement in 1948

TECHNICAL AWARD

CHARLES MESAK Don Lee Television for "PHASEFADER" in recognition of an outstanding advancement in the video field.

SPECIAL AWARD

LOUIS McMANUS For his original design of the Emmy

1949

BEST LIVE SHOW

ED WYNN (KTTV)
PANTOMIME QUIZ (KTTV)
YOUR WITNESS (KECA-TV)

BEST KINESCOPE SHOW

TEXACO STAR THEATRE (KNBH, NBC)
FRED WARING (KTTV, CBS)
THE GOLDBERGS (KTTV, CBS)
STUDIO ONE (KTTV, CBS)

BEST CHILDREN'S SHOW

TIME FOR BEANY (KTLA)
CYCLONE MALONE (KNBH)
KUKLA, FRAN and OLLIE (KNBH)

MOST OUTSTANDING LIVE PERSONALITY

ED WYNN (KTTV)
TOM HARMON (KFI-TV, KECA-TV, KTTV)
MIKE STOKEY (KTTV, KTLA)
BILL WELSH (KFI-TV, KTLA)

BEST FILM MADE FOR & VIEWED ON TELEVISION IN 1949

LIFE OF RILEY (KNBH)
GUIDING STAR (KTTV)
LONE RANGER (KECA-TV)
TIME BOMB (KNBH)
VAIN GLORY (KNBH)
YOUR SHOWTIME

MOST OUTSTANDING KINESCOPED PERSONALITY

MILTON BERLE (KNBH, NBC)
FRAN ALLISON (KNBH, NBC)
ARTHUR GODFREY (KTTV, CBS)

BEST PUBLIC SERVICE, CULTURAL OR EDUCATIONAL PROGRAM

CRUSADE IN EUROPE (KECA-TV & KTTV)
FORD NEWS & WEATHER (KNBH)
KATHY FISCUS RESCUE (KTLA)
MAN'S BEST FRIEND (KTLA)
NUREMBERG TRIALS (KTSL)
TELEFORUM (KTLA)

BEST SPORTS COVERAGE

WRESTLING (KTLA)
AMATEUR BOXING (KTLA)
BASEBALL (KLAC)
COLLEGE BASKETBALL (KTTV)
ICE HOCKEY (KTLA)
USC-UCLA FOOTBALL (KECA)

STATION ACHIEVEMENT

KTLA For outstanding overall achievement in 1949
Honorable mention to KECA-TV

BEST COMMERCIAL MADE FOR TELEVISION

LUCKY STRIKE N W Ayer & Son, Inc, for the American Tobacco Company

TECHNICAL AWARD

HAROLD W. JURY OF KTSL, LOS ANGELES For the synchronizing co-ordinator which allows superimposition from more than one location.

1950

BEST ACTOR

ALAN YOUNG (KTTV, CBS)
SID CAESAR (KNBH, NBC)
JOSE FERRER
STAN FREBERG as CECIL THE SEA SERPENT (KTLA)
CHARLES RUGGLES (KCEA-TV)

BEST ACTRESS

GERTRUDE BERG (KTTV, CBS)
JUDITH ANDERSON
IMOGENE COCA (KNBH, NBC)
HELEN HAYES (KECA-TV)
BETTY WHITE (KLAC)

MOST OUTSTANDING PERSONALITY
GROUCHO MARX (KNBH, NBC)
SID CAESAR (KNBH, NBC)
FAYE EMERSON (KTTV, KECA-TV)
DICK LANE (KTLA)
ALAN YOUNG (KTTV, CBS)

BEST PUBLIC SERVICE
CITY AT NIGHT (KTLA)
CLASSIFIED COLUMN (KTTV)
COMMUNITY CHEST KICKOFF
IN OUR TIME (KTTV)
MARSHALL PLAN (KECA-TV)
TELEFORUM (KTLA)

BEST CULTURAL SHOW
CAMPUS CHORUS AND ORCHESTRA (KTSL)
DESIGNED FOR WOMEN (KNBH)
SUNSET SERVICE (KNBH)
VIENNA PHILHARMONIC (KTTV)
THE WOMAN'S VOICE (KTTV)

SPECIAL EVENTS
DEPARTURE OF MARINES FOR KOREA (KFMB-TV San Diego & KTLA)
ARRIVAL OF CRUISER FROM KOREA (KTLA)
COMMISSIONING OF HOSPITAL SHIP HAVEN
ELECTION COVERAGE (KECA-TV)
TOURNAMENT OF ROSES (KECA-TV)

BEST SPORTS PROGRAM
RAMS FOOTBALL (KNBH)
COLLEGE BASKETBALL GAMES (KTTV, CBS)
COLLEGE FOOTBALL GAMES (KTTV, CBS)
HOLLYWOOD BASEBALL (KLAC)
LOS ANGELES BASEBALL (KFI-TV)

BEST VARIETY SHOW
THE ALAN YOUNG SHOW (KTTV, CBS)
FOUR STAR REVUE (KNBH, NBC)
KEN MURRAY (KTTV, CBS)
SHOW OF SHOWS (KNBH, NBC)
TEXACO STAR THEATRE (KNBH, NBC)

BEST EDUCATIONAL SHOW
KFI-TV UNIVERSITY (KFI-TV)
KIERAN'S KALEIDOSCOPE (KECA-TV)
KNOW YOUR SCHOOLS (KFI-TV)
MAGAZINE OF THE WEEK (KTLA)
ZOO PARADE (KNBH)

BEST CHILDREN'S SHOW
TIME FOR BEANY (KTLA)
CISCO KID (KNBH)
JUMP JUMP (KTTV)
KUKLA, FRAN AND OLLIE (KNBH, NBC)
LONE RANGER (KTLA)

BEST DRAMATIC SHOW
PULITZER PRIZE PLAYHOUSE (KECA-TV)
FIRESIDE THEATER (KTLA)
I REMEMBER MAMA (KTTV, CBS)
PHILCO TV PLAHOUSE (KNBH, NBC)
STUDIO ONE (KTTV, CBS)

BEST NEWS PROGRAM
KTLA NEWSREEL
CLETE ROBERTS (KLAC)
FLEETWOOD LAWTON (KTSL)
FORD NEWS AND WEATHER (KNBH)

BEST GAMES AND AUDIENCE PARTICIPATION SHOW
TRUTH OR CONSEQUENCES (KTTV, CBS)
KAY KYSER COLLEGE OF MUSICAL KNOWLEDGE (KNBH, NBC)
LIFE WITH LINKLETTER (KECA-TV)
PANTOMIME QUIZ (KTTV, CBS)
YOU BET YOUR LIFE (KNBH, NBC)

STATION ACHIEVEMENT
KTLA

TECHNICAL ACHIEVEMENT
ORTHOGRAM TV AMPLIFIER BY KNBH-NBC.

1951

BEST DRAMATIC SHOW
STUDIO ONE (CBS)
CELANESE THEATRE (ABC)
PHILCO-GOODYEAR TV PLAYHOUSE (NBC)
PULITZER PRIZE PLAYHOUSE (NBC)
ROBERT MONTGOMERY PRESENTS (NBC)

BEST COMEDY SHOW
RED SKELTON SHOW (NBC)
BURNS AND ALLEN (CBS)
GROUCHO MARX (NBC)
HERB SHRINER SHOW (ABC)
I LOVE LUCY (CBS)

BEST VARIETY SHOW
YOUR SHOW OF SHOWS (NBC)
ALL STAR REVUE (NBC)
COMEDY HOUR (NBC)
FRED WARING (CBS)
TOAST OF THE TOWN (CBS)

BEST ACTOR
SID CAESAR
WALTER HAMPDEN
CHARLTON HESTON
ROBERT MONTGOMERY
THOMAS MITCHELL
VAUGHN TAYLOR

BEST ACTRESS
IMOGENE COCA
HELEN HAYES
MARIA RIVA
MARY SINCLAIR
MARGARET SULLAVAN

BEST COMEDIAN OR COMEDIENNE
RED SKELTON (NBC)
LUCILLE BALL (CBS)
SID CAESAR (NBC)
IMOGENE COCA (NBC)
JIMMY DURATE (NBC)
MARTIN AND LEWIS (NBC)
HERB SHRINER (ABC)

SPECIAL ACHIEVEMENT AWARDS

U. S. SENATOR ESTES KEFAUVER For outstanding Public Service on Television
AMERICAN TELEPHONE & TELEGRAPH CO. For the transcontinental Micro-Wave Relay System
JACK BURRELL OF STATION KNBH, LOS ANGELES For the development of an independent TV transmission Mobile Unit.

1952

BEST DRAMATIC PROGRAM
ROBERT MONTGOMERY PRESENTS (NBC)
CELANESE THEATRE (ABC)
KRAFT TV THEATRE (NBC)
PHILCO-GOODYEAR TV PLAYHOUSE (NBC)
STUDIO ONE (CBS)

BEST VARIETY PROGRAM
YOUR SHOW OF SHOWS (NBC)
ARTHUR GODFREY AND HIS FRIENDS (CBS)
COLGATE COMEDY HOUR (NBC)
THE JACKIE GLEASON SHOW (CBS)
TOAST OF THE TOWN (CBS)

BEST PUBLIC AFFAIRS PROGRAM
SEE IT NOW (CBS)
BISHOP FULTON J. SHEEN (Syndicated)
CAMEL NEWS CARAVAN (NBC)
MEET THE PRESS (NBC)
VICTORY AT SEA (NBC)

BEST MYSTERY, ACTION OR ADVENTURE PROGRAM
DRAGNET (NBC)
BIG STORY (NBC)
FOREIGN INTRIGUE (Syndicated)
MARTIN KANE (NBC)
RACKET SQUAD (CBS)

BEST SITUATION COMEDY
I LOVE LUCY (CBS)
AMOS 'N' ANDY (CBS)
BURNS & ALLEN (CBS)
MR. PEEPERS (NBC)
OUR MISS BROOKS (CBS)
OZZIE AND HARRIET (ABC)

BEST AUDIENCE PARTICIPATION, QUIZ OR PANEL PROGRAM
WHAT'S MY LINE? (CBS)
DOWN YOU GO
THIS IS YOUR LIFE (NBC)
TWO FOR THE MONEY (CBS)
YOU BET YOUR LIFE (NBC)

BEST CHILDREN'S PROGRAM
TIME FOR BEANY (KTLA)
BIG TOP (CBS)
GABBY HAYES
HOWDY DOODY (NBC)
KUKLA, FRAN AND OLLIE (NBC)
SUPER CIRCUS (NBC)
ZOO PARADE (NBC)

BEST ACTOR
THOMAS MITCHELL
JOHN FORSYTHE
CHARLTON HESTON
JOHN NEWLAND
VAUGHN TAYLOR
JACK WEBB

BEST ACTRESS
HELEN HAYES
SARAH CHURCHILL
JUNE LOCKHART
MARIA RIVA
PEGGY WOOD

BEST COMEDIAN
JIMMY DURANTE (NBC)
SID CAESAR (NBC)
WALLY COX (NBC)
JACKIE GLEASON (CBS)
HERB SHRINER (ABC)

BEST COMEDIENNE
LUCILLE BALL (CBS)
EVE ARDEN (CBS)
IMOGENE COCA (NBC)
JOAN DAVIS (NBC)
MARTHA RAYE (NBC)

MOST OUTSTANDING PERSONALITY
BISHOP FULTON J. SHEEN (DUMONT)
LUCILLE BALL (CBS)
ARTHUR GODFREY (CBS)
JIMMY DURANTE (NBC)
EDWARD R. MURROW (CBS)
DONALD O'CONNOR (NBC)
ADLAI STEVENSON (NBC)

1953

BEST DRAMATIC PROGRAM
U.S. STEEL HOUR (ABC)
KRAFT TELEVISION THEATRE (NBC)
PHILCO-GOODYEAR TV PLAYHOUSE (NBC)
ROBERT MONTGOMERY PRESENTS (NBC)
STUDIO ONE (CBS)

BEST SITUATION COMEDY
I LOVE LUCY (CBS)
BURNS & ALLEN (CBS)
MR. PEEPERS (NBC)
OUR MISS BROOKS (CBS)
TOPPER (CBS)

BEST VARIETY PROGRAM
OMNIBUS (CBS)
COLGATE COMEDY HOUR (NBC)
JACKIE GLEASON SHOW (CBS)
YOUR SHOW OF SHOWS (NBC)
TOAST OF THE TOWN (CBS)

BEST PROGRAM OF NEWS OR SPORTS
SEE IT NOW (CBS)
CAMEL NEWS CARAVAN (NBC)
GILLETTE CAVALCADE OF SPORTS (NBC)
NCAA FOOTBALL GAMES (NBC)
PABST FIGHT (CBS)
PROFESSIONAL FOOTBALL (DUMONT)

BEST PUBLIC AFFAIRS PROGRAM
VICTORY AT SEA (NBC)
ADVENTURE AT SEA (NBC)
BISHOP FULTON J. SHEEN (Syndicated)
MEET THE PRESS (NBC)
PERSON TO PERSON (CBS)

BEST CHILDREN'S PROGRAM
KUKLA, FRAN AND OLLIE (NBC)
BIG TOP (CBS)
DING DONG SCHOOL (NBC)
SUPER CIRCUS (NBC)
ZOO PARADE (NBC)

BEST NEW PROGRAM
MAKE ROOM FOR DADDY (ABC)
U.S. STEEL HOUR (ABC)
ADVENTURE (NBC)
DING DONG SCHOOL (NBC)
LETTER TO LORETTA (NBC)
PERSON TO PERSON (CBS)

BEST MALE STAR OF REGULAR SERIES
DONALD O'CONNOR (Colgate Comedy Hour) (NBC)
SID CAESAR (Your Show of Shows) (NBC)
WALLY COX (Mr. Peepers) (NBC)
JACKIE GLEASON (Jackie Gleason Show) (CBS)
JACK WEBB (Dragnet) (NBC)

BEST FEMALE STAR OF REGULAR SERIES
EVE ARDEN (Our Miss Brooks) (CBS)
LUCILLE BALL (I Love Lucy) (CBS)
IMOGENE COCA (Your Show of Shows) (NBC)
DINAH SHORE (Dinah Shore Show) (NBC)
LORETTA YOUNG (Letter to Loretta) (NBC)

BEST SERIES SUPPORTING ACTOR
ART CARNEY (Jackie Gleason Show) (CBS)
BEN ALEXANDER (Dragnet) (NBC)
WILLIAM FRAWLEY (I Love Lucy) (CBS)
TONY RANDALL (Mr. Peepers) (NBC)
CARL REINER (Your Show of Shows) (NBC)

BEST SERIES SUPPORTING ACTRESS
VIVIAN VANCE (I Love Lucy) (CBS)
BEA BENEDARET (Burns & Allen) (CBS)
RUTH GILBERT (Milton Berle Show) (NBC)
MARION LORNE (Mr. Peepers) (NBC)
AUDREY MEADOWS (Jackie Gleason Show) (CBS)

BEST MYSTERY, ACTION OR ADVENTURE PROGRAM
DRAGNET (NBC)
FOREIGN INTRIGUE (NBC)
I LED THREE LIVES
SUSPENSE (CBS)
THE WEB (CBS)

BEST AUDIENCE PARTICIPATION, QUIZ OR PANEL PROGRAM
THIS IS YOUR LIFE (NBC)
WHAT'S MY LINE? (CBS)
I'VE GOT A SECRET (CBS)
TWO FOR THE MONEY (CBS)
YOU BET YOUR LIFE (NBC)

MOST OUTSTANDING PERSONALITY
EDWARD R. MURROW (CBS)
ARTHUR GODFREY (NBC)
MARTHA RAYE (NBC)
BISHOP FULTON J. SHEEN (Syndicated)
JACK WEBB (NBC).

1954

MOST OUTSTANDING NEW PERSONALITY
GEORGE GOBEL (NBC)
RICHARD BOONE (NBC)
WALT DISNEY (ABC)
TENNESSEE ERNIE FORD (CBS)
PRESTON FOSTER (Syndicated)
MICHAEL O'SHEA (NBC)
FESS PARKER (ABC)

BEST CULTURAL, RELIGIOUS OR EDUCATIONAL PROGRAM
OMNIBUS (CBS)
LIFE IS WORTH LIVING (DUMONT)
MEET THE PRESS (NBC)
PERSON TO PERSON (CBS)
SEE IT NOW (CBS)

BEST SPORTS PROGRAM
GILLETTE CAVALCADE OF SPORTS (NBC)
BLUE RIBBON BOUTS (CBS)
FOREST HILLS TENNIS MATCHES (NBC)
GREATEST MOMENTS IN SPORTS (NBC)
NCAA FOOTBALL (ABC)
PROFESSIONAL FOOTBALL (DUMONT)

BEST CHILDREN'S PROGRAM
LASSIE (CBS)
ART LINKLETTER AND THE KIDS (Syndicated)
DING DONG SCHOOL (NBC)
KUKLA, FRAN AND OLLIE (ABC)
TIME FOR BEANY (Syndicated)
ZOO PARADE (NBC)

BEST DAYTIME PROGRAM
ART LINKLETTER'S HOUSE PARTY (CBS)
BETTY WHITE SHOW (NBC)
BOB CROSBY SHOW (CBS)
GARRY MOORE SHOW (CBS)
ROBERT Q. LEWIS (CBS)

BEST WESTERN OR ADVENTURE SERIES
STORIES OF THE CENTURY (Syndicated)
ANNIE OAKLEY (Syndicated)
DEATH VALLEY DAYS (CBS)
ROY ROGERS SHOW (NBC)
WILD BILL HICKOK (Syndicated)

BEST NEWS REPORTER OR COMMENTATOR
JOHN DALY (ABC)
DOUGLAS EDWARDS (CBS)
CLETE ROBERTS (Syndicated)
ERIC SEVAREID (CBS)
JOHN CAMERON SWAYZE (NBC)

BEST AUDIENCE, GUEST PARTICIPATION OR PANEL PROGRAM
THIS IS YOUR LIFE (NBC)
MASQUERADE PARTY (ABC)
PEOPLE ARE FUNNY (NBC)
WHAT'S MY LINE? (CBS)
YOU BET YOUR LIFE (NBC)

BEST ACTOR IN A SINGLE PERFORMANCE
ROBERT CUMMINGS Twelve Angry Men (Studio One) (CBS)
FRANK LOVEJOY Double Indemnity (Lux Video Theatre) (CBS)
FREDERIC MARCH Christmas Carol (Shower of Stars) (CBS)
FREDERIC MARCH Royal Family (Best of Broadway) (CBS)
THOMAS MITCHELL Good Of His Soul (Ford Theatre) (NBC)
DAVID NIVEN The Answer (Four Star Playhouse) (CBS)

BEST ACTRESS IN A SINGLE PERFORMANCE
JUDITH ANDERSON Macbeth (Hallmark Hall of Fame) (NBC)
ETHEL BARRYMORE The 13th Chair (Climax) (CBS)
BEVERLY GARLAND White Is The Color (Medic) (NBC)
RUTH HUSSEY Craig's Wife (Lux Video Theatre) (NBC)
DOROTHY McGUIRE The Giaconda Smile (Climax) (CBS)
EVA MARIE SAINT Middle Of The Night (Philco TV Playhouse) (NBC)
CLAIRE TREVOR Ladies In Retirement (Lux Video Theatre) (NBC)

BEST MALE SINGER
PERRY COMO (CBS)
EDDIE FISHER (NBC)
FRANKIE LAINE (Syndicated)
TONY MARTIN (NBC)
GORDON MAC RAE (NBC)

BEST FEMALE SINGER
DINAH SHORE (NBC)
JANE FROMAN (CBS)
PEGGY KING (NBC)
GISELE MAC KENZIE (NBC)
JO STAFFORD (CBS)

BEST SUPPORTING ACTOR IN A REGULAR SERIES
ART CARNEY (Jackie Gleason Show) (CBS)
BEN ALEXANDER (Dragnet) (NBC)
DON DEFORE (The Adventures of Ozzie and Harriet) (ABC)
BILL FRAWLEY (I Love Lucy) (CBS)
GALE GORDON (Our Miss Brooks) (CBS)

BEST SUPPORTING ACTRESS IN A REGULAR SERIES
AUDREY MEADOWS (Jackie Gleason Show) (CBS)
BEA BENEDARET (Burns & Allen Show) (CBS)
JEAN HAGEN (Make Room For Daddy) (ABC)
MARION LORNE (Mr. Peepers) (NBC)
VIVIAN VANCE (I Love Lucy) (CBS)

BEST ACTOR STARRING IN A REGULAR SERIES
DANNY THOMAS (Make Room For Daddy) (ABC)
RICHARD BOONE (Medic) (NBC)
ROBERT CUMMINGS (My Hero) (Syndicated)
JACKIE GLEASON (Jackie Gleason Show) (CBS)
JACK WEBB (Dragnet) (NBC)

BEST ACTRESS STARRING IN A REGULAR SERIES
LORETTA YOUNG (Loretta Young Show) (NBC)
EVE ARDEN (Our Miss Brooks) (CBS)
GRACIE ALLEN (Burns & Allen Show) (CBS)
LUCILLE BALL (I Love Lucy) (CBS)
ANN SOUTHERN (Private Secretary) (CBS)

BEST MYSTERY OR INTRIGUE SERIES
DRAGNET (NBC)
FOREIGN INTRIGUE (NBC)
I LED THREE LIVES (Syndicated)
RACKET SQUAD (Syndicated)
WATERFRONT (Syndicated)

BEST VARIETY SERIES INCLUDING MUSICAL VARIETIES
DISNEYLAND (ABC)
GEORGE GOBEL SHOW (NBC)
JACK BENNY SHOW (CBS)
JACKIE GLEASON SHOW (CBS)
TOAST OF THE TOWN (CBS)
YOUR HIT PARADE (NBC)

BEST SITUATION COMEDY SERIES
MAKE ROOM FOR DADDY (ABC)
BURNS & ALLEN (CBS)
I LOVE LUCY (CBS)
MR. PEEPERS (NBC)
OUR MISS BROOKS (CBS)
PRIVATE SECRETARY (CBS)

BEST DRAMATIC SERIES
UNITED STATES STEEL HOUR (ABC)
FOUR STAR PLAYHOUSE (CBS)
MEDIC (NBC)
PHILCO TELEVISION PLAYHOUSE (NBC)
STUDIO ONE (CBS)

BEST INDIVIDUAL PROGRAM OF THE YEAR
OPERATION UNDERSEA (Disneyland) (ABC)
DIAMOND JUBILEE OF LIGHT (4 networks)
WHITE IS THE COLOR (Medic) (NBC)
A CHRISTMAS CAROL (Shower Of Stars) (CBS)
TWELVE ANGRY MEN (Studio One) (CBS)

BEST ART DIRECTION OF A LIVE SHOW
BOB MARKELL Mallory's Tragedy On Mt. Everest (You Are There) (CBS)
ROBERT TYLER LEE (Shower Of Stars) (CBS)
CARL MACAULEY (Space Patrol) (ABC)
WILLIAM T. MARTIN (Dinah Shore Show) (NBC)
JAMES VANCE (Climax) (CBS)

BEST ART DIRECTION OF A FILMED SHOW
RALPH BERGER and ALBERT PYKE A Christmas Carol (Shower Of Stars) (CBS)
DUNCAN CRAMER (Four Star Playhouse) (CBS)
FRANK DURLAUF (Ozzie and Harriet Show) (ABC)
CLAUDIO GUZMAN (Ray Bolger Show) (ABC)
SERGE KRIZMAN The Roman And The Renegade (Schlitz Playhouse Of Stars) (CBS)

BEST DIRECTION OF PHOTOGRAPHY
LESTER SHORR I Climb The Stairs (Medic) (NBC)
NORBERT BRODINE The Clara Schumann Story (Loretta Young Show) (NBC)
GEORGE T. CLEMENS The Roman And The Renegade (Schlitz Playhouse Of Stars) (CBS)
EDWARD COLMAN The Big Bible (Dragnet) (NBC)
HAROLD E. STINE Night Call (Cavalcade Of America) (Syndicated)
WALTER STRENGE (My Little Margie) (NBC)

BEST WRITTEN DRAMATIC MATERIAL
REGINALD ROSE Twelve Angry Men (Studio One) (CBS)
PADDY CHAYEFSKY (Philco Television Playhouse) (NBC)
DAVID DORTORT An Error In Chemistry (Climax) (CBS)
LEONARD FREEMAN The Answer (Four Star Playhouse) (CBS)
JAMES MOSER White Is The Color (Medic) (NBC)

BEST WRITTEN COMEDY MATERIAL
JAMES ALLARDICE, JACK DOUGLAS, HAL KANTER, HARRY WINKLER (George Gobel Show) (NBC)
GEORGE BALZER, MILT JOSEFSBERG, SAM PERRIN and JOHN TACKABERRY (Jack Benny Show) (CBS)
JAMES FRITZELL and EVERETT GREENBAUM (Mr. Peepers) (NBC)
JACKIE GLEASON and STAFF WRITERS (Jackie Gleason Show) (CBS)
JESS OPPENHEIMER, ROBERT G. CARROLL and MADELYN PUGH (I Love Lucy) (CBS)
DANNY THOMAS and STAFF WRITERS (Make Room For Daddy) (ABC)

BEST TECHNICAL ACHIEVEMENT
NBC, Color TV Policy and Burbank Color - JOHN WEST
CBS, West Coast Color TV Facilities - L.H. BOWMAN
Ozzie and Harriet Productions facilities - GEORGE E. H. HANSON.

BEST ENGINEERING EFFECTS
FOUR QUADRANT SCREEN - NBC - 1954 National Election Coverage - ROBERT SHELBY
ELECTRONIC EDITING "Background" (NBC) - JOHN GOETZ, WALTER O'MEARS and DANIEL ZAMPINO
JACKIE GLEASON SHOW - (CBS) - Jackie Gleason Enterprises
SPACE PATROL - ABC - CAMERON PIERCE

BEST TELEVISION SOUND EDITING
GEORGE NICHOLSON (Dragnet) (NBC)
CATHEY BURROW (Waterfront) (CBS)
JOHNNY BUSHELMAN (Ramar Of The Jungle) (Syndicated)
STANLEY CALLAHAN (Rin-Tin-Tin) (ABC)
JOSEF VON STROHEIM Red Christmas (Medic) (NBC)

BEST TELEVISION FILM EDITING
GRANT SMITH and LYNN HARRISON Operation Undersea (Disneyland) (ABC)
GEORGE AMY The Roman And The Renegade (Schlitz Playhouse Of Stars) (ABC)
SAMUEL E. BEETLEY The Answer (Four Star Playhouse) (CBS)
JODIE COPELAN White Is The Color (Medic) (NBC)
CHESTER W. SCHAEFFER Davy Crockett - Indian Fighter (Disneyland) (ABC)

BEST DIRECTION
FRANKLIN SCHAFFNER Twelve Angry Men (Studio One) (CBS)
ROBERT FLOREY The Clara Schumann Story (Loretta Young Show) (NBC)
CLARK JONES (Your Hit Parade) (NBC)
ROY KELLINO The Answer (Four Star Playhouse) (CBS)
TED POST Christmas On The Waterfront (Waterfront) (CBS)
ALEX SEGAL (U.S. Steel Hour) (ABC)

BEST ORIGINAL MUSIC COMPOSED FOR TV
WALTER SCHUMANN (Dragnet) (NBC)
BERNARD HERRMAN A Christmas Carol (Shower of Stars) (NBC)
GIAN CARLO MENOTTI Amahl and the Night Visitors (Hallmark Hall of Fame) (NBC)
VICTOR YOUNG Diamond Jubilee of Light (4 networks)
VICTOR YOUNG (Medic) (NBC)

BEST SCORING OF A DRAMATIC OR VARIETY PROGRAM
VICTOR YOUNG Diamond Jubilee of Light (4 networks)
BUDDY BREGMAN Anything Goes (Colgate Comedy Hour) (NBC)
GORDON JENKINS Shower of Stars (first show) (CBS)
NELSON RIDDLE Satins and Spurs
WALTER SCHARF Here Comes Donald (Texaco Star Theatre) starring Donald O'Connor (NBC)

BEST CHOREOGRAPHER
JUNE TAYLOR (Jackie Gleason Show) (CBS)
ROD ALEXANDER (Max Liebman Spectaculars) (NBC)
TONY CHARMOLI and BOB HERGET (Your Hit Parade) (NBC)
LOUIS DA PRON Here Comes Donald (Texaco Star Theatre) starring Donald O'Connor (NBC)

1955

BEST CHILDREN'S SERIES
LASSIE (CBS)
DING DONG SCHOOL (NBC)
HOWDY DOODY (NBC)
KUKLA, FRAN and OLLIE (ABC)
MICKEY MOUSE CLUB (ABC)
THE PINKY LEE SHOW (NBC)

BEST CONTRIBUTION TO DAYTIME PROGRAMMING
MATINEE THEATRE (NBC)
THE BOB CROSBY SHOW (CBS)
THE GARRY MOORE SHOW (CBS)
HOME - ARLENE FRANCIS (NBC)
TODAY - DAVE GARROWAY (NBC)

BEST SPECIAL EVENT OR NEWS PROGRAM
A-BOMB COVERAGE (CBS)
ACADEMY OF MOTION PICTURE ARTS & SCIENCES AWARDS (NBC)
ACADEMY OF TELEVISION ARTS & SCIENCES AWARDS (NBC)
FOOTBALL - ROSE BOWL - (NBC)
BASEBALL - WORLD SERIES - (NBC)

BEST DOCUMENTARY PROGRAM
(Religious, Informational, Educational Or Interview)
OMNIBUS (CBS)
MEET THE PRESS (NBC)
PERSON TO PERSON (CBS)
SEE IT NOW (CBS)
WIDE WIDE WORLD (NBC)

BEST AUDIENCE PARTICIPATION SERIES (QUIZ, PANEL, ETC.)

THE $64,000 QUESTION (CBS)
I'VE GOT A SECRET (CBS)
PEOPLE ARE FUNNY (NBC)
WHAT'S MY LINE? (CBS)
YOU BET YOUR LIFE (NBC)

BEST ACTION OR ADVENTURE SERIES

DISNEYLAND (Davy Crockett Series, etc.) (ABC)
ALFRED HITCHCOCK PRESENTS (CBS)
DRAGNET (NBC)
GUNSMOKE (CBS)
LINE-UP (CBS)

BEST COMEDY SERIES

PHIL SILVERS (You'll Never Get Rich) (CBS)
JACK BENNY SHOW (CBS)
BOB CUMMINGS SHOW (CBS)
CAESAR'S HOUR (NBC)
GEORGE GOBEL SHOW (NBC)
MAKE ROOM FOR DADDY (ABC)

BEST VARIETY SERIES

ED SULLIVAN SHOW (CBS)
DINAH SHORE SHOW (NBC)
FORD STAR JUBILEE (CBS)
PERRY COMO SHOW (NBC)
SHOWER OF STARS (CBS)

BEST MUSIC SERIES

YOUR HIT PARADE (NBC)
COKE TIME - EDDIE FISHER (NBC)
DINAH SHORE SHOW (NBC)
PERRY COMO SHOW (NBC)
VOICE OF FIRESTONE (CBS)

BEST DRAMATIC SERIES

PRODUCERS' SHOWCASE (NBC)
ALCOA-GOODYEAR TV PLAYHOUSE (NBC)
CLIMAX (CBS)
STUDIO ONE (CBS)
U. S. STEEL HOUR (CBS)

BEST SINGLE PROGRAM OF THE YEAR

PETER PAN Mary Martin (Producers' Showcase) (NBC)
THE AMERICAN WEST (Wide Wide World) (NBC)
CAINE MUTINY COURT MARTIAL (Ford Star Jubilee) (CBS)
DAVY CROCKETT AND RIVER PIRATES (Disneyland) (ABC)
NO TIME FOR SERGEANTS (U. S. Steel Hour) (CBS)
PETER PAN MEETS RUSTY WILLIAMS (Make Room For Daddy) (ABC)
THE SLEEPING BEAUTY (Producers' Showcase) (NBC)

BEST ACTOR - SINGLE PERFORMANCE

LLOYD NOLAN as CAPT. QUEEG Caine Mutiny Court Martial (Ford Star Jubilee) (CBS)
RALPH BELLAMY as FATHER Fearful Decision (U. S. Steel Hour) (CBS)
JOSE FERRER as CYRANO Cyrano de Bergerac (Producers' Showcase) (NBC)
EVERETT SLOANE as PRESIDENT Patterns (Kraft Theatre) (NBC)
BARRY SULLIVAN as DEFENSE ATTORNEY GREENWALD Caine Mutiny Court Martial (Ford Star Jubilee) (CBS)

BEST ACTRESS - SINGLE PERFORMANCE

MARY MARTIN as PETER Peter Pan (Producers' Showcase) (NBC)
JULIE HARRIS as SHEVAWN Wind from the South (U. S. Steel Hour) (CBS)
EVA MARIE SAINT as EMILY Our Town (Producers' Showcase) (NBC)
JESSICA TANDY as WIFE The Fourposter (Producers' Showcase) (NBC)
LORETTA YOUNG as SADIE Christmas Stopover (Loretta Young Show) (NBC)

BEST ACTOR - CONTINUING PERFORMANCE

PHIL SILVERS as SERGEANT BILKO (Phil Silvers Show, You'll Never Get Rich) (CBS)
BOB CUMMINGS as BOB COLLINS (Bob Cummings Show) (CBS)
JACKIE GLEASON as RALPH KRAMDEN (Honeymooners) (CBS)
DANNY THOMAS as DANNY WILLIAMS (Make Room for Daddy) (ABC)
ROBERT YOUNG as FATHER (Father Knows Best) (CBS)

BEST ACTRESS - CONTINUING PERFORMANCE

LUCILLE BALL as LUCY RICARDO (I Love Lucy) (CBS)
GRACIE ALLEN as GRACIE (Burns & Allen) (CBS)
EVE ARDEN as CONNIE BROOKS (Our Miss Brooks) (CBS)
JEAN HAGEN as MARGARET WILLIAMS (Make Room for Daddy) (ABC)
ANN SOTHERN as SUSIE MAC NAMARA (Private Secretary) (CBS)

BEST ACTOR IN A SUPPORTING ROLE

ART CARNEY as ED NORTON (Honeymooners) (CBS)
ED BEGLEY as ANDY SLOANE Patterns (Kraft Theatre) (NBC)
WILLIAM FRAWLEY as FRED MERTZ (I Love Lucy) (CBS)
CARL REINER in various roles (Caesar's Hour) (NBC)
CYRIL RITCHARD as Mr. DARLING and CAPT. HOOK Peter Pan (Producers' Showcase) (NBC)

BEST ACTRESS IN A SUPPORTING ROLE

NANETTE FABRAY in various roles (Caesar's Hour) (NBC)
ANN B. DAVIS as SCHULTZY Schultzy's Dream World (Bob Cummings Show) (CBS)
JEAN HAGEN as MARGARET WILLIAMS (Make Room for Daddy) (ABC)
AUDREY MEADOWS as Mrs. KRAMDEN (Honeymooners) (CBS)
THELMA RITTER as THE MOTHER A Catered Affair (Alcoa-Goodyear Playhouse) (NBC)

BEST COMEDIAN

PHIL SILVERS (CBS)
JACK BENNY (CBS)
SID CAESAR (NBC)
ART CARNEY (CBS)
GEORGE GOBEL (CBS)

BEST COMEDIENNE

NANETTE FABRAY (NBC)
GRACIE ALLEN (CBS)
EVE ARDEN (CBS)
LUCILLE BALL (CBS)
ANN SOTHERN (CBS)

BEST MALE SINGER

PERRY COMO (NBC)
HARRY BELAFONTE
EDDIE FISHER (NBC)
GORDON MAC RAE (NBC)
FRANK SINATRA (NBC)

BEST FEMALE SINGER
DINAH SHORE (NBC)
ROSEMARY CLOONEY (Syndicated)
JUDY GARLAND (CBS)
PEGGY LEE
GISELE MAC KENZIE (NBC)

BEST M.C. OR PROGRAM HOST - MALE OR FEMALE
PERRY COMO (NBC)
ALISTAIR COOKE (CBS)
JOHN DALY (CBS)
DAVE GARROWAY (NBC)
ALFRED HITCHCOCK (NBC)

BEST NEWS COMMENTATOR OR REPORTER
EDWARD R. MURROW (CBS)
JOHN DALY (ABC)
DOUGLAS EDWARDS (CBS)
CLETE ROBERTS (CBS)
JOHN CAMERON SWAYZE (NBC)

BEST SPECIALTY ACT - SINGLE OR GROUP
MARCEL MARCEAU (NBC)
HARRY BELAFONTE
VICTOR BORGE
SAMMY DAVIS, JR.
DONALD O'CONNOR (NBC)

BEST ORIGINAL TELEPLAY WRITING
ROD SERLING Patterns (Kraft TV Theatre) (NBC)
DAVID DAVIDSON Thunder Over Washington (Alcoa-Goodyear Playhouse) (NBC)
ROBERT ALAN AURTHUR A Man Is Ten Feet Tall (Philco Playhouse) (NBC)
PADDY CHAYEFSKY A Catered Affair (Alcoa-Goodyear Playhouse) (NBC)
CYRIL HUME & RICHARD MAIBAUM Fearful Decision (U. S. Steel Hour) (CBS)

BEST COMEDY WRITING
NAT HIKEN, BARRY BLITSER, ARNOLD AUERBACH, HARVEY ORKIN, VINCENT BOGERT, ARNOLD ROSEN, COLEMAN JACOBY, TONY WEBSTER & TERRY RYAN (Phil Silvers Show, You'll Never Get Rich) (CBS)
HAL KANTER, HOWARD LEEDS, EVERETT GREENBAUM & HARRY WINKLER (George Gobel Show) (NBC)
JESS OPPENHEIMER, MADELYN PUGH, BOB CARROLL, JR., BOB SCHILLER & BOB WEISKOPF L. A. At Last (I Love Lucy) (CBS)
SAM PERRIN, GEORGE BALZER, HAL GOLDMAN & AL GORDON (Jack Benny Show) (CBS)
MEL TOLKIN, SELMA DIAMOND, LARRY GELBART, MEL BROOKS & SHELDON KELLER (Caesar's Hour) (NBC)

BEST TELEVISION ADAPTATION
PAUL GREGORY & FRANKLIN SCHAFFNER Caine Mutiny Court Martial by Herman Wouk (Ford Star Jubilee) (CBS)
DAVID DORTORT The Ox-Bow Incident by Walter Van Tilberg Clark (20th Century Fox Hour) (CBS)
JOHN MONKS, JR. Miracle On 34th St. by Valentine Davies (20th Century Fox Hour) (CBS)
ROD SERLING The Champion by Ring Lardner (Climax) (CBS)
DAVID SHAW Our Town by Thornton Wilder (Producers' Showcase) (NBC)

BEST MUSICAL CONTRIBUTION
A Song from "Our Town" "Love and Marriage" by Sammy Cahn and James Van Heusen (Producers' Showcase) (NBC)
The Arranging of CAMARATA for "Together with Music" (Ford Star Jubilee) (Mary Martin & Noel Coward) (CBS)
The Score of "Our Town" by Sammy Cahn and James Van Heusen (Producers' Showcase) (NBC)
The Arranging of NELSON RIDDLE for "Our Town" (Producers' Showcase) (NBC)
The Series Scoring by David Broekman (Wide Wide World) (NBC)

BEST PRODUCER - LIVE SERIES
FRED COE (Producers' Showcase) (NBC)
HERBERT BRODKIN (Alcoa-Goodyear Playhouse) (NBC)
HAL KANTER (George Gobel Show) (NBC)
MARTIN MANULIS (Climax) (CBS)
THE THEATRE GUILD (U. S. Steel Hour) (CBS)
BARRY WOOD (Wide Wide World) (NBC)

BEST PRODUCER - FILM SERIES
WALT DISNEY (Disneyland) (ABC)
JAMES D. FONDA (You Are There) (CBS)
PAUL HENNING (Bob Cummings Show) (CBS)
NAT HIKEN (Phil Silver Show, You'll Never Get Rich) (CBS)
FRANK LA TOURETTE (Medic) (NBC)

BEST DIRECTOR - LIVE SERIES
FRANKLIN SCHAFFNER Caine Mutiny Court Martial (Ford Star Jubilee) (CBS)
JOHN FRANKENHEIMER Portrait in Celluloid (Climax) (CBS)
CLARK JONES Peter Pan (Producers' Showcase) (NBC)
DELBERT MANN Our Town (Producers' Showcase) (NBC)
ALEX SEGAL No Time for Sergeants (U. S. Steel Hour) (CBS)

BEST DIRECTOR - FILM SERIES
NAT HIKEN (Phil Silvers Show, You'll Never Get Rich) (CBS)
ROD AMATEAU Return of the Wolf (Bob Cummings Show) (CBS)
BERNARD GIRARD Grant & Lee at Appomatox (You Are There) (CBS)
ALFRED HITCHCOCK The Case of Mr. Pelham (Alfred Hitchcock Presents) (CBS)
SHELDON LEONARD (Make Room for Daddy) (ABC)
JACK WEBB Christmas Story (Dragnet) (NBC)

BEST ART DIRECTION - LIVE SERIES
OTIS RIGGS (Playwrights '56 and Producers' Showcase) (NBC)
CARL KENT (U. S. Steel Hour) (CBS)
JAN SCOTT (Hallmark Hall of Fame) (NBC)
DON SHIRLEY (Perry Como Show) (NBC)
WILLIAM CRAIG SMITH (Lux Video Theatre) (NBC)
JAMES D. VANCE (Climax) (CBS)

BEST ART DIRECTION - FILM SERIES
WILLIAM FERRARI (You Are There) (CBS)
DUNCAN CRAMER (Four Star Playhouse) (CBS)
ERNST FEGTE (Medic) (NBC)
SERGE KRIZMAN (Schlitz Playhouse)
PETER PROUD (Robin Hood)

BEST CINEMATOGRAPHY FOR TELEVISION
WILLIAM SCIKNER Black Friday (Medic) (NBC)
NORBERT BRODINE I Remember The Rani (Loretta Young Show) (NBC)
EDWARD COLMAN (Dragnet) (NBC)
GEORGE DISKANT The Collar (Four-Star Playhouse) (CBS)
ROBERT PITTACK (Private Secretary) (CBS)

BEST CAMERA WORK - LIVE SHOW
T. MILLER (Studio One) (CBS)
A. J. CUNNINGHAM (Climax) (CBS)
JOE STRAUSS (Lux Video Theatre) (NBC)
LES VAUGHT (Art Linkletter's House Party) (CBS)

BEST EDITING OF A TELEVISION FILM
EDWARD W. WILLIAMS Breakdown (Alfred Hitchcock Presents) (CBS)
SAMUEL E. BEETLEY The Collar (Four Star Playhouse) (CBS)
JASON H. BERNIE Operation 3 in 1 (Navy Log) (CBS)
STANLEY FRAZEN & GUY SCARPITTA Miss Coffee Break (Bob Cummings Show) (CBS)
DANIEL NATHAN Little Guy (Fireside Theatre, Jane Wyman) (NBC)

BEST CHOREOGRAPHER
TONY CHARMOLI Show Biz (Your Hit Parade) (NBC)
ROD ALEXANDER (Max Liebman Spectaculars) (NBC)
JEROME ROBBINS Peter Pan (Producers Showcase) (NBC)
JAMES STARBUCK (Max Liebman Presents) and (Shower of Stars with Ethel Merman) (NBC & CBS)
JUNE TAYLOR (Jackie Gleason Show) (CBS)

BEST ENGINEERING TECHNICAL ACHIEVEMENT
RCA TRICOLOR PICTURE TUBE which made the commercial color receiver practical
AUTOMATIC IRIS CONTROL for NBC pick-up of complete atom blast at Yucca Flats
COLOR WIPE AMPLIFIER developed by CBS Engineering
DUMONT ELECTRONICAM
ELECTRONIC EDITING MACHINE developed at the Disney Studios
ULTRA-VIOLET KINESCOPE RECORDING OF RCA which improved the quality of television recording

BEST COMMERCIAL CAMPAIGN
FORD
BANK OF AMERICA
CHRYSLER
HAMM'S BEER
PIEL'S BEER

GOVERNOR'S AWARD
(The first Presidential size Emmy to be awarded)
PRESIDENT DWIGHT D. EISENHOWER For his use and encouragement of television

1956

BEST SINGLE PROGRAM OF THE YEAR
REQUIEM FOR A HEAVYWEIGHT (Playhouse 90) (CBS)
A NIGHT TO REMEMBER Titanic (Kraft Television Theatre) (NBC)
LEONARD BERNSTEIN (Omnibus) (CBS)
SECRET LIFE OF DANNY KAYE (See It Now) (CBS)
VICTOR BORGE SHOW

BEST NEW PROGRAM SERIES
PLAYHOUSE 90 (CBS)
AIR POWER (CBS)
THE CHEVY SHOW Dinah Shore (NBC)
ERNIE KOVACS SHOW (NBC)
STEVE ALLEN SUNDAY SHOW (NBC)

BEST SERIES - HALF HOUR OR LESS
PHIL SILVERS SHOW (CBS)
ALFRED HITCHCOCK PRESENTS (CBS)
FATHER KNOWS BEST (NBC)
JACK BENNY SHOW (CBS)
PERSON TO PERSON (CBS)

BEST SERIES - ONE HOUR OR MORE
CAESAR'S HOUR (NBC)
CLIMAX (CBS)
ED SULLIVAN SHOW (CBS)
OMNIBUS (CBS)
PERRY COMO SHOW (NBC)

BEST PUBLIC SERVICE SERIES
SEE IT NOW (CBS)
MEET THE PRESS (NBC)
NBC OPERA (NBC)
WIDE WIDE WORLD (NBC)
YOU ARE THERE (CBS)

BEST COVERAGE OF A NEWSWORTHY EVENT
"YEARS OF CRISIS," Year-end report, Murrow and correspondents (CBS)
ANDREA DORIA SINKING, Live and Film (CBS)
ANDREA DORIA SURVIVORS ARRIVE IN NEW YORK (NBC)
NATIONAL POLITICAL CONVENTIONS (ABC)
NATIONAL POLITICAL CONVENTIONS (NBC)

BEST CONTINUING PERFORMANCE BY AN ACTOR IN A DRAMATIC SERIES
ROBERT YOUNG (Father Knows Best) (NBC)
JAMES ARNESS (Gunsmoke) (CBS)
CHARLES BOYER (Four Star Playhouse) (CBS)
DAVID NIVEN (Four Star Playhouse) (CBS)
HUGH O'BRIEN Wyatt Earp (Life and Legend of) (ABC)

BEST CONTINUING PERFORMANCE BY AN ACTRESS IN A DRAMATIC SERIES
LORETTA YOUNG (Loretta Young Show) (NBC)
JAN CLAYTON (Lassie) (CBS)
IDA LUPINO (Four Star Playhouse) (CBS)
PEGGY WOOD (I Remember Mama) (CBS)
JANE WYMAN (Jane Wyman Theatre) (NBC)

BEST CONTINUING PERFORMANCE BY A COMEDIAN IN A SERIES
SID CAESAR (Caesar's Hour) (NBC)
JACK BENNY (Jack Benny Show) (CBS)
BOB CUMMINGS (Bob Cummings Show) (CBS)
ERNIE KOVACS (Ernie Kovacs Show) (NBC)
PHIL SILVERS (Phil Silvers Show) (CBS)

BEST CONTINUING PERFORMANCE BY A COMEDIENNE IN A SERIES
NANETTE FABRAY (Caesar's Hour) (NBC)
EDIE ADAMS (Ernie Kovacs Show) (NBC)
GRACIE ALLEN (Burns & Allen) (CBS)
LUCILLE BALL (I Love Lucy) (CBS)
ANN SOTHERN (Private Secretary) (CBS)

BEST SINGLE PERFORMANCE BY AN ACTOR
JACK PALANCE as PRIZEFIGHTER Requiem for a Heavyweight (Playhouse 90) (CBS)
LLOYD BRIDGES as ALEC BEGGS Tragedy in a Temporary Town (Alcoa Hour-Goodyear Playhouse) (NBC)
FREDRIC MARCH as DODSWORTH Dodsworth (Producers' Showcase) (NBC)
SAL MINEO as DINO Dino (Studio One) (CBS)
RED SKELTON as BUDDY MC COY The Big Slide (Playhouse 90) (CBS)

BEST SINGLE PERFORMANCE BY AN ACTRESS
CLAIRE TREVOR as Mrs. DODSWORTH Dodsworth (Producers' Showcase) (NBC)
EDNA BEST as WIFE This Happy Breed (Ford Star Jubilee) (CBS)
GRACIE FIELDS as OLD LADY Old Lady Shows Her Medals (U.S. Steel Hour) (CBS)
NANCY KELLY as NUN The Pilot (Studio One) (CBS)
EVELYN RUDIE as ELOISE Eloise (Playhouse 90) (CBS)

BEST SUPPORTING PERFORMANCE BY AN ACTOR
CARL REINER Various Roles (Caesar's Hour) (NBC)
ART CARNEY as NORTON (Jackie Gleason Show) (CBS)
PAUL FORD as COLONEL (Phil Silvers Show) (CBS)
WILLIAM FRAWLEY as FRED MERTZ (I Love Lucy) (CBS)
ED WYNN as TRAINER Requiem for a Heavyweight (Playhouse 90) (CBS)

BEST SUPPORTING PERFORMANCE BY AN ACTRESS
PAT CARROLL Various Roles (Caesar's Hour) (NBC)
ANN B. DAVIS as SCHULTZY (Bob Cummings Show) (CBS)
AUDREY MEADOWS as ALICE KRAMDEN (Jackie Gleason Show) (CBS)
MILDRED NATWICK as MEDIUM Blithe Spirit (Ford Star Jubilee) (CBS)
VIVIAN VANCE as ETHEL MERTZ (I Love Lucy) (CBS)

BEST MALE PERSONALITY - CONTINUING PERFORMANCE
PERRY COMO (NBC)
STEVE ALLEN (NBC)
LEONARD BERNSTEIN (CBS)
TENNESSEE ERNIE FORD (NBC)
ALFRED HITCHCOCK (CBS)
BISHOP FULTON J. SHEEN (DUMONT)

BEST FEMALE PERSONALITY - CONTINUING PERFORMANCE
DINAH SHORE (NBC)
ROSEMARY CLOONEY (Syndicated)
FAYE EMERSON (CBS)
ARLENE FRANCIS (NBC)
GISELE MAC KENZIE (NBC)

BEST NEWS COMMENTATOR
EDWARD R. MURROW (CBS)
WALTER CRONKITE (CBS)
JOHN DALY (ABC)
DOUGLAS EDWARDS (CBS)
CHET HUNTLEY (NBC)

BEST TELEPLAY WRITING - HALF-HOUR OR LESS
JAMES P. CAVANAUGH Fog Closing In (Alfred Hitchcock Presents) (CBS)
MORTON FINE and DAVID FRIEDKIN Patrol (Frontier) (NBC)
RICHARD MORRIS The Pearl (Loretta Young Show) (NBC)
JOHN NESBITT Man with the Beard (Telephone Time) (ABC)
DAN ULLMAN The Buntline (Wyatt Earp) (ABC)

BEST TELEPLAY WRITING - ONE HOUR OR MORE
ROD SERLING Requiem for a Heavyweight (Playhouse 90) (CBS)
LOUIS PETERSON Joey (Alcoa Hour-Goodyear Playhouse) (NBC)
GEORGE ROY HILL and JOHN WHEDON A Night To Remember (Kraft Television Theatre) (NBC)
ELICK MOLL Sizeman and Son (Playhouse 90) (CBS)
REGINALD ROSE Tragedy in a Temporary Town (Alcoa Hour-Goodyear Playhouse) (NBC)

BEST COMEDY WRITING - VARIETY OR SITUATION COMEDY
NAT HIKEN, BILLY FRIEDBERG, TONY WEBSTER, LEONARD STERN, ARNOLD ROSEN, COLEMAN JACOBY (Phil Silvers Show) (CBS)
GOODMAN ACE, JAY BURTON, MORT GREEN, GEORGE FOSTER (Perry Como Show) (NBC)
ERNIE KOVACS, LOUIS M. HEYWARD, REX LARDNER, MIKE MARMER (Ernie Kovacs Show) (NBC)
SAM PERRIN, GEORGE ALZER, HAL GOLDMAN, AL GORDON (Jack Benny Show) (CBS)
MEL TOLKIN, GARY BELKIN, MEL BROOKS, SHELDON KELLER, NEIL SIMON, LARRY GELBART and MIKE STEWART (Caesar's Hour) (NBC)

BEST DIRECTION - HALF HOUR OR LESS
SHELDON LEONARD Danny's Comeback (Danny Thomas Show) (ABC)
GEORGE ARCHAINBAUD The Traitor (77th Bengal Lancers) (NBC)
HERSCHEL DAUGHERTY The Road That Led Afar (G. E. Theatre) (CBS)
WILLIAM RUSSELL First Moscow Purge Trail (You Are There) (CBS)
CLAY YURDIN As I Lay Dying (Camera Three) (CBS)

BEST DIRECTION - ONE HOUR OR MORE
RALPH NELSON Requiem for a Heavyweight (Playhouse 90) (CBS)
LEWIS ALLEN Child of the Regiment (20th Century-Fox Hour) (CBS)
BOB BANNER October 5 with Sinatra (Chevy Show - Dinah Shore) (NBC)
KIRK BROWNING La Boheme (NBC Opera Theatre) (NBC)
JOHN FRANKENHEIMER Forbidden Area (Playhouse 90) (CBS)
GEORGE ROY HILL A Night to Remember (Kraft Television Theatre) (NBC)

BEST ART DIRECTION - HALF HOUR OR LESS
PAUL BARNES (Your Hit Parade) (NBC)
WARREN CLYMER (Frontiers of Faith) (NBC)
GROVER COLE (Adventure) (CBS)
MARTIN OBZINA, JOHN ROBERT LLOYD, JOHN J. LLOYD, JOHN MEEHAN and GEORGE PATRICK (G. E. Theatre) (CBS)
FRANKLIN SWIG (Dinah Shore Show) (NBC)

BEST ART DIRECTION - ONE HOUR OR MORE
ALBERT HESCHONG Requiem for a Heavyweight (Playhouse 90) (CBS)
HENRY MAY (Omnibus) (CBS)
DUANE MC KINNEY (Kraft Television Theatre) (NBC)
JAN SCOTT (Kaiser Aluminum Hour) (NBC)
DON SHIRLEY (Perry Como Show) (NBC)

BEST CINEMATOGRAPHY FOR TELEVISION
NORBERT BRODINE The Pearl (Loretta Young Show) (NBC)
LLOYD AHERN Stranger in the Night (20th Century-Fox Hour) (CBS)
GEORGE E. DISKANT Tunnel of Fear (Four Star Playhouse) (CBS)
ROBERT W. PITTACK The Glorious Gift of Molly Malloy (G. E. Theatre) (CBS)
JOHN L. RUSSELL The Night Goes On (G. E. Theatre) (CBS)

BEST EDITING OF A FILM FOR TELEVISION
FRANK KELLER Our Mr. Sun (A.T.&T. Science Series) (CBS)
SAMUEL E. BEETLEY Tunnel of Fear (Four Star Playhouse) (CBS)
RICHARD FANTL Betty's Birthday (Father Knows Best) (NBC)
DANIEL A. NATHAN Between Jobs (Jane Wyman Theatre) (NBC)
ROBERT WATTS Bounty Killers (Cheyenne) (ABC)

BEST MUSICAL CONTRIBUTION FOR TELEVISION
LEONARD BERNSTEIN Composing Conducting (Omnibus) (CBS)
SIDNEY FINE Orchestrations of Victor Young's Music (Medic) (NBC)
NELSON RIDDLE Arrangement of Musical Score (Rosemary Clooney Show) (Syndicated)
WALTER SCHUMANN Vocal Arrangements (Tennessee Ernie Ford Show) (NBC)
OLIVER WALLACE Composing of Score (Disneyland TV Show) (ABC)

BEST LIVE CAMERA WORK
A NIGHT TO REMEMBER (Kraft Television Theatre) (NBC)
AN AMERICAN SUNDAY (Wide Wide World) (NBC)
JACK AND THE BEANSTALK (Producers' Showcase) (NBC)
REPUBLICAN CONVENTION (ABC-CBS-NBC Pool)
REQUIEM FOR A HEAVYWEIGHT (Playhouse 90) (CBS)

BEST ENGINEERING OR TECHNICAL ACHIEVEMENT
DEVELOPMENT OF VIDEO TAPE BY AMPEX and FURTHER DEVELOPMENT AND PRACTICAL APPLICATIONS BY CBS - DUAL ENTRY
APPLICATION OF LENTICULAR FILM TO RECORDING PROCESS FOR COLOR DELAYED RELEASE (NBC)
DEVELOPMENT OF THE TRULY PORTABLE "CREEPIE PEEPIE" FOR TELEVISION PICK-UP BY RCA
TELESCOPIC LENS WITH 100' FOCAL LENGTH ("BIG JAKE") DEVELOPED AND USED BY ABC
"WIDE WIDE WORLD," LIVE PICK-UP FROM HAVANA, CUBA (NBC)

1957

BEST SINGLE PROGRAM OF THE YEAR
May be either one of a series or an individual presentation, either entertainment, public service or coverage of a newsworthy event.
THE COMEDIAN (Playhouse 90) (CBS)
EDSEL SHOW (CBS)
GREEN PASTURES (Hallmark Hall of Fame) (NBC)
HELEN MORGAN STORY (Playhouse 90) (CBS)

BEST NEW PROGRAM SERIES OF THE YEAR
The most outstanding series of programs of any format presented originally in 1957.
SEVEN LIVELY ARTS (CBS)
LEAVE IT TO BEAVER (CBS)
MAVERICK (ABC)
TONIGHT - JACK PAAR (NBC)
WAGON TRAIN (NBC)

BEST DRAMATIC ANTHOLOGY SERIES
The most outstanding group of dramatic programs presented on a regular basis which employs individual stories and characters for each presentation, except comedy series which have a separate category.
PLAYHOUSE 90 (CBS)
ALFRED HITCHCOCK PRESENTS (CBS)
CLIMAX (CBS)
HALLMARK HALL OF FAME (NBC)
STUDIO ONE (CBS)

BEST DRAMATIC SERIES WITH CONTINUING CHARACTERS
The most outstanding group of dramatic programs presented multi-weekly, weekly, or from time to time on a regular basis and employing the same continuing characters; but excludes all comedy series which have a separate category.
GUNSMOKE (CBS)
LASSIE (CBS)
MAVERICK (ABC)
PERRY MASON (CBS)
WAGON TRAIN (NBC)

BEST COMEDY SERIES
The most outstanding group of comedy programs presented multi-weekly, weekly, or from time to time on a regular basis.
PHIL SILVERS SHOW (CBS)
BOB CUMMINGS SHOW (CBS & NBC)
CAESAR'S HOUR (NBC)
FATHER KNOWS BEST (NBC)
JACK BENNY SHOW (CBS)

BEST MUSICAL, VARIETY, AUDIENCE PARTICIPATION OR QUIZ SERIES
The most outstanding group of programs, not in the area of drama or comedy, presented multi-weekly, weekly, or from time to time on a regular basis.
DINAH SHORE - CHEVY SHOW (NBC)
ED SULLIVAN SHOW (CBS)
PERRY COMO SHOW (NBC)
STEVE ALLEN SHOW (NBC)
TONIGHT - JACK PAAR (NBC)

BEST PUBLIC SERVICE PROGRAM OR SERIES
OMNIBUS (ABC & NBC)
BELL TELEPHONE SCIENCE SERIES (NBC)
PERSON TO PERSON (CBS)
SEE IT NOW (CBS)
WIDE WIDE WORLD (NBC)

BEST COVERAGE OF AN UNSCHEDULED NEWSWORTHY EVENT

COVERAGE OF THE RIKERS ISLAND NEW YORK PLANE CRASH as presented on "World News Roundup" (CBS)
FOUR NEWSMEN INTERVIEW GOVERNOR ORVAL FAUBUS OF ARKANSAS IN LITTLE ROCK (ABC)
NEWS COVERAGE OF THE INTEGRATION STORY IN LITTLE ROCK AND OTHER SOUTHERN CITIES (NBC)
COVERAGE OF THE LITTLE ROCK SCHOOL RIOT, as presened on "Little Rock, 1957"(CBS)
NEWS COVERAGE OF FIRST RUSSIAN SPUTNIK, THE U.S. SATELLITE LAUNCHING EFFORTS AND VANGUARD FAILURE ON DEC. 6 (NBC)

BEST CONTINUING PERFORMANCE BY AN ACTOR IN A LEADING ROLE IN A DRAMATIC OR COMEDY SERIES

ROBERT YOUNG as JIM ANDERSON (Father Knows Best) (NBC)
JAMES ARNESS as MATT DILLON (Gunsmoke) (CBS)
BOB CUMMINGS as BOB COLLINS (Bob Cummings Show) (CBS & NBC)
PHIL SILVERS as BILKO (Phil Silvers Show) (CBS)
DANNY THOMAS as DANNY WILLIAMS (Danny Thomas Show) (ABC & CBS)

BEST CONTINUING PERFORMANCE BY AN ACTRESS IN A LEADING ROLE IN A DRAMATIC OR COMEDY SERIES

JANE WYATT as MARGARET ANDERSON (Father Knows Best) (NBC)
EVE ARDEN as LIZA HAMMOND (Eve Arden Show) (CBS)
SPRING BYINGTON as LILY RUSKIN (December Bride) (CBS)
JAN CLAYTON as AUNT ELLEN (Lassie) (CBS)
IDA LUPINO as EVE DRAKE (Mr. Adam and Eve) (CBS)

BEST CONTINUING PERFORMANCE (MALE) IN A SERIES BY A COMEDIAN, SINGER, HOST, DANCER, M.C., ANNOUNCER, NARRATOR, PANELIST, OR ANY PERSON WHO ESSENTIALLY PLAYS HIMSELF

JACK BENNY (Jack Benny Show) (CBS)
STEVE ALLEN (Steve Allen Show) (NBC)
SID CAESAR (Caesar's Hour) (NBC)
PERRY COMO (Perry Como Show) (NBC)
JACK PAAR (Tonight - Jack Paar) (NBC)

BEST CONTINUING PERFORMANCE (FEMALE) IN A SERIES BY A COMEDIENNE, SINGER, HOSTESS, DANCER, M.C., ANNOUNCER, NARRATOR, PANELIST, OR ANY PERSON WHO ESSENTIALLY PLAYS HERSELF

DINAH SHORE (Dinah Shore Chevy Show) (NBC)
GRACIE ALLEN (Burns and Allen Show) (CBS)
LUCILLE BALL (I Love Lucy) (CBS)
DODY GOODMAN (Tonight - Jack Paar) (NBC)
LORETTA YOUNG (Loretta Young Show) (NBC)

ACTOR - BEST SINGLE PERFORMANCE - LEAD OR SUPPORT

PETER USTINOV as SAMUEL JOHNSON The Life of Samuel Johnson (Omnibus) (NBC)
LEE J. COBB as PATHOLOGIST - DR. PEARSON No Deadly Medicine (Studio One) (CBS)
MICKEY ROONEY as SAMMY HOGARTH The Comedian (Playhouse 90) (CBS)
DAVID WAYNE as MENICK Heartbeat (Suspicion) (NBC)
ED WYNN as GRAMPS On Borrowed Time (Hallmark Hall of Fame) (NBC)

ACTRESS - BEST SINGLE PERFORMANCE - LEAD OR SUPPORT

POLLY BERGEN as HELEN MORGAN Helen Morgan Story (Playhouse 90) (CBS)
JULIE ANDREWS as CINDERELLA Cinderella (CBS)
HELEN HAYES as MRS. GILLING Mrs. Gilling and the Skyscraper (Alcoa Hour) (NBC)
PIPER LAURIE as RUTH CORNELIUS The Deaf Heart (Studio One) (CBS)
TERESA WRIGHT as ANNIE SULLIVAN The Miracle Worker (Playhouse 90) (CBS)

BEST CONTINUING SUPPORTING PERFORMANCE BY AN ACTOR IN A DRAMATIC OR COMEDY SERIES

CARL REINER Various Roles (Caesar's Hour) (NBC)
PAUL FORD as COLONEL HALL (Phil Silvers Show) (CBS)
BILL FRAWLEY as FRED MERTZ (I Love Lucy) (CBS)
LOUIS NYE as GORDON HATHAWAY (Steve Allen Show) (NBC)
DENNIS WEAVER as CHESTER (Gunsmoke) (CBS)

BEST CONTINUING SUPPORTING PERFORMANCE BY AN ACTRESS IN A DRAMATIC OR COMEDY SERIES

ANN B. DAVIS as SCHULTZY (Bob Cummings Show) (CBS & NBC)
PAT CARROLL Various Roles (Caesar's Hour) (NBC)
VERNA FELTON as HILDA CROCKER (December Bride) (CBS)
MARION LORNE as MRS. MABEL BANFORD (Sally) (NBC)
VIVIAN VANCE as ETHEL MERTZ (I Love Lucy) (CBS)

BEST NEWS COMMENTARY

EDWARD R. MURROW (See It Now) (CBS)
JOHN DALY News (ABC)
DOUGLAS EDWARDS News (CBS)
CHET HUNTLEY and DAVID BRINKLEY News (NBC)
ERIC SEVAREID World News Roundup (CBS)

BEST TELEPLAY WRITING - HALF HOUR OR LESS

PAUL MONASH The Lonely Wizard (Schlitz Playhouse of Stars) (CBS)
JOE CONNELLY and BOB MOSHER Beaver Gets Spelled (Leave it to Beaver) (CBS)
JOHN MESTON Born to Hang (Gunsmoke) (CBS)
ROSWELL ROGERS Margaret Hires a Gardener (Father Knows Best) (NBC)
MORTON WISHENGRAD A Chassidic Tale (Frontiers of Faith) (NBC)

BEST TELEPLAY WRITING - ONE HOUR OR MORE
ROD SERLING The Comedian (Playhouse 90) (CBS)
MARC CONNELLY Green Pastures (Hallmark Hall of Fame) (NBC)
WILLIAM GIBSON The Miracle Worker (Playhouse 90) (CBS)
ARTHUR HAILEY No Deadly Medicine (Studio One) (CBS)
JAMES LEE Life of Samuel Johnson (Omnibus) (NBC)

BEST COMEDY WRITING
NAT HIKEN, BILLY FRIEDBERG, PHIL SHARP, TERRY RYAN, COLEMAN JACOBY, ARNOLD ROSEN, SIDNEY ZELINKA, A.J. RUSSELL and TONY WEBSTER (Phil Silvers Show) (CBS)
ERNIE KOVACS No Dialogue Show (Ernie Kovacs Show) (NBC)
SAM PERRIN, GEORGE BALZER, AL GORDON, HAL GOLDMAN (Jack Benny Show) (CBS)
MEL TOLKIN, LARRY GELBART, MEL BROOKS, NEIL SIMON, SHELDON KELLER, MIKE STEWART, GARY BELKIN (Caesar's Hour) (NBC)
ROSWELL ROGERS and PAUL WEST (Father Knows Best) (NBC)

BEST DIRECTION - HALF HOUR OR LESS
ROBERT STEVENS The Glass Eye (Alfred Hitchcock Presents) (CBS)
BILL HOBIN (Your Hit Parade) (NBC)
CLARK JONES (Patrice Munsel Show) (ABC)
SHELDON LEONARD (Danny Thomas Show) (ABC & CBS)
PETER TEWKSBURY (Father Knows Best) (NBC)

BEST DIRECTION - ONE HOUR OR MORE
BOB BANNER Entire Series (Dinah Shore Chevy Show) (NBC)
JOHN FRANKENHEIMER The Comedian (Playhouse 90) (CBS)
GEORGE ROY HILL Helen Morgan Story (Playhouse 90) (CBS)
ARTHUR PENN The Miracle Worker (Playhouse 90) (CBS)
GEORGE SCHAEFER Green Pastures (Hallmark Hall of Fame) (NBC)

BEST ART DIRECTION
ROUBEN TER-ARUTUNIAN Twelfth Night (Hallmark Hall of Fame) (NBC)
BEULAH FRANKEL Don't Ever Come Back (Climax) (CBS)
HOWARD E. JOHNSON (Wagon Train) (NBC)
ROBERT KELLY (George Gobel Show) (NBC)
DON SHIRLEY (Perry Como Show) (NBC)

BEST CINEMATOGRAPHY FOR TELEVISION
HAROLD E. WELLMAN Hemo The Magnificent (Bell Telephone Science Series) (CBS)
NORBERT BRODINE Miss Ashley's Demon (Loretta Young Show) (NBC)
ROBERT DE GRASSE Entire Series (Danny Thomas Show) (ABC & CBS)
GEORGE E. DISKANT Voices in the Fog (Goodyear Theatre) (NBC)
WILLIAM MARGULIES Outlaw (Have Gun--Will Travel) (CBS)

BEST LIVE CAMERA WORK
PLAYHOUSE 90 (CBS)
ANNIE GET YOUR GUN (NBC)
CINDERELLA (CBS)
GENERAL MOTORS 50th ANNIVERSARY SHOW (NBC)
WIDE WIDE WORLD (NBC)

BEST EDITING OF A FILM FOR TELEVISION
Eligible in this category are motion pictures made primarily for television release, rather than theatrical pictures edited or adapted for use on television.
MIKE POZEN How to Kill a Woman (Gunsmoke) (CBS)
SAMUEL E. BEETLEY The Tinhorn (Goodyear Theatre) (NBC)
DANNY LANDRES Lonely Wizard (Schlitz Playhouse of Stars) (CBS)
MICHAEL R. MC ADAM Trail to Christmas (G. E. Theatre) (CBS)
ROBERT SPARR The Quick and the Dead (Maverick) (ABC)

BEST MUSICAL CONTRIBUTION FOR TELEVISION
LEONARD BERNSTEIN Conducting and Analyzing Music of Johann Sebastian Bach (Omnibus) (ABC)
MITCHELL AYRES Music Direction (Perry Como Show) (NBC)
ROBERT RUSSELL BENNETT Arranging and Conducting - The Innocent Years on Project 20 (NBC)
NELSON RIDDLE Arranging and Conducting (Frank Sinatra Show) (ABC)
RICHARD RODGERS Music Score Cinderella (CBS)

BEST ENGINEERING OR TECHNICAL ACHIEVEMENT
ENGINEERING AND CAMERA TECHNIQUES ON WIDE WIDE WORLD (NBC)
CHROMA KEY SYSTEM as developed by Frank Gaskins, Milt Altman, and Associates at NBC
COLOR MATTING AMPLIFIER (CBS)
DAGE VIDICON CAMERA adapted as a portable TV camera - Thompson Products Co.
LIVE PICK-UP FROM HAVANA OVER THE HORIZON (NBC)

TRUSTEES AWARD
JACK BENNY For his significant contributions to the television industry as a showman. For the high standard, for all to emulate, set by his personal skill and excellence as a performer. For the consistency, quality and good taste of his programs through may years and many media.

1958/59

MOST OUTSTANDING SINGLE PROGRAM OF THE YEAR
AN EVENING WITH FRED ASTAIRE (NBC)
CHILD OF OUR TIME (Playhouse 90) (CBS)
LITTLE MOON OF ALBAN (Hallmark Hall of Fame) (NBC)
THE OLD MAN (Playhouse 90) (CBS)

BEST DRAMATIC SERIES - ONE HOUR OR LONGER
PLAYHOUSE 90 (CBS)
U.S. STEEL HOUR (CBS)

BEST DRAMATIC SERIES - LESS THAN ONE HOUR
ALCOA-GOODYEAR THEATRE (NBC)
ALFRED HITCHCOCK PRESENTS (CBS)
GENERAL ELECTRIC THEATRE (CBS)
LORETTA YOUNG SHOW (NBC)
THE NAKED CITY (ABC)
PETER GUNN (NBC)

BEST COMEDY SERIES
JACK BENNY SHOW (CBS)
BOB CUMMINGS SHOW (NBC)
DANNY THOMAS SHOW (CBS)
FATHER KNOWS BEST (CBS & NBC)
PHIL SILVERS SHOW (CBS)
RED SKELTON SHOW (CBS)

BEST MUSICAL OR VARIETY SERIES
DINAH SHORE-CHEVY SHOW (NBC)
PERRY COMO SHOW (NBC)
STEVE ALLEN SHOW (NBC)

BEST WESTERN SERIES
MAVERICK (ABC)
GUNSMOKE (CBS)
HAVE GUN, WILL TRAVEL (CBS)
THE RIFLEMAN (ABC)
WAGON TRAIN (NBC)

BEST PUBLIC SERVICE PROGRAM OR SERIES
OMNIBUS (NBC)
BOLD JOURNEY (ABC)
MEET THE PRESS (NBC)
SMALL WORLD (CBS)
THE TWENTIETH CENTURY (CBS)
YOUNG PEOPLE'S CONCERTS - N.Y. PHILHARMONIC (CBS)

BEST NEWS REPORTING SERIES
HUNTLEY-BRINKLEY REPORT (NBC)
DOUGLAS EDWARDS WITH THE NEWS (CBS)
JOHN DALY AND THE NEWS (ABC)

BEST PANEL, QUIZ, OR AUDIENCE PARTICIPATION SERIES
WHAT'S MY LINE? (CBS)
I'VE GOT A SECRET (CBS)
KEEP TALKING (CBS)
THE PRICE IS RIGHT (NBC)
THIS IS YOUR LIFE (NBC)
YOU BET YOUR LIFE (NBC)

BEST SPECIAL DRAMATIC PROGRAM - ONE HOUR OR LONGER
LITTLE MOON OF ALBAN (Hallmark Hall of Fame) (NBC)
THE BRIDGE OF SAN LUIS REY (Du Pont Show of the Month) (CBS)
HAMLET (Du Pont Show of the Month) (CBS)
THE HASTY HEART (Du Pont Show of the Month) (CBS)
JOHNNY BELINDA (Hallmark Hall of Fame) (NBC)

BEST SPECIAL MUSICAL OR VARIETY PROGRAM - ONE HOUR OR LONGER
AN EVENING WITH FRED ASTAIRE (NBC)
ART CARNEY MEETS "PETER AND THE WOLF" (ABC)

BEST SPECIAL NEWS PROGRAM
FACE OF RED CHINA (CBS)
AMERICAN GI'S IN LEBANON (Outlook) (NBC)
ELECTION NIGHT RETURNS (CBS)
PROJECTION '59 (NBC)
THE STORY OF ATLAS 10B (Chet Huntley Reporting) (NBC)
WHERE WE STAND II (CBS)
YEARS OF CRISIS (CBS)

BEST ACTOR IN A LEADING ROLE (CONTINUING CHARACTER) IN A DRAMATIC SERIES
RAYMOND BURR as PERRY MASON (Perry Mason) (CBS)
JAMES ARNESS as MATT DILLON (Gunsmoke) (CBS)
RICHARD BOONE as PALADIN (Have Gun, Will Travel) (CBS)
JAMES GARNER as BRET MAVERICK (Maverick) (ABC)
CRAIG STEVENS as PETER GUNN (Peter Gunn) (NBC)
EFREM ZIMBALIST, JR. as STUART BAILEY (77 Sunset Strip) (ABC)

BEST ACTRESS IN A LEADING ROLE (CONTINUING CHARACTER) IN A DRAMATIC SERIES
LORETTA YOUNG as HOSTESS (Loretta Young Show) (NBC)
PHYLLIS KIRK as NORA CHARLES (The Thin Man) (NBC)
JUNE LOCKHART as MOTHER (Lassie) (CBS)
JANE WYMAN as HOSTESS (Jane Wyman Show) (NBC)

BEST ACTOR IN A LEADING ROLE (CONTINUING CHARACTER) IN A COMEDY SERIES
JACK BENNY as HIMSELF (Jack Benny Show) (CBS)
WALTER BRENNAN as "GRAMPA" (The Real McCoys) (ABC)
BOB CUMMINGS as BOB COLLINS (Bob Cummings Show) (NBC)
PHIL SILVERS as SGT. BILKO (Phil Silvers Show) (CBS)
DANNY THOMAS as DANNY WILLIAMS (Danny Thomas Show) (CBS)
ROBERT YOUNG as JIM ANDERSON (Father Knows Best) (CBS & NBC)

BEST ACTRESS IN A LEADING ROLE (CONTINUING CHARACTER) IN A COMEDY SERIES
JANE WYATT as MARGARET ANDERSON (Father Knows Best) (CBS & NBC)
GRACIE ALLEN as HERSELF (Burns & Allen) (CBS)
SPRING BYINGTON as LILY RUSKIN (December Bride) (CBS)
IDA LUPINO as EVE DRAKE (Mr. Adams and Eve) (CBS)
DONNA REED as DONNA STONE (Donna Reed Show) (ABC)
ANN SOTHERN as KATIE O'CONNOR (Ann Sothern Show) (CBS)

BEST SUPPORTING ACTOR (CONTINUING CHARACTER) IN A DRAMATIC SERIES
DENNIS WEAVER as CHESTER (Gunsmoke) (CBS)
HERSCHEL BERNARDI as LT. JACOBY (Peter Gunn) (NBC)
JOHNNY CRAWFORD as MARK MC CAIN (The Rifleman) (ABC)
WILLIAM HOPPER as PAUL DRAKE (Perry Mason) (CBS)

BEST SUPPORTING ACTRESS (CONTINUING CHARACTER) IN A DRAMATIC SERIES
BARBARA HALE as DELLA STREET (Perry Mason) (CBS)
LOLA ALBRIGHT as EDIE HART (Peter Gunn) (NBC)
AMANDA BLAKE as KITTY (Gunsmoke) (CBS)
HOPE EMERSON as MOTHER (Peter Gunn) (NBC)

BEST SUPPORTING ACTOR (CONTINUING CHARACTER) IN A COMEDY SERIES
TOM POSTON as MAN IN THE STREET, OTHERS (Steve Allen Show) (NBC)
RICHARD CRENNA as LUKE MC COY (The Real McCoys) (ABC)
PAUL FORD as COLONEL HALL (Phil Silvers Show) (CBS)
MAURICE GOSFIELD as PVT. DOBERMAN (Phil Silvers Show) (CBS)

BILLY GRAY as BUD ANDERSON (Father Knows Best) (CBS & NBC)
HARRY MORGAN as PETE (December Bride) (CBS)

BEST SUPPORTING ACTRESS (CONTINUING CHARACTER) IN A COMEDY SERIES

ANN B. DAVIS as SCHULTZY (Bob Cummings Show) (NBC)
ROSEMARY DE CAMP as MARGARET COLLINS (Bob Cummings Show) (NBC)
ELINOR DONAHUE as BETTY ANDERSON (Father Knows Best) (CBS & NBC)
VERNA FELTON as HILDA (December Bride) (CBS)
KATHY NOLAN as KATE MC COY (The Real McCoys) (ABC)
ZA SU PITTS as MISS NUGENT (Oh Susanna) (CBS)

BEST PERFORMANCE BY AN ACTOR (CONTINUING CHARACTER) IN A MUSICAL OR VARIETY SERIES

PERRY COMO (Perry Como Show) (NBC)
STEVE ALLEN (Steve Allen Show) (NBC)
JACK PAAR (Jack Paar Show) (NBC)

BEST PERFORMANCE BY AN ACTRESS (CONTINUING CHARACTER) IN A MUSICAL OR VARIETY SERIES

DINAH SHORE (Dinah Shore Chevy Show) (NBC)
PATTI PAGE (Patti Page Show) (ABC)

BEST SINGLE PERFORMANCE BY AN ACTOR

Any type or length program, live or film

FRED ASTAIRE as FRED ASTAIRE (An Evening with Fred Astaire) (NBC)
ROBERT CRAWFORD as TANGUY Child of our Time (Playhouse 90) (CBS)
PAUL MUNI as SAM ARLEN Last Clear Chance (Playhouse 90) (CBS)
CHRISTOPHER PLUMMER as KENNETH BOYD Little Moon of Alban (Hallmark Hall of Fame) (NBC)
MICKEY ROONEY as EDDIE Eddie (Alcoa-Goodyear Theatre) (NBC)
ROD STEIGER as HARVEY DENTON A Town Has Turned to Dust (Playhouse 90) (CBS)

BEST SINGLE PERFORMANCE BY AN ACTRESS

Any type or length program, live or film

JULIE HARRIS as BRIGID MARY Little Moon of Alban (Hallmark Hall of Fame) (NBC)
JUDITH ANDERSON as MARQUESA DE MONTEMAYOR Bridge of San Luis Rey (Du Pont Show of the Month) (CBS)
HELEN HAYES as MOTHER SERAPHIM One Red Rose for Christmas (U.S. Steel Hour) (CBS)
PIPER LAURIE as KIRSTEN CLAY Days of Wine and Roses (Playhouse 90) (CBS)
GERALDINE PAGE as THE YOUNG WOMAN The Old Man (Playhouse 90) (CBS)
MAUREEN STAPLETON as SADIE BURKE All the Kings Men (Kraft Theatre) (NBC)

BEST NEWS COMMENTATOR OR ANALYST

EDWARD R. MURROW (CBS)
JOHN DALY (ABC)
CHET HUNTLEY (NBC)

BEST DIRECTION OF A SINGLE PROGRAM OF A DRAMATIC SERIES - LESS THAN ONE HOUR

JACK SMIGHT Eddie (Alcoa-Goodyear Theatre) (NBC)
HERSCHEL DAUGHERTY One is a Wanderer (General Electric Theatre) (CBS)
BLAKE EDWARDS The Kill (Peter Gunn) (NBC)
ALFRED HITCHCOCK Lamb to the Slaughter (Alfred Hitchcock Presents) (CBS)
JAMES NEILSON Kid at the Stick (General Electric Theatre) (CBS)

BEST DIRECTION OF A SINGLE DRAMATIC PROGRAM - ONE HOUR OR LONGER

GEORGE SCHAEFER Little Moon of Alban (Hallmark Hall of Fame) (NBC)
JOHN FRANKENHEIMER A Town has Turned to Dust (Playhouse 90) (CBS)
GEORGE ROY HILL Child of our Time (Playhouse 90) (CBS)

BEST DIRECTION OF A SINGLE PROGRAM OF A COMEDY SERIES

PETER TEWKSBURY Medal for Margaret (Father Knows Best) (CBS)
HY AVERBACK Kate's Career (The Real McCoys) (ABC)
SEYMOUR BERNS Jack Benny Show with Gary Cooper (Jack Benny Show) (CBS)
RICHARD KINON The Interview (Mr. Adams and Eve) (CBS)
SHELDON LEONARD Pardon My Accent (Danny Thomas Show) (CBS)

BEST DIRECTION OF A SINGLE MUSICAL OR VARIETY PROGRAM

BUD YORKIN (An Evening with Fred Astaire) (NBC)
CLARK JONES Perry Como Show with Maureen O'Hara, Robert Preston (Perry Como Show) (NBC)
GOWER CHAMPION, JOE CATES Accent on Love (Pontiac Star Parade) (NBC)

BEST WRITING OF A SINGLE PROGRAM OF A DRAMATIC SERIES, LESS THAN ONE HOUR

ALFRED BRENNER, KEN HUGHES Eddie (Alcoa-Goodyear Theatre) (NBC)
ROALD DAHL Lamb to the Slaughter (Alfred Hitchcock Presents) (CBS)
BLAKE EDWARDS The Kill (Peter Gunn) (NBC)
CHRISTOPHER KNOPF The Loudmouth (Alcoa-Goodyear Theatre) (NBC)
SAMUEL TAYLOR One is a Wanderer (From story by James Thurber) (General Electric Theatre) (CBS)

BEST WRITING OF A SINGLE DRAMATIC PROGRAM - ONE HOUR OR LONGER

JAMES COSTIGAN Little Moon of Alban (Hallmark Hall of Fame) (NBC)
HORTON FOOTE The Old Man (From story by William Faulkner) (Playhouse 90) (CBS)
J.P. MILLER Days of Wine and Roses (Playhouse 90) (CBS)
IRVING GAYNOR NEIMAN Child of Our Time (From novel by Michael De Castillo) (Playhouse 90) (CBS)
ROD SERLING A Town Has Turned to Dust (Playhouse 90) (CBS)

BEST WRITING OF A SINGLE PROGRAM OF A COMEDY SERIES

SAM PERRIN, GEORGE BALZER, HAL GOLDMAN, AL GORDON Jack Benny Show with Ernie Kovacs (Jack Benny Show) (CBS)
BILLY FRIEDBERG, ARNIE ROSEN, COLEMAN JACOBY Bilko's Vampire (Phil Silvers Show) (CBS)
PAUL HENNING, DICK WESSON Grampa Clobbers the Air Force (Bob Cummings Show) (NBC)
BILL MANHOFF Once There Was a Traveling Salesman (The Real McCoys) (ABC)
ROSWELL ROGERS Medal for Margaret (Father Knows Best) (CBS)

BEST WRITING OF A SINGLE MUSICAL OR VARIETY PROGRAM

BUD YORKIN, HERBERT BAKER (An Evening with Fred Astaire) (NBC)
GOODMAN ACE, MORT GREEN, GEORGE FOSTER, JAY BURTON (Perry Como Show with Pier Angeli, Andy Griffith, Helen O'Connell) (NBC)
LARRY GELBART, WOODY ALLEN (Sid Caesar's Chevy Show with Shirley MacLaine, Art Carney, Jo Stafford (NBC)
A.J. RUSSELL Art Carney Meets "Peter and the Wolf" (ABC)
LEONARD STERN, STAN BURNS, HERB SARGENT, BILL DANA, DON HINKLEY, HAL GOODMAN, LARRY KLEIN (Steve Allen Show with Peter Ustinov, Louis Armstrong, Van Cliburn) (NBC)

BEST CINEMATOGRAPHY FOR TELEVISION

ELLIS W. CARTER Alphabet Conspiracy (Bell Telephone Special) (NBC)
FRED JACKMAN, JR. Corporal Hardy (Alcoa-Goodyear Theatre) (NBC)
WILLIAM MARGULIES Ella West (Have Gun, Will Travel) (CBS)
MACK STENGLER Day of Glory (Jane Wyman Show) (NBC)
HAROLD STINE Shady Deal at Sunny Acres (Maverick) (ABC)
RALPH WOOLSEY Diamond in the Rough (Maverick) (ABC)

BEST LIVE CAMERA WORK
Any type or length program

AN EVENING WITH FRED ASTAIRE (NBC)
BRIDGE OF SAN LUIS REY (DuPont Show of the Month) (CBS)
CHILD OF OUR TIME (Playhouse 90) (CBS)
THE OLD MAN (Playhouse 90) (CBS)
A TOWN HAS TURNED TO DUST (Playhouse 90) (CBS)

BEST ART DIRECTION IN A TELEVISION FILM
Any type or length program

CLAUDIO GUZMAN Bernadette (Westinghouse Desilu Playhouse) (CBS)
RALPH BERGER, CHARLES F. PYKE The Duchess of Denver (The Texan) (CBS)
JOHN MC CORMACK Corporal Hardy (Alcoa-Goodyear Theatre) (NBC)
ALBERT M. PYKE Man From Paris (The Californians) (NBC)
FRANK SYLOS Most Honorable Day (Loretta Young Show) (NBC)

BEST ART DIRECTION IN A LIVE TELEVISION PROGRAM
Any type or length

EDWARD STEPHENSON (An Evening with Fred Astaire) (NBC)
WARREN CLYMER Little Moon of Alban (Hallmark Hall of Fame) (NBC)
WALTER SCOTT HERNDON The Old Man (Playhouse 90) (CBS)
BOB MARKELL Hamlet (Du Pont Show of the Month) (CBS)
JAN SCOTT Hans Brinker or The Silver Skates (Hallmark Hall of Fame) (NBC)
ROBERT WADE Count of Monte Cristo (Du Pont Show of the Month) (CBS)

BEST EDITING OF A FILM FOR TELEVISION
Any type or length

SILVIO D'ALISERA Meet Mr. Lincoln (Project 20) (NBC)
ROBERT CRAWFORD Grandpa Clobbers the Air Force (Bob Cummings Show) (NBC)
RICHARD FANTL Eddie (Alcoa-Goodyear Theatre) (NBC)
DANNY B. LANDRES Long Distance (Schlitz Playhouse) (CBS)
ROBERT T. SPARR Rope of Cards (Maverick) (ABC)
RICHARD VAN ENGER Two Graves for Swan Valley (Bat Masterson) (NBC)
ROBERT WATTS Saga of Waco Williams (Maverick)

BEST MUSICAL CONTRIBUTION TO A TELEVISION PROGRAM
Regular or special, any length, live or film

DAVID ROSE Musical direction of An Evening with Fred Astaire (NBC)
FRANK DE VOL Musical direction of Lux Show starring Rosemary Clooney (NBC)
BERNARD GREEN Musical direction of Johnny Belinda on Hallmark Hall of Fame (NBC)
HENRY MANCINI Composing Peter Gunn theme (NBC)
EDDY MANSON Composing and conducting music for Harvey on Du Pont Show of the Month (CBS)
PAUL WESTON Composing and conducting music for Art Carney Meets "Peter and the Wolf" (ABC)

BEST CHOREOGRAPHY FOR TELEVISION
Any type or length program, live or film

HERMES PAN An Evening with Fred Astaire (NBC)
GENE KELLY Dancing is a Man's Game (Omnibus) (NBC)

BEST ENGINEERING OR TECHNICAL ACHIEVEMENT

Industry-wide improvement of editing of Video Tape as exemplified by ABC-CBS-NBC
Practical application of automation to TV program switching (NBC) Washington, D.C.
RCA Development of Color Video Tape

BEST ON-THE-SPOT COVERAGE OF A NEWS EVENT - ANY LENGTH, LIVE OR FILM

CBS Cuban Revolution. Live interview with new president. Jack Fern, Film Director; Correspondents, Stuart Novins and Richard Bate; Frank Donghi, Coordinator; Cameramen, Paul Rubenstein, Ralph Santos, Larry Smith.
CBS Lebanon Civil War Street Battle - Beirut. Frank Kearns, Correspondent; Paul Bruck, Cameraman.
NBC First Air Force attempt to probe the moon. Frank McGee of NBC News Washington, Roy Neal of NBC News Los Angeles; Producer Chet Hagen, NBC New York; Director, Jim Kitchell, NBC New York.
ABC Election of Pope John XXIII. John Secondari; Director, Marshall Diskin.
CBS Chicago Fire at Our Lady of Angels Parochial School. George Faber, Producer; Reporters, Joe Sauris, Hugh Hill, Frank Reynolds; Cameramen, Maury Bleckman, John Richardson, Irv Heberg, Wesley Marks.
CBS Crash of American Airlines Electra off LaGuardia into Flushing Bay. Paul Levitan, Producer; Don Hewitt, Director; Tom Costigan, Correspondent; Reporters Phil Scheffler, Charles Kuralt, Sam Jaffe, Bob Schakne; Cameramen, Arthur Kingham, George Snyder, Larry Racies, Lou Hutt, Mike Evdokimoff, Irving Heitzner.

TRUSTEES AWARD

BOB HOPE - Presented with appreciation and admiration for bringing the great gift of laughter to all peoples of all nations; for selflessly entertaining American troops throughout the world over many years; and for making television finer by these deeds and by the consistently high quality of his television programs through the years.

1959/60

OUTSTANDING PROGRAM ACHIEVEMENT IN THE FIELD OF HUMOR

A regular program, a special program, or a series, any length, live, tape or film

ART CARNEY SPECIAL (NBC)
DANNY THOMAS SHOW (CBS)
FATHER KNOWS BEST (CBS)
JACK BENNY SHOW (CBS)
RED SKELTON SHOW (CBS)

OUTSTANDING PROGRAM ACHIEVEMENT IN THE FIELD OF DRAMA

A regular program, a special program, or a series, any length, live, tape or film

PLAYHOUSE 90 (CBS)
ETHAN FROME (Du Pont Show of the Month) (CBS)
THE MOON AND SIXPENCE (NBC)
THE TURN OF THE SCREW (Ford Startime) (NBC)
THE UNTOUCHABLES (ABC)

OUTSTANDING PROGRAM ACHIEVEMENT IN THE FIELD OF VARIETY

A regular program, a special program, or a series, any length, live, tape or film

FABULOUS FIFTIES (CBS)
ANOTHER EVENING WITH FRED ASTAIRE (NBC)
DINAH SHORE CHEVY SHOW (NBC)
GARRY MOORE SHOW (CBS)
TONIGHT WITH BELAFONTE (Revlon Revue) (CBS)

OUTSTANDING PROGRAM ACHIEVEMENT IN THE FIELD OF NEWS

A regular program, a special program, or a series, any length, live, tape or film

HUNTLEY-BRINKLEY REPORT (NBC)
CHET HUNTLEY REPORTING (NBC)
DOUGLAS EDWARDS WITH THE NEWS (CBS)
JOURNEY TO UNDERSTANDING (NBC)
KHRUSHCHEV'S ARRIVAL, APPEARANCE AT NATIONAL PRESS CLUB, SPEECH TO THE NATION (Pool Coverage by NBC)

OUTSTANDING PROGRAM ACHIEVEMENT IN THE FIELD OF PUBLIC AFFAIRS AND EDUCATION

A regular program, a special program, or a series, any length, live, tape or film

TWENTIETH CENTURY (CBS)
MEET THE PRESS, (NBC)
THE POPULATION EXPLOSION (CBS Reports) (CBS)
SMALL WORLD (CBS)
WINTER OLYMPICS (CBS)

OUTSTANDING ACHIEVEMENT IN THE FIELD OF CHILDREN'S PROGRAMMING

A regular program, a special program, or a series, any length, live, tape or film

HUCKLEBERRY HOUND (Syndicated)
CAPTAIN KANGAROO (CBS)
LASSIE (CBS)
QUICK DRAW MC GRAW (Syndicated)
WATCH MR. WIZARD (NBC)

OUTSTANDING ACHIEVEMENT IN THE FIELD OF MUSIC

A regular program, a special program or a series, any length, live, tape or film, composing, arranging, conducting, etc.

LEONARD BERNSTEIN AND THE NEW YORK PHILHARMONIC (CBS)
BELL TELEPHONE HOUR (NBC)
GREEN PASTURES (Hallmark Hall of Fame) (NBC)
MUSIC OF GERSHWIN (Bell Telephone Hour) (NBC)
YOUNG PEOPLE'S CONCERTS Leonard Bernstein (CBS)

OUTSTANDING SINGLE PERFORMANCE BY AN ACTOR (LEAD OR SUPPORT)

Single performance only, any length, live, tape or film

LAURENCE OLIVIER The Moon and Sixpence (NBC)
LEE J COBB Project Immortality (Plahouse 90) (CBS)
ALEC GUINNES The Wicked Scheme of Jebal Deeks (Ford Startime) (NBC)

OUTSTANDING SINGLE PERFORMANCE BY AN ACTRESS (LEAD OR SUPPORT)

Single performance only, any length, live, tape or film

INGRID BERGMAN The Turn of the Screw (Ford Startime) (NBC)
JULIE HARRIS Ethan Frome (Du Pont Show of the Month) (CBS)
TERESA WRIGHT Margaret Bourke-White Story (Breck Sunday Showcase) (NBC)

OUTSTANDING PERFORMANCE BY AN ACTOR IN A SERIES (LEAD OR SUPPORT)

Continued performance only, any length, live, tape or film

ROBERT STACK (The Untouchables) (ABC)
RICHARD BOONE (Have Gun, Will Travel) (CBS)
RAYMOND BURR (Perry Mason) (CBS)

OUTSTANDING PERFORMANCE BY AN ACTRESS IN A SERIES (LEAD OR SUPPORT)

Continued performance only, any length, live, tape, or film

JANE WYATT (Father Knows Best) (CBS)
DONNA REED (Donna Reed Show) (ABC)
LORETTA YOUNG (Loretta Young Show) (NBC)

790 EMMYS

OUTSTANDING PERFORMANCE IN A VARIETY OR MUSICAL PROGRAM OR SERIES
Regular or special, any length, live, tape or film
HARRY BELAFONTE Tonight with Belafonte (Revlon Revue) (CBS)
FRED ASTAIRE Another Evening with Fred Astaire (NBC)
DINAH SHORE (Dinah Shore Chevy Show) (NBC)

OUTSTANDING WRITING ACHIEVEMENT IN DRAMA
Regular or special, any length, live, tape or film
ROD SERLING Various Episodes (Twilight Zone) (CBS)
JAMES COSTIGAN The Turn of the Screw (Ford Startime) (NBC)
LORI MANDEL Project Immortality (Plahouse 90) (CBS)

OUTSTANDING WRITING ACHIEVEMENT IN COMEDY
Regular or special, any length, live, tape or film
SAM PERRIN, GEORGE BALZER, AL GORDON, HAL GOLDMAN (Jack Benny Show) (CBS)
DOROTHY COOPER, ROSWELL ROGERS Various Episodes (Father Knows Best) (CBS)
NAT HIKEN Ballad of Louie The Louse (CBS)

OUTSTANDING WRITING ACHIEVEMENT IN THE DOCUMENTARY FIELD
Regular or special, any length, live, tape or film
HOWARD K. SMITH, AV WESTIN The Population Explosion (CBS)
JAMES BENJAMIN From Kaiser to Fuehrer (Twentieth Century) (CBS)
RICHARD F. HANSER Life in the Thirties (Project 20) (NBC)

OUTSTANDING DIRECTORIAL ACHIEVEMENT IN DRAMA
Regular or special, any length, live, tape or film
ROBERT MULLIGAN The Moon and Sixpence (NBC)
JOHN FRANKENHEIMER The Turn of the Screw (Ford Startime) (NBC)
PHIL KARLSON The Untouchables (Westinghouse-Desilu Playhouse) (CBS)

OUTSTANDING DIRECTORIAL ACHIEVEMENT IN COMEDY
Regular or special, any length, live, tape or film
RALPH LEVY, BUD YORKIN, (Jack Benny Hour Specials) (CBS)
SEYMOUR BERNS, (Red Skelton Show) (CBS)
SHELDON LEONARD (Danny Thomas Show) (CBS)

OUTSTANDING ACHIEVEMENT IN ART DIRECTION AND SCENIC DESIGN
Any type or length program or series
RALPH BERGER and FRANK SMITH The Untouchables (Westinghouse-Desilu Playhouse) (CBS)
CHARLES LISANBY (Garry Moore Show) (CBS)
JOHN J. LLOYD Various Episodes (Alfred Hitchcock Presents) (CBS)

OUTSTANDING ACHIEVEMENT IN CINEMATOGRAPHY FOR TELEVISION
Any type or length filmed program or series
CHARLES STRAUMER The Untouchables (Westinghouse-Desilu Playhouse) (CBS)
WILLIAM MARGULES The Morrison Story (The Lawless Years) (NBC)
RALPH WOOLSEY Secret Island (77 Sunset Strip) (ABC)

OUTSTANDING ACHIEVEMENT IN ELECTRONIC CAMERA WORK
Any type or length program or series
WINTER OLYMPICS (CBS)
PLAYHOUSE 90 (CBS)
THE TURN OF THE SCREW (Ford Startime) (NBC)

BEST ENGINEERING OR TECHNICAL ACHIEVEMENT
In picture, in sound, in development of technical equipment, etc.
THE NEW GENERAL ELECTRIC SUPERSENSITIVE CAMERA TUBE permitting colorcasting in no more light than is needed for black and white.
THE BRITISH BROADCASTING CORPORATION and THE NATIONAL BROADCASTING COMPANY for the development of the cable-film process speeding the transmission of overseas events.

OUTSTANDING ACHIEVEMENT IN FILM EDITING FOR TELEVISION
Any type or length filmed program
BEN H. RAY, ROBERT L. SWANSON (The Untouchables) (ABC)
DAN LANDRES The Patsy (General Electric Theatre) (CBS)
EDWARD WILLIAMS Man from the South (Alfred Hitchcock Presents) (CBS)

TRUSTEES AWARD
DR. FRANK STANTON, President, The Columbia Broadcasting System, Inc. by forthright and courageous action, has advanced immeasurably the freedom of television as an arm of the free press and in so doing has strengthened the total freedom of television.

TRUSTEES CITATION
THE AMPEX CORPORATION, THE RADIO CORPORATION OF AMERICA, MICHAEL R. GARGIULO, RICHARD GILLASPY In recognition of the cooperative effort of all phases of television production - For capturing on Videotape the Nixon-Khrushchev debate of July 25, 1959 in Moscow.

1960/61

OUTSTANDING PROGRAM ACHIEVEMENT IN THE FIELD OF HUMOR
A regular program, a special program, or a series, any length, live, tape or film
JACK BENNY SHOW (CBS)
ANDY GRIFFITH SHOW (CBS)
BOB HOPE BUICK SHOW (NBC)
CANDID CAMERA (CBS)
FLINTSTONES (ABC)

OUTSTANDING PROGRAM ACHIEVEMENT IN THE FIELD OF DRAMA
A regular program, a special program, or a series, any length, live, tape or film
MACBETH (Hallmark Hall of Fame) (NBC)
NAKED CITY (ABC)
SACCO-VANZETTI (NBC)
TWILIGHT ZONE (CBS)
THE UNTOUCHABLES (ABC)

OUTSTANDING PROGRAM ACHIEVEMENT IN THE FIELD OF VARIETY
A regular program, a special program, or a series, any length, live, tape or film
ASTAIRE TIME (NBC)
BELAFONTE, N.Y. 19 (CBS)
GARRY MOORE SHOW (CBS)
AN HOUR WITH DANNY KAYE (CBS)
JACK PAAR SHOW (NBC)

OUTSTANDING PROGRAM ACHIEVEMENT IN THE FIELD OF NEWS
A regular program, a special program, or a series, any length, live, tape or film
HUNTLEY-BRINKLEY REPORT (NBC)
CONVENTION COVERAGE (NBC)
DOUGLAS EDWARDS WITH THE NEWS (CBS)
EYEWITNESS TO HISTORY (CBS)
PRESIDENT KENNEDY'S LIVE NEWS CONFERENCES (ABC-CBS-NBC)

OUTSTANDING PROGRAM ACHIEVEMENT IN THE FIELD OF PUBLIC AFFAIRS AND EDUCATION
A regular program, a special program, or a series, any length, live, tape or film
THE TWENTIETH CENTURY (CBS)
CBS REPORTS (CBS)
PROJECT TWENTY (NBC)
THE U-2 AFFAIR (NBC White Paper) (NBC)
WINSTON CHURCHILL, THE VALIANT YEARS (ABC)

OUTSTANDING ACHIEVEMENT IN THE FIELD OF CHILDREN'S PROGRAMMING
A regular program, a special program, or a series, any length, live, tape or film
YOUNG PEOPLE'S CONCERT Aaron Copland's Birthday Party (CBS)
CAPTAIN KANGAROO (CBS)
HUCKLEBERRY HOUND (Syndicated)
SHARI LEWIS SHOW (NBC)
SHIRLEY TEMPLE SHOW (NBC)

OUTSTANDING SINGLE PERFORMANCE BY AN ACTOR IN A LEADING ROLE
Single performance only, any length, live, tape or film
MAURICE EVANS Macbeth (Hallmark Hall of Fame) (NBC)
CLIFF ROBERTSON The Two Worlds of Charlie Gordon (U.S. Steel Hour) (CBS)
ED WYNN The Man in the Funny Suit (Westinghouse-Desilu Playhouse) (CBS)

OUTSTANDING SINGLE PERFORMANCE BY AN ACTRESS IN A LEADING ROLE
Single performance only, any length, live, tape or film
JUDITH ANDERSON Macbeth (Hallmark Hall of Fame) (NBC)
INGRID BERGMAN 24 Hours in a Woman's Life (CBS)
ELIZABETH MONTGOMERY The Rusty Heller Story (The Untouchables) (ABC)

OUTSTANDING PERFORMANCE BY AN ACTOR IN A SERIES (LEAD)
Continued performance only, any length, live, tape or film
RAYMOND BURR (Perry Mason) (CBS)
JACKIE COOPER (Hennesey) (CBS)
ROBERT STACK (The Untouchables) (ABC)

OUTSTANDING PERFORMANCE BY AN ACTRESS IN A SERIES (LEAD)
Continued performance only, any length, live, tape or film
BARBARA STANWYCK (Barbara Stanwyck Show) (NBC)
DONNA REED (Donna Reed Show) (ABC)
LORETTA YOUNG (Loretta Young Show) (NBC)

OUTSTANDING PERFORMANCE IN A SUPPORTING ROLE BY AN ACTOR OR ACTRESS IN A SINGLE PROGRAM
Regular or special, any length, live tape or film
RODDY MC DOWALL Not Without Honor (Equitable's American Heritage) (NBC)
CHARLES BRONSON Memory in White (GE Theatre) (CBS)
PETER FALK Cold Turkey (The Law and Mr. Jones) (ABC)

OUTSTANDING PERFORMANCE IN A SUPPORTING ROLE BY AN ACTOR OR ACTRESS IN A SERIES
Continued performance only, any length, live, tape or film
DON KNOTTS as DEPUTY SHERIFF (Andy Griffith Show) (CBS)
ABBY DALTON as THE NURSE (Hennesey) (CBS)
BARBARA HALE as DELLA STREET (Perry Mason) (CBS)

OUTSTANDING PERFORMANCE IN A VARIETY OR MUSICAL PROGRAM OR SERIES
Regular or special, any length, live, tape or film
FRED ASTAIRE Astaire Time (NBC)
HARRY BELAFONTE Belafonte, N.Y. 19 (CBS)
DINAH SHORE (Dinah Shore Chevy Show) (NBC)

THE PROGRAM OF THE YEAR

That program, created originally or fully adapted for televison, which is considered to be the most outstanding presentation during the awards period. Such a program may be either one of a series or an individual presentation, either entertainment, public service or coverage of a newsworthy event, but may not include a duplicate or an approximate duplication of a presentation previously used in another medium.

MACBETH (Hallmark Hall of Fame) (NBC)
ASTAIRE TIME (NBC)
CONVENTION COVERAGE (NBC)
AN HOUR WITH DANNY KAYE (CBS)
SACCO-VANZETTI (NBC)

OUTSTANDING ACHIEVEMENT IN THE FIELD OF MUSIC FOR TELEVISION

Composing, arranging, conducting, etc, or a regular program, a special program, or a series any length, live, tape or film

LEONARD BERNSTEIN for (Leonard Bernstein and the New York Philharmonic) (CBS)
ANDRE PREVIN for the Donald O'Connor Show (NBC)
PETE RUGOLO, JERRY GOLDSMITH for The Thriller (NBC)

OUTSTANDING WRITING ACHIEVEMENT IN DRAMA

Regular or special, any length, live tape or film

ROD SERLING Various Episodes (The Twilight Zone) (CBS)
REGINALD ROSE Sacco-Vanzetti (NBC)
DALE WASSERMAN The Lincoln Murder Case (Du Pont of the Month) (CBS)

OUTSTANDING WRITING ACHIEVEMENT IN COMEDY

Regular or special, any length, live, tape or film

SHERWOOD SCHWARTZ, DAVE O'BRIEN, AL SCHWARTZ, MARTIN RAGAWAY, RED SKELTON Various Episodes (Red Skelton Show) (CBS)
RICHARD BAER Various Episodes (Hennesey) (CBS)
CHARLES STEWART, JACK ELINSON Various Episodes (The Danny Thomas Show) (CBS)

OUTSTANDING WRITING ACHIEVEMENT IN THE DOCUMENTARY FIELD

Regular or special, any length, live, tape or film

VICTOR WOLFSON Various Episodes (Winston Churchill, The Valiant Years) (ABC)
ARTHUR BARRON, AL WASSERMAN The U-2 Affair (NBC White Paper) (NBC)
FRED FRIENDLY, DAVID LOWE, EDWARD R. MURROW Harvest of Shame (CBS Reports) (CBS)

OUTSTANDING DIRECTORIAL ACHIEVEMENT IN DRAMA

Regular or special, any length, live, tape or film

GEORGE SCHAEFER Macbeth (Hallmark Hall of Fame) (NBC)
SIDNEY LUMET Sacco-Vanzetti (NBC)
RALPH NELSON The Man in the Funny Suit (Westinghouse-Desilu Playhouse) (CBS)

OUTSTANDING DIRECTORIAL ACHIEVEMENT IN COMEDY

Regular or special, any length, live, tape or film

SHELDON LEONARD (The Danny Thomas Show) (CBS)
JACK SHEA, RICHARD McDONOUGH (Bob Hope Buick Show) (NBC)
PETER TEWKSBURY (My Three Sons) (ABC)

OUTSTANDING ACHIEVEMENT IN ART DIRECTION AND SCENIC DESIGN

Regular or special, any length, live, tape or film

JOHN J. LLOYD Various Episodes (Checkmate) (CBS)
GARY SMITH Various Episodes (Perry Como's Kraft Music Hall) (NBC)
JAC VENZA 24 Hours in a Woman's Life (CBS)

OUTSTANDING ACHIEVEMENT IN CINEMATOGRAPHY FOR TELEVISION

Any type or length filmed program or series

GEORGE CLEMENS Various Episodes (Twilight Zone) (CBS)
WILLIAM MARGULIES Outrage at Pawnee Bend (Outlaws) (NBC)
WALTER STRENGE Sam Elder Story (Wagon Train) (NBC)

OUTSTANDING ACHIEVEMENT IN ELECTRONIC CAMERA WORK

Any type or length program or series

SOUNDS OF AMERICA (Bell Telephone Hour) (RED-EO-TAPE Mobile Unit for NBC)
DINAH SHORE CHEVY SHOW (NBC)
JOURNEY TO THE DAY (Playhouse 90) (CBS)
WRANGLER (KTLA-Hollywood Camera Crew for NBC)

OUTSTANDING ACHIEVEMENT IN FILM EDITING FOR TELEVISION

Any type or length filmed program or series

HARRY COSWICK, AARON NIBLEY, MILTON SHIFMAN Various Episodes (Naked City) (ABC)
RICHARD H. CAHOON, JOHN FAURE Various Episodes (Perry Mason) (CBS)
EDWARD W. WILLIAMS Incident in a Small Jail (Alfred Hitchcock Presents) (NBC)

OUTSTANDING ENGINEERING OR TECHNICAL ACHIEVEMENT

RADIO CORPORATION OF AMERICA and MARCONI'S WIRELESS TELEGRAPH COMPANY, LTD. - ENGLISH ELECTRIC VALVE COMPANY, LTD. for the independent development of the 4 1/2 inch image orthicon tube and cameras.

TRUSTEES' AWARD

NATIONAL EDUCATIONAL TELEVISION AND RADIO CENTER AND ITS AFFILIATED STATIONS - For its foresight and perseverence in promoting the development of Educational Television in the United States; and for its stimulation and transmission of the imaginative educational programs produced by the individual Educational Television Stations.

TRUSTEES' AWARD

MR. JOYCE C. HALL, PRESIDENT OF HALLMARK CARDS, INC. - For his personal interest in uplifting the standards of television through complete sponsorship over a ten-year period of Hallmark Hall of Fame, which has brought many enriching hours of entertainment to the viewing public; and or furthering the interests of young playwrights by establishing the Hallmark Teleplay-Writing Competition.

1961/62

OUTSTANDING PROGRAM ACHIEVEMENT IN THE FIELD OF HUMOR
A regular program, a special program, or a series, any length, live, tape or film
BOB NEWHART SHOW (NBC)
ANDY GRIFFITH SHOW (CBS)
CAR 54, WHERE ARE YOU? (NBC)
HAZEL (NBC)
RED SKELTON SHOW (CBS)

OUTSTANDING PROGRAM ACHIEVEMENT IN THE FIELD OF DRAMA
A regular program, a special program, or a series, any length, live, tape or film
THE DEFENDERS (CBS)
BEN CASEY (ABC)
DICK POWELL SHOW (NBC)
NAKED CITY (ABC)
PEOPLE NEED PEOPLE (Alcoa Premiere) (ABC)
VICTORIA REGINA (Hallmark Hall of Fame) (NBC)

OUTSTANDING PROGRAM ACHIEVEMENTS IN THE FIELDS OF VARIETY AND MUSIC
A regular program, a special program, or a series, any length, live, tape or film

VARIETY
GARRY MOORE SHOW (CBS)
HERE'S EDIE (ABC)
JUDY GARLAND SHOW (CBS)
PERRY COMO'S KRAFT MUSIC HALL (NBC)
WALT DISNEY'S WONDERFUL WORLD OF COLOR (NBC)

MUSIC
LEONARD BERNSTEIN AND THE NEW YORK PHILHARMONIC IN JAPAN (CBS)
BELL TELEPHONE HOUR (NBC)
NBC OPERA (NBC)
THE THIEF AND THE HANGMAN (ABC)

OUTSTANDING PROGRAM ACHIEVEMENT IN THE FIELD OF NEWS
A regular program, a special program, or a series, any length, live, tape or film
HUNTLEY-BRINKLEY REPORT (NBC)
CAPITAL CITIES BROADCASTING FOR THE EICHMANN TRIAL (Syndicated)
DOUGLAS EDWARDS WITH THE NEWS (CBS)
EYEWITNESS (with Walter Cronkite) (CBS)
NBC-TV GULF INSTANT NEWS SPECIALS (NBC)

OUTSTANDING PROGRAM ACHIEVEMENT IN THE FIELD OF EDUCATIONAL AND PUBLIC AFFAIRS PROGRAMMING
A regular program, a special program, or a series, any length, live, tape or film
DAVID BRINKLEY'S JOURNAL (NBC)
ABC'S WIDE WORLD OF SPORTS (ABC)
BELL AND HOWELL CLOSE-UP (ABC)
CBS REPORTS (CBS)
HOWARD K. SMITH-NEWS AND COMMENT (ABC)
NBC WHITE PAPER (NBC)

OUTSTANDING PROGRAM ACHIEVEMENT IN THE FIELD OF CHILDREN'S PROGRAMMING
A regular program, a special program, or a series, any length, live, tape or film
NEW YORK PHILHARMONIC YOUNG PEOPLE'S CONCERTS WITH LEONARD BERNSTEIN (CBS)
CAPTAIN KANGAROO (CBS)
1, 2, 3, GO! (NBC)
SHARI LEWIS SHOW (NBC)
UPDATE (NBC)
WALT DISNEY'S WONDERFUL WORLD OF COLOR (NBC)

OUTSTANDING SINGLE PERFORMANCE BY AN ACTOR IN A LEADING ROLE
Single performance only, any length, live, tape or film
PETER FALK as TRUCK DRIVER The Price of Tomatoes (Dick Powell Show) (NBC)
MILTON BERLE as DOYLE Doyle Against the House (Dick Powell Show) (NBC)
JAMES DONALD as PRINCE ALBERT Victoria Regina (Hallmark Hall of Fame) (NBC)
LEE MARVIN as SERGEANT HUGHES People Need People (Alcoa Premiere) (ABC)
MICKEY ROONEY as AUGIE MILLER Somebody's Waiting (Dick Powell Show) (NBC)

OUTSTANDING SINGLE PERFORMANCE BY AN ACTRESS IN A LEADING ROLE
Single performance only, any length, live or film
JULIE HARRIS as VICTORIA Victoria Regina (Hallmark Hall of Fame) (NBC)
GERALDINE BROOKS as KATHERINE BARNES Call Back Yesterday (Bus Stop) (ABC)
SUZANNE PLESHETTE as JULIE LAWLER Shining Image (Dr. Kildare) (NBC)
INGER STEVENS as ANNA The Price of Tomatoes (Dick Powell Show)(NBC)
ETHEL WATERS as JENNY HENDERSON Goodnight Sweet Blues (Route 66) (CBS)

OUTSTANDING CONTINUED PERFORMANCE BY AN ACTOR IN A SERIES (LEAD)
Continued performance only, any length, live, tape or film
E. G. MARSHALL as LAWRENCE PRESTON (The Defenders) (CBS)
PAUL BURKE as ADAM FLINT (Naked City) (ABC)
JACKIE COOPER as CHICK (Hennesey) (CBS)
VINCENT EDWARDS as DR. BEN CASEY (Ben Casey) (ABC)
GEORGE MAHARIS as BUZ (Route 66) (CBS)

OUTSTANDING CONTINUED PERFORMANCE BY AN ACTRESS IN A SERIES (LEAD)
Continued performance only, any length, live tape or film
SHIRLEY BOOTH as HAZEL (Hazel) (NBC)
GERTRUDE BERG as MRS. G. (Gertrude Berg Show) (CBS)
DONNA REED as DONNA STONE (Donna Reed Show) (ABC)
MARY STUART as JOANNE TATE (Search For Tomorrow) (CBS)
CARA WILLIAMS as GLADYS (Pete and Gladys) (CBS)

OUTSTANDING PERFORMANCE IN A SUPPORTING ROLE BY AN ACTOR
Regular or special any length, live, tape or film
DON KNOTTS as DEPUTY BARNEY FIFE (Andy Griffith Show) (CBS)
SAM JAFFE as DR. ZORBA (Ben Casey) (ABC)
BARRY JONES as DEAN Victoria Regina (Hallmark Hall of Fame) (NBC)
HORACE McMAHON as PARKER (Naked City) (ABC)
GEORGE C. SCOTT as KARL ANDERS I Remember a Lemon Tree (Ben Casey) (ABC)

OUTSTANDING PERFORMANCE IN A SUPPORTING ROLE BY AN ACTRESS
Regular or special any length, live, tape or film
PAMELA BROWN as DUCHESS OF KENT Victoria Regina (Hallmark Hall of Fame) (NBC)
JEANNE COOPER as LINDA But Linda Only Smiled (Ben Casey) (ABC)
COLLEEN DEWHURST as GERTRUDE HART Focus (NBC)
JOAN HACKETT as ELLEN PARKER A Certain Time, A Certain Darkness (Ben Casey) (ABC)
MARY WICKES as MAXFIELD (Gertrude Berg Show) (CBS)

OUTSTANDING PERFORMANCE IN A VARIETY OR MUSICAL PROGRAM OR SERIES
Regular or special any length, live, tape or film
CAROL BURNETT (Garry Moore Show) (CBS)
EDIE ADAMS Here's Edie (ABC)
PERRY COMO (Perry Como's Kraft Music Hall) (NBC)
JUDY GARLAND Judy Garland Show (CBS)
YVES MONTAND Yves Montand On Broadway (ABC)

OUTSTANDING DAYTIME PROGRAM (PROGRAM SPECIFICALLY CREATED FOR DAYTIME TELEVISION)
Regular or special any length, live, tape or film
PUREX SPECIALS FOR WOMEN (NBC)
ART LINKLETTER'S HOUSE PARTY (CBS)
CALENDAR (CBS)
TODAY (NBC)
VERDICT IS YOURS (CBS)

THE PROGRAM OF THE YEAR
That program, created originally or fully adapted for television, which is considered to be the most outstanding presentation during the awards period. Such a program may be either one of a series or an individual presentation, either entertainment, public service or coverage of a newsworthy event, but may not include a duplicate or an approximate duplication of a presentation previously used in another medium
VICTORIA REGINA (Hallmark Hall of Fame) (NBC)
BIOGRAPHY OF A BOOKIE JOINT (CBS Reports) (CBS)
JUDY GARLAND SHOW (CBS)
VINCENT VAN GOGH: A SELF PORTRAIT (NBC)
WALK IN MY SHOES (Bell and Howell Close-Up) (ABC)

OUTSTANDING ACHIEVEMENT IN ORIGINAL MUSIC COMPOSED FOR TELEVISION
A regular program, a special program, or a series, any lenght, live tape, or film
RICHARD RODGERS (Winston Churchill-The Valiant Years) (ABC)
JACQUES BELASCO Vincent Van Gogh: A Self Portrait (NBC)
ROBERT RUSSELL BENNETT (Project 20) (NBC)
LEITH STEVENS The Price of Tomatoes (Dick Powell Show) (NBC)
JOHN WILIAMS (Alcoa Premiere) (ABC)

OUTSTANDING WRITING ACHIEVEMENT IN DRAMA
A regular program, a special program, a series, or a single program of a series, any length, live, tape or film
REGINALD ROSE Various Episodes (The Defenders) (CBS)
HENRY F. GREENBERG People Need People (Alcoa Premiere) (ABC)
JACK LAIRD I Remember a Lemon Tree (Ben Casey) (ABC)
ROD SERLING Various Episodes (Twilight Zone) (CBS)
RICHARD ALAN SIMMONS The Price of Tomatoes (Dick Powell Show) (NBC)

OUTSTANDING WRITING ACHIEVEMENT IN COMEDY
A regular program, a special program, a series, or a single program of a series, any length, live, tape or film
CARL REINER (Dick Van Dyke Show) (CBS)
STAN FREBERG Chunking Chow Mein Hour (ABC)
NAT HIKEN, TONY WEBSTER, TERRY RYAN (Car 54, Where Are You?) (NBC)
ROLAND KIBBEE, BOB NEWHART, DON HINKLEY, MILT ROSEN, ERNIE CHAMBERS, DEAN HARGROVE, ROBERT KAUFMAN, NORM LIEBMAN, CHARLES SHERMAN, HOWARD SNYDER, LARRY SIEGEL (Bob Newhart Show) (NBC)
ED SIMMONS, DAVID O'BRIEN, MARTY RAGAWAY, ARTHUR PHILLIPS, AL SCHWARTZ, SHERWOOD SCHWARTZ, RED SKELTON (Red Skelton Show) (CBS)

OUTSTANDING WRITING ACHIEVEMENT IN THE DOCUMENTARY FIELD
A regular program, a special program, a series, or a single program of a series, any length, live, tape or film
LOU HAZAM Vincent Van Gogh; A Self Portrait (NBC)
ARTHUR HOLCH Walk In My Shoes (Bell and Howell Close-Up) (ABC)
GEORGE LEFFERTS (Purex Specials for Women) (NBC)
JAY McMULLEN Biography of a Bookie Joint (CBS Reports) (CBS)
AL WASSERMAN, ARTHUR ZEGART Battle for Newburgh (NBC White Paper) (NBC)

OUTSTANDING DIRECTORIAL ACHIEVEMENT IN DRAMA

A regular program, a special program, a series, or a single program of a series, any length, live, tape or film

FRANKLIN SCHAFFNER Various Episodes (The Defenders) (CBS)
ARTHUR HILLER Various Episodes (Naked City) (ABC)
BUZZ KULIK Shining Image (Dr. Kildare) (NBC)
GEORGE SCHAEFER Victoria Regina (Hallmark Hall of Fame) (NBC)
ALEX SEGAL People Need People (Alcoa Premiere) (ABC)
JACK SMIGHT Come Again to Carthage (Westinghouse Presents) (CBS)

OUTSTANDING DIRECTORIAL ACHIEVEMENT IN COMEDY

A regular program, a special program, a series, or a single program of a series, any length, live, tape or film

NAT HIKEN (Car 54, Where Are You?) (NBC)
SEYMOUR BERNS (Red Skelton Show) (CBS)
DAVE GEISEL (Garry Moore Show) (CBS)
JOHN RICH (Dick Van Dyke Show) (CBS)
BUD YORKIN Henry Fonda and the Family (CBS)

OUTSTANDING ACHIEVEMENT IN ART DIRECTION AND SCENIC DESIGN

A regular program, a special program, a series, or a single program of a series, any length, live, tape or film

GARY SMITH (Perry Como's Kraft Music Hall) (NBC)
PHILIP BARBER (Twilight Zone) (CBS)
CHARLES LISANBY (Garry Moore Show) (CBS)
JAN SCOTT (Theatre '62) (NBC)
BURR SMIDT The Power and the Glory (CBS)

OUTSTANDING ACHIEVEMENT IN CINEMATOGRAPHY FOR TELEVISION

Any type or length filmed program or series

JOHN S. PRIESTLEY (Naked City) (ABC)
GUY BLANCHARD Vincent Van Gogh: A Self Portrait (NBC)
WALTER CASTLE, HASKELL BOGGS (Bonanza) (NBC)
GEORGE CLEMENS (Twilight Zone) (CBS)
WALTER STRENGE (Wagon Train) (NBC)
TED VOIGTLANDER (Ben Casey) (ABC)

OUTSTANDING ACHIEVEMENT IN ELECTRONIC CAMERA WORK

Any type or length program or series, live or taped

ERNIE KOVACS Ernie Kovacs Shows (ABC)
LOU ONOFRIO Judy Garland Show (CBS)
HEINO RIPPE (Perry Como's Kraft Music Hall) (NBC)
O. TAMBURRI Victoria Regina (Hallmark Hall of Fame) (NBC)

OUTSTANDING ACHIEVEMENT IN FILM EDITING FOR TELEVISION

Any type or length filmed program or series

HUGH CHALOUPKA, AARON NIBLEY, CHARLES L. FREEMAN (Naked City) (ABC)
ARAM BOYAJIAN, ROBERT COLLINSON, BERNARD FRIEND, LORA HAYS, WALTER KATZ, LAWRENCE SILK, HAROLD SILVER, LEO ZOCHLING (Twentieth Century) (CBS)
MARSTON FAY, GENE PALMER (Wagon Train) (NBC)
CONSTANTINE GOCHIS U.S. #1: American Profile (NBC)
RICHARD L. VAN ENGER, A.C.E. (Bus Stop) (ABC)

OUTSTANDING ENGINEERING OR TECHNICAL ACHIEVEMENT

ABC VIDEO TAPE EXPANDER, or VTX-slow motion tape developed by ABC-Mr. Albert Malang, chief engineer, Video Facilities, ABC
AMTEC-device to correct timing faults on tape playbacks
INTERLEAVED SOUND-an NBC development which provides an emergency circuit available whenever there is a failure of the regular network television sound
SLOW MOTION KINESCOPE-as developed by CBS

TRUSTEES AWARD

CBS NEWS FOR THE SPECIAL PROGRAM-A TOUR OF THE WHITE HOUSE

TRUSTEES AWARD

MRS. JACQUELINE KENNEDY A Tour of the White House.

TRUSTEES AWARD

THE HEADS OF THE NEWS DEPARTMENTS OF ABC, CBS AND NBC John Glenn and Friendship VII space mission.

TRUSTEES AWARD

BRIGADIER GENERAL DAVID SARNOFF For his many years of vision and accomplishment.

1962/63

THE PROGRAM OF THE YEAR

That program, created originally or fully adapted for television, which is considered to be the most outstanding presentation during the awards period. Such a program may be either one of a series or an individual presentation, either entertainment, public service or coverage of a newsworthy event, but may not include a duplicate or an approximate duplication of a presentation previously used in another medium.

THE TUNNEL (NBC)
THE DANNY KAYE SHOW WITH LUCILLE BALL (NBC)
THE MADMAN (The Defenders) (CBS)
THE VOICE OF CHARLIE PONT (Premiere Presented by Fred Astaire) (ABC)

OUTSTANDING PROGRAM ACHIEVEMENT IN THE FIELD OF HUMOR

A regular program, a special program, or a series - any length; live, tape or film

THE DICK VAN DYKE SHOW (CBS)
THE BEVERLY HILLBILLIES (CBS)
THE DANNY KAYE SHOW WITH LUCILLE BALL (NBC)
MCHALE'S NAVY (ABC)

OUTSTANDING PROGRAM ACHIEVEMENT IN THE FIELD OF DRAMA

A regular program, a special program, or a series - any length; live, tape or film

THE DEFENDERS (CBS)
ALCOA PREMIERE/PREMIERE, PRESENTED BY FRED ASTAIRE (ABC)
THE DICK POWELL THEATRE (NBC)
THE ELEVENTH HOUR (NBC)
NAKED CITY (ABC)

OUTSTANDING PROGRAM ACHIEVEMENT IN THE FIELD OF MUSIC
A regular program, a special program, or a series - any length; live, tape or film
JULIE AND CAROL AT CARNEGIE HALL (CBS)
BELL TELEPHONE HOUR (NBC)
JUDY GARLAND AND HER GUESTS PHIL SILVERS AND ROBERT GOULET (CBS)
THE LIVELY ONES (NBC)
NBC OPERA (NBC)

OUTSTANDING PROGRAM ACHIEVEMENT IN THE FIELD OF VARIETY
A regular program, a special program, or a series - any length; live, tape or film
THE ANDY WILLIAMS SHOW (NBC)
CAROL AND COMPANY (CBS)
THE GARRY MOORE SHOW (CBS)
HERE'S EDIE (ABC)
THE RED SKELTON HOUR (CBS)

OUTSTANDING PROGRAM ACHIEVEMENT IN THE FIELD OF PANEL, QUIZ, OR AUDIENCE PARTICIPATION
A regular program, a special program, or a series - any length; live, tape or film
G-E COLLEGE BOWL (CBS)
PASSWORD (CBS)
TO TELL THE TRUTH (CBS)

OUTSTANDING PROGRAM ACHIEVEMENT IN THE FIELD OF CHILDREN'S PROGRAMMING
A regular program, a special program, or a series - any length; live, tape or film
WALT DISNEY'S WONDERFUL WORLD OF COLOR (NBC)
CAPTAIN KANGAROO (CBS)
DISCOVERY '62-'63 (ABC)
THE SHARI LEWIS SHOW (NBC)
UPDATE WITH ROBERT ABERNATHY (NBC)
WATCH MR. WIZARD (NBC)

OUTSTANDING ACHIEVEMENT IN THE FIELD OF DOCUMENTARY PROGRAMS
THE TUNNEL Produced by Reuven Frank (NBC)
EMERGENCY WARD (Du Pont Show of the Week) Produced by Irving Gitlin and Frank De Felitta; Written and Directed by Frank De Felitta (NBC)
HE IS RISEN (Project 20) Produced and Directed by Donald B Hyatt; Written by Richard Hanser (NBC)
THE RIVER NILE Produced and Written by Lou Hazam (NBC)
SHAKESPEARE: SOUL OF AN AGE Produced and Written by Lou Hazam (NBC)

OUTSTANDING PROGRAM ACHIEVEMENT IN THE FIELD OF NEWS
A regular program, a special program, or a series - any length; live, tape or film
HUNTLEY-BRINKLEY REPORT (NBC)
CBS NEWS EVENING REPORT WITH WALTER CRONKITE (CBS)
EYEWITNESS (CBS)
NBC SPECIAL NEWS REPORTS, GULF OIL CORPORATION (NBC)

OUTSTANDING PROGRAM ACHIEVEMENT IN THE FIELD OF NEWS COMMENTARY OR PUBLIC AFFAIRS
A regular program, a special program, or a series - any length; live, tape or film
DAVID BRINKLEY'S JOURNAL (NBC)
BELL & HOWELL CLOSE-UP! (ABC)
CBS REPORTS (CBS)
HOWARD K. SMITH, NEWS AND COMMENT (ABC)
TWENTIETH CENTURY (CBS)

OUTSTANDING ACHIEVEMENT IN INTERNATIONAL REPORTING OR COMMENTARY
Overseas Origination - Person or Program
PIERS ANDERTON, BERLIN CORRESPONDENT, NBC for The Tunnel, (NBC)
GERMANY: FATHERS AND SONS with John Rich, Produced by George A. Vicas (NBC)
MARVIN KALB, MOSCOW CORRESPONDENT, CBS for general reporting (CBS)
JAMES ROBINSON, SOUTHEAST ASIA, NBC for general reporting (NBC)
JOHN SECONDARI for The Vatican, Produced by Helen Jean Rogers (Bell & Howell Close-Up!) (ABC)

OUTSTANDING SINGLE PERFORMANCE BY AN ACTOR IN A LEADING ROLE
Single performance only - any length; live, tape or film
TREVOR HOWARD as DISRAELI The Invincible Mr. Disraeli (Hallmark Hall of Fame) (NBC)
BRADFORD DILLMAN as CHARLIE PONT The Voice of Charlie Pont (Premiere, Presented by Fred Astaire) (ABC)
DON GORDON as JOEY TASSILI The Madman (The Defenders) (CBS)
WALTER MATTHAU as MEREDITH Big Deal in Laredo (Du Pont Show of the Week) (NBC)
JOSEPH SCHILDKRAUT as RABBI GOTTLIEB Hear the Mellow Wedding Bells (Sam Benedict) (NBC)

OUTSTANDING SINGLE PERFORMANCE BY AN ACTRESS IN A LEADING ROLE
Single performance only - any length; live, tape or film
KIM STANLEY as FAITH PARSONS A Cardinal Act of Mercy (Ben Casey) (ABC)
DIAHANN CARROLL as RUBY JAY A Horse Has a Big Head, Let Him Worry (Naked City) (ABC)
DIANA HYLAND as LIZA LAURENTS The Voice of Charlie Pont (Premiere, Presented by Fred Astaire) (ABC)
ELEANOR PARKER as CONNIE FOLSOM Why Am I Grown So Cold? (The Eleventh Hour) (NBC)
SYLVIA SIDNEY as ADELA The Madman (The Defenders) (CBS)

OUTSTANDING CONTINUED PERFORMANCE BY AN ACTOR IN A SERIES (LEAD)
Continued performance only - any length; live, tape or film
E. G. MARSHALL as LAWRENCE PRESTON (The Defenders) (CBS)
ERNEST BORGNINE as LT. COMDR. QUINTON McHALE (McHale's Navy) (ABC)
PAUL BURKE as ADAM FLINT (Naked City) (ABC)
VIC MORROW as SGT. CHIP SAUNDERS (Combat) (ABC)
DICK VAN DYKE as ROB PETRIE (The Dick Van Dyke Show) (CBS)

OUTSTANDING CONTINUED PERFORMANCE BY AN ACTRESS IN A SERIES (LEAD)
Continued performance only - any length; live, tape or film

SHIRLEY BOOTH as HAZEL (Hazel) (NBC)
LUCILLE BALL as LUCY CARMICHAEL (The Lucille Ball Show) (CBS)
SHIRL CONWAY as LIZ THORPE (The Nurses) (CBS)
MARY TYLER MOORE as LAURA PETRIE (The Dick Van Dyke Show) (CBS)
IRENE RYAN as GRANNY (The Beverly Hillbillies) (CBS)

OUTSTANDING PERFORMANCE IN A SUPPORTING ROLE BY AN ACTOR
A regular program, a special program, or a series - any length; live, tape or film

DON KNOTTS as DEPUTY BARNEY FIFE (The Andy Griffith Show) (CBS)
TIM CONWAY as ENSIGN CHARLES PARKER (McHale's Navy) (ABC)
PAUL FORD as COLONEL PURDY Teahouse of the August Moon (Hallmark Hall of Fame) (NBC)
HURD HATFIELD as ROTHSCHILD The Invincible Mr. Disraeli (Hallmark Hall of Fame) (NBC)
ROBERT REDFORD as GEORGE LAURENTS The Voice of Charlie Pont (Premiere, Presented by Fred Astaire) (ABC)

OUTSTANDING PERFORMANCE IN A SUPPORTING ROLE BY AN ACTRESS
A regular program, a special program, or a series - any length; live, tape or film

GLENDA FARRELL as MARTHA MORRISON A Cardinal Act of Mercy (Ben Casey) (ABC)
DAVEY DAVISON as LAURA HUNTER Of Roses and Nightingales and Other Lovely Things (The Eleventh Hour) (NBC)
NANCY MALONE as LIBBY (Naked City) (ABC)
ROSE MARIE as SALLY ROGERS (The Dick Van Dyke Show) (CBS)
KATE REID as QUEEN VICTORIA The Invincible Mr. Disraeli (Hallmark Hall of Fame) April 4, 1963 (NBC)

OUTSTANDING PERFORMANCE IN A VARIETY OR MUSICAL PROGRAM OR SERIES
A regular program, a special program, or a series - any length; live, tape or film

CAROL BURNETT Julie and Carol at Carniege Hall (CBS) and Carol and Company (CBS)
EDIE ADAMS (Here's Edie) (ABC)
MERV GRIFFIN (The Merv Griffin Show) (NBC)
DANNY KAYE The Danny Kaye Show with Lucille Ball (NBC)
ANDY WILLIAMS (The Andy Williams Show) (NBC)

OUTSTANDING ACHIEVEMENT IN COMPOSING ORIGINAL MUSIC FOR TELEVISION
A regular program, a special program, or a series - any length; live, tape or film

ROBERT RUSSELL BENNETT He Is Risen (Project 20) (NBC)
EDDY MANSON The River Nile (NBC)
GIAN CARLO MENOTTI Labyrinth (NBC Opera) (NBC)
JOSEPH MULLENDORE (The Dick Powell Theatre) (NBC)
JOHNNY WILLIAMS (Alcoa Premiere/Premiere, Presented by Fred Astaire) (ABC)

OUTSTANDING ACHIEVEMENT IN ART DIRECTION AND SCENIC DESIGN
A regular program, a special program, or a series - any length; live, tape or film

CARROLL CLARK, MARVIN AUBREY DAVIS (Walt Disney's Wonderful World of Color) (NBC)
WARREN CLYMER (Hallmark Hall of Fame) (NBC)
WILLARD LEVITAS (The Defenders) (CBS)
HAL PEREIRA, EARL HENDRICK (Bonanza) (NBC)
GEORGE W. DAVIS, MERRILL PYE (The Eleventh Hour) (NBC)
JAN SCOTT various episodes (Du Pont Show of the Week) (NBC)

OUTSTANDING WRITING ACHIEVEMENT IN DRAMA
A regular program, a special program, or a series - any length; live, tape or film

ROBERT THOM, REGINALD ROSE The Madman (The Defenders) (CBS)
SIDNEY CARROLL Big Deal in Laredo (Du Pont Show of the Week) (NBC)
NORMAN KATKOV A Cardinal Act of Mercy (Ben Casey) (ABC)
JAMES LEE The Invincible Mr. Disraeli (Hallmark Hall of Fame) (NBC)
HALSTED WELLES The Voice of Charlie Pont (Premiere, Presented by Fred Astaire) (ABC)

OUTSTANDING WRITING ACHIEVEMENT IN COMEDY
A regular program, a special program, or a series - any length; live, tape or film

CARL REINER (The Dick Van Dyke Show) (CBS)
SAM PERRIN, GEORGE BALZER, HAL GOLDMAN, AL GORDON (The Jack Benny Program) (CBS)
PAUL HENNING (The Beverly Hillbillies) (CBS)
NAT HIKEN (Car 54, Where Are You?) (NBC)
ED SIMMONS, DAVE O'BRIEN, MARTIN A. RAGAWAY, ARTHUR PHILLIPS, LARRY RHINE, MORT GREENE, HUGH WEDLOCK, RED SKELTON, BRUCE HOWARD, RICK MITTLEMAN (The Red Skelton Hour) (CBS)

OUTSTANDING DIRECTORIAL ACHIEVEMENT IN DRAMA
A regular program, a special program, or a series - any length; live, tape or film

STUART ROSENBERG The Madman (The Defenders) (CBS)
FIELDER COOK Big Deal in Laredo (Du Pont Show of the Week) (NBC)
ROBERT ELLIS MILLER The Voice of Charlie Pont (Premiere, Presented by Fred Astaire) (ABC)
SYDNEY POLLACK A Cardinal Act of Mercy (Ben Casey) (ABC)
GEORGE SCHAEFER The Invincible Mr. Disraeli (Hallmark Hall of Fame) (NBC)

OUTSTANDING DIRECTORIAL ACHIEVEMENT IN COMEDY
A regular program, a special program, or a series - any length; live, tape or film

JOHN RICH (The Dick Van Dyke Show) (CBS)
SEYMOUR BURNS (The Red Skelton Hour) (CBS)
FREDERICK de CORDOVA (The Jack Benny Program) (CBS)
DAVID GEISEL (The Garry Moore Show) (CBS)
RICHARD WHORF (The Beverly Hillbillies) (CBS)

OUTSTANDING ACHIEVEMENT IN CINEMATOGRAPHY FOR TELEVISION
Any type or length filmed program or series
JOHN S. PRIESTLEY (Naked City) (ABC)
GUY BLANCHARD Shakespeare: Soul of An Age, and The River Nile (NBC)
GEORGE T. CLEMENS, ROBERT W. PITTACK (Twilight Zone) (CBS)
ROBERT HAUSER (Combat) (ABC)
JOE VADALA Comedian Backstage (Du Pont Show of the Week) (NBC)
WILLIAM HARTIGAN, EDMONDO RICCI The Vatican (Bell & Howell Close-Up!) (ABC)

OUTSTANDING ACHIEVEMENT IN ELECTRONIC CAMERA WORK
Any type or length program or series; live or tape
THE INVINCIBLE MR. DISRAELI (Hallmark Hall of Fame) (NBC)
HERE'S EDIE (ABC)
THE LIVELY ONES (NBC)
ABC'S WIDE WORLD OF SPORTS (ABC)

OUTSTANDING ACHIEVEMENT IN FILM EDITING FOR TELEVISION
Any type or length filmed program or series
SID KATZ (The Defenders) (CBS)
JAMES BALLAS, GEORGE BOEMLER, AL CLARK, MIKE POZEN, AARON STELL (Ben Casey) (ABC)
DAVID E. ROLAND Comedian Backstage (Du Pont Show of the Week) (NBC)
HUGH CHALOUPKA, AARON NIBLEY, CHARLES FREEMAN, HARRY COSWICK, JACK GLEASON (Naked City) (ABC)
HOWARD EPSTEIN, RICHARD BELDING, TONY MARTINELLI (Alcoa Premiere/Premiere, Presented by Fred Astaire) (ABC)

OUTSTANDING ELECTRONIC ENGINEERING ACHIEVEMENT
No Nominations

THE INTERNATIONAL AWARD
Judging by Special Committee of Former Emmy Award Winners of entries from countries throughout the world
WAR AND PEACE (Granada TV Network Ltd. of England)
THE BIRD (Steptoe and Son) (British Broadcasting Corporation)
CAESARIAN SECTION (Your Life in Their Hands) (British Broadcasting Corporation)
THE OFFSHORE ISLAND (Canadian Broadcasting Corporation)
TAKAJOH (English Title: YOUNG HAWK, OLD HAWK) (Nippon Television Network Corporation) Japan

THE STATION AWARD
Regional Winners judged by Committees at National Academy Chapters; Final Judging by Special Committee
SUPERFLUOUS PEOPLE (WCBS-TV, New York)
THE DARK CORNER (WBAL-TV, Baltimore)
SUSPECT (KING-TV, Seattle)
TIME'S MAN-(WKY-TV, Oklahoma City)
THE WASTED YEARS (WBBM-TV, Chicago)
OPERATION SOS (KMTV, Omaha)
BURDEN OF SHAME (KNXT, Los Angeles)
CONFORMITY (WCAU-TV, Philadelphia)

TRUSTEES AWARD
AMERICAN TELEPHONE AND TELEGRAPH COMPANY For conceiving and developing Telstar #1 and Telstar #2.

TRUSTEES AWARD
DICK POWELL In grateful memory of his conspicuous contributions to and reflections of credit upon the industry as an actor, director, producer and executive; and for his consistent and unselfish cooperation with and support of the Academy.

TRUSTEES CITATION
This citation is presented to the PRESIDENT OF THE UNITED STATES...JOHN F. KENNEDY. For making News Conferences available to television and participating in the program "Conversation with the President".

1963/64

THE PROGRAM OF THE YEAR
That program, created originally or fully adapted for television, which is considered to be the most outstanding presentation during the awards period. Such a program may be either one of a series or an individual presentation, either entertainment, public service or coverage of a newsworthy event.
THE MAKING OF THE PRESIDENT 1960 (ABC)
AMERICAN REVOLUTION OF '63 (NBC)
BLACKLIST (The Defenders) (CBS)
THE KREMLIN (NBC)
TOWN MEETING OF THE WORLD (CBS)

OUTSTANDING PROGRAM ACHIEVEMENT IN THE FIELD OF COMEDY
A special program, one of a series, or a series - any length; live, tape or film
THE DICK VAN DYKE SHOW (CBS)
THE BILL DANA SHOW (NBC)
THE FARMER'S DAUGHTER (ABC)
McHALE'S NAVY (ABC)
THAT WAS THE WEEK THAT WAS (NBC)

OUTSTANDING PROGRAM ACHIEVEMENT IN THE FIELD OF DRAMA
A special program, one of a series, or a series - any length; live, tape or film
THE DEFENDERS (CBS)
BOB HOPE PRESENTS THE CHRYSLER THEATRE (NBC)
EAST SIDE/WEST SIDE (CBS)
MR. NOVAK (NBC)
THE RICHARD BOONE SHOW (NBC)

OUTSTANDING PROGRAM ACHIEVEMENT IN THE FIELD OF MUSIC
A special program, one of a series, or a series - any length; live, tape or film
BELL TELEPHONE HOUR (NBC)
THE LIVELY ONES (NBC)
NEW YORK PHILHARMONIC YOUNG PEOPLE'S CONCERTS WITH LEONARD BERNSTEIN (CBS)

OUTSTANDING PROGRAM ACHIEVEMENT IN THE FIELD OF VARIETY

A special program, one of a series, or a series - any length; live, tape or film

THE DANNY KAYE SHOW (CBS)
THE ANDY WILLIAMS SHOW (NBC)
THE GARRY MOORE SHOW (CBS)
THE JUDY GARLAND SHOW (CBS)
THE TONIGHT SHOW STARRING JOHNNY CARSON (NBC)

OUTSTANDING PROGRAM ACHIEVEMENT IN THE FIELD OF CHILDREN'S PROGRAMMING

A special program, one of a series, or a series - any length; live, tape or film

DISCOVERY '63-'64 (ABC)
EXPLORING (NBC)
NBC CHILDREN'S THEATRE (NBC)
SCIENCE ALL STARS (ABC)
WILD KINGDOM (NBC)

OUTSTANDING ACHIEVEMENT IN THE FIELD OF DOCUMENTARY PROGRAMS

A special program, one of a series, or a series - any length; live, tape or film

THE MAKING OF THE PRESIDENT 1960 Produced by David L. Wolper and Mel Stuart; Written by Theodore H. White (ABC)
GREECE: THE GOLDEN AGE Produced and Written by Lou Hazam (NBC)
THE KREMLIN Produced by George Vicas; Written by Norman Borisoff, George Vicas, Aram Boyajian (NBC)
MANHATTAN BATTLEGROUND (DuPont Show of the Week) Produced and Written by William Jersey (NBC)
SAGA OF WESTERN MAN Produced by John H. Secondari and Helen Jean Rogers; Written by John H. Secondari (ABC)
THE TWENTIETH CENTURY Produced by Isaac Kleinerman (CBS)

OUTSTANDING PROGRAM ACHIEVEMENT IN THE FIELD OF NEWS REPORTS

A special program, one of a series, or a series - any length; live, tape or film

HUNTLEY-BRINKLEY REPORT (NBC)
CBS EVENING NEWS WITH WALTER CRONKITE (CBS)
NBC SPECIAL NEWS REPORTS (NBC)
RON COCHRAN WITH THE NEWS (ABC)

OUTSTANDING PROGRAM ACHIEVEMENT IN THE FIELD OF NEWS COMMENTARY OR PUBLIC AFFAIRS

A special program, one of a series, or a series - any length; live, tape or film

CUBA: PARTS I & II-THE BAY OF PIGS; THE MISSILE CRISIS (NBC White Paper) (NBC)
AMERICAN REVOLUTION OF '63 (NBC)
CBS REPORTS (CBS)
CHRONICLE (CBS)
TOWN MEETING OF THE WORLD (CBS)

OUTSTANDING SINGLE PERFORMANCE BY AN ACTOR IN A LEADING ROLE

Single performance only - any length; live, tape or film

JACK KLUGMAN as JOE LARCH Blacklist (The Defenders) (CBS)
JAMES EARL JONES as JOE Who Do You Kill? (EastSide/WestSide) (CBS)
RODDY McDOWALL as PAUL LeDOUX Journey Into Darkness (Arrest and Trial) (ABC)
JASON ROBARDS, JR. as ABE LINCOLN Abe Lincoln In Illinois (Hallmark Hall of Fame) (NBC)
ROD STEIGER as MIKE KIRSCH A Slow Fade To Black (Bob Hope Presents The Chrysler Theatre) (NBC)
HAROLD J. STONE as ELIHU KAMINSKY Nurse Is A Feminine Noun (The Nurses) (CBS)

OUTSTANDING SINGLE PERFORMANCE BY AN ACTRESS IN A LEADING ROLE

Single performance only - any length; live, tape or film

SHELLY WINTERS as JENNY DWORAK Two Is The Number (Bob Hope Presents The Chrysler Theatre) (NBC)
RUBY DEE as JENNY BISHOP Express Stop from Lenox Avenue (The Nurses) (CBS)
BETHEL LESLIE as ELLEN DUDLEY Statement of Fact (The Richard Boone Show) (NBC)
JEANETTE NOLAN as JESSIE McCOONY Vote No On 11! (The Richard Boone Show) (NBC)
DIANA SANDS as RUTH Who Do You Kill? (East Side/West Side) (CBS)

OUTSTANDING CONTINUED PERFORMANCE BY AN ACTOR IN A SERIES (LEAD)

Continued performance only - any length; live, tape or film

DICK VAN DYKE as ROB PETRIE (The Dick Van Dyke Show) (CBS)
RICHARD BOONE in various roles (The Richard Boone Show) (NBC)
DEAN JAGGER as ALBERT VANE (Mr. Novak) (NBC)
DAVID JANSSEN as DR RICHARD KIMBLE (The Fugitive) (ABC)
GEORGE C. SCOTT as NEIL BROCK (East Side/West Side) (CBS)

OUTSTANDING CONTINUED PERFORMANCE BY AN ACTRESS IN A SERIES (LEAD)

Continued performance only - any length; live, tape or film

MARY TYLER MOORE as LAURA PETRIE (The Dick Van Dyke Show) (CBS)
SHIRLEY BOOTH as HAZEL (Hazel) (NBC)
PATTY DUKE as PATTY LANE and CATHY LANE (The Patty Duke Show) (ABC)
IRENE RYAN as GRANNY (The Beverly Hillbillies) (CBS)
INGER STEVENS as KATIE HOLSTRUM (The Farmer's Daughter) (ABC)

OUTSTANDING PERFORMANCE IN A SUPPORTING ROLE BY AN ACTOR

A special program, one of a series, or a series - any length; live, tape or film

ALBERT PAULSEN as LIEUTENANT VOLKOVOI One Day In the Life of Ivan Denisovich (Bob Hope Presents the Chrysler Theatre) (NBC)
SORRELL BOOKE as JULIUS ORLOFF What's God to Julius? (Dr. Kildare) (NBC)
CONLAN CARTER as DOC The Hostages (Combat) (ABC)
CARL LEE as LONNIE HILL Express Stop From Lenox Avenue (The Nurses) (CBS)

OUTSTANDING PERFORMANCE IN A SUPPORTING ROLE BY AN ACTRESS

A special program, one of a series, or a series - any length; live, tape or film

RUTH WHITE as MRS. MANGAN Little Moon of Alban (Hallmark Hall of Fame) (NBC)
MARTINE BARTLETT as MIRANDA Journey Into Darkness (Arrest and Trial) (ABC)
ANJANETTE COMER as ANNABELLE Journey Into Darkness (Arrest and Trial) (ABC)
ROSE MARIE as SALLY ROGERS (The Dick Van Dyke Show) (CBS)
CLAUDIA McNEIL as MRS. HILL Express Stop From Lenox Avenue (The Nurses) (CBS)

OUTSTANDING PERFORMANCE IN A VARIETY OR MUSICAL PROGRAM OR SERIES

A special program, one of a series, or a series - any length; live, tape or film

DANNY KAYE (The Danny Kaye Show) (CBS)
JUDY GARLAND (The Judy Garland Show) (CBS)
BARBRA STREISAND (The Judy Garland Show) (CBS)
BURR TILLSTROM (That Was the Week That Was) various episodes (NBC)
ANDY WILLIAMS (The Andy Williams Show) (NBC)

OUTSTANDING ACHIEVEMENT IN COMPOSING ORIGINAL MUSIC FOR TELEVISION

A special program, one of a series, or a series - any length; live, tape or film

ELMER BERNSTEIN The Making of the President 1960 (ABC)
GEORGES AURIC The Kremlin (NBC)
JOHN BARRY Elizabeth Taylor in London (CBS)
KENYON HOPKINS (East Side/West Side) (CBS)
GEORGE KLEINSINGER Greece: The Golden Age (NBC)
ULPIO MINUCCI, JOE MOON, RAYBURN WRIGHT Saga of Western Man (ABC)

OUTSTANDING ACHIEVEMENT IN ART DIRECTION AND SCENIC DESIGN

A special program, one of a series, or a series - any length; live, tape or film

WARREN CLYMER (Hallmark Hall of Fame) (NBC)
ROBERT KELLY, GARY SMITH (The Judy Garland Show) (CBS)
JACK POPLIN (The Outer Limits) (ABC)
EDWARD STEPHENSON (The Danny Kaye Show) (CBS)

OUTSTANDING WRITING ACHIEVEMENT IN DRAMA - ORIGINAL

A special program or one of a series - any length; live, tape or film

ERNEST KINOY Blacklist (The Defenders) (CBS)
ARNOLD PERL Who Do You Kill? (East Side/West Side) (CBS)
DAVID RAYFIEL Something About Lee Wiley (Bob Hope Presents The Chrysler Theatre) (NBC)
ALLAN SLOANE And James Was A Very Small Snail (Breaking Point) (ABC)
ADRIAN SPIES What's God To Julius? (Dr. Kildare) (NBC)

OUTSTANDING WRITING ACHIEVEMENT IN DRAMA - ADAPTATION

A special program or one of a series - any length; live, tape or film

ROD SERLING It's Mental Work (Bob Hope Presents The Chrysler Theatre) From the story by John O'Hara (NBC)
JAMES BRIDGES The Jar (The Alfred Hitchcock Hour) From a short story by Ray Bradbury (CBS)
ROBERT HARTUNG The Patriots (Hallmark Hall of Fame) From the play by Sidney Kingsley (NBC)
WALTER BROWN NEWMAN The Hooligan (The Richard Boone Show) From a play by Anton Chekov (NBC)

OUTSTANDING WRITING ACHIEVEMENT IN COMEDY OR VARIETY

A special program, one of a series, or a series - any length; live, tape or film

CARL REINER, SAM DENOFF, BILL PERSKY (The Dick Van Dyke Show) various episodes (CBS)
HERBERT BAKER, MEL TOLKIN, ERNEST CHAMBERS, SAUL ILSON, SHELDON KELLER, PAUL MAZURSKY, LARRY TUCKER, GARY BELKIN, LARRY GELBART (The Danny Kaye Show) (CBS)
ROBERT EMMETT, GERALD GARDNER, SAUL TURTLETAUB, DAVID PANICH, TONY WEBSTER, THOMAS MEEHAN, ED SHERMAN (That Was the Week That Was) (NBC)
STEVEN GETHERS, JERRY DAVIS and LEE LOEB, JOHN McGREEVEY (The Farmer's Daughter) various episodes (ABC)

OUTSTANDING DIRECTORIAL ACHIEVEMENT IN DRAMA

A special program or one of a series - any length; live, tape or film

TOM GRIES Who Do You Kill? (East Side/West Side) (CBS)
PAUL BOGART Moment of Truth (The Defenders) (CBS)
SYDNEY POLLACK Something About Lee Wiley (Bob Hope Presents The Chrysler Theatre) (NBC)
STUART ROSENBERG Blacklist (The Defenders) (CBS)
GEORGE SCHAEFER The Patriots (Hallmark Hall of Fame) (NBC)

OUTSTANDING DIRECTORIAL ACHIEVEMENT IN COMEDY

A special program, one of a series, or a series - any length; live, tape or film

JERRY PARIS (The Dick Van Dyke Show) (CBS)
SIDNEY LANFIELD (McHale's Navy) (ABC)
PAUL NICKELL, WILLIAM RUSSELL, DON TAYLOR (The Farmer's Daughter) various episodes (ABC)
RICHARD WHORF (The Beverly Hillbillies) (CBS)

OUTSTANDING DIRECTORIAL ACHIEVEMENT IN VARIETY OR MUSIC

A special program, one of a series, or a series - any length; live, tape or film

ROBERT SCHEERER (The Danny Kaye Show) (CBS)
ROGER ENGLANDER A Tribute To Teachers (New York Philharmonic Young People's Concerts With Leonard Bernstein) (CBS)
BOB HENRY (The Andy Williams Show) (NBC)
MARSHALL JAMISON (That Was the Week That Was) (NBC)
CLARK JONES, SID SMITH (Bell Telephone Hour) various programs (NBC)

OUTSTANDING ACHIEVEMENT IN CINEMATOGRAPHY FOR TELEVISION
Any type or length filmed program or series

J. BAXTER PETERS The Kremlin (NBC)
JOHN S. PRIESTLEY (East Side/West Side) (CBS)
BRADFORD KRESS Greece: The Golden Age (NBC)
ELLIS F. THACKERY Once Upon a Savage Night (Kraft Suspense Theatre) (NBC)

OUTSTANDING ACHIEVEMENT IN ELECTRONIC PHOTOGRAPHY
Any type or length program or series, live or taped

THE DANNY KAYE SHOW (CBS)
BELL TELEPHONE HOUR (NBC)
THE LIVELY ONES (NBC)
RIDE WITH TERROR (DuPont Show of the Week) (NBC)

OUTSTANDING ACHIEVEMENT IN FILM EDITING FOR TELEVISION
Any type or length filmed program or series

WILLIAM T. CARTWRIGHT The Making of the President 1960 (ABC)
JAMES ALGIE, SAMUEL COHEN, HANS DUDELHEIM, WALTER ESSENFELD, ALEXANDER HAMILTON, EDWARD LEMPA, WALTER MORAN, NILS RASMUSSEN, JOHN ROBERTS, ROBERT SANDBO, EDWARD SHEA Saga of Western Man (ABC)
ARAM BOYAJIAN The Kremlin (NBC)
CONSTANTINE S. GOCHIS Greece: The Golden Age (NBC)
DANNY LANDRES, MILTON SHIFMAN, RICHARD WRAY Arrest and Trial (ABC)

THE INTERNATIONAL AWARD
Judged by Special Committee of former Emmy Award Winners of entries from countries throughout the world

LES RAISINS VERTS (Radiodiffusion Television Francais)
BUNRAKU DOLLS (NHK, Japan Broadcasting Corporation)
PALE HORSE, PALE RIDER (Canadian Broadcasting Corporation)

THE STATION AWARD
Regional Winners judged by Committees at National Academy Chapters; final judging by Special Committee

OPERATION CHALLENGE - A STUDY IN HOPE (KSD-TV, St. Louis)
THE CASE FOR THE LIMITED CHILD (KPIX San Francisco)
CHILD BEATING (WMAL-TV, Washington, D.C.)
DATE LINE: CHICAGO COMPOSITE (WNBQ, Chicago)
THE LAST PROM (WLW-T, Cincinnati)
THE NEXT REVOLUTION (WCBS-TV, New York)
POISON IN THE AIR (KNXT, Los Angeles)
WEDNESDAY'S CHILD (KGW-TV, Portland, Oregon)
WITHOUT VIOLENCE (WBRZ-TV, Baton Rouge)

1964/65

OUTSTANDING PROGRAM ACHIEVEMENTS IN ENTERTAINMENT

THE DICK VAN DYKE SHOW (CBS) Carl Reiner, Producer
THE MAGNIFICENT YANKEE (Hallmark Hall of Fame) (NBC) George Schaefer, Producer
MY NAME IS BARBRA (CBS) Richard Lewine, Producer
WHAT IS SONATA FORM? (New York Philharmonic Young People's Concerts with Leonard Bernstein) (CBS) Roger Englander, Producer
THE ANDY WILLIAMS SHOW (NBC) Bob Finkel, Producer
BOB HOPE PRESENTS THE CHRYSLER THEATRE (NBC) Dick Berg, Executive Producer
THE DEFENDERS (CBS) Bob Markell, Producer
HALLMARK HALL OF FAME (NBC) George Schaefer, Producer
THE MAN FROM U.N.C.L.E. (NBC) Sam Rolfe, Producer
MR. NOVAK (NBC) Leonard Freeman, Producer
PROFILES IN COURAGE (NBC) Robert Saudek, Executive Producer
WALT DISNEY'S WONDERFUL WORLD OF COLOR (NBC) Walt Disney, Executive Producer
THE WONDERFUL WORLD OF BURLESQUE (NBC) George Schlatter, Producer
XEROX SPECIALS (Based on the activities of the United Nations) "Carol For Another Christmas" (ABC) Joseph L. Mankiewicz, Producer; "Who Has Seen The Wind?" (ABC) George Sidney, Producer

OUTSTANDING INDIVIDUAL ACHIEVEMENTS IN ENTERTAINMENT

ACTORS AND PERFORMERS

LEONARD BERNSTEIN (New York Philharmonic Young People's Concerts with Leonard Bernstein) (CBS)
LYNN FONTANNE as FANNY DIXWELL HOLMES The Magnificent Yankee (Hallmark Hall of Fame) (NBC)
ALFRED LUNT as OLIVER WENDELL HOLMES The Magnificent Yankee (Hallmark Hall of Fame) (NBC)
BARBRA STREISAND My Name is Barbra (CBS)
DICK VAN DYKE as ROB PETRIE (The Dick Van Dyke Show) (CBS)
JULIE ANDREWS (The Andy Williams Show) (NBC)
JOHNNY CARSON (The Tonight Show Starring Johnny Carson) (NBC)
GLADYS COOPER as AUNT MARGARET (The Rogues) (NBC)
ROBERT COOTE as TIMMY ST. CLAIR (The Rogues) (NBC)
RICHARD CRENNA as SLATTERY (Slattery's People) (CBS)
JULIE HARRIS as FLORENCE NIGHTINGALE The Holy Terror (Hallmark Hall of Fame) (NBC)
BOB HOPE (Chrysler Presents A Bob Hope Comedy Special) (NBC)
DEAN JAGGER as ALBERT VANE (Mr. Novak) (NBC)
DANNY KAYE (The Danny Kaye Show) (CBS)
DAVID McCALLUM as ILLYA KURYAKIN (The Man From U.N.C.L.E.) (NBC)
RED SKELTON (The Red Skelton Hour) (CBS)

WRITERS

DAVID KARP The 700 Year Old Gang (The Defenders) (CBS)
WILLIAM BOARDMAN, DEE CARUSO, ROBERT EMMETT, DAVID FROST, GERALD GARDNER, BUCK HENRY, JOSEPH HURLEY, TOM MEEHAN, HERB SARGENT, LARRY SIEGEL, GLORIA STEINEM, JIM STEVENSON, CALVIN TRILLIN, SAUL TURTLETAUB (That Was The Week That Was) (NBC)
ROBERT HARTUNG Adaption of Emmet Laver's "The Magnificent Yankee" (Hallmark Hall of Fame) (NBC)
COLEMAN JACOBY, ARNEY ROSEN The Wonderful World of Burlesque (NBC)
CARL REINER Never Bathe On Saturday (The Dick Van Dyke Show) (CBS)

DIRECTORS

PAUL BOGART The 700 Year Old Gang (The Defenders) (CBS)
DWIGHT HEMION My Name is Barbra (CBS)
GEORGE SCHAEFER The Magnificent Yankee (Hallmark Hall of Fame) (NBC)

CONCEPTION, CHOREOGRAPHY AND STAGING

JOE LAYTON My Name is Barbra (CBS)

ART DIRECTORS AND SET DECORATORS

WARREN CLYMER The Holy Terror (Hallmark Hall of Fame) (NBC)
TOM JOHN, Art Director; BILL HARP, Set Decorator, My Name is Barbra (CBS)
GENE CALLAHAN, Art Director; JACK WRIGHT JR, Set Decorator, Carol For Another Christmas (Xerox Special) (ABC)

WARREN CLYMER The Magnificent Yankee (Hallmark Hall of Fame) (NBC)

COSTUME DESIGNER
NOEL TAYLOR The Magnificent Yankee (Hallmark Hall of Fame) (NBC)

MAKE-UP ARTIST
ROBERT O'BRADOVICH The Magnificent Yankee (Hallmark Hall of Fame) (NBC)

MUSICIANS
PETER MATZ, Music Director, My Name is Barbra (CBS)
HERBERT GROSSMAN, Music Director, The Fantasticks (Hallmark Hall of Fame) (NBC)

CINEMATOGRAPHERS
WILLIAM SPENCER (Twelve O'Clock High) (ABC)
HASKELL BOGGS, WILLIAM WHITLEY (Bonanza) (NBC)
FRED KOENEKAMP (The Man From U.N.C.L.E.) (NBC)

FILM EDITORS
HENRY BERMAN, JOSEPH DERVIN, WILL GULICK (The Man From U.N.C.L.E.) (NBC)

LIGHTING DIRECTOR
PHIL HYMES The Magnificent Yankee (Hallmark Hall of Fame) (NBC)

SPECIAL PHOTOGRAPHIC EFFECTS
L. B. ABBOTT (Voyage to the Bottom of the Sea) (ABC)

USE OF SPECIAL EFFECTS
PRODUCTION TEAM EFFORT (The Man from U.N.C.L.E.) (NBC)

COLOR CONSULTANT
EDWARD ANCONA (Bonanza) (NBC)

TECHNICAL DIRECTOR
CLAIR McCOY The Wonderful World of Burlesque (NBC)

OUTSTANDING PROGRAM ACHIEVEMENTS IN NEWS, DOCUMENTARIES, INFORMATION AND SPORTS
I, LEONARDO DA VINCI (Saga of Western Man) (ABC) John H. Secondari, Helen Jean Rogers, Producers
THE LOUVRE (NBC) Lucy Jarvis, Producer, John J. Sughrue, Co-Producer
NBC CONVENTION COVERAGE (NBC) Reuven Frank, Producer
THE DECISION TO DROP THE BOMB (NBC White Paper) (NBC) Fred Freed, Producer

OUTSTANDING INDIVIDUAL ACHIEVEMENTS IN NEWS, DOCUMENTARIES, INFORMATION AND SPORTS

NARRATORS
RICHARD BASEHART Let My People Go (Syndicated)
CHARLES BOYER The Louvre (NBC)

DIRECTORS
JOHN J. SUGHRUE The Louvre (NBC)
FRANK DE FELITTA Battle of the Bulge (NBC)
TOM PRIESTLEY John F. Kennedy Remembered (NBC)
HELEN JEAN ROGERS I, Leonardo da Vinci (Saga of Western Man) (ABC)

WRITERS
SIDNEY CARROLL The Louvre (NBC)
JOHN H. SECONDARI I, Leonardo da Vinci (Saga of Western Man) (ABC)

FILM EDITORS
ARAM BOYAJIAN The Louvre (NBC)
WALTER ESSENFELD, NILS RASMUSSEN I, Leonardo da Vinci (Saga of Western Man) (ABC)
ANGELO FARINA, BEN SCHILLER Battle of the Bulge (NBC)

CINEMATOGRAPHERS
TOM PRIESTLEY The Louvre (NBC)
DEXTER ALLEY, RICHARD NORLING The Journals of Lewis & Clark (NBC)
WILLIAM B. HARTIGAN I, Leonardo da Vinci (Saga of Western Man) (ABC)

MUSICIANS
NORMAN DELLO JOIO, Composer-Conductor, The Louvre (NBC)
ULPIO MINUCCI, Composer; RAYBURN WRIGHT, Conductor, I, Leonardo da Vinci (Saga of Western Man) (ABC)

THE INTERNATIONAL AWARD
Judged by Special Committee of former Emmy Award Winners of entries from countries throughout the world
LE BARBIER DE SEVILLE (Canadian Broadcasting Corporation, Canada)
ANTONIO E CLEOPATRA (RAI-Radiotelevisione Italiana, Italy)
BILDER AUS DER SOWJET-UNION: SIBIRIEN-TRAUM UND WIRKLICHKEIT (Norddeutscher Rundfunk, West Germany)
ISLAND YEARBOOK (Sveriges Radio, Sweden)
SEVEN-UP (Granada Television Limited, England)
SHOW BECAUD (Office de Radiodiffusion-Television Francaise, France)

THE STATION AWARD
Regional Winners judged by Committees at National Academy Chapters; Final judging by Special Committee
KU KLUX KLAN (WDSU-TV, New Orleans, La)
CONVERSATIONS WITH JAMES EMORY BOND (WBAL-TV, Baltimore, Md)
KOREAN LEGACY (KTLA, Los Angeles, Calif)
MY CHILDHOOD (WNEW-TV, New York, NY)
NO ROOM AT THE BOTTOM (KSD-TV, St. Louis, Mo)
THE OUTSIDERS (WOW-TV, Omaha, Neb)
ROSES HAVE THORNS (WOOD-TV, Grand Rapids, Mich)
STRANGERS IN THE SHADOWS (WBNS-TV, Columbus, Ohio)

1965/66

OUTSTANDING COMEDY SERIES
THE DICK VAN DYKE SHOW (CBS) Carl Reiner, Producer
BATMAN (ABC) Howie Horwitz, Producer
BETWITCHED (ABC) Jerry Davis, Producer
GET SMART! (NBC) Leonard Stern, Executive Producer
HOGAN'S HEROES (CBS) Edward H. Feldman, Producer

OUTSTANDING VARIETY SERIES
Awards to Producer and Star

THE ANDY WILLIAMS SHOW (NBC) Bob Finkel, Producer
THE DANNY KAYE SHOW (CBS) Bob Scheerer, Producer
THE HOLLYWOOD PALACE (ABC) William O. Harback and Nick Vanoff, Producers
THE RED SKELTON HOUR (CBS) Seymour Berns, Producer
THE TONIGHT SHOW STARRING JOHNNY CARSON (NBC) Art Stark, Producer

OUTSTANDING VARIETY SPECIAL
Awards to Producer and Star

CHRYSLER PRESENTS THE BOB HOPE CHRISTMAS SPECIAL (NBC) Bob Hope, Executive Producer
AN EVENING WITH CAROL CHANNING (CBS) Bud Yorkin, Producer
JIMMY DURANTE MEETS THE LIVELY ARTS (ABC) Alan Handley and Bob Wynn, Producers
THE JULIE ANDREWS SHOW (NBC) Alan Handley, Producer
THE SWINGING WORLD OF SAMMY DAVIS, JR. (Syndicated) Stan Greene, Producer

OUTSTANDING DRAMATIC SERIES

THE FUGITIVE (ABC) Alan Armer, Producer
BONANZA (NBC) David Dortort, Producer
I SPY (NBC) David Friedkin and Mort Fine, Producers
THE MAN FROM U.N.C.L.E. (NBC) Norman Felton, Executive Producer
SLATTERY'S PEOPLE (CBS) Irving Elman, Producer

OUTSTANDING DRAMATIC PROGRAM
A single program

AGES OF MAN (CBS) David Suskind and Daniel Melnick, Producers
EAGLE IN A CAGE (Hallmark Hall of Fame) (NBC) George Schaefer, Producer
INHERIT THE WIND (Hallmark Hall of Fame) (NBC) George Schaefer, Producer
RALLY 'ROUND YOUR OWN FLAG, MISTER (Slattery's People) (CBS) Irving Elman, Producer

OUTSTANDING MUSICAL PROGRAM
A special program, one of a series, or a series - Awards to Producer and Star

FRANK SINATRA: A MAN AND HIS MUSIC (NBC) Dwight Hemion, Producer
BELL TELEPHONE HOUR (NBC) Barry Wood, Executive Producer
THE BOLSHOI BALLET (Syndicated) Ted Mills, Producer
COLOR ME BARBRA (CBS) Joe Layton and Dwight Hemion, Producers
NEW YORK PHILHARMONIC YOUNG PEOPLE'S CONCERTS WITH LEONARD BERNSTEIN (CBS) Roger Englander, Producer

OUTSTANDING CHILDREN'S PROGRAM
A special program, one of a series, or a series

A CHARLIE BROWN CHRISTMAS (CBS) Lee Mendelson and Bill Melendez, Producers
CAPTAIN KANGAROO (CBS) Al Hyslop, Producer
DISCOVERY (ABC) Jules Power, Executive Producer
FURTHER ADVENTURES OF GALLEGHER (Walt Disney's Wonderful World of Color) (NBC) Walt Disney and Ron Miller, Producers
THE WORLD OF STUART LITTLE (NBC Children's Theatre) (NBC) George A. Heinemann, Producer

OUTSTANDING SINGLE PERFORMANCE BY AN ACTOR IN A LEADING ROLE IN A DRAMA

CLIFF ROBERTSON as QUINCEY PARKER The Game (Bob Hope Presents the Chrysler Theatre) (NBC)
ED BEGLEY as MATTHEW HARRISON BRADY Inherit The Wind (Hallmark Hall of Fame) (NBC)
MELVYN DOUGLAS as HENRY DRUMMOND Inherit The Wind (Hallmark Hall of Fame) (NBC)
TREVOR HOWARD as NAPOLEON Eagle In A Cage (Hallmark Hall of Fame) (NBC)
CHRISTOPHER PLUMMER as HAMLET Hamlet (Syndicated)

OUTSTANDING SINGLE PERFORMANCE BY AN ACTRESS IN A LEADING ROLE IN A DRAMA

SIGMONE SIGNORET as SARA LESCAUT A Small Rebellion (Bob Hope Presents The Chrysler Theatre) (NBC)
EARTHA KITT as ANGEL The Loser (I Spy) (NBC)
MARGARET LEIGHTON as CHRIS BECKER Behold The Great Man; A Life For A Life; Web of Hate; Horizontal Hero (Dr. Kildare) (NBC)
SHELLEY WINTERS as EDITH Back to Back (Bob Hope Presents the Chrysler Theatre) (NBC)

OUTSTANDING CONTINUED PERFORMANCE BY AN ACTOR IN A LEADING ROLE IN A DRAMATIC SERIES

BILL COSBY as ALEXANDER SCOTT (I Spy) (NBC)
RICHARD CRENNA as SLATTERY (Slattery's People) (CBS)
ROBERT CULP as KELLY ROBINSON (I Spy) (NBC)
DAVID JANSSEN as DR. RICHARD KIMBLE (The Fugitive) (ABC)
DAVID McCALLUM as ILLYA KURYAKIN (The Man From U.N.C.L.E.) (NBC)

OUTSTANDING CONTINUED PERFORMANCE BY AN ACTRESS IN A LEADING ROLE IN A DRAMATIC SERIES

BARBARA STANWYCK as VICTORIA BARKLEY (The Big Valley) (ABC)
ANNE FRANCIS as HONEY WEST (Honey West) (ABC)
BARBARA PARKINS as BETTY ANDERSON (Peyton Place) (ABC)

OUTSTANDING CONTINUED PERFORMANCE BY AN ACTOR IN A LEADING ROLE IN A COMEDY SERIES

DICK VAN DYKE as ROB PETRIE (The Dick Van Dyke Show) (CBS)
DON ADAMS as MAXWELL SMART (Get Smart!) (NBC)
BOB CRANE as COL. ROBERT HOGAN (Hogan's Heroes) (CBS)

OUTSTANDING CONTINUED PERFORMANCE BY AN ACTRESS IN A LEADING ROLE IN A COMEDY SERIES

MARY TYLER MOORE as LAURA PETRIE (The Dick Van Dyke Show) (CBS)
LUCILLE BALL as LUCY CARMICHAEL (The Lucy Show) (CBS)
ELIZABETH MONTGOMERY as SAMANTHA STEPHENS (Betwitched) (ABC)

OUTSTANDING PERFORMANCE BY AN ACTOR IN A SUPPORTING ROLE IN A DRAMA
A single program or series

JAMES DALY as DR. O'MEARA Eagle In A Cage (Hallmark Hall of Fame) (NBC)
DAVID BURNS as GREAT McGONIGLE (Trials Of O'Brien) (CBS)
LEO G. CARROLL as ALEXANDER WAVERLY (The Man From U.N.C.L.E.) (NBC)

OUTSTANDING PERFORMANCE BY AN ACTRESS IN A SUPPORTING ROLE IN A DRAMA
A single program or series

LEE GRANT as STELLA CHERNAK (Peyton Place) (ABC)
DIANE BAKER as RACHEL BROWN Inherit The Wind (Hallmark Hall of Fame) (NBC)
PAMELA FRANKLIN as BETSY BALCOMBE Eagle In A Cage (Hallmark Hall Of Fame) (NBC)
JEANETTE NOLAN as MAUDE MURDOCK The Conquest Of Maude Murdock (I Spy) (NBC)

OUTSTANDING PERFORMANCE BY AN ACTOR IN A SUPPORTING ROLE IN A COMEDY
A single program or series

DON KNOTTS as BARNEY FIFE The Return Of Barney Fife (The Andy Griffith Show) (CBS)
MOREY AMSTERDAM as BUDDY SORRELL (The Dick Van Dyke Show) (CBS)
FRANK GORSHIN as THE RIDDLER Hi Diddle Riddle (Batman) (ABC)
WERNER KLEMPERER as COL. WILHELM KLINK (Hogan's Heroes) (CBS)

OUTSTANDING PERFORMANCE BY AN ACTRESS IN A SUPPORTING ROLE IN A COMEDY
A single program or series

ALICE PEARCE as GLADYS KRAVITZ (Bewitched) (ABC)
AGNES MOOREHEAD as ENDORA (Bewitched) (ABC)
ROSEMARIE as SALLY ROGERS (The Dick Van Dyke Show) (CBS)

OUTSTANDING WRITING ACHIEVEMENT IN DRAMA
A special program or one of a series

MILLARD LAMPELL Eagle In A Cage (Hallmark Hall Of Fame) (NBC)
MORTON FINE, DAVID FRIEDKIN A Cup Of Kindness (I Spy) (NBC)
S. LEE POGOSTIN The Game (Bob Hope Presents The Chrysler Theatre) (NBC)

OUTSTANDING WRITING ACHIEVEMENT IN COMEDY
A special program, one of a series, or a series

BILL PERSKY, SAM DENOFF Coast To Coast Big Mouth (The Dick Van Dyke Show) (CBS)
MEL BROOKS, BUCK HENRY Mr. Big (Get Smart!) (NBC)
BILL PERSKY, SAM DENOFF The Ugliest Dog In The World (The Dick Van Dyke Show) (CBS)

OUTSTANDING WRITING ACHIEVEMENT IN VARIETY
A special program, one of a series, or a series

AL GORDON, HAL GOLDMAN, SHELDON KELLER An Evening With Carol Channing (CBS)
ERNEST CHAMBERS, PAT McCORMICK, RON FRIEDMAN, LARRY TUCKER, PAUL MAZURSKY, BILLIE BARNES, BERNARD ROTHMAN, NORMAN BARASCH, CARROL MOORE The Danny Kaye Show (CBS)
BILL PERSKY, SAM DENOFF The Julie Andrews Show (NBC)

OUTSTANDING DIRECTORIAL ACHIEVEMENT IN DRAMA
A special program or one of a series

SIDNEY POLLACK The Game (Bob Hope Presents The Chrysler Theatre) (NBC)
SHELDON LEONARD Hong Kong portions of: So Long, Patrick Henry; A Cup of Kindness; Carry Me Back To Old Tsing-Tao (I Spy) (NBC)
GEORGE SCHAEFER Eagle In A Cage (Hallmark Hall Of Fame) (NBC)
GEORGE SCHAEFER Inherit The Wind (Hallmark Hall Of Fame) (NBC)

OUTSTANDING DIRECTORIAL ACHIEVEMENT IN COMEDY
A special program, one of a series, or a series

WILLIAM ASHER Bewitched (ABC)
PAUL BOGART Diplomat's Daughter (Get Smart!) (NBC)
JERRY PARIS The Dick Van Dyke Show (CBS)

OUTSTANDING DIRECTORIAL ACHIEVEMENT IN VARIETY OR MUSIC
A special program, one of a series, or a series

ALAN HANDLEY The Julie Andrews Show (NBC)
GREG GARRISON The Dean Martin Show (NBC)
DWIGHT HEMION Frank Sinatra: A Man And His Music (NBC)
DWIGHT HEMION Color Me Barbra (CBS)
BOB HENRY The Andy Williams Show (NBC)

THE CRAFT AND PROGRAMMING AREAS
(Possibility of Multiple Awards)

ACHIEVEMENTS IN NEWS AND DOCUMENTARIES

PROGRAMS
AMERICAN WHITE PAPER: UNITED STATES FOREIGN POLICY (NBC) Fred Freed, Producer
KKK - THE INVISIBLE EMPIRE (CBS Reports) (CBS) David Lowe, Producer
SENATE HEARINGS ON VIETNAM (NBC) Chet Hagan, Producer
CBS REPORTS (CBS) Palmer Williams, Executive Producer
COVERAGE OF THE PAPEL VISIT (NBC) Chet Hagan, Producer
KTLA COVERAGE OF WATTS RIOTS (ABC, CBS and NBC) KTLA News Department
HUNTLEY-BRINKLEY REPORT (NBC) Robert Northshield, Executive Producer
THE MAKING OF THE PRESIDENT 1964 (CBS) David L. Wolper and Mel Stuart, Producers
MICHELANGELO: THE LAST GIANT (NBC) Louis Hazam, Producer
NATIONAL DRIVERS TEST (CBS) Warren V. Bush, Producer
TWENTIETH CENTURY (CBS) Isaac Kleinerman, Producer

INDIVIDUALS
WILLIAM BOARDMAN, LISA COMMAGER, DIANA FETTER, ROBERT RICKNER Researchers on Beethoven: Ordeal and Triumph (Saga Of Western Man) (ABC)
WALTER CRONKITE Commentator on CBS Evening News With Walter Cronkite (CBS)
LOU HAZAM Writer of Michelangelo: The Last Giant (NBC)
CHET HUNTLEY AND DAVID BRINKLEY Commentators on Huntley-Brinkley Report (NBC)
DAVID LOWE Writer of KKK - The Invisible Empire (CBS Reports) (CBS)
FRANK McGEE Commentator on The Frank McGee Report (NBC)
FRANK McGEE Commentator on The Papal Visit (NBC)
TOM PRIESTLEY Director of Michelangelo: The Last Giant (NBC)
HARRY REASONER Narrator of The Great Love Affair (CBS)
RICHARD SCHNEIDER Director of Papal Mass (ABC, CBS and NBC)

ERIC SEVAREID Commentator on CBS Evening News With Walter Cronkite (CBS)
HOWARD K. SMITH Commentator on United States Policy on Vietnam (Issues and Answers) (ABC)
MEL STUART Director of The Making Of The President 1964 (CBS)
PETER USTINOV Voice of Michelangelo on Michelangelo: The Last Giant (NBC)
THEODORE H. WHITE Writer of The Making Of the President 1964 (CBS)

ACHIEVEMENTS IN DAYTIME PROGRAMMING

PROGRAMS
CAMERA THREE (CBS) Dan Gallagher, Producer
MUTUAL OF OMAHA'S WILD KINGDOM (NBC) Don Meier, Producer
A TRIBUTE TO STEVENSON (Today) (NBC) Al Morgan, Producer

ACHIEVEMENTS IN SPORTS

PROGRAMS
ABC WIDE WORLD OF SPORTS (ABC) Roone Arledge, Executive Producer
CBS GOLF CLASSIC (CBS) Frank Chirkinian, Producer
SHELL'S WONDERFUL WORLD OF GOLF (NBC) Fred Raphael, Producer
NFL GAME OF THE WEEK (CBS) William C. Fitts III, Executive Producer
U.S.-RUSSIAN TRACK MEET (ABC) Chuck Howard, Producer

INDIVIDUAL
VIN SCULLY Sports Announcer on The World Series (NBC)

ACHIEVEMENTS IN EDUCATIONAL TELEVISION

PROGRAMS
AMERICA'S CRISIS: TROUBLE IN THE FAMILY (NET) Harold Mayer, Producer
AN HOUR WITH JOAN SUTHERLAND (NET) Curtis W. Davis, Producer
A ROOMFUL OF MUSIC (Festival Of Arts) (NET) David Sloss, Producer
BALDWIN VS. BUCKLEY (NET) Paul Bonner, Producer
HISTORY OF THE NEGRO PEOPLE (NET) Arthur Rabin, Producer
POLAND (Changing World) (NET) Richard Moore and Irving Saraf, Producers
THE DANCE THEATRE OF JOSE LIMON (Festival Of Arts) (NET) Jac Venza, Producer

INDIVIDUALS
JULIA CHILD Instructor and Hostess on The French Chef (NET)
KARL GENUS Writer and Director of Sibelius, A Symphony For Finland (NET)
LANE SLATE Director of The Creative Person - Robert Osborn (NET)
TOM WICKER, MAX FRANKEL, LESTER MARKEL Commentators on News In Perspective (NET)

INDIVIDUAL ACHIEVEMENTS IN MUSIC

COMPOSITION
LAURENCE ROSENTHAL Michelangelo: The Last Giant (NBC)
JERRY GOLDSMITH For original theme music on The Man From U.N.C.L.E. (NBC)
EARLE HAGEN I Spy (NBC)
DAVID ROSE Bonanza (NBC)
PETE RUGOLO Run For Your Life (NBC)
LALO SCHIFRIN The Making Of The President 1964 (CBS)
MORTON STEVENS Seven Hours To Dawn (Gunsmoke) (CBS)

CONDUCTING
MITCHELL AYRES The Hollywood Palace (ABC)
IRWIN KOSTAL The Julie Andrews Show (NBC)
GORDON JENKINS, NELSON RIDDLE Frank Sinatra: A Man And His Music (NBC)
ERICH LEINSDORF Beethoven: Ordeal And Triumph (Saga Of Western Man) (ABC)
LAURENCE ROSENTHAL Michelangelo: The Last Giant (NBC)
DONALD VOORHEES Bell Telephone Hour (NBC)

ARRANGING
JOE LIPMAN The Hollywood Palace (ABC)
MARTY PAICH Alice In Wonderland or What's A Nice Kid Like You Doing In A Place Like This? (ABC)

SPECIAL
RAY CHARLES Special vocal material for The Julie Andrews Show (NBC)
CLAUDE FRANK Pianist on Beethoven: Ordeal And Triumph (Saga Of Western Man) (ABC)

INDIVIDUAL ACHIEVEMENTS IN ART DIRECTION AND ALLIED CRAFTS

ART DIRECTION
JAMES TRITTIPO The Hollywood Palace (ABC)
CARROLL CLARK, WILLIAM TUNTKE Further Adventures of Gallegher (Walt Disney's Wonderful World Of Color) (NBC)
WILLIAM J. CREBER Voyage To The Bottom Of The Sea (ABC)
GEORGE DAVIS, MERRILL PYE, JAMES SULLIVAN The Man From U.N.C.L.E. (NBC)
TOM JOHN Color Me Barbra (CBS)
EDWARD STEPHENSON The Andy Williams Show (NBC)

SET DECORATION
HENRY GRACE, FRANCISCO LOMBARDO, JACK MILLS, CHARLES THOMPSON The Man From U.N.C.L.E. (NBC)
BILL HARP Color Me Barbra (CBS)
NORMAN ROCKETT Voyage to The Bottom Of The Sea (ABC)

COSTUME DESIGN
RAY AGHAYAN, BOB MACKIE Wonderful World of Burlesque II - Danny Thomas Special (NBC)

WARDROBE
ED SMITH The Hollywood Palace (ABC)

MAKE-UP
BOB O'BRADOVICH Inherit The Wind (Hallmark Hall Of Fame) (NBC)

SPECIAL
ARNOLD GOODE, BILL GRAHAM, BOB MURDOCK For creating the unusual props for The Man From U.N.C.L.E. (NBC)
ROBERT TAIT For the mechanical effects on Voyage to The Bottom Of The Sea (ABC)

INDIVIDUAL ACHIEVEMENTS IN CINEMATOGRAPHY

CINEMATOGRAPHY
WINTON C. HOCH Voyage to The Bottom Of the Sea (ABC)
HASKELL BOGGS, WILLIAM F. WHITLEY Bonanza (NBC)
FRED KOENEKAMP The Man From U.N.C.L.E. (NBC)
LIONEL LINDON The Cold, Cold War Of Paul Bryan (Run For Your Life) (NBC)
MEREDITH M. NICHOLSON The Fugitive (ABC)
TOM PRIESTLEY Michelangelo: The Last Giant (NBC)
TED VOIGTLANDER The Wild, Wild West (CBS)

SPECIAL
L. B. ABBOTT, HOWARD LYDECKER For photographic effects on Voyage To The Bottom Of The Sea (ABC)
L. B. ABBOTT, HOWARD LYDECKER For photographic effects on Lost In Space (CBS)
EDWARD ANCONA Color Co-ordinator on Bonanza (NBC)

INDIVIDUAL ACHIEVEMENTS IN FILM EDITING
DAVID BLEWITT, WILLIAM T. CARTWRIGHT The Making Of The President 1964 (CBS)
MARVIN COIL, EVERETT DOUGLAS, ELLSWORTH HOAGLAND Bonanza (NBC)
JAMES BAIOTTO, ROBERT BELCHER, RICHARD WORMELL Voyage to The Bottom Of The Sea (ABC)
HENRY BERMAN, JOSEPH DERVIN, WILLIAM GULICK The Man From U.N.C.L.E. (NBC)
LOFTUS McDONOUGH Michelangelo: The Last Giant (NBC)

INDIVIDUAL ACHIEVEMENTS IN SOUND EDITING
JAMES BOURGEOIS Mutual Of Omaha's Wild Kingdom (NBC)
ROBERT CORNETT, DON HALL, JR., DONALD HIGGINS, ELWELL JACKSON Voyage To The Bottom Of The Sea (ABC)
RICHARD LEGRAND, ROSS TAYLOR, HAROLD WOOLEY, RALPH HICKEY Batman (ABC)
JOHN J. LIPOW, WILLIAM RIVAL The Man From U.N.C.L.E. (NBC)

INDIVIDUAL ACHIEVEMENTS IN ELECTRONIC PRODUCTION

AUDIO ENGINEERING
LAURENCE SCHNEIDER Seventh Annual Young Performers Program (New York Philharmonic Young People's Concerts With Leonard Bernstein) (CBS)
WILLIAM COLE The Andy Williams Show (NBC)
HERMAN LEWIS Perry Mason (CBS)

VIDEO TAPE EDITING
CRAIG CURTIS, ART SCHNEIDER The Julie Andrews Show (NBC)
STAN CHLEBEK, CRAIG CURTIS, ART SCHNEIDER Lorne Greene's American West (NBC)

VIDEO CONTROL
ARNOLD DICK Bell Telephone Hour (NBC)

LIGHTING
LON STUCKY Frank Sinatra: A Man And His Music (NBC)
ROBERT BARRY Color Me Barbra (CBS)
JOHN FRESCHI The Andy Williams Show (NBC)
PHIL HYMES Bell Telephone Hour (NBC)

TECHNICAL DIRECTORS
O. TAMBURRI Inherit The Wind (Hallmark Hall Of Fame) (NBC)
KARL MESSERSCHMIDT The Dean Martin Show (NBC)

ELECTRONIC CAMERAMEN
MIKE ENGLISH, EMIL HUSNI, AL LORETO, JOHN LINCOLN The Strollin' 20's (CBS)

SPECIAL ELECTRONIC EFFECTS
MILT ALTMAN the Julie Andrews Show (NBC)

INDIVIDUAL ACHIEVEMENTS IN ENGINEERING DEVELOPMENT
Because of the unique nature of engineering developments all possible achievements in this awards year were considered by the Blue Ribbon Panel.
STOP ACTION PLAYBACK MVR Corporation and CBS
EARLY BIRD SATELLITE Hughes Aircraft Company and Communications Satellite Corporation

SPECIAL CLASSIFICATIONS OF INDIVIDUAL ACHIEVEMENTS
BURR TILLSTROM For his "Berlin Wall" hand ballet on That Was The Week That Was (NBC)
ART CARNEY For his performance as ED NORTON on The Adoption (The Jackie Gleason Show) (CBS)
NICK CASTLE Choreographer of The Andy Williams Show (NBC)
TONY CHARMOLI Choreograher of The Danny Kaye Show (CBS)
TONY CHARMOLI Choreographer of The Julie Andrews Show (NBC)
ROBERT HARTUNG For the adaption of Inherit The Wind (Hallmark Hall Of Fame) (NBC)
GENE KELLY For his performance on The Julie Andrews Show (NBC)
CARL REINER For the voices on Linus The Lionhearted (CBS)
CHARLES SCHULZ Writer of A Charlie Brown Christmas (CBS)

THE INTERNATIONAL AWARD

NON-FICTION
WYVERN AT WAR - NO. 2 "BREAKOUT" (Westward Television Limited, Plymouth, England)
THE HOUSE ON THE BEACH (Rediffusion Television Limited, London, England)
MOZART IN PRAGUE (Osterreichischer Rundfunk/Fernsehen, Vienna, Austria)

FICTION
STASERA RITA (RAI-Radiotelevisione Italiana, Rome, Italy)
THE SUCCESSOR (Anglia-Television Limited, Norwich, England)
THE TALE OF GENJI (Mainichi Broadcasting System, Inc., Osaka, Japan)

THE STATION AWARD
I SEE CHICAGO (WBBM-TV, Chicago, Illinois)
AS THEY LIKE IT (KGW-TV, Portland, Oregon)
THE CORNER (DTVI, St. Louis, Missouri)
GOVERNMENT BY GASLIGHT (WJXT-TV, Jacksonville, Florida)
GUNS ARE FOR KILLING (KPRC-TV, Houston, Texas)
MAKE A JOYFUL SOUND (WCBS-TV, New York, New York)
THE MINER'S STORY (WCAU-TV, Philadelphia, Pennsylvania)
NO DEPOSIT - NO RETURN (KRON-TV, San Francisco, California)
VIET NAM '65: A DISTANT CHRISTMAS (WWL-TV, New Orleans, Louisiana)

TRUSTEES AWARD
EDWARD R. MURROW Who brought together the highest qualities of broadcasting and journalism so that he became a symbol to colleagues and the public alike of the complete broadcast journalist.

TRUSTEES AWARD
XEROX CORPORATION
For its presentation of some of the finest art, news and historical documentaries.

1966/67

OUTSTANDING COMEDY SERIES
THE MONKEES (NBC) Bert Schneider and Bob Rafelson, Producers
BEWITCHED (ABC) William Froug, Producer
GET SMART! (NBC) Arnie Rosen, Producer
THE ANDY GRIFFITH SHOW (CBS) Bob Ross, Producer
HOGAN'S HEROES (CBS) Edward H. Feldman, Producer

OUTSTANDING VARIETY SERIES
Awards to Producer and Star

THE ANDY WILLIAMS SHOW (NBC) Edward Stephenson and Bob Finkel, Producers
THE DEAN MARTIN SHOW (NBC) Greg Garrison, Producer
THE JACKIE GLEASON SHOW (CBS) Ronald Wayne, Producer
HOLLYWOOD PALACE (ABC) Nick Vanoff and William O. Harbach, Producers
THE SMOTHERS BROTHERS COMEDY HOUR STARRING TOM AND DICK SMOTHERS (CBS) Saul Ilson and Ernest Chambers, Producers
THE TONIGHT SHOW STARRING JOHNNY CARSON (NBC) Art Stark, Producer

OUTSTANDING VARIETY SPECIAL
Awards to Producer and Star

THE SID CAESAR, IMOGENE COCA, CARL REINER, HOWARD MORRIS SPECIAL (CBS) Jack Arnold, Producer
CHRYSLER PRESENTS THE BOB HOPE CHRISTMAS SPECIAL (NBC) Bob Hope, Executive Producer
A TIME FOR LAUGHTER: A LOOK AT NEGRO HUMOR IN AMERICA (ABC Stage 67) Phil Stein, Producer
DICK VAN DYKE (CBS) Byron Paul and Jack Donohue, Producers

OUTSTANDING DRAMATIC SERIES
MISSION: IMPOSSIBLE (CBS) Joseph Gantman and Bruce Geller, Producers
THE AVENGERS (ABC) Julian Wintle, Executive Producer
I SPY (NBC) David Friedkin and Mort Fine, Producers
RUN FOR YOUR LIFE (NBC) Jo Swerling, Jr. Producer
STAR TREK (NBC) Gene Coon and Eugene Roddenberry, Producers

OUTSTANDING DRAMATIC PROGRAM
A single program or a series

DEATH OF A SALESMAN (CBS) David Susskind and Daniel Melnick, Producers
A CHRISTMAS MEMORY (ABC Stage 67) (ABC) Frank Perry, Producer
THE FINAL WAR OF OLLY WINTER (CBS Playhouse) (CBS) Fred Coe, Producer
THE GLASS MENAGERIE (CBS Playhouse) (CBS) Davis Susskind, Producer
THE LOVE SONG OF BARNEY KEMPINSKI (ABC Stage 67) (ABC) Marc Merson, Producer
MARK TWAIN TONIGHT! (CBS) David Susskind, Producer

OUTSTANDING MUSICAL PROGRAM
A special program, one of a series or a series - Awards to Producer and Star

BRIGADOON (ABC) Fielder Cook, Producer
FRANK SINATRA: A MAN AND HIS MUSIC PART II (CBS) Dwight Hemion, Producer
TOSCANINI: THE MAESTRO REVISTED (Bell Telephone Hour) (NBC)
Gerald Green, Producer

OUTSTANDING CHILDREN'S PROGRAM
A special program, one of a series or a series

JACK AND THE BEANSTALK (NBC) Gene Kelly, Producer
CHARLIE BROWN'S ALL STARS (CBS) Lee Mendelson and Bill Melendez, Producers
DISCOVERY '66-'67 (ABC) Jules Power, Executive Producer
IT'S THE GREAT PUMPKIN, CHRLIE BROWN (CBS) Lee Mendelson and Bill Melendez, Producers

OUTSTANDING SINGLE PERFORMANCE BY AN ACTOR IN A LEADING ROLE IN A DRAMA
PETER USTINOV as SOCRATES Barefoot in Athens (Hallmark Hall of Fame) (NBC)
ALAN ARKIN as BARNEY KEMPINSKI The Love Song of Barney Kempinski (ABC Stage 67) (ABC)
LEE J. COBB as WILLY LOMAN Death Of A Salesman (CBS)
IVAN DIXON as OLLY WINTER The Final War of Olly Winter (CBS Playhouse) (CBS)
HAL HOLBROOK as MARK TWAIN Mark Twain Tonight! (CBS)

OUTSTANDING SINGLE PERFORMANCE BY AN ACTRESS IN A LEADING ROLE IN A DRAMA
GERALDINE PAGE as SOOKIE A Christmas Memory (ABC Stage 67) (ABC)
SHIRLEY BOOTH as AMANDA The Glass Menagerie (CBS Playhouse) (CBS)
MILDRED DUNNOCK as LINDA LOMAN Death Of A Salesman (CBS)
LYNN FONTANNE as DOWAGER EMPRESS Anastasia (Hallmark Hall of Fame) (NBC)
JULIE HARRIS as ANASTASIA Anastasia (Hallmark Hall of Fame) (NBC)

OUTSTANDING CONTINUED PERFORMANCE BY AN ACTOR IN A LEADING ROLE IN A DRAMATIC SERIES
BILL COSBY as ALEXANDER SCOTT (I Spy) (NBC)
ROBERT CULP as KELLY ROBINSON (I Spy) (NBC)
BEN GAZZARA as PAUL BRYAN (Run For Your Life) (NBC)
DAVID JANSSEN as DR. RICHARD KIMBLE (The Fugitive) (ABC)
MARTIN LANDAU as ROLLIN HAND (Mission: Impossible) (CBS)

OUTSTANDING CONTINUED PERFORMANCE BY AN ACTRESS IN A LEADING ROLE IN A DRAMATIC SERIES
BARBARA BAIN as CINNAMON CARTER (Mission: Impossible) (CBS)
DIANA RIGG as MRS. EMMA PEEL (The Avengers) (ABC)
BARBARA STANWYCK as VICTORIA BARKLEY (The Big Valley) (ABC)

OUTSTANDING CONTINUED PERFORMANCE BY AN ACTOR IN A LEADING ROLE IN A COMEDY SERIES
DON ADAMS as MAXWELL SMART (Get Smart!) (NBC)
BOB CRANE as COL. ROBERT HOGAN (Hogan's Heroes) (CBS)
BRIAN KEITH as BILL DAVIS (Family Affair) (CBS)
LARRY STORCH as CORPORAL AGARN (F Troop) (ABC)

OUTSTANDING CONTINUED PERFORMANCE BY AN ACTRESS IN A LEADING ROLE IN A COMEDY SERIES

LUCILLE BALL as LUCY CARMICHAEL (The Lucy Show) (CBS)
ELIZABETH MONTGOMERY as SAMANTHA STEVENS (Bewitched) (ABC)
AGNES MOOREHEAD as ENDORA (Bewitched) (ABC)
MARLO THOMAS as ANN MARIE (That Girl) (ABC)

OUTSTANDING PERFORMANCE BY AN ACTOR IN A SUPPORTING ROLE IN A DRAMA
A single program or a series

ELI WALLACH as LOCARNO The Poppy Is Also A Flower (Xerox Special) (ABC)
LEO G. CARROLL as ALEXANDER WAVERLY (The Man From U.N.C.L.E.) (NBC)
LEONARD NIMOY as MR. SPOCK (Star Trek) (NBC)

OUTSTANDING PERFORMANCE BY AN ACTRESS IN A SUPPORTING ROLE IN A DRAMA
A single program or a series

AGNES MOOREHEAD as EMMA VALENTINE Night of the Vicious Valentine (The Wild, Wild West) (CBS)
TINA CHEN as VIETMANESE GIRL The Final War of Olly Winter (CBS Playhouse) (CBS)
RUTH WARRICK as HANNAH CORD (Peyton Place) (ABC)

OUTSTANDING PERFORMANCE BY AN ACTOR IN A SUPPORTING ROLE IN A COMEDY
A single program or a series

DON KNOTTS as BARNEY FIFE Barney Comes to Mayberry (The Andy Griffith Show) (CBS)
GALE GORDON as THEODORE MOONEY (The Lucy Show) (CBS)
WERNER KLEMPERER as COL. WILHELM KLINK (Hogan's Heroes) (CBS)

OUTSTANDING PERFORMANCE BY AN ACTRESS IN A SUPPORTING ROLE IN A COMEDY
A single program or a series

FRANCES BAVIER as AUNT BEE (The Andy Griffith Show) (CBS)
NANCY KULP as GRANNY (The Beverly Hillbillies) (CBS)
MARION LORNE as AUNT CLARA (Bewitched) (ABC)

OUTSTANDING WRITING ACHIEVEMENT IN DRAMA
A special program or one of a series

BRUCE GELLER (Mission: Impossible) (CBS)
ROBERT CULP The Warlord (I Spy) (NBC)
RONALD RIBMAN The Final War of Olly Winter (CBS Playhouse) (CBS)

OUTSTANDING WRITING ACHIEVEMENT IN COMEDY
A special program, one of a series or a series

BUCK HENRY, LEONARD STERN Ship of Spies (2 parts) (Get Smart!) (NBC)
EDMUND HARTMANN Buffy (Family Affair) (CBS)
SIDNEY SHELDON (I Dream of Jeannie) (NBC)

OUTSTANDING WRITING ACHIEVEMENT IN VARIETY
A special program, one of a series or a series

MEL BROOKS, SAM DENOFF, BILL PERSKY, CARL REINER, MEL TOLKIN The Sid Caesar, Imogene Coca, Carl Reiner, Howard Morris Special (CBS)
HARRY CRANE, RICH EUSTIS, LEE HALE, PAUL KEYES, AL ROGERS The Dean Martin Show (NBC)
MARVIN MARX, WALTER STONE, ROD PARKER The Jackie Gleason Show (CBS)

OUTSTANDING DIRECTORIAL ACHIEVEMENT IN DRAMA
A special program, one of a series or a series

ALEX SEGAL Death Of A Salesman (CBS)
PAUL BOGART The Final War of Olly Winter (CBS Playhouse) (CBS)
PAUL BOGART Mark Twain Tonight! (CBS)
GEORGE SCHAEFER Anastasia (Hallmark Hall of Fame) (NBC)

OUTSTANDING DIRECTORIAL ACHIEVEMENT IN COMEDY
A special program, one of a series or a series

JAMES FRAWLEY Royal Flush (The Monkees) (NBC)
WILLIAM ASHER (Bewitched)(ABC)
EARL BELLAMY One Of Our Bombs Is Missing (I Spy) (NBC)
WILLIAM RUSSELL (Family Affair) (CBS)
MAURY THOMPSON (The Lucy Show) (CBS)

OUTSTANDING DIRECTORIAL ACHIEVEMENT IN VARIETY OR MUSIC
A special program, one of a series or a series

FIELDER COOK Brigadoon (ABC)
GREG GARRISON The Dean Martin Show (NBC)
DWIGHT HEMION Frank Sinatra: A Man And His Music Part II (CBS)
BOB HENRY The Andy Williams Show (NBC)
BILL HOBIN The Sid Caesar, Imogene Coca, Carl Reiner, Howard Morris Special (CBS)

THE CRAFT AND PROGRAMMING AREAS
(Possibility of Multiple Awards)

PROGRAM AND INDIVIDUAL ACHIEVEMENTS IN NEWS AND DOCUMENTARIES

PROGRAMS

CHINA: THE ROOTS OF MADNESS (Syndicated) Mel Stuart, Producer
HALL OF KINGS (ABC) Harry Rasky, Producer
THE ITALIANS (CBS) Bernard Birnbaum, Producer
THE ANGRY VOICES OF WATTS (NBC) Stuart Schulberg, Producer
CBS REPORTS (CBS) Palmer Williams, Executive Producer
THE HOMOSEXUALS (CBS Reports) (CBS) Harry Morgan, Producer
IF IT'S TUESDAY, THIS MUST BE BELGIUM (CBS) J. C. Sheers, Producer
ORGANIZED CRIME IN AMERICA (American White Paper) (NBC) Fred

Freed, Executive Producer

INDIVIDUALS

THEODORE H. WHITE Writer of China: The Roots of Madness (Syndicated)
LUIGI BARZINI Narrator of The Italians (CBS)
LUIGI BARZINI AND PERRY WOLFF Writers of The Italians (CBS)
WALTER CRONKITE Commentator on CBS Evening News With Walter Cronkite (CBS)
CHET HUNTLEY AND DAVID BRINKLEY Commentators on Huntley-Brinkley Report (NBC)
JAMES MASON Narrator of Hall of Kings (ABC)
FRANK McGEE Commentator on The Frank McGee Report (NBC)
BUDD SCHULBERG Writer of The Angry Voices of Watts (NBC)
ERIC SEVAREID Commentator on CBS Evening News With Walter Cronkite (CBS)
HOWARD K. SMITH Commentator on Elections '66 (ABC)

INDIVIDUAL ACHIEVEMENTS IN ART DIRECTION AND ALLIED CRAFTS

ART DIRECTION

EARL G. CARLSON Set Decorator for Death Of A Salesman (CBS)
TOM JOHN Art Director for Death Of A Salesman (CBS)

COSTUME DESIGN

RAY AGHAYAN AND BOB MACKIE Alice Through The Looking Glass (NBC)

MAKE-UP

DICK SMITH Mark Twain Tonight! (CBS)
CLAUDE THOMPSON Alice Through The Looking Glass (NBC)

MECHANICAL SPECIAL EFFECTS

JIM RUGG Star Trek (NBC)
ROBERT TAIT Voyage To The Bottom Of The Sea (ABC)

INDIVIDUAL ACHIEVEMENTS IN CINEMATOGRAPHY

CINEMATOGRAPHY

HASKELL BOGGS, WILLIAM F. WHITELY Bonanza (NBC)

PHOTOGRAPHIC SPECIAL EFFECTS

L. B. ABBOTT The Time Tunnel (ABC)
L. B. ABBOTT Voyage To The Bottom Of The Sea (ABC)
DARRELL ANDERSON, LINWOOD G. DUNN, JOSEPH WESTHEIMER Star Trek (NBC)

INDIVIDUAL ACHIEVEMENTS IN FILM AND SOUND EDITING

PAUL KRASNY, ROBERT WATTS For Film Editing on Mission: Impossible (CBS)
DON HALL, DICK LEGRAND, DANIEL MANDELL, JOHN MILLS For Sound Editing on Voyage To The Bottom Of The Sea (ABC)
DOUGLAS H. GRINDSTAFF For Sound Editing on Star Trek (NBC)

INDIVIDUAL ACHIEVEMENTS IN ELECTRONIC PRODUCTION

TECHNICAL DIRECTORS

A. J. CUNNINGHAM Brigadoon (ABC)
A. J. CUNNINGHAM Death Of A Salesman (CBS)
KARL MESSERSCHMIDT The Dean Martin Show (NBC)
JOSEPH STRAUSS Frank Sinatra: A Man And His Music Part II (CBS)
O. TAMBURRI Damn Yankees (NBC)

LIGHTING DIRECTORS

LEARD DAVIS Brigadoon (ABC)
LEARD DAVIS Death Of A Salesman (CBS)
JOHN FRESCHI The Andy Williams Show (NBC)
LON STUCKY Frank Sinatra: A Man And His Music Part II (CBS)

VIDEO TAPE EDITING

JAMES E. BRADY Death Of A Salesman (CBS)
JAMES E. BRADY Brigadoon (ABC)
LEWIS W. SMITH The Red Skelton Hour (CBS)

AUDIO ENGINEERING

BILL COLE Frank Sinatra: A Man And His Music Part II (CBS)
RAY KEMPER Brigadoon (ABC)

SOUND RECORDING

FRED BOSCH The Cleveland Orchestra: One Man's Triumph (Bell Telephone Hour) (NBC)

ELECTRONIC CAMERAMEN

ROBERT DUNN, GORM ERICKSON, BEN WOLF, NICK DEMOS Brigadoon (ABC)
ROBERT DUNN, GORM ERICKSON, FRED GOUGH, JACK JENNINGS, DICK NELSON Death Of A Salesman (CBS)

INDIVIDUAL ACHIEVEMENTS IN ENGINEERING DEVELOPMENT

Because of the unique nature of engineering developments all possible achievements in this awards year were considered by the Blue Ribbon Panel.

PLUMBICON TUBE N. V. Philips Gloeilampenfabrieken
HIGH-BAND VIDEO TAPE RECORDER Ampex Company

SPECIAL CLASSIFICATIONS OF INDIVIDUAL ACHIEVEMENTS

ART CARNEY The Jackie Gleason Show (CBS)
TRUMAN CAPOTE AND ELEANOR PERRY For the adaption of A Christmas Memory (ABC Stage 67) (ABC)
ARTHUR MILLER For the adaption of Death Of a Salesman (CBS)
PETER GENNARO Choreograher of Brigadoon (ABC)
SHELDON KELLER AND GLENN WHEATON Writers of Frank Sinatra: A Man And His Music Part II (CBS)
BIL MELENDEZ Director of children's special It's The Great Pumpkin, Charlie Brown (CBS)
CHARLES SCHULZ Writer of children's special It's The Great Pumpkin, Charlie Brown (CBS)
CHARLES SCULZ Writer of children's special Charlie Brown's All Stars (CBS)
BURR TILLSTROM Puppeteer on Perry Como's Kraft Music Hall (NBC)

PROGRAM AND INDIVIDUAL ACHIEVEMENTS IN DAYTIME PROGRAMMING

PROGRAMS

MUTUAL OF OMAHA'S WILD KINGDOM (NBC) Don Meier, Producer
G. E. COLLEGE BOWL (NBC) John Cleary, Producer
THE MIKE DOUGLAS SHOW (Syndicated) Larry Rosen, Producer

INDIVIDUALS

MIKE DOUGLAS Master of Ceremonies on The Mike Douglas Show (Syndicated)
TOM KENNEDY Master of Ceremonies on You Don't Say (NBC)
GENE RAYBURN Master of Ceremonies on The Match Game (NBC)

PROGRAM AND INDIVIDUAL ACHIEVEMENTS IN SPORTS

PROGRAMS
ABC'S WIDE WORLD OF SPORTS (ABC) Roone Arledge, Executive Producer
PORTRAIT OF WILLIE MAYS (ABC) Robert Riger, Producer
SHELL'S WONDERFUL WORLD OF GOLF (NBC) Fred Raphael, Producer

INDIVIDUAL
JIM McKAY Sports Commentator on Fifth Anniversary Program (ABC's Wide World of Sports) (ABC)
CHRIS SCHENKEL Sports Commentator on Portrait of a Team (ABC)
CHRIS SCHENKEL Sports Commentator on NBA Basketball (ABC)

INDIVIDUAL ACHIEVEMENTS IN MUSIC

COMPOSITION
AARON COPLAND Thematic Music on CBS Playhouse (CBS)
EARLE HAGEN I Spy (NBC)
PETE RUGOLO Run For Your Life (NBC)
LALO SCHIFRIN Mission: Impossible (CBS)

CONDUCTORS
GORDON JENKINS AND NELSON RIDDLE Frank Sinatra: A Man And His Music Part II (CBS)

ARRANGERS
RAY ELLIS AND LENNIE HAYTON Lena (Syndicated)
GORDON JENKINS AND NELSON RIDDLE Frank Sinatra: A Man And His Music Part II (CBS)

MUSICAL ROUTINES AND CHORAL DIRECTION
TICKER FREEMAN AND GEORGE WYLE The Andy Williams Show (NBC)

SPECIAL AWARDS

THE INTERNATIONAL AWARD
Finalists judged by Special Committee of former Emmy Award Winners from countries throughout the world

DOCUMENTARY
BIG DEAL AT GOTHENBURG (Tyne Tees Television Limited, Newcastle-upon-Tyne, England)
DARWIN - "THE GALAPAGOS" (Canadian Broadcasting Corporation, Ottawa, Canada)
FAMILY OF MAN (RODZINA CZLOWIECZA) (Film Polski, Warsaw, Poland)

ENTERTAINMENT
THE CARETAKER (Rediffusion Television Limited, London, England)
D.H. LAWRENCE - "THE BLIND MAN" (Granada Television Network Limited, London, England)
PHEDRE (Office de Radiodiffusion Television Francaise, O.R.T.F., Paris, France)
BERNARD SHOW (Societe Suisse de Radiodiffusion et Television, Swiss Television, Zurich, Switzerland)

THE STATION AWARD
Regional Winners judged by Committees at National Academy Chapters; Final judging by Special Committee
THE ROAD TO NOWHERE (KLZ-TV, Denver, Colorado)
ASSIGNMENT: 1747 RANDOLPH STREET (WFIL-TV, Philadelphia, Pennsylvania)
A BABY IS A WONDERFUL THING (WBAL-TV, Baltimore, Maryland)
THE FACE OF GENIUS (WBZ-TV Boston, Massachusetts)
FIVE CIVILIZED TRIBES: AN UNFINISHED JOURNEY (KTUL-TV, Tulsa, Oklahoma)
THE GOLDEN CALF (KGW-TV, Portland, Oregon)
I SEE CHICAGO: THE ILLINOIS VOTER'S TEST (WBBM-TV, Chicago, Illinois)
THE LENGTHENING SHADOW (KSD-TV, St. Louis, Missouri)
MEDAL OF VALOR (KTTV, Hollywood, California)

TRUSTEES AWARD
SYLVESTER L. "PAT" WEAVER, JR.
"For his constant conviction that the American public deserves better than it gets on the television screen; for introducing the "special" to television, thus breathing new life into the weekly schedule; for providing us with TODAY and TONIGHT; but finally and most importantly, for the imagination, leadership, courage and integrity which he has brought to our medium during the eighteen years he has been a part of it."

1967/68

NEWS AND DOCUMENTARY PROGRAM AND INDIVIDUAL ACHIEVEMENTS
(Possibility of one Award, more than one Award, or no Award)

OUTSTANDING ACHIEVEMENT WITHIN REGULARLY SCHEDULED NEWS PROGRAMS

PROGRAMS
CRISIS IN THE CITIES (Public Broadcast Laboratory) (NET) Av Westin, Executive Producer
COVERAGE OF THE MILWAUKEE OPEN HOUSING CRISIS, FATHER GROPPI, DEMONSTRATIONS, RIOTS (The Huntley/Brinkley Report) (NBC) Robert J. Northshield, Executive Producer
IMMEDIATE AND ON-THE-SPOT COVERAGE OF THE TET ATTACKS (The Huntley/Brinkley Report) (NBC) Ron Steiman, Chief of NBC News' Saigon Bureau
POLICE CHIEF EXECUTING VC DURING TET ATTACK (The Huntley/Brinkley Report) (NBC) Robert J. Northshield, Executive Producer
SGT. SIMPSON: VIETNAM (Peter Jennings With The News) (ABC) Ken Gale and Sandy Goodman, Producers

INDIVIDUALS
JOHN LAURENCE AND KEITH KAY CBS News Correspondent and CBS News Cameraman, Respectively, For "Ist Cavalry," "Con Thien" And Other Segments (CBS Evening News With Walter Cronkite) (CBS)
DEAN BRELIS For Coverage of Attack on Hills 882 and 875 (The Huntley/Brinkley Report) (NBC)
KIRK BROWNING For Direction of "Crisis In The Cities" (Public Broadcast Laboratory) (NET)
WINSTON BURDETT CBS News Correspondent, For Middle East Coverage (CBS Evening News With Walter Cronkite and CBS News Special Reports) (CBS)
WALTER CRONKITE CBS News Correspondent, For Vietnam Coverage (CBS Evening News With Walter Cronkite and Report From Vietnam by Walter Cronkite) (CBS)
DAVID DOUGLAS DUNCAN For Still Photo Essays on the Marines Under Bombardment at Con Thien and Khesanh (ABC Evening News

With Bob Young) (ABC)
DON FARMER Correspondent, For Reports On The Black And White Communities Preparing For Another Apparently Long Hot Summer (ABC Evening News With Bob Young) (ABC)
PETER JENNINGS For Dramatic Report on Fred Esherick, a 15 Year-Old Boy Facing Death For Killing His Father (ABC Evening News With Bob Young) (ABC)
CHARLES KURALT AND JAMES WILSON CBS News Correspondent and CBS News Cameraman, Respectively, For "On The Road" (CBS Evening News With Walter Cronkite) (CBS)
WALTER LIPPMAN For Walter Lippman On Vietnam And Politics (Public Broadcast Laboratory)(NET)
EDWARD P. MORGAN Program Commentator, for Public Broadcast Laboratory (Series) And Particularly "A Conversation With Dean Acheson" (Public Broadcast Laboratory) (NET)
ERIC SEVAREID CBS News National Correspondent (CBS Evening News With Walter Cronkite) (CBS)
HOWARD K. SMITH, JOHN SCALI, WILLIAM H. LAWRENCE, JOSEPH C. HARSCH For Their Commentaries On Vietnam, Politics and Various Domestic Issues (Evening News) (ABC)
HOWARD TUCKNER For Reporting While Wounded in Vietnam (The Huntley/Brinkley Report) (NBC)
AV WESTIN Executive Producer For Public Broadcast Laboratory (Series) And Particularly "George Wallace's America" (Public Broadcast Laboratory) (NET)

OUTSTANDING ACHIEVEMENT IN COVERAGE OF SPECIAL EVENTS

PROGRAMS
NEWS ANALYSIS (State of the Union/68) (NET) Jim Karayn, Producer
CBS NEWS CONTINUOUS COVERAGE OF WAR IN MIDDLE EAST (CBS News Special Reports and Special Broadcasts) (CBS) Harold Haley, Ernest Leiser, Phillip Lewis, and Robert Wussler, Producers
CBS NEWS SPECIAL REPORT: VIETNAM PERSPECTIVE: THE ORDEAL OF CON THIEN (CBS) Burton Benjamin, Producer
COMPLETE LIVE COVERAGE OF THE UNITED NATIONS DURING THE MIDDLE EAST CRISIS (NBC) James Kitchell, Producer
COVERAGE OF THE MIDDLE EAST WAR AND OTHER SPECIALS FROM THE U.N. (War In The Middle East) (ABC) Walter Pfister, Jr., Executive Producer
SATELLITE COVERAGE OF ADENAUER'S FUNERAL (NBC) James Kitchell, Producer
SATELLITE COVERAGE OF POPE'S VISIT TO FATIMA (NBC) James Kitchell, Producer

INDIVIDUALS
FRANK McGEE For His Commentary on Satellite Coverage of Adenauer's Funeral (NBC)
WALTER CRONKITE CBS News Correspondent, For His Coverage of Apollo 4 (Saturn V) (CBS News Special Report: The Flight of Apollo 4) (CBS)

OUTSTANDING ACHIEVEMENT IN NEWS DOCUMENTARIES

PROGRAMS
AFRICA (ABC) James Fleming, Executive Producer
SUMMER '67: WHAT WE LEARNED (NBC) Fred Freed, Producer
ABC SCOPE: THE VIETNAM WAR Series (ABC) Arthur Holch, Executive Producer
CBS NEWS INQUIRY: THE WARREN REPORT (CBS News Hour) (CBS) Leslie Midgley, Producer
CBS NEWS SPECIAL: DESTINATION: NORTH POLE (CBS) Palmer Williams, Producer
CBS NEWS SPECIAL: VIET CONG (CBS News Hour) (CBS) James B. Faichney, Producer
CBS NEWS SPECIAL REPORT: MORLEY SAFER'S RED CHINA DIARY (CBS News Hour) (CBS) Morley Safer, Producer
CBS REPORTS: WHAT ABOUT RONALD REAGAN? (CBS News Hour) (CBS) Gene De Poris, Producer
ISRAEL: VICTORY OR ELSE (NBC) George Murray, Producer
KHRUSHCHEV IN EXILE (NBC) Lucy Jarvis, Producer
ON FACE VALUE (Your Dollar's Worth) (NET) Ofra Bikel, Producer
THE POOR PAY MORE (NET Journal) (NET) Morton Silverstein, Producer
SAME MUD, SAME BLOOD (NBC) Eliot Frankel, Producer
SOUTHERN ACCENTS, NORTHERN GHETTOS (ABC) William Peters, Producer
SOVIETS IN SPACE (NBC) George Vicas, Producer
SUMMER '67: WHAT WE LEARNED (NBC) Fred Freed, Producer
WAR IN THE SKIES (ABC) Lester Cooper, Producer
THE WAY IT IS (NET Journal) (NET) Harold Mayer, Producer
WHAT HARVEST FOR THE REAPER? (NET Journal) (NET) Morton Silverstein, Producer
WHERE IS PREJUDICE? (NET Journal) (NET) Richard McCutchen, Producer
WHO IN '68? (ABC) Paul Altmeyer, Producer

INDIVIDUALS
HARRY REASONER Writer of CBS Reports: What About Ronald Reagan? (CBS)
VO HUYNH Cameraman on Same Mud, Same Blood (NBC)
ETHEL HUBER For Music Supervision on CBS News Special: Road Signs On a Merry-Go-Round (CBS)
JOHN LAURENCE Correspondent on CBS News Special Report: Vietnam Perspective: The Ordeal Of Con Thien (CBS)
PETER McINTYRE Soundman on Same Mud, Same Blood (NBC)
MASAAKI SHIHARA Soundman on Same Mud, Same Blood (NBC)
JERI SOPANEN Cameraman on The Way It is (NET Journal) (NET)

OUTSTANDING ACHIEVEMENT IN CULTURAL DOCUMENTARIES

PROGRAMS
CBS NEWS SPECIAL: ERIC HOFFER: THE PASSIONATE STATE OF MIND (CBS News Hour) (CBS) Harry Morgan, Producer
CBS NEWS SPECIAL: GAUGUIN IN TAHITI: THE SEARCH FOR PARADISE (CBS News Hour) (CBS) Martin Carr, Producer
JOHN STEINBECK'S "AMERICA AND AMERICANS" (NBC) Lee Mendelson, Producer
DYLAN THOMAS: THE WORLD I BREATHE (NET Festival) (NET) Perry Miller Adato, Producer
AMERICAN PROFILE: MUSIC FROM THE LAND (American Profile) (NBC) Chet Hagan, Producer
AMERICAN PROFILE: THE NATIONAL GALLERY OF ART (American Profile) (NBC) Louis J. Hazam, Producer
AN EVENING AT TANGLEWOOD (NBC) George A. Heinemann, Producer
CAN YOU HEAR ME? (ABC) Lester Cooper, Producer
CBS NEWS SPECIAL: GALILEO GALILEI (CBS) Pamela Ilott, Producer
CBS NEWS SPECIAL: ROAD SIGNS ON A MERRY-GO-ROUND (CBS) Joseph Clement, Producer
DIALOGUE: MARTIN BUBER AND ISRAEL (NET) Michael Roemer and Robert Young, Producers
DUKE ELLINGTON: LOVE YOU MADLY (NET) Richard Moore and Ralph S. Gleason, Producers
EVERETT DIRKSEN'S WASHINGTON (ABC) James Benjamin, Producer
LIFE AND TIMES OF JOHN HUSTON, ESQUIRE (NET) Tom Slevin, Producer
MR. DICKENS OF LONDON (ABC) Daniel E. Wilson, Producer
ROBERT SCOTT AND THE RACE FOR THE SOUTH POLE (ABC) John H. Secondari and Helen Jean Rogers, Producers
THE LAW AND THE PROPHETS (Project 20) (NBC) Donald B. Hyatt, Producer
THE PURSUIT OF EXCELLENCE - THE VIENNA CHOIR BOYS (ABC) Ernest Pendrell, Producer
THE RISE AND FALL OF THE THIRD REICH (ABC) Mel Stuart, Executive Producer; Jack Kaufman, Producer
THE WYETH PHENOMENON ON "WHO, WHAT, WHEN, WHERE, WHY WITH HARRY REASONER" (CBS News Hour) (CBS) Harry Morgan, Producer

INDIVIDUALS

NATHANIEL DORSKY For His Art Photography For CBS News Special: "Gauguin In Tahiti: The Search For Paradise" (CBS News Hour) (CBS)
HARRY MORGAN Writer For the Wyeth Phenomenon On "Who, What, When, Where, Why With Harry Reasoner" (CBS News Hour) (CBS)
THOMAS A. PRIESTLEY AND ROBERT LOWEREE Director of Photography And Film Editor, Respectively, For John Steinbeck's "America and Americans" (NBC)
MARTIN CARR Writer For CBS News Special: "Gauguin In Tahiti: The Search For Paradise" (CBS News Hour) (CBS)
GERALD FRIED Composer For CBS News Special: 'Gauguin In Tahiti: The Search For Paradise" (CBS News Hour) (CBS)
WILLIAM B. HARTIGAN Director Of Photography For Robert Scott And The Race For The South Pole (ABC)
LOUIS J. HAZAM Writer For American Profile: The National Gallery Of Art (American Profile) (NBC)
PETER MOSELEY Film Editor For Life And Times Of John Huston, Esquire (NET)
ERIC SEVAREID Interviewer For CBS News Special: "Eric Hoffer: The Passionate State Of Mind" (CBS News Hour) (CBS)
JOHN WILCOX Cinematographer For CBS News Special: "Gauguin In Tahiti: The Search For Paradise" (CBS News Hour) (CBS)
ROBERT YOUNG Cinematographer For Dialogue: Martin Buber And Israel (NET)

OTHER NEWS AND DOCUMENTARY ACHIEVEMENTS

PROGRAMS

THE 21ST CENTURY (CBS) Isaac Kleinerman, Producer
SCIENCE AND RELIGION: WHO WILL PLAY GOD? (CBS News Special) (CBS) Ben Flynn, Producer
ANIMAL SECRETS Series (NBC) Edward Stanley, Producer
A CONVERSATION WITH SVETLANA ALLILUYEVA (NET Journal) (NET) Henry Morgenthau III, Producer
BOSTON POPS CONCERT FOR YOUNGSTERS (NBC) George A. Heinemann, Producer
DIRECTIONS Series (ABC) Wiley F. Hance, Executive Producer
DISCOVERY '68 Series (ABC) Jules Power, Executive Producer
THE LEARNING PROCESS (NBC) Craig Fisher, Producer
NEW MORALITY: CHALLENGE OF THE STUDENT GENERATION (CBS News Special) (CBS) Chalmers Dale, Producer
OUR WORLD (Global Telecast) (NET) Robert D. Squier, Executive Producer
THE SHEPARDES PLAYE (ABC) Wiley F. Hance, Producer

INDIVIDUAL

GEORGES DELERUE Composer For Our World (Global Telecast) (NET)

ENTERTAINMENT PROGRAM AND INDIVIDUAL ACHIEVEMENTS
(One Award only in each of the remaining Categories)

OUTSTANDING COMEDY SERIES

GET SMART (NBC) Burt Nodella, Producer
BEWITCHED (ABC) William Asher, Producer
FAMILY AFFAIR (CBS) Edmund Hartmann, Producer
HOGAN'S HEROES (CBS) Edward H. Feldman, Producer
THE LUCY SHOW (CBS) Tommy Thompson, Producer

OUTSTANDING DRAMATIC SERIES

MISSION: IMPOSSIBLE (CBS) Joseph E. Gantman, Producer
THE AVENGERS (ABC) Albert Fennell and Brian Clemens, Producers
I SPY (NBC) Morton Fine and David Friedkin, Producers
NET PLAYHOUSE (NET) Curtis Davis, Executive Producer
RUN FOR YOUR LIFE (NBC) Roy Huggins, Executive Producer
STAR TREK (NBC) Gene Roddenberry, Executive Producer

OUTSTANDING DRAMATIC PROGRAM

A single program of a series or a special program

ELIZABETH THE QUEEN (Hallmark Hall of Fame) (NBC) George Schaefer, Producer
DO NOT GO GENTLE INTO THAT GOOD NIGHT (CBS Playhouse) (CBS) George Schaefer, Producer
DEAR FRIENDS (CBS Playhouse) (CBS) Herbert Brodkin, Producer
THE STRANGE CASE OF DR. JEKYLL AND MR. HYDE (ABC) Dan Curtis, Producer
UNCLE VANYA (NET Playhouse) (NET) Sir Laurence Olivier, Producer
LUTHER (Xerox Special) (ABC) Michael Style and Trevor Wallace, Producers

OUTSTANDING MUSICAL OR VARIETY SERIES

Awards to producer and star (if applicable)

ROWAN AND MARTIN'S LAUGH-IN (NBC) George Schlatter, Producer
BELL TELEPHONE HOUR (NBC) Henry Jaffe, Executive Producer; Robert Drew, Michael Jackson and Mel Stuart, Producers
THE CAROL BURNETT SHOW (CBS) Joseph Hamilton, Producer
THE DEAN MARTIN SHOW (NBC) Greg Garrison, Producer
THE SMOTHERS BROTHERS COMEDY HOUR (CBS) Saul Ilson and Ernest Chambers, Producers

OUTSTANDING MUSICAL OR VARIETY PROGRAM

A special program or one of a series Awards to producer and star (if applicable)

ROWAN AND MARTIN'S LAUGH-IN SPECIAL (NBC) George Schlatter, Producer
A MAN AND HIS MUSIC ∎ ELLA ∎ JOBIM (NBC) Robert Sheerer, Producer
CHRYSLER PRESENTS THE BOB HOPE CHRISTMAS SPECIAL (Chrysler Presents the Bob Hope Show) (NBC) Bob Hope, Executive Producer
FIVE BALLETS OF THE FIVE SENSES (Lincoln Center/Stage 5 - Syndicated) (NET) Jac Venza, Producer
THE FRED ASTAIRE SHOW (NBC) Fred Astaire and Gil Rodin, Producers
HERB ALPERT AND THE TIJUANA BRASS (CBS) Gary Smith and Dwight Hemion, Producers

OUTSTANDING SINGLE PERFORMANCE BY AN ACTOR IN A LEADING ROLE IN A DRAMA

MELVYN DOUGLAS as PETER SCHERMAN Do Not Go Gentle Into That Good Night (CBS Playhouse) (CBS)
RAYMOND BURR as CHIEF IRONSIDE Ironside, World Premiere (NBC)
VAN HEFLIN as ROBERT SLOAN A Case of Libel (ABC)
GEORGE C. SCOTT as JOHN PROCTOR The Crucible (CBS)
ELI WALLACH as DOUG LAMBERT Dear Friends (CBS Playhouse) (CBS)

OUTSTANDING SINGLE PERFORMANCE BY AN ACTRESS IN A LEADING ROLE IN A DRAMA

MAUREEN STAPLETON as MARY O'MEAGHAN Among The Paths to Eden (Xerox Special) (ABC)
DAME JUDITH ANDERSON as ELIZABETH Elizabeth The Queen (Hallmark Hall of Fame) (NBC)
GENEVIEVE BUJOLD as JOAN Saint Joan (Hallmark Hall of Fame) (NBC)
COLLEEN DEWHURST as ELIZABETH PROCTOR The Crucible (CBS)
ANNE JACKSON as VIVIAN SPEARS Dear Friends (CBS Playhouse) (CBS)

OUTSTANDING CONTINUED PERFORMANCE BY AN ACTOR IN A LEADING ROLE IN A DRAMATIC SERIES

BILL COSBY as ALEXANDER SCOTT (I Spy) (NBC)
ROBERT CULP as KELLY ROBINSON (I Spy) (NBC)
RAYMOND BURR as CHIEF IRONSIDE (Ironside) (NBC)
BEN GAZZARA as PAUL BRYAN (Run For Your Life) (NBC)
MARTIN LANDAU as ROLLIN HAND (Mission: Impossible) (CBS)

OUTSTANDING CONTINUED PERFORMANCE BY AN ACTRESS IN A LEADING ROLE IN A DRAMATIC SERIES

BARBARA BAIN as CINNAMON CARTER (Mission: Impossble) (CBS)
DIANA RIGG as MRS. EMMA PEEL (The Avengers) (ABC)
BARBARA STANWYCK as VICTORIA BARKLEY (The Big Valley) (ABC)

OUTSTANDING CONTINUED PERFORMANCE BY AN ACTOR IN A LEADING ROLE IN A COMEDY SERIES

DON ADAMS as MAXWELL SMART (Get Smart) (NBC)
RICHARD BENJAMIN as DICK HOLLISTER (He and She) (CBS)
SEBASTIAN CABOT as FRENCH (Family Affair) (CBS)
BRIAN KEITH as BILL DAVIS (Family Affair) (CBS)
DICK YORK as DARRIN STEVENS (Bewitched) (ABC)

OUTSTANDING CONTINUED PERFORMANCE BY AN ACTRESS IN A LEADING ROLE IN A COMEDY SERIES

LUCILLE BALL as LUCY (The Lucy Show) (CBS)
BARBARA FELDON as AGENT '99' (Get Smart) (NBC)
ELIZABETH MONTGOMERY as SAMANTHA STEVENS (Bewitched) (ABC)
PAULA PRENTISS as PAULA HOLLISTER (He and She) (CBS)
MARLO THOMAS as ANN MARIE (That Girl) (ABC)

OUTSTANDING PERFORMANCE BY AN ACTOR IN A SUPPORTING ROLE IN A DRAMA

A single program of a series, a special program or a series

MILBURN STONE as DOC (Gunsmoke) (CBS)
JOSEPH CAMPANELLA as LEW WICKERSHAM (Mannix) (CBS)
LAWRENCE DOBKIN as GETTLINGER Do Not Go Gentle Into That Good Night (CBS Playhouse) (CBS)
LEONARD NIMOY as MR. SPOCK (Star Trek) (NBC)

OUTSTANDING PERFORMANCE BY AN ACTRESS IN A SUPPORTING ROLE IN A DRAMA

A single program of a series, a special program or a series

BARBARA ANDERSON as OFFICER EVE WHITFIELD (Ironside) (NBC)
LINDA CRISTAL as VICTORIA CANNON (The High Chaparral) (NBC)
TESSIE O'SHEA as TESSIE O'TOOLE The Strange Case of Dr. Jekyll and Mr. Hyde (ABC)

OUTSTANDING PERFORMANCE BY AN ACTOR IN A SUPPORTING ROLE IN A COMEDY

A single program of a series, a special program or a series

WERNER KLEMPERER as COL. WILHELM KLINK (Hogan's Heroes) (CBS)
JACK CASSIDY as OSCAR NORTH (He and She) (CBS)
WILLIAM DEMAREST as UNCLE CHARLEY (My Three Sons) (CBS)
GALE GORDON as THEODORE MOONEY (The Lucy Show) (CBS)

OUTSTANDING PERFORMANCE BY AN ACTRESS IN A SUPPORTING ROLE IN A COMEDY

A single program of a series, a special program or a series

MARION LORNE as AUNT CLARA (Bewitched) (ABC)
AGNES MOOREHEAD as ENDORA (Bewitched) (ABC)
MARGE REDMOND as SISTER JACQUELINE (The Flying Nun) (ABC)
NITA TALBOT as MARYA The Hostage (Hogan's Heroes) (CBS)

OUTSTANDING WRITING ACHIEVEMENT IN DRAMA

A special program or one of a series

LORING MANDEL Do Not Go Gentle Into That Good Night (CBS Playhouse) (CBS)
ALLAN BALTER AND WILLIAM READ WOODFIELD The Seal (Mission: Impossible) (CBS)
DON M. MANKIEWICZ Ironside, World Premiere (NBC)
REGINALD ROSE Dear Friends (CBS Playhouse) (CBS)

OUTSTANDING WRITING ACHIEVEMENT IN COMEDY

A special program or one of a series

ALLAN BURNS AND CHRIS HAYWARD The Coming Out Party (He and She) (CBS)
DANNY ARNOLD AND RUTH BROOKS FLIPPEN The Mailman Cometh (That Girl) (ABC)
MILT JOSEFSBERG AND RAY SINGER Lucy Gets Jack Benny's Account (The Lucy Show) (CBS)
LEONARD STERN AND ARNE SULTAN The Old Man And The She (He and She) (CBS)

OUTSTANDING WRITING ACHIEVEMENT IN MUSIC OR VARIETY

A special program or one of a series

CHRIS BEARD, PHIL HAHN, JACK HANRAHAN, COSLOUGH JOHNSON, PAUL KEYES, MARC LONDON, ALLAN MANNINGS, DAVID PANICH, HUGH WEDLOCK, DIGBY WOLFE Rowan and Martin's Laugh-In (NBC)
BILL ANGELOS, STAN BURNS, DON HINKLEY, BUZ KOHAN, MIKE MARMER, GAIL PARENT, ARNIE ROSEN, KENNY SOLMS, SAUL

TURTLETAUB The Carol Burnett Show (CBS)
LARRY HOVIS, PAUL W. KEYES, JIM MULLIGAN, DAVID PANICH, GEORGE SCHLATTER, DIGBY WOLFE Rowan and Martin's Laugh-In Special (NBC)
TED BERGMAN, ALLAN BLYE, SAM BOBRICK, ERNEST CHAMBERS, RON CLARK, GENE FARMER, HAL GOLDMAN, AL GORDON, SAUL ILSON, JERRY MUSIC, MASON WILLIAMS The Smothers Brothers Comedy Hour (CBS)

OUTSTANDING DIRECTORIAL ACHIEVEMENT IN DRAMA

A special program or one of a series

PAUL BOGART Dear Friends (CBS Playhouse) (CBS)
LEE H. KATZIN The Killing (Mission: Impossble) (CBS)
GEORGE SCHAEFER Do Not Go Gentle Into That Good Night (CBS Playhouse) (CBS)
ALEX SEGAL The Crucible (CBS)

OUTSTANDING DIRECTORIAL ACHIEVEMENT IN COMEDY

A special program or one of a series

BRUCE BILSON Maxwell Smart, Private Eye (Get Smart) (NBC)
DANNY ARNOLD The Apartment (That Girl) (ABC)
JAMES FRAWLEY The Devil and Peter Tork (The Monkees) (NBC)

OUTSTANDING DIRECTORIAL ACHIEVEMENT IN MUSIC OR VARIETY

A special program or one of a series

JACK HALEY, JR. Movin' With Nancy (NBC)
BILL R. FOSTER Rowan and Martin's Laugh-In Special (NBC)
GREG GARRISON The Dean Martin Show (NBC)
DWIGHT HEMION Herb Alpert and the Tijuana Brass (CBS)
GORDON W. WILES Rowan and Martin's Laugh-In, (NBC)

OUTSTANDING ACHIEVEMENT IN MUSICAL COMPOSITION

A special program or one of a series

EARLE HAGEN Laya (I Spy) (NBC)
BERNARD GREEN My Father and My Mother (CBS Playhouse) (CBS)
PETE RUGOLO Cry Hard, Cry Fast (Run For Your Life) (NBC)
LALO SCHIFRIN The Seal (Mission: Impossible) (CBS)
MORTON STEVENS Major Glory (Gunsmoke) (CBS)
HARRY SUKMAN The Champion of the Western World (The High Chaparral) (NBC)

OUTSTANDING ACHIEVEMENT IN ART DIRECTION AND SCENIC DESIGN

A special program or one of a series; Award to Art Director and Scenic Designer - and to Set Decorator (if applicable)

JAMES W. TRITTIPO Art Director for The Fred Astaire Show (NBC)
WARREN CLYMER Art Director for Elizabeth The Queen (Hallmark Hall Of Fame) (NBC)
ROMAIN JOHNSTON AND CHARLES KREINER Art Director and Set Decorator, Respectively, for The Smothers Brothers Comedy Hour (CBS)
WILLIAM P. ROSS Art Director for Echo Of Yesterday (Mission: Impossible) (CBS)
JAN SCOTT AND GEORGE GAINES Art Director and Set Decorator, Respectively, for Kismet (Armstrong Circle Theatre) (ABC)

OUTSTANDING ACHIEVEMENT IN CINEMATOGRAPHY

A special program or one of a series

RALPH WOOLSEY A Thief Is A Thief Is A Thief (It Takes A Thief) (ABC)
GORDON AVIL How To Escape From A Prison Camp Without Really Leaving (Hogan's Heroes) (CBS)
WINTON C. HOCH Raiders From Outerspace (Time Tunnel) (ABC)

OUTSTANDING ACHIEVEMENT IN ELECTRONIC CAMERAWORK

A special program or one of a series; Award to Technical Director, with Certificates to Cameramen

A. J. CUNNINGHAM, Technical Director; EDWARD CHANEY, ROBERT FONOROW, HARRY TATARIAN, BEN WOLFE, Cameramen, Do Not Go Gentle Into That Good Night (CBS Playhouse) (CBS)
CHUCK HOWARD Director of Program Productions, 10th Winter Olympic Games (ABC)
HEINO RIPP Technical Director, Herb Alpert and the Tijuana Brass (CBS)
JOE STRAUSS, Technical Director; RICHARD DURHAM, RAY FIGELSKI, ROY HOLM, ROBERT KEYS, CARL PITSCH, RON SHELDON, TONY YARLETT, Cameramen, The Fred Astaire Show (NBC)

OUTSTANDING ACHIEVEMENT IN FILM EDITING

A special program or one of a series

PETER JOHNSON The Sounds and Sights of Chicago (Bell Telephone Hour) (NBC)
RICHARD BROCKWAY, DONN CAMBERN, JOHN C. FULLER Chrysler Presents The Bob Hope Christmas Special (NBC)
PETER V. PUNZI Four Days To Omaha (NBC Experiment in Television) (NBC)
DONALD R. RODE The Doomsday Machine (Star Trek) (NBC)
DONALD D. WAGES The Photographer (Mission: Impossible) (CBS)
ROBERT WATTS The Traitor (Mission: Impossible) (CBS)

THE AREAS

(Possibility of one Award, more than one Award, or no Award)

OUTSTANDING ACHIEVEMENT IN CHILDREN'S PROGRAMMING

PROGRAMS

HE'S YOUR DOG, CHARLIE BROWN (CBS) Lee Mendelson and Bill Melendez, Producers
MISTEROGER'S NEIGHBORHOOD (NET) Fred Rogers, Producer
YOU'RE IN LOVE, CHARLIE BROWN (CBS) Lee Mendelson and Bill Melendez, Producers

INDIVIDUAL

FRED ROGERS Host on Misteroger's Neighborhood (NET)

OUTSTANDING ACHIEVEMENT IN DAYTIME PROGRAMMING

PROGRAMS

TODAY (NBC) Al Morgan, Producer
CAMERA THREE (CBS) Nick Havinga and James MacAllen, Producers
THE MIKE DOUGLAS SHOW (Syndicated) Roger E. Ailes, Producer

INDIVIDUALS

MacDONALD CAREY as DR. TOM HORTON Days of Our Lives (NBC)
JOAN BENNETT as ELIZABETH COLLINS STODDARD Dark Shadows

(ABC)
CELESTE HOLM as MRS. BERN Fat Hands and a Diamond Ring (Insight) (Syndicated)

OUTSTANDING ACHIEVEMENT IN SPORTS PROGRAMMING

PROGRAMS

ABC'S WIDE WORLD OF SPORTS (ABC) Roone P. Arledge, Executive Producer
THE AMERICAN SPORTSMAN (ABC) Lorne Hassan, Producer
THE FLYING FISHERMAN (Syndicated) Nicholas W. Russo, Executive Producer
10TH WINTER OLYMPIC GAMES (ABC) Roone P. Arledge, Executive Producer

INDIVIDUALS

JIM McKAY Sports Commentator on ABC's Wide World of Sports (ABC)
DICK BUTTON Sports Commentator on 10th Winter Olympic Games (ABC)
CHRISTOPHER SCHENKEL Sports Commentator on NCAA Football (ABC)

SPECIAL CLASSIFICATION OF INDIVIDUAL ACHIEVEMENTS

ART CARNEY for performances on The Jackie Gleason Show (CBS)
PAT PAULSEN for performances on The Smothers Brothers Comedy Hour (CBS)
THE WESTHEIMER COMPANY for Special Photographic Effects on Metamorphosis (Star Trek) (NBC)
JOSEPH G. SOROKIN Sound Editor of The Survivors (Mission: Impossible) (CBS)
CHARLES M. SCHULZ Writer of Children's Special, You're In Love, Charlie Brown (CBS)
BILL MELENDEZ Director of Children's Special, You're In Love, Charlie Brown (CBS)
DAVID WINTERS Choreographer of Movin' With Nancy (NBC)

OUTSTANDING INDIVIDUAL ACHIEVEMENT IN MUSIC

(Other than composer)
MITCHELL AYRES Conductor of The Hollywood Palace (ABC)
ARTHUR FIEDLER Conductor of A Boston Pops Concert for Youngsters (Children's Theatre) (NBC)
NEAL HEFTI Conductor of The Fred Astaire Show (NBC)
SAMMY CAHN Lyricist for The Legend of Robin Hood (NBC)
LEE HALE for Special Musical Material on The Dean Martin Christmas Show (The Dean Martin Show) (NBC)
ARTHUR MALVIN for Special Musical Material on A Man and His Music Ella Jobim (NBC)

OUTSTANDING INDIVIDUAL ACHIEVEMENT IN THE VISUAL ARTS

BERT GORDON for Graphic Design on The Strange Case of Dr. Jekyll and Mr. Hyde (ABC)
DICK SMITH for Make-Up on The Strange Case of Dr. Jekyll and Mr. Hyde (ABC)
DAN STRIEPEKE for Make-Up on The Space Destructors (Lost In Space) (CBS)

OUTSTANDING INDIVIDUAL ACHIEVEMENT IN ELECTRONIC PRODUCTION

ARTHUR SCHNEIDER Tape Editor of Rowan and Martin's Laugh-In Special (NBC)
WILLIAM M. KLAGES Lighting Director of Herb Alpert and The Tijuana Brass (CBS)
LON STUCKY Lighting Director of Carousel (Armstrong Circle Theatre) (ABC)
BILL COLE Audio Engineer of The Fred Astaire Show (NBC)
ROBERT H. GUHL Audio Engineer of Home to Judgement (I Spy) (NBC)
NICK V. GIORDANO Tape Editor of The Hollywood Palace (ABC)
JERRY SMITH for Video Control of Carousel (Armstrong Circle Theatre) (ABC)
HERB WEISS for Video Control of The Hollywood Palace (ABC)

SPECIAL AWARDS

THE TRUSTEES AWARD

DONALD H. McGANNON, President and Chairman of the Board of Directors of Group W (Westinghouse Broadcasting Company) "For his creative leadership of one of the most dynamic groups of radio and television stations in the United States; for innovating and encouraging the development by a Station Group of public service and entertainment programs of unparalleled scope and quality; and particularly for his early recognition of broadcasting's need to train and employ individuals from minority groups."

OUTSTANDING ACHIEVEMENT IN ENGINEERING DEVELOPMENT

BRITISH BROADCASTING CORPORATION For the "Electronic Field-Store Colour Television Standards Converter." By converting television pictures instantaneously from the 525-line/60-field NTSC system used in America and other countries to the 625-line/50-field PAL or SECAM systems used in Europe and in other parts of the world.

THE STATION AWARD

NOW IS THE TIME (WCAU-TV, Philadelphia, Pennsylvania)
OPERATION THANKS - PARTS I AND II (KFMB-TV, San Diego, California)
ALBINA: GHETTO OF THE MIND (KGW-TV, Portland, Oregon)
OUR KIND OF WORLD - EPISODE NO. 6 (KRMA-TV, Denver, Colorado)
WHAT'S A MAN WORTH? (KSD-TV, St. Louis, Missouri)
THE DROPOUT DRUGS (KUTV, Salt Lake City, Utah)
A MATTER OF LIFE (WNBC-TV, New York City, New York)
THE GIANTS AND THE COMMON MEN (WMAQ-TV, Chicago, Illinois)
THE OTHER WASHINGTON (WRC-TV, Washington, D.C.)

SPECIAL CITATION

THE OTHER SIDE OF THE SHADOW (WWL-TV, New Orleans, Louisiana)
THE OTHER WASHINGTON (WRC-TV, Wasington, D.C.)
TONY McBRIDE (KDKA-TV, Pittsburgh, Pennsylvania)
POVERTY'S CHILDREN ARE NOT ALIKE (KLZ-TV, Denver, Colorado)
THE INVISIBLE MINORITY (KNBC-TV, Los Angeles, California)
WHAT'S A MAN WORTH? (KSD-TV, St. Louis, Missouri)
SIX DAYS IN JULY (WWJ-TV, Detroit, Michigan)

THE INTERNATIONAL AWARD

DOCUMENTARY

LA SECTION ANDERSON (office de Radiodiffusion Television Francaise, O.R.T.F., Paris, France)
THE ENCHANTED ISLES (Anglia Television Limited, London, England)
HIGH STREET MAYFAIR (BOND STREET) (ATV Network Limited, London, England)
THE PRICE OF A RECORD (Four Companies Productions, Border Television Limited, Cumberland, England)
CONTRACT 736 (Scottish Television Limited, Glasgow, Scotland)
THE SERVANTS (Tyne Tees Television Limited, Newcastle upon Tyne, England)

ENTERTAINMENT

CALL ME DADDY (Armchair Theatre) (ABC Television Limited, Middlesex, England)
SWAN LAKE (Canadian Broadcasting Corporation, Ottawa, Canada)
THE GOOD AND FAITHFUL SERVANT (Rediffusion Television Limited, London, England)
RIEDAIGLIA (Sveriges Radio, Stockholm, Sweden)
DI OFARIMS (Westdeutscher Rundfunk, Cologne, Germany)

1968/69

OUTSTANDING ACHIEVEMENT WITHIN REGULARLY SCHEDULED NEWS PROGRAMS

PROGRAMS

COVERAGE OF HUNGER IN THE UNITED STATES (The Huntley-Brinkley Report) (NBC) Wallace Westfeldt, Executive Producer
DEBATE BETWEEN SENATOR ROBERT F. KENNEDY AND SENATOR EUGENE McCARTHY (Issues And Answers) (ABC) Peggy Whedon, Producer
RECAP OF SENATOR ROBERT F. KENNEDY FUNERAL (The ABC Weekend News) (ABC) Sid Darion, Executive Producer

INDIVIDUALS

CHARLES KURALT, JAMES WILSON, ROBERT FUNK Correspondent, Cameraman and Soundman, Respectively, For "On The Road" (CBS Evening News With Walter Cronkite) (CBS)
JOHN LAURENCE Correspondent for "Police After Chicago" (CBS Evening News With Walter
Cronkite) (CBS)
FRANK BOURGHOLTZER Reporter for "Coverage of Russian Naval Emergence in Mediterranean"
(The Frank McGee Report) (NBC)
FRED BRIGGS Reporter For "Coverage of the Campaign to Obtain Black Lung Compensation" (The Huntley-Brinkley Report) (NBC)
HEYWOOD HALE BROUN Special Correspondent For "Special Sports Reporting" (CBS Evening News With Roger Mudd-Saturday) (CBS)
JOHN CHANCELLOR Reporter For "Coverage of 1968 Political Campaign" (The Huntley-Brinkley Report) (NBC)
PETER JENNINGS For "Report on Slaughter of Baby Seals" (ABC News With Frank Reynolds) (ABC)
FRANK REYNOLDS For "Commentaries" (ABC Evening News With Frank Reynolds) (ABC)
MORLEY SAFER Correspondent For Coverage of "Nigerian-Biafran War" (CBS Evening News With Walter Cronkite) (CBS)
ERIC SEVARIED Correspondent For "Analysis" (CBS Evening News With Walter Cronkite) (CBS)
HOWARD K. SMITH For "Commentaries" (ABC Evening News With Frank Reynolds) (ABC)
LIZ TROTTA Reporter For Coverage of "Vietnam War" (The Huntley-Brinkley Report) (NBC)

OUTSTANDING ACHIEVEMENT IN COVERAGE OF SPECIAL EVENTS

PROGRAMS

COVERAGE OF MARTIN LUTHER KING ASSINATION AND AFTERMATH (CBS News Special Reports And Special Broadcasts) (CBS) Robert Wussler, Ernest Leiser, Burton Benjamin, Don Hewitt, Executive Producers
APOLLO: A JOURNEY TO THE MOON (FLIGHT NOS. VII, VIII AND IX) (NBC News Special) (NBC) James Kitchell, Producer
ASSASSINATION AND FUNERAL OF SENATOR ROBERT F. KENNEDY (ABC) Walter J. Pfister, Jr, Executive Producer
JULES BERGMAN AND RALPH LAPP DISCUSSIONS ON MANNED SPACE PROGRAMS-APPOLLO VIII (Space '68) (ABC) Walter J. Pfister, Jr, Executive Producer
CHICAGO DEMOCRATIC CONVENTION COVERAGE (NBC News Special) George Murray, Executive Producer
COVERAGE OF THE DEMOCRATIC CONVENTION AND SURROUNDING EVENTS (CBS News Special Reports and Special Broadcasts) (CBS) Robert Wussler, Executive Producer
COVERAGE OF ROBERT F. KENNEDY ASSASSINATION AND AFTERMATH (CBS News Special Reports and Special Broadcasts) (CBS) Ernest Leiser, William Small, Robert Wussler, Don Hewitt, Executive Producers
NEWS ANALYSIS (The President's Farewell) (NET) Ned Schnurman, Executive Producer
NEWS ANALYSIS (The Nixon Administration) (NET) Jim Karayn, Executive Producer
THE INVASION OF CZECHOSLOVAKIA (NBC News Special) (NBC) Robert Shafer, Producer
UNCONVENTIONAL CONVENTION COVERAGE (The Race To The White House) (ABC) Walter J. Pfister, Jr, Executive Producer

INDIVIDUALS

JULES BERGMAN Science Editor For Commentary "Space '68" (ABC)
WILLIAM BOYLE, DENNIS DALTON, GENE FARINET, ARTHUR LORD Writers For "Apollo: A Journey To The Moon" (Flight Nos. VII, VIII and IX) (NBC News Special) (NBC)
VERN DIAMOND Director For "Coverage Of The Democratic Convention And Surrounding Events" (CBS News Special Reports And Special Broadcasts) (CBS)
DELOS HALL Cameraman For "Coverage Of The Democratic Convention And Surrounding Events" (CBS News Special Reports And Special Broadcasts) (CBS)
CHET HUNTLEY, DAVID BRINKLEY, SANDY VANOCUR, JOHN CHANCELLOR, FRANK McGEE, EDWIN NEWMAN News Reporters For Team Coverage "Chicago Democratic Convention Coverage" (NBC News Special) (NBC)
WILLIAM H. LAWRENCE National Affairs Editor For Commentaries "Assassination And Funeral Of Senator Robert F. Kennedy" (ABC)
FRANK McGEE Reporter For "Apollo: A Journey To The Moon" (Flight Nos. VII, VII and IX) (NBC News Special) (NBC)
ANTHONY MESSURI Director For "Apollo: A Journey To The Moon" (Flight Nos. VII, VIII and IX) (NBC)
DAN RATHER Reporter For "Coverage Of The Democratic Convention And Surrounding Events" (CBS News Special Reports and Special Broadcasts) (CBS)
FRANK REYNOLDS Commentator For "Assassination And Funeral Of Senator Robert F. Kennedy" (ABC)
HOWARD K. SMITH Commmentator For "The Race To The White House" (ABC)
MIKE WALLACE Reporter For "Coverage Of The Democratic Convention And Surrounding Events" (CBS News Special Reports And Special Broadcasts) (CBS)

OUTSTANDING NEWS DOCUMENTARY PROGRAM ACHIEVEMENT

PROGRAMS

CBS REPORTS: HUNGER IN AMERICA (CBS News Hour) (CBS) Martin Carr, Producer
LAW AND ORDER (Public Broadcast Laboratory) (NET) Frederick Wiseman, Producer
APPALACHIA: RICH LAND, POOR PEOPLE (NET Journal) (NET) Jack Willis, Producer
BIAS AND THE MASS MEDIA, PART I (Time For Americans) (ABC) Hubbell Robinson, Stephen Fleischman, Executive Producers
CBS REPORTS: CAMPAIGN AMERICAN STYLE (CBS News Hour) (CBS) Jay McMullen, Producer
CITIES HAVE NO LIMITS (White Paper: The Ordeal Of The American City) (NBC) Fred Freed, Executive Producer
ELEGY AND MEMORY (ABC) Thomas Wolf, Executive Producer
FREE AT LAST (MARTIN LUTHER KING) (Public Broadcast Laboratory) (NET) Greg Shuker, Producer
HANOI: A REPORT BY CHARLES COLLINGWOOD (CBS News Hour) (CBS) Charles Collingwood, Producer
HEART ATTACK! (ABC) Lester Cooper, Producer
HOME COUNTRY, USA (American Profile) (NBC) Robert Rogers, Producer

ROBERT KENNEDY REMEMBERED (Guggenheim Productions, Inc) (ABC, CBS, NBC) Charles Guggenheim, Producer
OF BLACK AMERICA (CBS News Hour) Series (CBS) Perry Wolff, Executive Producer
RUSSIA IN THE MEDITERRANEAN (NBC News Special) (NBC) George Murray, Executive Producer
STILL A BROTHER (NET Journal) (NET) William Greaves, William Branch, Producers
THE CITIES: A CITY IS TO LIVE IN, DILEMMA IN BLACK AND WHITE, TO BUILD THE FUTURE (CBS News Hour) (CBS) Ernest Leiser, Executive Producer
VIEW FROM SPACE (ABC) James Benjamin, Producer
THE WHOLE WORLD IS WATCHING (Public Broadcast Laboratory) (NET) Av Westin, Executive Producer

INDIVIDUALS

PERRY WOLFF AND ANDY ROONEY Writers: "Black History: Lost, Stolen Or Strayed-Of Black America" (CBS News Hour) (CBS)
CHARLES AUSTIN, A.S.C. Cinematographer "Cities Have No Limits-White Paper: The Ordeal of the American City" (NBC)
MILI BONSIGNORI Film Editor "CBS Reports: Hunger In America" (CBS News Hour) (CBS)
MILI BONSIGNORI AND MORTON ROSENFELD Film Editors For 'View From Space" (ABC)
RENE'BRAS Animation For "View From Space" (ABC)
BILL BRAYNE Cameraman For "Law And Order" (Public Broadcast Laboratory) (NET)
CHARLES COLLINGWOOD Reporter For "Hanoi: A Report By Charles Collingwood" (CBS News Hour) (CBS)
DAVID CULHANE Reporter For "CBS Reports: Hunger In America" (CBS News Hour) (CBS)
JOSEPH LOUW Reporter For "Free At Last (Martin Luther King)" (Public Broadcast Laboratory) (NET)
DESMOND McELROY AND DAROLD MURRAY Film Editors "Home Country, USA-American Profile" (NBC)
DAROLD MURRAY Supervising Film Editor For "Cities Have No Limits-White Paper: The Ordeal Of The American City" (NBC)
RICHARD NORLING Cameraman For "Home Country, USA-American Profile" (NBC)
RICHARD ROY Cameraman For "Heart Attack!" (ABC)
FREDERICK WISEMAN Director "Law And Order" (Public Broadcast Laboratory) (NET)
FREDERICK WISEMAN Writer For "Law And Order" (Public Broadcast Laboratory) (NET)

OUTSTANDING CULTURAL DOCUMENTARY AND "MAGAZINE-TYPE" PROGRAM OR SERIES ACHIEVEMENT

PROGRAMS

DON'T COUNT THE CANDLES (CBS News Hour) (CBS) William K. McClure, Producer
JUSTICE BLACK AND THE BILL OF RIGHTS (CBS News Hour) (CBS) Burton Benjamin, Producer
MAN WHO DANCES: EDWARD VILLELLA (Bell Telephone Hour) (Drew Associates, Inc) (NBC) Robert Drew, Mike Jackson, Producers
THE GREAT AMERICAN NOVEL (CBS News Hour) (CBS) Arthur Barron, Producer
BIRTH AND DEATH (Public Broadcast Laboratory) (NET) Arthur and Evelyn Barron, Producers
BLACK JOURNAL NO. 1 (NET Journal) (NET) Alvin H. Perlmutter, Executive Producer
CHILDREN'S LETTERS TO GOD (Lee Mendelson Film Producers, Inc) (NBC) Lee Mendelson, Frank Buxton, Producers
COSMOPOLIS: BIG CITY, 2000 A.D. (Man And His Universe) (John H. Secondari Productions, Ltd) (ABC) John H. Secondari, Helen Jean Rogers, Producers
DOWN TO THE SEA IN SHIPS (Project XX) (NBC) Donald B. Hyatt, Producer
ECCE HOMO (The Southern Baptist Hour) (NBC) Doris Ann, Producer
FIRST TUESDAY (NBC) Eliot Frankel, Executive Producer
HEMINGWAY'S SPAIN-A LOVE AFFAIR (ABC) Lester Cooper, Producer
HOW LIFE BEGINS (ABC) Jules Power, Executive Producer
INGMAR BERGMAN INTERVIEW (Public Broadcast Laboratory) (NET) Lewis Freedman, Producer
JAZZ: THE INTIMATE ART (Bell Telephone Hour) (Drew Associates, Inc) (NBC) Robert Drew, Mike Jackson, Producers
JESSIE OWENS RETURNS TO BERLIN (Syndicated) (Cappy Productions, Inc) Bud Greenspan, Producer
JOHN STEINBECK'S TRAVELS WITH CHARLEY (Lee Mendelson Film Productions, Inc) (NBC) Lee Mendelson, Executive Producer
LOVE IN A SEXY SOCIETY (One Reach One) The Episcopal Radio-TV Foundation (Syndicated) Caroline Rakestraw, Executive Producer
MARGARET MEAD'S NEW GUINEA JOURNAL (NET Festival) (NET) Craig Gilbert, Producer
ONCE UPON A WALL--THE GREAT AGE OF FRESCO (CBS News Hour) (CBS) Peter Davis, Producer
ONE NATION INDIVISIBLE (Syndicated) (Westinghouse Broadcasting Company) Dick Hubert, Sr, Producer
ONE REACH ONE Series (Syndicated) (The Episcopal Radio-TV Foundation) Caroline Rakestraw, Executive Producer
REMBRANDT AND THE BIBLE (Directions) (ABC) Aram Boyajian, Producer
REPTILES AND AMPHIBIANS (National Geographic Special) (Metromedia Producers Corporation) (CBS) Walon Green, Producer; Robert Doyle, Executive Producer For National Geographic Society
60 MINUTES (CBS News Hour) Series (CBS) Don Hewitt, Executive Producer
SUNKEN TREASURE (The Undersea World Of Jacques Cousteau) (Metromedia Producers Corporation) (ABC) Alan Landsburg, Jacques Cousteau, Executive Producers
THE ACTOR (ABC) James Fleming, Producer
THE AMERICAN ALCOHOLIC (NBC News Special) (NBC) Len Giovannitti, Producer
THE BIG LITTLE WORLD OF ROMAN VISHNIAC (NBC News Special) (NBC) Craig Fisher, Producer
THE CONFRONTATION (ABC) Emile de Antonio, Producer
THE ENDLESS THREAD (One Reach One) The Episcopal Radio-TV Foundation (Syndicated) Caroline Rakestraw, Executive Producer
THE NEW VOICES OF WATTS (NBC Experiment In Television) (NBC) Stuart Schulberg, Producer
THE ROAD TO GETTYSBURG (The Saga Of Western Man) (John H. Secondari Productions, Ltd) (ABC) John H. Secondari, Helen Jean Rogers, Producers
THE SAVAGE HEART: A CONVERSATION WITH ERIC HOFFER (CBS News Hour) (CBS) Perry Wolff, Producer
THE SECRET OF MICHELANGELO: EVERY MAN'S DREAM (Capital Cities Broadcasting Corporation) (ABC) Milton A. Fruchtman, Producer
THE SENSE OF WONDER (ABC) Jules Power, Executive Producer
THE UNEXPECTED VOYAGE OF PEPITO AND CRISTOBAL (The Undersea World of Jacques Cousteau) (Metromedia Producers Corporation) (ABC) Warren V. Bush, Producer
WHALES (The Undersea World Of Jacques Cousteau) (Metromedia Productions Corporation) (ABC) Alan Landsburg, Jacques Cousteau, Executive Producers
WHAT COLOR IS THE WIND? (NBC Experiment In Television) (NBC) Allan Grant, Producer
WHAT MANNER OF MAN (Syndicated) (Shelby Storck and Company, Inc) Shelby Storck, Producer

INDIVIDUALS

WALTER DOMBROW AND JERRY SIMS Cinematographers For "The Great American Novel" (CBS News Hour) (CBS)
TOM PETIT Producer For "CBW: The Secrets Of Secrecy" Segment of "First Tuesday" (NBC)
LORD SNOWDON Cinematograher For "Don't Count The Candles" (CBS News Hour) (CBS)
RALPH BELLAMY Host For "One Reach One" Series (The Episcopal Radio-TV Foundation) (Syndicated)
WARREN V. BUSH Writer "Sunken Treasure" (The Undersea World of Jacques Cousteau) (Metromedia Producers Corporation) (ABC)
PATRICK CAREY, RON HEADFORD, JAMES GODFREY, LEWIS McLEOD Cameramen For "Hemingway's Spain-A Love Affair" (ABC)
WALT DeFARIA, SHELDON FAY, JR. Directors For "John Steinbeck's Travels With Charley" (Lee Mendelson Film Productions, Inc) (NBC)

WALTER ESSENFELD, NILS RASMUSSEN, SAMUEL COHEN Film Editors For "The Road To Gettysburg" (The Saga of Western Man) (John H. Secondari Productions, Ltd) (ABC)
JOSEPH FACKOVEC, REG BROWNE, PIERRE VACHO Film Editors For "What Manner Of Man" Shelby Storck and Company, Inc. (Syndicated)
SHELDON FAY, JR. Cameraman "John Steinbeck's Travels With Charley" (Lee Mendelson Film Production, Inc) (NBC)
ARTHUR FILLMORE, LASZLO PAL Cameramen "What Manner Of Man" Shelby Storck and Company, Inc. (Syndicated)
MILTON A. FRUCHTMAN Director "The Secret Of Michelangelo: Every Man's Dream" (Capital Cities Broadcasting Corporation) (ABC)
CRAIG GILBERT Director "Margaret Mead's New Guinea Journal" NET Festival (NET)
CRAIG GILBERT Writer for "Margaret Mead's New Guinea Journal" NET Festival (NET)
LEON GLUCKMAN Director For "The Actor" (ABC)
ALLEN GRANT Cameraman For "What Color Is The Wind?" (NBC Experiment In Television) (NBC)
MARSHALL FLAUM Writer For "What Color Is The Wind?" (NBC Experiment In Television) Allen Grant (NBC)
BUD GREENSPAN Director For "Jessie Owens Returns To Berlin" Cappy Productions, Inc. (Syndicated)
BUD GREENSPAN Writer For "Jessie Owens Returns To Berlin" Cappy Productions, Inc. (Syndicated)
WILLIAM B. HARTIGAN Cameraman For "The Road To Gettysburg" (The Saga of Western Man) (John H. Secondari Productions, Ltd) (ABC)
DICK HUBERT, SR. Writer For "One Nation Indivisible" Westinghouse Broadcasting Company (Syndicated)
MIKE JACKSON Director "Man Who Dances: Edward Villella" (Bell Telephone Hour) (Drew Associates, Inc) (NBC)
NORTON JUSTER, STUART HAMPLE Writers "Children's Letters To God" (Lee Mendelson Film Productions, Inc) (NBC)
ALAN LANDSBURG, WALON GREEN Writers "Reptiles And Amphibians" (National Geographic Special) (Metromedia Producers Corporation) (CBS)
JULES LAVENTHOL Film Editor For "Don't Count The Candles" (CBS News Hour) (CBS)
RICHARD LEITERMAN Director of Photography For "Margaret Mead's New Guinea Journal" NET Festival (NET)
ABBOT MILLS Cameraman "Man Who Dances: Edward Villella" (Bell Telephone Hour) (Drew Associates, Inc) (NBC)
JOHN OETTINGER, FRANK HOST, PAUL GALAN Film Editors For "One Nation Indivisible" Westinghouse Broadcasting Company (Syndicated)
LAURENCE D. SAVADOVE Writer For "Whales" (The Undersea World of Jacques Cousteau) (Metromedia Producer Corporation) (ABC)
JOHN H. SECONDARI Writer "Cosmopolis: Big City, 2000 A.D." (Man And His Universe) (John H. Secondari Productions, Ltd) (ABC)
JOHN H. SECONDARI Writer "The Road To Gettysburg" (The Saga of Western Man) (John H. Secondari Production, Ltd) (ABC)
JOHN SOH Film Editor For "Whales" And "Sunken Treasure" (The Undersea World of Jacques Cousteau) (Metromedia Producers Corporation) (ABC)
JOHN STEINBECK Writer "John Steinbeck's Travels With Charley" (Lee Mendelson Film Productions, Inc) (NBC)
SHELBY STORCK Narrator "What Manner Of Man" Shelby Storck and Company, Inc. (Syndicated)
SHELBY STORCK Writer For "What Manner Of Man" Shelby Storck and Company, Inc. (Syndicated)
WALKER STUART Director For "Hemingway's Spain - A Love Affair" (ABC)
JOHN TEEPLE Film Editor For "Ecce Homo" (The Southern Baptist Hour) (NBC)
THOMAS TOMIZAWA Producer For "College For The New Generation" Segment of (First Tuesday) (NBC)
KENNETH TYNAN Writer "The Actor" (ABC)
JOSEPH VADALA Photographer "Ecce Homo" (The Southern Baptist Hour) (NBC)
MIKE WALLACE, HARRY REASONER Reporters For "60 Minutes" (CBS News Hour) Series (CBS)

ENTERTAINMENT PROGRAM AND INDIVIDUAL ACHIEVEMENTS
(One Award Only in Each of the Remaining Categories)

OUTSTANDING COMEDY SERIES
GET SMART (NBC) Burt Nodella, Producer
BEWITCHED (ABC) William Asher, Producer
FAMILY AFFAIR (CBS) Edmund Hartmann, Producer
THE GHOST AND MRS. MUIR (NBC) Stanley Rubin, Producer
JULIA (NBC) Hal Kanter, Executive Producer

OUTSTANDING DRAMATIC SERIES
NET PLAYHOUSE (NET) Curtis Davis, Executive Producer
THE FBI (ABC) Charles Larson, Producer
IRONSIDE (NBC) Cy Chermak, Executive Producer
JUDD FOR THE DEFENSE (ABC) Harold Gast, Producer
THE NAME OF THE GAME (NBC) Richard Irving, Leslie Stevens, David Victor, Producers
MISSION: IMPOSSIBLE (CBS) Bruce Geller, Executive Producer

OUTSTANDING DRAMATIC PROGRAM
A single program of a series or a special program
TEACHER, TEACHER (NBC) (Hallmark Hall Of Fame) (NBC) George Lefferts, Producer
THE EXECUTION (Mission: Impossible) (CBS) William Read Woodfield, Allan Balter, Producers
HEIDI (NBC) Frederick Brogger, James Franciscus, Producers
A MIDSUMMER NIGHT'S DREAM (CBS) Lord Michael Birkett, Producer
THE PEOPLE NEXT DOOR (CBS Playhouse) (CBS) Herbert Brodkin, Producer
TALKING TO A STRANGER (NET Playhouse) Four Part Presentation (NET) Michael Blakewell, Producer

OUTSTANDING VARIETY OR MUSICAL SERIES
Award(s) To Producer and Star (If Applicable)
ROWAN AND MARTIN'S LAUGH-IN (NBC) Paul W. Keyes, Carolyn Rasin, Producers; Dan Rowan, Dick Martin, Stars
THE CAROL BURNETT SHOW (CBS) Joseph Hamilton, Producer; Carol Burnett, Star
THE DEAN MARTIN SHOW (NBC) Greg Garrison, Producer; Dean Martin, Star
THE SMOTHERS BROTHERS COMEDY HOUR (CBS) Allan Blye and George A. Sunga, Producers; Tom Smothers and Dick Smothers, Stars
THAT'S LIFE (ABC) Marvin Marx and Stan Harris, Producers; Robert Morse, Star

OUTSTANDING VARIETY OR MUSICAL PROGRAM
A Single program of a series or a special program. Award(s) To Producer and Star (If Applicable)
THE BILL COSBY SPECIAL (NBC) Roy Silver, Executive Producer; Bill Cosby, Star
BARBRA STREISAND: A HAPPENING IN CENTRAL PARK (CBS) Robert Scheerer, Producer; Barbra Streisand, Star
DUKE ELLINGTON CONCERT OF SACRED MUSIC (NET Playhouse) (NET) Richard Moore and Ralph J. Gleason, Producers; Duke Ellington, Star
FRANCIS ALBERT SINATRA DOES HIS THING (CBS) Saul Ilson and Ernest Chambers, Producers; Frank Sinatra, Star
THE RITE OF SPRING (NET Festival) (NET) Robert Foshko, Producer: Zubin Mehta, Conductor
ROWAN AND MARTIN'S LAUGH-IN (NBC) Paul W. Keyes and Carolyn Raskin, Producers; Dan Rowan, Dick Martin and Marcel Marceau, Stars

VLADIMIR HOROWITZ: A TELEVISION CONCERT AT CARNEGIE HALL (CBS) Roger Englander, Producer; Vladimir Horowitz, Pianist

OUTSTANDING SINGLE PERFORMANCE BY AN ACTOR IN A LEADING ROLE

A one-time appearance in a series or for a special program

PAUL SCOFIELD "Male Of The Species" (Prudential's On Stage) (NBC)
OSSIE DAVIS "Teacher, Teacher" (Hallmark Hall Of Fame) (NBC)
DAVID McCULLUM "Teacher, Teacher" (Hallmark Hall Of Fame) (NBC)
BILL TRAVERS "The Admirable Crichton" (Hallmark Hall Of Fame) (NBC)

OUTSTANDING SINGLE PERFORMANCE BY AN ACTRESS IN A LEADING ROLE

A one-time appearance in a series or for a special program

GERALDINE PAGE "The Thanksgiving Visitor" (ABC)
ANNE BAXTER "The Bobbie Currier Story" (The Name of the Game) (NBC)
LEE GRANT "The Gates of Cerberus" (Judd for the Defense) (ABC)

OUTSTANDING CONTINUED PERFORMANCE BY AN ACTOR IN A LEADING ROLE IN A DRAMATIC SERIES

CARL BETZ "Judd for the Defense" (ABC)
RAYMOND BURR "Ironside" (NBC)
PETER GRAVES "Mission: Impossible" (CBS)
MARTIN LANDAU "Mission: Impossible" (CBS)
ROSS MARTIN "The Wild, Wild West" (CBS)

OUTSTANDING CONTINUED PERFORMANCE BY AN ACTRESS IN A LEADING ROLE IN A DRAMATIC SERIES

BARBARA BAIN "Mission: Impossible" (CBS)
JOAN BLONDELL "Here Come The Brides" (ABC)
PEGGY LIPTON "The Mod Squad" (ABC)

OUTSTANDING CONTINUED PERFORMANCE BY AN ACTOR IN A LEADING ROLE IN A COMEDY SERIES

DON ADAMS "Get Smart" (NBC)
BRIAN KEITH "Family Affair" (CBS)
EDWARD MULHARE "The Ghost And Mrs. Muir" (NBC)
LLOYD NOLAN "Julia" (NBC)

OUTSTANDING CONTINUED PERFORMANCE BY AN ACTRESS IN A LEADING ROLE IN A COMEDY SERIES

HOPE LANGE "The Ghost And Mrs. Muir" (NBC)
DIAHANN CARROLL "Julia" (NBC)
BARBARA FELDON "Get Smart" (NBC)
ELIZABETH MONTGOMERY "Bewitched" (ABC)

OUTSTANDING SINGLE PERFORMANCE BY AN ACTOR IN A SUPPORTING ROLE

A one-time appearance in a series or for a special program (No Award Presented)
NED GLASS "A Little Chicken Soup Never Hurt Anybody" (Julia) (NBC)
HAL HOLBROOK "The Whole World Is Watching" (World Premiere) (NBC)
BILLY SCHULMAN "Teacher, Teacher" (Hallmark Hall Of Fame) (NBC)

OUTSTANDING SINGLE PERFORMANCE BY AN ACTRESS IN A SUPPORTING ROLE

A one-time appearance in a series or for a special program

ANNA CALDER-MARSHALL "Male Of The Species" (Prudential's On Stage) (NBC)
PAMELA BROWN "The Admirable Crichton" (Hallmark Hall Of Fame) (NBC)
IRENE HERVEY "The O'Casey Scandal" (My Three Sons) (CBS)
NANCY KOVACK "The Girl Who Came In With The Tide" (Mannix) (CBS)

OUTSTANDING CONTINUED PERFORMANCE BY AN ACTOR IN A SUPPORTING ROLE IN A SERIES

WERNER KLEMPERER "Hogan's Heroes" (CBS)
GREG MORRIS "Mission: Impossible" (CBS)
LEONARD NIMOY "Star Trek" (NBC)

OUTSTANDING CONTINUED PERFORMANCE BY AN ACTRESS IN A SUPPORTING ROLE IN A SERIES

SUSAN SAINT JAMES "The Name Of The Game" (NBC)
BARBARA ANDERSON "Ironside" (NBC)
AGNES MOOREHEAD "Bewitched" (ABC)

OUTSTANDING WRITING ACHIEVEMENT IN DRAMA

A single program or a series or a special program

JP MILLER "The People Next Door" (CBS Playhouse) (CBS)
ALLAN E. SLOANE "Teacher, Teacher" (Hallmark Hall Of Fame) (NBC)
ELLEN M. VIOLETT "The Experiment" (CBS Playhouse) (CBS)

OUTSTANDING WRITING ACHIEVEMENT IN COMEDY, VARIETY OR MUSIC

A single program or a series or a special program

ALLAN BLYE, BOB EINSTEIN, MURRAY ROMAN, CARL GOTTLIEB, JERRY MUSIC, STEVE MARTIN, CECIL TUCK, PAUL WAYNE, CY HOWARD, MASON WILLIAMS "The Smothers Brothers Comedy Hour" (CBS)
PAUL W. KEYES, HUGH WEDLOCK, JR, ALLAN S. MANINGS, CHRIS BEARD, DAVID PANICH, COSLOUGH H. JOHNSON, MARC LONDON, DAVID M. COX, JIM CARLSON, JACK MENDELSOHN, JAMES MULLIGAN, LORNE D. MICHAELS, HART POMERANTZ, PHIL HAHN, JACK HANRAHAN "Rowan And Martin's Laugh-In" (NBC)
ARNIE ROSEN, STAN BURNS, MIKE MARMER, HAL GOLDMAN, AL GORDON, DON HINKLEY, KENNY SOLMS, GAIL PARENT, BILL ANGELOS, ALAN KOHAN "The Carol Burnett Show" (CBS)

OUTSTANDING DIRECTORIAL ACHIEVEMENT IN DRAMA

A single program or a series or a special program

DAVID GREEN "The People Next Door" (CBS Playhouse) (CBS)
PAUL BOGART "Secrets" (CBS Playhouse) (CBS)
FIELDER COOK "Teacher, Teacher" (Hallmark Hall Of Fame) (NBC)

OUTSTANDING DIRECTORIAL ACHIEVEMENT IN COMEDY, VARIETY OR MUSIC (No Award Presented)

A single program or a series or a special program

GREG GARRISON "The Dean Martin Show" (NBC)
BILL HOBIN "The Bill Cosby Special" (NBC)
GORDON W. WILES "Rowan And Martin's Laugh-In" (NBC)

OUTSTANDING ACHIEVEMENT IN MUSICAL COMPOSITION

A single program or a series or a special program

JOHN T. WILLIAMS "Heidi" (NBC)
JACQUES BELASCO "Hemingway's Spain-A Love Affair" (ABC)
HUGO MONTENEGRO "Take Your Lover In The Ring" (The Outcasts) (ABC)
LALO SCHIFRIN "The Heir Apparent" (Mission: Impossible) (CBS)
MORTON STEVENS "Hawaii Five-O" (CBS Friday Night At The Movies) (CBS)

OUTSTANDING ACHIEVEMENT IN ART DIRECTION AND SCENIC DESIGN

A single program of a series or a special program. Award to Art Director and Scenic Designer, and to Set Decorator (If Applicable)

WILLIAM P. ROSS AND LOU HAFLEY Art Director and Set Decorator, Respectively, For "The Bunker" (Parts I and II), (Mission: Impossible) (CBS)
WALTER M. JEFFERIES, JR. AND JOHN DWYER Art Director and Set Decorator, Respectively, For "All Our Yesterdays" (Star Trek) (NBC)
KEN JOHNSON Art Director For "Rowan And Martin's Laugh-In" (NBC)

OUTSTANDING ACHIEVEMENT IN CINEMATOGRAPHY

GEORGE FOLSEY "Here's Peggy Fleming" (NBC)
FRANK PHILLIPS "Up-Tight" (Hawaii Five-O) (CBS)
ROBERT RIGER "19th Summer Olympic Games Special Reports" (ABC)
HOWARD SCHWARTZ "The Crash" (Land Of The Giants) (ABC)

OUTSTANDING ACHIEVEMENT IN ELECTRONIC CAMERAWORK

A single program of a series or a special program. Award to Technical Director, with Certificate to Cameramen

A.J. CUNNINGHAM Technical Director; NICK DeMOS, BOB FONAROW, FRED GOUGH, JACK JENNINGS, DICK NELSON, RICK TANZI, BEN WOLF Cameramen "The People Next Door" (CBS Playhouse) (CBS)
FRANK BIONDO Cameraman "Our First Fight" (That's Life) (ABC)
KARL MESSERSCHMIDT Technical Director; ROY HOLM, BOB KEYES, WAYNE NOSTAJA, TONY YARLETT Cameramen "Petula" (NBC)

OUTSTANDING ACHIEVEMENT IN FILM EDITING

A single program of a series or a special program

BILL MOSHER "An Elephant In A Cigar Box" (Judd For The Defense) (ABC)
JOHN C. FULLER, PATRICK KENNEDY, IGO KANTOR, FRANK McKELVEY 'Chrysler Presents The Bob Hope Christmas Special" (NBC)
SIDNEY KATZ "Teacher, Teacher" (Hallmark Hall Of Fame) (NBC)
DONALD R. RODE "Assignment: Earth" (Star Trek) (NBC)

THE AREAS

(Possibility of One Award, More Than One Award, or No Award)

OUTSTANDING ACHIEVEMENT IN CHILDREN'S PROGRAMMING

PROGRAMS

MISTEROGER'S NEIGHBORHOOD Series (NET) Fred Rogers, Producer
WALT DISNEY'S WONDERFUL WORLD OF COLOR Series (NBC) Ron Miller, Executive Producer

INDIVIDUALS

BOB KEESHAN "Captain Kangaroo" Series (CBS) (Performer)
BURR TILLSTROM "The Reluctant Dragon" (NBC Children's Theatre) (NBC) (Performer)

OUTSTANDING ACHIEVEMENT IN DAYTIME PROGRAMMING

PROGRAMS

THE DICK CAVETT SHOW Series (ABC) Don Silverman, Producer
HOLLYWOOD SQUARES Series (NBC) Merrill Heatter And Robert Quigley, Executive Producers

INDIVIDUALS

HUGH DOWNS "Concentration" Series (NBC) (Host)

OUTSTANDING ACHIEVEMENT IN SPORTS PROGRAMMING

PROGRAMS

19TH SUMMER OLYMPICS GAMES (ABC) Roone P. Arledge, Executive Producer
ABC'S WIDE WORLD OF SPORTS Series (ABC) Roone P. Arledge, Executive Producer

INDIVIDUALS

BILL BENNINGTON, MIKE FREEDMAN, MAC MEMION, ROBERT RIGER, MARV SCHLENKER, ANDY SIDARIS, LOU VOLPICELLI, DOUG WILSON "19th Summer Olympic Games" (ABC) (Directors)
CHRIS SCHENKEL "19th Summer Olympic Game" (ABC) (Commentator)

SPECIAL CLASSIFICATION ACHIEVEMENTS

PROGRAMS

FIRING LINE WITH WILLIAM F. BUCKLEY, JR. Series (Syndicated) Warren Steibel, Producer
MUTUAL OF OMAHA'S WILD KINGDOM Series (NBC) Don Meier, Producer
BROADWAY '68 - THE TONY AWARDS (NBC) Alexander Cohen, Pro-

ducer
1969 TOURNAMENT OF ROSES PARADE (CBS) Paul Levitan, Producer

INDIVIDUALS - (Variety Performances)
ARTE JOHNSON For "Rowan And Martin's Laugh-In" Series (NBC)
HARVEY KORMAN For "The Carol Burnett Show" Series (CBS)
RUTH BUZZI For "Rowan And Martin's Laugh-In" Series (NBC)
GOLDIE HAWN For "Rowan And Martin's Laugh-In" Series (NBC)

INDIVIDUALS - (Special Photographic Effects)
VAN DER VEER PHOTO EFFECTS, HOWARD A. ANDERSON COMPANY, THE WESTHEIMER COMPANY AND CINEMA RESEARCH For "The Tholian Web" (Star Trek) (NBC)

OUTSTANDING INDIVIDUAL ACHIEVEMENT IN MUSIC
MORT LINDSEY Musical Director "Barbra Streisand: A Happening In Central Park" (CBS)
TOM ADAIR AND JOHN SCOTT TROTTER Words and Music "Babar The Elephant" (NBC)
HERB ALPERT Arranger and Conductor "The Beat Of The Brass" (CBS)
BILLY BARNES Special Material "Rowan And Martin's Laugh-In" (NBC)

OUTSTANDING INDIVIDUAL ACHIEVEMENT IN THE VISUAL ARTS
RAY AGHAYAN Costume Designer For "Carol Channing And Pearl Bailey On Broadway" (ABC)
ANGEL G. ESPARZA Graphic Designer For "U.S.S. Pueblo Court Of Inquiry" (The Huntley-Brinkley Report) (NBC)
BOB MACKIE Costume Designer For "The Carol Burnett Show" (CBS)
CLAUDE THOMPSON Make-Up Artist For "And Debbie Makes Six" (ABC)

OUTSTANDING INDIVIDUAL ACHIEVEMENT IN ELECTRONIC PRODUCTION
BILL COLE Audio Engineer For "TCB" (NBC)
JOHN FRESCHI Lighting Director For "H. Andrew Williams Kaleidoscope Company" (NBC)
ROBERT GUHL, JIM STEWART, LARRY JONES Audio Engineers For "A Hint Of Darkness, A Hint Of Light" (The Mod Squad) (ABC)
ARTHUR SCHNEIDER Video Tape Editor For "Rowan And Martin's Laugh-In" (NBC)
BRUCE VERRAN AND JOHN TEELE Video Tape Editors For "Rowan And Martin's Laugh-In" (NBC)

SPECIAL AWARDS

A CITATION
BILLY SCHULMAN For recognition of an extraordinary achievement in the television drama, "Teacher, Teacher" presented by Hallmark Hall of Fame.

THE TRUSTEES AWARD
WILLIAM R. McANDREW, 1914-1968 Who shaped television news to be his permanent memorial by imposing on it early the American news tradition - honesty, bravery and public enlightment.
APOLLO VII, VIII, IX AND X SPACE MISSIONS Apollo VII Astronauts Walter Schirra, Donn Eisele, Walter Cunningham Apollo VIII Astronauts Frank Borman, James A Lovell, Jr, William A. Anders Apollo IX Astronauts James A. McDivitt, David R. Scott, Russel L. Schweickart Apollo X Astronauts Thomas B. Stafford, Eugene A. Cernan, John W. Young For sharing with the American public and the rest of the world the incredible experience of the unfolding of the mysteries of outer space and the surface of the moon via live television.

OUTSTANDING ACHIEVEMENT IN ENGINEERING DEVELOPMENT
EASTMAN KODAK COMPANY For the ME-4 Process, making it possible to develop color film with greater speed and sharper images than ever before.

CITATION
COLUMBIA BROADCASTING SYSTEM For the development of the Digital Control Technique used in the Minicam miniaturized television color camera, which provides a new degree of mobility by permitting control via a substantially smaller and more mobile connecting cable or, alternatively, a single wireless channel.

THE STATION AWARD
PRETTY SOON RUNS OUT (WHA-TV, Madison, Wisconsin)
APPALACHIAN HERITAGE (WLWT, Cincinnati, Ohio)
BEGGAR AT THE GATES (WBZ-TV, Boston, Massachusetts)
COLOR ME SOMEBODY (KING-TV, Seattle, Washington)
HEAL THE HURT CHILD (KSD-TV, St. Louis, Missouri)
JOB MAN CARAVAN (SCE-TV, Columbia, South Carolina)
MISTEROGERS SPECIAL PROGRAM FOR PARENTS (WQED, Pittsburgh, Pennsylvania)
OPERATION THANKS, Part I and II (KFMB-TV, San Diego, California)
SOMETHING FOR NOTHING (WFIL-TV, Philadelphia, Pennsylvania)
WE ARE ALL POLICEMEN (WNBC-TV, New York, New York)

SPECIAL CITATION
ASSIGNMENT: THE YOUNG GREATS (WFIL-TV, Philadelphia, Pennsylvania)
JOB MAN CARAVAN (SCE-TV, Columbia, South Carolina)
OPPORTUNITY LINE (KNXT-TV, Los Angeles, California)
PROJECT SUMMER (WMAL-TV, Washington, D.C.)
TELL IT LIKE IT IS (KPRC-TV, Houston, Texas)
THE NEW GENERATION AND THE ESTABLISHMENT (WHA-TV, Madison, Wisconsin)
THE SCHOOL THAT WOULD NOT DIE (WDSU-TV, New Orleans, Louisiana)
THE URBAN BATTLEGROUND (WIIC-TV, Pittsburg, Pennsylvania)
TO BE SOMEBODY (WTIC-TV, Hartford, Connecticut)
YA ES TIEMPO (IT'S ABOUT TIME) (WNJU-TV, Newark, New Jersey)

THE INTERNATIONAL AWARD

DOCUMENTARY
THE LAST CAMPAIGN OF ROBERT KENNEDY (Swiss Broadcasting and Television, Zurich, Switzerland)
AN EXPEDITION INTO THE STONE AGE (Nippon Television Network, Tokyo, Japan)
ARCHEOLOGY (Film Polski, Warsaw, Poland)
CHRISTMAS EVE IN BIAFRA (Independent Television News, London, England)
LIFE, DEATH AND JAPENESE MUSIC (Mainichi Broadcasting System, Osaka, Japan)

ENTERTAINMENT
A SCENT OF FLOWERS (Canadian Broadcasting Corporation, Ontario, Canada)
BLESSETH IS ONE (Hiroshima Telecasting Company, Ltd, Hiroshima City, Japan)
PAVONCELLO (Film Polski, Warsaw, Poland)
STAR QUALITY (Thames Television Limited, London, England)
THE CAESARS - CLAUDIUS (Granada Television Limited, London, England)

1969/70

NEWS AND DOCUMENTARY PROGRAM AND INDIVIDUAL ACHIEVEMENTS

(Possibility of one Award, more than one Award, or no Award)

OUTSTANDING ACHIEVEMENT WITHIN REGULARLY SCHEDULED NEWS PROGRAMS

PROGRAMS

AN INVESTIGATION OF TEENAGE DRUG ADDICTION - ODYSSEY HOUSE (The Huntley-Brinkley Report) (NBC) Wallace Westfeldt, Executive Producer; Les Crystal, Producer
CAN THE WORLD BE SAVED? (CBS Evening News With Walter Cronkite) (CBS) Ronald Bonn, Producer
CHICAGO CONSPIRACY TRIAL (CBS Evening News With Walter Cronkite) (CBS) Stanhope Gould, Producer
COVERAGE OF HURRICANE CAMILLE (ABC Evening News With Frank Reynolds And Howard K. Smith) (ABC) Avram Westin, Executive Producer; David Buksbaum, Producer
COVERAGE OF THE NIGERIAN/BIAFRAN CONFLICT (ABC Evening News With Frank Reynolds And Howard K. Smith) (ABC) Avram Westin, Executive Producer; David Buksbaum, Producer
THE HUNTLEY-BRINKLEY REPORT (NBC) Wallace Westfeldt, Executive Producer; Les Crystal, Producer
J. EDGAR HOOVER AND THE FBI (CBS Morning News With Joseph Benti) (CBS) Robert Markowitz, Producer
MAN AND HIS ENVIRONMENT (ABC Evening News With Frank Reynolds And Howard K. Smith) (ABC) Avram Westin, Executive Producer; David Buksbaum, Producer
MORATORIUM AND THE SILENT MAJORITY (ABC Evening News With Frank Reynolds And Howard K.Smith) (ABC) Avram Westin, Executive Producer; David Buksbaum, Producer

INDIVIDUALS

HEYWOOD HALE BROUN Special Correspondent For "Special Sports Reporting" (CBS Evening News With Roger Mudd) (CBS)
JOHN CHANCELLOR Correspondent For "Coverage of the Poison Grain Incident" (The Huntley-Brinkley Report) (NBC)
ROBERT GORALSKI Correspondent For "Investigation of the Green Beret Case" (The Huntley-Brinkley Report) (NBC)
CHET HUNTLEY Correspondent For "Coverage of the West German Elections" (The Huntley-Brinkley Report) (NBC)
FRANK REYNOLDS AND HOWARD K. SMITH For "News Commentaries" (ABC Evening News With Frank Reynolds And Howard K. Smith) (ABC)
MIKE WALLACE Correspondent For "Interviews With Meadlo And Medina" (CBS Evening News With Walter Cronkite) (CBS)

OUTSTANDING ACHIEVEMENT IN COVERAGE OF SPECIAL EVENTS

PROGRAMS

APOLLO: A JOURNEY TO THE MOON (APOLLO X, XI, XII) (NBC) James W. Kitchell, Executive Producer
SOLAR ECLIPSE: A DARKNESS AT NOON (NBC) Robert Northshield, Executive Producer; Walter Kravetz, Producer
COVERAGE OF THE ABM HEARINGS (NBC) Charles Jones, Producer
DWIGHT DAVID EISENHOWER: 1890-1969 (CBS) Ernest Leiser and Robert Wussler, Executive Producers
FOOTSTEPS ON THE MOON: THE FLIGHT OF APOLLO XI (ABC) Walter J. Pfister, Jr., Executive Producer; Robert Siegenthaler, Producer
MAN ON THE MOON: THE EPIC JOURNEY OF APOLLO XI (CBS) Robert Wussler, Executive Producer; Joan Richman, Clarence Cross, Producers
MR. NIXON IN ASIA (ABC) Walter J. Pfister, Jr., Executive Producer; Bob Rogow, Producer
SOLAR ECLIPSE: DARKNESS AT MIDDAY (ABC) Walter J. Pfister, Jr., Executive Producer; Robert Siegenthaler, Producer

INDIVIDUALS

WALTER CRONKITE Reporter For "Man On The Moon: The Epic Journey Of Apollo XI" (CBS)
JOEL BANOW Director For "Man On The Moon: the Epic Journey Of Apollo XI" (CBS)
JULES BERGMAN Co-Anchorman For "Footsteps On The Moon: The Flight Of Apollo XI" (ABC)
FRANK McGEE, CHET HUNTLEY AND DAVID BRINKLEY Reporters For "Apollo: A Journey To The Moon" (Apollo X, XI, XII) (NBC)
JOHN CHANCELLOR, FRANK McGEE AND JACK PERKINS Reporters For "Solar Eclipse: A Darkness At Noon" (NBC)
GENE FARINET, DENNIS DALTON, ARTHUR LORD AND KEN DONOAHUE Writers For "Apollo: A Journey To The Moon" (Apollo X, XI, XII) (NBC)
ROBERT J. LE DONNE News Editor For "Footsteps On The Moon: The Flight Of Apollo XI" (ABC)
LARRY PICKARD News Editor For "Footsteps On The Moon: The Flight Of Apollo XI" (ABC)
FRANK REYNOLDS Co-Anchorman For "Footsteps On The Moon: The Flight Of Apollo XI" (ABC)
FRED RHEINSTEIN Director For "Solar Eclipse: A Darkness At Noon" (Miahuatlan, Mexico, Segment) (NBC)
WALTER M. SCHIRRA, JR. Commentator For "Man On The Moon: The Epic Journey Of Apollo XI" (CBS)

OUTSTANDING ACHIEVEMENT IN NEWS DOCUMENTARY PROGRAMMING

PROGRAMS

HOSPITAL (NET Journal) (NET) Frederick Wiseman, Producer
THE MAKING OF THE PRESIDENT, 1978 (Metromedia Producers Corporation) (CBS) M.J. Rifkin, Executive Producer; Mel Stuart, Producer
ABORTION (Summer Focus) (ABC) Lester Cooper, Executive Producer; Ernest Pendrell, Producer
ADVENTURES AT THE JADE SEA (Metromedia Producers Corporation) (CBS) Harvey Bernhard, Executive Producer; David Seltzer, Producer
THE BATTLE OF EAST ST. LOUIS (CBS News Hours) (CBS) Perry Wolff, Executive Producer; Peter Davis, Producer
BLACK FIDDLER: PREJUDICE AND THE NEGRO (Summer Focus) (ABC) Stephen Fleischman, Executive Producer; Howard Enders, Producer
CBS REPORTS: A TIMETABLE FOR VIETNAM (CBS News Hour) (CBS) Ernest Leiser, Executive Producer; Bernard Birnbaum, Producer
DO YOU THINK A JOB IS THE ANSWER? (Public Broadcast Laboratory) (NET) Dave Dugan, Executive Producer; Gary Gilson, Producer
FASTEN YOUR SEATBELTS (NET Journal) (Document Associates, Inc.) (NET) Don Dixon, Executive Producer; Douglas Leiterman, Producer
FROM HERE TO THE SEVENTIES (NBC) Robert Northshield, Executive Producer; Mel Ferber, Producer
THE GREAT DOLLAR ROBBERY: CAN WE ARREST INFLATION? (ABC) Lester Cooper, Executive Producer; Herbert Dorfman, Producer
LBJ: WHY I CHOSE NOT TO RUN (CBS News Hour) (CBS) Burton Benjamin, Executive Producer; John Sharnik, Producer
THE NATURAL HISTORY OF OUR WORLD: THE TIME OF MAN (Metromedia Producers Corporation) (CBS) Marshall Flaum, Producer
THE ORDEAL OF THE AMERICAN CITY - CONFRONTATION (NBC White Paper) (NBC) Fred Freed, Executive Producer; Albert Waller, Producer
THE WAITING GAME (Lifewatch Six) Directors Group, Inc. (Syndicated) Walter King, Executive Producer; Ben Gradus, Producer
WHO INVITED US? (NET Journal) (NET) Alvin H. Perlmutter, Executive Producer; Alan M. Levin, Producer
WHO KILLED LAKE ERIE? (NBC) Fred Freed, Executive Producer
WHO SPEAKS FOR MAN? (NET Journal) (NET) Arthur Zegart, Producer
WILD RIVER (National Geographic Special) (Metromedia Producers

Corporation) (CBS) Robert C. Doyle, Executive Producer For National Geographic Society; Jack Kaufman, Executive Producer For Metromedia Producers Corporation; Ed Spiegel, Producer

INDIVIDUALS

FREDERICK WISEMAN Director For "Hospital" (NET Journal) (NET)
RICHARD BASEHART Narrator For "The Natural History Of Our World: The Time Of Man" (Metromedia Producers Corporation) (CBS)
CHARLES COLLINGWOOD Reporter For "CBS Reports: A Timetable For Vietnam" (CBS News Hour) (CBS)
WALTER CRONKITE Reporter "LBJ: Why I Chose Not To Run" (CBS News Hour) (CBS)
PETER DAVIS Writer For "The Battle Of East St. Louis" (CBS News Hour) (CBS)
MARSHALL FLAUM Writer For 'The Natural History Of Our World: The Time Of Man" (Metromedia Producers Corporation) (CBS)
GARY GILSON Reporter-Writer For "Do You Think A Job Is The Answer?" (Public Broadcast Laboratory) (NET)
DOUGLAS LEITERMAN Writer-Director For "Fasten Your Seatbelts" (Document Associates, Inc.) (NET)
FRANK McGEE Reporter For 'The Ordeal Of The American City - Confrontation" (NBC White Paper) (NBC)
FRANK McGEE Reporter For "Who Killed Lake Erie?" (NBC)
NBC NEWS TEAM Commentators For "From Here To The Seventies" (NBC)
ROBERT NORTHSHIELD Writer For "From Here To The Seventies" (NBC)
HUGHES RUDD Reporter For "The Battle Of East St. Louis" (CBS News Hour) (CBS)
LOUIS RUKEYSER Correspondent-Writer For "The Great Dollar Robbery: Can We Arrest Inflation?" (ABC)
DAVID SELTZER Writer For "Adventurers At The Jade Sea" (Metromedia Producers Corporation) (CBS)
ARTHUR ZEGART Writer-Director For "Who Speaks For Man?" (NET Journal) (NET)

OUTSTANDING ACHIEVEMENT IN MAGAZINE-TYPE PROGRAMMING

PROGRAMS

BLACK JOURNAL (Series) (NET) William Greaves, Executive Producer
60 MINUTES (Series) (CBS) Don Hewitt, Executive Producer
60 MINUTES November 25, 1969 (CBS) Don Hewitt, Executive Producer
SOME FOOTNOTES TO 25 NUCLEAR YEARS "Segment of First Tuesday" (NBC) Eliot Frankel, Executive Producer; William B. Hill, Producer
VOICES ON THE INSIDE "Segment of First Tuesday" (NBC) Eliot Frankel, Executive Producer; Len Giovannitti, Producer

INDIVIDUALS

TOM PETTIT Reporter-Writer For "Some Footnotes To 25 Nuclear Years" (Segment of First Tuesday) (NBC)
LEN GIOVANNITTI AND RAFAEL ABRAMOVITZ Directors For "Voices On The Inside" (Segment of First Tuesday) (NBC)
HARRY REASONER Reporter For "60 Minutes" (Series) (CBS)
MIKE WALLACE Reporter For "60 Minutes" (Series) (CBS)

OUTSTANDING ACHIEVEMENT IN CULTURAL DOCUMENTARY PROGRAMMING

PROGRAMS

ARTHUR RUBINSTEIN (NBC) George A. Vicas, Producer
FATHERS AND SONS (CBS News Hour) (CBS) Ernest Leiser, Executive Producer; Harry Morgan, Producer
THE JAPANESE (CBS News Hour) (CBS) Perry Wolff, Executive Producer; Igor Oganesoff, Producer
THE BALLAD OF THE IRON HORSE (John H. Secondari Productions, Ltd.) (ABC) John H. Secondari and Helen Jean Rogers, Producers
CHARLIE BROWN AND CHARLES SCHULZ (Lee Mendelson Film Productions, Inc.) (CBS) Lee Mendelson and Walt DeFaria, Executive Producers; Sheldon Fay, Jr., Producer
THE DESERT WHALES (The Undersea World Of Jacques Cousteau) (Metromedia Producers Corporation) (ABC) Warren Bush and Jacques Cousteau, Executive Producers
FERMENT AND THE CATHOLIC CHURCH (Summer Focus) (ABC) Lester Cooper, Executive Producer; James Benjamin, Producer
HOLLYWOOD: THE SELZNICK YEARS (Metromedia Producers Corporation) (NBC) M.J. Rifkin and Alan Landsburg, Executive Producers; Marshall Flaum, Producer
IN SEARCH OF REMBRANDT (NET Festival) (NET) Lane Slate, Executive Producer; Richard F. Siemanowski, Producer
THE JOURNEY OF ROBERT F. KENNEDY (Wolper Productions, Inc.) (ABC) David L. Wolper, Executive Producer; David Seltzer, Producer
THE MAN HUNTERS (MGM Documentary) (NBC) Irwin Rosten, Executive Producer; Nicolas Noxon, Producer
MODERN MAN: THE LOSER (Directions) (ABC) Wiley F. Hance, Producer
THE MYSTERY OF ANIMAL BEHAVIOR (National Geographic Special) (Metromedia Producers Cor⅛oration) (CBS) Robert C. Doyle, Executive Producer For National Geographic Society; Jack Kaufman, Executive Producer For Metromedia Producers Corporation; Walon Green, Producer
SAHARA: LA CARAVANE DU SEL (NBC) Lou Hazam, Producer
SIBERIA: THE ENDLESS HORIZON (National Geographic Special) (Metromedia Producers Corporation) (CBS) Robert C. Doyle, Executive Producer For National Geographic Society; Jack Kaufman, Executive Producer For Metromedia Producers Corporation; Larry Neiman, Producer
SURVIVAL ON THE PRAIRIE (NBC) Craig Fisher, Producer
THREE YOUNG AMERICANS IN SEARCH OF SURVIVAL (ABC) Stephen Fleischmen, Executive Producer
VOLCANO: BIRTH OF AN ISLAND (CBS News Hour) (CBS) Burton Benjamin, Executive Producer; Isaac Kleinerman, Producer
THE WARREN YEARS (NET) Jim Karayn, Executive Producer

INDIVIDUALS

EDWIN O. REISCHAUER Commentator For "The Japanese" (CBS News Hour) (CBS)
ARTHUR RUBINSTEIN Commentator For "Arthur Rubinstein" (NBC)
JAMES BENJAMIN Writer For "Ferment And The Catholic Church" (Summer Focus) (ABC)
WARREN BUSH Writer For "The Desert Whales" (The Undersea World of Jacques Cousteau) (Metromedia Producers Corporation) (ABC)
HUGH DOWNS Reporter For "Survival On The Prairie" (NBC)
MARSHALL FLAUM Writer For "Hollywood: The Selznick Years" (Metromedia Producers Corporation) (NBC)
MARSHALL FLAUM Director For "Hollywood: The Selznick Years" (Metromedia Producers Corporation) (NBC)
STEPHEN FLEISCHMAN Writer For "Three Young Americans In Search Of Survival" (ABC)
LOU HAZAM Writer For "Sahara: La Caravane Du Sel" (NBC)
JOHN HUSTON Narrator For "The Journey Of Robert F. Kennedy" (Wolper Productions, Inc.) (ABC)
CHARLES KURALT Reporter For "Volcano: Birth Of An Island" (CBS News Hour) (CBS)
JAMES MASON Host And Narrator For "In Search Of Rembrandt" (NET Festival) (NET)
HARRY MORGAN Writer For "Fathers And Sons" (CBS News Hour) (CBS)
NICOLAS NOXON Writer For "The Man Hunters" (MGM Documentary) (NBC)
NICOLAS NOXON Director For "The Man Hunters" (MGM Documentary) (NBC)
THOMAS A. PRIESTLEY Director For "Sahara: La Caravane Du Sel" (NBC)
HELEN JEAN ROGERS Director For "The Ballad Of The Iron Horse" (John H. Secondari Productions, Ltd.) (ABC)
ARTHUR SCHLESINGER, JR. Writer For "The Journey Of Robert F. Kennedy" (Wolper Productions, Inc.) (ABC)
JOHN H. SECONDARI Writer For "The Ballad Of The Iron Horse"

(John H. Secondari Productions, Ltd.) (ABC)
RICHARD F. SIEMANOWSKI Writer For "In Search Of Rembrandt" (NET Festival) (NET)
MEL STUART Director For "The Journey Of Robert F. Kennedy" (Wolper Productions, Inc.) (ABC)
BUD WISER Writer For "Siberia: The Endless Horizon" (National Geographic Special) (Metromedia Producers Corporation) (CBS)
PERRY WOLFF Writer For "The Japanese" (CBS News Hour) (CBS)

ENTERTAINMENT PROGRAM AND INDIVIDUAL ACHIEVEMENTS
(One Award Only In Each of the Remaining Categories)

OUTSTANDING COMEDY SERIES
Award(s) to Executive Producer(s) and Producer(s)
MY WORLD AND WELCOME TO IT (NBC) Sheldon Leonard, Executive Producer; Danny Arnold, Producer
THE BILL COSBY SHOW (NBC) William H. Cosby, Jr., Executive Producer; Marvin Miller, Producer
THE COURTSHIP OF EDDIE'S FATHER (ABC) James Komack, Producer
LOVE, AMERICAN STYLE (ABC) Arnold Margolin, Jim Parker, Executive Producers; Bill D' Angelo, Producer
ROOM 222 (ABC) Gene Reynolds, Producer

OUTSTANDING DRAMATIC SERIES
Award(s) to Executive Producer(s) and Producer(s)
MARCUS WELBY, M.D. (ABC) David Victor, Executive Producer; David J. O'Connell, Producer
THE FORSYTE SAGA (NET) Donald Wilson, Producer
IRONSIDE (NBC) Cy Chermak, Executive Producer; Douglas Benton, Winston Miller, Joel Rogosin, Albert Aley, Producers
THE MOD SQUAD (ABC) Danny Thomas, Aaron Spelling, Executive Producers; Tony Barrett, Harve Bennett, Producers
THE NAME OF THE GAME (NBC) Richard Irving, Executive Producer; George Eckstein, Dean Hargrove, Norman Lloyd, Boris Sagal, Producers
NET PLAYHOUSE (NET) Jac Venza, Executive Producer

OUTSTANDING DRAMATIC PROGRAM
A single program of a series or a special program
Award(s) to Executive Producer(s) and Producer(s)
A STORM IN SUMMER (NBC) (Hallmark Hall Of Fame) M.J. Rifkin, Executive Producer; Alan Landsburg, Producer
DAVID COPPERFIELD (NBC) Frederick Brogger, Producer
HELLO, GOODBYE, HELLO (ABC) (Marcus Welby, M.D.) David Victor, Executive Producer; David J. O'Connell, Producer
MY SWEET CHARLIE (NBC) (World Premiere) Bob Banner, Executive Producer; Richard Levinson, William Link, Producers

OUTSTANDING VARIETY OR MUSICAL SERIES
Award(s) to Executive Producer(s) and Producer(s) and Star (if applicable)
THE DAVID FROST SHOW (Syndicated) Peter Baker, Producer; David Frost, Star
THE CAROL BURNETT SHOW (CBS) Joe Hamilton, Producer; Carol Burnett, Star
THE DEAN MARTIN SHOW (NBC) Greg Garrison, Producer; Dean Martin, Star
THE DICK CAVETT SHOW (ABC) Jack Rollins, Executive Producer; Tony Converse, Producer; Dick Cavett, Star
ROWAN AND MARTIN'S LAUGH-IN (NBC) George Schlatter, Executive Producer; Carolyn Raskin, Paul Keyes, Producers; Dan Rowan and Dick Martin, Stars

OUTSTANDING VARIETY OR MUSICAL PROGRAM
A single program of a series or a special program
Award(s) to Executive Producer(s) and Producer(s) and Star (if applicable) A. Variety and Popular Music
ANNIE, THE WOMEN IN THE LIFE OF A MAN (CBS) Joseph Cates, Executive Producer; Martin Charnin, Producer; Anne Bancroft, Star
THE FRIARS CLUB "ROASTS" JACK BENNY (NBC) (Kraft Music Hall) Gary Smith, Dwight Hemion, Producers; Jack Benny, Star
THE SECOND BIL COSBY SPECIAL (NBC) Roy Silver, Executive Producer; Bruce Campbell, Roy Silver, Producers; Bill Cosby, Star
SINATRA (CBS) Frank Sinatra, Executive Producer; Carolyn Raskin, Producer; Frank Sinatra, Star
THE SOUND OF BURT BACHARACH (NBC) (Kraft Music Hall) Gary Smith, Dwight Hemion, Producers; Burt Bacharach, Star
B. Classical Music
CINDERELLA (NATIONAL BALLET OF CANADA) (NET) (NET Festival) John Barnes and Curtis Davis, Executive Producers; Norman Campbell, Producer
S. HUROK PRESENTS - PART III (CBS) Jim Krayer, Executive Producer; Roger Englander, Producer
SOUNDS OF SUMMER (The Blossom Music Center with Pierre Boulez) (NET) Craig Gilbert, Executive Producer; Jack Sameth, Producer
THE SWITCHED-ON SYMPHONY (NBC) Pierre Cossette, Burt Sugarman, Executive Producers; Jack Good, Producer

OUTSTANDING NEW SERIES
Award(s) to Executive Producer(s) and Producer(s)
ROOM 222 (ABC) Gene Reynolds, Producer
THE BILL COSBY SHOW (NBC) William H. Cosby, Jr., Executive Producer; Marvin Miller, Producer
THE FORSYTE SAGA (NET) Donald Wilson, Producer
MARCUS WELBY, M.D. (ABC) David Victor, Executive Producer; David J. O'Connell, Producer
SESAME STREET (NET) David D. Connell, Executive Producer; Sam Gibbon, Jon Stone, Lutrelle Horne, Producers

OUTSTANDING SINGLE PERFORMANCE BY AN ACTOR IN A LEADING ROLE
A one-time appearance in a series or for a special program
PETER USTINOV "A Storm In Summer" (Hallmark Hall Of Fame) (NBC)
AL FREEMAN, JR. "My Sweet Charlie" (World Premiere) (NBC)
SIR LAWRENCE OLIVIER "David Copperfield" (NBC)

OUTSTANDING SINGLE PERFORMANCE BY AN ACTRESS IN A LEADING ROLE
A one-time appearance in a series or for a special program
PATTY DUKE "My Sweet Charlie" (World Premiere) (NBC)
DAME EDITH EVANS "David Copperfield" (NBC)
SHIRLEY JONES "Silent Night, Lonely Night" (World Premiere) (NBC)

OUTSTANDING CONTINUED PERFORMANCE BY AN ACTOR IN A LEADING ROLE IN A DRAMATIC SERIES
ROBERT YOUNG "Marcus Welby, M.D." (ABC)
RAYMOND BURR "Ironside" (NBC)
MIKE CONNORS "Mannix" (CBS)
ROBERT WAGNER "It Takes A Thief" (ABC)

OUTSTANDING CONTINUED PERFORMANCE BY AN ACTRESS IN A LEADING ROLE IN A DRAMATIC SERIES

SUSAN HAMPSHIRE "The Forsyte Saga" (NET)
JOAN BLONDELL "Here Comes The Brides" (ABC)
PEGGY LIPTON "The Mod Squad" (ABC)

OUTSTANDING CONTINUED PERFORMANCE BY AN ACTOR IN A LEADING ROLE IN A COMEDY SERIES

WILLIAM WINDOM "My World And Welcome To It" (NBC)
BILL COSBY "The Bill Cosby Show" (NBC)
LLOYD HAYNES "Room 222" (ABC)

OUTSTANDING CONTINUED PERFORMANCE BY AN ACTRESS IN A LEADING ROLE IN A COMEDY SERIES

HOPE LANGE "The Ghost And Mrs. Muir" (ABC)
ELIZABETH MONTGOMERY "Bewitched" (ABC)
MARLO THOMAS "That Girl" (ABC)

OUTSTANDING PERFORMANCE BY AN ACTOR IN A SUPPORTING ROLE IN DRAMA

A continuing or one-time appearance in a series, or for a special program

JAMES BROLIN "Marcus Welby, M.D." (Series) (ABC)
TIGE ANDREWS "The Mod Squad" (Series) (ABC)
GREG MORRIS "Mission: Impossible" (Series) (CBS)

OUTSTANDING PERFORMANCE BY AN ACTRESS IN A SUPPORTING ROLE IN A DRAMA

A continuing or one-time appearance in a series, or for a special program

GAIL FISHER "Mannix" (Series) (CBS)
BARBARA ANDERSON "Ironside" (Series) (NBC)
SUSAN SAINT JAMES "The Name Of The Game" (Series) (NBC)

OUTSTANDING PERFORMANCE BY AN ACTOR IN A SUPPORTING ROLE IN COMEDY

A continuing or one-time appearance in a series, or for a special program

MICHAEL CONSTANTINE "Room 222" (Series) (ABC)
WERNER KLEMPERER "Hogan's Heroes" (Series) (CBS)
CHARLES NELSON REILLY "The Ghost And Mrs. Muir" (Series) (ABC)

OUTSTANDING PERFORMANCE BY AN ACTRESS IN A SUPPORTING ROLE IN COMEDY

A continuing or one-time appearance in a series, or for a special program

KAREN VALENTINE "Room 222" (Series) (ABC)
AGNES MOOREHEAD "Bewitched" (Series) (ABC)
LURENE TUTTLE "Julia" (Series) (NBC)

OUTSTANDING WRITING ACHIEVEMENT IN DRAMA

A single program of a series or a special program

RICHARD LEVINSON, WILLIAM LINK "My Sweet Charlie" (World Premiere) (NBC)
GEORGE BELLAK "Sadbird" (CBS Playhouse) (CBS)
DON M. MANKIEWICZ "Marcus Welby, M.D." (The ABC Wednesday Night Movie) (Pilot) (ABC)

OUTSTANDING WRITING ACHIEVEMENT IN COMEDY, VARIETY OR MUSIC

A single program of a series or a special program

GARY BELKIN, PETER BELLWOOD, HERB SARGENT, THOMAS MEEHAN, JUDITH VIORST "Annie, The Women In The Life Of A Man" (CBS)
PAUL W. KEYES, DAVID PANICH, MARC LONDON, COSLOUGH JOHNSON, JIM CARLSON, JIM MULLIGAN, JOHN CARSEY, GENE FARMER, JEREMY LLOYD, JOHN RAPPAPORT, STEPHEN SPEARS, JACK DOUGLAS, ALLAN MANNINGS "Rowan And Martin's Laugh-In" (with Buddy Hackett) (NBC)
ALLAN MANINGS, DAVID PANICH, COSLOUGH JOHNSON, JOHN CARSEY, STEPHEN SPEARS, JOHN RAPPAPORT, JIM CARLSON, MARC LONDON, CHET DOWLING, JIM ABELL, BARRY TOOK, JACK DOUGLAS, JIM MULLIGAN, GENE FARMER, JEREMY LLOYD "Rowan And Martin's Laugh-In" (with Nancy Sinatra) (NBC)

OUTSTANDING DIRECTORIAL ACHIEVEMENT IN DRAMA

A single program of a series or a special program

PAUL BOGART "Shadow Game" (CBS Playhouse) (CBS)
BUZZ KULIK "A Storm In Summer" (Hallmark Hall Of Fame) (NBC)
LAMONT JOHNSON "My Sweet Charlie" (World Premiere) (NBC)

OUTSTANDING DIRECTORIAL ACHIEVEMENT IN COMEDY, VARIETY OR MUSIC

A single program of a series or a special program

DWIGHT A. HEMION "The Sound Of Burt Bacharach" (Kraft Music Hall) (NBC)
SEYMOUR BERNS "The Second Bill Cosby Special" (NBC)
ROGER ENGLANDER "Berlioz Takes A Trip" (N.Y. Philharmonic Young People's Concerts) (CBS)

OUTSTANDING ACHIEVEMENT IN CHOREOGRAPHY

A single program of a series or a special program

NORMAN MAEN "This Is Tom Jones" (with Mary Hopkins, Jose Feliciano, Shelley Berman) (ABC)
TOM HANSEN "The Red Skelton Show" (with Walter Brennan) (Unidentified Flying Objects) (CBS)
DAVID WINTERS "Ann Margaret - From Hollywood With Love" (CBS)

OUTSTANDING ACHIEVEMENT IN MUSIC COMPOSITION

A. For a series or a single program of a series (in its first year only) (In the first year of original music's use only)

MORTON STEVENS "A Thousand Pardons, You're Dead" (Hawaii Five-O) (CBS)
QUINCY JONES "The Bill Cosby Show" (Series) (NBC)
FRANKLYN MARKS "Charlie, The Lonesome Cougar" (The Wonderful World of Disney) (NBC)

B. For a special program

PETE RUGOLO "The Challengers" (CBS Friday Night Movie) (CBS)

VAN ALEXANDER "Gene Kelley's Wonderful World Of Girls With 50 Girls, Count 'Em, 50" (NBC)
JACQUES BELASCO "'The Threshold" (Apollo: Journey To The Moon) (NBC)

OUTSTANDING ACHIEVEMENT IN MUSIC DIRECTION OF A VARIETY, MUSICAL OR DRAMATIC PROGRAM
A single program of a series or a special program
PETER MATZ "The Sound Of Burt Bacharach" (Kraft Music Hall) (NBC)
MORT LINDSEY "The Merv Griffin Show" (from Las Vegas with Chuck Connors, Joey Heatherton, Buddy Greco, Jack E. Leonard, Jerry Van Dyke) (CBS)
JOHNNIE SPENCE "This Is Tom Jones" (with Mary Hopkins, Shelley Berman, Jose Feliciano) (ABC)

OUTSTANDING ACHIEVEMENT IN MUSIC, LYRICS AND SPECIAL MATERIAL
A series or a single program of a series or a special program written for television
ARNOLD MARGOLIN, CHARLES FOX "Love, American Style" (Series) (ABC)
CHARLES AIDMAN, NAOMI C. HIRSHHORN "Spoon River" (CBS)
BILLY BARNES "Rowan And Martin's Laugh-In" (with Carol Channing) (NBC)

OUTSTANDING ACHIEVEMENT IN ART DIRECTION OR SCENIC DESIGN
For a dramatic program or feature length film made for television; for a series, a single program of a series or a special program
JAN SCOTT AND EARL CARLSON Art Director and Set Decorator Respectively, For "Shadow Game" (CBS Playhouse) (CBS)
GIBSON HOLLEY AND LUCIEN M. HAFLEY Art Director and Set Decorator Respectively, For "The Falcon" (3 Parts) (Mission: Impossible) (CBS)
HUGH GRAY RAISKY AND WESLEY LAWS Art Director and Set Decorator Respectively, For "Man On The Moon: The Epic Journey of Apollo XI" (CBS)
JAMES TRITTIPO Art Director For "The File On Devlin" (Hallmark Hall Of Fame) (NBC)
B. For a Musical or Variety single program of a series or a special program
E. JAY KRAUSE Art Director For "Mitzi's 2nd Special" (NBC)
PAUL BARNES AND BOB SANSOM; BILL HARP Art Directors and Set Decorator Respectively, For "The Carol Burnett Show" (with Steve Lawrence, Edward Villella) (CBS)
RENE LAGLER AND ROBERT CHECCHI Art Director and Set Decorator Respectively, For "The Glen Campbell Goodtime Hour" (with Tom Jones, Totie Fields, Jackie DeShannon) (CBS)

OUTSTANDING ACHIEVEMENT IN LIGHTING DIRECTION
A single program of a series or a special program, produced for electronic television only
LEARD DAVIS, ED HILL (Video: RICHARD SCOVEL, CLIVE BASSETT) "Appalachian Autumn" (CBS Playhouse) (CBS)
JOHN FRESCHI "The Switched-On Symphony" (NBC)
JIM KILGORE "The Johnny Cash Show" (with Rod McKuen, The Everly Brothers, Dusty Springfield) (ABC)
WILLIAM KLAGES "Kraft Music Hall" (with Petula Clark, Anthony Newley, Lou Rawls) (NBC)

OUTSTANDING ACHIEVEMENT IN COSTUME DESIGN
A single program of a series or a special program
BOB MACKIE "Diana Ross And The Supremes And The Temptations On Broadway" (NBC)
MICHAEL TRAVIS "Rowan And Martin's Laugh-In" (with Danny Kaye) (NBC)
GEORGE WHITTAKER "The Don Adams Special: Hooray For Hollywood" (CBS)

OUTSTANDING ACHIEVEMENT IN MAKE-UP
A single program of a series or a special program
RAY SEBASTIAN AND LOUIS A. PHILLIPPI "The Don Adams Special: Hooray For Hollywood" (CBS)
SHIRLEY MUSLIN AND MARIE ROCHE "This Is Tom Jones" (with Mary Hopkins, Jose Feliciano, Shelley Berman) (ABC)

OUTSTANDING ACHIEVEMENT IN CINEMATOGRAPHY FOR ENTERTAINMENT PROGRAMMING
A. For a series or a single program of a series
WALTER STRENGE "Hello, Goodbye, Hello" (Marcus Welby, M.D.) (ABC)
HARVEY GENKINS "N.Y.P.D." (Series) (ABC)
AL FRANCIS "The Amnesiac" (Mission: Impossible) (CBS)
B. For a special or feature length program made for television
LIONEL LINDON "Ritual Of Evil" (NBC Monday Night at the Movies) (NBC)
GENE POLITO "My Sweet Charlie" (World Premiere) (NBC)
HOWARD R. SCHWARTZ "The Immortal" (ABC Movie of the Week) (ABC)

OUTSTANDING ACHIEVEMENT IN CINEMATOGRAPHY FOR NEWS AND DOCUMENTARY PROGRAMMING
A. For a series, a single program of a series, a special program, program segments or elements within a regularly scheduled News program and coverage of Special Events
EDWARD WINKLE "Model Hippie" (The Huntley-Brinkley Report) (NBC)
CHARLES W. BOYLE "Middle Town U.S.A." (The Huntley-Brinkley Report) (NBC)
JAMES P. WATT, JR. "High School Profile" (The Huntley-Brinkley Report) (NBC)
B. Documentary, Magazine-type or Mini-documentary programs
THOMAS A. PRIESTLEY "Sahara: La Caravane due Sel" (NBC)
CHUCK AUSTIN, A.S.C. "The Ordeal of the American City - Confrontation" (NBC White Paper) (NBC)
RONALD W. VAN NOSTRAND "Hide And Go Seek" (First Tuesday) (NBC)

OUTSTANDING ACHIEVEMENT IN FILM EDITING FOR ENTERTAINMENT PROGRAMMING
A. For a series or a single program of a series
BILL MOSHER "Sweet Smell Of Failure" (Bracken's World) (NBC)
ARTHUR DAVID HILTON "The Falcon" (3 Parts) (Mission: Impossible) (CBS)
AXEL R. HUBERT "The Great Power Failure" (The Ghost And Mrs.

Muir) (ABC)
B. For a special or feature length program made for television
EDWARD M. ABROMS "My Sweet Charlie" (World Premiere) (NBC)
IGO KANTOR, JAMES HENRIKSON, STAN SIEGEL, TONY CARRAS, FRANK McKELVEY "Bob Hope Christmas Special" (NBC)
GENE PALMER "Marcus Welby, M.D." (ABC Wednesday Night Movie) (Pilot) (ABC)

OUTSTANDING ACHIEVEMENT IN FILM EDITING FOR NEWS AND DOCUMENTARY PROGRAMMING

A. For a series, a single program of a series, a special program, program segments or elements within a regularly scheduled News program and coverage of Special Events
MICHAEL C. SHUGRUE "The High School Profile" (The Huntley-Brinkley Report) (NBC)
RAYMOND L. ELBERFELD AND RICHARD A. HESSEL "Eisenhower Funeral" (The Huntley Brinkley Report) (NBC)
FRED FLAMENHAFT, MARTIN SHEPPARD, TOM DUNPHY, PAT MINERVA, KEN SHEA, GEORGE JOHNSON (The Huntley-Brinkley Report) (Series) (NBC)
B. Documentary, Magazine-type or Mini-documentary Programs
JOHN SOH "The Desert Whales" (The Undersea World Of Jacques Cousteau) (ABC)
PETER C. JOHNSON "The Mystery Of Animal Behavior" (CBS)
ROBERT B. LOWEREE AND HANK GRENNON "Arthur Rubinstein" (NBC)

OUTSTANDING ACHIEVEMENT IN FILM SOUND EDITING

A single program of a series or a special program
DOUGLAS H. GRINDSTAFF, ALEX BAMATTRE, MICHAEL COLGAN, BILL LEE, JOE KAVIGAN, JOSEF E. VON STROHEIM "The Immortal" (Movie of the Week) (ABC)
RICHARD E. RADERMAN AND NORMAN KARLIN "Charlie Noon" (Gunsmoke) (CBS)
DON HALL, JR., LARRY MEEK, WILLIAM HOWARD, JOHN KLINE, ROBERT CORNETT, FRANK R. WHITE "A Small War" (Land Of the Giants) (ABC)

OUTSTANDING ACHIEVEMENT IN FILM SOUND MIXING

A single program of a series or a special program
GORDON L. DAY AND DOMINICK GAFFEY "The Submarine" (Mission: Impossible) (CBS)
MELVIN M. METCALFE, SR., JOHN A. STRANSKY, JR., CLARENCE SELF, ROGER HEMAN "My Sweet Charlie" (World Premi re) (NBC)
ROGER GARY ANDREWS "Some Footnotes To K5 Nuclear Years" (First Tuesday) (NBC)

OUTSTANDING ACHIEVEMENT IN LIVE OR TAPE SOUND MIXING

A single program of a series or a special program
BILL COLE AND DAVE WILLIAMS "The Switched-On Symphony" (NBC)
MAHLON H. FOX "The Sound Of Burt Bacharach" (Kraft Music Hall) (NBC)
NEAL WEINSTEIN "The Jim Nabors Hour" (with Vikki Carr) (CBS)

OUTSTANDING ACHIEVEMENT IN VIDEO TAPE EDITING

A single program of a series or a special program
JOHN SHULTIS "The Sound Of Burt Bacharach" ("Pas de deaux" Segment and "Promises, Promises" Segment) (Kraft Music Hall) (NBC)
NICK GIORDANO "Finale" (The Hollywood Palace) (ABC)
ARMOND POITRAS "An Evening With Julie Andrews And Harry Belafonte" (NBC)

OUTSTANDING ACHIEVEMENT IN TECHNICAL DIRECTION AND ELECTRONIC CAMERAWORK

A single program of a series or a special program
HEINO RIPP, Technical Director; Al Camoin, Gene Martin, Donald Mulvaney, Cal Shadwell, Cameramen "The Sound Of Burt Bacharach" (Kraft Music Hall) (NBC)
CHARLES FRANKLIN AND KEN LAMKIN, Technical Directors; Robert Fonarow, Nick DeMos, Ben Wolf, Cameramen "A Storm In Summer" (Hallmark Hall Of Fame) (NBC)
O.TAMBURRI, Technical Director; Gene Schwarz, Robert Keyes, Kurt Tonnessen, Ronald Sheldon, Roy Holm, Wayne Osterhout, Cameramen "An Evening With Julie Andrews And Harry Belafonte" (NBC)

THE AREAS
(Possibility of One Award, More Than One Award, or No Award)

OUTSTANDING ACHIEVEMENT IN CHILDREN'S PROGRAMMING

PROGRAMS
SESAME STREET Series (NET) David D. Connell, Executive Producer; Sam Gibbon, Jon Stone, Lutrelle Horne, Producers
THE WONDERFUL WORLD OF DISNEY Series (NBC) Ron Miller, Executive Producer

INDIVIDUALS
JOE RAPOSO AND JEFFREY MOSS Music and Lyrics For "This Way to Sesame Street" (NBC)
JON STONE, JEFFREY MOSS, RAY SIPHERD, JERRY JUHL, DAN WILCOX, DAVE CONNELL, BRUCE HART, CAROLE HART, VIRGINIA SCHONE Writer For "Sally Sees Sesame Street" (Sesame Street) (NET)
MICHAEL LOEWENSTEIN Scenic Design For "Kukla, Fran And Ollie" (NET)

OUTSTANDING ACHIEVEMENT IN DAYTIME PROGRAMMING

PROGRAMS
TODAY Series (NBC) Stuart Schulberg, Producer
THE GALLOPING GOURMET Series (Syndicated) Treena Kerr, Producer; Graham Kerr, Host

INDIVIDUALS
HUGH DOWNS "Today" Series (NBC)
JOE GARAGIOLA "Today" Series (NBC)

828   EMMYS

OUTSTANDING ACHIEVEMENT IN SPORTS PROGRAMMING

PROGRAMS
THE NFL GAMES (CBS) William Fitts, Executive Producer
ABC'S WIDE WORLD OF SPORTS Series (ABC) Roone Arledge, Executive Producer
1969 WORLD SERIES (NBC) Lou Kusserow, Producer

INDIVIDUALS
ROBERT R. FORTE Film Editing For "Pre-Game Program" (Pro-Bowl Game) (CBS)
ROBERT RIGER Director For "International Ski Championships Val D'Isere, France" (ABC's Wide World of Sports) (ABC)

SPECIAL CLASSIFICATION OF OUTSTANDING PROGRAM AND INDIVIDUAL ACHIEVEMENT

PROGRAMS
MUTUAL OF OMAHA'S WILD KINGDOM Series (NBC) Don Meier, Producer
FELLINI - A DIRECTOR'S NOTEBOOK "NBC Experiment in Television" (NBC) Peter Goldfarb, Producer

INDIVIDUALS
GOLDIE HAWN "Rowan And Martin's Laugh-In" Series (NBC)
ARTE JOHNSON "Rowan And Martin's Laugh-In" Series (NBC)

OUTSTANDING ACHIEVEMENT IN ANY AREA OF CREATIVE TECHNICAL CRAFTS
JONNIE BURKE Special Visual Effects For "Time Bomb" (Mission: Impossible) (CBS)
HOWARD A. ANDERSON, JR., WILFRID CLINE, BILL HANSARD Special Photographic Effects For "Rally 'Round The Flag Boys" (My World And Welcome To It) (NBC)
EDIE J. PANDA Hair Styling For "The Don Adams Special - Hooray For Hollywood" (CBS)

SPECIAL AWARDS

OUTSTANDING ACHIEVEMENT IN ENGINEERING DEVELOPMENT
APOLLO COLOR TELEVISION FROM SPACE For the conceptual aspects, an Emmy to the Video Communications Division of NASA, and For development of the camera, an Emmy Award to the Westinghouse Electric Corporation.

CITATION
AMPEX CORPORATION For the development of the HS-200 Color Television Production System.

THE STATION AWARD
THE SLOW GUILLOTINE (KNBC-TV, Los Angeles, California)
CITY IN CRISIS (WDSU-TV, New Orleans, Louisiana)
JOB MAN CARAVAN (SCE-TV, Columbia, South Carolina)
JOURNEY TO A PINE BOX (WRC-TV, Washington, D.C.)
NEW VOICES IN THE WILDERNESS (WNBC-TV, New York, New York)
THE SAVAGE ROOT (WBZ-TV, Boston, Massachusetts)
URBAN MYTHOLOGY (WGTV, Athens, Georgia)
A VISIT TO ALLENVILLE (KOOL-TV, Phoenix, Arizona)
YOUNG, BLACK AND EXPLOSIVE (KOMO-TV, Seattle, Washington)

SPECIAL CITATION
THE OTHER AMERICANS (WJZ-TV, Baltimore, Maryland)
Honorable Mention - YOUNG, BLACK AND EXPLOSIVE (KOMO-TV, Seattle, Washington)
THE CHILDREN ARE WAITING (WBBM-TV, Chicago, Illinois)
THE FIRST STEP (WETK-TV, Winooski, Vermont)
SICKLE CELL ANEMIA (WABC-TV, New York, New York)
WHAT'S SO SPECIAL ABOUT WARRENDALE? (WIIC-TV, Pittsburgh, Pennsylvania)
WHOSE MUSEUM? (KPIX-TV, San Francisco, California)

THE TRUSTEES AWARD
To the Presidents of the News Divisions for "safeguarding the public's right to full information, at a time when the constitutional right of freedom of the press is under its strongest attack."

The Trustee Citation to the hundreds of men comprising the staff of NASA who "made it possible for hundreds of millions of people throughout the world to witness history being made 238,000 miles away."

The Trustee Citation to the 3M Company for "having presented some of the finest art, cultural, scientific, and entertainment programs in the public interest. This company has contributed significantly to upgrading the quality of television while presenting its sales message with modesty and taste."

1970/71

NEWS AND DOCUMENTARY PROGRAM AND INDIVIDUAL ACHIEVEMENTS
(Possibility of one Award, more than one Award, or no Award)

OUTSTANDING ACHIEVEMENT WITHIN REGULARLY SCHEDULED NEWS PROGRAMS

PROGRAMS
FIVE PART INVESTIGATION OF WELFARE (NBC Nightly News) (NBC) Wallace Westfeldt, Executive Producer; David Teitelbaum, Producer
COVERAGE OF THE INDO CHINA WAR (ABC Evening News) (ABC) Avram Westin, Executive Producer
COVERAGE OF THE PAKISTANI TIDAL WAVE DISASTER (NBC Nightly News) (NBC) Wallace Westfeldt, Executive Producer; David Teitelbaum, Producer
COVERAGE OF THE MIDDLE EAST PLANE HIJACKINGS (NBC Nightly News) (NBC) Wallace Westfeldt, Executive Producer; David Teitelbaum, Producer

INDIVIDUALS
BRUCE MORTON Correspondent For "Reports From The Lt. Calley Trial" (CBS Evening News With Walter Cronkite) (CBS)
PHIL BRADY Correspondent For "Investigation Of GI Drug Addiction In Vietnam" (NBC Nightly News) (NBC)

OUTSTANDING ACHIEVEMENT IN COVERAGE OF SPECIAL EVENTS

PROGRAMS
CBS NEWS SPACE COVERAGE FOR 1970-71: "Aquarius On The Moon: The Flight Of Apollo 13" and "Ten Yeas Later: The Flight Of Apollo 14" (CBS) Robert Wussler, Executive Producer; Joan Richman, Producer
EARTH DAY: A QUESTION OF SURVIVAL (CBS) Ernest Leiser, Executive Producer; Bernard Birnbaum, Phillip Scheffler and Paul Green-

berg, Producers
NBC NEWS COVERAGE OF THE SOUTHERN CALIFORNIA EARTHQUAKE (NBC) William B. Hill, Richard Fischer, Producers

INDIVIDUALS

WALTER CRONKITE Correspondent For "CBS News Space Coverage For 1970-71: Aquarius on the Moon: The Flight of Apollo 13" and "Ten Years Later: The Flight of Apollo 14" (CBS)
DOUGLAS KIKER Correspondent for "The War In Jordan" (NBC)

OUSTANDING ACHIEVEMENT IN NEWS DOCUMENTARY PROGRAMMING

PROGRAMS

THE SELLING OF THE PENTAGON (CBS News) Perry Wolff, Executive Producer; Peter Davis, Producer (CBS)
THE WORLD OF CHARLIE COMPANY (CBS News) Ernest Leiser, Executive Producer; Russ Bensley, Producer (CBS)
NBC WHITE PAPER: POLLUTION IS A MATTER OF CHOICE (NBC News) Fred Freed, Producer (NBC)

INDIVIDUALS

JOHN LAURENCE Correspondent For "The World Of Charlie Company" (CBS News) (CBS)
FRED FREED Writer For "NBC White Paper: Pollution Is A Matter of Choice" (NBC News) (NBC)
DENIS SANDERS AND ROBERT FRESCO Directors For "Trial: The City and County of Denver vs. Lauren R. Watson" (NET Journal) (PBS)

OUTSTANDING ACHIEVEMENT IN MAGAZINE-TYPE PROGRAMMING

PROGRAMS

GULF OF TONKIN SEGMENT "60 Minutes" Joseph Wershba, Producer (CBS)
THE GREAT AMERICAN DREAM MACHINE (Series) A. H. Perlmutter, Jack Willis, Executive Producers (PBS)
BLACK JOURNAL (Series) Tony Brown, Executive Producer; Phil Burton, Stan Lathan, Producers (PBS)

INDIVIDUALS

MIKE WALLACE Correspondent For "60 Minutes" (Series) (CBS)
MORLEY SAFER Correspondent For "Gulf Of Tonkin Segment" (60 Minutes) (CBS)
ELINOR BUNIN Director of Animated Film "The Great American Dream Machine" (PBS)

OUTSTANDING ACHIEVEMENT IN CULTURAL DOCUMENTARY PROGRAMMING

PROGRAMS

THE EVERGLADES (NBC News) Craig Fisher, Producer (NBC)
THE MAKING OF "BUTCH CASSIDY & THE SUNDANCE KID" (Penthouse Productions, Inc.) Ronald Preissman, Producer (NBC)
ARTHUR PENN, 1922-: THEMES AND VARIANTS (Robert Hughes Productions) Robert Hughes, Producer (PBS)
GERTRUDE STEIN: WHEN THIS YOU SEE, REMEMBER ME "Fanfare" Perry Miller Adato, Producer (PBS)
WHICH WAY, AMERICA? (KNBC Productions) John Gentri, Producer (NBC)

INDIVIDUALS

NANA MAHOMO Narrator For "A Black View Of South Africa" (CBS News) (CBS)
ROBERT GUENETTE AND THEODORE H. STRAUSS Writers For "They've Killed President Lincoln!" (Wolper Productions, Inc.) (NBC)
ROBERT YOUNG Director For "The Eskimo: Fight for Life" (Education Development Center) (CBS)
CRAIG GILBERT Director-Writer For "The Triumph Of Christy Brown" (Realities) (PBS)
GEORGE C. SCOTT Narrator For "A Man Named Lombardi" (Simon & Flynn, Inc.) (NBC)
JERRY IZENBERG Writer For "A Man Named Lombardi" (Simon & Flynn, Inc.) (NBC)
PERRY MILLER ADATO Director For "Gertrude Stein: When This You See, Remember Me" (Fanfare) (PBS)
NATHAN KROLL Director For "Helen Hayes - Portrait Of An American Actress" (Net Playhouse) (Kroll Productions, Inc.) (PBS)

ENTERTAINMENT PROGRAM AND INDIVIDUAL ACHIEVEMENTS

(One Award Only In Each Of The Remaining Categories)

OUTSTANDING SERIES - COMEDY

Award(s) to Executive Producer(s) and Producer(s)

ALL IN THE FAMILY (CBS) Norman Lear, Producer
ARNIE (CBS) Rick Mittleman, Producer
LOVE, AMERICAN STYLE (ABC) Arnold Margolin, Jim Parker, Executive Producers; Bill Idelson, Harvey Miller, William P. D'Angelo, Producers
THE MARY TYLER MOORE SHOW (CBS) James L. Brooks, Allan Burns, Executive Producers; David Davis, Producer
THE ODD COUPLE (ABC) Jerry Belson, Gary Marshall, Executive Producers; Jerry Davis, Producer

OUTSTANDING SERIES - DRAMA

Award(s) to Executive Producer(s) and Producers(s)

THE SENATOR - THE BOLD ONES (NBC) David Levinson, Producer
THE FIRST CHURCHILLS - MASTERPIECE THEATRE (PBS) Donald Wilson, Christopher Sarson, Producers
IRONSIDE (NBC) Cy Chermark, Executive Producer; Douglas Benton, Winston Miller, Joel Rogosin, Albert Aley, Producers
NET PLAYHOUSE (PBS) Jac Venza, Executive Producer
MARCUS WELBY, M.D. (ABC) David Victor, Executive Producer; David J. O'Connell, Producer

OUTSTANDING SINGLE PROGRAM - DRAMA OR COMEDY

A Single Program of a series or a special program
Award(s) to Executive Producer(s) and Producer(s)

THE ANDERSONVILLE TRIAL (PBS) (Hollywood Television Theatre) Lewis Freedman, Producer
HAMLET (NBC) (Hallmark Hall of Fame) Cecil Clarke, Executive Producer; George LeMaire, Producer
THE PRICE (NBC) (Hallmark Hall of Fame) David Susskind, Producer
THEY'RE TEARING DOWN TIM RILEY'S BAR (NBC) (Rod Serling's Night Gallery - Four-In-One) Jack Laird, Producer
VANISHED - PARTS I & II (NBC) (World Premiere Monday & Tuesday Night At The Movies) David Victor, Executive Producer; David J. O'Connell, Producer

OUTSTANDING VARIETY SERIES - MUSICAL

Award(s) to Executive Producer(s) and Producer(s) and Star (if applicable)

THE FLIP WILSON SHOW (NBC) Monte Kay, Executive Producer; Bob Henry, Producer; Flip Wilson, Star
THE CAROL BURNETT SHOW (CBS) Joe Hamilton, Executive Producer; Arnie Rosen, Producer; Carol Burnett, Star
ROWAN AND MARTIN'S LAUGH-IN (NBC) George Schlatter, Executive Producer; Carolyn Raskin, Producer; Dick Martin & Dan Rowan, Stars

OUTSTANDING VARIETY SERIES - TALK
Award(s) to Executive Producer(s) and Producer(s) and Star (if applicable)
THE DAVID FROST SHOW (Syndicated) Peter Baker, Producer; David Frost, Star
THE DICK CAVETT SHOW (ABC) Jack Rollins, Executive Producer; John Gilroy, Producer; Dick Cavett, Star
THE TONIGHT SHOW STARRING JOHNNY CARSON (NBC) Fred DeCordova and Rudy Tellez, Producers; Johnny Carson, Star

OUTSTANDING SINGLE PROGRAM - VARIETY OR MUSICAL
A single program of a series or a special program Award(s) to Executive Producer(s) and Producer(s) and Star (if applicable) A. Variety and Popular Music
SINGER PRESENTS BURT BACHARACH (CBS) Gary Smith, Dwight Hemion, Producers; Burt Bacharach, Star
ANOTHER EVENING WITH BURT BACHARACH (NBC) (Kraft Music Hall) Gary Smith, Dwight Hemion, Producers; Burt Bacharach, Star
HARRY AND LENA (ABC) Chiz Schultz, Producer; Harry Belafonte and Lena Horn, Stars
B. Classical Music
LEOPOLD STOKOWSKI (PBS) "Net Festival" Curtis W. Davis, Executive Producer; Thomas Slevin, Producer; Leopold Stokowski, Star
QUEEN OF SPADES (PBS) "Fanfare - NET Opera Theatre" Herman Adler, Producer
SWAN LAKE (PBS) "Fanfare" Curtis W. Davis, John Barnes, Executive Producers; Norman Campbell, Producer

OUTSTANDING NEW SERIES
Award(s) to Executive Producer(s) and Producer(s)
ALL IN THE FAMILY (CBS) Norman Lear, Producer
THE FLIP WILSON SHOW (NBC) Monte Kay, Executive Producer; Bob Henry, Producer
THE MARY TYLER MOORE SHOW (CBS) James L. Brooks, Allan Burns, Executive Producers; David Davis, Producer
THE ODD COUPLE (ABC) Jerry Belson, Gary Marshall, Executive Producers; Jerry Davis, Producer
THE SENATOR - THE BOLD ONES (NBC) David Levinson, Producer

OUTSTANDING SINGLE PERFORMANCE BY AN ACTOR IN A LEADING ROLE
A one-time appearance in a series or for a special program
GEORGE C. SCOTT "The Price" (Hallmark Hall of Fame) (NBC)
JACK CASSIDY "The Andersonville Trial" (Hollywood Television Theatre) (PBS)
HAL HOLBROOK 'A Clear And Present Danger" (World Premiere NBC Saturday Night At the Movies) (NBC)
RICHARD WIDMARK "Vanished, Parts I & II" (World Premiere NBC Monday & Tuesday Night At The Movies) (NBC)
GIG YOUNG "The Neon Ceiling" (World Premiere NBC Monday Night At The Movies) (NBC)

OUTSTANDING SINGLE PERFORMANCE BY AN ACTRESS IN A LEADING ROLE
A one-time appearance in a series or for a special program
LEE GRANT "The Neon Ceiling" (World Premiere NBC Monday Night At The Movies) (NBC)
COLLEEN DEWHURST "The Price" (Hallmark Hall of Fame) (NBC)
LEE GRANT "Ransom For A Dead Man" (World Premiere NBC Monday Night At The Movies) (NBC)

OUTSTANDING CONTINUED PERFORMANCE BY AN ACTOR IN A LEADING ROLE IN A DRAMATIC SERIES
HAL HOLBROOK (The Senator: The Bold ones) (NBC)
RAYMOND BURR (Ironside) (NBC)
MIKE CONNORS (Mannix) (CBS)
ROBERT YOUNG (Marcus Welby, M.D.) (ABC)

OUTSTANDING CONTINUED PERFORMANCE BY AN ACTRESS IN A LEADING ROLE IN A DRAMATIC SERIES
SUSAN HAMPSHIRE (The First Churchills) (Masterpiece Theatre) (PBS)
LINDA CRISTAL (The High Chaparral) (NBC)
PEGGY LIPTON (The Mod Squad) (ABC)

OUTSTANDING CONTINUED PERFORMANCE BY AN ACTOR IN A LEADING ROLE IN A COMEDY SERIES
JACK KLUGMAN (The Odd Couple) (ABC)
TED BESSELL (That Girl) (ABC)
BILL BIXBY (The Courtship Of Eddie's Father) (ABC)
CARROLL O'CONNOR (All In The Family) (CBS)
TONY RANDALL (The Odd Couple) (ABC)

OUTSTANDING CONTINUED PERFORMANCE BY AN ACTRESS IN A LEADING ROLE IN A COMEDY SERIES
JEAN STAPLETON (All In The Family) (CBS)
MARY TYLER MOORE (The Mary Tyler Moore Show) (CBS)
MARLO THOMAS (That Girl) (ABC)

OUTSTANDING PERFORMANCE BY AN ACTOR IN A SUPPORTING ROLE IN DRAMA
A continuing or one-time appearance in a series, or for a special program
DAVID BURNS "The Price" (Hallmark Hall of Fame) (NBC)
JAMES BROLIN (Marcus Welby, M.D.) (Series) (ABC)
ROBERT YOUNG "Vanished, Parts I & II" (World Premiere NBC Monday & Tuesday Night At The Movies) (NBC)

OUTSTANDING PERFORMANCE BY AN ACTRESS IN A SUPPORTING ROLE IN DRAMA
A continuing or one-time appearance in a series, or for a special program
MARGARET LEIGHTON "Hamlet" (Hallmark Hall of Fame) (NBC)
GAIL FISHER (Mannix) (Series) (CBS)
SUSAN SAINT JAMES (The Name Of The Game) (Series) (NBC)
ELENA VERDUGO (Marcis Welby, M.D.) (Series) (ABC)

OUTSTANDING PERFORMANCE BY AN ACTOR IN A SUPPORTING ROLE IN COMEDY
A continuing or one-time appearance in a series, or for a special program
EDWARD ASNER (The Mary Tyler Moore Show) (Series) (CBS)
MICHAEL CONSTANTINE (Room 222) (Series) (ABC)
GALE GORDON (Here's Lucy) (Series) (CBS)

OUTSTANDING PERFORMANCE BY AN ACTRESS IN A SUPPORTING ROLE IN COMEDY

A continuing or one-time appearance in a series, or for a special program

VALERIE HARPER (The Mary Tyler Moore Show) (Series) (CBS)
AGNES MOOREHEAD (Bewitched) (Series) (ABC)
KAREN VALENTINE (Room 222) (Series) (ABC)

OUTSTANDING DIRECTORIAL ACHIEVEMENT IN DRAMA

A single program of a series with continuing characters and/or theme

DARYL DUKE "The Day The Lion Died" (The Bold Ones - The Senator Segment) (NBC)
BOB SWEENEY "Over 50? Steal" (Hawaii Five-O) (CBS)
JOHN M. BADHAM "A Single Blow Of A Sword" (The Bold Ones - The Senator Segment) (NBC)

OUTSTANDING DIRECTORIAL ACHIEVEMENT IN DRAMA

A single program

FIELDER COOK "The Price" (Hallmark Hall of Fame) (NBC)
PETER WOOD "Hamlet" (Hallmark Hall of Fame) (NBC)
JOSEPH SARGENT "Tribes" (Move Of The Week On ABC) (ABC)
JAMES GOLDSTONE "A Clear And Present Danger" (World Premiere NBC Saturday Night At The Movies) (NBC)

OUTSTANDING DIRECTORIAL ACHIEVEMENT IN COMEDY

A single program of a series with continuing characters and/or theme

JAY SANDRICH "Toulouse Lautrec Is One Of My Favorite Artists" (The Mary Tyler Moore Show) (CBS)
ALAN RAFKIN "Support Your Local Mother" (The Mary Tyler Moore Show) (CBS)
JOHN RICH "Gloria's Pregnancy" (All In The Family) (CBS)

OUTSTANDING DIRECTORIAL ACHIEVEMENT IN VARIETY OR MUSIC

A single program of a series

MARK WARREN "Rowan And Martin's Laugh-In" (With Orson Welles) (NBC)
ART FISHER "Andy Williams Christmas Show" (The Andy Williams Show) (NBC)
TIM KILEY "The Flip Wilson Show" (With David Frost, James Brown and The Muppets) (NBC)

OUTSTANDING DIRECTORIAL ACHIEVEMENT IN COMEDY, VARIETY OR MUSIC

A special program

STERLING JOHNSON "Timex Presents Peggy Fleming At Sun Valley" (NBC)
WALTER C. MILLER, MARTIN CHARNIN "George M!" (Bell System Family Theatre) (NBC)
ROGER ENGLANDER "The Anatomy Of A Symphony Orchestra" (New York Philharmonic Young People's Concert) (CBS)

OUTSTANDING ACHIEVEMENT IN CHOREOGRAPHY

A single program of a series or a special program

ERNEST O. FLATT "The Carol Burnett Show" (With Nanette Fabray and Ken Berry) (CBS)
CLAUDE CHAGRIN "Hamlet" (Hallmark Hall of Fame) (NBC)
ALAN JOHNSON 'George M!" (Bell System Family Theatre) (NBC)

OUTSTANDING WRITING ACHIEVEMENT IN DRAMA

A single program of a series with continuing characters and/or theme

JOEL OLIANSKY "To Taste Of Death But Once" (The Bold Ones - The Senator Segment) (NBC)
DAVID W. RINTELS "A Continual Roar Of Musketry, Parts I & II" (The Bold Ones - The Senator Segment) (NBC)
JERROLD FREEDMAN "In Death's Other Kingdom" (The Psychiatrist, Four-In-One) (NBC)

OUTSTANDING WRITING ACHIEVEMENT IN DRAMA, ORIGINAL TELEPLAY

A single program

TRACY KEENAN WYNN, MARVIN SCHWARTZ "Tribes" (Movie Of The Week On ABC) (ABC)
WILLIAM READ WOODFIELD, ALLAN BALTER "San Francisco International Airport" (World Premiere NBC Tuesday Night At The Movies) (NBC)
DAVID KARP "The Brotherhood Of The Bell" (CBS Thursday Night Movies) (CBS)

OUTSTANDING WRITING ACHIEVEMENT IN DRAMA, ADAPTATION

A single program

SAUL LEVITT "The Andersonville Trial" (Hollywood Television Theatre) (PBS)
JOHN BARTON "Hamlet" (Hallmark Hall of Fame) (NBC)
DEAN RIESNER "Vanished" (World Premiere NBC Monday & Tuesday Night At The Movies) (NBC)

OUTSTANDING WRITING ACHIEVEMENT IN COMEDY

A single program of a series with continuing characters and/or theme

JAMES L. BROOKS, ALLAN BURNS "Support Your Local Mother" (The Mary Tyler Moore Show) (CBS)
NORMAN LEAR "Meet The Bunkers" (All In The Family) (CBS)
STANLEY RALPH ROSS "Oh, My Aching Back" (All In The Family) (CBS)
BOB CARROLL, JR., MADELYN DAVIS "Lucy Meets The Burtons" (Here's Lucy) (CBS)

OUTSTANDING WRITING ACHIEVEMENT IN VARIETY OR MUSIC

A single program of a series

HERBERT BAKER, HAL GOODMAN, LARRY KLEIN, BOB WEISKOPF, BOB SCHILLER, NORMAN STEINBERG, FLIP WILSON "The Flip Wilson Show" (With Lena Horne and Tony Randall) (NBC)
ARTHUR JULIAN, DON HINKLEY, JACK MENDELSOHN, STAN HART, LARRY SIEGEL, WOODY KLING, ROGER BEATTY, ARNIE ROSEN, KENNY SOLMS, GAIL PARENT "The Carol Burnett Show" (With Rita Hayworth) (CBS)
DANNY SIMON, MARTY FARRELL, NORMAN BARASCH, CARROLL MOORE, TONY WEBSTER, COLEMAN JACOBY, BOB ELLISON, "The Kopykats Kopy TV" (Kraft Music Hall) (NBC)

OUTSTANDING WRITING ACHIEVEMENT IN COMEDY, VARIETY OR MUSIC

A special program

BOB ELLISON, MARTY FARRELL "Singer Presents Burt Bacharach" **(CBS)**
HAL GOLDMAN, AL GORDON, HILLIARD MARKS, HUGH WEDLOCK, JR. "Timex Presents Jack Benny's 20th TV Anniversary Special" (NBC)
SAUL ILSON, ERNEST CHAMBERS, GARY BELKIN, ALEX BARRIS "The Doris Mary Anne Kappelhoff Special" (CBS)

OUTSTANDING ACHIEVEMENT IN MUSIC COMPOSITION

A. For a series or a single program of a series (In the first year of music's use only)

DAVID ROSE "The Love Child" (Bonanza) (NBC)
ROBERT PRINCE, BILLY GOLDENBERG "LA 2017" (The Name Of The Game) (Gene Barry Segment) (NBC)
FRANK COMSTOCK "Elegy For A Pig" (Adam-12) (NBC)
CHARLES FOX (Love, American Style) (Series) (ABC)

B. For a special program

WALTER SCHARF "The Tragedy Of The Red Salmon" (The Undersea World Of Jacques Cousteau) (ABC)
JOHN ADDISON "Hamlet" (Hallmark Hall of Fame) (NBC)
PETE RUGOLO "Do You Take This Stranger"(World Premiere NBC Monday Night At The Movies) (NBC)

OUTSTANDING ACHIEVEMENT IN MUSIC DIRECTION OF A VARIETY, MUSICAL OR DRAMATIC PROGRAM

A single program of a series or a special program

DOMINIC FRONTIERE "Swing Out, Sweet Land" (NBC)
JOHN ADDISON "Hamlet" (Hallmark Hall Of Fame) (NBC)
MORT LINDSEY "Big Band Salute, Parts I & II" (The Merv Griffin Show) (CBS)

OUTSTANDING ACHIEVEMENT IN MUSIC, LYRICS AND SPECIAL MATERIAL

A series or a single program of a series or a special program written for television

RAY CHARLES "The First Nine Months Are The Hardest" (NBC)
BILLY BARNES "Clairol Command Performance Presents...Pure Goldie" (NBC)
LEE HALE "The Dean Martin Show" (Series) (NBC)
WILLIAM GOLDENBERG, DAVID WILSON "All The Old Familiar Faces" (The Name of the Game) (Gene Barry Segment) (NBC)

OUTSTANDINDG ACHIEVEMENT IN CINEMATOGRAPHY FOR ENTERTAINMENT PROGRAMMING

A. For a series or a single program of a series

JACK MARTA "Cynthia Is Alive And Living In Avalon" (The Name of The Game) (Gene Barry Segment) (NBC)
TED VOIGTLANDER, A.S.C. "The Love Child" (Bonanza) (NBC)
WALTER STRENGE, A.S.C. "A Spanish Saying I Made Up" (Marcus Welby, M.D.) (ABC)

B. For a special or feature length program made for television

LIONEL LINDON, A.S.₃. "Vanished, Parts I & II" (World Premiere NBC Monday & Tuesday Night At The Movies) (NBC)
BOB COLLINS "Timex Presents Peggy Fleming At Sun Valley" (NBC)
RUSSELL L. METTY, A.S.C. "Tribes" (Movie Of The Week On ABC) (ABC)
EDWARD ROSSON "The Neon Ceiling" (World Premiere NBC Monday Night At The Movies) (NBC)

OUTSTANDING ACHIEVEMENT IN CINEMATOGRAPHY FOR NEWS AND DOCUMENTARY PROGRAMMING

For a series, a single program of a series, a special program, program segment or elements within: A. Regularly scheduled News programs and coverage of Special Events

LARRY TRAVIS "Los Angeles - Earthquake" (Sylmar V.A. Hospital) (CBS Evening News With Walter Cronkite) (CBS)
JAMES WATT "Cattle Drive Parts I & II" (The Huntley-Brinkley Report) (NBC)
HOUSTON HALL "They Paved Paradise" (The Huntley-Brinkley Report) (NBC)

B. Documentary, Magazine-type or Mini-documentary programs

JACQUES RENOIR "The Tragedy Of The Red Salmon" (The Undersea World of Jacques Cousteau) (ABC)
PHILIPPE COUSTEAU "Lagoon Of Lost Ships" (The Undersea World Of Jacques Cousteau) (ABC)
MICHEL DeLOIRE, JACQUES RENOIR "The Dragons Of Galapagos" (The Undersea World of Jacques Cousteau) (ABC)
JAMES S. WILSON, GUY ADENIS, GEORGE APOSTOLIDES, JOE BARDO-YESKO, TONY COGGANS, MICHAEL DUGAN, J. BARRY HERRON, ROBERT E. THOMAS, LARRY TRAVIS "Wildfire!" (GE Monogram Series) (NBC)

OUTSTANDING ACHIEVEMENT IN ART DIRECTION OR SCENIC DESIGN

A. For a dramatic program or feature length film; a single program of a series or a special program

PETER RODEN "Hamlet" (Hallmark Hall of Fame) (NBC)
JOHN J. LLOYD AND RUBY R. LEVITT Art Director and Set Decorator Respectively, "Vanished, Parts I & II" (World Premiere NBC Monday and Tuesday Night At The Movies) (NBC)
JAN SCOTT "Montserrat" (Hollywood Television Theatre) (PBS)
JOHN CLEMENTS "The Price" (Hallmark Hall of Fame) (NBC)
J.M. VAN TAMELEN AND FRED PRICE Art Director and Set Decorator Respectively, "The Mouse That Died" (Mannix) (CBS)

B. For a musical or variety single program of a series, or a special program

JAMES W. TRITTIPO AND GEORGE GAINES Art Director and Set Decorator Respectively, "Robert Young And The Family" (CBS)
RENE LAGLER AND ROBERT CHECCI Art Director and Set Decorator Respectively, "The Glen Campbell Goodtime Hour" (With Neil Diamond, Linda Ronstadt) (CBS)
ROMAIN JOHNSTON "The Flip Wilson Show" (With Robert Goulet and Lola Falana) (NBC)
FRED LUFF "Love Is" (Oral Roberts Valentine Special - Contact) (Syndicated)

OUTSTANDING ACHIEVEMENT IN COSTUME DESIGN

A single program of a series or a specal program

MARTIN BAUGH AND DAVID WALKER "Hamlet" (Hallmark Hall of Fame) (NBC)
ROBERT CARLTON "Bing Crosby - Cooling It" (NBC)
RET TURNER "Andy Williams Christmas Show" (The Andy Williams Show) (NBC)
PATRICIA SEGNAN "They've Killed President Lincoln!" (NBC)

OUTSTANDING ACHIEVEMENT IN MAKE-UP

A single program of a series or a special program

ROBERT DAWN 'Catafalque' (Mission: Impossible) (CBS)
MARIE ROCHE "Hamlet" (Hallmark Hall of Fame) (NBC)
ROLF J. MILLER "Samantha's Old Man" (Bewitched) (ABC)
PERC WESTMORE AND HARRY C. BLAKE "The Third Bill Cosby Special" (NBC)

OUTSTANDING ACHIEVEMENT IN FILM EDITING FOR ENTERTAINMENT PROGRAMMING

A. For a series or a single program of a series

MICHAEL ECONOMOU "A Continual Roar Of Musketry, Parts I & II" (The Bold Ones - The Senator Segment) (NBC)
ARTHUR DAVID HILTON "Over 50? Steal" (Hawaii Five-O) (CBS)
DOUGLAS STEWART "To Taste Of Death But Once" (The Bold Ones - The Senator Segment) (NBC)

B. For a special or feature length program made for television

GEORGE J. NICHOLSON "Longstreet" (Movie Of The Week On ABC) (ABC)
ROBERT F. SHUGRUE "The Neon Ceiling" (World Premier NBC Monday Night At The Movies) (NBC)
ROBERT WATTS "Vanished, Parts I & II" (World Premier NBC Monday and Tuesday Night At The Movies) (NBC)

OUTSTANDING ACHIEVEMENT IN FILM EDITING FOR NEWS AND DOCUMENTARY PROGRAMMING

For a series, a single program of a series, a special program, program segments or elements within: A. Regularly scheduled news programs and coverage of special events

GEORGE L. JOHNSON "Prison, Parts I Thru IV" (NBC Nightly News) (NBC)
MICHAEL C. SHUGRUE " The Welfare Worker" (NBC Nightly News) (NBC)
LOUIS BUCHIGNANI " L.A. Earthquake!" (ABC Evening News With Howard K. Smith And Harry Reasoner) (ABC)

B. Documentary, Magazine-type or Mini-documentary programs

ROBERT B. LOWEREE AND HENRY J. GRENNON "Cry Help! An NBC White Paper On Mentally Disturbed Youth" (NBC)
DAVID E. BLEWITT "The Tragedy Of The Red Salmon" (The Undersea World of Jacques Cousteau) (ABC)
DENA LEVITT "CBS Reports: The Selling Of The Pentagon" (CBS)
JOHN F. TEEPLE "The Prado" (The Southern Baptist Hour) (NBC)

OUTSTANDING ACHIEVEMENT IN FILM SOUND EDITING

A single program of a series or a special program

DON HALL, JR., JACK JACKSON, BOB WEATHERFORD, DICK JENSEN "Tribes" (Movie Of The Week On ABC) (ABC)
DOUGLAS H. GRINDSTAFF, FRANK R. WHITE, JOE KAVIGAN, DON CROSBY, CHUCK PERRY "The Blast" (Mission: Impossible) (CBS)
DOUGLAS H. GRINDSTAFF, EDWARD L. SANDLIN, JOSEF E. VON STROHEIM, SETH D. LARSEN, BILL RIVOL, BILLIE OWENS "Sunburst" (Mannix) (CBS)

OUTSTANDING ACHIEVEMENT IN FILM SOUND MIXING

A single program of a series or a special program

THEODORE SODERBERG "Tribes" (Movie Of The Week On ABC) (ABC)
JOEL F. MOSS AND DON RUSH "Sunburst" (Mannix) (CBS)
RONALD K. PIERCE AND JAMES Z. FLASTER "Vanished, Parts I & II" (World Premiere NBC Monday and Tuesday Night At The Movies) (NBC)
ROGER PARISH AND ROBERT L. HOYT "San Francisco International Airport" (World Premiere NBC Tuesday Night At The Movies) (NBC)

OUTSTANDING ACHIEVEMENT IN LIGHTING DIRECTION

A single program of a series or a special program produced for electronic television only

JOHN ROOK "Hamlet" (Hallmark Hall of Fame) (NBC)
KENNETH DETTLING "The Andersonville Trial" (Hollywood Television Theatre) (PBS)
JOHN FRESCHI "Andy Williams Christmas Show" (The Andy Williams Show) (NBC)
CARL GIBSON "Love Is" (Oral Roberts Valentine Special - Contact) (Syndicated)

OUTSTANDING ACHIEVEMENT IN LIVE OR TAPE SOUND MIXING

A single program of a series or a special program

HENRY BIRD "Hamlet" (Hallmark Hall of Fame) (NBC)
DAVE WILLIAMS "The Flip Wilson Show" (With Lena Horne and Tony Randall) (NBC)
MARSHALL KING "Swing Out, Sweet Land" (NBC)

OUTSTANDING ACHIEVEMENT IN VIDEO TAPE EDITING

A single program of a series or a special program

MARCO ZAPPIA "Hee-Haw" (With Roger Miller and Peggy Little) (CBS)
RAY KNIPE "Hamlet" (Hallmark Hall of Fame) (NBC)
STEVEN ORLAND AND MARTIN J. PETERS "Clairol Command Performance. . .Pure Goldie" (NBC)

OUTSTANDING ACHIEVEMENT IN TECHNICAL DIRECTION AND ELECTRONIC CAMERAWORK

A single program of a series or a special program

GORDON BAIRD; TOM ANCELL, RICK BENNEWITZ, LARRY BENTLEY, JACK READER Technical Director and Cameramen Respectively 'The Andersonville Trial" (Hollywood Television Theatre) (PBS)
LOUIS FUSARI; TONY YARLETT, RAY FIGELSKI, MARVIN AULT, JON OLSON Technical Director and Cameramen Respectively, 'Rowan And Martin's Laugh-In" (With Orson Welles) (NBC)
BILL SCHERTLE; BARNEY NEELEY, TOM McCONNELL, ALAN LATTER Technical Director and Cameramen Respectively, 'Apollo 14 Recovery Aboard The USS New Orleans" (Network Pool Coverage)

THE AREAS

(Possibility of One Award, More Than One Award, or No Award)

OUTSTANDING ACHIEVEMENT IN CHILDREN'S PROGRAMMING

PROGRAMS
SESAME STREET (Series) (PBS) David D. Connell, Executive Producer; Jon Stone, Lutrelle Horne, Producers
KUKLA, FRAN AND OLLIE (Series) (PBS) John J. Sommers, Richard Carter, Executive Producers

INDIVIDUALS
BURR TILLSTROM Performer "Kukla, Fran And Ollie" (Series) (PBS)
GEORGE W. RIESENBERGER Lighting Director "Sesame Street" (Series) (PBS)

OUTSTANDING ACHIEVEMENT IN DAYTIME PROGRAMMING

PROGRAMS
TODAY (Series) (NBC) Stuart Schulberg, Producer
THE GALLOPING GOURMET (Series) (Syndicated) Treena Kerr, Producer; Graham Kerr, Host

INDIVIDUALS
JAMES ANGERAME Technical Director "Love Is A Many Splendored Thing" (CBS)
VICTOR L. PAGANUZZI AND JOHN A. WENDELL Art Director and Set Decorator Respectively, "Love Is A Many Splendored Thing" (CBS)

OUTSTANDING ACHIEVEMENT IN SPORTS PROGRAMMNG

PROGRAMS
ABC'S WIDE WORLD OF SPORTS (Series) (ABC) Roone Arledge, Executive Producer
34TH MASTERS TOURNAMENT (CBS) Frank Chirkinian, Producer
NFL MONDAY NIGHT FOOTBALL (Series) (ABC) Roone Arledge, Executive Producer; Chet Forte, Producer

INDIVIDUALS
JIM McKAY Commentator "ABC's Wide World of Sports" (Series) (ABC)
DON MEREDITH Commentator "NFL Monday Night Football" (Series) (ABC)
WALT KUBILUS; DICK KERR, JOHN MORREALLE, MIKE REBICH, STUART GOODMAN, MORT LEVIN, SAL FOLINO, DON LANGFORD, ED PAYNE Technical Director and Cameramen Respectively, "NCAA Football" (Series) (ABC)

SPECIAL CLASSIFICATION OF OUTSTANDING PROGRAM AND INDIVIDUAL ACHIEVEMENT

PROGRAMS
THE WONDERFUL WORLD OF DISNEY (Series) (NBC) Ron Miller, Executive Producer
MUTUAL OF OMAHA'S WILD KINGDOM (Series) (NBC) Don Meier, Producer

INDIVIDUALS
HARVEY KORMAN Performer "The Carol Burnett Show" (Series) (CBS)
LILY TOMLIN Performer "Rowan And Martin's Laugh-In" (Series) (NBC)
ARTE JOHNSON Performer "Rowan And Martin's Laugh-In" (Series) (NBC)

OUTSTANDING ACHIEVEMENT IN ANY AREA OF CREATIVE TECHNICAL CRAFTS
LENWOOD B. ABBOTT, JOHN C. CALDWELL Special Photographic Effects "City Beneath The Sea" (World Premiere NBC Monday Night At The Movies) (NBC)
GENE WIDHOFF Graphic Art - Court Room Sketches 'Manson Trial" (The Huntley-Brinkley Report - NBC Nightly News) (NBC)
ALBERT J. WHITLOCK Special Photographic Effects "Vanished, Parts I & II" (World Premiere NBC Monday and Tuesday Night At The Movies) (NBC)

SPECIAL AWARDS

TRUSTEES AWARD
ED SULLIVAN For serving as a founder of The National Academy and its first National President; for pioneering in the variety format which has become a backbone of television programming; for having the foresight and courage to provide network exposure for minority performers; for bringing to millions of Americans cultural performances from ballet to opera to legitimate drama; for introducing performers from throughout the world to audiences who would otherwise never have known them; and, finally, for his showmanship, tastes and personal commitment in entertaining a nation for 23 years.

OUTSTANDING ACHIEVEMENT IN ENGINEERING DEVELOPMENT
THE COLUMBIA BROADCASTING SYSTEM For the development of the Color Corrector which can provide color uniformity between television picture segments and scenes shot and recorded under different conditions at different times and locations.

THE AMERICAN BROADCASTING COMPANY For the development of an "Open-Loop" Synchronizing System which enables the simultaneous synchronization of any number of color programs from remote locations.

CITATIONS
GENERAL ELECTRIC For development of the Portable Earth Station Transmitter.
STEFAN KUDELSKI For his design of the NAGARA IV Recorder.

THE STATION AWARD
IF YOU TURN ON (KNXT, Los Angeles, Calfornia)
ARE WE KILLING THE GULF? (KPRC-TV, Houston, Texas)
FATHER MOUNTAIN'S CHRISTMAS (KOOL-TV, Phoenix, Arizona)
HEY DOC (WCAU-TV, Philadelphia, Pennsylvania)
HOMES LIKE THESE (WLBT, Jackson, Mississippi)
THE LOST - THE LONELY (WJW-TV, Cleveland, Ohio)
NINE HEROES (WGBH, Educational Station, Allston, Massachusetts)
NO PLACE TO HIDE (WBBM-TV, Chicago, Illinois)
OUT CITY'S HISTORY - BOSTON: JUNE 1970 (WNAC-TV, Boston, Massachusetts)
TIMETABLE FOR DISASTER (WMC-TV, Memphis, Tennessee)

1971/72

NEWS AND DOCUMENTARY PROGRAM AND INDIVIDUAL ACHIEVEMENTS
(Possibility of One Award, More than One Award, or No Award)

OUTSTANDING ACHIEVEMENT WITHIN REGULARLY SCHEDULED NEWS PROGRAMS

PROGRAMS
DEFEAT OF DACCA (NBC Nightly News) Wallace Wesfeldt, Executive Producer; Robert Mulholland and David Teitelbaum, Producers (NBC)
COVERAGE OF PRESIDENT NIXON'S VISIT TO CHINA (NBC Nightly News) Wallace Westfeldt, Executive Producer; Les Crystal, Richard Fischer, Robert Mulholland, David Teitelbaum, Producers (NBC)
HOWARD HUGHES PHONE INTERVIEW (Segment) (NBC Nightly News) Wallace Westfeldt, Executive Producer; Richard Fischer, Bruce Sloan, Roy Neal, Producers (NBC)

INDIVIDUALS
PHIL BRADY, Reporter "Defeat of Dacca" (NBC Nightly News) (NBC)
BOB SCHIEFFER, PHIL JONES, DON WEBSTER, BILL PLANTE, Correspondents "The Air War" (CBS Evening News With Walter Cronkite) (CBS)
DAVID BRINKLEY, Correspondent "David Brinkley's Journal" (NBC Nightly News) (NBC)
JOHN CHANCELLOR, Correspondent "President Nixon's Visit to China" (NBC Nightly News) (NBC)

OUTSTANDING ACHIEVEMENT FOR REGULARLY SCHEDULED MAGAZINE-TYPE PROGRAMS

PROGRAMS
CHRONOLOG Eliot Frankel, Executive Producer (Series) (NBC)
THE GREAT AMERICAN DREAM MACHINE A. H. Perlmutter, Executive Producer (Series) (PBS)
60 MINUTES Don Hewitt, Executive Producer; Palmer Williams, Producer (Series) (CBS)

INDIVIDUALS
MIKE WALLACE, Correspondent "60 Minutes" (Series) (CBS)
TOM PETTIT, Reporter "The Business of Blood" (Segment) (Chronolog) (NBC)
ANDREW A. ROONEY, Writer "An Essay on War" (The Great American Dream Machine) (PBS)
MORLEY SAFER, Correspondent "60 Minutes" (Series) (CBS)

OUTSTANDING ACHIEVEMENT IN COVERAGE OF SPECIAL EVENTS

PROGRAMS
THE CHINA TRIP Av Westin and Wally Pfister, Executive Producers; Bill Lord, Producer (ABC)
JUNE 30, 1971, A DAY FOR HISTORY: THE SUPREME COURT AND THE PENTAGON PAPERS Lawrence E. Spivak, Executive Producer (NBC)
A RIDE ON THE MOON: THE FLIGHT OF APOLLO 15 Robert Wussler, Executive Producer; Joan Richman, Producer (CBS)
LOUIS ARMSTRONG 1900-1971 Robert Wussler, Executive Producer; Joan Richman, Producer (CBS)
THE PRESIDENT IN CHINA Robert Wussler and Ernest Leiser, Executive Producers (CBS)

INDIVIDUALS
JOEL BANOW, Director "Louis Armstrong 1900-1971" (CBS)
ANTHONY C. MESSURI, Director "The Flight of Apollo 15: A Journey To Hadley Rille" (NBC)

OUTSTANDING DOCUMENTARY PROGRAM ACHIEVEMENT

PROGRAMS - CURRENT SIGNIFICANCE
A NIGHT IN JAIL, A DAY IN COURT (CBS Reports) Burton Benjamin, Executive Producer; John Sharnik, Producer (CBS)
THIS CHILD IS RATED X: AN NBC NEWS WHITE PAPER ON JUVENILE JUSTICE Martin Carr, Producer (NBC)
JUSTICE IN AMERICA - Parts II and III (CBS Reports) Burton Benjamin, Executive Producer; John Sharnik and Harry Morgan, Producers (CBS)
SOME ARE MORE EQUAL THAN OTHERS "Justice in America" (CBS Reports) Burton Benjamin, Executive Producer; John Sharnik and Harry Morgan, Producers (CBS)
UNDER SURVEILLANCE (CBS Reports) Burton Benjamin, Executive Producer; Robert Chandler, Producer (CBS)

PROGRAMS - CULTURAL
HOLLYWOOD: THE DREAM FACTORY "The Monday Night Special" Nicolas Noxon, Executive Producer; Irwin Rosten and Bud Friedgen, Producers (ABC)
A SOUND OF DOLPHINS "The Undersea World of Jacques Cousteau" Jacques Cousteau and Marshall Flaum, Executive Producers; Andy White, Producer (ABC)
THE UNSINKABLE SEA OTTER "The Undersea World of Jacques Cousteau" Jacques Cousteau and Marshall Flaum, Executive Producers; Andy White, Producer (ABC)
THE AMERICAN WEST OF JOHN FORD Bob Banner, Executive Producer; Tom Egan, Dan Ford and Britt Lomond, Producers (CBS)
THE FORGOTTEN MERMAIDS "The Undersea World of Jacques Cousteau" Jacques Cousteau and Marshall Flaum, Executive Producers (ABC)
PICASSO IS 90 (CBS Reports) Burton Benjamin, Executive Producer; William K. McClure, Producer (CBS)

INDIVIDUALS
LOUIS J. HAZAM, Writer "Venice Be Damned!" (NBC)
ROBERT NORTHSHIELD, Writer "Suffer The Little Children - An NBC News White Paper on Northern Ireland" (NBC)
MARTIN CARR, Writer "This Child Is Rated X: An NBC White Paper on Juvenile Justice" (NBC)
FRED FLAMENHAFT, Director "Suffer The Little Children - An NBC News White Paper on Northern Ireland" (NBC)
ANDY WHITE, Writer "Octopus, Octopus" (The Undersea World of Jacques Cousteau) (ABC)

ENTERTAINMENT PROGRAM AND INDIVIDUAL ACHIEVEMENTS
(One Award Only In Each of the Remaining Categories)

OUTSTANDING SERIES - COMEDY
Award to Executive Producer(s) and/or Producer(s).
ALL IN THE FAMILY (CBS) Norman Lear, Producer
THE MARY TYLER MOORE SHOW (CBS) James L. Brooks and Allan Burns, Executive Producers; David Davis, Producer
THE ODD COUPLE (ABC) Jerry Belson and Garry Marshall, Executive Producers; Jerry Davis, Producer
SANFORD AND SON (NBC) Bud Yorkin, Executive Producer; Aaron Ruben, Producer

OUTSTANDING SERIES - DRAMA
Award to Executive Producer(s) and/or Producer(s).
ELIZABETH R (PBS) Masterpiece Theatre; Christopher Sarson, Executive Producer; Roderick Graham, Producer
COLUMBO (NBC) NBC Mystery Movie; Richard Levinson and William Link, Executive Producers; Everett Chambers, Producer
MANNIX (CBS) Bruce Geller, Executive Producer; Ivan Goff and Ben

Roberts, Producers
MARCUS WELBY, M.D. (ABC) David Victor, Executive Producer; David J. O'Connell, Producer
THE SIX WIVES OF HENRY VIII (CBS) Ronald Travers and Mark Shivas, Producers

OUTSTANDING SINGLE PROGRAM - DRAMA OR COMEDY

A single program of a series or a special program - Award to Executive Producer(s) and/or Producer(s)

BRIAN'S SONG (ABC) Movie of The Week; Paul Junger Witt, Producer
JANE SEYMOUR (CBS) The Six Wives of Henry VIII; Ronald Travers and Mark Shivas, Producers
THE LION'S CUB (PBS) Elizabeth R; Masterpiece Theatre; Christopher Sarson, Executive Producer; Roderick Graham, Producer
SAMMY'S VISIT (CBS) All In The Family; Norman Lear, Producer
THE SNOW GOOSE (NBC) Hallmark Hall of Fame; Frank O'Connor, Producer

OUTSTANDING VARIETY SERIES - MUSICAL

Award(s) to Executive Producer(s) and/or Producer(s) and Star (if applicable).

THE CAROL BURNETT SHOW (CBS) Joe Hamilton, Executive Producer; Arnie Rosen, Producer; Carol Burnett, Star
THE DEAN MARTIN SHOW (NBC) Greg Garrison, Producer; Dean Martin, Star
THE FLIP WILSON SHOW (NBC) Monte Kay, Executive Producer; Robert Henry, Producer; Flip Wilson, Star
THE SONNY & CHER COMEDY HOUR (CBS) Allan Blye and Chris Bearde, Producers; Sonny & Cher, Stars

OUTSTANDING VARIETY SERIES - TALK

Award(s) to Executive Producer(s) and/or Producer(s) and Star.

THE DICK CAVETT SHOW (ABC) John Gilroy, Producer; Dick Cavett, Star
THE DAVID FROST SHOW (Synd) Peter Baker, Producer; David Frost, Star
THE TONIGHT SHOW STARRING JOHNNY CARSON (NBC) Fred De Cordova, Producer; Johnny Carson, Star

OUTSTANDING SINGLE PROGRAM - VARIETY OR MUSICAL

A single program of a series or a special program - Award(s) to Executive Producer(s) and/or Producer(s) and Star (if applicable). A. Variety and Popular Music.

JACK LEMMON IN 'S WONDERFUL, 'S MARVELOUS, 'S GERSHWIN (NBC) Bell System Family Theatre; Joseph Cates, Executive Producer; Martin Charnin, Producer; Jack Lemmon, Star
THE FLIP WILSON SHOW (NBC) (with Sammy Davis Jr., Lily Tomlin and Ed McMahon) Monte Kay, Executive Producer; Robert Henry, Producer; Flip Wilson, Star
JULIE AND CAROL AT LINCOLN CENTER (CBS) Joe Hamilton, Producer; Julie Andrews and Carol Burnett, Stars
THE SONNY AND CHER COMEDY HOUR (CBS) (with Tony Randall) Allan Blye and Chris Bearde, Producers; Sonny and Cher, Stars
B. Classical Music.
BEETHOVEN'S BIRTHDAY: A CELEBRATION IN VIENNA WITH LEONARD BERNSTEIN (CBS) James Krayer, Executive Producer; Humphrey Burton, Producer; Leonard Bernstein, Star
HEIFETZ (NBC) Bell System Family Theatre; Lester Shurr, Executive Producer; Paul Louis, Producer; Jascha Heifetz, Star
THE PEKING BALLET: FIRST SPECTACULAR FROM CHINA (NBC) Lucy Jarvis, Producer
THE TRIAL OF MARY LINCOLN (PBS) NET Opera Theatre; Peter Herman Adler, Executive Producer; David Griffiths, Producer

OUTSTANDING NEW SERIES

Award to Executive Producer(s) and/or Producer(s).

ELIZABETH R (PBS) Masterpiece Theatre; Christopher Sarson, Executive Producer; Roderick Graham, Producer
COLUMBO (NBC) NBC Mystery Movie; Richard Levinson and William Link, Executive Producers; Everett Chambers, Producer
SANFORD AND SON (NBC) Bud Yorkin, Executive Producer; Aaron Ruben, Producer
THE SIX WIVES OF HENRY VIII (CBS) Ronald Travers and Mark Shivas, Producers
THE SONNY & CHER COMEDY HOUR (CBS) Allan Blye and Chris Bearde, Producers

OUTSTANDING SINGLE PERFORMANCE BY AN ACTOR IN A LEADING ROLE

A one-time appearance in a series or for a special program.

KEITH MICHELL "Catherine Howard" (The Six Wives of Henry VIII) (CBS)
JAMES CAAN "Brian's Song" (Movie of The Week) (ABC)
RICHARD HARRIS "The Snow Goose" (Hallmark Hall of Fame) (NBC)
GEORGE C. SCOTT "Jane Eyre" (Bell System Family Theatre) (NBC)
BILLY DEE WILLIAMS "Brian's Song" (Movie of The Week) (ABC)

OUTSTANDING SINGLE PERFORMANCE BY AN ACTRESS IN A LEADING ROLE

A one-time appearance in a series or for a special program.

GLENDA JACKSON "Shadow In The Sun" Elizabeth R (Masterpiece Theatre) (PBS)
GLENDA JACKSON "The Lion's Cub" Elizabeth R (Masterpiece Theatre) (PBS)
HELEN HAYES "Do Not Fold, Spindle or Mutilate" (Movie of The Week) (ABC)
PATRICIA NEAL "The Homecoming - A Christmas Story" (CBS)
SUSANNAH YORK "Jane Eyre" (Bell System Family Theatre) (NBC)

OUTSTANDING CONTINUED PERFORMANCE BY AN ACTOR IN A LEADING ROLE IN A DRAMATIC SERIES

PETER FALK "Columbo" (NBC Mystery Movie) (NBC)
RAYMOND BURR (Ironside) (NBC)
MIKE CONNORS (Mannix) (CBS)
KEITH MICHELL (The Six Wives of Henry VIII) (CBS)
ROBERT YOUNG (Marcus Welby, M.D.) (ABC)

OUTSTANDING CONTINUED PERFORMANCE BY AN ACTRESS IN A LEADING ROLE IN A DRAMATIC SERIES

GLENDA JACKSON Elizabeth R (Masterpiece Theatre) (PBS)
PEGGY LIPTON (The Mod Squad) (ABC)
SUSAN SAINT JAMES McMillan & Wife (NBC Mystery Movie) (NBC)

OUTSTANDING CONTINUED PERFORMANCE BY AN ACTOR IN A LEADING ROLE IN A COMEDY SERIES

CARROLL O'CONNOR (All in The Family) (CBS)
REDD FOXX (Sanford and Son) (NBC)
JACK KLUGMAN (The Odd Couple) (ABC)
TONY RANDALL (The Odd Couple) (ABC)

OUTSTANDING CONTINUED PERFORMANCE BY AN ACTRESS IN A LEADING ROLE IN A COMEDY SERIES

JEAN STAPLETON (All In The Family) (CBS)
SANDY DUNCAN (Funny Face) (CBS)
MARY TYLER MOORE (The Mary Tyler Moore Show) (CBS)

OUTSTANDING PERFORMANCE BY AN ACTOR IN A SUPPORTING ROLE IN DRAMA

A continuing or one-time appearance in a series, or for a special program.

JACK WARDEN (Brian's Song) (Movie of The Week) (ABC)
JAMES BROLIN (Marcus Welby, M.D.) (Series) (ABC)
GREG MORRIS (Mission: Impossible) (Series) (CBS)

OUTSTANDING PERFORMANCE BY AN ACTRESS IN A SUPPORTING ROLE IN DRAMA

A continuing or one-time appearance in a series, or for a special program.

JENNY AGUTTER (The Snow Goose) (Hallmark Hall of Fame) (NBC)
GAIL FISHER (Mannix) (Series) (CBS)
ELENA VERDUGO (Marcus Welby, M.D.) (Series) (ABC)

OUTSTANDING PERFORMANCE BY AN ACTOR IN A SUPPORTING ROLE IN COMEDY

A continuing or one-time appearance in a series, or for a special program.

EDWARD ASNER (The Mary Tyler Moore Show) (Series) (CBS)
TED KNIGHT (The Mary Tyler Moore Show) (Series) (CBS)
ROB REINER (All in The Family) (Series) (CBS)

OUTSTANDING PERFORMANCE BY AN ACTRESS IN A SUPPORTING ROLE IN COMEDY

A continuing or one-time appearance in a series, or for a special program.

VALERIE HARPER (The Mary Tyler Moore Show) (Series) (CBS)
SALLY STRUTHERS (All in The Family) (Series) (CBS)
CLORIS LEACHMAN (The Mary Tyler Moore Show) (Series) (CBS)

OUTSTANDING ACHIEVEMENT BY A PERFORMER IN MUSIC OR VARIETY

A continuing or one-time appearance in a series, or for a special program.

HARVEY KORMAN (The Carol Burnett Show) (Series) (CBS)
RUTH BUZZI (Rowan and Martin's Laugh-In) (Series) (NBC)
LILY TOMLIN (Rowan and Martin's Laugh-In) (Series) (NBC)

OUTSTANDING DIRECTORIAL ACHIEVEMENT IN DRAMA

A single program of a series with continuing characters and/or theme.

ALEXNDER SINGER "The Invasion of Kevin Ireland" (The Bold Ones - The Lawyers) (NBC)
EDWARD M. ABROMS "Short Fuse" (Columbo) (NBC Mystery Movie) (NBC)
DANIEL PETRIE "Hands of Love" (The Man and The City) (ABC)

OUTSTANDING DIRECTORIAL ACHIEVEMENT IN DRAMA

A single program.

TOM GRIES "The Glass House" (The New CBS Friday Night Movies) (CBS)
PAUL BOGART "Look Homeward, Angel" (CBS Playhouse 90) (CBS)
FIELDER COOK "The Homecoming - A Christmas Story" (CBS)
PATRICK GARLAND "The Snow Goose" (Hallmark Hall of Fame) (NBC)
BUZZ KULIK "Brian's Song" (Movie of The Week) (ABC)

OUTSTANDING DIRECTORIAL ACHIEVEMENT IN COMEDY

A single program of a series with continuing characters and/or theme.

JOHN RICH "Sammy's Visit" (All in The Family) (CBS)
PETER BALDWIN "Where There's Smoke, There's Rhoda" (The Mary Tyler Moore Show) (CBS)
JAY SANDRICH "Thoroughly Unmilitant Mary" (The Mary Tyler Moore Show) (CBS)

OUTSTANDING DIRECTORIAL ACHIEVEMENT IN VARIETY OR MUSIC

A single program of a series.

ART FISHER "The Sonny & Cher Comedy Hour" (with Tony Randall) (CBS)
TIM KILEY "The Flip Wilson Show" (with Petula Clark and Redd Foxx) (NBC)
DAVID P. POWERS "The Carol Burnett Show" (with Carol Channing and Steve Lawrence) (CBS)

OUTSTANDING DIRECTORIAL ACHIEVEMENT IN COMEDY, VARIETY OR MUSIC

A special program.

WALTER C. MILLER and MARTIN CHARNIN "Jack Lemmon in 'S Wonderful, 'S Marvelous, 'S Gershwin" (Bell System Family Theatre) (NBC)
ROGER ENGLANDER "Liszt and The Devil" (New York Philharmonic Young People's Concert) (CBS)
DAVID P. POWERS "Julie and Carol at Lincoln Center" (CBS)

OUTSTANDING ACHIEVEMENT IN CHOREOGRAPHY

A single program of a series or a special program.

ALAN JOHNSON "Jack Lemmon in 'S Wonderful, 'S Marvelous, 'S Gershwin" (Bell System Family Theatre) (NBC)
ERNEST O. FLATT "The Carol Burnett Show" (with Mel Torme and Nanette Fabray) (CBS)
TOM HANSEN "The Fabulous Fordies" (NBC)

OUTSTANDING WRITING ACHIEVEMENT IN DRAMA

A single program of a series with continuing characters and/or theme.

RICHARD L. LEVINSON and WILLIAM LINK "Death Lends A Hand" (Columbo) (NBC Mystery Movie) (NBC)
STEVE BOCHCO "Murder By The Book" (Columbo) (NBC Mystery Movie) (NBC)
JACKSON GILLIS "Suitable for Framing" (Columbo) (NBC Mystery Movie) (NBC)

OUTSTANDING WRITING ACHIEVEMENT IN DRAMA, ORIGINAL TELEPLAY

A single program.

ALLAN SLOANE "To All My Friends On Shore" (CBS)
JOHN D. F. BLACK "Thief" (Movie of The Weekend) (ABC)
JACK SHER "Goodbye, Raggedy Ann" (The New CBS Friday Night Movies) (CBS)

OUTSTANDING WRITING ACHIEVEMENT IN DRAMA, ADAPTATION

A single program.

WILLIAM BLINN "Brian's Song" (Movie of The Week) (ABC)
PAUL W. GALLICO "The Snow Goose" (Hallmark Hall of Fame) (NBC)
EARL HAMNER, JR. "The Homecoming - A Christmas Story" (CBS)
TRACY KEENAN WYNN "The Glass House" (The New CBS Friday Night Movies) (CBS)

OUTSTANDING WRITING ACHIEVEMENT IN COMEDY

A single program of a series with continuing characters and/or theme.

BURT STYLER "Edith's Problem" (All in The Family) (CBS)
BURT STYLER and NORMAN LEAR "The Saga of Cousin Oscar" (All in The Family) (CBS)
PHILIP MISHKIN and ALAN J. LEVITT "Mike's Problem" (All in The Family) (CBS)

OUTSTANDING WRITING ACHIEVEMENT IN VARIETY OR MUSIC

A single program of a series.

DON HINKLEY, STAN HART, LARRY SIEGEL, WOODY KLING, ROGER BEATTY, ART BAER, BEN JOELSON, STAN BURNS, MIKE MARMER and ARNIE ROSEN "The Carol Burnett Show" (with Tim Conway and Ray Charles) (CBS)
HERBET BAKER, HAL GOODMAN, LARRY KLEIN, BOB SCHILLER, BOB WEISKOPF, SID GREEN, DICK HILLS and FLIP WILSON "The Flip Wilson Show" (with Sammy Davis, Jr., Lily Tomlin and Ed McMahon) (NBC)
PHIL HAHN, PAUL WAYNE, GEORGE BURDITT, COSLOUGH JOHNSON, BOB ARNOTT, STEVE MARTIN, BOB EINSTEIN, ALLAN BLYE and CHRIS BEARDE "The Sonny & Cher Comedy Hour" (with Carroll O'Connor) (CBS)

OUTSTANDING WRITING ACHIEVEMENT IN COMEDY, VARIETY OR MUSIC

A special program.

ANNE HOWARD BAILEY "The Trial of Mary Lincoln" (NET Opera Theatre) (PBS)
MARTIN CHARNIN "Jack Lemmon in 'S Wonderful, 'S Marvelous, 'S Gershwin" (Bell System Family Theatre) (NBC)
BOB ELLISON, MARTY FARRELL and KEN and MITZI WELCH "Julie And Carol At Lincoln Center" (CBS)

OUTSTANDING ACHIEVEMENT IN MUSIC COMPOSITION

A. For a series or a single program of a series.

PETE RUGOLO "In Defense of Ellen McKay" (The Bold Ones - The Lawyers) (NBC)
CHARLES FOX "Love, American Style" (Series) (ABC)
WILLIAM GOLDENBERG "Lady In Waiting" (Columbo) (NBC Mystery Movie) (NBC)

B. For a special program.

JOHN T. WILLIAMS "Jane Eyre" (Bell System Family Theatre) (NBC)
CARL DAVIS "The Snow Goose" (Hallmark Hall of Fame) (NBC)
MICHEL LEGRAND "Brian's Song" (Movie of The Week) (ABC)

OUTSTANDING ACHIEVEMENT IN MUSIC DIRECTION OF A VARIETY, MUSICAL OR DRAMATIC PROGRAM

A single program of a series or a special program.

ELLIOT LAWRENCE "Jack Lemmon in 'S Wonderful, 'S Marvelous, 'S Gershwin" (Bell System Family Theatre) (NBC)
VAN ALEXANDER "The Golddiggers Chevrolet Show" (with Fess Parker) (Synd)
JAMES E. DALE "The Sonny & Cher Comedy Hour" (with Jean Stapleton and Mike Connors) (CBS)

OUTSTANDING ACHIEVEMENT IN MUSIC, LYRICS AND SPECIAL MATERIAL

A series or a single program of a special program written for television.

RAY CHARLES "The Funny Side of Marriage" (The Funny Side) (NBC)
BILLY BARNES "Rowan And Martin's Laugh-In" (with Liza Minnelli) (NBC)
EARL BROWN "The Sonny and Cher Comedy Hour" (Series) (CBS)

OUTSTANDING ACHIEVEMENT IN ART DIRECTION OR SCENIC DESIGN

A. For a dramatic program or feature length film made for television; a single program of a series or a special program.

JAN SCOTT "The Scarecrow" (Hollywood Television Theatre) (PBS)
BEN EDWARDS "Look Homeward, Angel" (CBS Playhouse 90) (CBS)
GIBSON HOLLEY, Art Director; LUCIEN HAFLEY, Set Decorator "Encore" (Mission: Impossible) (CBS)
STANLEY MORRIS "The Snow Goose" (Hallmark Hall of Fame) (NBC)

B. For a Musical or Variety single program of a series or a special program.

E. JAY KRAUSE "Diana!" (ABC)
PAUL BARNES and BOB SANSOM, Art Directors; BILL HARP, Set Decorator "The Carol Burnett Show" (with Vincent Price and Eydie Gorme) (CBS)
ROMAIN JOHNSTON "The Flip Wilson Show" (with Petula Clark and Redd Foxx) (NBC)
RENE LAGLER, Art Director; ROBERT CHECCHI, Set Decorator "The Glen Campbell Show" (with John Wayne) (CBS)

OUTSTANDING ACHIEVEMENT IN COSTUME DESIGN

A single program of a series or a special program.

ELIZABETH WALLER "The Lion's Cub" Elizabeth R (Masterpiece Theatre) (PBS)
BOB MACKIE and RET TURNER "The Sonny & Cher Comedy Hour" (with Art Carney) (CBS)
RET TURNER "The Fabulous Fordies" (NBC)

OUTSTANDING ACHIEVEMENT IN MAKE-UP

A single program of a series or a special program.

FRANK WESTMORE "Kung Fu" (Movie of The Week) (ABC)
HARRY C. BLAKE "Gideon" (Hallmark Hall of Fame) (NBC)
NICK MARCELLINO, LEONARD ENGELMAN and JOHN F. CHAMBERS "Pickman's Model" (Rod Serling's Night Gallery) (NBC)

OUTSTANDING ACHIEVEMENT IN CINEMATOGRAPHY FOR ENTERTAINMENT PROGRAMMING

A. For a series or a single program of a series.
LLOYD AHERN, A.S.C. "Blue Print For Murder" Columbo (NBC Mystery Movie) (NBC)
CHARLES G. CLARKE "The Only Way to Go" (Arnie) (CBS)
ROBERT L. MORRISON "Hawaii Five-O" (Series) (CBS)

B. For a special or feature length program made for television.
JOSEPH BIROC "Brian's Song" (Movie of The Week) (ABC)
RAY HENMAN "The Snow Goose" (Hallmark Hall of Fame) (NBC)
JACK A. MARTA "Duel" (Movie of The Weekend) (ABC)

OUTSTANDING ACHIEVEMENT IN CINEMATOGRAPHY FOR NEWS AND DOCUMENTARY PROGRAMMING

A. Regularly scheduled News programs and coverage of Special Events.
PETER McINTYRE and LIM YOUN CHOUL "Dacca" (NBC Nightly News) (NBC)
WILLIAM BRYAN "Pontiac Bussing" (NBC Nightly News) (NBC)
VO HUYNH "Beautiful Vietnam" (NBC Nightly News) (NBC)
KYUNG MO LEE "Seoul Hotel Fire" (NBC Nightly News) (NBC)
HOANG TRONG NGHIA and VO SUU "Viet Casualties" (NBC Nightly News) (NBC)
CHARLES A. RAY "West Virginia Flood" (NBC Nightly News) (NBC)
LARRY TRAVIS "Nitrogen Kills Columbia River Fish" (CBS Evening News With Walter Cronkite) (CBS)

B. Documentary, Magazine-type or Mini-documentary programs.
THOMAS PRIESTLEY "Venice Be Damned!" (NBC)
PHILIPPE COUSTEAU "Forgotten Mermaids" (The Undersea World of Jacques Cousteau) (ABC)
PHILIPPE COUSTEAU and MICHEL DELOIRE "The Unsinkable Sea Otter" (The Undersea World of Jacques Cousteau) (ABC)
MICHEL DELOIRE "Octopus, Octopus" (The Undersea World of Jacques Cousteau) (ABC)
JACQUES RENOIR "A Sound of Dolphins" (The Undersea World of Jacques Cousteau) (ABC)

OUTSTANDING ACHIEVEMENT IN FILM EDITING FOR ENTERTAINMENT PROGRAMMING

A. For a series or a single program of a series.
EDWARD M. ABROMS "Death Lends A Hand" Columbo (NBC Mystery Movie) (NBC)
RICHARD BRACKEN, GLORYETTE CLARK and TERRY WILLIAMS "The Bold Ones - The Lawyers" (Series) (NBC)
JOSEPH T. DERVIN, SR. "Spell Legacy Like Death" (Longstreet) (ABC)

B. For a special or feature length program made for television.
BUD S. ISAACS "Brian's Song" (Movie of The Week) (ABC)
GENE FOWLER "The Glass House" (The New CBS Friday Night Movies) (CBS)
KEN PEARCE "The Snow Goose" (Hallmark Hall of Fame) (NBC)

OUTSTANDING ACHIEVEMENT IN FILM EDITING FOR NEWS AND DOCUMENTARY PROGRAMMING

A. Regularly scheduled News programs and coverage of Special Events.
DAROLD MURRAY "War Song" (NBC Nightly News) (NBC)
GERALD C. BREESE "Native Hawaiians" (NBC Nightly News) (NBC)
GEORGE L. JOHNSON "Slaughter in East Pakistan Village of Subhadya" (NBC Nightly News) (NBC)

B. Documentary, Magazine-type or Mini-documentary programs.
SPENCER DAVID SAXON "Monkeys, Apes And Man" (National Geographic Society) (CBS)
SAMUEL COHEN and JAMES FLANAGAN "Earthquake!" (The Monday Night Special) (ABC)
JOHN SOH "The Forgotten Mermaids" (The Undersea World of Jacques Cousteau) (ABC)

OUTSTANDING ACHIEVEMENT IN FILM SOUND EDITING

A single program of a series or a special program.
JERRY CHRISTIAN, JAMES TROUTMAN, RONALD LaVINE, SIDNEY LUBOW, RICHARD RADERMAN, DALE JOHNSTON, SAM CAYLOR, JOHN STACY and JACK KIRSCHNER "Duel" (Movie of The Weekend) (ABC)
COLIN C. MOUAT, CHARLES L. CAMPBELL and ROGER A. SWORD "The Forgotten Mermaids" (The Undersea World of Jacques Cousteau) (ABC)
HAROLD E. WOOLEY, PAUL LAUNE, MARVIN KOSBERG, GEORGE EMICK, RALPH HICKEY, WAYNE FURY and MONTY PEARCE "Brian's Song" (Movie of The Week) (ABC)

OUTSTANDING ACHIEVEMENT IN FILM SOUND MIXING

A single program of a series or a special program.
THEODORE SODERBERG and RICHARD OVERTON "Fireball Forward" (The ABC Sunday Night Movie) (ABC)
WILLIAM J. MONTAGUE and ALFERD E. OVERTON "Brian's Song" (Movie of The Week) (ABC)
GEORGE PORTER, ROY GRANVILLE and ED NELSON "The Forgotten Mermaids" (The Undersea World of Jacques Cousteau) (ABC)

OUTSTANDING ACHIEVEMENT IN TECHNICAL DIRECTION AND ELECTRONIC CAMERAWORK

A single program of a series or a special program.
HEINO RIPP, Technical Director; ALBERT CAMOIN, FRANK GAETA, GENE MARTIN and DONALD MULVANEY, Cameramen "Jack Lemmon in 'S Wonderful, 'S Marvelous, 'S Gershwin" (Bell System Family Theatre) (NBC)
LOUIS FUSARI, Technical Director; RAY FIGELSKI, RICK LOMBARDO, WAYNE OSTERHOUDT and JON OLSON, Cameramen "The Flip Wilson Show" (with Petula Clark and Redd Foxx) (NBC)
O. TAMBURRI, Technical Director; DON MULVANEY, JON OLSON and BOB KEYS, Cameramen "Gideon" (Hallmark Hall of Fame) (NBC)

OUTSTANDING ACHIEVEMENT IN LIGHTING DIRECTION

A single program of a series or a special program, produced for electronic television only.
JOHN FRESCHI "Gideon" (Hallmark Hall of Fame) (NBC)
WILLIAM KLAGES "Good Vibrations from Central Park" (ABC)
JOHN R. NANCE "The Flip Wilson Show" (with Petula Clark and Redd Foxx) (NBC)

OUTSTANDING ACHIEVEMENT IN VIDEO TAPE EDITING
A single program of a series or a special program.
PAT McKENNA "Hogan's Goat" (Special of The Week) (PBS)
FRANK HEROLD "Paradise Lost - Part II" (NET Playhouse on The 30's) (PBS)
MIKE WENIG "The Twentieth Century Follies" (The ABC Comedy Hour) (ABC)

OUTSTANDING ACHIEVEMENT IN LIVE OR TAPE SOUND MIXING
A single program of a series or a special program.
NORMAN H. DEWES "The Elevator Story" (All in The Family) (CBS)
BILL COLE "Bing Crosby And His Friends" (NBC)
DAVE WILLIAMS "The Flip Wilson Show" (with Petula Clark and Redd Foxx) (NBC)

THE AREAS
(Possibility of One Award, More Than One Award, or No Award)

SPECIAL CLASSIFICATION OF OUTSTANDING PROGRAM AND INDIVIDUAL ACHIEVEMENT

GENERAL PROGRAMMING
THE PENTAGON PAPERS "PBS Special" David Prowitt, Executive Producer; Martin Clancy, Producer (PBS)
THE ADVOCATES Gregory G. Harney, Executive Producer; Russell Morash and Tom Burrows, Producers (Series) (PBS)
THE FRENCH CHEF Ruth Lockwood, Producer; Julia Child, Hostess (Series) (PBS)
MUTUAL OF OMAHA'S WILD KINGDOM Don Meier, Producer (Series) (Synd)
THE WONDERFUL WORLD OF DISNEY Ron Miller, Producer (Series) (NBC)

DOCU-DRAMA
THE SEARCH FOR THE NILE - PARTS I-VI Christopher Ralling, Producer (NBC)
THE PLOT TO MURDER HITLER "Appointment With Destiny" Robert Larson and Warren Bush, Executive Producers; Robert Guenette, Producer (CBS)

INDIVIDUALS
MICHAEL HASTINGS and DEREK MARLOW, Writers "The Search For The Nile - Parts I-VI" (NBC)
JESS PALEY, Cinematographer "The Plot to Murder Hitler" (Appointment With Destiny) (CBS)
BRIAN TUFANO and JOHN BAKER, Cinematographers "The Search For The Nile - Parts I-VI" (NBC)
GEORGE PORTER, DAVID RONNE, ROY GRANVILLE and EDWARD NELSON, Film Sound Mixers "Showdown At O.K. Corral" (Appointment With Destiny) (CBS)
WILLIAM MORRIS, Technical Director; ROBERT BERNSTEIN, PHILIP FONTANA, RICHARD KERR, JESSEL KOHN, MORTON LEVIN, JOHN MORREALE and MICHAEL REBICH, Cameramen, 25th Annual Antoinette Perry (Tony) Awards (ABC)

OUTSTANDING ACHIEVEMENT IN SPORTS PROGRAMMING

PROGRAMS
ABC'S WIDE WORLD OF SPORTS Roone Arledge, Executive Producer (Series) (ABC)
NFL MONDAY NIGHT FOOTBALL Roone Arledge, Executive Producer; Chet Forte and Dennis Lewin, Producers (Series) (ABC)
ROSE BOWL GAME Scotty Connal, Executive Producer; Lou Kusserow, Producer (NBC)
WORLD SERIES (Baseball) Lou Kusserow, Producer (NBC)
JACK PERKINS, Correspondent "The Perkins Piece" (XI Olympic Winter Games) (NBC)

INDIVIDUALS
WILLIAM P. KELLEY, Technical Director; JIM CULLEY, JACK BENNETT, BUDDY JOSEPH, MARIO CIARLO, FRANK MANFREDI, COREY LEIBLE, GENE MARTIN, CAL SHADWELL, BILLY BARNES and RON CHARBONNEAU, Cameramen "AFC Championship Game" (NBC)

OUTSTANDING ACHIEVEMENT IN CHILDREN'S PROGRAMMING

PROGRAMS
SESAME STREET David D. Connell, Executive Producer; Jon Stone, Producer (Series) (PBS)
THE ELECTRIC COMPANY David D. Connell, Executive Producer; Samuel Y. Gibbon Jr., Producer (Series) (PBS)

INDIVIDUALS
GEORGE W. RIESENBERGER, Lighting Director "Sesame Street" (Series) (PBS)
JOHN SCOTT TROTTER, Music Director "Play It Again, Charlie Brown" (CBS)

OUTSTANDING ACHIEVEMENT IN DAYTIME DRAMA

PROGRAMS
THE DOCTORS Allen Potter, Producer (Series) (NBC)
GENERAL HOSPITAL Jim Young, Producer (Series) (ABC)

INDIVIDUALS
JOHN L. COFFEY, Technical Director; SELWYN REED, LOUIS GERARD and GENE MARTIN, Cameramen "Another World" (NBC)
MEL HANDELSMAN, Lighting Director "All My Children" (ABC)

OUTSTANDING ACHIEVEMENT IN DAYTIME PROGRAMMING

PROGRAMS
DINAH'S PLACE Henry Jaffe, Executive Producer; Fred Tatashore, Producer; Dinah Shore, Star (Series) (NBC)
THE HOLLYWOOD SQUARES Merrill Heatter and Robert Quigley, Executive Producers; Bill Armstrong and Jay Redack, Producers (Series) (NBC)

INDIVIDUALS
PAUL LYNDE 'The Hollywood Squares" (Series) (NBC)
PETER MARSHALL "The Hollywood Squares" (Series) (NBC)

OUTSTANDING ACHIEVEMENT IN RELIGIOUS PROGRAMMING

PROGRAMS
INSIGHT Father Ellwood E. Kieser, Executive Producer; John Meredyth Lucas, Producer (Series) (Synd)
THIS IS THE LIFE Martin J. Neeb, Jr., Executive Producer; Stan Hersh and Melvin Hersh, Producers (Series) (Synd)

INDIVIDUALS

ALFRED ANTONINI, Music Director "And David Wept" (CBS)
LON STUCKY, Lighting Director "A City of The King" (Contact) (Synd)

OUTSTANDING ACHIEVEMENT IN ANY AREA OF CREATIVE TECHNICAL CRAFTS

PIERRE GOUPIL, MICHEL DELOIRE and YVES OMER, Underwater Cameramen "Secrets of the Sunken Caves" (The Undersea World of Jacques Cousteau) (ABC)
ROBERT GUENETTE, DAVID WOLPER, WARREN BUSH, NICHOLAS WEBSTER and ROBERT LARSON For re-creation of vintage film "The Plot To Murder Hitler," "The Last Days of John Dillinger," "Showdown at O.K. Corral" (Appointment With Destiny) (CBS)
EDIE PANDA, Hairstylist 'U.S.A." (Hollywood Television Theatre) (PBS)

TRUSTEES AWARDS

BILL LAWRENCE, NATIONAL AFFAIRS EDITOR, ABC NEWS (DECEASED) For dedicating more than four decades of his life to reporting the news of the nation, the last one of which was devoted to television; ranging from international politics to international affairs and global combat; with that degree of objectivity, that devotion to truth, that professional preeminence which can only serve as a model for all television newsmen.
DR. FRANK STANTON, PRESIDENT, CBS For his selfless leadership and unwavering principle in defense of our industry under attack, his outspoken stance and courageous posture in protecting the right of the people to know, frequently in the face of potential dangers, both personal and professional, from those many forces which have attempted to abridge or even to abolish that right.

OUTSTANDING ACHIEVEMENT IN ENGINEERING DEVELOPMENT

LEE HARRISON, III For the development of Scanimate, a unique electronic means of generating picture animation.

CITATIONS

RICHARD E. HILL and ELECTRONIC ENGINEERING COMPANY OF CALIFORNIA For the development of a time code and equipment to facilitate the editing of magnetic video tape.
NATIONAL BROADCASTING COMPANY For the development of the Hum Bucker, which provides a practical means to correct a picture transmission defect commonly encountered on remote pickups.

THE STATION AWARD

SICKLE CELL DISEASE: PARADOX OF NEGLECT (WZZM-TV) Grand Rapids, Michigan
ALL ABOUT WELFARE (WITF-TV) Hershey, Pennsylvania (Educational Station)
THE AWKWARD AGE (WCKT-TV) Miami, Florida
DRUG CRISES IN EAST HARLEM (WABC-TV) New York City, New York
INSIDE PARISH PRISON (WWL-TV) New Orleans, Louisiana
LOUISVILLE: OPEN CITY (WHAS) Louisville, Kentucky
MAKE NO MISTAKE ABOUT IT: THE PRESIDENT CAME TO IOWA (KDIN-TV) Des Moines, Iowa (Educational Station)
A PLACE FOR MUSIC (WHDH-TV) Boston, Massachusetts
PROBE. . .AND THROW AWAY THE KEY (WRC-TV) Washington, D.C.
. . .STILL GOT LIFE TO GO (WKY-TV) Oklahoma City, Oklahoma

1972/73

ENTERTAINMENT PROGRAM AND INDIVIDUAL ACHIEVEMENTS

(One Award Only In Each of the Following Categories)

OUTSTANDING COMEDY SERIES

Award to Executive Producer(s) and/or Producer(s).

ALL IN THE FAMILY Norman Lear, Executive Producer, John Rich, Producer (CBS)
THE MARY TYLER MOORE SHOW James L. Brooks and Allan Burns, Executive Producers; Ed Weinberger, Producer (CBS)
M*A*S*H Gene Reynolds, Producer (CBS)
MAUDE Norman Lear, Executive Producer; Rod Parker, Producer (CBS)
SANFORD AND SON Bud Yorkin, Executive Producer; Aaron Ruben, Producer (NBC)

OUTSTANDING DRAMA SERIES - CONTINUING

Award to Executive Producer(s) and/or Producer(s).

THE WALTONS Lee Rich, Executive Producer; Robert L. Jacks, Producer (CBS)
CANNON Quinn Martin, Executive Producer; Harold Gast and Aldrian Samish, Producers (CBS)
COLUMBO, NBC Sunday Mystery Movie; Dean Hargrove, Producer (NBC)
HAWAII FIVE-O Leonard Freeman, Executive Producer; Bob Sweeney and William Finnegan, Producers (CBS)
KUNG-FU Jerry Thorpe, Producer (ABC)
MANNIX Bruce Geller, Executive Producer; Ivan Goff and Ben Roberts, Producers (CBS)

OUTSTANDING DRAMA/COMEDY - LIMITED EPISODES

Award to Executive Producer(s) and/or Producer(s).

TOM BROWN'S SCHOOLDAYS Masterpiece Theatre: Parts I Through V; John D. McRae, Producer (PBS)
THE LAST OF THE MOHICANS Masterpiece Theatre: Parts I Through VIII; John D. McRae, Producer (PBS)
THE LIFE OF LEONARDO DA VINCI Parts I Through V; RAI Radiotelevisione Italiana, Executive Producer (CBS)

OUTSTANDING VARIETY MUSICAL SERIES

Award(s) to Executive Producer(s) and/or Producer(s) and Star(s) (if applicable).

THE JULIE ANDREWS HOUR Nick Vanoff and William O. Harbach, Producers; Julie Andrews, Star (ABC)
THE CAROL BURNETT SHOW Joe Hamilton, Executive Producer; Bill Angelos, Buz Kohan and Arnie Rosen, Producers; Carol Burnett, Star (CBS)
THE DICK CAVETT SHOW John Gilroy, Producer; Dick Cavett, Star (ABC)
THE FLIP WILSON SHOW Monte Kay, Executive Producer; Bob Henry, Producer; Flip Wilson, Star (NBC)
THE SONNY & CHER COMEDY HOUR Allan Blye and Chris Bearde, Producers; Sonny and Cher, Stars (CBS)

OUTSTANDING SINGLE PROGRAM - DRAMA OR COMEDY

A special program - Award to Executive Producer(s) and/or Producer(s).

A WAR OF CHILDREN The New CBS Tuesday Night Movies; Roger Gimbel, Executive Producer; George Schaefer, Producer (CBS)
LONG DAY'S JOURNEY INTO NIGHT Cecil Clarke, Executive Producer (ABC)
THE MARCUS-NELSON MURDERS The CBS Thursday Night Movies; Abby Mann, Executive Producer; Matthew Rapf, Producer (CBS)
THE RED PONY Bell System Family Theatre; Frederick W. Brogger, Producer (NBC)
THAT CERTAIN SUMMER Wednesday Movie Of The Week; Richard Levinson and William Link, Producers (ABC)

OUTSTANDING SINGLE PROGRAM - VARIETY AND POPULAR MUSIC

A special program - Award(s) to Executive Producer(s) and/or Producer(s) and Star(s) (if applicable).

SINGER PRESENTS LIZA WITH A "Z" Bob Fosse and Fred Ebb, Producers; Liza Minnelli, Star (NBC)
APPLAUSE Alexander Cohen, Executive Producer; Joseph Kipness, Lawrence Kasha, Dick Rosenbloom, Producers (CBS)
ONCE UPON A MATTRESS Joe Hamilton, Producer (CBS)

OUTSTANDING SINGLE PROGRAM - CLASSICAL MUSIC

A special program - Award(s) to Executive Producer(s) and/or Producer(s) and Star(s) (if applicable).

THE SLEEPING BEAUTY, J.W. Barnes and Robert Kotlowitz, Executive Producers; Norman Campbell, Producer (PBS)
BERNSTEIN IN LONDON Special Of The Week; Curtis W. Davis, Executive Producer; Mary Feldbauer and Brian Large, Producers; Leonard Bernstein, Star (PBS)
THE METROPOLITAN OPERA SALUTE TO SIR RUDOLF BING William Eliscu, Executive Producer; Charles E. Andrews, Producer (CBS)

OUTSTANDING NEW SERIES

Award to Executive Producer(s) and/or Producer(s).

AMERICA Michael Gill, Producer (NBC)
THE JULIE ANDREWS HOUR Nick Vanoff, Producer; Julie Andrews, Star (ABC)
KUNG FU Jerry Thorpe, Producer (ABC)
M*A*S*H Gene Reynolds, Producer (CBS)
MAUDE Norman Lear, Executive Producer; Rod Parker, Producer (CBS)
THE WALTONS Lee Rich, Executive Producer; Robert L. Jacks, Producer (CBS)

OUTSTANDING PROGRAM ACHIEVEMENT IN DAYTIME DRAMA

Award to Executive Producer(s) and/or Producer(s).

THE EDGE OF NIGHT Erwin Nicholson, Producer; Series (CBS)
DAYS OF OUR LIVES Betty Corday, Executive Producer; H. Wesley Kenney, Producer; Series (NBC)
THE DOCTORS Allen Potter, Producer; Series (NBC)
ONE LIFE TO LIVE Doris Quinlan and Agnes Nixon, Producers; Series (ABC)

OUTSTANDING PROGRAM ACHIEVEMENT IN DAYTIME

Award to Executive Producer(s) and/or Producer(s). An Award for program achievements which do not qualify as Daytime Drama.

DINAH'S PLACE Henry Jaffe, Executive Producer; Fred Tatasore, Producer; Dinah Shore, Star; Series (NBC)
THE HOLLYWOOD SQUARES Merrill Heatter and Robert Quigley, Executive Producers; Bill Armstrong and Jay Redack, Producers; Series (NBC)
JEOPARDY Robert H. Rubin, Producer; Series (NBC)
THE MIKE DOUGLAS SHOW Barry Sand, Producer; Mike Douglas, Star; Series (SYND)
PASSWORD Frank Wayne, Executive Producer; Howard Felsher, Producer; Series (ABC)

OUTSTANDING SINGLE PERFORMANCE BY AN ACTOR IN A LEADING ROLE

A single appearance in a "Continuing" or "Limited" Drama or Comedy Series; or for a special program.

LAWRENCE OLIVIER Long Day's Journey Into Night (ABC)
HENRY FONDA The Red Pony; Bell System Family Theatre (NBC)
HAL HOLBROOK That Certain Summer; Wednesday Movie Of The Week (ABC)
TELLY SAVALAS The Marcus-Nelson Murders; The CBS Thursday Night Movies (CBS)

OUTSTANDING SINGLE PERFORMANCE BY AN ACTRESS IN A LEADING ROLE

A single appearance in a "Continuing" or "Limited" Drama or Comedy Series; or for a special program.

CLORIS LEACHMAN A Brand New Life; Tuesday Movie Of The Week (ABC)
LAUREN BACALL Applause (CBS)
HOPE LANGE That Certain Summer; Wednesday Movie Of The Week (ABC)

OUTSTANDING CONTINUED PERFORMANCE BY AN ACTOR IN A LEADING ROLE

A. Drama Series - Continuing.

RICHARD THOMAS The Waltons (CBS)
DAVID CARRADINE Kung Fu (ABC)
MIKE CONNORS Mannix (CBS)
WILLIAM CONRAD Cannon (CBS)
PETER FALK Columbo; NBC Sunday Mystery Movie (NBC)

B. Drama/Comedy - Limited Episodes.

ANTHONY MURPHY Tom Brown's Schooldays; Masterpiece Theatre: Parts 1 Through V (PBS)
JOHN ABINERI The Last Of The Mohicans; Masterpiece Theatre: Parts I Through VIII (PBS)
PHILLIPE LeROY The Life Of Leonardo da Vinci (CBS)

OUTSTANDING CONTINUED PERFORMANCE BY AN ACTRESS IN A LEADING ROLE

A. Drama Series - Continuing

MICHAEL LEARNED The Waltons (CBS)
LINDA DAY GEORGE Mission: Impossible (CBS)
SUSAN SAINT JAMES McMillan & Wife; NBC Sunday Mystery Movie (NBC)

B. Drama/Comedy - Limited Episodes.

SUSAN HAMPSHIRE Vanity Fair; Masterpiece Theatre: Parts I Through V (PBS)
VIVIEN HEILBRON The Moonstone; Masterpiece Theatre: Parts I Through V (PBS)
MARGARET TYZACK Cousin Bette; Masterpiece Theatre: Parts I Through V (PBS)

OUTSTANDING CONTINUED PERFORMANCE BY AN ACTOR IN A LEADING ROLE IN A COMEDY SERIES

JACK KLUGMAN The Odd Couple (ABC)
ALAN ALDA M*A*S*H (CBS)
REDD FOXX Sanford And Son (NBC)
CARROLL O'CONNOR All In The Family (CBS)
TONY RANDALL The Odd Couple (ABC)

OUTSTANDING CONTINUED PERFORMANCE BY AN ACTRESS IN A LEADING ROLE IN A COMEDY SERIES

MARY TYLER MOORE The Mary Tyler Moore Show (CBS)
BEATRICE ARTHUR Maude (CBS)
JEAN STAPLETON All In The Family (CBS)

OUTSTANDING PERFORMANCE BY AN ACTOR IN A SUPPORTING ROLE IN DRAMA

A continuing or one-time appearance in a series, or for a special program.

SCOTT JACOBY That Certain Summer; Wednesday Movie Of The Week (ABC)
WILL GEER The Waltons; Series (CBS)
JAMES BROLIN Marcus Welby, M.D.; Series (ABC)

OUTSTANDING PERFORMANCE BY AN ACTRESS IN A SUPPORTING ROLE IN DRAMA

A continuing or one-time appearance in a series, or for a special program.

ELLEN CORBY The Waltons; Series (CBS)
GAIL FISHER Mannix; Series (CBS)
NANCY WALKER McMillan & Wife; NBC Sunday Mystery Movie; Series (NBC)

OUTSTANDING PERFORMANCE BY AN ACTOR IN A SUPPORTING ROLE IN COMEDY

A continuing or one-time appearance in a series, or for a special program.

TED KNIGHT The Mary Tyler Moore Show; Series (CBS)
EDWARD ASNER The Mary Tyler Moore Show; Series (CBS)
GARY BURGHOFF M*A*S*H; Series (CBS)
ROB REINER All In The Family; Series (CBS)
McLEAN STEVENSON M*A*S*H; Series (CBS)

OUTSTANDING PERFORMANCE BY AN ACTRESS IN A SUPPORTING ROLE IN COMEDY

A continuing or one-time appearance in a series, or for a special program.

VALERIE HARPER The Mary Tyler Moore Show; Series (CBS)
CLORIS LEACHMAN The Mary Tyler Moore Show; My Brother's Keeper (CBS)
SALLY STRUTHERS All In The Family; Series (CBS)

OUTSTANDING ACHIEVEMENT BY A SUPPORTING PERFORMER IN MUSIC OR VARIETY

A continuing or one-time appearance in a series, or for a special program.

TIM CONWAY The Carol Burnett Show (CBS)
HARVEY KORMAN The Carol Burnett Show; Series (CBS)
LIZA MINNELLI A Royal Gala Variety Performance In the Presence Of Her Majesty The Queen (ABC)
LILY TOMLIN Rowan And Martin's Laugh-In; Series (NBC)

OUTSTANDING DIRECTORIAL ACHIEVEMENT IN DRAMA

A single program of a series with combining characters and/or theme.

JERRY THORPE An Eye For An Eye; Kung Fu (ABC)
EDWARD M. ABROMS The Most Dangerous Match; Columbo; NBC Sunday Mystery Movie (NBC)
LEE PHILIPS The Love Story; The Waltons (CBS)

OUTSTANDING DIRECTORIAL ACHIEVEMENT IN DRAMA

A single program.

JOSEPH SARGENT The Marcus-Nelson Murders; The CBS Thursday Night Movies (CBS)
LAMONT JOHNSON That Certain Summer; Wednesday Movie Of The Week (ABC)
GEORGE SCHAEFER A War Of Children; The New CBS Thursday Night Movies (CBS)

OUTSTANDING DIRECTORIAL ACHIEVEMENT IN COMEDY

A single program of a series with continuing characters and/or theme.

JAY SANDRICH It's Whether You Win Or Lose; The Mary Tyler Moore Show (CBS)
GENE REYNOLDS, P-I-L-O-T; M*A*S*H (CBS)
JOHN RICH and BOB LA HENDRO The Bunkers And The Swingers; All In The Family (CBS)

OUTSTANDING DIRECTORIAL ACHIEVEMENT IN VARIETY OR MUSIC

A single program of a series.

BILL DAVIS The Julie Andrews Hour (with "Liza Doolittle" and "Mary Poppins") (ABC)
ART FISHER The Sonny & Cher Comedy Hour (with Mike Connors) (CBS)
TIM KILEY The Flip Wilson Show (with Roberta Flack and Burt Reynolds) (NBC)

OUTSTANDING DIRECTORIAL ACHIEVEMENT IN COMEDY, VARIETY OR MUSIC

A special program.

BOB FOSSE Singer Presents Liza With A "Z" (NBC)
MARTIN CHARNIN and DAVE WILSON Jack Lemmon - Get Happy (NBC)
STAN HARRIS Duke Ellington...We Love You Madly (CBS)
WALTER C. MILLER You're A Good Man, Charlie Brown; Hallmark Hall Of Fame (NBC)
DAVE POWERS and RON FIELD Once Upon A Mattress (CBS)

OUTSTANDING WRITING ACHIEVEMENT IN DRAMA

A single program of a series with continuing characters and/or theme.

JOHN McGREEVEY The Scholar; The Waltons (CBS)
STEVE BOCHCO Etude In Black; Columbo; NBC Sunday Mystery Movie (NBC)
EARL HAMNER, JR. The Love Story; The Waltons (CBS)

OUTSTANDING WRITING ACHIEVEMENT IN DRAMA, ORIGINAL TELEPLAY

A single program.

ABBY MANN The Marcus-Nelson Murders; The CBS Thursday Night Movies (CBS)
DAVID KARP Hawkins On Murder; The New CBS Tuesday Night Movies (CBS)
RICHARD LEVINSON and WILLIAM LINK That Certain Summer; Wednesday Movie Of The Week (ABC)

OUTSTANDING WRITING ACHIEVEMENT IN DRAMA, ADAPTATION

A single program.

ELEANOR PERRY The House Without A Christmas Tree (CBS)
ROBERT TOTTEN and RON BISHOP The Red Pony; Bell System Family Theatre (NBC)
ELLEN M. VIOLETT Go Ask Alice; Wednesday Movie Of The Week (ABC)

OUTSTANDING WRITING ACHIEVEMENT IN COMEDY

A single program of a series with continuing characters and/or theme.

MICHAEL ROSS, BERNIE WEST, and LEE KALCHEIM The Bunkers And The Swingers; All In The Family (CBS)
ALLAN BURNS and JAMES L. BROOKS The Good-Time News; The Mary Tyler Moore Show (CBS)
LARRY GELBART, P-I-L-O-T; M*A*S*H (CBS)

OUTSTANDING WRITING ACHIEVEMENT IN VARIETY OR MUSIC

A single program of a series.

STAN HART, LARRY SIEGEL, GAIL PARENT, WOODY KLING, ROGER BEATTY, TOM PATCHETT, JAY TARSES, ROBERT HILLIARD, ARNIE KOGEN, BILL ANGELOS and BUZ KOHAN The Carol Burnett Show (with Steve Lawrence And Lily Tomlin) (CBS)
HERBERT BAKER, MIKE MARMER, STAN BURNS, DON HINKLEY, DICK HILLS, SID GREEN, PAUL McCAULEY, PETER GALLAY and FLIP WILSON The Flip Wilson Show (with Sammy Davis, Jr., Ed Sullivan and Marilyn Michaels) (NBC)
BOB ELLISON, HAL GOODMAN, LARRY KLEIN, JAY BURTON, GEORGE BLOOM, LILA GARRETT, JOHN AYLESWORTH and FRANK PEPPIATT The Julie Andrews Hour (with "Eliza Doolittle" and "Mary Poppins") (ABC)

OUTSTANDING WRITING ACHIEVEMENT IN COMEDY, VARIETY OR MUSIC

A special program.

RENEE TAYLOR and JOSEPH BOLOGNA Acts Of Love - And Other Comedies (ABC)
FRED EBB Singer Presents Liza with a "Z" (NBC)
ALLAN MANNINGS, ANN ELDER, KARYL GELD, RICHARD PRYOR, JOHN RAPPAPORT, JIM RUSK, LILY TOMLIN, JANE WAGNER, ROD WARREN, and GORGE YANOK The Lily Tomlin Show (CBS)

OUTSTANDING ACHIEVEMENT IN CHOREOGRAPHY

A single program of a series or a special program.

BOB FOSSE Singer Presents Liza With A "Z" (NBC)
TONY CHARMOLI The Julie andrews Hour (with Robert Goulet And Joel Grey) (ABC)
ERNEST O. FLATT Family Show; The Carol Burnett Show (CBS)

OUTSTANDING ACHIEVEMENT IN MUSIC COMPOSITION

A. For a series or a single program of a series (in the first year of music's use only).

CHARLES FOX Love, American Style; Series (ABC)
ALEXANDER COURAGE Cycle Of Peril; Medical Center (CBS)
MARTY PAICH Ironside; Series (NBC)

B. For a special program.

JERRY GOLDSMITH The Red Pony; Bell System Family Theatre (NBC)
FRED EBB and JOHN KANDER Singer Presents Liza With A "Z" (NBC)
BILLY GOLDENBERG A Brand New Life; Tuesday Movie Of The Week (ABC)

OUTSTANDING ACHIEVEMENT IN MUSIC DIRECTION OF A VARIETY, MUSICAL OR DRAMATIC PROGRAM

A single program of a series or a special program.

PETER MATZ The Carol Burnett Show (with Anthony Newley and Bernadette Peters) (CBS)
VAN ALEXANDER The Wacky World Of Jonathan Winters (with Debbie Reynolds) (SYND)
IRWIN KOSTAL, Dr. Jekyll And Mr. Hyde (NBC)

OUTSTANDING ACHIEVEMENT IN MUSIC, LYRICS AND SPECIAL MATERIAL

A series or a single program of a series or a special program written for television.

FRED EBB and JOHN KANDER Singer Presents Liza With A "Z" (NBC)
EARL BROWN The Gloria Majestic Story; The Sonny And Cher Comedy Hour (with Jean Stapleton) (CBS)
BILLY GOLDENBERG and BOBBY RUSSELL The Marcus-Nelson Murders; The CBS Thursday Night Movies (CBS)

OUTSTANDING ACHIEVEMENT IN ART DIRECTION OR SCENIC DESIGN

A. For a dramatic program or feature length film made for television; for a series, a single program of a series or a special program.

TOM JOHN Much Ado About Nothing (CBS)
ROBERT BOYLE and JAMES HULSEY, Art Directors; JOHN KURL, Set Decorator; The Red Pony; Bell System Family Theatre (NBC)
WILLIAM CAMPBELL Night Of Terror; Tuesday Movie Of The Week (ABC)
GIBSON HOLLY, Art Director; LUCIEN M. HAFLEY, Set Decorator; Western; Mission: Impossible (CBS)
JAN SCOTT Another Part Of The Forest; Hollywood Television Theatre; Special Of The Week (PBS)
JAN M. VAN TAMELEN, Art Director; FRED R. PRICE, Set Decorator; Mannix; Series (CBS)

B. For a Musical or Variety single program of a series or a special program.

BRIAN BARTHOLOMEW and KEATON S. WALKER The Julie Andrews Hour (with "Eliza Doolittle" and "Mary Poppins") (ABC)
PAUL BARNES and BOB SANSOM, Art Directors; BILL HARP, Set Decorator; The Doily Sisters; The Carol Burnett Show (CBS)
ROMAIN JOHNSTON The Flip Wilson Show (with Burt Reynolds, Tim Conway and Roberta Flack) (NBC)

OUTSTANDING ACHIEVEMENT IN LIGHTING DIRECTION

A single program of a series or a special program, produced for electronic television only.

JOHN FRESCHI and JOHN CASAGRANDE 44th Annual Oscar Awards (NBC)
TRUCK KRONE Christmas Show; The Julie Andrews Hour (ABC)
JOHN R. BEAM The Sonny And Cher Comedy Hour (with William Conrad) (CBS)

OUTSTANDING ACHIEVEMENT IN COSTUME DESIGN

A single program of a series or a special program.

JACK BEAR The Julie Andrews Hour (with Ken Berry and Jack Cassidy) (ABC)
THEONI V. ALDREDGE Much Ado About Nothing (CBS)
GRADY HUNT Dagger Of The Mind; Columbo; NBC Sunday Mystery Movie (NBC)
EMMA PORTEOUS Dr. Jekyll And Mr. Hyde (NBC)
CHRISTINA VON HUMBOLDT Cortez and Montezuma; Appointment With Destiny (CBS)

OUTSTANDING ACHIEVEMENT IN MAKE-UP

A single program of a series or a special program.

DEL ARMSTRONG, ELLIS BURMAN and STAN WINSTON Gargoyles; The New CBS Tuesday Night Movies (CBS)
ROBERT A. SIDELL The Actress; The Waltons (CBS)
NEVILLE SMALLWOOD Dr. Jekyll & Mr. Hyde (NBC)
ALLAN SNYDER and RICHARD COBOS The Red Pony; Bell System Family Theatre (NBC)
FRANK C. WESTMORE Chains; Kung Fu (ABC)
MICHAEL WESTMORE and MARVIN WESTMORE Frankenstein - Parts I and II; ABC Wide World Of Entertainment (ABC)

OUTSTANDING ACHIEVEMENT IN CINEMATOGRAPHY FOR ENTERTAINMENT PROGRAMMING

A. For a series or a single program of a series.

JACK WOOLF An Eye For An Eye; Kung Fu (ABC)
SAM LEAVITT Banacek; NBC Wednesday Mystery Movie; Series (NBC)
RUSSELL L. METTY The Waltons; Series (CBS)

B. For a special or feature length program made for television.

HOWARD SCHWARTZ, A.S.C. Night Of Terror; Tuesday Movie Of The Week (ABC)
ANDREW JACKSON The Red Pony; Bell System Family Theatre (NBC)
OWEN ROIZMAN Singer Presents Liza With A "Z" (NBC)

OUTSTANDING ACHIEVEMENT IN FILM EDITING FOR ENTERTAINMENT PROGRAMMING

A. For a series or a single program of a series.

GENE FOWLER, JR., MARJORIE FOWLER, and ANTHONY WOLLNER The Literary Man; The Waltons (CBS)
DOUGLAS HINES The Mary Tyler Moore Show; Series (CBS)
STANFORD TISCHLER and FRED W. BERGER M*A*S*H; Series (CBS)

B. For a special or feature length program made for television

PETER C. JOHNSON and ED SPIEGEL Surrender At Appomattox; Appointment With Destiny (CBS)
HENRY BERMAN, A.C.E. Go Ask Alice; Wednesday Movie Of The Week (ABC)
ALAN HEIM Singer Presents Liza With A "Z" (NBC)

OUTSTANDING ACHIEVEMENT IN FILM SOUND EDITING

A single program of a series or a special program.

ROSS TAYLOR, FRED BROWN and DAVID MARSHALL The Red Pony; Bell System Family Theatre (NBC)
PETER BERKOS, JOHN SINGLETON, BRIAN COURCIER, GORDON ECKER, JOHN STACY, JAMES NOWNES, GEORGE LUCKENBACHER, WALTER JENEVEIN and SIDNEY LUBOW Short Walk to Daylight; Tuesday Movie Of The Week (ABC)
CHARLES L. CAMPBELL, ROGER A. SWORD, ROBERT H. CORNETT and JERRY R. STANFORD The Smile Of The Walrus; The Undersea World Of Jacques Cousteau (ABC)

OUTSTANDING ACHIEVEMENT IN FILM SOUND MIXING

A single program of a series or a special program.

RICHARD J. WAGNER, GEORGE E. PORTER, EDDIE J. NELSON and FRED LEROY GRANVILLE Surrender At Appomattox; Appointment With Destiny (CBS)
MELVIN M. METCALFE, SR. and THOM PIPER That Certain Summer; Wednesday Movie Of The Week (ABC)
GEORGE PORTER, EDDIE NELSON and HOPPY MEHTERIAN The Singing Whale; The Undersea World Of Jacques Cousteau (ABC)

OUTSTANDING ACHIEVEMENT IN LIVE OR TAPE SOUND MIXING

A single program of a series or a special program.

AL GRAMAGLIA and MAHLON FOX Much Ado About Nothing (CBS)
WILLIAM J. LEVITSKY 44th Annual Oscar Awards (NBC)
PHILIP RAMONE Duke Ellington. . .We Love You Madly (CBS)

OUTSTANDING ACHIEVEMENT IN VIDEO TAPE EDITING

A single program of a series or a special program.

NICK GIORDANO and ARTHUR SCHNEIDER The Julie Andrews Hour (with "Eliza Doolittle" and "Mary Poppins") (ABC)
WILLIAM H. BRESHEARS and ANDREW McINTYRE Ed Sullivan Presents The TV Comedy Years (CBS)
JAMES H. ROSE Burt Bacharach In Shangri-La (ABC)
CHARLES SHADEL and WALTER BALDERSON Democratic Convention Highlights; NBC Nightly News (NBC)
MIKE WENIG Love Is. . .Barbara Eden (ABC)

OUTSTANDING ACHIEVEMENTS IN TECHNICAL DIRECTION AND ELECTRONIC CAMERAWORK

A single program of a series or a special program.

ERNIE BUTTELMAN Technical Director; **ROBERT A. KEMP, JAMES ANGEL, JAMES BALDEN and DAVE HILMER**, Cameramen; The Julie Andrews Hour (with "Mary Poppins" And "Eliza Doolittle") (ABC)
CHARLES FRANKLIN, Technical Director; GORME ERICKSON, JACK JENNINGS, TOM McCONNELL, RICHARD NELSON and BARNEY NEELEY, Cameramen; The Sonny & Cher Comedy Hour (with Mike Connors) (CBS)
E.G. JOHNSON, Technical Director; SAM DRUMMY, Cameraman; Apollo 17 - Splashdown (Pool Coverage)

THE AREAS

(Possibility of One Award, More Than One Award, or No Award)

OUTSTANDING ACHIEVEMENT BY INDIVIDUALS IN DAYTIME DRAMA
MARY FICKETT, Performer; All My Children; Series (ABC)
MACDONALD CAREY, Performer; Days Of Our Lives; Series (NBC)
NORMAN HALL, Director; The Doctors; January 9, 1973 (NBC)
H. WESLEY KENNEY, Director; Days Of Our Lives; March 6, 1973 (NBC)
PETER LEVIN, Director; Love Is A Many Splendored Thing; July 17, 1972 (CBS)
DAVID PRESSMAN, Director; One Life To Live; January 23, 1973 (ABC)
VICTOR PAGANUZZI, Scenic Designer; JOHN A. WENDELL, Set Decorator; Love Is A Many Splendored Thing; Series (CBS)

OUTSTANDING ACHIEVEMENT BY INDIVIDUALS IN DAYTIME PROGRAMMING
An Award for individual achievements which do not qualify in Daytime Drama.
BILL CULLEN, Host; Three On A Match; Series (NBC)
PAUL LYNDE, Performer; The Hollywood Squares; Series (NBC)
PETER MARSHALL, Host; The Hollywood Squares; Series (NBC)

OUTSTANDING ACHIEVEMENT IN CHILDREN'S PROGRAMMING
An Award for programs and individual achievements. A. Entertainment/Fictional
SESAME STREET Jon Stone, Executive Producer; Bob Cunniff, Producer; Series (PBS)
ZOOM Christopher Sarson, Producer; Series (PBS)
TOM WHEDON, JOHN BONI, SARA COMPTON, TOM DUNSMUIR, THAD MUMFORD, JEREMY STEVENS and JIM THURMAN, Writers; The Electric Company (PBS)
THE ELECTRIC COMPANY Samuel Y. Gibbon, Jr. and David D. Connell, Executive Producers; Andy Ferguson, Producer; Series (PBS)
HENRY BEHAR, Director; The Electric Company (PBS)
ROBERT G. MYHRUM, Director; Sesame Street (PBS)
CHARLES M. SCHULZ, Writer; You're Elected, Charlie Brown (CBS)
JOE RAPOSO, Music Director; Sesame Street (PBS)
B. International/Factual
LAST OF THE CURLEWS The ABC Afterschool Special; William Hanna and Joseph Barbera, Producers (ABC)
SHARI LEWIS, Performer; A Picture Of Us; NBC Children's Theatre (NBC)
IN THE NEWS Joel Heller, Executive Producer; Pat Lynch and Judy Towers Reemtsma, Producers; Series (CBS)
MAKE A WISH Lester Cooper, Executive Producer; Tom Bywaters, Producer; Series (ABC)
JAMESON BREWER, Writer; Last Of The Curlews; The ABC Afterschool Special (ABC)

OUTSTANDING ACHIEVEMENT IN SPORTS PROGRAMMING
An Award for programs and for individuals contributing to the coverage of sporting events.
ABC'S WIDE WORLD OF SPORTS Roone Arledge, Executive Producer; Series (ABC)
1972 SUMMER OLYMPIC GAMES Roone Arledge, Executive Producer (ABC)
JOHN CROAK, CHARLES GARDNER, JAKOB HIERL, CONRAD KRAUS, EDWARD McCARTHY, NICK MAZUR, ALEX MOSKOVIC, JAMES PARKER, LOUIS RENDE, ROSS SKIPPER, ROBERT STEINBACK, JOHN DeLISA, GEORGE BOETTCHER, MERRIT ROESSER, LEO SCHARF, RANDY COHEN, VITO GERARDI, HAROLD BYERS, WINFIELD GROSS, PAUL SCOSKIE, PETER FRITZ, LEO STEPHAN, GERBER McBEATH, LOUIS TORINO, MICHAEL WENIG, TOM WIGHT and JAMES KELLEY, Video Tape Editors; 1972 Summer Olympic Games (ABC)
NCAA COLLEGE FOOTBALL Roone Arledge, Executive Producer; Chuck Howard, Producer; Series (ABC)
NFL MONDAY NIGHT FOOTBALL Roone Arledge, Executive Producer; Chet Forte and Dennis Lewin, Producers; Series (ABC)
SUPER BOWL VII Scotty Connal, Executive Producer; Roy Hammerman, Producer (NBC)
KEITH JACKSON, Commentator; 1972 Summer Olympic Games (ABC)
JIM McKAY, Commentator; 1972 Summer Olympic Games (ABC)

SPECIAL AWARDS

OUTSTANDING ACHIEVEMENT IN ENGINEERING DEVELOPMENT
Award to Sony for the development of the Trinitron, a picture tube providing good picture quality in color television receivers.

Award to CMX Systems, a CBS/Memorex company, for the development of a video tape editing system, utilizing a computer to aid the decision-making process, store the editing decisions and implement them in the final assembly of takes.

THE NATIONAL AWARD FOR COMMUNITY SERVICE
TAKE DES MOINES. . .PLEASE; KDIN-TV (Educational Station); Des Moines, Iowa
BARS TO PROGRESS; WMAR-TV; Baltimore, Maryland
CARRASCOLENDAS, KLRN-TV (Educational Station); Austin, Texas
EGYPT VALLEY - AN EPITAPH/A CALL TO CONSCIENCE (Montage); WKYC-TV; Cleveland, Ohio
THE GREEN GRASS OF HOME; KFDA-TV; Amarillo, Texas
IN A CLASS. . .ALL BY HIMSELF; KNBC-TV; Los Angeles, California
NEWSIGN 4; KRON-TV; San Francisco, California
ONE AND ONE IS. . .DOS; WZZM-TV; Grand Rapids, Michigan
A SEED OF HOPE; WTVJ-TV; Miami, Florida
WILLOWBROOK: THE LAST GREAT DISGRACE; WABC-TV; New York, New York

NEWS AND DOCUMENTARY PROGRAM AND INDIVIDUAL ACHIEVEMENTS
(Possibility of One Award, More than One Award, or No Award)

OUTSTANDING ACHIEVEMENT WITHIN REGULARLY SCHEDULED NEWS PROGRAMS
A. An Award for program segments, i.e. the presentation of individual stories (in single or multi-part) or elements within the program.
THE US/SOVIET WHEAT DEAL: IS THERE A SCANDAL? CBS Evening News with Walter Cronkite; Paul Greenberg and Russ Bensley, Executive Producers; Stanhope Gould and Linda Mason, Producers (CBS)
COVERAGE OF THE RETURN OF THE POW'S; NBC Nightly News; Robert Mulholland, Executive Producer; Richard Fischer, Producer (NBC)
COVERAGE OF THE SHOOTING OF GOVERNOR WALLACE; CBS Evening News With Walter Cronkite; Russ Bensley, Executive Producer; Ed Fouhy and John Lane, Producers (CBS)
THE TASADAY TRIBE OF THE PHILIPPINES; NBC Nightly News; Wallace Westfeldt, Executive Producer; Robert Mulholland and David Teitelbaum, Producers (NBC)
THE WATERGATE AFFAIR; CBS Evening News With Walter Cronkite; Paul Greenberg, Executive Producer; Stanhope Gould, Brian Healy, Ed Fouhy, Producers (CBS)
B. An Award for individuals contributing to the program segments.
WALTER CRONKITE, DAN RATHER, DANIEL SCHORR and JOEL BLOCKER, Correspondents; The Watergate Affair; CBS Evening

News With Walter Cronkite (CBS)
DAVID DICK, DAN RATHER, ROGER MUDD and WALTER CRONKITE, Correspondents; Coverage of the Shooting of Governor Wallace; CBS Evening News With Walter Cronkite (CBS)
ERIC SEVAREID, Correspondent; LBJ - The Man And The President;- CBS Evening News with Walter Cronkite (CBS)
JOHN CHANCELLOR, Correspondent; Coverage of President Nixon's Visit to Russia; NBC Nightly News (NBC)
JACK REYNOLDS, Reporter; The Tasaday Tribe Of The Philippines; NBC Nightly News (NBC)
ERIC SEVAREID, Correspondent; The Paradox Of Special Privilege: Executive Immunity And Shield Laws; CBS Evening News With Walter Cronkite (CBS)

OUTSTANDING ACHIEVEMENT FOR REGULARLY SCHEDULED MAGAZINE-TYPE PROGRAMS

A. An Award for programs, program segments or series.
THE POPPY FIELDS OF TURKEY - THE HEROIN LABS OF MARSEILLES - THE N.Y. CONNECTION; 60 Minutes; Don Hewitt, Executive Producer; William McClure, John Tiffin, Philip Scheffler, Producers (CBS)
THE SELLING OF COLONEL HERBERT; 60 Minutes; Don Hewitt, Executive Producer; Barry Lando, Producer (CBS)
60 MINUTES Don Hewitt, Executive Producer; Series (CBS)
FIRST TUESDAY Eliot Frankel, Executive Producer; Series (NBC)
TODAY Stuart Schulberg, Executive Producer; Douglas P. Sinsel, Gene Farinet, Producers; Series (NBC)
B. An Award for individuals contributing to the program, program segments or series achievements.
MIKE WALLACE, Correspondent; The Selling Of Colonel Herbert; 60 Minutes (CBS)
MIKE WALLACE, Correspondent; 60 Minutes; Series (CBS)
MORLEY SAFER, Correspondent; 60 Minutes; Series (CBS)
MIKE WALLACE, Correspondent; Dita Beard Interview; 60 Minutes (CBS)
EDWIN NEWMAN, Writer; No Contest; Today (NBC)

OUTSTANDING ACHIEVEMENT IN COVERAGE OF SPECIAL EVENTS

A. An Award for program achievements.
COVERAGE OF THE MUNICH OLYMPIC TRAGEDY; ABC Special; Roone Arledge, Executive Producer (ABC)
THE 1972 DEMOCRATIC NATIONAL CONVENTION; NBC News Special; George F. Murray, Executive Producer; Ray Lockhart, Producer (NBC)
ELECTION NIGHT '72; NBC News Special; Robert Northshield, Executive Producer (NBC)
JACKIE ROBINSON; CBS News Special; Robert Wussler, Executive Producer; Clarence Cross, Russ Bensley and Barry Jagoda, Producers (CBS)
THE RETURN OF THE POW'S; NBC News Special; Helen Marmor, Producer (NBC)
B. An Award for individuals contributing to the program achievement.
JIM McKAY, Commentator; Coverage Of The Munich Olympic Tragedy; ABC Special (ABC)
JOHN CHANCELLOR, DAVID BRINKLEY, EDWIN NEWMAN, CATHERINE MACKIN, DOUGLAS KIKER and GARRICK UTLEY, Correspondents; Election Night '72; NBC News Special (NBC)
HARRY REASONER and HOWARD K. SMITH Anchormen; Elections '72; ABC News Special (ABC)
DAVID FOX, Director; Apollo 17; Astronauts Splashdown in Pacific (Pool Coverage)
EDWIN NEWMAN, Writer; Decision '72: It Starts Tomorrow; NBC News Special (NBC)

OUTSTANDING DOCUMENTARY PROGRAM ACHIEVEMENT

A. An Award for documentary programs dealing with events or matters of current significance.
THE BLUE COLLAR TRAP; NBC News White Paper; Fred Freed, Producer (NBC)
THE MEXICAN CONNECTION; CBS Reports; Burton Benjamin, Executive Producer; Jay McMullen, Producer (CBS)
ONE BILLION DOLLAR WEAPON And Now the War Is Over - The American Military In the 70's; NBC Reports; Fred Freed, Executive Producer; Craig Leake, Producer (NBC)
IF YOU WANT US TO STAND DOWN, TELL US And Now the War Is Over - The American Military in The 70's; NBC Reports; Fred Freed, Executive Producer; Al Davis, Producer (NBC)
PENSIONS: THE BROKEN PROMISE; NBC Reports; Eliot Frankel, Executive Producer; David Schmerler, Producer (NBC)
B. An Award for documentary programs dealing with artistic, historical or cultural subjects.
AMERICA Michael Gill, Executive Producer; Series (NBC)
JANE GOODALL AND THE WORLD OF ANIMAL BEHAVIOR The Wild Dogs Of Africa; Marshall Flaum, Executive Producer; Hugo Van Lawick, Bill Travers, and James Hill, Producers (ABC)
THE CAVE PEOPLE OF THE PHILIPPINES; NBC Reports; Gerald Green, Producer (NBC)
THE INCREDIBLE FLIGHT OF THE SNOW GEESE Aubrey Buxton, Executive Producer (NBC)
IN SEARCH OF ANCIENT ASTRONAUTS Laurence Savadove, Executive Producer; Alan Landsburg, Producer (NBC)
C. An Award for individuals contributing to Documentary Programs.
ALISTAIR COOKE, Narrator; America; Series (NBC)
ALISTAIR COOKE, Writer; A Firebell In The Night; America (NBC)
HUGO VAN LAWICK, Director; Jane Goodall And The World Of Animal Behavior: The Wild Dogs Of Africa (ABC)
MARSHALL FLAUM And BILL TRAVERS, Writers; Jane Goodall And the World Of Animal Behavior; The Wild Dogs of Africa (ABC)
TOM PRIESTLEY, Director; The Forbidden City; NBC Reports (NBC)

SPECIAL CLASSIFICATION OF OUTSTANDING PROGRAM AND INDIVIDUAL ACHIEVEMENT

An Award for unique program and individual achievements, which does not fall into a specific category, or is not otherwise recognized.
THE ADVOCATES Greg Harney, Executive Producer; Tom Burrows, Russ Morash and Peter McGhee, Producers; Series (PBS)
VD BLUES Special Of The Week; Don Fouser, Producer (PBS)
LBJ: THE LAST INTERVIEW Burton Benjamin, Producer (CBS)
DICK CAVETT, Host; VD Blues; Special Of The Week (PBS)
WALTER CRONKITE, Correspondent; LBJ: The Last Interview; CBS News Special (CBS)

OUTSTANDING ACHIEVEMENT IN RELIGIOUS PROGRAMMING

An Award for programs and individual achievements.
DUTY BOUND Doris Ann, Executive Producer; Martin Hoade, Producer (NBC)
INSIGHT Father Ellwood Kieser, Executive Producer; John Meredyth Lucas and John Furia, Jr., Producers; Series (Synd)
MARTIN HOADE, Director; Duty Bound (NBC)
JOHN B. BOXER, Costume Designer; Duty Bound (NBC)

848 EMMYS

OUTSTANDING ACHIEVEMENT IN ANY AREA OF CREATIVE TECHNICAL CRAFTS

An Award for individual technical craft achievement which does not fall into a specific category, and is not otherwise recognized.

DONALD FELDSTEIN, ROBERT FONTANA and JOE ZUCKERMAN, Animation Layout of Da Vinci's Art; Leonardo: To Know How To See (NBC)
PHILIPPE COUSTEAU, Underwater Cameraman; The Singing Whale; The Undersea World of Jacques Cousteau (ABC)
BIDDY CHRYSTAL, Hairdresser; Dr. Jekyll And Mr. Hyde (NBC)

(One Award Only In Each of the Following Categories)

OUTSTANDING ACHIEVEMENT IN CINEMATOGRAPHY FOR NEWS AND DOCUMENTARY PROGRAMMING

A. Regularly scheduled News programs and coverage of Special Events.

LAURENS PIERCE Coverage of the Shooting of Governor Wallace; CBS Evening News With Walter Cronkite (CBS)
ISADORE BLECKMAN Roadside Garden; On The Road; CBS Evening News With Walter Cronkite (CBS)
DANG VAN MINH Vietnamese Orphans; ABC Evening News With Howard K. Smith And Harry Reasoner (ABC)

B. Documentary, Magazine-type or Mini-documentary programs.

DES and JEN BARTLETT The Incredible Flight Of The Snow Geese (NBC)
PHILIPPE COUSTEAU and JACQUES RENOIR The Smile Of The Walrus; The Undersea World Of Jacques Cousteau (ABC)
PHILIPPE COUSTEAU, FRANCOIS CHARLET and WALTER BAL The Singing Whale; The Undersea World Of Jacques Cousteau (ABC)

OUTSTANDING ACHIEVEMENT IN FILM EDITING FOR NEWS AND DOCUMENTARY PROGRAMMING

A. Regularly scheduled News programs and coverage of Special Events.

PATRICK MINERVA, MARTIN SHEPPARD, GEORGE JOHNSON, WILLIAM J. FREEDA, MIGUEL E. PORTILLO, ALBERT J. HELIAS, IRWIN GRAF, JEAN VENABLE, RICK HESSEL, LOREN BERRY, NICK WILKINS, GERRY BREESE, MICHAEL SHUGRUE, K. SU, EDWIN EINARSEN, THOMAS DUNPHY, RUSSEL MOORE and ROBERT MOLE; NBC Nightly News; Series (NBC)
MICHAEL C. SHUGRUE; I Am Woman; NBC Nightly News (NBC)
PATRICK MINERVA, THOMAS DUNPHY, JEAN VENABLE, EDWIN EINARSEN and GERALD BREESE Coverage Of President Nixon's Trip To Russia; NBC Nightly News (NBC)

Documentary, Magazine-type or Mini-documentary programs.

LES PARRY The Incredible Flight Of The Snow Geese (NBC)
CARL KRESS The Singing Whale; The Undersea World Of Jacques Cousteau (ABC)
JOHN SOH The Smile Of The Walrus; The Undersea World Of Jacques Cousteau (ABC)

1973/74

ENTERTAINMENT PROGRAM AND INDIVIDUAL ACHIEVEMENTS

(One Award Only In Each of the Following Categories)

OUTSTANDING COMEDY SERIES

Award to Executive Producer(s) and/or Producer(s)

M*A*S*H, Gene Reynolds, and Larry Gelbart, Producers (CBS)
THE MARY TYLER MOORE SHOW, James Brooks, and Allan Burns, Executive Producers; Ed Weinberger, Producer (CBS)
ALL IN THE FAMILY, Norman Lear, Executive Producer; John Rich, Producer (CBS)
THE ODD COUPLE, Garry Marshall, and Harvey Miller, Executive Producers; Tony Marshall, Producer (ABC)

OUTSTANDING DRAMA SERIES

Award to Executive Producer(s) and/or Producer(s)

UPSTAIRS, DOWNSTAIRS, Masterpiece Theatre; Rex Firkin, Executive Producer; John Hawkesworth, Producer (PBS)
KOJAK, Abby Mann, and Matthew Rapf, Executive Producers; James McAdams, Producer (CBS)
THE STREETS OF SAN FRANCISCO, Quinn Martin, Executive Producer; John Wilder, Producer (ABC)
POLICE STORY, David Gerber, Executive Producer; Stanley Kallis, Producer (NBC)
THE WALTONS, Lee Rich, Executive Producer; Robert L. Jacks, Producer (CBS)

OUTSTANDING MUSIC-VARIETY SERIES

Award to Executive Producer(s) and/or Producer(s) and Star (if applicable)

THE CAROL BURNETT SHOW, Joe Hamilton, Executive Producer; Ed Simmons, Producer; Carol Burnett, Star (CBS)
THE SONNY AND CHER COMEDY HOUR, Allan Blye, and Chris Bearde, Producers; Sonny and Cher, Stars (CBS)
THE TONIGHT SHOW STARRING JOHNNY CARSON, Fred de Cordova, Producer; Johnny Carson, Star (NBC)

OUTSTANDING LIMITED SERIES

Award to Executive Producer(s) and/or Producer(s)

COLUMBO, NBC Sunday Mystery Movie; Dean Hargrove, and Roland Kibbee, Executive Producers; Douglas Benton, Robert F. O'Neill, and Edward K. Dodds, Producers (NBC)
McCLOUD, NBC Sunday Mystery Movie; Glen Larson, Executive Producer; Michael Gleason, Producer (NBC)
THE BLUE KNIGHT, Lee Rich, Executive Producer; Walter Coblenz, Producer (NBC)

OUTSTANDING SPECIAL - COMEDY OR DRAMA

A Single Special Program Award to Executive Producer(s) and/or Producer(s)

THE AUTOBIOGRAPHY OF MISS JANE PITTMAN, Robert Christiansen, and Rick Rosenberg, Producers (CBS)
THE MIGRANTS, CBS Playhouse 90; Tom Gries, Producer (CBS)
THE EXECUTION OF PRIVATE SLOVIK, NBC Wednesday Night At The Movies; Richard Levinson, and William Link, Executive Producers; Richard Dubelman, Producer (NBC)
STEAMBATH, Hollywood Televison Theatre; Norman Lloyd, Executive Producer (PBS)
6 RMS RIV VU, Joe Hamilton, Producer (CBS)

OUTSTANDING COMEDY-VARIETY, VARIETY OR MUSIC SPECIAL

A Single Special Program Award to Executive Producer(s) and/or Producer(s) and Star (if applicable)

LILY, Irene Pinn, Executive Producer; Herb Sargent, and Jerry McPhie, Producers; Lily Tomlin, Star (CBS)
BARBRA STREISAND...AND OTHER MUSICAL INSTRUMENTS, Martin Erlichman, Executive Producer; Gary Smith, Dwight Hemion, and Joe Layton, Producers; Barbra Streisand, Star (CBS)
MAGNAVOX PRESENTS FRANK SINATRA, Howard W. Koch, Producer; Frank Sinatra, Star (NBC)
THE JOHN DENVER SHOW, Jerry Weintraub, Executive Producer; Rich Eustis, and Al Rogers, Producers; John Denver, Star (ABC)

OUTSTANDING CHILDREN'S SPECIAL

For programs which were broadcast during the evening
Award to Executive Producer(s) and Producer(s)

MARLO THOMAS AND FRIENDS IN FREE TO BE...YOU AND ME, Marlo Thomas, and Carole Hart, Producers; Marlo Thomas, Star (ABC)
THE BORROWERS, Hallmark Hall of Fame; Duane C. Bogie, Executive Producer; Walt DeFaria, and Warren Lockhart, Producers (NBC)
A CHARLIE BROWN THANKSGIVING, Lee Mendelson, and Bill Melendez, Producers (CBS)

BEST LEAD ACTOR IN A COMEDY SERIES

ALAN ALDA, M*A*S*H (CBS)
REDD FOXX, Sanford and Son (NBC)
JACK KLUGMAN, The Odd Couple (ABC)
CARROLL O'CONNOR, All In The Family (CBS)
TONY RANDALL, The Odd Couple (ABC)

BEST LEAD ACTOR IN A DRAMA SERIES

TELLY SAVALAS, Kojak (CBS)
WILLIAM CONRAD, Cannon (CBS)
KARL MALDEN, The Streets of San Francisco (ABC)
RICHARD THOMAS, The Waltons (CBS)

BEST LEAD ACTOR IN A LIMITED SERIES

WILLIAM HOLDEN, The Blue Knight (NBC)
PETER FALK, Columbo; NBC Sunday Mystery Movie (NBC)
DENNIS WEAVER, McCoud; NBC Sunday Mystery Movie (NBC)

BEST LEAD ACTOR IN A DRAMA

For a special program--Comedy or Drama; or a single appearance in a Drama or Comedy Series

HAL HOLBROOK, Pueblo; ABC Theatre (ABC)
DICK VAN DYKE, The Morning After; Wednesday Movie Of The Week (ABC)
LAURENCE OLIVIER, The Merchant Of Venice; ABC Theatre (ABC)
MARTIN SHEEN, The Execution of Private Slovik; NBC Wednesday Night At The Movies (NBC)
ALAN ALDA, 6 Rms Riv Vu (CBS)

ACTOR OF THE YEAR - SERIES

ALAN ALDA, M*A*S*H (CBS)

ACTOR OF THE YEAR - SPECIAL

HAL HOLBROOK, Pueblo; ABC Theatre (ABC)

BEST LEAD ACTRESS IN A COMEDY SERIES

MARY TYLER MOORE, The Mary Tyler Moore Show (CBS)
BEA ARTHUR, Maude (CBS)
JEAN STAPLETON, All In The Family (CBS)

BEST LEAD ACTRESS IN A DRAMA SERIES

MICHAEL LEARNED, The Waltons (CBS)
JEANETTE NOLAN, Dirty Sally (CBS)
JEAN MARSH, Upstairs, Downstairs; Masterpiece (PBS)

BEST LEAD ACTRESS IN A LIMITED SERIES

MILDRED NATWICK, The Snoop Sisters; NBC Tuesday Mystery Movie (NBC)
LEE REMICK, The Blue Knight (NBC)
HELEN HAYES, The Snoop Sisters; NBC Tuesday Mystery Movie (NBC)

BEST LEAD ACTRESS IN A DRAMA

For a special program--Comedy or Drama; or a single appearance in a Drama or Comedy Series

CICELY TYSON, The Autobiography of Miss Jane Pittman (CBS)
ELIZABETH MONTGOMERY, A Case of Rape; NBC Wednesday Night At The Movies (NBC)
KATHARINE HEPBURN, The Glass Menagerie (ABC)
CLORIS LEACHMAN, The Migrants; CBS Playhouse 90 (CBS)
CAROL BURNETT, 6 Rms Riv Vu (CBS)

ACTRESS OF THE YEAR - SERIES

MARY TYLER MOORE, The Mary Tyler Moore Show (CBS)

ACTRESS OF THE YEAR-SPECIAL

CICELY TYSON, The Autobiography of Miss Jane Pittman (CBS)

BEST SUPPORTING ACTOR IN COMEDY

For a special program, a one-time appearance in a series; or a continuing role

ROB REINER, All In The Family (CBS)
TED KNIGHT, The Mary Tyler Moore Show (CBS)
EDWARD ASNER, The Mary Tyler Moore Show (CBS)
GARY BURGHOFF, M*A*S*H (CBS)
McLEAN STEVENSON, M*A*S*H (CBS)

BEST SUPPORTING ACTOR IN DRAMA

For a special program; a one-time appearance in a series; or a continuing role

MICHAEL MORIARTY, The Glass Menagerie (ABC)
MICHAEL DOUGLAS, The Streets of San Francisco (ABC)
WILL GEER, The Waltons (CBS)
SAM WATERSTON, The Glass Menagerie (ABC)

BEST SUPPORTING ACTOR IN COMEDY-VARIETY, VARIETY OR MUSIC

For a special program; a one-time appearance in a series; or a continuing role

HARVEY KORMAN, The Carol Burnett Show (CBS)
TIM CONWAY, The Carol Burnett Show (with Tim Conway and Petula Clark) (CBS)
FOSTER BROOKS, The Dean Martin Comedy Hour (NBC)

SUPPORTING ACTOR OF THE YEAR

MICHAEL MORIARTY, The Glass Menagerie (ABC)

BEST SUPPORTING ACTRESS IN COMEDY
For a special program; a one-time appearance in a series; or a continuing role

CLORIS LEACHMAN, The Lars Affair; The Mary Tyler Moore Show (CBS)
VALERIE HARPER, The Mary Tyler Moore Show (CBS)
LORETTA SWIT, M*A*S*H (CBS)
SALLY STRUTHERS, All In The Family (CBS)

BEST SUPPORTING ACTRESS IN DRAMA
For a special program; a one-time appearance in a series; or a continuing role

JOANNA MILES, The Glass Menagerie (ABC)
ELLEN CORBY, The Waltons (CBS)
NANCY WALKER, McMillan And Wife; NBC Sunday Mystery Movie (NBC)

BEST SUPPORTING ACTRESS IN COMEDY-VARIETY, VARIETY OR MUSIC
For a special program; a one-time appearance in a series; or a continuing role

BRENDA VACCARO, The Shape Of Things (CBS)
VICKI LAWRENCE, The Carol Burnett Show (CBS)
LEE GRANT, The Shape of Things (CBS)
RUTH BUZZI, The Dean Martin Comedy Hour (NBC)

SUPPORTING ACTRESS OF THE YEAR
JOANNA MILES, The Glass Menagerie (ABC)

BEST DIRECTING IN DRAMA
A single program of a series with continuing characters and/or theme

ROBERT BUTLER, The Blue Knight, Part III (NBC)
HARRY HARRIS, The Journey; The Waltons (CBS)
PHILIP LEACOCK, The Thanksgiving Story; The Waltons (CBS)

BEST DIRECTING IN DRAMA
A single program--Comedy or Drama

JOHN KORTY, The Autobiography of Miss Jane Pittman (CBS)
TOM GRIES, The Migrants; CBS Playhouse 90 (CBS)
BORIS SAGAL, A Case of Rape; NBC Wednesday Night At The Movies (NBC)
ANTHONY PAGE, Pueblo; ABC Theatre (ABC)
LAMONT JOHNSON, The Execution of Private Slovik; NBC Wednesday Night At The Movies (NBC)

BEST DIRECTING IN COMEDY
A single program of a series with continuing characters and/or theme

JACKIE COOPER, Carry On, Hawkeye; M*A*S*H (CBS)
JAY SANDRICH, Lou's First Date; The Mary Tyler Moore Show (CBS)
GENE REYNOLDS, Deal Me Out; M*A*S*H (CBS)

BEST DIRECTING IN VARIETY OR MUSIC
A single program of a series

DAVE POWERS, The Australia Show; The Carol Burnett Show (CBS)
ART FISHER, The Sonny And Cher Comedy Hour (with Ken Berry and George Foreman) (CBS)
JOSHUA WHITE, In Concert (with Cat Stevens); ABC Wide World Of Entertainment (ABC)

BEST DIRECTING IN COMEDY-VARIETY, VARIETY OR MUSIC
A special program

DWIGHT HEMION, Barbra Streisand...And Other Musical Instruments (CBS)
MARTY PASETTA, Magnavox Presents Frank Sinatra (NBC)
TONY CHARMOLI, Mitzi...A Tribute To The American Housewife (CBS)
STERLING JOHNSON, Peggy Fleming Visits The Soviet Union; Bell System Family Theatre (NBC)

DIRECTOR OF THE YEAR - SERIES
ROBERT BUTLER, The Blue Knight, Part III (NBC)

DIRECTOR OF THE YEAR - SPECIAL
DWIGHT HEMION, Barbra Streisand...And Other Musical Instruments (CBS)

BEST WRITING IN DRAMA
A single program of a series with continuing characters and/or theme

JOANNA LEE, The Thanksgiving Story; The Waltons (CBS)
GENE R. KEARNEY, Death Is Not A Passing Grade; Kojak (CBS)
JOHN McGREEVEY, The Easter Story; The Waltons (CBS)

BEST WRITING IN DRAMA, ORIGINAL TELEPLAY
A single program--Comedy or Drama

FAY KANIN, Tell Me Where It Hurts; GE Theatre (CBS)
WILL LORIN, Cry Rape!; The New CBS Tuesday Night Movies (CBS)
LANFORD WILSON, The Migrants; CBS Playhouse 90 (CBS)

BEST WRITING IN DRAMA, ADAPTATION
A single program--Comedy or Drama

TRACY KEENAN WYNN, The Autobiography Of Miss Jane Pittman (CBS)
BRUCE JAY FRIEDMAN, Steambath; Hollywood Television Theare (PBS)
RICHARD LEVINSON, and WILLIAM LINK, The Execution Of Private Slovik; NBC Wednesday Night At The Movies (NBC)

BEST WRITING IN COMEDY
A single program of a series with continuing characters and/or theme

TREVA SILVERMAN, The Lou And Edie Story; The Mary Tyler Moore Show (CBS)
LINDA BLOODWORTH, and MARY KAY PLACE, Hot Lips And Empty Arms; M*A*S*H (CBS)
McLEAN STEVENSON, The Trial Of Henry Blake; M*A*S*H (CBS)

BEST WRITING IN VARIETY OR MUSIC
A Single program of a series

ED SIMMONS, GARY BELKIN, ROGER BEATTY, ARNIE KOGEN, BILL RICHMOND, GENE PERRET, RUDY DE LUCA, BARRY LEVINSON, DICK CLAIR, JENNA McMAHON, and BARRY HARMAN, The Carol Burnett Show (with Tim Conway and Bernadette Peters) (CBS)
CHRIS BEARDE, ALLAN BLYE, BOB ARNOTT, GEORGE BURDITT, BOB EINSTEIN, PHIL HAHN, COSLOUGH JOHNSON, JIM MULLIGAN, and PAUL WAYNE, The Sonny and Cher Comedy Hour (with Chuck Connors and Howard Cosell) (CBS)
STAN HART, LARRY SIEGEL, GAIL PARENT, WOODY KLING, ROGER BEATTY, TOM PATCHETT, JAY TARSES, ROBERT HILLIARD, ARNIE KOGEN, BUZ KOHAN, and BILL ANGELOS, The Family Show; The Carol Burnett Show (CBS)

BEST WRITING IN COMEDY-VARIETY, VARIETY OR MUSIC

A special program

HERB SARGENT, ROSALYN DREXLER, LORNE MICHAELS, RICHARD PRYOR, JIM RUSK, JAMES R. STEIN, ROBERT ILLES, LILY TOMLIN, GEORGE YANOK, JANE WAGNER, ROD WARREN, ANN ELDER, and KARYL GELD, Lily (CBS)
LARRY GELBART, MITZIE WELCH, and KEN WELCH, Barbra Streisand. . .And Other Musical Instruments (CBS)
RENEE TAYLOR, and JOSEPH BOLOGNA, Paradise (CBS)

WRITER OF THE YEAR - SERIES

TREVA SILVERMAN, The Lou And Edie Story; The Mary Tyler Moore Show (CBS)

WRITER OF THE YEAR - SPECIAL

FAY KANIN, Tell Me Where It Hurts; GE Theater (CBS)

OUTSTANDING ACHIEVEMENT IN CHOREOGRAPHY

A single program of a series or a special program

TONY CHARMOLI, Mitzi. . .A Tribute To The American Housewife (CBS)
ERNEST O. FLATT, The Australia Show; The Carol Burnett Show (CBS)
CARL JABLONSKI, Sammy Davis Starring In NBC Follies (with Milton Berle, Johnny Brown, Michael Landon and Carol Lawrence) (NBC)

BEST MUSIC COMPOSITION

A. For a series or a single program of a series (in the first year of music's use only)

MORTON STEVENS, Hookman; Hawaii Five-O (CBS)
DON B. RAY, Nightmare In Blue; Hawaii Five-O (CBS)
BRUCE BROUGHTON, The $100,000 Nickel; Hawaii Five-O (CBS)

B. For a special program

FRED KARLIN, The Autobiography Of Miss Jane Pittman (CBS)
BILLY GOLDENBERG, The Migrants; CBS Playhouse 90 (CBS)
LAURENCE ROSENTHAL, Portrait: A Man Whose Name Was John (ABC)

BEST SONG OR THEME

A series or a single program of a series or a special program written for television

MARTY PAICH and DAVID PAICH, "Light The Way"; Once More For Joey; Ironside (NBC)
FRED KARLIN "The Love That Lights Our Way"; The Autobiography Of Miss Jane Pittman (CBS)
BILLY GOLDENBERG, Kojak; Series (CBS)

BEST MUSIC DIRECTION OF A VARIETY, MUSICAL OR DRAMATIC PROGRAM

A single program of a series or a special program

JACK PARNELL, KEN WELCH and MITZIE WELCH, Barbra Streisand- . . .And Other Musical Instruments (CBS)
PETER MATZ, The Australia Show; The Carol Burnett Show (CBS)
MARTY PAICH, The Sonny And Cher Years; The Sonny And Cher Comedy Hour (CBS)

MUSICIAN OF THE YEAR

JACK PARNELL, KEN WELCH and MITZIE WELCH, Barbra Streisand- . . .And Other Musical Instruments (CBS)

BEST ART DIRECTION OR SCENIC DESIGN

A. For a dramatic program or feature length film made for television; for a series, a single program of a series, or a special program

JAN SCOTT, Art Director; CHARLES KREINER, Set Decorator; The Lie; CBS Playhouse 90 (CBS)
MICHAEL HALLER, The Autobiography Of Miss Jane Pittman (CBS)
WALTER H. TYLER, Art Director; RICHARD FRIEDMAN, Set Decorator; The Execution Of Private Slovik; NBC Wednesday Night At The Movies (NBC)

B. For a Musical or Variety single program of a series or a special program

BRIAN C. BARTHOLOMEW, Barbra Streisand. . .And Other Musical Instruments (CBS)
PAUL BARNES, and BOB SANSOM, Art Directors; BILL HARP, Set Decorator; The Carol Burnett Show (with Bernadette Peters and Tim Conway) (CBS)
RENE LAGLER, and LYNN GRIFFIN, Art Directors; The Andy Williams Christmas Show (NBC)

ART DIRECTOR AND SET DECORATOR OF THE YEAR

JAN SCOTT, Art Director; CHARLES KREINER, Set Decorator; The Lie; CBS Playhouse 90 (CBS)

OUTSTANDING ACHIEVEMENT IN COSTUME DESIGN

A single program of a series or a special program

BRUCE WALKUP and SANDY STEWART, The Autobiography Of Miss Jane Pittman (CBS)
GRADY HUNT, The Devil Made Me Do It; The Snoop Sisters; NBC Tuesday Mystery Movie (NBC)
BARBARA MURPHY, The New Treasure Hunt (Synd)
RET TURNER, and BOB MACKIE, The Sonny And Cher Years; The Sonny And Cher Comedy Hour (CBS)
CHARLES KNODE, Concluding Episode; War And Peace (PBS)

OUTSTANDING ACHIEVEMENT IN MAKE-UP

A single program of a series or a special program

STAN WINSTON, and RICK BAKER, The Autobiography Of Miss Jane Pittman (CBS)
NICK MARCELLINO, and JAMES LEE McCOY, Portrait: A Man Whose Name Was John (ABC)
BEN NYE II, Judgment--The Trial Of Julius And Ethel Rosenberg; ABC Theatre (ABC)
WILLIAM TUTTLE, The Phantom Of Hollywood; The New CBS Tuesday Night Movies (CBS)

BEST CINEMATOGRAPHY FOR ENTERTAINMENT PROGRAMMING

A. For a series or a single program of a series

HARRY WOLF, A.S.C., Any Old Port In A Storm; Columbo; NBC Sunday Mystery Movie (NBC)
GERALD PERRY FINNERMAN, A.S.C., Kojak (CBS)
ROBERT MORRISON, JACK WHITMAN, and BILL HUFFMAN, Hawaii Five-O (CBS)

B. For a special or feature length program made for television

TED VOIGTLANDER, A.S.C., It's Good To Be Alive; GE Theater (CBS)
RICHARD C. KRATINA, The Migrants; CBS Playhouse 90 (CBS)
WALTER STRENGE, A.S.C., Portrait: A Man Whose Name Was John (ABC)
ANDREW LASZLO, The Man Without A Country (ABC)
FRED MANDL, Trapped; Wednesday Movie Of The Week (ABC)

CINEMATOGRAPHER OF THE YEAR
TED VOIGTLANDER, A.S.C., It's Good To Be Alive; GE Theater (CBS)

BEST FILM EDITING FOR ENTERTAINMENT PROGRAMMING
A. For a series or a single program of a series
GENE FOWLER, JR., MARJORIE FOWLER, and SAMUEL E. BEETLEY, The Blue Knight (NBC)
DOUGLAS HINES, and BUD ISAACS, The Mary Tyler Moore Show (CBS)
STANFORD TISCHLER, and FRED W. BERGER, M*A*S*H (CBS)
B. For a special or feature length program made for television
FRANK MORRISS, The Execution Of Private Slovik; NBC Wednesday Night At The Movies (NBC)
RICHARD BRACKEN, A Case Of Rape; NBC Wednesday Night At The Movies (NBC)
SIDNEY LEVIN, The Autobiography Of Miss Jane Pittman (CBS)

FILM EDITOR OF THE YEAR
FRANK MORRISS, The Execution Of Private Slovik; NBC Wednesday Night At The Movies (NBC)

OUTSTANDING ACHIEVEMENT IN FILM SOUND EDITING
A single program of a series or a special program
BUD NOLAN, Pueblo; ABC Theatre (ABC)
SID LUBOW, SAM CAYLOR, JACK KIRSCHNER, RICHARD RADERMAN, STANLEY FRAZEN, and JOHN SINGLETON, Marker For A Dead Bookie; Kojak (CBS)
JERRY ROSENTHAL, RON ASHCROFT, AL KAJITA, RICHARD BURROW, JACK MILNER, TONY GARBER, WILLIAM M. ANDREWS, EDWARD L. SANDLIN, and MILTON C. BURROW, Collision Course; Police Story (NBC)

OUTSTANDING ACHIEVEMENT IN FILM OR TAPE SOUND MIXING
A single program of a series or a special program
ALBERT A. GRAMAGLIA, and MICHAEL SHINDLER, Pueblo; ABC Theatre (ABC)
JOHN K. KEAN, and THOM K. PIPER, The Execution Of Private Slovik; NBC Wednesday Night At The Movies (NBC)
CHARLES T. KNIGHT, and DON MINKLER, The Autobiography Of Miss Jane Pittman (CBS)

OUTSTANDING ACHIEVEMENT IN VIDEO TAPE EDITING
A single program of a series or a special program
ALFRED MULLER, Pueblo; ABC Theatre (ABC)
LEWIS W. SMITH, The Lie; CBS Playhouse 90 (CBS)
NICK V. GIORDANO, and GEORGE GURUNIAN, The John Denver Show (ABC)

OUTSTANDING ACHIEVEMENT IN TECHNICAL DIRECTION AND ELECTRONIC CAMERAWORK
A single program of a series or a special program
GERRY BUCCI, Technical Director; KENNETH TAMBURRI, DAVE HILMER, DAVE SMITH, JIM BALDEN, and RON BROOKS, Cameramen; In Concert (with Cat Stevens); ABC Wide World Of Entertainment (ABC)
PARKER ROE, Technical Director; LEW ADAMS, KEN LAMKIN, JOHN POLIAK, and GARY STANTON, Cameramen; Judgment--The Trial Of Julius And Ethel Rosenberg; ABC Theatre (ABC)
LOU MARCHAND, Technical Director; RICHARD KERR, MORRIS MANN, JOHN MORREALE, MICHAEL W. REBICH, and ROBERT WOLFF, Cameramen; Pueblo; ABC Theatre (ABC)

OUTSTANDING ACHIEVEMENT IN LIGHTING DIRECTION
A single program of a series or a special program, produced for electronic television only
WILLIAM M. KLAGES, The Lie; CBS Playhouse 90 (CBS)
JOHN FRESCHI, Mitzi. . .A Tribute To The American Housewife (CBS)
LON STUCKY, and JOHN NANCE, Dean Martin Presents Music Country (with Johnny Cash and Loretta Lynn) (NBC)

THE AREAS
(Possibility of One Award, More Than One Award, or No Award)

OUTSTANDING INDIVIDUAL ACHIEVEMENT IN CHILDRENS PROGRAMMING
CHARLES M. SCHULZ, Writer; A Charlie Brown Thanksgiving (CBS)
WILLIAM ZAHARUK, Art Director; PETER RAZMOFSKI, Set Decorator; The Borrowers; Hallmark Hall Of Fame (NBC)
DAME JUDITH ANDERSON, Performer; The Borrowers; Hallmark Hall Of Fame (NBC)
WALTER C. MILLER, Director; The Borrowers; Hallmark Hall Of Fame (NBC)
BILL DAVIS, Director; Marlo Thomas And Friends In Free To Be. . .You And Me (ABC)
JUUL HAALMEYER, Costume Designer; The Borrowers; Hallmark Hall Of Fame (NBC)

SPECIAL CLASSIFICATION OF OUTSTANDING PROGRAM AND INDIVIDUAL ACHIEVEMENT
An Award for unique program and individual achievements, which does not fall into a specific category, or is not otherwise recognized
THE DICK CAVETT SHOW, John Gilroy, Producer; Dick Cavett, Star; Series (ABC)
TOM SNYDER, Host; Tomorrow (NBC)
WARNER BROS. MOVIES--A 50 YEAR SALUTE, ABC Wide World Of Entertainment; Rick Rosner, Executive Producer; Lawrence Einhorn, Producer (ABC)
CBS ALL-AMERICAN THANKSGIVING DAY PARADE, Mike Gargiulo, Executive Producer (CBS)
PAUL LYNDE, Performer; The Hollywood Squares (NBC)
BETTE DAVIS, Hostess; Warner Bros. Movies--A 50 Year Salute; ABC Wide World Of Entertainment (ABC)

OUTSTANDING ACHIEVEMENT IN SPORTS PROGRAMMING
An Award for programs and for individuals contributing to the coverage of sporting events
ABC'S WIDE WORLD OF SPORTS, Roone Arledge, Executive Producer; Dennis Lewin, Producer (ABC)
JIM McKAY, Host; ABC'S Wide World Of Sports (ABC)
BOBBY RIGGS VS. BILLIE JEAN KING, TENNIS BATTLE OF THE SEXES, Roone Arledge, and Jackie Barnett, Executive Producers; Chuck Howard, Producer (ABC)
1973 WORLD SERIES, Allan B. Connal, Executive Producer; Roy Hammerman, Producer (NBC)
MONDAY NIGHT FOOTBALL, Roone Arledge, Executive Producer Don Ohlmeyer, Producer; (ABC)
HOWARD COSELL, Announcer; Monday Night Football (ABC)

FRANK GIFFORD, Announcer; Monday Night Football (ABC)
TONY VERNA, Director; The Triple Crown Of Racing: The Kentucky Derby, The Preakness And The Belmont Stakes (CBS)
HARRY COYLE, Director; 1973 World Series (NBC)

OUTSTANDING ACHIEVEMENT IN ANY AREA OF CREATIVE TECHNICAL CRAFTS

An Award for individual technical craft achievement which does not fall into a specific category, and is not otherwise recognized

LYNDA GURASICH, Hair Stylist; The Autobiography Of Miss Jane Pittman (CBS)
JORDON WHITELAW, Orchestral Treatment Director; Evening At Pops (with Ella Fitzgerald) (PBS)
RENA LEUSCHNER, Hairdresser; The Sonny And Cher Comedy Hour (with Paul Anka and Neil Sedaka) (CBS)

SPECIAL AWARDS

OUTSTANDING ACHIEVEMENT IN ENGINEERING DEVELOPMENT

CONSOLIDATED VIDEO SYSTEMS, INC. for the application of digital video technique to the Time Base Corrector, permitting use of smaller, lighter weight, more portable video tape equipment on news and other outside events in television broadcasting.
RCA for its leading role in the development of the quadraplex video tape cartridge equipment, providing improved production reliability and efficiency in broadcasting video taped program segments, promos, and commercials.
THE TELECOPTER To John D. Silva for the conception and expertise and To Golden West Broadcasters for its realization.

THE INTERNATIONAL AWARDS

NON-FICTION

HORIZON: THE MAKING OF A NATURAL HISTORY FILM, British Broadcasting Corporation, London, England
OMNIBUS: FIDELIO FINCKE, WHERE ARE YOU NOW?, British Broadcasting Corporation, London, England
GREY OWL, Canadian Broadcasting Corporation, Toronto, Ontario, Canada
BUNNY, Thames Television Limited, London, England
TOO LONG A WINTER, Yorkshire Television Ltd., London, England

FICTION

LA CABINA, Television Espanola, Madrid, Spain
HIGH SUMMER, Armchair Theatre; Thames Television Limited, London, England
COUNTRY MATTERS: THE LITTLE FARM, Granada Television, Ltd., Manchester, England
THE DUCHESS OF MALFI, British Broadcasting Corporation, London, England
SARAH, Yorkshire Television, Yorkshire, England

THE INTERNATIONAL DIRECTORATE EMMY AWARD

CHARLES CURRAN, President, European Broadcasting Union; Director-General, British Broadcasting Corporation

THE NATIONAL AWARD FOR COMMUNITY SERVICE

THROUGH THE LOOKING GLASS DARKLY, WKY-TV, Oklahoma City, Oklahoma
FROM PROTEST TO POLITICS, WXYZ-TV, Southfield, Michigan
THE RAPE OF PAULETTE, WBBM-TV, Chicago, Illinois
PROBE: UNCLE SAM IS A SLUMLORD, WRC-TV, Washington, D.C.
LIVING WITH DEATH, WCCO-TV, Minneapolis, Minnesota
FOCUS 30, KYTV, Springfield, Missouri
MEDICINE: WHERE DOES IT HURT? WNBC-TV, New York, New York
THE FRIGHTENING FEELING YOU'RE GOING TO DIE, WCVB-TV, Needham, Massachusetts
A MATTER OF LIFE AND DEBT, KOOL-TV, Phoenix, Arizona
WHAT HAPPENS TO ME?, KPEC-TV, Tacoma, Washington (Educational Station)
THE NINE-YEAR-OLD IN NORFOLK PRISON, WTIC-TV, Hartford, Connecticut
THE ELDERS, KDIN, Des Moines, Iowa (Educational Station)

DAYTIME PROGRAM AND INDIVIDUAL ACHIEVEMENTS

(One Award Only in Each of the Followig Categories)

OUTSTANDING DRAMA SERIES

Daytime Programming Award to Executive Producer(s) and/or Creator, and Producer(s)

THE DOCTORS, Joseph Stuart, Producer (NBC)
GENERAL HOSPITAL, Jim Young, Producer; Frank and Doris Hursley, Creators (ABC)
DAYS OF OUR LIVES, Betty Corday, Executive Producer; Ted Corday, Irna Phillips, and Allan Chase, Creators; H. Wesley Kenney, Producer (NBC)

OUTSTANDING DRAMA SPECIAL

Daytime Programming Award to Executive Producer(s) and Producer(s)

THE OTHER WOMAN, ABC Matinee Today; John Conboy, Producer (ABC)
A SPECIAL ACT OF LOVE, ABC Afternoon Playbreak; John Choy, Producer (ABC)
TIGER ON A CHAIN, CBS Daytime 90; Tony Converse, and Darryl Hickman, Executive Producers; Linda Fidler Wendell, Producer (CBS)

OUTSTANDING GAME SHOW

Daytime Programming Award to Executive Producer(s) and Producer(s)

PASSWORD, Frank Wayne, Executive Producer; Howard Felsher, Producer (ABC)
THE HOLLYWOOD SQUARES, Merrill Heatter and Robert Quigley, Executive Producers; Jay Redack, Producer (NBC)
JEOPARDY!, Robert H. Rubin, Producer (NBC)

OUTSTANDING TALK, SERVICE OR VARIETY SERIES

Daytime Programming Award to Executive Producer(s) and Producer(s)

THE MERV GRIFFIN SHOW, Bob Murphy, Producer (Synd)
DINAH'S PLACE, Henry Jaffe, Executive Producer; Fred Tatashore, Producer (NBC)
THE MIKE DOUGLAS SHOW, Woody Fraser, Producer (Synd)

OUTSTANDING ENTERTAINMENT CHILDREN'S SERIES

For programs which were broadcast during the daytime
Award to Executive Producer(s) and Producer(s)

ZOOM, Jim Crum, and Christopher Sarson, Producers (PBS)
CAPTAIN KANGAROO, Jim Krayer, Executive Producer; Jim Hirschfeld, Producer (CBS)
FAT ALBERT AND THE COSBY KIDS, Norman Prescott, and Lou Scheimer, Producers (CBS)
STAR TREK, Lou Scheimer, and Norman Prescott, Producers (NBC)

OUTSTANDING ENTERTAINMENT CHILDREN'S SPECIAL
For programs which were broadcast during the daytime
Award to Executive Producer(s) and Producer(s)

ROOKIE OF THE YEAR, The ABC Afterschool Special; Dan Wilson, Producer (ABC)
MY DAD LIVES IN A DOWNTOWN HOTEL, The ABC Afterschool Special; Gerald Isenberg, Executive Producer; Richard Marx, Producer (ABC)
THE SWISS FAMILY ROBINSON, Famous Classic Tales; Walter E. Hucker, Executive Producer (CBS)

BEST ACTOR IN DAYTIME DRAMA
A. For a Series

MACDONALD CAREY, Days Of Our Lives (NBC)
JOHN BERADINO, General Hospital (ABC)
PETER HANSEN, General Hospital (ABC)

B. For a Special Program

PAT O'BRIEN, The Other Woman; ABC Matinee Today (ABC)
PETER COFFIELD, Legacy Of Fear; CBS Daytime 90 (CBS)
DON PORTER, Mother Of The Bride; ABC Afternoon Playbreak (ABC)

DAYTIME ACTOR OF THE YEAR
PAT O'BRIEN, The Other Woman; ABC Matinee Today (ABC)

BEST ACTRESS IN DAYTIME DRAMA
A. For a Series

ELIZABETH HUBBARD, The Doctors (NBC)
MARY STUART, Search For Tomorrow (CBS)
RACHEL AMES, General Hospital (ABC)
MARY FICKETT, All My Children (ABC)

B. For a Special Program

CATHLEEN NESBITT, The Mask Of Love; ABC Matinee Today (ABC)
EVE ARDEN, Mother Of The Bride; ABC Afternoon Playbreak (ABC)
CONSTANCE TOWERS, Once In Her Life; CBS Daytime 90 (CBS)

DAYTIME ACTRESS OF THE YEAR
CATHLEEN NESBITT, The Mask Of Love; ABC Matinee Today (ABC)

BEST HOST OR HOSTESS IN A GAME SHOW
Daytime Programming

PETER MARSHALL, The Hollywood Squares (NBC)
ALLEN LUDDEN, Password (ABC)
ART FLEMING, Jeopardy! (NBC)

BEST HOST OR HOSTESS IN A TALK, SERVICE OR VARIETY SERIES
Daytime Programming

DINAH SHORE, Dinah's Place (NBC)
MIKE DOUGLAS, The Mike Douglas Show (Synd)
MERV GRIFFIN, The Merv Griffin Show (Synd)
BARBARA WALTERS, Not For Women Only (Synd)

DAYTIME HOST OF THE YEAR
PETER MARSHALL, The Hollywood Squares (NBC)

BEST INDIVIDUAL DIRECTOR FOR A DRAMA SERIES
Daytime Programming

H. WESLEY KENNEY, Days Of Our Lives (NBC)
HUGH McPHILLIPS, The Doctors (NBC)
NORMAN HALL, The Doctors (NBC)

BEST INDIVIDUAL DIRECTOR FOR A SPECIAL PROGRAM
Daytime Programming

H. WESLEY KENNEY, Miss Kline, We Love You; ABC Afternoon Playbreak (ABC)
PETER LEVIN, The Other Woman; ABC Matinee Today (ABC)
LELA SWIFT, The Gift Of Terror, ABC Afternoon Playbreak (ABC)
BURT BRINKERHOFF, The Mask Of Love; ABC Matinee Today (ABC)

BEST INDIVIDUAL DIRECTOR FOR A GAME SHOW
Daytime Programming

MIKE GARGIULO, Jackpot! (NBC)
JEROME SHAW, The Hollywood Squares (NBC)
STUART PHELPS, Password (with Carol Burnett and Elizabeth Montgomery) (ABC)

BEST INDIVIDUAL DIRECTOR FOR A TALK, SERVICE OR VARIETY PROGRAM
Daytime Programming

DICK CARSON, The Merv Griffin Show (with Rosemary Clooney, Helen O'Connell, Fran Warren and Kay Starr) (Synd)
RON A. APPLING, The Merv Griffin Show (with Clint Eastwood, Forrest Tucker and Stanley Myron Handleman) (Synd)
GLEN SWANSON, Dinah's Place (with Jose Feliciano) (NBC)

DAYTIME DIRECTOR OF THE YEAR
H. WESLEY KENNEY, Miss Kline, We Love You; ABC Afternoon Playbreak (ABC)

BEST WRITING FOR A DRAMA SERIES
Daytime Programming

HENRY SLESAR, The Edge Of Night (CBS)
EILEEN and ROBERT MASON POLLOCK, and JAMES LIPTON, The Doctors (NBC)
FRANK and DORIS HURSLEY, BRIDGET DOBSON, and DEBORAH HARDY, General Hospital (ABC)

BEST WRITING FOR A SPECIAL PROGRAM
Daytime Programming

LILA GARRETT, and SANDY KRINSKI, Mother Of The Bride; ABC Afternoon Playbreak (ABC)
ROBERT SHAW, Once In Her Life; CBS Daytime 90 (CBS)
ART WALLACE, Alone With Terror; ABC Matinee Today (ABC)

BEST WRITING FOR A GAME SHOW
Daytime Programming

JAY REDACK, HARRY FRIEDMAN, HAROLD SCHNEIDER, GARY JOHNSON, STEVE LEVITCH, RICK KELLARD, and ROWBY GOREN; The Hollywood Squares (NBC)
ROBERT SHERMAN, PATRICK NEARY, JOE NEUSTEIN, and DICK DeBARTOLO; Match Game '74 (CBS)
LYNETTE WILLIAMS, ELIZABETH M. CAMP, LESLIE COOPER, MARK EISMAN, G. ROSS PARKER, and JAMES J. THESING; Jeopardy! (NBC)

BEST WRITING FOR A TALK, SERVICE OR VARIETY PROGRAM
Daytime Programming

TONY GARAFALO, BOB MURPHY, and MERV GRIFFIN; The Merv Griffin Show (with Billie Jean King, Mark Spitz, Hank Aaron and Johnny Unitas) (Synd)
BILL WALKER, BOB HOWARD and FRED TATASHORE; The Child Abuse Show; Dinah's Place (NBC)
DON CORNELIUS, Soul Train (with Johnny Mathis) (Synd)

DAYTIME WRITER OF THE YEAR

LILA GARRETT, and SANDY KRINSKI, Mother Of The Bride; ABC Afternoon Playbreak (ABC)

OUTSTANDING MUSICAL DIRECTION
Daytime Programming

RICHARD CLEMENTS, A Special Act Of Love; ABC Afternoon Playbreak (ABC)
JOHN GELLER, The Doctors (NBC)
PAUL TAUBMAN, Edge Of Night (CBS)

OUTSTANDING ART DIRECTION OR SCENIC DESIGN
Daytime Programming

TOM TRIMBLE, Art Director; **BROCK BROUGHTON**, Set Decorator; The Young And The Restless (CBS)
OTIS RIGGS, JR., Another World (NBC)
VICTOR L. PAGANUZZI, Scenic Desiner; JOHN WENDELL, Set Decorator; Once In Her Life; CBS Daytime 90 (CBS)
LLOYD R. EVANS, Scenic Designer; TOM CUNNINGHAM, and JOHN WENDELL, Set Decorators; Love of Life; Series (CBS)

OUTSTANDING COSTUME DESIGN
Daytime Programming

BILL JOBE, The Mask Of Love; ABC Matinee Today (ABC)
LEWIS BROWN, Another World (NBC)
JULIA SZE, Somerset (NBC)
HAZEL ROY, All My Children; Series (ABC)

OUTSTANDING MAKE-UP
Daytime Programming

DOUGLAS D. KELLY, The Mask Of Love; ABC Matinee Today (ABC)
ANDREW EGER, The Edge of Night (CBS)
LEE BAYGAN, The Doctors (NBC)
SYLVIA LAWRENCE, All My Children (ABC)

OUTSTANDING TECHNICAL DIRECTION AND ELECTRONIC CAMERAWORK
Daytime Programming

LOU MARCHAND, Technical Director; **GERALD M. DOWD, FRANK MELCHIORRE, and JOHN MORRIS**, Cameramen; One Life To Live (ABC)
HAROLD SCHUTZMAN, Technical Director; HAL WELDON, WILLIAM UNKEL, and ROBERT TOERPER, Cameramen; The Edge Of Night (CBS)
A.J. CUNNINGHAM, Technical Director; RICK TANZI, JOE ARVIZU, JACK JENNINGS, and WAYNE ORR, Cameramen; The Price Is Right (CBS)
GORDON C. JAMES, Technical Director; GEORGE SIMPSON, GEORGE MEYER, and JOHN KULLMAN, Cameramen; Days Of Our Lives (NBC)
CLIVE BASSETT, Technical Director; PAUL JOHNSON, RICK TANZI, DICK OUDERKIRK, MARVIN DRESSER, and GORDON SWEENEY, Cameramen; The Young And The Restless (CBS)
J.J. LUPATKIN and BILL DEGENHARDT, Technical Directors; JOHN WOOD, FRANK ZUCCARO, JAMES WOODLE, JOE SOLOMITO, AL GIANETTA, and LEN GELARDI, Cameramen; All My Children (ABC)

OUTSTANDING LIGHTING DIRECTION
Daytime Programming

RICHARD HOLBROOK, The Young And The Restless (CBS)
ALAN E. SCARLETT, Days Of Our Lives (NBC)
RON HOLDEN, General Hospital (ABC)
MEL HANDLESMAN, All My Children (ABC)

OUTSTANDING SOUND MIXING
Daytime Programming

ERNEST DELLUTRI, Days Of Our Lives (NBC)
DICK ELLIS, General Hospital (ABC)
ALBIN S. LEMANSKI, All My Children (ABC)

OUTSTANDING EDITING
Daytime Programming

GARY ANDERSON, Miss Kline, We Love You; ABC Afternoon Playbreak (ABC)
JERRY GREENE, The Mask Of Love; ABC Matinee Today (ABC)
JEFF LAING, Once In Her Life; CBS Daytime 90 (CBS)

NEWS AND DOCUMENTARY

PROGRAM AND INDIVIDUAL ACHIEVEMENTS
(Possibility of One Award, More than One Award, or No Award)

OUTSTANDING ACHIEVEMENT WITHIN REGULARLY SCHEDULED NEWS PROGRAMS

For program segments, i.e. presentation of individual stories (in single or multi-part) or elements within the programs Emmy Awards may possibly be given to: Executive Producer(s), Producer(s), Broadcaster(s)

COVERAGE OF THE OCTOBER WAR FROM ISRAEL'S NORTHERN FRONT, CBS Evening News With Walter Cronkite; John Laurence, Correspondent (CBS)
THE AGNEW RESIGNATION, CBS Evening News With Walter Cronkite; Paul Greenberg, Executive Producer; Ron Bonn, Ed Fouhy, John Lane, Don Bowers, John Armstrong, and Robert Mean, Producers; Walter Cronkite, Robert Schakne, Fred Graham, Robert Pierpoint, Roger Mudd, Dan Rather, John Hart, and Eric Sevareid, Correspondents (CBS)
THE KEY BISCAYNE BANK CHARTER STRUGGLE, CBS Evening News With Walter Cronkite; Ed Fouhy, Producer; Robert Pierpoint, Correspondent (CBS)
REPORTS ON WORLD HUNGER, NBC Nightly News; Lester M. Crystal, Executive Producer; Richard Fisher and Joseph Angotti, Producers; Tom Streithorst, Phil Brady, John Palmer, and Liz Trotta, Correspondents (NBC)
INSIDE CHINA, ABC Evening News; Ted Koppel, and Steve Bell, Correspondents (ABC)
THE ARAB WORLD, ABC Evening News; Peter Jennings, and Barry Dunsmore, Correspondents (ABC)
DEPROGRAMMING: THE CLASH BETWEEN RELIGION AND CIVIL RIGHTS, CBS Evening News With Walter Cronkite; Roger Sims, Producer; Steve Young, Correspondent (CBS)

OUTSTANDING ACHIEVEMENT FOR REGULARLY SCHEDULED MAGAZINE-TYPE PROGRAMS

For program segments, i.e. the presentation of individual stories, individual segments, or a single program of a series Emmy Awards may possibly be given to: Executive Producer(s), Producer(s), Broadcaster(s)

AMERICA'S NERVE GAS ARSENAL, First Tuesday; Eliot Frankel, Executive Producer; William B. Hill, and Anthony Potter, Producers; Tom Pettit, Correspondent (NBC)
THE ADVERSARIES, Behind The Lines; Carey Winfrey, Executive Producer; Peter Forbath, Producer/Reporter; Brendan Gill, Host/Moderator (PBS)
A QUESTION OF IMPEACHMENT, Bill Moyers' Journal; Jerome Toobin, Executive Producer; Martin Clancy, Producer; Bill Moyers, Broadcaster (PBS)
IT'S ENOUGH TO MAKE YOU SICK, The Reasoner Report; Ernest Leiser, Executive Producer; Frank Reynolds, Correspondent (ABC)
THE END OF A SALESMAN, 60 Minutes; Don Hewitt, Executive Producer; Joseph Wershba, Producer; Morley Safer, Correspondent (CBS)
LOCAL NEWS AND THE RATING WAR, 60 Minutes; Don Hewitt, Executive Producer; Harry Moses, Producer; Mike Wallace, Correspondent (CBS)

OUTSTANDING ACHIEVEMENT IN COVERAGE OF SPECIAL EVENTS

For program achievements Emmy Awards may possibly be given to: Executive Producer(s), Producer(s), Broadcaster(s)

WATERGATE: THE WHITE HOUSE TRANSCRIPTS, Russ Bensley, Executive Producer; Sylvia Westerman, Barry Jagoda, Mark Harrington, and Jack Kelly, Producers; Walter Cronkite, Dan Rather, Barry Serafin, Bob Schieffer, Daniel Schorr, Nelson Benton, Bruce Morton, Roger Mudd, and Fred Graham, Correspondents (CBS)
WATERGATE COVERAGE, Martin Clancy, Executive Producer; The NPACT Staff, Producers; Jim Lehrer, Peter Kaye, and Robert MacNeil, Reporters (PBS)
ABC NEWS AT EASE, Walter J. Pfister, Producer; Howard K. Smith, and Harry Reasoner, Anchormen (ABC)
WATERGATE: THIS WEEK, Helen Marmor, Producer; John Chancellor, and Carl Stern, Correspondents (NBC)

OUTSTANDING DOCUMENTARY PROGRAM ACHIEVEMENTS

A. For documentary programs dealing with events or matters of current significance Emmy Awards may possibly be given to: Executive Producer(s), Producer(s), Broadcaster(s)

FIRE!, ABC News Close Up; Pamela Hill, Producer; Jules Bergman, Correspondent/Narrator (ABC)
CBS NEWS SPECIAL REPORT: THE SENATE AND THE WATERGATE AFFAIR, Leslie Midgley, Executive Producer; Hal Haley, Bernard Birnbaum, and David Browning, Producers; Dan Rather, Roger Mudd, Daniel Schorr, and Fred Graham, Correspondents (CBS)
ACTION BIOGRAPHY: HENRY KISSINGER, Ted Koppel, Producer; Howard K. Smith, Correspondent (ABC)
JUVENILE COURT, Special of the Week; Fred Wiseman, Producer (PBS)
THE UNQUIET DEATH OF JULIUS AND ETHEL ROSENERG, Special of the Week; Alvin Goldstein, Producer (PBS)
OIL: THE POLICY CRISIS, ABC News Close-up; Steven Fleischman, Producer (ABC)

OUTSTANDING DOCUMENTARY PROGRAM ACHIEVEMENTS

B. For documentary programs dealing with artistic, historial or cultural subjects Emmy Awards may possibly be given to: Executive Producer(s), Producer(s), (Broadcaster(s)

JOURNEY TO THE OUTER LIMITS, National Geographic Society; Nicholas Clapp, and Dennis Kane, Executive Producers; Alex Grasshoff, Producer (ABC)
THE WORLD AT WAR, Series; Jeremy Isaacs, Producer (Synd)
CBS REPORTS: THE ROCKEFELLERS, Burton Benjamin, Executive Producer; Howard Stringer, Producer; Walter Cronkite, Correspondent (CBS)
THE BABOONS OF GOMBE, Jane Goodall and The World of Animal Behavior; Marshall Flaum, Executive Producer; Hugo van Lawick, and Bill Travers, Producers (ABC)
CULTURE THIEVES, ABC News Close-up; Martin Carr, Producer; Howard K. Smith, Correspondent (ABC)
RAOUL WALSH, The Men Who Made The Movies; Richard Schickel, Producer (PBS)
POWER AND THE PRESIDENCY, The American Parade; Joel Heller, Executive Producer; Jack Willis, Producer (CBS)

OUTSTANDING INTERVIEW PROGRAM

For a single program or one entire program of a series produced by a network news division or dealing with public affairs exclusively Emmy Awards may possibly be given to: Executive Producer(s), Producer(s), Broadcaster(s)

SOLZHENITSYN, CBS News Special; Burton Benjamin, Producer; Walter Cronkite, Correspondent (CBS)
HENRY STEELE COMMAGER, Bill Moyers' Journal; Jerome Toobin, Executive Producer; Martin Clancy, Producer; Bill Moyers, Broadcaster (PBS)
WATERGATE: AN INTERVIEW WITH JOHN DEAN, CBS News Special Report; Ed Fouhy, Executive Producer; Don Bowers, Producer; Walter Cronkite, Correspondent (CBS)
CRISIS OF THE PRESIDENCY, ABC News Special; Ernest Leiser, Executive Producer; Arthur Holch and Joan Richman, Producers (ABC)

OUTSTANDING TELEVISION NEWS BROADCASTER

For achievements within program segments, one program of a series, or a single program; for reporting, interviewing, interpretation, commentary, analysis within Regularly Scheduled News programs, Magazine-type programs, Coverage of Special Events, interview programs, and Documentary programs dealing with events or matters of current significance. Emmy Award will be given to the News Broadcaster

HARRY REASONER, ABC News (ABC)
BILL MOYERS, Essay On Watergate; Bill Moyers' Journal (PBS)
MIKE WALLACE, 60 Minutes (CBS)
WALTER CRONKITE, CBS Evening News With Walter Cronkite and Various Specials (CBS)
CARL STERN, Coverage of Watergate and Justice Department; NBC Nightly News (NBC)
JOHN CHANCELLOR, NBC Nightly News (NBC)

OUTSTANDING INDIVIDUAL ACHIEVEMENT IN CHILDREN'S PROGRAMMING

RONALD BALDWIN, Art Director; NAT MONGIOI, Set Decorator; The Electric Company (PBS)
THE MUPPETS (JIM HENSON, FRANK OZ, CARROLL SPINNEY, JERRY NELSON, RICHARD HUNT, and FRAN BRILL), Performers; Sesame Street; Series (PBS)
JON STONE, JOSEPH A. BAILEY, JERRY JUHL, EMILY PERL KINGSLEY, JEFFREY MOSS, RAY SIPHERD, and NORMAN STILES, Writers; Sesame Street (PBS)
HENRY BEHAR, Director; The Electric Company (PBS)
THOMAS A. WHEDON, JOHN BONI, SARA COMPTON, TOM DUNSMUIR, THAD MUMFORD, JEREMY STEVENS, and JIM THURMAN, Writers; The Electric Company (PBS)

OUTSTANDING ACHIEVEMENT IN RELIGIOUS PROGRAMMING

KEN LAMKIN, Technical Director; SAM DRUMMY, GARY STANTON, and ROBERT HATFIELD, Cameramen; Gift Of Tears; This Is The Life (Synd)
JOHN WARD, Scenic Designer; MYRON BLEAM, Set Decorator; St Francis of Assisi, The Tower of Babel, David and Goliath; Marshall Efron's Illustrated, Simplified and Painless Sunday School (CBS)
HOLY LAND, Doris Ann, Producer (NBC)
DIRECTIONS, Sid Darion, Executive Producer (ABC)
CHRISTMAS IN WALES, Directions; Paul E. Wilson, Producer (ABC)

OUTSTANDING ACHIEVEMENT IN NEWS AND DOCUMENTARY DIRECTING

For program segments, one program of a series, or a single program; for Regularly Scheduled News programs, Magazine-type programs, Coverage of Special Events, Interview programs, Documentary programs dealing with events or matters of current significance, and Cultural Documentaries

PAMELA HILL, Fire!; ABC News Close-up (ABC)
VICTORIA HOCHBERG, The Right To Die; ABC News Close-up (ABC)
WILLIAM LINDEN, Watergate: The White House Transcripts; CBS News Special Report (CBS)

OUTSTANDING ACHIEVEMENT IN NEWS AND DOCUMENTARY WRITING

For program segments, one program of a series, or a single program; for Regularly Scheduled News programs, Magazine-type programs, Coverage of Special Events, Interview programs, Documentary programs dealing with events or matters of current significance, and Cultural Documentaries

ROBERT NORTHSHIELD, The Sins Of The Fathers; NBC Reports (NBC)
MARLENE SANDERS, The Right To Die; ABC News Close-up (ABC)
HOWARD STRINGER, and BURTON BENJAMIN, The Rockefellers; CBS Reports (CBS)
ALVIN H. GOLDSTEIN, The Unquiet Death of Julius and Ethel Rosenberg; Special Of The Week (PBS)

OUTSTANDING ACHIEVEMENT IN ANY AREA OF CREATIVE TECHNICAL CRAFTS

An Award for individual craft achievement which does not fall into a specific category, and is not otherwise recognized

PHILIPPE COUSTEAU, Under Ice Photography; Beneath the Frozen World; The Undersea World of Jacques Cousteau (ABC)
JOHN CHAMBERS, and TOM BURMAN, Make-up; Struggle for Survival; Primal Man (ABC)
AGGIE WHELAN, Courtroom Drawings; The Mitchell-Stans Trial; CBS Evening News with Walter Cronkite (CBS)
FRANCOIS CHARLET, Aerial Photography; Beneath the Frozen World; The Undersea World of Jacques Cousteau (ABC)
ROBERT R. DUNN, Cameraman; C. FRED GAYTON, Videotape Recorder Operator; Electronic Newsgathering using minicam; The Hearst Kidnapping; CBS Evening News (CBS)

(One Award Only In Each of the Following Categories)

OUTSTANDING INFORMATIONAL CHILDREN'S SERIES

MAKE A WISH, Lester Cooper, Executive Producer; Tom Bywaters, Producer (ABC)
THE ELECTRIC COMPANY, Samuel Y. Gibbon, Jr., Executive Producer; Andrew B. Ferguson, Jr., Producer (PBS)
IN THE NEWS, Joel Heller, Executive Producer; Judy Towers Reemtsma, Producer (CBS)

OUTSTANDING INFORMATIONAL CHILDREN'S SPECIAL

THE RUNAWAYS, Joseph Barbera and William Hanna, Executive Producers; Bill Schwartz, Producer (ABC)
WHAT'S IMPEACHMENT ALL ABOUT?, Joel Heller, Executive Producer; Walter Lister, Producer (CBS)
WHAT'S THE ENERGY CRISIS ALL ABOUT?, Joel Heller, Executive Producer; Walter Lister, Producer (CBS)

OUTSTANDING INSTRUCTIONAL CHILDREN'S PROGRAMMING

INSIDE/OUT, Larry Walcoff, Executive Producer (Synd)
MISTER ROGERS' NEIGHBORHOOD, Leland Hazard, Executive Producer; Fred Rogers, Producer; Series (PBS)
MULTIPLICATION ROCK, Tom Yohe, Executive Producer; Radford Stone, Producer; Series (ABC)
SESAME STREET, Jon Stone, Executive Producer; Bob Cunniff, Producer (PBS)

BEST CINEMATOGRAPHY FOR NEWS AND DOCUMENTARY PROGRAMMING

For a series, a single program of a series, a special program, program segments or elements within: A. Regularly scheduled News Programs and coverage of Special Events

DELOS HALL, Clanking Savannah Blacksmith; On The Road With Charles Kuralt; CBS Evening News with Walter Cronkite (CBS)
ROBERT O. BROWN, and ELIA RAVASZ, SLA Shootout, Los Angeles; CBS Evening News with Dan Rather (CBS)
ISADORE BLECKMAN, Bird Lady; On The Road With Charles Kuralt; CBS Evening News with Walter Cronkite (CBS)

B. Documentary, Magazine-type or Mini-documentary programs

WALTER DOMBROW, Ballerina; 60 Minutes (CBS)
PHILIPPE COUSTEAU, Beneath the Frozen World; The Undersea World of Jacques Cousteau (ABC)
JOHN J. LANDI, and RALPH MAYHER, Fire!; ABC News Close-up

(ABC)
DICK MINGALONE, Inside Attica; The Reasoner Report (ABC)

BEST MUSIC COMPOSITION
For a series, a single program of a series or a special program
WALTER SCHARF, Beneath the Frozen World; The Undersea World of Jacques Cousteau (ABC)
LYN MURRAY, Struggle For Survival; Primal Man (ABC)
BILLY GOLDENBERG, Journey to the Outer Limits; National Geographic Society (ABC)

BEST ART DIRECTION OR SCENIC DESIGN
For a series, a single program of a series or a special program
WILLIAM SUNSHINE, 60 Minutes; Series (CBS)
FRANK SKINNER, Soviet Prison Camps; NBC News Presents: Special Edition (NBC)
MERRILL SINDLER, The Cost of Living: Up, Up and Away; Today (NBC)

BEST FILM EDITING FOR NEWS AND DOCUMENTARY PROGRAMMING
For a series, a single program of a series, a special program, program segments or elements within: A. Regularly scheduled News programs and coverage of Special Events
WILLIAM J. FREEDA, Profile of Poverty in Appalachia; NBC Nightly News (NBC)
PATRICK MINERVA, THOMAS E. DUNPHY, WILLIAM J. FREEDA, IRWIN GRAF, ALBERT J. HELIAS, GEORGE JOHNSON, MIGUEL PORTILLO, MARTIN SHEPPARD, JEAN VENABLE, EDWIN EINARSEN, CONSTANTINE S. GOCHIS, LOFTUS McDONOUGH, DESMOND McELROY, ROBERT MOLE, RUSSELL MOORE, LOREN BERRY, TINA GRUETTNER, NICK WILKINS, GERRY BREESE, K TU-HUEI SU, MICHAEL SHUGRUE, and NINA JACKSON; NBC Nightly News (NBC)
GILBERT LeVEQUE, SLA Shootout; CBS Evening News with Dan Rather (CBS)

B. Documentary, Magazine-type or Mini-documentary programs
ANN CHEGWIDDEN, The Baboons of Gombe; Jane Goodall and The World of Animal Behavior (ABC)
DAVID H. NEWHOUSE, Journey to the Outer Limits National Geographic Society (ABC)
JOHN SOH, Beneath the Frozen World; The Undersea World of Jacques Cousteau (ABC)

BEST FILM OR TAPE SOUND MIXING
For a series, a single program of a series or a special program
PETER PILAFIAN, GEORGE E. PORTER, EDDIE J. NELSON, and ROBERT L. HARMAN; Journey to the Outer Limits; National Geographic Society (ABC)
ROBERT L. HARMAN, GEORGE E. PORTER, EDDIE J. NELSON, and GUY JOUAS; The Flight of the Penguins; The Undersea World of Jacques Cousteau (ABC)
GEORGE E. PORTER, EDDIE J. NELSON, and ROY GRANVILLE; South to Fire and Ice; The Undersea World of Jaques Cousteau (ABC)
ROBERT L. HARMAN, GEORGE E. PORTER, and EDDIE J. NELSON; The Baboons of Gombe; Jane Goodall and The World of Animal Behavior (ABC)

BEST FILM SOUND EDITING
For a series, a single program of a series or a special program
CHARLES L. CAMPBELL, ROBERT CORNETT, LARRY CAROW, LARRY KAUFMAN, COLIN MOUAT, DON WARNER, and FRANK R. WHITE, The Baboons of Gombe; Jane Goodall and The World of Animal Behavior (ABC)
STEPHEN E. PRICE, Bigger is Better; 60 Minutes (CBS)
CHARLES L. CAMPBELL, COLIN MOUAT, JERRY R. STANFORD, and LARRY CAROW; The Flight of the Penguins; The Undersea World of Jacques Cousteau (ABC)

BEST VIDEO TAPE EDITING
For a series, a single program of a series or a special program
GARY ANDERSON, Paramount Presents...ABC Wide World of Entertainment (ABC)
GEORGE KIYAK, ROBERT BAILEY, LLOYD CAMPBELL, JOSEPH D. COLVIN, DON DUNN, BUDDY FLECK, VINCENT GABRIELE, RICHARD LEIBLE, RALPH MARTUCCI, ARTHUR SCHWEIGER, MORTON SMITH, JERRY VALDIVIA, and RICHARD WEDEKING; Watergate: This Week; NBC News Special (NBC)
JACK STANLEY, and ERNEST ALLEN TOBIN, Watergate Hearings; CBS Evening News with Walter Cronkite (CBS)

BEST TECHNICAL DIRECTION AND ELECTRONIC CAMERAWORK
For a series, a single program of a series or a special program
CARL SCHUTZMAN, Technical Director; JOSEPH SCHWARTZ, and WILLIAM BELL, Cameramen; 60 Minutes (CBS)
DAVID FEE, Technical Director; STUART GOODMAN, RICHARD KERR, EUGENE WOOD, and PHIL FONTANA, Cameramen; Geraldo Rivera: Goodnight America; ABC Wide World of Entertainment (ABC)
MARTIN SOLOMON, Technical Director; HARRY HAIGOOD, DAVID DORSETT, and CASS GAYLORD, Cameramen; CBS Evening News with Walter Cronkie (CBS)

1974/75

THE CATEGORIES

Entertainment Program and Individual Achievements

OUTSTANDING COMEDY SERIES
Emmy(s) to Executive Producer(s) and/or Producer(s)
THE MARY TYLER MOORE SHOW, James L. Brooks and Allan Burns, Executive Producers; Ed Weinberger and Stan Daniels, Producers (CBS)
M*A*S*H, Gene Reynolds and Larry Gelbart, Producers (CBS)
ALL IN THE FAMILY, Don Nicholl, Executive Producer; Michael Ross and Bernie West, Producers (CBS)
RHODA, James L. Brooks and Allan Burns, Executive Producers; David Davis and Lorenzo Music, Producers (CBS)

OUTSTANDING DRAMA SERIES
Emmy(s) to Executive Producer(s) and/or Producer(s)
UPSTAIRS, DOWNSTAIRS, Masterpiece Theatre; Rex Firkin, Executive Producer; John Hawkesworth, Producer (PBS)
THE STREETS OF SAN FRANCISCO, Quinn Martin, Executive Producer; John Wilder and William Robert Yates, Producers (ABC)
POLICE STORY, Stanley Kallis and David Gerber, Executive Producers; Chris Morgan, Producer (NBC)
THE WALTONS, Lee Rich, Executive Producer; Robert L. Jacks, Producer (CBS)
KOJAK, Matthew Rapf, Executive Producer; Jack Laird and James

McAdams, Producers (CBS)

OUTSTANDING COMEDY-VARIETY OR MUSIC SERIES

Emmy(s) to Executive Producer(s) and/or Producer(s) and Star(s), if applicable

THE CAROL BURNETT SHOW, Joe Hamilton, Executive Producer; Ed Simmons, Producer; Carol Burnett, Star (CBS)
CHER, George Schlatter, Producer; Cher, Star (CBS)

OUTSTANDING LIMITED SERIES

Emmy(s) to Executive Producer(s) and/or Producer(s)

BENJAMIN FRANKLIN, Lewis Freedman, Executive Producer; George Lefferts and Glenn Jordan, Producers (CBS)
McCLOUD, NBC Sunday Mystery Movie; Glen A Larson, Executive Producer; Michael Gleason and Ronald Satlof, Producers (NBC)
COLUMBO, NBC Sunday Mystery Movie; Roland Kibbee and Dean Hargrove, Executive Producers; Everett Chambers and Edward K. Dodds, Producers (NBC)

OUTSTANDING SPECIAL - DRAMA OR COMEDY

Emmy(s) to Executive Producer(s) and/or Producer(s)

THE LAW, NBC World Premiere Movie; William Sackheim, Producer (NBC)
THE MISSILES OF OCTOBER, ABC Theatre; Irv Wilson, Executive Producer; Herbert Brodkin and Buzz Berger, Producers (ABC)
QUEEN OF THE STARDUST BALLROOM, Robert W. Christiansen and Rick Rosenberg, Producers (CBS)
LOVE AMONG THE RUINS, ABC Theatre; Allan Davis, Producer (ABC)
QB VII, Parts 1 & 2; ABC Movie Special; Douglas S. Cramer, Producer (ABC)

OUTSTANDING SPECIAL - COMEDY-VARIETY OR MUSIC

Emmy(s) to Executive Producer(s) and/or Producer(s) and Star(s) if applicable

AN EVENING WITH JOHN DENVER, Jerry Weintraub, Executive Producer; Al Rogers and Rich Eustis, Producers; John Denver, Star (ABC)
LILY, Irene Pinn, Executive Producer; Jane Wagner and Lorne Michaels, Producers; Lily Tomlin, Star (ABC)
SHIRLEY MacLAINE: IF THEY COULD SEE ME NOW, Bob Wells, Producer; Shirley MacLaine, Star (CBS)

OUTSTANDING CLASSICAL MUSIC PROGRAM

For a special program or for a series Emmy(s) to Executive Producer(s) and/or Producer(s) and Star(s), if applicable

PROFILE IN MUSIC: BEVERLY SILLS, Festival '75; Patricia Foy, Producer; Beverly Sills, Star (PBS)
RUBINSTEIN, Great Performances; Fritz Buttenstedt, Executive Producer; Helmut Bauer and David Griffiths, Producers; Artur Rubinstein, Star (PBS)
BERNSTEIN AT TANGLEWOOD, Great Performances; Klaus Hallig and Harry Kraut, Executive Producers; David Griffiths, Producer; Leonard Bernstein, Star (PBS)
EVENING AT POPS, William Cosel, Producer; Arthur Fiedler, Star; Series (PBS)

OUTSTANDING LEAD ACTOR IN A COMEDY SERIES

TONY RANDALL, The Odd Couple (ABC)
ALAN ALDA, M*A*S*H (CBS)
JACK ALBERTSON, Chico And The Man (NBC)
JACK KLUGMAN, The Odd Couple (ABC)
CARROLL O'CONNOR, All In The Family (CBS)

OUTSTANDING LEAD ACTOR IN A DRAMA SERIES

ROBERT BLAKE, Baretta (ABC)
KARL MALDEN, The Streets of San Francisco (ABC)
BARRY NEWMAN, Petrocelli (NBC)
TELLY SAVALAS, Kojak (CBS)

OUTSTANDING LEAD ACTOR IN A LIMITED SERIES

PETER FALK, Columbo; NBC Sunday Mystery Movie (NBC)
DENNIS WEAVER, McCloud; NBC Sunday Mystery Movie (NBC)

OUTSTANDING LEAD ACTOR IN A SPECIAL PROGRAM - DRAMA OR COMEDY

For a special program; or a single appearance in a Drama or Comedy Series

LAURENCE OLIVIER, Love Among The Ruins; ABC Theatre (ABC)
RICHARD CHAMBERLAIN, The Count Of Monte Cristo; Bell System Family Theatre (NBC)
WILLIAM DEVANE, The Missiles Of October; ABC Theatre (ABC)
CHARLES DURNING, Queen Of The Stardust Ballroom (CBS)
HENRY FONDA, IBM Presents Clarence Darrow (NBC)

OUTSTANDING LEAD ACTRESS IN A COMEDY SERIES

VALERIE HARPER, Rhoda (CBS)
MARY TYLER MOORE, The Mary Tyler Moore Show (CBS)
JEAN STAPLETON, All In The Family (CBS)

OUTSTANDING LEAD ACTRESS IN A DRAMA SERIES

JEAN MARSH, Upstairs, Downstairs; Masterpiece Theatre (PBS)
ANGIE DICKINSON, Police Woman (NBC)
MICHAEL LEARNED, The Waltons (CBS)

OUTSTANDING LEAD ACTRESS IN A LIMITED SERIES

JESSICA WALTER, Amy Prentiss; NBC Sunday Mystery Movie (NBC)
SUSAN SAINT JAMES, McMillan & Wife; NBC Sunday Mystery Movie (NBC)

OUTSTANDING LEAD ACTRESS IN A SPECIAL PROGRAM - DRAMA OR COMEDY

For a special program; or a single appearance in a Drama or Comedy Series

KATHARINE HEPBURN, Love Among The Ruins; ABC Theatre (ABC)
JILL CLAYBURGH, Hustling; Special World Premiere ABC Saturday Night Movie (ABC)
ELIZABETH MONTGOMERY, The Legend of Lizzie Borden; Special World Premiere ABC Monday Night Movie (ABC)
DIANA RIGG, In This House Of Brede; GE Theater (CBS)
MAUREEN STAPLETON, Queen of the Stardust Ballroom (CBS)

OUTSTANDING CONTINUING PERFORMANCE BY A SUPPORTING ACTOR IN A COMEDY SERIES
For a regular or limited series
ED ASNER, The Mary Tyler Moore Show (CBS)
ROB REINER, All In The Family (CBS)
TED KNIGHT, The Mary Tyler Moore Show (CBS)
GARY BURGHOFF, M*A*S*H (CBS)
McLEAN STEVENSON, M*A*SH (CBS)

OUTSTANDING CONTINUING PERFORMANCE BY A SUPPORTING ACTOR IN A DRAMA SERIES
For a regular or limited series
WILL GEER, The Waltons (CBS)
MICHAEL DOUGLAS, The Streets Of San Francisco (ABC)
J.D. CANNON, McCloud; NBC Sunday Mystery Movie (NBC)

OUSTANDING CONTINUING OR SINGLE PERFORMANCE BY A SUPPORTING ACTOR IN VARIETY OR MUSIC
For a continuing role in a regular or limited series; or a one-time appearance in a series; or a special
JACK ALBERTSON, Cher (CBS)
TIM CONWAY, The Carol Burnett Show (CBS)
JOHN DENVER, Doris Day Today (CBS)

OUTSTANDING SINGLE PERFORMANCE BY A SUPPORTING ACTOR IN A COMEDY OR DRAMA SPECIAL
ANTHONY QUALE, QB VII, Parts 1 & 2; ABC Movie Special (ABC
RALPH BELLAMY, The Missiles Of October; ABC Theatre (ABC)
TREVOR HOWARD, The Count of Monte Cristo; Bell System Family Theatre (NBC)
JACK HAWKINS, QB VII, Parts 1 & 2; ABC Movie Special (ABC)

OUTSTANDING SINGLE PERFORMANCE BY A SUPPORTING ACTOR IN A COMEDY OR DRAMA SERIES
For a one-time appearance in a regular or limited series
PATRICK McGOOHAN, By Dawn's Early Light; Columbo; NBC Sunday Mystery Movies (NBC)
LEW AYRES, The Vanishing Image; Kung Fu (ABC)
HAROLD GOULD, Fathers And Sons; Police Story (NBC)
HARRY MORGAN, The General Flipped At Dawn; M*A*S*H (CBS)

OUTSTANDING CONTINUING PERFORMANCE BY A SUPPORTING ACTRESS IN A COMEDY SERIES
For a regular or limited series
BETTY WHITE, The Mary Tyler Moore Show (CBS)
JULIE KAVNER, Rhoda (CBS)
NANCY WALKER, Rhoda (CBS)
LORETTA SWIT, M*A*S*H (CBS)

OUTSTANDING CONTINUING PERFORMANCE BY A SUPPORTING ACTRESS IN A DRAMA SERIES
For a regular or limited series
ELLEN CORBY, The Waltons (CBS)
NANCY WALKER, McMillan & Wife; NBC Sunday Mystery Movie (NBC)
ANGELA BADDELEY, Upstairs, Downstairs; Masterpiece Theatre (PBS)

OUTSTANDING CONTINUING OR SINGLE PERFORMANCE BY A SUPPORTING ACTRESS IN VARIETY OR MUSIC
For a continuing role in a regular or limited series; or a one-time appearance in a series; or a special
CLORIS LEACHMAN, Cher (CBS)
RITA MORENO, Out To Lunch (ABC)
VICKI LAWRENCE, The Carol Burnett Show (CBS)

OUTSTANDING SINGLE PERFORMANCE BY A SUPPORTING ACTRESS IN A COMEDY OR DRAMA SPECIAL
JULIET MILLS, QB VII, Parts 1 & 2; ABC Movie Special (ABC)
CHARLOTTE RAE, Queen of The Stardust Ballroom (CBS)
LEE REMICK, QB VII, Parts 1 & 2; ABC Movie Special (ABC)
EILEEN HECKART, Wedding Band; ABC Theatre (ABC)

OUTSTANDING SINGLE PERFORMANCE BY A SUPPORTING ACTRESS IN A COMEDY OR DRAMA SERIES
For a one-time appearance in a regular or limited series
CLORIS LEACHMAN, Phyllis Whips Inflation; The Mary Tyler Moore Show (CBS)
ZOHRA LAMPERT, Queen Of The Gypsies; Kojak (CBS)
SHELLEY WINTERS, The Barefoot Girls Of Bleecker Street; McCloud; NBC Sunday Mystery Movie (NBC)

OUTSTANDING DIRECTING IN A DRAMA SERIES
A single episode of a regular or limited series with continuing characters and/or theme
BILL BAIN, A Sudden Storm; Uptairs, Downstairs; Masterpiece Theatre (PBS)
HARRY FALK, The Mask Of Death; The Streets of San Francisco (ABC)
DAVID FRIEDKIN, Cross Your Heart And Hope to Die; Kojak (CBS)
TELLY SAVALAS, I Want To Report A Dream. . .;Kojak (CBS)
GLENN JORDAN, The Ambassador; Benjamin Franklin (CBS)

OUTSTANDING DIRECTING IN A COMEDY SERIES
A single episode of a regular or limited series with continuing characters and/or theme
GENE REYNOLDS, O.R.; M*A*S*H (CBS)
HY AVERBACK, Alcoholics Unanimous; M*A*S*H (CBS)
ALAN ALDA, Bulletin Board; M*A*S*H (CBS)

OUTSTANDING DIRECTING IN A COMEDY-VARIETY OR MUSIC SERIES
A single episode of a regular or limited series
DAVE POWERS, The Carol Burnett Show (with Alan Alda) (CBS)
ART FISHER, Cher (with Bette Midler, Flip Wilson and Elton John) (CBS)

OUTSTANDING DIRECTING IN A COMEDY-VARIETY OR MUSIC SPECIAL

BILL DAVIS, An Evening With John Denver (ABC)
ROBERT SCHEERER, Shirley MacLaine: If They Could See Me Now (CBS)
DWIGHT HEMION, Ann-Margret Olsson (NBC)

OUTSTANDING DIRECTING IN A SPECIAL PROGRAM - DRAMA OR COMEDY

GEORGE CUKOR, Love Among The Ruins; ABC Theatre (ABC)
JOHN BADHAM, The Law; NBC World Premiere Movie (NBC)
SAM O'STEEN, Queen Of The Stardust Ballroom (CBS)
TOM GRIES, QB VII, Parts 1 & 2; ABC Movie Special (ABC)
ANTHONY PAGE, The Missiles Of October; ABC Theatre (ABC)

OUTSTANDING WRITING IN A DRAMA SERIES

A single episode of a regular or limited series with continuing characters and/or theme

HOWARD FAST, The Ambassador; Benjamin Franklin (CBS)
ROBERT COLLINS, Robbery: 48 Hours; Police Story (NBC)
ALFRED SHAUGHNESSY, Miss Forrest; Upstairs, Downstairs; Masterpiece Theatre (PBS)
LORING MANDEL, The Whirlwind; Benjamin Franklin (CBS)
JOHN HAWKESWORTH, The Bolter; Upstairs, Downstairs; Masterpiece Theatre (PBS)

OUTSTANDING WRITING IN A COMEDY SERIES

A single episode of a regular or limited series with continuing characters and/or theme

ED WEINBERGER and STAN DANIELS, Mary Richards Goes To Jail; The Mary Tyler Moore Show (CBS)
DAVID LLOYD, Lou And That Woman; The Mary Tyler Moore Show (CBS)
NORMAN BARASCH, CARROLL MOORE, DAVID LLOYD, LORENZO MUSIC, ALLAN BURNS, JAMES L. BROOKS and DAVID DAVIS, Rhoda's Wedding; Rhoda (CBS)

OUTSTANDING WRITING IN A COMEDY-VARIETY OR MUSIC SERIES

A single episode of a regular or limited series

ED SIMMONS, GARY BELKIN, ROGER BEATTY, ARNIE KOGEN, BILL RICHMOND, GENE PERRET, RUDY DeLUCA, BARRY LEVINSON, DICK CLAIR and JENNA McMAHON, The Carol Burnett Show (with Alan Alda) (CBS)
DIGBY WOLFE, DON REO, ALAN KATZ, IRIS RAINER, DAVID PANICH, RON PEARLMAN, NICK ARNOLD, JOHN BONI, RAY TAYLOR and GEORGE SCHLATTER, Cher (with Raquel Welch, Tatum O'Neal and Wayne Rogers) (CBS)

OUTSTANDING WRITING IN A COMEDY-VARIETY OR MUSIC SPECIAL

BOB WELLS, JOHN BRADFORD and CY COLEMAN, Shirley MacLaine: If They Could See Me Now (CBS)
SYBIL ADELMAN, BARBARA GALLAGHER, GLORIA BANTA, PAT NARDO, STUART BIRNBAUM, MATT NEUMAN, LORNE MICHAELS, MARILYN MILLER, EARL POMERANTZ, ROSIE RUTHCHILD, LILY TOMLIN and JANE WAGNER, Lily (ABC)

OUTSTANDING WRITING IN A SPECIAL PROGRAM - DRAMA OR COMEDY - ORIGINAL TELEPLAY

JAMES COSTIGAN, Love Among The Ruins; ABC Theatre (ABC)
JEROME KASS, Queen Of The Stardust Ballroom (CBS)
STANLEY R. GREENBERG, The Missiles Of October; ABC Theatre (ABC)
FAY KANIN, Hustling; Special World Premiere ABC Saturday Night Movie (ABC)
JOEL OLIANSKY, Story by William Sackheim and Joel Oliansky; The Law; NBC World Premiere Movie (NBC)

OUTSTANDING WRITING IN A SPECIAL PROGRAM - DRAMA OR COMEDY - ADAPTATION

DAVID W. RINTELS, IBM Presents Clarence Darrow (NBC)
EDWARD ANHALT, QB VII, Parts 1 & 2; ABC Movie Special (ABC)

OUTSTANDING ACHIEVEMENT IN CHOREOGRAPHY

For a single episode of a series or a special program

MARGE CHAMPION, Queen Of The Stardust Ballroom (CBS)
ALAN JOHNSON, Shirley MacLaine: If They Could See Me Now (CBS)
DEE DEE WOOD, Cher (with Freddie Prinze and The Pointer Sisters) (CBS)

OUTSTANDING ACHIEVEMENT IN MUSIC COMPOSITION FOR A SERIES

Dramatic Underscore For a single episode of a regular or limited series

BILLY GOLDENBERG, The Rebel; Benjamin Franklin (CBS)
PAT WILIAMS, One Last Shot; The Streets Of San Francisco (ABC)

OUTSTANDING ACHIEVEMENT IN MUSIC COMPOSITION FOR A SPECIAL

Dramatic Underscore

JERRY GOLDSMITH, QB VII, Parts 1 & 2; ABC Movie Special (ABC)
BILLY GOLDENBERG, ALAN and MARILYN BERGMAN; Queen Of The Stardust Ballroom (CBS)

OUTSTANDING ACHIEVEMENT IN ART DIRECTION OR SCENIC DESIGN

For a single episode of a comedy, drama or limited series

CHARLES LISANBY, Art Director; ROBERT CHECCHI, Set Decorator; The Ambassador; Benjamin Franklin (CBS)
MICHAEL BAUGH, Art Director; JERRY ADAMS, Set Decorator; Playback; Columbo; NBC Sunday Mystery Movie (NBC)

OUTSTANDING ACHIEVEMENT IN ART DIRECTION OR SCENIC DESIGN

For a single episode of a comedy-variety or music series; or a comedy-variety or music special

ROBERT KELLY, Art Director; ROBERT CHECCHI, Set Decorator; Cher (with Bette Midler, Flip Wilson and Elton John) (CBS)
KEN JOHNSON and DWIGHT JACKSON, Art Directors; An Evening With John Denver (ABC)

OUTSTANDING ACHIEVEMENT IN ART DIRECTION OR SCENIC DESIGN
For a dramatic special or a feature length film made for television

CARMEN DILLON, Art Director; TESSA DAVIES, Set Decorator; Love Among The Ruins; ABC Theatre (ABC)
JACK DeSHEILDS, Art Director; HARRY GORDON, Set Decorator; The Legend Of Lizzie Borden; Special World Premiere; ABC Monday Night Movie (ABC)
ROSS BELLAH and MAURICE FOWLER, Art Directors; AUDREY BLESDEL-GODDARD and TERRY PARR, Set Decorators; QB VII, Parts 1 & 2; ABC Movie Special (ABC)

OUTSTANDING ACHIEVEMENT IN GRAPHIC DESIGN AND TITLE SEQUENCES
For a single episode of a series; or for a special program. This includes animation only when created for use in titling

PHILL NORMAN, QB VII, Parts 1 & 2; ABC Movie Special (ABC)
RICK ANDREOLI, The Tonight Show Starring Johnny Carson (NBC)
SUSAN CUSCUNA, The Tonight Show Starring Johnny Carson (NBC)

OUTSTANDING ACHIEVEMENT IN CINEMATOGRAPHY FOR ENTERTAINMENT PROGRAMMING FOR A SERIES
For a single episode of a regular or limited series

RICHARD C. GLOUNER, A.S.C., Playback; Columbo; NBC Sunday Mystery Movie (NBC)
WILLIAM JURGENSEN, Bombed; M*A*S*H (CBS)
VILIS LAPENIEKS, A.S.C. and SOL NEGRIN, A.S.C., Wall Street Gunslinger; Kojak (CBS)

OUTSTANDING ACHIEVEMENT IN CINEMATOGRAPHY FOR ENTERTAINMENT PROGRAMMING FOR A SPECIAL
For a special or feature length program made for television

DAVID M. WALSH, Queen Of the Stardust Ballroom (CBS)
HOWARD SCHWARTZ, A.S.C., Sad Figure, Laughing; Sandburg's Lincoln (NBC)
PAUL BEESON and ROBERT L. MORRISON, QB VII, Parts 1 & 2; ABC Movie Special (ABC)
MICHAEL CHAPMAN, Death Be Not Proud; Tuesday Movie of the Week (ABC)

OUTSTANDING FILM EDITING FOR ENTERTAINMENT PROGRAMMING FOR A SERIES
For a single episode of a comedy series

DOUGLAS HINES, An Affair To Forget; The Mary Tyler Moore Show (CBS)
STANFORD TISCHLER and FRED W. BERGER, The General Flipped At Dawn; M*A*S*H (CBS)

OUTSTANDING FILM EDITING FOR ENTERTAINMENT PROGRAMMING FOR A SERIES
For a single episode of a drama series

DONALD R. RODE, Mirror, Mirror On The Wall; Petrocelli (NBC)
RAY DANIELS, Cry Help!; The Streets Of San Francisco (ABC)
JERRY YOUNG, The Mask Of Death; The Streets Of San Francisco (ABC)

OUTSTANDING FILM EDITING FOR ENTERTAINMENT PROGRAMMING FOR A SPECIAL
For a special or film made for television

JOHN A. MARTINELLI, A.C.E., The Legend Of Lizzie Borden; Special World Premiere; ABC MMonday Night Movie (ABC)
BYRON "BUZZ" BRANDT and IRVING C. ROSENBLUM, QB VII, Parts 1 & 2; ABC Movie Special (ABC)
JERRY YOUNG, Attack on Terror: The FBI Versus The Ku Klux Klan, Parts 1 & 2 (CBS)

OUTSTANDING ACHIEVEMENT IN FILM SOUND EDITING
For a single episode of a regular or limited series; or for a special program

MARVIN I. KOSBERG, RICHARD BURROW, MILTON C. BURROW, JACK MILNER, RONALD ASHCROFT, JAMES BALLAS, JOSEF VON STROHEIM, JERRY ROSENTHAL, WILLIAM ANDREWS, EDWARD SANDLIN, DAVID HORTON, ALVIN KAJITA, TONY GARBER and JEREMY HOENACK, QB VII, Parts 1 & 2; ABC Movie Special (ABC)
DONALD ISAACS, DON HIGGINS, LARRY KAUFMAN, JACK KIRSCHNER, DICK LeGRAND, GARY VAUGHAN, GENE WAHRMAN, FRANK WHITE, and HAROLD WOOLEY, The Legend Of Lizzie Borden; Special World Premiere; ABC Monday Night Movie (ABC)

OUTSTANDING ACHIEVEMENT IN FILM OR TAPE SOUND MIXING
For a single episode of a regular or limited series; or for a special program

MARSHALL KING, The American Film Institute Salute To James Cagney (CBS)
DOUG NELSON, The Missiles Of October; ABC Theatre (ABC)
DOUG NELSON and NORM SCHWARTZ, California Jam; Wide World In Concert (ABC)

OUTSTANDING ACHIEVEMENT IN VIDEO TAPE EDITING
For a single episode of a regular or limited series; or for a special program

GARY ANDERSON and JIM McELROY, Judgement: The Court-Martial Of Lt. William Calley; ABC Theatre (ABC)
NICK V. GIORDANO and GEORGE GURUNIAN, California Jam; Wide World in Concert (ABC)
JERRY GREENE, The Missiles Of October; ABC Theatre (ABC)

OUTSTANDING ACHIEVEMENT IN TECHNICAL DIRECTION AND ELECTRONIC CAMERAWORK
For a single episode of a regular or limited series; or for a special program

ERNIE BUTTELMAN, Technical Director; JIM ANGEL, JIM BALDEN, RON BROOKS and ART LaCOMBE, Cameramen; The Missiles Of October; ABC Theatre (ABC)
HEINO RIPP, Technical Director; JON OLSON, BOB KEYS, JOHN

JAMES and KURT TONNESSEN, Cameramen; IBM Presents Clarence Darrow (NBC)
HEINO RIPP and LOU FUSARI, Technical Directors; ROY HOLM, TONY YARLETT, RICK LOMBARDO, BOB KEYS and RAY FIGELSKI, Cameramen; The Perry Como Christmas Show (CBS)

OUTSTANDING ACHIEVEMENT IN LIGHTING DIRECTION

For a single episode of a regular or limited series, or for a special program

JOHN FRESCHI, The Perry Como Christmas Show (CBS)
LON STUCKY, IBM Presents Clarence Darrow (NBC)

OUTSTANDING CHILDREN'S SPECIAL

For specials which were broadcast during the evening Emmy(s) to Executive Producer(s) and Producer(s)

YES, VIRGINIA, THERE IS A SANTA CLAUS, Burt Rosen, Executive Producer; Bill Melendez and Mort Green, Producers (ABC)
BE MY VALENTINE, CHARLIE BROWN, Lee Mendelson, Executive Producer; Bill Melendez, Producer (CBS)
DR. SEUSS' THE HOOBER-BLOOB HIGHWAY, David H. DePatie, Executive Producer; Friz Freleng and Ted Geisel, Producers (CBS)
IT'S THE EASTER BEAGLE, CHARLIE BROWN, Lee Mendelson, Executive Producer; Bill Melendez, Producer (CBS)

OUTSTANDING SPORTS EVENT

For a non-edited program (for a program which, when broadcast, was not edited)

JIMMY CONNORS VS. ROD LAVER TENNIS CHALLENGE, Frank Chirkinian, Executive Producer (CBS)
NFL MONDAY NIGHT FOOTBALL, Roone Arldedge, Executive Producer; Don Ohlmeyer, Producer (ABC)
NCAA FOOTBALL, Roone Arledge, Executive Producer; Chuck Howard, Producer (ABC)
ABC CHAMPIONSHIP GOLF, Roone Arledge, Executive Producer; Chuck Howard, Producer (ABC)
NBA CHAMPIONSHIP GAME, Chuck Milton, Producer (CBS)
NATIONAL FOOTBALL LEAGUE GAME - WASHINGTON VS. DALLAS, Chuck Milton and Tom O'Neill, Producers (CBS)
JACKIE GLEASON INVERRARY CLASSIC, John Koushouris, Executive Producer; Joe O'Rourke and Herb Kaplan, Producers (HTN)
ANDY WILLIAMS SAN DIEGO OPEN, John Koushouris, Producer (HTN)
MADISON SQUARE GARDEN EVENTS, Jack Simon, Producer (HTN)
1974 WORLD SERIES, Scotty Connal, Executive Producer; Roy Hammerman, Producer (NBC)
NBC MONDAY NIGHT BASEBALL, Scotty Connal, Executive Producer; Roy Hammerman, Producer (NBC)
AFC FOOTBALL PLAYOFFS, Scotty Connal, Executive Producer; Don Ellis and Ted Nathanson, Producers (NBC)
SPALDING INTERNATIONAL MIXED DOUBLES TENNIS CHAMPIONSHIP, Ron Devillier, Executive Producer; Renate Cole, Producer (PBS)
NATIONAL BICYCLE TRACK CHAMPIONSHIPS, Alf Steele, Executive Producer (PBS)
ATP SUMMER TENNIS TOUR, Greg Harney, Executive Producer (PBS)
WORLD FOOTBALL LEAGUE CHAMPIONSHIP, Edward Einhorn, Executive Producer; Joe Gallagher, Producer (TVS)
UCLA-NOTRE DAME BASKETBALL, Edward Einhorn, Executive Producer; Howard Zuckerman, Producer (TVS)
NCAA BASKETBALL, Edward Einhorn, Executive Producer; Howard Zuckerman, Producer (TVS)

OUTSTANDING SPORTS PROGRAM

For an edited program (for a program which, when broadcast, contained edited segments)

WIDE WORLD OF SPORTS, Roone Arledge, Executive Producer; Doug Wilson, Ned Steckel, Dennis Lewin, John Martin and Chet Forte, Producers (ABC)
THE SUPERSTARS, Roone Arledge, Executive Producer; Don Ohlmeyer, Producer (ABC)
THE AMERICAN SPORTSMAN, Roone Arledge, Executive Producer; Neil Cunningham, Pat Smith, Curt Gowdy, Bob Duncan, Neil Goodwin, Producers (ABC)
CBS SPORTS SPECTACULAR, Frank Chirkinian, Executive Producer; Perry Smith, Producer (CBS)
NFL ON CBS, William Fitts, Executive Producer; Tom O'Neill, Producer (CBS)
NBA ON CBS, Perry Smith and Chuck Milton, Producers (CBS)
THE BASEBALL WORLD OF JOE GARAGIOLA, Gates Brown-Parts 1 & 2; Joe Garagiola, Executive Producer; Don Ellis, Producer (NBC)
THE BASEBALL WORLD OF JOE GARAGIOLA, Old Ball Parks; Joe Garagiola, Executive Producer; Don Ellis, Producer (NBC)
SUPER BOWL IX PRE-GAME SHOW, Scotty Connal, Executive Producer; Dick Auerbach, Producer (NBC)
THE WAY IT WAS, Gerry Gross, Executive Producer (PBS)
VICTOR AWARDS, David Marmel, Executive Producer; Lou Rudolph, Producer (TVS)
USA-CHINA BASKETBALL HIGHLIGHTS, Edwards Einhorn, Executive Producer; Howard Zuckerman, Producer (TVS)

OUTSTANDING SPORTS BROADCASTER

JIM McKAY, Wide World Of Sports (ABC)
HOWARD COSELL, Monday Night Football (ABC)
KEITH JACKSON, NCAA Football (ABC)
FRANK GIFFORD, Monday Night Football (ABC)
CHRIS SCHENKEL, ABC Championship Golf (ABC)
VIN SCULLY, Jimmy Connors Vs. Rod Laver Tennis Challenge (CBS)
PAT SUMMERALL, NFL Football (CBS)
BRENT MUSBURGER, NBA Basketball (CBS)
JACK WHITAKER, NBA All Star Game (CBS)
KEN SQUIER, CBS Sports Spectacular (CBS)
CURT GOWDY, AFC Football Playoffs (NBC)
DON MEREDITH, Super Bowl IX (NBC)
JOE GARAGIOLA, The Baseball World of Joe Garagiola; Gates Brown-Parts 1 & 2 (NBC)
JIM SIMPSON, Wimbledon Tennis (NBC)
TIM RYAN, 1974 Stanley Cup Playoffs (NBC)
BUDD COLLINS, Spalding International Mixed Doubles Tennis Championship (PBS)
JUDY DIXON, Spalding International Mixed Doubles Tennis Championship (PBS)
CURT GOWDY, The Way It Was (PBS)

THE AREAS

(Possibility of One Award, More Than One Award, or No Award)

SPECIAL CLASSIFICATION OF OUTSTANDING PROGRAM AND INDIVIDUAL ACHIEVEMENT

An Award for unique program and individual achievements, which does not fall into a specific category, or is not otherwise recognized

THE AMERICAN FILM INSTITUTE SALUTE TO JAMES CAGNEY, George Stevens, Jr., Executive Producer; Paul W Keyes, Producer (CBS)
THE AMERICAN FILM INSTITUTE SALUTE TO ORSON WELLS, George Stevens, Jr., Executive Producer; Paul W Keyes, Producer (CBS)
ALISTAIR COOKE, Host, Masterpiece Theatre (PBS)
THE DICK CAVETT SHOW, John Gilroy, Producer; Dick Cavett, Star (ABC)
THAT'S ENTERTAINMENT: 50 YEARS OF MGM, ABC Wide World of Entertainment, Jack Haley, Jr., Executive Producer; Jimmie Baker, Producer (ABC)
86TH ANNUAL PASADENA TOURNAMENT OF ROSES PARADE, Dick Schneider, Producer (NBC)
TOM SNYDER, Host, Tomorrow (NBC)
JACK STEWART, Art Director; JOHN HUENERS, Set Decorator; Bicentennial Minutes (CBS)

OUTSTANDING ACHIEVEMENT IN SPECIAL MUSICAL MATERIAL

For a song (which must have both music and lyrics), a theme for a series, or special material for a variety program providing the first usage of this material was written expressly for television

ALAN and MARILYN BERGMAN, and BILLY GOLDENBERG, Queen Of The Stardust Ballroom (CBS)
CY COLEMAN and BOB WELLS, Shirley MacLaine: If They Could See Me Now (CBS)
MORTON STEVENS, Police Woman; Theme (NBC)
EARL BROWN and BILLY BARNES, Cher (with Bette Midler, Flip Wilson and Elton John) (CBS)
JOSE FELICIANO and JANNA MERLYN FELICIANO; Chico and The Man; Theme (NBC)

OUTSTANDING ACHIEVEMENT IN COSTUME DESIGN

For a single episode of a series; or for a special program

GUY VERHILLE, The Legend of Lizzie Borden; Special World Premiere; ABC Monday Night Movie (ABC)
MARGARET FURSE, Love Among The Ruins; ABC Theatre (ABC)
BRUCE WALKUP, Queen Of The Stardust Ballroom (CBS)
BOB MACKIE, Cher (with Bette Midler, Flip Wilson and Elton John) (CBS)
RET TURNER, The Sonny Comedy Revue (with McLean Stevenson and Joey Heatherton) (ABC)

OUTSTANDING ACHIEVEMENT IN MAKE-UP

For a single episode of a series; or for a special program

HARRY BLAKE, STAN WINSTON, JIM KAIL, RALPH GULKO, BOB OSTERMANN, TOM COLE and LARRY ABBOTT; Masquerade Party (Synd)
MARK R. BUSSAN, The Ambassador; Benjamin Franklin (CBS)
DAN STRIEPEKE and JOHN CHAMBERS, Twigs (CBS)

OUSTANDING ACHIEVEMENT IN ANY AREA OF CREATIVE TECHNICAL CRAFTS

An Award for individual technical craft achievement which does not fall into a specific category, and is not otherwise recognized

EDIE PANDA, Hairstylist; The Ambassador; Benjamin Franklin (CBS)
DOUG NELSON and NORM SCHWARTZ, Wide World In Concert; Double System Sound Editing and Synchronization For Stereophonic Broadcasting Of Television Programs; Series (ABC)
LARRY GERMAIN, Hairstylist; If I Should Wake Before I Die; Little House On The Prairie (NBC)

OUTSTANDING INDIVIDUAL ACHIEVEMENT IN SPORTS PROGRAMMING

For individuals who may be directors, writers, cinematographers, technical directors and electronic cameramen, sound mixers, film editors, video tape editors, lighting directors and graphic designers (for graphic design and title sequences)

GENE SCHWARZ, Technical Director; 1974 World Series (NBC)
HERB ALTMAN, Film Editor; The Baseball World Of Joe Garagiola (NBC)
COREY LEIBLE, LEN BASILE, JACK BENNETT, LOU GERARD and RAY FIGELSKI, Electronic Cameramen; 1974 Stanley Cup Playoffs (NBC)
JOHN PUMO, CHARLES D'ONOFRIO, FRANK FLORIO, Technical Directors; GEORGE KLIMCSAK, ROBERT KANIA, HAROLD HOFFMANN, HERMAN LANG, GEORGE DRAGO, WALT DENIEAR, STAN GOULD, AL DIAMOND, CHARLES ARMSTRONG, AL BRANTLEY, SIG MEYERS, FRANK McSPEDON, GEORGE F. NAEDER, JAMES MURPHY, JAMES McCARTHY, VERN SURPHLIS, AL LORETO, GORDON SWEENEY, JO SIDLO, WILLIAM HATHAWAY, GENE PESCALEK and CURLY FONOROW, Cameramen; Masters Tournament (CBS)
LARRY KAMM, LOU VOLPICELLI, BRICE WEISMAN, NED STECKEL, ANDY SIDARIS and CHET FORTE, Directors; WIDE WORLD OF SPORTS (ABC)
WERNER GUNTHER, JOHN BRODERICK and JOHN IRVINE, Technical Directors; ANDY ARMENTANI, DREW DeROSA, JIM HENEGHAN, JOHN MORREALE, JOE NESI, MIKE REBICH, JACK HIMELFARB, STEVE CILIBERTO, JESSE KOHN, JOE STEFANONI, STU GOODMAN, JOE SCHIAVO, BOB HAMMOND, ART PEFFER, DICK SPANOS, ART FERRARE, GENE WOOD, ROY HUTCHINGS, BILL KARVELAS, RONNIE STERCKX, JOE SAPIENZA, BOB WOLFE, JOHN CRONIN, CARL BROWN, ROBERT COPPER, DICK KERR, MORT LEVIN, BOB BERNSTEIN, JERRY DOUD and JACK DORFMAN, Cameramen; U.S. Open (ABC)
WILLIAM MORRIS and WERNER GUNTHER, Technical Directors; ANDY ARMENTANI, DREW DeROSA, JIM HENEGHAN, JOHN MORREALE, JOE NESI, MIKE REBICH, JACK HIMELFARB, STEVE CILIBERTO, JESSE KOHN, JOE STEFANONI, STU GOODMAN, JOE SCHIAVO, BILL SULLIVAN, STEVE NIKIFOR, JACK DORFMAN and BOB LOPES, Cameramen; Indianapolis 500 (ABC)
JOHN PETERSON and TONY ZACCARO, Film Editors; Wide World Of Sports (ABC)
JOHN CROAK, JOHN DeLISA, CHESTER PAWLAK, MARV GENCH, ALEX MOSKOVIC, JACK HIERL, TONY GRECO, ERSKINE ROBERTS, ART VOLK and HARVEY BEAL, Video Tape Editors; Wide World Of Sports (ABC)
JOHN CROAK, JOHN DeLISA, ART VOLK, RON ACKERMAN, MARV GENCH, ALEX MOSKOVIC and NICK MAZUR, Video Tape Editors; The Superstars (ABC)
PAT SMITH, Writer; The American Sportsman (ABC)
JACK SIMON, Director; New York Mets Baseball (HTN)
JOE O'ROURKE, Director; Professional Championship Golf (HTN)
HARRY COYLE, Director; 1974 World Series (NBC)
TED NATHANSON, Director; AFC Football Playoffs (NBC)
HOWARD NEEF and BARRY WINNIK, Cinematographers; The Baseball World Of Joe Garagiola; Gates Brown-Parts 1 & 2 (NBC)
MURRAY VECCHIO, BILL TOBEY, BILL ROSE, JOHN O'CONNOR, Videotape (Slow Motion) Editors; Orange Bowl (NBC)
SANDY BELL, FRANK VILOT, CHUCK FRANKLIN, JIM ANGERAMI and JOHN BURKHART, Technical Directors; DICK DOUGLAS, GEORGE KLIMCSAK, AL DIAMOND, FRANK McSPEDON, JOHN LINCOLN, PHIL WALSH, STAN GOULD, MIKE ENGLISH, ROBERT HELLER, DAVID GRAHAM, WALT DENIEAR, ROBERT CHANDLER, HAROLD HOFFMAN, GENE SAVITT, DAVE LEVENSON, GEORGE ERICKSON, CURLY FONAROW, TOM McCONNELL, FRED DANSEREAU, BOB FAETH, GEORGE DRAGO, JIM MURPHY, GEORGE F. NAEDER, JO SOKOTA, PAT McBRIDE, AL LORETO, DAVE LEAVEL, JERRY WEAVER, BOB CHANEY, FRED SCHULTZ, TONY BUTTS, DANNY IRELAND, Cameramen; NBA Basketball (CBS)
ANGEL J. GULINO, BOB BROWN, ED DAHLBERG, DICK OHLDACKER, SAM LANE, TOM DUFFY and FRANK HICKS, Sound Mixers; NBA Basketball (CBS)
PETE REED, Sound Mixer; Jimmy Connors Vs. Rod Laver Tennis Challenge (CBS)
SANDY GROSSMAN, Director; NBA Basketball (CBS)
BOB DAILEY, Director; Jimmy Connors Vs. Rod Laver Tennis Challenge (CBS)

SPECIAL AWARDS

OUTSTANDING ACHIEVEMENT IN ENGINEERING DEVELOPMENT

COLUMBIA BROADCASTING SYSTEM for spearheading the development and realization of the Electronic News Gathering System
NIPPON ELECTRIC COMPANY for development of digital television Frame Synchronizers
Citation to THE SOCIETY OF MOTION PICTURE AND TELEVISION

ENGINEERS for the technical development of the Unversal Video Tape Time Code

TRUSTEES AWARDS

ELMER LOWER, Vice President, Corporate Affairs, American Broadcastiing Companies, Inc.
DR. PETER GOLDMARK, President, Goldmark Laboratories, Stamford, Connecticut

THE NATIONAL AWARD FOR COMMUNITY SERVICE

THE WILLOWBROOK CASE: THE PEOPLE VS. THE STATE OF NEW YORK, WABC-TV, New York, New York
BREAST SURGERY: REBIRTH OR BETRAYAL, WXYZ-TV Detroit, Michigan
FOCUS 30, KYTV, Springfield, Missouri
GRANDPEOPLE, WPBT(Educational Station), No. Miami, Florida
THE OCCUPANT IN THE SINGLE ROOM, WNET (Educational Station), New York, New York
SENILITY, A STATE OF MIND, KSL, Salt Lake City, Utah
SMOKE AND STEEL, WKY-TV,Oklahoma City, Oklahoma
TROUBLE IN THE GHETTO, WAGA-TV, Atlanta, Georgia
WHY ME? KNXT, Los Angeles, California
WITHOUT FEAR, WKYC-TV, Cleveland, Ohio

THE 1973/74 INTERNATIONAL AWARDS

FICTION

MR AXELFORD'S ANGEL, Yorkshire Television Limited, Lonndon, England
DON JUAN, Television Espanola, Madrid, Spain
THE BENNY HILL SHOW, Thames Television Limited, London, England
SIX DAYS OF JUSTICE: THE COMPLAINT,Thames Televisin Limited, London, England
THE GOODIES AND THE BEANSTALK, British Broadcastig Corporation, London, England

NON-FICTION

AQUARIUS: HELLO DALI!, London Weekend Television, London, England
CTV INQUIRY: KEEP OUT OF THE REACH OF ADULTS, CTV Television Network, Limited, Ontario, Canada
KATARAGAMA: A GOD FOR ALL SEASONS, Granada Television Limited, Manchester, Great Britain
ELLESMERE LAND, Canadian Broadcasting Corporation, Ontario, Canada
UNTAMED WORLD: THE GREY GOOSE, CTV Television Network, Limited, Ontario, Canada

THE 1973/74 INTERNATIONAL DIRECTORATE EMMY AWARD

DR. JOSEPH V. CHARYK, President Communications Satellite Corporation

THE 1974/75 INTERNATIONAL AWARDS

FICTION

COMETS AMONG THE STARS, ATV Network Limited, Hertfordshire, England
MAD IN AUSTRIA, ORF, Vienna, Austria
JENNIE: HIS BORROWED PLUMES, Thames Television Limited, London, England
MR. SING MY HEARTS DELIGHT, Radio Telefis Eireann, Dublin, Ireland
THE EVACUEES, British Broadcasting Corporation, London, England
DE VERRASSING, Nederlandse Omroep Stichting, The Netherlands

NON-FICTION

TRAVELS THROUGH LIFE WITH LEACOCK, Canadian Broacasting Corporation, Ontario, Canada
AFTER 30 YEARS IN JUNGLE: HOMECOMING OF A JAPANESE SOLDIER, Fuji Telecasting Company, Limited, Tokyo, Japan
PILGER: MR. NIXON'S SECRET LEGACY, ATV Network Limited, Hertfordshire, England
INSIDE STORY: MAREK, British Broadcasting Corporation, London, England
THE SEARCH FOR THE SHINOHARA, Survival Anglia Limited, Lonndon, England

THE 1974/75 INTERNATIONAL DIRECTORATE AWARD

MR. JUNZO IMAMICHI, Chairman Of The Board Tokyo Broadcasting System, Inc

DAYTIME PROGRAM AND INDIVIDUAL ACHIEVEMENTS

(One Award Only in Each of the Following Categories)

OUTSTANDING DAYTIME DRAMA SERIES

Emmy(s) to Executive Producer(s) and/or Creator(s) and Producer(s)

THE YOUNG AND THE RESTLESS, John J. Conboy, Producer; William J. Bell and Lee Phillip Bell, Creators (CBS)
DAYS OF OUR LIVES, Mrs. Ted Corday, Executive Producer; Ted Corday, Irna Phillips and Allan Chase, Creators; Jack Herzberg, Producer (NBC)
ANOTHER WORLD, Paul Rauch, Executive Producer; Joe Rothenberger and Mary E. Bonner, Producers; Irna Phillips and William J. Bell, Creators (NBC)

OUTSTANDING DAYTIME DRAMA SPECIAL

Emmy(s) to Executive Producer(s) and Producer(s)

THE GIRL WHO COULDN'T LOSE, ABC Afternoon Playbreak; Ira Barmak, Executive Producer; Lila Garrett, Producer (ABC)
THE LAST RIDE OF SALEM, ABC Afternoon Playbreak; Robert Michael Lewis, Executive Producer; George Paris, Producer (ABC)

OUTSTANDING GAME OR AUDIENCE PARTICIPATION SHOW

Emmy(s) to Executive Producer(s) and Producer(s)

HOLLYWOOD SQUARES, Merrill Heatter and Bob Quigley, Executive Producers; Jay Redack, Producer (NBC)
THE $10,000 PYRAMID, Bob Stewart, Executive Producer; Anne Marie Schmitt, Producer (ABC)
JEOPARDY!, Robert H. Rubin, Executive Producer; Lynette Williams, Producer (NBC)
LET'S MAKE A DEAL, Stefan Hatos, Executive Producer; Alan Gilbert, Producer (ABC)

OUTSTANDING TALK, SERVICE OR VARIETY SERIES

Emmy(s) to Executive Producer(s) and Producer(s)

DINAH!, Henry Jaffe and Carolyn Raskin, Executive Producers; Fred Tatashore, Producer (Synd)
THE MIKE DOUGLAS SHOW, Jack Reilly, Executive Producer; Woody Fraser, Producer (Synd)
TODAY, Stuart Schulberg, Executive Producer; Douglas P. Sinsel and Gene Farinet, Producers (NBC)

OUTSTANDING ENTERTAINMENT CHILDREN'S SPECIAL

Emmy(s) to Executive Producer(s) and Producer(s)

HARLEQUIN, The CBS Festival Of Lively Arts For Young People; Edward Villella, Executive Poducer; Gardner Compton, Producer (CBS)
AILEY CELEBRATES ELLINGTON, The CBS Festival Of Lively Arts For Young People; Herman Krawitz, Executive Producer; Bob Weiner, Producer (CBS)
WHAT MAKES A GERSHWIN TUNE A GERSHWIN TUNE?, New York Philharmonic Young People's Concert; Roger Englander, Producer (CBS)

OUTSTANDING ENTERTAINMENT CHILDREN'S SERIES

Emmy(s) to Executive Producer(s) and Producer(s)

STAR TREK, Lou Scheimer and Norm Prescott, Producers (NBC)
CAPTAIN KANGAROO, Jimmy Hirshfeld, Producer (CBS)
THE PINK PANTHER, David H. DePatie and Friz Freleng, Producers (NBC)

OUTSTANDING ACTOR IN A DAYTIME DRAMA SERIES

MACDONALD CAREY, Days Of Our Lives (NBC)
JOHN BERADINO, General Hospital (ABC)
BILL HAYES, Days Of Our Lives (NBC)

OUTSTANDING ACTOR IN A DAYTIME DRAMA SPECIAL

BRADFORD DILLMAN, The Last Bride Of Salem; ABC Afternoon Playbreak (ABC)
JACK CARTER, The Girl Who Couldn't Lose; ABC Afternoon Playbreak (ABC)
BERT CONVY, Oh! Baby, Baby, Baby. . .;ABC Afternoon Playbreak (ABC)

OUTSTANDING ACTRESS IN A DAYTIME DRAMA SERIES

SUSAN FLANNERY, Days Of Our Lives (NBC)
RACHEL AMES, General Hospital (ABC)
SUSAN SEAFORTH, Days Of Our Lives (NBC)
RUTH WARRICK, All My Children (ABC)

OUTSTANDING ACTRESS IN A DAYTIME DRAMA SPECIAL

KAY LENZ, Heart In Hiding; ABC Afternoon Playbreak (ABC)
DIANE BAKER, Can I Save My Children?; ABC Afternoon Playbreak (ABC)
JULIE KAVNER, The Girl Who Couldn't Lose; ABC Afternoon Playbreak (ABC)
LOIS NETTLETON, The Last Bride Of Salem; ABC Afternoon Playbreak (ABC)

OUTSTANDING HOST IN A GAME OR AUDIENCE PARTICIPATION SHOW

PETER MARSHALL, The Hollywood Squares (NBC)
MONTY HALL, Let's Make A Deal (ABC)
GENE RAYBURN, Match Game '75 (CBS)

OUTSTANDING HOST OR HOSTESS IN A TALK, SERVICE OR VARIETY SERIES

BARBARA WALTERS, Today (NBC)
MIKE DOUGLAS, The Mike Douglas Show (Synd)
DINAH SHORE, Dinah! (Synd)
JIM HARTZ, Today (NBC)

OUTSTANDING INDIVIDUAL DIRECTOR FOR A DAYTIME DRAMA SERIES

For a single episode

RICHARD DUNLAP, The Young and The Restless (CBS)
IRA CIRKER, Another World (NBC)
JOSEPH BEHAR, Days Of Our Lives (NBC)

OUTSTANDING INDIVIDUAL DIRECTOR FOR A DAYTIME SPECIAL PROGRAM

MORT LACHMAN, The Girl Who Couldn't Lose; ABC Afternoon Playbreak (ABC)
WALTER C. MILLER, Can I Save My Children?; ABC Afternoon Playbreak (ABC)

OUTSTANDING INDIVIDUAL DIRECTOR FOR A GAME OR AUDIENCE PARTICIPATION SHOW

For a single episode

JEROME SHAW, The Hollywood Squares; October 28, 1974 (NBC)
JOSEPH BEHAR, Let's Make A Deal; March 6, 1975 (ABC)

OUTSTANDING INDIVIDUAL DIRECTOR FOR A DAYTIME VARIETY PROGRAM

For a single episode

GLEN SWANSON, Dinah!; Dinah Salutes Broadway (with Ethel Merman, Bobby Morse, Michelle Lee, Phil Silvers and Jack Cassidy) (Synd)
DICK CARSON, The Merv Griffin Show (with Robert Goulet, Louis Prima and Shecky Greene) (Synd)

OUTSTANDING WRITING FOR A DAYTIME DRAMA SERIES

For a single episode of a series; or for the entire series

HARDING LEMAY, TOM KING, CARLES KOZLOFF, JAN MERLIN and DOUGLAS MARLAND, Another World; Series (NBC)
WILLIAM J. BELL, The Young and The Restless; October 22, 1974 (CBS)
WILLIAM J. BELL, PAT FALKEN SMITH and BILL REGA; Days Of Our Lives; November 21, 1974 (NBC)

OUTSTANDING WRITING FOR A DAYTIME SPECIAL PROGRAM

AUDREY DAVIS LEVIN, Heart In Hiding; ABC Afternoon Playbreak (ABC)
RUTH BROOKS FLIPPEN, Oh! Baby, Baby, Baby. . .; ABC Afternoon Playbreak (ABC)
LILA GARRETT and SANFORD KRINSKI, The Girl Who Couldn't Lose; ABC Afternoon Playbreak (ABC)

THE DAYTIME AREAS
(Possibility of One Award, More Than One Award, or No Award)

OUTSTANDING INDIVIDUAL ACHIEVEMENT IN DAYTIME PROGRAMMING
For a single episode of a series or for a special program
PAUL LYNDE, Performer; The Hollywood Squares (NBC)
JAY REDACK, HARRY FRIEDMAN, GARY JOHNSON, HAROLD SCHNEIDER, RICK KELLARD and STEVE LEVITCH, Writers; The Hollywood Squares; November 22, 1974 (NBC)
STAS PYKA, Graphic Design and Title Sequence, How To Survive A Marriage (NBC)

OUTSTANDING INDIVIDUAL ACHIEVEMENT IN CHILDREN'S PROGRAMMING
For a single episode of a series; or for a special program
ELINOR BUNIN, Graphic Design and Title Sequences; Funshine Saturday & Sunday; Umbrella Title Animations For Saturday & Sunday Morning Children's Programming (ABC)
BOB KEESHAN, Performer; Captain Kangaroo (CBS)
BILL COSBY, Performer; Highlights Of Ringling Bros. Barnum & Bailey Circus; Bell System Family Theatre; (NBC)
CHARLES M. SCHULZ, Writer; Be My Valentine, Charlie Brown (CBS)

1975/76

THE CATEGORIES

Entertainment Program and Individual Achievements
(One Award Only In Each of the Following Categories)

OUTSTANDING COMEDY SERIES
Emmy(s) to Executive Producer(s) and/or Producer(s)
THE MARY TYLER MOORE SHOW; James L. Brooks and Allan Burns, Executive Producers; Ed Weinberger and Stan Daniels, Producers (CBS)
ALL IN THE FAMILY; Hal Kanter, Norman Lear and Woody Kling, Executive Producers; Lou Derman and Bill Davenport, Producers (CBS)
M*A*S*H; Gene Reynolds and Larry Gelbart, Producers (CBS)
WELCOME BACK KOTTER; James Komack, Executive Producer; Alan Sacks, George Yanok and Eric Cohen, Producers (ABC)
BARNEY MILLER; Danny Arnold, Executive Producer; Chris Hayward and Arne Sultan, Producers (ABC)

OUTSTANDING DRAMA SERIES
Emmy(s) to Executive Producer(s) and/or Producer(s)
POLICE STORY; David Gerber and Stanley Kallis, Executive Producers; Liam O'Brien and Carl Pingitore, Producers (NBC)
BARETTA; Bernard L. Kowalski, Executive Producer; Jo Swerling, Jr., Robert Harris, Howie Horwitz and Robert Lewin, Producers (ABC)
COLUMBO; NBC Sunday Mystery Movie; Everett Chambers, Producer (NBC)
THE STREETS OF SAN FRANCISCO; Quinn Martin, Executive Producer; William Robert Yates, Producer (ABC)

OUTSTANDING COMEDY-VARIETY OR MUSIC SERIES
Emmy(s) to Executive Producer(s) and/or Producer(s) and Star(s), if applicable
NBC'S SATURDAY NIGHT; Lorne Michaels, Producer (NBC)
THE CAROL BURNETT SHOW; Joe Hamilton, Executive Producer; Ed Simmons, Producer; Carol Burnett, Star (CBS)

OUTSTANDING LIMITED SERIES
Emmy(s) to Executive Producer(s) and/or Producer(s)
UPSTAIRS, DOWNSTAIRS; Masterpiece Theatre; Rex Firkin, Executive Producer; John Hawkesworth, Producer (PBS)
JENNIE: LADY RANDOLPH CHURCHILL; Great Performances; Stella Richman, Executive Producer; Andrew Brown, Producer (PBS)
RICH MAN, POOR MAN; Harve Bennett, Executive Producer; Jon Epstein, Producer (ABC)
THE ADAMS CHRONICLES; Jac Venza, Executive Producer; Virginia Kassel, Series Producer; Paul Bogart, Robert Costello, James Cellan Jones and Fred Coe, Producers (PBS)
THE LAW; William Sackheim, Producer (NBC)

OUTSTANDING SPECIAL - DRAMA OR COMEDY
Emmy(s) to Executive Producer(s) and/or Producer(s)
ELEANOR AND FRANKLIN; ABC Theatre; David Susskind, Executive Producer; Harry Sherman and Audrey Maas, Producers (ABC)
BABE; Norman Felton and Stanley Rubin, Producers (CBS)
A MOON FOR THE MISBEGOTTEN; ABC Theatre; David Suskind and Audrey Maas, Producers (ABC)
FEAR ON TRIAL; Alan Landsburg and Larry Savadove, Executive Producers; Stanley Chase, Producer (CBS)
THE LINDBERGH KIDNAPPING CASE; NBC World Premiere Movie; David Gerber, Executive Producer; Buzz Kulik, Producer (NBC)

OUTSTANDING SPECIAL - COMEDY-VARIETY OR MUSIC
Emmy(s) to Executive Producer(s) and/or Producer(s), and Star(s), if applicable
GYPSY IN MY SOUL; William O. Harbach, Executive Producers; Cy Coleman and Fred Ebb, Producers; Shirley MacLaine, Star (CBS)
THE MONTY PYTHON SHOW; Wide World: Special; Ian McNaughton, Producer (ABC)
JOHN DENVER ROCKY MOUNTAIN CHRISTMAS; Jerry Weintraub, Executive Producer; Al Rogers and Rich Eustis, Producers; John Denver, Star (ABC)
STEVE AND EYDIE: 'OUR LOVE IS HERE TO STAY'; Gary Smith, Executive Producer; Dwight Hemion, Producer; Steve Lawrence and Eydie Gorme, Stars (CBS)
LILY TOMLIN; Irene Pinn, Executive Producer; Jane Wagner and Lorne Michaels, Producers; Lily Tomlin, Star (ABC)

OUTSTANDING CLASSICAL MUSIC PROGRAM
For a special program or a series Emmy(s) to Executive Producers(s) and/or Producer(s) and Stars, if applicable
BERNSTEIN AND THE NEW YORK PHILHARMONIC; Great Performances; Klaus Hallig and Harry Kraut, Executive Producers; David Griffiths, Producer; Leonard Bernstein, Star (PBS)
THREE BY BALANCHINE WITH THE NEW YORK CITY BALLET; Great Performances; Dr. Reiner E. Moritz and Emile Ardolino, Producers (PBS)
ARTHUR RUBINSTEIN - CHOPIN; Great Performances; Fritz Buttenstedt, Executive Producer; Fritz Buttenstedt, and David Griffiths, Producers; Arthur Rubinstein, Star (PBS)
DANCE IN AMERICA: CITY CENTER JOFFREY BALLET; Jac Venza, Executive Producer; Merrill Brockway, Series Producer; Emile Ar-

dolino, Producer (PBS)
LIVE FROM LINCOLN CENTER; John Goberman, Executive Producer; David Griffiths and Ken Campbell, Producers; Andre Previn and Van Cliburn, Stars (PBS)

OUTSTANDING LEAD ACTOR IN A COMEDY SERIES
JACK ALBERTSON; Chico And The Man (NBC)
HAL LINDEN; Barney Miller (ABC)
ALAN ALDA; M*A*S*H (CBS)
HENRY WINKLER; Happy Days (ABC)

OUTSTANDING LEAD ACTOR IN A DRAMA SERIES
PETER FALK; Colombo, NBC Sunday Mystery Movie (NBC)
KARL MALDEN; The Streets Of San Francisco (ABC)
JAMES GARNER; The Rockford Files (NBC)

OUTSTANDING LEAD ACTOR IN A LIMITED SERIES
HAL HOLBROOK; Sandburg's Lincoln (NBC)
NICK NOLTE; Rich Man, Poor Man (ABC)
PETER STRAUSS; Rich Man, Poor Man (ABC)
GEORGE GRIZZARD; The Adams Chronicles (PBS)

OUTSTANDING LEAD ACTOR IN A DRAMA OR COMEDY SPECIAL
ANTHONY HOPKINS; The Lindbergh Kidnapping Case; NBC World Premiere Movie (NBC)
WILLIAM DEVANE; Fear On Trial (CBS)
JACK LEMMON; The Entertainer (NBC)
EDWARD HERRMANN; Eleanor And Franklin; ABC Theatre (ABC)
JASON ROBARDS; A Moon For The Misbegotten; ABC Theater (ABC)

OUTSTANDING LEAD ACTOR FOR A SINGLE APPEARANCE IN A DRAMA OR COMEDY SERIES
EDWARD ASNER; Rich Man, Poor Man (ABC)
ROBERT REED; The Fourth Sex; Medical Center, Parts 1 & 2 (CBS)
TONY MUSANTE; The Quality Of Mercy; Medical Story (NBC)
BILL BIXBY; Police Buff; The Streets Of San Francisco (ABC)

OUTSTANDING LEAD ACTRESS IN A COMEDY SERIES
MARY TYLER MOORE; The Mary Tyler Moore Show (CBS)
BEATRICE ARTHUR; Maude (CBS)
VALERIE HARPER; Rhoda (CBS)
LEE GRANT; Fay (NBC)
CLORIS LEACHMAN; Phyllis (CBS)

OUTSTANDING LEAD ACTRESS IN A DRAMA SERIES
MICHAEL LEARNED; The Waltons (CBS)
ANNE MEARA: Kate McShane (CBS)
ANGIE DICKINSON; Police Woman (NBC)
BRENDA VACCARO; Sara (CBS)

OUTSTANDING LEAD ACTRESS IN A LIMITED SERIES
ROSEMARY HARRIS; Notorious Woman; Masterpiece Theatre (PBS)
LEE REMICK; Jennie: Lady Randolph Churchill; Great Performances (PBS)
SUSAN BLAKELY; Rich Man, Poor Man (ABC)
JEAN MARSH; Upstairs, Downstairs; Masterpiece Theatre (PBS)

OUTSTANDING LEAD ACTRESS IN A DRAMA OR COMEDY SPECIAL
SUSAN CLARK; Babe (CBS)
COLLEEN DEWHURST; A Moon For The Misbegotten; ABC Theatre (ABC)
JANE ALEXANDER; Eleanor And Franklin; ABC Theatre (NBC)
SADA THOMPSON; The Entertainer (NBC)

OUTSTANDING LEAD ACTRESS FOR A SINGLE APPEARANCE IN A DRAMA OR COMEDY SERIES
KATHRYN WALKER; John Adams, Lawyer; The Adams Chronicles (PBS)
HELEN HAYES; Retire In Sunny Hawaii...Forever; Hawaii Five-O (CBS)
SHEREE NORTH; How Do You Know What Hurts Me?; Marcus Welby, M.D. (ABC)
PAMELA PAYTON-WRIGHT; John Quincy Adams, Diplomat; The Adams Chronicles (PBS)
MARTHA RAYE; Greed; McMillan & Wife; NBC Sunday Mystery Movie (NBC)

OUTSTANDING CONTINUING PERFORMANCE BY A SUPPORTING ACTOR IN A COMEDY SERIES
For a regular or limited series
TED KNIGHT; The Mary Tyler Moore Show (CBS)
GARY R. BURGHOFF; M*A*S*H (CBS)
ABE VIGODA; Barney Miller (ABC)
EDWARD ASNER; The Mary Tyler Moore Show (CBS)
HARRY MORGAN; M*A*S*H (CBS)

OUTSTANDING CONTINUING PERFORMANCE BY A SUPPORTING ACTOR IN A DRAMA SERIES
For a regular or limited series
ANTHONY ZERBE; Harry O (ABC)
WILL GEER; The Waltons (CBS)
RAY MILLAND; Rich Man, Poor Man (ABC)
ROBERT REED; Rich Man, Poor Man (ABC)
MICHAEL DOUGLAS; The Streets Of San Francisco (ABC)

OUTSTANDING CONTINUING OR SINGLE PERFORMANCE BY A SUPPORTING ACTOR IN VARIETY OR MUSIC
For a continuing role in a regular or limited series; or a one-time appearance in a series; or a special
CHEVY CHASE; NBC's Saturday Night, January 17, 1976 (NBC)
HARVEY KORMAN; The Carol Burnett Show, Series (CBS)
TIM CONWAY; The Carol Burnett Show, November 15, 1975 (CBS)

OUTSTANDING SINGLE PERFORMANCE BY A SUPPORTING ACTOR IN A COMEDY OR DRAMA SPECIAL
ED FLANDERS; A Moon For The Misbegotten; ABC Theatre (ABC)
ART CARNEY; Katherine; The ABC Sunday Night Movie (ABC)
RAY BOLGER; The Entertainer (NBC)

OUTSTANDING SINGLE PERFORMANCE BY A SUPPORTING ACTOR IN A COMEDY OR DRAMA SERIES
For a one-time appearance in a regular or limited series

GORDON JACKSON; The Beastly Hun; Upstairs, Downstairs; Masterpiece Theatre (PBS)
ROSCOE LEE BROWNE; The Escape Artist; Barney Miller (ABC)
BILL BIXBY; Rich Man, Poor Man (ABC)
NORMAN FELL; Rich Man, Poor Man (ABC)
VAN JOHNSON; Rich Man, Poor Man (ABC)

OUTSTANDING CONTINUING PERFORMANCE BY A SUPPORTING ACTRESS IN A COMEDY SERIES
For a regular or limited series

BETTY WHITE; The Mary Tyler Moore Show (CBS)
GEORGIA ENGEL; The Mary Tyler Moore Show (CBS)
NANCY WALKER; Rhoda (CBS)
JULIE KAVNER; Rhoda (CBS)
LORETTA SWIT; M*A*S*H (CBS)

OUTSTANDING CONTINUING PERFORMANCE BY A SUPPORTING ACTRESS IN A DRAMA SERIES
For a regular or limited series

ELLEN CORBY; The Waltons (CBS)
SUSAN HOWARD; Petrocelli (NBC)
ANGELA BADDELEY; Upstairs, Downstairs; Masterpiece Theatre (PBS)
DOROTHY McGUIRE; Rich Man, Poor Man (ABC)
SADA THOMPSON; Sandburg's Lincoln (NBC)

OUTSTANDING CONTINUING OR SINGLE PERFORMANCE BY A SUPPORTING ACTRESS IN A VARIETY OR MUSIC SHOW
For a continuing role in a regular or limited series; or a special

VICKI LAWRENCE; The Carol Burnett Show (CBS)
CLORIS LEACHMAN; Telly. . .Who Loves Ya Baby? (CBS)

OUTSTANDING SINGLE PERFORMANCE BY A SUPPORTING ACTRESS IN A COMEDY OR DRAMA SPECIAL

ROSEMARY MURPHY; Eleanor And Franklin; ABC Theatre (ABC)
IRENE TEDROW; Eleanor and Franklin; ABC Theatre (ABC)
LILIA SKALA; Eleanor And Franklin; ABC Theatre (ABC)
LOIS NETTLETON; Fear On Trial (CBS)

OUTSTANDING SINGLE PERFORMANCE BY A SUPPORTING ACTRESS IN A COMEDY OR DRAMA SERIES
For a one-time appearance in a regular or limited series

FIONNUALA FLANAGAN; Rich Man, Poor Man (ABC)
EILEEN HECKART; Mary's Aunt; The Mary Tyler Moore Show (CBS)
RUTH GORDON; Kiss Your Epaulets Goodbye; Rhoda (CBS)
KIM DARBY; Rich Man, Poor Man (ABC)
KAY LENZ; Rich Man, Poor Man (ABC)

OUTSTANDING DIRECTING IN A DRAMA SERIES
A single episode of a regular or limited series with continuing characters and/or theme

DAVID GREENE; Rich Man, Poor Man (ABC)
JAMES CELLAN JONES; Jennie: Lady Randolph Churchill, Part IV; Great Performances (PBS)
BORIS SAGAL; Rich Man, Poor Man, Episode 5 (ABC)
GEORGE SCHAEFER; Crossing Fox River; Sandburg's Lincoln (NBC)
FIELDER COOK; Beacon Hill; Pilot (CBS)
CHRISTOPHER HODSON; Women Shall Not Weep; Upstairs, Downstairs (PBS)

OUTSTANDING DIRECTING IN A COMEDY SERIES
A single episode of a regular or limited series with continuing characters and/or theme

GENE REYNOLDS; Welcome To Korea; M*A*S*H (CBS)
HAL COOPER; The Analyst; Maude (CBS)
JOAN DARLING; Chuckles Bites The Dust; The Mary Tyler Moore Show (CBS)
ALAN ALDA; The Kids; M*A*S*H (CBS)

OUTSTANDING DIRECTING IN A COMEDY-VARIETY OR MUSIC SERIES
A single episode of a regular or limited series

DAVE WILSON; NBC's Saturday Night (with host Paul Simon) (NBC)
DAVE POWERS; The Carol Burnett Show (with Maggie Smith) (CBS)
TIM KILEY; The Sonny And Cher Show; Premiere (CBS)

OUTSTANDING DIRECTING IN A COMEDY-VARIETY OR MUSIC SPECIAL

DWIGHT HEMION; Steve And Eydie: 'Our Love Is Here To Stay' (CBS)
BILL DAVIS; John Denver Rocky Mountain Christmas (ABC)
TONY CHARMOLI; Mitzi. . .Roarin' In The 20's (CBS)

OUTSTANDING DIRECTING IN A SPECIAL PROGRAM - DRAMA OR COMEDY

DANIEL PETRIE; Eleanor And Franklin; ABC Theatre (ABC)
LAMONT JOHNSON; Fear On Trial (CBS)
BUZZ KULIK; Babe (CBS)
JOSE QUINTERO and GORDON RIGSBY; A Moon For The Misbegotten; ABC Theatre (ABC)

OUTSTANDING WRITING IN A DRAMA SERIES
A single episode of a regular or limited series with continuing characters and/or theme

SHERMAN YELLEN; John Adams, Lawyer; The Adams Chronicles (PBS)
DEAN RIESNER; Rich Man, Poor Man (ABC)
JULIAN MITCHELL; Jennie: Lady Randolph Churchill; Great Performances (PBS)
JOEL OLIANSKY; Complaint Amended; The Law (NBC)
ALFRED SHAUGHNESSY; Another Year; Upstairs, Downstairs; Masterpiece Theatre (PBS)

OUTSTANDING WRITING IN A COMEDY SERIES
A single episode of a regular or limited series with continuing characters and/or theme

DAVID LLOYD; Chuckles Bites The Dust; The Mary Tyler Show (CBS)
DANNY ARNOLD and CHRIS HAYWARD; The Hero; Barney Miller (ABC)
JAY FOLB; The Analyst; Maude (CBS)
LARRY GELBART and GENE REYNOLDS; The More I See You; M*A*S*H (CBS)
LARRY GELBART and SIMON MUNTER; Hawkeye; M*A*S*H (CBS)

OUTSTANDING WRITING IN A COMEDY-VARIETY OR MUSIC SERIES
A single episode of a regular or limited series

ANNE BEATTS, CHEVY CHASE, AL FRANKEN, TOM DAVIS, LORNE MICHAELS, MARILYN SUZANNE MILLER, MICHAEL O'DONOGHUE, HERB SARGENT, TOM SCHILLER, ROSIE SCHUSTER and ALAN ZWEIBEL; NBC's Saturday Night (with Host Elliott Gould) (NBC)
ED SIMMONS, GARY BELKIN, ROGER BEATTY, BILL RICHMOND, GENE PERRET, ARNIE KOGEN, RAY JESSEL, RUDY DeLUCA, BARRY LEVINSON, DICK CLAIR and JENNA McMAHON; The Carol Burnett Show (with Jim Nabors) (CBS)
PHIL HAHN, BOB ARNOTT, JEANINE BURNIER, COSLOUGH JOHNSON, IRIS RAINER, STUART GILLARD, FRANK PEPPIATT, JOHN AYLESWORTH and TED ZEIGLER; The Sonny And Cher Show, Premiere (CBS)

OUTSTANDING WRITING IN A COMEDY-VARIETY OR MUSIC SPECIAL
JANE WAGNER, LORNE MICHAELS, ANN ELDER, CHRISTOPHER GUEST, EARL POMERANTZ, JIM RUSK, LILY TOMLIN, ROD WARREN and GEORGE YANOK; Lily Tomlin (ABC)
FRED EBB; Gypsy In My Soul (with Shirley Maclaine) (CBS)
DICK VAN DYKE, ALLAN BLYE, BOB EINSTEIN, JAMES STEIN, GEORGE BURDITT, ROBERT ILLES, STEVE MARTIN, JACK MENDELSOHN and RICK MITTLEMAN; Van Dyke And Company (NBC)
JERRY MAYER; Mitzi...Roarin' In The 20's (CBS)

OUTSTANDING WRITING IN A SPECIAL PROGRAM - DRAMA OR COMEDY - ORIGINAL TELEPLAY
JAMES COSTIGAN; Eleanor And Franklin; ABC Theatre (ABC)
JOANNA LEE; Babe (CBS)
J.P. MILLER; The Lindbergh Kidnapping Case; NBC World Premiere Movie (NBC)
NICHOLAS MEYER and ANTHONY WILSON; The Night That Panicked America; The ABC Friday Night Movie (ABC)
JEB ROSEBROOK and THEODORE STRAUSS; I Will Fight No More Forever; ABC Theatre (ABC)

OUTSTANDING WRITING IN A SPECIAL PROGRAM - DRAMA OR COMEDY - ADAPTATION
DAVID W. RINTELS; Fear On Trial (CBS)
JEANNE WAKATSUKI HOUSTON, JAMES D. HOUSTON and JOHN KORTY; Farewell To Manzanar; NBC World Premiere Movie (NBC)
ELLIOTT BAKER; The Entertainer (NBC)

OUTSTANDING CHILDREN'S SPECIAL
For specials which were broadcast during the evening
Emmy(s) to Executive Producer(s) and Producer(s)

YOU'RE A GOOD SPORT, CHARLIE BROWN; Lee Mendelson, Executive Producer; Bill Melendez, Producer (CBS)
HUCKLEBERRY FINN; Steven North, Producer (ABC)

OUTSTANDING LIVE SPORTS SPECIAL
Emmy(s) To Executive Producer(s) and Producer(s)

1975 WORLD SERIES; Scotty Connal, Executive Producer; Roy Hammerman, Producer (NBC)
NCAA BASKETBALL CHAMPIONSHIP; Scotty Connal, Executive Producer; Roy Hammerman, Producer (NBC)
ROSE BOWL; Scotty Connal, Executive Producer; Dick Auerbach, Producer (NBC)
THE SUPER BOWL TODAY AND SUPER BOWL X; Robert Wussler, Executive Producer; Robert Stenner, Producer (CBS)
1975 MASTERS GOLF TOURNAMENT; Frank Chirkinian, Producer (CBS)

OUTSTANDING LIVE SPORTS SERIES
Emmy(s) to Executive Producer(s) and Producer(s)

NFL MONDAY NIGHT FOOTBALL; Roone Arledge, Executive Producer; Don Ohlmeyer, Producer (ABC)
NCAA COLLEGE FOOTBALL; Roone Arledge, Executive Producer; Chuck Howard and Terry Jastrow, Producers (ABC)
ABC'S GOLF; Roone Arledge, Executive Producer; Chuck Howard, Producer (ABC)
NFL FOOTBALL ON CBS; Robert Wussler, Executive Producer (CBS)

OUTSTANDING EDITED SPORTS SPECIAL
Emmy(s) to Executive Producer(s) and Producer(s)

XII WINTER OLYMPICS GAMES; Roone Arledge, Executive Producer; Chuck Howard, Don Ohlmeyer, Geoff Mason, Chet Forte, Bob Goodrich, Ellie Riger, Brice Weisman, Doug Wilson, and John Wilcox, Producers (ABC)
TRIUMPH AND TRAGEDY...THE OLYMPIC EXPERIENCE; Roone Arledge, Executive Producer; Don Ohlmeyer, Producer (ABC)

OUTSTANDING EDITED SPORTS SERIES
Emmy(s) to Executive Producer(s) and Producer(s)

ABC's WIDE WORLD OF SPORTS; Roone Arledge, Executive Producer; Doug Wilson, Chet Forte, Ned Steckel, Brice Weisman, Terry Jastrow, Bob Goodrich, John Martin, Dennis Lewin, Chuck Howard and Don Ohlmeyer, Producers (ABC)
THE SUPERSTARS; Roone Arledge, Executive Producer; Don Ohlmeyer, Terry Jastrow and Chet Forte, Producers (ABC)
THE BASEBALL WORLD OF JOE GARAGIOLA; Joe Garagiola, Executive Producer; Don Ellis, Producer (NBC)
THE WAY IT WAS; Gerry Gross, Executive Producer; Dick Enberg and Dan Merrin, Producers (PBS)

OUTSTANDING SPORTS PERSONALITY
JIM MCKAY; ABC's Wide World Of Sports; ABC's XII Winter Olympics (ABC)
JOE GARAGIOLA; 1975 World Series--Game 6 (NBC)
FRANK GIFFORD; NFL Monday Night Football; ABC's XII Winter Olympics (ABC)
VIN SCULLY; Masters Golf (NBC)
HEYWOOD HALE BROUN; CBS Sports Programs (CBS)

THE NATIONAL AWARD FOR COMMUNITY SERVICE

FORGOTTEN CHILDREN; WBBM-TV Chicago, Illinois
A DAY WITHOUT SUUNSHINE; WPBT, North Miami, Florida
THE GIFT OF LIFE; KWTV, Oklahoma City, Oklahoma
BLOOD BANK; WCIX-TV Miami, Florida
CENTRE FOUR; WJXT-TV, Jacksonville, Florida
CLOSING THE GAP; WITF-TV, Hershey, Pennsylvania
BUDDY, CAN YOU SPARE A DIME?; WBAL-TV, Baltimore, Maryland
THE EDELIN CONVICTION; WGBH, Boston, Massachusetts

THE AREAS

(Possibility of One Award, More Than One Award, or No Award)

SPECIAL CLASSIFICATION OF OUTSTANDING PROGRAM AND INDIVIDUAL ACHIEVEMENT

An award for unique program and individual achievements, which does not fall into a specific category, or is not otherwise recognized

BICENTENNIAL MINUTES; Bob Markell, Executive Producer; Gareth Davies and Paul Waigner, Producers, Series (CBS)
THE TONIGHT SHOW STARRING JOHNNY CARSON; Fred De Cordova, Producer; Johnny Carson, Star, Series (NBC)
ANN MARCUS, JERRY ADELMAN and DANIEL GREGORY BROWNE, Writers; Mary Hartman, Mary Hartman, Pilot (Synd)
THE AMERICAN FILM INSTITUTE SALUTE TO WILLIAM WYLER; George Stevens, Jr., Executive Producer; Paul Keyes, Producer (CBS)
TOMORROW; Joel Tator, Pamela Burke and Bruce McKay, Producers (NBC)
MARY HARTMAN, MARY HARTMAN; Norman Lear, Executive Producer; Viva Knight, Producer (Synd)
TOM SNYDER, Host; Tomorrow (NBC)
LOUISE LASSER, Performer; Mary Hartman, Mary Hartman (Synd)
ARTIE MALVIN, KEN WELCH and MITZIE WELCH, Mini Musical - Irving Berlin Finale; The Carol Burnett Show (CBS)

OUTSTANDING INDIVIDUAL ACHIEVEMENT IN SPORTS PROGRAMMING

For a single episode of a series; or for a special program

ANDY SIDARIS, DON OHLMEYER, ROGER GOODMAN, LARRY KAMM, RONNIE HAWKINS and RALPH MELLANBY, Directors; XII Winter Olympic Games (ABC)

THE CREATIVE ARTS AWARDS

(One Award Only in Each of the Following Categories)

OUTSTANDING ACHIEVEMENT IN CHOREOGRAPHY

For a single episode of a series or a special program

TONY CHARMOLI; Gypsy In My Soul (with Shirley MacLaine) (CBS)
JAIME ROGERS; Mary's Incredible Dream (with Mary Tyler Moore) (CBS)
ERNEST O. FLATT; The Carol Burnett Show (with Roddy McDowell and Bernadette Peters) (CBS)
ROB ISCOVE; Ann-Margaret Smith; Bell System Family Theatre (NBC)
LESTER WILSON; Lola! (ABC)

OUTSTANDING ACHIEVEMENT IN MUSIC COMPOSITION FOR A SERIES

Dramatic Underscore For a single episode of a regular or limited series

ALEX NORTH; Rich Man, Poor Man (ABC)
JOHN CACAVAS; A Question Of Answers; Kojak (CBS)
JACK URBONT; Next Of Kin; Bronk (CBS)
DAVID ROSE; Remember Me (Parts 1 & 2); Little House On The Prairie (NBC)

OUTSTANDING ACHIEVEMENT IN MUSIC COMPOSITION FOR A SPECIAL

Dramatic Underscore

JERRY GOLDSMITH; Babe (CBS)
CY COLEMAN; Gypsy In My Soul (with Shirley MacLaine) (CBS)
BILL GOLDENBERG; Dark Victory (NBC)
JACK URBONT; Supercops; A CBS Friday Night Double Feature (CBS)

OUTSTANDING ACHIEVEMENT IN MUSIC DIRECTION

For a single episode of a series or a special program whether it be variety or music

SEIJI OZAWA; Central Park In The Dark/A Hero's Life; Evening At Symphony (PBS)
DON TRENNER, Conductor; CY COLEMAN, Arranger; Gypsy In My Soul (with Shirley MacLaine) (CBS)

OUTSTANDING ACHIEVEMENT IN ART DIRECTION OR SCENIC DESIGN

For a single episode of a comedy, drama or limited series

TOM JOHN, Art Director; JOHN WENDELL and WES LAWS, Set Decorators; Beacon Hill; Pilot (CBS)
ED WITTSTEIN, Art Director; The Adams Chronicles (PBS)
WILLIAM HINEY, Art Director; JOSEPH J. STONE, Set Decorator; Rich Man, Poor Man (ABC)
MICHAEL HALL and FRED PUSEY, Scenic Designers; Jennie: Lady Randolph Churchill; Great Performances (PBS)

OUTSTANDING ACHIEVEMENT IN ART DIRECTION OR SCENIC DESIGN

For a single episode of a comedy-variety or music series; or for a comedy-variety or music special

RAYMOND KLAUSEN, Art Director; ROBERT CHECCHI, Set Decorator; Cher (with Anthony Newley and Ike and Tina Turner) (CBS)
EUGENE T. McAVOY, Art Director; Mary's Incredible Dream (with Mary Tyler Moore) (CBS)
KEN JOHNSON, Art Director; John Denver (Rocky Mountain Christmas) (ABC)
PAUL BARNES and BOB SANSOM, Art Directors; BILL HARP, Set Decorator; The Carol Burnett Show (with The Pointer Sisters) (CBS)

OUTSTANDING ACHIEVEMENT IN ART DIRECTION OR SCENIC DESIGN

For a dramatic special or a feature length film made for television

JAN SCOTT, Art Director; ANTONY MONDELLO, Set Decorator; Eleanor And Franklin; ABC Theatre (ABC)
JACK F. DE SHIELDS, Art Director; REG ALLEN, Set Decorator; Barbary Coast; The ABC Sunday Night Movie (ABC)
ROY CHRISTOPHER, Art Director; FRANCISCO LOMBARDO, Set

Decorator; The Legendary Curse Of The Hope Diamond (CBS)

OUTSTANDING ACHIEVEMENT IN GRAPHIC DESIGN AND TITLE SEQUENCES

For a single episode of a series; or for a special program. This includes animation only when created for use in titling

NORMAN SUNSHINE; Addie And The King Of Hearts (CBS)
PHIL NORMAN; The New, Original Wonder Woman; The ABC Friday Night Movie Special Double Feature (ABC)
ANTHONY GOLDSCHMIDT; Eleanor And Franklin; ABC Theatre (ABC)
GIRSH BHARGAVA and BILL MANDEL; The Adams Chronicles (PBS)
EDIE BASKIN and BOB POOK; NBC's Saturday Night (with Host Buck Henry) (NBC)

OUTSTANDING ACHIEVEMENT IN COSTUME DESIGN FOR A DRAMA SPECIAL

JOE I. TOMPKINS; Eleanor And Franklin; ABC Theatre (ABC)
BOB CHRISTENSON and DENITA CAVETT; The Lindbergh Kidnapping Case; NBC World Premiere Movie (NBC)

OUTSTANDING ACHIEVEMENT IN COSTUME DESIGN FOR MUSIC-VARIETY

For a single episode of a series; or for a special program

BOB MACKIE; Mitzi. . .Roarin' In The 20's (CBS)
BOB MACKIE and RET TURNER; Cher (with Wayne Rogers and Nancy Walker) (CBS)

OUTSTANDING ACHIEVEMENT IN COSTUME DESIGN FOR A DRAMA OR COMEDY SERIES

For a single episode of a Drama, Comedy or Limited series

JANE ROBINSON and JILL SILVERSIDE; Recovery; Jennie: Lady Randolph Churchill; Great Performances (PBS)
CHARLES WALDO; Rich Man, Poor Man (ABC)
ALVIN COLT; John Adams, Diplomat; The Adams Chronicles (PBS)

OUTSTANDING ACHIEVEMENT IN MAKE-UP

For a single episode of a series or for a special program

DEL ARMSTRONG and MIKE WESTMORE; Eleanor And Franklin; ABC Theatre (ABC)
ALLAN WHITEY SNYDER; The 1975 Fashion Awards (ABC)
WILLIAM TUTTLE; Babe (CBS)

OUTSTANDING ACHIEVEMENT IN CINEMATOGRAPHY FOR ENTERTAINMENT PROGRAMMING FOR A SERIES

For a single episode of a regular or limited series

HARRY L. WOLF, A.S.C.; Keep Your Eye On The Sparrow; Baretta (ABC)
TED VOIGTLANDER, A.S.C.; Remember Me (Parts 1 & 2); Little House On The Prairie (NBC)
HOWARD SCHWARTZ; Rich Man, Poor Man (ABC)
SOLNEGRIN. A.S.C.; A Question Of Answers; Kojak (CBS)
WILLIAM JURGENSEN; Hawkeye; M*A*S*H (CBS)

OUTSTANDING ACHIEVEMENT IN CINEMATOGRAPHY FOR ENTERTAINMENT PROGRAMMING FOR A SPECIAL

For a special or feature length program made for television

PAUL LOHMANN and EDWARD R. BROWN, SR; Eleanor and Franklin; ABC Theatre (ABC)
CHARLES F. WHEELER. A.S.C.; Babe (CBS)
HIRO NARITA; Farewell To Manzanar; NBC World Premiere Movie (NBC)
RICHARD C. GLOUNER, A.S.C.; Griffin And Phoenix: A Love Story; The ABC Friday Night Movie (ABC)
JAMES CRABE; The Entertainer (NBC)

OUTSTANDING FILM EDITING FOR ENTERTAINMENT PROGRAMMING FOR A SERIES

For a single episode of a Comedy Series

STANFORD TISCHLER and FRED W. BERGER; Welcome To Korea; M*A*S*H (CBS)
DOUGLAS HINES; Chuckles Bites The Dust; The Mary Tyler Moore Show (CBS)

OUTSTANDING FILM EDITING FOR ENTERTAINMENT PROGRAMMING FOR A SERIES

For a single episode of a Drama or Limited Series

SAMUEL E. BEETLEY, A.C.E. and KEN ZEMKE; The Quality Of Mercy; Medical Story (NBC)
DOUGLAS STEWART; Rich Man, Poor Man (ABC)
DOUGLAS VAN ENGER, JR.; The Right To Die; Medical Story (NBC)
RICHARD BRACKEN; Rich Man, Poor Man (ABC)

OUTSTANDING FILM EDITING FOR ENTERTAINMENT PROGRAMMING FOR A SPECIAL

For a special or film made for television

MICHAEL KAHN; Eleanor And Franklin; ABC Theatre (ABC)
HENRY BERMAN; Babe (CBS)
BUD S. ISAACS, TONY RADECKI and GEORGE NICHOLSON, A.C.E; The Night That Panicked America; The ABC Friday Night Movie (ABC)
ROBERT K. LAMBERT; I Will Fight No More Forever; ABC Theatre (ABC)
RITA ROLAND, A.C.E.; The Lindbergh Kidnapping Case; NBC World Premiere Movie (NBC)

OUTSTANDING ACHIEVEMENT IN FILM SOUND EDITING

For a single episode of a regular or limited series

DOUGLAS H. GRINDSTAFF, AL KAJITA, MARVIN I. KOSBERG, HANS NEWMAN, LEON SELDITZ, DICK FRIEDMAN, STAN GILBERT, HANK SALERNO, LARRY SINGER and WILLIAM ANDREWS; The Quality Of Mercy; Medical Story (NBC)
JERRY CHRISTIAN, KEN SWEET, THOMAS M. PATCHETT, JACK JACKSON, DAVID A. SCHONLEBER, JOHN W. SINGLETON, DALE JOHNSTON, GEORGE E. LUCKENBACHER, WALTER JENEVEIN and DENNIS DILTZ; The Secret Of Bigfoot (Parts 1 & 2); The Six Million Dollar Man (ABC)
MARVIN I. KOSBERG, BOB HUMAN, HANS NEWMAN, LEON SELDITZ, JEREMY HOENACK, JACK MILNER, AL KAJITA, LUKE WOLFRAM, DICK FRIEDMAN, HANK SALERNO, LARRY SINGER, STAN GILBERT and WILLIAM ANDREWS; Task Force (Parts 1 & 2); Police Woman (NBC)

OUTSTANDING ACHIEVEMENT IN FILM SOUND EDITING

For a special program

CHARLES L. CAMPBELL, LARRY NEIMAN, COLIN MOUAT, LARRY CAROW, DON WARNER, JOHN SINGLETON, TOM McMULLEN, JOSEPH DiVITALE, CARL KRESS, JOHN KLINE and JOHN HANLEY; The Night That Panicked America; The ABC Friday Night Movie (ABC)
DON HALL, WILLIAM HARTMAN, MIKE CORRIGAN, ED ROSSI, DICK SPERBER, RON SMITH, JOHN JOLLIFFE, BOB PEARSON, JOHN KLINE, AL LA MASTRA and JAY ENGEL; Eleanor And Franklin; ABC Theatre (ABC)
MARVIN I. KOSBERG, LARRY KAUFMAN, JACK MILNER and WILLIAM ANDREWS; The Lindbergh Kidnapping Case; NBC World Premiere Movie (NBC)

OUTSTANDING ACHIEVEMENT IN FILM SOUND MIXING

For a single episode of a regular or limited series; or for a special program

DON BASSMAN and DON JOHNSON; Eleanor And Franklin (Parts 1 & 2); ABC Theatre (ABC)
CHARLES LEWIS, ROBERT L. HARMAN, GEORGE PORTER and EDDIE NELSON; Prairie Lawyer; Sandburg's Lincoln (NBC)

OUTSTANDING ACHIEVEMENT IN TAPE SOUND MIXING

For a single episode of a regular or limited series; or for a special program

DAVE WILLIAMS; Anniversary Show; The Tonight Show Starring Johnny Carson (NBC)
VERNON COLEMAN; New Year's Eve At Pops (Arthur Fiedler) (PBS)
JOHN F. PFEIFFER; Live From Lincoln Center (PBS)

OUTSTANDING ACHIEVEMENT IN VIDEO TAPE EDITING FOR A SERIES

For a single episode of a regular or limited series

GIRISH BHARGAVA and MANFORD SCHORN; The Adams Chronicles (PBS)
KEN DENISOFF and ROBERT VEATCH; Earthquake II; Sanford and Son (NBC)
SUSAN JENKINS and MANUEL MARTINEZ; The Telethon; Welcome Back, Kotter (ABC)
HOMER POWELL, FRED GOLAN and PAUL SCHATZKIN; Happy New Year; Barney Miller (ABC)

OUTSTANDING ACHIEVEMENT IN VIDEO TAPE EDITING FOR A SPECIAL

NICK V. GIORDANO; Alice Cooper-The Nightmare; Wide World: In Concert (ABC)
ROY STEWART; The Hemingway Play; Hollywood Television Theatre (PBS)
HAL COLLINS and DANNY WHITE; Texaco Presents A Quarter Century of Bob Hope On Television (NBC)
REX BAGWELL and FRANK PHILLIPS; Mitzi... Roarin' In The 20's (CBS)

OUTSTANDING ACHIEVEMENT IN TECHNICAL DIRECTION AND ELECTRONIC CAMERAWORK

For a single episode of a regular or limited series; or for a special program

LEONARD CHUMBLEY, Technical Director; WALTER EDEL, JOHN FEHER, STEVE ZINK, Cameramen; The Adams Chronicles (PBS)
KEN LAMKIN, Technical Director; LEW ADAMS, JOHN POLIAK, SAM-UEL E. DOWLEN and RONALD SHELDON, Cameramen; Mary's Incredible Dream (with Mary Tyler Moore) (CBS)
LOUIS FUSARI, Technical Director; JOHN OLSON, ROY HOLM, RICK LOMBARDO and IAN TAYLOR, Cameramen; Mitzi And A Hundred Guys (CBS)
JERRY WEISS, Technical Director; FRED DONELSON, BRUCE GRAY, GEORGE MEYER and ROY HOLM, Cameramen; Mitzi...Roarin' In The 20's (CBS)

OUTSTANDING ACHIEVEMENT IN LIGHTING DIRECTION

For a single episode of a regular or limited series; or for a special program

WILLIAM KLAGES and LON STUCKY; Mitzi And A Hundred Guys (CBS)
JOHN FRESCHI; Mitzi...Roarin' In The 20's (CBS)
BILLY KNIGHT and DICK WEISS; John Quincy Adams--Diplomat; The Adams Chronicles (PBS)

THE CREATIVE ARTS AREAS

(Possibility of One Award, More Than One Award or No Award)

OUTSTANDING ACHIEVEMENT IN SPECIAL MUSICAL MATERIAL

For a song (which must have both music and lyrics), a theme for a series, or special material for a variety program providing the first usage of this material was written expressly for television

KEN WELCH, MITZIE WELCH and ARTIE MALVIN; Cinderella Gets It On; The Carol Burnett Show (with The Pointer Sisters) (CBS)
CY COLEMAN and FRED EBB; Gypsy In My Soul (with Shirley MacLaine) (CBS)

OUTSTANDING ACHIEVEMENT IN ANY AREA OF CREATIVE TECHNICAL CRAFTS

An award for individual technical craft achievement which does not fall into a specific category and is not otherwise recognized

JEAN BURT REILLY and BILLIE LAUGHRIDGE, Hairstylists; Eleanor And Franklin; ABC Theatre (ABC)
DONALD SAHLIN, KERMIT LOVE, CAROLY WILCOX, JOHN LOVELADY and ROLLIE KREWSON, Costumes and Props for the Muppets; Sesame Street (PBS)
JOHN LEAY and MARK SCHUBIN, Live Stereo Simulcast Nationwide, First Stereo Simulcast Via Satellite; Live From Lincoln Center (Andre Previn/Van Cliburn) (PBS)
WERNER G. SHERER, Hairdresser; First Ladies' Diaries: Martha Washington (NBC)
LOUIS SCHMITT, SOPHIE QUINN and TRUDY PHILION, Animated Characters Designers; The Tiny Tree; Bell System Family Theatre (NBC)

OUTSTANDING INDIVIDUAL ACHIEVEMENT IN DAYTIME PROGRAMMING

For a single episode of a series; or for a special program

RENE LAGLER, Art Director; RICHARD HARVEY, Set Decorator; Dinah! (Synd)
STAS PYKA, Graphic Design and Title Sequence; First Ladies' Diaries: Edith Wilson (NBC)
LEE BAYGAN, Make-Up; First Ladies' Diaries: Martha Washington (NBC)
RICHARD W. WILSON, Tape Sound Mixer; The Merv Griffin Show (with Tony Bennett, Peggy Lee and Fred Astaire) (Synd)

OUTSTANDING INDIVIDUAL ACHIEVEMENT IN SPORTS PROGRAMMING

For a single episode of a series; or for a special program

JEFF COHAN, JOE ACETI, JOHN DELISA, LOU FREDERICK, JACK GALLIVAN, JIM JENNETT, CAROL LEHTI, HOWARD SHAPIRO, KATSUMI ASEADA, JOHN FERNANDEZ, PETER FRITZ, EDDIE C. JOSEPH, KEN KLINGBEIL, LEO STEPHAN, TED SUMMERS, MICHAEL WENIG, RON ACKERMAN, MICHAEL BONIFAZIO, BARBARA BOWMAN, CHARLIE BURNHAM, JOHN CROAK, CHARLES GARDNER, MARVIN GENCH, VICTOR GONZALES, JAKOB HIERL, NICK MAZUR, ED McCARTHY, ALEX MOSKOVIC, ARTHUR NACE, LOU RENDE, ERSKIN ROBERTS, MERRITT ROESSER, ARTHUR VOLK, ROGER HAENELT, CURT BRAND, PHIL MOLLICA, GEORGE BOETTCHER and HERB OHLANDT, Video Tape Editors; XII Winter Olympic Games (ABC)

DICK ROES, JACK KELLY, BILL SANDREUTER, FRANK BAILEY and JACK KESTENBAUM, Tape Sound Mixers; XII Winter Olympic Games (ABC)

LARRY CANSLER, Music Composition; Theme/CBS Sports Spectacular (CBS)

MIKE DELANEY, HARVEY HARRISON, HARRY HART, D'ARCY MARSH, BRUCE BUCKLEY, DON SHAPIRO and ERIC VAN HAREN NOMAN, Cameramen; XII Winter Olympic Games (ABC)

JOHN PETERSEN, TONY ZACCARO, DON SHOEMAKER, PETER SILVER, ALAN SPENCER, IRWIN KRECHAF and MARGARET MURPHY, Film Editors; XII Winter Olmpic Games (ABC)

OUTSTANDING ACHIEVEMENT IN RELIGIOUS PROGRAMMING

For a single episode of a series; or a special program

JOSEPH J. H. VADALA, Cinematographer; A Determining Force (NBC)
SHARON KAUFMAN, Film Sound Editor; The Will To Be Free (ABC)
HARVEY HOLOCKER, Make-Up; Good News; The Rex Humbard World Outreach Ministry (Synd)

OUTSTANDING INDIVIDUAL ACHIEVEMENT IN CHILDREN'S PROGRAMMING

For a single episode of a series; or for a special program

BUD NOLAN and JIM COOKMAN, Film Sound Editors; Bound For Freedom (NBC)
ROBERT L. HARMAN, TED GOMILLION and BILL EDMUNDSON, Film Sound Mixers; Papa And Me; Special Treat (NBC)
GERRI BRIOSO, Graphic Design; Sesame Street (PBS)
MICHAEL WESTMORE and LOUIS PHILLIPPI, Make-Up; Blackout; Land Of The Lost (NBC)

SPECIAL AWARDS

OUTSTANDING ACHIEVEMENT IN ENGINEERING DEVELOPMENT

SONY CORPORATION for the U-matic video cassette concept
EASTMAN KODAK for the development of Eastman Ektachrome Video News Film
Citation to TEKTRONIX for leadership in development of equipment for verifying television transmission performance in the vertical interval

DAYTIME PROGRAM AND INDIVIDUAL ACHIEVEMENTS

(One Award Only in Each of the Following Categories)

OUTSTANDING DAYTIME DRAMA SERIES

Emmy(s) to Executive Producer(s) and Producer(s)

ANOTHER WORLD; Paul Rauch, Executive Producer; Joe Rothenberger and Mary S. Bonner, Producers (NBC)
DAYS OF OUR LIVES; Mrs Ted Corday, Executive Producer; Jack Herzberg and Al Rabin, Producers (NBC)
THE YOUNG AND THE RESTLESS; John J. Conboy, Executive Producer; Patricia Wenig, Producer (CBS)
ALL MY CHILDREN; Bud Kloss, Producer (ABC)

OUTSTANDING DAYTIME DRAMA SPECIAL

Emmy(s) to Executive Producer(s) and Producer(s)

FIRST LADIES' DIARIES: EDITH WILSON; Jeff Young, Producer (NBC)
FIRST LADIES' DIARIES: RACHEL JACKSON; Paul Rauch, Producer (NBC)
FIRST LADIES' DIARIES: MARTHA WASHINGTON; Linda Wendell, Producer (NBC)

OUTSTANDING DAYTIME GAME OR AUDIENCE PARTICIPATION SHOW

Emmy(s) to Executive Producer(s) and Producer(s)

THE $20,000 PYRAMID; Bob Stewart, Executive Producer; Anne Marie Schmitt, Producer (ABC)
THE PRICE IS RIGHT; Frank Wayne, Executive Producer; Jay Wolpert, Producer (CBS)
MATCH GAME '75; Ira Skutch, Producer (CBS)
THE HOLLYWOOD SQUARES; Merrill Heatter and Bob Quigley, Executive Producers; Jay Redack, Producer (NBC)
LET'S MAKE A DEAL; Stefan Hatos, Executive Producer; Alan Gilert, Producer (ABC)

OUTSTANDING DAYTIME TALK, SERVICE OR VARIETY SERIES

Emmy(s) to Executive Producer(s) and Producer(s)

DINAH! Henry Jaffe and Carolyn Raskin, Executive Producers; Fred Tatashore, Producer (Synd)
GOOD MORNING, AMERICA; Mel Ferber, Executive Producer; George Merlis and Bob Lissit, Producers (ABC)
THE MIKE DOUGLAS SHOW; Jack Reilly, Executive Producer; Woody Fraser, Producer (Synd)

OUTSTANDING ENTERTAINMENT CHLDREN'S SERIES

Emmy(s) to Executive Producer(s) and Producer(s)

BIG BLUE MARBLE; Henry Fownes, Producer (Synd)
CAPTAIN KANGAROO; Jimmy Hirshfield, Producer (CBS)
ZOOM; Austin Hoyt, Executive Producer (PBS)
FAT ALBERT AND THE COSBY KIDS; Norman Prescott and Lou Scheimer, Producers (CBS)

OUTSTANDING ENTERTAINMENT CHILDREN'S SPECIAL

Emmy(s) to Executive Producer(s) and Producer(s)

DANNY KAYE'S LOOK-IN AT THE METROPOLITAN OPERA; The CBS Festival Of Lively Arts For Young People; Sylvia Fine, Executive Producer; Bernard Rothman, Jack Wohl and Herbert Bonis, Producers (CBS)
ME AND DAD'S NEW WIFE; ABC Afterschool Special; Daniel Wilson, Producer (ABC)

IT MUST BE LOVE ('CAUSE I FEEL SO DUMB!); ABC Afterschool Special; Arthur Barron and Evelyn Barron, Producers (ABC)
WHAT IS NOISE? WHAT IS MUSIC?; New York Philharmonic Young People's Concert; Roger Englander, Producer (CBS)
PAPA AND ME; Special Treat; William P. D'Angelo, Ray Allen and Harvey Bullock, Executive Producers; Michael McLean, Producer (NBC)

OUTSTANDING INFORMATIONAL CHILDREN'S SERIES

Emmy(s) to Executive Producer(s) and Producer(s)

GO; George A. Heinemann, Executive Producer; Rift Fournier, J. Philip Miller, William W. Lewis and Joan Bender, Producers (NBC)
THE ELECTRIC COMPANY; Andrew B. Ferguson, Producer (PBS)
MAKE A WISH; Lester Cooper, Executive Producer; Peter Weinberg, Producer (ABC)

OUTSTANDING INFORMATIONAL CHILDREN'S SPECIAL

Emmy(s) to Executive Producer(s) and Producer(s)

HAPPY ANNIVERSARY, CHARLIE BROWN; Lee Mendelson and Warren Lockhart, Producers (CBS)
WHAT ARE THE LOCH NESS AND OTHER MONSTERS ALL ABOUT?; Joel Heller, Executive Producer; Walter Lister, Producer (CBS)
WINNING AND LOSING: DIARY OF A CAMPAIGN; ABC Afterschool Special; Daniel Wilson, Producer (ABC)

OUTSTANDING INSTRUCTIONAL CHILDREN'S PROGRAMMING - SERIES AND SPECIALS

Emmy(s) to Executive Producer(s) and Producer(s)

GRAMMAR ROCK; Thomas G. Yohe, Executive Producer; Radford Stone, Producer (ABC)
MISTER ROGERS' NEIGHBORHOOD; Fred Rogers, Executive Producer; Bill Moates, Producer (PBS)
SESAME STREET; Jon Stone, Executive Producer; Dulcy Singer, Producer (PBS)

OUTSTANDING ACTOR IN A DAYTIME DRAMA SERIES

LARRY HAINES; Search For Tomorrow (CBS)
JOHN BERADINO; General Hospital (ABC)
BILL HAYES; Days Of Our Lives (NBC)
MacDONALD CAREY; Days Of Our Lives (NBC)
SHEPPERD STRUDWICK; One Life To Live (ABC)
MICHAEL NOURI; Search For Tomorrow (CBS)

OUTSTANDING ACTOR IN A DAYTIME DRAMA SPECIAL

GERALD GORDON; First Ladies' Diaries: Rachel Jackson (NBC)
JAMES LUISI; First Ladies' Diaries: Martha Washington (NBC)

OUTSTANDING ACTRESS IN A DAYTIME DRAMA SERIES

HELEN GALLAGHER; Ryan's Hope (ABC)
SUSAN SEAFORTH HAYES; Day Of Our Lives (NBC)
MARY STUART; Search For Tomorrow (CBS)
DENISE ALEXANDER; General Hospital (ABC)
FRANCES HEFLIN; All My Children (ABC)

OUTSTANDING ACTRESS IN A DAYTIME DRAMA SPECIAL

ELIZABETH HUBBARD; First Ladies' Diaries: Edith Wilson (NBC)
SUSAN BROWNING; First Ladies' Diaries: Martha Washington (NBC)

OUTSTANDING HOST OR HOSTESS IN A GAME OR AUDIENCE PARTICIPATION SHOW

ALLEN LUDDEN; Password (ABC)
PETER MARSHALL; The Hollywood Squares (NBC)
GEOFF EDWARDS; Jackpot (NBC)

OUTSTANDING HOST OR HOSTESS IN A TALK, SERVICE OR VARIETY SERIES

DINAH SHORE; Dinah! (Synd)
DAVID HARTMAN; Good Morning, America (ABC)
MIKE DOUGLAS; The Mike Douglas Show (Synd)
MERV GRIFFIN; The Merv Griffin Show (Synd)

OUTSTANDING INDIVIDUAL DIRECTOR FOR A DAYTIME DRAMA SERIES

For a single episode

DAVID PRESSMAN; One Life To Live (ABC)
HUGH McPHILLIPS; The Doctors (NBC)
RICHARD DUNLAP; The Young And The Restless (CBS)

OUTSTANDING INDIVIDUAL DIRECTOR FOR A DAYTIME SPECIAL PROGRAM

NICHOLAS HAVINGA; First Ladies' Diaries: Edith Wilson (NBC)
JOHN J. DESMOND; First Ladies' Diaries: Martha Washington (NBC)
IRA CIRKER; First Ladies' Diaries: Rachel Jackson (NBC)

OUTSTANDING INDIVIDUAL DIRECTOR FOR A GAME OR AUDIENCE PARTICIPATION SHOW

For a single episode

MIKE GARGIULO; The $20,000 Pyramid (ABC)
JEROME SHAW; The Hollywood Squares (NBC)

OUTSTANDING INDIVIDUAL DIRECTOR FOR A DAYTIME VARIETY PROGRAM

For a single episode

GLEN SWANSON; Dinah Salutes Tony Orlando and Dawn On Their 5th Anniversary; Dinah! (Synd)
DONALD R. KING; The Mike Douglas Show (with Fred Astaire and Gene Kelly) (Synd)

OUTSTANDING WRITING FOR A DAYTIME DRAMA SERIES

For a single episode of a series; or for the entire series

WILLIAM J. BELL, KAY LENARD, PAT FALKEN SMITH, BILL REGA, MARGARET STEWART, SHERI ANDERSON and WANDA COLEMAN; Days Of Our Lives; Series (NBC)
HENRY SLESAR; The Edge of Night; Series (ABC)
JEROME DOBSON, BRIDGET DOBSON and JEAN ROUVEROL; The Guiding Light (CBS)
WILLIAM J. BELL and KAY ALDEN; The Young And The Restless (CBS)
AGNES NIXON, WISNER WASHAM, KATHRYN McCABE, MARY K. WELLS and JACK WOOD; All My Children; Series (ABC)

OUTSTANDING WRITING FOR A DAYTIME SPECIAL PROGRAM

AUDREY DAVIS LEVIN; First Ladies' Diaries: Edith Wilson (NBC)
ETHEL FRANK; First Ladies' Diaries: Martha Washington (NBC)

THE DAYTIME AREAS
(Possibility of One Award, More Than One Award or No Award)

OUTSTANDING INDIVIDUAL ACHIEVEMENT IN DAYTIME PROGRAMMING
For a single episode of a series; or a special program
PAUL LYNDE, Performer; The Hollywood Squares (NBC)

OUTSTANDING INDIVIDUAL ACHIEVEMENT IN CHILDREN'S PROGRAMMING
For a single episode of a series; or for a special program
THE MUPPETS; Performers (JIM HENSON, FRANK OZ, JERRY NELSON, CARROLL SPINNEY and RICHARD HUNT); Sesame Street; April 25, 1975 (PBS)

1976/77

OUTSTANDING COMEDY SERIES
Award(s) to Executive Producer(s) and/or Producer(s)
THE MARY TYLER MOORE SHOW, Allan Burns and James L. Brooks, Executive Producers; Ed. Weinberger and Stan Daniels, Producers (CBS)
ALL IN THE FAMILY, Mort Lachman, Executive Producer; Milt Josefsberg, Producer (CBS)
BARNEY MILLER, Danny Arnold, Executive Producer; Roland Kibbee, Danny Arnold, Producers (ABC)
THE BOB NEWHART SHOW, Tom Patchett, Jay Tarses, Executive Producers; Michael Zinberg, Gordon Farr and Lynne Farr, Producers (CBS)
M*A*S*H, Gene Reynolds, Executive Producer; Allan Katz, Don Reo and Burt Metcalfe, Producers (CBS)

OUTSTANDING DRAMA SERIES
Award(s) to Executive Producer(s) and/or Producer(s)
UPSTAIRS, DOWNSTAIRS, Masterpiece Theatre; John Hawkesworth and Joan Sullivan, Producers (PBS)
BARETTA, Anthony Spinner, Bernard Kowalski and Leigh Vance, Executive Producers; Charles E. Dismukes, Producer (ABC)
COLUMBO, NBC Sunday Mystery Movie; Everett Chambers, Producer (NBC)
FAMILY, Aaron Spelling, Leonard Goldberg and Mike Nichols, Executive Producers; Nigel McKeand, Producer; (ABC)
POLICE STORY, David Gerber, Executive Producer; Liam O'Brien, Producer; Mel Swope, Co-Producer (NBC)

OUTSTANDING COMEDY-VARIETY OR MUSIC SERIES
Award(s) to Executive Producer(s) and/or Producer(s) and Star(s), if applicable
VAN DYKE AND COMPANY, Byron Paul, Executive Producer; Allan Blye and Bob Einstein, Producers; Dick Van Dyke, Star (NBC)
THE CAROL BURNETT SHOW, Joe Hamilton, Executive Producer; Ed Simmons, Producer; Carol Burnett, Star (CBS)
EVENING AT POPS, William Cosel, Producer; Arthur Fiedler, Star (PBS)
THE MUPPET SHOW, Jim Henson and David Lazer, Executive Producers; Jack Burns, Producer; The Muppets (Frank Oz, Richard Hunt, Dave Goelz, Eren Ozker, John Lovelady, and Jerry Nelson) Stars (SYND)
NBC's SATURDAY NIGHT, Lorne Michaels, Producer (NBC)

OUTSTANDING LIMITED SERIES
Award(s) to Executive Producer(s) and/or Producer(s)
ROOTS, ABC Novel For Television; David L. Wolper, Executive Producer; Stan Margulies, Producer (ABC)
THE ADAMS CHRONICLES, Jac Venza, Executive Producer; Virginia Kassel, Series Producer; Robert Costello, Coordinating Producer; Fred Coe and James Cellan-Jones, Producers (PBS)
CAPTAINS AND THE KINGS, NBC's Best Seller; Roy Huggins, Executive Producer; Jo Swerling, Jr., Producer (NBC)
MADAME BOVARY, Masterpiece Theatre; Richard Beynon, Producer (PBS)
THE MONEYCHANGERS, NBC World Premiere Movie; The Big Event; Ross Hunter and Jacque Mapes, Producers (NBC)

OUTSTANDING SPECIAL - DRAMA OR COMEDY
Award(s) to Executive Producer(s) and/or Producer(s)
ELEANOR AND FRANKLIN: THE WHITE HOUSE YEARS, ABC Theatre; David Susskind, Executive Producer; Harry R. Sherman, Producer (ABC)
SYBIL, NBC World Premiere Movie; The Big Event; Peter Dunne and Philip Capice, Executive Producers; Jacqueline Babbin, Producer (NBC)
HARRY S. TRUMAN: PLAIN SPEAKING, David Susskind, Producer (PBS)
RAID ON ENTEBBE, The Big Event; Edgar J. Scherick and Daniel H. Blatt, Executive Producers (NBC)
21 HOURS AT MUNICH, The ABC Sunday Night Movie; Edward S. Feldman, Executive Producer; Frank von Zerneck and Robert Greenwald, Producers (ABC)

OUTSTANDING SPECIAL - COMEDY-VARIETY OR MUSIC
Award(s) to Executive Producer(s) and/or Producer(s) and Star(s), if applicable
THE BARRY MANILOW SPECIAL, Miles Lourie, Executive Producer; Steve Binder, Producer; Barry Manilow, Star (ABC)
DOUG HENNING'S WORLD OF MAGIC, Jerry Goldstein, Executive Producer; Walter C. Miller, Producer; Doug Henning, Star (NBC)
THE NEIL DIAMOND SPECIAL, Jerry Weintraub, Executive Producer; Gary Smith and Dwight Hemion Producers; Neil Diamond, Star (NBC)
THE SHIRLEY MacLAINE SPECIAL: WHERE DO WE GO FROM HERE?, George Schlatter, Producer; Shirley MacLaine, Star (CBS)
SILLS AND BURNETT AT THE MET, Joe Hamilton, Producer; Beverly Sills and Carol Burnett, Stars (CBS)

OUTSTANDING CLASSICAL PROGRAM IN THE PERFORMING ARTS
For a special program, or for a series (excluding drama)
Award(s) to Executive Producer(s) and/or Producer(s) and Star(s), if applicable
AMERICAN BALLET THEATRE: SWAN LAKE, Live From Lincoln Center; Great Performances; John Goberman, Producer (PBS)
AMERICAN BALLET THEATRE; Dance In America; Great Performances; Jac Venza, Executive Producer; Emile Ardolino, Series Coordinating Producer; Merrill Brockway, Series Producer (PBS)
ARTHUR RUBINSTEIN AT 90, Great Performances; Jac Venza, Klaus Hallig and Herbert Kloiber, Executive Producers; David Griffiths and Fritz Buttenstadt, Producers; Arthur Rubinstein, Star (PBS)
THE BOLSHOI BALLET: ROMEO AND JULIET, Lothar Bock, Executive Producer; Alvin Cooperman, Producer (CBS)
MARTHA GRAHAM DANCE COMPANY, Dance In America; Great Performances; Jac Venza, Executive Producer; Emile Ardolino, Series Coordinating Producer; Merrill Brockway, Series Producer; Martha Graham, Star (PBS)

OUTSTANDING CHILDREN'S SPECIAL
For specials which were broadcast during the evening. Award(s) to Executive Producer(s) and Producer(s)

BALLET SHOES, PARTS 1 & 2, Piccadilly Circus; John McRae and Joan Sullivan, Producers (PBS)
IT'S ARBOR DAY, CHARLIE BROWN, Lee Mendelson, Executive Producer; Bill Melendez, Producer (CBS)
PETER PAN, Hallmark Hall Of Fame; The Big Event; Gary Smith and Dwight Hemion, Executive Producers; Gary Smith, Producer (NBC)
PINOCCHIO, Bernard Rothman and Jack Wohl, Producers (CBS)
THE LITTLE DRUMMER BOY, BOOK II, Arthur Rankin, Jr. and Jules Bass, Producers (NBC)

OUTSTANDING ACHIEVEMENT IN COVERAGE OF SPECIAL EVENTS - PROGRAMS
An Award for unique program achievement. A special event is a single program presented as live coverage; i.e., parades, pageants, awards presentations, salutes and coverage of other live events which were not covered by the news division. (Possibility of one Award, more than one Award, or no Award)

THE GOOD OLD DAYS OF RADIO, Loring d'Usseau, Producer (PBS)
GRAMMY AWARDS SHOW, Marty Pasetta, Producer (CBS)
THE 28th ANNUAL EMMY AWARDS, Norman Rosemont, Producer (ABC)
30th ANNUAL TONY AWARDS, Alexander H. Cohen, Producer (ABC)
48th ANNUAL OSCAR AWARDS, Howard W. Koch, Producer (ABC)

SPECIAL CLASSIFICATION OF OUTSTANDING PROGRAM ACHIEVEMENT
An Award for unique program achievement, which does not fall into a specific category, and is not otherwise recogniized. (Possibility of one Award, more than one Award, or no Award)

THE TONIGHT SHOW STARRING JOHNNY CARSON, Fred De Cordova, Producer; Johnny Carson, Star; Series (NBC)
BICENTENNIAL MINUTES, Bob Markell, Executive Producer; Series (CBS)
THE FIRST FIFTY YEARS, The Big Event; Greg Garrison, Executive Producer; Lee Hale, Chet Hagan, Producers (NBC)
LIFE GOES TO THE MOVIES, The Big Event; Jack Haley, Jr., Executive Producer; Mel Stuart, Richard Schickel, Malcolm Leo, Producers (NBC)
THE WONDERFUL WORLD OF DISNEY, Ron Miller, Executive Producer; Series (NBC)

OUTSTANDING LEAD ACTOR IN A COMEDY SERIES
CARROLL O'CONNOR, All In The Family (CBS)
JACK ALBERTSON, Chico and the Man (NBC)
ALAN ALDA, M*A*S*H (CBS)
HAL LINDEN, Barney Miller (ABC)
HENRY WINKLER, Happy Days (ABC)

OUTSTANDING LEAD ACTOR IN A DRAMA SERIES
JAMES GARNER, The Rockford Files (NBC)
ROBERT BLAKE, Baretta (ABC)
PETER FALK, Columbo (NBC)
JACK KLUGMAN, Quincy, M. E. (NBC)
KARL MALDEN, The Streets Of San Francisco (ABC)

OUTSTANDING LEAD ACTOR IN A LIMITED SERIES
CHRISTOPHER PLUMMER, The Moneychangers; NBC World Premiere Movie; The Big Event (NBC)
STANLEY BAKER, How Green Was My Valley; Masterpiece Theatre (PBS)
RICHARD JORDAN, Captains And The Kings; NBC's Best Seller (NBC)
STEVEN KEATS, Seventh Avenue; NBC's Best Seller (NBC)

OUTSTANDING LEAD ACTOR IN A DRAMA OR COMEDY SPECIAL
ED FLANDERS, Harry S. Truman: Plain Speaking (PBS)
PETER BOYLE, Tail Gunner Joe; NBC World Premiere Movie; The Big Event (NBC)
PETER FINCH, Raid On Entebbe; The Big Event (NBC)
EDWARD HERRMANN, Eleanor and Franklin: The White House Years; ABC Theatre (ABC)
GEORGE C. SCOTT, Beauty And The Beast; Hallmark Hall Of Fame (NBC)

OUTSTANDING LEAD ACTOR FOR A SINGLE APPEARANCE IN A DRAMA OR COMEDY SERIES
LOUIS GOSSETT, JR., Roots, Part 2 (ABC)
JOHN AMOS, Roots, Part 5 (ABC)
LEVAR BURTON, Roots, Part 1 (ABC)
BEN VEREEN, Roots, Part 6 (ABC)

OUTSTANDING LEAD ACTRESS IN A COMEDY SERIES
BEATRICE ARTHUR, Maude (CBS)
VALERIE HARPER, Rhoda (CBS)
MARY TYLER MOORE, The Mary Tyler Moore Show (CBS)
SUZANNE PLESHETTE, The Bob Newhart Show (CBS)
JEAN STAPLETON, All In The Family (CBS)

OUTSTANDING LEAD ACTRESS IN A DRAMA SERIES
LINDSAY WAGNER, The Bionic Woman (ABC)
ANGIE DICKINSON, Police Woman (NBC)
KATE JACKSON, Charlie's Angels (ABC)
MICHAEL LEARNED, The Waltons (CBS)
SADA THOMPSON, Family (ABC)

OUTSTANDING LEAD ACTRESS IN A LIMITED SERIES
PATTY DUKE ASTIN, Captains And The Kings; NBC's Best Seller (NBC)
SUSAN FLANNERY, The Moneychangers; NBC World Premiere Movie; The Big Event (NBC)
DORI BRENNER, Seventh Avenue; NBC's Best Seller (NBC)
EVA MARIE SAINT, How The West Was Won (ABC)
JANE SEYMOUR, Captains And The Kings; NBC's Best Seller (NBC)

OUTSTANDING LEAD ACTRESS IN A DRAMA OR COMEDY SPECIAL
SALLY FIELD, Sybil; NBC World Premiere Movie; The Big Event (NBC)
JANE ALEXANDER, Eleanor and Franklin: The White House Years; ABC Theatre (ABC)
SUSAN CLARK, Amelia Earhart; NBC Monday Night At The Movies, (NBC)
JULIE HARRIS, The Last Of Mrs. Lincoln; Hollywood Television Theatre (PBS)

JOANNE WOODWARD, Sybil; NBC World Premiere Movie; The Big Event (NBC)

OUTSTANDING LEAD ACTRESS FOR A SINGLE APPEARANCE IN A DRAMA OR COMEDY SERIES

BEULAH BONDI, The Waltons; The Pony Cart (CBS)
SUSAN BLAKELY, Rich Man, Poor Man, Book II, Ch. 1 (ABC)
MADGE SINCLAIR, Roots, Part 4 (ABC)
LESLIE UGGAMS, Roots, Part 6 (ABC)
JESSICA WALTER, The Streets of San Francisco; 'Til Death Us Do Part (ABC)

OUTSTANDING CONTINUING PERFORMANCE BY A SUPPORTING ACTOR IN A COMEDY SERIES

For a regular or limited series
GARY BURGHOFF, M*A*S*H (CBS)
EDWARD ASNER, The Mary Tyler Moore Show (CBS)
TED KNIGHT, The Mary Tyler Moore Show (CBS)
HARRY MORGAN, M*A*S*H (CBS)
ABE VIGODA, Barney Miller (ABC)

OUTSTANDING CONTINUING PERFORMANCE BY A SUPPORTING ACTOR IN A DRAMA SERIES

For a regular or limited series
GARY FRANK, Family (ABC)
NOAH BEERY, The Rockford Files (NBC)
DAVID DOYLE, Charlie's Angels (ABC)
TOM EWELL, Baretta (ABC)
WILL GEER, The Waltons (CBS)

OUTSTANDING CONTINUING OR SINGLE PERFORMANCE BY A SUPPORTING ACTOR IN VARIETY OR MUSIC

For a continuing role in a regular or limited series; or a one-time appearancce in a series; or a special
TIM CONWAY, The Carol Burnett Show; Series (CBS)
JOHN BELUSHI, NBC's Saturday Night (with Candice Bergen) (NBC)
CHEVY CHASE, NBC's Saturday Night (with Elliott Gould) (NBC)
HARVEY KORMAN, The Carol Burnett Show; Entire Series (CBS)
BEN VEREEN, The Bell Telephone Jubilee (NBC)

OUTSTANDING PERFORMANCE BY A SUPPORTING ACTOR IN A COMEDY OR DRAMA SPECIAL

BURGESS MEREDITH, Tail Gunner Joe; NBC World Premiere Movie; The Big Event (NBC)
MARTIN BALSAM, Raid On Entebbe; The Big Event (NBC)
MARK HARMON, Eleanor And Franklin: The White House Years; ABC Theatre (ABC)
YAPHET KOTTO, Raid On Entebbe; The Big Event (NBC)
WALTER McGINN, Eleanor And Franklin: The White House Years; ABC Theatre (ABC)

OUTSTANDING SINGLE PERFORMANCE BY A SUPPORTING ACTOR IN A COMEDY OR DRAMA SERIES

For a one-time appearance in a regular or limited series
EDWARD ASNER, Roots, Part 1 (ABC)
CHARLES DURNING, Captains And The Kings, Chapter 2; NBC's Best Seller (NBC)
MOSES GUNN, Roots, Part 1 (ABC)
ROBERT REED, Roots, Part 5 (ABC)
RALPH WAITE, Roots, Part 1 (ABC)

OUTSTANDING CONTINUING PERFORMANCE BY A SUPPORTING ACTRESS IN A COMEDY SERIES

For a regular or limited series
MARY KAY PLACE, Mary Hartman, Mary Hartman (SYND)
GEORGIA ENGEL, The Mary Tyler Moore Show (CBS)
JULIE KAVNER, Rhoda (CBS)
LORETTA SWIT, M*A*S*H (CBS)
BETTY WHITE, The Mary Tyler Moore Show (CBS)

OUTSTANDING CONTINUING PERFORMANCE BY A SUPPORTING ACTRESS IN A DRAMA SERIES

For a regular or limited series
KRISTY McNICHOL, Family (ABC)
MEREDITH BAXTER BIRNEY, Family (ABC)
ELLEN CORBY, The Waltons (CBS)
LEE MERIWETHER, Barnaby Jones (CBS)
JACQUELINE TONG, Upstairs, Downstairs; Masterpiece Theatre (PBS)

OUTSTANDING CONTINUING OR SINGLE PERFORMANCE BY A SUPPORTING ACTRESS IN VARIETY OR MUSIC

For a continuing role in a regular or limited series; or a one-time appearance in a series; or a special
RITA MORENO, The Muppet Show (SYND)
VICKI LAWRENCE, The Carol Burnett Show; Entire Series (CBS)
GILDA RADNER, NBC's Saturday Night (with Steve Martin) (NBC)

OUTSTANDING PERFORMANCE BY A SUPPORTING ACTRESS IN A COMEDY OR DRAMA SPECIAL

DIANA HYLAND, The Boy In The Plastic Bubble; The ABC Friday Night Movie (ABC)
RUTH GORDON, The Great Houdinis; The ABC Friday Night Movie (ABC)
ROSEMARY MURPHY, Eleanor And Franklin: The White House Years; ABC Theatre (ABC)
PATRICIA NEAL, Tail Gunner Joe; NBC World Premiere Movie; The Big Event (NBC)
SUSAN OLIVER, Amelia Earhart; NBC Monday Night At The Movies (NBC)

OUTSTANDING SINGLE PERFORMANCE BY A SUPPORTING ACTRESS IN A COMEDY OR DRAMA SERIES

For a one-time appearance in a regular or limited series

OLIVIA COLE, Roots, Part 8 (ABC)
SANDY DUNCAN, Roots, Part 5 (ABC)
EILEEN HECKART, The Mary Tyler Moore Show; Lou Proposes (CBS)
CICELY TYSON, Roots, Part 1 (ABC)
NANCY WALKER, Rhoda; The Separation (CBS)

OUTSTANDING WRITING IN A COMEDY SERIES

A single episode of a regular or limited series with continuing characters and/or theme

ALLAN BURNS, JAMES L. BROOKS, ED. WEINBERGER, STAN DANIELS, DAVID LLOYD and BOB ELLISON, The Mary Tyler Moore Show; The Last Show (CBS)
ALAN ALDA, M*A*S*H; Dear Sigmund (CBS)
DANNY ARNOLD, TONY SHEEHAN, Barney Miller; Quarantine, Part 2 (ABC)
DAVID LLOYD, The Mary Tyler Moore Show; Mary Midwife (CBS)
EARL POMERANTZ, The Mary Tyler Moore Show; Ted's Change Of Heart (CBS)

OUTSTANDING WRITING IN A DRAMA SERIES

A single episode of a regular or limited series with continuing characters and/or theme

ERNEST KINOY, WILLIAM BLINN, Roots, Part 2 (ABC)
JAMES LEE, Roots, Part 5 (ABC)
ROGER O. HIRSON, The Adams Chronicles; Charles Francis Adams: Minister To Great Britian (PBS)
M. CHARLES COHEN, Roots, Part 8 (ABC)
TAD MOSEL, The Adams Chronicles; John Quincy Adams: President (PBS)

OUTSTANDING WRITING IN A COMEDY-VARIETY OR MUSIC SERIES

A single episode of a regular or limited series

ANNE BEATTS, DAN AYKROYD, AL FRANKEN, TOM DAVIS, JAMES DOWNEY, LORNE MICHAELS, MARILYN SUZANNE MILLER, MICHAEL O'DONOGHUE, HERB SARGENT, TOM SCHILLER, ROSIE SHUSTER, ALAN ZWEIBEL, JOHN BELUSHI and BILL MURRAY, NBC's Saturday Night (with Sissy Spacek) (NBC)
JIM HENSON, JACK BURNS, MARC LONDON and JERRY JUHL, The Muppet Show (with Paul Williams) (SYND)
ANNE BEATTS, CHEVY CHASE, AL FRANKEN, TOM DAVIS, LORNE MICHAELS, MARILYN SUZANNE MILLER, MICHAEL O'DONOGHUE, HERB SARGENT, TOM SCHILLER, ROSIE SHUSTER and ALAN ZWEIBEL NBC's Saturday Night (with Elliott Gould) (NBC)
ED SIMMONS, ROGER BEATTY, ELIAS DAVIS, DAVID POLLOCK, RICK HAWKINS, LIZ SAGE, ADELE STYLER, BURT STYLER, TIM CONWAY, BILL RICHMOND, GENE PERRET, DICK CLAIR and JENNA McMAHON, The Carol Burnett Show (with Eydie Gorme) (CBS)
BOB EINSTEIN, ALLAN BLYE, GEORGE BURDITT, GARRY FERRIER, KEN FINKELMAN, MITCH MARKOWITZ, TOMMY McLOUGHLIN, DON NOVELLO, PAT PROFT, LEONARD RIPPS, MICKEY ROSE, AUBREY TADMAN, DICK VAN DYKE and PAUL WAYNE, Van Dyke & Company (with John Denver) (NBC)

OUTSTANDING WRITING IN A COMEDY-VARIETY OR MUSIC SPECIAL

ALAN BUZ KOHAN, TED STRAUSS, American Salutes Richard Rodgers: The Sound Of His Music (CBS)
ALAN THICKE, DON CLARK, SUSAN CLARK, RONNY PEARLMAN, STEVE BINDER, BARRY MANILOW and BRUCE VILANCH, The Barry Manilow Special (ABC)
BILL DYER, NTOZAKE SHANGE, An Evening With Diana Ross; The Big Event (NBC)
KEN WELCH, MITZIE WELCH, KENNY SOLMS and GAIL PARENT, Sills And Burnett At The Met (CBS)
DIGBY WOLFE and GEORGE SCHLATTER, John Denver And Friend (ABC)

OUTSTANDING WRITING IN A SPECIAL PROGRAM - DRAMA OR COMEDY - ORIGINAL TELEPLAY

LANE SLATE, Tail Gunner Joe; NBC World Premiere Movie; The Big Event (NBC)
BARRY BECKERMAN, Raid On Entebbe; The Big Event (NBC)
JAMES COSTIGAN, Eleanor And Franklin: The White House Years; ABC Theatre (ABC)
ERNEST KINOY, Victory At Entebbe (ABC)
DOUGLAS DAY STEWART, Teleplay; JOE MORGENSTERN and DOUGLAS DAY STEWART, Story; The Boy In The Plastic Bubble; The ABC Friday Night Movie (ABC)

OUTSTANDING WRITING IN A SPECIAL PROGRAM - DRAMA OR COMEDY - ADAPTATION

STEWART STERN, Sybil; NBC World Premiere Movie; The Big Event (NBC)
WILLIAM BAST, The Man In The Iron Mask; The Bell System Presents (NBC)
JOHN McGREEVEY, Judge Horton And The Scottsboro Boys; NBC World Premiere (NBC)
CAROL SOBIESKI, Harry S. Truman: Plain Speaking (PBS)
STEVEN GETHERS, A Circle Of Children (CBS)

OUTSTANDING DIRECTING IN A COMEDY SERIES

A single episode of a regular or limited series with continuing characters and/or theme

ALAN ALDA, M*A*S*H; Dear Sigmund (CBS)
PAUL BOGART, All In The Family; The Draft Dodger (CBS)
JOAN DARLING, M*A*S*H; The Nurses (CBS)
ALAN RAFKIN, M*A*S*H; Lt. Radar O'Reilly (CBS)
JAY SANDRICH, The Mary Tyler Moore Show; The Last Show (CBS)

OUTSTANDING DIRECTING IN A DRAMA SERIES

A single episode of a regular or limited series with continuing characters and/or theme

DAVID GREENE, Roots, Part 1 (ABC)
MARVIN CHOMSKY, Roots, Part 3 (ABC)
FRED COE, The Adams Chronicles; John Quincy Adams: President (PBS)
JOHN ERMAN, Roots, Part 2 (ABC)
GILBERT MOSES, Roots, Part 6 (ABC)

OUTSTANDING DIRECTING IN A SPECIAL PROGRAM - DRAMA OR COMEDY

DANIEL PETRIE, Eleanor And Franklin: The White House Years; ABC Theatre (ABC)
FIELDER COOK, Judge Horton And The Scottsboro Boys; NBC World Premiere Movie (NBC)
TOM GRIES, Helter Skelter (CBS)
IRVIN KERSHNER, Raid On Entebbe; The Big Event (NBC)
JUD TAYLOR, Tail Gunner Joe; NBC World Premiere Movie; The Big Event (NBC)

OUTSTANDING DIRECTING IN A COMEDY-VARIETY OR MUSIC SERIES
A single episode of a regular or limited series
DAVE POWERS, The Carol Burnett Show (with Eydie Gorme) (CBS)
JOHN C. MOFFITT, Van Dyke And Company (with John Denver) (NBC)
DAVE WILSON, NBC's Saturday Night (with Host Paul Simon) (NBC)

OUTSTANDING DIRECTING IN A COMEDY-VARIETY OR MUSIC SPECIAL
DWIGHT HEMION, America Salutes Richard Rodgers: The Sound Of His Music (CBS)
STEVE BINDER, The Barry Manilow Special (ABC)
TONY CHARMOLI, The Shirley MacLaine Special: Where Do We Go From Here? (CBS)
WALTER C. MILLER, Doug Henning's World Of Magic (NBC)
DAVID POWERS, Sills And Burnett At The Met (CBS)

OUTSTANDING ACHIEVEMENT IN COVERAGE OF SPECIAL EVENTS - INDIVIDUALS
An Award for unique program achievement. A special event is Oa a single program presented as live coverage; i.e., pageants, parades, awards presentations, salutes and coverage of other live events which were not covered by the news division. (Possibility of one Award, more than one Award, or no Award)
JOHN C. MOFFITT, Director; The 28th Annual Emmy Awards (ABC)
HELEN O'CONNELL, Hostess; Miss Universe Beauty Pageant (CBS)
MARTY PASETTA, Director; 48th Annual Oscar Awards (ABC)

OUTSTANDING DAYTIME TALK, SERVICE, OR VARIETY SERIES
Emmy(s) to Executive Producer(s) and Producer(s)
DINAH! Henry Jaffe and Carolyn Raskin, Executive Producers; Fred Tatashore, Producer (SYND)
THE GONG SHOW, Chuck Barris, Executive Producer; Gene Banks, Producer (NBC)
THE MERV GRIFFIN SHOW, Bob Murphy, Producer (SYND)
THE MIKE DOUGLAS SHOW, David Salzman, Executive Producer; Jack Reilly, Producer (SYND)

OUTSTANDING HOST OR HOSTESS IN A TALK, SERVICE OR VARIETY SERIES
PHIL DONAHUE, Donahue (SYND)
MIKE DOUGLAS, The Mike Douglas Show (SYND)
MERV GRIFFIN, The Merv Griffin Show (SYND)
DINAH SHORE, Dinah! (SYND)

OUTSTANDING INDIVIDUAL DIRECTOR FOR A DAYTIME VARIETY PROGRAM
For a single episode
DICK CARSON, The Merv Griffin Show; Merv Griffin in Israel (SYND)
JOHN DORSEY, The Gong Show (NBC)
DONALD R. KING, The Mike Douglas Show; Mike in Hollywood (with Ray Charles & Michel Le Grand) (SYND)
GLEN SWANSON, Dinah!; Dinah from Australia (SYND)

OUTSTANDING GAME OR AUDIENCE PARTICIPATION SHOW
For Daytime and Nightime Programs. Emmy(s) to Executive Producer(s) and Producer(s)
THE $20,000 PYRAMID, Bob Stewart, Executive Producer; Anne Marie Schmitt, Producer (ABC)
FAMILY FEUD, Howard Felsher, Producer (ABC)
HOLLYWOOD SQUARES, Robert Quigley and Merrill Heatter, Executive Producers; Jay Redack, Producer (NBC)
MATCH GAME '76, Ira Skutch, Producer (CBS)
TATTLETALES, Ira Skutch, Executive Producer; Paul Alter, Producer (CBS)

OUTSTANDING HOST OR HOSTESS IN A GAME OR AUDIENCE PARTICIPATION SHOW
For Daytime or Nighttime Programs
DICK CLARK, The $20,000 Pyramid (ABC)
BERT CONVY, Tattletales (CBS)
GENE RAYBURN, Match Game '76 (CBS)

OUTSTANDING INDIVIDUAL DIRECTOR FOR A GAME OR AUDIENCE PARTICIPATION SHOW
For a single episode of a Daytime or Nighttime Series
JOSEPH BEHAR, Let's Make a Deal (ABC)
MIKE GARGIULO, The $20,000 Pyramid (with Tony Randall & Jo Anne Worley) (ABC)

OUTSTANDING ENTERTAINMENT CHILDREN'S SERIES
Emmy(s) to Executive Producer(s) and Producer(s)
CAPTAIN KANGAROO, Jim Hirschfeld, Producer (CBS)
DAVID COPPERFIELD, Once Upon A Classic; Jay Rayvid, Executive Producer; John McRae and Don Coney, Producers (PBS)
HEIDI, Once Upon A Classic; Jay Rayvid, Executive Producer; John McRae and Don Coney, Producers (PBS)
THE PRINCE AND THE PAUPER; Once Upon A Classic; Jay Rayvid, Executive Producer; Barry Letts and Don Coney, Producers (PBS)
ZOOM! Cheryl Susheel Bibbs, Executive Producer; Monia Joblin and Mary Benjamin, Producers (PBS)

OUTSTANDING ENTERTAINMENT CHILDRENS SPECIAL
Emmy(s) to Executive Producer(s) and Producer(s)
BIG HENRY AND THE POLKA DOT KID, Special Treat; Linda Gottlieb, Producer (NBC)
BLIND SUNDAY, ABC Afterschool Specials; Daniel Wilson, Producer (ABC)
FRANCESCA BABY, ABC Afterschool Specials; Martin Tahse, Producer (ABC)
LUKE WAS THERE, Special Treat; Linda Gottlieb, Executive Producer; Richard Marquand, Producer (NBC)
THE ORIGINAL ROMPIN' STOMPIN' HOT AND HEAVY, COOL AND GROOVY ALL STAR JAZZ SHOW, The CBS Festival Of Lively Arts For Young People; Ron Kass and Edgar Bronfman, Jr., Executive Producers; Gary Keys, Producer (CBS)
P. J. AND THE PRESIDENT'S SON, ABC Afterschool Specials; Danny Wilson, Executive Producer; Fran Sears, Producer (ABC)

OUTSTANDING INFORMATIONAL CHILDREN'S SERIES
Emmy(s) to Executive Producer(s) and Producer(s)
ABC MINUTE MAGAZINE, Thomas H. Wolf, Producer (ABC)
AMERICA ROCK, Tom Yohe, Executive Producer; Radford Stone, Producer (ABC)
ANIMALS, ANIMALS, ANIMALS, Lester Cooper, Executive Producer; Peter Weinberg, Producer (ABC)
THE ELECTRIC COMPANY, Samuel Y. Gibbon, Jr., Executive Producer (PBS)

OUTSTANDING INFORMATIONAL CHILDREN'S SPECIAL
Emmy(s) to Executive Producer(s) and Producer(s)
HOW TO FOLLOW THE ELECTION, Sid Darion, Producer (ABC)
MY MOM'S HAVING A BABY, ABC Afterschool Specials; David H. DePatie and Friz Freleng, Executive Producers; Bob Chenault, Producer (ABC)

OUTSTANDING INSTRUCTIONAL CHILDREN'S PROGRAMMING - SERIES AND SPECIALS
Emmy(s) to Executive Producer(s) and Producer(s)
SESAME STREET, Jon Stone, Executive Producer; Dulcy Singer, Producer (PBS)
VILLA ALEGRE, Claudio Guzman, Executive Producer; Larry Gottlieb, Producer (PBS)

OUTSTANDING INDIVIDUAL DIRECTOR FOR A DAYTIME DRAMA SERIES
For a single episode
JOSEPH BEHAR, Days Of Our Lives (NBC)
IRA CIRKER, Another World (NBC)
PAUL E. DAVIS, LEONARD VALENTA, As The World Turns (CBS)
AL RABIN, Days Of Our Lives; Julie And Doug's Wedding (NBC)
JOHN SEDWICK, The Edge Of Night (ABC)
LELA SWIFT, Ryan's Hope (ABC)

OUTSTANDING DAYTIME DRAMA SERIES
Emmy(s) to Executive Producer(s) and Producer(s)
ALL MY CHILDREN, Bud Kloss and Agnes Nixon, Producers (ABC)
ANOTHER WORLD, Paul Rauch, Executive Producer; Mary S. Bonner and Joseph H. Rothenberger, Producers (NBC)
DAYS OF OUR LIVES, Mrs. Ted Corday, Executive Producer; H. Wesley Kenny and Jack Herzberg, Producers (NBC)
THE EDGE OF NIGHT, Erwin Nicholson, Producer (ABC)
RYAN'S HOPE, Paul Avila Mayer and Claire Labine, Executive Producers; Robert Costello, Producer (ABC)

THE INTERNATIONAL AWARDS
Awards presented at the Fourth Annual International Emmy and Directorate Awards

THE INTERNATIONAL DIRECTORATE EMMY AWARD
TALBOT DUCKMANTON, Chairman, and SIR CHARLES MOSES, Secretary-General, ASIAN BROADCASTING UNION

SPECIAL DIRECTORATE AWARD CITATIONS
Howard Thomas, Chairman of Thames Television, Ltd. and Dr. Roberto Marinho, President, TV-Globo Network of Brazil

FICTION
THE NAKED CIVIL SERVANT, Thames Television Limited, London, England
THE STANLEY BAXTER PICTURE SHOW PART III, London Weekend Television, London, England
FAWLTY TOWERS, British Broadcasting Corporation, London, England
LES LAVANDES ET LE RESEDA, Societe Nationale de Programme France Regions, Paris, France
IT'S A LOVELY DAY TOMORROW, ATV Network Limited, Hertfordshire, England

NON-FICTION
REACH FOR TOMORROW, Nippon Television Network, Tokyo, Japan
PROFESSOR MENGLEBERG, Nederlandse Omroep Stichting, The Netherlands
PINCHAS ZUKERMAN, British Broadcasting Corporation, London, England
THE BATTLE OF THE SOMME, British Broadcasting Corporation, London, England
W5-CHILDREN'S HOSPITAL, CTV Canada, Toronto, Ontario, Canada

THE NATIONAL AWARD FOR COMMUNITY SERVICE
RAPE (WGBH-TV) Boston, Massachusetts
EQUALITY, New Jersey Public Television, Trenton, New Jersey
BREAST CANCER: A FACT OF LIFE (KTBS-TV) Shreveport, Louisiana
EYEWITNESS NEWS: YEAR 2000 (KPIX) San Francisco, California
SIGHT AND SOUND: I AM OLD, I AM OLD (WNBC-TV) New York, New York
BEHIND THESE BARS (KAIT-TV) Jonesboro, Arkansas
THE NUCLEAR REACTION (KMGH-TV) Denver, Colorado
GENESIS, JUBA AND OTHER JEWELS (WTOP-TV) Washington, D.C.

OUTSTANDING ACTRESS IN A DAYTIME DRAMA SERIES
NANCY ADDISON, Ryan's Hope (ABC)
HELEN GALLAGHER, Ryan's Hope (ABC)
BEVERLEE McKINSEY, Another World (NBC)
MARY STUART, Search For Tomorrow (CBS)
RUTH WARRICK, All My Children (ABC)

OUTSTANDING ACHIEVEMENT IN DAYTIME DRAMA SPECIALS
The Academy's rules specify the possibility of no winners in this 'Area'. For this reason, the nominees' names have been omitted to spare any possible embarrassment in the event there are no winners.
"THE AMERICAN WOMAN: PORTRAITS OF COURAGE," Gaby Monet, Producer; Lois Nettleton, Performer; Writers, Gaby Monet, Anne Grant (ABC)

OUTSTANDING WRITING FOR A DAYTIME DRAMA SERIES
For a single episode of a series; or for the entire series
WILLIAM J. BELL, PAT FALKEN SMITH, WILLIAM REGA, KAY LENARD, MARGARET STEWART, Days of Our Lives; Series (NBC)
CLAIRE LABINE, PAUL AVILA MAYER, MARY MUNISTERI, Ryan's Hope; Series (ABC)
HARDING LEMAY, TOM KING, PETER SWET, BARRY BERG, JAN MERLIN, ARTHUR GIRON, KATHY CALLAWAY, Another World; Series (NBC)
AGNES NIXON, WISNER WASHAM, KATHRYN McCABE, MARY K. WELLS, JACK WOOD, All My Children; Series (ABC)

ROBERT SODERBERG, EDITH SOMMER, RALPH ELLIS, EUGENIE HUNT, THEODORE APSTEIN, GILLIAN SPENCER, As The World Turns; October 27, 1976 (CBS)

OUTSTANDING ACTOR IN A DAYTIME DRAMA SERIES

VAL DUFOUR, Search For Tomorrow (CBS)
FARLEY GRANGER, One Life to Live (ABC)
LARRY HAINES, Search For Tomorrow (CBS)
LAWRENCE KEITH, All My Children (ABC)
JAMES PRITCHETT, The Doctors (NBC)

CREATIVE ARTS IN TELEVISION

OUTSTANDING ART DIRECTION OR SCENIC DESIGN FOR A COMEDY SERIES

For a single episode of a regular or limited series

THOMAS E. AZZARI, Art Director; Fish; The Really Longest Day (ABC)
SEYMOUR KLATE, Art Director; MARY ANN BIDDLE, Set Decorator; Sirota's Court; The Happy Hooker (NBC) C. MURAWSKI, Art Director; Maude; Walter's Crisis (CBS) DON ROBERTS, Art Director; All In The Family; The Unemployment Story, Part 2 (CBS)
ROY CHRISTOPHER, Art Director; MARY ANN BIDDLE, Set Decorator; Mr. T & Tina; The Americanization of Michi (ABC)

OUTSTANDING ART DIRECTION OR SCENIC DESIGN FOR A DRAMA SERIES

For a single episode of a regular or limited series

TIM HARVEY, Scenic Designer; The Pallisers, Episode No. 1 (PBS)
JOHN CORSO, Art Director; JERRY ADAMS, Set Decorator; Captains And The Kings, Chapter 2; NBC's Best Seller (NBC)
JOSEPH R. JENNINGS, Art Director; SOLOMON BREWER, Set Decorator; Roots, Part 6 (ABC)
JAN SCOTT, Art Director; CHARLES BENNETT, Set Decorator; Roots, Part 2 (ABC)
ED WITTSTEIN, Production Designer; The Adams Chronicles; John Quincy Adams: Congressman (PBS)

OUTSTANDING ART DIRECTION OR SCENIC DESIGN FOR A COMEDY-VARIETY OR MUSIC SERIES

For a single episode of a regular or limited series

ROMAIN JOHNSTON, Art Director; The Mac Davis Show (with Susan St. James, The Pointer Sisters, and Shields & Yarnell) (NBC)
PAUL BARNES and BOB SANSOM, Art Directors; BILL HARP, Set Decorator; The Carol Burnett Show (with Glen Campbell) (CBS)
BILL BOHNERT, Art Director; JOHN TOLD, Set Decorator; Donny And Marie (with Chad Everett and Florence Henderson) (ABC)
EUGENE LEE, LEO YOSHIMURA and FRANNE LEE, NBC's Saturday Night (with Sissy Spacek) (NBC)

OUTSTANDING ART DIRECTION OR SCENIC DESIGN FOR A DRAMATIC SPECIAL

JAN SCOTT, Art Director; ANNE D. McCULLEY, Set Decorator; Eleanor And Franklin: The White House Years; ABC Theatre (ABC)
WILLIAM H. TUNTKE, Art Director; RICHARD FRIEDMAN, Set Decorator; Amelia Earhart; NBC Monday Night At The Movies (NBC)
ROY CHRISTOPHER, Art Director; BEULAH FRANKEL, Set Decorator; The Last Of Mrs. Lincoln; Hollywood Television Theatre (PBS)
TREVOR WILLIAMS, Art Director; ROBERT CHECCHI, Set Decorator; Eccentricities Of A Nightingale; Theater In America; Great Performances (PBS)

OUTSTANDING ART DIRECTION OR SCENIC DESIGN FOR A COMEDY-VARIETY OR MUSIC SPECIAL

ROBERT KELLY, Art Director; America Salutes Richard Rodgers: The Sound Of His Music (CBS)
JAC VENZA, Scenic Designer; American Ballet Theatre: Billy The Kid; Dance In America; Great Performances (PBS)
ROY CHRISTOPHER, Art Director; JOHN HUENERS, Set Decorator; The George Burns Comedy Special (CBS)
WILLIAM MICKLEY, Art Director; American Ballet Theatre: Les Painteurs; Dance In America; Great Performances (PBS)

OUTSTANDING ACHIEVEMENT IN CHOREOGRAPHY

For a single episode of a regular or limited series, or for a special program.

RON FIELD, America Salutes Richard Rodgers: The Sound Of His Music (CBS)
DAVID BLAIR, Swan Lake; Live From Lincoln Center; Great Performances (PBS)
ERNEST O. FLATT, The Carol Burnett Show (with The Pointer Sisters) (CBS)
ALAN JOHNSON, The Shirley MacLaine Special: Where Do We Go From Here? (CBS)
DONALD McKAYLE, Minstrel Man (CBS)

OUTSTANDING CINEMATOGRAPHY IN ENTERTAINMENT PROGRAMMING FOR A SERIES

For a single episode of a regular or limited series

RIC WAITE, Captains And The Kings, Chapter 1; NBC's Best Seller (NBC)
JOSEPH BIROC, The Moneychangers, Part 1; NBC World Premiere Movie; The Big Event (NBC)
JOHN J. JONES, Once An Eagle, Part 1; NBC's Best Seller (NBC)
WILLIAM JURGENSEN, M*A*S*H; Dear Sigmund (CBS)
SHERMAN KUNKEL, Baretta; Soldier In The Jungle (ABC)
STEVAN LARNER, Roots, Part 2 (ABC)
SOL NEGRIN, A.S.C., Kojak; Shield For Murder, Part 2 (CBS)
JOSEPH M. WILCOTS, Roots, Part 7 (ABC)

OUTSTANDING CINEMATOGRAPHY IN ENTERTAINMENT PROGRAMMING FOR A SPECIAL

WILMER C. BUTLER, Raid On Entebbe; The Big Event (NBC)
JAMES CRABE, Eleanor And Franklin: The White House Years; ABC Theatre (ABC)
MARIO TOSI, Sybil; NBC World Premiere Movie; The Big Event (NBC)
TED VOIGTLANDER, A.S.C., The Loneliest Runner (NBC)
RIC WAITE, Tail Gunner Joe; NBC World Premiere Movie; The Big Event (NBC)

OUTSTANDING ACHIEVEMENT IN COSTUME DESIGN FOR A DRAMA OR COMEDY SERIES

For a single episode of a regular or limited series

RAYMOND HUGHES, The Pallisers, Episode No. 1 (PBS)
ALVIN COLT, The Adams Chronicles; Henry Adams: Historian (PBS)
JACK F. MARTELL, Roots, Part 1 (ABC)
JOAN ELLACOTT, Madame Bovary, Episode No. 3; Masterpiece Theatre (PBS)

GRADY HUNT, The Quest; Prairie Woman (NBC)

OUTSTANDING ACHIEVEMENT IN COSTUME DESIGN FOR MUSIC-VARIETY

For a single episode of a regular or limited series, or for a special program

JAN SKALICKY, The Barber Of Seville; Live From Lincoln Center; Great Performances (PBS)
BILL HARGATE, Neil Sedaka Steppin' Out (NBC)
FRANK THOMPSON, America Salutes Richard Rodgers: The Sound Of His Music (CBS)
RET TURNER, BOB MACKIE, The Sonny & Cher Show (with Barbara Eden and The Smothers Brothers) (CBS)
BOB MACKIE, An Evening With Diana Ross; The Big Event (NBC)

OUTSTANDING ACHIEVEMENT IN COSTUME DESIGN FOR A DRAMA SPECIAL

JOE I. TOMPKINS, Eleanor And Franklin: The White House Years; ABC Theatre (ABC)
OLGA LEHMANN, The Man In The Iron Mask; A Bell System Special (NBC)
ALBERT WOLSKY, Beauty And The Beast; Hallmark Hall Of Fame (NBC)

OUTSTANDING FILM EDITING IN A COMEDY SERIES

For a single episode of a regular or limited series

DOUGLAS HINES, A.C.E., The Mary Tyler Moore Show; Murray Can't Lose (CBS)
SAMUEL E. BEETLEY, A.C.E., STANFORD TISCHLER, A.C.E., M*A*S*H; Dear Sigmund (CBS)

OUTSTANDING FILM EDITING IN A DRAMA SERIES

For a single episode of a regular or limited series

NEIL TRAVIS, Roots, Part 1 (ABC)
JAMES T. HECKERT, Roots, Part 8 (ABC)
PETER KIRBY, Roots, Part 3 (ABC)
JERROLD LUDWIG, Rich Man, Poor Man, Book II, Ch. 3 (ABC)
NEIL TRAVIS, JAMES HECKERT, Roots, Part 2 (ABC)

OUTSTANDING FILM EDITING FOR A SPECIAL

RITA ROLAND, A.C.E. and MICHAEL S. McLEAN, A.C.E., Eleanor And Franklin: The White House Years; ABC Theatre (ABC)
BYRON "BUZZ" BRANDT, A.C.E. and BUD ISAACS, A.C.E., Helter Skelter (CBS)
RONALD J. FAGAN, A.C.E., 21 Hours At Munich; The ABC Sunday Night Movie (ABC)
BUD S. ISAACS, A.C.E., ART SEID, A.C.E. and NICK ARCHER, A.C.E., Raid On Entebbe; The Big Event (NBC)
JOHN L. LOEFFLER, The Loneliest Runner (NBC)

OUTSTANDING ACHIEVEMENT IN FILM SOUND EDITING FOR A SERIES

For a single episode of a regular or limited series

LARRY CAROW, LARRY NEIMAN, DON WARNER, COLIN MOUAT, GEORGE FREDRICK, DAVE PETTIJOHN, and PAUL BRUCE RICHARDSON; Roots, Part 2 (ABC)
DALE JOHNSTON, JAMES A. BEAN, CARL J. BRANDON, JOE DiVITALE, DON TOMLINSON, DON WEINMAN and GENE CRAIG, The Six Million Dollar Man; The Return Of Bigfoot, Part 1 (ABC)
DOUGLAS H. GRINDSTAFF, RICHARD RADERMAN, SID LUBOW, HANS NEWMAN, AL KAJITA, LUKE WOLFRAM, DON V. ISAACS, HANK SALERNO, LARRY SINGER and STANLEY M. GILBERT, Fantastic Journey; Atlantium (NBC)
JERRY ROSENTHAL, WILLIAM L. STEVENSON and MICHAEL CORRIGAN, Charlie's Angels; The Mexican Connection (ABC)

OUTSTANDING ACHIEVEMENT IN FILM SOUND EDITING FOR A SPECIAL

BERNARD F. PINCUS, MILTON C. BURROW, GENE ELIOT, DON ERNST, TONY GARBER, DON V. ISAACS, LARRY KAUFMAN, WILLIAM L. MANGER, A. DAVID MARSHALL, RICHARD OSWALD, EDWARD L. SANDLIN and RUSS TINSLEY, Raid On Entebbe; The Big Event (NBC)
DOUGLAS H. GRINDSTAFF, DON V. ISAACS, LARRY KAUFMAN, BOB HUMAN, BUZZ COOPER, JACK A. FINLEY, MARVIN I. KOSBERG, HAROLD LEE CHANEY, DICK FRIEDMAN, BILL ANDREWS, RICHARD RADERMAN, LARRY SINGER, STANLEY M. GILBERT, HANK SALERNO, AL KAJITA and JACK MILNER, The Quest; NBC Thursday Night At The Movies (NBC)
RICHARD HARRISON, Eleanor And Franklin: The White House Years; ABC Theatre (ABC)
JERRY ROSENTHAL, WILLIAM PHILLIPS, JOHN STRAUSS, WILLIAM JACKSON, JAMES YANT, JERRY PIROZZI, and BRUCE BELL, The Boy In The Plastic Bubble; The ABC Friday Night Movie (ABC)

OUTSTANDING ACHIEVEMENT IN FILM SOUND MIXING

For a single episode of a regular or limited series, or for a special program

ALAN BERNARD, GEORGE E. PORTER, EDDIE J. NELSON and ROBERT L. HARMAN, The Savage Bees; NBC Monday Night At The Movies (NBC)
WILLIE D. BURTON, GEORGE E. PORTER, EDDIE J. NELSON and ROBERT L. HARMAN, Roots, Part 4 (ABC)
HOPPY MEHTERIAN, GEORGE E. PORTER, EDDIE J. NELSON and ARNOLD BRAUN, Roots, Part 7 (ABC)
GEORGE E. PORTER, EDDIE J. NELSON, ROBERT L. HARMAN and ARNOLD BRAUN, Roots, Part 8 (ABC)
RICHARD PORTMAN, DAVID RONNE, DONALD W. MAC DOUGALL and EDWARD "CURLY" THIRLWELL, Eleanor And Franklin: The White House Years; ABC Theatre (ABC)
BILL VARNEY, LEONARD PETERSON, ROBERT LITT and WILLIE D. BURTON, Roots, Part 1 (ABC)

OUTSTANDING ACHIEVEMENT IN GRAPHIC DESIGN AND TITLE SEQUENCES

For a single episode of a series, or for a special program. This includes animation only when created for use in titling

EYTAN KELLER, STU BERNSTEIN, Bell Telephone Jubilee (NBC)
PHILL NORMAN, The Moneychangers, Part 1; NBC World Premiere Movie; NBC Saturday Night At The Movies (NBC)
GENE PIOTROWSKY, Visions; The Gardener's Son (PBS)
MARTINE SHEON, DAVID SUMMERS, Previn And The Pittsburgh; Mozart As Keyboard Prodigy (PBS)

OUTSTANDING ACHIEVEMENT IN LIGHTING DIRECTION

For a single episode of a regular or limited series, or for a special program

WILLIAM M. KLAGES and PETER EDWARDS, The Dorothy Hamill Special (ABC)
IMERO FIORENTINO and SCOTT JOHNSON, The Neil Diamond Special (NBC)
GEORGE RIESENBERGER and WILLIAM KNIGHT, The Adams Chronicles; John Quincy Adams: President (PBS)
DICK WEISS and WILLIAM KNIGHT, The Adams Chronicles; Henry Adams: Historian (PBS)
KEN DETTLING and LEARD DAVIS, Visions; The Gold Watch (PBS)

OUTSTANDING ACHIEVEMENT IN MAKE-UP

For a single episode of a series, or for a special program

KEN CHASE, Make-Up Design; JOE DiBELLA, Make-up Artist; Eleanor And Franklin: The White House Years; ABC Theatre (ABC)
DEL ACEVEDO, JOHN CHAMBERS and DAN STRIEPEKE, Beauty And The Beast; Hallmark Hall Of Fame (NBC)
DICK SMITH, Harry S. Truman: Plain Speaking (PBS)
MICHAEL G. WESTMORE, ED BUTTERWORTH and CHARLIE SCHRAM, The Million Dollar Rip-Off; NBC World Premiere Movie; NBC Wednesday Night At The Movies (NBC)
STAN WINSTON, An Evening With Diana Ross; The Big Event (NBC)

OUTSTANDING ACHIEVEMENT IN MUSIC COMPOSITION FOR A SERIES (DRAMATIC UNDERSCORE)

For a single episode of a regular or limited series

QUINCY JONES, GERALD FRIED, Roots, Part 1 (ABC)
ELMER BERNSTEIN, Captains And The Kings, Chapter 8; NBC's Best Seller (NBC)
GERALD FRIED, Roots, Part 8 (ABC)
DICK DE BENEDICTIS, Police Story; Monster Manor (NBC)
JACK URBONT, Bronk; The Vigilante (CBS)

OUTSTANDING ACHIEVEMENT IN MUSIC COMPOSITION FOR A SPECIAL (DRAMATIC UNDERSCORE)

LEONARD ROSENMAN, ALAN BERGMAN and MARILYN BERGMAN, Sybil; NBC World Premiere Movie; The Big Event (NBC)
JOHN BARRY, Eleanor And Franklin: The White House Years; ABC Theatre (ABC)
FRED KARLIN, Minstrel Man (CBS)
DAVID SHIRE, Raid On Entebbe; The Big Event (NBC)
BILLY GOLDENBERG, Helter Skelter (CBS)

OUTSTANDING ACHIEVEMENT IN MUSIC DIRECTION

For a single episode of a series, or a special program, whether it be variety or music

IAN FRASER, America Salutes Richard Rodgers: The Sound Of His Music (CBS)
ANDRE PREVIN, Previn And The Pittsburgh; Mozart As Keyboard Prodigy (PBS)
JACK URBONT, Bronk; The Vigilante (CBS)
PETER MATZ, Sills And Burnett At The Met (CBS)
RAFAEL KUBELIK, New York Philharmonic: Rafael Kubelik; Live From Lincoln Center; Great Performances (PBS)

OUTSTANDING ACHIEVEMENT IN SPECIAL MUSICAL MATERIAL

For a song (which must have both music and lyrics), a theme for a series, or special material for a variety program providing that the first usage of this material was written expressly for television. (Possibility of one Award, more than one Award, or no Award)

BILL DYER and BILLY GOLDENBERG, An Evening with Diana Ross; The Big Event (NBC)
JERROLD IMMEL, How The West Was Won; Series Theme (ABC)
FRED KARLIN (Music) and MEG KARLIN (Lyrics), Minstrel Man; Song: "Early In The Morning" (CBS)
MORTON STEVENS (Music) and HERMINE HILTON (Lyrics), Police Woman; Killer Cowboys; Song: "Leave Me Tomorrow" (NBC)
LARRY GROSSMAN, America Salutes Richard Rodgers: The Sound Of His Music (CBS)

OUTSTANDING ACHIEVEMENT IN TAPE SOUND MIXING

For a single episode of a regular or limited series, or for a special program

DOUG NELSON, John Denver And Friend (ABC)
MICHAEL T. GANNON, JERRY CLEMANS, TOM HUTH and PHIL SERETTI, Police Story; Ice Time (NBC)
DOUG NELSON, NORMAN H. SCHWARTZ and JOHN BLACK, The American Music Awards (ABC)
EMIL NERODA, The Adams Chronicles; John Quincy Adams: President (PBS)

OUTSTANDING ACHIEVEMENT IN TECHNICAL DIRECTION AND ELECTRONIC CAMERAWORK

For a single episode of a regular or limited series, or for a special program

KARL MESSERSCHMIDT, Technical Director; JON OLSON, BRUCE GRAY, JOHN GUTIERREZ, JIM DODGE and WAYNE McDONALD, Cameramen, Doug Henning's World Of Magic (NBC)
ERNIE BUTTELMAN, Technical Director; DAVID HILMER, JAMES BALDEN, JACK DENTON, and MAYO PARTEE, Cameramen, A Special Olivia Newton-John (ABC)
GENE CROWE, Technical Director; SAMUEL ELDOWLEN, TOM DOAKES, LARRY HEIDER, BOB KEYS, WAYNE ORR, BILL PHILBIN and RON SHELDON, Cameramen, The Neil Diamond Special (NBC)
KEN LAMKIN, Technical Director; LEW ADAMS, MIKE KEELER, GARY STANTON and SAMUEL E. DOWLEN, ameramen, Victory At Entebbe (ABC)
KEN ANDERSON, Technical Director; ARTHUR G. VOGEL, JR., Cameraman, Harry S. Truman: Plain Speaking (PBS)

OUTSTANDING ACHIEVEMENT IN VIDEO TAPE EDITING FOR A SERIES

For a single episode of a regular or limited series

ROY STEWART, Visions; The War Widow (PBS)
TERRY PICKFORD, Meeting Of Minds, Episode No. 3 (PBS)
KEN DENISOFF and STOWELL WERDEN, C.P.O. Sharkey; Sharkey Boogies On Down (NBC)
JIMMY B. FRAZIER, Police Story; Ice Time (NBC)

OUTSTANDING ACHIEVEMENT IN VIDEO TAPE EDITING FOR A SPECIAL

GARY H. ANDERSON, American Bandstand's 25th Aniversary (ABC)
THOMAS KLEIN and BILL BRESHEARS, The Barry Manilow Special (ABC)
SUSAN JENKINS and MANUEL MARTINEZ, The Captain And Tennille Special (ABC)
JIMMY B. FRAZIER and DANNY WHITE, The Dorothy Hamill Special (ABC)
JAMES McELROY, MIKE GAVALDON and DAVID SAXON, Victory At Entebbe (ABC)
WILLIAM BRESHEARS and BARBARA BABCOCK, The Neil Diamond Special (NBC)

OUTSTANDING INDIVIDUAL ACHIEVEMENT IN ANY AREA OF CREATIVE TECHNICAL CRAFTS

An Award for individual technical craft achievement which does not fall into a specific category, and is not otherwise recognized. (Possibility of one Award, more than one Award, or no Award)

EMMA di VITTORIO (Hairstylist), VIVIENNE WALKER (Hairstylist), Eleanor and Franklin: The White House Years, ABC Theatre (ABC)
LARRY GERMAIN (Hairstylist), Little House on the Prairie, To Live with Fear (NBC)
NAOMI CAVIN (Hairstylist), The Great Houndinis; The ABC Friday Night Movie (ABC)
DICK WILSON (Live Sound Mixing), DOUG NELSON (Live Sound Mixing), The 28th Annual Emmy Awards (ABC)
ROBERT BIGGART (Tape Sound Editing), PATRICK SOMERSET (Tape Sound Editing), Victory At Entebbe (ABC)

SPECIAL CLASSIFICATION OF OUTSTANDING INDIVIDUAL ACHIEVEMENT

An Award for unique individual achievement which does not fall into a specific category, and is not otherwise recognized. (Possibility of one Award, more than one Award, or no Award)

ALLEN BREWSTER, BOB ROETHLE, WILLIAM LORENZ, MANUEL MARTINEZ, RON FLEURY, MIKE WELCH, JERRY BURLING, WALTER BALDERSON, CHUCK DROEGE (Video Tape Editing), The First Fifty Years; The Big Event (NBC)
GEORGE PITTS, CLAY CASSELL (Film Editing), The First Fifty Years; The Big Event (NBC)
ENZO MARTINELLI (Cinematography), Nancy Drew/Hardy Boys Mysteries; Mystery of the Haunted House (ABC)
ROBERT K. LAMBERT, PETER C. JOHNSON (Film Editing), Life Goes to the Movies; The Big Event (NBC)

OUTSTANDING INDIVIDUAL ACHIEVEMENT IN CHILDREN'S PROGRAMMING

For a single episode of a regular or limited series, or for a special program (Possibility of one Award, more than one Award, or no Award)

JEAN DE JOUX (Videoanimation), ELIZABETH SAVEL (Videoanimation), Peter Pan; Hallmark Hall of Fame; The Big Event (NBC)
BILL HARGATE (Costume Designer), Pinocchio (CBS)
JERRY GREENE (Video Tape Editor), Pinocchio (CBS)
MICHAEL TILSON THOMAS (Music Director), CBS Festival of Lively Arts For Young People; New York Philharmonic Young People's Concert; Making Pictures With Music (CBS)
STAN WINSTON (Make-up Artist), ED BUTTERWORTH (Make-up Artist) Pinocchio (CBS)

OUTSTANDING ACHIEVEMENT IN COVERAGE OF SPECIAL EVENT - INDIVIDUALS

An Award for individual achievement. A special event is a ingle program presented as live coverage; i.e., parades, pageants, awards presentations, salutes and coverage of other live events which were not covered by the news division. (Possibility of one Award, more than one Award, or no Award)

BRIAN C. BARTHOLOMEW, KEATON S. WALKER, ART Directors, The 28th Annual Emmy Awards (ABC)

OUTSTANDING ACHIEVEMENT IN BROADCAST JOURNALISM

ATAS Broadcast Journalism Awards to:

MacNEIL-LEHRER REPORT; ERIC SEVAREID; LEAGUE OF WOMEN VOTERS; 60 MINUTES

OUTSTANDING ACHIEVEMENT IN ENGINEERING DEVELOPMENT

An Award to an individual, a company or an organization for developments in engineering which are either so extensive an improvement on existing methods or so innovative in nature that they materially affect the transmission, recording or reception of television.

An Emmy was awarded to the AMERICAN BROADCASTING COMPANY for leadership in establishing Circularly Polarized Transmission to improve television reception, and a citation was awarded to VARIAN ASSOCIATES for improving the efficiency of UHF Klystrons.

1977/78

NIGHTTIME PROGRAMMING

OUTSTANDING COMEDY SERIES
Award(s) to Executive Producer(s) and/or Producer(s)

ALL IN THE FAMILY, Mort Lachman, Executive Producer; Milt Josefsberg, Producer (CBS)
BARNEY MILLER, Danny Arnold, Executive Producer; Tony Sheehan, Producer (ABC)
M*A*S*H, Burt Metcalfe, Producer (CBS)
SOAP, Paul Junger Witt, Tony Thomas, Executive Producers; Susan Harris, Producer (ABC)
THREE'S COMPANY, Don Nicholl, Michael Ross, Bernie West, Producers (ABC)

OUTSTANDING DRAMA SERIES
Award(s) to Executive Producer(s) and/or Producer(s)

THE ROCKFORD FILES, Meta Rosenberg, Executive Producer; Stephen J. Cannell, Supervising Producer; David Chase, Chas. Floyd Johnson, Producers (NBC)
COLUMBO, Richard Alan Simmons, Executive Producer (NBC)
FAMILY, Aaron Spelling, Leonard Goldberg, Executive Producers; Nigel McKeand, Producer (ABC)
LOU GRANT, James L Brooks, Allan Burns, Gene Reynolds, Executive Producers; Gene Reynolds, Producer (CBS)
QUINCY, Glen A. Larson, Jud Kinberg, Richard Irving, Executive Producers; B. W. Sandefur, Supervising Producer; Chris Morgan, Peter J. Thompson, Edward J. Montagne, Robert F. O'Neill, Producers; Michael Sloan, Associate Executive Producer (NBC)

SPECIAL ATAS GOVERNORS AWARD
TO LARRY STEWART, President of ATAS, 1975-1977.

OUTSTANDING COMEDY-VARIETY OR MUSIC SERIES
Award(s) to Executive Producer(s) and/or Producer(s) and Star(s), if applicable
THE MUPPET SHOW, David Lazer, Executive Producer; Jim Henson, Producer; The Muppets (Frank Oz, Jerry Nelson, Richard Hunt, Dave Goelz, Jim Henson), Stars (Synd)
AMERICA 2NIGHT, Alan Thicke, Producer (Synd)
THE CAROL BURNETT SHOW, Joe Hamilton, Executive Producer; Ed Simmons, Producer; Carol Burnett, Star (CBS)
EVENING AT POPS, Bill Cosel, Producer; Arthur Fiedler, Star (PBS)
NBC'S SATURDAY NIGHT LIVE, Lorne Michaels, Producer (NBC)

OUTSTANDING LIMITED SERIES
Award(s) to Executive Producer(s) and/or Producer(s)
HOLOCAUST, Herbert Brodkin, Executive Producer; Robert Berger, Producer (NBC)
KING, Edward S. Feldman, Executive Producer; Paul Maslansky, Producer; William Finnegan, Supervising Producer (NBC)
WASHINGTON: BEHIND CLOSED DOORS, Stanley Kallis, Executive Producer; Eric Bercovici, David W. Rintels, Supervising Producers; Norman Powell, Producer (ABC)
ANNA KARENINA, MASTERPIECE THEATRE, Ken Riddington, Executive Producer; Donald Wilson, Producer; Joan Sullivan, Series Producer (PBS)
I, CLAUDIUS, MASTERPIECE THEATRE, Joan Sullivan, Series Producer; Martin Lisemore, Producer (PBS)

FIRST ANNUAL ATAS GOVERNORS AWARD
To WILLIAM S. PALEY, Chairman of the Board, CBS

OUTSTANDING SPECIAL - DRAMA OR COMEDY
Award(s) to Executive Producer(s) and/or Producer(s)
THE GATHERING, Joseph Barbera, Executive Producer; Harry R. Sherman, Producer, (ABC)
A DEATH IN CANAAN, Robert W. Christiansen, Rick Rosenberg, Producers (CBS)
JESUS OF NAZARETH, Bernard J. Kingham, Executive Producer; Vincenzo Labella, Producer (NBC)
OUR TOWN, BELL SYSTEM SPECIAL, Saul Jaffe, Executive Producer; George Schaefer, Producer (NBC)
YOUNG JOE, THE FORGOTTEN KENNEDY, William McCutchen, Producer (ABC)

OUTSTANDING SPECIAL - COMEDY-VARIETY OR MUSIC
Award(s) to Executive Producer(s) and/or Producer(s) and Star(s), if applicable
BETTE MIDLER - OL' RED HAIR IS BACK, Aaron Russo, Executive Producer; Gary Smith, Dwight Hemion, Producers; Bette Midler, Star, (NBC)
DOUG HENNING'S WORLD OF MAGIC, Jerry Goldstein, Executive Producer; Walter C. Miller, Producer; Doug Henning, Star, (NBC)
THE GEORGE BURNS ONE-MAN SHOW, Irving Fein, Executive Producer; Stan Harris, Producer; George Burns, Star, (CBS)
NEIL DIAMOND: I'M GLAD YOU'RE HERE WITH ME TONIGHT, Jerry Weintraub, Executive Producer; Art Fisher, Producer; Neil Diamond, Star, (NBC)
THE SECOND BARRY MANILOW SPECIAL, Miles J. Lourie, Executive Producer; Ernest Chambers, Barry Manilow, Producers; Barry Manilow, Star, (ABC)

OUTSTANDING CLASSICAL PROGRAM IN THE PERFORMING ARTS
For a special program, or for a series (excluding drama). Award(s) to Executive Producer(s) and/or Producer(s) and Star(s), if applicable **AMERICAN BALLET THEATRE'S "GISELLE", Live From Lincoln Center; John Goberman, Producer (PBS)**
AMERICAN BALLET THEATRE, Live From Lincoln Center; John Goberman, Executive Producer; Emile Ardolino, Producer, (PBS)
DANCE IN AMERICA: CHOREOGRAPHY BY BALANCHINE; Jac Venza, Executive Producer; Emile Ardolino, Merrill Brockway, Producers, (PBS)
LA BOHEME, LIVE FROM THE MET; Michael Bronson, Executive Producer; John Goberman, Producer, (PBS)
THE NUTCRACKER (BARYSHNIKOV), Herman Krawitz, Executive Producer; Yanna Kroyt Brandt, Producer (CBS)

OUTSTANDING CHILDREN'S SPECIAL
For specials which were broadcast in the evening. Award(s) to Executive Producer(s) and/or Producer(s)
HALLOWEEN IS GRINCH NIGHT, David H. DePatie, Friz Freleng, Executive Producers; Ted Geisel, Producer (ABC)
A CONNECTICUT YANKEE IN KING ARTHUR'S COURT, Jay Rayvid, Executive Producer; Jay Rayvid, Chiz Schultz and Shep Greene, Producers (PBS)
THE FAT ALBERT CHRISTMAS SPECIAL, Lou Scheimer, Norm Prescott, Producers, (CBS)
ONCE UPON A BROTHERS GRIMM, Bernard Rothman, Jack Wohl, Producers, (CBS)
PETER LUNDY AND THE MEDICINE HAT STALLION Ed Friendly, Producer, (NBC)

OUTSTANDING INFORMATIONAL SERIES
Award(s) to Executive Producer(s) and/or Producer(s)
THE BODY HUMAN, Thomas W. Moore, Executive Producer; Alfred R. Kelman, Producer (CBS)
BETWEEN THE WARS, Alan Landsburg, Executive Producer; Anthony Potter, Series Producer (Synd)
COUSTEAU OASIS IN SPACE, Philippe Cousteau, Executive Producer; Andrew Solt, Producer (PBS)
MUTUAL OF OMAHA'S WILD KINGDOM, Don Meir, Producer (Synd)
NOVA, John Angier, Executive Producer (PBS)

OUTSTANDING INFORMATIONAL SPECIAL
Award(s) to Executive Producer(s) and/or Producer(s)
THE GREAT WHALES, NATIONAL GEOGRAPHIC, Thomas Skinner, Dennis B. Kane, Executive Producers; Nicolas Noxon, Producer, (PBS)
BING CROSBY: HIS LIFE AND LEGEND, Franklin Konigsberg, Executive Producer; Marshall Flaum, Producer, (ABC)
CALYPSO'S SEARCH FOR ATLANTIS, COUSTEAU ODYSSEY, Jacques Cousteau, Philippe Cousteau, Executive Producers; Andrew Solt, Producer, (PBS)
THE TREASURES OF TUTANKHAMUN, Donald Knox, Executive Producer; Valerie Gentile, Producer, (PBS)
TUT: THE BOY KING, George A. Heinemann, Executive Producer (NBC)

OUTSTANDING ACHIEVEMENT IN COVERAGE OF SPECIAL EVENTS - PROGRAMS
(Possibility of one Award, more than one Award, or no Award)
50th ANNUAL AWARDS OF THE ACADEMY OF MOTION PICTURE ARTS AND SCIENCES, Howard Koch, Producer (ABC)

SPECIAL CLASSIFICATION OF OUTSTANDING PROGRAM ACHIEVEMENT

(Possibility of one Award, more than one Award, or no Award)

THE TONIGHT SHOW STARRING JOHNNY CARSON, Fred de Cordova, Producer; Johnny Carson, Star (NBC)
THE AMERICAN FILM INSTITUTE SALUTE TO BETTE DAVIS, George Stevens, Jr., Executive Producer; Perry Lafferty, Supervising Producer; Robert Scheerer, Producer, (CBS)
THE AMERICAN FILM INSTITUTE SALUTE TO HENRY FONDA, George Stevens, Jr., Executive Producer; George Stevens, Jr., Eric Lieber, Producers, (CBS)
THE DICK CAVETT SHOW, Joan Konner, Executive Producer; Christopher Porterfield, Julie Rubenstein, Lynda Sheldon, Tom O'Malley, Producers, Dick Cavett; Star (PBS)
NBC: THE FIRST FIFTY YEARS - A CLOSER LOOK, Greg Garrison, Executive Producer; Lee Hale, Producer, (NBC)

OUTSTANDING LEAD ACTOR IN A COMEDY SERIES

CARROLL O'CONNOR, All In The Family (CBS)
ALAN ALDA, M*A*S*H (CBS)
HAL LINDEN, Barney Miller (ABC)
JOHN RITTER, Three's Company (ABC)
HENRY WINKLER, Happy Days (ABC)

OUTSTANDING LEAD ACTOR IN A DRAMA SERIES

EDWARD ASNER, Lou Grant (CBS)
JAMES BRODERICK, Family (ABC)
PETER FALK, Columbo (NBC)
JAMES GARNER, Rockford Files (NBC)
JACK KLUGMAN, Quincy (NBC)
RALPH WAITE, The Waltons (CBS)

OUTSTANDING LEAD ACTOR IN A LIMITED SERIES

MICHAEL MORIARTY, Holocaust (NBC)
HAL HOLBROOK, The Awakening Land (NBC)
JASON ROBARDS, JR., Washington: Behind Closed Doors (ABC)
FRITZ WEAVER, Holocaust (NBC)
PAUL WINFIELD, King (NBC)

OUTSTANDING LEAD ACTOR IN A DRAMA OR COMEDY SPECIAL

FRED ASTAIRE, A Family Upside Down, (NBC)
ALAN ALDA, Kill Me If You Can, (NBC)
HAL HOLBROOK, Our Town, Bell System, (NBC)
MARTIN SHEEN, Taxi!!!, Hallmark Hall of Fame, (NBC)
JAMES STACY, Just a Little Inconvenience, (NBC)

OUTSTANDING LEAD ACTOR FOR A SINGLE APPEARANCE IN A DRAMA OR COMEDY SERIES

BARNARD HUGHES, Lou Grant, Judge, (CBS)
DAVID CASSIDY, Police Story, A Chance to Live, (NBC)
WILL GEER, The Love Boat, The Old Man and the Runaway, (ABC)
JUDD HIRSCH, Rhoda, Rhoda Likes Mike, (CBS)
JOHN RUBINSTEIN, Family, And Baby Makes Three, (ABC)
KEENAN WYNN, Police Woman, Good Old Uncle Ben, (NBC)

OUTSTANDING LEAD ACTRESS IN A COMEDY SERIES

JEAN STAPLETON, All In The Family (CBS)
BEATRICE ARTHUR, Maude (CBS)
CATHRYN DAMON, Soap (ABC)
VALERIE HARPER, Rhoda (CBS)
KATHERINE HELMOND, Soap (ABC)
SUZANNE PLESHETTE, The Bob Newhart Show (CBS)

OUTSTANDING LEAD ACTRESS IN A DRAMA SERIES

SADA THOMPSON, Family (ABC)
MELISSA SUE ANDERSON, Little House On The Prairie (NBC)
FIONNULA FLANAGAN, How The West Was Won (ABC)
KATE JACKSON, Charlie's Angels (ABC)
MICHAEL LEARNED, The Waltons (CBS)
SUSAN SULLIVAN, Julie Farr, M.D. (ABC)

OUTSTANDING LEAD ACTRESS IN A LIMITED SERIES

MERYL STREEP, Holocaust (NBC)
ROSEMARY HARRIS, Holocaust (NBC)
ELIZABETH MONTGOMERY, The Awakening Land (NBC)
LEE REMICK, Wheels (NBC)
CICELY TYSON, King (NBC)

OUTSTANDING LEAD ACTRESS IN A DRAMA OR COMEDY SPECIAL

JOANNE WOODWARD, See How She Runs, GE Theatre (CBS)
HELEN HAYES, A Family Upside Down, (NBC)
EVA MARIE SAINT, Taxi!!!, Hallmark Hall of Fame, (NBC)
MAUREEN STAPLETON, The Gathering, (ABC)
SADA THOMPSON, Our Town, Bell System, (NBC)

OUTSTANDING LEAD ACTRESS FOR A SINGLE APPEARANCE IN A DRAMA OR COMEDY SERIES

RITA MORENO, The Rockford Files, The Paper Palace, (NBC)
PATTY DUKE ASTIN, Having Babies, Having Babies III, (ABC)
KATE JACKSON, James at 15/16, James at 15, (NBC)
JAYNE MEADOWS, Meeting of The Minds, Luther, Voltaire, Plato, Nightingale, (PBS)
IRENE TEDROW, James at 15/16, Ducks, (NBC)

OUTSTANDING CONTINUING PERFORMANCE BY A SUPPORTING ACTOR IN A COMEDY SERIES

For a regular or limited series

ROB REINER, All In The Family (CBS)
TOM BOSLEY, Happy Days (ABC)
GARY BURGHOFF, M*A*S*H (CBS)
HARRY MORGAN, M*A*S*H (CBS)
VIC TAYBACK, Alice (CBS)

OUTSTANDING CONTINUING PERFORMANCE BY A SUPPORTING ACTOR IN A DRAMA SERIES

For a regular or limited series

ROBERT VAUGHN, Washington: Behind Closed Doors (ABC)
OSSIE DAVIS, King (NBC)
WILL GEER, The Waltons (CBS)
SAM WANAMAKER, Holocaust (NBC)
DAVID WARNER, Holocaust (NBC)

OUTSTANDING CONTINUING OR SINGLE PERFORMANCE BY A SUPPORTING ACTOR IN VARIETY OR MUSIC
For a continuing role in a regular or limited series, or for a one-time appearance in a series or a special
TIM CONWAY, The Carol Burnett Show (Series) (CBS)
DAN AYKROYD, NBC'S Saturday Night Live (Series) (NBC)
JOHN BELUSHI, NBC'S Saturday Night Live (Series) (NBC)
LOUIS GOSSETT, JR. The Sentry Collection Presents Ben Vereen - His Roots, (ABC)
PETER SELLERS, The Muppet Show (Synd)

OUTSTANDING PERFORMANCE BY A SUPPORTING ACTOR IN A COMEDY OR DRAMA SPECIAL
HOWARD DA SILVA, Verna: USO Girl, Great Performances, (PBS)
JAMES FARENTINO, Jesus Of Nazareth, (NBC)
BURGESS MEREDITH, The Last Hurrah, Hallmark Hall Of Fame, (NBC)
DONALD PLEASENCE, The Defection of Simas Kudirka (CBS)
EFREM ZIMBALIST, JR., A Family Upside Down, (NBC)

OUTSTANDING SINGLE PERFORMANCE BY A SUPPORTING ACTOR IN A COMEDY OR DRAMA SERIES
For a one-time appearance in a regular or limited series
RICARDO MONTALBAN, How The West Was Won, Part II, (ABC)
WILL GEER, Eight Is Enough, Yes Nicholas. . .There Is A Santa Claus, (ABC)
LARRY GELMAN, Barney Miller, Goodbye Mr. Fish - Part II, (ABC)
HAROLD GOULD, Rhoda, Happy Anniversary, (CBS)
ABE VIGODA, Barney Miller, Goodbye Mr. Fish - Part II, (ABC)

OUTSTANDING CONTINUING PERFORMANCE BY A SUPPORTING ACTRESS IN A COMEDY SERIES
For a regular or limited series
JULIE KAVNER, Rhoda (CBS)
POLLY HOLLIDAY, Alice (CBS)
SALLY STRUTHERS, All In The Family (CBS)
LORETTA SWIT, M*A*S*H (CBS)
NANCY WALKER, Rhoda (CBS)

OUTSTANDING CONTINUING PERFORMANCE BY A SUPPORTING ACTRESS IN A DRAMA SERIES
For a regular or limited series
NANCY MARCHAND, Lou Grant (CBS)
MEREDITH BAXTER BIRNEY, Family (CBS)
TOVAH FELDSHUH, Holocaust (NBC)
LINDA KELSEY, Lou Grant (CBS)
KRISTY McNICHOL, Family (ABC)

OUTSTANDING CONTINUING OR SINGLE PERFORMANCE BY A SUPPORTING ACTRESS IN VARIETY OR MUSIC
For a continuing role in a regular or limited series, or for a one-time appearance in a series or a special
GILDA RADNER, NBC'S Saturday Night Live, (Series) (NBC)
BEATRICE ARTHUR, Laugh-In, (NBC)
JANE CURTIN, NBC'S Saturday Night Live (Series) (NBC)
DOLLY PARTON, Cher. . .Special, (ABC)
BERNADETTE PETERS, The Muppet Show (Synd)

OUTSTANDING PERFORMANCE BY A SUPPORTING ACTRESS IN A DRAMA OR COMEDY SPECIAL
EVA LE GALLIENNE, The Royal Family, (PBS)
PATTY DUKE ASTIN, A Family Upside Down, (NBC)
TYNE DALY, Intimate Strangers, (ABC)
MARIETTE HARTLEY, The Last Hurrah, Hallmark Hall Of Fame, (NBC)
CLORIS LEACHMAN, It Happed One Christmas, (ABC)
VIVECA LINDFORS, A Question Of Guilt, (CBS)

OUTSTANDING SINGLE PERFORMANCE BY A SUPPORTING ACTRESS IN A COMEDY OR DRAMA SERIES
For a one-time appearance in a regular or limited series
BLANCHE BAKER, Holocaust, Part I (NBC)
ELLEN CORBY, The Waltons, Grandma Comes Home, (CBS)
JEANETTE NOLAN, The Awakening Land, Part I, (NBC)
BEULAH QUO, Meeting Of The Minds, Douglass, Tz'u-Hsi, Beccaria, De Sade, (PBS)
BEATRICE STRAIGHT, The Dain Curse, Part I, (CBS)

OUTSTANDING WRITING IN A COMEDY SERIES
For a single episode of a regular or limited series with continuing characters and/or theme
BOB WEISKOPF and BOB SCHILLER, Teleplay, BARRY HARMAN and HARVE BROSTEN, Story; All In The Family, Cousin Liz, (CBS)
ALAN ALDA, M*A*S*H, Fallen Idol, (CBS)
MEL TOLKIN, LARRY RHINE, Teleplay, ERIK TARLOFF, Story; All In The Family, Edith's Crisis Of Faith - Part II, (CBS)
BOB WEISKOPF and BOB SCHILLER, All In The Family, Edith's 50th Birthday, (CBS)

OUTSTANDING WRITING IN A DRAMA SERIES
For an episode of a regular or limited series with continuing characters and/or theme
GERALD GREEN, Holocaust, (NBC)
STEVE ALLEN, Meeting of The Minds, (PBS)
ALAN AYCKBOURN, The Norman Conquests, (CBS)
ROBERT W. LENSKI, The Dain Curse, (CBS)
ABBY MANN, King, (NBC)

OUTSTANDING WRITING IN A COMEDY-VARIETY OR MUSIC SERIES
For an episode of a regular or limited series
ED SIMMONS, ROGER BEATTY, RICK HAWKINS, LIZ SAGE, ROBERT ILLES, JAMES STEIN, FRANELLE SILVER, LARRY SIEGEL, TIM CONWAY, BILL RICHMOND, GENE PERRET, DICK CLAIR and JENNA McMAHON, The Carol Burnett Show with Steve Martin, Betty White, (CBS)
ED SIMMONS, ROGER BEATTY, ELIAS DAVIS, DAVID POLLOCK, RICK

HAWKINS, LIZ SAGE, ADELE STYLER, BURT STYLER, TIM CONWAY, BILL RICHMOND, GENE PERRET, DICK CLAIR and JENNA McMAHON, The Carol Burnett Show with Ken Berry, (CBS)
JERRY JUHL, DON HINKLEY, JOSEPH BAILEY and JIM HENSON, The Muppet Show with Dom De Luise (Synd)
ALAN THICKE, JOHN BONI, NORMAN STILES, JEREMY STEVENS, TOM MOORE, ROBERT ILLES, JAMES STEIN, HARRY SHEARER, TOM DUNSMUIR and DAN WILCOX, America 2Night with Carol Burnett (Synd)
DAN AYKROYD, ANNE BEATTS, TOM DAVIS, JAMES DOWNEY, BRIAN DOYLE-MURRAY, AL FRANKEN, LORNE MICHAELS, MARILYN SUZANNE MILLER, DON NOVELLO, MICHAEL O'DONOGHUE, HERB SARGENT, TOM SCHILLER, ROSIE SHUSTER and ALAN ZWEIBEL, NBC's Saturday Night Live, Host Steve Martin (NBC)

OUTSTANDING WRITING IN A COMEDY-VARIETY OR MUSIC SPECIAL

LORNE MICHAELS, PAUL SIMON, CHEVY CHASE, TOM DAVIS, AL FRANKEN, CHARLES GRODIN, LILY TOMLIN and ALAN ZWEIBEL, The Paul Simon Special, (NBC)
ALAN BUZ KOHAN, ROD WARREN, PAT McCORMICK, TOM EYEN, JERRY BLATT, BETTE MIDLER and BRUCE VILANCH, Bette Midler - Ol' Red Hair Is Back, (NBC)
ELON PACKARD, FRED FOX and SEAMAN JACOBS The George Burns One-Man Show, (CBS)
ERNEST CHAMBERS and BARRY MANILOW, The Second Barry Manilow Special, (ABC)
MICHAEL H. KAGAN, The Sentry Collection Presents Ben Vereen - His Roots, (ABC)

OUTSTANDING WRITING IN A SPECIAL PROGRAM - DRAMA OR COMEDY - ORIGINAL TELEPLAY

GEORGE RUBINO, The Last Tenant, (ABC)
BRUCE FELDMAN, The Defection of Simas Kudirka, (CBS)
RICHARD LEVINSON and WILLIAM LINK, The Storyteller, (NBC)
LORING MANDEL, Breaking Up, (ABC)
JERRY McNEELY, Something For Joey, (CBS)
JAMES POE, The Gathering, (ABC)

OUTSTANDING WRITING IN A SPECIAL PROGRAM - DRAMA OR COMEDY - ADAPTATION

CARYL LEDNER, Mary White, (ABC)
BLANCHE HANALIS, A Love Affair: The Eleanor and Lou Gehrig Story (NBC)
ALBERT INNAURATO, Verna: USO Girl, Great Performances, (PBS)
JEROME LAWRENCE and ROBERT E. LEE, Actor, Hollywood Television Theatre (PBS)
BARBARA TURNER, The War Between The Tates, (NBC)

OUTSTANDING DIRECTING IN A COMEDY SERIES

For an episode of a regular or limited series with continuing characters and/or theme
PAUL BOGART, All In The Family, Edith's 50th Birthday (CBS)
HAL COOPER, Maude, Vivian's Decision, (CBS)
BURT METCALFE, ALAN ALDA, M*A*S*H, Comrades In Arms - Part I, (CBS)
JERRY PARIS, Happy Days, Richie Almost Dies, (ABC)
JAY SANDRICH, Soap, #24, (ABC)

OUTSTANDING DIRECTING IN A DRAMA SERIES

For an episode of a regular or limited series with continuing characters and/or theme
MARVIN J. CHOMSKY, Holocaust (NBC)
ABBY MANN, King (NBC)
GARY NELSON, Washington: Behind Closed Doors (ABC)
E. W. SWACKHAMER, The Dain Curse (CBS)
HERBERT WISE, I Claudius, Masterpiece Theatre (PBS)

OUTSTANDING DIRECTING IN A SPECIAL PROGRAM - DRAMA OR COMEDY

DAVID LOWELL RICH, The Defection of Simas Kudirka (CBS)
LOU ANTONIO, Something For Joey (CBS)
RANDAL KLEISER, The Gathering (ABC)
DELBERT MANN, Breaking Up (ABC)
RONALD MAXWELL, Verna: USO Girl, Great Performances (PBS)
GEORGE SCHAEFER, Our Town, Bell System (NBC)

OUTSTANDING DIRECTING IN A COMEDY-VARIETY OR MUSIC SERIES

For an episode of a regular or limited series
DAVE POWERS, The Carol Burnett Show with Steve Martin, Betty White, (CBS)
STEVE BINDER, Shields and Yarnell with John Aylesworth, (CBS)
PETER HARRIS, The Muppet Show with Elton John (Synd)
JOHN C. MOFFITT, The Richard Pryor Show with Paula Kelly (NBC)
DAVE WILSON, NBC's Saturday Night Live with Steve Martin (NBC)

OUTSTANDING DIRECTING IN A COMEDY-VARIETY OR MUSIC SPECIAL

DWIGHT HEMION, The Sentry Collection Presents Ben Vereen - His Roots (ABC)
TONY CHARMOLI, Mitzi...Zings Into Spring (CBS)
WALTER C. MILLER, Doug Henning's World of Magic (NBC)
GEORGE SCHAEFER, The Second Barry Manilow Special (ABC)
DAVE WILSON, The Paul Simon Special (NBC)

DAYTIME PROGRAMMING

OUTSTANDING HOST OR HOSTESS IN A TALK, SERVICE, OR VARIETY SERIES

JAMES CROCKETT Crockett's Victory Garden (PBS)
PHIL DONAHUE Donahue (Synd)
JIM NABORS The Jim Nabors Show (Synd)
DINAH SHORE Dinah! (Synd)

OUTSTANDING INDIVIDUAL DIRECTOR FOR A VARIETY PROGRAM

For a single episode
DONALD R. KING The Mike Douglas Show, Mike in Hollywood (Synd)
MARTIN HAIG MACKEY Over Easy (PBS)
GLEN SWANSON Dinah! Dinah and the Philadelphians (Synd)

OUTSTANDING TALK, SERVICE, OR VARIETY SERIES

Emmy(s) to Executive Producer(s) and Producer(s)
DINAH! Henry Jaffe, Executive Producer; Fred Tatashore, Producer (Synd)
MERV GRIFFIN SHOW Bob Murphy, Producer (Synd)
THE MIKE DOUGLAS SHOW Frank Miller, Executive Producer; Brad Lachman, Producer (Synd)
DONAHUE Richard Mincer, Executive Producer; Patricia McMillen,

Producer (Synd)

OUTSTANDING INDIVIDUAL DIRECTOR FOR A DAYTIME GAME OR AUDIENCE PARTICIPATION SHOW

For a single episode
PAUL ALTER, Family Feud, Valentine's Day Celebration Special (ABC)
MIKE GARGIULO, The $20,000 Pyramid (ABC)

OUTSTANDING HOST OR HOSTESS IN A GAME OR AUDIENCE PARTICIPATION SHOW

DICK CLARK, The $20,000 Pyramid (ABC)
RICHARD DAWSON, Family Feud (ABC)
GENE RAYBURN, Match Game (CBS)
CHUCK WOOLERY, SUSAN STAFFORD, Wheel of Fortune (NBC)

OUTSTANDING GAME OR AUDIENCE PARTICIPATION SHOW

Emmy(s) to Executive Producer(s) and Producer(s)
FAMILY FEUD, Howard Felsher, Producer (ABC)
HOLLYWOOD SQUARES, Merrill Heatter and Bob Quigley, Executive Producers; Jay Redack, Producer (NBC)
THE $20,000 PYRAMID, Bob Stewart, Executive Producer; Anne Marie Schmitt, Producer (ABC)

SPECIAL CLASSIFICATION OF OUTSTANDING PROGRAM ACHIEVEMENT

(Possibility of one Award, more than one Award or no Award)
CAMERA THREE John Musilli, Executive Producer; John Musilli, Roger Englander, Producers (CBS)
GOOD MORNING AMERICA, Woody Fraser, Executive Producer; George Merlis, Merrill Mazuer, Bob Blum, Producers (ABC)
LIVE FROM LINCOLN CENTER: RECITAL OF TENOR LUCIANO PAVAROTTI FROM THE MET John Goberman, Executive Producer (PBS)
MUTUAL OF OMAHA'S WILD KINGDOM, Don Meir, Executive Producer (Synd)

OUTSTANDING CHILDREN'S INFORMATIONAL SERIES

Emmy(s) to Executive Producer(s) and Producer(s)
ABC MINUTE MAGAZINE, Tom Wolf, Executive Producer (ABC)
ANIMALS, ANIMALS, ANIMALS, Lester Cooper, Executive Producer; Paul Weinberg, Producer (ABC)
VILLA ALEGRE, Claudio Guzman, Executive Producer; Larry Gotlieb, Producer (PBS)

OUTSTANDING CHILDREN'S INSTRUCTIONAL SERIES

Emmy(s) to Executive Producer(s) and Producer(s)
SCHOOLHOUSE ROCK, Tom Yohe, Executive Producer; Radford Stone, George Newall, Producers (ABC)
SESAME STREET, Al Hyslop, Producer (PBS)

OUTSTANDING CHILDREN'S ENTERTAINMENT SPECIAL

Emmy(s) to Executive Producer(s) and Producer(s)
A PIECE OF CAKE, Special Treat; Marilyn Olin, Lee Polk, Producers (NBC)
HEWITT'S JUST DIFFERENT, ABC Afterschool Special; Daniel Wilson, Executive Producer; Fran Sears, Producer (ABC) HOW THE BEATLES CHANGED THE WORLD, Special Treat; Charles E. Andrews, Ken Greengrass, Executive Producers (NBC)
I CAN, The Winners; Robert Guenette, Executive Producer; Paul Asselin, Diane Asselin, Producers (CBS)
JOURNEY TOGETHER, The Winners; Robert Guenette, Executive Producer; Paul Asselin and Diane Asselin, Producers (CBS)
MAN FROM NOWHERE, Once Upon A Classic; Jay Rayvid, Executive Producer; Ship Greene, Producer (PBS)
THE PINBALLS, ABC Afterschool Special; Martin Tahse, Producer (ABC)

OUTSTANDING CHILDREN'S ENTERTAINMENT SERIES

Emmy(s) to Executive Producer(s) and Producer(s)
CAPTAIN KANGAROO, Jim Hirschfeld, Producer (CBS)
ROBIN HOOD, Once Upon A Classic; Jay Rayvid, Executive Producer; Shep Greene, Producer (PBS)
ZOOM, Terri Payne Francis, Executive Producer; Bob Glover, Janet Weaver, Producers (PBS)

OUTSTANDING ACHIEVEMENT IN COVERAGE OF SPECIAL EVENTS

(Possibility of one Award, more than one Award or no Award)
ALL-AMERICAN THANKSGIVING DAY PARADE, Mike Gargiulo, Executive Producer; Vern Diamond, Clarence Schimmel, Jim Hirschfeld, Wilfred Feilding, Malachy Wienges, Producers (CBS)
TOURNAMENT OF ROSES PARADE AND PAGEANT, Mike Gargiulo, Executive Producer; Vern Diamond, Producer (CBS)
FOURTH ANNUAL DAYTIME EMMY AWARDS, Walter Miller, Producer (NBC)
MACY'S 51st ANNUAL THANKSGIVING DAY PARADE, Dick Schneider, Producer (NBC)
THE GREAT ENGLISH GARDEN PARTY - PETER USTINOV LOOKS AT 100 YEARS OF WIMBLEDON, Ken Ashton, Allison Hawkes, Pamela Moncur, Producers (NBC)

OUTSTANDING ACHIEVEMENT IN RELIGIOUS PROGRAMMING

(Possibility of one Award, more than one Award or no Award)
DIRECTIONS, Sid Darion, Executive Producer (ABC)
FRANCIS OF ASSISI: A SEARCH FOR THE MAN AND HIS MEANING, Doris Ann, Executive Producer; Martin Hoade, Producer (NBC)
WOMAN OF VALOR, Doris Ann, Executive Producer; Martin Hoade, Producer (NBC)

OUTSTANDING CHILDREN'S INFORMATIONAL SPECIAL

Emmmy(s) to Executive Producer(s) and Producer(s)
HENRY WINKLER MEETS WILLIAM SHAKESPEARE, CBS Festival of Lively Arts for Young People; Daniel Wilson, Producer (CBS)
VERY GOOD FRIENDS, ABC Afterschool Special; Matin Tahse, Producer (ABC)

OUTSTANDING WRITING FOR A DAYTIME DRAMA SERIES

For a single episode of a series; or for the entire series
WILLIAM J. BELL, KAY LENARD, BILL REGA, PAT FALKEN SMITH, MARGARET STEWART, Days of Our Lives (NBC)
JEROME and BRIDGET DOBSON, NANCY FORD, JEAN RUVEROL, ROBERT and PHYLLIS WHITE, The Guiding Light, Series (CBS)
CLAIRE LABINE, PAUL AVILA MAYER, MARY MUNISTERI, ALLAN LEICHT, JUDITH PINSKER, Ryan's Hope, Series (ABC)
AGNES NIXON, CATHY CHICOS, DORIS FRANKEL, KEN HARVEY, KATHRYN McCABE, WISNER WASHAM, MARY K. WELLS, JACK WOOD, All My Children, Series (ABC)

ANN MARCUS, RAY GOLDSTONE, JOYCE PERRY, MICHAEL ROBERT DAVID, LAURA OLSHER, ROCCI CHATFIELD, ELIZABETH HARROWER, Days of Our Lives, Series (NBC)

OUTSTANDING ACTOR IN A DAYTIME DRAMA SERIES
MATTHEW COWLES, All My Children (ABC)
LARRY KEITH, All My Children (ABC)
MICHAEL LEVIN, Ryan's Hope (ABC)
JAMES PRITCHETT, The Doctors (NBC)
ANDREW ROBINSON, Ryan's Hope (ABC)
MICHAEL STORM, One Life to Live (ABC)

OUTSTANDING INDIVIDUAL DIRECTOR FOR A DAYTIME DRAMA SERIES
For a single episode
IRA CIRKER, Another World, December 20, 1977 (NBC)
RICHARD DUNLAP, The Young and The Restless, March 3, 1978 (CBS)
RICHARD T. McCUE, As The World Turns, March 15, 1977 (CBS)
ROBERT MYHRUM, Love Of Life, August 31, 1977 (CBS)
AL RABIN, Days Of Our Lives, February 21, 1978 (NBC)
LELA SWIFT, Ryan's Hope, November 3, 1977 (ABC)

OUTSTANDING ACTRESS IN A DAYTIME DRAMA SERIES
MARY FICKETT, All My Children (ABC)
SUSAN SEAFORTH HAYES, Days Of Our Lives (NBC)
JENNIFER HARMON, One Life To Live (ABC)
LAURIE HEINEMAN, Another World (NBC)
SUSAN LUCCI, All My Children (ABC)
BEVERLEE Mc KINSEY, Another World (NBC)
VICTORIA WYNDHAM, Another World (NBC)

OUTSTANDING DAYTIME DRAMA SERIES
Emmy(s) to Executive Producer(s) and Producer(s)
ALL MY CHILDREN, Bud Kloss and Agnes Nixon, Producers (ABC)
DAYS OF OUR LIVES, Betty Corday and Wesley Kenny, Executive Producers; Jack Herzberg, Producer (NBC)
RYAN'S HOPE, Claire Labine and Paul Avila Mayer, Executive Producers; Robert Costello, Producer (ABC)
THE YOUNG AND THE RESTLESS, John Conboy, Executive Producer;

Patricia Wenig, Producer (CBS)

THE NATIONAL AWARD FOR COMMUNITY SERVICE FINALISTS
BUBBLE GUM DIGEST (WMAQ-TV) Chicago, Illinois
CO-OP CONSPIRACY: PYRAMID OF SHAME (KTVI-TV) St. Louis, Missouri
DYING TO GROW UP (WCVB-TV) Needham, Massachusetts
HOT SPOT: A REPORT ON ROCKY FLATS (KMGH-TV) Denver, Colorado
IS THERE ANY HOPE FOR HOPE STREET? (KAIT-TV) Jonesboro, Arkansas
MISERY, MONEY & WHITEWASH (KBTV) Denver, Colorado
ONE MAN'S STRUGGLE (WBAL-TV) Baltimore, Maryland
VOLUNTEER-A-THON (WRAL-TV) Raleigh, North Carolina
WATER (KOOL-TV) Phoenix, Arizona

THE INTERNATIONAL DIRECTORATE EMMY AWARD
ALPHONSE OUIMET, Chairman of the Board of TELESAT CANADA

THE INTERNATIONAL EMMY AWARDS

FICTION
THE COLLECTION, Granada Television Ltd. Manchester, England
THE LAST FLICKERS OF SUNSET, TV Asahi, Tokyo, Japan
SARAH, Canadian Broadcasting Corporation, Toronto, Canada
RED FLOWER, (NHK) Japan Broadcasting Corporation, Tokyo, Japan
ROGUE MALE, British Broadcasting Corporation, London, England

NON-FICTION
HENRY FORD'S AMERICA, Canadian Broadcasting Corporation, Torono, Canada
TIDES OF WAR, Global Communications Ltd., Don Mills, Canada
THE GOOD, BAD AND THE INDIFFERENT, Yorkshire Television Ltd., Leeds, England
HOMAGE TO CHAGALL, Canadian Broadcasting Corporation, Toronto, Canada
TWENTY-ONE, Granada Television Ltd., Manchester, England

CREATIVE ARTS IN TELEVISION

OUTSTANDING ART DIRECTION FOR A COMEDY SERIES
For a single episode of a regular or limited series
EDWARD STEPHENSON, Production Designer, ROBERT CHECCHI, Set Decorator, Soap, Episode #1 (ABC)
THOMAS E. AZZARI, A.E.S. Hudson Street, In The Black (ABC)
ROY CHRISTOPHER, Art Director, JAMES SHANAHAN, Art Director, Welcome Back, Kotter, Barbarino In Love, Part I (ABC)
PAUL SYLOS and EUGENE H. HARRIS, Art Directors, ROBERT SIGNORELLI and JOHN McCARTHY, Set Decorators, The Love Boat, (ABC)
C. MURAWSKI, Maude, The Wake (CBS)

OUTSTANDING ART DIRECTION FOR A DRAMA SERIES
For a single episode of a regular or limited series
TIM HARVEY, Art Director, I, Claudius, Masterpiece Theatre, Episode #1 (PBS)
JACK DE SHIELDS, Production Designer, JAMES F. CLAYTOR, Art Director, BARBARA KREIGER, Set Decorator, Washington: Behind Closed Doors-Episode #3 (ABC)
DEREK DODD, Anna Karenina, Masterpiece Theatre Episode #1 (PBS)
WILFRED J. SHINGLETON, Production Designer, THEO HARISCH, JURGEN KIEBACH, Art Directors, MAXI HAREITER, Set Decorator, Holocaust (NBC)

OUTSTANDING ART DIRECTION FOR A COMEDY-VARIETY OR MUSIC SERIES
For a single episode of a regular or limited series
ROY CHRISTOPHER, The Richard Pryor Show (NBC)
PAUL BARNES and BOB SANSOM Art Directors, BILL HARP, Set Decorator, The Carol Burnett Show, The Final Show (CBS)
BILL BOHNERT, Art Director, ARLENE ALEN, Set Decorator, Donny and Marie, Opening Show (ABC)
ROMAIN JOHNSTON, Captain and Tennille (ABC)
EUGENE LEE and LEO YOSHIMURA, Art Directors, FRANNE LEE and LEE MAYMAN, Set Decorators NBC's Saturday Night Live, host Steve Martin ((NBC)

OUTSTANDING ART DIRECTION FOR A DRAMATIC SPECIAL
JOHN DE CUIR, Production Designer, RICHARD C. GODDARD, Set Decorator, Ziegfeld: The Man And His Women (NBC)
ROY CHRISTOPHER, Production Designer, JAMES SHANAHAN, Set Decorator, Our Town, Bell System (NBC)
JOHN J. LLOYD, Art Director, HAL GAUSMAN, Set Decorator, It Happened One Christmas (ABC)
LOYD S. PAPEZ, Art Director, RICHARD FRIEDMAN, Set Decorator,

The Bastard (Synd)
JAN SCOTT, Art Director, ANNE D. McCULLEY, Set Decorator, The Gathering (ABC)

OUTSTANDING ART DIRECTION FOR A COMEDY-VARIETY OR MUSIC SPECIAL
ROMAIN JOHNSTON, Art Director, KERRY JOYCE, Set Decorator, The Sentry Collection Presents Ben Vereen - His Roots (ABC)
BRIAN C. BARTHOLOMEW, Art Director, Cher. . .Special (ABC)
ROY CHRISTOPHER, Art Director, DON REMACLE, Set Decorator, How To Survive the 70s and Maybe Even Bump Into Happiness (CBS)
ROMAIN JOHNSTON and JOHN DAPPER, Art Directors, ROBERT CHECCI, Set Decorator, They Said It With Music: Yankee Doodle To Ragtime (CBS)
ROBERT KELLY, Mitzi. . .Zings Into Spring (CBS)

OUTSTANDING ACHIEVEMENT IN CHOREOGRAPHY
For an episode of a regular or limited series
RON FIELD, The Sentry Collection Presents Ben Vereen - His Roots (ABC)
GEORGE BALANCHINE, ALEXANDRA DANILOVA, New York City Ballet: Coppelia, Live From Lincoln Center (PBS)
TONY CHARMOLI, Mitzi. . .Zings Into Spring (CBS)
ERNEST O. FLATT, The Carol Burnett Show, The Final Show (CBS)
MIRIAM NELSON, Ziegfeld: The Man And His Women (NBC)

OUTSTANDING CINEMATOGRAPHY IN ENTERTAINMENT PROGRAMMING FOR A SERIES
For a single episode of a regular or limited series
TED VOIGTLANDER, ASC, Little House On The Prairie, The Fighter (NBC)
LLOYD AHERN, The Love Boat, (The Inspector; A Very Special Girl; Until The Last Goodbye) (ABC)
JOSEPH BIROC, ASC, Washington: Behind Closed Doors, Part I (ABC)
ROBERT HAUSER, Roll Of Thunder, Hear My Cry (ABC)
MICHAEL HUGO, ASC, The Awakening Land (NBC)

OUTSTANDING CINEMATOGRAPHY IN ENTERTAINMENT PROGRAMMING FOR A SPECIAL
For a special or feature length program made for television
GERALD PERRY FINNERMAN, ASC, Ziegfeld: The Man And His Women (NBC)
JOSEPH BIROC, ASC, A Family Upside Down (NBC)
SOL NEGRIN, ASC, The Last Tenant (ABC)
HOWARD SCHWARTZ, ASC, The Ghost of Flight 401 (NBC)
RICHARD WAITE, The Life And Assassination Of The Kingfish (NBC)

OUTSTANDING ACHIEVEMENT IN COSTUME DESIGN FOR A DRAMA OR COMEDY SERIES
For a single episode of a regular or limited series
PEGGY FARRELL, EDITH ALMOSLINO, Holocaust (NBC)
DONFELD, The New Adventures of Wonder Woman, Anschluss '77 (CBS)
GRADY HUNT, Quark, The Emperor's Quasi Norms, Part II (NBC)
BILL JOBE, Testimony Of Two Men, Part III (Synd)
YVONNE WOOD, 79 Park Avenue (NBC)

OUTSTANDING ACHIEVEMENT IN COSTUME DESIGN FOR MUSIC-VARIETY
For a single episode of a regular or limited series, or for a special program
BOB MACKIE, RET TURNER, Mitzi. . .Zings Into Spring (CBS)
DAVID DOUCETTE, Dorothy Hamill Presents Winners (ABC)
BILL HARGATE, Doug Henning's World Of Magic (NBC)
WARDEN NEIL, The John Davidson Christmas Special (ABC)
SANDRA STEWART, Cindy (ABC)

OUTSTANDING ACHIEVEMENT IN COSTUME DESIGN FOR A DRAMA SPECIAL
NOEL TAYLOR, Actor, Hollywood Television Theatre (PBS)
JEAN-PIERRE DORLEAC, The Bastard (Synd)
GRADY HUNT, Ziegfeld: The Man And His Women (NBC)
BILL JOBE, The Dark Secret of Harvest Home (NBC)
OLGA LEHMANN, The Four Feathers, Bell System (NBC)

OUTSTANDING FILM EDITING IN A COMEDY SERIES
For a single episode of a regular or limited series
ED COTTER, Happy Days, Richie Almost Dies (ABC)
M. PAM BLUMENTHAL, The Bob Newhart Show, A Jackie Story (CBS)
STANFORD TISCHLER and LARRY L. MILLS, M*A*S*H, Fade Out, Fade In, (CBS)
NORMAN WALLERSTEIN, A.C.E. and Robert MOORE, A.C.E., Love Boat, (Masquerade; The Caper; Eyes Of Love; Hollywood Royalty) (ABC)

OUTSTANDING FILM EDITING IN A DRAMA SERIES
For a single episode of a regular or limited series
STEPHEN A. ROTTER, ROBERT M. REITANO, CRAIG McKAY, ALAN HEIM and BRIAN SMEDLEY-ASTON, Holocaust (NBC)
DAVID G. BLANGSTED, A.C.E., HOWARD TERRILL, A.C.E., Eight Is Enough, Yes Nicholas, There Is A Santa Claus (ABC)
BYRON "BUZZ" BRANDT, A.C.E., RICHARD MEYER and DAVID BERLATSKY, King (NBC)
JIM FARIS, Family, Acts Of Love, Part I (ABC)
BILL MOSHER, The Waltons, Grandma Comes Home (CBS)
ROBERT WATTS, Columbo, How To Dial A Murder (NBC)

OUTSTANDING FILM EDITING FOR A SPECIAL
For a drama, comedy or music-variety special or film made for television
JOHN A. MARTINELLI, A.C.E., The Defection of Simas Kudirka (CBS)
RONALD J. FAGAN, A.C.E., Young Joe, The Forgotten Kennedy (ABC)
LESLIE L. GREEN, Ziegfeld: The Man And His Women (NBC)
HARRY KAYE, A.C.E., DONALD RODE, To Kill A Cop (NBC)
KENNETH R. KOCH, Mary Jane Harper Cried Last Night (CBS)
BERNARD J. SMALL, Just A Little Inconvenience (NBC)
KEN ZEMKE, A Killing Affair (CBS)

OUTSTANDING ACHIEVEMENT IN FILM SOUND EDITING FOR A SERIES
For a single episode of a regular or limited series
DOUGLAS H. GRINDSTAFF, HANK SALERNO, LARRY SINGER, CHRISTOPHER CHULACK, RICHARD RADERMAN, DON CROSBY, H. LEE CHANEY, MARK DENNIS, DON V. ISAACS, STEVE OLSON and AL KAJITA, Police Story, River Of Promises (NBC)
LARRY CAROW, DAVID PETTIJOHN, DON WARNER, COLIN MOUAT, CHUCK MORAN and PIETER HUBBARD, Baa Baa Black Sheep/Black

Sheep Squadron, The Hawk Flies On Sunday (NBC)
TONY GARBER, DALE JOHNSTON and RON CLARK, Lou Grant, Nazi (CBS)
DOUGLAS H. GRINDSTAFF, LARRY SINGER, HANK SALERNO, CHRISTOPHER CHULACK, LUKE WOLFRAM, AL KAJITA, DWAYNE AVERY, RICHARD FRIEDMAN and DON V. ISAACS, Fantasy Island, Racer and Lady Of The Evening (ABC)
WILLIAM STEVENSON and RICHARD RADERMAN, Roll Of Thunder, Hear My Cry (ABC)

OUTSTANDING ACHIEVEMENT IN FILM SOUND EDITING FOR A SPECIAL

JERRY ROSENTHAL, MICHAEL CORRIGAN, JERRY PIROZZI, WILLIAM JACKSON, JAMES YANT, RICHARD LE GRAND, DONALD HIGGINS, JOHN STRAUSS and JOHN KLINE, The Amazing Howard Hughes (CBS)
DOUGLAS H. GRINDSTAFF, H. LEE CHANEY, DON V. ISAACS, LARRY KAUFMAN, STEVE OLSON, DON CROSBY, AL KAJITA, BOB HUMAN, HANK SALERNO and LARRY SINGER, The Last Hurrah, Hallmark Hall Of Fame (NBC)
DOUGLAS H. GRINDSTAFF, HANK SALERNO, LARRY SINGER, CHRISTOPHER CHULACK, MARK DENNIS, DON CROSBY, H. LEE CHANEY and DON V. ISAACS, To Kill A Cop, Part I (NBC)
DON HALL, DWAYNE AVERY, TOM BURKE and CHICK CAMERA, Standing Tall (NBC)
BERNARD F. PINCUS, PATRICK R. SOMERSET, JEFFREY BUSHELMAN, A. JEREMY HOENACK, JOHN BUSHELMAN, EDWARD L. SANDLIN, ROBERT A. BIGGART and JERRY ROSENTHAL, The Dark Secret Of Harvest Home (NBC)
DON WARNER, LARRY CAROW, COLIN MOUAT, DAVID PETTIJOHN, GARY VAUGHAN, CHUCK MORAN, PIETER HUBBARD and FRED STAFFORD, Tarantulas: The Deadly Cargo (CBS)

OUTSTANDING ACHIEVEMENT IN FILM SOUND MIXING

For a single episode of a regular or limited series, or for a special program

WILLIAM TEAGUE, GEORGE E. PORTER, EDDIE J. NELSON and ROBERT L. HARMAN, Young Joe, The Forgotten Kennedy (ABC)
ALAN BERNARD, GEORGE E. PORTER, EDDIE J. NELSON and HOPPY MEHTERIAN, Having Babies II (ABC)
EDDIE KNOWLES, GEORGE E. PORTER, EDDIE J. NELSON, and J. ROBERT PETTIS, Tarantulas: The Deadly Cargo, (CBS)
HOPPY MEHTERIAN, GEORGE E. PORTER, EDDIE J. NELSON and DEAN HODGES, A Sensitive, Passionate Man (NBC)
J. ROBERT PETTIS, GEORGE E. PORTER, EDDIE J. NELSON and CABELL SMITH, See How She Runs, G.E. Theatre (CBS)
TOMMY THOMPSON, GEORGE E. PORTER, EDDIE J. NELSON and HOPPY MEHTERIAN, In The Matter Of Karen Ann Quinlan (NBC)

OUTSTANDING ACHIEVEMENT IN GRAPHIC DESIGN AND TITLE SEQUENCES

For a single episode of a regular or limited series, or for a special program This includes animation only when created for use in titling.

BILL DAVIS, NBC: The First Fifty Years - A Closer Look - Variety (NBC)
EYTAN KELLER and STEWART BERNSTEIN, 50th Annual Awards of the Academy of Motion Picture Arts and Sciences (ABC)
MAURY NEMOY, ROBERT BRANHAM and JOHN DE CUIR, Ziegfeld: The Man And His Women (NBC)
PHILL NORMAN, Washington: Behind Closed Doors (ABC)

OUTSTANDING ACHIEVEMENT IN LIGHTING DIRECTION

For a single episode of a regular or limited series or for a special program

GREG BRUNTON, Cher. . .Special (ABC)
LEARD DAVIS, Lighting Designer, KEN DETTLING, Lighting Director, You Can Run But You Can't Hide, Visions (PBS)
IMERO FIORENTINO, The Neil Diamond Special: I'm Glad You're Here With Me Tonight (NBC) FRED MC KINNON and Carl J. VITELLI, JR., Happy Birthday, Las Vegas (ABC)
ALAN K. WALKER and BILL KLAGES, Olivia (ABC)
GEORGE RIESENBERGER, Best Of Families, The Great Trolley Strike of 1895 (PBS)

OUTSTANDING ACHIEVEMENT IN MAKE-UP

For a single episode of a series, or for a special program

RICHARD COBOS and WALTER SCHENCK, How The West Was Won, Part II (ABC)
HANK EDDS, ALLAN "WHITEY" SNYDER, Little House On The Prairie, The Fighter (NBC)
CHRISTINA SMITH, King (NBC)
FRANK C. WESTMORE and MICHAEL G. WESTMORE, A Love Affair: The Eleanor And Lou Gehrig Story (NBC)
MICHAEL G. WESTMORE, HANK EDDS and LYNN REYNOLDS, The Amazing Howard Hughes (CBS)

OUTSTANDING ACHIEVEMENT IN MUSIC COMPOSITION FOR A SERIES (DRAMATIC UNDERSCORE)

For a single episode of a regular or limited series

BILLY GOLDENBERG, King (NBC)
MORTON GOULD, Holocaust (NBC)
FRED KARLIN, The Awakening Land (NBC)
MORTON STEVENS, Wheels (NBC)
PATRICK WILLIAMS, Columbo, Try And Catch Me (NBC)

OUTSTANDING ACHIEVEMENT IN MUSIC COMPOSITION FOR A SPECIAL (DRAMATIC UNDERSCORE)

JIMMIE HASKELL, See How She Runs, G.E. Theatre (CBS)
DICK DE BENEDICTIS, Ziegfeld: The Man And His Women (NBC)
BILLY GOLDENBERG, Actor, Hollywood Television Theatre (PBS)
DAVID SHIRE, The Defection Of Simas Kudirka (CBS)

OUTSTANDING ACHIEVEMENT IN MUSIC DIRECTION

For a single episode of a regular or limited series, or a special program, whether it be variety or music

IAN FRASER, The Sentry Collection Presents Ben Vereen - His Roots (ABC)
JIMMIE HASKELL, The Second Barry Manilow Special (ABC)
ZUBIN MEHTA, The New York Philharmonic/Mehta, Live From Lincoln Center (PBS)
ANDRE PREVIN, Previn And The Pittsburgh, The Music That Made The Movies (PBS)

OUTSTANDING ACHIEVEMENT IN SPECIAL MUSICAL MATERIAL

For a song (which must have both music and lyrics), a theme for a series, or special material for a variety program providing that the first usage of this material was written expressly for television. (Possibility of one Award, more than one Award, or no Award)

STAN FREEMAN and ARTHUR MALVIN, Music and Lyrics The Carol Burnett Show, Mini Musical: "Hi-Hat", (CBS)
MITZIE WELCH and KEN WELCH, Music and Lyrics, The Sentry Collection Presents Ben Vereen - His Roots, Song: "See You Tomorrow In Class" (ABC)
EARL BROWN, The Donny And Marie Show, Song: "Leading Lady" (ABC)
BILL DYER, Lyrics, DICK DE BENEDICTIS, Music, Ziegfeld: The Man And His Women, Song: "Until The Music Ends" (NBC)
KENYON EMRYS-ROBERTS, Poldark, Masterpiece Theatre, Poldark Theme (PBS)

OUTSTANDING ACHIEVEMENT IN TAPE SOUND MIXING

For a single episode of a regular or limited series or for a special program

THOMAS J. HUTH, EDWARD J. GREENE and RON BRYAN, Bette Midler - Ol' Red Hair Is Back (NBC)
RON ESTES, Our Town, Bell System (NBC)
PHILLIP J. SERETTI, BOB GAUDIO, VAL GARAY, RICK RUGGIERI and JOHN WALKER, The Neil Diamond Special: I'm Glad You're Here With Me Tonight (NBC)
LARRY STEPHENS, THOMAS J. HUTH, RON BRYAN, ERIC LEVINSON and GROVER HELSLEY, Perry Como's Easter By The Sea (ABC)
DICK WILSON, The Lawrence Welk Show with Roger Williams at the Piano (Synd)

OUTSTANDING ACHIEVEMENT IN TECHNICAL DIRECTION AND ELECTRONIC CAMERAWORK

For a single episode of a regular or limited series, or for a special program

GENE CROWE, TD, WAYNE ORR, LARRY HEIDER, DAVE HILMER, BOB KEYS, Cameramen, The Sentry Collection Presents Ben Vereen - His Roots (ABC)
CHARLES FRANKLIN, TD, STEVE CUNNINGHAM, TD, HARRY TATARIAN, TD, MARK MILLER, TD, GORMAN ERICKSON, JOHN AGUIRRE, STANLEY ZITNICK, DAVID FINCH, RICHARD NELSON, HECTOR RAMIREZ, LOUIS SHORE, BEN WOLF, THOMAS BROWN, GORDON SWEENEY, ROBERT WELSH and BRIAN CUNNEEN, Cameramen, CBS: On The Air (CBS)
LOUIS FUSARI, TD, RODGER HARBAUGH, ROY HOLM, RICK LOMBARDO and PEGGY MAHONEY, Cameramen, Mitzi...What's Hot, What's Not (CBS)
KARL MESSERSCHMIDT, TD, JON OLSON, MIKE STRAMISKY, GEORGE LOOMIS, GEORGE FALARDEAU, MIKE HIGUERA and JIM DODGE, Cameramen, Doug Henning's World Of Magic (NBC)
O. TAMBURRI, TD, JON OLSON, ROY HOLM and REED HOWARD, Cameramen, Our Town, Bell System (NBC)

OUTSTANDING ACHIEVEMENT IN VIDEO TAPE EDITING FOR A SERIES

For a single episode of a regular or limited series

TUCKER WIARD, The Carol Burnett Show, The Final Show (CBS)
GARY H. ANDERSON, Soap, Episode #2 (ABC)
ED. J. BRENNAN, Laugh-In, Show #6 (NBC)
CHIP BROOKS, The Betty White Show, Pilot, (CBS)
JERRY DAVIS, Three's Company, Chrissy, Come Home (ABC)
MARCO ZAPPIA, Husbands, Wives & Lovers, The One Where Everybody Is Looking For A Little Action (CBS)

OUTSTANDING ACHIEVEMENT IN VIDEO TAPE EDITING FOR A SPECIAL

PAM MARSHALL and ANDY ZALL, The Sentry Collection Presents Ben Vereen - His Roots (ABC)
ED. J. BRENNAN, The Goldie Hawn Special (CBS)
CHIP BROOKS and HAL COLLINS, Texaco Presents Bob Hope In A Very Special Special - On The Road With Bing (NBC)
JIMMY B. FRAZIER, The Carpenters - Space Encounters (ABC)
MARCO ZAPPIA, TERRY GREENE, HARVEY BERGER and JIMMY B. FRAZIER, Superstunt (NBC)

OUTSTANDING INDIVIDUAL ACHIEVEMENT IN ANY AREA OF CREATIVE TECHNICAL CRAFTS

(Possibility of one Award, more than one Award, or no Award)

WILLIAM F. BROWNELL and JOHN H. KANTROWE, JR. (Sound Effects), Our Town, Bell System (NBC)
SUGAR BLYMER (Hairstylist), The Awakening Land, Part III (NBC)
LARRY GERMAIN and GLADYS WITTEN (Hairstylists), Little House On The Prairie, Here Come The Brides (NBC)
MARK SCHUBIN (Technical Designer), Live From Lincoln Center (Series) (PBS)
FRANK VAN DER VEER (Optical Effects), L. B. ABBOTT (Special Photographic Effects), The Return Of Captain Nemo (CBS)

SPECIAL CLASSIFICATION OF OUTSTANDING INDIVIDUAL ACHIEVEMENT

(Possibility of one Award, more than one Award or no Award)

WILLIAM PITKIN (Costume Designer), Romeo and Juliet (PBS)
MIKHAIL BARYSHNIKOV (Dancer), The Nutcracker (CBS)
WILLIAM T. CARTWRIGHT (Film Editor), JEFFREY WESTON (Film Editor), Oscar Presents The War Movies And John Wayne (ABC)
JAN SCOTT (Production Designer), EARL CARLSON (Set Decorator), CBS: On The Air (CBS)

OUTSTANDING INDIVIDUAL ACHIEVEMENT IN CHILDREN'S PROGRAMMING

(Possibility of one Award, more than one Award, or no Award)

KEN JOHNSON, Art Director, **ROBERT CHECCHI**, Set Decorator, Once Upon A Brothers Grimm (CBS)
BILL HARGATE (Costume Designer), Once Upon A Brothers Grimm (CBS)
JERRY GREENE (Video Tape Editor), Once Upon A Brothers Grimm (CBS)
NICHOLAS SPIES and ROBERT MILLSLAGLE (Video Tape Editors), A Connecticut Yankee In King Arthur's Court (PBS)
TOMMY COLE, LARRY ABBOTT, MICHAEL G. WESTMORE (Make-Up), Once Upon A Brothers Grimm (CBS)

OUTSTANDING ACHIEVEMENT IN COVERAGE OF SPECIAL EVENTS - INDIVIDUALS

(Possibility of one Award, more than one Award, or no Award)
RODGER HARBAUGH (Aerial Photography), The 29th Annual Emmy Awards Show (NBC)
WILLIAM W. LANDERS (Technical Direction and Electronic Camerawork), The 29th Annual Emmy Awards Show (NBC)
ALAN BUZ KOHAN (Music), 50th Annual Awards Of The Academy Of Motion Picture Arts And Sciences, Opening Production Number: "Look How Far We've Come" (ABC)
CLARK JONES (Director), Footlights: The 1978 Tony Awards (CBS)

OUTSTANDING ACHIEVEMENT IN BROADCAST JOURNALISM

ATAS Broadcast Journalism Awards
CHARLES KURALT, "On The Road" (CBS News).
BILL MOYERS (CBS Reports):
"THE FIRE NEXT DOOR" (CBS Reports), Howard Stringer, Executive Producer.
"EXPLODING GAS TANKS" (ABC News, 20/20 segment), Sylvia Chase, Correspondent, Stanhope Gould, Producer.

OUTSTANDING ACHIEVEMENT IN ENGINEERING DEVELOPMENT

An Award to an individual, a company or an organization for developments in engineering which are either so extensive an improvement on existing methods or so innovative in nature that they materially affect the transmission, recording or reception of television.

An Emmy was awarded to Petro Vlahos of Vlahos-Gottschalk Research Corporation for the invention and development of the ULTIMATTE video-matting device, and a citation was awarded to the Society of Motion Picture and Television Engineers for expeditiously achieving the difficult task of obtaining industry agreement on the One-Inch Type C Continuous Field Helical Recording Standards.

SPECIAL ATAS GOVERNORS MEDALLION

Frederick Wolcott, for his thirty years of service on the ATAS Engineering Awards Panel.

1978/79

NIGHTTIME PROGRAMMING

OUTSTANDING COMEDY SERIES

Emmy(s) to Executive Producer and/or Producer
TAXI, James L. Brooks, Stan Daniels, David Davis and Ed. Weinberger, Executive Producers; Glen Charles, Les Charles, Producers (ABC)
MORK & MINDY, Garry Marshall and Tony Marshall, Executive Producers; Dale McRaven, Bruce Johnson, Producers (ABC)
M*A*S*H, Burt Metcalfe, Producer (CBS)
BARNEY MILLER, Danny Arnold, Executive Producer; Tony Sheehan, Reinhold Weege, Co-Producers (ABC)
ALL IN THE FAMILY, Mort Lachman, Executive Producer; Milt Josefsberg, Producer (CBS)

OUTSTANDING COMEDY-VARIETY OR MUSIC PROGRAM

For a special or a series, Emmy(s) to Executive Producer and/or Producer and Star, if applicable
STEVE & EYDIE CELEBRATE IRVING BERLIN, Steve Lawrence, Gary Smith, Executive Producers; Gary Smith, Dwight Hemion, Producers; Steve Lawrence, Eydie Gorme, Stars (NBC)
SHIRLEY MacLAINE AT THE LIDO, Gary Smith, Dwight Hemion, Producers; Shirley MacLaine, Star (CBS)
NBC'S SATURDAY NIGHT LIVE, Lorne Michaels, Producer; Dan Aykroyd, John Belushi, Jane Curtin, Garrett Morris, Bill Murray, Laraine Newman, Gilda Radner, Stars; (NBC)
THE MUPPET SHOW, David Lazer, Executive Producer; Jim Henson, Producer; The Muppets (Frank Oz, Jerry Nelson, Richard Hunt, Dave Goelz, Jim Henson Stars) (Synd)
ARTHUR FIEDLER: JUST CALL ME MAESTRO, William Cosel, Producer; Arthur Fiedler, Star (PBS)

OUTSTANDING DRAMA SERIES

Emmy(s) to Executive Producer and/or Producer
LOU GRANT, Gene Reynolds, Executive Producer; Seth Freeman, Gary David Goldberg, Producers (CBS)
THE ROCKFORD FILES, Meta Rosenberg, Executive Producer; Stephen J. Cannell, Supervising Producer; Chas. Floyd Johnson, David Chase, Juanita Bartlett, Producers (NBC)
THE PAPER CHASE, Robert C. Thompson, Executive Producer; Robert Lewin, Albert Aley, Producers (CBS)

OUTSTANDING LIMITED SERIES

Emmy(s) to Executive Producer and/or Producer
ROOTS: THE NEXT GENERATIONS, David L. Wolper, Executive Producer; Stan Margulies, Producer (ABC)
BLIND AMBITION, David Susskind, Executive Producer; George Schaefer, Renee Valente, Producers (ABC)
BACKSTAIRS AT THE WHITE HOUSE, Ed Friendly, Executive Producer; Ed Friendly, Michael O'Herlihy, Producers (NBC)

OUTSTANDING DRAMA OR COMEDY SPECIAL

Emmy(s) to Executive Producer and/or Producer
FRIENDLY FIRE, Martin Starger, Executive Producer; Philip Barry, Producer; Fay Kanin, Co-Producer (ABC)
SUMMER OF MY GERMAN SOLDIER, Linda Gottlieb, Producer (NBC)
THE JERICHO MILE, Tim Zinnemann, Producer (ABC)
FIRST YOU CRY, Philip Barry, Producer (CBS)
DUMMY, Frank Konigsberg, Executive Producer; Sam Manners, Ernest Tidyman, Producers (CBS)

OUTSTANDING INFORMATIONAL PROGRAM

For a special or a series. Emmy(s) to Executive Producer and/or Producer
SCARED STRAIGHT!, Arnold Shapiro, Producer (Synd)
WHO ARE THE DEBOLTS--AND WHERE DID THEY GET 19 KIDS?, Henry Winkler, Executive Producer; John Korty, Warren Lockhart, Dan McCann, Producers (ABC)
THE BODY HUMAN: THE SEXES, Thomas W. Moore, Executive Producer; Alfred R. Kelman, Robert E. Fuisz, M.D., Producers; Vivian R. Moss, Charles A. Bangert, Co-Producers (CBS)

OUTSTANDING CLASSICAL PROGRAM IN THE PERFORMING ARTS

For a special or a series. Emmy(s) to Executive Producer and/or Producer and Star, if applicable
BALANCHINE IV, Dance In America; Great Performances; Jac Venza, Executive Producer; Merrill Brockway, Series Producer;

Emile Ardolino, Series Coordinating Producer; Judy Kinberg, Producer (PBS)
LIVE FROM LINCOLN CENTER (with Luciano Pavarotti and Joan Sutherland), John Goberman, Producer (PBS)
THE SLEEPING BEAUTY; The American Ballet Theatre; Live From Lincoln Center; John Goberman, Producer (PBS)
GIULINI'S BEETHOVEN'S 9TH LIVE - A GIFT FROM LOS ANGELES, Jeanne Mulcahy, Executive Producer; John Goberman, Producer (PBS)
BALANCHINE III, Dance In America; Great Performances; Jac Venza, Executive Producer; Merrill Brockway, Series Producer; Emile Ardolino, Series Coordinating Producer; Judy Kinberg, Producer (PBS)

OUTSTANDING ANIMATED PROGRAM

For a special or a series. Emmy(s) to Executive Producer and/or Producer (Possibility of one Award, more than one Award, or no Award)

THE LION, THE WITCH AND THE WARDROBE, David Connell, Executive Producer; Steve Melendez, Producer (CBS)
YOU'RE THE GREATEST, CHARLIE BROWN, Lee Mendelson, Executive Producer; Bill Melendez, Producer (CBS)
HAPPY BIRTHDAY, CHARLIE BROWN, Lee Mendelson, Producer (CBS)

OUTSTANDING CHILDREN'S PROGRAM

For a special or a series. Emmy(s) to Executive Producer and/or Producer (Possibility of one Award, more than one Award, or no Award)

CHRISTMAS EVE ON SESAME STREET, Jon Stone, Executive Producer; Dulcy Singer, Producer (PBS)
ONCE UPON A CLASSIC, Jay Rayvid, Executive Producer; Graham McDonald, James A. DeVinney, Producers; Series (PBS)
BENJI'S VERY OWN CHRISTMAS STORY, Joe Camp, Producer (ABC)
A SPECIAL SESAME STREET CHRISTMAS, Bob Banner, Executive Producer; Stephen Pouliot, Producer (CBS)

OUTSTANDING PROGRAM ACHIEVEMENT - SPECIAL EVENTS

Emmy(s) to Executive Producer and/or Producer. (Possibility of one Award, more than one Award, or no Award)

51ST ANNUAL AWARDS PRESENTATION OF THE ACADEMY OF MOTION PICTURE ARTS AND SCIENCES, Jack Haley, Jr., Producer (ABC)
GOOD LUCK TONIGHT - THE 1979 TONY AWARDS, Alexander H. Cohen, Executive Producer; Hildy Parks, Producer; Roy A. Somlyo, Co-Producer (CBS)
BARYSHNIKOV AT THE WHITE HOUSE, Gerald Slater, Executive Producer; Emille Ardolino, Producer (PBS)

OUTSTANDING PROGRAM ACHIEVEMENT - SPECIAL CLASS

Emmy(s) to Executive Producer and/or Producer and Star, if applicable. (Possibility of one Award, more than one Award, or no Award)

THE TONIGHT SHOW STARRING JOHNNY CARSON, Fred de Cordova, Producer; Johnny Carson, Star (NBC)
LIFELINE, Thomas W. Moore and Robert E. Fuisz, M.D., Executive Producers; Alfred Kelman, Producer; Geof Bartz, Co-Producer (NBC)
STEVE ALLEN'S MEETING OF MINDS, Loring d'Usseau, Producer; Steve Allen, Star (PBS)
THE DICK CAVETT SHOW, Chris Porterfield, Producer; Dick Cavett, Star (PBS)

OUTSTANDING SUPPORTING ACTRESS IN A COMEDY OR COMEDY-VARIETY OR MUSIC SERIES

For a continuing or single performance in a regular series

SALLY STRUTHERS, All In The Family, California Here We Are (CBS)
POLLY HOLLIDAY, Alice (CBS)
MARION ROSS, Happy Days (CBS)
LORETTA SWIT, M*A*S*H (CBS)

OUTSTANDING SUPPORTING ACTOR IN A COMEDY OR COMEDY-VARIETY OR MUSIC SERIES

For a continuing or single performance in a regular series

ROBERT GUILLAUME, Soap (ABC)
GARY BURGHOFF, M*A*S*H (CBS)
DANNY DE VITO, Taxi (ABC)
MAX GAIL, Barney Miller (ABC)
HARRY MORGAN, M*A*S*H (CBS)

OUTSTANDING SUPPORTING ACTRESS IN A DRAMA SERIES

For a continuing or single performance in a regular series

KRISTY McNICHOL; Family (ABC)
LINDA KELSEY; Lou Grant (CBS)
NANCY MARCHAND; Lou Grant (CBS)

OUTSTANDING SUPPORTING ACTOR IN A DRAMA SERIES

For a continuing or single performance in a regular series

STUART MARGOLIN, The Rockford Files (NBC)
MASON ADAMS, Lou Grant (CBS)
NOAH BEERY, The Rockford Files (NBC)
JOE SANTOS, The Rockford Files (NBC)
ROBERT WALDEN, Lou Grant (CBS)

OUTSTANDING SUPPORTING ACTRESS IN A LIMITED SERIES OR A SPECIAL

For a continuing role in a limited series, or for a single appearance in a limited series or a special

ESTHER ROLLE, Summer Of My German Soldier (NBC)
RUBY DEE, Roots: The Next Generations (ABC)
COLLEEN DEWHURST, Silent Victory: The Kitty O'Neil Story (CBS)
EILEEN HECKART, Backstairs At The White House (NBC)
CELESTE HOLM, Backstairs At The White House (NBC)

OUTSTANDING SUPPORTING ACTOR IN A LIMITED SERIES OR A SPECIAL

For a continuing role in a limited series, or for a single appearance in a limited series or a special

MARLON BRANDO, Roots: The Next Generations, Episode Seven (ABC)
ED FLANDERS, Backstairs At The White House, Book Two (NBC)
AL FREEMAN, JR., Roots: The Next Generations, Episode Seven (ABC)
ROBERT VAUGHN, Backstairs At the White House, Book One (NBC)
PAUL WINFIELD, Roots: The Next Generations, Episode Five (ABC)

OUTSTANDING LEAD ACTRESS IN A COMEDY SERIES

RUTH GORDON, Taxi, Sugar Mama (ABC)
KATHERINE HELMOND, Soap (ABC)
LINDA LAVIN, Alice (CBS)
ISABEL SANFORD, The Jeffersons (CBS)
JEAN STAPLETON, All In The Family (CBS)

OUTSTANDING LEAD ACTOR IN A COMEDY SERIES

For a continuing or single performance in a regular series

CARROLL O'CONNOR, All In The Family (CBS)
ALAN ALDA, M*A*S*H (CBS)
JUDD HIRSCH, Taxi (ABC)
HAL LINDEN, Barney Miller (ABC)
ROBIN WILLIAMS, Mork & Mindy (ABC)

OUTSTANDING LEAD ACTRESS IN A DRAMA SERIES

For a continuing or single performance in a regular series

MARIETTE HARTLEY, The Incredible Hulk, Married (CBS)
BARBARA BEL GEDDES, Dallas (CBS)
RITA MORENO, The Rockford Files, Rosendahl And Gilda Stern Are Dead (NBC)
SADA THOMPSON, Family (ABC)

OUTSTANDING LEAD ACTOR IN A DRAMA SERIES

For a continuing or single performance in a regular series

RON LEIBMAN, Kaz (CBS)
ED ASNER, Lou Grant (CBS)
JAMES GARNER, The Rockford Files (NBC)
JACK KLUGMAN, Quincy, M.E. (NBC)

OUTSTANDING LEAD ACTRESS IN A LIMITED SERIES OR A SPECIAL

For a continuing role in a limited series, or for a single appearance in a limited series or a special

BETTE DAVIS, Strangers: The Story of a Mother and Daughter (CBS)
CAROL BURNETT, Friendly Fire (ABC)
OLIVIA COLE, Backstairs At The White House (NBC)
KATHERINE HEPBURN, The Corn Is Green (CBS)
MARY TYLER MOORE, First You Cry (CBS)

OUTSTANDING LEAD ACTOR IN A LIMITED SERIES OR A SPECIAL

For a continuing role in a limited series, or for a single appearance in a limited series or a special

PETER STRAUSS, The Jericho Mile (ABC)
NED BEATTY, Friendly Fire (ABC)
LOUIS GOSSETT, JR., Backstairs At The White House (NBC)
KURT RUSSELL, Elvis (ABC)

OUTSTANDING DIRECTING IN A COMEDY OR COMEDY-VARIETY OR MUSIC SERIES

For a single episode of a regular series

NOAM PITLIK, Barney Miller, The Harris Incident (ABC)
ALAN ALDA, M*A*S*H; Dear Sis (CBS)
PAUL BOGART, All In The Family, California, Here We Are, Part II (CBS)
CHARLES DUBIN, M*A*S*H, Point Of View (CBS)
JAY SANDRICH, Soap, Episode 27 (ABC)

OUTSTANDING DIRECTING IN A DRAMA SERIES

For a single episode of a regular series

JACKIE COOPER, the White Shadow, Pilot (CBS)
BURT BRINCKERHOFF, Lou Grant, Schools (CBS)
MEL DAMSKI, Lou Grant, Murder (CBS)
GENE REYNOLDS, Lou Grant, Prisoner (CBS)

OUTSTANDING DIRECTING IN A LIMITED SERIES OR A SPECIAL

DAVID GREENE, Friendly Fire (ABC)
LOU ANTONIO, Silent Victory: The Kitty O'Neil Story (CBS)
GLENN JORDAN, Les Miserables (CBS)

OUTSTANDING WRITING IN A COMEDY OR COMEDY-VARIETY OR MUSIC SERIES

For a single episode of a regular series

ALAN ALDA, M*A*S*H, Inga (CBS)
DAN AYKROYD, ANNE BEATTS, TOM DAVIS, JAMES DOWNEY, BRIAN DOYLE-MURRAY, AL FRANKEN, BRIAN McCONNACHIE, LORNE MICHAELS, DON NOVELLO, HERB SARGENT, TOM SCHILLER, ROSIE SHUSTER, WALTER WILLIAMS, ALAN ZWEIBEL, NBC's Saturday Night Live, Host: Richard Benjamin (NBC)
MILT JOSEFSBERG, PHIL SHARP, BOB SCHILLER and BOB WEISKOPF, All In The Family, California Here We Are, Part Two (CBS)
MICHAEL LEESON, Taxi, Blind Date (ABC)
KEN LEVINE and DAVID ISAACS, M*A*S*H, Point of View (CBS)

OUTSTANDING WRITING IN A DRAMA SERIES

For a single episode of a regular series

MICHELE GALLERY, Lou Grant, Dying (CBS)
JIM BRIDGES, The Paper Chase, The Late Mr. Hart (CBS)
GENE REYNOLDS, Lou Grant, Marathon (CBS)
LEON TOKATYAN, Lou Grant, Vet (CBS)

OUTSTANDING WRITING IN A LIMITED SERIES OR A SPECIAL

For a single episode of a limited series, or for a special, whether the writing is an original teleplay or an adaptation

PATRICK NOLAN and MICHAEL MANN, The Jericho Mile (ABC)
GWEN BAGNI and PAUL DUBOV, Backstairs At The White House, Book One (NBC)
JANE HOWARD HAMMERSTEIN, Summer Of My German Soldier (NBC)
FAY KANIN, Friendly Fire (ABC)
ERNEST KINOY, Roots: The Next Generations, Episode One (ABC)

OUTSTANDING INDIVIDUAL ACHIEVEMENT - ANIMATION PROGRAM
(Possibility of one Award, more than one Award, or no Award)
BILL MELENDEZ and DAVID CONNELL, Writers; The Lion, The Witch and The Wardrobe (CBS)

OUTSTANDING INDIVIDUAL ACHIEVEMENT - INFORMATION PROGRAM
(Possibility of one Award, more than one Award, or no Award)
JOHN KORTY, Dicector; Who Are The Debolts–And Where Did They Get 19 Kids? (ABC)
ARNOLD SHAPIRO, Writer; Scared Straight! (Synd)

OUTSTANDING INDIVIDUAL ACHIEVEMENT - SPECIAL EVENTS
(Possibility of one Award, more than one Award, or no Award)
MIKHAIL BARYSHNIKOV, Baryshnikov At The White House (PBS)

A SPECIAL PRESENTATION
To MILTON BERLE, "Mr. Television"

SECOND ANNUAL ATAS GOVERNORS AWARD
To WALTER CRONKITE

ACADEMY TRIBUTE TO
DON HARRIS, ROBERT BROWN and BILL STEWART, news broadcasters who lost their lives in Guyana and Nicaragua

1978/79

DAYTIME PROGRAMMING

OUTSTANDING HOST OR HOSTESS IN A GAME OR AUDIENCE PARTICIPATION SHOW
BOB BARKER, The Price Is Right (CBS)
DICK CLARK, The $20,000 Pyramid (ABC)
PETER MARSHALL, The Hollywood Squares (NBC)

OUTSTANDING GAME OR AUDIENCE PARTICIPATION SHOW
Emmy(s) to Executive Produucer(s) and Producer(s)
FAMILY FEUD, Mark Goodson and Bill Todman, Executive Producers; Howard Felsher, Producer (ABC)
HOLLYWOOD SQUARES, Merrill Heatter, Bob Quigley, Executive Producers; Jay Redack, Producer (NBC)
THE $20,000 PYRAMID, Bob Stewart, Executive Producer; Anne Marie Schmitt, Producer (ABC)

OUTSTANDING HOST OR HOSTESS IN A TALK, SERVICE OR VARIETY SERIES
JOHN BENNETT-PERRY, Everyday (Synd)
PHIL DONAHUE, Donahue (Synd)
STEPHANIE EDWARDS, Everyday (Synd)

OUTSTANDING TALK, SERVICE OR VARIETY SERIES
Emmy(s) to Executive Producer(s) and Producer(s)
DINAH! Henry Jaffe, Executive Producer; Fred Tatashore, Producer (Synd)
DONAHUE, Richard Mincer, Executive Producer; Patricia McMillen, Producer (Synd)
GOOD MORNING AMERICA, George Merlis, Senior Producer; John Kippycash, Jack Reilly, Sonya Selby-Wright, Producers (ABC)
MIKE DOUGLAS SHOW, Frank R. Miller, Executive Producer; Vince Calandra, E.V. DiMassa, Jr., Producers (Synd)

SPECIAL CLASSIFICATION OF OUTSTANDING PROGRAM ACHIEVEMENT
(Possibility of one Award, more than one Award, or no Award)
A BEETHOVEN FESTIVAL, Jack Costello, Executive Producer (PBS)
CAMERA THREE, John Musilli, Executive Producer (CBS)
CINEMATIC EYE, Peter Anderson, Executive Producer; Benjamin Dunlap, Co-Producer; Ruth Sproat, Coordinating Producer; Sidney Palmer, Diana Weynand, Producers (PBS)

OUTSTANDING ACHIEVEMENT IN COVERAGE OF SPECIAL EVENTS
(Possibility of one Award, or more than one Award, or no Award)
THE FIFTH ANNUAL EMMY AWARDS FOR DAYTIME TELEVISION, William Carruthers, Joel Stein, Producers (ABC)
HOROWITZ: LIVE! Herbert Kloiber, Executive Producer; John Goberman, Producer (NBC)
LEONTYNE PRICE AT THE WHITE HOUSE, Hal Hutkoff, Producer (PBS)
ROSTROPOVICH AT THE WHITE HOUSE, Hal Hutkoff, Producer (PBS)

OUTSTANDING SUPPORTING ACTOR IN A DAYTIME DRAMA SERIES
LEWIS ARLT, Search for Tomorrow (CBS)
BERNARD BARROW, Ryan's Hope (ABC)
JOE GALLISON, Days of Our Lives (NBC)
RON HALE, Ryan's Hope (ABC)
PETER HANSEN, General Hospital (ABC)
MANDEL KRAMER, Edge of Night (ABC)

OUTSTANDING SUPPORTING ACTRESS IN A DAYTIME DRAMA SERIES
RACHEL AMES, General Hospital (ABC)
SUSAN BROWN, General Hospital (ABC)
LOIS KIBBEE, Edge of Night (ABC)
FRANCES REID, Days of Our Lives (NBC)
SUZANNE ROGERS, Days of Our Lives (NBC)

OUTSTANDING CHILDREN'S INFORMATIONAL SPECIAL
Emmy(s) to Executive Producer(s) and Producer(s)
RAZZMATAZZ, Joel Heller, Executive Producer; Vern Diamond, Producer (CBS)
THE SECRET OF CHARLES DICKENS, CBS Festival of Lively Arts for Young People; Daniel Wilson, Executive Producer; Linda Marmelstein, Producer (CBS)

OUTSTANDING CHILDREN'S INSTRUCTIONAL SERIES

Emmy(s) to Executive Producer(s) and Producer(s)
DEAR ALEX & ANNIE, (Kids Are People Too); Ken Greengrass and Phil Lawrence, Executive Producers; Lynn Ahrens, Producer (ABC)
METRIC MARVELS, George Newall, Tom Yohe, Producers (NBC)
SESAME STREET, David D. Connell, Vice President for Production; Al Hyslop, Producer (PBS)
SCIENCE ROCK, (Schoolhouse Rock); Tom Yohe, Executive Producer; George Newall, Radford Stone, Producers (ABC)

OUTSTANDING CHILDREN'S ENTERTAINMENT SERIES

Emmy(s) to Executive Producer(s) and Producer(s)
CAPTAIN KANGAROO, Frank Alesia, Joel Kosofsky, Producers (CBS)
JOHN HALIFAX: GENTLEMAN, Once Upon a Classic; Jay Rayvid, Executive Producer; James A. DeVinney, John McRae, Producers (PBS)
KIDS ARE PEOPLE TOO, Lawrence Einhorn, Executive Producer; Laura Schrock, Producer; Noreen Conlin, Co-Producer (ABC)
LORNA DOONE, Once Upon a Classic; Jay Rayvid, Executive Producer; Shep Greene, Barry Letts, Producers (PBS)
THE SECRET GARDEN, Once Upon a Classic; Jay Rayvid, Executive Producer; Dorothea Brooking, James A. DeVinney, Producers (PBS)

OUTSTANDING CHILDREN'S ENTERTAINMENT SPECIAL

Emmy(s) to Executive Producer(s) and Producer(s)
JOEY & REDHAWK, Daniel Wilson, Executive Producer; Fran Sears, Producer (CBS)
MAKE BELIEVE MARRIAGE, ABC Afterschool Special; Linda Gottlieb, Executive Producer; Evelyn Barron, Producer (ABC)
MOM AND DAD CAN'T HEAR ME, ABC Afterschool Special; Daniel Wilson, Executive Producer; Fran Sears, Producer (ABC)
NYC TOO FAR FROM TAMPA BLUES, Special Treat; Daniel Wilson, Executive Producer; Linda Marmelstein, Phyllis Minoff, Producers (NBC)
RODEO RED AND THE RUNAWAY, Special Treat; Linda Gottlieb, Executive Producer; Doro Bachrach, Producer (NBC)
THE TAP DANCE KID, Special Treat; Linda Gottlieb, Executive Producer; Evelyn Barron, Producer (NBC)

OUTSTANDING INDIVIDUAL DIRECTION FOR A GAME OR AUDIENCE PARTICIPATION SHOW

For a single episode
MIKE GARGIULO, The $20,000 Pyramid (ABC)
RICHARD SCHNEIDER, Jeopardy (NBC)
JEROME SHAW, The Hollywood Squares (NBC)

OUTSTANDING INDIVIDUAL DIRECTION FOR A VARIETY PROGRAM

For a single episode
RON WEINER, Donahue; Nazis and the Klan (Synd)
DONALD R. KING, America Alive (NBC)
GLEN SWANSON, Dinah!; The 5th Anniversary Show (Synd)

OUTSTANDING DIRECTION FOR A DAYTIME DRAMA SERIES

For the entire series
IRA CIRKER, MELVIN BERNHARDT, PAUL LAMMERS, ROBERT CALHOUN, Another World (NBC)
JACK COFFEY, DEL HUGHES, HENRY KAPLAN, All My Children (ABC)
RICHARD DUNLAP, BILL GLENN, The Young and The Restless (CBS)
JERRY EVANS, LELA SWIFT, Ryan's Hope (ABC)
AL RABIN, JOE BEHAR, FRANK PACELLI, Days of our Lives (NBC)
JOHN SEDWICK, RICHARD PEPPERMAN, The Edge of Night (NBC)

OUTSTANDING WRITING FOR A DAYTIME DRAMA SERIES

For the entire series
WILLIAM J. BELL, KAY ALDEN, ELIZABETH HARROWER, The Young and The Restless (CBS)
CLAIRE LABINE, PAUL AVILA MAYER, MARY MUNISTERI, JUDITH PINSKER, JEFFREY LANE, Ryan's Hope (ABC)
ANN MARCUS, MICHAEL ROBERT DAVID, RAYMOND E. GOLDSTONE, JOYCE PERRY, ELIZABETH HARROWER, ROCCI CHATFIELD, LAURA OLSHER, Days of Our Lives (NBC)
AGNES NIXON, WISNER WASHAM, JACK WOOD, MARY K. WELLS, KENNETH HARVEY, CATHY CHICOS, CAROLINE FRANZ, DORIS FRANKEL, WILLIAM DELLIGAN, All My Children (ABC)

OUTSTANDING ACTOR IN A DAYTIME DRAMA SERIES

JED ALLAN, Days of Our Lives (NBC)
NICHOLAS BENEDICT, All My Children (ABC)
JOHN CLARKE, Days of Our Lives (NBC)
JOEL CROTHERS, Edge of Night (ABC)
AL FREEMAN, JR., One Life to Live (ABC)
MICHAEL LEVIN, Ryan's Hope (ABC)

OUTSTANDING ACTRESS IN A DAYTIME DRAMA SERIES

NANCY ADDISON, Ryan's Hope (ABC)
IRENE DAILEY, Another World (NBC)
HELEN GALLAGHER, Ryan's Hope (ABC)
BEVERLEE McKINSEY, Another World (NBC)
SUSAN SEAFORTH HAYES, Days of Our Lives (NBC)
VICTORIA WYNDHAM, Another World (NBC)

OUTSTANDING DAYTIME DRAMA SERIES

Emmy(s) to Executive Producer(s) and Producer(s)
ALL MY CHILDREN, Agnes Nixon, Executive Producer; Bud Kloss, Producer (ABC)
DAYS OF OUR LIVES, Betty Corday, H. Wesley Kenney, Executive Producers; Jack Herzberg, Producer (NBC)
RYAN'S HOPE, Claire Labine, Paul Avila Mayer, Executive Producers; Ellen Barrett, Robert Costello, Producers (ABC)
THE YOUNG AND THE RESTLESS, John Conboy, Executive Producer; Ed Scott, Patricia Wenig, Producers (CBS)

OUTSTANDING CHILDREN'S INFORMATIONAL SERIES

Emmy(s) to Executive Producer(s) and Producer(s)
30 MINUTES, Joel Heller, Executive Producer; Madeline Amgott, Elliot Bernstein, JoAnn Caplin, Christine Huneke, Robert Rubin, Patti Obrow White, Producers (CBS)
ABC MINUTE MAGAZINE, Thomas H. Wolf, Producer (ABC)
ANIMALS, ANIMALS, ANIMALS, Lester Cooper, Executive Producer; Jake Haselkorn, Producer (ABC)
BIG BLUE MARBLE, Robert Wiemer, Executive Producer; Richard Berman, Producer (Synd)
IN THE NEWS, Joel Heller, Executive Producer; Susan Mills, Producer (CBS)
WHEN YOU TURN OFF THE SET, TURN ON A BOOK, Mary Alice Dwyer, Executive Producer; George Newall, Tom Yohe, Producers (NBC)

OUTSTANDING ACHIEVEMENT IN TECHNICAL EXCELLENCE FOR A DAYTIME DRAMA SERIES
Emmy(s) to Program Representative(s), Emmy Certificates to Respective Individuals
ALL MY CHILDREN, Technical Team (ABC)
ANOTHER WORLD, Technical Team (ABC)
THE EDGE OF NIGHT, Technical Team (ABC)
ONE LIFE TO LIVE, Technical Team (ABC)
RYAN'S HOPE, Technical Team (ABC)
THE YOUNG AND THE RESTLESS, Technical Team (CBS)

OUTSTANDING ACHIEVEMENT IN DESIGN EXCELLENCE FOR A DAYTIME DRAMA SERIES
Emmy(s) to Program Representatives, Emmy Certificates to Respective Individuals
DAYS OF OUR LIVES, Design Team (NBC)
LOVE OF LIFE, Design Team (CBS)
ONE LIFE TO LIVE, Design Team (ABC)
RYAN'S HOPE, Design Team (ABC)

THE NATIONAL AWARD FOR COMMUNITY SERVICE FINALISTS
1978 KENTUCKY GENERAL ASSEMBLY IN OPEN SESSION (KET NETWORK) Lexington, Kentucky
THE BIGGEST STING (KBTV) Denver, Colorado
A RACE WITH DEATH (WJLA-TV) Washington, D.C.
OLD AGE: DO NOT GO GENTLE (KGO-TV) San Francisco, California
NO ROOM IN SUBURBIA (WBZ-TV) Allston, Massachusetts
ZOOT SUIT: THE PLAY AND THE PROMISE (KNXT) Hollywood, California
THE DESERT PEOPLE (KOOL-TV) Phoenix, Arizona
SCANDAL AT C.E.T.A. (WPLG) Miami, Florida
WE THE VICTIMS (WCBS-TV) New York, New York
30 MINUTES (WIIC-TV) Pittsburgh, Pennsylvania
POISONS IN THE WIND (KMGH-TV) Denver, Colorado
THE UNIVERSITY OF THE THIRD AGE (KCST-TV) San Diego, California

CREATIVE ARTS IN TELEVISION

OUTSTANDING ACHIEVEMENT IN ENGINEERING DEVELOPMENT
EMMY AWARD to AMPEX CORPORATION, for the development of their Automatic Scan Tracking system for helical video tape equipment.
CITATION to MAGICAM, INC., for development of real time tracking of independent scenes.

OUTSTANDING ART DIRECTION FOR A SERIES
For a single episode of a regular series
HOWARD E. JOHNSON, Art Director, RICHARD B. GODDARD, Set Decorator, Little Women, Part I (NBC)
JOHN E. CHILBERG II, Art Director, MICKEY S. MICHAELS, Set Decorator, LOWELL CHAMBERS, Set Decorator, Battlestar Galactica, Saga Of A Star World (ABC)
RENE LAGLER, Art Director, EARL CARLSON, Set Decorator, The Mary Tyler Moore Hour (with Gene Kelly) (CBS)

OUTSTANDING ART DIRECTION FOR A LIMITED SERIES OR A SPECIAL
For a single episode of a regular or a limited series, or for a special program
JAN SCOTT, Art Director and Production Designer, BILL HARP, Set Decorator, Studs Lonigan, Part III (NBC)
MICHAEL BAUGH, Art Director, ROBERT CHECCHI, Set Decorator, ARTHUR JEPH PARKER, Set Decorator, Blind Ambition, Part 3 (CBS)
RICHARD Y. HAMAN, Art Director, ANNE D. McCULLEY, Set Decorator, Backstairs At The White House, Book One (NBC)
JAN SCOTT, Art Director and Production Designer, EDWARD J. McDONALD, Set Decorator, BILL HARP, Set Decorator, Studs Lonigan, Part I (NBC)
JACK SENTER, Production Designer, JOHN W. CORSO, Art Director, SHERMAN LOUDERMILK, Art Director, JOSPEH J. STONE, Set Decorator, JOHN M. DWYER, Set Decorator, ROBERT G. FREER, Set Decorator, Centennial, The Shepherds, Chapter Seven (NBC)

OUTSTANDING ACHIEVEMENT IN CHOREOGRAPHY
For a single episode of a regular or limited series, or for a special program
KEVIN CARLISLE, The 3rd Barry Manilow Special (ABC)
MARTHA GRAHAM, The Martha Graham Dance Company; Clytemnestra; Dance In America; Great Performances (PBS)
ANITA MANN, The Muppets Go Hollywood (CBS)

OUTSTANDING CINEMATOGRAPHY FOR A SERIES
For a single episode of a regular series
TED VOIGTLANDER, ASC, Little House On The Prairie, The Craftsman (NBC)
JOSEPH BIROC, Little Women, Part II (NBC)
WILLIAM W. SPENCER, ASC, Barnaby Jones, Memory Of A Nightmare (CBS)

OUTSTANDING CINEMATOGRAPHY FOR A LIMITED SERIES OR A SPECIAL
For a single episode of a limited series, or for a special program
HOWARD SCHWARTZ, ASC, Rainbow (NBC)
ARCH R. DALZELL (U.S.A.), FREDDIE YOUNG, B.S.C. (U.K.), Ike, Part II (ABC)
DENNIS DALZELL, the Winds Of Kitty Hawk (NBC)
DONALD M. MORGAN, Elvis (ABC)

OUTSTANDING COSTUME DESIGN FOR A SERIES
For a single episode of a regular series
JEAN-PIERRE DORLEAC, Battlestar Galactica, Furlon (ABC)
ALFRED E. LEHMAN, Laverne & Shirley, The Third Annual Shotz Talent Show (ABC)

OUTSTANDING COSTUME DESIGN FOR A LIMITED SERIES OR A SPECIAL
For a single episode of a limited series, or for a special program
ANN HOLLOWOOD, SUE LE CASH, CHRISTINE WILSON, Edward The King; King At Last (Synd)
BOB MACKIE, RET TURNER, Cher—. . .And Other Fantasies (NBC)
WARDEN NEIL, The John Davidson Christmas Show (ABC)
DAVID WALKER, The Corn Is Green (CBS)

OUTSTANDING FILM EDITING FOR A SERIES

For a single episode of a regular series

M. PAM BLUMENTHAL, Taxi, Paper Marriage (ABC)
FRED W. BERGER, A.C.E., Dallas, Reunion, Part II (CCBS)
JAMES GALLOWAY, A.C.E., Lou Grant, Hooker (CBS)
LARRY L. MILLS, STANFORD TISCHLER, M*A*S*H, The

OUTSTANDING FILM EDITING FOR A LIMITED SERIES OR A SPECIAL

For a single episode of a limited series, or for a special program

ARTHUR SCHMIDT, The Jericho Mile (ABC)
JAMES GALLOWAY, First You Cry (CBS)
JOHN A. MARTINELLI, A.C.E., The Winds of Kitty Hawk (NBC)
ROBERT WATTS, A.C.E., Centennial, Only The Rocks Live Forever, Chapter One (NBC)
JOHN M. WOODCOCK, A.C.E., BILL LENNY, PAUL DIXON, Ike, Part III (ABC)

OUTSTANDING ACHIEVEMENT IN FILM SOUND EDITING

For a single episode of a regular or limited series or for a special program

WILLIAM H. WISTROM, Friendly Fire (ABC)
DOUGLAS H. GRINDSTAFF, DON ISAACS, MARK DENNIS, BOB HUMAN, LARRY KAUFMAN, LARRY SINGER and HANK SALERNO, A Fire In The Sky (NBC)
LAWRENCE E. NEIMAN, CHARLES L. CAMPBELL, COLIN MOUAT, DON WARNER, DAVID PETTIJOHN, PIETER S. HUBBARD, GARY VAUGHAN, CHARLES E. MORAN, BOB CANTON and MARTIN VARNO, The Triangle Factory Fire Scandal (NBC)
MICHAEL REDBOURN, PETER HARRISON, RUSS TINSLEY, LINDA DOVE and LEONARD CORSO, Ike, Part II (ABC)

OUTSTANDING ACHIEVEMENT IN FILM SOUND MIXING

For a single episode of a regular or limited series, or for a special program

BILL TEAGUE, GEORGE E. PORTER, EDDIE J. NELSON, RAY WEST, The Winds Of Kitty Hawk(NBC)
STANLEY P. GORDON, GEORGE E. PORTER, EDDIE J. NELSON, HOPPY MEHTERIAN, A Christmas To Remember (CBS)
GEORGE E. PORTER, EDDIE J. NELSON, RAY WEST, MAURY HARRIS, The Triangle Factory Fire Scandal (NBC)
BILL TEAGUE, GEORGE E. PORTER, EDDIE J. NELSON, HOPPY MEHTERIAN, Ike, Part II (ABC)

OUTSTANDING ACHIEVEMENT IN GRAPHIC DESIGN AND TITLE SEQUENCES

For a single episode of a regular or limited series, or for a special program. This includes animation only when created for use in titling

STU BERNSTEIN, EYTAN KELLER, Cinderella At The Palace (CBS)
PHILL NORMAN, Vega$; Centerfold (ABC)

OUTSTANDING ACHIEVEMENT IN LIGHTING DIRECTION (ELECTRONIC)

For a single episode of a regular or limited series, or for a special program

GEORGE REISENBERGER, Lighting Consultant & Designer; ROY A. BARNETT, Director of Photography "E"; You Can't Take It With You (CBS)
WILLIAM M. KLAGES, GEORGE RIESENBERGER, A Salute To American Imagination (CBS)
WILLIAM KNIGHT, The Homecoming; Mourning Becomes Electra; Great Performances (PBS)
FRED McKINNON, Cinderella At The Palace (CBS)

OUTSTANDING ACHIEVEMENT IN MAKEUP

For a single episode of a regular or limited series, or for a special program

TOMMY COLE, MARK BUSSAN, RON WALTERS, Backstairs At The White House, Book Four (NBC)
KEN CHASE, Makeup Design; JOE DiBELLA, ZOLTAN ELEK, TOM MILLER, DAVID DITTMAR, Makeup Artists; Roots: The Next Generations, Episode Three (ABC)
LEO L. LOTITO, JR., NICK PAGLIARO, Lady Of The House (NBC)
MARVIN G. WESTMORE, Elvis (ABC)

OUTSTANDING ACHIEVEMENT IN HAIRSTYLING

For a single episode of a regular or limited series, or for a special program

JANICE D. BRANDOW, The Triangle Factory Fire Scandal (NBC)
SUSAN GERMAINE, LOLA KEMP, VIVIAN McATEER, Backstairs At The White House, Book Four (NBC)
JEAN BURT REILLY, Ike, Part III (ABC)

OUTSTANDING MUSIC COMPOSITION FOR A SERIES

(Dramatic underscore, theme, song, or special material - with or without lyrics) For a single episode of a regular series

DAVID ROSE, Little House On The Prairie, The Craftsman, (NBC)
DICK DeBENEDICTIS, DEAN DeBENEDICTIS, Dear Detective (CBS)
CHARLES FOX, NORMAN GIMBEL (Lyrics), The Paper Chase, A Day In The Life (CBS)
PATRICK WILLIAMS, Lou Grant, Prisoner (CBS)

OUTSTANDING MUSIC COMPOSITION FOR A LIMITED SERIES OR A SPECIAL

(Dramatic underscore, theme, song, or special material - with or without lyrics) For a single episode of a limited series, or for a special program

LEONARD ROSENMAN, Friendly Fire (ABC)
PETER MATZ, First You Cry (CBS)
ALEX NORTH, The Word (CBS)
KEN WELCH, MITZIE WELCH, The Hal Linden Special (ABC)

OUTSTANDING ACHIEVEMENT IN TAPE SOUND MIXING

For a single episode of a regular or limited series, or for a special program

ED GREENE, PHILLIP J. SERETTI, DENNIS S. SANDS, GARRY ULMER, Steve & Eydie Celebrate Irving Berlin (NBC)
ED GREENE, The Muppets Go Hollywood (CBS)
GORDON KLIMUCK, TOM HUTH, Perry Como's Early American Christmas (ABC)
DOUG NELSON, The 3rd Barry Manilow Special (ABC)
GEORJA SKINNER, PHILLIP J. SERETTI, Return Engagement, Hallmark Hall Of Fame (NBC)

OUTSTANDING ACHIEVEMENT IN TECHNICAL DIRECTION AND ELECTRONIC CAMERWORK

For a single episode of a regular or limited series, or for a special program

JERRY WEISS, TD, DON BARKER, PEGGY MAHONEY, REED HOWARD, KURT TONNESSEN, WILLIAM LANDERS, LOUIS CYWINSKI, GEORGE LOOMIS, BRIAN SHERRIFFE, Camerapersons, Dick Clark's Live Wednesday, Show #1 (NBC)
ROBERT G. HOLMES, TD, BRUCE BOTTONE, JIM HERRING, ROYDEN HOLM, BILL LANDERS, PEGGY MAHONEY, Camerapersons, The Midnight Special, Host Dolly Parton (NBC)
ROBERT C. JONES, TD, BARRY A. BROWN, LARRY HEIDER, WAYNE ORR, HANK GEVING, DIANNE BIEDERBECK, RICHARD PRICE, TOM KARNOWSKI, DAVE LEVISOHN, Camerapersons, You Can't Take It With You (CBS)
HEINO RIPP, TD, AL CAMOIN, PETER BASIL, TOM DE ZENDORF, JOHN PINTO, VINCE DI PIETRO, Camperpersons, NBC's Saturday Night Live, Host Richard Benjamin (NBC)

OUTSTANDING VIDEO TAPE EDITING FOR A SERIES

For a single episode of a regular series

ANDY ZALL, Stockard Channing In Just Friends, Pilot (CBS)
HAL COLLINS, HARVEY BERGER, The 200th Episode Celebration Of All In The Family (CBS)

OUTSTANDING VIDEO TAPE EDITING FOR A LIMITED SERIES OR A SPECIAL

For a single episode of a limited series, or for a special program

KEN DENISOFF, TUCKER WIARD, JANET McFADDEN, The Scarlet Letter, Part Two (PBS)
DARRYL SUTTON, The Muppets Go Hollywood (CBS)
ANDY ZALL, The Cheryl Ladd Special (ABC)
MARCO ZAPPIA, Liberace - A Valentine Special (CBS)

OUTSTANDING INDIVIDUAL ACHIEVEMENT - ANIMATION PROGRAM

(Possibility of one Award, more than one Award, or no Award)

JOHNNY BRADFORD (Lyrics), DOUG GOODWIN (Music), A Pink Christmas (main title song) (ABC)
DOUG GOODWIN (Music & Lyrics), A Pink Christmas (songs) (ABC)
PETER YARROW and DAVID CAMPBELL (Music & Lyrics), Puff The Magic Dragon (CBS)

OUTSTANDING INDIVIDUAL ACHIEVEMENT - CHILDREN'S PROGRAM

(Possibility of one Award, more than one Award, or no Award)

GERRI BRIOSO, Graphic Artist, Christmas Eve on Sesame Street (PBS)
TONY DI GIROLAMO, Lighting Director, DAVE CLARK, Lighting Director, Christmas Eve on Sesame Street (PBS)

OUTSTANDING INDIVIDUAL ACHIEVEMENT - CREATIVE TECHNICAL CRAFTS

(Possibility of one Award, more than one Award, or no Award)

JOHN DYKSTRA, Special Effects Coordinator, RICHARD EDLUND, Director of Miniature Photography, JOSEPH GOSS, Mechanical Special Effects, Battlestar Galactica, Saga Of A Star World (ABC)
TOM ANCELL (Live Stereo Sound Mixing), Giulini's Beethoven's 9th Live - A Gift From Los Angeles (PBS)
JOE UNSINN, Special Effects, Explosion and Destruction, Pyrotechnical Work, A Fire In The Sky (NBC)
DICK WILSON, (Sound Effects), Welcome Back Kotter, Barbarino's Baby (ABC)

OUTSTANDING INDIVIDUAL ACHIEVEMENT - INFORMATIONAL PROGRAM

(Possibility of one Award, more than one Award, or no Award)

ROBERT NEIMACK, Film Editor, Scared Straight! (Synd)

OUTSTANDING INDIVIDUAL ACHIEVEMENT - SPECIAL CLASS

(Possibility of one Award, more than one Award, or no Award)

HARRY BLAKE, BOB OSTERMANN and DAVID A. DITTMAR, Makeup Artists, General Electric's All-Star Aniversary (ABC)
WILLIAM M. KLAGES, Lighting Director, Rockette: A Holiday Tribute To Radio City Music Hall (NBC)
CARL VITELLI, Lighting Director, A Gift Of Song - The Music for UNICEF Special (NBC)
DAVE CLARK, Lighting Designer, MICHAEL ROSATTI and HARRY BOTTORF, Lighting Directors, Baryshnikov At The White House (PBS)
DAVID W. FOSTER and EDDIE C. JOSEPH, Videotape Editors, The Television Annual: 1978/1979 (ABC)

OUTSTANDING INDIVIDUAL ACHIEVEMENT - SPECIAL EVENTS

(Possibility of one Award, more than one Award, or no Award)

MICHAEL L. WENIG and TERRY PICKFORD, Videotape Editors, 51st Annual Awards Presentation of the Academy of Motion Picture Arts and Sciences (ABC)
ROY CHRISTOPHER, Art Director, 51st Annual Awards Presentation of the Academy of Motion Picture Arts and Sciences (ABC)

1979/80

PRIME TIME EMMY AWARDS

OUTSTANDING COMEDY SERIES

Emmy(s) to Executive Producer(s) and/or Producer(s)
BARNEY MILLER, Danny Arnold, Executive Producer; Tony Sheehan, Noam Pitlik, Producers; Gary Shaw, Co-Producer (ABC)
M*A*S*H, Burt Metcalfe, Executive Producer; Jim Mulligan, John Rappaport, Producers (CBS)
SOAP, Paul Junger Witt, Tony Thomas, Executive Producers; Susan Harris, Producer (ABC)
TAXI, James L. Brooks, Stan Daniels, Ed. Weinberger, Executive Producers; Glen Charles, Les Charles, Producers (ABC)
WKRP IN CINCINNATI, Hugh Wilson, Executive Producer; Rod Daniel, Bill Dial, Producers (CBS)

OUTSTANDING DRAMA SERIES

Emmy(s) to Executive Producer(s) and/or Producer(s)
DALLAS, Philip Capice, Lee Rich, Executive Producers; Leonard Katzman, Producer (CBS)
FAMILY, Aaron Spelling, Leonard Goldberg, Executive Producers; Edward Zwick, Producer (ABC)
LOU GRANT, Gene Reynolds, Executive Producer; Seth Freeman, Producer (CBS)
THE ROCKFORD FILES, Meta Rosenberg, Executive Producer; Ste-

phen J. Cannell, Supervising Producer; David Chase, Chas. Floyd Johnson, Juanita Bartlett, Producers (NBC)
THE WHITE SHADOW, Bruce Paltrow, Executive Producer; Mark Tinker, Producer (CBS)

OUTSTANDING LIMITED SERIES

Emmy(s) to Executive Producer(s) and/or Producer(s)
DISRAELI: PORTRAIT OF A ROMATIC, Masterpiece Theatre; OJoan Wilson, Series Producer; Cecil Clarke, Producer (PBS)
EDWARD & MRS. SIMPSON, Andrew Brown, Producer (Synd)
THE DUCHESS OF DUKE STREET II, Masterpiece Theatre; Joan Wilson, Series Producer; John Hawkesworth, Producer (PBS)
MOVIOLA, David L. Wolper, Executive Producer; Stan Margulies, Producer (NBC)

OUTSTANDING VARIETY OR MUSIC PROGRAM

For a special or a series Emmy(s) to Executive Producer(s) and/or Producer(s) and Star, if applicable
THE BENNY HILL SHOW, Dennis Kirkland, Keith Beckett, Mark Stuart, Producers (Synd)
GOLDIE AND LIZA TOGETHER, George Schlatter, Executive Producer; Don Mischer, Fred Ebb, Producers (CBS)
IBM PRESENTS BARYSHNIKOV ON BROADWAY, Herman Krawitz, Executive Producer; Gary Smith, Dwight Hemion, Producers (ABC)
THE MUPPET SHOW, David Lazer, Executive Producer; Jim Henson, Producer (Synd)
SHIRLEY MACLAINE...'EVERY LITTLE MOVEMENT' Gary Smith, Dwight Hemion, Producers (CBS)

OUTSTANDING DRAMA OR COMEDY SPECIAL

Emmy(s) to Executive Producer(s) and/or Producer(s)
ALL QUIET ON THE WESTERN FRONT (Hallmark Hall of Fame) Martin Starger, Executive Producer; Norman Rosemont, Producer (CBS)
AMBER WAVES, Philip Mandelker, Executive Producer; Stanley Kallis, Producer (ABC)
GIDEON'S TRUMPET (Hallmark Hall of Fame) John Houseman, Executive Producer; David W. Rintels, Producer (CBS)
GUYANA TRAGEDY: THE STORY OF JIM JONES, Frank Konigsberg, Executive Producer; Ernest Tidyman, Sam Manners, Producers (CBS)
THE MIRACLE WORKER, Raymond Katz, Sandy Gallin, Executive Producers; Fred Coe, Producer (NBC)

OUTSTANDING CLASSICAL PROGRAM IN THE PERFORMING ARTS

For a special or a series: Emmy(s) to Executive Producer(s) and/or Producer(s) and Star, if applicable
AGNES deMILLE AND THE JOFFREY BALLET IN CONVERSATIONS ABOUT THE DANCE Loring d'Usseau, Producer (PBS)
BEVERLY SILLS IN CONCERT, Thomas L. Merklinger, Executive Producer (PBS)
LIVE FROM STUDIO 8H: A TRIBUTE TO TOSCANINI, Judith De Paul, Alvin Cooperman, Producers (NBC)
LUCIANO PAVAROTTI AND THE NEW YORK PHILHARMONIC LIVE FROM LINCOLN CENTER, John Goberman, Producer (PBS)

OUTSTANDING INFORMATION PROGRAM

For a special or a series Emmy(s) to Executive Producer(s) and/or Producer(s)
BILL MOYERS' JOURNAL, Joan Konner, Executive Producer (PBS)
THE BODY HUMAN: THE BODY BEAUTIFUL, Thomas W. Moore, Executive Producer; Robert E. Fuisz, M.D., Alfred R. Kelman, Producers; Charles A. Bangert, Geof Bartz, Co-Producers (CBS)
THE BODY HUMAN: THE MAGIC SENSE, Thomas W. Moore, Executive Producer; Alfred R. Kelman, Robert E. Fuisz, M.D., Producers; Charles A. Bangert, Vivian R. Moss, Co-Producers (CBS)
THE NILE: THE COUSTEAU ODYSSEY, Jacques-Yves Cousteau, Philippe Cousteau, Executive Producers (PBS)
PICASSO--A PAINTER'S DIARY, George Page, Executive Producer; Perry Miller Adato, Producer (PBS)

OUTSTANDING PROGRAM ACHIEVEMENT - SPECIAL EVENTS

Emmy(s) to Executive Producer(s) and/or Producer(s) (Possibility of one Award, more than one Award, or no Award)
THE AMERICAN FILM INSTITUTE SALUTE TO JIMMY STEWART, George Stevens, Jr., Producer (CBS)
52nd ANNUAL AWARDS PRESENTATION OF THE ACADEMY OF MOTION PICTURE ARTS AND SCIENCES, Howard W. Koch, Producer (ABC)
THE KENNEDY CENTER HONORS: A CELEBRATION OF THE PERFORMING ARTS, George Stevens, Jr., Nick Vanoff, Producers (CBS)
THE 34th ANNUAL TONY AWARDS, Alexander H. Cohen, Executive Producer; Hildy Parks, Producer; Roy A. Somlyo, Co-Producer (CBS)

OUTSTANDING PROGRAM ACHIEVEMENT - SPECIAL CLASS

Emmy(s) to Executive Producer(s) and/or Producer(s) (Possibility of one Award, more than one Award or no Award)
FRED ASTAIRE: CHANGE PARTNERS AND DANCE, George Page, Jac Venza, Executive Producers; David Heeley, Producer (PBS)
FRED ASTAIRE: PUTTIN' ON HIS TOP HAT, George Page, Jac Venza, Executive Producers; David Heeley, Producer (PBS)
REAL PEOPLE, George Schlatter, Executive Producer; John Barbour, Bob Wynn, Producers (NBC)
THE TONIGHT SHOW STARRING JOHNNY CARSON, Fred de Cordova, Producer (NBC)
WINTER OLYMPICS '80 - THE WORLD COMES TO AMERICA Roone Arledge, Executive Producer; Don Wilson, Producer (ABC)

OUTSTANDING CHILDREN'S PROGRAM

For a special or a series. Emmy(s) to Executive Producer(s) and/or Producer(s) (Possibility of one Award, more than one Award, or no Award)
BENJI AT WORK, Joe Camp, Executive Producer; Fielder Baker, Producer (ABC)
THE HALLOWEEN THAT ALMOST WASN'T, Richard Barclay, Executive Producer; Gaby Monet, Producer (ABC)
SESAME STREET IN PUERTO RICO, Al Hyslop, Executive Producer (PBS)

OUTSTANDING ANIMATED PROGRAM

For a special or a series. Emmy(s) to Executive Producer(s) and/or Producer(s) (Possibility of one Award, more than one Award, or no Award)
CARLTON YOUR DOORMAN, Lorenzo Music, Barton Dean, Producers (CBS)
DR SEUSS' PONTOFFEL POCK, WHERE ARE YOU? David H. De Pattie, Friz Freleng, Executive Producers; Ted Geisel, Producer (ABC)
PINK PANTHER IN OLYM-PINKS, David H. De Patie, Friz Freleng, Producers (ABC)
SHE'S A GOOD SKATE, CHARLIE BROWN, Lee Mendelson, Executive Producer; Bill Melendez, Producer (CBS)

OUTSTANDING LEAD ACTOR IN A COMEDY SERIES
For a continuing or single performance in a regular series
ALAN ALDA; M*A*S*H (CBS)
ROBERT GUILLAUME; Benson (ABC)
JUDD HIRSCH; Taxi (ABC)
HAL LINDEN; Barney Miller (ABC)
RICHARD MULLIGAN; Soap (ABC)

OUTSTANDING LEAD ACTOR IN A DRAMA SERIES
For a continuing or single performance in a regular series
ED ASNER; Lou Grant (CBS)
JAMES GARNER; The Rockford Files (NBC)
LARRY HAGMAN; Dallas (CBS)
JACK KLUGMAN; Quincy, M.E. (NBC)

OUTSTANDING LEAD ACTOR IN A LIMITED SERIES OR A SPECIAL
For a continuing role in a limited series, or for a single appearance in a limited series or a special
POWERS BOOTHE; Guyana Tragedy: The Story of Jim Jones (CBS)
TONY CURTIS; Moviola, The Scarlett O'Hara War (NBC)
HENRY FONDA; Gideon's Trumpet (CBS)
JASON ROBARDS; F.D.R. The Last Year (NBC)

OUTSTANDING LEAD ACTRESS IN A COMEDY SERIES
For a continuing or single performance in a regular series
CATHRYN DAMON; Soap (ABC)
KATHERINE HELMOND; Soap (ABC)
POLLY HOLLIDAY; Flo (CBS)
SHEREE NORTH; Archie Bunker's Place (CBS)
ISABEL SANFORD; The Jeffersons (CBS)

OUTSTANDING LEAD ACTRESS IN A DRAMA SERIES
For a continuing or single performance in a regular series
LAUREN BACALL; The Rockford Files, Lions, Tigers, Monkeys and Dogs (NBC)
BARBARA BEL GEDDES; Dallas (CBS)
MARIETTE HARTLEY; The Rockford Files, Paradise Cove (CBS)
KRISTY McNICHOL; Family (ABC)
SADA THOMPSON; Family (ABC)

OUTSTANDING LEAD ACTRESS IN A LIMITED SERIES OR A SPECIAL
For a continuing role in a limited series, or for a single appearance in a limited series or a special
PATTY DUKE ASTIN; The Miracle Worker (NBC)
BETTE DAVIS; White Mama (CBS)
MELISSA GILBERT; The Miracle Worker (NBC)
LEE REMICK; Haywire (CBS)

OUTSTANDING SUPPORTING ACTOR IN A COMEDY OR VARIETY OR MUSIC SERIES
For a continuing or single performance in a regular series
MIKE FARRELL; M*A*S*H (CBS)
MAX GAIL; Barney Miller (ABC)
HOWARD HESSEMAN; WKRP in Cincinnati (CBS)
STEVE LANDESBERG; Barney Miller (ABC)
HARRY MORGAN; M*A*S*H (CBS)

OUTSTANDING SUPPORTING ACTOR IN A DRAMA SERIES
For a continuing or single performance in a regular series
MASON ADAMS; Lou Grant (CBS)
NOAH BERRY; The Rockford Files (NBC)
STUART MARGOLIN; The Rockford Files (NBC)
ROBERT WALDEN; Lou Grant (CBS)

OUTSTANDING SUPPORTING ACTOR IN A LIMITED SERIES OR A SPECIAL
For a continuing role in a limited series, or for a single appearance in a limited series or a special
ERNEST BORGNINE; All Quiet On The Western Front (Hallmark Hall of Fame) (CBS)
JOHN CASSAVETES; Flesh and Blood (CBS)
CHARLES DURNING; Attica (ABC)
HAROLD GOULD; Moviola, The Scarlett O'Hara War (NBC)
GEORGE GRIZZARD; The Oldest Living Graduate (NBC)

OUTSTANDING SUPPORTING ACTRESS IN A COMEDY OR VARIETY OR MUSIC SERIES
For a continuing or single performance in a regular series
LONI ANDERSON; WKRP In Cincinnati (CBS)
POLLY HOLLIDAY; Alice (CBS)
INGA SWENSON; Benson (ABC)
LORETTA SWIT; M*A*S*H (CBS)

OUTSTANDING SUPPORTING ACTRESS IN A DRAMA SERIES
For a continuing or single performance in a regular series
NINA FOCH; Lou Grant, Hollywood (CBS)
LINDA KELSEY; Lou Grant CBS)
NANCY MARCHAND; Lou Grant (CBS)
JESSICA WALTER; Trapper John, M.D. (CBS)

OUTSTANDING SUPPORTING ACTRESS IN A LIMITED SERIES OR A SPECIAL
For a continuing role in a limited series, or for a single appearance in a limited series or a special
EILEEN HECKART; F.D.R. The Last Year (NBC)
PATRICIA NEAL; All Quiet On The Western Front (Hallmark Hall of Fame) (CBS)
CARRIE NYE; Moviola, The Scarlett O'Hara War (NBC)
MARE WINNINGHAM; Amber Waves (ABC)

OUTSTANDING DIRECTING IN A COMEDY SERIES

For a single episode of a regular series
ALAN ALDA; M*A*S*H, Dreams (CBS)
JAMES BURROWS; Taxi, Louie And The Nice Girl (ABC)
CHARLES S. DUBIN; M*A*S*H, Period of Adjustment (CBS)
BURT METCALFE; M*A*S*H, Bottle Fatigue (CBS)
HARRY MORGAN; M*A*S*H, Stars And Stripe (CBS)

OUTSTANDING DIRECTING IN A DRAMA SERIES

For a single episode of a regular series
BURT BRINKERHOFF; Lou Grant, Hollywood (CBS)
PETER LEVIN; Lou Grant, Andrew Part II: Trial (CBS)
FRANK PERRY; Skag, Premiere (NBC)
GENE REYNOLDS; Lou Grant, Influence (CBS)
ROGER YOUNG; Lou Grant, Cop (CBS)

OUTSTANDING DIRECTING IN A VARIETY OR MUSIC PROGRAM

For a single episode of a regular or limited series or for a special
STEVE BINDER; The Big Show, with Mariette Hartley, Dean Martin (NBC)
TONY CHARMOLI; John Denver And The Muppets, A Christmas Get Together (ABC)
PETER HARRIS; The Muppet Show, with Liza Minnelli (Synd)
DWIGHT HEMION; IBM Presents Baryshnikov On Broadway (ABC)

OUTSTANDING DIRECTING IN A LIMITED SERIES OR A SPECIAL

For a single episode of a limited series, or for a special
MARVIN J. CHOMSKY; Attica (ABC)
JOHN ERMAN; Moviola, The Scarlett O'Hara War (NBC)
WILLIAM A. GRAHAM; Guyana Tragedy: The Story Of Jim Jones (CBS)
DELBERT MANN; All Quiet On The Western Front (CBS)
JOSEPH SARGENT; Amber Waves (ABC)

OUTSTANDING ACHIEVEMENT IN CHOREOGRAPHY

For a single episode of a regular or limited series, or for a special
RON FIELD; IBM Presents Baryshnikov On Broadway (ABC)
ALAN JOHNSON; Shirley MacLaine...'Every Little Movement' (CBS)
LESTER WILSON; Uptown - A Musical Comedy History Of Harlem's Apollo Theatre (NBC)

OUTSTANDING WRITING IN A COMEDY SERIES

For a single episode of a regular series
GLEN CHARLES, LES CHARLES; Taxi, Honor Thy Father (ABC)
BOB COLLEARY; Barney Miller, Photographer (ABC)
STAN DANIELS, ED. WEINBERGER; The Associates, The Censors (ABC)
DAVID ISAACS, KEN LEVINE; M*A*S*H, Goodbye, Radar, Part II (CBS)
MICHAEL LEESON, Teleplay; CHARLIE HAUCK, Story; The Associates, The First Day (ABC)

OUTSTANDING WRITING IN A DRAMA SERIES

For a single episode of a regular series
ALLAN BURNS, GENE REYNOLDS; Lou Grant, Brushfire (CBS)
STEPHEN J. CANNELL; Tenspeed And Brown Shoe, Pilot (ABC)
SETH FREEMAN; Lou Grant, Cop (CBS)
MICHELE GALLERY; Lou Grant, Lou (CBS)
ABBY MANN; Skag, Premiere (NBC)

OUTSTANDING WRITING IN A VARIETY OR MUSIC PROGRAM

For a single episode of a regular or limited series, or for a special
PETER AYKROYD, ANNE BEATTS, TOM DAVIS, JAMES DOWNEY, BRIAN DOYLE-MURRAY, AL FRANKEN, TOM GAMMELL, LORNE MICHAELS, MATT NEUMAN, DON NOVELLO, SARAH PALEY, MAX PROSS, HERB SARGENT, HARRY SHEARER, TOM SCHILLER, ROSIE SHUSTER, ALAN ZWEIBEL; Saturday Night Live, Host: Teri Garr (NBC)
FRED EBB; Goldie And Liza Together (CBS)
JIM HENSON, DON HINKLEY, JERRY JUHL, DAVID ODELL; The Muppet Show, Guest: Alan Arkin (Synd)
BUZ KOHAN; Shirley MacLaine...'Every Little Movement' (CBS)
BOB ARNOTT, ROGER BEATTY, DICK CLAIR, TIM CONWAY, ANN ELDER, ARNIE KOGEN, BUZ KOHAN, JENNA MC MAHON, KENNY SOLMS; Carol Burnett & Company, Guest: Sally Field (ABC)

OUTSTANDING WRITING IN A LIMITED SERIES OR A SPECIAL

For a single episode of a limited series, or for a special, whether the writing is an original teleplay or an adaptation
DAVID CHASE; Off The Minnesota Strip (ABC)
JAMES S. HENERSON; Attica (ABC)
JAMES LEE; Moviola, This Year's Blonde (NBC)
DAVID W. RINTELS; Gideon's Trumpet (Hallmark Hall of Fame) (CBS)
KEN TREVEY; Amber Waves (ABC)

CREATIVE CRAFT EMMY AWARDS

OUTSTANDING CINEMATOGRAPHY FOR A SERIES

For a single episode of a regular series
EMMETT BERGHOLZ; Fantasy Island, The Wedding (ABC)
ALRIC EDENS, A.S.C.; Quincy, M.E., Riot (NBC)
GERALD PERRY FINNERMAN, A.S.C.; From Here To Eternity, Pearl Harbor (NBC)
ENZO A. MARTINELLI, A.S.C.; The Contender, Breakthrough (CBS)
JOHN McPHERSON, A.S.C.; The Incredible Hulk, Broken Image (CBS)
TED VOIGTLANDER, A.S.C.; Little House On The Prairie, May We Make Them Proud (NBC)

OUTSTANDING CINEMATOGRAPHY FOR A LIMITED SERIES OR A SPECIAL

For a single episode of a limited series, or for a special
JOE BIROC, A.S.C.; Kenny Rogers As The Gambler CBS)
GAYNE RESCHER, A.S.C.; Moviola, The Silent Lovers (NBC)
TED VOIGTLANDER, A.S.C.; The Miracle Worker (NBC)
HARRY L. WOLF, A.S.C.; Brave New World (NBC)

OUTSTANDING ART DIRECTION FOR A SERIES

For a single episode of a regular series
JAMES J. AGAZZI, Art Director; PAUL SYLOS, Art Director BOB SIGNORELLI, Set Decorator; Hart To Hart, Man With Jade Eyes (ABC)

MICHAEL BAUGH, Production Designer; EDWARD McDONALD, Set Decorator; Beyond Westworld, Pilot (CBS)
JAMES D. BISSELL, Art Director; WILLIAM WEBB, Set Decorator; Palmerstown, U.S.A. The Old Sister (CBS)
HUB BRADEN, Art Director; FRED LUFF, Art Director; FRANK LOMBARDO, Set Decorator; Buck Rogers In The 25th Century; Ardala Returns (NBC)
DAVID MARSHALL, Art Director; WILLIAM CRAIG SMITH, Art Director; LEONARD MAZZOLA, Set Decorator; Skag, Premiere (NBC)

OUTSTANDING ART DIRECTION FOR A LIMITED SERIES OR A SPECIAL
For a single episode of a limited series, or for a special
MICHAEL BAUGH, Production Designer; JERRY ADAMS, Set Decorator; Moviola, The Silent Lovers (NBC)
JACK F. DE SHIELDS, Art Director; IRA BATES, Set Decorator; The Ordeal Of Dr. Mudd (CBS)
TOM H. JOHN, Art Director; MARY ANN BIDDLE, Set Decorator; Brave New World (NBC)
JAN SCOTT, Art Director & Production Designer; BILL HARP, Set Decorator; Orphan Train (CBS)
WILFRID SHINGLETON, Production Designer; JULIAN SACKS, Art Director; JEAN TAILLANDIER, Art Director; CHERYAL KEARNEY, Set Decorator; Gauguin The Savage (CBS)
JOHN STOLL, Production Designer; KAREL VACEK, Art Director; All Quiet On The Western Front (Hallmark Hall of Fame) (CBS)

OUTSTANDING ART DIRECTION FOR A VARIETY OR MUSIC PROGRAM
For a single episode of a single or regular series, or for a special
BRIAN C. BARTHOLOMEW, BOB KEENE, Production Designers; TONY BUGENHAGEN, Set Decorator; The Big Show, with Hosts Sarah Purcell, Flip Wilson (NBC)
ROMAIN JOHNSTON, Art Director; DEBE HENDRICKS, Set Decorator; Shirley MacLaine...'Every Little Movement' (CBS)
CHARLES LISANBY, Art Director; DWIGHT JACKSON, Set Decorator; IBM Presents Baryshnikov On Broadway (ABC)
MALCOLM STONE, Art Director; The Muppet Show, with Beverly Sills (Synd)

OUTSTANDING MUSIC COMPOSITION FOR A SERIES (DRAMATIC UNDERSCORE)
for a single episode of a regular series
BRUCE BROUGHTON; Dallas, The Lost Child (CBS)
JOHN CACAVAS; Eischied, Only The Pretty Girls Die - Part II (NBC)
BILLY GOLDENBERG; Skag, Premiere (NBC)
FRED KARLIN; Paris, Decisions (CBS)
PATRICK WILLIAMS; Lou Grant, Hollywood (CBS)

OUTSTANDING ACHIEVEMENT IN MUSIC COMPOSITION FOR A LIMITED SERIES OR A SPECIAL (DRAMATIC UNDERSCORE)
For a single episode of a limited series, or for a special
JERRY FIELDING; High Midnight (CBS)
GERALD FRIED; Moviola, The Silent Lovers (NBC)
PETE RUGOLO; The Last Convertible, Episode One (NBC)
HARRY SUKMAN; Salem's Lot (CBS)

OUTSTANDING ACHIEVEMENT IN MUSIC DIRECTION
For a single episode of a regular or limited series, or for a special, whether it be variety or music
ARTIE BUTLER; Barry Manilow - One Voice (ABC)
IAN FRASER, Music Director; RALPH BURNS AND BILLY BYERS, Principle Arrangers; IBM Presents Baryshnikov on Broadway (ABC)
NICK PERITO; The Big Show, hosts Steve Lawrence, Don Rickles (NBC)

OUTSTANDING COSTUME DESIGN FOR A SERIES
For a single episode of a regular series
JEAN-PIERRE DORLEAC; Galactica 1980, Starbuck's Great Journey (ABC)
CALISTA HENDRICKSON; The Muppet Show, with Guest Beverly Sills (Synd)
GRADY HUNT; Fantasy Island, Tatoo: The Love God/Magnolia Blossom (ABC)
ALFRED E. LEHMAN; Buck Rogers In The 25th Century Flight Of The War Witch, Part Two (NBC)
PETE MENEFEE; The Big Show, hosts Tony Randall, Herve Villechaize (NBC)

OUTSTANDING COSTUME DESIGN FOR A LIMITED SERIES OR A SPECIAL
For a single episode of a limited series, or for a special
BILL BELEW; The Carpenters, Music, Music, Music (ABC)
GRADY HUNT; The Dream Merchants (Synd)
BOB MACKIE; Ann-Margaret - Hollywood Movie Girls (ABC)
TRAVILLA; Moviola, The Scarlett O'Hara War (NBC)
RET TURNER; The Beatrice Arthur Special (ABC)

OUTSTANDING ACHIEVEMENT IN MAKEUP
For a single episode of a regular or limited series, or for a special
RICHARD BLAIR; Moviola, The Scarlett O'Hara War (NBC)
JOHN CHAMBERS, ROBERT A. SIDELL; Beyond Westworld, Pilot (CBS)
LORRAINE DAWKINS, ANITA HARRIS, SHEILA MANN, MARY SOUTHGATE, BRENDA YEWDELL; Disraeli: Portrait Of A Romantic, Masterpiece Theatre; Dizzy (PBS)
JACK FREEMAN; Haywire (CBS)
BEN LANE; JACK YOUNG, S.M.A.; Salem's Lot (CBS)

OUTSTANDING ACHIEVEMENT IN HAIRSTYLING
For a single episode of a regular or limited series, or for a special
NAOMA CAVIN, MARY HADLEY; Murder Can Hurt You! (ABC)
LEONARD DRAKE; Moviola, The Silent Lovers (NBC)
CAROLINE ELLIAS, BETTE IVERSON; Haywire (CBS)
LARRY GERMAIN, DONNA GILBERT; The Miracle Worker (NBC)
JOAN PHILLIPS; Fantasy Island, Dr. Jekyll and Ms. Hyde/Aphrodite (ABC)

OUTSTANDING ACHIEVEMENT IN GRAPHIC DESIGN AND TITLE SEQUENCES
For a single episode of a regular or limited series, or for a special, This includes animation only when created for use in titling
GENE KRAFT; Salem's Lot (CBS)
PHILL NORMAN; The French Atlantic Affair, Part I (ABC)

OUTSTANDING FILM EDITING FOR A SERIES
For a single episode of a regular series
M. PAM BLUMENTHAL; Taxi, Louie And The Nice Girl (ABC)
SIDNEY M. KATZ, A.C.E.; Skag, Premiere (NBC)
LARRY MILLS, STANFORD TISCHLER; M*A*S*H, The Yalu Brick Road (CBS)
LARRY STRONG, A.C.E.; Skag, The Working Girl, Part I (NBC)

OUTSTANDING FILM EDITING FOR A LIMITED SERIES OR A SPECIAL

For a single episode of a limited series, or for a special

BILL BLUNDEN, ALAN PATTILLO; All Quiet On The Western Front (Hallmark Hall Of Fame) (CBS)
PAUL LA MASTRA; Attica (ABC)
JERROLD L. LUDWIG, A.C.E.; Kenny Rogers As The Gambler (CBS)
JOHN A. MARTINELLI, A.C.E., RUSTY COPPLEMAN; S.O.S. Titanic (ABC)
DAVID NEWHOUSE, A.C.E.; Moviola, The Silent Lovers (NBC)
JOHN WOODCOCK, A.C.E.; When Hell Was In Session (NBC)

OUTSTANDING ACHIEVEMENT IN FILM SOUND EDITING

For a single episode of a regular or limited series, or for a special

MICHAEL L. HILKENE, TOM CORNWELL, DAVE ELLIOTT, DON ERNST, DIMITRY GORTINSKY, PETER HARRISON, ANDREW HERBERT, FRED JUDKINS, RUSS TINSLEY, CHRISTOPHER T. WELCH; The Plutonium Incident (CBS)
MICHAEL L. HILKENE, TOM CORNWELL, PETER HARRISON, ANDREW HERBERT, FRED JUDKINS, RUSS TINSLEY, JILL TAGGERT; Amber Waves (ABC)
MICHAEL REDBOURN, TOM CORNWELL, LINDA DOVE, DON ERNST, PETER HARRISON, ANDREW HERBERT, FRED JUDKINS, RUSS TINSLEY; Attica (ABC)
DON CROSBY, MARK DENNIS, TONY GARBER, DOUG GRINDSTAFF, DON V. ISAACS, HANK SALERNO, LARRY SINGER; Power, Part I (NBC)

OUTSTANDING ACHIEVEMENT IN FILM SOUND MIXING

For a single episode of a regular or limited series, or for a special

RAY BARONS, DAVID CAMPBELL, BOB PETTIS, JOHN REITZ; The Ordeal Of Dr. Mudd (CBS)
DAVID CAMPBELL, JOHN REITZ, BOB PETTIS, JACQUE NOSCO; Guyana Tragedy: The Story Of Jim Jones, Part II (CBS)
CHRISTOPHER LARGE, EDDIE NELSON, GEORGE E. PORTER, TERRY PORTER; Amber Waves (ABC)
WILLIAM L. MC CAUGHEY, DAVID E. DOCKENDORF, ROBERT L. HARMAN, JACK SOLOMON; Skag Premiere (NBC)
JOHN WILKENSON, ROBERT GLASS, JR., ROBERT THIRWELL, PATRICK MITCHELL; The Golden Moment: An Olympic Love Story (NBC)

OUTSTANDING ACHIEVEMENT IN TAPE SOUND MIXING

For a single episode of a regular or limited series, or for a special

BRUCE BURNS, JERRY CLEMANS; Sinatra: The First 40 Years (NBC)
JERRY CLEMANS, GORDON F. KLIMUCK, DOUG NELSON; Olivia Newton-John--Hollywood Nights (ABC)
JERRY CLEMANS, JUERGEN KOPPERS, DOUG NELSON; The Donna Summer Special (ABC)
JERRY CLEMANS, BILL SHERRILL; Kenny Rogers and the American Cowboy (CBS)
TERRY FARRIS, TOM HUTH, BLAKE NORTON; The Crystal Gayle Special (CBS)
DONALD WORSHAM; The Oldest Living Graduate (NBC)

OUTSTANDING VIDEO TAPE EDITING FOR A SERIES

For a single episode of a regular series

KEN DENISOFF, KEVIN MULDOON, ANDY ZALL; The Big Show, hosts Tony Randall, Herve Villechaize (NBC)
JOHN HAWKINS; The Muppet Show, with Guest Liza Minnelli (Synd)
TERRY PICKFORD; Fridays, Show #5, with Boz Scaggs (ABC)
MARCO ZAPPIA; A New Kind Of Family, I Do (ABC)

OUTSTANDING VIDEO TAPE EDITING FOR A LIMITED SERIES OR A SPECIAL

For a single episode of a limited series or for a special

TERRY CLIMER; The Donna Summer Special (ABC)
DANNY WHITE; Olivia Newton-John–Hollywood Nights (ABC)
ANDY ZALL; IBM Presents Baryshnikov On Broadway (ABC)
MARCO ZAPPIA; Perry Como's Christmas In New Mexico (ABC)

OUTSTANDING ACHIEVEMENT IN TECHNICAL DIRECTION AND ELECTRONIC CAMERWORK

For a single episode of a regular or limited series or for a special program

ROBERT G. HOLMES, TD, BRUCE BUTTONE, GEORGE FALARDEAU, BILL LANDERS, PEGGY MAHONEY, MIKE STRAMISKY, Camerapersons; The Midnight Special, Host: The Cars (NBC)
ROBERT A. KEMP, TD, RALPH ALCOCER, JIM ANGEL, DAVE BANKS, RON BROOKS, BUD HOLLAND, ART LA CONBE, DAN LANGFORD, Camerpersons; Goldie and Liza Together (CBS)
WAYNE PARSONS, TD, TOM GEREN, DEAN HALL, BOB HIGHTON, BILL LANDERS, RON SHELDON, Camerapersons; The Oldest Living Graduate (NBC)
JERRY WEISS, TD, LESLIE B. ATKINSON, ROY HOLM, PEGGY MAHONEY, MIKE STRAMISKY, Camerapersons; The Magic Of David Copperfield (CBS)
JERRY WEISS, TD, LARRY HEIDER, ROY HOLM, BILL LANDERS, PEGGY MAHONEY, WAYNE ORR, MIKE STRAMISKY, Camerapersons; A Christmas Special...With Love, Mac Davis (NBC)

OUTSTANDING ACHIEVEMENT IN LIGHTING DIRECTION (ELECTRONIC)

For a single episode of a regular or limited series, or for a special

TONY DI GIROLAMO; The Tender Land (PBS)
PETER G. EDWARDS, WILLIAM KNIGHT, PETER S. PASSAS; F.D.R. The Last Year (NBC)
DANIEL FLANNERY, Lighting Director; WILLIAM M. KLAGES, Lighting Consultant; Goldie And Liza Together (CBS)
WILLIAM M. KLAGES; The Big Show, hosts: Sarah Purcell, Flip Wilson (NBC)
FRED McKINNON, MARK PALIUS; The Cheryl Ladd Special: Souvenirs (ABC)
GEORGE W. RIESENBERGER, JOHN FRESCHI; The Unbroken Circle: A Tribute To Mother Maybelle Carter (CBS)

OUTSTANDING INDIVIDUAL ACHIEVEMENT - SPECIAL EVENTS

(Possibility of one Award, more than one Award, or no Award)

CARL VITELLI, Lighting Director; The 34th Annual Tony Awards (CBS)
DONALD O'CONNOR, Performer; 52nd Annual Awards Presentation Of The Academy Of Motion Picture Arts And Sciences (ABC)
LARRY GROSSMAN, Music, BUZ KOHAN, Lyrics; 52nd Annual Awards Presentation Of The Academy Of Motion Picture Arts And Sciences, "Dancin' On The Silver Screen" (ABC)
WALTER PAINTER, Choreographer; 52nd Annual Awards Presentation Of The Academy Of Motion Picture Arts And Sciences, "Dancin'

On The Silver Screen" (ABC)
RAY KLAUSEN, Art Director; 52nd Annual Awards Presentation Of The Academy Of Motion Picture Arts And Sciences (ABC)

OUTSTANDING INDIVIDUAL ACHIEVEMENT - INFORMATIONAL PROGRAM

(Possibility of one Award, more than one Award, or no Award)
DAVID CLARK, JOEL FEIN, ROBERT L. HARMAN, GEORGE E. PORTER, Film Sound Mixers; Dive To The Edge Of Creation, National Geographic Special (PBS)
BRYAN ANDERSON, BOB ELFSTROM, AL GIDDINGS, Cinematographers; Mysteries Of The Sea (ABC)
ROBERT E. FUISZ, M.D., LOUIS H. GORFAIN, Writers; The Body Human: The Body Beautiful (CBS)
HENRI COLPI, JOHN SOH, Film Editors; The Nile, The Cousteau Odyssey (PBS)
ROBERT EISENHARDT, HANK O'KARMA, JANE KURSON, Film Editors; The Body Human: The Body Beautiful (CBS)

OUTSTANDING INDIVIDUAL ACHIEVEMENT - SPECIAL CLASS

(Possibility of one Award, more than one Award or no Award)
HARRY BOTTORF, JOHN GISONDI, WILLIAM C. KNIGHT, DICK WEISS, Lighting; A Christmas Carol (PBS)
ORLAND TAMBURRI, Technical Director; READ HOWARD, WILLIAM LANDERS, VICTORIA WALKER, Camerapersons; Skinflint: A Country Christmas Carol (NBC)
GEOF BARTZ, Film Editor; Operation: Lifeline, Dr. James "Red" Duke, Trauma Surgeon (NBC)
DARRYL SUTTON, Video Tape Editor; Bob Hope's Overseas Christmas Tours: Around The World With The Troops (NBC)
CLIFFORD L. CHALLY, PAT ZINN, Costumes; The Dream Merchants (Synd)

OUTSTANDING INDIVIDUAL ACHIEVEMENT - CREATIVE TECHNICAL CRAFTS

(Possibility of one Award, more than one Award, or no Award)
SCOTT SCHACHTER, Live Audio Mixing; Live From Studio 8h: A Tribute To Toscanini (NBC)
ROY WHYBROW, Special Effects - Cinematography; All Quiet On The Western Front (Hallmark Hall of Fame) (CBS)
LESLIE ASCH, ED CHRISTIE, BARBARA DAVIS, FAZ FAZAKAS, NOMI FREDRICK, MICHAEL FRITH, AMY VAN GILDER, DAVE GOELZ, MARIANNE HARMS, LARRY JAMESON, MARI KAESTLE, ROLLIN KREWSON, TIM MILLER, ROBERT PAYNE, JAN ROSENTHAL, DON SAHLIN, CAROLY WILCOX, Muppet Design - Art Direction; The Muppet Show, with Guest Alan Arkin (Synd)
ED CHRISTIE, BARBARA DAVIS, FAZ FAZAKAS, NOMI FREDRICK, MICHAEL FRITH, AMY VAN GILDER, DAVE GOELZ, LARRY JAMESON, MARI KAESTLE, ROLLIN KREWSON, TIM MILLER, ROBERT PAYNE, JAN ROSENTHAL, DON SAHLIN, CAROLY WILCOX, Muppet Design - Art Direction; The Muppet Show, with Guest Kenny Rogers (Synd)
MARK SCHUBIN, Liveo Stereo Simulcast; Luciano Pavarotti And The New York Philharmonic; Live From Lincoln Center (PBS)

OUTSTANDING INDIVIDUAL ACHIEVEMENT - CHILDREN'S PROGRAM

(Possibility of one Award, more than one Award, or no Award)
ARTHUR GINSBURG, Film Editor; The Halloween That Almost Wasn't (ABC)
NAT MONGIOI, Art Director; Sesame Street in Puerto Rico (PBS)
BOB O'BRADOVICH, MakeUp; The Halloween That Almost Wasn't (ABC)
MARIETTE HARTLEY, Performer; The Halloween That Almost Wasn't (ABC)
OZZIE ALFONSO, Director; Sesame Street In Puerto Rico (PBS)

OUTSTANDING INDIVIDUAL ACHIEVEMENT - ANIMATION PROGRAM

(Possibility of one Award, more than one Award, or no Award)
FRIZ FRELENG, Director; Pink Panther In Olym-Pinks (ABC)
CHUCK JONES, Director; Bugs Bunny's Bustin' Out All Over (CBS)

NATIONAL DAYTIME EMMY AWARDS

OUTSTANDING DAYTIME DRAMA SERIES

Emmy(s) to Executive Producer(s) and Producer(s)
ALL MY CHILDREN, Agnes Nixon, Executive Producer; Jorn Winther, Producer (ABC)
ANOTHER WORLD, Paul Rauch, Executive Producer; Mary S. Bonner, Robert Costello, Producers (NBC)
GUIDING LIGHT, Allen M. Potter, Executive Producer; Leslie Kwartin, Joe Willmore, Producers (CBS)

OUTSTANDING GAME OR AUDIENCE PARTICIPATION SHOW

Emmy(s) to Executive Producer(s) and Producer(s)
FAMILY FEUD, Mark Goodson, Executive Producer; Howard Felsher, Producer (ABC)
HOLLYWOOD SQUARES, Merrill Heatter, Robert Quigley, Executive Producers; Jay Redack, Producer (NBC)
THE $20,000 PYRAMID, Bob Stewart, Executive Producer; Ann Marie Schmitt, Jane Rothchild, Producers (ABC)

OUTSTANDING TALK, SERVICE OR VARIETY SERIES

Emmy(s) to Executive Producer(s) and Producer(s)
DONAHUE, Richard Mincer, Executive Producer; Patricia McMillen, Senior Producer; Darlene Hayes, Sheri Singer, Producers (Synd)
GOOD MORNING AMERICA, George Merlis, Executive Producer; John Kippycash, Jack Reilly, Jan Rifkinson, Sonya Selby-Wright, Producers (ABC)
MIKE DOUGLAS SHOW, Frank Miller, Executive Producer; Vince Calandra, E.V. DiMassa, Jr., Producers (Synd)

OUTSTANDING ACTOR IN A DAYTIME DRAMA SERIES

JOHN GABRIEL; Ryan's Hope (ABC)
MICHAEL LEVIN; Ryan's Hope (ABC)
FRANC LUZ; The Doctors (NBC)
JAMES MITCHELL; All My Children (ABC)
WILLIAM MOONEY; All My Children (ABC)
DOUGLASS WATSON; Another World (NBC)

OUTSTANDING ACTRESS IN A DAYTIME DRAMA SERIES
JULIA BARR; All My Children (ABC)
LESLIE CHARLESON; General Hospital (ABC)
KIM HUNTER; The Edge Of Night (ABC)
JUDITH LIGHT; One Life To Live (ABC)
BEVERLEE McKINSEY; Another World (NBC)
KATHLEEN NOONE; All My Children (ABC)

OUTSTANDING PERFORMANCE BY AN ACTOR IN A SUPPORTING ROLE FOR A DAYTIME DRAMA SERIES
VASILI BOGAZIANOS; The Edge Of Night (ABC)
WARREN BURTON; All My Children (ABC)
LARRY HAINES; Search For Tomorrow (CBS)
RON HALE; Ryan's Hope (ABC)
JULIUS LAROSA; Another World (NBC)
SHEPPERD STRUDWICK; Love Of Life (CBS)

OUTSTANDING PERFORMANCE BY AN ACTRESS IN A SUPPORTING ROLE FOR A DAYTIME DRAMA SERIES
DEIDRE HALL; Days Of Our Lives (NBC)
FRANCESCA JAMES; All My Children (ABC)
LOIS KIBBEE; The Edge Of Night (ABC)
ELAINE LEE; The Doctors (NBC)
VALERIE MAHAFFEY; The Doctors (NBC)
LOUISE SHAFFER; Ryan's Hope (ABC)

OUTSTANDING GUEST/CAMEO APPEARANCE IN A DAYTIME DRAMA SERIES
For five or less appearances
SAMMY DAVIS, JR. One Life To Live (ABC)
JOAN FONTAINE Ryan's Hope (ABC)
KATHRYN HARROW; The Doctors (NBC)
HUGH McPHILLIPS; Days Of Our Lives (NBC)
ELI MINTZ; All My Children (ABC)

OUTSTANDING HOST OR HOSTESS IN A GAME OR AUDIENCE PARTICIPATION SHOW
RICHARD DAWSON; Family Feud (ABC)
PETER MARSHALL; The Hollywood Squares (NBC)

OUTSTANDING HOST OR HOSTESS IN A TALK, SERVICE OR VARIETY SERIES
PHIL DONAHUE; Donahue (Synd)
DINAH SHORE; Dinah! And Friends (Synd)

OUTSTANDING DIRECTION FOR A DAYTIME DRAMA SERIES
For the Entire Series
HENRY KAPLAN, JACK COFFEY, SHERRELL HOFFMAN, JORN WINTHER; All My Children (ABC)
IRA CIRKER, MELVIN BERNHARDT, ROBERT CALHOUN, BARNET KELLMAN, JACK HOFSISS, ANDREW WEYMAN; Another World (NBC)
JOHN SEDWICK, RICHARD PEPPERMAN; The Edge Of Night (ABC)
MARLENA LAIRD, ALAN PULTZ, PHIL SOGARD; General Hospital (ABC)
LARRY AUERBACH, ROBERT SCINTO; Love Of Life (CBS)
LELA SWIFT, JERRY EVANS; Ryan's Hope (ABC)

OUTSTANDING INDIVIDUAL DIRECTION FOR A GAME OR AUDIENCE PARTICIPATION SHOW
For a single episode
PAUL ALER; Family Feud 4/10/79 (ABC)
JEROME SHAW; The Hollywood Squares, 6/14/79 (NBC)

OUTSTANDING INDIVIDUAL DIRECTION FOR A TALK, SERVICE OR VARIETY SERIES
For a single episode
DUKE STRUCK; Henry Fonda Tribute, Good Morning America (ABC)
GLEN SWANSON Dinah! And Friends In Singapore (Synd) RON WEINER; Pimps, Donahue (Synd)

OUTSTANDING WRITING FOR A DAYTIME DRAMA SERIES
AGNES NIXON, WISNER WASHAM, JACK WOOD, CAROLINE FRANZ, MARY K. WELLS, CATHY CHICOS, CLARICE BLACKBURN, ANITA JAFFE, KEN HARVEY; All My Children (ABC) HENRY SLESAR, STEVE LEHRMAN; The Edge Of Night (ABC) GORDON RUSSELL, SAM HALL, PEGGY O'SHEA, DON WALLACE, LANIE BERTRAM, CYNTHIA BENJAMIN, MARISA GIOFFRE; One Life To Live (ABC)
CLAIRE LABINE, PAUL AVILA MAYER, MARY MUNISTERI, JUDITH PINSKER, JEFFREY LANE; Ryan's Hope (ABC)

OUTSTANDING ACHIEVEMENT IN TECHNICAL EXCELLENCE FOR A DAYTIME DRAMA SERIES
Emmys to individuals
JOSEPH SOLOMITO, HOWARD ZWEIG, Technical Directors; LAWRENCE HAMMOND, ROBERT AMBRICO, DIANE CATES-CANTRELL, CHRISTOPHER N MAURO, LARRY STRACK, VINCENT SENATORE, Electronic Camera; ALBIN S. LEMANSKI, Audio Engineer; LEN WALAS, Video Engineer; DIANA WENMAN, JEAN DADARIO, Associate Directors; ROGER HAENELT, JOHN L. GRELLA, Videotape Editors; IRVING ROBBIN, JIM REICHERT, Music Composers; TERI SMITH, Music Director; All My Children (ABC)
FRANK GAETA, STEVE CIMINO, FRANK DeRIENZO, Technical Directors; CARL ECKETT, DAVID WEINBERG, OLONZO ROBERTS, WAYNE NORMAN, Electronic Camera; PHILIP BERGE, MEL HENCH, Audio Engineers; ARNOLD DICK, HAROLD MOFSEN, Video Engineers; KEVIN KELLY, JOHN LIBRETTO, Associate Directors; LLOYD CAMPBELL, JOHN O'CONNOR, Videotape Editors; SCORE PRODUCTIONS; Music Composer/Director; Another World (NBC)
RAYMOND BARRETT, Technical Director; JACK DOLAN, STEVE JAMBECK, JAN KASSOFF, Electronic Camera; GEORGE CORRADO, Audio Engineer; FRANK VIERLING, Video Engineer; DAVID HANDLER, Associate Director; LEE GOLDMAN, Videotape Editor; BOB ISRAEL, Music Coordinator; JOHN GELLER, Music Director; The Doctors (NBC)
WILIAM EDWARDS, Technical Director; WILLIAM HUGHES, THOMAS STALLONE, ARIE HEFTER, Electronic Camera; EDWARD ATCHISON, Audio Engineer; ROBERT SAXON, Sound Effects; JOHN VALENTINO, Video Engineer; JOANNE GOODHART, Associate Director; STEPHEN SCOTT, LENNY DAVIDOWITZ, Videotape Editors; ELIOT LAWRENCE, Music Composer; BARBARA MILLER, Music Coordinator; The Edge Of Night (ABC)
DAVID SMITH, JOHN COCHRAN, Technical Directors; DAVE BANKS, LUIS ROJAS, CAROL WETOVICH, JAMES ANGEL, JACK DENTON, Electronic Camera; KEN QUAYLE, ZOLI OSAZE, Audio Engineers; NICK KLEISSAS, Sound Effects; SAM POTTER, Video Engineer; HAL ALEXANDER, GEORGE THOMPSON, Associate Directors; DAN BLEVENS, JACK MOODY, Videotape Editors; CHARLES PAUL, Music Composer/Director; General Hospital (ABC)
GEORGE WHITAKER, Technical Director; DICK KERR, MARY FLOOD, FRANK J MERKLEIN, Electronic Camera; WILLIAM deBLOCK, LEE M. GOLDMAN, Audio Engineers; RUDY PICARILLO, DICK WILLIAMS, LINDA WALLACH, Video Engineers; SUELLEN GOLDSTEIN, Associate Director; PAT MALIK, WALTER URBANSKI, Video Editors; CAREY

GOLD, Music Composer; SYBIL WEINBERGER, Music Supervisor; Ryan's Hope (ABC)

OUTSTANDING ACHIEVEMENT IN DESIGN EXCELLENCE FOR A DAYTIME DRAMA SERIES
Emmys to individuals
WILLIAM MICKLEY, Scenic Designer; WILLIAM ITKIN, DONNA LARSON, MEL HANDELSMAN, Lighting Directors; CAROL LUIKEN, Costume Designer; SYLVIA LAWRENCE, Make-up Designer; MICHAEL HUDDLE, Hair Designer; HY BLEY, Graphic Designer; All My Children (ABC)
ROBERT FRANKLIN, Art Director; RUSSELL CHRISTIAN, RICHARD HANKINS, Scenic Designers; LEO FARRENKOPF, MAURY VERSCHOORE, Lighting Designer; LEWIS BROWN, Costume Designer; FRANK RUBERTONE, Hair Designer; EDWARD JACKSON, Make-up Designer; Another World (NBC)
JIM ELLINGWOOD, MERCER BARROWS, Art Directors; GRANT VELIE, JOHN ZAK, TOM MARKLE, Lighting Directors; GEORGE WHITTAKER, Costume Designer; JAMES COLA, Make-up Designer; KATHY KOTARAKOS, Hair Designer; General Hospital (ABC)
SY TOMASHOFF, Scenic Designer; HERB GRUBER, Scenic Artist; JOHN CONNOLY, Lighting Director; BILL KELLARD, Costume Designer; JAMES COLA, Make-up Designer; JOHN K. QUINN, Hairdesigner; Ryan's Hope (ABC)

OUTSTANDING CHILDREN'S ENTERTAINMENT SERIES
Emmy(s) to Executive Producer(s) and Producer(s)
CAPTAIN KANGAROO, Robert Keeshan, Executive Producer; Joel Kosofsky, Producer (CBS)
HOT HERO SANDWICH, Bruce Hart, Carole Hart, Executive Producers; Howard G. Malley, Producer (NBC)
KIDS ARE PEOPLE TOO, Lawrence Einhorn, Executive Producer; Laura Schrock, Producer; Noreen Conlin, Co-Producer (ABC)

OUTSTANDING CHILDREN'S ENTERTAINMENT SPECIAL
Emmy(s) to Executive Producer(s) and Producer(s)
THE BOY WITH TWO HEADS, Once Upon A Classic; Jay Rayvid, Executive Producer; Frank Good, Producer (PBS)
THE HOUSE AT 12 ROSE STREET (NBC Special Treat) Daniel Wilson, Executive Producer; Fran Sears, Producer (NBC)
I DON'T KNOW WHO I AM (NBC Special Treat) Daniel Wilson, Executive Producer; Joanne A. Curley, Producer (NBC)
THE LATE GREAT ME: STORY OF A TEENAGE ALCOHOLIC, (ABC Afterschool Special) Daniel Wilson, Executive Producer; Linda Marmelstein, Producer (ABC)
THE ROCKING CHAIR REBELLION (NBC Special Treat) Daniel Wilson, Executive Producer; Phyllis Minoff, Producer (NBC)

OUTSTANDING CHILDREN'S ANTHOLOGY/DRAMATIC PROGRAMMING
Emmy(s) to Executive Producer(s) and Producer(s)
ANIMAL TALK (CBS Library) Diane Asselin, Executive Producer; Paul Asselin, Producer (CBS)
THE GOLD BUG (ABC Weekend Special) Linda Gottlieb, Executive Producer; Doro Bachrach, Producer (ABC)
LEATHERSTOCKING TALES Once Upon A Classic; Jay Rayvid, Executive Producer; Bob Walsh, Producer (PBS)
ONCE UPON A MIDNIGHT DREARY (CBS Library) Diane Asselin, Paul Asselin, Producers (CBS)
THE REVENGE OF RED CHIEF (ABC Weekend Special) Robert Chenault, Executive Producer (ABC)

OUTSTANDING CHILDREN'S INFORMATIONAL/INSTRUCTIONAL SERIES/SPECIAL
Emmy(s) to Executive Producer(s) and Producer(s)
MISTER ROGERS' NEIGHBORHOOD, Fred Rogers, Executive Producer; Hugh Martin, Producer (PBS)
SESAME STREET, Al Hyslop, Executive Producer; Dave Freyss, Producer (PBS)
THIRTY MINUTES, Joel Heller, Executive Producer; Madeline Amgott, Diego Echeverria, Horace Jenkens, Elizabeth Lawrence, Patti Obrow White, Robert Rubin, Producers (CBS)
MAKE 'EM LAUGH: A YOUNG PEOPLE'S COMEDY CONCERT (CBS Festival of Lively Arts For Young People) Jack Wohl, Bernard Rothman, Executive Producers; Robert Arnott, Sid Smith, Producers (CBS)
WHY A CONDUCTOR? (CBS Festival of Lively Arts For Young People) Kirk Browning, Executive Producer (CBS)

OUTSTANDING CHILDREN'S INFORMATION/INSTRUCTIONAL PROGRAMMING - SHORT FORMAT
Emmy(s) to Executive Producer(s) and Producer(s)
ABC SCHOOLHOUSE ROCK, Thomas Yohe, Executive Producer; George Newall, Radford Stone, Producers (ABC)
ASK NBC NEWS, Lester Crystal, Senior Executive Producer; Beryl Pfizer, Producer (NBC)
H.E.L.P.!!! (Dr. Henry's Emergency Lessons For People) Lynn Ahrens, Producer (ABC)
IN THE NEWS, Joel Heller, Executive Producer; Walter Lister, Producer (CBS)
WHEN YOU TURN OFF THE SET, TURN ON A BOOK, Mary Alice Dwyer, Executive Producer; George Newall, Tom Yohe, Producers (NBC)

OUTSTANDING INDIVIDUAL ACHIEVEMENT IN CHILDREN'S PROGRAMMING
For a single episode of a series or for a special program. (Possibility of one Award, more than one Award or no Award).

PERFORMERS:
MELISSA SUE ANDERSON; Which Mother Is Mine?, ABC Afterschool Special (ABC)
RENE AUBERJONOIS; Once Upon A Midnight Dreary, CBS Library (CBS)
MAIA DANZIGER; The Late Great Me: Story Of A Teenage Alcoholic, ABC Afterschool Special (ABC)
BOB KEESHAN; Captain Kangaroo (CBS)
BUTTERFLY McQUEEN; The Seven Wishes Of A Rich Kid, ABC Afterschool Special (ABC)
FRED ROGERS; Mister Rogers Goes To School, Mister Rogers' Neighborhood (PBS)

WRITERS:
MARY BATTEN; Forces/Friday, 3-2-1 Contact (PBS)
DAVID AXELROD, JOSEPH BAILEY, ANDY BRACKMAN, RICHARD CAMP, SHERRY COBEN, BRUCE HART, CAROLE HART, CAROLE HART, MARIANNE MEYER; Hot Hero Sandwich, #5 (NBC)
JAN HARTMAN; The Late Great Me: Story Of A Teenage Alcoholic, ABC Afterschool Special (ABC)
JOHN O'TOOLE; The Leatherstocking Tales, Once Upon A Classic (PBS)
FRED ROGERS; Mister Rogers Goes To School, Mister Rogers' Neighborhood (PBS)

DIRECTORS:
JOSEPH CONSENTINO; Divorce, Big Blue Marble (Synd)
ANTHONY LOVER; The Late Great Me: Story Of A Teenage Alcoholic, ABC Afterschool Special (ABC)
J. PHILIP MILLER; The Bloodhound Gang, 3-2-1 Contact (PBS)
ARTHUR ALLAN SEIDELMAN; Which Mother Is Mine? ABC Afterschool Special (ABC)
THOMAS TRBOVICH; Hot Hero Sandwich, #4 (NBC)

TECHNICAL DIRECTOR/ELECTRONIC CAMERA:
WILLIAM P. KELLEY, Technical Director;
GENE MARTIN, JOHN PINTO, VINCENT DiPIETRO, THOMAS C. DEZENDORF, EDWARD CORSI, DONALD MULVANEY, Electronic Camerapersons; Hot Hero Sandwich, #4 (NBC)
STEVEN ZINK, Director of Photography; Sesame Street, #1320 - Puerto Rico (PBS)

AUDIO:
GEORGE ALCH, Audio Engineer; A Special Gift, ABC Afterschool Special (ABC)
LEE DICHTER, Film Sound Mixer; Big Blue Marble, #105 (Synd)
PETER PAGE, Film Sound Mixer; Shark, Animals, Animals, Animals (ABC)
SCOTT A. SCHACHTER, JOEL G. SPECTOR, Tape Sound Mixers; Hot Hero Sandwich, #4 (NBC)

ASSOCIATE DIRECTION/VIDEO TAPE EDITING:
JEROME HAGGART, HARVEY BERGER, BILL BRESHEARS, Videotape Editors; Hot Hero Sandwich, #1 (NBC)
CHARLES J. LIOTTA, JOHN A. SERVIDIO, GEORGE A. MAGDA, Videotape Editors; Time Out (NBC)
DON SULLIVAN, Associate Director; JAN MORGAN, Videotape Editor; Fast/Slow, 3-2-1 Contact (PBS)

CINEMATOGRAPHY:
JOHN BEYMER, MIKE FASH; A Movie Star's Daughter, ABC Afterschool Special (ABC)
ROBERT COLLINS; Heartbreak Winner, ABC Afterschool Special (ABC)
TOM McDONOUGH; Mountan Climbing, Hot/Cold, 3-2-1 Contact (PBS)
DAVID SANDERSON; Once Upon A Midnight Dreary (CBS Library) (CBS)
ALEX THOMPSON; The Gold Bug, ABC Weekend Special (ABC)

FILM EDITING:
NORMAN GAY; Communication - Mets, 3-2-1 Contact (PBS)
JACK SHOLDER; Noisy/Quiet - Hearing, 3-2-1 Contact (PBS)
VINCENT SKLENA; The Late Great Me: Story Of A Teenage Alcoholic, ABC Afterschool Special (ABC)
MERLE WORTH; Fast/Slow - Speed Up/Slow Down, 3-2-1- Contact (PBS)

MUSIC COMPOSITION/DIRECTION:
TOM ANTHONY, Music Composer/Director; Theme, Noisy/Quiet, 3-2-1 Contact (PBS)
DANNY EPSTEIN, Music Director; Forces, 3-2-1 Contact (PBS)
WALT LEVINSKY, Music Composer; Forces, 3-2-1 Contact (PBS)
GLENN PAXTON, Music Composer; Which Mother Is Mine?, ABC Afterschool Special (ABC)
HOD DAVID SCHUDSON, Music Composer; Heartbreak Winner, ABC Afterschool Special (ABC)

ART DIRECTION/SCENIC DESIGN/SET DECORATION:
RONALD BALDWIN, Art Director; Growth/Decay, 3-2-1 Contact (PBS)
SHAWN CALLAHAN, HENRY HUBBERT, Set Decorators; Captain Kangaroo (CBS)
BIL MIKULEWICZ, Art Director/Scenic Designer; Space Chicken And The Disappearing Stars, Captain Kangaroo (CBS)
NAT MONGIOI, Set Decorator; Hot/Cold, 3-2-1 Contact (PBS)

LIGHTING DIRECTION:
TONY DiGIROLAMO, Lighting Director; Sesame Street, #1285 (PBS)

COSTUME/MAKE-UP/HAIR DESIGN:
STEVEN ATHA, Make-up/Hair Designer; The Gold Bug, ABC Weekend Special (ABC)
BILL GRIFFIN, Costume Designer; Captain Kangaroo, #791030 (CBS)
CONSTANCE WEXLER, Costume Designer; Growth/Decay, 3-2-1 Contact (PBS)

GRAPHIC DESIGN:
MICHAEL BAUGH; I Can Sing A Rainbow, Villa Alegre (PBS)
R. GREENBERG (Greenberg Associates); Noisy/Quiet, 3-2-1 Contact (PBS)
ROBERT POOK, Internal Graphics; Hot Hero Sandwich, #9 (NBC)

OUTSTANDING ACHIEVEMENT IN RELIGIOUS PROGRAMMING-SERIES/SPECIALS
Emmy(s) to Executive Producer(s) and Producer(s) (Possibility of one Award, more than one Award or no Award).

SERIES:
DIRECTIONS, Sid Darion, Executive Producer (ABC)
FOR OUR TIMES, Pamela Ilott, Executive Producer; Joseph Clement, Chalmers Dale, Marlene DiDonato, Ted Holmes, Producers (CBS)

SPECIALS:
AS WE WITH CANDLES DO, Doris Ann, Executive Producer (NBC)
A CONVERSATION ON PASSOVER: Renewing Ancient Traditions; Doris Ann, Executive Producer; Martin Hoade, Producer (NBC)
A TALENT FOR LIFE: Jews of the Italian Renaissance; Helen Marmor, Executive Producer; Martin Hoade, Producer (NBC)

OUTSTANDING INDIVIDUAL ACHIEVEMENT IN RELIGIOUS PROGRAMMING
For a single episode of a series or for a special program (Possibility of one Award, more than one Award or no Award).

PERFORMERS:
NORMAN ROSE, Narrator; A Talent For Life: Jews of the Italian Renaissance (NBC)
WILLIAM SCHALLERT; The Stableboy's CHRISTMAS, This Is The Life (Synd)
DEAN JAGGER; Independence And 76, This Is The Life (Synd)

WRITERS:
RICHARD F. MOREAN; If No Birds Sang, This Is The Life (Synd)
ALLAN E. SLOANE; As We With Candles Do (NBC)
ARTHUR ZEGARD; Aging In Venice, Directions (ABC)

DIRECTOR:
LYNWOOD KING; As We With Candles Do (NBC)

TECHNICAL DIRECTION/ELECTRONIC CAMERA:
HEINO RIPP, Technical Director; AL CAMOIN, GENE MARTIN, DON MULVANEY, Electronic Camerapersons; As We With Candles Do (NBC)

AUDIO:
JUSTUS TAYLOR, Sound Recordist; Seeds Of Revolution, Directions (ABC)

FILM EDITING:
EDWARD R. WILLIAMS; A Talent For Life: Jews of the Italian Renaissance (NBC)

MUSIC COMPOSITION/DIRECTION:
JOHN DUFFY, Music Composer/Director; A Talent For Life: Jews of The Italian Renaissance (NBC)

ART DIRECTION
THOMAS E. AZZARI; Stable Boy's Christmas, This Is The Life (Synd)

SPECIAL CLASSIFICATION OF OUTSTANDING PROGRAM ACHIEVEMENT
Emmy(s) to Executive Producer(s) and Producer(s)
AMERICAN BANDSTAND, Dick Clark, Executive Producer; Larry Klein, Producer; Barry Glazer, Co-Producer (ABC)
FYI (with Hal Linden) Yanna Kroyt Brandt, Producer (ABC)
GISELLE, E. Grigorian, Producer (for Gosteleradio - USSR) (NBC)
A MEMORIAL TRIBUTE TO JIM CROCKETT, Russell Marash, Producer (for WGBH - Boston) (PBS)

SPECIAL CLASSIFICATION OF OUTSTANDING INDIVIDUAL ACHIEVEMENT
(Possibility of one Award, more than one Award or no Award).

WRITERS:
JAY REDACK, HARRY FRIEDMAN, BRIAN POLLACK, GARY JOHNSON, STEVE KREINBERG, JUSTIN ANTONOW, PHIL KELLARD; The Hollywood Squares (NBC)

DIRECTOR:
MICHAEL R. GARGUILO; FYI (ABC)

CHOREOGRAPHER:
JOSEPH CAROW; Nightmare Ballet Sequence, Witch's Sister, Chapter 2, Big Blue Marble (Synd)

PUPPET DESIGN AND CONSTRUCTION:
DANNY SEAGREN; Miss Peach Of The Kelly School, The Annual Thanksgiving Turkey Day Raffle (Synd)

OUTSTANDING ACHIEVEMENT IN COVERAGE OF SPECIAL EVENTS
Possibility of one Award, more than one Award or no Award). Emmy(s) to Executive Producer(s) and Producer(s)
LA GIOCONDA, Jeanne Mulcahy, Executive Producer; John Goberman, Producer (For KCET - Los Angeles) (PBS)
MACY'S 53rd ANNUAL THANKSGIVING DAY PARADE, Dick Schneider, Producer (NBC)
91st TOURNAMENT OF ROSES PARADE, Dick Schneider, Producer (NBC)

OUTSTANDING INDIVIDUAL ACHIEVEMENT IN COVERAGE OF SPECIAL EVENTS
(Possibility of one Award, more than one Award or no Award).

PERFORMERS:
LUCIANO PAVAROTTI, La Gioconda (PBS)
RENATA SCOTTO, La Gioconda (PBS)

DIRECTOR:
KIRK BROWNING; La Gioconda (PBS)

TECHNICAL DIRECTION/ELECTRONIC CAMERA:
RON GRAFT, Technical Director; KENNETH PATTERSON, GARY EMRICK, LUIS A. FUERTE, DANIEL J. WEBB, Electronic Camerapersons; GREG HARMS, Video Engineer; La Gioconda (PBS)

AUDIO:
TOM ANCELL, Audio Mixer; La Gioconda (PBS)

ASSOCIATE DIRECTION/VIDEOTAPE EDITING:
VAL RIOLO, Associate Director; ROY STEWART, Videotape Editor; La Gioconda (PBS)

SCENIC DESIGN/SET DECORATION:
ZACK BROWN; La Gioconda (PBS)

LIGHTING DIRECTION:
KEN DETTLING; Lighting Director; La Gioconda (PBS)

COSTUME DESIGN:
ZACK BROWN; La Gioconda (PBS)

OUTSTANDING INDIVIDUAL ACHIEVEMENT IN ANY AREA OF CREATIVE TECHNICAL CRAFTS
(Possibility of one Award, more than one Award or no Award).

TECHNICAL DIRECTION/ELECTRONIC CAMERA:
MIKE MALOOF, Technical Director; DICK WATSON, GALEN WESTFALL, JOHN GILLIS, Electronic Camerapersons; Dinah! And Friends (Synd)

ASSOCIATE DIRECTION/VIDEOTAPE EDITING:
BECKY GREENLAW, Associate Director; GARY NESTRA, Videotape Editor; The Mike Douglas Show (Synd)

MUSIC COMPOSITION/DIRECTION:
JOE MASSIMINO, Music Composer/Director; The Mike Douglas Show (Synd)

LIVE SPORTS SPECIAL
Emmy(s) to Executive Producer(s) and Producer(s)
NCAA CHAMPIONSHIP BASKETBALL (Louisville vs. UCLA) - Don Ohlmeyer, Exec Producer; George Finkel, Producer (NBC)
SUPERBOWL XIV - Robert Stenner, Producer (CBS)
WIMBLEDON '80 - Don Ohlmeyer, Exec Producer; Geoffrey Mason, Producer; Ted Nathanson, Coproducer (NBC)
1980 WINTER OLYMPIC GAMES (Lake Placid, NY) - Roone Arledge, Exec Producer; Chuck Howard, Chet Forte, Dennis Lewin, Senior Producers; Bob Goodrich, Curt Gowdy Jr., Terry Jastrow, Terry O'Neil, Eleanor Riger, Ned Steckel, Doug Wilson, Producers; Jeff Ruhe, Coordinating Producer; Brice Weisman, Producer for "Up Close And Personals"; Robert Riger, Bud Greenspan, Special Projects Producers (ABC)
1979 WORLD SERIES (Baltimore Orioles vs. Pittsburgh Pirates) - Roone Arledge, Exec Producer; Chuck Howard, Producer (ABC)

LIVE SPORTS SERIES
Emmy(s) to Executive Producer(s) and Producer(s)
ABC'S NFL MONDAY NIGHT FOOTBALL - Roone Arledge, Exec Producer; Dennis Lewin, Producer (ABC)
NCAA BASKETBALL - Don Ohlmeyer, Exec Producer; George Finkel, Coordinating Producer; Ken Edmundson, Producer (NBC)
NCAA COLLEGE FOOTBALL - Roone Arledge, Exec Producer; Chuck Howard, Senior Producer; Bob Goodrich, Eleanor Riger, Curt Gowdy Jr., Dick Buffinton, Chris Carmody, Ned Steckel, Doug Wilson, Producers (ABC)
NFL FOOTBALL ON CBS - Bill Barnes, David Fox, Robert Stenner, Robert Rowe, Perry Smith, Chuck Will, Tom O'Neill, Howard Reifsynder, Producers (CBS)
PGA ON CBS - Frank Chirkinian, Exec Producer-Producer (CBS)

SPORTS SPECIAL EDITING
Emmy(s) to Executive Producer(s) and Producer(s)
GOSSAMER ALBATROSS-FLIGHT OF IMAGINATION - Eddie Einhorn, Exec Producer; Joesph A. Thompson, Producer (CBS)
1980 INDIANAPOLIS 500 - Roone Arledge, Exec Producer; Chuck Howard, Bob Goodrich, Producers (ABC)
OLYMPIC TRIALS - Don Ohlmeyer, Exec Producer; Don McGuire, Coordinating Producer; Peter Diamond, Bernie Hoffman, Linda Jonsson, Producers (NBC)
UPSETS AND UNDERDOGS, HOT DOGS AND HEROES: THE STORY OF THE 1979 NFL SEASON - Steve Sabol, Ed Sabol, Producers (NBC)
1980 WINTER OLYMPIC PREVIEW SPECIAL: ADIRONDACK GOLD RUSH - Roone Arledge, Exec Producer; Terry O'Neill, Producer (ABC)

SPORTS SERIES EDITING
Emmy(s) to Executive Producer(s) and Producer(s)
ABC'S WIDE WORLD OF SPORTS - Roone Arledge, Exec Producer; Dennis Lewin, Coordinating Producer; Chuck Howard, Chet Forte, Joe Aceti, Carol Lehti, Terry O'Neil, Ned Steckel, Doug Wilson, Bob Goodrich, Producers (ABC)
AMERICAN SPORTSMAN - Roone Arledge, Exec Producer; John Wilcox, Series Producer; Robert Duncan, Curt Gowdy, Robert Nixon, Producers (ABC)
CBS SPORTS SPECTACULAR - Eddie Einhorn, Exec Producer; Ed Goren, Coordinating Producer; David Fox, Ted Shaker, Perry Smith, Brad Schrieber, Charles Milton, Jim Silman, Michael Pearl, Dave Berman, Ken Squire, Sherman Eagan, Tom O'Neill, Tony Verna, Robert Stenner, Howard Reifsynder, Producers (CBS)
NFL GAME OF THE WEEK - Ed Sabol, Exec Producer; Steve Sabol, Producer (Synd)
THIS WEEK IN BASEBALL - Larry Parker, Exec Producer; Jody Shapiro, Geoff Belinfante, Supervising Producers; Tim Parker, Bill Brown, Producers (Synd)

SPORTS PERSONALITY
Emmy to sports personality for overall broadcasting achievement
HOWARD COSELL (ABC)
FRANK GIFFORD (ABC)
KEITH JACKSON (ABC)
AL McGUIRE (NBC)
JIM McKAY (ABC)
DON MEREDITH (ABC)
VIN SCULLY (CBS)
JACK WHITAKER (CBS)

DIRECTING IN SPORTS PROGRAMMING
Emmy(s) to Director(s) for a series, episode of a series of for a special
1980 WINTER OLYMPIC GAMES (Lake Placid, NY) - Joe Aceti, Roger Goodman, Coordinating Directors; Chet Forte, John DeLisa, Jack Gallivan, Mac Hemion, Craig Janoff, Jim Jennett, Larry Kamm, Bob Lanning, Raimo Piltz, Andy Sidaris, Ken Wolfe, Lou Volpicelli, Larry Cavolina, Ron Harrison, Directors (ABC)
THE MASTERS - Frank Chirkinian, Robert Dailey (CBS)
1979 WORLD SERIES - Chet Forte (ABC)
SUPER BOWL XIV - Sandy Grossman (CBS)
WIMBLEDON '80 (Men's Final-McEnroe vs. Borg) - Ted Nathanson (NBC)
NFL FOOTBALL ON CBS - Duke Struck, Robert Dailey, Sandy Grossman, Marvin Mews, Jim Silman, Robert Dunphy, Chris Erskine, Tony Verna, John McDonough (CBS)
ABC'S WIDE WORLD OF SPORTS (World Figure Skating Championships) - Doug Wilson (ABC)

FOLLOWING ARE AREAS WHERE THERE IS A POSSIBILITY OF ONE WINNER, MORE THAN ONE WINNER OR NO WINNER IN EACH AREA.

INDIVIDUAL ACHIEVEMENT IN SPORTS PROGRAMMING
Emmy(s) to individual(s) for a single episode of a series or for a special
ABC'S NFL MONDAY NIGHT FOOTBALL - Ron Ackerman, Tom Capace, Phil Mollica, Cyril Tywang, Videotape Editors (ABC)
NFL GAME OF THE WEEK - Bob Angelo, Ernie Ernst, Jay Gerber, Stan Leshner, Don Marx, Hank McElwee, Howard Neff, Jack Newman, Steve Sabol, Bob Smith, Art Spiller, Phil Tuckett, Cinematographers (Synd)
UP CLOSE AND PERSONALS (1980 Winter Olympic Games, Lake Placid, NY) - Angelo Bernarducci, Jon Day, Sam Fine, John Petersen, Vincent Reda, Anthony Scandiffio, Wayne Weiss, Ted Winterburn, Film Editors (ABC)
1980 WINTER OLYMPIC GAMES (Lake Placid, NY) - Barbara Bowman, Paul Fanelli, Charles Gardner, Marvin Gench, Roger Haenelt, Connie Kraus, Alex Moskovic, Lou Rende, Nathan Rogers, Erskine Roberts, Mario Schenchman, Ann Stone, Arthur Volk, Frank Guigliano, Videotape Editors (ABC)
UP CLOSE AND PERSONALS (1980 Winter Olympic Games, Lake Placid, NY) - Trevor Carless, George Hause, Jim Lynch, Jan Schulte, Location Sound Mixers (ABC)
ABC'S NFL MONDAY NIGHT FOOTBALL - Loren Coltran, Technical Manager; Bill Morris, Technical Director; Andrew J. Armentani, Jack Dorfman, Steve Nikifor, Joe Cotugno, Gary Donatelli, Jim Heneghan, Roy Hutchings, Tom O'Connell, Jack Savoy, Dick Spanos, Electronic

Cameramen (ABC)
1980 WINTER OLYMPIC GAMES (Lake Placid, NY) - Roger Goodman, Creative Director in charge; Hy Bley, Director of Graphic Arts; Maxwell Berry, Director of Electronic Graphics (ABC)
1980 WINTER OLYMPIC GAMES (Lake Placid, NY) - Mel Handelsman, Lighting Director (ABC)
UP CLOSE AND PERSONALS (1980 Winter Olympic Games, Lake Placid, NY) - Harvey Harrison, Harry Hart, Don Shapiro, Cinematographers (ABC)
1980 WINTER OLYMPIC GAMES (Lake Placid, NY) - Dick Horan, Robert Armbruster, Bill Blumel, Coach Coltran, Geoffrey Felger, Mike Jochim, Jacques Lesgards, Bill Maier, Joseph Polito, Elliott R. Reed, Martin Sandberg, Tony Versley, Mike Fisher, Joseph Kresnicka, B. Untiedt, Technical Managers; Les Weiss, Werner Gunther, Chester Mazurek, William Morris, Joseph Schiavo, Joe Nesi, E. Buttleman, J. Allen, G. Bucci, H. Falk, D. Smith, Technical Directors; Diane Cates, Gary Donatelli, Danny LaMothe, Charles Mitchell, Steve Nikifor, William Sullivan, Don Farnum, Rick Knipe, Morton Kipow, Joseph Montesano (minicam), Electronic Cameramen (ABC)
1980 WINTER OLYMPIC GAMES (Lake Placid, NY) - Carol Lehti, Rob Beiner, Jeff Cohan, Vince DeDario, Bob Dekas, Lou Frederick, Bob Hersh, Ronald Hawkins, Jean MacLean, Norm Samet, Howard Shapiro, Toni Slotkin, Stan Spiro, Doug Towey, Pat Tuite, Associate Directors (live-tape) (ABC)
1980 WINTER OLYMPIC GAMES (Lake Placid, NY, including original theme "Give It All You Got") - Chuck Mangione, Music Composer-Director (ABC)
1980 WINTER OLYMPIC GAMES (Lake Placid, NY) - Dick Roes, Jim Davis, Tom Glazner, Jack Hughes, George Meyer, Joe Vernum, Jonathan M. Lory, Gary Larson, D. Nelson, J. Eaton, R. Emerson, A. Morgenstern, Live-Tape Sound Mixers (ABC)
THE MASTERS - Lou Scannapieco, Arthur Tinn, Engineering Supervisors; Charles D'Onofrio, Sandy Bell, Technical Directors; George Klimcsak, George Rothweller, David Graham, Herman Lang, Hans Singer, Harry Haigood, Rick Blane, Frank McSpedon, Barry Drago, Jim Murphy, Mike Zwick, George Naeder, Jim McCarthy, Al Loreto, Al Diamond, Mike English, John Lincoln, Pat McBride, Stan Gould, Joe Sokota, Neil McCaffrey, Bob Welsh, David Finch, Gordon Sweeney, Gorm Erickson, Electronic Cameramen (CBS)

SPECIAL CLASSIFICATION OF PROGRAM AND INDIVIDUAL ACHIEVEMENT

Emmy(s) to Executive Producer(s) and Producer(s) for program; Emmy(s) to individual(s) for individual achievement; for programs and individual achievements which are so unique and different that they do not fall in any previous categories or areas

PROGRAM

A TRIBUTE TO THURMAN MUNSON - (Preempted regular Major League Baseball pregame programming - Terry Ewert, Producer (NBC)

INDIVIDUAL

JERRY P. CARUSO, HARRY SMITH, creators-developers of radio frequency golf cup mic - "Bob Hope Golf Classic" (NBC)

TOP 50 NIELSEN-RATED
TV SHOWS

SHOW	DATE	NET	TIME	%
Dallas (Who Shot J.R.?)	11/21/80	CBS	60	53.3
Roots	01/30/77	ABC	115	51.1
Gone with the Wind-Pt. 1 (Big Event Pt. 1)	11/07/76	NBC	179	47.7
Gone with the Wind-Pt. 2 (NBC Mon. Movie)	11/08/76	NBC	119	47.4
Super Bowl XII Game	01/15/78	CBS	218	47.2
Super Bowl XIII Game	01/21/79	NBC	230	47.1
Bob Hope Christmas Show	01/15/70	NBC	90	46.6
Super Bowl XIV Game	01/20/80	CBS	178	46.3
Roots	01/28/77	ABC	120	45.9
The Fugitive (Final Episode)	08/29/67	ABC	60	45.9
Roots	01/27/77	ABC	60	45.7
Bob Hope Christmas Show	01/14/71	NBC	90	45.0
Roots	01/25/77	ABC	60	44.8
Ed Sullivan	02/09/64	CBS	60	44.6
Super Bowl XI	01/09/77	NBC	204	44.4
Super Bowl VI	01/16/72	CBS	170	44.2
Roots	01/24/77	ABC	120	44.1
Beverly Hillbillies	01/08/64	CBS	30	44.0
Roots	01/16/77	ABC	60	43.8
Academy Awards	04/07/70	ABC	145	43.4
Ed Sullivan	02/16/64	CBS	60	43.2
Beverly Hillbillies	01/15/64	CBS	30	42.8
Super Bowl VII	01/14/73	NBC	185	42.7
Super Bowl IX	01/12/75	NBC	190	42.4
Beverly Hillbillies	02/26/64	CBS	30	42.4
Super Bowl X	01/18/76	CBS	200	42.3
Airport (Movie Special)	11/11/73	ABC	170	42.3
Love Story (ABC Sunday Movie)	10/01/72	ABC	120	42.3
Cinderella	02/22/65	CBS	90	42.3
Roots	01/29/77	ABC	60	42.3
Beverly Hillbillies	03/25/64	CBS	30	42.2
Super Bowl XII - Kickoff	01/15/78	CBS	15	42.1
Beverly Hillbillies	02/05/64	CBS	30	42.0
Beverly Hillbillies	01/29/64	CBS	30	41.9
Miss America Pageant	09/09/61	CBS	150	41.8
Beverly Hillbillies	01/01/64	CBS	30	41.8
Super Bowl VIII	01/13/74	CBS	160	41.6
Bonanza	03/08/64	NBC	60	41.6
Beverly Hillbillies	01/22/64	CBS	30	41.5
Bonanza	02/16/64	NBC	60	41.4
Academy Awards	04/10/67	ABC	150	41.2
Bonanza	02/09/64	NBC	60	41.0
Gunsmoke	01/28/61	CBS	30	40.9
Bonanza	03/28/65	NBC	60	40.8
Bonanza	03/07/65	NBC	60	40.7
All in the Family	01/08/72	CBS	30	40.7
Roots	01/23/77	ABC	120	40.5
Bonanza	02/02/64	NBC	60	40.5
Beverly Hillbillies	05/01/63	CBS	30	40.5
Gunsmoke	02/25/61	CBS	30	40.5

NOTE 1: Average Audience % Rankings Based on Reports July 1960 through Dec. 31, 1980. Data Represent Sponsored Programs, Telecast on Individual Networks.

NOTE 2: The largest television audience of all-time for a single event was the three-network coverage of the Apollo 11 Moon flight of July 29, 1969. The audience was estimated at 53,500,000 households, covering 93.9% of all U.S. TV.

BROADWAY PLAYS
Jan. 1, 1976–Dec. 31, 1980

A Broadway Musical

Norman Kean & Garth H Drabinsky presentation of a musical in a prolog and two acts (nine scenes, 15 numbers), with mus by Charles Strouse; lyr, Lee Adams; book by William F Brown. Prodn supv, Gower Champion; settings, Peter Wexler; cos, Randy Barcelo; light, John De Santis; mus cond, Kevin Farrell; orch, Robert M Freedman; mus supv-vocal arr, Donald Pippin; dance arr, Donald Johnston; snd, Abe Jacob; co-chor, George Bunt. GM, Marilyn S Miller; asso prod, Maria di Dia; publicity, Jeffrey Richards, Warren Knowlton; prodn coord, Barbara-Mae Phillips; stage mgrs, David Rubinstein, Judy Binus, Sherry Cohen. Opened Dec 21, '78, at the Lunt-Fontanne Theatre; $20 top weeknights, $22.50 weekend nights.

Nate Barnett, Irving Allen Lee, Warren Berlinger, Larry Riley, Jackee Harry, Alan Weeks, Patti Karr, Gwyda DonHowe, Christina Kumi Kimball, Maris Clement, Loretta Devince, Sydney Anderson, Michael Gallagher, Gwen Arment, Larry Marshall, Nate Barnett, Jo Ann Ogawa, Anne Francine, Albert Stephenson, Robert Melvin, Martin Rabbett, Tiger Haynes, Reggie Jackson, Prudence Darby, Don Edward Detrick, Sharon Ferrol, Scott Geralds, Maggy Gorrill, Leon Jackson, Carleton Jones, Michael Kubala, Karen Paskow, Marilyn Winbush, Brad Witsger.

Musical numbers: "Broadway, Broadway," "A Broadway Musical," "I Hurry Home to You," "Smoke and Fire," "Lawyers," "Yenta Power," "Let Me Sing My Song," "A Broadway Musical" (reprise), "Let Me Sing My Song" (reprise), "It's Time for a Cheer-Up Song," " You Gotta Have Dancing," "What You Go Through," "Don't Tell Me," "Together."
12/27/78B

A Day in Hollywood & A Night in the Ukraine

Alexander H Cohen & Hildy Parks presentation of a musical double-bill; book-lyrs, Dick Vosburgh; mus, Frank Lazarus; staged-chor, Tommy Tune; co-chor, Thommie Walsh; scenery, Tony Walton; light, Beverly Emmons; cos, Michel Stuart; snd, Otts Munderloh; mus dir-vocal-dance arrs, Wally Harper; co-prod-GM, Roy A Somlyo; asso prod, Philip M Getter; prodn asso, Seymour Herscher; publicity, Alpert-Levine; stage mgrs, Thomas Kelly, Christopher A Cohen. Opened May 1, '80, at the John Golden Theatre; $20 top.

Priscilla Lopez, David Garrison, Frank Lazarus, Stephen James, Peggy Hewett, Kate Draper, Niki Harris, Albert Stephenson.

Musical numbers: - "Just Go To The Movies," "Famous Feet," "The Best in the World," "I Love a Film Cliche," "It All Comes Out of the Piano," "Doin' the Production Code," "A Night in the Ukraine," "Samovar the Lawyer," "Just Like That," "Again," "A Duel, a Duel," "Natsha" and 14 standards.
05/07/80B

A History of the American Film

Judith Gordon & Richard S Bright presentation of a musical, book-lyr, Christopher Durang; mus, Mel Marvin. Staged, David Chambers; mus staging, Graciela Daniele; scenery, Tony Straiges; cos, Marjorie Slaiman; light, William Mintzer; snd, Lou Shapiro; mus dir, Clay Fullum; orch, Robert M Freedman; asso prods, Marc Howard, Sheila-Barbara-Dinah Prodns; GM, Dorothy Olim; publicity, David Powers, Barbara Carroll; company mgr, Gail Bell; stage mgrs, Ron Abbott, Gully Stanford, John Beven. Opened March 30, '78, at the ANTA Theatre; $16.50 top weeknights, $17.50 weekend nights.

Maureen Anderman, Gary Bayer, Walter Bobbie, Jeff Brooks, Bryan Clark, David Cromwell, David Garrison, Ben Halley Jr, Swoosie Kurtz, Kate McGregor-Stewart, Joan Pape, April Shawhan, Bent Spiner, Eric Weitz, Mary Catherine Wright.

Musical numbers: "The Silent Years," "Minstrel Song," "Shanty Town Romance," "They Can't Prohibit Love," "We're in a Salad," "Euphemism," "Ostende Nobis Tosca," "The Red, the White and the Blue," "Pretty Pin-Up," "Apple Blossom Victory," "Isn't It Fun to Be in the Movies," "Search for Wisdom."
04/05/78B

A Lesson From Aloes

Jay J Cohen & Richard Press, in ass'n with the Yale Repertory Theatre, presentation of a drama in two acts by Athol Fugard. Staged, Fugard; set, Michael H Yeargan; cos, Susan Hilferty; light, William Armstrong; exec prod, Ashton Springer; stage mgr, Laurence Rothenberg; publicity, Max Elsen, Irene Gandy. Opened Nov 17, '80, at the Playhouse Theatre; $20.50 top weeknights, $22.50 weekend nights.

Harris Yulin, Maria Tucci, James Earl Jones.
11/19/80B

A Life

Lester Osterman, Richard Horner, Hinks Shimberg & Freyberg-Cutler-Diamond Prodns presentation of a play in two acts, by Hugh Leonard. Staged, Peter Coe; scenery-cos, Robert Fletcher; light, Marc B Weiss; asso prod, Spencer Berlin; asso prod-casting, Lynne Stuart; GM, Malcolm Allen; publicity, Seymour Krawitz, Patricia McLean Krawitz, Martin Schwartz; stage mgrs, Elliott Woodruff, Eileen Haring. Opened Nov 2, '80, at the Morosco Theatre; $20 top weeknights, $22.50 weekend nights.

Roy Dotrice, Helen Stenborg, Aideen O'Kelly, Lauren Thompson, Adam Redfield, David Ferry, Pat Hingle, Dana Delany.
11/05/80B

A Matter Of Gravity

Robert Whitehead, Roger L Stevens & Konrad Matthaei prodn of a comedy in three acts, by Enid Bagnold. Staged, Noel Willman; set, Ben Edwards; cos, Jane Greenwood; light, Thomas Skelton. GM, Oscar E Olesen; publicity, Seymour Krawitz; asso, Patricia McLean Krawitz; company mgr, David Hedges; stage mgrs, Ben Strobach, Bill Becker; casting dir, Terry Fay; adv, Lawrence Weiner Associates (Hy Jacobs). Opened Feb. 3, '76, at the Broadhurst Theatre; $15 top. Charlotte Jones, Robert Moberly, Katharine Hepburn, Christopher Reeve, Elizabeth Lawrence, Paul Harding, Wanda Bimson, Daniel Tamm.
02/11/76B

A Meeting by the River

Terry Allen Kramer & Harry Rigby presentation of a three-act play by Christopher Isherwood and Don Bachardy, based on Isherwood's novel of the same title. Staged, Albert Marre; scenery, Robert Mitchell; light, Clarke W Thornton; cos, Marianne Custer; incidental mus, Glen Roven; asso prod, Jack Schlissel. GMs, Jack Schlissel, Jay Kingwill; publicity, Henry Luhrman, Bill Miller, Terry M Lilly; stage mgrs, Susie Cordon, Andy Bew, Ron Durbian. Opened March 28, '79 at the Palace Theatre; $17.50 top weeknights, $19.50 weekend nights.

Siobhan McKenna, Simon Ward, Keith Baxter, Meg Wynn-Owen, Gilbert Cole, Jonathan Epstein, Paul Collins, Ronald Bishop, Faizul Khan, Arjun Sajnani, Leslie Goldstein, Ed Kerrigan, Sam Jaffe, Harsha Nayyar, Keith McDermot.
04/04/79B

A Party With Betty Comden and Adolph Green

Arthur Cantor & Leonard Friedman presentation of a concert-revue in two parts; lyr, Betty Comden, Adolph Green; mus, various composers. Piano accompaniment, Paul Trueblood; Comden's gowns, des, Donald Brooks; execution, John Fitzpatrick. GMs, Jack Schlissel, Jay Kingwell; publicity, C George Willard; company mgr, Mark Bramble; stage mgr, Larry Bussard. Opened Feb. 10, '77, at the Morosco Theatre; $10 top weeknights; $12 weekend nights.

Betty Comden, Adolph Green, Paul Trueblood.
02/16/77B

A Remembrance: SEE Piaf

A Texas Trilogy: SEE Lu Ann Hampton Laverty Oberlander; The Last Meeting of the Knights of the White Magnolia; The Oldest Living Graduate)

A Touch of the Poet

Elliot Martin revival, by arrangement with the John F Kennedy Center for the Performing Arts, of a play in two acts, by Eugene O'Neill. Staged, Jose Quintero; sets-light, Ben Edwards; cos, Jane Greenwood. GM, Leonard A Mulhern; publicity, Seymour Krawitz; company mgr, Malcolm Allen; stage mgrs, Mitch Erickson, John Handy. Opened Dec 28, '77, at the Helen Hayes Theatre; $15 top weeknights, $16.50 weekend nights.

Barry Snider, Milo O'Shea, Kathryn Walker, Geraldine Fitzgerald, Jason Robards, Walter Flanagan, Dermot McNamara, Richard Hamilton, Betty Miller, George Ede.
01/11/78B

The Act

Shubert Organization presentation of a Cy Feuer & Ernest Martin prodn of a musical in two acts (13 numbers). Book, George Furth; mus, John Kander; lyr, Fred Ebb. Staged, Martin Scorsese (with an unbilled asst by Gower Champion); chor, Ron Lewis; scenery,

The Act
(Cont)

Tony Walton; light, Tharon Musser; cos, Halston; snd, Abe Jacob; mus dir, Stanley Lebowsky; orchs, Ralph Burns; dance mus arrs, Ronald Melrose; vocal-choral arrs, Earl Brown. GM, Joseph Harris, Ira Bernstein; publicity, Merle Debuskey, Leo Stern; stage mgrs, Phil Friedman, Robert Corpora, Richard Lombard. Opened Oct. 29, '77, at the Majestic Theatre; $20 top weeknights, $22.50 Friday nights, $25 Saturday nights, $35 opening.

Christopher Barrett, Liza Minnelli, Arnold Soboloff, Barry Nelson, Roger Minami, Mark Goddard, Gayle Crofoot. Gayle Crofoot, Carol Estey, Laurie Dawn Skinner.

Musical numbers: 'Shine It On,' 'It's the Strangest Thing,' 'Bobo's,' 'Turning (Shaker Hymn),' 'Little Do They Know,' 'Arthur in the Afternoon,' 'Hollywood, California,' 'The Money Tree,' 'City Lights,' 'There When I Need Him,' 'Hot Enough for You?' 'Little Do They Know' (reprise), 'My Own Space.' PO ancers: Wayne Cilento, Michael Leeds, Roger Minami, Albert Stephenson,
11/02/77B

Agamemnon

Joseph Papp presentation of a N Y Shakespeare Festival revival of a drama by Aeschylus; conceived, Andrei Serban, Elizabeth Swados, using fragments of the orig Greek and Edith Hamilton's trans. Staged, Andrei Serban; mus comp, Elizabeth Swados; scenery, Douglas W Schmidt; cos, Santo Loguasto; light, Jennifer Tipton; asso prod, Bernard Gersten. GM, Robert Kamlot; prodn mgr, Andrew Mihok; publicity, Merle Debuskey, Faith Geer. Opened May 18, '77, at the Vivian Beaumont Theatre; $10 top weeknights, $11 weekend nights.

Priscilla Smith, Jamil Zakkai, George Voskovec, Stuart Baker-Bergen, Patrick Ennis Burke, Suzanna Collins, Gretel Cummings, Jerry Cunliffe, Jon De Vries, Helena D Garcia, Natalie Gray, Kathleen Harris, C S Hayward, Rodney Hudson, Onni Johnson, Paul Kreppel, Paula Larke, Roger Lawson, Esther Levy, Mimi Locadio, Tom Matsusaka, Valois Mickens, Joseph Neal, William Parry, Justin Rashid, Peter Schlosser, Jai Oscar St John, Eron Tabor, John Watson, Beverly Wideman, Diane Lane.
05/25/77B

Ain't Misbehavin'

Emanuel Azenberg, Dasha Epstein, the Shubert Organization, Jane Gaynor & Ron Dante presentation of a musical show based on an idea by Murray Horwitz & Richard Maltby Jr, songs, Thomas (Fats) Waller, various others. Mus supv-orch-arr, Luther Henderson; staged, Richard Maltby Jr; mus staging, Arthur Faria; asso dir, Murray Horwitz; vocal arrs, William Elliot & Jeffrey Gutcheon; setting, John Lee Beatty; cos, Randy Barcelo; light, Pat Collins. Opened May 9, '78, at the Longacre Theatre; $15 top weeknights, $17.50 weekend nights and opening.

Nell Carter, Andre De Shields, Armelia McQueen, Ken Page, Charlaine Woodard; Luther Henderson (pianist).

Musical numbers: "Ain't Misbehavin'," "Lookin' Good, But Feelin' Bad," "T Ain't Nobody's Biz-ness If I Do," "Honeysuckle Rose," "Squeeze Me," "Handful of Keys," "I've Got a Feeling I'm Falling," "How Ya Baby," "The Jitterbug Waltz," "The Ladies Who Sing with the Band" (Yacht Club Swing," "When the Nylons Bloom Again," "Cash for Your Trash," "Off-Time"), "The Joint Is Jumpin," "Spreadin' Rhythm Around," "Lounging at the Waldorf," "The Viper's Drag," "Mean to Me," "Your Feet's Too Big," "Thank Ain't Right," "Keepin' Out of Mischief Now," "Find Out What They Like," "Fat and Greasy," "Black and Blue," "I'm Gonna Sit Right Down and Write Myself a Letter," "Two Sleepy People," "I've Got My Fingers Crossed," "I Can't Give You Anything But Love," "It's a Sin to Tell a Lie," "Honeysuckle Rose" (reprise).
05/17/78B

Amadeus

The Shubert Organization; Elizabeth I, McCann, Nelle Nugent, Roger S Berlind presentation of a play in two acts, by Peter Shaffer. Staged, Peter Hall; scenery, cos-light, John Bury; scenic asso, Ursula Belden; cos asso, John David Ridge; light asso, Beverly Emmons; mus dir-arr, Harrison Birtwistle. GM, Elizabeth I McCann, Nelle Nugent; publicity, Merle Debuskey; stage mgrs, Robert L Borod, Robert Charles, Richard Jay-Alexander. Opened Dec. 17, '80 at the Broadhurst Theatre; $26.50 top weeknights, $30 weekend nights.

Ian McKellen, Gordon Gould, Edward Zang, Victor Griffin, Haskell Gordon, Nicholas Kepros, Paul Harding, Patrick Hines, Louis Turenne, Michael McCarty, Russell Gold, Linda Robbins, Caris Corfman, Jane Seymour, Tim Curry, Philip Pleasants, Martin La Platney, Michele Farr, Warren Manzi, Ronald Bagden, Rick Hamilton, Richard Jay-Alexander, Peter Kingsley, Mark Nelson, Mark Torres.
12/24/80B

American Buffalo

Edgar Lansbury & Joseph Beruh presentation of a play in two acts, by David Mamet. Staged, Ulu Grosbard; set, Santo Loguasto; light, Jules Fisher. GM, Marvin A Krauss; company mgr, Al J Isaac; publicity, Gifford-Wallace; stage mgrs, Herb Vogler, Joel Tropper; asso prod, Nan Pearlman. Opened Feb. 16, '77, at the Ethel Barrymore Theatre; $13.50 top weeknights, $15 Saturday nights.

Kenneth McMillan, John Savage, Robert Duvall.
02/23/77B

The American Clock

Jack Garfein, Warner Theatre Prodns, Herbert Wasserman presentation of a Harold Clurman Theatre prodn of a drama in two acts by Arthur Miller. Staged, Vivian Matalon; settings, Karl Eigsti; light, Neil Peter Jampolis; cos, Robert Wojewodski; incidental mus, Robert Dennis; stage mgrs, Robert LoBianco, Jane Neufeld; GMs, Jack Schissel, Jay Kingwill; co mgr, Al Isaac; publicity, Joe Wohlandler Asso. Opened Nov 29, '80, at the Biltmore Theatre; $21 top weeknights, $25 weekend nights.

William Atherton, John Randolph, Joan Copeland, Donny Burks, Isaac Jerome, Frank Livermore, Ralph Drischell, Salem Ludwig, Francine Beers, Robert Harper, Alan North, Edward Seamon, Bill Smitrovich, David Chandler, Marilyn Caskey, Rosanna Carter, Susan Sharkey.
11/26/80B

An Almost Perfect Person

Burry Fredrik & Joel Key Rice presentation of a play in two acts (three scenes), by Judith Ross. Staged, Zoe Caldwell; set-light, Ben Edwards; cos, Jane Greenwood; asso prods, Sally Sears, Nadine Koval, William Livingston. GM, David Lawlor; publicity, Shirley Herz, Louise Weiner Ment; company mgr, Milton Moss; stage mgrs, Peter Lawrence, Robert Bruyr. Opened Oct. 27, '77, at the Belasco Theatre; $15 top.

Colleen Dewhurst, George Hearn, Rex Robbins, Gary Alexander Azerier.
11/02/77B

Angel

Philip Rose & Ellen Madison presentation of a musical in two acts (four scenes, 20 numbers); book, Ketti Frings, Peter Udell; mus, Gary Geld; lyr, Udell; based on Ketti Frings play, "Look Homeward, Angel," and the Thomas Wolfe original novel of the same title. Staged, Philip Rose; chor, Robert Tucker; scenery, Ming Cho Lee; light, John Gleason; cos, Pearl Somner; orch, Don Walker; dance mus arr, William Cox; asso prods, Karen Wald, Norman Main. GM, Helen Richards; publicity, Merle Debuskey, Leo Stern; company mgr, Charles Willard; stage mgrs, Steve Zweigbaum, Arturo E Porazzi, Paul Myrvold. Opened May 10, '78, at the Minskoff Theatre; $16 top weeknights, $17.50 weekend nights ($20 opening).

Donna Davis, Joel Higgins, Patti Allison, Grace Carney, Don Scardino, Frances Sternhagen, Elek Hartman, Rebecca Seay, Justine Johnson, Gene Masoner, Billy Beckham, Jayne Barnett, Leslie Ann Ray, Fred Gwynne, Daniel Keyes, Rex David Hays, Carl Nicholas, Norman Stotz, Patricia Englund.

Musical numbers: "Angel" Theme, "All the Comforts of Home," "Like the Eagles Fly," "Make a Little Sunshine," "Fingers and Toes," "Fatty," "Astoria Gloria," "Railbird," "If I Ever Loved Him," "A Dime Ain't Worth a Nickel," "I Got a Dream to Sleep On," "Drifting," "I Can't Believe It's You," "Feelin' Loved," "A Medley," "Tomorrow I'm Gonna Be Old," "Feelin' Loved" (reprise), "How Do You Say Goodbye," "Gant's Waltz," "Like the Eagles Fly" (reprise).
05/17/78B

Anna Christie

Alexander H Cohen, by arrangement with Gabriel Katzka & Edward L Schulman, revival of a play in four acts (with two intermissions), by Eugene O'Neill. Staged, Jose Quintero; scenery-light, Ben Edwards; cos, Jane Greenwood; co-prods, Hildy Parks, Roy A Somlyo. Prodn asso, Seymour Herscher; company mgr, George Martin, Alan Coleridge. Opened April 14, '77 at the Imperial Theatre.

Richard Hamilton, Edwin McDonough, Vic Polizos, Ken Harrison, Jack Davidson, Robert Donley, Mary McCarty, Liv Ullmann, John Lithgow.
04/20/77B

Annie
Mike Nichols presentation of an Irwin Meyer, Stephen R Friedman & Lewis Allen prodn of a musical in two acts (13 scenes, 19 numbers); book, Thomas Meehan; mus, Charles Strouse; lyr, Martin Charnin; based on comic-strip, "Little Orphan Annie." Staged, Martin Charnin; mus staging-chor, Peter Gennaro; set, David Mitchell; cos, Theoni V Aldredge; light, Judy Rasmuson. Exec prod, Michael P Price. GM, Gatchell & Neufeld; publicity, David Powers; company mgr, Drew Murphy; stage mgrs, Janet Beroza, Jack Timmers. Opened April 21, '77, at the Alvin Theatre; $15 top weeknights, $16.50 weekend nights.

Danielle Brisebois, Robyn Finn, Donna Graham, Janine Ruane, Diana Barrows, Shelley Bruce, Andrea McArdle, Dorothy Loudon, James Hosbein, Richard Ensslen, Sandy Faison, Edwin Bordo, Reid Shelton, Robert Fitch, Barbara Erwin, Donald Craig, Raymond Thorne, Steven Boockvor, Laurie Beechman, Edie Cowan, Penny Worth, Bob Freschi, Mari McMinn.

Musical numbers: "Maybe," "It's the Hard-Knock Life," "It's the Hard-Knock Life" (reprise), "Tomorrow," "We'd Like to Thank You," "Little Girls," "I Think I'm Gonna Like It Here," "N Y C," "Easy Street," "You Won't Be an Orphan for Long," "You're Never Fully Dressed Without a Smile" (reprise), "Easy Street" (reprise), "Tomorrow" (reprise), "Something Was Missing," "I Don't Need Anything But You," "Annie," "Maybe" (reprise), "A New Deal for Christmas."
04/27/77B

Appearing Nightly
Ron Delsener presentation of a solo show starring Lily Tomlin; wri-dirs, Jane Wagner, Lily Tomlin; addl material, Cynthia Buchanan, Lorne Michaels, Patrick Resnick, Jim Rusk. Staged, George Boyd; mus, Jerry Frankel; light, Daniel Adams; cos, J Allen Highfill; snd, Jack Mann; asso prod, George Boyd; exec prod, Michael Tannen. GM, Marvin A Krauss; company mgr, Robert I Goldberg; publicity, Sandra Manley, Cheryl Sue Dolby; stage mgr, Brian Meister. Opened March 24, '77, at the Biltmore Theatre; $13 top.
Lily Tomlin.
03/30/77B

The Bacchae
Circle in the Square revival of the Euripides drama; trans-staged, Michael Cacoyannis. Set-cos, John Conklin; light, Pat Collins; mus, Theodore Antoniou; publicity, Merle Debuskey, David Roggensack; stage mgrs, Randall Brooks, Rick Ralston. Opened Oct 2, '80, at the Circle in the Square Theatre; $18 top weeknights, $20 weekend nights.
Christopher Rich, Sheila Dabney, Elain Graham, Ernestine Jackson, Jodi Long, Karen Ludwig, Valois Mickens, Socorra, Santiago, Catherine Lee Smith, Michele-Denise Woods, Tom Klunis, Philip Bosco, John Noah Hertzler, Peter Efthymiou, Alfred Karl, Gary Tacon, Richard Kuss, Paul Perri, Irene Papas.
10/08/80B

Ballroom
Michael Bennett presentation of a musical without intermission (14 numbers), with book by Jerome Kass (based on his CBS-TV special, "Queen of the Stardust Ballroom"), mus-lyrs, Billy Goldenberg Alan, Marilyn Bergman. Staged-chor, Michael Bennett; company-chor, Bob Avian; scenery, Robin Wagner; cos, Theoni V Aldredge; light, Tharon Musser; orchestrations, Jonathan Tunick; snd, Otts Munderloh; mus dir, Don Jennings; co-prods, Bob Avian, Bernard Gersten, Susan MacNair. GM, Maurice Schaded; pub, Merle Debuskey, Leo Stern; company mgr, Sally Campbell; asst, Linda Cohen; stage mgrs, Jeff Hamlin, David Taylor, Pat Trott. Opened Dec 14, '78 at the Majestic Theatre; $22.50 top weeknights, $25 weekend nights.

Dorothy Loudon, Sally-Jane Heit, John Hallow, Dorothy Danner, Peter Alzado, Vincent Gardenia, Lynn Roberts, Bernie Knee, Patricia Drylie, Howard Parker, Barbara Erwin, Gene Kelton, Liz Sheridan, Michael Vita, Danny Carroll, Jayne Turner, Janet Stewart White, Roberta Haze, Victor Griffin, Adriana Keathley, Mary Ann Niles, Terry Violino, Svetlana McLee Grody, David Evans, Mavis Ray, Peter Gladke, Rudy Tronto, Marilyn Cooper, Dick Corrigan, Bud Fleming, Carol Flemming, Mickey Gunnerson, Alfred Karl, Dorothy D Lister, John J Martin, Joe Milan, Frank Pietri, Roberta Haze.
12/20/78B

Banjo Dancing
Stuart Oken, Jason Brett & Klezmer Corp presentation of a solo revue in two acts, devised by Stephen Wade, with Milton Kramer. Staged, Kramer; set, David Emmons; light, Dennis Parichy; stage mgr, Annette Kops; GM, Frank Scardino; publicity, Jeffrey Richards; asso prods, the Apollo Group, Jeffrey Wachtel. Opened Oct 20, '80, at the Century Theatre; $14 top weeknights, $15 weekends.
Stephen Wade.
10/29/80B

Barnum
Judy Gordon, Cy Coleman, Maurice & Lois F Rosenfield, in ass'n with Irvin & Kenneth Feld, presentation of a musical in two acts (14 numbers); mus, Cy Coleman; lyrs, Michael Stewart; book, Mark Bramble; staged-chor, Joe Layton; scenery, David Mitchell; cos, Theoni V Aldredge; light, Craig Miller; snd, Otts Munderloh; orchs, Hershy Kay; vocal arrs, Cy Coleman, Jeremy Stone; mus dir, Peter Howard; asso prods, Steven A Greenberg, Michael Scharf; GM, James Walsh; publicity, David Powers; stage mgrs, Mary Porter Hall, Marc Schlackman, Michael Mann. Opened Apr 30, '80, at the St James Theatre; $22.50 top weeknights, $25 weekend nights.

Jim Dale, Glenn Close, William C Witter, Terrence V Mann, Terri White, Kelly Walters, Catherine Carr, Barbara Nadel, Edward T Jacobs, Andy Teirstein, Dirk Lumbard, Sophie Schwab, Leonard John Crofoot, Karen Trott, William C Witter, Marianne Tatum, Steven Michael, Bruce Robertson, Robbi Morgan.

Musical numbers: - "There's a Sucker Born Ev'ry Minute," "Thank God I'm Old," "The Colors of My Life," "One Brick At a Time," "Museum Song," "I Like Your Style," "Bigger Isn't Better," "Love Makes Such Fools of Us," "Out There," "Come Follow the Band," "Black and White," "The Colors of My Life" (reprise), "The Prince of Humbug," "Join the Circus."
05/07/80B

The Basic Training of Pavlo Hummel
Moe Septee and Carmen F Zollo presentation of The Theatre Company of Boston revival of a play in two acts by David Rabe. Staged, David Wheeler; scenery, Robert Mitchell; cos, Domingo Rodriguez; light, David F Segal. GM, Laurel Ann Wilson; publicity, Max Eisen; stage mgrs, Patrick Horrigan, Barbara Diker. Opened April 24, '77, at the Longacre Theatre; $15-$16.50 top.

Al Pacino, Tisa Chang, Gustave Johnson, Joe Fields, Jack Kehoe, Max Wright, Larry Bryggman, Lance Henriksen, Paul Guilfoyle, John Aquino, Damien Leake, Gary Bolling, Michael Dinelli, Kevin Maung, Brad Sullivan, Ron Hunter, Andrea Masters, Rebecca Darke, Don Blakely, Anne Miyamoto, Richard Lynch, Sully Boyar, Tisa Chang.
04/27/77B

Bedroom Farce
Robert Whitehead, Roger L Stevens, George W George & Frank Milton presentation of a British National Theatre Co prodn of a two-act play by Alan Ayckbourn. Staged by the author and Peter Hall; scenery-cos, Timothy O'Brien, Tazenna Firth; light, Peter Radmore, scenery-light supv, Marc B Weiss. GM, Oscar E Olesen; publicity, Jeffrey Richards, Warren Knowlton; company mgr, Marshall Young; stage mgrs, Frederic De Wilde, Wayne Carson. Opened March 29, '79 at the Brooks Atkinson Theatre; $17.50 top weeknights, $18.50 weekend nights.
Michael Gough, Joan Hickson, Michael Stroud, Polly Adams, Derek Newark, Susan Littler, Stephen Moore, Delia Lindsay.
04/04/79B

The Belle of Amherst
Mike Merrick & Don Gregory presentation of a solo-play in two acts by William Luce, from material compiled by Timothy Helgeson. Staged, Charles Nelson Reilly; set-light, H R Poindexter; cos, Theoni V Aldredge. GM, James Awe; publicity, Seymour Krawitz, Patricia McLean Krawitz, Ted Goldsmith; stage mgrs, George Eckert, Berny Baker; adv, Lawrence Weiner agency. Opened April 28, '76 at the Longacre Theatre; $10 top weeknights, $12.50 weekend nights.
Julie Harris.
05/05/76B

Bent
Jack Schlissel & Steven Steinlauf presentation of a play in two acts, by Martin Sherman. Staged, Robert Allan Ackerman; settings, Santo Loquasto; light, Arden Fingerhut; cos, Robert Wojewodski; mus, Stanley Silverman; co-prods, Lee Minskoff, Patty Grubman. GM, Jay Kingwill; publicity, Jeffrey Richards Associates (Warren Knowlton, Alan Eichler, Bob Ganshaw, Helen Stern); company mgr, Al Isaac; stage mgrs, Robert Bennett, Donald Walters. Opened Dec. 2, '79, at the Apollo Theatre; $18 top weeknights, $19.50 weekend nights.

Bent
(Cont)
Richard Gere, David Marshall Grant, James Remar, Michael Gross, George Hall, Bryan E Clark, David Dukes, Ron Randell, Kai Wulff, Philip Kraus, John Synder.
12/05/79B

Best Friend
Marand Prodns, in ass'n with Rosemary Vuocolo & Nancy Davis, presentation of a play in two acts, by Michael Sawyer. Staged, Marty Jacobs; set, Andrew Greenhut; cos, Miles White; light, Richard Winkler. GM, Susan Bell; publicity, Lewis Harmon, Sol Jacobson; stage mgrs, Michael Wieben, Victor Raider-Wexler, Ingrid Sonnichsen. Opened Oct. 19, '76, at the Lyceum Theatre; $10 top weeknights, $12 weekend nights.
Barbara Baxley, Liz Sheridan, Mary Doyle, Michael M Ryan.
10/27/76B

"Bette! Divine Madness"
Ron Delsener presentation of a revue in two acts. Staged, Midler, Jerry Blatt; chor, Marla Blakey, Toni Basil; mus dir, Tony Berg, Randy Kerber; snd engr, Bill Darlington; light, Chip Monck; special material, Midler, Blatt, Bruce Vilanch. Opened Dec. 5, '79, at the Majestic Theatre; $25-$26 top, through Jan 6.
Bette Midler, The Staggering Harlettes (Franny Eisenberg, Linda Hart, Paulette McWilliams), Shabba-Doo
12/12/79B

Billy Bishop Goes to War
Mike Nichols & Lewis Allen presentation of a musical drama, wri-comp-staged, John Gray, Eric Peterson; co-prod, Vancouver East Cultural Center (Christopher Wootten, exec dir). Scenery, David Gropman; light, Jennifer Tipton; snd, Robert Kerzman; asso prods, Stephen Graham, Ventures West Capital, Inc; GM, Robert Fishko; publicity, David Powers; stage mgrs, George Gracey, T Schuyler Smith; company mgr, Harris Goldman. Opened May 29, '80, at the Morosco Theatre; $18 top weeknights, $20 weekend nights.
Eric Peterson, John Gray.
06/04/80B

Blackstone!
Columbia Artists Theatrical Corp and Blackstone Magik Enterprises presentation of a magic revue in two acts. Staged-chor, Kevin Carlisle; set, Peter Wolf; cos, Winn Morton; light, Martin Aronstein; magic prodn des, Jack Hart; mus supv-dir, Milton Sotzer; orchs, Richard Bellis; GM, Theatre Now Inc; stage mgr, Sam Clester; publicity, Alpert/LeVine; magic dir, Charles Reynolds; prodn supv, Jackie Schrock; company mgr, Hans Hortig. Opened May 19, '80, at the Majestic Theatre; $20 top weeknights, $22.50 weekend nights.
Harry Blackstone, Gay Blackstone, Becky Garrett, Elaine Barnes, Lynn Castles, Kevin Curlee, Ann McLean, Robbin McDowell, Mary McNamara, Reenie Moore, Richard Ruth, Bill Smith, Nikki Summerford, Jim Thompson, John Traub, Michael Weir, Jeffrey Streem.
05/21/80B

Bosoms and Neglect
Bernard Gersten & John Wulp, in ass'n with Marc Howard, presentation of a play in a prolog and two acts, by John Guare. Staged, Mel Shapiro; scenery, John Wulp, supv, Lynn Pecktal; cos, Willa Kim; light, Jennifer Tipton. GMs, Emanuel Azenberg, Max Allentuck; publicity, Merle Debuskey, Leo Stern; stage mgrs, Zane Weiner, Peter Von Mayhauser. Opened May 3, '79 at the Longacre Theatre; $17.50 weeknights, $19 weekend nights.
Paul Rudd, Kate Reid, Marian Mercer.
05/09/79B

Boy Meets Girl
Phoenix Theatre revival of a play in three acts (five scenes), by Bella and Sam Spewack. Staged, John Lithgow; scenery-light, James Tilton; cos, Clifford Capone; snd, David Rapkin; mus dir, Arthur Miller. Managing dir, T Edward Hambleton; GM, Marilyn S Miller; prodn mgr, Robert Beard; publicity, Gifford-Wallace; stage mgrs, Jonathan Penzner, Peter DeNicola; adv, Ash-LeDonne. Opened April 13, '76, at the Playhouse, $9 top weeknights, $10 weekend nights.
Lenny Baker, Frederick Coffin, Charles Kimbrough, Rex Robbins, Roy Poole, Ann McDonough, Alice Drummond, Don Scardino, Joe Grifasi, Moultrie Patten, Marybeth Hurt, Gwendolyn Brown, Stuart Warmflash, David Harris, Arthur Miller, Louise Stubbs, Jeffrey Jones.
04/21/76B

Break a Leg
Stephen R Friedman, Irwin Meyer & Kenneth D Laub in ass'n with Arthur Mogull, Jerold H Rubinstein & Warner Plays Inc, presentation of a play in two acts, by Ira Levin. Staged, Charles Nelson Reilly; scenery, Peter Larkin; cos, Theoni V Aldredge; light, Marc B Weiss; prodn asso, Claire Nichtern. GMs, R Tyler Gatchell Jr, Peter Neufeld; publicity, Solters & Roskin; company mgr, James G Mennen; stage mgrs, Peter Lawrence, Fred Chalfy, James Woolley. Opened April 29, '79 at the Palace Theatre; $17.50 weeknights, $18.50 weekend nights.
Jack Weston, Joseph Leon, Michael Connolly, David Margulies, Julie Harris, Rene Auberjonois, Patricia O'Connell, James Cahill, Timothy Lewis, Natalie Norwick.
05/02/79B

Brigadoon
Zev Bufman & the Shubert Organization presentation of a Wolf Trap revival of a musical in two acts (12 scenes, 23 numbers); book-lyrs, Alan Jay Lerner; mus, Fredrick Loewe; staged, Vivian Matalon; chor-mus staging, Agnes de Mille, recreated by James Jamieson; scenery, Michael J Hotopp, Paul de Pass; cos, Stanley Simmons; light, Thomas Skelton; mus dir-vocal arrs, Wally Harper; orchs, Mack Schlefer, Bill Brohn; snd, T Richard Fitzgerald; exec prod, Craig Hankenson; GM, Theatre Now (Willian Court Cohen, Edward H Davis, Norman E Rothstein; asso, Charlotte W Wilcox); publicity, Fred Nathan, Louse Winer Ment; stage mgrs, Joe Lorden, Jack Gianino, David Rosenberg. Opened Oct 16, '80, at the Majestic Theatre; $24.50 top weeknights, $26.50 Friday nights, $27.50 Saturday nights.
Martin Vidnovic, Mark Zimmerman, Kenneth Kantor, Casper Roos, Michael Cone, Marina Eglevsky, Elaine Hausman, John Curry, Jack Dabdoub, Meg Bussert, Mollie Smith, Stephen Lehew, Frank Hamilton, Mark Herrier, Betsy Craig.
Singers- Larry French, Linda Hohenfeld, Michael Hayward-Jones, Joseph Kolinski, Diane Pennington, Cheryl Russell, Linda Wonneberger.
Dancers: - Bill Badolato, Cherie Bower, Amy Danis, Tom Fowler, John Giffin, Mickey Gunnerson, Jennifer Henson, David Hughes, Phil LaDuca, Elena Malfitano, Susi McCarter, Jerry Mitchell, Eric Nesbitt, Holly Reeve, Dale Robbins, Harry Williams, Dandal Harris, Suzi Winson.
Musical numbers: - "Once in the Highlands," "Brigadoon," "Down on MacConnachy Square," "Watin' for My Dearie," "I'll Go Home with Bonnie Jean," "Bonnie Jean," "Heather on the Hill," "Rain Exorcism," "The Love of My Life," "Jeanie's Packing Up," "Come to Me," "Bend to Me," "Almost Like Being in Love," "Wedding Dance," "Sword Dance," "The Chase," "There But for You Go I," "Steps Stately," "Drunken Reel," "From This Day On," "Brigadoon" (reprise), "From This Day On" (reprise), "Brigadoon" (reprise).
10/22/80B

Bubbling Brown Sugar
J Lloyd Grant, Richard Bell, Robert M Cooper, Ashton Springer in ass'n with Moe Septee, Inc. presentation of the Media House prodn of a musical revue in two acts (34 numbers); book, Loften Mitchell, based on a concept by Rosetta LeNoire. Staged, Robert M Cooper; chor-mus staging, Billy Wilson; scenery, Clark Dunham; cos, Bernard Johnson; light, Barry Arnold; projections, Lucie D Grosvenor & Clarke Dunham; snd, Joel S Fichman; addl mus, Danny Holgate, Emme Kemp, & Lillian Lopez; choral arrs, Chapman Roberts; mus dir, Danny Holgage. GM, Ashton Springer; publicity, Max Eisen; stage mgr, Sam Ellis; adv, Lawrence Weiner & Assoc. Ltd. Opened March 2, '76, at the ANTA Theatre; $13 top weeknights, $15 weekend nights.
Lonnie McNeil, Vernon Washington, Newton Winters, Carolyn Byrd, Karen Grannum, Alton Lathrop, Dyann Robinson, Charlise Harris, Vivian Reed, Anthony Whitehouse, Josephine Premice, Avon Long, Joseph Attles, Chip Garnett, Ethel Beatty, Barbara Rubenstein, Barry Preston, Murphy Cross, Nedra Dixon, Emme Kemp, Stanley Ramsey.
03/10/76B

Bully
Don Saxon & Kevin Brown, with Kathy Raitt, presentation of a George Spotta-Four Star International prodn of a solo-play by Jerome Alden. Staged, Peter H. Hunt; set-cos, John Conklin; light, Peter H. Hunt; asso prod, Dan Lieberman. GM, Richard Horner; publicity, Faith Geer; company mgr, Jo Rosner; stage mgrs, Martha Knight, Leanna Lenhart. Opened Nov. 1, '77, at the 46th Street Theatre; $15 top.
James Whitmore.
11/09/77B

Buried Child

William Donnell, Burry Fredrik, Richard Humphrey & Rosita Sarnoff presentation of a comedy-drama in three acts by Sam Shepard. Staged, Robert Woodruff; set, Jonathan Putnam; light, John P Dodd; cos, Jess Goldstein; GM, David Lawlor; stage mgr, Ruth Kreshka; publicity, Shirley Herz, Jan Greenburg, Bruce Cohen. Opened Dec 5, '78, at Theatre de Lys, (Off Broadway): $8.95 top weeknights, $9.95 weekend nights.
Richard Hamilton, Jacqueline Brookes, Tom Noonan, Jay Sanders, Mary McDonnell, Christopher McCann, Bill Wiley.
12/13/78B

But Never Jam Today

Arch Nadler, Anita MacShane & the Urban Arts Theatre presentation of a musical in two acts (16 scenes, 8 numbers). Book by Vinnette Carroll and Bob Larimer; lyr, Larimer; mus, Bert Keyes and Larimer, adapted from the works of Lewis Carroll. Prodn devised, staged by Vinnette Carroll; chor, Talley Beatty; scenery-cos, William Schroder; light, Ken Billington; choral arr and vocal preparation, Cleavant Derricks; orch, Bert Keyes; special orch, H B Barnum, Larry Blank; mus dir, Donald Johnston; snd, T Richard Fitzgerald. Asso prods, Herb Hugel, Gene Messinger; GM, Elizabeth McCann, Nelle Nugent; pub, Michael Alpert, Marilyn LeVine; company mgr, James Kimo Gerald; stage mgr, Robert L Borod, Robert Charles. Opened July 31, '79, Longacre Theatre; $17.50 top weeknights, $20 weekends.
Marilynn Winbush, Cleavant Derricks, Lynne Thigpen, Brenda Braxton, Clayton Strange, Sharon K Brooks, Garry Q Lewis, Celestine DeSaussure, Jeffrey Anderson-Gunter, Lynne Clifton-Allen, Reginald Vel Johnson, Sheila Ellis, Jai Oscar St John, Charlene Harris.

Musical numbers: "Curiouser and Curiouser," "Twinkle Little Star," "Long Live The Queen," "A Real Life Lullabye," "The More I See People," "My Little Room," "But Never Jam Today," "Riding For A Fall," "All The Same To Me," "I've Got My Orders," "God Could Give Me Anything," "I Like To Win," "And They Call The Hatter Mad," "Jumping From Rock To Rock," "They."
08/08/79B

Caesar and Cleopatra

Elliott Martin & Gladys Rackmil, John F Kennedy Center for the Performing Arts, in ass'n with James Nederlander, revival of a play in two acts (six scenes), by George Bernard Shaw. Staged, Ellis Rabb; scenery, Ming Cho Lee; cos, Jane Greenwood; light, Thomas Skelton. GMs, Leonard A Mulhern, Maurice Shaded; publicity, Betty Lee Hunt, Maria Pucci; company mgr, James Mennen; stage mgrs, William Dodds, Michael Schaefer, Ian Stuart, Joseph Scalzo, Richard Delahanty. Opened Feb. 24, '77, at the Palace Theatre; $15 top weeknights, $17.50 weekend nights.
Rex Harrison, Elizabeth Ashley, Novella Nelson, Paul Hecht, Patrick Hines, William Robertson, Roger Campo, Mike Dantuqno, James Valentine, John Bergstrom, Edwin Owens, Thom Christopher, Charles Turner, Fiddle Viracola, Linda Lartin, Pawnee Sills, Cain Richards, Joseph Scalzo, Eric Booth, Paul Rosson, Ian Stuart.
03/02/77B

California Suite

Emanuel Azenberg & Robert Fryer presentation of a quadruple-bill of plays by Neil Simon. Staged, Gene Saks; set, William Ritman; cos, Jane Greenwood; light, Tharon Musser. M, Jose Vega; stage mgrs, Philip Cusack, Lani Sundsten; publicity, Bill Evans; adv, Blaine Thompson (Fred Golden, Matthew Serino, Regis Albrecht). Opened June 10, '76, at the Eugene O'Neill Theatre; $11 top weeknights, $13 weekend nights.
Visitor From New York- Tammy Grimes, George Grizzard.
Visitor From Philadelphia- Jack Weston, Leslie Easterbrook, Barbara Barrie.
Visitors From London- George Grizzard, Tammy Grimes.
Visitors From Chicago- Jack Weston, Barbara Barrie, George Grizzard, Tammy Grimes.
06/16/76B

Camelot

Mike Merrick & Don Gregory by arrangement with James M Nederlander, revival of a musical in two acts (two prologs, 14 scenes, 18 numbers); book-lyrs, Alan Jay Lerner; mus, Frederick Loewe, based on T H White's "The Once and Future King," Staged, Frank Dunlop (orig Bway prodn staged by Moss Hart); chor, Buddy Schwab; set-cos, Desmond Heeley; light, Thomas Skelton; mus dir, Franz Allers; orch cond, James Martin; mus coord, Robert Kreis; snd, John McClure; orchs, Robert Russell Bennett, Phil Lang; prodn supv, Jerry Adler; artistic cnsltnt, Stone Widney; asso prods, Steve Herman, John Cutler; publicity, Seymour Krawitz, Patricia McLean Krawitz; company mgr, James Awe; stage mgrs, Johnathan Weiss, Cathy Rice. Opened Jul 8, '80, at the N Y State Theatre; $25 top weeknights, $30 weekend nights.
Richard Burton, Andy McAvin, James Valentine, Christine Ebersole, Robert Fox, William Parry, Richard Muenz, Williams James, Paxton Whitehead, Thor Fields.
Court Ladies, Lords, Knights, Squires: - Robert Molnar, Nora Brennan, Deborah Magid, Davis Gaines, Steve Osborn, Herndon Lackey, Ken Henley, Gary Jaketic, Jack Starkey, Ronald Bennett Stratton, Jeanne Caryl, Melanie Clements, Stephanie Conlow, Van Craig, John Deyle, Debra Dickinson, Richard Dodd, Cecil Fulfer, Lisa Ann Grant, John Herrera, Kelby Kirk, Laura McCarthy, Patrice Pickering, Janelle Price, Nancy Rieth, Patrick Rogers, Deborah Roshe, D Paul Shannon, Sally Ann Swarm, Sally Williams, Lynn Keeton, Richard Maxon.
Musical numbers: - "Guenevere," "I Wonder What the Kind Is Doing Tonight," "The Simple Joys of Maidenhood," "Camelot," "Follow Me," "Camelot" (reprise), "C'Est Moi," "The Lusty Month of May," "How to Handle a Woman," "The Jousts," "Before I Gaze at You Again," "If Ever I Would Leave You," "The Seven Deadly Virtues," "What Do the Simple Folk Do?" "Fie on Goodness," "I Loved You Once in Silence," "Guenevere" (reprise), "Camelot" (reprise).
07/16/80B

Canterbury Tales

Equity Library Theatre revival of a musical in two acts; book, Martin Starkie, Nevill Coghill (based on a translation from Geoffrey Chaucer by Coghill); mus, Richard Hill, John Hawkins; lyr, Coghill. Staged, Robert Johanson; chor, Randy Hugill; mus dir, John Kroner; scenery, Michael Anania; cos, Sigrid Insull; light, Gregg Marriner; stage mgrs, M R Jacobs, Sarah Hayden; publicity, Lewis Harmon & Sol Jacobson. Opened Nov 29, '79, at the Equity Library Theatre (Off Bway); $4 admission. (Moved Feb 12, 1980 to the Rialto Theatre; $17.50 top weeknights, $19.50 weekend nights.
Earl McCarroll, David Asher, Robert Tetrick, Andy Ferrell, Mimi Sherwin, Melanie Vaughan, Kaylyn Dillehay, Tricia Witham, Krista Neumann, Andrew Traines, Vance Mizelle, Richard Stillman, Polly Pen, Win Atkins, Ted Houck, Maureen Sadusk, Kelly Walters, William Ryall, George Maguire.
12/26/79B

Carmelina

Roger L Stevens, J W Fisher, Joan Cullman & Jujamcyn Productions presentation of a musical in two acts (12 scenes, 15 numbers); book, Alan Jay Lerner, Joseph Stein; lyr, Lerner; mus, Burton Lane. Staged, Jose Ferrer; chor, Peter Gennaro; set, Oliver Smith; cos, Donald Brooks; light, Feder; snd, John McClure; orchs, Hershy Kay; mus cond, Don Jennings; vocal arr, Maurice Levine; dance music arr, David Krane. GM, Oscar E Olesen; publicity, Jeffrey Richards Associates (Warren Knowlton, Avivah Simon); company mgr, David Hedges; stage mgrs, William Dodds, Jay Adler, Dennis Honeycut. Opened Apr 8, '79, at the St James Theatre; $20 top weeknights, $22.50 weekend nights.
Marc Jordan, Gonzalo Madurga, Cesare Siepi, Grace Keagy, Ian Towers, Georgia Brown, Judy Sabo, Joseph d'Angerio, Frank Bouley, Jossie de Guzman, Gordon Ramsey, Howard Ross, John Michael King, Virginia Martin, Kita Bouroff, Caryl Tenney, David E Thomas.
Others: Kathryn Carter, Karen diBianco, Spence Ford, Ramon Galindo, Liza Gennaro, Laura Klein, Michael Lane, Morgan Richardson, Charles Spoerri, Kevin Wilson, Lee Winston.

Musical numbers: "It's Time for a Love Song," "Why Him?," "I Must Have Her," "Someone in April," "Signora Campbell," "Love Before Breakfast," "Yankee Doodles Are Coming to Town," "One More Walk Around the Garden," "All That He'd Want Me To Be," "It's Time for a Love Song," (reprise), "Carmelina," "The Image of Me," "I'm a Woman," "The Image of You," "It's Time for a Love Song," (reprise).
04/11/79B

Censored Scenes from King Kong

Michael White & Eddie Kulukundis presentation of a comedy with songs, in two acts; book-lyrs, Howard Schuman; mus, Andy Roberts; staged, Colin Bucksey; chor, David Toguri; set, Mike Porter; cos, Jennifer von Mayrhauser; light, Richard Nelson; snd, Robert Kerzman; stage mgr, Steven Zweigman; asso prod, Robert Fishko; GM, Harris Gold-

Censored Scenes
(Cont)
man; publicity, Front Page Enterprises (Elizabeth Rodman). Opened Mar 6, '80, at the Princess Theatre; $16 top weeknights, $18 weekend nights.
Stephen Collins, Nicky Mieholes, Pete Flasher, Peter Riegert, Carrie Fisher, Alma Cuervo, Chris Sarandon, Edward Love.
03/12/80B

Chapter Two
Emanuel Azenberg presentation of a play in two acts by neil Simon. Staged, Herbert Ross; scenery, William Ritman; cos, Noel Taylor; light, Tharon Musser. GM, Jose Vega; company mgr, Susan Bell; publicity, Bill Evans; stage mgrs, Charles Blackwell, Lani Sundsten. Opened Dec. 4, '77, at the Imperial Theatre; $15 top weeknights, $16.50 weekend nights.
Judd Hirsch, Cliff Gorman, Anita Gillette, Ann Wedgeworth.
12/07/77B

Charlie And Algernon
Kennedy Center, Isobel Robins Konecky, Fisher Theatre Foundation & Folger Theatre Group presentation of Michael Sheehan & Louis W Scheeder prodn of a musical in one act (21 numbers); book-lyrs, David Rogers; mus, Charles Strouse, based on novel, "Flowers for Algernon," by Daniel Keyes. Staged, Louis W Scheeder; chor, Virginia Freeman; mus dir-cond, Liza Redfield; orchs, Philip J Lang; scenery, Kate Edmunds; cos, Jess Goldstein; light, Hugh Lester; snd, William H Clements; GM, Theatre Now (William Court Cohen, Edward Davis, Norman Rothstein, Ralph Roseman); publicity, Michael Alpert, Marilynn LeVine; company mgr, Michael Lonergan; stage mgrs, Martha Knight, Peter Dowling, P'nenah Goldstein. Opened Sep 14, '80 at the Helen Hayes Theatre; $20 top weeknights, $22.50 weekend nights.
P J Benjamin, Sandy Faison, Edward Earle, Robert Sevra, Nancy Franklin, Loida Santos, Patrick Jude, Julienne Marie, Matthew Duda, Michael Vita.

Musical numbers: - "Have I the Right?" "I Got A Friend," "I Got a Friend" (reprise), "Some Bright Morning," "Jelly Donuts and Chocolate Cake," "Hey Look at Me," "Reading," "No Surprises," "Midnight Riding," "Dream Safe with Me," "Not Another Day Like This," "Somebody New," "I Can't Tell You," "Now," "Charlie and Algernon," "The Maze," "Whatever Time There Is," "Everything Was Perfect," "Charlie," "I Really Loved You," "Whatever Time There Is" (reprise).
09/17/80B

Charlotte
Eugene V Wolsk & Marc Howard, in ass'n with Marlene Mancini, presentation of a play in two acts, by Peter Hacks, trans-adapt from German, Herbert and Uta Berghof. Staged, Herbert Berghof; set, Lester Polakov; cos, Patricia Zipprodt; light, Pat Collins; GM, Manny Kladitis; publicity, Merle Debuskey, William Schelble; stage mgrs, Mitch Erickson, Timothy Farmer. Opened Feb 27, '80, at the Belasco Theatre; $18.50 top weeknights, $20 weekend nights.
Uta Hagen, Charles Nelson Reilly.
03/05/80B

Cheaters
Ken Marsolais, Philip M Getter & Leonard Soloway presentation of a play in two acts, by Michael Jacobs. Staged, Robert Drivas; scenery, Lawrence King; cos, Jane Greenwood; light, Ian Calderon; asso prods, Donald Tick, Martin Markinson. Publicity, Betty Lee Hunt, Maria Christina Pucci; company mgr, Robert L Wallner; stage mgrs, Larry Forde, Arlene Grayson, Steve Scott. Opened Jan 15, '78, at the Biltmore Theatre; $16 top weeknights, $17.50 weekend nights.
Rosemary Murphy, Lou Jacobi, Jack Weston, Doris Roberts, Roxanne Hart, Jim Staskel.
01/18/78B

Checking Out
Philip Mathias & Ken Myers presentation of a play in two acts (four scenes), by Allen Swift. Staged, Jerry Adler; set, David Jenkins; light, Ken Billington; cos, Carol Luiken. GM, Ken Myers; publicity, Susan Bloch; stage mgrs, Murray Gitlin, Ron Nguvu. Opened Sept. 14, '76, at the Longacre Theatre; $11 top weeknights, $13 weekend nights.
Joan Copeland, Hy Anzell, Allen Swift, Jonathan Moore, Mason Adams, Larry Bryggman, Tazewell Thompson, Michael Gorrin.
09/22/76B

The Cherry Orchard
Joseph Papp presentation of a N Y Shakespeare Festival revival of a play in four acts (with two intermissions), by Anton Chekhov; trans, Jean-Claude van Itallie. Staged, Andrei Serban; scenery-cos, Santo Loquasto; light, Jennifer Tipton; incidental mus, Elizabeth Swados; dance staging, Kathryn Posin; asso prod, Bernard Gersten. GM, Robert Kamlot; publicity, Merle Debuskey, Faith Geer; stage mgrs, Julia Gillett, Stephen McCorkle. Opened Feb. 17, '77, at the Vivian Beaumont Theatre; $10 top weeknights, $11 weekend nights.
Raul Julia, Meryl Streep, Max Wright, Marybeth Hurt, Irene Worth, Priscilla Smith, George Voskovec, Cathryn Damon, C K Alexander, Ben Masters, Dwight Marfield, Michael Cristofer, Jon DeVries, William Duff-Griffin, John Ahlburg, Suzanne Collins, Christine Estabrook, C S Hayward, Diane Lane, Jim Siering.

Standbys, understudies: Jacqueline Brooks, Gerry Bamman, Maury Cooper, Elizabeth Franz.
02/23/77B

Children of a Lesser God
Emanuel Azenberg, the Shubert Organization, Dasha Epstein & Ron Dante presentation of a Mark Taper Forum prodn of a play in two acts by Mark Medoff; staged, Gordon Davidson; set, Thomas A Walsh; cos, Nancy Potts; light, Tharon Musser; asso prods, William P Wingate, Kenneth Brecher; GM, Jose Vega; company mgr, Lilli Afan; publicity, Bill Evans, Howard Atlee; stage mgrs, Mark Wright, Jonathan Barlow Lee, Richard Kendall. Opened Mar 30, '80, at the Longacre Theatre; $20 top weeknights, $22.50 weekend nights.
Phyllis Frelich, John Rubinstein, Lewis Merkin, William Frankfather, Scotty Bloch, Julianne Gold, Lucy Martin.
04/02/80B

Clothes for a Summer Hotel
Elliot Martin, in ass'n with Donald Cecil & Columbia Pictures, presentation of a two-act play by Tennessee Williams. Staged, Jose Quintero; scenery, Oliver Smith; cos, Theoni V Aldredge; light, Marilyn Rennagel; orig mus, Michael Valenti; dance cnsltnt, Anna Sokolow; GM, Victor Samrock; company mgr, John Larson; publicity, Betty Lee Hunt, Maria Cristina Pucci; state mgrs, Robert L Borod, John Handy, Scott Palmer. Opened Mar 26, '80, at the Cort Theatre; $20 top weeknights, $22.50 weekend nights.
Madeleine le Roux, Kenneth Haigh, Geraldine Page, Michael Connolly, Mary Doyle, Robert Bays, Scott Palmer, Josephine Nichols, David Canary, Marilyn Rockafellow, Audree Rae, Michael Granger, Robert Black, Tanny McDonald, Weyman Thompson.
04/02/80B

Cold Storage
Claire Nichtern & Ashton Springer presentation, in ass'n with Irene Miller, of a play in two acts, by Ronald Ribman. Staged, Frank Corsaro; sets-cos, Karl Eigsti; light, William Mintzer. Publicity, Max Eisen, Judy Jacksina, Barbara Glenn; company mgr, Charles Willard; stage mgrs, Clint Jakeman, Ginny Friedman. Opened Dec 29, '77, at the Lyceum Theatre; $15 top weeknights, $17.50 weekend nights.
Len Cariou, Ruth Rivera, Martin Balsam.
01/11/78B

Comedians
Alexander H Cohen presentation, in ass'n with Gabriel Katzka & Edward L Schuman, of a play in three acts, by Trevor Griffiths. Staged, Mike Nichols; set, John Gunter; scenery-cos supv, James Tilton; light, Ron Wallace; co-prods, Hildy Parks, Roy Somlyo. Asso mgr, Seymour Herscher; publicity, Richard Hummler, Martha Mason; company mgr, Joel Wyman; stage mgrs, Nina Seely, Faizul Khan. Opened Nov. 28, '76, at the Music Box Theatre; $13.50 top weeknights, $15 weekend nights.
Norman Allen, Jonathan Price, Jeffrey DeMunn, Larry Lamb, David Margulies, Jarlath Conroy, Milo O'Shea, John Lithgow, Jayant Blue, Rex Robbins, Robert Gerringer, Armand Assante, Woody Kessler.
12/01/76B

Comin' Uptown
Ridgely Bullock & Albert W Selden, in ass'n with Columbia Pictures, presentation of a musical in two acts (13 scenes, 18 numbers); mus, Garry Sherman; book, Phillip Rose, Peter Udell; lyr, Peter Udell; based on Charles Dickens story, "A Christmas Carol"; staged, Philip Rose; chor, Michael Peters; scenery, Robin Wagner; cos, Ann Emonts; lightng, Gilbert V Hemsley Jr; snd, Jack Shearing; mus dir, Howard Roberts; vocal arrs, Garry Sherman; dance mus arrs, Timonthy Graphenreed; asso prod, Leslie K Bullock; GM, Jay Kingwill; publicity, Merle Debuskey, Leo Stern; stage mgrs, Mortimer Halpern, Nate Barnett, Lisa Blackwell. Opened Dec. 20, '79, at the Winter Garden Theatre; $22.50 top weeknights, $25 week-

Comin' Uptown
(Cont)
end nights.
Deborah Lynn Bridges, Deborah Burrell, Jenifer Lewis, Gregory Hines, John Russell, Larry Marshall, Saundra McClain, Robert Jackson, Tiger Haynes, Loretta Devine, Duane Davis, Vernal Polson, Ned Wright, Esther Marrow, Virginia McKinzie, Shirley Black-Brown, Allison R Manson, Carol Lynn Maillard, Kevin Babb, Roslyn Burrough, Barbara Christopher, Ronald Dunham, Milton Grayson, Linda James, Kevin Jeff, Frances Lee Morgan, Raymond Patterson, Gloria Suave, Eric Sawyer, Kiki Shepard, Faruma Williams.

Mus numbers: "Christmas Is Comin' Uptown", "Somebody's Gotta Be the Heavy", "Now I Lay Me Down to Sleep", "Get Your Act Together", "Lifeline", "What Better Time for Love", "It Won't Be Long", "Get Down, Brother, Get Down", "Sing a Christmas Song", "What Better Time for Love" (reprise), "Have I Finally Found My Heart?", "Nobody Really Do", "Goin' Gone", "One Way Ticket to Hell", "Nobody Really Do" (reprise), "Born Again" (reprise).
12/26/79B

Coquelico
Olivier Coquelin, in ass'n with Michael Butler, Gene Kelly and Alan Jay Lerner, presentation of the National Theatre of Prague prodn of a film and mime entertainment in two acts. Conceived-wri-staged, Josef Svoboda; film wri-dir, Evald Schorm; dances, Karel Vrtiska; mus-mus dir, O F Korte; GM, Ralph Lee; publicity, The Merlin Group (Becky Flora). Opened Feb. 22, '79 at the 22 Steps Theatre; $15 top weeknights, $17.50 weekend nights.
02/28/79B

The Crucifer of Blood
Lester Osterman, Richard Horner, Terry Allen Kramer & John Wulp presentation of a play in two acts (six scenes), by Paul Giovanni; based on an Arthur Conan Doyle story, "The Sign of Four." Staged, Paul Giovanni; set, John Wulp; cos, Ann Roth; light, Roger Morgan; scenery supv, Lynn Pecktal; snd, Leonard Will; sfx, Bran Ferrin. Publicity, Seymour Krawitz, Louie Weiner Ment; company mgr, Malcolm Allen; stage mgrs, Robert L Borod, Robert Charles, Alisa Jill Adler. Opened Sept 28, '78, at the Helen Hayes Theatre; $15 top weeknights, $16.50 weekend nights.

Dwight Schultz, Nicolas Surovy, Christopher Curry, Edward Zang, Tuck Milligan, Andrew David, Paxton Whitehead, Timothy Landfield, Glenn Close, Tuck Milligan, Roumel Reaux, Edward Zang, Melvin Lumm, Andrew Davis.
10/04/78B

Da
Lester Osterman, Marilyn Strauss & Marc Howard presentation of a Hudson Guild Theatre-Craig Anderson prodn of a play in two acts, by Hugh Leonard. Staged, Melvin Bernhardt; set, Marjorie Kellogg; cos, Jennifer von Mayrhauser; light, Arden Fingerhut. GM, Richard Horner; publicity, Howard Atlee, Becky Flora; company mgr, Bruce Laffey; stage mgr, Edward R Fitzgerald, David Naughton. Opened May 1, '78, at the Morosco Theatre; $15 top weeknights, $16.50 weekend nights.
Brian Murray, Ralph Williams, Barnard Hughes, Sylvia O'Brien, Richard Seer, Lester Rawlins, Mia Dillon, Lois de Banzie.
05/03/78B

Dancin'
Jules Fisher, the Shubert Organization & Columbia Pictures presentation of a Jules Fisher prodn of a musical in three acts (13 numbers); mus-lyr, Johann Sebastian Bach, Ralph Burns, George M Cohan, Neil Diamond, Bob Haggart, Ray Bauduc, Gil Rodin & Bob Crosby, Jerry Leiber & Mike Stoller, Johnny Mercer & Harry Warren, Louis Prima, John Philip Sousa, Carole Bayer Sager & Melissa Manchester, Barry Mann & Cynthia Weil, Felix Powell & George Asaf, Sigmund Romberg & Oscar Hammerstein II, Cat Stevens, Edgard Varese, Jerry Jeff Walker. Staged-chor, Bob Fosse; scenery, Peter Larkin; cos, Willa Kim; light, Jules Fisher; snd, Abe Jacob; mus arr-cond, Gordon Lowry Harrell; orch, Ralph Burns; asso prod, Patty Grubman. GM, Marvin A Krauss; publicity, Merle Debuskey, Susan L Schulman; company mgr G Warren McClane; management asso, Gary Gunas; stage mgrs, Phil Friedman, Perry Cline, Richard Korthaze. Opened March 27, '78 at the Broadhurst Theatre; $17.50-$18.50 top.
Gail Benedict, Sandahl Bergman, Karen G Burke, Rene Ceballos, Christopher Chadman, Wayne Cilento, Jill Cook, Gregory B Drotar, Vicki Frederick, Linda Haberman, Richard Korthaze, Edward Love, John Mineo, Ann Reinking, Blane Savage, Charles Ward.

Musicians: Art Baron, Lew Soloff, William Shadel, Peter Phillips, Allen Herman, David Moore.

Musical numbers: "Prologue (Hot August Night)," "Crunchy Granola Suite," "Mr. Bojangles," "Chaconne," "Ionisation," "I Wanna Be a Dancin' Man," "Big Noise from Winnetka," "It Feels Good, Let It Ride," "Easy," "I've Got Them Feelin' Too Good Today Blues," "Was Dog a Doughnut," "Sing, Sing, Sing," "Here You Come Again," "Yankee Doodle Dandy," "Gary Owen," "Stout Hearted Men," "Under the Double Eagle," "Dixie," "When Johnny Comes Marching Home," "Rally Round the Flag," "Pack Up Your Troubles in Your Old Kit Bag and Smile, Smile, Smile," "The Stars and Stripes Forever," "Yankee Doodle Disco," "Dancin'."
03/29/78B

Days in the Trees
Circle in the Square Theatre presentation of a play in two acts (three scenes), by Marguerite Duras; trans, Sonia Orwell. Staged, Stephen Porter; scenery-cos, Rouben Ter-Arutunian; light, Thomas Skelton; incidental mus, Robert Dennis. Art dir, Paul Libin; company mgr, William Conn; publicity, Merle Debuskey, Susan L Schulman; stage mgrs, James Bernardi, Donald Linahan. Opened Sept. 26, '76, at the Circle in the Square, $8.95 weeknights, $9.95 weekend nights.
Mildred Dunnock, Joseph Maher, Suzanne Lederer, Ed Setrakian, Helen Harrelson, Donald Linahan, Marlena Lustik.
09/29/76B

Days In The Trees: SEE Des Journees Entieres Dans Les Arbres

Deathtrap
Alfred de Liagre Jr & Roger L Stevens presentation of a play in two acts (six scenes), by Ira Levin. Staged, Robert Moore; sets, William Ritman; cos, Ruth Morley; light, Marc B Weiss. GM, Oscar F Olesen; publicity, Jeffrey Richards; company mgr, David Hedges; stage mgrs, Philip Cusack, Lani Sundsten. Opened Feb 26, '78, at the Music Box Theatre; $15 top weeknights, $17.50 weekend nights.
John Wood, Marian Seldes, Victor Garber, Marian Winters, Richard Woods.
03/01/78B

Des Journees Entieres Dans Les Arbres
(Days In The Trees)
French Government Artistic Action Assn & Jean de Rigault presentation in ass'n with the French Institute-French Alliance, of a Renaud-Barrault Co prodn of a play in three acts (four scenes), by Marguerite Duras (played without intermission). Staged, Jean-Louis Barrault; scenery-cos, Atelier du Theatre d'Orsay; Renaud's cos, Yves Saint Laurent; scenic-cos supv, Mason Arvold; light, Genevieve Soubirou; light supv, Martin Aronstein. GMs, Elizabeth McCann, Nelle Nugent; publicity, Michael Alpert, Marilynn LeVine, Warren Knowlton, Carl Samrock; adv, Blaine Thompson (Mike Mones). Opened May 6, '76, at the Ambassador Theatre; $12 top.
Madeleine Renaud, Jean-Pierre Aumont, Francoise Dorner, Jean Martin.
05/12/76B

Dirty Linen & New-Found-Land
Elliot Martin & Inter-Action Trust Ltd. presentation, by arrangement with the John F Kennedy Center for the Performing Arts, of a dual-bill by Tom Stoppard. Staged, Ed Berman; set-light-cos, Gabriella Falk; set-cos supv, Lawrence King, Michael H Yeargan; light supv, Martin Aronstein; prodn asso, Marjorie Martin. GM, Leonard A Mulhern; publicity, Seymour Krawitz; stage mgrs, Wally Peterson, Michael McCarty. Opened Jan. 11, '77, at the John Golden Theatre; $11 top weeknights, $13 weekend nights.
Dirty Linen- Cecilia Hart, Francis Bethencourt, Remak Ramsey, Michael Tolaydo, Merwin Goldsmith, Leila Blake, Stephen D Newman.

New-Found-Land- Jacob Brooke, Humphrey Davis.
01/19/77B

Diversions and Delights
Roger Berlind, Franklin R Levy & Mike Wise presentation of a solo-play by John Gay. Staged, Joseph Hardy; set-light des, H R Poindexter; light execution, Barry Arnold; cos, Noel Taylor. GMs, William C Cohen, Edward H Davis, Norman E Rothstein; publicity, Seymour Krawitz; asst GM, Charlotte Wilcox; stage mgrs, David Clive, Janyce Ann Wagner. Opened April 12, '78, at the Eugene O'Neill Theatre; $13 top weekday nights; $15 week-

Diversions and
(Cont)
end nights.
Vincent Price.
04/19/78B

Division Street
Emanuel Azenberg, the Shubert Organization, the Mark Taper Forum & Gordon Davidson presentation of a play in two acts by Steve Tesich. Staged, Tom Moore; set, Ralph Funicello; cos, Robert Blackman; light, Martin Aronstein; asso prods, William P Wingate, Kenneth Brecher; GM, Jose Vega; publicity, Bill Evans, Howard Atlee; asso mgr, Linda Cohen; stage mgrs, Franklin Keysar, Mary Michele Miner. Opened Oct 8, '80, at the Ambassador Theatre; $21 top weeknights, $24 weekend nights.
John Lithgow, Theresa Merritt, Keene Curtis, Justin Lord, Murphy Cross, Joe Regalbuto, Christine Lahti, Anthony Holland.
10/15/80B

Do You Turn Somersaults?
Kennedy Center presentation, in ass'n with Cheryl Crawford, by arrangement with the Royal Shakespeare Co, of a play in two acts (nine scenes), by Aleksei Arbuzov; trans, Ariadne Nicolaeff. Staged, Edwin Sherin; scenery, Oliver Smith; cos, Ann Roth; light, Ken Billington; incidental mus, Charles Gross. GM, Ralph Roseman; publicity, Michael Alpert, Marilynn LeVine; company mgr, James Awe; stage mgrs, Paul A Foley, Stephen Nasuta, Marc Schlackman. Opened Jan 9, '78, at the 46th St Theatre; $15 top weeknights, $16 weekend nights.
Mary Martin, Anthony Quayle.
01/11/78B

Dogg's Hamlet, Cahoot's Macbeth
British American Repertory Co presentation of two one-act comedies by Tom Stoppard. Staged, Ed Berman; scenery-cos, Norman Coates; light, Howard Eaton; asso prod, James Ware; GM, Ralph Roseman; prodn stage mgr, George Allison Elmer; publicity, Seymour Krawitz, Patricia McLean Krawitz. Opened Oct. 3, '79, at the 22 Steps Theatre; $15 top weeknights, $16.50 weekend nights.
John Challis, Alison Frazer, Ben Gotlieb, Peter Grayer, Davis Hall, Louis Haslar, Ruth Hunt, Stephen D Newman, John Straub, Alan Thompson, Sarah Venable, Peter Woodthorpe.
10/10/79B

Don't Step on My Olive Branch
Yael Co & Norman Kean presentation of a musical in one act; book, Harvey Jacobs; mus-lyr, Sander Hacker. Staged-chor, Jonatan Karmon; mus dir, David Krivoshei; snd, Sander Hacker; set-projections, James Tilton; light, William H Batchelder; cos, Pierre D'Alby. M, Charles Artesona; publicity, Max Eisen, Irene Gandy, Barbara Eisen, Judy Jacksina; stage mgrs, Daniel E Early, Karen Winer. Opened Nov. 1, '76, at the Playhouse, $14 top.
Rivka Raz, Ron Eliran, Ruthi Navon, Riki Gal, Hanan Goldblatt, Gail Benedict, Darleen Boudreaux, Donald Ronci, Karen DiBianco, Carla Farnsworth, David Kottke, Joel Robertson, Lisa Gould Rubin, Daniel Stewart, John Windsor.
Musical numbers: "Moonlight," "The World's Greatest Magical Act," "I Believe," "Only Love," "My Land," "We Love a Conference," "Come with Me," "Tired Heroes," "Have a Little Fun," "I Hear a Song," "I Live My Life in Color," "Young Days," "Somebody's Stepping on My Olive Branch," "It Was Worth It," "Jerusalem."
11/03/76B

The Double Dealer
National Theatre revival of a play in two acts by William Congreve. Staged, Peter Wood; set-cos, Tanya Moiseiwitsch; light, David Hersey. Opened Sept 27, '78, at the Olivier Theatre, London; $8.50 top.
John Harding, Dermot Crowley, Nicky Henson, Ralph Richardson, Michael Bryant, Nicholas Selby, Sara Kestelman, Robert Stephens, Judi Bowker, Brenda Blethyn, Dorothy Tutin, Craig Moss, Janet Whiteside, Daniel Thorndike, Dennis Tynsley, Ray Edwards, Alexander Allenby, Elliott Cooper, Adam Norton, Keith Skinner, Ian Anderson, Andrew Findon, Kevin Healey, Andrew Reed, David Roach, Henry Ward.
10/04/78B

Dracula
Jujamcyn Theatre, Elizabeth Ireland McCann, John Wulp, Victor Lurie, Nelle Nugent & Max Weitzenhoffer revival of a play in three acts, by Hamilton Deane, John L Balderston, based on Bram Stoker novel. Staged, Dennis Rosa; scenery-cos, Edward Gorey; scenery supv, Lynn Pecktal; cos supv, John David Ridge; light, Roger Morgan; prodn supv, John David Ridge. GM, Vincent Aleles; publicity, Solters & Roskin (Joshua Ellis, Milly Schoenbaum); company mgr, Susan Gustafson; stage mgrs, Charles Kindl, Tandy Cronyn. Opened Oct. 20, '77, at the Martin Beck Theatre; $15 top weeknights, $16.50 weekend nights.
Ann Sachs, Gretchen Oehler, Alan Coates, Dillon Evans, Jerome Dempsey, Richard Kavanaugh, Baxter Harris, Frank Langella.
10/26/77B

The Eccentricities of a Nightingale
Gloria Hope Sher, in ass'n with Neal Du Brock, presentation of a play in two acts (eight scenes and epilog) by Tennessee Williams. Staged, Edwin Sherin; scenery, William Ritman; cos, Theoni V Aldredge; light, Marc B Weiss; incidental mus, Charles Gross; produced in ass'n with Max W Jacobs. GM, C Edwin Knill; Seymour Krawitz, Louise Ment, Patricia M Krawitz; stage mgrs, Henry Banister, K Anna Moore. Opened Nov. 23, '76, at the Morosco Theatre; $12 top weeknights, $13.50 weekend nights.
Betsy Palmer, Shepperd Strudwick, Grace Carney, Nan Martin, David Selby, Peter Blaxill, Jen Jones, Patricia Guinan, W P Dremak, Thomas Stechschulte.
12/01/76B

The Effect of Gamma Rays on Man-in-the Moon Marigolds
Courtney Burr & Nancy Rosenthal rev of a play in two acts, by Paul Zindel. Staged, A J Antoon; sets-cos, Peter Harvey; light, Ian Calderon; incidental mus, Richard Peaslee; asso prods, William King, Charles Blum; prodn asso, Blossom Horrowitz. GM, Jerry Arrow; publicity, Max Eisen, Barbara Glenn; stage mgr, Murray Gitlin. Opened Mar 14, '78, at the Biltmore Theatre; $15 top weeknights, $16.50 weekend nights.
Carol Kane, Shelley Winters, Lori Shelle, Isabella Hoopes, Lolly Boroff.
03/22/78B

The Elephant Man
Richmond Crinkley, Elizabeth I McCann & Nelle Nugent presentation of an American National Theatre & Academy prodn of a play in two acts (21 scenes), by Bernard Pomerance. Staged, Jack Hofsiss; setting, David Jenkins; cos, Julie Weiss; light, Beverly Emmons; asso prods, Ray Larsen, Ted Snowdon. Publicity, Solters & Roskin (Joshua Ellis); company mgr, Susan Gustafson; prodn supv, Brent Peek; stage mgr, Pat De Rousie. Opened April 19, '79 at the Booth Theatre; $16.50 top weeknights, $18.50 weekend nights.
Kevin Conway, Richard Clarke, I M Hobson, Philip Anglim, John Neville-Andrews, Cordis Heard, Carole Shelley, Dannis Creaghan, David Heiss.
04/25/79B

Eubie
Ashton Springer, in ass'n with Frank C Pierson & Jay J Cohen, presentation of a revue in two acts (24 numbers), with mus, Eubie Blake, lyrs, Noble Sissle, Anzy Razaf, Johnny Brandon, FE Miller, Jim Europe. Conceived and staged, Julianne Boyd; musical supv-arrs, Danny Holgate; tap chor, Henry LeTang; musical staging, Billy Wilson; set, Karl Eigsti; cos, Bernard Johnson; light, William Mintzer; snd, Lou Gonzalez; choral arrs, Chapman Roberts; mus dir, Vicki Carter; prodn supv, Ron Abbott; assoc prod, John N Hart Jr; orchestrations, Neal Tate. Company mgr, Robert Ossenfort; stage mgrs, Clinton Turner Davis, Kimako, Terry Burrell; publicity, Max Eisen, Frances Trevens. Opened Sept 20, '78, at the Ambassador Theatre; $17.50 top weeknights, $20 weekend nights.
Ethel Beatty, Terry Burrell, Leslie Dockery, Lynnie Godfrey, Gregory Hines, Maurice Hines, Mel Johnson Jr, Lonnie McNeil, Janet Powell, Marion Ramsey, Alaina Reed, Jeffery V Thompson.
09/27/78B

Every Good Boy Deserves Favour
Kennedy Center & Metropolitan Opera presentation of a play for actors and orchestra, in one act by Tom Stoppard, with mus by Andre Previn; staged, Stoppard, from a concept by Trevor Nunn; settings-cos, Eldon Elder; light, Thomas Skelton; orch cond, David Gilbert; prod, Roger L Stevens; company mgr, John H Wilson; stage mgr, Mitchell

Every Good
(Cont)
Erickson; publicity, Marilynn LeVine, Alpert/LeVine. Opened July 30, '79 at the Metropolitan Opera House; $15 top.
Rene Auberjonois, Eli Wallach, Carol Teitel, Bobby Scott, Remak Ramsey, Carl Low.
08/01/79B

Evita
Robert Stigwood presentation, in assoc with David Land, of a mus in two acts (28 numbers), with lyrs by Tim Rice, mus, Andrew Lloyd Webber. Staged, Harold Prince; chor, Larry Fuller; orch, Hershy Kay, Andrew Lloyd Webber; mus dir, Rene Wiegert; scenery-cos, Timothy O'Brien, Tazeena Firth; light, David Hersey; snd, Abe Jacob; exec prods, R Tyler Gatchell Jr, Peter Neufeld. GM, Howard Haines; publicity, Mary Bryant, Patt Dale; company mgr, John Caruso; stage mgrs, George Martin, John Grigas, Andy Cadiff. Opened Sept. 25, '79, at the Broadway Theatre; $22.50 top weeknights; $25 weekend nights.
Patti LuPone, Terri Klausner (matinee alternate), Mandy Patinkin, Bob Gunton, Jane Ohringer, Mark Syers.
Argentine People: Seda Azarian, Dennis Birchall, Peppi Borza, Tom Carder, Robin Cleaver, Andy DeGange, Mark East, Teri Gill, Carlos Gorbea, Pat Gorman, Rex David Hays, Terri Klausner, Michael Lichtefield, Carol Lugenbeal, Paul Lynn, Morgan MacKay, Peter Marinos, Sal Mistretta, Jack Neubeck, Marcia O'Brien, Nancy Opel, Davia Sacks, James Sbano, David Staller, Michelle Stubbs, Robert Tanna, Clarence Teeters, Susan Terry, Phillip Tracy, David Vosburgh, Mark Waldrop, Sandra Wheeler, Brad Witsger, John Leslie Wolfe, Nancy Wood, John Yost.
Children: Megan Forste, Bridget Francis, Nicole Francis, Michael Pastryk, Christopher Wooten.
Musical numbers: "A Cinema In Buenos Aires: July 26, 1952," "Requiem for Evita," "Oh What a Circus," "On This Night of a Thousand Stars," "Eva Beware of the City," "Buenos Aires," "Goodnight and Thank You," "The Art of the Possible," "Charity Concert," "I'd Be Surprisingly Good for You," "Another Suitcase in Another Hall," "Peron's Latest Flame," "A New Argentina," Entr-Acte. "On the Balcony of the Casa Rosada," "Don't Cry for Me Argentina," "High Flying Adored," "Rainbow High," "Rainbow Tour," "The Actress Hasn't Learned (the lines you'd like to hear)," "And the Money Kept Rolling In (and out)," "Santa Evita," "Waltz for Eva and Che," "She Is a Diamond," "Dice Are Rolling," "Eva's Final Broadcast," "Montage," "Lament."
09/26/79B

Faith Healer
Morton Gottlieb presentation of a play in two acts (four scenes) by Brian Friel. Staged, Jose Quintero; set, John Lee Beatty; cos, Jane Greenwood; light, Marilyn Rennagel; asso prods, Ben Rosenberg, Warren Crane. GM, Ben Rosenberg, publicity, Solters & Roskin Inc (Milly Schoenbaum, Rima Corben); company mgr, Martin Cohen; stage mgrs, Warren Crane, John Handy. Opened Apr 5, '79, at the Longacre Theatre; $17.50 top weeknights, $19 weekend nights.
James Mason, Clarissa Kaye, Donal Donnelly.
04/11/79B

Fearless Frank
David Black & Robert Fabian, in ass'n with Oscar Lewenstein & Theodore P Donahue Jr, presentation of a musical comedy in two acts; book-lyrs, Andrew Davies; mus, Dave Brown. Staged, Robert Gillespie; mus staging, Michael Vernon; set, Martin Tilley; cos supv, Carrie F Robbins; light, Ruther Roberts; orchs, Michael Reed; mus dir-addl arrs, Michael Rose; GM, Theatre Now; publicity, Hunt-Pucci Associates; stage mgr, Larry Forde. Opened Jun 15, '80, at the Princess Theatre; $18.50 top weeknights, $20 Fri-Sat nights.
Niall Toibin, Alex Wipf, Valerie Mahaffey, Kristen Meadows, Steve Burney, Ann Hodapp, Olivier Pierre, Evalyn Baron.
Songs: - "The Man Who Made His Life Into a Work of Art," "The Examination Song," "Halted at the Very Gates of Paradise," "Come and Help Yourself to America," "Dandy Night Clerk," "Riding the Range," "Oh, Catch Me, Mr Harris, 'Cause I'm Falling," "My Poor Wee Lassie," "Evening News," "Le Maitre de Comte," "Oh, Mr Harris, You're a Naughty, Naughty Man," "Free Speech, Free Throught, Free Love," "Mr Harris, It's All Over Now," "Fearless Frank."
06/18/80B

Fiddler on the Roof
Shubert Organization, Nederlander Producing Co & John F Kennedy Center for the Performing Arts revival, in ass'n with Theatre Now, of a musical in two acts (16 numbers); book, Joseph Stein; mus, Jerry Bock; lyr, Sheldon Harnick; based on stories by Sholem Aleichem. Staged-chor, Jerome Robbins; re-produced, Ruth Mitchell; chor reproduced, Tom Abbott; set, Boris Aronson; cos, Patricia Zipprodt; light, Ken Billington; orchs, Don Alker; vocal arrs, Milton Greene; dance mus arrs, Betty Walberg; mus dir, Milton Rosenstock. GMs, William Court Cohen, Edward H Davis, Norman E Rothstein; publicity, Betty Lee Hunt, Maria Pucci; company mgr, Robb Lady; stage mgrs, Kenneth Porter, Tobias Mostel, Val Mayer, Wallace C Munro. Opened Dec. 28, '76, at the Winter Garden Theatre; $20 top.
Zero Mostel, Thelma Lee, Elizabeth Hale, Christopher Callan, Nancy Tompkins, Davia Sacks, Tiffany Bogart, Ruth Jaroslow, Irwin Pearl, Jeff Keller, Leon Spelman, Paul Lipson, Charles Mayer, Paul A Corman, Merrill Plaskow II, David Masters, Duane Bodin, Joyce Martin, Alexander Orfaly, Rick Friesen, Jeanne Grant, Tog Richards, Myron Curtis, Matthew Inge, Sammy Bayes, Don Tull, Glen McClaskey, Wallace Munro, Lynn Archer, David Horwitz, Patrick Quinn, Hope Katcher, Debra Timmons, Maureen Sadusky, Robert L Hultman, and Shelley Wolf.
Musical Numbers: "Tradition," "Matchmaker, Matchmaker," "If I Were a Rich Man," "Sabbath Prayer," "To Life," "Miracle of Miracles," "The Tailor, Motel Kamzoil," "Sunrise, Sunset," "Bottle Dance," "Wedding Dance," "Now I Have Everything," "Do You Love Me," "Far From the Home I Love," "Chava," "Anatevka," Epilog.
01/12/77B

Fifth of July
Jerry Arrow, Robert Lussier, Warner Theatres Inc, presentation of a play in two acts, by Lanford Wilson. Staged, Marshall W Mason; set, John Lee Beatty; cos, Laura Crow; light, Dennis Parichy; snd, Chuck London; GM, Belbrook Management; publicity, Max Eisen, Barbara Glenn; stage mgrs, Fred Reinglas, Jody Boese. Opened Nov 5, '80, at the Apollo Theatre; $22.50 top weeknights, $25 weekend nights.
Christopher Reeve, Jeff Daniels, Jonathan Hogan, Swoosie Kurtz, Joyce Reehling, Amy Wright, Mary Carver, Danton Stone.
11/12/80B

Filumena
Danny O'Donovan & Helen Montagu in ass'n with Mecca Prodns, presentation of a Franco Zeffirelli prod of a play in three acts, by Eduardo de Filippo, adapt, Keith Waterhouse, Willis Hall. Staged, Laurence Olivier; scenery-cos, Raimonda Gaetani; light, Thomas Skelton; GM, Theatre Now; publicity, Seymour Krawitz, Patricia Krawitz; company mgr, Terence Erkkila; stage mgrs, Larry Forde, Robert Rigamonti, Dorie Don Vito. Opened Feb 10, '80, at the St James Theatre; $17.50 top weeknights, $19.50 weekend nights.
Joan Plowright, Frank Finlay, Ernest Sarracino, Miriam Phillips, Gabor Morea, Bill Karnovsky, Donna Davis, Lisa Passero, Pierre Epstein, Dennis Boutsikaris, Stephen Schnetzer, Peter Iacangelo.
02/13/80B

First Monday In October
The Kennedy Center & Plumstead Theatre Society Inc (Martha Scott, Joel Spector, Bernard Wiesen) presentation of a play in two acts, by Jerome Lawrence and Robert E Lee. Staged by Edwin Sherin; set, Oliver Smith; light, Roger Morgan; cos, Ann Roth. Gen Management, Theatre Now Inc; publicity, John Springer, Louis Sica; stage mgrs, Frederic de Wilde, Robert Crawley, John Stewart, Eugene Stuckmann. Opened Oct 3, '78, at the Majestic Theatre; $18.00 top weeknights; $20 weekend nights.
John Stewart, P J Sidney, Larry Gates, Earl Sydnor, Maurice Copeland, Henry Fonda, John Wardwell, John Newton, Jane Alexander, Tom Stechschulte, Alexander Reed, Eugene Stuckmann, Patrick McCullough, Carol Mayo Jenkins, Ron Faber.
10/04/78B

For Colored Girls Who Have Considered Suicide/When the Rainbow is Enuf
Joseph Papp & Woodie King Jr presentation of a N Y Shakespeare Festival prodn, in ass'n with the Henry Street Settlement's New Federal Theatre, of a revue in one act, by Ntozake Shange. Staged, Oz Scott; scenery, Ming Cho Lee; light, Jennifer Tipton; cos, Judy Dearing; chor, Paula Moss; mus for song, "I Found God in Myself," Diana Wharton. GM, Robert Kamlot; publicity, Merle Debuskey, Leo Stern; company mgr, Robert Frissell; stage mgrs, John Beven, Fai Walker-Davis. Opened Sept. 15, '76, at the Booth Theatre; $11 top weeknights, $12 weekend nights.
Janet League, Aku Kadogo, Trazana Bever-

For Colored
(Cont)
ley, Paula Moss, Rise Collins, Laurie Carlos, Ntozake Shange.
09/22/76B

42d Street
David Merrick presentation of a musical in two acts (16 scenes, 17 numbers); songs, Harry Warren, Al Dubin; book, Michael Stewart, Mark Bramble; based on a novel by Bradford Ropes. Staged-chor, Gower Champion; scenery, Robin Wagner; cos, Theoni V Aldredge; light, Tharon Musser; mus dir-vocal arrs, John Lesko; orchs, Philip J Lang; dance mus arrs, Donald Johnston; snd, Richard Fitzgerald; GM, Helen L Nickerson; publicity, Fred Nathan; company mgr, Louise M Bayer; stage mgrs, Steve Zweigbaum, Arturo E Porazzi, Jane E Neufeld. Opened Aug 25, '80, at the Winter Garden Theatre; $25 top weekday nights, $30 weekend nights.

Danny Carroll, Robert Colston, Stan Page, Karen Prunczik, Carole Cook, Joseph Bova, Lee Roy Reams, Wanda Richert, Ginny King, Jeri Kansas, Jerry Orbach, Tammy Grimes, Dan Crabtree, James Congdon, Ron Schwinn, Bill Nabel, Stan Page.

Ensemble: - Carrole Banninger, Steve Belin, Robin Black, Joel Blum, Mary Cadorette, Ronny DeVito, Denise DiRenzi, Mark Dovey, Rob Draper, Brandt Edwards, Jon Engstrom, Sharon Ferrol, Cathy Greco, Dawn Herbert, Christine Jacobson, Teri Ann Kundrat, Shan Martin, Beth McVey, Maureen Mellon, Sandra Menhart, Bill Nabel, Tony Parise, Don Percassi, Jean Preece, Vicki Regan, Lars Rosager, Linda Sabatelli, Nikki Sahagen, Yvelin Semeria, Alison Sherve, Robin Stephens, David Storey, Karen Tamburrelli.

Musical numbers: - "Audition," "Young and Healthy," "Shadow Waltz," "Shadow Waltz" (reprise), "Go Into Your Dance," "You're Getting to Be a Habit with Me," "Getting Out of Town," "Dames," "I Know Now," "I Know Now" (reprise), "We're in the Money," "Sunny Side to Every Situation," "Lullaby of Broadway," "About a Quarter to Nine," "Overture," "Shuffle Off to Buffalo," "42d Street," "42d Street" (reprise).
08/27/80B

G. R. Point
Robert Fishko, Rick Hobard, Donald Warfield presentation of a drama in two acts by David Berry. Staged, William Devane; settings, Peter Larkin; light, Neil Peter Jampolis, Jane Reisman; company mgr, Harris Goldman; stage mgrs, Michael Frank, Johnny Willis; publicity, Milly Schoenbaum, Rima Corben. Opened April 16, '79 at the Playhouse Theatre; $16 top weeknights, $17.50 weekend nights.
Lazaro Perez, Howard Rollins Jr, Michael Jeter, Michael Moriarty, Mark Jenkins, Paul Espel, Mansoor Majee-Ullah, Lori Tan Chinn.
04/18/79B

Gemini
Jerry Arrow and Jay Broad representing Circle Repertory Company and PAF Playhouse presentation of a play in two acts by Albert Innaurato. Staged, Peter Mark Schifter; set, Christopher Nowak; cos, Ernest Allen Smith; light, Larry Crimmins; snd, Leslie A DeWeerdt Jr; Broadway prodn supv, Marshall W Mason; GM, Jerry Arrow; publicity, Rima Corben; stage mgr, Fred Reinglas. Opened May 20, '77, at the Little Theatre; $12 top.
Robert Picardo, Jessica James, Reed Birney, Carol Potter, Jonathan Hadary, Danny Aiello, Anne DeSalvo.
05/25/77B

The Gin Game
Shubert Organization presentation of a Hume Cronyn & Mike Nichols prodn of a play in two acts (four scenes), by D L Coburn. Staged, Mike Nichols; set, David Mitchell; cos, Bill Walker; light, Ronald Wallace. GMs, Elizabeth McCann, Nelle Nugent; company mgr, James Mennen; publicity, David Powers, Barbara Carroll; stage mgrs, Nina Seely, William Chance. Opened Oct. 6, '77, at the John Golden Theatre; $16 top weeknights, $17.50 weekend nights and opening.
Jessica Tandy, Hume Cronyn.
10/12/77B

Godspell
Edgar Lansbury, Stuart Duncan, Joseph Beruh & the Shubert Organization presentation of a musical in two acts (16 numbers); conceived-staged, John-Michael Tebelak; mus-lyr, Stephen Schwartz; light, Spencer Mosse; cos, Susan Tsu; prodn supv, Nina Faso; mus dir, Steve Reinhardt; snd, Robert Minor; asso prod, Charles Haid. GM, Marvin A Krauss Associates; publicity, Gifford-Wallace; exec supv, Al J Isaac, Gary Gunas; stage mgrs, Michael J Frank, Kitty Rea; adv, Blaine Thompson (Matthew Serino). Opened June 22, '76, at the Broadhurst Theatre; $13.50 top.
Lamar Alford, Laurie Faso, Lois Foraker, Robin Lamont, Elizabeth Lathram, Bobby Lee, Tom Rolfing, Don Scardino, Marley Sims, Valerie Williams.

Musical numbers: "Tower of Babble," "Prepare Ye the Way of the Lord," "Save the People," "Day by Day," "Learn Your Lessons Well," "Bless the Lord," "All for the Best," "All Good Gifts," "Light of the World," "Learn Your Lessons Well" (reprise), "Turn Back, O Man," "Alas for You," "By My Side," (lyr, Jay Hamburger, mus, Peggy Gordon), "We Beseech Thee," "On the Willows," Finale.
06/30/76B

Going Up
Ashton Springer, William Callahan, Stephens-Weitzenhoffer Prodns, in ass'n with Stephen R Friedman & Irwin Meyer, presentation of Goodspeed Opera House revival of a musical in two acts (four scenes, 16 numbers); book-lyr, Otto Harbach; mus, Louis A Hirsch, based on James Montgomery's play, "The Aviator." Staged, Billy Gile; chor-mus staging, Dan Siretta; mus dir-vocal arrs, Lynn Crigler; cos, David Toser; scenery-light supv, Edward Haynes; light, Peter M Ehrhardt; special cnsltnt, Alfred Simon; mus arr, Russell Warner. GM, Susan Chase; company mgr, Gino Giglio; publicity, Max Eisen, Irene Gandy, Barbara Glenn; stage mgrs, Ron Abbott, Larry McMillian. Opened Sept. 19, '76, at the Booth Theatre; $15 top.
Pat Lysinger, Calvin McRae, Larry Hyman, Stephen Bray, Kimberly Farr, Lee H Doyle, Michael Tartel, Walter Bobbie, Maureen Brennan, Noel Craig, Brad Blaisdell, Ronn Robinson, James Bontempo, Deborah Crowe, Michael Gallagher, Teri Gill, Barbara McKinley.

Musical numbers: "Paging Mr. Street," "I Want a Determined Boy," "If You Look in Her Eyes," "Going Up," "Hello, Frisco" (lyr, Gene Buck; from "The Ziegfeld Follies of 1915), "Down, Up, Left, Right," "Kiss Me," "The Tickle Toe," "Brand New Hero," "I'll Think of You" (lyr, Rennold Wolf; from "The Rainbow Girl"--1917-18), "I'll Think of You" (reprise), "Do It for Me," "My Sumurun Girl" (lyr, Al Jolson; from "The Whirl of Society"--1911-12), "Going Up" (reprise), "Down, Up, Left, Right" (reprise), "The Tickle Toe" (reprise).
09/22/76B

Golda
Theatre Guild presentation of Philip Langner, Armina Marshall & Marilyn Langner prodn of a play in two acts, by William Gibson, based on "My Life," the autobiography of Golda Meir. Staged, Arthur Penn; scenery-cos, Santo Loquasto; light-projections, Jules Fisher; visuals, Lucie D Grosvenor. GM, Victor Samrock; publicity, Joe Wolhandler, Peter Wolhandler, Sylvia Perchuk; stage mgrs, Andre St Jean, Wayne Carson, Peter Dowling. Opened Nov. 14, '77, at the Morosco Theatre; $18 top.
Anne Bancroft, James Tolkan, Richard Kuss, Ben Hammer, Nicholas La Padula, Harry Davis, Sam Schacht, Vivian Nathan, Zack Matalon, Frances Chaney, Justine Lichtman, Alice Golembo, Gerald Hiken, Ernest Graves, Eric Booth, Phillip Cates, Corinne Neuchateau, Sam Gray, Josh Freund, Michael Brown, Glenn Scarpelli, Rebecca Schull, David C Jones, Robert Levine, Judy Unger.
11/16/77B

Goodbye, Fidel
Martin Richards, Mary Lea Johnson & Bill Barnes, in ass'n with Sam Crothers & Allen Litke, presentation of a play in two acts (seven scenes) by Howard Sackler; staged, Edwin Sherin; scenery, Rouben Ter-Arutunian; cos, Florence Klotz; light, Toshiro Agawa; snd, Jack Shearing; GMs, R Tyler Gatchell Jr, Peter Neufeld; publicity, Betty Lee Hunt, Maria Cristina Pucci; prodn asso, Joel Brykman; stage mgrs, Steve Zweigbaum, Jonathan Penzner, Tony Diaz, Suzanne Toren. Opened Apr 23, '80, at the Ambassador Theatre; $20 top weeknights, $22.50 weekend nights.
Ralph Byers, Jane Alexander, Lee Richardson, Concetta Tomei, David Schramm, Curt Karibalis, Stephanie Cotsirlos, Kathy Bates, Tony Diaz, Guy Sorel, Gale Sondergaard, Florence Anglin, Christopher Cazenove, Pamela Brook, Raymundo Hidalgo-Gato, Arnaldo Santana, Vera Lockwood, Suzanne Toren, Bernie Passeltiner, Ivonne Coll.
04/30/80B

The Goodbye People
Joseph Kipness & Maurice Rosenfield revival of a play in two acts, by Herb Gardner. Staged, Jeff Bleckner; setting, Santo Loquasto; light, Jennifer Tipton; cos, Elizabeth Palmer; asso prods, Charlotte Dicker, Jamie Rosenfield. GM, Marvin A Krauss; publicity, the Merlin Group (Becky Flora); company

The Goodbye
(Cont)
mgr, Gary Gunas; stage mgrs, Fritz Holt, Judy Shafran. Opened April 30, '79 at the Belasco Theatre; $16 top weeknights, $17.50 weekend nights.
Ron Rifkin, Herschel Bernardi, Melanie Mayron, Marvin Lichterman, Michael Tucker, Sammy Smith.
05/02/79B

Gorey Stories
Terry Allen Kramer, Harry Rigby, Hale Matthews & John Wulp presentation of a two-part performance of 18 sketches with music, based on illustrated stories by Edward Gorey; adapted, Stephen Currens; score, David Aldrich. Staged, Tony Tanner; scenery supv, Lynn Pecktal; cos supv, David Murin; light, Roger Morgan; mus dir, Martin Silvestri. GMs, Jack Schlissel, Jay Kingwell; publicity, Henry Luhrman, Anne Obert Weinberg, Terry M Lilly; company mgr, Alan Wasser; stage mgrs, Franklin Keysar, Beth Prevor. Opened Oct 30, '78, at the Booth Theatre; $18.50 top weeknights, $20 weekend nights.
Gemze de Lappe, Sel Vitella, Julie Kurnitz, June Squibb, Leon Shaw, John Michalaski, Tobias Haller, Dennis McGovern, Susan Marchand.
11/01/78B

Got Tu Go Disco
Jerry Brandt & Gotta Dance Inc presentation of a musical in two acts (12 scenes, 16 numbers), with book by John Zodrow, mus-lyr, Kenny Lehman, John Davis, Ray Chew, Nat Adderley Jr, Thomas Jones, Wayne Morrison, Steve Boston, Eugene Narmore, Betty Rowland, Jerry Powell, Ashford & Simpson. Staged, Larry Forde; chor, Jo Jo Smith, Troy Garza; scenery, James Hamilton; light, Bobby Monk; cos, Joe Eula; mus supv-dir, Kenny Lehman, vocal dir, Kenny Lehman, Mitch Kerper; film seq, Robert Rabinowitz; snd, Lenny Will; prod in ass'n with Roy Rifkind, Julie Rifkind, Bill Spitalsky & WKTU Radio 92. GM, William Court Cohen, Edward H Davis, Norman E Rothstein, Ralph Roseman; publicity, Owen Levy-Valerie Warner, Connie DeNave; company mgr, Robb Lady; stage mgrs, Michael Turque, Arlene Grayson, John Fennessy, Les Magerman. Opened June 25, '79 at the Minskoff Theatre; $23 top weeknights, $25 weekend nights.
Irene Cara, Lisa Raggio, Rhetta Hughes, Laurie Dawn Skinner, Charlie Serrano, Gerri Griffen, Robin Lynn Beck, Patrick Jude, Justin Ross, Patti Karr, Jane Holzer, Joe Masiell, Marc Benecke, Bob Pettie.
Singers, dancers:- Gloria Covington, Jack Magradey, Billy Newton-David, Connie Marie Brazelton, Prudence Darby, Ronald Dunham, Miguel Gonz, Christine Jacobsen, Peter Kapetan, Jodi Moccia, Patrick Kinzer-Lau, Bronna Lipton, Mark Manley, Jamie Patterson, Dee Ranzweiler, Adrian Rosario, Willie Rosario, Sue Samuels, Julia Lema, Tony Constantine.
Musical numbers:- "Puttin' It On," "Disco Shuffle," "All I Need," "It Won't Work," "Trust Me," "In and Out," "Pleasure Pusher," "If That Didn't Do It, It Can't Be Done," "Hanging Over and Out," "Chic to Cheap," "Bad, Glad, Good and Had," "Cassie," "Takin' the Light," "Gettin' to the Top," "Dance Forever," "Got Tu Go Disco."
06/27/79B

The Grand Kabuki
Kazuko, Hillyer International, Inc. presentation with the assistance of the Japan Foundation; Prodn, Shochiku Co, Tokyo. Stage dir, Takeshiba Norio; GMs, Imai Masahiko, Suzuki Masako; stage mgr, Toshi Ogawa; company mgr, David Shapiro; publicity, Gurtman & Murtha. Opened Aug. 31, '77, at the Beacon Theatre.
Ennosuke Ichikawa III.
09/14/77B

The Grand Tour
James M Nederlander, Diana Shumlin, Jack Schlissel, in ass'n with Carol J Shorenstein & Stewart F Lane, presentation of a musical in two acts (13 scenes, 17 numbers), with mus-lyr by Jerry Herman; book by Michael Stewart and Mark Bramble, based on the original play, "Jacobowsky and the Colonel," by Franz Werfel, and the American comedy by S N Behrman. Staged, Gerald Freedman; chor, Donald Saddler; settings, Ming Cho Lee; cos, Theoni V Aldredge; light, Martin Aronstein; mus dir, Wally Harper; orch, Philip J Lang; dance mus arr, Peter Howard; vocal arr, Donald Pippin. GM, Jack Schlissel, Jay Kingwill; asso mgr, Charles Willard; publicity, Betty Lee Hunt, Maria Cristina Pucci; stage mgrs, Mary Porter Hall, Richard Elkow, Marc Schlackman, Debra Lyman. Opened Jan 11, '79, at the Palace Theatre; $20 top weeknights, $22.50 weekend nights.
Joel Grey, Grace Keagy, Jack Karcher, Mark Waldrop, Ron Holgate, Stephen Vinovich, Stan Page, George Reinholt, Chevi Colton, Florence Lacey, Gene Varrone, Travis Hudson, Kenneth Kantor, Jay Pierce, Jay Stuart, Jo Speros, Michelle Marshall, Bob Morrisey, Bjarne Buchtrup, Carol Dorian, Debra Lyman, Tina Paul, Linda Poser, Theresa Rakov, Paul Solen, Jeff Veazey, Bonnie Young, Bronna Lipton, Jeff Richards.
Musical numbers: "I'll Be Here Tomorrow," "For Poland," "I Belong Here," "Marianne," "We're Almost There," "Marianne" (reprise), "More and More, Less and Less," "One Extraordinary Thing," "One Extraordinary Thing" (reprise), "Mrs S L Jacobowsky," "Wedding Conversation," "Mazeltov," "I Think, I Think," "For Poland" (reprise), "You I Like," "I Belong Here" (reprise), "I'll Be Here Tomorrow" (reprise).
01/17/79B

Guys and Dolls
Moe Septee, in ass'n with Victor H Potamkin, revival of a musical in two acts (18 scenes, 20 numbers); mus-lyr, Frank Loesser; book, Jo Swerling, Abe Burrows, based on a story and characters by Damon Runyon. Staged-chor, Billy Wilson; scenery, Tom H John; cos, Bernard Johnson; light, Thomas Skelton; arrs-orchs, Danny Holgate, Horace Ott; mus dir-choral arr, Howard Roberts; snd, Sander Hacker; asso prods, Ashton Springer, Carmen F Zollo; prodn supv, Abe Burrows. GM, Laurel Ann Wilson; promotion cnsltnt, Norman Kean; publicity, Max Eisen, Barbara Glenn; company mgr, Donald Tirabassi; stage mgr, R Derek Swire, Clinton Jackson, Bonnie Sue Schloss; adv, Blaine Thompson agency (Matthew Serino). Opened July 21, '76, at the Broadway Theatre; $13 top weeknights, $15 weekend nights.
Ken Page, Christophe Pierre, Sterling McQueen, Ernestine Jackson, John Russell, Clark Morgan, Robert Guillaume, Jymie Charles, Norma Donaldson, James Randolph, Emett "Babe" Wallace, Irene Datcher, Bardell Conner, Marion Moore, Derrick Bell, Andy Torres, Prudence Darby, Edye Byrde, Walter White.
Singers, dancers: Toney Brealond, Nathan Jennings Jr, Bill Mackey, Eddie Wright Jr, Jacquelyn DuBois, Anna Maria Fowlkes, Helen Gelzer, Julia Lema, Jacqueline Smith-Lee.
07/28/76B

Hair
Michael Butler, in ass'n with K H Nezhad, revival of a musical in two acts (30 numbers); book-lyr, Gerome Ragni, James Rado; mus, Galt MacDermot. Staged, Tom O'Horgan; chor, Julie Arenal; asso prod, George Milman; scenery, Robin Wagner; light, Jules Fisher; cos, Nancy Potts; snd, Abe Jacob; mus dir, Denzil A Miller Jr; vocal dir, Patrick Flynn; GM, Eugene V Wolsk; publicity, Gifford-Wallace (Eileen McMahon); company mgr, Steven Suskin; stage mgrs, J Galen McKinley, Seth M M Sternberg, Eva Charney. Opened Aug. 4, '77 (press opening, Oct. 5, '77), at the Biltmore Theatre; $16.50 top weeknights, $20 weekend nights.
Randall Easterbrook, Michael Hoit, Scott Thornton, Cleavant Derricks, Ellen Foley, Iris Rosenkrantz, Alaina Reed, Kristen Vigard, Michael Leslie, Annie Golden, Louis Mattioli, Perry Arthur, James Rich, Eva Charney, Martha Wingate, Carl Woerner, Linda Myers, Byron Utley, Lori Wagner, James Rich, Emily Bindinger, Paul Binotto, Loretta Devine, Doug Katsaros, Raymond Paterson, James Sbano, Deborah Van Valkenburgh, Doug Wall, Charlaine Woodard.
Musical numbers: "Aquarius," "Donna," "Hashish," "Sodomy," "Colored Spade," "Manchester," "Ain't Got No," "Dead End," "I Believe in Love," "Air," "Initials," "I Got Life," "Going Down," "Hair," "My Conviction," "Easy to Be Hard," "Don't Put It Down," "Frank Mills," "Be-In," "Where Do I Go," "Electric Blues," "White Boys," "White Boys" (reprise), "Walking in Space," "Abie Baby," "Three-Five-Zero-Zero," "What a Piece of Work Is Man," "Good Morning Starshine," "The Bed," "The Flesh Failures."
10/12/77B

Happy End
Michael Harvey and The Chelsea Theatre Center (Robert Kalfin, artistic dir; Michael David, exec dir) presentation of a musical revival in two acts; mus, Kurt Weill; lyr, Bertolt Brecht; orig German play, Elisabeth Hauptmann; book-lyr adapt, Michael Feingold; Chelsea Theatre Center prodn newly conceived, Robert Kalfin. Staged, Robert Kalfin, Patricia Birch. Scenery, Robert U Taylor; cos, Carrie F Robbins; light, Jennifer Tipton; mus dir, Roland Gagnon; asso prod, Wilder Luke Burnap; stage mgrs, Mark Wright, Charles Kindl, Christopher Cara; GM, Jack Schlissel, Jay Kingwell; publicity, Susan Bloch. Opened May 16, '77, at the Martin Beck Theatre; $16 top weeknights, $17.50

Happy End
(Cont)
weekend night.

Christopher Lloyd, Benjamin Rayson, Tony Azito, John A Coe, Robert Weil, Raymond J Barry, Grayson Hall, Donna Emmanuel, Meryl Streep, Liz Sheridan, Joe Grifasi, Prudence Wright Holmes, Alexandra Borrie, Christopher Cara, Kristin Jolliff, Frank Kopyc, Tom Mardirosian, Martha Miller, Victor Pappas, David Pursley.

Songs: Prologue, "The Bilbao Song," "Lieutenants of the Lord," "March Ahead," "The Sailors' Tango," "Brother, Give Yourself A Shove," "Song of the Big Shot," "Don't Be Afraid," "In Our Childhood's Bright Endeavor," "The Liquor Dealer's Dream," "The Mandalay Song," "Surabaya Johnny," "Song of the Big Shot" (reprise), "Ballad of the Lily of Hell," "The Happy End" (finale).
06/08/77B

Happy New Year
Leonard Soloway, Allan Francis & Hale Matthews, in ass'n with Marble Arch Prodns, presentation of a musical in two acts (26 numbers), with book adapted by Burt Shevelove from Philip Barry's play, "Holiday," and songs by Cole Porter; edtr, Buster Davis; staged, Burt Shevelove; chor, Donal Saddler; scenery, Michael Egan; cos des, Pierre Balmain; cos supv, John Falabella; light, Ken Billington; snd, Tom Morse; asso prod, Dorothy Cherry; GMs, Leonard Soloway, Allan Francis; publicity, Sherley Herz, Jan Greenberg; prodn supv, David Taylor; stage mgrs, Nina Seely, Zane Weiner, Alan Mann. Opened Apr 27, '80, at the Morosco Theatre; $22.50 top weeknights, $25 weekend nights.

John McMartin, William Roerick, Richard Bekins, Kimberly Farr, Leslie Denniston, Michael Scott.

Seton Servants, Stork Club Set: - Roger Hamilton, Morgan Ensminger, J Thomas Smith, Tim Flavin, Richard Christopher, Lara Teeter, Lauren Goler, Mary Sue Finnerty, Bobbie Nord, Michelle Marshall.

Musical numbers: - "At Long Last Love," "Ridin' High," "Let's Be Buddies," "Boy, Oh, Boy," "East to Love," "You Do Something to Me," "Red, Hot and Blue," "Once Upon a Time," "Night and Day," "Let's Make It a Night," "Ours," "After You, Who?" "I Am Loved," "When Your Troubles Have Started."

Incidental numbers: - "Just One of Those Things," "It's De-Lovely," "Take Me Back to Manhattan," "Make It Another Old-Fashioned, Please," "They Couldn't Compare to You," "You've Got That Thing," "Every Time We Say Goodbye," "Let's Do It," "Where Have You Been?" "Let's Fly Away," "Girls," "What Is This Thing Called Love?"
04/30/80B

Harold and Maude
Frank Milton & Max Weitzenhoffer, in ass'n with Courtney Burr & Nancy Rosenthal, presentation of a play in two acts by Colin Higgins. Staged, Robert Lewis; scenery, Tony Straiges; cos, Florence Klotz; light, Neil Peter Jampolis; snd, Otts Munderloh; sfx, Chic Silber; mus-lyrs-snds, David Amram. GM, Richard Horner Associates; publicity, Solters & Roskin; company mgr, Malcolm Allen; stage mgrs, Ben Strobach, Valentine Mayer, Douglas Bergman. Opened Feb 7, '80, at the Martin Beck Theatre; $18.50 top weeknights, $20 weekend nights.

Keith McDermott, Ruth Ford, Berit Lagerwall, Chet Doherty, Janet Gaynor, Jack Bittner, Frank Ammirati, Denny Dillon, Jay Barney, Marc Jordan, Nonnie Weaver, Nita Novy, Valentine Mayer, Doug Bergman.

Mourners- Doug Bergman, Brian Brownlee, Catherine Bruno.
02/13/80B

Heartaches of a Pussycat
Kim d'Estainville presentation of a Group TSE prodn of a comic fantasy with incidental mus in two acts by Genevieve Serreau and James Lord, based on a story by Honore de Balzac and inspired by the drawings of J J Granville; staged, Alfredo Rodriguez Arias; masks, Rostislav Dobouninsy; cos, Claudie Gastine; set, Emilio Carcano; light, Beverly Emmons; orig light dsgn, Andre Diot; mus dir, Michel Sanvoisin; chor, Marilu Marini; asso prod, Jack Schlissel; GMs, Jack Schlissel, Jay Kingwill; publicity, Jeffrey Richards Asso; stage mgrs, Robert LoBianco, Jane E Neufeld; company mgr, Larry Goossen. Opened Mar 19, '80, at the ANTA Theatre; $18.50 top weeknights, $19.50 weekend nights.

Amelie Berg, Facundo Bo, Jean Jacques Guerolt, Larry Hager, Raquel Iruzunbieta, Zobeida Jaua, Jacques Jolivet, Marilu Marini, Jerome Nicolin, Horacio Pedrazzini, Joachin Riano, Alain Salomon.
03/26/80B

The Heiress
Steven Beckler & Thomas C Smith Revival of a play in two acts (seven scenes) by Ruth and Augustus Goetz, based on Henry James novel, "Washington Square." Produced for the Kennedy Center by Roger L Stevens and Richmond Crinkley, Kennedy Center and Xerox Corp. Staged, George Keathley; scenery, Oliver Smith; cos, Ann Roth; light, David F Segal; asso prod, Ken Morse. GM, Theatre Now, Inc., Edward H Davis, William C Cohen; publicity, Betty Lee Hunt, Maria Cristina Pucci; stage mgr, Joe Lorden; adv, Blaine Thompson (Matthew Serino). Opened April 20, '76, at the Broadhurst Theatre; $12 top weeknights, $13.50 weekend nights.

Sharon Laughlin, Richard Kiley, Jan Miner, Jane Alexander, Dorothy Blackburn, Roger Baron, Cecilia Hart, David Selby, Toni Darnay, William Gibberson.
04/28/76B

Hello, Dolly!
James M Nederlander & Houston Grand Opera revival of a musical in two acts (11 scenes, 16 numbers); book, Michael Stewart; mus-lyr, Jerry Herman, based on Thornton Wilder play, "The Matchmaker." Staged, Lucia Victor, from the orig chor staged, Gower Champion; chor, Jack Craig; scenery, Oliver Smith; cos, Freddy Wittop; light, Martin Aronstein; prodn supv, Jerry Herman; mus dir, John L DeMain; asso prod, Robert Buckley; dance-incidental mus arrs, Peter Howard. GM, Jack Schlissel, Jay Kingwill; publicity, Solters & Roskin (Milly Schoenbaum, Fred Nathan); company mgr, Morry Efron; stage mgrs, Pat Tolson, T L Boston, Judith Binus. Opened Mar 5, '78, at the Lunt-Fontanne Theatre; $16.50 top weeknights, $17.50 weekend nights.

Carol Channing, P J Nelson, Michael C Booker, Debra Pigliavento, Eddie Bracken, K T Baumann, Lee Roy Reams, Robert Lydiard, Alexandra Korey, Florence Lacey, Marilyn Hudgins, John Anania, Bill Bateman, Randolph Riscol.

Townspeople etc: Diane Abrams, JoEla Flood, Deborah Moldow, Janyce Nyman, Jacqueline Payne, Theresa Rakov, Barbara Ann Thompson, Richard Ammon, Kyle Cittadin, Ron Crofoot, Don Edward Detrick, Richard Dodd, Bob Draper, David Evans, Tom Garrett, Charlie Goeddertz, James Homan, Alex MacKay, Richard Maxon, Randy Morgan, Mark Waldrop, Coby Grossbart, Bubba Rambo.

Musical numbers: "I Put My Hand In," "It Takes a Woman," "Put on Your Sunday Clothes," "Put On Your Sunday Clothes" (reprise), "Ribbons Down My Back," "Motherhood," "Dancing," "Before the Parade Passes By," "Elegance," "The Waiters' Gallop," "Hello, Dolly!," "The Polka Contest," "It Only Takes a Moment," "So Long Dearie," "Hello, Dolly!" (reprise), "Finale."
03/08/78B

Herzl
Dore Schary presentation of a play in two acts (multi-scene), by Dore Schary and Amos Elon. Staged, J Ranelli; set, Douglas W Schmidt; cos, Pearl Somner; light, John Gleason. GM, Eugene V Wolsk; company mgr, Gino Giglio; publicity, John Springer Associates (Louis Sica, Suzanne Salter); stage mgrs, Frank Marino, Judith Binus. Opened Nov. 30, '76, at the Palace Theatre; $13.50 top weeknights, $15 weekend nights.

Paul Hecht, Louis Zorich, Stephan Mark Weyte, William Kiehl, John Michalski, Leo Bloom, Roy K Stevens, Linda Selman, Jack Axelrod, Eunice Anderson, Roger DeKoven, Judith Light, Rebecca Schull, Ralph Byers, Mitchell Jason, Richard Seff, Ellen Tovatt, Lester Rawlins, David Tress, Saylor Creswell.
12/08/76B

Hide and Seek
Michael Frazier & Bill McCutchen, in ass'n with Susan Madden Samson, presentation of a play in two acts (six scenes), Lezley Havard; staged, Melvin Bernhardt; set, John Lee Beatty; light, Arden Fingerhut; cos, Jennifer von Mayrhauser; snd, Gary Harris; GM, Theatre Now Inc; publicity, Betty Lee Hunt, Maria Cristina Pucci; stage mgrs, Frank Harenstein, Robert Townsend. Opened May 4, '80, at the Belasco Theatre; $20 top weeknights, $22.50 weekend nights.

Elizabeth Ashley, Peter Crombie, Sylvia Short, David Ackroyd, Christine Baranski, Tom Klunis, Alexandra Borrie, Michael Ayr, Robert Gerringer, Dana Barron.
05/07/80B

H.M.S Pinafore
Staged, Michael Heyland; set, Disley Jones; backdrop painted by Joseph and Phil Harker. Opened May 16, '76 at the Uris Theatre.

John Reed, Michael Rayner, Meston Reid, John Ayldon, Jon Ellison, Michael Buchan, Barbara Lilley, Patricia Leonard, Lyndsie Holland.
05/19/76B

Home

Elizabeth I McCann, Nelle Nugent, Gerald S Krone & Ray Larsen presentation of a Negro Ensemble Co prodn of a play without intermission by Sam-Art Williams. Staged, Douglas Turner Ward; scenery, Felix C Cochren; scenery supv, Lynn Pecktal; cos, Alvin B Perry; cos supv, Jeanne Button; light, Martin Aronstein; asso prod, Tommy DeMaio; publicity, Solters, Roskin, Friedman (Joshua Ellis); stage mgrs, Horacena J Taylor, Ron Nguvu. Opened May 7, '80, at the Cort Theatre; $18.50 weeknights, $19.50 weekend nights.

Charles Brown, L Scott Caldwell, Michele Shay.
05/14/80B

Home Sweet Homer

John F Kennedy for the Performing Arts presentation of a musical in 16 numbers, without intermission. Mus, Mitch Leigh; book, Roland Kibbee, Albert Marre; lyr, Charles Burr, Forman Brown. Staged, Marre; scenery-light, Howard Bay; cos, Bay, Ray Diffen; mus dir, Ross Reimueller; orchs, Buryl Red. GMs, Eugene Wolsk, Emanuel Azenberg; publicity, Ruth Cage; stage mgrs, Patrick Horgan, Gregory A Hirsch; adv, Blaine Thompson (Mike Mones). Opened Jan. 4, '75, at the Palace Theatre; $16 top weeknights, $17.50 weekend nights.

Yul Brynner, Joan Diener, Russ Thacker, Martin Vidnovic, Ian Sullivan, Bill Mackey, Daniel Brown, Brian Destazio, John Aristides, Bill Nabel, Les Freed, Shev Rodgers, Diana Davila, Suzanne Sponsler, Cecile Santos, Christine Uchida, Darel Glaser, P.J Mann.

Standbys, understudies: Linda Burne, Karen Shepard.
01/14/76B

Horowitz and Mrs Washington

Joel W Schenker, Jay J Cohen, Richard Press, Chester Gore, with Alan Silverman & Bernard Schwartz presentation of a play in two acts by Henry Denker; staged, Joshua Logan; scenery, Steven Rubin; cos, William Schroder; light, Marc B Weiss; GM, Victor Samrock; publicity, Max Eisen, Sol Jacobson; company mgr, David Payne; stage mgrs, Howard Whitfield, Skipp Lynch. Opened Apr 2, '80, at the John Golden Theatre; $20 top weeknights, $22.50 weekend nights.

Sam Levene, Theodore Sorel, Esther Rolle, Christopher Blount, Patricia Roe, Joe De Santis.
04/09/80B

I Have a Dream

Frank von Zerneck & Mike Wise, in ass'n with Frankie Herrett and the Shubert Organization, by arrangement with Mrs Coretta King and the Martin Luther King Jr Center For Social Change, presentation of a drama with mus; adapt, Josh Greenfeld; from the words of Martin Luther King Jr. Staged, Robert Greenwald; set, Donald Harris; cos, Terence Tam Soon; light, Martin Aronstein; mus dir, Fred Gripper; asso prods, Pat Lang & Theatre Now Inc. GM, James Walsh; company mgr, Ronald Bruguiere; publicity, Michael Alpert, Carl Samrock; stage mgrs, David Clive, Janyce Ann Wagner. Opened Sept. 20, '76, at the Ambassador Theatre; $13.50 top weeknights, $15 weekend nights.

Billy Dee Williams, Judy Ann Elder, Sheila Ellis, Leata Galloway, Ramona Brooks, Millie Foster, Clinton Derricks-Carroll.
09/22/76B

I Love My Wife

Terry Allen & Harry Rigby, by arrangement with Joseph Kipness, presentation of a musical in two acts (13 numbers); book-lyr, Michael Stewart; mus, Cy Coleman, from a Parisian comedy by Luis Rego. Staged, Gene Saks; mus staging, Onna White; scenery, David Mitchell; light, Gilbert V Hemsley Jr; cos, Ron Talsky; mus dir, John Miller; snd, Lou Gonzalez; asso prod, Frank Montalvo. GM, Jack Schlissel, Jay Kingwill; publicity, Henry Luhrman; stage mgrs, Bob Vandergriff, Tony Manzi. Opened April 17, '77, at the Ethel Barrymore Theatre; $14 top weeknights, $16 weekend nights.

Ilene Graff, Joanna Gleason, James Naughton, Michael Mark, Joseph Saulter, John Miller, Ken Bichel, Lenny Baker.

Musical numbers: "We're Still Friends," "Monica," "By Threes," "A Mover's Life," "Love Revolution," "Someone Wonderful I Missed," "Sexually Free," "Hey There, Good Times," "Lovers on Christmas Eve," "Scream," "Everybody Today Is Turning On," "Married Couple Seeks Married Couple," "I Love My Wife."
04/20/77B

I Ought to Be in Pictures

Emanuel Azenberg presentation of a play in two acts, by Neil Dimon. Staged, Herbert Ross; set, David Jenkins; cos, Nancy Potts; light, Tharon Musser; mgr, Jose Vega; publicity, Bill Evans, Howard Atlee; stage mgrs, Frank Marino, Arlene Grayson. Opened Apr 3, '80, at the Eugene O'Neill Theatre; $18.50 weeknights, $22 weekend nights.

Dinah Manoff, Joyce Van Patten, Ron Leibman.
04/09/80B

I Remember Mama

Alexander H Cohen & Hildy Parks presentation of a musical in two acts (15 numbers), with mus by Richard Rodgers, book by Thomas Meehan, lyr, Martin Charnin, addtl lyr, Raymond Jessel, based on the play, "I Remember Mama," by John Van Druten, and stories by Kathryn Forbes. Staged, Cy Feuer; mus staging, Danny Daniels; scenery, David Mitchell; cos, Theoni V Aldredge; light, Roger Morgan; snd, Otts Munderloh; orch, Philip J Lang; mus dir-vocal arr, Jay Blackton; co-prod, Roy A Somlyo; prodn supv, Jerry Adler. Publicity, David J Powers; company mgr, Charles Willard; stage mgrs, Robert Bennett, Christopher Cohen. Opened May 31, '79 at the Majestic Theatre; $22.50 weeknights, $25 weekend nights.

Maureen Silliman, Carrie Horner, Tara Kennedy, Kristen Vigard, Ian Ziering, George Hearn, Liv Ullmann, Dick Ensslen, Elizabeth Hubbard, Dolores Wilson, Betty Ann Grove, Armin Shimerman, George S Irving, Jenet McCall, Sigrid Heath, Stan Page, Myvanwy Jenn, Austin Colyer, John Dorrin, Mickey Gunnersen, Daniel Harnett, Danny Joel, Jan Kasni, Kevin Marcum, Richard Maxon, Marisa Morell, Frank Pietri, Elissa Wolfe.

Musical numbers: "I Remember Mama," "A Little Bit More," "A Writer Writes at Night," "Every Day" (Comes Something Beautiful), "The Hardangerfjord," "You Could Not Please Me More," "Uncle Chris," "Easy Come, Easy Go," "It Is Not the End of the World," "Mama Always Makes It Better," "Lars, Lars," "Fair Trade," "It's Going to Be Good to Be Gone," "Time," "I Remember Mama" (reprise).
06/06/79B

The Importance of Being Earnest

Circle in the Square revival of a comedy in three acts, by Oscar Wilde. Staged, Stephen Porter; scenery, Zack Brown; cos, Ann Roth; light, John McLain. Artistic dir, Paul Mann; managing dir, Paul Libin; publicity, Merle Debuskey, David Roggensack; company mgr, William Conn; stage mgrs, Randall Brooks, James Bernardi. Opened June 16, '77, at the uptown Circle in the Square, $9.95 top.

John Glover, Munson Hicks, James Valentine, Elizabeth Wilson, Patricia Conolly, Kathleen Widdoes, Mary Louise Wilson, G Wood, Thomas Ruisinger.
06/22/77B

The Innocents

Arthur Cantor & Rose Teed presentation of a play in one act by William Archibald, based on the Henry James story, "The Turn of the Screw." Staged, Harold Pinter; scenery, John Lee Beatty; cos, Deirdre Clancy; light, Neil Peter Jampolis; incidental mus, Harrison Birtwistle; cos supv, Mary McKinley; prodn mgr, Mitchell Erickson. Company mgr, Maurice Schaded; publicity, C George Willard; stage mgrs, John Handy, Paul Forste, Dino Laudicina. Opened Oct. 21, '76, at the Morosco Theatre; $12 top weeknights, $13.50 weekend nights.

Sara Jessica Parker, Pauline Flanagan, Claire Bloom, Michael MacKay, Dino Laudicina, Catherine Wolfe.
10/27/76B

The Inspector General

Circle in the Square revival of a play in two acts (four scenes), by Nicolai Gogol, translated by Betsy Hulick. Staged, Liviu Ciulei; set, Karen Schulz; cos, William Ivey Long; light, F Mitchell Dana. Circle in the Square artistic dir, Theodore Mann; m dir, Paul Libin; publicity, Merle Debuskey, David Roggensack; company mgr, William Conn; stage mgrs, Randall Brooks, Rick Ralston. Opened Sept 21, 78, at the uptown Circle in the Square Theatre; $11.95 top weeknights, $12.95 weekend nights.

Arnold Soboloff, Keith Perry, Bob Harper, Timothy Farmer, Thomas Toner, Peter Van Norden, Bill Nunnery, Jon DeVries, Renee Lippin, Warren Pincus, Theodore Bikel, Bill McIntyre, William Buell, Kenneth Welsh, Helen Burns, Christine Estabrook, Max Wright, Bob Balaban, Jon DeVries, Timothy Farmer, Keith Perry, Lynne Charnay, Mary Lou Rosato, Jean Barker.
09/27/78B

Iolanthe

James and Joseph Nederlander, in ass'n with City Center of Music and Drama Inc and the

Iolanthe
(Cont)

D'Oyly Carte Opera Trust, presentation of a comic opera in two acts with libretto by W S Gilbert and mus, Arthur Sullivan. Musical dir, Royston Nash; prodn dir, Leonard Osborn; prod, Michael Heyland; set-cos, Bruno Santini; light, Joe Davis (U S supervision, Martin Aronstein); chor, Virginia Mason; GM, Frederic Lloyd. Opened July 17, '78, at the NY State Theatre $17.50 top.

John Reed, John Ayldon, Geoffey Shovelton, Kenneth Sandford, Gareth Jones, Patricia Leonard, Jane Metcalfe, Suzanne O'Keeffe, Lorraine Dulcie Daniels, Patricia Ann Bennett, Barbara Lilley. Richard Brabrooke, Michael Buchan, Barry Clark, Malcolm Coy, Jon Ellison, Michael Farran-Lee, Guy Matthews, Richard Mitchell, Edwin Rolles, Thomas Scholey, Bryan Secombe, Alan Spencer, William Strachan, Kevin West, Patrick Wilkes, Susan Cochrane, Linda D'Arcy, Elizabeth Denham, Madeleine Hudson, Betti Lloyd-Jones, Roberta Morrell, Andrea Phillips, Patricia Rea, Suzanne Sloane, Gillian Swankie, Vivien Tierney, Alison West, Helene Witcombe.
07/19/78B

Ipi Tombi
A Deshe (Pashanel & Topol) presentation, by arrangement with Ray Cooney Prodns Ltd., Academy Theatre & Brooke Theatre, Johannesburg, of Bertha Egnos prodn of a musical; conceived-devised-comp-staged, Bertha Egnos; lyr, Gail Lakier. Chor, Sheila Wartski; addl chor, Neil McKay, cast members; scenery, Elizabeth MacLeish; light, Timothy Heale, John Wain; cos supv, Susan Wain; snd, Sander Hacker. GM, Ralph Roseman; publicity, Max Eisen, Barbara Glenn; stage mgrs, Patrick Horrigan, Barbara Dilker, Andre Love. Opened Jan. 12, '77, at the Harkness Theatre; $15 top weeknights, $16.50 weekend nights.

Count Wellington Judge, Martha Molefe, Daniel Pule, Dorcas Faku, Jabu Mbalo, Lydia Monamodi, Matthew Bodibe, Busi Dlamini, Gideon Bendile, Zelda Funani, Elliot Ngubane, Thembi Mtshali, Andrew Kau, Linda Tshabalala, Sam Hlatshwayo, Betty-Boo Hlela, Philip Gama, Dudu Nzimande, David Mthethwa, Coreen Pike, Shadrack Moyo, Nellie Khumalo, Junior Tshabalala, Simon Nkosi, Ali Lerefolo.
01/19/77B

It's So Nice To Be Civilized
Jay Julien, Arnon Milchan & Larry Kalish presentation of a musical comedy-drama in two acts; book-mus-lyrs, Micki Grant. Staged, Frank Corsaro; chor, Mabel Robinson; set, Charles Hoefler; cos, Ruth Morley; light, Charles Hoefler, Ralph Madero; asso prod, Danny Holgate; mus dir, Coleridge-Taylor Perkinson; orchs, Danny Holgate, Neal Tate; choral arrs, Tasha Thomas; dance arrs, Carl Maultsby; stage mgrs, Jack Gianino, Carloyn Greer, Paul Harman; snd, Palmer Shannon; GM, John Larson; publicity, Merlin Group (Cheryl Sue Dolby, Sandra Manley). Opened Jun 3, '80, at the Martin Beck Theatre; $22.50 top weeknights, $25 top Sat night. Obba Babatunde, Vivian Reed, Larry Stewart, Vickie D Chappell, Carol Lynn Maillard, Mabel King, Stephen Pender, Dan Strayhorn, Eugene Edwards, Deborah Burrell, Jaunita Grace Tyler.

Ensemble- Dara Atanian, Paul Binotto, Sharon K Brooks, P L Brown, Jean Cheek, Vondie Curtis-Hall, Paul Harman, Esther Marrow, Wellington Perkins, Dwayne Phelps.

Songs: - "Step Into My World," "Keep Your Eye on the Red," "Wake-Up, Sun," "Subway Rider," "God Help Us," "Who's Going to Teach the Children?," "Out on the Street," "Welcome, Mr Anderson," "Why Can't Me and You?," "Why Can't Me and You?" (reprise), "Out on the Street" (reprise), "When I Rise," "World Keeps Going Round," "Antiquity," "I've Still Got My Bite," "Look at Us," "Keep Your Eye on the Red" (reprise), "The American Dream," "Bright Lights," "Step Into My World" (reprise), "It's So Nice to Be Civilized," "Like a Lady," "Pass A Little Love Around."
06/11/80B

Jesus Christ Superstar
Hal Zeiger revival of a musical in two acts (24 numbers); mus, Andrew Lloyd Webber; lyr, Tim Rice. Staged, William Daniel Grey; chor, Kelly Carrol; mus dir, Peter Phillips. Opened Nov. 23, '77, at the Longacre Theatre; $12.50 top weeknights, $15 weekend nights.

Patrick Jude, William Daniel Grey, Barbara Niles, Doug Lucas, Richard Tolin, Christopher Cable, Steve Schochet, Bobby London, Randy Martin, Randy Wilson, D Bradley Jones, George Bernhard, Freida Ann Williams, Pauletta Pearson, Claudette Washington, Celeste Hogan, David Cahn, Ken Samuels, Lennie Del Duca, Mark Syers.

Musical numbers: "Heaven on Their Minds," "What's the Buzz," "Strange Thing Mystifying," "Everything's All Right," "This Jesus Must Die," "Hosanna," "Simon Zealotes," "Poor Jerusalem," "Pilate's Dream," "The Temple," "I Don't Know How to Love Him," "Damned for All Time," "The Last Supper," "Gethsemane," "The Arrest," "Peter's Denial," "Pilate and Christ," "King Herod's Song," "Could We Start Again, Please," "Judas' Death," "Trial Before Pilate," "Superstar," "John 19:41."
12/07/77B

John Gabriel Borkman
Circle in the Square (Theodore Mann, artistic dir; Paul Libin, M dir) revival of a drama in three acts (four scenes) by Henrik Ibsen, translated from the Norwegian by Rolf Fjelde. Staged, Austin Pendleton; sets, Andrew Jackness; cos, Jennifer von Mayrhauser; light, Paul Gallo; stage mgr, Randall Brooks; publicity, Merle Debuskey Associates (David Roggensack). Opened Dec. 18, '80 at the Circle in the Square; $18 top weeknights, $20 Saturday nights.

Rosemary Murphy, Brittain McGowin, Irene Worth, Patricia Cray Lloyd, Freddie Lehne, E G Marshall, Viveca Parker, Richard Kuss.
12/24/80B

The King and I
Lee Guber & Shelly Gross revival of a musical in two acts (18 numbers), mus, Richard Rodgers; book-lyr, Oscar Hammerstin 2d; based on Margaret Landon novel, "Anna and the King of Siam." Staged, Yuriko (orig chor, Jerome Robbins); set, Peter Wolf; cos, Stanley Simmons, based on orig des, Irene Sharaff; light, Thomas Skelton; mus supv, Milton Rosenstock; mus dir, John Lesko; snd, Richard Fitzgerald. GM, Theatre Now (William C Cohen, Edward H Davis, Norman E Rothstein); publicity, Solters & Roskin (Joshua Ellis, Milly Schoenbaum, Fred H Nathan); company mgr, Robb Lady; stage mgrs, Ed Preston, Conwell Worthington, Thomas H Rees. Opened May 2, '77, at the Uris Theatre; $15 top weeknights, $16.50 weekend nights.

Larry Swansen, Alan Amick, Constance Towers, Jae Woo Lee, Michael Kermoyan, Yul Brynner, June Angela, Hye-Young Choi, Gene Profanato, Julie Woo, Martin Vidnovic, John Michael King, Su Applegate, Jessica Chao, Lei-Lynne Doo, Dale Harimoto, Pamela Kalt, Susan Kikuchi, Diane Lam, Faye Fujisaki Mar, Sumiko Murashima, Libby Rhodes, Hope Sogawa, Mary Ann Teng, Patricia K Thomas, Clark Huang, Annie Lam, Connie Lam, Jennifer Lam, Paul Siu, Tim Waldrip, Kevan Weber, Kym Weber, Mary Woo, Sydney Smith, Marianne Tatum, Rebecca West, Kaipo Daniels, Barrett Hing, Ric Ornellas, Simeon Den, Chandra Tanna, Robert Vega.

Musical numbers: "I Whistle a Happy Tune," "My Lord and Master," "Hello, Young Lovers," "March of the Siamese Children," "A Puzzlement," "The Royal Bangkok Academy," "Getting to Know You," "We Kiss in a Shadow," "A Puzzlement" (reprise), "Shall I Tell You What I Think of You," "Something Wonderful," Finale, "Western People Funny," "I Have Dreamed," "Hello, Young Lovers" (reprise), "The Small House of Uncle Thomas," "Shall We Dance?" Finale.
05/04/77B

King of Hearts
Joseph Kipness & Patty Grubman, in ass'n with Jerome Minskoff, presentation of a musical in two acts (14 scenes, 14 numbers); book, Joseph Stein; mus, Peter Link; lyr, Jacob Brackman, based on an orig screenplay by Philippe de Broca, Maurice Bessy, Daniel Boulanger. Staged-chor, Ron Field; set, Santo Loquasto; cos, Patricia Zipprodt; light, Pat Collins; mus dir, Karen Gustafson; dance mus arr, Dorothea Freitag; orchs, Bill Brohn; snd, Jack Shearing; asso prods, Lee Minskoff, Charlotte Dicker. GM, Marvin A Krauss; asso, Gary Gunas; publicity, Merlin Group, Patt Dale; stage mgrs, Janet Beroza, Clint Jakeman, Robert Schear. Opened Oct 22, '78, at the Minskoff Theatre; $20 top.

Gary Morgan, Millicent Martin, Mitzi Hamilton, Marilyn d'Honau, Isabelle Farrell, Bob Gunton, Pamela Blair, Neva Rae Powers, Rex David Hays, Michael McCarty, Maria Guida, Gerrianne Raphael, Gordon J Weiss, Timothy Scott, David Thomas, Daniel Robinson, Bryan Nicholas, Julia Shelley, Will Roy, Donald Scardino, Jay Devlin, Robert Brubach, Harry Fawcett, John Scoullar, Jamie Haskins, Richard Christopher, Scott Allen, Alexander Orfaly, Scott Barnes, Roger Berdahl, Timothy Wallace, Karl Heist.

Musical numbers: "A Stain on the Name," "Deja Vu," "Promenade," "Turn Around," "Nothing, Only Love," "King of Hearts," "Close Upon the Hour," "A Brand New Day," "Le Grand Cirque de Provence," "Hey Look at Me, Mrs Draba," "Going Home Tomor-

King of
(Cont)
row," "Somewhere Is Here," "Nothing, Only Love" (reprise), "March, March, March."
10/25/78B

King of Schnorrers
Eric Krebs & Sam Landis presentation of a mus comedy in two acts; book-mus-lyr, Judd Woldin, based on a novel by Isreal Zangwill. Staged-chor, Grover Dale; settings, Adrianne Lobel; light, Richard Nelson; cos, Patricia Adshead; vocal arrs, Norman L Berman; mus dir, Hank Ross; prodn stage mgr, Jay Fox; GM, Linda Canavan; publicity, Shirley Herz, Jan Greenberg. Opened Oct. 9, '79, at the Harold Clurman Theatre; $10 top weeknights, $12 weekends (moved to Playhouse Theatre Nov. 28, '79; $16 top weeknights, $18 weekend nights).

Lloyd Battista, Sophie Schwab, Philip Casnoff, Angelina Reaux, Ralph Bruneau, Jerry Mayer, Rick McIlhiney, Paul Binotto, Ed Dixon, Thomas Lee Sinclair.
12/05/79B

The Kingfisher
Elliot Martin, with Hinks Shimberg, in ass'n with John Gale, presentation of a comedy in two acts (four scenes), by William Douglas Home. Staged, Lindsay Anderson; set, Alan Tagg; cos, Jane Greenwood; light, Thomas Skelton. GM, Victor Samrock; publicity, Seymour Krawitz, Louise Weiner Ment, Patricia McLean Krawitz; stage mgrs, Bill Weaver, Wally Peterson. Opened Dec 6, '78, at the Biltmore Theatre; $18.50 top weeknights, $19.50 weekend nights, $20 opening.

George Rose, Rex Harrison, Claudette Colbert.
12/13/78B

Knickerbocker Holiday
Richard Grayson & John Bowab presentation of a concert-style revival of a musical; book-lyr, Maxwell Anderson; score, Kurt Weill. Staged, John Bowab; mus dir, Bill Brohn; gowns, Donald Brooks; light, Ken Billington; prod in ass'n with Joseph Harris. Publicity, Betty Lee Hunt, Maria Pucci; company mgr, Gino Giglio; stage mgrs, Ben Sprecher, Frank Birt, Orrin Reilly. Opened April 19, '77, at Town Hall, $10 top.

Kurt Peterson, Gerard Russak, Genette Lane, John Dorrin, Gene Varrone, Elliott Savage, Eric Brotherson, Walter Charles, Edward Evanko, Maida Meyers, Alyson Bristol, Susan Rush, Clay Causey, Maureen Brennan, Richard Kiley, John Leslie Wolfe, Ed Dixon, Orrin Reiley.

Musical numbers: "Washington Irving Song," "Clickety-Clack," "Entrance of the Council," "Hush Hush," "There's Nowhere to Go But Up," "It Never Was You," "How Can You Tell an American?" "Will You Remember Me?" "Stuyvesant's Entrance," "One Touch of Alchemy," "The One Indispensable Man," "Young People Think About Love," "September Song," "All Hail, the Political Honeymoon," "Ballad of the Robbers," "Sitting in Jail," "We Are Cut in Twain," "There's Nowhere to Go But Up" (reprise), "The Army of New Amsterdam," "To War," "Our Ancient Liberties," "May and January," "The Scars," "Dirge for a Soldier," "No, Ve Vouldn't Gonto Do It," Finale.
04/27/77B

Knockout
Bill Sargent presentation of a play in two acts (nine scenes), by Louis La Russo II. Staged, Frank Corsaro; setting, Karl Eigsti; cos, Jane Greenwood; light, Neil Peter Jampolis; tech cnslt, Jose Torres; exec prod, Norman Maibaum. GMs, Leonard Soloway, Allan Francis; publicity, Seymour Krawitz, Louise Weiner Ment, Patricia McLean Krawitz; company mgr, Steven Suskin; stage mgrs, Jack Gianino, Brad Gordon, Shyler Nepveux. Opened May 6, '79 at the Helen Hayes Theatre; $17.50 top weeknights; $18.50 weekend nights.

Danny Aiello, David Patrick Kelly, Michael Aronin, Janet Sarno, Frank Bongiorno, Edward O'Neill, Margaret Warncke.
05/09/79B

La Guerre De Troie N'Aura Pas Lieu
(The Trojan War Will Not Take Place)
Le Treteau De Paris/Jean De Rigault in ass'n with 55th Street Dance Theatre Foundation presentation of Le Theatre De La Ville (Animateur-Directeur Jean Mercure) in a revival of a play in two acts by Jean Giraudoux. Staged, Jean Mercure; scenery-cos, Yannis Kokkos; incidental mus, Mark Wilkinson. GM, McCann & Nugent; publicity, Arthur Rubine; stage mgr, Alain Tartas. Opened April 20, '77, at the City Center Theatre.

Dominique Jayr, Isa Mercure, Virginia Duvernoy, Bernadette Lange, Helene Zanicoli, Jose-Maria Flotats, Bernard Giraudeau, Eugene Berthier, Jean-Marie Bon, Regis Outin, Maurice Chevit, Jandeline, Bernard Veron, Michel Salina, Anne-Laure Meury, Anny Duperey, Michel Feder, Jean-Luc Russier, Djanet Lachmet, Pascal Sellier, Angelo Bardi, Jean Mercure, Serge Peyrat, Lionel Baylac, Jean-Pierre Aumont, Lafleur, Coussonneau, Georges Joannon, Jenny Arasse.
04/27/77B

Ladies at the Alamo
Edgar Bronfman Jr, for Sagittarius Entertainment, presentation of a play in two acts by Paul Zindel. Staged, Frank Perry; set, Peter Larkin; cos, Ruth Morley; light, Marc B Weiss. GM, James Walsh; publicity, Michael Alpert, Warren Knowlton; stage mgrs, Marnel Sumner, Maureen Sadusk. Opened April 7, '77, at the Martin Beck Theatre; $13.50-$15 top.

Estelle Parsons, Eileen Heckart, Susan Peretz, Rosemary Murphy, Jan Farrand.
04/13/77B

The Lady From Dubuque
Richard Barr, Lester Osterman, Roger Berlind, Marc Howard, Spencer H Berlin & Hale Matthews presentation of a play in two acts by Edward Albee. Staged, Alan Schneider; set, Rouben Ter-Arutunian; cos, John Falabella; light, Richard Nelson; Irene Worth's cos, Pauline Trigere; GMs, Leonard Soloway, Allan Francis; publicity, Shirley Herz, Jan Greenberg, Bruce Cohen; company mgr, Michael Kasdan; stage mgrs, Julia Gillett, Dan Hild; asso prod, Leslie Strager. Opened Jan 31, '80, at the Morosco Theatre; $20 top weeknights, $22.50 weekend nights.

Celia Weston, Tony Musante, Frances Conroy, Baxter Harris, David Leary, Maureen Anderman, Earle Hyman, Irene Worth.
02/06/80B

The Lady from the Sea
Circle in the Square Theatre revival of a drama in two acts, by Henrik Ibsen; trans, Michael Meyer. Staged, Tony Richardson; scenery-cos, Rouben Ter-Arutunian; light, Thomas Skelton; mus-snd, Richard Peaslee. Artistic dir, Theodore Mann; managing dir, Paul Libin; publicity, Merle Debuskey, Susan L Schulman; stage mgr, Randall Brooks, James Bernardi; adv, Blaine Thompson (Don Josephson). Opened March 18, '76, at the Circle in the Square Theatre; $8.95 top.

George Ede, Kimberly Farr, Kipp Osborne, Allison Argo, Pat Hingle, John Heffernan, Vanessa Redgrave, Richard Lynch.
03/24/76B

Last Licks
The Shubert Organization, Eugene V Wolsk, Emanuel Azenberg & Dasha Epstein presentation of a play in two acts, by Frank D Gilroy. Staged, Tom Conti; setting, William Ritman; cos, Pearl Somner; light, Tharon Musser. Mgr, Jose Vega; company mgr, Manny Kladitis; publicity, Bill Evans, Howard Atlee; prodn supv, Jerry Adler; stage mgr, Jonathan Weiss. Opened Nov. 20, '79, at the Longacre Theatre; $18.50 top weeknights, $20 weekend nights.

Ed Flanders, J T Walsh, Susan Kellerman.
11/21/79B

The Last Meeting of the Knights of the White Magnolia
(A Texas Trilogy)
(For Credits see Lu Ann Hampton Laverty Oberlander). Opened Sept. 22, '76, at the Broadhurst Theatre.

John Marriott, Walter Flanagan, Thomas Toner, Patrick Hines, Henderson Forsythe, Graham Beckel, Fred Gwynne, Paul O'Keefe, Josh Mostel.
09/29/76B

Legend
Gladys Rackmil & Kennedy Center presentation of a Roger L Stevens prodn of a play in two acts (multi-scene), by Samuel Taylor. Staged, Robert Drivas; scenery, Santo Loquasto; cos, Florence Klotz; light, Thomas Skelton; orig mus, Dan Goggin; title song, Ronee Blakely. GMs, R Tyler Gatchell Jr & Peter Neufeld; publicity, Betty Lee Hunt, Maria Cristina Pucci, Maurice Turet; stage mgrs, Lorry Forde, Valentine Mayer, John Stuart; adv, Lawrence Weiner (Norman Weiner). Opened May 13, '76, at the Ethel Barrymore Theatre; $12 top weeknights, $13.50 weekend nights.

Munson Hicks, George Dzundza, F Murray Abraham, George Parry, Elizabeth Ashley, Stephen Clarke, Robert Anthony, James Carrington, Ben Slack, Ron Max, Chev Rodgers, Bill McIntyre, Wayne Maxwell, Sebastian Stuart, J J Quinn, Tom Flagg.

Legend
(Cont)
05/19/76B

Let My People Come
Phil Oesterman presentation of a revue in two acts (19 numbers). Staged, Oesterman; author unlisted. Chor, Charles Augins; set-light, Duane F Mazey; set-cos supv, Douglas W Schmidt; light supv, John Gleason; mus dir-vocal arrs, Norman Bergen; mus dir, Glen Roven. GM, Jay Kingwell; publicity, Saul Richman, Duane F Mazey, Robert Walter, Bob Blume; advertising, Great Scott (Lorraine Borden). Began previewing July 7, '76, at the Morosco Theatre; $12.50 top weeknights, $15 weekend nights.
Brandy Alexander, Joanne Baron, Pat Cleveland, Lorraine Davidson, Joelle Erasme, Paul Gillespie, Gloria Goldman, Tulane Howard, Bob Jockers, Empress Kilpatrick, Allan Lozito, Bryan Miller, Rod R Neves, Rozaa, Bryan Spencer, Sterling Saint-Jacques, Don Scotti, Dean Tait, Lori Wagner, Charles Whiteside.
09/08/76B

Lone Star and Pvt. Wars
Michael Harvey & Peter A Bobley, in ass'n with Columbia Pictures presentation of a dual bill by James McLure. "Pvt Wars," staged, Garland Wright; "Lone Star" staged, Stuart White. Settings, John Arnone; cos, Giva Taylor; light, Frances Aronson; asso prods, Stewart Lane, Jack Tantleff; GM, Albert Poland; prodn stage mgr, Susie Cordon; publicity, Hunt-Pucci Associates. Opened June 7, '79 at the Century Theatre; $12.95 top weeknights, $16.95 weekend nights.
Pvt Wars- Gregory Grove, Tony Campisi, Clifford Fetters
Lone Star- Powers Boothe, Leo Burmester, Clifford Fetters.
06/13/79B

Loose Ends
Circle in the Square (Theodore Mann, artistic dir; Paul Libin, m-dir) presentation of a play in two acts (eight scenes), by Michael Weller. Staged, Alan Schneider; scenery, Zack Brown; cos, Kristina Watson; light, David F Segal; pho projections, Cecilia Vettraino. Publicity, Merle Debuskey, Tom Trenkle; company mgr, William Conn; stage mgrs, Randall Brooks, James Bernardi. Opened June 6, '79 at the Circle in The Square Theatre; $14.95 top weeknights, $16.95 weekend nights.
Kevin Kline, Roxanne Hart, Patricia Richardson, Ernest Abuba, Jay O Sanders, Celia Weston, Steve Vinovich, Jodi Long, Michael Kell, Michael Lipton, Jeff Brooks.
06/13/79B

Lu Ann Hampton Laverty Oberlander
(A Texas Trilogy)
Robert Whitehead & Roger L Stevens presentation of a play in three acts by Preston Jones. Staged, Alan Schneider; scenery-light, Ben Edwards; cos, Jane Greenwood. GM, Oscar E Olesen; company mgr, James Walsh; publicity, Seymour Krawitz, Patricia McLean Krawitz, Louise Ment; stage mgrs, Charles Kindl, Stephen Nasuta. Opened Sept. 21, '76, at the Broadhurst Theatre; $9 top Sunday nights, $13.50 Monday-Friday nights, $15 Saturday nights.
Avril Gentles, Diane Ladd, James Staley, Graham Beckel, Everett McGill, Walter Flanagan, Thomas Toner, Patrick Hines, Baxter Harris, Josh Mostel, Kristin Griffith.
09/29/76B

Lu Ann Hampton Laverty Oberlander; The Last Meeting of the Knights of the White Magnolia; The Oldest Living Graduate:
SEE A Texas Trilogy

Lunch Hour
Robert Whitehead & Roger L Stevens presentation of a comedy in two acts by Jean Kerr. Staged, Mike Nichols; set, Oliver Smith; cos, Ann Roth; light, Jennifer Tipton; GM, Oscar E Olesen; publicity, Seymour Krawitz, Patricia Krawitz, Warren Knowlton. Opened Nov 12, '80, at the Ethel Barrymore Theatre; $20 top weeknights, $22.50 weekend nights.
Sam Waterston, Susan Kellerman, Gilda Radner, Max Wright, David Rasche.
11/19/80B

The Madwoman of Central Park West
Gladys Rackmil, Firtz Holt & Barry M Brown presentation of a solo musical with Phyllis Newman; book by Phyllis Newman and Arthur Laurents, mus-lyr, Peter Allan, Leonard Bernstein, Jerry Bock, Martin Charnin, John Clifton, Betty Comden, Fred Ebb, Jack Feldman, Adolph Green, Sheldon Harnick, John Kander, Ed Kleban, Barry Manilow, Phyllis Newman, Joe Raposo, Mary Rodgers, Carole Bayer Sager, Stephen Sondheim, Bruce Sussman. Staged, Arthur Laurents; scenery, Philipp Jung; cos, Theoni V Aldredge; light, Ken Billington; snd, Abe Jacob; orch, John Fliflon; mus dir, Herbert Kaplan; spec orch, Kirk Nurock; GM, Marvin A Krauss; asso, Eric Angelson; publicity, Shirley Herz; company mgr, Gary Gunas; stage mgrs, James Pentecost, Rick Ralston. Opened June 13, '79 at the 22 Steps Theatre; $17.50 top weeknights, $19 weekend nights.
Phyllis Newman.
Musical numbers:- "Up, Up, Up," "My Mother Was a Fortune Teller," "Cheerleader," "What Makes Me Love Him," "Don't Laugh," "No One's Toy," "Up, Up, Up" (reprise), "Better," "Don't Wish," "Copacabana (At the Copa)," "My New Friends," "List Song," "My Mother Was a Fortune Teller" (reprise).
06/20/79B

Major Barbara
Circle in the Square revival of a play in three acts (two intermissions), by George Bernard Shaw. Staged, Stephen Porter; scenery-cos, Zack Brown; light, John McLain; art dir, Theodore Mann; M dir, Paul Libin; publicity, Merle Debuskey, David Roggensack; company mgr, William Conn; stage mgrs, Nicholas Russiyan, Robert O'Rourke. Opened Feb 26, '80, at the Uptown Circle in the Square Theatre; $16 top weeknights, $18 weekend nights.
Rachel Gurney, Nicholas Walker, Donald Buka, Laurie Kennedy, Gina Franz, Nicholas Surovy, Rand Bridges, Philip Bosco, Paddy Croft, Norman Allen, Amanda Carlin, Frank Hamilton, Jon De Vries, Joan Croyden, Jamey Sheridan.
02/27/80B

Man and Superman
Circle in the Square uptown (Theodore Mann, artistic dir; Paul Libin, mng dir) revival of a play in three acts, incl the "Don Juan in Hell" scene as the second act, by George Bernard Shaw. Staged, Stephen Porter; scenery-cos, Zack Brown; light, F Mitchell Dana. Company mgr, Janet Spencer; publ, David Roggensack; stage mgrs, James Bernardi, Rick Ralston. Opened Dec 14, '78 (previews began Nov 24), at the Circle in the Square Theatre uptown, NY; $11.95 top weeknights, $12.95 weekend nights.
Richard Woods, Barbara Lester, Mark Lamos, George Grizzard, Ann Sachs, Kate Wilkinson, Bette Henritze, Laurie Kennedy, Nicholas Woodeson, Michael O'Hare, Philip Bosco, George Hall, Johnson Carroll, James Storm, David Berman, Robert Nicholas.
12/20/78B

Man Of La Mancha
Eugene V Wolsk revival of a musical; book, Dale Wasserman; mus, Mitch Leigh; lyr, Joe Darion; suggested by the life and works of Miguel de Cervantes y Saavedra, and presented without intermission. Prodn-mus staging, Albert Marre; set-light, Howard Bay; cos, Bay, Patton Campbell; mus arrs, Music Makers Inc; mus dir, Robert Brandzel. Company mgr, Chuck Eisler; publicity, John A Prescott; stage mgrs, Patrick Corrigan, Greg Hirsch, Kay Vance. Opened Sept. 15, '77, at the Palace Theatre; $16.50 top weeknights, $17.50 weekend nights.
Richard Kiley (Chev Rodgers at Wednesday matinees), Tony Martinez, Ben Vargas, Hector Mercado, Bob Wright, Marceline Decker, Chev Rodgers, Ted Forlow, Mark Holliday, Anthony DeVeechi, Edmond Varrato, David Wasson, Emily Yancy, Joan Susswein, Robin Polseno, Harriett Conrad, Margret Coleman, Taylor Reed, Ian Sullivan, Renato Cibelli, Michael St Paul.
09/21/77B

The Man Who Came to Dinner
Circle in the Square revival of a play in three acts by Moss Hart and George S Kaufman. Staged, Stephen Porter; scenery-cos, Zack Brown; light, Jeff Davis; publicity, Merle Debuskey, David Roggensack; stage mgrs, Randall Brooks, Nicholas Russiyan, Robert O'Rourke. Opened Jun 26, '80, at the uptown Circle in the Square: $16 top weeknights, $18 weekend nights.
Patricia O'Connell, Anita Dangler, Josh Clark, Amanda Carlin, Bill McCutcheon, Yolanda Childress, Dorothy Stinnette, Richard Woods, Maureen Anderman, Robert Nichols, Ellis Rabb, Kate Wilkinson, Peter Coffield, Nicholas Martin, Jason Jerrold, Jeffrey Rodman, George Spelvin, Robert O'Rourke, Carrie Nye, James Sheridan, Roderick Cook, Lilli

The Man
(Cont)
Syng, Leonard Frey, Charles Hardin.
07/02/80B

The Many Faces of Love
Town Hall presentation of a two-part program of dramatic readings by Hume Cronyn and Jessica Tandy of selections from the writings of Edward Albee, Richard Armour, Fyodor Dostoevsky, Benjamin Franklin, Robert Frost, James Goldman, Jan de Hartog, Samuel Hoffenstein, Richard Llewellyn, Phyllis McGinley, Edna St Vincent Millay, Ogden Nash, Dorothy Parker, Alan Paton, Rainer Maria Rilke, Bertrand Russell, William Shakespeare, Caitlin Thomas, James Thurber, Judith Viorst, Tennessee Williams, Thomas Wolfe and others. Material compiled-edtr, Eleanor Wolquitt; light, Michael Watson; prodn supv, Robert Walter. Presented Dec. 2, '76, at the Town Hall, NY.
12/08/76B

Mark Twain Tonight
Emanuel Azenberg & Dasha Epstein presentation of a solo-show, with material selected and arranged by Hal Holbrook from the stories, essays, letters and notes of Samuel Clemens. Prodn supv, Bennett Thomson; GM, Jose Vega; company mgr, Earl Shendell; publicity, Bill Evans. Opened March 15, '77, at the Imperial Theatre; $13.50 top weeknights, $15 weekend nights.
Hal Holbrook.
03/23/77B

The Merchant
The Shubert Organization, John F Kennedy Center for the Performing Arts, Roger Berlind & Eddie Kulukundis presentation, in ass'n with SRO Prodns, of a play by Arnold Wesker. Staged, John Dexter; scenery-cos, Jocelyn Herbert; light, Andy Phillips; light supv, Andrea Wilson. GM, Marvin A Krauss; publicity, Merle Debuskey, Susan L Schulman; company mgr, G Warren McClane; stage mgrs, Brent Peek, Pat De Rousie, Brian Meister, Mark Blum. Opened Nov. 15, '77, at the Plymouth Theatre; $17.50 top.
Joseph Leon, John Clements, Roberta Maxwell, Gloria Gifford, Julia Garfield, Marian Seldes, Boris Tumarin, John Seitz, Angela Wood, Nicolas Surovy, Riggs O'Hara, Everett McGill, Lieb Lensky, William Roerick, Rebecca Malka, Russ Banham, Mark Blum, Philip Carroll, James David Cromar, Brian Meister, John Tyrrell.
11/23/77B

The Mighty Gents
James Lipton Prodns, with the Shubert Organization & Ron Dante, presentation of a play by Richard Wesley. Staged, Harold Scott; incidental mus, Peter Link; scenery, Santo Loquasto; cos, Judy Dearing; light, Gilbert V Hemsley Jr; GM, Emanual Azenberg, Jose Vega; company mgr, Maurice Schaded; publicity, Howard Atlee; stage mgrs, David Taylor, Joseph DePauw. Opened April 16, '78, at the Ambassador Theatre; $15 top weeknights, $16.50 weekend nights.
Starletta DuPois, Dorian Harewood, Brent Jennings, Mansoor Najee-Ullah, Richard Gant, Morgan Freeman, Howard E Rollins, Frank Adu.
04/19/78B

The Mikado
James Nederlander presentation by arrangement with the D'Oyly Carte Opera Trust Ltd. and Bridget D'Oyly Carte, of a D'Oyly Carte revival of a comic opera in two acts; book-lyr, William S Gilbert; mus, Arthur Sullivan. Prodn dir, Michael Heyland; mus dir, Royston Nash; set, Disley Jones; cos, Charles Ricketts. GM, Frederic Lloyd; company mgr, Herbert Newby; adv, Blaine Thompson (Mike Mones). Opened May 5, '76, at the Uris Theatre $12.50 top weeknights, $15 weekend nights.
John Ayldon, Geoffrey Shovelton, John Reed, Kenneth Sandford, Michael Raynor, Jon Ellison, Julia Goss, Jane Metcalfe, Patricia Leonard, Lyndsie Holland.

Singers: Michael Buchan, Paul Burrows, Barry Clark, Malcolm Coy, Jon Ellison, Gareth Jones, Guy Matthews, William Palmerley, Edith Rolles, Thomas Scholey, Alan Spencer, William Strachan, Paul Waite, Michael Westbury, Caroline Baker, Patricia Ann Bennett, Gillian Burrows, Lorraine Dulcie-Daniels, Anne Eggkestone, Josephine Hichley, Beti Lloyd-Jones, Elsie McDougall, Roberta Morrell, Helen Houlder, Suzanne O'Keeffe, Glynis Prendergast, Patricia Rae, Vivian Tierney.
05/12/76B

Miss Margarida's Way
Joseph Papp presentation of a N Y Shakespeare Festival prodn of a solo play in two acts, by Roberto Athayde. Staged by author; scenery-cos, Santo Loquasto; light, Martin Tudor; asso prod, Bernard Gersten. GM, Robert Kamlot; company mgr, Bob MacDonald; publicity, Merle Debuskey, Sol Jacobson; stage mgrs, Penny Gebhard, Colin Garrey. Opened Sept. 16 (press opening Sept. 27), '77; $14 top weeknights, $15 weekend nights.
Estelle Parsons, Colin Garrey, Audience.
10/05/77B

Mrs. Warren's Profession
N Y Shakespeare Festival presentation of a Joseph Papp prodn of a play in four acts (two intermissions), by Bernard Shaw. Staged, Gerald Freedman; set, David Mitchell; cos, Theoni V Aldredge; light, Martin Aronstein; asso prod, Bernard Gersten. GM, Robert Kamlot; publicity, Merle Debuskey, Faith Geer; stage mgrs, Mary Porter Hall, John Beven; adv, Case & McGrath. Opened Feb. 18, '76, at the Vivian Beaumont Theatre; $9 top weeknights, $10 weekend nights.
Lynn Redgrave, Ron Randell, Ruth Gordon, Philip Bosco, Edward Herrmann, Milo O'Shea.
02/25/76B

Mister Lincoln
David Susskind presentation of Isabel Robins prodn of a solo-show in two acts, by Herbert Mitgang. Staged, Peter Coe; scenery-cos, David L Lovett; light, Allan Stitchbury; supv, Richard Winkler; company mgr, Louise M Bayer; publicity, Arlene and Frank Goodman; stage mgr, John Wilbur. Opened Feb 24, '80, at the Morosco Theatre; $18.50 top weeknights, $20 weekend nights.
Roy Dotrice.
02/27/80B

Mixed Couples
Frederick Brisson, in ass'n with the John F Kennedy Center for the Performing Arts, presentation of a play in two acts, by James Prideaux. Staged by George Schaefer; set, Oliver Smith; cos, Noel Taylor; light, Martin Aronstein. Prodn supv, Stone Widney; asst to prod, Dwight Frye; GM, Victor Samrock; publicity, Jeffrey Richards Associates (C George Willard, Robert Ganshaw, Ben Morse, Helen Stern); stage mgrs, Robert Townsend, Charles Kindl. Opened Dec. 28, '80, at the Brooks Atkinson Theatre; $22.50 top weeknights, $24 weekend nights.
John Stewart, Michael Higgins, Geraldine Page, Rip Torn, Julie Harris.
12/31/80B

Monteith and Rand
James Lipton presentation of a program of comedy sketches by and with James Monteith and Suzanne Rand, assisted by bill-boy russell. Light, Gilbert V Hemsley Jr; cos, Donald Brooks. GM, Max Allentuck; publicity, Bill Evans, Howard Atlee, Claudia McAllister, Greg Kilarjian; stage mgrs, Charles Gray, bill-boy russell. Opened Jan 2, '79, at the Booth Theatre; $17.50 top weeknights, $20 weekend nights.
John Monteith, Suzanne Rand, bill-boy russell.
01/10/79B

Morning's At Seven
Elizabeth I McCann, Nelle Nugent & Ray Larsen presentation of a revival of a comedy in three acts by Paul Osborn. Staged, Vivian Matalon; set, William Ritman; cos, Linda Fisher; light, Richard Nelson; company mgr, Barbara Darwall; stage mgrs, Marnel Summer, Ellen Raphael; publicity, Josh Ellis, Becky Flora (Solters/Roskin/Friedman). Opened Apr 10, '80, at the Lyceum Theatre; $17.50 top weeknights, $19.50 weekend nights.
Maurice Copeland, Teresa Wright, Elizabeth Wilson, Nancy Marchand, Richard Hamilton, David Rounds, Lois de Banzie, Maureen O'Sullivan, Gary Merrill.
04/16/80B

The Most Happy Fella
Sherwin M Goldman, in asso with the Michigan Opera Theatre, rev of a mus; book-mus-lyrs, Frank Loesser, based on the Sidney Howard play, "They Knew What They Wanted." Staged, Jack O'Brien; chor, Graciela Daniele; scenery, Douglas W Schmidt; cos, Nancy Potts; light, Gilbert V Hemsley Jr; mus dir, Andrew Meltzer. Asst prod, Virginia Hymes; GM, Mario de Maria; publicity, Cheryl Sue Dolby, Sandra Manley; stage mgrs, Herb Vogler, Ben Janney, Philip Jerry. Opened Oct. 11, '79, at the Majestic Theatre; $22.50 weeknights, $23.50 Friday nights, $25 Saturday nights.
Bill Hastings, Louisa Flaningam, Sharon Daniels (Linda Michel, matinee alternate), Karen Gionbetti, Tina Paul, D'Arcy Phifer, Smith Wordes, Tim Flavin, Dan O'Sullivan, Giorgio Tozzi (Frederick Burchinal, matinee alternate), Adrienne Leonetti, Steven Alex-Cole, Dennis Warning, Dean Badolato, David Miles, Kevin Wilson, Stephen Dubov, Richard Muenz, Gene Varrone, Darren Nimnicht, Franco

The Most
(Cont)
Spoto, Joe McGrath, Lawrence Asher, Melanie Helton, Dee Etta Rowe, Jane Warsaw, Sally Williams, Michael Capes.

Singers, Dancers: Richard Croft, D Michael Heath, Patrice Pickering, Candace Rogers, Bonnie Simmons, Richard White, Carla Wilkins.

Mus numbers: "Oh, My Feet," "Somebody Somewhere," "The Most Happy Fella," "Standing on the Corner," "Joey, Joey, Joey," "Rosabella," "Abbondanza," "Spozalizio," "Benevenuta," "Don't Cry," "Fresno Beauties," "Happy To Make Your Acquaintance," "Big D," "How Beautiful the Days," "Young People," "Warm All Over," "I Like Everybody," "My Heart Is So Full Of You," "Hoedown," "Mamma, Mamma," "Song of a Summer Night," "Please Let Me Tell You."
10/17/79B

Murder At The Howard Johnson's
Lee Guber & Shelly Gross presentation of a play in two acts (three scenes), by Ron Clark and Sam Bobrick. Staged, Marshall W Mason; setting, Karl Eigsti; cos, Sara Brook; light, Richard Nelson; asso prods, David S Newman, Fred Walker. Gm, Theatre Now; publicity, Solters & Roskin (Joshua Ellis, Rima Corben); company mgr, Stephen H Arnold; stage mgrs, Mortimer Halpern, Conwell Worthington.
Joyce Van Patten, Tony Roberts, Bob Dishy.
05/23/79B

Music Is
Richard Adler, Roger Berlind & Edward R Downe Jr presentation of a musical in two acts (14 scenes, 17 numbers); book-staged, George Abbott, mus, Richard Adler; lyr, Will Holt, based on Shakespeare's "Twelfth Night." Mus cond, Paul Gemignani; orchs, Hershy Kay; dance-vocal arrs, William Cox; scenery, Eldon Elder; cos, Lewis D Rampino; light, H R Poindexter. GM, William Court Cohen, Edward H Davis, Norman E Rothstein; publicity, Mary Bryant; stage mgrs, Bob Bernard, Elise Warner, Christopher Adler. Opened Dec. 20, '76, at the St James Theatre; $16 top weeknights, $17.50 weekend nights.
Daniel Ben-Zali, William McClary, David Holliday, David Brummel, Catherine Cox, Paul Michael, William Shakespeare, Laura Waterbury, David Sabin, Christopher Hewett, Sherry Mathis, Marc Jordan, Joel Higgins, Joe Ponazecki, Doug Carfrae, Helena Andreyko, Ann Crowley, Donald Hettinger (reeds), Steve Uscher (guitar), Jim Corti, Dennis Daniels, Dawn Herbert, Dana Kyle, Wayne Mattson, Jason McAuliffe, Carolann Page, Susan Elizabeth Scott, Denny Shearer, Melanie Vaughan, Mimi B Wallace.

Musical numbers: "Music Is," "When I First Saw My Lady's Face," "Lady's Choice," "The Time Is Ripe for Loving," "Should I Speak of Loving You," "Dance for Six," "Hate to Say Goodbye to You," "Big Bottom Betty," "Twenty One Chateaux," "Sudden Lilac," "Sing Hi," "Blindman's Buff" Dance, "The Tennis Song," "I Am It," "No Matter Where," "The Duel," "Please Be Human," "What You Will."
12/22/76B

The Music Man
James Nederlander, Raymond Lussa, Fred Walker revival of a musical; book-mus-lyr, Meredith Willson; book in collab with Franklin Lacey. Staged-chor, Michael Kidd; scenery, Peter Wolf; cos, Stanley Simmons; light, Marcia Madeira; snd, Barry Rimler; mus-vocal dir, Milton Rosenstock; orchs, Don Walker; GM, Jack Schlissel, James Walsh; publicity, Solters-Roskin-Friedman (Anne Obert Weinberg); stage mgrs, Conwell S Worthington II, John M. Galo, Charles Reif. Opened Jun 5, '80, at the City Center: $22.50 top weeknights, $25 weekend nights.
Jay Stuart, Peter Wandel, Dick Van Dyke, Iggie Wolfington, Ralph Braun, Randy Morgan, Larry Cahn, Lee Winston, Richard Warren Pugh, Calvin McRae, Meg Bussert, Carol Arthur, Lara Jill Miller, Christian Slater, Jen Jones, Christina Saffran, Marcia Brushingham, Mary Gaebler, P J Nelson, Mary Roche, Dennis Holland.

Salesmen, Townspeople, Kids: - Micheal J Rockne, Ralph Braun, Andy Hostettler, Dennis Batutis, Larry Cahn, Victoria Ally, Carol Ann Basch, David Beckett, Mark A Esposito, Liza Gennaro, Tony Jaeger, Wendy Kimball, Ara Marx, Darleigh Miller, Gail Pennington, Rosemary Rado, Coley Sohn.

Musical numbers: - "Rock Island," "Iowa Stubborn," "Trouble," "Piano Lesson," "Goodnight My Someone," "Seventy-Six Trombones," "Sincere," "The Sadder But Wiser Girl," "Pickalittle," "Goodnight, Ladies," "Marian the Librarian," "My White Knight," "Wells Fargo Wagon," "It's You," "Shipoopi," "Pickalittle" (reprise), "Lida Rose," "Will I Ever Tell You," "Gary, Indiana," "It's You" (reprise), "Till There Was You," "Seventy-Six Trombones" (reprise), "Goodnight My Someone" (reprise), "Till There Was You" (reprise).
06/11/80B

Musical Chairs
Lesley Savage & Bert Stratford presentation of a musical in two acts; book, Barry Berg, Ken Donnelly, Tom Savage; mus-lyrs, Tom Savage; based on orig story concept by Larry P Pontillo. Staged-chor, Rudy Tronto; scenery, Earnest Allen Smith; light, Peggy Clark; cos, Michael J Cesario; dir-asst chor, Susan Stroman; mus dir, Barry H Gordon; arrs-orchs, Ada Janik, Dick Lieb; stage mgrs, Douglas F Goodman, Douglas Walker; GM, Leonard A Mulhern; publicity, Jeffrey Richards, Warren Knowlton. Opened May 14, '80, at the Rialto Theatre; $20 top weeknights, $22.50 weekend nights.
Ron Holgate, Ellen McCabe, Douglas Walker, Scott Ellis, Enid Blaymore, Grace Keagy, Randall Easterbrook, Leslie-Anne Wolfe, Patti Karr, Brandon Maggart, Jess Richards, Joy Franz, Edward Earle, Tom Breslin, Rick Emery, Lee Meredith.
05/21/80B

My Fair Lady
Herman Levin revival of a musical in two acts (18 scenes, 17 numbers); book-lyr, Alan Jay Lerner; mus, Frederick Loewe, based on Bernard Shaw comedy, "Pygmalion." Staged, Jerry Adler, based on orig by Moss Hart; chor, Crandall Diehl, based on orig by Hanya Holm; scenery, Oliver Smith; cos, Cecil Beaton; light, John Gleason; special cos asst, R Robert Levine; mus dir, Theodore Saidenberg; mus arrs, Robert Russell Bennett, Phil Lang; dance mus arrs, Trude Rittman. GM, Philip Adler; publicity, Seymour Krawitz, Nicholas Russiyan, Ted Goldsmith, Patricia McLean Krawitz; company mgr, Malcolm Allen; stage mgrs, Russiyan, Alisa Jill Adler, Robert O'Rourke; adv, Lawrence Weiner (Herman Jacobs). Opened March 25, '76, at the St James Theatre; $15 top weeknights, $16 weekend nights.
Debra Lyman, Stan Picus, Ernie Pysher, Eleanor Phelps, Jerry Lanning, Christine Andreas, Robert Coote, Ian Richardson, Kevin Marcum, Jack Starkey, William James, Stan Page, Kevin Lane Dearinger, John Clarkson, Richard Neilson, George Rose, Sylvia O'Brien, Margaretta Warwick, Clifford Fearl, Sonja Anderson, Lynn Fitzpatrick, Karen Gibson, Vickie Patik, Brenda Forbes, Jack Karcher, Timothy Smith, Dru Alexandrine, Sonja Stuart.

Singers: Alyson Briton, Cynthia Meryl, Kevin Marcum.

Dancers: Sally Benoit, Marie Berry, Mari McMinn, Gina Ramsel, Catherine Rice, Bonnie Walker, Richard Ammon, Jeremy Blanton, David Evans, Richard Maxon, Rick Schneider.
03/31/76B

Night and Day
James M Nederlander, Kennedy Center & Michael Codron presentation of a play in two acts, by Tom Stoppard. Staged, Peter Wood; scenery-cos, Carl Toms; light, Neil Peter Jampolis; exec prods, Elizabeth I McCann, Nelle Nugent; publicity, Solters & Roskin (Joshua Ellis, Tom Trenkle); company mgr, Susan Gustafson; stage mgrs, William Dodds, Jay Adler, Leslie Lyles. Opened Nov. 27, '79 (review based on Nov. 24 review), at the ANTA Theatre; $18.50 weeknights, $19.50 weekend nights.
Dwight Schultz, Larry Riley, Maggie Smith, T J Scott, Paul Hecht, Peter Evans, Joseph Maher, Clarence Williams III.
11/28/79B

The Night of the Iguana
Circle in the Square Theatre revival of a play in two acts (three scenes), by Tennessee Williams. Staged, Joseph Hardy; scenery-light, H R Poindexter; cos, Noel Taylor. Artistic dir, Theodore Mann; managing dir, Paul Libin; publicity, Merle Debuskey, Susan L Schulman; company mgr, William Conn; stage mgrs, Randall Brooks, James Bernardi, Martin Rabbett. Opened Dec. 16, '76, at the uptown Circle in the Square Theatre; $9.95 top.
Richard Chamberlain, Gary Tacon, Sylvia Miles, William Paulson, Ben Van Vacter, Jennifer Savidge, John Rose, Amelia Laurenson, Matt Bennett, Barbara Caruso, Dorothy McGuire, Allison Argo, William Roerick, Benjamin Stewart.
12/22/76B

The Night of the Tribades
Burry Fredrik, Irwin Meyer & Stephen R Friedman, in ass'n with William Donnell, presentation of a play in two acts by Per Olov Enquist; trans, Ross Shideler; staged, Michael Kahn; scenery, Lawrence King; cos, Jane Greenwood; light, John McLain; asso prods, Sally Sears, Marilyn Strauss. GMs, Da-

The Night
(Cont)
vid Lawlor, Helen Nickerson; publicity, Shirley Herz, Louise Weiner Ment; stage mgrs, Suzanne Egan, Richard Humphrey. Opened Oct. 13, '77; $15 top.
Bibi Andersson, Max Von Sydow, Werner Klemperer, Eileen Atkins, Bill Moor.
10/19/77B

The 1940's Radio Hour
Jujamcyn Prods, Joseph P Harris, Ira Bernstein & Roger Berlind presentation of a musical without intermission, by Walton Jones, based on an idea by Jones, Carol Lees. Staged, Jones; mus staging, Thommie Walsh; scenery, David Gropman; light, Tharon Musser; cos, William Ivey Long; snd, Otts Munderloh; orch, Gary S Fagin; vocal arrs, Paul Schierhorn; mus supv, Stanley Lebowsky. GM, Frank Scardinol; publicity, Merlin Group (Cheryl Sue Dolby, Sandra Manley); company mgr, Susan Bell; stage mgrs, Edwin Aldridge, Craig Jacobs, James Lockhart. Opened Oct. 6, '79, at the St. James Theatre; $20 top weeknights, $22.50 weekend nights.
Arny Freeman, John Sloman, Josef Sommer, Stanley Lebowsky, Jack Hallett, Merwin Goldsmith, Jeff Zeller, Crissy Wilzak, Kathy Andrini, Stephen James, Joe Grifasi, Mary-Cleere Haran, Dee Dee Bridgewater, John Doolittle.
10/10/79B

No Man's Land
Roger L Stevens & Robert Whitehead presentation, in ass'n with Frank Milton, of a play in two acts, by Harold Pinter. Staged, Peter Hall; des, John Bury. GM, Oscar E Olesen; mgr, Marshall Young; publicity, Seymour Krawitz, Louise Ment, Patricia McLean Krawitz; stage mgrs, Paul A Foley, M B Miller. Opened Nov. 9, '76, at the Longacre Theatre; $15 top weeknights, $17.50 weekend nights.
Ralph Richardson, John Gielgud, Michael Kitchen, Terence Rigby, Peter Hall, John Bury.
11/17/76B

The November People
Shelly Beychok & Jim D'Spain presentation of a play in two acts, by Gus Weill. Staged, Arthur Sherman; sets, Kert Lundell; light, Thomas Skelton; cos, Joseph G Aulisi. GM, Dorothy Olim; publicity, Shirley Herz, William Schelble; company mgr, Gail Bell; stage mgrs, Alan Hall, Richard Elkow. Opened Jan 14, '78, at the Billy Rose Theatre; $15 top.
Cameron Mitchell, Jan Sterling, John Uecker, James Sutorius, Pamela Reed.
01/18/78B

Nuts
Stevie Phillips, in ass'n with Universal Pictures, presentation of a drama in three acts by Tom Topor; staged, Stephen Zuckerman; set, Tom Schwinn; light, Roger Morgan; cos, Christina Weppner, asso prods, Bonnie Champion, Danny Kreitzberg; GMs, Jack Schlissel, Jay Kingwill; company mgr, Larry Goossen; prodn stage mgr, Lola Shumlin. Opened Apr 28, '80, at the Biltmore Theatre; $19 top weeknights, $21 weekend nights.
Dave Florek, Richard Zobel, Gregory Abels, Linda Howes, Lenka Peterson, Hansford Rowe, Paul Stolarsky, Ed Van Nuys, Anne Twomey.
04/30/80B

Of the Fields, Lately
Patricia Flynn Peate presentation of a drama in two acts (four scenes) by David French. Staged, Jamie Brown; set, J Robin Modereger; cos, Dolores Gamba; light, Richard Dorfman; GM, Marilyn S Miller, Berenice Weiler; mgr, Barbara Carrellas; publicity, Jeffrey Richards Associates; stage mgrs, Brooke Allen, Larry Rosler. Opened May 27, '80, at the Century Theatre; $15 top weeknights, $17.50 weekend nights.
Christopher W Cooper, William Cain, Mary Fogarty, John Leighton.
05/28/80B

Oklahoma!
Zev Bufman & James M Nederlander, in ass'n with Donald C Carter, rev of a musical in two acts (six scenes, 17 numbers); mus, Richard Rodgers, book-lyr, Oscar Hammerstein II; based on the Lynn Riggs play, "Green Grow the Lilacs". Staged, William Hammerstein; chor, Agnes de Mille, recreated by Gemze de Lappe; mus dir, Jay Blackton; scenery, Michael J Hotopp, Paul de Pass; cos, Bill Hargate; light, Thomas Skelton; GM, Theatre Now Inc (William Court Cohen, Edward H Davis, Norman E Rothstein, Ralph Roseman); publicity, Fred Nathan; company mgr, James Awe; stage mgrs, Bob D Bernard, Elise Warner, Philip Rash. Opened Dec. 13, '79, at the Palace Theatre; $22.50 top weeknights, $25 weekend nights.
Laurence Guittard, Christine Andreas, Robert Ray, Stephen Crain, Harry Groener, Martin Vidnovic, Christine Ebersole, Bruce Adler, Martha Traverse, Philip Rash, Nick Jolley. Mary Wickes.
Dream Ballet: Louise Hickey, David Evans, Anthony Santiago, Judy Epstein, Patti Ross, Ilene Strickler, Susan Whelan, Sydney Underson, Tonda Hannum, Kristina Koebel, Leslie Morris, Eric Aaron, Brian Bullard, Phillip Candler, Joel T Myers, Michael Page, Kevin Ryan, Robert Sullivan.
Other singers, dancers: Lorraine Foreman, John Kildahl, Jessica Molaskey, M Lynne Wieneke, Gina Martin, Jerry Ziaja.
Musical numbers: "Oh, What a Beautiful Mornin' ", "The Surrey with the Fringe on Top", "Kansas City", "I Can't Say No", "Many a New Day", "It's a Scandal! It's an Outrage!", "People Will Say We're in Love", "Pore Jud Is Daid", "Lonely Room", "Out of My Dreams", "Laurey Makes Up Her Mind Ballet", "The Farmer and the Cowman", "All er Nothin' ", "People Will Say We're in Love" (reprise), "Oklahoma!", "Oh, What a Beautiful Mornin' " (reprise).
12/19/79B

The Oldest Living Graduate
(A Texas Trilogy)
(For Credits see Lu Ann Hampton Laverty Oberlander). Opened Sept. 23, '76, at the Broadhurst Theatre.
Fred Gwynne, Patricia Roe, Kristin Griffin, Ralph Roberts, Lee Richardson, Henderson Forsythe, William Le Massena, Paul O'Keefe, Avril Gentles.
09/29/76B

On the Twentieth Century
Producers Circle 2 Inc, in ass'n with Joseph Harris & Ira Bernstein, presentation of a musical in two acts (21 numbers); book-lyr, Betty Comden, Adolph Green; mus, Cy Coleman; based on plays by Ben Hecht, Charles MacArthur, Bruce Milholland. Staged, Harold Prince; mus staging, Larry Fuller; scenery, Robin Wagner; cos, Florence Klotz; light, Ken Billington; mus dir, Paul Gemignani; orch, Hershy Kay; asso prods, Sam Crothers, Andre Pastoria. GMs, Joseph Harris, Ira Bernstein; publicity, Bill Evans, Mary Bryant; bus mgr, Frank Scardino; stage mgrs, George Martin, E Bronson Platt, Gerald Teijelo, Andrew Cadiff. Opened Feb 19, '78, at the St James Theatre; $19.50 top weeknights, $22.50 weekend nights ($25 opening).
Ken Hilliard, Charles Rule, Ray Gill, Maris Clement, Carol Lurie, Hal Norman, George Coe, Dean Dittman, Keith Adams, Quitman Fludd III, Ray Stephens, Joseph Wise, Rufus Smith, Tom Batten, Stanley Simmonds, Imogene Coca, Mel Johnson Jr, Carol Lugenbeal, John Cullum, George Lee Andrews, Willi Burke, David Horwitz, Madeline Kahn, Sal Mistretta, Kevin Kline, Judy Kaye.
Singers: Susan Cella, Peggy Cooper, Karen Gibson, Melanie Vaughan, Linda Poser, Craig Lucas, David Vogel, Gerald Teijelo.
Musical numbers: "Stranded Again,", "On the Twentieth Century," "I Rise Again," "Indian Maiden's Lament," "Veronique," "I Have Written a Play," "Together," "Never," "Our Private World," "Repent," "Mine," "I've Got It All," "Entr' Acte," "Five Zeros," "She's a Nut," "Max Jacobs," "Babbette," "The Legacy," "Lily Oscar."
02/22/78B

On Golden Pond
Arthur Cantor & Greer Garson presentation of a Hudson Guild Theatre prodn of a play in two acts (five scenes), by Ernest Thompson. Staged, Craig Anderson; setting and cos, Steven Rubin; light, Craig Miller. Prod mgr, Harvey Elliott; company mgr, Jim Fiore; publicity, C George Willard, Kevin Patterson; stage mgrs, Daniel Morris, Judith Elizabeth Lowry. Opened Feb. 28, '79 at the Apollo Theatre; $15 top weeknights, $16.50 weekend nights.
Tom Aldredge, Frances Sternhagen, Ronn Carroll, Barbara Andres, Mark Bendo, Stan Lachow.
03/07/79B

On Golden Pond
Frank Gero, Frederick M Zollo & Mark Gero in assoc with Budd Block, revival of a play in two acts (five scenes) by Ernest Thompson. Staged, Craig Anderson; settings-cos, Steve Rubin; light, Craig Miller; stage mgr, Daniel Morris. GMs, Leonard Soloway, Allan Francis; publicity, Shirley Herz, Jan Greenburg; company mgr, Keith Waggoner. Opened Sept. 12, '79, at the Century Theatre; $15 top weeknights; $17.50 weekend nights.
Tom Aldredge, Frances Sternhagen, Ronn Carroll, Barbara Andres, Mark Bendo, Stan Lachow.
09/19/79B

Once a Catholic

Doris Cole Abrahams & Eddie Kulukundis, in ass'n with Leon Becker, presentation of a play in two acts, by Mary O'Malley. Staged, Mike Ockrent; scenery, William Ritman; cos, Patricia Adshead; light, Marc B Weiss. GM, R Tyler Gatchell Jr, Peter Neufeld; publicity, Michael Alpert, Marilynn LeVine; stage mgrs, Robert Vandergriff, Audrey Koran, Linda Beckett. Opened Oct. 10, '79, at the Helen Hayes Theatre; $18.50 top weeknights, $20 weekend nights.

Rachel Roberts, Peggy Cass, Pat Falkenhain, Joseph Leon, Roy Poole, Mia Dillon, Terry Calloway, Virginia Hut, Bonnie Hellman, Joyce Cohen, Christine Mitchell, Loretta Scott, Bill Buell, Charley Lang.
10/17/79B

Once in a Lifetime

Circle in the Square revival of a play in three acts (seven scenes), by Moss Hart and George S Kaufman. Staged, Tom Moore; scenery, Karl Eigsti; cos, Carol Luiken; light, F Mitchell Dana. Artistic dir, Theodore Mann; M-dir, Paul Libin; publicity, Merle Debuskey; stage mgrs, Randall Brooks, Rick Ralston. Opened June 15, '78, at the uptown Circle in the Square; $10.50 top weeknights, $11.50 weekend nights.

Michael Jeter, Richard Peterson, Jim Shankman, John Lithgow, Deborah May, Treat Williams, JayneMeadows Allen, Julia Duffy, Sydney Blake, Lee Meredith, Beverly May, Peter J Saputo, Jerry Zaks, Phyllis Somerville, George S Irving, Bella Jarrett, Max Wright, MacIntyre Dixon, Michael Brindidi, Eric Uhler, Jill P Rose, Elizabeth Kemp, Ellen March, Alma Cuervo, Bob Harper, Lance Davis, Sydney Blake, Keith Perry, Peter Bosche, Jack Straw, Lance Davis.
06/21/78B

Onward Victoria

John N Hart Jr in ass'n with Hugh J Hubbard & Robert M Brown presentation of a mus in two acts (16 scenes, 19 numbers), book-lyr, Charlotte Anker, Irene Rosenberg. Mus, Keith Herrmann. Staged, Julianne Boyd; mus staging, Michael Shawn; scenery, William Ritman; cos, Theoni V Aldredge; lighting, Richard Nelson; mus dir, Larry Blank; orchs, Michael Gibson; dance mus arr, Donald Johnston; vocal arr, Keith Herrmann, Larry Blank; snd, Lewis Mead. GM, Joseph Harris, Ira Bernstein; asso, Peter T Kulok; publicity, Shirley Herz, Jan Greenberg; stage Mgrs,, Ed Aldridge, Joseph Corby, Renee F Lutz. Opened Dec 14, '80, at Martin Beck Theatre; $25 top weeknights, $27.50 weekend nights.

Jill Eikenberry, Beth Austin, Marty McDonough, Dan Cronin, Ted Thurston,

Musical numbers: "The Only Sin Is Being Timid," "Magnetic Healing," "Curiosity," Carrie Wilder, Karen Gibson, Lora Jeanne Martens, Gordon Stanley, Marty McDonough, "Beecher's Processional," "I Depend On You," "Onward Victoria," "Changes," "A Taste of Forever," "Unescorted Women," "Love and Joy," "Everyday I Do Little Something John Kildahl, Carol Lurie, Dru Alexander, Scott Fless, Ian Michael Towers, Rex Hays, Martha Jean Sterner, Edmond Genest, Laura Waterbury, Lauren Goler, for the Lord," "It's Easy For Her," "You Cannot Drown the Dream," "Respectable," "Read It in the Weekly," "A Valentine for Beecher," "Beechers's Defense," "Another Life," Ken Waller, Michael Zaslow, Dorothy Holland, Linda Poser, Lenny Wolpe, Jim Jansen. "You Cannot Drown the Dream" (Reprise).
12/17/80B

Otherwise Engaged

James M Nederlander, Frank Milton & Michael Codron presentation of a play in two acts, by Simon Gray. Staged, Harold Pinter; set, Eileen Diss; cos, Jane Greenwood; scenic supv-light, Neil Peter Jampolis. GMs, Elizabeth McCann, Nell Nugent; company mgr, Susan Gustafson; publicity, Michael Alpert, Marilynn LeVine; stage mgrs, Ben Janney, Jeff Rubin. Opened Feb. 2, '77, at the Plymouth Theatre; $13.50 top weeknights, $15 weekend nights.

Tom Courtenay, John Christopher Jones, John Horton, Nicolas Coster, Lynn Milgrim, Michael Lombard, Carolyn Lagerfelt.
02/09/77B

Pacific Overtures

Harold Prince presentation, in ass'n with Ruth Mitchell, of a musical in two acts (12 numbers); mus, Stephen Sondheim; book, John Weidman; addl material by Hugh Wheeler. Staged, Harold Prince; chor, Patricia Birch; scenery, Boris Aronson; cos, Florence Klotz; light, Tharon Musser; orchs; Jonathan Tunick; mus dir, Paul Gemignani; dance mus, Daniel Troob; kabuki cnsltnt, Haruki Fujimoto; orig-cast album and takes, RCA Records. GM, Howard Haines; publicity, Mary Bryant; company mgr, Leo K Cohen; stage mgrs, George Martin, John Grigas, Carlos Goroea; adv, Ashe-LeDonne. Opened Jan. 11, '76, at the Winter Garden Theatre; $15 top.

Mako, Yuki Shimoda, Sab Shimono, James Dybas, Alvin Ing, Freddy Mao, Isao Sato, Soon-Teck Oh, Haruki Fujimoto, Jae Woo Lee, Timm Fujii, Conrad Yama, Mark Hsu Syers, Ernest Abuba, Larry Hama, Freda Foh Shen, Ernest Harada, Gedde Watanabe, Patrick Kinser-Lau, Leslie Watanabe, Tom Matsusaka.

Others: Susan Kikuchi, Diane Lam, Kim Miyori, Kenneth S Eiland, Joey Ginza, Tony Marinyo, Kevin Maung, Dingo Secretario.

Musicians: Fusako Yoshio (shamisen, vocals), Genji Ito (percussion).

Musical numbers: "The Advantages of Floating in the Middle of the Sea," "There Is No Other Way,", "Four Black Dragons," "Chrysanthemum Tea", "Poems," "Welcome to Kanagawa," "Someone in a Tree," "Lion Dance," "Please Hello," "A Bowler Hat," "Pretty Lady," "Next."
01/14/76B

Pal Joey

Circle in the Square revival of a musical in two acts (12 scenes, 15 numbers); mus, Richard Rodgers; lyr, Lorenz Hart; book, John O'Hara, based on O'Hara's New Yorker magazine sketches. Staged, Theodore Mann; chor, Margo Sappington; scenery, John J Moore; cos, Arthur Boccia; light, Ron Wallace; mus dir, Scott Oakley. Artistic dir, Theodore Mann; managing dir, Paul Libin; publicity, Merle Debuskey, Susan L Schulman; stage mgr, James Bernardi; adv, Blaine Thompson (Don Josephson). Opened June 27, '76, at the uptown Circle in the Square, $9.95 top.

Harold Gary, Christopher Chadman, Janie Sell, Boni Enten, Joan Copeland, Dixie Carter, Joe Sirola, Ralph Farnsworth.

Singers, dancers: Terri Treas, Gail Benedict, Murphy Cross, Rosamond Lynn, Marilu Henner, Deborah Geffner, David Hodo, Austin Colyer, Denny Martin Flinn, Michael Leeds, Kenn Scalice, Adam Petroski, Richard Dodd, Lisa Brown.
06/30/76B

Passione

John Wulp, Roger Berlind, Richard Horner, Hinks Shimberg presentation of a play in two acts by Albert Innaurato. Staged, Frank Langella; scenery, David Gropman; cos, William Ivey Long; light, Paul Gallo; orig off-off-Broadway showcase by Playwrights Horizons (Robert Moss, Andre Bishop); GM, Malcolm Allen; publicity, Bob Ullman; stage mgrs, Jay Adler, Charles Kindl. Opened Sep 23, '80, at the Morosco Theatre.

Peter Iacangelo, Richard Zavaglia, Daniel Keyes, Jerry Stiller, Sloane Shelton, Angela Paton, Dick Latessa, Laurel Cronin.
09/24/80B

Past Tense

Circle in the Square presentation of a drama in two scenes (played without intermission), by Jack Zineman; staged, Theodore Mann; scenery, Zack Brown; cos, Kirstina Watson; light, John McLain; Circle in the Square artistic dir, Theodore Mann; M dir, Paul Libin; publicity, Merle Debuskey, Leo Stern; stage mgrs, Nicholas Russiyan, Robert O'Rourke. Opened Apr 24, '80, at the Circle in the Square (Uptown): $16 top weeknights, $18 weekend nights.

Barbara Feldon, Laurence Luckinbill.
04/30/80B

Paul Robeson

Don Gregory presentation, by arrangement with Carmen F Zollo, of a play by Phillip Hayes Dean. Orig staging, Charles Nelson Reilly; staged, Lloyd Richards; sets, H R Poindexter; light, Ian Calderon; cos, Noel Taylor. GM, Leonard A Mulhern; publicity, Seymour Krawitz, Patricia McLean Krawitz, Louise Weiner Ment; company mgr, L Liberatore; stage mgrs, Phil Stein, Louis Mascolo. Opened Jan 19, '78, at the Lunt-Fontanne Theatre; $14 weeknights, $15 weekend nights.

James Earl Jones, Burt Wallace.
01/25/78B

Perfectly Frank

Gladys Rackmil and Fred Levinson, in asso with Emhan Inc, presentation of a revue in two acts of songs by Frank Loesser; other mus, Louis Alter, Remo Biondi, Hoagy Carmichael, Milton Delugg, Frederick Hollander, Gene Krupa, Burton Lane, Joseph J Lilley, Matt Malneck, Jimmy McHugh, Joseph Meyer, Alfred Newman, Victor Schertzinger, Arthur Schwartz, Manning Sherwin, Jule Styne and Lawrence Welk. Staged, Fritz Holt; chor, Tony Stevens; settings-cos, John Falabella; light, Ken Billington; mus dir, Yolanda Segovia; mus consultant, Larry Grossman; orchs, Bill Byers; dance arrs, Ronald Melrose; snd dsgn, Larry Spurgeon; GMs, Leonard

Perfectly Frank
(Cont)
Soloway, Al Francis; co mgr, Michael O'Rand; publicity, Shirley Herz Associates; stage mgrs, Lani Ball, T L Boston. Opened Nov 30, '80, at the Helen Hayes Theatre; $25 top weeknight, $27.50 weekend nights.
Andra Akers, Wayne Cilento, Jill Cook, Don Correia, David Holliday, David Ruprecht, Virginis Sandifur, Debbie Shapiro, Jo Sullivan, Jim Walton.
12/03/80B

Peter Pan
Zev Bufman & James M Nederlander, in assoc with Jack Molthen, Spencer Tandy & J Ronald Horowitz revival of musical in three acts (nine scenes, 20 numbers), with lyr by Carolyn Leigh; mus, Mark Charlap; additional lyrs, Betty Comden and Adolph Green; additional mus, Jule Styne, based on the play by James M Barrie. Staging-chor, Rob Iscove (original staging and chor by Jerome Robbins); orchestrations, Ralph Burns; dance arr, Wally Harper, David Krane; scenery, Peter Wolf; cos, Bill Hargate; light, Thomas Skelton; snd, Richard Fitzgerald; laser effects, Laser Media Inc.; flying, Foy; mus and vocal dir, Jack Lee. General management, Theatre Now; publicity, Solters & Roskin (Joshua Ellis, Rima Corben); company mgr, Camille Ranson; stage mgrs, Barbara-Mae Phillips, David Rubinstein, Nelson K Wilson. Opened Sept. 6, '79, at the Lunt-Fontanne Theatre; $20 top weeknights, $22.50 weekend nights.
Jonathan Ward, James Cook, Maggy Gorrill, Marsha Kramer, Alexander Winter, Beth Fowler, George Rose, Sandy Duncan, Jim Wolfe, Cleve Asbury, Reed Jones, Chris Farr, Michael Estes, Rusty Jacobs, Joey Abbott, Carl Tramon, Dennis Courney, Guy Stroman, Arnold Soboloff, Kevin McCready, Maria Pogee, Jon Vandertholen, Trey Wilson, Steve Yuhasz, Gary Daniel, Neva Rae Powers, William Carmichael, Dianna Hughes, Sharon-Ann Hill, David Storey, C J McCaffrey.
Musical numbers: "Tender Shepherd," "I've Got to Crow," "Neverland," "I'm Flying," "Morning to Neverland," "Pirate Song," "A Princely Scheme," "Indians," "Wendy," "Another Princely Scheme," "I Won't Grow Up," "Mysterious Lady," "Ugg-A-Wugg," "Distant Melody," "Hook's Waltz," "The Battle," "I've Got to Crow" (reprise), "Tender Shepherd" (reprise), "I Won't Grow Up" (reprise), "Neverland" (reprise).
09/12/79B

The Philadelphia Story
Lincoln Center Theatre Co presentation of a Richmond Crinkley revival of a play in two acts (four scenes), by Philip Barry. Staged, Ellis Rabb; set, John Conklin; cos, Nancy Potts; light, John Gleason; snd, Richard Fitzgerald; incidental mus, Claibe Richardson, played by Roslyn Artists String Quartet; prodn supv, Helaine Head; exec prods, Elizabeth I McCann, Nelle Nugent; publicity, Betty Lee Hunt, Maria Cristina Pucci; stage mgrs, Peter Glazer, Count Stovall. Opened Nov 14, '80, at the Vivian Beaumont Theatre; $21.50 top weeknights, $25 weekend nights.
Edward Fabry, Anne Sargent, Kim Beaty, Robert Burr, Cynthia Nixon, Blythe Danner, Meg Mundy, Micheal Gross, George Ede, Edward Herrmann, Mary Louise Wilson, Richard Council, Frank Converse, Douglass Watson, Count Stovall.
11/19/80B

Piaf
(A Remembrance)
Michael Ross & Eddie Vallone presentation of a play in two acts by David Cohen; conceived, Milli Janz. Staged, Lee Rachman; scenery-light, Ralph Alswang; cos, Robert Troie; mus arr-cond, John Marino. GM, David Lawlor; publicity, David Powers; stage mgrs, Robert J Bruyr, Amelia Haywood. Opened Feb. 14, '77, at the Playhouse Theatre; $12 top weeknights, $13 weekend nights.
Gregory Salata, Edmund Lyndeck, Lou Bedford, Juliette Koka, Douglas Andros, Donald Hampton.
02/16/77B

The Pirates Of Penzance
James Nederlander presentation by arrangement with the D'Oyly Carte Opera Trust Ltd. and Bridget D'Oyly Carte, of a D'Oyly Carte revival of a comic opera in two acts; book-lyr, William S Gilbert; mus, Arthur Sullivan. Prodn dir, Michael Heyland; mus dir, Royston Nash; set, Disley Jones; cos, Charles Ricketts; light supv, Martin Aronstein; GM, Frederic Lloyd; company mgr, Herbert Newby; publicity, Michael Alpert (Marilynn LeVine); adv, Blaine Thompson (Mike Mones). Opened May 6, '76, at the Uris Theatre; $12.50 top weeknights, $15 weekend nights.
James Conroy-Ward, John Ayldon, Jon Ellison, Meston Reid, Michael Rayner, Julia Goss, Jane Metcalfe, Caroline Baker, Patricia Ann Bennett, Lyndsie Holland.
05/19/76B

Platinum
Gladys Rackmil, Fritz Holt & Barry M Brown presentation of Joe Layton's prodn of a musical in two acts (12 numbers), with book by Will Holt and Bruce Vilanch,
11/15/78B mus, Gary William Friedman and lyrs, Will Holt, based on an idea by Will Holt. Staged and choreographed by Joe Layton; scenery, David Hays; light, John Gleason; cos, Bob Mackie; orchestrations, Fred Thaler, Jimmie Haskell; arrs, Fred Thaler, Jimmie Haskell and Gary William Friedman; musical dir, Fred Thaler; snd, PAR; multi-media, Sheppard Kerman. GM, Marvin A Krauss; co M, Sam Pagliaro; publicity, Shirley Herz; stage Ms, Frank Hartenstein, Charles Collins. Opened Nov 12, '78, at the Mark Hellinger Theatre; $19.50 top weeknights, $22.50 weekend nights.
Tony Shultz, Alexis Smith, Ronnie B Baker, Jonathan Freeman, John Hammil, Damita Jo Freeman, Robin Green, Avery Sommers, Stanley Kamel, Lisa Mordente, Richard Cox, Christine Faith, Wenndy Leigh Mackenzie, Jonathan Freeman, Fred Thaler, Gregory Bloch, Dick Frank, Steve Mack, Roy Markowitz, Alexis Smith, Alan Fairmont.

Players
The Kennedy Center & Eddie Kulukundis presentation of a play in two acts, by David Williamson. Staged, Michael Blakemore; scenery-cos, Hayden Griffin; prodn supv, Charles Vaughan III; light, Martin Aronstein. Publicity, Jeffrey Richards, Warren Knowlton; stage mgrs, Wayne Carson, Peter Lombard. Opened Sept 6, '78 at the Lyceum Theatre; $16 top weeknights, $17.50 weekend nights.
Gene Rupert, Thomas A Carlin, Rex Robbins, Tom Flagg, Fred Gwynne, Michael O'Hare.
09/13/78B

The Poison Tree
Emanuel Azenberg, William W Bradley, Marvin A Krauss & Irving Siders presentaton of a play in two acts (10 scenes), by Ronald Ribman. Staged, Charles Blackwell; set, Marjorie Kellogg; light, Martin Aronstein; cos, Judy Dearing. GM, Jose Vega; publicity, Merle Debuskey, Leo Stern; stage mgrs, Henry Velez, Robert St Clair, Steven Shaw, Gene O'Neill. Opened Jan. 8, '75, at the Ambassador Theatre; $10 top weeknights, $12 weekend nights.
Danny Meehan, Daniel Barton, Gene O'Neill, Peter Masterson, Robert Symonds, Charles Brown, Arlen Dean, Pat McNamara, Cleavon Little, Dick Anthony Williams, Moses Gunn, Northern J Calloway, Dennis Tate.
Understudies: Arthur French, Frank Hamilton, Charles Douglass.
01/14/76B

Poor Murderer
Kermit Bloomgarden, John Bloomgarden & Ken Marsolais presentation of a play in two acts, by Pavel Kohout. Staged, Herbert Berghof; scenery-light, Howard Bay; cos, Patricia Zipprodt; produced in ass'n with Don Mark Enterprises. GM, Max Allentuck; prodn asso, Dona D Vaughn; company mgr, Milton Moss; publicity, John Springer, Louis Sica; stage mgrs, Frederick A de Wilde, Harry Young, Timothy Farmer. Opened Oct. 20, '76, at the Ethel Barrymore Theatre; $13.50 top weeknights, $15 weekend nights.
Larry Gates, Laurence Luckinbill, Kevin McCarthy, Maria Schell, Paul Sparer, Ernest Graves, Peter Maloney, Julie Garfield, Ruth Ford, Felicia Montealegre, Barbara Coggin, Timothy Farmer, James Carruthers, Sean Griffin, Richard Vernon, Stanley Wietrzychowski, Brian Koonin, Alfonso Schiapano.
10/27/76B

Porgy and Bess
Sherwin M Goldman & The Houston Grand Opera revival of a musical in two acts (nine scenes, 30 numbers); mus, George Gershwin; libretto, DuBose Heyward; lyr, Heyward, Ira Gershwin, based on play, "Porgy," by Dorothy and DuBose Heyward. Staged, Jack O'Brien; mus dir-chorus master, John DeMain; set, Robert Randolph; cos, Nancy Potts; light, Gilbert V Hemsley Jr; chor-asst dir, Mabel Robinson. GM, Robert A Buckley; company mgr, Bill Liberman; stage mgrs, Helaine Head, Sally McCravey, William Gammon. Opened Sept. 25, '76, at the Uris Theatre; $17.50 top.
Ross Reimueller, Betty D Lane, Bernard Thacker, Curtis Dickson, Larry Marshall, Glover Parham, Wilma Shakesnider (Delores Ivory-David, alternate), Hartwell Mace, Mervin Wallace, Myra Merritt, Carol Brice, Alex Carrington, Donnie Ray Albert (Abraham Lind-Oquendo, Robert Mosley, alternates),

Porgy and
(Cont)
Andrew Smith (George Robert Merritt, alternate), Clamma Dale (Esther Hinds, Irene Oliver, alternates), Hansford Rowe, William Gammon, Cornel Richie, Shirley Baines, Raymond Bazemore, Kenneth Barry, Phyllis Bash, Steven Alex-Cole, John B Ross.

Ensemble: John D Anthony, Earl Baker, Kenneth Bates, Barbara Buck, Steven Alex-Cole, Ella Eure, Wilhelmena Fernandez, Elizabeth Graham, Earl Grandison, Kenneth Hamilton, Betty Harris, Loretta Holkmann, Alma Johnson, Cora Johnson, Roberta Long, Patricia McDermott, Naomi Moody, William Penn, Dwight Ransom, Rodrick Ross, Alexander B Smalls, Barbara Ann Webb, Wardell Woodard, Denice Woods, Barbara L Young.

Musical numbers: Introduction, "Brown Blues," "Summertime," "A Woman Is a Sometime Thing," "Here Come De Honey Man," "They Pass By Singin'," "Oh Little Stars," "Gone, Gone, Gone," "Overflow," "My Man's Gone Now," "Leavin' for the Promise' Lan'," "It Take a Long Pull To Get There," "I Got Plenty o' Nuttin'," "Buzzard Song," "Bess, You Is My Woman Now," "Oh, I Can't Sit Down," "I Ain't Got No Shame," "It Ain't Necessarily So," "What You Want Wid Bess?" "Oh, Doctor Jesus," "I Loves You, Porgy," " Oh, Hev'enly Father," "Oh, De Lawd Shake De Heavens," "Oh, Dere's Somebody Knockin' at de Do'," "A Red Headed Woman," "Clara, Clara," "There's a Boat Dat's Leavin' Soon for New York," "Good Mornin', Sistuh!" "Oh, Bess, Oh Where's My Bes?" "Oh, Lawd, I'm on My Way."
09/29/76B

Quick Change
Arthur Shafman Int'l Ltd presentation of a solo show in two acts; wris, Bruce M Belland, Roy M Rogosin, Michael McGiveney. Staged-mus, Rogosin; cos, Mary Wills; lyrs, Belland; company mgr, John Larson; publicity, Jeffrey Ricards Assocs; stage mgr, Ernie Guderjahn. Opened Oct 30, '80, at the Bijou Theatre; $16.50 top weeknights, $18.50 weekends.
Michael McGiveney.
11/05/80B

Reggae
Michael Butler & Eric Nezhad, in ass'n with David Cogan, presentation of a musical drama in two acts; book, Melvin Van Peebles, Kendrew Lascelles, Stafford Harrison; mus-lyrs, Ras Karbi, Michael Kamen, Kendrew Lascelles, Max Romeo, Randy Bishop, Jackie Mittoo, Stafford Harrison. Staged, Glenda Dickerson; addl staging, Gui Andrisano; chor, Mike Malone; set, Ed Burbridge; cos, Raoul Pene de Bois; light, Beverly Emmons; mus dir, Michael Kamen; dance cnsltnt, Rex Nettleford; snd dsgn, Lou Gonsalez; exec prod, Woodie King Jr; GM, Ken Myers; publicity, Merlin Group; company mgr, Dennis Purcell; stage mgrs, Robert Currie, Lee Murray. Opened Mar 27, '80, at the Biltmore Theatre; $22.50 top.
Alvin McDuffie, Sheryl Lee Ralph, Philip Michael Thomas, Obba Babatunde, Fran Salisbury, Louise Robinson, Calvin Lockhart, Ras Karbi, Charles Wisnet, Sam Harkness.

Ensemble: - Loretta Abbott, Breeha Clarke, Ralph Glenmore, Jeffrey Anderson Gunter, Thomas Pinnock, Louise Robinson, Kiki Shepard, Beth Shorter, Paul Cook Tarrt, Bruce Taylor, Ras-jawara Tesfa, Avond Testamark, Constance Thomas, Juanita Grace Tyler, Bryon Utley, Lewis Whitlock.

Musical numbers: - "Jamaica Is Waiting," "Rise Tafarii," "Farmer," "Hey Man," "Mash 'Em Up," "Mrs Brown," "Everything That Touches You," "Mash Ethiopia," "Son of Zion," "Reggae Music Got Soul," "Talkiin' 'Bout Reggae," "Everything That Touches You" (reprise), "Rise Up Jah-Jah Children," "No Sinners in Jah Yard," "Banana, Banana, Banana," "Promised Land," "Rasta Roll Call," "Ethiopian Pageant," "Rastafari," "Roots of the Tree," "I and II," "Gotta Take a Chance," "Star of Zion," "Chase the Devil," "Now I See It," "Now I See It " (reprise), "Everything That Touches You" (reprise), "Reggae Music Got Soul" (reprise), "Jamaica Is Waiting" (reprise).
04/02/80B

Rex
Richard Adler presentation, in ass'n with Roger Berlind & Edward R Downe Jr, of a musical in two acts (23 scenes, 22 numbers); mus, Richard Rodgers; lyr, Sheldon Harnick; book, Sherman Yellen. Staged, Edwin Sherin; chor, Dania Krupska; orchs, Irwin Kostal; mus dir, Jay Blackton; dance mus arrs, David Baker; scenery-cos, John Conklin; light, Jennifer Tipton. GMs, Edward H Davis, William Court Cohen; publicity, Jeffrey Richards; company mgr, Leo K Cohen; stage mgrs, Bob Bernard, Jack Timmers, Elise Warner; adv, Ash-LeDonne. Opened April 25, '76, at the Lunt-Fontanne Theatre; $15 top weeknights, $17.50 weekend nights.
Charles Rule, William Griffis, Tom Aldredge, Nicol Williamson, Ed Evanko, Glenn Close, Barbara Andres, April Shawhan, Stephen D Newman, Danny Ruvolo, Jeff Phillips, Martha Danielle, Penny Fuller, Keith Koppmeier, Merwin Goldsmith, Ken Henley, Dennis Daniels, Martha Danielle, Melanie Vaughan, Sparky Shapiro, Lillian Shelby, Gerald R Teijelo, Valerie Mahaffey, Michael John.

Singers, dancers: Harry Fawcett, Paul Forrest, Pat Gideon, Dawn Herbert, Robin Hoff, Don Johanson, Jim Litten, Craig Lucas, Carol Jo Lugenbeal, G Eugene Moose, Jo Speros, Gerald R Teijelo Jr, Candace Tovar, John Ulrickson.

Musical numbers: "Te Deum," "No Song More Pleasing," "Where Is My Son?" "The Field of Cloth of Gold," Basse Dance, "The Chase," "Away from You," "As Once I Loved You," "Elizabeth," "What Now?" "No Song More Pleasing" (reprise), "Away from You" (reprise), "Te Deum" (reprise), "Christmas at Hampton Court," "The Wee Golden Warrior," "Sword Dance and Morris Dance, "The Masque," "From Afar," "In Time," "In Time" (reprise), "Te Deum" (reprise").
04/28/76B

Richard III
The Shubert Organization, Victor Potamkin & Moe Septee revival of a play in three acts, by William Shakespeare. Staged, David Wheeler; scenery, Tony Straiges; light, Thomas Skelton; cos, Jeanne Button; incidental mus, Charles Gross. GM, Marvin A Krauss; company mgr, Mary Ellen Devery; publicity, Max Eisen, Robert Ganshaw; stage mgr, Bige- low Green. Opened June 10, '79 at the Cort Theatre; $18.50 weeknights, $20 weekend nights.
Bill Moor, Al Pacino, Richard Jamieson, Ronald Hunter, J T Walsh, Linda Selman, John Mahon, Judson Earney, Frederick C Neumann, Rex Robbins, Larry Bryggman, Paul Guilfoyle, Richard Bright, Max Wright, Penelope Allen, Jaime Sanchez, Harriet Rogers, Laura Harrington, Dominic Chianese, Glenn Scarpelli, Keith Gordon, Frederic Kimball, Bruce Waite, Dan Monahan, Daniel Zippi, Gary Bayer.
06/20/79B

The Roast
Paramount Pictures Corp presentation of a Joseph P Harris & Ira Bernstein prodn of a comedy in two acts by Jerry Belson and Garry Marshall; staged, Carl Reiner; scenery, William Ritman; cos, Alvin Colt; light, Tharon Musser; snd, Otts Munderloh; bus mgr, Peter T Kulok; publicity, Solters, Roskin, Friedman (Milly Schoenbaum); stage mgrs, Ed Aldridge, Victoria Merrill. Opened May 8, '80, at the Winter Garden Theatre; $22.50 top weeknights, $25 weekend nights.
Bill Macy, Larry Gelman, Barney Martin, Becky Gonzalez, John Arch-Carter, Doug McClure, David Huddleston, Antonio Fargas, Rob Reiner, Reynaldo Rey, Arny Freeman, Crissy Wilzak, Joe Silver, Peter Boyle.
05/14/80B

The Robber Bridegroom
John Houseman, Margot Harley & Michael B Kapon, by arrangement with the Acting Co., revival of a musical in one act (13 numbers); book-lyr, Alfred Uhry; mus comp-arr, Robert Waldman, based on Eudora Welty novella. Staged, Gerald Freedman; chor, Donald Saddler; scenery, Douglas W Schmidt; cos, Jeanne Button; light, David F Segal. GM, Elizabeth McCann, Nelle Nugent; publicity, Merlin group (Sandra Manley); stage mgrs, Mary Porter Hall, Bethe Ward. Opened Oct. 9, '76 at the Biltmore Theatre; $13 top weeknights, $15 weekend nights.
Barry Bostwick, Stephen Vinovich, Rhonda Coullet, Barbara Lang, Lawrence John Moss, Ernie Sabella, Trip Plymale, Susan Berger, Jana Schneider, Carolyn McCurry, George Deloy, Gary Epp, B J Hardin, Mary Murray, Melinda Tanner, Dennis Warning, Tom Westerman.

Musical numbers: "Once Upon the Natchez Trace," "Two Heads," "Steal with Style," "Rosamund's Dream," "The Pricklepear Bloom," "Nothin' Up," "Deeper in the Woods," "Riches," "Love Stolen," "Poor Tied Up Darlin'," "Goodbye Salome," "Sleepy Man," "Where Oh Where."
10/13/76B

Rockabye Hamlet
Lester Osterman Prodns & Joseph Kipness in ass'n with Martin Richards & Victor D'Arc, Marilyn Strauss presentation of a musical in two acts; book-mus-lyr, Cliff Jones, based on Shakespeare's "Hamlet." Staged-chor, Gower Champion; scenery, Kert F Lundell; cos, Joseph G Aulisi; light, Jules Fisher; snd, Abe Jacob; swordplay, Larry Carpenter; mus dir-vocal arrs, Gordon Lowry Harrell; asso cond, Bill Schneider; dance mus arr, Douglas Katsaros; co-chor, Tony Stevens. GM, Leon-

Rockabye Hamlet
(Cont)
ard Soloway; publicity, Betty Lee Hunt, Maria Pucci; stage mgrs, Bethe Ward, Tony Manzi; adv, Blaine Thompson. Opened Feb. 17, '76, at the Minskoff Theatre; $15 top weeknights, $17 weekend nights.

Rory Dodd, Larry Marshall, Alan Weeks, Leata Galloway, Meat Loaf, Randal Wilson, Beverly D'Angelo, Kim Milford, Christopher Chadman, Winston DeWitt Hemsley, Irving Lee, Judy Gibson, Tommy Aguilar, Steve Anthony, Terry Calloway, Prudence Darby, George Giraldo, Larry Hyman, Kurt Johnson, Clinton Keen, Paula Lynn, Joann Ogawa, Sandi Orcutt, Merle Poloway, Joseph Pugliese, Yolanda Raven, Michelle Stubbs, Dennis Williams,

Singers: James Braet, Judy DeAngelis, B G Gibson, Judy Gibson, Pat Gorman, Suzanne Lukather, Bruce Paine, William Parry. Roadies: Chet D'Elia, David Fredericks, David Lawson, Jeff Spielman.

Musical numbers: "Why Did He Have To Die?" "The Wedding," "That It Should Come To This," "Set It Right," "Hello-Hello," "Don't Unmask Your Beauty To The Moon," "If Not To You," 'Have I Got A Girl For You," 'Tis Pity, Tis True," "Shall We Dance," "All My Life," "Something's Rotten In Denmark," "Denmark Is Still," "Twist Her Mind," "Gentle Lover," "Where Is The Reason," "The Wart Song," "He Got It In The War," "It Is Done," "Midnight - Hot Blood," "Midnight Mass." "Hey . . .!," "Sing Along," "Your Daddy's Gone Away," "Rockabye Hamlet," "All By Yourself," "The Rosencrantz & Guildenstern Boogie," "Laertes Coercion," "The Last Blues," "Didn't She Do It For Love," "If My Morning Begins," "Swordfight."
02/18/76B

Romantic Comedy
Morton Gottieb presentation of a play in three acts (seven scenes) by Bernard Slade. Staged, Joseph Hardy; set, Douglas W Schmidt; cos, Jane Greenwood; light, Tharon Musser; GM, Ben Rosenberg; publicity, Solters & Roskin (Milly Schoenbaum); stage mgrs, Warren Crane, Wayne Carson; company mgr, Martin Cohen.

Anthony Perkins, Carole Cook, Mia Farrow, Holly Palance, Greg Mullavey, Deborah May.
11/14/79B

Romeo and Juliet
Circle in the Square revival of a play in two acts, by William Shakespeare. Staged, Theodore Mann; sword fight staging, Patrick Crean & Erik Fredericksen; scenery, Ming Cho Lee; cos, John Conklin; light, Thomas Skelton; incidental mus, Thomas Pasatieri. Circle in the Square artistic dir, Theodore Mann; managing dir, Paul Libin; publicity, Merle Debuskey, Davis Roggensack; stage mgrs, Randall Brooks, James Bernardi, K C Kelly. Opened March 17, '77, at the uptown Circle in the Square, $9.95 top.

Jim Broaddus, Christopher Loomis, Dennis Lipscomb, Dennis Patella, Peter Van Norden, Micheal Forella, Ray Wise, Armand Assante, Lester Rawlins, Delphi Harrington, Tom Klunis, Helen Harrelson, Richard Greene, Paul Rudd, John V Shea, Pamela Payton-Wright, Jan Miner, David Rounds, Lisa Pelikan, Erik Fredericksen, Jack Gwillim, K C Kelly, Daniel Ben-Zali, Mark Cohen, Ruth Livingston, Jennifer Savidge.
03/23/77B

Runaways
Joseph Papp presentation of a NY Shakespeare Festival prodn of a musical in two acts (41 numbers), wri-comp-dir, Elizabeth Swados. Scenery, Douglas W Schmidt, Woods Mackintosh; cos, Hilary Rosenfeld; snd, Bill Dreisbach; light, Jennifer Tipton; asso prod, Bernard Gersten. GM, Robert Kamlot; company mgrs, Bob MacDonald, Roger Gindi; publicity, Merle Debuskey, Richard Kornberg; stage mgrs, Gregory Meeh, Peter Glazer, Patricia Morinelli. Opened May 6 (press opening, May 13), '78, at the Plymouth Theatre; $17.50 top weeknights, $18.50 weekend nights.

Bruce Hlibok, Lorie Robinson, Carlo Imperato, Rachel Kelly, Ray Contreras, Nan-Lynn Nelson, Jossie de Guzman, Randy Ruiz, Jon Matthews, Bernie Allison, Venustra K Robinson, David Schechter, Evan H Miranda, Jonathan Feig, Kate Schellenbach, Leonard Brown, Mark Anthony Butler, Trini Alvarado, Karen Evans, Sheila Gibbs, Paula Anderson, Kenya Brome, Jerome Dekie, Karin Dekie, John Gallogly, Timmy Michaels, Toby Parker.

Musicians: Piano and Toy Piano, Judith Fleischer; String Bass, John Schimmel; Congas, Timbales, Bells, Sirens and Others, Leopoldo F Fleming; Traps, Triangle, Glass, Ratchet, David Sawyer; Saxophones, Flutes, Patience Higgins; Guitars, Elizabeth Swados.

Musical numbers: "You Don't Understand," "I Had to Go," "Parent-Kid Dance," "Appendectomy," "Where Do People Go," "Footstep," "Once Upon a Time," "Current Events," "Every Now and Then," "Out on the Street," "Minnesota Strip," "Song of a Child Prostitute," "Christmas Puppies," "Lazar's Heroes," "Find Me a Hero," "Scrynatchkielooaw," "The Undiscovered Son," "I Went Back Home," "This Is What I Do When I'm Angry," "The Basketball Song," "Spoons," "Lullaby for Luis," "We Are Not Strangers," "In the Sleeping Line," "Lullaby from Baby to Baby," "Tra Gog Voin Dein Whole" (I Will Not Tell a Soul), "Revenge Song," "Enterprise," "Sometimes," "Clothes," "We Are Not Strangers" (reprise), "Mr. Graffiti," "The Untrue Pigeon," "Senoras de la Noche," "We Have to Die?" "Where Are Those People Who Did 'Hair'?" "Appendectomy II," "Let Me Be a Kid," "To the Dead of Family Wars," "Problem After Problem," "Lonesome of the Road."
05/17/78B

The Runner Stumbles
Wayne Adams & Willard Morgan presentaton, by arrangement with the Hartman Theatre Co., of a play in two acts, by Milan Stitt. Staged, Austin Pendleton; set, Patricia Woodbridge; cos, James Berton Harris; light, Cheryl Thacker. GM, Dorothy Olim; publicity, Howard Atlee, Clarence Allsopp; stage mgrs, Peggy Peterson, David Lile; adv, Krone-Olim (Sheldon Baron). Opened May 18, '76, at the Little Theare, $9 top weeknights, $10 weekend nights.

Morrie Piersol, Stephen Joyce, Katina Commings, James Noble, Nancy Donohue, Sloane Shelton, Craig Richard Nelson, Joseph Mathewson, Marilyn Pfeiffer, Robert James Doran, David Lile, Monica Guglielmina.
05/26/76B

Saint Joan
Circle in the Square revival of a play in two acts and epilog, by George Bernard Shaw. Staged, John Clark; scenery, David Jenkins; cos, Zack Brown; light, John McLain. Artistic dir, Theodore Mann; managing dir, Paul Libin; publicity,, Merle Debuskey, David Roggensack; company mgr, William Conn; stage mgrs, Randall Brooks, James Bernardi. Opened Dec. 15, '77, at the Uptown Circle in the Square, $10.95 top weeknights, $11.95 weekend nights.

Roy Cooper, Armin Shimerman, Lynn Redgrave, Peter Van Norden, Pendleton Brown, Tom Aldredge, Tom Klunis, Kenneth Gray, Ed Setrakian, Robert LuPone, Gwendolyn Brown, Joseph Bova, Stephen Lang, Philip Bosco, Robert Gerringer, Paul Shyre, Paul Sparer, John Rose, Stephen Lang, Nicholas Hormann, Jim Broaddus.
12/21/77B

Sarava
Eugene V Wolsk presentation of Mitch Leigh prodn of a musical in two acts (17 scenes, 19 numbers), with book and lyrics by N Richard Nash, score by Mitch Leigh, based on "Dona Flor and Her Two Husbands," a novel by Jorge Amado, and a Brazilian-made film of the same title. Staged-chor, Rick Atwell; settings-cos, Santo Loquasto; light, David F Segal; mus dir and vocal arr, David Freidman; orch, Daniel Troob; dance mus arr, Dom Salvador; snd, Robert Kerzman. GM, Manny Kladitis; publicity, John A Prescott; stage mgrs, Douglas F Goodman, John Brigleb. Scheduled to open Feb. 23, '79 (caught at preview Feb. 9, '79) at the Mark Hellinger Theatre; $22.50 top weeknights, $25 weekend nights.

P J Benjamin, Tovah Feldshuh, Roderick Spencer Sibert, Doncharles Manning, Wilfredo Suarez, Jack Neubeck, Ken Waller, Carol Jean Lewis, Loyd Sannes, Gaetan Young, Betty Walker, Randy Graff, Alan Abrams, Michael Ingram, David Kottke, Steve J Ace, Frank Cruz, Donna Cyrus, Merlene Danielle, Adrienne Frimet, Brenda Garratt, Trudie Green, Jane Judge, Ivson Polk, Wynonna Smith, Michelle Stubbs, Freida Ann Williams.

Musical numbers: "Sarava," "Makulele," "Vadinho Is Gone," "Hosanna," "Nothing's Missing," "Nothing's Missing" (reprise), "I'm Looking for a Man," "A Simple Man," "Viva a Vida," "Muito Bom," "Nothing's Missing" (reprise), "Play the 'Which Way Do I Go?'" "Remember," "A Simple Man" (reprise), "You Do," "A Single Life," "Vadinho Is Gone" (reprise), "Sarava" (reprise).
02/14/79B

Secret Service
Phoenix Theatre revival of a play in three acts, by William Gillette. Staged, Daniel Freudenberger; scenery-light, James Tilton; cos, Clifford Capone. Managing dir, T Edward Hambleton; GM, Marilyn S Miller; prodn mgr, Robert Beard; publicity, Gifford-Wallace; stage mgrs, Jonathan Penzner, Peter DeNicola; adv, Ash-LeDonne. Opened April 12, '76, at the Playhouse, $9 top weeknights, $10 weekend nights.

Secret Service
(Cont)
Don Scardino, Louise Stubbs, Alice Drummond, Meryl Streep, David Harris, Frederick Coffin, John Lithgow, Marybeth Hurt, Charles Kimbrough, Joe Grifasi, Stuart Warmflash, Moultrie Patten, Lenny Baker, Jonathan Penzner, Rex Robbins, Hansford Rowe, Jeffrey Jones, Roy Poole, Arthur Miller.
04/14/76B

The Shadow Box
Lester Osterman, Ken Marsolais, Allan Francis & Leonard Soloway presentation of a Mark Taper Forum-Long Wharf Theatre prodn of a play in two acts by Michael Cristofer. Staged, Gordon Davidson; set, Ming Cho Lee; cos, Bill Walker; light, Ronald Wallace. Publicity, Betty Lee Hunt, Maria Cristina Pucci; company mgr, Robert H Wallner; stage mgrs, Franklin Keysar, Fred Hoot. Opened March 31, '77, at the Morosco Theatre; $12 top.
Josef Sommer, Simon Oakland, Vincent Stewart, Joyce Ebert, Lurence Luckinbill, Mandy Patinkin, Patricia Elliott, Rose Gregorio, Geraldine Fitzgerald.
04/06/77B

She Loves Me
Richard Grayson & John Bowab concert-version revival of a musical in two acts (24 numbers); book, Joe Masteroff; mus, Jerry Bock; lyr, Sheldon Harnick, based on a Hungarian play, "Parfumerie," by Miklos Laszlo. Staged, John Bowab; gowns, Donald Brooks; light, Ken Billington; mus dir, Wally Harper. Publicity, Betty Lee Hunt, Maria Pucci; company mgr, Gino Giglio; stage mgrs, Ben Sprecher, T L Boston, Michael Hayward-Jones. Opened March 29, '77, at Town Hall, $10 top.
Tom Batten, George David Connolly, Rita Moreno, Laurence Guittard, Barry Bostwick, George Rose, Bette Glenn, Marti Bucklew, Janet McCall, Madeline Kahn, Michael Hayward-Jones, John LaMotta, William James.
Musical number: "Good Morning, Good Day," "Sounds While Selling" "Days Gone By," "No More Candy," "Three Letters," "Tonight at Eight," "I Don't Know His Name," "Perspective," "Good Bye Georg," "Will He Like Me," "Ilona," "I Resolve," "A Romantic Atmosphere," "Tango Trangique," "Mr. Nowack Will You Please," "Dear Friend," "Try Me," "Where's My Shoe," "Vanilla Ice Cream," "She Loves Me," "A Trip to the Library," "Grand Knowing You," "Twelve Days to Christmas," Finale.
04/06/77B

Shelley Berman
Arthur Shafman Int'l Ltd presentation of a solo comedy act in two parts; wri-star, Shelley Berman; prodn supv, Kitzi Becker; GM, Christopher Dunlop; company mgr, John Larson; publicity, Jeffrey Richards Assocs. Opened Oct 2, '80, at the Bijou Theatre; $18.50 top nights, $15-$16.50 matinees.
Shelley Berman.
10/08/80B

Siamsa, The National Folk Theatre of Ireland
Brannigan-Eisler Performing Arts International, Inc. presentation of a folk entertainment in two acts. Devised-staged, Pat Ahern, Siamsa's artistic dir; des cnsltnt, Lona Moran; chor, Patricia Hanafin; ward supv, Phyllis O'Donoghue; company mgr, Martin Whelan; company secy, Christopher Fitz-Simon; tour coord, Dermond McCarthy; publicity, Dan Langan; stage mgr, Jimmy McDonnell. Opened Sept. 27, '76, at the Palace Theatre; $9.50 top.
Sean O'Mahony, Liam Heaslip, Sean Ahern, Patricia Hanafin, Jimmy Smith, Jerry Nolan, John McCarthy, Philomena Daly, Susan Rohan, Catherine Hurley, Michael O'Shea, Aidan O'Carroll, Mary Lyons, Marie O'Donoghue, Sandra O'Reilly, Catherine Spangler, Sean Heaslip, Oliver Hurley, John Fitzgerald, Pat Kennington, Gerard Buckley, Nicholas McAuliffe, Timmy O'Shea, Pierce Heaslip, Audrey O'Carroll.
09/29/76B

Side by Side by Sondheim
Harold Prince, in ass'n with Ruth Mitchell, by arrangement with the Incomes Co., Ltd., of a revue in two acts (30 numbers); lyr, Stephen Sondheim; mus, Sondheim, Leonard Bernstein, Mary Rodgers, Richard Rodgers, Jule Styne. Staged, Ned Sherrin; mus dir, Ray Cook; pianists, Daniel Troob, Albin Konopka; mus staging, Bob Howe; scenery, Peter Docherty; cos, Florence Klotz; light, Ken Billington; scenery supv, Jay Moore; mus supv, Paul Gemignani. GM, Howard Haines; publicity, Mary Bryant, Bruce Cohen; stage mgrs, John Grigas, Artie Masella. Opened April 17, '77, at the Music Box Theatre; $15 top weeknights, $17.50 weekend nights.
Millicent Martin, Julie N McKenzie, David Kernan, Ned Sherrin.
Musical numbers: "Comedy Tonight," "Love Is in the Air," "If Momma Was Married," "You Must Meet My Wife," "The Little Things You do Together," "Getting Married Today," "I Remember," "Can That Boy Foxtrot," "Company," "Another Hundred People," "Barcelona," "Marry Me a Little," "I Never Do Anything Twice," "Bring on the Girls," "Ah, Paree," "Buddy's Blues," "Broadway Baby," "You Could Drive a Person Crazy," "Everybody Says Don't," "Anyone Can Whistle," "Send in the Clowns," "We're Gonna Be All Right," "A Boy Like That," "I Have a Love," "The Boy From...," "Pretty Lady," "You Gotta Have a Gimmick," "Losing My Mind," "Could I Leave You," "I'm Still Here," "Conversation Piece," "Side by Side by Side."
04/20/77B

1600 Pennsylvania Avenue
Roger L Stevens & Robert Whitehead presentation of a musical in two acts (22 numbers); book-lyr, Alan Jay Lerner; mus, Leonard Bernstein. Staged-chor, Gilbert Moses, George Faison; scenery, Kert Lundell; light, Tharon Musser; cos, Whitney Blausen, Dona Granata; mus dir, Roland Gagnon; orchs, Sid Ramin, Hershey Kay; snd, John McClure. GM, Oscar E Olesen; company mgr, James Walsh; publicity, Seymour Krawitz, Patricia McLean Krawitz, Ted Goldsmith; casting-prodn coord, Doris Blum; casting dir, Terry Fay; stage mgrs, William Dodds, Marnel Sumner, Michael Turque; adv, Blaine Thompson (Mike Mones). Opened May 4, '76, at the Mark Hellinger Theatre; $15 top weeknights, $17.50 weekend nights.
Ken Howard, Patricia Routledge, Gilbert Price, Emily Yancy, Guy Costley, David E Thomas, Howard Ross, Reid Shelton, Ralph Farnsworth, J T Cromwell, Lee Winston, Richard Chappell, Walter Charles, Edwin Steffe, John Witham, Richard Muenz, Alexander Orfaly, Raymond Cox, Randolph Riscol, Raymond Bazemore, Urylee Leonardos, Carl Hall, Janette Moody, Cornel J Richie, Louise Heath, Bruce A Hubbard,
Singers, dancers: Elaine Bunse, Nancy Callman, Beth Fowler, Kris Karlowski, Joyce MacDonald, Charon Powers, Martha Thigpen, Jo-Ann Baldo, Clyde-Jaques Barrett, Joella Breedlove, Allyne DeChalus, Linda Griffin, Bob Heath, Michael Lichtefeld, Diana Mirras, Hector Jaime Mercado, Cleveland Pennington, Al Perryman, Renee Rose, Juliet Seignious, Thomas J Stanton, Clayton Strange, Mimi B Walace, Leah Randolph, Martial Rouman.
Musical numbers: "Rehearse!" "If I Was a Dove," "On Ten Square Miles by the Potomac River," "Welcome Home Miz Adams," "Take Care of This House," "The President Jefferson Sunday Luncheon Party March," "Seena," "Sonatina" ("The British"), "I Love My Wife," "Auctions," "The Little White Lie," "We Must Have a Ball," "The Ball," "Forty Acres and a Mule," "Bright and Black," "Duet for One" ("The First Lady of the Land"), "The Robber-Baron Minstrel Parade," "Pity the Poor," "The Red White and Blue," "I Love This Land," "Rehearse!" (reprise).
05/12/76B

Sly Fox
Lew Grade, Martin Starger & the Shubert Organization presentation of a play in two acts (seven scenes), by Larry Gelbart, based on Jonson's "Volpone." Staged, Arthur Penn; set-light, George Jenkins; cos, Albert Wolsky. GM, Eugene V Wolsk; company mgr, Manny Kladitis; publicity, Merle Debuskey, Susan L Schulman; stage mgrs, Henry Velez, Steven Shaw, Joel Simon. Opened Dec. 14, '76, at the Broadhurst Theatre; $15 top weeknights, $17.50 weekend nights.
Hector Elizondo, Jeffrey Tambor, Calvin Jung, George C Scott, John Heffernan, Jack Gilford, Bob Dishy, Gretchen Wyler, Trish Van Devere, Guy King, John Ramsey, James Gallery, Robb Webb, Willy Switkes, Joel Simon, Howland Chamberlin.
12/22/76B

So Long, 174th Street
Frederick Brisson presentation in ass'n with the Harkness Organization & Wyatt Dickerson, of a musical in 15 numbers (played without intermission); book, Joseph Stein; mus-lyr, Stan Daniels, based on Joseph Stein play, "Enter Laughing," from Carl Reiner's novel of that title. Staged, Burt Shevelove; chor, Alan Johnson; scenery, James Riley; cos, Stanley Simmons; light, Richard Nelson; mus dir, John Lesko; orchs, Luther Henderson; dance mus arrs, Wally Harper. GM, Ralph Roseman; prodn supv, Stoney Widney; publicity; Lee Solters, Bud Westman, Stanley F Kaminsky; company mgr, John A Caruso; stage mgrs, Bryan Young, Jack Magradey; adv, Blaine Thompson (Fred Golden, Mike Mones). Opened April 27, '76, at the Harkness Theatre; $15 top.

So Long,
(Cont)
Robert Morse, Joe Howard, Freda Soiffer, Gene Varrone, Robert Barry, Richard Marr, David Berk, Nancy Killmer, Mitchell Jason, Loni Ackerman, Lawrence John Moss, Sydney Blake, Chuck Beard, Michael Blue Aiken, Barbara Lang, George S Irving, Lee Goodman, James Brennan.

Singers, dancers: Jill Cook, Meribeth Kisner, Denise Mauthe, Rita Rudner, William Swiggard.

Musical numbers: "David Kolowitz, the Actor," "It's Like," "Undressing Girls with My Eyes," "Bolero on Rye," "Whoever You Are," "Say the Words," "My Son, the Druggist," "You Touched Her," "Men," "Boy Oh Boy," "The Butcher's Song," "Being with You," "If You Want to Break Your Family's Heart," "So Long, 174th Street," "David Kolowitz, the Actor" (reprise).
05/05/76B

Some Of My Best Friends
Arthur Whitelaw, Jack Schlissel & Leonard Soloway presentation of a play in two acts by Stanley Hart. Staged, Harold Prince; set, Eugene Lee; light, Ken Billington; cos, Franne Lee; asso prods, Donald Tick, Martin Markinson. GM, Jay Kinwill; publicity, Max Eisen; Judy Jacksina, Barbara Glenn; stage mgrs, Ben Strobach, Joseph Scalzo. Opened Oct. 25, '77, at the Longacre Theatre; $15 top weeknights, $16.50 weekend nights.
Ted Knight, Gavin Reed, Lee Wallace, Bob Balaban, Alice Drummond, Trish Hawkins, Ralph Williams, Joseph Scalzo.
11/02/77B

Something Old, Something New
Adela Holzer presentation of a play in three acts, by Henry Denker. Staged, Robert H Livingston; scenery-cos, Lawrence King, Michael H Yeargan; light, Clarke Dunham. GM, Leonard A Mulhern; company mgr, James Mennen; publicity, Michael Alpert; Marilynn LeVine, Warren Knowlton, Carl Samrock; stage mgrs, Martha Knight, Ken Sherber. Opened Jan. 1, '77 at the Morosco Theatre; $12 top weeknights. $13.50 weekend nights.
Holland Taylor, Dick Patterson, Hans Conried, Molly Picon, Lois Markle, Matthew Tobin, Ahvi Spindell, Cynthia Bostick.
01/12/77B

Something's Afoot
Emanuel Azenberg, Dasha Epstein - John Mason Kirby presentation of a musical; book-mus-lyr, James McDonald, David Vos, Robert Gerlach; addl mus, Ed Linderman. Staged-chor, Tony Tanner; scenery, Richard Seger, cos, Walter Watson, Clifford Capone; light, Richard Winkler; mus dir, Buster Davis; orch, Peter M Larson. GM, Marvin A Krauss; publicity, Cheryl Sue Dolby, Sandra Manley, Harriett Trachtenberg; company mgr, Robert Frissell; stage mgrs, Robert V Straus, Marilyn Wilt; adv, Blaine Thompson (Mike DeLuise). Opened May 27,'76, at the Lyceum Theatre; $13.50 top weeknights, $15 weekend nights.
Neva Small, Marc Jordan, Sel Vitella, Barbara Heuman, Jack Schmidt, Gary Beach, Liz Sheridan, Gary Gage, Tessie O'Shea, William Beckham.

Musical numbers: "A Marvelous Weekend," "Something's Afoot," "Carry On," "I Don't Know Why I Trust You (But I Do) "The Man with the Ginger Moustache," "Suspicious," "The Legal Heir," "You Fell Out of the Sky," "Dinghy," "I Owe It All," "New Day."
06/02/76B

Spokesong
Circle in the Square & Long Wharf Theatre presentation of a play with songs, with book and lyr by Stewart Paker, mus by Jimmy Kennedy. Staged, Kenneth Frankel; scenery, Marjorie Kellogg; cos, Bill Walker; light, John McLain; mus dir-pianist, Thomas Fay. Opened at the Uptown Circle in the Square Theatre; $11.95 top weeknights, $12.95 weekend nights.
Joseph Maher, John Lithgow, Virginia Vestoff, Josef Sommer, Maria Tucci, John Horton.
03/21/79B

Stages
Edgar Bronfman & Stuart Ostrow presentation of a Stuart Ostrow prodn of a play in two acts (five scenes), by Stuart Ostrow. Staged, Richard Foreman; sets, Douglas W Schmidt; cos, Patricia Zipprodt; light, Pat Collins; incidental mus, Stanley Silverman; snd, Roger Jay. GMs, Joseph Harris, Ira Bernstein; publicity, Betty Lee Hunt, Maria Cristina Pucci; stage mgrs, D W Koehler, Frank DeFilia. Opened Mar 19, '78, at the Belasco Theatre; $18 top.
Jack Warden, Roy Brocksmith, Philip Bosco, Diana Davila, Lois Smith, Tom Aldredge, Max Wright, Caroline Kava, Gretel Cummings, William Duell, Brenda Currin, Ralph Drischell, Howland Chamberlin, Manuel Martinez.
03/22/78B

Stop the World - I Want to Get Off
James Joseph Nederlander, in ass'n with the City Center of Music & Drama, presentation of Hillard Elkins' revival of a musical in two acts, with book, mus-lyrs, Leslie Bricusse and Anthony Newley. Staged, Mel Shapiro; chor-musical staging, Billy Wilson; scenery-cos, Santo Loquasto; light, Pat Collins; mus supv-arrs, Ian Fraser; mus dir, George Rhodes; orchestrations, Bill Byers, Joseph Lipman; assoc prod, Barbara Platoff. GM, Max Allentuck; publicity, Solters & Roskin (Fred Nathan); co M, Leo Cohen; stage M, Robert D Currie, Bernard Pollack, Jon R Hand. Opened Aug 3, '78, at the NY State Theatre; $17.50 top.
Sammy Davis Jr, Marian Mercer, Dennis Daniels, Donna Lowe, Debora Masterson, Joyce Nolan, Wendy Edmead, Patrick Kinser-Lau, Shelly Burch, Charles Willis Jr, Edwetta Little, Marcus B F Brown, Karen Gionbetti, Linda Griffin, Billy Newton-Davis, Robert Yori-Tanna.

Musical numbers: "I Wanna Be Rich," "Typically English," "Lumbered," "Welcome to Sludgeville," "Gonna Build a Mountain," "Glorious Russian," "Meilinki Meilchick," "Family Fugue," "Typische Deutsch," "Life Is a Woman," "All American," "Once in a Lifetime," "Mumbo Jumbo," "Welcome to Sunvale," "Someone Nice Like You," "What Kind of Fool Am I?"
08/09/78B

Strangers
Mike Merrick & Bill Wilson, in ass'n with Peter Owens, presentation of a play in two acts, by Sherman Yellen. Staged, Arvin Brown; settings, David Jenkins; cos, Ann Roth; light, Ronald Wallace. GMs, Joseph Harris, Ira Bernstein; publicity, Seymour Krawitz, Louise Weiner Ment, Patricia McLean Krawitz; bus mgr, Peter T Kulok; stage mgrs, Franklin Keysar, Dan Hild. Opened March 4, '79 at the John Golden Theatre; $18.50 top weeknights; $20 weekend nights.
Bruce Dern, Lois Nettleton, William Newman, Ellen Parker, Jean-Pierre Stewart.
03/07/79B

Strider: The Story of a Horse
Chelsea Theatre Center (Robert Kalfin, producing director) presentation of a fantasy in two acts by Mark Rozovsky, adapt from a story by Leo Tolstoy. English stage version, Robert Kalfin & Steve Brown, based on a translation from the Russian by Tamara Bering Sunguroff. Mus comp, M Rozovsky, S Vetkin; add'l mus, Norman L Berman. Orig Russian lyr, Uri Riashentsev; English lyr, Steve Brown; staged, Kalfin, Lynne Gannaway; mus dir-vocal & instrumental arrs, Norman Berman; scenery cnslt, Wolfgang Roth; cos, Andrew Marley; light, Robby Monk; snd, Gary Harris; prodn stage mgr, Zoya Wyeth; literary cnslt, Elinor Fuchs. Opened May 29, '79, at the Chelsea Westside Theatre; $12 top (moved to Helen Hayes Theatre Nov. 7, '79; $20 top weeknights, $22.50 weekends).
Roger DeKoven, Gordon Gould, Ronnie Newman, Pamela Burrell, Gerald Hiken, Katherine Mary Brown, Jeannine Khoutieff, Skip Lawing, Nina Dova, Benjamin Hendrickson, Igors Gavon, Charles Walker, John Brownlee, Nancy Kawalek, Karen Trott, Tad Ingram, Evan Handler, Steven Blane.
12/05/79B

Sugar Babies
Terry Allen Kramer & Harry Rigby presentation, in ass'n with Columbia Pictures, of a mus in two acts (25 numbers), conceived by Ralph G Allen and Rigby; sketches, Allen; mus, Jimmy McHugh; lyr, Dorothy Fields; addl mus-lyr, Arthur Malvin, Jay Livingstn, Ray Evans. Staged-chor, Ernest Flatt; sketch staging, Rudy Tronto; prodn supv, Flatt; asso prod, Jack Schlissel; scenery-cos, Raoul Pene du Bois; light, Gilbert V Hemsley Jr; vocal arrs, Arthur Malvin, Hugh Martin, Ralph Blane; mus dir, Glen Roven; orchs, Dick Hyman; dance mus arrs, Arnold Gross; prodn assos, Thomas Walton Associates & Frank Montalvo. GM, Jack Schlissel, Jay Kingwill; publicity, Henry Luhrman, Robert Pontarelli, Terry M Lilly, Kevin P McAnarney; company mgr, Alan Wasser; stage mgrs, Thomas Kelly, Bob Burland, Jay B Jacobson, David Campbell. Opened Oct. 8, '79, at the Mark Hellinger Theatre; $22.50 top weeknights, $25 weekend nights.
Mickey Rooney, Ann Miller, Sid Stone, Ann Jillian, Scot Stewart, Tom Boyd, Peter Leeds, Jack Fletcher, Jimmy Mathews, Bob Williams, Laura Booth, Christine Busini, Diane Duncan, Chris Elia, Debbie Gornay, Barbara Hanks, Jeri Kansas, Barbara Mandra, Robin Manus, Faye Fujisaki Mar, Linda Ravinsky, Michele

Sugar Babies
(Cont)
Rogers, Rose Scudder, Patti Watson, Laurie Sloan, Terpsie Toon, Jonathan Aronson, Eddie Pruett, Michael Radigan, Jeff Veazey, Hank Brunjes.

Mus numbers; "A Good Old Burlesque Show, " "Let Me Be Your Sugar Baby," "In Louisiana," "I Feel a Song Comin' On," "Goin' Back to New Orleans," "Sally," "Immigration Rose," "Don't Blame Me," "The Sugar Baby Bounce," "Down at the Gaiety Burlesque," "Mr Banjo Man," "I'm Keeping Myself Available for You," "Exactly Like You," "Warm and Willing," "Cuban Love Song," Every Day Another Tune," "I Can't Give You Anything But Love, Baby," "I'm Shooting High," "When You and I Were Young," "Maggie Blues," "On the Sunny Side of the Street," "You Can't Blame Your Uncle Sammy."
10/10/79B

The Suicide
Aurora Stage Wing Inc presentation of a play in two acts by Nikolai Erdman; trans, George Genereux Jr, Jacob Volkov; adapt, Trinity Square Repertory Co, Jonas Jurasas. Staged, Jurasas; set-cos, Santo Loquasto; light, F Mitchell Dana; snd, Jack Shearing; mus, Richard Weinstock; movement, Ara Fitzgerald; prod, Bill Dyer, Dick DeBenedictis; exec prods, James L Stewart, Richard Irvine; GMs, R Tyler Gatchell Jr, Peter Neufeld; asso, Douglas C Baker; publicity, Jeffrey Richards; stage mgrs, Peter Lawrence, Jim Woolley, Sarah Whitham. Opened Oct 9, '80, at the ANTA Theatre; $20 top weeknights, $22.50 weekend nights.

Derek Jacobi, Angela Pietropinto, Grayson Hall, Clarence Felder, Carol Mayo Jenkins, John Heffernan, John Christopher Jones, David Sabin, Chip Zien, William Myers, Laura Esterman, Mary Lou Rosato, Leda Siskind, Susan Edward, Cheryl Giannini, David Patrick Kelly, Derek Meader, Jeff Zinn, Bill Moersch, Andy Seligson.
10/15/80B

Sweeney Todd
Richard Barr, Charles Woodward, Robert Fryer, Mary Lea Johnson, Martin Richards presentation, in ass'n with Dean & Judy Manos, of a musical in two acts (26 numbers), with mus and lyr by Stephen Sondheim and book by Hugh Wheeler, based on a version of "Sweeney Todd," by Christopher Bond, from a 19th century melodrama by George Dibdin-Pitt. Staged, Harold Prince; chor, Larry Fuller; scenery, Eugene Lee; cos, Franne Lee; light, Ken Billington; orch, Jonathan Tunick; mus dir, Paul Gemignani. GMs, R Tyler Gatchell Jr, Peter Neufeld; publicity, Mary Bryant; stage mgrs, Alan Hall, Ruth E Rinklin, Arthur Maella; company mgr, Drew Murphy. Opened March 1, '79 at the Uris Theatre; $20 top weeknights, $22.50 weekend nights.

Victor Garber, Len Cariou, Merle Louise, Angela Lansbury, Edmund Lyndeck, Jack Eric Williams, Sarah Rice, Ken Jennings, Joaquin Romaguera, Robert Ousley, Duane Bodin, Walter Charles, Carole Doscher, Nancy Eaton, Mary-Pat Green, Cris Groenendaal, Skip Harris, Marthe Ihde, Betty Joslyn, Nancy Killmer, Frank Kopyc, Spain Logue, Craig Lucas, Pamela McLernon, Duane Morris, Richard Warren, Pugh Maggie Task, Heather B Withers, Robert Henderson.

Musical numbers: "The Ballad of Sweeney Todd," "No Place Like London," "The Barber and His Wife," "The Worst Pies in London," "Poor Thing," "My Friends," "Green Finch and Linnet Bird," "Ah, Miss," "Johanna," "Pirelli's Miracle Elixir," "The Contest," "Wait," "Kiss Me," "Ladies in Their Sensitivities," "Quartet," "Pretty Women," "Epiphany," "A Little Priest," "God, That's Good," "Johanna" (reprise), "By the Sea," "Not While I'm Around," "Parlor Songs," "City on Fire," "Final Sequence," "The Ballad of Sweeney Todd" (reprise).
03/07/79B

Talley's Folly
Circle Repertory Co (Marshal Mason, artistic dir) presentation of a comedy in one act by Lanford Wilson. Staged, Marshall Mason; set, John Lee Beatty; light, Dennis Parichy; cos, Jennifer von Mayrhauser; stage mgr, Fred Reinglas; snd, Chuck London; publicity, Richard Frankel. Opened May 3, '79, at the Circle Repertory Co, $8.50 top. (Off Broadway; moved to Brooks Atkinson Theatre 2/20/80 $18 top weeknights, $19.50 weekend nights).

Judd Hirsch, Trish Hawkins.
05/16/79B

Tartuffe
Circle in the Square revival of a comedy in two acts, by Moliere; English verse trans, Richard Wilbur. Staged, Stephen Porter; scenery-cos, Zack Brown; light, John McLain. Artistic dir, Theodore Mann; managing dir, Paul Libin; publicity, Merle Debuskey, David Roggensack; company mgr, William Conn; stage mgrs, Randall Brooks, James Bernardi. Opened Sept. 25, '77, at the uptown Circle in the Square Theatre; $10.95 top weeknights, $11.95 weekend nights.

Ruth Livingston, Patricia Elliott, Mildred Dunnock, Tammy Grimes, Swoosie Kurtz, Ray Wise, Peter Coffield, Stefan Gierasch, Victor Garber, John Wood, John Brocksmith, Jim Broaddus, Timothy Landfield.
09/28/77B

Teibele and Her Demon
Joseph Kipness, Jule Styne & Marvin A Krauss presentation of a Guthrie Theatre prodn of a play in two acts, by Isaac Bashevis Singer, Eve Friedman, from a Singer short story. Staged, Stephen Kanee; sets-cos, Desmond Heeley; light, Duane Schuler; mus, Richard Peaslee; asso prods, Charlotte & Dorothy Dicker; prodn supv, Fritz Holt; GM, Marvin Krauss, Gary Gunas; publicity, Seymour Krawitz, Patricia McLean Krawitz. Opened Dec. 16, '79, at the Brooks Atkinson Theatre; $18 top weeknights, $19.50 weekend nights.

F Murray Abraham, Barry Primus, Laura Esterman, Lee Lawson, Stefan Schnabel, Ron Perlman, Stephan Weyte.
12/19/79B

They Knew What They Wanted
Phoenix Theatre (T Edward Hambleton, managing dir) revival of a play in three acts, by Sidney Howard. Staged, Stephen Porter; set-light, James Tilton; cos, Albert Wolsky. GM, Marilyn S Miller; prodn mgr, Robert Beard; stage mgrs, Jonathan Penzner, Peter DeNicola; publicity, Gifford-Wallace (Tom Trenkle); adv, Ash-LeDonne. Opened Jan. 27, '76, at the Playhouse, $9 top weeknights, $10 weekend nights.

Barry Bostwick, Leonardo Cimino, Clavin Jung, Louis Zorich, Ben Kapen, Lois Nettleton, Clarence Felder, Joel Colodner, Rex Robbins.
02/04/76B

They're Playing Our Song
Emanuel Azenberg presentation of a musical in two acts (13 scenes, 10 numbers), with book by Neil Simon; mus, Marvin Hamlisch; lyr, Carole Bayer Sager. Staged, Robert Moore; musical staging, Patricia Birch; scenery-rojections, Douglas W Schmidt; cos, Ann Roth; light, Tharon Musser; mus dir, Larry Blank; orch, Ralph Burns, Richard Hazard, Gene Page. GM, Jose Vega; publicity, Bill Evans, Howard Atlee; company mgr, Susan Bell; stage mgrs, Robert D Currie, Philip Cusack, Bernard Pollock. Opened Feb. 11, '79 at the Imperial Theatre; $22.50 weeknights, $24 weekend nights.

Robert Klein, Lucie Arnaz, Wayne Mattson, Andy Roth, Greg Zadikov, Helen Castillo, Celia Celnik Matthau, Debbie Sharpiro, Philip Cusack.

Musical numbers: "Fallin'," "Workin' It Out," "If He Really Knew Me," "They're Playing Our Song," "If He Really Knew Me" (reprise), "Right," "Just for Tonight," "When You're in My Arms," "I Still Believe in Love." "Fill in the Words," "I Still Believe in Love" reprise sung by Johnny Mathis
02/14/79B

13 Rue de l'Amour
Circle in the Square presentation of a play in three acts, by Georges Feydeau, adapt-trans, Mawby Green, Ed Feilbert. Staged, Basil Langton; scenery-cos, Zack Brown; light, John McLain. Artistic dir, Theodore Mann; M dir, Paul Libin; stage mgrs, James Bernardi, John Shuman. Opened Mar 16, '78, at the Uptown Circle in the Square Theatre; $10.95 top weeknights, $11.95 weekend nights.

Jill P Rose, Jim Broaddus, Bernard Fox, Louis Jourdan, Patricia Elliott, Richard Pilcher, Laurie Main, Kathleen Freeman, Ian Trigger, John Shuman.
03/22/78B

Threepenny Opera
N Y Shakespeare Festival presentation of a Joseph Papp revival of a musical in three acts; book-lyr, Bertolt Brecht; mus, Kurt Weill; trans, Ralph Manheim, John Willett, based on "The Beggar's Opera," by John Gay. Staged, Richard Foreman; mus dir, Stanley Silverman; scenery, Douglas W Schmidt; cos, Theoni V Aldredge; light, Pat Collins. GM, Robert Kamlot; publicity, Merle Debuskey, Faith Greer; stage mgrs, D W Koehler, Michael Chambers, Frank Di Filia; adv, Case & McGrath. Opened May 1, '76, at the Vivian Beaumont Theatre; $9 top weeknights, $10 weekend nights.

Roy Brocksmith, Raul Julia, Ellen Greene, C K Alexander, Tony Azito, Ed Zang, Elizabeth

Threepenny Opera
(Cont)
Wilson, Ralph Drischell, Caroline Kava, William Duell, K C Wilson, Rik Colitti, Robert Schlee, Max Gulack, David Sabin, Glenn Kezer, Blair Brown, Pendleton Brown, M Patrick Hughes, George McGrath, Rick Petrucelli, John Ridge, Craig Rupp, Armin Shimerman, Jack Eric Williams, Ray Xifo, Penelope Bodry, Nancy Campbell, Gretel Cummings, Brenda Currin, Mimi Turque.
05/05/76B

Timbuktu
Luther Davis presentation of a musical in two acts (10 scenes, 16 numbers), mus-lyr, Robert Wright, George Forrest, from the themes of Alexander Borodin and African folk music; book, Luther Davis, based on musical by Charles Lederer, Luther Davis, from Edward Knoblauch's play. Staged-chor-cos, Geoffrey Holder; scenery, Tony Straiges; light, Ian Calderon; snd, Abe Jacob; mus dir-supv arr-incidental mus, Charles H Coleman; addl orch, Bill Brohn; prodn in ass'n with Sarnoff International Enterprises, William D Cunningham & John F Kennedy Center for the Performing Arts. GM, R Tyler Gatchell Jr, Peter Neufeld; publicity, Solters & Roskin (Joshua Ellis); company mgr, Drew Murphey; asso prod, Alan Eichler; stage mgrs, Donald Christy, Jeanna Belkin, Pat Trott. Opened Mar 1, '78, at the Mark Hellinger Theatre; $18.50 top weeknights, $19.50 weekend nights.
Obba Babatunde, Harold Pierson, Shezwae Powell, Lewis Tucker, Ira Hawkins, Melba Moore, Deborah Waller, Daniel Barton, Eleanor McCoy, George Bell, Bruce A Hubbard, Eartha Kitt, Deborah K Brown, Sharon Cuff, Patricia Lumpkin, Miguel Godreau, Gilbert Price, Luther Fontaine, Vanessa Shaw.
Singers, dancers: Gregg Baker, Joella Breedlove, Tony Carroll, Cheryl Cummings, Michael F Harrison, Dyane Harvey, Marzetta Jones, Jimmy Justice, Eugene Little, Joe Lynn, Tony Ndogo, Ray Pollard, Ronald Richardson, Renee Warren.
Music numbers: "Rhymes Have I," "Fate," "In the Beginning, Woman," "Baubles, Bangles and Beads," "Stranger in Paradise," "Gesticulate," "Night of My Nights," "The Mansa Marries Tonight," "My Magic Lamp," "Stranger In Paradise" (reprise), "Rahadlakum," "And This Is My Beloved," "Golden Land, Golden Life," "Night of My Nights" (reprise), "Sands of Time."
03/08/78B

Tintypes
Richmond Crinkley & Royal Pardon Prodns, Ivan Bloch, Larry J Silva, Eve Skina, in ass'n with Joan F Tobin, presentation of an American National Theatre & Academy prodn of a revue in two acts (48 numbers) conceived by Mary Kyte, with Mel Marvin and Gary Pearle. Staged, Gary Pearle; mus staging, Mary Kyte; set, Tom Lynch; cos, Jess Goldstein; light, Paul Gallo; snd, Jack Mann; mus-vocal arrs, Mel Marvin; orchs-vocal arrs, John McKinny; GM, Elizabeth I McCann, Nelle Nugent; prodn coord, Brent Peek; publicity, Betty Lee Hunt, Maria Cristina Pucci; stage mgrs, Steve Beckler, Bonnie Panson, Marie King. Opened Oct 23, '80, at the John Golden Theatre; $22.50 top weeknights, $25 weekend nights.
Carolyn Mignini, Lynne Thigpen, Trey Wilson, Mary Catherine Wright, Jerry Zaks; pianist-cond, Mel Marvin.
Musical numbers: - "Ragtime Nightingale," "The Yankee Doodle Boy," "Ta-Ra-Ra-Boom-De-Ay," "I Don't Care," "Come Take a Trip in My Airship," "Kentucky Babe," "A Hot Time in the Old Town Tonight," "Stars and Stripes Forever," "Electricity," "El Capitan," "Pastime Rag," "Meet Me in St Louis," "Solace," "Waltz Me Around Again, Willie," "Wabash Cannonball," "In My Merry Oldsmobile," "Wayfaring Stranger," "Sometimes I Feel Like a Motherless Child," "Aye, Lye, Lue, Lye," "I'll Take You Home Again, Kathleen," "America the Beautiful," "Wait for the Wagon," "What It Takes To Make Me Love You--You've Got It," "The Maiden with the Dreamy Eyes," "If I Were on the Stage," "Kiss Me Again," "Shortnin' Bread," "Nobody," "Elite Syncapations," "I'm Goin' to Live Anyhow, 'Til I Die," "The Ragtime Dance," "I Want What I Want When I Want It," "It's Delightful to Be Married," "Fifty-Fifty," "American Beauty," "Then I'd Be Satisfied with Life," "Narcissus," "Jonah Man," "When It's All Goin' Out and Nothing Comin' In," "We Shall Not Be Moved," "Hello, Ma Baby," "Teddy Da Roose," "A Bird in a Gilded Cage," "Bill Bailey, Won't You Please Come Home?" "She's Gettin' More Like the Whites Folks Every Day "You're a Grand Old Flag," "The Yankee Doodle Boy," "Toyland," "Smiles."
10/29/80B

Tribute
Morton Gottlieb presentation of a play in two acts, by Bernard Slade. Staged, Arthur Storch; scenery, William Ritman; cos, Lowell Detweiler; light, Tharon Musser; asso prods, Ben Rosenberg, Warren Crane. GM, Ben Rosenberg; publicity, Solters & Roskin (Milly Schoenbaum); company mgr, Martin Cohen; stage mgrs, Warren Crane, Tom Capps, Laura Beattie. Opened Jun 1, '78, at the Brooks Atkinson Theatre; $16 top weeknights, $17.50 weekend and opening nights.
A Larry Haines, Tresa Hughes, Jack Lemmon, Catherine Hicks, Rosemary Prinz, Robert Picardo, Joan Welles, Ann Dodge.
06/07/78B

Trick
Joshua Logan presentation of a play in two acts (five scenes), by Larry Cohen. Staged by the author; setting, Raymond C Recht; light, Marshall S Spiller; cos, Judy Dearing. Asso prods, Paul B Berkowsky, Sheila Tronn Cooper; publicity, the Merlin Group; stage mgrs, Tom Kelly, John Barrett. Opened Feb. 4, '79 at the Playhouse; $13.50 top weeknights, $15 weekend nights.
Tammy Grimes, Donald Madden, Lee Richardson.
02/07/79B

Tricks of the Trade
Gilbert Cates, in ass'n with Matthew Alexander, presentation of a play in two acts (10 scenes), by Sidney Michaels. Staged, Cates; set-light, Peter Dohanos; cos, Albert Wolskey; incidental mus, Charles Fox; snd, Peter Berger; GM, Paul Libin; publicity, Merle Debuskey, Leo Stern; stage mgrs, Martin Gold, Carlos Gorbea; prodn asso, Tom Folino.
Opened Nov 6, '80, at the Brooks Atkinson Theatre; $22.50 top weeknights, $24 weekend nights.
George C Scott, Trish Van Devere, Lee Richardson, Geoffrey Pierson.
11/12/80B

The Trip Back Down
Philip Rose, Gloria & Louis K Sher presentation of a play in two acts, by John Bishop. Staged, Terry Schreiber; set, Hal Tine; cos, Pearl Somner; light, Richard Nelson. GM, Helen Richards; company mgr, Steven Suskin; publicity, Merle Debuskey, Leo Stern; stage mgrs, Mortimer Helpern, Dean Vallas. Opened Jan. 4, '76, at the Longacre Theatre; $12 top weeknights, $13.50 weekend nights.
John Cullum, John Randolph Jones, William Andrews, Charles Brant, Arlen Dean Snyder, Doris Belack, William Andrews, Anthony Call, Gwendolyn Brown, Gordon Oas-Heim, Jill Andre, Edward Seamon, Alexa Spencer, Carol Chanco, Andrew Jarkowsky, Blaise Bulfair.
01/12/77B

The Trojan War Will Not Take Place: SEE La Guerre De Troie N'Aura Pas Lieu

27 Wagons Full Of Cotton & A Memory Of Two Mondays
Phoenix Theatre (T Edward Hambleton, managing dir) presentation of a double-bill of one-act plays, "27 Wagons Full of Cotton," by Tennessee Williams, and "A Memory of Two Mondays," by Arthur Miller. Staged, Arvin Brown; scenery-light, James Tilton; cos, Albert Wolsky. GM, Marilyn S Miller; prodn mgr, Robert Beard; stage mgrs, Jonathan Penzner, Peter DeNicola; publicity, Gifford-Wallace (Tom Trenkle) adv, Ashe-LeDonne. Opened Jan. 26, '75, at the Playhouse, $9 top weeknights, $10 weekend nights.
27 Wagons Full of Cotton; Roy Poole, Meryl Streep, Tony Musante.
A Memory of Two Mondays; Thomas Hulce, Pierre Epstein, Alice Drummond, Meryl Streep, Roy Poole, Leonardo Cimino, John Lithgow, Tony Musante, Joseph Grifasi, Joel Colodner, Calvin Jung, Rex Robbins, Clarence Felder, Ben Kapen.
01/28/76B

Unexpected Guests
Charles Grodin presentation of a play in two acts, by Jordan Crittenden. Staged, Charles Grodin; set, Stuart Wurtzel; cos, Joseph G Aulisi; light, Cheryl Thacker. Prodn supv, Richard Scanga; company mgr, John Corkill; publicity, Michael Alpert, Marilynn LeVine; stage mgrs, John Brigleb, Ellsworth Wright. Opened March 2, '77, at the Little Theatre; $12 top weeknights, $13.50 weekend nights.
Frank Piazza, Jerry Stiller, Bill Lazarus, Michael Vale, Anne Ives, Loney Lewis, Constance Forslund, Zohra Lampert, Robert Costanzo, Robert Earl Jones.
03/09/77B

The Utter Glory of Morrissey Hall

Arthur Whitelaw, Albert W Selden & H Ridgely Bullock in ass'n with Marc Howard, presentation of a musical in two acts (overture and 17 numbers), with book by Clark Gesner and Nagle Jackson, mus-lyr, Clark Gesner. Staged, Nagle Jackson; mus-dance staging, Buddy Schwab; settings-light, Howard Bay; cos, David Graden; mus dir, John Lesko; orch, Jay Blackton, Russell Warner; dance mus arr, Allen Cohen; asso prod, Sandy Stern. GMs, Jack Schlissel, Jay Kingwill; publicity, Betty Lee Hunt, Maria Cristina Pucci; stage mgrs, Mark S Krause, Bryan Young, Gail Pearson. Opened May 13, '79 at the Mark Hellinger Theatre; $20 top weeknights, $22.50 weekend nights.

Celeste Holm, Marilyn Caskey, Patricia Falkenhain, Laurie Franks, Taina Elg, Karen Gibson, John Wardwell, Mary Saunders, Gina Franz, Adrienne Alexander, Jill P Rose, Kate Kelly, Polly Pen, Cynthia Parva, Beck McSpadden, Dawn Jeffory, Bonnie Hellman, Anne Kaye, Lauren Shub, Willard Beckham, John Gallogly, Robert Lanchester.

Musical numbers: Overture ("At the Fair"), "Promenade," "Proud, Erstwhile, Upright, Fair," "Elizabeth's Song," "Lost," "Morning," "The Letter," "Oh Sun," "Give Me That Key," "Duet," "Interlude and Gallop," "You Will Know When the Time Has Arrived," "You Would Say," "See the Blue," "Dance of Resignation," "The War," "Oh Sun" (reprise).
05/16/79B

Vieux Carre

Golden Eagle Prodns, Inc and George R Nice in ass'n with Ruth Hercolani presentation of a drama in two acts by Tennessee Williams. Staged, Arthur Allan Seidelman; set-light, James Tilton; cos, Jane Greenwood; incidental mus, Galt MacDermot; asso prods, Milton Justice, Eleanor Fortus, May Grindrod, Christopher Rote, Myles Spector. GM, C Edwin Knill; publicity, David Lipsky; stage mgrs, Lee Murray, William Pomeroy, Robert Colson. Opened May 11, '77, at the Martin Beck Theatre; $13.50-$15 top.

Richard Alfieri, Sylvia Sidney, Gertrude Jeanette, Diane Kagan, Tom Aldredge, Reb Brownell, Grace Carney, Iris Whitney, Olive Deering, John William Reilly, Jed Cooper, Bill Perley, Robert Colson, Toni Darnay, Lois Holmes, Sharon Morrison.
05/18/77B

The Water Engine

Joseph Papp presentation of a NY Shakespeare Festival prodn of a one-act play and curtain-raiser by David Memet. Staged, Steven Schacter; scenery, John Lee Beatty; cos, Laura Crow; light, Dennis Parichy; mus, Alaric Jans; asso prod, Bernard Gersten. GM, Robert Kamlot; publicity, Merle Debuskey, William Schelble; company mgr, Bob MacDonald; stage mgrs, Jason La Padura, Harold Apter. Opened Mar 6, '78, at the Plymouth Theatre; $15 top.

Charles Kimbrough, Dwight Schultz, Patti LuPone, David Sabin, Bill Moor, Barbara Tarbuck, Dominic Chianese, Michael J Miller, Colin Stinton, Eric Loeb, Paul Milikin, Alaric Janes.
03/08/78B

West Side Story

Gladys Rackmil, the John F Kennedy Center & James M Nederlander, in ass'n with Zev Bufman revival of a musical in two acts (17 numbers); book, Arthur Laurents; mus, Leonard Bernstein, lyrs, Stephen Sondheim; staged-chor, Jerome Robbins; book staging, Gerald Freedman; co-chor, Peter Gennaro; mus dirs, John DeMain, Donald Jennings; scenery, Oliver Smith; cos, Irene Sharaff; light, Jean Rosenthal; orchs, Leonard Bernstein, Sid Ramin, Irwin Lostal; asso prods, Allan Tessler, Steven Jacobson, Stewart Lane; GM, Theatre Now; publicity, Betty Lee Hunt, Maria Cristina Pucci; stage mgrs, Patrick Horrigan, Brenna Krupa, Arlene Grayson. Opened Feb 14, '80, at the Minskoff Theatre; $20 top weeknights, $22.50 weekend nights.

James J Mellon, Ken Marshall, Hector Jaime Mercado, Jossie de Guzman, Debbie Allen, Missy Whitchurch.

Jets: - Mark Bove, Todd Lester, Brian Kaman, Tim O'Keefe (opening night substitute), Cleve Asbury, Reed Jones, Brent Barrett, G Russell Weilandich, Stephen Bogardus, Mark Fotopoulos.

Their Girls: - Georganna Mills, Heather Lee Gerdes, Frankie Wade, Charlene Gehm, Nancy Louise Chismar.

Sharks: - Ray Contreras, Michael Rivera, Darryl Tribble, Adrian Rosario, Michael de Lorenzo, Willie Rosario, Michael Franks, Mark Morales, Gary-Michael Davies.

Their Girls: - Yamil Borges, Nancy Ticotin, Harolyn Blackwell, Stephanie E Williams, Marlene Danielle, Amy Lester. Sammy Smith, Arch Johnson, John Bentley, Jake Turner.

Musical numbers: - Prologue, "Jet Song," "Something's Coming," "The Dance at the Gym," "Maria," "Tonight," "America," "Cool," "One Hand, One Heart," "Tonight" (reprise), "The Rumble," "I Feel Pretty," "Somewhere," "Gee, Officer Krupke," "A Boy Like That," "I Have a Love," "Taunting," "Finale."
02/20/80B

Wheelbarrow Closers

Tony Conforti, in ass'n with Howard Efron & George Tunick, presentation of a play in two acts, by Louis La Russo II. Staged, Paul Sorvino; set, Charles Carmello Jr; supv, Ken Billington; light, Leon Di Leone; cos, Jan Wallace; supv, Carol Luiken; prodn assos, David Silberg, Diane Matthews; asso prods, Michael Bash, Howard Wesson, Irving Warhaftig. Publicity, Max Eisen, Barbara Glenn, Irene Gandy; stage mgrs, Gary Stein, Jane Barish. Opened Oct. 11, '76, at the Bijou Theatre.

Norah Foster, Ray Serra, Harvey Siegel, Frances Helm, James Allan Bartz, Danny Aiello, Tom Degidon.
10/13/76B

Who's Afraid of Virginia Woolf?

Ken Marsolais & James Scott Prodns Inc., in ass'n with MPL Ltd., by arrangement with Richard Barr & Clinton Wilder, revival of a drama in three acts, by Edward Albee. Staged by author; set-light, William Ritman; cos, Jane Greenwood. GM, Leonard Soloway; publicity, Betty Lee Hunt, Maria Cristina Pucci; stage mgrs, Mark Wright, Wayne Carson; company mgr, Terry Grossman; adv, Blaine Thompson (Don Josephson). Opened April 1, '76 at the Music Box Theatre; $11 top weeknights, $13 weekend nights.

Colleen Dewhurst, Ben Gazzara, Maureen Anderman, Richard Kelton.
04/07/76B

Whoopee

Ashton Springer, Frank C Pierson & Michael P Price revival of a musical in two acts (12 scenes, 16 numbers), with book by William Anthony McGuire, lyr, Gus Kahn, mus, Walter Donaldson, based on the play, "The Nervous Wreck," by Owen Davis, taken from a short story, "The Wreck," by E J Rath. Staged, Frank Corsaro; chor-mus staging, Dan Siretta; mus dir, Lynn Crigler; scenery, John Lee Beatty; cos, David Toser; light, Peter M Ehrhardt; snd, Warren E Jenkins; prodn supv, Ron Abbott; mus cnslt, Alfred Simon; prodn cnslt, G William Oakley; orch-dance arr, Russell Warner; asso prods, Martin Markinson, Joseph Harris, Donald Tick, company mgr, Alexander Holt; publicity, Max Eisen; stage mgrs, John J Bonanni, John Beven, Joann Cifala. Opened Feb. 14, '79 at the ANTA Theatre; $19.50 top weeknights, $22.50 weekend nights.

J Kevin Scannell, Carol Swarbrick, Bob Allen, Beth Austin, Charles Repole, Franc Luz, Leonard Drum, Garrett M Brown, Catherine Cox, Peter Boyden, Vic Polizos, Bill Rowley, Al Micacchion, Steven Gelfer, Rick Pessagno, Paul M Elkin, Brent Saunders, Candy Darling, Susan Stroman, Robin Black, Diane Epstein, Teri Corcoran, Jo-Ann, Jonathan Aronson.

Musical numbers: "Let's All Make Whoopee Tonight," "Makin' Whoopee," "I'm Bringing a Red, Red Rose," "Go Get 'Im", "Until You Get Somebody Else", "Go Get 'Im" (reprise), "Love Me or Leave Me", "I'm Bringing a Red, Red Rose" (reprise), "My Baby Just Cares for Me", "Go Get 'Im" (reprise), "Out of the Dawn", "The Tapanoe Tap," "Reaching for Someone," "You," "Yes, Sir, That's My Baby." "Makin' Whoopeee" (reprise).
02/21/79B

Whose Life Is It Anyway?

Emanuel Azenberg, James M Nederlander & Ray Cooney presentation, by arrangement with Mermaid Theatre Trust, of a play in two-acts, by Brian Clark. Staged, Michael Lindsay-Hogg; setting, Alan Tagg; cos, Pearl Somner; light, Tharon Musser. GM, Jose Vega company mgr, Laurel Ann Wilson; publicity, Bill Evans, Howard Atlee; stage mgrs, Martin Herzer, Cathy B Blaser; Dianne Trulock. Opened April 17, '79 at the Trafalgar Theatre; $18 top weeknights, $19.50 weekend nights.

Tom Conti, Beverly May, Pippa Pearthree, Damien Leake, Jean Marsh, Philip Bosco, Veronica Castang, Kenneth Welsh, Peter McRobbie, Russell Leib, Edmond Genest, Richard de Fabees, James Higgins.
04/25/79B

Wings

Kennedy Center presentation, in ass'n with Claus von Bulow, of a play in one act, by Arthur Kopit. Staged, John Madden; scenery, Andrew Jackness; cos, Jeanne Button; light, Tom Schraeder; snd, Tom Voegeli. GM, Wil-

Wings
(Cont)
liam C Cohen, Edward H Davis, Norman E Rothstein, Ralph Roseman; publicity, Jeffrey Richards, Helen Stern, Warren Knowlton; company mgr, Michael Lonergan; stage mgrs, Patrick Horrigan, Brian Meister. Opened Jan. 28, '79 at the Lyceum Theatre; $17.50 top weeknights, $20 weekend nights.
Constance Cummings, Mary-Joan Negro, Roy Steinberg, Ross Petty, Gina Franz, Mary Michele Rutherford, James Tolkan, Carl Don, Betty Pelzer.
02/07/79B

Working
Stephen R Friedman & Irwin Meyer, in ass'n with Joseph Harris, presentation of a musical; songs, Craig Carnelia, Micki Grant, Mary Rodgers, Susan Birkenhead, Stephen Schwartz, James Taylor; adapt, Schwartz; from Studs Terkel book of the same title. Staged, Schwartz; dances-mus staged, Onna White; settings, David Mitchell; cos, Marjorie Slaiman; light, Ken Billington; mus dir-vocal arr, Stephen Reinhardt; orch, Kirk Nurock; dance-incidental mus, Michele Brourman. GMs, R Tyler Gatchell Jr, Peter Neufeld; publicity, Betty Lee Hunt, Maria Cristina Pucci; company mgr, Douglas C Baker; stage mgrs, Alan Hall, Ruth E Rinklin, Richard Elkow. Opened May 14, '78, at the 46th Street Theatre; $19 top weeknights, $20 weekend nights.
Susan Bigelow, Steven Boockvor, Rex Everhart, Arny Freeman, Bob Gunton, David Patrick Kelly, Robin Lamont, Matt Landers, Bobo Lewis, Patti LuPone, Joe Mantegna, Matthew McGrath, Lenora Nemetz, David Langston Smyrl, Brad Sullivan, Lynn Thigpen, Terri Treas.
Musical numbers: "All the Livelong Day," "Lovin' Al," "The Mason," "Neat to Be a Newsboy," "Nobody Tells Me How," "Treasure Island Trio," "Un Mejor Dia Vendra," "Just a Housewife," "Millwork," "Night Skate," "Joe," "If I Could've Been," "It's an Art," "Brother Trucker," "Husbands and Wives," "Fathers and Sons," "Cleanin' Women," "Something to Point To."
05/17/78B

Your Arms Too Short To Box With God
Frankie Hewett & the Shubert Organization presentation, in ass'n with Theatre Now Inc, of a Ford's Theatre prodn of a musical with 27 numbers, presented without intermission. Conceived, Vinnette Carroll from the Book of Matthew; mus-lyr, Alex Bradford; addl mus-lyr, Micki Grant. Staged, Carroll; chor, Talley Beattly; set-cos, William Schroder; scenic supv, Michael Hotopp; light, Gilbert V Hemsley Jr; orchs, H B Burnam; choral arrs-dir, Chapman Roberts. GMs, William Court Cohen, Edward H Davis, Norman E Rothstein; publicity, Henry Luhrman; stage mgrs, Haig Shepherd, Robert Charles, Steve Goldstein. Opened Dec. 22, '76, at the Lyceum Theatre; $15 top.
Salome Bey, Clinton Derricks-Carroll, David St Charles, Sheila Ellis, Dolores Hall, William Hardy Jr, Hector Jaime Mercado, Mabel Robinson, William Thomas Jr, Deborah Lynn Bridges, Sharon Brooks, Thomas Jefferson Fouse Jr, Michael Gray, Cardell Hall, Bobby Hill, Lidell Jackson, Edna Krider, Leon Washington, Marilyn Winbush.
Musical numbers: "Beatitudes," "We're Gonna Have a Good Time," "There's a Stranger in Town," "Do You Know Jesus? He's a Wonder," "Just a Little Bit of Jesus Goes a Long Way," "We Are the Priests and Elders," "Something Is Wrong in Jerusalem," "It Was Alone," "I Know I Have to Leave Here," "Be Careful Whom You Kiss," "It's Too Late," "Judas Dance," "Your Arms Too Short to Box with God," "Give Us Barrabas," "See How They Done My Lord," "Come on Down," "Can't No Grave Hold My Body Down," "Beatitudes" (reprise), "Didn't I Tell You," "Me and Jesus," "When the Power Comes," "As Long As I Live," "Everybody Has His Own Way," "On That Day," "I Left My Sins Behind Me," "I Love You So Much Jesus," "The Band."
12/29/76B

Your Arms Too Short To Box With God
Tom Mallow in ass'n with James Janek presentation of musical in two acts conceived from the Book of St Matthew by Vinnette Carroll; mus-lyrs, Alex Bradford; addl mus-lyrs, Micki Grant. Staged, Vinnette Carroll; chor, Talley Beatty; scenery-cos, William Schroder; light, Richard Winkler; snd, Abe Jacob; mus dir, Michael Powell; orchs-dance mus, H B Barnum; prod supvs, Jerry R Moore, Richard Martini; artistic prodn coord, Ralph Farrington; orig prod, Urban Arts Theatre (Anita MacShane, prod dir); GM, James Janek, publicity, Max Eisen. Opened Jun 2, '80, at the Ambassador Theatre; $20 top weeknights, $22.50 top weekend nights.
Julius Richard Brown, Cleavant Derricks, Sheila Ellis, Ralph Farrington, Jamil K Garland, Elijah Gill, William-Keebler Hardy Jr, Jennifer-Yvette Holliday, Garry Q Lewis, Linda Morton, Jai Oscar St John, Kiki Shepard, Leslie Hardesty Sisson, Ray Stephens, Quincella Swyningan, Faruma S Williams, Marilynn Winbush, Linda E Young, Adrian Bailey, Linda James.
06/18/80B

Zalmen, Or The Madness Of God
Moe Septee presentation of a play in two acts, by Elie Wisel, stage adaptation by Marion Wisel. Staged, Alan Schneider; set, William Ritman; light, Richard Nelson; cos, Marjorie Slaiman. GM, Laurel Ann Wilson; company mgr, Donald Tirabassi; publicity, Max Eisen; asso, Barbara Glenn; stage mgrs, R Derek Swire, Ted Harris, Michael Haney; adv, Blaine Thompson (Matthew Serino). Opened March 17, '76, at the Lyceum Theatre; $10 top weeknights, $12 weekend nights.
Richard Bauer, Joseph Wiseman, Paul Sparer, Edwin Bordo, Sanford Seeger, Carl Don, David Reinhardsen, Warren Pincus, David Margulies, Lee Wallace, Polly Adams, David Little, Rodman Flender, John B Jellison, Michael Haney, Irwin Atkins, Nancy Dutton, Michael Gottin, Zviah Igdalsky.
03/24/76B

Zoot Suit
The Shubert Organization, Center Theatre Group of LA & Gordon Davidson presentation of Mark Taper Forum prodn of a play in two acts (multi-scenes), by Luis Valdez with orig mus-lyr, Lalo Guerrero, Daniel Valdez. Staged by the author; chor, Patricia Birch; setting, Thomas A Walsh, Roberto Morales; cos, Peter J Hall; light, Dawn Chiang; snd, Abe Jacob; mus seq prodn, Daniel Valdez; prodn asso, Kenneth S Brecher. GM, Max Allentuck; publicity, Merle Debuskey, Owen Levy; company mgr, Leo K Cohen; stage mgrs, Milt Commons, Bethe Ward, Miguel Delgado. Opened March 25, '79 at the Winter Garden Theatre; $19.50 top weeknights, $22.50 weekend nights.
Edward James Olmos, Daniel Valdez, Abel Franco, Lupe Ontiveros, Roberta Delgado Esparza, Tony Plana, Charles Aidman, Karen Hensel, Rose Portillo, Geno Silva, Mike Gomez, Paul Mace, Julie Carmen, Angela Moya, Dennis Stewart, Kim Miyori, Lewis Whitlock, Darlene Bryan, Miguel Delgado, Lee Mathis, Richard Jay-Alexander, Luis Manuel, Gela Jacobson, Helen Andreyko, Michele Mais, Vincent Duke Milana, Raymond Barry, Arthur Hammer.
03/28/79B

PLAYS ABROAD

Jan. 1, 1976–Dec. 31, 1980

A Bedfull of Foreigners
(London)
Duncan C Weldon & Louis I. Michaels for Triumph Theatre Prodn presentation, in ass'n with Louis Benjamin, of a play in two-acts by Dave Freeman. Staged, Roger Redfarn; set, Terry Parsons; light, Andrew A Gardner. Opened April 12, '76, at the Victoria Palace, London; $3.75 top.
Peter Bland, Colin Jeavons, Julia Sutton, Terry Scott, June Whitfield, Dennis Ramsden, Lynda Baron.
05/05/76A

A Cheery Soul
(Sydney)
Sydney Theatre Co presentation of a Paris Theatre Co prodn of a play in three acts by Patrick White. Staged, Jim Sharman; des, Brian Thomson; cos, Anna Senior; mus, Cameron Allen; light, John Hoenig; chor, Keith Bain. Opened Jan. 17, '79, at the Sydney Opera House Drama Theatre, Sydney; $7.50 top.
Robyn Nevin, Peter Carroll, Pat Bishop, Maggie Kirkpatrick, John Paramor, Claire Crowther, Deborah Kennedy, Linden Wilkinson, Paul Johnstone, Jan Hamilton, Paul Chubb, Sharon Calcraft, Annie Byron.
01/31/79A

A Chorus Line
(London)
Michael White presentation of The New York Shakespeare Festival's prodn (produced in New York by Joseph Papp with Plum Prodns) of a musical without intermission (13 numbers); conceived-chor-staged, Michael Bennett; book, James Kirkwood, Nicholas Dante; mus, Marvin Hamlisch. Lyr, Edward Kleban. Co-chor, Bob Avian; set, Robin Wagner; cos, Theoni V Aldredge; light, Tharon Musser; snd, Art Jacob; orchs, Bill Byers, Hershey Kay, Jonathan Tunick; mus coord, Robert Thomas; mus dir, Ray Cook; vocal arrs, Don Pippin; asst cond, Grant Cossack; asso prod (New York) Bernard Gersten, (London) Robert Fox. Opened July 22, '76 at Theatre Royal, Drury Lane, London,; $8 top.
Tommy Aguilar, Steve Baumann, Jean Fraser, Eivind Harum, Ron Kurowski, Yvette Mathews, T Michael Reed, Timothy Scott, Jane Summerhays, Michael Austin, Nancy Dafgek, Troy Garza, Jeff Hyslop, Jennifer Ann Lee, Gina Paglia, Ken Rogers, Donn Simione, Miriam Welch, Ronald Young, Christine Baker, Mark Dovey, Mitzi Hamilton, Loida Iglesias, Wendy Mansfield, A William Peekins, Sandy Roveta, Ronald Stafford, Nancy Wood.
Musical numbers: "I Hope I Get It," "I Can Do That," "And. . .," "At the Ballet," "Sing!," "Hello Twelve, Hello Thirteen, Hello Love," "Nothing," "Dance: Ten; Looks; Three," "The Music and the Mirror," "One," "The Tap Combination," "What I Did For Love." "One" (Reprise).
08/04/76A

A Day In Hollywood & A Night In The Ukraine
(London)
Danny O'Donovan & Helen Montague (for Backstage Productions) & Michael Winner presentation (by arrangement with Richard Jackson & Buddy Dalton) of a New End Theatre prodn of a revue, with sketches by Dick Vosburgh; mus, Frank Lazarus; lyr, Vosburgh; and a one act comedy by Vosburgh. Staged, Ian Davidson; set, Barry Parman; light, Bill Graham. Opened Mar 28, '79, at the Mayfair Theatre, London; $10 top.
Paddie O'Neil, Frank Lazarus, Sheila Steafel, John Bay, Maureen Scott, Jon Glover, Alexandra Sebastian.
04/11/79A

A Deadly Dream: SEE Ein Toedlicher Traum

A Fair Quarrel
(London)
National Theatre revival of a comedy in two acts by Thomas Middleton and William Rowley. Staged, William Gaskill; scenery-cos, Hayden Griffin; light, Andy Phillips; mus, George Fenton; fight staging, William Hobbs. Opened Feb. 8, '79, at the Olivier Theatre, London; $9.85 top.
Ian Ireland, Marjorie Yates, Bruce Alexander, Paul Freeman, Fred Pearson, Nicky Henson, Christian Burgess, Harriet Walter, Roger Gartland, Mark Wing-Davey, Peter Hugo Daley, Dermot Crowley, Gil Brailey, Ned Vukovic, Marty Cruickshank, Chloe Salaman.
02/21/79A

A Family
(London)
Duncan C Weldon and Louis I Michaels presentation of drama in two acts by Ronald Harwood. Staged, Casper Wrede. Setting, Peter Bennion; light, Joe Davis; snd, Tim Foster and George Glossop. Opened July 6, '78, at the Haymarket Theatre, London; $9.40 top.
Paul Scofield, Celia Gregory, Eleanor Bron, Irene Handl, Trevor Peacock, Sally Bazely, Gary Waldhorn, Harry Andrews.
07/12/78A

A Hole in the Head: SEE 'S Loch im Chopf

A Life
(Dublin)
Abbey Theatre presentation of two-act drama by Hugh Leonard. Staged, Joe Dowling; setting-cos, Wendy Shea; light, Tony Wakefield. Opened Oct. 4, '79, at the Abbey Theatre, Dublin; $7 top.
Cyril Cusack, Daphne Carroll, Maureen Toal, Philip O'Flynn, Dearbhla Molloy, Garrett Keogh, Stephen Brennan, Ingrid Craigie.
10/24/79A

A l'Ombre de Gatsby
(In Gatsby's Shadow)
(Brussels)
Yvan Baudouin presentation of a play in one act by Jeannine Monsieur. Staged, Baudouin; set, Chris Cornil; cos, Lesly Bunton, Cornil, Sylvie Van Loo. Opened April 19, '77, at the Theatre Yvan Baudouin, Brussels.
Yvan Baudouin, Lesly Bunton, Pierre Gilmar, Fernande Claude.
06/01/77A

A Manual of Trench Warfare
(Sydney)
Australian Elizabeth Theatre Trust presentation of the State Theatre Co of South Australia prodn of a drama in two acts by Clem Gorman. Staged, Colin George; dsgn, Richard Roberts; light, Nigel Levings; movement, Michael Fuller. Opened May 31, '79, at the Seymour Centre's York Theatre, Sydney: $8.90 top.
Colin Friels, Edwin Hodgeman, Neil Fitzpatrick, Wayne Jarratt.
06/27/79A

A Murder is Announced
(London)
Peter Saunders presentation of drama in two acts; adapt, Leslie Darbon; from the book by Agatha Christie. Staged, Robert Chetwyn; decor-cos, Anthony Holland; light; Robert Bryan. Opened Sept. 22, '77, at the Vaudeville Theatre, London; $6.50 top.
Patricia Brake, Dinah Sheridan, Eleanor Summerfield, Christopher Scoular, Mia Nadasi, Dulcie Gray, Barbara Flynn, Nancy Nevinson, Gareth Armstrong, Michael Dyerball, James Grout, Michael Fleming.
10/19/77A

A Night with Dame Edna
(London)
Bestall Reynolds (UK) Ltd presentation of a one-man show by Barry Humphries and with Barry Humphries. Staged, Ian Davidson; set, Diane Millstead; cos, Kenneth Everage, Jane Hamilton, Zandra Rhodes. Piano accompaniment, Alan Clare. Opened Dec 13, '78, at the Piccadilly Theatre, London; $10 top.
Barry Humphries.
12/20/78A

A Song of Scandal
(Dublin)
Ardenza Prodns Ltd. presentation of musical by Maureen Charlton and Annette Perry; add'l mus, Michael Swallow; based on Richard Brinsley Sheridan's "The School for Scandal." Staged, Alice Dalgarno; set, Ewa Gargulinska; cos, Derry O'Donovan. Opened Sept. 26, '76, at the Pavilion Theatre, Dun Laoire, Dublin; $3 top.
Louise Studley, Barbara McCaughey, Kevin Hough, Philip O'Brien, Theresa O'Dwyer, Rachel Burrows, Jim Tinkler, Bill Brown, Adrian Vale, Paul Wilson, Frank Cullinan.
10/06/76A

A Toast to Melba
(Melbourne)
Australian Performing Group presentation of play by Jack Hibberd; staged, Hibberd. mus, Lorraine Milne; set, Kelvin Gedye, John Koning. Opened April 1, '76, at The National Theatre, Melbourne; $6.25 top.
Evelyn Krape, Paul Hampton, Jack Weiner, Tony Taylor, Claire Dobbin, Peter Finlay, Max Gillies, Fay Mokotow.
04/21/76A

A Toast to Melba
(Sydney)
Univ. of New South Wales Drama Foundation presentation of the Old Tote Theatre Co. in a two-act comedy with music by Jack Hibberd. Staged, Mick Rodger; decor, Hugh Colman; light, Jerry Luke; mus dir, Sandra McKenzie. Opened Sept. 30, '76, at the Parade Theatre, Sydney; $6.90 top.
Jennifer McGregor, John Allen, Terry Bader, Christine Collins, Ralph Cotterill, Drew For-

A Toast
(Cont)
sythe, Anne Grigg, Mario Merino.
10/20/76A

A Very Good Year
(Sydney)
King O'Malley Theatre Co presentation of a play by Bob Ellis; mus, Patrick Flynn, Philip Scott, Mervyn Drake, Ian Hutchinson, Ludwig von Beethoven; lyr, Bob Ellis, Lord Byron, Robert Frost, Phillip Scott, Ian Hutchinson, Malcolm Fraser, Rudyard Kipling, Mad Tom o'Bedlam. Staged, Mick Rodger; des, Mike Bridges; mus dir, Mervyn Drake; chor, David Atkins. Opened Dec. 9, '80 at the Stables Theatre, Sydney; $6 top.
Terry Bader, John Clayton, Anne Grigg, Lorna Lesley, Mervyn Drake.
12/31/80A

A Visit with the Family
(Sydney)
Nimrod Theatre Co presentation of a play in two acts, by Greg Bunbury. Staged, Richard Wherrett; des, Larry Eastwood; light, Grahame Murray. Opened Oct 14, '78, at the Nimrod Theatre, Sydney; $7.50 top.
Brian Young, Tom Farley, Robyn Nevin, Helen Morse, Brandon Burke, Gillian Jones, Lou Brown, Margo Lee.
11/01/78A

A World of Wisdom
(London)
John Farrow (for Impresarios Ltd), in ass'n with Jimmy Jacobs, presentation of a variety show by Norman Wisdom. Chor, Samantha Stevens; chor for Wisdom's routines, Fred Peters. Opened June 19, '79 at the Drury Lane Theatre, London; $8 top.
Norman Wisdom, Tony Fayne, Samantha Stevens Dancers, Colin Norman Orchestra.
06/27/79A

Acapulco Madame
(Paris)
Yvonne Printemps presentation of a comedy in two acts by Yves Jamiaque. Staged, Yves Gasc; set, Pace. Opened Sept. 14, '76, at the Theatre De La Michodiere, Paris; $8 top.
Micheline Boudet, Philippe Nicaud, Ariele Semenoff, Henry Courseaux, Jaime Gomez.
10/06/76A

Adventures of a Bear Called Paddington
(Sydney)
Clem Dirago & Partners Ltd presentation of a play in two acts by Alfred Bradley and Michael Bond. Staged, Geoffrey Williams; chor, Robina Beard; dsgn, Michael Salmon. Opened May 5, '80, at the Regent Theatre, Sydney; $6.50 top adults, $4.50 children.
Hugh Munro, Peter Rowley, Anne Grigg, Carole Skinner, Gordon McDougall, Brian Harrison.
05/28/80A

Affluence
(Dublin)
Irish Theatre Co presentation of two-act play by Wesley Burrowes. Staged, Christopher Fitzsimon; set, Monica Frawley; light, Julian Erskine. Opened Sep 29, '80, at the Oscar Theatre, Dublin: $6 top.
Eric Erskine, John Olohan, Godfrey Quigley, Louis Rolston, Liam Sweeney, Conor McDermottroe, Joseph O'Byrne, James Lancaster, Edward Byrne, J J Murphy, Alan Stanford, Maire Hastings, Stella McCusker.
10/29/80A

After Me the Deluge: SEE El Diluvio Que Viene

After Shave
(London)
Cameron Mackintosh presentation of a musical revue in two acts (24 numbers); lyr, Stephen Wyatt; mus, Nic Rowley. Staged-chor, Christie Dickason; mus dir-arrs, Nic Rowley; des, Clive Lavagna; light, Brian Harris; snd, Malcolm Blackmoor. Opened Aug. 24, '77, at the Apollo Theatre, London; $6.95 top.
Sue Aldred, Linda Dobell, Nicolette Marvin, Caroline Noh, Belinda Sinclair.
08/31/77A

Ain't Misbehavin'
(London)
Michael White, Ray Cooney & Stoll Prodns presentation of a musical show, based on idea by Murray Horowitz & Richard Maltby Jr; songs, Thomas (Fats) Waller and various others. Mus supv-orch-arr, Luther Henderson; staged, Richard Maltby Jr; mus staging, Arthur Faria; asso dir, Murray Horowitz; vocal arr-dir, William Elliott; setting, John Lee Beatty; cos, Randy Barcelo; light, Pat Collins; asso prod, Robert Fox; prodn supv, Andrew Treagus. Opened March 22, '79, at Her Majesty's Theatre, London; $14.25 top.
Evan Bell, Andre De Shields, Annie Joe Edwards, Jozella Reed, Charlaine Woodard; Luther Henderson, pianist.
Musical numbers: "Ain't Misbehavin'," "Lookin' Good but Feelin' Bad," "'T Ain't Nobody's Biz-ness If I Do," "Honeysuckle Rose," "Squeeze Me," "Handful of Keys," "I've Got a Feeling I'm Falling," "How Ya Baby," "The Jitterbug Waltz," "The Ladies Who Sing With the Band" ("Yacht Club Swing," "When the Nylons Bloom Again," "Cash For Your Trash," "Off-Time"), "The Joint Is Jumpin'," "Spreadin' Rhythm Around," "Lounging at The Waldorf," "The Viper's Drag," "Mean to Me," "Your Feet's Too Big," "That Ain't Right," "Keeping Out of Mischief Now," "Find Out What They Like," "Fat and Greasy," "Black and Blue," "I'm Gonna Sit Right Down and Write Myself a Letter," "Two Sleepy People," "I've Got My Fingers Crossed," "I Can't Give You Anything But Love," "It's a Sin to Tell a Lie," "Honeysuckle Rose"(reprise).
04/04/79A

Alex - Or the Automatic Trial
(Sydney)
Griffin Theatre Co & New South Wales Theatre of the Deaf presentation of a drama in two acts, adapted by Ian Watson from the Anthony Burgess novel, "A Clockwork Orange." Staged, Ian Watson; des, Astrid Spielman; light, Tony Rossiter; mus dir, Struan Smith. Opened Aug. 29, '79, at the Stables Theatre, Sydney; $4.50 top.
Stewart Chalmers, Ingle Knight, Rosemarie Lenzo, George Leppard, Andrew Lindsay, Susan Winter.
09/26/79A

Alice's Boys
(London)
Michael Codron presentation of a play in two acts by Felicity Browne and Jonathan Hales. Staged, Lindsay Anderson; setting, Alan Tagg; light, David Colmer; cos, Lindy Hemming. Opened May 10, '78, at the Savoy Theatre, London; $9.15 top.
Michael Gambon, Michael Jayston, Sam Davies, Joanna van Gyseghem, Gary Bond, Ralph Richardson, Geoffrey Keen.
05/24/78A

All You Need Is Love
(Dublin)
National Theatre presentation of a two-act drama by John Lynch. Staged, Patrick Laffan; scenery, Frank Conway; light, Tony Wakefield; snd, Kevin Mullery. Opened Nov. 11, '76 at the Peacock Theatre, Dublin; $2 top.
Stephen Brennan, Ingrid Craigie, Larry Murphy, Marie Ni Ghrainne, Philip O'Sullivan, Raymond Hardie, Martina Stanley, Ronan Paterson, Shay Whelan, Fiona MacAnna.
11/24/76A

Amadeus
(London)
Nat'l Theatre presentation. Staged, Peter Hall. Set-light, John Bury; mus dir, Harrison Birtwistle. Opened Nov 2, '79 at the Olivier Theatre, London; $10.95 top.
Dermot Crowley, Donald Gee, Philip Locke, Paul Scofield, Basil Henson, Andrew Cruickshank, Nicholas Selby, Felicity Kendal, Simon Callow, William Sleigh, John Normington, David Morris, Nik Forster, Louis Selwyn, Steven Slater, Glyn Baker, Nigel Bellairs, Leo Dove, Jane Evers, Susan Gilmore, Robin McDonald, Peggy Marshall, Robin Meredith, Ann Sedgwick, Glenn Williams.
11/14/79A

An Evening with Adolf Hitler
(Sydney)
An Actors Co presentation of a drama in two acts by Jennifer Compton and Matthew O'Sullivan. Staged, Matthew O'Sullivan. Opened at the Actors Co Theatre, Ultimo, Sydney, Sept 28. $7 top.
Matthew O'Sullivan, Beverly Blankenship.
10/18/78A

An Evening with Dave Allen
(London)
Danny O'Donovan, Alan Cluer and Helen Montagu (for Backstage Prdctns) presentation of a solo show in two acts with Dave Allen; light, Joe Davis. Opened Oct 4, '78, at the Vaudeville Theatre, London; $9.95 top.
10/18/78A

An Evening with Tommy Steele
(London)
Bernard Delfont & Richard Mills presentation of a revue. Staged-light, Dick Huran; mus dir, Alan Bence. Opened Oct. 11, '79, at Prince of Wales Theatre, London; $13.98 top.
Tommy Steele.
10/31/79A

An Evening With Margaret Rutherford
(Sydney)
John Howitt Enterprises presentation of a solo show by Tracey Lee. Staged, John Howitt; mus arr, Chic Perryman; accompanist, Bill Palmer; cos, Bill Robinson. Opened April 27, '79, at the 269 Playhouse, Sydney; $6.80 top.
Tracey Lee.
05/09/79A

Anastasia
(London)
Robert Sidaway & Mark Furness revival of a drama in three acts, by Marcelle Maurette, Guy Bolton. Staged, Tony Craven; set, Pamela Ingram; cos, Hugh Durrant; light, Howard Eaton. Opened Sept. 22, '76, at the Cambridge Theatre, London; $5.15 top.
David Nettheim, David Griffin, Peter Wyngarde, Ron Alexander, Nyree Dawn Porter, Ray Gatenby, Brian Poyser, Jeanette Lewis, John Locke, Jo Anderson, Elspeth March.
09/29/76A

And a Nightingale Sang
(London)
Archie Stirling & Howard Panter presentation of a play in two acts (six scenes) by C P Taylor; staged, Mike Ockrent; settings, Geoffrey Scott; light, Leonard Tucker; mus supv, Peter Skellern. Opened July 17, '79, at the Queen's Theatre, London; $13.65 top.
Gemma Jones, Arthur Blake, Roger Avon, Veronica Sowerby, Patricia Routledge, Christian Rodska, Ray Brooks.
07/25/79A

Annie
(London)
Michael White presentation of Mike Nichols prodn of a musical in two acts (13 scenes, 19 numbers), book, Thomas Meehan; mus, Charles Strouse; lyr, Martin Charnin, based on comic strip "Little Orphan Annie." Staged, Martin Charnin; mus staging-chor, Peter Gennaro; settings, David Mitchell; cos, Theoni V Aldredge; light, Richard Pilbrow; dance mus arrs, Peter Howard; orch, Philip J Lang; mus dir, Ray Cook; asso prod, Robert Fox. Opened May 3, '78, at the Victoria Palace Theatre, London; $11 top.
Hayley Milton, Deborah Clarke, Stacy Golding, Melanie Rose, Michelle Freeman, Denise Brompton, Andrea McArdle, Sheila Hancock, Harry Ditson, Richard Manuel, Edward Harbour, Andy Mulligan, Beatrice Aston, Judith Paris, Jay Denyer, Lynne Williamson, Colette Hiller, Sue Aldred, Stratford Johns, Kenneth Nelson, Clovissa Newcombe, Matt Zimmerman, Brian Ellis, Archie T Tridmorten, Damon Sanders, Gerry Tebbutt.
    Musical numbers: "Maybe," "It's the Hard Knock Life," "It's the Hard Knock Life" (reprise), "Tomorrow," "We'd Like To Thank You," "Little Girls," "I Think I'm Gonna Like It Here," "N.Y.C.," "Easy Street," "You Won't Be an Orphan For Long," "You're Never Fully Dressed Without a Smile," "You're Never Fully Dressed Without a Smile" (reprise), "Easy Street" (reprise), "Tomorrow" (reprise), "Something Was Missing," "I Don't Need Anything But You," "Annie," "Maybe" (reprise), "A New Deal for Christmas."
05/10/78A

Antony and Cleopatra
(London)
Prospect Theatre Co. revival of a play in two acts by William Shakespeare. Staged, Toby Robertson; des, Nicholas Georgiadis; mus, Donald Fraser; light, Keith Edmundson; chor, William Louther. Opened Nov. 16, '77, at the Old Vic Theatre, London; $6.35 top.
Alec McCowen, Derek Jacobi, John Nettleton, Rupert Frazer, Kenneth Gilbert, John Rowe, Paul Vaughan Teague, John Bowe, David Shaughnessy, Robert Eddison, Jeffery Daunton, Philip York, Neil McCaul, Michael Howarth, Philip Bloomfield, Andrew Seear, Terence Wilton, Dorothy Tutin, Bernice Stegers, Zoe Hicks, Rosamond Freeman-Attenwood, Graeme Elder, Clive Gibertson, Paul Cartwright, Stephen Jennifer, Laurence Joyce, Alan Lawrence.
12/07/77A

Antony and Cleopatra
(Stratford-On-Avon)
Royal Shakespeare Co revival of a drama in two acts by William Shakespeare. Staged, Peter Brook; set-cos, Sally Jacobs; mus, Richard Peaslee; light, Nick Chelton. Opened Oct 10, '78, at the Shakespeare Memorial Theatre, Stratford-upon-Avon; $13.95 top.
Alan Howard, Jonathan Pryce, Paul Brooke, Marjorie Bland, David Lyon, John Bowe, Patrick Stewart, John Nettles, Paul Whitworth, Hilton McRae, Dennis Clinton, Paul Webster, Alan Cody, John Nettles, Alan Rickman, Dennis Clinton, David Bradley, David Suchet, George Raistrick, Paul Moriarity, Glenda Jackson, Paola Dionisotti, Juliet Stevenson, Philip McGough, David Bradley, Raymond Westwell, Richard Griffiths, John Riley, Ian Reynolds, Robert Pritchard, Glenn Coleman, David Statham, Peter Morris, Gareth Richards, Robin Weatherall, Tony McVey.
10/18/78A

Antoss Fur Claudia
(Kickoff for Claudia)
(Gera, East Germany)
Gera Theater presentation of a musical in two acts. Book-lyr, Hans-Georg Albig; mus, Friedrich-Wilhelm Tiller; dir, Lothar Arnold; Gera Theater Orchestra cond, Rainer Eichorn; chor, Ranier Uhlig; set des, Lothar Gopfert; cos, Romi Wallat; Orchs, Tiller; artistic cnsltnt, Ursula Sternberg. Opened May 5, 1977, at the Gera Theater, German Democratic Republic.
Peter Meyer, Angelika Poser, Gunter Grunschneder, Peter Tshaplik, Jurgen Kurth, Klaus Winter, Nils Giesecke, Eleonore Udet, Jugo Wieg, Werner Junghams, Jurgen Mutze, Ekkehard Kaminiarz, Wolfgang Grimmer, Emil Hirschleber, Barbara Zitzmann.
    Music, Gera State Orchestra, Jena Philharmonic.
05/25/77A

The Apple Cart
(London)
Duncan C Weldon and Louis I Michaels, by arrangement with Anthony Chardet Prodns, presentation of a revival of a comedy in two acts by George Bernard Shaw. Staged, Patrick Garland. Sets, Eileen Diss; cos, Raymond Hughes; light, Bill Bray. Opened Nov. 7, '77, at the Phoenix Theatre, London; $8.15 top.
Jerry Harte, John Newton, Paul Hardwick, Keith Michell, Brigite Khan, Nigel Stock, Rony Robinson, Charles Lloyd Pack, Peter Sugden, Philip Anthony, Jo Warne, June Jago, Penelope Keith, Jeannette Sterke, Paul Maxwell, Michael Booth, Michael Cogan.
11/16/77A

The Arbor
(London)
English Stage Co presentation of a play in two acts by Andrea Dunbar. Staged, Max Stafford-Clark. Scenery, Peter Hartwell; cos, Gemma Jackson; light, Gareth Jones. Opened Jun 24, '80, at the Royal Court Theatre, London: $10.50 top.
Kathryn Pogson, Jeff Rawle, Mia Soterious, Dave Hill, Jane Wood, Ron Cook, David Haig, Paul Barber, Lynda Rooke.
07/09/80A

Are You Now or Have You Ever Been
(London)
Robert Sherman, Douglas Goldie & Archie Sterling presentation of a play in two acts by Eric Bentley. Staged, Anton Rodgers; des, Saul Radomsky. Opened Sep 29, '77 at the Mayfair Theatre, London; $6.10 top.
Marcella Markham, Thick Wilson, Robert Sheedy, Weston Gavin, Ramsay Williams, Hal Galili, Peter Banks, Robert Whelan, Bob Sherman, Christopher L Muncke, Thomas Baptiste.
11/02/77A

Aristocrats
(Dublin)
National Theatre presentation of three-act drama by Brian Friel. Staged, Joe Dowling; setting, Wendy Shea; light, Leslie Scott; piano, Veronica McSwiney. Opened March 8, '79, at the Abbey Theatre, Dublin; $6 top.
Niall O'Brien, Kevin McHugh, Bill Foley, John Kavanagh, Dearbhla Molloy, Stephen Rea, Ingrid Craigie, Kate Flynn, Geoff Golden, Kathleen Barrington.
04/25/79A

Arsenic and Old Lace
(London)
Walter Jokel revival of a comedy in three acts (five scenes) by Joseph Kesselring. Staged, Hugh Goldie; set, John Page; light, Trevor Mitchell. Opened May 19, '77, at the Whitehall Theatre, London; $6.05 top.
Barbara Mullen, Lennard Pearce, Brian Poyser, Grahame Mallard, Alan Leith, Joyce Heron, Toria Fuller, Julian Holloway, Barry J Gordon, Jonathan Adams, Derek Royle, Stan Pretty.
06/15/77A

Aspects Of Max Wall
(London)
Peter Saunders presentation of a solo show by Max Wall. Mus accompaniment, William Blezard, piano; Tony Parkinson, drums. Opened Feb. 7, '79, at the Vaudeville Theatre, London; $9 top.
02/21/79A

Backyard
(Sydney)
Nimrod Street Theatre Co Ltd, presentation of a drama in two acts by Janis Balodis. Staged, Terence Clarke; des, Stephen Curtis; light, Margie Wright. Opened July 31 at the Nimrod Downstairs Theatre, Sydney. $7 top.
Bryan Brown, Julie McGregor, David Atkins, Michele Fawdon, Joan Sydney, David Slingsby.
08/20/80A

Baggage
(London)
Michael White presentation of a comedy in two acts by Lee Langley. Staged, Val May. Sets, Graham Brown; light, Andrew A Gardner; add'l cos, Sue Blaine. Opened June 17, '76, at the Vaudeville Theatre, London; $5,80 top.
Gerald Harper, Hannah Gordon, Una Stubbs, Ian Marter, Prunella Gee, David Warwick, Judy Buxton.
06/30/76A

Banana Ridge
(London)
Ray Cooney, H M Tennent Ltd. & Eddie Kulukundis revival of a farce in three acts (five scenes) by Ben Travers. Staged, Val May; set, Robin Archer; light, Joe Davis. Opened July 19, '76, at the Savoy Theatre, London; $6.30 top.
Jan Holden, Roy Hepworth, Viviene Martin, Robert Morley, George Cole, Geoffrey Burridge, Beth Morris, Michael Malnick, Joan Sanderson, Anthony Dawes, Anthony Baird.
07/28/76A

Bar Mitzvah Boy
(London)
Wolverstow Ltd presentation of a Peter Witt prodn of a musical in two acts (14 scenes, 19 numbers); book, Jack Rosenthal; mus, Jule Styne; lyr, Don Black; based on an orig television play by Rosenthal. Staged, Martin Charnin; chor, Peter Gennaro; set, Robin Don; cos, Gaelle Allen; light, David Hersey; mus dir, Alexander Fiars; dance arr, Ray Holder; orchs-arr, Irwin Kostal. Opened Oct 31, '78, at Her Majesty's Theatre, London; $12.35 top.
Barry Andel, Ashley Knight, Zelah Clarke, Kerry Shale, Sharon Lee Hill, Gordon Faith, Peter Whitman, Harry Towb, Leonie Cosman, Ray C Davis, Joyce Blair, Vivienne Martin, Raymond Brody, Benny Lee, Barry Martin, Mostyn Evans, David Hitchen.
Others: Raymond Brody, Jonathan Courage, Joan Hall, Jeannie Harris, David Hitchen, Maurice Lane, Albin Pahernick, Barbara Rosenblat, Buster Skeggs, Carole Star, Brent Verdon, Giselle Wolf, Erica Yorke.
Musical numbers: "Why?" "If Only a Little Bit Sticks," "The Bar Mitzvah of Eliot Green," "This Time Tomorrow," "Thou Shalt Not," "The Harolds of This World," "We've Done Alright," "The Bar Mitzvah of Eliot Green" (reprise), "Simchas," "You Wouldn't Be You," "The Bar Mitzvah," "Rita's Request," "Where is the Music Coming From?" "Victor's Request," "If Only a Little Bit Sticks" (reprise), "The Sun Shines Out of Your Eyes," "The Sun Shines Out of Your Eyes" (reprise), "I've Just Begun," "We've Done Alright" (reprise).
11/08/78A

Barnardo
(London)
Gold Star Prodns presentation of a mus in two acts (18 numbers), with book, mus-lyr, Ernest Maxin. Staged, Maxin; settings, Jim Clay, Peter Higgins; cos, Michael Endacott; chor, Alain Dehay; mus dir, Barry Westcott. Opened May 22, '80, at the Royalty Theatre, London: $19.90 top.
Jonathan Courage, Nicky Bird, Chris Connah, Mark V York, Timothy Carlton, James Smillie, Adrian Cale, Tommy Barnett, Bobby Collins, Alastair King, Fiona Fullerton, Marisa Campbell, Eleanor Moir, Richard Majewsky, Paul Medford, Jason Norman, Chris Poole, Sarah Anderson, Lucy Baker, Kathy Barnett, Lisa Evans, Mandy Hanson, Debbie Norris, Justine Page, Ursula Stammer.
Musical nuumbers: - "London's East End," "Oy Vey," "The Midnight Waltz," "Lovely Ot Pies," "There's a First Time," "Snuggle Up," "What Children Will Do," "You're the Man," "Tosh," "Welcome to Dreamlan," "Girls," "Cor," "I Feel Sorry For You," "I'm a Winner," "My Son," "Why Don't We Try Again," "Who Needs a Man?," "Am I Running Out of Time?," Alastair King, Gillian Scotland, Jacob Witkin, Matthew Peters,- Raymond Begley, Nicky Bird, Eloise Ritchie, Mark Holmes, Richard Mitchell, Ian Oliver, Hugo Bower, Richard Brookes, Tracy Hall, Catherine Murphy, Michelle Welch, Gerry Dolan, Jane Hardy, John Arnatt, Lyndon Miles, Jayford Cameron, Jenny Beamish, Damien Nash
Singers, dancers, east end kids: - Debbish Blackett, Frances Carr-Boyd, Hilary Evans, Lisa Westcott,
06/18/80A

The Bastard From the Bush
(Sydney)
Nimrod Theatre Co Ltd presentation of a solo show by Robin Ramsay and Rodney Fisher, from writings of Henry Lawson. Staged, Rodney Fisher; decor-light, Margie Wright. Opened March 16, '79, at the Nimrod Downstairs Theatre, Sydney; $5 top.
Robin Ramsay.
04/25/79A

Beatlemania
(London)
Ray Cooney, in ass'n with Capital Radio, Brian Rix and Paul Elliott, presentation of a multimedia revue in two acts with songs by John Lennon, Paul McCartney; editorial, Robert Rabinowitz, Bob Gill, Lynda Obst; images, Rabinowitz, Gill, Shep Kerman, Kathleen Rabinowitz. Orig concept, Steven Leber, David Krebs, Jules Fisher; prodn supv, Fisher; (orig Broadway prodn, Krebs, Leber); visuals dir, Charles E Hoefler; mus supv, Sandy Yaguda; mus supv (London), Donna Johnson; mus dir, Rodney Mendoza; scenery, Robert D Mitchell; light, Fisher; snd, Abe Jacob; media engr, Mary McGregor. Opened Oct. 18, '79, at the Astoria Theatre, London; $13.75.
Peter McGann, James Cushing, Peter Santora, Bobby Taylor.
Offstage musicians: Rodney Mendoza, Cliff Haines, Stanley Lishak, John Franca, Barry Graham, Ted Beament, Alan Waterson.
10/31/79A

Bedroom Farce
(London)
National Theatre presentation of a comedy in two acts by Alan Ayckbourn. Staged, Ayckbourn, Peter Hall; set, Timothy O'Brien, Tazeena Firth; light, Peter Radmore. Opened March 16, '77, at the Lyttleton Theatre, London; $7.75 top.
Michael Gough, Joan Hickson, Michael Kitchen, Polly Adams, Derek Newark, Susan Littler, Stephen Moore, Maria Aitken.
03/23/77A

Beecham
(London)
Eddie Kulukundis, Michael White & Archie Stirling presentation of a play in two acts by Caryl Brahms and Ned Sherrin. Staged, Patrick Garland; scenery, Richard Marks; cos, Barbara Wilson; light, Kevin Flynn; mus dir, Colin Purbrook. Opened Jan 29, '80, at the Apollo Theatre, London: $13.60 top.
Timothy West, Terry Wale.
02/13/80A

Beetles & Buckman
(London)
Stella Richman prodn of a revue with 35 songs and sketches. Staged, David Reid; light, Peter Sutton. David O'Brien, pianist. Opened Feb. 3, '76, at the Mayfair Theatre, London; $5 admission.
Chris Beetles, Rob Buckman, David Tate, Tina Parry; David O'Brien, pianist.
Musical numbers: "One Glove Love," "A Far from the Sea Shanty," "Mean Man Blues," Catchy Little Number," "The Blues Blues," "Sniff and Snuffle Shuffle," "Blue River," "J.L. Slug," "Filthy and Greedy."
02/11/76A

Before the Party
(London)
H M Tennent, with Myriad Prodns in association with Sunshine Ltd, presentation of an Oxford Playhouse Prodn of a revival of a comedy-drama by Rodney Ackland based on a short story by W Somerset Maugham. Staged, Tom Conti; set, Tanya McCallins; cos, Angela Butterfield; light, David Colmer. Opened Mar 13, '80, at the Queen's, London.
Jane Asher, Michael Gough, Phyllis Calvert, Jayne Tottman, Miles Anderson, Louise Breslin.
04/02/80A

The Belle of Amherst
(London)
Peter Witt presentation of a Mike Merrick-Don Gregory prodn of a solo play in two acts by William Luce, compiled by Timothy Helgeson from poems and correspondence of Emily Dickenson. Staged, Charles Nelson Reilly; set-light, H.R. Poindexter; cos, Theoni V. Aldredge. Opened Sept. 14, '77, at the Phoenix Theatre, London; $6.80 top.
Julie Harris.
09/21/77A

The Bells of Hell
(London)
Michael Codron presentation of a comedy in two acts by John Mortimer. Staged, John

The Bells
(Cont)
Tydeman; scenery, Peter Rice; light, Nick Chelton. Opened July 27, '77, at the Garrick Theatre, London $7 top.
Phyllida Law, Peter Woodthorpe, Tony Britton, Derek Thompson, Lesley Duff, Trevor Baxter.
08/03/77A

Bent
(London)
Royal Court Theatre & Eddie Kulukundis (by arrangement with Jack Schlissel) presentation of an English Stage Co prodn of a play in two acts by Martin Sherman. Staged, Robert Chetwyn; set-cos, Alan Tagg; light, Robert Bryan; mus, Andy Roberts. Opened May 3, '79, at the Royal Court Theatre, London; $7 top.
Ian McKellen, Jeff Rawle, Simon Shepherd, Haydn Wood, Jeremy Arnold, Ken Shorter, Roger Dean, Richard Gale, Tom Bell, Gregory Martyn, John Francis, Peter Cellier.
05/23/79A

Betrayal
(London)
National Theatre presentation of a play in two acts (nine scenes) by Harold Pinter. Staged, Peter Hall; set-light, John Bury. Opened Nov 15, '78, at the Lyttelton Theatre, London; $8.50 top.
Michael Gambon, Penelope Wilton, Daniel Massey, Artro Morris, Glenn Williams.
11/22/78A

Beyond The Rainbow
(London)
Harold Fielding, Bernard Delfont & Richard M Mills, by arrangement with Universal Pictures, presentation of a Harry Bernsen prodn of a musical in two acts (24 scenes, 17 numbers); book, Iaia Fiastri (English version, David Forrest); mus, Armando Trovaioli; lyr, Leslie Bricusse, based on the novel "After Me, the Deluge," by David Forrest. Staged, Pietro Garinei; chor, Gino Landi; set-cos, Giulio Coltellacci; mus dir, Michael Reed; choral dir, John McCarthy. Opened Nov 9, '78, at the Adelphi Theatre, London; $11.85 top.
Johnny Dorelli, Roy Kinnear, Dorothy Vernon, Lesley Duff, Geoffrey Burridge, Janet Mahoney, Franco Ricchio, Noel Johnson.
Dancers, singers: Roy Ashby, Josie Ashcroft, Neil Boyle, Emma Bryant, Frankie Cull, Paul Easom, Natalie Forbes, Nicky Goodchap, Lynne Hayworth, David Hepburn, Nicola Kimber, Stuart Lock, Penny Stevenson, Rebecca Wilson, Susan Gene, Jane Hardy, Jan Hartley, Linda Lovell, Simon Masterton Smith, Iain Parkinson, Geoff Thomas, David Urwin.
Musical numbers: "Come Join Us at the Table," "Pity," "Ding Dong Song," "Throw It Away," "A Time For Love," "Consolation," "A Time For Love" (reprise), "Love, According to Me," " A Tiny Ant," "San Crispino," "Pity" (reprise), Clementina," "I Want You," "I Want You," "Beyond the Rainbow," "Love According to You," "Come Join Us at the Table" (reprise).
11/22/78A

Big and Little: SEE Gross Und Klein

Big Toys
(Sydney)
Univ. of New South Wales Drama Foundation presentation of the Old Tote Theatre Co. prodn of a play in three acts by Patrick White. Staged, Jim Sharman; des, Brian Thomson; light, Jerry Luke; cos, Victoria Alexander. Opened July 27, '77, at the Parade Theatre, Sydney; $7.30 top.
Arthur Dignam, Kate Fitzpatrick, Max Cullen.
08/24/77A

The Biograph Girl
Harold Fielding presentation of a musical in two acts (18 numbers); book-lyrs, Warner Brown; mus, David Heneker. Staged, Victor Spinetti; mus numbers staged, Irving Davies; mus dir, Michael Reed; scenery, John Pascoe; cos, Graham Brown; light, Eric Delzenne; snd, Edward Fardell. Opened Nov 19, '80, at the Phoenix Theatre, London: $19.10 top.
Kate Revill, Sally Brelsford, Michelle Fine, Sheila White, Jane Hardy, Bruce Barry, Ron Berglas, Richard Kates, Guy Siner.
Musical Numbers: - "The Moving Picture Show," "Working in Flickers," "That's What I Get All Day," "Working in Flickers" (reprise), "Diggin' Gold Dust," "Every Lady Needs a Master," "I Just Wanted to Make Him Laugh," "I Like to be the Way I Am in My Own Front Parlor," "Beyond Babel," "A David Griffith Show," "More Than A Man," "The Industry," "Gentle Fade," "Nineteen Twenty-Five," "The Biograph Girl," "One of the Pioneers," "Put It in the Tissue Paper," "Working In Flickers" (reprise).
11/26/80A

Blithe Spirit
(London)
National Theatre revival of a comedy in three acts (seven scenes) by Noel Coward. Staged, Harold Pinter; set, Eileen Diss; cos, Robin Fraser Paye; light, Richard Pilbrow. Opened June 24, '76, at the Lyttelton Theatre, London; $4.20 top.
Susan Williamson, Rowena Cooper, Richard Johnson, Geoffrey Chater, Joan Hickson, Elizabeth Spriggs, Maria Aitken.
07/07/76A

The Blue Macushla
(Dublin)
National Theatre Society presentation of comedy-drama in two acts by Thomas Murphy. Staged, Jim Sheridan; setting, Brian Collins; cos, Ib Jorgensen; light, Richard Caswell. Opened Mar 6, '80, at Abbey Theatre, Dublin: $8 top.
Donal McCann, Stephen Rea, Deirdre Donnelly, Emmet Bergin, Barry McGovern, Peadar Lamb, Des Nealon, Michael O'Briain, Fidelma Cullen, Pat Leavy, Paddy Long, Patric Laffan, Paul Brennan.
04/02/80A

Bodies
(London)
Ray Cooney, by arrangement with the Hampstead Theatre, presentation of a drama in two acts by James Saunders. Staged, Robin Lefevre; setting, Tanya McCallin; cos, Lindy Hemming; light, Alan O'Toole, Gerry Jenkinson. Opened April 23, '79, at the Ambassadors Theatre, London; $10.40 top.
Gwen Watford, Angela Down, David Burke, Dinsdale Landen.
05/02/79A

Born in the Gardens
(London)
Eddie Kulukundis, John Walbank, Archie Stirling & Howard Panter presentation of a play in two acts by Peter Nichols. Staged, Clifford Williams; setting, John Gunter; light, Mark Pritchard. Opened Jan 23, '80, at the Globe Theatre, London; $13.75 top.
Beryl Reid, Barry Foster, Peter Bowles, Jan Waters.
01/30/80A

Boy's Own McBeth
(Sydney)
Dunsinane Enterprises presentation of a comedy in three acts by Grahame Bond and Jim Burnett; mus, Bond. Staged, Bond and Mark Gould; dir, Rory O'Donoghue. Opened July 11, '79, Kirk Gallery, Sydney, $8.50 top.
Nick Lathouris, Rory O'Donoghue, Paul Johnstone, Grahame Bond, Nicholas Lyon, Bjarne Ohlin, Elizabeth Wilder.
08/29/79A

Braeker
(Zurich)
Schauspielhaus presentation of a comedy-drama in eight scenes by Herbert Meier. Staged, Roberto Guicciardini; set-cos, Lorenzo Ghiglia; incidental mus, George Gruntz, Tarot; tech dir, Rene Wartmann; light, Robert Egli; snd, Margret Nonhoff. Opened Sep 21, '78, at the Schauspielhaus, Zurich; $20 top.
Peter Brogle, Anne-Marie Dermon, Alfred Pfeifer, Michael Rittermann, Ingrit Seibert, Robert Tessen, Fred Tanner, Bernd Rumpf, Peter Ehrlich, Erwin Parker, Otto Dornbierer.
Musicians: Doris Hug, Annemarie Wiesner, Christoph Marthaler, Pepe Solbach.
10/25/78A

Brand
(London)
National Theatre rev of a drama in two acts by Henrik Ibsen, adapt, Geoffrey Hill. Staged, Christopher Morahan; sets, Ralph Koltai; cos, Koltai, Gaelle Allen; light, David Hersey; mus, Harrison Birtwistle. Opened April 25, '78, at the Olivier Theatre, London; $7.65 top.
Michael Bryant, Anthony Douse, Jeremy Ewing, Dermot Crowley, Lynn Farleigh, Tamara Hinchco, Timothy Block, Robert Stephens, Stanley Lloyd, Dennis Tynsley, Margaret Ford, Roger Gartland, Patience Collier, Daniel Thorndike, Brian Kent, Martin Howells, Anna Manahan, Gawn Grainger, Peter Needham, Nicholas Selby, Peter Rocca, Jane Evers, Brenda Dowsett, Peggy Marshall, Marianne Morley, Keith Skinner, Richard Perkins.
05/03/78A

Brasil Tropical
(London)
Tropicana Theatre Productions S A presentation, in ass'n with Richard Graham (by arrangement with Ray Cooney Prods Ltd.), of an Eberhard Radisch and Gino Askanasy pro-

Brasil Tropical
(Cont)
duction of a musical. Staged, Edvaldo Carneiro and Domingos Campos; chor, Campos, Claudette Walker; mus dir, Fliel Nogueria; decor, Miguel H; cos, Campos, Paco Rabanne, Jose Moura; carnival cos, Evandro Castro Lima. Opened May 29, '79, at the Drury Lane Theatre, London; $12 top.
　　Solo Dancers - Inaicyra, Telma, Jocely
　　Singers - Ana Teresa, Dalila, Jorge
　　Dancers - Cristina, Dina, Betty, Lissa, Leda, Angela, Neli, Regina, Marcia, Rosangela, Gracinha, Marlene, Rose, Gil, Flescha, Gato, Negao, Jacinto, Juvenal, Leleco, Sarigue, Adelson, Carlos, Alva, Shellei, Jose Maria.
06/13/79A

Breezeblock Park
(London)
Mermaid Theatre, in ass'n with Michael Codron, presentation of a play in two acts by Willy Russell. Staged, Alan Dossor; scenery-cos, Adrian Vaux; light, Joe Davis; cos supv, Valerie Metheringham. Opened Sept. 12, '77, at the Mermaid Theatre, London; $6 top.
Wendy Craig, Ken Jones, Emma Jean Richards, Julie Walters, Peter Postlewaite, Eileen Kennally, Norman Rossington, David Neilson, Ian Redford.
09/21/77A

The Bride of Gospel Place
(Sydney)
National Institute of Dramatic Art presentation of a drama in four acts by Louis Esson. Staged, Aubrey Mellor; des, Stephen Gow; light, Michael Triggs; snd, Lorraine Drennan; movement, Keith Bain; fights, George Sparkes; mus dir, Roma Conway. Opened Jun 17, '80, at the Jane Street Theatre, Sydney; $7 top.
Barry Otto, Barry Lovett, Peter Blackwell, Anthony Martin, Mark Ferguson, Georgia Campbell, Helen Jones, John Hannan, Fay Mokotow, Mervyn Drake, Tim Burns, Angela Punch McGregor, Craige Cronin, Deidre Rubenstein, Vivienne Garrett.
07/16/80A

The Browning Version & Harlequinade
(Britain)
British National Theatre Revival of two Terence Ratigan plays. Staged, Michael Rudman; settings, Carl Toms; light, Brian Ridley. Opened May 13, '80, at the Lytellton Playhouse, $13.55 top.
Alec McCowen, Geraldine McEwan, Nicky Henson, Graeme Henderson, Ellen Pollock, Heather Tobias, Kay Adshead.
05/21/80A

Bruderlichkeit
(Fraternity)
(Zurich)
Schauspielhaus presentation of a comedy-drama in one act by Juerg Federspiel. Staged, Max-Peter Ammann; set, Jiri Kotlar; cos, Heinz Berner; mus, George Gruntz; chor, Roy Bosier, Daisy Stuerm; tech dir, Bruno Zaugg; mus dir, Pierre Favre, Mario Beretta; light, Christian Scheifele, Hans-Joerg Huber; snd, Margret Nonhoff. Opened Nov. 5, '77, at the Studio Tiefenbrunnen, Zurich; $4.55 admission.
Helen Vita, Alfred Pfeifer, Kurt Sobotka, Barbara-Magdalena Ahren, Bettina Lindtberg, Heinz Berner, Jon Laxdal, Roy Bosier, Walo Luond, Bruno Zaugg.
12/07/77A

Bubbling Brown Sugar
(London)
Jack Levin & David A Barber presentation, in ass'n with Dan Wright and Ken Myers, of a musical in two acts (34 numbers); book, Loften Mitchell; based on concept by Rosetta LeNoire; score including standard numbers plus new songs by Danny Holgate, Emme Kemp and Lillian Lopez. Staged, Charles Augins; chor-mus staging, Billy Wilson; scenery, Clarke Dunham; cos, Bernard Johnson; light, Francis Reid; projections, Lucie D Grosvenor, Clarke Dunham; snd, Autograph; coral arr, Chapman Roberts; mus supv-arr, Holgate; mus dir, Richard Leonard. Opened Sep 28, '77, at the Royalty Theatre, London; $8.70 top.
Charles Augins, Newton Winters, Pepsi Maycock, Dawn Hope, Ray Collins, Beverly Butler, David Cameron, Rosita Yarboy, Helen Gelzer, Clarke Peters, Amii Stewart, Keith Hodiak, Alan Harding, Mel Taylor, Miguel Brown, Pinky Steede, Elaine Delmar, Billy Daniels, Lon Satton, Stephanie Lawrence, Alan Harding, Bernard Sharpe, Liz White.
10/19/77A

Bullie's House
(Sydney)
Nimrod Street Theatre Co presentation of a drama in two acts by Thomas Keneally. Staged, Ken Horler; dsgn, Michael Pearce; light, Keith Edmundson; special props, Brian Hosking; mus, Philip Lanley. Opened Feb 6, '80, at the Nimrod Theatre, Sydney; $8 top.
Athol Compton, Bob Maza, Bill Conn, Kevin Smith, Justine Saunders, Don Reid, Martin Harris, Philip Lanley.
03/05/80A

Bunraku
(National Puppet Theatre of Japan)
(Edinburgh)
Edinburgh International Festival presentation of the National Puppet Theatre of Japan, in "Heike Nyogonoshima," ("The Priest in Exile") and "Sonezaki Shinju" ("The Double Suicide at Sonezaki"). Opened Aug. 31, '76, at the Royal Lyceum Theatre, Edinburgh; $6 top.
10/20/76A

Burlesco
(Sydney)
Nimrod Street Theatre Co Ltd presentation of Sideshow in a mime fantasy in two acts. Staged, Michael Matou; mus, Martin Raphael; light, Barbara Williams. Opened Dec 12, '79, at the Nimrod Downstairs Theatre, Sydney; $6 top.
Michael Matou, Kevin English, Fifi L'Amor, Simon Reptile, Cigarette.
02/06/80A

Bus Stop
(London)
Veronica Flint-Shipman & Paul Elliott revival of a comedy-drama in three acts by William Inge. Staged, Vivian Matalon; set, Saul Radomsky; light, Nick Chelton; cos, Jane Robinson. Opened May 12, '76, at the Phoenix Theatre, London; $7.50 top.
Jenny Quayle, Miriam Karlin, Roy Purcell, Lee Remick, Alfred Marks, John Church, Don Fellows, Keir Dullea.
05/26/76A

Buster
(London)
Prospect Theatre presentation of a revue, with 13 numbers, by Jane McCulloch and David Fraser. Staged, Toby Robertson; scenery-cos, Hugh Durrant; light, Keith Edmundson; stage mgr, Trevor Ingman. Opened Sept. 14, '77, at the Old Vic Theatre, London; $7.65 top.
Max Wall, Jan Waters.
　　Musical numbers: "Born in a Trunk," "Walking Down Broadway," "The Movie Game," "He'd a Villa, Kids and Wife," "The Company's on Location," "Vaudeville," "Everybody's Talkin' 'bout the Talkies," "Sing the Hollywood Blues," "I Still Can't Believe," "Buster Keaton, They've Sent You A Wire," "Sad Clown," "The Cards Are on the Table," "Little Funny Man," "It's Been a Long, Long Climb."
09/21/77A

Cabaret
(Berlin)
Theater des Westens presentation of a musical in two acts with book by Joe Masteroff (based on play, "I Am a Camera," by John van Druten and "The Berlin Stories" by Christopher Isherwood); mus, John Kander; lyr, Fred Ebb, and German text by Robert Gilbert. Staged, Karl Vibach; mus dir, Wolfgang Peters; chor, John Grant; scenery (based on New York prodn), Margarete Ruijgrok; cos, Patricia Zipprodt, Ilse-Marianne Wittneben. Opened Dec. 30, '78, at the Theater des Westens, West Berlin; $15 top.
Horst Buchholz, Joachim Kemmer, Jutta Boll, Tatjiana Sais, Manfred Lichtenfeld, Helge Roeske, Gerhard Garbers, Regina Heiden, Gundula Petrovska, Rolf Decker. Original ladies orchestra--Gloria Roberts (piano), Lisa Gordanier (tenor sax), Anne-marie Roelof, (trombone), Iris Surma (drums).
01/10/79A

The Cakeman
(Sydney)
Aboriginal Arts Board of the Australia Council presentation, in ass'n with Robert J Merritt & Brian Syron, of a drama in two acts by Robert J Merritt. Staged, George Ogilvie; set, Wendy Dickson; mus, Michael Carlos; light, Simon Jenkins; film segments dir, Gillian Armstrong. Opened April 29, '77, at the Bondi Pavillion Theatre, Sydney, $5 top.
Brian Syron, Justine Saunders, Teddy Phillips (Shona Bernard), Max Cullen, George Shevtsov, Robert Faggetter.
06/15/77A

Can You Hear Me at the Back?
(London)
John Gale & Mark Shivas presentation of a play in two acts by Brian Clark. Staged, Barry Davis; setting, Carmen Dillon; light, Howard Eaton. Opened May 30, '79, at the Piccadilly Theatre, London; $11.40 top.
Peter Barkworth, Hannah Gordon, Edward Hardwicke, Michael Maloney, Stephanie Beacham.
06/13/79A

Canaries
(Dublin)
National Theatre Society presenation of two-act play by Bernard Farrell. Staged, Patrick Mason; sets, Frank Conway; cos, Jo Taylor; light, Brian Collins. Opened Oct 2, '80, at Abbey Theatre, Dublin; $8 top.
May Cluskey, Ingrid Craigie, Eamonn Morrissey, Stephen Brennan, David Kelly, Eileen Colgan, Desmond Perry, Clive Geraghty, Fiona MacAnnan, Anita Reeves, Desmond Cave.
12/10/80A

Candida
(London)
Eddie Kulukundis & Bill Freedman revival of a comedy in three acts by George Bernard Shaw. Staged, Michael Blakemore; set, Alan Tagg; light, Leonard Tucker. Opened June 23, '77, at the Albery Theatre, London; $7.60 top.
Maureen Lipman, Denis Quilley, Simon Jones, Leslie Sands, Deborah Kerr, Patrick Ryecart.
07/06/77A

Canterbury Tales
(London)
Chanticleer Prodns (by arrangement with Classic Presentations) presentation of a revival of a musical in two acts (24 numbers), by Neville Coghill and Martin Starkie; mus, Richard Hill, John Hawkins; lyrs, Coghill, adapted from works of Geoffrey Chaucer. Staged, Martin Starkie; cos, Loudon Sainthill; set, Derek Cousins; chor, Hugh Halliday; mus dir, Denys Rawson. Opened April 24, '79, at the Shaftesbury Theatre, London; $10.25 top.
Jessie Evans, Anna Sharkey, Percy Herbert, Buddy Elias, Dudley Owen, Michael Logan, Peter Forest, Ian Steele, Susan Begley, Barbara Miller, Philip Blaine, Jonathan Darvill, Michael Jones, Nigel Hughes, Michael Barbour, Simon Clark, John Howard, Joanna Gale, Bridget de Courcy, Sally Brelesford, Tricia Deighton, John Alasdair, Beverley Kay, Kim Mendez, Roland Brine, Shaun Johnstone, Paul Madden, Steve Whatley, Leonie Palette.

Musical numbers: "Song of Welcome," "Good Night Hymn," "Canterbury Day," "I Have a Noble Cock," "Darling Let Me Teach You How to Kiss," "There's the Moon," "Gorgeous Lady," "My Little Feathery Lady," "My Husband is so Clever," "Top of the Cocks," "April Song," "Love Will Conquer All," "Fill Your Glass," "Canterbury Day" (reprise), "Come on and Marry Me Honey," "Beer, Beer, Beer," "Where Are the Girls of Yesterday?" "Wedding Song," "If She Has Never Loved Before," "I'll Give My Love a Ring," "Sing in Praise of Women's Virtue," "I Am All Ablaze," "April Song" (reprise), "Love Will Conquer All" (reprise).
05/02/79A

Captive Audience
(Dublin)
Edwards-MacLiammoir Dublin Gate Theatre Prodns presentation of two-act drama by Desmond Forristal. Staged, Hilton Edwards; setting, Robert Heade. Opened Oct. 10, '79, at the Gate Theatre, Dublin; $6.
Liz Bono, Michael Lawlor, Gerard McSorley.
10/31/79A

Carte Blanche
(London)
Michael White and Richard Pilbrow presentation of a Hillard Elkins prodn of a sexual adventure (2 acts; 18 scenes) in words and mus put together by Kenneth Tynan, Clifford Williams; staged, Williams; material by Robert Cohan, Peter Darrell, Rudy de Luca and Barry Levinson, Alistair Eliot, Robin Hughes, Eugene Ionesco, Pat McCormick, Robert North, Molly Parkin, The Earl of Rochester, Frantz Salieri, Kenneth Tynan, Paul Verlaine, Keith Waterhouse, Michael Weller, Clifford Williams; mus-lyr, Alan Blaikley, Bob Downes, Ken Howard, Dee Shipman, Roger Webb, Marc Wilkinson; prodn des, Abdel Farrah, Judith Bland; light, Andrew Bridge; snd, David Collinson; mus supv, Marc Wilkinson; mus dir, Nic Rowley. Opened at Phoenix Theatre, London Sept. 30, '76. $8.10 top.
Sue Aldred, Robin Courbet, Fiona Douglas Stewart, Caroline Grenville, Philip Hatton, Rodney Madden, Michael Manning, Natasha Morgan, Sue Rittman, Peter Van de Wouw, Edwin van Wyk, Jean Warren, Michael Watkins, Josephine Welcome.
10/06/76A

The Case of the Oily Levantine
(London)
Bestall Reynolds Ltd presentation of a play in two acts by Anthony Shaffer. Staged, Patrick Dromgoole; setting, Hayden Griffin; cos, Anne Sinclair; light, Howard Eaton. Opened Sept. 13, '79, at Her Majesty's Theatre, London; $13.20 top.
William Squire, Anna Quayle, Adrienne Posta, Paul Angelis, Gwen Nelson, Hywel Bennett, Roger Leach, Wolfe Morris, Bernard Archard.
09/19/79A

The Case of Katherine Mansfield
(Sydney)
Nimrod Theatre Co presentation of a one-woman documentary compiled, edited and performed by Cathy Downes. Voice of Middleton Murry by Stuart Devinnie; light, Kim Newell; mus, Michael Houston. Opened Jun, '80, at the Nimrod Downstairs Theatre, Sydney: $7.60 top.
Cathy Downes.
06/25/80A

The Cassidy Album
(Sydney)
Seymour Centre presentation, by arrangement with the Adelaide Festival of Arts Inc, of a trilogy (A Hard God, Furtive Love, An Eager Hope) by Peter Kenna. Staged, John Tasker; des, Ian Robinson; light, Christine Dunstan, Patrick Whelan. Opened March 29, '78, at the York Theatre, Sydney; $7.40 top.
Vic Rooney, Maggie Kirkpatrick, Tony Sheldon, Alan Wilson, Phillip Ross, Janice Finn, Ray Meagher.
04/19/78A

Cause Celebre
(London)
John Gale presentation of a drama in two acts by Terence Rattigan. Staged, Robin Midgley. Scenery, Adrian Vaux; light, Joe Davis; cos, Brian Castle. Opened July 4, '77, at Her Majesty's Theatre, London; $6.90 top.
Glynis Johns, Anthony Pedley, Matthew Ryan, Sheila Grant, Neil Daglish, Helen Lindsay, Jeremy Hawk, Adam Richardson, Angela Browne, Kevin Hart, Patrick Barr, Kenneth Griffith, Bernard Archard, Darryl Forbes-Dawson, Phillip Bowen, David Glover, Peggy Aitchison, Anthony Howard, David Masterman.
07/13/77A

The Chairman
(London)
Michael White presentation of a comedy in two acts by Philip Mackie. Staged, Gareth Davies; set, Stuart M Stanley; light, Jack Raby. Opened March 10, '76, at the Globe Theatre, London; $6 top.
Peter Blythe, David Firth, Sarah Atkinson, Reginald Marsh, Barrie Cookson, Jill Melford, Tony Britton, Michael Malnick.
03/17/76A

The Changeling
(London)
Royal Shakespeare Co revival of a play in two acts by Thomas Middleton and William Rowley. Staged, Terry Hands; set-cos, Judith Bland; mus, Guy Woolfenden. Opened Oct 16, '78, at the Aldwych Theatre, London; $8.95 top.
James Laurenson, Philip Dunbar, Roger Martin, David Shaw-Parker, Diana Quick, Jill Baker, Emrys James, Bernard Brown, Arthur Whybrow, Barrie Rutter, David Hobbs, John McEnery, Julian Glover, Charles Dance, Charlotte Cornwell, Stephen Jenn.

Asylum immates: Michele Copsey, Rory Edwards, David Hobbs, Kenneth McClellan, Roger Martin, David Shaw-Parker, Peter Tullo.
11/01/78A

The Cherry Orchard
(London)
National Theatre rev of a play in four acts by Anton Chekhov, translated by Michael Frayn. Staged, Peter Hall; sets, John Bury; light, David Hersey; mus, Harrison Birtwistle, Dominic Muldowney. Opened Feb. 14, '78, at the Olivier Theatre, London; $8.15 top.
Albert Finney, Susan Littler, Nicky Henson, Ralph Richardson, Judi Bowker, Dorothy Tutin, Susan Fleetwood, Robert Stephens, Helen Ryan, Terence Rigy, Derek Thompson, Ben Kingsley, Peter Needham, Daniel Thorndike, Brian Kent, Norman Claridge, Edna Dore, Irene Gorst, Tamara Hinchco, Martin Howells, Marianne Morley, Richard Perkins, Peter Rocca, Keith Skinner, Dennis Tynsley,

The Cherry
(Cont)
Janet Whiteside.
03/29/78A

Chers Zoiseaux
(Dear Birdies)
(Paris)
Claude Sainval presentation of a comedy in two acts by Jean Anouilh. Staged, Anouilh, Roland Pietri; set, Jean-Demis Malcles. Opened Dec. 15, '76, at the Comedie-Des-Champs-Elysees Theatre, Paris; $12 top.
Guy Trejan, Herve Bellon, Uta Taeger, Annick Le Goff, Gerard Dournel, Gilberte Geniat, Francoise Brion, Michel Lonsdale, Odile Mallet, Jacques Castelot.
12/29/76A

Chicago
(London)
Ray Cooney & Larry Parnes, by arrangement with the Crucible Theatre Trust, presentation of a musical in two acts (20 numbers), with book by Fred Ebb and Bob Fosse, mus, John Kander; lyr, Fred Ebb; based on the play of the same title by Maurine Dallas Watkins. Staged, Peter James; chor, Gillian Gregory; settings, Roger Glossop; cos, Anne Sinclair; light, Peter Barham; prodn cnslt, Tony Stevens; mus dir, David Firman. Opened April 10, '79, at the Cambridge Theatre, London; $13.65 top.
Jenny Logan, Antonia Ellis, Richard Fox, Don Fellows, Erick Ray Evans, Jacquie Toye, Liz Whiting, Rachel Izen, Philippa Boulter, Tracie Hart, Hope Jackman, Okon Jones, Mark Jefferis, Martin Baker, Ben Cross, Kenn Oldfield, G Lyons, Linda Dobell.
Singers, dancers, others - Dawn Hope, Ellie Smith, Buster Skeggs, Jenny McGusty, Colin Bennett, Hugh Spight.
Musical numbers - "All That Jazz," "Funny Honey," "Cell Block Tango," "When You're Good to Mama," "Tap Dance," "All I Care About," "A Little Bit of Good," "We Both Reached for the Gun," "Roxie," "I Can't Do It Alone," "Chicago After Midnight," "My Own Best Friend," "I Know a Girl," "Me and My Baby," "Mister Cellophane," "When Velma Takes the Stand," "Razzle Dazzle," "Class," "Nowadays," "Nowadays," (reprise).
04/18/79A

Chidley
(Melbourne)
Hoopla Prodns, by arrangement with the Melbourne Theatre Co., presentation of a play in two acts by Alma de Groen. Staged, Garrie Hutchinson; des, Peter Corrigan; light, John Beckett. Opened Dec. 15, '76, at the Grant Street Theatre, Melbourne; $4.50 top.
Graeme Blundell, Carol Burns, Peter Cummins, Carillo Gantner, Robert Hewett.
12/29/76A

Children of the Sun
(London)
Royal Shakespeare Co presentation of a revival of a play in two acts by Maxim Gorky. English adaptation, Jeremy Brooks and Kitty Hunter Blair. Staged by Terry Hands; settings, Chris Dyer.
John Burgess, Norman Rodway, Sinead Cusack, Valerie Lush, Edward Peel, Alan Howard, Natasha Parry, Susan Dury, Arthur White, Brian Abbott, Carmen Du Sautoy, John Shrapnel, Paul Webster, Jenny Lipman, Kate Fitzgerald, Dennis Edwards.
Townspeople and peasants- Eileen Carrdus, Philip Fox, Jimmy Gardner, Joseph Greig, Peter Holmes, Arthur Kohn, Valerie Testa, Stuart Organ, Diana Van Fossen.
10/24/79A

The Circle
(London)
Duncan C Weldon & Louis Michaels revival of a play in three acts by W. Somerset Maugham. Staged, Peter Dews; set, Finlay James; light, Mich Hughes. Opened Oct. 13, '76, at the Haymarket Theatre, London; $5.80 top.
Martin Jarvis, Martin Chamberlain, Lee Hudson, Susan Hampshire, Clive Francis, John McCallum, Alan Haywood, Googie Withers.
10/20/76A

City of Broken Promises
(Hong Kong)
Hong Kong Arts Festival presentation of Garrison Players prodn of a musical in two acts, adapt, Brenda Davies; book, Austin Coates; mus, Judi Elman; lyr, Elman, Davies, June Armstrong-Wright. Staged, June Armstrong-Wright; mus-arr-orch, Vic Cristobal; mus dir, John Barham; scenery, Brian Tilbrook; cos, Rachel Day; light, Brian Smith; stage mgr, Andrew Ritchie. Opened Feb 6, '78, at the Shouson Theatre, Hong Kong; $5 top.
Yvonne Chow, Peter Rumsey, Bob McPherson, Mel Tobias, Timothy Kwok, Molly Fernley, Peter Atkins, Miranda Szeto, Tim Conway, Robert Fluhr, Eaon Jackson, Hugh Gailey, Alec Reeve, Patricia Garcia Clancy, Gill Taylor, Amy Lau, Agnes Po, Brenda Davies, Shield Self, Lannie Lee, Patric, Mok, Kevin Kwan, Elton Kwang, Zachary NG, Paul Yau, Dominic Lee.
03/15/78A

City Sugar
(London)
Michael White presentation of a drama in two acts by Stephen Poliakoff. Staged, Hugh Thomas; set, Robert Harris; light, Rory Dempster; cos, Sue Blane. Opened March 4, '76, at the Comedy Theatre, London; $6 top.
Adam Faith, James Aubrey, Lynne Miller, Natasha Pyne, Alan Hay, Hilary Gasson, Michael Tarn.
03/17/76A

Close of Play
(London)
National Theatre presentation of a play in two acts by Simon Gray. Staged, Harold Pinter; setting, Eileen Diss; cos, Elizabeth Waller; light, Leonard Tucker. Opened May 24, '79, at the Lyttelton Theatre, London; $10.90 top.
Michael Redgrave, Annie Leon, Zena Walker, Lynn Farleigh, John Standing, Michael Gambon, Anna Massey, Adam Godley.
05/30/79A

The Closed Door
(Dublin)
National Theatre Co presentation of play in two acts by J Graham Reid. Staged, Art O'Briain; setting, Bronwen Casson; light, Tony Wakefield. Opened Apr 24, '80, at Peacock Theatre, Dublin; $4 top.
Kevin Mc Hugh, Kathleen Barrington, Trudy Kelly, Colm Meaney, Desmond Perry, Catherine Gibson, Derek Lord, Noel O'Donovan, Marcus O'Higgins.
05/21/80A

Cloud Nine
(London)
English Stage Co presentation of a Joint Stock Theatre Group prodn of a play in two acts by Caryl Churchill. Staged, Max Stafford-Clark; settings, Peter Hartwell; light, Robin Myerscough-Walker; cos, Sylvia Kennedy. Opened March 29, '79, at the Royal Court Theatre, London; $7.20 top.
Anthony Sher, Jim Hooper, Julie Covington, Miriam Margoyles, Tony Rohr, Carole Hayman, William Hoyland.
04/18/79A

Cloud Nine
(London)
Joint Stock Theatre Group-English Stage Co presentation of a play in two acts, by Caryl Churchill. Staged, Max Stafford-Clark, Les Waters; set, Peter Hartwell; mus dir, Andy Roberts; light, Robin Myerscough-Walker. Opened Sep 4, '80, at the Royal Court Theatre, London; $12 top.
Graeme Garden, Ron Cook, Anthony O'Donnell, Harriet Walter, Anna Nygh, Maggie Steed, Hugh Fraser.
09/17/80A

Clouds
(London)
Ray Cooney, in ass'n with Hampstead Theatre Ltd, presentation of a comedy in two acts by Michael Frayn. Staged, Michael Rudman. Set, Sue Plummer; light, Gerry Jenkinson; cos, Lindy Hemmings. Opened Nov. 1, '78, at the Duke of York's Theatre, London; $10 top.
Tom Courtenay, Felicity Kendal, Mark Kingston, Paul Chapman, Mark Heath.
11/15/78A

The Club
(Melbourne)
Melbourne Theatre Co. presentation of a play in two acts by David Williamson. Staged, Rodney Fisher; des, Shaun Gurton. Opened May 26, '77, at the Russell Street Theatre, Melbourne; A $6 top.
Frank Gallacher, Gerard Maguire, Terence Donovan, Harold Hopkins, Frank Wilson, John Walton.
06/15/77A

Cock-a-Doodle Dandy
(Dublin)
Abbey Theatre Co. presentation of play in three acts by Sean O'Casey. Staged, Tomas MacAnna; set, Brian Collins; cos, Maebh Browne; light, Tony Wakefield. Opened Aug. 11, '77, at the Abbey Theatre, Dublin; $5 top.
M. Stanley, Edward Golden, Michael OhAonghusa, Maire Ni Ghrainne, Bernadette Shortt, Angela Harding, Bill Foley, Nial O'Brien, Emmett Bergin, Geoffrey Golden, Clive Geraghty, Larry Murphy, Maire O'Neill, Macdara O Fatharta, Stephen Brennan, Michael O

Cock-a-Doodle Dandy
(Cont)
Briain, Desmond Perry, Ronan Paterson, Liz Bono, Se Phelan, Angela Lynch, Maureen Mythen.
08/24/77A

Colette
(London)
H M Tennent by arrangement with Laurie Mansfield & Bernard Sandler, presentation of a musical in two acts (24 numbers); book-mus-lyrs, John Dankworth; Staged, Wendy Toye; scenery, Tim Goodchild; light, David Hersey; snd, Derrick Bunn; mus dir, Richard Holmes. Opened Sep 24, '80, at the Comedy Theatre, London; $18 top.
John Moffatt, Cleo Laine, Kenneth Nelson.

Musical numbers: - "You Can Be Sure of Spring," "He's a Captain," "I'm Special," "Ambitious," "Paree!" "Our Relationship," "Alone with Myself," "Attention Will Wander," "You've Got to Do," "We'll Stick Together," "I'm Special" (reprise), "I Never Make the Same Mistake," "Little Girl," "He's a Captain" (reprise), "Alone with Myself" (reprise), "Nothing Special," "I Never Make the Same Mistake" (reprise), "A Little Touch of Powder," "Love with Someone Younger," "Will He Ever Be Back?" "Paree!" (reprise), "Little Red Room," "You Can Be Sure of Spring" (reprise), "Little Red Room" (reprise).
10/08/80A

Come Into My Bed
(London)
Paul Raymond presentation of a comedy in two acts by Andre Launay. Staged, Victor Spinetti; light, Kevin P Savage. Opened Jan. 26, '76, at the Whitehall Theatre, London; $6.70 top.
Fiona Richmond, Barry Britten, Karen Bland, Julia Bond, Kevan Sheehan, Caroline Grenville, Wendy Gilmore, Michael Walker, Neil Phelps.
02/11/76A

The Comedians
(London)
Prospect Theatre Co. presentation of the Nottingham Playhouse revival of a comedy-drama in three acts by Trevor Griffiths. Staged, Richard Eyre; set, John Gunter; light, Steffan Adderton. Opened Aug. 10, '77, at the Old Vic Theatre, London; $5.95 top.
Bill Dean, David Beames, Bill Stewart, Sam Dale, Arthur Kohn, Alan Barry, Jimmy Jewel, Philip Jackson, Moti Makan, Ralph Nossek, William Maxwell, A James Smith.
08/17/77A

Comedy, Comedy
(Sydney)
Ensemble Productions, in association with The Festival of Sydney, presentation of a double-bill of comedies by Graeme Nixon. Staged, Fred Simms; des, Richard Heller; light-snd, Joddi Speight. Opened Jan 15, '80, at the Ensemble-at-the-Stables Theatre, Sydney; $5 top.
Les Asmussen, Denise Otto, Terry Byrnes, Sharon Flanagan, Greg Radford, Lucy Charles, Shauna O'Grady, Michael Ross.
02/06/80A

Conference of the Birds:
SEE La Conference des Oiseaux

Confusions
(London)
Michael Codron presentation of five playlets by Alan Ayckbourn. Staged, Alan Strachan; set, Alan Tagg; cos, Susan Yelland; light, David Colmer. Opened May 19, '76, at the Apollo Theatre, London; $6.35 top.
Mother Figure- Pauline Collins, Sheila Gish, Derek Fowlds.
Drinking Companion- John Alderton, Pauline Collins, Sheila Gish, James Cossins.
Between Mouthfuls- John Alderton, James Cossins, Sheila Gish, Derek Fowlds, Pauline Collins.
Gosforth's Fete- Sheila Gish, Pauline Collins, John Alderton, James Cossins, Derek Fowlds.
A Talk In The Park- John Alderton, Pauline Collins, James Cossins, Sheila Gish, Derek Fowlds.
05/26/76A

Cop Out!
(Melbourne)
Melbourne Theatre Co. presentation, in ass'n with the Australia Council, Victoria Ministry of the Arts and Melbourne City Council, of a play in two acts, by Cliff Green. Staged, Paul Karo; des, Steve Nolan; cos, Betty Druitt; light, Jamie Lewis. Opened Nov. 24, '77, at the Russell Street Theatre, Melbourne; $6.30 top weeknights, $6.60 Saturday night.
Maureen Edwards, Gerard Maguire, Frank Wilson, Lachlan Macdonald, Frank Gallacher, Jonathan Hardy.
12/14/77A

The Correction: SEE Die Korrektur

Counting the Ways
(London)
National Theatre of Great Britain presentation of a play in one act (no intermission), by Edward Albee. Staged, Bill Bryden; decor, John Bury. Opened Dec. 6, '76, at the Olivier Theatre, London; $4.45 top.
Michael Gough, Beryl Reid.
12/15/76A

The Country Wife
(London)
National Theatre presentation of a revival of a comedy in two acts by William Wycherley. Staged, Peter Hall, with Stewart Trotter; set-cos, John Bury; light, Leonard Tucker; mus, Harrison Birtwistle. Opened Nov. 29, '77, at the Olivier Theatre, London; $8.75 top.
Albert Finney, Nicholas Selby, Paul Henley, Robin Bailey, Elizabeth Spriggs, Ann Beach, Kenneth Cranham, Gawn Grainger, Ben Kingsley, Richard Johnson, Susan Littler, Polly Adams, Helen Ryan, Tel Stevens, Madoline Thomas, Edna Dore, Ray Edwards, Jane Evers, Irene Gorst, Peter Jolley, Stanley Lloyd, Peggy Marshall, Marianne Morley, Peter Pacey, Richard Perkins, Peter Rocca, Keith Skinner, Daniel Thorndike, Dennis Tynsley, Janet Whiteside.

Cousin Vladimir
(London)
Royal Shakespeare Co presentation of a play in two acts (seven scenes) by David Mercer. Staged, Jane Howell; set, Hayden Griffin, with Eamon D'Arcy; light, Rory Dempster. Opened Sept 22, '78, at the Aldwych Theatre, London; $8.85 top.
Walter Brown, Mark Dignam, Susan Engel, George Baker, Geoffrey Chater, Gaye Brown, Julian Glover, Sheila Reid, Glen Walford, Michael Bertenshaw, Edward Jewesbury.
10/04/78A

Crooked in the Car Seat
(Dublin)
Gemini Prodns presentation of two-act (seven scenes) drama by Brian Lynch. Staged, Donald Taylor Black; setting, Alan Pleass; light, Patrick Scanlon. Opened Oct. 9, '79, at the Eblana Theatre, Dublin; $5 top.
Deirdre Donnelly, Oliver Maguire, Kevin McHugh, Ronan Smith, Bob Carlile, Paul Murphy, Maria McDermottroe.
10/31/79A

The Crucifer of Blood
(London)
Louis I Michaels & Duncan C Weldon presentation of a play in two acts (six scenes) by Paul Giovanni; based on Arthur Conan Doyle story, "The Sign of the Four." Staged, Paul Giovanni; set, John Wulp; cos, Judith Bland; light, David Hersey and Mark Pritchard; scenery supv, Lynn Pecktal; snd-sfx, Brian Ferren. Opened March 21, '79, at the Haymarket Theatre, London; $11.20 top.
John Quentin, Edward Petherbridge, Nicholas Day, John Cater, Billy McColl, Geoffrey Snell, Keith Michell, Denis Lill, Susan Hampshire, Reis Etan, Klim Leh T'Chei, James Curran.
04/04/79A

Curse of the Starving Class
(London)
English Stage Co. (by arrangement with the New York Shakespeare Festival) presentation of a drama in three acts by Sam Shepard. Staged, Nancy Meckler; set, Sue Plummer; light, Jack Raby. Opened April 21, '77, at the Royal Court Theatre, London; $5.20 top.
Annette Crosbie, Brian Deacon, Patti Love, John Ratzenberger, Dudley Sutton, Ray Hassett, Michael Ensign, Michael Walker, Tony Sibbald.
04/27/77A

Cyrano de Bergerac
(Sydney)
Sydney Theatre Co presentation of a comedy in five acts by Edmond Rostand; trans, Louis Nowra. Staged, Richard Wherrett; set, John Stoddart; cos, Luciana Arrighi; light, Keith Edmundson; mus, Sarah de Jong; fights, George Whaley. Opened July 24, '80, at Sydney Opera House Drama Theatre, $9.20 top.
John Bell, Robin Ramsay, Helen Morse, Andrew McFarlane, Vic Rooney, Peter Whitford, George Shevtsov, Maggie Blinco, Brandon Burke, Robin Blowering, Peter Flett, Robert van Mackelenberg, Stuart Campbell, Andrew Tighe, Alan Tobin, Wilfred Last, John Sheerin, Bill McClusky, Jon Blake, Ian Kenny, Craig Ashley, Jennifer West, Linda Cropper, Greg

Cyrano de
(Cont)
Ford, Philip Parr.
08/27/80A

The Dance of Death
(London)
Royal Shakespeare Co revival of a play in two acts by August Strindberg, English adaptation by Michael Meyer. Staged, John Caird; settings, Mary Moore; light, Leo Leibovici. Opened June 15, '78, at the Aldwych Theatre, London; $8.30 top.
Emrys James, Sheila Allen, Deirdra Morris, Myrtle Moss, Alan David, Lynsey Baxter, Richard Derrington, Michael Bertenshaw.
06/28/78A

Dancing Partners & Animal, Vegetable and Mineral
(Sydney)
Ensemble Prodns presentation of a Megan Fry prodn of a dual-bill of plays by Graeme Nixon. Staged by Fred Simms; scenery and costumes, Doug Anderson; light, Peter Critchley; snd, Rod Dyson. Opened Jan. 16, '79, at the Ensemble-at-the Stables, Sydney; $4 top.
Dancing Partners-Michael Ross, Lesley Larkum, Matthew Larkum, Sharon Flanagan.
Animal, Vegetable and Mineral-Julie Herbert, Shauna O'Grady, James Moss, David Webb, James C Steele, Terry Byrnes, Anne E Morgan, Harold Jones, Michael Ross, Michael O'Brien, Richard Hughes.
01/31/79A

Dangerous Corner
(London)
Revival of a play by J B Priestley. Staged, Robert Gillespie. Set Robin Archer. Opened at the Ambassador's Theatre, London, Dec. 17, '80.
Peter Dennis, Ann Lynn.
12/31/80A

The Danny La Rue Show
(Sydney)
Sadleir Bros Int'l presentation of a variety show. Staged, Freddie Carpenter; wris, Bryan Blackburn, Mike Goddard; chor, Keith Little; decor-cos, Berkeley Sutcliffe, Danny La Rue; cos, Mark Canter; mus dir, Derek New. Opened April 19, '79, at the Regent Theatre, Sydney; $11.90 top.
Danny La Rue, Wayne King, The Rosettis, David Ellen, Cristina Avery.
05/16/79A

The Dark Horse
(London)
Colin Brough (for the Lupton Theatre Co) presentation of a play in two acts by Rosemary Anne Sisson. Staged, Val May; settings, Voytek; light, James Baird. Opened Aug 3, '78, at the Comedy Theatre, London; $9.65 top.
Edward Woodward, Peter Woodward, Peter Cellier, Peter Walmsley, Geoffrey Lumsden, George Selway, Roger Leach, Tony Haygarth, Barbara Jefford, Michael Barrington, Deborah Fairfax, Stacy Dorning, Murray Melvin, Robert Lister, Rex Robinson, Jamie Cowell-Parker, Francis Lloyd.
08/16/78A

Das Ende von Venedig
(The End of Venice)
(Zurich)
Schauspielhaus presentation of drama in one act by Juerg Amann. Staged, Carsten Bodinus; light, Christian Scheifele; snd, Margret Nonhoff. Opened Nov. 24, '76, set, Heinz Kriesi; cos, Renate Kalanke; tech dir, Bruno Zaugg; at the Studio Tiefenbrunnen, Zurich; $3.85 admission.
Joerg Cossardt, Gert Westphal, Anne-Marie Dermon, Erwin Parker, Franz Keller, Ulrich Bodamer, Otto Dornbierer, Peter Holliger, Diethelm Stix, Luzius Versell.
12/08/76A

Das Nest
(The Nest)
(Zurich)
Theatre am Neumarkt presentation of a comedy-drama in three acts (18 scenes) by Franz Xaver Kroetz. Staged, Jochen Foelster; set-cos, Hans Georg Schaefer; tech dir, Georges Nagy; snd-light, Peter Brodbeck, Twist Sopek. Opened March 6, '76, at the Theatre am Neumarkt, Zurich; $6.90 top.
Mathias Gnaedinger, Rosalinde Renn.
03/17/76A

Days of The Commune
(London)
Royal Shakespeare Co. presentation of a drama in two acts by Bertolt Brecht, trans, Clive Barker, Arno Reinfrank. Staged, Howard Davies; scenery-cos, Chris Dyer; mus, Douglas Jarman, David Keefe; light, Brian Harris; film effects, Joost Hunningher, John Holland; snd, John A Leonard. Opened Nov. 4, '77, at Aldwych Theatre, London; $7.25 top.
Paul Moriarty, David Lyon, Alfred Molina, Alan Cody, Bob Peck, Nickolas Grace, Mike Gwilym, Christopher Whitehouse, Marie Kean, Greg Hicks, Ian McKellan, Frances Viner, Cherie Lunghi, Paola Dionisotti, Margaret Ashcroft, Ruby Wax, Denyse Alexander, Lynda Rooke, John Brown, David Howey, Kim Begley, Paul Whitworth, Paul Shelley, Keith Taylor, Ian McDiarmid, Richard Griffiths, Leon Tanner, Jesse Birdsall, Steve Fletcher, Bryan Keenan, Jeremy Barlow, Tony McVey.
11/23/77A

Dead Eyed Dicks
(Dublin)
Eamonn Andrews Studios, H M Tennent Ltd. & Butler Fergusson presentation of a play in two acts by Peter King. Staged, Lionel Harris; set, J Hutchinson Scott; chor, Wayne Sleep; mus arr, Grant Hossack; mus, Kay Furst. Opened Oct. 7, '76, at the Gaiety Theatre, Dublin; $6 top.
Richard Vernon, Lally Bowers, Graham Crowden, Madeleine Cannon, Sheila Ruskin, June Brown, Declan Mulholland, John Standing, Peter O'Toole.
10/27/76A

Dean
(London)
Steven Bentinck presentation of a musical in two acts (21 numbers); book, John Howlett; mus-lyr, Robert Campbell. Staged, Robert H. Livingston; mus numbers staged, Noel Tovey; scenery, Terry Parsons; light, Nick Chelton; snd, Pinaki Dutt-Roy; mus dir, Clive Chaplin; mus arrs, John Bell. Opened Aug. 30, '77, at the Casino Theatre, London; $7.85 top.
Peter Karrie, Murray Kash, John Blythe, Anna Nicholas, Jill Jarress, Robert Booth, Betty Benfield, Alastair Kerr, Marlene Mackey, Jane Egan, Oscar James, Marc Anthony, Ken Caswell, Beverley Elman, Lesley Hand, Matt Zimmerman, Anthony O'Keeffe, Dudley Rogers, Glenn Conway.

Musical numbers: "The Ballad of James Dean," "Song 55," "Sounds of New York," "What Price Gold?," "I Scream," "Say Hello to Your Mother," "Lullaby," "Gonna Make Him a Star," "I Didn't Mean You," "Girl in Times Square," "Just One Knock On That Door," "Lost in L.A.," "Running Out of Time," "Happy New Year Kid," "Hollywood Dreams," "I Scream" (reprise), "Play That Song Again," "That Boy," "Misery, Mystery," "Texas," "Song 55" (reprise).
09/07/77A

Dear Birdies: SEE Chers
Zoiseaux

Dear Daddy
(London)
Simon Clarke in ass'n with Ray Cooney presentation of a comedy-drama in two acts by Denis Cannan. Staged, David William; scenery, Hutchinson Scott; light, Joe Davis. Opened Oct. 20, '76, at the Ambassadors Theatre, London; $5.75 top.
Nigel Patrick, Isabel Dean, Jennifer Hilary, Joseph Blatchley, David Crosse, Patrick Drury, Rosalind March, Phyllis Calvert.
10/27/76A

Death of a Salesman
(London)
Nat'l Theatre revival of a drama in two acts by Arthur Miller. Staged, Michael Rudman; settings, John Gunter; cos, Lindy Hemming; light, Mick Hughes; mus, John White. Opened Sept. 20, '79, at the Lyttelton Theatre, London; $11.45 top.
Doreen Mantle, Warren Mitchell, David Baxt, Stephen Grief, Ursula Smith, Michael J Jackson, Harry Towb, Harold Kasket, Jerry Harte, Mandie Joel, Ronnie Letham, Carole Harrison, Liz Goulding, Jeffrey Chiswick.
10/03/79A

The Death of Humpty Dumpty
(Dublin)
Abbey Players presentation of two-act drama by J Graham Reid. Staged, Patrick Mason; setting-cos, Juliet Watkinson; light, Tony Wakefield. Opened Sept. 6, '79, at Peacock Theatre, Dublin; $4 top.
Clive Geraghty, Kate Flynn, James Lancaster, Martina Stanley, Bill Foley, Dearbhla Molloy, Colm Meaney, Liam Neeson, Fedelma Cullen, Fiona MacAnna, Barry McGovern, Sharon O'Doherty.
10/03/79A

Deathtrap
(London)
Michael White in ass'n with Alfred de Liagre Jr & Roger L Stevens, presentation of a melodrama in two acts (six scenes) by Ira Levin.

Deathtrap
(Cont)
Staged, Michael Blakemore; set, William Ritman; light, Spike Gaden. Opened Oct 26, '78, at the Garrick Theatre, London; $10.25 top.
Denis Quilley, Rosemary McHale, Philip Sayer, Joyce Grant, David Healy.
11/08/78A

Demand
(Sydney)
Ensemble Productions presentation of a Megan Fry prodn of a drama in two acts by Derek Mortimer. Staged, Gary Baxter; light, Peter Critchley; dsgn, Doug Anderson; snd, Rod Dyson. Opened Jan. 23, '79, at Ensemble-at-the-Stables, Sydney; $4 top.
Andrew Inglis, Michael Pentecost, Damien Corrigan, John O'Brien, Craig Lambert, James Moss, Richard Hughes, Tony Auckland, Gary Daniels, Guy Malcolm, Rod McNeil, Graeme Rudd, Julie Bailue.
02/07/79A

Der Liebe Augustin
(Zurich)
Schauspielhaus presentation of a drama in six scenes by Hansjoerg Schneider. Staged, Hans Gratzer; setting-cos, Wolfgang Mai; incidental mus, George Gruntz; tech dir, Bruno Zaugg; light, Hans-Joerg Huber; snd, Robert Stalder; mus dir, Mario Beretta. Opened March 15, '79, at the Keller im Schauspielhaus, Zurich; $7 admission.
Matthias Habich, Ingrit Seibert, Susanne Bialucha, Sibylle Courvoisier, Klaus Knuth, Heinrich Trimbur, Juergen Cziesla, Bernd Rumpf, Christian Spatzek, Wernher Buck.
04/25/79A

The Devil's Disciple
(London)
Royal Shakespeare Co. presentation of a revival of a comedy in three acts by George Bernard Shaw. Staged, Jack Gold. Sets, Roger Butlin; light, Stewart Leviton; mus, Carl Davis. Opened July 13, '76, at the Aldwych Theatre, London; $5.95 top.
Patience Collier, Tom Conti, Tony Haygarth, Larry Hoodekoff, Eve Pearce, Alan Tilvern, Ann Way, Zoe Wanamaker, T P McKenna, Estelle Kohler, Richard Simpson, Peter Tilbury, Valerie Colgan, Lynsey Baxter, John Wood, Patrick Godfrey, Bob Hoskins, Steven Beard, Ian Lowe, Joe Dunlop, Norman Tipton, Manning Redwood, Karl Held, Raymond Marlowe.
07/21/76A

Devil's Island
(London)
English Stage Co. presentation of a Joint Stock Theatre Group prodn of a drama without intermission by Tony Bicat. Staged, David Hare; des, Hayden Griffin; light, Rory Dempster. Opened Feb. 24, '77, at the Royal Court Theatre, London; $5.15 top.
Gillian Barge, Suzanne Bertish, Simon Callow, Philip Donaghy, David Rintoul, Jane Wood.
03/02/77A

The Devil's Own People
(Dublin)
Dublin Theatre Festival in ass'n with Gemini Prodns presentation of play in two acts by Patrick Galvin. Staged-des, James D Waring; mus dir, Peter O'Brien. Opened Sept. 27, '76 at the Gaiety Theatre, Dublin; $6 top.
Ray McAnally, Des Keogh, Eileen Colgan, Anne Bushnell, Pat Leavy, Phyl O'Doherty, Brenda Doyle, Derry Power, Dearbhla Molloy, Robert Carrickford, Patrick Dawson, Eoin White, Joe MacArland, Gerald Fitzmahoney, Con O'Connor, Sheila Byrne, William Kiernan, Alan Gilsenan, Bernise Toolan, Marie Hegarty, Frances Fitzpatrick, Tom Lawlor.
10/20/76A

Die Korrektur
(The Correction)
(Zurich)
Schauspielhaus presentation of a drama in four scenes by Juerg Amann. Staged, Gudrun Orsky; setting-cos, Ambrosius Humm; tech dir, Bruno Zaugg; light, Christoph Ausfeld; snd, Werner Baumann. Opened Mar 7, '80, at the Keller im Schauspielhaus: $6.85 admission.
Jodoc Seidel, Bernd Rumpf, Hilke Ruthner, Horst Warning, Dietrich Boden, Peter Holliger, Istvan Kelemen, Angelica Arndts, Edzard Wuestendoerfer.
04/02/80A

Die Lehrerin Verspricht der Negerin Waermere Traenen
(The Teacher Promises the Negress Warmer Tears)
(Zurich)
Schauspielhaus presentation of a one-act solo drama by Juerg Laederach. Staged, Rolf Stahl; setting-cos, Wolfgang Mai; tech dir, Bruno Zaugg; light, Hans-Joerg Huber; snd, Alexander Hiltebrand. Opened Dec. 14, '78, at the Keller in Schauspielhaus, Zurich; $7.50 top.
Rosel Schaefer.
01/24/79A

Die Letzte Adresse
(The Last Address)
(Zurich)
Schauspielhaus presentation of drama in 18 scenes by Walter Matthias Diggelmann. Staged, Hans Gerd Kuebel; set, Jiri Kotlar; tech adv, Urs Ullmann; tech dir, Bruno Zaugg; light, Christian Scheifele, Hans Stamm; snd, Marget Nonhoff, Beat Hodel. Opened June 3, '76, at the Studio Tiefenbrunnen, Zurich; $3.85 admission.
Walo Luond, Anne-Marie Blanc, Alexander Pelz, Ingold Wildenauer, Christian Reiner, Paul Am Acher, Anne-Marie Dermon, Claudine Rajchman, Alfred Pfeifer, Ulrich Kuhlman, Oskar Hoby, Luzious Versell, Wernher Buck, Bettina Lindtberg.
06/16/76A

Dimetos
(London)
Oscar Lewenstein & Eddie Kulukundis presentation of a drama in two acts by Athol Fugard. Staged, Fugard; scenery-cos, Douglas Heap; light, Brian Thomas. Opened May 23, '76, at the Comedy Theatre, London; $6.30 top.
Celia Quicke, Paul Scofield, Yvonne Bryceland, Ben Kingsley.
06/09/76A

Don't Bother To Dress
(London)
Robin A Ellis, with Trip Prodns, presentation of a play in two acts by Neville Siggs. Staged, Victor Spinetti; asso dir, Anthony Collin. Opened Sept. 20, '77, at the Victoria Palace Theatre, London; $6 top.
Ingrid Pitt, Nick Tate, Tim Barrett, Eunice Gayson, Sabina Franklyn, Stewart Permutt.
09/28/77A

Don't Piddle Against The Wind, Mate
(Sydney)
National Institute of Dramatic Art presentation of a play in two acts by Kenneth G Ross. Staged, John Tasker; des, Bill Pritchard; light, Bryon Jones. Opened Aug. 3, '77, at the Jane Street Theatre, Sydney; $4 top.
John Clayton, Ron Graham, Noni Hazlehurst, John Paramor, Maggie Kirkpatrick, Michael Ferguson.
08/24/77A

Donkey's Years
(London)
Michael Codron presentation of a comedy in three acts by Michael Frayn. Staged, Michael Rudman; set, Alan Tagg; light, Ken Miller. Opened July 15, '76, at the Globe Theatre, London; $6.30 top.
A J Brown, Peter Barkworth, Peter Jeffrey, Andrew Robertson, Julian Curry, Harold Innocent, Jeffry Wickham, John Harding, Penelope Keith.
07/28/76A

Dorothy
(Dublin)
Dublin Theatre Festival presentation of a play in two acts (seven scenes), by J Graham Reid. Staged, Kevin McHugh; set, Robert Lane; light, Paul Mercier. Opened Oct 14, '80, at the Oscar Theatre, Dublin: $6 top.
Joan O'Hara, Godfrey Quigley, Ena May, Maurie Taylor, Derek Lord, Gerard McSorley, Denis Staunton.
12/03/80A

The Double Dealer
(London)
National Theatre revival of a play in two acts by William Congreve. Staged, Peter Wood; set-cos, Tanya Moiseiwitsch; light, David Hersey. Opened Sep 27, '78, at the Olivier Theatre, London; $8.50 top.
John Harding, Dermot Crowley, Nicky Henson, Ralph Richardson, Michael Bryant, Nicholas Selby, Sara Kestelman, Robert Stephens, Judi Bowker, Brenda Blethyn, Dorothy Tutin, Craig Moss, Janet Whiteside, Daniel Thorndike, Dennis Tynsley, Ray Edwards, Alexander Allenby, Elliott Cooper, Adam Norton, Keith Skinner.
Musicians: Ian Anderson, Andrew Findon, Kevin Healey, Andrew Reed, David Roach, Henry Ward.
10/04/78A

Dracula
(London)
Pip Simmons Theatre group presentation of a musical in two acts by Pip Simmons, adapt from book by Bram Stoker. Staged, Pip Simmons; mus, Chris Jordan; prodn mgr, Joan Oliver; cos, Laura Crowe; light, Dick Johnson. Opened Dec. 7, '76, at Royal Court Theatre, London; $3.50 top.
Peter Oliver, Rod Beddall, Sheila Burnett, Meirav Gary, Ben Bazell, Emil Wolk, Peter Jonfield, Roderic Leigh, Chris Jordan.
12/29/76A

Dracula
(London)
Michael White revival of a play in three acts (four scenes), by Hamilton Deane and John L Balderston, based on the novel by Bram Stoker. Staged, Dennis Rosa; scenery-cos, Edward Gorey; scenery supv, Lynn Peektal; cos supv, John David Ridge; light, Graham Large, based on orig light by Roger Morgan. Opened Sept 13, '78, at the Shaftesbury Theatre, London; $9.75 top.
Rosalind Ayres, Marilyn Galsworthy, Rupert Frazer, Barrie Cookson, Derek Godfrey, Nickolas Grace, Shaun Curry, Terence Stamp.
09/20/78A

The Dragon Variation
(London)
Paul Elliott & Bernard Jay presentation of a drama in two acts (three scenes) by Robert King. Staged, Marc Miller; set, Hutchinson Scott; cos, Brian Castle; light, Nick Chelton. Opened Oct 4, '77 at the Duke of York's Theatre, London; $6.15 top.
Nyree Dawn Porter, Roy Dotrice, Anthony Andrews.
10/26/77A

Drake's Dream
(London)
Sue and Martin Gates Presentation of a Worthing Connaught Theatre Prodn of a musical in two acts (23 numbers); book, Simon Brett; mus-lyr, Lynne, Richard Riley. Staged, Nicolas Young. Des, Angela Muhl; light, Terence Caughell; mus dir, Peter Martin; asso prod, Ian Liston; orig stage conception, Martin Gates. Opened Dec 7, '77 at the Shaftesbury Theatre, London; $7.25 top.
Paul Jones, Bill Pearson, Tricia Deighton, Donald Scott, Bill Bradley, Nicholas Denney, Stanley Fleet, Richard Tate, Earl Jordan, Janet Shaw, David Burt, Caro Gurney, Anne Sedgewick.
01/25/78A

The Dresser
(London)
Michael Codron presentation of a Royal Exchange Theatre Co production of a play in two acts by Ronald Harwood. Staged, Michael Elliott; set, Laurie Dennett; cos, Stephen Doncaster; light, Mark Henderson; snd, Ian Gibson. Opened Apr 30, '80, at the Queen's Theatre, London; $14.70 top.
Tom Courtenay, Jane Wenham, Jacqueline Tong, Janet Henfrey, Freddie Jones, Lockwood West, Geoffrey McGivern, Rex Arundel, David Browning, Peter O'Dwyer, Kenneth Oxtoby, Trevor Griffiths.
05/21/80A

Duet for One
(London)
Ray Cooney presentation, in ass'n with Ian B Albery and Herbert Jay, of a play in two acts (six scenes) by Tom Kempinski. Staged, Roger Smith; set, Caroline Beaver; light, Mick Hughes. Opened Sep 23, '80, at the Duke of York's Theatre, London; $15.60 top.
Frances de la Tour, David de Keyser.
10/15/80A

Dunant
(Zurich)
Schauspielhaus presentation of a drama in 14 scenes by Herbert Meier. Staged, Joerg Cossardt; set, Heinz Kriesi; cos, Renate Kalanke; tech dir, Bruno Zaugg; light, Kurt Janser, Christian Scheifele; snd, Robert Stalder. Opened March 5, '76, at the Studio Tiefenbrunnen, Zurich; $3.85 admission.
Gert Westphal, Angelica Arndts, Fred Tanner, Gerd Dorfer, Walo Luond, Erwin Kohlund, Joerg Cossardt, Klaus Knuth, Elmar Schulte, Renate Schroeter, Wernher Buck, Walter Morath, Gerhart Wilhelm, John Laxdal, Michael Schulmeyer, Alexander Pelz, Wolfgang Warncke, Hanna Burgwitz, Ingold Wildenauer, Edzard Wuestendoerfer, Jodoc Seidel, Sibylle Courvoisier.
03/31/76A

Dusa, Fish, Stas & Vi
(London)
Michael Codron presentation of a comedy-drama by Pam Gems; staged, Nancy Meckler. Scenery, Tanya McCallin; cos, Lindy Hemming; light, Gerry Jenkinson. Opened Feb. 10, '77, at the Mayfair Theatre, London, $6 top.
Brigit Forsyth, Alison Fiske, Diane Fletcher, Mary Maddox.
02/23/77A

Dylan Thomas Growing Up
(London)
A revival of a one-man show, based on the works of Dylan Thomas. Opened Mar 3, '80 at the Ambassadors, London: $11.25 top.
Emlyn Williams.
04/02/80A

Early Days
(London)
Duncan C Weldon & Louis I Michaels presentation of a National Theatre prodn of a drama in two acts by David Storey. Staged, Lindsay Anderson; scenery, Jocelyn Herbert; lighting, Joe Davis; mus, Alan Price. Opened Dec 11, '80 at the Comedy Theatre, London; $13.80 top.
Ralph Richardson, Edward Judd, Sheila Ballantine, Gerald Flood, Michael Bangerter, Marty Cruickshank, Peter Machin.
12/17/80A

Eclipse
(London)
English Stage Co presentation of a drama in two acts by Leigh Jackson. Staged, Stuart Burge; set, Nadine Baylis; light, Jack Raby. Opened Aug 2, '78, at the Royal Court Theatre, London; $5.80 top.
Paul Rogers, Leonard Fenton, James Cossins, Ann Bell, Peter Bowles.
08/16/78A

Edith Piaf, Je Vous Aime
(London)
Michael Cooper & Dan Crawford presentation of a musical in two acts. Devised-prod, Libby Morris. Staged, John Heawood; set, Barry Parman; cos, Yuki; light, Seymour Grey; English lyr, Fran Landesman, Ronnie Bridges, Peter Reeves; arrs, Chuck Mallet, Frank Stafford, Southern Music Publishing; mus dir, Mallet. Opened June 21, '77, at the Shaftesbury Theatre, London; $5.15 top.
Libby Morris, Peter Reeves, Maureen Scott, Clifton Todd.
07/13/77A

Ein Pestalozzi
(Zurich)
Schauspielhaus presentation of a drama in two parts by Heinz Stalder. Staging, Werner Dueggelin; setting-cos, Wolfgang Mai; tech dir, Ali Sadigh-Behsadi; light, Robert Egli; snd, Eugen Stieger. Opened Nov. 29, '79, at the Schauspielhaus, Zurich; $18.75 top.
Hubert Kronlachner, Annelore Sarbach, Lorli Fischer, Rene Scheibli, Renate Schroeter, Klaus Knuth, Bernd Rumpf, Anne-Marie Dermon, Jodoc Seidel, Rosel Schaefer.
12/26/79A

Ein Toedlicher Traum
(A Deadly Dream)
(Zurich)
Schauspielhaus presentation of a play in three parts by Fred Tanner, in collab with Ulrich Bodamer and Gilles Tschudi. Based on the novel, "Geschwister Tanner," and other prose by Robert Walser. Staged, Tanner; setting, Ambrosius Humm; cos, Gina Zeh, Manfred Fonfara, Othmar Zehnder; incidental mus, Mario Beretta; tech dir, Bruno Zaugg; light, Christoph Ausfeld; snd, Rico Maag. Opened May 2, '80, at the Keller im Schauspielhaus: $6.85 admission.
Gilles Tschudi, Markus Mislin, Jodoc Seidel, Ingrit Seibert, Susanne Bialucha, Sibylle Courvoisier, Wernher Buck, Peter Holliger, Edzard Wuestendoerfer, Dagma Loubier, Heinrich Trimbur, Edwin Maechler, Ines Wellauer, Susanne Naegeli.
06/25/80A

El Diluvio Que Viene
(After Me the Deluge)
(Madrid)
Ramon Riba and Antonio Riba presentation of musical comedy by Garinei and Giovannini. Wri, Iaia Fiastri; based on David Forrest musical. Mus, Armando Trovaioli; chor. Gino Landi; sets, Giulio Coletellacci; dir, Garinei and Giovannini; Spanish adapt, Ramon and Antonio Riba; mus arrs, Renato Serio, Angel Gatti; mus dir, Rafael Ibarbia; trans, Giorgi; cos, Hermanas Capistros, Pedro Riu; light. Giancarlo Bottone. Opened March 12, '77 at the Teatro Monumental, Madrid; $5 top.
Lorenzo Valverde, Maria Elias, Manolo Zarzo, Josefina Guell, Franz Joham, Lia Uya, Franco Ricchio. Plus Bluebell ballet and the Men's Ballet and Choir.
03/23/77A

El Gran Deschave
(The Great Outburst)
(Buenos Aires)
Carlos A Petit & Enrique J Muscio presentation of a play in two acts, by Armando Chulak and Sergio De Cecco. Staged, Carlos Gandolfo; scenery, cos-light, Carlos Cytrynowski; mus, Horacio Della Rocca. At the Regina Theatre, Buenos Aires; $1.50 top.
Federico Luppi, Haydee Padilla, Nora Cullen, Beto Gianola, Hector Bidonde, Mario Fortuna.
01/21/76A

El Gran Deschave
(The Great Unburdening)
(Madrid)
A Carlos A Petit prodn of a play in two acts by Sergio de Cecco, Armando Chulak. Staging-light-cos, Carlos Cytrynowski. Dir, Carlos Gandolfo. Opened Jan 19, '78 at Teatro Arniches (Madrid). Top $4.88.
Federico Luppi, Haydee Padilla, Nora Cullen, Roberto Pieri, Jose Maria Rivara, Jorge Murano.
02/15/78A

The Elephant Man
(London)
National Theatre Co presentation of a drama in two acts (21 scenes) by Bernard Pomerance. Staged, Roland Rees, scenery, Tanya McCallin; cos, Lindy Hemming; light, Gerry Jenkinson. Opened Jul 15, '80, at the Lyttelton Theatre, London: $14.15 top.
Peter McEnery, Peter Howell, Arthur Blake, David Schofield, Dallas Cavell, Karina Knight, Heather Tobias, Peter Bourke, Anthony Falkingham, Heather Tobias, Jennie Stoller, Audrey Noble, Karina Knight.
Others: - Dan Meaden, Iain Rattray, Penny Ryder, Charles Spicer, Charles Wegner.
07/30/80A

The Elocution of Benjamin Franklin
(Sydney)
Nimrod Theatre presentation of a two-act comedy drama by Steve J Spears. Staged, Richard Wherrett; scenery, Larry Eastwood; stage mgr, Maxine le Guier; ward, Charlotte Fairweather, Debbie Eastwood. Reviewed Sept. 5, '76, at the Nimrod Theatre Downstairs, Sydney, Australia; $5.50 top.
Gordon Chater.
10/27/76A

The Elocution of Benjamin Franklin
(London)
Dorothy Hammerstein - Frank Milton in ass'n with Backstage Prodns Ltd, presentation of Nimrod Theatre of Australia prodn of a solo play in two acts, by Steve J Spears. Staged, Richard Wherrett; scenery, Larry Eastwood; light, Joe Davis. Opened Feb 7, '78, at the Mayfair Theatre, London; $4.90 top.
Gordon Chater.
03/15/78A

Elvis
(London)
A Ray Cooney presentation of a multimedia musical in two parts devised by Jack Good and Ray Cooney. Staged, Good; des, Patrick Robertson; light, David Hersey; cos, Rosemary Vercoe; mus supv, Harry Robinson; mus dir, Keith Strachan; asst dir, Annabel Leventon; chor, Carole Todd; snd, Autograph. Opened Nov. 28, '77, at the Astoria Theatre, London; $10 top.
James Proby, Shakin' Stevens, Timothy Whitnall, Helen Baker, Tanith Banbury, Anna Macleod, Yael O'Dwyer, Richard Ashley, Paul Felber, Stephen Leigh, Richard Piper, Shaun Simon.
12/21/77A

Emigres
(London)
National Theatre Co. presentation of a drama in two acts by Slawomir Mrozek; trans, Maciej and Teresa Wrona, Robert Holman. Staged, Kevin Billington; set, John Halle; light, Stephen Wentworth. Opened July 5, '76, at the Young Vic Theatre, London; $2.25 top.
Brian Cox, Jim Norton.
07/14/76A

The Emperor of Ice-Cream
(Dublin)
Abbey Theatre presentation of two-act play by Bill Morrison, based on a novel by Brian Moore. Staged, Tomas MacAnna; set, Wendy Shea; light, Leslie Scott; cos, Maebh Browne. Opened April 28, '77, at the Abbey Theatre, Dublin; $5 top.
Stephen Brennan, Bryan Murray, Desmond Perry, Maire Ni Dhomhnaill, May Cluskey, Peadar Lamb, Geoffrey Golden, Bob Carlile, Patrick Laffan, Clive Geraghty, Michael O hAonghusa, Niall O'Brien, Fedelma Cullen, Maire Ni Ghrianne, Kathleen Barrington, Micheal O'Briain, Larry Murphy, Fionna MacAnna, Brid Ni Neachtain, Angela Lynch, Noel McGee, Andrina Wafer.
05/25/77A

The End of Venice: SEE Das Ende von Venedig

Endgame
(London)
English Stage Co. revival of a play in one act by Samuel Beckett. Staged, Donald McWhinnie; set, Andrew Sanders; light, Jack Raby. Opened May 6, '76, at the Royal Court Theatre, London; $6 top.
Patrick Magee, Stephen Rea, Leslie Sarony, Rose Hill.
05/26/76A

Enjoy
(London)
Michael Codron presentation of a play in two acts by Alan Bennett. Staged, Ronald Eyre; set, Douglas Heap; light, Nick Chelton; cos, Deirdre Clancy. Opened Oct 15, '80, at the Vaudeville Theatre, London: $16.80 top.
Colin Blakely, Joan Plowright, Philip Sayer, Susan Littler, Roger Alborough, Julian Ronnie, Stephen Flynn, Liz Smith, Graham Wyles, Michael Hughes, Marc Sinden, Simon Painter, Gareth Price.
10/22/80A

Errol Flynn's Great Big Adventure Book for Boys
(Sydney)
King O'Malley Theatre Co presentation of a comedy with mus in two acts by Rob George; mus, Mervyn Drake; staged, Lex Marinos; chor, Nancye Hayes; des, Patrick Cook, Jenny Coopes; swordfights, Tex Clark; light, Russell Boyd. Opened Sep 4, '80, at the Stables Theatre, Sydney: $6 top.
Sean Scully, Ros Speirs, Mervyn Drake, Belinda Giblin, Anne Grigg, John Hannan, Robert Hughes.
10/15/80A

Every Good Boy Deserves Favor
06/21/78A
(London)
Mermaid Theatre presentation of an opus for symphony orchestra and six actors by Tom Stoppard, with mus by Andre Previn. Staged, Trevor Nunn; settings, Ralph Koltai; mus dir, Michael Lankester. Opened June 14, '78, at the Mermaid Theatre, London; $7.35 top.
John Woodvine, Ian McDiarmid, Sam Monck, Rowena Cooper, Frank Windsor, John Carlisle.

Everyman
(Sydney)
Nimrod Theatre Co presentation of a play by Rudi Krausmann. Staged, John Bell; light, Margie Wright; mus, Nicholas Enright, Jennifer McGregor. Preceded by "Marxisma" and "Stubble," mus sketches, Moya Henderson. Opened Feb. 11, '78, at the Nimrod Theatre, Sydney; $6 top.
Nicholas Enright, Jennifer McGregor, John McTernan, Anna Volska,
04/19/78A

Evita
(London)
Robert Stigwood, in ass'n with David Land, presentation of musical in two acts (27 numbers); mus, Andrew Lloyd Webber; lyr, Tim Rice. Staged, Harold Prince; chor, Larry Fuller; settings, Timothy O'Brien and Tazeena Firth; light, David Hersey; orch, Hershy Kay; orig orch-vocal arr, Andrew Lloyd Webber; mus dir, Anthony Bowles; exec prod, Bob Swash. Opened June 21, '78 at the Prince Edward Theatre, London; $11.10 top.
David Essex, Elaine Paige, Joss Ackland, Siobhan McCarthy, Mark Ryan.
Singers-- Joshua Bancel, Derek Beard, Michele Breeze, Chris Brooke, Jo Cameron Brown, Jimmy Cassidy, Derek Damon, Jeni Evans, Colin Fay, Susannah Fellows, Stanley Fleet, Stewart Mackintosh, Robin Merrill, Nigel Planer, Claire Rimmer, Ken Robson, Myra Sands, Wendy Schoemann, Janet Shaw, David Taegar, Christina Thornton, Edwin van Wyk.
Dancers-- Peppi Borza, Christine Cartwright, Andrea Chance, Teresa Codling, Margaret Ede, Anthony Edge, Susan Hayes, Gerard Jouanneau, Julie Kirk, Connel Miles, Phillip Needs, David Shelmerdine, Nancy Wood, John Yost.
Musical numbers: "A Cinema in Buenos Aires," "Requiem," "Oh What a Circus," "On

Evita
(Cont)
This Night of a Thousand Stars," "Eva Beware of the City," "Buenos Aires," "Goodnight and Thank You," "The Art of the Possible," "Charity Concert," "I'd Be Surprisingly Good for You," "Another Suitcase in Another Hall," "Peron's Latest Flame," "A New Argentine," "On the Balcony of the Casa Rosada," "Don't Cry For Me Argentina," "High Flying Adored," "Rainbow High," "Rainbow Tour," "The Actress Hasn't Learned," "And the Money Kept Rolling In," "Santa Evita," "Waltz for Eva and Che," "She is a Diamond," "Dice Are Rolling," "Eva's Final Broadcast," "Montage," "Lament."
06/28/78A

Fair Slaughter
(London)
English Stage Co. presentation of a drama in two acts, by Howard Barker. Staged, Stuart Burge; set, Patrick Robertson, Rosemary Vercoe; light, Jack Raby. Opened June 13, '77, at the Royal Court Theatre, London $5.15 top.
Max Wall, John Thaw, Nick Edmett, Tony Mathews, David Jackson, Judith Liebert, Robert Gary, Jan Chappell, Tony Halfpenny, Robin Meredith.
06/22/77A

The Fall Guy
(Melbourne)
Melbourne Theatre Co. presentation of a play in two acts by Linda Aronson. Staged-des, Mick Rodger; chor, Jon Finlayson. Opened March 31, '77, at the Russell Street Theatre, Melbourne; A$6 top.
Norman Kaye, Terence Donovan, Mervyn Drake, Stephen Oldfield.
04/27/77A

The Family Dance
(London)
H.M. Tennent Ltd. presentation of a drama in two acts by Felicity Browne. Staged, Jonathan Hales. Set, Eileen Diss; light, Leonard Tucker; cos, Robin Fraser-Paye. Opened June 5, '76, at the Criterion Theatre, London; $6.40 top.
Alec McCowen, Michael Bryant, Helen Lindsay, Annette Crosbie, Judy Parfitt, James Warwick, Anthony Nash.
06/23/76A

The Family Reunion
(London)
Peter Saunders, in ass'n with the Royal Exchange Theatre Co., revival of a verse drama in two acts by T S Eliot. Staged, Michael Elliott; sets, Laurie Dennett; cos, Clare Jeffery; light, Michael Williams, Mark Henderson; snd, Ian Gibson. Opened June 19, '79 at the Vaudeville Theatre, London; $11.70 top.
Pauline Jameson, Daphne Oxenford, Constance Chapman, Avril Elgar, Jeffry Wickham, William Fox, Joanna David, Edward Fox, Harry Walker, Esmond Knight, Hilda Schroder.
06/27/79A

Filumena
(London)
Danny O'Donovan, Alan Cluer & Helen Montagu, in ass'n with Mecca Prodns, presentation of a comedy in three acts by Eduardo de Fillippo; adapt, Keith Waterhouse, Willis Hall. Staged, Franco Zeffirelli; set, Raimonda Gaetani; light, Joe Davis. Opened Nov. 2, '77, at the Lyric Theatre, London; $8.10 top.
Joan Plowright, Colin Blakely, Larry Noble, Patricia Hayes, Sharon Mughan, Jane Gurnett, Christopher Guard, Trevor Eve, Larry Lamb, David Graham, Linda Polan, Trevor Griffiths, Edward Duke.
11/16/77A

Find the Lady
(Dublin)
Peacock Workshop Prodn of drama in two acts by Tom McIntyre. Staged, Patrick Mason; set, Frank Conway; light, Tony Wakefield; mus, Jolyon Jackson, Garvan Gallagher, Greg Boland. Opened May 9, '77 at the Peacock Theatre, Dublin; $1.50 top.
Philip O'Sullivan, Raymond Hardie, Desmond Cave, Martina Stanley, Billie Morton, Ingrid Craigie, Macdara O Fatharta, Se Phelan, Ronan Paterson.
06/01/77A

Fire Angel
(London)
Ray Cooney presentation of a musical in two acts (18 numbers); book-lyr, Paul Bentley; mus, Roger Haines, based on Shakespeare's "The Merchant of Venice." Staged, Braham Murray; chor, Arlene Phillips; scenery-cos, Johanna Bryant; light, Robert Bryan; snd, Ian Gibson; orchs-mus supv, Anthony Bowles; mus dir, David Firman. Opened March 24, '77, at Her Majesty's Theatre, London; $8.60 top.
Gaye Brown, Belinda Nash, Libby Rose, Wanda Rokicki, Mark Tyme, Keith Hodiak, Anthony Wood, Julian Littman, Ludovico Romano, Richard Roman, Larrington Walker, Joshua Bancel, Terence Hillyer, Peter Karrie, David Wheldon-Williams, Colin Fay, Helen Baker, Jeni Evans, Myra Sands, Megg Nicol, Paulette Hegney, Pauline Crawford, Ian Burford, Stanley Fleet, Helen Chappelle, Linda Kendrick, C T Wilkinson, Derek Smith.
Musical numbers: "Don Piranha's Boys," "Daddy's Girl," "My Body's Weary," "African Ice," "Satan Baby," "Morning Psalm," "Moonlight Quartet," "Carnival," "Shining Moon," "Diarrhoea Dave," "Sun Man," "Ell Nekomoss," "Fire Angel," "Brother, Be Right," "Sun Man" (reprise), "Shining Moon" (reprise), "Getting Together," "The Mercy Song."
03/30/77A

The Fire That Consumes
(London)
Mermaid Theatre presentation of a play in three acts by Henry de Montherlant. English version, Vivian Cox, Bernard Miles. Staged, Miles; scenery-cos, Adrian Vaux; light, Peter Sutton; company stage mgr, Nigel Wilson. Opened Oct 13, '77 at the Mermaid Theatre, London; $6.20 top.
Nigel Hawthorne, Dai Bradley, Adam Bareham, David William, George Tarry, David Woodcock.
11/02/77A

Flexitime
(Sydney)
Clifford Hocking presentation, in ass'n with the Arts Councils of South Australia and Victoria, of a Peter Canavan prodn of a play in four acts by Roger Hall. Staged, Don Mackay; des, Sandra Matlock; light, Ian McGrath. Opened Jun 23, '80, at the Everest Theatre, Seymour Centre, Sydney: $11.90 top.
Michael Carman, Sydney Conabere, Hu Pryce, Anne Phelan, Chris Connelly, Terry McDermott, Denzil Howson.
07/16/80A

Flowers for Algernon
(London)
Michael White, in ass'n with Isobel Robins Konecky, presentation of a musical in 18 numbers, with no intermission, with mus by Charles Strouse, book and lyr by David Rogers, based on a Daniel Keyes novel of the same title. Staged, Peter Coe; settings, Lawrence Schafer; cos, Ingeborg; chor, Rhoda Levine; light, Spike Gaden; snd, Philip Clifford; mus arr, Philip J Lang; prodn supv, Andrew Treagus; mus dir, Alexander Faris; asso prod, Robert Fox. Opened June 14, '79, at the Queen's Theatre, London; $14.70 top.
Cheryl Kennedy, Audrey Woods, Ralph Nossek, Michael Crawford, Jason Ash, Jeanna L'Esty, Richard Owens, Betty Benfield, Sharon Lee Hill, George Harris, Amanda Holmes, Brian Honeyball, Betty Turner, Barry Wade.
Musical numbers - "His Name is Charlie Gordon," "I Got a Friend," "Some Bright Morning," "Our Boy Charlie," "Hey Look at Me," "Reading," "No Surprises," "Midnight Riding," "Dream Safe With Me," "I Can't Tell You," "Now," "Charlie and Algernon," "The Maze," "Whatever Time There Is," "Charlie," "Charlie and Algernon" (reprise)," "I Really Loved You," "Whatever Time There Is" (reprise).
06/20/79A

Flying Blind
(London)
English Stage Co, in ass'n with Bill Freedman & Eddie Kulukundis, presentation of a play in two acts by Bill Morrison. Staged, Alan Dossor; setting, John Gunter; light, Jack Raby. Opened June 20, '78 at the Royal Court Theatre, London; $5.60 top.
Peter Postlethwaite, Valerie Lilley, Patrick Drury, Simon Callow, Rachel Bell, Sharman MacDonald, Sid Livingstone, James Duggan, Walter McMonagle, Alan Devlin, Andrew Byatt, Christopher Whitehouse, Maggie Shevlin, Ewan Stewart.
06/28/78A

For Colored Girls Who Have Considered Suicide/When The Rainbow is Enuf
(London)
Woodie King Jr, in assoc with Dellgray Ltd presentation of a revue in two acts by Ntozake Shange. Staged, Avery Brookes; scenery, Ming Cho Lee; light, John Coffey; cos, Judy Dearing; chor, Paula Moss. Opened Oct. 10, '79, at the Royalty Theatre, London; $11.90 top.
Queene Cavette, Denise Marcia, Elizabeth Van Dyke, Linda Thomas Wright, Joyce Han-

For Colored
(Cont)
ley, Lynn Whitfield, Ruthanna Graves.
10/24/79A

For King and Country
(London)
Mermaid Theatre Trust presentation of a revival of a drama in three acts by John Wilson (based on an episode in the novel "Return To The Wood" by J L Hodson). Staged, Bernard Miles, Ron Pember; scenery, Adriane Vaux; light, Peter Sutton. Opened Sept. 24, '76, at the Mermaid Theatre, London; $4.60 top.
Paul Copley, Ron Pember, Anthony Smee, John Nolan, Seymour Matthews, Roy Purcell, Stephen Boswell, Rob Edwards, Jestyn Phillips, David Horovitch, Frank Moorey, Geoffrey Freshwater, Michael Cashman, David Purcell.
10/06/76A

For Services Rendered
(London)
National Theatre revival of a play in three acts by W Somerset Maugham. Staged, Michael Rudman; set-cos, Carl Toms; light, Gerry Jenkinson. Opened May 1, '79, at the Lyttelton Theatre, London; $10.90 top.
Jean Anderson, Pamela Sholto, Harold Innocent, Barbara Ferris, Phyllida Law, Elizabeth Romilly, Peter Jeffrey, Alison Fiske, John Quayle, Leslie Sands, Robin Bailey, Ian Hogg.
05/16/79A

The Force of Habit
(London)
National Theatre presentation of a comedy-drama in two acts by Thomas Bernhard (English trans, Neville and Stephen Plaice); staged, Elijah Moshinsky. Scenery, Timothy O'Brien, Tazeena Firth; light, David Hersey. Opened Nov. 9, '76, at the Lyttleton Theatre, London; $7.50 top.
Philip Locke, Gawn Grainger, Brenda Blethyn, Oliver Cotton, Warren Clarke.
11/24/76A

Foreskin's Lament
(Auckland)
Theatre Corporate presentation of a play by Greg McGee. Staged, Roger McGill; decor, John Verryt. Opened Oct. 30, '80 at the Theatre Corporate, Auckland, N.Z.; $5 top.
John Watson, Gregory Naughton, Philip Holder, Geoffrey Snell, Roy Billing, Grant McFarland, Christopher White, Judy Gibson, Alison Quigan.
12/31/80A

Forty Love
(London)
Paul Elliott presentation of a comedy in two acts (four scenes) by Leslie Randall. Staged, Val May; setting, Tony Hemmings; light, James Baird. Opened Feb. 21, '79, at the Comedy Theatre, London; $9 top.
Joyce Blair, Leslie Randall, Norman Rossington, Stella Tanner.
02/28/79A

Fraternity: SEE Bruderlichkeit

Frau von Kauenhofen
(Zurich)
Schauspielhaus presentation of a drama in four acts by Hartmut Lange. Staged, Lange setting-cos, Jan Schlubach; mus collab, Mario Beretta; tech dir, Rene Wartmann; light, Hans-Joerg Huber; snd, Alex Hildebrand. Opened April 12, '79 at the Schauspielhaus, Zurich; $17.60 top.
Marianne Hoppe, Charles Regnier, Rainer Goernemann, Brigitte Karner, Kurt Conradi.
05/23/79A

The French Have a Song For It
(London)
Nathan Joseph presentation of a revue in two parts, devised by Peter Reeves. Staged, Eleanor Fazan; set, Ted Tuersley; cos, Gilly Hebden; light, Robert Ornbo; mus arr, David Wykes; addl mus arr, Paul Reade; mus dir, Clive Chaplin. Opened May 2, '79, at the Piccadilly Theatre, London; $12.50 top.
Helen Shapiro, Amanda Barrie, Sonja Kristina, Stephen Tate, Peter Reeves.
05/16/79A

Friday the Thirteenth
(Sydney)
New Theatre presentation of a drama in two acts by Kevin Barry Morgan. Staged, John Armstrong; asst dir, Frank Branes; dsgnr, Marguerite Edwards; light, David McQuire; ward, Jill Sargeant. Opened June 24, '78, at the New Theatre, Sydney; $3.50 top.
Lorrie Cruikshank, Tony Parr, Bill Webb, Kevin Morgan, Hugh Watson, Marty O'Neill, Trevor Lobb, Stan Ashmore-Smith, Kevin Williams, John Birt, Wayne van Heekeren, Peter Talmacs.
07/12/78A

Fringe Benefits
(London)
Ray Cooney & Brian Rix, in ass'n with Duncan Weldon and Louis I. Michaels, presentation of a play in two acts (three scenes) by Peter Yeldham and Donald Churchill. Staged-light, Wallace Douglas. Opened Aug. 26, '76, at the Whitehall Theatre, London; $5.30 top.
Jane Downs, Brian Rix, Terence Alexander, Barbara Kinghorne, Sally Harrison, Jean Perkins, Richard Latham.
09/15/76A

The Fruits of Enlightenment
(London)
National Theatre revival of a play in two acts (four scenes) by Leo Tolstoy; adapted, Michael Frayn. Staged, Christopher Morahan; set-cos-light, John Bury. Opened Mar 14, '79, at the Olivier Theatre, London; $10.80 top.
Glyn Grain, Brenda Blethyn, John Harding, Robin Meredith, Daniel Thorndike, Brian Kent, Peter Copley, Peter Needham, Dennis Tynsley, Andrew Cruickshank, Michael Beint, Anthony Douse, Ralph Richardson, David Pugh, Selina Cadell, Irene Gorst, Greg Hicks, Joyce Redman, Tamara Hinchco, Donald Gee, Harry Lomax, Sara Kestelman, Kitty Fitzgerald, John Atkinson, Nicholas Selby, Stanley Lloyd, Martyn Whitby, Peggy Marshalll, Jane Evers, Marianne Morley.
03/28/79A

Funny Peculiar
(London)
Mermaid Theatre Trust, in ass'n with Michael Codron, presentation of a comedy in two acts by Mike Stott. Staged, Alan Dossor; set, Patrick Robertson; cos, Rosemary Vercoe; light, Peter Sutton. Opened Jan. 22, '76, at the Mermaid Theatre, London; $5.05 top.
Julie Walters, Nicholas Woodeson, Richard Beckinsale, Nick Stringer, Matthew Kelly, Eileen O'Brien, Suzan Cameron, David Casey, Peter Postlethwaite, Nicholas Woodeson.
02/04/76A

Further Prospects: SEE Journey Into Happiness & Further Prospects

Gaslight
(London)
Danny O'Donovan & Alan Cluer revival of a drama in two acts (three scenes) by Patrick Hamilton. Staged, Robert Young; set, Saul Radomsky; light, Joe Davis, Robert Bryan. Opened March 24, '76, at the Criterion Theatre, London; $7 top.
Anton Rodgers, Nicola Pagett, Carolyn Moody, Louise Hall-Taylor, Peter Vaughan, Stephen Lester, Trevor Griffiths.
04/07/76A

George and Mildred
(Sydney)
Stephan Bell & Mark Furness presentation of a farce in two acts by Johnnie Mortimer and Brian Cooke. Staged, Tony Clayton; des, Terry Parsons. Opened Aug 14, '79, Theatre Royal, Sydney, $10.50 top.
Yootha Joyce, Brian Murphy, Wendy Blacklock, Ron Hackett, Carol Adams, Liza Marshall.
08/29/79A

Gershwin
(Melbourne)
Total Theatre Pty. Ltd. presentation of "Gershwin", a musical entertainment written and conceived by John Diedrich and John O'May. Mus, George Gershwin; lyr, Ira Gershwin, B G De Sylva, Irving Caesar. artistic dir-chor, Tony Bart; mus dir, Michael Tyack; staging, Trina Parker; light, Jamie Lewis. Opened Total Theatre, Melbourne, Feb. 21, '76. $7 top.
John Diedrich, Caroline Gillmer, Natalie Mosco, John O'May.
03/03/76A

Getting Away With Murder
(London)
Knightsbridge Theatrical Prodns Ltd. presentation of a Peter Witt Prodn of a drama in two acts by J Lee Thompson. Staged, Robert Chetwyn. Set, Hutchinson Scott; light, David Hersey. Opened at Comedy Theatre, London, July 21, '76, $6.25 top.
Ernest Clark, Anthony Bate, Barry Foster, Hildegard Neil, Robert Ralph.
07/28/76A

The Ghost Train
(London)
James Verner, in ass'n with Hermes Prodns Ltd., presentation of a revival of a melodrama

The Ghost
(Cont)
in three acts by Arnold Ridley. Staged, Bill Hays; set, Michael Annals; light, Leonard Tucker. Opened Nov. 18, '76, at the Old Vic Theatre, London; $5.90 top.
Wilfrid Brambell, James Villiers, Veronica Strong, Martin Turley, Judy Buxton, Gwen Nelson, Geoffrey Davies, Louise Purnell, Patrick Newell, Allan Cuthbertson, Carl Davies, Chris Morton.
12/01/76A

The Giant Lobelia
(Dublin)
Dublin Theatre Festival in ass'n with Gemini Prodns presentation of two-act drama by Harry Barton. Staged, Barry Cassin: set, Alan Pleass. Opened Oct. 5, '76, at the Eblana Theatre, Dublin; $3 top.
Angela Vale, Brian de Salvo, Veronica Duffy, Beryl Fagan, Aiden Grennell, Jonathan White, Michael Grennell.
10/20/76A

Gimme Shelter
(London)
The Network presentation of a Soho Poly prodn of three short plays by Barrie Keeffe. Staged, Keith Washington; decor, Mary Moore; light, Nick Chelton. Opened March 23, '77, at the Royal Court Theatre, London; $5.16 top.
Phillip Joseph, Ian Sharp, Sharman MacDonald, Roger Leach, Philip Davis, Peter Hughes.
04/20/77A

The Gin Game
(London)
Shubert Organization Ltd presentation in ass'n with Hume Cronyn & Mike Nichols of a play in two acts (four scenes) by D L Coburn. Staged, Mike Nichols; set, David Mitchell; cos, Bill Walker; light, Ronald Wallace. Opened Jul 31, '79, at the Lyric Theatre, London; $14 top.
Jessica Tandy, Hume Cronyn.
08/08/79A

The Glad Hand
(London)
English Stage Co presentation of a play in two acts by Snoo Wilson. Staged, Max Stafford-Clark; settings, Peter Hartwell; light, Jack Raby; snd, John Del'Nero. Opened May 11, '78, at the Royal Court Theatre, London; $5.50 top.
Olivier Pierre, Rachel Bell, Nick LePrevost, Will Knightley, Anthony Sher, Tony Rohr, Alan Devlin, Gwyneth Strong, Manning Redwood, Julian Hough, Julie Walters, Di Patrick, Thomas Baptiste.
05/24/78A

The Glass Menagerie
(London)
Revival of Tennessee Williams play; staged, Peter James; set, Poppy Mitchell; light, Tim Thornalley. Opened Nov. '79, the Roundhouse Theatre, London.
Gloria Grahame, Veronica Roberts, Malcolm Ingram, Clive Arrindell.
12/05/79A

Gloo Joo
(London)
Eddie Kulukundis & Oscar Lewenstein presentation of a Hampstead Theatre prodn of a play in two acts by Michael Hastings. Staged, Michael Rudman; setting, Poppy Mitchell; cos, Lindy Hemming; light, Gerry Jenkinson. Opened Nov. 10, '78, at the Criterion Theatre, London; $8.85 top.
Oscar James, Heather Tobias, Antony Brown, Dave Hill, Edward Halsted, Akosua Busia.
11/29/78A

Going Home
(Melbourne)
Melbourne Theatre Co. presentation of comedy-drama in three acts by Alma De Groen. Staged, John Sumner; set, William Passmore. Opened March 11, '76, at the Russell Street Theatre, Melbourne; $7.50 top.
Max Cullen, Berys Marsh, Gerard Maguire, Carole Skinner, Simon Chilvers.
03/24/76A

The Golden Oldies
(Melbourne)
Hoopla Prodns presentation by arrangement with Melbourne Theatre Company of a play in two acts by Dorothy Hewett. Staged, Graeme Blundell; des, Peter Corrigan; light, John Beckett. Opened Jan. 19, '77 at Grant Street Theatre, Melbourne; $4.50 top.
Maggie Millar, Marion Edward.
02/09/77A

The Golden Oldies
(Sydney)
Goethe Institute Sydney & Australian Theatre Studies Program presentation of a Greenroom Co prodn, in assoc with the Australian Elizabethan Theatre Trust, of a drama in two acts by Dorothy Hewett. Staged, John Tasker; des, Tom Bannerman; light-snd, G A C Lawson. Opened Sept. 12, '79, at the Jane Street Theatre, Sydney; $6 top.
Michele Fawdon, Carole Skinner.
09/26/79A

Golden Pathway Through Europe
(Sydney)
Ensemble Theatre Co presentation of a play in two acts by Rod Milgate. Staged, Brian Young; dsgn, Yoshi Tosa; light, Mel Conder. Opened Oct 27, '80, at the Ensemble Theatre, Sydney: $7.50 top.
Alex Pinder, Roger Carroll, Judy Ferris, Kati Edwards, Harold Jones, Frank Haines, Jenny Ludlam.
12/03/80A

Gone With Hardy
(Sydney)
Nimrod Street Theatre Co presentation of a play in two acts, by David Allen. Staged, Richard Wherrett; scenery-cos, Anthony Babicci; light, Margie Wright; chor, Keith Bain; mus dir, Terence Clarke. Opened Dec 2, '78, at the Nimrod Theatre Downstairs, Sydney; $7.50 top.
Drew Forsythe, Kerry Walker, Henri Szeps, Terence Clarke.
12/27/78A

The Good Woman Of Setzuan
(London)
English Stage Company, Duncan C Weldon and Louis I Michaels for Triumph Theatre Productions Ltd revival of a play in two acts by Bertolt Brecht. Staged, Keith Hack; des, Sally Gardner; light, Phil Rowe; snd, John Del-Nero; graphics, Pip Paton-Walker; mus, Stephen Oliver; asst dir, Jonathan Holloway; prodn mgr, John Leonard. Opened Oct 10, '77 at the Royal Court Theatre in London; $5.25 top.
Janet Suzman, Richard Ireson, Jonathan Kent, Mary Sheen, Gillian Martell, Frank Vincent, Philip McGough, Constantin de Goguel, Fred Pearson, Renee Goddard, Karen Pidgeon, Perry Benson, Mark Burdis, Stephen Oliver, Perry Mason, John Head.
10/26/77A

The Gorky Brigade
(London)
English Stage Co presentation of a play in two acts by Nicholas Wright. Staged, William Gaskill; settings, Eamon D'Arcy; cos, Pippy Bradshaw; light, Andy Phillips. Opened at the Royal Court Theatre, London; $8.95.
Jane Wood, Richard Mayes, Philip Davis, Daniel Peacock, June Page, Peter-Hugo Daly, Elizabeth Estensen, Jonathan Moore, Gary Olsen, Paul Curran, Stuart Wilde.
09/19/79A

The Government Inspector
(London)
Old Vic Co revival of a play in two acts by Nicolai Gogol, English version by Edward O Marsh and Christopher Selbie. Staged, Toby Robertson; settings, Robin Archer; light, Mick Hughes, Bill Wardroper; mus, Donald Fraser. Opened Sept. 3, '79, at the Old Vic Theatre, London; $9.50 top.
Hugh Sullivan, Trevor Martin, Ralph Michael, Robert Putt, Ray Callaghan, Michael Gardiner, Colin Bruce, Ronnie Stevens, Steven Beard, Ian Richardson, John Cording, Barbara Jefford, Nini Pitt, Sheila Mitchell, Maroussia Frank, Pamela Manson, Mark Buffery, Rob Middleton, Michael Thomas, Richard Harradine, Keith Bartlett, Roger Blake, Paul Toothill, Art Malik.
09/26/79A

The Great Outburst: SEE El Gran Deschave

The Great Unburdening: SEE El Gran Deschave

The Greeks
(London)
Royal Shakespeare Co presentation of a trilogy adapted by John Barton and Kenneth Cavander, mainly from Euripides, with additional material from Homer. Aeschylus and Sophocles. Staged, Barton; scenery, John Napier; light, David Hersey; mus, Nick Bicat; movement, Sheila Falconer. Opened Feb 2, '80, at the Aldwych Theatre, London: $14.15 top.
John Shrapnel, Oliver Ford Davies, Tony Church, Edwin Richfield, Judy Buxton, Janet Suzman, Mike Gwilym, Peter Woodward,

The Greeks
(Cont)
Peter Holmes, Stuart Organ, Annie Lambert, Susan Drury, Jenny Lipman, Diana Berriman, Avril Carson, Jocelyn Cunningham, Lynn Dearth, Susannah Fellows, Celia Gregory, Judith Harte, Darlene Johnson, Deirdra Morris, Eliza Ward, Billie Whitelaw, Rupert Baderman, Hugo Simpson, Cassian Castle, Edward George.
02/20/80A

Gross Und Klein
(Big and Little)
(Berlin)
Schaubuehne am Halleschen Ufer presentation of a play in two acts (10 scenes) by Botho Strauss. Staged, Peter Stein; settings, Karl Ernst Herrman; cos, Moidele Bickel. Opened Dec. 6, '78, at the CCC Film Studio, Spandau, West Berlin; $10 top.
Edith Clever, Willem Menne, Elke Petri, Hildegard Wensch, Johanna Hofer, Gerhard Bienert, Udo Samel, Gunter Berger, Jutta Lampe, Meray Uelgen, Tina Engel, Hans Madin.
01/24/79A

The Guardsman
(London)
National Theatre revival of a comedy in three acts by Ferenc Molnar, English version by Frank Marcus. Staged, Peter Wood; sets, Ralph Koltai; cos, David Walker; light, David Hersey. Opened Jan 3, '77, at the Lyttleton Theatre, London; $9 top.
Richard Johnson, Diana Rigg, Philip Stone, Madoline Thomas, Brenda Blethyn, David Schofield, Diana Payan, Anne Leon, Tom Durham, Peter Jolley, Robert Ralph, Andrew Tourell.
03/01/78A

Half-Life
(London)
National Theatre Co presentation of a drama in three acts by Julian Mitchell. Staged, Waris Hussein; sets, Jane Martin; light, Stephen Wentworth; cos, Judy Moorcroft. Opened March 2, '78, at the Duke of York's Theatre, London; $8.15 top.
Lockwood West, John Gielgud, Richard Pearson, Avril Elgar, Malcolm Ingram, Hugh Padidck, Isabel Dean, Diane Fletcher.
03/29/78A

The Half-Promised Land
(Dublin)
Dublin Theatre Festival presentation of two-act drama, by Maeve Binchy. Staged, Patrick Laffan; setting, Bronwen Casson; light, Leslie Scott. Opened Oct. 11, '79, at Peacock Theatre, Dublin; $4 top.
Fiona MacAnna, Maire Ni Ghrainne, Maire Hastings, Desmond Cave, Kathleen Barrington, Emmet Bergin, Bernadette McKenna, Bill Foley, Barry McGovern.
10/31/79A

Hamlet
(London)
English Stage Co revival of Shakespeare's play. Staged, Richard Eyre; scenery, William Dudley. Opened Apr 2, '80, at the Royal Court, London.
Jonathan Pryce, Michael Elphick, Jill Bennett, Harriet Walter, Geoffrey Chater.
04/23/80A

Hancock's Last Half Hour
(Sydney)
Nimrod Street Theatre Co presentation of Hoopla Foundation prodn of solo play in one act, by Heathcote Williams. Staged, Graeme Blundell; decor, Peter Corrigan. Opened Feb. 10, '79, at the Nimrod Downstairs Theatre, Sydney; $4 top.
Bruce Miles.
03/14/79A

Handle With Care
(Ghent)
Jacques Veys presentation of a musical in two acts (13 numbers); book, Andre Ernotte, Elliot Tiber; mus, Claude Lombard; Flemish lyr, Ernst van Altena. Staged, Ernotte; chor, Lily De Munter; scenery-cos, Jacques Berwouts; light, Jaak Van de Velde. Opened Sep 14, '77 at the Arena Theatre, Ghent, Belgium.
Linda Lepomme, Maryn Devalck, Tony Boast, Jean-Pierre Claeys, Etienne Delaruye, Jacky Eddy, Marc Van Herzeele, Clement Van Hove, Erna Palsterman, Jakob Beks, Wim Huys.
10/19/77A

Hans Andersen
(London)
Harold Fielding presentation of a musical in two parts; book, Beverly Cross; based on motion picture "Hans Christian Andersen," produced by Samuel Goldwyn with mus-lyr, Frank Loesser. Staged, Tommy Steele; mus dir, Michael Reed; choral dir, John McCarthy; light, Eric Delzenne, Molly Friedel; scenic-cos des, Tim Goodchild; chor, Irving Davies. Opened Dec. 19, '77, at the Palladium, London; $8.25 top.
Tommy Steele, Bob Todd, Lila Kaye, Anthony Valentine, John Baskcomb, Geoffrey Toone, Sally Ann Howes, Patricia Hall, Valeria Bader, Simon Adams or Stephen James Dean, David Vickers, Goeffrey Saunders, Wallace Stephenson, Sandra Snook, Graham Tudor Phillips, Hugh Spight, Michele Anne Hunt.
12/28/77A

Happy Birthday
(London)
John Gale presentation of a comedy in two acts by Marc Camoletti, English adaptation, Beverley Cross. Staged, Roger Redfarn; setting, Peter Rise; light, Joe Davis. Opened April 18, '79, at the Apollo Theatre, London; $11.45 top.
Elizabeth Counsell, Ian Lavender, Christopher Timothy, Julia Foster, Malou Cartwright.
05/02/79A

Happy Days
(London)
Royal Court Theatre revival of a play in two acts by Samuel Beckett. Staged, Beckett; scenery, Jocelyn Herbert; light, Jack Raby; snd, John Del'Nero. Opened June 7, '79, at the Royal Court Theatre, London; $7 top.
Billie Whitelaw, Leonard Fenton.
06/20/79A

Harry Lauder
(Glasgow)
Citizens Theatre presentation of a solo show by Jack House. Staged, Kenny McBain; decor, John Byrne; mus dir, Peggy O'Keefe; mus arrs, Ian Gourlay; light, Keith Russell; chor, Judy Gridley; cos, Heather Gorman. Opened May 11, '76, at the Citizens Theatre, Glasgow.
Peter Kelly.
06/09/76A

Haus Vaterland
(Berlin)
Schiller Theatre, Werkstatt, Berlin, presentation of a cabaret revue in one act, based on cabaret shows in Haus Vaterland around 1930, gathered together by Dieter Hildebrandt. Staged, Stefan Wigger; set, Bert Kistner; cos, Gaby Frey; mus arrs-dir, Wolfgang de Gelmini. Opened Jan. 10, '76 at Schiller Theatre Werkstatt, $6 tops.
Karin Remsing, Edith Robbers, Gisela Schneeberger, Egon Blader, Till Hoffmann, Holger Madin, Heinz Rabe, Stefan Wigger.
03/09/77A

Hedda Gabler
(London)
Duncan C Weldon & Louis I Michaels revival of a drama in four acts by Henrik Ibsen, adapt, David Essinger from trans by Vicky Carlstrand. Staged, Keith Hack; set, Maria Bjornson; light, Vic Lockwood. Opened June 15, '77, at the Duke of York's Theatre, London; $6.05 top.
Renee Goddard, Gwen Nelson, John Shrapnel, Janet Suzman, Ian Bannen, Rosemary McHale, Jonathan Kent.
06/22/77A

Heinrich Heine Revue
(Duesseldorf)
Kammerspiele Duesseldorf presentation of a theatrical revue by Claus Bremer and Rolf Becker, based on Heinrich Heine's "Dichter unbekann." Prod, Peter Thomas; staged, Guenther Buech; mus, Peter Janssens; chor, Marlis Gruenberg; sets, Lioba Winterhalder; mus dir, Peter Frass-Wolfsburg; light, Manfred Boelke; snd, Georg Gerhards; cos, Erika Huelsmann; assts, Hans Hoffmann, Werner Raeune. Opened Dec. 13, '77, at the Kammerspiele, Duesseldorf; $10 top.
Katrin Schoenermark, Dagmar Soerensen, Ilona Wiedem, Georg Cadalbert, Klaus Jaegel, Manfred Repp, Michael Thiele.
03/29/78A

Hello, Dolly
(London)
Ray Cooney, in ass'n with Paul Elliott, revival of a musical in two acts (14 numbers), with book by Michael Stewart and score and lyr by Jerry Herman, based on Thornton Wilder's comedy "The Matchmaker". Staged, Lucia Victor; chor, Ron Crofoot (based on the orig prodn dir-chor by Gower Champion); settings-cos, Oliver Smith; light, Joe Davis; mus dir, Clive Chaplin; snd, Hardware House Ltd; prodn supv, Jerry Herman. Opened at the Drury Lane Theatre, London; $17.30 top.
Carol Channing, Eddie Bracken, Tudor Davies, Maureen Scott, Mandy More, Richard Drabble, Veronica Clifford, Angela Curran,

Hello, Dolly
(Cont)
Mike Fields, Ian Burford, Lucille Gaye, David Wheldon Williams.

Dancers- Jo Scott Baker, Carol Ball, Emma Bryant, Janet Date, Mandy Mason, Gail Rolfe, Marc Arnall, Roy Ashby, Adrian Barnes, Frankie Cull, Derek Knight, Peter Loury, Paul Madden, Clive Packham, Grahame Turner, Roland A Wollens.

Singers- Les Ames, Richard Mitchell, Christopher Molloy, David Wheldon Williams, Audrey Duggan, Marie Jackson, Debra Jansen, Dianne Margaret.

Mus numbers- "I Put My Hand In," "It Takes A Woman," "Put On Your Sunday Clothes," "Put On Your Sunday Clothes," (reprise), "Ribbons Down My Back," "Motherhood," "Dancing," "Before the Parade Passes By," "Elegance," "The Waiters' Gallop," "Hello, Dolly!" "It Only Takes a Moment," "So Long Dearie," "Hello, Dolly!" (reprise).
10/03/79A

High as a Kite
(Wellington, NZ)
Downstage Theatre presentation of a play by Robert Lord; staged, Alyson Baker; decor, Doug Simpson; light, Tony Forster. Opened Oct 20, '79 at the Hannah Playhouse, Wellington, NZ; $10 top dinner and show.
John Banas, Philippa Campbell, Janet Fisher, Stephen Tozer.
11/07/79A

Hinge & Bracket
(London)
Michael Codron presentation of a musical revue; wri-staged-perf, Patrick Fyffe, George Logan. Opened Oct 22, '80, at the Globe Theatre, London: $15.80 top.
George Logan, Patrick Fyffe.
11/05/80A

The Homecoming
(London)
Michael Codron revival of a drama in two acts by Harold Pinter. Staged, Kevin Billington; setting, Eileen Diss; light, Mick Hughes; cos, Lindy Hemmings. Opened May 1, '78, at the Garrick Theatre, London; $9.10 top.
Timothy West, Michael Kitchen, Charles Kay, Roger Lloyd Pack, Oliver Cotton, Gemma Jones.
05/10/78A

The Hothouse
(London)
Ian B Albery, in asso with the Hampstead Theatre, presentation of a play in two acts by Harold Pinter. Staged, Pinter; set, Eileen Diss; cos, Elizabeth Waller; light, Gerry Jenkinson; snd, Dominic Muldowney. Opened Jun 25, '80, at the Ambassadors Theatre, London: $14 top.
Derek Newark, James Grant, Roger Davidson, Angela Pleasence, Robert East, Michael Forrest, Edward De Souza.
07/02/80A

The House Of The Deaf Man
(Sydney)
Nimrod Street Theatre Ltd presentation of a drama in two acts by John Anthony King. Staged, John Bell; dsgn, Kim Carpenter; light, Keith Edmundsen. Opened Mar 12, '80, at the Nimrod Theatre Upstairs, Sydney: $8.50 top.
Brian McDermott, Kerry Walker, Vivienne Garrett, Paul Bertram, Deborah Kennedy, Joseph Furst, Brian Fitzsimmons.
04/02/80A

Housewife - Superstar
(London)
Michael White presentation of a one-man show. Staged, Ian Davidson; set, Brian Thomson; light, Rory Dempster. Opened March 16, '76, at the Apollo Theatre, London; $5.50 top.
Barry Humphries, assisted by Iris Mason.
04/07/76A

How Sleep The Brave
(Sydney)
Ensemble Productions presentation of a drama in two acts by Phillip Mann. Staged, Stanley Walsh; prod, Megan Fry; dsgn, Doug Anderson; light, Peter Critchley; snd, Rod Dyson. Opened Jan. 2, '78, at the Ensemble-at-the Stables, Sydney; $4 top.
Guy Malcolm, Don Carter, Frank Haines, Damien Corrigan, Ross Hohnen, Gary Daniels, George Leppard, Craig Lambert.
01/10/79A

Hunting
(Wellington, NZ)
Circa Theater presentation of a play by Joseph Musaphia. Staged, Musaphia; decor, Barbara Collinson-Smith; light, Ian McMinn. Opened April 18, '79, at Circa Theatre, Wellington, NZ; $4.50 top.
Arthur Ranford, Adele Chapman, Alice Fraser, Michael Haigh.
05/09/79A

I Do! I Do!
(London)
Veronica Flint-Shipman & Paul Elliott presentation of a musical comedy in two acts (16 numbers); book-lyr, Tom Jones; mus, Harvey Schmidt, based on the Jan de Hartog play. "The Fourposter." Staged, Lowell Purvis (orig staging, Gower Champion); scenery, Oliver Smith; cos, Bob Mackie; light, Nick Chelton; mus dir, Ian MacPherson; asso prod, Bernard Jay. Opened Jan. 21, '76, at the Phoenix Theatre, London.
Juliet Prowse, Rock Hudson.
Musical numbers: "All the Dearly Beloved," "Together Forever," "I Do! I Do!" "Good Night," "I Love My Wife," "Something Has Happened," "My Cup Runneth Over," "Love Isn't Everything," "Nobody's Perfect," "A Well Known Fact," "Flaming Agnes," "The Honeymoon is Over," "Where Are the Snows?" "When the Kids Get Married," "The Father of the Bride," "What Is a Woman?" "Someone Needs Me," "Roll Up the Ribbons," "This House."
02/04/76A

I Do Not Like Thee, Dr Fell
(Dublin)
Abbey Theatre presentation of a play in two acts by Bernard Farrell. Staged, Paul Brennan; setting, Frank Conway. Opened March 15, '79, at the Peacock Theatre, Dublin, $3 top.
Garrett Keogh, John Molloy, Billie Morton, Eileen Colgan, Tom Hickey, Liam Neeson, Kathleen Barrington.
04/25/79A

I Gotta Shoe
(London)
H M Tennent presentation of a D & J Arlon prodn of a musical in one act (nine numbers); book-lyr, Caryl Brahms, Ned Sherrin; mus, Peter Knight, John Cameron Ron Grainer; based on fairy tale, "Cinderella." Staged, Sherrin, David Toguri; mus staging, Toguri; des, Berkeley Sutcliffe; light, John Wood; mus dir, Fiachra Trench. Opened Dec. 15, '76, at the Criterion Theatre, London; $6.70 top.
Linda Lewis, Clarke Peters, Felix Rice, Eric Roberts, Elisabeth Welch.
Musical numbers: "Shine Shine Shoe," "Lord Didn't It Rain," "In Cabaret," "Look on Me with a Loving Eye," "Cindy-Ella," "Crumpet Voluntary," "The First Time," "Never Been a Night," "Gettin' Wed."
12/29/76A

I Love My Wife
(London)
Harold Fielding presentation by arrangement with Joseph Kipness, of a musical in two acts (13 numbers); book-lyr, Michael Stewart; mus, Cy Coleman, from Parisian comedy by Luis Rego. Staged, Gene Saks; mus staging, Onna White; scenery, David Mitchell; light, Eric Delzenne; snd, Edward Fardell. Opened Oct. 6, '77, at the Prince of Wales Theatre, London; $7.95 top.
Deborah Fallender, Liz Robertson, Ben Cross, Adrian Brown, Bob Emmines, Simon Woolf, David Brown, Richard Beckinsale.
Musical numbers: "We're Still Friends," "Monica," "By Threes," "A Mover's Life," "Love Revolution," "Someone Wonderful I Missed," "Sexually Free," "Hey There, Good Times," "Lovers on Christmas Eve," "Scream," "Everybody Today Is Turning On," "Married Couple Seeks Married Couple," "I Love My Wife."
10/19/77A

I Love, You Love
(Sydney)
Studio Australia Productions presentation of a trilogy of one-acters by Leila Blake. Staged, Blake; decor, Ron Ferrier; light-snd, Peter Critchley. Opened at the Ensemble-at-the-Stables, Sydney, Jan. 31, '79; $4.50 top.
Leila Blake, Colin Taylor.
02/21/79A

The Iceman Cometh
(London)
Royal Shakespeare Co. revival of a drama in four acts (played with two intermissions) by Eugene O'Neill. Staged, Howard Davies; set, Chris Dyer; light, David Hersey. Opened May 25, '76, at the Aldwych Theatre, London; $5.90 top.

The Iceman
(Cont)
Norman Rodway, Harry Towb, Raymond Marlowe, Bob Hoskins, David Daker, Hal Galili, Richard Simpson, John Warner, Cy Grant, Patrick Stewart, Patrick Godfrey, Gary Bond, Kenneth Cranham, Patti Love, Paola Dionisotti, Lynda Marchal, Alan Tilvern, Larry Hoodekoff, Karl Held.
07/07/76A

If You're Good Looking, You're A Dope: SEE Si T'es Beau, T'es Con

The Ik
(London)
Royal Shakespeare Co. presentation of the International Centre of Theatre Research prodn of a documentary-drama in one act by Denis Cannan and Colin Higgins, based on book, "The Mountain People," by Colin Turnbull. Staged, Peter Brook; decor, George Wakhevitch, Jeanne Wakhevitch; tech adv, Joseph Towles. Opened Jan. 15, '76, at the Roundhouse Theatre, London; $5.10 top.
Malick Bagayogo, Michele Collison, Miriam Goldschmidt, Bruce Myers, Katsuhiro Oida, Andreas Katsulas, Davidson Knight, Kelvin Omarde, Philip Calender, Hubert Clarke, Adrian Phillips.
01/28/76A

Il Campiello
(London)
National Theatre presentation of a revival of a comedy in two acts by Carlo Goldoni (English adapt, Susanna Graham-Jones, Bill Bryden); staged, Bill Bryden. Set, Hayden Griffin; cos, Deirdre Clancy; light, Rory Dempster; mus, Michael Nyman. Opened Oct. 26, '76, at the Olivier Theatre, London; $6.80 top.
Morag Hood, Beryl Reid, Patti Love, Peggy Mount, Jeananne Crowley, June Watson, Andrew Byatt, Stephen Rea, Michael Gough, Derek Newark, Trevor Ray, John Gill, Jonathan Battersby, Peter Needham, Liam O'Callaghan, Rose Power, Pitt Wilkinson.
11/03/76A

Ils
(They)
(Paris)
Centre Dramatique National de Nanterre & Theatre National Populaire de Villeurbanne presentation of a play in two acts by Stanislaw Ignacy Witkiewicz, adapted into French by Georges Lisowki. Staged, Andrzej Wajda; settings, Krystyna Zachwatowicz; cos, Zachwatowicz, Jacques Schmidt; chor, Barbara Pierce. Opened Feb 5, '80, at the Theatre des Amandiers, Nanterre: $10 top.
Wojciech Pszoniak, Andrezej Seweryn, Christine Gagnieux, Anne Alvaro.
04/02/80A

In the Red
(London)
Allan Davis presentation of a comedy in two acts by William Douglas-Home. Staged, Davis; set, Carmen Dillon; cos, John Cavanagh; light, Andrew Bridge. Opened March 25, '77, at the Whitehall Theatre, London; $6 top.
Dinah Sheridan, Gerald Harper, Bruce Montague, Norman Rossington, Fiona Mollison, Adam Richardson, M J Hemingway.
04/20/77A

In Gatsby's Shadow: SEE A l'Ombre de Gatsby

Inadmissible Evidence
(London)
English Stage Co revival of a drama in two acts by John Osborne, staged by the author. Setting, John Gunter; light, Jack Raby. Opened Sept 13, '78, at the Royal Court Theatre, London; $6.85 top.
Nicol Williamson, Clive Swift, Paul Greenwood, Deborah Norton, Rowena Roberts, Marjorie Yates, Julie Peasgood, Elizabeth Bell.
09/20/78A

Inside the Island
(Sydney)
Nimrod Street Theatre Co Ltd presentation of a drama in two acts, by Neil Armfield; des, Bill Haycock; mus, Sarah de Jong; light, Keith Edmundson; Opened Aug 13, '80 at Nimrod Upstairs Theatre, Sydney: $8.50 top.
Martin Vaughan, John McTernan, Dinah Shearing, Judy Davis, Tony Blackett, Paul Chubb, Annie Byron, Tyler Coppin, Bill Conn, Colin Friels, Martin Harris, Warren Coleman.
09/10/80A

Irene
(London)
Harold Fielding revival of a musical comedy in two acts (15 scenes, 20 numbers); book, Hugh Wheeler, Joseph Stein; from Harry Rigby adapt; based on orig libretto by James Montgomery; mus, Harry Tierney; lyr, Joseph McCarthy; addl lyr-mus, Charles Gaynor, Otis Clements; plus songs by Jack Lloyd & Wally Harper, McCarthy & Fred Fisher, McCarthy & James Monaco; Irving Kahal & Sammy Fain; Norman Newell & Michael Reed. Staged, Freddie Carpenter; mus staging, Norman Maen; scenery-cos, Kenneth Rowell; light, Richard Pilbrow, Howard Eldridge; choral dir, John McCarthy; mus dir, Michael Reed. Opened June 15, '76, at the Adelphi Theatre, London; $6.75 top.
Jessie Evans, Janet Mahoney, Jenny Logan, Julie Anthony, Helen Christie, Chris Dyson, Eric Flynn, Damon Sanders, Jon Pertwee, Madeleine Orr.
Singers, dancers: Josie Ashcroft, Aubrey Budd, Christine Cartwright, Bill Drysdale, Mary Dunne, Debbie Hearnden, Gerry Hunt, Geraldine Long, Francesca Lucy, Jenny Lyons, Peter Pantelic, Anne Pryce, Bruce Scott, Penny Stevenson, Lesley Summers, Trevor Willis, Chris Dyson, Mercia Glossop, Kevin Quarmby, Jacqui Linley, Georgina Rourke, Rex Taylor-Craig, Gerry Tebbutt, David Urwin, Kay Williams.
Musical numbers: "What Do You Want to Make Those Eyes at Me For," "The World Must Be Bigger Than an Avenue," "The Family Tree," "Alice Blue Gown," "They Go Wild, Simply Wild, Over Me," "An Irish Girl," "Point Your Toe," "Mother, Angel, Darling," "I Can Dream, Can't I," "Riviera Rage," "I'm Always Chasing Rainbows," " Last Part of Ev'ry Party," "We're Getting Away with It," "If Only He Knew," "Irene," "Up There On Park Avenue," "The Great Lover Tango," "You Made Me Love You," "You Made Me Love You" (reprise), "Alice Blue Gown" (reprise).
06/23/76A

Irma La Douce
(London)
Paul Elliott, in asso with Ray Cooney, Brian Rix & Brian Hewitt-Jones, revival of a musical with score by Marguerite Monnot; lyr, Julian More, David Heneker, Monty Norman; staging-chor, Billy Wilson; settings, Voytek. Opened Nov. 27, '79, at the Shaftesbury Theatre, London; $14 top.
Helen Gelzer, Charles Dance, Bernard Spear.
12/05/79A

It's All Right If I Do It
(London)
Bernard Delfont and Richard M Mills presentation of a comedy in two acts by Terence Frisby. Staged, Robert Chetwyn; scenery, Patrick Robertson; light, Robert Bryan; cos, Rosemary Vercoe. Opened March 2, '77, at the Mermaid Theatre, London; $5.15 top.
John Stride, Prunella Scales, Tony Haygarth, Toni Palmer, Jonathan Coy, Jennie Anderson, John J Carney, Primula Cotton.
03/09/77A

It's Magic
(London)
Bernard Delfont & Richard M Mills presentation of a variety show with staging and lighting by Dick Hurran; chor, Fred Peters; scenery, Tod Kingman; mus dir, Paul Burnett. Opened Dec 10, '80 at the Prince of Wales Theatre, London; $17.60 top.
Paul Daniels, Jean-Claude & Yvette, Campagnie Philippe Genty, Karen Kay, Fred Peters Dancers.
12/17/80A

Ivanov
(London)
Royal Shakespeare Co. revival of a play in four acts by Anton Chekhov; adapt, Jeremy Brooks, Kitty Hunter-Blair. Staged, David Jones; set, William Dudley; light, Stewart Leviton; mus, Carl Davis. Opened Sept. 7, '76, at the Aldwych Theatre, London; $5.90 top.
John Wood, Bob Hoskins, Estelle Kohler, Sebastian Shaw, Joe Dunlop, Norman Rodway, Carol Gillies, Mia Farrow, Valerie Colgan, Larry Hoodekoff, Kenneth Cranham, Zoe Wanamaker, Patrick Godfrey, Patience Collier, Richard Simpson, Raymond Marlowe, Doyne Byrd, Steven Beard, Diana Rowan, Clare Shenstone, Norman Tipton.
09/15/76A

Jeeves Takes Charge
(London)
Bernard Theobald, Cameron Mackintosh Ltd & the Really Useful Co presentation of a one-man show in two acts by P G Wodehouse; adapt-devised-perf by Edward Duke. Staged, Gillian Lynne; scenery, Claire Lyth, Francis Butler; cos, Una-Mary Parker; mus dir, Roger Haines; chor, Susan Holderness; light, Hugh Wooldridge; incidental mus, Brian Rust, John Wadley. Opened Sep 30, '80, at the Fortune Theatre, London: $14 top.

Jeeves Takes
(Cont)
Edward Duke.
10/22/80A

Joking Apart
(London)
Michael Codron presentation of a comedy in two acts (four scenes) by Alan Ayckbourn. Staged, Ayckbourn; set, Alan Tagg; light, Richard Pilbrow; cos, Lindy Hemming. Opened March 7, '79, at the Globe Theatre, London; $11.25 top.
Christopher Cazenove, Alison Steadman, Julian Fellowes, Marcia Warren, Robert Austin, Jennifer Piercey, John Price, Diane Bull.
03/14/79A

Journey Into Happiness & Further Prospects: SEE Reise ins Glueck & Weitere Aussichten

Julius Caesar
(London)
National Theatre revival of a play in two acts by William Shakespeare. Staged, John Schlesinger; set, John Bury; light, David Hersey; mus, Harrison Birtwistle. Opened March 22, '77, at the Olivier Theatre, London; $7.75 top.
John Gielgud, Brian Cox, Ronald Pickup, Gawn Grainger, Oliver Cotton, Pitt Wilkinson, Peter Needham, Michael Beint, Norman Claridge, Mark McManus, Ian Charleson, Liam O'Callaghan, Glyn Grain, Tom Wilkinson, Martin Friend, Peter Carlisle, John Gill, Rowena Cooper, Ann Firbank, Keith Skinner, Edna Dore, Paul Henley, Daniel Thorndike, Andrew Hilton, Trevor Ray, Timothy Block, Ray Edwards, Shane Connaughton, Brian Kent, Olu Jacobs, Stanley Lloyd, Dennis Tynsley, Chris Hunter, Jonathan Battersby, Shulie Bannister, Vivienne Burgess, Imogen Claire, Irene Gorst, Marianne Morley, Peter Rocca.
03/30/77A

Juno and The Paycock
(London)
Royal Shakespeare Co revival of a play by Sean O'Casey. Staged, Trevor Nunn; set, John Gunter; cos, Lindy Hemmings; light, David Hersey. Opened at the Aldwych, London, Oct 8, '80.
Norman Rodway, Judi Dench, Dearbhla Molloy, Frank Grimes, Gerard Murphy, John Roga; Doreen Keogh.
11/12/80A

Just Between Ourselves
(London)
Michael Codron presentation of a play in two acts (four scenes) by Alan Ayckbourn. Staged, Alan Strachan. Set, Patrick Robertson; light, Nick Chelton. Opened April 20, '77, at the Queen's Theatre, London; $6.55 top.
Colin Blakely, Rosemary Leach, Michael Gambon, Constance Chapman, Stephanie Turner.
04/27/77A

Kickoff for Claudia: SEE
Antoss Fur Claudia

The King and I
(London)
Tom Arnold Associates & Ross Taylor, in ass'n with Lee Guber & Shelly Gross, revival of a musical in two acts (19 numbers), with mus by Richard Rodgers, book and lyr by Oscar Hammerstein 2d, based on the Margaret Landon novel "Anna and the King of Siam." Staged, Yuriko (original chor by Jerome Robbins, reproduced by Susan Kikuchi); settings, Peter Wolf; cos, Irene Sharaff; light, David Hersey; mus dir, Cyril Ornadel; snd, Bruce Elliott. Opened June 12, '79, at the Palladium, London; $15.75 top.
Nick Burnell, Kevin Heuston, Virginia McKenna, Maurice Chong, John Bennett, Yul Brynner, Susan Kikuchi, Marty Rhone, June Angela, Hye-Young Choi, Gene Profanato, Paul Williamson, Shirley Cantrell, Carolyn Choa, Diana Choy, Ran Hamilton, Seeta Indrani, Kathy Lee, San Lee, Suzie Leong, Claire Lutter, Makuini Menehira, Sureen Osler, Pamela Quinn, Eileen Battye, Deborah Jackson, Donna Louise, Glenda Nicholls, Susan Varley, Yuzo Asai, Frankie Au, Jeffrey van der Byl, Lyndon Brown, Serve Julien, Kenneth Kwong, Louise Tam, Rocky Gibbs, Suzanne Tan, Joanne Kwong, Joanne Perry, Rachael Shek, Richard Eastgate, Jerry Loy, Clair Long, Samantha Cook, Simon Tan, Alvin Lee, Chichi Kadijono, Chua Kah Joo.
Musical numbers - "I Whistle a Happy Tune," "My Lord and Master," "Hello Young Lovers," "March of the Siamese Children," "A Puzzlement," "The Royal Bangkok Academy," "Getting to Know You," "We Kiss in a Shadow," "A Puzzlement", (reprise), "Shall I Tell You What I Think of You?", "Something Wonderful," "Western People Funny," "I Have Dreamed," "Hello Young Lovers" (reprise), "The Small House of Uncle Thomas," "Song of King," "Shall We Dance?", Finale.
06/20/79A

King Lear
(London)
Prospect Theatre Co revival of a play by William Shakespeare. Staged, Toby Robertson; set, Alan Barrett; light, Keith Edmundson; mus, Donald Fraser; chor, Charles Augins; fights, Ian McKay. Opened Oct. 24, '78, at the Old Vic Theatre, London; $8 top.
Anthony Quayle, Paul Ridley, James Stephens, Kenneth Gilbert, John Rye, Trevor Martin, Ralph Michael, James Aubrey, Christopher Neame, Andrew Secombe, Enn Reitel, Barry J Gordon, Matthew Guiness, Jeremy Gittins, Carol Gillies, Isla Blair, Mel Martin, Tom Fahy, James Murray, Colin Kaye, Kevin Whatley.
11/15/78A

The Kingfisher
(London)
John Gale presentation of a comedy in two acts (four scenes) by William Douglas Home. Staged, Lindsay Anderson. Set, Alan Tagg; light, Joe Davis; incidental mus, Alan Price. Opened May 4, '77, at the Lyric Theatre, London; $6.90 top.
Alan Webb, Ralph Richardson, Celia Johnson.
05/25/77A

Kings and Clowns
(London)
Duncan C Weldon & Louis I Michaels presentation of a Hillard Eikins prodn of a musical in two acts (28 numbers); book-mus-lyr, Leslie Bricusse. Staged, Mel Shapiro; chor, Gillian Gregory; scenery, John Napier; cos, Napier, Ann Curtis; light, Richard Pilbrow, Graham Large; snd, David Collison; mus dir, Ed Coleman; asso prod, Marcelle Garfield. Opened March 1, '78, at the Phoenix Theatre, London; $9.70 top.
Frank Finlay, Elizabeth Counsell, Dilys Watling, Maureen Scott, Anna Quayle, Colette Gleeson, Sally Mates, Ray C Davis, Michael Heath, Michael Napier Brown, Charles West, Richard Ratcliff, Richard Walsh, Philip Griffiths, Jeanna L'Esty, Dorcas Jones, June Shand.
Musical numbers: "Kings and Clowns," "Henry Tudor," "Good Times," "To Love One Man," "Get Rid Of Her!," "I'm Not," "The Grape and the Vine," "A Woman Is a Wonderful Thing," "In Bed," "My Son," "The Grape and the Vine" (reprise), "Young Together," "Henry Tudor" (reprise), "Tomorrow with Me," "Kings and Clowns" (reprise), "Could Anything Be More Beautiful," "Bitch," "The Perfect Woman," "Henry Tudor" (reprise), "Is Sad," "Ten Wishes," "Henry Tudor" (reprise), "Good Times" (reprise), "The End of Love," "A Man is About to Be Born," "Sextet," "Young Together" (reprise), "Good Times" (reprise).
03/29/78A

Kismet
(London)
Stanley Picker, in ass'n with Richard Pilbrow, presentation of a rev of a musical in two acts (16 numbers); book, Charles Lederer, Luther Davis, based on Edward Knoblauch play of the same title; mus-lyr, Robert Wright, George Forrest, adapt from themes by Alexander Borodin. Staged, Albert Marre; chor, Bonnie Evans (based on orig routines by Jack Cole); sets, Oliver Smith; cos, Frank Thompson; light, Robert Bryan; snd, David Collison; orig orch, Arthur Kay, adapt-mus dir, Alexander Faris. Opened March 21, '78, at the Shaftesbury Theatre, London; $11.40 top.
Paul Bacon, John Reardon, Lorna Dallas, Michael Jones, Denis Carey, Jane Darling, Christopher Hewett, Joan Diener, Sheila O'Neill, Anita Pashley, Shaune Powell, Didi Watts, Jane Darling, Elizabeth Suggars.
Singers, dancers, others: Minoo Golvala, Alan-Charles Thomas, Kevin A J Ranson, David Wheldon-Williams, Mason Taylor, Kenneth Caswell, Roland A Wollens, Joe MacKlaine, Roy Stewart, David Hampshire, Steve Payne, Margo Harris, Antoinette Howlett, Rosemary Ashe, Frank Olegario, Barnaby Noel-Hines, Wallace Stephenson, David Bacon, Lynda Bainbridge, Frances Maria De'arth, Lynn Brotchie, Angie Harwood, Sue Rittman, Alison Temple Savage, Didi Watts, Shirley Lee, Marie Lorraine, Michael Hartley, Carolyn Allen, Jan Hartley.
Musical numbers: "Sands of Time," "Rhymes Have I," "Fate," "Bazaar of the Caravans," "Not Since Nineveh," " Baubles, Bangles and Beads," "Stranger in Paradise," "Gesticulate," "Fate" (reprise), "Night of My Nights," "The Olive Tree," "Was I Wazir,"

Kismet
(Cont)
"Rahadlakum," "And This is My Beloved," "Presentation of Princesses," "Sands of Time" (reprise).
03/29/78A

Krapp's Last Tape
(Berlin)
Prodn of the Berlin DAAD Academic Exchange Program, in collaboration with the Berliner Festchen, Academy of Fine Arts, and the Kuenstlerhaus Bethanien, of the tragicomedy in one act by Samuel Beckett. Staged, Beckett. Snd, Richard S. Bailey; set-props, Richard Riddell; cos, Tere Garcia; motion technique, John L. Jenkins; light, Bud Thore; mgr, Carroll Hauptle; asst, Michael Haerdter. Opened at Academy of Fine Arts, Berlin, Sept. 27, '77; $4 top.
Rick Cluchey.
12/14/77A

La Conference des Oiseaux
(Conference of the Birds)
(Paris)
Centre Int'l de Creations Theatrales presentation of a theatre piece by Jean-Claude Carriere, based on a 12th century Persian poem by Farid Uddin Attar. Preceded by "The Bone" by Carriere & Malick Bowens, based on an African story by Birago Diop. Staged, Peter Brook; science elements-cos, Sally Jacobs. Opened Oct. 7, '79, at the Bouffes du Nord, Paris; $6 top.
Maurice Benichou, Urs Bihler, Malik Bowens, Miriam Goldschmidt, Andreas Katsulas, Arnault Lecarpentier, Mireille Maalouf, Alain Maratrat, Bruce Myers, Yoshi Oida, Jean-Claude Perrin, Tapa Sudana. Musicians: Blaise Catala, Linda Daniel, Toshi Tsuchitori.
11/21/79A

La Culotte
(Paris)
Pierre Franck presentation of a comedy in two acts (four scenes) by Jean Anouilh. Staged by Roland Pietri, Anouilh. Set, Jean-Denis Malcles. Opened Sept 25, '78, at Theatre Atelier, Paris, $12 top.
Jean-Pierre Marielle, Ariane Carletti, Madeleine Cheminat, Gilberte Geniat, Marco Perrin, Jacqueline Jehanneuf, Christian Marin, Odette Mallet.
10/18/78A

Laburnum Grove
(London)
Duncan C Weldon & Louis I Michaels presentation of a revival of a comedy in three acts (four scenes) by J B Priestly. Staged, Hugh Goldie. Set, Hutchinson Scott; light, James Baird. Opened Oct 27, '77 at the Duke of York's Theatre, London; $6.20 top.
Honour Shepherd, Deborah Watling, Simon Merrick, Arthur Lowe, Rob Edwards, Sam Kydd, Joan Cooper, Dermot Walsh, Eric Longworth.
11/02/77A

The Lady or the Tiger
(London)
John Gale & David Conville presentation of a Richmond Fringe Orange Tree Prodn of a musical in two acts (19 numbers); book, Jeremy Paul, Michael Richmond; mus, Nola York; lyr-staged, Richmond; based on short story by Frank Stockton. Dances, Tony Kinnie; mus arrs, Keith Strachan; des, Mary Moore; cos, Shirley Reid; light, Roger Needham. Opened Feb. 3, '76, at the Fortune Theatre, London; $5.70 top.
Kate Crutchley, Vernon Joyner, Gordon Reid, John Morton.
Musical numbers: "Ours is the Kingdom," "The Bow Song," "Daddy's Little Girl," "Lady Evadne," "Sophistication," "Money in My Hat," "The Lady or the Tiger," "Childish Things," "Everything Around Me," "You Know What I Mean," "Sing It Along," "Light a Convenient Candle," "Minstrel Music," "Chariot Wheels," "Angelo," "Good Goodbye," "Here's Gold," "What Would You Do?" "Better Than a Man."
02/11/76A

The Lady From Maxim's
(London)
National Theatre revival of a comedy in three acts by Georges Feydeau, trans, John Mortimer. Staged, Christopher Morahan; set-cos, Michael Annals; light, Leonard Tucker, Annals. Opened Oct 18, '77, at the Lyttelton Theatre, London; $8.50 top.
Edward Hardwicke, John Normington, Stephen Moore, Sara Kestelman, Morag Hood, Michael Bryant, Michael Beint, Martin Friend, Ruth Kettlewell, Barbara Ogilvie, Yvonne D'Alpra, Rose Power, Anne Leon, Diana Payan, Rosamund Greenwood, Robert Ralph, Michael Stroud, Peter Tilbury, Jeananne Crowley, Harry Lomax, Brian Kent, Timothy Davies, Antony Higginson, John Falconer, Louis Haslar, Elizabeth Benson, Christopher Good, Liz Bagley, Shiela Beckett, Brenda Dowsett, Robert Howard, Andrew Tourell.
11/02/77A

Lady Harry
(London)
Ray Cooney presentation of a play in two acts (seven scenes) by Norman Krasna. Staged, Alexander Dore; sets, Peter Williams; light, Chris Ellis. Opened Feb. 23, '78, at the Savoy Theatre, London; $7.80 top.
Terence Budd, John Fraser, Paul Foulds, Corinne Hollingworth, Eileen Erskin, Roy Hepworth, Delia Lindsay, Anthony Woodruff, Jeremy Sinden, Frank Gatliff.
03/29/78A

The Lady's Not For Burning
(London)
Prospect Theatre Co revival of a play in three acts by Christopher Fry. Staged, George Baker; setting, Sally Gardner; light, Keith Edmundson; mus, Donald Fraser. Opened July 3, '78, at the Old Vic Theatre, London; $7.50 top.
Michael Thomas, Derek Jacobi, Kate Nicholls, Clive Arrindell, Brenda Bruce, Oz Clarke, Michael Dennison, Eileen Atkins, Robert Eddison, John Savident, Ronnie Stevens.
07/12/78A

Lamb of God
(Sydney)
Ensemble Prodns presentation of a comedy-drama in two acts by John Summons. Staged, Hayes Gordon; prod, Judy Ferris; dsgn, Brian Tucker; light, Kim Hague-Smith; snd, Rod Dyson. Opened, Aug 10, '78, at the Ensemble Theatre, Sydney; $7.50 top.
Nick Hedstrom, Michael Smith, Patricia Jones, Martin Vaughan.
09/06/78A

Lancelot and Guinevere
(London)
Old Vic Co presentation of a play in two acts by Gordon Honeycombe (based on "Le Morte d'Arthur," by Thomas Malory). Staged, Martin Jenkins; set, Anthony Dean; light, Brian Harris; mus, David Cain. Opened Sep 10, '80, at the Old Vic Theatre, London; $14.40 top.
Timothy West, David Sumner, Maureen O'Brien, Bryan Marshall, Philip Sully, Ron Meadows, Stephen Jenn, Christopher Fulford, Kevin Quarmby, Bernard Archard, Lois Butlin, Jane Cussons, Peter Marinker, John Hug, Peter Roberts, Bernard Bresslaw.
09/24/80A

The Last Address: SEE Die Letzte Adresse

The Last of Mrs Cheyney
(London)
Duncan C Weldon, Louis I Michaels and Bob Mahoney revival of a play by Fredrick Lonsdale. Staged, Nigel Patrick; cos, Pippy Bradshaw; set, Anthony Holland. Opened at the Cambridge Theatre, London, Oct 23, '80: $18.40 top.
Joan Collins, James Villiers, Simon Williams, Michael Aldridge, Elspeth March, Moyra Fraser, Ian Masters, Judi Maynard, Pamela Merrick.
11/05/80A

Last of The Red Hot Lovers
(London)
Ian Albery-Eddie Kulukundis presentation of Neil Simon's comedy. Staged, Eric Thompson; set, Laurie Dennett. Opened Nov. 13, '79, at the Criterion Theatre, London; $12.60 top.
Lee Montagu, Susan Engel, Georgina Hale, Bridget Turner.
11/21/79A

Laughter
(London)
English Stage Co presentation of a play in two acts by Peter Barnes. Staged, Charles Marowitz. Sets, Patrick Robertson, Rosemary Vercoe; light, Leonard Tucker; chor, Stuart Hopps. Opened Jan 27, '78, at the Royal Court Theatre, London; $5.85 top.
Roger Kemp, Paul Bentall, Timothy West, Neil Boorman, Stuart Rayner, Patricia Leach, Patrick Connor, Barry Stanton, David Suchet, Derek Francis, Francis de la Tour.
02/01/78A

Leading Lady
(Melbourne)
Eric Dare & William Orr presentation of musical revue by John McKellar. Staged, William Orr; chor, Robina Beard; cos, Bill Goodwin; mus dir, Phillip Scott. Opened March 12, '77, at St. Martin's Theatre, Melbourne; $6.90 top.
Jill Perryman, Bryan Daires, Darrell Hilton.
03/23/77A

Leave Him To Heaven
(London)
Roger Clifford for London Plays Ltd., & Bill Wellings, by arrangement with Watford Palace Theatre, musical in three acts (44 numbers), by Ken Lee. Staged, Philip Hedley; chor, Pat Adams; set, Ken Lee; mus arrs, Neil McArthur, Brian Protheroe; light, David Lindsey; mus dir, McArthur. Opened June 2, '76, at the New London Theatre, London; $5.13 top.
Brian Protheroe, Larry Dann, Ken Shorter, Paul Felber, Colin Copperfield, Steven Pacey, Cindy Wells, Sue Bond, Anita Dobson, Nicky Croydon, Liz White.
Musical numbers: "Good Evening Friends," "Payola Blues," "Wonderful World," "Great Pretender," "Stay," "Chantilly Lace," "Blue Moon," "At the Hop," "Waitin' in School," "Teen Angel," "Teenager in Love," "Venus in Blue Jeans," "Wooden Heart," "Ya Ya," "Singing the Blues," "Poetry in Motion," "I Can Never Go Home," "My Prayer," "Walk Hand in Hand," "Where or When," "I Believe," "The Book," "Ten Commandments," "Book of Love," "Garden of Eden," "Give Him a Great Big Kiss," "Little Darlin'," "Little Star," "Three Stars," "Ebony Eyes," "Terry," "Tell Laura I Love Her," "Endless Sleep," "Duke of Earl," "Steadfast, Loyal and True," "Tutti Frutti," "Rock Around the Clock," "Great Balls of Fire," "Rockin' Robin," "Ready Teddy," "Girl Can't Help It," "Lovers Never Say Goodbye," "Everybody Rock," "Rock'n Roll Is Here to Say."
06/16/76A

Le Scenario
(The Script)
(Paris)
Georges Herbert & Pierre Franck presentation of a play in two acts by Jean Anouilh. Staged, Anouilh, Roland Pietri; set, Jean-Denis Malcles. Opened Sept. 23, '76, at the Theatre De L'Oeuvre, Paris; $10 top.
Daniel Gelin, Jacques Fabbri, Jean Barney, Sylvie Favre, Sabine Azema, Alexandre Crecq, Karine Lafabrie, Florence Blin, Jean Amos, Jean-Simon Prevost.
10/20/76A

Les Miserables
(Paris)
Europe I, Spectacles ALAP-Lumbroso, Palais des Sports presentation of a musical drama in 18 scenes, based on novel by Victor Hugo. Libretto, Alain Boublil, Claude-Michel Schonberg; mus, Schonberg; text, Boublil, Jean-Marc Natel. Staged, Robert Hossein; mus arr, John Cameron; mus dir, Jean-Michel Defaye; sets, Jean Mandaroux; cos, Sylvie Poulet; light, Hossein; snd, Claude Wargnier; chor, Arthur Plasschaert. Opened Sep 22, '80, at the Palais des Sports, Paris.
Rose Laurens, Maurice Barrier, Jean Vallee, Yvan Dautin, Marie-France Roussel, Marianne Mille, Marius.
12/10/80A

Let The Good Stones Roll
(London)
Charles Ross & Steven Craven presentation of a musical in two acts by Rayner Bourton; sngs, Mick Jagger, Keith Richard; orig material-sngs, Steve Dawson. Staged, Tony Craven; chor, Albin Pahernik; des, Martin Johns; light, David Tate; mus dir, Keith Strachan. Opened March 29, '78, at the Ambassadors Theatre, London; $8.40 top.
Louis Selwyn, Sara Coward, James Bate, Joss Buckley, Colin Copperfield, David Gretton, Martin Smith.
04/19/78A

The Life and Adventures of Nicholas Nickleby
(London)
Royal Shakespeare Co presentation of a two-part play by David Edgar, adapt from Charles Dickens novel. Staged, Trevor Nunn, John Caird; sets-cos, John Napier, Dermot Hayes; light, David Hersey; mus-lyr, Stephen Oliver. Opened Jun 5-6, '80, at the Aldwych Theatre, London: $17.50 top.
Roger Rees, Susan Littler, John Woodvine, Jane Downs, Edward Petherbridge, Clare Travers-Deacon, Rose Hill, David Lloyd Meredith, Terence Harvey, Patrick Godfrey, Ben Kingsley, Timothy Kightley, Andrew Hawkins, Timothy Spall, William Maxwell, Janet Dale, Stephen Rashbrook, John McEnery, Clyde Pollitt, Thelma Whiteley, Griffith Jones, Sharon Bower, Shirley King, Lila Kaye, David Threlfall, Cathryn Harrison, Suzanne Bertish, Bob Peck, Julie Peasgood, Alan Gill, Christopher Rabenscroft, Mark Tandy, Nicholas Gecks, John Mashikiza, Teddy Kempner, Juliet Hammon-Hill, Ian East, Neil Phillips, Jeffery Dench, Roderick Horn, Graham Crowden, Hubert Rees, Norman Tyrrell.
07/02/80A

The Life of Galileo
(London)
National Theatre revival of a drama in three acts by Bertolt Brecht; trans, Howard Brenton. Staged, John Dexter; scenery-cos, Jocelyn Herbert, Stephen Skaptason; light, Andy Phillips; mus, Hanns Eisler. Opened Aug 13, '80, at the Olivier Theatre, London; $14.15 top.
Robert Oates, Michael Gambon, Marc Brenner, Yvonne Bryceland, Elliott Cooper, Andrew Cruickshank, Nicholas Selby, Norman Rutherford, Nigel Bellairs, Selina Cadell, Timothy Norton, Edmond Bennett, Gordon Whiting, Daniel Thorndike, Michael Beint, James Hayes, Peggy Marshall, Jill Stanford, Artro Morris, Roger Gartland, Peter Needham, Robert Howard, Adam Norton, Glenn Williams, Harry Lomax, Robert Ralph, Brian Kent, Simon Callow, Peter Harding, Peter Dawson, Melvyn Bedford, Basil Henson, Mark Dignam, Stephen Moore, Michael Thomas, Peter Land, Sandra Fehr, William Sleigh, Kenneth Mackintosh, Adam Stafford, David Stone, Terry Diab, Jane Evers, Michael Fenner, Michelle Middleton, Stephen Rooney, Janet Whiteside.
08/20/80A

Lionel
(London)
David L Shaw presentation of an Allan Warren prodn of a musical in two acts (32 numbers); conceived, Allan Warren; book, John Welles; based on the career and works of Lionel Bart. Staged, Gillian Gregory; mus concept-orchs, John Cameron; des, Brian Thomson; cos, Sue Blane; mus dir, Roy Moore. Opened May 16, '77, at the New London Theatre, London; $6.50 top.
Todd Carty, Clarke Peters, Avis Bunnage, Adrienne Posta, Hugh Futcher, Marian Montgomery, Aubrey Woods, Valerie Bader, David Brenchlay, Peter Durkin, Elaine Holland, Richard Merson, Chris Nietto, Pamela Scott, Carole Ball.
Musical numbers: "Mirror Man," "Down the Lane," "Jellied Eels," "Who Will Buy?" "Business as Usual," "What Makes a Star?" "Big Times," "It's Yourself," "I'd Do Anything," "Consider Yourself," "When Does the Ravishing Begin?" "Sparrers Can't Sing," "You've Gotta Pick a Pocket or Two," "Butterfingers," "In the Land of Promises," "Do You Mind?" " Rock with the Caveman," "Livin' Doll," "To Be a Performer," "Putting' Out the Flags," "Easy Going Me," "Opposites," "Unseen Hands," "Fings Ain't Wot They Used to Be," "Handful of Songs," "The Day After Tomorrow," "Where is Love?" "Living in Dreamland," "To Be a Performer" (reprise), "Handful of Songs" (reprise).
05/25/77A

Living Quarters
(Dublin)
Abbey Theatre, in ass'n with Oscar Lewenstein, presentation of two-act drama by Brian Friel. Staged, Joe Dowling; set, Wendy Shay; light, Tony Wakefield. Opened March 24, '77, at the Abbey Theatre, Dublin; $2.50 top.
Clive Geraghty, Ray McAnally, Fedelma Cullen, Maire Hastings, Stephen Brennan, Bernadette Shortt, Michael OhAonghusa, Niall O'Brien, Dearbhla Molloy.
04/13/77A

Liza of Lambeth
(London)
John Fenston & Ben Arbeid, in ass'n with John French, presentation of a musical in two acts (27 numbers); book-lyr, William Rushton, Berny Stringle; score, Cliff Adams, based on the novel, "Liza of Lambeth," by Somerset Maugham. Staged, Stringle; chor, Michele Hardy; scenery, Christopher Morley; light, Joe Aveline; cos, Ann Curtiss; mus dir, John Burrows; mus arrs, Harry Roberts; snd, David Collison. Opened June 8, '76, at the Shaftesbury Theatre, London; $6.30 top.
Maggie Vickers, Peggy Ann Jones, Pamela Cundell, Stella Tanner, Jean Reeve, Christopher Neil, Patricia Hayes, Brian Hall, Michael Robbins, Tony Hughes, Dudley Stevens, Kenneth Caswell, Angela Richards, Tina Martin, Jan Todd, Frank Coda, Bryan Marshall, Kate Williams, Paddy Glynn, David Rayner, Ron Pember, Eric Shilling, David Bowman, Jeannie Harris, Richard Merson.
Musical numbers: "Husbands," "Liza," "Gawd Bless Yer," "I Come Down from Wigan," "Liza of Lambeth's Mum," "Liza Ballet," "Prince of Wales," "Is This All," "Watch It," "Red Jollop," "Good Bad Time," "Who in His Right Mind," "Dirty Bertie," "Tricky Finish," "Going Down to Chingford on a Chara," "Whatever Happens to a Man," "Liza Outing," "Beautiful Colors," "What's the Use of Killing Yourself," "Gilbert and Sullivan," "Why Can't We Choose," "I Know I Shouldn't Like It," "Between Ourselves," "A Little Bit on the Side," "Is This All" (reprise), "Whatever Happens to a Man" (reprise), "Liza" (reprise).

Liza of
(Cont)
06/16/76A

The London Cuckolds
(London)
English Stage Co revival of a comedy in two acts by Edward Ravenscroft. Staged, Stuart Burge; set, Robin Archer; light, Jack Raby; mus, Alastair McLachlan. Opened Feb. 27, '79, at the Royal Court Theatre, London; $7 top.

Alan Dobie, Roger Kemp, Barry Stanton, Deborah Norton, Cherith Mellor, Michael Elphick, Kenneth Cranham, Christopher Hancock, Stephanie Beacham, Susan Porrett, Brian Protheroe, Nina Thomas, Ann Dyson, Annie Hulley, David Claridge, Reynold Silva, Roger Frost, James Saxon, Alastair McLachlan.
03/28/79A

Look After Lulu
(London)
Duncan C Weldon & Louis I Michaels revival of a comedy in three acts (four scenes) by Noel Coward; adapted from a French farce by Georges Feydeau. Staged, Patrick Garland; set, Carl Toms; light, Mick Hughes. Opened Oct 9, '78, at the Haymarket Theatre, London; $9.95 top.

Geraldine McEwan, Martin Milman, Kate Percival, Shelley Borkum, Janice Halsey, Tom Karol, Michael Hughes, John Haden, Gary Raymond, Martin Chamberlain, George Howe, Fenella Fielding, Clive Francis, Paul Hardwick, Nigel Stock, John Haden, Peter Bowles, Yvette Byrne, Petra, Robert Perceval.
10/25/78A

Lost to the Devil
(Sydney)
George F Miller presentation of a musical melodrama in two acts by Stanley Walsh. Staged, Walsh; decor, Tom Lingwood; light, John Simmonds; mus dir, Don Harvie; chor, Michael O'Reilly. Opened Feb. 16, '79, at the Music Hall, Sydney; $16 minimum.

Terry Bader, Trevor McCosker, Sandra Griffin, Jenni Anderson, David Atkins, Alan Wilson, Karen Johnson, Bob Mercer, Ron Haddrick, Jenny Ludeke, Des Rolfe, Trevor Prior, Eileen Colocott, Malcolm Pink.
03/14/79A

The Love of a Good Man
(London)
English Stage Co presentation of a play in two acts by Howard Barker. Staged, Nicolas Kent; setting, Stephanie Howard; light, David Colmer. Opened Jan 14, '80, at the Royal Court Theatre, London; $9.10 top.

Daniel Gerroll, Peter Howell, Peter Jonfield, Ian McDiarmid, Anthony Pedley, Edward Jewesbury, Nigel Gregory, Peter Kinley, Kevin Costello, Diane Fletcher, Laura Davenport, Graham Lines.
01/23/80A

Macbeth
(London)
National Theatre revival of a play by William Shakespeare. Staged, Peter Hall and John Russell Brown; settings-light, John Bury; mus, Dominic Muldowney. Opened June 6, '78, at the Olivier Theatre, London; $8.80 top.

Elizabeth Spriggs, Rosamund Greenwood, Yvonne Bryceland, Nicholas Selby, Nicky Henson, Terence Rigby, Glyn Grain, James Grant, Albert Finney, Robin Bailey, Michael Beint, Dorothy Tutin, Paul Henley, Daniel Massey, Martin Howells, Judy Bowker, Brian Kent, Dinah Stabb, Jeremy Dimmick, Alexander Allenby, Daniel Thorndike, Richard Perkins, Norman Claridge, Ray Edwards, Peter Jolley, Louisa Livingstone, Sheraton Blount, Alan Ford, Janet Whiteside, Keith Skinner, Anthony Douse, Dermet Crowley, Peggy Marshall, Jane Evers, Brenda Dowsett, Stanley Lloyd, Roger Gartland, Harry Meacher, Adam Norton, David Pugh, Dennis Tynsley.
06/14/78A

Macbeth
(London)
Old Vic Company revival of a play by William Shakespeare; staged, Bryan Forbes; set, Keith Wilson; light, Brian Harris; snd, John Leonard. Opened Sep 3, '80, at the Old Vic Theatre, London, $14.50 top.

Peter O'Toole, Brian Blessed, Frances Tomelty, Marjorie Bland.
09/10/80A

The Madras House
(London)
National Theatre revival of a comedy-drama in four acts by Harley Granville Barker. Staged, William Gaskill; set, Hayden Griffin; cos, Deirdre Clancy; light, Rory Dempster. Opened June 22, '77, at the Olivier Theatre, London; $7.75 top.

Maya Kemp, Oliver Cotton, Ronald Pickup, Tamara Hincho, Janet Whiteside, Tel Stevens, Brenda Blethyn, Elspeth March, Paul Rogers, Jane Hylton, Margaret Ford, Jane Evers, Marianne Morley, Mark McManus, Barbara Hicks, Dinah Stabb, Paul Henley, Helen Ryan, Joss Ackland, Michael Medwin, Shulie Bannister, Imogen Claire, Lucinda Macdonald, Paul Scofield, Irene Gorst.
07/06/77A

Maggie
(London)
Cushingham Ltd. & Neville Meyer presentation of a musical in two acts (17 numbers); book-mus-lyr, Michael Wild, adapted from play, "What Every Woman Knows," by J M Barrie. Staged, Tom Hawkes; mus staging, Sally Gilpin; scenery, Malcolm Pride; light, Nick Chelton; mus dir, John White. Opened Oct. 12, '77, at the Shaftesbury Theatre, London; $7.05 top.

Leonard Fenton, Clifton Todd, Mark Brackenbury, Anna Sharkey, Peter Gale, Anna Neagle, Briony McRoberts, Barry Sinclair, David Hitchen, Brian Pulman, Joan Lawrence, Jeanna L'Esty, Tobina Mahon Brown, Gill Offord, James McClure, Alan Woodhouse, John Haden, Stephen Ward.

Musical numbers: "Charm," "I Never Laughed in My Life," "Three Hundred Pounds," "Scottish Lullaby," "Shand," "Maggie," "Reprise," "The London Waltz," "If I Ever Really Love," "Do You Remember," "Till the End of Time," "I Can See the Stars," "Dougal Drummonds Railway," "Soliloquy," "Just an Idea," "Till the End of Time" (reprise), "I Just Took a Look at Me."
10/19/77A

Make and Break
(London)
Michael Codron presentation of a play in two acts by Michael Frayn. Staged, Michael Blakemore; setting, Michael Annals; cos, Robin Don; light, Spike Gaden. Opened Apr 24, '80, at the Haymarket Theatre, London: $13.60 top.

Ian Gray, Gary Fairhall, Anthony Roye, Catherine Neilson, Leonard Rossiter, David Graham, Donald Morley, Paul Gregory. James Grout, Peter Blythe, Glyn Grain, Prunella Scales, Ray Edwards,
05/07/80A

Man and Superman
(London)
Royal Shakespeare Co. and Eddie Kulukundis presentation of a revival of a comedy in three acts by George Bernard Shaw. Staged, Clifford Williams. Set, Carl Toms; light, John B Read; mus, Marc Wilkinson. Opened Aug. 16, '77, at the Savoy Theatre, London; $7.30 top.

James Cossins, Ginnette Clarke, Nigel Havers, Richard Pasco, Susan Hampshire, Renee Asherson, Janet Henfrey, Beth Morris, Nicky Henson, Mark Capri, Harry Towb.
08/31/77A

Mardi Gras
(London)
Bernard Delfont & Richard M. Mills presentation of a musical in two acts (16 numbers); book, Melvyn Bragg; mus-lyr, Alan Blaikley, Ken Howard. Staged, Clifford Williams; chor, Paddy Stone; set-cos, Abd'Elkader Farrah; light, Andy Phillips; mus dir, Ray Cook; orchs, Kenny Woodman, Dave Lindup, Fred Tomlinson, Peter Knight, Burt Rhodes, Keith Amos, Ted Brennan; vocal arrs, Fred Tomlinson. Opened March 18, '76, at the Prince of Wales Theatre, London; $7 top.

Morgan Sheppard, Pepsi Maycock, Nicky Henson, Dana Gillespie, Lon Satton, Gaye Brown, Miquel Brown, Don Staiton, Gregory Munroe, Aubrey Woods, Marsha Hunt, Robert Arditti, Leonard Bickley, Sancra Carrier, Queenie Cavette, Tony Cyrus, Joycea Gobern, Maggie Goodwin, Keith Hodiak, Joanna Horlock, Grace Hutchinson, Michael Jaimeson, Jacqui Leatherby, Vince Logan, Robert Narain, Lorna Nathan, Pauline Peters, Wendy Pollock, Felix Rice, Eric Roberts, Jo-Anne Robinson, Gail Rolfe, Ludovico Romano, Barrie Stevens, Betty Winsett, Jeannette Tavernier.

Musical numbers: "Mardi Gras," "Everything About You," "From Now On," "Isn't It a Nice Sensation?" "I Call the Tune," "That's That," "The Second Line," "New Orleans," "Love Keeps No Season," "I Can See It All," "Everybody's Moving," "Make Jazz," "Celandine's Blues," "When I Feel the Spirit Move Me," "The Calinda," "Love's Fool."
03/24/76A

Mary Barnes
(London)
English Stage Co presentation of a play in three acts by David Edgar. Staged, Peter Farago; scenery-cos, Christopher Morley; light, Jack Raby. Opened Jan. 10, '79, at the

Mary Barnes
(Cont)
Royal Court Theatre, London; $7 top.
Patti Love, Donald Sumpter, Simon Callow, Tim Hardy, Ann Mitchell, Colin Bennett, Katherine Kitovitz, Timothy Spall, Judy Monahan, David Gant, Teddy Kempner, Judith Harte, Roger Allam.
01/24/79A

The Matchmaker
(London)
Stoll Prodns presentation of a Cambridge Theatre Co. revival of a comedy in four acts (one intermission) by Thornton Wilder. Staged, Jonathan Lynn; settings-cos, Saul Radomsky; light, Michael Ryan. Opened Aug 30, '78, at Her Majesty's Theatre, London; $9.75 top.
Bernard Spear, Frank Lazarus, Jack Klaff, Nancy Mitchell, Angus MacInnes, Christina Nagy, Richard Simpson, Maria Charles, Tom Kleh, Leueen Willoughby, Jennie Anderson, Dicken Ashworth, David Hayward, Mary Henry.
09/13/78A

Mate!
(London)
Walter Jokel presentation of a comedy in two acts (four scenes) by C Scott Forbes. Staged, James Roose-Evans; set, Bruno Santini; light, Mick Hughes. Opened Dec 12, '78, at the Comedy Theatre, London; $9.85 top.
Britt Ekland, Julian Holloway, Mark York, Timothy Carlton, Matthew Evans.
12/20/78A

McCormack
(Dublin)
Dublin City Theatre presentation of play in two acts by G P Gallivan, prodn script, Thomas MacAnna. Staged, Alan Simpson; setting, Bronwen Casson; mus dir, Eily O'Grady. Opened May 15, '80, at Pavilion Theatre, Dun Laoghaire, Dublin: $6 top.
Frank Patterson, Des Keogh, Brian McGrath, Lana McDonnell, Ann Manahan, Vernon Hayden, Malcolm Douglas.
05/28/80A

Medea
(Athens)
State Theatre of Northern Greece presentation of the classic drama by Euripides, staged-trans into modern Greek, Minos Volanakis. Set, Robert Mitchel; cos, Deni Vachlioti. Mus, Theodore Antonious. Opened Aug. 14, '76 in Thessaloniki and moved over for two performances in Athens at the Lycabettus open air theatre.
Melina Mercouri, Demetris Papamichael, Nicos Vrettos, Despo Diamantidou, Eleane Apergui, Demetris Karellis, Phedon Georgitsis, Christos Tsangas, Costas Matsokas, Nelson Moraetopoulos, Elenitsa Constandinides, Akis Moesiades.
09/29/76A

Memoir
(London)
Quest Prodns Ltd presentation of a play in two acts by John Murrell. Staged, William Chappell; scenery, Mervyn Rowe; light, Leslie Scott. Opened Jan 11, '78, at the Ambassadors Theatre, London; $7.75 top.
Siobhan McKenna, Niall Buggy.
01/25/78A

Mensch Meier
(Zurich)
Theatre am Neumarkt presentation of a play in 22 scenes by Franz Xaver Kroetz. Staged, Horst Mendroch; setting, Ambrosius Humm; cos, Renate Kalanke; tech dir, Georges Nagy; light, Twist Sopek; snd, Jiri Vohralik. Opened Feb. 3, '79, at the Theatre am Neumarkt, Zurich; $10.60 top.
Iris Erdmann, Henning Heers, Marcus Lachmann.
02/21/79A

The Merchant
(Stockholm)
Royal Dramatic Theater presentation of a play by Arnold Wesker. Staged, Staffan Roos; sets, Goran Wassberg; cos, Marik Vos. Opened Oct. 8, '76 at Royal Dramatic Theatre, Stockholm
Ingvar Kjellson, Malin Ek, Gunn Wallgreen, Ulf Johanson, Ponten, Lars Amble, Rolf Skoglund, Anita Wall.
10/20/76A

Middle Age Spread
(Auckland, NZ)
Mercury Theatre presentation of a play in two acts, by Roger Hall. Staged, Roy Hope; decor, Pat Templeton; light, Don Jowsey. Opened May 24, '78, at the Mercury Theatre, Auckland, NZ, $6 top.
David Weatherley, Helen Dorward, Paul Robinson, Helen Smith, Chris Sheil, Ilona Rogers.
06/14/78A

Middle Age Spread
(London)
John Gale presentation of a play in two acts (10 scenes) by Roger Hall. Staged, Robert Kidd; sets, Alan Tagg; light, Howard Eaton. Opened Oct. 17, '79, at the Lyric Theatre, London; $12.90 top.
Marjie Lawrence, Richard Briers, Sheila Grant, Paul Eddington, Judy Loe, Tom Chadbon.
10/31/79A

The Millionairess
(London)
Louis I Michaels & Duncan C Weldon revival of a play in two acts (four scenes) by George Bernard Shaw. Staged, Michael Lindsay-Hogg; settings, Alan Tagg; cos, Robin Fraser Paye; light, Joe Davis. Opened Dec 14, '78, at the Haymarket Theatre, London; $10 top.
Nigel Hawthorne, Penelope Keith, Ian Ogilvy, Angharad Rees, Simon Jones, Charles Kay, Ronald Govey, Lucy Griffiths, Jonathan Elsom.
12/27/78A

Mr. Laurel and Mr. Hardy
(London)
Jack Hockett & Oakley Entertainment Ltd. presentation of a musical play in two acts by Tom McGrath. Staged, Robert Walker; set, Miki van Zwanenberg; chor, Pat Lovett; light, Alastair McArthur. Opened Nov. 15, '76 at the Mayfair Theatre, London; $4.95 top.
John Shedden, Ian Ireland, Michael Wild.
11/24/76A

Mishima
(Hong Kong)
University Players Club presentation of a play by Gus Wong. Staged, Jack Lowcock; set, Gus Wong, Lowcock; light, Anthony Hung, Frederick Wong; film sequences, Fong Ling Ching; snd, Lana Ng; adapted from the writings of Yukio Mishima and biographies by John Nathan and Henry Scott-Stokes. Opened Jan. 12, '79, at Studio Theatre, Hong Kong.
Gregory Leong, Louis Ho, Selina Kan, Elizabeth Wu, Augustine Wong.
02/07/79A

Molly
(London)
H M Tennent Ltd in ass'n with Grosvenor Entertainment & Shineline Ltd presentation of a drama in two acts (five scenes) by Simon Gray. Staged, Stephen Hollis; set, Christopher Morley; cos, Ann Curtis; light, Peter Sutton. Opened Oct 25, '78, at the Comedy Theatre, London; $10.25 top.
Billie Whitelaw, T P McKenna, Barbara Atkinson, Anthony Allen, Michael Shannon, David Telfer.
11/08/78A

More Than A Sentimental Bloke
(Sydney)
Festival of Sydney presentation of a solo program of readings of the poems, letters and other writing of Clarence James Dennis. Staged, George Whaley and Wal Cherry. Opened Jan 4, '80, in the Recording Hall, Sydney Opera House; $5 top.
John Derum.
01/23/80A

Motherdear
(London)
Geoffrey Rose & Donald Bodley presentation of a play in two acts (seven scenes) by Royce Ryton. Staged, Frith Banbury; setting, Geoffrey Scott; cos, Anthony Holland; light, Robert Ornbo. Opened May 12, '80, at the Ambassadors Theatre, London: $13.70 top.
Norma Streader, Polly James, Margaret Lockwood, William Eedle, Dorothy Primrose, Zulema Dene, Chris Johnston, Francis Lloyd, Margaret Diamond, Sheila Burrell, Frank Barrie.
05/21/80A

Mother's Day
(London)
Royal Court Theatre presentation of a play in two acts by David Storey. Staged, Robert Kidd; set, Harry Waistnage; light, Jack Raby; cos, Robert Dein. Opened, Sept. 22, '76 at Royal Court Theatre, London; $4.45 top.
Jane Carr, Patricia Healey, Susan Porrett, Betty Marsden, Alun Armstrong, Bryan Pringle, Colin Farrell, Gorden Kaye, David Ryall, Peter Myers, Dorothea Phillips.
09/29/76A

Murder Among Friends
(London)
John Gale presentation of a play in two acts (four scenes) by Bob Barry. Staged, Roger Redfarn; sets, Peter Rice; light, Joe Davis. Opened Feb 21, '78, at the Comedy Theatre, London; $8.75 top.

Murder Among
(Cont)
Moira Lister, Tony Britton, Barry Stokes, Margaret Courtenay, Dermot Walsh, Robert Swales.
03/01/78A

My Astonishing Self
(Dublin)
Dublin Theatre Festival in ass'n with St. Lawrence Prodns presentation of an entertainment devised by Michael Voysey from writings of George Bernard Shaw. Staged, Bil Keating; scenery, Robert Heade; cos, Derry O'Donovan. Opened at Gate Theatre, Dublin, Sept. 27, '76; $5 top.
Donal Donnelly.
10/20/76A

My Fair Lady
(London)
Cameron Mackintosh presentation of a revival of a musical in two acts (23 numbers); with mus, Frederick Loewe. Book-lyrs, Alan Jay Lerner. (Based on the play, "Pygmalion," by Bernard Shaw) with additional mus, Trude Rittman. Staged, Robin Midgley; chor, mus staging, Gillian Lynne; settings, Adrian Vaux; cos, Tim Goodchild; light, Joe Davis; mus arr, Robert Russell Bennett, Phil Lang; mus dir, Ray Cook; snd, Edward Fardell; prodn supv, Robert West. Opened Oct 25, '79 at the Adelphi Theatre, London; $16.95 top.
Tony Britton, Liz Robertson, Peter Bayliss, Anna Neagle, Richard Caldicot, Betty Paul, Peter Land, Kalman Glass, Eddie Davies, Roy Sone, Joan Ryan, Peggy Ashby, Bob Appleby, Jack Gunn, Frank Lee White, Josie Ashcroft, Bill Boazman, Peter Durkin, Shirley Greenwood, Jillian Mack, Bronwen Stanway, David Farrow, Brian Pullman, Anita Joannou, Gil Offord, Jack Gunn, Deirdre Laird, David Hepburn, Robert Austin-Moore, Penny Stevenson, David Oakley, Anita Pashley, Kevin A J Ranson, Arthur Tolcher, Frank Lee White.
Musical numbers: - "Why Can't the English?" "Wouldn't It Be Loverly?" "With a Little Bit of Luck," (reprise), "Just You Wait," "Poor Prof Higgins," "The Rain in Spain," "I Could Have Danced All Night," "Ascot Gavotte," "On the Street Where You Live," (reprise), "On the Street Where You Live" (reprise), "Show Me," "Wouldn't It Be Loverly?" (reprise), "Get Me To The Church on Time" (reprise), "Why Can't a Woman be More Like a Man?" "Why Can't a Woman Be More Like a Man" (reprise), "Without You" "I've Grown Accustomed To Her Face."
11/07/79A

National Puppet Theatre of Japan: SEE Bunraku

The Naval Officer
(Auckland)
Mercury Theatre presentation of a play in two acts by Brian McNeill; staged, Ian Mullins and the author; scenery, Jan Mullins, John McKay, Tom Wilson; cos, Arthur Thompson; light, John McKay. Opened July 4, '79, at the Mercury Theatre, Auckland, NZ; $6.50 top.
John Givins, Alastair Browning, Sidney Jackson, George Pensotti, Brian McNeill, Damian Corrigan, Waric Slyfield, Claire Oberman, Paul Robinson, Graeme Anderson, Marion Parry, Faye Flegg, Norman Forsey, Grant McFarland.
07/25/79A

Ned Kelly
(Sydney)
Adelaide Festival Center Trust & Eric Dare, in ass'n with the Australian Elizabethan Theatre Trust, presentation of a musical by Reg Livermore; des-staged, Livermore; mus, Patrick Flynn; arr-dir, Michael Carlos; chor, Keith Bain; light-sfx, Martin Smith; snd, Jands. Opened Feb 4, '78, at Her Majesty's Theatre, Sydney; $10.40 top.
Nick Turbin, Doug Parkinson, Stephen Thomas, Ric Herbert, Jeremy Paul, Arthur Dignam, Geraldine Turner, Beverley Evans, Paul Smyth, Graham Lowndes, Timothy Bean, Robert McKell.
03/01/78A

Nepal
(Zurich)
Theatre am Neumarkt presentation of a comedy-drama in two parts by Urs Widmer. Staged, Peter Schweiger; set-cos, Ambrosius Humm; tech dir, Georges Nagy; light, Paul Flury; snd, Alex Hiltebrand. Opened Oct. 21, '77, at the Theatre am Neumarkt, Zurich; $8,30 top.
Karl Ghirardelli, Walo Luond.
12/21/77A

The Nest: SEE Das Nest

Night and Day
(London)
Michael Codron presentation of a play in two acts by Tom Stoppard. Staged, Peter Wood; set, Carl Toms; light, Robert Bryan. Opened Nov. 8, '78, at the Phoenix Theatre London; $9.90 top.
William Marlowe, George Harris, Diana Rigg, Jon Bentley, John Thaw, Peter Machin, David Langton, Olu Jacobs.
11/15/78A

Nightshade
(Dublin)
Peacock Theatre, in ass'n with the Dublin Theatre Festival Ltd, presentation of a two-act play by Stewart Parker. Staged, Chris Parr; setting, Bronwen Casson; lighting, Tony Wakefield; magic consultant, Tony Sadar; wrestling sequences, Pat Whelan; dances arr, Bernie Keogh. Opened Oct 9, '80 at the Peacock Theatre, Dublin; $5 top.
T P McKenna, Lise-Ann McLaughlin, Colm Meaney, Niall O'Brien, Geoff Golden, Kate Flynn, Maureen Toal, Michael Duffy, Joan Sheehy, Condy Conarian.
12/17/80A

No Names. . .No Pack Drill
(Sydney)
Sydney Theatre Co presentation of a play in three acts by Bob Herbert. Staged, George Ogilvie; scenery, Kristian Fredrikson; light, Keith Edmundson; cos, Anna French. Opened Apr 15, '80, at Sydney Opera House Drama Theatre; $9.20 top.
Mel Gibson, Noni Hazlehurst, Brandon Burke, Julie Hamilton, Al Thomas, Janice Finn, Ron Falk, Andrew Tighe, John Sheerin, Jon Blake.
04/23/80A

No Room for Dreamers
(Sydney)
Ensemble Productions, in association with the Festival of Sydney presentation of a drama in two acts by George Hutchinson. Staged, Lex Marinos; des, Richard Heller; light and snd, Joddi Speight; mus dir, Mervyn Drake. Opened Jan 1, '80, at the Stables Theatre, Sydney; $5 top.
Terry Bader, Alan Becher, Peter Corbett, Laurel McGowan, Shaunna O'Grady, Peter Rowley, Sonja Talis.
01/23/80A

Not Quite Jerusalem
(London)
English Stage Co presentation of a play in two acts by Paul Kember. Staged, Les Waters; sets, Peter Hartwell; light, Dick Johnson; snd, Charles Wright. Opened Dec 2, '80, at the Royal Court Theatre, London; $11.75 top.
Bernard Strother, Philip Davis, Annie Hayes, Kevin McNally, Bruce Alexander, Leslee Udwin.
12/10/80A

Notre Dame de Paris
(Paris)
Spectacles ALAP, Spectacles Lumbroso and Palais des Sports presentation of a play in two acts; adapted, Alain Decaux, Robert Hossein, Georges Soria; from the novel by Victor Hugo. Staged-light, Hossein; set, Jean Mandaroux; cos, Sylvie Poulet; snd, Michel Asline; mus, Bernard Guillaumat; laser effects, Trapeze; stunts-combats, Guy di Rigo. Opened Sep 25, '78, at Palais des Sports, Paris; $18.50 top.
Michel Creton, Jean de Conninck, Max Montavon, Rene Dupre, Pierre Negre, Annie Monnange, Gerard Boucaron, Jean-Pierre Bernard, Anne Fontaine, Rachel Salik, Marcel Guegan, Bernard Lanneau, Albert Michel, Claude Petit.
10/25/78A

Obsessive Behaviour In Small Spaces
(Sydney)
University of New South Wales Drama Foundation presentation of The Old Tote Theatre Co. in a play in two acts, by Ian Stocks and Robert Trebor Lang, from idea by Richard Weight. Staged, Rodney Fisher; des, Tony Tripp; light, Jerry Luke. Opened Nov. 16, '77, at the Parade Theatre, Sydney; $7.30 top.
Michele Fawdon, Ross Thompson, Neil Redfern, John Jarratt, Liddy Clark.
12/07/77A

Oh, Mr Porter
(London)
Mermaid Theatre Trust, in ass'n with Michael Codron, presentation of a musical in two acts (40 numbers). Book, Benny Green; mus-lyrs, Cole Porter. Staged-chor, Wendy Toye; set, Alan Barrett; light, Andrew A Gardner; mus dir, Ken Moule. Opened Apr 27, '77 at the Mermaid Theatre, London; $5.20 top.
Jacqueline Clarke, Tudor Davies, Richard Denning, Don Fellows, Graham James, Eleanor McCready, Kenneth Nelson, Su Pollard, Jeanette Ranger, Una Stubbs.
Musical Numbers: "Let's Do It," "Let's Be

Oh, Mr
(Cont)
Buddies," "But in the Morning No," "Little Skipper From Heaven Above," "You'd Be So Nice to Come Home To," "Friendship," "All of You," "My Heart Belongs to Daddy," "Easy to Love," "Let's Not Talk About Love," "Do I Love You?" "I'm In Love Again," "Cherry Pie Ought to Be You," "Riding High," "After You Who?" "I've Got You On My Mind," "Nobody's Chasin' Me," "Ladies in Waiting," "Introduced," "They Couldn't Compare to You," "I Love You," "Begin the Beguine," "Jungle Drums," "Did You Evah?" "It Ain't Etiquette," "How's Your Romance," "What Shall I Do?" "Miss Otis Regrets," "The Tale of an Oyster," "I Concentrate On You," "When Your Troubles Have Started," "You're Just Too Too," "I've Still Got My Health," "I'll Always Be True to You Darling in My Fashion," "I Hate Men," "After All I'm Only a School Girl," "Rap Tap on Wood," "I've Got You Under My Skin," "All through the Night."
05/11/77A

Oklahoma!
Cameron Mackintosh presentation of a revival of a musical by Richard Rodgers, Oscar Hammerstein. Staged, James Hammerstein. Dance routines re-staged, Gemze de Lappe. Sets, Tim Goodchild; light, Richard Pilbrow; snd, Paul Farrah; mus dir, Ray Cook. Opened at the Palace Theatre, London, Sept 17, '80.
Rosamund Shelley, John Diedrich, Madge Ryan, Linal Haft, Robert Bridges, Brent Verdon, Mark White, Jillian Mack, Alfred Molina.
09/24/80A

The Old Country
(London)
Michael Codron presentation of a play in two acts by Alan Bennett. Staged, Clifford Williams; des, John Gunter; light, Leonard Tucker. Opened Sept. 7, '77, at the Queens Theatre, London; $7.65 top.
Alec Guinness, Rachel Kempson, Bruce Bould, Heather Canning, John Phillips, Faith Brook.
09/21/77A

Old Flames
(London)
Eddie Kulukundis & S. Spencer Davids presentation of comedy-drama in two acts by E A Whitehead. Staged, Jonathan Hales; set, Sue Plummer; light, Robert Bryan. Opened Feb. 19, '76, at the Arts Theatre, London; $5 top.
Katherine Fahy, Gary Bond, Barbara Ewing, Judy Cornwell, Anne Dyson.
03/03/76A

Old Movies
(London)
National Theatre presentation of a comedy in two acts (six scenes) by Bill Bryden. Staged, Bryden; set, Geoffrey Scott; light, Peter Radmore. Opened June 16, '77, at the Cottesloe Theatre, London; $4.30 top.
E G Marshall, Kenneth Cranham, Fulton MacKay, Deborah Fallender, Trevor Ray, Rowena Cooper, Glyn Grain, Chris Hunter, Olu Jacobs.
07/06/77A

Old World
(London)
Royal Shakespeare Co. presentation of a play in two acts (nine scenes) by Aleksei Arbuzov; English trans, Ariadne Nicolaeff. Staged, Terry Hands; set, Ralph Koltai; light, Stewart Leviton; mus, Ian Kellam. Opened Oct. 12, '76, at the Aldwych Theatre, London; $5.45 top.
Peggy Ashcroft, Anthony Quayle.
10/20/76A

Oliver
(London)
Cameron Mackintosh (by arrangement with Donald Albery) presentation of a rev of a musical comedy in two acts (21 numbers); book-mus-lyr, Lionel Bart, adapt, from Charles Dickens novel "Oliver Twist." Staged, Robin Midgley, Larry Oaks; decor, Sean Kenny; light, Chris Ellis; orch, Eric Rogers; snd, Rod Mead; mus dir, Chris Walker. Opened Dec 21, '77, at the Albery Theatre, London; $9.25 top.
Paul Ainsworth, Robert Bridges, Joan Turner, Graham Hamilton, Jill Fletcher, Kim Smith, Marilynn Cutts, Stephen Kebell, Roy Hudd, Gillian Burns, Annabelle Lanyon, Michael Attwell, Jack Allen, Leslie Glazer, Elaine Garreau, Eileen Bell, Maggie Ryder, Paul Peters, Richard Drabble, Carol Brook, Bronwen Stanway, Simon Clark, Richard Merson, Will Howard, Geoffrey Ferris, Neil France, Robert McCulley, Jessica Higgs.
Workhouse Boys and Fagin's Gang: John Ahmet, Tommy Barnett, Nick Berry, Barry Cracknell, Adam Dyke, Derek Ganley, Perry Fenwick, Joe James, Wayne Kerbell, Romain de Kerckhove, Gary Love, Graham Mills, Robert Northwood, Mike Samuels, Kevin Sullivan, Stuart Smitherman, Lee Towsey, Ian Turnbull, Chris Wilkinson, Paul Wilson.
Musical numbers: "Food," "Oliver!" "I Shall Scream," "Boy for Sale," "That's Your Funeral," "Where is Love?," "Consider Yourself," "Pick a Pocket," "Fine Life," "I'd Do Anything," "Be Back Soon," "Oom-Pah-Pah," "My Name," "As Long As He Needs Me," "Reviewing the Situation," "Oliver" (reprise), "As Long As He Needs Me" (reprise), "Reviewing the Situation" (reprise).
01/25/78A

On Approval
(London)
Duncan C Weldon & Louis I Michaels revival of a comedy in two acts (three scenes) by Frederick Londsdale. Staged, Frith Banbury; scenery, Anthony Holland; light, Charles Peyton. Opened June 28, '77, at the Vaudeville Theatre, London; $6.50 top.
Carolyn Seymour, Patricia Routledge, Kenneth More, Moray Watson.
07/06/77A

On Our Selection
(Sydney)
National Institute of Dramatic Art presentation of a comedy in four acts, adapted by George Whaley from Bert Bailey's dramatization of Steele Rudd's books; staged, Whaley; dsgn, Kim Carpenter; mus dir, Roma Conway; chor, Keith Bain; light, Timothy Clark. Opened June 30, '79, at the Jane Street Theatre, Sydney; $6 top.
Don Crosby, Kerry Walker, Sally Cahill, Vivienne Garrett, Geoffrey Rush, Jon Blake, John Clayton, Noni Hazlehurst, Mel Gibson, Barry Otto, John Smythe, Robert Menzies.
07/25/79A

On the Rope, or The Ghost Train Ballad
(Zurich)
Schauspielhaus presentation of drama in one act by Fernando Arrabal. German trans Elke Kummer. Staged, Peter Lotschak; set-cos, Gian-Maurizio Fercioni; light, Hans Stamm; snd, Georg Luedeke. Opened Sept. 25, '76, at the Studio Tiefenbrunnen, Zurich; $3.85 admission.
Robert Tessen, Peter Brogle, Alexander Pelz.
10/06/76A

On The Twentieth Century
(London)
Harold Fielding presentation of a musical with book and lyrics by Betty Comden and Adoph Green, mus, Cy Coleman, based on play by Ben Hecht, Charles MacArthur and Bruce Mulholland. Staged, Peter Coe; mus staging, Larry Fuller reprod, Gerald Teijelo; scenery, Robert Wagner; cos, Florence Klotz; mus dir, Ray Cook; orchs, Hershy Kay. Opened Mar 20, '80 at Her Majesty's Theatre, London; $17.60 top.
Keith Michell, Julia McKenzie, Mark Wynter, Ann Beach, David Healey, Fred Evans, Valerie Leon, Chris Melville, Richard Manuel, Ricardo Sibelo, Ewart Walters, Johnny Worthy.
04/02/80A

Once A Catholic
(London)
English Stage Co. presentation of a comedy in two acts by Mary O'Malley. Staged, Mike Ockrent; des, Poppy Mitchell; light, Jack Raby; snd, John Del'Nero. Opened Aug. 10, '77, at the Royal Court Theatre, London; $5 top.
Pat Heywood, Jeanne Watts, Doreen Keogh, John Boswall, John Rogan, Jane Carr, June Page, Anna Keaveney, Kim Clifford, Lilian Rostkowska, Sally Watkins, Rowena Roberts, Daniel Gerroll, Mike Grady.
08/17/77A

Once in a Lifetime
(London)
Royal Shakespeare Co revival of a comedy in three acts by Moss Hart and George S Kaufman. Staged, Trevor Nunn, Gillian Lynne; settings, John Napier; cos, Andreane Neofitou; light, Robert Bryan; mus arr, Jim Parker. Opened Sept. 4, '79, at the Aldwych Theatre, London; $12.25 top.
Richard Griffiths, Zoe Wanamaker, Peter McEnery, Keith Hodiak, Gaye Brown, Toria Fuller, Susannah Fellows, Helen Brammer, Allan Hendrick, Michael Bertenshaw, Kate Fitzgerald, George Raistrick, Darlene Johnson, Cheryl Hall, Diana Van Fossen, Ian Reddington, Brian Abott, Susan Dury, Jocelyn Cunningham, Philip McGough, Valerie Lush, John Nettles, Arthur White, Geoffrey Freshwater, Juliet Stevenson, David Suchet, David Bradley, Carmen du Sautoy, Bill Buffery, Alan Barker, Ian Charleson, Paul Boroke, Stuart Organ, Michael Siberry.
09/19/79A

Once In May: SEE Wie Einst Im Mai

One Man's Meat
(Dublin)
Oscar Productions presentation of a two-act comedy by Lee Dunne. Staged, Dunne. Set, Robert Lane; light, Richard Johnstone. Opened Apr 23, '80, at Oscar Theatre, Dublin: $6 top.
Vincent Smith, Brenda Doyle, James Caffrey, Madelyn Erskine.
05/21/80A

One More Time
(Tel Aviv)
Amnon Berenson presentation of a Gil Shiva Prodn. Conceived-wri, Ehud Manor; staging and chor, Donald McKayle; settings, Tom Walsh; cos, Rita Weissman; light, Ken Billington; mus supv, orchestration and vocal arr, Howard Roberts. Opened Nov 11, '79 at the Habimah National Theatre, Tel Aviv; $12 top.
Wilbur Archie, Priscilla Baskerville, Elaine Beener, Gregg Burge, Pi Douglas, Yolanda Graves, Bonita Jackson, Jaime Patterson.
11/14/79A

Oor Wullie
(Aberdeen, Scotland)
Overground Theatre of England presentation, under licence from D C Thompson & Co Ltd of a musical comedy in two acts, with book and lyr by Alan Bryce; mus comp-arr, Milton Reame-James. Staged, Mario Riccio; mus dir, Liz Kean; des, Opened Sept. 10, '79, at Her Majesty's Theatre, Aberdeen; $4 top. Stuart M Stanley; chor, Angela Hardcastle.
Pat Doyle, David Christie, Vernon Nurse, Clare Dow, Fiona MacArthur, Ann Tobin, William Garrity, David Peate.
10/10/79A

Operation: Shield Rock
(Dublin)
Icelandic Theatre Company presentation of two-act comedy by Jonas Arnason. Staged, Anthony Matheson; set, Steinthor Sigurdsson. Opened Sept. 27, '76 at Peacock Theatre, Dublin; $2 top.
Gunnar Eyjolfsson, Jonina Olafsdottir, Jestyne Phillips, Graham Swannell, Arni Ibsen, Ingibjorg Asgeirsdottir.
10/20/76A

Orfeus-Biografie eines Halbstarken
(Orfeus-Biography of a Young Misfit)
(Zurich)
Theatre am Neumarkt presentation of a drama in 22 scenes by Peter Greiner. Staged, Helmut Palitsch; set-cos, Thomas Kierlinger; tech dir, Georges Nagy; light, Franz Windlin; snd, Jiri Vohralik. Opened Feb 20, '79, at the Theatre am Neumarkt, Zurich; $10.60 top.
Johann Adam Oest, Peter Bollag, Lilo Geyger, Olga Strub, Iris Erdman, Beat Faeh.
03/28/79A

Orfeus-Biography of a Young Misfit: SEE
Orfeus-Biografie eines Halbstarken

Othello
(London)
National Theatre Company presentation of a play by Willian Shakespeare, dir, Peter Hall; settings, John Bury; cos, Sue Jenkinsn; light, David Hersey. Opened Mar 20, '80 at the Olivier, London: $13.10 top.
Paul Scofield, Michael Bryant, Felicity Kendal, Yvonne Bryceland, Basil Henson, Stephen Moore, Michael Cambon.
04/02/80A

The Other Side of the Swamp
(London)
Phoenix Theatre Prodns revival of a play in two acts by Royce Ryton. Staged, Joan Kemp-Welch; light, Roy Prosho. Opened Jun 18, '80, at the Phoenix Theatre, London: $10.50 top.
Royce Ryton, Paul Jerricho.
06/25/80A

Other Times
(Melbourne)
Melbourne Theatre Co. presentation of a play in three acts (6 scenes) by Ray Lawler. Staged, John Sumner; scenery, Anne Fraser. Opened Dec. 16, '76, at the Russell Street Theatre, Melbourne; $6 top.
Irene Inescort, Peter Curtin, Christine Amor, Carole Skinner, Bruce Myles, Sandy Gore, David Downer.
12/29/76A

Out On a Limb
(London)
John Gale and Cameron Mackintosh presentation of a comedy in two acts (five scenes) by Joyce Rayburn. Staged, James Grout; scenery, Hutchinson Scott; light, Andrew Bridge; cos, Penny Lowe. Opened Oct. 21, '76, at the Vaudeville Theatre, London; $5.60 top.
Ian Carmichael, Phyllida Law, Julia Lockwood, Michael Fleming, Jacqueline Lacey, Hugh Paddick.
11/03/76A

Outside Edge
(London)
Eddie Kulukundis, by arrangement with Hampstead Theatre Prodns, presentation of a play in two acts by Richard Harris. Staged, Robin Lefevre; setting, Grant Hicks; light, Alan O'Toole; cos, Lindy Hemmings. Opened Sept. 11, '79 at the Queen's Theatre, London; $13.50 top.
Julia McKenzie, Richard Kane, John Kane, Julian Curry, Maureen Lipman, Ian Trigger, Susan Carpenter, Martin Wimbush, Natalie Forbes.
09/19/79A

Pal Joey
(London)
Ian B Albery presentation, in association with Christopher Malcolm and Capital Radio, of a revival of a musical by John O'Hara; mus-lyr, Richard Rodgers, Lorenz Hart. Staged, Robert Walker; chor, Stuart Hopps; sets, Mick Bearwish; light, Gerry Jenkinson; cos, Anthony McDonald, Iona McLeish. Opened Sep 25, '80 at the Albery Theatre, London: $18.95 top.
Sian Phillips, Denis Lawson, Christopher Muncke, Danielle Carson, Darlene Johnson, Alan Tilvern.
10/22/80A

Pandora's Cross
(Sydney)
Paris Theatre Co presentation of musical play in two acts by Dorothy Hewett. Mus, Ralph Tyrrell. Staged, Jim Sharman; scenery, Brian Thomson; cos, Luciana Arrighi; mus dir, Roy Ritchie; chor, Graeme Watson; light, Bill Walker. Opened June 29, '78, at the Paris Theatre, Sydney; $7.50 top.
Arthur Dignam, Jennifer Claire, John Gaden, Julie McGregor, John Paramor, Geraldine Turner, Steve J Spears, Robyn Nevin, Neil Redfern.
Mus numbers: "Pandora's Cross," "Good News," "Malley's Back," "Pandora," "Pig in a Wig," "Rudi Roderigo," "Jack of Hearts," "Across the Western Suburbs," "Sine in My Feathers," "I'm Wrapped in You," "Striptease You," " Hooker on the Game," "Waltzing Punk," " Pyjama Girl."
07/12/78A

Parcel Post
(London)
English Stage Co. presentation of a comedy in two acts by Yemi Ajibade. Staged, Donald Howarth; set, David Short; light, Jack Raby. Opened March 16, '76, at the Royal Court Theatre, London; $6 top.
Yemi Ajibade, Taiwo Ajai, Rudolph Walker, Willie Payne, Christopher Asante, Flenna Forster-Jones, Muriel Odunton, Ilarrio Bisi Pedro, Johnny Briggs, Stuart Rayner, Gordon Case.
03/24/76A

The Passion of Dracula
(London)
Backstage Prodns, in association with Miriam Bienstock, presentation of a play in three acts by Bob Hall and David Richmond. Staged, Clifford Williams; setting, Farrah; light, David Hersey and Mark Pritchard; mus, Mark Wilkinson. Opened Aug 23, '78 at the Queen's Theatre, London; $9.75 top.
Richard Vernon, Richard Moore, Roy Dotrice, Geraldine James, James Villiers, Michael Feast, Beth Morris, Tom Marshall, George Chakiris.
09/06/78A

Patrick Gulliver
(Dublin)
Peacock Theatre, in assn with the Dublin Comedy Theatre, presentation of one-man show by Eamon Morrissey based on the works of Jonathan Swift. Staged, Joe Dowling; light, Tony Wakefield. Opened June 21, '78 at the Peacock Theater, Dublin; $4 top.
Eamon Morrissey.
07/12/78A

Paul Robeson
(London)
Robert Stigwood presentation of Don Gregory prodn of a play by Phillip Hayes Dean. Original staging by Charles Nelson Reilly, staged, Lloyd Richards; setting, H R Poindexter; light, Ian Calderon; cos, Noel Taylor. Opened July 27, '78, at Her Majesty's Theatre, London; $9.70 top.
James Earl Jones, Burt Wallace.
08/16/78A

The Philanderer
(London)
National Theatre Co revival of play in two acts (four scenes) by George Bernard Shaw. Staged, Christopher Morahan; settings, Eileen Diss; cos, Pamela Howard; light, Leonard Tucker. Opened Sept 7, '78, at the Lyttleton Theatre, London; $7.20 top.
Dinsdale Landen, Polly Adams, Penelope Wilton, Frederick Treves, Basil Henson, Perry Benson, John Standing, Barbara Flynn.
09/20/78A

Pillars of the Community
(London)
Royal Shakespeare Co. revival of a drama in four acts by Henrik Ibsen. Staged, John Barton; des, Michael Annals; mus, James Walker. Opened Aug. 1, '77, at the Aldwych Theatre, London.
Ian McKellen, Eliza Ward, Howard Taylor, Paola Dionisotti, Mike Gwilym, Judi Dench, Paul Brooke, Tony Church, Ivan Beavis, Griffith Jones, Leon Tanner, Marjorie Bland, Duncan Preston, David Waller, Marie Kean, Denyse Alexander, Carmen Du Sautoy, Avril Carson, Bobbie Brown, Kim Begley, Alan Cody.
08/10/77A

Pirates at the Barn
(Sydney)
A Nimrod Theatre & Festival of Sydney presentation of a comedy in two acts by Eleanor Witcombe. Staged, Neil Armfield; des, Wendy Dickson. Opened Jan 1, '80, on Clark Island, Sydney Harbor; $6 top for adults, $4.50 for children.
Louise le Nay, Maggie Kirkpatrick, Paul Bertram, Brian Blain, Leo Bradney-George, Tony Taylor, Simon Burke, Russel Newman, Stuart Campbell, Peter Fisher.
01/23/80A

The Pleasure of His Company
(London)
Veronica Flint-Shipman & Paul Elliott revival of a comedy in two acts (four scenes) by Samuel Taylor. Staged, Peter Dews; set-cos, Terry Parsons; light, Nick Chelton. Opened July 7, '76, at the Phoenix Theatre, London; $5.40 top.
John A Tinn, Douglas Fairbanks Jr., Belinda Carroll, Dinah Sheridan, David Langton, Wilfrid Hyde-White, Michael Howarth.
07/14/76A

Plenty
(London)
National Theatre presentation of a drama in two acts (12 scenes) by David Hare; staged, Hare. Settings, Hayden Griffin; cos, Deirdre Clancy; light, Rory Dempster; mus, Nick Bicat. Opened April 12, '78, at the Lyttelton Theatre, London; $8.95 top.
Kate Nelligan, Julie Covington, Stephen Moore, Paul Freeman, Robert Ralph, Basil Henson, David Schofield, Gil Brailey, Kristopher Kum, Me Me Lai, Lindsay Duncan, Tom Durham, Frederick Treves, Timothy Davies.
04/19/78A

The Plough And The Stars
(London)
National Theatre revival of a drama in two acts by Sean O'Casey. Staged, Bill Bryden; scenery, Geoffrey Scott; light, Leonard Tucker; cos, Deirdre Clancy; mus dir, Dominic Muldowney; staff dir, Nikolas Simmonds; prodn mgr, Richard Bullimore; snd, Sue Ayliff. Opened Sep 20, '77, at the Olivier Theatre, London; $5.80 top.
Tony Doyle, Susan Fleetwood, J G Devlin, Bryan Murray, Anna Manahan, Carmel McSharry, Nora Connolly, Cyril Cusack, Dermot Crowley, Oliver Maguire, Gawn Grainger, Glyn Grain, Brenda Fricker, Harry Webster, Peggy Marshall, James Green, Tommy Makem.
10/19/77A

Plunder
(London)
National Theatre revival of a comedy in three acts (six scenes) by Ben Travers. Staged, Michael Blakemore; set, Michael Annals; light, Leonard Tucker. Opened Jan. 14, '76, at the Old Vic Theatre, London; $6.60 top.
Trevor Ray, Diana Quick, Dandy Nichols, Paul Dawkins, Frank Finlay, Catherine Harding, Polly Adams, Dinsdale Landen, Michael Beint, Brenda Kaye, Michael Keating, Carol Frazer, Ray Edwards, Desmond Adams, Michael Stroud, Barbara Keogh, Daniel Thorndike, Derek Newark, Andrew Hilton, Glyn Grain, Patrick Monckton, Peter Rocca, Rose Power, Brenda Blethyn, Nora Connolly, Jeananne Crowley, Rynagh O'Grady.
01/21/76A

The Point
(London)
Mermaid Theatre Trust, in ass'n with Nilsson House Music Inc. & Murakami-Wolf Prodns Inc., presentation of a musical in two acts by Harry Nilsson; adapt, Ron Pember, Bernard Miles. Set-cos, Peter Whiteman; light, Mick Hughes; chor, Wayne Sleep, Graham Powell; mus dir, Mike McNaught; vocal dir, Derek Damon. Opened Dec. 16, '76, at the Mermaid Theatre, London; $4.50 top.
Wayne Sleep, Bernard Miles, Colin Bennett, Kenneth Caswell, Christina Avery, Jo Warne, David Delve, Paul Aylett, Alan Bodenham, Oscar James, Peggy Ann Jones, Richard Merson, Raymond Skipp,
01/19/77A

Prayer For My Daughter
(London)
English Stage Co presentation of a play in two acts by Thomas Babe. Staged, Max Stafford-Clark; setting, Jeeda Barford, John Gunter, Margaret Martin, Chris Townsend; light, Robin Myerscough-Walker. Opened Nov. 14, '78, at Royal Court Theatre, London; $7 top.
Donal McCann, Antony Sher, Kevin McNally, John Dicks.
11/29/78A

Prisoners of Mother England
(Wellington, NZ)
Downstage Theatre presentation of a play by Roger Hall. Staged, Anthony Taylor; settings, Raymond Boyce; light, Tony Forster. Opened Sept. 27, '79, at the Hannah Playhouse, Wellington, NZ; $10 top dinner and show.
Prue Langbein, Lloyd Scott, Frances Edmond, Bruce Phillips, Helen Moulder, David McKenzie, Kathryn Rawlings, Michael McGrath, John McDavitt, Ashley Sumner, Kate Harcourt, Dulcie Smart, Paul Baeyertz.
10/17/79A

Privates on Parade
(London)
Royal Shakespeare Co. presentation of a comedy in two acts (23 scenes) by Peter Nichols. Staged, Michael Blakemore; set, Michael Annals; light, Robert Bryan; mus, Denis King; chor, Eleanor Fazan. Opened Feb. 22, '77, at the Aldwych Theatre, London; $5.65 top.
Nigel Hawthorne, Denis Quilley, David Daker, Emma Williams, Ben Cross, Joe Melia, Tim Wylton, Simon Jones, Ian Gelder, John Venning, Richard Rees.
03/02/77A

The Provk'd Wife
(London)
National Theatre revival of a play by John Vanbrugh. Staged, Peter Wood. Sets-cos, Carl Toms. Lighting, Robert Bryan; mus effects, Dominic Muldowney. Opened Oct 28, '80 at the Lyttleton Theatre, London.
John Wood, Geraldine McEwan, Nickey Henson, Dorothy Tutin, Michael Kitchen, Lindsay Duncan, Brenda Blethyn.
12/17/80A

Proxapera
(Dublin)
Edwards-MacLiammoir Dublin Gate Theatre Prdctns presentation of a drama in two acts by Peter Luke, adapted from a novel by Benedict Kiely. Staged, Hilton Edwards; set, Robert Heade. Opened Oct 3, '78 at the Gate Theatre, Dublin; $5 top.
Tony Malone, Michael Duffy, Stephen Nealon, Gathleen Nealon, Gerard Delany, Gerard McSorley, Des Nealon, Maria McDermotroe, Gerry Alexander, Derek Lord, Conor Evans.
10/18/78A

The Purging and The Singer
(London)
James Verner presentation of a double bill by Georges Feydeau and Frank Wedekind; adapt-staged, Peter Barnes; set, Michael Annals; light, Leonard Tucker. Opened Oct 11, '76, at the Old Vic Theatre, London; $5.80 top.
The Purging---Leonard Rossiter, Joan Morrow, Dilys Laye, John Phillips, Adam Armstrong, William Sleigh.
The Singer---Ashley Knight, Earl Robinson, John Stride, Joan Morrow, Leonard Rossiter, Allyson Rees, Dilys Laye, John Phillips.
10/20/76A

Rattle of a Simple Man
(London)
Duncan C Weldon, Louis I Michaels and Bob Mahoney, in ass'n with Nems Prodns, presentation of a revival of a play by Charles Dyer. Staged, Peter Egan; sets, Tanya McCallin. Opened at the Savoy Theatre, London, Sep 18, '80.
Pauline Collins, John Alderton, John Challis.
10/15/80A

The Rear Column
(London)
Michael Codron presentation of a play in three acts (six scenes plus epilog), by Simon Gray. Staged, Harold Pinter; sets, Eileen Diss; light, Nick Chelton; cos, Elizabeth Waller. Opened Feb 22, '78, at the Globe Theatre, London; $8.60 top.
Donald Gee, Jeremy Irons, Simon Ward, Clive Francis, Barry Foster, Riba Akabusi, Dorrett Thompson, Michael Forrest.
03/01/78A

The Red Devil Battery Sign
(Vienna)
Franz Schafranek presentation of a play in two parts by Tennessee Williams. Staged, Schafranek. Cos, Prof W F Adlmuller. Co-dirs; Lola Braxton, Jeremy Young. Chor, Braxton. Mus, Ingrid Fessler, Mario Ramos. Set, Tamare, Peter Kodera, Jean Veenenbos. Projections prod by Silberberger, Weiss. Opened Jan. 20, 1976, at the English Theater of Vienna.
Declan Mulholland, David McConeghey, David Powell, Ruth Brinkman, Walter Fara, Mario Ramos, Alejandro Vasquez, Alfonso Herrera, Keith Baxter, Maria Britneva, Colin Thatcher, Lois Baxter, Jeremy Young, Lance Lumsden, Nicola Filippelli, Michael Gliksmann, Russel Bittner, Michael Marinucci, Neal Bull, Rita Steinmuller.
03/03/76A

The Red Devil Battery Sign
(London)
Gene Persson presentation of a drama in three acts (nine scenes) by Tennessee Williams. Staged, Keith Baxter, David Leland; set, Bob Ringwood, Kate Owen; light-projections, David Hersey; orig mus, Mario Ramos. Opened July 7, '77, at the Phoenix Theatre, London; $6.50 top.
Ken Shorter, Michael Ensign, Garry McDermott, Glenn Williams, Don Staiton, Simon Walsh, Deborah Benzimra, Estelle Kohler, Mario Ramos, Alejandro Vasquez, Alfonso Salazar, Peter Lucas, Keith Baxter, Maria Britneva, Pierce Brosnan, Nitza Saul, Robert Henderson, Raad Rawi. Tony Garner, Tony London, Kelvin Omard, Elvis Payne, Mario Renzullo.
07/20/77A

Reflections
(London)
Louis I Michael and Duncan C Weldon presentation of a play in two acts by John Peacock, staged, Keith Hack. Sets, Voytek; cos, Judith Bland; light, Nick Chelton. Opened March 13, '80, at the Haymarket Theatre, London; $13.30 top.
Dorothy Tutin, Donald Pleasence, Gordon Gostelow, Peter Jonfield, Jeffery Kissoon, Margery Mason, Moir Leslie.
03/26/80A

Reise ins Glueck & Weitere Aussichten
(Journey Into Happiness & Further Prospects)
(Zurich)
Theatre am Neumarkt presentation of two one-act plays by Franz Xaver Kroetz. Staged, Ruediger List; set, Hanspeter Waelchili; cos, Isolde Hahn; tech dir, Georges Nagy; snd, Peter Brodbeck; light, Enzo Scanzi, Twist Sopek. Opened Oct. 15, '76, at the Theatre am Neumarkt, Zurich; $7.20 top.
Renate Steiger.
10/27/76A

Richard III
(London)
Rustaveli Company of Soviet Georgia revival (in Russian) of Shakespeare's play. Staged, Robert Sturua; translation, K Kidnadze; mus, Gia Kancheli. At the Roundhouse Theatre, London, Jan 1980.
Ramaz Chkhikvadze, Avto Makharadze, Kakhi Kavsadze, Nana Paschuasvili.
02/13/80A

Ride, Ride
(London)
Aldersgate Prodns Ltd. presentation of a musical in two acts (18 numbers); book-lyr, Alan Thornhill; mus, Penelope Thwaites; addl songs, Joe Griffiths. Staged, Peter Coe; set, Cameron Johnson; cos, Ingeborg; light, John Harrison; mus arrs, Joe Griffiths; mus dir, Ray Bishop. Opened May 24, '76, at the Westminster Theatre, London; $5.40 top.
Jane Martin, Peter Honri, Sarah Ross, Kim Goody, Raymond Skipp, Gregory Kane, Eileen Lowes, Caroline High, Jeremy Anthony, Richard Warner, Kathy Dunkerley, Jon C P Mattocks, Abby Hadfield, Richard Owens, Robert Lister, Anthony Dunston, Martin Wimbush, Chris Channer, Julia Nelson, Rosemary Jenner, Paul Large, Pauline Menear.
Musical numbers: "The Whole Wide World," "It's Exciting to be Alive," "Fiercer Than Coal," "Which is Which?" "Sweet William" "You Can't Make a Living," "Strange City," "Jehovah Reigns," "The Garden of England," "Why Me?" "He Knows My Name," "The Pillars of Society," "A Nice Little Change of Air," "One by One," "Everyone's Needed," "What Thou Hast Done," "Ride! Ride!" "Travellers' Blessing."
06/09/76A

The Ripper Show (And How They Wrote It)
(Sydney)
National Theatre Institute of Dramatic Art presentation of a play with music. Book, Frank Hatherley; mus, Jeremy Barlow. Staged, Stanley Walsh; chor, Robins Beard; scenery, Bill Pritchard; mus dir, Roma Conway; light, Moss Cooper. Opened June 15, '77, at the Jane Street Theatre, Sydney; $4 top.
Ron Graham, Maggie Kirkpatrick, Noni Hazlehurst, John Paramor, Don Reid.
06/29/77A

Rolls Hyphen Royce
(London)
Martin Gibson (in ass'n with Clement Scott, Gilbert, Richard Schulman & David Prole) presentation of a play in two acts by William Douglas Home. Staged, Allan Davis; set, Martin Johns; cos, Anthony Mendleson; light, Andrew Bridge; mus-snd effects, John Dalby. Opened May 11, '77, at the Shaftesbury Theatre, London; $6.55 top.
Wilfrid Hyde-White, Jean Holness, Hilary Wontner, Peter Egan, Leon Eagles, Derek Wright, Alister Cameron, David Bedard, Barry Justice, Richard Leech, Alfred Marks, John Paul, Maggie Petersen, Natalie Caron, David Masterman, John Atterbury, Paul Toothill, Shelly Power, Jane Downs, Simon Barry, Charles Rogers,
06/01/77A

The Romans in Britain
(London)
National Theatre presentation of a play in two acts by Howard Brenton. Staged, Michael Bogdanov; set, Martin Johns; cos, Stephanie Howard; light, Chris Ellis; snd, Rob Barnard. Opened Oct 16, '80, at the Olivier Theatre, London: $14.30 top.
John Normington, James Carter, Jill Stanford, Greg Hicks, Michael Fenner, Roger Gartland, Yvonne Bryceland, James Hayes, Peter Dawson, Malachi Bogdanov, Loraine Sass, Susan Williamson, Chloe Needham, Gordon Whiting, Anna Carteret, Terry Diab, Jane Evers, Elliott Cooper, Peter Needham, Michael Beint, Robert Ralph, Robert Oates, Peter Sproule, Michael Bryant, Nigel Bellairs, Artro Morris, William Sleigh, Colin Rae, Glenn Williams, Brian Kent, Peter Harding, Peter Dawson, James Hayes, Melvyn Bedford, Stephen Moore.
10/22/80A

Rookery Nook
(London)
H M Tennent revival of a farce by Ben Travers; staged, Frank Dunlop; setting, Michael Annals. Opened Nov. 20, '79, at Her Majesty's Theatre, London; $13.10 top.
Nicky Henson, Josephine Tewson, Andrew Robertson, Dora Bryan, Terence Frisby, Geoffrey Lumsden, Nina Thomas, Peter Schofield, Cherith Mellor.
11/28/79A

Rosalinda
(Johannesburg)
Performing Arts Council of the Transvaal presentation of a ballet in two acts, based on the Johann Strauss operetta, "Die Fledermaus." Chor, Ronald Hynd; mus arr, John Lanchbery; settings-cos, Peter Dogherty; light, Nick Michaletos; orch dir, Terence Kern. Opened April 24, '78, at the Johannesburg Civic Theatre; $8 top.
Eugene Christensen, Faye Daniel, Gwen Morris, Edgardo Hartley, James Riveros, Geoffrey Sutherland, Bruce Simpson.
05/31/78A

Rose
(London)
Colin Brough presentation of a play in two acts by Andrew Davies. Staged, Alan Dossor; settings, John Gunter; light, Andy Phillips;

Rose
(Cont)
cos, Lindy Hemmings. Opened Feb 28, '80, at the Duke of York's Theatre, London: $14.90 top.
Glenda Jackson, Jean Heywood, Stephanie Cole, Gillian Martell, Tom Georgeson, Diana Davies, Richard Vanstone, David Daker.
03/05/80A

Rosmersholm
(London)
Duncan C Weldon & Louis I Michaels revival of a drama in four acts by Henrik Ibsen; adapt, Jeremy Brooks. Staged, Clifford Williams; set, Ralph Koltai; light, James Baird. Opened Oct 19, '77, at the Haymarket Theatre, London; $7.80 top.
Claire Bloom, Constance Chapman, Michael Aldridge, Daniel Massey, Frank Middlemass, Terrence Hardiman.
10/26/77A

Rudi
(Berlin)
Schaubuehne and Halleschen Ufer presentation of a dramatic reading in one act, based on the Berlin novel of same name by Bernard von Brentano. Staged, Klaus Michael Grueber; set, Antonio Recalcati; cos, Dagmar Niefind; dramatic advisors, Ellen Hammer, Bernard Paultrat. Opened Jun 20, '79, at the Hotel Esplanade, West Berlin; $10 top.
Paul Burian, Ellfriede Falke, Alexander Schubart.
08/08/79A

Rum an Coca-Cola
(London)
English Stage Co. presentation of a play in two acts by Mustapha Matura. Staged, Donald Howarth; set, Jocelyn Herbert; light, Jack Raby. Opened Nov. 3, '76, at the Royal Court Theatre, London; $5.65 top.
Norman Beaton, Trevor Thomas.
11/17/76A

Rum for Your Money
(Sydney)
Marian St Theatre presentation of a musical in two acts, with book and some lyrics by David Nettheim, based on an outline by Timothy Bean and Peter James from an idea by Alastair Duncan, based on "January the Twenty-Sixth," a recording commissioned by the Bank of New South Wales with book by Jon Kingsmill, lyr, John McKellar and Kingsmill; mus, Leo Breen, Sybil Graham, John Shaw, Frank Smith, James Wallett and Bob Young. Additional mus by mus dir Guy Simpson. Staged, Alastair Duncan; dsgn, Michael O'Kane; chor, Keith Little, cos, Ann Lidstone; light, Michael Ney. Opened May 8, '80, at the Marian St Theatre, Sydney: $9 top.
Peter Whitford, Valerie Bader, Roy Dunbar, Ray Duparc, Roland Hill, Arthur Pickering, Stephen Thomas, Carmen Tanti.
05/28/80A

Sacred Cow
(Sydney)
Eric Dare presentation, in ass'n with J C Wiliamson Prodns, of a solo revue devised-dir-performed, Reg Livermore. Staged, Peter Batey; color, Martin Smith; cos, Garry Cox; chor, Karen Johnson; projected cartoons, Bruce Petty; mus dir, Peter Kenny. Opened Feb. 14, '79, at Her Majesty's Theatre, Sydney; $9.80 top.
Reg Livermore.
02/28/79A

Saki
(London)
John de Lannoy, for Planned Theatre Ltd, presentation of a one-man show by Emlyn Williams from the stories of Saki. Staged, Peter Woodthorpe; light, Joe Davis. Opened Sep 22, '77 at the Apollo Theatre, London. $7 top.
Emlyn Williams.
10/19/77A

Salad Days
(London)
David Conville, in ass'n with Gordon Faith and Jeffrey Freilich, revival of a musical in two acts (16 scenes, 13 numbers); book-lyr, Dorothy Reynolds, Julian Slade; mus, Slade. Staged, David Conville; chor, Wayne Sleep; set, Tim Goodchild; light, Brian Benn; mus dir, Neil Rhoden. Opened April 14, '76, at the Duke of York's Theatre, London; $6.50 top.
Bill Kerr, Christina Matthews, Adam Bareham, Sheila Steafel, David Morton, Tricia George, Elizabeth Seal, David Alder, Colette Kelly, Ian Talbot, Louis Hammond, Osmund Bullock, Malcolm Rennie, Melanie Parr.
Musical numbers; "The Things That Are Done by a Don," "We Said We Wouldn't Look Back," "Find Yourself Something to Do," "I Sit in the Sun," "Oh Look at Me," "It's Hush-Hush," "Out of Breath," "Cleopatra," "Sand in My Eyes," "It's Easy to Sing," "We're Looking For a Piano," "The Time of My Life," "We Don't Understand Our Children."
05/05/76A

Same Time, Next Year
(London)
Michael Linnit presentation of Morton Gottlieb's prodn of a play in two acts (six scenes) by Bernard Slade; staged, Eric Thompson (orig New York prodn staged, Gene Saks); cos, Michael Stennet; des, Alan Tagg; light, Mick Hughes. Opened at Prince of Wales Theatre, London, Sept. 23, '76; $5.90 top.
Michael Crawford, Frances Cuka.
10/13/76A

Saratoga
(London)
Royal Shakespeare Co revival of a comedy in five-acts (one intermission), by Bronson Howard. Staged, Ronald Eyre; scenery, Jocelyn Herbert; cos, David Walker; mus arr, Carl Davis; chor, David Toguri; light, Brian Harris. Opened Dec. 21, '78, at the Aldwych Theatre, London; $9 top.
Dennis Waterman, James Laurenson, Brian Hayes, Jeffery Dench, James Berwick, Alan David, Paul Imbusch, Michael Bertenshaw, Bille Brown, Stephen Jenn, Keith Hodiak, Reginald Tsiboe, Kelvin Omard, David Shaw-Parker, Polly James, Cherie Lunghi, Sheila Reid, Joanna McCallum, Maxine Audley, Denyse Alexander, Shirley King, Roger Martin, Deirdra Morris, Peter Tullo.
01/10/79A

Scanlan
(Sydney)
Nimrod Street Theatre Co Ltd, presentation of a comedy in one act by Barry Oakley. Staged, Neil Armfield. Opened July 31 at Nimord Downstairs Theatre, $4.00 top.
Max Gilliese.
08/27/80A

The Script: SEE Le Scenario

Sentenced To Life
(London)
Aldersgate Productions presentation of a play in two acts by Malcolm Muggeridge and Alan Thornhill. Staged, David William; setting, Alan Barlow; light, Basil Soper. Opened May 17, '78, at the Westminster Theatre, London; $6.40 top.
Denys Hawthorne, Ruth Goring, John Byron, Susan Colverd, Robin Wentworth, Mary Wimbush.
05/24/78A

Sergeant Ola and His Followers
(London)
English Stage Co presentation of a play in two acts by David Lan. Staged, Max Stafford-Clark. Settings, Peter Hartwell; light, Jack Raby; mus, Gasper Lawal, Andy Roberts. Opened Oct. 23, '79, at Royal Court Theatre, London; $8.45 top.
Ben Tomas, Bruce Alexander, Mia Soterious, Sarah Lam, Will Knightley, Norman Beaton, Paul Kember, Burt Caesar, David Rintoul, Jimmy Findley, Joseph Charles.
10/31/79A

Sextet
(London)
John Gale presentation of a comedy in two acts (four scenes) by Michael Pertwee. Staged, Robin Midgley; set, Hutchinson Scott; light, Chris Ellis; cos, Clive Lavagna. Opened April 13, '77, at the Criterion Theatre, London; $6.70 top.
Peter Blythe, Gareth Gwyn-Jones, Angela Scoular, Julia Lockwood, Julian Fellowes, Leslie Phillips, Carol Hawkins.
04/20/77A

Show Boat
(West Berlin)
Theater des Westens prodn of a musical in two acts by Oscar Hammerstein 2d, based on the novel by Edna Ferber; mus, Jerome Kern; staged, Edward M Greenberg; mus dir, Wolfgang Peters; chor, Sharon Halley; settings, Grady Larkens; cos, Marianne Kuehnel; German translation, Jane Furch-Allers. Opened Oct. 19, '79, at the Theatre des Westens, West Berlin; $15 top.
Uwe Helfrich, Lutz Riedel, Eddy Tilman, Vera Little, Ilse Kuenkele, Heinz Fabian, Irene Ziedek, Silvio Francesco, Georg Tryphon, Margarita Cantero, Joachim Kammer, Guenther Kieslich, Jutta-Renate Ihloff, Gilbert Price, Rudolf Lasch.
11/28/79A

Shut Your Eyes And Think Of England
(London)
John Gale presentation of a comedy in two acts by Anthony Marriott and John Chapman. Staged, Patrick Garland. Set, Peter Rice; light, Joe Davis. Opened Nov. 15, '77, at the Apollo Theatre, London; $8 top.
Frank Thornton, Madeline Smith, Donald Sinden, Jan Holden, Willoughby Goddard, Peter Bland, Patsy Rowlands, Ken Wynne, Robin Parkinson.
11/23/77A

Side by Side by Sondheim
(London)
Mermaid Theatre, in ass'n with H M Tennent & Cameron Mackintosh, presentation of a revue based on the mus-lyr of Stephen Sondheim (add'l mus, Leonard Bernstein, Mary Rodgers, Richard Rodgers, Jule Styne). Staged, Ned Sherrin; mus staging, Bob Howe; mus supv, Ray Cook; mus dirs, Tim Higgs, Stuart Pedlar; cos, Gina Fratini; light, John Wood. Opened May 4, '76, at the Mermaid Theatre, London; $5 top.
Millicent Martin, Julia McKenzie, David Kernan, Ned Sherrin.
05/26/76A

Side By Side By Sondheim
(Sydney)
H M Tennent Ltd and Cameron Mackintosh Productions with Globe Theatre Productions Pty Ltd by arrangement, with Incomes Co (Theatre) Ltd and The MLC Theatre Royal Co presentation of a musical entertainment in two acts. Exec prod, Len Evans; prod, Helen Montagu; staged, Bill Cronshaw; mus dir, Ray Cook; mus staging, Robina Beard; des, Peter Docherty; stage dir, Walter Van Nieuwkuyk. Opened Sep 27, '77 at Theatre Royal, Sydney; $8.40 top.
Jill Perryman, Geraldine Morrow, Bartholomew John, John Laws.
10/19/77A

The Siege of Frank Sinatra
(Sydney)
King O'Malley Theatre Co presentation of a comedy-drama in two acts by Denis Whitburn. Staged, Lex Marinos; des, Axel Bartz; light, Grant Fraser. Opened Nov 7, '80 at the Stables Theatre, Sydney: $6 top.
Max Cullen, Lou Brown, Penny Cook.
12/03/80A

Signed and Sealed
(London)
H.M. Tennent presentation of a farce in three acts; trans-adapt, Christopher Hampton from "Le Mariage de Barillon," by Georges Feydeau and Maurice Desvallieres. Staged, Patrick Garland; set, Stefanos Lazaridis; cos, Beatrice Dawson; light, David Hersey. Opened June 23, '76, at the Comedy Theatre, London; $6.25 top.
Peter Glaze, Barry Stanton, Gerald James, Kenneth Williams, Alun Lewis, Peggy Mount, Jane Carr, Paul Hardwick, Floella Benjamyin, Neil France, Bryan Pringle, Sue Aldred, Matthew Francis, Roy Purkiss.
07/07/76A

Sisterly Feelings
(London)
National Theatre presentation of a play in two acts (four scenes) by Alan Ayckbourn. Staged, Ayckbourn, Christopher Morahan; setting, Alan Tagg; cos, Lindy Hemming; light, David Hersey. Opened Jun 3, '80, at the Olivier Theatre, London: $13.90 top.
Andrew Cruickshank, Michael Bryant, Susan Williamson, Penelope Wilton, Michael Gambon, Anna Carteret, Simon Callow, Greg Hicks, Selina Cadell, Stephen Moore, Gordon Whiting, Michael Fenner.
06/11/80A

Si T'es Beau, T'es Con
(If You're Good Looking, You're A Dope)
(Paris)
Patrick Barroux presentation of a comedy in four acts by Francoise Dorin. Staged, Jacques Rosny; set, Hubert Monloup; cos, Phillippe Venet, Francesco Smalto. Opened Sept. 20, '77, at the Theatre Des Arts, Paris; $12 top.
Jean-Claude Brialy, Nicolle Chollet, Paul Le Person, Andre Falcon, Sabine Azema, Serge Maillat, Jacques Jouanneau, Madeleine Cheminat, Emmanuelle Bondeville.
09/28/77A

Sleak
(London)
Sammy Sphincter presentation, for Harami League & Blackhill Enterprises, of a play with mus in two acts by C.P. Lee. Staged, Charlie Hanson; light, Jack Raby; snd, John Del'Nero. Opened Sept. 12, '77, at the Royal Court Theatre, London; $4 top.
Jimmy Hibbert, Judy Lloyd, Michael Deeks, Bob Harding, Gordon Kaye, Arthur Kelly, C.P. Lee, Bruce Mitchell, Les Prior.
09/21/77A

Sleuth
(London)
Ray Cooney, in ass'n with Michael White, rev of a play in two acts by Anthony Shaffer. Staged, Hugh Goldie; sets, John Page; light, Neil Goodwill. Opened March 7, '78, at the Savoy Theatre, London; $7.70 top.
Patrick Cargill, Tony Anholt, Robert Dexter, Peter Stannage, Jack Francis.
04/05/78A

'S Loch im Chopf
(A Hole in the Head)
(Zurich)
Theatre am Neumarkt presentation of a comedy in five acts by Wolfgang Deichsel, based on "L'Affaire de la Rue de Lourcine" by Eugene Labiche. Swiss dialect adapt, Rene Scheibli. Staged, Dieter Bitterli; set-cos, Ambrosius Humm; tech dir, Georges Nagy; light, Twist Sopek, Enzo Scanzi; snd, Peter Brodbeck, Alex Hiltebrand. Opened Jan. 28, '77, at the Theatre am Neumarkt, Zurich; $7.20 top.
Mathias Ghadedinger, Renate Steiger, Katja Frueh, Urs Bihler, Herbert Leiser, Bernd Spitzer.
02/09/77A

Small Change
(London)
English Stage Co. presentation of a drama in two acts by Peter Gill. Staged, Gill; scenery, William Dudley; cos, Deirdre Clancy, Pippy Bradshaw; light, Gareth Jones. Opened July 8, '76, at the Royal Court Theatre, London; $5.40 top.
James Hazeldine, June Watson, Phillip Joseph, Marjorie Yates.
07/21/76A

Some Great Fools From History
(Sydney)
Australian Elizabethan Theatre Trust presentation, in ass'n with the Festival of Perth, of a solo-show with Nola Rae. Staged, Chris Harris; dsgn, Matthew Ridout. Opened May '79, at the Everest Theatre, Sydney; $7.50 top.
05/23/79A

Some of My Best Friends Are Women
(Melbourne)
Melbourne Theatre Company presentation of entertainment in two parts written by Therese and Leonard Radic. Staged, Ray Lawler; scenery, Tony Tripp. Opened, July 15, '76 at St Martin's Theatre, Melbourne, $7.50 top.
Patricia Kennedy, Frederick Parslow, Jan Friedl, Gary Down, Christine Amor.
07/28/76A

Something's Afoot
(London)
Danny O'Donovan & Alan Cluer presentation of a musical in two acts (11 numbers); book-mus-lyr, James McDonald, David Vos, Robert Gerlach; addl mus, Ed Linderman. Staged-chor, Tony Tanner; scenery, Richard Seger; light, Robert Bryan; mus dir, Ian MacPherson. Opened June 16, '77, at the Ambassadors Theatre, London; $6.90 top.
Ruth Madoc, Peter Rutherford, Michael Bevis, Sally Smith, Robert Dorning, Dudley Stevens, Joyce Grant, Peter Bayliss, Sheila Bernette, Martin Smith.
Musical numbers: "A Marvellous Weekend," "Something's Afoot," "Carry On," "I Don't Know Why I Trust You (But I Do)," "The Man With the Ginger Moustache," "Suspicious," "The Legal Heir," "You Fell Out of the Sky," "Dinghy," "I Owe It All," "New Day."
06/22/77A

Songbook
(London)
Jack Gill by arrangement with Stoll Productions & The Cambridge Theatre Co presentation of a musical in two acts (33 numbers); mus, Monty Norman; lyr, Julian More, book, Norman and More; staged, Jonathan Lynn; mus staging, Gillian Lynne; mus dirs, Ray Cook, Grant Hossack; vocal arr, Cook; setting, Saul Radomsky; light, Joe Davis. Opened July 28, '79, at the Globe Theatre, London; $16 top.
Anton Rodgers, Gemma Craven, Diane Langton, Andrew C Wadsworth, David Healy, Harold Prince (voice).
Musical numbers: "Songbook," "East River Rhapsody," "Talking Picture Show," "Such Sweet Poison," "Mister Destiny,"

Songbook
(Cont)
"Your Time Is Different to Mine," "Pretty Face," "Je Vous Aime, Milady," "Les Halles," "Olympics Song," "Nazi Party Pooper," "I'm Gonna Take Him Home to Momma," "Bumpity-Bump," "The Girl in the Window," "Victory V," "April in Wisconsin," "Songbook" (reprise), "Happy Hickory," "Lovely Sunday Mornin'," "Rusty's Dream Ballet," "A Storm in My Heart," "The Pokenhatchit Protest Committee," "Happy Hickory" (reprise), "I Accuse," "Messages I," "Messages II," "I Found Love," "Don't Play That Lovesong Any More," "Golden Oldie," "Climbin'," "Nostalgia," "Don't Play That Lovesong Any More" (reprise), "Songbook" (reprise).
08/01/79A

Son Of Betty
(Melbourne)
Eric Dare presentation of a revue in two parts. Staged, Peter Batey; cos, Garry Cox; chor, Karen Johnson; light, Graham Beatty; AV, Jim Mann. Opened Feb 29, '80, at Her Majesty's Theatre, Melbourne.
Reg Livermore; Wellington Bewts Burlesk Bank dir by Peter Kenny.
04/02/80A

Son Of Betty
(Sydney)
Eric Dare & J C Williamson Prodn Ltd presentation of a solo show in two acts, devised and dsgn, and with all spoken material written by Reg Livermore; staged, Peter Batey; cos, Garry Cox; chor, Karen Johnson; mus dir, Peter Kenny. Opened May 14, '80 at Her Majesty's Theatre, Sydney; $11.20 top.
Reg Livermore.
05/28/80A

Songs From Sideshow Alley
(Sydney)
Classic Corp presentation of a musical in two acts, mus-lyr, Robyn Archer. Staged, Rodney Fisher; set, Ian Robinson; cos, Ron Williams; chor, Keith Bain; light, Peter Holderness. Opened Oct. 29, '80 at the Paris Theatre, Sydney; $10.50 top.
Nancye Hayes, Maggie Kirkpatrick, Andrew de Teliga, John Summers, Peter Deane-Butcher.
Musical numbers: "The Song of the Spruikers," "The Song of Answering Back," "Solidarity in the Alley," "The Justification Song," "Whaddya Call a Good Time?" "A Chorus of Cocky Domination," "The Song of Unfashionable Anklets," "The Backyard Abortion Waltz," "Wha' ha Gonna Do With Your Last Two Dollars?" "The Song of Increasing Dicates," "Puttin on a Show," "Saturday Night in the Alley," "When Your Timing's Right."
12/31/80A

Songs My Mother Didn't Teach Me
(Sydney)
Australian Elizabethan Theatre Trust presentation of a musical in two acts, with book and additional lyr by Peter Batey, mus-lyr, John Mulder. Staged, Peter Batey; chor, Karen Johnson. Opened Jan 22, '80, at Bondi Pavilion Theatre, Sydney, $8.50 top.
Liz Harris, Karen Johnson, John Mulder.
01/30/80A

The Sower and the Reaper
(Sydney)
Ensemble Prodns in association with the Festival of Sydney, presentation of a drama in two acts by John Summers. Staged, Gary Baxter; scenery and cos, Richard Heller; light, Joddi Speight. Opened Jan 22 '80, at the Ensemble-at-the-Stables Theatre, Sydney: $5 top.
Angela Bennie, John Hageman, Patricia Jones, Michael Ross, Denise Otto, Anthony Martin.
02/13/80A

So Who Needs Men!
(London)
Grosvenor Entertainments presentation of a play in two acts by John Briley. Staged, Briley; scenery-cos, Pamela Ingram; light, Christopher Norman. Opened Oct. 7, '76, at the New London Theatre, London; $5.60 top.
Katy Manning, Primmi Townsend, Grahame Mallard, Peter Denyer, Jeff Rawle, Malcolm Bullivant, Harold Kasket, Thelma Ruby, Daphne Goddard.
10/20/76A

Spinechiller
(London)
Robert S Fishko & Stockton Briggle, in ass'n with Charles J Davis, Dennis Zorn and Ray Cooney, presentation of a melodrama in two acts by George Baxt. Staged, Stockton Briggle; sets, Hugh Durrant; light, Robert Ornbo. Opened Jan 5, '78, at the Duke of York's Theatre, London; $7.15 top.
Sian Phillips, Liz Gebhardt, Gerard Hely, Christine Shaw, Peter Small, Samuel E Wright, Thomasine Heiner, Caroline Wilkins, Michael Malnick, Harry Ditson, Paul Daneman, Gretchen Franklin, Nigel McLauchlan, Joshua Bancel.
02/01/78A

Spokesong
(London)
Jimmy Jacobs & Dan Crawford presentation of a play in two acts by Stewart Parker; songs, Jimmy Kennedy. Staged, Robert Gillespie; set, John Scully; cos, Maggie Smith; light, Molly Friedel; mus arrs, John Holbrooke. Opened Feb. 16, '77, at the Vaudeville Theatre, London; $6 top.
Robert Bridges, Niall Buggy, Annabel Leventon, Patrick Waldron, Valerie Hermanni, Donald MacIver.
03/02/77A

Stage Struck
(London)
Michael Codron presentation of a play in two acts (three scenes) by Simon Gray. Staged, Stephen Hollis; setting, Carl Toms; light, Mick Hughes. Opened Nov. 21, '79, at the Vaudeville Theatre, London; $14.20 top.
Andrew Sharp, Alan Bates, Sheila Ballantine, Nigel Stock.
11/28/79

Starmania
(Paris)
Roland Hubert-Perrier-Europe 1 presentation of a rock-opera in two acts (28 numbers); book-lyr-mus, Michel Berger, Luc Plamondon. Staged, Tom O'Horgan; cos, Randy Barcelo; set, Bill Stabile; light, John MacLain; snd, Abe Jacob; movement, Serge Gubel Mann; mus dir, Michel Bernholc. Opened April 10, '79, at the Palais des Congres, Paris; $20 top.
France Gall, Diane Dufresne, Daniel Balavoine, Nanette Workman, Rene Joly, Etienne Chicot, Gregory Ken, 70 actors, singers, dancers.
Musical numbers: "Il Se Passe Quelque Chose a Monopolis," "Quand on Arrive en Ville," "Travesti," "Banlieue Nord," "La Complainte de la Serveuse Automate," "Le Blues du Businessman," "Starmania, Starmania," "Un Garcon Pas Comme les Autres," "La Chanson de Ziggy," "Un Enfant de la Pollution," "Au Secours, J'ai Besoin d'Amour," "Paranoia," "Le Reve de Stella Starlight," "Les Adieux d'un Sex Symbol," "Je suis Avec Johnny Rockfort a la Vie, a la Mort," "S O S d'Un Terrien en Detresse," "Si Vous Voulez un Homme Nouveau, Zero C'Est l'Homme Qu'Il Vous Faut," "Sex Shops, Cinemas, Pornos," "On Etait des Vieux si heureux," "Quand on n'a Plus Rien a Perdre," "Les Uns Contre Les Autres," "Ego Trip," "Petite Musique Terrienne," "Monopolis," "Disc-Jockey's Song," "Ce Soir on Dance au Naziland," "Le Tango de l'Amour et de la Mort," "Le Monde est Stone."
05/30/79A

The Star Turns Red
(Dublin)
National Theatre Society presentation of two-act drama by Sean O'Casey. Staged, Tomas MacAnna; sets-cos, Bronwen Casson; mus, Peter O'Brien; light, Tony Wakefield. Opened Feb. 2, '78 at Abbey Theatre, Dublin; $5 top.
Desmond Perry, May Cluskey, Niall O'Brien, Ronan Paterson, Bernadette Shortt, Larry Murphy, Gerard Walsh, Bill Foley, Patrick Laffan, Michael O'Briain, Mick Lally, Geoff Golden, Micheal O'hAonghusa, Peadar Lamb, Raymond Hardie, Pat Abernethy, Philip O'Flynn, Edward Golden, Conal Kearney, Macdara O'Fatharta, Maire O'Neill, Michael O'Sullivan, Se Phelan, Raymond Hardie, Frank Melia, Bob Carlile, Kate Flynn, Sean Lawlor.
04/05/78A

State of the Play
(Wellington, NZ)
Downstage Theatre presentation of a play by Roger Hall. Staged, Anthony Taylor; decor, Paul Shirriffs; light, Malcolm Savage. Opened June 8, '78, at the Hannah Playhouse, Wellington, NZ; $9.50 top, dinner and show.
Peter Vere-Jones, Ray Henwood, Penny Downie, Anne Budd, Stephen Gledhill, Michael McGrath.
08/16/78A

State of the Play
(Auckland, NZ)
Mercury Theatre presentation of a play in three acts by Roger Hall. Staged, Anne Flannery; scenery-cos, Arthur Thompson; light, John McKay. Opened at the Mercury 2 Theatre, Auckland, NZ; $4 top.
David Weatherley, John Atha, Claire Oberman, Donna Akersten, Arthur Wright, Clifford Wallace.
05/23/79A

State of Revolution
(London)
National Theatre presentation of a drama in two acts by Robert Bolt. Staged, Christopher Morahan; set, Ralph Koltai; light, David Hersey. Opened May 26, '77, at the Lyttleton Theatre, London; $7.75 top.
Stephen Moore, John Normington, Michael Bryant, John Blessed, Sara Kestelman, Trevor Martin, Terence Rigby, Anthony Douse, Catherine Harding, Michael Stroud, Godfrey James, John Labanowski, Louis Haslar, Antony Higginson, John Pollendine, James Leith, June Watson, Peter Tilbury, Michael Kitchen, Peter Gordon, Edwin Brown, Sarah Simmons, Julian Battersby, Roger Gartland, Julia Pascal, Diana Payan, Robert Ralph, Andrew Tourell, Drew Wood.
06/01/77A

Stevie
(London)
Duncan C Weldon and Louis I Michaels presentation of a drama in two acts by Hugh Whitemore. Staged, Clifford Williams; set, John Gunter; light, Andy Phillips. Opened March 23, '77, at the Vaudeville Theatre, London; $6 top.
Glenda Jackson, Mona Washbourne, Peter Eyre.
03/30/77A

The Story Goes. . .
(Dublin)
Irish National Theatre presentation of one-man show by Eamon Kelly; staged, Michael Colgan; setting, Maebh Browne; light, Leslie Scott. Opened July 3, '79, at the Peacock Theatre, Dublin; $4 top.
Eamon Kelly.
08/01/79A

The Streets of London
(London)
Archie Stirling in association with Stoll Prodns, revival of a melodrama in five acts (13 mus numbers) by Dion Boucicault; mus, Gary Carpenter; lyr, Ian Barnett; staged, Diane Cilento; mus staging, Noel Tovey; set, Hayden Griffin, Peter Hartwell; cos, Frances Tempest; light, Howard Eaton; mus dir, Roger Moffatt. Opened Oct 21, '80, at Her Majesty's Theatre, London: $17.10 top.
William Squire, Royce Mills, Michael Carter, David Mallinson, Shaun Curry, Diana Martin, Debra Jansen, Bruce Green, Max Latimer, June Shand, John Denton, Joy Graham, John Scott Martin, Stephen Kebell, Jean Reeve, Sally Hall, Chris Cummings, Chris Hale, Helen Cherry, Susannah Fellows, Richard Walsh, John Watts, Jane Wymark, Peter Spraggon, Patsy Byrne, Kim Smith.
Musical number: - "Gold!" "Not on Your Life," "When Livingstone Makes Me His Wife," "Fare Thee Well," "Winter Music," "Miss Crotchetty Quaver," "Second Flooring," "Australia!" "The Salons of the Wealthy," "The Streets of London Gallop," "Fortune's Ruin," "Fortune's Ruin" (reprise), "Gold! (reprise).
10/29/80A

Strife
(London)
Nat'l Theatre Co revival of a drama in two acts (four scenes) by John Galsworthy. Staged by Christopher Morahan; settings, John Bury; costumes, Deirdre Clancy; light, David Hersey. Opened Nov 30, '78, at the Olivier Theatre, London; $8.40 top.
Andrew Cruickshank, John Harding, Peter Copley, Nicholas Selby, Daniel Thorndike, Peter Needham, Glyn Grain, Sara Kestelman, Brian Kent, Donald Gee, Michael Bryant, Anthony Douse, Roger Gartland, Stanley Lloyd, Michael Beint, Tamara Hinchco, Brenda Blethyn, Madoline Thomas, Edna Dore, Marianne Morley, William Smoker, Ned Vukovic, Elliott Cooper, David Pugh, John Rees, William Sleigh, John Atkinson, Philip Croskin, Martyn Whitby, Timothy Norton, Irene Gorst, Nik Forster, Robin Meredith, Jane Evers, Peggy Marshall, Michael Howley, Dennis Tynsley.
12/06/78A

Sugar and Spice
(London)
English Stage Co prodn of a play in two acts by Nigel Williams. Staged, Bill Alexander; scenery, Mary Moore; light, Jack Raby; snd, Charles Wright; Opened Oct 13, '80, at the Royal Court Theatre, London: $12 top.
Carole Hayman, Tammi Jacobs, Toyah Willcox, Caroline Quentin, Gwyneth Strong, John Fowler, Daniel Peacock, Tony London, Leroi Samuels.
11/05/80A

The Sunny South
(Sydney)
Sydney Theatre Co presentation of a play in five acts (one intermission) by George Darrell. Staged, Richard Wherrett; scenery, Ian Robinson; cos, Vicki Feitscher; light, Jerry Luke; mus arr, Terence Clarke; chor, Robyn Moase; fight arr, Tex Clarke. Opened Jan 1, '80, at the Sydney Opera House Drama Theatre; $9.20 top.
John Hargreaves, John Frawley, Peter Carroll, George Spartels, Robin Ramsay, John Allen, Ronald Falk, John McTernan, John Gaden, Brandon Burke, Andrew Tighe, Geoffrey Clendon, Bob Baxter, Robert Alexander, Lynette Curran, Geraldine Turner, Janice Finn.
02/06/80A

Swann With Topping
(London)
Harold Fielding presentation of an Upstream Theatre Club prodn of a revue wri-comp-perf, Donald Swann, Frank Topping. Scenery, Charlotte Goodfield; light, Erid Delzenne; snd, Edward Fardell. Opened Oct 2, '80, at the Ambassadors Theatre, London; $13.20 top.
Donald Swann, Frank Topping.
10/22/80A

Sweeney Todd
(London)
Robert Stigwood, in ass'n with David Land by arrangement with Richard Barr, Charles Woodward, Robert Fryer, Mary Lea Johnson & Martin Richards, presentation of a musical in two acts (25 numbers); mus-lyr, Stephen Sondheim; book, Hugh Wheeler, based on a version of "Sweeney Todd" by Christopher Bond, from a 19th century melodrama by George Didbin-Pitt. Staged, Harold Prince; chor, Larry Fuller; scenery, Eugene Lee; cos, Franne Lee; light, Ken Billington; orch, Jonathan Tunick; mus dir, Ray Cook. Opened Jul 2, '80, at the Drury Lane Theatre, London: $24 top.
Denis Quilley, Sheila Hancock, Dilys Watling, Michael Staniforth, Andrew C Wadsworth, Mandy More, Austin Kent, David Wheldon-Williams,
Others: - Sylvia Beamish, Michael Bulman, Simon Butteriss, Linda D'Arcy, John Aron, Oz Clarke. Victoria Duncan, Katherine Dyson, Mercia Glossop, Andrew Golder, Stuart Haycock, Stephen Hill, Marie Jackson, Diane Mansfield, Neil Michael, William Relton, Myra Sands, Suzanne Sloan, Grant Smith, Rex Taylor, Craig, David Urwin.
Musical numbers: - "The Ballad of Sweeney Todd," "No Place Like London," "The Barber and His Wife," "The Worst Pies in London," "Poor Things," "My Friends," "Green Finch and Linnet Bird," "Ah, Miss," "Johanna," "Pirelli's Miracle Elixir," "The Contest," "Wait," "Kiss Me," "Ladies in Their Sensitivities," "Quartet," "Pretty Women," "Epiphany," "A Little Priest," "God, That's Good!" "Johanna"(reprise), "By the Sea," "Not While I'm Around," "City on Fire!" "Final Sequence," "Ballad of Sweeney Todd" (reprise).
07/09/80A

Syndrome
(Sydney)
Ensemble Theatre Co presentation of a play in three acts by Ken Hayles. Staged, Tony Ingersent; prod, Megan Fry; dsgnr, Doug Anderson; light, Peter Critchley; snd, Rod Dyson. Opened Jan. 9, '79, at the Ensemble-at-the Stables, Sydney; $4 top.
Sonja Tallis, Jyoti Mukherjee, Jenifer Dwyer, Allan Penney, Gillian Levett.
01/24/79A

Taking Steps
(London)
Michael Codron presentation of play in two acts by Alan Ayckbourn. Staged, Michael Rudman; scenery, Alan Tagg; cos, Lindy Hemming; light, Gerry Jenkinson. Opened Sep 2, '80, at the Lyric Theatre, London: $16.80 top.
Nicola Pagett, Paul Chapman, Michael Maloney, Dinsdale Landen, Richard Kane, Wendy Murray.
09/10/80A

Talbot's Box
(London)
English Stage Co. presentation of an Abbey Theatre Co. prodn of a play in two acts by Thomas Kilroy. Staged, Patrick Mason; set-cos, Wendy Shea; light, Tony Wakefield. Opened Nov. 23, '77, at the Royal Court Theatre, London; $5.50 top.
John Molloy, Stephen Brennan, Clive Geraghty, Ingrid Craigie, Eileen Colgan.
11/30/77A

Tales From the Vienna Woods
(London)
National Theatre presentation of a revival of a drama in two acts by Odon von Horvath (English trans, Christopher Hampton); staged, Maximilian Schell. Set, Timothy O'Brien, Tazeena Firth; light, David Hersey; mus arr-dir, Robert Stewart. Opened Jan. 26, '77, at the Olivier Theatre, London; $7.90 top.

Susan Williamson, Stephen Rea, Madoline Thomas, Oliver Cotton, Elizabeth Spriggs, Pitt Wilkinson, Warren Clarke, Nicholas Selby, Vivienne Burgess, Kate Nelligan, Paul Rogers, Rosamund Greenwood, Ann Way, Struan Rodger, Rowena Shah, Toyah Willcox, Sylvia Coleridge, Anne Leon, Ellen Pollock, John Gill, Brenda Blethyn, Timothy Block, Peter Carlisle, Trevor Ray.

With: Diane Bates, Nicholas Frith, Trevor Goodall, Shulie Bannister, Imogen Claire, Irene Gorst, Maya Kemp, Lucinda Macdonald, Jonathan Battersby, Michael Beint, Edna Dore, Ray Edwards, Martin Friend, Glyn Grain, Brian Kent, Marianne Morley, Peter Needham, Rose Power, Daniel Thorndike.
02/02/77A

Tamburlaine The Great
(London)
National Theatre presentation of a revival of a drama in two parts by Christopher Marlowe. Staged, Peter Hall. Set-cos, John Bury; light, David Hersey; mus, Harrison Birtwistle (mus dir, Dominic Muldowney). Opened Oct. 4, '76, at the Olivier Theatre, London; $7.70 top.

Robert Eddison, Philip Locke, Philip Stone, Nicholas Selby, Brian Cox, Michael Beint, Kenneth Mackintosh, Harry Lomax, Albert Finney, Susan Fleetwood, Harry Webster, Oliver Cotton, Gawn Grainger, John Nettleton, Glyn Grain, Peter Needham, Peter Rocca, Denis Quilley, Norman Claridge, John Gill, Michael Melia, Daniel Thorndike, Barbara Jefford, Brenda Blethyn, Angela Galbraith, Michael Gough, Timothy Block, Michael Keating, Andrew Hilton, Carol Frazer, Jeananne Crowley, Pitt Wilkinson, Desmond Adams, Jonathan Battersby, Ray Edwards, Brian Kent, Stanley Lloyd, Patrick Monckton, Virginia Moore, Jeffrey Morgan, Liam O'Callaghan, Catherine Riding, Ray Roberts, Sarah Simmons, Dennis Tynsley. Struan Rodger, Mark McManus, Jim Norton, Derek Newark, Diana Quick, Gerard Salih.
10/13/76A

Tea and Sex and Shakespeare
(Dublin)
National Theatre Society presentation of two-act play by Thomas Kilroy. Staged, Max Stafford-Clark; set, Bronwen Casson; light, Tony Wakefield. Opened Oct. 6, '76, at the Abbey Theatre, Dublin; $10 top.

Donal McCann, Aideen O'Kelly, Kathleen Barrington, Desmond Perry, May Cluskey, Angela Harding, Kevin McHugh.
10/20/76A

The Teacher Promises the Negress Warmer Tears: SEE
Die Lehrerin Verspricht der Negerin Waermere Traenen

Tell
(Zurich)
Tell Musical AG & Good News Zurich prodn of a musical in two acts (13 scenes); book-lyr, Beat Hirt; mus, Tommy Fortmann. Staged, Klaus Ueberall; chor, Jimmie James; mus dir, Armand Volker; set, Gerd Burla; cos, Anita Burla; light, Christian Scheiffele; snd, Erwin Bircher, Ivor Barnett. Opened July 31, '77, at the Scheutzenhaus Albisguetli, Zurich; $15-$20 top.

Toni Vescoli, Henriette Kammerl, Ronnie Lee Williams, Alexis Korner, Bruno Ferrari, Iren Indra, John Ward, Walter Luthi, Markus Gehrig, Urs Schaerz, Jens van Harten, Rolf Frei, Reinhard Mueller, Ronald Baumann.

Musical numbers: "Tell Us," "Guitar Song," "Heroes," "Tell's Song," "Rock Tell," "Amigo," "Our World Always Wants to See Winners," "Shots," "Tell, What Would Have Happened?," "Tell's Escape," "Tell's Escape" (reprise), "Women's Rock," "Heroes" (reprise), "Gessler's Song," "Heroes" (reprise), "Wilhelm Tell."
08/24/77A

Ten Times Table
(London)
Michael Codron presentation of a comedy in two acts (five scenes) by Alan Ayckbourn. Staged, Ayckbourn; sets, Patrick Robertson; light, Leonard Tucker. Opened April 5, '78 at the Globe Theatre, London; $9.40 top.

Paul Eddington, Benjamin Whitrow, Julia McKenzie, Stephanie Fayerman, John Salthouse, Matyelok Gibbs, Tenniel Evans, Christopher Godwin, Diane Bull, Rob Stuart.
04/12/78A

That's The Way It Is
(Sydney)
Lee-Grey Creative Services Pty Ltd & Dineil Management presentation of a musical in two acts; book-lyr-mus, Calvin DeGrey, Roderic Lee. Staged, DeGrey; mus dir, Lee; chor, Jacque DePaul; des, Ken Healey, Stephen Churm; cos, Billy Robinson; light, David Kinsey, Mark Williams; snd, Colin Abrahams. Opened May 11, '78 at the 269 Playhouse, Sydney; $6.50 top.

Anna Thomas, Dave Lamb, Lester Bishop, Garry Rowe, Katrina Valkenburg, Brian Phillips, Christo Hayze, Richard Kodet, Calvin DeGrey, Vicki O'Neile, Leigh Jane Welsh, David Cohen, Gail Crowley.
05/24/78A

Thee and Me
(London)
National Theatre Co presentation of a play in two acts by Philip Martin. Staged, Michael Rudman; setting, Sue Plummer; cos, Lindy Hemmings; light, Gerry Jenkinson. Opened Feb 26, '80, at the Lyttelton Theatre, London: $12.10 top.

Billy McColl, Kay Adshead, Leonard Maguire, Ian Hogg, Mary Maddox, George Sweeney, Gillian Barge, Don Warrington.
03/03/80A

There Were Giants In Those Days & The Job
(Sydney)
Nimrod Street Theatre Co presentation of a dual-bill of one-act plays, "There Were Giants in Those Days," by Steve J Spears, and "The Job" by Lloyd Sutter. Staged, Ken Horler; scenery-light, Anthony Babicci; light, Margie Wright. Opened Sep 2, '78, at the Nimrod Downstairs, Sydney; $7.50 top.

THERE WERE GIANTS IN THOSE DAYS: John Clayton, David Argue, Basie Bonkowski.
THE JOB: David Argue, John Clayton.
11/01/78A

They: SEE Ils

They're Playing Our Song
(London)
Ray Cooney, by arrangement with Emanuel Azenberg in association with Tony Aljoe, Francine Lefrak and Ron Dante, prodn of a musical; book, Neil Simon; mus, Marvin Hamlisch; lyrs, Carole Bayer Sager; staged, David Taylor; set, Douglas W Schmidt; chor, Lani Sundsten. Opened Oct 1, '80, at the Shaftesbury Theatre, London, $19 top.

Gemma Craven, Tom Conti.
10/15/80A

13 Rue De l'Amour
(London)
Veronica Flint-Shipman & Paul Elliott, in ass'n with Duncan C Weldon & Louis I. Michaels, revival of a comedy in three acts by Georges Feydeau. Staged, Peter Dews; set, Finlay James; light, Nick Chelton. Opened March 17, '76, at the Phoenix Theatre, London; $6 top.

Louis Jourdan, Glynis Johns, James Grout, Mandy Cuthbert, Michael Cochrane, David Stoll, Margaret Courtenay, John Baddeley, Robert Vowles, Paul Marks.
03/24/76A

The Thoughts of Chairman Alf
(London)
Donald & Ian Albery presentation of a solo show in two acts, by Johnny Speight. Mus dir, Ronnie Cass. Opened Nov. 11, '76, at the Criterion Theatre, London; $6.55 top.

Warren Mitchell.
12/01/76A

Three Solo Pieces For Actresses
(Sydney)
Nimrod Theatre Co Ltd, presentation of three one-act plays: "Not I," by Samuel Beckett; cos, Lindy Ward; light, Neil Simpson. "Vicki Madison Clocks Out," by Alex Buzo, and "Potiphar's Wife," by Margot Hilton. Staged, Ken Horler, with Helen Morse and Julie McGregor; des, Neil Simpson, Sally Toone; Opened Oct 17, '79 at the Nimrod Theatre Downstairs, Sydney; $6 top.
11/07/79A

Time Was
(Dublin)
National Theatre Society presentation of comedy in two acts, by Hugh Leonard.

Time Was
(Cont)
Staged, Kevin McHugh, Tomas MacAnna; set, Wendy Shea; cos, Nigel Boyd; light, Tony Wakefield; snd, Jim Colgan. Opened at the Abbey Theatre, Dublin, Dec. 21, '76; $5 top.
Godfrey Quigley, Kate Flynn, Desmond Perry, Dearbhla Molloy, May Cluskey, Raymond Hardie, Larry Murphy, John Molloy, Michael O hAonghusa.
01/19/77A

Time's Wing'd Chariot
(Sydney)
Peter Williams Prodns presentation, in ass'n with the Festival of Sydney, of a solo show in two parts. Staged, Ida Marchant. Opened Jan. 5, '77, at the St. James Playhouse, Sydney; $3.50 top.
Alexander Archdale.
02/02/77A

Tishoo
(London)
Michael Codron presentation of a play in two acts by Brian Thompson. Staged, Ronald Eyre. Set, John Gunter; light, Brian Harris. Opened Oct. 24, '79, at the Wyndham's Theatre, London; $13.80 top.
Tony Selby, Penelope Wilton, Alec McCowen, Diane Bull, Geoffrey Palmer.
10/31/79A

Tom Foolery
(London)
Cameron Mackintosh, in association with Omega Stage Ltd & Capital Radio, presentation of a revue in two acts with words, mus and lyr by Tom Lehrer, adapted by Mackintosh and Robin Ray. Staged, Gillian Lynne; setting, Adrian Vaux; snd, Paul Farrah; light, Andrew Bridge; arr and mus dir, Chris Walker. Opened Jun 5, '80, at the Criterion Theatre, London: $17.50 top.
Robin Ray, Jonathan Adams, Martin Connor, Tricia George.
06/18/80A

Tommy
(London)
The Who, in conjunction with Danny O'Donovan, Alan Cluer & Helen Montagu, presentation of a rock musical in two acts (22 numbers); score-lyr, Pete Townshend; add'l songs, Sonny Boy Williamson, John Entwhistle. Devised, staged, Paul Tomlinson, John Hole; chor, Tudor Davies; set, David Knapman; cos, Harry Waistnage; mus dir-orch, Simon Webb; arr, Paul Herbert, Webb; light, Stanley Osborne White; snd, Bob Pridden; projection cnslt, Robert Ornbo; lasers, John Woolf. Opened Feb. 6, '79, at the Queen's Theatre, London; $12 top.
Anna Nicholas, Colin Copperfield, Steve Devereaux, Peter Straker, Sue Bond, Daniel Dobson, Bob Grant, Philip Carvosso, Kevin Williams, Eric Danot, Lorelei Lynn, Vivien Stokes, Allan Love.
 Dancers: Howard Miller, Jan Reynolds.
 Singers: Denise Alonzo, Debbi Angland, Martin Barnbrook, Gina Berry, Margaret Biggins, Angela Buckland, Gillian Burton, Deborah Dobson, Paul Gilbert, Laura Girling, Sarah Hague, Sarah Hobbs, Kathryn Horton, Cheryl Kerr, Helen Leversedge, Tony McBride, Esme Ockmore, Carol Osborne, Sally Reeves, Anne Spurway, Ian Storey, Jacquie Sullivan, Deborah Tee, Yvette Tinworth, Ian Turner, Toni Webber, Michelle Gill, Garry Love.
 Musical numbers: "Prologue," "It's a Boy, Mrs Walker," "Fifty-One," "The Amazing Journey," "Sparks," "Christmas," "Cousin Kevin," "Uncle Ernie," "Eyesight to the Blind," "The Acid Queen," "The Underture," "Pinball Wizard," "A Man I've Found," "Go to the Mirror Boy," "I'm Free," "Mother and Son," "I'm a Sensation," "Extra Extra," "Sally Simpson," "Come to My House," "Tommy's Holiday Camp," "Welcome to the Camp."
02/21/79A

Tonight: Lola Blau
(Sydney)
Adelaide Festival Centre Trust & ACG-Paradine Entertainments presentation by arrangement with Josef Weinberger Ltd of an entertainment in one act by George Kreisler. Staged, Ted Robinson; mus-orig text, George Kreisler; English text, Don White; mus dir, Dale Ringland; des, Silvia Jansons; cos, Sonia Fory; light, Alan Knox. Opened Sept. 13, '79, at the Seymour Centre's York Theatre, Sydney; $8.50 top.
Robyn Archer.
10/03/79A

Touched
(London)
Old Vic, by arrangement with the Royal Victoria Hall Foundation, presentation of a play in two acts by Stephen Lowe. Staged, Richard Eyre; des, William Dudley; cos, Pippy Bradshaw; light, Rory Dempster; snd-light, Malcolm Gelsthorpe. Opened Sept. 28, '77, at the Old Vic Theatre, London; $6.10 top.
Marjorie Yates, Lorraine Peters, Kay Adshead, David Beames, Donna Owen, Natasha Lewer, Susan Tracy, Annie Hayes, Malcolm Storry, Dave Hill, Kristine Howarth.
10/19/77A

The Training Run
(Sydney)
Evening Star Prodns presentation of a play in three acts, by Mervyn Rutherford. Staged, Max Cullen. Opened Jan 4. '77, at the Bondi Pavilion Theatre, Sydney; $5 top.
Cul Cullen, John Hargreaves, Julie Dawson, John Clayton, Gordon Piper, Barney Leeman.
02/02/77A

Traitors
(Sydney)
Nimrod Street Theatre Co Ltd Presentation of a play in three acts, with prolog and epilog, by Stephen Sewell. Staged, Neil Armfield; dsgn, Bill Haycock; light, Grahame Murray; mus, Michael Barkl. Opened Feb 20, '80, at the Nimrod Downstairs Theatre, Sydney: $6 top.
Michele Fawdon, Noni Hazlehurst, Judi Farr, Colin Friel, Barry Otto, Max Gillies.
04/02/80A

Translations
(Dublin)
Field Day Theatre Co presentation of two-act drama by Brian Friel. Staged, Art O'Brien; set, Consolata Boyle; light, Rupert Murray. Opened Oct 6, '80 at the Gate Theatre, Dublin; $6 top.
Mick Lally, Ann Hasson, Roy Hanlon, Nuala Hayes, Liam Neeson, Brendan Scallon, Ray McAnally, Stephen Rea, David Heap, Shaun Scott.
12/31/80A

The Travelling Music Show
(London)
Duncan C Weldon, Louis I Michaels, Marthill E Ltd and S Spencer Davids presentation of the Hillard Elkins prodn of a musical in two acts (37 numbers) with mus-lyr, Anthony Newley, Leslie Bricusse, Herbert Kretzmer. Staged, Burt Shevelove; chor, Norman Maen; sets, John Napier, Terry Parsons; cos, Ann Curtis; mus arrs, David Lindup; snd, David Collison; mus dir, Don Hunt. Opened March 28, '78, at Her Majesty's Theatre, London; $10.40 top.
Bruce Forsyth, Valerie Walsh, Katie Budd, Derek Griffiths, Tony Maiden, Mary Ann Onymous.
 Musical numbers: "After Today," "Candy Man," "Father Christmans," "Feeling Good," "Fill the World With Love," "Goldfinger," "Gonna Build a Mountain," "The Good Old Bad Old Days," "Good Times," "I Wanna Be Rich," "If I Ruled the World," "It's a Musical World," "The Joker," "King of the Castle," "The Ladies Love Me," "London is London," "Look At That Face," "Lumbered," "My Kind of Girl," "My Way," "Nothing Can Stop Me Now," "On the Boards," "Once in a Lifetime," "Schooldays," "Someone Nice Like You," "Stop the World," "Sweet Beginning," "Talk to the Animals," "Talk Your Way Out of It," "Thank You Very Much," "This Dream," "Typically English," "What Kind Of Fool Am I?," "When You Gotta Go," "Who Can I Turn To?," "A Wonderful Day Like Today," "You and I."
04/05/78A

Travelling North
(Sydney)
Nimrod Theatre Co Ltd presentation of a comedy in two acts by David Williamson. Staged, John Bell; des, Ian Robinson; light, Peter Holderness. Opened Aug. 22, '79, at the Nimrod Theatre, Sydney; $8 top.
Frank Wilson, Carol Raye, Jennifer Hagan, Julie Hamilton, Deborah Kennedy, Graham Rouse, Henri Szeps, Anthony Ingersent.
09/05/79A

Treadmill
(Sydney)
Ensemble Prodns Ltd presentation of a play in two acts by Lorna Bol. Staged, Mary Amoore; des, Doug Anderson; light, Peter Critchley. Opened at the Ensemble-at-the-Stables Theatre, Sydney, Feb 2, '78; $4 top.
Ros Forrest, Anne E Morgan, Angela Bennie.
03/15/78A

Treats
(London)
English Stage Co., in ass'n with Michael Codron, presentation of a comedy in two acts by Christopher Hampton. Staged, Robert Kidd; set, Andrew Sanders; light, Jack Raby. Opened Feb. 5, '76, at the Royal Court Theatre, London; $6.05 top.
Jane Asher, Stephen Moore, James Bolam.
02/18/76A

Trespassers Will Be Prosecuted
(Sydney)
A National Institute of Dramatic Art presentation of a two-act drama by Peter Kenna. Dir, George Whaley; des, Eamon D'Arcy; light, David Glover, Cheryl Noonan; snd, Rosemary James, Mike Simons; cos, Anne Heath. At Jane Street Theatre, Sydney, Australia, July 21, '76; $2.50 top.
Willie Fennell, Terry Peck.
08/04/76A

Troubadour
(London)
Michael Lombardi, in association with General Entertainment Investments Ltd, presentation of a musical in two acts (16 numbers), with book and lyr by Michael Lombardi; mus, Ray Holder. Staged, James Fortune; chor, David Drew; orch, Ken Thorne; mus dir, Denys Rawson; settings, Tim Goodchild; light, David Hersey; exec prod, John F Oakley. Opened Dec 19, '78, at the Cambridge Theatre, London; $12 top.
Clive Packham, Dudley Owen, John Watts, Sandra Berkin, Michael G Jones, Kim Braden, Saba Milton, Gordon Whiting, Tim Brown, Wallace Stephenson, Andrew Wadsworth, Ian Steele, Neil Anthony, Debbie Astell, Robert Barrington, Sylvia Byrne, Jenny Challenor, Janet Date, Chris Dyson, Hilary Anne Evans, Mary Evelegh, Richard Harradine, Phillip Harrison, Alistair Horne, Shaun Johnstone, Moir Leslie, Pamela Maguire, Andrew Matthews, Lyndon Miles, Gilbert O'Brien, Susannah Page, Dawn Tolhurst, Alison Thomas, Anna Vincent, David Wheldon-Williams, Richard Wherlock, Lyndsey Williams
Musical numbers: "Wife-Beating Song," "Troubadour," "One Only Rose," "Woman Is a Cheat," "Can Anyone Assist Me?" "Panic in the Palace," "Loneliness of Power," "Melancholy Lover," "Onward to Jerusalem" "We Must Have Jerusalem," "Mary's Child," "We Must Have Jerusalem" (reprise), "Ave Maris Stella," "If There Is Love," "Kalenda Maya," "If There Is Love" (reprise).
12/27/78A

The 20's And All That Jazz
(Melbourne)
J C Williamson Productions Ltd & Michael Edgley Int'l Pty Ltd presenation of a musical wri-staged, John Diedrich, Caroline Gillmer, John O'May. Mus dir, Michael Tyack; chor, Jilian Fitzgerald; set, Trina Parker. Opened Apr 16, '77, at Her Majesty's Theatre, Melbourne; $7 top.
John Diedrich, Caroline Gillmer, John O'May.
05/11/77A

The Two Ronnies
(Sydney)
Michael Edgley Int'l Pty Ltd & J C Williamson Prodns Ltd presentation of Harold Fielding's London Palladium prodn of a variety show in two parts; staged, David Kerr, from orig staging of Terry Hughes; mus dir, Anthony Howard Williams; wris, Gerald Wiley, Eddie Braben, Donald Groves, Spike Mullins, Neil Shand; des, Michael Knight; cos, Berkeley Sutcliffe; light, Eric Delzenne; snd, Edward Fardell. Opened June 16, '79, at the Regent Theatre, Sydney; $13.50 top.
Ronnie Barker, Ronnie Corbett, Fred Evans, Sam Kelly, John Pratt, Peter Ford, Kris Schumacher, Jennie Martell, Omar Pasha, Steve Bor, Jade.
07/04/79A

T.Zee
(London)
Royal Court Theatre and Michael White presentation of musical in one act by Richard O'Brien, Richard Hartley. Staged, Nicholas Wright; mus arrs, Hartley; art dir, Brian Thomson; cos, Sue Blane; light, Jack Raby. Opened at Royal Court Theatre, London, Aug. 10, '76, $4.65 top.
Richard O'Brien, Belinda Sinclair, Warren Clarke, Paul Nicholas, Diane Langton, Arthur Dignam, Jim Sweeney, Kimi Wong, Gilyan Jones, Julian Littman, Charles Nowosielski.
08/18/76A

The Umbrellas Of Cherbourg
(London)
Jack Levin, Derek Rawden, Roy Rogosin presentation for Partus Enterprises, of a musical by Michel LeGrand and Jacques Demy; text translated by Sheldon Harnick. Staged, Andrei Serban; scenery, Michael Yeargan. Opened Apr 10, '80, at the Phoenix, London: $15.75 top.
usan Gene, Martin Smith, Simon Masterston-Smith, Michele Summers, Sheila Matthews.
04/23/80A

Uncle Vanya
(Dublin)
National Theatre Society presentation of a drama in two acts by Anton Chekhov. Dir, Vladimir Monakhov; set, Bronwen Casson; light, Leslie Scott. Opened at Abbey Theatre, Dublin, Oct 4, '78; $6 top.
Bill Foley, Fidelma Cullen, Maire Ni Ghrainne, May Cluskey, Cyril Cusack, Clive Geraghty, Peadar Lamb, Kathleen Barrington, Larry Murphy.
11/01/78A

Under Milk Wood
(London)
Nicholas Newton revival, in association with Topaz Prodn & Gordon Prior, of a play in two acts, by Dylan Thomas. Staged, Malcolm Taylor; setting, Martin Morley; light, Denis Crompton and Steve Kemp. Opened June 29, '78, at the Mayfair Theatre, London; $8.30 top.
Richard Davies, John Francis.
07/12/78A

Under The Greenwood Tree
(London)
John Gale presentation of a play with songs, in two acts (10 scenes) by Patrick Garland; adapted from Thomas Hardy novel; mus comp-arr, Chris Littlewood. Staged, Patrick Garland; set, Neville Dewis; cos, Barbara Wilson; light, Kevin Flynn. Opened Dec 6, '78, at the Vaudeville Theatre, London; $8.80 Top.
Richard Cottan, Geoffrey Kirkness, Jack Le White, Richard Evans, George Gabriel, Terence Conoley, David Bacon, Charmain May, Frank Shelley, George Parsons, Suzan Crowley, Gilbert Wynne, Sonia Woolley, Patricia Macrae, Trevor Nichols, Pauline Menear, Trevor Clarke, Adrian Casey.
12/20/78A

The Undertaking
(London)
Bill Kenwright presentation of a play by Trevor Baxter; staged, Donald MacKechnie; setting, Saxon Lucas;; light, Jon Daly. Opened Oct 31, '79 at the Fortune Theatre, London; $13.50 top.
Annette Crosbie, John Barron, Miriam Karlin, Gerald Flood, Steven Grives, Kenneth Williams, Lorraine Chase.
11/07/79A

The Undiscovered Country
(London)
National Theatre revival of a play in five acts by Arthur Schnitzler, adapted by Tom Stoppard. Staged, Peter Wood; settings, William Dudley; cos, David Walker; light, Robert Bryan; mus, John White. Opened June 20, '79 at the Olivier Theatre, London; $11.30 top.
Dorothy Tutin, Janet Whiteside, Sara Kestelman, Emma Piper, Greg Hicks, Michael Byrne, John Wood, John Harding, Anna Carteret, Glyn Grain, Brian Kent, Joyce Redman, Peter Needham, Elliott Cooper, William Sleigh, Mark Farmer, David Browning, Jane Evers, Roger Gartland, Michael Bryant, Fiona Gaunt, Anne Sedgwick, Dermot Crowley, Susan Gilmore, Nik Forster, Martyn Whitby, Adam Norton, Marjorie Yates, Marianne Morley, Grant Warnock, Sandra Osborn, Graham McGrath, Catherine Devitt.
06/27/79A

The Unvarnished Truth
(London)
Michael Codron, by arrangement with the Cambridge Theatre Co, presentation of a comedy in two acts (three scenes) by Royce Ryton. Staged, Jonathan Lynn; sets, Robin Archer; light, Michael J Ryan. Opened April 13, '78, at the Phoenix Theatre, London; $8.40 top.
Tim Brooke-Taylor, Jo Kendall, Graeme Garden, Gabrielle Hamilton, Royce Ryton, Gwyneth Owen, Ivor Roberts, Morar Kennedy, Joyce Donaldson.
04/19/78A

Upside Down at the Bottom of the World
(Sydney)
Nimrod Street Theatre Co presentation of a comedy drama in two acts by David Allen. Staged, Neil Armfield; des, Edie Kurzer; light, Michael Manuel. Opened Aug 8, '79, Nimrod Theatre, Sydney, $7 top.
Barry Otto, Kerry Walker, Paul Bertram, Sally Cahill.
08/29/79A

Upstarts
(Dublin)
National Theatre Society presentation of two-act drama by Neil Donnelly. Staged, Patrick Laffan; set, Juliet Watkinson; light, Tony Wakefield. Opened Aug 7, '80, at the Peacock Theatre, Dublin; $6.25 top.
Kevin McHugh, Clive Geraghty, Macdara O'Fatharta, Eileen Colgan, Fiona MacAnna, Ste-

Upstarts
(Cont)
phen Brennan, Desmond Perry, Pat Leavy, James O'Mahony.
08/20/80A

The Venetian Twins
(Sydney)
Sydney Theatre Co presentation of a Nimrod Theatre Co Ltd. Prodn of a musical based on a Carlo Goldoni play, with book-lyrs, Nick Enright; mus, Terence Clark; staged, John Bell; chor, Nance Hayes, Keith Bain; des, Stephen Curtis; light, Grahame Murphy; fights, Tex Clarke. Opened Oct 26, '79 at the Sydney Opera House Theatre; $7.50 top.
Valerie Bader, Annie Byron, John Frawley, Barry Lovett, Drew Forsythe, Jon Ewing, Jennifer McGregor, Tony Sheldon, Tony Taylor, John McTernan.
Musical numbers: - Overture, "Twins," "Give Me Your Hand," "Hiss the Villain," "Recitative and Rivalry Trio," "Never Cross a Man Like Me," "Except," "Better Dead Than Wed," "Gypsy Love," "A Little Man," "A Little Mate," "My Hand," "Finaletto," "Jindyworoback," "Little Girl at the Window," "Beatrice's Mad Scene," "Rest In Peace," "Zanetto's Farewell," "The Ballad of Middle-Classe Propriety," "The Day of Judgment," "Finale."
11/07/79A

Very Good Eddie
(London)
Donald Ian Albery presentation of the Goodspeed Opera House revival of a musical comedy in two acts (three scenes, 19 numbers). Book, Guy Bolton; mus, Jerome Kern; lyr, Schuyler Green, based on a farce by Phillip Bartholomae; add'l lyr, Elsie Janis, P.G Wodehouse, Anne Caldwell, Frank Craven, Harry Graham, Harry B Smith, Herbert Reynolds, John E Hazzard. Staged, Bill Gile; mus staging, Dan Siretta; mus dir, Derek Taverner; arrs, Russell Warner; scenery, Fred Voelpel; cos, David Toser; light, Francis Reid. Opened March 23, '76, at the Piccadilly Theatre, London; $7.50 top.
John Blythe, Robert Swann, Gita Denise, Mary Barrett, Teddy Green, Cookie Weymouth, Richard Freeman, Nigel Williams, Prue Clarke, Vonya Carlton, Vicky Spencer, Miranda Fellows, Pam Scott, Carol Hoffman, Jack Gunn, Adrian Barnes, Roy Durbin, Guy Lutman, Peter Sutherland.
Musical numbers: "We're on Our Way," "Some Sort of Somebody," "Thirteen Collar," "Bungalow in Quogue," "Isn't It Great to be Married," "Good Night Boat," "Left All Alone Again Blues," "Hot Dog," "I'd Like to Have a Million in the Bank," "If You're a Friend of Mine," "Wedding Bells Are Calling Me," "Honeymoon Inn," "I've Got to Dance," "Moon of Love," "Old Boy Neutral," "Babes in the Wood," "Katy-Did," "Nodding Roses," finale.
03/31/76A

Vieux Carre
(London)
Nottingham Playhouse prodn of a play in two acts by Tennessee Williams. Staged, Keith Hack; settings, Voytek; light, Francis Reid; cos, Maria Bjornson; mus, Jeremy Nicholas. Opened Aug 15, '78, at the Piccadilly Theatre, London, after a season at the Nottingham Playhouse.
Sylvia Miles, Nadia Cattouse, Karl Johnson, Sheila Gish, Richard Kane, Betty Hardy, Judith Fellows, Jonathan Kent, Robin McDonald, Jack Elliott.
08/23/78A

Vinci Avait Raison
(Vinci Was Right)
(Brussels)
Roger Domany presentation of a new play in one act by Roland Topor. Staged-set, Topor; prodn coord, Roland Mahauden. Opened Dec. 22, '76 at Theatre de Poche, Brussels.
Fernand Abel, Suzy Falk, Patrick Poecks, Roland De Manez, Colette Emmanuelle, Veronique Peynet.
02/02/77A

Vinci Was Right: SEE Vinci Avait Raison

Visions
(Sydney)
Paris Co presentation of a drama in two acts (20 scenes), by Louis Nowra. Staged, Rex Cramphorn; dsgn, Jono Enemark and Melody Cooper; mus, Sarah de Jong; mus dir, Cameron Allen; chor, Keith Bain; light, Bill Walker. Opened Aug 17, '78 at the Paris Theatre, Sydney; $7.50 top.
John Gaden, Kate Fitzpatrick, Claire Crowther, Mary-Lou Stewart, Jennifer Claire, Tim Hughes, John Paramor, Peter Corbett, Geoffrey Glendon, Judy Davis.
09/06/78A

Viva Indonesia
(Sydney)
Popular Theatre Troupe presentation of a musical documentary in two parts, wristaged by Richard Fotheringham. Mus, Jane Ahlquist, Frank Millward. Opened May 30, '79, at the Stables Theatre, Sydney; $4 top.
Clare McKenna, Theresa Collie, Jane Ahlquist, Kathryn Porril, Roger Allen, Roger Prosser, Ken McLeod.
06/13/79A

Volpone
(London)
National Theatre revival of a comedy in two acts by Ben Jonson. Staged, Peter Hall; set, John Bury; cos, Deirdre Clancy; light, David Hersey. Opened Apr 26, '77, at the Olivier Theatre, London; $7.75 top.
Paul Scofield, Ben Kingsley, David Rappaport, Imogen Claire, John-Angelo Messana, Paul Rogers, Hugh Paddick, Michael Medwin, John Gielgud, Ian Charleson, Morag Hood, Ray Edwards, Warren Clarke, Elizabeth Spriggs, Brenda Blethyn, Lucinda Macdonald, Nicholas Selby, Peter Needham, Brian Kent, Daniel Thorndike, Norman Claridge, Michael Beint, Martin Friend, Stanley Lloyd, Jonathan Battersby, Irene Gorst, Chris Hunter, Liam O'Callaghan, Peter Rocca, Dennis Tynsley.
05/11/77A

Waiting for Godot: SEE Warten Auf Godot

The Wall is Mama
(Berlin)
Quartier Latin presentation of a play in two acts by Rick Cluchey. Staged, John Jenkins and Rick Cluchey; scenery, Cork Marcheschi; cos, Lee Gates; light, Bud Thorpe; snd, Carroll Hauptle. Opened June 29, '78, at the Schaubuehne am Halleschen Ufer, West Berlin; $10 top.
Nadja Brouwers, Java, Bud Thorpe, Arthur Graham, Lee Gates, Carroll Hauptle, Teri Garcia Suro, Rick Cluchey, John Jenkins.
08/16/78A

The Warhorse
(Sydney)
King O'Malley Theatre Co presentation of a play in two acts by John Upton. Staged, Stephen Wallace; des, Edie Kurzer. Opened Oct 10, '80, at the Stables Theatre, Sydney; $6 top.
ORobert Hughes. Willie Fennell, Patricia Hill, Mervyn Drake, Victoria Battese, John Hannan.
12/03/80A

Warten Auf Godot
(Waiting for Godot)
(Berlin)
Schiller Theatre, Berlin, presentation of a tragicomedy in two acts by Samuel Beckett. German adapt, Elmar Tophoven, with changes by Beckett. Dir, Beckett. Set-cos, Matias. Program and assistance, Walter D Asmus. Lighting, Heinz Hohenwald. Make-up, Hans Dublies. Tech collaboration, Julian Herrey, Hans Bohrer. Opened in repertory March 8, 1975. $10 top.
Horst Bollmann, Stefan Wigger, Klaus Herm, Carl Raddatz, Torsten Sense.
03/09/77A

Watch It Come Down
(London)
National Theatre Co. presentation of a drama in two acts by John Osborne. Staged, Bill Bryden; set, Hayden Griffin; cos, Deirdre Clancy; light, Andy Phillips. Opened Feb. 24, '76, at the Old Vic Theatre. London; $6.50 top.
Jill Bennett, Frank Finlay, Michael Feast, Michael Gough, Angela Galbraith, Susan Fleetwood, Rowena Cooper, Peter Needham.
03/03/76A

Watch on the Rhine
(London)
National Theatre Company revival of a play by Lillian Hellman. Staged, Mike Ockrent; sets, Eileen Diss; cos, Jessica Gwynne; light, Leonard Tucker; Opened Sep 16, '80, at the Lyttelton Theatre, London.
David Burke, Susan Engel, Peggy Ashcroft, John Quayle, Sandor Eles, Deborah Grant, Timothy Breeze.
10/15/80A

Waters of the Moon
(London)
Duncan C Weldon & Louis I Michaels rev of a play in two acts (five scenes) by N C Hunter. Staged, Patrick Garland; sets, Alan Tagg; cos, Finlay James; light, Joe Davis; mus arr, Richard Kayne. Opened Jan 26, '78, at the Haymarket Theatre, London; $9.75 top.
Paul Geoffrey, Frances Cuka, Wendy Hiller,

Waters of
(Cont)
Charles Lloyd Pack, Carmen Silvera, Doris Hare, Derek Godfrey, Ingrid Bergman, Brigitte Kahn, Paul Hardwick.
02/15/78A

Weapons of Happiness
(London)
National Theatre presentation of a drama in two acts by Howard Brenton. Staged, David Hare. Set, Hayden Griffin; light, Rory Dempster. Opened July 14, '76, at the Lyttleton Theatre, London; $4.20 top.
Frank Finlay, Michael Medwin, Derek Thompson, Billy Colvill, Nick Brimble, Julie Covington, Annie Hayes, Frederick Radley, Thelma Whiteley, Bernard Gallagher, Maurice O'Connell, Matthew Guinness, William Russell, Pat Connell, Martin Friend, Shaun Scott, Jeremy Truelove, Geoffrey Bateman, Chris Hunter.
07/21/76A

Weitere Aussichten
(Reise ins Glueck & Weitere Aussichten)
10/27/76A

What's a Nice Country Like U.S. Doing in a State Like This?
(London)
Ray Cooney, by arrangement with Michael Quinn McAloney Prodns, presentation of a revue in two acts, with sketches by Ira Gasman and Cary Hoffman; mus, Cary Hoffman; lyr, Ira Gasman, based on idea by Ira Gasman, Cary Hoffman, Bernie Travis. Staged, Michael Quinn McAloney; mus dir, Richard Leonard; set, Deborah Mitchell; light, Dave Bond; chor, Jane Darling. Opened May 27, '76, at the Mayfair Theatre, London; $5.40 top.
Peter Blake, Billy Boyle, Niel McCaul, Jacquie Toy, Leueen Willoughby.
06/02/76A

When We Are Married
(London)
Revival of a play by JB Priestley. Staged, Robin Legevre. Scenery, Eileen Diss. Cos, Jessica Gwynne. Opened Dec 12, '79 at Lyttleton Theatre, London: $13.10 top.
Leslie Sands, Pat Heywood, Robin Bailey, Joan Sanderson, Harold Innocent, Barbara Ferris, Mary Maddox, Liz Smith, Peter Jeffrey.
02/06/80A

The White Devil
(London)
Bullfinch Prodns presentation of a revival of a drama in two acts by John Webster (adapt, Edward Bond). Staged, Michael Lindsay-Hogg. Set, John Gunter; cos, Deirdre Clancy; light, Andy Phillips. Opened July 12, '76, at the Old Vic Theatre, London; $6.30 top.
Patrick Magee, John Kane, James Villiers, Jonathan Scott-Taylor, Jonathan Pryce, Colin Campbell, Tom Chadbon, Jack Shepherd, Jarlath Conroy, Dennis Burgess, John Grillo, Frances de la Tour, Glenda Jackson, Madge Ryan, Miriam Margoyles, Anna Welsh, Sean Scanlan, Edward Phillips, Kit Thacker, Fidelis Morgan, Patricia Donovan, Rodger Croucher.
07/21/76A

The White Guard
(London)
Royal Shakespeare Co revival of a play in three acts (seven scenes), by Mikhail Bulgakov, adapted by Michael Glenny. Staged, Barry Kyle; settings, Christopher Morley; light, Brian Harris; mus arr, John Riley. Opened May 29, '79, at the Aldwych Theatre, London; $10.90 top.
John Nettles, Allan Hendrick, Juliet Stevenson, Richard Griffiths, Patrick Stewart, Geoffrey Freshwater, Michael Pennington, John Bowe, Bill Dean, George Raistrick, Donald Douglas, Dennis Edwards, Dennis Clinton, Philip McGough, Malcolm Storry, Alan Barker, James Griffin, Bill Buffery, Conrad Asquith, Brian Abbot, Michael Bertenshaw, Ian Reddington, James Adams, Sebastian Allen, Danny Brooks, Eric Carlson, John Fortnum, Simon Grigsby, Philip Inman, Adam Shaw, Nicholas Turner, James Wolfe.
06/13/79A

White Suit Blues
(London)
Old Vic in arrangement with the Royal Victoria Hall Foundation presentation of a musical in two acts (nine songs); book, Adrian Mitchell; mus, Mike Westbrook; lyr, Mark Twain; adapt, Adrian Mitchell. Staged, Richard Eyre; scenery-cos, Pamela Howard; light, Geoffrey Mersereau. Opened Sept. 21, '77, at the Old Vic Theatre, London; $6.55 top.
Trevor Peacock, Kay Adshead, David Beames, Helen Brammer, Duncan Faber, Annie Hayes, Robert Hickson, Arthur Kohn, Sylveste McCoy, Malcolm Storry, Larry Walker, Polly Warren, Lola Young.
Musical numbers: "Swing Low Sweet Chariot," "He Done His Level Best," "This Planet Is a Strange Place," "I Swear I Saw the Soul of Mark Twain," "I Can Call it All Back," "Apple Pie," "The Song of One," "I'm 'bout Satisfied,"
09/28/77A

Who Killed 'Agatha' Christie?
(London)
Bill Kenwright presentation of a melodrama in two acts (three scenes) by Tudor Gates. Staged, John Dove; set, Pamela Ingram; light, Durham Marenghi. Opened Oct 18, '78, at the Ambassadors Theatre, London; $9.95 top.
James Bolam, Gerald Flood, Hugh James, Juliette Kaplan.
11/01/78A

Whose Life Is It Anyway?
(London)
Mermaid Theatre Trust, in ass'n with Ray Cooney, presentation of a play in two acts by Brian Clark. Staged, Michael Lindsay-Hogg; sets, Alan Tagg; light, Andy Phillips. Opened March 6, '78, at the Mermaid Theatre, London; $6.80 top.
Tom Conti, Jennie Goossens, Phoebe Nicholls, Trevor Thomas, Jane Asher, Rona Anderson, Richard Ireson, Edward Lyon, Alan Brown, Peter Honri, Robert Gary, Sebastian Shaw.
04/05/78A

Wie Einst Im Mai
(Once In May)
(Berlin)
Theater des Westens presentation of an operetta in two acts with book by Willi Kollo and Walter Lieck (based on the original 1913 "Farce with Songs" version by Rudolf Schanzer and Rudolf Bernauer) and mus by Walter and Willi Kollo (revised by Kollo). Staged, Karl Vibach; mus dir, Wolfgang Peters; chor, Hans Knuetter; mus rearr, Guenther Guersch; scenery, Paul Walter; cos, Ilse Marianne Wittneber. Opened April 5, '79, at the theater des Westens, West Berlin; $15 top.
Kurt Waitzmann, Angela Muethel, Wolker Brandt, Iska Geri, Wolfgang Ziffer, Silvio Francesco, Marilyn Found, Friedrich Schoenfelder, Jo Herbst, Kurt von Ruffin, Margo Rothweiler.
06/06/79A

Wild Oats
(London)
Royal Shakespeare Co. revival of a comedy in two acts by John O'Keefe. Staged, Clifford Williams; set, Ralph Koltai; cos, Judith Bland; light, Robert Ornbo. Opened Dec. 14, '76, at the Aldwych Theatre, London; $5.55 top.
Joe Melia, Norman Rodway, Patrick Godfrey, Lisa Harrow, Simon Jones, Doyne Bird, Jeremy Irons, Alan Howard, Raymond Westwell, Tim Wylton, Zoe Wanamaker, John Bott, Tim Barlow, James Cormack, Raymond Marlowe, Joe Dunlop, Richard Simpson, Emma Williams, Diana Rowan, Eve Pearce, Billie Brown, Ben Cross.
12/29/76A

The Woman
(London)
National Theatre Co presentation of a drama in two acts by Edward Bond, staged by the author. Settings, Hayden Griffin; light, Andy Phillips; cos, Hayden Griffin and Stephen Skaptason; songs, Hans Werner Henze. Opened Aug 10, '78, at the Olivier Theatre, London, $8.45 top.
Nicky Henson, Susan Fleetwood, Andrew Cruikshank, James Grant, Dawn Grainger, Brian Kent, Norman Claridge, Peter Jolley, Peter Needham, Ray Edwards, Irene Gorst, Derek Thompson, Michael Beint, Glyn Grain, Harry Meacher, Chris Hallam, Keith Skinner, Richard Perkins, Yvonne Bryceland, Dermot Crowley, Dinah Stabb, Timothy Norton, Anthony Douse, Stanley Lloyd, Alexander Allenby, Margaret Ford, Marianne Morley, Tel Stevens.
08/16/78A

Women Behind Bars
(London)
Debbie Raymond & Fiona Richmond presentation of a play in one act by Tom Eyen. Staged, Ron Link; set, Stanley Moore; light, Steve Kemp. Opened June 22, '77, at the Whitehall Theatre, London; $6.80 top.
Divine, Sweet William, Jennifer Granville, Sally Sagoe, Ruby Buchanan, Debbie Arnold, Zoe Gonord, Annie Lambert, Mavourneen Bryceland, Fiona Richmond, Andy Pan-

Women Behind
(Cont)
telidou.
07/06/77A

WonderWoman
(Sydney)
Dare Properties Pty Ltd. and Livermore Nominees Pty Ltd. presentation of Reg Livermore in a two-act, one-man musical; devised-wri-des, Reg Livermore. Prod, Eric Dare; dir, Peter Batey; mus dir, Mike Wade; chor, Keith Bain; cos, The Costume and Ballet Centre, Perth. Reviewed at Balmain Bijour Theatre, Sydney, Sept. 23, 1976, $7.50 top.
Reg Livermore.
10/27/76A

Wren, Pepys & Charlie Too
(London)
Musical comedy; book-lyr, David Adams; mus, Chuck Mallett, Adams; addl material, Ken Hill; staged, David Adams; chor, Gillian Gregory; mus dir, David Green; sets, Derek Cousins; cos, Colin Wild; light-snd, Theatre Projects; stage mgr, Patrick Durkin. Opened July 4, '79, Park Lane Hotel, London, $40 package price for Champagne, Dinner and Show.
Brian Ralph, Ian Hanham, Benny Lee, John Gower, Carol Cleveland, Maggie Vickers, Wendy Walsh, Lisa Westcott, Jacob Witkin.

Musicians-- David Green (piano), Mick Taylor (flute), Ninian Perry (bass), Simon Limbrick (percussion).

Musical numbers: "In Praise of Man," "Will You Build a Little Church for Me," "Turn Ye to Me," "Inventions," "Saints and Soldiers," "The Three Knaves," "A Country to Love," "I Will Get Through," "Monarchy Madness," "The Corn Hop Dance," "As I Make Love to Thee," "Love for All," "Keep a Watch on My Heart," "I Will Arise," "Out of Our Minds," "Dreaming Spires."
07/11/79A

Yahoo
(London)
Michael Codron presentation of a revue in two acts, devised by Alec Guinness and Alan Strachan, based on life and writings of Jonathan Swift. Staged, Strachan; set, Bernard Culshaw; light, Nick Chelton; mus, Stephen Oliver. Opened Oct. 6, '76, at the Queen's Theatre, London; $5.80 top.
Alec Guinness, Nicola Pagett, Mark Kingston, Angela Thorne.
10/13/76A

You and the Night and The Housewine
(Sydney)
Nimrod Street Theatre Co Ltd presentation of a revue in two parts devised, wri-staged by the performers. Des, Roger Kirk; light, Margie Wright; mus dir, Max Lambert. Opened Nov 5, '80 at the Nimrod Theatre Downstairs, Sydney: $7 top.
Robyn Moase, Deidre Rubenstein, Tony Sheldon, Tony Taylor.
12/03/80A

Young Mo
(Sydney)
Nimrod Theatre presentation, in ass'n with the Festival of Sydney by arrangement with the Rock Theatre of Paris and the Adelaide Festival Center Trust, of a musical by Steve J Spears. Staged, Richard Wherrett; decor, Vicki Feitscher; chor, Pamele Gibbons; mus dir, Roy Ritchie; piano arrs, Marlene Dale; light, Grahame Murray. Opened Jan. 28, '77, at the Nimrod Theatre, Sydney; $5.50 top.
Garry McDonald, Glorie Dawn, Sue Walker, Willie Fennell, John Gaden, John McTernan, Marlene Dale, Gary Cosham, Roy Ritchie.
02/16/77A

Zykovs
(London)
Royal Shakespeare Co. presentation of a drama in four acts by Maxim Gorky. Staged, David Jones; set, Timothy O'Brien, Tazeena Firth; light, David Hersey. Opened April 28, '76, at the Aldwych Theatre, London; $6.50 top.
Paul Rogers, Sheila Allen, Mike Gwilym, David Daker, Patrick Godfrey, Lynsey Baxter, Janet Whiteside, Mia Farrow, Valerie Colgan, Norman Rodway, Gary Bond.
05/05/76A

TONYS

NOTE: Tonys were awarded without prior nominations through 1956.

1947

Actors (Dramatic)
Jose Ferrer, Cyrano de Bergerac
Fredric March, Years Ago

Actresses (Dramatic)
Ingrid Bergman, Joan of Lorraine
Helen Hayes, Happy Birthday

Actress, Supporting or Featured (Dramatic)
Patricia Neal, Another Part of the Forest

Actor, Supporting or Featured (Musical)
David Wayne, Finian's Rainbow

Director
Elia Kazan, All My Sons

Costumes
Lucinda Ballard, Happy Birthday/Another Part of the Forest/Street Scene/John Loves Mary/The Chocolate Soldier
David Ffolkes, Henry VIII

Choreographers
Agnes de Mille, Brigadoon
Michael Kidd, Finian's Rainbow

Special Awards
Dora Chamberlain
Mr. and Mrs. Ira Katzenberg
Jules Leventhal
Burns Mantle
P. A. MacDonald
Arthur Miller
Vincent Sardi, Sr.
Kurt Weill

1948

Actors (Dramatic)
Henry Fonda, Mister Roberts
Paul Kelly, Command Decision
Basil Rathbone, The Heiress

Actresses (Dramatic)
Judith Anderson, Medea
Katherine Cornell, Antony and Cleopatra
Jessica Tandy, A Streetcar Named Desire

Actor (Musical)
Paul Hartman, Angel in the Wings

Actress (Musical)
Grace Hartman, Angel in the Wings

Play
Mister Roberts by Thomas Heggen and Joshua Logan, based on the Thomas Heggen novel

Producer
Leland Hayward, Mister Roberts

Authors
Thomas Heggen and Joshua Logan, Mister Roberts

Costumes
Mary Percy Schenck, The Heiress

Scenic Designer
Horace Armistead, The Medium

Choreographer
Jerome Robbins, High Button Shoes

Stage Technicians
George Gebhardt
George Pierce

Special Awards
Vera Allen
Paul Beisman
Joe E. Brown
Robert Dowling
Experimental Theatre, Inc.
Rosamond Gilder
June Lockhart
Mary Martin
Robert Porterfield
James Whitmore

1949

Actor (Dramatic)
Rex Harrison, Anne of the Thousand Days

Actress (Dramatic)
Martita Hunt, The Madwoman of Chaillot

Actor, Supporting or Featured (Dramatic)
Arthur Kennedy, Death of a Salesman

Actress, Supporting or Featured (Dramatic)
Shirley Booth, Goodbye, My Fancy

Actor (Musical)
Ray Bolger, Where's Charley?

Actress (Musical)
Nanette Fabray, Love Life

Play
Death of a Salesman by Arthur Miller

Producers (Dramatic)
Kermit Bloomgarden and Walter Fried, Death of a Salesman

Author
Arthur Miller, Death of a Salesman

Director
Elia Kazan, Death of a Salesman

Musical
Kiss Me Kate, music and lyrics by Cole Porter, book by Bella and Samuel Spewack

Producers (Musical)
Saint-Subber and Lemuel Ayers, Kiss Me Kate

Authors (Musical)
Bella and Samuel Spewack, Kiss Me Kate

Composer and Lyricist
Cole Porter, Kiss Me Kate

Costumes
Lemuel Ayers, Kiss Me Kate

Scenic Designer
Jo Mielziner, Sleepy Hollow/Summer and Smoke/Anne of the Thousand Days/Death of a Salesman/South Pacific

Choreographer
Gower Champion, Lend An Ear

Conductor and Musical Director
Max Meth, As The Girls Go

1950

Actor (Dramatic)
Sidney Blackmer, Come Back, Little Sheba

Actress (Dramatic)
Shirley Booth, Come Back, Little Sheba

Actor (Musical)
Ezio Pinza, South Pacific

Actress (Musical)
Mary Martin, South Pacific

Actor, Supporting or Featured (Musical)
Myron McCormick, South Pacific

Actress, Supporting or Featured (Musical)
Juanita Hall, South Pacific

Play
The Cocktail Party by T. S. Eliot

Producer (Dramatic)
Gilbert Miller, The Cocktail Party

Author (Dramatic)
T. S. Eliot, The Cocktail Party

Director
Joshua Logan, South Pacific

Musical
South Pacific, music by Richard Rodgers, lyrics by Oscar Hammerstein II, book by Oscar Hammerstein II and Joshua Logan

Producers (Musical)
Richard Rodgers, Oscar Hammerstein II, Leland Hayward and Joshua Logan, South Pacific

Authors (Musical)
Oscar Hammerstein II and Joshua Logan, South Pacific

Composer
Richard Rodgers, South Pacific

Costumes
Aline Bernstein, Regina

Scenic Designer
Jo Mielziner, The Innocents

Choreographer
Helen Tamiris, Touch and Go

Conductor and Musical Director
Maurice Abravanel, Regina

Stage Technician
Joe Lynn, master propertyman, Miss Liberty

Special Awards
Maurice Evans
Mrs. Eleanor Roosevelt presented a special award to a volunteer worker of the American Theatre Wing's hospital program.

1951

Actor (Dramatic)
Claude Rains, Darkness At Noon

Actress (Dramatic)
Uta Hagen, The Country Girl

Actor, Supporting or Featured (Dramatic)
Eli Wallach, The Rose Tattoo

Actress, Supporting or Featured (Dramatic)
Maureen Stapleton, The Rose Tattoo

Actor (Musical)
Robert Alda, Guys and Dolls

Actress (Musical)
Ethel Merman, Call Me Madam

Actor, Supporting or Featured (Musical)
Russell Nype, Call Me Madam

Actress, Supporting or Featured (Musial)
Isabel Bigley, Guys and Dolls

Play
The Rose Tattoo by Tennessee Williams

Producer (Dramatic)
Cheryl Crawford, The Rose Tattoo

Author (Dramatic)
Tennessee Williams, The Rose Tattoo

Director
George S. Kaufman, Guys and Dolls

Musical
Guys and Dolls, music and lyrics by Frank Loesser, book by Jo Swerling and Abe Burrows

Producers (Musical)
Cy Feuer and Ernest H. Martin, Guys and Dolls

Authors (Musical)
Jo Swerling and Abe Burrows, Guys and Dolls

Composer and Lyricist
Frank Loesser, Guys and Dolls

Costumes
Miles White, Bless You All

Scenic Designer
Boris Aronson, The Rose Tattoo/The Country Girl/Season In The Sun

Choreographer
Michael Kidd, Guys and Dolls

Conductor and Musical Director
Lehman Engel, The Consul

Stage Technician
Richard Raven, The Autumn Garden

Special Award
Ruth Green

1952

Actor (Dramatic)
Jose Ferrer, The Shrike

Actress (Dramatic)
Julie Harris, I Am a Camera

Actress (Musical)
Gertrude Lawrence, The King & I

Actor (Musical)
Phil Silvers, Top Banana

Actor, Supporting or Featured (Dramatic)
John Cromwell, Point of No Return

Actress, Supporting or Featured (Dramatic)
Marian Winters, I Am a Camera

Actor, Supporting or Featured (Musical)
Yul Brynner, The King & I

Actress, Supporting or Featured (Musical)
Helen Gallagher, Pal Joey

Play
The Fourposter by Jan de Hartog

Musical
The King & I, book and lyrics by Oscar Hammerstein II, music by Richard Rodgers

Director
Jose Ferrer, The Shrike/The Fourposter/Stalag 17

Costumes
Irene Sharaff, The King & I

Scenic Designer
Jo Mielziner, The King & I

Choreographer
Robert Alton, Pal Joey

Conductor and Musical Director
Max Meth, Pal Joey

Stage Technician
Peter Feller, master carpenter for Call Me Madam

Special Awards
Edward Kook
Judy Garland
Charles Boyer

1953

Actor (Dramatic)
Tom Ewell, The Seven Year Itch

Actress (Dramatic)
Shirley Booth, Time of the Cuckoo

Actor, Supporting or Featured (Dramatic)
John Williams, Dial M for Murder

Actress, Supporting or Featured (Dramatic)
Beatrice Straight, The Crucible

Actor (Musical)
Thomas Mitchell, Hazel Flagg

Actress (Musical)
Rosalind Russell, Wonderful Town

Actor, Supporting or Featured (Musical)
Hiram Sherman, Two's Company

Actress, Supporting or Featured (Musical)
Sheila Bond, Wish You Were Here

Play
The Crucible by Arthur Miller

Producer (Dramatic)
Kermit Bloomgarden, The Crucible

Author (Dramatic)
Arthur Miller, The Crucible

Director
Joshua Logan, Picnic

Musical
Wonderful Town, book by Joseph Fields and Jerome Chodorov, music by Leonard Bernstein, lyrics by Betty Comden and Adolph Green

Producer (Musical)
Robert Fryer, Wonderful Town

Authors (Musical)
Joseph Fields and Jerome Chodorov, Wonderful Town

Composer
Leonard Bernstein, Wonderful Town

Costume Designer
Miles White, Hazel Flagg

Scenic Designer
Raoul Pene du Bois, Wonderful Town

Choreographer
Donald Saddler, Wonderful Town

Conductor and Musical Director
Lehman Engel, Wonderful Town and Gilbert and Sullivan Season

Stage Technician
Abe Kurnit, Wish You Were Here

Special Awards
Beatrice Lillie
Danny Kaye
Equity Community Theatre

1954

Actor (Dramatic)
David Wayne, The Teahouse of the August Moon

Actress (Dramatic)
Audrey Hepburn, Ondine

Actor, Supporting or Featured (Dramatic)
John Kerr, Tea and Sympathy

Actress, Supporting or Featured (Dramatic)
Jo Van Fleet, The Trip to Bountiful

Actor (Musical)
Alfred Drake, Kismet

Actress (Musical)
Dolores Gray, Carnival in Flanders

Actor, Supporting or Featured (Musical)
Harry Belafonte, John Murray Anderson's Almanac

Actress, Supporting or Featured (Musical)
Gwen Verdon, Can-Can

Play
The Teahouse of the August Moon by John Patrick

Producer (Dramatic)
Maurice Evans and George Schaefer, The Teahouse of the August Moon

Author (Dramatic)
John Patrick, The Teahouse of the August Moon

Director
Alfred Lunt, Ondine

Musical
Kismet, book by Charles Lederer and Luther Davis, music by Alexander Borodin, adapted and with lyrics by Robert Wright and George Forrest

Producer (Musical)
Charles Lederer, Kismet

Author (Musical)
Charles Lederer and Luther Davis, Kismet

Composer
Alexander Borodin, Kismet

Costume Designer
Richard Whorf, Ondine

Scenic Designer
Peter Larkin, Ondine and The Teahouse of the August Moon

Choreographer
Michael Kidd, Can-Can

Musical Conductor
Louis Adrian, Kismet

Stage Technician
John Davis, Picnic

1955

Actor (Dramatic)
Alfred Lunt, Quadrille

Actress (Dramatic)
Nancy Kelly, The Bad Seed

Actor, Supporting or Featured (Dramatic)
Francis L. Sullivan, Witness for the Prosecution

Actress, Supporting or Featured (Dramatic)
Patricia Jessel, Witness for The Prosecution

Actor (Musical)
Walter Slezak, Fanny

Actress (Musical)
Mary Martin, Peter Pan

Actor, Supporting or Featured (Musical)
Cyril Ritchard, Peter Pan

Actress, Supporting or Featured (Musical)
Carol Haney, The Pajama Game

Play
The Desperate Hours by Joseph Hayes

Producers (Dramatic)
Howard Erskine and Joseph Hayes, The Desperate Hours

Author (Dramatic)
Joseph Hayes, The Desperate Hours

Director
Robert Montgomery, The Desperate Hours

Musical
The Pajama Game, book by George Abbott and Richard Bissell, music and lyrics by Richard Adler and Jerry Ross

Producers (Musical)
Frederick Brisson, Robert Griffith and Harold S. Prince, The Pajama Game

Authors (Musical)
George Abbott and Richard Bissell, The Pajama Game

Composer and Lyricist
Richard Adler and Jerry Ross, The Pajama Game

Costume Designer
Cecil Beaton, Quadrille

Scenic Designer
Oliver Messel, House of Flowers

Choreographer
Bob Fosse, The Pajama Game

Conductor and Musical Director
Thomas Schippers, The Saint of Bleecker Street

Stage Technician
Richard Rodda, Peter Pan

Special Award
Proscenium Productions

1956

Actor (Dramatic)
Ben Gazzara, A Hatful of Rain
Boris Karloff, The Lark
Paul Muni, Inherit the Wind
Michael Redgrave, Tiger at the Gates
Edward G. Robinson, The Middle of the Night

Actress (Dramatic)
Barbara Bel Geddes, Cat on a Hot Tin Roof
Gladys Cooper, The Chalk Garden
Ruth Gordon, The Matchmaker
Julie Harris, The Lark
Siobhan McKenna, The Chalk Garden
Susan Strasberg, The Diary of Anne Frank

Actor, Supporting or Featured (Dramatic)
Ed Begley, Inherit the Wind
Anthony Franciosa, A Hatful of Rain
Andy Griffith, No Time for Sergeants
Anthony Quayle, Tamburlaine the Great
Fritz Weaver, The Chalk Garden

Actress, Supporting or Featured (Dramatic)
Diane Cilento, Tiger at the Gates
Anne Jackson, The Middle of the Night
Una Merkel, The Ponder Heart
Elaine Stritch, Bus Stop

Actor (Musical)
Stephen Douglass, Damn Yankees
William Johnson, Pipe Dream
Ray Walston, Damn Yankees

Actress (Musical)
Carol Channing, The Vamp
Gwen Verdon, Damn Yankees
Nancy Walker, Phoenix '55

Actor, Supporting or Featured (Musical)
Russ Brown, Damn Yankees
Mike Kellin, Pipe Dream
Will Mahoney, City Center Finian's Rainbow
Scott Merrill, The Threepenny Opera

Actress, Supporting or Featured (Musical)
Rae Allen, Damn Yankees
Pat Carroll, Catch a Star
Lotte Lenya, The Threepenny Opera
Judy Tyler, Pipe Dream

Play
Bus Stop by William Inge; Producers Robert Whitehead and Roger L. Stevens
Cat on a Hot Tin Roof by Tennessee Williams; Producer The Playwrights' Company
The Diary of Anne Frank by Frances Goodrich and Albert Hackett; Producer Kermit Bloomgarden
Tiger at the Gates by Jean Giraudoux, adapted by Christopher Fry; Producers Robert L. Joseph, The Playwrights' Company and Henry M. Margolis
The Chalk Garden by Enid Bagnold; Producer Irene Mayer Selznick

Authors (Dramatic)
Frances Goodrich and Albert Hackett, The Diary of Anne Frank

Producer (Dramatic)
Kermit Bloomgarden, The Diary of Anne Frank

Director
Joseph Anthony, The Lark
Harold Clurman, Bus Stop/Pipe Dream/Tiger at the Gates
Tyrone Guthrie, *The Matchmaker/Six Characters in Search of an Author/Tamburlaine the Great
Garson Kanin, The Diary of Anne Frank
Elia Kazan, Cat on a Hot Tin Roof
Albert Marre, The Chalk Garden
Herman Shumlin, Inherit the Wind

Musical
Damn Yankees by George Abbott and Douglass Wallop. Music by Richard Adler and Jerry Ross; Producers Frederick Brisson, Robert Griffith, Harold S. Prince in association with Albert B. Taylor
Pipe Dream. Book and lyrics by Oscar Hammerstein II, music by Richard Rodgers; Producers Rodgers and Hammerstein

Authors (Musical)
George Abbott and Douglass Wallop, Damn Yankees

Producers (Musical)
Frederick Brisson, Robert Griffith, Harold S. Prince in association with Albert B. Taylor, Damn Yankees

Composer and Lyricist
Richard Adler and Jerry Ross, Damn Yankees

Conductor and Musical Director
Salvatore Dell'Isola, Pipe Dream
Hal Hastings, Damn Yankees
Milton Rosenstock, The Vamp

Scenic Designer
Boris Aronson, The Diary of Anne Frank/Bus Stop/Once Upon a Tailor/A View from the Bridge
Ben Edwards, The Ponder Heart/Someone Waiting/The Honeys
Peter Larkin, Inherit the Wind/No Time for Sergeants
Jo Mielziner, Cat on a Hot Tin Roof/The Lark/The Middle of the Night/Pipe Dream
Raymond Sovey, The Great Sebastians

Costume Designer
Mainbocher, The Great Sebastians
Alvin Colt, The Lark/Phoenix '55/*Pipe Dream
Helene Pons, The Diary of Anne Frank/Heavenly Twins/A View from the Bridge

Choreographer
Robert Alton, The Vamp
Bob Fosse, Damn Yankees
Boris Runanin, Phoenix '55/Pipe Dream
Anna Sokolow, Red Roses for Me

Stage Technician
Larry Bland, carpenter, The Middle of the Night/The Ponder Heart/Porgy and Bess

Harry Green, electrician and sound man, The Middle of the Night/Damn Yankees

Special Awards
The Threepenny Opera
The Theatre Collection of the N. Y. Public Library

1957

Actor (Dramatic)
Maurice Evans, The Apple Cart
Wilfred Hyde-White, The Reluctant Debutante
Fredric March, Long Day's Journey Into Night
Eric Portman, Separate Tables
Ralph Richardson, The Waltz Of The Toreadors
Cyril Ritchard, A Visit To A Small Planet

Actress (Dramatic)
Florence Eldridge, Long Day's Journey Into Night
Margaret Leighton, Separate Tables
Rosalind Russell, Auntie Mame
Sybil Thorndike, The Potting Shed

Actor, Suporting or Featured (Dramatic)
Frank Conroy, The Potting Shed
Eddie Mayehoff, A Visit To A Small Planet
William Podmore, Separate Tables
Jason Robards, Jr., Long Day's Journey Into Night

Actress, Supporting or Featured (Dramatic)
Peggy Cass, Auntie Mame
Anna Massey, The Reluctant Debutante
Beryl Measor, Separate Tables
Mildred Natwick, The Waltz Of The Toreadors
Phyllis Neilson-Terry, Separate Tables
Diana Van Der Vlis, The Happiest Millionaire

Actor (Musical)
Rex Harrison, My Fair Lady
Fernando Lamas, Happy Hunting
Robert Weede, The Most Happy Fella

Actress (Musical)
Julie Andrews, My Fair Lady
Judy Holliday, Bells Are Ringing
Ethel Merman, Happy Hunting

Actor, Supporting or Featured (Musical)
Sydney Chaplin, Bells Are Ringing
Robert Coote, My Fair Lady
Stanley Holloway, My Fair Lady

Actress, Supporting or Featured (Musical)
Edith Adams, Li'l Abner
Virginia Gibson, Happy Hunting
Irra Petina, Candide
Jo Sullivan, The Most Happy Fella

Play
Long Day's Journey Into Night by Eugene O'Neill; Producers Leigh Connell, Theodore Mann and Jose Quintero
Separate Tables by Terence Rattigan; Producers The Producers Theatre and Hecht-Lancaster
The Potting Shed by Graham Greene; Producers Carmen Capalbo and Stanley Chase
The Waltz Of The Toreadors by Jean Anouilh, translated by Lucienne Hill; Producer The Producers Theatre (Robert Whitehead)

Author (Dramatic)
Eugene O'Neill, Long Day's Journey Into Night

Producer (Dramatic)
Leigh Connell, Theodore Mann and Jose Qintero, Long Day's Journey Into Night

Director
Joseph Anthony, A Clearing in the Woods/The Most Happy Fella
Harold Clurman, The Waltz of the Toreadors
Peter Glenville, Separate Tables
Moss Hart, My Fair Lady
Jose Quintero, Long Day's Journey Into Night

Musical
Bells Are Ringing. Book and lyrics by Betty Comden and Adolph Green, music by Jule Styne; Producer The Theatre Guild
Candide. Book by Lillian Hellman, music by Leonard Bernstein, lyrics by Richard Wilbur; Producer Ethel Linder Reiner in association with Lester Osterman, Jr.
My Fair Lady. Book and lyrics by Alan Jay Lerner, music by Frederick Loewe; Producer Herman Levin
The Most Happy Fella. Book, music and lyrics by Frank Loesser; Producers Kermit Bloomgarden and Lynn Loesser

Author (Musical)
Alan Jay Lerner, My Fair Lady

Producer (Musical)
Heman Levin, May Fair Lady

Composer
Frederick Loewe, My Fair Lady

Conductor and Musical Director
Franz Allers, My Fair Lady
Herbert Greene, The Most Happy Fella
Samuel Krachmalnick, Candide

Scenic Designer
Boris Aronson, A Hole In The Head/Small War on Murray Hill
Ben Edwards, The Waltz Of The Toreadors
George Jenkins, The Happiest Millionaire/Too Late The Phalarope
Donald Oenslager, Major Barbara
Oliver Smith, A Clearing in the Woods/Candide/Auntie Mame/*My Fair Lady/Eugenia/A Visit To A Small Planet

Costume Designer
Cecil Beaton, Little Glass Clock/*My Fair Lady
Alvin Colt, Li'l Abner/The Sleeping Prince
Dorothy Jeakins, Major Barbara/Too Late The Phalarope
Irene Sharaff, Candide/Happy Hunting/Shangri La/Small War on Murray Hill

Choreographer
Hanya Holm, My Fair Lady
Michael Kidd, Li'l Abner
Dania Krupska, The Most Happy Fella
Jerome Robbins and Bob Fosse, Bells Are Ringing

Stage Technician
Thomas Fitzgerald, sound man, Long Day's Journey Into Night
Joseph Harbach, carpenter, Auntie Mame
Howard McDonald (posthumous), carpenter, Major Barbara

Special Awards
American Shakespeare Festival
Jean-Louis Barrault French Repertory
Robert Russell Bennett
William Hammerstein
Paul Shyre

1958

Actor (Dramatic)
Ralph Bellamy, Sunrise At Campobello
Richard Burton, Time Remembered
Hugh Griffith, Look Homeward, Angel
Laurence Olivier, The Entertainer
Anthony Perkins, Look Homeward, Angel
Peter Ustinov, Romanoff and Juliet
Emlyn Williams, A Boy Growing Up

Actress (Dramatic)
Wendy Hiller, A Moon For The Misbegotten
Eugenie Leontovich, The Cave Dwellers
Helen Hayes, Time Remembered
Siobhan McKenna, The Rope Dancers
Mary Ure, Look Back In Anger
Jo Van Fleet, Look Homeward, Angel

Actor, Supporting or Featured (Dramatic)
Henry Jones, Sunrise At Campobello

Actress, Supporting or Featured (Dramatic)
Anne Bancroft, Two For The Seesaw

Actor (Musical)
Ricardo Montalban, Jamaica
Robert Preston, The Music Man
Eddie Foy, Jr., Rumple
Tony Randall, Oh, Captain!

Actress (Musical)
Thelma Ritter, New Girl In Town
Lena Horne, Jamaica
Beatrice Lillie, Ziegfeld Follies
Gwen Verdon, New Girl In Town

Actor, Supporting or Featured (Musical)
David Burns, The Music Man

Actress, Supporting or Featured (Musical)
Barbara Cook, The Music Man

Play
The Rope Dancers by Morton Wishengrad
Two For The Seesaw by William Gibson
Time Remembered by Jean Anouilh. English version by Patricia Moyes
The Dark at the Top of the Stairs by William Inge
Look Back In Anger by John Osborne
Romanoff and Juliet by Peter Ustinov
Sunrise At Campobello by Dore Schary

Author (Dramatic)
Dore Schary, Sunrise At Campobello

Producers (Dramatic)
Lawrence Langner, Theresa Helburn, Armina Marshall and Dore Schary, Sunrise At Campobello

Director (Dramatic)
Vincent J. Donehue, Sunrise At Campobello

Musical
West Side Story. Book by Arthur Laurents, music by Leonard Bernstein, lyrics by Stephen Sondheim
New Girl In Town. Book by George Abbott, music and lyrics by Bob Merrill
The Music Man. Book by Meredith Willson and Franklin Lacey, music and lyrics by Meredith Willson
Oh, Captain!. Book by Al Morgan and Jose Ferrer, music and lyrics by Jay Livingston and Ray Evans
Jamaica. Book by E. Y. Harburg and Fred Saidy, music by Harold Arlen, lyrics by E. Y. Harburg

Author (Musical)
Meredith Willson and Franklin Lacey, The Music Man

Producer (Musical)
Kermit Bloomgarden, Herbert Greene, Frank Productions, The Music Man

Composer and Lyricist
Meredith Willson, The Music Man

Conductor and Musical Director
Herbert Greene, The Music Man

Scenic Designer
Oliver Smith, West Side Story

Costume Designer
Motley, The First Gentleman

Choreographer
Jerome Robbins, West Side Story

Stage Technician
Harry Romar, Time Remembered

Special Awards
The New York Shakespeare Festival
Mrs. Martin Beck

1959

Actor (Dramatic)
Cedric Hardwicke, A Majority of One
Alfred Lunt, The Visit
Christopher Plummer, J. B.
Cyril Ritchard, The Pleasure of His Company
Jason Robards, Jr., The Disenchanted
Robert Stephens, Epitaph for George Dillon

Actress (Dramatic)
Gertrude Berg, A Majority of One
Claudette Colbert, The Marriage-Go-Round
Lynn Fontanne, The Visit
Kim Stanley, A Touch of the Poet
Maureen Stapleton, The Cold Wind and the Warm

Actor, Supporting or Featured (Dramatic)
Marc Connelly, Tall Story
George Grizzard, The Disenchanted
Walter Matthau, Once More, With Feeling
Robert Morse, Say, Darling
Charlie Ruggles, The Pleasure of His Company
George Scott, Comes a Day

Actress, Supporting or Featured (Dramatic)
Maureen Delany, God and Kate Murphy
Dolores Hart, The Pleasure of His Company
Julie Newmar, The Marriage-Go-Round
Nan Martin, J. B.
Beatrice Reading, Requiem for a Nun

Actor (Musical)
Larry Blyden, Flower Drum Song
Richard Kiley, Redhead

Actress (Musical)
Miyoshi Umeki, Flower Drum Song
Gwen Verdon, Redhead

Actor, Supporting or Featured (Musical)
Russell Nype, Goldilocks
Leonard Stone, Redhead
Cast of La Plume de Ma Tante

Actress, Supporting or Featured (Musical)
Julienne Marie, Whoop-Up
Pat Stanley, Goldilocks
Cast of La Plume de Ma Tante

Play
A Touch of the Poet by Eugene O'Neill; Producers The Producers Theatre, Robert Whitehead and Roger L. Stevens
Epitaph for George Dillon by John Osborne and Anthony Creighton; Producer David Merrick and Joshua Logan
J. B. by Archibald MacLeish; Producer Alfred de Liagre, Jr.
The Disenchanted by Budd Schulberg and Harvey Breit; Producers William Darrid and Eleanor Saidenberg
The Visit by Friedrich Duerrenmatt, adapted by Maurice Valency; Producer The Producers Theatre

Author (Dramatic)
Archibald MacLeish, J. B.

Producer (Dramatic)
Alfred de Liagre, Jr., J. B.

Director
Peter Brook, The Visit
Robert Dhery, La Plume de Ma Tante
William Gaskill, Epitaph for George Dillon
Peter Glenville, Rashomon
Elia Kazan, J. B.
Cyril Ritchard, The Pleasure of His Company
Dore Schary, A Majority of One

Musical
Flower Drum Song, book by Oscar Hammerstein II and Joseph Fields, lyrics by Oscar Hammerstein II, music by Richard Rodgers
La Plume de Ma Tante, written, devised and directed by Robert Dhery, music by Gerard Calvi, English lyrics by Ross Parker. (David Merrick and Joseph Kipness present the Jack Hylton Production)
Redhead by Herbert and Dorothy Fields, Sidney Sheldon and David Shaw, music by Albert Hague, lyrics by Dorothy Fields

Authors (Musical)
Herbert and Dorothy Fields, Sidney Sheldon and David Shaw, Redhead

Producers (Musical)
Robert Fryer and Lawrence Carr, Redhead

Composer
Albert Hague, Redhead

Conductor and Musical Director
Jay Blackston, Redhead
Salvatore Dell'Isola, Flower Drum Song
Lehman Engel, Goldilocks
Gershon Kingsley, La Plume de Ma Tante

Scenic Designer
Boris Aronson, J. B.
Ballou, The Legend of Lizzie
Ben Edwards, Jane Eyre
Oliver Messel, Rashomon
Donald Oenslager, A Majority of One
Teo Otto, The Visit

Costume Designer
Castillo, Goldilocks
Dorothy Jeakins, The World of Suzie Wong
Oliver Messel, Rashomon
Irene Sharaff, Flower Drum Song
Rouben Ter-Arutunian, Redhead

Choreographer
Agnes de Mille, Goldilocks
Bob Fosse, Redhead
Carol Haney, Flower Drum Song
Onna White, Whoop-Up

Stage Technician
Thomas Fitzgerald, Who Was That Lady I Saw You With?
Edward Flynn, The Most Happy Fella (City Center Revival)
Sam Knapp, The Music Man

Special Awards
John Gielgud
Howard Lindsay and Russel Crouse

1960

Actor (Dramatic)
Melvyn Douglas, The Best Man
Lee Tracy, The Best Man
Jason Robards, Jr., Toys in the Attic
Sidney Poitier, A Raisin in the Sun
George C. Scott, The Andersonville Trial

Actress (Dramatic)
Anne Bancroft, The Miracle Worker
Margaret Leighton, Much Ado About Nothing
Claudia McNeil, A Raisin in the Sun
Geraldine Page, Sweet Bird of Youth
Maureen Stapleton, Toys in the Attic
Irene Worth, Toys in the Attic

Actor, Supporting or Featured (Dramatic)
Warren Beatty, A Loss of Roses
Harry Guardino, One More River
Roddy McDowall, The Fighting Cock
Rip Torn, Sweet Bird of Youth
Lawrence Winters, The Long Dream

Actress, Supporting or Featured (Dramatic)
Leora Dana, The Best Man
Jane Fonda, There Was a Little Girl
Sarah Marshall, Goodbye, Charlie
Juliet Mills, Five Finger Exercise
Anne Revere, Toys in the Attic

Actor (Musical)
Jackie Gleason, Take Me Along
Robert Morse, Take Me Along
Walter Pidgeon, Take Me Along
Andy Griffith, Destry Rides Again
Anthony Perkins, Greenwillow

Actress (Musical)
Carol Burnett, One Upon a Mattress
Dolores Gray, Destry Rides Again
Eileen Herlie, Take Me Along
Mary Martin, The Sound of Music
Ethel Merman, Gypsy

Actor, Supporting or Featured (Musical)
Theodore Bikel, The Sound of Music
Kurt Kasznar, The Sound of Music
Tom Bosley, Fiorello!
Howard Da Silva, Fiorello!
Jack Klugman, Gypsy

Actress, Supporting or Featured (Musical)
Sandra Church, Gypsy
Pert Kelton, Greenwillow
Patricia Neway, The Sound of Music
Lauri Peters, The Sound of Music
The Children, The Sound of Music

Play
A Raisin in the Sun by Lorraine Hansberry; Producers Philip Rose and David J. Cogan
The Best Man by Gore Vidal; Producer The Playwrights' Company
The Miracle Worker by William Gibson. Produced by Fred Coe
The Tenth Man by Paddy Chayefsky; Producers Saint-Subber and Arthur Cantor
Toys in the Attic by Lillian Hellman; Producer Kermit Bloomgarden

Author (Dramatic)
William Gibson, The Miracle Worker

Producer (Dramatic)
Fred Coe, The Miracle Worker

Director (Dramatic)
Joseph Anthony, The Best Man
Tyrone Guthrie, The Tenth Man
Elia Kazan, Sweet Bird of Youth
Arthur Penn, The Miracle Worker
Lloyd Richards, A Raisin in the Sun

Musical
Fiorello! by Jerome Weidman and George Abbott. Lyrics by Sheldon Harnick, music by Jerry Bock; Producers Robert E. Griffith and Harold S. Prince.
Gypsy by Arthur Laurents. Lyrics by Stephen Sondheim, music by Jule Styne; Producers David Merrick and Leland Hayward
Once Upon a Mattress, book by Jay Thompson, Marshall Barer, Dean Fuller, lyrics by Marshall Barer, music by Mary Rodgers; Producers T. Edward Hambleton, Norris Houghton, William and Jean Eckart
Take Me Along. Book by Joseph Stein and Robert Russell, lyrics and music by Bob Merrill; Producer David Merrick.
The Sound of Music. Book by Howard Lindsay and Russel Crouse, lyrics by Oscar Hammerstein II, music by Richard Rodgers; Producers Leland Hayward, Richard Halliday, Rodgers and Hammerstein

Authors (Musical)
Jerome Weidman and George Abbott, Fiorello!
Howard Lindsay and Russel Crouse, The Sound of Music

Producer (Musical)
Robert Griffith and Harold Prince, Fiorello!
Leland Hayward and Richard Halliday, The Sound of Music

Director (Musical)
George Abbott, Fiorello!
Vincent J. Donehue, The Sound of Music
Peter Glenville, Take Me Along
Michael Kidd, Destry Rides Again
Jerome Robbins, Gypsy

Composers
Jerry Bock, Fiorello!
Richard Rodgers, The Sound of Music

Conductor and Musical Director
Abba Bogin, Greenwillow
Frederick Dvonch, The Sound of Music
Lehman Engel, Take Me Along
Hal Hastings, Fiorello!
Milton Rosenstock, Gypsy

Scenic Designer (Dramatic)
Will Steven Armstrong, Caligula
Howard Bay, Toys in the Attic
David Hays, The Tenth Man
George Jenkins, The Miracle Worker
Jo Mielziner, The Best Man

Scenic Designer (Musical)
Cecil Beaton, Saratoga
William and Jean Eckart, Fiorello!
Peter Larkin, Greenwillow
Jo Mielziner, Gypsy
Oliver Smith, The Sound of Music

Costume Designer
Cecil Beaton, Saratoga
Alvin Colt, Greenwillow
Raoul Pene Du Bois, Gypsy
Miles White, Take Me Along

Choreographer
Peter Gennaro, Fiorello!
Michael Kidd, Destry Rides Again
Joe Layton, Greenwillow
Lee Scott, Happy Town
Onna White, Take Me Along

Stage Technician
Al Alloy, chief electrician, Take Me Along
James Orr, chief electrician, Greenwillow
John Walters, chief carpenter, The Miracle Worker

Special Awards
John D. Rockefeller III
James Thurber and Burgess Meredith, A Thurber Carnival

1961

Actor (Dramatic)
Hume Cronyn, Big Fish, Little Fish
Sam Levene, The Devil's Advocate
Zero Mostel, Rhinoceros
Anthony Quinn, Becket

Actress (Dramatic)
Tallulah Bankhead, Midgie Purvis
Barbara Baxley, Period of Adjustment
Barbara Bel Geddes, Mary, Mary
Joan Plowright, A Taste of Honey

Actor, Supporting or Featured (Dramatic)
Philip Bosco, The Rape of the Belt
Eduardo Ciannelli, The Devil's Advocate
Martin Gabel, Big Fish, Little Fish
George Grizzard, Big Fish, Little Fish

Actress, Supporting or Featured (Dramatic)
Colleen Dewhurst, All the Way Home
Eileen Heckart, Invitation to a March
Tresa Hughes, The Devil's Advocate
Rosemary Murphy, Period of Adjustment

Actor (Musical)
Richard Burton, Camelot
Phil Silvers, Do Re Mi
Maurice Evans, Tenderloin

Actress (Musical)
Julie Andrews, Camelot
Carol Channing, Show Girl
Elizabeth Seal, Irma la Douce
Nancy Walker, Do Re Mi

Actor, Supporting or Featured (Musical)
Clive Revill, Irma la Douce
Dick Gautier, Bye, Bye Birdie
Ron Husmann, Tenderloin
Dick Van Dyke, Bye, Bye Birdie

Actress, Supporting or Featured (Musical)
Nancy Dussault, Do Re Mi
Tammy Grimes, The Unsinkable Molly Brown
Chita Rivera, Bye, Bye Birdie

Play
All the Way Home by Tad Mosell; Producer Fred Coe in association with Arthur Cantor
Becket by Jean Anouilh, translated by Lucienne Hill; Producer David Merrick
The Devil's Advocate by Dore Schary; Producer Dore Schary
The Hostage by Brendan Behan; Producers S. Field and Caroline Burke Swann

Author (Dramatic)
Jean Anouilh, Becket

Producer (Dramatic)
David Merrick, Becket

Director (Dramatic)
Joseph Anthony, Rhinoceros
Sir John Gielgud, Big Fish, Little Fish
Joan Littlewood, The Hostage
Arthur Penn, All the Way Home

Musical
Bye, Bye Birdie. Book by Michael Stewart, music by Charles Strouse, lyrics by Lee Adams; Producer Edward Padula in association with L. Slade Brown
Do Re Mi. Book by Garson Kanin, music by Jules Styne, lyrics by Betty Comden and Adolph Green; Producer David Merrick
Irma la Douce. Book and lyrics by Alexandre Breffort, music by Marguerite Monnot. English book and lyrics by Julian More, David Heneker and Monty Norman. Producer David Merrick in association with Donald Albery and H. M. Tennent, Ltd.

Author (Musical)
Michael Stewart, Bye, Bye Birdie

Producer (Musical)
Edward Padula, Bye, Bye Birdie

Director (Musical)
Peter Brook, Irma la Douce
Gower Champion, Bye, Bye Birdie
Garson Kanin, Do Re Mi

Conductor and Musical Director
Franz Allers, Camelot
Pembroke Davenport, 13 Daughters
Stanley Lebowsky, Irma la Douce
Elliott Lawrence, Bye, Bye Birdie

Scenic Designer (Dramatic)
Roger Furse, Duel of Angels
David Hays, All the Way Home
Jo Mielziner, The Devil's Advocate
Oliver Smith, Becket
Rouben Ter-Arutunian, Advise and Consent

Scenic Designer (Musical)
George Jenkins, 13 Daughters
Robert Randolph, Bye, Bye Birdie
Oliver Smith, Camelot

Costume Designer (Dramatic)
Theoni V. Aldredge, The Devil's Advocate
Motley, Becket
Raymond Sovey, All the Way Home

Costume Designer (Musical)
Adrian, and Tony Duquette, Camelot
Rolf Gerard, Irma la Douce
Cecil Beaton, Tenderloin

Choreographer
Gower Champion, Bye, Bye Birdie
Onna White, Irma la Douce

Stage Technician
Teddy Van Bemmel, Becket

Special Awards
David Merrick
The Theatre Guild

1962

Actor (Dramatic)
Fredric March, Gideon
John Mills, Ross
Donald Pleasence, The Caretaker
Paul Scofield, A Man for All Seasons

Actress (Dramatic)
Gladys Cooper, A Passage to India
Colleen Dewhurst, Great Day in the Morning
Margaret Leighton, Night of the Iguana
Kim Stanley, A Far Country

Actor, Supporting or Featured (Dramatic)
Godfrey M. Cambridge, Purlie Victorious
Joseph Campanella, A Gift of Time
Walter Matthau, A Shot in the Dark
Paul Sparer, Ross

Actress, Supporting or Featured (Dramatic)
Elizabeth Ashley, Take Her, She's Mine
Zohra Lampert, Look: We've Come Through
Janet Margolin, Daughter of Silence
Pat Stanley, Sunday in New York

Actor (Musical)
Ray Bolger, All American
Alfred Drake, Kean
Richard Kiley, No Strings
Robert Morse, How to Succeed in Business Without Really Trying

Actress (Musical)
Anna Maria Alberghetti, Carnival
Diahann Carroll, No Strings
Molly Picon, Milk and Honey
Elaine Stritch, Sail Away

Actor, Supporting or Featured (Musical)
Orson Bean, Subways Are for Sleeping
Severn Darden, From the Second City
Pierre Olaf, Carnival
Charles Nelson Reilly, How to Succeed...

Actress, Supporting or Featured (Musical)
Elizabeth Allen, The Gay Life
Barbara Harris, From the Second City
Phyllis Newman, Subways Are for Sleeping
Barbra Streisand, I Can Get It for You Wholesale

Play
A Man for All Seasons by Robert Bolt; Producers Robert Whitehead and Roger L. Stevens
Gideon by Paddy Chayefsky; Producers Fred Coe and Arthur Cantor
The Caretaker by Harold Pinter; Producers Roger L. Stevens, Frederick Brisson and Gilbert Miller
The Night of the Iguana by Tennessee Williams; Producers Charles Bowden and Viola Rubber

Author (Dramatic)
Robert Bolt, A Man for All Seasons

Producer (Dramatic)
Charles Bowden and Viola Rubber, Night of the Iguana
Fred Coe and Arthur Cantor, Gideon
David Merrick, Ross
Robert Whitehead and Roger L. Stevens, A Man for All Seasons

Director (Dramatic)
Tyrone Guthrie, Gideon
Donald McWhinnie, The Caretaker
Jose Quintero, Great Day In the Morning
Noel Willman, A Man for All Seasons

Musical
Carnival. Book by Michael Stewart and Helen Deutsch, music and lyrics by Bob Merrill; Producer David Merrick
How to Succeed in Business Without Really Trying. Book by Abe Burrows, Jack Weinstock and Willie Gilbert, music and lyrics by Frank Loesser; Producers Cy Feuer and Ernest Martin
Milk and Honey. Book by Don Appell, lyrics and music by Jerry Herman; Producer Gerard Oestreicher.
No Strings. Book by Samuel Taylor, music and lyrics by Richard Rodgers; Producer Richard Rodgers in association with Samuel Taylor.

Author (Musical)
Abe Burrows, Jack Weinstock and Willie Gilbert, How to Succeed...
Michael Stewart and Helen Deutsch, Carnival

Producer (Musical)
Helen Bonfils, Haila Stoddard and Charles Russell, Sail Away
Cy Feuer and Ernest Martin, How to Succeed...
David Merrick, Carnival
Gerard Oestreicher, Milk and Honey

Director (Musical)
Abe Burrows, How to Succeed...
Gower Champion, Carnival
Joe Layton, No Strings
Joshua Logan, All American

Composer
Richard Adler, Kwamina
Jerry Herman, Milk and Honey
Frank Loesser, How to Succeed...
Richard Rodgers, No Strings

Conductor and Musical Director
Pembroke Davenport, Kean
Herbert Greene, The Gay Life
Elliot Lawrence, How to Succeed...
Peter Matz, No Strings

Scenic Designer
Will Steven Armstrong, Carnival
Rouben Ter-Arutunian, A Passage to India
David Hays, No Strings
Oliver Smith, The Gay Life

Costume Designer
Lucinda Ballard, The Gay Life
Donald Brooks, No Strings
Motley, Kwamina
Miles White, Milk and Honey

Choreographer
Agnes de Mille, Kwamina
Michael Kidd, Subways Are for Sleeping
Dania Krupska, The Happiest Girl in the World
Joe Layton, No Strings

Stage Technician
Al Alloy, Ross
Michael Burns, A Man for All Seasons

Special Awards
Brooks Atkinson
Franco Zeffirelli
Richard Rodgers

1963

Actor (Dramatic)
Charles Boyer, Lord Pengo
Paul Ford, Never Too Late
Arthur Hill, Who's Afraid of Virginia Woolf?
Bert Lahr, The Beauty Part

Actress (Dramatic)
Hermione Baddeley, The Milk Train Doesn't Stop Here Anymore
Uta Hagen, Who's Afraid of Virginia Woolf?
Margaret Leighton, Tchin-Tchin
Claudia McNeill, Tiger, Tiger Burning Bright

Actor, Supporting or Featured (Dramatic)
Alan Arkin, Enter Laughing
Barry Gordon, A Thousand Clowns
Paul Rogers, Photo Finish
Frank Silvera, The Lady of the Camellias

Actress, Supporting or Featured (Dramatic)
Sandy Dennis, A Thousand Clowns
Melinda Dillon, Who's Afraid of Virginia Woolf?
Alice Ghostley, The Beauty Part
Zohra Lampert, Mother Courage and Her Children

Actor (Musical)
Sid Caesar, Little Me
Zero Mostel, A Funny Thing Happened on the Way to the Forum
Anthony Newley, Stop the World - I Want to Get Off
Clive Revill, Oliver!

Actress (Musical)
Georgia Brown, Oliver!
Nanette Fabray, Mr. President
Sally Ann Howes, Brigadoon
Vivien Leigh, Tovarich

Actor, Supporting or Featured (Musical)
David Burns, A Funny Thing Happened on the Way to the Forum
Jack Gilford, A Funny Thing Happened on the Way to the Forum
David Jones, Oliver!
Swen Swenson, Little Me

Actress, Supporting or Featured (Musical)
Ruth Kobart, A Funny Thing Happened on the Way to the Forum
Virginia Martin, Little Me
Anna Quayle, Stop the World - I Want to Get Off
Louise Troy, Tovarich

Play
A Thousand Clowns by Herb Gardner; Producers Fred Coe and Arthur Cantor
Mother Courage and Her Children by Bertolt Brecht, adapted by Eric Bentley; Producers Cheryl Crawford and Jerome Robbins
Tchin-Tchin by Sidney Michaels; Producer David Merrick.
Who's Afraid of Virginia Woolf? by Edward Albee; Producers Theatre 1963, Richard Barr and Clinton Wilder

Producer (Dramatic)
The Actors Studio Theatre, Strange Interlude
Richard Barr and Clinton Wilder, Theatre 1963, Who's Afraid of Virginia Woolf?
Cheryl Crawford and Jerome Robbins, Mother Courage and Her Children
Paul Vroom, Buff Cobb and Burry Fredrik, Too True To Be Good

Director (Dramatic)
George Abbott, Never Too Late
John Gielgud, The School for Scandal
Peter Glenville, Tchin-Tchin
Alan Schneider, Who's Afraid of Virginia Woolf?

Musical
A Funny Thing Happened on the Way to the Forum. Book by Burt Shevelove and Larry Gelbart, music and lyrics by Stephen Sondheim; Producer Harold Prince
Little Me. Book by Neil Simon, music by Cy Coleman, lyrics by Carolyn Leigh; Producers Cy Feuer and Ernest Martin
Oliver!. Book, music and lyrics by Lionel Bart; Producers David Merrick and Donald Albery
Stop the World - I Want to Get Off. Book, music and lyrics by Leslie Bricusse and Anthony Newley; Producer David Merrick in association with Bernard Delfont

Author (Musical)
Lionel Bart, Oliver!
Leslie Bricusse and Anthony Newley, Stop the World - I Want to Get Off
Burt Shevelove and Larry Gelbart, A Funny Thing Happened on the Way to the Forum
Neil Simon, Little Me

Producer (Musical)
Cy Feuer and Ernest Martin, Little Me
David Merrick and Donald Albery, Oliver!
Harold Prince, A Funny Thing Happened on the Way to the Forum

Director (Musical)
George Abbott, A Funny Thing Happened Happened on the Way to the Forum
Peter Coe, Oliver!
John Fearnley, Brigadoon
Cy Feuer and Bob Fosse, Little Me

Composer and Lyricist
Lionel Bart, Oliver!
Leslie Bricusse and Anthony Newley, Stop the World - I Want to Get Off
Cy Coleman and Carolyn Leigh, Little Me
Milton Schafer and Ronny Graham, Bravo Giovanni

Conductor and Musical Director
Jay Blackton, Mr. President
Anton Coppola, Bravo Giovanni
Donald Pippin, Oliver!
Julius Rudel, Brigadoon

Scenic Designer
Will Steven Armstrong, Tchin-Tchin
Sean Kenny, Oliver!
Anthony Powell, The School for Scandal
Franco Zeffirelli, The Lady of the Camellias

Costume Designer
Marcel Escoffier, The Lady of the Camellias
Robert Fletcher, Little Me
Motley, Mother Courage and Her Children
Anthony Powell, The School for Scandal

Choreographer
Bob Fosse, Little Me
Carol Haney, Bravo Giovanni

Stage Technician
Solly Pernick, Mr. President
Milton Smith, Beyond the Fringe

Special Awards
W. McNeil Lowry
Irving Berlin
Alan Bennett
Peter Cook
Jonathan Miller
Dudley Moore

1964

Actor (Dramatic)
Richard Burton, Hamlet
Albert Finney, Luther
Alec Guinness, Dylan
Jason Robards, Jr, After the Fall

Actress (Dramatic) Play
Elizabeth Ashley, Barefoot in the Park
Sandy Dennis, Any Wednesday
Colleen Dewhurst, The Ballad of the Sad Cafe
Julie Harris, Marathon '33

Actor, Supporting or Featured (Dramatic)
Lee Allen, Marathon '33
Hume Cronyn, Hamlet
Michael Dunn, The Ballad of the Sad Cafe
Larry Gates, A Case of Libel

Actress, Supporting or Featured (Dramatic)
Barbara Loden, After the Fall
Rosemary Murphy, Any Wednesday
Kate Reid, Dylan
Diana Sands, Blues for Mister Charlie

Actor (Musical)
Sydney Chaplin, Funny Girl
Bob Fosse, Pal Joey (City Center revival)
Bert Lahr, Foxy
Steve Lawrence, What Makes Sammy Run?

Actress (Musical)
Carol Channing, Hello, Dolly!
Beatrice Lillie, High Spirits
Barbra Streisand, Funny Girl
Inga Swenson, 110 in the Shade

Actor, Supporting or Featured (Musical)
Jack Cassidy, She Loves Me
Will Geer, 110 in the Shade
Danny Meehan, Funny Girl
Charles Nelson Reilly, Hello, Dolly!

Actress, Supporting or Featured (Musical)
Julienne Marie, Foxy
Kay Medford, Funny Girl
Tessie O'Shea, The Girl Who Came to Supper
Louise Troy, High Spirits

Play
The Ballad of the Sad Cafe by Edward Albee; Producers Lewis Allen and Ben Edwards
Barefoot in the Park by Neil Simon; Producer Saint Subber
Dylan by Sidney Michaels; Producers George W. George and Frank Granat
Luther by John Osborne; Producer David Merrick

Author (Dramatic)
John Osborne, Luther

Producer (Dramatic)
Lewis Allen and Ben Edwards, The Ballad of the Sad Cafe
George W. George and Frank Granat, Dylan
Herman Shumlin, The Deputy
Saint Subber, Barefoot in the Park

Director (Dramatic)
June Havoc, Marathon '33
Mike Nichols, Barefoot in the Park
Alan Schneider, The Ballad of the Sad Cafe
Herman Shumlin, The Deputy

Musical
Funny Girl. Book by Isobel Lennart, music by Jule Styne, lyrics by Bob Merrill; Producer Ray Stark
Hello, Dolly! Book by Michael Stewart, music and lyrics by Jerry Herman; Producer David Merrick
High Spirits. Book, lyrics and music by Hugh Martin and Timothy Gray; Producers Lester Osterman, Robert Fletcher and Richard Horner
She Loves Me. Book by Joe Masteroff, music by Jerry Bock, lyrics by Sheldon Harnick; Producer Harold Prince in association with Lawrence N. Kasha and Philip C. McKenna

Author (Musical)
Noel Coward and Harry Kurnitz, The Girl Who Came To Supper
Joe Masteroff, She Loves Me
Hugh Martin and Timothy Gray, High Spirits
Michael Stewart, Hello, Dolly!

Producer (Musical)
City Center Light Opera Company, West Side Story
David Merrick, Hello, Dolly!
Harold Prince, She Loves Me
Ray Stark, Funny Girl

Director (Musical)
Joseph Anthony, 110 in the Shade
Gower Champion, Hello, Dolly!
Noel Coward, High Spirits
Harold Prince, She Loves Me

Composer and Lyricist
Jerry Herman, Hello, Dolly!
Hugh Martin and Timothy Gray, High Spirits
Harvey Schmidt and Tom Jones, 110 in the Shade
Jule Styne and Bob Merrill, Funny Girl

Conductor and Musical Director
Shepard Coleman, Hello, Dolly!
Lehman Engel, What Makes Sammy Run?
Charles Jaffe, West Side Story
Fred Werner, High Spirits

Scenic Designer
Raoul Pene Du Bois, The Student Gypsy
Ben Edwards, The Ballad of the Sad Cafe
David Hays, Marco Millions
Oliver Smith, Hello, Dolly!

Costume Designer
Irene Sharaff, The Girl Who Came To Supper
Beni Montresor, Marco Millions
Rouben Ter-Arutunian, Arturo Ui
Freddy Wittop, Hello, Dolly!

Choreographer
Gower Champion, Hello, Dolly!
Danny Daniels, High Spirits
Carol Haney, Funny Girl
Herbert Ross, Anyone Can Whistle

Special Award
Eva Le Gallienne

1965

Actor (Dramatic)
John Gielgud, Tiny Alice
Walter Matthau, The Odd Couple
Donald Pleasence, Poor Bitos
Jason Robards, Hughie

Actress (Dramatic)
Marjorie Rhodes, All In Good Time
Beah Richards, The Amen Corner
Diana Sands, The Owl and the Pussycat
Irene Worth, Tiny Alice

Actor, Supporting or Featured (Dramatic)
Jack Albertson, The Subject Was Roses
Murray Hamilton, Absence of a Cello
Martin Sheen, The Subject Was Roses
Clarence Williams III, Slow Dance on the Killing Ground

Actress, Supporting or Featured (Dramatic)
Rae Allen, Traveller Without Luggage
Alexandra Berlin, All In Good Time
Carolan Daniels, Slow Dance on the Killing Ground
Alice Ghostley, The Sign in Sidney Brustein's Window

Actor (Musical)
Sammy Davis, Golden Boy
Zero Mostel, Fiddler On The Roof
Cyril Ritchard, The Roar of the Greasepaint - The Smell of the Crowd
Tommy Steele, Half A Sixpence

Actress (Musical)
Elizabeth Allen, Do I Hear A Waltz?
Nancy Dussault, Bajour
Liza Minnelli, Flora, the Red Menace
Inga Swenson, Baker Street

Actor, Supporting or Featured (Musical)
Jack Cassidy, Fade Out - Fade In
James Grout, Half A Sixpence
Victor Spinetti, Oh, What A Lovely War!
Jerry Orbach, Guys and Dolls

Actress, Supporting or Featured (Musical)
Maria Karnilova, Fiddler On The Roof
Luba Lisa, I Had A Ball
Carrie Nye, Half A Sixpence
Barbara Windsor, Oh, What A Lovely War!

Play
Luv by Murray Schisgal; Producer Claire Nichtern
The Odd Couple by Neil Simon; Producer Saint-Subber
The Subject Was Roses by Frank Gilroy; Producer Edgar Lansbury
Tiny Alice by Edward Albee; Producers Theatre 1965, Richard Barr, Clinton Wilder

Author (Dramatic)
Edward Albee, Tiny Alice
Frank Gilroy, The Subject Was Roses
Murray Schisgal, Luv
Neil Simon, The Odd Couple

Producer (Dramatic)
Hume Cronyn, Allen-Hogdon Inc., Stevens Productions Inc., Bonfils-Seawell Enterprises, Slow Dance on the Killing Ground
Claire Nichtern, Luv
Theatre 1965, Richard Barr, Clinton Wilder, Tiny Alice
Robert Whitehead, Tartuffe

Director (Dramatic)
William Ball, Tartuffe
Ulu Grosbard, The Subject Was Roses
Mike Nichols, Luv/The Odd Couple
Alan Schneider, Tiny Alice

Musical
Fiddler On The Roof. Book by Joseph Stein, music by Jerry Bock, lyrics by Sheldon Harnick; Producer Harold Prince
Golden Boy. Book by Clifford Odets and William Gibson, music by Charles Strouse, lyrics by Lee Adams; Producer Hillard Elkins
Half A Sixpence. Book by Beverly Cross, music and lyrics by David Heneker; Producers Allen Hodgdon, Stevens Productions and Harold Fielding
Oh, What A Lovely War! Devised by Joan Littlewood for Theatre Workshop, Charles Chilton and Members of the Cast; Producers David Merrick and Gerry Raffles

Author (Musical)
Jerome Coopersmith, Baker Street
Beverly Cross, Half A Sixpence
Sidney Michaels, Ben Franklin In Paris
Joseph Stein, Fiddler On The Roof

Producer (Musical)
Allen Hodgdon, Stevens Productions and Harold Fielding, Half A Sixpence
Hillard Elkins, Golden Boy
David Merrick, The Roar of the Greasepaint - The Smell of the Crowd
Harold Prince, Fiddler On The Roof

Director (Musical)
Joan Littlewood, Oh, What A Lovely War!
Anthony Newley, The Roar of the Greasepaint - The Smell of the Crowd
Jerome Robbins, Fiddler On The Roof
Gene Saks, Half A Sixpence

Composer and Lyricist
Jerry Bock and Sheldon Harnick, Fiddler On The Roof
Leslie Bricusse and Anthony Newley, The Roar of the Greasepaint - The Smell of The Crowd
David Heneker, Half A Sixpence
Richard Rodgers and Stephen Sondheim, Do I Hear A Waltz?

Scenic Designer
Boris Aronson, Fiddler On The Roof and Incident At Vichy
Sean Kenny, The Roar of the Greasepaint - The Smell of the Crowd
Beni Montresor, Do I Hear A Waltz?
Oliver Smith, *Baker Street/Luv/The Odd Couple

Costume Designer
Jane Greenwood, Tartuffe
Motley, Baker Street
Freddy Wittop, The Roar of the Greasepaint - The Smell of the Crowd
Patricia Zipprodt, Fiddler On The Roof

Choreographer
Peter Gennaro, Bajour
Donald McKayle, Golden Boy
Jerome Robbins, Fiddler On The Roof
Onna White, Half A Sixpence

Special Awards
Gilbert Miller
Oliver Smith

1966

Actor (Dramatic)
Roland Culver, Ivanov
Donald Donnelly and Patrick Bedford, Philadelphia, Here I Come!
Hal Holbrook, Mark Twain Tonight!
Nicol Williamson, Inadmissible Evidence

Actress (Dramatic)
Sheila Hancock, Entertaining Mr. Sloan
Rosemary Harris, The Lion in Winter
Kate Reid, Slapstick Tragedy
Lee Remick, Wait Until Dark

Actor, Supporting or Featured (Dramatic)
Burt Brinckerhoff, Cactus Flower
A. Larry Haines, Generation
Eamon Kelly, Philadelphia
Patrick Magee, Marat/Sade

Actress, Supporting or Featured
Zoe Caldwell, Slapstick Tragedy
Glenda Jackson, Marat/Sade
Mairin D. O'Sullivan, Philadelphia
Brenda Vaccaro, Cactus Flower

Actor (Musical)
Jack Cassidy, Superman
John Cullum, On A Clear Day You Can See Forever
Richard Kiley, Man of La Mancha
Harry Secombe, Pickwick

Actress (Musical)
Barbara Harris, On A Clear Day
Julie Harris, Skyscraper
Angela Lansbury, Mame
Gwen Verdon, Sweet Charity

Actor, Supporting or Featured (Musical)
Roy Castle, Pickwick
John McMartin, Sweet Charity
Frankie Michaels, Mame
Michael O'Sullivan, Superman

Actress, Supporting or Featured (Musical)
Beatrice Arthur, Mame
Helen Gallagher, Sweet Charity
Patricia Marand, Superman
Charlotte Rae, Pickwick

Play
Inadmissible Evidence by John Osborne; Producer The David Merrick Arts Foundation
Marat/Sade by Peter Weiss. English version by Geoffrey Skelton; Producer The David Merrick Arts Foundation
Philadelphia, Here I Come! by Brian Friel; Producer The David Merrick Arts Foundation
The Right Honourable Gentleman by Michael Dyne; Producers Peter Cookson, Amy Lynn and Walter Schwimmer

Director (Dramatic)
Peter Brook, Marat/Sade
Hilton Edwards, Philadelphia
Ellis Rabb, You Can't Take It With You
Noel Willman, The Lion in Winter

Musical
Mame. Book by Jerome Lawrence and Robert E. Lee, music and lyrics by Jerry Herman. Producers Sylvia and Joseph Harris, Robert Fryer and Lawrence Carr
Man of La Mancha. Book by Dale Wasserman, music by Mitch Leigh, lyrics by Joe Darion. Producers Albert W. Selden and Hal James
Skyscraper. Book by Peter Stone, music by James Van Heusen, lyrics by Sammy Cahn. Producers Cy Feuer and Ernest M. Martin
Sweet Charity. Book by Neil Simon, music by Cy Coleman, lyrics by Dorothy Fields. Producers Sylvia and Joseph Harris, Robert Fryer and Lawrence Carr

Director (Musical)
Cy Feuer, Skyscraper
Bob Fosse, Sweet Charity
Albert Marre, Man of La Mancha
Gene Saks, Mame

Composer and Lyricist
Cy Coleman and Dorothy Fields, Sweet Charity
Jerry Herman, Mame
Mitch Leigh and Joe Darion, Man of La Mancha
Burton Lane and Alan Jay Lerner, On A Clear Day

Scenic Designer
Howard Bay, Man of La Mancha
William and Jean Eckart, Mame
David Hays, Drat! The Cat!
Robert Randolph, Anya/Skyscraper/Sweet Charity

Costume Designer
Loudon Sainthill, The Right Honourable Gentleman
Howard Bay and Patton Campbell, Man of La Mancha
Irene Sharaff, Sweet Charity
Gunilla Palmstierna-Weiss, Marat/Sade

Choreographer
Jack Cole, Man of La Mancha
Bob Fosse, Sweet Charity
Michael Kidd, Skyscraper
Onna White, Mame

Special Award
Helen Menken (posthumous)

1967

Actor (Dramatic)
Hume Cronyn, A Delicate Balance
Donald Madden, Black Comedy
Donald Moffat, Right You Are and The Wild Duck
Paul Rogers, The Homecoming

Actress (Dramatic)
Eileen Atkins, The Killing of Sister George
Vivien Merchant, The Homecoming
Rosemary Murphy, A Delicate Balance
Beryl Reid, The Killing of Sister George

Actor, Supporting or Featured (Dramatic)
Clayton Corzatte, The School for Scandal
Stephen Elliott, Marat/Sade
Ian Holm, The Homecoming
Sydney Walker, The Wild Duck

Actress, Supporting or Featured (Dramatic)
Camila Ashland, Black Comedy
Brenda Forbes, The Loves of Cass McGuire
Marian Seldes, A Delicate Balance
Maria Tucci, The Rose Tattoo

Actor (Musical)
Alan Alda, The Apple Tree
Jack Gilford, Cabaret
Robert Preston, I Do! I Do!
Norman Wisdom, Walking Happy

Actress (Musical)
Barbara Harris, The Apple Tree
Lotte Lenya, Cabaret
Mary Martin, I Do! I Do!
Louise Troy, Walking Happy

Actor, Supporting or Featured (Musical)
Leon Bibb, A Hand is on the Gate
Gordon Dilworth, Walking Happy
Joel Grey, Cabaret
Edward Winter, Cabaret

Actress, Supporting or Featured (Musical)
Peg Murray, Cabaret
Leland Palmer, A Joyful Noise
Josephine Premice, A Hand is on the Gate
Susan Watson, A Joyful Noise

Play
A Delicate Balance, by Edward Albee; Producers Theatre 1967, Richard Barr and Clinton Wilder
Black Comedy, by Peter Shaffer; Producer Alexander H. Cohen
The Homecoming, by Harold Pinter; Producer Alexander Cohen
The Killing of Sister George by Frank Marcus; Producers Helen Bonfils and Morton Gottlieb

Director (Dramatic)
John Dexter, Black Comedy
Donald Driver, Marat/Sade
Peter Hall, The Homecoming
Alan Schneider, A Delicate Balance

Musical
Cabaret. Book by Joe Masteroff, music by John Kander, lyrics by Fred Ebb; Producer Harold Prince in association with Ruth Mitchell
I Do! I Do! Book and lyrics by Tom Jones, music by Harvey Schmidt. Producer David Merrick
The Apple Tree. Book by Sheldon Harnick and Jerry Bock, music by Jerry Bock, lyrics by Sheldon Harnick; Producer Stuart Ostrow
Walking Happy. Book by Roger O. Hirson and Ketti Frings, music by James Van Heusen, lyrics by Sammy Cahn; Producers Cy Feuer and Ernest M. Martin

Director (Musical)
Gower Champion, I Do! I Do!
Mike Nichols, The Apple Tree
Jack Sydow, Annie Get Your Gun
Harold Prince, Cabaret

Composer and Lyricist
Jerry Bock and Sheldon Harnick, The Apple Tree
Sammy Cahn and James Van Heusen, Walking Happy
Tom Jones and Harvey Schmidt, I Do! I Do!
John Kander and Fred Ebb, Cabaret

Scene Designer
Boris Aronson, Cabaret
John Bury, The Homecoming
Oliver Smith, I Do! I Do!
Alan Tagg, Black Comedy

Choreographer
Michael Bennett, A Joyful Noise
Danny Daniels, Walking Happy/Annie Get Your Gun
Ronald Field, Cabaret
Lee Theodore, The Apple Tree

Costume Designer
Nancy Potts, The Wild Duck/The School for Scandal
Tony Walton, The Apple Tree
Freddy Wittop, I Do! I Do!
Patricia Zipprodt, Cabaret

1968

Actor (Dramatic)
Martin Balsam, You Know I Can't Hear You When the Water's Running
Albert Finney, Joe Egg
Milo O'Shea, Staircase
Alan Webb, I Never Sang for My Father

Actress (Dramatic)
Zoe Caldwell, The Prime of Miss Jean Brodie
Colleen Dewhurst, More Stately Mansions
Maureen Stapleton, Plaza Suite
Dorothy Tutin, Portrait of a Queen

Actor, Supporting or Featured (Dramatic)
Paul Hecht, Rosencrantz and Guildenstern Are Dead
Brian Murray, Rosencrantz and Guildenstern Are Dead
James Patterson, The Birthday Party
John Wood, Rosencrantz and Guildenstern Are Dead

Actress, Supporting or Featured (Dramatic)
Pert Kelton, Spofford
Zena Walker, Joe Egg
Ruth White, The Birthday Party
Eleanor Wilson, Weekend

Actor (Musical)
Robert Goulet, The Happy Time
Robert Hooks, Hallelujah, Baby!
Anthony Roberts, How Now, Dow Jones
David Wayne, The Happy Time

Actress (Musical)
Melina Mercouri, Illya, Darling
Patricia Routledge, Darling of the Day
Leslie Uggams, Hallelujah, Baby!
Brenda Vacarro, How Now, Dow Jones

Actor, Supporting or Featured (Musical)
Scott Jacoby, Golden Rainbow
Nikos Kourkoulos, Illya, Darling
Mike Rupert, The Happy Time
Hiram Sherman, How Now, Dow Jones

Actress, Supporting or Featured (Musical)
Geula Gill, The Grand Music Hall of Israel
Julie Gregg, The Happy Time
Lillian Hayman, Hallelujah, Baby!
Alice Playten, Henry, Sweet Henry

Play
Joe Egg, by Peter Nichols; Producers Joseph Cates and Henry Fownes
Plaza Suite, by Neil Simon; Producer Saint-Subber
Rosencrantz and Guildenstern Are Dead, by Tom Stoppard; Producer The David Merrick Arts Foundation
The Price, by Arthur Miller; Producer Robert Whitehead

Producer (Dramatic)
The David Merrick Arts Foundation, Rosencrantz and Guildenstern Are Dead

Director (Dramatic)
Michael Blakemore, Joe Egg
Derek Goldby, Rosencrantz and Guildenstern Are Dead
Mike Nichols, Plaza Suite
Alan Schneider, You Know I Can't Hear You When the Water's Running

Musical
Hallelujah, Baby! Book by Arthur Laurents, music by Jule Styne, lyrics by Betty Comden and Adolph Green; Producers Albert Selden, Hal James, Jane C. Nusbaum, and Harry Rigby
The Happy Time. Book by N. Richard Nash, music by John Kander, lyrics by Fred Ebb; Producer David Merrick
How Now, Dow Jones. Book by Max Shulman, music by Elmer Bernstein, lyrics by Carolyn Leigh; Producer David Merrick
Illya, Darling. Book by Jules Dassin, music by Manos Hadjidakis, lyrics by Joe Darion; Producer Kermit Bloomgarden

Producer (Musical)
Albert Selden, Hal James, Jane C. Nusbaum and Harry Rigby, Hallelujah, Baby!

Director (Musical)
George Abbott, How Now, Dow Jones
Gower Champion, The Happy Time
Jules Dassin, Illya, Darling
Burt Shevelove, Hallelujah, Baby!

Composer and Lyricist
Elmer Bernstein and Carolyn Leigh, How Now, Dow Jones
Manos Hadjidakis and Joe Darion, Illya, Darling
John Kander and Fred Ebb, The Happy Time
Jule Styne, Betty Comden and Adolph Green, Hallelujah, Baby!

Scenic Designer
Boris Aronson, The Price
Desmond Heeley, Rosencrantz and Guildenstern Are Dead
Robert Randolph, Golden Rainbow
Peter Wexler, The Happy Time

Costume Designer
Jane Greenwood, More Stately Mansions
Desmond Heeley, Rosencrantz and Guildenstern Are Dead
Irene Sharaff, Hallelujah, Baby!
Freddy Wittop, The Happy Time

Choreographer
Michael Bennett, Henry, Sweet Henry
Kevin Carlisle, Hallelujah, Baby!
Gower Champion, The Happy Time
Onna White, Illya, Darling

Special Awards
Audrey Hepburn
Carol Channing
Pearl Bailey
David Merrick
Maurice Chevalier
APA-Phoenix Theatre
Marlene Dietrich

1969

Actor (Dramatic)
Art Carney, Lovers
James Earl Jones, The Great White Hope
Alec McCowen, Hadrian VII
Donald Pleasence, The Man in the Glass Booth

Actress (Dramatic)
Julie Harris, Forty Carats
Estelle Parsons, Seven Descents of Myrtle
Charlotte Rae, Morning, Noon and Night
Brenda Vaccaro, The Goodbye People

Actor, Supporting or Featured (Dramatic)
Al Pacino, Does a Tiger Wear a Necktie?
Richard Castellano, Lovers and Other Strangers
Anthony Roberts, Play It Again, Sam
Louis Zorich, Hadrian VII

Actress, Supporting or Featured (Dramatic)
Jane Alexander, The Great White Hope
Diane Keaton, Play It Again, Sam
Lauren Jones, Does a Tiger Wear a Necktie?
Anna Manahan, Lovers

Actor (Musical)
Herschel Bernardi, Zorba
Jack Cassidy, Maggie Flynn
Joel Grey, George M!
Jerry Orbach, Promises, Promises

Actress (Musical)
Maria Karnilova, Zorba
Angela Lansbury, Dear World
Dorothy Loudon, The Fig Leaves Are Falling
Jill O'Hara, Promises, Promises

Actor, Supporting or Featured (Musical)
A. Larry Haines, Promises, Promises
Ronald Holgate, 1776
Edward Winter, Promises, Promises

Actress, Supporting or Featured (Musical)
Sandy Duncan, Canterbury Tales
Marian Mercer, Promises, Promises
Lorraine Serabian, Zorba
Virginia Vestoff, 1776

Play
The Great White Hope by Howard Sackler; Producer Herman Levin
Hadrian VII by Peter Luke; Producers Lester Osterman Productions, Bill Freedman, Charles Kasher
Lovers by Brian Friel; Producers Helen Bonfils and Morton Gottlieb
The Man in the Glass Booth by Robert Shaw; Producers Glasshouse Productions and Peter Bridge, Ivor David Balding & Associates Ltd. and Edward M. Meyers with Leslie Ogden

Director (Dramatic)
Peter Dews, Hadrian VII
Joseph Hardy, Play It Again Sam
Harold Pinter, The Man in the Glass Booth
Michael A. Schultz, Does a Tiger Wear a Necktie?

Musical
Hair. Book by Gerome Ragni and James Rado, music by Galt MacDermot, lyrics by James Rado; Producer Michael Butler
Promises, Promises. Book by Neil Simon, music and lyrics by Burt Bacharach; Producer David Merrick
1776. Book by Peter Stone, music and lyrics by Sherman Edwards; Producer Stuart Ostrow
Zorba. Book by Joseph Stein, music by John Kander, lyrics by Fred Ebb; Producer Harold Prince

Director (Musical)
Peter Hunt, 1776
Robert Moore, Promises, Promises
Tom O'Horgan, Hair
Harold Prince, Zorba

Scenic Designer
Boris Aronson, Zorba
Derek Cousins, Canterbury Tales
Jo Mielziner, 1776
Oliver Smith, Dear World

Costume Designer
Michael Annals, Morning, Noon and Night
Robert Fletcher, Hadrian VII
Louden Sainthill, Canterbury Tales
Patricia Zipprodt, Zorba

Choreographer
Sammy Bayes, Canterbury Tales
Ronald Field, Zorba
Joe Layton, George M!
Michael Bennett, Promises, Promises

Special Awards
The National Theatre Company of Great Britain
The Negro Ensemble Company
Rex Harrison
Leonard Bernstein
Carol Burnett

1970

Actor (Dramatic)
James Coco, Last of the Red Hot Lovers
Frank Grimes, Borstal Boy
Stacy Keach, Indians
Fritz Weaver, Child's Play

Actress (Dramatic)
Geraldine Brooks, Brightower
Tammy Grimes, Private Lives (Revival)
Helen Hayes, Harvey (Revival)

Actor, Supporting or Featured (Dramatic)
Joseph Bova, The Chinese and Dr. Fish
Ken Howard, Child's Play
Dennis King, A Patriot for Me

Actress, Supporting or Featured (Dramatic)
Blythe Danner, Butterflies Are Free
Alice Drummond, The Chinese and Dr. Fish
Eileen Heckart, Butterflies Are Free
Linda Lavin, Last of the Red Hot Lovers

Actor (Musical)
Len Cariou, Applause
Cleavon Little, Purlie
Robert Weede, Cry For Us All

Actress (Musical)
Lauren Bacall, Applause
Katharine Hepburn, Coco
Dilys Watling, Georgy

Actor, Supporting or Featured (Musical)
Rene Auberjonois, Coco
Brandon Maggart, Applause
George Rose, Coco

Actress, Supporting or Featured (Musical)
Bonnie Franklin, Applause
Penny Fuller, Applause
Melissa Hart, Georgy
Melba Moore, Purlie

Play
Borstal Boy by Frank McMahon; Producers Michael McAloney, Burton C. Kaiser
Child's Play by Robert Marasco; Producer David Merrick
Indians by Arthur Kopit; Producers Lyn Austin, Oliver Smith, Joel Schenker, Roger L. Stevens
Last of the Red Hot Lovers by Neil Simon; Producer Saint-Subber

Director (Dramatic)
Joseph Hardy, Child's Play
Milton Katselas, Butterflies Are Free
Tomas MacAnna, Borstal Boy
Robert Moore, Last of the Red Hot Lovers

Musical
Applause. Book by Betty Comden and Adolph Green, music by Charles Strouse, lyrics by Lee Adams; Producers Joseph Kipness and Lawrence Kasha
Coco. Book and lyrics by Alan Jay Lerner, music by Andre Previn; Producer Frederick Brisson
Purlie. Book by Ossie Davis, Philip Rose, Peter Udell, music by Gary Geld, lyrics by Peter Udell; Producer Philip Rose

Director (Musical)
Mitchell Benthall, Coco
Ron Field, Applause
Philip Rose, Purlie

Scenic Designer
Howard Bay, Cry for Us All
Ming Cho Lee, Billy
Jo Mielziner, Child's Play
Robert Randolph, Applause

Costume Designer
Ray Aghayan, Applause
Cecil Beaton, Coco
W. Robert Lavine, Jimmy
Freddy Wittop, A Patriot for Me

Choreographer
Michael Bennett, Coco
Grover Dale, Billy
Ron Field, Applause
Louis Johnson, Purlie

Lighting Designer
Jo Mielziner, Child's Play
Tharon Musser, Applause
Thomas Skelton, Indians

Special Awards
Noel Coward
Alfred Lunt and Lynn Fontanne
The New York Shakespeare Festival
Barbra Streisand

1971

Actor (Dramatic)
Brian Bedford, The School for Wives
John Gielgud, Home
Alec McCowen, The Philanthropist
Ralph Richardson, Home

Actress (Dramatic)
Estelle Parsons, And Miss Reardon Drinks a Little
Diana Rigg, Abelard and Heloise
Marian Seldes, Father's Day
Maureen Stapleton, Gingerbread Lady

Actor, Supporting or Featured (Dramatic)
Ronald Radd, Abelard and Heloise
Donald Pickering, Conduct Unbecoming
Paul Sand, Story Theatre
Ed Zimmermann, The Philanthropist

Actress, Supporting or Featured (Dramatic)
Rae Allen, And Miss Reardon Drinks a Little
Lili Darvas, Les Blancs
Joan Van Ark, The School for Wives
Mona Washbourne, Home

Actor (Musical)
David Burns, Lovely Ladies, Kind Gentlemen
Larry Kert, Company
Hal Linden, The Rothschilds
Bobby Van, No, No, Nanette (Revival)

Actress (Musical)
Susan Browning, Company
Sandy Duncan, The Boy Friend
Helen Gallagher, No, No, Nanette
Elaine Stritch, Company

Actor, Supporting or Featured (Musical)
Keene Curtis, The Rothschilds
Charles Kimbrough, Company
Walter Willison, Two By Two

Actress, Supporting or Featured (Musical)
Barbara Barrie, Company
Patsy Kelly, No, No, Nanette
Pamela Myers, Company

Play
Home by David Storey; Producer Alexander H. Cohen
Sleuth by Anthony Shaffer; Producers Helen Bonfils, Morton Gottlieb and Michael White
Story Theatre by Paul Sills; Producer Zev Bufman
The Philanthropist by Christopher Hampton; Producers David Merrick and Byron Goldman

Producer (Dramatic)
Alexander H. Cohen, Home
David Merrick, The Philanthropist
Helen Bonfils, Morton Gottlieb and Michael White, Sleuth
Zev Bufman, Story Theatre

Director (Dramatic)
Lindsay Anderson, Home
Peter Brook, Midsummer Night's Dream
Stephen Porter, The School for Wives
Clifford Williams, Sleuth

Musical
Company; Producer Harold Prince
The Me Nobody Knows; Producer Jeff Britton
The Rothschilds. Producers Lester Osterman and Hillard Elkins

Producer (Musical)
Harold Prince, Company
Jeff Britton, The Me Nobody Knows
Hillard Elkins and Lester Osterman, The Rothschilds

Director (Musical)
Michael Kidd, The Rothschilds
Robert H. Livingston, The Me Nobody Knows
Harold Prince, Company
Burt Shevelove, No, No, Nanette

Book (Musical)
George Furth, Company
Robert H. Livingston and Herb Schapiro, The Me Nobody Knows
Sherman Yellen, The Rothschilds

Lyrics (Musical)
Sheldon Harnick, The Rothschilds
Will Holt, The Me Nobody Knows
Stephen Sondheim, Company

Score (Musical)
Jerry Bock, The Rothschilds
Gary William Friedman, The Me Nobody Knows
Stephen Sondheim, Company

Scenic Designer
Boris Aronson, Company
John Bury, The Rothschilds
Sally Jacobs, Midsummer Night's Dream
Jo Mielziner, Father's Day

Costume Designer
Raoul Pene Du Bois, No, No, Nanette
Jane Greenwood, Hay Fever/Les Blancs
Freddy Wittop, Lovely Ladies, Kind Gentlemen

Choreographer
Michael Bennett, Company
Michael Kidd, The Rothschilds
Donald Saddler, No, No, Nanette

Lighting Designer
Robert Ornbo, Company
H. R. Poindexter, Story Theatre
William Ritman, Sleuth

Special Awards
Elliot Norton
Ingram Ash
Playbill
Roger L. Stevens

1972

Actor (Dramatic)
Tom Aldredge, Sticks and Bones
Donald Pleasence, Wise Child
Cliff Gorman, Lenny
Jason Robards, The Country Girl

Actress (Dramatic)
Eileen Atkins, Vivat! Vivat Regina!
Colleen Dewhurst, All Over
Rosemary Harris, Old Times
Sada Thompson, Twigs

Actor, Supporting or Featured (Dramatic)
Vincent Gardenia, The Prisoner of Second Avenue
Douglas Rain, Vivat! Vivat Regina!
Lee Richardson, Vivat! Vivat Regina!
Joe Silver, Lenny

Actress, Supporting or Featured (Dramatic)
Cara Duff-MacCormick, Moonchildren
Mercedes McCambridge, The Love Suicide at Schofield Barracks
Frances Sternhagen, The Sign in Sidney Brustein's Window (Revival)
Elizabeth Wilson, Sticks and Bones

Actor (Musical)
Clifton Davis, Two Gentlemen of Verona
Barry Bostwick, Grease
Raul Julia, Two Gentlemen of Verona
Phil Silvers, A Funny Thing Happened on the Way to the Forum (Revival)

Actress (Musical)
Jonelle Allen, Two Gentlemen of Verona
Dorothy Collins, Follies
Mildred Natwick, '70 Girls '70
Alexis Smith, Follies

Actor, Supporting or Featured (Musical)
Larry Blyden, A Funny Thing Happened on the Way to the Forum (Revival)
Timothy Meyers, Grease
Gene Nelson, Follies
Ben Vereen, Jesus Christ Superstar

Actress, Supporting or Featured (Musical)
Adrienne Barbeau, Grease
Linda Hopkins, Inner City
Bernadette Peters, On The Town (Revival)
Beatrice Wind, Ain't Supposed to Die a Natural Death

Play
Old Times by Harold Pinter; Producer Roger L. Stevens
The Prisoner of Second Avenue by Neil Simon; Producer Saint-Subber
Sticks and Bones by David Rabe; Producer The New York Shakespeare Festival - Joseph Papp
Vivat! Vivat Regina! by Robert Bolt; Producers David Merrick and Arthur Cantor

Director (Dramatic)
Jeff Bleckner, Sticks and Bones
Gordon Davidson, The Trial Of The Catonsville Nine
Peter Hall, Old Times
Mike Nichols, The Prisoner of Second Avenue

Musical
Ain't Supposed to Die a Natural Death; Producers Eugene V. Wolsk, Charles Blackwell, Emanuel Azenberg, Robert Malina
Follies. Producer Harold Prince
Two Gentlemen of Verona. Producer The New York Shakespeare Festival - Joseph Papp
Grease. Producers Kenneth Waissman and Maxine Fox

Director (Musical)
Gilbert Moses, Ain't Supposed to Die a Natural Death
Harold Prince and Michael Bennett, Follies
Mel Shapiro, Two Gentlemen of Verona
Burt Shevelove, A Funny Thing Happened on the Way to the Forum

Book (Musical)
Ain't Supposed to Die a Natural Death by Melvin Van Peebles
Follies by James Goldman
Grease by Jim Jacobs and Warren Casey
Two Gentlemen of Verona by John Guare and Mel Shapiro

Score
Ain't Supposed to Die a Natural Death. Composer: Melvin Van Peebles. Lyricist: Melvin Van Peebles
Follies. Composer: Stephen Sondheim. Lyricist: Stephen Sondheim
Jesus Christ Superstar. Composer: Andrew Lloyd Webber. Lyricist: Tim Rice
Two Gentlemen of Verona. Composer: Galt MacDermot. Lyricist: John Guare

Scenic Designer
Boris Aronson, Follies
John Bury, Old Times
Kert Lundell, Ain't Supposed to Die a Natural Death
Robin Wagner, Jesus Christ Superstar

Costume Designer
Theoni V. Aldredge, Two Gentlemen of Verona
Randy Barcelo, Jesus Christ Superstar
Florence Klotz, Follies
Carrie F. Robbins, Grease

Choreographer
Michael Bennett, Follies
Patricia Birch, Grease
Jean Erdman, Two Gentlemen of Verona

Lighting Designer
Martin Aronstein, Ain't Supposed to Die a Natural Death
John Bury, Old Times
Jules Fisher, Jesus Christ Superstar
Tharon Musser, Follies

Special Awards
The Theatre Guild-American Theatre Society
Richard Rodgers
Fiddler on the Roof
Ethel Merman

1973

Actor (Dramatic)
Jack Albertson, The Sunshine Boys
Alan Bates, Butley
Wilfrid Hyde White, The Jockey Club Stakes
Paul Sorvino, That Championship Season

Actress (Dramatic)
Jane Alexander, 6 Rms Riv Vu
Colleen Dewhurst, Mourning Becomes Electra
Julie Harris, The Last of Mrs. Lincoln
Kathleen Widdoes, Much Ado About Nothing

Actor, Supporting or Featured (Dramatic)
Barnard Hughes, Much Ado About Nothing
John Lithgow, The Changing Room
John McMartin, Don Juan
Hayward Morse, Butley

Actress, Supporting or Featured (Dramatic)
Maya Angelou, Look Away
Leora Dana, The Last of Mrs. Lincoln
Katherine Helmond, The Great God Brown
Penelope Windust, Elizabeth I

Actor (Musical)
Len Cariou, A Little Night Music
Robert Morse, Sugar
Brock Peters, Lost in the Stars
Ben Vereen, Pippin

Actress (Musical)
Glynis Johns, A Little Night Music
Leland Palmer, Pippin
Debbie Reynolds, Irene (Revival)
Marcia Rodd, Shelter

Actor, Supporting or Featured (Musical)
Laurence Guittard, A Little Night Music
George S. Irving, Irene
Avon Long, Don't Play Us Cheap
Gilbert Price, Lost in the Stars

Actress, Supporting or Featured (Musical)
Patricia Elliot, A Little Night Music
Hermione Gingold, A Little Night Music
Patsy Kelly, Irene
Irene Ryan, Pippin

Play
Butley by Simon Gray; Producers Lester Osterman and Richard Horner
That Championship Season by Jason Miller; Producer The New York Shakespeare Festival - Joseph Papp
The Changing Room by David Storey; Producers Charles Bowden, Lee Reynolds, Isobel Robins
The Sunshine Boys by Neil Simon; Producers Emanuel Azenberg and Eugene V. Wolsk

Director (Dramatic)
A. J. Antoon, That Championship Season
A. J. Antoon, Much Ado About Nothing
Alan Arkin, The Sunshine Boys
Michael Rudman, The Changing Room

Musical
A Little Night Music. Producer Harold Prince
Don't Bother Me, I Can't Cope; Producers Edward Padula and Arch Lustberg
Pippin. Producer Stuart Ostrow
Sugar. Producer David Merrick

Director (Musical)
Vinnette Carroll, Don't Bother Me, I Can't Cope
Gower Champion, Sugar
Bob Fosse, Pippin
Harold Prince, A Little Night Music

Book (Musical)
A Little Night Music by Hugh Wheeler
Don't Bother Me, I Can't Cope by Micki Grant
Don't Play Us Cheap by Melvin Van Peebles
Pippin by Roger O. Hirson

Score (Musical)
A Little Night Music. Music and lyrics: Stephen Sondheim
Don't Bother Me, I Can't Cope. Music and Lyrics: Micki Grant
Much Ado About Nothing. Music: Peter Link
Pippin. Music and Lyrics: Stephen Schwartz

Scenic Designer
Boris Aronson, A Little Night Music
David Jenkins, The Changing Room
Santo Loquasto, That Championship Season
Tony Walton, Pippin

Costume Designer
Theoni V. Aldredge, Much Ado About Nothing
Florence Klotz, A Little Night Music
Miles White, Tricks
Patricia Zipprodt, Pippin

Choreographer
Gower Champion, Sugar
Bob Fosse, Pippin
Peter Gennaro, Irene
Donald Saddler, Much Ado About Nothing

Lighting Designer
Martin Aronstein, Much Ado About Nothing
Ian Calderon, That Championship Season
Jules Fisher, Pippin
Tharon Musser, A Little Night Music

Special Awards
John Lindsay
Actor's Fund of America
Shubert Organization

1974

Actor (Dramatic)
Michael Moriarty, Find Your Way Home
Zero Mostel, Ulysses in Nighttown
Jason Robards, A Moon for the Misbegotten (Revival)
George C. Scott, Vanya (Revival)
Nicol Williamson, Uncle Vanya

Actress (Dramatic)
Jane Alexander, Find Your Way Home
Colleen Dewhurst, A Moon for the Misbegotten (Revival)
Julie Harris, The Au Pair Man
Madeline Khan, In The Boom Boom Room
Rachel Roberts, performances with The New Phoenix Repertory Company

Actor, Supporting or Featured (Dramatic)
Rene Auberjonois, The Good Doctor
Ed Flanders, A Moon for the Misbegotten (Revival)
Douglas Turner Ward, The River Niger
Dick A. Williams, What the Wine-Sellers Buy

Actress, Supporting or Featured (Dramatic)
Regina Baff, Veronica's Room
Fionnuala Flanagan, Ulysses in Nighttown
Charlotte Moore, Chemin de Fer
Roxie Roker, The River Niger
Frances Sternhagen, The Good Doctor

Actor (Musical)
Alfred Drake, Gigi
Joe Morton, Raisin
Christopher Plummer, Cyrano
Lewis J. Stadlen, Candide

Actress (Musical)
Virginia Capers, Raisin
Carol Channing, Lorelei
Michele Lee, Seesaw

Actor, Supporting or Featured (Musical)
Mark Baker, Candide
Ralph Carter, Raisin
Tommy Tune, Seesaw

Actress, Supporting or Featured (Musical)
Leigh Berry, Cyrano
Maureen Brennan, Candide
June Gable, Candide
Ernestine Jackson, Raisin
Janie Sell, Over Here!

Play
In The Boom Boom Room by David Rabe; Producer Joseph Papp
The Au Pair Man by Hugh Leonard; Producer Joseph Papp
The River Niger by Joseph A. Walker; Producer The Negro Ensemble Co., Inc.
Ulysses in Nighttown by Marjorie Barkentin; Producers Alexander H. Cohen and Bernard Delfont

Director (Dramatic)
Burgess Meredith, Ulysses in Nighttown
Mike Nichols, Uncle Vanya
Stephen Porter, Chemin de Fer
Jose Quintero, A Moon for the Misbegotten (Revival)
Edwin Sherin, Find Your Way Home

Musical
Over Here! Producers Kenneth Waissman and Maxine Fox
Raisin. Producer Robert Nemiroff
Seesaw. Producers Joseph Kipness, Lawrence Kasha, James Nederlander, George M. Steinbrenner III, Lorin E. Price

Director (Musical)
Michael Bennett, Seesaw
Donald McKayle, Raisin
Harold Prince, Candide
Tom Moore, Over Here!

Book (Musical)
Candide by Hugh Wheeler
Raisin by Robert Nemiroff and Charlotte Zaltzberg
Seesaw by Michael Bennett

Score
Gigi. Music: Frederick Loewe. Lyrics: Alan Jay Lerner
The Good Doctor. Music: Peter Link. Lyrics: Neil Simon
Raisin. Music: Judd Woldin. Lyrics: Robert Brittan
Seesaw. Music: Cy Coleman. Lyrics: Dorothy Fields

Scenic Designer
John Conklin, The Au Pair Man
Franne and Eugene Lee, Candide
Santo Loquasto, What the Wine-Sellers Buy
Oliver Smith, Gigi
Ed Wittstein, Ulysses in Nighttown

Costume Designer
Theoni V. Aldredge, The Au Pair Man
Finlay James, Crown Matrimonial
Franne Lee, Candide
Oliver Messel, Gigi
Carrie F. Robbins, Over Here!

Choreographer
Michael Bennett, Seesaw
Patricia Birch, Over Here!
Donald McKayle, Raisin

Lighting Designer
Martin Aronstein, In The Boom Boom Room
Ken Billington, The Visit (Revival)
Ben Edwards, A Moon for the Misbegotten (Revival)
Jules Fisher, Ulysses in Nighttown
Tharon Musser, The Good Doctor

Special Awards
Liza Minnelli
Bette Midler
Peter Cook and Dudley Moore, Good Evening
A Moon for the Misbegotten (Revival)
Candide
Actor's Equity Association
Theatre Development Fund
John F. Wharton
Harold Friedlander

1975

Actor (Dramatic)
James Dale, Scapino
Peter Firth, Equus
Henry Fonda, Clarence Darrow
Ben Gazzara, Hughie & Duet
John Kani & Winston Ntshona, Sizwe Banzi Is Dead & The Island
John Wood, Sherlock Holmes

Actress (Dramatic)
Elizabeth Ashley, Cat On A Hot Tin Roof
Ellen Burstyn, Same Time, Next Year
Diana Rigg, The Misanthrope
Maggie Smith, Private Lives
Liv Ullman, A Doll's House

Actor, Supporting or Featured (Dramatic)
Larry Blyden, Absurd Person Singular
Leonard Fry, The National Health
Frank Langella, Seascape
Philip Locke, Sherlock Holmes
George Rose, My Fat Friend
Dick Anthony Williams, The Black Picture Show

Actress, Supporting or Featured (Dramatic)
Linda Miller, The Black Picture Show
Rita Moreno, The Ritz
Geraldine Page, Absurd Person Singular
Carole Shelley, Absurd Person Singular
Elizabeth Spriggs, London Assurance
Frances Sternhagen, Equus

Actor (Musical)
John Cullum, Shenandoah
Joel Grey, Goodtime Charley
Raul Julia, Where's Charley?
Eddie Mekka, The Lieutenant
Robert Preston, Mack and Mabel

Special Awards
Neil Simon
Al Hirschfeld

Actress (Musical)
Lola Falana, Doctor Jazz
Angela Lansbury, Gypsy
Bernadette Peters, Mack and Mabel
Ann Reinking, Goodtime Charley

Actor, Supporting or Featured (Musical)
Tom Aldredge, Where's Charley?
John Bottoms, Dance With Me
Douglas Henning, The Magic Show
Gilbert Price, The Night That Made America Famous
Ted Ross, The Wiz
Richard B. Shull, Goodtime Charley

Actress, Supporting or Featured (Musical)
Dee Dee Bridgewater, The Wiz
Susan Browning, Goodtime Charley
Zan Charisse, Gypsy
Taina Elg, Where's Charley?
Kelly Garrett, The Night That Made America Famous
Donna Theodore, Shenandoah

Play
Equus, by Peter Shaffer; producers Kermit Bloomgarden and Doris Cole Abrahams
Same Time, Next Year, by Bernard Slade; producer Morton Gottlieb
Seascape, by Edward Albee; producers Richard Barr, Charles Woodward and Clinton Wilder
Short Eyes, by Miguel Pinero; producer Joseph Papp
Sizwe Banzi Is Dead & The Island, by Athol Fugard, John Kani and Winston Ntshona; producers Hillard Elkins, Lester Osterman Prodns, Bernard Delfont, Michael White
The National Health, by Peter Nichols; producer Circle In the Square Inc.

Director (Dramatic)
Arvin Brown, The National Health
John Dexter, Equus
Frank Dunlop, Scapino
Ronald Eyre, London Assurance
Athol Fugard, Sizwe Banzi Is Dead & The Island
Gene Saks, Same Time, Next Year

Musical
Mack and Mabel, producer David Merrick
Shenandoah, producers Philip Rose, Gloria and Louis K. Sher
The Lieutenant, producers Spofford Beadle and Joseph Kutrzeba
The Wiz, producer Ken Harper

Director (Musical)
Gower Champion, Mack and Mabel
Grover Dale, The Magic Show
Geoffrey Holder, The Wiz
Arthur Laurents, Gypsy

Book (Musical)
Mack and Mabel, Michael Stewart
Shenandoah, James Lee Barrett
The Lieutenant, Gene Curty, Nitra Scharfman, Chuck Strand
The Wiz, William F. Brown

Score
A Letter for Queen Victoria, Music and Lyrics, Alan Lloyd
Shenandoah, Music and Lyrics, Gary Geld
The Lieutenant, Music and Lyrics, Gene Curty, Nitra Scharfman, Chuck Strand
The Wiz, Music and Lyrics, Charlie Smalls

Scenic Designer
Scott Johnson, Dance With Me
Tanya Moiseiwitsch, The Misanthrope
William Ritman, God's Favorite
Rouben Ter-Arutunian, Goodtime Charley
Carl Toms, Sherlock Holmes
Robert Wagner, Mack and Mabel

Costume Designer
Arthur Boccia, Where's Charley?
Raoul Pene du Bois, Doctor Jazz
Geoffrey Holder, The Wiz
Willa Kim, Goodtime Charley
Tanya Moiseiwitsch, The Misanthrope
Patricia Zipprodt, Mack and Mabel

Choreographer
Gower Champion, Mack and Mabel
George Faison, The Wiz
Donald McKayle, Doctor Jazz
Margo Sappington, Where's Charley?
Robert Tucker, Shenandoah
Joel Zwick, Dance With Me

Lighting Designer
Chip Monck, The Rocky Horror Show
Abe Feder, Goodtime Charley
Neil Patrick Jampolis, Sherlock Holmes
Andy Phillips, Equus
Thomas Skelton, All God's Chillun
James Tilton, Seascape

1976

Actor (Dramatic)
Moses Gunn, The Poison Tree
George C. Scott, Death of a Salesman
Donald Sinden, Habeas Corpus
John Wood, Travesties

Actress (Dramatic)
Tovah Feldshuh, Yentl
Rosemary Harris, The Royal Family
Lynn Redgrave, Mrs. Warren's Profession
Irene Worth, Sweet Bird of Youth

Actor, Featured Role (Dramatic)
Barry Bostwick, They Knew What They Wanted
Gabriel Dell, Lamppost Reunion
Edward Herrmann, Mrs. Warren's Profession
Daniel Seltzer, Knock Knock

Actress, Featured Role (Dramatic)
Marybeth Hurt, Trelawny of the 'Wells'
Shirley Knight, Kennedy's Children
Lois Nettleton, They Knew What They Wanted
Meryl Streep, 27 Wagons Full of Cotton

Actor (Musical)
Mako, Pacific Overtures
Jerry Orbach, Chicago
Ian Richardson, My Fair Lady
George Rose, My Fair Lady

Actress (Musical)
Donna McKechnie, A Chorus Line
Vivian Reed, Bubbling Brown Sugar
Chita Rivera, Chicago
Gwen Verdon, Chicago

Actor, Featured Role (Musical)
Robert LuPone, A Chorus Line
Charles Repole, Very Good Eddie
Isao Sato, Pacific Overtures
Sammy Williams, A Chorus Line

Actress, Featured Role (Musical)
Carole Bishop, A Chorus Line
Priscilla Lopez, A Chorus Line
Patti LuPone, The Robber Bridegroom
Virginia Seidel, Very Good Eddie

Play
First Breeze of Summer, by Leslie Lee; producer Negro Ensemble Company
Knock Knock, by Jules Feiffer; producers Harry Rigby & Terry Allen Kramer
Lamppost Reunion, by Louis La Russo II; producer Joe Garofalo
Travesties, by Tom Stoppard; producers David Merrick, Doris Cole Abrahams, Burry Fredrik

Director (Dramatic)
Arvin Brown, Ah, Wilderness!
Marshall W. Mason, Knock Knock
Ellis Rabb, The Royal Family
Peter Wood, Travesties

Musical
A Chorus Line, producer Joseph Papp
Bubbling Brown Sugar, producers J. Lloyd Grant, Richard Bell, Robert M. Cooper & Ashton Springer
Chicago, producers Robert Fryer, James Cresson
Pacific Overtures, producer Harold Prince

Director (Musical)
Michael Bennett, A Chorus Line
Bob Fosse, Chicago
Bill Gile, Very Good Eddie
Harold Prince, Pacific Overtures

Book (Musical)
A Chorus Line, James Kirkwood & Nicholas Dante
Chicago, Fred Ebb & Bob Fosse
Pacific Overtures, John Weidman
The Robber Bridegroom, Alfred Uhry

Score
A Chorus Line, Music Marvin Hamlish; Lyrics Edward Kleban
Chicago, Music John Kandler; Lyrics Fred Ebb
Pacific Overtures, Music & Lyrics, Stephen Sondheim
Treemonisha, Music & Lyrics, Scott Joplin

Scenic Designers
Boris Aronson, Pacific Overtures
Ben Edwards, A Matter of Gravity
David Mitchell, Trelawny of the 'Wells'
Tony Walton, Chicago

Costume Designers
Theoni V. Aldredge, A Chorus Line
Florence Klotz, Pacific Overtures
Ann Roth, The Royal Family
Patricia Zipprodt, Chicago

Lighting Designer
Ian Calderon, Trelawny of the 'Wells'
Jules Fisher, Chicago
Tharon Musser, A Chorus Line
Tharon Musser, Pacific Overtures

Choreographer
Michael Bennett & Bob Avian, A Chorus Line
Patricia Birch, Pacific Overtures
Bob Fosse, Chicago
Billy Wilson, Bubbling Brown Sugar

Special Awards
Mathilde Pincus
Circle in the Square
Thomas H. Fitzgerald
The Arena Stage

1977

Actor (Dramatic)
Tom Courtenay, Otherwise Engaged
Ben Gazzara, Who's Afraid of Virginia Woolf?
Al Pacino, The Basic Training of Pavlo Hummel
Ralph Richardson, No Man's Land

Actress (Dramatic)
Colleen Dewhurst, Who's Afraid of Virginia Woolf?
Julie Harris, The Belle of Amherst
Liv Ullmann, Anna Christie
Irene Worth, The Cherry Orchard

Actor, Featured Role (Dramatic)
Bob Dishy, Sly Fox
Joe Fields, The Basic Training of Pavlo Hummel
Laurence Luckinbill, The Shadow Box
Jonathan Pryce, Comedians

Actress, Featured Role (Dramatic)
Trazana Beverley, For Colored Girls Who Have Considered Suicide/When The Rainbow Is Enuf
Patricia Elliott, The Shadow Box
Rose Gregorio, The Shadow Box
Mary McCarty, Anna Christie

Actor (Musical)
Barry Bostwick, The Robber Bridegroom
Robert Guillaume, Guys and Dolls
Raul Julia, The Threepenny Opera
Reid Shelton, Annie

Actress (Musical)
Clamma Dale, Porgy and Bess
Ernestine Jackson, Guys and Dolls
Dorothy Loudon, Annie
Andrea McArdle, Annie

Actor, Featured Role (Musical)
Lenny Baker, I Love My Wife
David Kernan, Side By Side By Sondheim
Larry Marshall, Porgy and Bess
Ned Sherrin, Side By Side By Sondheim

Actress, Featured Role (Musical)
Ellen Greene, The Threepenny Opera
Delores Hall, Your Arms Too Short To Box With God
Millicent Martin, Side By Side By Sondheim
Julie N. McKenzie, Side By Side By Sondheim

Play
For Colored Girls Who Have Considered Suicide/When The Rainbow Is Enuf, by Ntozake Shange; producer Joseph Papp
Otherwise Engaged, by Simon Gray; producers Michael Codron, Frank Milton and James M. Nederlander
The Shadow Box, by Michael Cristofer; producers Allan Francis, Ken Marsolais, Lester Osterman, Leonard Soloway
Streamers, by David Rabe; producer Joseph Papp

Director (Dramatic)
Gordon Davidson, The Shadow Box
Ulu Grosbard, American Buffalo
Mike Nichols, Comedians
Mike Nichols, Streamers

Musical
Annie, producers Lewis Allen and Mike Nichols
Happy End, producers Michael Harvey and Chelsea Theatre Centre
I Love My Wife, producers Terry Allen Kramer and Harry Rigby
Side By Side By Sondheim, producer Harold Prince

Director (Musical)
Vinette Carroll, Your Arms Too Short To Box With God
Martin Charnin, Annie
Jack O'Brien, Porgy and Bess
Gene Saks, I Love My Wife

Book (Musical)
Annie, Thomas Meehan
Happy End, Elisabeth Hauptmann
I Love My Wife, Michael Stewart
Your Arms Too Short To Box With God, Vinnette Carroll

Score
Annie, Music Charles Strouse; Lyrics Martin Charnin
Happy End, Music Kurt Weill; Lyrics Bertolt Brecht
Godspell, Music and Lyrics, Stephen Schwartz
I Love My Wife, Music Cy Coleman; Lyrics Michael Stewart

Scenic Designer
Santo Loquasto, American Buffalo
Santo Loquasto, The Threepenny Opera
David Mitchell, Annie
Robert Randolph, Porgy and Bess

Costume Designer
Theoni V. Aldredge, Annie
Theoni V. Aldredge, The Threepenny Opera
Santo Loquasto, The Cherry Orchard
Nancy Potts, Porgy and Bess

Lighting Designer
John Bury, No Man's Land
Pat Collins, The Threepenny Opera
Neil Peter Jampolis, The Innocents
Jennifer Tipton, The Cherry Orchard

Choreographer
Talley Beatty, Your Arms Too Short To Box With God
Patricia Birch, Music Is
Peter Gennaro, Annie
Onna White, I Love My Wife

Most Innovative Production Of A Revival
The Cherry Orchard
Guys and Dolls
Porgy and Bess
The Threepenny Opera

Special Awards
Lily Tomlin
Barry Manilow
Diana Ross
National Theatre For The Deaf
Mark Taper Forum
Equity Library Theatre

1978

Actor (Dramatic)
Hume Cronyn, The Gin Game
Barnard Hughes, Da
Frank Langella, Dracula
Jason Robards, A Touch of the Poet

Actress (Dramatic)
Anne Bancroft, Golda
Anita Gillette, Chapter Two
Estelle Parsons, Miss Margarida's Way
Jessica Tandy, The Gin Game

Actor, Featured Role (Dramatic)
Morgan Freeman, The Mighty Gents
Victor Garber, Deathtrap
Cliff Gorman, Chapter Two
Lester Rawlins, Da

Actress, Featured Role (Dramatic)
Starletta DuPois, The Mighty Gents
Swoosie Kurtz, Tartuffe
Marian Seldes, Deathtrap
Ann Wedgeworth, Chapter Two

Actor (Musical)
Eddie Bracken, Hello, Dolly!
John Cullum, On The Twentieth Century
Barry Nelson, The Act
Gilbert Price, Timbuktu!

Actress (Musical)
Madeline Kahn, On The Twentieth Century
Eartha Kitt, Timbuktu!
Liza Minnelli, The Act
Frances Sternhagen, Angel

Actor, Featured Role (Musical)
Steven Boockvor, Working
Wayne Cilento, Dancin'
Rex Everhart, Working
Kevin Kline, On The Twentieth Century

Actress, Featured Role (Musical)
Nell Carter, Ain't Misbehavin'
Imogene Coca, On The Twentieth Century
Ann Reinking, Dancin'
Charlaine Woodard, Ain't Misbehavin'

Play
Chapter Two, by Neil Simon; producer Emanuel Azenberg
Da, by Hugh Leonard; Hudson Guild Theatre prodn presented by Lester Osterman, Marilyn Strauss and Marc Howard
Deathtrap, by Ira Levin, presented by Alfred de Liagre Jr., and Roger L. Stevens
The Gin Game, by D.L. Coburn; Shubert Organization Presentation of Mike Nichols and Hume Cronyn prodn

Director (Dramatic)
Melvin Bernhardt, Da
Robert Moore, Deathtrap
Mike Nichols, The Gin Game
Dennis Rosa, Dracula

Musical
Ain't Misbehavin', Manhattan Theatre Club Prodn
Dancin', Jules Fisher, Shubert Organization and Columbia Pictures presentation of Jules Fisher prodn
On The Twentieth Century, Producers Circle 2 Inc. prodn in association with Joseph Harris and Ira Bernstein
Runaways, New York Shakespeare Festival Production

Director (Musical)
Bob Fosse, Dancin'
Richard Maltby, Jr., Ain't Misbehavin'
Harold Prince, On The Twentieth Century
Elizabeth Swados, Runaways

Book (Musical)
A History Of The American Film, Christopher Durang
On The Twentieth Century, Betty Comdem & Adolph Green
Runaways, Elizabeth Swados
Working, Stephen Schwartz

Score
The Act, Music and Lyrics John Kander & Fred Ebb
On The Twentieth Century, Music Cy Coleman; Lyrics Comden & Green
Runaways, Music and Lyrics, Elizabeth Swados
Working, Music and Lyrics Craig Cornelia, Micki Grant, Mary Rodgers Susan Birkenhead, Stephen Schwartz, James Taylor

Scenic Designer
Zack Brown, The Importance of Being Earnest
Edward Gorey, Dracula
David Mitchell, Working
Robin Wagner, On The Twentieth Century

Costume Designer
Edward Gorey, Dracula
Halston, The Act
Geoffrey Holder, Timbuktu!
Willa Kim, Dancin'

Lighting Designer
Jules Fisher, Beatlemania
Jules Fisher, Dancin'
Tharon Musser, The Act
Ken Billington, Working

Choreographer
Arthur Faria, Ain't Misbehavin'
Bob Fosse, Dancin'
Ron Lewis, The Act
Elizabeth Swados, Runaways

Most Innovative Production Of A Revival
Dracula
Tartuffe
Timbuktu!
A Touch of the Poet

Special Award
The Long Wharf Theatre

1979

Actor (Dramatic)
Phillip Anglim, The Elephant Man
Tom Conti, Whose Life Is It Anyway?
Jack Lemmon, Tribute
Alex McCowen, St. Mark's Gospel

Actress (Dramatic)
Jane Alexander, First Monday In October
Constance Cummings, Wings
Carole Shelley, The Elephant Man
Frances Sternhagen, On Golden Pond

Actor, Featured Role (Dramatic)
Bob Balaban, The Inspector General
Michael Gough, Bedroom Farce
Joseph Maher, Spokesong
Edward James Olmos, Zoot Suit

Actress, Featured Role (Dramatic)
Joan Hickson, Bedroom Farce
Laurie Kennedy, Man and Superman
Susan Littler, Bedroom Farce
Mary-Joan Negro, Wings

Actor (Musical)
Len Cariou, Sweeney Todd
Vicent Gardenia, Ballroom
Joel Grey, The Grand Tour
Robert Klein, They're Playing Our Song

Actress (Musical)
Tovah Feldshuh, Sarava
Angela Lansbury, Sweeney Todd
Dorothy Loudon, Ballroom
Alexis Smith, Platinum

Actor, Featured Role (Musical)
Richard Cox, Platinum
Henderson Forsythe, The Best Little Whorehouse In Texas
Gregory Hines, Eubie!
Ron Holgate, The Grand Tour

Actress, Featured Role (Musical)
Joan Ellis, The Best Little Whorehouse In Texas
Carlin Glynn, The Best Little Whorehouse In Texas
Millicent Martin, King Of Hearts
Maxine Sullivan, My Old Friends

Play
Bedroom Farce by Alan Ayckbourn; producers Robert Whitehead, Roger L. Stevens, George W. George, Frank Milton
The Elephant Man by Bernard Pomerance; producers Richmond Crinkley, Elizabeth I. McCann, Nelle Nugent
Whose Life Is It Anyway? by Brian Clark; producers Emanuel Azenberg, James Nederlander, Ray Cooney
Wings by Arthur Kopit; producer Kennedy Center for the Performing Arts

Director (Dramatic)
Alan Ayckbourn & Peter Hall, Bedroom Farce
Paul Giovanni, The Crucifer Of Blood
Jack Hofsiss, The Elephant Man
Michael Lindsay-Hogg, Whose Life Is It Anyway?

Musical
Ballroom, producers Michael Bennett, Bob Avian, Bernard Gersten, Susan MacNair
Sweeney Todd, producers Richard Barr, Charles Woodward, Robert Fryer, Mary Lea Johnson, Martin Richards
The Best Little Whorehouse In Texas, producer Universal Pictures
They're Playing Our Song, producer Emanuel Azenberg

Director (Musical)
Michael Bennett, Ballroom
Peter Masterson & Tommy Tune, The Best Little Whorehouse In Texas
Robert Moore, They're Playing Our Song
Harold Prince, Sweeney Todd

Book (Musical)
Ballroom, Jerome Kass
Sweeney Todd, Hugh Wheeler
The Best Little Whorehouse In Texas, Larry L. King, Peter Masterson
They're Playing Our Song, Neil Simon

Score
Carmelina, Music Alan Jay Lerner; Lyrics Burton Lane
Eubie!, Music and Lyrics, Eubie Blake
Sweeney Todd, Music and Lyrics, Stephen Sondheim
The Grand Tour, Music and Lyrics, Jerry Herman

Scenic Designer
Karl Eigsti, Knockout
David Jenkins, The Elephant Man
Eugene Lee, Sweeney Todd
John Wulp, The Crucifer Of Blood

Costume Designer
Theoni V. Aldredge, Ballroom
Franne Lee, Sweeney Todd
Ann Roth, The Crucifer Of Blood
Julie Weiss, The Elephant Man

Lighting Designer
Ken Billington, Sweeney Todd
Beverly Emmons, The Elephant Man
Roger Morgan, The Crucifer Of Blood
Tharon Musser, Ballroom

Choreographer
Michael Bennett & Bob Avian, Ballroom
Henry LeTang & Billy Wilson, Eubie!
Dan Siretta, Whoopee!
Tommy Tune, The Best Little Whorehouse In Texas

Special Awards
Henry Fonda
Walter F. Diehl
Eugene O'Neill Memorial Theatre Center
American Conservatory Theatre

1980

Actor (Dramatic)
Charles Brown, Home
Gerald Hiken, Strider
Judd Hirsch, Talley's Folly
John Rubinstein, Children Of a Lesser God

Actress (Dramatic)
Blythe Danner, Betrayal
Phyllis Frelich, Children Of a Lesser God
Maggie Smith, Night And Day
Anne Twomey, Nuts

Actor, Featured Role (Dramatic)
David Dukes, Bent
George Hearn, Watch On The Rhine
Earle Hyman, The Lady From Dubuque
Joseph Maher, Night And Day
David Rounds, Morning's At Seven

Actress, Featured Role (Dramatic)
Maureen Anderman, The Lady From Dubuque
Pamela Burrell, Strider
Lois de Banzie, Morning's At Seven
Dinah Manoff, I Ought To Be In Pictures

Actor (Musical)
Jim Dale, Barnum
Gregory Hines, Comin' Uptown
Mickey Rooney, Sugar Babies
Giorgio Tozzi, The Most Happy Fella

Actress (Musical)
Christine Andreas, Oklahoma!
Sandy Duncan, Peter Pan
Patti LuPone, Evita
Ann Miller, Sugar Babies

Actor, Featured Role (Musical)
David Garrison, A Day In Hollywood, A Night In The Ukraine
Harry Groener, Oklahoma!
Bob Gunton, Evita
Mandy Patinkin, Evita

Actress, Featured Role (Musical)
Debbie Allen, West Side Story
Glenn Close, Barnum
Jossie de Guzman, West Side Story
Priscilla Lopez, A Day In Hollywood, A Night In The Ukraine

Play
Bent, by Martin Sherman; producers, Jack Schissel, Steven Steinlauf
Children Of a Lesser God, by Mark Medoff; producers, Emanuel Azenberg, The Shubert Organization, Dasha Epstein, Ron Dante
Home, by Samm-Art Williams; producers, Elizabeth I. McCann, Nelle Nugent, Gerald S. Krone, Ray Larsen
Talley's Folly, by Lanford Wilson; producers, Nancy Cooperstein, Porter Van Zandt, Marc Howard

Director (Dramatic)
Gordon Davidson, Children Of A Lesser God
Peter Hall, Betrayal
Marshall W. Mason, Talley's Folly
Vivian Matalon, Morning's At Seven

Musical
A Day In Hollywood, A Night In The Ukraine, producers, Alexander H. Cohen, Hildy Parks
Barnum, producers, Judy Gordon, Cy Coleman, Lois Rosenfield, Maurice Rosenfield
Evita, producer, Robert Stigwood
Sugar Babies, producers, Terry Allen Kramer, Harry Rigby

Director (Musical)
Ernest Flatt, Rudy Tronto, Sugar Babies
Joe Layton, Barnum
Harold Prince, Evita
Tommy Tune, A Day In Hollywood, A Night In The Ukraine

Book (Musical)
A Day In Hollywood, A Night In The Ukraine, Dick Vosburgh
Barnum, Mark Bramble
Evita, Tim Rice
Sugar Babies, Ralph G. Allen and Harry Rigby

Score
A Day In Hollywood, A Night In The Ukraine, Music, Frank Lazarus; Lyrics, Dick Vosburgh
Barnum, Music, Cy Coleman; Lyrics, Michael Stewart
Evita, Music, Andrew Lloyd Webber; Lyrics, Tim Rice
Sugar Babies, Music, Arthur Malvin; Lyrics, Arthur Malvin

Scenic Designer
John Lee Beatty, Talley's Folly
David Mitchell, Barnum
Timothy O'Brien, Tazeena Firth, Evita
Tony Walton, A Day In Hollywood, A Night In The Ukraine

Costume Designer
Theoni V. Aldredge, Barnum
Pierre Balmain, Happy New Year
Timothy O'Brien, Tazeena Firth, Evita
Raoul Pene du Bois, Sugar Babies

Lighting Designer
Beverly Emmons, A Day In Hollywood, A Night In The Ukraine
David Hersey, Evita
Craig Miller, Barnum
Dennis Parichy, Talley's Folly

Choreographer
Ernest Flatt, Sugar Babies
Larry Fuller, Evita
Joe Layton, Barnum
Tommy Tune, Thommie Walsh, A Day In Hollywood, A Night In The Ukraine

Reproduction Of A Play Or Musical
Major Barbara, producer, Circle in the Square
Morning's At Seven, producers, Elizabeth I. McCann, Nelle Nugent, Ray Larsen
Peter Pan, producers, Zev Bufman, James M. Nederlander
West Side Story, producers, Gladys Rackmil, John F. Kennedy Center, James M. Nederlander, Ruth Mitchell

Special Awards
Actors Theatre of Louisville
Goodspeed Opera House
Mary Tyler Moore

Lawrence Langner Award
Helen Hayes

Theatre Award '80
Richard Fitzgerald
Hobe Morrison

PULITZER PRIZE PLAYS

1917 None

1918 WHY MARRY? Jesse Lynch Williams

1919 None

1920 BEYOND THE HORIZON Eugene O'Neill

1921 MISS LULU BETT Zona Gale

1922 ANNA CHRISTIE Eugene O'Neill

1923 ICEBOUND Owen Davis

1924 HELL-BENT FOR HEAVEN Hatcher Hughes

1925 THEY KNEW WHAT THEY WANTED Sidney Howard

1926 CRAIG'S WIFE George Kelly

1927 IN ABRAHAM'S BOSOM Paul Green

1928 STRANGE INTERLUDE Eugene O'Neill

1929 STREET SCENE Elmer L. Rice

1930 THE GREEN PASTURES Marc Connelly

1931 ALISON'S HOUSE Susan Glaspell

1932 OF THEE I SING George S. Kaufman, Morrie Ryskind, Ira Gershwin. Music by George Gershwin

1933 BOTH YOUR HOUSES Maxwell Anderson

1934 MEN IN WHITE Sidney Kingsley

1935 THE OLD MAID Zoe Akins

1936 IDIOT'S DELIGHT Robert E. Sherwood

1937 YOU CAN'T TAKE IT WITH YOU Moss Hart and George S. Kaufman

1938 OUR TOWN Thornton Wilder

1939 ABE LINCOLN IN ILLINOIS Robert E. Sherwood

1940 THE TIME OF YOUR LIFE William Saroyan

1941 THERE SHALL BE NO NIGHT Robert E. Sherwood

1942 None

1943 THE SKIN OF OUR TEETH Thornton Wilder

1944 None SPECIAL CITATION Richard Rodgers and Oscar Hammerstein II for the musical OKLAHOMA!

1945 HARVEY Mary Chase

1946 STATE OF THE UNION Russel Crouse and Howard Lindsay

1947 None

1948 A STREETCAR NAMED DESIRE Tennessee Williams

1949 DEATH OF A SALESMAN Arthur Miller

1950 SOUTH PACIFIC Richard Rodgers, Oscar Hammerstein II and Joshua Logan

1951 None

1952 THE SHRIKE Joseph Kramm

1953 PICNIC William Inge

1954 THE TEAHOUSE OF THE AUGUST MOON John Patrick

1955 CAT ON A HOT TIN ROOF Tennessee Williams

1956 DIARY OF ANNE FRANK Albert Hackett and Frances Goodrich

1957 LONG DAY'S JOURNEY INTO NIGHT Eugene O'Neill

1958 LOOK HOMEWARD ANGEL Ketti Frings

1959 J.B. Archibald MacLeish

1960 FIORELLO! book by Jerome Weidman and George Abbott, music by Jerry Bock, lyrics by Sheldon Harnick

1961 ALL THE WAY HOME Tad Mosel

1962 HOW TO SUCCEED IN BUSINESS WITHOUT REALLY TRYING Frank Loesser and Abe Burrows

1963 None

1964 None

1965 THE SUBJECT WAS ROSES Frank D. Gilroy

1966 None

1967 A DELICATE BALANCE Edward Albee

1968 None

1969 THE GREAT WHITE HOPE Howard Sackler

1970 NO PLACE TO BE SOMEBODY Charles Gordone

1971 THE EFFECT OF GAMMA RAYS ON MAN-IN-THE-MOON MARIGOLDS Paul Zindel

1972 None

1973 THAT CHAMPIONSHIP SEASON Jason Miller

1974 None

1975 SEASCAPE Edward Albee

1976 A CHORUS LINE Michael Bennett, James Kirkwood, Nicholas Dante, Marvin Hamlisch, Edward Kleban

1977 THE SHADOW BOX Michael Christofer

1978 THE GIN GAME D. L. Coburn

1979 BURIED CHILD Sam Shepard

1980 TALLEY'S FOLLY Lanford Wilson

LONG-RUNNING BROADWAY PLAYS
As of June 1, 1980

SHOW	PERFS.
Grease (M)	3,388 (a)
Fiddler on the Roof (M)	3,242 (b)
Life with Father (P)	3,224
Tobacco Road (P)	3,182
Hello, Dolly (M)	2,844 (c)
My Fair Lady (M)	2,717
Man of LaMancha (M)	2,329
Abie's Irish Rose (P)	2,327
Oklahoma (M)	2,212
A Chorus Line (M)	1,995 (*)
South Pacific (M)	1,925
Pippin (M)	1,908 (d)
Magic Show (M)	1,859
Harvey (P)	1,775
Hair (M)	1,742
Wiz (M)	1,672
Born Yesterday (P)	1,642
Mary, Mary (P)	1,572
Voice of the Turtle (P)	1,557
Oh, Calcutta (M) (revival)	1,550 (*)
Barefoot in the Park (P)	1,532
Mame (M)	1,503
Arsenic and Old Lace (P)	1,444
Same Time Next Year (P)	1,444
Sound of Music (M)	1,443
How to Succeed in Business (M)	1,417
Hellzapoppin (M)	1,404
Music Man (M)	1,375
Funny Girl (M)	1,348
Oh, Calcutta (M) (original)	1,316
Annie (M)	1,301 (*)
Angel Street (P)	1,295
Lightin' (P)	1,291
Promises, Promises (M)	1,281
King and I (M)	1,246
Cactus Flower (P)	1,234
Sleuth (P)	1,222
1776 (M)	1,217
Equus (P)	1,209
Guys and Dolls (M)	1,200
Cabaret (M)	1,166
Mister Roberts (P)	1,157
Annie Get Your Gun (M)	1,147
Seven Year Itch (P)	1,141
Butterflies Are Free (P)	1,128
Pins and Needles (M)	1,108
Plaza Suite (P)	1,097
Equus (P)	1,091
Kiss Me, Kate (M)	1,071
Don't Bother Me, I Can't Cope (M)	1,065
Pajama Game (M)	1,063
Shenandoah (M)	1,050
Teahouse of the August Moon (P)	1,027
Damn Yankees (M)	1,019
Never Too Late (P)	1,007

Note: (a) The run of "Grease" includes 128 performances played at the Eden Theatre, a downtown house classified as Broadway, before the show moved uptown. Similarly, the original "Oh, Calcutta" played 710 performances at the same theatre before transferring uptown.

(b) The 3,242 performance run of "Fiddler on the Roof" was set by the original production of 1964-65. As with such other longrun shows as "My Fair Lady," "The King and I" and "Guys and Dolls," the performance figure does not include performances played by any revival of the show.

(c) The run of "Hello Dolly" was interrupted for an out-of-town engagement. The same was true of "South Pacific" and "Don't Bother Me, I Can't Cope."

(d) The total for "Pippin" is a corrected figure.

Designations: (P) Play, (M) Musical, (*) Show still running. Figures indicate number of performances played.

GRAMMYS

1958

RECORD OF THE YEAR
CATCH A FALLING STAR - Perry Como (RCA)
THE CHIPMUNK SONG - David Seville (Lib)
FEVER - Peggy Lee (Cap)
NEL BLU DIPINTO DI BLU (VOLARE) - Domenico Modugno (Decca)
WITCHCRAFT - Frank Sinatra (Cap)

ALBUM OF THE YEAR
ELLA FITZGERALD SINGS THE IRVING BERLIN SONG BOOK - Ella Fitzgerald (Verve)
COME FLY WITH ME - Frank Sinatra (Cap)
THE MUSIC FROM PETER GUNN - Henry Mancini (Victor)
ONLY THE LONELY - Frank Sinatra (Cap)
TCHAIKOVSKY: CONCERTO NO. 1, IN B FLAT MINOR OP. 23 - Van Cliburn (Victor)

SONG OF THE YEAR
(Songwriter's Award)
CATCH A FALLING STAR - Paul Vance and Lee Pockriss (Victor)
FEVER - Johnny Davenport and Eddie Cooley (Cap)
GIGI - Alan J. Lerner and Frederick Lowe (MGM)
NEL BLU DIPINTO DI BLU (VOLARE) - Domenico Modugno (Decca)
WITCHCRAFT - Cy Coleman and Carolyn Leigh (Cap)

BEST VOCAL PERFORMANCE, FEMALE
ELLA FITZGERALD SINGS THE IRVING BERLIN SONG BOOK - Ella Fitzgerald (Verve)
EVERYBODY LOVES A LOVER - Doris Day (Col)
EYDIE IN LOVE - Eydie Gorme (Am-Par)
FEVER - Peggy Lee (Cap)
I WISH YOU LOVE - Keely Smith (Cap)

BEST VOCAL PERFORMANCE, MALE
CATCH A FALLING STAR - Perry Como (RCA)
COME FLY WITH ME - Frank Sinatra (Cap)
HAWAIIAN WEDDING SONG - Andy Williams (Cadence)
NEL BLU DIPINTO DI BLU (VOLARE) - Domenico Modugno (Decca)
WITCHCRAFT - Frank Sinatra (Cap)

BEST PERFORMANCE BY AN ORCHESTRA
BURNISHED BRASS - George Shearing (Cap)
CROSS COUNTRY SUITE - Buddy DeFranco (Dot)
PETER GUNN - Henry Mancini (RCA)
I WANT TO LIVE - Johnny Mandel (UA)
KANE IS ABLE - Jack Kane (Coral)
BILLY MAY'S BIG FAT BRASS - Billy May (Cap)
OTHER WORLDS, OTHER SOUNDS - Esquivel (RCA)
YOUNG MAN'S LAMENT - David Rose & His Orchestra with Andre Previn (MGM)

BEST PERFORMANCE BY A DANCE BAND
BASIE - Count Basie (Roulette)
BAUBLES, BANGLES & BEADS - Jonah Jones (Cap)
PETER GUNN - Ray Anthony (Cap)
PATRICIA - Perez Prado (RCA)
TEA FOR TWO CHA CHA - Warren Covington & The Tommy Dorsey Orchestra (Decca)

BEST PERFORMANCE BY A VOCAL GROUP OR CHORUS
BAUBLES, BANGLES AND BEADS - Kirby Stone Four (Col)
TOM DOOLEY - Kingston Trio (Cap)
IMAGINATION - The King Sisters (Cap)
SING A SONG OF BASIE - Lambert, Henricks, & Ross (Am-Par)
THAT OLD BLACK MAGIC - Louis Prima, Keely Smith (Cap)

BEST JAZZ PERFORMANCE (INDIVIDUAL)
BAUBLES, BANGLES & BEADS - Jonah Jones (Cap)
BURNISHED BRASS - George Shearing (Cap)
DIXIELAND STORY - Matty Matlock (WB)
ELLA FITZGERALD SINGS THE DUKE ELLINGTON SONG BOOK - Ella Fitzgerald (Verve)
JUMPIN' WITH JONAH - Jonah Jones (Cap)

BEST JAZZ PERFORMANCE (GROUP)
BASIE - Count Basie (Roulette)
BAUBLES, BANGLES & BEADS - Jonah Jones (Cap)
BURNISHED BRASS - George Shearing (Cap)
FOUR FRESHMAN IN PERSON (Cap)
SING A SONG OF BASIE - Basie Rhythm Section, Dave Lambert Singers (Am-Par)

BEST COMEDY PERFORMANCE
BEST OF THE STAN FREBERG SHOWS - Stan Freberg (Cap)
CHIPMUNK SONG - David Seville (Lib)
THE FUTURE LIES AHEAD - Mort Sahl (Verve)
GREEN CHRISTMAS - Stan Freberg (Cap)
IMPROVISATIONS TO MUSIC - Mike Nichols & Elaine May (Merc)

BEST COUNTRY & WESTERN PERFORMANCE
ALL I HAVE TO DO IS DREAM - Everly Brothers (Cadence)
BIRD DOG - Everly Brothers (Cadence)
TOM DOOLEY - Kingston Trio (Cap)
OH LONESOME ME - Don Gibson (Victor)
OH, OH, I'M FALLING IN LOVE AGAIN - Jimmie Rodgers (Roulette)

BEST RHYTHM & BLUES PERFORMANCE
BELAFONTE SINGS THE BLUES - Harry Belafonte (Victor)
THE END - Earl Grant (Decca)
LOOKING BACK - Nat King Cole (Cap)
PATRICIA - Perez Prado (Victor)
TEQUILA - Champs (Challenge)

BEST ARRANGEMENT
(Arranger's Award)
COME FLY WITH ME (Frank Sinatra) - Billy May (Cap)
FEVER (Peggy Lee) - Jack Marshall (Cap)
THE MUSIC FROM PETER GUNN - Henry Mancini (RCA)
BILLY MAY'S BIG FAT BRASS - Billy May (Cap)
WITCHCRAFT (Frank Sinatra) - Nelson Riddle (Cap)

BEST ENGINEERED RECORD (CLASSICAL)
(Engineer's Award)
DUETS WITH A SPANISH GUITAR (Almeida & Terri) Eng: Sherwood Hall III (Cap)
GAIETE PARISIENNE (Felix Slatkin) Eng: Sherwood Hall III (Cap)
PROKOFIEFF: LIEUTENANT KIJI/STRAVINSKY; SONG OF THE NIGHTINGALE (Fritz Reiner) (Victor)
STRAVINSKY: RITE OF SPRING (Bernstein) (Col)

BEST ENGINEERED RECORDING (OTHER THAN CLASSICAL)
(Engineer's Award)
THE CHIPMUNK SONG (David Seville) Eng: Ted Keep (Lib)
COME FLY WITH ME (Frank Sinatra) Eng: Luis P. Valentin (Cap)
BILLY MAY'S BIG FAT BRASS (Billy May) Eng: Hugh Davies (Cap)
OTHER WORLDS, OTHER SOUNDS (Esquivel) Eng: Rafael O. Valentin (Victor)
WITCHCRAFT (Frank Sinatra) Eng: Luis P. Valentin (Cap)

BEST ALBUM COVER
(Art Director's Award)
COME FLY WITH ME (Frank Sinatra) Art Dir: Marvin Schwartz (Cap)
FOR WHOM THE BELLS TOLL (Ray Heindorf) Photog: Paramount Pictures Corp., Ray Rennahan, A.S.C. (WB)
IRA IRONSTRINGS PLAY MUSIC FOR PEOPLE WITH $3.98 - Art Dir: David Rose (WB)
JULIE (Julie London) Art Dir: Charles Ward (Lib)
ONLY THE LONELY (Frank Sinatra) Art Dir: Frank Sinatra (Cap)

BEST MUSICAL COMPOSITION FIRST RECORDED AND RELEASED IN 1958 (OVER 5 MINS. DURATION)
(Samuel) BARBER: VANESSA (Victor)
CROSS COUNTRY SUITE - Nelson Riddle
I WANT TO LIVE - Johnny Mandel (UA)
(Richard) RODGERS: VICTORY AT SEA, VOL. III (Victor)
KURT WEILL: MAHOGONNY (Col)

BEST ORIGINAL CAST ALBUM (BROADWAY OR TV)
FLOWER DRUM SONG - Orig. Cast Album, Salvatore dell'Isola, Musical Dir. Richard Rodgers, Music (Col)
THE MUSIC MAN - Orig. Broadway Cast, Meredith Willson (Cap)
SOUND OF JAZZ - from CBS TV "Seven Lively Arts" with Basie, Giuffre, Holiday, etc. (Col)
VICTORY AT SEA VOL. 11 - from NBC TV prod. RCA Victor Sym. Orch., Richard Rodgers (RCA)
PETER GUNN - Henry Mancini (RCA)

BEST SOUND TRACK ALBUM–DRAMATIC PICTURE SCORE OR ORIGINAL CAST
AUNTIE MAME SOUND TRACK - Ray Heindorf Orchestra (WB)
THE BRIDGE ON THE RIVER KWAI - Malcolm Arnold (Col)
GIGI - Orig. Motion Picture Sound Track, Andre Previn (MGM)
I WANT TO LIVE - Johnny Mandel (UA)
SOUTH PACIFIC - Orig. Sound Track Orch. cond. Alfred Newman (Victor)

BEST PERFORMANCE–DOCUMENTARY OR SPOKEN WORD
THE BEST OF THE STAN FREBERG SHOWS (Cap)
GREAT AMERICAN SPEECHES - Melvyn Douglas, Vincent Price, Carl Sandburg, Ed Begley (Caedmon)
GREEN CHRISTMAS - Stan Freberg (Cap)
IMPROVISATIONS TO MUSIC - Mike Nichols, Elaine May (Merc)
TWO INTERVIEWS OF OUR TIME - Henry Jacobs, Woody Leafer (Fantasy)
THE LADY FROM PHILADELPHIA - Marion Anderson (Rupp, Morrow) (Victor)

BEST RECORDING FOR CHILDREN
CHILDREN'S MARCHING SONG - Cyril Stapleton (London)
THE CHIPMUNK SONG - David Seville (Lib)
FUN IN SHARILAND - Shari Lewis (Victor)
MOMMY, GIVE ME A DRINKA WATER - Danny Kaye (Cap)
TUBBY THE TUBA - Jose Ferrer (MGM)
THE WITCH DOCTOR - David Seville (Lib)

BEST CLASSICAL PERFORMANCE - ORCHESTRAL
BARBER: MEDITATION AND DANCE OF VENGEANCE - Charles Munch, Boston Symphony (Victor)
BEETHOVEN: SYMPHONY No. 6 IN F MAJOR - Bruno Walter, Columbia Symphony Orch. (Col)
GAIETE PARISIENNE - Felix Slatkin, Hollywood Bowl Symphony (Cap)
MAHLER: SYMPHONY No. 2 IN C MINOR (Emilia Cundari, Maureen Forrester, Westminster Choir) - Bruno Walter, N.Y. Philharmonic (Col)
PROKOFIEV: SYMPHONY No. 5 IN B FLAT MAJOR - Eugene Ormandy, Philadelphia Orchestra (Col)
RIMSKY-KORSAKOFF: SCHEHEREZADE - Pierre Monteux, London Symphony (Victor)
STRAVINSKY: LE SACRE DU PRINTEMPS - Leonard Bernstein, N.Y. Philharmonic (Col)

BEST CLASSICAL PERFORMANCE - INSTRUMENTAL (WITH CONCERTO SCALE ACCOMPANIMENT)
BARTOK: CONCERTO FOR VIOLIN - Isaac Stern (Bernstein, cond. N.Y. Philharmonic) (Col)
BRAHMS: PIANO CONCERTO No. 2 - Emil Gilels (Fritz Reiner, cond. Chicago Symphony) (Victor)
RACHMANINOFF: RHAPSODY ON A THEME OF PAGANINI - Leonard Pennario (Cap)
SAINT-SAENS: PIANO CONCERTO No. 2 - Artur Rubinstein (Wallenstein, cond. Symphony of the Air) (Victor)
(Andres) SEGOVIA GOLDEN JUBILEE (last record in set) (Decca)
TCHAIKOVSKY: CONCERTO No. 1 IN B FLAT MINOR, OP. 23 - Van Cliburn (Kondrashin Symphony) (Victor)

BEST CLASSICAL PERFORMANCE - INSTRUMENTALIST (OTHER THAN CONCERTO SCALE ACCOMPANIMENT)
ART OF THE HARPSICHORD - Wanda Landowska (RCA)
BEETHOVEN SONATA No. 9 AND SONATA No. 8 - Nathan Milstein (Cap)
HOROWITZ PLAYS CHOPIN - Vladimir Horowitz (Victor)
MUSIC FOR THE HARP - Marcel Grandjany (Cap)
SEGOVIA GOLDEN JUBILEE - Andres Segovia (Decca)

BEST CLASSICAL PERFORMANCE - CHAMBER MUSIC (INCLUDING CHAMBER ORCHESTRA)
BEETHOVEN QUARTET 130 - Hollywood String Quartet (Cap)
BEETHOVEN: TRIO IN E FLAT, OP. 3 - Jascha Heifetz, William Primrose, Gregor Piatigorsky (Victor)
BEETHOVEN: TRIO IN E FLAT MAJOR; TRIO IN D MAJOR - Pablo Casals, Eugene Istomin, Fuchs (Col)
BEETHOVEN: TRIO IN G, OP. 9, NO. 1; TRIO IN C MINOR, OP. 9, NO. 3 - Jascha Heifetz, William Primrose, Gregor Piatigorsky (Victor)
RAVEL: QUARTET IN F MAJOR; DEBUSSY: QUARTET IN G MINOR - The Budapest String Quartet (Col)

BEST CLASSICAL PERFORMANCE - VOCAL SOLOIST (WITH OR WITHOUT ORCHESTRA)
CHERUBINI: MEDEA - Maria Callas (Merc)
DUETS FOR SPANISH GUITAR - Salli Terri (Cap)
EILEEN FARRELL AS MEDEA - Eileen Farrell (Col)
OPERATIC RECITAL - Renata Tebaldi (London)
WAGNER: PRELUDE & LIEBESTOD/"TRISTAN & ISOLDE", BRUNNHILDE'S IMMOLATION, DIE GOTTERDAMERUNG - Eileen Farrell (Munch, Boston Symphony) (Victor)

BEST CLASSICAL PERFORMANCE - OPERATIC OR CHORAL
BARBER: VANESSA - Dimitri Mitropoulos, Metropolitan Opera Chorus & Orch. (Steber, Elias, Resnick, Gedda, Nagy, Cehanovsky, Tozzi) (Victor)
DONIZETTI: LUCIA DE LAMMERMOOR - Erich Leinsdorf, Rome Opera House Chorus & Orch. (Peters, Pace, Carlin, Palma, Peerce, Maero, Tozzi) (Victor)
PUCCINI: MADAME BUTTERFLY - Erich Leinsdorf, Rome Opera House

Chorus & Orch. (Cifferi, Mattioli, Moffo, Zeri, Elias, Pace, Carlin, Valletti, Catalani Cesari, Mineo, Corena, Monreale) (Victor)
ROSSINI: BARBER OF SEVILLE - Maria Callas, Tito Gobbi (Angel)
VICTORIA: REQUIEM MASS - Dom David Nicholson, Dir., Choir of the Abbey of Mt. Angel/C. Robert Zimmerman, Dir., Portland Symphony Choir (Victor)
VIRTUOSO - Roger Wagner Chorale (Cap)

1959

RECORD OF THE YEAR
A FOOL SUCH AS I - Elvis Presley (RCA)
HIGH HOPES - Frank Sinatra (Cap)
LIKE YOUNG - Andre Previn (MGM)
MACK THE KNIFE - Bobby Darin (Atco)
THE THREE BELLS - The Browns (RCA)

ALBUM OF THE YEAR
BELAFONTE AT CARNEGIE HALL - Harry Belafonte (RCA)
COME DANCE WITH ME - Frank Sinatra (Cap)
MORE MUSIC FROM PETER GUNN - Henry Mancini (RCA)
RACHMANINOFF PIANO CONCERTO No. 3 - Van Cliburn, Kiril Kondrashin (RCA)
VICTORY AT SEA, VOL. I - Robert Russell Bennett (Remake) (RCA)

SONG OF THE YEAR
(Songwriter's Award)
BATTLE OF NEW ORLEANS - Jimmy Driftwood
HIGH HOPES - Sammy Cahn, Jimmy van Heusen
I KNOW - Karl Stutz, Edith Lindeman
LIKE YOUNG - Paul Francis Webster, Andre Previn
SMALL WORLD - Jule Styne, Stephen Sondheim

BEST VOCAL PERFORMANCE, FEMALE
ALRIGHT, OKAY - Peggy Lee (Cap)
BROADWAY '59 - Pat Suzuki (RCA)
BUT NOT FOR ME - Ella Fitzgerald (Verve)
LA STRADA DEL AMORE - Caterina Valente (RCA)
PORGY AND BESS - Lena Horn (RCA)

BEST VOCAL PERFORMANCE, MALE
AN EVENING WITH LERNER AND LOWE - Robert Merrill (RCA)
BELAFONTE AT CARNEGIE HALL - Harry Belafonte (RCA)
COME DANCE WITH ME - Frank Sinatra (Cap)
GUESS WHO - Jesse Belvin (RCA)
MACK THE KNIFE - Bobby Darin (Atco)

BEST PERFORMANCE BY A DANCE BAND
ANATOMY OF A MURDER - Duke Ellington (Col)
BREAKFAST DANCE AND BARBECUE - Count Basie (Roulette)
FOR THE VERY FIRST TIME - Glenn Miller (RCA)
NEW SOUNDS AT THE ROOSEVELT - Larry Elgart (RCA)
POPS AND PRADO - Perez Prado (RCA)
SOUND SPECTACULAR - Ray Anthony (Cap)

BEST PERFORMANCE BY AN ORCHESTRA
JUST FOR KICKS - Bob Thompson & Orch.
LIKE YOUNG - David Rose & Orch. with Andre Previn (MGM)
MORE MUSIC FROM PETER GUNN - Henry Mancini (RCA)
MUSIC FROM M SQUAD - Stanley Wilson (RCA)
STRINGS AFLAME - Esquivel (RCA)
TWO SIDES OF WINTERHALTER - Hugo Winterhalter

BEST PERFORMANCE BY A VOCAL GROUP OR CHORUS
AMES BROTHERS SING FAMOUS HITS OF FAMOUS QUARTETS - Ames Brothers (RCA)
BATTLE HYMN OF THE REPUBLIC - Mormon Tabernacle Choir, Richard Condi, Cond. (Col)
KINGSTON TRIO AT LARGE - Kingston Trio (Cap)
THE THREE BELLS - The Browns (RCA)
THE STEPHEN FOSTER SONG BOOK - Robert Shaw Chorale (RCA)

BEST JAZZ PERFORMANCE - SOLOIST
BEST OF NEW BROADWAY SHOW HITS - Urbie Green (RCA)
BOBBY TROUP AND HIS STARS OF JAZZ - Bobby Troup (RCA)
EASY NOW - Ruby Braff (RCA)
ELLA SWINGS LIGHTLY - Ella Fitzgerald (Verve)
LIKE YOUNG - Andre Previn (MGM)
RED NORVO IN HI-FI - Red Norvo (RCA)

BEST JAZZ PERFORMANCE - GROUP
CHANCES ARE IT SWINGS - Shorty Rogers (RCA)
I DIG CHICKS - Jonah Jones (Cap)
MORE MUSIC FROM PETER GUNN - Henry Mancini (RCA)
RED NORVO IN HI-FI - Red Norvo (RCA)
ELLINGTON JAZZ PARTY - Duke Ellington (Col)

BEST CLASSICAL PERFORMANCE - ORCHESTRA
BEETHOVEN: SYMPHONY No. 6 - Pierre Monteux cond. Vienna Philharmonic (RCA)
DEBUSSY: IMAGES FOR ORCHESTRA - Charles Munch cond. Boston Symphony (RCA)
ROSSINI: OVERTURES - Fritz Reiner cond. Chicago Symphony (RCA)
TCHAIKOVSKY: CAPRICCIO ITALIEN; RIMSKY-KORSAKOV: CAPRICCIO ESPAGNOL - Kiril Kondrashin cond. RCA Victor Symphony (RCA)
TCHAIKOVSKY: 1812 OVERTURE/RAVEL: BOLERO - Morton Gould & His Orch. (RCA)

BEST CLASSICAL PERFORMANCE - CONCERTO OR INSTRUMENTAL SOLOIST (WITH FULL ORCHESTRAL ACCOMPANIMENT)
BRAHMS: VIOLIN CONCERTO IN D - Henryk Szeryng (Monteux cond. London Symphony) (RCA)
BRAHMS: PIANO CONCERTO No. 2 - Artur Rubinstein (J. Kripps cond. RCA Victor Symphony) (RCA)
MENDELSSOHN: VIOLIN CONCERTO No. 2 IN E MINOR OP. 64; PROKOFIEFF: VIOLIN CONCERTO No. 2 IN G MINOR - Jascha Heifetz (Munch cond. Boston Symphony) (RCA)
RACHMANINOFF: PIANO CONCERTO No. 3 - Van Cliburn (Kondrashin cond. Symphony of the Air) (RCA)
TCHAIKOVSKY: PIANO CONCERTO No. 1 - Vladimir Horowitz (Toscanini cond. NBC Symphony) (RCA)

BEST CLASSICAL PERFORMANCE - OPERA CAST OR CHORAL
MOZART: THE MARRIAGE OF FIGARO - Erich Leinsdorf, Vienna Philharmonic (Peters, London, Della, Casa) (RCA)
ROSSINI: THE BARBER OF SEVILLE - Erich Leinsdorf, Metropolitan Orch. & Chorus (Peters, Valetti, Merrill, Tozzi) (RCA)
SAINT-SAENS: SAMPSON AND DELILAH - Fausto Cleva cond. Metropolitan Opera Orch. & Chorus (Stevens, Del Monago) (RCA)
THE BELOVED CHORUSES - Mormon Tabernacle Choir, Richard Condie cond. (Col)
VERDI: THE FORCE OF DESTINY - Fernado Previtali cond. Accademia de Santa Cecilia, Rome, Orch. & Chorus (Milanov, Tozzi) (RCA)

BEST CLASSICAL PERFORMANCE - VOCAL SOLOIST (WITH OR WITHOUT ORCHESTRA)
A BRAHMS/SCHUMANN RECITAL - Maureen Forrester (Decca)
BJOERLING IN OPERA - Jussi Bjoerling (London)
MARIA CALLAS PORTRAYS VERDI HEROINES - Maria Callas (Angel)
MILANOV OPERATIC ARIAS - Zinka Milanov (RCA)
THE ART OF SONG - Cesare Valletti (RCA)

BEST CLASSICAL PERFORMANCE - CHAMBER MUSIC
BEETHOVEN: SONATA No. 21, IN C OP. 53/"WALDSTEIN" SONATA NO. 18 IN E FLAT OP. 53 NO. 3 - Artur Rubinstein (RCA)
BEETHOVEN: PIANO QUARTET IN E FLAT OP. 16; SCHUMAN PIANO QUARTET IN E FLAT OP. 47 - The Festival Quartet (RCA)
CELLO GALAXY - Felix Slatkin (Cap)
FOUR ITALIAN SONATAS - Nathan Milstein (Cap)
VILLA LOBOS: STRING QUARTET - Felix Slatkin (Cap)

BEST CLASSICAL PERFORMANCE - INSTRUMENTAL SOLOIST WITHOUT ORCHESTRAL ACCOMPANIMENT
BEETHOVEN: SONATA NO. 21 IN C OP. 53/"WALDSTEIN" SONATA NO. 18 IN E FLAT OP. 53 NO. 3 - Artur Rubinstein (RCA)
DANZAS - Laurindo Almeida (Cap)
FOUR ITALIAN SONATAS - Nathan Milstein (Cap)
BERG: SONATA FOR PIANO, OP. 1; KRENEK: SONATA NO. 3, OP. 92 NO 4; SCHOENBERG: THREE PIANO PIECES OP. 11 - Glenn Gould (Col)
PENNARIO PLAYS - Leonard Pennario (Cap)
PRESENTING JAIME LAREDO - Jaime Laredo (RCA)

BEST MUSICAL COMPOSITION (MORE THAN 5 MIN.)
ANATOMY OF A MURDER - Duke Ellington
MORE MUSIC FROM PETER GUNN - Henry Mancini
PROKOFIEFF: THE OVERTURE RUSSE OP. 72 - Serge Prokofieff
ST. LAWRENCE SUITE - Morton Gould
SHOSTAKOVITCH: CONCERTO NO. 2 FOR PIANO AND ORCH., OP. 101 - Dimitri Shostakovitch

BEST SOUND TRACK ALBUM - BACKGROUND SCORE FROM MOTION PICTURE OR TELEVISION
ANATOMY OF A MURDER - Duke Ellington (Col)
MORE MUSIC FROM PETER GUNN - Henry Mancini (RCA)
PETE KELLY'S BLUES - Dick Cathcart (WB)
THE MUSIC FROM M SQUAD - Stanley Wilson (RCA)
THE NUN'S STORY - Franz Waxman (WB)

BEST SOUND TRACK ALBUM--ORIGINAL CAST, MOTION PICTURE OR TELEVISION
FOR THE FIRST TIME - Mario Lanza (RCA)
PORGY AND BESS - Andre Previn, Ken Darby (Col)
SLEEPING BEAUTY (Disneyland)
SOME LIKE IT HOT (U.A.)
THE FIVE PENNIES (Dot)

BEST BROADWAY SHOW ALBUM
A PARTY WITH BETTY COMDEN AND ADOLPH GREEN - Betty Comden, Adolph Green (Cap)
AGES OF MAN - Sir John Gielgud (Col)
GYPSY - Ethel Merman (Col)
ONCE UPON A MATTRESS - Hal Hastings, cond. (Kapp)
REDHEAD - Gwen Verdon (RCA)

BEST COMEDY PERFORMANCE - SPOKEN WORD
HAMLET - Andy Griffith (Cap)
INSIDE SHELLEY BERMAN - Shelley Berman (Verve)
LOOK FORWARD IN ANGER - Mort Sahl (Verve)
SICK HUMOR - Lenny Bruce (Fantasy)
STAN FREBERG WITH ORIGINAL CAST - Stan Freberg (Cap)

BEST COMEDY PERFORMANCE - MUSICAL
A PARTY WITH BETTY COMDEN AND ADOLPH GREEN - Betty Comden, Adolph Green (Cap)
CHARLIE WEAVER SINGS FOR HIS PEOPLE - Cliff Arquette (Col)
MONSTER RALLY - Hans Conreid, Alice Pearce
MUSICALLY MAD - Bernie Green (RCA)
THE BATTLE OF KOOKAMONGA - Homer & Jethro (RCA)

BEST PERFORMANCE - DOCUMENTARY, SPOKEN WORD
A LINCOLN PORTRAIT - Carl Sandburg (Col)
AGES OF MAN - Sir John Gielgud (Col)
BASIL RATHBONE READS SHERLOCK HOLMES - Basil Rathbone (Audio Book)
MARK TWAIN TONIGHT - Hal Holbrook (Col)
NEW YORK TAXI DRIVER - Tony Schwartz (Col)

BEST PERFORMANCE BY "TOP 40" ARTIST
A BIG HUNK O'LOVE - Elvis Presley (RCA)
BROKEN HEARTED MELODY - Sarah Vaughan (Merc)
CHARLIE BROWN - The Coasters (Atco)
MAKIN' LOVE - Floyd Robinson (RCA)
MIDNIGHT FLYER - Nat King Cole (Cap)
NEIL SEDAKA - Neil Sedaka (RCA)

BEST COUNTRY AND WESTERN PERFORMANCE
BATTLE OF NEW ORLEANS - Johnny Horton (Col)
DON'T TELL ME YOUR TROUBLES - Don Gibson (RCA)
HOME - Jim Reeves (RCA)
SET HIM FREE - Skeeter Davis (RCA)
TENNESSEE STUD - Eddy Arnold (RCA)

BEST RHYTHM AND BLUES PERFORMANCE
A BIG HUNK O'LOVE - Elvis Presley (RCA)
CHARLIE BROWN - The Coasters (Atco)
GUESS WHO - Jesse Belvin (RCA)
MIDNIGHT FLYER - Nat King Cole (Cap)
WHAT A DIFFERENCE A DAY MAKES - Dinah Washington (Merc)

BEST PERFORMANCE - FOLK
BELAFONTE AT CARNEGIE HALL - Harry Belafonte (RCA)
KINGSTON TRIO AT LARGE - Kingston Trio (Cap)
TENNESSEE STUD - Eddy Arnold (RCA)
ATHE WILD WILD WEST - Ralph Hunter Choir (RCA)
THE WILDERNESS ROAD - Jimmy Driftwood (RCA)

BEST RECORDING FOR CHILDREN
HANSEL AND GRETEL - Franz Allers (RCA)
PETER AND THE WOLF - Peter Ustinov (von Karajan, Philharmonia Orch.) (Angel)
POPEYE'S FAVORITE SEA CHANTIES - Capt. Allen Swift
THE ARABIAN NIGHTS - Marla Ray (RCA)
THREE TO MAKE MUSIC/CINDERELLA - Mary Martin (RCA)

BEST ARRANGEMENT
AN EVENING WITH LERNER & LOWE - Johnny Green (RCA)
COME DANCE WITH ME - Billy May (Frank Sinatra) (Cap)
MACK THE KNIFE - Richard Wess (Bobby Darin) (Atco)
MORE MUSIC FROM PETER GUNN - Henry Mancini (RCA)
STRINGS AFLAME - Esquivel (RCA)
VICTORY AT SEA, VOL. 1 (Re-make) - Robert Russell Bennett cond. RCA Symphony Orch. (RCA)

BEST ENGINEERED RECORDING, CLASSICAL
(Engineer's Award)
DOUBLING IN BRASS - Lewis W. Layton (Morton Gould) (RCA)
ROSSINI OVERTURES - Lewis W. Layton (Fritz Reiner) (RCA)
TCHAIKOVSKY: CAPRICCIO ITALIEN; RIMSKY KORSAKOV: CAPRICCIO ESPAGNOL - Lewis W. Layton (Kiril Kondrashin) (RCA)
TCHAIKOVSKY: 1812 OVERTURE; RAVEL: BOLERO - Lewis W. Layton (Morton Gould) (RCA)
VICTORY AT SEA, VOL. 1 - Lewis W. Layton (Robert Russell Bennett) (RCA)

BEST ENGINEERING - NOVELTY RECORDING
(Engineer's Award)
ALVIN'S HARMONICA - Ted Keep (David Seville) (Cap)
ORIENTA - Thorne Nogar (Markko Polo Adventurers) (RCA)
SUPERSONICS IN FLIGHT - Robert Simpson (Billy Mure) (RCA)
THE BAT - Luis P. Valentin (Alvino Rey) (Cap)
THE WILD WILD WEST - Robert Simpson (Ralph Hunter Choir) (RCA)

BEST ENGINEERING CONTRIBUTION - OTHER THAN CLASSICAL OR NOVELTY
(Engineer's Award)
BELAFONTE AT CARNEGIE HALL - Robert Simpson (RCA)
BIG BAND GUITAR - Robert Simpson (Buddy Morrow) (RCA)
COMPULSION TO SWING - Robert Simpson (Henri Rene) (RCA)
NEW SOUNDS AT THE ROOSEVELT - Robert Simpson (Larry Elgart) (RCA)
STRINGS AFLAME - Ernest Oelrich (Esquivel) (RCA)

BEST ALBUM COVER
(Art Director's Award)
ANATOMY OF A MURDER - Saul Bass (Duke Ellington) (Col)
FOR LP FANS ONLY - Col. Tom Parker (Elvis Presley) (RCA)
PORGY AND BESS - Acy R. Lehman (Lena Horne, Harry Belafonte) (RCA)
SHOSTAKOVICH: SYMPHONY NO. 5 - Robert M. Jones (Howard Mitchell) (RCA)
THE SOUTH SHALL RISE AGAIN - Robert L. Yorke, Acy R. Lehmann (Phil Harris) (RCA)

BEST NEW ARTIST OF 1959
EDD BYRNES
BOBBY DARIN
MARK MURPHY
JOHNNY RESTIVO
MAVIS RIVERS

SPECIAL TRUSTEES AWARDS FOR ARTISTS & REPERTOIRE CONTRIBUTION
Record of the Year, MACK THE KNIFE, Bobby Darin; A & R Producer, Ahmet Ertegun (ATCO).
Album of the Year, COME DANCE WITH ME, Frank Sinatra; A & R Producer; Dave Cavanaugh (Cap).

1960

RECORD OF THE YEAR
ARE YOU LONESOME TONIGHT? - Elvis Presley (RCA)
GEORGIA ON MY MIND - Ray Charles (ABC)
MACK THE KNIFE - Ella Fitzgerald (Verve)
NICE N' EASY - Frank Sinatra (CAP)
THEME FROM A SUMMER PLACE - Percy Faith (Col)

ALBUM OF THE YEAR
BELAFONTE RETURNS TO CARNEGIE HALL - Harry Belafonte (RCA)
BRAHMS: CONCERTO NO. 2 IN B FLAT - Sviatoslav Richter (RCA)
BUTTON DOWN MIND - Bob Newhart (WB)
NICE N' EASY - Frank Sinatra (Cap)
PUCCINI: TURANDOT - Erich Leinsdorf (RCA)
WILD IS LOVE - Nat King Cole (Cap)

SONG OF THE YEAR
(Songwriter's Award)
HE'LL HAVE TO GO - Charles Grean, Joe Allison, Audrey Allison
NICE N' EASY - Lew Spence, Marilyn Keith, Alan Bergman
SECOND TIME AROUND - Sammy Cahn, Jimmy Van Heusen
THEME FROM A SUMMER PLACE - Max Steiner
THEME FROM EXODUS - Ernest Gold

BEST VOCAL PERFORMANCE FEMALE - SINGLE OR TRACK
SOUND OF MUSIC - Doris Day (Col)
I'VE GOTTA RIGHT TO SING THE BLUES - Eileen Farrell (Col)
MACK THE KNIFE - Ella Fitzgerald (Verve)
I'M SORRY - Brenda Lee (Decca)
I'M GONNA GO FISHIN' - Peggy Lee (Cap)

BEST VOCAL PERFORMANCE, FEMALE - ALBUM
CLAP HANDS, HERE COMES ROSIE - Rosemary Clooney (Col)
MACK THE KNIFE/ELLA IN BERLIN - Ella Fitzgerald (Verve)
LATIN ALA LEE - Peggy Lee (Cap)
MIRIAM MAKEBA - Miriam Makeba (RCA)
DELLA - Della Reese (RCA)

BEST VOCAL PERFORMANCE MALE - SINGLE OR TRACK
GEORGIA ON MY MIND - Ray Charles (ABC)
MISTY - Johnny Mathis (Col)
ARE YOU LONESOME TONIGHT? - Elvis Presley (RCA)
HE'LL HAVE TO GO - Jim Reeves (RCA)
NICE N' EASY - Frank Sinatra (Cap)

BEST VOCAL PERFORMANCE MALE - ALBUM
BELAFONTE RETURNS TO CARNEGIE HALL - Harry Belafonte (RCA)
GENIUS OF RAY CHARLES - Ray Charles (Atl)
WILD IS LOVE - Nat King Cole (Cap)
G.I. BLUES - Elvis Presley (RCA)
NICE N' EASY - Frank Sinatra (Cap)

BEST PERFORMANCE BY A BAND FOR DANCING
DANCE WITH BASIE - Count Basie (Roulette)
BANDLAND - Les Brown (Col)
THE BLUES AND THE BEAT - Henry Mancini (RCA)
GIRLS & BOYS ON BROADWAY - Billy May (Cap)
BIG HITS BY PRADO - Perez Prado (RCA)

BEST ARRANGEMENT
(Arranger's Award)
THEME FROM THE APARTMENT (Ferrante/Teicher) Arr: Don Costa (UA)
THEME FROM A SUMMER PLACE - Arr: Percy Faith (Col)
I'M GONNA GO FISHING' (Gerry Mulligan) Arr: Bill Holman (Verve)
LET THE GOOD TIMES ROLL (Ray Charles) Arr: Quincy Jones (Atl)
MR. LUCKY - Arr: Henry Mancini (RCA)
HONEYSUCKLE ROSE (Shearing) Arrs: George Shearing, Billy May (Cap)
NICE N' EASY (Frank Sinatra) Arr: Nelson Riddle (Cap)
WILD PERCUSSION AND HORNS A'PLENTY (Dick Schory) Arr: Dick Schory (RCA)

BEST PERFORMANCE BY AN ORCHESTRA
COUNT BASIE STORY - Count Basie (Roulette)
INFINITY IN SOUND - Esquivel (RCA)
THEME FROM A SUMMER PLACE - Percy Faith (Col)
MR. LUCKY - Henry Mancini (RCA)
THE CONCERT JAZZ BAND - Gerry Mulligan (Verve)

BEST PERFORMANCE BY A VOCAL GROUP
GREENFIELDS - The Brothers Four (Col)
WE GOT US - Eydie Gorme, Steve Lawrence (ABC)
ALL OVER THE PLACE - The Hi Los (Col)
HERE WE GO AGAIN - Kingston Trio (Cap)
SCANDINAVIAN SHUFFLE - Swe-Danes (WB)

BEST PERFORMANCE BY A CHORUS
BELAFONTE RETURNS TO CARNEGIE HALL - Belafonte Folk Singers (RCA)
DEEP NIGHT - Ray Charles Singers (Decca)
MY FAVORITE THINGS - Pete King Chorale (Kapp)
SONGS OF THE COWBOY - Norman Luboff Choir (Col)
WHAT WONDROUS LOVE - Robert Show Choral (RCA)

BEST JAZZ PERFORMANCE - SOLO OR SMALL GROUP
JAZZ TRACK - Miles Davis (Col)
BACK TO BACK - Duke Ellington, Johnny Hodges (Verve)
THE GREATEST TRUMPET OF THEM ALL - Dizzy Gillespie and his Octet (Verve)
THE HOTTEST NEW GROUP IN JAZZ - Lambert, Hendricks and Ross (Col)
WEST SIDE STORY - Andre Previn (Contempo)
WHITE SATIN - George Shearing (Cap)
GREATEST PIANO OF THEM ALL - Art Tatum (Verve)
PYRAMID - Modern Jazz Quartet (Atl)

BEST JAZZ PERFORMANCE - LARGE GROUP
THE COUNT BASIE STORY - Count Basie (Roulette)
SKETCHES OF SPAIN - Miles Davis, Gil Evans (Col)
THE GREAT WIDE WORLD OF QUINCY JONES - Quincy Jones (Merc)
BLUES AND THE BEAT - Henry Mancini (RCA)
I'M GONNA GO FISHIN' - Gerry Mulligan (Verve)
SPIRITUALS TO SWING CONCERT - The Recording Artists (Vanguard)

BEST CLASSICAL PERFORMANCE - ORCHESTRA
HAYDN: SALOMON SYMPHONIES VOL. 2 - Sir Thomas Beecham cond. Royal Philharmonic (Cap)
IVES: SYMPHONY NO. 2 - Leonard Bernstein cond. New York Philharmonic (Col)
COPLAND: APPALACHIAN SPRING - Aaron Copland cond. Boston Symphony (RCA)
GROFE: GRAND CANYON SUITE - Morton Gould cond. Morton Gould Orchestra (RCA)
SCHUBERT: SYMPHONY NO. 9 - Josef Krips cond. London Symphony (London)
STRAVINSKY: PETROUCHKA - Pierre Monteux cond. Boston Symphony (RCA)
TCHAIKOVSKY: SIXTH SYMPHONY - Eugene Ormandy cond. Philadelphia Symphony (Col)
BARTOK: MUSIC FOR STRINGS, PERCUSSION AND CELESTE - Fritz Reiner cond. Chicago Symphony (RCA)

BEST CLASSICAL PERFORMANCE - VOCAL OR INSTRUMENTAL - CHAMBER MUSIC
CONVERSATIONS WITH THE GUITAR - Laurindo Almeida (Cap)
SCHUBERT: "TROUT" QUINTET - Clifford Curzon and Vienna Octet (London)
BRAHMS: HORN TRIO; BEETHOVEN: SONATA FOR HORN AND PIANO - Joseph Eger, Henryk Szeryng, Victor Babin (RCA)
HAYDN: QUARTETS, OPUS 71 and 74 - Griller Quartet (Vanguard)
DEBUSSY AND RAVEL QUARTETS - Juilliard Quartet (RCA)
BACH: THE COMPLETE BRANDENBURG CONCERTI - Yehudi Menuhin and Bach Festival Chamber Orchestra (Cap)
BACH: CANTATA NO. 4; CHRIST LAG IN TODESBADEN - Robert Shaw Chorale (RCA)
JANACEK STRING QUARTETS Nos. 1 and 2 - Smetana Quartet (Artia)

BEST CLASSICAL PERFORMANCE - CONCERTO OR INSTRUMENTAL SOLOIST
SCHUMANN: PIANO CONCERTO IN A - Van Cliburn (Reiner cond. Chicago Symphony) (RCA)
MOZART: CLARINET CONCERTO - Gervase De Peyer (Maag cond. London Symphony) (London)
PROKOFIEFF: CONCERTO NO. 2 - Malcolm Frager (Leibowitz cond. Paris Conservatoire) (RCA)
BRAHMS: DOUBLE CONCERTO (CONCERTO FOR VIOLIN AND CELLO IN A MINOR) - Zino Francescatti, Pierre Fournier (Walter cond. Columbia Symphony) (Col)
BACH: CONCERTO NO. 5 - Glenn Gould (Golschmann cond. Columbia Symphony) (Col)
SIBELIUS: VIOLIN CONCERTO IN D - Jascha Heifetz (Hendl cond. Chicago Symphony) (RCA)
BRAHMS: PIANO CONCERTO No. 2 IN B-FLAT - Sviatoslav Richter (Leinsdorf cond. Chicago Symphony) (RCA)
BRAHMS: PIANO CONCERTO No. 2 - Rudolf Serkin (Ormandy cond. Philadelphia Symphony) (Col)

BEST CLASSICAL PERFORMANCE - INSTRUMENTAL SOLOIST OR DUO (OTHER THAN WITH ORCHESTRA)
THE SPANISH GUITARS OF LAURINDO ALMEIDA - Laurindo Almeida (Cap)
THE ART OF JULIAN BREAM - Julian Bream (RCA)
PICTURES AT AN EXHIBITION - Vladimir Horowitz (RCA)
HAYDN...LANDOWSKA - Wanda Landowska (RCA)
BACH: PARTITA No. 3 In E; BRAHMS: SONATA No. 3 IN D MINOR - Jaime Laredo (RCA)
BRAHMS: KEYBOARD MUSIC OF THE FRENCH COURT - Paul Maynard (Am. Soc Concerts in Home)
PROKOFIEFF: SONATA No. 7 AND PICTURES AT AN EXHIBITION - Sviatoslav Richter (Artia)
CHOPIN: BALLADES - Artur Rubinstein (RCA)

BEST CLASSICAL PERFORMANCE - VOCAL SOLOIST
CONVERSATIONS WITH THE GUITAR - Salli Terri (Cap)
ARIAS IN GREAT TRADITION - Eileen Farrell (Col)
SCHUBERT: SONGS, ALBUM 3 - Dietrich Fischer-Dieskau (Angel)
MAHLER: KINDERTOTENLIEDER - Maureen Forrester (RCA)
BRITTEN: NOCTURNE - Peter Pears (London)
A PROGRAM OF SONG - Leontyne Price (RCA)
HANDEL: ARIAS - Joan Sutherland (Oiseau-Lyre)
SCHUMANN: DICHTERLIEBE - Cesare Valletti (RCA)

BEST CLASSICAL OPERA PRODUCTION
VERDI: AIDA - Herbert von Karajan (Solos: Tebaldi, Bergonzi, Simionato, Corena) (London)
PUCCINI: LA BOHEME - Tullio Serafin (Solos: Tebaldi, Bergonzi, Bastianini, Corena) (London)
MOZART: DON GIOVANNI - Josef Krips (Solos: Siepi, Danco, Dermote, Corena) (London)
VERDI: SHAKESPEARE: MACBETH - Erich Leinsdorf (Solos: Warren, Hines, Rysanek, Bergonzi) (RCA)
BOITA: MEFISTOFELE - Tullio Serafin (Solos: Siepi, Tebaldi, Del Monaco) (London)
BRITTEN: PETER GRIMES - Benjamin Britten (Solos: Pears, Pease, Watson) (London)
VERDI: LA TRAVIATA - Tullio Serafin (Solos: de los Angeles, Del Monte, Sereni) (Cap)
PUCCINI: TURANDOT - Erich Leinsdorf (Solos: Tebaldi, Nilsson, Bjoerling, Tozzi) (RCA)
POULENC, COCTEAU: LA VOIX HUMAINE - Georges Pretre cond. Paris Opera Comique & National Theatre Orch. (Solos: Duval) (RCA)

BEST CONTEMPORARY CLASSICAL COMPOSITION
SYMPHONY NO. 1 - Easley Blackwood (RCA)
ORCHESTRAL SUITE FROM TENDER LAND SUITE - Aaron Copland (RCA)
SONATA FOR CELLO AND PIANO - Paul Hindemith (RCA)
SYMPHONY No. 2 - Charles Ives (Col)
LA VOIX HUMAINE - Francis Poulenc (RCA)
SYMPHONY No. 1 - Roger Sessions (Comp. Rcds)
THRENI - Igor Stravinsky (Col)
DENSITY 21.5 - Edgard Varese (Col)

BEST CLASSICAL PERFORMANCE - CHORAL
HANDEL: THE MESSIAH - Sir Thomas Beecham cond. Royal Philharmonic & Chorus (Solos: Vyvyan, Sinclair, Vicki, Tozzi) (RCA)
ARIAS, ANTHEMS AND CHORALES OF AMERICAN MORAVIANS, VOL. 1 - Moravian Festival Chorus (Col)
BERLIOZ: REQUIEM - Charles Munch & The New England Conservatory Chorus (RCA)
VERDI: REQUIEM - Fritz Reiner, Vienna Philharmonic Society of Friends of Music of Vienna (RCA)
BACH: MOTET No. 3 "JESU MEINE FREUDE" - Robert Shaw Chorale (RCA)
DVORAK: REQUIEM - Maria Stader, Sieglinde Wagner, Hans Ernst Haefliger, Kim Borg (DGG)
VAUGHAN WILLIAMS: MASS IN G MINOR; BACH: CHRIST LAY IN THE BONDS OF DEATH - Roger Wagner Chorale (Cap)

BEST SOUND TRACK ALBUM OR RECORDING OF MUSIC SCORE FROM MOTION PICTURE OR TV
(Composer's Award)
THE APARTMENT - Comp: Adolph Deutch (S-T) (UA)
BEN HUR - Comp: Dr. Miklos Rozsa (S-T) (MGM)
EXODUS - Comp: Ernest Gold (S-T) (RCA)
MR. LUCKY - Comp: Henry Mancini (RCA)
THE UNTOUCHABLES - Comp: Nelson Riddle (Cap)

BEST SOUND TRACK ALBUM OR RECORDING OF ORIGINAL CAST FROM MOTION PICTURE OR TV
(Composer's Award)
BELLS ARE RINGING (Judy Holiday, Dean Martin, Orig. Cast) Comps: Betty Comden, Adolph Green, Jule Styne (Cap)
CAN CAN (Frank Sinatra, Orig. Cast) Comp: Cole Porter (Cap)
G.I. Blues - Elvis Presley (RCA)
LI'L ABNER (S-T) - Comp: Nelson Riddle (Col)

BEST SHOW ALBUM (ORIGINAL CAST)
(Composer's Award)
BYE BYE BIRDIE - Charles Strouse, Lee Adams (Col)
CAMELOT - Alan Lerner, Fred Lowe (Col)
FIORELLO! - Jerry Bock, Sheldon Harnick (Cap)
THE SOUND OF MUSIC - Richard Rodgers, Oscar Hammerstein (Col)
THE UNSINKABLE MOLLY BROWN - Meredith Willson (Cap)

BEST COMEDY PERFORMANCE - SPOKEN WORD
THE EDGE OF SHELLEY BERMAN - Shelley Berman (Verve)
BUTTON DOWN MIND STRIKES BACK - Bob Newhart (WB)
2,000 YEAR OLD MAN - Carl Reiner and Mel Brooks (World Pac.)
THE WONDERFUL WORLD OF JONATHAN WINTERS - Jonathan Winters (Verve)

BEST COMEDY PERFORMANCE - MUSICAL
JONATHAN AND DARLENE EDWARDS IN PARIS - Paul Weston, Jo Stafford (Col)
THE OLD PAYOLA ROLL BLUES - Stan Freberg (Cap)
HOMER AND JETHRO AT THE COUNTRY CLUB - Homer and Jethro (RCA)
AN EVENING WASTED WITH TOM LEHRER - Tom Lehrer (Lehrer)
ALVIN FOR PRESIDENT - David Seville (Lib)

BEST PERFORMANCE - DOCUMENTARY OR SPOKEN WORD
AGES OF MAN, VOL. 2 (ONE MAN IN HIS TIME) PART TWO--SHAKESPEARE - Sir John Gielgud (Col)
VOICES OF THE TWENTIETH CENTURY - Henry Fonda (Decca)
J.B. - Archibald MacLeish (RCA)
F.D.R. SPEAKS - Franklin D. Roosevelt, Robert Bialek, A&R Prod. (Wash.)

BEST PERFORMANCE BY A POP SINGLE ARTIST
GEORGIA ON MY MIND - Ray Charles (ABC)
MACK THE KNIFE - Ella Fitzgerald (Verve)
HEART - Peggy Lee (Cap)
ARE YOU LONESOME TONIGHT? - Elvis Presley (RCA)
NICE N' EASY - Frank Sinatra (Cap)

BEST COUNTRY AND WESTERN PERFORMANCE
NORTH TO ALASKA - Johnny Horton (Col)
WINGS OF A DOVE - Ferlin Husky (Cap)
PLEASE HELP ME, I'M FALLING - Hank Locklin (RCA)
HE'LL HAVE TO GO - Jim Reeves (RCA)
EL PASO - Marty Robbins (Col)

BEST RHYTHM AND BLUES PERFORMANCE
SHAKE A HAND - LaVerne Baker (Atl)
FINGER POPPIN' TIME - Hank Ballard (King)
LET THE GOOD TIMES ROLL - Ray Charles (Atl)
WALKIN' AND TALKIN' - Bo Diddley (Checker)
TRAVELIN' - John Lee Hooker (VeeJay)
ALL I COULD DO WAS CRY - Etta James (Argo)
GOT MY MOJO WORKING - Muddy Waters (Chess)
LONELY TEARDROPS - Jackie Wilson (Brunswick)

BEST PERFORMANCE - FOLK
SWING DAT HAMMER - Harry Belafonte (RCA)
CHEERS - Belafonte Singers (RCA)
GREENFIELDS - The Brothers Four (Col)
SONGS OF BILLY YANK AND JOHNNY REB - Jimmy Driftwood (RCA)
HERE WE GO AGAIN - Kingston Trio (Cap)
SOUTHERN FOLK HERITAGE SERIES - Alan Lomax (Atl)
SONGS OF ROBERT BURNS - Ewan MacColl (Flkwy)
MIRIAM MAKEBA - Miriam Makeba (RCA)

BEST ALBUM CREATED FOR CHILDREN
ADVENTURES IN MUSIC, GRADE 3, VOLUME 1 - Howard Mitchell (RCA)
LET'S ALL SING WITH THE CHIPMUNKS - David Seville (Lib)
DR. SEUSS PRESENTS: BARTHOLOMEW AND THE OOBLECK - Dr. Seuss (Camden)
FOLK SONGS FOR YOUNG PEOPLE - Pete Seeger (Flkways)
MOTHER GOOSE NURSERY RHYMES - Sterling Holloway (Disneyland)
STORIES AND SONGS OF THE CIVIL WAR - Ralph Bellamy (RCA)

BEST ENGINEERING CONTRIBUTION - CLASSICAL
(Engineer's Award)
PROKOFIEFF: ALEXANDER NEVSKY (Reiner cond. Chicago Symphony) Eng: Lewis Layton (RCA)
BARTOK: MUSIC FOR STRINGS, PERCUSSION AND CELESTE (Reiner cond. Chicago Symphony) Eng: Lewis Layton (RCA)
BERLIOZ: REQUIEM (Munch cond. New England Conservatory Chorus & Boston Symphony) Eng: Lewis Layton (RCA)
R. STRAUSS: DON QUIXOTE (Reiner cond. Chicago Symphony) Eng: Lewis Layton (RCA)
SPANISH GUITARS OF LAURINDO ALMEIDA (Laurindo Almeida) Eng: Hugh Davies (Cap)
THE TWO PIANOS OF LEONARD PENNARIO (Leonard Pennario) Eng: John Kraus (Cap)
PUCCINI: TURANDOT (Tebaldi, Nilsson, Bjoerling, Tozzi, Leinsdorf, cond.) Eng: Lewis Layton (RCA)

BEST ENGINEERING CONTRIBUTION - POPULAR
(Engineer's Award)
BELAFONTE RETURNS TO CARNEGIE HALL (Harry Belafonte) Eng: Robert Simpson (RCA)
LOUIS BELLSON SWINGS JULE STYNE - Eng: Luis P. Valentin (Verve)
ELLA FITZGERALD SINGS THE GEORGE AND IRA GERSHWIN SONG BOOK - Eng: Luis P. Valentin (Verve)
INFINITY IN SOUND (Esquivel) Eng: John Norman (RCA)
PERSUASIVE PERCUSSION NO. 2 (Terry Snyder & the All Stars) Eng: Robert Fine (Cmmd)
WILD IS LOVE (Nat King Cole) Eng: John Kraus (Cap)
WILD PERCUSSION AND HORNS A'PLENTY (Dick Schory) Eng: Robert Simpson (RCA)

BEST ENGINEERING CONTRIBUTION - NOVELTY
(Engineer's Award)
ALVIN FOR PRESIDENT (David Seville & the Chipmunks) Eng: Ted Keep (Lib)
JUNE NIGHT (Jack Cookerly) Eng: John Kraus (Cap)
LET'S ALL SING WITH THE CHIPMUNKS (David Seville) Eng: Ted Keep (Lib)
MR. CUSTER (Larry Verne) Eng: George Fernandez (Era)
NEW SOUNDS AMERICA LOVES BEST (John Klein) Engs: Robert Simpson, John Crawford, Tony Salvatore (RCA)
THE OLD PAYOLA ROLL BLUES (Stan Freberg) Eng: John Kraus (Cap)
SPIKE JONES IN HI-FI - Eng: Thorne Nogar (WB)

BEST ALBUM COVER
(Art Director's Award)
PROKOFIEFF: ALEXANDER NEVSKY (Reiner cond. Chicago Symphony) Art Dir: Bob Jones (RCA)
BEAN BAGS (Milt Jackson) Art Dir: Marvin Israel (Atl)
CARLOS MONTOYA - Art Dir: Bob Jones (RCA)
ELLA FITZGERALD SINGS THE GEORGE AND IRA GERSHWIN SONG BOOK - Art Dir: Sheldon Marks (Verve)
LATIN ALA LEE (Peggy Lee) Art Dir: Marvin Schwartz (Cap)
NOW! FRED ASTAIRE - Art Dir: Irving Werbin (Kapp)
TCHAIKOVSKY: NUTCRACKER SUITE EXCERPTS (Reiner, Chicago Symphony) Art Dir: Bob Jones (RCA)
STRAVINSKY: PETROUCHKA (Monteux, Boston Symphony) Art Dir: Bob Jones (RCA)
WILD PERCUSSION AND HORNS A'PLENTY (Dick Schory) Art Dir: Bob Jones (RCA)

BEST NEW ARTIST OF 1960
THE BROTHERS FOUR (Col)
MIRIAM MAKEBA (RCA)
BOB NEWHART (WB)
LEONTYNE PRICE (RCA)
JOANIE SOMMERS (WB)

BEST JAZZ COMPOSITION OF MORE THAN FIVE MINUTES DURATION
(Composer's Award)
BLUE RONDO A LA TURK - Dave Brubeck (Col)
BLUES SUITE - Bob Brookmeyer (Atl)
IDIOM '59 (FESTIVAL SESSION) - Duke Ellington (Col)
NEWPORT SUITE - Maynard Ferguson (Roulette)
SKETCH FROM THIRD STREAM MUSIC - John Lewis (Atl)
SKETCHES OF SPAIN - Miles Davis, Gil Evans (Col)
WESTERN SUITE - Jimmy Giuffre (Atl)

SPECIAL NATIONAL TRUSTEES AWARDS FOR ARTISTS AND REPERTOIRE CONTRIBUTION.
Record Of The Year, THEME FROM A SUMMER PLACE, A&R Prod: Ernest Altschuler (Col).
BUTTON DOWN MIND, A&R Prod: George Avakian (WB).

1961

RECORD OF THE YEAR
BIG BAD JOHN - Jimmy Dean (Col)
UP A LAZY RIVER - Si Zentner (Lib)
MOON RIVER - Henry Mancini (RCA)
THE SECOND TIME AROUND - Frank Sinatra (Rep)
TAKE FIVE - Dave Brubeck (Col)

ALBUM OF THE YEAR - (NON-CLASSICAL)
BREAKFAST AT TIFFANY'S - Henry Mancini (RCA)
GENIUS SOUL JAZZ - Ray Charles (Impulse)
GREAT BAND WITH GREAT VOICES - Si Zentner, Johnny Mann Singers (Lib)
JUDY AT CARNEGIE HALL - Judy Garland (Cap)
THE NAT COLE STORY - Nat King Cole (Cap)
WEST SIDE STORY (Soundtrack) - Johnny Green, Music Director (Col)

ALBUM OF THE YEAR - CLASSICAL
THE ART OF THE PRIMA DONNA - Joan Sutherland, (Molinari - Pradelli, Royal Opera House Orch.) (London)
BLOCK: SACRED SERVICE - Leonard Bernstein, New York Philharmonic (Col)
BRAHMS: SYMPHONY NO. 2 - William Steinberg, Pittsburgh Symphony (Command)
REVERIE FOR SPANISH GUITARS - Laurindo Almeida (Cap)
STRAVINSKY CONDUCTS, 1960: LE SACRE DU PRINTEMPS; PETROUCHKA - Igor Stravinsky cond. Columbia Symphony (Col)

SONG OF THE YEAR
(Songwriter's Award)
A LITTLE BITTY TEAR - Hank Cochran (Decca)
BIG BAD JOHN - Jimmy Dean (Col)
LOLLIPOPS AND ROSES - Tony Velona (Kapp)
MAKE SOMEONE HAPPY - Jule Styne, Betty Comden, Adolph Green
MOON RIVER - Henry Mancini, Johnny Mercer (RCA)

BEST INSTRUMENTAL THEME OR INSTRUMENTAL VERSION OF SONG
(Composer's Award)
AFRICAN WALTZ - Galt MacDermott (Roulette)
THE GUNS OF NAVARONE - Dimitri Tiomkin (Col)
LA DOLCE VITA - Nino Rota (RCA)
PARIS BLUES - Duke Ellington (Col)
THEME FROM "CARNIVAL" - Robert Merrill (MGM)

BEST SOLO VOCAL PERFORMANCE - FEMALE
(Following are all album nominations)
BASIN STREET EAST - Peggy Lee (Cap)
THE ESSENTIAL BILLIE HOLIDAY (CARNEGIE HALL CONCERT) - Billie Holiday (Verve)
JUDY AT CARNEGIE HALL - Judy Garland (Cap)
LENA AT THE SANDS - Lena Horne (RCA)
MR. PAGANINI - Ella Fitzgerald (Verve)

BEST SOLO VOCAL PERFORMANCE - MALE
(Following are all single nominations)
A LITTLE BITTY TEAR - Burl Ives (Decca)
BIG BAD JOHN - Jimmy Dean (Col)
DANNY BOY - Andy Williams (Col)
LOLLIPOPS AND ROSES - Jack Jones (Kapp)
PORTRAIT OF MY LOVE - Steve Lawrence (UA)

BEST JAZZ PERFORMANCE - SOLOIST OR SMALL GROUP (INSTRUMENTAL)
ANDRE PREVIN PLAYS HAROLD ARLEN - Andre Previn (Contemporary)
BILL EVANS AT THE VILLAGE VANGUARD - Bill Evans Trio (Riverside)
DREAMSTREET - Erroll Garner (Am-Par)
EUROPEAN CONCERT - The Modern Jazz Quartet (Atl)
THE GREATEST HORN IN THE WORLD - Al Hirt (RCA)

BEST JAZZ PERFORMANCE - LARGE GROUP (INSTRUMENTAL)
A TOUCH OF ELEGANCE - Andre Previn (Col)
BASIE AT BIRDLAND - Count Basie & Orch. (Roulette)
GILLESPIANA - Dizzy Gillespie (Verve)
OUT OF THE COOL - Gil Evans (ABC)
WEST SIDE STORY - Stan Kenton (Cap)

BEST ORIGINAL JAZZ COMPOSITION
(Composer's Award)
A TOUCH OF ELEGANCE - Andre Previn (Col)
AFRICAN WALTZ - Galt MacDermott (Rvrsde)
GILLESPIANA - Lalo Schifrin (Verve)
PERCEPTIONS - J.J. Johnson (Verve)
UNSQUARE DANCE - Dave Brubeck (Col)

BEST PERFORMANCE BY AN ORCHESTRA - FOR DANCING
CALCUTTA - Lawrence Welk (Dot)
I DIG DANCERS - Quincy Jones (Merc)
UP A LAZY RIVER - Si Zentner (Lib)
THE LERNER AND LOEWE BANDBOOK - Les Brown (Col)
MR. LUCKY GOES LATIN - Henry Mancini (RCA)
SHALL WE SWING? - Glen Gray, Billy May (Cap)

BEST PERFORMANCE BY AN ORCHESTRA (OTHER THAN DANCING)
A CONCERT IN JAZZ - Gerry Mulligan (Verve)
A TOUCH OF ELEGANCE - Andre Previn (Col)
BREAKFAST AT TIFFANY'S - Henry Mancini (RCA)
THE GREATEST HORN IN THE WORLD - Al Hirt (RCA)
WEST SIDE STORY - Stan Kenton (Cap)

BEST ARRANGEMENT
(Arranger's Award)
ALL ABOUT ROSIE - George Russell (Mulligan) (Verve)
UP A LAZY RIVER - Bob Florence (Si Zentner) (Lib)
MOON RIVER - Henry Mancini (RCA)
NEW PIANO IN TOWN - Peter Nero (RCA)
PERCEPTIONS - J.J. Johnson (Dizzy Gillespie) (Verve)

BEST PERFORMANCE BY A VOCAL GROUP
CLOSE UP - Kingston Trio (Cap)
HIGH FLYING - Lambert, Hendricks & Ross (Col)
THE SLIGHTLY FABULOUS LIMELITERS - The Limeliters (RCA)
VOICES IN FUN - Four Freshmen (Cap)
THE WAY YOU LOOK TONIGHT - The Lettermen (Cap)

BEST PERFORMANCE BY A CHORUS
A SONG AT TWILIGHT - Roger Wagner Chorale (Cap)
BELAFONTE FOLK SINGERS AT HOME AND ABROAD - Belafonte Folk Singers (RCA)
GREAT BAND WITH GREAT VOICES (Si Zentner Orch) Johnny Mann Singers (Lib)
HEY, LOOK ME OVER - The Pete King Chorale (Kapp)
THIS IS NORMAN LUBOFF - Norman Luboff Choir (RCA)

BEST SOUND TRACK ALBUM OR RECORDING OF SCORE FROM MOTION PICTURE OR TELEVISION
BREAKFAST AT TIFFANY'S - Henry Mancini (RCA)
CHECKMATE - Johnny Williams (Col)
THE GUNS OF NAVARONE - Dimitri Tiomkin (Col)
LA DOLCE VITA - Nino Rota (RCA)
PARIS BLUES - Duke Ellington, Louis Armstrong (UA)

BEST SOUND TRACK ALBUM OR RECORDING OF ORIGINAL CAST FROM MOTION PICTURE OR TELEVISION
BABES IN TOYLAND - Tutti Camarata (Buena Vista)
BLUE HAWAII - Elvis Presley (RCA)
FLOWER DRUM SONG - Alfred Newman, Ken Darby (Decca)
PARENT TRAP - Tutti Camarata (Buena Vista)
WEST SIDE STORY - Johnny Green, Saul Chaplin, Sid Ramin, Irwin Kostal (Col)

BEST ORIGINAL CAST SHOW ALBUM
(Composer's Award)
CARNIVAL - Robert Merrill (MGM)
DO RE MI - Jule Styne, Betty Comden, Adolph Green (RCA)
HOW TO SUCCEED IN BUSINESS WITHOUT REALLY TRYING - Frank Loesser (RCA)
MILK AND HONEY - Jerry Herman (RCA)
WILDCAT - Cy Coleman, Carolyn Leigh (RCA)

BEST COMEDY PERFORMANCE
AN EVENING WITH MIKE NICHOLS AND ELAINE MAY - Mike Nichols, Elaine May (Merc)
HERE'S JONATHAN - Jonathan Winters (Verve)
JOSE JIMENEZ THE ASTRONAUT - Bill Dana (Kapp)
STAN FREBERG PRESENTS THE UNITED STATES OF AMERICA - Stan Freberg (Cap)
2001 YEARS WITH CARL REINER AND MEL BROOKS - Carl Reiner, Mel Brooks (Cap)

BEST DOCUMENTARY OR SPOKEN WORD RECORDING
THE COMING OF CHRIST - Alexander Scourby, Robert Russell Bennett, cond. (Decca)
HUMOR IN MUSIC - Leonard Bernstein, cond. New York Philharmonic (Col)
MORE OF HAL HOLBROOK IN MARK TWAIN TONIGHT! - Hal Holbrook (Col)
WISDOM, VOL. 1 (Sandburg, Shapley, Nehru, Lipschitz) Milt Gabler, Prod. (Decca)
WORLD OF DOROTHY PARKER - Dorothy Parker (Verve)

BEST ENGINEERING CONTRIBUTION - POPULAR RECORDING
(Engineer's Award)
BREAKFAST AT TIFFANY'S (Henry Mancini) Eng: Al Schmitt (RCA)
COZY (Steve Lawrence, Eydie Gorme) Eng: Bill MacMeekin (UA)
GREAT BAND WITH GREAT VOICES (Johnny Mann Singers) Eng: Al Schmitt (Lib)
JUDY AT CARNEGIE HALL (Judy Garland) Eng: Robert Arnold (Cap)
STEREO 35/MM. (Enoch Light) Eng: Robert Fine (Command)

BEST ENGINEERING CONTRIBUTION - NOVELTY
(Engineer's Award)
THE ALVIN SHOW (David Seville) Eng: Ted Keep (lib)
CARTOONS IN STEREO (Bob Prescott) Eng: Bruno Vineis (Audio Fld.)
THE SOUPY SALES SHOW - Eng: Eddie Brackett (Rep)
STAN FREBERG PRESENTS THE UNITED STATES OF AMERICA - Eng: John Kraus (Cap)
X-15 AND OTHER SOUNDS: ROCKETS MISSILES & JETS - Eng: Rafael O. Valentin (Rep)

BEST ALBUM COVER
(Other than Classical) (Art Director's Award)
A TOUCH OF ELEGANCE (Andre Previn) Art Dir: Bob Cato (Col)
BREAKFAST AT TIFFANY'S (Henry Mancini) Art Dir: Robert Jones (RCA)
JACKIE'S BAG (Jackie McLean) Art Dir: Reid Miles (Blue Note)
JUDY AT CARNEGIE HALL (Judy Garland) Art Dir: Jim Silke (Cap)
NEW ORLEANS - THE LIVING LEGEND (Peter Bocage) Art Dir: Ken Deardoff (Rvrsd)

BEST RECORDING FOR CHILDREN
GOLDEN TREASURY OF GREAT MUSIC AND LITERATURE - Arthur Shimkin, Producer (Golden)
101 DALMATIONS - Tutti Carmarata, Prod. (Disney)
PROKOFIEV: PETER AND THE WOLF - Leonard Bernstein, New York Philharmonic (Col)
THE SOUPY SALES SHOW - Soupy Sales (Rep)
YOUNG ABE LINCOLN - Arthur Shimkin, Producer (Original Broadway Cast) (Golden)

BEST ROCK AND ROLL RECORDING
GOODBYE CRUEL WORLD - James Darren (Colpix)
I LIKE IT LIKE THAT - Chris Kenner (Instnt)
IT'S GONNA WORK OUT FINE - Ike & Tina Turner (Sue)
LET'S TWIST AGAIN - Chubby Checker (Pkwy)
THE LION SLEEPS TONIGHT - The Tokens (RCA)

BEST COUNTRY AND WESTERN RECORDING
A LITTLE BITTY TEAR - Burl Ives (Decca)
BIG BAD JOHN - Jimmy Dean (Col)
HELLO WALLS - Faron Young (Cap)
HILLBILLY HEAVEN - Tex Ritter (Cap)
WALK ON BY - Leroy Van Dyke (Merc)

BEST RHYTHM & BLUES RECORDING
BRIGHT LIGHTS, BIG CITY - Jimmy Reed (Vee Jay)
FOOL THAT I AM - Etta James (Argo)
HIT THE ROAD JACK - Ray Charles (Am-Par)
MOTHER IN LAW - Ernie K-Doe (Minit)
SAVED - LaVerne Baker (Atl)

BEST FOLK RECORDING
BELAFONTE FOLK SINGERS AT HOME AND ABROAD - Belafonte Folk Singers (RCA)
THE BIG BILL BROONZY STORY - Bill Broonzy (Verve)
THE CLANCY BROTHERS AND TOMMY MAKEM - The Clancy Brothers and Tommy Makem (Col)
FOLK SONGS OF BRITAIN, VOL. 1 - Alan Lomax (Caedmon)
THE SLIGHTLY FABULOUS LIMELITERS - The Limeliters (RCA)

BEST GOSPEL OR OTHER RELIGIOUS RECORDING

EVERYTIME I FEEL THE SPIRIT - Mahalia Jackson (Col)
HYMNS AT HOME - Tennessee Ernie Ford (Cap)
JESUS KEEP ME NEAR THE CROSS - Prof. Alex Bradford (Choice)
LINCOLN HYMNS - Tex Ritter (Cap)
SWING LOW - Staple Singers (VeeJay)

BEST NEW ARTIST OF 1961

ANN-MARGRET (RCA)
DICK GREGORY (Colpix)
THE LETTERMEN (Cap)
PETER NERO (RCA)
TIMI YURO (Lib)

BEST CLASSICAL PERFORMANCE - ORCHESTRA

BARTOK: MUSIC FOR STRING INSTRUMENTS, PERCUSSION & CELESTA; HINDEMITH: MATHIS DER MAHLER - Herbert von Karajan cond. Philharmonia (Angel)
BRUCKNER: SYMPHONY NO. 4 IN E FLAT MAJOR; WAGNER: TANNHAUSER OVERTURE & VENUSBERG MUSIC - Bruno Walter cond. Boston Symphony (Col)
RAVEL: DAPHNIS ET CHLOE - Charles Munch cond. Boston Symphony (RCA)
R. STRAUSS: DON JUAN; DEBUSSY: LA MER - Fritz Reiner cond. Chicago Symphony (RCA)
R. STRAUSS: DON QUIXOTE - George Szell cond. Cleveland Orchestra (Epic)

BEST CLASSICAL PERFORMANCE - CHAMBER MUSIC

BEETHOVEN: SERENADE, OP. 8; KODALY: DUO FOR VIOLIN & CELLO, OP. 7 - Jascha Heifetz, Gregor Piatigorsky, William Primrose (RCA)
BERG: LYRIC SUITE; SEBERN: 5 PIECES FOR STRING QUARTET, OP. 5, 6 BAGATELLES, OP. 9 - Juilliard String Quartet (RCA)
FAURE: FIRST QUARTET, OP. 15; SCHUMANN: CLAVIER QUARTET, OP. 47 - Leonard Pennario, Eudice Shapiro, Sanford Schonbach, Victor Gottlieb (Cap)
FAURE: SONATA NO. 1; DEBUSSY: SONATA NO. 3 - Gary Graffman, Berl Senofsky (RCA)
FRANCK AND MOZART SONATAS - Erica Morini, Rudolf Firkusny (Decca)

BEST CLASSICAL PERFORMANCE - INSTRUMENTAL SOLOIST (WITH ORCHESTRA)

BARTOK: CONCERTO NO. 1 FOR VIOLIN & ORCH. - Isaac Stern (Ormandy, Philadelphia Orchestra) (Col)
BEETHOVEN: EMPEROR CONCERTO - Leon Fleisher (Szell cond. Cleveland Orchestra) (Epic)
BOCCHERINI, CASSADO: CONCERTO FOR GUITAR - Andres Segovia (Jorda cond. Symphony of Air) (Decca)
BRAHMS: DOUBLE CONCERTO (CONCERTO IN A FOR VIOLIN & CELLO) - Jascha Heifetz, Gregor Piatigorsky (Wallenstein cond.) (RCA)
R. STRAUSS: DON QUIXOTE - Pierre Founier (Szell cond. Cleveland Orchestra) (Epic)

BEST CLASSICAL PERFORMANCE - INSTRUMENTAL SOLOIST (WITHOUT ORCHESTRA)

BACH: SUITE NO. 3 - Andres Segovia (Decca)
BARTOK, HINDEMITH, PROKOFIEFF: SOLO VIOLIN SONATAS - Ruggerio Ricci (London)
BEETHOVEN: APPASSIONATA SONATAS, FUNERAL MARCH SONATA - Sviatoslav Richter (RCA)
HOMAGE TO LISZT - Vladimir Horowitz (RCA) REVERIE FOR SPANISH GUITARS - Laurindo Almeida (Cap)

BEST OPERA RECORDING
(Conductor's Award)

DONIZETTI: LUCIA DI LAMMERMOOR - John Pritchard cond. Chorus & Orch. of L'Accademia di Santa Cecilia (Sutherland, Cioni, Merrill, Siepi) (London)
MOZART: THE MARRIAGE OF FIGARO - Carlo Maria Giulini cond. Philharmonic Orchestra & Chorus (Schwarzkopf, Moffo, Taddei, Wachter, Cossotto) (Angel)
PUCCINI: MADAME BUTTERFLY - Gabriele Santini cond. Rome Opera Chorus & Orch. (de Los Angeles, Bjoerling, Piarzzini, Serini) (Cap)
R. STRAUSS: ELEKTRA - Karl Bohm cond. Orch & Chorus of Dresden State Opera (Borkh, Schech, Madeira, Fischer-Dieskau, Uhl) (DGG)
WAGNER: THE FLYING DUTCHMAN - Antal Dorati cond. Royal Opera House Orchestra (London, Rysanek, Tozzi, Elias, Liebl, Lewis) (RCA)

BEST CLASSICAL PERFORMANCE - CHORAL (OTHER THAN OPERA)

BACH: B MINOR MASS - Robert Shaw Chorale, Robert Shaw cond. (RCA)
BEETHOVEN: MISSA SOLEMNIS - Westminster Choir, Warren Martin, Dir; Leonard Bernstein cond. New York Philharmonic (Col)
BERLIOZ: L'ENFANCE DU CHRIST - St. Anthony Singers w/Pears, Morrison; Goldsbrough Orch., Colin Davis, cond. (Oiseau-Lyre)
POULENC: GLORIA IN G MAJOR FOR SOPRANO SOLO, CHORUS & ORCHESTRA - French Natl Radio-TV Chorus & Orch., Yvonne Gouverne, dir., Georges Pretre cond. (Angel)
RESPIGHI: LAUD TO THE NATIVITY; MONTEVERDI: MAGNIFICAT - Rober Wagner Chorale, Roger Wagner, dir., Alfred Wallenstein cond. LA Philharmonic (Cap)
WALTON: BELSHAZZAR'S FEAST - Rutgers Univ. Choir, F. Austin Walter, dir., Eugene Ormandy cond. Philadelphia Orchestra (Col)

BEST CLASSICAL PERFORMANCE - VOCAL SOLOIST

THE ART OF THE PRIMA DONNA - Joan Sutherland (Molinari-Pradelli cond. Royal Opera House Orch.) (London)
BACH: CANTATAS NO. 58 & NO. 202 - Eileen Farrell, Bach Aria Group Orch. (Decca)
THE FABULOUS VICTORIA DE LOS ANGELES - Victoria de los Angeles, (Moore, pianist) (Angel)
OPERATIC ARIAS - Leontyne Price (deFabrutis and Rome Opera House Orch.) (RCA)
TRIMBLE: FOUR FRAGMENTS FROM THE CANTERBURY TALES - Adele Addison (Conant, Russo, Orenstein) (Col)

BEST CONTEMPORARY CLASSICAL COMPOSITION
(Composer's Award)

DISCANTUS - Laurindo Almeida (Cap)
GLORIA IN G MAJOR - Francis Poulenc (Angel)
MOVEMENTS FOR PIANO AND ORCHESTRA - Igor Stravinsky (Col)
MUSIC FOR BRASS QUINTET - Gunther Schuller (Comp. Recordings)
STRING QUARTET NO. 2 - Elliott Carter (RCA)

BEST ENGINEERING CONTRIBUTION - CLASSICAL RECORDING
(Engineer's Award)

BRAHMS: SYMPHONY NO. 2 (Steinberg cond. Pittsburgh Symphony) Eng: Robert Fine (Cmmnd)
POULENC: CONCERTO IN G FOR ORGAN, STRINGS AND TIMPANI (Durufle, soloist; Pretre cond. French Natl Radio-TV Orch.) Engs: Paul Vavasseur, Walter Ruhlmann (Angel)

PROKOFIEV: CONCERTO NO. 3 (Browning, solo; Leinsdorf Philharmonia Orch.) Eng: Chris Parker (Cap)
RAVEL: DAPHNIS ET CHLOE (Munch cond. Boston Symphony) Eng: Lewis W. Layton (RCA)
R. STRAUSS: ELEKTRA (Borkh, Schech, Madeira, Fischer-Dieskau, Uhl; Bohm cond. Orch. & Chorus of Dresden State Opera) Eng: Heinrich Keiholtz (DGG)

BEST ALBUM COVER - CLASSICAL
(Art Director's Award)
ALBENIZ: IBERIA; RAVEL: RAPSODIE ESPAGNOLE (Morel cond. Paris Conservatory Orch.) Art Dir: Robert Jones (RCA)
BEETHOVEN: NINE SYMPHONIES (Klemperer cond. Philharmonia Orch.) Art Dir: Marvin Schwartz (Angel)
GOLDEN AGE OF ENGLISH LUTE MUSIC (Julian Bream) Art Dir: Meyer Miller (RCA)
GOULD BALLET MUSIC: FALL RIVER LEGEND, INTERPLAY, LATIN AMERICAN SYMPHONETTE (Gould & his Orch.) Art Dir: Robert Jones (RCA)
PUCCINI: MADAME BUTTERFLY (de los Angeles, Bjoerling, Pirazzini, Serini; Santini cond. Rome Opera Chorus & Orch.) Art Dir: Marvin Schwartz (RCA)

1962

RECORD OF THE YEAR
DESAFINADO - Stan Getz, Charlie Byrd (Verve)
FLY ME TO THE MOON BOSSA NOVA - Joe Harnell & His Orchestra (Kapp)
I CAN'T STOP LOVING YOU - Ray Charles (ABC)
I LEFT MY HEART IN SAN FRANCISCO - Tony Bennett (Col)
RAMBLIN' ROSE - Nat King Cole (Cap)
WHAT KIND OF FOOL AM I - Sammy Davis, Jr. (Reprise)

ALBUM OF THE YEAR
(Other than Classical)
THE FIRST FAMILY - Vaughn Meader (Cadence)
I LEFT MY HEART IN SAN FRANCISCO - Tony Bennett (Col)
JAZZ SAMBA - Stan Getz, Charlie Byrd (Verve)
MODERN SOUNDS IN COUNTRY & WESTERN MUSIC - Ray Charles (ABC)
MY SON, THE FOLK SINGER - Allan Sherman (WB)

ALBUM OF THE YEAR - CLASSICAL
BACH: ST. MATTHEW PASSION - Otto Klemperer cond. Philharmonia Orch. & Choir (Angel)
Columbia Records Presents VLADIMIR HOROWITZ - Vladimir Horowitz (Col)
THE HEIFETZ - PIATIGORSKY CONCERTS WITH PRIMROSE, PENNARIO AND GUESTS - Jascha Heifetz, Gregor Piatigorsky, William Primrose (RCA)
MAHLER: SYMPHONY NO. 9 IN D MINOR - Bruno Walter cond. Columbia Symphony (Col)
STRAVINSKY: THE FIREBIRD BALLET - Igor Stravinsky cond. Columbia Symphony (Col)

SONG OF THE YEAR
(Songwriter's Award)
AS LONG AS HE NEEDS ME - Lionel Bart (RCA)
I LEFT MY HEART IN SAN FRANCISCO - Douglass Cross, George Cory (Col)
MY COLORING BOOK - John Kander, Fred Ebb (Colpix)
THE SWEETEST SOUNDS - Richard Rodgers (Cap)
WHAT KIND OF FOOL AM I - Leslie Bricusse, Anthony Newley (London)

BEST INSTRUMENTAL THEME
(Composer's Award)
A TASTE OF HONEY - Bobby Scott, Ric Marlow (Reprise)
BABY ELEPHANT WALK - Henry Mancini (RCA)
ROUTE 66 THEME - Nelson Riddle (Cap)
STRANGER ON THE SHORE - Acker Bilk, Robert Mellin (Atco)
THE STRIPPER - David Rose (MGM)
WALK ON THE WILD SIDE - Elmer Bernstein, Mack David (Ava)

BEST SOLO VOCAL PERFORMANCE - FEMALE
ELLA SWINGS BRIGHTLY WITH NELSON RIDDLE - Ella Fitzgerald (album) (Verve)
I'M A WOMAN - Peggy Lee (single) (Cap)
LENA...LOVELY AND ALIVE - Lena Horne (album) (RCA)
LOVE LETTERS - Ketty Lester (album) (Era)
MY COLORING BOOK - Sandy Stewart (single) (Colpix)
NO STRINGS - Diahann Carroll (album) (Cap)
SLIGHTLY OUT OF TUNE (DESAFINADO) - Pat Thomas (Verve)

BEST SOLO VOCAL PERFORMANCE - MALE
COMIN' HOME BABY - Mel Torme (album) (Atl)
I CAN'T STOP LOVING YOU - Ray Charles (album) (ABC)
I LEFT MY HEART IN SAN FRANCISCO - Tony Bennett (album) (Col)
WHAT KIND OF FOOL AM I - Sammy Davis, Jr. (album) (Reprise)
WHAT KIND OF FOOL AM I - Anthony Newley (single) (London)

BEST JAZZ PERFORMANCE - SOLOIST OR SMALL GROUP (INSTRUMENTAL)
A TASTE OF HONEY - Eddie Cano (Reprise)
DESAFINADO - Stan Getz (Verve)
NAT KING COLE SINGS, GEORGE SHEARING PLAYS - George Shearing Quintet (Cap)
TIJUANA MOODS - Charlie Mingus (RCA)
UNDERCURRENT - Bill Evans, Jim Hall (UA)
VIVA BOSSA NOVA! - Laurindo Almeida (Cap)
WEST SIDE STORY - Oscar Peterson Trio (Verve)

BEST JAZZ PERFORMANCE - LARGE GROUP (INSTRUMENTAL)
ADVENTURES IN JAZZ - Stan Kenton (Cap)
BIG BAND BOSSA NOVA - Stan Getz, Gary McFarland (Verve)
CARNEGIE HALL CONCERT - Dizzy Gillespie (Verve)
FIRST TIME! - Duke Ellington, Count Basie (Col)
THE LEGEND - Count Basie (Roulette)
MILES DAVIS AT CARNEGIE HALL - Miles Davis, Gil Evans (Orch.) (Col)
WALK ON THE WILD SIDE - Jimmy Smith (Verve)

BEST ORIGINAL JAZZ COMPOSITION
(Composer's Award)
CAST YOUR FATE TO THE WINDS - Vince Guaraldi (Fantasy)
DESMOND BLUE - Paul Desmond (RCA)
FOCUS - Eddie Sauter (Verve)
QUINTESSENCE - Quincy Jones (Impulse)
SOUNDS OF HATARI - Henry Mancini (RCA)
TIJUANA MOODS - Charlie Mingus (RCA)
TUNISIAN FANTASY - Lalo Schifrin (Verve)

BEST PERFORMANCE BY AN ORCHESTRA - FOR DANCING
BIG BAND BOSSA NOVA - Stan Getz, Gary McFarland (Verve)
BIG BAND BOSSA NOVA - Quincy Jones (Merc)
FLY ME TO THE MOON BOSSA NOVA - Joe Harnell (Kapp)
JAZZ POPS - Neal Hefti (Reprise)
THE STRIPPER - David Rose (MGM)
VIVA BOSSA NOVA! - Laurindo Almeida (Cap)

BEST PERFORMANCE BY AN ORCHESTRA OR INSTRUMENTALIST WITH ORCHESTRA - NOT JAZZ OR DANCING
THE COLORFUL PETER NERO - Peter Nero (RCA)
HATARI! - Henry Mancini (RCA)
HOEDOWN! - Felix Slatkin (Lib)
STRANGER ON THE SHORE - Acker Bilk (Atco)
WALK ON THE WILD SIDE - Elmer Bernstein (Ava)

BEST INSTRUMENTAL ARRANGEMENT
(Arranger's Award)

BABY ELEPHANT WALK (Mancini & Orch.) Arr: Henry Mancini (RCA)
FLY ME TO THE MOON BOSSA NOVA (Harnell & Orch.) Arr: Joe Harnell (Kapp)
FOCUS (Stan Getz) Arr: Eddie Sauter (Verve)
QUINTESSENCE (Jones) Arr: Quincy Jones (ABC)
ROUTE 66 THEME (Riddle & His Orch.) Arr: Nelson Riddle (Cap)
SENSUOUS STRINGS OF ROBERT FARNON (Farnon & Orch.) Arr: Robert Farnon (Merc.)
THE STRIPPER (Rose & Orch.) Arr: David Rose (MGM)

BEST BACKGROUND ARRANGEMENT
(Arranger's Award)

BORN TO LOSE (Ray Charles) Arr: Marty Paich (ABC)
GO AWAY LITTLE GIRL (Steve Lawrence) Arr: Marion Evans (Col)
I CAN'T STOP LOVING YOU (Ray Charles) Arr: Marty Paich (Impulse)
I LEFT MY HEART IN SAN FRANCISCO (Tony Bennett) Arr: Marty Manning (Col)
JOAO GILBERTO (Joao Gilberto) Arr: Antonio Carlos Jobim (Cap)
MY SHIP (Carol Sloane) Arr: Bill Finegan (Col)
WHAT KIND OF FOOL AM I? (Sammy Davis, Jr.) Arr: Marty Paich (Reprise)

BEST PERFORMANCE BY A VOCAL GROUP
A SONG FOR YOUNG LOVE - The Lettermen (Cap)
THE HI-LO'S HAPPEN TO FOLK SONGS - The Hi-Lo's (Reprise)
IF I HAD A HAMMER - Peter, Paul & Mary (WB)
THE SWINGERS - The Four Freshmen (Cap)
THROUGH CHILDREN'S EYES - The Limeliters (RCA)

BEST PERFORMANCE BY A CHORUS
A CHORAL SPECTACULAR - Norman Luboff (RCA)
CONSIDER YOURSELF - Pete King Chorale (Kapp)
GREAT BAND WITH GREAT VOICES SWING THE GREAT VOICES OF THE GREAT BAND - Johnny Mann Singers, Si Zentner Orch. (Lib)
PRESENTING THE NEW CHRISTY MINSTRELS - The New Christy Minstrels (Col)
THE WARING BLEND - Fred Waring and the Pennsylvanians (Cap)

BEST ORIGINAL CAST SHOW ALBUM
(Composer's Award)

A FUNNY THING HAPPENED ON THE WAY TO THE FORUM (Orig. Broadway Cast) Comp: Stephen Sondheim (Cap)
BEYOND THE FRINGE (Alan Bennett, Peter Cook, Jonathan Miller, Dudley Moore) Comp: Dudley Moore (Cap)
NO STRINGS (Orig. Broadway Cast) Comp: Richard Rodgers (Cap)
OLIVER! (Orig. Broadway Cast Recording) Comp: Lionel Bart (RCA)
STOP THE WORLD - I WANT TO GET OFF (Anthony Newley, Anna Quayle & Cast) Comps: Leslie Bricusse, Anthony Newley (London)

BEST CLASSICAL PERFORMANCE - ORCHESTRA
BRUCKNER: SYMPHONY No. 7 IN E MAJOR - Otto Klemperer cond. Philharmonia Orch. (Angel)
MAHLER: SYMPHONY No. 3 IN D MINOR - Leonard Bernstein cond. New York Philharmonic (Col)
MAHLER: SYMPHONY No. 9 IN D MINOR - Bruno Walter cond. Columbia Symphony (Col)
R. STRAUSS: ALSO SPRACH ZARATHUSTRA, OP. 30 - Fritz Reiner cond. Chicago Symphony (RCA)
STRAVINSKY: THE FIREBIRD BALLET - Igor Stravinsky cond. Columbia Symphony (Col)

BEST CLASSICAL PERFORMANCE - CHAMBER MUSIC
BACH: SONATAS FOR VIOLIN & HARPSICHORD - Yehudi Menuhin, George Malcolm (Angel)
BARTOK: COMPLETE QUARTETS - Hungarian Quartet (DGG)
BEETHOVEN: THE LATE QUARTETS - The Budapest String Quartet (Col)
THE HEIFETZ-PIATIGORSKY CONCERTS WITH PRIMROSE, PENNARIO AND GUESTS - Jascha Heifetz, Gregor Piatigorsky, William Primrose (RCA)
THE INTIMATE BACH - Laurindo Almeida, Virginia Majewski, Vincent De Rosa (Cap)
RUBINSTEIN and SZERYNG VIOLIN SONATAS, BRAHMS: SONATA NO. 1; BEETHOVEN: SONATA No. 8 OP. 30, No. 3 - Artur Rubinstein, Henryk Szeryng (RCA)

BEST CLASSICAL PERFORMANCE - INSTRUMENTAL SOLOIST(S) (WITH ORCHESTRA)
BRAHMS: CONCERTO IN D FOR VIOLIN - David Oistrakh (Klemperer cond. French Natl Radio Orch.) (Angel)
BRUCH: SCOTTISH FANTASY, VIEUXTEMPS: CONCERTO No. 5 - ascha Heifetz (Sargent cond. New Symphony Orch. of London) (RCA)
LISZT: CONCERTOS 1 AND 2 FOR PIANO & ORCH. - Svitoslav Richter (Kondrashin cond. London Symphony) (Merc.)
RACHMANINOFF: CONCERTO NO. 2 - Van Cliburn (Reiner cond. Chicago Symphony) (RCA)
STRAVINSKY: CONCERTO IN D FOR VIOLIN - Isaac Stern (Stravinsky cond. Columbia Symphony) (Col)

BEST CLASSICAL PERFORMANCE - INSTRUMENTAL SOLOIST OR DUO (WITHOUT ORCHESTRA)
THE ART OF LEON GOOSSENS - Leon Goossens (Angel)
BACH: THE ART OF THE FUGUE, VOL. 1 - Glenn Gould (Col)
BACH: THE SIX SONATAS & PARTITAS FOR VIOLIN UNACCOMPANIED - Joseph Szigeti (Vanguard)
BEETHOVEN: SONATA No. 22 FOR PIANO - Sviatoslav Richter (RCA)
Columbia Records Presents VLADIMIR HOROWITZ - Vladimir Horowitz (Col)
Five Pieces from PLATERO AND I - Andres Segovia (Decca)
FRENCH PIANO MUSIC--FOUR HANDS - Robert and Gaby Casadesus (Col)
HIGHLIGHTS OF RUBINSTEIN AT CARNEGIE HALL RECORDED DURING THE HISTORIC TEN RECITALS OF 1961 - Artur Rubinstein (RCA)

BEST OPERA RECORDING
(Conductor's Award)

BEETHOVEN: FIDELIO - Otto Klemperer cond. Philharmonia Orch. & Chorus (Solos: Ludwig, Vickers, Frick, Hallstein, Berry) (Angel)
BIZET: THE PEARL FISHERS - Pierre Dervaux cond. Chorus & Orch. of Theatre Natl de l'Opera Comique (Solos: Micheau, Gedda) (Angel)

PUCCINI: LA BOHEME - Erich Leinsdorf cond. Rome Opera House Orch. & Chorus (Solos: Moffo, Tucker, Costa, Merrill, Tozzi, Maero) (RCA)
R. STRAUSS: SALOME - Georg Solti cond. Vienna Philharmonic (Solos: Nilsson, Wachter, Stolze) (London)
VERDI: AIDA - Georg Solti cond. Rome Opera House Orch. & Chorus (Solos: Price, Vickers, Gorr, Merrill, Tozzi) (RCA)
WAGNER: DIE WALKURE - Erich Leinsdorf cond. London Symphony (Solos: Nilsson, Brouwenstien, Gorr, Vickers, London, Ward) (RCA)

BEST CLASSICAL PERFORMANCE - CHORAL (OTHER THAN OPERA)

BACH: ST. MATTHEW PASSION - Philharmonia Choir, Wilhelm Pitz, Choral Director, Otto Klemperer cond. Philharmonic Orch. (Angel)
BERLIOZ: ROMEO AND JULIET - New England Conservatory Chorus, Lorna Cooke de Varon, Dir. Charles Munch cond. Boston Symphony (RCA)
FAURE: REQUIEM - Roger Wagner Chorale; Orch. de la Societe des Concerts du Conservatoire de Paris, Roger Wagner, cond. (Cap)
HONEGGER: KING DAVID (Le Roi David) - Univ. of Utah Chorus, Ardean Watts, Dir. Maurice Abravanel cond. Utah Symphony (Vanguard)
MAHLER: SYMPHONY No. 3 IN D MINOR - Women's Chorus of Schola Cantorum, Hugh Ross, Dir. Boy's Choir, Church of Transfiguration, Stuart Gardner, Dir. Leonard Bernstein cond. New York Philharmonic (Col)
PROKOFIEV: ALEXANDER NEVSKY, OP. 78 - Westminster Choir, Warren Martin, Dir. Thomas Schippers cond. New York Philharmonic (Col)

BEST CLASSICAL PERFORMANCE - VOCAL SOLOIST (WITH OR WITHOUT ORCHESTRA)

FOSS: TIME CYCLE - Adele Addison (Bernstein cond. New York Philharmonic) (Col)
GREAT ARIAS FROM FRENCH OPERA - Maria Callas (Pretre cond. Orch. Natl de la Radio Diffusion Francaise) (Angel)
SCHUBERT: DIE SCHONE MULLERIN - Dietrich Fischer-Dieskau (Moore, piano) (Angel)
SPANISH SONGS OF THE 20th CENTURY - Victoria de los Angeles (Soriano, piano) (Angel)
R. STRAUSS: SALOME - Birgit Nilsson (Solti cond. Vienna Philharmonic) (London)
WAGNER: GOTTERDAMERUNG, BRUNNHILDE'S IMMOLATION SCENE; WESENDONCK: SONGS - Eileen Farrell (Bernstein cond. New York Philharmonic) (Col)

BEST CLASSICAL COMPOSITION BY CONTEMPORARY COMPOSER

ARCANA - Comp: Edgard Varese (Col)
CONNOTATIONS FOR ORCHESTRA - Comp: Aaron Copland (Col)
THE FLOOD - Comp: Igor Stravinsky (Col)
NOYE'S FLUDDE - Comp: Benjamin Britten (London)
SONG OF SONGS - Comp: Lukas Foss (Col)
SYMPHONY No. 2 - Comp: Sir William Walton (Epic)
TIME CYCLE - Comp: Lukas Foss (Col)

BEST ENGINEERING CONTRIBUTION - CLASSICAL RECORDING
(Engineer's Award)

Columbia Records Presents VLADIMIR HOROWITZ - Eng: Fred Plaut (Col)
COPLAND: BILLY THE KID; APPALACHIAN SPRING (Dorati cond. London Symphony) Eng: Robert Fine (Merc)
HOLST: THE PLANETS (Karajan cond. Vienna Philharmonic) Eng: London Recording Team (col)
MAHLER: SYMPHONY No. 3 IN D MINOR - (Bernstein cond. New York Philharmonic) Eng: Fred Plaut (Col)
MAHLER: SYMPHONY No. 9 IN D MINOR (Walter cond. Columbia Symphony Orch.) Eng: William Britten (Col)
PROKOFIEV: CONCERTO No. 3 FOR PIANO; RACHMANINOFF: CONCERTO No. 1 FOR PIANO (Janis, piano; Kondrashin cond. Moscow Philharmonic) Eng: Robert Fine (Merc)
STRAUSS: ALSO SPRACH ZARATHUSTRA OP. 30 (Reiner cond. Chicago Symphony) Eng: Lewis W. Layton (RCA)

BEST ALBUM COVER - CLASSICAL
(Art Director's Award)

BARTOK: THE MIRACULOUS MANDARIN; SHOSTAKOVICH: THE AGE OF GOLD (Irving cond. Philharmonia Orchestra) Art Dir: Jim Silke (Cap)
BEETHOVEN: FIDELIO (Klemperer cond. Philharmonia Orch. & Chorus) Art Dir: Marvin Schwartz (Angel)
FAURE: REQUIEM (Wagner cond. Roger Wagner Chorale & Orch. de la Societe des Conservatoire de Paris) Art Dir: Marvin Schwartz (Cap)
THE INTIMATE BACH (Almeida, Majewski, de Rosa) Art Dir: Marvin Schwartz (Cap)
OTTO KLEMPERER CONDUCTS (WEILL: THREE PENNY OPERA SUITE and others) (Klemperer cond. Philharmonia Orch.) Art Dir: Marvin Schwartz (Angel)
WAGNER: PRELUDE AND LOVE DEATH; R. STRAUSS DEATH AND TRANSFIGURATION (Leinsdorf cond. Los Angeles Philharmonic) Art Dir: Marvin Schwartz (Cap)

BEST COMEDY PERFORMANCE

ANOTHER DAY, ANOTHER WORLD - Jonathan Winters (Verve)
BEYOND THE FRINGE - Alan Bennett, Peter Cook, Jonathan Miller, Dudley Moore (Cap)
THE FIRST FAMILY - Vaughn Meader (Cadence)
MY SON, THE FOLKSINGER - Allan Sherman (WB)
NICHOLS AND MAY EXAMINE DOCTORS - Elaine May and Mike Nichols (Merc)

BEST DOCUMENTARY OR SPOKEN WORD RECORDING

CARL SANDBURG READING HIS POETRY - Carl Sandburg (Caedmon)
ENOCH ARDEN (MUSIC BY R. STRAUSS; POEM BY ALFRED TENNYSON) - Claude Rains, reader; Glenn Gould, pianist (Col)
FIRST PERFORMANCE: LINCOLN CENTER FOR THE PERFORMING ARTS - New York Philharmonic, Leonard Bernstein, cond. (Col)
MAMA SANG A SONG - Stan Kenton (Cap)
SIR MICHAEL REDGRAVE READS "THE HARMFULNESS OF TOBACCO", "A TRANSGRESSION", "THE FIRST CLASS PASSENGER" BY ANTON CHEKHOV - Sir Michael Redgrave (Spoken Arts)
SIX MILLION ACCUSE - Yehuda Lev, narr. (UA)
THE STORY-TELLER: A SESSION WITH CHARLES LAUGHTON - Charles Laughton (Cap)
THIS IS MY BELOVED - Laurence Harvey (Atl)

BEST ENGINEERING CONTRIBUTION - OTHER THAN NOVELTY OR CLASSICAL
(Engineer's Award)

ADVENTURES IN JAZZ (Stan Kenton) Eng: Carson C. Taylor (Cap)
GREAT BAND WITH GREAT VOICES SWING THE GREAT VOICES OF THE GREAT BANDS (Si Zentner Orch., Johnny Mann Singers) Eng: Al Schmitt (Lib)
HATARI! (Henry Mancini) Eng: Al Schmitt (RCA)
I CAN'T STOP LOVING YOU (Ray Charles) Eng: Bill Putnam (ABC)
JONAH JONES AND GLEN GRAY - Eng: Hugh Davies (Cap)
ROUTE 66 THEME (Nelson Riddle) Eng: John Kraus (Cap)
STEREO SPECTACULAR (Various Artists) Eng: William Hamilton (Audio Fld.)

BEST ENGINEERING CONTRIBUTION - NOVELTY
(Engineer's Award)
THE CHIPMUNK SONGBOOK (David Seville) Eng: Al Schmitt (Lib)
THE CIVIL WAR, VOL. 1 (Fennell cond. Eastman Wind Ensemble; Martin Gabel, narr.) Eng: Robert Fine (Merc)
THE FIRST FAMILY (Vaughn Meader) Eng: John Quinn (Cadence)
MY SON, THE FOLK SINGER (Allan Sherman) Eng: Lowell Frank (WB)
PEPINO, THE ITALIAN MOUSE (Lou Monte) Eng: Eddie Smith (Reprise)

BEST ALBUM COVER (OTHER THAN CLASSICAL)
(Art Director's Award)
THE COMEDY (The Modern Jazz Quartet) Art Dir: Loring Eutemey (Atl)
THE FIRST FAMILY (Vaughn Meader) Art Dir: Bill Longcore (Cadence)
THE GREAT YEARS (Frank Sinatra) Art Dir: Jim Silke (Cap)
JAZZ SAMBA (Stan Getz) Art Dir: John Murello (Verve)
LENA. . .LOVELY AND ALIVE (Lena Horne) Art Dir: Robert Jones (RCA)
LONELY WOMAN (The Modern Jazz Quartet) Art Dir: Loring Eutemey (Atl)
MY SON, THE FOLK SINGER (Allan Sherman) Art Dir: Ken Kim (WB)
POTPOURRI PAR PIAF (Edith Piaf) Art Dir: Ed Thrasher (Cap)

BEST RECORDING FOR CHILDREN
THE CAT WHO WALKED BY HERSELF - Boris Karloff (Caedmon)
THE CHIPMUNK SONGBOOK - David Seville (Lib)
GRIMM'S FAIRY TALES - Danny Kaye (Golden)
SAINT-SAEN'S: CARNIVAL OF THE ANIMALS; BRITTEN: YOUNG PERSON'S GUIDE TO THE ORCHESTRA - Leonard Bernstein (Col)
SHARI IN STORYLAND - Shari Lewis (RCA)
THROUGH CHILDREN'S EYES - The Limeliters (RCA)
YOU READ TO ME, I'LL READ TO YOU - John Ciardi (Spoken)

BEST ROCK AND ROLL RECORDING
ALLEY CAT - Bent Fabric (Atco)
BIG GIRLS DON'T CRY - Four Seasons (VeeJay)
BREAKING UP IS HARD TO DO - Neil Sedaka (RCA)
TWISTIN' THE NIGHT AWAY - Sam Cooke (RCA)
UP ON THE ROOF - The Drifters (Atl)
YOU BEAT ME TO THE PUNCH - Mary Wells (Motown)

BEST COUNTRY AND WESTERN RECORDING
DEVIL WOMAN - Marty Robbins (Col)
FUNNY WAY OF LAUGHIN' - Burl Ives (Decca)
IT KEEPS RIGHT ON A-HURTIN' - Johnny Tillotson (Cadence)
P.T. 109 - Jimmy Dean (Col)
SHE STILL THINKS I CARE - George Jones (UA)
WOLVERTON MOUNTAIN - Claude King (Col)

BEST RHYTHM AND BLUES RECORDING
BRING IT ON HOME TO ME - Sam Cooke (RCA)
COMIN' HOME BABY - Mel Torme (Atl)
I CAN'T STOP LOVING YOU - Ray Charles (ABC)
LOCO-MOTION - Little Eva (Dimension)
NUT ROCKER - B. Bumble and the Stingers (Rendezvous)
WHAT'D I SAY - Bobby Darin (Atco)

BEST FOLK RECORDING
THE BALLAD OF JED CLAMPETT - Flatt and Scruggs (Col)
BOB DYLAN - Bob Dylan (Col)
IF I HAD A HAMMER - Peter, Paul & Mary (WB)
JOAN BAEZ IN CONCERT - Joan Baez (Vanguard)
THE MIDNIGHT SPECIAL - Harry Belafonte (RCA)
PRESENTING THE NEW CHRISTY MINSTRELS - The New Christy Minstrels (Col)
SOMETHING SPECIAL - Kingston Trio (Cap)

BEST GOSPEL OR OTHER RELIGIOUS RECORDING
BLACK NATIVITY - Prof. Alex Bradford (Marion Williams & Stars of Faith) (VeeJay)
GREAT SONGS OF LOVE AND FAITH - Mahalia Jackson (Col)
HYMNS AT SUNSET - Ralph Carmichael (Cap)
I LOVE TO TELL THE STORY - Tennessee Ernie Ford (Cap)
INSPIRATION - GREAT MUSIC FOR CHORUS & ORCHESTRA - Norman Luboff Choir, Leopold Stokowki cond. New Symphony Orch. of London (RCA)
MARIAN ANDERSON - HE'S GOT THE WHOLE WORLD IN HIS HANDS, AND 18 OTHER SPIRITUALS - Marian Anderson (Franz Rupp, piano) (RCA)
SAME ME - The Clefs of Calvary (True Sound)

BEST NEW ARTIST OF 1962
FOUR SEASONS (VeeJay)
ROBERT GOULET (Col)
VAUGHN MEADER (Cadence)
THE NEW CHRISTY MINSTRELS (Col)
PETER, PAUL AND MARY (WB)
ALLAN SHERMAN (WB)

1963

RECORD OF THE YEAR
THE DAYS OF WINE AND ROSES - Henry Mancini (RCA)
DOMINIQUE - Soeur Sourire (Philips)
HAPPY DAYS ARE HERE AGAIN - Barbra Streisand (Col)
I WANNA BE AROUND - Tony Bennett (Col)
WIVES AND LOVERS - Jack Jones (Kapp)

ALBUM OF THE YEAR--OTHER THAN CLASSICAL
BACH'S GREATEST HITS - The Swingle Singers (Philips)
THE BARBRA STREISAND ALBUM - Barbra Streisand (Col)
THE DAYS OF WINE AND ROSES - Andy Williams (Col)
HONEY IN THE HORN - Al Hirt (RCA)
THE SINGING NUN - Soeur Sourire (Philips)

ALBUM OF THE YEAR - CLASSICAL
BRITTEN: WAR REQUIEM - Benjamin Britten cond. London Sym. Orch. & Chorus (Soloists: Vishnevskaya, Pears, Fischer-Dieskau; David Willocks, Dir. Bach Choir; Edward Chapman, Dir. Highgate School Choir (London)
DEBUSSY: LA MER; RAVEL: DAPHNIS AND CHLOE - George Szell cond. Cleveland Orch. (Epic)
GREAT SCENES FROM GERSHWIN'S PORGY & BESS - Leontyne Price and William Warfield (Skitch Henderson cond. RCA Sym. Orch. & Chorus) (RCA)
PUCCINI: MADAMA BUTTERFLY - Erich Leinsdorf cond. RCA Italiana Opera Orch. & Chorus (Soloists: Price, Tucker, Elias) (RCA)
THE SOUND OF VLADIMIR HOROWITZ (Works of Schumann, Scarlatti, Schubert, Scriabin) Vladimir Horowitz (Col)

SONG OF THE YEAR
(Composer's Award)
CALL ME IRRESPONSIBLE - Comps: Sammy Cahn, Jimmy Van Heusen (Reprise)
THE DAYS OF WINE AND ROSES - Comps: Johnny Mercer, Henry Mancini (RCA)
THE GOOD LIFE - Comps: Sacha Distel, Jack Reardon (Jay Gee)
I WANNA BE AROUND - Comps: Sadie Vimmerstedt, Johnny Mercer (Col)
WIVES AND LOVERS - Comps: Burt Bacharach, Hal David (Kapp)

BEST INSTRUMENTAL THEME
(Composer's Award)
BLUESETTE - Comp: Jean "Toots" Theilmans (ABC-Para)
GRAVY WALTZ - Comps: Ray Brown, Steve Allen (Dot)
LAWRENCE OF ARABIA - Comp: Maurice Jarre (Colpix)
MORE (THEME FROM "MONDO CANE") - Comps: Riz Ortolani, Nino Oliviero, Norman Newell (UA)
WASHINGTON SQUARE - Comps: Bob Goldstein, David Shire (Epic)

BEST VOCAL PERFORMANCE - FEMALE
THE BARBRA STREISAND ALBUM - Barbra Streisand (Col)
BLAME IT ON THE BOSSA NOVE - Eydie Gorme (single) (Col)
DOMINIQUE - Soeur Sourire (The Singing Nun) (single) (Philips)
I'M A WOMAN - Peggy Lee (album) (Cap)
THE WORLD OF MIRIAM MAKEBA - Miriam Makeba (album) (RCA)

BEST VOCAL PERFORMANCE - MALE
BUSTED - Ray Charles (single) (ABC-Para)
CATCH A RISING STAR - John Gary (album) (RCA)
THE DAYS OF WINE AND ROSES - Andy Williams (album) (Col)
I WANNA BE AROUND - Tony Bennett (single) (Col)
WIVES AND LOVERS - Jack Jones (single) (Kapp)

BEST INSTRUMENTAL JAZZ PERFORMANCE - SOLOIST OR SMALL GROUP
CONVERSATIONS WITH MYSELF - Bill Evans (Verve)
CRISS-CROSS - Thelonious Monk (Col)
DAVE BRUBECK AT CARNEGIE HALL - Dave Brubeck Quartet (Col)
4 TO GO! - Andre Previn, with Ray Brown, Herb Ellis, Shally Manne (Col)
OUR MAN IN NEW ORLEANS - Al Hirt (RCA)
PETER NERO IN PERSON - Peter Nero (RCA)
SEVEN STEPS TO HEAVEN - Miles Davis (Col)

BEST INSTRUMENTAL JAZZ PERFORMANCE - LARGE GROUP
ENCORE: WOODY HERMAN, 1963 - Woody Herman Band (Philips)
FULL NELSON - Oliver Nelson Orch. (Verve)
GERRY MULLIGAN '63 - Gerry Mulligan Concert Jazz Band (Verve)
OUR MAN IN NEW ORLEANS - Al Hirt (RCA)
QUINCY JONES PLAYS THE HIP HITS - Quincy Jones (Mercury)
SEVEN STEPS TO HEAVEN - Miles Davis (Col)

BEST ORIGINAL JAZZ COMPOSITION
(Composer's Award)
BLACK SAINT AND THE SINNER LADY - Comp: Charlie Mingus (Impulse)
EAST SIDE-WEST SIDE - Comp: Kenyon Hopkins (Backbone Hill)
GRAVY WALTZ - Comp: Ray Brown, Steve Allen (Dot)
LITTLE BIRD - Comps: Dick Grove, Pete Jolly, Tommy Wolf (Ava)
MEDITATION - Comps: Newton Mendonco, Antonio Carlos Jobim (Riverside)
TAKE TEN - Comp: Paul Desmond (RCA)

BEST PERFORMANCE BY AN ORCHESTRA - FOR DANCING
ENCORE: WOODY HERMAN, 1963 - Woody Herman (Philips)
FLY ME TO THE MOON AND THE BOSSA NOVA POPS - Joe Harnell (Kapp)
THE PAGE 7...AN EXPLOSION IN POP MUSIC - Page Cavanaugh (RCA)
QUINCY JONES PLAYS THE HIP HITS - Quincy Jones (Mercury)
RICHARD RODGERS BANDBOOK - Les Brown (Col)
THIS TIME BY BASIE! HITS OF THE 50'S AND 60'S - Count Basie (Reprise)

BEST PERFORMANCE BY AN ORCHESTRA OR INSTRUMENTALIST WITH ORCHESTRA - NOT JAZZ OR DANCING
ANDRE PREVIN IN HOLLYWOOD - Andre Previn (Col)
HAIL THE CONQUERING NERO - Peter Nero (RCA)
JAVA - Al Hirt (RCA)
MORE - Kai Winding (Verve)
OUR MAN IN HOLLYWOOD - Henry Mancini (RCA)
THEMES FOR YOUNG LOVERS - Percy Faith (Col)

BEST INSTRUMENTAL ARRANGEMENT
(Arranger's Award)
GRAVY WALTZ (Steve Allen) Arr: Robert N. Enevoldsen (Dot)
I CAN'T STOP LOVING YOU (Count Basie) Arr: Quincy Jones (Reprise)
MORE (Kai Winding) Arr: Claus Ogerman (Verve)
MOUNTAIN GREENERY (Peter Nero) Arrs: Peter Nero & Marty Gold (RCA)
WASHINGTON SQUARE (The Village Stompers) Arr: Joe Sherman (Epic)

BEST BACKGROUND ARRANGEMENT
(Arranger's Award)
BLAME IT ON THE BOSSA NOVA (Eydie Gorme) Arr: Marion Evans (Col)
BUSTED (Ray Charles) Arr: Benny Carter (ABC)
CALL ME IRRESPONSIBLE (Frank Sinatra) Arr: Nelson Riddle (Reprise)
THE DAYS OF WINE AND ROSES (Henry Mancini) Arr: Henry Mancini (RCA)
TELL ME THE TRUTH (Nancy Wilson) Arr: Gerald Wilson (Cap)
WIVES AND LOVERS (Jack Jones) Arr: Pete King (Kapp)

BEST PERFORMANCE BY A VOCAL GROUP
BLOWIN' IN THE WIND - Peter, Paul and Mary (WB)
HEY LOOK US OVER! - The J's with Jamie (Col)
THE HI LO'S HAPPEN TO BOSSA NOVA - The Hi Lo's (Reprise)
LIKE SING - JACKIE AND ROY KRAL - Jackie and Roy Kral (Col)
WAITIN' FOR THE EVENING TRAIN - Anita Kerr Singers (RCA)

BEST PERFORMANCE BY A CHORUS
BACH'S GREATEST HITS - Swingle Singers (Philips)
CHARADE - Henry Mancini and his Orchestra with Chorus (RCA)
GREEN, GREEN - The New Christy Minstrels (Col)
THE JOY OF CHRISTMAS - The Mormon Tabernacle Choir, Richard P. Condie, Director; Leonard Bernstein cond. New York Phil. (Col)
THE MANY MOODS OF CHRISTMAS - Robert Shaw Chorale, RCA Orchestra, Robert Shaw cond.

BEST ORIGINAL SCORE FROM A MOTION PICTURE OR TELEVISION
(Composer's Award)
CLEOPATRA - Comp: Alex North (20th Cen. Fox)
LAWRENCE OF ARABIA - Comp: Maurice Jarre (Colpix)
MONDO CANE - Comps: Riz Ortolani, Nino Oliviero (UA)
TOM JONES - Comp: John Addison (UA)

BEST SCORE FROM AN ORIGINAL CAST SHOW ALBUM
(Composer's Award)
HERE'S LOVE (Original Cast with Janis Paige, Craig Stevens, Laurence Naismith; Elliot Lawrence) Musical Director - Comp: Meredith Willson (Col)
JENNIE (Mary Martin, Original Cast with Ethel Shutta, George Wallace, Jack DeLon, Robbin Bailey) Comps: Arthur Schwartz, Howard Deitz (RCA)
110 IN THE SHADE (Original Cast with Robert Horton, Inga Swenson, Stephen Douglass, Will Peer, Steve Roland, Scooter Teague, Lesley Warren; Orchestra conducted by Donald W. Pippin) Comps: Harvey Schmidt, Tom Jones (RCA)
SHE LOVES ME (Original Cast with Barbara Cook, Daniel Massey, Jack Cassidy) Comps: Jerry Bock, Sheldon Harnick (MGM)
TOVARICH (Original Cast with Vivien Leigh, Jean-Pierre Aumont) Comps: Lee Pockriss, Anne Croswell (Cap)

BEST CLASSICAL PERFORMANCE - ORCHESTRA
BARTOK: CONCERTO FOR ORCHESTRA - Erich Leinsdorf cond. Boston Sym. Orch. (RCA)
BEETHOVEN: THE NINE SYMPHONIES (COMPLETE) - Herbert von Karajan cond. Berlin Philharmonic (DGG)
BEETHOVEN: SYMPHONY No. 6 IN F MAJOR, OP. 68 ("PASTORALE") - Fritz Reiner cond. Chicago Symphony (RCA)
MAHLER: SYMPHONY No. 1 IN D MAJOR ("THE TITAN") - Bruno Walter cond. Columbia Symphony (Col)
RAVEL: DAPHNIS AND CHLOE - George Szell cond. the Cleveland Orchestra (Epic)
SCHUBERT: SYMPHONY No. 9 IN C MAJOR ("THE GREAT") - Arturo Toscanini cond. Philadelphia Symphony (RCA)

BEST CLASSICAL PERFORMANCE - CHAMBER MUSIC
BEETHOVEN: QUARTET No. 11 IN F MINOR, OP. 95; QUARTET NO. 16 IN F MAJOR, OP. 135 - Juilliard String Quartet (RCA)
BEETHOVEN: SONATAS FOR VIOLIN & PIANO (NOS. 3, 4 & 5) - Zino Francescatti, Violinist; Robert Casadesus, Pianist (Col)
BRAHMS: LIEBESLIEDER WALTZES; SCHUMANN: SPANISCHE LIEBESLIEDER - Arthur Gold and Robert Fizdale (with vocalists) (Col)
AN EVENING OF ELIZABETHAN MUSIC - Julian Bream Consort (RCA)
MOZART: WIND MUSIC, VOLS. 1-5 - London Wind Soloists (London)
SCHUBERT: QUINTET IN A MAJOR FOR PIANO & STRINGS, OP. 114 ("TROUT") - Members of Budapest String Quartet with Mieczyslaw Horszowski and Julius Levine (Col)

BEST CLASSICAL PERFORMANCE - INSTRUMENTAL SOLOIST(S) (WITH ORCHESTRA)
BARTOK: CONCERTO No. 1 FOR PIANO & ORCHESTRA - Rudolf Serkin (Szell cond. Columbia Symphony) (Col)
BRUCH: CONCERTO No. 1 IN G MINOR FOR VIOLIN, OP. 26; MOZART: CONCERTO No. 4 IN D MAJOR, FOR VIOLIN, K 218 - Jascha Heifetz (Sargent cond. New Symphony Orchestra of London) (RCA)
HINDEMITH: CONCERTO FOR VIOLIN - David Oistrakh (Hindemith cond. London Symphony) (London)
LISZT: CONCERTO No. 1 FOR PIANO & ORCHESTRA - Andre Watts (Bernstein cond. New York Philharmonic) (Col)
RACHMANINOFF: CONCERTO No. 3 IN D MINOR FOR PIANO - Vladimir Ashkenazy (Fistoulari cond. London Symphony) (London)
RAVEL: CONCERTO IN G FOR PIANO & ORCHESTRA; DELLO JOIO: FANTASY & VARIATIONS FOR PIANO & ORCHESTRA - Lorin Hollander (Leinsdorf cond. Boston Symphony) (RCA)
TCHAIKOVSKY: CONCERTO No. 1 IN B-FLAT MINOR FOR PIANO & ORCHESTRA - Artur Rubinstein (Leinsdorf cond. Boston Symphony) (RCA)

BEST CLASSICAL PERFORMANCE - INSTRUMENTAL SOLOIST OR DUO (WITHOUT ORCHESTRA)
BACH: THE SIX PARTITAS - Glenn Gould (Col)
BEETHOVEN: THREE FAVORITE SONATAS (SONATA NO. 8 "PATHETIQUE"; SONATA NO. 14 "MOONLIGHT"; SONATA NO. 23 "APPASSIONATA") - Rudolf Serkin (Col)
GRANADA (ALBENIZ): "GRANADA"; GRANADOS: "SPANISH DANCE IN E MINOR"; PONCE, TANSMAN, AGUADO: "EIGHT LESSONS FOR THE GUITAR"; SOR: "FOUR STUDIES") - Andres Segovia (Decca)
SCHUMANN: CARNAVAL; FANTASIESTUCKE - Artur Rubinstein (RCA)
THE SOUND OF HOROWITZ (Works of Schumann, Scarlatti, Schubert, Scriabin) - Vladimir Horowitz (Col)

BEST OPERA RECORDING
(Conductor's Award, Plaques to Principal Soloists)
BARTOK: BLUEBEARD'S CASTLE - Eugene Ormandy cond. Philadelphia Orchestra (Soloists: Elias, Hines) (Col)
MOZART: COSI FAN TUTTE - Eugen Jochum cond. RIAS Chamber Chorus, Berlin Philharmonic (Soloists: Seefried, Merriman, Koth, Haefliger, Prey, Fischer-Dieskau) (DGG)
MUSSORGSKY: BORIS GODOUNOV - Andre Cluytens cond. Paris Conservatoire Orchestra & Chorus of National Opera of Sofia (Soloist: Boris Christoff) (Angel)
PUCCINI: MADAMA BUTTERFLY - Erich Leinsdorf cond. RCA Italiana Orchestra & Chorus (Soloists: Price, Tucker, Elias) (RCA)
PUCCINI: TOSCA - Herbert von Karajan cond. Vienna Philharmonic (Soloists: Price, DiStefano, Taddei) (RCA)
WAGNER: SIEGFRIED - Georg Solti cond. Vienna Philharmonic (Soloists: Nilsson, Windgassen, Hotter, Stolze, Hoffgen, Neidlinger, Sutherland) (London)

BEST CLASSICAL PERFORMANCE - CHORAL (OTHER THAN OPERA)
BACH: ST. MATTHEW PASSION - Abraham Kaplan, Dir. Collegiate Chorale; Stuart Gardner, Dir. Boy's Choir, Church of Transfiguration; Leonard Bernstein cond. New York Philharmonic (Col)
BRAHMS: A GERMAN REQUIEM - Richard Condie Dir. Mormon Tabernacle Choir; Eugene Ormandy cond. Philadelphia Orchestra (Col)
BRITTEN: WAR REQUIEM - David Willcocks, Dir. Bach Choir; Edward Chapman, Dir. Highgate School Choir; Benjamin Britten cond. London Symphony Orchestra & Chorus (London)
HAYDN: "NELSON MASS" (MASS No. 9 IN D MINOR, MISSA SOLEMNIS) - David Willcocks cond. Choir of King's College & London Symphony (London)
MILHAUD: LES CHOEPHORES - Hugh Ross, Dir. Schola Cantorum of New York; Leonard Bernstein cond. New York Philharmonic (Col)
ROBERT SHAW CHORALE "ON TOUR" (Ives, Schoenberg, Mozart, Ravel) - Robert Shaw cond. Robert Shaw Chorale & Orch. (RCA)
STRAVINSKY: OEDIPUS REX - Igor Stravinsky cond. Chorus & Orch. of Opera Society of Washington (Col)

BEST CLASSICAL PERFORMANCE - VOCAL SOLOIST
A VERDI COLLABORATION - Anna Moffo (Ferrara cond. RCA Italiana Sym. Orch.) (RCA)
CANTELOUBE: SONGS OF THE AUVERGNE, VOL. 2 Netania Davrath (Orch. cond. by Pierre de la Roche) (Vanguard)
COMMAND PERFORMANCE - Joan Sutherland (Bonynge cond. London Symphony) (London)

GREAT SCENES FROM GERSHWIN'S PORGY & BESS - Leontyne Price (RCA)
MAHLER: DES KNABEN WUNDERHORN - Maureen Forrester (Prohaska cond. Symphony Orchestra of Vienna Festival) (Vanguard)
MELODIES DE FRANCE (Ravel, Debussy, Duparc) - Victoria de los Angeles (Pretre cond. Paris Conservatoire Orch.) (Angel)
RAVEL: SCHEHERAZADE; BERLIOZ: CLEOPATRE (Scene Lyrique) - Jennie Tourel (Bernstein cond. New York Philharmonic) (Col)
SCHUBERT: SCHWANENGESANG - Dietrich Fischer-Dieskau (Moore, Pianist) (Col)
STRAVINSKY: OEDIPUS REX - Shirley Verrett (Stravinsky cond. Chorus & Orch. of the Washington Opera Society) (Col)

BEST CLASSICAL COMPOSITION BY CONTEMPORARY COMPOSER

(Composer's Award)
ANDROMACHE'S FAREWELL, OP. 39 - Comp: Samuel Barber (Col)
CONCERTO FOR PIANO - Comp: John LaMontaine (Composers Recordings)
CONCERTO No. 2 FOR CELLO & ORCHESTRA - Comp: Heitor Villa-Lobos (Westminster)
SYMPHONY No. 4, OP. 43 - Comp. Dimitri Shostakovich (Col)
SYMPHONY No. 8 - Comp. William Schuman (Col)
WAR REQUIEM - Comp. Benjamin Britten (London))

BEST ENGINEERED RECORDING - CLASSICAL

(Engineer's Award))
BERNSTEIN CONDUCTS TCHAIKOVSKY (Bernstein cond. New York Philharmonic) - Eng: Fred Plaut (Col)
BRITTEN: WAR REQUIEM (Britten cond. London Symphony Orch. & Chorus) - Eng: Kenneth Wilkenson (London)
GREAT SCENES FROM GERSHWIN'S PORGY & BESS (Price & Warfield) - Eng: Lewis Layton (RCA)
MAHLER: SYMPHONY No. 1 IN D ("THE TITAN") (Leinsdorf cond. Boston Symphony) - Eng: Lewis Layton (RCA)
PUCCINI: MADAME BUTTERFLY (Leinsdorf cond. RCA Italiana Orch. & Chorus) - Eng: Lewis Layton (Price, Tucker, Elias) (RCA)
WAGNER: SIEGFRIED (Solti cond. Vienna Philharmonic. Soloists: Nilsson, Windgassen, Hotter, Stolze, Hoffgen, Neidlinger, Sutherland) - Eng: Gordon Parry (London)

BEST ALBUM COVER - CLASSICAL

(Art Director's Award)
BEETHOVEN: SYMPHONY NO. 5 IN C MINOR, OP. 67 (Bernstein cond. New York Philharmonic) Art Dir: John Berg (Col)
BEETHOVEN: SYMPHONY No. 6 IN F MAJOR, OP. 68 ("PASTORALE") (Reiner cond. Chicago Sym. Orch.) Art Dir: Robert Jones (RCA)
EVENING OF ELIZABETHAN MUSIC (Julian Bream Consort) Art Dir: Dorle Soria (RCA)
PUCCINI: MADAMA BUTTERFLY (Leinsdorf cond. RCA Italiana Orch. & Chorus) Art Dir: Robert Jones (RCA)
PUCCINI: TOSCA (von Karajan cond. Vienna Philharmonic Orch.) Art Dir: Dorle Soria (RCA)
GRANADA (Albeniz: "Granada; Granados: "Spanish Dance in E Minor"; Ponce, Tansman, Aguado: "8 Lessons for Guitar"; Sor: "Four Studies") (Andres Segovia) Art Dir: Vladimir Bobri (Decca)
R. STRAUSS: DON QUIXOTE (Ormandy cond. Philadelphia Orch.) Art Dir: Bob Cato (Col)

MOST PROMISING NEW CLASSICAL RECORDING ARTIST

THE ABBEY SINGERS (Vocalists) (Decca)
REGINE CRESPIN (Vocalist) (London)
COLIN DAVIS (Conductor) (Angel)
ALIRIO DIAZ (Guitarist) (Vanguard)
JOHN OGDON (Pianist) (Angel)
FOU TS'ONG (Pianist) (Westminster)
ANDRE WATTS (Pianist) (Col)

BEST COMEDY PERFORMANCE

BILL COSBY IS A VERY FUNNY FELLOW, RIGHT! - Bill Cosby (WB)
CARL REINER AND MEL BROOKS AT THE CANNES FILM FESTIVAL - Carl Reiner, Mel Brooks (Cap)
HELLO MUDDUH, HELLO FADDAH - Allan Sherman (WB)
I AM THE GREATEST! - Cassius Clay (Col)
THINK ETHNIC - The Smothers Bros. (Merc)

BEST DOCUMENTARY, SPOKEN WORD OR DRAMA RECORDING (OTHER THAN COMEDY)

THE BADMEN (Pete Seeger and others) Goddard Lieberson, Producer (Col)
BRECHT ON BRECHT (Original Cast with Dane Clark, Anne Jackson, Lotte Lenya, Viveca Lindfors, George Voskovec, Michael Wager) Berthold Brecht, Playwright (Col)
JOHN F. KENNEDY - THE PRESIDENTIAL YEARS (David Teig, Narr) Norman Weiser, Producer (four Corners)
STRANGE INTERLUDE - Eugene O'Neill (Original Broadway Cast: Betty Field, Jane Fonda, Ben Gazzara, Pat Hingle, Geoff Horne, William Prince, Geraldine Page, Richard Thomas, Franchot Tone) (Col)
WE SHALL OVERCOME (The March on Washington. . .August 28, 1963) - Dr. Martin Luther King, Jr. (with Joan Baez, Marian Anderson, Odetta, Rabbi Joachim Prinz, Bob Dylan, Whitney M. Young, Jr., John Lewis, Roy Wilkins, Walter Reuther, Peter, Paul and Mary, Bayard Rustin, A. Philip Randolph) (United Civil Rights)
WHO'S AFRAID OF VIRGINIA WOOLF? - Edward Albee, Playwright (Original Cast: Uta Hagen, Arthur Hill, George Grizzard, with Melinda Dillon) (WB)

BEST ENGINEERED RECORDING - OTHER THAN CLASSICAL

(Engineer's Award)
THE BARBRA STREISAND ALBUM (Barbra Streisand) Eng: Frank Laico (Col)
CHARADE (Henry Mancini Orch. & Chorus) Eng: James A. Malloy (RCA)
ELLA AND BASIE (Ella Fitzgerald, Count Basie) Eng: Luis P. Valentin (Verve)
EXOTIC SOUNDS OF BALI (Mantle Hood, Dir.) Eng: Harold Chapman (Col)
THE MANY MOODS OF CHRISTMAS (Robert Shaw Chorale) Eng: Anthony J. Salvatore (RCA)
OUR MAN IN HOLLYWOOD (Henry Mancini) Eng: Albert H. Schmitt (RCA)
POLITELY PERCUSSIVE (Dick Schory) Eng: Ronald A. Steele (RCA)
THE SECOND BARBRA STREISAND ALBUM (Barbra Streisand) Eng: Frank Laico (Col)
SUPERCUSSION (Dick Schory) Eng: Ronald A. Steele (RCA)

BEST ENGINEERED RECORDING - SPECIAL OR NOVEL EFFECTS

(Engineer's Award)
CHEYENNE FRONTIER DAYS (Hank Thompson) Eng: John Kraus (Cap)
CIVIL WAR VOL. 2 (Frederick Fennell) Eng: Robert Fine (Mercury)
FAST, FAST, FAST RELIEF FROM TV COMMERCIALS (Bill McFadden, Bryna Rayburn) Eng: William Hamilton (Audio Fid.)
FOUR IN THE FLOOR (The Shut Downs) Engs: Scotty Shackner, Bob MacMeekin (Dimension)
HEARTSTRINGS (Dean Elliott) Engs: John Kraus, Hugh B. Davies (Cap)
PEPINO'S FRIEND PASQUALE (Lou Monte) Eng: Phil Macy, Al Weintraub (Reprise)
ZOUNDS! WHAT SOUNDS (Dean Elliott) Eng: John Kraus (Cap)

BEST ALBUM COVER - OTHER THAN CLASSICAL
(Art Director's Award)
ALOHA FROM NORMAN LUBOFF (The Norman Luboff Choir) Art Dir: Robert Jones (RCA)
BACH'S GREATEST HITS (The Swingle Singers) Art Dir: Jim Ladwing (Philips)
THE BARBRA STREISAND ALBUM (Barbra Streisand) Art Dir: John Berg (Col)
CARL REINER AND MEL BROOKS AT THE CANNES FILM FESTIVAL (Carl Reiner and Mel Brooks) Art Dir: Edward L. Thrasher (WB)
HOLLYWOOD MY WAY (Nancy Wilson) Art Dir: Jim Silke (Cap)
HONEY IN THE HORN (Al Hirt) Art Dir: Robert Jones (RCA)
NIGHT TRAIN (Oscar Peterson) Art Dir: John Murello (Verve)

BEST ALBUM NOTES
(Annotator's Award)
THE AMAZING AMANDA AMBROSE (Amanda Ambrose) Ann: Bob Bollard (RCA)
THE BADMEN (Pete Seeger and others) Ann: B.A. Botkin, Sylvester L. Vigilante, Harold Preece, James L. Horan (Col)
THE BARBRA STREISAND ALBUM (Barbra Streisand) Ann: Harold Arlen (Col)
THE ELLINGTON ERA (Duke Ellington) Ann: Leonard Feather, Stanley Dance (Col)
EVENING OF ELIZABETHAN MUSIC (Julian Bream Consort) Ann: Sidney Bock (RCA)
WHO'S AFRAID OF VIRGINIA WOOLF? (Original Cast) Ann: Edward Albee, Harold Clurman (Col)

BEST RECORDING FOR CHILDREN
ADDITION AND SUBTRACTION - Rica Owen Moore (Disney)
BERNSTEIN CONDUCTS FOR YOUNG PEOPLE - Leonard Bernstein cond. New York Phil. (Col)
CHILDREN'S CONCERT - Pete Seeger (Col)
LET'S GO TO THE ZOO - Fred V. Grunfeld, Producer (Various Artists) (Decca)
ON TOP OF SPAGHETTI - Tom Glazer (and The Do Re Mi Children's Chorus) (Kapp)
PUFF (THE MAGIC DRAGON) - Peter, Paul and Mary (WB)
WINNIE THE POOH - Jack Gilford (Golden)

BEST ROCK AND ROLL RECORDING
ANOTHER SATURDAY NIGHT - Sam Cooke (RCA)
DEEP PURPLE - Nino Tempo, April Stevens (Atco)
I WILL FOLLOW HIM - Little Peggy March (RCA)
IT'S MY PARTY - Lesley Gore (Merc)
OUR DAY WILL COME - Ruby & The Romantics (Kapp)
TEEN SCENE - Chet Atkins (RCA)

BEST COUNTRY AND WESTERN RECORDING
DETROIT CITY - Bobby Bare (RCA)
FLATT & SCRUGGS AT CARNEGIE HALL - Flatt & Scruggs (Col)
LOVE'S GONNA LIVE HERE - Buck Owens (Cap)
NINETY MILES AN HOUR (DOWN A DEAD END STREET) - Hank Snow (RCA)
THE PORTER WAGONER SHOW - Porter Wagoner (RCA)
RING OF FIRE - Johnny Cash (Col)
SAGINAW, MICHIGAN - Lefty Frizzell (Col)

BEST RHYTHM AND BLUES RECORDING
BUSTED - Ray Charles (ABC-Para)
FRANKIE AND JOHNNY - Sam Cooke (RCA)
(LOVE IS LIKE A) HEAT WAVE - Martha & The Vandellas (Gordy)
HEY, LITTLE GIRL - Major Lance (Okeh)
HELLO STRANGER - Barbara Lewis (Atl)
PART TIME LOVE - Little Johnny Taylor (Galaxy)
SINCE I FELL FOR YOU - Lenny Welch (Cadence)

BEST FOLK RECORDING
BLOWIN' IN THE WIND - Peter, Paul & Mary (WB)
GREEN, GREEN - The New Christy Minstrels (Col)
JUDY COLLINS No. 3 - Judy Collins (Elektra)
ODETTA SINGS FOLK SONGS - Odetta (RCA)
WALK RIGHT IN (album) - The Rooftop Singers (Vanguard))
WE SHALL OVERCOME - Pete Seeger (Col)
THE WORLD OF MIRIAM MAKEBA - Mariam Makeba (RCA)

BEST GOSPEL OR OTHER RELIGIOUS RECORDING (MUSICAL)
DOMINIQUE - Soeur Sourire (The Singing Nun) (Philips)
THE EARTH IS THE LORD'S (AND THE FULLNESS THEREOF) - George Beverly Shea (RCA)
MAKE A JOYFUL NOISE - Mahalia Jackson (Col)
MAKIN' A JOYFUL NOISE - The Limeliters (RCA)
PIANO IN CONCERT - Charles Magnuson and Fred Bock (Sacred)
RECORDED LIVE! - Bessie Griffin and the Gospel Pearls (Epic)
STEPPIN' RIGHT IN - Kings of Harmony (Kings of Harmony)
THE STORY OF CHRISTMAS - Tennessee Ernie Ford; The Roger Wagner Chorale (Col)

BEST NEW ARTIST OF 1963
VIKKI CARR (Lib)
JOHN GARY (RCA)
J'S WITH JAMIE (Col)
TRINI LOPEZ (Reprise)
SWINGLE SINGERS (Philips)

1964

RECORD OF THE YEAR
DOWNTOWN - Petula Clark (WB)
THE GIRL FROM IPANEMA - Stan Getz, Astrud Gilberto (Verve)
HELLO, DOLLY! - Louis Armstrong (Kapp)
I WANT TO HOLD YOUR HAND - The Beatles (Cap)
PEOPLE - Barbra Streisand (Col)

ALBUM OF THE YEAR
COTTON CANDY - Al Hirt (RCA)
FUNNY GIRL - Robert Merrill, Jule Styne (Cap)
GETZ/GILBERTO - Stan Getz, Joao Gilberto (Verve)
PEOPLE - Barbra Streisand (Col)
THE PINK PANTHER - Henry Mancini (RCA)

ALBUM OF THE YEAR - CLASSICAL
BERNSTEIN: SYMPHONY No. 3 ("KADDISH") - Leonard Bernstein cond. New York Philharmonic (Col)
BIZET: CARMEN - Herbert von Karajan cond. Vienna Philharmonic (Soloists: Price, Corelli, Merrill, Freni) (RCA)
MAHLER: SYMPHONY No. 5; BERG: WOZZECK EXCERPTS (Phyllis Curtin) - Erich Leinsdorf cond. Boston Symphony (RCA)
VERDI: FALSTAFF - Georg Solti cond. RCA Italiana Opera Orch. & Chorus (Soloists: Evans, Merrill, Kraus, Simionato, Ligabue, Elias, others) (RCA)
VERDI: REQUIEM MASS - Carlo Maria Giulini cond. Philharmonia Orch. (Soloists: Schwarzkopf, Gedda, Ludwig, Ghiaurov) (Angel)

SONG OF THE YEAR
(Songwriter's Award)
A HARD DAY'S NIGHT - Songwrs: John Lennon, Paul McCartney (Cap)
DEAR HEART - Songwrs: Henry Mancini, Ray Evans, Jay Livingston (RCA)
HELLO, DOLLY! - Songwr: Jerry Herman (Kapp)
PEOPLE - Songwrs: Jule Styne, Bob Merrill (Col)
WHO CAN I TURN TO - Songwrs: Leslie Bricusse, Anthony Newley (Col)

BEST INSTRUMENTAL COMPOSITION (OTHER THAN JAZZ)
(Composer's Award)
COTTON CANDY - Comp: Russ Daymon (RCA)
THE PINK PANTHER THEME - Comp: Henry Mancini (RCA)
SUGAR LIPS - Comp: Buddy Killen, Billy Sherrill (RCA)
THEME FROM GOLDEN BOY - Comps: Charles Strouse, Lee Adams (Decca)
THEME FROM "THE MUNSTERS" - Comp: Jack Marshall (Cap)

BEST VOCAL PERFORMANCE - FEMALE
DOWNTOWN - Petula Clark (single) (WB)
THE GIRL FROM IPANEMA - Astrud Giberto (single) (Verve)
HOW GLAD I AM - Nancy Wilson (single) (Cap)
PEOPLE - Barbra Streisand (single) (Col)
WE'LL SING IN THE SUNSHINE - Gale Garnett (single) (RCA)

BEST VOCAL PERFORMANCE - MALE
CALL ME IRRESPONSIBLE - Andy Williams (album) (Col)
EVERYBODY LOVES SOMEBODY - Dean Martin (album) (Reprise)
GETZ/GILBERTO - Joao Gilberto (album) (Verve)
HELLO, DOLLY! - Louis Armstrong (single) (Kapp)
WHO CAN I TURN TO? - Tony Bennett (single) (Col)

BEST INSTRUMENTAL JAZZ PERFORMANCE - SMALL GROUP OR SOLOIST WITH SMALL GROUP
COLLABORATION - The Modern Jazz Quartet with Laurindo Almeida (Atl)
GETZ/GILBERTO - Stan Getz (Verve)
MILES DAVIS IN EUROPE - Miles Davis (Col)
MUMBLES - Oscar Peterson and Clark Terry (Merc)
MY FAIR LADY - Andre Previn (Col)
SWEET SEPTEMBER (album) - Pete Jolly (Ava)

BEST INSTRUMENTAL JAZZ PERFORMANCE - LARGE GROUP OR SOLOIST WITH LARGE GROUP
DYNAMIC SOUND PATTERNS OF THE ROD LEVITT ORCHESTRA - Rod Levitt (Riverside)
GUITAR FROM IPANEMA - Laurindo Almeida (Cap)
THE INDIVIDUALISM OF GIL EVANS - Gil Evans (Verve)
MY FAIR LADY WITH THE UNORIGINAL CAST - Shelly Manne (Cap)
OSCAR PETERSON--NELSON RIDDLE - Oscar Peterson and Nelson Riddle (Verve)
QUIET NIGHTS - Miles Davis and Gil Evans (Col)
QUINCY JONES EXPLORES THE MUSIC OF HENRY MANCINI - Quincy Jones (Merc)
WOODY HERMAN '64 - Woody Herman (Phillips)

BEST ORIGINAL JAZZ COMPOSITION
(Composer's Award)
THE CAT - Comp: Lalo Schifrin (Verve)
HERE AND NOW - Comp: Bob Florence (Lib)
NIGHT CREATURE - Comp: Duke Ellington (Rep)
PACO - Comp: Gerald Wilson (World Pac.)
THEME FROM MR. BROADWAY - Comp: Dave Brubeck (Col)
THE WITCHING HOUR - Comp: Quincy Jones (Merc)

BEST INSTRUMENTAL PERFORMANCE - NON-JAZZ
AS LONG AS HE NEEDS ME - Peter Nero (RCA)
THE BEATLES SONG BOOK (Hollyridge Strings) Stu Phillips (Cap)
COTTON CANDY - Al Hurt (RCA)
GOLDEN BOY (string version) Quincy Jones (Merc)
PINK PANTHER - Henry Mancini (RCA)

BEST INSTRUMENTAL ARRANGEMENT
(Arranger's Award)
A SPOONFUL OF SUGAR - Duke Ellington - Arr: Billy Strayhorn (Reprise)
GOLDEN BOY (string version) - Quincy Jones - Arr: Quincy Jones (Merc)
I WANT TO HOLD YOUR HAND - Arthur Fiedler & the Boston Pops - Arr: Richard Hayman (RCA)
THEME FROM "THE LONG SHIPS" - Arr: Hugo Montenegro (RCA)
PINK PANTHER - Arr: Henry Mancini (RCA)
THE SONG IS YOU - Arr: Bob Florence (Lib)
SUGAR LIPS - Al Hirt - Arr: Anita Kerr (RCA)

BEST ACCOMPANIMENT ARRANGEMENT FOR VOCALIST(S) OR INSTRUMENTALIST(S)
(Arranger's Award)
HOW GLAD I AM - Nancy Wilson - Arr: Oliver Nelson (Cap)
PEOPLE - Barbra Streisand - Arr: Peter Matz (Col)
RINGO - Lorne Green - Arr: Don Ralke (RCA)
WE'LL SING IN THE SUNSHINE - Gale Garnett - Arr: Sid Bass (RCA)
WHERE LOVE HAS GONE - Jack Jones - Arr: Pete King (Kapp)
WHO CAN I TURN TO - Tony Bennett - Arr: George Siravo (Col)

BEST PERFORMANCE BY A VOCAL GROUP
A HARD DAY'S NIGHT - The Beatles (Cap)
THE DOUBLE SIX SING RAY CHARLES - The Double Six of Paris (Philips)
GRAND OLE OPRY FAVORITES - The Browns (RCA)
MORE FOUR FRESHMEN AND FIVE TROMBONES - Four Freshmen (Cap)
PETER PAUL AND MARY IN CONCERT - Peter, Paul and Mary (WB)

BEST PERFORMANCE BY A CHORUS
ARTISTRY IN VOICES & BRASS - Stan Kenton Orchestra: Chorus by Pete Rugolo (Cap)
DEAR HEART - Henry Mancini Orchestra & Chorus (RCA)
DON'T LET THE RAIN COME DOWN (CROOKED LITTLE MAN) - The Serendipity Singers (Philips)
LOVE ME WITH ALL YOUR HEART - The Ray Charles Singers (Col)
THE SWINGLE SINGERS GOING BAROQUE - The Swingle Singers (Philips)

BEST ORIGINAL SCORE WRITTEN FOR A MOTION PICTURE OR TV SHOW
(Composer's Award)
A HARD DAY'S NIGHT - The Beatles - Comps: John Lennon, Paul McCartney (UA)
GOLDFINGER - John Barry Cond. - Comp: John Barry (UA)
MARY POPPINS - Julie Andrews, Dick Van Dyke, David Tomlinson, Glynis Johns, Ed Wynn - Comp: Richard M. Sherman, Robert B. Sherman (Buena Vista)
THE PINK PANTHER - Henry Mancini cond. - Comp: Henry Mancini (RCA)
ROBIN AND THE SEVEN HOODS - Frank Sinatra, Dean Martin, Bing Crosby, Sammy Davis, Jr. - Comps: Sammy Cahn, Jimmy Van Heusen (Reprise)

BEST SCORE FROM ORIGINAL CAST SHOW ALBUM
(Composer's Award)
FIDDLER ON THE ROOF - Orig. Cast w/Zero Mostel, Tanya Everett, Joanna Merlin - Comps: Jerry Bock, Sheldon Harnick (RCA)
FUNNY GIRL - Barbra Streisand and Orig. Cast - Comps: Jule Styne, Bob Merrill (Cap)

ELLO DOLLY! - Carol Channing and Orig. Cast - Comp: Jerry Herman (RCA)
HIGH SPIRITS - Beatrice Lillie, Tammy Grimes, Edward Woodward and Orig. Cast - Comps: Hugh Martin, Timothy Gray (ABC)
WHAT MAKES SAMMY RUN? - Steve Lawrence and Orig. Cast - Comp: Ervin Drake (Col)

BEST COMEDY PERFORMANCE
FOR SWINGIN' LIVERS ONLY! - Allan Sherman (WB)
I STARTED OUT AS A CHILD - Bill Cosby (WB)
READY OR NOT, HERE COMES GODFREY CAMBRIDGE - Godfrey Cambridge (Epic)
WHISTLE STOPPING - Jonathan Winters (Verve)
WOODY ALLEN - Woody Allen (Colpix)

BEST DOCUMENTARY, SPOKEN WORD OR DRAMA RECORDING (OTHER THAN COMEDY)
BBC TRIBUTE TO JOHN F. KENNEDY - "That was The Week That Was" Cast (Decca)
DIALOGUE HIGHLIGHTS FROM "BECKET" - Richard Burton, Peter O'Toole (RCA)
DYLAN - Original Cast with Sir Alec Guinness and Kate Reid
THE KENNEDY WIT - John F. Kennedy, narrated by David Brinkley, introduction by Adlai Stevenson (RCA)
SHAKESPEARE: HAMLET - Richard Burton (Orig. Cast: Hume Cronyn, John Gielgud, Alfred Drake, George Voskovec, Ellen Herlie, William Redfield, George Ross) (Col)
SHAKESPEARE: OTHELLO - National Theatre of Great Britain Prod. - Sir Laurence Olivier (w/Maggie Smith, Joyce Redman, Frank Finlay) (RCA)

BEST ENGINEERED RECORDING
(Engineer's Award)
ARTISTRY IN VOICES & BRASS - Stan Kenton - Eng: John Kraus (Cap)
GETZ/GILBERTO - Stan Getz, Joao Gilberto - Eng: Phil Ramona (Verve)
THE PINK PANTHER - Henry Mancini - Eng: James Malloy (RCA)
POPS GOES THE TRUMPET - Al Hirt, Arthur Fiedler & the Boston Pops - Eng: Bernie Keville (RCA)
SUGAR LIPS - Al Hirt - Eng: Chuck Seitz (RCA)
WHO CAN I TURN TO - Tony Bennett - Eng: George Kneurr, Frank Laico (Col)

BEST ENGINEERED RECORDING - SPECIAL OR NOVEL EFFECTS
(Engineer's Award)
THE BIG SOUNDS OF THE SPORT CARS - Eng: Bill Robinson
THE CHIPMUNKS SING THE BEATLES - The Chipmunks - Eng: Dave Hassinger (Lib)
LES POUPEES DE PARIS - Various Artists - Eng: John Norman (RCA)
MAIN THEME: THE ADDAMS FAMILY - Vic Mizzy - Eng: James Malloy (RCA)
WALKIN' IN THE RAIN - The Ronettes - Eng: Larry Levine (Phillies)

BEST ALBUM COVER
(Awards to Art Director, Photographer or Graphic Artist)
GETZ/GILBERTO - Stan Getz, Joao Gilberto - Art Dir: Acy Lehman; Graphic: Olga Albizu (Verve)
GUITAR FROM IPANEMA - Laurindo Almeida - Art Dir: George Osaki; Photographer: George Jerman (Cap)
OSCAR PETERSON PLAYS MY FAIR LADY - Art Dir: Acy Lehman; Graphic: Tom Daly (Verve)
PEOPLE - Barbra Streisand - Art Dir: Robert Cato; Photog: Don Bronstien (Col)
POITIER MEETS PLATO - Art Dir: Ed Thrasher (WB)
THE SOUND OF HARLEM - Various Artists - Art Dir: Robert Cato; Graphic: Milton Glaser (Col)

BEST RECORDING FOR CHILDREN
A SPOONFUL OF SUGAR - Mary Martin and the Do-Re-Mi Children's Chorus (Kapp)
BRITTEN: YOUNG PERSON'S GUIDE TO THE ORCHESTRA - Hugh Downs, narrator: Arthur Fiedler cond. the Boston Pops Orch. (RCA)
BURL IVES CHIM CHIM CHEREE AND OTHER CHILDREN'S CHOICES - Burl Ives and Children's Chorus (Buena Vista)
DANIEL BOONE - Fess Parker (RCA)
MARY POPPINS - Julie Andrews and Dick Van Dyke (w/David Tomlinson, Glynis Johns, Ed Wynn) (Buena Vista)

BEST ROCK AND ROLL RECORDING
A HARD DAY'S NIGHT - The Beatles (Cap)
DOWNTOWN - Petula Clark (WB)
MR. LONELY - Bobby Vinton (Epic)
OH, PRETTY WOMAN - Roy Orbison (Monument)
YOU'VE LOST THAT LOVIN' FEELING - The Righteous Brothers (Phillies)

BEST RHYTHM AND BLUES RECORDING
BABY LOVE - The Supremes (Motown)
GOOD TIMES - Sam Cooke (RCA)
HOLD WHAT YOU'VE GOT - Joe Tex (Dial Lat)
HOW GLAD I AM - Nancy Wilson (Cap)
KEEP ON PUSHING - The Impressions (ABC)
WALK ON BY - Dionne Warwicke (Scepter)

BEST FOLK RECORDING
BELAFONTE AT THE GREEK THEATRE - Harry Belafonte (RCA)
PETER, PAUL AND MARY IN CONCERT - Peter, Paul and Mary (RCA)
THE TIMES, THEY ARE A'CHANGIN' - Bob Dylan (Col)
TODAY - The New Christy Minstrels (Col)
THE VOICE OF AFRICA - Miriam Makeba (RCA)
WE'LL SING IN THE SUNSHINE - Gale Garnett (RCA)
WOODY GUTHRIE: LIBRARY OF CONGRESS RECORDINGS - Woody Guthrie (Nonesuch)

BEST GOSPEL OR OTHER RELIGIOUS RECORDING (MUSICAL)
FAMILY ALBUM OF HYMNS - Roger Williams (Kapp)
GREAT GOSPEL SONGS - Tennessee Ernie Ford (Cap)
GREGORIAN CHANT - Dominican Nuns of Fichermont (Philips)
GEORGE BEVERLY SHEA SINGS HYMNS OF SUNRISE AND SUNSET - George Beverly Shea (RCA)
SWEET HOUR OF PRAYER - Jo Stafford (Cap)
STANDIN' ON THE BANKS OF THE RIVER - James Cleveland & The Angelic Choir (Savoy)
THIS I BELIEVE - Fred Waring (Cap)

BEST NEW ARTIST OF 1964
THE BEATLES (Cap)
PETULA CLARK (WB)
ASTRUD GILBERTO (Verve)
ANTONIO CARLOS JOBIM (WB)
MORGANA KING (Mainstream)

BEST COUNTRY & WESTERN SINGLE
DANG ME - Roger Miller (Smash)
FOUR STRONG WINDS - Bobby Bare (RCA)
HERE COMES MY BABY - Dottie West (RCA)
ONCE A DAY - Connie Smith (RCA)
YOU'RE THE ONLY WORLD I KNOW - Sonny James (Cap)

BEST COUNTRY & WESTERN ALBUM
THE BEST OF BUCK OWENS - Buck Owens (Cap)
THE BEST OF JIM REEVES - Jim Reeves (RCA)
BITTER TEARS - Johnny Cash (Col)
DANG ME/CHUG-A-LUG - Roger Miller (Smash)
GUITAR COUNTRY - Chet Atkins (RCA)
HANK WILLIAMS, JR. SINGS SONGS OF HANK WILLIAMS - Hank Williams, Jr. (MGM)

BEST COUNTRY & WESTERN VOCAL PERFORMANCE - FEMALE
HE SAYS THE SAME THING TO ME (track) - Skeeter Davis (RCA)
HERE COMES MY BABY (single) - Dottie West (RCA)
ONCE A DAY (single) - Connie Smith (RCA)
SECOND FIDDLE (single) - Jean Shepard (Cap)
TWO SIDES OF WANDA JACKSON (album) - Wanda Jackson (Cap)

BEST COUNTRY & WESTERN VOCAL PERFORMANCE - MALE
DANG ME (single) - Roger Miller (Smash)
FORT WORTH, DALLAS OR HOUSTON (album) - George Hamilton IV (RCA)
FOUR STRONG WINDS (single) - Bobby Bare (RCA)
HANK LOCKLIN SINGS HANK WILLIAMS (album) - Hank Locklin (RCA)
I WALK THE LINE (album) - Johnny Cash (Col)
MY HEART SKIPS A BEAT (single) - Buck Owens (Cap)
YOU'RE THE ONLY WORLD I KNOW (single) - Sonny James (Cap)

BEST COUNTRY & WESTERN SONG
(Songwriter's Award)
DANG ME - Roger Miller (Smash)
HERE COMES MY BABY - Dottie West, Bill West (RCA)
ONCE A DAY - Bill Anderson (RCA)
WINE, WOMEN AND SONG - Betty Sue Perry (Decca)
YOU'RE THE ONLY WORLD I KNOW - Sonny James, Bob Tubert (Cap)

BEST NEW COUNTRY & WESTERN ARTIST OF 1964
CHARLIE LOUVIN (Cap)
ROGER MILLER (Smash)
CONNIE SMITH (RCA)
DOTTIE WEST (RCA)
HANK WILLIAMS, JR. (MGM)

BEST ALBUM NOTES
(Annotator's Award)
BEYOND THE FRINGE '64 - Orgiinal Cast - Ann: Alexander Cohen (Cap)
THE DEFINITIVE PIAF - Edith Piaf - Ann: Rory Guy (Cap)
GETZ/GILBERTO - Stan Getz, Joao Gilberto - Anns: Stan Getz, Joao Gilberto, Gene Lees (Verve)
MAHLER: SYMPHONY NO. 5; BERG: WOZZECK EXCERPTS (Phyllis Curtin) - Erich Leinsdorf cond. Boston Symphony - Ann: Neville Cardus (RCA)
MEXICO (LEGACY COLLECTION) - Carlos Chavez - Anns: Stanton Catlin, Carleton Beals (Col)
QUINCY JONES EXPLORES THE MUSIC OF HENRY MANCINI - Quincy Jones - Ann: Jack Tracy (Merc)
THE YOUNG CHEVALIER - Maurice Chevalier - Ann: George Sponholtz (Cap)

BEST CLASSICAL PERFORMANCE - ORCHESTRA
BARTOK: CONCERTO FOR ORCHESTRA - Eugene Ormandy cond. Philadelphia Orchestra (Col)
HANDEL: CONCERTI GROSSI (12), OP. 6 - Yehudi Menuhin cond. Bath Festival Chamber Orchestra (Angel)
HAYDN: SYMPHONY No. 95 IN C MINOR, SYMPHONY No. 101 IN D MAJOR ("CLOCK") - Fritz Reiner cond. Chicago Symphony (RCA)
MAHLER: SYMPHONY No. 2 IN C ("RESURRECTION") - Leonard Bernstein cond. New York Philharmonic (Col)
MAHLER: SYMPHONY No. 5 IN C SHARP MINOR; BERG: WOZZECK EXCERPTS (Phyllis Curtin) - Erich Leinsdorf cond. Boston Symphony (RCA)
MOZART: LAST SIX SYMPHONIES - Bruno Walter cond. Columbia Symphony (Col)
R. STRAUSS: SYMPHONIA DOMESTICA - George Szell cond. Cleveland Orchestra (Col)

BEST CHAMBER PERFORMANCE - INSTRUMENTAL
BEETHOVEN: QUARTET No. 15 IN A MINOR OP. 132 - Juilliard String Quartet (RCA)
BEETHOVEN: SONATAS (5) FOR PIANO & CELLO (Complete) - Sviatoslav Richter, Mstislav Rostropovich (Philips)
BEETHOVEN: TRIO No. 1 IN E FLAT, OP. 1, No. 1, - Jascha Heifetz, Gregor Piatigorsky (Jacob Lateiner, piano) (RCA)
BRAHMS: QUINTET IN F MINOR FOR PIANO AND STRINGS - Rudolph Serkin w/the Budapest Quartet (Col)
MOZART: THE COMPLETE FLUTE SONATAS - Jean-Pierre Rampal, Robert Veyron-Lacroix (Epic)
STRAVINSKY: L'HISTOIRE DU SOLDAT - Igor Markevich cond. Chamber Group (w/narrators Jean Cocteau, Peter Ustinov, Jean-Marie Fertey, Anne Tonietti) (Philips)

BEST CHAMBER MUSIC PERFORMANCE - VOCAL
DUFAY MOTETS - Le Petit Ensemble Vocal de Montreal (Vox)
IT WAS A LOVER AND HIS LASS (MORLEY, BYRD AND OTHERS) - New York Pro Musica, Noah Greenberg cond. (Decca)
MUSIC FOR VOICES AND VIOLS IN THE TIME OF SHAKESPEARE - Golden Age Singers (Westminster)
MUSIC OF THE RENNAISSANCE (DES PREZ, MORLEY) - Vocal Arts Ensemble (Counterpoint)
MUSIC OF MEDIEVAL FRANCE, 1200-1400,SACRED AND SECULAR - Deller Consort (Vanguard)
WALTON: FACADE - Hermione Gingold, Russell Oberlin, Thomas Dunn cond. (Decca)

BEST CLASSICAL PERFORMANCE - INSTRUMENTAL SOLOIST(S) (WITH ORCHESTRA)
BARBER: CONCERTO FOR PIANO & ORCHESTRA, OP. 38 - John Browning (Szell cond. Cleveland Orchestra) (Col)
BEETHOVEN: CONCERTO NO. 5 IN E FLAT - Artur Rubinstein (Leinsdorf cond. Boston Symphony) (RCA)
BLOCH: CONCERTO FOR VIOLIN - Yehudi Menuhin (Kletzki cond. Philharmonia Orchestra) (Angel)
BRAHMS: CONCERTO No. 1 IN D MINOR FOR PIANO - Van Cliburn (Leinsdorf cond. Boston Symphony) (RCA)
MOZART: SINFONIA CONCERTANTE IN E FLAT MAJOR FOR VIOLIN, VIOLA & ORCHESTRA - Rafael Druian and Abraham Skernick (Szell Cond. Cleveland Orchestra) (Col)
PROKOFIEFF: CONCERTO No. 1 IN D MAJOR FOR VIOLIN - Isaac Stern (Ormandy cond. Philadelphia Orchestra) (Col)
RODRIGO: CONCIERTO DE ARANJUEZ FOR GUITAR & ORCHESTRA; VIVALDI: CONCERTO IN D FOR LUTE & STRINGS - Julian Bream (Davis cond. Melos Chamber Orchestra) (RCA)

BEST CLASSICAL PERFORMANCE - INSTRUMENTAL SOLOIST (WITHOUT ORCHESTRA)

A FRENCH PROGRAM (RAVEL, POULENC, FAURE, CHABRIER) - Artur Rubinstein (RCA)
BACH: TWO AND THREE PART INVENTIONS - Glenn Gould (Col)
FRENCH BAROQUE MUSIC FOR HARPSICHORD (COUPERIN, RAMEAU & BOISMORTIER) - Igor Kipnis (Epic)
POPULAR CLASSICS FOR SPANISH GUITAR (VILLA-LOBOS, FALLA, etc.) - Julian Beam (RCA)
RICHTER PLAYS SCHUBERT (SONATA IN A MAJOR FOR PIANO, "WANDERER" FANTASIA FOR PIANO) - Sviatoslav Richter (Angel)
VLADIMIR HOROWITZ PLAYS BEETHOVEN, DEBUSSY, CHOPIN (BEETHOVEN: SONATA No. 8 "PATHETIQUE"; DEBUSSY; PRELUDES; CHOPIN: ETUDES & SCHERZOS 1 THROUGH 4) - Vladimir Horowitz (Col)

BEST OPERA RECORDING
(Conductor's Award)

BIZET: CARMEN - Herbert Von Karajan cond. Vienna Philharmonic & Chorus (Soloists: Price, Corelli, Merrill, Freni) (RCA)
MUSSORGSKY: BORIS GODOUNOV - Alexander Melik-Pachaev cond. Orchestra & Chorus of the Bolshoi Theatre (Soloists: London, Arkhipova) (Col)
PUCCINI: LA BOHEME - Thomas Schippers cond. Orchestra & Chorus of Opera House, Rome (Soloists: Freni, Gedda, Adani, Sereni) (Angel)
SMETANA: THE BARTERED BRIDE - Rudolf Kempe cond. Bamberg Symphony (Soloists: Lorengar, Wunderlich, Frick) (Angel)
WAGNER: LOHENGRIN - Rudolf Kempe cond. Vienna Philharmonic, Chorus of Vienna State Opera. (Soloists: Thomas, Grummer, Fischer-Dieskau, Ludwig) (Angel)
VERDI: FALSTAFF: - Georg Solti cond. RCA Italiana Opera Orchestra & Chorus (Soloists: Evan, Merrill, Kraus, Simionato, Ligabue, Elias, Freni) (RCA)

BEST CHORAL PERFORMANCE (OTHER THAN OPERA)
(Awards to Choral and Orchestra Conductors)

BRITTEN: A CEREMONY OF CAROLS - The Robert Shaw Chorale, Robert Shaw cond. (RCA)
MOZART: REQUIEM MASS IN D MINOR - Harvard Glee Club, Radcliffe Choral Society, Elliott Forbes cond.; Chorus Pro Musica, Alfred Nash Patterson cond.; New England Conservatory Chorus, Lorna Cooke de Varon cond.; St. John's Seminary Choir, Rt. Rev. Russell H. Davis cond.; Erich Leinsdorf cond. Boston Symphony (RCA)
POULENC: STABAT MATTER - Rene Duclos Chorus, Rene Duclos cond.; Georges Pretre & Paris Conservatoire (Angel)
STRAVINSKY: SYMPHONY OF PSALMS - Toronto Festival Chorus, Elmer Iseler cond.; Igor Stravinsky cond. Canadian Broadcasting Corp. Orchestra (Col)
VERDI: REQUIEM MASS - Philharmonia Chorus, Wilhelm Pitz, dir.; Carlo Maria Giulini cond. Philharmonia Orchestra (Angel)
VERDI: REQUIEM MASS - Westminster Choir, George Lynn, dir.; Eugene Ormandy cond. Philadelphia Orchestra (Col)

BEST CLASSICAL VOCAL SOLOIST PERFORMANCE (WITH OR WITHOUT ORCHESTRA)

THE AGE OF BEL CANTO: OPERATIC SCENES - Joan Sutherland (Bonygne cond. London Symphony & New Symphony of London)
BERLIOZ: NUITS D'ETE (SONG CYCLE) - Regine Crespin (Ansermet cond. Suisse Romande Orchestra) (London)
BERLIOZ: NUITS D'ETE (SONG CYCLE); FALLA: EL AMOR BRUJO - Leontyne Price (Reiner cond. Chicago Symphony) (RCA)
BRITTEN: SERENADE FOR TENOR, HORN & STRINGS - Peter Pears (Britten cond. London Symphony) (London)
CALLAS SINGS VERDI - Maria Callas (Rescigno cond. Paris Conservatoire) (Angel)
SHUBERT DIE WINTERREISE - Dietrich Fischer-Dieskau (Angel)
TSARS AND KINGS (OPERA ARIAS) - Boris Christoff (Cluytens cond. Paris Conservatoire Orchestra) (Angel)

BEST COMPOSITION BY A CONTEMPORARY COMPOSER
(Composer's Award)

A FRENCHMAN IN NEW YORK - Darius Milhaud (RCA)
NEW ENGLAND HOLIDAYS - Charles E. Ives
PANIO CONCERTO - Samuel Barber (Col)
SERMON, NARRATIVE AND PRAYER - Igor Stravinsky (Col)
SYMPHONY No. 3 ("KADDISH") - Leonard Bernstein (Col)

BEST ENGINEERED RECORDING
(Engineer's Award)

BRITTEN: YOUNG PERSON'S GUIDE TO THE ORCHESTRA - Carlo Maria Giulini cond. Philharmonia Orchestra - Eng: Douglas Larter (Angel)
MAHLER: SYMPHONY No. 2 IN C MINOR ("RESURRECTION") - Leonard Bernstein cond. New York Philharmonic - Eng: Fred Plaut (Col)
MAHLER: SYMPHONY No. 5 IN C SHARP MINOR - Erich Leinsdorf cond. Boston Symphony - Eng: Lewis Layton (RCA)
PROKOFIEFF: SYMPHONY No. 5, OP. 100 - Erich Leinsdorf cond. Boston Symphony - Eng: Lewis Layton (RCA)
VLADIMIR HOROWITZ PLAYS BEETHOVEN, DEBUSSY, CHOPIN - Vladimir Horowitz - Eng: Fred Plaut (Col)

BEST ALBUM COVER - CLASSICAL
(Awards to Art Director, Photographer or Graphic Artist)

COURT AND CEREMONIAL MUSIC OF THE 16TH CENTURY - Roger Blanchard Ensemble with the Poulteau Consort - Art Dir: Bill Harvey; Graphic: Lionel Kalish (Nonesuch)
MAHLER: SYMPHONY No. 5 IN C SHARP MINOR - Erich Leinsdorf cond. Boston Symphony - Art Dir: Robert Jones; Photog: David Hecht (RCA)
MEXICO: (LEGACY COLLECTION) - Carlos Chavez - Art Dir: Robert Cato (Col)
SAINT-SAENS: CARNIVAL OF THE ANIMALS; BRITTEN: YOUNG PERSON'S GUIDE TO THE ORCHESTRA - Arthur Fiedler cond. Boston Pops - Art Dir: Robert Jones; Graphic: Jan Balet (RCA)
R. STRAUSS: ALSO SPRACH ZARATHUSTRA - Eugene Ormandy cond. Philadelphia Orchestra - Art Dir: John Berg; Designer: Henrietta Condak (Col)
VERDI: REQUIEM MASS - Giulini cond. Philharmonia Orchestra - Art Dir: Marvin Schwartz (Angel)

MOST PROMISING NEW CLASSICAL RECORDING ARTIST

MIRELLA FRENI, Soprano (Angel)
MARILYN HORNE, Mezzo-Soprano (London)
IGOR KIPNIS, Harpsichord (Epic)
JUDITH RASKIN, Soprano (Decca)
JESS THOMAS, Tenor (DGG)

1965

RECORD OF THE YEAR
(Grammys to Artist and A&R Producer)

A TASTE OF HONEY - Herb Alpert & the Tijuana Brass - A&R: Herb Alpert, Jerry Moss (A&M)
THE "IN" CROWD - Ramsey Lewis Trio - A&R: Esmond Edwards (Cadet)
KING OF THE ROAD - Roger Miller - A&R: Jerry Kennedy (Smash)
THE SHADOW OF YOUR SMILE (LOVE THEME FROM THE SANDPIPER) - Tony Bennett - A&R: Ernie Altschuler, Al Stanton (Col)
YESTERDAY - Paul McCartney - A&R: George Martin (Cap)

ALBUM OF THE YEAR
(Grammys to Artist and A&R Producer)
HELP! - The Beatles - A&R: George Martin (Cap)
MY NAME IS BARBRA - Barbra Steisand - A&R: Bob Mersey (Col)
MY WORLD - Eddy Arnold - A&R: Chet Atkins
SEPTEMBER OF MY YEARS - Frank Sinatra - A&R: Sonny Burke (Reprise)
SOUND OF MUSIC - Julie Andrews and Cast - A&R: Neely Plumb (RCA)
WHIPPED CREAM & OTHER DELIGHTS - Herb Alpert & the Tijuana Brass - A&R: Herb Alpert and Jerry Moss (A&M)

ALBUM OF THE YEAR - CLASSICAL
(Awards to the Artist and A&R Producer)
BERG: WOZZECK - Karl Bohm cond. Orchestra of German Opera, Berlin - A&R: Otto Gerdes (DGG)
CHOPIN: 8 POLONAISES, 4 IMPROMPTUS - Artur Rubinstein - A&R: Max Wilcox (RCA)
HOROWITZ AT CARNEGIE HALL, An Historic Return - Vladimir Horowitz - A&R: Thomas Frost (Col)
IVES: SYMPHONY NO. 4 - Leopold Stokowski cond. American Symphony - A&R: John McClure (Col)
STRAUSS: SALOME (DANCE OF THE SEVEN VEILS, INTERLUDE & FINAL SCENE); THE EGYPTIAN HELEN (AWAKENING SCENE) - Leontyne Price; Erich Leinsdorf cond. Boston Symphony - A&R: Richard Mohr (RCA)

SONG OF THE YEAR
(Songwriter's Award)
I WILL WAIT FOR YOU (THEME FROM "UMBRELLAS OF CHERBOURG") - Michel Legrand, Norman Gimbel, Jacques Demy (Philips)
KING OF THE ROAD - Roger Miller (Smash)
SEPTEMBER OF MY YEARS - Jimmy Van Heusen, Sammy Cahn (Reprise)
THE SHADOW OF YOUR SMILE (LOVE THEME FROM "THE SANDPIPER") - Paul Francis Webster, Johnny Mandel (Mercury)
YESTERDAY - John Lennon, Paul McCartney (Cap)

BEST VOCAL PERFORMANCE - FEMALE
THE ASTRUD GILBERTO ALBUM - Astrud Gilberto (Verve)
DOWNTOWN (album) - Petula Clark (WB)
GENTLE IS MY LOVE (album) - Nancy Wilson (Cap)
MY NAME IS BARBRA (album) - Barbra Streisand (Col)
WHAT THE WORLD NEEDS NOW IS LOVE (single) - Jackie DeShannon (Imperial)

BEST VOCAL PERFORMANCE - MALE
BABY THE RAIN MUST FALL (album) - Glenn Yarbrough (RCA)
IT WAS A VERY GOOD YEAR (single) - Frank Sinatra (Reprise)
KING OF THE ROAD (single) - Roger Miller (Smash)
THE SHADOW OF YOUR SMILE (LOVE THEME FROM "THE SANDPIPER") (single) - Tony Bennett (Col)
YESTERDAY (single) - Paul McCartney (Cap)

BEST INSTRUMENTAL PERFORMANCE, NON-JAZZ
A TASTE OF HONEY - Herb Alpert & the Tijuana Brass (A&M)
GIRL TALK - Neal Hefti (Col)
THE GREAT RACE - Henry Mancini (RCA)
WALK IN THE BLACK FOREST - Horst Jankowski (Merc)
YAKETY AXE - Chet Atkins (RCA)

BEST PERFORMANCE BY A VOCAL GROUP
FLOWERS ON THE WALL - The Statler Bros (Col)
HELP! - The Beatles (Cap)
MRS. BROWN YOU'VE GOT A LOVELY DAUGHTER - Herman's Hermits (MGM)
WE DIG MANCINI - Anita Kerr Singers (RCA)
YOU WERE ON MY MIND - We Five (A&M)

BEST PERFORMANCE BY A CHORUS
ANYONE FOR MOZART? - The Swingle Singers (Philips)
CHIM CHIM CHER-EE & OTHER HAPPY SONGS - New Christy Minstrels (Col)
DEAR HEART & OTHER SONGS ABOUT LOVE - Henry Mancini Chorus and Orchestra (RCA)
JAZZ SUITE ON THE MASS TEXTS - Paul Horn and Chorus (RCA)
ROBERT SHAW CHORALE & ORCHESTRA ON BROADWAY - Robert Shaw Chorale and Orchestra (RCA)

BEST ORIGINAL SCORE WRITTEN FOR A MOTION PICTURE OR TV SHOW
(Composer's Award)
HELP! (The Beatles) John Lennon, Paul McCartney, George Harrison, Ken Thorne (Cap)
THE MAN FROM U.N.C.L.E. (Hugo Montenegro Orch.) Lalo Schifrin, Mort Stevens, Walter Scharf, Jerry Goldsmith (RCA)
THE SANDPIPER (Robert Armbruster Orch.) Johnny Mandel (Mercury)
THE UMBRELLAS OF CHERBOURG (Michel Legrand Orch.) Michel Legrand, Jacques Demy (Philips)
ZORBA THE GREEK (M. Theodorakis Orch.) Mikis Theodorakis (20th)

BEST SCORE FROM AN ORIGINAL CAST SHOW
(Composer's Award)
BAJOUR - Walter Marks (Col)
BAKER STREET - Marian Grudeff, Raymond Jessell (MGM)
DO I HEAR A WALTZ - Richard Rodgers, Stephen Sondheim (Col)
HALF A SIXPENCE - David Heneker (RCA)
ON A CLEAR DAY - Alan Lerner, Burton Lane (RCA)

BEST COMEDY PERFORMANCE
MOM ALWAYS LIKED YOU BEST - Smothers Bros. (Merc)
THEM COTTON PICKIN' DAYS IS OVER - Godfrey Cambridge (Epic)
WELCOME TO THE L.B.J. RANCH - Earl Doud & Allen Robin (Cap)
WHY IS THERE AIR? - Bill Cosby (WB)
YOU DON'T HAVE TO BE JEWISH - Various Artists written by Bob Booker & George Foster (Kapp)

BEST SPOKEN WORD OR DRAMA RECORDING
A PERSONAL CHOICE - Sir Alec Guinness (RCA)
A TIME TO KEEP: 1964 - Chet Huntley and David Brinkley (RCA)
THE BRONTES - Margaret Webster (Vanguard)
JOHN F. KENNEDY: AS WE REMEMBER HIM - Produced by Goddard Lieberson (Col)
MUCH ADO ABOUT NOTHING - National Theatre of Great Britain (RCA)
THE VOICE OF THE UNCOMMON MAN - Adlai Stevenson (Produced by Mort Nasatir) (MGM)

BEST NEW ARTIST
THE BYRDS (Col)
HERMAN'S HERMITS (MGM)
HORST JANKOWSKI (Merc)
TOM JONES (Parrot)
MARILYN MAYE (RCA)
SONNY & CHER (Atco)
GLENN YARBROUGH (RCA)

BEST RECORDING FOR CHILDREN
DR. SEUSS PRESENTS "FOX IN SOX"; "GREEN EGGS AND HAM" - Marvin Miller (RCA)
LOVE SONGS FOR CHILDREN: "A" YOU'RE ADORABLE - Diahann Carroll (Golden)

PATRICK MULDOON & HIS MAGIC BALLOON - Carmel Quinn (RCA)
SUPERCALIFRAGELISTIC EXPIALIDOCIOUS - The Chipmunks (David Seville) (Lib)
WINNIE THE POOH & THE HONEY TREE - Sterling Holloway, Sebastian Cabot (Disney)

BEST ALBUM NOTES
(Annotator's Award)
BERG: WOZZECK - Karl Bohm cond. Orchestra of German Opera - Anns: Gustav Rudolf Sellner, Otto Gerdes (DGG)
FATHER & SON: HANK WILLIAMS & HANK WILLIAMS, JR. - Ann: Charles Lamb (MGM)
GRAND TERRACE BAND - Earl Hines - Ann: Stanley Dance (RCA)
SEPTEMBER OF MY YEARS - Frank Sinatra - Ann: Stan Cornyn (Reprise)
THE VOICE OF THE UNCOMMON MAN - Adlai Stevenson - Ann: Dom Cerulli (MGM)

BEST INSTRUMENTAL JAZZ PERFORMANCE - SMALL GROUP OR SOLOIST WITH SMALL GROUP
A LOVE SUPREME - John Coltrane (Imp)
CYCLE - Paul Horn (RCA)
GLAD TO BE UNHAPPY - Paul Desmond, Jim Hall (RCA)
THE "IN" CROWD - Ramsey Lewis Trio (Cadet)
THE POWER OF POSITIVE SWINGING - Clark Terry & Bob Brookmeyer Quintet (Mainstream)
SOFT SAMBA - Gary McFarland Group (Verve)
SOUL SAUCE - Cal Tjader (Verve)
TRIO '65 - Bill Evans Trio (Verve)

BEST INSTRUMENTAL JAZZ PERFORMANCE - LARGE GROUP OR SOLOIST WITH LARGE GROUP
BUMPIN' - Wes Montgomery w/String Orch. (Verve)
ELLINGTON '66 - Duke Ellington Orch. (Rep)
INSIGHT - Rod Levitt (RCA)
JAZZ SUITE ON THE MASS TEXTS - Paul Horn (RCA)
KENNY BURRELL: GUITAR FORMS - Kenny Burrell and Gil Evans Orch. (Verve)
LOVE THEME FROM "THE SANDPIPER" - Dizzy Gillespie (Fuller, Monterey Jazz Fest.) (World Pac)
MICKEY ONE - Stan Getz (Verve)

BEST ORIGINAL JAZZ COMPOSITION
(Composer's Award)
A LOVE SUPREME - John Coltrane (Imp)
BUMPIN' - Wes Montgomery (Verve)
CANADIANA SUITE - Oscar Peterson (Limelite)
JAZZ SUITE ON THE MASS TEXTS - Lalo Schifrin (RCA)
MICKEY ONE - Eddie Sauter (MGM)
VIRGIN ISLANDS SUITE - Duke Ellington and Billy Strayhorn (Reprise)

BEST INSTRUMENTAL ARRANGEMENT
(Arranger's Award)
A HARD DAY'S NIGHT (Fiedler, Boston Pops) Arr: Jack Mason (RCA)
A TASTE OF HONEY (Alpert & Tijuana Brass) Arr: Herb Alpert (A&M)
GIRL TALK (Neal Hefti) Arr: Neal Hefti (Col)
MISSION TO MOSCOW (Si Zentner Orch.) Arr: Bob Florence (RCA)
THE SHADOW OF YOUR SMILE (Armbruster Orch.) Arr: Johnny Mandel (Merc)
WALK IN THE BLACK FOREST (Jankowski Orch.) Arr: Horst Jankowski (Merc)

BEST ARRANGEMENT ACCOMPANYING VOCALIST OR INSTRUMENTALIST
(Arranger's Award)
DAY BY DAY (Astrud Gilberto) Arr: Claus Ogerman (Verve)
EVERYTHING I'VE GOT (Vikki Carr) Arr: Bob Florence (Lib)
GREENSLEEVES (Kenny Burrell) Arr: Gil Evans (Verve)
HE TOUCHED ME (Barbra Streisand) Arr: Don Costa (Col)
IT WAS A VERY GOOD YEAR (Frank Sinatra) Arr: Gordon Jenkins (Reprise)
IT'S NOT UNUSUAL (Tom Jones) Arr: Les Reed (Parrot)
WHAT THE WORLD NEEDS NOW IS LOVE (Jackie DeShannon) Arr: Burt Bacharach (Imp)
YESTERDAY (The Beatles) Arr: George Martin (Cap)

BEST CONTEMPORARY (R&R) SINGLE
BABY THE RAIN MUST FALL - Glenn Yarbrough (RCA)
IT'S NOT UNUSUAL - Tom Jones (Parrot)
KING OF THE ROAD - Roger Miller (Smash)
WHAT THE WORLD NEEDS NOW IS LOVE - Jackie DeShannon (Imp)
YESTERDAY - Paul McCartney (Cap)

BEST CONTEMPORARY (R&R) VOCAL PERFORMANCE - FEMALE
BABY I'M YOURS - Barbara Lewis (Atl)
I KNOW A PLACE - Petula Clark (WB)
RESCUE ME - Fontella Bass (Chess)
SUNSHINE, LOLLIPOPS AND RAINBOWS - Lesley Gore (Merc)
WHAT THE WORLD NEEDS NOW IS LOVE - Jackie DeShannon (Imp)

BEST CONTEMPORARY (R&R) VOCAL PERFORMANCE - MALE
HEARTACHES BY THE NUMBER - Johnny Tillotson (MGM)
KING OF THE ROAD - Roger Miller (Smash)
1-2-3 - Len Barry (Decca)
WHAT'S NEW PUSSYCAT - Tom Jones (Parrot)
YESTERDAY - Paul McCartney (Cap)

BEST CONTEMPORARY (R&R) PERFORMANCE - GROUP (VOCAL OR INSTRUMENTAL)
FLOWERS ON THE WALL - The Statler Brothers (Col)
HELP! - The Beatles (Cap)
MRS. BROWN YOU'VE GOT A LOVELY DAUGHTER - Herman's Hermits (MGM)
STOP IN THE NAME OF LOVE - The Supremes (Motown)
WOOLY BULLY - Sam the Sham & The Pharaohs (MGM)

BEST RHYTHM & BLUES RECORDING
IN THE MIDNIGHT HOUR - Wilson Pickett (Alt)
MY GIRL - The Temptations (Motown)
PAPA'S GOT A BRAND NEW BAG - James Brown (King)
SHAKE - Sam Cooke (RCA)
SHOTGUN - Jr. Walker & the All Stars (Soul)

BEST FOLK RECORDING
A SONG WILL RISE - Peter, Paul & Mary (WB)
AN EVENING WITH BELAFONTE/MAKEBA - Harry Belafonte, Miriam Makeba (RCA)
MAKEBA SINGS - Miriam Makeba (RCA)
ROSCOE HOLCOMB: THE HIGH LONESOME SOUND - Roscoe Holcomb (Folkways)
STRANGERS AND COUSINS - Pete Seeger (Col)
THERE BUT FOR FORTUNE - Joan Baez (Vanguard)
THE WOMENFOLK AT THE HUNGRY I - Womenfolk (RCA)

BEST GOSPEL OR OTHER RELIGIOUS RECORDING
ALL DAY SING AND DINNER ON THE GROUND - The Statesmen Quartet w/Hovie Lister (RCA)
BOB ASHTON'S SONGS OF LIVING FAITH - Ralph Carmichael Singers and Orchestra (Stylist)
HOW GREAT THOU ART - Kate Smith (RCA)
JUST KEEP ON SINGING - Marian Anderson (RCA)
LET ME WALK WITH THEE - Tennessee Ernie Ford (Cap)
SOMETHING OLD, SOMETHING NEW - Blackwood Bros. (RCA)
SOUTHLAND FAVORITES - George Beverly Shea and Anita Kerr Singers (RCA)
WHAT A HAPPY TIME - Happy Goodman Family (Word)

BEST COUNTRY & WESTERN SINGLE
FLOWERS ON THE WALL - The Statler Bros. (Col)
IS IT REALLY OVER - Jim Reeves (RCA)
KING OF THE ROAD - Roger Miller (Smash)
MAKE THE WORLD GO AWAY - Eddy Arnold (RCA)
MAY THE BIRD OF PARADISE FLY UP YOUR NOSE - "Little" Jimmy Dickens (Col)
YAKETY AXE - Chet Atkins (RCA)

BEST COUNTRY & WESTERN ALBUM
FATHER & SON: HANK WILLIAMS & HANK WILLIAMS, JR (MGM)
THE JIM REEVES WAY - Jim Reeves (RCA)
MORE OF THAT GUITAR COUNTRY - Chet Atkins (RCA)
MY WORLD - Eddy Arnold (RCA)
THE RETURN OF ROGER MILLER - Roger Miller (Smash)

BEST COUNTRY & WESTERN VOCAL PERFORMANCE - FEMALE
BABY - Wilma Burgess (Decca)
BEFORE THE RING ON YOUR FINGER TURNS GREEN - Dottie West (RCA)
QUEEN OF THE HOUSE - Jody Miller (Cap)
SINGLE GIRL AGAIN - Molly Bee (MGM)
SUNGLASSES - Skeeter Davis (RCA)

BEST COUNTRY & WESTERN VOCAL PERFORMANCE - MALE
CRYSTAL CHANDELIER - Carl Belew (RCA)
IS IT REALLY OVER - Jim Reeves (RCA)
KING OF THE ROAD - Roger Miller (Smash)
MAKE THE WORLD GO AWAY - Eddy Arnold (RCA)
TALK ME SOME SENSE - Bobby Bare (RCA)

BEST COUNTRY & WESTERN SONG
(Songwriter's Award)
CRYSTAL CHANDELIER - Ted Harris (RCA)
FLOWERS ON THE WALL - Lewis DeWitt (Col)
KING OF THE ROAD - Roger Miller (Smash)
MAY THE BIRD OF PARADISE FLY UP YOUR NOSE - Neal Merritt (Col)
WHAT'S HE DOING IN MY WORLD - Carl Belew, B.J. Moore, Eddie Busch (RCA)

BEST NEW COUNTRY & WESTERN ARTIST
WILMA BURGESS (Decca)
JODY MILLER (Cap)
NORMA JEAN (RCA)
DEL REEVES (UA)
STATLER BROTHERS (Col)

BEST ENGINEERED RECORDING
(Engineer's Award)
A TASTE OF HONEY (Alpert & Tijuana Brass) - Eng: Larry Levine (A&M)
MORE OF THAT GUITAR COUNTRY (Chet Atkins) - Engs: Al Pachucki, Chuck Seitz (RCA)
LATIN SOUND OF HENRY MANCINI (Mancini) - Eng: Richard Bogert, James Malloy (RCA)
MY NAME IS BARBRA (Barbra Streisand) - Eng: Frank Laico (Col)
SEPTEMBER OF MY YEARS (Frank Sinatra) - Eng: Lowell Frank (Reprise)
THAT HONEY HORN SOUND (Al Hirt) - Eng: Chuck Seitz, Wm. Vandevort (RCA)

BEST ENGINEERED RECORDING, CLASSICAL
(Engineer's Award)
GOULD: SPIRITUALS FOR ORCH./COPLAND: DANCE SYMPHONY (Gould, Chicago Sym.) - Eng: Bernard Keville (RCA)
HOROWITZ AT CARNEGIE HALL - An Historic Return (Vladimir Horowitz) - Eng: Fred Plaut (Col)
IVES: SYMPHONY NO. 4 (Stokowski cond. American Symphony Orch.) - Eng: Edward T. Graham (Col) Anthony Salvatore (RCA)
STRAUSS: SALOME/THE EGYPTIAN HELEN (Leontyne Price, Leinsdorf cond. Boston Sym.) - Eng: Anthony Salvatore (RCA)
STRAVINSKY: SYMPHONY OF PSALMS (Robert Shaw Chorale, RCA Sym.) - Eng: Bernard Keville (RCA)

BEST ALBUM COVER - PHOTOGRAPHY
(Awards to Art Director and Photographer)
THE AZNAVOUR STORY (Charles Aznavour) - Art Dir: Ed Thrasher - Photog: Sherman Weisburd (Reprise)
BRINGING IT ALL BACK HOME - (Bob Dylan) - Art Dir: John Berg - Photog: Dan Kramer (Col)
JAZZ SUITE ON THE MASS TEXTS (Paul Horn) - Art Dir: Bob Jones - Photog: Ken Whitmore (RCA)
KENNY BURRELL/GUITAR FORMS (Kenny Burrell) - Art Dir: Acy Lehman - Photog: Rudolph Regname (Verve)
MONK (Thelonious Monk) - Art Dir: Jerry Smokler - Photog: W. Eugene Smith (Col)
MY NAME IS BARBRA (Barbra Streisand) - Art Dir: Robert Cato - Photog: Sheldon Streisand (Col)
WHIPPED CREAM & OTHER DELIGHTS (Herb Alpert & the Tijuana Brass) - Art Dir. & Photog: Peter Whorf (A&M)

BEST ALBUM COVER - GRAPHIC ARTS
(Awards to Art Director and Graphic Artist)
BARTOK: CONCERTO NO. 2 FOR VIOLIN/STRAVINSKY: CONCERTO FOR VIOLIN (Silverstein, Leinsdorf, Boston Sym.) - Art Dir: George Estes - Graphic: James Alexander (RCA)
CONCERT IN THE VIRGIN ISLANDS (Duke Ellington) Art Dir: Ed Thrasher - Graphic: Patrick Blackwell (Reprise)
GOULD: SPIRITUALS FOR ORCH./COPLAND: DANCE SYMPHONY (Gould, Chicago Symphony) - Art Dir: George Estes - Graphic: Charles White (RCA)
HOROWITZ AT CARNEGIE HALL (Horowitz) - Art Dir. & Graphic: John Berg (Col)
SOLO MONK (Thelonious Monk) - Art Dir: Jerry Smokler - Graphic: Paul Davis (Col)
WILLIAM TELL & OTHER FAVORITE OVERTURES (Bernstein, New York Philharmonic) - Art Dir. & Graphic: John Berg (Col)

BEST CLASSICAL PERFORMANCE - ORCHESTRA
(Conductor's Award)
BACH: BRANDENBURG CONCERTOS - Herbert von Karajan cond. Berlin Philharmonic (DGG)
BERLIOZ: ROMEO AND JULIET - Arturo Toscanini cond. NBC Symphony (RCA)

GOULD: SPIRITUALS FOR ORCHESTRA/COPLAND: DANCE SYMPHONY - Morton Gould cond. Chicago Symphony (RCA)
IVES: SYMPHONY NO. 4 - Leopold Stokowski cond. American Symphony (Col)
PROKOFIEFF: SYMPHONY NO. 6 IN E-FLAT MINOR - Erich Leinsdorf cond. Boston Symphony (RCA)
RAVEL: DAPHNIS & CHLOE SUITE NO. 2/ROUSSEL: BACCHUS AND ARIADNE, SUITE NO. 2 - Jean Martinon cond. Chicago Symphony (RCA)

BEST CLASSICAL CHAMBER MUSIC PERFORMANCE INSTRUMENTAL OR VOCAL
A PURCELL ANTHOLOGY - Yehudi Menuhin and Members of Bath Festival Orch. (Angel)
BACH: THE SIX SONATAS FOR VIOLIN & HARPSICHORD - Erick Friedman, Bruce Prince-Joseph (RCA)
BARTOK: THE SIX STRING QUARTETS - Juilliard String Quartet (Col)
MOZART/SCHUMANN RECITAL - Vladimir Ashkenazy, Malcolm Frager (London)
SCHUBERT: TRIO NO. 1 IN B-FLAT FOR PIANO - Isaac Stern, Eugene Istomin, Leonrad Rose (Col)
SONATA RECITAL BY SZIGETI & BARTOK (BARTOK/BEETHOVEN/DEBUSSY) - Joseph Szigeti, Bela Bartok (Vanguard)

BEST CLASSICAL PERFORMANCE - INSTRUMENTAL SOLOIST(S) (WITH ORCHESTRA)
BARBER: CONCERTO FOR VIOLIN & ORCHESTRA/HINDEMITH: CONCERTO FOR VIOLIN & ORCH. Isaac Stern (Bernstein cond. New York Philharmonic) (Col)
BEETHOVEN: CONCERTO NO. 4 IN G MAJOR FOR PIANO AND ORCHESTRA - Artur Rubinstein (Leinsdorf cond. Boston Symphony) (RCA)
BEETHOVEN: CONCERTO NO. 4 IN G MAJOR FOR PIANO AND ORCHESTRA - Rudolf Serkin (Toscanini cond. NBC Symphony) (RCA)
BEETHOVEN: TRIPLE CONCERTO - Isaac Stern, Leonard Rose, Eugene Istomin (Ormandy cond. Philadelphia Orchestra) (Col)
RACHMANINOFF: CONCERTO NO. 1 IN F SHARP FOR PIANO/CONCERTO NO. 4 IN G MINOR FOR PIANO - Leonard Pennario (Previn cond. Royal Philharmonic) (RCA)
TCHAIKOVSKY: CONCERTO NO. 2 IN G MAJOR FOR PIANO & ORCH/CONCERTO NO. 3 IN E-FLAT MAJOR FOR PIANO & ORCH. - Gary Graffman (Ormandy, Philadelphia Orchestra) (Col)

BEST CLASSICAL PERFORMANCE - INSTRUMENTAL SOLOIST (WITHOUT ORCHESTRA)
ALKAN: PIANO MUSIC - Raymond Lewenthal (RCA)
BACH: WELL TEMPERED CLAVIER, BOOK 1, VOL. 3 (17-24) - Glenn Gould (Col)
CHOPIN BALLADES (1,2,3,4,) - Vladimir Ashkenazy (London)
CHOPIN: 8 POLONAISES AND 4 IMPROMPTUS - Artur Rubinstein (RCA)
HOROWITZ AT CARNEGIE HALL - An Historic Return - Vladimir Horowitz (Col)
JULIAN BREAM IN CONCERT - Julian Bream (RCA)

BEST OPERA RECORDING
(Conductor's Award)
BELLINI: NORMA - Richard Bonynge cond. London Symphony & Chorus (Soloists: Sutherland, Horne, Alexander, Cross) (RCA)
BERG: WOZZECK - Karl Bohm cond. Orchestra of German Opera, Berlin (Soloists: Fischer-Dieskau, Lear, Wunderlich) (DGG)
VERDI: LA FORZA DEL DESTINO - Thomas Schippers cond. RCA Italiana Opera Orchestra & Chorus (Soloists: Price, Tucker, Verrett, Merrill, Tozzi, Flagello) (RCA)
VERDI: LUISA MILLER - Fausto Cleva cond. RCA Italiana Opera Orchestra & Chorus (Soloists: Moffo, Bergonzi, Verrett, MacNeil, Tozzi, Flagello) (RCA)
WAGNER: GOTTERDAMMERUNG - Georg Solti cond. Vienna Philharmonic (Soloists: Nilsson, Windgassen, Fischer-Dieskau) (London)

BEST CHORAL PERFORMANCE (OTHER THAN OPERA)
BERLIOZ: REQUIEM - Robert Page cond. Temple University Choir/Eugene Ormandy cond. Philadelphia Orchestra (Col)
BRAHMS: GERMAN REQUIEM - Herbert von Karajan cond. Vienna Singverein & Berlin Philharmonic (DGG)
BRITTEN: CANTATA MISERICORDIUM - Benjamin Britten cond. London Symphony Chorus & Orchestra (London)
HANDEL: MESSIAH - Wilhelm Pitz, Chorus Master, The Philharmonia Chorus/Otto Klemperer cond. Philharmonia Orchestra (Angel)
SCHOENBERG: GURRE LIEDER - Wolfgang Schubert cond. Bavarian Radio Symphony Chorus/Rafael Kubelik cond. Bavarian Radio Symphony (DGG)
STRAVINSKY: SYMPHONY OF PSALMS/POULENC: GLORIA - Robert Shaw cond. Robert Shaw Chorale, RCA Victor Symphony (RCA)

BEST CLASSICAL VOCAL SOLOIST PERFORMANCE
CANTELOUBE: SONGS OF THE AUVERGNE/RACHMANINOFF: VOCALISE/VILLA LOBOS: BACHIANAS BRASILEIRAS NO. 5 - Anna Moffo (Stokowski cond. American Symphony) (RCA)
FALLA: SEVEN POPULAR SPANISH SONGS - Shirley Verrett
MIRELLA FRENI - OPERATIC ARIAS - Mirella Freni (Ferraris cond. Rome Opera House Orchestra) (Angel)
MOUSSORGSKY: SONGS - Galina Vishnevskaya (Markevitch cond. Russian State Symphony)
RUSSIAN & FRENCH ARIAS - Nicolai Ghiaurov (Downes cond. London Symphony) (London)
SCHUMANN: LIEDERKREIS - Dietrich Fischer-Dieskau (Moore, Pianist) (Angel)
STRAUSS: SALOME (DANCE OF THE SEVEN VEILS INTERLUDE, FINAL SCENE)/THE EGYPTIAN HELEN (AWAKENING SCENE) - Leontyne Price (Leinsdorf cond. Boston Symphony) (RCA)

BEST COMPOSITION BY A CONTEMPORARY CLASSICAL COMPOSER
(Composer's Award)
CANTATA MISERICORDIUM - Benjamin Britten, (London)
CHICHESTER PSALMS - Leonard Bernstein, (London)
STRING QUARTET NO. 4 - David Diamond, (Epic)
SYMPHONY NO. 4 - Charles Ives, (Col)
VARIATIONS ON A THEME BY HINDEMITH - William Walton, (Col)
WORLD WAR I SUITE - Morton Gould, (RCA)

MOST PROMISING NEW CLASSICAL RECORDING ARTIST
NICOLAI GHIAUROV, Bass (London)
EVELYN LEAR, Soprano (DGG)
RAYMOND LEWENTHAL, Pianist (RCA)
PETER SERKIN, Pianist (RCA)
SHIRLEY VERRETT, Soprano (RCA)

1966

RECORD OF THE YEAR
(Awards to the Artist and A&R Producer)
ALMOST PERSUADED - David Houston - A&R: Billy Sherrill (Epic)
MONDAY, MONDAY - The Mamas & The Papas - A&R: Lou Adler (Dunhill)
STRANGERS IN THE NIGHT - Frank Sinatra - A&R: Jimmy Bowen (Reprise)
WHAT NOW MY LOVE - Herb Alpert & the Tijuana Brass - A&R: Herb Alpert and Jerry Moss (A&M)

WINCHESTER CATHEDRAL - New Vaudeville Band - A&R: Geoff Stephens (Fontana)

ALBUM OF THE YEAR
(Awards to the Artist and A&R Producer)
COLOR ME BARBRA - Barbra Streisand - A&R: Bob Mersey (Col)
DR. ZHIVAGO (Soundtrack) - Maurice Jarre - A&R: Jesse Kaye (MGM)
REVOLVER - The Beatles - A&R: George Martin (Cap)
SINATRA: A MAN & HIS MUSIC - Frank Sinatra - A&R: Sonny Burke (Reprise)
WHAT NOW MY LOVE - Herb Alpert & the Tijuana Brass - A&R: Herb Alpert and Jerry Moss (A&M)

SONG OF THE YEAR
(Songwriter's Award)
BORN FREE - John Barry, Don Black (MGM)
THE IMPOSSIBLE DREAM - Mitch Leigh, Joe Darion (Kapp)
MICHELLE - John Lennon, Paul McCartney (Cap)
SOMEWHERE MY LOVE (Lara's Theme from Dr. Zhivago) - Paul Francis Webster,
Maurice Jarre (MGM)
STRANGERS IN THE NIGHT - Bert Kaempfert, Charles Singleton, Eddie Snyder (Reprise)

BEST INSTRUMENTAL THEME
(Composer's Award)
ARABESQUE - Henry Mancini (RCA)
BATMAN THEME - Neal Hefti (RCA)
PRISSY - Priscilla Hubbard (RCA)
TRUMPET PICKIN' - D.J. Edwards (RCA)
WHO'S AFRAID - Alex North (WB)

BEST VOCAL PERFORMANCE - FEMALE
BORN A WOMAN (Single) - Sandy Posey (MGM)
COLOR ME BARBRA (album) - Barbra Streisand (Col)
ELLA AT DUKE'S PLACE (album) - Ella Fitzgerald (Verve)
IF HE WALKED INTO MY LIFE (single) - Eydie Gorme (Col)
THESE BOOTS ARE MADE FOR WALKIN' (single) - Nancy Sinatra (Reprise)

BEST VOCAL PERFORMANCE - MALE
ALMOST PERSUADED (single) - David Houston (Epic)
DISTANT DRUMS (single) - Jim Reeves (RCA)
ELEANOR RIGBY (single) - Paul McCartney (Cap)
THE IMPOSSIBLE DREAM (single) Jack Jones (Kapp)
THE SHADOW OF YOUR SMILE (album) - Andy Williams (Col)
STRANGERS IN THE NIGHT (single) - Frank Sinatra (Reprise)

BEST INSTRUMENTAL PERFORMANCE (OTHER THAN JAZZ)
BATMAN THEME - Neal Hefti (RCA)
BORN FREE - Roger Williams (Kapp)
CHET ATKINS PICKS ON THE BEATLES - Chet Atkins (RCA)
DR. ZHIVAGO (Soundtrack) Maurice Jarre (MGM)
WHAT NOW MY LOVE - Herb Alpert & the Tijuana Brass (A&M)

BEST PERFORMANCE BY A VOCAL GROUP
A MAN AND A WOMAN - Anita Kerr Singers (WB)
CHERISH - THE ASSOCIATION (Valiant)
GOOD VIBRATIONS - THE Beach Boys (Cap)
GUANTANAMERA - The Sandpipers (A&M)
MONDAY, MONDAY - The Mamas & The Papas (Dunhill)

BEST PERFORMANCE BY A CHORUS
A MAN AND A WOMAN - The Johnny Mann Singers (Lib)
BASIE SWINGIN', VOICES SINGIN' - The Alan Copeland Singers (With Count Basie) (ABC)
HENRY MANCINI PRESENTS THE ACADEMY AWARD SONGS - Henry Mancini, Orch. & Chorus (RCA)
ROCOCO A' GO GO - Swingle Singers (Philips)
SOMEWHERE, MY LOVE (Lara's Theme from Dr. Zhivago) - Ray Conniff & Singers (Col)

BEST ORIGINAL SCORE WRITTEN FOR A MOTION PICTURE OR TELEVISION SHOW
(Composer's Award)
ARABESQUE - Henry Mancini (RCA)
BORN FREE - John Barry (MGM)
DR. ZHIVAGO - Maurice Jarre (MGM)
ORIGINAL MUSIC FROM THE SCORE "ALFIE" - Sonny Rollins (Impulse)
WHO'S AFRAID OF VIRGINIA WOOLF? - Alex North (WB)

BEST SCORE FROM AN ORIGINAL CAST SHOW ALBUM
(Composer's Award)
THE APPLE TREE - Jerry Bock, Sheldon Harnick (Col)
MAME - Jerry Herman (Col)
MAN OF LA MANCHA - Mitch Leigh, Joe Darion (Kapp)
SKYSCRAPER - Jimmy Van Heusen, Sammy Cahn (Cap)
SWEET CHARITY - Cy Coleman, Dorothy Fields (Col)

BEST COMEDY PERFORMANCE
DOWNTOWN - Mrs. Miller (Cap)
FUNNY WAY TO MAKE AN ALBUM - Don Bowman (RCA)
HAVE A LAUGH ON ME - Archie Campbell (RCA)
WANTED FOR MURDER - Homer and Jethro (RCA)
WONDERFULNESS - Bill Cosby (WB)

BEST SPOKEN WORD, DOCUMENTARY OR DRAMA
DAY FOR DECISION - Johnny Sea (WB)
DEATH OF A SALESMAN - Lee J. Cobb, Mildred Dunnock (Caedmon)
EDWARD R. MURROW - A REPORTER REMEMBERS - VOL. I THE WAR YEARS - Edward R. Murrow (Col)
HISTORY REPEATS ITSELF - Buddy Starcher (Decca)
THE STEVENSON WIT - Adlai Stevenson, David Brinkley, narrator (RCA)

BEST RECORDING FOR CHILDREN
ALICE THROUGH THE LOOKING GLASS - Orig. Cast- Moose Charlap & Elsie Simmons, Score (RCA)
THE CHRISTMAS THAT ALMOST WASN'T - Paul Tripp & Cast (RCA)
DR. SEUSS PRESENTS: "IF I RAN THE ZOO" AND "SLEEP BOOK" - Marvin Miller (RCA)
FOR THE CHILDREN OF THE WORLD ART LINKLETTER NARRATES "THE BIBLE" - Art Linkletter (RCA)
HAPPINESS IS - Marty Gold cond. Do-Re-Mi Children's Chorus (Kapp)

BEST ALBUM NOTES
(Annotator's Award)
BEN COLDER STRIKES AGAIN - Harvey Cowen (MGM)
DR. ZHIVAGO - Nelson Lyon (Maurice Jarre)
EDWARD R. MURROW - A REPORTER REMEMBERS - VOL. I THE WAR YEARS - Fred Friendly (Col)
THE ELLINGTON ERA, VOL. II - Stanley Dance, Ralph Gleason (Col)
SINATRA AT THE SANDS - Stan Cornyn (Reprise)

BEST INSTRUMENTAL JAZZ PERFORMANCE - GROUP OR SOLOIST WITH GROUP
AT THE "GOLDEN CIRCLE" - Ornette Coleman Trio (Blue Note)
BILL EVANS TRIO WITH SYMPHONY ORCHESRTA - Bill Evans Trio (Verve)
CONCERT OF SACRED MUSIC - Duke Ellington Orch. (RCA)
GOIN' OUT OF MY HEAD - Wes Montgomery (Verve)
INTERMODULATION - Bill Evans, Jim Hall (Verve)
JOHN HANDY RECORDED LIVE AT THE MONTEREY JAZZ FESTIVAL - John Handy Quintet (Col)
STAN KENTON CONDUCTS THE LOS ANGELES NEOPHONIC ORCHESTRA - Stan Kenton (Cap)
WOODY'S WINNERS - Woody Herman Orchestra (Col)

BEST ORIGINAL JAZZ COMPOSITION
(Composer's Award)
ABC BLUES - Bob Brookmeyer (Solid State)
IF ONLY WE KNEW - John Handy (Col)
IN THE BEGINNING GOD - Duke Ellington (RCA)
JAZZ SAMBA - Claus Ogerman (Verve)
MARQUIS DE SADE - Lalo Schifrin (Verve)
TIME REMEMBERED - Bill Evans (Rvrsd)

BEST CONTEMPORARY (R&R) RECORDING
CHERISH - The Association (Valiant)
ELEANOR RIGBY - Paul McCartney (Cap)
GOOD VIBRATIONS - The Beach Boys (Cap)
LAST TRAIN TO CLARKSVILLE - The Monkees (Colgems)
MONDAY, MONDAY - The Mamas & The Papas (Dunhill)
WINCHESTER CATHEDRAL - New Vaudeville Band (Fontana)

BEST CONTEMPORARY (R&R) SOLO VOCAL PERFORMANCE - MALE OR FEMALE
BORN A WOMAN - Sandy Posey (MGM)
ELEANOR RIGBY - Paul McCartney (Cap)
IF I WERE A CARPENTER - Bobby Darin (Atl)
THESE BOOTS ARE MADE FOR WALKIN' - Nancy Sinatra (Reprise)
YOU DON'T HAVE TO SAY YOU LOVE ME - Dusty Springfield (Philips)

BEST CONTEMPORARY (R&R) GROUP PERFORMANCE - VOCAL OR INSTRUMENTAL
CHERISH - The Association (Valiant)
GOOD VIBRATIONS - The Beach Boys (Cap)
GUANTANAMERA - The Sandpipers (A&M)
LAST TRAIN TO CLARKSVILLE - The Monkees (Colgm)
MONDAY, MONDAY - The Mamas & The Papas (Dunhill)

BEST RHYTHM & BLUES RECORDING
CRYING TIME - Ray Charles (ABC-Par)
IT'S A MAN'S MAN'S MAN'S WORLD - James Brown (King)
LOVE IS A HURTIN' THING - Lou Rawls (Cap)
UPTIGHT - Stevie Wonder (Tamla)
WHEN A MAN LOVES A WOMAN - Percy Sledge (Atl)

BEST RHYTHM & BLUES SOLO VOCAL PERFORMANCE - MALE OR FEMALE
CRYING TIME - Ray Charles (ABC-Par)
IT'S A MAN'S MAN'S MAN'S WORLD - James Brown (King)
LOVE IS A HURTIN' THING - Lou Rawls (Cap)
UPTIGHT - Stevie Wonder (Tamla)
WHEN A MAN LOVES A WOMAN - Percy Sledge (Alt)

BEST RHYTHM & BLUES GROUP PERFORMANCE - VOCAL OR INSTRUMENTAL
COOL JERK - Capitols (Atco)
HOLD IT RIGHT THERE - Ramsey Lewis (Cadet)
HOLD ON, I'M COMIN' - Sam & Dave (Stax)
I'M YOUR PUPPET - James & Bobby Purify (Bell)
SPANISH HARLEM - King Curtis (Atco)

BEST FOLK RECORDING
BLUES IN THE STREET - Cortelia Clark (RCA)
GOD BLESS THE GRASS - Pete Seeger (Col)
HURRY SUNDOWN - Peter, Paul & Mary (WB)
LEADBELLY - Leadbelly (Elektra)
OLIVER SMITH - Oliver Smith (Elektra)
REFLECTIONS IN A CRYSTAL WIND - Mimi & Richard Farina (Vanguard)
SOUND OF THE SITAR - Ravi Shankar (Wrld Pac)
VIOLETS OF DAWN - Mitchell Trio (Merc)

BEST SACRED RECORDING (MUSICAL)
BIGGER "N" BETTER - Happy Goodman Family (Canaan)
CONNIE SMITH SINGS GREAT SACRED SONGS - Connie Smith (RCA)
GRAND OLD GOSPEL - Porter Wagoner & the Blackwood Bros. (RCA)
HOW BIG IS GOD - The Blackwood Bros. (RCA)
THE OAK RIDGE BOYS AT THEIR BEST - The Oak Ridge Boys (UA)
SOUTHLAND SONGS THAT LIFT THE HEART - George Beverly Shea (RCA)

BEST COUNTRY & WESTERN RECORDING
ALMOST PERSUADED - David Houston (Epic)
DISTANT DRUMS - Jim Reeves (RCA)
DON'T TOUCH ME - Jeannie Seely (Monument)
I'M A NUT - Leroy Pullins (Kapp)
THERE GOES MY EVERYTHING - Jack Greene (Decca)

BEST COUNTRY & WESTERN VOCAL PERFORMANCE - FEMALE
AIN'T HAD NO LOVING - Connie Smith (RCA)
DON'T COME HOME A DRINKIN' - Loretta Lynn (Decca)
DON'T TOUCH ME - Jeannie Seely (Monument)
EVIL ON YOUR MIND - Jan Howard (Decca)
WOULD YOU HOLD IT AGAINST ME - Dottie West (RCA)

BEST COUNTRY & WESTERN VOCAL PERFORMANCE - MALE
ALMOST PERSUADED - David Houston
ALMOST PERSUADED NO. 2 - Ben Colder (Verve)
DISTANT DRUMS - Jim Reeves (RCA)
JUST BETWEEN YOU AND ME - Charley Pride (RCA)
THERE GOES MY EVERYTHING - Jack Greene (Decca)

BEST COUNTRY & WESTERN SONG
(Songwriter's Award)
ALMOST PERSUADED - Bill Sherrill, Glenn Sutton (Epic)
DON'T TOUCH ME - Hank Cochran (Monument)
HUSBANDS AND WIVES - Roger Miller (Smash)
STREETS OF BALTIMORE - Tompall Glaser, Harlan Howard (RCA)
THERE GOES MY EVERYTHING - Dallas Frazier (Decca)

BEST INSTRUMENTAL ARRANGEMENT
(Arranger's Award)
ARABESQUE - (Henry Mancini) - Arr: Henry Mancini (RCA)
BATMAN THEME (Neal Hefti) - Arr: Neal Hefti (RCA)
BORN FREE (track from soundtrack album) (John Barry) Arr: John Barry (MGM)
MICHELLE (Bud Shank) - Arr: Bob Florence (World Pac.)
WHAT NOW MY LOVE (Herb Alpert & the Tijuana Brass) Arr: Herb Alpert (A&M)

BEST ARRANGEMENT ACCOMPANYING A VOCALIST OR INSTRUMENTALIST
(Arranger's Award)
ELEANOR RIGBY (Paul McCartney, Beatles) Arr: George Martin (Cap)
GOIN' OUT OF MY HEAD (Wes Montgomery) Arr: Oliver Nelson (Verve)
GOOD VIBRATIONS (Beach Boys) Arr: Brian Wilson (Cap)
IF HE WALKED INTO MY LIFE (Eydie Gorme) Arr: Don Costa (Col)
STRANGERS IN THE NIGHT (Frank Sinatra) Arr: Ernie Freeman (Reprise)
THESE BOOTS ARE MADE FOR WALKIN' (Nancy Sinatra) Arr: Billy Strange (Reprise)

BEST ENGINEERED RECORDING—NON-CLASSICAL
(Engineer's Award)
ARABESQUE - Henry Mancini - Eng: Dick Bogert (RCA)
JOE WILLIAMS & THAD JONES - MEL LEWIS & THE JAZZ ORCHESTRA - - Eng: Phil Ramone (Sid. St.)
THE LAST WORD IN LONESOME IS ME (Eddy Arnold) Eng: James Malloy (RCA)
PRESENTING THAD JONES - MEL LEWIS & THE JAZZ ORCHESTRA - Eng: Phil Ramone (Sid. St)
STRANGERS IN THE NIGHT (Frank Sinatra) (album) Engrs: Eddie Brackett, Lee Herschberg (Reprise)

BEST ENGINEERED RECORDING - CLASSICAL
(Engineer's Award)
IVES: SYMPHONY NO. 1 IN D MINOR (Gould cond. Chicago Symphony) - Eng: Bernard Keville (RCA)
MAHLER: SYMPHONY NO. 6 IN A MINOR (Leinsdorf cond. Boston Symphony) - Eng: Anthony Salvatore (RCA)
VARESE: ARCANA (Martinon cond. Chicago Symphony) - Eng: Bernard Keville (RCA)
VIVALDI: GLORIA IN D (Robert Shaw Orch. & Chorus) - Eng: Ernest Oelrich (RCA)
WAGNER: LOHENGRIN (Leinsdorf cond. Boston Symphony Pro Musica Chorus & Soloists) - Eng: Anthony Salvatore (RCA)

BEST ALBUM COVER, PHOTOGRAPHY
(Awards to the Art Director and Photographer)
BLONDE ON BLONDE (Bob Dylan) Art Dirs: Bob Cato and John Berg - Photog: Gerald Schatsberg (Col)
CONFESSIONS OF A BROKEN MAN (Porter Wagoner) Art Dir: Robert Jones - Photog: Les Leverette (RCA) GUANTANAMERA (Sandpipers) Art Dir. & Photog: Peter Whorf (A&M) SAMMY DAVIS, JR SINGS - LAURINDO ALMEIDA PLAYS - Art Dir: Ed Thrasher - Photog: Tom Tucker (Reprise)
THE TIME MACHINE (Gary Burton) Art Dir: Robert Jones - Photog: Tom Zimmerman (RCA)
TURN! TURN! TURN! (The Byrds) Art Dirs: Bob Cato And John Berg - Photog: Guy Webster (Col)
WHAT NOW MY LOVE (Herb Alpert & The Tijuana Brass) Art Dir: Peter Whorf - Photog: George Jerman (A&M)

BEST ALBUM COVER, GRAPHIC ARTS
(Awards to the Art Director and Graphic Artist)
BAROQUE FANFARES & SONATAS FOR BRASS (London Brass Players, Joshua Rifkin dir.) Art Dir: William S. Harvey - Graphic: Gordon Kibbee (Nonesuch)
CHARLIE BYRD CHRISTMAS CAROLS FOR SOLO GUITAR - Art Dirs: Bob Cato and John Berg - Graphic: Allen Weinberg (Col)
COLOR ME BARBRA (Barbra Streisand) Art Dirs: Bob Cato and John Berg - Graphic: Elinor Bunin (Col)
IVES: SYMPHONY NO. 1 IN D MINOR (Gould cond. Chicago Symphony) Art Dir: George Estes - Graphic: Mozelle Thompson (RCA)
REVOLVER (The Beatles) Graphic: Klaus Voormann (Cap)
STAN KENTON CONDUCTS THE LOS ANGELES NEOPHONIC ORCHESTRA - Art Dir: George Osaki - Graphic: Rod Dyer (Cap)
TALK THAT TALK (The Jazz Crusaders) Art Dir: Woody Woodward - Graphic - Peter Whorf (Pac. Jazz)

ALBUM OF THE YEAR - CLASSICAL
(Awards to the Artist and A&R Producer)
AARON COPLAND CONDUCTS (Copland: Music for a Great City, Statements) - Aaron Copland cond. London Symphony - A&R: John McClure (Col)
HANDEL: MESSIAH - Colin Davis cond. London Symphony Orch. & Choir - A&R: Harold Lawrence (Philips)
HENZE: SYMPHONIES (1 thru 5) - H.W. Henze cond. Berlin Philharmonic - A&R: Otto Gerdes (DGG)
IVES: SYMPHONY NO. 1 IN D MINOR - Morton Gould cond. Chicago Symphony - A&R: Howard Scott (RCA)
MAHLER: SYMPHONY NO. 6 IN A MINOR - Erich Leinsdorf cond. Boston Symphony - A&R: Richard Mohr (RCA)
MAHLER: SYMPHONY NO. 10 - Eugene Ormandy cond. Philadelphia Orchestra - A&R: Thomas Frost (Col)
OPENING NIGHTS AT THE MET - Various Artists - A&R: Peter Delheim (RCA)
PRESENTING MONTSERRAT CABALLE (Bellini & Donizetti Arias) - Montserrat Caballe - A&R: C. Gerhardt (RCA)
WAGNER: DIE WALKURE - Georg Solti cond. Vienna Philharmonic (Soloists: Nilsson, Crespin, Ludwig, King, Hotter, Frick) A&R: John Culshaw (London)

BEST CLASSICAL PERFORMANCE - ORCHESTRA
BARTOK: CONCERTO FOR ORCHESTRA - George Szell cond. Cleveland Orchestra (Col)
BOULEZ: LE SOLEIL DES EAUX; MESSIAEN: CHRONOCHROMIE; KOECHLIN: LES BANDAR-LOG (Angel) Pierre Boulez cond. BBC Symphony; Antal Dorati cond. BBC Symphony
IVES: FOURTH OF JULY - Leonard Bernstein cond. New York Philharmonic (Colv)
IVES: SYMPHONY NO. 1 IN D MINOR - Morton Gould cond. Chicago Symphony (RCA)
MAHLER: SYMPHONY NO. 6 IN A MINOR - Erich Leinsdorf cond. Boston Symphony (RCA)
MAHLER: SYMPHONY NO. 10 - Eugene Ormandy cond. Philadelphia Orchestra (Col)
RAVEL: DAPHNIS AND CHLOE - Ernest Ansermet cond. L'Orchestre de la Suisse Romande (London)
VARESE: ARCANA/MARTIN: CONCERTO FOR SEVEN WIND INSTRUMENTS, TIMPANI, PERCUSSION & STRING ORCHESTRA - Jean Martinon cond. Chicago Symphony (RCA)

BEST CHAMBER MUSIC PERFORMANCE INSTRUMENTAL OR VOCAL
ARENSKY: TRIO IN D MINOR FOR VIOLIN, CELLO & PIANO/MARTINU: DUO FOR VIOLIN & CELLO - Jascha Heifetz, Gregor Piatigorsky with Leonard Pennario (RCA)
BEETHOVEN: TRIO NO. 6 IN B FLAT, OP. 97 ("ARCHDUKE") - Eugene Istomin, Isaac Stern, Leonard Rose (Col)
BOSTON SYMPHONY CHAMBER PLAYERS (Selections by Mozart, Brahms, Beethoven, Fine, Copland, Carter, Piston) Boston Symphony Chamber Players (RCA)

FRANCK: SONATA IN A MAJOR FOR VIOLIN & PIANO/DEBUSSY: SONATA IN G MINOR FOR VIOLIN & PIANO - Erick Friedman, Andre Previn (RCA)
HAYDN: QUARTETS (OP. 33) - Weller Quartet (London)
MOZART: THE SIX QUINTETS FOR STRING QUARTET & VIOLA - Walter Trampler & Budapest Quartet (Col)
PROKOFIEV: SONATA FOR CELLO & PIANO, OP. 119/CHOPIN: SONATA IN G MINOR FOR PIANO & CELLO, OP. 65 - Gregor Piatigorsky and Rudolf Firkusny (RCA)
SCHUBERT: QUINTET IN C MAJOR - Vienna Philharmonic Quartet (London)

BEST CLASSICAL PERFORMANCE - INSTRUMENTAL SOLOIST(S) (WITH OR WITHOUT ORCHESTRA)

BAROQUE GUITAR (Bach, Sanz, Weiss, Etc.) Julian Bream (RCA)
CHOPIN: NOCTURNES - Ivan Moravec (Conn.Soc)
DVORAK: CONCERTO IN A MINOR FOR VIOLIN - Isaac Stern, Soloist (Eugene Ormandy cond. Philadelphia Orchestra) (Col)
ELGAR: CONCERTO FOR VIOLIN - Yehudi Menuhin, Soloist (Sir Adrian Boult cond. New Philharmonia Orchestra) (Angel)
OPERATIC LISZT - Raymond Lewenthal (RCA)
PROKOFIEV: CONCERTO NO. 1 IN D FLAT MAJOR FOR PIANO/CONCERTO NO. 2 IN G MINOR FOR PIANO - John Browning, Soloist (Erich Leinsdorf cond. Boston Symphony) (RCA)
RODRIGO: CONCIERTO DE ARANJUEZ FOR GUITAR & ORCHESTRA/CASTELNUOVO - TEDESCO: CONCERTO IN D MAJOR FOR GUITAR - John Williams, Soloist (Eugene Ormandy cond. Philadelphia Orchestra) (Col)
RUBINSTEIN & CHOPIN (Bolero, Tarentelle, Fantasie in F Minor Barcarolle, Bercuse & 3 Nouvelles Etudes) - Artur Rubinstein (RCA)

BEST OPERA RECORDING
(Conductor's Award)
BARTOK: BLUEBEARD'S CASTLE - Istvan Kertesz cond. London Symphony (Soloists: Ludwig, Berry) (London)
COPLAND: THE TENDER LAND - Aaron Copland cond. Choral Arts Society & New York Philharmonic (Soloists: Clements, Turner, Cassilly, Treigle, Fredericks) (Col)
PUCCINI: TURANDOT - Francesco Molinari - Pradelli cond. Rome Opera Chorus & Orchestra (Soloists: Nilsson, Corelli) (Angel)
WAGNER: DIE WALKURE - Georg Solti cond. Vienna Philharmonic (Soloists: Nilsson, Crespin, Ludwig, King, Hotter) (London)
WAGNER: LOHENGRIN - Erich Leinsdorf cond. Boston Symphony (Soloists: Konya, Amarca, Gorr, Dooley) (RCA)

BEST CLASSICAL CHORAL PERFORMANCE (OTHER THAN OPERA)
BEETHOVEN: MISSA SOLEMNIS IN D MAJOR - Wilhelm Pitz cond. New Philharmonia Chorus Otto Klemperer cond. New Philharmonia Orchestra (Angel)
BLESS THIS HOUSE - Richard Condie, Dir., Mormon Tabernacle Choir - Eugene Ormandy cond. Philadelphia Orchestra (Col)
HANDEL: MESSIAH - Colin Davis cond. London Symphony Orchestra & Choir (Philips)
HANDEL: MESSIAH - Robert Shaw cond. Robert Shaw Chorale & Orchestra (RCA)
IVES: MUSIC FOR CHORUS (Gen. Wm. Booth Enters Into Heaven, Serenity, The Circus Band, etc.) Gregg Smith cond. Columbia Chamber Orchestra, Gregg Smith Singers, Ithaca College Concert Choir - George Bragg cond. Texas Boys Choir (Col)
ORFF: CARMINA BURANA - Wilhelm Pitz cond. New Philharmonia Chorus - Rafael Fruhbeck de Burgos cond. New Philharmonia Orch. (Angel)
VAUGHAN WILLIAMS: HODIE - David Willcocks cond. Bach Choir & Choristers of Westminster Abbey/London Symphony (Angel)
VERDI: REQUIEM - Alfred Nash Patterson, Dir., Boston Symphony Chorus/Erich Leinsdorf cond. Boston Symphony Orchestra (RCA)

BEST CLASSICAL VOCAL SOLOIST PERFORMANCE (WITH OR WITHOUT ORCHESTRA)
MAHLER: SYMPHONY NO. 4 IN G MAJOR - Judith Raskin, Soloist (Szell cond. Cleveland Orchestra) (Col)
MAHLER: THE YOUTH'S MAGIC HORN (Das Knaben Wunderhorn) - Janet Baker, Solo. (Wyn Morris cond. London Philharmonic) (Angel)
PRESENTING MONTSERRAT CABALLE (Bellini & Donizetti Arias) - Montserrat Caballe (Carlo Felice Cilario, cond.) (RCA)
PRIMA DONNA (Barber, Purcell, etc.) Leontyne Price, Soloist (Molinari-Pradelli cond. RCA Italiana Opera Orchestra) (RCA)
SCHUMANN: DICHTERLIEBE - Dietrich Fischer-Dieskau, Soloist (DGG)
STRAUSS: FOUR LAST SONGS - Elisabeth Schwarzkopf, Soloist (Szell cond. Berlin Radio Symphony) (Angel)

1967

RECORD OF THE YEAR
(Awards to the Artist and A&R Producer)
BY THE TIME I GET TO PHOENIX - Glen Campbell - A&R: Al de Lory (Cap)
MY CUP RUNNETH OVER - Ed Ames - A&R: Jim Fogelsong, Joe Reisman (RCA)
ODE TO BILLIE JOE - Bobbie Gentry - A&R: Bobby Paris, Kelly Gordon (Cap)
SOMETHIN' STUPID - Nancy and Frank Sinatra - A&R: Jimmy Bowen, Lee Hazelwood (Reprise)
UP, UP AND AWAY - 5th Dimension - A&R: Marc Gordon, Johnny Rivers (Soul City)

ALBUM OF THE YEAR
(Awards to the Artist and A&R Producer)
FRANCIS ALBERT SINATRA/ANTONIO CARLOS JOBIM - Francis Albert Sinatra, Antonio Carlos Jobim - A&R: Sonny Burke (Reprise)
IT MUST BE HIM - Vikki Carr - A&R: Dave Pell, Tommy Oliver (Lib)
MY CUP RUNNETH OVER - Ed Ames - A&R: Jim Fogelsong (RCA)
ODE TO BILLIE JOE - Bobbie Gentry - A&R: Bobby Paris, Kelly Gordon (Cap)
SGT. PEPPER'S LONELY HEARTS CLUB BAND - The Beatles - A&R: George Martin (Cap)

SONG OF THE YEAR
(Songwriter's Award)
BY THE TIME I GET TO PHOENIX - Jim Webb (Cap)
GENTLE ON MY MIND - John Hartford (RCA)
MY CUP RUNNETH OVER - Tom Jones, Harvey Schmidt (RCA)
ODE TO BILLIE JOE - Bobbie Gentry (Cap)
UP, UP AND AWAY - Jim Webb (Soul City)

BEST INSTRUMENTAL THEME
(Composer's Award)
A BANDA - Chico Buarque De Hollanda (A&M)
CASINO ROYALE - Burt Bacharach, Hal David (A&M)
HURRY SUNDOWN - Hugo Montenegro (MGM)
MERCY, MERCY, MERCY - Joe Zawinul (Cap)
MISSION: IMPOSSIBLE - Lalo Schifrin (Dot)

BEST VOCAL PERFORMANCE - FEMALE
ALFIE (single) - Dionne Warwick (Scepter)
DON'T SLEEP IN THE SUBWAY (single) Petula Clark (WB)
IT MUST BE HIM (album) - Vikki Carr (Lib)
ODE TO BILLIE JOE (single) Bobbie Gentry (Cap)
RESPECT (single) Aretha Franklin (Atl)

BEST VOCAL PERFORMANCE - MALE
BY THE TIME I GET TO PHOENIX (single) Glen Campbell (Cap)
CAN'T TAKE MY EYES OFF YOU (single) Frankie Valli (Philips)
FRANCIS ALBERT SINATRA/ANTONIO CARLOS JOBIM - Francis Albert Sinatra (Reprise)
MY CUP RUNNETH OVER (album) - Ed Ames (RCA)
YESTERDAY (single) Ray Charles (ABC)

BEST INSTRUMENTAL PERFORMANCE
CASINO ROYALE - Herb Alpert & the Tijuana Brass (A&M)
CHET ATKINS PICKS THE BEST - Chet Atkins (RCA)
MERCY, MERCY, MERCY - Cannonball Adderley Quintet (Cap)
MISSION: IMPOSSIBLE - Lalo Schifrin (Dot)
MUSIC TO WATCH GIRLS BY - Bob Crewe Generation (DynoVoice)

BEST PERFORMANCE BY A VOCAL GROUP
I'M A BELIEVER - The Monkees (Colgems)
THE LETTER - The Box Tops (Bell)
NEVER MY LOVE - The Association (WB)
SGT. PEPPER'S LONELY HEARTS CLUB BAND - The Beatles (Cap)
UP, UP AND AWAY - 5th Dimension (Soul City)

BEST PERFORMANCE BY A CHORUS
BLAME IT ON ME - Ray Charles Singers (Command)
ENCOUNTER - Swingle Singers - with the Modern Jazz Quartet (Philips)
UP, UP AND AWAY - Johnny Mann Singers (Lib)
WINDY - Percy Faith Chorus and Orch. (Col)
WISH ME A RAINBOW - Living Voices - Ethel Gabriel, conductor (RCA)

BEST ORIGINAL SCORE WRITTEN FOR A MOTION PICTURE OR TV SHOW
(Composer's Award)
CASINO ROYALE (Various Artists, Bacharach cond.) Comp: Burt Bacharach (RCA)
DOCTOR DOOLITTLE (Rex Harrison & motion picture cast, Lionel Newman cond.) Comp: Leslie Bricusse (20th)
IN THE HEAT OF THE NIGHT (Quincy Jones cond.) Comp: Quincy Jones (UA)
MISSION: IMPOSSIBLE (Lalo Schifrin Orch.) Comp: Lalo Schifrin (Dot)
TO SIR WITH LOVE (Soundtrack W/Lulu & the Mindbenders) Comps: Ron Grainer, Don Black, Mark London (Fontana)

BEST SCORE FROM AN ORIGINAL CAST SHOW ALBUM
(Awards to Composers & A&R Producer)
CABARET - Fred Ebb & John Kander - A&R: Goddard Lieberson (Col)
HALLELUJAH, BABY - Jule Styne, Betty Comden, Adolph Green - A&R: Edward Kleban (Col)
I DO! I DO! - Harvey Schmidt & Tom Jones - A&R: Andy Wiswell (RCA)
WALKING HAPPY - Sammy Cahn & Jimmy Van Heusen - A&R: Richard C. Jones (Cap)
YOU'RE A GOOD MAN, CHARLIE BROWN - Clark Gesner - A&R: Bob Morgan, Herb Galewitz (MGM)

BEST COMEDY RECORDING
THE COCKFIGHT AND OTHER TALL TALES - Archie Campbell (RCA)
COWBOYS AND COLORED PEOPLE - Flip Wilson (Atl)
LENNY BRUCE IN CONCERT - Lenny Bruce (UA)
REVENGE - Bill Cosby (WB)
TAKE-OFFS AND PUT-ONS - George Carlin (RCA)

BEST NEW ARTIST
LANA CANTRELL (RCA)
5TH DIMENSION (Soul City)
BOBBIE GENTRY (Cap)
HARPERS BIZARRE (WB)
JEFFERSON AIRPLANE (RCA)

BEST INSTRUMENTAL JAZZ PERFORMANCE - SMALL GROUP OR SOLOIST WITH SMALL GROUP
(7 or less Persons)
DUSTER - Gary Burton Quartet (RCA)
FURTHER CONVERSATIONS WITH MYSELF - Bill Evans (Verve)
HAPPENINGS - Bobby Hutcherson (Blue Note)
MERCY, MERCY, MERCY - Cannonball Adderley Quintet (Cap)
MILES SMILES - Miles Davis (Col)
SWEET RAIN - Stan Getz (Verve)

BEST INSTRUMENTAL JAZZ PERFORMANCE - LARGE GROUP OR SOLOIST WITH LARGE GROUP
(8 or more Persons)
BIG SWING FACE - Buddy Rich (Pac. Jazz)
FAR EAST SUITE - Duke Ellington (RCA)
LIVE AT MONTEREY - Don Ellis Big Band (Pac. Jaz)
LIVE AT THE VILLAGE VANGUARD - Thad Jones and Mel Lewis (UA)
WOODY LIVE - EAST AND WEST - Woody Herman (Col)

BEST CONTEMPORARY SINGLE
(Awards to the Artist and A&R Producer)
BY THE TIME I GET TO PHOENIX - Glen Campbell - A&R: Al de Lory (Cap)
DON'T SLEEP IN THE SUBWAY - Petula Clark - A&R: Tony Hatch (WB)
ODE TO BILLIE JOE - Bobbie Gentry - A&R: Bobby Paris, Kelly Gordon (Cap)
UP, UP AND AWAY - 5th Dimension - A&R: Marc Gordon, Johnny Rivers (Soul City)
YESTERDAY - Ray Charles - A&R: Sid Feller, Tangerine Records (ABC)

BEST CONTEMPORARY ALBUM
(Awards to the Artist and A&R Producer)
INSIGHT OUT - The Association - A&R: Bones Howe (WB)
IT MUST BE HIM - Vikki Carr - A&R: Dave Pell, Tommy Oliver (Lib)
ODE TO BILLIE JOE - Bobbie Gentry - A&R: Bobby Paris, Kelly Gordon (Cap)
SGT. PEPPER'S LONELY HEARTS CLUB BAND - The Beatles - A&R: George Martin (Cap)
UP, UP AND AWAY - 5th Dimension - A&R: Marc Gordon, Johnny Rivers (Soul City)

BEST CONTEMPORARY FEMALE SOLO PERFORMANCE--VOCAL
DON'T SLEEP IN THE SUBWAY - Petula Clark (WB)
I SAY A LITTLE PRAYER - Dionne Warwicke (Scptr)
IT MUST BE HIM - Vikki Carr (album) (Lib)
A NATURAL WOMAN - Aretha Franklin (Atl)
ODE TO BILLIE JOE - Bobbie Gentry (Cap)

BEST CONTEMPORARY MALE SOLO PERFORMANCE—VOCAL
BY THE TIME I GET TO PHOENIX - Glen Campbell (Cap)
CAN'T TAKE MY EYES OFF YOU - Frankie Valli (Philips)
CHILD OF CLAY - Jimmie Rodgers (A&M)
SAN FRANCISCO (Be Sure to Wear Some Flowers in Your Hair) - Scott McKenzie (Col)
YESTERDAY - Ray Charles (ABC)

BEST CONTEMPORARY GROUP PERFORMANCE (VOCAL OR INST.)
I'M A BELIEVER - The Monkees (Colgems)
THE LETTER - Box Tops (Bell)
SGT. PEPPER'S LONELY HEARTS CLUB BAND - The Beatles (Cap)
UP, UP AND AWAY - 5th Dimension (Soul City)
A WHITER SHADE OF PALE - Procul Harum (Deram)
WINDY - The Association (WB)

BEST RHYTHM & BLUES RECORDING
(Awards to the Artist and A&R Producer)
DEAD END STREET - Lou Rawls - A&R: David Axelrod (Cap)
RESPECT - Aretha Franklin - A&R: Jerry Wexler (Atl)
SKINNY LEGS AND ALL - Joe Tex - A&R: Buddy Killen (Dial)
SOUL MAN - Sam & Dave - A&R: David Porter & Isaac Hayes (Stax)
TRY A LITTLE TENDERNESS - Otis Redding - A&R: Steve Cropper (Atco)

BEST RHYTHM & BLUES SOLO VOCAL PERFORMANCE - FEMALE
I HEARD IT THROUGH THE GRAPEVINE - Gladys Knight & The Pips (Soul)
THE QUEEN ALONE - Carla Thomas (Stax)
RESPECT - Aretha Franklin (Atl)
TELL MAMA - Etta James (Cadet)
(YOU'LL) GO TO HELL - Nina Simone (RCA)

BEST RHYTHM & BLUES SOLO VOCAL PERFORMANCE - MALE
DEAD END STREET - Lou Rawls (Cap)
FUNKY BROADWAY - Wilson Pickett (Atl)
HIGHER AND HIGHER - Jackie Wilson (Brnswck)
SKINNY LEGS AND ALL - Joe Tex (Dial)
TRY A LITTLE TENDERNESS - Otis Redding (Atco)

BEST RHYTHM & BLUES GROUP PERFORMANCE - VOCAL OR INSTRUMENTAL
AIN'T NO MOUNTAIN HIGH ENOUGH - Marvin Gaye & Tammi Terrell (Tamla)
HIP HUG-HER - Booker T. & the M.G.'s (Stax)
THE KING & QUEEN - Carla Thomas and Otis Redding (Stax)
SOUL MAN - Sam & Dave (Stax)
I SECOND THAT EMOTION - Smokey Robinson & the Miracles (Tamla)

BEST SACRED PERFORMANCE
DOTTIE WEST SINGS SACRED BALLADS - Dottie West (RCA)
HOW GREAT THOU ART - Elvis Presley (RCA)
THE OLD COUNTRY CHURCH - The Browns (RCA)
SONGS FOR THE SOUL - Red Foley (Decca)
SURELY GOODNESS AND MERCY - George Beverly Shea & the Blackwood Bros. Quartet (RCA)

BEST GOSPEL PERFORMANCE
THE BLACKWOOD BROS. QUARTET SINGS FOR JOY - The Blackwood Bros. Quartet (RCA)
GOOD N' HAPPY - Happy Goodman Family (Canaan)
MORE GRAND OLD GOSPEL - Porter Wagoner & The Blackwood Bros. Quartet (RCA)
THE OAK RIDGE BOYS - Oak Ridge Boys (Heartwarming)
THE SINGING RAMBOS - GOSPEL BALLADS - The Singing Rambos (Heartwarming)

BEST FOLK PERFORMANCE
ALBUM 1700 - Peter, Paul & Mary (WB)
ALICE'S RESTAURANT - Arlo Guthrie (Reprise)
GENTLE ON MY MIND - John Hartford (RCA)
IN MY LIFE - Judy Collins (Elektra)
JANIS IAN - Janis Ian (Verve)
WAIST DEEP IN THE BIG MUDDY - Pete Seeger (Col)

BEST COUNTRY & WESTERN RECORDING
(Awards to the Artist and A&R Producer)
COLD HARD FACTS OF LIFE - Porter Wagoner - A&R: Bob Ferguson (RCA)
DOES MY RING HURT YOUR FINGER - Charley Pride - A&R: Chet Atkins, Jack Clement, and Felton Jarvis (RCA)
GENTLE ON MY MIND - Glen Campbell - A&R: Al de Lory (Cap)
POP A TOP - Jim Ed Brown - A&R: Felton Jarvis (RCA)
THROUGH THE EYES OF LOVE - Tompall & the Glaser Bros - A&R: Jack Clement (MGM)

BEST COUNTRY & WESTERN SOLO VOCAL PERFORMANCE - FEMALE
CINCINNATI, OHIO - Connie Smith (RCA)
I DON'T WANNA PLAY HOUSE - Tammy Wynette (Epic)
MAMA SPANK - Liz Anderson (RCA)
PAPER MANSIONS - Dottie West (RCA)
WHAT DOES IT TAKE - Skeeter Davis (RCA)

BEST COUNTRY & WESTERN SOLO VOCAL PERFORMANCE - MALE
ALL THE TIME - Jack Greene (Decca)
COLD HARD FACTS OF LIFE - Porter Wagoner (RCA)
DOES MY RING HURT YOUR FINGER - Charley Pride (RCA)
GENTLE ON MY MIND - Glen Campbell (Cap)
POP A TOP - Jim Ed Brown (RCA)

BEST COUNTRY & WESTERN PERFORMANCE DUET, TRIO OR GROUP (VOCAL OR INSTRUMENTAL)
CHET'S TUNE - Some of Chet's Friends (RCA)
GAME OF TRIANGLES - Liz Anderson, Bobby Bare, Norma Jean (RCA)
JACKSON - Johnny Cash, June Carter (Col)
THE LONESOME RHODES - The Lonesome Rhodes (RCA)
MY CUP RUNNETH OVER - The Blue Boys (RCA)
MY ELUSIVE DREAMS - David Houston, Tammy Wynette (Epic)
OUR WAY OF LIFE - Bobby Goldsboro, Del Reeves (UA)
THROUGH THE EYES OF LOVE - Tompall & the Glaser Bros. (MGM)

BEST COUNTRY & WESTERN SONG
(Songwriter's Award)
BREAK MY MIND - John Loudermilk (RCA)
COLD HARD FACTS OF LIFE - Bill Anderson (RCA)
DOES MY RING HURT YOUR FINGER - Don Robertson, John Crutchfield, Doris Clement (RCA)
GENTLE ON MY MIND - John Hartford (RCA)
IT'S SUCH A PRETTY WORLD TODAY - Dale Noe (Cap)

BEST SPOKEN WORD, DOCUMENTARY OR DRAMA RECORDING
THE BALCONY - Patrick Magee, Cyril Cusack (Caedmon)
THE EARTH - Rod McKuen (WB)
GALLANT MEN - Sen. Everett M. Dirksen (Cap)
A MAN FOR ALL SEASONS - Paul Scofield, Wendy Hiller, Robert Shaw (RCA)
MARK TWAIN TONIGHT, VOL. 3 - Hal Holbrook (Col)
AN OPEN LETTER TO MY TEENAGE SON - Victor Lundberg (Lib)
POEMS OF JAMES DICKEY - James Dickey (Spoken Arts)

BEST RECORDING FOR CHILDREN
THE CARNIVAL OF THE ANIMALS - Verses by Ogden Nash, narrated by Tutti Camarata (Symphonie-Orchester Graunke) (Buena Vista)
DR. SEUSS: HOW THE GRINCH STOLE CHRISTMAS (TV Soundtrack) - Boris Karloff (MGM)
A HAPPY BIRTHDAY PARTY WITH WINNIE THE POOH - Sterling Holloway (Disneyland)
THE JUNGLE BOOK - Motion Picture Cast (Phil Harris, Louis Prima, Sterling Holloway, Sebastian Cabot, George Saunders) Tutti Camarata, A&R Prod. (Disney)
JUNGLE BOOKS - Richard Kiley (MGM)
MAGIC FISHBONE/HAPPY PRINCE/POTTED PRINCESS - Julie Harris, Richard Kiley (MGM)

BEST INSTRUMENTAL ARRANGEMENT
(Arranger's Award)
ALFIE (Burt Bacharach Orch.) - Arr: Burt Bacharach (A&M)
CASINO ROYALE (Herb Alpert & the Tijuana Brass) Arr: Burt Bacharach (A&M)
MUSIC TO WATCH GIRLS BY (Bob Crewe Generation) Arr: Hutch Davie (Philips)
NORWEGIAN WOOD (Buddy Rich Orch.) Arr: Bill Holman (Pac. Jazz)
WAVE (Antonio Carlos Jobim) Arr: Claus Ogerman (A&M)
WEST SIDE MEDLEY (Buddy Rich Orch.) Arr: Bill Reddie (Pac. Jazz)

BEST ARRANGEMENT ACCOMPANYING VOCALIST(S) OR INSTRUMENTALIST(S)
(Arranger's Award)
BY THE TIME I GET TO PHOENIX (Glen Campbell) Arr: Al de Lory (Cap)
A DAY IN THE LIFE (The Beatles) Arr: The Beatles & George Martin (Cap)
DON'T SLEEP IN THE SUBWAY (Petula Clark) Arr: Tony Hatch (WB-7 Arts)
ODE TO BILLIE JOE (Bobbie Gentry) Arr: Jimmie Haskell (Cap)
WINDY (The Association) Arr: Bill Holman, Bones Howe, Ray Pohlman (WB-7 Arts)

BEST ENGINEERED RECORDING, NON-CLASSICAL
(Engineer's Award)
CHET'S TUNE (Some of Chet's Friends) Eng: William Vandevort (RCA)
HOW GREAT THOU ART (Elvis Presley) Eng: James Malloy (RCA)
MISSION: IMPOSSIBLE (Lalo Schifrin) Eng: Hank Cicalo (Dot)
ODE TO BILLIE JOE (Bobbie Gentry) Eng: Joe Polito (Cap)
SGT. PEPPER'S LONELY HEARTS CLUB BAND (The Beatles) Eng: G.E. Emerick (Cap)

BEST ENGINEERED RECORDING - CLASSICAL
(Engineer's Award)
THE GLORIOUS SOUND OF BRASS (Philadelphia Brass Ensemble) Eng: Edward T. Graham (Col)
MAHLER: DAS LIED VON DER ERDE (Bernstein, Vienna Philharmonic & Soloists) Eng: Gordon Parry (London)
MAHLER: SYMPHONY NO. 2 IN C MINOR ("RESURRECTION") (Solti cond. London Symphony Chorus & Orch.; Harper, Watts) Eng: Gordon Parry (London)
MAHLER: SYMPHONY NO. 3 IN D MINOR (Leinsdorf cond. Boston Symphony) Eng: Edwin Begley (RCA Red Seal)
MAHLER: SYMPHONY NO. 8 IN E FLAT (Bernstein cond. London Symphony) Eng: Hellmuth Kolbe (Col)
RACHMANINOFF: SYMPHONY NO. 1 IN D (Ormandy cond. Philadelphia Orchestra) Eng: Edward T. Graham (Col)
WAGNER: TRISTAN & ISOLDE "LIVE" (Bohm cond. Bayreuth Festival Orchestra/Nilsson, Windgassen) Eng: Gunter Hermanns (DGG)

BEST ALBUM COVER - PHOTOGRAPHY
(Awards to Art Director and Photographer)
BOB DYLAN'S GREATEST HITS (Bob Dylan) Art Dirs: John Berg and Bob Cato - Photog: Roland Scherman (Col)
BRAVO, BRAVO, AZNAVOUR (Charles Aznavour) Art Dir. & Photog: Ken Kim (Monument)
THE DOORS (The doors) Art Dir: Bill Harvey - Photogs: Guy Webster, Joel Brodsky (Elektra)
EARTHWORDS & MUSIC (John Harford) Art Dir: Robert Jones - Photog: New World Photography (RCA)
FROM MEXICO WITH LAUGHS (Don Bowman) Art Dir: Robert Jones - Photog: Howard Cooper (RCA)
SUBURBAN ATTITUDES IN COUNTRY VERSE (John Loudermilk) Art Dir: Bob Jones - Photog: Jimmy Moore (RCA)
THAT MAN, ROBERT MITCHUM, SINGS - Art Dir. & Photog: Ken Kim (Monument)

BEST ALBUM COVER - GRAPHIC ARTS
(Awards to Art Director and Graphic Artist)
THE GOLD STANDARD COLLECTION (Hank Thompson) Art Dir: Ed Thrasher - Graphic: Charles White (WB-7)
HAYDN: SYM. NO. 84 IN E FLAT MAJOR: SYM. NO. 85 IN B FLAT MAJOR "LA REINE" (Bernstein cond. New York Philharmonic) Art Dirs: John Berg and Bob Cato - Graphic: Henrietta Condak (Col)
MONK/STRAIGHT, NO CHASER (Thelonious Monk) Art Dirs: John Berg and Bob Cato - Graphic: Laslo Kubinyi (Col)
NASHVILLE CATS (Homer & Jethro) Art Dir: Robert Jones - Graphic: Jack Davis (RCA)
SGT. PEPPER'S LONELY HEARTS CLUB BAND (The Beatles) Art Dirs: Peter Blake & Jann Haworth (Cap)
UP, UP AND AWAY (5th Dimension) Art Dir: Woody Woodward - Graphic: Wayne Kimball (Soul City)

BEST ALBUM NOTES
(Annotator's Award)
THE EARTH (Rod McKuen, Music by Anita Kerr) Ann: Rod McKuen (WB)
EXTRA SPECIAL (Peggy Lee) Ann: Rory Guy (Cap)
THE FAR EAST SUITE (Duke Ellington) Ann: Stanley Dance (RCA)
FRANCIS ALBERT SINATRA/ANTONIO CARLOS JOBIM - Ann: Stan Cornyn (Reprise)
LISTEN! (Gary Lewis & the Playboys) Ann: Richard Oliver (Lib)
SUBURBAN ATTITUDES IN COUNTRY VERSE (John Loudermilk) Ann: John D. Loudermilk (RCA)

ALBUM OF THE YEAR - CLASSICAL
(Awards to the Artist and A&R Producer)
BERG: WOZZECK - Pierre Boulez Cond. Orch. & Chorus of Paris National Opera (Solos: Berry, Strauss, Uhl, Doench)–A&R: Thomas Shepard (Col)
HOROWITZ IN CONCERT - Vladimir Horowitz--A&R: Thomas Frost (Col)
MAHLER: DAS LIED VON DER ERDE - Leonard Bernstein cond. Vienna Philharmonic (James King and Dietrich Fischer-Dieskau)--A&R: John Culshaw (London)
MAHLER: SYMPHONY NO. 8 IN E FLAT MAJOR ("SYMPHONY OF A THOUSAND") - Leonard Bernstein cond. London Symphony with soloists and choruses - A&R: John McClure (Col)
PUCCINI: LA RONDINE Francesco Molinari-Pradelli cond. RCA Italiana

Opera Orch. & Chorus (Soloists: Moffo, Barioni, Sereni, Sciutti, De Palma)--A&R: Richard Mohr (RCA)
THE WORLD OF CHARLES IVES - Robert Browning Overture - Leopold Stokowski cond. American Symphony/Washington's Birthday - Leonard Bernstein cond. New York Philharmonic - A&R: John McClure, Thomas Frost (Col)

BEST CLASSICAL PERFORMANCE - ORCHESTRA
(Conductor's Award)
HOLST: THE PLANETS - Sir Adrian Boult cond. New Philharmonia Orch. (Angel)
IVES: ORCHESTRAL SET NO. 2/ROBERT BROWNING OVERTURE/ PUTNAM'S CAMP - Morton Gould cond. Chicago Symphony (RCA)
MAHLER: DAS LIED VON DER ERDE - Leonard Bernstein cond. Vienna Philharmonic (with James King & Dietrich Fischer-Dieskau) (London)
MAHLER: SYMPHONY NO. 2 IN C MINOR ("RESURRECTION") - Georg Solti cond. London Symphony (London)
SHOSTAKOVICH: SYMPHONY NO. 10 IN E MINOR - Herbert von Karajan cond. Berlin Philharmonic (DGG)
STRAVINSKY: FIREBIRD & PETROUCHKA SUITES - Igor Stravinsky cond. Columbia Symphony (Col)

BEST CHAMBER MUSIC PERFORMANCE
BEETHOVEN: QUARTET NO. 15 IN A MINOR, OP. 132 - Yale Quartet (Vanguard)
BRAHMS: QUINTET IN F MINOR FOR PIANO, OP. 34 - Artur Rubinstein & Guarneri Quartet (RCA)
BRAHMS: (THE) TRIOS FOR PIANO, VIOLIN & CELLO (Nos. 1, 2, & 3) - Eugene Istomin, Isaac Stern, Leonard Rose (Col)
THE GLORIOUS SOUND OF BRASS - Philadelphia Brass Ensemble (Col)
IVES: QUARTETS NOS.1 & 3 - Juilliard Quartet (Col)
WEST MEETS EAST - Ravi Shankar and Yehudi Menuhin (Angel)

BEST CLASSICAL PERFORMANCE - INSTRUMENTAL SOLOIST(S) (WITH OR WITHOUT ORCHESTRA)
CHOPIN: NOCTURNES - Artur Rubinstein (RCA)
GRANADOS: GOYESCAS Complete/ESCENAS ROMANTICAS - Alicia de Larrocha (Epic)
HOROWITZ IN CONCERT - Vladimir Horowitz (Col)
IVES: SONATA NO. 1 FOR PIANO - William Masselos (RCA)
SEGOVIA ON STAGE - Andres Segovia (Decca)
20TH CENTURY GUITAR (Works by Brindle, Britten, Villa-Lobos, Martin, Henze) Julian Bream (RCA)

BEST OPERA RECORDING
(Awards to the Artist and A&R Producer)
BERG: WOZZECK - Pierre Boulez cond. orch. & Chorus of Paris National Opera (Soloists: Berry, Strauss, Uhl, Doench) A&R: Thomas Shepard (Col)
HANDEL: JULIUS CAESAR - Julius Rudel cond. New York City Opera Chorus & Orch. (Soloists: Treigle, Sills, Forrester, Wolff) A&R: Peter Dellheim (RCA) PUCCINI: LA RONDINE - Francesco Molinari-Pradelli cond. RCA Italiana Opera Orch. & Chorus (Soloists: Moffo, Barioni, Sereni Sciutti, De Palma) A&R: Richard Mohr (RCA)
PUCCINI: MADAME BUTTERFLY - Sir John Barbirolli cond. Rome Opera Orch. & Chorus (Soloists: Scotto, Bergonzi) A&R: Kinloch Anderson (Angel)
VERDI: FALSTAFF - Leonard Bernstein cond. Vienna Philharmonic Orch. & Chorus (Soloists: Fischer-Dieskau, Ligabue, Sciutti, Resnik) A&R: Erik Smith (Col)
WAGNER: DIE WALKURE - Herbert von Karajan cond. Berlin Philharmonic (Soloists: Crespin, Janowitz, Veasey, Vickers, Stewart, Talvela) A&R: Otto Gerdes (DGG)
WAGNER: TRISTAN & ISOLDE "LIVE" - Karl Bohm cond. Bayreuth Festival Chorus & Orch. (Soloists: Nilsson, Windgassen, Ludwig, Talvela, Wachter) A&R: Otto Gerdes, Hans Hirsch (DGG)

BEST CLASSICAL CHORAL PERFORMANCE (OTHER THAN OPERA)
(Awards to Choral and Orchestra Conductors)
THE CHORAL MUSIC OF ARNOLD SCHOENBERG - Gregg Smith Singers (Everest)
COPLAND: IN THE BEGINNING, LARK, LAS AGACHADAS - Aaron Copland cond. New England Conservatory Chorus (CBS)
HANDEL: MESSIAH - John McCarthy cond. Ambrosian Singers - Charles Mackerras cond. English Chamber Orch. (Angel)
HAYDN: THE SEASON - Karl Bohm cond. Vienna Singverein & Vienna Symphony (DGG)
MAHLER: SYMPHONY NO. 8 IN E FLAT MAJOR ("SYMPHONY OF A THOUSAND") - Leonard Bernstein cond. London Symphony Chorus & Orch. Soloists & Chorus (Col)
ORFF: CATULLI CARMINA - Robert Page cond. Temple Univ. Chorus - Eugene Ormandy cond. Philadelphia Orch. (Col)
PENDERECKI: PASSION ACCORDING TO ST. LUKE - Janusz Przybylski & Jozef Suwara, cond. Boys Chorus of Cracow; Henryk Czyz cond. Cracow Philharmonic (Philips)

BEST CLASSICAL VOCAL SOLOIST PERFORMANCE
AN ELISABETH SCHWARZKOPF SONGBOOK - Elisabeth Schwarzkopf (Gerald Moore, Pianist) (Angel)
BEETHOVEN: SONGS - Dietrich Fischer-Dieskau (Jorg Demus, Pianist) (DGG)
COPLAND: 12 POEMS OF EMILY DICKENSON - Adele Addison (Aaron Copland, Pianist) (CBS)
PRIMA DONNA, VOLUME 2 - Leontyne Price (Molinari-Pradelli cond. RCA Italiana Opera Orch.) (RCA)
SCHUBERT: DIE SCHOENE MUELLERIN - Fritz Wunderlich (Hubert Giesen, Pianist) (DGG)
SCHUBERT: DIE WINTERREISE - Peter Pears (Benjamin Britten, Pianist) (London)
SHEPHERD ON THE ROCK & OTHER SONGS - Christa Ludwig (with Instrumental Ensemble) (Angel)
VICTORIA DE LOS ANGELES SINGS DEBUSSY AND RAVEL AND OTHER FRENCH SONGS - Victoria de los Angeles (Gonzalo Soriano, Pianist) (Angel)

1968

RECORD OF THE YEAR
(Awards to the Artist and A&R Producer)
HARPER VALLEY P.T.A. - Jeannie C. Riley - A&R: Shelby S. Singleton, Jr. (Plantation)
HEY JUDE - The Beatles - A&R: George Martin (Cap)
HONEY - Bobby Goldsboro - A&R: Bob Montgomery, Bobby Goldsboro (UA)
MRS. ROBINSON - Simon & Garfunkel - A&R: Paul Simon, Art Garfunkel, Roy Halee (Col)
WICHITA LINEMAN - Glen Campbell - A&R: Al de Lory (Cap)

ALBUM OF THE YEAR
(Awards to the Artist and A&R Producer)
BOOKENDS - Simon & Garfunkel - A&R: Paul Simon, Art Garfunkel, Roy Halee (Col)
BY THE TIME I GET TO PHOENIX - Glen Campbell - A&R: Al de Lory (Cap)
FELICIANO! - Jose Feliciano - A&R: Rick Jarrard (RCA)
MAGICAL MYSTERY TOUR - The Beatles - A&R: George Martin (Cap)
A TRAMP SHINING - Richard Harris - A&R: Jim Webb (Dunhill)

SONG OF THE YEAR
(Songwriter's Award)
HARPER VALLEY P.T.A. - Tom T. Hall (Plantation)
HONEY - Bobby Russell (UA)
HEY JUDE - John Lennon, Paul McCartney (Cap)
LITTLE GREEN APPLES - Bobby Russell (Col)
MRS. ROBINSON - Paul Simon (Col)

BEST NEW ARTIST OF 1968
CREAM (Atco)
JOSE FELICIANO (RCA)
GARY PUCKETT & THE UNION GAP (Col)
JEANNIE C. RILEY (Plantation)
O.C. Smith (Col)

BEST INSTRUMENTAL ARRANGEMENT
(Arranger's Award)
BAROQUE-A-NOVA (Mason Williams) Arr: Al Capps (WB)
CLASSICAL GAS (Mason Williams) Arr: Mike Post (WB)
THE GOOD, THE BAD AND THE UGLY (Hugo Montenegro) Arr: Hugo Montenegro (RCA)
SCARBOROUGH FAIR (Wes Montgomery) Arr: Don Sebesky (A&M)
THE WINDMILLS OF YOUR MIND (Michel Legrand) Arr: Michel Legrand (UA)

BEST ARRANGEMENT ACCOMPANYING VOCALIST(S)
(Arranger's Award)
FOOL ON THE HILL (Sergio Mendes & Brasil '66) Arr: Dave Grusin (A&M)
LIGHT MY FIRE (Jose Feliciano) Arr: George Tipton (RCA)
MAC ARTHUR PARK (Richard Harris) Arr: Jim Webb (Dunhill)
WICHITA LINEMAN (Glen Campbell) Arr: Al de Lory (Cap)
YESTERDAY I HEARD THE RAIN (Tony Bennett) Arr: Torrie Zito (Col)

BEST ENGINEERED RECORDING (OTHER THAN CLASSICAL)
(Engineer's Award)
DAKTARI (album) (Shelly Manne) Eng: Dave Wiechman (Atl)
THE GOOD, THE BAD AND THE UGLY (album) (Hugo Montenegro) Eng: Richard Bogert (RCA)
MAN OF LA MANCHA (London Orig. Cast) (album) Engs: Jerry Boys, Peter Vince (Decca)
ROTARY CONNECTION TRIP I (album) (Rotary Connection) Eng: Doug Brand (Concept)
WICHITA LINEMAN (single) (Glen Campbell) Engs: Joe Polito, Hugh Davies (Cap)

BEST ALBUM COVER
(Awards to the Art Director, Photographer and/or Graphic Artist)
IVES; HOLIDAYS SYMPHONY (Bernstein cond. New York Philharmonic) Art Dirs: John Berg and Bob Cato - Des: Ron Coro - Photog: Don Huntstein (CBS)
RHINOCEROS (Rhinoceros) Art Dir: William S. Harvey - Graphic: Gene Szafran (Elektra)
ROAD SONG (Wes Montgomery) Art Dir: Sam Antupit - Photog: Pete Turner (A&M)
UNDERGROUND (Thelonius Monk) Art Dirs: John Berg, Richard Mantel - Photog: Horn/Griner Studio (Col)
WOW (Moby Grape) Art Dir. & Graphic: Bob Cato (Col)

BEST ALBUM NOTES
(Annotator's Award)
ANTHOLOGY OF INDIAN MUSIC, VOLUME ONE (Ravi Shankar, Ali Akbar Khan, Balachander) Ann: Richard Oliver (World Pacific)
ETHEL WATERS ON STAGE & SCREEN 1925-40 - Ann: Miles Kreuger (Col)
FRANCIS A. & EDWARD K. (Francis Albert Sinatra, Edward Kennedy Ellington) Ann: Stan Cornyn (Reprise)
JOHNNY CASH AT FOLSOM PRISON (Johnny Cash) Ann: Johnny Cash (Col)
PETE SEEGER'S GREATEST HITS (Pete Seeger) Ann: Pete Seeger (Col)

BEST CONTEMPORARY - POP VOCAL PERFORMANCE - FEMALE
ANGEL OF THE MORNING (single) Merrilee Rush (Bell)
DO YOU KNOW THE WAY TO SAN JOSE (single) Dionne Warwicke (Scepter)
FUNNY GIRL (album) Barbra Streisand (Col)
I SAY A LITTLE PRAYER (single) Aretha Franklin (Atlantic)
THOSE WERE THE DAYS (single) Mary Hopkin (Cap)

BEST CONTEMPORARY - POP VOCAL PERFORMANCE - MALE
HONEY (single) Bobby Goldsboro (UA)
LIGHT MY FIRE (single) Jose Feliciano (RCA)
LITTLE GREEN APPLES (single) O.C. Smith (CBS)
MAC ARTHUR PARK (single) Richard Harris (Dunhill)
WICHITA LINEMAN (single) Glen Campbell (Cap)

BEST CONTEMPORARY - POP PERFORMANCE, VOCAL DUO OR GROUP
CHILD IS FATHER TO THE MAN - Blood, Sweat & Tears (Col)
FOOL ON THE HILL - Sergio Mendes & Brasil '66 (A&M)
GOIN' OUT OF MY HEAD/CAN'T TAKE MY EYES OFF YOU (medley) The Lettermen (Cap)
HEY JUDE - The Beatles (Cap)
MRS. ROBINSON - Simon & Garfunkel (Col)
WOMAN, WOMAN (album) Gary Puckett & the Union Gap (Col)

BEST CONTEMPORARY - POP PERFORMANCE - CHORUS
ANGEL OF THE MORNING - Percy Faith Chorus and Orchestra (Col)
HONEY - Ray Conniff & the Singers (Col)
MAC ARTHUR PARK - Ray Charles Singers (Command)
MISSION IMPOSSIBLE/NORWEGIAN WOOD (medley) Alan Copeland Singers (ABC)
THIS GUY'S IN LOVE WITH YOU - Johnny Mann Singers (Lib)

BEST CONTEMPORARY - POP PERFORMANCE INSTRUMENTAL
CLASSICAL GAS - Mason Williams (WB)
ELEANOR RIGBY - Wes Montgomery (A&M)
THE GOOD, THE BAD AND THE UGLY - Hugo Montenegro (RCA)
GRAZING IN THE GRASS - Hugh Masekela (Uni)
HERE, THERE AND EVERYWHERE - Jose Feliciano (RCA)

BEST RHYTHM & BLUES VOCAL PERFORMANCE - FEMALE
CHAIN OF FOOLS (single) Aretha Franklin (Atlantic)
HE CALLED ME BABY (single) Ella Washington (S.Stg7)
LOVE MAKES A WOMAN (single) Barbara Acklin (Brnswc)
PIECE OF MY HEART (single) Erma Franklin (Shout)
SECURITY (single) Etta James (Cadet)

BEST RHYTHM & BLUES VOCAL PERFORMANCE - MALE

(SITTIN' ON) THE DOCK OF THE BAY (single) Otis Redding (Volt)
FOR ONCE IN MY LIFE (single) Stevie Wonder (Tamla)
(YOU KEEP ME) HANGIN' ON (single) Joe Simon (Sd. Stge 7)
I HEARD IT THROUGH THE GRAPEVINE (single) Marvin Gaye (Tamla)
WHO'S MAKING LOVE (single) Johnnie Taylor (Stax)

BEST RHYTHM & BLUES PERFORMANCE BY A DUO OR GROUP - VOCAL OR INSTRUMENTAL

CLOUD NINE - The Temptations (Gordy)
I THANK YOU - Sam & Dave (Stax)
PICKIN' WILD MOUNTAIN BERRIES - Peggy Scott and Jo Jo Benson (Plantation)
SWEET INSPIRATION - The Sweet Inspiration (Atlantic)
TIGHTEN UP - Archie Bell & The Drells (Atlantic)

BEST RHYTHM & BLUES SONG

(Songwriter's Award)
CHAIN OF FOOLS - Don Covay (Atlantic)
(SITTIN' ON) THE DOCK OF THE BAY - Otis Redding and Steve Cropper (Volt)
I WISH IT WOULD RAIN - Norman Whitfield, Barrett Strong, Roger Penzabene (Gordy)
PICKIN' WILD MOUNTAIN BERRIES - Edward Thomas, Bob McRee, Clifton Thomas (Plantation)
WHO'S MAKING LOVE - Homer Banks, Bettye Crutcher, Raymond Jackson, Donald Davis (Stax)

BEST COUNTRY VOCAL PERFORMANCE - FEMALE

BIG GIRLS DON'T CRY (single) Lynn Anderson (Chart)
COUNTRY GIRL (single) Dottie West (RCA)
D-I-V-O-R-C-E (single) Tammy Wynette (Epic)
HARPER VALLEY P.T.A. (single) Jeannie C. Riley (Plantation)
MY SON (single) Jan Howard (Decca)

BEST COUNTRY VOCAL PERFORMANCE - MALE

THE CARROLL COUNTY ACCIDENT (single) Porter Wagoner (RCA)
FOLSOM PRISON BLUES (single) Johnny Cash (Col)
I WANNA LIVE (single) Glen Campbell (Cap)
LITTLE GREEN APPLES (single) Roger Miller (Smash)
SKIP A ROPE (single) Henson Cargill (Monument)

BEST COUNTRY PERFORMANCE, DUO OR GROUP VOCAL OR INSTRUMENTAL

FOGGY MOUNTAIN BREAKDOWN - Flatt & Scruggs (Col)
IT'S MY TIME - The Everly Brothers (WB)
THE LOVERS - Bill Wilbourne and Kathy Morrison (UA)
MOUNTAIN DEW - Nashville Brass (RCA)
THROUGH THE EYES OF LOVE - Tompall & the Glaser Bros. (MGM)

BEST COUNTRY SONG

(Songwriter's Award)
D-I-V-O-R-C-E - Curly Putman and Bobby Braddock (Col)
HARPER VALLEY P.T.A. - Tom T. Hall (Plantation)
HONEY - Bobby Russell (Verve)
LITTLE GREEN APPLES - Bobby Russell (Smash)
SKIP A ROPE - Glenn Tubb, Jack Moran (Monument)

BEST SACRED PERFORMANCE

BEAUTIFUL ISLE OF SOMEWHERE - Jake Hess (RCA)
HOW GREAT THOU ART - Anita Bryant (Col)
I'LL FLY AWAY - Jim Bohi (Supreme)
102 STRINGS, VOL. 2 - Ralph Carmichael (Word)
WHISPERING HOPE - George Beverly Shea (RCA)
YOU'LL NEVER WALK ALONE (album) Elvis Presley (RCA)

BEST GOSPEL PERFORMANCE

THE FLORIDA BOYS SING KINDA COUNTRY - Florida Boys Quartet (Word)
FOR GOODNESS SAKE - Thrasher Bros. (Anchor)
A GREAT DAY - Oak Ridge Boys (Hrtwrmg)
THE HAPPY GOSPEL OF THE HAPPY GOODMANS - Happy Goodman Family (Word)
YOURS FAITHFULLY - Blackwood Bros. Quartet (RCA)

BEST SOUL GOSPEL PERFORMANCE

BREAD OF HEAVEN, Parts 1 & 2 - James Cleveland & Angelic Choir (Savoy)
LONG WALK TO D.C. - Staple Singers (Stax)
ONLY BELIEVE - Swan Silvertones (Scepter)
THE SOUL OF ME - Dottie Rambo (Hrtwrmg)
WAIT A LITTLE LONGER - Davis Sisters (Savoy)
WILLA DORSEY: THE WORLD'S MOST EXCITING GOSPEL SINGER - Willa Dorsey (Word)

BEST FOLK PERFORMANCE

BOTH SIDES NOW - Judy Collins (Elektra)
DID SHE MENTION MY NAME - Gordon Lightfoot (UA)
THE HANGMAN'S BEAUTIFUL DAUGHTER - The Incredible String Band (Elektra)
JOHN WESLEY HARDING - Bob Dylan (Col)
LATE AGAIN - Peter, Paul & Mary (WB-7)
THE UNICORN - Irish Rovers (Decca)

BEST INSTRUMENTAL THEME

(Composer's Award)
CLASSICAL GAS - Mason Williams (WB)
THE GOOD, THE BAD AND THE UGLY - Hugo Montenegro, Ennio Morricone (RCA)
THE ODD COUPLE - Neal Hefti (Dot)
ROSEMARY'S BABY - Christopher Komeda (Dot)
THEME FROM "THE FOX" - Lalo Schifrin (WB-7)

BEST ORIGINAL SCORE WRITTEN FOR A MOTION PICTURE OR TV SPECIAL

(Composer's Award)
BONNIE AND CLYDE - Charles Strouse (WB-7)
THE FOX - Lalo Schifrin (WB-7)
THE GRADUATE - Paul Simon, Dave Grusin (Col)
THE ODD COUPLE - Neal Hefti (Dot)
VALLEY OF THE DOLLS - Andre Previn (20th)

BEST SCORE FROM AN ORIGINAL CAST SHOW ALBUM

(Awards to the Composer and A&R Producer)
GEORGE M! - George M. Cohan - A&R: Thomas Shepard (Col)
HAIR - Gerome Ragni, James Rado, Galt MacDermott - A&R: Andy Wiswell (RCA)
THE HAPPY TIME - Fred Ebb. John Kander - A&R: George R. Marek, Andy Wiswell (RCA)
JACQUES BREL IS ALIVE AND WELL AND LIVING IN PARIS - Jacques Brel - A&R: Ed Kleban (Col)
YOUR OWN THING - Hal Hester, Danny Apolinar - A&R: George R. Marek, Andy Wiswell (RCA)

BEST COMEDY RECORDING
W.C. FIELDS ORIGINAL VOICE TRACKS FROM GREAT MOVIES - Produced by Gil Rodin (Decca)
FLIP WILSON, YOU DEVIL YOU - Flip Wilson (Atlantic)
HELLO DUMMY! Don Rickles (WB-7)
ROWAN & MARTIN LAUGH-IN - Dan Rowan and Dick Martin (Epic)
TO RUSSELL, MY BROTHER, WHOM I SLEPT WITH - Bill Cosby (WB-7)

BEST SPOKEN WORD RECORDING
THE CANTERBURY PILGRIMS - Martin Starkie (DGG)
I HAVE A DREAM - Rev. Martin Luther King, Jr. (20)
KENNEDY-NIXON: THE GREAT DEBATES, 1960 - Produced by Joel Heller (Col)
LONESOME CITIES (album) Rod McKuen (WB-7)
MURDER IN THE CATHEDRAL - Paul Scofield (Caedmon)

BEST INSTRUMENTAL JAZZ PERFORMANCE - SMALL GROUP OR SOLOIST WITH SMALL GROUP
BILL EVANS AT THE MONTREUX JAZZ FESTIVAL - Bill Evans Trio (Verve)
COMPADRES - Dave Brubeck, Gerry Mulligan (Col)
THE ELECTRIFYING. . .EDDIE HARRIS - Eddie Harris (Atl)
GARY BURTON QUARTET IN CONCERT - Gary Burton (RCA)
JAZZ FOR A SUNDAY AFTERNOON, VOL. 1 - Produced by Sonny Lester (Various) (Solid St.)
MILES IN THE SKY - Miles Davis, Herbie Hancock (Col)

BEST INSTRUMENTAL JAZZ PERFORMANCE - LARGE GROUP OR SOLOIST WITH LARGE GROUP
AND HIS MOTHER CALLED HIM BILL Duke Ellington (RCA)
CONCERTO FOR HERD - Woody Herman (Verve)
DOWN HERE ON THE GROUND - Wes Montgomery (A&M)
ELECTRIC BATH - Don Ellis (Col)
MERCY,MERCY - Buddy Rich (World Pac.)
UP IN ERROLL'S ROOM - Erroll Garner (Verve)

BEST CLASSICAL PERFORMANCE - ORCHESTRA
(Conductor's Award)
BACH: FOUR SUITES FOR ORCHESTRA - Nikolaus Harnoncourt cond. Concentus Musicus of Vienna (Telef)
BOULEZ CONDUCTS DEBUSSY - Pierre Boulez cond. New Philharmonia Orch. (Col)
MAHLER: SYMPHONY NO.6 IN A MINOR & SYMPHONY NO.9 IN D MAJOR - Leonard Bernstein cond. New York Philharmonic (Col)
MESSIAEN: TURANGALILA/TAKEMITSU: NOVEMBER STEPS - Seiji Ozawa cond. Toronto Symphony (RCA)
PROKOFIEFF: ROMEO & JULIET - Erich Leinsdorf cond. Boston Symphony (RCA)
RIMSKY-KORSAKOV: SCHEHERAZADE - Andre Previn cond. London Symphony (RCA)
STRAVINSKY: RITE OF SPRING - Seiji Ozawa cond. Chicago Symphony (RCA)

BEST CHAMBER MUSIC PERFORMANCE
BEETHOVEN: THE FIVE MIDDLE QUARTETS - Guarneri Quartet (RCA)
BEETHOVEN: TRIO NO. 3 IN C MINOR & MENDELSSOHN: TRIO NO. 1 IN D MINOR - Eugene Istomin, Isaac Stern, Leonard Rose (Col)
GABRIELI: CANZONI FOR BRASS, WINDS, STRINGS & ORGAN - E. Power Biggs with Edward Tarr Brass Ensemble & Gabrieli Consort, Vittorio Negri, cond. (Col)
HINDEMITH: SONATA FOR VIOLA & PIANO - Walter Trampler & Ronald Turini (RCA)
JULIAN BREAM AND HIS FRIENDS - Julian Bream & Cremona String Quartet (RCA)
MOZART: QUINTET K. 515/MENDELSSOHN: TRIO NO. 2 IN C MINOR - Jascha Heifetz, Gregor Piatigorsky, William Primrose, Leonard Pennario (RCA)
WORKS BY MOZART, BRAHMS, SCHUBERT, POULENC, HAIEFF, VILLA-LOBOS, COLGRASS - Boston Symphony Chamber Players (RCA)

BEST OPERA RECORDING
(Awards to Conductor and A&R Producer)
BERG: LULU - Karl Bohm cond. Orchestra of German Opera, Berlin (Soloists: Lear, Fischer-Dieskau) A&R: Dr. Hans Hirsch (DGG)
GINASTERA: BOMARZO - Julius Rudel cond. Opera Society of Washington (Soloists: Novoa, Turner, Penagos, Simon) A&R: Thomas Shepard (Col)
MOZART: COSI FAN TUTTE - Erich Leinsdorf cond. New Philharmonia Orch. & Ambrosian Opera Chorus (Soloists: Price, Troyanos, Raskin, Milnes, Shirley, Flagello) A&R: Richard Mohr (RCA)
STRAUSS: ELEKTRA - Georg Solti cond. Vienna Philharmonic (Soloists: Nilsson, Resnik, Collier, Krause, Stolze) A&R: John Culshaw (London)
WAGNER: DAS RHEINGOLD - Herbert von Karajan cond. Berlin Philharmonic (Soloists: Fischer-Dieskau, Stolze, Mitalvela, Veasey, Grobe, Keleman, Dominguez) A&R: Otto Gerdes (DGG)

BEST PERFORMANCE - INSTRUMENTAL SOLOIST(S) (CLASSICAL)
BERG: CONCERTO FOR VIOLIN & ORCHESTRA - Arthur Grumiaux (Markevitch cond. Concertgebouw Orch.) (Philips)
BUSONI: CONCERTO FOR PIANO WITH MALE CHORUS - John Ogdon (Daniell Revenaugh cond. Royal Philharmonic) (Angel)
CARTER: CONCERTO FOR PIANO - Jacob Lateiner (Leinsdorf cond. Boston Symphony) (RCA)
DANCES OF DOWLAND - Julian Bream (RCA)
HOROWITZ ON TELEVISION - Vladimir Horowitz (Col)
RACHMANINOFF: CONCERTO NO. 3 IN D MINOR FOR PIANO & ORCHESTRA - Alexis Weissenberg (Pretre cond. Chicago Symphony) (RCA)
SCHUMANN: CONCERTO IN A MINOR FOR PIANO & ORCHESTRA - Artur Rubinstein (Giulini cond. Chicago Symphony) (RCA)

BEST CHORAL PERFORMANCE (OTHER THAN OPERA)
(Awards to Choral and Orchestra Conductors)
BERLIOZ: REQUIEM - Charles Munch cond. Bavarian Radio Chorus & Symphony (DGG)
THE GLORY OF GABRIELI - Vittorio Negri cond./Gregg Smith Singers/Texas Boys Choir, George Bragg, Dir./Edward Tarr Ensemble (with E. Power Biggs) (Col)
HANDEL: SOLOMON - Stephen Simon cond. Vienna Jeunesse Chorus & Vienna Volksoper Orch (with Shirley-Quirk, Endich, Brooks, Young) (RCA)
HAYDN: THE CREATION - Abraham Kaplan cond. Camerata Singers/Leonard Bernstein cond. New York Philharmonic (Col)
MOZART: REQUIEM - Colin Davis cond. John Alldis Choir & B.B.C. Symphony (Philips)
ORFF: CARMINA BURANA - Eugen Jochum cond. Schoenberg Children's Chorus/Chorus & Orch. of German Opera, Berlin (DGG)
PFITZNER: VON DEUTSCHER SEELE - Joseph Keilberth cond. Bavarian Symphony Chorus and Orch. (DGG)
SHOSTAKOVICH: SYMPHONY NO. 2 IN C MAJOR & SYMPHONY NO. 3 IN E FLAT MAJOR - John McCarthy cond. Ambrosian Singers/Morton Gould cond. Royal Philharmonia (RCA)

BEST VOCAL SOLOIST PERFORMANCE - CLASSICAL
MAHLER: KINDERTOTENLIEDER & SONGS OF A WAYFARER - Janet Baker (Barbirolli cond. Halle Orch.) (Angel)
ROSSINI RARITIES - Montserrat Caballe (Cillario cond. RCA Italiana Opera Orch. & Chorus) (RCA)
SCHUMANN: SONGS - Dietrich Fischer-Dieskau (Jorg Demus, Pianist)

(DGG)
SONGS OF POULENC - Gerard Souzay (Dalton Baldwin, Pianist) (RCA)
SONGS OF ANDALUCIA - Victoria de los Angeles (ARS Musicae Ensemble of Barcelona) (Angel)
VERRETT IN OPERA - Shirley Verrett (Pretre cond. RCA Italiana Opera Orch.) (RCA)

BEST ENGINEERED RECORDING - CLASSICAL
(Engineer's Award)
BRITTEN: BILLY BUDD (Britten cond. London Symphony/Soloists: Glossop, Pears, Shirley-Quirk, Brannigan) Engs: Gordon Parry, Kenneth Wilkenson (London)
MAHLER: SYMPHONY NO. 9 IN D MAJOR - (Georg Solti cond. London Symphony) Eng: Gordon Parry (London)
MESSIAEN: TURANGALILA/TAKEMITSU: NOVEMBER STEPS (Ozawa cond. Toronto Symphony) Eng: Bernard Keville (RCA)
PROKOFIEFF: ROMEO & JULIET (Leinsdorf cond. Boston Symphony) Eng: Anthony Salvatore (RCA)
RACHMANINOFF: CONCERTO NO. 3 IN D MINOR FOR PIANO & ORCHESTRA (Weissenberg/Pretre cond. Chicago Symphony) Eng: Michael Moran (RCA)
STRAVINSKY: RITE OF SPRING (Ozawa cond. Chicago Symphony) Eng: Bernard Keville (RCA)
VERDI: ERNANI (Schippers cond. RCA Italiana Opera Orch. & Chorus) Eng: Anthony Salvatore (RCA)

1969

RECORD OF THE YEAR
(Awards to the Artist and A&R Producer)
AQUARIUS/LET THE SUNSHINE IN - 5th Dimension - A&R: Bones Howe (Soul City)
A BOY NAMED SUE - Johnny Cash - A&R: Bob Johnston (Col)
IS THAT ALL THERE IS - Peggy Lee - A&R: Jerry Leiber, Mike Stoller (Cap)
LOVE THEME FROM ROMEO & JULIET - Henry Mancini - A&R: Joe Reisman (RCA)
SPINNING WHEEL - Blood, Sweat & Tears - A&R: James William Guercio (Col)

ALBUM OF THE YEAR
(Awards to the Artist and A&R Producer)
ABBEY ROAD - The Beatles - A&R: George Martin (Apple)
THE AGE OF AQUARIUS - 5th Dimension - A&R: Bones Howe (Soul City)
BLOOD, SWEAT & TEARS - Blood, Sweat & Tears - A&R: James William Guercio (Col)
CROSBY, STILLS & NASH - Crosby, Stills & Nash - A&R: David Crosby, Stephen Stills, Graham Nash (Atl)
JOHNNY CASH AT SAN QUENTIN - Johnny Cash - A&R: Bob Johnston (Col)

SONG OF THE YEAR
(Songwriter's Award)
GAMES PEOPLE PLAY - Joe South
L'LL NEVER FALL IN LOVE AGAIN - Burt Bacharach, Hal David
RAINDROPS KEEP FALLIN' ON MY HEAD - Burt Bacharach, Hal David
SPINNING WHEEL - David Clayton Thomas
A TIME FOR US (LOVE THEME FROM ROMEO & JULIET) - Larry Kusik, Eddie Snyder, Nino Rota

BEST NEW ARTIST OF 1969
CHICAGO (Col)
CROSBY, STILLS & NASH (Atl)
LED ZEPPELIN (Atl)
OLIVER (Crewe)
NEON PHILHARMONIC (WB)

BEST INSTRUMENTAL ARRANGEMENT
(Arranger's Award)
LOVE THEME FROM ROMEO & JULIET (Mancini) Arr: Henry Mancini (RCA)
MIDNIGHT COWBOY (Ferrante & Teicher) Arrs: Arthur Ferrante, Lou Teicher (Lib)
WALKING IN SPACE (Quincy Jones) Arr: Quincy Jones (A&M)
VARIATIONS ON A THEME BY ERIC SATIE (Blood, Sweat & Tears) Arr: Dick Halligan (Col)

BEST ARRANGEMENT ACCOMPANYING VOCALIST(S)
(Arranger's Award)
AQUARIUS/LET THE SUNSHINE IN (5th Dimension) Arrs: Bill Holman, Bob Alcivar, Bones Howe (Soul City)
IS THAT ALL THERE IS (Peggy Lee) Arr: Randy Newman (Cap)
I'VE GOTTA BE ME (Tony Bennett) Arr: Torrie Zito (Col)
SPINNING WHEEL (Blood, Sweat & Tears) Arr: Fred Lipsius (Col)
YOU'VE MADE ME SO VERY HAPPY (Blood, Sweat & Tears) Arrs: Al Kooper, Fred Lipsius (Col)

BEST ENGINEERED RECORDING (OTHER THAN CLASSICAL)
(Engineer's Award)
ABBEY ROAD (The Beatles) Engs: Geoff Emerick, Phillip McDonald (Apple)
THE AGE OF AQUARIUS (5th Dimension) Eng: Bones Howe (Soul City)
BLOOD, SWEAT & TEARS (Blood, Sweat & Tears) Eng: Roy Halee, Fred Catero (Col)
MOOG GROOVE (Electronic Concept Orch.) Engs: Bruce Swedien, Doug Brand, Hans Wurman, Chuck Lishon (Limelight)
VELVET VOICES & BOLD BRASS (Anita Kerr Singers) Engs: Lee Herschberg, Larry Cox, Chuck Britz (Para)

BEST ALBUM COVER
(Awards to the Art Director, Photographer and/or Graphic Artist)
AMERICA THE BEAUTIFUL (Gary McFarland) Painting: Evelyn J. Kelbish - Graphics: David Stahlberg (Skye)
BLIND FAITH (Blind Faith) Art Dir. & Photog: Bob Seideman (Atco)
LED ZEPPELIN II (Led Zeppelin) Art Work by David Juniper (Atl)
PIDGEON (Pidgeon) Art Dir: Tom Lazarus - Photog: Gene Brownell - Des: Bill Gordon (Decca)
RICHARD PRYOR (Richard Pryor) Art Dir: Gary Burden - Photog: Henry Diltz (Dove)

BEST ALBUM NOTES
(Annotator's Award)
CHICAGO MESS AROUND (Johnny Dodds) Ann: John Dodds, II (Milestone)
DAVID'S ALBUM (Joan Baez) Ann: Joan Baez (Vanguard)
JOHN HARTFORD (J. Hartford) Ann: John Hartford (RCA)
MABEL MERCER & BOBBY SHORT AT TOWN HALL - Ann: Rex Reed (Atl)
NASHVILLE SKYLINE (Bob Dylan) Ann: Johnny Cash (Col)

BEST CONTEMPORARY VOCAL PERFORMANCE - FEMALE
IS THAT ALL THERE IS (single) Peggy Lee (Cap)
JOHNNY ONE TIME (single) Brenda Lee (Decca)
PUT A LITTLE LOVE IN YOUR HEART (single) Jackie DeShannon (Lib-UA)
SON OF A PREACHER MAN (single) Dusty Springfield (Atl)
THIS GIRL'S IN LOVE WITH YOU (single) Dionne Warwicke (Scepter)
WITH PEN IN HAND (single) Vikki Carr (Lib)

BEST CONTEMPORARY VOCAL PERFORMANCE - MALE
EVERYBODY'S TALKIN' (track) Harry Nilsson (UA)
GAMES PEOPLE PLAY (single) Joe South (Cap)
GITARZAN (single) Ray Stevens (Monument)
MY WAY (single) Frank Sinatra (WB)
RAINDROPS KEEP FALLIN' ON MY HEAD (single) B.J. Thomas (Scepter)

BEST CONTEMPORARY VOCAL PERFORMANCE BY A GROUP
ABBEY ROAD - The Beatles (Apple)
BLOOD, SWEAT & TEARS - Blood, Sweat & Tears (Col)
AQUARIUS/LET THE SUNSHINE IN - 5th Dimension (Sl Cty)
CROSBY, STILLS & NASH - Crosby, Stills & Nash (Atl)
MORNING GIRL - Neon Philharmonic (WB)

BEST CONTEMPORARY PERFORMANCE BY A CHORUS
ANGEL OF THE MORNING - Living Voices (RCA)
JEAN - Ray Conniff & the Singers (Col)
LOVE THEME FROM ROMEO & JULIET - Percy Faith Orch. & Chorus (Col)
MAC ARTHUR PARK - Brooks Arthur Ensemble (Verve)
SLICES OF LIFE - Ray Charles Singers (Command)

BEST CONTEMPORARY INSTRUMENTAL PERFORMANCE
AREA CODE 615 - Area Code 615 (Polydor)
LOVE THEME FROM ROMEO & JULIET - Henry Mancini (RCA)
MIDNIGHT COWBOY - Ferrante & Teicher (Lib-UA)
WITH LOVE - Boots Randolph (Monument)
VARIATIONS ON A THEME BY ERIC SATIE - Blood, Sweat & Tears (Col)

BEST CONTEMPORARY SONG
(Songwriter's Award)
GAMES PEOPLE PLAY - Joe South
IN THE GHETTO - Mac Davis
JEAN - Rod McKuen
RAINDROPS KEEP FALLIN' ON MY HEAD - Burt Bacharach, Hal David
SPINNING WHEEL - David Clayton Thomas

BEST R&B VOCAL PERFORMANCE, FEMALE
FOOLISH FOOL (single) Dee Dee Warwick (Merc)
THE HUNTER (album) Tina Turner (Blue Thumb)
SHARE YOUR LOVE WITH ME (single) Aretha Franklin (Atl)
YESTERDAY (single) Ruth Brown (Skye)
YOU GOTTA PAY THE PRICE (single) Gloria Taylor (Silver Fox)

BEST R&B VOCAL PERFORMANCE, MALE
DOING HIS THING (single) Ray Charles (Tang)
THE CHOKIN' KIND (single) Joe Simon (Sd. Stg.)
ICE MAN COMETH (album) Jerry Butler (Merc)
LIVE & WELL (album) B.B. King (ABC)
YOUR GOOD THING (IS ABOUT TO END) (single) Lou Rawls (Cap)

BEST R&B VOCAL PERFORMANCE BY A DUO OR GROUP
BACKFIELD IN MOTION - Mel & Tim (Scepter)
FRIENDSHIP TRAIN - Gladys Knight & The Pips (Mtn)
IT'S YOUR THING - The Isley Brothers (T-Neck)
COLOR HIM FATHER - The Winstons (Metromedia)
SOULSHAKE - Peggy Scott, Jo Jo Benson (SSS)

BEST R&B INSTRUMENTAL PERFORMANCE
A BLACK MAN'S SOUL - Ike Turner (Pompeii)
GAMES PEOPLE PLAY - King Curtis (Atco)
TRASH TALKIN' - Albert Collins (Imperial)
WHAT DOES IT TAKE - Walker & The All Stars (Soul)
WORKIN' ON A GROOVY THING - Richard "Groove" Holmes (World Pac.)

BEST R&B SONG
(Songwriter's Award)
BACKFIELD IN MOTION - Herbert McPherson, Melvin Harden
COLOR HIM FATHER - Richard Spencer
I'D RATHER BE AN OLD MAN'S SWEETHEART - Clarence Carter, George Jackson, Raymond Moore
IT'S YOUR THING - Rudolph Isley, O. Kelly Isley, Jr., Ronnie Isley
ONLY THE STRONG SURVIVE - Kenny Gamble, Leon Huff, Jerry Butler

BEST SOUL GOSPEL
CASSIETTA - Cassietta George (Audio Gosp.)
COME ON AND SEE ABOUT ME - James Cleveland and the Southern California Choir (Savoy)
GUIDE ME, O THOU GREAT JEHOVAH - Mahalia Jackson (Col)
PRECIOUS MEMORIES - Sister Rosetta Tharpe (Savoy)
OH HAPPY DAY - Edwin Hawkins Singers (Buddah)

BEST COUNTRY VOCAL PERFORMANCE, FEMALE
BACK SIDE OF DALLAS (single) Jeannie C. Riley (Plantation)
I FALL TO PIECES (single) Diana Trask (Par)
RIBBON OF DARKNESS (single) Connie Smith (RCA)
STAND BY YOUR MAN (album) Tammy Wynette (Epic)
THAT'S A NO NO (single) Lynn Anderson (Chart)

BEST COUNTRY VOCAL PERFORMANCE, MALE
ALL I HAVE TO OFFER YOU IS ME (single) Charley Pride (RCA)
ARE YOU FROM DIXIE (single) Jerry Reed (RCA)
A BOY NAMED SUE (single) Johnny Cash (Col)
FROM HEAVEN TO HEARTACHE (single) Bobby Lewis (UA)
SPRING (single) Clay Hart (Metromedia)

BEST COUNTRY PERFORMANCE BY A DUO OR GROUP
CALIFORNIA GIRL - Tompall & Glaser Bros. (MGM)
JUST SOMEONE I USED TO KNOW - Porter Wagoner & Dolly Parton (RCA)
MAC ARTHUR PARK - Waylon Jennings & The Kimberlys (RCA)
RINGS OF GOLD - Dottie West & Don Gibson (RCA)
WISH I DIDN'T HAVE TO MISS YOU - Jack Greene & Jeannie Seely (Decca)

BEST COUNTRY INSTRUMENTAL PERFORMANCE
THE HITS OF CHARLEY PRIDE - Tommy Allsup & The Nashville Survey (Metromedia)
LOVIN' SEASON - Floyd Cramer (RCA)
THE NASHVILLE BRASS FEATURING DANNY DAVIS PLAY MORE NASHVILLE SOUNDS - Danny Davis & The Nashville Brass (RCA)
NASHVILLE SKYLINE RAG - Bob Dylan (Col)
SOLID GOLD '69 - Chet Atkins (RCA)

BEST COUNTRY SONG
(Songwriter's Award)
ALL I HAVE TO OFFER YOU IS ME - Dallas Frazier, A.L. Owens
A BOY NAMED SUE - Shel Silverstein
STAND BY YOUR MAN - Tammy Wynette, Billy Sherrill
THE THINGS THAT MATTER - Don Sumner
YOU GAVE ME A MOUNTAIN - Marty Robbins

BEST SACRED PERFORMANCE
(Non-Classical)
AIN'T THAT BEAUTIFUL SINGING - Jake Hess (RCA)
HE TOUCHED ME - Bill Gaither Trio (Hrtwrmg)
HOLY, HOLY, HOLY - Tennessee Ernie Ford (Cap)
I BELIEVE - George Beverly Shea (RCA)
WHISPERING HOPE - Connie Smith & Nat Stuckey (RCA)

BEST GOSPEL PERFORMANCE
THE BEST IS YET TO COME - The LeFevres (Canaan)
IN GOSPEL COUNTRY - Porter Wagoner & the Blackwood Bros. (RCA)
IT'S HAPPENING - The Oak Ridge Boys (Hrtwrmg)
THIS HAPPY HOUSE - Happy Goodman Family (Word)
THIS IS MY VALLEY - The Singing Rambos (Hrtwrmg)

BEST FOLK PERFORMANCE
ANY DAY NOW - Joan Baez (Vanguard)
ATLANTIS - Donovan (Epic)
BIRD ON A WIRE - Judy Collins (Elektra)
CLOUDS - Joni Mitchell (WB)
DAY IS DONE - Peter, Paul & Mary (WB)
YOUNG VS. OLD - Pete Seeger (Col)

BEST INSTRUMENTAL THEME
(Composer's Award)
GROOVY GRUBWORM - Harlow Wilcox, Bobby Warren
MACKENNA'S GOLD - Quincy Jones
MEMPHIS UNDERGROUND - Herbie Mann
MIDNIGHT COWBOY - John Barry
QUENTIN'S THEME - Robert Cobert

BEST ORIGINAL SCORE WRITTEN FOR A MOTION PICTURE OR TV SPECIAL
(Composer's Award)
BUTCH CASSIDY & THE SUNDANCE KID - Burt Bacharach (A&M)
THE LOST MAN - Quincy Jones (Uni)
MACKENNA'S GOLD - Quincy Jones (RCA)
ME, NATALIE - Henry Mancini (Col)
YELLOW SUBMARINE - John Lennon, Paul McCartney, George Harrison, George Martin (Cap)

BEST SCORE FROM AN ORIGINAL CAST SHOW ALBUM
(Awards to Composers and A&R Producer)
DAMES AT SEA - George Haimsohn, Robin Miller, Jim J. Wise - A&R: Thomas Shepard (Col)
OH! CALCUTTA! - Robert Dennis, Stanley Walden, Peter Schickle - A&R: Henry Jerome (Aidart)
PROMISES, PROMISES - Burt Bacharach, Hal David - A&R: Henry Jerome, Phil Ramone (Lib)
1776 - Sherman Edwards - A&R: Thomas Shepard (Col)
ZORBA - John Kander, Fred Ebb - A&R: Richard C. Jones (Cap)

BEST RECORDING FOR CHILDREN
CHITTY CHITTY BANG BANG - Do-Re-Mi Chorus (Kapp)
FOLK TALES OF THE TRIBES OF AFRICA - Eartha Kitt (Caedmon)
FOR ALL MY LITTLE FRIENDS - Tiny Tim (WB)
PETER, PAUL & MOMMY - Peter, Paul & Mary (WB)
YELLOW SUBMARINE - Richard Wolfe Children's Chorus (RCA)

BEST COMEDY RECORDING
BERKELEY CONCERT - Lenny Bruce (WB)
BILL COSBY - Bill Cosby (Uni)
DON RICKLES SPEAKS! - Don Rickles (WB)
LAUGH-IN '69 - Carolyn Raskin, Producer (WB)
W.C. FIELDS ON RADIO - Bruce Lundvall, A&R Producer (Col)

BEST SPOKEN WORD RECORDING
THE GREAT WHITE HOPE - James Earl Jones (Tetra.)
HOME TO THE SEA - Jesse Pearson, Narrator (WB)
MAN ON THE MOON - Walter Cronkite (WB)
ROBERT F. KENNEDY: A MEMORIAL - A&R: Thomas Shepard and Joel Heller (Col)
WE LOVE YOU, CALL COLLECT - Art Linkletter & Diane (Word/Cap)

BEST INSTRUMENTAL JAZZ PERFORMANCE - SMALL GROUP OR SOLOIST WITH SMALL GROUP
(7 or less)
THE 86 YEARS OF EUBIE BLAKE - Eubie Blake (Col)
THE GREAT OSCAR PETERSON ON PRESTIGE - Oscar Peterson (Prestige)
IN A SILENT WAY - Miles Davis (Col)
MEMPHIS UNDERGROUND - Herbie Mann (Atl)
VIOLIN SUMMIT - Stephane Grappelly, Stuff Smith, Sven Asmussen, Jean Luc-Ponty (Prestige)
WHAT'S NEW - Bill Evans, Jeremy Steig (Verve)
WILLOW WEEP FOR ME - Wes Montgomery (Verve)

BEST INSTRUMENTAL JAZZ PERFORMANCE LARGE GROUP OR SOLOIST WITH LARGE GROUP
(8 or more)
AMERICA THE BEAUTIFUL - Gary McFarland (Skye)
BUDDY & SOUL - Buddy Rich Orch. (World Pac)
CENTRAL PARK NORTH - Thad Jones, Mel Lewis (SISt)
LIGHT MY FIRE - Woody Herman (Cadet)
THE NEW DON ELLIS BAND GOES UNDERGROUND - Don Ellis (Col)
THE MUSIC OF HOAGY CARMICHAEL - Bob Wilber (Monmouth)
STANDING OVATION - Count Basie (Para)
WALKING IN SPACE - Quincy Jones (A&M)

ALBUM OF THE YEAR, CLASSICAL
(Awards to the Artist and A&R Producer)
BERIO: SINFONIA - Luciano Berio cond. New York Philharmonic & Swingle Singers - A&R: Thomas Z. Shepard (Col)
BOULEZ CONDUCTS BERG (THREE PIECES FOR ORCHESTRA/CHAMBER CONCERTO/ALTENBERG LIEDER) Pierre Boulez cond. BBC Symphony (Baremboim, Gawriloff, Lukomska) A&R: Thomas Z. Shepard (Col)
BOULEZ CONDUCTS DEBUSSY, VOL.2 "IMAGES POUR ORCHESTRE" - Pierre Boulez cond. Cleveland Orch. - A&R: Thomas Z. Shepard (Col)

GABRIELI: ANTIPHONAL MUSIC OF GABRIELI (CANZONI FOR BRASS CHOIRS) - The Philadelphia, Cleveland and Chicago Brass Ensembles - A&R: Andrew Kazdin (Col)
STRAUSS: ALSO SPRACH ZARATHUSTRA - Zubin Mehta cond. Los Angeles Philharmonic - A&R: Raymond Minshull (London)
SWITCHED-ON BACH (Virtuoso Electronic Performance of BRANDENBURG CONCERTO NO. 3/AIR ON A G STRING/JESU, JOY OF MAN'S DESTINY, etc.) - performed on Moog Synthesizer - Walter Carlos - A&R: Rachel Elkind (Col)

BEST CLASSICAL PERFORMANCE, ORCHESTRA
(Conductor's Award)
BARTOK: MUSIC FOR STRINGS, PERCUSSION & CELESTA - Pierre Boulez cond. BBC Symphony (Col)
BOULEZ CONDUCTS DEBUSSY, VOL.2 "IMAGES POUR ORCHESTRE" - Pierre Boulez cond. Cleveland Orchestra (Col)
RAVEL: RAPSODIE ESPAGNOLE/MOTHER GOOSE SUITE/ALBORADA DEL GRACIOSO/INTRODUCTION & ALLEGRO - Jean Martinon cond. Chicago Symphony (RCA)
STRAUSS: ALSO SPRACH ZARATHUSTRA - Zubin Mehta cond. Los Angeles Philharmonic (London)
WAGNER: GREAT ORCHESTRAL HIGHLIGHTS FROM "THE RING OF THE NIBELUNGS" - George Szell cond. Cleveland Orchestra (Col)

BEST CHAMBER MUSIC PERFORMANCE
BACH & VIVALDI SONATAS FOR LUTE & HARPSICHORD - Julian Bream, George Malcolm (RCA)
BEETHOVEN: TRIOS FOR STRINGS - Grumiaux Trio (Philips)
BRAHMS: QUARTETS FOR PIANO & STRINGS (3)/SCHUMANN: QUINTET IN E FLAT MAJOR FOR PIANO & STRINGS - Artur Rubinstein & Guarneri Quartet (RCA)
BRAHMS: SONATAS IN E MINOR & F MAJOR FOR CELLO AND PIANO - Jacqueline De Pre and Daniel Barenboim (Angel)
GABRIELI: ANTIPHONAL MUSIC OF GABRIELI (CANZONI FOR BRASS CHOIRS) - The Philadelphia, Cleveland and Chicago Brass Ensembles (Col)
PROKOFIEV: SONATAS FOR VIOLIN & PIANO - Itzhak Perlman, Vladimir Ashkenazy (RCA)
SHOSTAKOVICH: STRING QUARTETS (COMPLETE) Borodin Quartet (Seraphim)

BEST CLASSICAL PERFORMANCE - INSTRUMENTAL SOLOIST(S) (WITH OR WITHOUT ORCHESTRA)
BACH: SONATAS & PARTITAS FOR SOLO VIOLIN - Henryk Szeryng (DGG)
DVORAK: CONCERTO IN B MINOR FOR CELLO - Mstislav Rostropovich, Cello (Karajan cond. Berlin Philharmonic) (DGG)
GILELS AT CARNEGIE HALL - Emil Gilels (Melyd)
IVES: SONATA NO.2 "CONCORD MASS." - John Kirkpatrick (Col)
RAVEL: INTRODUCTION & ALLEGRO FOR HARP & STRINGS - Edward Druzinsky, Harp (Martinon cond. Chicago Symphony) (RCA)
SWITCHED-ON BACH - Walter Carlos, Moog Synthesizer (Col)

BEST OPERA RECORDING
(Awards to Conductor and A&R Producer)
CAVALLI: L'ORMINDO - Raymond Leppard cond. London Philharmonic (Soloists: Wakefield, van Bork, Howells, Berbie, Cuenod; Glyndebourne Festival Opera) A&R: Michael Bremner (Argo)
MOZART: THE MARRIAGE OF FIGARO - Karl Bohm cond. Chorus & Orch. of German Opera (Soloists: Prey, Mathis, Janowitz, Fischer-Dieskau) A&R: Gustav Rudolf Sellner (DGG)
STRAUSS: ARIADNE AUF NAXOS - Rudolf Kempe cond. Dresden State Opera (Soloists: Janowitz, King, Zylis-Gara, Geszty, Adam) A&R: R. Kinloch Anderson and Eberhard Geiler (Angel)
STRAUSS: SALOME - Erich Leinsdorf cond. London Symphony (Soloists: Caballe, Milnes, Lewis, Resnik, King) A&R: Richard Mohr (RCA)
VERDI: LA TRAVIATA - Lorin Maazel cond. Orch. & Chorus of Deutsche Opera Berlin (Soloists: Lorengar, Aragall, Fischer-Dieskau) A&R: John Mordler (London)
VERDI: OTELLO - Sir John Barbirolli cond. New Philharmonia Orch. & Chorus (Soloists: McCracken, Fischer-Dieskau, Jones, Di Stasio) A&R: R. Kinloch Anderson (Angel)
WAGNER: SIEGFRIED - Herbert von Karajan cond. Berlin Philharmonic (Soloists: Thomas, Stewart, Stolze, Dernesch, Keleman, Dominguez, Gayer, Ridderbusch) A&R: Otto Gerdes (DGG)

BEST CHORAL PERFORMANCE. (OTHER THAN OPERA)
(Grammys to Conductor and Choral Director)
BACH: MASS IN B MINOR - Vienna Boys Choir & Chorus Viennensis - Hans Gillesberger, cond./Concentus Musicus - Nikolaus Harnoncourt, cond. (Telefunken)
BERIO: SINFONIA - Swingle Singers, Ward Swingle, Choral Master/New York Philharmonic, Luciano Berio, cond. (Col)
BERLIOZ: ROMEO ET JULIETTE - John Alldis Choir, London Symphony Orchestra & Chorus - Colin Davis, cond. (Philips)
BILLINGS: THE CONTINENTAL HARMONY - Gregg Smith Singers, Gregg Smith, cond. (Col)
DELIUS: SONGS OF SUNSET - Royal Liverpool Philharmonic Choir; Edmund Walters, cond. Royal Liverpool Philharmonic Orch.; Charles Groves cond. (Angel)
HENZE: THE RAFT OF THE FRIGATE "MEDUSA" Choirs of North German Radio/Berlin Radio/Boy's Chorus of St. Nicolai & North German Radio Symphony - Hans Werner Henze, cond. (DGG)
VAUGHAN WILLIAMS: SYMPHONY NO.1 (A SEA SYMPHONY) London Philharmonic Choir - Frederick Jackson, Choral Master/London Philharmonic - Adrian Boult, cond. (Angel)

BEST VOCAL SOLOIST PERFORMANCE, CLASSICAL
BACH & HANDEL ARIAS (EXCERPTS FROM MAGNIFICAT, CHRISTMAS ORATORIO, ST. MATTHEW PASSION, MESSIAH, RODELINDA) - Marilyn Horne (Lewis cond. Vienna Cantata Orch.) (London)
BARBER: TWO SCENES FROM "ANTONY & CLEOPATRA"/KNOXVILLE: SUMMER OF 1915 - Leontyne Price (Schippers cond. New Philharmonia) (RCA)
BERG: ALTENBERG LIEDER - Halina Lukomska (Boulez cond. London Symphony in album "Boulez Conducts Berg") (Col)
BRAHMS: FOUR SERIOUS SONGS - Sherrill Milnes (From BRAHMS: REQUIEM recording by Erich Leinsdorf and Boston Symphony) (RCA)
BRITTEN: HOLY SONNETS OF DONNE, SONGS & PROVERBS OF BLAKE - Peter Pears, Dietrich Fischer-Dieskau (London)
MAHLER: DES KNABEN WUNDERHORN - Elisabeth Schwarzkopf & Dietrich Fischer-Dieskau (Szell cond. London Symphony) (Angel)
A MOST UNUSUAL SONG RECITAL (Beethoven, Rossini, Brahms, Reger, R. Strauss) Christa Ludwig, Walter Berry (Moore, Accom.) (Seraphim)
SCENES & ARIAS FROM FRENCH OPERA Beverly Sills (Mackerras cond. Royal Philharmonic) (Westminster)
STRAUSS (RICHARD): NINETEEN EARLY SONGS Dietrich Fischer-Dieskau (Gerald Moore, accomp.) (Angel)

BEST ENGINEERED RECORDING, CLASSICAL
(Engineer's Award)
BERIO: SINFONIA (Berio cond. New York Philharmonic, Swingle Singers) Engs: Fred Plaut, Ed Michalski (Col)
BOULEZ CONDUCTS DEBUSSY, VOL.2 "IMAGES POUR ORCHESTRE" (Boulez cond. Cleveland Orchestra) Engs: Edwart T. Graham, Arthur Kendy (Col)
GABRIELI: ANTIPHONAL MUSIC OF GABRIELI (CANZONI FOR BRASS CHOIRS) (Philadelphia, Cleveland & Chicago Brass Ensembles) Engs: Edward T. Graham, Milton Cherin (Col/Odyssey)
KHACHATURIAN: SYMPHONY NO.3/RIMSKY-KORSAKOV: RUSSIAN EASTER OVERTURE (Stokowski cond. Chicago Symphony) Eng: Paul Goodman (RCA)
MAHLER: SYMPHONY NO.1 (Ormandy cond. Philadelphia Symphony) Eng: Edwin Begley (RCA)

SWITCHED-ON BACH (Walter Carlos) Eng: Walter Carlos (Col)

1970

RECORD OF THE YEAR
(Grammys to the Artist and A&R Producer)

BRIDGE OVER TROUBLED WATER - Simon & Garfunkel - A&R; Paul Simon, Art Garfunkel, Roy Halee (Col)
CLOSE TO YOU - Carpenters - A&R: Jack Daugherty (A&M)
EVERYTHING IS BEAUTIFUL - Ray Stevens - A&R: Ray Stevens (Barnaby)
FIRE AND RAIN - James Taylor - A&R: Peter Asher (WB)
LET IT BE - The Beatles - A&R: George Martin (Apple)

ALBUM OF THE YEAR
(Grammys to the Artist and A&R Producer)

BRIDGE OVER TROUBLED WATER - Simon & Garfunkel - A&R: Paul Simon, Art Garfunkel, Roy Halee (Col)
CHICAGO - Chicago - A&R: James William Guercio (Col)
CLOSE TO YOU - Carpenters - A&R: Jack Daugherty (A&M)
DEJA VU - Crosby, Stills, Nash & Young - A&R: Crosby, Stills, Nash & Young (A&M)
ELTON JOHN - Elton John - A&R: Gus Dudgeon (Uni)
SWEET BABY JAMES - James Taylor - A&R: Peter Asher (WB)

SONG OF THE YEAR
(Songwriter's Award)

BRIDGE OVER TROUBLED WATER - Paul Simon
EVERYTHING IS BEAUTIFUL - Ray Stevens
FIRE AND RAIN - James Taylor
LET IT BE - John Lennon, Paul McCartney
WE'VE ONLY JUST BEGUN - Roger Nichols, Paul Williams

BEST NEW ARTIST OF THE YEAR

CARPENTERS (A&M)
ELTON JOHN (Uni)
MELBA MOORE (Merc)
ANNE MURRAY (Cap)
THE PARTRIDGE FAMILY (Bell)

BEST INSTRUMENTAL ARRANGEMENT
(Arranger's Award)

BITCHES BREW (M. Davis) Arr: Miles Davis (Col)
GULA MATARI (Q. Jones) Arr: Quincy Jones (A&M)
THE MAGIC BUS ATE MY DONUT (Don Ellis) Arr: Fred Selden (Col)
OVERTURE FROM TOMMY (Assembled Multitude) Arr: Tom Sellers (Atl)
THEME FROM MEDICAL CENTER (Lalo Schifrin) Arr: Lalo Schifrin (MGM)
THEME FROM Z (Mancini) Arr: Henry Mancini (RCA)

BEST ARRANGEMENT ACCOMPANYING VOCALIST(S)
(Arranger's Award)

BRIDGE OVER TROUBLED WATER (Simon & Garfunkel) Arr: Paul Simon, Art Garfunkel, Jimmie Haskell, Ernie Freeman, Larry Knechtel (Col)
CLOSE TO YOU (Carpenters) Arr: Richard Carpenter (A&M)
EVERYTHING IS BEAUTIFUL - Ray Stevens, arr: (Barnaby)
LUCRETIA MAC EVIL (Blood, Sweat & Tears) arr: Dick Halligan (Col)

BEST ENGINEERED RECORDING
(Engineer's Award)

BRIDGE OVER TROUBLED WATER (Simon & Garfunkel) Eng: Roy Halee (Col)
CLOSE TO YOU (Carpenters) Engs: Ray Gerhardt, Dick Bogert (A&M)
THE KAEMPFERT TOUCH (B. Kaempfert & Orch.) Eng: Peter Klemt (Decca)
TAP ROOT MANUSCRIPT (Neil Diamond) Eng: Armin Steiner (Uni)
TO OUR CHILDREN'S CHILDREN'S CHILDREN (The Moody Blues) Engs: Derek Varnals, Adrian Martins, Robin Thompson (Threshold)

BEST ALBUM COVER
(Awards to Art Director, Photographer and/or Graphic Artist)

CHICAGO (Chicago) Cover: John Berg - Cover Art: Nick Fasciano (Col)
HAND MADE (Mason Williams) Art Dir: Ed Thrasher - Design: Dave Bhang (WB)
INDIANOLA MISSISSIPPI SEEDS (B.B. King) - Design: Robert Lockart-Photog:Ivan Nagy (ABC)
MASON PROFFIT (Mason Profit) Photog: Peter Whorf - Designer: Martin Donald - Art Dir: Christopher Whorf (Happy Tiger)
THE NAKED CARMEN (Various) Art Dir: Desmond Strobel-Design: John Craig (Merc)
SCHUBERT "UNFINISHED" SYMPHONY - BEETHOVEN : FIFTH SYMPHONY (Philharmonic Symphony Orchestra of London, Rodzinski, cond.) Art Dir: Peter Whorf - Design: Christopher Whorf - Photog: Fred Poore (Westminster Gold)
UNCLE CHARLIE & HIS DOG TEDDY (Nitty Gritty Dirt Band) Art Dir: Woody Woodward - Photog: William E. McEuen - Album Design: Dean O. Torrence (UA) THE WORLD'S GREATEST BLUES SINGER (Bessie Smith) Art Dir: John Berg - Cover Art: Philip Hays - Album Design: Lloyd Ziff (Col)

BEST ALBUM NOTES
(Annotator's Award)

AS I SEE IT (Jack Moran) Ann: Billy Edd Wheeler (Athena)
BITCHES BREW (Miles Davis) Ann: Ralph J. Gleason (Col)
THE WORLD'S GREATEST BLUES SINGER (Bessie Smith) Ann: Chris Albertson (Col)
HOLD BACK THE WORLD (Alexander's Greyhound Brass) Ann: Rod McKuen (Stanyan)
I DO NOT PLAY NO ROCK 'N ROLL (Mississippi Fred McDowell) Ann: Anthony d'Oberoff (Cap)
JUDY. LONDON. 1969 (Judy Garland) Ann: Rex Reed (Juno)
SIXTEEN ALL TIME GREATEST HITS (Bill Monroe & Blue Grass Boys) Ann: James Goodfriend (Col)
THEY SHOOT HORSES, DON'T THEY? (John Green Orch.) Ann: Arthur Knight (ABC)

BEST CONTEMPORARY VOCAL PERFORMANCE - FEMALE

AIN'T NO MOUNTAIN HIGH ENOUGH (single) Diana Ross (Motown)
FANCY (album) Bobbie Gentry (Cap)
I'LL NEVER FALL IN LOVE AGAIN (album) Dionne Warwick (Scepter)
LONG LONG TIME (album) Linda Ronstadt (Cap)
SNOWBIRD (single) Anne Murray (Cap)

BEST CONTEMPORARY VOCAL PERFORMANCE - MALE

ELTON JOHN (album) Elton John (Uni)
EVERYTHING IS BEAUTIFUL (single) Ray Stevens (Barnaby)
MAD DOGS & ENGLISHMEN (album) Joe Cocker (A&M)
RAINY NIGHT IN GEORGIA (single) Brook Benton (Cotillion)
SWEET BABY JAMES (album) James Taylor (WB)

BEST CONTEMPORARY VOCAL PERFORMANCE BY A DUO, GROUP OR CHORUS
ABC - Jackson 5 (Motown)
BRIDGE OVER TROUBLED WATER - Simon & Garfunkel (Col)
CHICAGO - Chicago (Col)
CLOSE TO YOU - Carpenters (A&M)
LET IT BE - The Beatles (Apple)

BEST CONTEMPORARY INSTRUMENTAL PERFORMANCE
AIRPORT LOVE THEME - Vincent Bell (Decca)
OVERTURE FROM TOMMY - Assembled Multitude (Atl)
STAR SPANGLED BANNER - Jimi Hendrix (Cot)
SOUL FLOWER - Quincy Jones (UA)
THEME FROM Z AND OTHER FILM MUSIC - Henry Mancini (RCA)

BEST CONTEMPORARY SONG
(Songwriter's Award)
BRIDGE OVER TROUBLED WATER - Paul Simon
EVERYTHING IS BEAUTIFUL - Ray Stevens
FIRE AND RAIN - James Taylor
LET IT BE - John Lennon, Paul McCartney
WE'VE ONLY JUST BEGUN - Roger Nichols, Paul Williams

BEST R&B VOCAL PERFORMANCE - FEMALE
BLACK GOLD - Nina Simone (album) (RCA)
DON'T PLAY THAT SONG (single) Aretha Franklin (Atl)
SET ME FREE (single) Esther Phillips (Atl)
SHE DIDN'T KNOW (single) Dee Dee Warwick (Atco)
STAND BY YOUR MAN (single) Candi Staton (Fame)

BEST R&B VOCAL PERFORMANCE - MALE
ENGINE NO. 9 (single) Wilson Pickett (Atl)
PATCHES (single) Clarence Carter (Atl)
SIGNED, SEALED, DELIVERED (single) Stevie Wonder (Tamla)
THE THRILL IS GONE (single) B.B. King (ABC)
WAR (single) Edwin Starr (Gordy)

BEST R&B PERFORMANCE BY A DUO OR GROUP, VOCAL OR INSTRUMENTAL
DIDN'T I (BLOW YOUR MIND THIS TIME) The Delfonics (Philly Groove)
EXPRESS YOURSELF - Charles Wright & The Watts 103RD Street Rhythm Band (WB)
5-10-15-20 (25-30 YEARS OF LOVE) The Presidents (Buddah)
IT'S ALL IN THE GAME - Four Tops (Motown)
SOMEBODY'S BEEN SLEEPING IN MY BED - 100 Proof (Buddah)

BEST RHYTHM & BLUES SONG
(Songwriter's Award)
DIDN'T I (BLOW YOUR MIND THIS TIME) Thom Bell and William Hart (Phly Groove)
GROOVY SITUATION - Russell Lewis and Herman Davis (Merc)
PATCHES - Ronald Dunbar, General Johnson (Atl)
SIGNED, SEALED, DELIVERED - Stevie Wonder, Lee Garrett, Syreeta Wright, Lulu Hardaway (Tamla)
SOMEBODY'S BEEN SLEEPING IN MY BED Greg Perry, General Johnson, Angelo Bond (Buddah)

BEST SOUL GOSPEL PERFORMANCE
AMAZING GRACE - James Cleveland (Savoy)
CHRISTIAN PEOPLE - Andrae Crouch (Lib)
EVERY MAN WANTS TO BE FREE - Edwin Hawkins Singers (Buddah)
GOD GAVE ME A SONG - Myrna Summers (Cot)
HELLO SUNSHINE - Jessy Dixon (Savoy)

BEST COUNTRY VOCAL PERFORMANCE - FEMALE
MULE SKINNER BLUES - Dolly Parton (single) (RCA)
ROSE GARDEN - Lynn Anderson (single) (Col)
RUN WOMAN, RUN - Tammy Wynette (single) (Epic)
THEN HE TOUCHED ME - Jean Shepart (single) (Cap)
A WOMAN LIVES FOR LOVE - Wanda Jackson (single) (Cap)

BEST COUNTRY VOCAL PERFORMANCE - MALE
AMOS MOSES - Jerry Reed (single) (RCA)
CHARLEY PRIDE'S 10TH ALBUM - Charley Pride (Col)
FOR THE GOOD TIMES - Ray Price (single) (Col)
OKIE FROM MUSKOGEE - Merle Haggard (album) (Cap)
SUNDAY MORNING COMING DOWN - Johnny Cash (single) (Col)

BEST COUNTRY VOCAL PERFORMANCE BY A DUO OR GROUP
BED ROSES - Statler Brothers (Merc)
DADDY WAS AN OLD-TIME PREACHER MAN - Porter Wagoner & Dolly Parton (RCA)
IF I WERE A CARPENTER - Johnny Cash & June Carter (Col)
SUSPICIOUS MINDS - Waylon Jennings & Jessi Colter (RCA)
TENNESSEE BIRDWALK - Jack Blanchard & Misty Morgan (Wayside)

BEST COUNTRY INSTRUMENTAL PERFORMANCE
DRIVIN' HOME - Jerry Smith (Decca)
ME & JERRY - Chet Atkins, Jerry Reed (RCA)
STREET SINGER - Merle Haggard and the Stranger (Cap)
YESTERGROOVIN' - Chet Atkins (RCA)
YOU AIN'T HEARD NOTHIN' YET - Danny Davis & the Nashville Brass (RCA)

BEST COUNTRY SONG
(Songwriter's Award)
THE FIGHTIN' SIDE OF ME - Merle Haggard (Cap)
HELLO DARLIN' - Conway Twitty (Decca)
IS ANYBODY GOIN' TO SAN ANTONE - Glenn Martin & Dave Kirby (RCA)
MY WOMAN, MY WOMAN, MY WIFE - Marty Robbins (Col)
WONDER COULD I LIVE THERE ANYMORE - Bill Rice (RCA)

BEST SACRED PERFORMANCE (MUSICAL)
THE CENTURION - Ralph Carmichael Orch & Chorus (Light)
EVERYTHING IS BEAUTIFUL - Jake Hess (RCA)
GOD OF OUR FATHERS - Richard Condie, cond. - Mormon Tabernacle Choir (Col)
RAPTURE - Pat Boone (Supreme)
THERE IS MORE TO LIFE - George Beverly Shea (RCA)

BEST GOSPEL PERFORMANCE (OTHER THAN SOUL GOSPEL)
FANTASTIC THRASHERS AT FANTASTIC CAVERNS - Thrasher Brothers (Canaan)
THE LEFEVRES/MOVING UP - The LeFevres (Canaan)
THE MANY MOODS OF THE FLORIDA BOYS - The Florida Boys (Canaan)

TALK ABOUT THE GOOD TIMES - Wendy Bagwell & The Sunliters (Canaan)
TALK ABOUT THE GOOD TIMES - Oak Ridge Boys (Heartwarming)

BEST ETHNIC OR TRADITIONAL RECORDING (INCLUDING TRADITIONAL BLUES)
BLACK MUSIC OF SOUTH AMERICA - David Lewisohn (Nonesuch)
FOLK FIDDLING FROM SWEDEN - Bjorn Stabi and Ole Hjorth (Nonesuch)
GOOD FEELIN' - T-Bone Walker (Polydor)
I DO NOT PLAY NO ROCK N' ROLL - Mississippi Fred McDowell (Cap)
SAIL ON - Muddy Waters (Chess)
SHREE RAG - Ali Akbar Khan, accomp. by Shankar Ghosh, Tabla (Conn Soc)

BEST INSTRUMENTAL COMPOSITION
(Composer's Award)
AIRPORT LOVE THEME - Alfred Newman (Decca)
BITCHES BREW - Miles Davis (Col)
GULA MATARI - Quincy Jones (A&M)
LOVE THEME FROM SUNFLOWER - Henry Mancini (RCA)
THEME FROM MEDICAL CENTER - Lalo Schifrin (MGM)

BEST ORIGINAL SCORE WRITTEN FOR A MOTION PICTURE OR TV SPECIAL
(Composer's Award)
AIRPORT - Alfred Newman (Decca)
DARLING LILI - Johnny Mercer, Henry Mancini (RCA)
LET IT BE - John Lennon, Paul McCartney, George Harrison, Ringo Starr (Apple)
M*A*S*H* - Johnny Mandel (Col)
THE STERILE CUCKOO - Fred Karlin (Para)

BEST SCORE FROM AN ORIGINAL CAST SHOW ALBUM
(Grammys to Composers and A&R Producer)
APPLAUSE - Charles Strouse, Lee Adams - A&R: Bob Arnold (ABC)
COCO - Alan Lerner, Andre Previn - A&R: Andy Wiswell (Para)
COMPANY - Stephen Sondheim, - A&R: Thomas Z. Shepard (Col)
JOY - Oscar Brown, Jr., Jean Pace, Sivuca - A&R: Ernie Altschuler (RCA)
PURLIE - Gary Geld, Peter Udell - A&R: Andy Wiswell (Ampex)

BEST RECORDING FOR CHILDREN
ARISTOCATS - Tutti Camarata, Musical Prod. (Camarata, Holloway, Harris, Lester, Mike Sammes Singers) (Disneyland)
A BOY NAMED CHARLIE BROWN (Soundtrack) A&R Prod. & Musical Dir: John Scott Trotter (Col)
RUBBER DUCKIE - Jim Henson (Col)
SESAME STREET (Sesame Street TV Cast) Children's TV Workshop, Joan Cooney, Producer (Col)
SUSAN SINGS SONGS FROM SESAME STREET - Loretta Long (Scepter)

BEST COMEDY RECORDING
THE BEGATTING OF THE PRESIDENT - Orson Welles (Mediarts)
DADDY PLAYED FIRST BASE - Homer & Jethro (RCA)
THE DEVIL MADE ME BUY THIS DRESS - Flip Wilson (Little David)
I AM THE PRESIDENT - David Frye (Elektra)
LIVE AT MADISON SQUARE GARDEN - Bill Cosby (Uni)

BEST SPOKEN WORD RECORDING
EVERETT DIRKSEN'S AMERICA - Everett Dirksen (Bell)
GROVER HENSON FEELS FORGOTTEN - Bill Cosby (Uni)
IN THE BEGINNING - Robert Cotterell, A&R Prod. (Apollo 8, 11, 12 Astronauts, Pres. Kennedy & Nixon) (Creative Sound)
POEMS AND BALLADS FROM 100-PLUS AMERICAN POETS - Paul Molloy, A&R Prod. (Ambrose, Dryden, Hecht, Molloy, Seeger) (Scholastic)
THE SOFT SEA - Jesse Pearson (WB)
WHY I OPPOSE THE WAR IN VIETNAM - Rev. Martin Luther King, Jr. (Black Forum)

BEST JAZZ PERFORMANCE - SMALL GROUP OR SOLOIST WITH SMALL GROUP
(7 or less)
ALONE - Bill Evans (MGM)
COLTRANE LEGACY - John Coltrane (Atl)
FAT ALBERT ROTUNDA - Herbie Hancock (WB)
FEELING IS BELIEVING - Erroll Garner (Octv)
GOOD-VIBES - Gary Burton (Atl)
SWISS MOVEMENT - Les McCann, Eddie Harris (Atl)
THAT'S THE WAY IT IS - Milt Jackson Quintet with Ray Brown (Impulse)

BEST JAZZ PERFORMANCE - LARGE GROUP OR SOLOIST WITH LARGE GROUP
(8 or more)
BITCHES BREW - Miles Davis (Col)
BRIDGE OVER TROUBLED WATER - Paul Desmond (A&R)
CONSUMMATION - Thad Jones & Mel Lewis (Ble/Nt)
DON ELLIS AT FILLMORE - Don Ellis (Col)
DUKE ELLINGTON - 70TH BIRTHDAY CONCERT - Duke Ellington (Solid State)
GULA MATARI - Quincy Jones (A&M)
LIVE AT THE ROOSEVELT GRILL - World's Greatest Jazzband (Atl)
THREE SHADES OF BLUE - Johnny Hodges (Flying Dutchman)

ALBUM OF THE YEAR, CLASSICAL
(Grammys to Artist and A&R Producer)
BEETHOVEN EDITION 1970 (Karajan, Berlin Philharmonic, Oistrakh, Anda, Kempf, Goossens, Leitner, etc.) A&R: Dr. Wilfried Daenicke (DGG)
BERLIOZ: LES TROYENS - Colin Davis cond. Royal Opera House Orchestra & Chorus (Solos: Vickers, Veasey Lindholm) A&R: Erik Smith (Philips)
BRAHMS: DOUBLE CONCERTO (CONCERTO IN A MINOR FOR VIOLIN & CELLO) David Oistrakh & Mstislav Rostropovich (Szell cond. Cleveland Orchestra) A&R: Peter Andry (Angel)
IVES: THREE PLACES IN NEW ENGLAND/RUGGLES: SUN TREADER - Michael Tilson Thomas cond. Boston Symphony - A&R: Tom Mowrey (DGG)
SHOSTAKOVICH: SYMPHONY NO. 13 - Eugene Ormandy cond. Philadelphia Symphony (Krause, baritone/Male Chorus of Mendelssohn Club of Philadelphia, R. Page, dir.) - A&R: Peter Dellheim (RCA)
STRAVINSKY: LE SACRE DU PRINTEMPS - Pierre Boulez cond. Cleveland Orchestra - A&R: Thomas Z. Shepard (Col)

BEST CLASSICAL PERFORMANCE, ORCHESTRA
(Conductor's Award)
BARTOK: CONCERTO FOR ORCHESTRA - Seiji Ozawa cond. Chicago Symphony (Angel)
BERLIOZ: ROMEO & JULIET - Carlo Maria Giulini cond. Chicago Symphony (Angel)
BRUCKNER: SYMPHONY NO. 8 IN C MINOR - George Szell cond. Cleveland Orchestra (Col)
DVORAK: SYMPHONY NO. 8 IN G MAJOR - George Szell cond. Cleveland Orchestra (Angel)
IVES: THREE PLACES IN NEW ENGLAND/RUGGLES: SUN TREADER

- Michael Tilson Thomas cond. Boston Symphony (DGG)
MAHLER: SYMPHONY NO. 2 IN C MINOR "RESURRECTION" - Eugene Ormandy cond. Philadelphia Symphony (RCA)
MAHLER: SYMPHONY NO. 6 IN A MINOR - Georg Solti cond. Chicago Symphony (London)
STRAVINSKY: LE SACRE DU PRINTEMPS - Pierre Boulez cond. Cleveland Orchestra (Col)

BEST CLASSICAL PERFORMANCE - INSTRUMENTAL SOLOIST(S) (WITH OR WITHOUT ORCHESTRA)

BACH: WELL TEMPERED CLAVIER BOOK 2, NOS. 9-16 - Glenn Gould (CBS)
BARTOK: CONCERTO NO. 2 FOR PIANO - Alexis Weissenberg (Ormandy cond. Philadelphia Symphony) (RCA)
BEETHOVEN: SONATAS NO. 26 OP. 81a ("LES ADIEUX") & NO. 15, OP. 28 ("PASTORAL") Ivan Moravec (Conn Soc)
BRAHMS: CONCERTO IN D MAJOR FOR VIOLIN - David Oistrakh (Szell Cond. Cleveland Orchestra) (Angel)
BRAHMS: DOUBLE CONCERTO (CONCERTO IN A MINOR FOR VIOLIN & CELLO) - David Oistrakh & Mstislav Rostropovich (Szell cond. Cleveland Orchestra) (Angel)
BRITTEN: SUITES FOR CELLO (2) - Mstislav Rostropovich (Britten cond.) (London)
CHOPIN: CONCERTO NO. 1 IN E MINOR FOR PIANO - Van Cliburn (Ormandy cond. Philadelphia Symphony) (RCA)
SCHUMANN: KREISLERIANA-Vladimir Horowitz (Col)
WELL-TEMPERED SYNTHESIZER - Walter Carlos (Col)

BEST CHAMBER MUSIC PERFORMANCE
(Inst. or Vocal)

BEETHOVEN: THE COMPLETE PIANO TRIOS - Eugene Istomin, Isaac Stern, Leonard Rose (Col)
BEETHOVEN: THE FIVE LATE QUARTETS - Guarneri Quartet (RCA)
CARTER: QUARTETS NOS. 1 & 2 FOR STRINGS - Composers Quartet (Nonesuch)
FRANCK: SONATA IN A MAJOR FOR VIOLIN & PIANO/BRAHMS: SONATA NO. 3 IN D MINOR - Sviatoslav Richter, David Oistrakh (Angel)
(GRAINGER) SALUTE TO PERCY GRAINGER - Benjamin Britten cond. English Chamber Orchestra & Ambrosian Singers (London)
IVES: CALCIUM LIGHT NIGHT - Gunther Schuller (CBS)
SCHUBERT: TRIO NO. 1 IN B FLAT MAJOR, MILHAUD: PASTORALE FOR OBOE, CLARINET & BASSOON/HINDEMITH: KLEINE KAMMER-MUSIK - The Boston Symphony Chamber Players (RCA)

BEST OPERA RECORDING
(Grammys to Conductor and A&R Producer)

BERLIOZ: LES TROYENS - Colin Davis cond. Royal Opera House Orchestra & Chorus (Solos: Vickers, Veasey, Lindholm) A&R: Erik Smith (Philips)
DEBUSSY: PELLEAS ET MELISANDE - Pierre Boulez cond. Orchestra of Royal Opera House (Solos: McIntyre, Shirley, Soederstroem, David, Ward, etc.) A&R: Paul Myers (Col)
R. STRAUSS: DER ROSENKAVALIER - Georg Solti cond. Vienna Philharmonic (Solos: Crespin, Minton, Donath, Jungwirth) A&R: Christopher Raeburn (London)
VERDI: IL TROVATORE - Zubin Mehta cond. New Philharmonia Orchestra, Ambrosian Opera Chorus (Solos: Price, Domingo, Milnes, Cossotto) A&R: Richard Mohr (RCA)
WAGNER: GOTTERDAMMERUNG - Herbert von Karajan cond. Berlin Philharmonic, Deutsche Opera Chorus (Solos: Brilioth, Stewart, Keleman, Dernesch, Janowitz, Ludwig, Chookasian) A&R: Otto Gerdes (DGG)

BEST VOCAL SOLOIST PERFORMANCE, CLASSICAL

BERLIOZ: THE TROJANS - FINAL SCENES "DEATH OF CLEOPATRA" - Janet Baker (Gibson cond. London Symphony) (Angel)
MAHLER: DES KNABEN WUNDERHORN - Christa Ludwig & Walter Berry (Bernstein cond. New York Philharmonic) (Col)
MAHLER: KINDERTOTENLIEDER/WAGNER: WESENDONCK LIEDER - Marilyn Horn (Henry Lewis cond.) (London)
MOZART & STRAUSS ARIAS - Beverly Sills (Ceccato cond. London Philharmonic) (Audio Treasury)
PRIMA DONNA VOLUME III - Leontyne Price (Downes cond. London Symphony) (RCA)
SCHUBERT: LIEDER - Dietrich Fischer-Dieskau (Gerald Moore, accomp.) (DGG)

BEST CHORAL PERFORMANCE (OTHER THAN OPERA)
(Grammys to Conductor and Choral Director)

HAYDN: THE CREATION - Herbert von Karajan cond. Berlin Philharmonic/Reinhold Schmid & Helmut Froschauer cond. Vienna Singverien (DGG)
(IVES) NEW MUSIC OF CHARLES IVES - Gregg Smith cond. Gregg Smith Singers and Columbia Chamber Ensemble (Col)
MAHLER: DAS KLAGENDE LIED - Arthur Oldham cond. London Symphony Orchestra Chorus - Pierre Boulez cond. London Symphony (Col)
ORFF: CARMINA BURANA - Lorna Cooke de Varon, dir, New England Conservatory Chorus; Katherine Edmonds Pusztai, cond. Children's Chorus of New England Conservatory; Seiji Ozawa cond. Boston Symphony (RCA)
SHOSTAKOVICH: SYMPHONY NO. 13 - Eugene Ormandy cond. Philadelphia Symphony; Robert E. Page, dir., Male Chorus of Mendelssohn Club (RCA)
(STRAVINSKY): THE NEW STRAVINSKY - Gregg Smith cond. Ithaca College Concert Choir/Robert Craft cond. Columbia Symphony (Col)
VAUGHAN WILLIAMS: FIVE TUDOR PORTRAITS - Bach Choir & New Philharmonia - David Willcocks, cond. (Angel)

BEST ENGINEERED RECORDING, CLASSICAL
(Engineer's Award)

BRAHMS: DOUBLE CONCERTO (CONCERTO IN A MINOR FOR VIOLIN & CELLO) (Oistrakh & Rostropovich/Szell cond. Cleveland Orchestra - Eng: Carson C. Taylor (Angel)
IVES: THREE PLACES IN NEW ENGLAND/RUGGLES: SUN TREADER (Thomas cond. Boston Symphony) Eng: Gunter Hermanns (DGG)
SHOSTAKOVICH: SYMPHONY NO. 6 AND AGE OF GOLD (Stokowski cond. Chicago Symphony) Eng: Paul Goodman (RCA)
SHOSTAKOVICH: SYMPHONY NO. 13 (Ormandy cond. Philadelphia Symphony) Eng: Bernard Keville (RCA)
R. STRAUSS: DER ROSENKAVALIER (Solti cond. Vienna Philharmonic/Crespin, Minton) Engs: Gordon Parry, James Locke (London)
STRAVINSKY: LE SACRE DU PRINTEMPS (Boulez cond. Cleveland Orchestra) Engs: Fred Plaut, Ray Moore, Arthur Kendy (Col)
WELL-TEMPERED SYNTHESIZER (Walter Carlos) Eng: Walter Carlos (Col)

1971

RECORD OF THE YEAR
(Grammys to the Artist and A&R Producer)

IT'S TOO LATE - Carole King - A&R: Lou Adler (Ode)
JOY TO THE WORLD - Three Dog Night - A&R: Richard Podolor (Dunhill)
MY SWEET LORD - George Harrison - A&R: George Harrison, Phil Spector (Apple)
THEME FROM SHAFT - Isaac Hayes - A&R: Isaac Hayes (Enterprise)
YOU'VE GOT A FRIEND - James Taylor - A&R: Peter Asher (WB)

ALBUM OF THE YEAR
(Grammys to the Artist and A&R Producer)
ALL THINGS MUST PASS - George Harrison - A&R: George Harrison and Phil Spector (Apple)
CARPENTERS - Carpenters - A&R: Jack Daugherty (A&M)
JESUS CHRIST SUPERSTAR - London Production - A&R: Andrew Lloyd Webber, Tim Rice (Decca)
SHAFT - Isaac Hayes - A&R: Isaac Hayes (Enterprise)
TAPESTRY - Carole King - A&R: Lou Adler (A&M)

SONG OF THE YEAR
(Songwriter's Award)
HELP ME MAKE IT THROUGH THE NIGHT - Kris Kristofferson
IT'S IMPOSSIBLE - Sid Wayne, Armando Manzanero
ME & BOBBY MC GEE - Kris Kristofferson, Fred Foster
ROSE GARDEN - Joe South
YOU'VE GOT A FRIEND - Carole King

BEST NEW ARTIST OF THE YEAR
CHASE (Epic)
EMERSON, LAKE & PALMER (Cot)
HAMILTON, JOE FRANK & REYNOLDS (Dunhill)
CARLY SIMON (Elektra)
BILL WITHERS (Sussex)

BEST INSTRUMENTAL ARRANGEMENT
(Arranger's Award)
EARTH - Arr: Michel Colombier (A&M)
NIGHTINGALE II - Arr: Joshua Rifkin (Elektra)
THE RITE OF SPRING (Hubert Laws) Arr: Don Sebesky (CTI)
THEME FROM SHAFT - Arrs: Isaac Hayes, Johnny Allen (Enterprises)
THEME FROM SUMMER OF '42 - Arr: Michel Legrand (WB)

BEST ARRANGEMENT ACCOMPANYING VOCALIST(S)
(Arranger's Award)
FREEDOM AND FEAR (Bill Medley) Arr: Michel Colombier (A&M)
LONG AGO TOMORROW (B.J. Thomas) Arrs: Burt Bacharach, Pat Williams (Scepter)
SUPERSTAR (Carpenters) Arr: Richard Carpenter (A&M)
UNCLE ALBERT/ADMIRAL HALSEY (Paul & Linda McCartney) Arr: Paul McCartney (Apple)
WHAT'S GOING ON (Marvin Gaye) Arr: David Van DePitte (Tamla)

BEST ENGINEERED RECORDING (NON-CLASSICAL)
(Engineer's Award)
CARPENTERS (Carpenters) Engs: Ray Gerhardt, Dick Bogert (A&M)
THE 5TH DIMENSION/LIVE! (5th Dimension) Eng: Bones Howe (Bell)
STONES (Neil Diamond) (single) Eng: Armin Steiner (Uni)
THEME FROM SHAFT (Isaac Hayes) Engs: Dave Purple, Henry Bush, Ron Capone (Enterprise)
WINGS (Michel Colombier) Engs: Larry Levine, Roger Roche (A&M)

BEST ALBUM COVER
(Awards to Art Director, Photographer and/or Graphic Artist)
B, S & T; 4 (Blood, Sweat & Tears) Art Dir: John Berg - Design: Robert Lockart - Photos and Art: Norman Seeff (Col)
BARK (Jefferson Airplane) Concept & Design: Acy Lehman - Photog: Nick Sangiamo (Grunt)
BLACK PEARL (Jimmy McGriff) Art Dir: Norman Seeff - Cover: John Van Hamersveld (UA)
HOT PLATTERS (Various) Art Dir: Ed Thrasher - Design: John Van Hamersveld (WB)
THE MUSIC OF ERIK SATIE: THROUGH A LOOKING GLASS (Camarata Contemporary Chamber Orch.) Art Dir: Vincent J. Biondi - Ilustration: Susan Obrant (Dream)
POLLUTION (Pollution) Art Dir: Gene Brownell - Design: Dean O. Torrance (Prophesy)
SHAREPICKERS (Mason Williams) Art Dir: Ed Thrasher - Photo: Terry Paul (WB)
STICKY FINGERS (The Rolling Stones) Photog: Andy Warhol - Graphics: Craigbraun (Rolling Stones)

BEST ALBUM NOTES
(Annotator's Award)
THE GENIUS OF LOUIS ARMSTRONG (Armstrong) Ann: Don DeMicheal (Col)
HONKY TONKIN' WITH CHARLIE WALKER (Walker) Ann: Tom West (Epic)
LOUIS ARMSTRONG JULY 4, 1900 - JULY 6, 1971 (Armstrong) Ann: Nat Hentoff (RCA)
MILES DAVIS (Davis) Ann: Colman Andrews (UA)
MUSIC OF VARESE (Simonovitch cond. Paris Instrumental Ensemble) Ann: James Lyons (Angel)
PIANO RAGS BY SCOTT JOPLIN (Rifkin) Ann: Joshua Rifkin (Nonesuch)
SAM HARD AND HEAVY (Samudio) Ann: Sam Samudio (Atlantic)
THIS IS BENNY GOODMAN (Goodman) Ann: George T. Simon (RCA)

BEST POP VOCAL PERFORMANCE, FEMALE
GYPSYS, TRAMPS & THIEVES - Cher (Kapp)
ME & BOBBY MC GEE - Janis Joplin (Col)
THE NIGHT THEY DROVE OLD DIXIE DOWN - Joan Baez (Vanguard)
TAPESTRY - Carole King (Ode)
THAT'S THE WAY I'VE ALWAYS HEARD IT SHOULD BE - Carly Simon (Elektra)

BEST POP VOCAL PERFORMANCE, MALE
AIN'T NO SUNSHINE - Bill Withers (Sussex)
I AM, I SAID - Neil Diamond (Uni)
IF YOU COULD READ MY MIND - Gordon Lightfoot (Reprise)
IT'S IMPOSSIBLE - Perry Como (RCA)
YOU'VE GOT A FRIEND - James Taylor (WB)

BEST POP VOCAL PERFORMANCE BY A DUO, GROUP OR CHORUS
ALL I EVER NEED IS YOU - Sonny & Cher (Kapp)
CARPENTERS - Carpenters (A&M)
HOW CAN YOU MEND A BROKEN HEART - Bee Gees (Atco)
JESUS CHRIST SUPERSTAR - London Production - Andrew Lloyd Webber, Geoffrey Mitchell, Alan Doggett, Horace James (Decca)
JOY TO THE WORLD - Three Dog Night (Dunhill)

BEST POP INSTRUMENTAL PERFORMANCE
BURT BACHARACH - Burt Bacharach (A&M)
SMACKWATER JACK - Quincy Jones (A&M)
THEME FROM LOVE STORY - Henry Mancini (RCA)
THEME FROM SUMMER OF '42 - Michel Legrand (WB)
THEME FROM SUMMER OF '42 - Peter Nero (Col)

BEST R&B VOCAL PERFORMANCE, FEMALE
BRIDGE OVER TROUBLED WATER - Aretha Franklin (Atlantic)
CONTACT - Freda Payne (Invictus)
I LOVE YOU (CALL ME) Diana Ross (Motown)
MR. BIG STUFF - Jean Knight (Stax)
PEARL - Janis Joplin (Col)

BEST R&B VOCAL PERFORMANCE, MALE
AIN'T NOBODY HOME - B.B. King (ABC)
INNER CITY BLUES (MAKE ME WANNA HOLLER) - Marvin Gaye (Tamla)
A NATURAL MAN - Lou Rawls (MGM)
NEVER CAN SAY GOODBYE - Isaac Hayes (Enterprise)
WE CAN WORK IT OUT - Stevie Wonder (Tamla)

BEST R&B PERFORMANCE BY A DUO OR GROUP, VOCAL OR INSTRUMENTAL
IF I WERE YOUR WOMAN - Gladys Knight and The Pips (Soul)
PROUD MARY - Ike and Tina Turner (UA)
RESPECT YOURSELF - Staple Singers (Stax)
THEME FROM SHAFT - Isaac Hayes (Enterprise)
YOU'VE GOT A FRIEND - Roberta Flack, Donny Hathaway (Atlantic)

BEST RHYTHM & BLUES SONG
(Songwriter's Award)
AIN'T NO SUNSHINE - Bill Withers
IF I WERE YOUR WOMAN - Clay McMurray, Laverne Ware, Pamela Sawyer
MR. BIG STUFF - Joseph Broussard, Ralph Williams, Carrol Washington
NEVER CAN SAY GOODBYE - Clifton Davis
SMILING FACES SOMETIMES - Norman Whitfield, Barrett Strong

BEST SOUL GOSPEL PERFORMANCE
THE FIVE BLIND BOYS OF ALABAMA - Blind Boys of Alabama (Hob)
GREAT MOMENTS IN GOSPEL - Clara Ward (Hob)
PASS ME NOT - Dottie Rambo (Heartwarming)
PUT YOUR HAND IN THE HAND OF THE MAN FROM GALILEE - Shirley Caesar (Hob)
THERE IS A GOD - Valerie Simpson (Tamla)

BEST COUNTRY VOCAL PERFORMANCE, FEMALE
GOOD LOVIN' - Tammy Wynette (Epic)
HELP ME MAKE IT THROUGH THE NIGHT - Sammi Smith (Mega)
HE'S SO FINE - Jody Miller (Epic)
HOW CAN I UNLOVE YOU - Lynn Anderson (Col)
JOSHUA - Dolly Parton (RCA)

BEST COUNTRY VOCAL PERFORMANCE, MALE
EASY LOVING - Freddie Hart (Capitol)
I WON'T MENTION IT AGAIN - Ray Price (Col)
KISS AN ANGEL GOOD MORNING - Charley Pride (RCA)
SHE'S ALL I GOT - Johnny Paycheck (Col)
WHEN YOU'RE HOT, YOU'RE HOT - Jerry Reed (RCA)

BEST COUNTRY VOCAL PERFORMANCE BY A DUO OR GROUP
AFTER THE FIRE IS GONE Conway Twitty and Loretta Lynn (Decca)
BETTER MOVE IT ON HOME - Porter Wagoner and Dolly Parton (RCA)
I SAW THE LIGHT - Roy Acuff with the Nitty Gritty Dirt Band (UA)
NO NEED TO WORRY - Johnny Cash and June Carter (Col)
RINGS - Tompall & The Glaser Bros. (MGM)

BEST COUNTRY INSTRUMENTAL PERFORMANCE
FOR THE GOOD TIMES - Floyd Cramer (RCA)
JERRY KENNEDY PLAYS: WITH ALL DUE RESPECT TO KRIS KRISTOFFERSON - Jerry Kennedy (Mer)
ROSE GARDEN - Bakersfield Brass (Capitol)
RUBY, DON'T TAKE YOUR LOVE TO TOWN - Danny Davis & The Nashville Brass (RCA)
SNOWBIRD - Chet Atkins (RCA)

BEST COUNTRY SONG
(Songwriter's Award)
EASY LOVING - Freddie Hart
FOR THE GOOD TIMES - Kris Kristofferson
HELP ME MAKE IT THROUGH THE NIGHT - Kris Kristofferson
ME & BOBBY MC GEE - Kris Kristofferson, Fred Foster
ROSE GARDEN - Joe South

BEST SACRED PERFORMANCE (MUSICAL)
ABIDE WITH ME - Anita Bryant (Word)
AMAZING GRACE - George Beverly Shea (RCA)
DID YOU THINK TO PRAY - Charley Pride (RCA)
GOLDEN STREETS OF GLORY - Dolly Parton (RCA)
PAT BOONE FAMILY - Pat Boone Family (Word)

BEST GOSPEL PERFORMANCE (OTHER THAN SOUL GOSPEL)
HE'S STILL KING OF KINGS - Blackwood Bros. (RCA)
JESUS CHRIST, WHAT A MAN - Oak Ridge Boys (Impact)
LET ME LIVE - Charley Pride (RCA)
PUT YOUR HAND IN THE HAND - Hovie Lister with the Statesmen (Skylite)
TIME TO GET IT TOGETHER The Imperials (Impact)

BEST ETHNIC OR TRADITIONAL RECORDING (INCLUDING TRADITIONAL BLUES)
18TH CENTURY TRADITIONAL MUSIC OF JAPAN - Keiko Matsuo (Everest)
THE ESSO TRINIDAD STEEL BAND - Esso Trinidad Steel Band (WB)
JAVANESE COURT GAMELAN - Javanese Players, Robert E. Brown, Producer (Nonesuch)
MESSAGE TO THE YOUNG - Howlin' Wolf (Chess)
MISSISSIPPI FRED MC DOWELL - Mississippi Fred McDowell (Everest)
STORMY MONDAY BLUES - T-Bone Walker (Blues-Time)
THEY CALL ME MUDDY WATERS - Muddy Waters (Chess)

BEST INSTRUMENTAL COMPOSITION
(Composer's Award)
HILL WHERE THE LORD HIDES - Chuck Mangione (Mercury)
NEW ORLEANS SUITE - Duke Ellington (Atl)
THEME FROM LOVE STORY - Francis Lai (Par)
THEME FROM SHAFT - Isaac Hayes (Enterprise)
THEME FROM SUMMER OF '42 - Michel Legrand (WB)

BEST ORIGINAL SCORE WRITTEN FOR A MOTION PICTURE OR A TELEVISION SPECIAL
(Composer's Award)
BLESS THE BEASTS & CHILDREN - Barry DeVorzon, Perry Botkin, Jr. (A&M)
FRIENDS - Elton John, Bernie Taupin (Par)
LOVE STORY - Francis Lai (Par)
RYAN'S DAUGHTER - Maurice Jarre (MGM)
SHAFT - Isaac Hayes (MGM)

BEST SCORE FROM AN ORIGINAL CAST SHOW ALBUM
(Awards to Composers and A&R Producer)
FOLLIES - Stephen Sondheim - A&R: Richard C. Jones (Capitol)
GODSPELL - Composed and Produced by Stephen Schwartz (Bell)
THE ROTHSCHILDS - Jerry Bock, Sheldon Harnick - A&R: Thomas Z.

Shepard (Col)
TOUCH - Kenn Long, Jim Crozier - A&R: Glenn Osser (Ampex)
TWO BY TWO - Richard Rodgers, Martin Charnin - A&R: Thomas Z. Shepard (Col)

BEST RECORDING FOR CHILDREN
BILL COSBY TALKS TO KIDS ABOUT DRUGS - Bill Cosby (Uni)
SESAME ST., RUBBER DUCKIE & OTHER SONGS FROM SESAME ST. - Richard Wolfe Children's Chorus (Camden)
SEX EXPLAINED FOR CHILDREN - Dr. Stanley Daniels (Carapan)
THE STORY OF SCHEHERAZADE - Julie Harris (Caedmon)
WILLY WONKA & THE CHOCOLATE FACTORY - Golden Orch. & Chorus, Peter Moore, Conductor (Golden)

BEST COMEDY RECORDING
AJAX LIQUOR STORE - Hudson & Landry (Dore)
CHEECH & CHONG - Cheech & Chong (Ode)
FLIP - THE FLIP WILSON SHOW - Flip Wilson (Little David)
THIS IS A RECORDING - Lily Tomlin (Polydor)
WHEN I WAS A KID - Bill Cosby (Uni)

BEST SPOKEN WORD RECORDING
DESIDERATA - Les Crane (WB)
HAMLET - Richard Chamberlain (RCA)
I CAN HEAR IT NOW - THE SIXTIES - Walter Cronkite (Col)
LONG DAY'S JOURNEY INTO NIGHT - Stacy Keach, Robert Ryan, Geraldine Fitzgerald (Caedmon)
WILL ROGERS' U.S.A. - James Whitmore (Col)

BEST JAZZ PERFORMANCE BY A SOLOIST
THE BILL EVANS ALBUM - Bill Evans (Col)
CARMEN MCRAE - Carmen McRae (Mainstream)
GYPSY QUEEN - Larry Coryell (Flying Dutchman)
PHIL WOODS & HIS EUROPEAN RHYTHM MACHINE AT THE FRANKFURT JAZZ FESTIVAL - Phil Woods -(Embryo)
PORTRAIT OF JENNY - Dizzy Gillespie (Perceptn)
QUINTESSENTIAL RECORDING SESSION - Earl Hines (Chiaroscuro)
THE YOU AND ME THAT USED TO BE - Jimmy Rushing (RCA)

BEST JAZZ PERFORMANCE BY A GROUP
THE BILL EVANS ALBUM - Bill Evans Trio (Col)
GARY BURTON & KEITH JARRETT (Atl)
GIANTS - Dizzy Gillespie, Bobby Hackett, Mary Lou Williams (Perception)
MILES DAVIS AT THE FILLMORE - Miles Davis (Col)
MWANDISHI - Herbie Hancock (WB)
THE NIFTY CAT - Roy Eldridge (Master Jazz)
PHIL WOODS & HIS EUROPEAN RHYTHM MACHINE AT THE FRANKFURT JAZZ FESTIVAL - Phil Woods (Embryo)

BEST JAZZ PERFORMANCE BY A BIG BAND
AFRIQUE - Count Basie (Flying Dutchman)
A DIFFERENT DRUMMER - Buddy Rich (RCA)
MAYNARD FERGUSON - M.F. HORN - Maynard Ferguson (Col)
NEW ORLEANS SUITE - Duke Ellington (Atl)
WOODY - Woody Herman (Cadet)

ALBUM OF THE YEAR, CLASSICAL
(Grammys to the Artist and A&R Producer)
BERLIOZ: REQUIEM - Colin Davis cond. London Symphony/Russell Burgess cond. Wandsworth School Boys Choir/Arthur Oldham cond. London Symphony Chorus - A&R: Vittorio Negri (Philips)
BOULEZ CONDUCTS BOULEZ: PLI SELON PLI - Pierre Boulez cond. BBC Symphony -A&R: Paul Myers (Col)
CRUMB: ANCIENT VOICES OF CHILDREN - Jan DeGaetani & Michael Dash/Arthur Weisberg cond. Contemporary Chamber Ensemble - A&R: Teresa Sterne (Nonesuch)
HAYDN: SYMPHONIES NOS. 65-72 (Vol. I) Antal Dorati cond. Philharmonia Hungarica - A&R: James Mallinson (London)
HOROWITZ PLAYS RACHMANINOFF (Etudes - Tableaux, Piano Music, Sonatas) - Vladimir Horowitz - A&R: Richard Killough, Thomas Frost (Col.)
JANACEK: SINFONIETTA/LUTOSLAVSKI: CONCERTO FOR ORCHESTRA - Seiji Ozawa cond. Chicago Symphony - A&R: Peter Andry (Angel)
MAHLER: SYMPHONY NO. 1 IN D MAJOR - Carlo Maria Giulini cond. Chicago Symphony - A&R: Christopher Bishop (Angel)
PENDERECKI: UTRENJA, THE ENTOMBMENT OF CHRIST - Eugene Ormandy cond. Philadelphia Orchestra/Robert Page, Dir., Temple University Choirs - A&R: Peter Dellheim (RCA)
SHOSTAKOVICH: SYMPHONY NO. 14 - Phyllis Curtin, Simon Estes; Eugene Ormandy cond. Philadelphia Orchestra - A&R: Max Wilcox (RCA)
TIPPETT: THE MIDSUMMER MARRIAGE - Colin Davis cond. Royal Opera House Orchestra Covent Garden - A&R: Erik Smith (Philips)

BEST CLASSICAL PERFORMANCE - ORCHESTRA
(Conductor's Award)
BOULEZ CONDUCTS BOULEZ: PLI SELON PLI - Pierre Boulez cond. The BBC Symphony(Col)
BOULEZ CONDUCTS RAVEL - Pierre Boulez cond. The Cleveland Orchestra (Col)
HAYDN: SYMPHONIES NOS. 65-72 (Vol. I) - Antal Dorati cond. Philharmonia Hungarica (London)
HOLST: THE PLANETS - Bernard Haitink cond. London Philharmonic (Philips)
MAHLER: SYMPHONY NO. 1 IN D MAJOR - Carlo Maria Giulini cond. Chicago Symphony (Angel)
MAHLER: SYMPHONY NO. 3 IN D MIN. - Jascha Horenstein cond. London Symphony (Nonesuch)
RESPIGHI: THE FOUNTAINS OF ROME/THE PINES OF ROME - Eugene Ormandy cond Philadelphia Orchestra (Col)
VAUGHAN WILLIAMS: SYMPHONY NO. 4 IN F MINOR - Andre Previn cond. London Symphony (RCA)

BEST CLASSICAL PERFORMANCE - INSTRUMENTAL SOLOIST OR SOLOISTS (WITH ORCHESTRA)
BACH: COMPLETE CONCERTOS FOR HARPSICHORD & ORCHESTRA - Igor Kipnis (Marriner cond. London Strings) (Col)
BEETHOVEN: TRIPLE CONCERTO (CONCERTO IN C MAJOR FOR VIOLIN, PIANO & CELLO, OP. 56) David Oistrakh, Mstislav Rostropovich, Sviatoslav Richter (von Karajan cond. Berlin Philharmonic) (Angel)
BERG: CONCERTO FOR VIOLIN & ORCHESTRA/MARTINON: CONCERTO FOR VIOLIN - Henryk Szeryng (Kubelik cond. Bavarian Symphony) (DGG)
DVORAK: CONCERTO IN B MINOR FOR CELLO - Jacqueline du Pre (Barenboim cond. Chicago Symphony) (Angel)
RACHMANINOFF: RHAPSODY ON A THEME OF PAGANINI/LISZT: CONCERTO NO. 2 IN A MAJOR - Van Cliburn (Ormandy cond. Philadelphia Orchestra) (RCA)
SCHUMAN, WILLIAM: CONCERTO FOR VIOLIN - Paul Zukofsky (Thomas cond. Boston Symphony) (DGG)
SIBELIUS: CONCERTO IN D MINOR FOR VIOLIN/TCHAIKOVSKY: CONCERTO IN D MAJOR FOR VIOLIN - Kyung-Wha Chung (Previn cond. London Symphony) (London)
VILLA-LOBOS: CONCERTO FOR GUITAR - Julian Bream (Previn cond. London Symphony) (RCA)
WALTON: CONCERTO FOR VIOLIN & ORCHESTRA/CONCERTO FOR VIOLA & ORCHESTRA - Yehudi Menuhin (Walton cond. New Philharmonia) (Angel)

BEST CLASSICAL PERFORMANCE - INSTRUMENTAL SOLOIST OR SOLOISTS (WITHOUT ORCHESTRA)

ALICIA DE LARROCHA PLAYS SPANISH PIANO MUSIC OF THE 20TH CENTURY - Alicia de Larrocha (London)
BACH: WELL-TEMPERED CLAVIER, BOOK 2, VOL. 3 PRELUDES & FUGUES 17-24 - Glenn Gould (Col)
BARBER: SONATA FOR PIANO/PROKOFIEFF: SONATA NO. 6 IN A MAJOR - Van Cliburn (RCA)
BARTOK: MIKROKOSMOS, VOL. 6/OUT OF DOORS SUITE/SONATINA - Stephen Bishop (Philips)
BEETHOVEN: SONATA NO. 29 IN B FLAT OP. 106 "HAMMERKLAVIER" - Rudolf Serkin (Col.)
THE BRAHMS I LOVE - Artur Rubinstein (RCA)
HOROWITZ PLAYS RACHMANINOFF (Etudes - Tableaux, Piano Music, Sonatas) Vladimir Horowitz (Col.)
PIANO RAGS BY SCOTT JOPLIN - Joshua Rifkin (Nonesuch)
SATIE: PIANO MUSIC OF ERIK SATIE, Vol. 5 - Aldo Ciccolini (Angel)

BEST CHAMBER MUSIC PERFORMANCE

CRUMB: ANCIENT VOICES OF CHILDREN - Jan DeGaitani, Michael M Dash; Arthur Weisberg cond. Contemporary Chamber Ensemble (Nonesuch)
DEBUSSY: QUARTET IN G MINOR/RAVEL: QUARTET IN F MAJOR - Juilliard Quartet (Col.)
DVORAK: PIANO TRIOS (Complete) Beaux Arts Trio (Philips)
FUX-SCHMELZER: MUSIC IN THE HAPSBURG PALACE - Nikolaus Harnoncourt cond. Concentus Musicus (Telefunken)
IVES: CHAMBER MUSIC - Paul Zukofsky, Gilbert Kalish, Charles Russo, Robert Sylvester (N.Y. String Quartet) (Col.)
THE MOZART QUARTETS FOR FLUTE - Jean-Pierre Rampal, Isaac Stern, Alexander Schneider, Leonard Rose (Col.)
SCHUBERT: FANTAISIE IN C MAJOR FOR VIOLIN (& PIANO) Op. 159 - Jascha Heifetz, - Brooks Smith (RCA)

BEST OPERA RECORDING

(Grammys to Conductor and A&R Producer)

MASSENET: MANON - Julius Rudel cond. New Philharmonia & Ambrosian Opera Chorus/(Solos: Sills, Gedda, Souzay, Bacquier) A&R: Michael Williamson (Audio Treas.)
MOZART: THE MAGIC FLUTE - Georg Solti cond. Vienna Philharmonic (Solos: Prey, Lorengar, Burrows, Fischer-Dieskau, Deutekom, Talvela) - A&R: Christopher Raeburn (London)
PUCCINI: IL TABARRO - Erich Leinsdorf cond. New Philharmonia; John Alldis Choir (Solos: Price, Domingo, Milnes) A&R: Richard Mohr (RCA)
TIPPETT: THE MIDSUMMER MARRIAGE - Colin Davis cond. Royal Opera House, Covent Garden (Solos: Remedios, Carlyle, Burrows, Herincx, Harwood) A&R: Erik Smith (Philips)
VERDI: AIDA - Erich Leinsdorf cond, London Symphony, John Alldis Choir (Solos: Price, Domingo, Milnes, Bumbry, Raimondi) A&R: Richard Mohr (RCA)
VERDI: DON CARLO - Carlo Maria Giulini cond. Orchestra of Royal Opera House, Covent Garden & Ambrosian Opera Chorus (Solos: Domingo, Caballe, Raimondi, Milnes, Verrett) A&R: Christopher Bishop (Angel)
WAGNER: DIE MEISTERSINGER VON NURNBERG - Herbert von Karajan cond. Dresden State Opera Orchestra & Choruses of Dresden State Opera & Leipzig Radio (Solos: Adam, Donath, Kollo, Evans, Schreider) A&R: R. Kinloch Anderson, Diether Gerhardt Worm (Angel)
WAGNER: PARSIFAL - Pierre Boulez cond. Bayreuth Festival Orchestra & Chorus (Solos: Stewart, Ridderbusch, Crass, King, Jones, McIntyre) A&R: Dr. Hans Hirsch (DGG)

BEST CLASSICAL VOCAL SOLOIST PERFORMANCE

AN EVENING OF DUETS - Janet Baket & Dietrich Fischer-Dieskau (Angel)
BERIO: EPIFANIE - Cathy Berberian (Berio cond. The B.B.C. Symphony) (RCA)
HAYDN & MOZART ARIAS - Dietrich Fischer-Dieskau (Peters cond. Vienna Haydn Orchestra) (London)
IVES: AMERICAN SCENES/AMERICAN POETS - Evelyn Lear, Thomas Stewart (Col.)
LEONTYNE PRICE SINGS ROBERT SCHUMANN - Leontyne Price (Garvey, accomp.) (RCA)
SHOSTAKOVICH: SYMPHONY NO. 14 - Phyllis Curtin, Simon Estes (Ormandy cond. Philadelphia Orchestra) (RCA)
WOLF: SONGS (Salzburg Festival 1953) Elisabeth Schwarzkopf (Furtwangler accomp.) (Seraphim)

BEST CHORAL PERFORMANCE CLASSICAL (OTHER THAN OPERA)

(Grammys to Conductor and Choral Director)

BERLIOZ: REQUIEM - Colin Davis cond. London Symphony/Russell Burgess cond. Wandsworth School Boys Choir/Arthur Oldham cond. London Symphony Chorus (Philips)
PENDERECKI: UTRENJA, THE ENTOMBMENT OF CHRIST - Robert Page, Dir., Temple University Choirs/Eugene Ormandy cond. Philadelphia Orchestra (RCA)
PROKOFIEV: SEVEN, THEY ARE SEVEN - Gennady Rozhdestvensky cond. Moscow Radio Chorus & Moscow Radio Symphony (Melodia/Angel)
SIBELIUS: KULLERVO, OP. 7 - Ensti Pohjola cond. Helsinki University Men's Choir; Paavo Berglund cond. Bournemout Symphony (Angel)
STOCKHAUSEN: STIMMUNG - Wolfgang Fromme cond. Collegium Vocale of Cologne (DGG)
VERDI: FOUR SACRED PIECES - Roger Wagner cond. Los Angeles Master Chorale/Zubin Mehta cond. Los Angeles Philharmonic (London)

BEST ENGINEERED RECORDING, CLASSICAL

(Engineer's Award)

BERLIOZ: REQUIEM - Colin Danis cond. London Symphony/Russell Burgess cond. Wandsworth School Boys Choir/Arthur Oldham cond. London Symphony - Eng: Vittorio Negri (Philips)
BEETHOVEN: EGMONT - COMPLETE INCIDENTAL MUSIC - Georg Szell cond. Vienna Philharmonic - Eng: Gordon Parry (London)
CRUMB: ANCIENT VOICES OF CHILDREN - Jan de Gaetani, Michael Dash, Weisberg cond. Contemporary Chamber Ensemble - Eng: Marc J. Aubort (Nonesuch)
HOLST: THE PLANETS - William Steinberg cond. Boston Symphony - Eng: Gunter Hermanns (DGG)
JANACEK: SINFONIETTA - Seiji Ozawa cond. Chicago Symphony - Eng: Carson C. Taylor (Angel)
MAHLER: SYMPHONY NO. 1 IN D MAJOR - Carlo Maria Giulini cond. Chicago Symphony - Eng: Carson C. Taylor (Angel)
TCHAIKOVSKY: 1812 OVERTURE/BEETHOVEN: WELLINGTON'S VICTORY - Eugene Ormandy cond. Philadelphia Orchestra - Eng: Paul Goodman (RCA)

1972

RECORD OF THE YEAR

(Grammys to the Artist and A&R Producer)

ALONE AGAIN (NATURALLY) - Gilbert O'Sullivan - Prod: Gordon Mills (MAM/London)
AMERICAN PIE - Don McLean - Prod: Ed Freeman (UA)
THE FIRST TIME EVER I SAW YOUR FACE - Roberta Flack - Prod: Joel Dorn (Atlantic)
SONG SUNG BLUE - Neil Diamond - Prods: Tom Catalano & Neil Diamond (Uni)

WITHOUT YOU - Nilsson - Prod: Richard Perry (RCA)

ALBUM OF THE YEAR
(Grammys to the Artist and A&R Producer)
AMERICAN PIE - Don McLean - Prod: Ed Freeman (UA)
THE CONCERT FOR BANGLA DESH - George Harrison & Friends (Ravi Shankar, Bob Dylan, Leon Russell, Ringo Starr, Billy Preston, Eric Clapton, Klaus Voormann, others) - Prods: George Harrison & Phil Spector (Apple)
JESUS CHRIST SUPERSTAR - Orginial Broadway Cast - Composers: Andrew Lloyd Webber & Tim Rice - Prod: Tom Morgan (Decca)
MOODS - Neil Diamond - Prods: Tom Catalano & Neil Diamond (Uni)
NILSSON SCHMILSSON - Nilsson - Prod: Richard Perry (RCA)

SONG OF THE YEAR
(Songwriter's Award)
ALONE AGAIN (NATURALLY) - Gilbert O'Sullivan
AMERICAN PIE - Don McLean
THE FIRST TIME EVER I SAW YOUR FACE - Ewan MacColl
SONG SUNG BLUE - Neil Diamond
THE SUMMER KNOWS - Marilyn & Alan Bergman & Michel Legrand

BEST NEW ARTIST OF THE YEAR
AMERICA (WB)
HARRY CHAPIN (Elektra)
EAGLES (Asylum/Atl.)
LOGGINS & MESSINA (Columbia)
JOHN PRINE (Atlantic)

BEST INSTRUMENTAL ARRANGEMENT
(Arranger's Award)
FLAT BAROQUE - Carpenters - Arr: Richard Carpenter (A&M)
LONELY TOWN - Freddie Hubbard - Arr: Don Sebesky (CTI)
MONEY RUNNER - Quincy Jones - Arr: Quincy Jones (Reprise)
THEME FROM THE FRENCH CONNECTION - Don Ellis Arr: Don Ellis (Columbia)
THEME FROM THE MANCINI GENERATION - Henry Mancini - Arr: Henry Mancini (RCA)

BEST ARRANGEMENT ACCOMPANYING VOCALIST(S)
(Arranger's Award)
BETCHA BY GOLLY, WOW - Stylistics - Arr: Thom Bell (Avco)
DAY BY DAY - Jackie & Roy - Arr: Don Sebesky (CTI)
LAZY AFTERNOON - Jackie & Roy - Arr: Don Sebesky (CTI)
THE SUMMER KNOWS - Sarah Vaughan - Arr: Michel Legrand (Mainstream)
WHAT ARE YOU DOING THE REST OF YOUR LIFE - Sarah Vaughan - Arr: Michel Legrand (Mainstream)

BEST ENGINEERED RECORDING
(Engineer's Award)
BABY I'M-A WANT YOU - Bread - Eng: Armin Steiner (album) (Elektra)
FRAGILE - Yes - Eng: Eddy Offord (album) (Atlantic)
HONKY CHATEAU - Elton John - Eng: Ken Scott (album) (Uni)
MOODS - Neil Diamond - Eng: Armin Steiner (album) (Uni)
SONG OF SCHMILSSON - Nilsson - Eng: Robin Cable, Ken Scott and Phillip Mac Donald (album) (RCA)

BEST ALBUM COVER
(Award to Art Director, Photographer and/or Graphic Artist)
CHIEF (Dewey Terry) Album Design & Cover Art: Aaron Schumaker for Tumbleweed Graphics (Tumbleweed)
FIVE DOLLAR SHOES (Five Dollar Shoes) Art Director: Ron Levine, Concept & Design: Pacific - Eye & Ear--Illustrations: Robert Rodriguez (Neighborhood/Famous)
FLASH (Flash) - Art Direction & Design: Hipgnosis - Photographer: Poe (Capitol)
HISTORICAL FIGURES AND ANCIENT HEADS - Canned Heat - Art Director & Cover Photog: Norman Seeff (UA)
SCHOOL'S OUT (Alice Cooper) Album Design: Wilkes & Braun, Inc. - Photog: Robert Otter (Desk, outside) - Jacket Concept: Sound Packaging Corp. (WB)
THE SIEGEL-SCHWALL BAND (The Siegel-Schwall Band) Art Director: Acy Lehman -Artist: Harvey Dinnerstein (Wooden Nickel)
SUNSET RIDE (Zephyr) Art Directors: Ed Thrasher and Chris Wolf/Illustrator: Dave Willardson - Graphic: John & Barbara Casado (WB)
VIRGIN (The Mission) Art Director: Bill Levy - Design: Fred Marcellino (Paramount)

BEST ALBUM NOTES
(Annotator's Award)
BUNNY BERIGAN, HIS TRUMPET & HIS ORCHESTRA, VOLUME I (Bunny Berigan) Ann: Dan Morgenstern (Vintage)
LENNY BRUCE/CARNEGIE HALL (Lenny Bruce) Ann: Albert Goldman (UA)
TOM T. HALL'S GREATEST HITS (Tom T. Hall) Ann. Tom T. Hall (Mercury)
LET MY CHILDREN HEAR MUSIC (Charles Mingus) Ann: Charles Mingus (Col.)
SUPER CHIEF (Count Basie) Ann: Michael Brooks (Col.)

BEST JAZZ PERFORMANCE BY A SOLOIST
ALONE AT LAST - Gary Burton (album) (Atlantic)
GREAT SCOTT - Tom Scott - (album) (A&M)
THE HUB OF HUBBARD - Freddie Hubbard (album) (MPS/BASF)
SAHARA - McCoy Tyner (album) (Milestone)
TUNE-UP! - Sonny Stitt (album) (Cobblestone)

BEST JAZZ PERFORMANCE BY A GROUP
(All nominations are albums)
THE CHUCK MANGIONE QUARTET - Chuck Mangione (Mercury)
FIRST LIGHT - Freddie Hubbard (CTI)
I SING THE BODY ELECTRIC - Weather Report (Col.)
OUTBACK - Joe Farrell (CTI)
SAHARA - McCoy Tyner (Milestone)
WHITE RABBIT - George Benson (CTI)

BEST JAZZ PERFORMANCE BY A BIG BAND
(All nominations are albums)
THE AGE OF STEAM - Gerry Mulligan (A&M)
ALL SMILES - Kenny Clark - Francy Boland Big Band (MPS/BASF)
CONNECTION - - Don Ellis (Col.)
M.F. HORN TWO - Maynard Ferguson (Col.)
TOGO BRAVA SUITE - Duke Ellington (U.A.)

BEST POP VOCAL PERFORMANCE, FEMALE
ANTICIPATION - Carly Simon (album) (Elektra)
DAY DREAMING - Aretha Franklin (single) (Atl.)
I AM WOMAN - Helen Reddy (single) (Cap.)
QUIET FIRE - Roberta Flack (album) (Atl.)
SWEET INSPIRATION/WHERE YOU LEAD - Barbra Streisand (single) (Col.)

BEST POP VOCAL PERFORMANCE, MALE
(All nominations are singles)
ALONE AGAIN (NATURALLY) Gilbert O'Sullivan (MAM/London)
AMERICAN PIE - Don McLean (UA)
BABY, DON'T GET HOOKED ON ME - Mac Davis (Col.)
CANDY MAN - Sammy Davis, Jr. (MGM)
WITHOUT YOU - Nilsson (RCA)

BEST POP VOCAL PERFORMANCE BY A DUO, GROUP OR CHORUS
BABY I'M-A WANT YOU - Bread (album) (Elektra)
A HORSE WITH NO NAME - America (single) (WB)
I'D LIKE TO TEACH THE WORLD TO SING (IN PERFECT HARMONY) - New Seekers (single) (Elektra)
SUMMER BREEZE - Seals & Crofts (single) (W.B.)
WHERE IS THE LOVE - Roberta Flack & Donny Hathaway (single) (Atlantic)

BEST POP INSTRUMENTAL PERFORMANCE BY AN INSTRUMENTAL PERFORMER
AMAZING GRACE - Pipes & Drums & Military Band of the Royal Scots Dragoon Guards (album) (RCA)
DOC - Doc Severinsen (album) (RCA)
THE INNER MOUNTING FLAME - Mahavishnu Orchestra with John McLaughlin (album) (Col.)
JOY - Apollo 100 (single) (Mega)
OUTA-SPACE - Billy Preston (single) (A&M)

BEST POP INSTRUMENTAL PERFORMANCE BY AN ARRANGER, COMPOSER, ORCHESTRA AND/OR CHORAL LEADER
BLACK MOSES - Isaac Hayes (album) (Enterprise)
BRASS ON IVORY - Henry Mancini and Doc Severinsen (Album) (RCA)
CARAVANSERAI - Santana (album) (Col.)
MONEY RUNNER - Quincy Jones (single) (Reprise)
PICTURES AT AN EXHIBITION - Emerson, Lake and Palmer (album) (Cotillion/Atl.)
THEME FROM THE GARDEN OF THE FINZI CONTINIS - Cy Coleman (single) (London)

BEST R&B VOCAL PERFORMANCE, FEMALE
CLEAN UP WOMAN - Betty Wright (single) (Alston/Atl)
FROM A WHISPER TO A SCREAM - Esther Phillips (album) (Kudu/CTI)
IN THE GHETTO - Candi Staton (single) (Fame)
OH, NO NOT MY BABY - Merry Clayton (single) (Ode)
YOUNG, GIFTED & BLACK - Aretha Franklin (album) (Atlantic)

BEST R&B VOCAL PERFORMANCE, MALE
(All nominations are for singles)
DROWNING IN THE SEA OF LOVE - Joe Simon (Spring)
FREDDIE'S DEAD - Curtis Mayfield (Curtom)
I GOTCHA - Joe Tex (Dial/Merc.)
ME & MRS. JONES - Billy Paul (PIR)
WHAT HAVE THEY DONE TO MY SONG MA - Ray Charles (Tangerine)

BEST R&B VOCAL PERFORMANCE BY A DUO, GROUP OR CHORUS
(All nominations are singles)
HELP ME MAKE IT THROUGH THE NIGHT - Gladys Knight & The Pips (Soul/Motown)
IF YOU DON'T KNOW ME BY NOW - Harold Melvin & The Blue Notes (PIR)
I'LL BE AROUND - The Spinners (Atlantic)
I'LL TAKE YOU THERE - The Staple Singers (Stax)
PAPA WAS A ROLLING STONE - The Temptations (Gordy/Motown)

BEST R&B INSTRUMENTAL PERFORMANCE
CRUSADERS I - Crusaders (album) (Blue Thumb)
EVERYBODY'S TALKIN' - King Curtis (album) (Atco)
JUNKIE CHASE - Curtis Mayfield (Track) (Curtom)
LET'S STAY TOGETHER - Isaac Hayes (single) (Enterprise)
PAPA WAS A ROLLING STONE - The Temptations & Paul Riser, cond. (single) (Gordy/Motown)

BEST RHYTHM & BLUES SONG
(Songwriter's Award)
BACK STABBERS - Leon Huff, Gene McFadden and John Whitehead
EVERYBODY PLAYS THE FOOL - Rudy Clark, J.R. Bailey and Kenny Williams
FREDDIE'S DEAD - Curtis Mayfield
ME & MRS. JONES - Ken Gambel, Leon Huff and Cary Gilbert
PAPA WAS A ROLLING STONE - Barrett Strong and Norman Whitfield

BEST SOUL GOSPEL PERFORMANCE
AMAZING GRACE - Aretha Franklin (album) (Atlantic)
JESU - The Edwin Hawkins Singers - (single) (Buddah)
LAST MILE OF THE WAY - Clara Ward (single) (Nashboro)
MY SWEET LORD - The B.C. & M. Choir (album) (Creed)
PRECIOUS MEMORIES - Aretha Franklin & James Cleveland (track) (Atlantic)

BEST COUNTRY VOCAL PERFORMANCE, FEMALE
(All nominations are singles)
DELTA DAWN - Tanya Tucker (Col.)
HAPPIEST GIRL IN THE WHOLE USA - Donna Fargo (Dot)
MY MAN - Tammy Wynette (Epic)
ONE TIN SOLDIER - Skeeter Davis (RCA)
ONE'S ON THE WAY - Loretta Lynn (Decca)
TOUCH YOUR WOMAN - Dolly Parton (RCA)

BEST COUNTRY VOCAL PERFORMANCE, MALE
CHANTILLY LACE - Jerry Lee Lewis (single) (Mercury)
CHARLEY PRIDE SINGS HEART SONGS - Charley Pride (album) (RCA)
GOOD HEARTED WOMAN - Waylon Jennings (single) (RCA)
I TAKE IT ON HOME - Charlie Rich (single) (Epic)
IT'S NOT LOVE (BUT IT'S NOT BAD) - Merle Haggard (single) (Capitol)

BEST COUNTRY VOCAL PERFORMANCE BY A DUO OR GROUP
CLASS OF '57 - The Statler Bros (single) (Mercury)
IF I HAD A HAMMER - Johnny Cash & June Carter (single) (Col)
LEAD ME ON - Conway Twitty & Loretta Lynn (album) (Decca)
TAKE ME - George Jones & Tammy Wynette (single) (Epic)
WILL THE CIRCLE BE UNBROKEN - Mother Maybelle Carter, Earl Scruggs, Doc Watson, Roy Acuff, Merle Travis, Jimmy Martin, The Nitty Gritty Dirt Band (album) (UA)

BEST COUNTRY INSTRUMENTAL PERFORMANCE
CHET ATKINS PICKS ON THE HITS - Chet Atkins (album) (RCA)
FLOWERS ON THE WALL - Danny Davis & The Nashville Brass (album) (RCA)
FOGGY MOUNTAIN BREAKDOWN - Lester Flatt (single) (RCA)
ME AND CHET - Chet Atkins & Jerry Reed (Album) (RCA)
CHARLIE MC COY/THE REAL MC COY - Charlie McCoy (album) (Monument)

BEST COUNTRY SONG
(A Songwriter's Award)
DELTA DAWN - Alex Harvey & Larry Collins
FUNNY FACE - Donna Fargo
HAPPIEST GIRL IN THE WHOLE USA - Donna Fargo
KISS AN ANGEL GOOD MORNIN' - Ben Peters
WOMAN (SENSUOUS WOMAN) Gary S. Paxton

BEST INSPIRATIONAL PERFORMANCE
(Non-classical)
AMAZING GRACE - The Pipes & Drums & Military Band of the Royal Scots - Dragoon Guards (track) (RCA)
AWARD WINNING GUITAR - Little Jimmy Dempsey (album) (Skylite)
THE GREATEST HITS OF CHRISTMAS - Eugene Ormandy cond. Philadelphia Orchestra and Chorus (album) (RCA)
HE TOUCHED ME - Elvis Presley (album) (RCA)
LAND OF MANY CHURCHES - Merle Haggard (album) (Capitol)
LOVE LIFTED ME - Ray Stevens (single) (Barnaby)
SPREAD A LITTLE LOVE AROUND - Danny Lee & The Children of Truth (album) (RCA)

BEST GOSPEL PERFORMANCE (OTHER THAN SOUL GOSPEL)
(All nominations are albums)
AMERICA SINGS - The Thrasher Bros. (Canaan)
BY YOUR REQUEST - Wendy Bagwell & the Sunliters (Canaan)
LIGHT - Oak Ridge Boys (Heartwarming)
L-O-V-E - Blackwood Bros. (RCA)
SOUL IN THE FAMILY - The Rambos (Heartwarming)

BEST ETHNIC OR TRADITIONAL RECORDING (INCLUDING TRADITIONAL BLUES)
(All nominations are albums)
BLUES PIANO ORGY - Little Brother Mongomery, Roosevelt Sykes, Sunnyland Slim, Speckled Red, Otis Spann, Curtis Jones - Prod: Robert G. Koester (Delmark)
LIGHTNIN' STRIKES - Lightnin' Hopkins (Tradition/Everest)
LIVE AT SOLEDAD PRISON - John Lee Hooker (ABC)
THE LONDON MUDDY WATERS SESSION - Muddy Waters (Chess)
WALKING THE BLUES - Otis Spann (Barnaby)

BEST RECORDING FOR CHILDREN
(All nominations are albums)
THE ELECTRIC COMPANY - Lee Chamberlin, Bill Cosby, Rita Moreno (WB)
KUKLA, FRAN & OLLIE - Kukla, Fran & Ollie (RCA/Camden)
THE MUPPET ALPHABET ALBUM - Muppets (Jim Henson) (Col. Children's Album)
SESAME STREET II - Original TV Cast - Prods: Joe Raposo & Jeffrey Moss (WB)
SNOOPY, COME HOME - Original Cast - Composers: Robert B. & Richard M. Sherman (Columbia)

BEST COMEDY RECORDING
(All nominations are albums)
ALL IN THE FAMILY - The Bunkers (Carroll O'Connor, Jean Stapleton, Sally Struthers, Robert Reiner) (Atlantic)
AND THAT'S THE TRUTH - Lily Tomlin (Polydor)
BIG BAMBU - Cheech & Chong (Ode)
FM & AM - George Carlin (Little David)
GERALDINE - Flip Wilson (Little David)

BEST SPOKEN WORD RECORDING
(All nominations are albums)
ANGELA DAVIS SPEAKS - Angela Davis (Folkways)
CANNONBALL ADDERLEY PRESENTS SOUL ZODIAC - Narrator: Rick Holmes (Capitol)
LENNY - Original Cast - Prod: Bruce Botnick (Blue Thumb)
THE WORD - Rod McKuen (Discus/Stanyan)
YEVTUSHENKO - Yevtushenko (Col.)

BEST INSTRUMENTAL COMPOSITION
(Composer's Award)
BRASS ON IVORY - Henry Mancini (RCA)
BRIAN'S SONG - Michel Legrand (Bell)
OUTA-SPACE - Billy Preston & Joe Greene (A&M)
THEME FROM FRENCH CONNECTION - Don Ellis (Col.)
THEME FROM THE GODFATHER - Nino Rota (Paramount)

BEST ORIGINAL SCORE WRITTEN FOR A MOTION PICTURE OR A TELEVISION SPECIAL
(Composer's Award)
$ SOUNDTRACK - Quincy Jones (Reprise)
THE GARDEN OF THE FINZI CONTINIS - Manuel DeSica (RCA)
THE GODFATHER - Nino Rota (Paramount)
NICHOLAS AND ALEXANDRA - Richard Rodney Bennett (Bell)
SUPERFLY - Curtis Mayfield (Curtom)

BEST SCORE FROM THE ORIGINAL CAST SHOW ALBUM
(Grammys to the Composers and A&R Producer)
AIN'T SUPPOSED TO DIE A NATURAL DEATH - Comp: Melvin Van Peebles - Prod: Melvin Van Peebles (A&M)
DON'T BOTHER ME I CAN'T COPE - Comp: Micki Grant - Prod: Jerry Ragavoy (Polydor)
GREASE - Comps: Warren Casey & Jim Jacobs - Prod: Arnold Maxin (MGM)
SUGAR - Comps: Jule Styne & Bob Merrill - Prod: Mitch Miller (UA)
TWO GENTLEMEN OF VERONA - Comps: John Guare & Galt MacDermott - Prods: Harold Wheeler & Galt MacDermott & Lee Young (ABC)

ALBUM OF THE YEAR, CLASSICAL
(Grammys to the Artist and Producer; Certificates to the Engineer)
BERLIOZ: BENVENUTO CELLINI - Colin Davis cond. BBC Symphony Chorus of Covent Garden (Gedda, Eda-Pierre, Soyer, Berbie) Prod: Erik Smith (Philips)
BERNSTEIN: MASS - Leonard Bernstein cond. Choirs & Orchestra - Prods: John McClure & Richard Killough (Col.)
BRAHMS: CONCERTO NO. 2 IN B FLAT MAJOR FOR PIANO - Artur Rubinstein; Eugene Ormandy cond. Philadelphia Orchestra - Prod: Max Wilcox (RCA)
HOROWITZ PLAYS CHOPIN (Pol. in A-Flat Major Intro & Rondo, OP. 16, Etc.) Vladimir Horowitz - Prods: Richard Killough & Thomas Frost (Col.)
MAHLER: SYMPHONY NO. 8 IN E FLAT MAJOR ("SYMPHONY OF A THOUSAND") - Georg Solti cond. Chicago Symphony, Vienna Boys Choir, Vienna State Opera Chorus, Vienna Singverein Chorus & Soloists - Prod: David Harvey (London)
WAGNER: TANNHAUSER - Georg Solti cond. Vienna Philharmonic (Kollo, Dernesch, Ludwig, Braun, Sotin) Prod: Ray Munshull (London)

BEST CLASSICAL PERFORMANCE - ORCHESTRA
(A Conductor's Award)

BOULEZ CONDUCTS BARTOK/THE MIRACULOUS MANDARIN & DANCE SUITE - Pierre Boulez cond. New York Philharmonic (Col.)
GLIERE: ILYA MUROMETZ (SYMPHONY NO. 3) Eugene Ormandy cond. Philadelphia Orchestra (RCA)
HAYDN: SYMPHONIES (COMPLETE) VOL. 4 & 5 Antal Dorati cond. Philharmonia Hungarica (London)
IVES: ORCHESTRAL SET NO. 2 - Leopold Stokowski cond. London Symphony (London)
MAHLER: SYMPHONY NO. 7 IN E MINOR - Georg Solti cond. Chicago Symphony (London)
SCHUMANN: SYMPHONIES (4) Herbert von Karajan cond. Berlin Philharmonic (DG)
SHOSTAKOVICH: SYMPHONY NO. 15 - Maksim Shostakovich cond. Moscow Radio Symphony (Mel/Angel)
STRAVINSKY: RITE OF SPRING (SACRE DU PRINTEMPS) - Michael Tilson Thomas cond. Boston Symphony (DG)

BEST OPERA RECORDING
(Grammys to Conductor & Producer)

BERLIOZ: BENVENUTO CELLINI - Colin Davis cond. BBC Symphony/Chorus of Covent Garden/Prin. Solos: Nicolai Gedda, Christiane Eda-Pierre, Roger Soyer, Jeanne Berbie - Prod: Erik Smith (Philips)
BRITTEN: OWEN WINGRAVE - Benjamin Britten cond. English Chamber Orchestra/Prin. Solos: J. Baker, P. Pears, B. Luson, H. Harper - Prod: David Harvey (London)
MUSSORGSKY: BORIS GODUNOV - Herbert von Karajan cond. Vienna Philharmonic Vienna Boys Choir, Vienna State Opera Chorus/Prin. Solos: Nicolai Ghaiurov, Galina Vishnevskaya, Ludovic Spiess, Martti Talvela, Aleksei Maslennikov - Prod: Ray Minshull (London)
STRAUSS: DER ROSENKAVALIER - Leonard Bernstein cond. Vienna State Opera Chorus/Vienna Philharmonic/Prin. Solos: Christa Ludwig, Walter Berry, Lucia Popp, Jones - Prod: John Culshaw (Columbia)
WAGNER: THE RING OF THE NIBELUNG - Wilhelm Furtwangler cond. Rome Symphony/RAI Chorus/Prin. Solos: Martha Modl, Ludwig Suthaus, Ferdinand Frantz - Prods: J.D. Bicknell & Radiotelevisione Italiana (Seraphim)
WAGNER: TANNHAUSER - Georg Solti cond. Vienna Philharmonic/Prin. Solos: Rene Kollo, Helga Dernesch, Christa Ludwig, Victor Braun, Hans Sotin - Prod: Ray Minshull (London)

BEST CHORAL PERFORMANCE, CLASSICAL (OTHER THAN OPERA)
(Grammys to the Conductor and Choral Director)

BERNSTEIN: MASS - Leonard Bernstein cond, the Orchestra and Norman Schribner and Berkshire Boys Choirs (Col.)
DELIUS: A MASS OF LIFE - Charles Groves cond. the London Philharmonic Choir and Orchestra (Angel)
THE GLORY OF VENICE (GABRIELI IN SAN MARCO - Music for Multiple Choirs, Brass & Organ) E. Power Biggs, Gregg Smith Singers, Texas Boys Choir, Gregg Smith/Tarr Brass Ensemble, Vittorio Negri, cond. (Col.)
MAHLER: SYMPHONY NO. 8 IN E FLAT MAJOR ("SYMPHONY OF A THOUSAND") - Georg Solti cond. Vienna State Opera chorus, Vienna Singverein Chorus, Vienna Boys Choir, Chicago Symphony & Soloists (London)
MONTEVERDI: MADRIGALS, Books 8, 9 and 10 Raymond Leppard cond. Glyndebourne Opera Chorus/Ambrosian Singers/English Chamber Orchestra (Philips)
PROKOFIEV: ALEXANDER NEVSKY - Andre Previn cond. London Symphony Chorus and Orchestra (Angel)

BEST CHAMBER MUSIC PERFORMANCE

BARTOK: SONATAS NO. 1 & 2 FOR VIOLIN AND PIANO - Isaac Stern & Alexander Zakin (Col.)
DVORAK: QUINTET IN A MAJOR FOR PIANO - Artur Rubinstein & Guarneri Quartet (RCA)
JULIAN & JOHN (Sel. by Lawes, Carulli, Albeniz, Granados) Julian Bream & John Williams (RCA)
MUSIC FOR GUITAR & HARPSICHORD (Works by Straube, Ponce & Dodgson) John Williams & Rafael Puyana (Col.)
MUSIC FOR TWO HARPSICHORDS (Mozart, Byrd, Farnably, etc.) Igor Kipnis & Turston Dart (Col.)
SCHUBERT: QUARTET NO. 13 IN A MINOR - Guarneri Quartet (RCA)
SHOSTAKOVICH: SONATA FOR VIOLIN & PIANO - David Oistrakh & Sviatoslav Richter (Mel/Angel)
STRING QUARTETS OF THE NEW VIENNESE SCHOOL - La Salle Quartet (DG)

BEST CLASSICAL PERFORMANCE - INSTRUMENTAL SOLOIST OR SOLOISTS (WITH ORCHESTRA)

BRAHMS: CONCERTO NO. 2 IN B FLAT MAJOR FOR PIANO - Artur Rubinstein (Ormandy cond. Philadelphia Orchestra) (RCA)
MOZART: COMPLETE WORKS FOR VIOLIN & ORCHESTRA - David Oistrakh (Berlin Philharmonic) (Angel)
MOZART: THE FOUR HORN CONCERTOS - Barry Tuckwell (Marriner cond. Academy of St. Martin-In-Fields) (Angel)
MUSIC FOR ORGAN, BRASS & PERCUSSION - E. Power Biggs (Peress cond. Col. Brass Percussion Ensemble) (Col)
RAVEL: CONCERTO IN D MAJOR FOR LEFT HAND - Philippe Entremont (Boulez cond. Cleveland Orchestra) (Col)
STRAUSS: CONCERTO IN D MAJOR FOR OBOE - Heinz Holliger (DeWaart cond. New Philharmonia) (Philips)

BEST CLASSICAL PERFORMANCE - INSTRUMENTAL SOLOIST OR SOLOISTS (WITHOUT ORCHESTRA)

THE ART OF LAURINDO ALMEIDA - Laurindo Almeida (Orion)
BEETHOVEN: THE LATE SONATAS FOR PIANO - Charles Rosen (Col.)
COUPERIN: HARPSICHORD PIECES - Rafael Puyana (Philips)
DEBUSSY: IMAGES, BOOKS 1 & 2 CHILDREN'S CORNER SUITE - Arturo Benedetti Michelangeli (DG)
HOROWITZ PLAYS CHOPIN - Vladimir Horowitz (Col)
JANACEK: PIANO WORKS (COMPLETE) - Rudolf Firkusny (DG)
PAGANINI: THE 24 CAPRICES - Itzhak Perlman (Angel)
SCHUMANN: DAVIDSBUNDLERTANZE/BRAHMS: SONATA NO. 1 - William Masselos (RCA)

BEST CLASSICAL VOCAL SOLOIST PERFORMANCE

BRAHMS: DIE SCHONE MAGELONE - Dietrich Fischer-Dieskau (Accom: Richter) (Angel)
ELGAR: SEA PICTURES - Janet Baker (Barbirolli cond. London Symphony) (Angel)
FIVE GREAT OPERATIC SCENES (Verdi: Traviata, Don Carlo/Tchaikovsky: Onegin/Strauss: Ariadne, etc.) - Leontyne Price (Cleva cond. London Symphony) (RCA)
SONGS BY STEPHEN FOSTER - Jan de Gaetani (Accom: Kalish) (Nonesuch)
SONGS OF DEBUSSY - Anna Moffo (accomp: Robert Casadesus) (RCA)
WAGNER: WESENDONCK LIEDER - Birgit Nilsson (Davis cond. London Symphony) (Philips)

BEST ALBUM NOTES (CLASSICAL)
(Annotator's Award)

BERLIOZ: BENVENUTO CELLINI - Davis cond. BBC Symphony - Ann: David Cairns (Philips)
HAYDN: SYMPHONIES (COMPLETE) VOLS. 4 & 5 - Dorati cond. Philharmonia Hungarica - Ann: H. C. Robbins Landon (London)
JOHN OGDON PLAYS ALKAN - John Ogdon - Ann: Sacheverell Sitwell (RCA)
JULIAN & JOHN - Julian Bream & John Williams - Ann: Tom Eastwood (RCA)
MICHAEL RABIN - IN MEMORIAM - Michael Rabin - Ann: Karolynne Gee (Seraphim)
STRING QUARTETS OF THE NEW VIENNESE SCHOOL - La Salle Quar-

tet - Ann: Dr. Ursula Von Rauchhaupt (DG)
VAUGHAN WILLIAMS: SYMPHONY NO. 2 ("A LONDON SYMPHONY") - Previn cond. London Symphony - ann: James Lyons (RCA)

BEST ENGINEERED RECORDING (CLASSICAL)
(Engineer's Award)
BERNSTEIN: MASS - Bernstein cond. Orchestra & Choir - Eng: Don Puluse (Col.)
BERLIOZ: BENVENUTO CELLINI - Davis cond. BBC Symphony/Chorus of Covent Garden - Eng: Hans Lauterslager (Philips)
BOULEZ CONDUCTS STRAVINSKY (PETRUSHKA) - Boulez cond. New York Philharmonic - Engs: Raymond Moore & Edward Graham (Col.)
BOULEZ CONDUCTS BARTOK/THE MIRACULOUS MANDARIN (Complete) & DANCE SUITE - Boulez cond. New York Philharmonic - Hugh Ross, Dir., Schola Cantorum - Engs: Edward Graham & Raymond Moore (Col.)
GLIERE: ILYA MUROMETZ (SYMPHONY NO. 3) Ormandy cond. Philadelphia Orchestra - Eng: Paul Goodman (RCA)
MAHLER: SYMPHONY NO. 8 ("SYMPHONY OF A THOUSAND") - Solti cond. Chicago Symphony - Engs: Gordon Parry & Kenneth Wilkinson
WAGNER: TANNHAUSER - Solti cond. Vienna Philharmonic - Engs: Gordon Parry, James Lock & Colin Moorfoot (London)

1973

RECORD OF THE YEAR
(Grammys to the Artist and A&R Producer)
BAD, BAD LEROY BROWN - Jim Croce - Terry Cashman & Tommy West, Producers (ABC)
BEHIND CLOSED DOORS - Charlie Rich - Bill Sherrill, Producer (EPIC/Col.)
KILLING ME SOFTLY WITH HIS SONG - Roberta Flack - Joel Dorn, Producer (Atlantic)
YOU ARE THE SUNSHINE OF MY LIFE Stevie Wonder - Stevie Wonder, Producer (Tamla/Motown)
YOU'RE SO VAIN - Carly Simon - Richard Perry, Producer (Elektra)

ALBUM OF THE YEAR
(Grammys to the Artist and A&R Producer)
BEHIND CLOSED DOORS - Charlie Rich - Billy Sherrill, Producer (Epic/Col.)
THE DIVINE MISS M - Bette Midler - Joel Dorn, Barry Manilow, Geoffrey Haslam & Ahmet Ertegun, Producers (Atlantic)
INNERVISIONS - Stevie Wonder - Stevie Wonder, Producer (Tamla/Motown)
KILLING ME SOFTLY - Roberta Flack - Joel Dorn, Producer (Atlantic)
THERE GOES RHYMIN' SIMON - Paul Simon - Paul Simon, Phil Ramone, Paul Samwell-Smith, Roy Halee and M.S.S. Rhythm Studio, Producers (Col)

SONG OF THE YEAR
(A Songwriter's Award)
BEHIND CLOSED DOORS - Kenny O'Dell
KILLING ME SOFTLY WITH HIS SONG - Norman Gimbel, Charles Fox
TIE A YELLOW RIBBON ROUND THE OLE OAK TREE - Irwin Levine, L. Russell Brown
YOU ARE THE SUNSHINE OF MY LIFE - Stevie Wonder
YOU'RE SO VAIN - Carly Simon

BEST NEW ARTIST OF THE YEAR
EUMIR DEODATO (CTI)
MAUREEN McGOVERN (20th Century)
BETTE MIDLER (Atlantic)
MARIE OSMOND (MGM)
BARRY WHITE (20th Century)

BEST INSTRUMENTAL ARRANGEMENT
(An Arranger's Award)
THE DAILY DANCE - Stan Kenton & His Orchestra - Bill Holman, Arranger (Creative World)
EASY LIVING/AIN'T NOBODY'S BUSINESS IF I DO (Medley) - Grover Washing, Jr. - Bob James, Arranger (Kudu/CTI)
PROLOGUE/CRUNCHY GRANOLA SUITE - Neil Diamond - Lee Holdridge, Arranger (MCA)
SPAIN - Chick Corea and Return to Forever - Chick Corea, Arranger (Polydor)
SUMMER IN THE CITY - Quincy Jones - Quincy Jones, Arranger (A&M)

BEST ARRANGEMENT ACCOMPANYING VOCALIST
(An Arranger's Award)
LADY LOVE - Jon Lucien - Dave Grusin, Arranger (RCA)
LIVE AND LET DIE - Paul McCartney & Wings - George Martin, Arranger (Apple/Capitol)
MICHELLE - The Singers Unlimited - Gene Puerling, Arranger (MPS/BASF)
RASHIDA - Jon Lucien - Dave Grusin, Arranger (RCA)
SING - Carpenters - Richard Carpenter, Arranger (A&M)
TOUCH ME IN THE MORNING - Diana Ross - Tom Baird & Gene Page, Arrangers (Motown)

BEST ENGINEERED RECORDING (NON-CLASSICAL)
(An Engineer's Award)
THE DARK SIDE OF THE MOON - Pink Floyd - Alan Parson, Engineer (album) (Harvest/Capitol)
GOODBYE YELLOW BRICK ROAD - Elton John - David Hentschel, Engineer (album) (MCA)
INNERVISIONS - Stevie Wonder - Robert Margouleff & Malcolm Cecil Engineers (album) (Tamla/Motown)
LONG TRAIN RUNNIN' - The Doobie Brothers - Donn Landee, Engineer (track) (WB)
NO SECRETS - Carly Simon - Robin Geoffrey Cable & Bill Schnee, Engineers (album) (Elektra)

BEST ALBUM PACKAGE
(Grammy to Art Director)
BILLION DOLLAR BABIES (Alice Cooper) Pacific Eye and Ear, Art Director (WB)
CHICAGO VI - (Chicago) John Berg, Art director (Col)
CHUBBY CHECKER'S GREATEST HITS - (Chubby Checker) Al Steckler, Art director (ABKCO)
HOUSES OF THE HOLY - (Led Zeppelin) Hipgnosis, Art Director (Atl)
LOS COCHINOS - (Cheech & Chong) - Ode Visuals, Inc., Art Director (Ode/A&M)
OOH LA LA - (Faces) Jim Ladwig - AGI, Art Director (WB)
TOMMY - (London Symphony/Chambre Choir) Wilkes & Braun, Inc., Art Director (Ode/A&M)
THE WORLD OF IKE & TINA - (Ike & Tina Turner) Mike Salisbury, Art Director (UA)

BEST ALBUM NOTES
(An Annotator's Award)
GOD IS IN THE HOUSE - (Art Taum); Ann - Dan Morgenstern (Onyx)
LONESOME, ON'RY AND MEAN - (Waylon Jennings); Ann - Chet Flippo (RCA)

OL' BLUE EYES IS BACK - (Frank Sinatra); Ann - Stan Cornyn (Reprise/W.B.)
REMEMBER MARILYN - (Marilyn Monroe); Ann - Lionel Newman (20th Century)
THIS IS JIMMIE RODGERS - (Jimmie Rodgers); Ann - William Ivey (RCA)

BEST JAZZ PERFORMANCE BY A SOLOIST
THE BEGINNING AND THE END - Clifford Brown (Album) (Col)
GOD IS IN THE HOUSE - Art Tatum (album) (Onyx)
IN A MIST - Freddie Hubbard (track) (CTI)
MORNING STAR - Hubert Laws (Album) (CTI)
THE VERY THOUGHT OF YOU - Ray Brown (Milt Jackson Quintet) (track) (Impulse/ABC)

BEST JAZZ PERFORMANCE BY A GROUP
ALONE TOGETHER - Jim Hall, Ron Carter (album) (Milestone)
INSIDE STRAIGHT - Cannonball Adderley Quintet (album) (Fantasy)
LIGHT AS A FEATHER - Chick Corea and Return to Forever (album) (Polydor)
MUSIC OF ANOTHER PRESENT ERA - Oregon (album) (Vanguard)
SUPERSAX PLAYS BIRD - Supersax (album) (Cap)

BEST JAZZ PERFORMANCE BY A BIG BAND
GIANT STEPS - Woody Herman (album) (Fantasy)
SOARING - Don Ellis (album) (MPS/BASF)
SVENGALI - Gil Evans (album) (Atl)
SWISS SUITE - Oliver Nelson (album) (Flying Dutchman)
TANJAH - Randy Weston (album) (Polydor)

BEST POP VOCAL PERFORMANCE, FEMALE
BOOGIE WOOGIE BUGLE BOY - Bette Midler (single) (Atl)
DANNY'S SONG - Anne Murray (single) (Cap)
KILLING ME SOFTLY WITH HIS SONG - Roberta Flack (single) (Atl)
TOUCH ME IN THE MORNING - Diana Ross (singe) (Motown)
YOU'RE SO VAIN - Carly Simon (single) (Elektra)

BEST POP VOCAL PERFORMANCE, MALE
AND I LOVE YOU SO - Perry Como (single) (RCA)
BAD, BAD LEROY BROWN - Jim Croce (single) (ABC)
DANIEL - Elton John (single) (MCA)
THERE GOES RHYMIN' SIMON - Paul Simon (album) (Col)
YOU ARE THE SUNSHINE OF MY LIFE - Stevie Wonder (single) (Tamla/Motown)

BEST POP VOCAL PERFORMANCE BY A DUO, GROUP OR CHORUS
DIAMOND GIRL Seals & Crofts (track) (WB)
LIVE AND LET DIE - Paul McCartney & Wings (single) (Apple/Capitol)
NEITHER ONE OF US (WANTS TO BE THE FIRST TO SAY GOODBYE) - Gladys Knight & the Pips (single) (Soul/Motown)
SING - Carpenters (single) (A&M)
TIE A YELLOW RIBBON ROUND THE OLE OAK TREE - Dawn Featuring Tony Orlando (single) (Bell)

BEST POP INSTRUMENTAL PERFORMANCE
ALSO SPRACH ZARATHUSTRA (2001) Eumir Deodato (single) (CTI)
BIRD OF FIRE - Mahavishnu Orchestra (track) (Col)
FRANKENSTEIN - Edgar Winter (single) (Epic/Col.)
SPACE RACE - Billy Preston (single) (A&M)
YOU'VE GOT IT BAD GIRL (instrumental portions of album) Quincy Jones (A&M)

BEST R&B VOCAL PERFORMANCE, FEMALE
ALONE AGAIN (NATURALLY) Esther Phillips (album) (Kudu/CTI)
ETTA JAMES - Etta James (album) (Chess)
I CAN'T STAND THE RAIN - Ann Peebles (single) (Hi/London)
MASTER OF EYES - Aretha Franklin (single) (Atl)
PILLOW TALK - Sylvia (single) (Vibration)

BEST R&B VOCAL PERFORMANCE, MALE
CALL ME (COME BACK HOME) Al Green (single) (Hi/London)
I'M GONNA LOVE YOU JUST A LITTLE MORE BABY - Barry White (single) (20th Cent.)
KEEP ON TRUCKIN' - Eddie Kendricks (single) (Tamla/Motown)
LET'S GET IT ON - Marvin Gaye (album) (Motown)
SUPERSTITION - Stevie Wonder (track) (Tamla/Motown)

BEST R&B VOCAL PERFORMANCE BY A DUO, GROUP OR CHORUS
BE WHAT YOU ARE - The Staple Singers (single) (Stax)
THE CISCO KID - War (single) (UA)
COULD IT BE I'M FALLING IN LOVE - The Spinners (single) (Atl)
LOVE TRAIN - The O'Jays (single) (Phila. Int'l/Col)
MIDNIGHT TRAIN TO GEORGIA - Gladys Knight & The Pips (single) (Buddah)

BEST R&B INSTRUMENTAL PERFORMANCE
BLACK BYRD - Donald Byrd (album) (Blue Note/UA)
HANG ON SLOOPY - Ramsey Lewis (single) (Col)
2ND CRUSADE - The Crusaders (album) (Blue Thumb)
SOUL MAKOSSA - Manu Dibango (album) (Atl)
YES WE CAN CAN - Young-Holt Unlimited (track) (Atl)

BEST RHYTHM & BLUES SONG
(A Songwriter's Award)
THE CISCO KID - War
FAMILY AFFAIR - Sylvester Stewart
LOVE TRAIN - Ken Gamble, Leon Huff
MIDNIGHT TRAIN TO GEORGIA - Jim Weatherly
SUPERSTITION - Stevie Wonder

BEST SOUL GOSPEL PERFORMANCE
DOWN MEMORY LANE - James Cleveland (track) (Savoy)
HE AIN'T HEAVY - Jessy Dixon (track) (Gospel/Savoy)
LOVES ME LIKE A ROCK - Dixie Hummingbirds (single) (ABC)
NEW WORLD - Edwin Hawkins Singers (album) (Buddah)
YOU'VE GOT A FRIEND - Swan Silvertones (album) (Hob/Scepter)

BEST COUNRY VOCAL PERFORMANCE, FEMALE
COUNTRY SUNSHINE - Dottie West (single) (RCA)
KIDS SAY THE DARNDEST THINGS - Tammy Wynette (single) (Epic/Col.)
LET ME BE THERE - Olivia Newton-John (single) (MCA)
PAPER ROSES - Marie Osmond (single) (MGM)
TEDDY BEAR SONG - Barbara Fairchild (single) (Columbia)

BEST COUNTRY VOCAL PERFORMANCE, MALE
AMAZING LOVE - Charley Pride (single) (RCA)
BEHIND CLOSED DOORS - Charlie Rich (single) (Epic/Col.)
(OLD DOGS.xxx . .CHILDREN AND) WATERMELON WINE Tom T. Hall (single) (Mercury)
REDNECKS, WHITE SOCKS & BLUE RIBBON BEER - Johnny Russell (single) (RCA)
WHY ME - Kris Kristofferson (single) (Monument)

BEST COUNTRY VOCAL PERFORMANCE BY A DUO OR GROUP
CARRY ME BACK - Statler Brothers (album) (Mercury)
FROM THE BOTTLE TO THE BOTTOM - Kris Kristofferson, Rita Coolidge (track) (A&M)
IF TEARDROPS WERE PENNIES - Dolly Parton, Porter Wagoner (single) (RCA)
LOUISIANA WOMAN, MISSISSIPPI MAN - Conway Twitty, Loretta Lynn (single) (MCA)
WE'RE GONNA HOLD ON - Tammy Wynette, George Jones (single) (Epic/Col.)

BEST COUNTRY INSTRUMENTAL PERFORMANCE
DUELING BANJOS - Eric Weissberg, Steve Mandell (track) (WB)
FIDDLIN' AROUND - Chet Atkins (track) (RCA)
GOOD TIME CHARLIE - Charlie McCoy (album) (Monument)
I'LL FLY AWAY - Dann Davis & The Nashville Brass (album) (RCA)
SUPERPICKERS - Chet Atkins (album) (RCA)

BEST COUNTRY SONG
(A Songwriter's Award)
BEHIND CLOSED DOORS Kenny O'Dell
COUNTRY SUNSHINE - Billy Davis & Dottie West
THE MOST BEAUTIFUL GIRL - Rory Bourke, Billy Sherill & Norris Wilson
(OLD DOGS...,CHILDREN AND) WATERMELON WINE - Tom T. Hall
WHY ME - Kris Kristofferson

BEST INSPIRATIONAL PERFORMANCE
ALL THE PRAISES - Connie Smith (album) (RCA)
ANITA BRYANT...NATURALLY - Anita Bryant (album) (Myrrh/Word)
IN THE SWEET BY AND BY - Roy Rogers & Dale Evans (album) (Word)
LET'S JUST PRAISE THE LORD - Bill Gaither Trio (album) (Impact/Hrtwarming)
THERE'S SOMETHING ABOUT THAT NAME - George Beverly Shea (album) (RCA)

BEST GOSPEL PERFORMANCE (OTHER THAN SOUL GOSPEL)
I BELIEVE IN JESUS - Statesmen (album) (Artistic)
JUST ANDRAE - Andrae Crouch (album) (light/Word)
LIVE - The Imperials (album) (Impact/Hrtwarming)
RELEASE ME (FROM MY SIN) - Blackwood Brothers (album) (Skylite)
STREET GOSPEL - Oak Ridge Boys (album) (Heartwarming)

BEST ETHNIC OR TRADITIONAL RECORDING
BLUES AT MONTREAUX - King Curtis & Champion Jack Dupree (album) (Atl)
CAN'T GET NO GRINDIN' - Muddy Waters (album) (Chess)
JOHN LEE HOOKER'S DETROIT (1948-1952) John Lee Hooker (album) (UA)
LEADBELLY (LIVE IN CONCERT) - Leadbelly (album) (Playboy)
THEN AND NOW - Doc Watson (album) (UA)

BEST RECORDING FOR CHILDREN
FREE TO BE...YOU AN ME - Marlo Thomas and Friends (album) (Bell)
THE LITTLE PRINCE - Peter Ustinov (album) (Argo)
MULTIPLICATION ROCK - Bob Dorough, Grady Tate, Blossom Dearie (album) (Cap)
SESAME STREET LIVE - Sesame Street Cast (album) - Joe Roposo, Producer (Col)
SONGS FROM the Electric Co. TV Show Conducted by Buddy Baker, with Vocalists (album) (Disneyland)

BEST COMEDY RECORDING
LOS COCHINOS - Cheech & Chong (album) (Ode/A&M)
FAT ALBERT - Bill Cosby (album) (MCA)
OCCUPATION: FOOLE - George Carlin (album) (Little David/Atl.)
RICHARD NIXON: A FANTASY - David Frye (album) (Buddah)
LEMMINGS - National Lampoon (album) (Banana/Blue Thumb)
CHILD OF THE 50's) - Robert Klein (album) (Brut/Buddah)

BEST SPOKEN WORD RECORDING
AMERICA, WHY I LOVE HER - John Wayne (album) (RCA)
JONATHAN LIVINGSTON SEAGULL - Richard Harris (album) (Dunhill/ABC)
SLAUGHTERHOUSE-FIVE - Kurt Vonnegut, Jr. (album) (Caedmon)
SONGS & CONVERSATIONS - Billie Holiday (album) (Paramount)
WITCHES GHOSTS & GOBLINS - Vincent Price (album) (Caedmon)

BEST INSTRUMENTAL COMPOSITION
(A Composer's Award)
FRANKENSTEIN - Edgar Winter
HOCUS POCUS - Thijs van Leer and Jan Akkerman
LAST TANGO IN PARIS - Gato Barbieri
SOUL MAKOSSA - Manu Dibanog
SPACE RACE - Billy Preston

ALBUM OF BEST ORIGINAL SCORE WRITTEN FOR A MOTION PICTURE OR A TELEVISION SPECIAL
(A Composer's Award)
JONATHAN LIVINGSTON SEAGULL - Neil Diamond (Col)
LAST TANGO IN PARIS - Gato Barbieri (UA)
LIVE AND LET DIE - Paul & Linda McCartney & George Martin (UA)
PAT GARRETT & BILLY THE KID - Bob Dylan (Col)
SOUNDER - Taj Mahal (Col)

BEST SCORE FROM THE ORIGINAL CAST SHOW ALBUM
CYRANO - Anthony Burgess, Michael J. Lewis, Composers; Jerry Moss, Phil Ramone, Producers (A&M)
A LITTLE NIGHT MUSIC - Stephen Sondheim, Composer; Goddard Lieberson, Producer (Col)
MAN FROM THE EAST - Stomu Yamashta, Composer; Stomu Yamashta, Producer (Island/Cap)
PIPPIN - Stephen Schwartz Composer; Stephen Schwartz, Phil Ramone, Producers (Motown)
SEESAW - Cy Coleman, Dorothy Fields, Composer; Cy Coleman, Producer (Buddah)

ALBUM OF THE YEAR, CLASSICAL
(Grammys to the Artist and Producer)
BARTOK: CONCERTO FOR ORCHESTRA - Pierre Boulez cond. New York Philharmonic - Thomas Z. Shepard, Producer (Col)
BEETHOVEN: CONCERTI (5) FOR PIANO & ORCHESTRA (Vladimir Ashkenazy/Georg Solti cond. Chicago Symphony - David Harvey, Producer (London)
BIZET: CARMEN - Leonard Bernstein cond. Metropolitan Opera Orchestra/Manhattan Opera Chorus/Soloists: M. Horne, J. McCracken, A. Maliponte, T. Krause - Thomas W. Mowrey, Producer (D.G./Polydor)
JOPLIN: THE RED BACK BOOK - Gunther Schuller cond. NE Conservatory Ragtime Ensemble - George Sponhaltz, Producer (Angel/Cap)
PROKOFIEV: ROMEO AND JULIET - Lorin Maazel cond. Cleveland Orchestra - Michael Woolcock, Producer (London)
PUCCINI: HEROINES (La Boheme, La Rondine, Tosca, Manon, Lescaut) - Leontyne Price/Downes cond. New Philharmonia) Richard Mohr, Producer (RCA)
(RACHMANINOFF) THE COMPLETE RACHMANINOFF - Vols. 1, 2, 3 - Sergei Rachmaninoff - John Pfeiffer, Greg Benko, Producers (RCA)

RACHMANINOFF: CONCERTO NO. 2 IN C MINOR FOR PIANO - Artur Rubinstein/Eugene Ormandy cond. Philadelphia Orchestra - Max Wilcox, Producer (RCA)

BEST CLASSICAL PERFORMANCE - ORCHESTRA
(A Conductor's Award)

BARTOK: CONCERTO FOR ORCHESTRA - Pierre Boulez cond. New York Philharmonic (Col)
BEETHOVEN: SYMPHONY NO. 9 IN D MINOR - Georg Solti cond. Chicago Symphony (London)
BERLIOZ: SYMPHONIE FANTASTIQUE - Seiji Ozawa cond. Boston Symphony (E.G./Polydor)
HOLST: THE PLANETS - Leonard Bernstein cond. New York Philharmonic (Col)
PROKOFIEV: ROMEO AND JULIET - Lorin Maazel cond. Cleveland Orchestra (London)
PROKOFIEV: ROMEO AND JULIET (COMPLETE BALLET) - Andre Previn cond. London Symphony (Angel/Cap)
RUSSO: THREE PIECES FOR BLUES BAND AND ORCHESTRA - Seiji Ozawa cond. San Francisco Symphony (Seigel-Schwall Band) (D.G./Polydor)
SIBELIUS: SYMPHONY NO. 2 IN D MAJOR - Eugene Ormandy cond. Philadelphia Orchestra (RCA)

BEST OPERA RECORDING
(Grammys to the Conductor and Producer)

BIZET: CARMEN - Leonard Bernstein cond. Metropolitan Opera Orchestra, Manhattan Opera Chorus/Prin. Solos: M. Horne, J. McCracken, A. Maliponte, T. Krause; Thomas W. Mowrey, Producer (D.G./Poly)
DELIUS: A VILLAGE ROMEO AND JULIET - Meredith Davies cond. Royal Philharmonic/John Alldis Choir/Prin. Solos: Robert Tear, Elizabeth Harwood; Christopher Bishop, Producer (Angel/Cap.)
PUCCINI: TURANDOT - Zubin Mehta cond. London Philharmonic, John Alldis Choir & Wandsworth School Choir/Prin. Solos: Sutherland, Pavarotti, Caballe, Ghaiurov, Krause, Pears; Ray Minshull, Producer (London)
WAGNER: DER RING DES NIBELUNGEN - Karl Bohm cond. Bayreuth Festival Orchestra/Prin Solos: Nilsson, Rysanek, Burmeister, Windgassen, King, Wohlfart, Adam, Stewart, Talvela, Greindl, Neidlinger; Wolfgang Lohse, Producer (Philips/Merc.)
WAGNER: PARSIFAL - George Solti cond. Vienna Philharmonic, Vienna State Opera Chorus/Vienna Boys Choir/Prin. Solos: Kollo, Ludwig, Fischer-Dieskau, Frick, Keleman, Hotter; Christopher Raeburn, Producer (London)
WAGNER: TRISTAN UND ISOLDE - Herbert von Karajan cond. Berlin Philharmonic/Prin. Solos: Vickers, Dernesch; Michael Glotz, Producer (Angel/Cap.)

BEST CHORAL PERFORMANCE, CLASSICAL (OTHER THAN OPERA)
(Grammys to the Conductor and Choral Director)

BACH: ST. MATTHEW PASSION - Helmuth Froschauer cond. Vienna Singverein/Herbert von Karajan cond. Berlin Philharmonic (D.G./Polydor)
BEETHOVEN: MISSA SOLEMNIS - Eugen Jochum cond. Netherlands Radio Chorus & Concertgoebouw Orchestra/Giebel, Hoffgen, Haefliger, Ridderbusch (Phil.)
ELGAR: THE DREAM OF GERONTIUS - David Willcocks cond. Choir of King's College, Cambridge/Benjamin Britten cond. London Symphony (London)
HAYDN: MASS IN TIME OF WAR (Leonard Bernstein's Concert for Peace) - Norman Scribner Choir Norman Scribner, Dir./Orchestra cond. by Leonard Bernstein (Col)
HAYDN: THE SEASON - Herbert von Karajan cond. Chorus of the Deutsche Oper, Berlin & Berlin Philharmonic (Angel/Cap.)
MONTEVERDI: MADRIGALS, BOOKS 3 & 4 - Raymond Leppard cond. Glyndebourne Opera Chorus (Philip)
WALTON: BELSHAZZAR'S FEAST - Andre Previn cond. London Symphony & Arthur Oldham cond. London Symphony Orchestra Chorus (Angel/Cap)

BEST CHAMBER MUSIC PERFORMANCE

BENNETT: CONCERTO FOR GUITAR & CHAMBER ENSEMBLE - Julian Bream/Melos Ensemble of London, David Atherton (RCA)
BRAHMS: QUARTETS FOR STRINGS (COMPLETE) The Cleveland Quartet (RCA)
DVORAK: PIANO QUARTET IN E FLAT MAJOR, OP. 87 - Artur Rubinstein/Guarneri Quartet (RCA)
EARLY AMERICAN VOCAL MUSIC - Western Wind Vocal Ensemble (Nonesuch)
JOPLIN: THE RED BACK BOOK - Gunther Schuller & New England Ragtime Ensemble (Angel/Cap.)
ROCHBERG: QUARTET NO. 3 FOR STRINGS - Concord String Quartet (Nonesuch)
SCHUBERT: DUETS - Janet Baker, Dietrich Fischer-Dieskau (D.G./Polydor)

BEST CLASSICAL PERFORMANCE - INSTRUMENTAL SOLOIST OR SOLOISTS (WITH ORCHESTRA)

BEETHOVEN: CONCERTI (5) FOR PIANO & ORCHESTRA - Vladimir Shkenazy (Solti cond. Chicago Symphony) (London)
BRAHMS: CONCERTO NO. 1 IN D MINOR FOR PIANO & ORCHESTRA & CONCERTO NO. 2 IN B FLAT MAJOR FOR PIANO & ORCHESTRA - Emil Gilels (Jochum cond. Berlin Philharmonic) (D.G./Pol)
MOZART: CONCERTO NO. 21 IN C MAJOR & CONCERTO NO. 25 IN C MAJOR - Stephen Bishop (C. Davis cond. London Symphony) (Philips/Merc.)
PREVIN: CONCERTO FOR GUITAR & ORCHESTRA/PONCE: CONCIERTO DEL SUR FOR GUITAR & ORCHESTRA - John Williams (Previn cond. London Symphony) (Col)
RACHMANINOFF: CONCERTO NO. 2 IN C MINOR FOR PIANO - Artur Rubinstein (Ormandy cond. Philadelphia Orchestra) (RCA)
SAINT-SAENS: CONCERTI FOR PIANO (COMPLETE) Aldo Ciccolini (Baudo cond. Orchestre de Paris) (Seraphim/Cap.)
VIVALDI: FOUR SEASONS - Pinchas Zukerman - (Zukerman cond. English Chamber Orchestra) (Col)

BEST CLASSICAL PERFORMANCE - INSTRUMENTAL SOLOIST OR SOLOISTS (WITHOUT ORCHESTRA)

BACH: FRENCH SUITES 1 - 4 Glenn Gould (Col)
BACH: WELL-TEMPERED KLAVIER - Sviatoslav Richter (Melodiya/Angel)
CHOPIN: ETUDES - Maurizio Pollini (D.G.Poly)
HEAVY ORGAN AT CARNEGIE HALL - Virgil Fox (RCA)
SCHUBERT: SONATA IN B FLAT, OP. 960 - Alfred Brendel (Philips/Merc.)
(SCRIABIN) HOROWITZ PLAYS SCRIABIN - Vladimir Horowitz (Col)
THE WOODS SO WILD - Julian Bream (RCA)

BEST CLASSICAL VOCAL SOLOIST PERFORMANCE

BERG: SEVEN EARLY SONGS - Heather Harper (Boulez cond. BBC Symphony) (Col)
BERIO: RECITAL 1 (FOR CATHY) - Cathy Berberian (Berio cond. London Sinfonietta) (RCA)
LA VOCE D'ORO - Placido Domingo (Santi cond. New Philharmonia) (RCA)
MAHLER: DAS LIED VON DER ERDE - Yvonne Minton, Rene Kollo (Solti cond. Chicago Symphony) (London)
MARILYN HORNE SINGS ROSSINI (Excerpts from Siege of Corinth & La Donna del Lago) - Marilyn Horne (Lewis cond. Royal Philharmonic) (London)
MARTTI TALVELA - A LIEDER RECITAL (Schumann) Martti Talvela; (Irwin Gage, Accomp.) (London)
PUCCINI: HEROINES (La Boheme, La Rondine, Tosca, Manon Lescaut) - Leontyne Price (Downes cond. New Philharmonia) (RCA)
SCHUBERT: SONGS - Janet Baker; (Gerald Moore, accomp.) (Sera-

phim/Cap.)

BEST ALBUM NOTES - CLASSICAL
(An Annotator's Award)
BACH: BRANDENBURG CONCERTI - Marriner cond. Acad. of St. Martin-in-the Fields - Ann: Erik Smith (Philips/Merc.)
BERIO: RECITAL 1 (FOR CATHY) Berberian, Berio cond. London Sinfonietta - Ann: Misha Donat (RCA)
BIZET: CARMEN - Bernstein cond. Metropolitan Opera Orchestra, Horne, McCracken, Maliponte, Krause - Ann: Harvey Phillips (D.G.)
DEBUSSY: LA MER/PRELUDE A L'APRES MIDI D'UN FAUNE & RAVEL: DAPHNIS & CHLOE SUITE NO. 2 - Ormandy cond. Philadelphia Orchestra - Ann: Clair Van Ausdall (RCA)
DVORAK: PIANO QUARTET IN E FLAT MAJOR, OP. 87 - Guarneri Quartet/Artur Rubinstein - Ann: Irving Kolodin (RCA)
HINDEMITH: SONATAS FOR PIANO (COMPLETE) Glenn Gould - Ann: Glenn Gould (Col.)
HAYDN: SYMPHONY NO. 36 - SYMPHONY NO. 48 - Dorati cond. Philharmonica Hungarica - Ann: H.C. Robbins Landon (London)
HAYDN: SYMPHONY NO. 20 IN C MAJOR TO SYMPHONY NO. 35 IN B FLAT MAJOR - Dorati cond. Philharmonica Hungarica - Ann: H.C. Robbins Landon (London)
RACHMANINOFF: CONCERTO NO. 2 IN C MINOR FOR PIANO - Rubinstein/Ormandy cond. Philadelphia Orchestra - Ann: Alan Rich (RCA)
THE WOODS SO WILD - Julian Bream - Ann: Tom Eastwood (RCA)

BEST ENGINEERED RECORDING - CLASSICAL
(An Engineer's Award)
BACH'S GREATEST FUGUES - Ormandy cond. Philadelphia Orchestra - Paul Goodman, Eng. (RCA)
BARTOK: CONCERTO FOR ORCHESTRA - Boulez cond. New York Philharmonic - Edward T. Graham, Raymond Moore, Engs. (Columbia)
BERLIOZ: SYMPHONIE FANTASTIQUE - Ozawa cond. Boston Symphony - Hans Schweigmann, Eng. (E.G./Poly.)
BIZET: CARMEN - Bernstein cond. Metropolitan Opera Orchestra & Soloists - Gunther Hermanns, Eng. (D.G./Poly.)
HOLST: THE PLANETS - Bernstein cond. New York Philharmonic - Edward T. Graham, Larry Keyes, Engs. (Columbia)
PROKOFIEV: ROMEO AND JULIET - Maazel cond. Cleveland Orchestra - Jack Law, Colin Moorfoot, Gordon Parry, Engs. (London)
PUCCINI: HEROINES - Leontyne Price/Downes cond. New Philharmonia - Tony Salvatore, Eng. (RCA)
WAGNER: PARSIFAL - Solti cond. Vienna Philharmonic & Soloists - Kenneth Wilkinson, Gordon Parry, Engs. (London)

1974 HALL OF FAME WINNERS
BODY AND SOUL - Coleman Hawkins - Bluebird #B-10523-A Released in 1939
THE CHRISTMAS SONG - Nat "King" Cole - Capitol #311 Released in 1946
GERSHWIN: RHAPSODY IN BLUE - Paul Whiteman with George Gershwin - Victor #35822-A Released in 1927
WEST END BLUES - Louis Armstrong - Okeh #8597 Released in 1928
WHITE CHRISTMAS - Bing Crosby - Decca #18429-A Released in 1942

1974

RECORD OF THE YEAR
(Grammys to the Artist and A&R Producer) (Certificates to the Arranger, Engineer and Songwriter)
DON'T LET THE SUN GO DOWN ON ME - Elton John - Gus Dudgeon, Producer (MCA)
FEEL LIKE MAKIN' LOVE - Roberta Flack - Roberta Flack, Producer (Atl.)
HELP ME - Joni Mitchell - Joni Mitchell & Henry Lewy, Producers (Asylum)
I HONESTLY LOVE YOU - Olivia Newton-John - John Farrar, Producer (MCA)
MIDNIGHT AT THE OASIS - Maria Muldaur - Lenny Waronker & Joe Boyd, Producers (Reprise/WB)

ALBUM OF THE YEAR
(Grammys to the Artist and A&R Producer) (Certificates to the Arrangers and Engineer)
BACK HOME AGAIN - John Denver - Milton Okun, Producer (RCA)
BAND ON THE RUN - Paul McCartney & Wings - Paul McCartney, Producer (Apple/Cap)
CARIBOU - Elton John - Gus Dudgeon, Producer (MCA)
COURT AND SPARK - Joni Mitchell - Joni Mitchell & Henry Lewy, Producers (Asylum)
FULFILLINGNESS' FIRST FINALE - Stevie Wonder - Stevie Wonder, Producer (Tamla/Motown)

SONG OF THE YEAR
(A Songwriter's Award)
FEEL LIKE MAKIN' LOVE - Eugene McDaniels
I HONESTLY LOVE YOU - Jeff Barry & Peter Allen
MIDNIGHT AT THE OASIS - David Nichtern
THE WAY WE WERE - Marilyn & Alan Bergman, Marvin Hamlisch
YOU AN ME AGAINST THE WORLD - Paul Williams & Ken Ascher

BEST NEW ARTIST OF THE YEAR
(This category is for an artist or organized group whose first recording was released during the Eligibility Period.)
BAD COMPANY (Swan Song)
JOHNNY BRISTOL (MGM)
DAVID ESSEX (Col.)
GRAHAM CENTRAL STATION (WB)
MARVIN HAMLISCH (MCA)
PHOEBE SNOW (Shelter)

BEST INSTRUMENTAL ARRANGEMENT
(An Arranger's Award for a specific arrangement released on either a single or a track from an album)
CIRCUMVENT - Les Hooper Big Band - Les Hooper, Arranger (Creative Wrld)
FIREBIRD/BIRDS OF FIRE - Don Sebesky - Don Sebesky, Arranger (CTI)
LOOK WHAT THEY'VE DONE - Les Hooper Big Band - Les Hooper, Arranger (Creative Wrld)
NIGHT ON BALD MOUNTAIN - Bob James - Bob James, Arranger (CTI)
THRESHOLD - Pat Williams - Pat Williams, Arranger (Capitol)

BEST ARRANGEMENT ACCOMPANYING VOCALISTS
(An Arranger's Award for a specific arrangement released on either a single or a track from an album)
DOWN TO YOU - Joni Mitchell - Joni Mitchell & Tom Scott, Arrangers (Asylum)
LAND OF MAKE BELIEVE - Esther Satterfield (Chuck Mangione, Hamilton Philharmonic) - Chuck Mangione, Arranger (Mercury)
SMILE OF THE BEYOND - Carol Shive (Mahavishnu Orch., with London Symphony) Michael Gibbs, Arranger (Col.)
WE'VE ONLY JUST BEGUN - The Singers Unlimited - Gene Puerling & Les Hooper, Arrangers (MPS/BASF)
WHERE IS LOVE - The Singers Unlimited - Gene Puerling, Arranger (MPS/BASF)

BEST ENGINEERED RECORDING (NON-CLASSICAL)
(An Engineer's Award)
BAND ON THE RUN - Paul McCartney & Wings - Geoff Emerick, Engineer (album) (Apple/Cap.)
CRIME OF THE CENTURY - Supertramp - Ken Scott & John Jansen, Engineers (album) (A&M)
LINCOLN MAYORGA AND DISTINGUISHED COLLEAGUES VOLUME III - Lincoln Mayorga - Bill Schnee, Engineer (album) (Sheffield)
POWERFUL PEOPLE - Gino Vannelli - Tommy Vicari & Larry Forkner, Engineers (album) (A&M)
SOUTHERN COMFORT - The Crusaders - Rik Pekkonen & Peter Granet, Engineers (album) (Blue Thumb)

BEST ALBUM PACKAGE
(Grammys to Art Director. Certificates to Designer(s), Photographer(s), Illustrator(s), etc. where applicable)
CHEECH & CHONG'S WEDDING ALBUM - Cheech & Chong - Ode Visuals, Art Director (Ode)
COME & GONE - Mason Proffit - Ed Thrasher & Christopher Whorf, Art Directors (WB)
IS IT IN - Eddie Harris - Bob Defrin & Basil Pao, Art Directors (Atl.)
ON STAGE - Loggins and Messina - Ron Coro, Art Director (Col.)
QUADROPHENIA - The Who - Ethan A. Russell, Art Director (MCA)
RIDE 'EM COWBOY - Paul Davis - Eddie Biscoe, Art Director (Bang)
SANTANA'S GREATEST HITS - Santana - John Berg, Art Director (Col.)
THAT'S A PLENTY - The Pointer Sisters - Herb Greene, Art Director (Blue Thumb)

BEST ALBUM NOTES
(An Annotator's Award)
50 YEARS OF FILM MUSIC - Original Motion Picture Soundtrack Recordings - Rudy Behlmer, Annotator (WB)
FOR THE LAST TIME - Bob Wills and His Texas Playboys - Charles R. Townsend, Annotator (UA)
THE HAWK FLIES - Coleman Hawkins - Dan Morgenstern, Annotator (Milestone)
THE PIANIST - Duke Ellington - Ralph J. Gleason, Annotator (Fantasy)
THE WORLD IS STILL WAITING FOR THE SUNRISE - Les Paul & Mary Ford - J.R. Young, Annotator (Capitol)

BEST PRODUCER OF THE YEAR
(A Producer's Award for consistently outstanding creativity in producing. Listed below are examples of the producer's activities. (A)Album; (S)Single; (T)Track.)
THOM BELL - "Mighty Love" (S) - Spinners - "You Make Me Feel Brand New" (S) - Stylistics; "Then Came You" (S) - Dionne Warwick & Spinners; "Love Don't Love Nobody" (S) - Spinners; "I'm Coming Home" (S) - Johnny Mathis; "Mighty Love"(A) - Spinners; "Rockin' Roll Baby" (A) - Stylistics
RICK HALL - "You're Having My Baby" (S) - Paul Anka; "One Hell Of A Woman" (S) - Mac Davis; "As Long As He Takes Care Of Home" (T) - Candi Staton
BILLY SHERRILL - "Woman To Woman" (S) - Tammy Wynette; "The Grand Tour" (S) - George Jones; "I Love My Friend" (S) - Charlie Rich; "Very Special Love Songs" (A) - Charlie Rich; "Would You Lay With Me" (A) - Tanya Tucker
LENNY WARONKER - "Carefree Highway" (S) - Gordon Lightfoot; "Waitress In A Donut Shop" (A) - Maria Muldaur (co-prod.: Joe Boyd); "Good Old Boys " (A) - Randy Newman (co-prod.: Russ Titleman); "Sundown" (A) - Gordon Lightfoot; "Midnight At The Oasis" (S) - Maria Muldaur (co-prod.: Joe Boyd)
STEVIE WONDER - "Fulfillingness' First Finale" (A) - Stevie Wonder; "You Haven't Done Nothin' " (S) - Stevie Wonder; "Boogie On Reggae Woman" (S) - Stevie Wonder; "Spinnin' & Spinnin' " (T) - Syretta Wright

BEST JAZZ PERFORMANCE BY A SOLOIST
(This category is for a solo performance with or without a group or band.)
FIRST RECORDINGS! - Charlie Parker (album) (Onyx)
HIGH ENERGY - Freddie Hubbard (album) (Col.)
IN THE BEGINNING - Hubert Laws (album) (CTI)
NAIMA - McCoy Tyner (track) (Milestone)
SOLO-CONCERTS - Keith Jarrett (album) (ECM/Poly)

BEST JAZZ PERFORMANCE BY A GROUP
(All nominations are albums)
HIGH ENERGY - Freddie Hubbard (Col.)
SALT PEANUTS - Supersax (Capitol)
SAMA LAYUCA - McCoy Tyner (Milestone)
THE TOKYO CONCERT - Bill Evans (Fantasy)
THE TRIO - Oscar Peterson, Joe Pass, Niels Pedersen (Pablo)

BEST JAZZ PERFORMANCE BY A BIG BAND
(All nominations are albums)
GIANT BOX - Don Sebesky (CTI)
LAND OF MAKE BELIEVE - Chuck Mangione (with Hamilton Philharmonic Orch.) (Mercury)
LOOK WHAT THEY'VE DONE - Les Hooper Big Band (Creative Wrld)
THUNDERING HERD - Woody Herman (Fantasy)
THRESHOLD - Pat Williams (Capitol)

BEST POP VOCAL PERFORMANCE, FEMALE
(This category is for pop, rock and folk.)
CLEO LAINE LIVE AT CARNEGIE HALL - Cleo Laine (album) (RCA)
COURT AND SPARK - Joni Mitchell (album) (Asylum)
FEEL LIKE MAKIN' LOVE - Roberta Flack (single) (Atl.)
I HONESTLY LOVE YOU - Olivia Newton-John (single) (MCA)
JAZZMAN - Carole King (track) (Ode)

BEST POP VOCAL PERFORMANCE, MALE
(This category is for pop, rock and folk.)
CAT'S IN THE CRADLE - Harry Chapin (track) (Elektra)
DON'T LET THE SUN GO DOWN ON ME - Elton John (single) (MCA)
FULFLLINGNESS' FIRST FINALE - Steve Wonder (album) (Tamla/Motown)
NOTHING FROM NOTHING - Billy Preston (track) (A&M)
PLEASE COME TO BOSTON - Dave Loggins (single) (Epic/Col.)

BEST POP VOCAL PERFORMANCE BY A DUO, GROUP OR CHORUS
(This category is for pop, rock and folk. All recordings on which the group receives artist billing on the label are eligible here even though the vocal may feature only one member of the group.)
BAND OF THE RUN - Paul McCartney & Wings (single) (Apple/Cap.)
BODY HEAT - Quincy Jones (album) (A&M)
RIKKI DON'T LOSE THAT NUMBER - Steely Dan (single) (ABC)
THEN CAME YOU - Dionne Warwick & Spinners (single) (Atl.)
YOU MAKE ME FEEL BRAND NEW - Stylistics (track) (Avco)

BEST POP INSTRUMENTAL PERFORMANCE

(This category is for pop, rock and folk. All recordings are for either pure instrumentals or instrumentals with vocal coloring.)

ALONG CAME BETTY - Quincy Jones (track) (A&M)
THE ENTERTAINER - Marvin Hamlisch (single) (MCA)
HEAD HUNTERS - Herbie Hancock (album) (Col.)
JOURNEY TO THE CENTRE OF THE EARTH - Rick Wakeman (album) (A&M)
RHAPSODY IN WHITE - Love Unlimited Orchestra (album) (20th Cent.)

BEST R & B VOCAL PERFORMANCE, FEMALE

AIN'T NOTHING LIKE THE REAL THING - Aretha Franklin (single) (Atl.)
IF LOVING YOU IS WRONG I DON'T WANT TO BE RIGHT - Millie Jackson (track) (Spring)
ST. LOUIS BLUES - Etta James (track) (Chess)
TINA TURNS THE COUNTRY ON! - Tina Turner (album) (UA)
WOMAN TO WOMAN - Shirley Brown (single) (Truth/Stax)
(YOU KEEP ME) HANGIN' ON - Ann Peebles (track) (Hi/London)
YOU'VE BEEN DOING WRONG FOR SO LONG - Thelma Houston (single) (Motown)

BEST R & B VOCAL PERFORMANCE, MALE

BOOGIE DOWN - Eddie Kendricks (single) (Tamla/Motown)
BOOGIE ON REGGAE WOMAN - Stevie Wonder (track) (Tamla/Motown)
HANG ON IN THERE BABY - Johnny Bristol (single) ((MGM)
MARVIN GAYE - LIVE - Marvin Gaye (album) (Tamla/Motown)
ROCK YOUR BABY - George McCrae (single) (T.K.)

BEST R & B VOCAL PERFORMANCE BY A DUO, GROUP OR CHORUS

(All recordings on which the group receives artist billing on label are eligible here even though the vocal may feature only one member of the group. All nominations are singles.)

DANCING MACHINE - Jackson Five (Motown)
FOR THE LOVE OF MONEY - The O'Jays (Phila. Int./Epic)
I FEEL A SONG (IN MY HEART) - Gladys Knight & The Pips (Buddah)
MIGHTY LOVE - Spinners (Atl.)
TELL ME SOMETHING GOOD - Rufus (ABC)

BEST R & B INSTRUMENTAL PERFORMANCE

LIGHT OF WORLDS - Kool & The Gang (album) (De-Lite)
PICK UP THE PIECES - Average White Band (track) (Atl.)
SCRATCH - The Crusaders (album) (Blue Thumb)
STRUTTIN' - Billy Preston (track) (A&M)
TSOP (THE SOUND OF PHILADELPHIA) - MFSB (single) (Phila. Int./Epic)

BEST RHYTHM & BLUES SONG

(A Songwriter's Award)

DANCING MACHINE - Harold Davis, Don Fletcher & Dean Parts
FOR THE LOVE OF MONEY - Ken Gamble, Leon Huff & Anthony Jackson
LIVING FOR THE CITY - Stevie Wonder
ROCK YOUR BABY - Henry Wayne Casey & Richard Finch

BEST SOUL GOSPEL PERFORMANCE

EDWIN HAWKINS SINGERS LIVE - Edwin Hawkins Singers (album) (Buddah)
FATHER ALONE - Ike Turner (single) (UA)
THE GOSPEL ACCORDING TO IKE AND TINA - Ike & Tina Turner (album) (UA)
IN THE GHETTO - James Cleveland and the Southern California Community Choir (album) (Savoy)
MY DESIRE - Five Blind Boys (album) (Peacock/ABC)

BEST COUNTRY VOCAL PERFORMANCE, FEMALE

JOLENE - Dolly Parton (track) (RCA)
LAST TIME I SAW HIM - Dottie West (single) (RCA)
LOVE SONG - Anne Murray (album) (Capitol)
WOMAN TO WOMAN - Tammy Wynette (single) (Epic)
WOULD YOU LAY WITH ME (IN A FIELD OF STONE) - Tanya Tucker (single) (Col.)

BEST COUNTRY VOCAL PERFORMANCE, MALE

BONAPARTE'S RETREAT - Glen Campbell (single) (Capitol)
COUNTRY FEELIN' - Charley Pride (album) (RCA)
THE ENTERTAINER - Roy Clark (album) (Dot)
I'M A RAMBLIN' MAN - Waylon Jennings (single) (RCA)
PLEASE DON'T TELL ME HOW THE STORY ENDS - Ronnie Milsap (single) (RCA)

BEST COUNTRY VOCAL PERFORMANCE BY A DUO OR GROUP

AFTER THE FIRE IS GONE - Willie Nelson & Tracy Nelson (single) (Atl.)
DADDY WHAT IF - Bobby Bare, Bobby Bare Jr. (single) (RCA)
FAIRYTALE - The Pointer Sisters (track) (Blue Thumb)
LOVING ARMS - Kris Krisofferson & Rita Coolidge (single) (A&M)
WHATEVER HAPPENED TO RANDOLPH SCOTT - The Statler Brothers (single) (Mercury)

BEST COUNTRY INSTRUMENTAL PERFORMANCE

THE ATKINS -TRAVIS TRAVELING SHOW - Chet Atkins & Merle Travis (album) (RCA)
BOOGIE WOOGIE (A/K/A T.D.'S BOOGIE WOOGIE) - Charlie McCoy & Barefoot Jerry (single) (Monument)
NASHVILLE BRASS IN BLUE GRASS COUNTRY - Danny Davis & The Nashville Brass (album) (RCA)
THE NASHVILLE HIT MAN - Charlie McCoy (album) (Monument)
THE YOUNG AND THE RESTLESS - Floyd Cramer (album) (RCA)

BEST COUNTRY SONG

(A Songwriter's Award)

A VERY SPECIAL LOVE SONG - Norris Wilson & Billy Sherrill
FAIRYTALE - Anita Pointer and Bonnie Pointer
IF WE MAKE IT THROUGH DECEMBER - Merle Haggard
I'M A RAMBLIN' MAN - Ray Pennington
PAPER ROSES - Janice Torre and Fred Spielman

BEST INSPIRATIONAL PERFORMANCE

(Non-classical)

HOW GREAT THOU ART - Elvis Presley (track) (RCA)
LISTEN - Bill Pursell (album) (Word)
THE LORD'S PRAYER - Sister Janet Mead (single) (A&M)
MAKE A JOYFUL NOISE - Tennessee Ernie Ford (album) (Capitol)
THANKS FOR SUNSHINE - The Bill Gaither Trio (album) (Impact)

BEST GOSPEL PERFORMANCE (OTHER THAN SOUL GOSPEL)
THE BAPTISM OF JESSE TAYLOR - Oak Ridge Boys (single) (Col.)
THE CARPENTER'S TOOL - Wendy Bagwell & The Sunliters (album) (Canaan)
FOLLOW THE MAN WITH THE MUSIC - Imperials (album) (Impact)
STEPPING ON THE CLOUDS - The LeFevres (album) (Canaan)
THERE HE GOES - The Blackwood Brothers (album) (Skylite)

BEST ETHNIC OR TRADITIONAL RECORDING (INCLUDING TRADITIONAL BLUES AND PURE FOLK)
(All nominations are albums)
THE BACK DOOR WOLF - Howlin' Wolf (Chess)
BIG DADDY - Bukka White (Biograph)
CATALYST - Willie Dixon (Ovation)
LONDON REVISITED - Muddy Waters & Howlin' Wolf (Chess)
TWO DAYS IN NOVEMBER - Doc & Merle Watson (U.A.)

BEST RECORDING FOR CHILDREN
(All nominations are albums)
AMERICA SINGS - Burl Ives, Others, Orch. & Chorus - Buddy Baker cond. (Disneyland)
ELI WALLACH READS ISAAC BASHEVIS SINGER - Eli Wallach (Newbery)
NEW ADVENTURES OF BUGS BUNNY VOLUME II - Mel Blanc (Peter Pan)
ROBIN HOOD - Various Artists, narrated by Roger Miller (Disneyland)
WINNIE THE POOH & TIGGER TOO - Sebastian Cabot, Sterling Holloway, Paul Winchell (Disneyland)

BEST COMEDY RECORDING
(All nominations are albums)
BOOGA! BOOGA! - David Steinberg (Col.)
CHEECH & CHONG'S WEDDING ALBUM - Cheech & Chong (Ode)
MIND OVER MATTER - Robert Klein (Brut/Buddah)
MISSING WHITE HOUSE TAPES - National Lampoon (Blue Thumb)
THAT NIGGER'S CRAZY - Richard Pryor (Partee/Stax)

BEST SPOKEN WORD RECORDING
AN EAR TO THE SOUNDS OF OUR HISTORY - Eric Sevareid (album) (Col.)
AUTUMN - Rod McKuen (track) (Stanyan/WB)
GOOD EVENING - Peter Cook & Dudley Moore (album) (Island)
SENATOR SAM AT HOME - Sam Ervin (album) (Col.)
WATERGATE VOLUME THREE: "I HOPE THE PRESIDENT IS FORGIVEN" (John W. Dean III Testifies) - Compiled by Don Molner (Folkways)

BEST INSTRUMENTAL COMPOSITION
(This is a Composer's Award for an original composition with or without lyrics which first gained recognition as an instrumental)
ALONG CAME BETTY - Benny Golson
BARRY'S THEME - Barry White
CHAMELEON - Herbie Hancock, Paul Jackson, Bennie Maupin and Harvey Mason
RHAPSODY IN WHITE - Barry White
TUBULAR BELLS (THEME FROM "THE EXORCIST") - Mike Oldfield

ALBUM OF BEST ORIGINAL SCORE WRITTEN FOR A MOTION PICTURE OR A TELEVISION SPECIAL
(A Composer's Award)
DEATH WISH - Herbie Hancock (Col.)
QB VII - Jerry Goldsmith (ABC)
SERPICO - Mikis Theodorakis (Paramount/ABC)
THE THREE MUSKETEERS - Michel Legrand (Bell)
THE WAY WE WERE - Marvin Hamlisch, Alan & Marilyn Bergman (Col.)

BEST SCORE FROM THE ORIGINAL CAST SHOW ALBUM
(Grammys to the Composers and A&R Producers)
LET MY PEOPLE COME - Earl Wilson, Jr., & Phil Oesterman Composers; Henry Jerome, Producer (Libra)
THE MAGIC SHOW - Stephen Schwartz, Composer; Phil Ramone & Stephen Schwartz, Producers (Bell)
OVER HERE - Richard M. Sherman & Robert B. Sherman, Composers; Charles Koppelman & Teo Macero, Producers (Col.)
RAISIN - Judd Woldin & Robert Brittan, Composers; Thomas Z. Shepard, Producer (Col.)
THE ROCKY HORROR SHOW - Richard O'Brien, Composer; Lou Adler, Producer (Ode)

ALBUM OF THE YEAR, CLASSICAL
(Grammys to the Artist and Producer; Certificates to the Engineer)
BERLIOZ: THE DAMNATION OF FAUST - Colin Davis cond. London Symphony Orchestra & Chorus/Ambrosian Singers/Wandsworth School Boys' Choir/Soloists: Gedda, Bastin, Veasey, Van Allan - Erik Smith, Producer (Philips)
BERLIOZ: SYMPHONIE FANTASTIQUE - Georg Solti cond. Chicago Symphony - David Harvey, Producer (London)
IVES: THE 100TH ANNIVERSARY - Various Orchestras, Conductors, Soloists, etc. - Leroy Parkins & Vivian Perlis, Producers (Col.)
MAHLER: SYMPHONY NO. 2 IN C MINOR ("RESURRECTION") Leonard Bernstein cond. London Symphony/Edinburgh Festival Chorus/Soloists: Baker, Armstrong/ John McClure, Producer (Col.)
SCHUMANN: FAUST - Benjamin Britten cond. English Chamber Orchestra/Soloists: Fischer-Dieskau, Pears, Shirley-Quirk - Christopher Raeburn & Michael Woolcock, Procucers (London)
"SNOWFLAKES ARE DANCING" - Isao Tomita - Isao Tomita, Producer (RCA)
WEBER: DER FREISCHUTZ - Carlos Kleiber cond. Dresden State Orchestra/Leipzig Radio Chorus/Soloists: Mathis, Janowitz,Schreier, Adam, etc. - Dr. Ellen Hickmann, Producer (DG)

BEST CLASSICAL PERFORMANCE - ORCHESTRA
(A Conductor's Award)
BARTOK: CONCERTO FOR ORCHESTRA - Herbert von Karajan cond. Berlin Philharmonic (Angel)
BERLIOZ: SYMPHONIE FANTASTIQUE - Georg Solti cond. Chicago Symphony (London)
BERNSTEIN CONDUCTS RAVEL - Leonard Bernstein cond. New York Philharmonic (Col.)
HOLST: THE PLANETS - Andre Previn cond. London Symphony (Angel)
IVES: SYMPHONY NO. 4 - Jose Serebrier cond. London Philharmonic (RCA)
MAHLER: SYMPHONY NO. 2 IN C MINOR - Leonard Bernstein cond. London Symphony (Col.)

BEST OPERA RECORDING
(Grammys to the Conductor and Producer; special Plaques to the Principal Soloists)

HUMPERDINCK: HANSEL & GRETEL - Kurt Eichhorn cond. Bavarian Radio Orchestra/Soloists: Moffo, Ludwig, Fischer-Dieskau/Fritz Ganss, Theodor Holzinger (RCA)
MOZART: COSI FAN TUTTE - Georg Solti cond. London Philharmonic/Soloists: Lorengar, Berganza, Berbie, Davies, Krause, Bacquier - Christopher Raeburn, Producer (London)
MOZART: DON GIOVANNI - Colin Davis cond. Chorus & Orchestra Royal Opera House, Covent Garden/Soloists: Wixell, Ganzarolli, Arroyo, Te Kenawa, Freni, Burrows/Erik Smith, Producer (Philips)
PFITZNER: PALESTRINA - Rafael Kubelik cond. Bavarian Radio Chorus & Orchestra/Soloists: Donath, Fassbaender, Gedda, Fischer-Dieskau, Prey - Dr. Rudolf Werner, Producer (DG)
PUCCINI: LA BOHEME - Georg Solti cond. London Philharmonic/Soloists: Caballe, Domingo, Milnes, Blegen, Raimondi/Richard Mohr, Producer (RCA)
VERDI: I VESPRI SICILIANI - James Levine cond. New Philharmonia/John Alldis Choir/Soloists: Arroyo, Domingo, Milnes, Raimondi - Richard Mohr, Producer, (RCA)
WEBER: DER FREISCHUTZ - Carlos Kleiber cond. Dresden State Orchestra/Leipzig Radio Chorus/Soloists: Mathis, Janowitz, Schreier, Adam, Crass, Weikl - Dr. Ellen Hickman, Producer (DGw)

BEST CHORAL PERFORMANCE, CLASSICAL (OTHER THAN OPERA)
(Grammys to the Conductor and Choral Director)

BERLIOZ: THE DAMNATION OF FAUST - Colin Davis cond. London Symphony Orchestra & Chorus/Ambrosian Singers/Wandsworth School Boys' Choir/Gedda, Bastin, Veasey, Van Allan (Philips)
HOLST: CHORAL SYMPHONY - Sir Adrian Boult cond. London Philharmonic Choir & Orchestra (Angel)
JANACEK: GLAGOLITIC MASS (SLAVONIC MASS) - Rudolf Kempe cond. Royal Philharmonic & Brighton Festival Chorus (London)
PENDERECKI: UTRENJA - Andrzej Markowski cond. Symphony Orchestra of National Philharmonic/Chorus of National Philharmonic Warsaw-Jozef Bok, Chorus Master/Pioneer Choir - Wladyslaw Skoraczewski, Chorus Master (Philips)
RACHMANINOFF: THE BELLS - Eugene Ormandy cond. Philadelphia Orchestra/Temple University Choirs, Robert Page, Director (RCA)
RACHMANINOFF: VESPERS (MASS) OP. 37 - Aleksander Sveshnikov cond. U.S.S.R. Russian Chorus (Mel. Angel)
SCHUMANN: FAUST - Russell Burgess cond. Aldeburgh Festival Singers/Wandsworth School Choir/Benj. Britten cond. English Chamber Orchestra (London)
VAUGHAN WILLIAMS: DONA NOBIS PACEM - Sir Adrian Boult, cond./John Alldis, Chorus Master/London Philharmonic Choir & Orchestra (Angel)

BEST CHAMBER MUSIC PERFORMANCE
(Instrumental or Vocal)

BEETHOVEN: LATE QUARTETS - Juilliard Quartet (Col.)
BRAHMS: TRIOS (COMPLETE)/SCHUMANN: TRIO NO. 1 IN D MINOR - Artur Rubinstein, Henryk Szeryng, Pierre Fournier (RCA)
COPLAND: APPALACHIAN SPRING - Aaron Copland cond. Columbia Chamber Orchestra (Col.)
HAYDN: STRING QUARTETS, OP. 50 NO. 1 & 2 Tokyo String Quartet (DG)
IVES: VIOLIN SONATAS NOS. 1 - 4 Paul Zukofsky, Gilbert Kalish (Nonesuch)
JOPLIN: PALM LEAF RAG - Ralph Grierson with George Sponholtz & The Southland Stingers (Angel)
JULIAN & JOHN, VOL. 2 (Albeniz, Giuliani, Granados, etc.) - Julian Bream & John Williams (RCA)

BEST CLASSICAL PERFORMANCE INSTRUMENTAL SOLOIST OR SOLOISTS (WITH ORCHESTRA)

BARTOK: VIOLIN CONCERTO NO. 2 - Itzhak Perlman (Previn cond. London Symphony) (Angel)
BRAHMS: PIANO CONCERTO NO. 2 IN B FLAT MAJOR Alfred Brendel (Haitink cond. Concertgebouw Orchestra) (Philips)
CHOPIN: VARIATIONS ON "LA CI DAREM LA MANO"/FANTASY ON POLISH AIRS, OP. 13/ANDANTE SPIANATO & GRANDE POLONAISE BRILLANTE IN E FLAT, OP. 22 Claudio Arrau (Inbal cond. London Philharmonic) (Philips)
LISZT: TODTENTANZ FOR PIANO & ORCH./FRANCK: SYMPHONIC VARIATIONS FOR PIANO & ORCH. Andre Watts (Leinsdorf cond. London Symphony) (Col.)
SHOSTAKOVICH: VIOLIN CONCERTO NO. 1 - David Oistrakh (M. Shostakovich cond. New Philharmonic) (Angel)
STRAUSS: HORN CONCERTO NO. 2 IN E FLAT MAJOR Norbert Hauptmann (von Karajan cond. Berlin Philharmonic) (DG)
WALTON: VIOLIN CONCERTO/STRAVINSKY: VIOLIN CONCERTO IN D MAJOR - Kyung-Wha Chung (Previn cond. London Symphony) (London)
WEBER: CONCERTINO IN E MINOR FOR HORN & ORCH. Barry Tuckwell (Marriner cond. Academy of St. Martin-in-the-Fields) (Angel)

BEST CLASSICAL PERFORMANCE INSTRUMENTAL SOLOIST OR SOLOISTS (WITHOUT ORCHESTRA)

ALBENIZ: IBERIA - Alicia de Larrocha (London)
BACH: FRENCH SUITES, VOL. 2 NOS. 5 & 6 - Glenn Gould (Col.)
BEETHOVEN: PIANO SONATAS NOS. 21 IN C MAJOR ("WALDSTEIN") & 23 IN F MINOR ("APPASSIONATA") - Vladimir Horowitz (Col.)
CRUMB: MAKRO KOSMOS - David Burge (Nonesuch)
PERPETUAL MOTION - Itzhak Perlman (Angel)
RAVEL & DEBUSSY: MUSIC FOR TWO PIANOS/4 HANDS - Alfons & Aloys Kontarsky (DG)
SNOWFLAKES ARE DANCING - Isao Tomita (RCA)

BEST CLASSICAL VOCAL SOLOIST PERFORMANCE

AMAZING GRACE (Agnus Dei, Bless the Lord, O My Soul, etc.) - Sherrill Milnes (RCA)
BRAHMS: ALTO RHAPSODY - Janet Baker (Angel)
CATHY BERBERIAN AT THE EDINBURGH FESTIVAL - Cathy Berberian (RCA)
CRUMB: NIGHT OF THE FOUR MOONS - Jan DeGaetani (Col.)
DAVIES: EIGHT SONGS FOR A MAD KING - Julius Eastman (Nonesuch)
FRENCH AND SPANISH SONGS - Marilyn Horne (London)
SCHUBERT: GOETHE-LIEDER - Elly Ameling (Philips)
(R. STRAUSS) LEONTYNE PRICE SINGS RICHARD STRAUSS - Leontyne Price (RCA)
THERE'S A MEETING HERE TONIGHT - Martina Arroyo (Angel)
WAGNER: DUETS FROM PARSIFAL & DIE WALKURE - Birgit Nilsson, Helge Briiloth (Philips)

BEST ALBUM NOTES - CLASSICAL
(An Annotator's Award)

BERLIOZ: THE DAMNATION OF FAUST - Davis cond. London Symphony; Ann - David Cairns (Philips)
HERRMANN: CITIZEN KANE - Gerhardt cond. National Philharmonic; Ann - Christopher Palmer (RCA) HUMPERDINCK: HANSEL & GRETEL- Eichhorn cond. Bavarian Radio/Moffo, Donath; Ann - George Jellinek (RCA)
KORNGOLD: THE CLASSIC ERICH WOLFGANG KORNGOLD - Hoelscher/Mattes, cond; Ann - Rory Guy (Angel)
MAHLER: SYMPHONY NO. 10 - Morris cond. New Philharmonia Orch; Ann - Deryck Cooke (Philips)
MOZART: DON GIOVANNI - Davis cond. Royal Opera House Chorus

& Orchestra; Ann - Erik Smith (Philips)
RACHMANINOFF: THE BELLS & THREE RUSSIAN SONGS - Ormandy cond./Curtin, Shirley, Devlin/Temple University Choirs, Page; Ann - Clair W. Van Ausdall (RCA)
SCRIABIN: PIANO MUSIC (COMP.) VOL. II - Ponti; Ann - Donald Garvelmann (Vox)
VERDI: I VESPRI SICILIANI - Levine, New Philharmonia; Ann - Irving Kolodin (RCA)
WEBER: DER FREISCHUTZ - Kleiber cond. Mathis, Janowitz, etc; Ann - Wolfram Schwinger (DG)

BEST ENGINEERED RECORDING - CLASSICAL

(An Engineer's Award)
BERLIOZ: SYMPHONIE FANTASTIQUE - Solti cond. Chicago Symphony; Eng - Kenneth Wilkinson (London)
BERNSTEIN: CANDIDE - Original Cast; Engs - Bud Graham and Ray Moore (Col.)
COPLAND: APPALACHIAN SPRING - Copland cond. Columbia Chamber Players; Engs - Stanley Tonkel, Ray Moore and Milt Cherin (Col.)
IVES: SYMPHONY NO. 4 - Serebrier cond. London Philharmonic; Engs - Paul Goodman & Robert Auger (RCA)
PERCUSSION MUSIC - New Jersey Percussion Ensemble; Engs - Marc Aubort & Joanna Nickrenz (Nonesuch)
PUCCINI: LA BOHEME - Solti cond. London Philharmonic/Domingo, Caballe; Eng - Anthony Salvatore (RCA)
SNOWFLAKES ARE DANCING - Isao Tomita; Eng - Isao Tomita (RCA)

1975 HALL OF FAME WINNERS

BEETHOVEN: PIANO SONATAS (32) (12 Albums) Artur Schnabel - Beethoven Sonata Society/HMV Vols. I-XII - Released 1932-1938
CARNEGIE HALL JAZZ CONCERT (Album) - Benny Goodman - Columbia #OSL 160 - Released in 1950
I CAN'T GET STARTED - Bunny Berigan - Victor #36208-A - Released in 1937
LEONCAVALLO: PAGLIACCI, ACT 1: VESTI LA GIUBBA - Enrico Caruso - Victrola #88061 - Released in 1907
MOOD INDIGO - Duke Ellington - Brunswick #80003-A - Released in 1931

1975

RECORD OF THE YEAR

(Grammys to the Artist and A&R Producer. Certificates to Arranger, Engineer and Songwriter)
AT SEVENTEEN - Janis Ian - Brooks Arthur, Producer (Col.)
LOVE WILL KEEP US TOGETHER - Captain & Tennille - Daryl Dragon, Producer (A&M)
LYIN' EYES - Eagles - Bill Szymczyk, Producer (Asylum)
MANDY - Barry Manilow - Clive Davis, Barry Manilow & Ron Dante, Producers (Arista)
RHINESTONE COWBOY - Glen Campbell - Dennis Lambert & Brain Potter, Producers (Capitol)

ALBUM OF THE YEAR

(Grammys to the Artist and A&R Producer. Certificates to the Arranger and Engineer)
BETWEEN THE LINES - Janis Ian - Brooks Arthur, Producer (Col.)
CAPTAIN FANTASTIC AND THE BROWN DIRT COWBOY - Elton John - Gus Dudgeon, Producer (MCA)
HEART LIKE A WHEEL - Linda Ronstadt - Peter Asher, Producer (Capitol)
ONE OF THESE NIGHTS - Eagles - Bill Szymczyk, Producer (Asylum)
STILL CRAZY AFTER ALL THESE YEARS - Paul Simon - Paul Simon & Phil Ramone, Producers (Col.)

SONG OF THE YEAR

(A Songwriter's Award)
AT SEVENTEEN - Janis Ian
FEELINGS - Morris Albert
LOVE WILL KEEP US TOGETHER - Neil Sedaka & Howard Greenfield
RHINESTONE COWBOY - Larry Weiss
SEND IN THE CLOWNS - Stephen Sondheim

BEST NEW ARTIST OF THE YEAR

(This category is for an artist or organized group whose first recording was released during the Eligibility Period)
MORRIS ALBERT (RCA)
AMAZING RHYTHM ACES (RCA)
BRECKER BROS. (Arista)
NATALIE COLE (Capitol)
K.C. & THE SUNSHINE BAND (T.K.)

BEST INSTRUMENTAL ARRANGEMENT

(An Arranger's Award for a specific arrangement released on either a single or a track from an album)
CHILDREN OF LIMA - Woody Herman - Alan Broadbent, Arranger (Fantasy)
LIVING FOR THE CITY - Thad Jones & Mel Lewis - Thad Jones, Arranger (PIR)
NO SHOW - Blood, Sweat & Tears - Ron McClure, Arranger (Col.)
THE ROCKFORD FILES - Mike Post - Mike Post, Pete Carpenter, Arrangers (MGM)
SOME SKUNK FUNK - The Brecker Bros. - Randy Brecker, Arranger (Arista)
THEME FOR "JAWS" - John Williams - Herbert Spencer, Arranger (MCA)

BEST ARRANGEMENT ACCOMPANYING VOCALISTS

(An Arranger's Award for a specific arrangement released on either a single or a track from an album)
APRIL IN PARIS - The Singers Unlimited - Gene Puerling, Arranger (MPS)
AUTUMN IN NEW YORK - The Singers Unlimited - Gene Puerling, Arranger (MPS)
GERSHWIN MEDLEY - Mel Torme - Mel Torme, Arranger (Atlantic)
KILLING ME SOFTLY WITH HIS SONG - The Singers Unlimited - Gene Puerling, Arranger (MPS)
MISTY - Ray Stevens - Ray Stevens, Arranger (Barnaby)

BEST ENGINEERED RECORDING (NON-CLASSICAL)

(An Engineer's Award) (all nominations are albums)
AMBROSIA - Ambrosia; Engs - Chuck Johnson, Freddie Piro, Billy Taylor, Tom Trefethen, & Alan Parson (20th Century)
BETWEEN THE LINES - Janis Ian; Engs - Brooks Arthur, Larry Alexander & Russ Payne (Col.)
I'VE GOT THE MUSIC IN ME - Thelma Houston & Pressure Cooker; Eng - Bill Schnee (Sheffield)
THE ORIGINAL SOUNDTRACK - 10cc; Eng - Eric Stewart (Mercury)
STORM AT SUNUP - Gino Vannelli; Eng - Tommy Vicari (A&M)

BEST ALBUM PACKAGE

(Grammy to Art Director. Certificates to Designer(s), Photographer(s), Illustrator(s), etc. where applicable)
ATLANTIC CROSSING - Rod Stewart - John Kosh, Art Director (WB)
DREAM - Nitty Gritty Dirt Band - William E. McEuen, Art Director (UA)
HONEY - Ohio Players - Jim Ladwig, Art Director (Mercury)
ONE OF THESE NIGHTS - Eagles - Gary Burden, Art Director (Asylum)
PHYSICAL GRAFFITI - Led Zeppelin - AGI, Art Director (Swan Song/Atl)
PLAYING POSSUM - Carly Simon - Gene Christensen, Art Director

(Elktra)
SOLO PIANO - Phineas Newborn, Jr. - Bob Defrin, Art Director (Atlantic)
STEPPIN' - The Pointer Sisters - Mick Haggerty, Art Director (Blue Thumb)
WISH YOU WERE HERE - Pink Floyd - Hipgnosis, Art Director (Col.)

BEST ALBUM NOTES
(An Annotator's Award)
BLOOD ON THE TRACKS - Bob Dylan; Ann - Pete Hamill (Col.)
GREATEST HITS, VOL. 2 - Tom T. Hall; Ann - Tom T. Hall (Mercury)
A LEGENDARY PERFORMER - Glenn Miller and His Orchestra; Ann - George T. Simon (RCA)
THE REAL LENNY BRUCE - Lenny Bruce; Ann - Ralph J. Gleason (Fantasy)
THE TATUM SOLO MASTERPIECES - Art Tatum; Ann - Benny Green, Annotator (Pablo)

BEST PRODUCER OF THE YEAR
(A Producer's Award for consistently outstanding creativity in producing.) Listed below are examples of the producer's activities. (A)Album, (S)Single, (T)Track
PETER ASHER - " Heart Like A Wheel" (A) - Linda Ronstadt; "Heat Wave" (S) - Linda Ronstadt "It Doesn't Matter Any More" (S) - Linda Ronstadt; "Prisoner In Disguise" (A) - Linda Ronstadt "When Will I Be Loved" (S) - Linda Ronstadt; "You're No Good" (S) - Linda Ronstadt
GUS DUDGEON - "Captain Fantastic and the Brown Dirt Cowboy" (A) - Elton John; "How Glad I Am" (S) - Kicci Dee; "Island Girl" (S) - Elton John; "Philadelphia Freedom" (S) - Elton John Band; "Someone Saved My Life Tonight" (S) - Elton John
DENNIS LAMBERT and BRIAN POTTER - "Estate of Mind" (A) - Evie Sands; "I Love Makin' Love To You" (S) - Evie Sands; "It Only Takes A Minute" (S) - Tavares; "Rhinestone Cowboy" (A) - Glen Campbell; "Rhinestone Cowboy" (S) - Glen Campbell; "Yesterday Can't Hurt Me" (T) - Evie Sands; "You Brought the Woman Out of Me" (S) - Evie Sands
ARIF MARDIN - "Cut the Cake" (A) - Average White Band; "If I Ever Lose This Heaven" (T) - Average White Band; "Jive Talkin' " (S) - Bee Gees; "Judith" (A) - Judy Collins; "Main Course" (A) - Bee Gees; "Mama's Pride" (A) - Mama's Pride; "The Prophet" (A) - Richard Harris
BILL SZYMCZYK - "Hotline" (A) - The J. Geils Band - (Album with Co-Producer); "Lyin' Eyes" (S) - Eagles; "One Of These Nights" (A) - Eagles; "One Of These Nights" (S) - Eagles

BEST JAZZ PERFORMANCE BY A SOLOIST
(This category is for a solo performance with or without a group or band.)
CONCIERTO - Jim Hall - (album) (CTI)
GIANT STEPS - (first release of alternate take) - John Coltrane (track) (Atlantic)
IMAGES - Phil Woods - (album) (Gryphon/RCA)
OSCAR PETERSON AND DIZZY GILLESPIE - Dizzy Gillespie - (album) (Pablo)
SOLO PIANO - Phineas Newborn, Jr. (album) (Atlantic)

BEST JAZZ PERFORMANCE BY A GROUP
BASIE JAM - Count Basie (album) (Pablo)
DIZZY GILLESPIE'S BIG 4 - Dizzy Gillespie Quartet (album) (Pablo)
GIANT STEPS - (first release of alternate take) - John Coltrane Quartet (track) (Atlantic)
NO MYSTERY - Return to Forever featuring Chick Corea (album) (Polydor)
SUPERSAX PLAYS BIRD WITH STRINGS - Supersax - (album) (Capitol)

BEST JAZZ PERFORMANCE BY A BIG BAND
(All nominations are albums)
CLARK TERRY'S BIG B-A-D BAND LIVE AT THE WICHITA JAZZ FESTIVAL - Clark Terry (Vanguard)
IMAGES - Phil Woods with Michel Legrand and His Orchestra (Gryphon/RCA)
LAB '75 - North Texas State University Lab Band - Leon Breeden, Director (NTSU)
POTPOURRI - Thad Jones & Mel Lewis (PIR)
THE TIGER OF SAN PEDRO - Bill Watrous and the Manhattan Wildlife Refuge (Col.)

BEST POP VOCAL PERFORMANCE, FEMALE
(This category is for pop, rock and folk.)
AIN'T NO WAY TO TREAT A LADY - Helen Reddy (single) (Capitol)
AT SEVENTEEN - Janis Ian (single) (Columbia)
HAVE YOU NEVER BEEN MELLOW - Olivia Newton-John (single) (MCA)
HEART LIKE A WHEEL - Linda Ronstadt (album) (Capitol)
SEND IN THE CLOWNS - Judy Collins (single) (Elektra)

BEST POP VOCAL PERFORMANCE, MALE
(This category is for pop, rock and folk.)
BAD BLOOD - Neil Sedaka (single) (Rocket/MCA)
CAPTAIN FANTASTIC AND THE BROWN DIRT COWBOY - Elton John (album) (MCA)
FEELINGS - Morris Albert (single) (RCA)
RHINESTONE COWBOY - Glen Campbell (single) (Capitol)
STILL CRAZY AFTER ALL THESE YEARS - Paul Simon (album) (Columbia)

BEST POP VOCAL PERFORMANCE BY A DUO, GROUP OR CHORUS
(This category is for pop, rock and folk. All recordings on which the group receives artist billing on the label are eligible here even though the vocal may feature only one member of the group.)
A CAPELLA 2 - The Singers Unlimited (album) (MPS)
LOVE WILL KEEP US TOGETHER - Captain & Tennille (single) (A&M)
LYIN' EYES - Eagles (single) (Asylum)
MY LITTLE TOWN - Simon & Garfunkel (single) (Columbia)
THE WAY WE WERE/TRY TO REMEMBER - Gladys Knight & The Pips (single) (Buddah)

BEST POP INSTRUMENTAL PERFORMANCE
(This category is for pop, rock and folk. All recordings are for either pure instrumentals or instrumentals with vocal coloring.)
BRAZIL - The Ritchie Family (single) (20th Century)
CHASE THE CLOUDS AWAY - Chuck Mangione (album) (A&M)
THE HUSTLE - Van McCoy and the Soul City Symphony (single) (AVCO)
THE ROCKFORD FILES - Mike Post (single) (MGM)
TOM CAT - Tom Scott & The L.A. Express (album) (Ode)

BEST R & B VOCAL PERFFORMANCE, FEMALE
NEVER CAN SAY GOODBYE - Gloria Gaynor (album) (MGM)
ROCKIN' CHAIR - Gwen McCrae (single) (Cat/T.K.)
SHAME, SHAME, SHAME - Shirley (and Company) (single) (Vibration)
THIS WILL BE - Natalie Cole (single) (Capitol)
WHAT A DIFF'RENCE A DAY MAKES - Esther Phillips (album) (Kudu/

CTI)

BEST R & B VOCAL PERFORMANCE, MALE
CHOCOLATE CHIP - Isaac Hayes (album) (Hot Buttered Soul)
LIVING FOR THE CITY - Ray Charles (single) (Crossover)
L-O-V-E (LOVE) - Al Green (single) (Hi/London)
LOVE WON'T LET ME WAIT - Major Harris (single) (Atlantic)
SUPERNATURAL THING - PART I - Ben E. King (single) (Atlantic)

BEST R & B VOCAL PERFORMANCE BY A DUO, GROUP OR CHORUS
(All recordings on which the group receives artist billing on label are eligible here even though the vocal may feature only one member of the group.)
CUT THE CAKE - Average White Band (album) (Atlantic)
FIRE - Ohio Players (album) (Mercury)
GET DOWN TONIGHT - K.C. & The Sunshine Band (single) (T.K.)
HOW LONG (BETCHA' GOT A CHICK ON THE SIDE) - The Pointer Sisters (single) (Blue Thumb)
SHINING STAR - Earth, Wind & Fire (single) (Columbia)

BEST R & B INSTRUMENTAL PERFORMANCE
(All recordings are for either pure instrumentals or instrumentals with vocal coloring.)
DISCO BABY - Van McCoy and the Soul City Symphony (album) (AVCO)
FLY, ROBIN, FLY - Silver Convention (single) (Midland/RCA)
HANG UP YOUR HANGUPS - Herbie Hancock (single) (Columbia)
SNEAKIN' UP BEHIND YOU - Brecker Bros. (single) (Arista)
EXPRESS - B. T. Express (single) (Scepter)

BEST RHYTHM & BLUES SONG
(A Songwriter's Award)
EASE ON DOWN THE ROAD - Charlie Small
GET DOWN TONIGHT - H.W. Casey & Richard Finch
THAT'S THE WAY (I LIKE IT) - H.W. Casey & Richard Finch
WALKING IN RHYTHM - Barney Perry
WHERE IS THE LOVE - H.W. Casey, Richard Finch, Willie Clarke, Betty Wright

BEST SOUL GOSPEL PERFORMANCE
GOD HAS SMILED ON ME - James Cleveland with Voices of Tabernacle (album) (Savoy)
JESUS IS THE BEST THING - James Cleveland & Chas. Fold Singers (track) (Savoy)
THE STORM IS PASSING OVER - The 21st Century (album) (Creed)
TAKE ME BACK - Andrae Crouch and the Disciples (album) (Light)
TO THE GLORY OF GOD - James Cleveland & Southern California Community Choir (album) (Savoy)

BEST COUNTRY VOCAL PERFORMANCE, FEMALE
I CAN'T HELP IT (IF I'M STILL IN LOVE WITH YOU) - Linda Ronstadt (single) (Capitol)
IF I COULD ONLY WIN YOUR LOVE - Emmylou Harris (single) (Reprise)
I'M NOT LISA - Jessi Colter (single) (Capitol)
JOLENE (track from "In Concert") - Dolly Parton (track) (RCA)
THE PILL - Loretta Lynn (single) (MCA)

BEST COUNTRY VOCAL PERFORMANCE, MALE
(All nominations are singles)
ARE YOU SURE HANK DONE IT THIS WAY? - Waylon Jennings (RCA)
BEFORE THE NEXT TEARDROP FALLS - Freddy Fender (Dot/ABC)
BLUE EYES CRYING IN THE RAIN - Willie Nelson (Columbia)
COUNTRY BOY (YOU GOT YOUR FEET IN L.A.) - Glen Campbell (Capitol)
MISTY - Ray Stevens (Barnaby)
THANK GOD I'M A COUNTRY BOY - John Denver (RCA)

BEST COUNTRY VOCAL PERFORMANCE BY A DUO OR GROUP
FEELINS' - Conway Twitty & Loretta Lynn (single) (MCA)
I'LL GO TO MY GRAVE LOVING YOU - Statler Brothers (single) (Mercury)
LIVE YOUR LIFE BEFORE YOU DIE - The Pointer Sisters (single) (Blue Thumb)
LOVER PLEASE - Kris Kristofferson & Rita Coolidge (single) (Monument)
TEXAS GOLD - Asleep At The Wheel (album) (Capitol)

BEST COUNTRY INSTRUMENTAL PERFORMANCE
CHARLIE MY BOY - Charlie McCoy (album) (Monument)
COLONEL BOGEY - Chet Atkins & Jerry Reed (track) (RCA)
THE ENTERTAINER - Chet Atkins (track) (RCA)
FAT BOY RAG - Asleep At The Wheel (track) (Capitol)
VASSAR CLEMENTS - Vassar Clements (album) (Mercury)

BEST COUNTRY SONG
(A Songwriter's Award)
BEFORE THE NEXT TEARDROP FALLS - Vivian Keith & Ben Peters
BLUE EYES CRYING IN THE RAIN - Fred Rose
(HEY WON'T YOU PLAY) ANOTHER SOMEBODY DONE SOMEBODY WRONG SONG - Chips Moman & Larry Butler
I'M NOT LISA - Jessi Colter
THANK GOD I'M A COUNTRY BOY - John Martin Sommers

BEST INSPIRATIONAL PERFORMANCE
(Non-classical)
AMAZING GRACE - Larry Hart (track) (Cam)
GENTLE AS MORNING - Anita Kerr (album) (Word)
JESUS, WE JUST WANT TO THANK YOU - The Bill Gaither Trio (album) (Impact)
SOMETHING GOOD IS ABOUT TO HAPPEN - The Speers (album) (Heartwarming)
THIS TIME LORD - Ray Price (album) (Myrrh)

BEST GOSPEL PERFORMANCE (OTHER THAN SOUL GOSPEL)
(All nominations are albums)
CONNIE SMITH SINGS HANK WILLIAMS GOSPEL - Connie Smith (Columbia)
HAPPY GOODMAN FAMILY HOUR - Happy Goodman Family (Canaan)
HOLY BIBLE - NEW TESTAMENT - Statler Brothers (Mercury)
JOHNNY CASH SINGS PRECIOUS MEMORIES - Johnny Cash (Columbia)
NO SHORTAGE - Imperials (Impact)

BEST ETHNIC OR TRADITIONAL RECORDING (INCLUDING TRADITIONAL BLUES AND PURE FOLK)
(All nominations are albums)
I GOT WHAT IT TAKES - Koko Taylor (Alligator)
MEMPHIS BLUES (first U.S release) - Memphis Slim (Olympic)
THE MUDDY WATERS WOODSTOCK ALBUM - Muddy Waters (Chess)
MUSIC OF GUATEMALA - San Lucas Band, Kathryn King, Producer (ABC/Command)
WAKE UP DEAD MAN - Black Convict Work Songs Recorded & Edited by Bruce Jackson (Rounder)

BEST LATIN RECORDING
AFRO-INDIO - Mongo Santamaria (album) (Fania)
BARRETTO - Ray Barretto (album) (Fania)
FANIA ALL-STARS LIVE AT YANKEE STADIUM, VOL.I - Fania All-Stars (album) (Fania)
THE GOOD, THE BAD & THE UGLY - Willie Colon (album) (Fania)
QUIERES SER MI AMANTE - Camilo Sesto (single) (Pronto)
PAUNETTO'S POINT - Bobby Paunetto (album) (Pathfinder)
SUN OF LATIN MUSIC - Eddie Palmieri (album) (Coco)

BEST RECORDING FOR CHILDREN
BERT & ERNIE SING-ALONG - Bert & Ernie (CRA)
THE LITTLE PRINCE - Richard Burton, Narrator (featuring Jonathan Winters, Billy Simpson) (PIP)
MERRY CHRISTMAS FROM SESAME STREET - Sesame Street Cast (CRA)
MR. POPPER'S PENGUINS - Jim Backus (Newbery Award)
REALLY ROSIE - Carole King (Ode)
SESAME STREET MONSTERS - Jim Henson's Sesame Street Monsters (CRA)

BEST COMEDY RECORDING
(All nominations are albums)
AN EVENING WITH WALLY LONDO FEATURING BILL SLASZO - George Carlin (Little David)
IS IT SOMETHING I SAID? - Richard Pryor (Reprise)
MATCHING TIE & HANDKERCHIEF - Monty Python (Arista)
MODERN SCREAM - Lily Tomlin (Polydor)
A STAR IS BOUGHT - Albert Brooks (Asylum)

BEST SPOKEN WORD, DOCUMENTARY OR DRAMA RECORDING
(All nominations are albums)
THE AUTOBIOGRAPHY OF MISS JANE PITTMAN - Claudia McNeil (Caedmon)
GIVE 'EM HELL HARRY - James Whitmore (U.A.)
IMMORTAL SHERLOCK HOLMES MERCURY THEATER ON THE AIR - Orson Wells (Radiola)
THE PROPHET - Richard Harris (Atlantic)
TALK ABOUT AMERICA - Alistair Cooke (Pye)
TO KILL A MOCKINGBIRD - Maureen Stapleton (Miller-Brody)

BEST INSTRUMENTAL COMPOSITION
(This is a Composer's Award for an original composition with or without lyrics which first gained recognition as an instrumental)
CHASE THE CLOUDS AWAY - Chuck Mangione
FLY, ROBIN, FLY - Silvester Levay, Stephan Praeger
THE HUSTLE - Van McCoy
IMAGES - Michel Legrand
THE ROCKFORD FILES - Mike Post, Pete Carpenter

ALBUM OF BEST ORIGINAL SCORE WRITTEN FOR A MOTION PICTURE OR A TELEVISION SPECIAL
(A Composer's Award)
JAWS - John Williams (MCA)
MURDER ON THE ORIENT EXPRESS - Richard Rodney Bennett (Capitol)
NASHVILLE - Carradine, Blakley, Baskin, Reicheg, Gibson, Black (ABC)
THE RETURN OF THE PINK PANTHER - Henry Mancini (RCA)
THE WIND AND THE LION - Jerry Goldsmith (Artista)

BEST CAST SHOW ALBUM
(Grammys to the Composers and A&R Producer)
CHICAGO - John Kander, Fred Ebb, Composers - Phil Ramone, Producer (Artist)
A CHORUS LINE - Marvin Hamlisch, Edward Kleban, Composers - Goddard Lieberson, Producer (Columbia)
A LITTLE NIGHT MUSIC (Original London Cast) Stephen Sondheim, Composer - Thomas Z. Shepard, Producer (RCA)
SHENANDOAH - Gary Geld, Peter Udell, Composers - Gary Geld, Peter Udell, Philip Rose, Producers (RCA)
THE WIZ - Charlie Smalls, Composer - Jerry Wexler, Producer

ALBUM OF THE YEAR, CLASSICAL
(Grammys to the Artist and Producer. Certificates to the Engineer(s).)
BEETHOVEN: SYMPHONIES (9) COMPLETE - Sir Georg Solti cond. Chicago Symphony - Ray Minshull, Producer (London)
BEETHOVEN: SYMPHONY NO. 5 IN C MINOR- Carlos Kleiber cond. Vienna Philharmonic - Werner Mayer, Producer (DG)
MOZART: COSI FAN TUTTE - Colin Davis cond. Royal Opera House, Covent Garden/Prin. Solos: Caballe, Baker, Gedda, Ganzarolli, Cotrubas, Van Allen - Erik Smith, Producer (Philips)
ORFF: CARMINA BURANA - Micheal Tilson Thomas cond. Cleveland Orchestra/Robert Page Dir. Cleveland Orchestra Chorus & Boys Choir/Soloists: Blegen, Riegel, Bindery - Andrew Kazdin, Producer (Columbia)
PENDERECKI: MAGNIFICAT - Kryzysztof Penderecki cond. Polish Radio National Symphony & Chorus - David Mottley, Producer (Angel)
RAVEL: DAPHNIS ET CHLOE (Complete Ballet) - Pierre Boulez cond. New York Philharmonic/Camarata Singers - Andrew Kazdin, Producer (Columbia)
ROSSINI: THE SIEGE OF CORINTH - Thomas Schippers cond. London Symphony & Ambrosian Opera Chorus/Prin. Solos: Sills, Verrett, Diaz, Theyard - John Mordler, Producer (Angel)

BEST CLASSICAL PERFORMANCE - ORCHESTRA
(A Conductor's Award)
BARTOK: CONCERTO FOR ORCHESTRA - Rafael Kubelik cond. Boston Symphony (DG)
BEETHOVEN: SYMPHONIES (9) COMPLETE - Sir Georg Solti cond. Chicago Symphony (London)
BEETHOVEN: SYMPHONY NO. 5 IN C MINOR - Carlos Kleiber cond. Vienna Philharmonic (DG)
BEETHOVEN: SYMPHONY NO. 9 IN D MINOR - Seiji Ozawa cond. New Philharmonic Orchestra (Philips)
BERLIOZ: SYMPHNOIE FANTASTIQUE - Colin Davis cond. Concertgebouw Orchestra, Amsterdam (Philips)
MAHLER: SYMPHONY NO. 4 IN G MAJOR - James Levine cond. Chicago Symphony (RCA)
MAHLER: SYMPHONY NO. 5 IN C SHARP MINOR - Herbert von Karajan cond. Berlin Philharmonic (DG)
RAVEL: DAPHNIS ET CHLOE (Complete Ballet) - Pierre Boulez cond. New York Philharmonic (Columbia)

BEST OPERA RECORDING
(Grammys to the Conductor and Producer; special plaques to the Principal Soloists)
DALLAPICCOLA: IL PRIGIONIERO - Antal Dorati cond. National Symphony Orchestra of Washington, D.C./University of Maryland Chorus, Paul Traver, Dir./Prin. Solos: Mazzieri, Barrera, Emili - James Mallinson, Producer (London)
KORNGOLD: DIE TOTE STADT - Erich Leinsdorf cond. Munich Radio Orchestra/Bavarian Radio Chorus/Prin. Solos: Kollo, Neblett, Prey, Luxon - Charles Gerhardt, Producer (RCA)
MOZART: COSI FAN TUTTE - Colin Davis cond. Royal Opera House, Covent Garden/Prin. Solos: Caballe, Baker, Gedda, Ganzarolli, Van Allen, Cotrubas - Erik Smith, Producer (Philips)
ROSSINI: THE BARBER OF SEVILLE - James Levine cond. London Symphony & John Alldis Choir/Prin. Solos: Sills, Milnes, Gedda - Christopher Bishop, Producer (Angel)
ROSSINI: THE SIEGE OF CORINTH - Thomas Schippers cond. London Symphony Orchestra & Ambrosian Opera Chorus/Prin. Solos: Sills, Verrett, Diaz, Theyard/John Mordler, Producer (Angel)
SCHOENBERG: MOSES AND AARON - Michael Gielen cond. Orchestra & Chorus of the Austrian Radio/Prin. Solos: Reich, Devos, Csapo, Obrowsky, Lucas - Abkauf Von Orf, Producer (Philips)
VAUGHAN WILLIAMS: SIR JOHN IN LOVE - Meredith Davis cond. New Philharmonia Orchestra/John Alldis Choir/Prin. Solos: Herincx, Palmer, Tear - Christopher Bishop, Producer (Angel)

BEST CHORAL PERFORMANCE, CLASSICAL (OTHER THAN OPERA)
(Grammys to the Conductor and Choral Director)
BEETHOVEN: MISSA SOLEMNIS - Vienna Singverein & Berlin Philharmonic - Herbert von Karajan, cond. (Angel)
BERLIOZ: LA DAMNATION DE FAUST - Tanglewood Festival Chorus - John Oliver, Chorus Master/Boston Boy Choir - Theodore Marier, Chorus Master/Boston Symphony Orchestra - Seiji Ozawa, cond. (DG)
CHERUBINI: REQUIEM IN D MINOR FOR MALE CHORUS & ORCHESTRA - Ambrosian Singers - John McCarthy, Dir./New Philharmonia Orchestra - Riccardo Muti, cond. (Angel)
HAYDN: HARMONIEMESSE - Westminster Choir & New York Philharmonic - Leonard Bernstein, cond. (Columbia)
ORFF: CARMINA BURANA - Cleveland Orchestra Chorus & Boys Choir - Robert Page, Dir./Cleveland Orchestra - Michael Tilson Thomas, cond./Soloists: Blegen, Binder, Riegel (Columbia)
PENDERECKI: MAGNIFICAT - Polish Radio Chorus of Krakow - Tadeusz Dobrzanski, Chorus Master/Soloists & Boys Chorus from Krakow Philharmonic Chorus - Palka & Wietrzny, Chorus Masters/Polish Radio National Symphony - Krzysztof Penderecki, cond.(Angel)
SCHOENBERG: GURRE-LIEDER - BBC Symphony Chorus/Goldsmith's Choral Union/Gentlemen of London Philharmonic Choir/BBC Symphony - Pierre Boulez, cond./Soloists: Napier, Minton Thomas (Columbia)

BEST CHAMBER MUSIC PERFORMANCE
(Instrumental or Vocal)
BAROQUE OBOE RECITAL: WORKS BY BACH, COUPERIN & MARAIS - Heinz Holliger, Christiane Jaccottet, Marcal Cervera (Philips)
BOLLING: SUITE FOR FLUTE & PIANO - Jean Pierre Rampal, Claude Bolling (Columbia)
GERSHWIN: GERSHWIN'S WONDERFUL' (Side 1: America In Paris, 3 Preludes) - Ralph Grierson & Artie Kane (Angel)
IVES: QUARTETS NOS. 1 & 2 - Concord Quartet (Nonesuch)
JOPLIN: THE EASY WINNERS & OTHER RAG-TIME MUSIC OF SCOTT JOPLIN - Itzhak Perlman & Andre Previn (Angel)
RAVEL: TRIO FOR VIOLIN, CELLO & PIANO - Jaime Laredo, Ruth Laredo & Jeffery Solow (Columbia)
SCHUBERT: TRIOS NOS. 1 IN B FLAT MAJOR OPP. 99 & 2 IN E FLAT MAJOR, OP. 100 (THE TRIOS) Artur Rubinstein, Henryk Szeryng, Pierre Fournier (RCA)
R. STRAUSS: SONATA IN F FOR CELLO & PIANO Mstislav Rostropovich & Vasso Devetzi (Angel)

BEST CLASSICAL PERFORMANCE INSTRUMENTAL SOLOIST OR SOLOISTS (WITH ORCHESTRA)
BERKELEY: GUITAR CONCERTO/RODRIGO: CONCIERTO DE ARANJUEZ FOR GUITAR - Julian Bream (Gardiner cond. Monteverdi Orchestra) (RCA)
DVORAK: CONCERTO IN B MINOR FOR CELLO - Lynn Harrell (Levine cond. London Symphony) (RCA)
FOUR TRUMPET CONCERTOS BY VIVALDI, TELEMANN, MOZART, HUMMEL - Maurice Andre (von Karajan cond. Berlin Philharmonic) (Angel)
MENDELSSOHN: CONCERTO NO. 1 IN G MINOR FOR PIANO & NO. 2 IN D MINOR FOR PIANO - Murray Perahia (Marriner cond. Academy of St. Martin-in-the-Fields) (Columbia)
MOZART: CONCERTOS FOR PIANO & ORCHESTRA COMPOSED IN 1784 (6) (NOS. 14 - 19) - Peter Serkin (Schneider cond. English Chamber Orchestra) (RCA)
MOZART: CONCERTOS NOS. 18 IN B FLAT MAJOR & 27 IN B FLAT MAJOR FOR PIANO & ORCHESTRA - Alfred Brendel (Marriner cond. Academy of St. Martin-in-the-Fields) (Philips)
RAVEL: CONCERTO FOR LEFT HAND & CONCERTO FOR PIANO IN G MAJOR/FAURE: FANTAISIE FOR PIANO & ORCHESTRA Alicia de Larrocha (De Burgos cond. London Philharmonic - Faure/Foster cond. London Philharmonic - Ravel) (London)
SAINT-SAENS: INTRODUCTION & RONDO CAPRICCIOSO, HAVANAISE/CHAUSSON: POEME/RAVEL: TZIGANE - Itzhak Perlman (Martinon cond. Orchestre de Paris) (Angel)

BEST CLASSICAL PERFORMANCE INSTRUMENTAL SOLOIST OR SOLOISTS (WITHOUT ORCHESTRA)
BACH: SONATAS & PARTITAS FOR VIOLIN UNACCOMPANIED Nathan Milstein (DG)
BACH: SUITES FOR LUTE - John Williams (Columbia)
CHOPIN: ETUDES, OP. 10 & 25 - Vladimir Ashkenazy (London)
FALLA: "MUSIC OF FALLA" (Three Cornered Hat, El Amor Brujo, etc.) - Alicia de Larrocha (London)
MESSIAEN: VINGT REGARDS SUR L'ENFANT JESUS - Peter Serkin (RCA)
SCHUMAN: CARNAVAL, OP. 9 - Arturo Benedetti Michelangeli (Angel)

BEST CLASSICAL VOCAL SOLOIST PERFORMANCE
AFTER THE BALL (A Treasury of Turn-of-the-Century Popular Songs) - Joan Morris (Bolcom, accomp.)
CANTELOUBE: SONGS OF THE AUVERGNE, ALBUM 2 - Victoria de los Angeles (Jacquillat cond. Lamoureux Concerts Orchestra) (Angel)
CLEO LAINE SINGS PIERROT LUNAIRE & SONGS BY IVES - Cleo Laine (Nash Ensemble, Howarth/Hymas, piano) (RCA)
MAHLER: KINDERTOTENLIEDER - Janet Baker (Bernstein cond. Israel Philhamonic) (Columbia)
SCHUMANN: FRAUENLIEBE UND LEBEN - Elly Ameling (Baldwin, accomp.) (Philips)
SCHUMANN: FRAUENLIEBE UND LEBEN, OP. 42 - Elisabeth Schwarzkopf (Parsons, accomp.) (Angel)
VERDI & PUCCINI DUETS (Othello, Ballo en Maschera, Manon Lescaut, Madame Butterfly) Leontyne Price & Placido Domingo (Santi cond. New Philharmonic) (RCA)

BEST ALBUM NOTES, CLASSICAL
(An Annotator's Award)
THE ENGLISH HARPSICHORD (Byrd, Farnaby, etc.) -Igor Kipnis - Judith Robison, Annotator (Angel)
"FOOTLIFTERS" (A Century of American Marches - Sousa, Joplin, Ives) - Gunther Schuller cond. All-Star Band - Gunther Schuller, Annotator (Columbia)
GAGLIANO: LA DAFNE - Paul Vorwerk cond. Musica Pacifica - James H. Moore, Annotator (ABC/Command)

GERSHWIN: "GERSHWIN'S WONDERFUL" - Ralph Grierson & Artie Kane - Rory Guy, Annotator (Angel)
HAYDN: SYMPHONIES 93 - 104 - Dorati cond. Philharmonia Hungarica - H.C. Robbins-Landon, Annotator (London)
JOPLIN: THE COMPLETE WORKS OF SCOTT JOPLIN - Dick Hyman - Rudi Blesh, Annotator (RCA)
JOPLIN: THE EASY WINNERS - Itzhak Perlman/Andre Previn - Rory Guy and Itzhak Perlman, Annotators (Angel)
KODALY: ORCHESTRAL WORKS (Complete) - Antal Dorati cond. Hungarian Phil. - Laszlo Eosze, Annotator (London)
KORNGOLD: DIE TOTE STADT - Leinsdorf cond. Munich Radio Orchestra/Kollo, Neblett, Prey, Luxon - Christopher Palmer, Annotator (RCA)

BEST ENGINEERED RECORDING, CLASSICAL

(An Engineer's Award)
BARTOK: CONCERTO FOR ORCHESTRA - Rafael Kubelik cond. Boston Symphony - Heinz Wildhagen, Engineer (DG)
BEETHOVEN: SYMPHONIES (9) COMPLETE - Sir Georg Solti cond. Chicago Symphony - Kenneth Wilkinson, Engineer (London)
BEETHOVEN: SYMPHONY NO. 5 IN C MINOR - Carlos Kleiber cond. Vienna Philharmonic - H.P. Schweigmann, Engineer (DG)
ORFF: CARMINA BURANA - Thomas cond. Cleveland Orchestra/Cleveland Chorus & Boys Choir, Page/Soloists: Blegen, Riegel, Binder - Edward Graham & Raymond Moore, Engineers (Columbia)
RAVEL: DAPHNIS & CHLOE - Maazel cond. Cleveland Orchestra - Gordon Parry & Colin Moorfoot, Engineers (London)
RAVEL: DAPHNIS ET CHLOE (Complete Ballet) - Boulez cond. New York Philharmonic - Bud Graham, Ray Moore & Milton Cherin, Engineers (Columbia)
STRAVINSKY: RITE OF SPRING - Sir George Solti cond. Chicago Symphony - James Lock & Kenneth Wilkinson, Engineers (London)

1976 HALL OF FAME WINNERS

GERSHWIN: PORGY & BESS (Opera) (Album) - Lehman Engel, Conductor; Cast: Lawrence Winters, Camilla Williams and others. Columbia #SL-162. Released in 1951
GOD BLESS THE CHILD - Billie Holiday. Okeh #6270. Released in 1941
OKLAHOMA! (Album) - Original Broadway Cast with Alfred Drake, Orchestra & Chorus directed by Jay Blackton. Decca #A 359. Released in 1943
RACHMANINOFF: PIANO CONCERTO NO. 2 IN C MINOR (Album) Sergei Rachmaninoff (Piano); Philadelphia Orchestra. Victrola #M 58. Released in 1929
TAKE THE "A" TRAIN - Duke Ellington & his Orchestra Victor #27380-A. Released in 1941.

1976

RECORD OF THE YEAR

(Grammys to the Artist & Producer.) (This category is for singles. An album track released as a single during the Eligibility Year is eligible provided that the track itself did not receive a previous nomination or award.)
AFTERNOON DELIGHT - Starland Vocal Band - Milt Okun, Producer (Windsong/RCA)
50 WAYS TO LEAVE YOUR LOVER - Paul Simon - Paul Simon, Phil Ramone, Producers (Columbia)
I WRITE THE SONGS - Barry Manilow - Ron Dante, Barry Manilow, Producers (Arista)
IF YOU LEAVE ME NOW - Chicago - James William Guercio, Producer (Columbia)
THIS MASQUERADE - George Benson - Tommy Lipuma, Producer (Warner Bros.)

ALBUM OF THE YEAR

(Grammys to the Artist and Producer. This category is for non-classical albums.)
BREEZIN' - George Benson - Tommy Lipuma, Producer (Warner Bros.)
CHICAGO X - Chicago - James William Guercio, Producer (Columbia)
FRAMPTON COMES ALIVE - Peter Frampton - Peter Frampton, Producer (A&M)
SILK DEGREES - Boz Scaggs - Joe Wissert, Producer (Columbia)
SONGS IN THE KEY OF LIFE - Stevie Wonder - Stevie Wonder, Producer (Tamla)

SONG OF THE YEAR

(A Songwriter's Award.) (Any song is eligible if a new recording of it has been released during the Eligibility Year, provided it was not a previous final nomination in a songwriting category.)
AFTERNOON DELIGHT - Bill Danoff
BREAKING UP IS HARD TO DO - Neil Sedaka, Howard Greenfield
I WRITE THE SONGS - Bruce Johnston
THIS MASQUERADE - Leon Russell
THE WRECK OF THE EDMUND FITZGERALD - Gordon Lightfoot

BEST NEW ARTIST OF THE YEAR

(This category is for an artist or organized group whose first recording was released during the Eligibility Year.)
BOSTON (Epic)
DR. BUZZARD'S ORIGINAL "SAVANNAH" BAND (RCA)
THE BROTHERS JOHNSON (A&M)
STARLAND VOCAL BAND (Windsong/RCA)
WILD CHERRY (Epic)

BEST INSTRUMENTAL ARRANGEMENT

(An Arranger's Award. This category is for a specific arrangement released for the first time during the Eligibility Year on either a single or an album track.)
THE DISASTER MOVIE SUITE - Henry Mancini cond. - London Symphony - Henry Mancini, John Williams, Herb Spencer & Al Woodbury, Arrangers (RCA)
LEPRECHAUN'S DREAM - Chick Corea - Chick Corea, Arranger (Polydor)
LIFE IS JUST A GAME - Stanley Clarke - Stanley Clarke, Arranger (Emperor/Atlantic)
SAUDADE DO BRAZIL - Antonio Carlos Jobim - Claus Ogerman, Arranger (Warner Bros.)
WESTCHESTER LADY - Bob James - Bob James, Arranger (CTI)

BEST ARRANGEMENT ACCOMPANYING VOCALISTS

(An Arranger's Award. This category is for a specific arrangement released for the first time during the Eligibility Year on either a single or an album track.)
BOTO (PORPOISE) - Antonio Carlos Jobim - Claus Ogerman, Arranger (Warner Bros.)
GREEN DOLPHIN STREET - The Singers Unlimited - Clare Fischer, Arranger (MPS)
IF YOU LEAVE ME NOW - Chicago - Jimmie Haskell & James Wm. Guercio, Arrangers (Columbia)
LET 'EM IN - Wings - Paul McCartney, Arranger (Capitol)
SENTIMENTAL JOURNEY - The Singers Unlimited - Robert Farnon, Arranger (MPS)

BEST ARRANGEMENT FOR VOICES (DUO, GROUP OR CHORUS)

(An Arranger's Award.) (This category is for a specific arrangement released for the first time during the Eligibility Year on either a single or an album track. This category covers all voices on a recording excluding a featured soloist and includes a cappella and voices with instrumental accompaniment.)

AFTERNOON DELIGHT - Starland Vocal Band - Starland Vocal Band, Arrangers (Windsong/RCA)
AIN'T MISBEHAVIN' - Quire - Christian Chevallier, Arranger (RCA)
BOHEMIAN RHAPSODY - Queen - Queen, Arrangers (Elektra)
CAN'T HIDE LOVE - Earth, Wind & Fire - Earth, Wind & Fire, Arrangers (Columbia)
I GET ALONG WITHOUT YOU VERY WELL - The Singers Unlimited - Gene Puerling, Arranger (MPS)

BEST ENGINEERED RECORDING (NON-CLASSICAL)

(An Engineer's Award.) (All nominations are albums)

BREEZIN' - George Benson - Al Schmitt, Engineer (Warner Bros.)
THE DREAM WEAVER - Gary Wright - Jay Lewis, Engineer (Warner Bros.)
THE KING JAMES VERSION - Harry James and his Big Band - Ron Hitchcock, Engineer (Sheffield Lab)
SOMEWHERE I'VE NEVER TRAVELLED - Ambrosia - Alan Parsons & Tom Trefethen, Engineers (20th Cent.)
TALES OF MYSTERY AND IMAGINATION - EDGAR ALLAN POE - The Alan Parsons Project - Alan Parsons, Engineer (20th Cent.)

BEST ALBUM PACKAGE

(An Art Director's Award. This category is for either classical or non-classical single-jacket albums or multiple pocket album packages.)

BELLAVIA - Chuck Mangione - Roland Young, Art Director (A&M)
CHICAGO X - Chicago - **John Berg, Art Director (Columbia)**
CONEY ISLAND BABY - Lou Reed - Acy Lehman, Art Director (RCA)
THE END OF THE BEGINNING - Richie Havens - Roland Young, Art Director (A&M)
MIRRORS - Peggy Lee - Roland Young, Art Director (A&M)
PRESENCE - Led Zeppelin - Hipgnosis and Hardie, Art Directors (Swan Song)
SCHUMANN: SYMPHONY #1 IN B-FLAT, OP. 38; MANFRED: OVERTURE, Op. 115 - Charles Munch cond. Boston Symphony - J. Stelmach, Art Director (RCA)
SILK DEGREES - Boz Scaggs - Ron Coro & Nancy Donald, Art Directors (Columbia)

BEST ALBUM NOTES

(An Annotator's Award.) (This category is for original writing for a specific album. Either classical or non-classical albums qualify.)

BEETHOVEN: THE FIVE PIANO CONCERTOS - Rubinstein, Baremboim cond. London Philharmonic - George R. Marek, Annotator (RCA)
THE BLUE SKY BOYS (BILL & EARL BOLICK) - Douglas B. Green, Annotator (RCA)
CARUSO - A LEGENDARY PERFORMER - Enrico Caruso - Francis Robinson, Annotator (RCA)
THE CHANGING FACE OF HARLEM, THE SAVOY SESSIONS - Various Artists - **Dan Morgenstern, Annotator (Savoy)**
THE COMPLETE TOMMY DORSEY, VOLUME I/1935 - Mort Goode, Annotator (RCA)

BEST PRODUCER OF THE YEAR

(A Producer's Award for consistently outstanding creativity in producing. Listed below are examples of the producer's activities.) (A)Album (S)Single (T)Track

KENNETH GAMBLE & LEON HUFF: "Enjoy Yourself" (S) - The Jacksons; "Family Reunion" (A) - The O'Jays; "Message In The Music" (A) - The O'Jays; "Wake Up Everybody" (A) & (S) - Melvin & The Bluenotes; "All Things In Time" (A) - Lou Rawls; "You'll Never Find Another Love Like Mine" (S) - Lou Rawls; "Groovy People" (S) - Lou Rawls; "Living For The Weekend" (S) - The O'Jays
RICHARD PERRY: "Burton Cummings" (A) - Burton Cummings; "Stand Tall" (S) - Burton Cummings; "The Coming Out" (A) - Manhattan Transfer
LENNIE WARONKER: "Gord's Gold" (Album One) - Gordon Lightfoot; "Summertime Dream" (A) - Gordon Lightfoot; "Shower The People" (S) - James Taylor; "In The Pocket" (A) - James Taylor; "Sweet Harmony" (A) - Maria Muldaur; "The Wreck Of The Edmund Fitzgerald" (S) - Gordon Lightfoot (above product with co-producers)
JOE WISSERT: "It's Over" (S) - Boz Scaggs; "Silk Degrees" (A) - Boz Scaggs; "Lowdown" (S) - Boz Scaggs; "Music, Music" (A) - Helen Reddy; "I Can't Hear You No More" (S) - Helen Reddy; "Gratitude" (A) - Earth, Wind & Fire (with co-producers)
STEVIE WONDER: "Songs In The Key Of Life" (A) - Stevie Wonder

BEST JAZZ VOCAL PERFORMANCE

(This category is for a soloist, duo or group.) (All nominations are albums)

FITZGERALD & PASS. . .AGAIN - Ella Fitzgerald (Pablo)
MORE SARAH VAUGHAN LIVE IN JAPAN - Sarah Vaughan (Mainstream)
PORGY AND BESS - Ray Charles and Cleo Laine (RCA)
QUIRE - Quire (RCA)
WHERE IS LOVE? - Irene Kral (Choice)

BEST JAZZ PERFORMANCE BY A SOLOIST

(This category is for a solo instrumental performance with or without a group or band.)

BASIE & ZOOT - Count Basie (album) (Pablo)
COMMITMENT - Jim Hall (album) (Horizon/A&M)
DONNA LEE - Jaco Pastorius (track) (Epic)
CLARK TERRY AND HIS JOLLY GIANTS - Clark Terry (album) (Vanguard)
THE NEW PHIL WOODS ALBUM - Phil Woods (album) (RCA)
WORKS OF ART - Art Tatum (album) (Jazz)

BEST JAZZ PERFORMANCE BY A GROUP

(This category is for an instrumental group.) (All nominations are albums)

BASIE & ZOOT - Count Basie & Zoot Sims (Pablo)
THE PAUL DESMOND QUARTET LIVE - Paul Desmond Quartet (Horizon/A&M)
THE LEPRECHAUN - Chick Corea (Polydor)
JACO PASTORIUS - Jaco Pastorius (Epic)
SINCE WE MET - The Bill Evans Trio (Fantasy)

BEST JAZZ PERFORMANCE BY A BIG BAND

(This category is primarily for a big band sound.) (All nominations are albums)

AFRO-CUBAN JAZZ MOODS - Dizzy Gillespie and Machito (Pablo)
THE ELLINGTON SUITES - Duke Ellington (Pablo)
LONG YELLOW ROAD - Toshiko Akiyoshi-Lew Tabackin Big Band (RCA)
NEW LIFE - Thad Jones, Mel Lewis (Horizon/A&M)
THE NEW PHIL WOODS ALBUM - Phil Woods (RCA)

BEST POP VOCAL PERFORMANCE, FEMALE

(This category is for a solo performance in either pop, rock or folk.)
HASTEN DOWN THE WIND - Linda Ronstadt (album) (Asylum)
HERE, THERE AND EVERYWHERE - Emmylou Harris (track) (Reprise)
THE HISSING OF SUMMER LAWNS - Joni Mitchell (album) (Asylum)
NATALIE - Natalie Cole (album) (Capitol)
TURN THE BEAT AROUND - Vicki Sue Robinson (single) (RCA)

BEST POP VOCAL PERFORMANCE, MALE

(This category is for a solo performance in either pop, rock or folk.)
SILK DEGREES - Boz Scaggs (album) (Columbia)
SONGS IN THE KEY OF LIFE - Stevie Wonder (album) (Tamla)
THIS MASQUERADE - George Benson (track) (Warner Bros.)
THE WRECK OF THE EDMUND FITZGERALD - Gordon Lightfoot (single) (Reprise)
YOU'LL NEVER FIND ANOTHER LOVE LIKE MINE - Lou Rawls (single) (PIR)

BEST POP VOCAL PERFORMANCE BY A DUO, GROUP OR CHORUS

(This category is for pop, rock and folk. All recordings on which the group receives artist billing on the label are eligible here even though the vocal may feature only one member of the group.) (All nominations are singles)
AFTERNOON DELIGHT - Starland Vocal Band (Windsong/RCA)
BOHEMIAN RHAPSODY - Queen (Elektra)
DON'T GO BREAKING MY HEART - Elton John & Kiki Dee (Rocket/MCA)
I'D REALLY LOVE TO SEE YOU TONIGHT - England Dan and John Ford Coley (Big Tree)
IF YOU LEAVE ME NOW - Chicago (Columbia)

BEST POP INSTRUMENTAL PERFORMANCE

(This category is for pop, rock and folk. All recordings are for either pure instrumentals or instrumentals with vocal coloring.)
BACK TO BACK - The Brecker Brothers Band (album) (Arista)
BREEZIN' - George Benson (album) (Warner Bros.)
CONTUSION - Stevie Wonder (track) (Tamla)
A FIFTH OF BEETHOVEN - Walter Murphy & The Big Apple Band (Pri. Stock)
WIRED - Jeff Beck (album) (Epic)

BEST R & B VOCAL PERFORMANCE, FEMALE

(This category is for a solo performance.) (All nominations are singles)
LEAN ON ME - Melba Moore (Buddah)
LOVE HANGOVER - Diana Ross (Motown)
MISTY BLUE - Dorothy Moore (Malaco)
SOMETHING HE CAN FEEL - Aretha Franklin (Atlantic)
SOPHISTICATED LADY (SHE'S A DIFFERENT LADY) - Natalie Cole (Capitol)

BEST R & B VOCAL PERFORMANCE, MALE

(This category is for a solo performance.)
DISCO LADY - Johnnie Taylor (single) (Columbia)
GROOVY PEOPLE - Lou Rawls (track) (PIR)
I NEED YOU, YOU NEED ME - Joe Simon (single) (Spring)
I WANT YOU - Marvin Gaye (album) (Tamla)
I WISH - Stevie Wonder (track) (Tamla)
LOWDOWN - Boz Scaggs (single) (Columbia)

BEST R & B VOCAL PERFORMANCE BY A DUO, GROUP OR CHORUS

(All recordings on which the group receives artist billing on the label are eligible here even though the vocal may feature only one member of the group.)
GRATITUDE - Earth, Wind & Fire (album) (Columbia)
PLAY THAT FUNKY MUSIC - Wild Cherry (track) (Epic)
RUBBERBAND MAN - Spinners (single) (Atlantic)
(SHAKE, SHAKE, SHAKE) SHAKE YOUR BOOTY - KC & The Sunshine Band (single) (T.K.)
YOU DON'T HAVE TO BE A STAR (TO BE IN MY SHOW) - Marilyn McCoo, Billy Davis Jr. (single) (ABC)

BEST R & B INSTRUMENTAL PERFORMANCE

(All recordings are for either pure instrumentals or instrumentals with vocal coloring.)
AFTER THE DANCE - Marvin Gaye (track) (Tamla)
BRASS CONSTRUCTION - Brass Construction (album) (U.A.)
DOIN' IT - Herbie Hancock (single) (Columbia)
HOPE THAT WE CAN BE TOGETHER SOON - Stanley Turrentine (single) (Fantasy)
KEEP THAT SAME OLD FEELING - The Crusaders (single) (Blue Thumb)
THEME FROM GOOD KING BAD - George Benson (track) (CTI)

BEST RHYTHM & BLUES SONG

(A Songwriter's Award.) (Any song is eligible if a new recording of it has been released during the Eligibility Year, provided it was not a previous final nomination in a songwriting category.)
DISCO LADY - Harvey Scales, Al Vance, Don Davis
LOVE HANGOVER - Pam Sawyer, Marilyn McLeod
LOWDOWN - Boz Scaggs, David Paich
MISTY BLUE - Bob Montgomery
(SHAKE, SHAKE, SHAKE) SHAKE YOUR BOOTY - Harry Wayne Casey, Richard Finch

BEST SOUL GOSPEL PERFORMANCE

(All nominations are albums)
GIVE IT TO ME - James Cleveland & The Southern California Community Choir (Savoy)
HOW I GOT OVER - Mahalia Jackson (Columbia)
THIS IS ANOTHER DAY - Andrae Crouch and the Disciples (Light)
TOUCH ME - VOLUME II - James Cleveland & The Charles Fold Singers (Savoy)
WAR ON SIN - Inez Andrews (Songbird)

BEST COUNTRY VOCAL PERFORMANCE, FEMALE

(This category is for a solo performance)
ALL I CAN DO - Dolly Parton (album) (RCA)
ELITE HOTEL - Emmylou Harris (album) (Reprise)
I'LL GET OVER YOU - Crystal Gayle (single) (U.A.)
'TIL I CAN MAKE IT ON MY OWN - Tammy Wynette (single) (Epic)
TONITE! AT THE CAPRI LOUNGE LORETTA HAGGERS - Mary Kay Place (album) (Columbia)

BEST COUNTRY VOCAL PERFORMANCE, MALE

(This category is for a solo performance)
ARE YOU READY FOR THE COUNTRY - Waylon Jennings (album) (RCA)
BROKEN LADY - Larry Gatlin (single) (Monument)
FOREVER LOVERS - Mac Davis (album) (Columbia)
I'D HAVE TO BE CRAZY - Willie Nelson (single) (Columbia)
(I'M A) STAND BY MY WOMAN MAN - Ronnie Milsap (single) (RCA)

BEST COUNTRY VOCAL PERFORMANCE BY A DUO OR GROUP

(All nominations are singles)
THE END IS NOT IN SIGHT (THE COWBOY TUNE) - Amazing Rhythm Aces (ABC)
GOLDEN RING - George Jones, Tammy Wynette (Epic)
THE LETTER - Loretta Lynn, Conway Twitty (MCA)
ROUTE 66 - Asleep At The Wheel (Capitol)
YOUR PICTURE IN THE PAPER - The Statler Bros. (Mercury)

BEST COUNTRY INSTRUMENTAL PERFORMANCE

(This category is for an Orchestra, Group or Soloist and is for either pure instrumentals or instrumentals with vocal coloring.)
BLUE EYES CRYING IN THE RAIN - Ace Cannon (single) (Hi)
CHESTER & LESTER - Chet Atkins, Les Paul (album) (RCA)
I'M THINKING TONIGHT OF MY BLUE EYES - Floyd Cramer (single) (RCA)
LONG HARD RIDE - Marshall Tucker Band (single) (Capricorn)
TEXAS - Danny Davis and the Nashville Brass (album) (RCA)

BEST COUNTRY SONG

(A Songwriter's Award.) (Any song is eligible if a new recording of it has been released during the Eligibility Year, provided it was not a previous final nomination in a songwriting category.)
BROKEN LADY - Larry Gatlin
THE DOOR IS ALWAYS OPEN - Bob McDill, Dickey Lees
DROPKICK ME, JESUS - Paul Craft
EVERY TIME YOU TOUCH ME (I GET HIGH) - Charlie Rich, Billy Sherrill
HANK WILLIAMS, YOU WROTE MY LIFE - Paul Craft

BEST INSPIRATIONAL PERFORMANCE

(This category is for non-classical recordings.)
AMAZING GRACE - Willie Nelson (track) (Columbia)
THE ASTONISHING, OUTRAGEOUS, AMAZING, INCREDIBLE, UNBELIEVABLE, DIFFERENT WORLD OF GARY S. PAXTON - Gary S. Paxton (album) (Newpax)
HAVE A TALK WITH GOD - Stevie Wonder (track) (Tamla)
JUST A CLOSER WALK WITH THEE - Sonny James (track) (Columbia)
PRECIOUS MEMORIES - Ray Price (album) (Word)
SILVER LININGS - Charlie Rich (album) (Epic)
SOMETHING SUPER NATURAL - Pat Boone (album) (Lamb & Lion)

SUNDAY MORNING WITH CHARLEY PRIDE - Charley Pride (album) (RCA)

BEST GOSPEL PERFORMANCE (OTHER THAN SOUL GOSPEL)

BETWEEN THE CROSS AND HEAVEN (THERE'S A WHOLE LOT OF LIVING GOING ON) - The Speers (album) (Heartwarming)
HERE THEY COME - The Florida Boys (album) (Canaan)
JUST BECAUSE - Imperials (album) (Impact)
LEARNING TO LEAN - The Blackwood Brothers (album) (Skylight)
WHERE THE SOUL NEVER DIES - Oak Ridge Boys (single) (Columbia)

BEST ETHNIC OR TRADITIONAL RECORDING

(This category includes traditional blues and pure folk recordings.) (All nominations are albums)
BAGPIPE MARCHES AND MUSIC OF SCOTLAND - Shotts & Dykehead Caledonia Pipe Band (Olympic)
BEWARE OF THE DOG - Hound Dog Taylor (Alligator)
IF YOU LOVE THESE BLUES, PLAY 'EM AS YOU PLEASE - Michael Bloomfield (Guitar Player)
MARK TWANG - John Hartford (Flying Fish)
PROUD EARTH - Chief Dan George, Arliene Nofchissey Williams, Rick Brosseau (Salt City)

BEST LATIN RECORDING

(This category is for pure Latin music.) (All nominations are albums)
COCINANDO LA SALSA - Joe Cuba (Tico)
EL MAESTRO - Johnny Pacheco (Fania)
LA GORME - Eydie Gorme (Gala)
"SALSA" SOUNDTRACK - Fania All-Stars (Fania)
SOFRITO - Mongo Santamaria (Vaya)
UNFINISHED MASTERPIECE - Eddie Palmieri (Coco)

BEST RECORDING FOR CHILDREN

(This category is intended for recordings created specifically for children.)
THE ADVENTURES OF ALI AND HIS GANG VS. MR. TOOTH DECAY - Muhammed Ali & His Gang (album) (St. John's Fruits & Vegetables)
DICKENS' CHRISTMAS CAROL - Mickey Mouse & Scrooge McDuck (album) (Disneyland)
PROKOFIEV: PETER AND THE WOLF; SAINT SAENS: CARNIVAL OF THE ANIMALS - Hermione Gingold, Bohm cond. Vienna Philharmonic (album) (D.G.)
SNOW WHITE AND THE SEVEN DWARFS - Original Soundtrack (album) (Buena Vista)
WINNIE THE POOH FOR PRESIDENT (CAMPAIGN SONG) - Sterling Holloway, Larry Groce (single) (Disneyland)

BEST COMEDY RECORDING

(Either spoken word or musical performances are eligible here.) (All nominations are albums)
BICENTENNIAL NIGGER - Richard Pryor (Warner Bros.)
BILL COSBY IS NOT HIMSELF THESE DAYS - RAT OWN, RAT OWN, RAT OWN - Bill Cosby (Capitol)
GOODBYE POP - National Lampoon (Epic)
SLEEPING BEAUTY - Cheech & Chong (Ode)
YOU GOTTA WASH YOUR ASS - Redd Foxx (Atlantic)

BEST SPOKEN WORD RECORDING
(This category is for spoken word, documentary or drama recordings.) (All nominations are albums)
ASIMOV: FOUNDATION - THE PSYCHOHISTORIANS - William Shatner (Caedmon)
DICKENS: A TALE OF TWO CITIES - James Mason (Caedmon)
FAHRENHEIT 451 - Ray Bradbury (Listening Library)
GREAT AMERICAN DOCUMENTS - Orson Welles, Henry Fonda, Helen Hayes, James Earl Jones (CBS)
HEMINGWAY: THE OLD MAN AND THE SEA - Charlton Heston (Caedmon)

BEST INSTRUMENTAL COMPOSITION
(A Composer's Award for an original, non-classical composition with or without lyrics which first gained recognition as an instrumental.)
BELLAVIA - Chuck Mangione
CONTUSION - Stevie Wonder
EARTH, WIND & FIRE - Maurice White, Skip Scarbrough
LEPRECHAUN'S DREAM - Chick Corea
MIDNIGHT SOUL PATROL - Quincy Jones, Louis Johnson, Dave Grusin
THE WHITE DAWN - Henry Mancini

ALBUM OF BEST ORIGINAL SCORE WRITTEN FOR A MOTION PICTURE OR A TELEVISION SPECIAL
(A Composer's Award for an original background score or original songs written specifically for the or motion picture television special.)
CAR WASH - Norman Whitfield (MCA)
THE OMEN - Jerry Goldsmith (Tattoo/RCA)
ONE FLEW OVER THE CUCKOO'S NEST - Jack Nitzsche (Fantasy)
RICH MAN, POOR MAN - Alex North (MCA)
TAXI DRIVER - Bernard Herrmann (Arista)
3 DAYS OF THE CONDOR - Dave Grusin (Capitol)

BEST CAST SHOW ALBUM
(Awards to the Composers and Album Producers.) (Original cast albums, albums by road casts, or working casts, including show revival casts, are eligible.)
BUBBLING BROWN SUGAR - Razaf, Goodman, Sampson, Webb, Strayhorn, Holgate, Kemp, Lopez, Rogers, Williams, Mills, Parish, Ellington, Hines, Sissle, Blake, Pinkard, Waller, Overstreet, Higgins, Herzog, Webster, Holiday, Comps. - Hugo and Luigi, Producers (H&L)
MY FAIR LADY - 20th Anniversary Production - Alan Jay Lerner, Frederick Lowe, Composers - Goddard Lieberson, Producer (Columbia)
PACIFIC OVERTURES - Stephen Sondheim, Composer - Thomas Z. Shepard, Producer (RCA)
REX - Richard Rodgers, Sheldon Harnick, Composers - Thomas Z. Shepard, Producer (RCA)
SIDE BY SIDE BY SONDHEIM - Stephen Sondheim, Composer - Thomas Z. Shepard, Producer (RCA)

ALBUM OF THE YEAR CLASSICAL
(Grammys to the Artist and Producer. Certificates to the Engineer(s).)
THE ART OF COURTLY LOVE (Machaut & His Age - 14th Century Avant-Garde - The Court of Burgundy) - David Munrow cond. The Early Music Consort of London - Christopher Bishop, Producer (Seraphim)
BEETHOVEN: (THE) FIVE PIANO CONCERTOS - Artur Rubinstein & Daniel Barenboim cond. London Philharmonic - Max Wilcox, Producer (RCA)
BIZET: CARMEN - Sir Georg Solti (cond. London Philharmonic - Prin. Solos: Troyanos, Domingo, Kanawa, Van Dam) - Christopher Raeburn, Producer (London)
GERSHWIN: PORGY & BESS - Lorin Maazel (cond. Cleveland Orchestra - Prin. Solos: Mitchell, White) - Michael Woolcock, Producer (London)
GERSHWIN: RHAPSODY IN BLUE - George Gershwin - (1925 Piano Roll) & Michael Tilson Thomas cond. Columbia Jazz Band; GERSHWIN: AN AMERICAN IN PARIS - Michael Tilson Thomas cond. New York Philharmonic - Andrew Kazdin, Producer (Columbia)
HOROWITZ CONCERTS 1975/76 (Schumann, Scriabin) Vladimir Horowitz - John Pfeiffer, Producer (RCA)
JOPLIN: TREEMONISHA - Gunther Schuller (cond. Original Cast Orchestra & Chorus - Prin. Solos: Balthrop, Allen, White) - Tom Mowrey, Producer (DGw)
ARTURO TOSCANINI - THE PHILADELPHIA ORCHESTRA - (First Release of the Legendary 1941-42 Recording - Schubert, Debussy, Berlioz, Respighi, etc.) - Arturo Toscanini cond. The Philadelphia Orchestra - John Pfeiffer, Producer (RCA)

BEST CLASSICAL ORCHESTRAL PERFORMANCE
(Grammys to the Conductor and Producer. Certificates to the classical orchestra committee.)
BERLIOZ: SYMPHONIE FANTASTIQUE - Jean Martinon cond. Orchestra National of the ORFT - Rene Challan, Producer (Angel)
BRAHMS: SYMPHONY NO. 1 IN C MINOR - James Levine cond. Chicago Symphony - Thomas Z. Shepard & Jay David Saks, Producer (RCA)
ELGAR: SYMPHONY NO. 2 IN E FLAT MAJOR - Sir Georg Solti cond. London Philharmonic - Ray Minshull, Producer (London)
FALLA: THREE CORNERED HAT (Boulez Conducts Falla) Pierre Boulez cond. New York Philharmonic - Andrew Kazdin, Producer (Columbia)
THE FOURTH OF JULY! (Ives: Sym. No. 2, Var. on America/Copland: Appalachian Spring/Bernstein: Over. to Candide/Gershwin: Amer. In Paris) Zubin Mehta cond. Los Angeles Philharmonic - Ray Minshull, Producer (London)
GERSHWIN: RHAPSODY IN BLUE - Michael Tilson Thomas cond. Columbia Jazz Band (with Gershwin 1925 Piano Roll) - Andrew Kazdin, Producer (Columbia)
RAVEL: DAPHNIS ET CHLOE (Complete Ballet) - Jean Martinon cond. Orchestre de Paris - Rene Challan, Producer (Angel)
STRAUSS: ALSO SPRACH ZARATHUSTRA - Sir Georg Solti cond. Chicago Symphony - Ray Minshull, Producer (London)

BEST OPERA RECORDING
(Grammys to the Conductor and Producer; special plaques to the Principal Soloists.)
BIZET: CARMEN - Sir Georg Solti (cond. London Philharmonic - Prin. Solos: Tatiana Troyanos, Placido Domingo, Kiri Te Kanawa, Jose Van Dam) - Christopher Raeburn, Producer (London)
GERSHWIN: PORGY & BESS - Lorin Maazel (cond. Cleveland Orchestra & Chorus - Prin. Solos: Leona Mitchell, Willard White) - Michael Woolcock, Producer (London)
JOPLIN: TREEMONISHA - Gunther Schuller (cond. Original Cast Orchestra & Chorus - Prin. Solos: Carmen Balthrop, Betty Allen, Willard White) - Tom Mowrey, Producer (DG)
MASSENET: THAIS - Lorin Maazel (cond. New Philharmonia Orchestra, John Alldis Choir - Prin. Solos: Beverly Sills, Sherrill Milnes, Nicolai Gedda) - Christopher Bishop, Producer (Angel)
SCHOENBERG: MOSES AND AARON - Pierre Boulez (cond. BBC Symphony, BBC Symphony Singers, Orpheus Boys Choir - Prin. Solos: Gunther Reich, Richard Cassilly, Richard Angus, Felicity Palmer, Roland Hermann) - Paul Myers, Producer (Columbia)
VERDI: MACBETH - Claudio Abbado (cond. Chorus & Orchestra of La Scala - Prin. Solos: Shirley Verrett, Placido Domingo, Nicolai Ghiaurov) - Rainer Brock, Producer (DG)

BEST CHORAL PERFORMANCE, CLASSICAL (OTHER THAN OPERA)

(Grammys to the Conductor and Choral Director)

BEETHOVEN: MISSA SOLEMNIS - Walter Hagen-Groll (Chorus Master of New Philharmonia Chorus) - Carlo Maria Giulini (cond. London Philharmonic) (Angel)
BERLIOZ: REQUIEM - Leonard Bernstein (cond. Choeurs de Radio France, Orchestre National de France & Orchestre Philharmonique de Radio France - w/Burrows, Tenor) (Columbia)
BERNSTEIN: CHICHESTER PSALMS; BRITTEN: REJOICE IN THE LAMB - Phillip Ledger (cond. Kings College Choir, Cambridge) (Angel)
ELGAR: THE KINGDOM, OP. 51 - Sir Adrian Boult (cond. London Philharmonic Chorus & London Philharmonic Orchestra) (Connoisseur Society)
FAURE: REQUIEM - Franz Muller (Chorus Master of Netherlands Radio Chorus) - Jean Fournet (cond. Rotterdam Philharmonic) (Philips)
GREGORIAN CHANT - Dom Jean Claire (Director of Choir of the Monks of Saint-Pierre de Solesmes Abbey) (London)
RACHMANINOFF: THE BELLS - Arthur Oldham (Chorus Master of London Symphony Chorus) - Andre Previn (cond. London Symphony) (Angel)
TIPPETT: A CHILD OF OUR TIME - Colin Davis (cond. BBC Singers & Choral Society and BBC Symphony) (Philips)
VERDI: OPERA CHORUSES (From Nabucco, Il Trovatore, Otello, Aida, etc.) - Romano Gandolfi (Chorus Master of Chorus of La Scala, Milan) - Claudio Abbado (cond. Orchestra of La Scala, Milan) (DG)

BEST CHAMBER MUSIC PERFORMANCE

(Instrumental or Vocal)

THE ART OF COURTLY LOVE (Machaut & His Age - 14th Century Avant Garde - The Court of Burgundy) - David Munrow cond. The Early Music Consort of London (Seraphim)
BARBER: QUARTET FOR STRINGS, OP. 11, IVES: QUARTET NO. 2 FOR STRINGS (TWO AMERICAN MASTERPIECES) - The Cleveland Quartet (RCA)
BEETHOVEN: SONATAS FOR CELLO (Complete) - Jacqueline du Pre & Daniel Barenboim (Angel)
DVORAK: QUARTETS, OPP. 96 & 105 - Prague String Quartet (DG)
THE HEIFETZ PIATIGORSKY CONCERTS (Dvorak: Trio in F Min. for Piano w/Leonard Pennario, Stravinsky: Suite Italienne for Violin & Cello, Gliere: Duo for Violin & Cello, etc.) - Jascha Heifetz & Gregor Piatigorsky (Columbia)
HINDEMITH: SONATAS FOR BRASS & PIANO (Complete) - Glenn Gould & Philadelphia Brass Ensemble (Columbia)
MESSIAEN: QUARTET FOR THE END OF TIME - Tashi (Peter Serkin, Fred Sherry, Ida Kavafian, Richard Stoltzman) (RCA)
SCHUBERT: QUINTET IN C, OP. 163 - Thomas Igloi & Alberni Quartet (CRD)
SHOSTAKOVICH: QUARTET NO. 14 IN F SHARP MAJOR - Fitzwilliam Quartet (Oiseau Lyre)

BEST CLASSICAL PERFORMANCE-- INSTRUMENTAL SOLOIST OR SOLOISTS (WITH ORCHESTRA)

BARTOK: CONCERTI FOR PIANO NOS. 1 & 3 - Stephen Bishop, Piano (David cond. London Symphony) (Philips)
BEETHOVEN: THE FIVE PIANO CONCERTOS - Artur Rubinstein, Piano (Barenboim cond. London Philharmonic) (RCA)
BRAHMS: CONCERTO IN D MAJOR FOR VIOLIN - Nathan Milstein, Violin (Jochum cond. Vienna Philharmonic) (DG)
PROKOFIEV: THE FIVE PIANO CONCERTOS - Vladimir Ashkenazy, Piano (Previn cond. London Symphony) (London)
RAVEL: CONCERTO IN G MAJOR FOR PIANO & ORCH. & CONCERTO IN D MAJOR FOR LEFT HAND - Aldo Ciccolini, Piano (Martinon cond. Orchestre de Paris) (Angel)
STRAUSS: DON QUIXOTE - Mstislav Rostropovich, Cello (Karajan cond. Berlin Philharmonic) (Angel)

BEST CLASSICAL PERFORMANCE-- INSTRUMENTAL SOLOIST OR SOLOISTS (WITHOUT ORCHESTRA)

CHOPIN: PRELUDES, OP. 28 - Maurizio Pollini, Piano (DG)
(GERSHWIN) "WATTS BY GEORGE": ANDRE WATTS PLAYS GEORGE GERSHWIN (Rhapsody in Blue, Preludes for Piano (3), 13 Songs from Gershwin Songbook) - Andre Watts, Piano (Columbia)
HOROWITZ CONCERTS 1975/76 (Schumann, Scriabin) - Vladimir Horowitz, Piano (RCA)
THE INTIMATE GUITAR/2 (Bach, Sor, Albeniz, Molleda, San Sebastian, Samazeuilh) - Andres Segovia, Guitar (RCA)
(KREISLER) ITZHAK PERLMAN PLAYS FRITZ KREISLER - (Caprice Viennois, Andantino in the Style of Martini, Allegretto in the Style of Boccherini, La Gitana) - Itzhak Perlman, Violin (Angel)
LISZT: LEGENDARY SOVIET PIANIST - LAZAR BERMAN PLAYS LISZT - Lazar Berman, piano (Everest)
RACHMANINOFF: 23 PRELUDES - Vladimir Ashkenazy, Piano (London)
SCHUBERT: SONATA IN A MINOR, OP. 42 & HUNGARIAN MELODY IN B MINOR (D 817) - Alfred Brendel, Piano (Philips)

BEST CLASSICAL VOCAL SOLOIST PERFORMANCE

CLASSICAL BARBRA (Debussy: Beau Soir, Canteloube: Berceuse, Wolf: Verschwiegene, etc.) - Barbra Streisand - (Ogerman cond. Columbia Symphony) (Columbia)
(HERBERT) MUSIC OF VICTOR HERBERT (Kiss in The Dark, Italian Street Song, Kiss Me Again etc.) - Beverly Sills (Kostelanetz cond. London Symphony) (Angel)
IVES: SONGS - Jan de Gaetani (Gilbert Kalish, Accomp.) (Nonesuch)
MAHLER: DAS LIED VON DER ERDE - Janet Baker & James King - (Haitink cond. Concertgebouw Orchestra) (Philips)
MOZART: ARIAS (La Clemenza di Tito, Die Entfuhrung aus dem Serail, Nozze di Figaro, etc.) - Margaret Price - (Lockhart cond. English Chamber Orchestra) (RCA)
SCHOENBERG: NINE EARLY SONGS; THE CABARET SONGS OF ARNOLD SCHOENBERG - Marni Nixon (Leonard Stein, Accomp.) (RCA)
(VERDI) CARLO BERGONZI SINGS VERDI - Carlo Bergonzi (Santi cond. New Philharmonia & Gardelli cond. Royal Philharmonic) (Philips)
WOLF: MORIKE LIEDER - Dietrich Fischer-Dieskau (Sviatoslav Richter, Accomp.) (DG)

BEST ENGINEERED RECORDING, CLASSICAL

(An Engineer's Award)

BEYOND THE SUN: AN ELECTRONIC PORTRAIT OF HOLST'S "THE PLANETS" - Patrick Gleeson - Patrick Gleeson, Skip Shimmin, Neil Schwartz, Seth Dworken, Engineers (Mercury)
BRAHMS: SYMPHONY NO. 1 IN C MINOR - James Levine cond. Chicago Symphony - Paul Goodman, Engineer (RCA)
BRITTEN: FOUR SEA INTERLUDES & PASSACAGLIA FROM "PETER GRIMES" - Previn cond. London Symphony - Christopher Parker, Engineer (Angel)
FALLA: THREE CORNERED HAT (BOULEZ CONDUCTS FALLA) - Boulez cond. New York Philharmonic/de Gaetani - E. T. (Bud) Graham, Ray Moore, Milton Cherin, Engineers (Columbia)
GERSHWIN: PORGY & BESS - Maazel cond. Cleveland Orchestra/ Mitchell, White - James Lock, Arthur Lilley, Colin Moorfoot, Michael Mailes, Engineers (London)
GERSHWIN: RHAPSODY IN BLUE - George Gershwin (1925 Piano Roll) & Thomas cond. Columbia Jazz Band - E. T. (Bud) Graham, Ray Moore, Milt Cherin, Engineers (Columbia)
MAHLER: SYMPHONY NO. 2 IN C MINOR ("RESURRECTION") - Mehta cond. Vienna Philharmonic - James Lock, Colin Moorfoot, Jack Law, Engineers (London)
SAINT-SAENS: SYMPHONY NO. 3 IN C MINOR ("ORGAN") - Barenboim cond. Chicago Symphony - Klaus Scheibe, Engineer (DG)
STRAUSS: AN ALPINE SYMPHONY - Mehta cond. Los Angeles Philharmonic - James Lock, Engineer (London)

1977 HALL OF FAME WINNERS
BACH: THE WELL TEMPERED CLAVIER (Complete) (Albums) Wanda Landowska - RCA Victor #LM1017, #LM1107, #LM1136 - Released 1949-1954
BEETHOVEN: SYMPHONIES (9) (Albums) - Arturo Toscanini conducting the NBC Symphony - RCA Victor #LM6009, #LM1723, #LM1042, #LM1755, #LM1756, #LM1757, #LM6009 - Released 1950-1953
BEGIN THE BEGUINE - Artie Shaw - Bluebird #B7746 - Released in 1938
MY FAIR LADY (Album) - Original Broadway Cast with Rex Harrison and Julie Andrews - Columbia #OL5090 - Released in 1956
SINGIN' THE BLUES - Frankie Trumbauer & His Orchestra, featuring Bix Beiderbecke on Cornet - Okeh #40772 - Released in 1927

1977

RECORD OF THE YEAR
(Grammys to the Artist and A&R Producer. Certificates to the Arranger, Engineer and Songwriter)
BLUE BAYOU - Linda Ronstadt - Peter Asher, Producer (Asylum)
DON'T IT MAKE MY BROWN EYES BLUE - Crystal Gayle - Allen Reynolds, Producer (UA)
HOTEL CALIFORNIA - Eagles - Bill Szymczyk, Producer (Asylum)
LOVE THEME FROM A STAR IS BORN (EVERGREEN) - Barbra Streisand - Barbra Streisand, Phil Ramone, Producers (Columbia)
YOU LIGHT UP MY LIFE - Debby Boone - Joe Brooks, Producer (WB/Curb)

ALBUM OF THE YEAR
(Grammys to the Artist and A&R Producer. Certificates to the Arranger and Engineer)
AJA - Steely Dan - Gary Katz, Producer (ABC)
HOTEL CALIFORNIA - Eagles - Bill Szymczyk, Producer (Asylum)
J T - James Taylor - Peter Asher, Producer (Columbia)
RUMOURS - Fleetwood Mac - Fleetwood Mac, Richard Dashut, Ken Caillat, Producers (W.B.)
STAR WARS - London Symphony - John Williams, Conductor - George Lucas, Producer (20th Cent.)

SONG OF THE YEAR
(A Songwriter's Award)
DON'T IT MAKE MY BROWN EYES BLUE - Richard Leigh
HOTEL CALIFORNIA - Don Felder, Don Henley, Glenn Frey
LOVE THEME FROM A STAR IS BORN (EVERGREEN) - Barbra Streisand, Paul Williams
NOBODY DOES IT BETTER - Marvin Hamlisch, Carole Bayer Sager
SOUTHERN NIGHTS - Allen Toussaint
YOU LIGHT UP MY LIFE - Joe Brooks

BEST NEW ARTIST OF THE YEAR
(This category is for an artist or organized group whose first recording was released during the Eligibility Period)
STEPHEN BISHOP (ABC)
DEBBY BOONE (WB/CURB)
SHAUN CASSIDY (WB/CURB)
FOREIGNER (Atlantic)
ANDY GIBB (RSO)

BEST INSTRUMENTAL ARRANGEMENT
(An Arranger's Award for a specific arrangement released on either a single or album track)
FREE AS THE WIND - The Crusaders - The Crusaders, Arrangers (ABC)
MUSICMAGIC - Return to Forever - Chick Corea, Arranger (Columbia)
NADIA'S THEME (THE YOUNG AND THE RESTLESS) - (Barry De Vorzon) - Harry Betts, Perry Botkin, Jr., Barry De Vorzon, Arrangers (Arista)
ROOTS MURAL THEME - Quincy Jones - Herb Spencer, Arranger (A&M)
SCHEHEREZADE - Hubert Laws - Bob James, Arranger (CTI)

BEST ARRANGEMENT ACCOMPANYING VOCALIST(S)
(An Arranger's Award for a specific arrangement released on either a single or an album track)
BESAME MUCHO - Joao Gilberto - Claus Ogerman, Arranger (W. B.)
CALLING OCCUPANTS OF INTERPLANETARY CRAFT - Carpenters - Richard Carpenter, Arranger (A & M)
THE DEVIL IS A LIAR - Seawind - Seawind, Arranger (CTI)
LOVE THEME FROM A STAR IS BORN (EVERGREEN) - (Barbra Streisand) - Ian Freebairn-Smith, Arranger (Columbia)
NATURE BOY - George Benson - Claus Ogerman, Arranger (W. B.)

BEST ARRANGEMENT FOR VOICES
(An Arranger's Award for a specific arrangement released on either a single or an album track)
ALL YOU DO IS DIAL - Heatwave - Heatwave, Arrangers (Epic)
BABY, I'LL GIVE IT TO YOU - Seals & Crofts - Jim Seals, Arranger (W. B.)
GO YOUR OWN WAY - Fleetwood Mac - Fleetwood Mac, Arrangers (W. B.)
NEW KID IN TOWN - Eagles - Eagles, Arrangers (Asylum)
OH LORD, COME BY HERE - Quincy Jones - Quincy Jones, James Cleveland, John Mandel, Arrangers (A & M)

BEST ENGINEERED RECORDING (non-Classical)
(An Engineer's Award.) (All nominations are albums)
AJA - Steely Dan - Roger Nichols, Elliot Scheiner, Bill Schnee, Al Schmitt, Engineers (ABC)
DISCOVERED AGAIN! - Dave Grusin - Bill Schnee, Engineer (Sheffield Lab)
J T - James Taylor - Val Garay, Engineer (Columbia)
RUMOURS - Fleetwood Mac - Ken Caillat, Richard Dashut, Engineers (W. B.)
SIMPLE DREAMS - Linda Ronstadt - Val Garay, Engineer (Asylum)

BEST ALBUM PACKAGE
(Grammy to Art Director. Certificates to Designer, Photographer, Illustrator, etc. where applicable.)
COLOR AS A WAY OF LIFE (Lou Donaldson) Abie Sussman, Bob Defrin, Art Directors (Cotillion/Atlantic)
GINSENG WOMAN (Eric Gale) Paula Scher, Art Director (Columbia)
HEJIRA (Joni Mitchell) Glen Christensen, Art Director (Asylum)
LOVE NOTES (Ramsey Lewis) John Berg, Art Director (Columbia)
SIMPLE DREAMS (Linda Ronstadt) Kosh, Art Director (Asylum)
SINGIN' (Melissa Manchester) Kosh, Art Director (Arista)
WINGS OVER AMERICA (Wings) MPL/Hipgnosis, Art Director (Capitol)
YARDBIRDS FAVORITES (Yardbirds) Paula Scher, Art Director (Epic)

BEST ALBUM NOTES
(An Annotator's Award for original writing for a specific album.)
BING CROSBY: A LEGENDARY PERFORMER - George T. Simon, Ann (RCA)
GUY LOMBARDO: A LEGENDARY PERFORMER - George T. Simon, Ann (RCA)
JEFFERSON AIRPLANE - FLIGHT LOG - Jefferson Airplane, Patrick Snyder, Ann (Grunt/RCA)
THE LESTER YOUNG STORY VOL. I - Michael Brooks, Ann (Columbia)
STORMY BLUES - Billie Holiday, Chris Albertson, Ann (Verve/Polydor)

BEST PRODUCER OF THE YEAR

(A Producer's Award for consistently outstanding creativity in producing. Listed below are examples of the producer's activities.) AAlbum SSingle TTrack

PETER ASHER: "Handy Man" (S) - James Taylor; "JT" (A) - James Taylor; "Lonely Boy" (S) - Andrew Gold; "What's Wrong With This Picture" (A) - Andrew Gold; "Simple Dreams" (A) - Linda Ronstadt; "Blue Bayou" (S) - Linda Ronstadt
THE BEE GEES, ALBHY GALUTEN, KARL RICHARDSON: "Here at Last. . .Bee Gees Live" (A) - Bee Gees
KENNETH GAMBLE & LEON HUFF: "The Jacksons" (A) - The Jacksons; "See You When I Git There" (S) - Lou Rawls; "Teddy Pendergrass" (A) - Teddy Pendergrass; "Travelin' At The Speed of Thought" (A) - The O'Jays; "Unmistakably Lou" (A) - Lou Rawls
RICHARD PERRY: "Baby It's Me" (A) - Diana Ross; "Endless Flight" (A) - Leo Sayer; "How Much Love" (S) - Leo Sayer; "Nobody Does It Better" (S) - Carly Simon; "Thunder In My Heart" (S) - Leo Sayer; "When I Need You" (S) - Leo Sayer; "You Make Me Feel Like Dancing" (S) - Leo Sayer
BILL SZYMCZYK; "Hotel California" (A) - Eagles; "Hotel California" (S) - Eagles; "Hurry Sundown" (A) - Outlaws; "Life In The Fast Lane" (S) - Eagles

BEST JAZZ VOCAL PERFORMANCE

(This category is for a soloist, duo or group.) (All nominations are albums)
AMOROSO - Joao Gilberto (W. B.)
CARMEN MCRAE AT THE GREAT AMERICAN MUSIC HALL - Carmen McRae (Blue Note/U.A.)
HELEN MERRILL - JOHN LEWIS - Helen Merrill (Mercury)
KRAL SPACE - Irene Kral (Catalyst)
LOOK TO THE RAINBOW - Al Jarreau (W. B.)

BEST JAZZ PERFORMANCE BY A SOLOIST

(This category is for a solo instrumental performance with or without a group or band.)(All nominations are albums)
AFRO BLUE IMPRESSIONS - John Coltrane (Pablo)
'BOP REDUX - Hank Jones (Muse)
THE GIANTS - Oscar Peterson (Pablo)
HEAVY WEATHER - Jaco Pastorius (Col.)
THE PHIL WOODS SIX - LIVE FROM THE SHOWBOAT - Phil Woods (RCA)

BEST JAZZ PERFORMANCE BY A GROUP

(This category is for an instrumental group.) (All nominations are albums)
AFRO BLUE IMPRESSIONS - John Coltrane (Pablo)
ECLYPSO - Tommy Flanagan Trio (Inner City)
HOMECOMING - LIVE AT THE VILLAGE VANGUARD - Dexter Gordon (Columbia)
MEL LEWIS & FRIENDS - Mel Lewis (Horizon/A & M)
THE PHIL WOODS SIX - LIVE FROM THE SHOWBOAT - Phil Woods (RCA)

BEST JAZZ PERFORMANCE BY A BIG BAND

(This category is primarily for a big band sound.) (All nominations are albums)
BUDDY RICH PLAYS AND PLAYS AND PLAYS - Buddy Rich (RCA/Gryphon)
THE 40TH ANNIVERSARY, CARNEGIE HALL CONCERT - Woody Herman (RCA)
LAB '76 - North Texas State University Lab Band, Leon Breeden, director (NTSU Lab Jazz)
PRIME TIME - Count Basie and his Orchestra (Pablo)
ROAD TIME - Toshiko Akiyoshi-Lew Tabackin Big Band (RCA)

BEST POP VOCAL PERFORMANCE, FEMALE

(This category is for a solo performance in either pop, rock or folk.) (All nominations are singles)
BLUE BAYOU - Linda Ronstadt (Asylum)
HERE YOU COME AGAIN - Dolly Parton (RCA)
LOVE THEME FROM A STAR IS BORN (EVERGREEN) - Barbra Streisand (Columbia)
NOBODY DOES IT BETTER - Carly Simon (Elektra)
YOU LIGHT UP MY LIFE - Debby Boone (WB/Curb)

BEST POP VOCAL PERFORMANCE, MALE

(This category is for a solo performance in either pop, rock or folk.)
AFTER THE LOVIN' (album) - Engelbert Humperdinck (Epic)
HANDY MAN (single) - James Taylor (Columbia)
I JUST WANT TO BE YOUR EVERYTHING (single) - Andy Gibb (RSO)
ON AND ON (single) - Stephen Bishop (ABC)
WHEN I NEED YOU (single) - Leo Sayer (W. B.)

BEST POP VOCAL PERFORMANCE BY A DUO, GROUP OR CHORUS

(This category is for pop, rock or folk. All recordings on which the group received artist billing on the label are eligible here even though the vocal may feature only one member of the group.)
AJA - Steely Dan (album) (ABC)
CSN - Crosby, Stills & Nash (album) (Atlantic)
HOTEL CALIFORNIA - Eagles (album) (Asylum)
HOW DEEP IS YOUR LOVE - Bee Gees (single) (RSO)
RUMOURS - Fleetwood Mac (album) (W. B.)

BEST POP INSTRUMENTAL RECORDING

(This category is for pop, rock or folk. All recordings are for either pure instrumentals or instrumentals with vocal coloring.)
GONNA FLY NOW (THEME FROM "ROCKY") - Bill Conti (single) (UA)
GONNA FLY NOW (THEME FROM "ROCKY") - Maynard Ferguson (single) (Columbia)
NADIA'S THEME (THE YOUNG AND THE RESTLESS) - Barry De Vorzon (album) (Arista)
STAR WARS - London Symphony, John Williams, conductor (album) (20th Century)
STAR WARS THEME/CANTINA BAND - Meco (single) (Millennium)

BEST R & B VOCAL PERFORMANCE, FEMALE

(This category is for a solo performance.)
BREAK IT TO ME GENTLY - Aretha Franklin (single) (Atlantic)
DON'T LEAVE ME THIS WAY - Thelma Houston (single) (Motown)
I BELIEVE YOU - Dorothy Moore (single) (Malaco)
I'VE GOT LOVE ON MY MIND - Natalie Cole (single) (Capitol)
YOUR LOVE IS SO GOOD FOR ME - Diana Ross (track) (Motown)

BEST R & B PERFORMANCE, MALE

(This category is for a solo performance.)
AIN'T GONNA BUMP NO MORE (WITH NO BIG FAT WOMAN) - Joe Tex (single) (Epic)
GOT TO GIVE IT UP (PART I) - Marvin Gaye (single) (Motown)
IT'S JUST A MATTER OF TIME - B. B. King (track) (ABC)
A REAL MOTHER FOR YA - Johnny "Guitar" Watson (track) (DJM)
UNMISTAKABLY LOU - Lou Rawls (album) (PIR/Epic)

BEST R & B VOCAL PERFORMANCE BY A DUO, GROUP OR CHORUS
(All recordings on which the group receives artist billing on the label are eligible here even though the vocal may feature only one member of the group.)
ASK RUFUS - Rufus featuring Chaka Khan (album) (ABC)
BABY DON'T CHANGE YOUR MIND - Gladys Knight and the Pips (track) (Buddah)
BEST OF MY LOVE - Emotions (track) (Columbia)
BOOGIE NIGHTS - Heatwave (single) (Epic)
EASY - Commodores (single) (Motown)

BEST R & B INSTRUMENTAL PERFORMANCE
(All recordings are for either pure instrumentals or instrumentals with vocal coloring.)
FUNKY SEA, FUNKY DEW - Brecker Brothers (track) (Arista)
GETAWAY - Salsoul Orchestra (single) (Salsoul)
MORE STUFF - Stuff (album) (W. B.)
Q - Brothers Johnson (track) (A & M)
THE UNFINISHED BUSINESS - The Blackbyrds (track) (Fantasy)

BEST RHYTHM & BLUES SONG
(A Songwriter's Award.) (Any song is eligible if a new recording of it has been released during the Eligibility Year.)
BEST OF MY LOVE - Maurice White, Al McKay
BRICK HOUSE - Milan Williams, Walter Orange, Thomas McClary, William King, Lionel Richie, Ronald LaPread
DON'T LEAVE ME THIS WAY - Kenny Gamble, Leon Huff, Carry Gilbert
EASY - Lionel Richie
YOU MAKE ME FEEL LIKE DANCING - Leo Sayer, Vini Poncia

BEST GOSPEL PERFORMANCE, CONTEMPORARY OR INSPIRATIONAL
(All nominations are albums)
ADAM AGAIN - Michael Omartian (Myrrh/Word)
HART AND SOUL - Larry Hart & The Soul Singers (Genesis)
MIRROR - Evie Tornquist (Word)
MORE, FROM THE ASTONISHING, OUTRAGEOUS, AMAZING, INCREDIBLE, UNBELIEVABLE GARY S. PAXTON - Gary S. Paxton (New Pax) REBA/LADY - Reba Rambo Gardner (Greentree)
SAIL ON - Imperials (Dayspring/Word)

BEST GOSPEL PERFORMANCE, TRADITIONAL
BILL GAITHER SONGS - Blackwood Brothers (album) (Skylite)
CORNERSTONE - The Speers (album) (Heartwarming)
HAVE A LITTLE TALK WITH JESUS - Oak Ridge Boys (track) (Rockland Road)
NATURALLY - The Rambos (album) (Heartwarming)
THEN AND NOW - The Cathedral Quartet (album) (Canaan)
TILL HE COMES - The Lefevres (album) (Canaan)

BEST SOUL GOSPEL PERFORMANCE, CONTEMPORARY
BORN AGAIN - Jessy Dixon (single) (Light)
GOD IS NOT DEAD - Mighty Clouds of Joy (track) (ABC)
HE IS KING - Danniebelle (album) (Light)
MORE - Larnelle Harris (album) (Word)
WONDERFUL! - Edwin Hawkins & The Edwin Hawkins Singers (album) (Birthright)

BEST SOUL GOSPEL PERFORMANCE, TRADITIONAL
I'M JUST ANOTHER SOLDIER - Five Blind Boys of Mississippi (single) (Jewel)
JAMES CLEVELAND LIVE AT CARNEGIE HALL - James Cleveland (album) (Savoy)
THE LORD IS MY LIFE - James Cleveland & The Greater Metropolitan Church of Christ Choir (album) (Savoy)
SATISFACTION GUARANTEED - Rev. Cleavant Derricks & Family (album) (Canaan)
STAND UP FOR JESUS - The Savannah Choir & Rev. Issac Douglas (album) (Creed)

BEST INSPIRATIONAL PERFORMANCE
HOME WHERE I BELONG - B. J. Thomas (album) (Myrrh/Word)
HOW GREAT THOU ART - Ray Price (album) (Word)
OH LORD, COME BY HERE - Quincy Jones & James Cleveland conducting the Wattsline Choir (track) (A & M)
TELL ALL THE WORLD ABOUT LOVE - Carol Lawrence (album) (Word)
YOUR ARMS TOO SHORT TO BOX WITH GOD - Salome Bey, Clinton Derricks-Carroll, Sheila Ellis, Delores Hall, William Hardy, Jr., Hector Jaime Mercado, Stanley Perryman, Mabel Robinson, William Thomas, Jr. (album) (ABC)

BEST COUNTRY VOCAL PERFORMANCE, FEMALE
(This category is for a solo performance.)
AFTER THE LOVIN' - Barbara Mandrell (track) (ABC/DOT)
DON'T IT MAKE MY BROWN EYES BLUE - Crystal Gayle (single) (U. A.)
MAKING BELIEVE - Emmylou Harris (single) (W. B.)
WHAT'RE YOU DOING TONIGHT - Janie Fricke (single) (Columbia)
(YOUR LOVE HAS LIFTED ME) HIGHER AND HIGHER - Dolly Parton (track) (RCA)

BEST COUNTRY VOCAL PERFORMANCE, MALE
(This category is for a solo performance.)
I DON'T WANNA CRY - Larry Gatlin (single) (Monument)
IT WAS ALMOST LIKE A SONG - Ronnie Milsap (single) (RCA)
LUCILLE - Kenny Rogers (single) (UA)
LUCKENBACH, TEXAS - Waylon Jennings (single) (RCA)
MR. BOJANGLES - Jerry Jeff Walker (single) (MCA)

BEST COUNTRY VOCAL PERFORMANCE BY A DUO OR GROUP
DYNAMIC DUO - Loretta Lynn, Conway Twitty (album) (MCA)
HEAVEN'S JUST A SIN AWAY - The Kendalls (single) (Ovation)
NEAR YOU - George Jones, Tammy Wynette (single) (Epic)
THE WHEEL - Asleep At The Wheel (album) (Capitol)
Y'ALL COME BACK SALOON - Oak Ridge Boys (single) (ABC/Dot)

BEST COUNTRY INSTRUMENTAL PERFORMANCE
(This category is for an Orchestra, Group or Soloist and is for either pure instrumentals or instrumentals with vocal coloring.)
CHET, FLOYD & DANNY - Chet Atkins, Floyd Cramer, Danny Davis (album) (RCA)
COUNTRY INSTRUMENTALIST OF THE YEAR - Hargus "Pig" Robbins (album) (Elektra)
ME & MY GUITAR - Chet Atkins (album) (RCA)
RAGTIME ANNIE - Asleep At The Wheel (track) (Capitol)
WEST BOUND AND DOWN - Jerry Reed (track) (MCA)

BEST COUNTRY SONG

(A Songwriter's Award.) (Any song is eligible if a new recording of it has been released during the Eligibility Year.)

DESPERADO - Glenn Frey, Don Henley
DON'T IT MAKE MY BROWN EYES BLUE - Richard Leigh
IT WAS ALMOST LIKE A SONG - Archie Jordan, Hal David
LUCILLE - Roger Bowling, Hal Bynum
LUCKENBACH, TEXAS - Bobby Emmons, Chips Moman

BEST ETHNIC OR TRADITIONAL RECORDING

(This category includes traditional blues and pure folk recordings.) (All nominations are albums)

BLUES HIT BIG TOWN - Junior Wells (Delmark)
HARD AGAIN - Muddy Waters (Blue Sky/CBS)
RIGHT PLACE, WRONG TIME - Otis Rush (Bullfrog)
THINGS THAT I USED TO DO - Joe Turner (Pablo)
WHAT HAPPENED TO MY BLUES - Willie Dixon (Ovation)

BEST LATIN RECORDING

(This category is for pure Latin music.) (All nomintations are albums)

DAWN - Mongo Santamaria (Vaya)
FIREWORKS - Machito Orchestra with Lalo Rodriguez
LA LEYENDA - Tito Puente (Tico/Fania)
MUY AMIGOS/CLOSE FRIENDS - Eydie Gorme & Danny Rivera (Gala/Coco)
TOMORROW: BARRETTO LIVE - Ray Barretto Band (Atlantic)

BEST RECORDING FOR CHILDREN

(This category is intended for recordings created specifically for children.)

AREN'T YOU GLAD YOU'RE YOU - Sesame Street Cast & Muppets (album) (Sesame Street)
A CHARLIE BROWN CHRISTMAS - Various (Written by Charles M. Schulz) (Charlie Brown Records) (7' 1p)
DOPE! THE DOPE KING'S LAST STAND - Various Artists (Lily Tomlin, Muhammad Ali, Pres. Jimmy Carter, etc.) Arther Morrison, Producer (album) (Cornucopia)
RUSSELL HOBAN: THE MOUSE AND HIS CHILD - Read by Peter Ustinov (album) (Caedmon)
THE SESAME STREET FAIRY TALE ALBUM - Jim Henson's Muppets (album) (Sesame Street)

BEST COMEDY RECORDING

(Either spoken word or musical performances are eligible here.) (All nominations are albums)

ARE YOU SERIOUS??? - Richard Pryor (Laff)
THE ERNIE KOVACS ALBUM - Ernie Kovacs (Columbia)
LET'S GET SMALL - Steve Martin (W. B.)
ON THE ROAD - George Carlin (Little David)
SATURDAY NIGHT LIVE - NBC's Saturday Night Live Cast (Arista)

BEST SPOKEN WORD RECORDING

(This category is for spoken word, documentary or drama) (All nominations are albums)

ALEX HALEY TELLS THE STORY OF HIS SEARCH FOR ROOTS - Alex Haley (W. B.)
THE BELLE OF AMHERST - Julie Harris (Credo)
FOR COLORED GIRLS WHO HAVE CONSIDERED SUICIDE/WHEN THE RAINBOW IS ENUF - (Original Cast) Ntozake Shange, writer (Buddah)
J.R.R. TOLKIEN: THE SILMARILLION OF BEREN AND LUTHIEN - Read by Christopher Tolkien (Caedmon)
THE TRUMAN TAPES - Harry Truman speaking with Ben Gradus (Caedmon)

BEST INSTRUMENTAL COMPOSITION

(A Composer's Award for an original, non-classical composition with or without lyrics which first gained recognition as an instrumental.)

BIRDLAND - Joe Zawinul
BOND '77/JAMES BOND THEME - Marvin Hamlisch
GONNA FLY NOW (THEME FROM "ROCKY") - Bill Conti, Carol Connors, Ann Robbins
MAIN TITLE FROM STAR WARS - John Williams
"ROOTS" MEDLEY (MOTHERLAND, ROOTS MURAL THEME) - Quincy Jones, Gerald Fried

BEST ORIGINAL SCORE WRITTEN FOR A MOTION PICTURE OR A TELEVISION SPECIAL

(A Composer's Award for an original background score or original songs written specifically for the motion picture or television special.

ROCKY - Bill Conti (UA)
THE SPY WHO LOVED ME - Marvin Hamlisch (UA)
A STAR IS BORN - Kenny Ascher, Alan & Marilyn Bergman, Rupert Holmes, Leon Russell, Barbra Streisand, Donna Weiss, Paul Williams, Kenny Loggins (Columbia)
STAR WARS - John Williams (20th Century)
YOU LIGHT UP MY LIFE - Joe Brooks (Arista)

BEST CAST SHOW ALBUM

(Awards to the Composers and Album Producers.) (Original cast albums, albums by road casts or working casts, including show revival casts, are eligible.)

ANNIE - Charles Strouse, Martin Charnin, Composers - Larry Morton, Charles Strouse, Producers (Columbia)
GUYS AND DOLLS - Frank Loesser, Composer - William Goldstein, Producer (Motown)
I LOVE MY WIFE - Cy Coleman, Michael Stewart, Composers - Cy Coleman, Producer (Atlantic)
STARTING HERE, STARTING NOW - Richard Maltby, Jr., David Shire, Composers - Jay David Saks, Producer (RCA)
YOUR ARMS TOO SHORT TO BOX WITH GOD - Micki Grant, Alex Bradford, Composers Esmond Edwards, Producer (ABC)

ALBUM OF THE YEAR CLASSICAL

(Grammys to the Artist and Producer.) (Certificates to the Engineer(s).

CONCERT OF THE CENTURY - (Recorded Live at Carnegie Hall May 18, 1976) - Leonard Bernstein, Vladimir Horowitz, Isaac Stern, Mstislav Rostropovich, Dietrich Fischer-Dieskau, Yehudi Meuhin, Lyndon Woodside - Thomas Frost, Producer (Columbia)
GERSHWIN: PORGY & BESS - John De Main (cond. Houston Grand Opera Production - Prin. Solos: Dale, Smith, Shakesnider, Lane, Brice, Smalls) - Thomas Z. Shepard, Producer (RCA)
HAYDN: ORLANDO PALADINO - Antal Dorati (cond. Orchestre de Chambre de Lausanne/Auger, Ameling, Killebrew, Ahnsjo, Luxon, Trimarchi, Shirley - Erik Smith, Producer (Philips)
MAHLER: SYMPHONY NO. 9 IN D MAJOR - Carlo Maria Giulini (cond. Chicago Symphony) - Gunther Breest, Producer (DG)
PARKENING AND THE GUITAR - Christopher Parkening - Patti Laursen, Producer (Angel)
RAVEL: BOLERO/DEBUSSY: LA MER & APRES MIDI D'UN FAUNE - Sir Georg Solti (cond. Chicago Symphony) - Ray Mishull, Producer (London)

BEST CLASSICAL ORCHESTRAL PERFORMANCE

(Grammys to the Conductor and Producer. Certificates to the classical orchestra committee.)
BARTOK: THE WOODEN PRINCE - Pierre Boulez cond. New York Philharmonic - Andrew Kazdin, Producer (Columbia)
BRUCKNER: SYMPHONY NO. 8 IN C MINOR - Herbert von Karajan cond. Berlin Philharmonic - Hans Hirsch, Producer (DG)
MAHLER: SYMPHONY NO. 3 IN D MINOR - James Levine cond. Chicago Symphony - Thomas Z. Shepard, Jay David Saks, Producers (RCA)
MAHLER: SYMPHONY NO. 9 IN D MAJOR - Carlo Maria Giulini cond. Chicago Symphony - Gunther Breest, Producer (DG)
RAVEL: BOLERO - Sir Georg Solti cond. Chicago Symphony - Ray Minshull, Producer (London)
TCHAIKOVSKY: SWAN LAKE - Andre Previn cond. London Symphony - Christopher Bishop, Producer (Angel)

BEST OPERA RECORDING

(Grammys to the Conductor and Producer; special plaques to the Principal Soloists.)
GERSHWIN: PORGY & BESS - John De Main (cond. Houston Grand Opera Production - Prin. Solos: Albert, Dale, Smith, Shakesnider, Lane, Brice, Smalls); Thomas S. Shepard, Producer (RCA)
HAYDN: ORLANDO PALADINO - Antal Dorati (cond. Orchstre de Chambre de Lausanne - Prin. Solos: Auger, Ameling, Killbrew, Ahnsjo, Luxon, Shirley, Trimarchi); Erik Smith, Producer (Philips)
JANACEK: KATYA KABANOVA - Charles Mackerras (cond. Vienna Philharmonic - Prin. Solos: Soderstrom, Knіplova, Dvorsky); James Mallinson, Producer (London)
MUSSORGSKY: BORIS GODUNOV - Jerzy Semkow (cond. Polish National Radio Symphony Orchestra & Chorus - Prin. Solos: Talvela, Gedda); David Mottley, Producer (Angel)
PUCCINI: TOSCA - Colliin Davis (cond. Chorus & Orchestra of Royal Opera House, Covent Garden - Prin. Solos: Caballe, Carreras, Wixell, Ramey); Erik Smith, Producer (Philips)
WAGNER: DIE MEISTERSINGER VON NURNBERG - Eugen Jochum cond. (Deutsche Oper Berlin Orchestra & Chorus - Prin. Solos: Fischer-Dieskau, Domingo, Ludwig, Ligendza) - Gunther Breest, Producer (DG)
WAGNER: THE FLYING DUTCHMAN - Sir Georg Solti (cond. Chicago Symphony Orchestra & Chorus - Prin. Solos: Bailey, Martin, Talvela, Kollo, Krenn, Jones); Ray Minshull, Producer (London)
WEILL: THREE PENNY OPERA - Original Cast (New York Shakespeare Festival, Stanley Silverman, cond. - Prin. Solos: Raul Julia, C.K. Alexander, Ellen Greene) - Larry Morton, Producer (Columbia)

BEST CHORAL PERFORMANCE, CLASSICAL (OTHER THAN OPERA)

(Grammys to the Conductor and Choral Director)
BERLIOZ: L'ENFANCE DU CHRIST - Colin Davis (cond. John Alldis Choir; London Symphony) (Philips)
BRITTEN: SAINT NICHOLAS - David Willcocks (cond. King's College Choir, Cambridge; Academy of St. Martin-in-the-Fields) (Seraphim)
BRUCKNER: TE DEUM - Herbert von Karajan (cond. Vienna Singverein; Berlin Philharmonic) (DG)
DVORAK: STABAT MATER - Rafael Kubelik (cond. Chorus of Bavarian Radio & Bavarian Radio Symphony) (DG)
PURCELL: FUNERAL MUSIC FOR QUEEN MARY - Philip Ledger (cond. King's College Choir, Cambridge; Academy of St. Martin-in-the-Fields) (Angel)
ROUSSEL: PSALM 80, FOR TENOR, CHORUS & ORCHESTRA - Serge Baudo, Cond. (Stephen Caillat Chorus & Orchestre de Paris) (Conn. Soc.)
VERDI: REQUIEM - Sir Georg Solti, Conductor - Margret Hillis, Choral Director (Chicago Symphony Chorus & Orchestra) (RCA)

BEST CHAMBER MUSIC PERFORMANCE

(Instrumental or vocal)
BARTOK: QUARTETS FOR STRINGS (6) - Guarneri Quartet. (RCA)
A CONTEMPORARY ELIZABETHAN CONCERT (Works of Dowland, Williams, Purcell, etc.) David Munrow cond. Early Music Consort of London (Angel)
DVORAK: QUARTETS NO. 8 IN E MAJOR, OP 80 & NO. 10 IN E FLAT MAJOR, OP. 51 - Prague String Quartet. (DG)
DVORAK: QUINTET FOR PIANO IN A MAJOR, OP. 81 - Emanuel Ax & Cleveland Quartet (RCA)
IMPROVISATIONS - WEST MEETS EAST - ALBUM 3 - Ravi Shankar, Yehudi Menuhin, Jean-Pierre Rampal, Martine Geliot, Alla Rakha (Angel)
RACHMANINOFF: SONATA FOR CELLO & PIANO IN G MINOR, OP. 19 - ANDANTE/TCHAIKOVSKY:
TRIO FOR PIANO IN A MINOR, OP. 50 - PEZZO ELEGIACO - Vladimir Horowitz, Isaac Stern, Mstislav Rostropovich (Columbia)
SCHOENBERG: QUARTETS FOR STRINGS (COMPLETE) - Juilliard Quartet (Columbia)

BEST CLASSICAL PERFORMANCE INSTRUMENTAL SOLOIST OR SOLOISTS (WITH ORCHESTRA)

BEETHOVEN: CONCERTI FOR PIANO (5) - Alfred Brendel, Piano (Haitink cond. London Philharmonic) (Philips)
BEETHOVEN: CONCERTO FOR PIANO NO. 4 IN G MAJOR - Maurizio Pollini, Piano (Bohm cond. Vienna Philharmonic) (DG)
BRAHMS: CONCERTO FOR PIANO NO. 2 IN B FLAT MAJOR, OP. 83 - Solomon, Piano (Dobrowen cond. Philharmonic) (Vox)
CONCERTOS FROM SPAIN - (Surinach: Piano Concerto Montsalvatge; Concerto Breve) - Alicia de Larrocha, Piano (De Burgos cond. Royal Philharmonic) (London)
ELGAR: CONCERTO FOR CELLO, OP. 85 - Jacqueline Du Pre, Cello (Barenboim cond. Philadelphia Orchestra) (Columbia)
RACHMANINOFF: CONCERTO FOR PIANO NO. 3 IN D MINOR - Lazar Berman, Piano (Abbado, London Symphony) (Columbia)
SCHUMANN: CONCERTO FOR CELLO & ORCHESTRA IN A MINOR - BLOCH: SCHELOMO - Mstislav Rostropovich, Cello (Bernstein cond. Orchestra National de France) (Angel)
VIVALDI: THE FOUR SEASONS - Itzhak Perlman, Violin (Perlman cond. London Philharmonic) (Angel)

BEST CLASSICAL PERFORMANCE INSTRUMENTAL SOLOIST OR SOLOISTS (WITHOUT ORCHESTRA)

BACH: THE ENGLISH SUITES (Complete) - Glenn Gould, Piano (Columbia)
BACH: PARTITAS FOR HARPSICHORD NOS. 1 IN B FLAT MAJOR & 2 IN C MINOR - Igor Kipnis, Harpsichord (Angel)
BEETHOVEN: SONATA FOR PIANO NO. 18 IN E FLAT MAJOR, OP. 31 NO. 3 - SCHUMANN: FANTASIESTUCKE, OP. 12 - Arthur Rubinstein, Piano (RCA)
GRAINGER: PIANO MUSIC OF PERCY GRAINGER - Daniel Adni, Piano (Seraphim)
GRANADOS: GOYESCAS - Alicia de Larrocha, Piano (London)
KREISLER: ITZHAK PERLMAN PLAYS FRITZ KREISLER: ALBUM 2 - Itzhak Perlman, Violin (Angel)
MESSAIEN: 20 REGARDS DE L'ENFANT JESUS - Michel Beroff, Piano (Conn. Soc.)

BEST CLASSICAL VOCAL SOLOIST PERFORMANCE

BACH: ARIAS - Janet Baker (Marriner cond. Academy of St. Martin-in-the-Fields) (Angel)
BUT YESTERDAY IS NOT TODAY (Songs by Barber, Bowles, Copland, Chanler, etc.) - Donald Gramm (Hassard, accomp.) (New World)
FAURE: SONGS (Complete) - Gerard Souzay (Baldwin, Accomp.) (Conn. Soc.)
IVES: SONGS - Dietrich Fischer-Dieskau (Ponti, accomp.) (DG)

LUCIANO PAVAROTTI - O HOLY NIGHT (O Holy Night, Sanctus, Schubert: Ave Maria, etc.) - Luciano Pavarotti (Adler cond. National Philharmonic) (London)
RACHMANINOFF: SONGS - Volume Two - Elisabeth Soderstrom (Ashkenazy, accomp.) (London)
ROSSINI/MOZART: OPERA ARIAS - Frederica von Stade (de Waart cond. Rotterdam Philharmonic) (Philips)
SCHUBERT ON STAGE - Elly Ameling (de Waart cond. Rotterdam Philharmonic) (Philips)
SHOSTAKOVICH: SYMPHONY NO. 14 - Galina Vishnevskaya, Soprano - Mark Reshetin, Bass (Rostropovich cond. Moscow Philharmonic) (Columbia)

BEST ENGINEERED RECORDING, CLASSICAL

(An Engineer's Award)
BARTOK: THE WOODEN PRINCE - Boulez cond. N.Y. Philharmonic - Bud Graham, Ray Moore & Milt Cherin, Engineers (Columbia)
BERLIOZ: L'ENFANCE DU CHRIST - Davis cond. London Symphony - S.J.W. Witteveen, Dick van Dijk, Engineers (Philips)
GERSHWIN: PORGY & BESS - De Main cond. Houston Grand Opera - Paul Goodman, Anthony Salvatore, Engineers (RCA)
MAHLER: SYMPHONY NO. 2 IN C MINOR ("RESURRECTION") - Abbado cond. Chicago Symphony - Heinz Wildhagen, Engineer (DG)
MAHLER: SYMPHONY NO. 9 IN D MAJOR - Giulini cond. Chicago Symphony - Klaus Schiebe, Engineer (DG)
RAVEL: BOLERO - Solti cond. Chicago Symphony - Kenneth Wilkinson, Engineer (London)

1978 HALL OF FAME WINNERS

BACH-STOKOWSKI: TOCCATA & FUGUE IN D MINOR - Leopold Stokowski conducting Philadelphia Orchestra - Victrola #6751 - Released in 1927
THE GENIUS OF ART TATUM, VOLS. 1-13 (Albums) Art Tatum - Clef #MGC612, #MGC613, #MGC614, #MGC615, #MGC618, #MGC643, #MGC657, #MGC658, #MGC659, #MGC660, #MGC661, #MGC679, #MGC712 - Released 1954 through 1955
I CAN HEAR IT NOW, VOLS. 1-3 (Albums) - Edward R. Murrow - Columbia - #ML4095, #ML4261, #ML4340 - Released 1948 through 1950
MY BLUE HEAVEN - Gene Austin - Victor #20964 - Released in 1928
STRANGE FRUIT - Billie Holiday - Commodore #CMS526 - Released in 1939

1978

RECORD OF THE YEAR

(Grammys to the Artist and Producer.) (Certificates to the Arranger, Engineer, Songwriter, Musicians and Background Singers.)
BAKER STREET - Gerry Rafferty - Hugh Murphy, Gerry Rafferty, Producers (UA)
FEELS SO GOOD - Chuck Mangione - Chuck Mangione, Producer (A&M)
JUST THE WAY YOU ARE - Billy Joel - Phil Ramone, Producer (Columbia)
STAYIN' ALIVE - The Bee Gees - The Bee Gees, Karl Richardson, Albhy Galuten, Producers (RSO)
YOU NEEDED ME - Anne Murray - Jim Ed Norman, Producer (Capitol)

ALBUM OF THE YEAR

(Grammys to the Artist and Producer.) (Certificates to the Arranger, Engineer and Songwriter.)
EVEN NOW - Barry Manilow - Barry Manilow, Ron Dante, Producers (Arista)
GREASE (ORIGINAL SOUNDTRACK) - John Travolta, Olivia Newton-John, Frankie Valli, Frankie Avalon, Stockard Channing, Jeff Conaway, Cindy Bullens, Sha-Na-Na, Louis St. Louis - Barry Gibb, John Farrar, Louis St. Louis, Albhy Galuten, Karl Richardson, Producers (Arista)
RUNNING ON EMPTY - Jackson Browne - Jackson Browne, Producer (Asylum)
SATURDAY NIGHT FEVER (MOTION PICTURE SOUNDTRACK) - The Bee Gees, David Shire, Yvonne Elliman, Tavares, Kool & The Gang, K.C. & The Sunshine Band, MFSB, Trammps, Walter Murphy, Ralph MacDonald - The Bee Gees, Karl Richardson, Albhy Galuten, Freddie Perren, Bill Oakes, David Shire, Arif Mardin, Thomas J. Valentino, Ralph MacDonald, W. Walter, K.G. Productions, H.W. Casey, Richard Finch, obby Martin, Broadway Eddie, Ron Kersey, Producers (RSO)
SOME GIRLS - The Rolling Stones - The Glimmer Twins, Producers

SONG OF THE YEAR

(A Songwriter's Award.)
JUST THE WAY YOU ARE - Billy Joel
STAYIN' ALIVE - Barry Gibb, Robin Gibb, Maurice Gibb
THREE TIMES A LADY - Lionel Richie
YOU DON'T BRING ME FLOWERS - Neil Diamond, Alan Bergman, Marilyn Bergman
YOU NEEDED ME - Randy Goodrum

BEST NEW ARTIST OF THE YEAR

(This category is for an artist or organized group whose first recording was released during the Eligibility Period)
THE CARS (Elektra)
ELVIS COSTELLO (Columbia)
CHRIS REA (UA)
A TASTE OF HONEY (Capitol)
TOTO (CBS)

BEST POP VOCAL PERFORMANCE, FEMALE

(This category is for a solo performance in either pop, rock or folk.)
HOPELESSLY DEVOTED TO YOU - Olivia Newton-John (single) (RSO)
MAC ARTHUR PARK - Donna Summer (single) (Casablanca)
YOU BELONG TO ME - Carly Simon (single) (Elektra)
YOU DON'T BRING ME FLOWERS - (Solo version, not duet) - Barbra Streisand (track) (Columbia)
YOU NEEDED ME - Anne Murray (single) (Capitol)

BEST POP VOCAL PERFORMANCE, MALE

(This category is for a solo performance in either pop, rock or folk.)
BAKER STREET - Gerry Rafferty (single) (UA)
COPACABANA (AT THE COPA) - Barry Manilow (single) (Arista)
I JUST WANNA STOP - Gino Vannelli (single) (A&M)
RUNNING ON EMPTY - Jackson Browne (album) (Asylum)
SOMETIMES WHEN WE TOUCH - Dan Hill (single) (20th Century)

BEST POP VOCAL PERFORMANCE BY A DUO, GROUP OR CHORUS

(This category is for pop, rock, or folk. All recordings on which the group received artist billing on the label are eligible here even though the vocal may feature only one member of the group.)
THE CLOSER I GET TO YOU - Roberta Flack, Donny Hathaway (single) (Atlantic)
FM (NO STATIC AT ALL) - Steely Dan (single) (MCA)
GOT TO GET YOU INTO MY LIFE - Earth, Wind & Fire (single) (Columbia)
SATURDAY NIGHT FEVER - The Bee Gees (album) (RSO)
THREE TIMES A LADY - Commodores (single) (Motown)

BEST POP INSTRUMENTAL PERFORMANCE

(This category is for pop, rock or folk. All recordings are for either pure instrumentals or instrumentals with vocal coloring.)
CHILDREN OF SANCHEZ - Chuck Mangione Group (album) (A&M)
CLOSE ENCOUNTERS OF THE THIRD KIND (ORIGINAL MOTION PICTURE SOUNDTRACK) - John Williams (album) (Arista)
GUITAR MONSTERS - Chet Atkins, Les Paul (album) (RCA)
THE PINK PANTHER THEME ('78) - Henry Mancini (single) (UA)
STAR WARS AND CLOSE ENOUNTERS OF THE THIRD KIND - Zubin Mehta cond. The Los Angeles Philharmonic (London)

BEST R&B VOCAL PERFORMANCE, FEMALE

(This category is for a solo performance.)
ALMIGHTY FIRE - Aretha Franklin (album) (Atlantic)
I LOVE THE NIGHTLIFE (DISCO ROUND) - Alicia Bridges (single) (Polydor)
I'M EVERY WOMAN - Chaka Khan (single) (WB)
LAST DANCE - Donna Summer (single) (Casablanca)
OUR LOVE - Natalie Cole (single) (Capitol)

BEST R&B VOCAL PERFORMANCE, MALE

(This category is for a solo performance.)
CLOSE THE DOOR - Teddy Pendergrass (single) (PIR)
DANCE WITH ME - Peter Brown (single) (T.K.Prod.)
I CAN SEE CLEARLY NOW - Ray Charles (single) (Atlantic)
ON BROADWAY - George Benson (single) (WB)
WHEN YOU HEAR LOU, YOU'VE HEARD IT ALL - Lou Rawls (album) (PIR/Columbia)

BEST R&B VOCAL PERFORMANCE BY A DUO, GROUP OR CHORUS

(All recordings on which the group receives artist billing on the label are eligible here even though the vocal may feature only one member of the group.)
ALL 'N ALL - Earth, Wind & Fire (album) (Columbia)
BOOGIE OOGIE OOGIE - A Taste of Honey (single) (Capitol)
EASE ON DOWN THE ROAD - Diana Ross & Michael Jackson (single) (MCA)
NATURAL HIGH - Commodores (album) (Motown)
USE TA BE MY GIRL - O'Jays (track) (Columbia)

BEST R&B INSTRUMENTAL PERFORMANCE

(All recordings are for either pure instrumentals or instrumentals with vocal coloring.)
IMAGES - The Crusaders (album) (ABC)
MODERN MAN - Stanley Clarke (album) (Nemperor)
RUNNIN' - Earth, Wind & Fire (track) (Columbia)
STREETWAVE - Brothers Johnson (track) (A&M)
SWEET & SOUR - Average White Band (track) (Atlantic)

BEST RHYTHM & BLUES SONG

(A Songwriter's Award.) (Any song is eligible if a new recording of it has been released during the Eligibility Year.)
BOOGIE OOGIE OOGIE - Perry Kibble, Janice Johnson
DANCE, DANCE, DANCE - Bernard Edwards, Kenny Lehman, Nile Rogers
FANTASY - Maurice White, Eddie de Barrio, Verdine White
LAST DANCE - Paul Jabara
USE TA BE MY GIRL - Kenneth Gamble, Leon Huff

BEST COUNTRY VOCAL PERFORMANCE, FEMALE

(This category is for a solo performance.)
HERE YOU COME AGAIN - Dolly Parton (album) (RCA)
QUARTER MOON IN A TEN CENT TOWN - Emmylou Harris (album) (WB)
SLEEPING SINGLE IN A DOUBLE BED - Barbara Mandrell (single) (ABC)
TALKIN' IN YOUR SLEEP - Crystal Gayle (single) (UA)
WALK RIGHT BACK - Anne Murray (single) (Capitol)

BEST COUNTRY VOCAL PERFORMANCE, MALE

(This category is for a solo performance.)
GEORGIA ON MY MIND - Willie Nelson (single) (Columbia)
I'VE ALWAYS BEEN CRAZY - Waylon Jennings (album) (RCA)
LET'S TAKE THE LONG WAY AROUND THE WORLD - Ronnie Milsap (single) (RCA)
LOVE OR SOMETHING LIKE IT - Kenny Rogers (album) (UA)
SOFTLY, AS I LEAVE YOU - Elvis Presley (single) (RCA/Victory)
TAKE THIS JOB AND SHOVE IT - Johnny Paycheck (single) (Epic)

BEST COUNTRY VOCAL PERFORMANCE BY A DUO OR GROUP

ANYONE WHO ISN'T ME TONIGHT - Kenny Rogers and Dottie West (single) (UA)
CRYIN' AGAIN - Oak Ridge Boys (single) (ABC)
DO YOU KNOW YOU ARE MY SUNSHINE - Statler Brothers (single) (Mercury)
IF THE WORLD RAN OUT OF LOVE TONIGHT - Jim Ed Brown, Helen Cornelius (single) (RCA)
MAMAS DON'T LET YOUR BABIES GROW UP TO BE COWBOYS - Waylon Jennings and Willie Nelson (single) (RCA)
ON MY KNEES - Charlie Rich with Janie Fricke (single) (Epic)

BEST COUNTRY INSTRUMENTAL PERFORMANCE

(This category is for an Orchestra, Group or Soloist and is for either pure instrumentals or instrumentals with vocal coloring.)
BANJO BANDITS - Roy Clark and Buck Trent (album) (ABC)
COOKIN' COUNTRY - Danny Davis & The Nashville Brass (album) (RCA)
ONE O'CLOCK JUMP - Asleep At The Wheel (track) (Capitol)
STEEL GUITAR RAG - Roy Clark (track) (Dot/ABC)
UNDER THE DOUBLE EAGLE - Doc Watson & Merle Watson (single) (UA)

BEST COUNTRY SONG

(A Songwriter's Award.) (Any song is eligible if a new recording of it has been released during the Eligibility Year.)
EVERY TIME TWO FOOLS COLLIDE - Jan Dyer and Jeffrey Tweel
THE GAMBLER - Don Schlitz
LET'S TAKE THE LONG WAY AROUND THE WORLD - Archie Jordan and Naomi Martin
MAMAS DON'T LET YOUR BABIES GROW UP TO BE COWBOYS - Ed and Patsy Bruce
TAKE THIS JOB AND SHOVE IT - David A. Coe

BEST GOSPEL PERFORMANCE, CONTEMPORARY OR INSPIRATIONAL
COME ON, RING THOSE BELLS - Evie (album) (Word)
COSMIC COWBOY - Barry McGuire (album) (Sparrow)
DESTINED TO BE YOURS - McGuire (album) (Greentree)
IMPERIALS LIVE - Imperials (album) (DaySpring)
THE LADY IS A CHILD - Reba (album) (Greentree/Heartwarming)
WHAT A FRIEND - Larry Hart (track) (Genesis)

BEST GOSPEL PERFORMANCE, TRADITIONAL
(All nominations are albums)
ELVIS' FAVORITE GOSPEL SONGS - J.D. Sumner & The Stamps Quartet (RCA)
HIS AMAZING LOVE - Blackwood Brothers (Skylite Sing)
THE OLD RUGGED CROSS - George Beverly Shea (Word)
REFRESHING - The Happy Goodman Family (Canaan)
SUNSHINE & ROSES - Cathedral Quartet (Canaan)

BEST SOUL GOSPEL PERFORMANCE, CONTEMPORARY
BECAUSE HE'S JESUS - Highland Park Community Choir, Inc. (track) (Davida)
DANNIEBELLE LIVE IN SWEDEN WITH CHORALERNA - Danniebelle and The Choralerna (album) (Sparrow)
LIVE IN LONDON - Andrae Crouch & The Disciples (album) (Light)
LOVE ALIVE II - Walter Hawkins (album) (Light)
REACH OUT AND TOUCH - Shirley Caeser (track) (Hob/Roadshow)
YOU LIGHT UP MY LIFE - Loleatta Holloway (track) (Gold Mine)

BEST SOUL GOSPEL PERFORMANCE, TRADITIONAL
AMAZING GRACE - Gladys McFadden & Loving Sisters (track) (ABC)
I DON'T FEEL NOWAYS TIRED - James Cleveland & The Salem Inspirational Choir, dir. by Doretha Wade (album) (Savoy) (ABC)
LIVE AND DIRECT - Mighty Clouds of Joy (album) (ABC)
SPECIAL APPEARANCE - Rev. Isaac Douglas, featuring the San Francisco Community Singers and the 21st Century Singers (album) (Creed/Nashboro)
TOMORROW - James Cleveland and the Charles Fold Singers, dir. by CCharles Fold (album) (Savoy)

BEST INSPIRATIONAL PERFORMANCE
(All nominations are albums)
BEHOLD - Billy Preston (Myrrh)
FIRST CLASS - The Boones (Lamb & Lion)
GOIN' UP IN SMOKE - Larry Hart (Genesis)
HAPPY MAN - B. J. Thomas (Myrrh)
HE TOUCHED ME - Tennessee Ernie Ford (Word)
PRECIOUS MEMORIES - Anita Kerr (Word)

BEST ETHNIC OR TRADITIONAL RECORDING
(This category includes traditional blues and pure folk recordings.) (All nominations are albums)
CHICAGO BLUES AT HOME - Louis Myers, John Littlejohn, Eddie Taylor, Jimmy Rogers, Johnny Shines, Homesick James Williamson, Bob Myers (Advent)
CLIFTON CHENIER AND HIS RED HOT LOUISIANA BAND IN NEW ORLEANS - Clifton Chenier (Dixieland/Jubilee)
I HEAR SOME BLUES DOWNSTAIRS - Fenton Robinson (Alligator)
I'M READY - Muddy Waters (Blue Sky)
U.S.A. - Memphis Slim & His House Rockers, featuring Matt "Guitar" Murphy (Pearl)

BEST LATIN RECORDING
(This category is for pure Latin music. It is not for Latin oriented or Latin influenced recordings.)
CORO MIYARE - Fania All Stars (track) (Columbia)
LAURINDO ALMEIDA TRIO - Laurindo Almeida (album) (Dobre)
HOMENAJE A BENY MORE - Tito Puente (album) (Tico)
LA RAZA LATINA - Orchestra Harlow (album) (Fania)
LUCUMI, MACUMBA, VOODOO - Eddie Palmieri (album) (Epic)
MONGO A LA CARTE - Mongo Santamaria (album) (Vaya)

BEST RECORDING FOR CHILDREN
(This category is intended for recordings created specifically for children.) (All nominations are albums)
CHARLIE BROWN'S ALL-STARS (TV SPECIAL) - Warren Lockhart & Jymn Magon, Producers (Charlie Brown Productions)
THE HOBBIT (SOUNDTRACK) - Orson Bean, John Huston, Hans Conried (Buena Vista/Disneyland)
THE MUPPET SHOW - The Muppets (Arista)
PETER AND THE WOLF - David Bowie & Eugene Ormandy cond. the Philadelphia Orchestra (RCA)
SESAME STREET FEVER - The Muppets & Robin Gibb (Sesame St.)

BEST COMEDY RECORDING
(Either spoken word or musical performances are eligible here.) (All nominations are albums)
THE RUTLES (ALL YOU NEED IS CASH) - The Rutles (WB)
ON STAGE - Lily Tomlin (Arista)
SEX AND VIOLINS - Martin Mull (ABC)
A WILD AND CRAZY GUY - Steve Martin (WB)
THE WIZARD OF COMEDY - Richard Pryor (Laff)

BEST SPOKEN WORD RECORDING
(This category is for spoken word, documentary or drama.) (All nominations are albums)
CITIZEN KANE (ORIGINAL MOTION PICTURE SOUNDTRACK) Orson Welles (Mark 56)
JOHN STEINBECK: THE GRAPES OF WRATH (EXCERPTS) - Read by Henry Fonda (Caedmon)
THE NIXON INTERVIEWS WITH DAVID FROST - Richard Nixon & David Frost (Polydor)
ROOTS (ORIGINAL SOUNDTRACK FOR TV) - Stan Cornyn, Producer (WB)
WUTHERING HEIGHTS - Dame Judith Anderson, Claire Bloom, James Mason, George Rose, Gordon Gould (Caedmon)

BEST INSTRUMENTAL COMPOSITION
(A Composer's Award for an original, non-classical composition with or without lyrics which first gained recognition as an instrumental.)
THE CAPTAIN'S JOURNEY - Lee Ritenour
CONSUELO'S LOVE THEME - Chuck Mangione
END OF THE YELLOW BRICK ROAD - Quincy Jones, Nick Ashford, Valerie Simpson
FRIENDS - Chick Corea
THEME FROM "CLOSE ENCOUNTERS OF THE THIRD KIND" - John Williams

BEST ALBUM OF ORIGINAL SCORE WRITTEN FOR A MOTION PICTURE OR A TELEVISION SPECIAL

(A Composer's and/or Songwriter's Award for an original score or original songs written specifically for the motion picture or television special.)
BATTLESTAR GALACTICA - Stu Phillip, John Tartaglia, Sue Collins, Glen Larson, Composers (MCA)
CLOSE ENCOUNTERS OF THE THIRD KIND - John Williams, Composer (Arista)
HOLOCAUST: THE STORY OF THE FAMILY WEISS - Morton Gould, Composer (RCA Red Seal)
MIDNIGHT EXPRESS - Giorgio Moroder, Chris Bennett, David Castle, Wiliam Hayes, Oliver Stone, Composers (Casablanca)
REVENGE OF THE PINK PANTHER - Henry Mancini, Composer - Leslie Bricusse, Lyricist (UA)

BEST CAST SHOW ALBUM

(Awards to the Composers and Album Producers.) (Original cast albums, albums by road casts or working casts, including show revival casts, are eligible.)
AIN'T MISBEHAVIN' - Thomas Fats Waller & Others, Composers - Thomas Z. Shepard, Producer (RCA Red Seal)
THE BEST LITTLE WHOREHOUSE IN TEXAS - Carol Hall, Composer - John Simon, Producer (MCA)
BEATLEMANIA - John Lennon, Paul McCartney, George Harrison, Ringo Starr, Composers - Sandy Yaguda, Kenny Laguna, Producers (RCA Red Seal)
THE KING AND I - Richard Rodgers, Oscar Hammerstein II, Composers - Thomas Z. Shepard, Producer (RCA Red Seal)
ON THE TWENTIETH CENTURY - Adolph Green, Betty Comden, Cy Coleman, Composers - Cy Coleman, Producer (Columbia)

BEST JAZZ VOCAL PERFORMANCE

(All nominations are albums)
ALL FLY HOME - Al Jarreau (WB)
GENTLE RAIN - Irene Kral (Choice)
HOW LONG HAS THIS BEEN GOING ON - Sarah Vaughan (Pablo)
THE MAIN MAN - Eddie Jefferson (Inner City)
TOGETHER AGAIN - FOR THE FIRST TIME - Mel Torme (Gryphon/Century)
TRUE TO LIFE - Ray Charles (Atlantic)

BEST JAZZ INSTRUMENTAL PERFORMANCE, SOLOIST

(All nominations are albums)
HEAVY LOVE (Al Cohn & Jimmy Rowles) - Al Cohn (Xanadu)
MONTREUX '77 - OSCAR PETERSON JAM - Oscar Peterson (Pablo)
ROSEWOOD - Woody Shaw (Columbia)
SOPHISTICATED GIANT - Dexter Gordon (Columbia)
STAN GETZ GOLD - Stan Getz (Inner City)

BEST JAZZ INSTRUMENTAL PERFORMANCE, GROUP

(All nominations are albums)
FRIENDS - Chick Corea (Polydor)
HEAVY LOVE - Al Cohn and Jimmy Rowles (Xanadu)
THE PEACOCKS - Stan Getz and Jimmy Rowles (Columbia)
ROSEWOOD - Woody Shaw Concert Ensemble (Columbia)
SONG FOR SISYPHUS - The Phil Woods Quintet (Gryphon/Century)

BEST JAZZ INSTRUMENTAL PERFORMANCE, BIG BAND

(All nominations are albums)
BIG BAND JAZZ - Rob McConnell & The Boss Brass (Umbrella)
INSIGHTS - Toshiko Akiyoshi, Lew Tabackin Big Band (RCA)
LIVE IN MUNICH - Thad Jones and Mel Lewis (Horizon/A&M)
SOPHISTICATED GIANT - Dexter Gordon & Orchestra (Columbia)
THAD JONES GREETINGS & SALUTATIONS - Thad Jones (Biograph)

BEST INSTRUMENTAL ARRANGEMENT

(An Arranger's Award for a specific arrangement released on either a single or album track.)
AJA - Woody Herman Band - Alan Broadbent, Arranger (Century)
GREEN EARRINGS - Woody Herman Band - Joe Roccisano, Arranger (Century)
MAD HATTER RHAPSODY - Chick Corea - Chick Corea, Arranger (Polydor)
MAIN TITLE (OVERTURE PART ONE) - Wiz Original Soundtrack - Quincy Jones & Robert Freedman, Arrangers (MCA)
RUNNIN' - Earth, Wind & Fire - Tom Tom 84, Arranger (Columbia)

BEST ARRANGEMENT ACOMPANYING VOCALIST(S)

(An Arranger's Award for a specific arrangement released on either a single or album track.)
FALLING ALICE - Chick Corea - Chick Corea, Arranger (Polydor)
FANTASY - Earth, Wind & Fire - Tom Tom 84, Arranger (Columbia)
GOT TO GET YOU INTO MY LIFE - Earth, Wind & Fire - Maurice White, Arranger (RSO)
IT HAPPENS VERY SOFTLY - Andrea Marcovicci - Robert Freedman, Arranger (Take Home Tunes)
WE THREE KINGS - Christmas Festival Choracle & Orchestra - William Pursell, Arranger (National Geographic)

BEST ARRANGEMENT FOR VOICES

(An Arranger's Award for a specific arrangement released on either a single or album track.)
CRY ME A RIVER - The Singers Unlimited - Gene Puerling. Arranger (MPS/Capitol)
HIGH CLOUDS - Vocal Jazz Incorporated - Ira Shankman, Arranger (Grapevine)
ROTUNDA - McCoy Tyner - McCoy Tyner, Arranger (Milestone)
STAYIN' ALIVE - The Bee Gees - The Bee Gees, Arranger (RSO)
STUFF LIKE THAT - Quincy Jones - Quincy Jones, Valerie Simpson, Nick Ashford, Arrangers (A&M)

BEST ALBUM PACKAGE

(Grammy to Art Director. Certificates to Designer, Photographer, Illustrator, etc. where applicable.)
BOYS IN THE TREES - Carly Simon - Johnny Lee & Tony Lane, Art Directors (Elektra)
BRUCE ROBERTS - Bruce Roberts - Tony Lane, Art Director (Elektra)
THE CARS - The Cars - Ron Coro, Art Director (Elektra)
CHILDREN OF SANCHEZ - Chuck Mangione - Juni Osaki, Art Director (A&M)
HEADS - Bob James - John Berg & Paula Scher, Art Directors (Columbia)
LAST KISS - Fandango - Gribbitt/Tim Bryant, Art Director (RCA)
NON-FICTION - Steve Kuhn - Barbara Wojirsch, Art Director (ECM)
OUT OF THE WOODS - Oregon - Ron Coro & Johnny Lee, Art Directors (Elektra)

BEST ALBUM NOTES

(An Annotator's Award for original writing for a specific album.)

BEETHOVEN: 9 SYMPHONIES - von Karajan; Berlin Philharmonic - Irving Kolodin & Bill Bender, Annotators (Polydor)
A BING CROSBY COLLECTION, VOL. I & II - Michael Brooks, Annotator (Columbia)
ELLINGTON AT CARNEGIE HALL 1943 - Leonard Feather, Annotator (Prestige)
GEORGIA SEA ISLAND SONGS - Various artists - Alan Lomax, Annotator (New World)
THE INDIVIDUALISM OF PEE WEE RUSSELL - Dan Morgenstern, Annotator (Savoy)
WORKS OF CARPENTER/GILBERT/WEISS/POWELL - L.A. Philharmonic - Phil David Baker & R.D. Darrell, Annotators (New World)

BEST HISTORICAL REPACKAGE ALBUM

(Grammy to the Repackage Album Producer. Certificates to Designer, Annotator, Engineer, etc.)

A BING CROSBY COLLECTION, VOLS. I & II - Michael Brooks, Producer (Columbia)
THE FIRST RECORDED SOUNDS 1888 TO 1929 - Edison - George Garabedian, Producer (Mark 56)
THE GREATEST GROUP OF THEM ALL - The Ravens - Bob Porter, Producer (Savoy)
LA DIVINA - Maria Callas - Peter Andry & Walter Legge, Producers (Angel)
LESTER YOUNG STORY VOL. 3 - Michael Brooks, Producer (Columbia)

BEST ENGINEERED RECORDING

(Non-Classical) (An Engineer's Award.)

ALL 'N ALL - Earth, Wind & Fire - George Massenberg, Engineer (album) (Columbia)
CLOSE ENCOUNTERS OF THE THIRD KIND - John Williams - John Neal, Engineer (album) (Arista)
FM (NO STATIC AT ALL) - Steely Dan - Roger Nichols, Al Schmitt, Engineers (track) (MCA)
PYRAMID - The Alan Parsons Project - Alan Parsons, Engineer (album) (Arista)
SOUNDS...AND STUFF LIKE THAT - Quincy Jones - Bruce Swedien, Engineer (album) (A&M)
A TRIBUTE TO ETHEL WATERS - Diahann Carroll - Allen Sides & John Neal, Engineers (album) (Orinda)

PRODUCER OF THE YEAR

(A Producer's Award for consistently outstanding creativity in producing. Listed below are examples of producer's activities. AAlbum; SSingle; TTrack)

THE BEE GEES, ALBHY GALUTEN, KARL RICHARDSON: "More Than A Woman" (T); "Night Fever" (S); "Stayin' Alive" (S) - The Bee Gees
PETER ASHER: "Living in The U.S.A." (A); "Back In The U.S.A." (S) - Linda Rondstadt
QUINCY JONES: "Blam" (A) - Bros. Johnson; "Ease On Down The Road" (S) - Diana Ross, Michael Jackson; "Sounds...And Stuff Like That" (A) - Quincy Jones; "The Wiz" (A) - Original Soundtrack
ALAN PARSONS: "Time Passages" (A) - Al Stewart; "Pyramid" (A) - The Alan Parsons Project
PHIL RAMONE - "Hot Streets" (A); "Alive Again" (T); "No Tell Lover" (T) - Chicago

ALBUM OF THE YEAR CLASSICAL

(Grammys to the Artist and Producer. Certificates to the Engineer(s) and Classical Orchestra Comitee.)

BACH: MASS IN B MINOR - Neville Marriner (cond. Academy of St. Martin-in-the-Fields) - Vittorio Negri, Producer (Philips)
BEETHOVEN: SYMPHONIES (9) Complete - Herbert von Karajan (cond. Berlin Philharmonic) - Michel Glotz, Producer (DG)
BRAHMS: CONCERTO FOR VIOLIN IN D MAJOR - Itzhak Perlman with Carlo Maria Giulini (cond. Chicago Symphony) - Christopher Bishop, Producer (Angel)
DVORAK: SYMPHONY NO. 9 IN E MINOR ("NEW WORLD") - Carlo Maria Giulini (cond. Chicago Symphony) - Gunther Breest, Producer (DG)
MAHLER: SYMPHONY NO. 4 IN G MAJOR - Claudio Abbado (cond. Vienna Philharmonic) - Rainer Brock, Producer (DG)
NIELSEN: MASKARADE - John Frandsen (cond. Danish Radio Symphony Orchestra & Chorus/Prin. Solos: Hansen, Landy, Johansen, Plesner, Bastian, Sorens) - Peter Willemoes, Producer (Unicorn)
RACHMANINOFF: CONCERTO NO. 3 IN D MINOR FOR PIANO (HOROWITZ GOLDEN JUBILEE) - Vladimir Horowitz with Eugene Ormandy (cond. New York Philharmonic) - John F. Pfeiffer, Producer (RCA)
SIBELIUS: SYMPHONIES (Complete) - Colin Davis (cond. Boston Symphony) (Philips)

BEST CLASSICAL ORCHESTRAL PERFORMANCE

(Grammys to the Conductor and Producer. Certificate to Classical Orchestra Comittee.)

BEETHOVEN: SYMPHONIES (9) Complete - Herbert von Karajan cond. Berlin Philharmonic - Michel Glotz, Producer (DG)
BRUCKNER: SYMPHONY NO. 9 IN D MINOR - Carlo Maria Giulini cond. Chicago Symphony - Christopher Bishop, Producer (Angel)
HOLST: THE PLANETS - Neville Marriner cond. Concertgebouw Orchestra - Vittorio Negri, Producer (Philips)
MAHLER: SYMPHONY NO. 9 IN D MAJOR - Claudio Abbado cond. Vienna Philharmonic - Rainer Brock, Producer (DG)
MEDELSSOHN: SYMPHONIES (5) Complete - Kurt Masur cond. Leipzig Gewandhaus Orchestra - Rainer Brock, Producer (Vanguard)
MESSIAEN: TURANGALILA SYMPHONY - Andre Previn cond. London Symphony Orchestra - Christopher Bishop, Producer (Angel)
RACHMANINOFF: SYMPHONY NO. 1 IN D MINOR - Leonard Slatkin cond. St. Louis Symphony - Marc Auboit & Joanna Nickrenz, Producers (Candide)
SHOSTAKOVICH: SYMPHONY NO. 5 - Andre Previn cond. Chicago Symphony - Christopher Bishop, Producer (Angel)
STRAVINSKY: RITE OF SPRING - Zubin Mehta cond. New York Philharmonic - Andrew Kazdin, Producer (Columbia)
VARESE: AMERIQUES/ARCANA/IONISATION (BOULEZ CONDUCTS VARESE) - Pierre Boulez cond. New York Philharmonic - Andrew Kazdin, Producer (Columbia)

BEST OPERA RECORDING

(Grammys to the Conductor and Producer.) (Special plaques to the Principal Soloists.)

CHARPENTIER: LOUISE - Julius Rudel (cond. Chorus & Orchestra of Paris Opera - Prin. Solos: Sills, Gedda) - Christopher Bishop, Producer (Angel)
LEHAR: THE MERRY WIDOW - Julius Rudel (cond. New York City Opera Orchestra & Chorus - Prin. Solos: Sills, Titus) - George Sponhaltz & John Coveney, Producers (Angel)
MOZART: LA CLEMENZA DI TITO - Colin Davis (cond. Orchestra & Chorus of Royal Opera House, Covent Garden - Prin. Solos: Baker, Popp, Minton, von Stade, Burrows) (Philips)
NIELSEN: MASKARADE - John Frandsen (cond. Danish Radio Symphony Orchestra & Chorus - Prin. Solos: Hansen, Landy, Johansen, Plesner, Bastian, Sorensen) - Peter Willemoes, Producer (Unicorn)
PUCCINI: LA FANCIULLA DEL WEST - Zubin Mehta (cond. Chorus & Orchestra of Royal Opera House, Covent Garden - Prin. Solos: Neblett, Domingo, Milnes) - Gunther Breest, Producer (DG)
SHOSTAKOVICH: THE NOSE - Gennady Rozhdestvensky (cond. Chorus & Orchestra of Moscow Chamber Opera with soloists) - Severin Pazukhin, Producer (Columbia)
(R.) STRAUSS: SALOME - Herbert von Karajan (cond. Berlin Philharmonic - Prin. Solos: Behrens, van Dam) - Michel Glotz, Producer (Angel)
VERDI: LA TRAVIATA - Carlos Kleiber (cond. Bavarian State Opera Chorus & Orchestra - Prin. Solos: Cotrubas, Domingo, Milnes) - Dr. Hans Hirsch, Producer (DG)

BEST CHORAL PERFORMANCE, CLASSICAL (OTHER THAN OPERA)

(Grammys to the Conductor and Choral Director.)
BACH: MASS IN B MINOR - Neville Marriner (cond. Chorus & Academy of St. Martin-in-the-Fields) (Philips)
BEETHOVEN: MISSA SOLEMNIS - Sir Georg Solti, cond.; Margaret Hillis, Choral Director (Chicago Symphony Orchestra & Chorus) (London)
BLOCH: SACRED SERVICE - Maurice Abravanel (cond. Utah Chorale & Symphony Orchestra) (Angel)
HAYDN: MASS NO. 9 IN D MINOR ("LORD NELSON MASS") - Leonard Bernstein, Cond.; Joseph Flummerfelt, Choral Dir. (Westminster Choir & New York Philharmonic) (Columbia)
PROKOFIEV: ALEXANDER NEVSKY - Leonard Slatkin, Cond.; Thomas Peck, Choral Dir. (St. Louis Symphony Chorus & Orchestra) (Candide)
STRAVINSKY: LES NOCES & MASS - Leonard Bernstein (cond. Trinity Boys' Choir, English Bach Festival Chorus & English Bach Festival Orchestra) (DG)
VIVALDI: GLORIA IN D MAJOR & MAGNIFICAT - Riccardo Muti, Cond.; Norbert Balatsch, Choral Dir. (New Philharmonia Chorus & Orchestra) (Angel)
WALTON: BELSHAZZAR'S FEAST - Sir Georg Solti, Cond.; John Alldis, Choral Dir. (London Philharmonic Choir & Orchestra) (London)

BEST CHAMBER MUSIC PERFORMANCE

(Instrumental or vocal)
THE ART OF THE RECORDER - David Munrow cond. David Munrow Recorder Consort & Members of the Early Music Consort of London (Angel)
BARTOK: QUARTET NO. 2 FOR STRINGS, OP 17 & QUARTET NO. 6 - Tokyo String Quartet (DG)
BARTOK: SONATA FOR 2 PIANOS & PERCUSSION/MOZART: ANDANTE WITH 5 VARIATIONS FOR PIANO, 4 HANDS/DEBUSSY: EN BLANC ET NOIR FOR 2 PIANOS - Stephen Bishop-Kovacevich & Martha Argerich (Philips)
BEETHOVEN: SONATAS FOR VIOLIN & PIANO (Complete) - Itzhak Perlman & Vladimir Ashkenazy (London)
DUETS FOR TWO VIOLINS - Itzhak Perlman & Pincas Zukerman (Angel)
JOHN WILLIAMS & FRIENDS - John Williams, Carlos Bonell, Brian Gascoigne, Morris Pert, Keith Marjoram (Columbia)
MOZART: QUARTETS FOR PIANO & STRINGS - Artur Rubinstein & Members of Guarneri Quartet (RCA)
SCHUBERT: QUINTET IN C MAJOR FOR STRINGS - Melos Quartet with Mstislav Rostropovich (DG)

BEST CLASSICAL PERFORMANCE INSTRUMENTAL SOLOIST(S) (WITH ORCHESTRA)

BRAHMS: CONCERTO FOR VIOLIN IN D MAJOR - Itzhak Perlman, Violin (Giulini cond. Chicago Symphony) (Angel)
CHOPIN: CONCERTO NO. 2 IN F MINOR FOR PIANO - Emanuel Ax, Piano (Ormandy cond. Philadelphia Orchestra) (RCA)
DVORAK: CONCERTO FOR CELLO IN B MINOR/SAINT-SAENS: CONCERTO FOR CELLO NO. 1 IN A MINOR - Mstislav Rostropovich, Cello (Giulini cond. London Philharmonic) (Angel)
MOZART: CONCERTOS FOR PIANO NOS. 21 IN C MAJOR & 9 IN E FLAT MAJOR - Murray Perahia, Piano (Perahia cond. English Chamber Orchestra) (Columbia)
RACHMANINOFF: CONCERTO NO. 3 IN D MINOR FOR PIANO (HOROWITZ GOLDEN JUBILEE) - Vladimir Horowitz, Piano (Ormandy cond. Philadelphia Orchestra) (RCA)
VAUGHAN WILLIAMS: CONCERTO FOR TUBA - Arnold Jacobs, Tuba (Barenboim cond. Chicago Symphony) (DG)

BEST CLASSICAL PERFORMANCE INSTRUMENTAL SOLOIST(S) (WITHOUT ORCHESTRA)

BACH: ITALIAN CONCERTO/CHORAL PRELUDE/PRELUDE,S922/ CHROMATIC FANTASY & FUGUE/FANTASY & FUGUE - Alfred Brendel, Piano (Philips)
BEETHOVEN: THE LATE PIANO SONATAS - Maurizio Pollini, Piano (DG)
BEETHOVEN: VARIATIONS ON A WALTZ BY DIABELLI - Charles Rosen, Piano (Peters)
DEBUSSY: PRELUDES FOR PIANO, BOOKS I & II - Paul Jacobs, Piano (Nonesuch)
THE HOROWITZ CONCERTS 1977/78 - Vladimir Horowitz, Piano (RCA)
LISZT: 12 TRANSCENDENTAL ETUDES & 3 ETUDES DE CONCERT - Claudio Arrau, Piano (Philips)
RUDOLF SERKIN ON TELEVISION - Rudolf Serkin, Piano (Columbia)

BEST CLASSICAL VOCAL SOLOIST PERFORMANCE

BRAHMS: ALTO RHAPSODY - Christa Ludwig (Bohm cond. Vienna Philharmonic) (DG)
LUCIANO PAVAROTTI - HITS FROM LINCOLN CENTER - Luciano Pavarotti (various Accomp.) (London)
MARIA CALLAS/THE LEGEND The Unreleased Recordings - Maria Callas (various Conds. & Orchs.) (Angel)
MUSSORGSKY: SONGS & DANCES OF DEATH - Galina Vishnevskaya (Rostropovich cond. London Philharmonic) (Angel)
RAVEL: SHEHERAZADE - Marilyn Horne (Bernstein cond. Orchestre Nationale de France) (Columbia)
TERESA BERGANZA - FAVORITE ZARZUELA ARIAS - Teresa Berganza (Asensio cond. English Chamber Orchestra) (Zambra)
WAGNER: ARIAS - Dietrich Fischer-Dieskau (Kubelik cond. Bavarian Radio Orchestra) (Angel)

BEST ENGINEERED RECORDING - CLASSICAL

(An Engineer's Award.)
BACH: MASS IN B MINOR - Marriner cond. Chorus & Academy of St. Martin-in-the-Fields (Philips)
BEETHOVEN: SYMPHONIES (9) Complete - von Karajan cond. Berlin Philharmonic - Gunter Hermann, Engineer (DG)
BERLIOZ: SYMPHONIE FANTASTIQUE - Ormandy cond. Philadelphia Orchestra - Paul Goodman, Engineer (RCA)
BRUCKNER: SYMPHONY NO. 5 IN B FLAT MAJOR - von Karajan cond. Berlin Philharmonic - Gunter Hermann, Engineer (DG)
FREDRICK FENNELL - CLEVELAND SYMPHONIC WINDS - Jack Renner, Engineer (Telarc)
HOLST: THE PLANETS - Marriner cond. Concertgebouw Orchestra (Philips)
MESSIAEN: TURANGALILA SYMPHONY - Previn cond. London Symphony - Chris Parker, Engineer (Angel)
PROKOFIEV: ALEXANDER NEVSKY - Slatkin cond. St. Louis Symphony & Chorus - Marc Aubort, Engineer (Candide)
VARESE: AMERIQUES/ARCANA/IONISATION (BOULEZ CONDUCTS VARESE) - Boulez cond. New York Philharmonic - Bud Graham, Arthur Kendy & Ray Moore, Engineers (Columbia)
WAGNER: DIE WALKURE: RIDE OF THE VALKYRIES/TRISTAN: PRELUDE ACT I/GOTTERDAMMERUNG: SIEGFRIED'S FUNERAL MUSIC/ SIEGFRIED: FOREST MURMURS - Leinsdorf cond. Los Angeles Philharmonic - Doug Sax & Bud Wyatt, Engineers (Sheffield Lab)

1979 HALL OF FAME WINNERS

HOW HIGH THE MOON - Les Paul & Mary Ford - Capitol #1451 - Released in 1951
ONE O'CLOCK JUMP - Count Basie - Decca #1363 - Released in 1937
RACHMANINOFF: RHAPSODY ON A THEME OF PAGANINI (Album) - Sergei Rachmaninoff (Piano); Philadelphia Orchestra, Leopold Sto-

kowski, Conductor - RCA Victor #M250 - Released in 1935

1979

RECORD OF THE YEAR
(Grammy to the Artist and Producer if other than the Artist.) (Certificates to the Arranger, Engineer, Songwriter, Musicians and Background Singers.)
AFTER THE LOVE HAS GONE - Earth, Wind & Fire - Maurice White, Producer (ARC-CBS)
THE GAMBLER - Kenny Rogers - Larry Butler, Producer (UA)
I WILL SURVIVE - Gloria Gaynor - Dino Fekaris, Freddie Perren, Producers (Polydor)
WHAT A FOOL BELIEVES - The Doobie Brothers - Ted Templeman, Producer (WB)
YOU DON'T BRING ME FLOWERS - Barbra Streisand and Neil Diamond - Bob Gaudio, Producer (Columbia)

ALBUM OF THE YEAR
(Grammys to the Artist and Producer if other than the Artist.) (Certificates to the Arranger, Engineer and Songwriter.)
BAD GIRLS - Donna Summer - Giorgio Moroder, Pete Bellotte, Producers (Casablanca)
BREAKFAST IN AMERICA - Supertramp - Supertramp, Peter Henderson, Producers (A&M)
52ND STREET - Billy Joel - Phil Ramone, Producer (Columbia)
THE GAMBLER - Kenny Rogers - Larry Butler, Producer (UA)
MINUTE BY MINUTE - The Doobie Brothers - Ted Templeman, Producer (WB)

SONG OF THE YEAR
(A Songwriter's Award)
AFTER THE LOVE HAS GONE - David Foster, Jay Graydon, Bill Champlin
CHUCK E.'S IN LOVE - Rickie Lee Jones
HONESTY - Billy Joel
I WILL SURVIVE - Dino Fekaris, Freddie Perren
MINUTE BY MINUTE - Lester Abrams, Michael McDonald
REUNITED - Dino Fekaris, Freddie Perren
SHE BELIEVES IN ME - Steve Gibb
WHAT A FOOL BELIEVES - Kenny Loggins, Michael McDonald

BEST NEW ARTIST
(This Category is for an artist or organized group whose first recording was released during the Eligibility Period)
BLUES BROTHERS (Atlantic)
DIRE STRAITS (WB)
RICKIE LEE JONES (WB)
THE KNACK (Capitol)
ROBIN WILLIAMS (Casablanca)

BEST POP VOCAL PERFORMANCE, FEMALE
(This Category is for a solo performance)
BAD GIRLS - Donna Summer (Album) (Casablanca)
CHUCK E.'S IN LOVE - Rickie Lee Jones (Track) (WB)
DON'T CRY OUT LOUD - Melissa Manchester (Single) (Arista)
I WILL SURVIVE - Gloria Gaynor (Track) (Polydor)
I'LL NEVER LOVE THIS WAY AGAIN - Dionne Warwick (Single) (Arista)

BEST POP VOCAL PERFORMANCE, MALE
(This category is for a solo performance)
DA YA THINK I'M SEXY? - Rod Stewart (Single) (WB)
52ND STREET - Billy Joel (Album) (Columbia)
SAD EYES - Robert John (Single) (EMI-America)
SHE BELIEVES IN ME - Kenny Rogers (Single) (UA)
UP ON THE ROOF - James Taylor (Single) (Columbia)

BEST POP VOCAL PERFORMANCE BY A DUO, GROUP OR CHORUS
(All recordings on which the group receives artist billing on the label are eligible here even though the vocal may feature only one member of the group.)
BREAKFAST IN AMERICA - Supertramp (Album) (A&M)
LONESOME LOSER - Little River Band (Single) (Capitol)
MINUTE BY MINUTE - The Doobie Brothers (Album) (WB)
SAIL ON - Commodores (Track) (Motown)
YOU DON'T BRING ME FLOWERS - Barbra Streisand & Neil Diamond (Single) (Columbia)

BEST POP INSTRUMENTAL PERFORMANCE
(All recordings are for either pure instrumentals or instrumentals with vocal coloring.)
AN EVENING OF MAGIC - Chuck Mangione (Album) (A&M)
MANHATTAN (Music From The Film) - Zubin Mehta & The New York Philharmonic (Album - Side 2) (CBS)
MUSIC BOX DANCER - Frank Mills (Track) (Polydor)
RISE - Herb Alpert (Single) (A&M)
THEME FROM SUPERMAN (MAIN TITLE) - John Williams (Track) (WB)

BEST ROCK VOCAL PERFORMANCE, FEMALE
(This category is for a solo performance)
HOT STUFF - Donna Summer (Single) (Casablanca)
THE LAST CHANCE TEXACO - Rickie Lee Jones (Track) (WB)
SURVIVOR - Cindy Bullens (Single) (UA)
TNT - Tanya Tucker (Album) (MCA)
VENGEANCE - Carly Simon (Single) (Elektra)
YOU'RE GONNA GET WHAT'S COMING - Bonnie Raitt (Track) (WB)

BEST ROCK VOCAL PERFORMANCE, MALE
(This category is for a solo performance)
BAD CASE OF LOVING YOU (DOCTOR, DOCTOR) - Robert Palmer (Track) (Island/W.B.)
BLONDES (HAVE MORE FUN) - Rod Stewart (Track) (WB)
DANCIN' FOOL - Frank Zappa (Track) (Zappa)
GOTTA SERVE SOMEBODY - Bob Dylan (Single) (Columbia)
IS SHE REALLY GOING OUT WITH HIM? - Joe Jackson (Single) (A&M)

BEST ROCK VOCAL PERFORMANCE BY A DUO OR GROUP
(All recordings on which the group receives artist billing on the label are eligible here even though the vocal may feature only one member of the group.)
BRIEFCASE FULL OF BLUES - Blues Brothers (Album) (Atlantic)
CANDY-O - Cars (Album) (Elektra)
CORNERSTONE - Styx (Album) (A&M)
HEARTACHE TONIGHT - Eagles (Single) (Asylum)
MY SHARONA - The Knack (Single) (Capitol)
SULTANS OF SWING - Dire Straits (Single) (WB)

BEST ROCK INSTRUMENTAL PERFORMANCE

(All recordings are for either pure instrumentals or instrumentals with vocal coloring.)
HIGH GEAR - Neil Larsen (Single) (A&M)
NIGHT OF THE LIVING DREGS - Dixie Dregs (Album) (Capricorn)
PEGASUS - The Allman Brothers Band (Track) (Capricorn)
RAT TOMAGO - Frank Zappa (Track) (Zappa)
ROCKESTRA THEME - Wings (Track) (Columbia)

BEST R & B VOCAL PERFORMANCE, FEMALE

(This category is for a solo performance)
DEJA VU - Dionne Warwick (Track) (Arista)
DIM ALL THE LIGHTS - Donna Summer (Single) (Casablanca)
I LOVE YOU SO - Natalie Cole (Album) (Capitol)
KNOCK ON WOOD - Amii Stewart (Single) (Ariola)
MINNIE - Minnie Ripperton (Album) (Capitol)
RING MY BELL - Anita Ward (Single) (Juana)

BEST R & B VOCAL PERFORMANCE, MALE

(This category is for a solo performance.)
CRUISIN' - Smokey Robinson (Single) (Motown)
DON'T LET GO - Isaac Hayes (Single) (Polydor)
DON'T STOP 'TILL YOU GET ENOUGH - Michael Jackson (Single) (Epic)
LOVE BALLAD - George Benson (Track) (WB)
MAMA CAN'T BUY YOU LOVE - Elton John (Single) (MCA)
SOME ENCHANTED EVENING - Ray Charles (Single) (Atlantic)

BEST R&B VOCAL PERFORMANCE BY A DUO, GROUP OR CHORUS

(All recordings on which the group receives artist billing on the label are eligible here even though the vocal may feature only one member of the group.)
AFTER THE LOVE HAS GONE - Earth, Wind & Fire (Track) (ARC-CBS)
AIN'T NO STOPPIN' US NOW - McFadden & Whitehead (Single) (Philips International)
MIDNIGHT MAGIC - Commodores (Album) (Motown)
REUNITED - Peaches & Herb (Single) (Polydor)
WE ARE FAMILY - Sister Sledge (Single) (Atlantic)

BEST R&B INSTRUMENTAL PERFORMANCE

(All recordings are for either pure instrumentals or instrumentals with vocal coloring.)
BOOGIE WONDERLAND (Instrumental) - Earth, Wind & Fire (Single) (ARC-CBS)
LAND OF PASSION - Hubert Laws (Track) (Columbia)
READY OR NOT - Herbie Hancock (Track) (Columbia)
WAVE - Harvey Mason (Track) (Arista)
WISHING ON A STAR - Jr. Walker (Single) (Whitfield/W.B.)

BEST RHYTHM & BLUES SONG

(A Songwriter's Award.) (Any song is eligible if a new recording of it has been released during the eligibility year, provided it was not a previous final nomination in a songwriting category.)
AFTER THE LOVE HAS GONE - David Foster, Jay Graydon, Bill Champlin
AIN'T NO STOPPIN' US NOW - Gene McFadden, John Whitehead, Jerry Cohen
DEJA VU - Isaac Hayes, Adrienne Anderson
REUNITED - Dino Fekaris, Freddie Perren
WE ARE FAMILY - Nile Rodgers, Bernard Edwards

BEST DISCO RECORDING

(One Grammy to the Artist; one Grammy to the Producer if other than the Artist. This category is for singles, albums or tracks.)
BOOGIE WONDERLAND - Earth, Wind & Fire and The Emotions - Maurice White & Al McKay, Producers (Single) (ARC-CBS)
BAD GIRLS - Donna Summer - Giorgio Moroder & Pete Bellotte, Producers (Album) (Casablanca)
DA YA THINK I'M SEXY? - Rod Stewart - Tom Dowd, Producer (Single) (WB)
DON'T STOP 'TIL YOU GET ENOUGH - Michael Jackson - Quincy Jones, Producer (Single) (Epic)
I WILL SURVIVE - Gloria Gaynor - Dino Fekaris, Freddie Perren, Producers (Single) (Polydor)

BEST COUNTRY VOCAL PERFORMANCE, FEMALE

(This category is for a solo performance.)
BLUE KENTUCKY GIRL - Emmylou Harris (Album) (WB)
I WILL SURVIVE - Billie Jo Spears (Single) (UA)
JUST FOR THE RECORD - Barbara Mandrell (Album) (MCA)
TELL ME WHAT IT'S LIKE - Brenda Lee (Single) (MCA)
WE SHOULD BE TOGETHER - Crystal Gayle (Album) (UA)

BEST COUNTRY VOCAL PERFORMANCE, MALE

(This category is for a solo performance.)
BURGERS AND FRIES/WHEN I STOP LEAVING (I'LL BE GONE) - Charley Pride (Album) (RCA)
EVERY WHICH WAY BUT LOOSE - Eddie Rabbitt (Single) (Elektra)
FAMILY TRADITION - Hank Williams, Jr. (Album) (Elektra)
THE GAMBLER - Kenny Rogers (Single) (UA)
WHISKEY RIVER - Willie Nelson (Single) (Columbia)

BEST COUNTRY VOCAL PERFORMANCE BY A DUO OR GROUP

(All recordings on which the group receives artist billing on the label are eligible here even though the vocal may feature only one member of the group.) (All nominations are singles)
ALL I EVER NEED IS YOU - Kenny Rogers & Dottie West (UA)
ALL THE GOLD IN CALIFORNIA - Larry Gatlin and The Gatlin Brothers Band (Columbia)
THE DEVIL WENT DOWN TO GEORGIA - Charlie Daniels Band (Epic)
HEARTBREAK HOTEL - Willie Nelson & Leon Russell (Columbia)
IF I SAID YOU HAVE A BEAUTIFUL BODY WOULD YOU HOLD IT AGAINST ME - Bellamy Brothers (WB)

BEST COUNTRY INSTRUMENTAL PERFORMANCE

(This category is for an orchestra, group or soloist, and is for either pure instrumentals or instrumentals with vocal coloring.)
BIG SANDY/LEATHER BRITCHES - Doc & Merle Watson (Track) (UA)
BLUEGRASS CONCERTO - The Osborne Brothers (Album) (CMH)
FANTASTIC PICKIN' - Lester Flatt's Nashville Grass (Album) (CMH)
IN CONCERT - Floyd Cramer (Album) (RCA)
LIVE FROM AUSTIN CITY LIMITS - Nashville Super Pickers (Album) (Flying Fish)
NASHVILLE JAM - Vassar Clements, Doug Jernigan, Jesse McReynolds, Buddy Spicher (Album) (Flying Fish)

BEST COUNTRY SONG

(A Songwriter's award.) (Any song is eligible if a new recording of it has been released during the eligibility year, provided it was not a previous final nomination in a songwriting category.)

ALL THE GOLD IN CALIFORNIA - Larry Gatlin
BLUE KENTUCKY GIRL - Johnny Mullins
EVERY WHICH WAY BUT LOOSE - Steve Dorff, Milton Brown, Snuff Garrett
IF I SAID YOU HAVE A BEAUTIFUL BODY WOULD YOU HOLD IT AGAINST ME - David Bellamy
YOU DECORATED MY LIFE - Bob Morrison, Debbie Hupp

BEST GOSPEL PERFORMANCE, CONTEMPORARY OR INSPIRATIONAL

(This category is for contemporary-flavored gospel recordings.) (All nominations are albums)

ALL THINGS ARE POSSIBLE - Dan Peek (MCA/Songbird)
FOLLOWING YOU - Andrus, Blackwood & Co. (Greentree)
HEED THE CALL - Imperials (Dayspring)
MY FATHER'S EYES - Amy Grant (Myrrh)
NEVER THE SAME - Evie Tornquist (Word)

BEST GOSPEL PERFORMANCE, TRADITIONAL

(All nominations are albums)

A CHORAL CONCERT OF LOVE - Dottie Rambo Choir (Heartwarming)
BREAKOUT - The Mercy River Boys (Canaan)
FEELINGS - Rex Nelon Singers (Canaan)
LIFT UP THE NAME OF JESUS - The Blackwood Brothers (Skylite)
YOU AIN'T HEARD NOTHING YET! - The Cathedral Quartet (Canaan)

BEST SOUL GOSPEL PERFORMANCE, CONTEMPORARY

CASSIETTA IN CONCERT - Cassietta George (Album) (Audio Arts)
GIVE ME SOMETHING TO HOLD ON TO - Myrna Summers (Album) (Savoy)
I'LL BE THINKING OF YOU - Andrae Crouch (Album) (Light)
MORE THAN MAGIC - Bili Thedford (Album) (Good News)
PUSH FOR EXCELLENCE - Rev. Jesse L. Jackson, Walter Hawkins & Family, Edwin Hawkins, Push Choir, Jackie Verdell, Dannibelle, Bili Thedford, Jessy Dixon, Andrae Crouch (Myrrh)
THANK YOU - Kevin Yancy directing the Fountain of Life Joy Choir (Single) (Gospel Roots)

BEST SOUL GOSPEL PERFORMANCE, TRADITIONAL

(All nominations are albums)

CHANGING TIMES - Mighty Clouds of Joy (Epic)
FOR THE WRONG I'VE DONE - Willie Banks & The Messengers (HSE)
IN GOD'S OWN TIME - James Cleveland & Triboro Mass Choir, Albert Jamison, Dir. (Savoy)
IT'S A NEW DAY - James Cleveland and the So. California Community Choir (Savoy)
TRY JESUS - Troy Ramey and The Soul Searchers (Nashboro)

BEST INSPIRATIONAL PERFORMANCE

(This category is for religious recordings by other than regular gospel recording artists.)

BAND AND BODYWORKS - Noel Paul Stookey (Album) (New World)
I SAW THE LIGHT - Willie Nelson & Leon Russell (Track) (Columbia)
I'LL SING THIS SONG FOR YOU - Mike Douglas (Album) (Word)
JUST THE WAY I AM - Pat Boone (Album) (Lamb & Lion)
YOU GAVE ME LOVE (WHEN NOBODY GAVE ME A PRAYER) - B. J. Thomas (Album) (Myrrh)

BEST ETHNIC OR TRADITIONAL RECORDING

(This category includes traditional blues and pure folk recordings.) (All nominations are albums)

THE CHIEFTAINS 7 - The Chieftains (Columbia)
ICE PICKIN' - Albert Collins (Alligator)
LAUGH YOUR BLUES AWAY - Uncle Dave Macon (Rounder)
LIVING CHICAGO BLUES, VOL. 1 - The Jimmy Johnson Blues Band, Eddie Shaw & The Wolf Gang, Left Hand Frank & His Blues Band (Alligator)
LIVING CHICAGO BLUES, VOL. 3 - Lonnie Brooks Blues Band, Pinetop Perkins & Sons of the Blues (Alligator)
MUDDY "MISSISSIPPI" WATERS LIVE - Muddy Waters (Blue Sky-CBS)
NEW ENGLAND TRADITIONAL FIDDLING - Paul F. Wells, Producer (John Edwards Memorial Foundation)
NEW ORLEANS JAZZ & HERITAGE FESTIVAL - Eubie Blake, Charles Mingus, Roosevelt Sykes, Clifton Chenier (Flying Fish)
SO MANY ROADS - Otis Rush (Delmark)

BEST LATIN RECORDING

(This category is for pure Latin music.) (All nominations are albums)

CROSS OVER - Fania All Stars (Columbia)
ETERNOS - Celia Cruz & Johnny Pacheco (Vaya)
IRAKERE - Irakere (Columbia)
TOUCHING YOU, TOUCHING ME - Airto Moreira (WB)

BEST RECORDING FOR CHILDREN

(This category is intended for recordings created specifically for children.) (All nominations are albums)

THE MUPPET MOVIE - Jim Henson, Creator - Paul Williams, Producer (Atlantic)
ANNE MURRAY SINGS FOR THE SESAME STREET GENERATION - Anne Murray (Sesame St.)
SESAME DISCO! - Jim Henson, Creator - Joe Raposo & Michael Delugg, Producers (Sesame St.)
THE STARS COME OUT ON SESAME STREET - Jim Henson, Creator - Jon Stone, Producer - Jim Timmens, Record Editor (Sesame St.)
YOU'RE IN LOVE, CHARLIE BROWN - Jymn Magon & Lee Mendelson, Producers (Charlie Brown)

BEST COMEDY RECORDING

(Either spoken word or musical performances are eligible here.)

COMEDY IS NOT PRETTY - Steve Martin (Album) (WB)
I NEED YOUR HELP BARRY MANILOW - Ray Stevens (Track) (WB)
REALITY...WHAT A CONCEPT - Robin Williams (Album) (Casablanca)
RUBBER BISCUIT - Blues Brothers (Track) (Atlantic)
WANTED - Richard Pryor (Album) (WB)

BEST SPOKEN WORD, DOCUMENTARY OR DRAMA RECORDING

(This category is for non-musical show albums including comedy show albums.)

APOCALYPSE NOW Original Motion Picture Soundtrack - (Elektra)
AGES OF MAN (READINGS FROM SHAKESPEARE) - Sir John Gielgud (Caedmon)
AN AMERICAN PRAYER - Jim Morrison (Elektra)
THE OX-BOW INCIDENT - Henry Fonda (Caedmon)
STARE WITH YOUR EARS - Ken Nordine (Snail)
ORSON WELLES/HELEN HAYES AT THEIR BEST - Orson Welles & Helen Hayes (Mark 56)

BEST INSTRUMENTAL COMPOSITION

(A Composer's Award for an original non-classical composition with or without lyrics which first gained recognition as an instrumental.)
AMBIANCE - Marian McPartland
ANGELA (THEME FROM "TAXI") - Bob James
CENTRAL PARK - Chick Corea
MAIN TITLE THEME FROM "SUPERMAN" - John Williams
RISE - Andy Armer, Randy Badazz

BEST ALBUM OF ORIGINAL SCORE WRITTEN FOR A MOTION PICTURE OR A TELEVISION SPECIAL

(A Composer's award for an original background score or original songs written specifically for the motion picture or television special.)
ALIEN - Jerry Goldsmith, Composer (RCA)
APOCALYPSE NOW - Carmine Coppola, Francis Coppola, Composers (Elektra)
ICE CASTLES - Alan Parsons, Eric Woolfson, Marvin Hamlisch, Composers - Carole Bayer Sager, Lyrics (Arista)
THE MUPPET MOVIE - Paul Williams & Kenny Ascher, Composers and Lyricists (Atlantic)
SUPERMAN - John Williams, Composer (WB)

BEST CAST SHOW ALBUM

(Awards to the Composer(s), Lyricist(s) and Album Producer. Original cast albums, albums by road casts, or working casts, including show revival casts, are eligible.)
BALLROOM - Billy Goldenberg, Comp - Alan & Marilyn Bergman, Lyrs - Larry Morton, Producer (Columbia)
THE GRAND TOUR - Jerry Herman, Comp/Lyr - Mike Berniker & Jerry Herman, Producers (Columbia)
I'M GETTING MY ACT TOGETHER AND TAKING IT ON THE ROAD - Gretchen Cryer & Nancy Ford, Comps - Edward Kleban, Producer (Columbia)
SWEENEY TODD - Stephen Sondheim, Comp/Lyr - Thomas Z. Shepard, Producer (RCA)
THEY'RE PLAYING OUR SONG - Marvin Hamlisch, Comp - Carole Bayer Sager, Lyr - Brooks Arthur, Carole Bayer Sager, Marvin Hamlisch, Producers (Casablanca)

BEST JAZZ FUSION PERFORMANCE, VOCAL OR INSTRUMENTAL

(This category is for any type of borderline jazz performance, rock, pop, R&B, classical, etc.) (All nominations are albums)
BETCHA - Stanley Turrentine (Elektra)
CHICK COREA/SECRET AGENT - Chick Corea Group (Polydor)
8:30 - Weather Report (ARC-CBS)
LIVIN' INSIDE YOUR LOVE - George Benson (WB)
THREE WORKS FOR JAZZ SOLOISTS & SYMPHONY ORCHESTRA - Don Sebesky with Jazz Quintet & Soloists and Symphony Orchestra (Gryphon)

BEST JAZZ VOCAL PERFORMANCE

(This category is for a soloist, duo or group.) (All nominations are albums)
FINE AND MELLOW - Ella Fitzerald (Pablo)
I LOVE BRAZIL - Sarah Vaughan (Pablo)
THE LIVE-LIEST - Eddie Jefferson (Muse)
PREZ AND JOE - Joe Williams (GNP/Crescendo)
SNEAKIN' AROUND - Helen Humes (Classic Jazz)

BEST JAZZ INSTRUMENTAL PERFORMANCE, SOLOIST

(This category is for a solo instrumental performance with or without a group or band.) (All nominations are albums)
MANHATTAN SYMPHONIE - Dexter Gordon (Columbia)
JOUSTS - Oscar Peterson (Pablo)
PAUL DESMOND - Paul Desmond (Artists House)
REFLECTORY - Pepper Adams (Muse)
WARM TENOR - Zoot Sims (Pablo)

BEST JAZZ INSTRUMENTAL PERFORMANCE, GROUP

(This category is for an instrumental group.) (All nominations are albums)
AFFINITY - Bill Evans/Toots Thielemans (WB)
ARNETT COBB & THE MUSE ALL STARS/LIVE AT SANDY'S - Arnett Cobb (Muse)
DUET - Gary Burton & Chick Corea (ECM/WB)
THE GIFTED ONES - Dizzy Gillespie/Count Basie (Pablo)
LOVE FOR SALE - The Great Jazz Trio (Hank Jones, Buster Williams, Tony Williams (Inner City)
WARM TENOR - Zoot Sims (Pablo)

BEST JAZZ INSTRUMENTAL PERFORMANCE, BIG BAND

(This category is primarily for a big band sound.) (All nominations are albums)
AT FARGO, 1940 LIVE - Duke Ellington (Book of the Month Club)
KOGUN - Toshiko Akiyoshi/Lew Tabackin Big Band (RCA)
NATURALLY - Mel Lewis & The Jazz Orchestra (Telarc)
NOTE SMOKING - Louie Bellson & The Explosion (Discwasher)
THAD JONES/MEL LEWIS & UMO - Thad Jones, Mel Lewis & UMO (RCA)

BEST INSTRUMENTAL ARRANGEMENT

(An Arranger's Award. This category is for a specific arrangement released for the first time during the eligibility year on either a single or an album track.)
SABOTAGE - John Serry - John Serry, Arr (Chrysalis)
LAZY AFTERNOON - Freddie Hubbard - Claus Ogerman, Arr (CBS)
SEBASTIAN'S THEME - Don Sebesky - Don Sebesky, Arr (Gryphon)
SOULFUL STRUT - George Benson - Claus Ogerman, Arr (WB)
WAVE - Harvey Mason - Jeremy Lubbock & Harvey Mason, Arrs (Arista)

BEST ARRANGEMENT ACCOMPANYING VOCALIST(S)

(An Arranger's Award. This category is for a specific arrangement released for the first time during the eligibility year on either a single or an album track.)
AFTER THE LOVE HAS GONE - Earth, Wind & Fire - Jerry Hey & David Foster, Arrs (ARC-CBS)
EVERYTHING MUST CHANGE - Benard Ighner - Byron Olson, Arr (Alfa)
I'LL NEVER LOVE THIS WAY AGAIN - Dionne Warwick - Artie Butler & Barry Manilow, Arrs (Arista)
ROUND MIDNIGHT - Richard Evans - Richard Evans, Arr (Horizon)
SEPTEMBER - Earth, Wind & Fire - Tom Tom 84, Arr (ARC-CBS)
WHAT A FOOL BELIEVES - The Doobie Brothers - Michael McDonald, Arr (WB)

BEST ALBUM PACKAGE

(An Art Director's Award. This category is for either classical or non-classical single-jacket or multiple pocket album packages.)

BREAKFAST IN AMERICA - Supertramp - Mike Doud & Mick Haggerty, Art Dir (A&M)
CHICAGO 13 - Chicago - Tony Lane, Art Dir (Columbia)
FEAR OF MUSIC - Talking Heads - John Gillespie, Art Dir (Sire)
IN THROUGH THE OUT DOOR - Led Zeppelin - Hipgnosis, Art Dir (Swan Song)
LOOK SHARP - Joe Jackson - Michael Ross, Art Dir (A&M)
MORNING DANCE - Spyro Gyra - Peter Corriston, Art Dir (Infinity)
NEAR PERFECT/PERFECT - Martin Mull - Ron Coro/Johnny Lee, Art Dirs (Elektra)
RAMSEY - Ramsey Lewis - John Berg, Art Dir (Columbia)
WITH SOUND REASON - Sonny Fortune - Lynne Dresse Breslin, Art Dir (Atlantic)

BEST ALBUM NOTES

(An Annotator's Award. This category is for original writing for a specific album. Either classical or non-classical albums qualify.)

BILLIE HOLIDAY (GIANTS OF JAZZ) - Melvin Maddocks, Ann (Time - Life)
DUKE ELLINGTON (GIANTS OF JAZZ) - Dan Morgenstern & Stanley Dance, Anns (Time - Life)
HOAGY CARMICHAEL - A LEGENDARY PERFORMER AND COMPOSER - Richard M. Sudhalter, Ann (RCA)
THE MAGICAL MUSIC OF WALT DISNEY - Dick Schory, Ann (Ovation)
CHARLIE PARKER: THE COMPLETE SAVOY SESSIONS - Bob Porter & James Patrick, Anns (Savoy)

BEST HISTORICAL REISSUE

(Grammy to the Reissue Album Producer(s).)

ONE NEVER KNOWS, DO ONE? THE BEST OF FATS WALLER - George Spitzer, Chick Crumpacker, Producers (Book of the Month Records)
BILLIE HOLIDAY (GIANTS OF JAZZ) - Jerry Korn, Producer (Time - Life)
DUKE ELLINGTON (GIANTS OF JAZZ) - Jerry Korn, Producer (Time - Life)
THE MAGICAL MUSIC OF WALT DISNEY - Dick Schory, Producer (Ovation)
A TRIBUTE TO E. POWER BIGGS - Andrew Kazdin, Producer (Columbia)

BEST ENGINEERED RECORDING

(Non-Classical) (An Engineer's Award.) (All nominations are albums)

BREAKFAST IN AMERICA - Supertramp - Peter Henderson, Eng (A&M)
EVE - The Alan Parsons Project - Alan Parsons, Eng (Arista)
JUST FRIENDS - LA-4 - Phil Edwards, Eng (Concord Jazz)
RICKIE LEE JONES - Rickie Lee Jones - Lee Herschberg, Loyd Clifft, Tom Knox, Roger Nichols, Engs (W.B.)
CORNERSTONE - Styx - Gary Loizzo, Eng (A&M)

PRODUCER OF THE YEAR

(Non-Classical) (A Producer's Award for consistently outstanding creativity in producing.) Listed below are examples of producer's activities. (A) Album; (S) Single; (T) Track

LARRY BUTLER: "The Gambler" (S) & (A), "She Believes In Me" (S), "You Decorated My Life" (S), "Kenny" (A), - Kenny Rogers
MIKE CHAPMAN: "Stumblin' In" (S) - Suzie Quatro & Chris Norman; "My Sharona" (T), "Get The Knack" (A) - The Knack; "One Way Or Another" (S) - Blondie
QUINCY JONES: "Don't Stop 'Til You Get Enough" (S), "Rock With You" (T) - Michael Jackson; "Do You Love What You Feel" (S), "Master Jam" (A) - Rufus & Chaka
TED TEMPLEMAN: "Van Halen II" (A) - Van Halen; "What A Fool Believes" (S), "Minute By Minute" (S) & (A) - The Doobie Brothers
MAURICE WHITE: "Walking The Line" (S) - The Emotions; "After The Love Has Gone" (S), "I Am" (A), "September" (S) - Earth, Wind & Fire

BEST CLASSICAL ALBUM

(Grammys to the Artists, and to the Producer if other than the artist.) (Certificates to the Engineer(s) and Classical Orchestra Committee.)

BRAHMS: SYMPHONIES (4) COMPLETE - Sir Georg Solti cond. Chicago Symphony Orchestra - James Mallinson, Producer (London)
BRITTEN: PETER GRIMES - Colin Davis cond. Orchestra & Chorus of Royal Opera House, Covent Garden/Prin. Solos: Vickers, Harper, Summers - Vittorio Negri, Producer (Philips)
THE HOROWITZ CONCERTS 1978/79 - Vladimir Horowitz - John Pfeiffer, Producer (RCA)
MUSSORGSKY-RAVEL: PICTURES AT AN EXHIBITION; STRAVINSKY: THE FIREBIRD SUITE - Riccardo Muti cond. The Philadelphia Orchestra - Christopher Bishop, Producer (Angel)
SHOSTAKOVICH: LADY MACBETH OF MTSENSK - Mstislav Rostropovich cond. London Philharmonic/Ambrosian Opera Chorus/Prin. Solos: Vishnevskaya, Gedda - Suvi Raj Grubb, Producer (Angel)
WEBERN: THE COMPLETE WORKS OF ANTON WEBERN, VOLUME 1 - Pierre Boulez cond. Ensemble - Paul Myers, Producer (Columbia)

BEST CLASSICAL ORCHESTRAL RECORDING

(Grammys to the Conductor and Producer. Certificate to the Classical Orchestra Committee.)

BRAHMS: SYMPHONIES (4) COMPLETE - Sir Georg Solti cond. Chicago Symphony - James Mallinson, Producer (London)
HOLST: THE PLANETS - Sir Georg Solti cond. London Philharmonic - James Mallinson, Producer (London)
IVES: THREE PLACES IN NEW ENGLAND - Dennis Russell Davies cond. St. Paul Chamber Orchestra - Tom Voegeli, Producer (Sound 80)
MAHLER: SYMPHONY NO. 4 IN G MAJOR - Andre Previn cond. Pittsburgh Symphony - Suvi Raj Grubb, Producer (Angel)
RACHMANINOFF: SYMPHONIES NOS. 2 IN E MINOR & 3 IN A MINOR - Leonard Slatkin cond. St Louis Symphony - Marc Aubort & Joanna Nickrenz, Producers (Vox Box)
SIBELIUS: FOUR LEGENDS FROM THE "KALEVALA" - Eugene Ormandy cond. The Philadelphia Orchestra - John Willan, Producer (Angel)
ZELENKA: ORCHESTRAL WORKS (COMPLETE) - Alexander Van Wijnkoop Cond. Camerata Bern - Dr. Andreas Holschneider, Producer (DG)

BEST OPERA RECORDING

(Grammys to the Conductor and Producer; special plaques to the Principal Soloists.

BRITTEN: PETER GRIMES - Colin Davis (cond. Orchestra & Chorus of the Royal Opera House, Covent Garden - Prin. Solos: Vickers, Harper, Summers) Vittorio Negri, Producer (Philips)
HINDEMITH: MATHIS DER MALER - Rafael Kubelik (cond. Bavarian Radio Symphony & Bavarian Radio Chorus - Prin. Solos: Fischer-Dieskau, King) - Friedrich Welz & John Willan, Producers (Angel)
SHOSTAKOVICH: LADY MACBETH OF MTSENSK - Mstislav Rostropovich (cond. London Philharmonic, Ambrosian Opera Chorus - Prin. Solos: Vishnevskaya, Gedda) Suvi Raj Grubb, Producer (Angel)
VERDI: OTELLO - James Levine (cond. National Philharmonic - Prin. Solos: Domingo, Scotto, Milnes) Richard Mohr, Producer (RCA)
VERDI: RIGOLETTO - Julius Rudel (cond. Philharmonia Orchestra & Ambrosian Opera Chorus - Prin. Solos: Sills, Kraus, Milnes) John Fraser, Producer (Angel)

BEST CHORAL PERFORMANCE, CLASSICAL (OTHER THAN OPERA)
(Grammys to the Conductor and Choral Director)
AMERICAN MUSIC FOR CHORUS - John Oliver (cond. Tanglewood Festival Chorus) (DG)
BEETHOVEN: "CHORAL FANTASY", ELEGIAC SONG & "CALM SEA AND PROSPEROUS VOYAGE" - Jerzy Semkow, Cond.; Thomas Peck, Choral Dir. (St. Louis Symphony Chorus & Orchestra) (Candide)
BEETHOVEN: MISSA SOLEMNIS - Leonard Bernstein (cond. Radio Chorus of the N.O.S. Hilversum & Concertgebouworkest) (DG)
BERLIOZ: LA DAMNATION DE FAUST - Daniel Barenboim (cond. Chorus of Orchestre de Paris & Orchestre de Paris) (DG)
BERLIOZ: REQUIEM - Lorin Maazel, Cond.; Robert Page, Choral Dir. (Cleveland Orchestra & Chorus) (London)
BRAHMS: A GERMAN REQUIEM - Sir Georg Solti, Cond.; Margaret Hillis, Choral Dir. (Chicago Symphony & Chorus) (London)
BRITTEN: SPRING SYMPHONY - Andre Previn, Cond.; Richard Hickox, Chorus Master; Keith Walters, Choral Director (London Symphony Chorus/St. Clement Danes School Boys' Choir & London Symphony) (Angel)
STRAVINSKY: SYMPHONY OF PSALMS - Maurice Abravanel, Cond.: Newell B. Weight, Choral Dir. (Utah Chorale & Utah Symphony) (Angel)

BEST CHAMBER MUSIC PERFORMANCE
(Instrumental or Vocal.)
BERG: CHAMBER CONCERTO FOR PIANO & VIOLIN/FOUR PIECES FOR CLARINET & PIANO - Pierre Boulez, Daniel Barenboim, Pinchas Zukerman/Pay & Ensemble Inter-Contemporain (DG)
BOLLING: SUITE FOR VIOLIN & JAZZ PIANO - Pinchas Zukerman & Claude Bolling with Max Hediguer & Marcel Sabiani (Columbia)
COPLAND: APPALACHIAN SPRING - Davis cond. St. Paul Chamber Orchestra (Sound 80)
DEBUSSY: QUARTET IN G MINOR/RAVEL: QUARTET IN F - Tokyo Quartet (Columbia)
DOHNANYI: SERENADE, OP. 10/BEETHOVEN: SERENADE, OP. 8 - Itzhak Perlman, Lynn Harrell, Pinchas Zukerman (Columbia)
SHOSTAKOVICH: QUARTETS NOS. 5 & 6 - Fitzwilliam Quartet (L'Oiseau Lyre)
TELEMANN: 6 SONATAS FOR 2 FLUTES - Michael Debost & James Galway (Seraphim)
VIVALDI: FOUR FLUTE CONCERTOS - KOTO FLUTE - Ransom Wilson & The New Koto Ensemble of Tokyo - Yoshikazu Fukumura, Conductor (Angel)

BEST CLASSICAL PERFORMANCE - INSTRUMENTAL SOLOIST OR SOLOISTS (WITH ORCHESTRA)
ANNIE'S SONG & OTHER GALWAY FAVORITES - James Galway (Gerhardt cond. National Philharmonic) (RCA)
BARTOK: CONCERTOS FOR PIANO NOS. 1 & 2 - Maurizio Pollini (Abbado cond. Chicago Symphony) (DG)
CHOPIN: CONCERTO FOR PIANO NO. 1 IN E MINOR - Krystian Zimerman (Giulini cond. Los Angeles Philharmonic) (DG)
HORN CONCERTOS BY JOSEPH HAYDN & MICHAEL HAYDN - Barry Tuckwell (English Chamber Orchestra) (Angel)
ISAAC STERN & JEAN-PIERRE RAMPAL PLAY VIVALDI & TELEMANN - Isaac Stern & Jean-Pierre Rampal (Jerusalem Music Center Chamber Orchestra) (Columbia)
MOZART: CONCERTOS FOR VIOLIN NO. 3 IN G MAJOR & NO. 5 IN A MAJOR - Anne Sophie Mutter (von Karajan cond. Berlin Philharmonic) (DG)
TRUMPET CONCERTOS BY HAYDN, TELEMANN, ALBINONI & MARCELLO - Maurice Andre (Lopez-Cobos cond. London Philharmonic) (Angel)

BEST CLASSICAL PERFORMANCE - INSTRUMENTAL SOLOIST OR SOLOISTS (WITHOUT ORCHESTRA)
BACH: GOLDBERG VARIATIONS - Rosalyn Tureck (Columbia)
BACH: TOCCATAS, VOLUME 1 - Glenn Gould (Columbia)
BOULEZ: SONATA FOR PIANO NO. 2 - Maurizio Pollini (DG)
DEBUSSY: ESTAMPES, IMAGES, BOOKS 1 & 2 - Paul Jacobs (Nonesuch)
FRANCK: PRELUDE, CHORALE & FUGUE FOR PIANO/BACH-BUSONI: CHACONNE/MOZART: RONDO IN A MINOR - Artur Rubinstein (RCA)
THE HOROWITZ CONCERTS 1978/79 - Vladimir Horowitz (RCA)
RZEWSKI: THE PEOPLE UNITED WILL NEVER BE DEFEATED - Ursula Oppens (Vanguard)
SCARLATTI: SONATAS (12) - Igor Kipnis (Angel)
VILLA-LOBOS: ETUDES (12) & SUITE POPULAIRE BRASILIENNE - Julian Bream (RCA)

BEST CLASSICAL VOCAL SOLOIST PERFORMANCE
FREDERICA VON STADE SONG RECITAL - Frederica von Stade (Martin Katz, Accomp.) (Columbia)
LIEDER BY SCHUBERT & RICHARD STRAUSS - Leontyne Price (David Garvey, Accomp.) (Angel)
MOZART: LIEDER - Elly Ameling (Dalton Baldwin, Accomp.) (Philips)
MUSSORGSKY: SONGS - Yevgeny Nesterenko (Shenderovich & Krainev, Accomps.) (Col./Mel.)
O SOLE MIO (Favorite Neapolitan Songs) - Luciano Pavarotti (Bologna Orchestra) (London)
SCHUBERT: LIEDER - Dietrich Fischer-Dieskau (Svjatoslav Richter, Accomp.) (DG)
RAVEL: CHANSONS MADECASSES - Jan de Gaetani (Dunkel, Anderson, Kalish, Accomps.) (Nonesuch)
VICTORIA DE LOS ANGELES IN CONCERT - Victoria de los Angeles (Gerald Moore, Accomp.) (Angel)

BEST ENGINEERED RECORDING, CLASSICAL
(An Engineer's Award.)
BARTOK: CONCERTOS FOR PIANO NOS. 1 & 2 - Maurizio Pollini/Abbado cond. Chicago Symphony - Klaus Hiemann, Engineer (DG)
THE BERMUDA TRIANGLE - Isao Tomita - Isao Tomita, Engineer (RCA)
BRITTEN: PETER GRIMES - Davis cond. Royal Opera House, Covent Garden/Prin. Solos: Vickers, Harper, Summers - Vittorio Negri, Engineer (Philips)
COPLAND: APPALACHIAN SPRING/IVES: THREE PLACES IN NEW ENGLAND - Davis cond. St. Paul Chamber Orchestra - Tom Jung, Engineer (Sound 80)
HINDEMITH: CONCERT MUSIC FOR STRINGS & BRASS/SYMPHONIC METAMORPHOSIS ON THEMES BY WEBER - Ormandy cond. The Philadelphia Orchestra - John Kurlander, Engineer (Angel)
MUSSORGSKY-RAVEL: PICTURES AT AN EXHIBITION - Maazel cond. The Cleveland Orchestra - Jack Renner, Engineer (Telarc)
PROKOFIEV: SCYTHIAN SUITE/LT. KIJE - Abbado cond. Chicago Symphony - Klaus Hiemann, Engineer (DG)
RACHMANINOFF: SYMPHONIES NOS. 2 & 3 - Slatkin cond. St Louis Symphony - Marc Aubort & Joanna Nickrenz, Engineers (Vox Box)
SIBELIUS: FOUR LEGENDS FROM THE "KALEVALA" - Ormandy cond. Philadelphia Orchestra - John Kurlander, Engineer (Angel)
SONDHEIM: SWEENEY TODD - Original Cast - Anthony Salvatore, Engineer (RCA)
STRAVINSKY: THE FIREBIRD SUITE/BORODIN: PRINCE IGOR - Shaw cond. Atlanta Symphony Orchestra & Chorus - Jack Renner, Engineer (Telarc)

CLASSICAL PRODUCER OF THE YEAR

(A Producer's Award for consistently outstanding creativity in producing. Listed below are examples of producer's activities.)

MARC AUBORT & JOANNA NICKRENZ: BEETHOVEN: CHORAL FANTASY, ELEGIAC SONG, CALM SEAS & PROSPEROUS VOYAGE, RONDO IN B FLAT - Semkow & Peck/St. Louis Orchestra & Chorus (Candide); BEETHOVEN: QUINTET IN E-FLAT MAJOR FOR PIANO & WINDS - Simon, Woodhams, Silfies, Berry Pandolfi (Turnabout); BRAHMS: QUINTET IN B MINOR FOR CLARINET & STRINGS - Banes, Sant'Ambrogio, Silfies, Korman, Beiler (Turnabout); RACHMANINOFF: SYMPHONIES NOS. 2 & 3 - Slatkin cond. St. Louis Symphony (Vox Box)

ANDREW KAZDIN: BACH: TOCCATAS, VOLUME 1 - Glenn Gould (Columbia); LALO: SYMPHONIE ESPAGNOLE FOR VIOLIN & ORCHESTRA - Zukerman/Mehta cond. Los Angeles Philharmonic (Columbia); MANHATTAN (Music from the Film) - Graffman/Mehta cond. New York Philharmonic (Columbia); MENOTTI: THE TELEPHONE - Mester cond. Louisville Orchestra/Seibel, Orth (Louisville); SCHOENBERG: VERKLARTE NACHT - Boulez cond. New York Philharmonic (Columbia); TCHAIKOVSKY: CONCERTO FOR VIOLIN & ORCHESTRA IN D MAJOR - Stern/Rostropovich cond. National Symphony (Columbia)

JAMES MALLINSON: BERLIOZ: REQUIEM - Maazel cond. Cleveland Orchestra & Chorus (London); BRAHMS: SYMPHONIES (4) COMPLETE - Solti cond. Chicago Symphony (London); HOLST: THE PLANETS - Solti cond. London Philharmonic (London); NEW YEAR'S IN VIENNA - Boskovsky cond. Vienna Philharmonic (London); PUCCINI: TOSCA - Rescigno cond./Freni, Pavarotti (London); TCHAIKOVSKY: 1812 OVERTURE - Dorati cond. Detroit Symphony (London)

PAUL MYERS: BEETHOVEN: SYMPHONIES (9) - Maazel cond. Cleveland Orchestra (Columbia); FAURE: REQUIEM - Davis cond. Ambrosian Singers & Philharmonic Orchestra (Columbia); FREDERICA VON STADE SONG RECITAL - Frederica von Stade (Columbia); JOHN WILLIAMS PLAYS GUITAR MUSIC FORM ENGLAND, JAPAN, BRAZIL, VENEZUELA, ARGENTINA & MEXICO - John Williams (Columbia); PUCCINI: MADAME BUTTERFLY - Maazel cond./Scotto, Domingo (Columbia); WEBERN: COMPLETE WORKS - Boulez cond. Ensemble (Columbia)

VITTORIO NEGRI: BRITTEN: PETER GRIMES - Davis cond./Vickers, Harper, Summers (Philips); DVORAK: SYMPHONY NO. 8 IN G MAJOR - Davis cond. Concertgebouw Orchestra (Philips); STRAVINSKY: THE FIREBIRD (COMPLETE) - Davis cond. Concertgebouw Orchestra (Philips)

THOMAS Z. SHEPARD: SONDHEIM: SWEENEY TODD - Original Cast (RCA)

ROBERT WOODS: CHOPIN: PIANO MUSIC - Frager (Telarc); MUSSORGSKY-RAVEL: PICTURES AT AN EXHIBITION - Maazel cond. The Cleveland Orchestra (Telarc); STRAVINSKY: THE FIREBIRD SUITE - Shaw cond. Atlanta Symphony (Telarc)

1980 HALL OF FAME WINNERS

BALLAD FOR AMERICANS (Album) - Paul Robeson - Victor #P20 - Released in 1940
IN A MIST - Bix Beiderbacke (Piano Solo) - Okeh # - Released in 1927
JELLY ROLL MORTON: THE SAGA OF MR. JELLY LORD (The Library of Congress Recordings) (12 Albums) - Ferdinand "Jelly Roll" Morton - Circle Sound 1-12 - Released 1949-1950

PLATINUM RECORDS
1976–1980

ARTIST—TITLE	LABEL

1976

ALBUMS

Aerosmith —Rocks	Columbia
Average White Band —Soul Searching	Atlantic
Bad Company —Run With The Pack	Swan Song
The Beatles —Rock 'N' Roll Music	Capitol
Bee Gees —Children of the World	RSO
George Benson —Breezin'	Warner Bros.
Boston —Boston	Epic
Brass Construction —Brass Construction	United Artists
The Brothers Johnson —Look Out for #1	A & M
Captain & Tennille —Song of Joy	A & M
Chicago —Chicago X	Columbia
John Denver —Spirit	RCA
Neil Diamond —Beautiful Noise	Columbia
Doobie Brothers —Best of the Doobies	Warner Bros.
Bob Dylan —Desire	Columbia
Eagles —Eagles - Their Greatest Hits	Asylum
Eagles —Hotel California	Asylum
Earth, Wind & Fire —Spirit	Columbia
The Electric Light Orchestra —A New World Record	United Artists
Peter Frampton —Frampton Comes Alive!	A & M
Heart —Dreamboat Annie	Mushroom
Jefferson Starship —Spitfire	Grunt
Elton John —Blue Moves	MCA/Rocket
Kiss —Destroyer	Casablanca
Led Zeppelin —Presence	Swan Song
Led Zeppelin —The Song Remains the Same	Swan Song
Lynyrd Skynyrd —One More For From The Road	MCA
Steve Miller Band —Fly Like An Eagle	Capitol
The Outlaws - Waylon Jennings, Willie Nelson, Jessi Colter, Tompall Glaser —The Outlaws	RCA
Parliament —Mothership Connection	Casablanca
The Rolling Stones —Black and Blue	Rolling Stone
Linda Ronstadt —Hasten Down the Wind	Asylum
Boz Scaggs —Silk Degrees	Columbia
Rod Stewart —A Night on the Town	Warner Bros.
Wild Cherry —Wild Cherry	Epic/Sweet City
Wings —Wings at the Speed of Sound	Capitol
Wings —Wings Over America	Capitol

SINGLES

Rick Dees & His Cast of Idiots —Disco Duck	RSO
The Manhattans —Kiss and Say Goodbye	Columbia
Wild Cherry —Play that Funky Music	Epic/Sweet City
Johnnie Taylor —Disco Lady	Columbia

1977

ALBUMS

Aerosmith —Draw The Line	Columbia
The Beatles —The Beatles At The Hollywood Bowl	Capitol
Bee Gees —Here At Last. . .Bee Gees. . .Live	Polydor/RSO
George Benson —In Flight	Warner Bros.
Debby Boone —You Light Up My Life	Warner Bros.
Brothers Johnson —Right On Time	A & M
Jackson Browne —The Pretender	Elektra/Asylum
Jimmy Buffett —Changes In Latitudes, Changes In Attitudes	ABC
Shaun Cassidy —Born Late	Warner Bros.
Shaun Cassidy —Shaun Cassidy	Warner Bros.
Chicago —Chicago XI	Columbia
Natalie Cole —Unpredictable	Capitol
Rita Coolidge —Anytime. . .Anywhere	A & M
Crosby, Stills & Nash —CSN	Atlantic
Neil Diamond —I'm Glad You're Here With Me Tonight	Columbia
Neil Diamond —Love At The Greek	Columbia
Earth, Wind & Fire —All 'N' All	Columbia
Electric Light Orch. —Out Of The Blue	United Artists/Jet
Emotions —Rejoice	Columbia
Fleetwood Mac —Rumours	Warner Bros.
The Floaters —The Floaters	ABC
Foghat —Foghat Live	Warner/Bearsville
Foreigner —Foreigner	Atlantic
Peter Frampton —I'm In You	A & M
Heart —Little Queen	Columbia/Portrait
Heatwave —Too Hot To Handle	CBS/Epic
Engelbert Humperdinck —After The Lovin'	CBS/Epic
Isley Brothers —Go For Your Guns	Columbia/T-Neck
Waylon Jennings —Ol' Waylon	RCA
Elton John —Elton John's Greatest Hits, Vol. II	MCA
Kansas —Leftoverture	Columbia/Kirshner
Kansas —Point Of Know Return	Columbia/Kirshner
Kiss —Kiss Alive II	Casablanca
Kiss —Love Gun	Casablanca
Kiss —Rock And Roll Over	Casablanca
Lynyrd Skynyrd —Street Survivors	MCA
Barry Manilow —Barry Manilow Live	Arista
Barry Manilow —This One's For You	Arista
Steve Miller Band —Book Of Dreams	Capitol
Olivia Newton-John —Greatest Hits	MCA
Ted Nugent —Cat Scratch Fever	CBS/Epic
Ted Nugent —Free For All	CBS/Epic
Original Soundtrack —Rocky	United Artists
Original Soundtrack —Star Wars	20th Century
Pink Floyd —Animals	Columbia
Elvis Presley —Elvis Sings The Wonderful World Of Christmas	RCA
Elvis Presley —In Concert	RCA
Elvis Presley —Moody Blue	RCA

PLATINUM RECORDS

ARTIST—TITLE	LABEL
Queen —News Of The World	Elektra
Lou Rawls —All Things In Time	Phila. International
Linda Ronstadt —Greatest Hits	Elektra/Asylum
Linda Ronstadt —Simple Dreams	Elektra/Asylum
Rose Royce —In Full Bloom	Warner Bros./Whitfield
Rufus - featuring Chaka Khan —Ask Rufus	ABC
Leo Sayer —Endless Flight	Warner Bros.
Boz Scaggs —Down Two Then Left	Columbia
Bob Seger & The Silver Bullet Band —'Live' Bullet	Capitol
Bob Seger & The Silver Bullet Band —Night Moves	Capitol
Steely Dan —Aja	ABC
Al Stewart —Year Of The Cat	GRT/Janus
Rod Stewart —Foot Loose & Fancy Free	Warner Bros.
Barbra Streisand & Kris Kristofferson —A Star Is Born	Columbia
Barbra Streisand —Superman	Columbia
Styx —The Grand Illusion	A & M
James Taylor —James Taylor's Greatest Hits	Columbia
James Taylor —J.T.	Warner Bros.
War —Greatest Hits	United Artists
Barry White —Barry White Sings For Someone You Love	20th Century

SINGLES

Debby Boone —You Light Up My Life	Warner Bros.
Heatwave —Boogie Nights	CBS/Epic
Rose Royce —Car Wash	MCA

1978

ALBUMS

ARTIST—TITLE	LABEL
Abba —Greatest Hits	Atlantic
Abba —The Album	Atlantic
Aerosmith —Live Bootleg	Columbia
Atlanta Rhythm Section —Champagne Jam	Polydor
Bee Gees —Saturday Night Fever	Polydor/RSO
George Benson —Weekend in L.A.	Warner Bros.
Blue Oyster Cult —Agents Of Fortune	Columbia
Boston —Don't Look Back	CBS/Epic
Brothers Johnson —Blam	A & M
Jackson Browne —Running On Empty	Asylum
Jimmy Buffett —Son Of A Son Of A Sailor	ABC
Cars —The Cars	Elektra
Shaun Cassidy —Under Wraps	Warner/Curb
Chic —C'est Chic	Atlantic
Chicago —Hot Streets	Columbia
Eric Clapton —Backless	Polydor/RSO
Eric Clapton —Slowhand	Polydor/RSO
Natalie Cole —Thankful	Capitol
Commodores —Natural High	Motown
Peter Criss —Kiss - Peter Criss	Casablanca
John Denver —I Want To Live	RCA
Neil Diamond —You Don't Bring Me Flowers	Columbia
Doobie Brothers —Takin' It To The Streets	Warner Bros.
Earth, Wind & Fire —The Best Of Earth, Wind & Fire - Volume I	Columbia/ARC
Dan Fogelberg & Tim Weisberg —Twin Sons Of Different Mothers	CBS/Epic/Full Moon
Foreigner —Double Vision	Atlantic
Ace Frehley —Kiss - Ace Frehley	Casablanca
Funkadelic —One Nation Under A Groove	Warner Bros.
FM —Original Soundtrack	MCA
Crystal Gayle —We Must Believe In Magic	United Artists
Andy Gibb —Flowing Rivers	Polydor/RSO
Andy Gibb —Shadow Dancing	Polydor/RSO
Original Soundtrack —Grease	Polydor/RSO
Heart —Dog And Butterfly	Mushroom
Heart —Magazine	CBS/Portrait
Heatwave —Central Heating	CBS/Epic
Isley Brothers —Showdown	CBS/T-Neck
Jefferson Starship —Earth	RCA/Grunt
Waylon Jennings & Willie Nelson —Waylon & Willie	RCA
Jethro Tull —M.U. - The Best Of Jethro Tull	Chrysalis
Billy Joel —52nd Street	Columbia
Billy Joel —The Stranger	Columbia
Elton John —A Single Man	MCA
Quincy Jones —Sounds . . . And Stuff Like That	A & M
Journey —Infinity	Columbia
Kiss —Double Platinum	Casablanca
L.T.D. —Togetherness	A & M
Kenny Loggins —Nightwatch	Columbia
Lynyrd Skynyrd —Skynyrd's First And. . .Last	MCA
Chuck Mangione —Feels So Good	A & M
Barry Manilow —Even Now	Arista
Barry Manilow —Greatest Hits	Arista
Steve Martin —A Wild & Crazy Guy	Warner Bros.
Steve Martin —Let's Get Small	Warner Bros.
Johnny Mathis —You Light Up My Life	Columbia
Paul McCartney & Wings —London Town	Capitol
Meat Loaf —Bat Out Of Hell	CBS/Epic/Cleveland International
Meco —Star Wars And Other Galactic Funk	Millenium
Steve Miller Band —The Steve Miller Band's Greatest Hits 1974-78	Capitol
Anne Murray —Let's Keep It That Way	Capitol
Willie Nelson —Stardust	Columbia
Olivia Newton-John —Totally Hot	MCA
Ted Nugent —Double Live Gonzo	CBS/Epic
Ted Nugent —Weekend Warriors	CBS/Epic
O'Jays —So Full Of Love	CBS/Phila. Int'l.
Pablo Cruise —Worlds Away	A & M
Parliament —Funkentelechy vs. The Placebo Syndrome	Casablanca
The Alan Parsons Project —I Robot	Arista
Dolly Parton —Here You Come Again	RCA
Teddy Pendergrass —Life Is A Song Worth Singing	CBS/Phila. Int'l.

ARTIST—TITLE	LABEL
Teddy Pendergrass — Teddy Pendergrass	CBS/Phila. Int'l.
Queen —Jazz	Elektra
Gerry Rafferty —City To City	United Artists
Kenny Rogers —Ten Years Of Gold	United Artists
Rolling Stones —Some Girls	Atlantic/Rolling Stones
Linda Ronstadt —Living In The USA	Asylum
REO Speedwagon —You Get What You Play For	CBS/Epic
Bob Seger & The Silver Bullet Band —Stranger In Town	Capitol
Sgt. Pepper's Lonely Hearts Club Band —Original Soundtrack	Polydor/RSO
Gene Simmons —Kiss - Gene Simmons	Casablanca
Carly Simon —Boys In The Trees	Elektra
Paul Simon —Greatest Hits, Etc.	Columbia
Bruce Springsteen —Darkness On The Edge Of Town	Columbia
Paul Stanley —Kiss - Paul Stanley	Casablanca
Steely Dan —Steely Dan's Greatest Hits	ABC
Rod Stewart —Blondes Have More Fun	Warner Bros.
Barbra Streisand —Barbra Steisand's Greatest Hits Volume II	Columbia
Barbra Streisand —Songbird	Columbia
Styx —Pieces Of Eight	A & M
Donna Summer —Live And More	Casablanca
A Taste Of Honey —A Taste Of Honey	Capitol
Thank God It's Friday —Original Soundtrack	Casablanca
Marshall Tucker Band —Carolina Dreams	Capricorn
Van Halen —Van Halen	Warner Bros.
Village People —Cruisin'	Casablanca
Village People —Macho Man	Casablanca
Joe Walsh —But Seriously, Folks	Asylum
Bob Welch —French Kiss	Capitol
Barry White —Barry White, The Man	20th Century
The Who —Who Are You	MCA
Wings —Wings Greatest	Capitol
Yes —Tormato	Atlantic

SINGLES

ARTIST—TITLE	LABEL
Bee Gees —Night Fever	Polydor/RSO
Bee Gees —Stayin' Alive	Polydor/RSO
Chic —Le Freak	Atlantic
Andy Gibb —Shadow Dancing	Polydor/RSO
Meco —Star Wars Theme/Cantina Band	Millenium
Queen —We Are The Champions	Elektra
Samantha Sang —Emotion	Private Stock
Taste of Honey —Boogie Oogie Oogie	Capitol
John Travolta & Olivia Newton-John —You're the One That I Want	Polydor/RSO
Frankie Valli —Grease	Polydor/RSO

1979

ALBUMS

ARTIST—TITLE	LABEL
Bad Company —Desolation Angels	Swan Song
Bee Gees —Spirits Having Flown	RSO
Blondie —Parallel Lines	Chrysalis
Blues Bros. —Briefcase Full Of Blues	Atlantic
The Cars —Candy-o	Elektra
Cheap Trick —Live At Budokan	Epic
Chic —Risque	Atlantic
Charlie Daniels Band —Million Mile Reflection	Epic
Dire Straits —Dire Straits	Warner Bros.
Doobie Bros. —Minute By Minute	Warner Bros.
Earth, Wind & Fire —I Am	ARC/Columbia
Electric Light Orchestra —Discovery	JET/CBS
Firefall —Elan	Atlantic
Dan Fogelberg —Nether Lands	CBS
G.Q. —Disco Nights	Arista
Gloria Gaynor —Love Tracks	Polydor
Michael Jackson —Off The Wall	CBS
The Jacksons —Destiny	Epic
Waylon Jennings —Greatest Hits	RCA
Rickie Lee Jones —Rickie Lee Jones	Warner Bros.
Journey —Evolution	CBS
Kansas —Two For The Show	CBS/Kirshner
Kiss —Dynasty	Casablanca
Knack —Get The Knack	Capitol
Little River Band —First Under The Wire	Harvest
Little River Band —Sleeper Catcher	Capitol
Eddie Money —Eddie Money	CBS
Moody Blues —Octave	London
O'Jays —Identify Yourself	Phila. Int'l.
Peaches & Herb —2 Hot	Polydor
Teddy Pendergrass —Teddy	Phila. Int'l.
Kenny Rogers —The Gambler	United Artists
Sister Sledge —We Are Family	Atlantic
Al Stewart —Time Passages	Arista
Donna Summer —Bad Girls	Casablanca
Supertramp —Breakfast In America	A & M
Toto —Toto	Columbia
Van Halen —Van Halen II	Warner Bros.
Gino Vanelli —Brother To Brother	A & M
Village People —Go West	Casablanca
The Who —The Kids Are Alright Movie Soundtrack	MCA
Wings —Back To The Egg	CBS

SINGLES

ARTIST—TITLE	LABEL
Bee Gees —Too Much Heaven	RSO
Bee Gees —Tragedy	RSO
Gloria Gaynor —I Will Survive	Polydor
Nick Gilder —Hot Child In The City	Chrysalis
The Jacksons —Shake Your Body	Epic
Mc Fadden & Whitehead —Ain't No Stopping Us Now	Phila. Int'l.
Peaches & Herb —Reunited	Polydor
Amii Stewart —Knock On Wood	Ariola America
Rod Stewart —Do Ya Think I'm Sexy	Warner Bros.
Donna Summer —Bad Girls	Casablanca

PLATINUM RECORDS

ARTIST—TITLE	LABEL
Donna Summer —Hot Stuff	Casablanca
Village People —Y.M.C.A.	Casablanca

1980

ALBUMS

ARTIST—TITLE	LABEL
Herb Alpert —Rise	A & M
AC/DC —Back In Black	Atlantic
AC/DC —Highway To Hell	Atlantic
Bee Gees —Bee Gees Greatest	RSO
Pat Benatar —Crimes Of Passion	Chrysalis
Pat Benatar —In The Heat Of The Night	Chrysalis
George Benson —Give Me The Night	Warner Bros.
Blondie —Eat To The Beat	Chrysalis
Brothers Johnson —Light Up The Night	A & M
Jackson Browne —Hold Out	Elektra
The Cars —Panorama	Elektra
The Charlie Daniels Band —Full Moon	Epic
Cheap Trick —Dream Police	Epic
Christopher Cross —Christopher Cross	Warner Bros.
John Denver & The Muppets —A Christmas Together	RCA
Neil Diamond —September Morn	Columbia
Doobie Brothers —One Step Closer	Warner Bros.
Bob Dylan —Slow Train Coming	Columbia
The Eagles —The Long Run	Asylum
Electric Light Orchestra —ELO's Greatest Hits	Jet
Fleetwood Mac —Tusk	Warner Bros.
Dan Fogelberg —Phoenix	Epic
Foreigner —Head Games	Atlantic
The Isley Brothers —Go All The Way	T-Neck
The Jacksons —Triumph	Epic
Billy Joel —Glass Houses	Columbia
Journey —Departure	Columbia
Kool and the Gang —Ladies Night	Phonogram
Led Zeppelin —In Through The Out Door	Atlantic
Gordon Lightfoot —Summertime Dream	Reprise
Kenny Loggins —Celebrate Me Home	Columbia
Lynyrd Skynyrd —Gold And Platinum	MCA
Barry Manilow —One Voice	Arista
Mickey Mouse —Mickey Mouse Disco	Disneyland
Bette Midler —"The Rose"-Original Soundtrack	Atlantic
Molly Hatchet —Flirtin' With Disaster	Epic
Molly Hatchet —Molly Hatchet	Epic
Anne Murray —Greatest Hits	Capitol
Willie Nelson —Willie Nelson & Family Live	Columbia
Olivia Newton-John & Electric Light Orchestra —From The Original Motion Picture Soundtrack "Xanadu"	MCA
Original Soundtrack —Honeysuckle Rose	Columbia
Original Cast Album —Annie	Columbia
Pablo Cruise —A Place In The Sun	A & M
Teddy Pendergrass —TP	Phila Intl.
Tom Petty & The Heartbreakers —Damn The Torpedoes	MCA
Pink Floyd —The Wall	Columbia
Prince —Prince	Warner Bros.
Queen —The Game	Elektra
Kenny Rogers —Gideon	United Artists
Kenny Rogers —Greatest Hits	United Artists
Kenny Rogers —Kenny	Capitol
The Rolling Stones —Emotional Rescue	Atlantic
Linda Ronstadt —Mad Love	Asylum
REO Speedwagon —You Can Tune A Piano, But You Can't Tuna Fish	Epic
Bob Seger & The Silver Bullet Band —Against The Wind	Capitol
Bruce Springsteen —The River	Columbia
Rod Stewart —Rod Stewart's Greatest Hits	Warner Bros.
Barbra Streisand —Guilty	Columbia
Barbra Streisand —Wet	Columbia
Styx —Cornerstone	A & M
Donna Summer —On The Radio, Vol. I & II	Casablanca
Van Halen —Women And Children First	Warner Bros.
Original Soundtrack —Urban Cowboy	Asylum
Dionne Warwick —Dionne	Arista
The Whispers —The Whispers	Solar
Neil Young —Rust Never Sleeps	Warner Bros.

SINGLES

ARTIST—TITLE	LABEL
Lipps, Inc. —Funkytown	Casablanca
Queen —Another One Bites The Dust	Elektra
S.O.S. Band —Take Your Time (Do It Right)	Tabu

NECROLOGY
Jan. 1, 1976–Dec. 31, 1980

ABAS, Nathan: Conductor. Jun 1, 1980 (83).

ABEL, Alan: Writer-Musician-Producer. Jan 1, 1980 (50).

ABOTT, Merriel: Choreographer-Director. Nov 6, 1977 (84).

ACKER, Jean: Silent screen star. Aug 16, 1978 (85).

ADA MAY (Ada May Weeks): Musicomedy star. Apr 25, 1978 (80).

ADAM, Kenneth: TV pioneer. Oct 18, 1978 (70).

ADAM, Ronald: Actor-Paywright. Mar 27, 1979 (82).

ADAMS, Claire: Silent screen actress. Sep 25, 1978.

ADAMSON, Harold: Lyricist. Aug 17, 1980 (73).

ADAMSON, Joy: Writer. Jan 3, 1980 (69).

ADDINSELL, Richard: Composer. Nov 15, 1977 (73).

ADDISS, Justus: Director. Oct 26, 1979 (62).

ADLER, Jay: Actor. Sep 23, 1978 (82).

ADLER, Kurt: Conductor. Sep 21, 1977 (70).

AGADATI, Itchak: Executive-Documentary Producer. Oct 9, 1980 (77).

AGER, Milton: Songwriter. Apr 6, 1979 (86).

AHN, Philip: Actor. Feb 28, 1978 (72).

ALDEN, Hortense: Actress. Apr 2, 1978 (76).

ALEXANDER, C K: Actor-Director. Sep 2, 1980 (57).

ALLBRITTON, Louise: Actress. Feb 16, 1979 (59).

ALLEN, Charme: Actress. Oct 4, 1980 (89).

ALLEN, Dea: Singer-Entertainer. Jul 14, 1980 (63).

ALLWYN, Astrid: Actress. Mar 31, 1978 (67).

ALSOP, Mary O'Hara: Writer. Oct 15, 1980 (94).

ALSWANG, Ralph: Stage Designer. Feb 15, 1979 (62).

ALTER, Louis. Composer. Nov 5, 1980 (78).

ALVIN, Joseph: Publicist. Oct 9, 1980 (72).

AMATI, Giovanni: Exhibitor. Jun 30, 1980 (74).

AMES, Vic: Singer. Jan 23, 1978 (51).

AMMON, Alicia: Comedienne. Feb 24, 1980 (94).

ANDERSON, Bruce: Actor-Singer. Sep 14, 1979 (73).

ANDERSON, Eddie (Rochester): Actor. Feb 28, 1977 (71).

ANDERSON, Warner: Actor. Aug 26, 1976 (65).

ANDREWS, Robert Hardy: Writer. Nov 11, 1976 (73).

ANSON, Jay: Writer. Mar 12, 1980 (58).

ARDREY, Robert: Writer. Jan 14, 1980 (71).

ARENA, Maurizio: Actor. Nov 21, 1979 (46).

ARENA, Rodolfo: Actor. Aug 31, 1980 (69).

ARKIN, David: Composer. Oct 8, 1980 (73).

ARLEN, Richard: Actor. Mar 28, 1976 (75).

ARMADORI, Luis Cesar: Playwright-Director. Jun, 1977 (74).

ARMITAGE, Buford: Actor. Nov 3, 1978 (80).

ARONSON, Boris: Designer. Nov 16, 1980 (81).

ARVAN, Jan: Actor. May 24, 1979 (66).

ARZNER, Dorothy: Director. Oct 1, 1979 (82).

ASTIE, Odee (BiBi O'Deal): Stunt Woman. Nov 14, 1980 (40).

ASTOR, Gertrude: Silent screen star. Nov 9, 1977 (90).

ATLASS, Ralph L: Radio Pioneer. Jun 20, 1979 (76).

AUDRY, Jacqueline: Director. Jun 30, 1977 (69).

AUGUST, Jan: Pianist. Jan 17, 1976 (71).

AURTHUR, Robert Alan: Writer-Producer. Nov 20, 1978 (56).

AVERY, Tex: Animator. Aug 26, 1980 (71).

AYLMER, Sir Felix: Actor. Sep 2, 1979 (80).

AYRES, Bert: Producer. Mar 14, 1978 (79).

BABB, Kroger: Producer. Jan 28, 1980 (73).

BACHAUER, Gina: Pianist. Aug 22, 1976 (63).

BADDELEY, Angela: Actress. Feb 22, 1976 (71).

BAER, Abel: Songwriter. Oct 5, 1976 (83).

BAGNALL, George L: Executive. Mar 13, 1978 (81).

BAILEY, Bill: Dancer. Dec 12, 1978 (66).

BAILEY, Edwin: Producer. Jul 17, 1977 (50s).

BAIN, Bessie: Actress. Dec 6, 1978 (76).

BAIRD, John: Director. Apr 5, 1978.

BAKER, Mary: Agent. Jul 29, 1976 (67).

BAKER, Sir Stanley: Actor. Jun 28, 1976 (49).

BALCON, Sir Michael: Producer. Oct 16, 1977 (81).

BALDWIN, Faith: Writer. Mar 18, 1978 (84).

BALLARD, Florence: Singer. Feb 22, 1976 (32).

BALLIN, Robert Walden: Producer. Mar 21, 1977 (73).

BALLINGER, Bill S: Writer-Producer. Mar 23, 1980 (68).

BANNERMAN, Margaret: Actress. Apr 25, 1976 (79).

BARBOSA, Haroldo: Composer-Humorist. Sep 1979 (64).

BARNETT, Vince: Comedian. Aug 10, 1977 (75).

BARR, Leonard: Comic. Oct 28, 1980 (77).

BARRES, Madeleine: Actress. Apr 10, 1978 (70).

BARRETT, Edith: Actress. Feb 22, 1977 (64).

BARRETT, Sheila: Actress-Singer. Aug 10, 1980 (71).

BARRIE, Wendy: Actress. Feb 2, 1978 (65).

BARRINGER, Ned (Spencer Edward Barringer): Silent film Actor-Writer. Feb 13, 1976 (87).

BARRY, Donald (Red): Actor. Jul 17, 1980 (69).

BARRY, John: Production Designer. May 31, 1979 (43).

BARRY, Merna: Singer. Oct 31, 1976 (51).

BARTLETT, Sy: Producer-Writer. May 29, 1978 (78).

BARTON, Elsie: Former Vaudevillian. Oct 29, 1980 (82).

BARTON, Lucy: Costume Designer. May 14, 1979 (87).

BASSE, Eli: Writer. Dec 20, 1979 (74).

BATES, Albert S: Film editor. Apr 23, 1976 (68).

BATES, Bill: Composer-Producer. Nov 21, 1978.

BATES, Michael: Actor. Jan 11, 1978 (57).

BATSON, George D: Playwright. Jul 25, 1977 (61).

BAUKHAGE, Hilmar R: Commentator. Feb 1, 1976 (87).

BAUMER, Marie: Playwright. Jul 31, 1977 (76).

BAVA, Mario: Director. Apr 27, 1980 (66).

BAXTER, Alan: Actor. May 8, 1976 (67).

BAYES, Sarah Carter: Singer. Jan 8, 1979 (80).

BEADLE, Sir Gerald C: Broadcast pioneer. Nov 6, 1976 (77).

BEARUP, Thomas W: Broadcast pioneer. Jun 16, 1980 (82).

BEASLEY, Irene: Singer-Writer-Producer. Jan 7, 1980 (76).

BEATON, Sir Cecil: Designer. Jan 18, 1980 (76).

BECKETT, Adam: Producer. Feb 26, 1979 (29).

BECKLEY, Tony: Actor. Apr 19, 1980 (mid 40s).

BELASCO, Arthur: Actor. Nov 8, 1979 (81).

BELASCO, William: Producer. Feb 26, 1976 (41).

BELLAH, James Warner: Writer. Sep 22, 1976 (77).

BEN-AMI, Jacob: Actor. Jul 2, 1977 (86).

BEN-YOSSEF, Avraham: Actor. Dec 1, 1980 (73).

BENHAM, Earl: Singer. Mar 21, 1976 (89).

BENJAMIIN, Robert S: Executive. Oct 22, 1979 (70).

BENNETT, Cyril: Producer. Nov 7, 1976 (48).

BENNETT, Litka K: Vaudevillian-Actress. Nov 15, 1979 (71).

BENNETT, Vivienne: Actress. Nov 11, 1978 (73).

BERGEN, Edgar: Ventriloquist. Sep 30, 1978 (75).

BERKELEY, Busby: Director. Mar 14, 1976 (80).

BERMAN, Henry: Producer. Jun 12, 1979 (65).

BERNARD, Raymond: Director. Dec, 1977 (86).

BERNHARDT, Russ: Actor. Oct 9, 1978 (53).

BETZ, Carl: Actor. Jan 18, 1978 (56).

BIBERMAN, Abner: Actor-Director. Jun 20, 1977 (69).

BIGARD, Barney: Jazz musician. Jun 27, 1980 (74).

BIGELOW, Joe: Writer. Feb 20, 1976 (66).

BIGGS, E Power: Organist. Mar 1, 1977 (70).

BILLER, Hal: Writer. Dec 7, 1979 (60).

BILLS, Elmer E Sr: Exhibitor. May 12, 1977 (70).

BINYON, Claude: Writer-Director. Feb 14, 1978 (72).

BIOW, Milton: Advertising exec and Broadcast pioneer. Feb 1, 1976 (83).

BIRDWELL, Russell: Publicist-Director. Dec 15, 1977 (74).

BISSELL, Richard: Playwright. May 4, 1977 (63).

BIXBY, Carl: Writer. Jun 29, 1978 (83).

BIXIO, Cesare Andrea: Lyricist-Composer. Mar 5, 1978 (82).

BLAIR, David: Dancer-Choreographer. Apr 1, 1976 (43).

BLAKE, Howard: Writer-Producer. Aug 25, 1979 (75).

BLONDELL, Joan: Actress. Dec 25, 1979 (70).

BLOOMGARDEN, Kermit: Producer. Sep 20, 1976 (73).

BLUE, James: Documentary maker. Jun 14, 1980 (49).

BOGERT, Vin: Writer. Nov 28, 1978 (64).

BOHNSACK, Alan M: Exhibitor. Jul 4, 1979 (53).

BOLES, Jim: Actor. May 26, 1977 (63).

BOLTON, Guy: Playwright. Sep 5, 1979 (96).

BOND, Johnny: Singer-Actor. Jun 12, 1978 (62).

BONELLI, Richard: Operatic baritone. Jun 7, 1980 (91).

BONHAM, John: Led Zeppelin Drummer. Sep 25, 1980 (33).

BONSTELLE, Helen: Actress. Jul 26, 1979 (61).

BOREN, Charles: Executive. Sep 10, 1978 (71).

BOSWELL, Connee: Singer. Oct 10, 1976 (68).

BOULANGER, Nadia: Teacher of Composition. Oct 22, 1979 (92).

BOURBON, Diana: Producer-Actress. Mar 19, 1978 (78).

BOURNEUF, Philip: Actor. Mar 23, 1979 (71).

BOWER, Roger: Broadcaster. May 17, 1979 (75).

BOWMAN, Lee: Actor. Dec 25, 1979 (64).

BOYD, Stephen: Actor. Jun 2, 1977 (48).

BOYER, Charles: Actor. Aug 26, 1978 (78).

BOYLE, Edward G: Set decorator. Feb 17, 1977.

BOZZACCO, Enrico: Musician. Jan 30, 1979 (91).

BRACHO, Julio: Director. Apr 26, 1978 (69).

BRACKETT, Leigh: Writer. Mar 18, 1978 (60).

BRAILOWSKY, Alexander: Concert pianist. Apr 25, 1976 (80).

BRANDWYNNE, Nat: Bandleader. Mar, 1978 (67).

BRAY, John R: Pioneer animation producer. Oct 10, 1978 (81).

BRECHER, Leo: Exhibitor. Feb 5, 1980 (90).

BREL, Jacques: Songwriter. Oct 9, 1978 (49).

BRENT, Earl K: Songwriter-Producer. Jul 8, 1977 (63).

BRENT, George: Actor. May 26, 1979 (75).

BRENT, Romney: Actor. Sep 24, 1976 (74).

BRESLER, Jerry: Producer. Aug 23, 1977 (65).

BRICE, Eugene: Opera Singer-Teacher. Oct 31, 1980 (67).

BRILL, Leighton: Producer. Jul 26, 1977 (84).

BRILL, Richard: Producer. Sep 8, 1979 (58).

BRITT, Jim: Sportscaster. Dec 31, 1980 (70).

BRITTEN, Benjamin: Composer. Dec 4, 1976 (63).

BRITTON, Barbara: Actress. Jan 16, 1980 (59).

BRODER, Jane: Agent. Jun 16, 1977 (83).

BROGAN, Harry: Actor. May 20, 1977 (72).

BROOKS, Geraldine: Actress. Jun 19, 1977 (52).

BROPHY, Thomas J: Producer-Actor. Feb 22, 1979.

BROWN, George Frame: Actor. Nov 19, 1979 (83).

BROWN, Hiram S Jr: Producer-Advertising Executive. Jul 17, 1979 (70).

BROWN, Joe David Sr: Writer. Apr 22, 1976 (60).

BROWN, Sydney: Actor. Mar 1, 1979 (80).

BROWN, Zara Cully: Actress. Feb 28, 1978 (86).

BROWNE, E Martin: Actor-Director. Apr 27, 1980 (80).

BRUNTON, Dorothy: Musicomedy star. Jun 5, 1977.

BRYANT, Dorothy: Chorus Equity Executive. Jun 24, 1979 (83).

BRYANT, Marie: Choreographer. May 23, 1978 (59).

BRYLAWSKI, A Julian: Executive. May 15, 1977 (94).

BUCHANAN, Edgar: Actor. Apr 4, 1979 (76).

BUCKNER, Milt: Jazz pianist. Jul 27, 1977 (62).

BUCKWHEAT (Billy Thomas): Actor. Oct 10, 1980 (49).

BUFFUM, Ray: Producer-Writer. Dec 13, 1980 (76).

BUNETTA, Frank: Director. Mar 30, 1978 (62).

BUNN, Alden (Tarheel Slim): Blues singer. Aug 21, 1977 (52).

BURKE, Hilda (Hilda Korins): Operatic soprano. Apr 6, 1978 (73).

BURKE, Kathleen: Actress. Apr 9, 1980 (66).

BURKHARD, Paul: Composer. Sep 6, 1977 (65).

BURNETTE, Dorsey: C&W Singer-Songwriter. Aug 19, 1979 (46).

BURR, Donald: Actor-Singer-Director. Feb 27, 1979 (71).

BURTON, John W: Producer. Jun 1, 1978 (71).

BURTON, Martin: Actor. Aug 4, 1976 (71).

BURWELL, Cliff: Songwriter. Oct 10, 1976 (78).

BUSCH, Ernst: Actor-Balladeer. Jun 8, 1980 (80).

BUSCH, Lou (Joe "Fingers" Carr): Musician. Sep 19, 1979 (69).

BUTCHER, Blayne R: Radio Producer. Oct 13, 1980 (77).

BUTLER, David: Director. Jun 21, 1979 (84).

BUTTERWORTH, Peter: Actor. Jan 16, 1979 (59).

BYRAM, John: Producer. Nov 20, 1977 (76).

BYRD, Henry Roeland (Prof Longhair): Composer-Pianist. Jan 30, 1980 (61).

BYRNE, Grace Nelson: Singer. Nov 15, 1978 (86).

CABOT, Sebastian: Actor. Aug 23, 1977 (59).

CAIN, James M: Writer. Oct 27, 1977 (85).

CAIROLI, Charlie: Circus clown. Feb 17, 1980 (70).

CALVERT, Eddie: Musician. Aug 7, 1978 (56).

CAMBRIDGE, Godfrey: Comedian-Actor. Nov 29, 1976 (43).

CAMPBELL, Flora: Actress. Nov 6, 1978 (67).

CANDULI, Joe: Bandleader. Feb 15, 1977 (75).

CANTWELL, Alexander: Producer-Writer. Apr 18, 1979 (57).

CAPEHART, Homer E: Executive. Sep 3, 1979 (82).

CAPLAN, Rupert: Writer-Director. Mar 24, 1979 (82).

CAPURRO, Arturo (Arthur Kent): Metropolitan Opera Singer. Dec 3, 1980 (74).

CARLINI, Paolo: Actor. Nov 1979 (53).

CARLSON, Richard: Actor. Nov 25, 1977 (65).

CARPENTER, Claude E: Set Decorator. Feb 18, 1976 (71).

CARR, Joe "Fingers" (Lou Busch): Musician. Sep 19, 1979 (69).

CARR, John Dickson: Writer. Feb 27, 1977 (70).

CARRE, Ben: Art director. May 28, 1978 (95).

CARROLL, Dee: Actress. Apr 28, 1980 (54).

CARROLL, John: Actor. Apr 24, 1979 (71).

CARSON, Robert: Actor. Jun 2, 1979 (69).

CARTER, Maybelle (Mother): Singer. Oct 23, 1978 (60).

CARTER, Richard: Producer. Apr 9, 1978 (58).

CARTOLA (Angenor de Oliveira): Composer. Nov 30, 1980 (72).

CASE, Nelson: Pioneer Announcer. Mar 24, 1976 (66).

CASEY, Rosemary: Playwright. Mar 22, 1976 (70).

CASSIDY, Jack: Actor. Dec 12, 1976 (49).

CASTLE, William: Producer. May 31, 1977 (63).

CASTOLDI, Alex J: Exhibition Exec. Sep 10, 1980.

CAZALE, John: Actor. Mar 12, 1978 (42).

CEBALLOS, Larry: Dance director. Sep 12, 1978 (90).

CECILIA (Eva Sobrido): Singer. Aug 2, 1976 (26)

CERF, Kurt: Actor. Oct 27, 1979 (69).

CHALFEN, Morris: Impresario. Nov 4, 1979 (72).

CHAMBERLAIN, Gifford: Executive. Jul 20, 1976 (73).

CHAMPION, Gower: Director-Choreographer. Aug 25, 1980 (60).

CHANDLER, Joan: Actress. May 11, 1979 (55).

CHAPLIN, Charlie: Actor-Writer-Producer-Director- Composer. Dec 25, 1977 (88).

CHARISSE, Pierre: Dancer. Sep 18, 1978 (69).

CHARLES, Lewis: Actor. Nov 9, 1979 (63).

CHASE, Ilka: Actress-Writer. Feb 15, 1978 (72).

CHAVANCE, Louis: Writer. Sep 21, 1979 (72).

CHAVEZ, Carlos: Composer. Aug 2, 1978 (79).

CHERNIAVSKY, Alex: Impresario. Nov 8, 1978 (82).

CHERRY, Ralph: Musician. Jan 1, 1979 (73).

CHRISTIE, Agatha: Writer. Jan 12, 1976 (85).

CHUITO el de BAYAMON (Jesus Sanchez Erazo): Singer. Jan 26, 1979 (78).

CHURCH, Arthur: Broadcast pioneer. Sep 22, 1978 (82).

CIERKES, Vincent (Dantini the Magnificent): Magician. Mar 14, 1979 (73).

CLARKE, Jackie: Comedian. Jul 1, 1979 (51).

CLAYTON, Bob: Actor-Announcer. Nov 1, 1979 (57).

CLOONEY, Betty: Singer. Aug 5, 1976 (45).

CLOUZOT, Henri-Georges: Director. Jan 12, 1977 (69).

CLURMAN, Harold: Director-Producer-Critic. Sep 9, 1980 (78).

COBB, Lee J: Actor. Feb 11, 1976 (64).

COCHRANE, Percival: Writer. Sep 29, 1980 (73).

COE, Fred: Producer-Director. Apr 29, 1979 (64).

COGHILL, Nevill: Producer. Nov 8, 1980 (81).

COHEN, Emanuel: Executive. Sep 9, 1977 (85).

COHEN, Maury: Writer-Producer. May 15, 1979 (65).

COLIZZI, Giuseppe: Director. Aug 23, 1978 (53).

COLLIER, John: Writer. Apr 6, 1980 (78).

COLLINS, Hal: Writer-Inventor of Off-Line Videotape Editing. Nov 7, 1980 (60).

COLLINS, Jerry (Jerry Joseph Cohen): Comedian. Jan 26, 1976 (50).

COLLINSON, Peter: Director. Dec 16, 1980 (44).

COLT, Ethel Barrymore: Singer-Actress. May 22, 1977 (65).

COMBS, George Hamilton Jr: Commentator. Nov 29, 1977 (78).

COMPTON, Fay: Actress. Dec 12, 1978 (84).

CONNELLY, Marc: Playwright. Dec 21, 1980 (90).

CONSTANDUROS, Denis: Writer. Oct 23, 1978 (68).

COOPER, Maudie Prickett: Actress. Apr 14, 1976 (61).

COOPER, Wyatt E: Writer. Jan 5, 1978 (50).

COQUATRIX, Bruno: Impresario-Songwriter. Apr 1, 1979.

CORBETT, Margaret: Vaudevillian. May 12, 1979 (74).

CORCORAN, Corky (Gene Patrick Corcoran): Musician. Oct 3, 1979 (55).

CORRIGAN, Ray: Actor. Aug 10, 1976 (73).

CORTEZ, Ricardo: Actor. Apr 28, 1977 (77).

CORWIN, Sherrill C: Exhibitor. May 8, 1980 (71).

CORY, George: Lyricist. Apr 11, 1978 (55).

COSTELLO, Dolores: Silent Screen Star. Mar 1, 1979 (73).

COTSWORTH, Staats: Actor. Apr 9, 1979 (71).

COUGHLIN, Father Charles E: Radio Personality. Oct 27, 1979 (88).

COUGHLIN, Kevin: Actor. Jan 19, 1976 (30).

COURTENEIDGE, Cicely: Actress. Apr 28, 1980 (87).

COURTNEY, Alan: Broadcast personality. Sep 16, 1978 (65).

COUSTEAU, Philippe: Cinematographer. Jun 28, 1979 (38).

COWAN, Louis G: Producer-Network exec. Nov 18, 1976 (67).

CRABTREE, Paul: Writer-Producer-Director. Mar, 1979 (60).

CRAIG, Harry: Writer. Oct 23, 1978 (57).

CRANE, Bob: Actor. Jun 29, 1978 (49).

CRAWFORD, Joan: Actress. May 10, 1977 (69).

CREE, Sam: Playwright. Oct 25, 1980 (52).

CRESWELL, John: Dancer. Oct 13, 1979 (42).

CRIDER, Dorothy Ellen: Actress. Jul 3, 1980 (62).

CRISTIANA, Emma: Aerialist. Jan 6, 1979 (92).

CROFOOT, Alan: Operatic Tenor. Mar 5, 1979 (49).

CROMWELL, John: Director. Sep 26, 1979 (91).

CROMWELL, John: Actor-Playwright. Sep 1, 1979 (65).

CROSBY, Bing (Harry Lillis Crosby): Singer-Actor. Oct 14, 1977 (76).

CROWE, Eileen (Eileen Judge): Actress. May 8, 1978 (79).

CUENCA, Carlos Fernandez: Director. May, 1979 (75).

CURRAN, Sir Charles: Broadcast executive. Jan 9, 1980 (58).

CURZON, George: Actor. May 10, 1976 (77).

CUSHMAN, Nancy: Actress. Sep 26, 1979. (65).

DAILEY, Dan: Dancer-Actor. Oct 16, 1978 (62).

DALLAMANO, Massimo: Director. Nov, 1976 (59).

DALTON, Emmet: Producer. Mar 4, 1978 (80).

DALY, James: Actor. Jul 4, 1978 (59).

DALY, Patricia Joiner: Actress-AFTRA executive. Oct 30, 1978 (49).

DAMEREL, Myrtle: Actress. Sep 18, 1978 (90).

DAN, Zhao: Actor-Director. Oct 10, 1980 (66).

DANCIGERS, Oscar: Producer. Feb 27, 1976 (74).

DANTINI THE MAGNIFICENT (Vincent Cierkes): Magician. Mar 14, 1979 (73).

DAQUIN, Louis: Director. Oct 2, 1980 (72).

DARRO, Frankie: Actor. Dec 25, 1976 (59).

DARVAS, Nicholas: Dancer. Jun 3, 1977 (53).

DASSIN, Joe: Singer. Aug 21, 1980 (42).

DAUPHIN, Claude: Actor. Nov 16, 1978 (75).

DAVENPORT, Doris: Actress. Jun 18, 1980 (63).

DAVES, Delmer: Producer-Director. Aug 17, 1977 (73).

DAVID, Thayer: Actor. Jul 17, 1978 (51).

DAVIES, Rupert: Actor. Nov 22, 1976 (59).

DAVIS, Benny: Songwriter-Vaudevillian. Dec 20, 1979 (84).

DAVIS, Hal C: AFM President. Jan 11, 1978 (63).

DAVIS, Meyer: Orchestra leader. Apr 5, 1976 (83).

DAVIS, Roger: Actor. Mar 3, 1980 (96).

DAWN, Gloria: Musicomedy star. Apr 2, 1978 (49).

DAWSON, Basil: Writer. Apr 1979 (65).

DAY, Josette: Actress. Jun 29, 1978 (63).

DAYKARHANOVA, Tamara: Actress-Coach. Aug 2, 1980 (91).

de ABREU, Gilda: Singer-Actress. Jun 1979 (74).

DEAN, Basil: Actor-Writer-Producer. Apr 22, 1978 (89).

DEASE, John: Actor. Feb 1, 1979 (72).

DeCICCO, Pasquale (Pat): Agent-Producer. Oct 24, 1978 (68).

DeFILIPPO, Peppino: Actor-Playwright-Director. Jan 26, 1980 (76).

DeHAVEN, Carter: Actor. Jul 20, 1977 (90).

DeHAVEN, Carter Jr: Producer. Mar 1, 1979 (68).

DEHN, Paul: Writer. Sep 30, 1976 (63).

DELANNOY, Monique: TV Personality. Apr 25, 1979 (42).

DeLEO, Don: Actor. Aug 14, 1979 (74).

DELL, Peggy (Peg Tisdall): Singer-Pianist. Apr 30, 1979 (74).

DELLER, Alfred: Singer. Jul 16, 1979 (67).

DELTGEN, Rene: Actor. Jan 28, 1979 (70).

del VILLAR, Francisco: Producer-Director. Sep 1, 1978 (58).

DELYSIA, Alice: Actress-Singer. Feb 9, 1979 (90).

DeMARNEY, Derrick: Actor-Producer-Director. Feb 18, 1978 (71).

deMORAES, Vinicius: Lyricist. Jul 9, 1980.

DENNIS, Patrick (Edward Tanner 3d): Writer. Nov 6, 1976 (55).

de OLIVEIRA, Angenor (Cartola): Composer. Nov 30, 1980 (72).

de PHILIPPE, Edis: Opera singer. Jul 16, 1978 (66).

DePIRRO, Nicola: Executive. Jul 3, 1979 (81).

DERMAN, Lou: Writer. Feb 15, 1976 (61).

DeROCHEMONT, Louis: Producer. Dec 23, 1978 (79).

DERODE, Julian: Producer. May 11, 1979 (65).

DeSIMONE, Robert: Musician. Jul 6, 1977 (66).

DESMOND, Paul: Musician. May 30, 1977 (52).

DESSAU, Paul: Composer. Jun 28, 1979 (84).

DEUTSCH, Adolph: Composer. Jan 1, 1980 (82).

DEVINE, Andy: Actor. Feb 18, 1977 (70).

DEVORE, Dorothy: Comedienne. Sep 10, 1976 (77).

DeWITT, George: TV Personality. Jul 14, 1979 (56).

DIAMOND, David: Producer. Nov 9, 1979 (79).

DIXON, Dean: Conductor. Nov 3, 1976 (61).

DOHERTY, Marie: Actress-Singer. Mar 22, 1977 (83).

DONALD, Peter: Actor. Apr 20, 1979 (60).

DONATI, Ermanno: Production Executive. Jul 9, 1979 (59).

DONOVAN, Mary Thompson: Musicomedy star. Nov 18, 1978 (88).

DORAN, D A: Executive. Mar 5, 1978 (80).

DORZIAT, Gabrielle: Actress. Nov 30, 1979 (99).

DOUGLAS, Helen Gahagan: Actress. Jun 28, 1980 (79).

DOWLING, Eddie (Joseph Nelson Goucher): Actor-Writer-Director-Producer. Feb 18, 1976 (81).

DOWNS, Bill: Network correspondent. May 3, 1978 (63).

DRAGONETTE, Jessica: Soprano. Mar 18, 1980 (71).

DREBEN, Stan: Writer. Feb 16, 1980 (61).

DREYER, Marien: Playwright. Jan 16, 1980 (71).

DRUTMAN, Irving: Writer-Songwriter. Sep 20, 1978 (68).

DUBINSKY, H William: Exhibitor. Sep 23, 1980 (76).

DUBOV, Paul: Writer-Producer. Sep 20, 1979.

DUFFIELD, Brainerd: Writer. Apr 5, 1979 (62).

DUFFY, Albert J: Writer. Sep 15, 1976 (73).

DUNCAN, Ted: Arranger. Mar 9, 1976 (74).

DUNLAP, Florence: Actress. May 3, 1977 (94).

DUNN, Liam: Actor. Apr 11, 1976 (59).

DUPRAY, Gaston: Actor. Dec 12, 1976 (91).

DURANTE, Jimmy: Performer. Jan 28, 1980 (86).

DVORAK, Ann: Actress. Dec 10, 1979 (67).

DYER, Bonar: Executive. Oct 3, 1979 (74).

DZIGAN, Shimon: Comic. Apr 14, 1980 (74).

EBERLE, Ray: Band Singer. Aug 25, 1979 (60).

EBERT, Carl: Director. May 14, 1980 (93).

EDELMAN, Louis F: Producer. Jan 6, 1976 (75).

EDMONSON, Edward E (Professor Backwards): Vaudevillian. Jan 29, 1976 (65).

EDMONSON, William: Actor. May 28, 1979 (76).

EDOUART, Farciot: Cinematographer. Mar 17, 1980 (85).

EDWARDS, Leo: Songwriter. Jul 12, 1978 (92).

EDWARDS, Webley: Pioneer broadcaster. Oct 5, 1977 (71).

EGLEVSKY, Andre: Dancer. Dec 4, 1977 (60).

EILERS, Sally: Actress. Jan 5, 1978 (69).

ELIOT, Jean: Dancer. Apr 20, 1978 (45).

ELLINGTON, Richard: Writer. Dec 5, 1980 (66).

ELLIS, Don: Musician-Composer. Dec 17, 1978 (44).

ELLSWORTH, Whitney: Producer. Sep 7, 1980 (71).

EMERLING, Ernest: Executive. May 18, 1979 (74).

EMNEY, Fred: Comedian. Dec 25, 1980 (80).

ENRIGHT, Josephine: Actress. Feb 24, 1976 (72).

ERAZO, Jesus Sanchez (Chuito el de Bayamon): Singer. Jan 26, 1979 (78).

ERNST, Morris L: Attorney-Writer. May 21, 1976 (87).

ESCUDERO, Vicente: Flamenco Dancer. Dec 4, 1980 (91).

ESTABROOK, Howard: Writer-Director. Jul 16, 1978 (94).

ESTRADA, Noel: Composer. Dec 1, 1979 (62).

ETTING, Ruth: Actress-Singer. Sep 24, 1978 (81).

EUARD, Opal: Actress. May 13, 1980 (80s).

EUBANKS, Gene (Cody): Actor-Producer. Jul 10, 1976 (81).

EUSTREL, Anthony: Actor. Jul 2, 1979 (76).

EVANS, Bill: Musician. Sep 15, 1980 (51).

EVANS, Dame Edith: Actress. Oct 14, 1976 (88).

EVANS, Tolchard: Songwriter. Mar 12, 1978 (77).

EVELYN, Clara: Musicomedy star. May 22, 1980 (99).

FABBRI, Diego: Playwright. Aug 1980 (69).

FAIRE, Virginia Brown: Silent screen star. Jun 30, 1980 (75).

FAIRMAN, Derek: Actor. May 19, 1979 (73).

FAITH, Percy: Conductor. Feb 9, 1976 (67).

FALLIS, Barbara: Dancer. Sep 5, 1980 (56).

FANCEY, Edwin J: Producer-Distributor. Oct 28, 1980 (79).

FARINA (Alan Hoskins): Actor. Jul 26, 1980 (59).

FARRAND, Jan: Actress. Nov 4, 1980 (52).

FAYE, Herbie: Comedian. Jun 28, 1980 (81).

FEGTE, Ernst: Art director. Dec 15, 1976 (76).

FENTON, Leslie C: Actor-Director-Producer. Mar 25, 1978 (76).

FERGUSON, Helen: Silent film actress-Publicist. Mar 14, 1977 (76).

FERNANDEZ, Royes: Dancer. Mar 3, 1980 (50).

FERREIRA, Procopio: Actor-Playwright. Jun 18, 1979 (80).

FEUERRING, Jacob: Concert Pianist. Sep 30, 1979 (67).

FIEDLER, Arthur: Conductor. Jul 10, 1979 (83).

FIELDER, Frank: Actor-Manager. Dec 24, 1980 (96).

FIELDING, Jerry: Composer-Conductor. Feb 17, 1980 (57).

FIELDS, Dame Gracie: Performer. Sep 27, 1979 (81).

FIELDS, Totie: Comedienne. Aug 2, 1978 (48).

FINCH, Peter: Actor. Jan 14, 1977 (60).

FINKE, Jack: Writer. Sep 1, 1979 (61).

FINKLEHOFFE, Fred F: Playwright-Producer. Oct 5, 1977 (67).

FINN, Adelaide: Actress. Jan 20, 1978 (84).

FINOS, Philopoemen: Producer. Jan 26, 1977 (69).

FINSTON, Nathaniel: Conductor. Dec 19, 1979 (89).

FISHER, Steve: Writer. Mar 27, 1980 (67).

FISHER, Terence: Director. Jun 18, 1980 (76).

FITZGERALD, Walter: Actor. Dec 20, 1976 (80).

FITZPATRICK, James: Producer. Jun 12, 1980 (86).

FLAHERTY, George: IATSE Executive. May 25, 1979 (84).

FLATT, Lester: Singer-Guitarist. May 11, 1979 (64).

FLAVIN, James: Actor. Apr 23, 1976 (69).

FLEISCHER, Dave: Animation Pioneer. Jun 25, 1979 (84).

FLEISCHMAN, Theo: Belgian Radio Pioneer. Feb 27, 1979 (86).

FLICKENSCHILD, Elisabeth: Actress. Oct, 1977 (72).

FLOREY, Robert: Director. May 16, 1979 (78).

FLYNN, Bernard F: Producer. Jul 1, 1980 (60).

FODOR, Andre: Producer. August, 1978.

FOGLE, George L: Producer-Director. Sep 29, 1976 (76).

FONTAINE, Frank: Comic. Aug 4, 1978 (58).

FORAN, Dick: Actor. Aug 10, 1979 (69).

FORD, Cecil: Producer. Mar 27, 1980 (69).

FORD, Mary: Singer. Sep 30, 1977 (53).

FORMAN, Celia Adler: Actress. Jan 31, 1979 (89).

FORST, Willi: Actor-Writer-Director-Producer. Aug 12, 1980 (77).

FOSTER, George: Writer-Producer. Aug 19, 1980 (59).

FOSTER, Norman: Actor-Director. Jul 7, 1976 (72).

FOSTER, Sidney: Concert pianist. Feb 7, 1977 (59).

FOX, Sidney S: Broadcast pioneer. Mar 3, 1980 (91).

FOX, Virgil Keen: Organist. Oct 25, 1980 (68).

FOY, Bryan: Producer. Apr 20, 1977 (82).

FRANCEN, Victor: Actor. Nov, 1977 (88).

FRANCIS, Eve: Actress. Dec 6, 1980 (84).

FRANK, Allan: Actor. Aug 9, 1979 (64).

FRANK, Benno D: Director. Mar, 1980 (72).

FRANK, Fredric M: Writer. May 9, 1977 (65).

FRANKENFELD, Peter: TV Personality. Jan 3, 1979 (65).

FRANKLIN, Alberta (Levy): Silent film actress. Mar 14, 1976 (79).

FRANKLIN, Paul: Writer. May 15, 1980 (80).

FRANKS, Ollie: Comedienne. Jan 29, 1976 (56).

FREEDMAN, Bill: Writer. Jun 26, 1977 (70).

FRENCH, Hugh: Producer. Nov 2, 1976 (66).

FRICK (Hans Mauch): Comedy Skater. Jun 5, 1979 (60).

FRIEDKIN, David: Writer-Director. Oct 15, 1976 (64).

FRIEDMAN, Joel: Executive. Nov 8, 1977 (52).

FRIEDMAN, Leopold (Lep): Executive. Dec 18, 1978 (91).

FRIEND, Ted: Writer-Broadcaster. Feb 26, 1978 (78).

FRITZELL, Jim: Writer. Mar 16, 1979 (58).

FROESCHEL, George: Writer. Nov 22, 1979 (88).

FROMAN, Jane: Singer. Apr 22, 1980 (72).

FROMKESS, Leon: Producer. Mar 11, 1977 (69).

FRUEH, Kurt: Director. Mar 24, 1979 (64).

FUETER, Heinrich: Producer. Oct 14, 1979 (68).

FULLER, Frances: Actress. Dec 18, 1980 (73).

FUNK, Larry: Bandleader. Jul 15, 1977 (71).

FUNT, Julian: Writer. Apr 8, 1980 (73).

GABIN, Jean: Actor. Nov 15, 1976 (72).

GABRIELSON, Frank W: Writer. Jan 24, 1980 (69).

GALE, Alan: Comedian. May 26, 1980 (72).

GALE, Tim: Manager. Apr 20, 1976 (70).

GALLICO, Paul: Writer. Jul 16, 1976 (78).

GARBER, Jan: Bandleader. Oct 5, 1977 (82).

GARCIA, Sara: Actress. Nov 21, 1980 (85).

GARDINER, James W: Producer. Nov 6, 1976 (57).

GARDINER, Reginald: Actor. Jul 7, 1980 (77).

GARGAN, William: Actor. Feb 16, 1979 (73).

GARLAND, Edward (Montudie): Musician. Jan 22, 1980 (95).

GARMES, Lee: Cinematographer. Aug 31, 1978 (80).

GARNER, Erroll: Jazz pianist. Jan 2, 1977 (53).

GARNETT, Tay: Director. Oct 3, 1977 (83).

GARY, Romain: Writer. Nov 2, 1980 (66).

GATESON, Marjorie: Actress. Apr 17, 1977 (86).

GEAR, Luella: Comedienne. Apr 3, 1980 (80).

GEER, Will: Actor. Apr 22, 1978 (76).

GELLER, Bruce: Producer-Writer. May 21, 1978 (47).

GENN, Leo: Actor. Jan 26, 1978 (72).

GENSLER, Lewis: Songwriter. Jan 15, 1978 (81).

GENTRY, Stephen: Network executive. May 21, 1978 (37).

GERING, Marion: Director-Producer. Apr 19, 1977 (73).

GHIRINGHELLI, Antonio: Opera Executive. Jul, 1979 (76).

GILBERT, Jody: Actress. Feb 3, 1979.

GILBERT, Lou: Actor. Nov 6, 1978 (69).

GILBERT, Paul: Comedian. Feb 12, 1976 (58).

GILBERT, Ray: Composer. Mar 3, 1976 (63).

GILBERT, Willie: Writer. Dec 2, 1980 (64).

GILKEY, Stanley: Producer. Nov 3, 1979 (79).

GILLESPIE, A Arnold: SFX expert. May 3, 1978 (79).

GILLIS, Don: Composer. Jan 10, 1978 (65).

GINSBERG, Henry: Producer. Jun 10, 1979 (82).

GLUCKMAN, Leon: Actor-Producer-Director. Mar 7, 1978 (55).

GLUCKSMAN, Ernest D: Writer-Producer-Director. Jul 7, 1979 (77).

GODFREY, Freda: Actress. Sep 5, 1980 (91).

GOETZ, Ben: Executive. Aug 22, 1979 (88).

GOETZ, Harry M: Executive. Dec 19, 1978 (90).

GOFF, Norris: Actor. Jun 7, 1978 (72).

GOLDBECK, Willis: Director-Producer. Sep 17, 1979 (80).

GOLDBERG, Leonard J: Producer-Distributor. Apr 25, 1979 (33).

GOLDMAN, Richard Franko: Conductor. Jan 19, 1980 (69).

GOLDMARK, Dr Peter Carl: Engineer. Dec 7, 1977 (71).

GOLDSTEIN, Morey (Razz): Distribution executive. Jul 1, 1980 (77).

GOLDSTEIN, Shmulik: Comedian. Nov 23, 1978 (70).

GOLDWYN, Frances Howard: Actress. Jun 2, 1976 (73).

GOODLIFFE, Michael: Actor. Mar 22, 1976 (61).

GORDON, Gray: Orchestra leader. Jul 23, 1976 (72).

GORDON, Lou: Commentator. May 24, 1977 (60).

GORDON, Max: Producer. Nov 2, 1978 (86).

GORDON, Mildred: Writer. Feb 3, 1979 (73).

GOUREVITCH, Boris: Exhibitor. Jun 3, 1980 (83).

GRADE, Leslie: Agent. Oct 15, 1979 (63).

GRAHAM, Fred: Actor. Oct 10, 1979 (61).

GRANT, Arnold M: Executive. Nov 15, 1980 (72).

GRANT, Morton: Writer. Jul 25, 1980 (76).

GRAUER, Ben: Pioneer announcer. May 31, 1977 (68).

GRAVES, Ralph: Actor. Feb 18, 1977 (75).

GRAY, Billy: Comedian. Jan 4, 1978 (73).

GRAY, Jerry: Orchestra leader-Composer. Aug 10, 1976 (61).

GRAYSON, Mitchell: Producer-Director. Feb 8, 1979 (63).

GRECO, Dea Carroll: Singer. Oct 30, 1978 (53).

GREENBERGER, Leo: Exhibitor. Oct 22, 1979 (79).

GREENE, Angela: Actress. Feb 9, 1978 (55).

GREENE, Madeline: Singer. May 30, 1976 (55).

GREENE, Paul: Writer. Jan 1, 1977 (70).

GREENWOOD, Charlotte: Musicomedy star. Jan 18, 1978 (87).

GREGORY, Euphemia G: Lyric Soprano. Jan 15, 1979 (83).

GRENFELL, Joyce: Actress. Nov 30, 1979 (69).

GRETLER, Heinrich: Actor. Sep 30, 1977 (80).

GRIES, Tom: Writer-Director. Jan 3, 1977 (53).

GRIFFITH, Corinne: Silent Screen Star. Jul 13, 1979 (81).

GRIFFITH, Hugh: Actor. May 14, 1980 (67).

GRIGAITIS, Walter (Mother Gates): Composer. Nov 20, 1977 (65).

GROSS, Ben: Radio-TV Columnist. Aug 13, 1979 (87).

GUNTHER, Robert J: Animator. Jan 19, 1979 (62).

HACKETT, Bobby: Jazz musician. Jun 7, 1976 (61).

HACKETT, Jeanette: Vaudevillian. Aug 16, 1979 (81).

HAENSCHEN, Gus: Bandleader. Mar 27, 1980 (90).

HAGEN, Jean: Actress. Aug 29, 1977 (54).

HAKIM, Raymond: Producer. Aug 14, 1980 (70).

HALE, Lionel: Playwright. May 15, 1977 (67).

HALEY, Jack: Actor. Jun 6, 1979 (79).

HALFF, Alma Murphy: Actress. Dec 16, 1978 (89).

HALFI, Avraham: Actor. Jun 8, 1980 (76).

HALL, Arch: Producer-Writer. Apr 28, 1978 (69).

HALL, Bob Z: Critic-Publicist. Dec 13, 1980 (74).

HALL, Jon: Actor. Dec 13, 1979 (64).

HALLE, Cliff: Actor. Apr 3, 1976 (57).

HALLIDAY, Brett (Davis Dresser): Writer. Feb 4, 1977 (72).

HALOP, Billy: Actor. Nov 9, 1976 (56).

HALPRIN, Sol: Cinematographer. May 4, 1977 (75).

HAMILTON, Fred: Agent-former child actor. Sep 9, 1980 (65).

HAMMOND, Kay: Actress. May 4, 1980 (71).

HANIGHEN, Bernie: Songwriter. Oct 19, 1976 (68).

HANNA, Betty: Actress. Oct 5, 1976 (73).

HANNEMAN, Frederick G: Exhib-former child actor. Oct 3, 1980 (66).

HARBIN, Robert: Illusionist. Jan 12, 1978 (68).

HARDIN, Tim: Folk Singer-Songwriter. Dec 29, 1980 (40).

HARE, J Robertson: Actor. Jan 25, 1979 (87).

HARMON, Francis S: Executive. Apr 27, 1977 (82).

HARNLEY, Leslie: Music Director. Nov 11, 1980 (62).

HARPER, Ethel Ernestine: Singer-Actress. Mar 31, 1979 (75).

HARRINGTON, Kate: Actress. Nov 23, 1978 (75).

HARRIS, Jed: Producer-Director. Nov 15, 1979 (79).

HARRIS, Roy: Composer. Oct 1, 1979 (81).

HART, Winifred Westover: Silent screen actress. Mar 19, 1978 (78).

HARTFORD-DAVIS, Robert: Producer-Director. Jun 12, 1977 (54).

HASSALL, Imogen: Actress. Nov 16, 1980 (38).

HASSE, O E: Actor. Sep 12, 1978 (75).

HASTINGS, Sue: Puppeteer. Jun 30, 1977 (93).

HATHAWAY, Donny: Singer. Jan 13, 1979 (33).

HAWKS, Howard: Director. Dec 26, 1977 (81).

HAWLEY, William E: Actor. Aug 22, 1976 (66).

HAYES, Edgar: Bandleader. Jun 28, 1979 (77).

HAYES, Gertrude Jr: Actress. Dec 13, 1980 (78).

HAYES, Leslie W: Broadcast pioneer. Nov 1, 1976 (80).

HAYES, Margaret: Actress. Jan, 1977 (61).

HAYES, Roland: Concert tenor. Dec 25, 1976 (89).

HAYMES, Dick: Singer. Mar 28, 1980 (61).

HAYNES, Dick: Radio Personality. Nov 25, 1980 (69).

HAYWARD, Lillie: Writer. Jun 29, 1977 (86).

HAYWOOD, Billie: Singer-Comedienne. Jul 8, 1979 (75)

HEARN, Julia Knox: Actress. May 1, 1976 (92).

HEARNE, Richard (Mr Pastry): Dancer-Comedian. Aug 25, 1979 (70).

HEIDT, Charles P: Producer. Jan 24, 1977 (82).

HEIMS, Jo: Writer. Apr 27, 1978 (48).

HEINDORF, Ray: Composer-Conductor. Feb 3, 1980 (71).

HEISLER, Stuart R: Director. Aug 21, 1979 (82).

HENABERRY, Joseph E: Actor-Director. Feb 18, 1976 (88).

HENKE, Mel: Composer-Pianist. Mar 31, 1979 (63).

HENRY, Charlotte: Actress. Apr 11, 1980 (65).

HERRICK, Margaret: AMPAS Secretary. Jun 21, 1976 (73).

HEYNE, Joe: Songwriter. Jun, 1978 (73).

HIBLER, Winston: Producer. Aug 8, 1976 (65).

HILO HATTIE (Clara Nelson): Singer-Dancer. Dec 12, 1979 (78).

HILTON, Arthur David: Director. Oct 15, 1979 (82).

HITCHCOCK, Alfred: Director. Apr 29, 1980 (80).

HOCH, Winton C: Cinematographer. Mar 20, 1979 (73).

HODGE, Al: Actor. Mar 19, 1979 (66).

HOFFMAN, Bern: Actor. Dec 15, 1979 (66).

HOFFMAN, John Ivan: Director. Jan 6, 1980 (75).

HOGAN, Henry S: Vaudevillian. Apr 23, 1980 (108).

HOLLAND, Herbert L (Peanuts): Musician. Feb 7, 1979 (69).

HOLLANDER, Friedrich: Composer. Jan 18, 1976 (79).

HOLM, Wilton: Cinematographer-Engineer. Oct 18, 1979 (65).

HOLMAN, Russell: Executive. May 1, 1979 (85).

HOLME, Thea: Actress-Writer. Dec, 1980 (76).

HOLMES, Edward: Actor. Jul 12, 1977 (66).

HOLMES, John William: Film editor. Feb 2, 1978 (73).

HOLT, Nick: Actor. Oct 6, 1979 (45).

HOLTZ, Lou: Comedian. Sep 22, 1980 (87).

HOLTZMANN, Fanny Elizabeth: Attorney. Feb 5, 1980 (77).

HOLZER, Lou: Songwriter. Apr 6, 1977 (63).

HOMOLKA, Oscar: Actor. Jan 27, 1978 (79).

HOOD, Darla: Actress. Jun 13, 1979 (48).

HOPKINS, David J: Executive. Oct 12, 1980 (66).

HORNBLOW, Arthur Jr: Producer. Jul 17, 1976 (83).

HORVATH, Charles: Actor. Jul 23, 1978 (57).

HORWITZ, Howie: Producer. Jun 25, 1976 (58).

HOSKINS, Alan (Farina): Actor. Jul 26, 1980 (59).

HOUSTON, Renee: Actress. Feb 9, 1980 (77).

HOWARD, Johnny: Comedian. Jan 21, 1976 (70s).

HOWE, James Wong: Cinematographer. Jul 12, 1976 (76).

HOWE, Quincy: Commentator. Feb 17, 1977 (76).

HUBLEY, John: Animator. Feb 21, 1977 (62).

HUEMER, Richard Martin: Animator. Nov 30, 1979 (81).

HUG, Armand: Composer-Jazz pianist. Mar 19, 1977 (66).

HUGHES, Howard: Producer-Director. Apr 5, 1976 (70).

HUGHES, Richard: Writer. Apr 28, 1976 (76).

HUISMAN, Jacqueline: Actress. Mar 28, 1978 (56).

HULBERT, Jack: Light comedian. Mar 25, 1978 (85).

HULL, Henry: Actor. Mar 8, 1977 (86).

HUNNICUTT, Arthur: Actor. Sep 27, 1979 (68).

HUNT, Walter (Pee Wee): Musician. Jun 22, 1979 (72).

HUSTON, Philip: Actor. Jul 25, 1980 (72).

HUTTON, Jim: Actor. Jun 2, 1979 (45).

HYAMS, Leila: Actress. Dec 4, 1977 (72).

HYDE-CHAMBERS, Derek: Film editor-Director. Feb 2, 1980 (66).

HYDE, Donald: Agent-Packager. Jan 21, 1980 (62).

HYLAND, Diana: Actress. Mar 21, 1977 (41).

HYLTON, Jane: Actress. Feb 28, 1979 (50).

HYMAN, Eliot: Executive. Jul 23, 1980 (75).

HYMAN, Joseph M: Producer. Feb 25, 1977 (80).

IMHOF, Marcelle: Vaudevillian. Jan 15, 1977 (88).

IMPERIO, Pastora: Flamenco Dancer. Sep 27, 1979 (90).

INESCORT, Frieda: Actress. Feb 21, 1976 (75).

INFASCELLI, Roberto: Producer. Aug 18, 1977 (37).

INGSTER, Boris: Writer-Director. Jul 2, 1978 (74).

IRVINE, Richard F: Executive. Mar 30, 1976 (65).

IRVING, Jules: Producer-Director. Jul 28, 1979 (54).

IRWIN, Lou: Agent. Aug 4, 1978 (83).

ISLEY, Phil: Exhibitor. May 27, 1976 (83).

ITURBI, Jose: Conductor-Pianist. Jun 28, 1980 (84).

IVES, Anne: Actress. May 15, 1979 (92).

JACKSON, Butter (Quentin): Musician. Oct 2, 1976 (67).

JACKSON, Eddie: Singer-Dancer. Jul 15, 1980 (84).

JACKSON, Irene Williams: Opera Singer. Dec 6, 1980 (94).

JACOBS, Alexander: Writer. Oct 26, 1979 (51).

JACOBS, Newton P: Executive. Nov 6, 1980 (80).

JACQUES, Hattie: Actress. Sep 6, 1980 (56).

JAMEYSON, Howard: Exhibitor. Jun 13, 1979 (84).

JANNEY, Leon: Actor. Oct 28, 1980 (63).

JANSSEN, David: Actor. Feb 13, 1980 (49).

JARDIN, Pascal: Writer. Jul 31, 1980 (45).

JASON, Leigh: Director. Feb 19, 1979 (74).

JEFFERSON, Eddie: Lyricist. May 9, 1979 (60).

JEROME, M K: Songwriter. Jan 8, 1977 (83).

JOHNSON, Buddy (Woodrow Wilson Johnson): Composer-Bandleader. Feb 9, 1977 (62).

JOHNSON, Nunnally: Writer-Director-Producer. Mar 25, 1977 (79).

JOHNSON, Winnie: Singer-Dancer. Oct 15, 1980 (62).

JOHNSTON, Agnes Christine: Writer. Jul 19, 1978 (82).

JOLLEY, I Stanford: Actor. Dec 7, 1978 (78).

JONAY, Roberta: Actress. Apr 19, 1976 (55).

JONES, Anissa: Actress. Aug 28, 1976 (18).

JONES, Blanche Calloway: Singer-Bandleader. Dec 16, 1978 (76).

JONES, Freda M: Actress. Oct 24, 1976 (79).

JONES, James: Writer. May 9, 1977 (55).

JONES, Preston: Playwright. Sep 19, 1979 (43).

JOOSS, Kurt: Choreographer. May 22, 1979 (78).

JORY, Jean Inness: Actress. Dec 27, 1978.

JOSEPH, Kenneth: Executive. Feb 18, 1978 (55).

JOSHI, Pravin: Actor-Playwright. Jan 19, 1979 (45).

KADAR, Jan: Director. Jun 1, 1979 (61).

KAHN, Kermit: Writer. Dec 20, 1976 (62).

KALCHEIM, Nat: Agent. Jan 13, 1980 (82).

KALLMAN, Richard: Actor. Feb 22, 1980 (46).

KAMEN, Milt: Comedian. Feb 24, 1977 (55).

KAMERN, Lee: Distribution Executive. Sep 24, 1979 (67).

KAMINSKA, Ida: Actress. May 21, 1980 (80).

KANTOR, MacKinlay: Writer. Oct 11, 1977 (73).

KANTZ, Ruth: Songwriter. Mar 6, 1977.

KAPLER, Aleksei Y: Writer. Aug, 1979 (75).

KARGER, Frederick M: Composer-Bandleader. Aug 5, 1979 (63).

KARIAT, Ramu: Director. Feb 10, 1979 (51).

KARMEN, Roman: Director. Apr, 1978 (71).

KARNES, Robert: Actor. Dec 4, 1979 (62).

KARP, Jack: Executive. Oct 12, 1980 (77).

KARSAVINA, Tamara: Ballerina. May 26, 1978 (93).

KASZNAR, Kurt: Actor. Aug 6, 1979 (65).

KAUFMAN, Boris: Cinematographer. Jun 24, 1980 (83).

KAUHI, Richard H: Singer. Jan 21, 1979 (40).

KAUTNER, Helmut: Director. Apr 20, 1980 (72).

KAYE, Sidney M: Copyright Attorney. Aug 27, 1979 (79).

KEARNEY, Gene R: Writer-Director-Producer. Nov 4, 1979 (49).

KELLER, Father James: Broadcast personality. Feb 7, 1977 (76).

KELLER, Frank P: Film editor. Dec 25, 1977.

KELLER, Grete: Singer-Actress. Nov 4, 1977 (75).

KELLOGG, Ray: SFX Creator. Jul 5, 1976 (70).

KELLY, Emmett: Clown. Mar 28, 1979 (80).

KENNEDY, Gertrude: Vaudevillian. Nov 20, 1978 (86).

KENNEY, Douglas: Writer-Producer. Sep 3, 1980 (33).

KENNY, Bill: Singer. Mar 23, 1978 (63).

KENT, Arthur (Arturo Capurro): Metropolitan Opera Singer. Dec 3, 1980 (74).

KENTON, Erle C: Director. Jan 28, 1980 (83).

KENTON, Stan: Bandleader. Aug 25, 1979 (67).

KERRIDGE, Sir Robert: Exhibitor. Apr 26, 1979 (78).

KERZ, Leo: Actor. Nov 4, 1976 (64).

KHACHATURIAN, Aram: Composer. Apr, 1978 (74).

KIDO, Shiro: Film executive. Apr 18, 1977 (82).

KILIAN, Victor: Actor. Mar 11, 1979 (81).

KIMBLE, Lawrence: Writer. Sep 3, 1977 (72).

KING, Matty: Choreographer. Aug 19, 1978 (72).

KING, Maurice: Producer. Sep 2, 1977 (62).

KING, Philip: Playwright. Feb 9, 1979 (74).

KING, Teddi: Jazz singer. Nov 18, 1977 (48).

KING, William Strickland: Advertising Exec. Sep 18, 1980 (72).

KINTNER, Robert E: Executive. Dec 20, 1980 (73).

KIPNIS, Alexander: Operatic basso. May 14, 1978 (87).

KLEINER, Arthur: Musical director-Composer. Mar 31, 1980 (77).

KNAPP, Max: Actor. Dec 16, 1979 (80).

KNUDSEN, Peggy (Jordan): Actress. Jul 11, 1980 (57).

KOBAYASHI, Setsutaro: Executive. Aug 12, 1977 (77).

KOENIG, Lester: Writer-Disk executive. Nov 20, 1977 (58).

KOPLAN, Rosemary LaPlanche: Actress. May 6, 1979 (54).

KORDA, Vincent: Art Director. Jan 4, 1979 (81).

KORJUS, Miliza: Singer. Aug 26, 1980 (72).

KOSTELANETZ, Andre: Conductor. Jan 13, 1980 (78).

KOUDRIAVTZEFF, Nicolas: Impresario. Sep 1980 (84).

KOUTAIE, Ari: Actor. Sep 30, 1980 (80).

KRAMER, Karl: Executive. Oct 14, 1980 (81).

KRELLBERG, Sherman S: Producer-Distributor. Jan 10, 1979 (87).

KRESEL, Lee: Writer. Dec 25, 1980 (62).

KRIMSKY, John: Producer. Oct 7, 1980 (74).

KRIPS, Alfred: Concertmaster. Sep 9, 1979 (79).

KRONENBERGER, Louis: Writer-Critic. Apr 30, 1980 (75).

KRUEGER, Emmy: Operatic soprano. Mar 13, 1976 (89).

KRUMGOLD, Joseph: Writer. Jul 10, 1980 (72).

KURENKO, Maria: Opera singer. May 17, 1980 (89).

KYVELI (Papandreou, Kyveli): Actress. May 25, 1978 (92).

LACEY, Catherine: Actress. Sep 23, 1979 (75).

LACKEY, Kenneth: Former vaudevillian. Apr 16, 1976 (74).

LADD, Francetta Malloy: Musicomedy and Vaudeville headliner. Jul 17, 1978 (71).

LAEMMLE, Carl Jr: Producer-Executive. Sep 24, 1979 (71).

LAING, Alfred B: Silent film actor. Aug 3, 1976 (86).

LAIRE, Judson: Actor. Jul 5, 1979 (76).

LaMONACA, Caesar: Bandleader. Aug 21, 1980 (94).

LAMPIN, Georges: Actor-Director. May, 1979 (78).

LaMURE, Pierre: Composer-Playwright. Dec 28, 1976.

LANDERS, Muriel R: Comedienne. Feb 19, 1977 (55).

LANG, Fritz: Director. Aug 2, 1976 (85).

LANGLOIS, Henri: Film historian. Jan 12, 1977 (62).

LANGTON, Paul: Actor. Apr 15, 1980 (65).

LARSEN, Roy: Time-Life Executive. Sep 9, 1979 (80).

LARSON, Kent: Musician. Nov 3, 1979 (48).

LATINOVITS, Zolta: Actor. Jun, 1976 (44).

LAUCK, Chester H (Lum): Actor. Feb 21, 1980 (79).

LAUREN, S K: Writer. Dec 4, 1979 (87).

LAURIE, John: Actor. Jun 23, 1980 (83).

LAW, Warner: Writer. Jan 10, 1979 (60).

LAWRENCE, Dorothea Dix: Opera Singer. May 29, 1979 (79).

LAWRENCE, Marjorie: Dramatic Soprano. Jan 13, 1979 (71).

LAWRENCE, Richard: Executive. Nov 22, 1977 (51).

LAWSON, John Howard: Writer. Aug 12, 1977 (82).

LAWSON, Kate Drain: Costume Designer. Nov 14, 1977 (83).

LAZAGA, Pedro: Director. Nov 30, 1979.

LAZOWSKI, Yurek: Dancer-Choreographer. Jul 6, 1980 (66).

LE CALLAHAN, Lillian Hill: Comedienne. Jun 29, 1976 (78).

LEDERER, Charles: Writer. Mar 5, 1976 (65).

LEE, Joanna: Actress. Jan 31, 1980 (104).

LEHMANN, Beatrix: Actress. Aug 1, 1979 (76).

LEHMANN, Lotte: Operatic soprano. Aug 26, 1976 (88).

LEIGHTON, Margaret: Actress. Jan 13, 1976 (53).

LEMMER, Ruby Ada: Dancer. Jun 27, 1977 (93).

LENGSFELDER, Hans Jan: Feb 6, 1979 (75).

LENNON, John: Founder member of the Beatles. Dec 8, 1980 (40).

LEONETTI, Tommy: Singer. Sep 15, 1979 (50).

LEONI, Eraldo: Executive. Apr 11, 1980 (58).

LERNER, Irving: Producer-Director. Dec 25, 1976 (67).

LERT, Richard: Conductor. Apr 25, 1980 (94).

LESLIE, Adam: Writer. Apr 25, 1979 (62).

LESLIE, Edgar: Songwriter. Jan 22, 1976 (90).

LESSER, Sol: Film industry pioneer. Sep 19, 1980 (90).

LEVENE, Sam: Actor. Dec 28, 1980 (75).

LEVENSON, Sam: Humorist. Aug 27, 1980 (68).

LEVIN, Dan: Director. Jul 29, 1980 (58).

LEVITT, Alan J: Writer-Producer. Feb 20, 1980 (50s).

LEVITT, Saul: Playwright. Sep 30, 1977 (66)

LEVY, Leon: Broadcast pioneer. Aug 9, 1978 (83).

LEVY, Melvin: Writer. Dec 1, 1980 (78).

LEWIS, Albert: Producer. Apr 5, 1978 (93).

LEWIS, Gene: Writer. Mar 27, 1979 (91).

LEWIS, George Q: Comedian-Writer. Oct 4, 1979 (65).

LEWIS, Philip C: Writer. Sep 3, 1979 (75).

LEWIS, Sir Edward: Recording executive. Jan 29, 1980 (79).

L'HERBIER, Marcel: Director. Nov 26, 1979 (91).

LHEVINNE, Rosina: Pianist. Nov 9, 1976 (96).

LIEBERSON, Goddard: Musicologist. May 29, 1977 (66).

LIEVEN, Tatiana: Actress-Director. Nov 30, 1978 (69).

LIGHT, Enoch: Bandleader. Jul 31, 1978 (71).

LIGHTSTONE, Leonard: Executive. Nov 11, 1977 (61).

LINDEN, Robert: Casting Director-Production Associate. Nov 1, 1980 (66).

LIPPERT, Robert L: Exhibitor-Producer. Nov 16, 1976 (67).

LISEMORE, Martin: Producer. Feb 3, 1977 (36).

LITZ, Katherine: Choreographer. Dec 19, 1978 (66).

LIVESEY, Roger: Actor. Feb 5, 1976 (69).

LLOYD, Jack: Writer. May 21, 1976 (53).

LOCKHART, Kathleen: Actress. Feb 17, 1978 (84).

LOCOCO, Clemente: Exhibitor. Jan, 1980 (87).

LODEN, Barbara: Actress-Director-Writer. Sep 5, 1980 (48).

LOEB, Lee: Writer. Oct 25, 1978 (58).

LOEB, Marx B: Producer. Aug 26, 1980 (80).

LOEW, Arthur M: Executive. Sep 6, 1977 (79).

LOMBARDO, Guy: Bandleader. Nov 5, 1977 (75).

LONGFORD, Christine: Playwright. May 14, 1980 (80).

LORD, Robert: Writer-Producer. Apr 5, 1976 (75).

LOTITO, Louis A: Producer-Theatre owner. Feb 12, 1980 (79).

LOVELY, Louis: Silent screen actress. Mar 18, 1980 (84).

LOVSKY, Celia: Actress. Oct 12, 1979 (82).

LOWRY, Judith: Actress. Nov 29, 1976 (86).

LUAHINE, Iolani: Dancer. Dec 10, 1978 (63).

LUBIN, Ernest: Composer. Mar 15, 1977 (60).

LUM (Chester H Lauck): Actor. Feb 21, 1980 (79).

LUMET, Julia: Dancer-Choreographer. Oct 15, 1976 (68).

LUNT, Alfred: Actor. Aug 3, 1977 (84).

LUSTIG, Jan: Writer. Apr, 1979 (77).

LUSTY, Lou: Producer. Nov 24, 1980.

LUTHER, Frank: Writer-Songwriter-Singer. Nov 16, 1980 (80).

LYON, Ben: Actor. Mar 22, 1979 (78).

LYONS, Leonard: Columnist. Oct 7, 1976 (70).

LYTELL, Grace Menken: Actress. Aug 14, 1978 (86).

MACARIO, Erminio: Vaudevillian. Mar 26, 1980 (78).

MacDonald, Philip: Writer. Dec 10, 1980 (80).

MacDONALD, Wallace: Actor-Producer. Oct 30, 1978 (87).

MacDonnell, Norman S: Producer. Nov 28, 1979 (63).

MACHARG, Eddie: Personal Manager-Music Publisher. Nov 29, 1980 (77).

MACHIN, Antonio: Singer. Aug 4, 1977 (74).

MACK, Austin: Pianist. Oct 15, 1980 (86).

MACK, Jennie: Dancer. Apr 18, 1977 (100).

MACK, Ted: Emcee. Jul 12, 1976 (72).

MACKEY, Bernard: Singer-Guitarist. Mar 5, 1980 (70).

MacLIAMMOIR, Michael: Actor-Playwright. Mar 6, 1978 (78).

MAHONEY, Wilkie: Writer. Jul 30, 1976 (78).

MAINWARING, Daniel: Writer. Jan 31, 1977 (74).

MALRAUX, Andre: Writer. Nov 23, 1976 (75).

MANHEIM, Lucie: Actress-Director. Jul 28, 1976 (77).

MANN, Gene: Producer. Aug 6, 1978 (72).

MANN, Robert J: Writer-Producer. May 21, 1980 (66).

MANNI, Ettore: Actor. Jul 27, 1979 (52).

MANNING, Knox: Announcer. Aug 26, 1980 (76).

MANSFIELD, Michael: Writer. May 31, 1979 (55).

MANTOVANI, Annunzio Paolo: Conductor. Mar 29, 1980 (74).

MARAIS, Josef: Composer-Singer. Apr 27, 1978 (72).

MARCH, Joseph Moncure: Writer. Feb 14, 1977 (78).

MARCIO, Flavio: Playwright. May 23, 1979.

MARCUS, Sol: Songwiter. Feb 5, 1976 (63).

MARION, Charles R: Writer. Sep 29, 1980 (65).

MARKEY, Gene: Writer-Producer. May 1, 1980 (85).

MARKOV, Georgio: Playwright. Sep 10, 1978 (49).

MARRIOTT, John: Actor. Apr 5, 1977 (83).

MARSHALL, Mort: Actor. Feb 1, 1979 (60).

MARSHALL, Norman: Producer-Director. Nov 7, 1980 (78).

MARTELL, Marty: Actor-Singer-Director. May 7, 1979 (79).

MARTERIE, Ralph: Bandleader. Oct 8, 1978 (63).

MARTIN, Sobey: Director. Jul 27, 1978 (69).

MARTIN, Strother: Actor. Aug, 1980 (61).

MARTINEZ, Pedro: Actor. Dec 25, 1978 (33).

MARTINI, Nino: Operatic tenor. Dec 10, 1976 (72).

MARX, Groucho: Comedian. Aug 19, 1977 (86).

MARX, Gummo: Agent-former Comedian. Apr 21, 1977 (84).

MARX, Zeppo: Agent. Nov 29, 1979 (79).

MASON, Mary (Betty Wharton): Actress. Oct 13, 1980 (69).

MASON, Shirley: Silent Film Star. Jul 27, 1979 (79).

MASSINE, Leonide: Choreographer. Mar 16, 1979 (83).

MASTIN, Will: Dancer-Singer. Mar 1, 1979 (99).

MATHONET, Georges: Vaudeville producer. Oct 19, 1978 (66).

MATHY-FRISDANE, Marianne Kahn: Opera singer-Teacher. Oct 18, 1978 (88).

MATLOCK, Julian (Matty): Musician. Jun 14, 1978 (71).

MATRAY, Ernst: Choreographer-Director. Nov, 1978 (87).

MATTHEWS, Dorothy: Actress. May 18, 1977 (65).

MAUCH, Hans (Frick): Comedy Skater. Jun 5, 1979 (60).

MAUDE, Margery: Actress. Aug 7, 1979 (90).

MAXWELL, Robert E: Producer-Cinematographer. Dec 22, 1978 (54).

MAY, Mia: Silent Screen Actress. Nov, 1980 (96).

MAYPOLE, Roy: Actor-Producer. Jul 4, 1976 (62).

McBRIDE, Mary Margaret: Talk show hostess. Apr 7, 1976 (76).

McCANN, John: Playwright. Feb 23, 1980 (75).

McCARTY, Mary: Actress. Apr 3, 1980 (56).

McCAULEY, Jack: Dancer-Singer. Jun 13, 1980 (79).

McCORD, Ted: Cinematographer. Jan 19, 1976 (75).

McCOY, Tim: Screen cowboy. Jan 29, 1978 (86).

McCOY, Van: Musician. Jul 6, 1979 (35).

McCULLOCH, Jimmy: Musician. Sep 17, 1979 (26).

McDANIEL, William A: Executive. Nov 26, 1980 (62).

McDERMOTT, Pat: Producer. Mar 26, 1976 (53).

McDEVITT, Ruth: Actress. Mar 27, 1976 (80).

McDONAGH, Paulette: Director. Sep, 1978.

McDONALD, Frank: Director. Mar 8, 1980 (80).

McEVEETY, Joseph L: Writer-Producer. Oct 15, 1976 (50).

McGANN, William: Director. Nov 15, 1977 (84).

McGEE, Pat: Exhibitor-Distributor. Sep 24, 1980 (74).

McGINN, Walter: Actor. Mar 31, 1977 (40).

McGOWAN, John P: Playwright. May 28, 1977 (81).

McGRATH, Paul: Actor. Apr 13, 1978 (74).

McGRAW, Charles: Actor. Jul 29, 1980 (66).

McGUIRE, Kathryn: Silent screen star. Oct 10, 1978.

McGUIRE, Ken: Writer. May 27, 1978 (55).

McKELWAY, St Clair: Writer. Jan 10, 1980 (74).

McLARTY, James E: Writer-Actor. Apr 16, 1979 (48).

McMILLAN, Roddy: Actor. Jul 9, 1979 (56).

McNAMARA, Maggie: Actress. Feb 18, 1978 (48).

McNULTY, Harold: Actor. Jun 6, 1978 (75).

McQUADE, John: Actor. Sep 21, 1979 (63).

McQUEEN, Steve: Actor. Nov 7, 1980 (50).

MEDFORD, Harold: Writer. Oct 26, 1977 (66).

MEDFORD, Kay: Actress. Apr 10, 1980 (59).

MELL, Joseph: Actor. Aug 31, 1977 (62).

MELLOR, Maggi: Actress-Director. Dec 31, 1978 (46).

MELMAN, Marian: Actress. Oct 30, 1978 (78).

MERCER, David: Writer. Aug 8, 1980 (52).

MERCER, Johnny: Songwriter. Jun 25, 1976 (66).

MERMAN, Lewis (Doc): Production Executive. Sep 7, 1979 (79).

MERRICK, Lawrence: Playwright-Producer. Jan 26, 1977 (50).

MESSEL, Oliver: Designer. Jul 13, 1978 (74).

MEURISSE, Paul: Actor. Jan 19, 1979 (66).

MEYER, Eve: Actress-Producer. Mar 27, 1977 (44).

MEYER, Johannes: Director. Jan 25, 1976.

MIDDLETON, Robert: Actor. Jun 14, 1977 (66).

MIELZINER, Jo: Stage designer. Mar 15, 1976 (74).

MIGNONE, Carolina (Milly): Singer. Sep 1980 (75).

MIHURA, Miguel: Playwright. Oct 28, 1977 (72).

MILAN, Frank: Actor. Apr 8, 1977 (71).

MILESTONE, Lewis: Director. Sep 25, 1980 (84).

MILGRAM, David E: Exhibitor. Nov 23, 1980 (73).

MILLER, Bettye: Jazz pianist-Singer. Feb 28, 1977 (49).

MILLER, Eddie: Songwriter. Apr 10, 1977 (57).

MILLER, Henry: Writer. Jun 7, 1980 (88).

MILLER, Jack: Writer. Jan 12, 1980 (45).

MILLS, Jack: Music Publisher. Mar 23, 1979 (87).

MILLS, Jim: Actor. Apr 24, 1980 (60).

MILLY (Mignone, Carolina): Singer. Sep, 1980 (75).

MINEO, Sal: Actor. Feb 12, 1976 (37).

MINGUS, Charles: Jazz Bassist. Jan 5, 1979 (56).

MIRELL, Leon I: Producer. Dec 7, 1977 (54).

MISHKIN, Leo: Critic. Dec 27, 1980 (74).

MITCHELL, Blue: Musician. May 21, 1979 (49).

MITCHELL, George A: Inventor. Apr 16, 1980 (91).

MITCHELL, Yvonne: Actress. Mar 24, 1979 (53).

MOCHRIE, Robert H: Executive. Aug 19, 1980 (86).

MOCKRIDGE, Cyril J: Composer. Jan 18, 1979 (82).

MOGUY, Leonide: Producer. Apr 21, 1976 (77).

MOLINA, Mercedes: Dancer. Nov 30, 1978 (44).

MONCRIEFF, Gladys: Musicomedy star. Feb 8, 1976 (83).

MONTGOMERY, Robert B: Composer. Sep 15, 1978 (56).

MOORE, Carroll B: Playwright. Feb 5, 1977 (63).

MOREHOUSE, Chauncey: Jazz Drummer. Oct 31, 1980 (78).

MORELL, Andre: Actor. Nov, 1978 (69).

MORELLI, Rina: Actress. Jul 17, 1976 (67).

MOREY, Edward: Executive. Jul 14, 1977 (84).

MORGAN, Kenneth R: Sound Pioneer. Mar 15, 1979 (81).

MORRIS, Lee: Songwriter. Oct 18, 1978 (66).

MORRIS, Lloyd W: Exhibitor. Jul 7, 1979 (75).

MORRISON, Ann: Actress. Apr 18, 1978 (62).

MORRISON, Bret: Actor. Sep 25, 1978 (66).

MORRISON, Paul: Designer. Dec 29, 1980 (74).

MOSS, Charles B Sr: Exhibitor. Jul 30, 1979 (66).

MOSS, Tom: Comedian-Producer. Jan, 1980 (87).

MOSTEL, Zero: Actor. Sep 8, 1977 (62).

MOUSSOURIS, Coast: Actor-Director-Producer. Dec 7, 1976 (73).

MR PASTRY (Richard Hearne): Dancer-Comedian. Aug 25, 1979 (70).

MUELLER, Merrill: Print-TV Newsman. Nov 30, 1980 (64).

MULHALL, Jack: Silent Screen Star. Jun 1, 1979 (91).

MULLEN, Barbara: Actress. Mar 9, 1979 (64).

MULLEN, Frank E: Pioneer broadcast executive. Feb 20, 1977 (80).

MURCOTT, Joel: Writer. Feb 16, 1978 (62).

MURPHY, Maurice: Actor. Nov 23, 1978 (65).

MUSE, Clarence: Actor-Composer-Singer. Oct 13, 1979 (89).

MUSTIN, Burt: Actor. Jan 28, 1977 (92).

MUSU, Antonio: Producer. Nov 1979 (63).

MYERS, Carmel: Actress. Nov 9, 1980 (80).

MYERS, Richard: Composer-Producer. Mar 12, 1977 (75).

MYRTILE, Odette: Actress-Singer. Nov 18, 1978 (80).

NABOKOV, Nicolas: Composer-Writer. Apr 6, 1978 (75).

NABOKOV, Vladimir: Writer. Jul 2, 1977 (78).

NANCE, Ray: Jazz musician. Jan 28, 1976 (62).

NASH, Mary: Actress. Dec 3, 1976 (92).

NATHAN, Paul: Producer. Nov 16, 1977 (64).

NATHANSON, Don Paul: Writer-Executive. Dec 24, 1980 (66).

NATHANSON, Paul Louis: Exhibitor. Nov 13, 1980 (67).

NAZZARI, Amedeo: Actor. Nov 7, 1979 (72).

NEAL, Harold L Jr: Broadcast executive. Feb 28, 1980 (55).

NEBEL, Long John: Broadcast personality. Apr 10, 1978 (66).

NEIBURG, A J: Songwriter. Jul 11, 1978 (75).

NEILSON, James: Director. Dec 9, 1979 (70).

NELSON, Clara (Hilo Hattie): Singer-Dancer. Dec 12, 1979 (78).

NESBITT, Ann Greenway: Lyric soprano. Jun 26, 1977 (78).

NEVEN-DU MONT, Juergen: Documentary Maker. Jul 14, 1979 (57).

NEWELL, David: Actor. Jan 25, 1980 (75).

NEWHOUSE, Samuel I: Executive. Aug 29, 1979 (84).

NEWKIRK, Van C: Broadcast Pioneer. Jan 6, 1979 (75).

NEWMAN, Angela: Actress. Apr 15, 1979 (49).

NEWMAN, Charles: Lyricist. Jan 9, 1978 (76).

NICHOLL, Don: Writer-Producer. Jul 5, 1980 (54).

NICHOLS, Barbara: Actress. Oct 5, 1976 (47).

NIELSEN, Arthur Charles: Executive. Jun 1, 1980 (83).

NIELSON-TERRY, Phyllis: Actress. Sep 25, 1977 (84).

NILES, John Jacob: Folksinger. Mar 1, 1980 (87).

NIMURA, Yeichi: Dancer-Choreographer. Apr 3, 1979 (82).

NOBLE, Ray: Songwriter-Bandleader. Apr 3, 1978 (71).

NOLAN, Bob: C&W composer-Singer. Jun 16, 1980 (72).

NORMAN, Frank: Playwright. Dec 23, 1980 (49).

NORTH, Robert: Producer. Aug 13, 1976 (92).

NOSCHESE, Alighiero: Actor. Dec 3, 1979 (47).

NOVACK, Shelly: Actor. May 27, 1978 (30).

NOVAES, Guiomar: Pianist. Mar 7, 1979 (83).

NUATJIM, Chamroon: Actor. May 9, 1979 (65).

NUGENT, Elliot: Playwright-Producer-Actor. Aug 9, 1980 (83).

NUGENT, Norma Lee: Actress. Dec 12, 1980 (81).

OAKIE, Jack: Comic. Jan 23, 1978 (74).

OAKLAND, Ben: Songwriter. Aug 26, 1979 (71).

OBERON, Merle: Actress. Nov 22, 1979 (68).

O'BRIEN-MOORE, Erin: Actress. May 3, 1979 (77).

O'DEA, Denis: Actor. Nov 5, 1978 (75).

O'DEAL, BiBi (Odee Astie): Stunt Woman. Nov 14, 1980 (40).

ODLUM, Floyd B: Financier. Jun 17, 1976 (84).

O'HARA, Barry J: Actor-Singer. Sep 5, 1979 (53).

O'HARA, Shirley: Actress. May 5, 1979 (68).

OLIVER, Eddie: Bandleader. Mar 19, 1976 (69).

OLIVIERO, Nino: Songwriter. Feb, 1980 (62).

O'MALLEY, Rex: Actor. May 1, 1976 (75).

O'MOORE, Mary: Actress. May 27, 1980 (77).

O'NEILL, Barbara: Actress. Sep 3, 1980 (70).

O'NEILL, James L: Actor. Jul 18, 1977 (93).

OPPENHEIMER, George: Writer. Aug 14, 1977 (77).

ORCHARD, Julian: Actor. Jun 21, 1979 (49).

ORFALY, Alexander: Actor. Jan 22, 1979 (43).

ORNSTEIN, George H (Bud): Executive. Sep 2, 1978 (61).

ORTEGA, Santos: Actor. Apr 10, 1976 (76).

OSTROFF, Manning: Former Producer-Director. Dec 30, 1980 (73).

OTTENHEIMER, Albert M: Actor. Jan 25, 1980 (75).

OTTOLINA, Renny: TV personality. Mar 16, 1978 (49).

PAGLIERO, Marcello: Actor-Writer-Director. Dec 16, 1980 (73).

PAL, George: Producer-Director. May 2, 1980 (72).

PALMER, Ernest: Cinematographer. Feb 22, 1978 (92).

PAPPAOUTSAKIS, James: Flutist. Jan 7, 1979 (68).

PARAMOR, Norrie: Bandleader. Sep 9, 1979 (65).

PARANJPE, Raja: Director. Feb 9, 1979 (69).

PARKS, Gordon Jr: Director. Apr 2, 1979 (44).

PARNELL, Emory: Actor. Jun 22, 1979 (86).

PASO, Alphonso: Playwright-Actor-Director. Jul 10, 1978 (51).

PASSER, Dirch: Actor-Comedian. Sep, 1980 (54).

PATERSON, Pat: Actress. Aug 24, 1978 (67).

PATRICK, Gail: Actress-Producer. Jul 6, 1980 (69).

PAUL, Bernard: Director. Dec 6, 1980 (50).

PAUL, Norman: Writer-Producer. Jul 1, 1979 (65).

PAYNE, Percival (Sonny): Musician. Jan 29, 1979 (52).

PAYNE, Virginia: Actress. Feb 10, 1977 (66).

PEARL, Irwin: Actor-Director. Nov 13, 1980 (35).

PEARSON, Mack: Vaudevillian. Jun 19, 1977 (75).

PEDERSON, Bert: Musician. Aug 23, 1977 (56).

PEPPER, Jack: Vaudevillian. Mar 31, 1979 (76).

PERELMAN, S J: Writer. Oct 17, 1979 (75).

PERKINS, Voltaire: Actor. Oct 10, 1977 (80).

PERRY, Al Keahola: Singer-Musical Director. Sep 24, 1979 (78).

PERRYMAN, Diana: Actress. Jan 10, 1979 (54).

PERRYMAN, Lloyd: Singer. May 31, 1977 (60).

PESKAY, Edward J: Exhibitor-Producer. Aug 25, 1978 (79).

PETERS, Richard: IATSE Executive. Feb 23, 1979 (47).

PETROVA, Olga: Actress-Writer. Nov 30, 1977 (93).

PEZZULO, Ted: Playwright-Actor. Nov 10, 1979 (43).

PHILLIPS, Alex, Sr: Cinematographer. Jun 14, 1977 (77).

PHILLPOTTS, Ambrosine: Actress. Oct 12, 1980 (68).

PHIPPS, Nicholas: Actor-Writer. Apr 11, 1980 (66).

PHIPPS, Sally (Byrnece Beutler): Silent film actress. Mar 17, 1978 (67).

PIATIGORSKY, Gregor: Cellist. Aug 6, 1976 (73).

PICKFORD, Mary: Silent Screen Star. May 28, 1979 (86).

PICKLES, Wilfred: TV personality. Mar 27, 1978 (73).

PIERCE, Joan Standing: Actress. Feb 3, 1979 (76).

PIERCE, Sam: Producer. Jan 6, 1979 (67).

PINCUS, Norman: Producer. Oct 30, 1978.

PINKHAM, Eleanor: Executive. Nov 22, 1979 (70).

PIOUS, Minerva: Actress. Mar 17, 1979 (75).

PISTON, Walter: Composer. Nov 12, 1976 (82).

PISU, Mario: Actor. Jul, 1976 (66).

POE, James: Writer. Jan 24, 1980 (58).

POINTDEXTER, H R: Set and lighting designer. Sep 24, 1977 (41).

POLESIE, Herbert S: Producer-Director. Jun 8, 1979 (79).

POLLOCK, Nancy: Actress. Jun 20, 1979 (77).

PONS, Lily: Colaratura soprano. Feb 13, 1976 (71).

PORTER, Julio: Director-Writer. Nov 1979 (63).

PORTER, Katherine Anne: Writer. Sep 18, 1980 (90).

POTTER, H C: Director. Aug 31, 1977 (73).

POTTLE, Samuel H: Composer. Jul 4, 1978 (44).

POWELL, Robert: Dancer. Oct 24, 1977 (38).

POWELL, Rudy: Musician. Oct 30, 1976 (69).

POWERS, James D: Newspaperman. Jul 4, 1980 (61).

POWERS, John Robert: Model agency pioneer. Jul 19, 1977 (84).

PRADA, Jose Maria: Actor. Aug 13, 1978 (53).

PREAGER, Lou: Bandleader. Nov 14, 1978 (72).

PREJEAN, Albert: Actor. Nov 1, 1979 (85).

PRENTISS, Eleanor: Actress. Aug 14, 1979 (67).

PRESLEY, Elvis Aaron: Singer. Aug 16, 1977 (42).

PREVERT, Jacques: Writer. Apr 11, 1977 (77).

PREVOST, Jeanne: Actress. Nov 24, 1980 (93).

PRIMA, Louis: Bandleader. Aug 24, 1978 (67).

PRINCESS WHITE: Singer-Dancer. Mar 20, 1976 (95).

PRINTEMPS, Yvonne: Singer-Actress. Jan 18, 1977 (82).

PRINZE, Freddie: Actor. Jan 29, 1977 (22).

PROFESSOR BACKWARDS (Edward E Edmonson): Jan 29, 1976 (65).

PROFESSOR LONGHAIR (Henry Roeland Byrd): Composer-Pianist. Jan 30, 1980 (61).

PUCK, Eva: Vaudevillian-Musicomedy Star. Oct 24, 1979 (87).

PULMAN, Jack: Writer. May 20, 1979 (50).

PURCELL, Harold: Songwriter. May 28, 1977 (69).

RACKIN, Martin: Writer-Producer. Apr 15, 1976 (58).

RADD, Ronald: Actor. Apr 23, 1976 (47).

RADOK, Alfred: Director. Jun, 1976 (62).

RAFT, George: Actor. Nov 24, 1980 (85).

RAINE, Jack: Actor. May 30, 1979 (83).

RAKSIN, Ruby: Composer. May 16, 1979 (63).

RAMSAY, G Clark: Executive. Nov 29, 1977 (62).

RAND, Sally: Dancer. Aug 31, 1979 (75).

RANDAX, Georges: Actor. Jan 30, 1979 (81).

RANDOLPH, Lillian: Actress. Sep 12, 1980 (65).

RASKIN, Milt: Composer-Pianist. Oct 16, 1977 (61).

RASSER, Alfred: Actor. Aug 18, 1977 (71).

RATTIGAN, Sir Terence: Playwright. Nov 30, 1977 (66).

RAUH, Stanley E: Writer. Sep 12, 1979 (81).

RAV-NOF, Zeev: Director. Mar 23, 1979 (53).

RAY, Nicholas: Director. Jun 16, 1979 (67).

REDFIELD, William: Actor. Aug 17, 1976 (49).

REDMAN, George: Conductor. May 8, 1979 (80).

REED, Alan (Teddy Bergman): Actor. Jun 14, 1977 (69).

REED, Marshall: Actor-Director-Producer-Writer. Apr 15, 1980 (52).

REED, Sir Carol: Director. Apr 25, 1976 (69).

REID, Dorothy Davenport: Silent film star. Oct 12, 1977 (81).

REID, Mary: Actress. Jul 18, 1979 (83).

REMEY, Ethel: Actress. Feb 28, 1979.

RENALDO, Duncan: Actor. Sep 3, 1980 (76).

RENNAHAN, Ray: Cinematographer. May 19, 1980 (84).

RENNERT, Guenther: Opera director. Jul 31, 1978 (67).

RENOIR, Jean: Director. Feb 13, 1979 (84).

RETHBERG, Elisabeth: Opera singer. Jun 6, 1976 (81).

RHEINER, Samuel: Executive. Dec 22, 1980 (80).

RHODES, Lila: Actress. Oct 5, 1980 (90).

RHODES, Marjorie: Actress. Jul 4, 1979 (76).

RICCI, Nora: Actress. Apr 15, 1976 (51).

RICHARDS, Cully: Writer-Comedian. Jun 17, 1978 (68).

RICHARDS, Stanley: Playwright. Jul 26, 1980 (62).

RICHARDSON, Clair: Impresario. Sep 12, 1980 (59).

RICHTER, Hans: Director. Feb 1, 1976 (87).

RIPERTON, Minnie: Singer. Jul 12, 1979 (31).

RITCHARD, Cyril: Actor-Singer. Dec 18, 1977 (79).

RITTS, Paul: Actor-Director. Oct 18, 1980 (60).

RIVERO, Julian: Actor. Feb 24, 1976 (85).

ROBBINS, Gale: Actress-Singer. Feb 18, 1980 (58).

ROBBINS, Penny: Actress-Singer. Nov 4, 1980 (50).

ROBERTS, Rachel: Actress. Nov 27, 1980 (53).

ROBERTSON, William: Actor. Mar 16, 1980 (71).

ROBESON, Paul: Singer-Actor. Jan 23, 1976 (77).

ROBINSON, BIG JIM (Nathan): Musician. May 4, 1976 (86).

ROBINSON, Casey: Writer. Dec 6, 1979 (76).

ROBINSON, Charles Knox: Playwright-Producer. Jun 4, 1980 (79).

ROBINSON, Francis: Opera executive. May 14, 1980 (70).

ROBISON, David Victor: Writer. Nov 30, 1978 (67).

ROBSON, Mark: Director. Jun 20, 1978 (64).

ROCHA, Aurimar: Writer-Actor-Director-Producer. May 16, 1979 (46).

ROCKWELL, George L (Doc): Comedian. Mar 2, 1978 (89).

RODGERS, Richard: Composer-Producer. Dec 30, 1979 (77).

RODGERS, Robert: Writer. Oct 10, 1976 (52).

RODRIGUES, Nelson: Playwright. Dec 21, 1980 (68).

ROGERS, Lela: Writer. May 25, 1977 (86).

ROLFE, Des: Actor. Oct 26, 1979 (68).

ROLLI, Paola: Casting Director. Nov 1, 1980 (48).

ROOM, Abram M: Director. Jul, 1976 (82).

ROONEY, Pat 3rd: Vaudevillian. Nov 5, 1979.

ROSE, Irving: Dancer-Actor. Sep 9, 1977 (81).

ROSE, Jane: Actress. Jun 29, 1979 (66).
ROSE, Tom: Writer. Feb 19, 1976 (51).

ROSEN, Arnie: Writer-Producer. Jan 30, 1980 (58).

ROSEN, Kenneth M: Writer-Producer. Jul 2, 1976 (47).

ROSENBERG, Aaron: Producer. Sep 1, 1979 (67).

ROSENBLOOM, Maxie: Comedian and former Fighter. Mar 6, 1976 (71).

ROSENHAUS, Matthew B: Financier. Aug 26, 1980 (69).

ROSENTHAL, Andrew: Playwright-Composer. Nov 11, 1979 (61).

ROSNER, Ady: Musician. Aug 8, 1976 (67).

ROSNER, Jo: Producer. Sep 21, 1980 (65).

ROSS, Lenny (Leonardo Del Rossi): Comedian. Jan 25, 1976 (71).

ROSSELLINI, Roberto: Director. Jun 3, 1977 (71).

ROTA, Nino: Composer. Apr 10, 1979 (68).

ROTH, Jack: Drummer. Feb 12, 1980 (81).

ROTH, Lillian: Actress-Singer. May 12, 1980 (69).

ROUSE, Ethel S: Writer. Nov 11, 1979 (62).

ROVINA, Hanna: Actress. Feb 2, 1980.

ROY, Jahar: Actor. Aug 11, 1977 (58).

ROY, Mike: TV personality. Jun 26, 1976 (63).

ROYAL, John F: Broadcast pioneer. Feb 13, 1978 (91).

ROYCE, Riza: Actress-Writer. Oct 20, 1980 (72).

ROZANSKA, Elektra: Opera singer-Actress. Jul 3, 1978 (87).

RULOWA, Shura: Dancer. Oct 10, 1979.

RUPERT, Gene: Actor-Singer. May 14, 1979 (47).

RUSKIN, Shimen: Actor. Apr 23, 1976 (69).

RUSSELL, Evelyn: Actress. Feb 4, 1976 (49).

RUSSELL, Rosalind: Actress. Nov 28, 1976 (64).

RYDGE, Sir Norman: Executive. May 14, 1980 (79).

SACKHEIM, Jerry: Writer. May 13, 1979 (74).

SAFIER, Morris: Distribution executive. Jun 24, 1980 (88).

SAIDENBERG, Eleanor: Producer. Feb 14, 1978 (66).

SALINGER, Paul: Director. Jul 17, 1978 (37).

SALUSSE, Jean: Opera executive. Jul 23, 1977 (46).

SAMISH, Adrian: Producer. Oct 14, 1976 (66).

SAMUELS, Lesser: Writer. Dec 22, 1980 (86).

SAMUELS, Rae: Vaudevillian. Oct 23, 1979 (93).

SANCHEZ TELLO, Alfonso: Director. Apr 18, 1979.

SANDRINI, Luis: Actor. Jul 5, 1980 (75).

SANDS, Dorothy: Actress. Sep 11, 1980 (87).

SANTILLO, Frank: Film editor. Jun 30, 1978 (65).

SAPSAMRUAY, Somchit: Actress. Jul 7, 1980 (56).

SARTRE, Jean-Paul: Playwright. Apr 15, 1980 (74).

SATTERWHITE, Collen Gray: Songwriter. Feb 6, 1978 (57).

SAUBERLICH, Lu: Actress. Oct, 1976 (64).

SAVIAN, Nick: Actor. Nov 8, 1980 (56).

SAVILLE, Victor: Director-Producer. May 8, 1979 (83).

SAWYER, Gordon E: Sound director. May 15, 1980 (75).

SAYRE, Joel: Writer. Sep 9, 1979 (78).

SCARPITTA, Guy: Director. Jul 6, 1978 (63).

SCHAFER, Kermit: Producer-Writer. Mar 8, 1979 (64).

SCHARY, Dore: Writer-Producer-Director-Executive. Jul 6, 1980 (74).

SCHERTZER, Hymie: Musician. Mar 22, 1977 (67).

SCHIPPERS, Thomas: Conductor. Dec 16, 1977 (47).

SCHLAGER, Sig: Executive. Nov 27, 1980 (81).

SCHLAIFER, Edward M: Executive. Nov 20, 1980 (85).

SCHMIDT, Wolf: Actor-Writer-Producer. Jan 17, 1977 (64).

SCHNEIDER, Benno: Director-Talent executive. Aug 13, 1977 (75).

SCHNITZER, Henriette: Actress. May 4, 1979 (84).

SCHOLLAR, Ludmilla: Ballerina. Jul 10, 1978.

SCHOUTEN, Richard: Producer. Jul 3, 1977 (47).

SCHRAMM, Karla: Silent screen actress. Jan 17, 1980 (89).

SCHREIBER, Taft: Executive. Jun 14, 1976 (68).

SCHUDSON, Hod David: Composer-Record Producer Nov 17, 1980 (38).

SCHULBERG, Adeline: Agent. Jul 15, 1977 (83).

SCHULBERG, Stuart: Producer. Jun 28, 1979 (56).

SCHWARTZ, Samuel H: Producer. Jul 11, 1977 (69).

SCOTT, Esther Mae: Singer-Composer. Oct 16, 1979 (86).

SCOTT, Linda: Singer. Nov 10, 1978 (28).

SCULLY, William A: Executive. May 20, 1978 (84).

SEATON, George: Writer-Director. Jul 28, 1979 (68).

SEBASTIAN, John: Harmonicist. Aug 18, 1980 (65).

SEBERG, Jean: Actress. Sep 8, 1979 (40).

SEGAL, Alex: Director. Aug 22, 1977 (62).

SEITZ, John F: Cinematographer. Feb 27, 1979 (86).

SEKELY, Steve: Director. Mar 9, 1979 (80).

SELANDER, Lesley: Director. Dec 5, 1979 (79).

SELBY, Sarah: Actress. Jan 7, 1980 (74).

SELLERS, Peter: Actor. Jul 24, 1980 (54).

SELTZER, Frank N: Producer. Apr 7, 1977 (77).

SELVIN, Ben: Bandleader-Disk executive. Jul 15, 1980 (82).

SELZNICK, Howard: Former Agent. Dec 4, 1980 (82).

SEMMLER, Alexander: Composer. Apr 24, 1977 (76).

SEN YUNG, Victor: Actor. Nov 9, 1980 (65).

SERVAIS, Jean: Actor. Feb 22, 1976 (65).

SEWELL, Theodore W: Producer. Jan 13, 1979 (67).

SEYMOUR, James: Writer. Jan 29, 1976 (80).

SHACKLETON, Allan: Distribution Executive. Oct 13, 1979 (42).

SHAND, Terry: Songwriter. Nov 11, 1977.

SHANKAR, Uday: Dancer. Sep 26, 1977 (76).

SHAPIRO, Samuel: Exhibitor. May 18, 1977 (78).

SHAPIRO, Ted: Composer-Musician. May 26, 1980 (81).

SHAW, Robert: Actor-Playwright. Aug 26, 1978 (51).

SHAY, Dorothy: Singer. Oct 22, 1978 (57).

SHEAR, Barry: Director. Jun 13, 1979 (56).

SHEEKMAN, Arthur: Writer. Jan 12, 1978 (76).

SHEEN, Archbishop Fulton J: Clerical TV Personality. Dec 10, 1979 (84).

SHELLEY, Norman: Actor. Aug 22, 1980 (77).

SHEPITKO, Larissa: Director. Jul 2, 1979 (40).

SHERIDAN, Cecil: Comedian. Jan 4, 1980 (70).

SHERMAN, Charles: Producer-Playwright. Dec 25, 1976 (77).

SHERMAN, Edward: Personal manager. Feb 20, 1980 (77).

SHINDLER, Benjamin: Exhibitor. Oct 26, 1978 (91).

SHOEMAKER, Ann: Actress. Sep 18, 1978 (87).

SHOR, Toots (Bernard): Restauranteur. Jan 23, 1977 (73).

SHREWSBURY, Lillian: Actress. Jun 15, 1979 (90).

SHUFTAN, Eugene: Cinematographer. Sep 6, 1977 (91).

SHUKEN, Leo: Composer. Jul 24, 1976 (69).

SHUMLIN, Herman: Producer-Director. Jun 4, 1979 (80).

SHURLOCK, Geoffrey: Executive. Apr 26, 1976 (81).

SHUTTA, Ethel: Singer-Actress. Feb 5, 1976 (79).

SIDNEY, Jack Sr: Vaudevillian. May 15, 1977 (88).

SIEBER, Rudolph: Director. Jun 24, 1976 (77).

SIEGEL, Seymour N: Broadcast executive. Jul 15, 1978 (69).

SILLS, Doris Kenyon: Silent Screen Star. Sep 1, 1979 (81).

SILVERHEELS, Jay: Actor. Mar 5, 1980 (67).

SIM, Alastair: Actor. Aug 19, 1976 (75).

SIMPSON, Alan: Director. May 15, 1980 (59).

SINATRA, Ray Dominic: Orchestra Leader. Nov 1, 1980 (76).

SINGER, George: Conductor. Oct 1, 1980 (76).

SINGER, Jacques: Conductor. Aug 11, 1980 (70).

SINGER, Werner: Concert Pianist. Apr 29, 1979 (76).

SIRCAR, Birendranath: Producer. Nov 28, 1980 (80).

SISK, J Kelly: Executive. Nov 6, 1980 (67).

SJOBERG, Alf: Actor-Director. Apr 17, 1980 (77).

SJOBERG, Tore: Producer. May 29, 1980 (65).

SKALL, William V: Cinematographer. Mar 22, 1976 (78).

SKINNER, Cornelia Otis: Actress. Jul 9, 1979 (78).

SKINNER, Jane: Writer-Producer. Sep 16, 1976 (54).

SLATE, Syd: Singer-Actor. May 2, 1976 (68).

SLATER, Barney: Writer. Nov 29, 1978 (55).

SLATTERY, Jack: Announcer. Oct 29, 1979 (62).

SMALL, Edward: Producer. Jan 25, 1977 (85).

SMITH, H Allen: Writer. Feb 25, 1976 (69).

SMITH, Paul J: Animator. Nov 16, 1980 (74).

SMITH, Queenie: Actress. Aug 5, 1978 (80).

SMITH, Robert Paul: Playwright. Jan 30, 1977 (61).

SMITH, Ruby: Singer. Mar 24, 1977 (73).

SNIDER, Richard: Director. Jun 4, 1977 (48).

SNYDER, Sam: Producer. Nov 4, 1980 (79).

SOBOLOFF, Arnold: Actor. Oct 28, 1979 (48).

SOLDEVILLA, Laly: Actress. Sep 12, 1979 (46).

SOLMSEN, Rudi: Producer. May 23, 1980 (72).

SOO, Jack: Actor. Jan 11, 1979 (63).

SORIA, Dario: Recording executive. Mar 28, 1980 (67).

SPEAKS, Margaret: Soprano. Jul 16, 1977 (72).

SPIVEY, Victoria: Singer. Oct 3, 1976 (68).

STABILE, Dick: Bandleader. Sep 25, 1980 (71).

STAMBLER, Robert: Producer. Nov 7, 1979.

STAPP, Jack: Music Publisher. Dec 22, 1980 (68).

STARKE, Pauline: Silent screen star. Feb 3, 1977 (76).

STEELE, Joseph Henry: Publicist-Executive. Sep 21, 1980 (85).

STEINBERG, William: Music director. May 16, 1978 (78).

STEVENS, Onslow: Actor. Jan 5, 1977 (70).

STEWART, Bill: TV Newsman. Jun 20, 1979 (37).

STEWART, Donald Ogden: Writer. Aug 2, 1980 (85).

STEWART, Hal D: Playwright-Director. May, 1979 (80).

STEWART, Sophie: Actress. Jun, 1977 (69).

STILL, William Grant: Composer-Conductor. Dec 3, 1978 (83).

STILLMAN, Al: Lyricist. Feb 17, 1979 (73)

STODEL, Capt Jack: Exective. Oct 8, 1979 (80).

STOKES, Sewell: Writer. Nov 2, 1979 (76).

STOKOWSKI, Leopold: Conductor. Sep 13, 1977 (95).

STOLOFF, Morris: Conductor. Apr 16, 1980 (mid 80s).

STOLPER, Alexander: Director. Jan 1979 (71).

STONE, Milburn: Actor. Jun 12, 1980 (75).

STONEMAN, Hatti: Singer. Jul 22, 1976 (75).

STRAUSBERG, Solomon M: Exhibitor. Dec 6, 1980 (73).

STREET, Mel: Singer. Oct 21, 1978 (43).

STREETER, Edward: Writer. Mar 31, 1976 (84).

STRONG, Michael: Actor. Sep 17, 1980 (mid-50's).

STROUT, Dick: Television personality. Apr 23, 1978 (47).

STUART, Gil: Actor. Jun 8, 1977 (58).

STUART, John: Actor. Oct 18, 1979 (81).

STUDEBAKER, Hugh: Actor. May 6, 1978 (77).

STUECKGOLD, Grete: Operatic soprano. Sep 13, 1977 (82).

SUBRAMANIAN, P: Producer. Sep, 1978 (71).

SULLIVAN, Frank: Writer. Feb 19, 1976 (83).

SULLIVAN, Joseph B: Vaudevillian. Dec 8, 1980 (79).

SUMMERS, Hope: Actress. Jul 22, 1979 (78).

SUSSMAN, Carol Levine: Executive. Oct 14, 1979 (59).

SUTER, Karl: Director. Dec 31, 1977 (51).

SWANN, Russell: Magician. Mar 16, 1980 (76).

SWANSON, Howard: Composer. Nov 12, 1978 (71).

SWEET, Marion: Actress. Jul 17, 1978 (62).

SWEETSER, Norman: Actor-Director. Aug 28, 1980 (86).

SWENSON, Karl: Actor. Oct 8, 1978 (70).

SWEZEY, Robert D: Broadcasting Executive. Sep 25, 1979 (72).

SWOPE, John: Producer. May 11, 1979 (70).

SYRJALA, Sointu: Costume Designer. Apr 10, 1979.

TAFFLER, Sydney: Actor. Nov 8, 1979 (63).

TALIAFERRO, Hal (aka Wally Wales): Actor. Feb 12, 1980 (84).

TALIAFERRO, Mabel: Actress. Jan 24, 1979 (91).

TALLMAN, Frank: Stuntman-Pilot. Apr 16, 1978 (59).

TAMARIN, Alfred H: Advertising-Publicity executive. Aug 18, 1980 (67).

TANNER, Pearl King: Actress. Jul 16, 1980 (100).

TARCAI, Mary: Actress. Sep 22, 1979 (72).

TARHEEL Slim (Alden Bunn): Blues singer. Aug 21, 1977 (52).

TAUB, Sam: Sportscaster. Jul 11, 1979 (92).

TAYLOR, Davidson: Broadcast Executive. Jul 27, 1979 (72).

TCHEREPNIN, Alexander: Composer-Pianist. Sep 29, 1977 (78).

TCHERKASSY, Alexis: Baritone. Dec 14, 1980 (76).

TEAL, Ray: Actor. Apr 2, 1976 (74).

TEMPLETON, Olive: Actress. May 29, 1979 (96).

TERNENT, Billy: Bandleader. Mar 25, 1977 (77).

TETZEL, Joan: Actress. Oct 31, 1977 (56).

TEYTE, Maggie: Singer. May 27, 1976 (88).

THOM, Robert: Writer. May 8, 1979 (49).

THOMAS, Billy (Buckwheat): Actor. Oct 10, 1980 (49).

THOMAS, Harry H: Film executive. Aug 25, 1976 (84).

THOMPSON, Frank: Costume designer. Jun 4, 1977 (57).

THOMSON, Alden Gay: Actress. Apr 1, 1979 (80).

THOR, Larry: Actor-Writer. Mar 15, 1976 (59).

THORNDIKE, Dame Sybil: Actress. Jun 9, 1976 (93).

THURN-TAXIS, Alexis: Producer-Director. Jul 26, 1979 (88).

TIOMKI, Dimitri: Composer. Nov 11, 1979 (80).

TOBIAS, George: Actor. Feb 27, 1980 (78).

TODARO, Tony: Composer. Jul 28, 1976 (61).

TODMAN, William S: TV Packager. Jul 29, 1979 (62).

TOKAR, Norman: Director. Apr 6, 1979 (59).

TORRE NILSSON, Leopoldo: Director. Sep 8, 1978 (54).

TOTHEROH, Dan: Writer. Dec 3, 1976 (82).

TOURNEUR, Jacques: Director. Dec 22, 1977 (73).

TOURTELLOT, Arthur B: Executive. Oct 18, 1977 (64).

TOVROV, Orin: Writer. Aug 16, 1980 (69).

TOWNE, Gene: Writer. Mar 17, 1979 (74).

TOZZI, Fausto: Actor. Dec 10, 1978 (57).

TRABER, Alfredo: Highwire Artist. Oct 2, 1980 (75).

TRAVERS, Ben: Playwright. Dec 18, 1980 (94).

TRESMAND, Ivy: Actress. Nov 2, 1980 (81).

TREVOR, Austin: Actor. Jan 22, 1978 (80).

TRIESAULT, Ivan: Dancer-Actor. Jan 3, 1980 (80).

TROUTMAN, Ivy: Actress. Jan 12, 1979 (96).

TRUMBO, Dalton: Writer. Sep 10, 1976 (79).

TUMARIN, Boris: Actor. Jan 28, 1979 (68).

TWERP, Joe: Comedian-Writer. Dec 15, 1980 (70).

TWIST, Derek: Director. Aug 15, 1979 (74).

TWIST, John: Writer-Producer. Feb 11, 1976 (77).

TYNAN, Kenneth: Writer-Critic. Jul 26, 1980 (53).

TZAVELLAS, George: Director. Oct 19, 1976 (60).

ULLMAN, Daniel: Writer. Oct 23, 1979 (61).

UNDERWOOD, Cecil: Producer. Sep 27, 1976 (76).

UNSWORTH, Geoffrey: Cinematographer. Nov, 1978 (63).

URQUHART, Molly: Actress. Oct 6, 1977 (71).

URZI, Saro: Actor. Nov 2, 1979 (66).

VALLI, Romolo: Actor. Feb 1, 1980 (55).

VALORI, Bice: Comedienne. Mar 17, 1980 (52).

VAN, Bobby: Dancer-Entertainer. Jul 31, 1980 (51).

VANCE, Nina: Producer. Feb 18, 1980 (65).

VANCE, Vivian: Actress. Aug 17, 1979

VANDERIC, Georges: Comedian. Aug 1, 1979 (78).

VANDERKAR, Robert: Cameraman. Nov 19, 1980 (33).

Van DYKE, Philip: Director. May 4, 1979 (75).

Van ENGER, Charles J Sr: Cinematographer. Jul 4, 1980 (89).

Van GYSEGHEM, Andre: Actor-Director. Oct 13, 1979 (73).

VARCONI, Victor: Actor. Jun 16, 1976 (80).

VEIGA, Jorge: Composer-Singer. Jun 29, 1979 (68).

VEMBO, Sophia: Singer. Mar 12, 1978 (66).

VENTURA, Ray: Songwriter-Producer. Apr 3, 1979 (71).

VENUTI, Joe: Musician. Aug 14, 1978 (81).

VERSOIS, Odile: Actress. Jun 23, 1980 (50).

VICIOUS, Sid (John Simon Ritchie): Punk Rock Musician. Feb 2, 1979 (21).

VIDOR, Doris Warner: Executive. Aug 28, 1978.

VIDOR, Florence (Florence Arto): Silent screen star. Nov 3, 1977 (82).

VILLA, Mario: Exhibitor. Dec, 1980 (83).

VISCONTI, Luchino: Director. Mar 17, 1976 (69).

VOLPI, Giacomo Lauri: Operatic Tenor. Mar 17, 1979 (86).

von CUBE, Irmgard: Writer. Jul 25, 1977 (77).

VORKAPICH, Slavko: Director-Montage expert. Oct 20, 1976 (84).

VYE, Murvyn: Actor. Aug 17, 1976 (62)

WAGENHEIM, Charles: Actor. Mar 6, 1979 (84).

WAINER, Lee Writer-Composer. Nov 11, 1979 (74).

WALES, Wally (aka Hal Taliaferro): Actor. Feb 12, 1980 (84).

WALKER, Ray: Actor. Oct 6, 1980 (76).

WALLACE, Regina Katherine: Actress. Feb 13, 1978 (86).

WALLENDA, Karl: Highwire artist. Mar 22, 1978 (73).

WALSH, Raoul: Pioneer Director. Dec 31, 1980 (93).

WALSH, Sammy: Comedian. Oct 5, 1980 (75).

WALTERS, Lou: Nitery operator. Aug 15, 1977 (81).

WARD, Richard: Actor. Jul 1, 1979 (64).

WARNER, Jack L: Film producer and Pioneer. Aug 13, 1978 (86).

WARNER, Rae: Dancer. Jan 15, 1978 (80).

WARREN, Eda: Film editor. Jul 15, 1980 (76).

WASHINGTON, Ned: Lyricist. Dec 20, 1976 (75).

WATERS, Ethel: Singer-Actress. Sep 1, 1977 (80).

WATKINS, Linda: Actress. Oct 31, 1976.

WATSON, Charles: Singer. Jan 8, 1979 (65).

WATSON, Lula B: Singer. Mar 6, 1979 (104).

WATTS, Queenie: Actress. Jan 25, 1980 (53).

WAYNE, Frances: Singer. Feb 6, 1978 (50s).

WAYNE, John: Actor. Jun 11, 1979 (72).

WAYNE, Mabel: Songwriter-Pianist. Jun 19, 1978 (86).

WEDGE, Maura K: Actress. Nov 9, 1979 (40).

WEEKS, Ranny: Bandleader. Apr 26, 1979 (72).

WEISS, Rudolph: Actor. Apr 5, 1978 (77).

WEISS, Sam: Drummer. Dec 18, 1977 (67).

WELCH, William Addams: Writer. Feb 2, 1976 (61).

WEST, Mae: Actress-Writer. Nov 22, 1980 (87).

WHARTON, Betty (Mary Mason): Actress. Oct 13, 1980 (69).

WHITCUP, Leonard: Composer-Lyricist. Apr 6, 1979 (75).

WHITE, Alice: Dancer. Jun 26, 1977 (75).

WHITE, Frank K: Executive. Nov 12, 1979 (80).

WHITE, Princess: Singer-Dancer. Mar 20, 1976 (95).

WHITLEY, Ray: Singer-Composer. Feb 21, 1979 (77).

WIGFALL, James: Actor. Jul 24, 1978 (36).

WILCOX, Herbert: Producer-Director. May 15, 1977 (85).

WILDER, Alec: Composer. Dec 24, 1980 (73).

WILDING, Michael: Actor. Jul 8 1979 (66).

WILLAT, Irvin V: Director. Apr 17, 1976 (84).

WILLI, Arthur: Talent executive. Mar 31, 1977 (81).

WILLIAMS, Annie Laurie: Agent. May 17, 1977 (80s).

WILLIE, Raymond: Exhibitor. Oct 20, 1978 (77).

WILLING, Foy: Singer. Jul 24, 1978 (63).

WILLS, Chill: Actor. Dec 15, 1978 (76).

WILLSON, Henry: Agent. Nov 2, 1978 (67).

WILSON, Michael: Writer. Apr 9, 1978 (63).

WILSON, Paul: Film executive. Sep 13, 1976 (76).

WINKLER, Gerd: Director. Aug 8, 1978 (49).

WINOGRADOFF, Anatol: Actor. Apr 27, 1980 (89).

WINTERS, Marian: Actress. Nov 3, 1978 (54).

WINTLE, Julian: Producer. Nov 8, 1980 (67).

WISE, David E: Executive. Dec 19, 1980 (73).

WOLF, Loraine: Singer. Feb 28, 1978 (57).

WOLF, Stephen A: Promoter. Nov 21, 1977 (34).

WOLF, Tommy: Composer. Jan 8, 1979 (53).

WOLFE, Robert S: Distribution executive. Feb 24, 1980 (83).

WOLFSON, Louis 2d: Exhibitor. Oct 11, 1979 (52).

WOLFSON, P J: Writer-Producer-Director. Apr 16, 1979 (75).

WOOD, Georgie: Comic. Feb 19, 1979 (83).

WOOD, Peggy: Actress. Mar 18, 1978 (86).

WOOD, Randall: Recording Executive. Oct 6, 1980 (50).

WOOD, Ross: Newsreel Cameraman. Oct 3, 1980 (64).

WOODARD, Bronte: Writer. Aug 6, 1980 (39).

WOODFORD, Jack: Director-Speech Coach. Nov 15, 1980 (67).

WOOLNER, Bernie: Producer. Feb 21, 1977 (66).

WORTH, Stan: Composer-Conductor. Aug 31, 1980 (48).

WRIGHT, O V: R & B Singer. Nov 16, 1980 (41).

WRIGHT, William H: Producer. Jul 23, 1980 (78).

YOSHIWARA, Kyonosuke: Actor. Nov 30, 1979 (79).

YOUNG, Collier: Writer-Producer. Dec 25, 1980 (72).

YOUNG, Gig: Actor. Oct 19, 1978 (60).

YOUNG, John Shaw: TV pioneer. Jan 12, 1976 (74).

YOUNG, Zillah S: Conductor. Mar 29, 1979 (33).

ZANUCK, Darryl F: Producer-Writer. Dec 22, 1979 (77).

ZELZER, Harry: Impresario. Jun 14, 1979 (82).

ZOLA, Jean-Pierre: Jan 17, 1979 (63).

ZUCKMAYER, Carl: Playwright. Jan 18, 1977 (80).

ZUKOR, Adolph: Film pioneer. Jun 10, 1976 (103).